Peterson's
Four-Year
Colleges
2012

PETERSON'S

Publishing

PETERSON'S
Publishing

About Peterson's Publishing

Peterson's Publishing provides the accurate, dependable, high-quality education content and guidance you need to succeed. No matter where you are on your academic or professional path, you can rely on Peterson's print and digital publications for the most up-to-date education exploration data, expert test-prep tools, and top-notch career success resources—everything you need to achieve your goals.

Visit us online at **www.petersonspublishing.com** and let Peterson's help you achieve your goals.

For more information, contact Peterson's Publishing, 2000 Lenox Drive, Lawrenceville, NJ 08648; 800-338-3282 Ext. 54229; or find us on the World Wide Web at www.petersonspublishing.com.

Bernadette Webster, Director of Publishing; Jill C. Schwartz, Editor; John Wells, Research Project Manager; Cathleen Fee, Research Associate; Phyllis Johnson, Programmer; Ray Golaszewski, Publishing Operations Manager; Linda M. Williams, Composition Manager; Karen Mount, Fulfillment Coordinator; Danielle Vreeland, Shannon White, Client Relations Representatives; Charlotte Thomas, Richard Woodland, Contributing Authors

ISSN 1544-2330
ISBN-13: 978-0-7689-3279-9
ISBN-10: 0-7689-3279-3

Printed in the United States of America

10 9 8 7 6 5 4 3 2 1   13 12 11

Forty-second Edition

Contents

A Note from the Peterson's Editors

For nearly fifty years, Peterson's has given students and parents the most comprehensive, up-to-date information on undergraduate institutions in the United States and Canada. *Peterson's Four-Year Colleges 2012* features advice and tips on the college search and selection process, such as how to consider the factors that truly make a difference during your search, how to understand the application process, and how to get financial aid. Each year, Peterson's researches the data published in *Peterson's Four-Year Colleges*. The information is furnished by the colleges and is accurate at the time of publishing.

Opportunities abound for students, and this guide can help you find what you want in a number of ways:

- For application and admissions advice and guidance, just head to **THE ADVICE CENTER**. Within the **Search, Find, Select** section, the "College Admissions Countdown Calendar" outlines pertinent month-by-month milestones. "Choosing Your Top Ten Colleges" gets you started on putting together the most important top ten list you have ever made. "Surviving Standardized Tests" describes frequently used tests and what you need to know to succeed on them. Of course, part of the college selection process involves visiting the schools themselves, and "The Whys and Whats of College Visits" is just the planner you need to make those trips well worth your while. Next, "Applying 101" provides advice on how best to approach the application phase of the process. If you can't make sense out of the early decision/early action conundrum, "The Early Decision Decision" can help clarify it for you. Finally, "What International Students Need to Know About Admission to U.S. Colleges and Universities" has tips on college admissions for non–U.S. citizens and can also be useful to U.S. citizens. Up next is the **Money, Money, Money** section, which provides all the essential information on how to meet your education expenses, starting with the "Financial Aid Countdown Calendar" and followed by articles covering "Who's Paying for This? Financial Aid Basics" and "Middle Income Families: Making the Financial Aid Process Work." And be sure to check out our **Options, Options, Options** section for some sneak peeks into specific institutions and programs that may be just right for you, including the latest on honors programs, public versus private colleges, women's colleges, and online learning. Finally, you'll want to read through the **How to Use This Guide** section, which explains the information presented for each individual college, how Peterson's collects its data, and how Peterson's determines eligibility for inclusion in this guide.

- Next up is the **PROFILES** section. Here you'll find our unparalleled college profiles, arranged alphabetically by state. They provide need-to-know information about accredited four-year colleges—including entrance difficulty, campus setting, total enrollment, student-faculty ratio, application deadlines, expenses, most frequently chosen baccalaureate fields, and academic programs. All the information you need to apply is placed together at the conclusion of each college profile. Display ads, which appear near some of the institutions' profiles, have been provided and paid for by those colleges or universities that wished to supplement their profile data with additional information about their institution.

- And if you still thirst for even more information, over 400 two-page narrative descriptions appear as **COLLEGE CLOSE-UPS**—descriptions written by admissions or college officials that provide great detail about each school. They are edited to provide a consistent format across entries for your ease of comparison.

- If you already have specifics in mind, such as a particular major or institution, turn to the **INDEXES** section. Here you can search for a school based on major, entrance difficulty, cost ranges, and geography. If you already have colleges in mind that pique your interest, you can use the "Alphabetical Listing of Colleges and Universities" to search for these schools. Page numbers referring to all information presented about a college are conveniently referenced.

Join the college conversation on Facebook® and Twitter™ at www.facebook.com/find.colleges and www.twitter.com/find_colleges and receive additional college search tips and advice. Peterson's resources are available to help you do your best in finding the right school!

Peterson's publishes a full line of books—college and grad guides, education exploration, test preparation, financial aid, and career preparation. Peterson's publications can be found at high school guidance offices, college libraries and career centers, and your local bookstore and library. Peterson's books are now also available as eBooks.

We welcome any comments or suggestions you may have about this publication. Your feedback will help us make educational dreams possible for you—and others like you.

Colleges will be pleased to know that Peterson's helped you in your selection. Admissions staff members are more than happy to answer questions, address specific problems, and help in any way they can. The editors at Peterson's wish you great success in your college search!

The Advice Center

College Admissions Countdown Calendar

This practical month-by-month calendar is designed to help you stay on top of the process of applying to college. For most students, the process begins in September of the junior year of high school and ends in June of the senior year. You may want to begin considering financial aid options, reviewing your academic schedule, and attending college fairs before your junior year.

JUNIOR YEAR

September
- Check with your counselor to make sure your course credits will meet college requirements.
- Be sure you are involved in one or two extracurricular activities.
- Begin building your personal list of colleges.

October
- Register for and take the PSAT.

November
- Strive to get the best grades you can. A serious effort will provide you with the most options during the application process.

December
- Get involved in a community service activity.
- Begin to read newspapers and a weekly news magazine.
- Buy *Peterson's Master the SAT, Peterson's Ultimate ACT Tool Kit,* or *The Real ACT Prep Guide* (published by Peterson's) and begin to study for the tests.

January
- With your school counselor, decide when to take the ACT, SAT, and SAT Subject Tests (and which Subject Tests to take). If English is not your primary language and you are planning on attending a college in North America, decide when to take the TOEFL.
- Keep your grades up!

February
- Plan a challenging schedule of classes for your senior year.
- Think about which teachers you will ask to write recommendations.
- Check http://www.nacacnet.org/EVENTSTRAINING/ COLLEGEFAIRS/Pages/default.aspx for schedules and locations of college fairs.

March
- Register for the tests you will take in the spring (ACT, SAT, SAT Subject Tests, or the TOEFL).
- Meet with your school counselor to discuss college choices.
- Review your transcript and test scores with your counselor to determine how competitive your range of choices should be.
- Develop a preliminary list of fifteen to twenty colleges and universities.
- Start scheduling campus visits. The best time is when school is in session (but never during final exams). Summers are OK but will not show you what the college is really like. If possible, save your top college choices for the fall. Be aware, however, that fall is the busiest visit season, and you will need advance planning. Don't forget to write thank you letters to your interviewers.

April
- Take any standardized tests for which you have registered.
- Create a list of your potential college choices and begin to record personal and academic information that can be transferred later to your college applications.

May
- Plan college visits and make appointments.
- Structure your summer plans to include advanced academic work, travel, volunteer work, or a job.
- Confirm your academic schedule for the fall.

Summer
- Write to any colleges on your list that do not accept the Common Application to request application forms.
- Begin working on your application essays

SENIOR YEAR

September

- Register for the ACT, SAT, SAT Subject Tests, or TOEFL, as necessary.
- Check with your school counselor for the fall visiting schedule of college reps.
- Ask appropriate teachers if they would write recommendations for you. Don't forget to write thank you letters when they accept.
- Meet with your counselor to compile your final list of colleges.

October

- Mail or send early applications electronically after carefully checking them to be sure they are completely filled out.
- Photocopy or print extra copies of your applications to use as a backup.
- Take the tests for which you have registered.
- Don't be late! Keep track of all deadlines for transcripts, recommendations, financial aid, etc.

November

- Be sure that you have requested your ACT and SAT scores be sent to your colleges of choice.
- Complete and submit all applications. Print or photocopy an extra copy for your records.

December

- Take any necessary tests: ACT, SAT, SAT Subject Tests, or TOEFL.
- Meet with your counselor to verify that all is in order and that transcripts are out to colleges.

January

- Prepare the Free Application for Federal Student Aid (FAFSA), available at www.fafsa.ed.gov or through your school counseling office. An estimated income tax statement (which can be corrected later) can be used. The sooner you apply for financial aid, the better your chances.

February

- Send in your FAFSA via the Web or U.S. mail.
- Be sure your midyear report has gone out to the colleges to which you've applied.
- Let colleges know of any new honors or accomplishments that were not in your original application.

March

- Register for any Advanced Placement (AP) tests you might take.
- Be sure you have received a FAFSA acknowledgment.

April

- Review the acceptances and financial aid offers you receive.
- Go back to visit one or two of your top-choice colleges.
- Notify your college of choice that you have accepted its offer (and send in a deposit by May 1).
- Notify the colleges you have chosen not to attend of your decision.

May

- Take AP tests.

June

- Graduate! Congratulations and best of luck.

Choosing Your Top Ten Colleges

By using all the information in the various sections of this guide, you will find colleges worthy of the most important top-ten list on the planet—yours.

The first thing you will need to do is decide what type of institution of higher learning you want to attend. Each of the thousands of four-year colleges and universities in the United States is as unique as the people applying to it. Although listening to the voices and media hype around you can make it sound as though there are only a few elite schools worth attending, this simply is not true. By considering some of the following criteria, you will soon find that the large pool of interesting colleges can be narrowed down to a more reasonable number.

SIZE AND CATEGORY

Schools come in all shapes and sizes, from tiny rural colleges of 400 students to massive state university systems serving 100,000 students or more. If you are coming from a small high school, a college with 3,500 students may seem large to you. If you are currently attending a high school with 3,000 students, selecting a college of a similar size may not feel like a new enough experience. Some students coming from very large impersonal high schools are looking for a place where they will be recognized from the beginning and offered a more personal approach. If you don't have a clue about what size might feel right to you, try visiting a couple of nearby colleges of varying sizes. You do not have to be seriously interested in them; just feel what impact the number of students on campus has on you.

Large Universities

Large universities offer a wide range of educational, athletic, and social experiences. Universities offer a full scope of undergraduate majors and award master's and doctoral degrees as well. Universities are usually composed of several smaller colleges. Depending on your interest in a major field or area of study, you would likely apply to a specific college within the university. Each college has the flexibility to set its own standards for admission, which may differ from the overall average of the university. The colleges within a university system also set their own course requirements for earning a degree.

Universities may be public or private. Some large private universities, such as Harvard, Yale, Princeton, University of Pennsylvania, New York University, Northwestern, and Stanford, are well-known for their high entrance standards, the excellence of their education, and the success rates of their graduates. These institutions place a great deal of emphasis on research and compete aggressively for grants from the federal government to fund these projects. Large public universities,

such as the State University of New York (SUNY) System, University of Michigan, University of Texas, University of Illinois, University of Washington, and University of North Carolina, also support excellent educational programs, compete for and win research funding, and have successful graduates. Public universities usually offer substantially lower tuition rates to in-state students, although their tuition rates for out-of-state residents are often comparable to those of private institutions.

At many large universities, sports play a major role on campus. Athletics can dominate the calendar and set the tone year-round at some schools. Alumni travel from far and wide to attend their alma mater's football or basketball games, and the campus, and frequently the entire town, grinds to a halt when there is a home game. Athletes are heroes and dominate campus social life.

What are some other features of life on a university campus? Every kind of club imaginable, from literature to bioengineering and chorus to politics, can be found on most college campuses. You will be able to play the intramural version of almost every sport in which the university fields interscholastic teams and join fraternities, sororities, and groups dedicated to social action. You can become a member of a band, an orchestra, or perhaps a chamber music group or work on the newspaper, the literary magazine, or the Web site. The list can go on and on. You may want to try out a new interest or two or pursue what you have always been interested in and make like-minded friends along the way.

Take a look at the size of the classrooms in the larger universities and envision yourself sitting in that atmosphere. Would this offer a learning environment that would benefit you?

Liberal Arts Colleges

If you have considered large universities and come to the conclusion that all that action could be a distraction, a small liberal arts college might be right for you. Ideally tucked away on a picture-perfect campus, a liberal arts college generally has fewer than 5,000 students. The mission of most liberal arts schools is learning for the sake of learning, with a strong emphasis on creating lifelong learners who will be able to apply their education to any number of careers. This contrasts with objectives of the profession-based preparation of specialized colleges.

Liberal arts colleges cannot offer the breadth of courses provided by the large universities. As a result, liberal arts colleges try to create a niche for themselves. For instance, a college may place its emphasis on its humanities departments, whose professors are all well-known published authors and international presenters in their areas of expertise. A college may highlight its science departments by providing state-of-the-art-facilities where undergraduates conduct research side by side with top-notch professors and copublish their findings in the most prestigious scientific journals in the country. The personal approach is very important at liberal arts colleges. Whether in advisement, course selection, athletic programs tailored to students' interests, or dinner with the department head at her home, liberal arts colleges emphasize that they get to know their students.

If they are so perfect, why doesn't everyone choose a liberal arts college? Well, the small size limits options. Fewer people may mean less diversity. The fact that many of these colleges encourage a study-abroad option (a student elects to spend a semester or a year studying in another country) reduces the number of students on campus even further. Some liberal arts colleges have a certain reputation that does not appeal to some students. You should ask yourself questions about the campus life that most appeals to you. Will you fit in with the campus culture? Will the small size mean that you go through your social options quickly? Check out the activities listed on the Student Center bulletin board. Does the student body look diverse enough for you? Will what is happening keep you busy and interested? Do the students have input into decision making? Do they create the social climate of the school?

Small Universities

Smaller universities often combine stringent admissions policies, handpicked faculty members, and attractive scholarship packages. These institutions generally have undergraduate enrollments of about 4,000 students. Some are more famous for their graduate and professional schools but have also established strong undergraduate colleges. Smaller universities balance the great majors options of large universities with a smaller campus community. They offer choices but not to the same extent as large universities. On the other hand, by limiting admissions and enrollment, they manage to cultivate some of the characteristics of a liberal arts college. Like a liberal arts college, a small university may emphasize a particular program and go out of its way to draw strong candidates in a specific area, such as premed, to its campus. Universities such as The Johns Hopkins University, University of Notre Dame, Vanderbilt University, Washington University in St. Louis, and Wesleyan University in Connecticut are a few examples of this category.

Technical or Specialized Colleges

Another alternative to the liberal arts college or large university is the technical or otherwise specialized college. Their goal is to offer a specialized and saturated experience in a particular field of study. Such an institution might limit its course offerings to engineering and science, the performing or fine arts, or business. Schools such as California Institute of Technology, Carnegie Mellon University, Massachusetts Institute of Technology, and Rensselaer Polytechnic Institute concentrate on attracting the finest math and science students in the country. At other schools, like Bentley College in Massachusetts or Bryant College in Rhode Island, students eat, sleep, and breathe business. These institutions are purists at heart and strong believers in the necessity of focused, specialized

study to produce excellence in their graduates' achievements. If you are certain about your chosen path in life and want to immerse yourself in subjects such as math, music, or business, you will fit right in.

Religious Colleges

Many private colleges have religious origins, and many of these have become secular institutions with virtually no trace of their religious roots. Others remain dedicated to a religious way of education. What sets religious colleges apart is the way they combine faith, learning, and student life. Faculty members and administrators are hired with faith as a criterion as much as their academic credentials.

Single-Gender Colleges

There are strong arguments that being able to pursue one's education without the distraction, competition, and stress caused by the presence of the opposite sex helps a student evolve a stronger sense of her or his self-worth; achieve more academically; have a more fulfilling, less pressured social schedule; and achieve more later in life. For various historic, social, and psychological reasons, there are many more all-women than all-men colleges. A strict single-sex environment is rare. Even though the undergraduate day college adheres to an all-female or all-male admissions policy, coeducational evening classes or graduate programs and coordinate facilities and classes shared with nearby coed or opposite-sex institutions can result in a good number of students of the opposite sex being found on campus. If you want to concentrate on your studies and hone your leadership qualities, a single-gender school is an option.

LOCATION

Location and distance from home are two other important considerations. If you have always lived in the suburbs, choosing an urban campus can be an adventure, but after a week of the urban experience, will you long for a grassy campus and open space? On the other hand, if you choose a college in a rural area, will you run screaming into the Student Center some night looking for noise, lights, and people? The location—urban, rural, or suburban—can directly affect how easy or how difficult adjusting to college life will be for you.

Don't forget to factor in distance from home. Everyone going off to college wants to think he or she won't be homesick, but sometimes it's nice to get a home-cooked meal or to do the laundry in a place that does not require quarters. Even your kid sister may seem like less of a nuisance after a couple of months away.

Here are some questions you might ask yourself as you go through the selection process: In what part of the country do I want to be? How far away from home do I want to be? What is the cost of returning home? Do I need to be close to a city? How close? How large of a city? Would city life distract me? Would I concentrate better in a setting that is more rural or more suburban?

ENTRANCE DIFFICULTY

Many students will look at a college's entrance difficulty as an indicator of whether or not they will be admitted. For instance, if you have an excellent academic record, you might wish to primarily consider those colleges that are highly competitive. Although entrance difficulty does not translate directly to quality of education, it indicates which colleges are attracting large numbers of high-achieving students. A high-achieving student body usually translates into prestige for the college and its graduates. Prestige has some advantages but should definitely be viewed as a secondary factor that might tip the scales when all the other important factors are equal. Never base your decision on prestige alone!

The other principle to keep in mind when considering this factor is to not sell yourself short. If everything else tells you that a college might be right for you, but your numbers just miss that college's average range, apply there anyway. Your numbers—grades and test scores—are undeniably important in the admissions decision, but there are other considerations. First, lower grades in honors or AP courses will impress colleges more than top grades in regular-track courses because they demonstrate that you are the kind of student willing to accept challenges. Second, admissions directors are looking for different qualities in students that can be combined to create a multifaceted class. For example, if you did poorly in your freshman and sophomore years but made a great improvement in your grades in later years, this usually will impress a college. If you are likely to contribute to your class because of your special personal qualities, a strong sense of commitment and purpose, unusual and valuable experiences, or special interests and talents, these factors can outweigh numbers that are weaker than average. Nevertheless, be practical. Overreach yourself in a few applications, but put the bulk of your effort into gaining admission to colleges where you have a realistic chance for admission.

THE PRICE OF AN EDUCATION

The price tag for higher education continues to rise, and it has become an increasingly important factor for people. While it is necessary to consider your family's resources when choosing a list of colleges to which you might apply, never eliminate a college solely because of cost. There are many ways to pay for college, including loans, and a college education will never depreciate in value, unlike other purchases. It is an investment in yourself and will pay back the expense many times over in your lifetime.

Surviving Standardized Tests

WHAT ARE STANDARDIZED TESTS?

Colleges and universities in the United States use tests to help evaluate applicants' readiness for admission or to place them in appropriate courses. The tests that are most frequently used by colleges are the ACT of American College Testing, Inc., and the College Board's SAT. In addition, the Educational Testing Service (ETS) offers the TOEFL test, which evaluates the English-language proficiency of nonnative speakers. The tests are offered at designated testing centers located at high schools and colleges throughout the United States and U.S. territories and at testing centers in various countries throughout the world.

Upon request, special accommodations for students with documented visual, hearing, physical, or learning disabilities are available. Examples of special accommodations include tests in Braille or large print and such aids as a reader, recorder, magnifying glass, or sign language interpreter. Additional testing time may be allowed in some instances. Contact the appropriate testing program or your guidance counselor for details on how to request special accommodations.

THE ACT

The ACT is a standardized college entrance examination that measures knowledge and skills in English, mathematics, reading, and science reasoning and the application of these skills to future academic tasks. The ACT consists of four multiple-choice tests.

Test 1: English
- 75 questions, 45 minutes
- Usage and mechanics
- Rhetorical skills

Test 2: Mathematics
- 60 questions, 60 minutes
- Pre-algebra
- Elementary algebra
- Intermediate algebra
- Coordinate geometry
- Plane geometry
- Trigonometry

Test 3: Reading
- 40 questions, 35 minutes
- Prose fiction
- Humanities
- Social studies
- Natural sciences

Test 4: Science
- 40 questions, 35 minutes
- Data representation

- Research summary
- Conflicting viewpoints

Each section is scored from 1 to 36 and is scaled for slight variations in difficulty. Students are not penalized for incorrect responses. The composite score is the average of the four scaled scores. The ACT Plus Writing includes the four multiple-choice tests and a writing test, which measures writing skills emphasized in high school English classes and in entry-level college composition courses.

To prepare for the ACT, ask your guidance counselor for a free guidebook called "Preparing for the ACT." Besides providing general test-preparation information and additional test-taking strategies, this guidebook describes the content and format of the four ACT subject area tests, summarizes test administration procedures followed at ACT test centers, and includes a practice test. Peterson's publishes *The Real ACT* that includes five official ACT tests.

THE SAT

The SAT measures developed critical reading and mathematical reasoning abilities as they relate to successful performance in college. It is intended to supplement the secondary school record and other information about the student in assessing readiness for college. There is one unscored, experimental section on the exam, which is used for equating and/or pretesting purposes and can cover either the mathematics or critical reading area.

Critical Reading
- 67 questions, 70 minutes
- Sentence completion
- Passage-based reading

DON'T FORGET TO . . .

☐ Take the SAT or ACT before application deadlines.

☐ Note that test registration deadlines precede test dates by about six weeks.

☐ Register to take the TOEFL test if English is not your native language and you are planning on studying at a North American college.

☐ Practice your test-taking skills with *Peterson's Master the SAT, Peterson's Ultimate ACT Tool Kit, The Real ACT* (published by Peterson's), *Peterson's Master TOEFL Reading Skills, Peterson's Master TOEFL Vocabulary,* and *Peterson's Master TOEFL Writing Skills.*

☐ Contact the College Board or American College Testing, Inc., in advance if you need special accommodations when taking tests.

Mathematics

- 54 questions, 70 minutes
- Multiple-choice
- Student-produced response (grid-ins)

Writing

- 49 questions plus essay, 60 minutes
- Identifying sentence errors
- Improving paragraphs
- Improving sentences
- Essay

Students receive one point for each correct response and lose a fraction of a point for each incorrect response (except for student-produced responses). These points are totaled to produce the raw scores, which are then scaled to equalize the scores for slight variations in difficulty for various editions of the test. The critical reading, writing, and mathematics scaled scores range from 200–800 per section. The total scaled score range is from 600–2400.

SAT SUBJECT TESTS

Subject Tests are required by some institutions for admission and/or placement in freshman-level courses. Each Subject Test measures one's knowledge of a specific subject and the ability to apply that knowledge. Students should check with each institution for its specific requirements. In general, students are required to take three Subject Tests (one English, one mathematics, and one of their choice).

Subject Tests are given in the following areas: biology, chemistry, Chinese, French, German, Italian, Japanese, Korean, Latin, literature, mathematics, modern Hebrew, physics, Spanish, U.S. history, and world history. These tests are 1 hour long and are primarily multiple-choice tests. Three Subject Tests may be taken on one test date.

Scored like the SAT, students gain a point for each correct answer and lose a fraction of a point for each incorrect answer. The raw scores are then converted to scaled scores that range from 200 to 800.

THE TOEFL INTERNET-BASED TEST (IBT)

The Test of English as a Foreign Language Internet-Based Test (TOEFL iBT) is designed to help assess a student's grasp of English if it is not the student's first language. Performance on the TOEFL test may help interpret scores on the critical reading sections of the SAT. The test consists of four integrated sections: speaking, listening, reading, and writing. The TOEFL iBT emphasizes integrated skills. The paper-based versions of the TOEFL will continue to be administered in certain countries where the Internet-based version has not yet been introduced. For further information, visit www.toefl.org.

WHAT OTHER TESTS SHOULD I KNOW ABOUT?

The AP Program

This program allows high school students to try college-level work and build valuable skills and study habits in the process. Subject matter is explored in more depth in AP courses than in other high school classes. A qualifying score on an AP test—which varies from school to school—can earn you college

credit or advanced placement. Getting qualifying grades on enough exams can even earn you a full year's credit and sophomore standing at more than 1,500 higher-education institutions. There are more than thirty AP courses across multiple subject areas, including art history, biology, and computer science. Speak to your guidance counselor for information about your school's offerings.

College-Level Examination Program (CLEP)

The CLEP enables students to earn college credit for what they already know, whether it was learned in school, through independent study, or through other experiences outside of the classroom. More than 2,900 colleges and universities now award credit for qualifying scores on one or more of the 33 CLEP exams. The exams, which are 90 minutes in length and are primarily multiple choice, are administered at participating colleges and universities. For more information, check out the Web site at www.collegeboard.com/clep.

WHAT CAN I DO TO PREPARE FOR THESE TESTS?

Know what to expect. Get familiar with how the tests are structured, how much time is allowed, and the directions for each type of question. Get plenty of rest the night before the test and eat breakfast that morning.

There are a variety of products, from books to software to videos, available to help you prepare for most standardized tests. Find the learning style that suits you best. As for which products to buy, there are two major categories— those created by the test makers and those created by private companies. The best approach is to talk to someone who has been through the process and find out which product or products he or she recommends.

Some students report significant increases in scores after participating in coaching programs. Longer-term programs (40 hours) seem to raise scores more than short-term programs (20 hours), but beyond 40 hours, score gains are minor. Math scores appear to benefit more from coaching than critical reading scores.

Resources

There is a variety of ways to prepare for standardized tests— find a method that fits your schedule and your budget. But you should definitely prepare. Far too many students walk into these tests cold, either because they find standardized tests frightening or annoying or they just haven't found the time to study. The key is that these exams are standardized. That means these tests are largely the same from administration to administration; they always test the same concepts. They have to, or else you couldn't compare the scores of people who took the tests on different dates. The numbers or words may change, but the underlying content doesn't.

So how do you prepare? At the very least, you should review relevant material, such as math formulas and commonly used vocabulary words, and know the directions for each question type or test section. You should take at least one practice test and review your mistakes so you don't make them again on the test day. Beyond that, you know best how much preparation you need. You'll also find lots of material in libraries or bookstores to help you: books and software from the test makers and from other publishers (including Peterson's) or live courses that range from national test-preparation companies to teachers at your high school who offer classes.

Top 10 Ways Not to Take the Test

10. Cramming the night before the test.

9. Not becoming familiar with the directions before you take the test.

8. Not becoming familiar with the format of the test before you take it.

7. Not knowing how the test is graded.

6. Spending too much time on any one question.

5. Second-guessing yourself.

4. Not checking spelling, grammar, and sentence structure in essays.

3. Writing a one-paragraph essay.

2. Forgetting to take a deep breath to keep from—

1. Losing It!

The Whys and Whats of College Visits

Dawn B. Sova, Ph.D.

The campus visit should not be a passive activity for you and your parents. Take the initiative and gather information beyond that provided in the official tour. You will see many important indicators during your visit that will tell you more about the true character of a college and its students than the tour guide will reveal. Know what to look for and how to assess the importance of such indicators.

WHAT SHOULD YOU ASK AND WHAT SHOULD YOU LOOK FOR?

Your first stop on a campus visit is the visitor center or admissions office, where you will probably have to wait to meet with a counselor. Colleges usually plan to greet visitors later than the appointed time in order to give them the opportunity to review some of the campus information that is liberally scattered throughout the visitor waiting room. Take advantage of the time to become even more familiar with the college by arriving 15 to 30 minutes before your appointment to observe the behavior of staff members and to browse through the yearbooks and student newspapers that will be available.

If you prepare in advance, you will have already reviewed the college catalog and map of the campus. These materials familiarize you with the academic offerings and the physical layout of the campus, but the true character of the college and its students emerges in other ways.

Begin your investigation with the visitor center staff members. As a student's first official contact with the college, they should make every effort to welcome prospective students and project a friendly image.

- How do they treat you and other prospective students who are waiting? Are they friendly and willing to speak with you, or do they try their hardest to avoid eye contact and conversation?

- Are they friendly with each other and with students who enter the office, or are they curt and unwilling to help?

- Does the waiting room have a friendly feeling or is it cold and sterile?

If the visitor center staff members seem indifferent to prospective students, there is little reason to believe that they will be warm and welcoming to current students. View such behavior as a warning to watch very carefully the interaction of others with you during the tour. An indifferent or unfriendly reception in the admissions office may be simply the first of many signs that attending this college will not be a pleasant experience.

Look through several yearbooks and see the types of activities that are actually photographed, as opposed to the activities that colleges promise in their promotional literature. Some questions are impossible to answer if the college is very large, but for small and moderately sized colleges the yearbook is a good indicator of campus activity.

- Has the number of clubs and organizations increased or decreased in the past five years?

- Do the same students appear repeatedly in activities?

- Do sororities and fraternities dominate campus activities?

- Are participants limited to one sex or one ethnic group, or is there diversity?

- Are all activities limited to the campus, or are students involved in activities in the community?

Use what you observe in the yearbooks as a means of forming a more complete understanding of the college, but don't base your entire impression on just one facet. If time permits, look through several copies of the school newspaper, which should reflect the major concerns and interests of the students. The paper is also a good way to learn about the campus social life.

- Does the paper contain a mix of national and local news?

- What products or services are advertised?

- How assertive are the editorials?

- With what topics are the columnists concerned?

- Are movies and concerts that meet your tastes advertised or reviewed?

- What types of ads appear in the classified section?

The newspaper should be a public forum for students, and, as such, should reflect the character of the campus and of the student body. A paper that deals only with seemingly safe and well-edited topics on the editorial page and in regular feature columns might indicate administrative censorship. A lack of ads for restaurants might indicate either a lack of good places to eat or that area restaurants do not welcome student business. A limited mention of movies, concerts, or other entertainment might reveal a severely limited campus social life. Even if ads and reviews are included, you should still balance how such activities reflect your tastes.

You will have only a limited amount of time to ask questions during your initial meeting with the admissions counselor, for very few schools include a formal interview in the initial campus visit or tour. Instead, this brief meeting is often just a nicety that allows the admissions office to begin a file for the student and to record some initial impressions. Save your questions for the tour guide and for students on campus you meet along the way.

HOW CAN YOU ASSESS THE TRUE CHARACTER OF A COLLEGE AND ITS STUDENTS?

Colleges do not train their tour guides to deceive prospective students, but they do caution guides to avoid unflattering topics and campus sites. Does this mean that you will see only a sugarcoated version of life on a particular college campus? Not at all, especially not if you are observant.

Most organized campus visits include such campus facilities as dormitories, dining halls, libraries, student activity and recreation centers, and the health and student services centers. Some may only be pointed out, while you will walk through others. Either way, you will find that many signs of the true character of the college emerge if you keep your eyes open.

Bulletin boards in dormitories and student centers contain a wealth of information about campus activities, student concerns, and campus groups. Read the posters, notices, and messages to learn what *really* interests students. Unlike ads in the school newspaper, posters put up by students advertise both on-and off-campus events, so they will give you an idea of what is also available in the surrounding community.

Review the notices, which may cover either campuswide events or events that concern only small groups of students. The catalog may not mention a performance group, but an individual dormitory with its own small theater may offer regular productions. Poetry readings, jam sessions, writers' groups, and other activities may be announced and show diversity of student interests.

Even the brief bulletin board messages offering objects for sale and noting objects that people want to purchase reveal a lot about a campus. Are most of the items computer related? Or do the messages specify audio equipment or musical instruments? Are offers to trade goods or services posted? Don't ignore the "ride wanted" messages. Students who want to share rides home during a break may specify widely diverse geographical locations. If so, then you know that the student body is not limited to only the immediate area or one locale. Other messages can also enhance your knowledge of the true character of the campus and its students.

As you walk through various buildings, examine their condition carefully.

- Is the paint peeling, and do the exteriors look worn?
- Are the exteriors and interiors of the building clean?
- Is the equipment in the classrooms up-to-date or outdated?

Pay particular attention to the dormitories, especially to factors that might affect your safety. Observe the appearance of the structure, and ask about the security measures in and around the dormitories.

- Are the dormitories noisy or quiet?
- Do they seem crowded?
- How good is the lighting around each dormitory?
- Are the dormitories spread throughout the campus or are they clustered in one main area?
- Who has access to the dormitories in addition to students?
- How secure are the means by which students enter and leave the dormitory?

While you are on the subject of dormitory safety, you should also ask about campus safety. Don't expect that the guide will rattle off a list of crimes that have been committed in the past year. To obtain that information, access the recent year of issues of *The Chronicle of Higher Education* and locate its yearly report on campus crime. Also ask the guide about safety measures that the campus police take and those that students have initiated.

- Can students request escorts to their residences late at night?
- Do campus shuttle buses run at frequent intervals all night?
- Are "blue-light" telephones liberally placed throughout the campus for students to use to call for help?
- Do the campus police patrol the campus regularly?

If the guide does not answer your questions satisfactorily, wait until after the tour to contact the campus police or traffic office for answers.

Campus tours usually just point out the health services center without taking the time to walk through. Even if you don't see the inside of the building, you should take a close look at the location of the health services center and ask the guide questions about services.

- How far is the health center from the dormitories?
- Is a doctor always on call?
- Does the campus transport sick students from their dormitories or must they walk?
- What are the operating hours of the health center?
- Does the health center refer students to a nearby hospital?

If the guide can't answer your questions, visit the health center later and ask someone there.

Most campus tours take pride in showing students their activities centers, which may contain snack bars, game rooms, workout facilities, and other means of entertainment. Should you scrutinize this building as carefully as the rest? Of course. Outdated and poorly maintained activity equipment contributes to your total impression of the college. You should also ask about the hours, availability, and cost (no, the activities are usually not free) of using the bowling alleys, pool tables, air hockey tables, and other ammenities.

As you walk through campus with the tour, also look carefully at the appearance of the students who pass. The way in which both men and women groom themselves, the way they dress, and even their physical bearing communicate a lot more than any guidebook can. If everyone seems to conform to the same look, you might feel that you would be uncomfortable at the college, however nonconformist that look might be. On the other hand, you might not feel comfortable on a campus that stresses diversity of dress and behavior, and your observations now can save you discomfort later.

- Does every student seem to wear a sorority or fraternity t-shirt or jacket?
- Is everyone of your sex sporting the latest fad haircut?
- Do all of the men or the women seem to be wearing expensive name-brand clothes?
- Do most of the students seem to be working hard to look outrageous with regards to clothing, hair color, and body art?
- Would you feel uncomfortable in a room full of these students?

Is appearance important to you? If it is, then you should consider very seriously if you answer yes to any of the above questions. You don't have to be the same as everyone else on campus, but standing out too much may make you unhappy.

As you observe the physical appearance of the students, also listen to their conversations as you pass them. What are they talking about? How are they speaking? Are their voices and accents all the same, or do you hear diversity in their speech? Are you offended by their language? Think how you will feel if surrounded by the same speech habits and patterns for four years.

WHERE SHOULD YOU VISIT ON YOUR OWN?

Your campus visit is not over when the tour ends because you will probably have many questions yet to be answered and many places to still be seen. Where you go depends upon the extent to which the organized tour covers the campus. Your tour should take you to view residential halls, health and student services centers, the gymnasium or field house, dining halls, the library, and recreational centers. If any of the facilities on this list have been omitted, visit them on your own and ask questions of the students and staff members you meet. In addition, you should step off campus and gain an impression of the surrounding community. You will probably become bored with life on campus and spend at least some time off campus. Make certain that you know what the surrounding area is like.

The campus tour leaves little time to ask impromptu questions of current students, but you can do so after the tour. Eat lunch in one of the dining halls. Most will allow visitors to pay cash to experience a typical student meal. Food may not be important to you now while you are living at home and can

simply take anything you want from the refrigerator at any time, but it will be when you are away at college with only a meal ticket to feed you.

- How clean is the dining hall? Consider serving tables, floors, and seating.
- What is the quality of the food?
- How big are the portions?
- How much variety do students have at each meal?
- How healthy are the food choices?

While you are eating, try to strike up a conversation with students and tell them that you are considering attending their college. Their reactions and advice can be eye-opening. Ask them questions about the academic atmosphere and the professors.

- Are the classes large or small?
- Do the majority of the professors only lecture or are tutorials and seminars common?
- Is the emphasis of the faculty career-oriented or abstract?
- Are the teaching methods innovative and stimulating or boring and dull?
- Is the academic atmosphere pressured, lax, or somewhere in between?
- Which are the strong majors? The weak majors?
- Is the emphasis on grades or social life or a mix of both at the college?
- How hard do students have to work to receive high grades?

Current students can also give you the inside line on the true nature of the college social life. You may gain some idea through looking in the yearbook, in the newspaper, and on the bulletin boards, but students will reveal the true highs and lows of campus life. Ask them about drug use, partying, dating, drinking, and anything else that may affect your life as a student.

- Which are the most popular club activities?
- What do students do on weekends? Do most go home?
- How frequently do concerts occur on campus? Who has recently performed?
- How can you become involved in specific activities (name them)?
- How strictly are campus rules enforced and how severe are penalties?
- What counseling services are available?
- Are academic tutoring services available?
- Do they feel that the faculty really cares about students, especially freshmen?

You will receive the most valuable information from current students, but you will only be able to speak with them after the tour is over. And you might have to risk rejection as you try to initiate conversations with students who might not want to reveal how they feel about the campus. Still, the value of this information is worth the chance.

If you have the time, you should also visit the library to see just how accessible research materials are and to observe the physical layout. The catalog usually specifies the days and hours of operation, as well as the number of volumes contained in the library and the number of periodicals to which it subscribes. A library also requires accessibility, good lighting, an adequate number of study carrels, and lounge areas for students. Many colleges have created 24-hour study lounges for students who find the residence halls too noisy for studying, although most colleges claim that they designate areas of the residences as "quiet study" areas. You may not be interested in any of this information, but when you are a student you will have to make frequent use of the campus library so you should know what is available. You should at least ask how extensive their holdings are in your proposed major area. If they have virtually nothing, you will have to spend a lot of time ordering items via interlibrary loan or making copies, which can become expensive. The ready answer of students that they will obtain their information from the Internet is unpleasantly countered by professors who demand journal articles with documentation.

Make a point of at least driving through the community surrounding the college because you will be spending time there shopping, dining, working in a part-time job, or attending events. Even the largest and best-stocked campus will not meet all of your social and personal needs. If you can spare the time, stop in several stores to see if they welcome college students.

- Is the surrounding community suburban, urban, or rural?
- Does the community offer stores of interest, such as bookstores, craft shops, and boutiques?
- Do the businesses employ college students?
- Does the community have a movie or stage theater?
- Are there several types of interesting restaurants?
- Do there seem to be any clubs that court a college clientele?
- Is the center of activity easy to walk to, or do you need other transportation?

You might feel that a day is not enough to answer all of your questions, but even answering some questions will provide you with a stronger basis for choosing a college. Many students visit a college campus several times before making their decision. Keep in mind that for the rest of your life you will be associated with the college that you attend. You will spend four years of your life at this college. The effort of spending several days to obtain the information to make your decision is worthwhile.

Dawn B. Sova, Ph.D., is a former newspaper reporter and columnist, as well as the author of more than eight books and numerous magazine articles. She teaches creative and research writing, as well as scientific and technical writing, newswriting, and journalism.

Applying 101

The words "applying yourself" have several important meanings in the college application process. One meaning refers to the fact that you need to keep focused during this important time in your life, keep your priorities straight, and know the dates that your applications are due so you can apply on time. The phrase might also refer to the person who is really responsible for your application—you.

You are the only person who should compile your college application. You need to take ownership of this process. The guidance counselor is not responsible for completing your applications, and neither are your parents. College applications must be completed in addition to your normal workload at school, college visits, and SAT, ACT, or TOEFL testing.

THE APPLICATION

The application is your way of introducing yourself to a college admissions office. As with any introduction, you want to make a good first impression. The first thing you should do in presenting your application is to find out what the college or university needs from you. Read the application carefully to find out the application fee and deadline, required standardized tests, number of essays, interview requirements, and anything else you can do or submit to help improve your chances for acceptance.

Completing college applications yourself helps you learn more about the schools to which you are applying. The information a college asks for in its application can tell you much about the school. State university applications often tell you how they are going to view their applicants. Usually, they select students based on GPAs and test scores. Colleges that request an interview, ask you to respond to a few open-ended questions, or require an essay are interested in a more personal approach to the application process and may be looking for different types of students than those sought by a state school.

In addition to submitting the actual application, there are several other items that are commonly required. You will be responsible for ensuring that your standardized test scores and your high school transcript arrive at the colleges to which you apply. Most colleges will ask that you submit teacher recommendations as well. Select teachers who know you and your abilities well and allow them plenty of time to complete the recommendations. When all portions of the application have been completed and sent in, whether electronically or by mail, make sure you follow up with the college to ensure their receipt.

FOLLOW THESE TIPS WHEN FILLING OUT YOUR APPLICATIONS

- **Follow the directions to the letter.** You don't want to be in a position to ask an admissions officer for exceptions due to your inattentiveness.
- **Proofread all parts of your application,** including your essay. Again, the final product indicates to the admissions staff how meticulous and careful you are in your work.
- **Submit your application as early as possible,** provided all of the pieces are available. If there is a problem with your application, this will allow you to work through it with the admissions staff in plenty of time. If you wait until the last minute, it not only takes away that cushion but also reflects poorly on your sense of priorities.
- **Keep a copy of the completed application,** whether it is a photocopy or a copy saved on your computer.

THE APPLICATION ESSAY

Whereas the other portions of your application—your transcript, test scores, and involvement in extracurricular activities—are a reflection of what you've accomplished up to this point, your application essay is an opportunity to present yourself in the here and now. The essay shows your originality and verbal skills and how you approach a topic or problem and express your opinion.

Some colleges may request one essay or a combination of essays and short-answer topics to learn more about who you are and how well you can communicate your thoughts. Common essay topics cover such simple themes as writing about yourself and your experiences or why you want to attend that particular school. Other colleges will ask that you show your imaginative or creative side by writing about a favorite author, for instance, or commenting on a hypothetical situation. In such cases, they will be looking at your thought processes and level of creativity.

Admissions officers, particularly those at small or mid-size colleges, use the essay to determine how you, as a student, will fit into life at that college. The essay, therefore, is a critical component of the application process. Here are some tips for writing a winning essay:

- Colleges are looking for an honest representation of who you are and what you think. Make sure that the tone of the essay reflects enthusiasm, maturity, creativity, the ability to communicate, talent, and your leadership skills.

- Be sure you set aside enough time to write the essay, revise it, and revise it *again.* Running "spell check" will only detect a fraction of the errors you probably made on your first pass at writing it. Take a break and then come back to it and reread it. You will probably notice other style, content, and grammar problems—and ways that you can improve the essay overall.

- Always answer the question that is being asked, making sure that you are specific, clear, and true to your personality.

- Enlist the help of reviewers who know you well— friends, parents, teachers—since they are likely to be the most honest and will keep you on track in the presentation of your true self.

THE PERSONAL INTERVIEW

Although it is relatively rare that a personal interview is required, many colleges recommend that you take this opportunity for a face-to-face discussion with a member of the admissions staff. Read through the application materials to determine whether or not a college places great emphasis on the interview. If they strongly recommend that you have one, it may work against you to forego it.

In contrast to a group interview and some alumni interviews, which are intended to provide information about a college, the personal interview is viewed both as an information session and as further evaluation of your skills and strengths. You will meet with a member of the admissions staff who will be assessing your personal qualities, high school preparation, and your capacity to contribute to undergraduate life at the institution. On average, these meetings last about 45 minutes—a relatively short amount of time in which to gather information and leave the desired impression—so here are some suggestions on how to make the most of it.

Scheduling Your Visit

Generally, students choose to visit campuses in the summer or fall of their senior year. Both times have their advantages. A summer visit, when the campus is not in session, generally allows for a less hectic visit and interview. Visiting in the fall, on the other hand, provides the opportunity to see what campus life is like in full swing. If you choose the fall, consider arranging an overnight trip so that you can stay in one of the college dormitories. At the very least, you should make your way around campus to take part in classes, athletic events, and social activities. Always make an appointment and avoid scheduling more than two college interviews on any given day. Multiple interviews in a single day hinder your chances of making a good impression, and your impressions of the colleges will blur into each other as you hurriedly make your way from place to place.

Preparation

Know the basics about the college before going for your interview. Read the college catalog and Web site in addition to this guide. You will be better prepared to ask questions that are not answered in the literature and that will give you a better understanding of what the college has to offer. You should also spend some time thinking about your strengths and weaknesses and, in particular, what you are looking for in a college education. You will find that as you get a few interviews under your belt, they will get easier. You might consider starting with a college that is not a top contender on your list, so that the stakes are not as high.

Asking Questions

Inevitably, your interviewer will ask you, "0Do you have any questions?" Not having one may suggest that you're unprepared or, even worse, not interested. When you do ask questions, make sure that they are ones that matter to you and that have a bearing on your decision about whether or not to attend that college. The questions that you ask will give the interviewer some insight into your personality and priorities. Avoid asking questions that are answered in the college literature—again, a sign of unpreparedness. Although the interviewer will undoubtedly pose questions to you, the interview should not be viewed merely as a question-andanswer session. If a conversation evolves out of a particular question, so much the better. Your interviewer can learn a great deal about you from how you sustain a conversation. Similarly, you will be able to learn a great deal about the college in a conversational format.

Separate the Interview from the Interviewer

Many students base their feelings about a college solely on their impressions of the interviewer. Try not to characterize a college based only on your personal reaction, however, since your impressions can be skewed by whether you and your interviewer hit it off. Pay lots of attention to everything else that you see, hear, and learn about a college. Once on campus, you may never see your interviewer again.

In the end, remember to relax and be yourself. Your interviewer will expect you to be somewhat nervous, which will relieve some of the pressure. Don't drink jitters-producing caffeinated beverages prior to the interview, and suppress nervous fidgets like leg-wagging, finger-drumming, or bracelet jangling. Consider your interview an opportunity to put forth your best effort and to enhance everything that the college knows about you up to this point.

THE FINAL DECISION

Once you have received your acceptance letters, it is time to go back and look at the whole picture. Provided you received more than one acceptance, you are now in a position to compare your options. The best way to do this is to compare your original list of important college-ranking criteria with what you've discovered about each college along the way. In addition, you and your family will need to factor in the financial aid component. You will need to look beyond these cost issues and the quantifiable pros and cons of each college, however, and know that you have a good feeling about your final choice. Before sending off your acceptance letter, you need to feel confident that the college will feel like home for the next four years. Once the choice is made, the only hard part will be waiting for an entire summer before heading off to college!

The Early Decision Decision

SEARCH, FIND, SELECT

Maybe a senior you knew last year didn't get into the college he wanted. He said it was because he didn't apply early decision. Maybe your friend's mom told your mom that unless students apply early decision, their chances of getting into top schools are slim to none, even though they have great grades and spectacular essays. Maybe you figure you'd better get in on the early decision action.

All of the above are true—well, sort of—because many students applying to college get the term "early decision" backwards. High school guidance and college counselors run into this kind of thinking all the time and suggest putting "decision" before "early"—as in making a wise decision about committing to a college before applying early. For some students, early decision is a great option. For others, early decision is loaded with pitfalls and dangers.

"When students come back in the fall of their senior year, I often hear 'I know I want to apply early. Can you help me choose the school?'" says Kathy Cleaver, Director of College Counseling at Durham Academy in Durham, North Carolina. She compares that to saying, "I know I want to get married, please help me pick the man." Continues Cleaver, "First you have to fall in love with the school and know it's your first choice and then join the circus for early decision." She's referring to the media hype flying around high school halls about early decision—it's easy to fall prey to the early decision madness. Hot competition to get into "top" schools creates early decision anxiety. Michael "Mickey" Gilbert, Guidance Counselor at Passaic High School in Passaic, New Jersey, throws out some scary numbers that confirm that, yes, the competition for admittance to top schools is white-hot. There are about 30,000 high schools in the United States, and although the majority of high school seniors apply to institutions in their own states, there are still limited spaces in the "top" schools and the eight Ivy League schools. "No wonder kids think that early decision is the way to go," speculates Gilbert. Early decision panic sets in because students are convinced that if they get their applications in early, they have an edge. Sometimes early decision might make the difference, but there are many issues to consider before taking the early decision leap.

EARLY THIS, EARLY THAT

With all the buzz about early decision, do you really know what it means along with all the other early options, such as early action and early notification? And what about the variations of early decision? Each institution can have its own version of early decision, meaning that deadlines and criteria are different. There's the early decision that notifies students by December, there's the early decision round two, and then there is the early action/single choice.

Seeing the confusion, the National Association for College Admission Counseling (NACAC) developed a standard set of definitions. NACAC is an education association of secondary school counselors, college and university admissions and financial aid officers, counselors, and other individuals who work with students as they transition from high school to college. While each institution has its own variations of each early option, an understanding of the basic differences can help. The list that follows was adapted from the definitions found on the NACAC Web site (www.nacacnet.org).

Early Decision

- Early decision is the application process in which students make a commitment to a first-choice institution where, if admitted, they definitely will enroll. Should a student who applies for financial aid not be offered an award that makes attendance possible, the student may decline the offer of admission and be released from the early decision commitment.

- While pursuing admission under an early decision plan, students may apply to other institutions, but may have only one early decision application pending at any time.

- The institution must notify the applicant of the decision within a reasonable and clearly stated period of time after the early decision deadline. Usually, a nonrefundable deposit must be made well in advance of May 1.

- A student applying for financial aid must adhere to institutional early decision aid application deadlines.

- The institution will respond to an application for financial aid at or near the time of an offer of admission.

- The early decision application supercedes all other applications. Immediately upon acceptance of an offer of admission, a student must withdraw all other applications and make no subsequent applications.

- The application form will include a request for a parent and a counselor signature, in addition to the student's signature, indicating an understanding of the early decision commitment and agreement to abide by its terms.

Early Action

- Early action is the application process in which students make application to an institution of preference and receive a decision well in advance of the institution's regular response date. Students who are admitted under early action are not obligated to accept the institution's offer of admission or to submit a deposit until the regular reply date (not prior to May 1).

- A student may apply to other colleges without restriction.

- The institution must notify the applicant of the decision within a reasonable and clearly stated period of time after the early action deadline.

- A student applying for financial aid must adhere to institutional aid application deadlines.

- A student admitted under an early action plan may not be required to make a commitment prior to May 1, but may be encouraged to do so as soon as a final college choice is made. Colleges that solicit commitments to offers of early action admission and/or financial assistance prior to May 1 may do so provided those offers include a clear statement that written requests for extensions until May 1 will be granted, and that such requests will not jeopardize a student's status for admission or financial aid.

Regular Decision

- Regular decision is the application process in which a student submits an application to an institution by a specified date and receives a decision within a reasonable and clearly stated period of time, but not later than April 15.

- A student may apply to other colleges without restriction.

- The institution will state a deadline for completion of applications and will respond to completed applications by a specified date.

- A student applying for financial aid must adhere to institutional aid application deadlines.

- A student admitted under a regular decision plan may not be required to make a commitment prior to May 1, but may be encouraged to do so as soon as a final college choice is made. Colleges that solicit commitments to offers of admission and/or financial assistance prior to May 1 may do so provided those offers include a clear statement that written requests for extensions until May 1 will be granted, and that such requests will not jeopardize a student's status for admission or financial aid.

Rolling Admission

- Rolling admission is the application process in which an institution reviews applications as they are completed and renders admission decisions to students throughout the admission cycle.

- A student may apply to other colleges without restriction.

- The institution will respond to completed applications in a timely manner.

- A student applying for financial aid must adhere to institutional aid application deadlines.

- A student admitted under a rolling admission plan may not be required to make a commitment prior to May 1, but may be encouraged to do so as soon as a final college choice is made. Colleges that solicit commitments to offers of admission and/or financial assistance prior to May 1 may do so provided those offers include a clear statement that written requests for extensions until May 1 will be granted, and that such requests will not jeopardize a student's status for admission or financial aid.

Wait List

- Wait list is an admission decision option utilized by institutions to protect against shortfalls in enrollment. Wait lists are sometimes made necessary because of the uncertainty of the admission process, as students submit applications for admission to multiple institutions and may receive several offers of admission. By placing a student on the wait list, an institution does not initially offer or deny admission, but extends to a candidate the possibility of admission in the future before the institution's admission cycle is concluded.

- The institution will ensure that a wait list, if necessary, is of reasonable length and is maintained for a reasonable period of time, but never later than August 1.

- In the letter offering a wait list position, the institution should provide a past wait list history, which describes the number of students placed on the wait list(s), the number offered admission from the wait list, and the availability of financial aid. Students should be given an indication of when they can expect to be notified of a final admission decision.

- An institution must resolve final status and notify wait list candidates as soon after May 1 as possible.

- The institution will not require students to submit deposits to remain on a wait list or pressure students for a commitment to enroll prior to sending an official offer of admission in writing.

There is one more option, called early action/single choice (EASC), that some highly selective schools such as Harvard, Yale, and Stanford have begun using. Early action/single choice is a nonbinding early admission option for freshman applicants that replaces early decision. With this change, students learn about their admission decision in December without being required to reply until May 1. This option allows students to apply to as many colleges as they want under a regular admission time frame. The difference is that the early action/single choice option does not allow a candidate to apply to other schools under any type of early action, early decision, or early notification program. Students are asked to sign a statement in their application agreeing to file only one early application.

Each of these options has variations, depending on the institution using them. Some schools have a November 1 deadline for early decision round one. Smaller schools have a deadline of November 15, while others have a December 1 deadline. Then there's an early decision round two. To make matters even more complicated, some schools with early decision say that students can't apply to other institutions if they've sent in an early decision application to their admissions office. Others say it's okay to apply to other schools at the same time you're applying early decision to them, but if they send you an acceptance, you must withdraw the other applications.

Just because two institutions have an application process called early decision or early action doesn't mean that their policies are identical. "There is no common terminology, even among the colleges that have early decision," says Christoph Guttentag, Dean of Undergraduate Admissions at Duke University in Durham, North Carolina. He also points out that just when you think you've got the definitions figured out, institu-

PARENTS, SOME ADVICE FOR YOU

Though guidance counselors stress that high school students should make the final decision about which college to attend, they also say that parents are a very important part of the decision equation. Parents can help as organizers of all the information and provide the support needed to make a good choice. "Little things like setting up file folders and keeping track of deadlines can keep a student on track," advises David Gibson, College Advisor at St. Mary's Parish in Annapolis, Maryland.

Along with their children, parents also need to understand the basics of early option terminology as it applies to each institution being considered. Five different colleges might have five different early decision criteria. Read the fine print, and make note of deadlines.

What really will help—you, your child, and your wallet—is to understand the basics about financial aid. Says Shawn Leftwich, Director of Undergraduate Admissions at Wheaton College in Illinois, "Have an in-depth discussion with the financial aid officer so that you are aware of the ramifications, restrictions, and implications of the financial aid offer."

If possible, make an appointment to visit with a financial aid officer at the college while your child is visiting the campus. Bring your tax forms and discuss the prospects of financial aid. "Financial aid people are straight shooters. It's not in their best interest to tell you one thing to get your foot in the door and then turn around and pull the rug out from under you," says Bill McClintick, Director of College Counseling at Mercerburg Academy. "Parents might not like the answer they get from the financial aid officer, but they will get a candid assessment of their eligibility for financial aid."

Leftwich suggests having an honest discussion with your child early in the college selection process. Talk about what you can realistically afford, what colleges will appropriately challenge him or her, if location is a factor, and what kind of environment best suits your child. Whichever option your child uses to apply, you both will know the decision is an informed one.

tions change them. "Colleges are always balancing the needs of their institution and the needs of students," he comments.

EARLY DECISION: A MATCHMAKING TOOL OR A CLEVER STRATEGY?

Despite the differences in what actually constitutes early decision, it has become more of a strategy than a matchmaking tool, according to Bill McClintick, Director of College Counseling at Mercersburg Academy in Mercersburg, Pennsylvania. He also chairs the national steering committee on admissions standards for NACAC. The focus of early decision used to be on matching the student with the college and letting the admissions office know that that institution is where the student wants to be above all others. Today, early decision is

misunderstood and misused. High school seniors think that they must use the early decision tactic to get an edge. The result, says McClintick is "at many of the top places, early decision applications have gone through the roof."

Though high school students may have exaggerated ideas of how much early decision can really help them, it is true that it does give a small segment of students applying at highly selective schools an advantage. Generally, the more selective the institution, the more small differences matter. "Even if it's a small increase, you need everything you can get," states John Latting, Dean of Undergraduate Admissions at The Johns Hopkins University in Baltimore, Maryland.

"Remember," cautions McClintick, "we're only talking about a small slice of kids in the grand scheme of things." He mentions 5 percent of high school seniors nationally who aspire to the "top" institutions. State colleges and universities fill a much lower percentage of their freshman class with early decision applications. "I don't believe that more kids are chasing the same number of spots," says Jon Reider, Director of College Counseling at San Francisco University High School in San Francisco, California. "Students are applying to more and more schools, even with the early decision option on the side. This is inflating the selectivity of some colleges beyond what it used to be." In reality, 90 percent of students apply regular admission. Interest in early decision comes from a relatively small segment of the college applicant pool.

THE BENEFITS OF EARLY DECISION

There are clear benefits for students who apply for early decision. Aside from the fact that early decision does play a role in acceptance rates for a relatively small percentage of students at a small number of schools, early decision is a good option. The caveat is that students must know, without a shred of doubt, that one institution, above all others, is the best match for their goals and their likes and dislikes, and that based on grades and test scores, they solidly match the institution's criteria for admission. The option to go early decision should be taken after extensive research, multiple visits to the campus, and talking to a lot of people. "Early decision is for those who can put their hearts and souls into one application," advises Cleaver.

There are other advantages. You have to make only one choice, and you will know by December if you've been accepted. You have to fill out only one application. You are not chewing your nails over your list of possibilities during the Christmas holiday. Instead, you know where you're going and can sit back and enjoy the rest of your senior year, while others in your class are madly filling out applications, writing essays, and agonizing over the thin envelopes that arrive in the mail. Says Guttentag, "The advantage of having that challenging process over with is not insignificant."

Early decision is helpful for admissions officers at selective colleges because it allows them to make decisions between well-qualified students and select those who really want to be at their institution. As Shawn Leftwich, Director of Undergraduate Admissions at Wheaton College in Illinois, points out, early decision is for the students who are strongly committed. "We like you. You like us. We know you're coming, and we can fill our freshman class." However, on the flip side, she adds that some students aren't so sure about which college they want to attend, and early decision only makes the process more stressful.

Before you decide to go with early decision, consider early action. Many high school counselors lean toward early action, which is another good option. With early action you're able to apply later in the process. This means you will be able to take the SATs again. Your first-semester grades and AP classes taken in the first semester of your senior year can be used to evaluate your eligibility. You have September and October to visit several campuses while they are in session and plenty of time to do the research to put more than one school on your list.

THE PITFALLS OF EARLY DECISION

Though early decision has benefits, before you jump into it, look at the ramifications of that option. Advises Gilbert, "Early decision might give you an edge, but the tradeoff is not so great."

Perhaps the most compelling reason why students should seriously examine early decision before jumping at it is because they are bound by an agreement to attend that school if accepted. Students sign a pledge to attend that institution and are required to withdraw applications from all other schools. They also are obligated to accept the financial aid award that the institution gives them. An early decision is a binding decision. "Regardless," advises David Gibson, College Advisor at St. Mary's Parish in Annapolis, Maryland, "students don't learn about their financial aid awards until March or April, and if the award funding is not at all acceptable because the family's financial need was not met, they need to decline the offer and begin searching for a new college. March or April is not a good time to start applying to new colleges."

How binding is binding? Though no school can force a student to attend if they've signed an early decision agreement, students who decide not to attend that school hurt others with that decision. High school counselors have to sign the binding agreement, along with parents, and must state that they will not send out transcripts to other institutions. Many institutions will not accept the application of a student who applied early decision elsewhere and backed out of the agreement. Admissions officers may find out in May that an early decision student is not coming, so they'll call the counselor and ask if the student applied to another school. If so, often a phone call to the other institution is made and acceptance denied. Sometimes the counselor loses a good reputation with that institution, putting applicants who follow in subsequent years at a disadvantage.

After the consequences of signing a binding agreement, the financial aspect of early decision is the next biggest pitfall. "You can't compare financial aid offers," says Latting. "You have only one offer." Students won't know if they're eligible for Pell grants or merit scholarships. Government FAFSA forms are not submitted until January, and students might not find out how much aid they can get until March or April, long

QUESTIONS TO ASK YOURSELF BEFORE APPLYING EARLY DECISION

What if you don't get accepted early decision—then what? Speaking from the experience of seeing students deal with early decision rejection letters, Reider says, "Some of your friends are getting acceptance letters, and you get one thin envelope and the pain of rejection. You've given the early decision institution your best shot and you lost." Cleaver has seen kids in her high school end up thinking they won't get in anywhere. "This is the first time they've faced a big rejection and news they don't want to hear," she says, noting that because of the timetable of early decision, letters often come right around exam time in December.

When students apply regular decision, meaning they wait until well into their senior year and apply to several different institutions, it's "all or some," quips Latting. "With early decision, it's all or nothing." Many application deadlines for regular decision are in January. If you get that rejection letter from the school you were counting on, that doesn't give you much time to apply to other schools, much less visit them.

Are you ready to make such a drastic decision so early in your senior year? A lot can change in how you think about your future between the beginning of your senior year and graduation. With six or seven months behind you as a senior, you might be in a better position to compare colleges in April than you were back in September. Think about it—you're making the decision about where you want to spend the next four years of your life in early October of your senior year!

Have you given yourself enough time to pick one college above all others? If you want to apply early decision, you should start making plans to do so in your junior year. In order to apply early decision, you must have your ACTs or SATs taken, campus visits done, a final choice made, a dynamite essay written, a stellar application filled out, and teacher recommendation letters collected. That's a lot to cram into the end of your junior year and a few months into your senior year.

Have you given an admissions office enough information to make a decision about you? The more information the admissions office has about grades and classes you took and activities and leadership positions you held, the better they can decide if you're a good match for them. Do you really want decisions being made about you based on sophomore and junior grades and activities? What happens to that AP English class you finally felt ready to take the beginning of your senior year? What about that calculus class you aced in the first semester of your senior year? Admissions won't be able to assess that on an early decision application.

after the early decision agreement was signed and sealed. "This means that if they are accepted, they are then obligated to a college that might not fund them to the level of their financial need," says Gibson. Students who apply early action or regular decision are in a better position to negotiate financial aid packages.

EARLY DECISION REJECTION

In case you haven't heard, fat is good, thin is bad. Thin envelopes from college admissions offices usually mean a single-page letter saying good luck, we wish you the best, but you're not going to be attending our school next fall. However stated, it's hard to be rejected, especially when you've applied early decision, which states to the college and to yourself that this is the college you've decided is the only one you really, really want to attend above all others.

But thin envelopes don't mean the end of the world. Cleaver advises to not let early decision get control of you. "There are too many choices of colleges for you not to get into college. You might not get into Princeton, but there are many other wonderful schools if you do the research to look for a good match. Early decision is a tool to use to apply, but it is not always the best tool."

Objecting to the term "perfect match," Reider asks, "Does it really matter what kind of car you drive? There are twenty different colleges that can get you where you want to go. You'll be successful in most places."

HOW TO DO EARLY DECISION THE RIGHT WAY

Taking the early decision option requires more than gathering information, filling out an application, writing an essay, and waiting for an envelope to come in the mail or an e-mail to hit your In Box. If you're going to be serious about early decision, the time to start is in your junior year.

Research the institutions at the top of your list. Think through what you want out of college—not just in terms of a future career, but also factors such as location, size, distance from home, sports, and other activities. Think about who you want to be. "It has to be a love connection," says Cleaver. Tune out all the early decision talk and do your homework about each college. Then ask yourself if one stands out above all the others you've researched. Is this the one to which you can

commit to a binding agreement? Are you in the competition to be admitted? Will you have the funds to attend this college?

"Admissions can tell if your application is from the heart," Cleaver cautions. Students ask her how to make their applications "look like they want to go there." She replies that what they put on an application and in an essay has to pour out of their hearts. Students who visit the campus and sit in on a class or a campus organization have the edge if something really clicked with them. They will write a convincing application. Perhaps they'll tell about how exciting the professor they heard was or how wonderful it is that the college has a chess club. Cleaver observes that kids usually write about an institution's sports team or about the ivy-covered walls of the campus on their application essay instead of writing about some interesting aspect of the university that spoke to them, which takes research, time, and reflection. "Don't make the mistake of chasing a name and not being a good consumer," cautions McClintick. Part of being a good consumer is to make sure you are a reasonably competitive applicant. This means looking at the school's admission criteria and statistics. What percentage of the freshman class is filled with early decision and early action students? If it's a high percentage, then you might want to reconsider where that school falls on your wish list. How many students return for their sophomore year? If more than 10 percent leave after their freshman year, that should tell you something about student satisfaction—and ultimately yours.

One of the most important ways to choose the right school is to visit the campus, perhaps multiple times and preferably with students on campus. "Campus visits are a critical time to talk with undergraduates and to find out what the academic, social, and physical climate is like," advises Guttentag. If you're staying in a dorm on Tuesday night during a visit, you can tell how serious kids are about their work. What kinds of conversations are they having? "Are these the kind of kids you want to spend four years of your life with?" asks McClintick.

After you've thoroughly investigated all the aspects of a college and decided it's at the absolute top of your list, after you are familiar with the early decision requirements at that institution, and after you've determined that you have a good chance of getting into that institution, then you can say early decision is for you. For those who are not so sure, fortunately, colleges and universities have plenty of other options for admission.

What International Students Need to Know About Admission to U.S. Colleges and Universities

Kitty M. Villa

There are two principles to remember about admission to a university in the United States. First, applying is almost never a one-time request for admission but an ongoing process that may involve several exchanges of information between applicant and institution. "Admission process" or "application process" means that a "yes" or "no" is usually not immediate, and requests for additional information are to be expected. To successfully manage this process, you must be prepared to send additional information when requested and then wait for replies. You need a thoughtful balance of persistence to communicate regularly and effectively with your selected universities and patience to endure what can be a very long process.

The second principle involves a marketplace analogy. The most successful applicants are alert to opportunities to create a positive impression that sets them apart from other applicants. They are able to market themselves to their target institution. Institutions are also trying to attract the highest-quality student that they can. The admissions process presents you with the opportunity to analyze your strengths and weaknesses as a student and to look for ways to present yourself in the most marketable manner.

FIRST STEP—SELECTING INSTITUTIONS

With thousands of institutions of higher education in the United States, how do you begin to narrow your choices down to the institutions that are best for you? There are many factors to consider, and you must ultimately decide which factors are most important to you.

Location

You may spend several years studying in the United States. Do you prefer an urban or rural campus? Large or small metropolitan area? If you need to live on campus, will you be unhappy at a university where most students commute from off-campus housing? How do you feel about extremely hot summers or cold winters? Eliminating institutions that do not match your preferences in terms of location will narrow your choices.

Recommendations from Friends, Professors, or Others

There are valid academic reasons to consider the recommendations of people who know you well and have firsthand knowledge about particular institutions. Friends and contacts may be able to provide you with "inside information" about the campus or its academic programs to which published sources have no access. You should carefully balance anecdotal information with your own research and your own impressions. However, current and former students, professors, and others may provide excellent information during the application process.

Your Own Academic and Career Goals

Consideration of your academic goals is more complex than it may seem at first glance. All institutions do not offer the same academic programs. The application form usually provides a definitive listing of the academic programs offered by an institution. A course catalog describes the degree program and all the courses offered. In addition to printed sources, there is a tremendous amount of institutional information available on the Web. Program descriptions, even course descriptions and course syllabi, are often available to peruse online.

You may be interested in the rankings of either the university or of a program of study. Keep in mind, however, that rankings usually assume that quality is quantifiable. Rankings are usually based on presumptions about how data relate to quality and are likely to be unproven. It is important to carefully consider the source and the criteria of any ranking information before believing and acting upon it.

Your Own Educational Background

You may be concerned about the interpretation of your educational credentials, since your country's degree nomenclature and the grading scale may differ from those in the United States. Universities use reference books about the educational systems of other countries to help them understand specific educational credentials. Generally, these credentials are interpreted by each institution; there is not a single interpretation that applies to every institution. The lack of uniformity is good news for most students, since it means that students from a wide variety of educational backgrounds can find a U.S. university that is appropriate to their needs.

To choose an appropriate institution, you can and should do an informal self-evaluation of your educational background. This self-analysis involves three important questions:

1. How Many Years of Study Have You Completed?

Completion of secondary school with at least twelve total years of education usually qualifies students to apply for undergraduate (bachelor's) degree programs. Completion of a university degree program that involves at least sixteen years of total education qualifies one to apply for admission to graduate (master's) degree programs in the United States.

2. Does the Education That You Have Completed in Your Country Provide Access to Further Study in the United States?

Consider the kind of institution where you completed your previous studies. If educational opportunities in your country are limited, it may be necessary to investigate many U.S. institutions and programs in order to find a match.

3. Are Your Previous Marks or Grades Excellent, Average, or Poor?

Your educational record influences your choice of U.S. institutions. If your grades are average or poor, it may be advisable to apply to several institutions with minimally difficult or non-competitive entrance levels.

YOU are one of the best sources of information about the level and quality of your previous studies. Awareness of your educational assets and liabilities will serve you well throughout the application process.

SECOND STEP—PLANNING AND ASSEMBLING THE APPLICATION

Planning and assembling a university application can be compared to the construction of a building. First, you must start with a solid foundation, which is the application form itself. The application, often available online as well as in paper form, usually contains a wealth of useful information, such as deadlines, fees, and degree programs available at that institution. To build a solid application, it is best to begin well in advance of the application deadline.

How to Obtain the Application Form

Application forms and links to institutional Web sites may also be available at a U.S. educational advising center associated with the American Embassy or Consulate in your country. These centers are excellent resources for international students and provide information about standardized test administration, scholarships, and other matters to students who are interested in studying in the United States. Your local U.S. Embassy or Consulate can guide you to the nearest educational advising center.

What Are the Key Components of a Complete Application?

Institutional requirements vary, but the standard components of a complete application include the following:

- Transcript
- Required standardized examination scores
- Evidence of financial support
- Letters of recommendation
- Application fee

Transcript

A complete academic record or transcript includes all courses completed, grades earned, and degrees awarded. Most universities require an official transcript to be sent directly from the school or university. In many other countries, however, the practice is to issue official transcripts and degree certificates directly to the student. If you have only one official copy of your transcript, it may be a challenge to get additional certified copies that are acceptable to U.S. universities. Some institutions will issue additional official copies for application purposes.

If your institution does not provide this service, you may have to seek an alternate source of certification. As a last resort, you may send a photocopy of your official transcript, explain that you have only one original, and ask the university for advice on how to deal with this situation.

Required Standardized Examination Scores

Arranging to take standardized examinations and earning the required scores seem to cause the most anxiety for international students.

The university application form usually indicates which examinations are required. The standardized examination required most often for undergraduate admission is the Test of English as a Foreign Language (TOEFL). Institutions may also require the SAT of undergraduate applicants. These standardized examinations are administered by the Educational Testing Service (ETS).

These examinations are offered in almost every country of the world. It is advisable to begin planning for standardized examinations at least six months prior to the application deadline of your desired institutions. Test centers fill up quickly, so it is important to register as soon as possible. Information about the examinations is available at U.S. educational advising centers associated with embassies or consulates.

Most universities require that the original test scores, not a student copy, be sent directly by the testing service. When you register for the test, be sure to indicate that the testing service should send the test scores directly to the universities.

You should begin your application process before you receive your test scores. Delaying submission of your application until the test scores arrive may cause you to miss deadlines and negatively affect the outcome of your application. If you want to know your scores in order to assess your chances of admission to an institution with rigorous admission standards, you should take the tests early.

Many universities in the United States set minimum required scores on the TOEFL or other standardized examinations. Test scores are an important factor, but most institutions also look at a number of other factors in their consideration of a candidate for admission.

For More Information

Questions about test formats, locations, dates, and registration may be addressed to:

ETS Corporate Headquarters
Rosedale Road
Princeton, New Jersey 08541
Web sites: http://www.ets.org
http://www.ets.org/toefl/
Phone: 609-921-9000
Fax: 609-734-5410

Evidence of Financial Support

Evidence of financial support is required to issue immigration documents to admitted students. This is part of a complete application package but usually plays no role in determining admission. Most institutions make admissions decisions without regard to the source and amount of financial support.

Letters of Recommendation

Most institutions require one or more letters of recommendation. The best letters are written by former professors, employers, or others who can comment on your academic achievements or professional potential.

Some universities provide a special form for the letters of recommendation. If possible, use the forms provided. If you are applying to a large number of universities, however, or if your recommenders are not available to complete several forms, it may be necessary for you to duplicate a general recommendation letter.

Application Fee

Most universities also require an application fee, ranging from $25 to $100, which must be paid to initiate consideration of the application.

Completing the Application Form

Whether sent by mail or electronically, the application form must be neat and thoroughly filled out. Although parts of the application may not seem to apply to you or your situation, do your best to answer all the questions.

Remember that this is a process. You provide information, and your proposed university then may request clarification and further information. If you have questions, it is better to initiate the entire process by submitting the application form rather than asking questions before you apply. The university will be better able to respond to you after it has your application. Always complete as much as you can. Do not permit uncertainty about the completion of the application form to cause unnecessary delays.

THIRD STEP—DISTINGUISH YOUR APPLICATION

To distinguish your application—to market yourself successfully—is ultimately the most important part of the application process. As you select your prospective universities, begin to analyze your strengths and weaknesses as a prospective student. As you complete your application, you should strive to create a positive impression and set yourself apart from other applicants, to highlight your assets and bring these qualities to the attention of the appropriate university administrators and professors. Applying early is a very easy way to distinguish your application.

Deadline or Guideline?

The application deadline is the last date that an application for a given semester will be accepted. Often, the application will specify that all required documents and information be submitted before the deadline date. To meet the deadlines, start the application process early. This also gives you more time to take—and perhaps retake and improve—the required standardized tests.

Admissions deliberations may take several weeks or months. In the meantime, most institutions accept additional information, including improved test scores, after the posted deadline.

Even if your application is initially rejected, you may be able to provide additional information to change the decision. You can request reconsideration based on additional information, such as improved test scores, strong letters of recommendation, or information about your class rank. Applying early allows more time to improve your application. Also, some students may decide not to accept their offers of admission, leaving room for offers to students on a waiting list. Reconsideration of the admission decisions can occur well beyond the application deadline.

Think of the deadline as a guideline rather than an impermeable barrier. Many factors—the strength of the application, your research interests, the number of spaces available at the proposed institution—can override the enforcement of an application deadline. So, if you lack a test score or transcript by the official deadline, you may still be able to apply and be accepted.

Statement of Purpose

The statement of purpose is your first and perhaps best opportunity to present yourself as an excellent candidate for admission. Whether or not a personal history essay or statement of purpose is required, always include a carefully written statement of purpose with your applications. A compelling statement of purpose does not have to be lengthy, but it should include some basic components:

- Part One—Introduce yourself and describe your educational background. This is your opportunity to describe any facet of your educational experience that you wish to emphasize. Perhaps you attended a highly ranked secondary school or university in your home country. Mention the name and any noteworthy characteristics of the secondary school or university from which you graduated. Explain the grading scale used at your university. Do not forget to mention your rank in your graduating class and any honors you may have received. This is not the time to be modest.

- Part Two—Describe your current academic and career interests and goals. Think about how these will fit into those

SEARCH, FIND, SELECT

of the institution to which you are applying, and mention the reasons why you have selected that institution.

- Part Three—Describe your long-term goals. When you finish your program of study, what do you plan to do next? If you already have a job offer or a career plan, describe it. Give some thought to how you'll demonstrate that studying in the United States. will ultimately benefit others.

Use Personal Contacts When Possible

Appropriate and judicious use of your own network of contacts can be very helpful. Friends, former professors, former students of your selected institutions, and others may be willing to advise you during the application process and provide you with introductions to key administrators or professors. If suggested, you may wish to contact certain professors or administrators by mail, phone, or e-mail. A personal visit to discuss your interest in the institution may be appropriate. Whatever your choice of communication, try to make the encounter pleasant and personal. Your goal is to make a positive impression, not to rush the admission decision.

There is no single right way to be admitted to U.S. universities. The same characteristics that make the educational choice in the United States so difficult—the number of institutions and the variety of programs of study—are the same attributes that allow so many international students to find the institution that's right for them.

Kitty M. Villa is the former Assistant Director, International Office, at the University of Texas at Austin.

Financial Aid Countdown Calendar

JUNIOR YEAR

Fall

Now is the time to get serious about the colleges in which you are interested. Meet with your guidance counselor to help you narrow down your choices. Hopefully by the spring, your list will have five to ten solid choices. College visits are always a great idea—remember this will be the place you will call home for four years, so start your campus visits soon!

❑ Register for the PSAT/NMSQT.

❑ Check out local financial aid nights in the area. Be sure to attend these valuable sessions, especially if this is the first time your family is sending someone off to college. Try to become familiar with common financial aid terms. Start reviewing the literature available and begin to familiarize yourself with the various programs. A good booklet is published by the U.S. Department of Education, "Funding Education Beyond High School: The Guide to Federal Student Aid" and is available at any financial aid office or on the Web at http://studentaid.ed.gov/students/attachments/siteresources/Funding_Education_Beyond_HS_2011-12.pdf.

❑ In October, take the PSAT/NMSQT.

❑ Do some Web browsing! There are many free scholarship search engines, such as Petersons.com. Also, head to the bookstore or library and pick up a copy of *Peterson's Scholarships, Grants & Prizes,* which features details on billions of dollars of aid from private sources, or *Best Scholarships for the Best Students,* which offers great info on scholarships, fellowships, and experiential learning programs for top students.

❑ Ask your parents to contact their employers, unions, and any religious and fraternal organizations with which they have a connection to learn about possible scholarship opportunities.

❑ Check with your high school guidance counselor for the qualifications and deadlines of local scholarship awards. Many guidance counselors report that there are few applicants for these awards.

Winter

❑ Keep checking for scholarships! Remember that this is the one area over which you have control. The harder you work, the better your chances for success!

❑ Register and study for the ACT or SAT and SAT Subject Tests.

Spring

❑ Spring Break—a great time to visit colleges. Remember your top ten list? Time to start narrowing it down.

❑ Review the requirements for local scholarships. What can you do now and over the summer to improve your chances?

❑ Take the ACT or SAT. Good luck!

❑ Look for a summer job, especially one that ties in with your college plans. For example, if you want to major in premed, why not try to get a job at a hospital or with a laboratory?

Summer

❑ College visit time! Ask: Is this where I see myself getting my undergraduate degree? Can I adjust to the seasons, the town surrounding the campus, the distance from home, the college size? Does this school feel right for me?

❑ Why not get a jump on college (and maybe save some money!) and enroll for a college course at the local community college? Or, better yet, do some extra prep work for the ACT or SAT!

MONEY, MONEY, MONEY

SENIOR YEAR

Fall

How's the college list coming? Can you get your list down to five or six choices? Your guidance counselor can help with this process. Once you have your top choices, make a list of what each college requires for admission and financial aid. Be sure your list includes all deadlines. Attend a financial aid night presentation with your parents. Some of these sessions offer help in completing forms; others offer a broader view of the process. Contact the presenter (usually a local college financial aid professional) to be sure you are getting the information you need.

❑ Do any of these colleges require the CSS/Financial Aid PROFILE® financial aid application? Many private colleges use this form for institutional aid. You need to file this comprehensive form in late September or early October. For more information or to find out which colleges use this supplemental form, go to http://profileonline.collegeboard.com/index.jsp. (Web site registration is free; however, PROFILE is a fee-based application).

❑ Don't falter now in your scholarship search. Get the applications filed by the published deadlines.

❑ Register now if you are planning to retake the SAT.

❑ Most important, start completing your college applications—the earlier, the better! If you are interested in early decision or early action, now is the time! Remember, accuracy and completeness are a must!

Winter

❑ Ensure all college applications are completed.

❑ Get the Free Application for Federal Student Aid (FAFSA). This is the key form for financial aid for every school across the country. Remember, watch your deadlines, but do not file until after January 1. Be sure to keep a copy of the form, whether you file electronically or with the paper application. Do you have some questions? Call the local financial aid office. Many states have special toll-free call-in programs in January and February, Financial Aid Awareness Month. Be sure that you have completed each school's required forms.

❑ As the letters of admission start to arrive, the financial aid award letters should be right behind them. Important question for parents: What is the bottom line? Remember, aid at a lower-cost state school will be less than a higher-cost private college. But what will you be required to pay? This can be confusing, so consider gift aid (scholarships and grants), student loans, and parent loans. The school with the lowest sticker price (tuition, fees, and room and board) might not be the best bargain when you look at the overall financial aid package.

Spring

❑ Still not sure where to go? The financial aid package at your top choice just not enough? Call the financial aid office and the admissions office. Talk it over. While schools don't like to bargain, they are usually willing to take a second look. Is there something unusual about your family's financial situation that might impact your parents' ability to pay?

❑ By May 1, you must make your final decision. Notify your chosen college and find out what you need to do next. Tell the other colleges you are not accepting their offers of admission and financial aid.

Summer

❑ Time to crunch the numbers. Parents, get information from the college on the total charges for the coming fall term. Deduct the aid package and then plan for how the balance will be paid. Contact the college financial aid office for the best parental loan program. If you want to arrange for a payment plan, contact the business office for further information. Most schools have deferred payment plans available for a nominal fee.

Congratulations! Remember that you need to reapply for aid every year!

Who's Paying for This?
Financial Aid Basics

A college education can be expensive—costing more than $150,000 for four years at some of the higher priced private colleges and universities. Even at the lower cost state colleges and universities, the cost of a four-year education can approach $60,000. Determining how you and your family will come up with the necessary funds to pay for your education requires planning, perseverance, and learning as much as you can about the options that are available to you. But before you get discouraged, College Board statistics show that 53 percent of full-time students attend four-year public and private colleges with tuition and fees less than $9000, while 20 percent attend colleges that have tuition and fees more than $36,000. College costs tend to be less in the western states and higher in New England.

Paying for college should not be looked at as a four-year financial commitment. For many families, paying the total cost of a student's college education out of current income and savings is usually not realistic. For families that have planned ahead and have financial savings established for higher education, the burden is a lot easier. But for most, meeting the cost of college requires the pooling of current income and assets and investing in longer-term loan options. These family resources, together with financial assistance from state, federal, and institutional sources, enable millions of students each year to attend the institution of their choice.

FINANCIAL AID PROGRAMS

There are three types of financial aid:

1. Gift-aid—Scholarships and grants are funds that do not have to be repaid.

2. Loans—Loans must be repaid, usually after graduation; the amount you have to pay back is the total you've borrowed plus any accrued interest. This is considered a source of self-help aid.

3. Student employment—Student employment is a job arranged for you by the financial aid office. This is another source of self-help aid.

The federal government has four major grant programs—the Federal Pell Grant, the Federal Supplemental Educational Opportunity Grant, Academic Competitiveness Grants (ACG), and SMART grants. ACG and SMART grants are limited to students who qualify for a Pell grant and are awarded to a select group of students. Overall, these grants are targeted to low-to-moderate income families with significant financial need. The federal government also sponsors a student employment program called the Federal Work-Study Program, which offers jobs both on and off campus, and several loan programs, including those for students and for parents of undergraduate students.

There are two types of student loan programs: subsidized and unsubsidized. The subsidized Federal Direct Loan and the Federal Perkins Loan are need-based, government-subsidized loans. Students who borrow through these programs do not have to pay interest on the loan until after they graduate or leave school. The unsubsidized Federal Direct Loan and the Federal Direct PLUS Loan Program are not based on need, and borrowers are responsible for the interest while the student is in school. These loans are administered by different methods. Once you choose your college, the financial aid office will guide you through this process.

After you've submitted your financial aid application and you've been accepted for admission, each college will send you a letter describing your financial aid award. Most award letters show estimated college costs, how much you and your family are expected to contribute, and the amount and types of aid you have been awarded. Most students are awarded aid from a combination of sources and programs. Hence, your award is often called a financial aid "package."

SOURCES OF FINANCIAL AID

Millions of students and families apply for financial aid each year. Financial aid from all sources exceeds $143 billion per year. The largest single source of aid is the federal government, which will award more than $100 billion this year.

The next largest source of financial aid is found in the college and university community. Most of this aid is awarded to students who have a demonstrated need based on the Federal Methodology. Some institutions use a different formula, the Institutional Methodology (IM), to award their own funds in conjunction with other forms of aid. Institutional aid may be either need-based or non-need based. Aid that is not based on need is usually awarded for a student's academic performance (merit awards), specific talents or abilities, or to attract the type of students a college seeks to enroll.

Another source of financial aid is from state government. All states offer grant and/or scholarship aid, most of which is need-based. However, more and more states are offering substantial merit-based aid programs. Most state programs award aid only to students attending college in their home state.

Other sources of financial aid include:

- Private agencies
- Foundations
- Corporations
- Clubs
- Fraternal and service organizations

- Civic associations
- Unions
- Religious groups that award grants, scholarships, and low-interest loans
- Employers that provide tuition reimbursement benefits for employees and their children

More information about these different sources of aid is available from high school guidance offices, public libraries, college financial aid offices, directly from the sponsoring organizations, and on the Web at www.petersons.com and www.finaid.org.

HOW NEED-BASED FINANCIAL AID IS AWARDED

When you apply for aid, your family's financial situation is analyzed using a government-approved formula called the Federal Methodology. This formula looks at five items:

1. Demographic information of the family
2. Income of the parents
3. Assets of the parents
4. Income of the student
5. Assets of the student

This analysis determines the amount you and your family are expected to contribute toward your college expenses, called your Expected Family Contribution or EFC. If the EFC is equal to or more than the cost of attendance at a particular college, then you do not demonstrate financial need. However, even if you don't have financial need, you may still qualify for aid, as there are grants, scholarships, and loan programs that are not need-based.

If the cost of your education is greater than your EFC, then you do demonstrate financial need and qualify for assistance. The amount of your financial need that can be met varies from school to school. Some are able to meet your full need, while others can only cover a certain percentage of need. Here's the formula:

$$\begin{aligned} &\text{Cost of Attendance} \\ -\ &\underline{\text{Expected Family Contribution}} \\ =\ &\text{Financial Need} \end{aligned}$$

The EFC remains constant, but your need will vary according to the costs of attendance at a particular college. In general, the higher the tuition and fees at a particular college, the higher the cost of attendance will be. Expenses for books and supplies, room and board, transportation, and other miscellaneous items are included in the overall cost of attendance. It is important to remember that you do not have to be "needy" to qualify for financial aid. Many middle and upper-middle income families qualify for need-based financial aid.

APPLYING FOR FINANCIAL AID

Every student must complete the Free Application for Federal Student Aid (FAFSA) to be considered for financial aid. The FAFSA is available from your high school guidance office, many public libraries, colleges in your area, or directly from the U.S. Department of Education.

Students are encouraged to apply for federal student aid on the Web. The electronic version of the FAFSA can be accessed at http://www.fafsa.ed.gov. Both the student and at least one parent must apply for a federal PIN at http:// www.pin.ed.gov. The PIN serves as your electronic signature when applying for aid on the Web.

To award their own funds, some colleges require an additional application, the CSS/Financial Aid PROFILEt form. The PROFILE asks supplemental questions that some colleges and awarding agencies feel provide a more accurate assessment of the family's ability to pay for college. It is up to the college to decide whether it will use only the FAFSA or both the FAFSA and the PROFILE. PROFILE applications are available from the high school guidance office and on the Web. Both the paper application and the Web site list those colleges and programs that require the PROFILE application.

If Every College You're Applying to for Fall 2012 Requires the FAFSA

. . . then it's pretty simple: Complete the FAFSA after January 1, 2012, being certain to send it in before any college-imposed deadlines. (You are not permitted to send in the 2012–13 FAFSA before January 1, 2012.) Most college FAFSA application deadlines are in February or early March. It is easier if you have all your financial records for the previous year available, but if that is not possible, you are strongly encouraged to use estimated figures.

After you send in your FAFSA, either with the paper application or electronically, you'll receive a Student Aid Report (SAR) that includes all of the information you reported and shows your EFC. If you provided an e-mail address, the SAR is sent to you electronically; otherwise, you will receive a paper copy in the mail. Be sure to review the SAR, checking to see if the information you reported is accurately represented. If you used estimated numbers to complete the FAFSA, you may have to resubmit the SAR with any corrections to the data. The college(s) you have designated on the FAFSA will receive the information you reported and will use that data to make their decision. In many instances, the colleges to which you've applied will ask you to send copies of your and your parents' federal income tax returns for 2011, plus any other documents needed to verify the information you reported.

If a College Requires the PROFILE

Step 1: Register for the CSS/Financial Aid PROFILE in the fall of your senior year in high school. You can apply for the PROFILE online at http://profileonline.collegeboard.com/ prf/index.jsp. Registration information with a list of the colleges that require the PROFILE is available in most high school guidance offices. There is a fee for using the Financial Aid PROFILE application ($25 for the first college, which includes the $9 application fee, and $16 for each additional college). You must pay for the service by credit card when you register. If you do not have a credit card, you will be billed. A limited number of fee waivers are automatically granted to first-time applicants based on the financial information provided on the PROFILE.

Step 2: Fill out your customized CSS/Financial Aid PROFILE. Once you register, your application will be immediately available online and will have questions that all students must complete, questions which must be completed by the student's parents (unless the student is independent and the colleges or programs selected do not require parental information), and *may* have supplemental questions needed by one or more of your schools or programs. If required, those will be found in Section Q of the application.

In addition to the PROFILE application you complete online, you may also be required to complete a Business/ Farm Supplement via traditional paper format. Completion of this form is not a part of the online process. If this form is required, instructions on how to download and print the supplemental form are provided. If your biological or adoptive parents are separated or divorced and your colleges and programs require it, your noncustodial parent may be asked to complete the Non-custodial PROFILE.

Once you complete and submit your PROFILE application, it will be processed and sent directly to your requested colleges and programs.

IF YOU DON'T QUALIFY FOR NEED-BASED AID

If you are not eligible for need-based aid, you can still find ways to lessen your burden.

Here are some suggestions:

- Search for merit scholarships. You can start at the initial stages of your application process. College merit awards are increasingly important as more and more colleges award these to students they especially want to attract. As a result, applying to a college at which your qualifications put you at the top of the entering class may give you a larger merit award. Another source of aid to look for is private scholarships that are given for special skills and talents. Additional information can be found at and at www.finaid.org.

- Seek employment during the summer and the academic year. The student employment office at your college can help you locate a school-year job. Many colleges and local businesses have vacancies remaining after they have hired students who are receiving Federal Work-Study Program financial aid.

- Borrow through the unsubsidized Federal Direct Loan program. This is generally available to all students. The terms and conditions are similar to the subsidized loans. The biggest difference is that the borrower is responsible for the interest while still in college, although the government permits students to delay paying the interest right away and add the accrued interest to the total amount owed. You must file the FAFSA to be considered.

- After you've secured what you can through scholarships, working, and borrowing, you and your parents will be expected to meet your share of the college bill (the Expected Family Contribution). Many colleges offer monthly payment plans that spread the cost over the academic year. If the monthly payments are too high, parents can borrow through the Federal Direct PLUS Loan Program, through one of the many private education loan programs available, or through home equity loans and lines of credit. Families seeking assistance in financing college expenses should inquire at the financial aid office about what programs are available at the college. Some families seek the advice of professional financial advisers and tax consultants.

Middle-Income Families: Making the Financial Aid Process Work

Richard Woodland

A report from the U.S. Department of Education's National Center for Education Statistics took a close look at how middle-income families finance a college education. The report, *Middle Income Undergraduates: Where They Enroll and How They Pay for Their Education,* was one of the first detailed studies of these families. Even though 31 percent of middle-income families have the entire cost of attendance covered by financial aid, there is widespread angst among middle-income families that, while they earn too much to qualify for grant assistance, they are financially unable to pay the spiraling costs of higher education.

First, we have to agree on what constitutes a "middle-income" family. For the purposes of the federal study, middle income is defined as those families with incomes between $35,000 and $70,000. The good news is that 52 percent of these families received grants, while the balance received loans. Other sources of aid, including work-study, also helped close the gap.

So how do these families do it? Is there a magic key that will open the door to significant amounts of grants and scholarships?

The report found some interesting trends. One way families can make college more affordable is by choosing a less expensive college. In fact, in this income group, 29 percent choose to enroll in low-to moderate-cost schools. These include schools where the total cost is less than $8,500 per year. In this sector, we find the community colleges and lower-priced state colleges and universities. But almost half of these middle-income families choose schools in the upper-level tier, with costs ranging from $8,500 to $16,000. The remaining 23 percent enrolled at the highest-tier schools, with costs above $16,000. Clearly, while cost is a factor, middle-income families are not limiting their choices based on costs alone.

The report shows that families pay these higher costs with a combination of family assets, current income, and long-term borrowing. This is often referred to as the "past-present-future" model of financing. In fact, just by looking at the Expected Family Contributions, it is clear that there is a significant gap in what families need and what the financial aid process can provide. Families are closing this gap by making the financial sacrifices necessary to pay the price at higher-cost schools, especially if they think their child is academically strong. The report concludes that parents are more likely to pay for a higher-priced education if their child scores high on the SAT.

The best place for middle-income families to start is with the high school guidance office. This office has information on financial aid and valuable leads on local scholarships. Most guidance officers report that there are far fewer applicants for these locally based scholarships than one would expect. So read the information they send home and check on the application process. A few of those $500–$1000 scholarships can add up!

Plan to attend a financial aid awareness program. If your school does not offer one, contact your local college financial aid office and see when and where they will be speaking. You can get a lot of "inside" information on how the financial aid process works.

Next, be sure to file the correct applications for aid. Remember, each school can have a different set of requirements. For example, many higher-cost private colleges will require the CSS/Financial Aid PROFILE® application, filed in September or October of the senior year. Other schools may have their own institutional aid application. All schools will require the Free Application for Federal Student Aid (FAFSA). Watch the deadlines! It is imperative that you meet the school's published application deadline. Generally, schools are not flexible about this, so be sure to double-check the due date of all applications.

Finally, become a smart educational consumer. Peterson's has a wide range of resources available to help you understand the process. Be sure to also check your local library, bookstore, and of course, the Internet. A great Web site to check is www.finaid.org.

Once admitted to the various colleges and universities, you will receive an award notice outlining the aid you are eligible to receive. If you feel the offer is not sufficient, or if you have some unique financial circumstances, call the school's financial aid office to see if you can have your application reviewed again. The financial aid office is your best source for putting the pieces together and finding financial solutions.

The financial aid office will help you determine the "net price." This is the actual out-of-pocket cost that you will need to cover. Through a combination of student and parent loans, most families are able to meet these expenses with other forms of financial aid and family resources.

Many students help meet their educational expenses by working while in school. While this works for many students, research shows that too many hours spent away from your studies will negatively impact your academic success. Most experts feel that working 10 to 15 hours a week is optimal.

An overlooked source of aid is the tax credits given to middle-income families. Rather than extending eligibility for traditional sources of grant assistance to middle-income families, the federal tax system has built in a number of significant tax benefits, known as the Hope Scholarship and Lifetime Learning tax credit, for middle-income families. While it may be seven or eight months before you see the tax credit, most families in this income group can count on this benefit, usually between $1500 to $2000 per student. This is real money in your pocket. You do not need to itemize your deductions to qualify for this tax credit.

A tool to help families get a handle on the ever-rising costs of college is to assume that you can pay one third of the "net charges" from savings, another third from available (non-retirement) assets, and the rest from parent borrowing. If any one of these "thirds" is not available, shift that amount to one of the other resources. However, if it looks like you will be financing most or all of the costs from future income (borrowing), it may be wise to consider a lower-cost college.

Millions of middle-income families send their children to colleges and universities every year. Only 8 percent attend the lowest-priced schools. By using the concept of past-present-future financing, institutional assistance, federal and state aid, meaningful targeted tax relief, and student earnings, you can afford even the highest-cost schools.

Richard Woodland is the former Director of Financial Aid at Rutgers University–Camden.

MONEY, MONEY, MONEY

Honors Programs and Colleges: Smart Choices for an Undergraduate Education

Dr. Joan Digby

In general, students and their parents are guided toward a narrow selection of colleges and universities based on reputation, conversations with friends, or promotional material. Few people think to approach the college search focused on honors opportunities. As a result, students with extraordinary talents and interests miss out on a rich variety of untapped financial resources and exciting college experiences.

The smarter approach is to seek out a distinctive education that caters to students' great diversity of intellectual and creative strengths. If you are a strong student filled with ideas, longing for creative expression and ready to take on career-shaping challenges, then an honors education is just for you. Honors programs and colleges offer some of the finest undergraduate degrees available at U.S. colleges and do it with students in mind. The essence of honors is personal attention, top faculty, enlightening seminars, illuminating study-travel experiences, research options, and career-building internships—all designed to enhance a classic education and prepare you for life achievements. And here is an eye-opening bonus: Honors program and colleges may reward your past academic performance by giving you scholarships that will help you pay for your higher education!

Take your choice of institutions: community college, state or private, two-or four-year, college or large research university. There are honors opportunities in each. What they share is an unqualified commitment to academic excellence. Honors education teaches students to think and write clearly, be excited by ideas, and become independent, creative, self-confident learners. It prepares exceptional students for professional choices in every imaginable sphere of life: arts and sciences, engineering, business, health, education, medicine, theater, music, film, journalism, media, law, politics—invent your own professional goal and honors will guide you to it! Whichever honors program or college you choose, you can be sure to enjoy an extraordinarily fulfilling undergraduate education.

WHO ARE HONORS STUDENTS?

Who are you? Perhaps a high school junior filling out your first college application, a community college student seeking to transfer to a four-year college, or possibly a four-year college student doing better than you had expected. You might be an international student, a varsity athlete, captain of the debate team, or second violin in the orchestra. Whether you are the first person in your family to attend college or an adult with a grown family seeking a new career, honors might well be right for you. Honors programs admit students with every imaginable background and educational goal.

How does honors satisfy students and give them something special? Read what students in some honors programs and colleges say. Although they refer to particular honors colleges or programs, their experiences are typical of what students find exciting about honors education on hundreds of campuses around the country.

> "Being an honors program student has been a life-changing experience for me. I have gained tremendously in knowledge, experience, and self-esteem. I have learned so much more in the program than any textbook could teach about the value of encouraging support and positive thinking."

> —*Cheri Becker, Mount Wachusett Community College*

> "I've been in a healing ceremony in Ecuador and have performed music on stage. I've guided my peers and Navajo children, hiked the Grand Canyon, and so much more. Sometimes, experience speaks for itself; always, it creates paths, opens eyes, and helps us find our places. Thanks to my honors program, I've experienced these wonders and accomplishments. Now I know that there are no greater lessons than how to learn and love discovery."

> —*April Fisher, University of North Florida*

> "The Honors College has been my home away from home. In the midst of a diverse, fairly large university, it has provided me with the intimacy that I needed...My freshman-year living situation on the honors floor... allowed me to find like-minded students early in my college career."

> —*Brian Leech, Davidson Honors College, University of Montana*

"I was able to transition from an honors program at a two-year institution into an honors program at a four-year institution without any reservations or tribulations."

—*Rachel Jones Williams, Harrisburg Area Community College*

"Every single professor is in love with what they do and it shows in their research, their amazing teaching, and their interaction with students outside of the classroom. The undergraduate journey can be very difficult at times, but as an Honors College student, you're sure to have plenty of support every step of the way."

—*Walteria Tucker, Wilkes Honors College, Florida Atlantic University*

"The class size is perfect and I've been able to make some of my closest relationships with students and teachers through the program. The majority of honors faculty I have encountered have been overwhelmingly helpful...and my favorite courses have been honors classes."

—*Ellen Daschler, Eastern Illinois University*

"Our professor met us at a local restaurant the last evening of class and we shared a wonderful dinner. It had such a familiar feel to it because these are students I have known throughout my four years in the program."

—*Betsy Porter, University of La Verne*

"For the last two years, I have investigated new synthetic methods under the direction of a professor emeritus. Through the University Honors College, I am able to pursue this interest in chemistry and other academic endeavors . . . that have allowed me to develop my academic potential and contribute to the scientific body of knowledge."

—*Justin Chalker, University of Pittsburgh*

"The most rewarding part of being a member of the honors program is the joy of doing creative, meaningful projects with faculty I love."

—*Meleia Egger, Hartwick College*

"I would... like to add a word of praise for the way the curriculum is structured. It has deepened and enriched my thinking and helped me develop tools to negotiate the complex world we live in."

—*Monideepa Talukdar, Southeastern Louisiana University*

"We have a better time...our discussions get rather heated. In a lot of classes, only one or two students will speak up, but in the honors classes, it's a free-for-all."

—*Jonathan Post, Reinhardt College*

"My internship at a major international bank gave me an in-depth look into the world of investment and accounting. Funded by the Honors College, I was able to study business and culture in Shanghai, China, for a month. These valuable experiences are helping me to develop professionally, academically, and personally."

—*Jenny Lam, Honors College, The College of Staten Island, CUNY*

"The honors thesis was the key factor during the selection process at my future employer....It helped me to get the job and have an advantage over others. It is a lot of work but, in the end, it is worth it."

—*Olgierd Hinz, Lee Honors College, Western Michigan University*

These portraits don't tell the whole story, but they should give you a sense of what it means to be part of an honors program or college. One of the great strengths of honors programs and colleges is that they are nurturing environments that encourage students to be well-rounded and help students make life choices.

WHAT IS AN HONORS PROGRAM?

An honors program is a sequence of courses designed specifically to encourage independent and creative learning. For more than half a century, honors education—given definition by the National Collegiate Honors Council—has been an institution on U.S. campuses. Although honors programs have many different designs, there are typical components. At two-year colleges, the programs often concentrate on special versions of general education courses and may have individual capstone projects that come out of students' special interests. At four-year colleges and universities, honors programs are generally designed for students of almost every major in every college on campus. In growing numbers, they are given additional prominence as honors colleges. Whether a program or a college, honors often includes a general education or "core" component followed by advanced courses (often called colloquia or seminars). Some programs have honors contracts that shape existing courses into honors components to suit the needs of individual students. Many have interdisciplinary or collaborative seminars that bring students of different majors together to discuss a complex topic with faculty members from different disciplines. A good number have final thesis, capstone, or creative projects, which may or may not be in the departmental major. Almost always, honors curriculum is incorporated within whatever number of credits is required of every student for graduation. Honors very rarely requires students to take additional credits. Students who complete an honors program or honors college curriculum frequently receive transcript and diploma notations as well as certificates, medallions, or other citations at graduation ceremonies.

In every case, catering to the student as an individual plays a central role in honors course design. Most honors classes are small (fewer than 20 students); most are discussion-oriented, giving students a chance to present their own interpretations of ideas and even teach a part of the course. Many classes are interdisciplinary, which means they are taught by faculty members from two or more departments, providing different perspectives on a subject. All honors classes help students develop and articulate their own perspectives by cultivating both verbal and written style. They help students mature intel-

OPTIONS, OPTIONS, OPTIONS

OPTIONS, OPTIONS, OPTIONS

lectually, preparing them to engage in their own explorations and research. Some programs even extend the options for self-growth to study abroad and internships in science, government, the arts, or business related to the major. Other programs encourage or require community service as part of the honors experience. In every case, honors is an experiential education that deepens classroom learning and extends far beyond.

Despite their individual differences, all honors programs and honors colleges rely on faculty members who enjoy working with bright, independent students. The ideal honors faculty members are open-minded, encouraging master teachers. They want to see their students achieve at their highest capacity and are glad to spend time with students in discussions and laboratories, on field trips and at conferences, or online in e-mail. They often influence career decisions, are inspiring role models, and remain friends long after they have served as thesis advisers.

WHERE ARE HONORS PROGRAMS AND HONORS COLLEGES LOCATED?

Because honors programs and honors colleges include students from many different departments or colleges, they usually have their own offices and space on campus. Some have their own buildings. Most programs have honors centers or lounges, where students gather together for informal conversations, luncheons, discussions, lectures, and special projects.

Many honors students have cultivated strong personal interests that have nothing to do with classes. They may be multilingual; they may be fine artists or poets, musicians or racing car enthusiasts, mothers or fathers. Some volunteer in hospitals or do landscape gardening to pay for college. Many work in retail stores and catering. Some are avid sports enthusiasts, while others collect antiques. When they get together in honors lounges, there is always an interesting mixture of ideas!

In the honors center, you will also find the honors director or dean. The honors director often serves as a personal adviser to all of the students in the program. Many programs also have peer counselors and mentors who are upperclass honors students and know the ropes from a student's perspective and experience. Some have specially assigned honors advisers who guide honors students through their degrees, assist in registration, and answer every imaginable question. The honors office area usually is a good place to meet people, ask questions, and solve problems.

In general, honors provides an environment in which students feel free to talk about their passionate interests and ideas knowing that they will find good listeners and, sometimes, even arguers. There is no end to conversations among honors students. Like many students in honors, you may feel a great relief in finding a sympathetic group that respects your intelligence and creativity. In honors, you can be eccentric; you can be yourself! Some lifelong friendships, even marriages, are the result of social relationships developed in honors programs.

ARE YOU READY FOR HONORS?

Admission to honors programs and honors colleges is generally based on a combination of several factors: high school or previous college grades, experience taking AP or IB courses, SAT or ACT scores, personal essay, and extracurricular achievements. To stay in honors, students need to maintain a certain grade point average (GPA) and show progress toward the completion of the specific honors program or college requirements. Since you have probably exceeded admissions standards all along, maintaining your GPA will not be as big a problem as it sounds. Your professors and your honors director are there to help you succeed in the program. Most honors programs have very low attrition rates because students enjoy classes and do well.

Of course, you must be careful about how you budget your time for studying. Honors encourages well-rounded, diversified students, so you should play a sport, work at the radio station, join clubs of interest, or pledge a sorority or fraternity. You might find a job in the student center or library that will help you pay for your car expenses and that also is reasonable. But remember, each activity takes time, and you must strike the balance that leaves you enough time to do your homework, write papers, prepare for seminar discussions, do your research, and do well on exams. Choose the jobs and activities that attract you, but never let them overshadow your primary purpose—which is to be a student.

Sometimes even the very best students who apply for admission into an honors program or college are frightened by the thought of speaking in front of a group, giving seminar papers, or writing a thesis. But if you understand how the programs work, you will see that there is nothing to fear. The basis of honors is confidence in the student and building the student's self-confidence. Admittance to an honors program means you have already demonstrated your academic achievement in high school or college classes. Once in the honors environment, you learn how to formulate and structure ideas so that you can apply critical judgment to sets of facts and opinions. In small seminar classes, you practice discussion and arguments, so by the time you come to the senior thesis or project, the method is second nature. For most honors students, the senior thesis, performance, or portfolio presentation is the project that gives them the greatest fulfillment and pride. In many honors programs and colleges, students present their work either to other students or to faculty members in their major departments. Students often present their work at regional and national honors conferences. Some students even publish their work jointly with their faculty mentors. These are great achievements, and they come naturally with the training. There is nothing to fear. Honors will prepare you for life.

Dr. Joan Digby is Director of the Honors Program and Merit Fellowship at Long Island University, C.W. Post Campus. She was also President of the National Collegiate Honors Council from 1999 to 2000.

Public and Private Colleges and Universities— How to Choose

Debra Humphreys

As you survey the thousands of four-year colleges in the country and weigh the options before you, it is important to be aware of how colleges differ and what kind of educational experience each college offers you. In every state in the country, you will find both public and private colleges and universities. What are the differences between public and private colleges, and how should you approach the decision to attend one or the other? What are some common misconceptions regarding both public and private colleges that you should know about before you eliminate an entire category of institution from your list of prospective schools?

WHAT ARE THE BASIC CHARACTERISTICS OF PUBLIC AND PRIVATE INSTITUTIONS?

Over the course of the nation's history, what began as a small group of mostly church-affiliated colleges has grown in both size and complexity. Over the years, education in the United States became increasingly democratized, and more and more state-sponsored institutions and state systems of higher education emerged. These included small colleges, sometimes called "normal schools," designed to train school teachers for the expanding public school system; land-grant colleges and universities brought into existence with federal support in the mid-nineteenth century in order to prepare workers to expand the nation's agricultural and technological capacity; and large state systems that evolved in the twentieth century and now include two-year colleges, basic four-year institutions, and large research universities, all supported at least in part by state revenues.

While there are some clear distinctions to be made, even some of the core characteristics of public and private colleges vary from state to state. In general, a public institution receives at least part of its operating budget from state tax revenues, operates with a mandate and mission from the state where it is located, and is accountable to the elected officials of that state. Most private colleges and universities are independent, not-for-profit institutions. They operate with revenues from tuition, income from endowments, private gifts and bequests, and federal, private, or corporate foundation grants. These institutions are primarily accountable to a board of trustees, usually made up of local or national business and community leaders and esteemed alumni.

There are also a small but growing number of for-profit colleges whose operating revenues include tuition dollars but also might include investor financing. Some of these colleges are owned and operated by publicly traded corporations. Most of the following generalizations about private institutions however refer to the more familiar not-for-profit independent college previously described.

While the distinction between public and private institutions might seem clear at first, these two kinds of colleges and universities actually share many characteristics. All accredited colleges and universities in the country—whether public or private, for profit or not—are entitled to receive public funds from the federal government in the form of direct grants and loans for eligible students, support for student work-study programs, and competitive grants to support research or campus programs. In exchange for this federal support, all schools undergo a peer-reviewed accreditation process by a regional accreditor authorized by the federal government's Department of Education.

Whether a college is public or private, you should know if it is accredited and therefore an institution whose students are eligible for all available federal financial aid. Accreditation status also provides you with assurance that the school operates in a fiscally responsible manner and that its academic programs have been deemed sound by an outside group of educators from its peer institutions.

HOW ARE PUBLIC AND PRIVATE COLLEGES AND UNIVERSITIES RUN?

In many ways, your experience as a student will not differ significantly based on what type of governance system a college or university uses. However, some knowledge of this might be useful in making choices among the various options. Private colleges and universities tend to have more independence and autonomy in how they are run, with boards of trustees that oversee financial and other program and life on campus at these schools. Public colleges and universities often have more complex governing structures with boards of regents or other types of oversight committees made up of politically appointed or elected officials exercising more or less oversight and intrusion into their day-to-day operations. New York, for instance, has a board of regents that oversees the system's campuses and is more actively involved in reviewing and revising curricular requirements that apply to institutions throughout the system. Other states have multiple public colleges, each with its own board overseeing each campus' operations with more or less intrusion into day-to-day operations.

Whether an institution is public or private, you will want to ask lots of questions about campus climate and academic programs in order to help you determine if a school is right for you. Being aware of some facts about public and private institutions will help you frame these questions to get truly useful answers.

ARE ALL PUBLIC COLLEGES AND UNIVERSITIES BIG AND IMPERSONAL?

Like private institutions, public colleges come in all shapes and sizes. Some are large institutions offering multiple degrees and majors to both undergraduate and graduate students alike. These institutions offer students many curricular options as well as access to leading scholars and an environment where cutting-edge academic research is conducted. While an institution of this size and scope might seem intimidating at first, remember that there are large institutions that do take very seriously their undergraduate programs. While you may receive less customized attention at a larger institution, many large public and private research universities offer options such as smaller honors programs, academic learning communities with smaller cohorts of students, or theme residence halls that can minimize the potential that you will get lost in the crowd.

If you are considering a large research institution— whether it is public or private—you should ask questions about the undergraduate program. What is the student-faculty ratio for undergraduates? What is the average class size, especially for introductory first-year courses? How many courses are taught by graduate students, and what sort of teacher training do those students receive? Are there opportunities for undergraduate students to participate in research projects with university faculty members?

In addition to the large, public research universities, there are many other smaller, state-funded regional institutions that still offer a wide range of both liberal arts and sciences fields as well as professional fields of study. Many states also offer small, public liberal arts colleges that share many of the defining characteristics of traditional, private liberal arts colleges. In 1987, some of these institutions formed the Council of Public Liberal Arts Colleges (COPLAC). COPLAC schools pride themselves on providing students of high ability and from all backgrounds access to a quality liberal education. These colleges and universities have been nationally recognized as outstanding in many ways. They offer small classes, innovations in teaching, personal interactions with faculty members, opportunities for faculty-supervised research, and supportive atmospheres. Most of them are located on campuses in rural or small-town settings. In addition to offering rigorous and well-integrated undergraduate programs, these institutions often charge far less tuition than many private colleges do. More information can be found at http://www.coplac.org.

These public liberal arts colleges, along with more traditional private liberal arts institutions, do offer unique learning environments that research suggests often lead to higher levels of student achievement. Liberal arts colleges tend to offer a high degree of student-faculty interaction, high levels of student engagement with both in-class and out-of-class experiences, and lots of opportunities for collaborative and innovative learning practices. Businesses are also increasingly asking for exactly the set of skills and capacities that a liberal education provides, whether offered in a traditional liberal arts college setting or within a larger university that grants degrees in both liberal arts and other fields. Many public liberal arts and more comprehensive colleges and universities also now offer students a rigorous liberal education while integrating liberal learning into professional degree programs, for instance in health sciences, engineering, or education.

ARE PUBLIC COLLEGES CHEAPER THAN PRIVATE COLLEGES?

The cost of college is not easy to calculate and is not limited simply to the advertised price of tuition. It is absolutely not the case that attending a public college will always cost a student less money than attending a private institution. It is true that the basic tuition for in-state or out-of-state students attending public colleges is on average less expensive than the advertised tuition rate at private institutions. It is very important, however, to note that many private colleges and universities offer significant amounts of financial aid—often beyond the basic federal loans and grants available to all students. Many, but not all, private colleges have large endowments that allow them to effectively discount the standard, published tuition rates for a great number of their students. The National Association of College and University Business Officers sampled a small group of private colleges and discovered that only 10 percent of entering students were paying the full, advertised tuition. Ninety percent of their students received price discounts in the form of scholarships or financial aid. In other words, don't write off a college simply because its tuition looks extremely high relative to other institutions.

Both private and public institutions, however, have been fiscally stressed in recent years because of declining values of stock portfolios in endowments or because of declining state revenues resulting from the deteriorating economy. It is safe to say that for many students in the coming years, it will become increasingly difficult to get large amounts of financial aid. Many institutions, however, remain committed to widening access to more students from less economically privileged backgrounds. In addition, students demonstrating high levels of academic achievement are being rewarded at both private and public institutions—both in terms of admission and financial aid.

It is important to look carefully at the tuition and the financial aid requirements and availability at each school you are considering, private or public. In-state and out-of-state tuitions and the difference between them varies substantially from state to state. Out-of-state tuition also varies from state to state but still tends to be lower than average private tuition levels.

Policies vary as well for determining state residency status. In many states, the policy for dependent students requires that their parents must have lived in the state for at least twelve months prior to attendance in order to qualify for in-state tuition. For independent students, the requirement of twelve months residence prior to enrollment applies to the student. Independent status must be verified and generally entails proof that a student receives no support from parents or other relatives living in or out of the state in question. As budgets have increasingly tightened, states have over the past several years made it increasingly difficult to establish in-state residence after matriculating at a school. Exceptions are sometimes made, however, for students from migrant, refugee, or military families.

IS IT EASIER TO GAIN ADMISSION TO A PUBLIC INSTITUTION ESPECIALLY AS A STATE RESIDENT?

Few public colleges and universities automatically admit students who graduate from a public high school in their state. Many, however, give preference in admissions and financial assistance to in-state residents. Moreover, some states have implemented policies that guarantee admission to at least one of the state's public institutions for all students graduating in a top percentage of their high school classes.

There are, indeed, more highly selective private than public institutions. Many public colleges and universities, however, do admit very few applicants. These highly selective institutions might draw their students from a national pool of applicants and can be among the most selective in the country. However, the national universities and liberal arts colleges with the lowest acceptance rates in the country are mostly all private institutions.

While some public institutions offer virtually open admissions to state residents, it is important for all prospective students to realize that even an open-admission institution will require incoming students to meet certain academic standards before being admitted to credit-bearing courses. In most cases, public and private institutions give incoming students a series of placement exams that determines at what level the student can begin his or her course work. Depending on the results of these exams, a student may be required to take and pass one or more remedial courses before being admitted to courses that will actually count towards a degree.

Since each state's requirements are different and shift often, you should not assume that, regardless of your academic background, admission is automatic to your local state college. In the current climate—with costs rising and competition across systems tightening—admission rates are dropping at many public institutions.

IS THE CLIMATE ON A PUBLIC COLLEGE CAMPUS SIGNIFICANTLY DIFFERENT THAN THAT ON A PRIVATE COLLEGE CAMPUS?

The social and academic climate at colleges and universities varies substantially, and public institutions do not necessarily offer a distinctively different climate than private institutions do. You can find, at some public institutions, the small, residential environment traditionally associated with private liberal arts colleges. You will also find the presence of fraternities and sororities at both public and private institutions. You should look carefully at whether a school in which you are interested has fraternities and sororities and how much influence the Greek system has on college life. At some institutions, fraternities and sororities dominate the entire social life of the campus.

One campus environment that can only be found at a private institution is a highly religious environment. Many early colleges and universities were founded by churches or religious orders. Some of these institutions no longer retain a strong affiliation with one church or denomination. Others do retain a strong affiliation, and church traditions can heavily influence the climate of these institutions. Usually, these campuses will admit a student from any religious background, but they may require students to attend chapel services and/or take religion or theology courses to graduate. In addition, some college missions and curricula are influenced by their religious affiliations. For instance, many Catholic institutions have a strong commitment to community service and social justice. Students may find, at these institutions, curricula related to social justice issues and requirements that they complete a community-service learning activity or course to graduate. Institutions with a strong mission are also often able to develop more coherent, cohesive, and innovative curricula for their students.

Finally, other important climate factors to consider include whether a college or university is in an urban or rural setting; what the diversity of the student body is in terms of geographic, religious, or racial/ethnic background; if most students live on campus or commute from home; and finally if the college dominates the life of the community in which it is located. Each of these options has advantages and disadvantages you will want to weigh in making your decisions.

ARE PRIVATE COLLEGES MORE ACADEMICALLY RIGOROUS THAN PUBLIC COLLEGES?

Private colleges and universities are not necessarily more academically rigorous than public institutions. You will find rigorous, intellectually challenging, and innovative academic programs at both private and public institutions. There is also a common misconception that schools that are more highly selective have the most effective or engaging academic programs. Research suggests that there is no connection between the selectivity of an institution and the presence of effective or innovative teaching and learning practices. There is, however, preliminary research that suggests that the academic quality of

Questions to Ask as You Evaluate Prospective Colleges and Universities

- Does the college offer a distinctive first-year experience?
- Does the college offer a small-size freshman seminar for all students?
- Are all students required to complete a senior project or assignment that allows them to integrate all that they have learned and demonstrate acquired skills and knowledge?
- Are students encouraged or required to completeinternships and/or service learning courses?
- Are students encouraged to study abroad? Is support for study abroad provided to all students and are study abroad experiences integrated into a student's overall curricula?
- Does the college offer learning communities, especially in the student's early years?
- Are students required to complete rigorous writing courses not only in the freshman year but also across the curriculum in whatever major he or she chooses to pursue?
- Are there opportunities for students to pursue independent research or creative projects under the supervision of a senior faculty member?

one's peers does seem to have an impact on the grade point averages of fellow students.

Nothing could be more important in your decision-making process than evaluating the nature of academic programs at prospective colleges or universities. Across both public and private institutions, there have been exciting and important changes in how colleges and universities are organizing undergraduate curricula. Many promising programs have been proven to result in higher levels of student retention, graduation, satisfaction, and academic achievement.

Many colleges and universities also now participate in the National Survey of Student Engagement. This survey asks students in both their first and last years about a series of effective educational practices and the degree to which they are engaged in the academic life of their school. Issues that are examined in the survey include the level of academic challenge, active and collaborative learning opportunities, the nature of student-faculty interactions, the number of enriching educational experiences available, and the supportive nature of the campus environment. Ask if the school you are considering participates in this survey and if you can see the results from recent classes of students.

THE PRIVATE/PUBLIC CHOICE

While there are distinct differences between public and private colleges and universities you should not limit your choice— whatever your background—to only one type of institution. There are wonderful opportunities at many different kinds of schools. The availability of many kinds of financial aid may bring private institutions with high-tuition levels within reach for you, whatever your financial background. Whether a school is highly selective or has open admissions, you should also be able to find a college or university that will challenge you academically and provide you with a supportive environment in which to live, learn, and pursue a college degree of lasting value.

Debra Humphreys is Vice President for Communications and Public Affairs for the Association of American Colleges and Universities.

Distance Education—
It's Closer Than You Think

Y ou may not realize it, but as an incoming college student, you are joining a revolution that is radically changing education. It's called distance learning. From kindergarten up to postgraduate degrees, distance learning is fast becoming an essential teaching tool. Most of the colleges and universities you are considering for a bachelor's degree offer distance learning in one form or another. Most likely you will be a distance learner at some point, whether during college or graduate school or throughout your career.

In case you're not familiar with distance learning—or asynchronous learning, online learning, or distance education—it means you don't sit in a classroom facing a teacher. You can be hundreds of miles or minutes from the teacher and other students. Most often you connect through the Internet to the teacher, fellow students, and study materials. However, increasingly sophisticated technologies, such as virtual laboratories, simulations, and interactive multimedia, are also used. You may run across the term "blended learning." Many institutions incorporate online learning into their face-to-face classes. In fact, a number of colleges require that a part of all classes is online.

FROM SNAIL-MAIL COURSES TO LEADING-EDGE TECHNOLOGY

Talk about change. Distance education began in the late 1800s, when schools mailed correspondence courses to farmers who wanted to learn how to grow better crops. Since technology came along, distance learning has become accessible and widespread. At first educators were skeptical, but as name-plate universities began to incorporate it into their teaching methodology, distance education became accepted.

When brick-and-mortar colleges and universities first considered distance education, the goal was to make it as good as face-to-face education. Now, says Ray Schroeder, Professor Emeritus of Communication and Director of the Center for Online Learning, Research, and Service (COLRS), at the University of Illinois at Springfield, "Field research shows that online learning technologies are better than face-to-face learning in a number of ways." Having taught online, he has seen firsthand how students participate more in discussions and learn from one another. Peg Miller, Ph.D., former Coordinator of Academic Support for Distributed Learning, University of Central Florida, cites a survey she conducted every other semester that compares face-to-face and distance learners at her institution. She has found that students from face-to-face and online classes were almost identical in the grades they earned and in their satisfaction with the classes.

ON THE UPSWING

Many reasons have caused the phenomenal growth of distance education. It's convenient and user-friendly, plus the scope of classes is stunning. Not that you'll likely begin your college years with classes in forensics or grading diamonds, but they are offered and indicate the enormous variety of courses. Along with many others in education, Michael P. Lambert, Secretary and Executive Director of the Distance Education Training Council, feels that online learning has transformed how people learn. "You no longer sit in a box with 35 other people where you might never raise your hand," he says. Adds Gerald Heeger, former President of the University of Maryland University College (UMUC), "Online learning gets rid of the limitations of geography and time. And as bandwidth increases, we will do more and more."

PROCEED WITH CAUTION

Now that you're convinced that distance education sounds great, sign me up, it's only fair to warn you that perhaps you shouldn't start your bachelor's degree totally online. Distance learning changes how you study, respond to your teachers, participate in class discussions, and take exams. If you're not prepared for the differences, you can easily fall behind and even fail. Though the age of online students continues to drop, most are older, have had some life experience since graduating from high school, and have the self-discipline, maturity, and self-motivation, that distance education demands. The average age of distance students is in the mid-30s, and 95 percent of them work full-time. They know what they want from college and are willing to meet the rigors of online learning, which are considerable.

Of course, some students straight from high school do successfully start college as distance learners because they've already had some online learning experience. Some take online classes in high school or advanced-placement and college courses. At Stevens Institute of Technology's Web Campus, incoming freshmen brush up on math and precalculus online before their first fall semester. At first, Nathan Kahl, former instructor for the Euclid Program at Stevens Institute of Technology Web Campus, was skeptical that high school graduates could succeed in the online courses he taught, but he saw that "everyone quickly got into the swing of things." He admits that he underestimated the students' ability to learn online. Heeger agrees "There's no reason why a bright junior in high school who is ready to take college freshmen courses can't do it."

The University of Phoenix Online (parent company: Apollo Group, Inc.) has developed a bachelor's degree program specifically for incoming freshmen of any age—including those just out of high school. In today's job market, a college education is a necessity, yet many students have life situations that prevent them from attending. Notes former president of Apollo Group, Inc., Brian Mueller about the accommodations their program makes for students who are new to higher education, "It is our experience that if you create an online classroom, it must have all the features that incoming students need, which are small, highly interactive, and collaborative classes." Their freshman classes average 15 and require that the instructor has consistent contact with the students. New freshmen also get a tremendous amount of support in writing, math, and online research skills and have the help of an academic counselor who closely tracks them for ten weeks into their first semester. "We think there are more students coming out of high school who must have jobs, so we took the model for working adults and created an environment for traditional students that combines education and work," says Mueller.

However, not all educators have the same experience with incoming freshmen. Jimmy Reeves, Ph.D., Professor and Chair, Department of Chemistry and Biochemistry at the University of North Carolina at Wilmington, teaches both online and face-to-face classes and knows how students can react. Freshmen who fail his face-to-face class sometimes ask to take his class online. He says no because the discipline required is rare among 19-year-old students. "Junior and senior college students do well, but it has more to do with their level of maturity and the reasons why they're in college," he says, referring to the fact that many incoming college students want to experiment or come because their parents demand it. "Without any real desire to learn or sense of why they're in college, it's easy to get distracted in online classes," he notes. You can't hide in the back of a lecture hall half asleep on Monday morning and hope for the best on multiple-choice questions. In online classes, your active participation is noticed and taken into account for final grades.

Attending college isn't just about acquiring knowledge in a particular field in order to get a job. It's also about learning social skills and meeting people with different ideas from diverse backgrounds. "If you want to live in a dorm and have bull sessions on the meaning of life with the kids down the hall, then being a fully online freshman student isn't for you," advises Cynthia Davis, Associate Dean of Academic Affairs in the School of Undergraduate Studies at the University of Maryland University College (UMUC). She adds that sometimes students mistakenly think getting a bachelor's degree online will take less time than physically attending classes or won't require as much work. But as she points out, online classes demand the same amount of effort, if not more than face-to-face classes.

WHAT'S IT GOING TO BE LIKE?

Blended learning or mixed-mode classes, combining face-to-face and online instruction, are becoming a permanent fixture in higher education. Students might sit in a classroom on Monday but take the remaining two classes for that week online. Professors routinely post the syllabus, class calendar, or PowerPoint lectures. Reeves says that it's rare to see college classes without some Web-based materials. Davis

comments that UMUC routinely Web-enhances all of its face-to-face classes with companion Web classrooms. Students can have optional online discussions or print copies of class materials.

"We find more students use online technology to enhance their studies and get better grades," comments Schroeder. Educators see a trend of students enrolling in one university and taking courses from other institutions. For instance, say you're in an art class but want to study German cathedral architecture, which your university doesn't have but another one offers online. It's only a matter of time before this will be a standard option for college students.

LOTS TO LOOK FOR, LOTS TO AVOID, LOTS TO ASK

Though much of distance education depends on the Internet, you can't just type in "distance education" and see what comes up in a search for a college. You must seriously research and do background checks to make sure a diploma mill doesn't hand you a bachelor's degree that isn't credible. There are plenty of places to get information. Petersons.com offers a database of colleges and universities that have online courses, as well as totally online distance education providers. "You have to be a good consumer," recommends Heeger. "It's no different from getting a loan. You don't borrow money from people you never heard of. You shouldn't get degrees from people you never heard of." Schroeder suggests checking the course completion of online programs, their enrollment, and growth of programs. "Just as one checks with friends and colleagues about the quality of consumer services, such as computers and cars, one should check with students who are enrolled in online programs," he advises.

Is the Institution Accredited by a Valid Accrediting Body?

There are several kinds of accrediting organizations:

- The six regional accrediting agencies recognized by the U.S. Department of Education
- The Council for Higher Education Accreditation (www.chea.org)
- Other institutional accrediting agencies, such as the Accrediting Council for Independent Colleges and Schools and the Distance Education and Training Council
- Specialized accrediting agencies that cover schools offering everything from acupuncture to veterinary medicine
- Other discipline-based accrediting organizations, such as those for law and business schools

Can You Transfer Credits Received Online from One Institution to Another?

Policies vary greatly among universities and colleges. Though distance education is widely accepted, there are so many places where students can take bogus online courses that institutions are justifiably cautious. If students do decide they want to get a bachelor's degree completely online, they need to be sure the campus-based program and distance education program offer the same degree. At most institutions both on-campus and online degrees are the same, but others do differ-

Test-Drive an Online Class

Just like face-to-face instruction, online classes are different, depending on the course material and how each teacher chooses to structure the course, but here's a typical scenario of what it's like to be a distance learner.

Getting started. First you'll want to get to the general information page for the class, which you'll visit often. The professor's contact information, the class calendar, the syllabus, and announcements on quizzes and tests or links to other pages on which you'll find posted discussion questions may be found here. Some teachers will ask you to tell something about yourself to the other students in the class. Be sure to read the syllabus, which will outline the course and tell you when assignments are due and how grades are determined.

Responding to discussion questions. Those students who never raised their hands will get a shock in online courses. Responding with thoughtful answers to online discussion groups is mandatory. Usually the teacher will assign reading material and then post a discussion question. The material might be from your textbook or Web sites. You must respond to the question and possibly to the postings of other students in the class. Teachers will gauge your participation in the class and how well you learn the material.

Interacting with fellow students and your teacher. Ray Schroeder, Professor Emeritus of Communication and Director of the Center for Online Learning, Research, and Service (COLRS) at the University of Illinois at Springfield, gives talks about distance education. Often he'll ask his audience to recall their favorite class from elementary school up to college and what made it so memorable. Was it the textbook? The actual classroom? The view out the window? When he asks if it was the interaction among students and with the teacher, the audience realizes that's what made the class good. "Both in person and online, learning takes place in the interaction," says Schroeder. "Otherwise, we would do just as well to read a book or watch a video to learn." In online classes, interaction between you and the professor and other students is an enormous part of your success.

Nathan Kahl, former instructor for the Euclid Program at Stevens Institute of Technology Web Campus, explains, "Distance students expect that their teachers will be online at least as much as they are." The level of interaction expected from you will vary by school and course, but you should know that in online courses, you must be an active participant. On the flip side, teachers carefully monitor discussions to make sure the more talkative students don't dominate. Keith W. Miller, Professor of Computer Science at the University of Illinois at Springfield, interacts with his students in a variety of ways. "I make announcements to the whole class on the homepage. I send e-mails to the whole class. I enter into the electronic discussions on the bulletin board forums, and post daily reminders and assignments to the course calendar. The students interact with me using e-mail, notes in their assignments, and via the bulletin boards. Now and then someone calls me at my office on the phone, but that's rare." He likes to answer his e-mails at least once a day, which means that his students get much more feedback than they would if he were physically in a classroom with them.

As do most online teachers, Cynthia Davis, Associate Dean of Academic Affairs in the School of Undergraduate Studies at the University of Maryland University College, gets students to participate with a weekly discussion topic. "If we're reading a novel," she says, "I ask them to discuss the role of the narrator or analyze a passage. The students respond individually and then respond to other students' comments."

Attending virtual lectures. Some online courses allow you to hear and see the professor or other guest speakers who are also online. If you want to ask a question, there's a button to indicate you want to speak. Everyone else can hear you as if you all were in the same room. Other professors add voice to PowerPoint lectures, which you can view when you want to, not at some prearranged time.

Taking quizzes and tests. No more waiting weeks to get your tests back. Online technology in some courses instantly zaps back the corrected test and notes that you missed question six and need to study page 54 of the textbook. Just like in face-to-face classes, you have an allotted amount of time to take the quiz. Some online courses may have automated components, such as instant quizzes and animated and interactive practice sessions. Others have mandatory proctored exams at a nearby community college or learning center for students who are off campus.

entiate in the degrees conferred, and it will show up on your diploma.

What Kind of Refund Policy Does the University Have for Distance Learners?

It might become painfully apparent for students that online learning is not for them, and they want to drop out. Find out ahead of time about the refund policy for online classes. What happens if you're ill during an online class? How can you make up the work? Even before taking any classes, you should

find out if you're suited for online learning. Many institutions offer self-assessment tests on their Web sites.

What Online Services Does the College Provide?

Is the dorm wired? Can you get an e-mail address from the university? What about browsers and computer compatibility? Ask how the Internet is part of face-to-face classes. To what extent is the library online, and is it available 24/7 for research? Ask about writing and math labs and help-desk support. Look for online tutorials that show students how to use the school's specific software. Is there a tech fee?

IF YOU'RE LEARNING ONLINE, YOU BETTER HAVE THESE

Since online learning is part of college, it's helpful to know what to expect ahead of time, rather than three weeks into the class, when you feel like throwing your laptop out the window and would happily settle for sitting in the back row of the nearest classroom. Here are the five skills and abilities that successful online students must have:

1. You must have the self-discipline to do things you don't want to do when you don't want to do them.

If you're a procrastinator, you'll find the catch-up tactics that served you well in face-to-face classes won't work online. "Students get the idea they can whiz by without studying, or they came from high schools where they weren't pushed," cautions Heeger. "Maybe they never got Fs in high school, but they do here." That's because they don't realize they're responsible for learning the material on their own. The burden is on you to keep up with the homework. It doesn't take long to fall far behind in online classes.

Typically, students in face-to-face and online classes need 2 hours for work outside of class for every hour in class. But online students often forget to add that hour. For every hour they would have to sit in a traditional classroom, they should be listening, studying, thinking, writing, responding to discussions, and getting ready for tests, plus the 2 hours outside of class. Three classes a week—that's 9 to 10 hours for one class. Online teachers keep students on track with weekly quizzes and homework assignments. If students start lagging, they're likely to get an e-mail from the professor asking what's going on. Claudine SchWeber, Ph.D., Chair of the Doctor of Management Program at the University of Maryland University College, has taught online for years and states, "My classes are structured by weekly readings, activities, and discussions. Students can't decide to get around to doing the work when they feel like it. It must be done at the instructor's pace. The first shot of online can be a shock to their system."

2. You must have the ability to manage your time without anyone telling you do your homework NOW.

In high school, students usually can put off studying until the weekend. "That doesn't work in college. You can't write complex papers the night before," says Karen L. Kirkendall, Ph.D., Associate Professor of Liberal and Integrative Studies and Director of the Capitol Scholars Honors Program at the University of Illinois at Springfield. She teaches both online and face-to-face classes and has seen first-time online students who have never failed before start to slip and suddenly realize they are in big trouble. "My online classes are extraordinarily structured so I pretty much know when students aren't engaged, which I monitor by seeing how much they participate in online discussions," she notes.

Distance Learning Myths

As distance education becomes more accepted, people will readily discard some of the myths on this list. But for now, they persist.

Distance learning is for people on ranches 200 miles from the nearest freeway. Geography is not a factor. Many distance learners who are located across the campus or a few miles away just don't want to deal with the commute or have a work schedule that conflicts with being in a class at a certain time. They appreciate the flexibility that distance education gives them.

Distance learning is easier than face-to-face classes. Once you start an online class, you'll knock that myth off the list. Still, some students think it will be easier. When they realize they must not only respond to discussion questions but also comment on the responses from other students, they wonder why they ever thought distance education was going to be easy. Online teachers normally keep track of how their students progress with frequent monitoring and quizzes.

I'll get a better education in face-to-face classes. Much research has been conducted comparing the two and consistently, online learning is equivalent or better. Teachers of online courses now have plenty of precedents to follow, training and research to help them teach better, and technology to prepare for classes and keep up with their students' progress.

I'll talk to a computer all day. Yes, you are in front of a computer as a distance learner, but you also interact with professors and other students much more than you ever would in a core freshman class of 200. Teachers have sophisticated software to facilitate interaction. Even though you don't physically see your teachers, they put a great deal of effort into class preparation and reading e-mails. Some get as many as 3,000 e-mails in a ten-week class. Distance learners often get to know fellow students much more easily online than they would walking in and out of a class.

I need to be a computer geek. If you can handle the simplest maneuvers around a computer, such as attaching documents to e-mails or going to a specified Web address, you can be a distance learner. And you'll have tech support to help out if you run into problems.

Distance education is cheaper than face-to-face. Too bad this is a myth. It costs the same as a traditional college if you attend a recognized institution. Most students pay for distance education through student loans.

3. You must have the skills to communicate your thoughts in writing.

"Online participation in class discussions isn't instant messaging. You are what you write in online classes," advises SchWeber. Most of the work in online classes is written, whether it's participation in discussions, homework, quizzes, papers, or tests.

Since you'll communicate by e-mail and post your thoughts, netiquette is essential. You need to think differently online than when speaking on the phone or face-to-face. "You can't write a report that sounds like you are hanging out with friends," advises SchWeber. "When you are totally online, the only image people (including your professor) have of you is how you write." Kirkendall has reprimanded students who sent e-mails showing disrespect to the teacher because they were upset about something. Probably they would never respond that way if face-to-face. "Never hit the submit button when you're angry," Kirkendall cautions.

4. You must have the ability to research worthwhile information on the Web.

You need to know what's junk and what's reliable. In addition, professors take plagiarism very seriously, especially because it's so easy to do.

5. You must have some computer skills and know some computer-speak.

Those who design the software and set up how a distance learning class is taught are careful to make sure the technology doesn't get in the way of learning; however, you should know the basics. "In some classes, certain downloads are required, such as Adobe Acrobat, but in general, the skills are not beyond the abilities used daily by most elementary school children," says Schroeder, pointing out that if distance programs use expensive or exotic technology, they defeat the purpose. He reports that most computers that are five years old have the speed, memory, and capability to support online learning. Some classes might require a microphone. You should be familiar with some of the computer jargon so that if you're asked to post something or use a drop box, add an attachment, or take part in a threaded discussion, you'll know what what you need to do. Just about every distance learning provider has online tutorials to familiarize you with their particular online software. If you run into technical problems, help-desk support is available.

Why Not Women's Colleges?

Before we start talking about the many advantages that women's colleges offer, let's get some myths out of the way. It is almost certain that the minute you hear "women's colleges" in the same sentence with "choosing colleges" you immediately think: no boys, no fun, no way!

Maybe that is why some girls who visit Joan Jaffe's office at Mills College in San Francisco, California, rush in to tell her that they just saw some guys on the campus of this women's college. Jaffe, Associate Dean of Admission, frequently gets this reaction from the young women who visit the campus. That's because many think that if they go to a women's college they are never going to see a guy within 2 miles of the campus gates, which, by the way, will clang shut behind them, leaving them secluded inside a heavily guarded male-free zone.

KISS MYTH NUMBER ONE GOOD-BYE

Forget iron gates. The first myth to get rid of is the one that assumes attending a women's college means kissing your social life good-bye. In fact, as Patricia Gibbs, Vice President for Student Affairs, Dean of Students at Wesleyan College in Macon, Georgia, points out, "If you were a guy looking for a date, where would you go?" Not only that, the majority of women's colleges are near, if not next to, coed campuses. Most share activities with other colleges and universities, and many have reciprocal agreements so that guys can take classes at the women's college and vice versa.

When it comes to dating, women's colleges offer the best of both worlds. You can hang out with guys when you want to and then retreat to your own lovely environment (women's dorms usually are beautiful) and hang out with the girls. Julie Binder, who transferred from the University of Wisconsin to all-women's Barnard College in New York City, notes that there is open registration with Columbia University, which just happens to be right next door. "Campus life is shared. Sports are shared," she says.

As you dig deeper into this myth, you will find that attending a women's college is not about isolation, it's about options. You get to choose if you want to be in classes, clubs, and organizations only with women or mingle with the men.

SCRATCH MYTH NUMBER TWO

Myth Number Two: Women's colleges are just a bunch of catty, competitive females waiting for the right moment to scratch each other's eyes out. Scratch that myth, too. Instead, women's colleges cultivate an environment of sisterhood—women who look out for one another. Most women's colleges encourage women in the upper-level classes to help their younger classmates. Talking to their "big sisters," newcomers can find out what classes to take and which professors are best, and they find a sympathetic ear for the problems that most first-year college students face.

The Rich Traditions in Women's Colleges

Tradition plays an important part of the experience women have in women's colleges. They run the gamut from solemn ceremonies of passing along the bond of sisterhood to the fun of secret surprises. "Women's colleges have a strong sense of tradition," says Amy Shaver, former Academic Dean at Stephens College in Columbia, Missouri. It's also a wonderful way to help women from all social, economic, religious, and ethnic backgrounds to share a common experience and pass it on to the next generation of students. "Traditions bond women over the generations," says Jennifer Rickard, Dean of Admissions and Financial Aid at Bryn Mawr College, who notes that it's not unusual at all to have students today singing songs and participating in ceremonies that the class of 1945 did and which will be the same when today's students have their twenty-year reunion.

Here's a sampling of the many traditions you'll find on women's college campuses:

Lantern Night At Bryn Mawr's Lantern Night, women gather around a fountain on campus. Each woman is given a lantern as a symbol of knowledge and learning. Each class has a color, and as the lanterns are passed from the sophomores to the first-year students, songs are sung in Greek that are the same as the ones sung 100 years ago around the same fountain.

Senior Paint Night Mills College seniors get the okay to paint the campus in their class color. Along with brushes and cans of paint, they are given a few guidelines as to what can and cannot be painted, but the rest is up to them.

The Crossing of the Bridge As women students come to Stephens to begin their college education, they cross over a bridge on campus in a ceremony symbolizing their entrance into the world of academia. At graduation, they cross over another bridge on campus and are welcomed into the alumnae society.

Candlelight Induction Ceremony Spelman students dressed in white dresses and black shoes light candles and hear the charge to be the best they can be. While the candles are still lit, they sing the Spelman hymn.

Midnight Breakfast At Barnard, the night before finals, the president of the college, deans, and professors make breakfast for the students.

"The sense of community is very strong at women's colleges," observes Fran Samuels, former Director of College Counseling at The Master's School in Dobbs Ferry, New York. "The myth is that a women's college will be cliquish. In truth, the women are supportive of each other." The strong bonds of sisterhood that naturally develop connect students to their college, its history, and its students, past, present, and future. Many women's colleges designate a rotating color for each incoming class. For example, if the freshman class you enter is dubbed the golden hearts, by the time you graduate, you are connected to all the golden hearts who graduated ahead of you and all the golden hearts who will graduate after you.

TOSS MYTH NUMBER THREE

Another myth that should be tossed out is that women's colleges don't prepare you for the "real world." Well, try saying that to the 12 women members of Congress who graduated from women's colleges. Or to the 15 women on *Business Week*'s list of the rising stars in corporate America. Although you are not in a totally coed situation, on the other hand you are in an environment in which you can gain skills to think critically and learn to meet challenges. Becky Marsh, Director of Advancement at Whitfield School, in St. Louis, Missouri, points out that when you first ride a bike, training wheels allow you to learn how to balance. Once you are ready to race down the street, you take them off. Same with women's colleges. The focus is on your education and your strengths, and who you are. You graduate ready to take on the obstacles of the real world. "In high school, I had the feeling that boys were given more opportunities to share their knowledge. It was harder and more intimidating for me to share my opinions in a coed class," says Brittany Johnson, from Spelman College in Atlanta, Georgia. "Now I feel like I can do anything."

Graduates of women's colleges feel empowered and willing to confront any limits to their abilities. While in college, they have many opportunities to assume leadership roles and see women in leadership positions as professors and deans. "They don't doubt whether they can do anything. Instead, they ask, 'Why can't I do it now?'" reports Amy Shaver, former Academic Dean at Stephens College in Columbia, Missouri. Women can find their own voices and establish their own ways of approaching things that will ultimately make them successful in a male-dominated world. They learn from seeing other women students and professors engaged in the intellectual process.

THE ADVANTAGES

As more young women find out about the advantages that women's colleges offer them, they like what they see. Maybe that is why attendance at women's colleges is growing. Learning leadership skills tops the list of advantages. Says Shaver, "Women in a same-sex environment are more likely to take risks and speak up in class. They are more willing to stand up and voice an opinion." If you think about it, students get plenty of practice at a women's college because all the leadership roles go to women. From day one on a women's campus, you will see women leading the entire college or involved in interesting and significant research. You get more exposure to what leadership is and what to expect as a leader. "Leadership becomes ingrained," notes Jennifer Fondiller, Dean of Admissions and Financial Aid at Barnard College in New York City.

You might not realize it, but women react differently in classrooms with all women. They tend to speak up with confidence and to test their ideas more readily when they are not competing with men. Researchers find that even as early as the fifth grade, girls are taught differently than boys. Teachers call on boys more frequently and don't ask girls the more thought-provoking questions or to critically analyze problems. In coed situations, the more aggressive and competitive guys take over, whereas in all-female classes, research indicates there is much more give-and-take and exchange of ideas.

Coming from a coed public school, Johnson realized that more attention was given to the guys in her classes, but at Spelman, she says, "Everyone is on the same path." Arlene Cash, Vice President for Enrollment Management at Spelman, notes that women don't have to vie for attention or retreat into the intellectual background in all-women classes. In a coed class, the environment becomes more adversarial. "Women feel they have to perform. In women's colleges they become more academically involved and interact with faculty members more frequently," says Debbie Greenberg, former College Counselor at Whitfield School. Speaking of the rich interaction that occurs in her classes at Barnard, Binder says, "The diversity of experience around the discussion table is unparalleled."

YOU CAN SUCCEED

Shaver characterizes the environment in women's colleges as one in which there is no fear of failing when the social pressures and dynamics of men and women are removed from the classroom. Women's colleges give women the opportunity to explore different avenues without the fear of failing. "We challenge them to become what they want to become," says Gibbs from Wesleyan. "No one says, 'You can't do that because you are a woman.'" At the same time, you are interacting with other women who have the same goals as you, which reinforces who you are. Or, as Jennifer Rickard, Dean of Admissions and Financial Aid at Bryn Mawr College, in Bryn Mawr, Pennsylvania, points out, women are not just sitting in classes to do well on exams and get good grades. They also are figuring out what they want to do with their education. "There's less expectation to conform to an external measure," she says.

Many women's colleges foster self-government and give their students responsibilities they might not find in a coed institution. At Bryn Mawr, for instance, students pay a self-government association fee as part of their tuition. This is put into a fund that is controlled by a student government that takes ownership of how the students want to govern themselves. "This isn't student government making only recommendations to the administration as to how to allocate the budget to the different student groups vying for funds," notes Rickard. "You have students dealing with real-world management issues, such as resource allocation."

Since women's colleges are smaller than big coed universities, women receive all the benefits that students get from a small liberal arts college in addition to the advantages that only a women's college offers. A big plus is interaction with professors and staff, which is hard to achieve when you are one of 200 students in a lecture hall taught by a graduate student.

What Made You Choose a Women's College?

When she got to the point of choosing which college to attend, Wisambi Loundu had plenty of options. Coming from San Diego, the California universities were a logical choice. Women's colleges were not on her list. In fact, she hardly knew they existed. Her first thought when someone suggested a women's college to her was, "I'm not going to a school full of girls minus boys." Her second thought was just as negative. "If it's all girls, they will always be fighting." The third and fourth thoughts assumed that a women's college wouldn't prepare her for the real world, plus she would be isolated.

But then her math teacher's daughter told her about Bryn Mawr, and as Wisambi started exploring the possibility, the advantages of a women's college started lining up. However, it wasn't until she visited Bryn Mawr that she really began to see herself there. "I fell in love with the campus," says Wisambi. "It was like nothing I'd ever seen before." Her stay in the dorm added to her steadily growing thoughts that Bryn Mawr might be it. "The girls I stayed with in the dorm were so friendly. At first I was suspicious, but I saw it was not a front. Plus, there were girls from all over the world."

But Wisambi didn't make her final decision just yet. She decided to look at other schools, like Wellesley and the University of California schools, as well as Stanford. Meanwhile, her friend told her more about Bryn Mawr. "She said I'd make lasting friends and she talked about how the academics would train me for the outside world even if there were no men on campus. Bryn Mawr would build my identity as a woman."

She still wasn't convinced and made a second visit, along with visits to Wellesley and Stanford, which she says were nice, but too big. It would be too hard to make friends there, she thought. When the time came to make her final selection, she chose Bryn Mawr.

Now at BrynMawr, how does Wisambi feel about her choice? The academics are more challenging than she anticipated but doable, and she is excited about the internships she will be able to access. She also finds that the staff and teachers at Bryn Mawr go out of their way to make her feel at home. "They match us up with a mentor and professor," she says.

How about dating? Since Bryn Mawr is part of a tri-college community, guys are around, though Wisambi says you have to make an effort to meet people on other campuses.

Talking to seniors who are getting ready to head out to the "real world," Wisambi can see that they are full of confidence and don't think for a minute that they won't do well. "And that's a positive," she says.

Women's colleges tend to foster seminar-style classes taught by full professors, many of them women. "You have an expert teaching you," says Gibbs. Faculty members get to know their students and can challenge them intellectually on an individual basis. "Within two days, all my teachers knew my name," recalls Johnson, who says she was given each professor's e-mail address, home phone number, and all the contact information she needed and was encouraged to reach out to them.

Women are encouraged to achieve their intellectual goals. Professors often will point out specific programs that they know suit the student's interests. Add to this the opportunities to conduct research with a professor, and in many cases actually present research findings to a professional society, and you can see why women graduate with a terrific resume before they even start their careers. Rickard mentions the opportunity that Bryn Mawr students have to work on funded projects with professors during the summer and then present the results along with them at conferences. "It's a window into the academic world and the world of the intellectual," she notes. It's no surprise that women in women's colleges major in math and science at a higher national average than women in coed institutions.

Paid and unpaid internships, too, are more available for women at women's colleges, mainly because of the network of women graduates in business and industry who want to help their "sisters" at their alma maters. "I'm getting my professional edge now," says Binder, who is interested in TV production and had a paid internship as a production assistant while a sophomore at Barnard. "You will have an amazing resume by the time you graduate," she says.

Peggy Hock, Ph.D., former College Counselor at Notre Dame High School in San Jose, California, points out that colleges naturally rely on their alumni to come forward with networking opportunities for students; however, the alumnae of women's colleges tend to be more loyal and willing to give of their time. This translates into many more opportunities for internships, mentoring, and job possibilities. At Barnard, for example, the career office has an alumna mentor network. Students can call, ask questions, and get advice about career choices. At alumnae events, current students mix with the graduates. Binder takes full advantage of the Web log of women who are working all over the world and willing to spend time online with Barnard students. She applied for a job at a public relations firm in New York after contacting a fellow Barnard graduate working there. She met with her and subsequently got a letter of recommendation.

HOW TO CHOOSE

Choosing a women's college isn't any different from choosing a coed college. You should definitely visit the campus and don't be afraid to ask lots of questions—even the ones that might make you uncomfortable. Because women's colleges are similar to small coed liberal arts colleges, make sure that you don't compare a women's campus to a big university.

Janet Ashley, former Interim Director for Admissions at Spelman College, advises high school women to ask what a women's college can give them academically. "Their choice depends on what their goals are," she says.

If you're worried about the dating scene, ask about the levels of interaction with guys and how close the relationships are with neighboring institutions.

"Look at the individuality of each women's college," suggests Rickard, "because each has its own personality."

Look at the school before looking at the fact that it's a women's college, and on the flip side, don't rule out a school just because it is a women's college. "So many students make quick decisions about where to apply," warns Fondiller, noting that sometimes the decision hinges on what schools a friend is applying to rather than if that institution really fits the student. Many women's colleges specialize in certain fields like science, math, or theater.

Famous Firsts From Women's Colleges

Quick, from which college did the first woman to be named Secretary of State graduate? Or the woman scientist who identified the Hong Kong flu? Or the first woman executive vice president of the American Stock Exchange? Here's a big clue. They were all graduates of women's colleges.

SENATOR
- Barbara Mikulski (MD)—Mount Saint Agnes College

REPRESENTATIVES
- Tammy Baldwin (WI)—Smith College
- Donna Christian-Christensen (VI)—St. Mary's College
- Rosa DeLauro (CT)—Marymount College
- Jane Harman (CA)—Smith College
- Gabrielle Giffords (AZ)—Scripps College
- Eddie Bernice Johnson (TX)—Saint Mary's College
- Barbara Lee (CA)—Mills College
- Nita Lowey (NY)—Mount Holyoke College
- Betty McCollum (MN)—College of Saint Catherine
- Nancy Pelosi (CA), first woman elected as Speaker of the House of Representatives—Trinity College
- Allyson Schwartz (PA)—Simmons College

SECRETARY OF STATE
- Hillary Rodham Clinton (NY)—Wellesley College

OTHER FAMOUS WOMEN FIRSTS
- Madeleine Albright, first woman to be named Secretary of State in the United States, appointed in 1997—Wellesley
- Jane Amsterdam, first woman editor, the New York Post—Cedar Crest College
- Emily Green Balch, first woman to receive the Nobel Peace Prize in 1946—Bryn Mawr College
- Catherine Brewer Benson, first woman to receive a college bachelor's degree—Wesleyan College

- Earla Biekert, first scientist to identify the Hong Kong flu virus—Wesleyan College
- Cathleen Black, first woman leader of the American Newspaper Publishers Association—Trinity Washington University
- Sarah Porter Boehmler, first woman executive vice president of American Stock Exchange—Sweet Briar College
- Jane Matilda Bolin, first African American woman judge in the United States—Wellesley College
- Dorothy L. Brown, first African American woman general surgeon in the South—Bennett College for Women
- Pearl S. Buck, first American woman to win the Nobel Prize in Literature—Randolph-Macon Woman's College
- Ila Burdett, Georgia's first female Rhodes Scholar—Agnes Scott College
- Dorothy Vredenburgh Bush, first woman secretary of the Democratic National Party—Mississippi University for Women
- Hon. Audrey J. S. Carrion, first Hispanic woman judge Circuit Court for Baltimore City—College of Notre Dame of Maryland
- Rachel Carson, first environmentalist who awakened public consciousness through her book, *Silent Spring*—Chatham University
- Barbara Cassani, first woman CEO of a commercial airline—Mount Holyoke College
- Elaine L. Chao, U.S. Secretary of Labor, 2001; First Asian American woman appointed to a President's cabinet—Mount Holyoke College

Adapted from the Web site of the Women's College Coalition at http://www.womenscolleges.org.

How to Use This Guide

PROFILES

The **PROFILES** section contains basic data in capsule form for quick review and comparison. The following outline of the format shows the section headings and the items that each section covers. Any item that does not apply to a particular college or for which no information was supplied is omitted from that college's listing. Display ads, which appear near some of the institutions' profiles, have been provided and paid for by those colleges and universities that chose to supplement their profile with additional information.

Category Overviews

Type of Institution

Private institutions are designated as independent (nonprofit), proprietary (profit-making), or independent with a specific religious denomination or affiliation. Nondenominational or interdenominational religious orientation is possible and would be indicated. Public institutions are designated by the source of funding. Designations include federal, state, province, commonwealth (Puerto Rico), territory (U.S. territories), county, district (an educational administrative unit often having boundaries different from units of local government), city, state and local (local may refer to county, district, or city), or state-related (funded primarily by the state but administratively autonomous). *Religious affiliation* may follow, along with year founded. Each institution is classified as one of the following:

- Primarily two-year: Awards baccalaureate degrees but majority of students are enrolled in two-year programs.

- Four-year: Awards baccalaureate degrees; may also award associate degrees; does not award graduate (postbaccalaureate) degrees.

- Five-year: Awards a five-year baccalaureate in a professional field such as architecture or pharmacy; does not award graduate degrees.

- Upper-level: Awards baccalaureate degrees, but entering students must have at least two years of previous college-level credit; may also offer graduate degrees.

- Comprehensive: Awards baccalaureate degrees; may also award associate degrees; offers graduate degree programs, primarily at the master's, specialist's, or professional level, although one or two doctoral programs may be offered.

- University: Offers four years of undergraduate work, plus graduate degrees through the doctorate in more than two academic or professional fields.

Setting

Designated as *urban* (located within a major city), *suburban* (a residential area within commuting distance of a major city), *small town* (a small but compactly settled area not within commuting distance of a major city), or *rural* (a remote and sparsely populated area).

Endowment

The total dollar value of funds and/or property donated to the institution or the multicampus educational system of which the institution is a part.

Student body

An institution is *coed* (coeducational—admits men and women), *primarily* (80 percent or more) *women, primarily men, women only,* or *men only.* A few schools are designated as *undergraduate: women only; graduate: coed* or *undergraduate: men only; graduate: coed.*

Entrance

The five levels of entrance difficulty *(most difficult, very difficult, moderately difficult, minimally difficult,* and *noncompetitive)* are based on the percentage of applicants who were accepted for fall 2010 freshman admission (or, in the case of upper-level schools, for entering-class admission) and on the high school class rank and standardized test scores of the accepted freshmen who actually enrolled in fall 2010. The colleges were asked to select the level that most closely corresponds to their entrance difficulty, according to these guidelines.

Undergraduates

Percentages of undergraduates who are part-time or full-time students; transfers in; live on campus; out-of-state; Black or African American, non-Hispanic/Latino; Hispanic/Latino; Asian, non-Hispanic/Latino; Native Hawaiian or other Pacific Islander, non-Hispanic/Latino; American Indian or Alaska Native, non-Hispanic/Latino are given. *Retention:* The percentage of freshmen (or, for upper-level institutions, entering students) who returned the following year for the fall term.

Freshmen

Admission: Figures are given for the number of students who applied for fall 2010 admission, the number of those who were admitted, and the number who enrolled. *Average high school GPA:* Freshman statistics include the average high school GPA. *Test scores:* Percentage of freshmen who took the SAT and received critical reading, math, and writing scores above 500, above 600, and above 700; as well as percentage of freshmen taking the ACT who received a composite score of 18 or higher, 24 or higher, and 30 or higher.

Faculty

Total: The total number of faculty members; percentage of full-time faculty members as of fall 2010; and percentage of total faculty members who hold terminal degrees. *Student/faculty ratio:* School's estimate of the ratio of matriculated undergraduate students to faculty members teaching undergraduate courses.

Academics

Calendar: Most colleges indicate one of the following: 4-1-4, 4-4-1, or a similar arrangement (two terms of equal length plus an abbreviated winter or spring term, with the numbers referring to months); semesters; trimesters; quarters; 3-3 (three courses for each of three terms); modular (the academic year is divided into small blocks of time; courses of varying lengths are assembled according to individual programs); or standard year (for most Canadian institutions). *Degrees:* This names the full range of levels of certificates, diplomas, and degrees, including prebaccalaureate, baccalaureate, graduate, and professional, that are offered by this institution: *Special study options:* Details on study options available at each college, such as accelerated degree program, academic remediation for entering students, Advanced Placement credit, cooperative education programs, distance learning, double majors, English as a second language (ESL), and external degree programs. *ROTC:* Army, Naval, or Air Force Reserve Officers' Training Corps programs offered either on campus, at a branch campus [designated by a (b)], or at a cooperating host institution [designated by (c)].

Computers on Campus

Information is provided on the numbers of computers/terminals available on campus for general student use, what computer technology is accessible to students, and availability of a campuswide network and wireless campus network.

Student Life

Housing options: Institution's policy about whether students are permitted to live off-campus or are required to live on campus for a specified period; whether freshmen only, coed, single-sex, cooperative, and disabled student housing options are available; whether campus housing is leased by the school and/or provided by a third party; whether freshman applicants are given priority for college housing. "College housing not available" indicates that no college-owned or -operated housing facilities are provided for undergraduates and that noncommuting students must arrange for their own accommodations. *Activities and organizations:* Information on clubs and organizations, including sororities and fraternities. *Campus security:* Campus safety measures including 24-hour emergency response devices (phones and alarms) and patrols by trained security personnel, student patrols, late-night transport-escort service, and controlled dormitory access (key, security card, etc.). *Student services:* Information indicates services offered to students by the college, such as legal services, health clinics, personal-psychological counseling, and women's centers.

Athletics

Membership in one or more of the following athletic associations is indicated by initials: NCAA: National Collegiate Athletic Association; NAIA: National Association of Intercollegiate Athletics; NCCAA: National Christian College Athletic Association; USCAA: United States Collegiate Athletic Association; and CIS: Canadian Interuniversity Sport. The overall NCAA division in which all or most intercollegiate teams compete is designated by I, II, or III. All teams that do not compete in this division are listed as exceptions.

Sports offered by the college are divided into two groups: *Intercollegiate* ("M" or "W" following the name of each sport indicates that it is offered for men or women) and *Intramural.* An "s" in parentheses following an "M" or "W" for an intercollegiate sport indicates that athletic scholarships (or grants-in-aid) are offered for men or women in that sport, and a "c" indicates a club team as opposed to a varsity team.

Standardized Tests

The most commonly required standardized tests are the ACT, SAT, and SAT Subject Tests. These and other standardized tests may be used for selective admission, as a basis for counseling or course placement, or for both purposes. This section notes if a test is used for admission or placement and whether it is required, required for some, or recommended. In addition to the ACT and SAT, the following standardized entrance and placement examinations are referred to by their initials: ABLE (Adult Basic Learning Examination); ACT ASSET (ACT Assessment of Skills for Successful Entry and Transfer); ACT PEP (ACT Proficiency Examination Program); CAT (California Achievement Tests); CELT (Comprehensive English Language Test); CPAt (Career Programs Assessment); CPT (Computerized Placement Test); DAT (Differential Aptitude Test); LSAT (Law School Admission Test); MAPS (Multiple Assessment Program Service); MCAT (Medical College Admission Test); MMPI (Minnesota Multiphasic Personality Inventory); OAT (Optometry Admission Test); PAA (Prueba de Aptitud Académica—Spanish-language version of SAT); PCAT (Pharmacy College Admission Test); PSAT/NMSQT (Preliminary SAT/National Merit Scholarship Qualifying Test); SCAT (Scholastic College Aptitude Test); TABE (Test of Adult Basic Education); TASP (Texas Academic Skills Program); TOEFL (Test of English as a Foreign Language); WPCT (Washington Pre-College Test).

Costs

Costs are given for the 2011–12 academic year or for the 2010–11 academic year if 2011–12 figures were not yet available. Annual expenses may be expressed as a comprehensive fee (including full-time tuition, mandatory fees, and college room and board) or as separate figures for full-time tuition, fees, room and board, or room only. For public institutions where tuition differs according to residence, separate figures are given for area or state residents and for nonresidents. Part-time tuition is expressed in terms of a per-unit rate (per credit, per semester hour, etc.).

The tuition structure at some institutions is complex in that freshmen and sophomores may be charged a different rate from that for juniors and seniors, a professional or vocational division may have a different fee structure from the liberal arts division of the same institution, or part-time tuition may be prorated on a sliding scale according to the number of credit hours taken. Tuition and fees may vary according to academic program, campus/location, class time (day, evening, weekend), course/credit load, course level, degree level, reciprocity agreements, and student level. *Room and board* charges are reported as an average for one academic year and may vary according to the board plan selected, campus/location, type of housing facility, or student level. *Payment plans* may include tuition prepayment, installment payments, and deferred payment. A tuition prepayment plan gives a student the option of locking in the current tuition rate for the entire term of enrollment by paying the full amount in advance rather than year by year. *Waivers:* availability of full or partial undergraduate tuition waivers to minority students, children of alumni, employees or their children, adult students, and senior citizens may be listed.

Financial Aid

This information represents aid awarded to undergraduates for the available academic year. Figures are given for the number of undergraduates who applied for aid, the number who were judged to have need, and the number who had their need met. The number of Federal Work-Study Programs and/or part-time jobs and average earnings are listed, as well as the number of non-need-based awards. The *Average percent of need met* for those determined to have need, *Average financial aid package* awarded to undergraduates (the amount of scholarships, grants, work-study payments, or loans in the institutionally administered financial aid package divided by the number of students who received any financial aid-amounts used to pay the officially designated Expected Family Contribution (EFC), *Average need-based loan, Average need-based gift aid,* and *Average non-need-based aid* are given. *Average indebtedness upon graduation,* which is the average per-borrower indebtedness of the last graduating undergraduate class from amounts borrowed at this institution through any loan programs, excluding parent loans, is listed last.

Applying

Application and admission *Options* include the following: Early admission—(highly qualified students may matriculate before graduating from high school); Early action—admission plan that allows students to apply and be notified of an admission decision well in advance of the regular notification dates (If accepted, the candidate is not committed to enroll; students may reply to the offer under the college's regular reply policy); Deferred entrance—practice of permitting accepted students to postpone enrollment, usually for a period of one academic term or year; Early decision deadline—plan that permits students to apply and be notified of an admission decision (and financial aid offer, if applicable) well in advance of the regular notification date, and. applicants agree to accept an offer of admission and to withdraw their applications from other colleges. *Application fee:* The fee required with an application is noted. *Required, Required for some,* and *Recommended:* Other application requirements are grouped into three categories and may include an essay, standardized test scores, a high school transcript, a minimum high school grade point average (expressed as a number on a scale of 0 to 4.0, where 4.0 equals A, 3.0 equals B, etc.), letters of recommendation, an interview on campus or with local alumni, and, for certain types of schools or programs, special requirements such as a musical audition or an art portfolio. *Application deadlines and Notification:* Admission application deadlines and dates for notification of acceptance or rejection are given either as specific dates or as rolling and continuous. Rolling means that applications are processed as they are received, and qualified students are accepted as long as there are openings. Continuous means that applicants are notified of acceptance or rejection as applications are processed up until the date indicated or the actual beginning of classes. The application deadline and the notification date for transfers are given if they differ from the dates for freshmen. Early decision and early action application deadlines and notification dates are also indicated when relevant.

Freshman Application Contact

The name, title, mailing address, and phone number of the person to contact for further information are given at the end of the profile. The fax number, e-mail address, and Web site may also be provided.

Additional Information

Each school that has a College Close-Up in this guide will have a cross-reference with the page number of the Close-Up.

COLLEGE CLOSE-UPS

The over 400 two-page descriptions provide an inside look at colleges and universities. The descriptions provide a wealth of information that is crucial in the college decision-making process—components such as tuition, financial aid, and major fields of study. Prepared exclusively by college officials, the descriptions are designed to help give students a better sense of the individuality of each institution, in terms that include campus environment, student activities, and lifestyle. The absence of any college or university does not constitute an editorial decision on the part of Peterson's. In essence, these descriptions are an open forum for colleges and universities, on a voluntary basis, to communicate their particular message to prospective college students. The colleges included have paid a fee to Peterson's to provide this information. The **College Close-Ups** are edited to provide a consistent format across entries for your ease of comparison.

INDEXES

Here you'll find easy-to-use breakdowns of schools' majors, entrance difficulty, and cost ranges. We've also provided an "Advertisers Index," a "Geographical Listing of College Close-Ups," and an "Alphabetical Listing of Colleges and Universities."

Majors

This listing presents hundreds of undergraduate fields of study that are currently offered, according to the colleges' responses on *Peterson's Annual Survey of Undergraduate Institutions*. The majors appear in alphabetical order, each followed by an alphabetical list of the schools that offer a bachelor's-level program in that particular field. Liberal Arts and Studies indicates a general program with no specified major.

The terms used are those of the U.S. Department of Education Classification of Instructional Programs (CIP). Many institutions, however, use different terms. Although the term major is used in this guide, some colleges may use other terms, such as concentration, program of study, or field.

Entrance Difficulty

This listing groups colleges by their own assessment of their entrance difficulty level. The colleges were asked to select the level that most closely corresponds to their entrance difficulty. Institutions for which high school class rank and/or standardized test scores do not apply as admission criteria were asked to select the level that best indicates their entrance difficulty as compared to other institutions.

Cost Ranges

Colleges are grouped into thirteen price ranges, from under $2000 to $30,000 and over.

Institutional Changes Since Peterson's Four-Year Colleges 2011

The following is an alphabetical listing of institutions that have closed, merged with other institutions, or changed their names or status since *Peterson's Four-Year Colleges 2011*.

American InterContinental University (Houston, TX): *name changed to American InterContinental University Houston.*

American InterContinental University Buckhead Campus (Atlanta, GA): *closed.*

American InterContinental University Dunwoody Campus (Atlanta, GA): *name changed to American InterContinental University Atlanta.*

American InterContinental University–London (London, United Kingdom): *name changed to American InterContinental University London.*

Antioch University McGregor (Yellow Springs, OH): *name changed to Antioch University Midwest.*

Arkansas State University - Jonesboro (State University, AR): *name changed to Arkansas State University.*

Belhaven College (Maitland, FL): *name changed to Belhaven University.*

Belhaven College (Memphis, TN): *name changed to Belhaven University.*

Bridgewater State College (Bridgewater, MA): *name changed to Bridgewater State University.*

Clarke College (Dubuque, IA): *name changed to Clarke University.*

College of Santa Fe (Santa Fe, NM): *name changed to Santa Fe University of Art and Design.*

Collins College: A School of Design and Technology (Tempe, AZ): *name changed to Collins College.*

Columbia College (Yauco, PR): *name changed to Columbia Centro Universitario.*

Cox College of Nursing and Health Sciences (Springfield, MO): *name changed to Cox College.*

Crichton College (Memphis, TN): *name changed to Victory University.*

Dana College (Blair, NE): *closed.*

Deree College, The American College of Greece (Athens, Greece): *name changed to DEREE - The American College of Greece.*

ECPI Technical College (Roanoke, VA): *name changed to Skyline College.*

Embry-Riddle Aeronautical University (Prescott, AZ): *name changed to Embry-Riddle Aeronautical University–Prescott.*

Embry-Riddle Aeronautical University (Daytona Beach, FL): *name changed to Embry-Riddle Aeronautical University–Daytona.*

Embry-Riddle Aeronautical University Worldwide (Daytona Beach, FL): *name changed to Embry-Riddle Aeronautical University–Worldwide.*

Emily Carr Institute of Art + Design (Vancouver, BC, Canada): *name changed to Emily Carr University of Art + Design.*

Eugene Bible College (Eugene, OR): *name changed to New Hope Christian College.*

Fitchburg State College (Fitchburg, MA): *name changed to Fitchburg State University.*

Florida Culinary Institute (West Palm Beach, FL): *name changed to Lincoln Culinary Institute.*

Framingham State College (Framingham, MA): *name changed to Framingham State University.*

Hannibal-LaGrange College (Hannibal, MO): *name changed to Hannibal-LaGrange University.*

John Wesley College (High Point, NC): *name changed to Laurel University.*

Medical College of Georgia (Augusta, GA): *name changed to Georgia Health Sciences University.*

Meritus University (Fredericton, NB, Canada): *closed.*

Montana State University–Billings (Billings, MT): *name changed to Montana State University Billings.*

Mount Mercy College (Cedar Rapids, IA): *name changed to Mount Mercy University.*

National College (Bayamón, PR): *name changed to National University College.*

Patricia Stevens College (St. Louis, MO): *name changed to Stevens Institute of Business & Arts.*

Polytechnic University of the Americas–Miami Campus (Miami, FL): *name changed to Polytechnic University of Puerto Rico, Miami Campus.*

Polytechnic University of the Americas–Orlando Campus (Winter Park, FL): *name changed to Polytechnic University of Puerto Rico, Orlando Campus.*

Reinhardt College (Waleska, GA): *name changed to Reinhardt University.*

Saint Luke's College (Kansas City, MO): *name changed to Saint Luke's College of Health Sciences.*

Salem State College (Salem, MA): *name changed to Salem State University.*

Santa Fe Community College (Gainesville, FL): *name changed to Santa Fe College.*

Southwestern College (Phoenix, AZ): *name changed to Arizona Christian University.*

Strayer University - Central Austin Campus (Austin, TX): *name changed to Strayer University - North Austin Campus.*

Strayer University - Garner Campus (Raleigh, NC): *name changed to Strayer University - South Raleigh Campus.*

Strayer University - New Brunswick Campus (Piscataway, NJ): *name changed to Strayer University - Piscataway Campus.*

University of Arkansas at Fort Smith (Fort Smith, AR): *name changed to University of Arkansas–Fort Smith.*

University of Colorado at Boulder (Boulder, CO): *name changed to University of Colorado Boulder.*

University of Phoenix–Wisconsin Campus (Madison, WI): *name changed to University of Phoenix–Madison Campus.*

Wesley College (Florence, MS): *closed.*

Western New England College (Springfield, MA): *name changed to Western New England University.*

Westfield State College (Westfield, MA): *name changed to Westfield State University.*

West Suburban College of Nursing (Oak Park, IL): *name changed to Resurrection University.*

William and Catherine Booth College (Winnipeg, MB, Canada): *name changed to Booth University College.*

DATA COLLECTION PROCEDURES

The data contained in the **PROFILES** and **INDEXES** sections were researched between winter 2010 and spring 2011 through *Peterson's Annual Survey of Undergraduate Institutions*. Questionnaires were sent to the more than 2,700 colleges and universities that met the outlined inclusion criteria. All data included in this edition have been submitted by officials (usually admissions and financial aid officers, registrars, or institutional research personnel) at the colleges. Some of the institutions that submitted data were contacted directly by the Peterson's research staff to verify unusual figures, resolve discrepancies, or obtain additional data. All usable information received in time for publication has been included. The omission of any particular item from the **PROFILES** and **INDEXES** sections signifies that the information is either not applicable to that institution or not available. Because of Peterson's comprehensive editorial review and because all material comes directly from college officials, we believe that the information presented is accurate. You should check with a specific college or university at the time of application to verify such figures as tuition and fees, which may have changed since this guide's publication.

CRITERIA FOR INCLUSION IN THIS BOOK

The term "four-year college" is the commonly used designation for institutions that grant the baccalaureate degree. Four years is the expected amount of time required to earn this degree, although some bachelor's degree programs may be completed in three years, others require five years, and part-time programs may take considerably longer. Upper-level institutions offer only the junior and senior years and accept only students with two years of college-level credit. Therefore, "four-year college" is a conventional term that accurately describes most of the institutions included in this guide, but should not be taken literally in all cases.

To be included in this guide, an institution must have full accreditation or be a candidate for accreditation (preaccreditation) status by an institutional or specialized accrediting body recognized by the U.S. Department of Education or the Council for Higher Education Accreditation (CHEA). Institutional accrediting bodies, which review each institution as a whole, include the six regional associations of schools and colleges (Middle States, New England, North Central, Northwest, Southern, and Western), each of which is responsible for a specified portion of the United States and its territories. Other institutional accrediting bodies are national in scope and accredit specific kinds of institutions (e.g., Bible colleges, independent colleges, and rabbinical and Talmudic schools). Program registration by the New York State Board of Regents is considered to be the equivalent of institutional accreditation, since the board requires that all programs offered by an institution meet its standards before recognition is granted. A Canadian institution must be chartered and authorized to grant degrees by the provincial government, affiliated with a chartered institution, or accredited by a recognized U.S. accrediting body. This guide also includes institutions outside the United States that are accredited by these U.S. accrediting bodies. There are recognized specialized or professional accrediting bodies in more than forty different fields, each of which is authorized to accredit institutions or specific programs in its particular field. For specialized institutions that offer programs in one field only, we designate this to be the equivalent of institutional accreditation. A full explanation of the accrediting process and complete information on recognized, institutional (regional and national) and specialized accrediting bodies can be found online at www.chea.orgoratwww.ed.gov/admins/finaid/accred/index.htm.

NOTICE: Certain portions of or information contained in this book have been submitted and paid for by the educational institution identified, and such institutions take full responsibility for the accuracy, timeliness, completeness and functionality of such content. Such portions or information include (i) each display ad in the "Profiles" section from pages 54 through 983 that comprises a half or full page of information covering a single educational institution, and (ii) each two-page description in the "College Close-Up" section from pages 986 through 1797."

Profiles

ALABAMA

Alabama Agricultural and Mechanical University

Huntsville, Alabama

- **State-supported** university, founded 1875
- **Suburban** 2001-acre campus
- **Endowment** $29.3 million
- **Coed** 4,940 undergraduate students, 93% full-time, 52% women, 48% men
- **Minimally difficult** entrance level, 51% of applicants were admitted

Undergraduates 4,592 full-time, 348 part-time. 31% are from out of state; 96% Black or African American, non-Hispanic/Latino; 0.3% Hispanic/Latino; 0.2% Asian, non-Hispanic/Latino; 0.1% American Indian or Alaska Native, non-Hispanic/Latino; 0.4% Race/ethnicity unknown; 0.9% international; 4% transferred in. *Retention:* 75% of full-time freshmen returned.

Freshmen *Admission:* 5,363 applied, 2,725 admitted, 1,119 enrolled. *Test scores:* SAT critical reading scores over 500: 13%; SAT math scores over 500: 17%; SAT writing scores over 500: 13%; ACT scores over 18: 47%; SAT critical reading scores over 600: 1%; SAT math scores over 600: 1%; ACT scores over 24: 4%.

Faculty *Total:* 290, 100% full-time, 34% with terminal degrees. *Student/faculty ratio:* 20:1.

Academics *Calendar:* semesters. *Degrees:* bachelor's, master's, doctoral-research/scholarship, and post-master's certificates. *Special study options:* academic remediation for entering students, adult/continuing education programs, advanced placement credit, cooperative education, distance learning, double majors, honors programs, independent study, internships, off-campus study, part-time degree program, services for LD students, study abroad, summer session for credit. *ROTC:* Army (b). *Unusual degree programs:* 3-2 nursing.

Computers on Campus 1,000 computers/terminals are available on campus for general student use. Campuswide network is available.

Student Life *Housing:* on-campus residence required through sophomore year. *Options:* men-only, women-only. Campus housing is university owned. *Activities and organizations:* drama/theater group, student-run newspaper, radio and television station, choral group, marching band, University Voices Gospel Choir, University Choir and Band, Elementary/Early Childhood Club, National Alliance of Business Students, national fraternities, national sororities. *Campus security:* 24-hour patrols, late-night transport/escort service, controlled dormitory access. *Student services:* health clinic, personal/psychological counseling.

Athletics Member NCAA. All Division I except football (Division I-AA). *Intercollegiate sports:* baseball M(s), basketball M(s)/W(s), cross-country running M(s)/W(s), golf M(s), soccer M(s), tennis M/W, track and field M(s)/W(s), volleyball W(s). *Intramural sports:* basketball M/W, cross-country running M/W, football M, golf M, soccer M, table tennis M/W, tennis M/W, track and field M/W, volleyball W.

Standardized Tests *Required:* ACT (for admission).

Costs (2011–12) *Tuition:* state resident $4872 full-time, $203 per credit part-time; nonresident $9744 full-time, $406 per credit part-time. Full-time tuition and fees vary according to course load. Part-time tuition and fees vary according to course load. *Required fees:* $928 full-time. *Room and board:* $6200; room only: $3090. Room and board charges vary according to board plan, housing facility, and location. *Payment plan:* installment. *Waivers:* employees or children of employees.

Financial Aid Of all full-time matriculated undergraduates who enrolled in 2009, 3,784 applied for aid, 3,293 were judged to have need, 371 had their need fully met. In 2009, 233 non-need-based awards were made. *Average percent of need met:* 12%. *Average financial aid package:* $10,342. *Average need-based gift aid:* $7405. *Average non-need-based aid:* $8605. *Average indebtedness upon graduation:* $31,863.

Applying *Options:* electronic application, deferred entrance. *Application fee:* $10. *Required:* high school transcript, minimum 2 GPA. *Recommended:* 1 letter of recommendation. *Application deadlines:* 6/15 (freshmen), rolling (transfers). *Notification:* continuous (freshmen), continuous (transfers).

Freshman Application Contact Dr. Evelyn Ellis, Interim Director of Admissions, Alabama Agricultural and Mechanical University, 4900

Meridian Street, Huntsville, AL 35811. *Phone:* 256-372-5245. *Toll-free phone:* 800-553-0816. *Fax:* 256-851-9747. *Web site:* http://www.aamu.edu/.

Alabama State University

Montgomery, Alabama

- **State-supported** comprehensive, founded 1867, part of Alabama Commission on Higher Education
- **Urban** 172-acre campus
- **Coed** 4,882 undergraduate students, 92% full-time, 59% women, 41% men
- **Minimally difficult** entrance level, 44% of applicants were admitted

Undergraduates 4,506 full-time, 376 part-time. 32% are from out of state; 95% Black or African American, non-Hispanic/Latino; 0.4% Hispanic/Latino; 0.1% Native Hawaiian or other Pacific Islander, non-Hispanic/Latino; 3% Race/ethnicity unknown; 0.5% international; 6% transferred in; 45% live on campus. *Retention:* 65% of full-time freshmen returned.

Freshmen *Admission:* 8,231 applied, 3,641 admitted, 1,101 enrolled. *Average high school GPA:* 3.0. *Test scores:* SAT critical reading scores over 500: 15%; SAT math scores over 500: 12%; ACT scores over 18: 38%; SAT critical reading scores over 600: 2%; SAT math scores over 600: 2%; ACT scores over 24: 3%.

Faculty *Total:* 407, 62% full-time, 50% with terminal degrees. *Student/faculty ratio:* 17:1.

Academics *Calendar:* semesters. *Degrees:* bachelor's, master's, doctoral-professional, doctoral-research/scholarship, post-master's, and postbachelor's certificates. *Special study options:* academic remediation for entering students, advanced placement credit, cooperative education, distance learning, double majors, freshman honors college, honors programs, independent study, internships, part-time degree program, student-designed majors, summer session for credit. *ROTC:* Army (c), Air Force (b).

Computers on Campus Students can access the following: computer help desk, free student e-mail accounts, online (class) grades, online (class) registration, online (class) schedules. Campuswide network is available. Wireless service is available via entire campus.

Student Life *Housing options:* men-only, women-only, disabled students. Campus housing is university owned. *Activities and organizations:* drama/theater group, student-run newspaper, radio station, choral group, marching band, national fraternities, national sororities. *Campus security:* 24-hour emergency response devices and patrols, late-night transport/escort service, self-defense education, well-lit campus. *Student services:* health clinic, personal/psychological counseling.

Athletics Member NCAA. All Division I. *Intercollegiate sports:* baseball M(s), basketball M(s)/W(s), bowling W, cheerleading M/W, cross-country running M(s)/W(s), football M(s), golf M(s)/W(s), soccer W(s), softball W(s), tennis M(s)/W(s), track and field M(s)/W(s), volleyball W(s). *Intramural sports:* baseball M, basketball M/W, softball M/W, swimming and diving M/W, tennis M/W, track and field M/W, volleyball M/W, weight lifting M/W.

Standardized Tests *Required:* SAT or ACT (for admission).

Costs (2010–11) *One-time required fee:* $150. *Tuition:* state resident $6312 full-time, $263 per credit hour part-time; nonresident $12,624 full-time, $526 per credit hour part-time. *Required fees:* $852 full-time, $213 per term part-time. *Room and board:* $4800; room only: $2460. Room and board charges vary according to board plan and housing facility. *Payment plan:* deferred payment. *Waivers:* employees or children of employees.

Financial Aid Of all full-time matriculated undergraduates who enrolled in 2009, 4,467 applied for aid, 4,038 were judged to have need, 527 had their need fully met. In 2009, 42 non-need-based awards were made. *Average percent of need met:* 68%. *Average financial aid package:* $14,148. *Average need-based loan:* $3782. *Average need-based gift aid:* $14,148. *Average non-need-based aid:* $7280. *Average indebtedness upon graduation:* $31,317.

Applying *Options:* electronic application, early admission, deferred entrance. *Application fee:* $25. *Required:* high school transcript, minimum 2 GPA. *Recommended:* essay or personal statement, interview. *Application deadlines:* 7/31 (freshmen), 7/31 (transfers). *Notification:* continuous (freshmen), continuous (transfers).

Freshman Application Contact Director of Admissions and Recruitment, Alabama State University, 915 South Jackson Street, Montgomery, AL 36101-0271. *Phone:* 334-229-4291. *Toll-free phone:* 800-253-5037. *Fax:* 334-229-4984. *E-mail:* admissions@alasu.edu. *Web site:* http://www.alasu.edu/.

Amridge University
Montgomery, Alabama

- **Independent** university, founded 1967, affiliated with Church of Christ
- **Urban** 9-acre campus
- **Endowment** $750,000
- **Coed** 370 undergraduate students, 64% full-time, 54% women, 46% men
- **Minimally difficult** entrance level

Undergraduates 237 full-time, 133 part-time. Students come from 48 states and territories; 75% are from out of state; 34% Black or African American, non-Hispanic/Latino; 3% Hispanic/Latino; 0.8% Asian, non-Hispanic/Latino; 27% Race/ethnicity unknown; 96% transferred in. *Retention:* 60% of full-time freshmen returned.

Freshmen *Admission:* 4 enrolled.

Faculty *Total:* 78, 50% full-time, 100% with terminal degrees. *Student/faculty ratio:* 11:1.

Academics *Calendar:* semesters. *Degrees:* associate, bachelor's, master's, and doctoral-other. *Special study options:* accelerated degree program, adult/continuing education programs, advanced placement credit, distance learning, double majors, external degree program, internships, part-time degree program, services for LD students, summer session for credit.

Computers on Campus 5 computers/terminals are available on campus for general student use. Students can access the following: online (class) registration, access to over 20 million monographs and journals online. Campuswide network is available.

Student Life *Housing:* college housing not available.

Costs (2011–12) *Tuition:* $7620 full-time, $330 per semester hour part-time. Full-time tuition and fees vary according to course load. Part-time tuition and fees vary according to course load. *Required fees:* $800 full-time, $400 per term part-time. *Waivers:* employees or children of employees.

Financial Aid Of all full-time matriculated undergraduates who enrolled in 2008, 330 applied for aid, 300 were judged to have need, 275 had their need fully met. In 2008, 20 non-need-based awards were made. *Average percent of need met:* 85%. *Average financial aid package:* $8500. *Average need-based loan:* $5500. *Average need-based gift aid:* $6500. *Average non-need-based aid:* $4000. *Average indebtedness upon graduation:* $18,000.

Applying *Options:* electronic application. *Application fee:* $75. *Required:* high school transcript, minimum 2 GPA. *Application deadlines:* rolling (freshmen), rolling (out-of-state freshmen), rolling (transfers).

Freshman Application Contact Mrs. Ora Davis, Admissions Officer, Amridge University, 1200 Taylor Road, Montgomery, AL 36117. *Phone:* 334-387-3877 Ext. 7524. *Toll-free phone:* 800-351-4040 Ext. 213. *Fax:* 334-387-3878. *E-mail:* oradavis@amridgeuniversity.edu. *Web site:* http://www.amridgeuniversity.edu/.

See page 994 for the College Close-Up.

Andrew Jackson University
Birmingham, Alabama

- **Private** comprehensive, founded 1994
- **Suburban** campus with easy access to Birmingham
- **Coed** 230 undergraduate students, 31% women, 69% men
- **Noncompetitive** entrance level, 87% of applicants were admitted

Undergraduates 230 part-time. 95% are from out of state.

Freshmen *Admission:* 115 applied, 100 admitted.

Faculty *Total:* 50, 90% with terminal degrees. *Student/faculty ratio:* 11:1.

Academics *Degrees:* certificates, associate, bachelor's, master's, and doctoral-other (offers primarily external degree programs). *Special study options:* accelerated degree program, adult/continuing education programs, advanced placement credit, distance learning, external degree program, independent study, off-campus study, part-time degree program, summer session for credit.

Computers on Campus Campuswide network is available.

Student Life *Housing:* college housing not available.

Costs (2010–11) *Tuition:* Full-time tuition and fees vary according to course load. Part-time tuition and fees vary according to course load. No tuition increase for student's term of enrollment. students have sponsored tuition. *Required fees:* $700 full-time, $350 per term part-time. *Payment plans:* installment, deferred payment. *Waivers:* employees or children of employees.

Applying *Options:* electronic application. *Application fee:* $75. *Required:* interview. *Required for some:* essay or personal statement, high school transcript.

Freshman Application Contact Ms. Tammy J. Kassner, Director of Admissions, Andrew Jackson University, 2919 John Hawkins Parkway, Birmingham, AL 35244. *Phone:* 205-871-9288 Ext. 107. *Fax:* 800-871-9294. *E-mail:* admissions@aju.edu. *Web site:* http://www.aju.edu/.

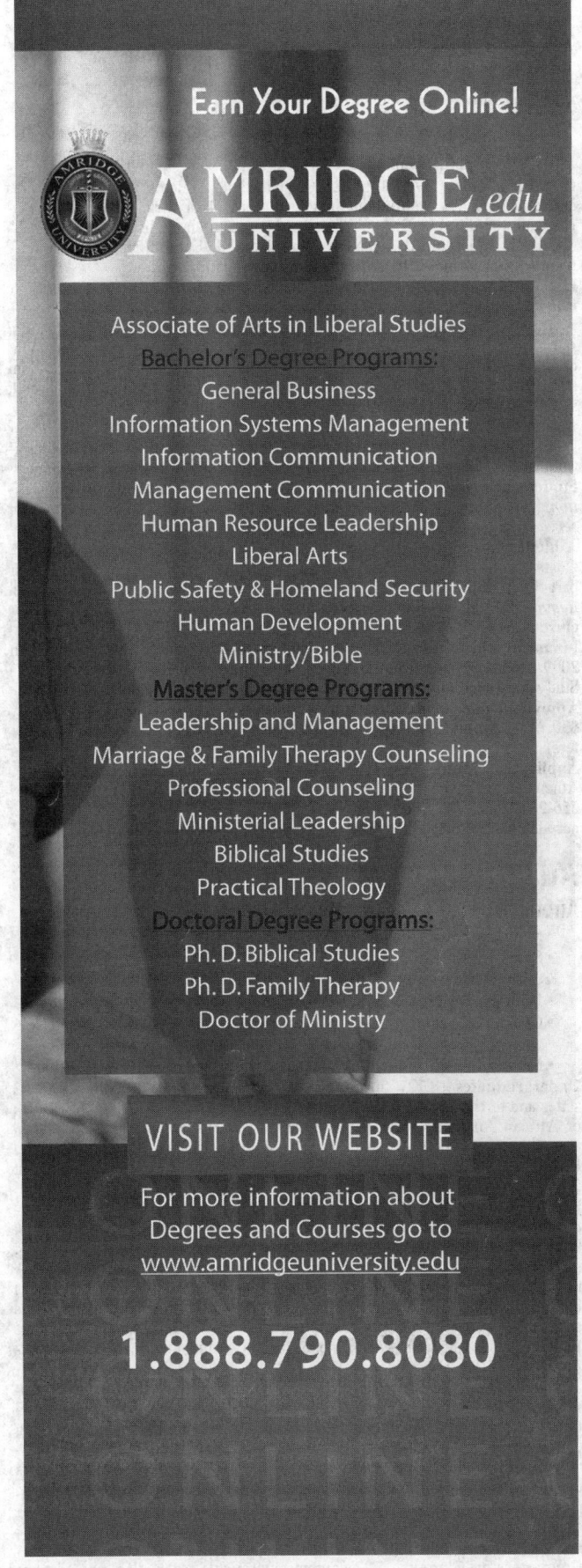

Athens State University

Athens, Alabama

- **State-supported** upper-level, founded 1822, part of Alabama College System
- **Small-town** 45-acre campus
- **Coed** 3,621 undergraduate students, 44% full-time, 65% women, 35% men
- **Noncompetitive** entrance level

Undergraduates 1,598 full-time, 2,023 part-time. Students come from 7 states and territories; 4% are from out of state; 12% Black or African American, non-Hispanic/Latino; 1% Hispanic/Latino; 1% Asian, non-Hispanic/Latino; 3% American Indian or Alaska Native, non-Hispanic/Latino; 2% Race/ethnicity unknown; 0.6% international; 21% transferred in.
Faculty *Total:* 210, 41% full-time, 32% with terminal degrees. *Student/faculty ratio:* 18:1.
Academics *Calendar:* semesters. *Degree:* certificates and bachelor's. *Special study options:* adult/continuing education programs, advanced placement credit, cooperative education, distance learning, double majors, independent study, internships, off-campus study, part-time degree program, study abroad, summer session for credit.
Computers on Campus 210 computers/terminals are available on campus for general student use. Students can access the following: online (class) registration, grades, transcripts, schedules, e-mail. Campuswide network is available.
Student Life *Housing:* college housing not available. *Activities and organizations:* drama/theater group, student-run newspaper, national sororities. *Student services:* personal/psychological counseling.
Athletics *Intramural sports:* table tennis M/W, volleyball M/W.
Costs (2010–11) *Tuition:* state resident $4110 full-time, $137 per credit hour part-time; nonresident $8220 full-time, $274 per credit hour part-time. *Required fees:* $750 full-time, $25 per credit hour part-time. *Waivers:* senior citizens and employees or children of employees.
Financial Aid Of all full-time matriculated undergraduates who enrolled in 2009, 1,058 applied for aid, 657 were judged to have need. 15 Federal Work-Study jobs (averaging $6100). In 2009, 10 non-need-based awards were made.
Applying *Options:* electronic application, deferred entrance. *Application fee:* $30. *Application deadline:* rolling (transfers). *Notification:* continuous (transfers).
Application Contact Ms. Necedah Henderson, Coordinator of Admissions, Athens State University, 300 North Beaty Street, Athens, AL 35611. *Phone:* 256-233-8217. *Toll-free phone:* 800-522-0272. *Fax:* 256-233-6565. *E-mail:* necedah.henderson@athens.edu. *Web site:* http://www.athens.edu/.

Auburn University

Auburn University, Alabama

- **State-supported** university, founded 1856
- **Small-town** 1875-acre campus with easy access to Atlanta and Birmingham
- **Endowment** $365.2 million
- **Coed** 20,221 undergraduate students, 93% full-time, 49% women, 51% men
- **Moderately difficult** entrance level, 79% of applicants were admitted

Undergraduates 18,727 full-time, 1,494 part-time. Students come from 53 states and territories; 43 other countries; 39% are from out of state; 8% Black or African American, non-Hispanic/Latino; 3% Hispanic/Latino; 2% Asian, non-Hispanic/Latino; 0.7% American Indian or Alaska Native, non-Hispanic/Latino; 1% Race/ethnicity unknown; 0.7% international; 6% transferred in; 20% live on campus. *Retention:* 87% of full-time freshmen returned.
Freshmen *Admission:* 15,784 applied, 12,417 admitted, 4,204 enrolled. *Average high school GPA:* 3.78. *Test scores:* SAT critical reading scores over 500: 90%; SAT math scores over 500: 93%; SAT writing scores over 500: 86%; ACT scores over 18: 100%; SAT critical reading scores over 600: 46%; SAT math scores over 600: 57%; SAT writing scores over 600: 43%; ACT scores over 24: 80%; SAT critical reading scores over 700: 14%; SAT math scores over 700: 15%; SAT writing scores over 700: 9%; ACT scores over 30: 30%.
Faculty *Total:* 1,357, 88% full-time, 59% with terminal degrees. *Student/faculty ratio:* 18:1.
Academics *Calendar:* semesters. *Degrees:* bachelor's, master's, doctoral-professional, doctoral-research/scholarship, post-master's, and postbachelor's certificates. *Special study options:* accelerated degree program, adult/continuing education programs, advanced placement credit, cooperative education, distance learning, double majors, English as a second language, freshman honors college, honors programs, independent study, internships, off-campus study, part-time degree program, services for LD students, study abroad, summer session for credit. *ROTC:* Army (b), Navy (b), Air Force (b). *Unusual degree programs:* 3-2 engineering.
Computers on Campus 1,722 computers/terminals are available on campus for general student use. Students can access the following: computer help desk,

free student e-mail accounts, online (class) grades, online (class) registration, pay Bursar online, course materials available online. Campuswide network is available. 100% of college-owned or -operated housing units are wired for high-speed Internet access. Wireless service is available via entire campus.
Student Life *Housing options:* coed, men-only, women-only, disabled students. Campus housing is university owned. *Activities and organizations:* drama/theater group, student-run newspaper, radio and television station, choral group, marching band, Student Government Association, University Program Council, IMPACT (volunteer opportunities), International Student Organization, student media (AU Plainsman newspaper, WEGL radio, Glomerata yearbook, Eagle Eye television, AU Circle literary journal), national fraternities, national sororities. *Campus security:* 24-hour emergency response devices and patrols, late-night transport/escort service, controlled dormitory access. *Student services:* health clinic, personal/psychological counseling.
Athletics Member NCAA. All Division I except football (Division I-A). *Intercollegiate sports:* baseball M(s), basketball M(s)/W(s), cross-country running M(s)/W(s), equestrian sports W(s), golf M(s)/W(s), gymnastics W(s), soccer W(s), softball W(s), swimming and diving M(s)/W(s), tennis M(s)/W(s), track and field M(s)/W(s), volleyball W(s). *Intramural sports:* badminton M/W, basketball M/W, bowling M/W, crew M(c)/W(c), football M/W, golf M/W, ice hockey M(c), lacrosse M(c)/W(c), racquetball M/W, rugby M(c)/W(c), sailing M(c)/W(c), soccer M/W, softball M/W, swimming and diving M/W, table tennis M/W, tennis M/W, track and field M/W, ultimate Frisbee M/W, volleyball M/W, water polo M(c)/W(c), wrestling M(c)/W(c).
Standardized Tests *Required:* SAT or ACT (for admission).
Costs (2010–11) *Tuition:* state resident $7008 full-time, $292 per semester hour part-time; nonresident $21,024 full-time, $876 per semester hour part-time. Full-time tuition and fees vary according to program and reciprocity agreements. Part-time tuition and fees vary according to course load, program, and reciprocity agreements. *Required fees:* $892 full-time, $446 per term part-time. *Room and board:* $9630; room only: $4780. Room and board charges vary according to board plan and housing facility. *Payment plan:* installment. *Waivers:* employees or children of employees.
Financial Aid Of all full-time matriculated undergraduates who enrolled in 2009, 9,590 applied for aid, 5,504 were judged to have need, 911 had their need fully met. 346 Federal Work-Study jobs (averaging $2521). In 2009, 2336 non-need-based awards were made. *Average percent of need met:* 54%. *Average financial aid package:* $8740. *Average need-based loan:* $4373. *Average need-based gift aid:* $5419. *Average non-need-based aid:* $4600. *Average indebtedness upon graduation:* $22,232.
Applying *Options:* electronic application, early admission, early action, deferred entrance. *Application fee:* $50. *Required:* essay or personal statement, high school transcript, minimum 2 GPA. *Required for some:* minimum 3 GPA. *Recommended:* minimum 3 GPA. *Application deadlines:* 2/1 (freshmen), 2/1 (out-of-state freshmen), rolling (transfers), 10/1 (early action). *Notification:* 2/15 (freshmen), continuous (transfers), 10/15 (early action).
Freshman Application Contact Ms. Cindy Singley, Director, University Recruitment, Auburn University, Auburn University, AL 36849. *Phone:* 334-844-4080. *Toll-free phone:* 800-AUBURN9. *E-mail:* admissions@auburn.edu. *Web site:* http://www.auburn.edu/.

Auburn University Montgomery

Montgomery, Alabama

- **State-supported** comprehensive, founded 1967, part of Auburn University
- **Suburban** 500-acre campus
- **Coed** 4,812 undergraduate students, 67% full-time, 62% women, 38% men
- **Moderately difficult** entrance level, 83% of applicants were admitted

Undergraduates 3,233 full-time, 1,579 part-time. 5% are from out of state; 34% Black or African American, non-Hispanic/Latino; 1% Hispanic/Latino; 2% Asian, non-Hispanic/Latino; 0.5% American Indian or Alaska Native, non-Hispanic/Latino; 3% Race/ethnicity unknown; 3% international; 9% transferred in; 13% live on campus. *Retention:* 57% of full-time freshmen returned.
Freshmen *Admission:* 2,118 applied, 1,763 admitted, 915 enrolled. *Average high school GPA:* 2.96. *Test scores:* ACT scores over 18: 80%; ACT scores over 24: 15%; ACT scores over 30: 1%.
Faculty *Total:* 315, 57% full-time. *Student/faculty ratio:* 19:1.
Academics *Calendar:* semesters. *Degrees:* bachelor's, master's, doctoral-other, and post-master's certificates. *Special study options:* academic remediation for entering students, adult/continuing education programs, advanced placement credit, cooperative education, distance learning, double majors, English as a second language, honors programs, independent study, internships, off-campus study, part-time degree program, services for LD students, study abroad, summer session for credit. *ROTC:* Army (b), Air Force (c).
Computers on Campus Students can access the following: campus intranet, computer help desk, free student e-mail accounts, online (class) grades, online (class) registration, online (class) schedules. Campuswide network is available. 100% of college-owned or -operated housing units are wired for high-speed

Internet access. Wireless service is available via classrooms, computer labs, libraries, student centers.

Student Life *Housing options:* coed, disabled students. Campus housing is university owned. *Activities and organizations:* drama/theater group, student-run newspaper, choral group, national fraternities, national sororities. *Campus security:* 24-hour emergency response devices and patrols, student patrols, late-night transport/escort service, controlled dormitory access. *Student services:* health clinic, personal/psychological counseling.

Athletics Member NAIA. *Intercollegiate sports:* baseball M(s), basketball M(s)/W(s), cheerleading M(s)/W(s), soccer M(s)/W(s), softball W(s), tennis M(s)/W(s). *Intramural sports:* badminton M/W, basketball M/W, bowling M/W, football M/W, soccer M/W, softball W, table tennis M/W, tennis M/W, volleyball M/W, wrestling M.

Standardized Tests *Required:* ACT (for admission). *Recommended:* SAT (for admission).

Costs (2010–11) *Tuition:* state resident $6730 full-time, $206 per credit hour part-time; nonresident $18,286 full-time, $618 per credit hour part-time. Full-time tuition and fees vary according to course load. Part-time tuition and fees vary according to course load. *Required fees:* $550 full-time, $8 per semester hour part-time, $155 per term part-time. *Room only:* $3820. Room and board charges vary according to housing facility. *Waivers:* employees or children of employees.

Financial Aid Of all full-time matriculated undergraduates who enrolled in 2009, 2,284 applied for aid, 1,638 had their need fully met. 46 Federal Work-Study jobs (averaging $3888). *Average need-based loan:* $3958. *Average need-based gift aid:* $4693.

Applying *Options:* electronic application, deferred entrance. *Application fee:* $25. *Required:* high school transcript. *Application deadlines:* rolling (freshmen), rolling (transfers). *Notification:* continuous (freshmen), continuous (transfers).

Freshman Application Contact Mr. Ronnie McKinney, Director of Recruitment, Auburn University Montgomery, PO Box 244023, Montgomery, AL 36124-4023. *Phone:* 334-244-3615. *Toll-free phone:* 800-227-2649. *Fax:* 334-244-3795. *E-mail:* rmckinne@aum.edu. *Web site:* http://www.aum.edu/.

Birmingham-Southern College
Birmingham, Alabama

- **Independent Methodist** comprehensive, founded 1856
- **Urban** 196-acre campus with easy access to Birmingham
- **Endowment** $56.6 million
- **Coed** 1,521 undergraduate students, 99% full-time, 49% women, 51% men
- **Moderately difficult** entrance level, 66% of applicants were admitted

Undergraduates 1,504 full-time, 17 part-time. Students come from 32 states and territories; 15 other countries; 37% are from out of state; 8% Black or African American, non-Hispanic/Latino; 3% Hispanic/Latino; 4% Asian, non-Hispanic/Latino; 0.7% American Indian or Alaska Native, non-Hispanic/Latino; 1% Two or more races, non-Hispanic/Latino; 1% Race/ethnicity unknown; 2% transferred in; 84% live on campus. *Retention:* 82% of full-time freshmen returned.

Freshmen *Admission:* 2,217 applied, 1,474 admitted, 368 enrolled. *Average high school GPA:* 3.49. *Test scores:* SAT critical reading scores over 500: 88%; SAT math scores over 500: 84%; SAT writing scores over 500: 80%; ACT scores over 18: 100%; SAT critical reading scores over 600: 50%; SAT math scores over 600: 45%; SAT writing scores over 600: 36%; ACT scores over 24: 80%; SAT critical reading scores over 700: 12%; SAT math scores over 700: 9%; SAT writing scores over 700: 10%; ACT scores over 30: 23%.

Faculty *Total:* 134, 78% full-time, 81% with terminal degrees. *Student/faculty ratio:* 13:1.

Academics *Calendar:* 4-1-4. *Degree:* bachelor's. *Special study options:* advanced placement credit, cooperative education, double majors, honors programs, independent study, internships, off-campus study, part-time degree program, student-designed majors, study abroad, summer session for credit. *ROTC:* Army (c), Air Force (c). *Unusual degree programs:* 3-2 engineering with Auburn University, Columbia University, Washington University in St. Louis, University of Alabama at Birmingham; nursing with Vanderbilt University; environmental studies with Duke University.

Computers on Campus 306 computers/terminals and 306 ports are available on campus for general student use. Students can access the following: campus intranet, computer help desk, free student e-mail accounts, online (class) grades, online (class) registration, online (class) schedules. Campuswide network is available. 100% of college-owned or -operated housing units are wired for high-speed Internet access. Wireless service is available via entire campus.

Student Life *Housing:* on-campus residence required through sophomore year. *Options:* coed, men-only, women-only, disabled students. Campus housing is university owned. *Activities and organizations:* drama/theater group, student-run newspaper, choral group, marching band, Black Student Union, Southern Bouldering Club, Student Government Association, MCAO, BSC Chapter of Habitat for Humanity, national fraternities, national sororities. *Campus secu-*

rity: 24-hour emergency response devices and patrols, late-night transport/ escort service, controlled dormitory access, vehicle safety inspections for students, emergency phone stations throughout campus. *Student services:* health clinic, personal/psychological counseling.

Athletics Member NCAA. All Division III. *Intercollegiate sports:* baseball M, basketball M/W, cheerleading M/W, cross-country running M/W, football M, golf M/W, lacrosse M/W, soccer M/W, softball W, tennis M/W, track and field M/W, volleyball W. *Intramural sports:* basketball M/W, football M/W, racquetball M/W, soccer M/W, softball M, table tennis M/W, tennis M/W, ultimate Frisbee M/W, volleyball M/W, water polo M/W.

Standardized Tests *Required:* SAT or ACT (for admission).

Costs (2010–11) *One-time required fee:* $200. *Comprehensive fee:* $37,210 includes full-time tuition ($26,900), mandatory fees ($990), and room and board ($9320). Full-time tuition and fees vary according to program and reciprocity agreements. Part-time tuition: $4483 per course. Part-time tuition and fees vary according to course load, program, and reciprocity agreements. *Required fees:* $495 per term part-time. *College room only:* $5450. Room and board charges vary according to board plan, housing facility, and location. *Payment plan:* installment. *Waivers:* employees or children of employees.

Financial Aid Of all full-time matriculated undergraduates who enrolled in 2009, 994 applied for aid, 841 were judged to have need, 227 had their need fully met. 178 Federal Work-Study jobs (averaging $1351). 281 state and other part-time jobs (averaging $1213). In 2009, 598 non-need-based awards were made. *Average percent of need met:* 82%. *Average financial aid package:* $27,468. *Average need-based loan:* $3935. *Average need-based gift aid:* $5341. *Average non-need-based aid:* $9987. *Average indebtedness upon graduation:* $28,157.

Applying *Options:* electronic application, deferred entrance. *Application fee:* $40. *Required:* essay or personal statement, high school transcript, minimum 2 GPA, 1 letter of recommendation. *Required for some:* interview. *Recommended:* interview. *Application deadlines:* rolling (freshmen), rolling (transfers). *Notification:* continuous (freshmen), continuous (transfers).

Freshman Application Contact Mr. Tyler Peterson, Director of Recruitment, Birmingham-Southern College, Box 549008, Birmingham, AL 35254. *Phone:* 205-226-4696. *Toll-free phone:* 800-523-5793. *Fax:* 205-226-3074. *E-mail:* tpeterso@bsc.edu. *Web site:* http://www.bsc.edu/.

See page 1124 for the College Close-Up.

Brown Mackie College–Birmingham

Birmingham, Alabama

- **Proprietary** 4-year
- **Coed**

Academics *Degrees:* diplomas, associate, and bachelor's.

Freshman Application Contact Brown Mackie College–Birmingham, 105 Vulcan Road, Suite 400, Birmingham, AL 35209. *Phone:* 205-909-1500. *Toll-free phone:* 888-299-4699. *Web site:* http://www.brownmackie.edu/birmingham.

See page 1138 for the College Close-Up.

Columbia Southern University

Orange Beach, Alabama

- **Proprietary** comprehensive, founded 1993, administratively affiliated with Waldorf College; Mayes Education
- **Small-town** campus
- **Coed** 18,183 undergraduate students, 100% full-time, 31% women, 69% men
- **Noncompetitive** entrance level, 100% of applicants were admitted

Undergraduates 18,183 full-time. Students come from 52 states and territories; 61 other countries; 95% are from out of state; 18% Black or African American, non-Hispanic/Latino; 6% Hispanic/Latino; 2% Asian, non-Hispanic/Latino; 0.1% Native Hawaiian or other Pacific Islander, non-Hispanic/Latino; 0.7% American Indian or Alaska Native, non-Hispanic/Latino; 0.7% Two or more races, non-Hispanic/Latino; 23% Race/ethnicity unknown; 0.1% international. *Retention:* 84% of full-time freshmen returned.

Freshmen *Admission:* 10,520 applied, 10,520 admitted.

Faculty *Total:* 240, 15% full-time, 39% with terminal degrees.

Academics *Calendar:* modular. *Degrees:* certificates, diplomas, associate, bachelor's, master's, doctoral-research/scholarship, and postbachelor's certificates (offers only distance learning degree programs). *Special study options:* academic remediation for entering students, adult/continuing education programs, distance learning, external degree program, part-time degree program.

Computers on Campus Students can access the following: computer help desk, online (class) grades, online (class) registration, online (class) schedules.

Student Life *Housing:* college housing not available.

Costs (2011–12) *Tuition:* $200 per credit part-time. *Waivers:* employees or children of employees.

Applying *Options:* electronic application. *Application fee:* $25. *Required for some:* high school transcript. *Application deadlines:* rolling (freshmen), rolling (transfers).

Freshman Application Contact Director of Admissions, Columbia Southern University, 21982 University Lane, Orange Beach, AL 36561. *Phone:* 251-981-3771 Ext. 521. *Toll-free phone:* 800-977-8449. *Fax:* 251-224-0540. *E-mail:* admissions@columbiasouthern.edu. *Web site:* http://www.columbiasouthern.edu/.

Concordia College

Selma, Alabama

Freshman Application Contact Ms. Phyllis Richardson, Director, STARS, Concordia College, 1804 Green Street, Selma, AL 36701. *Phone:* 334-874-5700 Ext. 102. *Fax:* 334-874-5755. *E-mail:* prichrdson@concordiaselma.edu. *Web site:* http://www.concordiaselma.edu/.

Faulkner University

Montgomery, Alabama

- **Independent** comprehensive, founded 1942, affiliated with Church of Christ
- **Urban** 75-acre campus
- **Endowment** $14.4 million
- **Coed** 2,562 undergraduate students, 78% full-time, 62% women, 38% men
- **Minimally difficult** entrance level, 51% of applicants were admitted

Undergraduates 1,986 full-time, 576 part-time. Students come from 27 states and territories; 17 other countries; 11% are from out of state; 27% Black or African American, non-Hispanic/Latino; 0.8% Hispanic/Latino; 0.3% Asian, non-Hispanic/Latino; 0.4% American Indian or Alaska Native, non-Hispanic/Latino; 0.7% Two or more races, non-Hispanic/Latino; 43% Race/ethnicity unknown; 1% international; 2% transferred in. *Retention:* 59% of full-time freshmen returned.

Freshmen *Admission:* 1,152 applied, 583 admitted, 254 enrolled. *Average high school GPA:* 2.9. *Test scores:* SAT critical reading scores over 500: 45%; SAT math scores over 500: 41%; SAT writing scores over 500: 40%; ACT scores over 18: 82%; SAT critical reading scores over 600: 16%; SAT math scores over 600: 14%; SAT writing scores over 600: 16%; ACT scores over 24: 17%; SAT critical reading scores over 700: 5%; SAT writing scores over 700: 5%; ACT scores over 30: 1%.

Faculty *Total:* 339, 38% full-time, 38% with terminal degrees. *Student/faculty ratio:* 12:1.

Academics *Calendar:* semesters. *Degrees:* associate, bachelor's, master's, and doctoral-professional. *Special study options:* academic remediation for entering students, accelerated degree program, adult/continuing education programs, advanced placement credit, distance learning, double majors, English as a second language, freshman honors college, honors programs, independent study, internships, off-campus study, part-time degree program, services for LD students, study abroad, summer session for credit. *ROTC:* Army (c), Air Force (c).

Computers on Campus 228 computers/terminals and 150 ports are available on campus for general student use. Students can access the following: campus intranet, computer help desk, free student e-mail accounts, online (class) grades, student account access. Campuswide network is available. 100% of college-owned or -operated housing units are wired for high-speed Internet access. Wireless service is available via entire campus.

Student Life *Housing:* on-campus residence required through junior year. *Options:* men-only, women-only, disabled students. Campus housing is university owned. Freshman campus housing is guaranteed. *Activities and organizations:* drama/theater group, student-run newspaper, choral group, marching band, student government, Senators, Christians in Action, acappella chorus. *Campus security:* 24-hour emergency response devices and patrols, student patrols, late-night transport/escort service. *Student services:* health clinic, personal/psychological counseling.

Athletics Member NAIA, NCCAA. *Intercollegiate sports:* baseball M(s), basketball M(s)/W(s), cheerleading M(c)/W(c), football M(s), golf M(s)/W(s), soccer M(s)/W(s), softball W(s), volleyball W(s). *Intramural sports:* basketball M/W, bowling M/W, golf M/W, racquetball M/W, soccer M/W, softball M/W, table tennis M/W, ultimate Frisbee M/W, volleyball M/W.

Standardized Tests *Required:* SAT or ACT (for admission).

Costs (2010–11) *Comprehensive fee:* $21,380 includes full-time tuition ($13,740), mandatory fees ($1070), and room and board ($6570). Full-time tuition and fees vary according to location and program. Part-time tuition: $480 per semester hour. Part-time tuition and fees vary according to location. *Required fees:* $270 per semester hour part-time, $60 per term part-time. *Room and board:* Room and board charges vary according to board plan and housing facility. *Payment plan:* installment. *Waivers:* adult students, senior citizens, and employees or children of employees.

Applying *Options:* electronic application, early admission, deferred entrance. *Application fee:* $25. *Required:* high school transcript, minimum 2 GPA. *Recommended:* essay or personal statement, 2 letters of recommendation, interview. *Application deadlines:* rolling (freshmen), rolling (out-of-state freshmen), rolling (transfers). *Notification:* continuous (freshmen), continuous (out-of-state freshmen), continuous (transfers).

Freshman Application Contact Mr. Keith Mock, Director of Admissions, Faulkner University, 5345 Atlanta Highway, Montgomery, AL 36109-3398. *Phone:* 334-386-7200. *Toll-free phone:* 800-879-9816. *Fax:* 334-386-7137. *E-mail:* admissions@faulkner.edu. *Web site:* http://www.faulkner.edu/.

Heritage Christian University

Florence, Alabama

- **Independent** comprehensive, founded 1971, affiliated with Church of Christ
- **Small-town** 43-acre campus
- **Endowment** $4.2 million
- **Coed, primarily men** 81 undergraduate students, 56% full-time, 10% women, 90% men
- **Noncompetitive** entrance level

Undergraduates 45 full-time, 36 part-time. Students come from 14 states and territories; 1 other country; 48% are from out of state; 25% transferred in; 60% live on campus. *Retention:* 33% of full-time freshmen returned.

Freshmen *Admission:* 9 applied, 15 enrolled.

Faculty *Total:* 20, 25% full-time, 40% with terminal degrees.

Academics *Calendar:* semesters. *Degrees:* associate, bachelor's, and master's. *Special study options:* academic remediation for entering students, accelerated degree program, adult/continuing education programs, cooperative education, distance learning, external degree program, independent study, internships, part-time degree program, summer session for credit.

Computers on Campus 12 computers/terminals are available on campus for general student use. Students can access the following: free student e-mail accounts, online (class) grades, online (class) registration, online (class) schedules. Campuswide network is available. 100% of college-owned or -operated housing units are wired for high-speed Internet access. Wireless service is available via entire campus.

Student Life *Housing options:* men-only, women-only, disabled students. Campus housing is university owned. *Activities and organizations:* drama/theater group, Missions Club, Preachers Club, Student Government Association, Christian Ladies Organization, HCU Skit Team. *Student services:* personal/psychological counseling.

Athletics *Intramural sports:* softball M/W.

Standardized Tests *Required for some:* International students must meet the same admission policy and procedures as students from the United States. In addition, they must take and pass the TOEFL (Test of English as a Foreign Language) exam to demonstrate proficiency in English before enrolling at Heritage Christian University.

Costs (2010–11) *One-time required fee:* $300. *Comprehensive fee:* $17,265 includes full-time tuition ($11,360), mandatory fees ($480), and room and board ($5425). Part-time tuition: $355 per credit hour. *Required fees:* $20 per credit hour part-time. *College room only:* $3000. Room and board charges vary according to housing facility. *Payment plans:* installment, deferred payment. *Waivers:* employees or children of employees.

Applying *Options:* early admission, deferred entrance. *Application fee:* $25. *Required:* high school transcript, minimum 2 GPA, 3 letters of recommendation. *Recommended:* interview. *Application deadlines:* rolling (freshmen), rolling (transfers). *Notification:* 7/1 (freshmen), continuous (transfers).

Freshman Application Contact Mr. Cory Collins, Dean of Students, Heritage Christian University, PO Box HCU, Florence, AL 35630. *Phone:* 256-766-6610. *Toll-free phone:* 800-367-3565. *Fax:* 256-766-9289. *E-mail:* ccollins@hcu.edu. *Web site:* http://www.hcu.edu/.

Herzing University

Birmingham, Alabama

Director of Admissions Ms. Tess Anderson, Admissions Coordinator, Herzing University, 280 West Valley Avenue, Birmingham, AL 35209. *Phone:* 205-916-2800. *E-mail:* admiss@bhm.herzing.edu. *Web site:* http://www.herzing.edu/birmingham/.

Huntingdon College

Montgomery, Alabama

- **Independent United Methodist** 4-year, founded 1854
- **Suburban** 71-acre campus with easy access to Birmingham
- **Endowment** $38.8 million
- **Coed** 1,107 undergraduate students, 80% full-time, 51% women, 49% men
- **Moderately difficult** entrance level, 62% of applicants were admitted

Undergraduates 886 full-time, 221 part-time. Students come from 18 states and territories; 6 other countries; 14% are from out of state; 18% Black or African American, non-Hispanic/Latino; 2% Hispanic/Latino; 0.2% Asian, non-Hispanic/Latino; 0.1% Native Hawaiian or other Pacific Islander, non-Hispanic/Latino; 0.5% American Indian or Alaska Native, non-Hispanic/Latino; 1% Two or more races, non-Hispanic/Latino; 15% Race/ethnicity unknown; 0.7% international; 8% transferred in; 43% live on campus. *Retention:* 59% of full-time freshmen returned.

Freshmen *Admission:* 1,261 applied, 784 admitted, 272 enrolled. *Average high school GPA:* 3.28. *Test scores:* SAT critical reading scores over 500: 52%; SAT math scores over 500: 46%; SAT writing scores over 500: 33%; ACT scores over 18: 91%; SAT critical reading scores over 600: 6%; SAT math scores over 600: 6%; SAT writing scores over 600: 10%; ACT scores over 24: 32%; ACT scores over 30: 6%.

Faculty *Total:* 123, 38% full-time, 59% with terminal degrees. *Student/faculty ratio:* 13:1.

Academics *Calendar:* semesters. *Degree:* bachelor's. *Special study options:* academic remediation for entering students, accelerated degree program, adult/continuing education programs, advanced placement credit, double majors, honors programs, independent study, internships, off-campus study, part-time degree program, services for LD students, student-designed majors, study abroad, summer session for credit. *ROTC:* Army (c), Air Force (c). *Unusual degree programs:* 3-2 engineering with Auburn University.

Computers on Campus 13 computers/terminals are available on campus for general student use. Students can access the following: campus intranet, free student e-mail accounts, online (class) grades, online (class) schedules, online library, student web hosting. Campuswide network is available. 100% of college-owned or -operated housing units are wired for high-speed Internet access. Wireless service is available via classrooms, dorm rooms, learning centers, libraries.

Student Life *Housing:* on-campus residence required through junior year. *Options:* coed, disabled students. Campus housing is university owned. Freshman campus housing is guaranteed. *Activities and organizations:* student-run newspaper, choral group, marching band, Alpha Omicron Pi, Sigma Nu, Campus Ministries, Student Government Association, Campus Activities Board, national fraternities, national sororities. *Campus security:* 24-hour emergency response devices and patrols, student patrols, late-night transport/escort service, controlled dormitory access, electronic video surveillance. *Student services:* health clinic.

Athletics Member NCAA. All Division III. *Intercollegiate sports:* baseball M, basketball M/W, cross-country running M/W, football M, golf M/W, soccer M/W, softball W, tennis M/W, volleyball W. *Intramural sports:* basketball M/W, bowling M/W, cheerleading M(c)/W(c), football M/W, soccer M/W, softball M/W, table tennis M/W, tennis M/W, ultimate Frisbee M/W, volleyball M/W.

Standardized Tests *Required:* SAT or ACT (for admission).

Costs (2010–11) *Comprehensive fee:* $28,990 includes full-time tuition ($19,990), mandatory fees ($1000), and room and board ($8000). Full-time tuition and fees vary according to course load, program, and student level. Part-time tuition: $830 per credit hour. Part-time tuition and fees vary according to course load and program. No tuition increase for student's term of enrollment. *Room and board:* Room and board charges vary according to housing facility. *Payment plan:* deferred payment. *Waivers:* children of alumni and employees or children of employees.

Financial Aid Of all full-time matriculated undergraduates who enrolled in 2009, 716 applied for aid, 642 were judged to have need, 128 had their need fully met. 99 Federal Work-Study jobs (averaging $970). In 2009, 229 non-need-based awards were made. *Average percent of need met:* 74%. *Average financial aid package:* $15,853. *Average need-based loan:* $4164. *Average need-based gift aid:* $12,556. *Average non-need-based aid:* $9652. *Average indebtedness upon graduation:* $17,993.

Applying *Options:* electronic application, deferred entrance. *Required:* high school transcript, minimum 2.25 GPA. *Required for some:* essay or personal statement, 3 letters of recommendation, interview, auditions for music students; portfolios for art. *Application deadlines:* 8/15 (freshmen), 8/15 (transfers). *Notification:* continuous until 9/7 (freshmen), continuous until 9/7 (transfers).

Freshman Application Contact Office of Admission, Huntingdon College, 1500 East Fairview Avenue, Montgomery, AL 36106-2148. *Phone:* 334-833-4497. *Toll-free phone:* 800-763-0313. *Fax:* 334-833-4347. *E-mail:* admiss@huntingdon.edu. *Web site:* http://www.huntingdon.edu/.

ITT Technical Institute
Bessemer, Alabama

- **Proprietary** primarily 2-year, founded 1994, part of ITT Educational Services, Inc.
- **Suburban** campus
- **Coed**
- **Minimally difficult** entrance level

Academics *Calendar:* quarters. *Degrees:* associate and bachelor's.
Student Life *Housing:* college housing not available. *Campus security:* 24-hour emergency response devices.
Freshman Application Contact Director of Recruitment, ITT Technical Institute, 6270 Park South Drive, Bessemer, AL 35022. *Phone:* 205-497-5700. *Toll-free phone:* 800-488-7033. *Web site:* http://www.itt-tech.edu/.

ITT Technical Institute
Madison, Alabama

- **Proprietary** primarily 2-year, part of ITT Educational Services, Inc.
- **Coed**
- **Minimally difficult** entrance level

Academics *Degrees:* associate and bachelor's.
Student Life *Housing:* college housing not available.
Freshman Application Contact Director of Recruitment, ITT Technical Institute, 9238 Madison Boulevard, Suite 500, Madison, AL 35758. *Phone:* 256-542-2900. *Toll-free phone:* 877-210-4900. *Web site:* http://www.itt-tech.edu/.

ITT Technical Institute
Mobile, Alabama

- **Proprietary** primarily 2-year, part of ITT Educational Services, Inc.
- **Coed**
- **Minimally difficult** entrance level

Academics *Degrees:* associate and bachelor's.
Student Life *Housing:* college housing not available.
Freshman Application Contact Director of Recruitment, ITT Technical Institute, Office Mall South, 3100 Cottage Hill Road, Building 3, Mobile, AL 36606. *Phone:* 251-472-4760. *Toll-free phone:* 877-327-1013. *Web site:* http://www.itt-tech.edu/.

Jacksonville State University
Jacksonville, Alabama

- **State-supported** comprehensive, founded 1883
- **Small-town** 459-acre campus with easy access to Birmingham
- **Coed** 8,100 undergraduate students, 76% full-time, 57% women, 43% men
- **Minimally difficult** entrance level, 84% of applicants were admitted

Undergraduates 6,140 full-time, 1,960 part-time. Students come from 43 states and territories; 73 other countries; 18% are from out of state; 28% Black or African American, non-Hispanic/Latino; 1% Hispanic/Latino; 0.6% Asian, non-Hispanic/Latino; 0.6% American Indian or Alaska Native, non-Hispanic/Latino; 6% Race/ethnicity unknown; 2% international; 9% transferred in; 23% live on campus. *Retention:* 68% of full-time freshmen returned.
Freshmen *Admission:* 2,794 applied, 2,348 admitted, 1,272 enrolled. *Average high school GPA:* 3.11. *Test scores:* SAT critical reading scores over 500: 39%; SAT math scores over 500: 41%; ACT scores over 18: 83%; SAT critical reading scores over 600: 11%; SAT math scores over 600: 13%; ACT scores over 24: 31%; SAT critical reading scores over 700: 2%; ACT scores over 30: 2%.
Faculty *Total:* 475, 69% full-time. *Student/faculty ratio:* 20:1.
Academics *Calendar:* semesters. *Degrees:* bachelor's, master's, post-master's, and postbachelor's certificates. *Special study options:* academic remediation for entering students, accelerated degree program, adult/continuing education programs, advanced placement credit, cooperative education, distance learning, double majors, honors programs, independent study, internships, part-time degree program, services for LD students, summer session for credit. *ROTC:* Army (b).
Computers on Campus 350 computers/terminals are available on campus for general student use. Students can access the following: computer help desk, free student e-mail accounts, online (class) grades, online (class) registration, online (class) schedules. Campuswide network is available.
Student Life *Housing options:* coed, men-only, women-only, disabled students. Campus housing is university owned. *Activities and organizations:* drama/theater group, student-run newspaper, radio and television station, choral group, marching band, Student Government Association, Archaeology Club, Campus Fellowship Clubs, Computer Science Club, Biology Club,

national fraternities, national sororities. *Campus security:* 24-hour emergency response devices and patrols, student patrols, late-night transport/escort service, controlled dormitory access, night security officer in female residence halls. *Student services:* health clinic, personal/psychological counseling.
Athletics Member NCAA. All Division I except football (Division I-AA). *Intercollegiate sports:* baseball M(s), basketball M(s)/W(s), cross-country running M(s)/W(s), golf M(s)/W(s), riflery M(s)/W(s), soccer W(s), softball W(s), tennis M(s)/W(s), volleyball W(s). *Intramural sports:* badminton M(c)/W(c), basketball M(c)/W(c), bowling M(c)/W(c), football M(c), golf M(c)/W(c), racquetball M(c)/W(c), soccer M(c)/W(c), softball M(c)/W(c), table tennis M(c)/W(c), tennis M(c)/W(c), volleyball M(c)/W(c).
Standardized Tests *Required:* SAT or ACT (for admission).
Costs (2010–11) *Tuition:* state resident $6780 full-time, $226 per credit hour part-time; nonresident $13,560 full-time, $452 per credit hour part-time. *Room and board:* $6162. Room and board charges vary according to board plan and housing facility. *Payment plan:* installment. *Waivers:* employees or children of employees.
Financial Aid Of all full-time matriculated undergraduates who enrolled in 2008, 4,765 applied for aid. 224 Federal Work-Study jobs (averaging $1302). *Average financial aid package:* $6563. *Average need-based loan:* $3889. *Average need-based gift aid:* $3878.
Applying *Options:* electronic application, early admission, deferred entrance. *Application fee:* $30. *Required:* high school transcript. *Application deadlines:* rolling (freshmen), rolling (out-of-state freshmen), rolling (transfers). *Notification:* continuous (freshmen), continuous (out-of-state freshmen), continuous (transfers).
Freshman Application Contact Mr. Andrew Green, Director of Admission, Jacksonville State University, 700 Pelham Road North, Jacksonville, AL 36265. *Phone:* 256-782-5363. *Toll-free phone:* 800-231-5291. *Fax:* 256-782-5291. *E-mail:* info@jsu.edu. *Web site:* http://www.jsu.edu/.

Judson College
Marion, Alabama

- **Independent Baptist** 4-year, founded 1838
- **Rural** 118-acre campus with easy access to Birmingham
- **Endowment** $12.9 million
- **Coed, primarily women** 322 undergraduate students, 83% full-time, 96% women, 4% men
- **Moderately difficult** entrance level, 82% of applicants were admitted

Undergraduates 266 full-time, 56 part-time. Students come from 25 states and territories; 2 other countries; 25% are from out of state; 11% Black or African American, non-Hispanic/Latino; 2% Hispanic/Latino; 0.6% Asian, non-Hispanic/Latino; 1% American Indian or Alaska Native, non-Hispanic/Latino; 2% Two or more races, non-Hispanic/Latino; 0.3% international; 6% transferred in; 67% live on campus. *Retention:* 68% of full-time freshmen returned.
Freshmen *Admission:* 298 applied, 243 admitted, 94 enrolled. *Average high school GPA:* 3.4. *Test scores:* SAT critical reading scores over 500: 57%; SAT math scores over 500: 43%; ACT scores over 18: 96%; SAT critical reading scores over 600: 14%; ACT scores over 24: 38%; ACT scores over 30: 6%.
Faculty *Total:* 50, 44% full-time, 56% with terminal degrees. *Student/faculty ratio:* 9:1.
Academics *Calendar:* semesters plus 2-month term. *Degrees:* associate and bachelor's. *Special study options:* academic remediation for entering students, accelerated degree program, adult/continuing education programs, advanced placement credit, distance learning, double majors, external degree program, honors programs, independent study, internships, off-campus study, part-time degree program, services for LD students, student-designed majors, study abroad, summer session for credit. *ROTC:* Army (c).
Computers on Campus 54 computers/terminals and 54 ports are available on campus for general student use. Students can access the following: campus intranet, computer help desk, free student e-mail accounts, online (class) grades, online (class) schedules. Campuswide network is available. 100% of college-owned or -operated housing units are wired for high-speed Internet access. Wireless service is available via dorm rooms, student centers.
Student Life *Housing:* on-campus residence required through senior year. *Options:* women-only. Campus housing is university owned. Freshman campus housing is guaranteed. *Activities and organizations:* drama/theater group, student-run newspaper, choral group, marching band, Student Government Association, Campus Ministries, Faith-Based Service Learning Activities, Ambassadors, Science Club. *Campus security:* 24-hour emergency response devices and patrols, late-night transport/escort service, controlled dormitory access. *Student services:* personal/psychological counseling.
Athletics Member USCAA. *Intercollegiate sports:* basketball W(s), equestrian sports W, soccer W(s), softball W(s), tennis W(s), volleyball W(s). *Intramural sports:* basketball W, field hockey W, softball W, tennis W, volleyball W.
Standardized Tests *Required:* SAT or ACT (for admission).
Costs (2011–12) *One-time required fee:* $160. *Comprehensive fee:* $22,970 includes full-time tuition ($13,600), mandatory fees ($820), and room and

board ($8550). Part-time tuition: $450 per semester hour. *Payment plans:* installment, deferred payment. *Waivers:* employees or children of employees.
Financial Aid Of all full-time matriculated undergraduates who enrolled in 2009, 209 applied for aid, 196 were judged to have need, 25 had their need fully met. In 2009, 18 non-need-based awards were made. *Average percent of need met:* 76%. *Average financial aid package:* $13,259. *Average need-based loan:* $3926. *Average need-based gift aid:* $9855. *Average non-need-based aid:* $8859. *Average indebtedness upon graduation:* $17,563.
Applying *Options:* electronic application, early admission, deferred entrance. *Application fee:* $35. *Required:* high school transcript, minimum 2 GPA. *Application deadlines:* rolling (freshmen), rolling (out-of-state freshmen), rolling (transfers). *Notification:* continuous (freshmen), continuous (out-of-state freshmen), continuous (transfers).
Freshman Application Contact Mrs. Charlotte S. Clements, Vice President for Admissions and Financial Aid, Judson College, 302 Bibb Street, Marion, AL 36756. *Phone:* 334-683-5110. *Toll-free phone:* 800-447-9472. *Fax:* 334-683-5282. *E-mail:* admissions@judson.edu. *Web site:* http://www.judson.edu/.

Miles College
Fairfield, Alabama

Freshman Application Contact Mr. Charlotte S. Clements Mr. Christopher Robertson, Director of Admissions and Recruitment, Miles College, 5500 Myron Massey Boulevard, Bell Building, Fairfield, AL 35064. *Phone:* 205-929-1657. *Toll-free phone:* 800-445-0708. *Fax:* 205-929-1627. *E-mail:* admissions@miles.edu. *Web site:* http://www.miles.edu/.

Oakwood University
Huntsville, Alabama

- **Independent Seventh-day Adventist** comprehensive, founded 1896
- **1200-acre campus**
- **Coed**
- **Minimally difficult** entrance level

Faculty *Student/faculty ratio:* 14:1.
Academics *Calendar:* semesters. *Degrees:* associate, bachelor's, master's, and postbachelor's certificates.
Student Life *Campus security:* 24-hour patrols, student patrols, late-night transport/escort service.
Standardized Tests *Required:* SAT or ACT (for admission).
Costs (2010–11) *Comprehensive fee:* $22,238 includes full-time tuition ($13,434), mandatory fees ($816), and room and board ($7988). *College room only:* $3374. Room and board charges vary according to board plan and housing facility.
Financial Aid Of all full-time matriculated undergraduates who enrolled in 2001, 1,422 applied for aid, 1,422 were judged to have need, 131 had their need fully met. *Average percent of need met:* 77. *Average financial aid package:* $6500. *Average need-based loan:* $4500. *Average need-based gift aid:* $2500. *Average non-need-based aid:* $2000. *Average indebtedness upon graduation:* $15,000.
Applying *Options:* early action, deferred entrance. *Application fee:* $25. *Required:* high school transcript, minimum 2 GPA. *Required for some:* essay or personal statement.
Freshman Application Contact Mr. Jason McCracken, Director of Enrollment Management, Oakwood University, 7000 Adventist Boulevard, NW, Huntsville, AL 35896. *Phone:* 256-726-7354. *Toll-free phone:* 800-358-3978. *Fax:* 256-726-7154. *E-mail:* admission@oakwood.edu. *Web site:* http://www.oakwood.edu/.

Remington College–Mobile Campus
Mobile, Alabama

Freshman Application Contact Remington College–Mobile Campus, 828 Downtowner Loop West, Mobile, AL 36609-5404. *Phone:* 251-343-8200. *Toll-free phone:* 800-866-0850. *Web site:* http://www.remingtoncollege.edu/.

Samford University
Birmingham, Alabama

- **Independent Baptist** university, founded 1841
- **Suburban** 180-acre campus
- **Coed** 2,938 undergraduate students, 94% full-time, 64% women, 36% men
- **Moderately difficult** entrance level, 87% of applicants were admitted

Undergraduates 2,757 full-time, 181 part-time. Students come from 39 states and territories; 11 other countries; 61% are from out of state; 4% transferred in; 68% live on campus. *Retention:* 86% of full-time freshmen returned.
Freshmen *Admission:* 2,435 applied, 2,111 admitted, 715 enrolled. *Average high school GPA:* 3.66. *Test scores:* SAT critical reading scores over 500: 84%; SAT math scores over 500: 82%; ACT scores over 18: 99%; SAT critical reading scores over 600: 44%; SAT math scores over 600: 38%; ACT scores over 24: 69%; SAT critical reading scores over 700: 9%; SAT math scores over 700: 5%; ACT scores over 30: 18%.
Faculty *Total:* 439, 67% full-time, 82% with terminal degrees. *Student/faculty ratio:* 12:1.
Academics *Calendar:* 4-1-4. *Degrees:* certificates, associate, bachelor's, master's, doctoral-professional, doctoral-research/scholarship, and post-master's certificates. *Special study options:* accelerated degree program, adult/continuing education programs, advanced placement credit, cooperative education, distance learning, double majors, honors programs, independent study, internships, off-campus study, part-time degree program, services for LD students, study abroad, summer session for credit. *ROTC:* Army (c), Air Force (b). *Unusual degree programs:* 3-2 engineering with The University of Alabama at Birmingham, Auburn University, and Mercer University (Georgia).
Computers on Campus 330 computers/terminals and 400 ports are available on campus for general student use. Students can access the following: campus intranet, computer help desk, free student e-mail accounts, online (class) grades, online (class) registration, online (class) schedules, free online storage and tech support. Campuswide network is available. 100% of college-owned or -operated housing units are wired for high-speed Internet access. Wireless service is available via entire campus.
Student Life *Housing:* on-campus residence required through sophomore year. *Options:* men-only, women-only, disabled students. Campus housing is university owned. Freshman campus housing is guaranteed. *Activities and organizations:* drama/theater group, student-run newspaper, radio and television station, choral group, marching band, Alpha Delta Pi sorority, Phi Mu sorority, Chi Omega sorority, Zeta Tau Alpha sorority, Pi Kappa Phi, national fraternities, national sororities. *Campus security:* 24-hour emergency response devices and patrols, late-night transport/escort service, Self defense education, security escort services, and lighted pathways / sidewalks. *Student services:* health clinic, personal/psychological counseling.
Athletics Member NCAA. All Division I except football (Division I-AA). *Intercollegiate sports:* baseball M(s), basketball M(s)/W(s), cross-country running M(s)/W(s), golf M(s)/W(s), soccer M(c)/W(s), softball W(s), tennis M(s)/W(s), track and field M(s)/W(s), volleyball W(s). *Intramural sports:* basketball M/W, bowling M/W, football M/W, rock climbing M/W, soccer M/W, softball M/W, ultimate Frisbee M(c)/W(c), volleyball M/W.
Standardized Tests *Required:* SAT or ACT (for admission).
Costs (2011–12) *Comprehensive fee:* $32,090 includes full-time tuition ($23,422), mandatory fees ($510), and room and board ($8158). Full-time tuition and fees vary according to course load, location, and program. Part-time tuition and fees vary according to course load, location, and program. *Room and board:* Room and board charges vary according to board plan and housing facility. *Waivers:* employees or children of employees.
Financial Aid Of all full-time matriculated undergraduates who enrolled in 2009, 1,637 applied for aid, 941 were judged to have need, 201 had their need fully met. 541 Federal Work-Study jobs (averaging $1975). 482 state and other part-time jobs (averaging $1632). In 2009, 591 non-need-based awards were made. *Average percent of need met:* 75%. *Average financial aid package:* $16,310. *Average need-based loan:* $3859. *Average need-based gift aid:* $12,791. *Average non-need-based aid:* $7742. *Average indebtedness upon graduation:* $20,328.
Applying *Options:* electronic application, early admission, deferred entrance. *Application fee:* $35. *Required:* essay or personal statement, 1 letter of recommendation. *Required for some:* high school transcript. *Application deadlines:* rolling (freshmen), rolling (out-of-state freshmen), 7/1 (transfers). *Notification:* continuous (freshmen), continuous (out-of-state freshmen).
Freshman Application Contact Mr. Jason E. Black, Director of Orientation and Visits, Samford University, 800 Lakeshore Drive, Samford Hall, Birmingham, AL 35229-0002. *Phone:* 205-726-3673. *Toll-free phone:* 800-888-7218. *Fax:* 205-726-2171. *E-mail:* jjblack@samford.edu. *Web site:* http://www.samford.edu/.

See page 1590 for the College Close-Up.

Southeastern Bible College
Birmingham, Alabama

- **Independent nondenominational** 4-year, founded 1935
- **Suburban** 10-acre campus
- **Coed** 189 undergraduate students, 84% full-time, 49% women, 51% men

Undergraduates 159 full-time, 30 part-time. Students come from 8 states and territories; 7% are from out of state; 36% Black or African American, non-Hispanic/Latino; 0.5% Hispanic/Latino; 5% Race/ethnicity unknown; 6% transferred in; 28% live on campus. *Retention:* 56% of full-time freshmen returned.
Freshmen *Admission:* 13 enrolled. *Average high school GPA:* 3.09.
Faculty *Total:* 29, 24% full-time, 45% with terminal degrees. *Student/faculty ratio:* 12:1.

Academics *Calendar:* semesters. *Degrees:* diplomas, associate, and bachelor's. *Special study options:* academic remediation for entering students, adult/continuing education programs, advanced placement credit, double majors, independent study, internships, part-time degree program, services for LD students, summer session for credit.

Computers on Campus 30 computers/terminals are available on campus for general student use. Students can access the following: free student e-mail accounts. Wireless service is available via entire campus.

Student Life *Housing options:* men-only, women-only. Campus housing is university owned. *Activities and organizations:* choral group, Student Council, Student Missions Fellowship, chorale. *Campus security:* controlled dormitory access.

Standardized Tests *Required:* SAT or ACT (for admission).

Costs (2010–11) *Tuition:* $11,250 full-time, $375 per semester hour part-time. Full-time tuition and fees vary according to course load and program. Part-time tuition and fees vary according to course load and program. *Required fees:* $350 full-time, $175 per term part-time. *Room only:* $2550. *Payment plan:* installment. *Waivers:* employees or children of employees.

Applying *Options:* electronic application, deferred entrance. *Application fee:* $30. *Required:* essay or personal statement, high school transcript, minimum 1.5 GPA, 2 letters of recommendation. *Required for some:* interview.

Freshman Application Contact Ms. Deidra Whitfield, Admissions Counselor, Southeastern Bible College, 2545 Valleydale Road, Birmingham, AL 35244. *Phone:* 205-970-9210. *Toll-free phone:* 800-749-8878. *Fax:* 205-970-9207. *E-mail:* deidra.whitfield@sebc.edu. *Web site:* http://www.sebc.edu/.

South University
Montgomery, Alabama

- **Proprietary** comprehensive, founded 1887, part of Education Management Corporation
- **Coed**

Academics *Calendar:* quarters. *Degrees:* associate, bachelor's, and master's.

Costs (2010–11) *Tuition:* Information about tuition and fees can be obtained by contacting the South University Admissions Office.

Freshman Application Contact South University, 5355 Vaughn Road, Montgomery, AL 36116-1120. *Phone:* 334-395-8800. *Toll-free phone:* 866-629-2962. *Web site:* http://www.southuniversity.edu/montgomery/.

See page 1620 for the College Close-Up.

Spring Hill College
Mobile, Alabama

- **Independent Roman Catholic (Jesuit)** comprehensive, founded 1830
- **Suburban** 450-acre campus
- **Coed** 1,383 undergraduate students, 92% full-time, 62% women, 38% men
- **Moderately difficult** entrance level, 53% of applicants were admitted

Undergraduates 1,266 full-time, 117 part-time. Students come from 36 states and territories; 8 other countries; 55% are from out of state; 19% Black or African American, non-Hispanic/Latino; 7% Hispanic/Latino; 1% Asian, non-Hispanic/Latino; 0.8% American Indian or Alaska Native, non-Hispanic/Latino; 0.7% Two or more races, non-Hispanic/Latino; 3% Race/ethnicity unknown; 0.6% international; 2% transferred in; 76% live on campus. *Retention:* 77% of full-time freshmen returned.

Freshmen *Admission:* 4,778 applied, 2,531 admitted, 401 enrolled. *Average high school GPA:* 3.48. *Test scores:* SAT critical reading scores over 500: 70%; SAT math scores over 500: 67%; SAT writing scores over 500: 72%; ACT scores over 18: 99%; SAT critical reading scores over 600: 26%; SAT math scores over 600: 23%; SAT writing scores over 600: 24%; ACT scores over 24: 53%; SAT critical reading scores over 700: 1%; SAT math scores over 700: 1%; SAT writing scores over 700: 1%; ACT scores over 30: 5%.

Faculty *Total:* 140, 56% full-time, 65% with terminal degrees. *Student/faculty ratio:* 14:1.

Academics *Calendar:* semesters. *Degrees:* certificates, bachelor's, master's, post-master's, and postbachelor's certificates. *Special study options:* academic remediation for entering students, accelerated degree program, adult/continuing education programs, advanced placement credit, distance learning, double majors, honors programs, independent study, internships, off-campus study, part-time degree program, services for LD students, student-designed majors, study abroad, summer session for credit. *ROTC:* Army (c), Air Force (c). *Unusual degree programs:* 3-2 engineering with Marquette University, University of Alabama at Birmingham, University of Florida, Auburn University, Texas A&M University.

Computers on Campus 194 computers/terminals and 250 ports are available on campus for general student use. Students can access the following: campus intranet, computer help desk, free student e-mail accounts, online (class)

grades, online (class) registration, online (class) schedules. Campuswide network is available. 100% of college-owned or -operated housing units are wired for high-speed Internet access. Wireless service is available via computer centers, computer labs, libraries, student centers.

Student Life *Housing:* on-campus residence required through senior year. *Options:* coed, men-only, women-only. Campus housing is university owned. Freshman campus housing is guaranteed. *Activities and organizations:* drama/theater group, student-run newspaper, choral group, Student Government Association, Student Nurses Association, SHORES, Campus Programming Board, SHAPe Community (Spring Hill Awakening Program), national fraternities, national sororities. *Campus security:* 24-hour emergency response devices and patrols, late-night transport/escort service, controlled dormitory access. *Student services:* health clinic, personal/psychological counseling.

Athletics Member NAIA. *Intercollegiate sports:* baseball M(s), basketball M(s)/W(s), cross-country running M(s)/W(s), golf M(s)/W(s), soccer M(s)/W(s), softball W(s), tennis M(s)/W(s), volleyball W(s). *Intramural sports:* basketball M/W, cheerleading W(c), football M/W, racquetball M/W, rugby M(c), soccer M/W, softball M/W, ultimate Frisbee M/W, volleyball M/W, weight lifting M/W.

Standardized Tests *Required:* SAT or ACT (for admission).

Costs (2010–11) *Comprehensive fee:* $36,980 includes full-time tuition ($25,110), mandatory fees ($1620), and room and board ($10,250). Part-time tuition: $890 per credit hour. *Required fees:* $50 per credit hour part-time. *College room only:* $5350. Room and board charges vary according to board plan and housing facility. *Payment plan:* installment. *Waivers:* employees or children of employees.

Financial Aid Of all full-time matriculated undergraduates who enrolled in 2009, 1,023 applied for aid, 879 were judged to have need, 179 had their need fully met. In 2009, 349 non-need-based awards were made. *Average percent of need met:* 87%. *Average financial aid package:* $27,679. *Average need-based loan:* $3813. *Average need-based gift aid:* $20,941. *Average non-need-based aid:* $14,071. *Average indebtedness upon graduation:* $26,325.

Applying *Options:* electronic application, early admission, deferred entrance. *Application fee:* $25. *Required:* essay or personal statement, high school transcript, 1 letter of recommendation. *Recommended:* minimum 2.5 GPA, interview. *Application deadlines:* 7/15 (freshmen), 7/15 (out-of-state freshmen), rolling (transfers). *Notification:* continuous (freshmen), continuous (out-of-state freshmen), continuous (transfers).

Freshman Application Contact Ms. Ellen G. Richardson, Admissions Office, Spring Hill College, 4000 Dauphin Street, Mobile, AL 36608-1791. *Phone:* 251-380-3030. *Toll-free phone:* 800-SHC-6704. *Fax:* 251-460-2186. *E-mail:* admit@shc.edu. *Web site:* http://www.shc.edu/.

Stillman College
Tuscaloosa, Alabama

- **Independent** 4-year, founded 1876, affiliated with Presbyterian Church (U.S.A.)
- **Urban** 100-acre campus with easy access to Birmingham
- **Endowment** $15.6 million
- **Coed**
- **Minimally difficult** entrance level

Faculty *Student/faculty ratio:* 18:1.

Academics *Calendar:* semesters. *Degree:* bachelor's.

Student Life *Campus security:* 24-hour patrols, 24-hour patrols by trained campus police.

Athletics Member NCAA. All Division II.

Standardized Tests *Required:* SAT or ACT (for admission), SAT and SAT Subject Tests or ACT (for admission). *Recommended:* SAT (for admission), ACT (for admission), SAT Subject Tests (for admission).

Costs (2010–11) *Comprehensive fee:* $20,988 includes full-time tuition ($12,524), mandatory fees ($1940), and room and board ($6524). Part-time tuition: $518 per credit hour. *Required fees:* $1940 per term part-time. *Room and board:* Room and board charges vary according to housing facility.

Financial Aid *Of all full-time matriculated undergraduates who enrolled in 2009,* 1,009 applied for aid, 956 were judged to have need, 534 had their need fully met. 172 Federal Work-Study jobs (averaging $1086). *In 2009,* 64 non-need-based awards were made. *Average financial aid package:* $18,804. *Average need-based loan:* $5500. *Average need-based gift aid:* $6000. *Average non-need-based aid:* $6489. *Average indebtedness upon graduation:* $32,188. *Financial aid deadline:* 6/1.

Applying *Options:* electronic application, early admission, early decision, deferred entrance. *Application fee:* $50. *Required:* high school transcript, minimum 2 GPA. *Recommended:* essay or personal statement, interview.

Freshman Application Contact Stillman College, PO Drawer 1430, 3600 Stillman Boulevard, Tuscaloosa, AL 35403-9990. *Phone:* 205-366-8837. *Toll-free phone:* 800-841-5722. *Web site:* http://www.stillman.edu/.

Strayer University - Birmingham Campus

Birmingham, Alabama

- **Proprietary** comprehensive
- **Coed**

Academics *Degrees:* certificates, diplomas, associate, bachelor's, master's, and postbachelor's certificates.

Costs (2010–11) *Tuition:* $13,635 full-time, $1590 per course part-time.

Freshman Application Contact Strayer University - Birmingham Campus, 3570 Grandview Parkway, Suite 200, Birmingham, AL 35243. *Web site:* http://www.strayer.edu/birmingham/.

Strayer University - Huntsville Campus

Huntsville, Alabama

- **Proprietary** comprehensive
- **Coed**

Academics *Degrees:* certificates, diplomas, associate, bachelor's, master's, and postbachelor's certificates.

Costs (2010–11) *Tuition:* $13,635 full-time, $1590 per course part-time.

Freshman Application Contact Strayer University - Huntsville Campus, 4955 Corporate Drive, NW, Suite 200, Huntsville, AL 35805. *Web site:* http://www.strayer.edu/huntsville/.

Talladega College

Talladega, Alabama

- **Independent** 4-year, founded 1867
- **Small-town** 130-acre campus with easy access to Birmingham
- **Coed** 706 undergraduate students, 92% full-time, 57% women, 43% men
- **Moderately difficult** entrance level, 51% of applicants were admitted

Undergraduates 650 full-time, 56 part-time. Students come from 31 states and territories; 3 other countries; 39% are from out of state; 89% Black or African American, non-Hispanic/Latino; 2% Hispanic/Latino; 0.4% Asian, non-Hispanic/Latino; 2% Race/ethnicity unknown; 80% live on campus. *Retention:* 54% of full-time freshmen returned.

Freshmen *Admission:* 1,771 applied, 906 admitted, 245 enrolled. *Average high school GPA:* 2.6.

Faculty *Total:* 43, 79% full-time, 42% with terminal degrees. *Student/faculty ratio:* 18:1.

Academics *Calendar:* semesters. *Degree:* bachelor's. *Special study options:* academic remediation for entering students, accelerated degree program, adult/continuing education programs, cooperative education, double majors, English as a second language, independent study, internships, off-campus study, part-time degree program, study abroad. *ROTC:* Army (c).

Computers on Campus 105 computers/terminals are available on campus for general student use. Students can access the following: computer help desk, free student e-mail accounts. Campuswide network is available. 100% of college-owned or -operated housing units are wired for high-speed Internet access. Wireless service is available via entire campus.

Student Life *Housing options:* men-only, women-only. Campus housing is university owned. *Activities and organizations:* drama/theater group, student-run newspaper, choral group, Student Government Association, Crimson Ambassadors, Students in Free Enterprise (SIFE), Talladega College Choir, Social Work Club, national fraternities, national sororities. *Campus security:* 24-hour patrols, late-night transport/escort service, campus police. *Student services:* health clinic, personal/psychological counseling.

Athletics Member USCAA. *Intercollegiate sports:* golf M, softball W, tennis W. *Intramural sports:* baseball M, basketball M/W, volleyball W.

Standardized Tests *Recommended:* SAT or ACT (for admission).

Costs (2010–11) *Comprehensive fee:* $16,996 includes full-time tuition ($10,175), mandatory fees ($936), and room and board ($5885). Full-time tuition and fees vary according to course load. Part-time tuition: $308 per credit hour. *Payment plans:* tuition prepayment, installment. *Waivers:* employees or children of employees.

Financial Aid Of all full-time matriculated undergraduates who enrolled in 2003, 407 applied for aid, 375 were judged to have need, 100 had their need fully met. 141 Federal Work-Study jobs (averaging $691). *Average percent of need met:* 90%. *Average financial aid package:* $5000. *Average need-based loan:* $5335. *Average need-based gift aid:* $3025. *Average non-need-based aid:* $5774. *Average indebtedness upon graduation:* $12,790. *Financial aid deadline:* 6/30.

Applying *Options:* electronic application, early admission. *Application fee:* $25. *Required:* essay or personal statement, high school transcript, minimum 2 GPA, 1 letter of recommendation. *Application deadlines:* rolling (freshmen), rolling (transfers). *Notification:* continuous (freshmen), continuous (transfers).

Freshman Application Contact Talladega College, 627 West Battle Street, Talladega, AL 35160-2354. *Phone:* 256-761-6415. *Toll-free phone:* 800-762-2468 (in-state); 800-633-2440 (out-of-state). *Web site:* http://www.talladega.edu/.

Troy University

Troy, Alabama

- **State-supported** comprehensive, founded 1887, part of Troy University System
- **Small-town** 877-acre campus
- **Coed** 22,245 undergraduate students, 50% full-time, 61% women, 39% men
- **Moderately difficult** entrance level, 71% of applicants were admitted

Undergraduates 11,085 full-time, 11,160 part-time. Students come from 50 states and territories; 47 other countries; 41% Black or African American, non-Hispanic/Latino; 3% Hispanic/Latino; 0.9% Asian, non-Hispanic/Latino; 0.1% Native Hawaiian or other Pacific Islander, non-Hispanic/Latino; 1% American Indian or Alaska Native, non-Hispanic/Latino; 0.2% Two or more races, non-Hispanic/Latino; 7% Race/ethnicity unknown; 2% international; 11% transferred in; 30% live on campus. *Retention:* 66% of full-time freshmen returned.

Freshmen *Admission:* 6,530 applied, 4,667 admitted, 2,989 enrolled.

Faculty *Total:* 1,469, 38% full-time, 49% with terminal degrees. *Student/faculty ratio:* 28:1.

Academics *Calendar:* semesters. *Degrees:* associate, bachelor's, master's, doctoral-professional, and post-master's certificates. *Special study options:* academic remediation for entering students, accelerated degree program, advanced placement credit, distance learning, double majors, English as a second language, honors programs, independent study, internships, part-time degree program, services for LD students, summer session for credit. *ROTC:* Army (b), Air Force (b).

Computers on Campus 1,908 computers/terminals and 4,927 ports are available on campus for general student use. Students can access the following: campus intranet, computer help desk, free student e-mail accounts, online (class) grades, online (class) registration, online (class) schedules. Campuswide network is available. Wireless service is available via classrooms, dorm rooms, libraries.

Student Life *Housing:* on-campus residence required for freshman year. *Options:* coed, men-only, women-only. Campus housing is university owned. Freshman campus housing is guaranteed. *Activities and organizations:* drama/theater group, student-run newspaper, television station, choral group, marching band, T-Day/Athletic Events, Activities Council, Pep Rallies, national fraternities, national sororities. *Campus security:* 24-hour emergency response devices and patrols, student patrols, late-night transport/escort service, controlled dormitory access. *Student services:* health clinic, personal/psychological counseling.

Athletics Member NCAA. All Division I except football (Division I-A). *Intercollegiate sports:* baseball M(s), basketball M(s)/W(s), cross-country running M(s)/W(s), golf M(s)/W(s), soccer W(s), softball W(s), tennis M(s)/W(s), track and field M(s)/W(s), volleyball W(s). *Intramural sports:* basketball M/W, bowling M/W, cross-country running M/W, football M, golf M/W, soccer W, softball W, tennis M/W, track and field M/W, volleyball W.

Standardized Tests *Required:* SAT or ACT (for admission).

Costs (2010–11) *Tuition:* state resident $6480 full-time, $216 per credit hour part-time; nonresident $12,960 full-time, $432 per credit hour part-time. Full-time tuition and fees vary according to location and program. Part-time tuition and fees vary according to location and program. *Required fees:* $720 full-time, $8 per credit hour part-time, $50 per term part-time. *Room and board:* $6570. Room and board charges vary according to board plan and housing facility. *Payment plan:* installment. *Waivers:* employees or children of employees.

Financial Aid Of all full-time matriculated undergraduates who enrolled in 2009, 7,764 applied for aid, 7,753 were judged to have need. In 2009, 1134 non-need-based awards were made. *Average financial aid package:* $4667. *Average need-based loan:* $4726. *Average need-based gift aid:* $4611. *Average non-need-based aid:* $5198.

Applying *Options:* electronic application, deferred entrance. *Application fee:* $30. *Required:* high school transcript. *Recommended:* interview. *Application deadlines:* rolling (freshmen), rolling (transfers).

Freshman Application Contact Mr. Buddy Starling, Dean of Enrollment Management, Troy University, University Avenue, Troy, AL 36082. *Phone:* 334-670-3243. *Toll-free phone:* 800-551-9716. *Fax:* 334-670-3733. *E-mail:* bstar@troy.edu. *Web site:* http://www.troy.edu/.

Tuskegee University

Tuskegee, Alabama

- **Independent** comprehensive, founded 1881
- **Small-town** 5000-acre campus
- **Coed** 2,479 undergraduate students, 97% full-time, 56% women, 44% men
- **Moderately difficult** entrance level, 64% of applicants were admitted

Undergraduates 2,411 full-time, 68 part-time. Students come from 44 states and territories; 19 other countries; 72% are from out of state; 84% Black or African American, non-Hispanic/Latino; 0.3% Hispanic/Latino; 0.1% American Indian or Alaska Native, non-Hispanic/Latino; 14% Race/ethnicity unknown; 1% international; 6% transferred in; 63% live on campus. *Retention:* 71% of full-time freshmen returned.

Freshmen *Admission:* 2,471 applied, 1,584 admitted, 701 enrolled. *Average high school GPA:* 3.2. *Test scores:* SAT critical reading scores over 500: 86%; SAT math scores over 500: 98%; ACT scores over 18: 321%; SAT critical reading scores over 600: 13%; SAT math scores over 600: 21%; ACT scores over 24: 64%; SAT critical reading scores over 700: 1%; SAT math scores over 700: 1%; ACT scores over 30: 3%.

Faculty *Total:* 294, 93% full-time, 78% with terminal degrees. *Student/faculty ratio:* 12:1.

Academics *Calendar:* semesters. *Degrees:* bachelor's, master's, doctoral-other, and doctoral-professional. *Special study options:* academic remediation for entering students, cooperative education, English as a second language, honors programs, internships, off-campus study, part-time degree program, summer session for credit. *ROTC:* Army (b), Air Force (b). *Unusual degree programs:* 3-2 forestry with Auburn University, Iowa State University of Science and Technology, University of Michigan, Idaho State University.

Computers on Campus 1,000 computers/terminals are available on campus for general student use. Students can access the following: online (class) registration. Campuswide network is available.

Student Life *Housing:* on-campus residence required through sophomore year. *Options:* coed, men-only, women-only. Freshman applicants given priority for college housing. *Activities and organizations:* drama/theater group, student-run newspaper, choral group, marching band, national fraternities, national sororities. *Campus security:* 24-hour emergency response devices and patrols, late-night transport/escort service. *Student services:* health clinic, personal/psychological counseling.

Athletics Member NCAA. All Division II. *Intercollegiate sports:* baseball M(s), basketball M(s)/W(s), cross-country running M/W, football M(s), golf M(s), riflery M/W, soccer M, tennis M(s)/W(s), track and field M(s)/W(s), volleyball W(s). *Intramural sports:* badminton M/W, basketball M/W, football M, golf M, gymnastics M/W, riflery M/W, soccer M, swimming and diving M/W, tennis M/W, track and field M/W, volleyball M/W.

Standardized Tests *Required:* SAT or ACT (for admission).

Costs (2010–11) *Comprehensive fee:* $24,320 includes full-time tuition ($16,100), mandatory fees ($650), and room and board ($7570). Full-time tuition and fees vary according to course load and program. Part-time tuition: $665 per credit hour. Part-time tuition and fees vary according to course load and program. *Room and board:* Room and board charges vary according to housing facility. *Payment plan:* installment. *Waivers:* employees or children of employees.

Financial Aid Of all full-time matriculated undergraduates who enrolled in 2009, 2,519 applied for aid, 2,147 were judged to have need, 1,379 had their need fully met. 525 Federal Work-Study jobs (averaging $1879). 424 state and other part-time jobs (averaging $4628). In 2009, 597 non-need-based awards were made. *Average percent of need met:* 85%. *Average financial aid package:* $19,250. *Average need-based loan:* $6006. *Average need-based gift aid:* $8000. *Average non-need-based aid:* $6000. *Average indebtedness upon graduation:* $28,575.

Applying *Options:* electronic application, early admission. *Application fee:* $25. *Required:* high school transcript, minimum 2 GPA. *Application deadlines:* 4/15 (freshmen), 4/15 (transfers).

Freshman Application Contact Tuskegee University, Tuskegee, AL 36088. *Phone:* 334-727-8500. *Toll-free phone:* 800-622-6531. *Web site:* http://www.tuskegee.edu/.

United States Sports Academy

Daphne, Alabama

- **Independent** upper-level, founded 1972
- **Suburban** 10-acre campus
- **Coed**

Faculty *Student/faculty ratio:* 18:1.

Academics *Calendar:* continuous. *Degrees:* bachelor's, master's, and doctoral-research/scholarship.

Applying *Application fee:* $50.

Application Contact United States Sports Academy, One Academy Drive, Daphne, AL 36526-7055. *Toll-free phone:* 800-223-2668. *Web site:* http://www.ussa.edu/.

The University of Alabama

Tuscaloosa, Alabama

- **State-supported** university, founded 1831, part of University of Alabama System
- **Suburban** 1000-acre campus with easy access to Birmingham
- **Endowment** $631.9 million
- **Coed** 24,882 undergraduate students, 92% full-time, 52% women, 48% men
- **Moderately difficult** entrance level, 54% of applicants were admitted

Undergraduates 22,866 full-time, 2,016 part-time. Students come from 50 states and territories; 58 other countries; 31% are from out of state; 12% Black or African American, non-Hispanic/Latino; 2% Hispanic/Latino; 1% Asian, non-Hispanic/Latino; 0.5% American Indian or Alaska Native, non-Hispanic/Latino; 0.5% Two or more races, non-Hispanic/Latino; 0.2% Race/ethnicity unknown; 1% international; 6% transferred in; 30% live on campus. *Retention:* 85% of full-time freshmen returned.

Freshmen *Admission:* 20,112 applied, 10,790 admitted, 5,519 enrolled. *Average high school GPA:* 3.5. *Test scores:* SAT critical reading scores over 500: 72%; SAT math scores over 500: 76%; SAT writing scores over 500: 68%; ACT scores over 18: 100%; SAT critical reading scores over 600: 30%; SAT math scores over 600: 32%; SAT writing scores over 600: 27%; ACT scores over 24: 61%; SAT critical reading scores over 700: 13%; SAT math scores over 700: 9%; SAT writing scores over 700: 7%; ACT scores over 30: 21%.

Faculty *Total:* 1,555, 73% full-time, 80% with terminal degrees. *Student/faculty ratio:* 19:1.

Academics *Calendar:* semesters. *Degrees:* bachelor's, master's, doctoral-professional, doctoral-research/scholarship, and post-master's certificates. *Special study options:* academic remediation for entering students, accelerated degree program, adult/continuing education programs, advanced placement credit, cooperative education, distance learning, double majors, English as a second language, external degree program, freshman honors college, honors programs, independent study, internships, off-campus study, part-time degree program, services for LD students, student-designed majors, study abroad, summer session for credit. *ROTC:* Army (b), Air Force (b).

Computers on Campus 2,200 computers/terminals are available on campus for general student use. Students can access the following: campus intranet, computer help desk, free student e-mail accounts, online (class) grades, online (class) registration, online (class) schedules. Campuswide network is available. 100% of college-owned or -operated housing units are wired for high-speed Internet access. Wireless service is available via classrooms, computer centers, dorm rooms, libraries, student centers.

Student Life *Housing:* on-campus residence required for freshman year. *Options:* coed, men-only, women-only, disabled students. Campus housing is university owned and leased by the school. Freshman campus housing is guaranteed. *Activities and organizations:* drama/theater group, student-run newspaper, radio station, choral group, marching band, SOURCE Board of Governors, Residence Hall Association, International Student Association, Student Government Association, Black Student Union, national fraternities, national sororities. *Campus security:* 24-hour emergency response devices and patrols, late-night transport/escort service, controlled dormitory access, 24 hour patrols by University of Alabama Police (UAPD), certified law enforcement personnel. *Student services:* health clinic, personal/psychological counseling, women's center, legal services.

Athletics Member NCAA. All Division I except football (Division I-A). *Intercollegiate sports:* baseball M(s), basketball M(s)/W(s), bowling M(c)/W(c), cheerleading M(s)/W(s), crew M(c)/W(s), cross-country running M(s)/W(s), golf M(s)/W(s), gymnastics W(s), ice hockey M(c), lacrosse M(c)/W(c), racquetball M(c)/W(c), rugby M(c)/W(c), soccer M(c)/W(s), softball W(s), swimming and diving M(s)/W(s), table tennis M(c)/W(c), tennis M(s)/W(s), track and field M(s)/W(s), ultimate Frisbee M(c), volleyball M(c)/W(s), water polo M(c)/W(c), wrestling M(c). *Intramural sports:* badminton M/W, basketball M/W, bowling M/W, football M/W, golf M/W, racquetball M/W, soccer M/W, softball M/W, swimming and diving M/W, table tennis M/W, tennis M/W, ultimate Frisbee M/W, volleyball M/W.

Standardized Tests *Required:* SAT or ACT (for admission).

Costs (2010–11) *Tuition:* state resident $7900 full-time; nonresident $20,500 full-time. Full-time tuition and fees vary according to course load. Part-time tuition and fees vary according to course load. *Room and board:* $8214; room only: $4700. Room and board charges vary according to board plan and housing facility. *Payment plans:* installment, deferred payment. *Waivers:* employees or children of employees.

Financial Aid Of all full-time matriculated undergraduates who enrolled in 2008, 11,204 applied for aid, 8,520 were judged to have need, 1,143 had their need fully met. 450 Federal Work-Study jobs (averaging $2299). In 2008, 4322 non-need-based awards were made. *Average percent of need met:* 53%.

Average financial aid package: $9536. *Average need-based loan:* $4190. *Average need-based gift aid:* $6680. *Average non-need-based aid:* $407. *Average indebtedness upon graduation:* $26,701.

Applying *Options:* electronic application, early admission. *Application fee:* $40. *Required:* essay or personal statement, high school transcript. *Required for some:* interview. *Application deadlines:* 2/1 (freshmen), 2/1 (out-of-state freshmen), 3/1 (transfers). *Notification:* continuous (freshmen), continuous (out-of-state freshmen), continuous (transfers).

Freshman Application Contact Ms. Mary K. Spiegel, Executive Director of Undergraduate Admissions, The University of Alabama, Box 870132, Tuscaloosa, AL 35487. *Phone:* 205-348-5666. *Toll-free phone:* 800-933-BAMA. *Fax:* 205-348-9046. *E-mail:* admissions@ua.edu. *Web site:* http://www.ua.edu/.

The University of Alabama at Birmingham
Birmingham, Alabama

- **State-supported** university, founded 1969, part of University of Alabama System
- **Urban** 187-acre campus with easy access to Birmingham
- **Coed** 11,028 undergraduate students, 74% full-time, 58% women, 42% men
- **Moderately difficult** entrance level, 82% of applicants were admitted

Undergraduates 8,204 full-time, 2,824 part-time. 7% are from out of state; 27% Black or African American, non-Hispanic/Latino; 2% Hispanic/Latino; 4% Asian, non-Hispanic/Latino; 0.1% Native Hawaiian or other Pacific Islander, non-Hispanic/Latino; 0.3% American Indian or Alaska Native, non-Hispanic/Latino; 1% Two or more races, non-Hispanic/Latino; 3% Race/ethnicity unknown; 2% international; 12% transferred in; 20% live on campus. Retention: 82% of full-time freshmen returned.

Freshmen *Admission:* 4,667 applied, 3,847 admitted, 1,571 enrolled. *Average high school GPA:* 3.5. *Test scores:* ACT scores over 18: 100%; ACT scores over 24: 53%; ACT scores over 30: 9%.

Faculty *Total:* 931, 93% full-time, 85% with terminal degrees. *Student/faculty ratio:* 17:1.

Academics *Calendar:* semesters. *Degrees:* certificates, bachelor's, master's, doctoral-other, doctoral-professional, doctoral-research/scholarship, post-master's, and postbachelor's certificates. *Special study options:* academic remediation for entering students, accelerated degree program, adult/continuing education programs, advanced placement credit, cooperative education, distance learning, double majors, English as a second language, freshman honors college, honors programs, independent study, internships, off-campus study, part-time degree program, services for LD students, student-designed majors, study abroad, summer session for credit. *ROTC:* Army (b), Air Force (c). *Unusual degree programs:* 3-2 engineering with Biomedical Engineering 5th Year Master's Program; Fast-Track Program - Civil Engineering, Electrical Engineering, Materials Engineering, and Mechanical Engineering; BS / MS in Biology; BS/MS in Computer Science; Public Health Fifth Year Master's Program, and Fast-Track Programs in Mathematics and Accounting.

Computers on Campus Students can access the following: campus intranet, computer help desk, free student e-mail accounts, online (class) grades, online (class) registration, online (class) schedules, transcript requests. Campuswide network is available. 100% of college-owned or -operated housing units are wired for high-speed Internet access. Wireless service is available via classrooms, computer labs, dorm rooms, learning centers, libraries, student centers.

Student Life *Housing options:* coed, disabled students. Campus housing is university owned and is provided by a third party. Freshman applicants given priority for college housing. *Activities and organizations:* drama/theater group, student-run newspaper, radio station, choral group, marching band, campus ministries, service-oriented groups, sports-affiliated groups, national fraternities, national sororities. *Campus security:* 24-hour emergency response devices and patrols, late-night transport/escort service, controlled dormitory access. *Student services:* health clinic, personal/psychological counseling, women's center.

Athletics Member NCAA. All Division I except football (Division I-A). *Intercollegiate sports:* baseball M(s), basketball M(s)/W(s), cross-country running W(s), golf M(s)/W(s), riflery M/W, soccer M(s)/W(s), softball W(s), tennis M(s)/W(s), track and field W(s), volleyball W(s). *Intramural sports:* badminton M/W, basketball M/W, bowling M/W, football M/W, racquetball M/W, skiing (downhill) M/W, soccer M/W, softball M/W, swimming and diving M/W, table tennis M/W, tennis M/W, track and field M/W, ultimate Frisbee M/W, volleyball M/W, water polo M/W, wrestling M.

Standardized Tests *Required:* SAT or ACT (for admission).

Costs (2010–11) *Tuition:* state resident $5472 full-time, $228 per credit hour part-time; nonresident $12,864 full-time, $536 per credit hour part-time. Full-time tuition and fees vary according to program. Part-time tuition and fees vary according to program. *Required fees:* $784 full-time, $167 per term part-time. *Room and board:* $8810; room only: $5000. Room and board charges vary according to board plan and housing facility. *Payment plan:* installment. *Waivers:* employees or children of employees.

Financial Aid Of all full-time matriculated undergraduates who enrolled in 2009, 5,217 applied for aid, 4,140 were judged to have need, 601 had their need fully met. In 2009, 1283 non-need-based awards were made. *Average percent of need met:* 50%. *Average financial aid package:* $9334. *Average need-based loan:* $4394. *Average need-based gift aid:* $5063. *Average non-need-based aid:* $6449. *Average indebtedness upon graduation:* $21,670.

Applying *Options:* electronic application, early admission, deferred entrance. *Application fee:* $30. *Required:* high school transcript, minimum 2.25 GPA. *Application deadlines:* rolling (freshmen), 5/1 (transfers). *Notification:* continuous (freshmen), continuous (transfers).

Freshman Application Contact Ms. Chenise Ryan, Director of Undergraduate Admissions, The University of Alabama at Birmingham, 1530 3rd Avenue South, HUC 260, Birmingham, AL 35294-1150. *Phone:* 205-934-8221. *Toll-free phone:* 800-421-8743. *Fax:* 205-975-7114. *E-mail:* undergradadmit@uab.edu. *Web site:* http://www.uab.edu/.

The University of Alabama in Huntsville
Huntsville, Alabama

- **State-supported** university, founded 1950, part of University of Alabama System
- **Suburban** 400-acre campus
- **Endowment** $48.6 million
- **Coed** 6,005 undergraduate students, 76% full-time, 47% women, 53% men
- **Moderately difficult** entrance level, 66% of applicants were admitted

Undergraduates 4,539 full-time, 1,466 part-time. Students come from 42 states and territories; 75 other countries; 10% are from out of state; 15% Black or African American, non-Hispanic/Latino; 3% Hispanic/Latino; 3% Asian, non-Hispanic/Latino; 1% American Indian or Alaska Native, non-Hispanic/Latino; 2% Two or more races, non-Hispanic/Latino; 2% Race/ethnicity unknown; 3% international; 11% transferred in; 21% live on campus. *Retention:* 75% of full-time freshmen returned.

Freshmen *Admission:* 1,846 applied, 1,221 admitted, 622 enrolled. *Average high school GPA:* 3.54. *Test scores:* SAT critical reading scores over 500: 81%; SAT math scores over 500: 77%; ACT scores over 18: 100%; SAT critical reading scores over 600: 38%; SAT math scores over 600: 43%; ACT scores over 24: 69%; SAT critical reading scores over 700: 9%; SAT math scores over 700: 12%; ACT scores over 30: 19%.

Faculty *Total:* 480, 63% full-time, 68% with terminal degrees. *Student/faculty ratio:* 16:1.

Academics *Calendar:* semesters. *Degrees:* bachelor's, master's, doctoral-professional, doctoral-research/scholarship, post-master's, and postbachelor's certificates. *Special study options:* academic remediation for entering students, advanced placement credit, cooperative education, distance learning, double majors, English as a second language, honors programs, independent study, internships, off-campus study, part-time degree program, services for LD students, study abroad, summer session for credit. *ROTC:* Army (c). *Unusual degree programs:* 3-2 engineering with Oakwood College, Morehouse College, Clark Atlanta University, Spelman College.

Computers on Campus 1,213 computers/terminals and 3,174 ports are available on campus for general student use. Students can access the following: campus intranet, computer help desk, free student e-mail accounts, online (class) grades, online (class) registration, online (class) schedules. Campuswide network is available. 100% of college-owned or -operated housing units are wired for high-speed Internet access. Wireless service is available via classrooms, computer centers, computer labs, dorm rooms, learning centers, libraries, student centers.

Student Life *Housing:* on-campus residence required through sophomore year. *Options:* coed, cooperative, disabled students. Campus housing is university owned. Freshman campus housing is guaranteed. *Activities and organizations:* drama/theater group, student-run newspaper, choral group, Black Student Association, Chinese Students and Scholars Association, Baptist Campus Ministry, Indian Student Organization, American Society of Civil Engineers, national fraternities, national sororities. *Campus security:* 24-hour emergency response devices and patrols, late-night transport/escort service, controlled dormitory access, Sworn Police Department with state certified police officers; 24/7 dispatch center; community policing efforts. *Student services:* health clinic, personal/psychological counseling.

Athletics Member NCAA. All Division II except ice hockey (Division I). *Intercollegiate sports:* badminton M(c)/W(c), baseball M(s), basketball M(s)/W(s), bowling M(c)/W(c), cheerleading M(s)/W(s), crew M(c)/W(c), cross-country running M(s)/W(s), ice hockey M(s), soccer M(s)/W(s), softball W(s), tennis M(s)/W(s), track and field M(s)/W(s), volleyball W(s). *Intramural sports:* basketball M/W, football M/W, soccer M/W, softball M/W, tennis M/W, ultimate Frisbee M/W, volleyball M/W.

Standardized Tests *Required:* SAT or ACT (for admission).

Costs (2010–11) *Tuition:* state resident $7492 full-time, $260 per credit hour part-time; nonresident $17,986 full-time, $630 per credit hour part-time. Full-time tuition and fees vary according to course load. Part-time tuition and fees vary according to course load. *Required fees:* $38 per credit hour part-time. *Room and board:* $7540; room only: $5290. Room and board charges vary according to board plan and housing facility. *Payment plan:* installment. *Waivers:* employees or children of employees.

Financial Aid Of all full-time matriculated undergraduates who enrolled in 2009, 3,642 applied for aid, 2,395 were judged to have need, 258 had their need fully met. 72 Federal Work-Study jobs (averaging $4282). In 2009, 745 non-need-based awards were made. *Average percent of need met:* 57%. *Average financial aid package:* $8940. *Average need-based loan:* $7555. *Average need-based gift aid:* $6033. *Average non-need-based aid:* $5312. *Average indebtedness upon graduation:* $19,852. *Financial aid deadline:* 7/31.

Applying *Options:* electronic application. *Application fee:* $30. *Required:* high school transcript. *Application deadlines:* 8/19 (freshmen), 8/19 (out-of-state freshmen), 8/19 (transfers). *Notification:* continuous (freshmen), continuous (transfers).

Freshman Application Contact Ms. Sandra Ranae Barinowski, Director of Admissions, The University of Alabama in Huntsville, Enrollment Services, 301 Sparkman Drive, Huntsville, AL 35899. *Phone:* 256-824-6070. *Toll-free phone:* 800-UAH-CALL. *Fax:* 256-824-4539. *E-mail:* admitme@email.uah.edu. *Web site:* http://www.uah.edu/.

University of Mobile
Mobile, Alabama

- **Independent Southern Baptist** comprehensive, founded 1961
- **Suburban** 830-acre campus
- **Endowment** $13.2 million
- **Coed** 1,480 undergraduate students, 90% full-time, 68% women, 32% men
- **Moderately difficult** entrance level, 75% of applicants were admitted

Undergraduates 1,333 full-time, 147 part-time. Students come from 28 states and territories; 24 other countries; 16% are from out of state; 24% Black or African American, non-Hispanic/Latino; 1% Hispanic/Latino; 0.4% Asian, non-Hispanic/Latino; 2% American Indian or Alaska Native, non-Hispanic/Latino; 0.7% Two or more races, non-Hispanic/Latino; 7% Race/ethnicity unknown; 2% international; 11% transferred in; 38% live on campus. *Retention:* 70% of full-time freshmen returned.

Freshmen *Admission:* 886 applied, 661 admitted, 235 enrolled. *Average high school GPA:* 3.33. *Test scores:* SAT critical reading scores over 500: 70%; SAT math scores over 500: 58%; SAT writing scores over 500: 54%; ACT scores over 18: 90%; SAT critical reading scores over 600: 17%; SAT math scores over 600: 13%; SAT writing scores over 600: 29%; ACT scores over 24: 26%; SAT critical reading scores over 700: 3%; ACT scores over 30: 3%.

Faculty *Total:* 181, 45% full-time, 40% with terminal degrees. *Student/faculty ratio:* 12:1.

Academics *Calendar:* semesters. *Degrees:* associate, bachelor's, and master's. *Special study options:* academic remediation for entering students, accelerated degree program, adult/continuing education programs, advanced placement credit, double majors, honors programs, independent study, internships, part-time degree program, services for LD students, summer session for credit. *ROTC:* Army (c), Air Force (c). *Unusual degree programs:* 3-2 engineering with Auburn University and University of South Alabama.

Computers on Campus 110 computers/terminals are available on campus for general student use. Students can access the following: campus intranet, computer help desk, free student e-mail accounts, online (class) grades, online (class) registration, online (class) schedules. Campuswide network is available. 100% of college-owned or -operated housing units are wired for high-speed Internet access. Wireless service is available via classrooms, computer centers, computer labs, dorm rooms, learning centers, libraries, student centers.

Student Life *Housing:* on-campus residence required for freshman year. *Options:* men-only, women-only. Campus housing is university owned. Freshman campus housing is guaranteed. *Activities and organizations:* drama/theater group, choral group, Campus Activity Board, Baptist Campus Ministry, Student Government Association, Fellowship of Christian Athletes. *Campus security:* 24-hour emergency response devices and patrols, controlled dormitory access, text alerts. *Student services:* health clinic, personal/psychological counseling.

Athletics Member NAIA. *Intercollegiate sports:* baseball M(s), basketball M(s)/W(s), cheerleading W(s), cross-country running M(s)/W(s), golf M(s)/W(s), soccer M(s)/W(s), softball W(s), tennis M(s)/W(s), track and field M(s)/W(s), volleyball W(s). *Intramural sports:* basketball M/W, golf M/W, soccer M/W, softball M/W, tennis M/W, track and field M/W, volleyball M/W.

Standardized Tests *Required:* SAT or ACT (for admission). *Recommended:* SAT and SAT Subject Tests or ACT (for admission), SAT Subject Tests (for admission).

Costs (2010–11) *Comprehensive fee:* $23,900 includes full-time tuition ($15,590), mandatory fees ($530), and room and board ($7780). Full-time tuition and fees vary according to course load. Part-time tuition: $555 per credit hour. Part-time tuition and fees vary according to course load. *Required fees:* $163 per degree program part-time. *College room only:* $4590. Room and board charges vary according to housing facility. *Payment plan:* installment. *Waivers:* employees or children of employees.

Financial Aid Of all full-time matriculated undergraduates who enrolled in 2009, 962 applied for aid, 862 were judged to have need. 65 Federal Work-Study jobs (averaging $2175). In 2009, 79 non-need-based awards were made. *Average percent of need met:* 58%. *Average financial aid package:* $12,985. *Average need-based loan:* $5049. *Average need-based gift aid:* $6569. *Average non-need-based aid:* $5420. *Average indebtedness upon graduation:* $16,660.

Applying *Options:* electronic application, deferred entrance. *Application fee:* $50. *Required:* high school transcript, minimum 3.33 GPA. *Required for some:* interview. *Application deadlines:* rolling (freshmen), rolling (transfers). *Notification:* continuous (freshmen), continuous (transfers).

Freshman Application Contact Mrs. Charity Wittner, Director of Enrollment, University of Mobile, 5735 College Parkway, Mobile, AL 36613-2842. *Phone:* 251-442-2507. *Toll-free phone:* 800-946-7267. *Fax:* 251-442-2498. *E-mail:* cwittner@umobile.edu. *Web site:* http://www.umobile.edu/.

University of Montevallo
Montevallo, Alabama

- **State-supported** comprehensive, founded 1896
- **Small-town** 160-acre campus with easy access to Birmingham
- **Endowment** $2.1 million
- **Coed** 2,512 undergraduate students, 89% full-time, 66% women, 34% men
- **Moderately difficult** entrance level

Undergraduates 2,232 full-time, 280 part-time. Students come from 26 states and territories; 23 other countries; 5% are from out of state; 15% Black or African American, non-Hispanic/Latino; 2% Hispanic/Latino; 0.4% Asian, non-Hispanic/Latino; 0.5% American Indian or Alaska Native, non-Hispanic/Latino; 0.8% Two or more races, non-Hispanic/Latino; 4% Race/ethnicity unknown; 2% international; 8% transferred in; 45% live on campus. *Retention:* 72% of full-time freshmen returned.

Freshmen *Admission:* 432 enrolled. *Average high school GPA:* 3.34. *Test scores:* ACT scores over 18: 97%; ACT scores over 24: 42%; ACT scores over 30: 7%.

Faculty *Total:* 211, 62% full-time. *Student/faculty ratio:* 17:1.

Academics *Calendar:* semesters. *Degrees:* bachelor's, master's, and post-master's certificates. *Special study options:* academic remediation for entering students, accelerated degree program, advanced placement credit, double majors, honors programs, independent study, internships, part-time degree program, services for LD students, study abroad, summer session for credit. *ROTC:* Army (c), Air Force (c). *Unusual degree programs:* 3-2 engineering with Auburn University, University of Alabama at Birmingham.

Computers on Campus 340 computers/terminals are available on campus for general student use. Students can access the following: campus intranet, computer help desk, free student e-mail accounts, online (class) grades, online (class) registration, online (class) schedules. Campuswide network is available. 100% of college-owned or -operated housing units are wired for high-speed Internet access. Wireless service is available via classrooms, computer centers, computer labs, dorm rooms, libraries, student centers.

Student Life *Housing:* on-campus residence required for freshman year. *Options:* coed, men-only, women-only. Campus housing is university owned. Freshman campus housing is guaranteed. *Activities and organizations:* drama/theater group, student-run newspaper, television station, choral group, Student Government Association, University Programming Council, Campus Ministries, Greek Life, Environmental Club, national fraternities, national sororities. *Campus security:* 24-hour emergency response devices and patrols, late-night transport/escort service, controlled dormitory access. *Student services:* health clinic, personal/psychological counseling.

Athletics Member NCAA. All Division II. *Intercollegiate sports:* baseball M(s), basketball M(s)/W(s), golf M(s)/W(s), soccer M(s)/W(s), tennis W(s), volleyball W(s). *Intramural sports:* basketball M/W, bowling M, football M, golf M, tennis M/W, volleyball M/W.

Standardized Tests *Required:* SAT or ACT (for admission). *Recommended:* ACT (for admission).

Costs (2010–11) *Tuition:* state resident $7230 full-time, $241 per credit hour part-time; nonresident $14,460 full-time, $482 per credit hour part-time. Full-time tuition and fees vary according to course load. Part-time tuition and fees vary according to course load. *Required fees:* $520 full-time. *Room and board:* $4924. Room and board charges vary according to housing facility. *Payment plan:* installment. *Waivers:* employees or children of employees.

Financial Aid Of all full-time matriculated undergraduates who enrolled in 2009, 1,559 applied for aid, 1,287 were judged to have need, 341 had their

need fully met. 90 Federal Work-Study jobs (averaging $1775). In 2009, 356 non-need-based awards were made. *Average percent of need met:* 64%. *Average financial aid package:* $9191. *Average need-based loan:* $4092. *Average need-based gift aid:* $6340. *Average non-need-based aid:* $6715. *Average indebtedness upon graduation:* $12,712.

Applying *Options:* electronic application, early admission, deferred entrance. *Application fee:* $30. *Required:* high school transcript, minimum 2 GPA. *Recommended:* interview. *Application deadlines:* 8/1 (freshmen), rolling (transfers). *Notification:* 9/1 (freshmen).

Freshman Application Contact Mr. Ira Lynn Gurganus, Director of Admissions, University of Montevallo, University of Montevallo, Office of Admissions, Station 6030, Montevallo, AL 35115-6030. *Phone:* 205-665-6030. *Toll-free phone:* 800-292-4349. *Fax:* 205-665-6032. *E-mail:* admissions@montevallo.edu. *Web site:* http://www.montevallo.edu/.

University of North Alabama

Florence, Alabama

- **State-supported** comprehensive, founded 1830
- **Urban** 200-acre campus
- **Coed**
- **Minimally difficult** entrance level

Faculty *Student/faculty ratio:* 22:1.

Academics *Calendar:* semesters. *Degrees:* bachelor's, master's, and post-master's certificates.

Student Life *Campus security:* 24-hour emergency response devices and patrols, student patrols, late-night transport/escort service, controlled dormitory access.

Athletics Member NCAA. All Division II.

Standardized Tests *Required:* SAT or ACT (for admission).

Costs (2010–11) *Tuition:* state resident $5550 full-time, $185 per credit hour part-time; nonresident $11,100 full-time, $370 per credit hour part-time. Full-time tuition and fees vary according to course load and program. Part-time tuition and fees vary according to course load and program. *Required fees:* $1118 full-time. *Room and board:* $5012. Room and board charges vary according to board plan and housing facility.

Financial Aid *Of all full-time matriculated undergraduates who enrolled in 2009,* 3,465 applied for aid, 2,487 were judged to have need, 1,749 had their need fully met. 124 Federal Work-Study jobs (averaging $1373). 386 state and other part-time jobs (averaging $1397). *In 2009,* 899 non-need-based awards were made. *Average percent of need met:* 61. *Average financial aid package:* $7357. *Average need-based loan:* $3726. *Average need-based gift aid:* $4625. *Average non-need-based aid:* $1072. *Average indebtedness upon graduation:* $29,200.

Applying *Options:* electronic application, early admission, deferred entrance. *Application fee:* $25. *Required:* high school transcript.

Freshman Application Contact Mrs. Kim O. Mauldin, Director of Admissions, University of North Alabama, One Harrison Plaza, Florence, AL 35632-0001. *Phone:* 256-765-4680. *Toll-free phone:* 800-TALKUNA. *Fax:* 256-765-4329. *E-mail:* admissions@una.edu. *Web site:* http://www.una.edu/.

University of South Alabama

Mobile, Alabama

- **State-supported** university, founded 1963
- **Suburban** 1225-acre campus
- **Endowment** $95.0 million
- **Coed** 11,658 undergraduate students, 74% full-time, 57% women, 43% men
- **Moderately difficult** entrance level, 86% of applicants were admitted

Undergraduates 8,681 full-time, 2,977 part-time. Students come from 51 states and territories; 101 other countries; 18% are from out of state; 9% transferred in; 24% live on campus. *Retention:* 66% of full-time freshmen returned.

Freshmen *Admission:* 4,369 applied, 3,777 admitted, 1,772 enrolled. *Test scores:* ACT scores over 18: 89%; ACT scores over 24: 35%; ACT scores over 30: 4%.

Faculty *Total:* 816, 63% full-time. *Student/faculty ratio:* 22:1.

Academics *Calendar:* semesters. *Degrees:* certificates, bachelor's, master's, doctoral-other, doctoral-professional, doctoral-research/scholarship, post-master's, and postbachelor's certificates. *Special study options:* academic remediation for entering students, accelerated degree program, adult/continuing education programs, advanced placement credit, cooperative education, distance learning, double majors, English as a second language, external degree program, freshman honors college, honors programs, part-time degree program, services for LD students, study abroad, summer session for credit. *ROTC:* Army (b), Air Force (b).

Computers on Campus 500 computers/terminals are available on campus for general student use. Students can access the following: campus intranet, computer help desk, free student e-mail accounts, online (class) grades, online (class) registration, online (class) schedules. Campuswide network is available. 100% of college-owned or -operated housing units are wired for high-speed Internet access. Wireless service is available via entire campus.

Student Life *Housing options:* coed, disabled students. Campus housing is university owned and is provided by a third party. *Activities and organizations:* drama/theater group, student-run newspaper, television station, choral group, marching band, Student Government Association, African American Student Association, Council of International Student Organizations, Alpha Epsilon Delta Pre-Health Professions, Panhellenic Council, national fraternities, national sororities. *Campus security:* 24-hour emergency response devices and patrols, late-night transport/escort service. *Student services:* health clinic, personal/psychological counseling, legal services.

Athletics Member NCAA. All Division I. *Intercollegiate sports:* baseball M(s), basketball M(s)/W(s), cross-country running M(s)/W(s), fencing M(c)/W(c), football M(c), golf M/W, soccer W(s), tennis M(s)/W(s), track and field M(s)/W(s), volleyball W(s). *Intramural sports:* badminton M/W, basketball M/W, bowling M/W, cheerleading M(c)/W(c), golf M/W, racquetball M/W, sailing M(c)/W(c), soccer M/W, softball M/W, table tennis M/W, tennis M/W, volleyball M/W, water polo M/W.

Standardized Tests *Required for some:* SAT or ACT (for admission).

Costs (2011–12) *Tuition:* state resident $6810 full-time, $227 per hour part-time; nonresident $13,620 full-time, $454 per hour part-time. Full-time tuition and fees vary according to class time, course level, course load, degree level, and program. Part-time tuition and fees vary according to class time, course level, course load, degree level, and program. *Required fees:* $398 per term part-time. *Room and board:* $5608; room only: $2908. Room and board charges vary according to board plan, housing facility, location, and student level. *Payment plan:* installment. *Waivers:* employees or children of employees.

Financial Aid Of all full-time matriculated undergraduates who enrolled in 2009, 5,584 applied for aid, 4,421 were judged to have need, 477 had their need fully met. 92 Federal Work-Study jobs (averaging $2600). In 2009, 914 non-need-based awards were made. *Average percent of need met:* 60%. *Average financial aid package:* $8471. *Average need-based loan:* $4378. *Average need-based gift aid:* $5682. *Average non-need-based aid:* $4121.

Applying *Options:* electronic application, early admission. *Application fee:* $35. *Required:* high school transcript. *Recommended:* minimum 2 GPA. *Application deadlines:* 7/15 (freshmen), 8/10 (transfers). *Notification:* continuous until 8/18 (freshmen), continuous until 8/18 (transfers).

Freshman Application Contact Mr. Christopher A. Lynch, Director, New Student Recruitment, University of South Alabama, Mobile, AL 36688-0002. *Phone:* 251-460-6141. *Toll-free phone:* 800-872-5247. *E-mail:* admiss@usouthal.edu. *Web site:* http://www.southalabama.edu/.

The University of West Alabama

Livingston, Alabama

- **State-supported** comprehensive, founded 1835
- **Small-town** 595-acre campus
- **Endowment** $421,639
- **Coed**
- **Minimally difficult** entrance level

Faculty *Student/faculty ratio:* 19:1.

Academics *Calendar:* semesters. *Degrees:* associate, bachelor's, and master's.

Student Life *Campus security:* 24-hour patrols.

Athletics Member NCAA. All Division II.

Standardized Tests *Required:* SAT or ACT (for admission).

Costs (2010–11) *Tuition:* state resident $5060 full-time, $215 per semester hour part-time; nonresident $10,120 full-time, $430 per semester hour part-time. Full-time tuition and fees vary according to course load, degree level, and program. Part-time tuition and fees vary according to course load, degree level, and program. *Required fees:* $470 full-time. *Room and board:* $4466. Room and board charges vary according to board plan and housing facility.

Financial Aid *Of all full-time matriculated undergraduates who enrolled in 2009,* 982 applied for aid, 878 were judged to have need, 513 had their need fully met. 112 Federal Work-Study jobs (averaging $3336). *In 2009,* 144 non-need-based awards were made. *Average percent of need met:* 68. *Average need-based loan:* $2961. *Average need-based gift aid:* $3729. *Average non-need-based aid:* $1739. *Average indebtedness upon graduation:* $17,406.

Applying *Options:* electronic application, early admission, deferred entrance. *Application fee:* $50. *Required:* high school transcript, minimum 2 GPA.

Freshman Application Contact Mr. Danny Buckalew, The University of West Alabama, Station 4, Livingston, AL 35470. *Phone:* 205-652-3581. *Toll-free phone:* 800-621-7742 (in-state); 800-621-8044 (out-of-state). *Fax:* 205-652-3522. *E-mail:* db@uwa.edu. *Web site:* http://www.uwa.edu/.

Virginia College at Birmingham

Birmingham, Alabama

Director of Admissions Director of Admissions, Virginia College at Birmingham, 488 Palisades Boulevard, Birmingham, AL 35209. *Phone:* 205-802-1200. *Web site:* http://www.vc.edu/.

Virginia College at Huntsville

Huntsville, Alabama

Freshman Application Contact Director of Admission, Virginia College at Huntsville, 2800-A Bob Wallace Avenue, Huntsville, AL 35805. *Phone:* 256-533-7387. *Fax:* 256-533-7785. *Web site:* http://www.vc.edu/.

ALASKA

Alaska Bible College

Glennallen, Alaska

Freshman Application Contact Alaska Bible College, Box 289, Glennallen, AK 99588-0289. *Phone:* 907-822-3201. *Toll-free phone:* 800-478-7884. *Web site:* http://www.akbible.edu/.

Alaska Pacific University

Anchorage, Alaska

- **Independent** comprehensive, founded 1959
- **Urban** 170-acre campus
- **Endowment** $32.5 million
- **Coed**
- **Moderately difficult** entrance level

Faculty *Student/faculty ratio:* 10:1.

Academics *Calendar:* semesters. *Degrees:* certificates, associate, bachelor's, master's, and postbachelor's certificates.

Student Life *Campus security:* 24-hour emergency response devices, student patrols, late-night transport/escort service, controlled dormitory access.

Standardized Tests *Required:* SAT or ACT (for admission).

Costs (2010–11) *Comprehensive fee:* $35,660 includes full-time tuition ($26,250), mandatory fees ($110), and room and board ($9300). Full-time tuition and fees vary according to class time, course load, degree level, location, program, and reciprocity agreements. Part-time tuition: $1100 per semester hour. Part-time tuition and fees vary according to class time, course load, degree level, location, and program. No tuition increase for student's term of enrollment. *Required fees:* $55 per term part-time. *College room only:* $4400. Room and board charges vary according to board plan and housing facility. *Payment plans:* installment, deferred payment.

Financial Aid *Of all full-time matriculated undergraduates who enrolled in 2009,* 213 applied for aid, 196 were judged to have need, 4 had their need fully met. *In 2009,* 8 non-need-based awards were made. *Average percent of need met:* 92. *Average financial aid package:* $15,100. *Average need-based loan:* $4570. *Average need-based gift aid:* $7900. *Average non-need-based aid:* $9570. *Average indebtedness upon graduation:* $43,392.

Applying *Options:* electronic application, deferred entrance. *Application fee:* $25. *Required:* essay or personal statement, high school transcript, minimum 2.5 GPA, 2 letters of recommendation. *Required for some:* interview.

Freshman Application Contact Ms. Jennifer Jensen, Director of Admissions, Alaska Pacific University, 4101 University Drive, Anchorage, AK 99508. *Phone:* 907-564-8248. *Toll-free phone:* 800-252-7528. *Fax:* 907-564-8317. *E-mail:* admissions@alaskapacific.edu. *Web site:* http://www.alaskapacific.edu/.

Charter College

Anchorage, Alaska

Director of Admissions Ms. Lily Sirianni, Vice President, Charter College, 2221 East Northern Lights Boulevard, Suite 120, Anchorage, AK 99508. *Phone:* 907-277-1000. *Toll-free phone:* 800-279-1008. *Web site:* http://www.chartercollege.edu/.

University of Alaska Anchorage

Anchorage, Alaska

- **State-supported** comprehensive, founded 1954, part of University of Alaska System
- **Urban** 428-acre campus
- **Coed**
- **Noncompetitive** entrance level

Academics *Calendar:* semesters. *Degrees:* certificates, associate, bachelor's, master's, post-master's, and postbachelor's certificates.

Student Life *Campus security:* 24-hour emergency response devices and patrols, student patrols, late-night transport/escort service, controlled dormitory access.

Athletics Member NCAA. All Division II.

Standardized Tests *Required:* SAT or ACT (for admission).

Costs (2010–11) *Tuition:* state resident $4410 full-time, $147 per credit part-time; nonresident $15,000 full-time, $500 per credit part-time. Full-time tuition and fees vary according to course level and location. Part-time tuition and fees vary according to course level and location. *Required fees:* $686 full-time, $26 per course part-time, $31 per term part-time. *Room and board:* Room and board charges vary according to board plan and housing facility. *Payment plans:* installment, deferred payment.

Financial Aid *Of all full-time matriculated undergraduates who enrolled in 2009,* 4,356 applied for aid, 3,190 were judged to have need, 517 had their need fully met. *In 2009,* 217 non-need-based awards were made. *Average percent of need met:* 73. *Average financial aid package:* $10,055. *Average need-based loan:* $4042. *Average need-based gift aid:* $4088. *Average non-need-based aid:* $2932. *Average indebtedness upon graduation:* $22,043.

Applying *Options:* deferred entrance. *Application fee:* $50. *Required:* minimum 2 GPA. *Required for some:* high school transcript.

Freshman Application Contact Enrollment Services, University of Alaska Anchorage, PO Box 141629, 3901 Old Seward Highway, Anchorage, AK 99508-8046. *Phone:* 907-786-1480. *Fax:* 907-786-4888. *E-mail:* enroll@uaa.alaska.edu. *Web site:* http://www.uaa.alaska.edu/.

University of Alaska Fairbanks

Fairbanks, Alaska

- **State-supported** university, founded 1917, part of University of Alaska System
- **Small-town** 2250-acre campus
- **Endowment** $60.0 million
- **Coed** 8,652 undergraduate students, 44% full-time, 58% women, 42% men
- **Minimally difficult** entrance level, 77% of applicants were admitted

Undergraduates 3,787 full-time, 4,865 part-time. Students come from 50 states and territories; 53 other countries; 12% are from out of state; 6% transferred in; 20% live on campus. *Retention:* 76% of full-time freshmen returned.

Freshmen *Admission:* 2,012 applied, 1,547 admitted, 1,077 enrolled. *Average high school GPA:* 3.19. *Test scores:* SAT critical reading scores over 500: 64%; SAT math scores over 500: 62%; SAT writing scores over 500: 53%; ACT scores over 18: 74%; SAT critical reading scores over 600: 27%; SAT math scores over 600: 20%; SAT writing scores over 600: 15%; ACT scores over 24: 30%; SAT critical reading scores over 700: 4%; SAT math scores over 700: 2%; SAT writing scores over 700: 1%; ACT scores over 30: 3%.

Faculty *Total:* 1,049, 33% full-time, 43% with terminal degrees. *Student/faculty ratio:* 9:1.

Academics *Calendar:* semesters. *Degrees:* certificates, associate, bachelor's, master's, doctoral-research/scholarship, and postbachelor's certificates. *Special study options:* academic remediation for entering students, accelerated degree program, advanced placement credit, cooperative education, distance learning, double majors, external degree program, honors programs, independent study, internships, off-campus study, part-time degree program, services for LD students, student-designed majors, study abroad, summer session for credit. *ROTC:* Army (b). *Unusual degree programs:* 3-2 engineering; computer science.

Computers on Campus 125 computers/terminals and 22 ports are available on campus for general student use. Students can access the following: campus intranet, computer help desk, free student e-mail accounts, online (class) grades, online (class) registration, online (class) schedules, university portal, campus wireless access. Campuswide network is available. 100% of college-owned or -operated housing units are wired for high-speed Internet access. Wireless service is available via entire campus.

Student Life *Housing options:* coed, disabled students. Campus housing is university owned. Freshman applicants given priority for college housing. *Activities and organizations:* drama/theater group, student-run newspaper, radio and television station, choral group, Alaska Alpine Club, American Indian Science & Engineering Society, Golden Key International Honor Society, Great Alaskan Accounting People, National Society of Collegiate Scholars, national fraternities, national sororities. *Campus security:* 24-hour emergency response devices and patrols, student patrols, late-night transport/escort service, controlled dormitory access, ID check at door of residence halls, crime prevention and safety workshops. *Student services:* health clinic, personal/psychological counseling, women's center, legal services.

Athletics Member NCAA. All Division II except ice hockey (Division I). *Intercollegiate sports:* basketball M(s)/W(s), cross-country running M(s)/W(s), ice hockey M(s), riflery M(s)/W(s), skiing (cross-country) M(s)/W(s), volleyball W(s). *Intramural sports:* archery M(c)/W(c), basketball M/W, bowling M/W, fencing M(c)/W(c), ice hockey M/W, lacrosse M/W, rugby W(c), soccer M/W, swimming and diving M(c)/W(c), ultimate Frisbee M/W, volleyball M/W, water polo M/W.

Standardized Tests *Required:* SAT or ACT (for admission).

Costs (2011–12) *Tuition:* state resident $5115 full-time, $154 per credit part-time; nonresident $16,755 full-time, $542 per credit part-time. Full-time tuition and fees vary according to course level, course load, location, and reciprocity agreements. Part-time tuition and fees vary according to course level, course load, location, and reciprocity agreements. *Required fees:* $960 full-time. *Room and board:* $6960; room only: $3610. Room and board charges vary according to board plan and housing facility. *Payment plan:* installment. *Waivers:* children of alumni, senior citizens, and employees or children of employees.

Financial Aid Of all full-time matriculated undergraduates who enrolled in 2008, 2,402 applied for aid, 1,577 were judged to have need, 527 had their need fully met. 42 Federal Work-Study jobs (averaging $2938). In 2008, 965 non-need-based awards were made. *Average percent of need met:* 57%. *Average financial aid package:* $10,723. *Average need-based loan:* $9105. *Average need-based gift aid:* $5462. *Average non-need-based aid:* $7620. *Average indebtedness upon graduation:* $29,534. *Financial aid deadline:* 7/1.

Applying *Options:* electronic application, deferred entrance. *Application fee:* $50. *Required:* high school transcript, minimum 2.5 GPA. *Application deadlines:* 7/1 (freshmen), 7/1 (out-of-state freshmen), 7/1 (transfers). *Notification:* continuous (freshmen), continuous (out-of-state freshmen), continuous (transfers).

Freshman Application Contact Mike Earnest, Director of Admissions, University of Alaska Fairbanks, PO Box 757480, Fairbanks, AK 99775-7480.

Phone: 907-474-7500. *Toll-free phone:* 800-478-1823. *Fax:* 907-474-5379. *E-mail:* admissions@uaf.edu. *Web site:* http://www.uaf.edu/.

See page 1684 for the College Close-Up.

University of Alaska Southeast
Juneau, Alaska

- **State-supported** comprehensive, founded 1972, part of University of Alaska System
- **Small-town** 198-acre campus
- **Coed** 3,073 undergraduate students, 28% full-time, 65% women, 35% men
- **Noncompetitive** entrance level

Undergraduates 860 full-time, 2,213 part-time. Students come from 42 states and territories; 7 other countries; 11% are from out of state; 8% transferred in; 17% live on campus. *Retention:* 61% of full-time freshmen returned.

Freshmen *Admission:* 655 applied, 294 enrolled. *Average high school GPA:* 2.94. *Test scores:* SAT critical reading scores over 500: 57%; SAT math scores over 500: 59%; SAT writing scores over 500: 49%; SAT critical reading scores over 600: 16%; SAT math scores over 600: 24%; SAT writing scores over 600: 19%; SAT critical reading scores over 700: 8%; SAT math scores over 700: 3%; SAT writing scores over 700: 3%.

Faculty *Total:* 229, 45% full-time, 27% with terminal degrees. *Student/faculty ratio:* 9:1.

Academics *Calendar:* semesters. *Degrees:* certificates, associate, bachelor's, master's, and post-master's certificates. *Special study options:* academic remediation for entering students, adult/continuing education programs, advanced placement credit, cooperative education, distance learning, double majors, independent study, internships, off-campus study, part-time degree program, services for LD students, student-designed majors, study abroad, summer session for credit.

Computers on Campus Students can access the following: campus intranet, computer help desk, free student e-mail accounts, online (class) grades, online (class) registration, online (class) schedules. Campuswide network is available. 100% of college-owned or -operated housing units are wired for high-speed Internet access. Wireless service is available via entire campus.

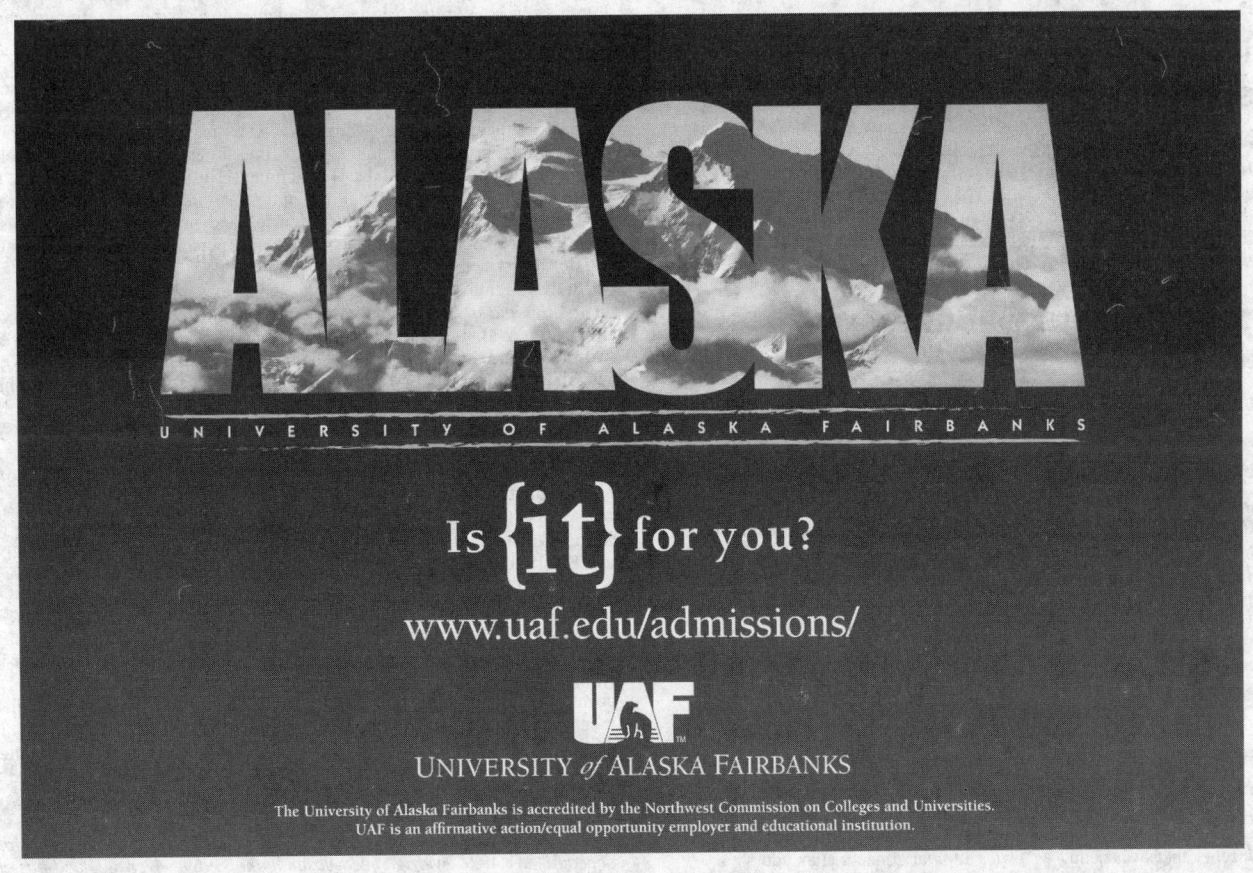

Student Life *Housing options:* coed. Campus housing is university owned. Freshman applicants given priority for college housing. *Activities and organizations:* student-run newspaper, radio station, Wooch.een, Native Student Club, Sustainability Club, Alpha Phi Omega, The Beatniks, UAS Improv Club. *Campus security:* 24-hour emergency response devices and patrols, late-night transport/escort service, controlled dormitory access. *Student services:* health clinic, personal/psychological counseling.

Athletics *Intercollegiate sports:* riflery M(c)/W(c). *Intramural sports:* basketball M/W, rock climbing M(c)/W(c), skiing (cross-country) M(c)/W(c), skiing (downhill) M(c)/W(c), soccer M/W, softball M/W, ultimate Frisbee M/W, volleyball M/W.

Standardized Tests *Recommended:* SAT or ACT (for admission).

Costs (2010–11) *Tuition:* state resident $4410 full-time, $147 per semester hour part-time; nonresident $15,000 full-time, $500 per semester hour part-time. Full-time tuition and fees vary according to course level, course load, and location. Part-time tuition and fees vary according to course level, course load, and location. *Required fees:* $729 full-time, $13 per semester hour part-time, $5 per term part-time. *Room and board:* $8165; room only: $4285. Room and board charges vary according to housing facility and location. *Payment plans:* tuition prepayment, installment. *Waivers:* children of alumni, senior citizens, and employees or children of employees.

Financial Aid Of all full-time matriculated undergraduates who enrolled in 2008, 506 applied for aid, 290 were judged to have need, 21 had their need fully met. 35 Federal Work-Study jobs. In 2008, 48 non-need-based awards were made. *Average percent of need met:* 45%. *Average financial aid package:* $5458. *Average need-based loan:* $2026. *Average need-based gift aid:* $1290. *Average non-need-based aid:* $1196.

Applying *Options:* electronic application, deferred entrance. *Application fee:* $50. *Required:* high school transcript, minimum 2 GPA. *Required for some:* essay or personal statement. *Application deadlines:* 9/9 (freshmen), 9/9 (out-of-state freshmen), 9/9 (transfers). *Notification:* continuous (freshmen), continuous (out-of-state freshmen), continuous (transfers).

Freshman Application Contact Ms. Deema Ferguson, Admissions Clerk, University of Alaska Southeast, 11120 Glacier Highway, Juneau, AK 99801-8625. *Phone:* 907-796-6294 Ext. 6100. *Toll-free phone:* 877-796-4827. *Fax:* 907-796-6365. *E-mail:* admissions@uas.alaska.edu. *Web site:* http://www.uas.alaska.edu/.

ARIZONA

American Indian College of the Assemblies of God, Inc.

Phoenix, Arizona

Director of Admissions Sandra Gonzales, Director of Enrollment Management, American Indian College of the Assemblies of God, Inc., 10020 North Fifteenth Avenue, Phoenix, AZ 85021-2199. *Phone:* 602-944-3335 Ext. 226. *Toll-free phone:* 800-933-3828. *E-mail:* sgonzales@aicag.edu. *Web site:* http://www.aicag.edu/.

Argosy University, Phoenix

Phoenix, Arizona

- **Proprietary** university, founded 1997
- **Urban** campus
- **Coed**

Academics *Calendar:* semesters. *Degrees:* bachelor's, master's, and doctoral-professional.

Costs (2010–11) *Tuition:* Tuition varies by program. Students should contact Argosy University for tuition information.

Freshman Application Contact Argosy University, Phoenix, 2233 West Dunlap Avenue, Phoenix, AZ 85021. *Phone:* 602-216-2600. *Toll-free phone:* 866-216-2777. *Web site:* http://www.argosy.edu/phoenix/.

See page 1002 for the College Close-Up.

Arizona Christian University

Phoenix, Arizona

Freshman Application Contact Rebekah Dubina, Admissions Advisor, Arizona Christian University, 2625 East Cactus Road, Phoenix, AZ 85032. *Phone:* 602-386-4106. *Toll-free phone:* 800-247-2697. *Fax:* 602-404-2159. *E-mail:* rebekah@swcaz.edu. *Web site:* http://arizonachristian.edu/.

Arizona State University

Tempe, Arizona

- **State-supported** university, founded 1885, part of Arizona State University System
- **Urban** 1965-acre campus with easy access to Phoenix
- **Coed** 56,562 undergraduate students, 83% full-time, 51% women, 49% men
- **Moderately difficult** entrance level, 87% of applicants were admitted

Undergraduates 46,994 full-time, 9,568 part-time. Students come from 53 states and territories; 98 other countries; 21% are from out of state; 5% Black or African American, non-Hispanic/Latino; 18% Hispanic/Latino; 6% Asian, non-Hispanic/Latino; 0.1% Native Hawaiian or other Pacific Islander, non-Hispanic/Latino; 2% American Indian or Alaska Native, non-Hispanic/Latino; 1% Two or more races, non-Hispanic/Latino; 3% Race/ethnicity unknown; 3% international; 11% transferred in; 21% live on campus. *Retention:* 84% of full-time freshmen returned.

Freshmen *Admission:* 29,771 applied, 25,795 admitted, 9,544 enrolled. *Average high school GPA:* 3.39. *Test scores:* SAT critical reading scores over 500: 70%; SAT math scores over 500: 74%; ACT scores over 18: 92%; SAT critical reading scores over 600: 28%; SAT math scores over 600: 35%; ACT scores over 24: 51%; SAT critical reading scores over 700: 5%; SAT math scores over 700: 7%; ACT scores over 30: 9%.

Faculty *Total:* 2,705, 94% full-time, 84% with terminal degrees. *Student/faculty ratio:* 24:1.

Academics *Calendar:* semesters. *Degrees:* certificates, bachelor's, master's, doctoral-professional, doctoral-research/scholarship, post-master's, and post-bachelor's certificates (profile includes data for the West, Polytechnic and Downtown Phoenix campuses). *Special study options:* accelerated degree program, adult/continuing education programs, advanced placement credit, cooperative education, distance learning, double majors, English as a second language, freshman honors college, honors programs, independent study, internships, off-campus study, part-time degree program, services for LD students, study abroad, summer session for credit. *ROTC:* Army (b), Navy (b), Air Force (b). *Unusual degree programs:* 3-2 BA/MA Global Health; BA/MA Political Science; BS/MS Biological Science.

Computers on Campus 4,250 computers/terminals are available on campus for general student use. Students can access the following: campus intranet, computer help desk, free student e-mail accounts, online (class) grades, online (class) registration, online (class) schedules. Campuswide network is available. 100% of college-owned or -operated housing units are wired for high-speed Internet access. Wireless service is available via classrooms, computer centers, computer labs, dorm rooms, learning centers, libraries, student centers.

Student Life *Housing:* on-campus residence required for freshman year. *Options:* coed. Campus housing is university owned and leased by the school. Freshman applicants given priority for college housing. *Activities and organizations:* drama/theater group, student-run newspaper, radio and television station, choral group, marching band, Interfraternity Council, Panhellenic Council, Undergraduate Student Government, Business School Council, Residence Hall Association, national fraternities, national sororities. *Campus security:* 24-hour emergency response devices and patrols, late-night transport/escort service. *Student services:* health clinic, personal/psychological counseling, legal services.

Athletics Member NCAA. All Division I except football (Division I-A). *Intercollegiate sports:* baseball M(s), basketball M(s)/W(s), cross-country running M(s)/W(s), golf M(s)/W(s), gymnastics W(s), soccer W(s), softball W(s), swimming and diving M(s)/W(s), tennis W(s), track and field M(s)/W(s), volleyball W(s), water polo W(s), wrestling M(s). *Intramural sports:* badminton M/W, baseball M(c), basketball M/W, cheerleading M(c)/W(c), crew M(c)/W(c), equestrian sports M(c)/W(c), fencing M(c)/W(c), field hockey M(c)/W(c), gymnastics M(c), ice hockey M(c), lacrosse M(c)/W(c), racquetball M(c)/W(c), rugby M(c)/W(c), sailing M(c)/W(c), soccer M(c)/W(c), softball M/W, table tennis M/W, tennis M(c)/W(c), track and field M/W, ultimate Frisbee M(c)/W(c), volleyball M(c)/W, water polo M(c).

Standardized Tests *Required for some:* SAT or ACT (for admission), SAT and SAT Subject Tests or ACT (for admission).

Costs (2010–11) *Tuition:* state resident $7793 full-time, $557 per credit hour part-time; nonresident $20,257 full-time, $844 per credit hour part-time. Full-time tuition and fees vary according to program. Part-time tuition and fees vary according to program. *Required fees:* $339 full-time, $110 per term part-time. *Room and board:* $9706; room only: $5640. Room and board charges vary according to board plan, housing facility, and location. *Payment plan:* installment. *Waivers:* employees or children of employees.

Financial Aid Of all full-time matriculated undergraduates who enrolled in 2008, 26,685 applied for aid, 22,890 were judged to have need, 3,884 had their need fully met. 954 Federal Work-Study jobs (averaging $2087). 6,235 state and other part-time jobs (averaging $3338). In 2008, 6008 non-need-based awards were made. *Average percent of need met:* 60%. *Average financial aid package:* $11,482. *Average need-based loan:* $3969. *Average need-based gift*

aid: $8016. *Average non-need-based aid:* $7722. *Average indebtedness upon graduation:* $18,542.

Applying *Options:* electronic application. *Application fee:* $50. *Required:* high school transcript, minimum 3 GPA. *Required for some:* application fee is $65 for nonresidents. *Application deadlines:* rolling (freshmen), rolling (transfers). *Notification:* continuous (freshmen), continuous (transfers).

Freshman Application Contact Arizona State University, PO Box 870112, Tempe, AZ 85287-0112. *Phone:* 480-965-7788. *Fax:* 480-965-3610. *E-mail:* admissions@asu.edu. *Web site:* http://www.asu.edu/.

The Art Center Design College
Tucson, Arizona

- **Proprietary** 4-year, founded 1983
- **Suburban** campus with easy access to Tucson
- **Coed**
- **Moderately difficult** entrance level

Academics *Calendar:* semester with a full summer program. *Degrees:* associate and bachelor's.

Standardized Tests *Required for some:* ACT ASSET.

Costs (2010–11) *One-time required fee:* $125. *Tuition:* $18,360 full-time, $765 per credit hour part-time. Full-time tuition and fees vary according to course load, location, and program. Part-time tuition and fees vary according to location and program. No tuition increase for student's term of enrollment. *Payment plans:* tuition prepayment, installment.

Applying *Application fee:* $25. *Required:* essay or personal statement, high school transcript, interview.

Freshman Application Contact Sarah LaVetter, Director of Admissions, The Art Center Design College, 2525 North Country Club Road, Tucson, AZ 85716-2505. *Phone:* 520-325-0123. *Toll-free phone:* 800-825-8753. *Fax:* 520-325-5535. *Web site:* http://www.theartcenter.edu/.

The Art Institute of Phoenix
Phoenix, Arizona

- **Proprietary** 4-year, founded 1995, part of Education Management Corporation
- **Suburban** campus
- **Coed**

Academics *Calendar:* quarters. *Degrees:* diplomas, associate, and bachelor's.

Costs (2010–11) *Tuition:* Tuition cost varies by program. Prospective students should contact the school for current tuition costs. Other charges include a starting kit for all first-quarter students. Kits vary in price, depending on the program of study.

Freshman Application Contact The Art Institute of Phoenix, 2233 West Dunlap Avenue, Phoenix, AZ 85021-2859. *Phone:* 602-331-7500. *Toll-free phone:* 800-474-2479. *Web site:* http://www.artinstitutes.edu/phoenix/.

See page 1056 for the College Close-Up.

The Art Institute of Tucson
Tucson, Arizona

- **Proprietary** 4-year, founded 2007
- **Coed**

Academics *Degrees:* associate and bachelor's.

Costs (2010–11) *Tuition:* Tuition cost varies by program. Prospective students should contact the school for current tuition costs. Other charges include a starting kit for all first-quarter students. Kits vary in price, depending on the program of study.

Freshman Application Contact The Art Institute of Tucson, 5099 East Grant Road, Suite 100, Tucson, AZ 85712. *Phone:* 520-318-2700. *Toll-free phone:* 866-690-8850. *Web site:* http://www.artinstitutes.edu/tucson/.

See page 1074 for the College Close-Up.

Brookline College
Phoenix, Arizona

- **Proprietary** 4-year, founded 1979
- **Urban** campus with easy access to Phoenix
- **Coed** 1,072 undergraduate students, 100% full-time, 81% women, 19% men
- **Noncompetitive** entrance level

Undergraduates 1,072 full-time.

Faculty *Total:* 43, 51% full-time, 14% with terminal degrees. *Student/faculty ratio:* 25:1.

Academics *Calendar:* continuous. *Degrees:* certificates, diplomas, associate, and bachelor's. *Special study options:* accelerated degree program, distance learning, part-time degree program.

Computers on Campus 25 computers/terminals are available on campus for general student use. Students can access the following: campus intranet, computer help desk. Campuswide network is available.

Student Life *Housing:* college housing not available. *Campus security:* 24-hour emergency response devices.

Costs (2011–12) *Tuition:* $13,000 full-time. Full-time tuition and fees vary according to degree level and program. No tuition increase for student's term of enrollment. *Payment plan:* installment.

Applying *Options:* electronic application. *Required:* interview. *Application deadlines:* rolling (freshmen), rolling (out-of-state freshmen), rolling (transfers). *Notification:* continuous (freshmen), continuous (out-of-state freshmen), continuous (transfers).

Freshman Application Contact Ms. Theresa Dean, Director of Admissions, Brookline College, 2445 West Dunlap Avenue, Suite 100, Phoenix, AZ 85021. *Phone:* 602-242-6265. *Toll-free phone:* 800-793-2428. *Fax:* 602-973-2572. *E-mail:* tdean@brooklinecollege.edu. *Web site:* http://brooklinecollege.edu/.

Brookline College
Tempe, Arizona

- **Proprietary** 4-year, founded 1982
- **Urban** campus with easy access to Phoenix
- **Coed** 415 undergraduate students, 100% full-time, 78% women, 22% men
- **Noncompetitive** entrance level

Undergraduates 415 full-time.

Faculty *Total:* 37, 41% full-time, 14% with terminal degrees. *Student/faculty ratio:* 11:1.

Academics *Calendar:* continuous. *Degree:* diplomas and associate. *Special study options:* accelerated degree program, part-time degree program.

Computers on Campus 20 computers/terminals are available on campus for general student use. Students can access the following: campus intranet, computer help desk. Campuswide network is available.

Student Life *Housing:* college housing not available. *Campus security:* 24-hour emergency response devices.

Costs (2011–12) *Tuition:* $13,000 full-time. Full-time tuition and fees vary according to degree level and program. No tuition increase for student's term of enrollment. *Payment plan:* installment.

Applying *Options:* electronic application. *Required:* interview. *Application deadlines:* rolling (freshmen), rolling (out-of-state freshmen), rolling (transfers). *Notification:* continuous (freshmen), continuous (out-of-state freshmen), continuous (transfers).

Freshman Application Contact Ms. Cheryl Kindred, Campus Director, Brookline College, 1140-1150 South Priest Drive, Tempe, AZ 85281. *Phone:* 480-545-8755. *Toll-free phone:* 888-886-2428. *Fax:* 480-926-1371. *E-mail:* ckindred@brooklinecollege.edu. *Web site:* http://brooklinecollege.edu/.

Brookline College
Tucson, Arizona

- **Proprietary** 4-year, founded 1979
- **Urban** campus with easy access to Tucson
- **Coed** 645 undergraduate students, 100% full-time, 69% women, 31% men
- **Noncompetitive** entrance level

Undergraduates 645 full-time.

Faculty *Total:* 41, 56% full-time, 5% with terminal degrees. *Student/faculty ratio:* 16:1.

Academics *Calendar:* continuous. *Degree:* diplomas and associate. *Special study options:* accelerated degree program, part-time degree program.

Computers on Campus 25 computers/terminals are available on campus for general student use. Students can access the following: campus intranet, computer help desk. Campuswide network is available.

Student Life *Housing:* college housing not available. *Campus security:* 24-hour emergency response devices.

Costs (2011–12) *Tuition:* $13,000 full-time. Full-time tuition and fees vary according to degree level and program. No tuition increase for student's term of enrollment. *Payment plan:* installment.

Applying *Options:* electronic application. *Required:* interview. *Application deadlines:* rolling (freshmen), rolling (out-of-state freshmen), rolling (transfers). *Notification:* continuous (freshmen), continuous (out-of-state freshmen), continuous (transfers).

Freshman Application Contact Ms. Leigh Anne Pechota, Campus Director, Brookline College, 5441 East 22nd Street, Suite 125, Tucson, AZ 85711. *Phone:* 520-748-9799. *Toll-free phone:* 888-292-2428. *Fax:* 520-748-9355. *E-mail:* lpechota@brooklinecollege.edu. *Web site:* http://brooklinecollege.edu/.

Brown Mackie College–Phoenix

Phoenix, Arizona

- **Proprietary** primarily 2-year, part of Education Management Corporation
- **Coed**

Academics *Degrees:* diplomas, associate, and bachelor's.

Costs (2010–11) *Tuition:* Tuition varies by program. Students should contact Brown Mackie College for tuition information.

Freshman Application Contact Brown Mackie College–Phoenix, 13430 North Black Canyon Highway, Suite 190, Phoenix, AZ 85029. *Phone:* 602-337-3044. *Toll-free phone:* 866-824-4793. *Web site:* http://www.brownmackie.edu/phoenix/.

See page 1158 for the College Close-Up.

Brown Mackie College–Tucson

Tucson, Arizona

- **Proprietary** primarily 2-year, founded 1972, part of Education Management Corporation
- **Suburban** campus
- **Coed**

Academics *Degrees:* diplomas, associate, and bachelor's.

Costs (2010–11) *Tuition:* Tuition varies by program. Students should contact Brown Mackie College for tuition information.

Freshman Application Contact Brown Mackie College–Tucson, 4585 East Speedway, Suite 204, Tucson, AZ 85712. *Phone:* 520-319-3300. *Web site:* http://www.brownmackie.edu/tucson/.

See page 1166 for the College Close-Up.

CollegeAmerica–Flagstaff

Flagstaff, Arizona

- **Proprietary** primarily 2-year
- **Coed** 300 undergraduate students
- **Noncompetitive** entrance level

Undergraduates *Retention:* 60% of full-time freshmen returned.

Faculty *Student/faculty ratio:* 33:1.

Academics *Degrees:* associate and bachelor's.

Freshman Application Contact CollegeAmerica–Flagstaff, 3012 East Route 66, Flagstaff, AZ 86004. *Phone:* 928-213-6060. *Toll-free phone:* 800-622-2894. *Web site:* http://www.collegeamerica.edu/.

College of the Humanities and Sciences, Harrison Middleton University

Tempe, Arizona

- **Independent** comprehensive, founded 1998
- **Suburban** campus with easy access to Phoenix
- **Coed** 100 undergraduate students, 100% full-time, 54% women, 46% men

Undergraduates 100 full-time.

Faculty *Total:* 23, 74% full-time, 43% with terminal degrees.

Academics *Calendar:* continuous. *Degrees:* diplomas, associate, bachelor's, master's, doctoral-other, and doctoral-professional. *Special study options:* advanced placement credit, distance learning, double majors, independent study, student-designed majors, summer session for credit.

Costs (2010–11) *One-time required fee:* $350. *Tuition:* $250 per credit hour part-time. *Payment plan:* installment.

Applying *Options:* electronic application. *Application fee:* $50. *Required:* high school transcript, interview. *Application deadlines:* rolling (freshmen), rolling (out-of-state freshmen), rolling (transfers). *Notification:* continuous (freshmen), continuous (out-of-state freshmen), continuous (transfers).

Freshman Application Contact College of the Humanities and Sciences, Harrison Middleton University, 1105 East Broadway, Tempe, AZ 85282. *Toll-free phone:* 877-248-6724. *Web site:* http://www.hmu.edu/.

Collins College

Tempe, Arizona

- **Proprietary** 4-year, founded 1978, part of Career Education Corporation
- **Urban** 3-acre campus with easy access to Phoenix
- **Coed** 1,287 undergraduate students, 100% full-time, 23% women, 77% men

Undergraduates 1,287 full-time. Students come from 52 states and territories; 2 other countries.

Academics *Calendar:* trimesters. *Degrees:* associate and bachelor's.

Computers on Campus Students can access the following: computer help desk. Wireless service is available via entire campus.

Standardized Tests *Recommended:* SAT and SAT Subject Tests or ACT (for admission).

Financial Aid Of all full-time matriculated undergraduates who enrolled in 2007, 935 applied for aid, 935 were judged to have need, 27 had their need fully met. 65 Federal Work-Study jobs (averaging $3000). In 2007, 4 non-need-based awards were made. *Average percent of need met:* 65%. *Average financial aid package:* $5287. *Average need-based loan:* $3513. *Average need-based gift aid:* $3014. *Average non-need-based aid:* $750.

Applying *Options:* early admission, deferred entrance. *Application fee:* $50. *Required:* high school transcript, interview. *Application deadlines:* rolling (freshmen), rolling (transfers). *Notification:* continuous (freshmen), continuous (transfers).

Freshman Application Contact Admissions Department, Collins College, 4750 South 44th Place, Phoenix, AZ 85040. *Phone:* 480-966-3000. *Toll-free phone:* 800-876-7070. *Fax:* 480-966-2599. *E-mail:* contact@collinscollege.edu. *Web site:* http://www.collinscollege.edu/.

DeVry University

Mesa, Arizona

Admissions Office Contact DeVry University, 1201 South Alma School Road, Mesa, AZ 85210-2011. *Web site:* http://www.devry.edu/.

DeVry University

Phoenix, Arizona

- **Proprietary** comprehensive, founded 1967, part of DeVry University
- **Urban** 18-acre campus
- **Coed** 1,634 undergraduate students, 50% full-time, 29% women, 71% men
- **Minimally difficult** entrance level

Undergraduates 822 full-time, 812 part-time. 5% are from out of state; 7% Black or African American, non-Hispanic/Latino; 25% Hispanic/Latino; 3% Asian, non-Hispanic/Latino; 0.5% Native Hawaiian or other Pacific Islander, non-Hispanic/Latino; 3% American Indian or Alaska Native, non-Hispanic/Latino; 0.6% Two or more races, non-Hispanic/Latino; 20% Race/ethnicity unknown; 0.2% international; 22% transferred in.

Freshmen *Admission:* 395 enrolled.

Faculty *Total:* 120, 29% full-time. *Student/faculty ratio:* 19:1.

Academics *Calendar:* semesters. *Degrees:* associate, bachelor's, and master's. *Special study options:* academic remediation for entering students, accelerated degree program, adult/continuing education programs, advanced placement credit, distance learning, part-time degree program, services for LD students, summer session for credit.

Computers on Campus Students can access the following: online (class) registration. Campuswide network is available.

Student Life *Housing:* college housing not available. *Campus security:* 24-hour emergency response devices, student patrols, late-night transport/escort service, trained security personnel on duty, lighted pathways/sidewalks.

Costs (2010–11) *Tuition:* $14,766 full-time, $580 per credit hour part-time. Full-time tuition and fees vary according to course load. Part-time tuition and fees vary according to course load. *Required fees:* $60 full-time, $30 per term part-time. *Payment plans:* installment, deferred payment. *Waivers:* employees or children of employees.

Financial Aid Of all full-time matriculated undergraduates who enrolled in 2007, 435 applied for aid, 414 were judged to have need, 32 had their need fully met. In 2007, 34 non-need-based awards were made. *Average percent of need met:* 43%. *Average financial aid package:* $13,557. *Average need-based loan:* $8565. *Average need-based gift aid:* $6253. *Average non-need-based aid:* $15,538. *Average indebtedness upon graduation:* $20,667.

Applying *Options:* electronic application, early admission, deferred entrance. *Application fee:* $50. *Required:* high school transcript, interview. *Application deadlines:* rolling (freshmen), rolling (transfers). *Notification:* continuous (freshmen), continuous (transfers).

Freshman Application Contact DeVry University, 2149 West Dunlap Avenue, Phoenix, AZ 85021-2995. *Phone:* 602-870-9222. *Web site:* http://www.devry.edu/.

Dunlap-Stone University

Phoenix, Arizona

- **Proprietary** 4-year, founded 1995
- **Urban** campus with easy access to Phoenix
- **Coed**

Faculty *Student/faculty ratio:* 15:1.

Academics *Calendar:* semesters 3 semesters per year (fall, spring, summer). *Degrees:* certificates, associate, and bachelor's.

Costs (2010–11) *Tuition:* $7800 full-time, $310 per credit hour part-time. Full-time tuition and fees vary according to course level, course load, degree level, and program. Part-time tuition and fees vary according to course level, course load, degree level, and program. No tuition increase for student's term of enrollment. *Required fees:* $50 full-time.

Applying *Options:* electronic application, deferred entrance.

Freshman Application Contact Dunlap-Stone University, 11225 North 28th Drive, Suite B-201, Phoenix, AZ 85029. *Phone:* 602-648-5750. *Toll-free phone:* 800-474-8013. *Web site:* http://www.dunlap-stone.edu/.

Embry-Riddle Aeronautical University–Prescott

Prescott, Arizona

- **Independent** comprehensive, founded 1978
- **Small-town** 547-acre campus with easy access to Phoenix
- **Endowment** $63.9 million
- **Coed** 1,654 undergraduate students, 93% full-time, 17% women, 83% men
- **Moderately difficult** entrance level, 82% of applicants were admitted

Undergraduates 1,541 full-time, 113 part-time. Students come from 49 states and territories; 27 other countries; 75% are from out of state; 2% Black or African American, non-Hispanic/Latino; 9% Hispanic/Latino; 6% Asian, non-Hispanic/Latino; 0.5% Native Hawaiian or other Pacific Islander, non-Hispanic/Latino; 1% American Indian or Alaska Native, non-Hispanic/Latino; 4% Two or more races, non-Hispanic/Latino; 7% Race/ethnicity unknown; 4% international; 8% transferred in; 45% live on campus. *Retention:* 78% of full-time freshmen returned.

Freshmen *Admission:* 1,439 applied, 1,179 admitted, 354 enrolled. *Average high school GPA:* 3.55. *Test scores:* SAT critical reading scores over 500: 70%; SAT math scores over 500: 79%; ACT scores over 18: 94%; SAT critical reading scores over 600: 27%; SAT math scores over 600: 47%; ACT scores over 24: 69%; SAT critical reading scores over 700: 4%; SAT math scores over 700: 7%; ACT scores over 30: 18%.

Faculty *Total:* 111, 73% full-time, 58% with terminal degrees. *Student/faculty ratio:* 17:1.

Academics *Calendar:* semesters. *Degrees:* bachelor's and master's. *Special study options:* academic remediation for entering students, accelerated degree program, adult/continuing education programs, advanced placement credit, cooperative education, distance learning, double majors, English as a second language, honors programs, independent study, internships, part-time degree program, services for LD students, student-designed majors, study abroad, summer session for credit. *ROTC:* Army (b), Air Force (b).

Computers on Campus 470 computers/terminals are available on campus for general student use. Students can access the following: campus intranet, computer help desk, free student e-mail accounts, online (class) grades, online (class) registration, online (class) schedules. Campuswide network is available. 100% of college-owned or -operated housing units are wired for high-speed Internet access. Wireless service is available via entire campus.

Student Life *Housing:* on-campus residence required for freshman year. *Options:* coed. Campus housing is university owned. Freshman campus housing is guaranteed. *Activities and organizations:* student-run newspaper, radio and television station, Hawaii Club, Strike Eagles, Theta XI, American Institute of Aeronautics and Astronautics (AIAA), Arnold Air Society, national fraternities, national sororities. *Campus security:* 24-hour emergency response devices and patrols, student patrols, late-night transport/escort service. *Student services:* health clinic, personal/psychological counseling.

Athletics Member NAIA. *Intercollegiate sports:* soccer M(s)/W(s), volleyball W(s), wrestling M(s). *Intramural sports:* basketball M/W, bowling M/W, racquetball M/W, soccer M/W, softball M/W, table tennis M/W, tennis M/W, volleyball M/W.

Standardized Tests *Required:* SAT and SAT Subject Tests or ACT (for admission).

Costs (2011–12) *Comprehensive fee:* $38,572 includes full-time tuition ($28,860), mandatory fees ($812), and room and board ($8900). Part-time tuition: $1195 per credit hour. *College room only:* $5000. Room and board charges vary according to board plan and housing facility. *Payment plans:* installment, deferred payment. *Waivers:* employees or children of employees.

Financial Aid Of all full-time matriculated undergraduates who enrolled in 2009, 1,143 applied for aid, 1,014 were judged to have need. 69 Federal Work-Study jobs (averaging $1077). 448 state and other part-time jobs (averaging $1378). *Average financial aid package:* $20,161. *Average need-based loan:* $4970. *Average need-based gift aid:* $11,989.

Applying *Options:* electronic application, deferred entrance. *Application fee:* $50. *Required:* high school transcript, minimum 2 GPA, 2 letters of recommendation, medical examination for flight students. *Required for some:* minimum 3 GPA. *Recommended:* essay or personal statement, interview. *Application deadlines:* rolling (freshmen), rolling (transfers). *Notification:* continuous (freshmen), continuous (transfers).

Freshman Application Contact Debra Cates-Foster, Director of Admissions, Embry-Riddle Aeronautical University–Prescott, 3700 Willow Creek Road, Prescott, AZ 86301-3720. *Phone:* 928-777-6600. *Toll-free phone:* 800-888-3728. *Fax:* 928-777-6606. *E-mail:* pradmit@erau.edu. *Web site:* http://www.embryriddle.edu/.

Everest College

Phoenix, Arizona

Freshman Application Contact Mr. Jim Askins, Director of Admissions, Everest College, 10400 North 25th Avenue, Suite 190, Phoenix, AZ 85021. *Phone:* 602-942-4141. *Fax:* 602-943-0960. *E-mail:* jaskins@cci.edu. *Web site:* http://www.everest.edu/.

Everest Online

Tempe, Arizona

Admissions Office Contact Everest Online, 8150 South Hardy Drive #102, Tempe, AZ 85284-1117. *Web site:* http://www.everestonline.edu/.

Grand Canyon University

Phoenix, Arizona

- **Independent Southern Baptist** comprehensive, founded 1949
- **Urban** 90-acre campus with easy access to Phoenix
- **Coed**
- **Moderately difficult** entrance level

Undergraduates 40% live on campus.

Freshmen *Admission:* 841 admitted.

Academics *Calendar:* semesters. *Degrees:* bachelor's, master's, doctoral-research/scholarship, and post-master's certificates. *Special study options:* academic remediation for entering students, accelerated degree program, adult/continuing education programs, advanced placement credit, cooperative education, distance learning, double majors, English as a second language, freshman honors college, honors programs, independent study, internships, off-campus study, part-time degree program, study abroad, summer session for credit. *ROTC:* Army (b), Air Force (c).

Computers on Campus 65 computers/terminals are available on campus for general student use. Students can access the following: campus intranet, computer help desk, free student e-mail accounts, online (class) grades, online (class) registration, online (class) schedules. Campuswide network is available. 100% of college-owned or -operated housing units are wired for high-speed Internet access. Wireless service is available via classrooms, computer centers, computer labs, dorm rooms, learning centers, libraries, student centers.

Student Life *Housing:* on-campus residence required through sophomore year. *Options:* men-only, women-only, disabled students. Campus housing is university owned and leased by the school. *Activities and organizations:* drama/theater group, choral group, International Student Association, Fellowship of Christian Athletes, Student Nurses Association, Canyon Crazies, AZ Hosa. *Campus security:* 24-hour emergency response devices and patrols, late-night transport/escort service, controlled dormitory access. *Student services:* health clinic, personal/psychological counseling.

Athletics Member NCAA. All Division II. *Intercollegiate sports:* baseball M(s), basketball M(s)/W(s), cross-country running M(s)/W(s), golf M(s)/W(s), lacrosse M(c), soccer M(s)/W(s), softball W(s), swimming and diving M(s)/W(s), tennis W(s), volleyball M(s)/W(s), wrestling M(s). *Intramural sports:* basketball M/W, football M/W, softball M/W, volleyball M/W.

Standardized Tests *Recommended:* SAT or ACT (for admission).

Costs (2011–12) *Comprehensive fee:* $30,000 includes full-time tuition ($16,500), mandatory fees ($1500), and room and board ($12,000). Full-time tuition and fees vary according to course load and location. Part-time tuition: $688 per credit. Part-time tuition and fees vary according to course load and location. *Room and board:* Room and board charges vary according to board plan and housing facility. *Payment plan:* installment. *Waivers:* employees or children of employees.

Financial Aid Of all full-time matriculated undergraduates who enrolled in 2007, 1,102 applied for aid, 942 were judged to have need, 155 had their need fully met. *Average financial aid package:* $3371. *Average need-based loan:* $3701. *Average need-based gift aid:* $3360.

Applying *Options:* electronic application, early admission, deferred entrance. *Required:* high school transcript, minimum 2.25 GPA. *Application deadlines:* rolling (freshmen), rolling (transfers). *Notification:* continuous (freshmen), continuous until 9/1 (transfers).
Freshman Application Contact Enrollment, Grand Canyon University, 3300 West Camelback Road, PO Box 11097, Phoenix, AZ 86017-3030. *Phone:* 800-486-7085. *Toll-free phone:* 800-800-9776. *E-mail:* admissionsonline@ gcu.edu. *Web site:* http://www.gcu.edu/.

High-Tech Institute

Phoenix, Arizona

Freshman Application Contact Mr. Glen Husband, Vice President of Admissions, High-Tech Institute, 1515 East Indian School Road, Phoenix, AZ 85014-4901. *Phone:* 602-279-9700. *Web site:* http://www.high-techinstitute.com/.

International Baptist College

Chandler, Arizona

Freshman Application Contact Director of Admissions, International Baptist College, 2211 West Germann Road, Chandler, AZ 85286. *Phone:* 480-245-7970. *Toll-free phone:* 800-422-4858. *E-mail:* admissions@ibconline.edu. *Web site:* http://www.ibconline.edu/ibc/.

ITT Technical Institute

Phoenix, Arizona

- **Proprietary** primarily 2-year, founded 1972, part of ITT Educational Services, Inc.
- **Urban** campus
- **Coed**
- **Minimally difficult** entrance level

Academics *Calendar:* quarters. *Degrees:* associate and bachelor's.
Student Life *Housing:* college housing not available.
Financial Aid Of all full-time matriculated undergraduates who enrolled in 2009, 10 Federal Work-Study jobs (averaging $4000).
Freshman Application Contact Director of Recruitment, ITT Technical Institute, 10220 North 25th Avenue, Suite 100, Phoenix, AZ 85021. *Phone:* 602-749-7900. *Toll-free phone:* 877-221-1132. *Web site:* http://www.itt-tech.edu/.

ITT Technical Institute

Tempe, Arizona

- **Proprietary** 4-year, founded 1963, part of ITT Educational Services, Inc.
- **Coed**
- **Minimally difficult** entrance level

Academics *Degrees:* associate and bachelor's.
Student Life *Housing:* college housing not available.
Freshman Application Contact Director of Recruitment, ITT Technical Institute, 5005 S. Wendler Drive, Tempe, AZ 85282. *Phone:* 602-437-7500. *Toll-free phone:* 800-879-4881. *Web site:* http://www.itt-tech.edu/.

ITT Technical Institute

Tucson, Arizona

- **Proprietary** primarily 2-year, founded 1984, part of ITT Educational Services, Inc.
- **Urban** campus
- **Coed**
- **Minimally difficult** entrance level

Academics *Calendar:* quarters. *Degrees:* associate and bachelor's.
Student Life *Housing:* college housing not available.
Freshman Application Contact Director of Recruitment, ITT Technical Institute, 1455 West River Road, Tucson, AZ 85704. *Phone:* 520-408-7488. *Toll-free phone:* 800-870-9730. *Web site:* http://www.itt-tech.edu/.

National Paralegal College

Phoenix, Arizona

Freshman Application Contact Admissions Office, National Paralegal College, 6516 N 7th Street, Suite 103, Phoenix, AZ 85014. *Phone:* 845-371-9101. *Toll-free phone:* 800-371-6105. *Fax:* 866-347-2744. *E-mail:* info@ nationalparalegal.edu. *Web site:* http://nationalparalegal.edu/.

Northcentral University

Prescott Valley, Arizona

- **Proprietary** comprehensive
- **Coed** 402 undergraduate students, 100% full-time, 55% women, 45% men
- **Minimally difficult** entrance level

Undergraduates 402 full-time. Students come from 45 states and territories; 8 other countries.
Faculty *Total:* 470, 5% full-time, 89% with terminal degrees. *Student/faculty ratio:* 19:1.
Academics *Calendar:* continuous. *Degrees:* certificates, bachelor's, master's, doctoral-professional, doctoral-research/scholarship, and post-master's certificates (offers only distance learning programs). *Special study options:* accelerated degree program, distance learning, external degree program, services for LD students.
Computers on Campus Students can access the following: campus intranet, computer help desk, online (class) grades, online (class) registration, online (class) schedules. Campuswide network is available.
Costs (2011–12) *Tuition:* $8800 full-time. *Payment plans:* tuition prepayment, installment. *Waivers:* employees or children of employees.
Applying *Options:* electronic application. *Required:* essay or personal statement, high school transcript. *Application deadlines:* rolling (freshmen), rolling (transfers). *Notification:* continuous (freshmen), continuous (transfers).
Freshman Application Contact Northcentral University, 10000 East University Drive, Prescott Valley, AZ 86314. *Phone:* 888-327-2877 Ext. 8083. *Toll-free phone:* 888-327-2877. *Web site:* http://www.ncu.edu/.

Northern Arizona University

Flagstaff, Arizona

- **State-supported** university, founded 1899, part of Arizona State University System, under the Arizona Board of Regents
- **Small-town** 740-acre campus
- **Endowment** $79.4 million
- **Coed** 20,194 undergraduate students, 85% full-time, 58% women, 42% men
- **Moderately difficult** entrance level, 65% of applicants were admitted

Undergraduates 17,081 full-time, 3,113 part-time. Students come from 52 states and territories; 54 other countries; 22% are from out of state; 3% Black or African American, non-Hispanic/Latino; 16% Hispanic/Latino; 2% Asian, non-Hispanic/Latino; 0.5% Native Hawaiian or other Pacific Islander, non-Hispanic/Latino; 5% American Indian or Alaska Native, non-Hispanic/Latino; 2% Two or more races, non-Hispanic/Latino; 1% Race/ethnicity unknown; 4% international; 11% transferred in; 35% live on campus. *Retention:* 71% of full-time freshmen returned.
Freshmen *Admission:* 31,773 applied, 20,724 admitted, 4,132 enrolled. *Average high school GPA:* 3.4. *Test scores:* SAT critical reading scores over 500: 65%; SAT math scores over 500: 67%; SAT writing scores over 500: 52%; ACT scores over 18: 90%; SAT critical reading scores over 600: 21%; SAT math scores over 600: 23%; SAT writing scores over 600: 8%; ACT scores over 24: 44%; SAT critical reading scores over 700: 3%; SAT math scores over 700: 2%; SAT writing scores over 700: 1%; ACT scores over 30: 4%.
Faculty *Total:* 1,501, 56% full-time. *Student/faculty ratio:* 20:1.
Academics *Calendar:* semesters. *Degrees:* certificates, bachelor's, master's, doctoral-professional, doctoral-research/scholarship, and postbachelor's certificates. *Special study options:* accelerated degree program, advanced placement credit, cooperative education, distance learning, double majors, English as a second language, freshman honors college, honors programs, independent study, internships, off-campus study, part-time degree program, services for LD students, study abroad, summer session for credit. *ROTC:* Army (b), Air Force (b).
Computers on Campus 400 computers/terminals are available on campus for general student use. Students can access the following: campus intranet, computer help desk, free student e-mail accounts, online (class) grades, online (class) registration, online (class) schedules. Campuswide network is available. 100% of college-owned or -operated housing units are wired for high-speed Internet access. Wireless service is available via entire campus.
Student Life *Housing options:* coed, men-only, women-only. Campus housing is university owned. Freshman campus housing is guaranteed. *Activities and organizations:* drama/theater group, student-run newspaper, radio and television station, choral group, marching band, national fraternities, national sororities. *Campus security:* 24-hour emergency response devices and patrols, late-night transport/escort service, controlled dormitory access. *Student services:* health clinic, personal/psychological counseling.
Athletics Member NCAA. All Division I. *Intercollegiate sports:* basketball M(s)/W(s), cheerleading M/W, cross-country running M(s)/W(s), football M(s), golf W(s), soccer W(s), swimming and diving W(s), tennis M(s)/W(s), track and field M(s)/W(s), volleyball W(s). *Intramural sports:* baseball M(c),

basketball M/W, cross-country running M/W, fencing M(c)/W(c), football M/W, gymnastics M(c)/W(c), ice hockey M(c), lacrosse M(c)/W(c), racquetball M(c)/W(c), rugby M(c)/W(c), skiing (downhill) M(c)/W(c), soccer M/W, softball M/W, swimming and diving M/W, tennis M/W, ultimate Frisbee M/W, volleyball M/W, water polo M(c)/W(c), weight lifting M/W, wrestling M(c).

Standardized Tests *Required for some:* SAT (for admission), ACT (for admission), SAT or ACT (for admission), SAT and SAT Subject Tests or ACT (for admission), SAT Subject Tests (for admission), ACT/SAT test scores required for home-schooled students.

Costs (2010–11) *Tuition:* state resident $6964 full-time, $497 per credit part-time; nonresident $19,364 full-time, $807 per credit part-time. Full-time tuition and fees vary according to degree level, location, and program. Part-time tuition and fees vary according to course load, degree level, location, and program. No tuition increase for student's term of enrollment. *Required fees:* $703 full-time, $6 per credit part-time, $282 per term part-time. *Room and board:* $8072; room only: $4480. Room and board charges vary according to board plan and housing facility. *Payment plan:* installment. *Waivers:* employees or children of employees.

Financial Aid Of all full-time matriculated undergraduates who enrolled in 2008, 9,621 applied for aid, 7,118 were judged to have need, 1,040 had their need fully met. In 2008, 2263 non-need-based awards were made. *Average percent of need met:* 65%. *Average financial aid package:* $8729. *Average need-based loan:* $3947. *Average need-based gift aid:* $5592. *Average non-need-based aid:* $3443. *Average indebtedness upon graduation:* $16,703.

Applying *Options:* electronic application, deferred entrance. *Application fee:* $25. *Required:* high school transcript, minimum 3 GPA. *Application deadlines:* rolling (freshmen), rolling (out-of-state freshmen), rolling (transfers). *Notification:* continuous (freshmen), continuous (out-of-state freshmen), continuous (transfers).

Freshman Application Contact James Casebeer, Associate Director, Northern Arizona University, PO Box 4084, Flagstaff, AZ 86011. *Phone:* 928-523-6080. *Toll-free phone:* 888-MORE-NAU. *Fax:* 928-523-1230. *E-mail:* Undergraduate.Admissions@nau.edu. *Web site:* http://www.nau.edu/.

Northern Arizona University–Yuma

Yuma, Arizona

Director of Admissions Eileen Knight, Associate Director of Admissions, Northern Arizona University–Yuma, 2020 South Avenue 8E, PO Box 6236, Yuma, AZ 85365. *Phone:* 928-317-6431. *Toll-free phone:* 888-NAU-Yuma. *E-mail:* eileen.knight@nau.edu. *Web site:* http://www.yuma.nau.edu/.

Penn Foster College

Scottsdale, Arizona

- **Proprietary** 4-year
- **Coed**

Faculty *Total:* 63, 49% full-time.

Academics *Degrees:* certificates, associate, and bachelor's. *Special study options:* academic remediation for entering students, accelerated degree program, cooperative education, distance learning, external degree program, independent study, internships, off-campus study, part-time degree program, services for LD students.

Computers on Campus Students can access the following: online (class) grades, online (class) registration.

Costs (2011–12) *One-time required fee:* $200. *Tuition:* $90 per credit part-time. Part-time tuition and fees vary according to course load and student level. *Payment plan:* installment.

Applying *Options:* electronic application. *Application fee:* $75. *Required:* high school transcript. *Application deadlines:* rolling (freshmen), rolling (out-of-state freshmen).

Freshman Application Contact Admissions, Penn Foster College, 14300 North Northsight Boulevard, Suite 120, Scottsdale, AZ 85260. *Phone:* 480-315-4950. *Toll-free phone:* 800-471-3232. *Web site:* http://www.pennfostercollege.edu/.

Pima Medical Institute

Mesa, Arizona

- **Proprietary** primarily 2-year, founded 1985, part of Vocational Training Institutes, Inc.
- **Urban** campus
- **Coed** 958 undergraduate students
- **Minimally difficult** entrance level

Academics *Calendar:* modular. *Degrees:* certificates, associate, and bachelor's. *Special study options:* distance learning.

Student Life *Housing:* college housing not available.

Standardized Tests *Required:* Wonderlic aptitude test (for admission).

Applying *Required:* interview. *Required for some:* high school transcript.

Freshman Application Contact Admissions Office, Pima Medical Institute, 957 South Dobson Road, Mesa, AZ 85202. *Phone:* 480-644-0267 Ext. 225. *Toll-free phone:* 888-898-9048. *Web site:* http://www.pmi.edu/.

Pima Medical Institute

Tucson, Arizona

- **Proprietary** primarily 2-year, founded 1972, part of Vocational Training Institutes, Inc.
- **Urban** campus
- **Coed** 900 undergraduate students
- **Minimally difficult** entrance level

Academics *Calendar:* modular. *Degrees:* certificates, associate, and bachelor's. *Special study options:* academic remediation for entering students, accelerated degree program, adult/continuing education programs, cooperative education, distance learning, internships.

Computers on Campus Campuswide network is available.

Student Life *Housing:* college housing not available.

Standardized Tests *Required:* Wonderlic Scholastic Level Exam (for admission).

Applying *Options:* early admission. *Required:* interview. *Required for some:* high school transcript.

Freshman Application Contact Admissions Office, Pima Medical Institute, 3350 East Grant Road, Tucson, AZ 85716. *Phone:* 520-326-1600 Ext. 5112. *Toll-free phone:* 888-898-9048. *Web site:* http://www.pmi.edu/.

Prescott College

Prescott, Arizona

- **Independent** comprehensive, founded 1966
- **Small-town** 6-acre campus
- **Endowment** $844,290
- **Coed** 780 undergraduate students, 84% full-time, 59% women, 41% men
- **Moderately difficult** entrance level, 99% of applicants were admitted

Undergraduates 658 full-time, 122 part-time. Students come from 51 states and territories; 5 other countries; 68% are from out of state; 2% Black or African American, non-Hispanic/Latino; 6% Hispanic/Latino; 1% Asian, non-Hispanic/Latino; 0.1% Native Hawaiian or other Pacific Islander, non-Hispanic/Latino; 2% American Indian or Alaska Native, non-Hispanic/Latino; 4% Two or more races, non-Hispanic/Latino; 3% Race/ethnicity unknown; 0.8% international; 22% transferred in; 4% live on campus. *Retention:* 64% of full-time freshmen returned.

Freshmen *Admission:* 363 applied, 361 admitted, 76 enrolled. *Average high school GPA:* 2.9. *Test scores:* SAT critical reading scores over 500: 80%; SAT math scores over 500: 68%; SAT writing scores over 500: 79%; ACT scores over 18: 95%; SAT critical reading scores over 600: 55%; SAT math scores over 600: 20%; SAT writing scores over 600: 36%; ACT scores over 24: 55%; SAT critical reading scores over 700: 10%; SAT math scores over 700: 7%; SAT writing scores over 700: 5%; ACT scores over 30: 10%.

Faculty *Total:* 136, 54% full-time, 65% with terminal degrees. *Student/faculty ratio:* 7:1.

Academics *Calendar:* quarters (4-week blocks followed by 10-week terms for each quarter). *Degrees:* bachelor's, master's, doctoral-research/scholarship, post-master's, and postbachelor's certificates. *Special study options:* adult/continuing education programs, advanced placement credit, double majors, external degree program, independent study, internships, off-campus study, services for LD students, student-designed majors, summer session for credit.

Computers on Campus 50 computers/terminals and 20 ports are available on campus for general student use. Students can access the following: campus intranet, computer help desk, free student e-mail accounts. Campuswide network is available. 100% of college-owned or -operated housing units are wired for high-speed Internet access. Wireless service is available via classrooms, computer centers, computer labs, dorm rooms, libraries.

Student Life *Housing options:* coed. Campus housing is university owned. Freshman applicants given priority for college housing. *Activities and organizations:* drama/theater group, student-run newspaper, Student Union, Catalyst, WEB (Women's Empowerment Breakthrough), HUB (Helping Understand Bikes), Aztlan Center. *Campus security:* 24-hour emergency response devices. *Student services:* personal/psychological counseling.

Standardized Tests *Required:* SAT or ACT (for admission).

Costs (2010–11) *Tuition:* $24,864 full-time, $1036 per credit hour part-time. Full-time tuition and fees vary according to course load, degree level, and reciprocity agreements. Part-time tuition and fees vary according to course load, degree level, and reciprocity agreements. *Required fees:* $2401 full-time, $1035 per term part-time. *Room only:* $3810. Room and board charges vary according to housing facility. *Payment plans:* installment, deferred payment. *Waivers:* employees or children of employees.

Financial Aid Of all full-time matriculated undergraduates who enrolled in 2009, 499 applied for aid, 457 were judged to have need, 16 had their need

fully met. 187 Federal Work-Study jobs (averaging $1398). In 2009, 118 non-need-based awards were made. *Average percent of need met:* 54%. *Average financial aid package:* $16,686. *Average need-based loan:* $5240. *Average need-based gift aid:* $11,307. *Average non-need-based aid:* $6370. *Average indebtedness upon graduation:* $15,182.

Applying *Options:* electronic application, early decision, deferred entrance. *Application fee:* $25. *Required:* essay or personal statement, 1 letter of recommendation. *Required for some:* high school transcript, interview. *Application deadlines:* 8/15 (freshmen), 8/15 (out-of-state freshmen), 8/15 (transfers). *Early decision deadline:* 12/1. *Notification:* continuous (freshmen), continuous (out-of-state freshmen), continuous (transfers), 12/15 (early decision).

Freshman Application Contact Nancy Simmons, Receptionist, Prescott College, 220 Grove Avenue, Prescott, AZ 86301. *Phone:* 928-350-2100. *Toll-free phone:* 800-628-6364. *Fax:* 928-776-5242. *E-mail:* admissions@prescott.edu. *Web site:* http://www.prescott.edu/.

Scottsdale Culinary Institute

Scottsdale, Arizona

Director of Admissions Scottsdale Culinary Institute, 8100 East Camelback Road, Suite 1001, Scottsdale, AZ 85251-3940. *Toll-free phone:* 800-848-2433. *Web site:* http://www.scichefs.com/.

University of Advancing Technology

Tempe, Arizona

- **Proprietary** comprehensive, founded 1983

- **Urban** campus

- **Coed, primarily men** 1,013 undergraduate students, 100% full-time, 8% women, 92% men

Undergraduates 1,013 full-time. 7% Black or African American, non-Hispanic/Latino; 7% Hispanic/Latino; 3% Asian, non-Hispanic/Latino; 0.3% Native Hawaiian or other Pacific Islander, non-Hispanic/Latino; 0.7% American Indian or Alaska Native, non-Hispanic/Latino; 6% Two or more races, non-Hispanic/Latino; 14% Race/ethnicity unknown; 2% international; 22% live on campus.

Freshmen *Admission:* 140 enrolled. *Average high school GPA:* 2.5.

Faculty *Total:* 60, 52% full-time, 10% with terminal degrees. *Student/faculty ratio:* 14:1.

Academics *Calendar:* semesters. *Degrees:* associate, bachelor's, and master's. *Special study options:* cooperative education, distance learning, double majors, independent study, internships, summer session for credit.

Computers on Campus 400 computers/terminals and 300 ports are available on campus for general student use. Students can access the following: campus intranet, free student e-mail accounts, online (class) grades, online (class) registration, online (class) schedules. Campuswide network is available. 100% of college-owned or -operated housing units are wired for high-speed Internet access. Wireless service is available via entire campus.

Student Life *Housing:* on-campus residence required for freshman year. *Options:* coed. Campus housing is university owned, leased by the school and is provided by a third party. *Activities and organizations:* student-run newspaper, television station, Web Club, Gaming Club, Animation Club, Video Club, student government. *Campus security:* 24-hour patrols.

Athletics *Intramural sports:* fencing M/W, softball M/W.

Standardized Tests *Required for some:* SAT or ACT (for admission).

Costs (2011–12) *Comprehensive fee:* $30,426 includes full-time tuition ($19,400), mandatory fees ($100), and room and board ($10,926). *College room only:* $7346. Room and board charges vary according to board plan. *Payment plan:* installment. *Waivers:* employees or children of employees.

Applying *Options:* electronic application. *Required:* essay or personal statement, high school transcript. *Required for some:* minimum 2.5 GPA. *Application deadline:* rolling (freshmen).

Freshman Application Contact Admissions Office, University of Advancing Technology, 2625 West Baseline Road, Tempe, AZ 85283-1042. *Phone:* 602-383-8228. *Toll-free phone:* 800-658-5744. *Fax:* 602-383-8222. *E-mail:* admissions@uat.edu. *Web site:* http://www.uat.edu/.

See page 1682 for the College Close-Up.

The University of Arizona

Tucson, Arizona

- **State-supported** university, founded 1885, part of Arizona Board of Regents
- **Urban** 362-acre campus
- **Coed** 30,592 undergraduate students, 88% full-time, 52% women, 48% men
- **Moderately difficult** entrance level, 75% of applicants were admitted

Undergraduates 26,909 full-time, 3,683 part-time. 29% are from out of state; 4% Black or African American, non-Hispanic/Latino; 19% Hispanic/Latino; 7% Asian, non-Hispanic/Latino; 0.6% Native Hawaiian or other Pacific Islander, non-Hispanic/Latino; 3% American Indian or Alaska Native, non-Hispanic/Latino; 2% Race/ethnicity unknown; 4% international; 6% transferred in; 20% live on campus. *Retention:* 77% of full-time freshmen returned.

Freshmen *Admission:* 26,629 applied, 20,068 admitted, 7,025 enrolled. *Average high school GPA:* 3.36. *Test scores:* SAT critical reading scores over 500: 68%; SAT math scores over 500: 74%; ACT scores over 18: 92%; SAT critical reading scores over 600: 29%; SAT math scores over 600: 34%; ACT scores over 24: 52%; SAT critical reading scores over 700: 6%; SAT math scores over 700: 7%; ACT scores over 30: 9%.

Faculty *Total:* 1,972, 77% full-time, 82% with terminal degrees. *Student/faculty ratio:* 20:1.

Academics *Calendar:* semesters. *Degrees:* bachelor's, master's, doctoral-professional, doctoral-research/scholarship, post-master's, and postbachelor's certificates. *Special study options:* accelerated degree program, adult/continuing education programs, advanced placement credit, cooperative education, distance learning, double majors, English as a second language, external degree program, freshman honors college, honors programs, independent study, internships, off-campus study, part-time degree program, services for LD students, study abroad, summer session for credit. *ROTC:* Army (b), Navy (b), Air Force (b). *Unusual degree programs:* 3-2 business administration with American Graduate School of International Management.

Computers on Campus Students can access the following: campus intranet, computer help desk, free student e-mail accounts, online (class) grades, online (class) registration, online (class) schedules. Campuswide network is available. Wireless service is available via classrooms, computer centers, computer labs, dorm rooms, learning centers, libraries, student centers.

Student Life *Housing options:* coed, women-only, disabled students. Campus housing is university owned and leased by the school. Freshman applicants given priority for college housing. *Activities and organizations:* drama/theater group, student-run newspaper, radio and television station, choral group, marching band, national fraternities, national sororities. *Campus security:* 24-hour patrols, student patrols, late-night transport/escort service, emergency telephones. *Student services:* health clinic, personal/psychological counseling, women's center, legal services.

Athletics Member NCAA. All Division I except football (Division I-A). *Intercollegiate sports:* baseball M(s), basketball M(s)/W(s), cross-country running M(s)/W(s), golf M(s)/W(s), gymnastics W(s), ice hockey M(c), lacrosse M(c)/W(c), rock climbing M(c)/W(c), soccer M(c)/W(c), softball W(s), swimming and diving M(s)/W(s), tennis M(s)/W(s), track and field M(s)/W(s), volleyball M(c)/W(s), wrestling M(c). *Intramural sports:* badminton M/W, basketball M/W, bowling M/W, cross-country running M/W, football M/W, golf M/W, racquetball M/W, soccer M/W, softball M/W, swimming and diving M/W, table tennis M/W, tennis M/W, track and field M/W, volleyball M/W, water polo M/W, weight lifting M/W, wrestling M.

Standardized Tests *Recommended:* SAT or ACT (for admission).

Costs (2010–11) *Tuition:* state resident $8237 full-time, $544 per credit hour part-time; nonresident $24,597 full-time, $999 per credit hour part-time. Full-time tuition and fees vary according to course level, course load, and program. Part-time tuition and fees vary according to course level, course load, and program. *Required fees:* $623 full-time, $61 per credit hour part-time. *Room and board:* $9024. Room and board charges vary according to board plan and housing facility. *Waivers:* employees or children of employees.

Financial Aid Of all full-time matriculated undergraduates who enrolled in 2008, 14,614 applied for aid, 10,709 were judged to have need, 1,111 had their need fully met. In 2008, 6364 non-need-based awards were made. *Average percent of need met:* 64%. *Average financial aid package:* $10,021. *Average need-based loan:* $4325. *Average need-based gift aid:* $7849. *Average non-need-based aid:* $5064. *Average indebtedness upon graduation:* $18,712.

Applying *Options:* electronic application, early admission. *Application fee:* $50. *Required:* essay or personal statement, high school transcript. *Required for some:* minimum 3 GPA, interview. *Application deadlines:* 5/1 (freshmen), rolling (transfers). *Notification:* continuous (freshmen).

Freshman Application Contact The University of Arizona, Tucson, AZ 85721. *Phone:* 520-621-3705. *Web site:* http://www.arizona.edu/.

University of Phoenix

Phoenix, Arizona

Freshman Application Contact Ms. Audra McQuarie, Registrar/Executive Director, University of Phoenix, 4035 South Riverpoint Parkway, Mail Stop CF-L101, Phoenix, AZ 85040. *Phone:* 480-557-6151. *Toll-free phone:* 800-776-4867 (in-state); 800-228-7240 (out-of-state). *Fax:* 480-643-3068. *E-mail:* audra.mcquarie@phoenix.edu. *Web site:* http://www.uopxonline.com/.

University of Phoenix–Phoenix Campus

Phoenix, Arizona

Freshman Application Contact Ms. Audra McQuarie, Registrar/Executive Director, University of Phoenix–Phoenix Campus, 4035 South Riverpoint Parkway, Mail Stop CF-L101, Phoenix, AZ 85040. *Phone:* 480-557-6151. *Toll-free phone:* 800-776-4867 (in-state); 800-228-7240 (out-of-state). *Fax:* 480-643-3068. *E-mail:* audra.mcquarie@phoenix.edu. *Web site:* http://www.phoenix.edu/.

University of Phoenix–Southern Arizona Campus

Tucson, Arizona

Freshman Application Contact Ms. Audra McQuarie, Registrar/Executive Director, University of Phoenix–Southern Arizona Campus, 4035 South Riverpoint Parkway, Mail Stop CF-L101, Phoenix, AZ 85040-1958. *Phone:* 480-557-6151. *Toll-free phone:* 800-776-4867 (in-state); 800-228-7240 (out-of-state). *Fax:* 480-643-3068. *E-mail:* audra.mcquarie@phoenix.edu. *Web site:* http://www.phoenix.edu/.

Western International University

Phoenix, Arizona

- **Proprietary** comprehensive, founded 1978
- **Urban** 4-acre campus
- **Coed** 2,369 undergraduate students, 100% full-time, 64% women, 36% men
- **Moderately difficult** entrance level

Undergraduates 2,369 full-time. 15% Black or African American, non-Hispanic/Latino; 12% Hispanic/Latino; 3% American Indian or Alaska Native, non-Hispanic/Latino; 2% Two or more races, non-Hispanic/Latino; 15% Race/ethnicity unknown; 0.9% international.

Freshmen *Admission:* 84 enrolled.

Faculty *Total:* 228, 7% with terminal degrees. *Student/faculty ratio:* 31:1.

Academics *Calendar:* continuous. *Degrees:* associate, bachelor's, master's, and postbachelor's certificates. *Special study options:* academic remediation for entering students, accelerated degree program, adult/continuing education programs, advanced placement credit, distance learning, double majors, honors programs, independent study, part-time degree program, study abroad, summer session for credit.

Computers on Campus Students can access the following: campus intranet, computer help desk, free student e-mail accounts, online (class) grades, online (class) registration, online (class) schedules. Campuswide network is available. Wireless service is available via entire campus.

Student Life *Housing:* college housing not available. *Campus security:* 24-hour emergency response devices and patrols, late-night transport/escort service.

Costs (2010–11) *Tuition:* $9600 full-time, $425 per credit hour part-time. Full-time tuition and fees vary according to student level. Part-time tuition and fees vary according to student level. *Required fees:* $25 full-time.

Financial Aid *Average financial aid package:* $3321. *Average indebtedness upon graduation:* $5285.

Applying *Options:* electronic application, deferred entrance. *Application fee:* $25. *Required:* high school transcript, minimum 2.5 GPA. *Application deadlines:* rolling (freshmen), rolling (transfers).

Freshman Application Contact Ms. Karen Janitell, Executive Director of Enrollment, Western International University, 9215 North Black Canyon Highway, Phoenix, AZ 85021-2718. *Phone:* 602-429-1063. *E-mail:* karen.janitell@west.edu. *Web site:* http://www.west.edu.

ARKANSAS

Arkansas Baptist College
Little Rock, Arkansas

Freshman Application Contact Arkansas Baptist College, 1621 Dr. Martin Luther King, Jr. Drive, Little Rock, AR 72202-6067. *Phone:* 501-244-5104 Ext. 5124. *Web site:* http://www.arkansasbaptist.edu/.

Arkansas State University
Jonesboro, Arkansas

- **State-supported** comprehensive, founded 1909, part of Arkansas State University System
- **Small-town** 1374-acre campus with easy access to Memphis
- **Endowment** $35.4 million
- **Coed** 10,051 undergraduate students, 77% full-time, 58% women, 42% men
- **Moderately difficult** entrance level, 70% of applicants were admitted

Undergraduates 7,789 full-time, 2,262 part-time. Students come from 35 states and territories; 48 other countries; 10% are from out of state; 18% Black or African American, non-Hispanic/Latino; 1% Hispanic/Latino; 0.5% Asian, non-Hispanic/Latino; 0.4% American Indian or Alaska Native, non-Hispanic/Latino; 2% Two or more races, non-Hispanic/Latino; 6% Race/ethnicity unknown; 4% international; 10% transferred in; 28% live on campus. *Retention:* 71% of full-time freshmen returned.
Freshmen *Admission:* 4,568 applied, 3,201 admitted, 1,716 enrolled. *Average high school GPA:* 3.28. *Test scores:* SAT critical reading scores over 500: 48%; SAT math scores over 500: 68%; SAT writing scores over 500: 44%; ACT scores over 18: 89%; SAT critical reading scores over 600: 16%; SAT math scores over 600: 20%; SAT writing scores over 600: 8%; ACT scores over 24: 37%; SAT math scores over 700: 8%; SAT writing scores over 700: 4%; ACT scores over 30: 3%.
Faculty *Total:* 650, 74% full-time, 49% with terminal degrees. *Student/faculty ratio:* 19:1.
Academics *Calendar:* semesters. *Degrees:* certificates, associate, bachelor's, master's, doctoral-professional, doctoral-research/scholarship, post-master's, and postbachelor's certificates. *Special study options:* academic remediation for entering students, accelerated degree program, advanced placement credit, distance learning, double majors, English as a second language, honors programs, independent study, internships, off-campus study, part-time degree program, services for LD students, study abroad, summer session for credit. *ROTC:* Army (b).
Computers on Campus 510 computers/terminals and 5,268 ports are available on campus for general student use. Students can access the following: campus intranet, computer help desk, free student e-mail accounts, online (class) grades, online (class) registration, online (class) schedules. Campuswide network is available. 99% of college-owned or -operated housing units are wired for high-speed Internet access. Wireless service is available via entire campus.
Student Life *Housing:* on-campus residence required for freshman year. *Options:* coed, men-only, women-only. Campus housing is university owned. *Activities and organizations:* drama/theater group, student-run newspaper, radio and television station, choral group, marching band, Baptist Collegiate Ministries, Black Student Association, Japanese Student Organization, Honors College Association, Indian Student Association, national fraternities, national sororities. *Campus security:* 24-hour emergency response devices and patrols, student patrols, late-night transport/escort service, controlled dormitory access, check-in desk; video surveillance cameras. *Student services:* health clinic, personal/psychological counseling.
Athletics Member NCAA. All Division I except football (Division I-A). *Intercollegiate sports:* baseball M(s), basketball M(s)/W(s), bowling W(s), cross-country running M(s)/W(s), golf M(s)/W(s), soccer W(s), tennis W(s), track and field M(s)/W(s), volleyball W(s). *Intramural sports:* badminton M/W, basketball M/W, bowling M/W, football M/W, golf M/W, racquetball M/W, rugby M(c), soccer M/W, softball M/W, table tennis M/W, tennis M/W, ultimate Frisbee M/W, volleyball M/W.
Standardized Tests *Required:* SAT or ACT (for admission). *Required for some:* ACT ASSET or ACT COMPASS. *Recommended:* ACT (for admission).
Costs (2010–11) *Tuition:* state resident $5100 full-time, $170 per credit hour part-time; nonresident $13,320 full-time, $444 per credit hour part-time. Full-time tuition and fees vary according to course load, location, and program. Part-time tuition and fees vary according to course load, location, and program. *Required fees:* $1540 full-time, $49 per credit hour part-time, $25 per term part-time. *Room and board:* $6544. Room and board charges vary according to board plan, housing facility, and student level. *Payment plan:* installment. *Waivers:* senior citizens and employees or children of employees.

Financial Aid Of all full-time matriculated undergraduates who enrolled in 2009, 7,468 applied for aid, 5,947 were judged to have need, 1,529 had their need fully met. 200 Federal Work-Study jobs (averaging $3000). 300 state and other part-time jobs (averaging $3500). In 2009, 650 non-need-based awards were made. *Average percent of need met:* 50%. *Average financial aid package:* $12,100. *Average need-based loan:* $8600. *Average need-based gift aid:* $6000. *Average non-need-based aid:* $6500. *Average indebtedness upon graduation:* $19,000. *Financial aid deadline:* 7/1.
Applying *Options:* electronic application, early admission, deferred entrance. *Application fee:* $15. *Required:* high school transcript, minimum 2.5 GPA, ACT composite score of 19, immunization, selective service. *Application deadlines:* rolling (freshmen), rolling (transfers). *Notification:* continuous (freshmen), continuous (transfers).
Freshman Application Contact Ms. Tammy Fowler, Director of Admissions, Arkansas State University, PO Box 1630, State University, AR 72467. *Phone:* 870-972-3024. *Toll-free phone:* 800-382-3030. *Fax:* 870-972-3406. *E-mail:* admissions@astate.edu. *Web site:* http://www.astate.edu/.

Arkansas Tech University
Russellville, Arkansas

- **State-supported** comprehensive, founded 1909
- **Small-town** 542-acre campus
- **Endowment** $17.2 million
- **Coed** 9,138 undergraduate students, 74% full-time, 52% women, 48% men
- **Moderately difficult** entrance level, 91% of applicants were admitted

Undergraduates 6,801 full-time, 2,337 part-time. Students come from 41 states and territories; 38 other countries; 5% are from out of state; 5% transferred in; 31% live on campus. *Retention:* 74% of full-time freshmen returned.
Freshmen *Admission:* 3,621 applied, 3,291 admitted, 1,825 enrolled. *Average high school GPA:* 3.11. *Test scores:* SAT critical reading scores over 500: 42%; SAT math scores over 500: 75%; ACT scores over 18: 86%; SAT critical reading scores over 600: 17%; SAT math scores over 600: 33%; ACT scores over 24: 36%; ACT scores over 30: 3%.
Faculty *Total:* 463, 63% full-time, 44% with terminal degrees. *Student/faculty ratio:* 18:1.
Academics *Calendar:* semesters. *Degrees:* certificates, associate, bachelor's, master's, and post-master's certificates. *Special study options:* academic remediation for entering students, adult/continuing education programs, advanced placement credit, distance learning, double majors, English as a second language, honors programs, independent study, internships, part-time degree program, services for LD students, summer session for credit. *ROTC:* Army (c).
Computers on Campus 700 computers/terminals are available on campus for general student use. Students can access the following: campus intranet, computer help desk, free student e-mail accounts, online (class) grades, online (class) registration, online (class) schedules. Campuswide network is available. 100% of college-owned or -operated housing units are wired for high-speed Internet access. Wireless service is available via classrooms, computer centers, computer labs, dorm rooms, learning centers, libraries, student centers.
Student Life *Housing:* on-campus residence required through sophomore year. *Options:* coed, men-only, women-only, disabled students. Campus housing is university owned. Freshman campus housing is guaranteed. *Activities and organizations:* drama/theater group, student-run newspaper, radio and television station, choral group, marching band, national fraternities, national sororities. *Campus security:* 24-hour patrols, late-night transport/escort service, controlled dormitory access. *Student services:* health clinic, personal/psychological counseling.
Athletics Member NCAA. All Division II. *Intercollegiate sports:* baseball M(s), basketball M(s)/W(s), cheerleading M(s)/W(s), cross-country running W(s), football M(s), golf M(s)/W(s), softball W(s), tennis W(s), volleyball W(s). *Intramural sports:* basketball M/W, bowling M/W, football M/W, racquetball M/W, softball M/W, table tennis M/W, tennis M/W, ultimate Frisbee M/W, volleyball M/W.
Standardized Tests *Required:* SAT or ACT (for admission).
Costs (2010–11) *Tuition:* state resident $5100 full-time, $170 per credit hour part-time; nonresident $10,200 full-time, $340 per credit hour part-time. Full-time tuition and fees vary according to course load and location. Part-time tuition and fees vary according to course load and location. *Required fees:* $808 full-time, $14 per credit hour part-time, $388 per term part-time. *Room and board:* $5270; room only: $3144. Room and board charges vary according to board plan, housing facility, and location. *Payment plans:* installment, deferred payment. *Waivers:* senior citizens and employees or children of employees.
Financial Aid Of all full-time matriculated undergraduates who enrolled in 2008, 4,943 applied for aid, 4,100 were judged to have need, 799 had their need fully met. In 2008, 1045 non-need-based awards were made. *Average percent of need met:* 72%. *Average financial aid package:* $8635. *Average*

need-based loan: $3756. *Average need-based gift aid:* $4884. *Average non-need-based aid:* $7183. *Average indebtedness upon graduation:* $16,363.
Applying *Options:* electronic application, early action, deferred entrance. *Required:* high school transcript, minimum 2 GPA. *Notification:* continuous (freshmen), continuous (transfers).
Freshman Application Contact Ms. Shauna Donnell, Director of Enrollment Management, Arkansas Tech University, Doc Bryan Student Services Building, Suite 141, Russellville, AR 72801. *Phone:* 479-968-0343. *Toll-free phone:* 800-582-6953. *Fax:* 479-964-0522. *E-mail:* tech.enroll@atu.edu. *Web site:* http://www.atu.edu/.

Central Baptist College
Conway, Arkansas
- **Independent Baptist** 4-year, founded 1952
- **Small-town** 11-acre campus
- **Endowment** $1.5 million
- **Coed**
- **Minimally difficult** entrance level

Faculty *Student/faculty ratio:* 21:1.
Academics *Calendar:* semesters. *Degrees:* associate and bachelor's.
Athletics Member NCCAA.
Standardized Tests *Required:* ACT (for admission).
Costs (2010–11) *Comprehensive fee:* $16,480 includes full-time tuition ($9750), mandatory fees ($930), and room and board ($5800).
Applying *Options:* electronic application, early admission. *Application fee:* $25. *Required:* essay or personal statement, high school transcript, minimum 2.5 GPA, 2 letters of recommendation.
Freshman Application Contact Ms. Rachel Waymire, Admissions Counselor, Central Baptist College, 1501 College Avenue, Conway, AR 72034. *Phone:* 501-329-6872 Ext. 197. *Toll-free phone:* 800-205-6872. *Fax:* 501-329-2941. *E-mail:* rwaymire@cbc.edu. *Web site:* http://www.cbc.edu/.

Ecclesia College
Springdale, Arkansas
- **Independent religious** 4-year, founded 1995
- **Suburban** 200-acre campus
- **Coed**
- **Noncompetitive** entrance level

Faculty *Student/faculty ratio:* 10:1.
Academics *Calendar:* semesters. *Degrees:* associate and bachelor's.
Student Life *Campus security:* student patrols.
Athletics Member NCCAA.
Standardized Tests *Required:* SAT or ACT (for admission), COMPASS (for admission).
Applying *Application fee:* $35. *Required:* essay or personal statement, high school transcript, minimum 2 GPA, interview.
Freshman Application Contact Ecclesia College, 9653 Nations Drive, Springdale, AR 72762. *Phone:* 479-248-7236 Ext. 223. *Toll-free phone:* 800-735-9926. *Web site:* http://www.ecollege.edu/.

Harding University
Searcy, Arkansas
- **Independent** university, founded 1924, affiliated with Church of Christ
- **Small-town** 275-acre campus with easy access to Little Rock
- **Endowment** $87.2 million
- **Coed** 4,173 undergraduate students, 93% full-time, 53% women, 47% men
- **Moderately difficult** entrance level, 73% of applicants were admitted

Undergraduates 3,888 full-time, 285 part-time. Students come from 49 states and territories; 49 other countries; 72% are from out of state; 4% Black or African American, non-Hispanic/Latino; 3% Hispanic/Latino; 0.5% Asian, non-Hispanic/Latino; 0.1% Native Hawaiian or other Pacific Islander, non-Hispanic/Latino; 0.6% American Indian or Alaska Native, non-Hispanic/Latino; 2% Two or more races, non-Hispanic/Latino; 0.7% Race/ethnicity unknown; 6% international; 5% transferred in; 77% live on campus. *Retention:* 80% of full-time freshmen returned.
Freshmen *Admission:* 2,015 applied, 1,464 admitted, 992 enrolled. *Average high school GPA:* 3.5. *Test scores:* SAT critical reading scores over 500: 72%; SAT math scores over 500: 73%; ACT scores over 18: 95%; SAT critical reading scores over 600: 35%; SAT math scores over 600: 37%; ACT scores over 24: 61%; SAT critical reading scores over 700: 12%; SAT math scores over 700: 8%; ACT scores over 30: 17%.
Faculty *Total:* 463, 56% full-time, 51% with terminal degrees. *Student/faculty ratio:* 16:1.

Academics *Calendar:* semesters. *Degrees:* bachelor's, master's, doctoral-professional, doctoral-research/scholarship, and post-master's certificates. *Special study options:* academic remediation for entering students, accelerated degree program, adult/continuing education programs, advanced placement credit, cooperative education, distance learning, double majors, English as a second language, freshman honors college, honors programs, independent study, internships, part-time degree program, services for LD students, student-designed majors, study abroad, summer session for credit.
Computers on Campus 482 computers/terminals and 2,400 ports are available on campus for general student use. Students can access the following: campus intranet, computer help desk, free student e-mail accounts, online (class) grades, online (class) registration, online (class) schedules. Campus-wide network is available. 100% of college-owned or -operated housing units are wired for high-speed Internet access. Wireless service is available via entire campus.
Student Life *Housing:* on-campus residence required through senior year. *Options:* men-only, women-only, disabled students. Campus housing is university owned. Freshman campus housing is guaranteed. *Activities and organizations:* drama/theater group, student-run newspaper, radio and television station, choral group, marching band, Bisons for Christ, Harding in Action, Spring Break Campaigns, HUmanity. *Campus security:* 24-hour emergency response devices and patrols, student patrols, late-night transport/escort service, controlled dormitory access. *Student services:* health clinic, personal/psychological counseling.
Athletics Member NCAA. All Division II. *Intercollegiate sports:* baseball M(s), basketball M(s)/W(s), cheerleading W, cross-country running M(s)/W(s), football M(s), golf M(s)/W(s), lacrosse M(c), rugby M(c), soccer M(s)/W(s), tennis M(s)/W(s), track and field M(s)/W(s), ultimate Frisbee M(c)/W(c), volleyball W(s). *Intramural sports:* basketball M/W, cross-country running M/W, football M/W, golf M/W, racquetball M/W, soccer M/W, softball M/W, swimming and diving M/W, table tennis M/W, tennis M/W, track and field M/W, ultimate Frisbee M/W, volleyball M/W, weight lifting M/W.
Standardized Tests *Required:* SAT or ACT (for admission).
Costs (2010–11) *Comprehensive fee:* $19,962 includes full-time tuition ($13,590), mandatory fees ($450), and room and board ($5922). Full-time tuition and fees vary according to course load. Part-time tuition: $453 per credit hour. Part-time tuition and fees vary according to course load. *Required fees:* $23 per credit hour part-time. *College room only:* $2934. Room and board charges vary according to board plan and housing facility. *Payment plans:* tuition prepayment, installment. *Waivers:* senior citizens and employees or children of employees.
Financial Aid Of all full-time matriculated undergraduates who enrolled in 2008, 2,800 applied for aid, 2,227 were judged to have need, 556 had their need fully met. 439 Federal Work-Study jobs (averaging $935). 1,327 state and other part-time jobs (averaging $1556). In 2008, 429 non-need-based awards were made. *Average percent of need met:* 70%. *Average financial aid package:* $12,219. *Average need-based loan:* $5106. *Average need-based gift aid:* $7457. *Average non-need-based aid:* $5443. *Average indebtedness upon graduation:* $33,989.
Applying *Options:* electronic application, early admission, early action, deferred entrance. *Application fee:* $40. *Required:* essay or personal statement, high school transcript, 2 letters of recommendation. *Application deadlines:* rolling (freshmen), rolling (out-of-state freshmen), rolling (transfers). *Notification:* continuous (freshmen), continuous (out-of-state freshmen), continuous (transfers).
Freshman Application Contact Mr. Glenn Dillard, Assistant Vice President for Enrollment Management, Harding University, Box 12255, Searcy, AR 72149-2255. *Phone:* 501-279-4407. *Toll-free phone:* 800-477-4407. *Fax:* 501-279-4129. *E-mail:* admissions@harding.edu. *Web site:* http://www.harding.edu/.

Henderson State University
Arkadelphia, Arkansas
- **State-supported** comprehensive, founded 1890
- **Small-town** 151-acre campus with easy access to Little Rock
- **Coed**
- **Moderately difficult** entrance level

Faculty *Student/faculty ratio:* 18:1.
Academics *Calendar:* semesters. *Degrees:* certificates, associate, bachelor's, master's, and postbachelor's certificates.
Student Life *Campus security:* 24-hour emergency response devices and patrols, controlled dormitory access.
Athletics Member NCAA. All Division II.
Standardized Tests *Required:* SAT or ACT (for admission). *Recommended:* ACT (for admission).
Costs (2010–11) *Tuition:* state resident $5340 full-time, $178 per credit hour part-time; nonresident $10,680 full-time, $356 per credit hour part-time. Full-time tuition and fees vary according to course load. Part-time tuition and fees vary according to course load. *Required fees:* $1104 full-time. *Room and*

board: $5084. Room and board charges vary according to board plan and housing facility.

Financial Aid *Of all full-time matriculated undergraduates who enrolled in 2009, 3,026 applied for aid, 2,535 were judged to have need, 24 had their need fully met. In 2009, 95 non-need-based awards were made. Average percent of need met:* 83. *Average financial aid package:* $10,648. *Average need-based loan:* $3984. *Average need-based gift aid:* $11,908. *Average non-need-based aid:* $9096. *Average indebtedness upon graduation:* $16,529.

Applying *Options:* electronic application, deferred entrance. *Required:* high school transcript. *Required for some:* essay or personal statement, 3 letters of recommendation. *Recommended:* minimum 2.5 GPA.

Freshman Application Contact Ms. Vikita Hardwrick, Director of University Relations/Admissions, Henderson State University, 1100 Henderson Street, PO Box 7560, Arkadelphia, AR 71999-0001. *Phone:* 870-230-5028. *Toll-free phone:* 800-228-7333. *Fax:* 870-230-5066. *E-mail:* hardwrv@hsu.edu. *Web site:* http://www.hsu.edu/.

Hendrix College
Conway, Arkansas

- **Independent United Methodist** comprehensive, founded 1876
- **Suburban** 65-acre campus with easy access to Little Rock
- **Endowment** $146.4 million
- **Coed** 1,454 undergraduate students, 99% full-time, 57% women, 43% men
- **Very difficult** entrance level, 83% of applicants were admitted

Undergraduates 1,443 full-time, 11 part-time. Students come from 42 states and territories; 13 other countries; 50% are from out of state; 3% Black or African American, non-Hispanic/Latino; 4% Hispanic/Latino; 3% Asian, non-Hispanic/Latino; 0.1% Native Hawaiian or other Pacific Islander, non-Hispanic/Latino; 0.6% American Indian or Alaska Native, non-Hispanic/Latino; 2% Two or more races, non-Hispanic/Latino; 6% Race/ethnicity unknown; 4% international; 1% transferred in; 86% live on campus. *Retention:* 86% of full-time freshmen returned.

Freshmen *Admission:* 1,554 applied, 1,288 admitted, 404 enrolled. *Average high school GPA:* 3.89. *Test scores:* SAT critical reading scores over 500: 95%; SAT math scores over 500: 95%; ACT scores over 18: 100%; SAT critical reading scores over 600: 75%; SAT math scores over 600: 67%; ACT scores over 24: 94%; SAT critical reading scores over 700: 29%; SAT math scores over 700: 16%; ACT scores over 30: 56%.

Faculty *Total:* 139, 78% full-time, 83% with terminal degrees. *Student/faculty ratio:* 12:1.

Academics *Calendar:* semesters. *Degrees:* bachelor's and master's. *Special study options:* advanced placement credit, cooperative education, double majors, English as a second language, independent study, internships, off-campus study, services for LD students, student-designed majors, study abroad. *ROTC:* Army (c). *Unusual degree programs:* 3-2 engineering with Columbia University, Vanderbilt University, Washington University in St. Louis; public health BA/MPH with University of Arkansas Medical School.

Computers on Campus 75 computers/terminals are available on campus for general student use. Students can access the following: campus intranet, computer help desk, free student e-mail accounts, online (class) grades, online (class) registration, online (class) schedules. Campuswide network is available. 100% of college-owned or -operated housing units are wired for high-speed Internet access. Wireless service is available via entire campus.

Student Life *Housing:* on-campus residence required through senior year. *Options:* coed, men-only, women-only. Campus housing is university owned. Freshman campus housing is guaranteed. *Activities and organizations:* drama/theater group, student-run newspaper, radio station, choral group, Volunteer Action Center, student government, Music ensembles, Multicultural Development Committee, Social Committee. *Campus security:* 24-hour emergency response devices and patrols, late-night transport/escort service, controlled dormitory access. *Student services:* health clinic, personal/psychological counseling.

Athletics Member NCAA. All Division III. *Intercollegiate sports:* baseball M, basketball M/W, cross-country running M/W, field hockey W, golf M/W, lacrosse M, soccer M/W, softball W, swimming and diving M/W, tennis M/W, track and field M/W, volleyball W. *Intramural sports:* basketball M/W, cheerleading M/W, football M/W, racquetball M/W, soccer M/W, softball M/W, table tennis M/W, tennis M/W, ultimate Frisbee M/W.

Standardized Tests *Required:* SAT or ACT (for admission).

Costs (2011–12) *Comprehensive fee:* $43,944 includes full-time tuition ($33,930), mandatory fees ($300), and room and board ($9714). Full-time tuition and fees vary according to course load. Part-time tuition: $4279 per course. Part-time tuition and fees vary according to course load. *College room only:* $4968. Room and board charges vary according to board plan and housing facility. *Payment plan:* installment. *Waivers:* employees or children of employees.

Financial Aid Of all full-time matriculated undergraduates who enrolled in 2009, 1,152 applied for aid, 888 were judged to have need, 333 had their need

fully met. 561 Federal Work-Study jobs (averaging $1389). 254 state and other part-time jobs (averaging $1229). In 2009, 555 non-need-based awards were made. *Average percent of need met:* 83%. *Average financial aid package:* $22,498. *Average need-based loan:* $4919. *Average need-based gift aid:* $18,080. *Average non-need-based aid:* $14,775. *Average indebtedness upon graduation:* $17,641.

Applying *Options:* electronic application, deferred entrance. *Application fee:* $40. *Required:* essay or personal statement, high school transcript. *Required for some:* interview. *Recommended:* 1 letter of recommendation. *Application deadlines:* 6/1 (freshmen), 7/1 (transfers). *Notification:* continuous (freshmen), continuous (transfers).

Freshman Application Contact Ms. Laura E. Martin, Director of Admission, Hendrix College, 1600 Washington Avenue, Conway, AR 72032. *Phone:* 501-450-1362. *Toll-free phone:* 800-277-9017. *Fax:* 501-450-3843. *E-mail:* martinl@hendrix.edu. *Web site:* http://www.hendrix.edu/.

ITT Technical Institute
Little Rock, Arkansas

- **Proprietary** primarily 2-year, founded 1993, part of ITT Educational Services, Inc.
- **Urban** campus
- **Coed**
- **Minimally difficult** entrance level

Academics *Calendar:* quarters. *Degrees:* associate and bachelor's.

Student Life *Housing:* college housing not available.

Freshman Application Contact Director of Recruitment, ITT Technical Institute, 4520 South University Avenue, Little Rock, AR 72204. *Phone:* 501-565-5550. *Toll-free phone:* 800-359-4429. *Web site:* http://www.itt-tech.edu/.

John Brown University
Siloam Springs, Arkansas

- **Independent interdenominational** comprehensive, founded 1919
- **Small-town** 200-acre campus
- **Endowment** $55.5 million
- **Coed** 1,710 undergraduate students, 87% full-time, 55% women, 45% men
- **Moderately difficult** entrance level, 71% of applicants were admitted

Undergraduates 1,485 full-time, 225 part-time. Students come from 39 states and territories; 45 other countries; 71% are from out of state; 3% Black or African American, non-Hispanic/Latino; 4% Hispanic/Latino; 0.9% Asian, non-Hispanic/Latino; 0.3% Native Hawaiian or other Pacific Islander, non-Hispanic/Latino; 1% American Indian or Alaska Native, non-Hispanic/Latino; 2% Two or more races, non-Hispanic/Latino; 1% Race/ethnicity unknown; 6% international; 4% transferred in; 68% live on campus. *Retention:* 75% of full-time freshmen returned.

Freshmen *Admission:* 1,033 applied, 732 admitted, 323 enrolled. *Average high school GPA:* 3.56. *Test scores:* SAT critical reading scores over 500: 63%; SAT math scores over 500: 71%; SAT writing scores over 500: 75%; ACT scores over 18: 99%; SAT critical reading scores over 600: 25%; SAT math scores over 600: 31%; SAT writing scores over 600: 27%; ACT scores over 24: 65%; SAT critical reading scores over 700: 6%; SAT math scores over 700: 6%; SAT writing scores over 700: 6%; ACT scores over 30: 13%.

Faculty *Total:* 131, 53% full-time, 49% with terminal degrees. *Student/faculty ratio:* 14:1.

Academics *Calendar:* semesters. *Degrees:* associate, bachelor's, and master's. *Special study options:* accelerated degree program, adult/continuing education programs, distance learning, double majors, English as a second language, external degree program, honors programs, independent study, internships, services for LD students, study abroad. *ROTC:* Army (c), Air Force (c).

Computers on Campus 100 computers/terminals are available on campus for general student use. Students can access the following: campus intranet, computer help desk, free student e-mail accounts, online (class) grades, online (class) registration, online (class) schedules. Campuswide network is available. 100% of college-owned or -operated housing units are wired for high-speed Internet access. Wireless service is available via classrooms, dorm rooms, learning centers, libraries, student centers.

Student Life *Housing:* on-campus residence required through junior year. *Options:* coed, men-only, women-only. Campus housing is university owned. Freshman campus housing is guaranteed. *Activities and organizations:* drama/theater group, student-run newspaper, radio station, choral group, Student Government Association, Student Ministries Organization, Student Activities Club, Student Missionary Fellowship. *Campus security:* 24-hour emergency response devices and patrols, late-night transport/escort service, controlled dormitory access. *Student services:* health clinic, personal/psychological counseling.

Athletics Member NAIA. *Intercollegiate sports:* basketball M(s)/W(s), cheerleading M(s)/W(s), cross-country running M(s)/W(s), golf M(s), soccer M(s)/W(s), tennis M(s)/W(s), volleyball W(s). *Intramural sports:* baseball M, basketball M/W, football M/W, golf M, racquetball M/W, rugby M, soccer M/W, softball M/W, table tennis M/W, tennis M/W, ultimate Frisbee M/W, volleyball M/W.

Standardized Tests *Required:* SAT or ACT (for admission).

Costs (2011–12) *Comprehensive fee:* $28,328 includes full-time tuition ($19,834), mandatory fees ($932), and room and board ($7562). Full-time tuition and fees vary according to course load. Part-time tuition: $628 per credit. Part-time tuition and fees vary according to course load. *Room and board:* Room and board charges vary according to board plan and housing facility. *Payment plan:* installment. *Waivers:* employees or children of employees.

Financial Aid Of all full-time matriculated undergraduates who enrolled in 2009, 1,161 applied for aid, 1,034 were judged to have need, 317 had their need fully met. In 2009, 178 non-need-based awards were made. *Average percent of need met:* 1%. *Average financial aid package:* $18,376. *Average need-based loan:* $9177. *Average need-based gift aid:* $12,620. *Average non-need-based aid:* $6700. *Average indebtedness upon graduation:* $19,500.

Applying *Options:* electronic application, deferred entrance. *Application fee:* $25. *Required:* essay or personal statement, high school transcript, minimum 2.5 GPA, 2 letters of recommendation. *Recommended:* interview. *Application deadlines:* rolling (freshmen), rolling (transfers). *Notification:* continuous (freshmen), continuous (transfers).

Freshman Application Contact Mr. Jared Burgess, Director of Visitation Program, John Brown University, 2000 West University, Siloam Springs, AR 72761. *Phone:* 479-524-7190. *Toll-free phone:* 877-JBU-INFO. *Fax:* 479-524-4196. *E-mail:* JBurgess@jbu.edu. *Web site:* http://www.jbu.edu/.

Lyon College
Batesville, Arkansas

- **Independent Presbyterian** 4-year, founded 1872
- **Small-town** 136-acre campus
- **Endowment** $39.8 million
- **Coed** 651 undergraduate students, 97% full-time, 56% women, 44% men
- **Moderately difficult** entrance level, 65% of applicants were admitted

Undergraduates 630 full-time, 21 part-time. Students come from 27 states and territories; 8 other countries; 26% are from out of state; 4% Black or African American, non-Hispanic/Latino; 1% Hispanic/Latino; 2% Asian, non-Hispanic/Latino; 1% American Indian or Alaska Native, non-Hispanic/Latino; 7% Race/ethnicity unknown; 2% international; 9% transferred in; 79% live on campus. *Retention:* 65% of full-time freshmen returned.

Freshmen *Admission:* 1,108 applied, 717 admitted, 200 enrolled. *Average high school GPA:* 3.49. *Test scores:* SAT critical reading scores over 500: 73%; SAT math scores over 500: 77%; SAT writing scores over 500: 70%; ACT scores over 18: 100%; SAT critical reading scores over 600: 42%; SAT math scores over 600: 54%; SAT writing scores over 600: 39%; ACT scores over 24: 67%; SAT critical reading scores over 700: 15%; SAT math scores over 700: 12%; SAT writing scores over 700: 4%; ACT scores over 30: 16%.

Faculty *Total:* 63, 65% full-time. *Student/faculty ratio:* 13:1.

Academics *Calendar:* semesters. *Degree:* bachelor's. *Special study options:* accelerated degree program, advanced placement credit, double majors, independent study, internships, part-time degree program, student-designed majors, study abroad, summer session for credit. *Unusual degree programs:* 3-2 engineering with University of Missouri-Rolla, University of Arkansas, University of Minnesota.

Computers on Campus 101 computers/terminals are available on campus for general student use. Students can access the following: campus intranet, computer help desk, free student e-mail accounts, online (class) grades, online (class) registration, online (class) schedules. Campuswide network is available. 100% of college-owned or -operated housing units are wired for high-speed Internet access. Wireless service is available via entire campus.

Student Life *Housing:* on-campus residence required through junior year. *Options:* coed, men-only, women-only. Campus housing is university owned and leased by the school. Freshman campus housing is guaranteed. *Activities and organizations:* drama/theater group, student-run newspaper, choral group, Baptist Christian Ministry, Student Activities Council, Pre-Med Club, national fraternities, national sororities. *Campus security:* 24-hour patrols, late-night transport/escort service. *Student services:* health clinic, personal/psychological counseling.

Athletics Member NAIA. *Intercollegiate sports:* baseball M(s), basketball M(s)/W(s), cross-country running M(s)/W(s), golf M(s)/W(s), soccer M(s)/W(s), softball W(s), volleyball W(s). *Intramural sports:* badminton M/W, basketball M/W, football M/W, softball M/W, table tennis M/W, tennis M/W, ultimate Frisbee M/W, volleyball M/W.

Standardized Tests *Required:* SAT or ACT (for admission).

Costs (2011–12) *Comprehensive fee:* $30,246 includes full-time tuition ($22,682), mandatory fees ($224), and room and board ($7340). Part-time

tuition: $790 per credit hour. *Room and board:* Room and board charges vary according to board plan. *Payment plan:* installment. *Waivers:* employees or children of employees.

Financial Aid Of all full-time matriculated undergraduates who enrolled in 2009, 557 applied for aid, 498 were judged to have need, 71 had their need fully met. 202 Federal Work-Study jobs (averaging $1054). 6 state and other part-time jobs (averaging $1051). In 2009, 128 non-need-based awards were made. *Average percent of need met:* 78%. *Average financial aid package:* $20,828. *Average need-based loan:* $3883. *Average need-based gift aid:* $16,364. *Average non-need-based aid:* $14,039. *Average indebtedness upon graduation:* $18,180.

Applying *Options:* electronic application, early admission, early action, deferred entrance. *Application fee:* $25. *Required:* high school transcript, minimum 2.5 GPA. *Required for some:* essay or personal statement, 2 letters of recommendation. *Application deadlines:* rolling (freshmen), rolling (transfers). *Notification:* continuous (freshmen), continuous (transfers).

Freshman Application Contact Office of Enrollment Services, Lyon College, 2300 Highland Road, Batesville, AR 72501. *Phone:* 870-307-7250. *Toll-free phone:* 800-423-2542. *Fax:* 870-307-7542. *E-mail:* admissions@lyon.edu. *Web site:* http://www.lyon.edu/.

Ouachita Baptist University
Arkadelphia, Arkansas

- **Independent Baptist** 4-year, founded 1886
- **Small-town** 200-acre campus with easy access to Little Rock
- **Endowment** $77.2 million
- **Coed** 1,504 undergraduate students, 98% full-time, 54% women, 46% men
- **Moderately difficult** entrance level, 63% of applicants were admitted

Undergraduates 1,477 full-time, 27 part-time. Students come from 33 states and territories; 46 other countries; 46% are from out of state; 7% Black or African American, non-Hispanic/Latino; 0.8% Hispanic/Latino; 0.5% Asian, non-Hispanic/Latino; 0.1% Native Hawaiian or other Pacific Islander, non-Hispanic/Latino; 1% American Indian or Alaska Native, non-Hispanic/Latino; 0.1% Two or more races, non-Hispanic/Latino; 3% international; 4% transferred in; 92% live on campus. *Retention:* 81% of full-time freshmen returned.

Freshmen *Admission:* 1,849 applied, 1,161 admitted, 451 enrolled. *Average high school GPA:* 3.57. *Test scores:* SAT critical reading scores over 500: 74%; SAT math scores over 500: 78%; ACT scores over 18: 97%; SAT critical reading scores over 600: 32%; SAT math scores over 600: 33%; ACT scores over 24: 56%; SAT critical reading scores over 700: 9%; SAT math scores over 700: 3%; ACT scores over 30: 14%.

Faculty *Total:* 139, 78% full-time, 68% with terminal degrees. *Student/faculty ratio:* 12:1.

Academics *Calendar:* semesters. *Degree:* bachelor's. *Special study options:* academic remediation for entering students, accelerated degree program, advanced placement credit, cooperative education, distance learning, double majors, English as a second language, honors programs, independent study, internships, off-campus study, part-time degree program, study abroad, summer session for credit. *ROTC:* Army (b). *Unusual degree programs:* 3-2 engineering with University of Arkansas at Fayetteville.

Computers on Campus 275 computers/terminals and 1,301 ports are available on campus for general student use. Students can access the following: campus intranet, computer help desk, free student e-mail accounts, online (class) grades, online (class) schedules, student Web portal. Campuswide network is available. 100% of college-owned or -operated housing units are wired for high-speed Internet access. Wireless service is available via entire campus.

Student Life *Housing:* on-campus residence required through senior year. *Options:* men-only, women-only, disabled students. Campus housing is university owned and leased by the school. Freshman campus housing is guaranteed. *Activities and organizations:* drama/theater group, student-run newspaper, television station, choral group, marching band, Phi Beta Lambda, Campus Activities Board, Student Education Association, Student Foundation, International Club. *Campus security:* 24-hour emergency response devices and patrols, controlled dormitory access. *Student services:* health clinic, personal/psychological counseling.

Athletics Member NCAA. All Division II. *Intercollegiate sports:* baseball M(s), basketball M(s)/W(s), cheerleading M/W, cross-country running W(s), football M(s), golf M(s)/W(s), soccer M(s)/W(s), softball W(s), swimming and diving M(s)/W(s), tennis M(s)/W(s), volleyball W(s), wrestling M(s). *Intramural sports:* basketball M/W, football M/W, soccer M, softball M/W, table tennis M/W.

Standardized Tests *Required:* SAT or ACT (for admission).

Costs (2011–12) *Comprehensive fee:* $26,670 includes full-time tuition ($20,160), mandatory fees ($470), and room and board ($6040). Part-time tuition: $580 per semester hour. *Room and board:* Room and board charges vary according to housing facility. *Payment plans:* installment, deferred payment. *Waivers:* employees or children of employees.

Financial Aid Of all full-time matriculated undergraduates who enrolled in 2009, 1,173 applied for aid, 930 were judged to have need, 493 had their need fully met. 300 Federal Work-Study jobs (averaging $1800). In 2009, 501 non-need-based awards were made. *Average percent of need met:* 89%. *Average financial aid package:* $18,065. *Average need-based loan:* $4659. *Average need-based gift aid:* $12,062. *Average non-need-based aid:* $8999. *Average indebtedness upon graduation:* $15,970. *Financial aid deadline:* 6/1.

Applying *Options:* deferred entrance. *Required:* high school transcript, minimum 2.75 GPA. *Recommended:* interview. *Application deadlines:* 8/15 (freshmen), 8/15 (transfers). *Notification:* continuous (freshmen), continuous (transfers).

Freshman Application Contact Mrs. Lori Motl, Director of Admissions Counseling, Ouachita Baptist University, OBU Box 3776, Arkadelphia, AR 71998-0001. *Phone:* 870-245-5110. *Toll-free phone:* 800-342-5628. *Fax:* 870-245-5500. *E-mail:* motll@obu.edu. *Web site:* http://www.obu.edu/.

Philander Smith College
Little Rock, Arkansas

Freshman Application Contact Mr. George Gray, Director of Recruitment and Admissions, Philander Smith College, 812 West 13th Street, Little Rock, AR 72202-3799. *Phone:* 501-370-5310. *Toll-free phone:* 800-446-6772. *Fax:* 501-370-5225. *E-mail:* ggray@philander.edu. *Web site:* http://www.philander.edu/.

Southern Arkansas University–Magnolia
Magnolia, Arkansas

- **State-supported** comprehensive, founded 1909, part of Southern Arkansas University System
- **Small-town** 781-acre campus
- **Endowment** $20.7 million
- **Coed** 2,944 undergraduate students, 85% full-time, 57% women, 43% men
- **Moderately difficult** entrance level, 67% of applicants were admitted

Undergraduates 2,516 full-time, 428 part-time. Students come from 25 states and territories; 24 other countries; 22% are from out of state; 31% Black or African American, non-Hispanic/Latino; 2% Hispanic/Latino; 0.8% Asian, non-Hispanic/Latino; 0.7% Native Hawaiian or other Pacific Islander, non-Hispanic/Latino; 0.4% American Indian or Alaska Native, non-Hispanic/Latino; 3% international; 9% transferred in; 42% live on campus. *Retention:* 62% of full-time freshmen returned.

Freshmen *Admission:* 2,392 applied, 1,591 admitted, 645 enrolled. *Average high school GPA:* 3.16. *Test scores:* SAT critical reading scores over 500: 36%; SAT math scores over 500: 58%; ACT scores over 18: 76%; SAT critical reading scores over 600: 8%; SAT math scores over 600: 16%; ACT scores over 24: 27%; SAT math scores over 700: 5%; ACT scores over 30: 3%.

Faculty *Total:* 220, 74% full-time, 42% with terminal degrees. *Student/faculty ratio:* 16:1.

Academics *Calendar:* semesters. *Degrees:* certificates, associate, bachelor's, and master's. *Special study options:* academic remediation for entering students, accelerated degree program, adult/continuing education programs, advanced placement credit, distance learning, double majors, freshman honors college, honors programs, independent study, internships, part-time degree program, services for LD students, study abroad, summer session for credit.

Computers on Campus 194 computers/terminals and 194 ports are available on campus for general student use. Students can access the following: campus intranet, computer help desk, free student e-mail accounts, online (class) grades, online (class) registration, online (class) schedules. Campuswide network is available. 100% of college-owned or -operated housing units are wired for high-speed Internet access. Wireless service is available via computer centers, computer labs, dorm rooms, libraries, student centers.

Student Life *Housing:* on-campus residence required through sophomore year. *Options:* coed, men-only, women-only. Campus housing is university owned and is provided by a third party. Freshman campus housing is guaranteed. *Activities and organizations:* drama/theater group, student-run newspaper, radio station, choral group, marching band, Student Government Association, Student Activities Board, Resident Hall Association, Residential College, International Student Association, national fraternities, national sororities. *Campus security:* 24-hour emergency response devices, student patrols, late-night transport/escort service, controlled dormitory access. *Student services:* health clinic, personal/psychological counseling.

Athletics Member NCAA. All Division II. *Intercollegiate sports:* baseball M(s), basketball M(s)/W(s), cross-country running M/W(s), football M(s), golf M, softball W(s), tennis W(s), track and field M/W, volleyball W(s). *Intramural sports:* badminton M/W, basketball M/W, football M, golf M, softball M/W, swimming and diving M/W, table tennis M/W, tennis M/W, volleyball M/W.

Standardized Tests *Required:* SAT or ACT (for admission). *Recommended:* ACT (for admission).

Costs (2010–11) *Tuition:* state resident $5340 full-time, $178 per hour part-time; nonresident $8100 full-time, $270 per hour part-time. Full-time tuition and fees vary according to course load. Part-time tuition and fees vary according to course load. *Required fees:* $1086 full-time, $35 per hour part-time, $18 per term part-time. *Room and board:* $4570; room only: $2290. Room and board charges vary according to board plan and housing facility. *Payment plan:* installment. *Waivers:* children of alumni, senior citizens, and employees or children of employees.

Financial Aid Of all full-time matriculated undergraduates who enrolled in 2009, 1,959 applied for aid, 1,766 were judged to have need, 1,187 had their need fully met. 1,250 Federal Work-Study jobs (averaging $3097). 303 state and other part-time jobs (averaging $4268). In 2009, 284 non-need-based awards were made. *Average percent of need met:* 100%. *Average financial aid package:* $7679. *Average need-based loan:* $3692. *Average need-based gift aid:* $4106. *Average non-need-based aid:* $5891. *Average indebtedness upon graduation:* $15,672.

Applying *Options:* electronic application, early admission, deferred entrance. *Required:* high school transcript. *Required for some:* interview. *Application deadlines:* 8/27 (freshmen), 8/27 (transfers).

Freshman Application Contact Southern Arkansas University–Magnolia, 100 East University, Magnolia, AR 71753. *Phone:* 870-235-4040. *Toll-free phone:* 800-332-7286. *Web site:* http://www.saumag.edu/.

Strayer University - Little Rock Campus
Little Rock, Arkansas

- **Proprietary** comprehensive
- **Coed**

Academics *Degrees:* bachelor's and master's.

Costs (2010–11) *Tuition:* $13,635 full-time, $1590 per course part-time.

Freshman Application Contact Strayer University - Little Rock Campus, 10825 Financial Centre Parkway, Suite 131, Little Rock, AR 72211. *Web site:* http://www.strayer.edu/little_rock.

University of Arkansas
Fayetteville, Arkansas

- **State-supported** university, founded 1871, part of University of Arkansas System
- **Suburban** 410-acre campus
- **Endowment** $673.1 million
- **Coed** 17,247 undergraduate students, 87% full-time, 48% women, 52% men
- **Moderately difficult** entrance level, 60% of applicants were admitted

Undergraduates 15,001 full-time, 2,246 part-time. Students come from 50 states and territories; 120 other countries; 30% are from out of state; 5% Black or African American, non-Hispanic/Latino; 5% Hispanic/Latino; 3% Asian, non-Hispanic/Latino; 0.1% Native Hawaiian or other Pacific Islander, non-Hispanic/Latino; 2% American Indian or Alaska Native, non-Hispanic/Latino; 2% Two or more races, non-Hispanic/Latino; 0.4% Race/ethnicity unknown; 3% international; 9% transferred in; 30% live on campus. *Retention:* 83% of full-time freshmen returned.

Freshmen *Admission:* 14,019 applied, 8,468 admitted, 3,810 enrolled. *Average high school GPA:* 3.56. *Test scores:* SAT critical reading scores over 500: 79%; SAT math scores over 500: 84%; ACT scores over 18: 100%; SAT critical reading scores over 600: 33%; SAT math scores over 600: 43%; ACT scores over 24: 70%; SAT critical reading scores over 700: 7%; SAT math scores over 700: 7%; ACT scores over 30: 19%.

Faculty *Total:* 1,026, 92% full-time, 84% with terminal degrees. *Student/faculty ratio:* 18:1.

Academics *Calendar:* semesters. *Degrees:* bachelor's, master's, doctoral-professional, doctoral-research/scholarship, post-master's, and postbachelor's certificates. *Special study options:* accelerated degree program, advanced placement credit, cooperative education, distance learning, double majors, English as a second language, freshman honors college, honors programs, independent study, internships, part-time degree program, services for LD students, study abroad, summer session for credit. *ROTC:* Army (b), Air Force (b). *Unusual degree programs:* 3-2 law.

Computers on Campus 3,014 computers/terminals are available on campus for general student use. Students can access the following: computer help desk, free student e-mail accounts, online (class) grades, online (class) registration, online (class) schedules. Campuswide network is available. 100% of college-owned or -operated housing units are wired for high-speed Internet access. Wireless service is available via entire campus.

Student Life *Housing:* on-campus residence required for freshman year. *Options:* coed, men-only, women-only, disabled students. Campus housing is university owned. Freshman campus housing is guaranteed. *Activities and organizations:* drama/theater group, student-run newspaper, radio and television station, choral group, marching band, Gamma Beta Phi, University Baptist Collegiate Ministry, Associated Student Government, Black Students Association, Hot Pink Ribbon Club, national fraternities, national sororities. *Campus security:* 24-hour emergency response devices and patrols, student patrols, late-night transport/escort service, controlled dormitory access, RAD (Rape Aggression Defense program). *Student services:* health clinic, personal/psychological counseling, women's center, legal services.

Athletics Member NCAA. All Division I except football (Division I-A). *Intercollegiate sports:* baseball M(s), basketball M(s)/W(s), cross-country running M(s)/W(s), golf M(s)/W(s), gymnastics W(s), soccer W(s), softball W(s), swimming and diving W(s), tennis M(s)/W(s), track and field M(s)/W(s), volleyball W(s). *Intramural sports:* badminton M/W, basketball M/W, bowling M/W, cheerleading M(c)/W(c), crew M(c)/W(c), football M, golf M/W, racquetball M/W, rugby M(c)/W(c), soccer M/W, softball M/W, tennis M/W, ultimate Frisbee M/W, volleyball M(c)/W(c), water polo M/W.

Standardized Tests *Required:* SAT or ACT (for admission).

Costs (2010–11) *Tuition:* state resident $5211 full-time, $174 per credit hour part-time; nonresident $14,443 full-time, $481 per contact hour part-time. Full-time tuition and fees vary according to course load and program. Part-time tuition and fees vary according to course load and program. *Required fees:* $1557 full-time. *Room and board:* $8042; room only: $5096. Room and board charges vary according to board plan and housing facility. *Payment plan:* installment. *Waivers:* senior citizens and employees or children of employees.

Financial Aid Of all full-time matriculated undergraduates who enrolled in 2009, 7,428 applied for aid, 5,508 were judged to have need, 1,002 had their need fully met. In 2009, 2354 non-need-based awards were made. *Average percent of need met:* 64%. *Average financial aid package:* $9030. *Average need-based loan:* $4306. *Average need-based gift aid:* $6343. *Average non-need-based aid:* $5315. *Average indebtedness upon graduation:* $20,171.

Applying *Options:* electronic application, early admission, early action. *Application fee:* $40. *Required:* high school transcript. *Recommended:* minimum 3 GPA. *Application deadlines:* 8/1 (freshmen), 8/1 (transfers), 11/15 (early action). *Notification:* continuous until 9/1 (freshmen), continuous (transfers), 12/15 (early action).

Freshman Application Contact University of Arkansas, 232 Silas H. Hunt Hall, Office of Admissions, Fayetteville, AR 72701-1201. *Phone:* 479-575-5346. *Toll-free phone:* 800-377-5346 (in-state); 800-377-8632 (out-of-state). *Fax:* 479-575-7515. *E-mail:* uofa@uark.edu. *Web site:* http://www.uark.edu/.

University of Arkansas at Little Rock

Little Rock, Arkansas

- **State-supported** university, founded 1927, part of University of Arkansas System
- **Urban** 150-acre campus
- **Endowment** $7.6 million
- **Coed**
- **Minimally difficult** entrance level

Faculty *Student/faculty ratio:* 16:1.

Academics *Calendar:* semesters. *Degrees:* certificates, associate, bachelor's, master's, doctoral-professional, doctoral-research/scholarship, post-master's, and postbachelor's certificates.

Student Life *Campus security:* 24-hour emergency response devices, student patrols, late-night transport/escort service.

Athletics Member NCAA. All Division I.

Standardized Tests *Required:* ACT (for admission).

Costs (2010–11) *Tuition:* state resident $5228 full-time, $174 per credit hour part-time; nonresident $14,175 full-time, $473 per credit hour part-time. Full-time tuition and fees vary according to program. Part-time tuition and fees vary according to program. *Required fees:* $1415 full-time, $47 per credit hour part-time. *Room only:* $3255. Room and board charges vary according to housing facility.

Financial Aid *Average financial aid package:* $7190.

Applying *Options:* early admission, deferred entrance. *Required:* high school transcript, minimum 2.5 GPA, proof of immunization.

Freshman Application Contact Ms. Tammy Harrison, Director of Admissions, University of Arkansas at Little Rock, 2801 South University Avenue, Little Rock, AR 72204-1099. *Phone:* 501-569-3127. *Toll-free phone:* 800-482-8892. *Fax:* 501-569-8956. *E-mail:* twharrison@ualn.edu. *Web site:* http://www.ualr.edu/.

University of Arkansas at Monticello

Monticello, Arkansas

- **State-supported** comprehensive, founded 1909, part of University of Arkansas System
- **Small-town** 1600-acre campus
- **Endowment** $1.9 million
- **Coed**
- **Noncompetitive** entrance level

Faculty *Student/faculty ratio:* 15:1.

Academics *Calendar:* semesters. *Degrees:* certificates, associate, bachelor's, master's, and postbachelor's certificates.

Student Life *Campus security:* 24-hour emergency response devices and patrols.

Athletics Member NCAA. All Division II.

Standardized Tests *Recommended:* used for placement.

Costs (2010–11) *Tuition:* state resident $3510 full-time, $117 per semester hour part-time; nonresident $7770 full-time, $259 per semester hour part-time. Full-time tuition and fees vary according to location and program. Part-time tuition and fees vary according to location and program. *Required fees:* $1240 full-time, $41 per semester hour part-time. *Room and board:* Room and board charges vary according to board plan and housing facility.

Financial Aid *Of all full-time matriculated undergraduates who enrolled in 2006,* 166 Federal Work-Study jobs (averaging $1159). 292 state and other part-time jobs (averaging $1388).

Applying *Options:* early admission, deferred entrance. *Required:* high school transcript, proof of immunization.

Freshman Application Contact Ms. Mary Whiting, Director of Admissions, University of Arkansas at Monticello, Monticello, AR 71656. *Phone:* 870-460-1026. *Toll-free phone:* 800-844-1826. *E-mail:* admissions@uamont.edu. *Web site:* http://www.uamont.edu/.

University of Arkansas at Pine Bluff

Pine Bluff, Arkansas

- **State-supported** comprehensive, founded 1873, part of University of Arkansas System
- **Urban** 327-acre campus
- **Coed** 3,283 undergraduate students, 91% full-time, 56% women, 44% men
- **30%** of applicants were admitted

Undergraduates 3,002 full-time, 281 part-time. Students come from 37 states and territories; 20 other countries; 37% are from out of state; 5% transferred in; 46% live on campus. *Retention:* 57% of full-time freshmen returned.

Freshmen *Admission:* 4,988 applied, 1,505 admitted, 802 enrolled. *Test scores:* SAT critical reading scores over 500: 20%; SAT math scores over 500: 18%; ACT scores over 18: 29%; SAT critical reading scores over 600: 7%; SAT math scores over 600: 8%; ACT scores over 24: 2%.

Faculty *Total:* 234, 73% full-time, 51% with terminal degrees. *Student/faculty ratio:* 17:1.

Academics *Calendar:* semesters. *Degrees:* certificates, associate, bachelor's, and master's. *Special study options:* academic remediation for entering students, accelerated degree program, adult/continuing education programs, advanced placement credit, cooperative education, distance learning, double majors, English as a second language, external degree program, honors programs, independent study, internships, off-campus study, part-time degree program, services for LD students, summer session for credit. *ROTC:* Army (b). *Unusual degree programs:* 3-2 engineering with University of Arkansas at Fayetteville.

Computers on Campus 1,000 computers/terminals and 1,400 ports are available on campus for general student use. Students can access the following: campus intranet, computer help desk, free student e-mail accounts, online (class) grades, online (class) registration, online (class) schedules. Campus-wide network is available. Wireless service is available via classrooms, computer centers, computer labs, learning centers, libraries.

Student Life *Housing options:* men-only, women-only. Campus housing is university owned. *Activities and organizations:* drama/theater group, student-run newspaper, choral group, marching band, Pre-Alumni Club, Honors College, national fraternities, national sororities. *Campus security:* 24-hour emergency response devices and patrols. *Student services:* health clinic, personal/psychological counseling.

Athletics Member NCAA, NAIA. All NCAA Division I except football (Division I-AA). *Intercollegiate sports:* baseball M, basketball M(s)/W(s), cross-country running M/W, golf M(s), track and field M/W, volleyball W(s). *Intramural sports:* baseball M, basketball M, bowling M/W, cross-country running M, football M/W, golf M/W, gymnastics M/W, racquetball M/W, softball M/W, swimming and diving M/W, table tennis M/W, tennis M/W, track and field M/W, volleyball M/W, weight lifting M/W.

Standardized Tests *Required:* SAT or ACT (for admission).

Costs (2010–11) *Tuition:* state resident $3750 full-time, $125 per credit hour part-time; nonresident $8700 full-time, $290 per credit hour part-time. Full-time tuition and fees vary according to course level, degree level, and location. Part-time tuition and fees vary according to course level, degree level, and location. *Required fees:* $1230 full-time, $8 per credit hour part-time, $23 per term part-time. *Room and board:* Room and board charges vary according to board plan and housing facility. *Waivers:* senior citizens and employees or children of employees.

Financial Aid Of all full-time matriculated undergraduates who enrolled in 2005, 2,825 applied for aid, 2,825 were judged to have need, 1,200 had their need fully met. 328 Federal Work-Study jobs (averaging $1000). *Average percent of need met:* 70%. *Average financial aid package:* $8121. *Average need-based loan:* $4500. *Average need-based gift aid:* $1000.

Applying *Options:* electronic application, early admission, deferred entrance. *Required:* high school transcript, minimum 2 GPA. *Application deadline:* rolling (freshmen). *Notification:* continuous (freshmen), continuous (transfers).

Freshman Application Contact University of Arkansas at Pine Bluff, 1200 North University Drive, Pine Bluff, AR 71601-2799. *Phone:* 870-575-8461. *Toll-free phone:* 800-264-6585. *Web site:* http://www.uapb.edu/.

University of Arkansas for Medical Sciences

Little Rock, Arkansas

- **State-supported** university, founded 1879, part of University of Arkansas System
- **Urban** 5-acre campus with easy access to Little Rock
- **Endowment** $31.0 million
- **Coed** 944 undergraduate students, 79% full-time, 80% women, 20% men

Undergraduates 749 full-time, 195 part-time. 12% are from out of state.

Academics *Calendar:* semesters. *Degrees:* certificates, associate, bachelor's, master's, doctoral-professional, doctoral-research/scholarship, and postbachelor's certificates (bachelor's degree is upper-level). *Special study options:* part-time degree program, services for LD students. *ROTC:* Army (c).

Computers on Campus Students can access the following: campus intranet, computer help desk, free student e-mail accounts, online (class) grades. Campuswide network is available. 100% of college-owned or -operated housing units are wired for high-speed Internet access. Wireless service is available via entire campus.

Student Life *Housing options:* coed. Campus housing is university owned. *Campus security:* 24-hour emergency response devices and patrols, late-night transport/escort service, controlled dormitory access. *Student services:* health clinic, personal/psychological counseling.

Athletics *Intercollegiate sports:* ultimate Frisbee M/W, volleyball M/W. *Intramural sports:* basketball M/W, football M, golf M, ultimate Frisbee M/W, volleyball M/W.

Costs (2011–12) *Tuition:* state resident $6600 full-time; nonresident $15,576 full-time. Full-time tuition and fees vary according to course load, degree level, location, program, and reciprocity agreements. Part-time tuition and fees vary according to course load, degree level, location, program, and reciprocity agreements. *Required fees:* $256 full-time. *Room only:* $5900. *Waivers:* senior citizens and employees or children of employees.

Financial Aid Of all full-time matriculated undergraduates who enrolled in 2005, 734 applied for aid, 686 were judged to have need. 9 Federal Work-Study jobs (averaging $1201). *Average percent of need met:* 62%. *Average financial aid package:* $3000. *Average need-based loan:* $4000. *Average need-based gift aid:* $500. *Average indebtedness upon graduation:* $7000.

Freshman Application Contact University of Arkansas for Medical Sciences, 4301 West Markham, Little Rock, AR 72205-7199. *Phone:* 501-686-5730. *Web site:* http://www.uams.edu/.

University of Arkansas–Fort Smith

Fort Smith, Arkansas

- **State and locally supported** 4-year, founded 1928, part of University of Arkansas System
- **Suburban** 120-acre campus
- **Endowment** $54.7 million
- **Coed** 7,751 undergraduate students, 67% full-time, 58% women, 42% men
- **Minimally difficult** entrance level, 58% of applicants were admitted

Undergraduates 5,221 full-time, 2,530 part-time. Students come from 35 states and territories; 16 other countries; 10% are from out of state; 6% transferred in; 6% live on campus. *Retention:* 64% of full-time freshmen returned.

Freshmen *Admission:* 3,884 applied, 2,271 admitted, 1,422 enrolled. *Average high school GPA:* 3.15. *Test scores:* ACT scores over 18: 86%; ACT scores over 24: 29%; ACT scores over 30: 2%.

Faculty *Total:* 426, 53% full-time, 42% with terminal degrees. *Student/faculty ratio:* 20:1.

Academics *Calendar:* semesters. *Degrees:* certificates, associate, and bachelor's. *Special study options:* academic remediation for entering students, accelerated degree program, adult/continuing education programs, advanced placement credit, cooperative education, distance learning, double majors, English as a second language, external degree program, honors programs, internships, off-campus study, part-time degree program, services for LD students, study abroad, summer session for credit. *ROTC:* Army (c), Air Force (c).

Computers on Campus 914 computers/terminals and 2,000 ports are available on campus for general student use. Students can access the following: campus intranet, computer help desk, free student e-mail accounts, online (class) grades, online (class) registration, online (class) schedules, online subscription databases, information portal, online course management system and online courses. Campuswide network is available. 100% of college-owned or -operated housing units are wired for high-speed Internet access. Wireless service is available via classrooms, computer centers, computer labs, dorm rooms, learning centers, libraries, student centers.

Student Life *Housing options:* coed, disabled students. Campus housing is university owned. *Activities and organizations:* drama/theater group, student-run newspaper, choral group, Campus Activities Board, Phi Beta Lambda, Drama Club, Non-Traditional Students, Baptist Collegiate Ministry, national fraternities, national sororities. *Campus security:* 24-hour emergency response devices and patrols, student patrols, late-night transport/escort service, controlled dormitory access, Student patrols operate on varying hours throughout the semester. The new dormitory facilities have electronic card readers entrances. *Student services:* health clinic, personal/psychological counseling.

Athletics Member NCAA. All Division II. *Intercollegiate sports:* baseball M(s), basketball M(s)/W(s), cross-country running M(s)/W(s), golf M(s)/W(s), tennis M(s)/W(s), volleyball W(s). *Intramural sports:* badminton M/W, basketball M/W, bowling M/W, cheerleading M/W, football M/W, riflery M(c)/W(c), soccer M/W, softball M/W, table tennis M/W, ultimate Frisbee M/W, volleyball M/W.

Standardized Tests *Required:* SAT or ACT (for admission), COMPASS (in lieu of SAT or ACT) (for admission).

Costs (2011–12) *Tuition:* state resident $3570 full-time, $119 per credit hour part-time; nonresident $9540 full-time, $318 per credit hour part-time. Full-time tuition and fees vary according to course load and program. Part-time tuition and fees vary according to course load and program. *Required fees:* $1348 full-time, $40 per term part-time, $68 per term part-time. *Room only:* $4000. Room and board charges vary according to board plan and housing facility. *Payment plan:* installment. *Waivers:* senior citizens and employees or children of employees.

Financial Aid Of all full-time matriculated undergraduates who enrolled in 2004, 2,564 applied for aid, 2,232 were judged to have need, 215 had their need fully met. 110 Federal Work-Study jobs (averaging $3000). 94 state and other part-time jobs (averaging $3000). In 2004, 350 non-need-based awards were made. *Average percent of need met:* 62%. *Average financial aid package:* $5568. *Average need-based loan:* $3183. *Average need-based gift aid:* $3504. *Average non-need-based aid:* $2643. *Average indebtedness upon graduation:* $7339.

Applying *Options:* electronic application, early admission, deferred entrance. *Required:* high school transcript. *Application deadlines:* rolling (freshmen), rolling (transfers).

Freshman Application Contact Office of Admissions and School Relations, University of Arkansas–Fort Smith, 5210 Grand Avenue, PO Box 3649, Fort Smith, AR 72913-3649. *Phone:* 479-788-7120. *Toll-free phone:* 888-512-5466. *Fax:* 479-788-7016. *E-mail:* information@uafortsmith.edu. *Web site:* http://www.uafortsmith.edu/.

University of Central Arkansas

Conway, Arkansas

Freshman Application Contact Penny Hatfield, Interim Director of Admissions, University of Central Arkansas, 201 Donaghey Avenue, Bernard 100, Conway, AR 72035. *Phone:* 501-450-346. *Toll-free phone:* 800-243-8245. *Fax:* 501-450-5228. *E-mail:* phatfield@uca.edu. *Web site:* http://www.uca.edu/.

University of Phoenix–Little Rock Campus

Little Rock, Arkansas

Freshman Application Contact Ms. Audra McQuarie, Registrar/Executive Director, University of Phoenix–Little Rock Campus, 4035 South Riverpoint Parkway, Mail Stop CF-L101, Phoenix, AZ 85040. *Phone:* 480-557-6151. *Toll-free phone:* 800-776-4867 (in-state); 800-228-7240 (out-of-state). *Fax:*

480-643-3068. *E-mail:* audra.mcquarie@phoenix.edu. *Web site:* http://www.phoenix.edu/.

University of the Ozarks
Clarksville, Arkansas

- **Independent Presbyterian** 4-year, founded 1834
- **Small-town** 56-acre campus with easy access to Little Rock
- **Endowment** $76.5 million
- **Coed** 630 undergraduate students, 97% full-time, 55% women, 45% men
- **Moderately difficult** entrance level, 59% of applicants were admitted

Undergraduates 611 full-time, 19 part-time. Students come from 21 states and territories; 17 other countries; 30% are from out of state; 4% Black or African American, non-Hispanic/Latino; 6% Hispanic/Latino; 0.6% Asian, non-Hispanic/Latino; 2% American Indian or Alaska Native, non-Hispanic/Latino; 1% Two or more races, non-Hispanic/Latino; 0.6% Race/ethnicity unknown; 14% international; 3% transferred in; 72% live on campus. *Retention:* 64% of full-time freshmen returned.

Freshmen *Admission:* 1,372 applied, 814 admitted, 204 enrolled. *Average high school GPA:* 3.31. *Test scores:* SAT critical reading scores over 500: 55%; SAT math scores over 500: 52%; ACT scores over 18: 92%; SAT critical reading scores over 600: 14%; SAT math scores over 600: 17%; ACT scores over 24: 39%; SAT critical reading scores over 700: 2%; SAT math scores over 700: 2%; ACT scores over 30: 4%.

Faculty *Total:* 66, 74% full-time, 52% with terminal degrees. *Student/faculty ratio:* 11:1.

Academics *Calendar:* semesters. *Degree:* bachelor's. *Special study options:* academic remediation for entering students, advanced placement credit, cooperative education, double majors, English as a second language, independent study, internships, off-campus study, part-time degree program, services for LD students, study abroad, summer session for credit. *Unusual degree programs:* 3-2 engineering with University of Arkansas; theology with University of Dubuque, marine biology with University of Southern Mississippi.

Computers on Campus 120 computers/terminals are available on campus for general student use. Students can access the following: campus intranet, computer help desk, free student e-mail accounts. Campuswide network is available. 100% of college-owned or -operated housing units are wired for high-speed Internet access. Wireless service is available via libraries.

Student Life *Housing:* on-campus residence required through sophomore year. *Options:* coed, men-only, women-only. Campus housing is university owned. Freshman campus housing is guaranteed. *Activities and organizations:* drama/theater group, student-run newspaper, radio and television station, choral group, Phi Beta Lambda, Planet Club, Student Government Association, Student Foundation Board, Baptist Campus Ministries. *Campus security:* 24-hour emergency response devices and patrols, late-night transport/escort service. *Student services:* health clinic.

Athletics Member NCAA. All Division III. *Intercollegiate sports:* baseball M, basketball M/W, cheerleading M/W, cross-country running M/W, soccer M/W, softball W, tennis M/W. *Intramural sports:* badminton M/W, basketball M/W, bowling M/W, football M/W, racquetball M/W, soccer M, softball M/W, table tennis M/W, tennis M/W, ultimate Frisbee M/W, volleyball M/W, weight lifting M/W.

Standardized Tests *Required:* SAT or ACT (for admission).

Costs (2011–12) *Comprehensive fee:* $28,550 includes full-time tuition ($21,450), mandatory fees ($600), and room and board ($6500). Part-time tuition: $900 per credit hour. *College room only:* $3000. Room and board charges vary according to board plan and housing facility. *Payment plan:* installment. *Waivers:* children of alumni and employees or children of employees.

Financial Aid Of all full-time matriculated undergraduates who enrolled in 2009, 389 applied for aid, 354 were judged to have need, 65 had their need fully met. 133 Federal Work-Study jobs (averaging $1130). 23 state and other part-time jobs (averaging $5370). In 2009, 191 non-need-based awards were made. *Average percent of need met:* 77%. *Average financial aid package:* $18,877. *Average need-based loan:* $10,173. *Average need-based gift aid:* $13,990. *Average non-need-based aid:* $16,569. *Average indebtedness upon graduation:* $18,425.

Applying *Options:* electronic application, deferred entrance. *Application fee:* $30. *Required:* minimum 2 GPA. *Required for some:* essay or personal statement, high school transcript, interview. *Application deadlines:* rolling (freshmen), rolling (transfers). *Notification:* continuous (freshmen), continuous (transfers).

Freshman Application Contact Ms. Kim Myrick, Vice President for Enrollment Management, University of the Ozarks, 415 North College Avenue, Clarksville, AR 72830-2880. *Phone:* 479-979-1227. *Toll-free phone:* 800-264-8636. *Fax:* 479-979-1417. *E-mail:* admiss@ozarks.edu. *Web site:* http://www.ozarks.edu/.

Williams Baptist College
Walnut Ridge, Arkansas

Freshman Application Contact Mrs. Angela Flippo, Vice President for Enrollment, Williams Baptist College, 60 West Fulbright Avenue, Walnut Ridge, AR 72476. *Phone:* 870-759-4117. *Toll-free phone:* 800-722-4434. *Fax:* 870-886-3924. *E-mail:* admissions@wbcoll.edu. *Web site:* http://www.wbcoll.edu/.

CALIFORNIA

Academy of Art University
San Francisco, California

- **Proprietary** comprehensive, founded 1929
- **Urban** 3-acre campus
- **Coed**
- **Noncompetitive** entrance level

Faculty *Student/faculty ratio:* 20:1.

Academics *Calendar:* semesters. *Degrees:* certificates, diplomas, associate, bachelor's, and master's.

Student Life *Campus security:* 24-hour emergency response devices and patrols, late-night transport/escort service, controlled dormitory access, ID check at all buildings.

Athletics Member NCAA. All Division II.

Costs (2010–11) *Comprehensive fee:* $31,450 includes full-time tuition ($17,760), mandatory fees ($290), and room and board ($13,400). Full-time tuition and fees vary according to course load. Part-time tuition: $740 per credit. Part-time tuition and fees vary according to course load. *Room and board:* Room and board charges vary according to housing facility.

Financial Aid Of all full-time matriculated undergraduates who enrolled in 2008, 3,558 applied for aid, 3,144 were judged to have need. 105 Federal Work-Study jobs (averaging $2717). *Average financial aid package:* $7037. *Average need-based loan:* $3930. *Average need-based gift aid:* $5787.

Applying *Options:* electronic application, early admission, deferred entrance. *Application fee:* $100. *Required:* high school transcript. *Recommended:* minimum 2 GPA, interview, portfolio.

Freshman Application Contact Admissions, Academy of Art University, 79 New Montgomery Street, San Francisco, CA 94105. *Phone:* 800-544-2787. *Toll-free phone:* 800-544-ARTS. *Fax:* 415-618-6287. *E-mail:* info@academyart.edu. *Web site:* http://www.academyart.edu/.

Academy of Couture Art
West Hollywood, California

Admissions Office Contact Academy of Couture Art, Pacific Design Center, 8687 Melrose Avenue, Suite G520, West Hollywood, CA 90069. *Web site:* http://www.academyofcoutureart.com/.

Alliant International University
San Diego, California

- **Independent** university, founded 1952, part of Alliant International University
- **Suburban** 60-acre campus with easy access to San Diego
- **Coed**

Faculty *Student/faculty ratio:* 13:1.

Academics *Calendar:* semesters. *Degrees:* certificates, bachelor's, master's, doctoral-professional, doctoral-research/scholarship, and postbachelor's certificates.

Student Life *Campus security:* 24-hour emergency response devices and patrols, student patrols, late-night transport/escort service.

Costs (2010–11) *Comprehensive fee:* $23,974 includes full-time tuition ($16,350), mandatory fees ($220), and room and board ($7404). Full-time tuition and fees vary according to course load. Part-time tuition: $600 per semester hour. Part-time tuition and fees vary according to course load. *Room and board:* Room and board charges vary according to board plan.

Financial Aid Of all full-time matriculated undergraduates who enrolled in 2009, 101 applied for aid, 101 were judged to have need. 12 Federal Work-Study jobs (averaging $2000). 5 state and other part-time jobs (averaging $3000). In 2009, 31 non-need-based awards were made. *Average percent of need met:* 62. *Average financial aid package:* $13,550. *Average need-based loan:* $5500. *Average need-based gift aid:* $6750. *Average non-need-based aid:* $1700.

Applying *Options:* electronic application, deferred entrance. *Application fee:* $45. *Required:* high school transcript, minimum 2 GPA.

Allied American University

Laguna Hills, California

Director of Admissions Lindsay Oglesby, Admissions Director, Allied American University, 22952 Alcade Drive, Laguna Hills, CA 92653. *Phone:* 888-384-0849. *Toll-free phone:* 888-384-0849. *Fax:* 949-707-2978. *E-mail:* info@allied.edu. *Web site:* http://allied.edu/.

American Jewish University

Bel Air, California

- **Independent Jewish** comprehensive, founded 1947
- **Suburban** 28-acre campus with easy access to Los Angeles
- **Endowment** $21.1 million
- **Coed** 131 undergraduate students, 96% full-time, 55% women, 45% men
- **Moderately difficult** entrance level, 98% of applicants were admitted

Undergraduates 126 full-time, 5 part-time. Students come from 14 states and territories; 6 other countries; 17% are from out of state; 3% Black or African American, non-Hispanic/Latino; 6% Hispanic/Latino; 2% Asian, non-Hispanic/Latino; 3% American Indian or Alaska Native, non-Hispanic/Latino; 37% Race/ethnicity unknown; 0.8% international; 19% transferred in; 59% live on campus.
Freshmen *Admission:* 46 applied, 45 admitted, 20 enrolled. *Average high school GPA:* 3.15. *Test scores:* SAT critical reading scores over 500: 62%; SAT math scores over 500: 54%; SAT writing scores over 500: 61%; ACT scores over 18: 100%; SAT critical reading scores over 600: 23%; SAT math scores over 600: 23%; SAT writing scores over 600: 15%; ACT scores over 24: 25%.
Faculty *Total:* 78, 14% full-time, 51% with terminal degrees. *Student/faculty ratio:* 8:1.
Academics *Calendar:* semesters. *Degrees:* bachelor's and master's. *Special study options:* academic remediation for entering students, adult/continuing education programs, advanced placement credit, cooperative education, double majors, independent study, internships, part-time degree program, services for LD students, student-designed majors, study abroad, summer session for credit. *Unusual degree programs:* 3-2 business administration; education.
Computers on Campus 38 computers/terminals and 10 ports are available on campus for general student use. Students can access the following: campus intranet, free student e-mail accounts, online (class) grades, online (class) schedules. Campuswide network is available. 100% of college-owned or -operated housing units are wired for high-speed Internet access. Wireless service is available via computer centers, computer labs, dorm rooms, libraries, student centers.
Student Life *Housing options:* coed. Campus housing is university owned. Freshman campus housing is guaranteed. *Activities and organizations:* drama/theater group, student-run newspaper, choral group, Associate Students of American Jewish University, AJU is but a Dream, Bio-Ethics Association, Drama Club. *Campus security:* 24-hour emergency response devices and patrols, controlled dormitory access. *Student services:* health clinic, personal/psychological counseling.
Standardized Tests *Required:* SAT or ACT (for admission).
Costs (2011–12) *One-time required fee:* $200. *Comprehensive fee:* $38,052 includes full-time tuition ($24,744), mandatory fees ($944), and room and board ($12,364). Full-time tuition and fees vary according to course load and degree level. Part-time tuition: $1031 per unit. Part-time tuition and fees vary according to course load and degree level. *Room and board:* Room and board charges vary according to board plan and housing facility. *Payment plan:* installment. *Waivers:* employees or children of employees.
Financial Aid Of all full-time matriculated undergraduates who enrolled in 2009, 136 applied for aid, 136 were judged to have need, 120 had their need fully met. 35 Federal Work-Study jobs (averaging $929). In 2009, 56 non-need-based awards were made. *Average percent of need met:* 96%. *Average financial aid package:* $24,500. *Average need-based loan:* $6500. *Average need-based gift aid:* $9238. *Average non-need-based aid:* $2000. *Average indebtedness upon graduation:* $28,000.
Applying *Options:* electronic application, deferred entrance. *Application fee:* $35. *Required:* essay or personal statement, high school transcript, 2 letters of recommendation. *Recommended:* interview. *Application deadlines:* 5/31 (freshmen), 5/31 (out-of-state freshmen), 5/31 (transfers). *Notification:* continuous (freshmen), continuous (out-of-state freshmen), continuous (transfers).
Freshman Application Contact Mr. Matt Spooner, Director of Undergraduate Admissions, American Jewish University, Familian Campus, 15600 Mulholland Drive, Los Angeles, CA 90077-1599. *Phone:* 310-440-1250. *Toll-free phone:* 888-853-6763. *Fax:* 310-471-3657. *E-mail:* admissions@ajula.edu. *Web site:* http://www.ajula.edu/.

American Musical and Dramatic Academy, Los Angeles

Los Angeles, California

Freshman Application Contact Karen Jackson, Director of Admission, American Musical and Dramatic Academy, Los Angeles, 6305 Yucca Street, Los Angeles, CA 90028. *Phone:* 323-469-3300. *Toll-free phone:* 866-374-5300. *Fax:* 323-469-5246. *E-mail:* kjackson@amda.edu. *Web site:* http://www.amda.edu/.

Antioch University Los Angeles

Culver City, California

Application Contact Admissions, Antioch University Los Angeles, 400 Corporate Pointe, Culver City, CA 90230. *Phone:* 310-578-1080 Ext. 100. *Toll-free phone:* 800-7ANTIOCH. *Fax:* 310-822-4824. *E-mail:* admissions@antiochla.edu. *Web site:* http://www.antiochla.edu/.

Antioch University Santa Barbara

Santa Barbara, California

- **Independent** upper-level, founded 1977, part of Antioch University
- **Small-town** campus with easy access to Los Angeles
- **Coed**

Faculty *Student/faculty ratio:* 12:1.
Academics *Calendar:* quarters. *Degrees:* bachelor's, master's, and doctoral-research/scholarship.
Student Life *Campus security:* late-night transport/escort service.
Costs (2010–11) *Tuition:* $16,314 full-time, $546 per unit part-time. *Required fees:* $300 full-time.
Financial Aid *Of all full-time matriculated undergraduates who enrolled in 2003,* 23 Federal Work-Study jobs (averaging $2120).
Applying *Options:* electronic application, deferred entrance. *Application fee:* $60.
Application Contact Antioch University Santa Barbara, 801 Garden Street, Santa Barbara, CA 93101-1581. *Phone:* 805-962-8179 Ext. 152. *Web site:* http://www.antiochsb.edu/.

Argosy University, Inland Empire

San Bernardino, California

- **Proprietary** university, founded 2006
- **Coed**

Academics *Degrees:* bachelor's, master's, and doctoral-professional.
Costs (2010–11) *Tuition:* Tuition varies by program. Students should contact Argosy University for tuition information.
Freshman Application Contact Argosy University, Inland Empire, 636 East Brier Drive, Suite 120, San Bernardino, CA 92408. *Phone:* 909-915-3800. *Toll-free phone:* 866-217-9075. *Web site:* http://www.argosy.edu/inlandempire/.

See page 1002 for the College Close-Up.

Argosy University, Los Angeles

Santa Monica, California

- **Proprietary** university
- **Coed**

Academics *Degrees:* bachelor's, master's, and doctoral-professional.
Costs (2010–11) *Tuition:* Tuition varies by program. Students should contact Argosy University for tuition information.
Freshman Application Contact Argosy University, Los Angeles, 5230 Pacific Concourse, Suite 200, Santa Monica, CA 90045. *Phone:* 310-866-4000. *Toll-free phone:* 866-505-0332. *Web site:* http://www.argosy.edu/santamonica/.

See page 1002 for the College Close-Up.

Argosy University, Orange County

Orange, California

- **Proprietary** university
- **Urban** campus
- **Coed**

Academics *Calendar:* semesters. *Degrees:* associate, bachelor's, master's, and doctoral-professional.
Costs (2010–11) *Tuition:* Tuition varies by program. Students should contact Argosy University for tuition information.

Freshman Application Contact Argosy University, Orange County, 601 South Lewis Street, Orange, CA 92868. *Phone:* 714-620-3700. *Toll-free phone:* 800-716-9598. *Web site:* http://www.argosy.edu/orangecounty/.

See page 1002 for the College Close-Up.

Argosy University, San Diego

San Diego, California

- **Proprietary** university
- **Coed**

Academics *Degrees:* bachelor's, master's, and doctoral-professional.

Costs (2010–11) *Tuition:* Tuition varies by program. Students should contact Argosy University for tuition information.

Freshman Application Contact Argosy University, San Diego, 1615 Murray Canyon Road, Suite 100, San Diego, CA 92108. *Phone:* 619-321-3000. *Toll-free phone:* 866-505-0333. *Web site:* http://www.argosy.edu/sandiego/.

See page 1002 for the College Close-Up.

Argosy University, San Francisco Bay Area

Alameda, California

- **Proprietary** university, founded 1998, part of Education Management Corporation
- **Coed**

Academics *Calendar:* semesters. *Degrees:* bachelor's, master's, and doctoral-professional.

Costs (2010–11) *Tuition:* Tuition varies by program. Students should contact Argosy University for tuition information.

Freshman Application Contact Argosy University, San Francisco Bay Area, 1005 Atlantic Avenue, Alameda, CA 94501. *Phone:* 510-217-4700. *Toll-free phone:* 866-215-2777. *Web site:* http://www.argosy.edu/sanfrancisco/.

See page 1002 for the College Close-Up.

Art Center College of Design

Pasadena, California

- **Independent** comprehensive, founded 1930
- **Suburban** 175-acre campus with easy access to Los Angeles
- **Coed** 1,554 undergraduate students, 86% full-time, 45% women, 55% men
- **Very difficult** entrance level, 82% of applicants were admitted

Undergraduates 1,330 full-time, 224 part-time. Students come from 28 states and territories; 34 other countries; 23% are from out of state; 3% Black or African American, non-Hispanic/Latino; 10% Hispanic/Latino; 37% Asian, non-Hispanic/Latino; 0.8% Native Hawaiian or other Pacific Islander, non-Hispanic/Latino; 0.1% American Indian or Alaska Native, non-Hispanic/Latino; 0.5% Two or more races, non-Hispanic/Latino; 2% Race/ethnicity unknown; 20% international; 12% transferred in.

Freshmen *Admission:* 308 applied, 254 admitted, 160 enrolled. *Average high school GPA:* 3.27. *Test scores:* SAT critical reading scores over 500: 64%; SAT math scores over 500: 64%; ACT scores over 18: 100%; SAT critical reading scores over 600: 31%; SAT math scores over 600: 34%; ACT scores over 24: 22%; SAT critical reading scores over 700: 3%; SAT math scores over 700: 10%.

Faculty *Total:* 366, 23% full-time.

Academics *Calendar:* trimesters. *Degrees:* bachelor's and master's. *Special study options:* academic remediation for entering students, advanced placement credit, independent study, internships, off-campus study, services for LD students, study abroad, summer session for credit.

Computers on Campus 250 computers/terminals are available on campus for general student use. Students can access the following: campus intranet, computer help desk, free student e-mail accounts, online (class) grades, online (class) registration, online (class) schedules. Campuswide network is available. Wireless service is available via entire campus.

Student Life *Housing:* college housing not available. *Activities and organizations:* student-run radio station, Out Network, Art Center International Student Organization, Eco-Council, Art Center Student Government, Working Title. *Campus security:* 24-hour emergency response devices and patrols. *Student services:* personal/psychological counseling.

Standardized Tests *Required for some:* SAT or ACT (for admission).

Costs (2011–12) *Tuition:* $32,592 full-time. *Payment plan:* installment. *Waivers:* employees or children of employees.

Financial Aid Of all full-time matriculated undergraduates who enrolled in 2005, 1,090 applied for aid. 150 Federal Work-Study jobs (averaging $2000). *Average percent of need met:* 60%. *Average financial aid package:* $13,708. *Average need-based loan:* $5283. *Average need-based gift aid:* $8227. *Average indebtedness upon graduation:* $70,000.

Applying *Options:* electronic application, deferred entrance. *Application fee:* $50. *Required:* essay or personal statement, high school transcript, Portfolio. *Recommended:* interview. *Application deadlines:* rolling (freshmen), rolling (out-of-state freshmen), rolling (transfers). *Notification:* continuous (freshmen), continuous (out-of-state freshmen), continuous (transfers).

Freshman Application Contact Ms. Kit Baron, Vice President, Admissions and Enrollment Management, Art Center College of Design, 1700 Lida Street, Pasadena, CA 91103. *Phone:* 626-396-2322. *Fax:* 626-795-0578. *E-mail:* kit.baron@artcenter.edu. *Web site:* http://www.artcenter.edu/.

The Art Institute of California–Hollywood

North Hollywood, California

- **Proprietary** 4-year, founded 1992, part of Education Management Corporation
- **Urban** campus
- **Coed**

Academics *Calendar:* quarters. *Degrees:* associate and bachelor's.

Costs (2010–11) *Tuition:* Tuition cost varies by program. Prospective students should contact the school for current tuition costs. Other charges include a starting kit for all first-quarter students. Kits vary in price, depending on the program of study.

Freshman Application Contact The Art Institute of California–Hollywood, 5250 Lankershim Boulevard, North Hollywood, CA 91601. *Phone:* 818-299-5100. *Toll-free phone:* 877-468-6232. *Web site:* http://www.artinstitutes.edu/hollywood/.

See page 1012 for the College Close-Up.

The Art Institute of California–Inland Empire

San Bernardino, California

- **Proprietary** 4-year, part of Education Management Corporation
- **Suburban** campus
- **Coed**

Academics *Degrees:* associate and bachelor's.

Costs (2010–11) *Tuition:* Tuition cost varies by program. Prospective students should contact the school for current tuition costs. Other charges include a starting kit for all first-quarter students. Kits vary in price, depending on the program of study.

Freshman Application Contact The Art Institute of California–Inland Empire, 674 East Brier Drive, San Bernardino, CA 92408. *Phone:* 909-915-2100. *Toll-free phone:* 800-353-0812. *Web site:* http://www.artinstitutes.edu/inlandempire/.

See page 1014 for the College Close-Up.

The Art Institute of California–Los Angeles

Santa Monica, California

- **Proprietary** 4-year, part of Education Management Corporation
- **Urban** campus
- **Coed**

Academics *Calendar:* quarters. *Degrees:* diplomas, associate, and bachelor's.

Costs (2010–11) *Tuition:* Tuition cost varies by program. Prospective students should contact the school for current tuition costs. Other charges include a starting kit for all first-quarter students. Kits vary in price, depending on the program of study.

Freshman Application Contact The Art Institute of California–Los Angeles, 2900 31st Street, Santa Monica, CA 90405-3035. *Phone:* 310-752-4700. *Toll-free phone:* 888-646-4610. *Web site:* http://www.artinstitutes.edu/losangeles/.

See page 1016 for the College Close-Up.

The Art Institute of California–Orange County

Santa Ana, California

- **Proprietary** 4-year, founded 2000, part of Education Management Corporation
- **Urban** campus with easy access to Orange County
- **Coed**

Academics *Calendar:* quarters. *Degrees:* diplomas, associate, and bachelor's.
Costs (2010–11) *Tuition:* Tuition cost varies by program. Prospective students should contact the school for current tuition costs. Other charges include a starting kit for all first-quarter students. Kits vary in price, depending on the program of study.
Freshman Application Contact The Art Institute of California–Orange County, 3601 West Sunflower Avenue, Santa Ana, CA 92704. *Phone:* 714-830-0200. *Toll-free phone:* 888-549-3055. *Web site:* http://www.artinstitutes.edu/orangecounty/.

See page 1018 for the College Close-Up.

The Art Institute of California– Sacramento

Sacramento, California

- **Proprietary** 4-year
- **Coed**

Academics *Degrees:* diplomas, associate, and bachelor's.
Costs (2010–11) *Tuition:* Tuition cost varies by program. Prospective students should contact the school for current tuition costs. Other charges include a starting kit for all first-quarter students. Kits vary in price, depending on the program of study.
Freshman Application Contact The Art Institute of California–Sacramento, 2850 Gateway Oaks Drive, Suite 100, Sacramento, CA 95833. *Phone:* 916-830-6320. *Toll-free phone:* 800-477-1957. *Web site:* http://www.artinstitutes.edu/sacramento/.

See page 1020 for the College Close-Up.

The Art Institute of California– San Diego

San Diego, California

- **Proprietary** 4-year, founded 1981, part of Education Management Corporation
- **Urban** campus
- **Coed**

Academics *Calendar:* quarters. *Degrees:* associate and bachelor's.
Costs (2010–11) *Tuition:* Tuition cost varies by program. Prospective students should contact the school for current tuition costs. Other charges include a starting kit for all first-quarter students. Kits vary in price, depending on the program of study.
Freshman Application Contact The Art Institute of California–San Diego, 7650 Mission Valley Road, San Diego, CA 92108. *Phone:* 858-598-1200. *Toll-free phone:* 866-275-2422. *Web site:* http://www.artinstitutes.edu/sandiego/.

See page 1022 for the College Close-Up.

The Art Institute of California– San Francisco

San Francisco, California

- **Proprietary** comprehensive, founded 1939, part of Education Management Corporation
- **Urban** campus
- **Coed**

Academics *Calendar:* quarters. *Degrees:* diplomas, associate, bachelor's, and master's.
Costs (2010–11) *Tuition:* Tuition cost varies by program. Prospective students should contact the school for current tuition costs. Other charges include a starting kit for all first-quarter students. Kits vary in price, depending on the program of study.
Freshman Application Contact The Art Institute of California–San Francisco, 1170 Market Street, San Francisco, CA 94102. *Phone:* 415-865-0198. *Toll-free phone:* 888-493-3261. *Web site:* http://www.artinstitutes.edu/sanfrancisco/.

See page 1024 for the College Close-Up.

The Art Institute of California– Sunnyvale

Sunnyvale, California

- **Proprietary** 4-year
- **Coed**

Academics *Degrees:* associate and bachelor's.
Costs (2010–11) *Tuition:* Tuition cost varies by program. Prospective students should contact the school for current tuition costs. Other charges include a starting kit for all first-quarter students. Kits vary in price, depending on the program of study.
Freshman Application Contact The Art Institute of California–Sunnyvale, 1120 Kifer Road, Sunnyvale, CA 94086. *Phone:* 408-962-6400. *Toll-free phone:* 866-583-7961. *Web site:* http://www.artinstitutes.edu/sunnyvale/.

See page 1026 for the College Close-Up.

Azusa Pacific University

Azusa, California

- **Independent nondenominational** university, founded 1899
- **Small-town** 60-acre campus with easy access to Los Angeles
- **Endowment** $39.2 million
- **Coed** 5,511 undergraduate students, 85% full-time, 65% women, 35% men
- **Moderately difficult** entrance level, 83% of applicants were admitted

Undergraduates 4,708 full-time, 803 part-time. Students come from 52 states and territories; 15 other countries; 19% are from out of state; 5% Black or African American, non-Hispanic/Latino; 15% Hispanic/Latino; 8% Asian, non-Hispanic/Latino; 0.4% Native Hawaiian or other Pacific Islander, non-Hispanic/Latino; 0.5% American Indian or Alaska Native, non-Hispanic/Latino; 0.1% Two or more races, non-Hispanic/Latino; 15% Race/ethnicity unknown; 2% international; 13% transferred in; 59% live on campus. *Retention:* 86% of full-time freshmen returned.
Freshmen *Admission:* 7,807 applied, 6,441 admitted, 1,197 enrolled. *Average high school GPA:* 3.66. *Test scores:* SAT critical reading scores over 500: 75%; SAT math scores over 500: 70%; ACT scores over 18: 98%; SAT critical reading scores over 600: 26%; SAT math scores over 600: 25%; ACT scores over 24: 52%; SAT critical reading scores over 700: 3%; SAT math scores over 700: 2%; ACT scores over 30: 9%.
Faculty *Total:* 393, 87% full-time, 70% with terminal degrees. *Student/faculty ratio:* 12:1.
Academics *Calendar:* semesters. *Degrees:* bachelor's, master's, doctoral-professional, and doctoral-research/scholarship. *Special study options:* academic remediation for entering students, accelerated degree program, adult/continuing education programs, advanced placement credit, cooperative education, distance learning, double majors, English as a second language, freshman honors college, honors programs, independent study, internships, off-campus study, part-time degree program, services for LD students, study abroad, summer session for credit. *ROTC:* Army (c).
Computers on Campus Students can access the following: campus intranet, computer help desk, free student e-mail accounts, online (class) grades, online (class) registration. Campuswide network is available. Wireless service is available via entire campus.
Student Life *Housing options:* coed, men-only, women-only. Campus housing is university owned and leased by the school. Freshman applicants given priority for college housing. *Activities and organizations:* drama/theater group, student-run newspaper, radio and television station, choral group, marching band, community service groups, choir, outreach ministries groups, Habitat for Humanity, Multi-Ethnic Student Alliance (MESA). *Campus security:* 24-hour emergency response devices and patrols, student patrols, late-night transport/escort service, controlled dormitory access. *Student services:* health clinic, personal/psychological counseling.
Athletics Member NAIA. *Intercollegiate sports:* baseball M(s), basketball M(s)/W(s), cross-country running M(s)/W(s), football M(s), golf M(s), soccer M(s)/W(s), softball W(s), tennis M(s), track and field M(s)/W(s), volleyball M/W(s). *Intramural sports:* basketball M/W, football M/W, golf M/W, skiing (downhill) M/W, soccer W, volleyball M/W.
Standardized Tests *Required:* SAT or ACT (for admission).
Costs (2010–11) *Comprehensive fee:* $35,882 includes full-time tuition ($28,000), mandatory fees ($800), and room and board ($7082). *College room only:* $4076.
Financial Aid Of all full-time matriculated undergraduates who enrolled in 2008, 3,793 applied for aid, 2,594 were judged to have need, 641 had their need fully met. In 2008, 1048 non-need-based awards were made. *Average percent of need met:* 64%. *Average financial aid package:* $21,269. *Average need-based loan:* $6235. *Average need-based gift aid:* $13,386. *Average non-need-based aid:* $5755. *Financial aid deadline:* 7/1.

Applying *Options:* early admission, early action, deferred entrance. *Application fee:* $45. *Required:* essay or personal statement, high school transcript, minimum 2.8 GPA, 2 letters of recommendation. *Required for some:* interview. *Application deadlines:* 6/1 (freshmen), 6/1 (transfers), 11/15 (early action). *Notification:* continuous (freshmen), continuous (transfers), 1/15 (early action).
Freshman Application Contact Ms. Lynnette Barnes, Processing Coordinator, Azusa Pacific University, 901 East Alosta Avenue, PO Box 7000, Undergraduate Admissions, 7221, Azusa, CA 91702-7000. *Phone:* 626-815-6000 Ext. 3419. *Toll-free phone:* 800-TALK-APU. *E-mail:* admissions@apu.edu. *Web site:* http://www.apu.edu/.

Bethany University
Scotts Valley, California

- **Independent Assemblies of God** comprehensive, founded 1919
- **Small-town** 40-acre campus with easy access to San Francisco and San Jose
- **Endowment** $947,613
- **Coed**
- **Minimally difficult** entrance level

Faculty *Student/faculty ratio:* 12:1.
Academics *Calendar:* semesters. *Degrees:* certificates, associate, bachelor's, and master's.
Student Life *Campus security:* 24-hour emergency response devices and patrols, late-night transport/escort service, controlled dormitory access.
Athletics Member NAIA.
Standardized Tests *Required:* SAT or ACT (for admission).
Costs (2010–11) *One-time required fee:* $100. *Comprehensive fee:* $26,300 includes full-time tuition ($18,300), mandatory fees ($550), and room and board ($7450). Full-time tuition and fees vary according to degree level and program. Part-time tuition: $735 per unit. Part-time tuition and fees vary according to course load, degree level, and program. *Required fees:* $275 per term part-time. *Room and board:* Room and board charges vary according to housing facility.
Financial Aid *Of all full-time matriculated undergraduates who enrolled in 2003,* 370 applied for aid, 331 were judged to have need, 50 had their need fully met. 38 Federal Work-Study jobs (averaging $2011). *In 2003,* 15 non-need-based awards were made. *Average percent of need met:* 39. *Average financial aid package:* $10,250. *Average need-based loan:* $4570. *Average need-based gift aid:* $7423. *Average non-need-based aid:* $6000. *Average indebtedness upon graduation:* $21,000.
Applying *Options:* electronic application, early admission, deferred entrance. *Application fee:* $35. *Required:* essay or personal statement, high school transcript, minimum 2 GPA, Christian commitment.
Freshman Application Contact Bethany University, 800 Bethany Drive, Scotts Valley, CA 95066-2820. *Phone:* 831-438-3800 Ext. 3900. *Toll-free phone:* 800-843-9410. *Fax:* 831-438-4517. *E-mail:* info@bethany.edu. *Web site:* http://www.bethany.edu/.

Bethesda Christian University
Anaheim, California

Director of Admissions Jacquie Ha, Director of Admission, Bethesda Christian University, 730 North Euclid Street, Anaheim, CA 92801. *Phone:* 714-517-1945. *Fax:* 714-517-1948. *E-mail:* admission@bcu.edu. *Web site:* http://www.bcu.edu/.

Biola University
La Mirada, California

- **Independent interdenominational** university, founded 1908
- **Suburban** 95-acre campus with easy access to Los Angeles
- **Endowment** $60.0 million
- **Coed** 4,106 undergraduate students, 94% full-time, 61% women, 39% men
- **Moderately difficult** entrance level, 78% of applicants were admitted

Undergraduates 3,853 full-time, 253 part-time. Students come from 49 states and territories; 20 other countries; 23% are from out of state; 3% Black or African American, non-Hispanic/Latino; 15% Hispanic/Latino; 11% Asian, non-Hispanic/Latino; 0.8% Native Hawaiian or other Pacific Islander, non-Hispanic/Latino; 0.6% American Indian or Alaska Native, non-Hispanic/Latino; 3% Two or more races, non-Hispanic/Latino; 1% Race/ethnicity unknown; 1% international; 9% transferred in; 68% live on campus. *Retention:* 86% of full-time freshmen returned.
Freshmen *Admission:* 2,951 applied, 2,294 admitted, 883 enrolled. *Average high school GPA:* 3.54. *Test scores:* SAT critical reading scores over 500: 76%; SAT math scores over 500: 74%; SAT writing scores over 500: 73%; ACT scores over 18: 93%; SAT critical reading scores over 600: 35%; SAT

math scores over 600: 34%; SAT writing scores over 600: 32%; ACT scores over 24: 58%; SAT critical reading scores over 700: 7%; SAT math scores over 700: 5%; SAT writing scores over 700: 5%; ACT scores over 30: 14%.
Faculty *Total:* 493, 46% full-time, 35% with terminal degrees. *Student/faculty ratio:* 16:1.
Academics *Calendar:* 4-1-4. *Degrees:* certificates, bachelor's, master's, doctoral-other, doctoral-research/scholarship, post-master's, and postbachelor's certificates. *Special study options:* double majors, English as a second language, honors programs, internships, off-campus study, part-time degree program, services for LD students, study abroad, summer session for credit. *ROTC:* Army (c), Air Force (c). *Unusual degree programs:* 3-2 engineering.
Computers on Campus Students can access the following: campus intranet, computer help desk, free student e-mail accounts, online (class) grades, online (class) registration, online (class) schedules. Campuswide network is available. Wireless service is available via entire campus.
Student Life *Housing:* on-campus residence required for freshman year. *Options:* coed, men-only, women-only, disabled students. Campus housing is university owned. Freshman campus housing is guaranteed. *Activities and organizations:* drama/theater group, student-run newspaper, radio and television station, choral group, Social Justice Ministry, Guerilla Film Society, Community Bike Riders, Xopoc Dance Team, Biola Cheese Society. *Campus security:* 24-hour emergency response devices and patrols, late-night transport/escort service, controlled dormitory access. *Student services:* health clinic, personal/psychological counseling.
Athletics Member NAIA. *Intercollegiate sports:* baseball M(s), basketball M(s)/W(s), cross-country running M(s)/W(s), golf M(s)/W(s), soccer M(s)/W(s), softball W(s), swimming and diving M(s)/W(s), tennis M(s)/W(s), track and field M(s)/W(s), volleyball W(s). *Intramural sports:* basketball M/W, cheerleading W(c), football M/W, lacrosse M(c), soccer M/W, softball M/W, ultimate Frisbee M/W, volleyball M/W.
Standardized Tests *Required:* SAT or ACT (for admission).
Costs (2010–11) *Comprehensive fee:* $36,897 includes full-time tuition ($28,852), mandatory fees ($45), and room and board ($8000). Full-time tuition and fees vary according to course load. Part-time tuition and fees vary according to course load. *College room only:* $4500. Room and board charges vary according to board plan, housing facility, and location. *Payment plan:* installment.
Financial Aid Of all full-time matriculated undergraduates who enrolled in 2009, 2,688 applied for aid, 2,367 were judged to have need, 2,366 had their need fully met. 642 Federal Work-Study jobs (averaging $1390). In 2009, 355 non-need-based awards were made. *Average percent of need met:* 70%. *Average financial aid package:* $33,123. *Average need-based loan:* $1339. *Average need-based gift aid:* $12,955. *Average non-need-based aid:* $14,829. *Average indebtedness upon graduation:* $29,075.
Applying *Options:* electronic application, early action, deferred entrance. *Application fee:* $45. *Required:* essay or personal statement, high school transcript, minimum 3 GPA, 1 letter of recommendation, The student must be an evangelical believer in the Christian faith. *Required for some:* interview. *Application deadlines:* 3/1 (freshmen), 3/1 (out-of-state freshmen), 11/15 (transfers), 11/15 (early action). *Notification:* 4/1 (freshmen), 4/1 (out-of-state freshmen), 1/15 (transfers), 1/15 (early action).
Freshman Application Contact Mr. Andre Stephens, Director of Undergraduate Admissions, Biola University, 13800 Biola Avenue, La Mirada, CA 90639. *Phone:* 562-903-4752. *Toll-free phone:* 800-652-4652. *E-mail:* admissions@biola.edu. *Web site:* http://www.biola.edu/.

Brooks Institute
Santa Barbara, California

Freshman Application Contact Admissions Office, Brooks Institute, 27 East Cota Street, Santa Barbara, CA 93101. *Phone:* 805-966-3888. *Toll-free phone:* 888-276-4999. *Fax:* 805-565-1386. *E-mail:* admissions@brooks.edu. *Web site:* http://www.brooks.edu/.

California Baptist University
Riverside, California

- **Independent Southern Baptist** comprehensive, founded 1950
- **Suburban** 110-acre campus with easy access to Los Angeles
- **Endowment** $11.0 million
- **Coed** 3,798 undergraduate students, 88% full-time, 63% women, 37% men
- **Minimally difficult** entrance level, 71% of applicants were admitted

Undergraduates 3,353 full-time, 445 part-time. Students come from 36 states and territories; 28 other countries; 6% are from out of state; 13% transferred in; 52% live on campus. *Retention:* 75% of full-time freshmen returned.
Freshmen *Admission:* 2,373 applied, 1,679 admitted, 819 enrolled. *Average high school GPA:* 3.4. *Test scores:* SAT critical reading scores over 500: 47%; SAT math scores over 500: 49%; SAT writing scores over 500: 47%; ACT

scores over 18: 79%; SAT critical reading scores over 600: 12%; SAT math scores over 600: 14%; SAT writing scores over 600: 9%; ACT scores over 24: 23%; SAT critical reading scores over 700: 1%; SAT math scores over 700: 1%; SAT writing scores over 700: 1%; ACT scores over 30: 2%.

Faculty *Total:* 334, 51% full-time, 39% with terminal degrees. *Student/faculty ratio:* 22:1.

Academics *Calendar:* 2-4-4-2. *Degrees:* bachelor's and master's. *Special study options:* accelerated degree program, adult/continuing education programs, advanced placement credit, distance learning, double majors, English as a second language, honors programs, independent study, internships, off-campus study, part-time degree program, study abroad, summer session for credit. *ROTC:* Army (b), Air Force (c).

Computers on Campus 279 computers/terminals are available on campus for general student use. Students can access the following: campus intranet, computer help desk, free student e-mail accounts, online (class) grades, online (class) registration, online (class) schedules. Campuswide network is available. Wireless service is available via classrooms, computer labs.

Student Life *Housing:* on-campus residence required for freshman year. *Options:* men-only, women-only. Campus housing is university owned. Freshman applicants given priority for college housing. *Activities and organizations:* drama/theater group, student-run newspaper, choral group, CBU CRAZIES, University Place-Men, University Place-Women, Student Leadership Groups, Commuter Students. *Campus security:* 24-hour emergency response devices and patrols, student patrols, late-night transport/escort service, controlled dormitory access. *Student services:* personal/psychological counseling.

Athletics Member NAIA. *Intercollegiate sports:* baseball M(s), basketball M(s)/W(s), cheerleading M(s)/W(s), cross-country running M(s)/W(s), golf M(s)/W(s), soccer M(s)/W(s), softball W(s), swimming and diving M(s)/W(s), track and field M(s)/W(s), volleyball M(s)/W(s), water polo M(s)/W(s), wrestling M(s). *Intramural sports:* basketball M/W, bowling M/W, football M/W, softball M/W, table tennis M/W, ultimate Frisbee M/W, volleyball M/W.

Standardized Tests *Required:* SAT or ACT (for admission).

Costs (2010–11) *Comprehensive fee:* $33,024 includes full-time tuition ($22,854), mandatory fees ($1800), and room and board ($8370). Full-time tuition and fees vary according to class time and program. Part-time tuition: $879 per semester hour. Part-time tuition and fees vary according to class time and program. *Required fees:* $235 per term part-time. *College room only:* $4160. Room and board charges vary according to board plan and housing facility. *Payment plan:* installment. *Waivers:* employees or children of employees.

Financial Aid Of all full-time matriculated undergraduates who enrolled in 2009, 2,576 applied for aid, 1,894 were judged to have need, 1,605 had their need fully met. 178 Federal Work-Study jobs (averaging $888). In 2009, 449 non-need-based awards were made. *Average percent of need met:* 58%. *Average financial aid package:* $8651. *Average need-based loan:* $2298. *Average need-based gift aid:* $4677. *Average non-need-based aid:* $3656. *Average indebtedness upon graduation:* $34,650.

Applying *Options:* electronic application, early admission, early action, deferred entrance. *Application fee:* $45. *Required:* essay or personal statement, high school transcript, minimum 2 GPA, 2 letters of recommendation. *Recommended:* interview. *Application deadlines:* rolling (freshmen), rolling (out-of-state freshmen), rolling (transfers), 12/1 (early action). *Notification:* continuous until 9/6 (freshmen), continuous until 6/9 (out-of-state freshmen), continuous (transfers), 12/20 (early action).

Freshman Application Contact Mr. Allen Johnson, Director, Undergraduate Admissions, California Baptist University, 8432 Magnolia Avenue, Riverside, CA 92504-3297. *Phone:* 951-343-4212. *Toll-free phone:* 877-228-8866. *Fax:* 951-343-4525. *E-mail:* admissions@calbaptist.edu. *Web site:* http://www.calbaptist.edu/.

California Christian College

Fresno, California

- **Independent religious** 4-year
- **Urban** 5-acre campus
- **Endowment** $122,093
- **Coed** 20 undergraduate students, 85% full-time, 45% women, 55% men
- **Noncompetitive** entrance level, 100% of applicants were admitted

Undergraduates 17 full-time, 3 part-time. Students come from 1 other state; 1 other country; 20% Black or African American, non-Hispanic/Latino; 40% Hispanic/Latino; 10% Asian, non-Hispanic/Latino; 5% international; 10% transferred in; 25% live on campus.

Freshmen *Admission:* 3 applied, 3 admitted, 5 enrolled. *Average high school GPA:* 3.04.

Faculty *Total:* 5, 20% with terminal degrees. *Student/faculty ratio:* 4:1.

Academics *Calendar:* semesters. *Degrees:* associate and bachelor's. *Special study options:* academic remediation for entering students, cooperative education, distance learning, independent study, part-time degree program.

Computers on Campus 5 computers/terminals are available on campus for general student use. Students can access the following: wireless Internet access. Campuswide network is available. 100% of college-owned or -operated housing units are wired for high-speed Internet access. Wireless service is available via entire campus.

Student Life *Housing:* on-campus residence required through sophomore year. *Options:* men-only, women-only. Campus housing is university owned. *Student services:* personal/psychological counseling.

Standardized Tests *Required:* standardized Bible content tests (for admission). *Recommended:* SAT or ACT (for admission).

Costs (2011–12) *Comprehensive fee:* $11,760 includes full-time tuition ($7080), mandatory fees ($530), and room and board ($4150). *Payment plan:* installment.

Financial Aid Of all full-time matriculated undergraduates who enrolled in 2008, 22 applied for aid, 20 were judged to have need. *Average percent of need met:* 62%. *Average financial aid package:* $12,030. *Average need-based loan:* $6797. *Average need-based gift aid:* $6641. *Average indebtedness upon graduation:* $4500.

Applying *Options:* electronic application. *Application fee:* $40. *Required:* essay or personal statement, high school transcript, minimum 2 GPA, 2 letters of recommendation, statement of faith, moral/ethical statement. *Recommended:* interview. *Application deadlines:* rolling (freshmen), rolling (transfers). *Notification:* continuous (freshmen), continuous (transfers).

Freshman Application Contact California Christian College, 4881 East University Avenue, Fresno, CA 93703-3533. *Phone:* 559-251-5571. *Web site:* http://www.calchristiancollege.org/.

California Coast University

Santa Ana, California

Director of Admissions Damien McMenamin, Director of Admission, California Coast University, 925 North Spurgeon Street, Santa Ana, CA 92701. *Phone:* 714-547-9625. *Toll-free phone:* 888-CCU-UNIV. *Fax:* 714-547-5777. *E-mail:* admissions@calcoast.edu. *Web site:* http://www.calcoast.edu/.

California College

San Diego, California

Director of Admissions Tana Sanderson, Director of Admission, California College, 2820 Camino del Rio South, Suite 300, San Diego, CA 92108. *Phone:* 619-295-5785. *Toll-free phone:* 800-622-3188. *E-mail:* tana.sanderson@cc-sd.edu. *Web site:* http://www.cc-sd.edu/.

California College of the Arts

San Francisco, California

- **Independent** comprehensive, founded 1907
- **Urban** 4-acre campus with easy access to San Francisco and Oakland
- **Endowment** $28.6 million
- **Coed** 1,410 undergraduate students, 93% full-time, 61% women, 39% men
- **Moderately difficult** entrance level, 76% of applicants were admitted

Undergraduates 1,312 full-time, 98 part-time. Students come from 37 states and territories; 39 other countries; 21% are from out of state; 5% Black or African American, non-Hispanic/Latino; 12% Hispanic/Latino; 19% Asian, non-Hispanic/Latino; 0.8% American Indian or Alaska Native, non-Hispanic/Latino; 10% Race/ethnicity unknown; 11% international; 13% transferred in; 15% live on campus. *Retention:* 75% of full-time freshmen returned.

Freshmen *Admission:* 1,287 applied, 976 admitted, 233 enrolled. *Average high school GPA:* 3.17. *Test scores:* SAT critical reading scores over 500: 66%; SAT math scores over 500: 65%; SAT writing scores over 500: 66%; ACT scores over 18: 91%; SAT critical reading scores over 600: 26%; SAT math scores over 600: 25%; SAT writing scores over 600: 24%; ACT scores over 24: 46%; SAT critical reading scores over 700: 4%; SAT math scores over 700: 5%; SAT writing scores over 700: 1%.

Faculty *Total:* 524, 16% full-time, 64% with terminal degrees. *Student/faculty ratio:* 9:1.

Academics *Calendar:* semesters. *Degrees:* bachelor's and master's. *Special study options:* academic remediation for entering students, advanced placement credit, cooperative education, double majors, English as a second language, honors programs, independent study, internships, off-campus study, services for LD students, student-designed majors, study abroad, summer session for credit.

Computers on Campus 346 computers/terminals and 33 ports are available on campus for general student use. Students can access the following: computer help desk, free student e-mail accounts, online (class) grades, online (class) registration, online (class) schedules. Campuswide network is available. 100% of college-owned or -operated housing units are wired for high-speed

Internet access. Wireless service is available via classrooms, computer centers, computer labs, dorm rooms, learning centers, libraries.

Student Life *Housing options:* coed. Campus housing is university owned. Freshman applicants given priority for college housing. *Activities and organizations:* Alpha Rho Rho (Allied ARB Fraternity), Queer/Straight Alliance (QSA), Future Action Reclamation Mob (FARM), Alliance for Multiculturalism in Architecture (NOMAS), Ceramics Guild. *Campus security:* 24-hour emergency response devices and patrols, late-night transport/escort service. *Student services:* personal/psychological counseling.

Standardized Tests *Recommended:* SAT or ACT (for admission).

Costs (2011–12) *Tuition:* $34,872 full-time, $1453 per unit part-time. Full-time tuition and fees vary according to degree level. Part-time tuition and fees vary according to course load and degree level. *Required fees:* $350 full-time. *Room only:* $7000. Room and board charges vary according to housing facility. *Payment plan:* installment. *Waivers:* employees or children of employees.

Financial Aid Of all full-time matriculated undergraduates who enrolled in 2009, 943 applied for aid, 886 were judged to have need, 35 had their need fully met. 845 Federal Work-Study jobs (averaging $2926). 71 state and other part-time jobs (averaging $3238). In 2009, 169 non-need-based awards were made. *Average percent of need met:* 56%. *Average financial aid package:* $22,923. *Average need-based loan:* $4772. *Average need-based gift aid:* $18,202. *Average non-need-based aid:* $7905. *Average indebtedness upon graduation:* $24,677.

Applying *Options:* electronic application, deferred entrance. *Application fee:* $60. *Required:* essay or personal statement, high school transcript, 2 letters of recommendation, Portfolio of creative work and statement of artistic and professional goals required. *Required for some:* interview. *Application deadlines:* 2/1 (freshmen), rolling (transfers). *Notification:* continuous (freshmen), continuous (transfers).

Freshman Application Contact Ms. Robynne Royster, Director of Admissions, California College of the Arts, 1111 Eighth Street, San Francisco, CA 94107. *Phone:* 415-703-9523 Ext. 9532. *Toll-free phone:* 800-447-1ART. *Fax:* 415-703-9539. *E-mail:* enroll@cca.edu. *Web site:* http://www.cca.edu/.

See page 1176 for the College Close-Up.

California Institute of Integral Studies
San Francisco, California

Application Contact Admissions Department, California Institute of Integral Studies, 1453 Mission Street, San Francisco, CA 94103. *Phone:* 415-575-6156. *Fax:* 415-575-1268. *E-mail:* admissions@ciis.edu. *Web site:* http://www.ciis.edu/.

California Institute of Technology
Pasadena, California

- **Independent** university, founded 1891
- **Suburban** 124-acre campus with easy access to Los Angeles
- **Endowment** $1.5 billion
- **Coed** 967 undergraduate students, 100% full-time, 40% women, 60% men
- **Most difficult** entrance level, 13% of applicants were admitted

Undergraduates 967 full-time. 65% are from out of state; 0.7% transferred in; 95% live on campus. *Retention:* 98% of full-time freshmen returned.

Freshmen *Admission:* 4,859 applied, 610 admitted, 222 enrolled. *Test scores:* SAT critical reading scores over 500: 100%; SAT math scores over 500: 100%; SAT writing scores over 500: 100%; ACT scores over 18: 100%; SAT critical reading scores over 600: 98%; SAT math scores over 600: 100%; SAT writing scores over 600: 99%; ACT scores over 24: 100%; SAT critical reading scores over 700: 79%; SAT math scores over 700: 99%; SAT writing scores over 700: 83%; ACT scores over 30: 100%.

Faculty *Total:* 317, 95% full-time, 97% with terminal degrees. *Student/faculty ratio:* 3:1.

Academics *Calendar:* 3 ten-week terms. *Degrees:* bachelor's, master's, doctoral-research/scholarship, and post-master's certificates. *Special study options:* cooperative education, double majors, English as a second language, independent study, off-campus study, services for LD students, student-designed majors, study abroad. *ROTC:* Army (c), Air Force (c). *Unusual degree programs:* 3-2 engineering.

Computers on Campus Students can access the following: computer help desk, free student e-mail accounts, online (class) registration. Campuswide network is available. 100% of college-owned or -operated housing units are wired for high-speed Internet access. Wireless service is available via entire campus.

Student Life *Housing:* on-campus residence required for freshman year. *Options:* coed. Campus housing is university owned. Freshman campus housing is guaranteed. *Activities and organizations:* drama/theater group, student-run newspaper, choral group, Instrumental music groups, Entrepreneur's Club, Glee Club, theater arts, Ultimate Disc Club. *Campus security:* 24-hour emergency response devices and patrols, late-night transport/escort service, controlled dormitory access. *Student services:* health clinic, personal/psychological counseling, women's center.

Athletics Member NCAA. All Division III. *Intercollegiate sports:* baseball M, basketball M/W, cross-country running M/W, fencing M/W, ice hockey M(c), rugby M(c), soccer M/W(c), swimming and diving M/W, tennis M/W, track and field M/W, volleyball M(c)/W, water polo M/W. *Intramural sports:* badminton M/W, baseball M, basketball M/W, cross-country running M/W, fencing M/W, football M/W, ice hockey M, racquetball M, soccer M/W, softball M/W, squash M/W, swimming and diving M/W, table tennis M/W, tennis M/W, track and field M/W, ultimate Frisbee M/W, volleyball M/W, water polo M/W.

Standardized Tests *Required:* SAT or ACT (for admission), SAT Subject Tests (for admission).

Costs (2011–12) *One-time required fee:* $500. *Comprehensive fee:* $49,380 includes full-time tuition ($36,387), mandatory fees ($1317), and room and board ($11,676). *College room only:* $6570. *Payment plans:* installment, deferred payment. *Waivers:* employees or children of employees.

Financial Aid Of all full-time matriculated undergraduates who enrolled in 2009, 602 applied for aid, 513 were judged to have need, 513 had their need fully met. 325 Federal Work-Study jobs (averaging $2763). 76 state and other part-time jobs (averaging $2502). In 2009, 23 non-need-based awards were made. *Average percent of need met:* 100%. *Average financial aid package:* $34,928. *Average need-based loan:* $3442. *Average need-based gift aid:* $31,030. *Average non-need-based aid:* $40,888. *Average indebtedness upon graduation:* $10,760.

Applying *Options:* electronic application, early admission, early action, deferred entrance. *Application fee:* $65. *Required:* essay or personal statement, high school transcript, 2 letters of recommendation. *Application deadlines:* 1/1 (freshmen), 2/15 (transfers), 11/1 (early action). *Notification:* 4/1 (freshmen), 5/1 (transfers), 12/15 (early action).

Freshman Application Contact Mr. Jarrid James Whitney, Director of Admissions, California Institute of Technology, 383 South Hill Avenue, Mail Code 10-90, Pasadena, CA 91125. *Phone:* 626-395-6341. *Fax:* 626-683-3026. *Web site:* http://www.caltech.edu/.

California Institute of the Arts
Valencia, California

- **Independent** comprehensive, founded 1961
- **Suburban** 60-acre campus with easy access to Los Angeles
- **Endowment** $101.6 million
- **Coed** 895 undergraduate students, 99% full-time, 49% women, 51% men
- **Very difficult** entrance level, 31% of applicants were admitted

Undergraduates 887 full-time, 8 part-time. Students come from 42 states and territories; 23 other countries; 51% are from out of state; 8% Black or African American, non-Hispanic/Latino; 12% Hispanic/Latino; 11% Asian, non-Hispanic/Latino; 0.1% Native Hawaiian or other Pacific Islander, non-Hispanic/Latino; 0.7% American Indian or Alaska Native, non-Hispanic/Latino; 4% Two or more races, non-Hispanic/Latino; 1% Race/ethnicity unknown; 7% international; 16% transferred in; 40% live on campus. *Retention:* 79% of full-time freshmen returned.

Freshmen *Admission:* 1,237 applied, 378 admitted, 151 enrolled.

Faculty *Total:* 314, 51% full-time, 54% with terminal degrees. *Student/faculty ratio:* 7:1.

Academics *Calendar:* semesters. *Degrees:* bachelor's, master's, doctoral-other, and postbachelor's certificates. *Special study options:* advanced placement credit, cooperative education, double majors, independent study, internships, services for LD students, student-designed majors, study abroad.

Computers on Campus 42 computers/terminals and 1,000 ports are available on campus for general student use. Students can access the following: campus intranet, computer help desk, free student e-mail accounts, online (class) grades, online (class) registration, online (class) schedules. Campuswide network is available. 100% of college-owned or -operated housing units are wired for high-speed Internet access. Wireless service is available via libraries, student centers.

Student Life *Housing options:* coed, disabled students. Campus housing is university owned. Freshman applicants given priority for college housing. *Activities and organizations:* drama/theater group, student-run radio and television station, choral group, Student Council, FISK - Graphic Arts Club, Soccer Club, Korean Bible Study, Black Student Union. *Campus security:* 24-hour emergency response devices and patrols, late-night transport/escort service, controlled dormitory access. *Student services:* health clinic, personal/psychological counseling.

Costs (2011–12) *Comprehensive fee:* $47,886 includes full-time tuition ($37,684), mandatory fees ($576), and room and board ($9626). Part-time tuition and fees vary according to course load. *College room only:* $5450. Room and board charges vary according to board plan, housing facility, and location. *Payment plan:* installment. *Waivers:* employees or children of employees.

PROFILES

Financial Aid Of all full-time matriculated undergraduates who enrolled in 2009, 734 applied for aid, 655 were judged to have need, 36 had their need fully met. 236 Federal Work-Study jobs (averaging $2515). 4 state and other part-time jobs (averaging $1500). In 2009, 59 non-need-based awards were made. *Average percent of need met:* 74%. *Average financial aid package:* $30,448. *Average need-based loan:* $9445. *Average need-based gift aid:* $16,573. *Average non-need-based aid:* $7043. *Average indebtedness upon graduation:* $50,017.

Applying *Options:* electronic application. *Application fee:* $70. *Required:* essay or personal statement, high school transcript, 2 letters of recommendation, portfolio or audition. *Required for some:* interview. *Application deadlines:* 1/5 (freshmen), 1/5 (transfers). *Notification:* continuous until 4/1 (freshmen), continuous until 4/1 (transfers).

Freshman Application Contact Molly Ryan, Director of Admissions, California Institute of the Arts, 24700 McBean Parkway, Valencia, CA 91355-2340. *Phone:* 661-255-1050. *Toll-free phone:* 800-545-2787. *Fax:* 661-253-7710. *E-mail:* admiss@calarts.edu. *Web site:* http://www.calarts.edu/.

See page 1178 for the College Close-Up.

California Intercontinental University

Diamond Bar, California

Director of Admissions John Ramsay, Director of Admission, California Intercontinental University, 1470 Valley Vista Drive, Suite 150, Diamond Bar, CA 91765. *Phone:* 909-396-6090. *Toll-free phone:* 866-687-2258. *Fax:* 909-804-5151. *E-mail:* admissions@caluniversity.com. *Web site:* http://caluniversity.edu/.

California Lutheran University

Thousand Oaks, California

- **Independent Lutheran** comprehensive, founded 1959
- **Suburban** 290-acre campus with easy access to Los Angeles
- **Endowment** $54.0 million
- **Coed**
- **Moderately difficult** entrance level

Faculty *Student/faculty ratio:* 15:1.

Academics *Calendar:* semesters. *Degrees:* certificates, bachelor's, master's, doctoral-professional, post-master's, and postbachelor's certificates.

Student Life *Campus security:* 24-hour emergency response devices and patrols, late-night transport/escort service, controlled dormitory access, escort service; shuttle service.

Athletics Member NCAA. All Division III.

Standardized Tests *Required:* SAT or ACT (for admission).

Costs (2010–11) *Comprehensive fee:* $41,580 includes full-time tuition ($30,750), mandatory fees ($250), and room and board ($10,580). Part-time tuition: $990 per unit. *Required fees:* $250 per year part-time. *College room only:* $5690. Room and board charges vary according to board plan.

Financial Aid *Of all full-time matriculated undergraduates who enrolled in 2009,* 1,809 applied for aid, 1,590 were judged to have need, 266 had their need fully met. 189 Federal Work-Study jobs (averaging $2500). 440 state and other part-time jobs (averaging $2500). *In 2009,* 734 non-need-based awards were made. *Average percent of need met:* 70. *Average financial aid package:* $22,580. *Average need-based loan:* $4430. *Average need-based gift aid:* $18,150. *Average non-need-based aid:* $11,400. *Average indebtedness upon graduation:* $23,900.

Applying *Options:* electronic application, early action, deferred entrance. *Application fee:* $45. *Required:* essay or personal statement, high school transcript, minimum 2.8 GPA, 1 letter of recommendation. *Recommended:* minimum 3 GPA, interview.

Freshman Application Contact Mr. Matthew Ward, Dean of Undergraduate Enrollment, California Lutheran University, Office of Admission, #1350, Thousand Oaks, CA 91360. *Phone:* 805-493-3135. *Toll-free phone:* 877-258-3678. *Fax:* 805-493-3114. *E-mail:* cluadm@clunet.edu. *Web site:* http://www.callutheran.edu/.

See page 1180 for the College Close-Up.

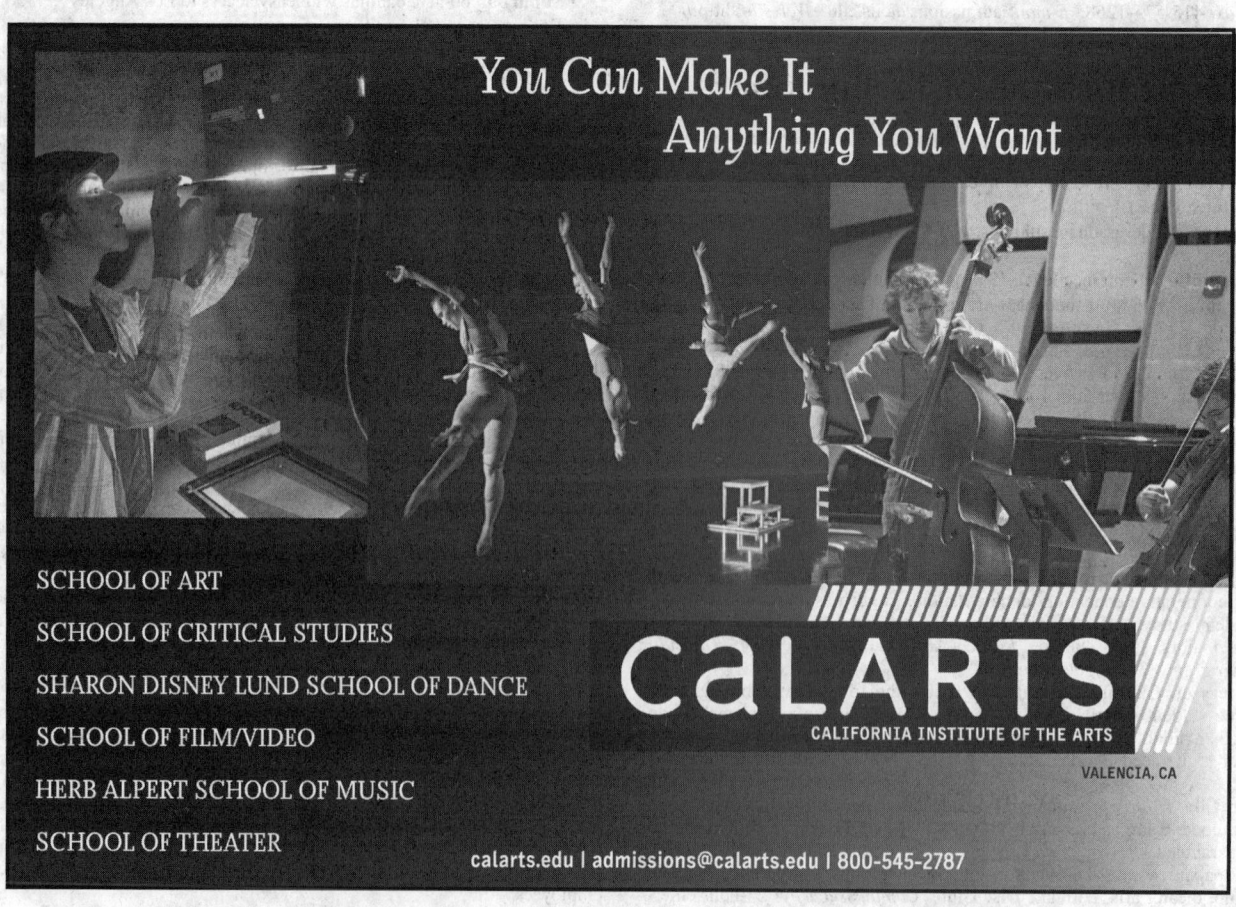

California Maritime Academy

Vallejo, California

- **State-supported** 4-year, founded 1929, part of California State University System
- **Suburban** 64-acre campus with easy access to San Francisco
- **Coed**
- **Moderately difficult** entrance level

Faculty *Student/faculty ratio:* 22:1.

Academics *Calendar:* semesters. *Degree:* bachelor's.

Student Life *Campus security:* 24-hour patrols, student patrols.

Athletics Member NAIA.

Standardized Tests *Required:* SAT or ACT (for admission).

Costs (2010–11) *Tuition:* state resident $0 full-time; nonresident $11,160 full-time. *Required fees:* $5294 full-time. *Room and board:* $9740.

Applying *Options:* electronic application. *Application fee:* $55. *Required:* high school transcript, minimum 2 GPA, health form.

Freshman Application Contact California Maritime Academy, 200 Maritime Academy Drive, Vallejo, CA 94590. *Phone:* 707-654-1330. *Toll-free phone:* 800-561-1945. *Web site:* http://www.csum.edu/.

California Miramar University

San Diego, California

Director of Admissions Jean Van Slyke, Director of Admissions, California Miramar University, 9750 Miramar Road, Suite 180, San Diego, CA 92126. *Phone:* 858-653-3000. *Toll-free phone:* 877-570-5678. *Fax:* 858-653-6786. *E-mail:* admissions@calmu.edu. *Web site:* http://www.calmu.edu/.

California National University for Advanced Studies

Northridge, California

Freshman Application Contact Ms. Stephanie Smith, Registrar, California National University for Advanced Studies, Admissions, 8550 Balboa Boulevard, Suite 210, Northridge, CA 91325. *Phone:* 818-830-2411. *Toll-free phone:* 800-744-2822 (in-state); 800-782-2422 (out-of-state). *Fax:* 818-830-2418. *E-mail:* cnuadms@mail.cnuas.edu. *Web site:* http://www.cnuas.edu/.

California Polytechnic State University, San Luis Obispo

San Luis Obispo, California

- **State-supported** comprehensive, founded 1901, part of California State University System
- **Suburban** 6000-acre campus
- **Coed** 17,332 undergraduate students, 97% full-time, 45% women, 55% men
- **Moderately difficult** entrance level, 33% of applicants were admitted

Undergraduates 16,744 full-time, 588 part-time. 6% are from out of state; 0.7% Black or African American, non-Hispanic/Latino; 12% Hispanic/Latino; 10% Asian, non-Hispanic/Latino; 0.1% Native Hawaiian or other Pacific Islander, non-Hispanic/Latino; 0.5% American Indian or Alaska Native, non-Hispanic/Latino; 4% Two or more races, non-Hispanic/Latino; 7% Race/ethnicity unknown; 0.9% international; 3% transferred in; 36% live on campus. *Retention:* 91% of full-time freshmen returned.

Freshmen *Admission:* 33,627 applied, 10,944 admitted, 3,524 enrolled. *Average high school GPA:* 3.84. *Test scores:* SAT critical reading scores over 500: 89%; SAT math scores over 500: 95%; ACT scores over 18: 99%; SAT critical reading scores over 600: 46%; SAT math scores over 600: 68%; ACT scores over 24: 83%; SAT critical reading scores over 700: 7%; SAT math scores over 700: 19%; ACT scores over 30: 23%.

Faculty *Total:* 1,220, 66% full-time, 64% with terminal degrees. *Student/faculty ratio:* 19:1.

Academics *Calendar:* quarters. *Degrees:* bachelor's and master's. *Special study options:* academic remediation for entering students, advanced placement credit, cooperative education, distance learning, double majors, English as a second language, honors programs, internships, off-campus study, part-time degree program, services for LD students, study abroad, summer session for credit. *ROTC:* Army (b).

Computers on Campus Students can access the following: campus intranet, free student e-mail accounts, online (class) grades, online (class) registration, online (class) schedules. Campuswide network is available. Wireless service is available via classrooms, computer centers, computer labs, learning centers, libraries, student centers.

Student Life *Housing options:* coed, disabled students. Campus housing is university owned. *Activities and organizations:* drama/theater group, student-run newspaper, radio and television station, choral group, marching band, national fraternities, national sororities. *Campus security:* 24-hour emergency response devices and patrols, student patrols, late-night transport/escort service, controlled dormitory access. *Student services:* health clinic, personal/psychological counseling, women's center, legal services.

Athletics Member NCAA. All Division I except football (Division I-AA). *Intercollegiate sports:* baseball M(s), basketball M(s)/W(s), cross-country running M(s)/W(s), golf M(s)/W(s), soccer M(s)/W(s), softball W(s), swimming and diving M(s)/W(s), tennis M(s)/W(s), track and field M(s)/W(s), volleyball W(s), wrestling M(s). *Intramural sports:* basketball M/W, football M/W, racquetball M/W, soccer M/W, softball M/W, table tennis M/W, tennis M/W, volleyball M/W.

Standardized Tests *Required:* SAT or ACT (for admission).

Costs (2010–11) *Tuition:* state resident $0 full-time; nonresident $11,160 full-time, $248 per unit part-time. Full-time tuition and fees vary according to course load, degree level, and program. Part-time tuition and fees vary according to course load, degree level, and program. *Required fees:* $6480 full-time, $1432 per term part-time. *Room and board:* $9992; room only: $5653. Room and board charges vary according to board plan and housing facility. *Payment plan:* installment. *Waivers:* employees or children of employees.

Financial Aid Of all full-time matriculated undergraduates who enrolled in 2008, 9,764 applied for aid, 6,642 were judged to have need, 403 had their need fully met. In 2008, 561 non-need-based awards were made. *Average percent of need met:* 59%. *Average financial aid package:* $9396. *Average need-based loan:* $3593. *Average need-based gift aid:* $2824. *Average non-need-based aid:* $2126.

Applying *Options:* electronic application, early admission, early decision. *Application fee:* $55. *Required:* high school transcript. *Application deadlines:* 11/30 (freshmen), 11/30 (transfers). *Early decision deadline:* 10/31. *Notification:* 4/1 (freshmen), 4/1 (transfers), 12/15 (early decision).

Freshman Application Contact Mr. James Maraviglia, Assistant Vice President of Admissions, Recruitment, and Financial Aid, California Polytechnic State University, San Luis Obispo, Admissions Office, 1 Grand Avenue, San Luis Obispo, CA 93407-0031. *Phone:* 805-756-2311. *Fax:* 805-756-5911. *E-mail:* admissions@calpoly.edu. *Web site:* http://www.calpoly.edu/.

California State Polytechnic University, Pomona

Pomona, California

- **State-supported** comprehensive, founded 1938, part of California State University System
- **Urban** 1400-acre campus with easy access to Los Angeles
- **Endowment** $33.2 million
- **Coed** 18,727 undergraduate students, 85% full-time, 43% women, 57% men
- **Moderately difficult** entrance level, 45% of applicants were admitted

Undergraduates 15,942 full-time, 2,785 part-time. Students come from 47 states and territories; 39 other countries; 1% are from out of state; 3% Black or African American, non-Hispanic/Latino; 33% Hispanic/Latino; 26% Asian, non-Hispanic/Latino; 0.3% Native Hawaiian or other Pacific Islander, non-Hispanic/Latino; 0.3% American Indian or Alaska Native, non-Hispanic/Latino; 2% Two or more races, non-Hispanic/Latino; 6% Race/ethnicity unknown; 4% international; 8% transferred in; 12% live on campus. *Retention:* 91% of full-time freshmen returned.

Freshmen *Admission:* 23,396 applied, 10,447 admitted, 2,019 enrolled. *Average high school GPA:* 3.41. *Test scores:* SAT critical reading scores over 500: 62%; SAT math scores over 500: 75%; ACT scores over 18: 91%; SAT critical reading scores over 600: 20%; SAT math scores over 600: 38%; ACT scores over 24: 52%; SAT critical reading scores over 700: 2%; SAT math scores over 700: 7%; ACT scores over 30: 4%.

Faculty *Total:* 955, 53% full-time, 54% with terminal degrees. *Student/faculty ratio:* 26:1.

Academics *Calendar:* quarters. *Degrees:* bachelor's and master's. *Special study options:* academic remediation for entering students, adult/continuing education programs, advanced placement credit, cooperative education, distance learning, double majors, English as a second language, honors programs, internships, off-campus study, part-time degree program, services for LD students, study abroad, summer session for credit. *ROTC:* Army (b).

Computers on Campus 1,875 computers/terminals are available on campus for general student use. Students can access the following: campus intranet, computer help desk, free student e-mail accounts, online (class) grades, online (class) registration, online (class) schedules. Campuswide network is available. 100% of college-owned or -operated housing units are wired for high-speed Internet access. Wireless service is available via entire campus.

Student Life *Housing:* on-campus residence required for freshman year. *Options:* coed, disabled students. Campus housing is university owned and is provided by a third party. Freshman applicants given priority for college housing. *Activities and organizations:* drama/theater group, student-run newspaper, choral group, Rose Float Club, Ridge Runners Ski Club, Barkada (Asian club), American Marketing Association, Cal Poly Society of Accountants, national fraternities, national sororities. *Campus security:* 24-hour emergency response devices and patrols, student patrols, late-night transport/escort service, controlled dormitory access, video camera surveillance. *Student services:* health clinic, personal/psychological counseling, women's center.

Athletics Member NCAA. All Division II. *Intercollegiate sports:* baseball M(s), basketball M(s)/W(s), cross-country running M(s)/W(s), soccer M(s)/W(s), tennis M(s)/W(s), track and field M(s)/W(s), volleyball W(s). *Intramural sports:* basketball M/W, bowling M/W, football M/W, softball M/W, tennis M/W, volleyball M/W.

Standardized Tests *Required:* SAT or ACT (for admission).

Costs (2011–12) *Tuition:* state resident $0 full-time; nonresident $11,160 full-time, $248 per unit part-time. Full-time tuition and fees vary according to degree level and program. Part-time tuition and fees vary according to course load, degree level, and program. *Required fees:* $4806 full-time, $3301 per year part-time. *Room and board:* $10,011; room only: $6327. Room and board charges vary according to board plan and housing facility. *Payment plans:* installment, deferred payment. *Waivers:* employees or children of employees.

Financial Aid Of all full-time matriculated undergraduates who enrolled in 2009, 11,142 applied for aid, 9,642 were judged to have need, 1,487 had their need fully met. 231 Federal Work-Study jobs (averaging $2564). In 2009, 17 non-need-based awards were made. *Average percent of need met:* 72%. *Average financial aid package:* $11,309. *Average need-based loan:* $4058. *Average need-based gift aid:* $8982. *Average non-need-based aid:* $3516. *Average indebtedness upon graduation:* $16,736.

Applying *Options:* electronic application. *Application fee:* $55. *Required:* high school transcript, minimum 2 GPA. *Application deadlines:* 11/30 (freshmen), 11/30 (transfers). *Notification:* continuous until 10/2 (freshmen), 5/1 (transfers).

Freshman Application Contact Mr. Scott J. Duncan, Director, Admissions, California State Polytechnic University, Pomona, 3801 West Temple Avenue, Pomona, CA 91768-2557. *Phone:* 909-869-3258. *Fax:* 909-869-4529. *E-mail:* admissions@csupomona.edu. *Web site:* http://www.csupomona.edu/.

California State University, Bakersfield
Bakersfield, California

- **State-supported** comprehensive, founded 1970, part of California State University System
- **Urban** 575-acre campus
- **Coed** 6,525 undergraduate students, 87% full-time, 62% women, 38% men
- **Moderately difficult** entrance level, 66% of applicants were admitted

Undergraduates 5,657 full-time, 868 part-time. 2% are from out of state; 15% transferred in; 5% live on campus. *Retention:* 69% of full-time freshmen returned.

Freshmen *Admission:* 5,300 applied, 3,513 admitted, 1,030 enrolled. *Average high school GPA:* 2.98. *Test scores:* SAT critical reading scores over 500: 23%; SAT math scores over 500: 23%; ACT scores over 18: 55%; SAT critical reading scores over 600: 3%; SAT math scores over 600: 4%; ACT scores over 24: 8%; SAT math scores over 700: 1%.

Academics *Calendar:* quarters. *Degrees:* bachelor's and master's. *Special study options:* academic remediation for entering students, accelerated degree program, adult/continuing education programs, advanced placement credit, distance learning, double majors, English as a second language, external degree program, freshman honors college, honors programs, independent study, internships, off-campus study, part-time degree program, services for LD students, student-designed majors, study abroad, summer session for credit.

Computers on Campus Students can access the following: online (class) registration. Campuswide network is available.

Student Life *Housing options:* coed, disabled students. *Activities and organizations:* drama/theater group, student-run newspaper, choral group, national fraternities, national sororities. *Campus security:* 24-hour emergency response devices and patrols, late-night transport/escort service. *Student services:* health clinic, personal/psychological counseling, women's center.

Athletics Member NCAA. All Division II except wrestling (Division I). *Intercollegiate sports:* basketball M(s), golf M(s), soccer M(s), softball W(s), swimming and diving M(s)/W(s), tennis M(s)/W(s), track and field M(s)/W(s), volleyball W(s), water polo W(s), wrestling M(s). *Intramural sports:* archery M/W, badminton M/W, baseball M/W, basketball M/W, fencing M/W, football M/W, golf M/W, gymnastics M/W, racquetball M/W, riflery M/W, soccer M, softball M/W, swimming and diving M/W, tennis W, volleyball M/W, weight lifting M/W, wrestling M/W.

Standardized Tests *Required for some:* SAT or ACT (for admission).

Costs (2010–11) *Tuition:* state resident $0 full-time; nonresident $11,160 full-time, $248 per unit part-time. Full-time tuition and fees vary according to course load, degree level, and reciprocity agreements. Part-time tuition and fees vary according to course load, degree level, and reciprocity agreements. *Required fees:* $5314 full-time, $3538 per year part-time. *Room and board:* $7041; room only: $3500. Room and board charges vary according to board plan. *Payment plan:* installment. *Waivers:* senior citizens and employees or children of employees.

Financial Aid Of all full-time matriculated undergraduates who enrolled in 2007, 4,288 applied for aid, 3,869 were judged to have need, 621 had their need fully met. In 2007, 365 non-need-based awards were made. *Average percent of need met:* 78%. *Average financial aid package:* $9026. *Average need-based loan:* $5259. *Average need-based gift aid:* $6199. *Average non-need-based aid:* $2402. *Average indebtedness upon graduation:* $5727.

Applying *Options:* electronic application, deferred entrance. *Application fee:* $55. *Required:* high school transcript. *Application deadlines:* 3/1 (freshmen), rolling (transfers). *Notification:* continuous (freshmen).

Freshman Application Contact Debra Blowers, Assistant Director, Admissions and Evaluations, California State University, Bakersfield, 9001 Stockdale Highway, Balersfield, CA 93311-1099. *Phone:* 661-664-3036. *Toll-free phone:* 800-788-2782. *E-mail:* admissions@csub.edu. *Web site:* http://www.csub.edu/.

California State University Channel Islands
Camarillo, California

Freshman Application Contact Ms. Ginger Reyes, California State University Channel Islands, One University Drive, Camarillo, CA 93012. *Phone:* 805-437-8520. *Fax:* 805-437-8519. *E-mail:* prospective.student@csuci.edu. *Web site:* http://www.csuci.edu/.

California State University, Chico
Chico, California

- **State-supported** comprehensive, founded 1887, part of California State University System
- **Small-town** 119-acre campus
- **Endowment** $39.0 million
- **Coed** 14,758 undergraduate students, 93% full-time, 51% women, 49% men
- **Moderately difficult** entrance level, 67% of applicants were admitted

Undergraduates 13,661 full-time, 1,097 part-time. Students come from 38 states and territories; 36 other countries; 2% are from out of state; 2% Black or African American, non-Hispanic/Latino; 15% Hispanic/Latino; 5% Asian, non-Hispanic/Latino; 0.3% Native Hawaiian or other Pacific Islander, non-Hispanic/Latino; 0.8% American Indian or Alaska Native, non-Hispanic/Latino; 3% Two or more races, non-Hispanic/Latino; 9% Race/ethnicity unknown; 3% international; 9% transferred in; 1% live on campus. *Retention:* 85% of full-time freshmen returned.

Freshmen *Admission:* 13,381 applied, 8,935 admitted, 1,900 enrolled. *Average high school GPA:* 3.28. *Test scores:* SAT critical reading scores over 500: 57%; SAT math scores over 500: 63%; ACT scores over 18: 85%; SAT critical reading scores over 600: 14%; SAT math scores over 600: 19%; ACT scores over 24: 38%; SAT critical reading scores over 700: 1%; SAT math scores over 700: 2%; ACT scores over 30: 2%.

Faculty *Total:* 857, 55% full-time, 61% with terminal degrees. *Student/faculty ratio:* 23:1.

Academics *Calendar:* semesters. *Degrees:* certificates, bachelor's, master's, post-master's, and postbachelor's certificates. *Special study options:* academic remediation for entering students, adult/continuing education programs, advanced placement credit, cooperative education, distance learning, double majors, English as a second language, external degree program, honors programs, independent study, internships, off-campus study, part-time degree program, services for LD students, student-designed majors, study abroad, summer session for credit.

Computers on Campus 1,212 computers/terminals and 1,205 ports are available on campus for general student use. Students can access the following: campus intranet, computer help desk, free student e-mail accounts, online (class) grades, online (class) registration, online (class) schedules, student account information, calendar, transcripts. Campuswide network is available. 100% of college-owned or -operated housing units are wired for high-speed Internet access. Wireless service is available via entire campus.

Student Life *Housing options:* coed, women-only, disabled students. Campus housing is university owned. Freshman applicants given priority for college housing. *Activities and organizations:* drama/theater group, student-run newspaper, radio station, choral group, Scour and Devour, Panhellenic Council, The Edge Campus Christian Fellowship, Golden Key International Honor Society, Music and Entertainment Industry, national fraternities, national sororities.

Campus security: 24-hour emergency response devices and patrols, student patrols, late-night transport/escort service, controlled dormitory access, crime prevention workshops, RAD self-defense program, Chico Safe Rides, blue light emergency phones, freshmen safety orientation. *Student services:* health clinic, personal/psychological counseling, women's center, legal services.

Athletics Member NCAA. All Division II. *Intercollegiate sports:* baseball M(s), basketball M(s)/W(s), cross-country running M(s)/W(s), field hockey W(c), golf M(s)/W(s), racquetball M(c)/W(c), rugby M(c), soccer M(s)/W(s), softball W(s), tennis M(c)/W(c), track and field M(s)/W(s), ultimate Frisbee M(c), volleyball W(s), water polo M(c)/W(c). *Intramural sports:* basketball M/W, bowling M/W, football M/W, soccer M/W, softball M/W, volleyball M/W.

Standardized Tests *Required:* SAT or ACT (for admission).

Costs (2011–12) *Tuition:* state resident $0 full-time; nonresident $11,160 full-time, $372 per unit part-time. Full-time tuition and fees vary according to degree level. Part-time tuition and fees vary according to course load and degree level. *Required fees:* $5620 full-time, $1922 per term part-time. *Room and board:* $11,138; room only: $6746. Room and board charges vary according to board plan and housing facility. *Payment plans:* installment, deferred payment. *Waivers:* senior citizens and employees or children of employees.

Financial Aid Of all full-time matriculated undergraduates who enrolled in 2008, 8,947 applied for aid, 7,285 were judged to have need, 1,134 had their need fully met. In 2008, 595 non-need-based awards were made. *Average percent of need met:* 89%. *Average financial aid package:* $11,706. *Average need-based loan:* $4475. *Average need-based gift aid:* $8982. *Average non-need-based aid:* $1978.

Applying *Options:* electronic application, deferred entrance. *Application fee:* $55. *Required:* high school transcript, GPA of 10th /11th grade college preparatory courses only. *Required for some:* minimum 2 GPA. *Application deadlines:* 11/30 (freshmen), 11/30 (transfers). *Notification:* 3/1 (freshmen), 3/1 (transfers).

Freshman Application Contact California State University, Chico, Chico, CA 95929-0722. *Phone:* 530-898-4428. *Toll-free phone:* 800-542-4426. *Fax:* 530-898-6456. *Web site:* http://www.csuchico.edu/.

California State University, Dominguez Hills

Carson, California

- **State-supported** comprehensive, founded 1960, part of California State University System
- **Urban** 350-acre campus with easy access to Los Angeles
- **Endowment** $7.9 million
- **Coed** 10,823 undergraduate students, 66% full-time, 65% women, 35% men
- **Moderately difficult** entrance level, 85% of applicants were admitted

Undergraduates 7,103 full-time, 3,720 part-time. Students come from 22 states and territories; 34 other countries; 1% are from out of state; 22% Black or African American, non-Hispanic/Latino; 45% Hispanic/Latino; 9% Asian, non-Hispanic/Latino; 0.5% Native Hawaiian or other Pacific Islander, non-Hispanic/Latino; 0.3% American Indian or Alaska Native, non-Hispanic/Latino; 3% Two or more races, non-Hispanic/Latino; 6% Race/ethnicity unknown; 2% international; 20% transferred in; 5% live on campus. *Retention:* 69% of full-time freshmen returned.

Freshmen *Admission:* 8,213 applied, 6,999 admitted, 1,037 enrolled. *Average high school GPA:* 3.07. *Test scores:* SAT critical reading scores over 500: 16%; SAT math scores over 500: 18%; SAT writing scores over 500: 16%; ACT scores over 18: 41%; SAT critical reading scores over 600: 2%; SAT math scores over 600: 3%; SAT writing scores over 600: 2%; ACT scores over 24: 5%.

Faculty *Total:* 645, 40% full-time, 53% with terminal degrees. *Student/faculty ratio:* 26:1.

Academics *Calendar:* semesters. *Degrees:* bachelor's, master's, post-master's, and postbachelor's certificates. *Special study options:* academic remediation for entering students, accelerated degree program, advanced placement credit, cooperative education, distance learning, double majors, external degree program, honors programs, independent study, internships, off-campus study, part-time degree program, services for LD students, student-designed majors, study abroad, summer session for credit. *ROTC:* Army (b), Air Force (c).

Computers on Campus 256 computers/terminals and 200 ports are available on campus for general student use. Students can access the following: free student e-mail accounts, online (class) grades, online (class) registration, online (class) schedules. Campuswide network is available. Wireless service is available via classrooms, computer labs, dorm rooms, libraries, student centers.

Student Life *Housing options:* coed. Campus housing is university owned. *Activities and organizations:* drama/theater group, student-run newspaper, radio station, choral group, Latino Business Students Association, Black Business Student Association, Espirito de Nuestro Futuro, Organization of African

Studies, Recreation Club, national fraternities, national sororities. *Campus security:* 24-hour emergency response devices, student patrols, late-night transport/escort service, campus police. *Student services:* health clinic, personal/psychological counseling, women's center.

Athletics Member NCAA. All Division II. *Intercollegiate sports:* baseball M(s), basketball M(s)/W(s), cross-country running W(s), golf M, soccer M(s)/W(s), softball W(s), track and field W(s), volleyball W(s). *Intramural sports:* basketball M/W, cross-country running M/W, football M/W, golf M/W, soccer M/W, softball M/W, swimming and diving M/W, tennis M/W, track and field M(c)/W(c), volleyball M/W, water polo M/W, weight lifting M/W.

Standardized Tests *Required for some:* SAT or ACT (for admission).

Costs (2010–11) *Tuition:* state resident $0 full-time; nonresident $11,160 full-time, $372 per unit part-time. *Required fees:* $4849 full-time, $1539 per term part-time. *Room and board:* $10,085; room only: $5693. Room and board charges vary according to housing facility. *Payment plan:* installment. *Waivers:* senior citizens and employees or children of employees.

Financial Aid Of all full-time matriculated undergraduates who enrolled in 2008, 4,684 applied for aid, 4,449 were judged to have need, 97 had their need fully met. 189 Federal Work-Study jobs (averaging $1920). In 2008, 165 non-need-based awards were made. *Average percent of need met:* 34%. *Average financial aid package:* $5457. *Average need-based loan:* $2401. *Average need-based gift aid:* $4310. *Average non-need-based aid:* $3165. *Average indebtedness upon graduation:* $12,786.

Applying *Options:* electronic application. *Application fee:* $55. *Required:* high school transcript. *Application deadlines:* rolling (freshmen), rolling (transfers). *Notification:* continuous (freshmen), continuous (transfers).

Freshman Application Contact Information Center, California State University, Dominguez Hills, 1000 East Victoria Street, Carson, CA 90747-0001. *Phone:* 310-243-3696. *Web site:* http://www.csudh.edu/.

California State University, East Bay

Hayward, California

- **State-supported** comprehensive, founded 1957, part of California State University System
- **Suburban** 343-acre campus with easy access to San Francisco Bay Area
- **Endowment** $9.2 million
- **Coed**
- **Moderately difficult** entrance level

Faculty *Student/faculty ratio:* 24:1.

Academics *Calendar:* quarters. *Degrees:* certificates, bachelor's, master's, doctoral-professional, and postbachelor's certificates.

Student Life *Campus security:* 24-hour emergency response devices and patrols, late-night transport/escort service.

Athletics Member NCAA, NAIA. All NCAA Division III.

Standardized Tests *Required for some:* SAT or ACT (for admission).

Costs (2010–11) *Tuition:* state resident $0 full-time; nonresident $13,800 full-time. *Required fees:* $4872 full-time. *Room and board:* $10,029.

Financial Aid *Of all full-time matriculated undergraduates who enrolled in 2009,* 4,842 applied for aid, 4,695 were judged to have need, 60 had their need fully met. 699 Federal Work-Study jobs (averaging $2400). *Average percent of need met:* 55. *Average financial aid package:* $10,823. *Average need-based loan:* $7097. *Average need-based gift aid:* $9027. *Average indebtedness upon graduation:* $15,958.

Applying *Options:* electronic application. *Application fee:* $55. *Required:* high school transcript, minimum 2 GPA, California State University eligibility index.

Freshman Application Contact Dr. Colin Ormsby, Interim Executive Director of Undergraduate Admissions, California State University, East Bay, 25800 Carlos Bee Boulevard, Hayward, CA 94542-3000. *Phone:* 510-885-2784. *Fax:* 510-885-4059. *E-mail:* admissions@csueastbay.edu. *Web site:* http://www.csueastbay.edu/.

California State University, Fresno

Fresno, California

- **State-supported** comprehensive, founded 1911, part of California State University System
- **Urban** 1399-acre campus
- **Endowment** $87.5 million
- **Coed**
- **Minimally difficult** entrance level

Faculty *Student/faculty ratio:* 20:1.

Academics *Calendar:* semesters. *Degrees:* certificates, bachelor's, master's, and doctoral-other.

Student Life *Campus security:* 24-hour emergency response devices and patrols, late-night transport/escort service, controlled dormitory access.

Athletics Member NCAA. All Division I except football (Division I-A).

Standardized Tests *Required:* SAT or ACT (for admission).

Costs (2010–11) *Tuition:* state resident $0 full-time; nonresident $11,160 full-time. *Required fees:* $4230 full-time. *Room and board:* $10,200. Room and board charges vary according to board plan.

Financial Aid *Of all full-time matriculated undergraduates who enrolled in 2009,* 11,721 applied for aid, 10,746 were judged to have need, 1,324 had their need fully met. 320 Federal Work-Study jobs (averaging $3197). *In 2009,* 151 non-need-based awards were made. *Average percent of need met:* 71. *Average financial aid package:* $11,251. *Average need-based loan:* $4058. *Average need-based gift aid:* $9380. *Average non-need-based aid:* $2843. *Average indebtedness upon graduation:* $12,670.

Applying *Options:* electronic application. *Application fee:* $55. *Required:* high school transcript, minimum 2 GPA.

Freshman Application Contact Mr. Andy Hernandez, Admissions Officer, California State University, Fresno, 5150 North Maple Avenue, M/S JA 57, Fresno, CA 93740-8026. *Phone:* 559-278-6115. *Fax:* 559-278-4812. *E-mail:* andyhe@csufresno.edu. *Web site:* http://www.csufresno.edu/.

California State University, Fullerton

Fullerton, California

- **State-supported** comprehensive, founded 1957, part of California State University System
- **Suburban** 236-acre campus with easy access to Los Angeles
- **Endowment** $18.7 million
- **Coed** 29,962 undergraduate students, 76% full-time, 57% women, 43% men
- **Moderately difficult** entrance level, 45% of applicants were admitted

Undergraduates 22,754 full-time, 7,208 part-time. Students come from 35 states and territories; 62 other countries; 1% are from out of state; 3% Black or African American, non-Hispanic/Latino; 33% Hispanic/Latino; 22% Asian, non-Hispanic/Latino; 0.4% American Indian or Alaska Native, non-Hispanic/Latino; 2% Two or more races, non-Hispanic/Latino; 7% Race/ethnicity unknown; 4% international; 14% transferred in; 3% live on campus. *Retention:* 84% of full-time freshmen returned.

Freshmen *Admission:* 33,565 applied, 15,153 admitted, 3,912 enrolled. *Average high school GPA:* 3.27. *Test scores:* SAT critical reading scores over 500: 47%; SAT math scores over 500: 57%; ACT scores over 18: 83%; SAT critical reading scores over 600: 10%; SAT math scores over 600: 17%; ACT scores over 24: 25%; SAT critical reading scores over 700: 1%; SAT math scores over 700: 2%; ACT scores over 30: 1%.

Faculty *Total:* 1,680, 50% full-time, 77% with terminal degrees. *Student/faculty ratio:* 26:1.

Academics *Calendar:* semesters. *Degrees:* bachelor's, master's, doctoral-other, post-master's, and postbachelor's certificates. *Special study options:* academic remediation for entering students, adult/continuing education programs, advanced placement credit, cooperative education, distance learning, double majors, English as a second language, freshman honors college, honors programs, independent study, internships, off-campus study, part-time degree program, services for LD students, student-designed majors, study abroad, summer session for credit. *ROTC:* Army (b).

Computers on Campus 2,000 computers/terminals are available on campus for general student use. Students can access the following: campus intranet, computer help desk, free student e-mail accounts, online (class) grades, online (class) registration, online (class) schedules. Campuswide network is available. Wireless service is available via entire campus.

Student Life *Housing options:* coed. Campus housing is university owned. *Activities and organizations:* drama/theater group, student-run newspaper, radio station, choral group, Pan-Hellenic Council, American Marketing Association, Lacrosse Club, Samaritans (volunteer service club), Human Services Student Association, national fraternities, national sororities. *Campus security:* 24-hour emergency response devices and patrols, student patrols, late-night transport/escort service, controlled dormitory access. *Student services:* health clinic, personal/psychological counseling, women's center, legal services.

Athletics Member NCAA. All Division I. *Intercollegiate sports:* baseball M(s), basketball M(s)/W(s), cross-country running M(s)/W(s), golf M(s)/W(s), gymnastics W(s), soccer M(s)/W(s), softball W(s), tennis W(s), track and field M(s)/W(s), volleyball W(s), wrestling M(s). *Intramural sports:* archery M(c)/W(c), badminton M/W, basketball M/W, bowling M/W, equestrian sports M(c)/W(c), football M/W, gymnastics W, ice hockey M(c)/W(c), lacrosse M/W(c), racquetball M/W, rugby M/W(c), sailing M(c)/W(c), skiing (downhill) M/W, soccer M/W, softball M/W, swimming and diving M/W, table tennis M/W, tennis M/W, ultimate Frisbee M(c)/W(c), volleyball M/W, water polo M(c)/W(c), wrestling M.

Standardized Tests *Required:* SAT (for admission), SAT or ACT (for admission).

Costs (2011–12) *Tuition:* state resident $0 full-time; nonresident $11,160 full-time, $3837 per term part-time. Full-time tuition and fees vary according to course load. Part-time tuition and fees vary according to course load. *Required fees:* $4971 full-time, $1605 per term part-time. *Room and board:* $9632;

room only: $6122. *Payment plans:* installment, deferred payment. *Waivers:* senior citizens and employees or children of employees.

Financial Aid Of all full-time matriculated undergraduates who enrolled in 2009, 15,531 applied for aid, 12,126 were judged to have need, 10,851 had their need fully met. 456 Federal Work-Study jobs (averaging $2577). In 2009, 1210 non-need-based awards were made. *Average percent of need met:* 53%. *Average financial aid package:* $10,023. *Average need-based loan:* $6522. *Average need-based gift aid:* $8412. *Average non-need-based aid:* $7024. *Average indebtedness upon graduation:* $14,989.

Applying *Options:* electronic application. *Application fee:* $55. *Required:* high school transcript, minimum 2 GPA. *Application deadlines:* 11/30 (freshmen), 11/30 (transfers). *Notification:* continuous (freshmen), continuous (transfers).

Freshman Application Contact Ms. Nancy J. Dority, Assistant Vice President of Enrollment Services, California State University, Fullerton, Office of Admissions and Records, PO Box 34080, Fullerton, CA 92834-9480. *Phone:* 657-278-2370. *Fax:* 657-278-2356. *E-mail:* admissions@fullerton.edu. *Web site:* http://www.fullerton.edu/.

California State University, Long Beach

Long Beach, California

- **State-supported** comprehensive, founded 1949, part of California State University System
- **Suburban** 320-acre campus with easy access to Los Angeles
- **Endowment** $36.6 million
- **Coed** 27,436 undergraduate students, 82% full-time, 59% women, 41% men
- **Moderately difficult** entrance level, 34% of applicants were admitted

Undergraduates 22,533 full-time, 4,903 part-time. Students come from 47 states and territories; 82 other countries; 1% are from out of state; 4% Black or African American, non-Hispanic/Latino; 31% Hispanic/Latino; 19% Asian, non-Hispanic/Latino; 4% Native Hawaiian or other Pacific Islander, non-Hispanic/Latino; 0.6% American Indian or Alaska Native, non-Hispanic/Latino; 2% Two or more races, non-Hispanic/Latino; 7% Race/ethnicity unknown; 5% international; 8% transferred in; 30% live on campus. *Retention:* 88% of full-time freshmen returned.

Freshmen *Admission:* 47,673 applied, 16,428 admitted, 3,988 enrolled. *Average high school GPA:* 3.44. *Test scores:* SAT critical reading scores over 500: 53%; SAT math scores over 500: 62%; ACT scores over 18: 80%; SAT critical reading scores over 600: 15%; SAT math scores over 600: 23%; ACT scores over 24: 33%; SAT critical reading scores over 700: 1%; SAT math scores over 700: 3%; ACT scores over 30: 3%.

Faculty *Total:* 1,886, 50% full-time, 58% with terminal degrees. *Student/faculty ratio:* 21:1.

Academics *Calendar:* semesters. *Degrees:* bachelor's, master's, doctoral-research/scholarship, and postbachelor's certificates. *Special study options:* academic remediation for entering students, accelerated degree program, adult/continuing education programs, advanced placement credit, distance learning, double majors, English as a second language, honors programs, independent study, internships, off-campus study, part-time degree program, services for LD students, student-designed majors, study abroad, summer session for credit. *ROTC:* Army (b).

Computers on Campus 2,000 computers/terminals are available on campus for general student use. Campuswide network is available.

Student Life *Housing options:* coed. *Activities and organizations:* drama/theater group, student-run newspaper, radio and television station, choral group, national fraternities, national sororities. *Campus security:* 24-hour emergency response devices and patrols, student patrols, late-night transport/escort service. *Student services:* health clinic, personal/psychological counseling, women's center, legal services.

Athletics Member NCAA. All Division I. *Intercollegiate sports:* archery M(c)/W(c), badminton M(c)/W(c), basketball M(s)/W(s), bowling M(c)/W(c), crew M(c)/W(c), cross-country running M(s)/W(s), fencing M(c)/W(c), golf M/W, rugby M(c), sailing M(c)/W(c), skiing (downhill) M(c)/W(c), soccer M(c)/W(c), softball W(s), table tennis M(c), tennis W(s), track and field M(s)/W(s), volleyball M(s)/W(s), water polo M(s)/W(s). *Intramural sports:* basketball M/W, gymnastics M/W, racquetball M/W, softball W, swimming and diving M/W, table tennis W(c), tennis W, track and field M(c)/W(c), volleyball M/W.

Standardized Tests *Required:* SAT or ACT (for admission).

Costs (2011–12) *Tuition:* state resident $0 full-time; nonresident $11,160 full-time. Full-time tuition and fees vary according to program. Part-time tuition and fees vary according to course load and program. *Required fees:* $5464 full-time. *Room and board:* $11,294. Room and board charges vary according to board plan. *Payment plan:* installment. *Waivers:* senior citizens and employees or children of employees.

Financial Aid Of all full-time matriculated undergraduates who enrolled in 2009, 17,032 applied for aid, 16,141 were judged to have need, 8,011 had their need fully met. In 2009, 1075 non-need-based awards were made. *Average percent of need met:* 83%. *Average financial aid package:* $12,981. *Average need-based loan:* $3436. *Average need-based gift aid:* $5444. *Average non-need-based aid:* $2478. *Average indebtedness upon graduation:* $10,787.
Applying *Options:* electronic application. *Application fee:* $55. *Required:* high school transcript. *Required for some:* minimum 2 GPA, minimum GPA of 2.4 for nonresidents. *Application deadlines:* 11/30 (freshmen), 11/30 (transfers). *Notification:* continuous (freshmen), continuous (transfers).
Freshman Application Contact Mr. Thomas Enders, Director of Enrollment Services, California State University, Long Beach, Brotman Hall, 1250 Bellflower Boulevard, Long Beach, CA 90840. *Phone:* 562-985-4641. *Web site:* http://www.csulb.edu/.

California State University, Los Angeles

Los Angeles, California

- **State-supported** comprehensive, founded 1947, part of California State University System
- **Urban** 173-acre campus
- **Endowment** $14.0 million
- **Coed** 15,952 undergraduate students, 83% full-time, 59% women, 41% men
- **Moderately difficult** entrance level, 57% of applicants were admitted

Undergraduates 13,186 full-time, 2,766 part-time. Students come from 27 states and territories; 82 other countries; 1% are from out of state; 6% Black or African American, non-Hispanic/Latino; 52% Hispanic/Latino; 18% Asian, non-Hispanic/Latino; 0.1% American Indian or Alaska Native, non-Hispanic/Latino; 10% Race/ethnicity unknown; 5% international; 16% transferred in; 4% live on campus. *Retention:* 83% of full-time freshmen returned.
Freshmen *Admission:* 22,731 applied, 12,996 admitted, 2,061 enrolled. *Average high school GPA:* 3.13. *Test scores:* SAT critical reading scores over 500: 23%; SAT math scores over 500: 29%; SAT writing scores over 500: 22%; ACT scores over 18: 44%; SAT critical reading scores over 600: 3%; SAT math scores over 600: 6%; SAT writing scores over 600: 2%; ACT scores over 24: 9%; SAT math scores over 700: 1%; ACT scores over 30: 1%.
Faculty *Total:* 1,029, 55% full-time. *Student/faculty ratio:* 23:1.
Academics *Calendar:* quarters. *Degrees:* bachelor's, master's, and doctoral-research/scholarship. *Special study options:* academic remediation for entering students, accelerated degree program, adult/continuing education programs, advanced placement credit, cooperative education, distance learning, double majors, English as a second language, honors programs, independent study, internships, off-campus study, part-time degree program, services for LD students, student-designed majors, study abroad, summer session for credit. *ROTC:* Army (c), Air Force (c). *Unusual degree programs:* 3-2 nursing.
Computers on Campus 1,500 computers/terminals are available on campus for general student use. Students can access the following: campus intranet, computer help desk, free student e-mail accounts, online (class) grades, online (class) registration, online (class) schedules. Campuswide network is available. 100% of college-owned or -operated housing units are wired for high-speed Internet access. Wireless service is available via classrooms, computer centers, computer labs, dorm rooms, learning centers, libraries, student centers.
Student Life *Housing options:* coed. Campus housing is university owned. *Activities and organizations:* drama/theater group, student-run newspaper, choral group, Society of Hispanic Engineering and Science Students, Institute of Electrical and Electronics Engineer, Sigma Delta PI, Asian Unified, Society of Automotive Engineers, national fraternities, national sororities. *Campus security:* 24-hour emergency response devices, student patrols, late-night transport/escort service. *Student services:* health clinic, personal/psychological counseling, women's center, legal services.
Athletics Member NCAA. All Division II. *Intercollegiate sports:* baseball M(s), basketball M(s)/W(s), cross-country running W(s), soccer M(s)/W(s), tennis W(s), track and field M(s)/W(s), volleyball W(s). *Intramural sports:* basketball M/W, bowling M/W, gymnastics M/W, racquetball M/W, skiing (cross-country) M/W, soccer M/W, softball M/W, swimming and diving M/W, tennis M/W, track and field M/W, volleyball M/W, water polo M/W, wrestling M.
Standardized Tests *Required for some:* SAT or ACT (for admission).
Costs (2010–11) *Tuition:* state resident $0 full-time; nonresident $8928 full-time, $248 per unit part-time. Full-time tuition and fees vary according to course level and course load. Part-time tuition and fees vary according to course level and course load. *Required fees:* $4846 full-time, $1025 per term part-time. *Room and board:* $9105. Room and board charges vary according to housing facility. *Payment plan:* installment. *Waivers:* employees or children of employees.

Financial Aid Of all full-time matriculated undergraduates who enrolled in 2008, 9,412 applied for aid, 8,916 were judged to have need, 1,449 had their need fully met. In 2008, 95 non-need-based awards were made. *Average percent of need met:* 66%. *Average financial aid package:* $9484. *Average need-based loan:* $5002. *Average need-based gift aid:* $7561. *Average non-need-based aid:* $4048.
Applying *Options:* electronic application, early admission. *Application fee:* $55. *Required:* high school transcript. *Application deadlines:* 6/15 (freshmen), 6/15 (transfers). *Notification:* 11/1 (freshmen), 11/1 (transfers).
Freshman Application Contact Mr. Vince Lopez, Director of Outreach and Recruitment, California State University, Los Angeles, 5151 State University Drive, Los Angeles, CA 90032-8530. *Phone:* 323-343-3839. *E-mail:* admission@calstatela.edu. *Web site:* http://www.calstatela.edu/.

California State University, Monterey Bay

Seaside, California

- **State-supported** comprehensive, founded 1994, part of California State University System
- **Small-town** 1387-acre campus with easy access to San Jose
- **Endowment** $9.6 million
- **Coed** 4,422 undergraduate students, 93% full-time, 60% women, 40% men
- **Moderately difficult** entrance level, 52% of applicants were admitted

Undergraduates 4,100 full-time, 322 part-time. Students come from 29 states and territories; 12 other countries; 2% are from out of state; 4% Black or African American, non-Hispanic/Latino; 29% Hispanic/Latino; 5% Asian, non-Hispanic/Latino; 0.9% Native Hawaiian or other Pacific Islander, non-Hispanic/Latino; 0.8% American Indian or Alaska Native, non-Hispanic/Latino; 5% Two or more races, non-Hispanic/Latino; 8% Race/ethnicity unknown; 0.7% international; 11% transferred in; 52% live on campus. *Retention:* 76% of full-time freshmen returned.
Freshmen *Admission:* 10,263 applied, 5,364 admitted, 829 enrolled. *Average high school GPA:* 3.19. *Test scores:* SAT critical reading scores over 500: 44%; SAT math scores over 500: 44%; SAT writing scores over 500: 42%; ACT scores over 18: 76%; SAT critical reading scores over 600: 10%; SAT math scores over 600: 10%; SAT writing scores over 600: 7%; ACT scores over 24: 24%; SAT math scores over 700: 1%; SAT writing scores over 700: 1%; ACT scores over 30: 2%.
Academics *Calendar:* semesters. *Degrees:* bachelor's and master's. *Special study options:* academic remediation for entering students, advanced placement credit, cooperative education, distance learning, double majors, independent study, internships, part-time degree program, services for LD students, student-designed majors, study abroad, summer session for credit.
Computers on Campus 980 computers/terminals are available on campus for general student use. Students can access the following: campus intranet, computer help desk, free student e-mail accounts, online (class) grades, online (class) registration, online (class) schedules. Campuswide network is available. 100% of college-owned or -operated housing units are wired for high-speed Internet access. Wireless service is available via entire campus.
Student Life *Housing:* on-campus residence required through sophomore year. *Options:* coed, disabled students. Campus housing is university owned. Freshman applicants given priority for college housing. *Activities and organizations:* drama/theater group, student-run newspaper, radio station, choral group, Otter Dance Team, Disc Golf Team, First Year Council, M.E.Ch.A, Electronic Music Culture (E=MC2), national fraternities, national sororities. *Campus security:* 24-hour emergency response devices and patrols, student patrols, late-night transport/escort service, controlled dormitory access. *Student services:* health clinic, personal/psychological counseling.
Athletics Member NCAA. All Division II. *Intercollegiate sports:* baseball M(s), basketball M(s)/W(s), cross-country running M(s)/W(s), golf M(s)/W(s), sailing M/W, soccer M(s)/W(s), softball W(s), volleyball W(s), water polo W(s). *Intramural sports:* basketball M/W, bowling M/W, soccer M/W, volleyball M/W.
Standardized Tests *Required for some:* SAT or ACT (for admission), ELM/EPT.
Costs (2010–11) *Tuition:* state resident $0 full-time; nonresident $11,160 full-time, $372 per unit part-time. Full-time tuition and fees vary according to degree level. Part-time tuition and fees vary according to degree level. No tuition increase for student's term of enrollment. *Required fees:* $4721 full-time, $1473 per term part-time. *Room and board:* $8440; room only: $5440. Room and board charges vary according to board plan and housing facility. *Payment plan:* installment. *Waivers:* senior citizens and employees or children of employees.
Financial Aid Of all full-time matriculated undergraduates who enrolled in 2009, 2,814 applied for aid, 2,221 were judged to have need, 369 had their need fully met. *Average percent of need met:* 74%. *Average financial aid*

package: $9181. *Average need-based loan:* $4138. *Average need-based gift aid:* $7782. *Average indebtedness upon graduation:* $15,254.

Applying *Options:* electronic application, deferred entrance. *Application fee:* $55. *Required:* high school transcript, minimum 2 GPA. *Application deadlines:* 11/30 (freshmen), 11/30 (out-of-state freshmen), 11/30 (transfers). *Notification:* continuous (freshmen), continuous (out-of-state freshmen), continuous (transfers).

Freshman Application Contact Mr. John Larsen, Assistant Director of Recruitment, California State University, Monterey Bay, 100 Campus Center, Seaside, CA 93955. *Phone:* 831-582-3738. *Fax:* 831-582-3783. *E-mail:* admissions@csumb.edu. *Web site:* http://www.csumb.edu/.

California State University, Northridge
Northridge, California

- **State-supported** comprehensive, founded 1958, part of California State University System
- **Urban** 356-acre campus with easy access to Los Angeles
- **Coed** 29,880 undergraduate students, 77% full-time, 56% women, 44% men
- **Moderately difficult** entrance level, 74% of applicants were admitted

Undergraduates 22,991 full-time, 6,889 part-time. 4% are from out of state; 8% Black or African American, non-Hispanic/Latino; 34% Hispanic/Latino; 11% Asian, non-Hispanic/Latino; 0.4% Native Hawaiian or other Pacific Islander, non-Hispanic/Latino; 0.2% American Indian or Alaska Native, non-Hispanic/Latino; 2% Two or more races, non-Hispanic/Latino; 10% Race/ethnicity unknown; 6% international; 15% transferred in. *Retention:* 75% of full-time freshmen returned.

Freshmen *Admission:* 23,015 applied, 16,926 admitted, 5,195 enrolled. *Average high school GPA:* 3.15. *Test scores:* SAT critical reading scores over 500: 35%; SAT math scores over 500: 38%; SAT critical reading scores over 600: 7%; SAT math scores over 600: 10%; SAT critical reading scores over 700: 1%; SAT math scores over 700: 1%.

Faculty *Total:* 1,833, 43% full-time. *Student/faculty ratio:* 25:1.

Academics *Calendar:* semesters. *Degrees:* bachelor's and master's. *Special study options:* academic remediation for entering students, adult/continuing education programs, advanced placement credit, distance learning, double majors, English as a second language, independent study, internships, off-campus study, part-time degree program, services for LD students, student-designed majors, study abroad, summer session for credit. *ROTC:* Army (c), Air Force (c).

Computers on Campus 723 computers/terminals are available on campus for general student use. Students can access the following: online (class) registration. Campuswide network is available.

Student Life *Activities and organizations:* drama/theater group, student-run newspaper, radio station, choral group, national fraternities, national sororities. *Campus security:* 24-hour emergency response devices, late-night transport/escort service. *Student services:* health clinic, personal/psychological counseling, women's center.

Athletics Member NCAA. All Division I except football (Division II). *Intercollegiate sports:* baseball M(s), basketball M(s)/W(s), cross-country running M(s)/W(s), football M(s), golf M(s), soccer M(s), softball W(s), swimming and diving M(s)/W(s), tennis W(s), track and field M(s)/W(s), volleyball M(s)/W(s). *Intramural sports:* baseball M, basketball M/W, bowling M(c)/W(c), cross-country running M/W, football M/W, golf M, ice hockey M(c), racquetball M/W, rugby M(c), sailing M(c)/W(c), skiing (downhill) M(c)/W(c), soccer M/W, swimming and diving M/W, table tennis M(c)/W(c), tennis W, track and field M/W, volleyball M/W.

Standardized Tests *Required:* SAT or ACT (for admission).

Costs (2010–11) *Tuition:* state resident $0 full-time; nonresident $11,160 full-time. *Required fees:* $5076 full-time. *Room and board:* $12,414. Room and board charges vary according to board plan and housing facility. *Payment plan:* installment. *Waivers:* senior citizens and employees or children of employees.

Financial Aid Of all full-time matriculated undergraduates who enrolled in 2008, 15,508 applied for aid, 14,475 were judged to have need. 501 Federal Work-Study jobs (averaging $2726). In 2008, 1022 non-need-based awards were made. *Average financial aid package:* $12,547. *Average need-based loan:* $6000. *Average need-based gift aid:* $9690. *Average non-need-based aid:* $1615. *Average indebtedness upon graduation:* $14,691.

Applying *Options:* electronic application. *Application fee:* $55. *Required:* high school transcript. *Application deadlines:* 11/30 (freshmen), 11/30 (transfers). *Notification:* continuous (freshmen), continuous (transfers).

Freshman Application Contact Ms. Mary Baxton, Associate Director of Admissions and Records, California State University, Northridge, 18111 Nordhoff Street, Northridge, CA 91330-8207. *Phone:* 818-677-3777. *Fax:* 818-677-3766. *E-mail:* admissions.records@csun.edu. *Web site:* http://www.csun.edu/.

California State University, Sacramento
Sacramento, California

- **State-supported** comprehensive, founded 1947, part of California State University System
- **Urban** 300-acre campus
- **Coed**
- **Moderately difficult** entrance level

Faculty *Student/faculty ratio:* 26:1.

Academics *Calendar:* semesters. *Degrees:* bachelor's, master's, and doctoral-research/scholarship.

Student Life *Campus security:* 24-hour emergency response devices and patrols, student patrols, late-night transport/escort service, controlled dormitory access.

Athletics Member NCAA. All Division I except football (Division I-AA).

Standardized Tests *Required:* SAT or ACT (for admission).

Costs (2010–11) *Tuition:* state resident $0 full-time; nonresident $11,160 full-time, $372 per unit part-time. Full-time tuition and fees vary according to degree level. Part-time tuition and fees vary according to degree level. *Required fees:* $5194 full-time, $1709 per term part-time. *Room and board:* $9512. Room and board charges vary according to board plan and housing facility.

Financial Aid *Of all full-time matriculated undergraduates who enrolled in 2008,* 15,970 applied for aid, 14,865 were judged to have need, 1,604 had their need fully met. *In 2008,* 62 non-need-based awards were made. *Average percent of need met:* 90. *Average financial aid package:* $7030. *Average need-based loan:* $4072. *Average need-based gift aid:* $5716. *Average non-need-based aid:* $1250. *Average indebtedness upon graduation:* $12,473.

Applying *Options:* electronic application, early action, deferred entrance. *Application fee:* $55. *Required:* minimum 2 GPA. *Required for some:* high school transcript.

Freshman Application Contact Mr. Emiliano Diaz, Director of University Outreach Services, California State University, Sacramento, 6000 J Street, Lassen Hall, Sacramento, CA 95819-6048. *Phone:* 916-278-3901. *Fax:* 916-278-5603. *E-mail:* admissions@csus.edu. *Web site:* http://www.csus.edu/.

California State University, San Bernardino
San Bernardino, California

- **State-supported** comprehensive, founded 1965, part of California State University System
- **Suburban** 430-acre campus with easy access to Los Angeles
- **Coed** 13,680 undergraduate students, 87% full-time, 64% women, 36% men
- **Moderately difficult** entrance level

Undergraduates 11,909 full-time, 1,771 part-time. 10% Black or African American, non-Hispanic/Latino; 46% Hispanic/Latino; 7% Asian, non-Hispanic/Latino; 0.4% Native Hawaiian or other Pacific Islander, non-Hispanic/Latino; 0.5% American Indian or Alaska Native, non-Hispanic/Latino; 3% Two or more races, non-Hispanic/Latino; 7% Race/ethnicity unknown; 3% international; 13% transferred in; 10% live on campus. *Retention:* 86% of full-time freshmen returned.

Freshmen *Admission:* 10,728 applied, 1,773 enrolled. *Average high school GPA:* 3.24. *Test scores:* SAT critical reading scores over 500: 27%; SAT math scores over 500: 30%; SAT writing scores over 500: 26%; ACT scores over 18: 20%; SAT critical reading scores over 600: 4%; SAT math scores over 600: 5%; SAT writing scores over 600: 3%; ACT scores over 24: 3%.

Faculty *Total:* 795, 54% full-time. *Student/faculty ratio:* 25:1.

Academics *Calendar:* quarters. *Degrees:* bachelor's, master's, and doctoral-research/scholarship. *Special study options:* accelerated degree program, cooperative education, distance learning, double majors, honors programs, independent study, internships, off-campus study, part-time degree program, services for LD students, student-designed majors, study abroad, summer session for credit. *ROTC:* Army (b), Air Force (b).

Computers on Campus 1,300 computers/terminals are available on campus for general student use. Students can access the following: computer help desk, free student e-mail accounts, online (class) grades, online (class) registration, online (class) schedules. Campuswide network is available. Wireless service is available via entire campus.

Student Life *Housing options:* coed, women-only. Campus housing is university owned and is provided by a third party. *Activities and organizations:* drama/theater group, student-run newspaper, radio and television station, choral group, national fraternities, national sororities. *Campus security:* 24-hour emergency response devices and patrols, student patrols, late-night transport/escort service, residence staff on call 24 hours. *Student services:* health clinic, personal/psychological counseling, women's center, legal services.

PROFILES

Athletics Member NCAA. All Division II. *Intercollegiate sports:* baseball M(s), basketball M(s)/W(s), cross-country running W, golf M(s), soccer M(s)/W(s), softball W(s), swimming and diving M(s)/W(s), tennis W, volleyball W(s), water polo M/W. *Intramural sports:* basketball M/W, field hockey M/W, football M/W, soccer M/W, softball M, volleyball M/W.

Standardized Tests *Required:* SAT or ACT (for admission).

Costs (2011–12) *Tuition:* state resident $0 full-time; nonresident $11,160 full-time. Part-time tuition and fees vary according to course load. *Required fees:* $5189 full-time. *Room and board:* Room and board charges vary according to board plan and housing facility. *Waivers:* employees or children of employees.

Financial Aid Of all full-time matriculated undergraduates who enrolled in 2009, 9,715 applied for aid, 9,003 were judged to have need, 962 had their need fully met. 345 Federal Work-Study jobs (averaging $3911). In 2009, 145 non-need-based awards were made. *Average percent of need met:* 68%. *Average financial aid package:* $10,958. *Average need-based loan:* $3499. *Average need-based gift aid:* $8235. *Average non-need-based aid:* $3728. *Average indebtedness upon graduation:* $23,791.

Applying *Options:* electronic application, early admission, early action. *Application fee:* $55. *Required:* high school transcript, minimum 2 GPA. *Application deadlines:* rolling (freshmen), rolling (transfers). *Notification:* continuous (freshmen), continuous (transfers).

Freshman Application Contact Ms. Julie Mellen, Assistant Director of Admissions and Evaluations, California State University, San Bernardino, 5500 University Parkway, University Hall, Room 107, San Bernardino, CA 92407-2397. *Phone:* 909-537-5211. *Fax:* 909-537-7034. *E-mail:* moreinfo@mail.csusb.edu. *Web site:* http://www.csusb.edu/.

California State University, San Marcos

San Marcos, California

- **State-supported** comprehensive, founded 1990, part of California State University System
- **Suburban** 304-acre campus with easy access to San Diego
- **Coed** 8,841 undergraduate students, 75% full-time, 61% women, 39% men
- **Moderately difficult** entrance level

Undergraduates 6,657 full-time, 2,184 part-time. 1% are from out of state; 3% Black or African American, non-Hispanic/Latino; 29% Hispanic/Latino; 11% Asian, non-Hispanic/Latino; 0.7% American Indian or Alaska Native, non-Hispanic/Latino; 3% Two or more races, non-Hispanic/Latino; 9% Race/ethnicity unknown; 2% international; 15% transferred in; 6% live on campus. *Retention:* 78% of full-time freshmen returned.

Freshmen *Admission:* 9,936 applied, 1,256 enrolled. *Average high school GPA:* 3.18. *Test scores:* SAT critical reading scores over 500: 39%; SAT math scores over 500: 49%; SAT critical reading scores over 600: 7%; SAT math scores over 600: 10%; SAT critical reading scores over 700: 1%; SAT math scores over 700: 1%.

Faculty *Total:* 528, 42% full-time. *Student/faculty ratio:* 24:1.

Academics *Calendar:* semesters. *Degrees:* bachelor's and master's. *Special study options:* academic remediation for entering students, adult/continuing education programs, advanced placement credit, distance learning, double majors, English as a second language, independent study, internships, off-campus study, part-time degree program, services for LD students, student-designed majors, study abroad, summer session for credit. *ROTC:* Army (c), Navy (c), Air Force (c).

Computers on Campus 1,400 computers/terminals are available on campus for general student use. Students can access the following: computer help desk, free student e-mail accounts, online (class) registration, online (class) schedules. Campuswide network is available.

Student Life *Housing options:* disabled students. Campus housing is provided by a third party. *Activities and organizations:* drama/theater group, student-run newspaper, choral group, Accounting Club, Liberal Studies Club, MECHA, Sigma IOTA Epsilon, national fraternities, national sororities. *Campus security:* 24-hour emergency response devices and patrols, student patrols, late-night transport/escort service. *Student services:* health clinic, personal/psychological counseling, women's center.

Athletics Member NAIA. *Intercollegiate sports:* baseball M, cross-country running M/W, golf M/W, soccer M/W, track and field M/W. *Intramural sports:* softball W.

Standardized Tests *Recommended:* SAT or ACT (for admission).

Costs (2010–11) *Tuition:* state resident $0 full-time; nonresident $9508 full-time, $372 per unit part-time. Part-time tuition and fees vary according to course load. *Required fees:* $5044 full-time. *Room only:* $7500. Room and board charges vary according to housing facility. *Waivers:* senior citizens and employees or children of employees.

Financial Aid Of all full-time matriculated undergraduates who enrolled in 2007, 2,799 applied for aid, 2,208 were judged to have need. 156 Federal Work-Study jobs (averaging $1962). *Average financial aid package:* $6924.

Average need-based loan: $4001. *Average need-based gift aid:* $4013. *Average indebtedness upon graduation:* $14,584.

Applying *Options:* electronic application. *Application fee:* $55. *Required:* high school transcript, minimum 3 GPA. *Application deadlines:* 11/30 (freshmen), 11/30 (transfers). *Notification:* continuous (freshmen), continuous (transfers).

Freshman Application Contact Darren Bush, Director of Admissions, California State University, San Marcos, 333 South Twin Oaks Valley Road, San Marcos, CA 92096-0001. *Phone:* 760-750-4848. *Fax:* 760-750-3248. *E-mail:* apply@csusm.edu. *Web site:* http://www.csusm.edu/.

California State University, Stanislaus

Turlock, California

- **State-supported** comprehensive, founded 1957, part of California State University System
- **Small-town** 228-acre campus
- **Endowment** $8.9 million
- **Coed** 6,970 undergraduate students, 80% full-time, 64% women, 36% men
- **Moderately difficult** entrance level, 34% of applicants were admitted

Undergraduates 5,559 full-time, 1,411 part-time. Students come from 20 states and territories; 26 other countries; 0.4% are from out of state; 3% Black or African American, non-Hispanic/Latino; 34% Hispanic/Latino; 11% Asian, non-Hispanic/Latino; 1% Native Hawaiian or other Pacific Islander, non-Hispanic/Latino; 0.8% American Indian or Alaska Native, non-Hispanic/Latino; 4% Two or more races, non-Hispanic/Latino; 6% Race/ethnicity unknown; 2% international; 14% transferred in; 9% live on campus. *Retention:* 86% of full-time freshmen returned.

Freshmen *Admission:* 4,896 applied, 1,643 admitted, 1,029 enrolled. *Average high school GPA:* 3.3. *Test scores:* SAT critical reading scores over 500: 31%; SAT math scores over 500: 39%; SAT writing scores over 500: 35%; ACT scores over 18: 68%; SAT critical reading scores over 600: 6%; SAT math scores over 600: 8%; SAT writing scores over 600: 6%; ACT scores over 24: 16%; SAT critical reading scores over 700: 1%; ACT scores over 30: 2%.

Faculty *Total:* 438, 59% full-time, 63% with terminal degrees. *Student/faculty ratio:* 21:1.

Academics *Calendar:* 4-1-4. *Degrees:* bachelor's, master's, doctoral-other, post-master's, and postbachelor's certificates. *Special study options:* academic remediation for entering students, adult/continuing education programs, advanced placement credit, cooperative education, distance learning, double majors, English as a second language, honors programs, independent study, internships, off-campus study, part-time degree program, services for LD students, student-designed majors, study abroad, summer session for credit.

Computers on Campus 200 computers/terminals are available on campus for general student use. Students can access the following: computer help desk, free student e-mail accounts, online (class) grades, online (class) registration, online (class) schedules. Campuswide network is available. 100% of college-owned or -operated housing units are wired for high-speed Internet access. Wireless service is available via entire campus.

Student Life *Housing options:* coed. Campus housing is university owned and leased by the school. *Activities and organizations:* drama/theater group, student-run newspaper, radio station, choral group, Alpha Xi Delta, Phi Sigma Sigma, Kappa Sigma, Delta Phi Gamma, Nu Alpha Kappa Inc., national fraternities, national sororities. *Campus security:* 24-hour emergency response devices and patrols, student patrols, late-night transport/escort service, controlled dormitory access. *Student services:* health clinic, personal/psychological counseling, women's center.

Athletics Member NCAA. All Division II. *Intercollegiate sports:* baseball M, basketball M/W, cheerleading M(c)/W(c), cross-country running M/W, golf M, soccer M/W, softball W, tennis W, track and field M/W, volleyball W. *Intramural sports:* basketball M/W, football M/W, soccer M/W, ultimate Frisbee M/W, volleyball M/W.

Standardized Tests *Required for some:* SAT or ACT (for admission).

Costs (2010–11) *One-time required fee:* $55. *Tuition:* state resident $0 full-time; nonresident $8928 full-time, $372 per unit part-time. Full-time tuition and fees vary according to course load, degree level, reciprocity agreements, and student level. Part-time tuition and fees vary according to course load, degree level, reciprocity agreements, and student level. *Required fees:* $5302 full-time, $1763 per term part-time. *Room and board:* $8880; room only: $6038. Room and board charges vary according to board plan and housing facility. *Payment plans:* installment, deferred payment. *Waivers:* adult students, senior citizens, and employees or children of employees.

Financial Aid Of all full-time matriculated undergraduates who enrolled in 2009, 4,431 applied for aid, 4,064 were judged to have need, 178 had their need fully met. 168 Federal Work-Study jobs (averaging $3478). In 2009, 26 non-need-based awards were made. *Average percent of need met:* 56%. *Average financial aid package:* $10,247. *Average need-based loan:* $5402. *Average need-based gift aid:* $6103. *Average non-need-based aid:* $4238. *Average indebtedness upon graduation:* $16,500.

PROFILES

Applying Options: electronic application. *Application fee:* $55. *Required:* high school transcript. *Required for some:* interview. *Recommended:* minimum 3 GPA. *Application deadlines:* 11/30 (freshmen), 11/30 (transfers). *Notification:* continuous (freshmen), continuous (transfers).
Freshman Application Contact Student Outreach, California State University, Stanislaus, One University Circle, Turlock, CA 95382. *Phone:* 209-667-3122. *Toll-free phone:* 800-300-7420. *Fax:* 209-667-3788. *E-mail:* outreach_help_desk@csustan.edu. *Web site:* http://www.csustan.edu/.

Chapman University

Orange, California

- **Independent** comprehensive, founded 1861, affiliated with Christian Church (Disciples of Christ), administratively affiliated with Brandman University
- **Suburban** 78-acre campus with easy access to Los Angeles
- **Coed** 4,910 undergraduate students, 95% full-time, 58% women, 42% men
- **Very difficult** entrance level, 50% of applicants were admitted

Undergraduates 4,678 full-time, 232 part-time. Students come from 48 states and territories; 62 other countries; 28% are from out of state; 2% Black or African American, non-Hispanic/Latino; 12% Hispanic/Latino; 9% Asian, non-Hispanic/Latino; 0.2% Native Hawaiian or other Pacific Islander, non-Hispanic/Latino; 0.4% American Indian or Alaska Native, non-Hispanic/Latino; 3% Two or more races, non-Hispanic/Latino; 9% Race/ethnicity unknown; 3% international; 7% transferred in; 42% live on campus. *Retention:* 93% of full-time freshmen returned.
Freshmen *Admission:* 8,056 applied, 3,996 admitted, 1,174 enrolled. *Average high school GPA:* 3.66. *Test scores:* SAT critical reading scores over 500: 92%; SAT math scores over 500: 94%; SAT writing scores over 500: 95%; ACT scores over 18: 99%; SAT critical reading scores over 600: 48%; SAT math scores over 600: 59%; SAT writing scores over 600: 55%; ACT scores over 24: 83%; SAT critical reading scores over 700: 8%; SAT math scores over 700: 12%; SAT writing scores over 700: 10%; ACT scores over 30: 20%.
Faculty *Total:* 696, 52% full-time. *Student/faculty ratio:* 14:1.
Academics *Calendar:* 4-1-4. *Degrees:* bachelor's, master's, doctoral-professional, doctoral-research/scholarship, and postbachelor's certificates. *Special study options:* academic remediation for entering students, adult/continuing education programs, advanced placement credit, distance learning, double majors, English as a second language, honors programs, independent study, internships, off-campus study, part-time degree program, services for LD students, student-designed majors, study abroad, summer session for credit. *ROTC:* Army (c), Air Force (c). *Unusual degree programs:* 3-2 business administration; engineering with University of California, Irvine.
Computers on Campus Students can access the following: campus intranet, computer help desk, free student e-mail accounts, online (class) grades, online (class) registration, online (class) schedules. Campuswide network is available. 100% of college-owned or -operated housing units are wired for high-speed Internet access. Wireless service is available via entire campus.
Student Life *Housing options:* coed, disabled students. Campus housing is university owned. Freshman campus housing is guaranteed. *Activities and organizations:* drama/theater group, student-run newspaper, radio station, choral group, Gamma Beta Phi, Alpha Kappa Psi Professional Business Fraternity, Public Relations Student Society of America, Black Student Union, Disciples on Campus, national fraternities, national sororities. *Campus security:* 24-hour emergency response devices and patrols, late-night transport/escort service, controlled dormitory access, full safety education program. *Student services:* health clinic, personal/psychological counseling.
Athletics Member NCAA. All Division III. *Intercollegiate sports:* baseball M, basketball M/W, cheerleading M(c)/W(c), crew M(c)/W, cross-country running M/W, football M, golf M, lacrosse M(c)/W(c), sailing M(c)/W(c), soccer M/W, softball W, swimming and diving M(c)/W, tennis M/W, track and field W, volleyball W, water polo M/W. *Intramural sports:* basketball M/W, soccer M/W, tennis M/W, volleyball M/W.
Standardized Tests *Required:* SAT or ACT (for admission). *Recommended:* SAT Subject Tests (for admission).
Costs (2011–12) *Comprehensive fee:* $53,191 includes full-time tuition ($39,200), mandatory fees ($1034), and room and board ($12,957). Part-time tuition: $1220 per credit. Part-time tuition and fees vary according to course load. *College room only:* $9255. Room and board charges vary according to board plan and housing facility. *Payment plans:* tuition prepayment, installment, deferred payment. *Waivers:* employees or children of employees.
Financial Aid Of all full-time matriculated undergraduates who enrolled in 2009, 3,778 applied for aid, 2,652 were judged to have need, 2,652 had their need fully met. 828 Federal Work-Study jobs (averaging $2186). In 2009, 727 non-need-based awards were made. *Average percent of need met:* 100%. *Average financial aid package:* $27,771. *Average need-based loan:* $4511. *Average need-based gift aid:* $24,076. *Average non-need-based aid:* $17,256. *Average indebtedness upon graduation:* $23,917.

Applying Options: electronic application, early action. *Application fee:* $60. *Required:* essay or personal statement, high school transcript, 1 letter of recommendation. *Recommended:* interview. *Application deadlines:* 1/15 (freshmen), 3/15 (transfers), 11/15 (early action). *Notification:* 3/15 (freshmen), 4/15 (transfers), 1/10 (early action).
Freshman Application Contact Ms. Marcela Mejia-Martinez, Assistant Vice Chancellor and Chief Admission Officer, Chapman University, One University Drive, Orange, CA 92866. *Phone:* 714-997-6711. *Toll-free phone:* 888-CUAPPLY. *Fax:* 714-997-6713. *E-mail:* admit@chapman.edu. *Web site:* http://www.chapman.edu/.

See page 1210 for the College Close-Up.

Charles Drew University of Medicine and Science

Los Angeles, California

- **Independent** comprehensive, founded 1966
- **Urban** campus with easy access to Los Angeles
- **Coed**
- **Moderately difficult** entrance level

Faculty *Student/faculty ratio:* 9:1.
Academics *Calendar:* semesters. *Degrees:* associate, bachelor's, master's, and doctoral-research/scholarship.
Standardized Tests *Recommended:* SAT or ACT (for admission).
Costs (2010–11) *Tuition:* $11,232 full-time, $468 per unit part-time. Full-time tuition and fees vary according to course level, course load, degree level, program, and student level. Part-time tuition and fees vary according to course level, course load, degree level, program, and student level.
Financial Aid *Financial aid deadline:* 7/31.
Applying *Application fee:* $35. *Required:* essay or personal statement, high school transcript, minimum 2 GPA, 3 letters of recommendation, interview. *Required for some:* pre-admission assessment exams.
Freshman Application Contact Ms. Yvette Lane, Associate Director, Student Service, Charles Drew University of Medicine and Science, 1731 East 120th Street, Los Angeles, CA 90059. *Phone:* 323-563-4922. *Fax:* 323-563-4923. *E-mail:* yvettelane@cdrewu.edu. *Web site:* http://www.cdrewu.edu/.

Claremont McKenna College

Claremont, California

- **Independent** comprehensive, founded 1946, part of The Claremont Colleges Consortium
- **Small-town** 50-acre campus with easy access to Los Angeles
- **Endowment** $466.4 million
- **Coed** 1,261 undergraduate students, 100% full-time, 46% women, 54% men
- **Most difficult** entrance level, 17% of applicants were admitted

Undergraduates 1,256 full-time, 5 part-time. Students come from 45 states and territories; 29 other countries; 56% are from out of state; 3% Black or African American, non-Hispanic/Latino; 8% Hispanic/Latino; 12% Asian, non-Hispanic/Latino; 0.1% Native Hawaiian or other Pacific Islander, non-Hispanic/Latino; 0.1% American Indian or Alaska Native, non-Hispanic/Latino; 2% Two or more races, non-Hispanic/Latino; 20% Race/ethnicity unknown; 7% international; 2% transferred in; 95% live on campus. *Retention:* 95% of full-time freshmen returned.
Freshmen *Admission:* 4,264 applied, 729 admitted, 314 enrolled. *Test scores:* SAT critical reading scores over 500: 100%; SAT math scores over 500: 100%; SAT critical reading scores over 600: 89%; SAT math scores over 600: 94%; SAT critical reading scores over 700: 52%; SAT math scores over 700: 55%.
Faculty *Total:* 148, 86% full-time, 95% with terminal degrees. *Student/faculty ratio:* 9:1.
Academics *Calendar:* semesters. *Degrees:* bachelor's and master's. *Special study options:* advanced placement credit, double majors, English as a second language, independent study, internships, off-campus study, services for LD students, student-designed majors, study abroad, summer session for credit. *ROTC:* Army (b), Air Force (c). *Unusual degree programs:* 3-2 engineering with Stanford University, Harvey Mudd College, Columbia University, University of California System schools, University of Southern California.
Computers on Campus 220 computers/terminals are available on campus for general student use. Students can access the following: campus intranet, computer help desk, free student e-mail accounts, online (class) grades, online (class) registration, online (class) schedules. Campuswide network is available. 100% of college-owned or -operated housing units are wired for high-speed Internet access. Wireless service is available via entire campus.
Student Life *Housing:* on-campus residence required for freshman year. *Options:* coed, disabled students. Campus housing is university owned. Freshman campus housing is guaranteed. *Activities and organizations:* drama/theater group, student-run newspaper, radio station, choral group, The Forum -

student newspaper, ASCMC - student government, Debate/Forensics Club, Amnesty International, Civitas (community service club). *Campus security:* 24-hour emergency response devices and patrols, student patrols, late-night transport/escort service, controlled dormitory access. *Student services:* health clinic, personal/psychological counseling, women's center.

Athletics Member NCAA. All Division III. *Intercollegiate sports:* archery M(c)/W(c), baseball M, basketball M/W, cheerleading M(c)/W(c), cross-country running M/W, equestrian sports M(c)/W(c), fencing M(c)/W(c), field hockey M(c)/W(c), football M, golf M/W, lacrosse M(c)/W(c), rugby M(c)/W(c), sailing M(c)/W(c), skiing (downhill) M(c)/W(c), soccer M/W, softball W, swimming and diving M/W, tennis M/W, track and field M/W, volleyball M(c)/W, water polo M/W. *Intramural sports:* basketball M/W, bowling M/W, crew M/W, football M, soccer M/W, squash M/W, table tennis M/W, tennis M/W, ultimate Frisbee M/W, volleyball M/W, water polo M/W, weight lifting M/W.

Standardized Tests *Required:* SAT or ACT (for admission).

Costs (2011–12) *Comprehensive fee:* $55,600 includes full-time tuition ($42,245), mandatory fees ($235), and room and board ($13,120). Full-time tuition and fees vary according to reciprocity agreements. Part-time tuition: $6666 per course. Part-time tuition and fees vary according to course load and reciprocity agreements. *College room only:* $7166. Room and board charges vary according to board plan and housing facility. *Payment plan:* installment. *Waivers:* employees or children of employees.

Financial Aid Of all full-time matriculated undergraduates who enrolled in 2009, 607 applied for aid, 537 were judged to have need, 537 had their need fully met. 280 Federal Work-Study jobs (averaging $1850). In 2009, 86 non-need-based awards were made. *Average percent of need met:* 100%. *Average financial aid package:* $35,177. *Average need-based gift aid:* $34,276. *Average non-need-based aid:* $12,591. *Average indebtedness upon graduation:* $9259.

Applying *Options:* electronic application, early decision, deferred entrance. *Application fee:* $60. *Required:* essay or personal statement, high school transcript, 3 letters of recommendation. *Recommended:* interview. *Application deadlines:* 1/2 (freshmen), 4/1 (transfers). *Early decision deadline:* 11/15 (for plan 1), 1/2 (for plan 2). *Notification:* 4/1 (freshmen), 5/15 (transfers), 12/15 (early decision plan 1), 2/15 (early decision plan 2).

Freshman Application Contact Mr. Richard C. Vos, Vice President/Dean of Admission and Financial Aid, Claremont McKenna College, Bauer Center, 500 East 9th Street, Claremont, CA 91711. *Phone:* 909-621-8088. *Fax:* 909-621-8516. *E-mail:* admission@claremontmckenna.edu. *Web site:* http://www.claremontmckenna.edu/.

Cleveland Chiropractic College– Los Angeles Campus

Los Angeles, California

- **Independent** comprehensive, founded 1911, administratively affiliated with Cleveland Chiropractic College-Kansas City
- **Urban** campus
- **Coed** 94 undergraduate students, 50% full-time, 47% women, 53% men
- **Minimally difficult** entrance level, 50% of applicants were admitted

Undergraduates 47 full-time, 47 part-time. Students come from 13 states and territories; 6 other countries; 16% are from out of state; 11% Black or African American, non-Hispanic/Latino; 12% Hispanic/Latino; 9% Asian, non-Hispanic/Latino; 1% American Indian or Alaska Native, non-Hispanic/Latino; 5% Two or more races, non-Hispanic/Latino; 22% Race/ethnicity unknown; 5% international; 76% transferred in. *Retention:* 88% of full-time freshmen returned.

Freshmen *Admission:* 2 applied, 1 admitted, 2 enrolled. *Average high school GPA:* 3.61.

Faculty *Total:* 35, 71% full-time, 94% with terminal degrees. *Student/faculty ratio:* 7:1.

Academics *Calendar:* trimesters. *Degrees:* associate, bachelor's, master's, and doctoral-professional. *Special study options:* academic remediation for entering students, accelerated degree program, adult/continuing education programs, advanced placement credit, cooperative education, distance learning, part-time degree program, services for LD students, summer session for credit.

Computers on Campus 30 computers/terminals and 30 ports are available on campus for general student use. Students can access the following: campus intranet, free student e-mail accounts, online (class) grades, online (class) schedules, Internet. Campuswide network is available. 100% of college-owned or -operated housing units are wired for high-speed Internet access. Wireless service is available via classrooms, computer centers, learning centers, libraries, student centers.

Student Life *Housing:* college housing not available. *Activities and organizations:* SCCA, SACA, Gonstead Club, Student Council, SICA. *Campus secu-*

rity: 24-hour emergency response devices. *Student services:* health clinic, personal/psychological counseling.

Standardized Tests *Required for some:* SAT or ACT (for admission).

Costs (2011–12) *Tuition:* $6465 full-time, $268 per credit part-time. Full-time tuition and fees vary according to program. Part-time tuition and fees vary according to program. *Required fees:* $270 full-time, $90 per year part-time. *Payment plan:* installment.

Applying *Options:* electronic application. *Application fee:* $50. *Required:* minimum 2.5 GPA. *Required for some:* high school transcript. *Application deadlines:* 8/29 (freshmen), 8/29 (out-of-state freshmen), 8/29 (transfers). *Notification:* 8/30 (freshmen), 8/30 (out-of-state freshmen), 8/30 (transfers).

Freshman Application Contact Ms. Sunshine Garcia, Director of Admissions, Cleveland Chiropractic College–Los Angeles Campus, 590 North Vermont, Los Angeles, CA 90004. *Phone:* 323-906-2162. *Toll-free phone:* 800-446-CCLA. *Fax:* 323-906-2094. *E-mail:* la.admissions@cleveland.edu. *Web site:* http://www.clevelandchiropractic.edu/.

Cogswell Polytechnical College

Sunnyvale, California

- **Independent** 4-year, founded 1887
- **Suburban** 2-acre campus with easy access to San Francisco and San Jose
- **Coed, primarily men** 238 undergraduate students, 57% full-time, 19% women, 81% men
- **Moderately difficult** entrance level, 100% of applicants were admitted

Undergraduates 135 full-time, 103 part-time. Students come from 13 states and territories; 3 other countries; 14% are from out of state; 3% Black or African American, non-Hispanic/Latino; 12% Hispanic/Latino; 10% Asian, non-Hispanic/Latino; 2% Native Hawaiian or other Pacific Islander, non-Hispanic/Latino; 3% Two or more races, non-Hispanic/Latino; 17% Race/ethnicity unknown; 3% international; 33% transferred in; 18% live on campus. *Retention:* 64% of full-time freshmen returned.

Freshmen *Admission:* 36 applied, 36 admitted, 32 enrolled. *Average high school GPA:* 3.04. *Test scores:* SAT critical reading scores over 500: 66%; SAT math scores over 500: 66%; SAT writing scores over 500: 55%; ACT scores over 18: 33%; SAT critical reading scores over 600: 44%; SAT math scores over 600: 33%; SAT writing scores over 600: 44%; ACT scores over 24: 33%; SAT critical reading scores over 700: 22%; SAT math scores over 700: 11%; SAT writing scores over 700: 11%; ACT scores over 30: 33%.

Faculty *Total:* 49, 20% full-time, 18% with terminal degrees. *Student/faculty ratio:* 7:1.

Academics *Calendar:* semesters. *Degrees:* bachelor's and master's. *Special study options:* advanced placement credit, distance learning, double majors, internships, part-time degree program, student-designed majors, study abroad, summer session for credit.

Computers on Campus 224 computers/terminals are available on campus for general student use. Students can access the following: computer help desk, free student e-mail accounts, online (class) grades, online (class) registration, online (class) schedules. Campuswide network is available. Wireless service is available via entire campus.

Student Life *Housing options:* coed. Campus housing is provided by a third party. *Activities and organizations:* student-run radio station, ASB, Game Development club, Audio Production and Engineering club, CPC radio, Film Critics club. *Campus security:* 24-hour emergency response devices. *Student services:* personal/psychological counseling.

Standardized Tests *Recommended:* SAT or ACT (for admission).

Costs (2011–12) *Tuition:* $18,744 full-time, $781 per credit hour part-time. Full-time tuition and fees vary according to course load. Part-time tuition and fees vary according to course load. *Required fees:* $180 full-time. *Room only:* $8200. Room and board charges vary according to housing facility. *Payment plan:* deferred payment. *Waivers:* employees or children of employees.

Financial Aid Of all full-time matriculated undergraduates who enrolled in 2007, 111 applied for aid, 111 were judged to have need. 15 Federal Work-Study jobs (averaging $3000). In 2007, 6 non-need-based awards were made. *Average financial aid package:* $10,099. *Average need-based loan:* $4827. *Average need-based gift aid:* $2441. *Average non-need-based aid:* $1108. *Average indebtedness upon graduation:* $35,032.

Applying *Options:* electronic application, deferred entrance. *Application fee:* $55. *Required:* essay or personal statement, high school transcript, minimum 2.7 GPA. *Required for some:* interview, portfolio. *Application deadlines:* 3/1 (freshmen), 3/1 (transfers). *Notification:* continuous (freshmen), continuous (transfers).

Freshman Application Contact Mr. Debbie Pinheiro, Director of New Student Enrollment, Cogswell Polytechnical College, 1175 Bordeaux Drive, Sunnyvale, CA 94089-1299. *Phone:* 408-541-0100. *Toll-free phone:* 800-264-7955. *Fax:* 408-747-0764. *E-mail:* dpinheiro@cogswell.edu. *Web site:* http://www.cogswell.edu/.

The Colburn School Conservatory of Music

Los Angeles, California

- **Independent** 4-year, founded 1980
- **Urban** campus with easy access to Los Angeles
- **Coed** 67 undergraduate students, 100% full-time, 55% women, 45% men
- **Most difficult** entrance level, 11% of applicants were admitted

Undergraduates 67 full-time. Students come from 18 states and territories; 10 other countries; 4% transferred in; 100% live on campus. *Retention:* 95% of full-time freshmen returned.

Freshmen *Admission:* 227 applied, 25 admitted, 15 enrolled.

Faculty *Total:* 29, 28% full-time, 14% with terminal degrees. *Student/faculty ratio:* 4:1.

Academics *Calendar:* semesters. *Degrees:* certificates, diplomas, bachelor's, and postbachelor's certificates. *Special study options:* English as a second language.

Computers on Campus 12 computers/terminals are available on campus for general student use. Students can access the following: campus intranet, computer help desk, free student e-mail accounts. Campuswide network is available. 100% of college-owned or -operated housing units are wired for high-speed Internet access. Wireless service is available via classrooms, computer centers, computer labs, dorm rooms, libraries.

Student Life *Housing:* on-campus residence required through junior year. *Options:* coed. Campus housing is university owned. Freshman campus housing is guaranteed. *Campus security:* 24-hour emergency response devices and patrols, controlled dormitory access. *Student services:* personal/psychological counseling.

Standardized Tests *Recommended:* SAT or ACT (for admission).

Costs (2011–12) *One-time required fee:* $500. *Comprehensive fee:* The Colburn School does not charge its Conservatory students for tuition, room or board.

Applying *Options:* electronic application, deferred entrance. *Application fee:* $110. *Required:* essay or personal statement, high school transcript, 2 letters of recommendation, interview, pre-screening DVD, in-person audition by invitation. *Application deadlines:* 1/15 (freshmen), 1/15 (transfers). *Notification:* 4/1 (freshmen), 4/1 (transfers).

Freshman Application Contact Ms. Kathleen Tesar, Associate Dean, The Colburn School Conservatory of Music, 200 South Grand Avenue, Los Angeles, CA 90012. *Phone:* 213-621-4534. *Fax:* 213-625-0371. *E-mail:* admissions@colburnschool.edu. *Web site:* http://www.colburnschool.edu/.

Coleman University

San Diego, California

Freshman Application Contact Admissions Department, Coleman University, 7380 Parkway Drive, La Mesa, CA 91942-1532. *Phone:* 619-465-3990. *E-mail:* jschafer@cts.com. *Web site:* http://www.coleman.edu/.

Coleman University

San Marcos, California

Director of Admissions Senior Admissions Officer, Coleman University, 1284 West San Marcos Boulevard, San Marcos, CA 92078. *Phone:* 760-747-3990. *Fax:* 760-752-9808. *Web site:* http://www.coleman.edu/.

Columbia College Hollywood

Tarzana, California

Freshman Application Contact Carmen Munoz, Admissions Director, Columbia College Hollywood, 18618 Oxnard Street, Tarzana, CA 91356. *Phone:* 818-345-8414. *Toll-free phone:* 800-785-0585. *Fax:* 818-345-9053. *E-mail:* admissions@columbiacollege.edu. *Web site:* http://www.columbiacollege.edu/.

Concordia University

Irvine, California

- **Independent** comprehensive, founded 1972, affiliated with Lutheran Church–Missouri Synod, part of The Concordia University System
- **Suburban** 70-acre campus with easy access to Los Angeles
- **Endowment** $10.3 million
- **Coed** 1,558 undergraduate students, 95% full-time, 61% women, 39% men
- **Moderately difficult** entrance level, 64% of applicants were admitted

Undergraduates 1,477 full-time, 81 part-time. Students come from 39 states and territories; 14 other countries; 15% are from out of state; 2% Black or African American, non-Hispanic/Latino; 15% Hispanic/Latino; 3% Asian, non-Hispanic/Latino; 0.1% Native Hawaiian or other Pacific Islander, non-Hispanic/Latino; 0.6% American Indian or Alaska Native, non-Hispanic/Latino; 22% Race/ethnicity unknown; 2% international; 12% transferred in; 60% live on campus. *Retention:* 75% of full-time freshmen returned.

Freshmen *Admission:* 1,916 applied, 1,221 admitted, 308 enrolled. *Average high school GPA:* 3.3. *Test scores:* SAT critical reading scores over 500: 54%; SAT math scores over 500: 56%; SAT writing scores over 500: 56%; ACT scores over 18: 85%; SAT critical reading scores over 600: 16%; SAT math scores over 600: 14%; SAT writing scores over 600: 16%; ACT scores over 24: 31%; SAT critical reading scores over 700: 3%; SAT math scores over 700: 1%; SAT writing scores over 700: 1%; ACT scores over 30: 5%.

Faculty *Total:* 314, 23% full-time, 39% with terminal degrees. *Student/faculty ratio:* 17:1.

Academics *Calendar:* semesters. *Degrees:* associate, bachelor's, and master's (associate's degree for international students only). *Special study options:* academic remediation for entering students, accelerated degree program, adult/continuing education programs, advanced placement credit, distance learning, double majors, honors programs, independent study, internships, off-campus study, part-time degree program, services for LD students, study abroad, summer session for credit. *ROTC:* Army (c).

Computers on Campus 103 computers/terminals are available on campus for general student use. Students can access the following: computer help desk, free student e-mail accounts, online (class) grades, online (class) registration, online (class) schedules. Campuswide network is available. 100% of college-owned or -operated housing units are wired for high-speed Internet access. Wireless service is available via entire campus.

Student Life *Housing:* on-campus residence required for freshman year. *Options:* coed, disabled students. Campus housing is university owned. Freshman campus housing is guaranteed. *Activities and organizations:* drama/theater group, student-run newspaper, choral group, intramurals, Screaming Eagles, Lacrosse, abbey west, student activities. *Campus security:* 24-hour emergency response devices and patrols, student patrols, late-night transport/escort service, Lighted walkways, 24-hour dispatch. *Student services:* health clinic, personal/psychological counseling.

Athletics Member NAIA. *Intercollegiate sports:* baseball M(s), basketball M(s)/W(s), cross-country running M(s)/W(s), lacrosse M(c), soccer M(s)/W(s), softball W(s), swimming and diving M(s)/W(s), tennis M(s)/W(s), track and field M(s)/W(s), volleyball W(s), water polo M(s)/W(s). *Intramural sports:* basketball M/W, bowling M/W, football M/W, soccer M/W, softball M/W, track and field M/W, ultimate Frisbee M/W, volleyball M/W.

Standardized Tests *Required:* SAT or ACT (for admission).

Costs (2011–12) *Comprehensive fee:* $35,890 includes full-time tuition ($26,700), mandatory fees ($600), and room and board ($8590). Full-time tuition and fees vary according to course load. Part-time tuition: $815 per unit. Part-time tuition and fees vary according to course load. *Required fees:* $300 per term part-time. *College room only:* $4900. Room and board charges vary according to board plan and housing facility. *Payment plan:* installment. *Waivers:* employees or children of employees.

Financial Aid Of all full-time matriculated undergraduates who enrolled in 2009, 1,214 applied for aid, 1,026 were judged to have need, 248 had their need fully met. 39 Federal Work-Study jobs (averaging $2199). 18 state and other part-time jobs (averaging $1750). In 2009, 273 non-need-based awards were made. *Average percent of need met:* 74%. *Average financial aid package:* $21,699. *Average need-based loan:* $4302. *Average need-based gift aid:* $14,237. *Average non-need-based aid:* $6699. *Average indebtedness upon graduation:* $23,465. *Financial aid deadline:* 3/2.

Applying *Options:* electronic application, early action, deferred entrance. *Application fee:* $50. *Required:* essay or personal statement, high school transcript, 2 letters of recommendation. *Required for some:* interview. *Recommended:* minimum 2.8 GPA. *Application deadlines:* rolling (freshmen), rolling (transfers), 12/1 (early action). *Notification:* continuous (freshmen), continuous (transfers), 12/15 (early action).

Freshman Application Contact Mr. Rick Hardy, Associate Vice President for Enrollment Management, Concordia University, 1530 Concordia West, Irvine, CA 92612-3299. *Phone:* 949-214-3147. *Toll-free phone:* 800-229-1200. *Fax:* 949-854-6894. *E-mail:* admission@cui.edu. *Web site:* http://www.cui.edu/.

Design Institute of San Diego

San Diego, California

Director of Admissions Ms. Paula Parrish, Director of Admissions, Design Institute of San Diego, 8555 Commerce Avenue, San Diego, CA 92121-2685. *Phone:* 858-566-1200. *Toll-free phone:* 800-619-4337. *Fax:* 858-566-2711. *E-mail:* admissions@disd.edu. *Web site:* http://www.disd.edu/.

DeVry University
Alhambra, California

Admissions Office Contact DeVry University, Unit 100, Building A-11, First Floor, 1000 South Fremont Avenue, Alhambra, CA 91803. *Web site:* http://www.devry.edu/.

DeVry University
Anaheim, California

Admissions Office Contact DeVry University, 1900 South State College Boulevard, Suite 150, Anaheim, CA 92806-6136. *Web site:* http://www.devry.edu/.

DeVry University
Bakersfield, California

Admissions Office Contact DeVry University, 3000 Ming Avenue, Bakersfield, CA 93304-4136. *Web site:* http://www.devry.edu/.

DeVry University
Daly City, California

Admissions Office Contact DeVry University, 2001 Junipero Serra Boulevard, Suite 161, Daly City, CA 94014-3899. *Web site:* http://www.devry.edu/.

DeVry University
Elk Grove, California

Admissions Office Contact DeVry University, Sacramento Center, 2216 Kausen Drive, Elk Grove, CA 95758. *Toll-free phone:* 866-573-3879. *Web site:* http://www.devry.edu/.

DeVry University
Fremont, California

- **Proprietary** comprehensive, founded 1998, part of DeVry University
- **Suburban** 17-acre campus with easy access to San Francisco
- **Coed**
- **Minimally difficult** entrance level

Faculty *Student/faculty ratio:* 10:1.
Academics *Calendar:* semesters. *Degrees:* associate, bachelor's, and master's.
Student Life *Campus security:* 24-hour emergency response devices and patrols, late-night transport/escort service, lighted pathways/sidewalks.
Costs (2010–11) *Tuition:* $14,766 full-time, $580 per credit hour part-time. Full-time tuition and fees vary according to course load. Part-time tuition and fees vary according to course load. *Required fees:* $60 full-time, $30 per term part-time. *Payment plans:* installment, deferred payment.
Financial Aid *Of all full-time matriculated undergraduates who enrolled in 2007,* 505 applied for aid, 483 were judged to have need, 6 had their need fully met. *In 2007,* 34 non-need-based awards were made. *Average percent of need met:* 37. *Average financial aid package:* $12,445. *Average need-based loan:* $7034. *Average need-based gift aid:* $7847. *Average non-need-based aid:* $17,920. *Average indebtedness upon graduation:* $70,191.
Applying *Options:* electronic application, early admission, deferred entrance. *Application fee:* $50. *Required:* high school transcript, interview.
Freshman Application Contact DeVry University, 6600 Dumbarton Circle, Fremont, CA 94555. *Web site:* http://www.devry.edu/.

DeVry University
Irvine, California

Admissions Office Contact DeVry University, 430 Exchange, Suite 250, Irvine, CA 92602-1303. *Web site:* http://www.devry.edu/.

DeVry University
Long Beach, California

- **Proprietary** comprehensive, founded 1984, part of DeVry University
- **Urban** 23-acre campus with easy access to Los Angeles
- **Coed**
- **Minimally difficult** entrance level

Faculty *Student/faculty ratio:* 14:1.
Academics *Calendar:* semesters. *Degrees:* associate, bachelor's, and master's.

Student Life *Campus security:* 24-hour emergency response devices and patrols, late-night transport/escort service, motion detectors, closed hours.
Costs (2010–11) *Tuition:* $14,766 full-time, $580 per credit hour part-time. Full-time tuition and fees vary according to course load. Part-time tuition and fees vary according to course load. *Required fees:* $60 full-time, $30 per term part-time. *Payment plans:* installment, deferred payment.
Financial Aid *Of all full-time matriculated undergraduates who enrolled in 2007,* 221 applied for aid, 213 were judged to have need, 5 had their need fully met. *In 2007,* 14 non-need-based awards were made. *Average percent of need met:* 44. *Average financial aid package:* $14,244. *Average need-based loan:* $8555. *Average need-based gift aid:* $8196. *Average non-need-based aid:* $16,538. *Average indebtedness upon graduation:* $36,961.
Applying *Options:* electronic application, early admission, deferred entrance. *Application fee:* $50. *Required:* high school transcript, interview.
Freshman Application Contact DeVry University, 3880 Kilroy Airport Way, Long Beach, CA 90806. *Web site:* http://www.devry.edu/.

DeVry University
Oakland, California

Admissions Office Contact DeVry University, 505 14th Street, Oakland, CA 94612. *Web site:* http://www.devry.edu/.

DeVry University
Palmdale, California

Director of Admissions Admissions Office, DeVry University, One 39115 Trade Center Drive, Suite 100, Palmdale, CA 93551. *Toll-free phone:* 866-986-9388. *Web site:* http://www.devry.edu/.

DeVry University
Pomona, California

- **Proprietary** comprehensive, founded 1983, part of DeVry University
- **Urban** 15-acre campus with easy access to Los Angeles
- **Coed** 2,934 undergraduate students, 40% full-time, 36% women, 64% men
- **Minimally difficult** entrance level

Undergraduates 1,176 full-time, 1,758 part-time. 3% are from out of state; 9% Black or African American, non-Hispanic/Latino; 40% Hispanic/Latino; 9% Asian, non-Hispanic/Latino; 0.7% Native Hawaiian or other Pacific Islander, non-Hispanic/Latino; 0.6% American Indian or Alaska Native, non-Hispanic/Latino; 0.6% Two or more races, non-Hispanic/Latino; 20% Race/ethnicity unknown; 0.4% international; 24% transferred in.
Freshmen *Admission:* 537 enrolled.
Faculty *Total:* 111, 19% full-time. *Student/faculty ratio:* 38:1.
Academics *Calendar:* semesters. *Degrees:* associate, bachelor's, and master's. *Special study options:* academic remediation for entering students, accelerated degree program, adult/continuing education programs, advanced placement credit, distance learning, part-time degree program, services for LD students, summer session for credit.
Computers on Campus Students can access the following: online (class) registration. Campuswide network is available.
Student Life *Housing:* college housing not available. *Campus security:* 24-hour emergency response devices, late-night transport/escort service.
Costs (2010–11) *Tuition:* $14,766 full-time, $580 per credit hour part-time. Full-time tuition and fees vary according to course load. Part-time tuition and fees vary according to course load. *Required fees:* $60 full-time, $30 per term part-time. *Payment plans:* installment, deferred payment. *Waivers:* employees or children of employees.
Financial Aid *Of all full-time matriculated undergraduates who enrolled in 2007,* 414 applied for aid, 394 were judged to have need, 6 had their need fully met. *In 2007,* 50 non-need-based awards were made. *Average percent of need met:* 36%. *Average financial aid package:* $12,689. *Average need-based loan:* $7876. *Average need-based gift aid:* $8289. *Average non-need-based aid:* $16,971. *Average indebtedness upon graduation:* $33,385.
Applying *Options:* electronic application, early admission, deferred entrance. *Application fee:* $50. *Required:* high school transcript, interview. *Application deadlines:* rolling (freshmen), rolling (transfers). *Notification:* continuous (freshmen), continuous (transfers).
Freshman Application Contact DeVry University, 901 Corporate Center Drive, Pomona, CA 91768-2642. *Phone:* 909-622-8866. *Web site:* http://www.devry.edu/.

DeVry University
San Diego, California

Admissions Office Contact DeVry University, 2655 Camino Del Rio North, Suite 201, San Diego, CA 92108-1633. *Web site:* http://www.devry.edu/.

DeVry University

Sherman Oaks, California

- **Proprietary** comprehensive
- **Coed**

Faculty *Student/faculty ratio:* 23:1.

Academics *Degrees:* associate, bachelor's, and master's.

Costs (2010–11) *Tuition:* $14,766 full-time, $580 per credit hour part-time. Full-time tuition and fees vary according to course load. Part-time tuition and fees vary according to course load. *Required fees:* $60 full-time, $30 per term part-time. *Payment plans:* installment, deferred payment.

Financial Aid *Of all full-time matriculated undergraduates who enrolled in 2007, 120 applied for aid, 108 were judged to have need, 4 had their need fully met. In 2007, 19 non-need-based awards were made. Average percent of need met:* 39. *Average financial aid package:* $11,834. *Average need-based loan:* $8480. *Average need-based gift aid:* $6691. *Average non-need-based aid:* $17,847. *Average indebtedness upon graduation:* $31,200.

Applying *Options:* electronic application, early admission, deferred entrance. *Application fee:* $50.

Freshman Application Contact DeVry University, 15301 Ventura Boulevard, D-100, Sherman Oaks, CA 91403. *Toll-free phone:* 888-610-0800. *Web site:* http://www.devry.edu/.

Dominican University of California

San Rafael, California

- **Independent** comprehensive, founded 1890, affiliated with Roman Catholic Church
- **Suburban** 85-acre campus with easy access to San Francisco
- **Endowment** $19.4 million
- **Coed** 1,586 undergraduate students, 82% full-time, 73% women, 27% men
- **Moderately difficult** entrance level, 52% of applicants were admitted

Undergraduates 1,299 full-time, 287 part-time. Students come from 28 states and territories; 14 other countries; 6% are from out of state; 5% Black or African American, non-Hispanic/Latino; 18% Hispanic/Latino; 21% Asian, non-Hispanic/Latino; 1% Native Hawaiian or other Pacific Islander, non-Hispanic/Latino; 1% American Indian or Alaska Native, non-Hispanic/Latino; 4% Two or more races, non-Hispanic/Latino; 13% Race/ethnicity unknown; 2% international; 7% transferred in; 47% live on campus. *Retention:* 84% of full-time freshmen returned.

Freshmen *Admission:* 2,774 applied, 1,456 admitted, 338 enrolled. *Average high school GPA:* 3.44. *Test scores:* SAT critical reading scores over 500: 56%; SAT math scores over 500: 61%; ACT scores over 18: 91%; SAT critical reading scores over 600: 10%; SAT math scores over 600: 34%; ACT scores over 24: 28%; SAT critical reading scores over 700: 2%; SAT math scores over 700: 8%; ACT scores over 30: 1%.

Faculty *Total:* 346, 26% full-time, 46% with terminal degrees. *Student/faculty ratio:* 12:1.

Academics *Calendar:* semesters. *Degrees:* bachelor's, master's, and post-bachelor's certificates. *Special study options:* academic remediation for entering students, adult/continuing education programs, advanced placement credit, double majors, English as a second language, external degree program, honors programs, independent study, internships, off-campus study, part-time degree program, services for LD students, student-designed majors, study abroad, summer session for credit. *Unusual degree programs:* 3-2 occupational therapy.

Computers on Campus 200 computers/terminals and 700 ports are available on campus for general student use. Students can access the following: computer help desk, free student e-mail accounts, online (class) grades, online (class) registration, online (class) schedules, Microsoft Office Applications (Word, Excel, PowerPoint). Campuswide network is available. 100% of college-owned or -operated housing units are wired for high-speed Internet access. Wireless service is available via classrooms, computer centers, computer labs, dorm rooms, learning centers, libraries, student centers.

Student Life *Housing options:* coed. Campus housing is university owned. Freshman applicants given priority for college housing. *Activities and organizations:* drama/theater group, student-run newspaper, radio station, choral group, Students Promoting Dominican Islands, Perceptions, Science Club, Filipino Club, Scripture Union. *Campus security:* 24-hour emergency response devices and patrols, late-night transport/escort service, controlled dormitory access. *Student services:* health clinic, personal/psychological counseling.

Athletics Member NCAA. All Division II. *Intercollegiate sports:* basketball M(s)/W(s), golf M(s)/W(s), lacrosse M(s), soccer M(s)/W(s), softball W(s), tennis W(s), volleyball W(s). *Intramural sports:* cheerleading W.

Standardized Tests *Required:* SAT or ACT (for admission).
Costs (2011–12) *Comprehensive fee:* $51,810 includes full-time tuition ($36,900), mandatory fees ($450), and room and board ($14,460). Full-time tuition and fees vary according to course load, degree level, and program. Part-time tuition: $1560 per unit. Part-time tuition and fees vary according to degree level and program. *College room only:* $8400. Room and board charges vary according to board plan. *Payment plan:* installment. *Waivers:* senior citizens and employees or children of employees.
Financial Aid Of all full-time matriculated undergraduates who enrolled in 2008, 934 applied for aid, 862 were judged to have need, 72 had their need fully met. 200 Federal Work-Study jobs (averaging $1778). 46 state and other part-time jobs (averaging $5412). In 2008, 72 non-need-based awards were made. *Average percent of need met:* 55%. *Average financial aid package:* $22,418. *Average need-based loan:* $4458. *Average need-based gift aid:* $18,314. *Average non-need-based aid:* $10,528. *Average indebtedness upon graduation:* $32,314.
Applying *Options:* electronic application, deferred entrance. *Application fee:* $40. *Required:* essay or personal statement, high school transcript, 1 letter of recommendation. *Recommended:* interview. *Application deadlines:* 2/1 (freshmen), 2/1 (transfers). *Notification:* continuous (freshmen), continuous (transfers).
Freshman Application Contact Ms. Rebecca Finn Kenney, Director of Undergraduate Admissions, Dominican University of California, 50 Acacia Avenue, San Rafael, CA 94901-2298. *Phone:* 415-485-3204. *Toll-free phone:* 888-323-6763. *Fax:* 415-485-3214. *E-mail:* enroll@dominican.edu. *Web site:* http://www.dominican.edu/.

See page 1258 for the College Close-Up.

Emmanuel Bible College

Pasadena, California

Director of Admissions Admissions, Emmanuel Bible College, 1605 East Elizabeth Street, Pasadena, CA 91104. *Phone:* 626-446-0300. *E-mail:* info@ebcministry.edu. *Web site:* http://www.ebcministry.edu/.

Epic Bible College

Sacramento, California

Director of Admissions Ms. Sheila Knoll, Assistant Director of Records, Epic Bible College, 5225 Hillsdale Boulevard, Sacramento, CA 95842. *Phone:* 916-348-4689. *E-mail:* kclarke@tlbc.edu. *Web site:* http://epic.edu/.

Everest College

Ontario, California

Freshman Application Contact Admissions Office, Everest College, 1819 South Excise Avenue, Ontario, CA 91761. *Phone:* 909-484-4311. *Fax:* 909-484-1162. *Web site:* http://www.everest.edu/campus/ontario/.

Ex'pression College for Digital Arts

Emeryville, California

Admissions Office Contact Ex'pression College for Digital Arts, 6601 Shellmound Street, Emeryville, CA 94608. *Toll-free phone:* 877-833-8800. *Web site:* http://www.expression.edu/.

FIDM/The Fashion Institute of Design & Merchandising, Los Angeles Campus

Los Angeles, California

- **Proprietary** primarily 2-year, founded 1969, part of The Fashion Institute of Design and Merchandising/FIDM
- **Urban** campus
- **Coed** 4,424 undergraduate students, 87% full-time, 88% women, 12% men
- **Moderately difficult** entrance level, 67% of applicants were admitted

Undergraduates 3,849 full-time, 575 part-time. Students come from 45 states and territories; 10 other countries; 37% are from out of state; 6% Black or African American, non-Hispanic/Latino; 22% Hispanic/Latino; 12% Asian, non-Hispanic/Latino; 0.9% Native Hawaiian or other Pacific Islander, non-Hispanic/Latino; 0.7% American Indian or Alaska Native, non-Hispanic/Latino; 2% Two or more races, non-Hispanic/Latino; 10% Race/ethnicity unknown; 0.9% international; 18% transferred in. *Retention:* 91% of full-time freshmen returned.

Freshmen *Admission:* 1,720 applied, 1,151 admitted, 846 enrolled. *Average high school GPA:* 2.75.
Faculty *Total:* 366, 19% full-time. *Student/faculty ratio:* 16:1.
Academics *Calendar:* quarters. *Degrees:* associate and bachelor's (also includes Orange County Campus). *Special study options:* academic remediation for entering students, adult/continuing education programs, advanced placement credit, cooperative education, distance learning, English as a second language, independent study, internships, part-time degree program, services for LD students, study abroad, summer session for credit.
Computers on Campus Students can access the following: campus intranet, online (class) grades, online (class) registration, online (class) schedules. Campuswide network is available. Wireless service is available via computer centers, learning centers, libraries, student centers.
Student Life *Activities and organizations:* student-run newspaper, ASID (student chapter), Design Council, Phi Theta Kappa Honor Society, Student Council, MODE. *Campus security:* 24-hour emergency response devices and patrols, late-night transport/escort service. *Student services:* personal/psychological counseling.
Standardized Tests *Recommended:* SAT or ACT (for admission).
Costs (2010–11) *Tuition:* $27,635 full-time. Full-time tuition and fees vary according to program. Part-time tuition and fees vary according to program. No tuition increase for student's term of enrollment. *Required fees:* $525 full-time. *Payment plans:* tuition prepayment, installment. *Waivers:* employees or children of employees.
Financial Aid Of all full-time matriculated undergraduates who enrolled in 2009, 88 Federal Work-Study jobs (averaging $2935).
Applying *Options:* electronic application, deferred entrance. *Application fee:* $225. *Required:* essay or personal statement, high school transcript, minimum 2 GPA, 3 letters of recommendation, interview, major-determined project. *Application deadlines:* rolling (freshmen), rolling (out-of-state freshmen), rolling (transfers).
Freshman Application Contact Ms. Susan Aronson, Director of Admissions, FIDM/The Fashion Institute of Design & Merchandising, Los Angeles Campus, Los Angeles, CA 90015. *Phone:* 213-624-1201. *Toll-free phone:* 800-624-1200. *Fax:* 213-624-4799. *E-mail:* saronson@fidm.com. *Web site:* http://www.fidm.edu/.

Fresno Pacific University

Fresno, California

Freshman Application Contact Fresno Pacific University, 1717 South Chestnut Avenue, #2005, Fresno, CA 93727. *Phone:* 800-660-6089. *Toll-free phone:* 800-660-6089. *Fax:* 559-453-2007. *E-mail:* ugadmis@fresno.edu. *Web site:* http://www.fresno.edu/.

Golden Gate University

San Francisco, California

Freshman Application Contact Mr. Louis D. Riccardi Jr., Director of Enrollment Services, Golden Gate University, 536 Mission Street, San Francisco, CA 94105-2968. *Phone:* 415-442-7800. *Toll-free phone:* 800-448-3381. *Fax:* 415-442-7807. *E-mail:* info@ggu.edu. *Web site:* http://www.ggu.edu/.

Harvey Mudd College

Claremont, California

- **Independent** 4-year, founded 1955, part of The Claremont Colleges Consortium
- **Suburban** 33-acre campus with easy access to Los Angeles
- **Endowment** $208.1 million
- **Coed** 773 undergraduate students, 100% full-time, 42% women, 58% men
- **Most difficult** entrance level, 25% of applicants were admitted

Undergraduates 771 full-time, 2 part-time. Students come from 47 states and territories; 18 other countries; 60% are from out of state; 0.9% Black or African American, non-Hispanic/Latino; 7% Hispanic/Latino; 19% Asian, non-Hispanic/Latino; 0.4% American Indian or Alaska Native, non-Hispanic/Latino; 5% Two or more races, non-Hispanic/Latino; 5% Race/ethnicity unknown; 5% international; 99% live on campus. *Retention:* 98% of full-time freshmen returned.
Freshmen *Admission:* 2,508 applied, 638 admitted, 195 enrolled. *Test scores:* SAT critical reading scores over 500: 100%; SAT math scores over 500: 100%; SAT writing scores over 500: 100%; ACT scores over 18: 100%; SAT critical reading scores over 600: 98%; SAT math scores over 600: 100%; SAT writing scores over 600: 95%; ACT scores over 24: 100%; SAT critical reading scores over 700: 66%; SAT math scores over 700: 91%; SAT writing scores over 700: 63%; ACT scores over 30: 94%.

Faculty *Total:* 103, 84% full-time, 100% with terminal degrees. *Student/faculty ratio:* 9:1.

Academics *Calendar:* semesters. *Degree:* bachelor's. *Special study options:* double majors, internships, off-campus study, services for LD students, student-designed majors, study abroad. *ROTC:* Army (c), Air Force (b). *Unusual degree programs:* 3-2 economics/engineering with Claremont McKenna College and /engineering with Scripps College.

Computers on Campus 120 computers/terminals and 860 ports are available on campus for general student use. Students can access the following: campus intranet, computer help desk, free student e-mail accounts, online (class) grades, online (class) registration, online (class) schedules. Campuswide network is available. 100% of college-owned or -operated housing units are wired for high-speed Internet access. Wireless service is available via entire campus.

Student Life *Housing:* on-campus residence required for freshman year. *Options:* coed. Campus housing is university owned. Freshman campus housing is guaranteed. *Activities and organizations:* drama/theater group, student-run newspaper, radio station, choral group, Ballroom Dancing, Delta-H (outdoors club), Intervarsity Christian Fellowship, Science Bus, SWE (Society of Women Engineers). *Campus security:* 24-hour emergency response devices and patrols, late-night transport/escort service. *Student services:* health clinic, personal/psychological counseling, women's center.

Athletics Member NCAA. All Division III. *Intercollegiate sports:* baseball M, basketball M/W, cross-country running M/W, football M, golf M, lacrosse W, soccer M/W, softball W, swimming and diving M/W, tennis M/W, track and field M/W, volleyball W, water polo M/W. *Intramural sports:* badminton M(c)/W(c), equestrian sports M(c)/W(c), fencing M(c)/W(c), football M/W, ice hockey M(c), lacrosse M(c), rock climbing M(c)/W(c), rugby M(c)/W(c), sailing M(c)/W(c), soccer M/W, swimming and diving M/W, table tennis M(c)/W(c), tennis M/W, ultimate Frisbee M(c)/W(c), volleyball M/W, water polo M.

Standardized Tests *Required:* SAT or ACT (for admission), SAT Subject Tests (for admission), SAT or ACT and the SAT Subject Test in Math 2C and a second SAT II subject exam (for admission).

Costs (2010–11) *Comprehensive fee:* $53,588 includes full-time tuition ($40,133), mandatory fees ($257), and room and board ($13,198). Part-time tuition: $1194 per credit hour. *College room only:* $6935. Room and board charges vary according to board plan. *Payment plan:* installment. *Waivers:* employees or children of employees.

Financial Aid Of all full-time matriculated undergraduates who enrolled in 2009, 478 applied for aid, 415 were judged to have need, 415 had their need fully met. 238 Federal Work-Study jobs (averaging $2197). 17 state and other part-time jobs (averaging $6470). In 2009, 183 non-need-based awards were made. *Average percent of need met:* 100%. *Average financial aid package:* $33,470. *Average need-based loan:* $4895. *Average need-based gift aid:* $29,588. *Average non-need-based aid:* $10,452. *Average indebtedness upon graduation:* $21,806. *Financial aid deadline:* 2/1.

Applying *Options:* electronic application, early admission, early decision, deferred entrance. *Application fee:* $60. *Required:* essay or personal statement, high school transcript, 3 letters of recommendation. *Recommended:* interview. *Application deadlines:* 1/2 (freshmen), 4/1 (transfers). *Early decision deadline:* 11/15 (for plan 1), 1/2 (for plan 2). *Notification:* 4/1 (freshmen), 5/15 (transfers), 12/15 (early decision plan 1), 2/15 (early decision plan 2).

Freshman Application Contact Mr. Peter Osgood, Director of Admission, Harvey Mudd College, 301 Platt Boulevard, Claremont, CA 91711. *Phone:* 909-621-8011. *Fax:* 909-607-7046. *E-mail:* admission@hmc.edu. *Web site:* http://www.hmc.edu/.

Henley-Putnam University

San Jose, California

Director of Admissions Nancy Reggio, Director of Admissions, Henley-Putnam University, 25 Metro Drive, Suite 500, San Jose, CA 95110. *Phone:* 408-453-9900. *Toll-free phone:* 888-852-8746. *Fax:* 408-453-9700. *E-mail:* nreggio@henley-putnam.edu. *Web site:* http://www.henley-putnam.edu/.

Holy Names University

Oakland, California

- **Independent Roman Catholic** comprehensive, founded 1868
- **Urban** 60-acre campus with easy access to San Francisco
- **Endowment** $9.8 million
- **Coed, primarily women** 758 undergraduate students, 79% full-time, 74% women, 26% men
- **Moderately difficult** entrance level, 70% of applicants were admitted

Undergraduates 597 full-time, 161 part-time. 52% live on campus. *Retention:* 65% of full-time freshmen returned.

Freshmen *Admission:* 543 applied, 381 admitted, 113 enrolled. *Average high school GPA:* 3.18. *Test scores:* SAT critical reading scores over 500: 29%; SAT math scores over 500: 37%; SAT writing scores over 500: 33%; ACT

scores over 18: 62%; SAT critical reading scores over 600: 5%; SAT math scores over 600: 4%; SAT writing scores over 600: 4%; ACT scores over 24: 13%.

Faculty *Total:* 138, 28% full-time, 32% with terminal degrees. *Student/faculty ratio:* 14:1.

Academics *Calendar:* semesters. *Degrees:* certificates, bachelor's, master's, post-master's, and postbachelor's certificates. *Special study options:* academic remediation for entering students, accelerated degree program, adult/continuing education programs, advanced placement credit, distance learning, double majors, English as a second language, honors programs, independent study, internships, part-time degree program, services for LD students, student-designed majors, study abroad, summer session for credit. *ROTC:* Army (c), Air Force (c). *Unusual degree programs:* 3-2 business administration.

Computers on Campus 92 computers/terminals are available on campus for general student use. Students can access the following: computer help desk, free student e-mail accounts, online (class) grades, online (class) registration, online (class) schedules. Campuswide network is available. Wireless service is available via entire campus.

Student Life *Housing options:* coed. Campus housing is university owned. Freshman campus housing is guaranteed. *Activities and organizations:* drama/theater group, choral group, Drama Club, Latinos Unidos, Black Student Union, Biology Club, Hiking Club. *Campus security:* 24-hour emergency response devices, late-night transport/escort service, controlled dormitory access, 24-hour security main gate. *Student services:* personal/psychological counseling.

Athletics Member NAIA. *Intercollegiate sports:* basketball M(s)/W(s), cross-country running M(s)/W(s), golf M(s), soccer M(s)/W(s), softball W(s), volleyball M(s)/W(s).

Standardized Tests *Required:* SAT or ACT (for admission).

Costs (2011–12) *Comprehensive fee:* $40,650 includes full-time tuition ($30,050), mandatory fees ($340), and room and board ($10,260). Full-time tuition and fees vary according to course load and reciprocity agreements. Part-time tuition: $995 per credit hour. Part-time tuition and fees vary according to course load and reciprocity agreements. *Room and board:* Room and board charges vary according to board plan and housing facility. *Payment plan:* installment. *Waivers:* employees or children of employees.

Financial Aid Of all full-time matriculated undergraduates who enrolled in 2006, 373 applied for aid, 247 were judged to have need, 58 had their need fully met. 50 Federal Work-Study jobs (averaging $1699). 53 state and other part-time jobs (averaging $1750). In 2006, 77 non-need-based awards were made. *Average percent of need met:* 43%. *Average financial aid package:* $15,554. *Average need-based loan:* $4154. *Average need-based gift aid:* $13,258. *Average non-need-based aid:* $10,557. *Average indebtedness upon graduation:* $10,500. *Financial aid deadline:* 6/30.

Applying *Options:* electronic application, deferred entrance. *Required:* essay or personal statement, high school transcript. *Required for some:* interview. *Application deadlines:* 8/15 (freshmen), 8/5 (out-of-state freshmen), 8/15 (transfers). *Notification:* continuous (freshmen), continuous (out-of-state freshmen), continuous (transfers).

Freshman Application Contact Holy Names University, 3500 Mountain Boulevard, Oakland, CA 94619-1699. *Phone:* 510-436-1195. *Toll-free phone:* 800-430-1321. *Web site:* http://www.hnu.edu/.

Hope International University

Fullerton, California

Freshman Application Contact Ms. Midge Madden, Office Manager, Hope International University, 2500 East Nutwood Avenue, Fullerton, CA 92831-3138. *Phone:* 714-879-3901. *Toll-free phone:* 800-762-1294. *Fax:* 714-681-7423. *E-mail:* mfmadden@hiu.edu. *Web site:* http://www.hiu.edu/.

Humboldt State University

Arcata, California

- **State-supported** comprehensive, founded 1913, part of California State University System
- **Rural** 161-acre campus
- **Endowment** $15.6 million
- **Coed** 7,222 undergraduate students, 92% full-time, 54% women, 46% men
- **Moderately difficult** entrance level

Undergraduates 6,630 full-time, 592 part-time. Students come from 50 states and territories; 38 other countries; 15% are from out of state; 4% Black or African American, non-Hispanic/Latino; 15% Hispanic/Latino; 3% Asian, non-Hispanic/Latino; 0.7% Native Hawaiian or other Pacific Islander, non-Hispanic/Latino; 2% American Indian or Alaska Native, non-Hispanic/Latino; 7% Two or more races, non-Hispanic/Latino; 10% Race/ethnicity unknown; 1% international; 11% transferred in; 27% live on campus. *Retention:* 74% of full-time freshmen returned.

Freshmen *Admission:* 9,205 applied, 1,310 enrolled. *Average high school GPA:* 3.16. *Test scores:* SAT critical reading scores over 500: 60%; SAT math scores over 500: 57%; SAT writing scores over 500: 54%; ACT scores over 18: 82%; SAT critical reading scores over 600: 21%; SAT math scores over 600: 16%; SAT writing scores over 600: 14%; ACT scores over 24: 33%; SAT critical reading scores over 700: 3%; SAT math scores over 700: 1%; SAT writing scores over 700: 2%; ACT scores over 30: 4%.

Faculty *Total:* 499, 46% full-time, 87% with terminal degrees. *Student/faculty ratio:* 24:1.

Academics *Calendar:* semesters. *Degrees:* bachelor's, master's, post-master's, and postbachelor's certificates. *Special study options:* academic remediation for entering students, adult/continuing education programs, advanced placement credit, cooperative education, distance learning, double majors, English as a second language, honors programs, independent study, internships, off-campus study, part-time degree program, services for LD students, student-designed majors, study abroad, summer session for credit.

Computers on Campus 1,098 computers/terminals are available on campus for general student use. Students can access the following: computer help desk, free student e-mail accounts, online (class) grades, online (class) registration, online (class) schedules. Campuswide network is available. 100% of college-owned or -operated housing units are wired for high-speed Internet access. Wireless service is available via entire campus.

Student Life *Housing options:* coed. Campus housing is university owned. Freshman applicants given priority for college housing. *Activities and organizations:* drama/theater group, student-run newspaper, radio station, choral group, marching band, student radio station, Student Environmental Action Coalition, Youth Educational Services, Ballet Folklorico, International Student Union, national fraternities, national sororities. *Campus security:* 24-hour emergency response devices and patrols, late-night transport/escort service, controlled dormitory access. *Student services:* health clinic, personal/psychological counseling, women's center.

Athletics Member NCAA. All Division II. *Intercollegiate sports:* basketball M(s)/W(s), cheerleading W(c), crew M(c)/W, cross-country running M(s)/W(s), football M(s), lacrosse M(c), soccer M(s)/W(s), softball W(s), track and field M(s)/W(s), volleyball W(s). *Intramural sports:* baseball M(c), basketball M/W, fencing M(c)/W(c), rugby M(c)/W(c), soccer M/W, ultimate Frisbee M(c)/W(c), volleyball M(c), water polo M(c).

Standardized Tests *Required for some:* SAT or ACT (for admission).

Costs (2011–12) *Tuition:* state resident $0 full-time; nonresident $17,656 full-time, $372 per unit part-time. Full-time tuition and fees vary according to degree level. Part-time tuition and fees vary according to course load and degree level. *Required fees:* $6496 full-time, $2048 per term part-time. *Room and board:* $10,486; room only: $5302. Room and board charges vary according to board plan and housing facility. *Payment plan:* installment. *Waivers:* employees or children of employees.

Financial Aid Of all full-time matriculated undergraduates who enrolled in 2009, 4,966 applied for aid, 4,300 were judged to have need, 28 had their need fully met. 325 Federal Work-Study jobs (averaging $2600). In 2009, 75 non-need-based awards were made. *Average percent of need met:* 66%. *Average financial aid package:* $11,206. *Average need-based loan:* $4201. *Average need-based gift aid:* $8793. *Average non-need-based aid:* $1558. *Average indebtedness upon graduation:* $17,444.

Applying *Options:* electronic application. *Application fee:* $55. *Required:* high school transcript, minimum 2 GPA. *Application deadlines:* 11/30 (freshmen), 11/30 (out-of-state freshmen), 11/30 (transfers). *Notification:* continuous (freshmen), continuous (out-of-state freshmen), continuous (transfers).

Freshman Application Contact Ms. Rhonda Geldin, Assistant Director of Admissions, Humboldt State University, 1 Harpst Street, Arcata, CA 95521. *Phone:* 707-826-4402. *Fax:* 707-826-6190. *E-mail:* hsuinfo@humboldt.edu. *Web site:* http://www.humboldt.edu/.

Humphreys College
Stockton, California

Director of Admissions Director of Admission, Humphreys College, 6650 Inglewood Avenue, Stockton, CA 95207-3896. *Phone:* 209-235-2901. *E-mail:* ugadmission@humphreys.edu. *Web site:* http://www.humphreys.edu/.

Interior Designers Institute
Newport Beach, California

- **Proprietary** comprehensive, founded 1984
- **Suburban** 1-acre campus with easy access to Los Angeles and San Diego
- **Coed**

Academics *Degrees:* certificates, associate, bachelor's, and master's.
Costs (2010–11) *Tuition:* $15,950 full-time.
Applying *Application fee:* $95. *Required:* high school transcript.

Freshman Application Contact Interior Designers Institute, 1061 Camelback Road, Newport Beach, CA 92660. *Web site:* http://www.idi.edu/.

International Technological University
Santa Clara, California

Director of Admissions Manisha Pai, Director of Admissions and Registrar, International Technological University, 1650 Warburton Avenue, Santa Clara, CA 95050. *Phone:* 408-331-1014. *Fax:* 408-331-1026. *E-mail:* mpai@itu.edu. *Web site:* http://www.itu.edu/.

ITT Technical Institute
Anaheim, California

- **Proprietary** primarily 2-year, founded 1982, part of ITT Educational Services, Inc.
- **Suburban** campus
- **Coed**
- **Minimally difficult** entrance level

Academics *Calendar:* quarters. *Degrees:* associate and bachelor's.
Student Life *Housing:* college housing not available.
Financial Aid Of all full-time matriculated undergraduates who enrolled in 2009, 20 Federal Work-Study jobs (averaging $5000).
Freshman Application Contact Director of Recruitment, ITT Technical Institute, 4000 West Metropolitan Drive, Suite 100, Anaheim, CA 92801-9938. *Phone:* 714-941-2400. *Web site:* http://www.itt-tech.edu/.

ITT Technical Institute
Clovis, California

- **Proprietary** 4-year, founded 2005, part of ITT Educational Services, Inc.
- **Coed**
- **Minimally difficult** entrance level

Academics *Calendar:* quarters. *Degrees:* associate and bachelor's.
Student Life *Housing:* college housing not available.
Freshman Application Contact Director of Recruitment, ITT Technical Institute, 362 North Clovis Avenue, Clovis, CA 93612. *Phone:* 559-325-5400. *Toll-free phone:* 800-564-9771. *Web site:* http://www.itt-tech.edu/.

ITT Technical Institute
Concord, California

- **Proprietary** 4-year, part of ITT Educational Services, Inc.
- **Coed**
- **Minimally difficult** entrance level

Academics *Calendar:* quarters. *Degrees:* associate and bachelor's.
Freshman Application Contact Director of Recruitment, ITT Technical Institute, 1140 Galaxy Way, Suite 400, Concord, CA 94520. *Phone:* 925-674-8200. *Toll-free phone:* 800-211-7062. *Web site:* http://www.itt-tech.edu/.

ITT Technical Institute
Corona, California

- **Proprietary** 4-year
- **Coed**
- **Minimally difficult** entrance level

Academics *Degrees:* associate and bachelor's.
Freshman Application Contact Director of Recruitment, ITT Technical Institute, 4160 Temescal Canyon Road, Suite 100, Corona, CA 92883. *Phone:* 951-277-5400. *Toll-free phone:* 877-764-9661. *Web site:* http://www.itt-tech.edu/.

ITT Technical Institute
Lathrop, California

- **Proprietary** primarily 2-year, founded 1997, part of ITT Educational Services, Inc.
- **Coed**
- **Minimally difficult** entrance level

Academics *Calendar:* quarters. *Degrees:* associate and bachelor's.
Student Life *Housing:* college housing not available.
Freshman Application Contact Director of Recruitment, ITT Technical Institute, 16916 South Harlan Road, Lathrop, CA 95330. *Phone:* 209-858-0077. *Toll-free phone:* 800-346-1786. *Web site:* http://www.itt-tech.edu/.

ITT Technical Institute
Oxnard, California

- **Proprietary** primarily 2-year, founded 1993, part of ITT Educational Services, Inc.
- **Urban** campus
- **Coed**
- **Minimally difficult** entrance level

Academics *Calendar:* quarters. *Degrees:* associate and bachelor's.

Student Life *Housing:* college housing not available.

Freshman Application Contact Director of Recruitment, ITT Technical Institute, 2051 Solar Drive, Suite 150, Oxnard, CA 93036. *Phone:* 805-988-0143. *Toll-free phone:* 800-530-1582. *Web site:* http://www.itt-tech.edu/.

ITT Technical Institute
Rancho Cordova, California

- **Proprietary** primarily 2-year, founded 1954, part of ITT Educational Services, Inc.
- **Urban** campus
- **Coed**
- **Minimally difficult** entrance level

Academics *Calendar:* quarters. *Degrees:* associate and bachelor's.

Student Life *Housing:* college housing not available.

Freshman Application Contact Director of Recruitment, ITT Technical Institute, 10863 Gold Center Drive, Rancho Cordova, CA 95670-6034. *Phone:* 916-851-3900. *Toll-free phone:* 800-488-8466. *Web site:* http://www.itt-tech.edu/.

ITT Technical Institute
San Bernardino, California

- **Proprietary** primarily 2-year, founded 1987, part of ITT Educational Services, Inc.
- **Urban** campus
- **Coed**
- **Minimally difficult** entrance level

Academics *Calendar:* quarters. *Degrees:* associate and bachelor's.

Student Life *Housing:* college housing not available.

Freshman Application Contact Director of Recruitment, ITT Technical Institute, 670 East Carnegie Drive, San Bernardino, CA 92408. *Phone:* 909-806-4600. *Toll-free phone:* 800-888-3801. *Web site:* http://www.itt-tech.edu/.

ITT Technical Institute
San Diego, California

- **Proprietary** primarily 2-year, founded 1981, part of ITT Educational Services, Inc.
- **Suburban** campus
- **Coed**
- **Minimally difficult** entrance level

Academics *Calendar:* quarters. *Degrees:* associate and bachelor's.

Student Life *Housing:* college housing not available.

Freshman Application Contact Director of Recruitment, ITT Technical Institute, 9680 Granite Ridge Drive, San Diego, CA 92123. *Phone:* 858-571-8500. *Toll-free phone:* 800-883-0380. *Web site:* http://www.itt-tech.edu/.

ITT Technical Institute
San Dimas, California

- **Proprietary** primarily 2-year, founded 1982, part of ITT Educational Services, Inc.
- **Suburban** campus
- **Coed**
- **Minimally difficult** entrance level

Academics *Calendar:* quarters. *Degrees:* associate and bachelor's.

Student Life *Housing:* college housing not available.

Financial Aid Of all full-time matriculated undergraduates who enrolled in 2009, 20 Federal Work-Study jobs (averaging $4500).

Freshman Application Contact Director of Recruitment, ITT Technical Institute, 650 West Cienega Avenue, San Dimas, CA 91773. *Phone:* 909-971-2300. *Toll-free phone:* 800-414-6522. *Web site:* http://www.itt-tech.edu/.

ITT Technical Institute
Sylmar, California

- **Proprietary** primarily 2-year, founded 1982, part of ITT Educational Services, Inc.
- **Urban** campus
- **Coed**
- **Minimally difficult** entrance level

Academics *Calendar:* quarters. *Degrees:* associate and bachelor's.

Student Life *Housing:* college housing not available.

Freshman Application Contact Director of Recruitment, ITT Technical Institute, 12669 Encinitas Avenue, Sylmar, CA 91342-3664. *Phone:* 818-364-5151. *Toll-free phone:* 800-363-2086. *Web site:* http://www.itt-tech.edu/.

ITT Technical Institute
Torrance, California

- **Proprietary** primarily 2-year, founded 1987, part of ITT Educational Services, Inc.
- **Urban** campus
- **Coed**
- **Minimally difficult** entrance level

Academics *Calendar:* quarters. *Degrees:* associate and bachelor's.

Student Life *Housing:* college housing not available.

Financial Aid Of all full-time matriculated undergraduates who enrolled in 2009, 6 Federal Work-Study jobs (averaging $4000).

Freshman Application Contact Director of Recruitment, ITT Technical Institute, 20050 South Vermont Avenue, Torrance, CA 90502. *Phone:* 310-380-1555. *Web site:* http://www.itt-tech.edu/.

John F. Kennedy University
Pleasant Hill, California

Director of Admissions Ms. Jen Miller-Hogg, Director of Admissions, John F. Kennedy University, 100 Ellinwood Way, Pleasant Hill, CA 94523-4817. *Phone:* 925-969-3584. *Toll-free phone:* 800-696-JFKU. *E-mail:* jmhogg@jfku.edu. *Web site:* http://www.jfku.edu/.

The King's College and Seminary
Van Nuys, California

Freshman Application Contact Mrs. Marilyn J. Chappell, Director of Admissions, The King's College and Seminary, 14800 Sherman Way, Van Nuys, CA 91405-8040. *Phone:* 818-779-8040. *Toll-free phone:* 888-779-8040. *Fax:* 818-779-8429. *E-mail:* mchappell@kingscollege.edu. *Web site:* http://www.kingscollege.edu/.

LA College International
Los Angeles, California

- **Proprietary** 4-year, founded 1981
- **Urban** with easy access to Los Angeles
- **Coed** 530 undergraduate students, 100% full-time, 90% women, 10% men
- **Noncompetitive** entrance level

Undergraduates 530 full-time. Students come from 35 states and territories; 16% are from out of state; 5% transferred in.

Freshmen *Admission:* 109 enrolled.

Faculty *Total:* 93, 4% full-time, 98% with terminal degrees. *Student/faculty ratio:* 14:1.

Academics *Calendar:* quarters. *Degrees:* associate and bachelor's. *Special study options:* accelerated degree program, cooperative education, distance learning, independent study, services for LD students.

Computers on Campus 72 computers/terminals are available on campus for general student use. Students can access the following: computer help desk. Wireless service is available via entire campus.

Student Life *Housing:* college housing not available. *Campus security:* 24-hour emergency response devices.

Costs (2010–11) *Tuition:* $43,365 full-time, $565 per credit hour part-time. Full-time tuition and fees vary according to program. *Payment plan:* installment. *Waivers:* employees or children of employees.

Applying *Options:* electronic application. *Required:* high school graduate or hold a General Equivalency (Education) Diploma (GED). Complete the Jump Start Orientation Seminar.

Freshman Application Contact LA College International, 3200 Wilshire Boulevard, # 400, Los Angeles, CA 90010-1308. *Toll-free phone:* 800-57 GO ICT. *Web site:* http://www.lac.edu/.

Laguna College of Art & Design
Laguna Beach, California

Director of Admissions Mike Rivas, Vice President of Enrollment, Laguna College of Art & Design, 2222 Laguna Canyon Road, Laguna Beach, CA 92651-1136. *Phone:* 949-376-6000 Ext. 232. *Toll-free phone:* 800-255-0762. *Web site:* http://www.lagunacollege.edu/.

La Sierra University
Riverside, California

- **Independent Seventh-day Adventist** comprehensive, founded 1922, administratively affiliated with WASC (Western Association of Schools and Colleges)
- **Suburban** 100-acre campus with easy access to Los Angeles
- **Endowment** $15.8 million
- **Coed**
- **Moderately difficult** entrance level

Faculty *Student/faculty ratio:* 13:1.

Academics *Calendar:* quarters. *Degrees:* bachelor's, master's, doctoral-other, post-master's, and postbachelor's certificates.

Student Life *Campus security:* 24-hour emergency response devices and patrols, student patrols, late-night transport/escort service.

Athletics Member NCAA. All Division III.

Standardized Tests *Required:* SAT or ACT (for admission).

Costs (2010–11) *Comprehensive fee:* $33,231 includes full-time tuition ($24,840), mandatory fees ($1041), and room and board ($7350). Full-time tuition and fees vary according to course load and location. Part-time tuition: $690 per quarter hour. Part-time tuition and fees vary according to course load and location. *Room and board:* Room and board charges vary according to board plan and housing facility.

Financial Aid *Of all full-time matriculated undergraduates who enrolled in 2006,* 1,114 applied for aid, 1,019 were judged to have need, 117 had their need fully met. 269 Federal Work-Study jobs (averaging $2314). *In 2006,* 373 non-need-based awards were made. *Average percent of need met:* 64. *Average financial aid package:* $15,006. *Average need-based loan:* $4856. *Average need-based gift aid:* $11,281. *Average non-need-based aid:* $5847. *Average indebtedness upon graduation:* $28,876.

Applying *Options:* electronic application, deferred entrance. *Application fee:* $30. *Required:* essay or personal statement, high school transcript, 2 letters of recommendation. *Required for some:* interview.

Freshman Application Contact La Sierra University, 4500 Riverwalk Parkway, Riverside, CA 92515. *Phone:* 951-785-2176. *Toll-free phone:* 800-874-5587. *Web site:* http://www.lasierra.edu/.

Life Pacific College
San Dimas, California

Freshman Application Contact Ms. Dorienne Elston, Director of Admissions, Life Pacific College, 1100 Covina Boulevard, San Dimas, CA 91773-3298. *Phone:* 909-599-5433 Ext. 314. *Toll-free phone:* 877-886-5433 Ext. 314. *Fax:* 909-706-3070. *E-mail:* adm@lifepacific.edu. *Web site:* http://www.lifepacific.edu/.

Lincoln University
Oakland, California

- **Independent** comprehensive, founded 1919
- **Urban** 2-acre campus
- **Coed**
- **Minimally difficult** entrance level

Faculty *Student/faculty ratio:* 14:1.

Academics *Calendar:* semesters. *Degrees:* certificates, associate, bachelor's, and master's.

Student Life *Campus security:* 24-hour emergency response devices.

Costs (2010–11) *Tuition:* $8845 full-time, $355 per unit part-time. Full-time tuition and fees vary according to course level and degree level. Part-time tuition and fees vary according to course level and degree level. *Required fees:* $350 full-time.

Applying *Options:* electronic application, deferred entrance. *Application fee:* $75. *Required:* high school transcript, minimum 2 GPA. *Required for some:* essay or personal statement, interview.

Freshman Application Contact Ms. Reenu Shrestha, Admissions Officer, Lincoln University, 401 15th Street, Oakland, CA 94612. *Phone:* 510-628-8010 Ext. 8030. *Fax:* 510-628-8012. *E-mail:* admissions@lincolnuca.edu. *Web site:* http://www.lincolnuca.edu/.

Loma Linda University
Loma Linda, California

Freshman Application Contact Admissions Office, Loma Linda University, Loma Linda, CA 92350. *Phone:* 909-558-1000. *Web site:* http://www.llu.edu/.

Loyola Marymount University
Los Angeles, California

- **Independent Roman Catholic** comprehensive, founded 1911
- **Suburban** 142-acre campus with easy access to Los Angeles
- **Endowment** $376.5 million
- **Coed** 5,951 undergraduate students, 95% full-time, 57% women, 43% men
- **Very difficult** entrance level, 54% of applicants were admitted

Undergraduates 5,675 full-time, 276 part-time. Students come from 52 states and territories; 41 other countries; 26% are from out of state; 5% Black or African American, non-Hispanic/Latino; 21% Hispanic/Latino; 9% Asian, non-Hispanic/Latino; 0.3% Native Hawaiian or other Pacific Islander, non-Hispanic/Latino; 0.2% American Indian or Alaska Native, non-Hispanic/Latino; 7% Two or more races, non-Hispanic/Latino; 4% international; 5% transferred in; 55% live on campus. *Retention:* 89% of full-time freshmen returned.

Freshmen *Admission:* 10,192 applied, 5,498 admitted, 1,378 enrolled. *Average high school GPA:* 3.74. *Test scores:* SAT critical reading scores over 500: 93%; SAT math scores over 500: 93%; SAT writing scores over 500: 94%; ACT scores over 18: 99%; SAT critical reading scores over 600: 50%; SAT math scores over 600: 58%; SAT writing scores over 600: 57%; ACT scores over 24: 89%; SAT critical reading scores over 700: 9%; SAT math scores over 700: 11%; SAT writing scores over 700: 11%; ACT scores over 30: 20%.

Faculty *Total:* 1,053, 49% full-time. *Student/faculty ratio:* 11:1.

Academics *Calendar:* semesters. *Degrees:* certificates, bachelor's, master's, doctoral-professional, doctoral-research/scholarship, post-master's, and post-bachelor's certificates. *Special study options:* academic remediation for entering students, accelerated degree program, advanced placement credit, cooperative education, distance learning, double majors, English as a second language, honors programs, independent study, internships, part-time degree program, services for LD students, student-designed majors, study abroad, summer session for credit. *ROTC:* Army (c), Navy (c), Air Force (b). *Unusual degree programs:* engineering.

Computers on Campus 780 computers/terminals and 2,000 ports are available on campus for general student use. Students can access the following: campus intranet, computer help desk, free student e-mail accounts, online (class) grades, online (class) registration, online (class) schedules. Campuswide network is available. 100% of college-owned or -operated housing units are wired for high-speed Internet access. Wireless service is available via entire campus.

Student Life *Housing options:* coed, men-only, women-only, disabled students. Campus housing is university owned. Freshman applicants given priority for college housing. *Activities and organizations:* drama/theater group, student-run newspaper, radio and television station, choral group, Greeks, Intramurals, Christian Life Communities, Black Student Union, Serve LA, national fraternities, national sororities. *Campus security:* 24-hour emergency response devices and patrols, late-night transport/escort service, controlled dormitory access. *Student services:* health clinic, personal/psychological counseling.

Athletics Member NCAA. All Division I. *Intercollegiate sports:* baseball M(s), basketball M(s)/W(s), cheerleading M/W, crew M/W(s), cross-country running M(s)/W(s), golf M(s), soccer M(s)/W(s), softball W(s), swimming and diving W(s), tennis M(s)/W(s), track and field M/W, volleyball W(s), water polo M(s)/W(s). *Intramural sports:* baseball M(c), basketball M/W(c), football M/W, ice hockey M(c), lacrosse M(c), rugby M(c), skiing (downhill) M(c)/W(c), soccer M(c)/W(c), tennis M(c)/W(c), volleyball M(c)/W(c), water polo W(c).

Standardized Tests *Required:* SAT or ACT (for admission).

Costs (2010–11) *One-time required fee:* $218. *Comprehensive fee:* $50,334 includes full-time tuition ($35,740), mandatory fees ($664), and room and board ($13,930). Full-time tuition and fees vary according to reciprocity agreements. Part-time tuition: $1490 per credit hour. Part-time tuition and fees vary according to course load. *Required fees:* $5 per credit hour part-time, $60 per term part-time. *College room only:* $9530. Room and board charges vary according to board plan and housing facility. *Payment plans:* installment, deferred payment. *Waivers:* employees or children of employees.

Financial Aid Of all full-time matriculated undergraduates who enrolled in 2007, 3,654 applied for aid, 2,834 were judged to have need, 611 had their need fully met. In 2007, 305 non-need-based awards were made. *Average percent of need met:* 80%. *Average financial aid package:* $14,617. *Average need-based loan:* $4879. *Average non-need-based aid:* $11,665. *Average indebtedness upon graduation:* $28,548. *Financial aid deadline:* 7/30.

Applying *Options:* electronic application, early admission, early action, deferred entrance. *Application fee:* $60. *Required:* essay or personal statement, high school transcript, 1 letter of recommendation. *Required for some:* portfolios or auditions for animation, dance, music, or theatre arts majors. *Recommended:* interview. *Application deadlines:* 1/15 (freshmen), 3/15 (transfers), 11/1 (early action). *Notification:* continuous (freshmen), continuous (transfers), 12/20 (early action).

Freshman Application Contact Loyola Marymount University, One LMU Drive, Los Angeles, CA 90045-2659. *Phone:* 310-338-2750. *Toll-free phone:* 800-LMU-INFO. *Web site:* http://www.lmu.edu/.

See page 1392 for the College Close-Up.

Marymount College, Palos Verdes, California

Rancho Palos Verdes, California

- **Independent Roman Catholic** 4-year, founded 1932
- **Suburban** 26-acre campus with easy access to Los Angeles
- **Endowment** $7.7 million
- **Coed** 793 undergraduate students, 98% full-time, 52% women, 48% men
- **Minimally difficult** entrance level, 47% of applicants were admitted

Undergraduates 774 full-time, 19 part-time. Students come from 20 states and territories; 26 other countries; 9% are from out of state; 4% Black or African American, non-Hispanic/Latino; 16% Hispanic/Latino; 4% Asian, non-Hispanic/Latino; 0.8% Native Hawaiian or other Pacific Islander, non-Hispanic/Latino; 3% Two or more races, non-Hispanic/Latino; 44% Race/ethnicity unknown; 7% international; 13% transferred in; 52% live on campus. *Retention:* 67% of full-time freshmen returned.

Freshmen *Admission:* 3,075 applied, 1,440 admitted, 447 enrolled. *Average high school GPA:* 2.68. *Test scores:* SAT critical reading scores over 500: 33%; SAT math scores over 500: 25%; SAT writing scores over 500: 38%; ACT scores over 18: 56%; SAT critical reading scores over 600: 8%; SAT math scores over 600: 13%; SAT writing scores over 600: 4%; ACT scores over 24: 11%; SAT math scores over 700: 4%.

Faculty *Total:* 81, 40% full-time, 44% with terminal degrees. *Student/faculty ratio:* 16:1.

Academics *Calendar:* semesters. *Degrees:* associate and bachelor's. *Special study options:* academic remediation for entering students, adult/continuing education programs, advanced placement credit, English as a second language, honors programs, independent study, internships, part-time degree program, services for LD students, study abroad, summer session for credit.

Computers on Campus 90 computers/terminals are available on campus for general student use. Students can access the following: campus intranet, computer help desk, free student e-mail accounts, online (class) grades. Campuswide network is available. 100% of college-owned or -operated housing units are wired for high-speed Internet access. Wireless service is available via entire campus.

Student Life *Housing options:* coed. Campus housing is university owned. *Activities and organizations:* drama/theater group, student-run newspaper, radio station, choral group. *Campus security:* 24-hour emergency response devices and patrols, late-night transport/escort service, controlled dormitory access. *Student services:* health clinic, personal/psychological counseling.

Athletics Member NAIA. *Intercollegiate sports:* golf M/W, soccer M(s), tennis M(s)/W(s). *Intramural sports:* archery M, basketball M/W, golf M/W, lacrosse M/W, soccer M/W, softball M/W, swimming and diving M/W, tennis M/W, volleyball M/W.

Standardized Tests *Recommended:* SAT or ACT (for admission).

Costs (2011–12) *Comprehensive fee:* $39,971 includes full-time tuition ($27,396), mandatory fees ($500), and room and board ($12,075). Part-time tuition: $1035 per unit. *Room and board:* Room and board charges vary according to housing facility. *Payment plan:* installment. *Waivers:* employees or children of employees.

Financial Aid Of all full-time matriculated undergraduates who enrolled in 2009, 40 Federal Work-Study jobs (averaging $2000).

Applying *Options:* electronic application, early admission. *Application fee:* $40. *Required:* high school transcript. *Required for some:* essay or personal statement, interview. *Application deadlines:* 7/1 (freshmen), 8/15 (transfers). *Notification:* continuous until 9/1 (freshmen), continuous until 9/1 (transfers).

Freshman Application Contact Ms. Paula Avery, Director of Admissions, Marymount College, Palos Verdes, California, 30800 Palos Verdes Drive East, Rancho Palos Verdes, CA 90275-6299. *Phone:* 310-377-5501 Ext. 211. *Fax:*

310-265-0962. *E-mail:* admissions@marymountpv.edu. *Web site:* http://www.marymountpv.edu/.

The Master's College and Seminary

Santa Clarita, California

- **Independent nondenominational** comprehensive, founded 1927
- **Suburban** 110-acre campus with easy access to Los Angeles
- **Endowment** $10.9 million
- **Coed** 1,053 undergraduate students, 91% full-time, 47% women, 53% men
- **Moderately difficult** entrance level, 69% of applicants were admitted

Undergraduates 959 full-time, 94 part-time. Students come from 41 states and territories; 30 other countries; 33% are from out of state; 12% transferred in; 75% live on campus. *Retention:* 81% of full-time freshmen returned.

Freshmen *Admission:* 632 applied, 439 admitted, 211 enrolled. *Average high school GPA:* 3.6. *Test scores:* SAT critical reading scores over 500: 77%; SAT math scores over 500: 67%; ACT scores over 18: 91%; SAT critical reading scores over 600: 36%; SAT math scores over 600: 31%; ACT scores over 24: 66%; SAT critical reading scores over 700: 7%; SAT math scores over 700: 3%; ACT scores over 30: 17%.

Faculty *Total:* 199, 33% full-time, 34% with terminal degrees. *Student/faculty ratio:* 10:1.

Academics *Calendar:* semesters. *Degrees:* certificates, bachelor's, master's, doctoral-professional, and doctoral-research/scholarship. *Special study options:* academic remediation for entering students, accelerated degree program, adult/continuing education programs, advanced placement credit, cooperative education, distance learning, double majors, external degree program, independent study, internships, part-time degree program, services for LD students, study abroad, summer session for credit.

Computers on Campus 57 computers/terminals are available on campus for general student use. Students can access the following: free student e-mail accounts, online (class) grades, online (class) registration, online (class) schedules. Campuswide network is available. Wireless service is available via entire campus.

Student Life *Housing:* on-campus residence required through junior year. *Options:* men-only, women-only. Campus housing is university owned. Freshman campus housing is guaranteed. *Activities and organizations:* drama/theater group, choral group, College Chorale, Summer Missions, intramurals, Church Ministries, Drama Club. *Campus security:* 24-hour patrols. *Student services:* health clinic, personal/psychological counseling.

Athletics Member NAIA, NCCAA. *Intercollegiate sports:* baseball M(s), basketball M(s)/W(s), cross-country running M(s)/W(s), golf M(s), soccer M(s)/W(s), tennis W(s), track and field M(s)/W(s), volleyball W(s). *Intramural sports:* basketball M/W, football M/W, soccer M/W, volleyball M/W.

Standardized Tests *Required:* SAT or ACT (for admission).

Costs (2011–12) *Comprehensive fee:* $35,280 includes full-time tuition ($26,260), mandatory fees ($620), and room and board ($8400). Full-time tuition and fees vary according to course load, degree level, and program. Part-time tuition: $1100 per credit hour. Part-time tuition and fees vary according to course load, degree level, and program. *Required fees:* $1100 per credit hour part-time. *College room only:* $7362. Room and board charges vary according to board plan. *Payment plan:* installment. *Waivers:* employees or children of employees.

Financial Aid Of all full-time matriculated undergraduates who enrolled in 2009, 950 applied for aid, 854 were judged to have need, 124 had their need fully met. 65 Federal Work-Study jobs (averaging $2676). 191 state and other part-time jobs (averaging $532,750). In 2009, 66 non-need-based awards were made. *Average percent of need met:* 65%. *Average financial aid package:* $18,723. *Average need-based loan:* $4719. *Average need-based gift aid:* $14,120. *Average non-need-based aid:* $7178. *Average indebtedness upon graduation:* $12,842.

Applying *Options:* electronic application, early admission, early action, deferred entrance. *Application fee:* $40. *Required:* essay or personal statement, high school transcript, minimum 2.75 GPA, 2 letters of recommendation. *Recommended:* interview. *Application deadlines:* 9/1 (freshmen), 9/1 (out-of-state freshmen), 9/1 (transfers), 11/15 (early action). *Notification:* 3/15 (freshmen), 3/15 (transfers), 12/22 (early action).

Freshman Application Contact Ms. Hollie Gorsh, Director of Admissions, The Master's College and Seminary, 21726 Placerita Canyon Road, Santa Clarita, CA 91321. *Phone:* 661-259-3540 Ext. 3369. *Toll-free phone:* 800-568-6248. *Fax:* 661-288-1037. *E-mail:* admissions@masters.edu. *Web site:* http://www.masters.edu/.

Menlo College

Atherton, California

- **Independent** 4-year, founded 1927
- **Small-town** 45-acre campus with easy access to San Francisco
- **Endowment** $6.9 million
- **Coed** 590 undergraduate students, 96% full-time, 34% women, 66% men
- **Moderately difficult** entrance level, 36% of applicants were admitted

Undergraduates 568 full-time, 22 part-time. Students come from 21 states and territories; 24 other countries; 21% are from out of state; 6% Black or African American, non-Hispanic/Latino; 15% Hispanic/Latino; 8% Asian, non-Hispanic/Latino; 4% Native Hawaiian or other Pacific Islander, non-Hispanic/Latino; 7% Two or more races, non-Hispanic/Latino; 10% Race/ethnicity unknown; 13% international; 12% transferred in; 63% live on campus. *Retention:* 71% of full-time freshmen returned.

Freshmen *Admission:* 3,396 applied, 1,206 admitted, 152 enrolled. *Average high school GPA:* 3.29. *Test scores:* SAT critical reading scores over 500: 35%; SAT math scores over 500: 56%; SAT writing scores over 500: 36%; ACT scores over 18: 72%; SAT critical reading scores over 600: 6%; SAT math scores over 600: 13%; SAT writing scores over 600: 4%; ACT scores over 24: 18%; SAT math scores over 700: 1%; SAT writing scores over 700: 1%; ACT scores over 30: 5%.

Faculty *Total:* 72, 36% full-time, 54% with terminal degrees. *Student/faculty ratio:* 14:1.

Academics *Calendar:* semesters. *Degree:* bachelor's. *Special study options:* accelerated degree program, adult/continuing education programs, advanced placement credit, cooperative education, double majors, English as a second language, independent study, internships, part-time degree program, services for LD students, student-designed majors, study abroad, summer session for credit. *ROTC:* Army (c), Air Force (c).

Computers on Campus 152 computers/terminals are available on campus for general student use. Students can access the following: campus intranet, computer help desk, free student e-mail accounts, online (class) grades, online (class) registration, online (class) schedules. Campuswide network is available. 100% of college-owned or -operated housing units are wired for high-speed Internet access. Wireless service is available via classrooms, computer centers, computer labs, dorm rooms, learning centers, libraries, student centers.

Student Life *Housing:* on-campus residence required through sophomore year. *Options:* coed, men-only, women-only. Campus housing is university owned. *Activities and organizations:* student-run newspaper, radio station, International Club, Residence Hall Association, SERV, Women Club, Hawaiian Club. *Campus security:* 24-hour emergency response devices and patrols, controlled dormitory access. *Student services:* personal/psychological counseling, women's center.

Athletics Member NAIA. *Intercollegiate sports:* baseball M, basketball M/W, cross-country running M/W, football M, golf M, soccer M/W, softball W, volleyball W, wrestling M/W. *Intramural sports:* basketball M(c)/W(c), cheerleading W(c), skiing (downhill) M(c)/W(c).

Standardized Tests *Required:* SAT or ACT (for admission).

Costs (2011–12) *Comprehensive fee:* $46,200 includes full-time tuition ($34,500), mandatory fees ($400), and room and board ($11,300). Full-time tuition and fees vary according to program. Part-time tuition: $1438 per credit hour. Part-time tuition and fees vary according to program. *Room and board:* Room and board charges vary according to housing facility. *Payment plan:* installment. *Waivers:* employees or children of employees.

Financial Aid Of all full-time matriculated undergraduates who enrolled in 2009, 386 applied for aid, 368 were judged to have need, 27 had their need fully met. 293 Federal Work-Study jobs (averaging $1000). In 2009, 162 non-need-based awards were made. *Average percent of need met:* 71%. *Average financial aid package:* $28,412. *Average need-based loan:* $3824. *Average need-based gift aid:* $24,378. *Average non-need-based aid:* $10,815. *Average indebtedness upon graduation:* $28,333.

Applying *Options:* electronic application, early admission, early action, deferred entrance. *Application fee:* $40. *Required:* essay or personal statement, high school transcript, 1 letter of recommendation. *Recommended:* minimum 2.5 GPA, interview. *Application deadlines:* rolling (freshmen), rolling (out-of-state freshmen), rolling (transfers), 12/1 (early action). *Notification:* continuous (freshmen), continuous (out-of-state freshmen), continuous (transfers), 12/15 (early action).

Freshman Application Contact Cindy McGrew, Director, Enrollment Management Operations, Menlo College, 1000 El Camino Real, Atherton, CA 94027. *Phone:* 650-543-3940. *Toll-free phone:* 800-556-3656. *Fax:* 650-543-4496. *E-mail:* admissions@menlo.edu. *Web site:* http://www.menlo.edu/.

See page 1420 for the College Close-Up.

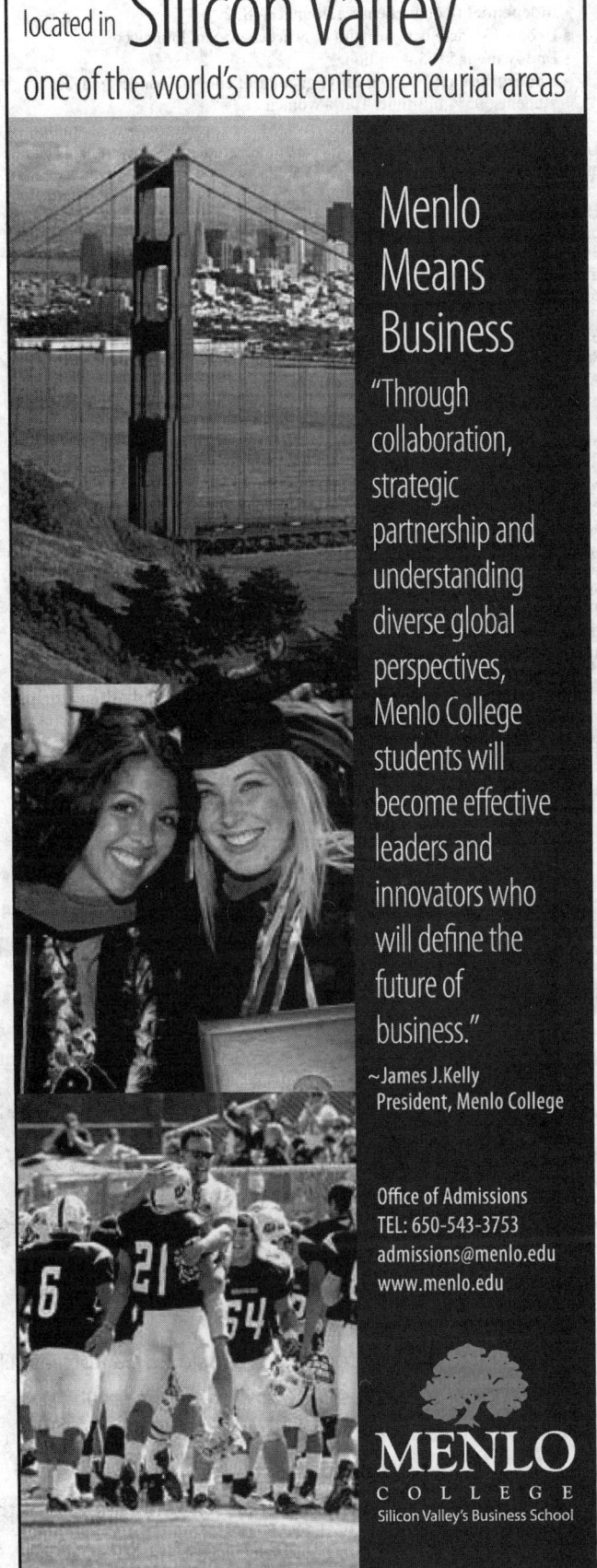

Mills College

Oakland, California

- **Independent** comprehensive, founded 1852
- **Urban** 135-acre campus with easy access to San Francisco
- **Endowment** $165.4 million
- **Undergraduate: women only; graduate: coed** 957 undergraduate students, 95% full-time, 100% women
- **Moderately difficult** entrance level, 57% of applicants were admitted

Undergraduates 912 full-time, 45 part-time. Students come from 44 states and territories; 15 other countries; 20% are from out of state; 8% Black or African American, non-Hispanic/Latino; 18% Hispanic/Latino; 8% Asian, non-Hispanic/Latino; 0.4% Native Hawaiian or other Pacific Islander, non-Hispanic/Latino; 1% American Indian or Alaska Native, non-Hispanic/Latino; 4% Two or more races, non-Hispanic/Latino; 18% Race/ethnicity unknown; 2% international; 11% transferred in; 58% live on campus. *Retention:* 81% of full-time freshmen returned.

Freshmen *Admission:* 2,129 applied, 1,220 admitted, 207 enrolled. *Average high school GPA:* 3.67. *Test scores:* SAT critical reading scores over 500: 86%; SAT math scores over 500: 74%; SAT writing scores over 500: 81%; ACT scores over 18: 99%; SAT critical reading scores over 600: 45%; SAT math scores over 600: 29%; SAT writing scores over 600: 38%; ACT scores over 24: 53%; SAT critical reading scores over 700: 10%; SAT math scores over 700: 4%; SAT writing scores over 700: 5%; ACT scores over 30: 14%.

Faculty *Total:* 200, 51% full-time, 72% with terminal degrees. *Student/faculty ratio:* 11:1.

Academics *Calendar:* semesters. *Degrees:* certificates, bachelor's, master's, doctoral-research/scholarship, and postbachelor's certificates. *Special study options:* accelerated degree program, adult/continuing education programs, advanced placement credit, double majors, English as a second language, honors programs, independent study, internships, off-campus study, part-time degree program, services for LD students, student-designed majors, study abroad. *ROTC:* Army (c). *Unusual degree programs:* 3-2 business administration; engineering; education; public policy.

Computers on Campus 345 computers/terminals and 8 ports are available on campus for general student use. Students can access the following: campus intranet, computer help desk, free student e-mail accounts, online (class) grades, online (class) registration, online (class) schedules, online degree audit.

Campuswide network is available. 100% of college-owned or -operated housing units are wired for high-speed Internet access. Wireless service is available via entire campus.

Student Life *Housing options:* coed, women-only, cooperative, disabled students. Campus housing is university owned. Freshman campus housing is guaranteed. *Activities and organizations:* drama/theater group, student-run newspaper, radio station, choral group, Mujeres Unidas, Black Women's Collective, Student Athlete Advisory Committee, Women's Health Resource Center, Phi Alpha Delta Pre-Law Fraternity. *Campus security:* 24-hour emergency response devices and patrols, late-night transport/escort service, controlled dormitory access. *Student services:* health clinic, personal/psychological counseling, women's center.

Athletics Member NCAA, NAIA. All NCAA Division III. *Intercollegiate sports:* crew W, cross-country running W, soccer W, swimming and diving W, tennis W, volleyball W. *Intramural sports:* badminton W, basketball W, soccer W, softball W, tennis W, volleyball W.

Standardized Tests *Required:* SAT or ACT (for admission). *Recommended:* SAT Subject Tests (for admission).

Costs (2010–11) *Comprehensive fee:* $49,249 includes full-time tuition ($36,428), mandatory fees ($1177), and room and board ($11,644). Full-time tuition and fees vary according to course load. Part-time tuition: $6072 per course. Part-time tuition and fees vary according to course load. *Required fees:* $1177 per year part-time. *Room and board:* Room and board charges vary according to board plan and housing facility. *Payment plan:* installment. *Waivers:* employees or children of employees.

Financial Aid Of all full-time matriculated undergraduates who enrolled in 2008, 821 applied for aid, 770 were judged to have need, 377 had their need fully met. 299 Federal Work-Study jobs (averaging $3010). 261 state and other part-time jobs (averaging $3489). In 2008, 103 non-need-based awards were made. *Average percent of need met:* 83%. *Average financial aid package:* $31,932. *Average need-based loan:* $5375. *Average need-based gift aid:* $23,274. *Average non-need-based aid:* $16,774. *Average indebtedness upon graduation:* $28,914.

Applying *Options:* electronic application, early action, deferred entrance. *Application fee:* $50. *Required:* high school transcript, 2 letters of recommendation, essay or graded paper. *Recommended:* interview. *Application deadlines:* 2/1 (freshmen), 3/1 (transfers), 11/15 (early action). *Notification:* 3/30 (freshmen), 4/1 (transfers), 12/1 (early action).

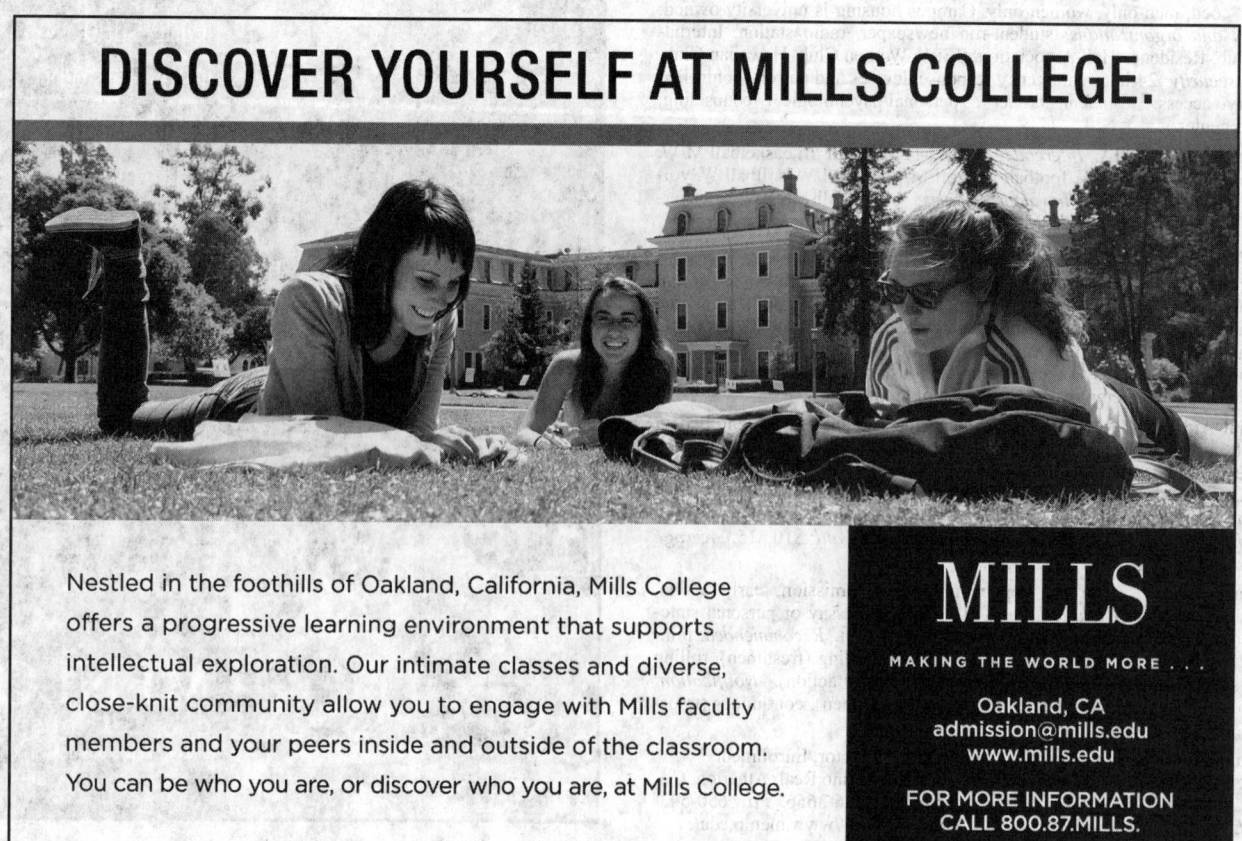

Freshman Application Contact Ms. Giulietta Aquino, Vice President of Enrollment Management, Mills College, 5000 MacArthur Boulevard, Oakland, CA 94613-1301. *Phone:* 510-430-2135. *Toll-free phone:* 800-87-MILLS. *Fax:* 510-430-3314. *E-mail:* admission@mills.edu. *Web site:* http://www.mills.edu/.

See page 1436 for the College Close-Up.

Mount St. Mary's College

Los Angeles, California

- **Independent Roman Catholic** comprehensive, founded 1925, administratively affiliated with Sister of St. Joseph Carondelet
- **Urban** 71-acre campus with easy access to Los Angeles
- **Endowment** $79.6 million
- **Coed, primarily women** 2,288 undergraduate students, 79% full-time, 92% women, 8% men
- **Moderately difficult** entrance level, 73% of applicants were admitted

Undergraduates 1,803 full-time, 485 part-time. Students come from 13 states and territories; 3 other countries; 2% are from out of state; 11% transferred in; 29% live on campus. *Retention:* 84% of full-time freshmen returned.

Freshmen *Admission:* 1,799 applied, 1,309 admitted, 528 enrolled. *Test scores:* SAT critical reading scores over 500: 30%; SAT math scores over 500: 29%; SAT writing scores over 500: 35%; ACT scores over 18: 58%; SAT critical reading scores over 600: 4%; SAT math scores over 600: 4%; SAT writing scores over 600: 5%; ACT scores over 24: 7%; ACT scores over 30: 1%.

Faculty *Total:* 375, 25% full-time, 38% with terminal degrees. *Student/faculty ratio:* 12:1.

Academics *Calendar:* semesters. *Degrees:* associate, bachelor's, master's, doctoral-professional, and post-master's certificates. *Special study options:* academic remediation for entering students, accelerated degree program, advanced placement credit, distance learning, double majors, English as a second language, freshman honors college, honors programs, independent study, internships, off-campus study, part-time degree program, services for LD students, student-designed majors, study abroad, summer session for credit. *Unusual degree programs:* 3-2 nursing.

Computers on Campus Students can access the following: campus intranet, computer help desk, free student e-mail accounts, online (class) grades, online (class) registration, online (class) schedules. Campuswide network is available. 100% of college-owned or -operated housing units are wired for high-speed Internet access. Wireless service is available via entire campus.

Student Life *Housing options:* men-only, women-only. Campus housing is university owned. Freshman applicants given priority for college housing. *Activities and organizations:* drama/theater group, student-run newspaper, choral group, Na Pua O Ka Aina, Pangkat Pilipino, Latinas Unidas, California Nursing Student Association, Associated Student Body. *Campus security:* 24-hour emergency response devices and patrols, late-night transport/escort service, controlled dormitory access. *Student services:* health clinic, personal/psychological counseling, women's center.

Athletics *Intramural sports:* basketball M/W, volleyball W.

Standardized Tests *Required:* SAT or ACT (for admission).

Costs (2011–12) *Comprehensive fee:* $41,751 includes full-time tuition ($30,696), mandatory fees ($930), and room and board ($10,125). Full-time tuition and fees vary according to course load, degree level, and program. Part-time tuition: $1218 per unit. Part-time tuition and fees vary according to course load, degree level, and program. *Room and board:* Room and board charges vary according to board plan and housing facility. *Payment plan:* installment. *Waivers:* employees or children of employees.

Financial Aid Of all full-time matriculated undergraduates who enrolled in 2009, 1,626 applied for aid, 1,573 were judged to have need, 113 had their need fully met. In 2009, 194 non-need-based awards were made. *Average percent of need met:* 79%. *Average financial aid package:* $28,700. *Average need-based loan:* $5500. *Average need-based gift aid:* $10,500. *Average non-need-based aid:* $10,978. *Average indebtedness upon graduation:* $26,500.

Applying *Options:* electronic application, early action. *Application fee:* $50. *Required:* essay or personal statement, high school transcript, minimum 2.5 GPA, 1 letter of recommendation. *Recommended:* 2 letters of recommendation, interview. *Application deadlines:* 2/15 (freshmen), 3/15 (transfers), 12/1 (early action). *Notification:* continuous (freshmen), continuous (transfers), 1/1 (early action).

Freshman Application Contact Yvonne Berumen, Director of Admissions, Mount St. Mary's College, 12001 Chalon Road, Los Angeles, CA 90049-1599. *Phone:* 310-954-4250. *Toll-free phone:* 800-999-9893. *Fax:* 310-954-4259. *E-mail:* admissions@msmc.la.edu. *Web site:* http://www.msmc.la.edu/.

Mt. Sierra College

Monrovia, California

Freshman Application Contact Mt. Sierra College, 101 East Huntington Drive, Monrovia, CA 91016. *Phone:* 888-486-9818. *Toll-free phone:* 888-828-8800. *Web site:* http://www.mtsierra.edu/.

Musicians Institute

Hollywood, California

- **Proprietary** 4-year, founded 1976
- **Urban** campus
- **Coed** 1,528 undergraduate students
- **Minimally difficult** entrance level

Freshman *Admission:* 1,048 applied.

Faculty *Total:* 125. *Student/faculty ratio:* 12:1.

Academics *Calendar:* quarters. *Degrees:* certificates, diplomas, associate, and bachelor's. *Special study options:* internships, part-time degree program, services for LD students, summer session for credit.

Computers on Campus Students can access the following: campus intranet, computer help desk, free student e-mail accounts, online (class) grades, online (class) schedules. Wireless service is available via entire campus.

Student Life *Housing:* college housing not available. *Campus security:* 24-hour emergency response devices and patrols. *Student services:* personal/psychological counseling.

Standardized Tests *Required for some:* SAT or ACT (for admission).

Costs (2011–12) *Tuition:* $24,000 full-time. Full-time tuition and fees vary according to course load and degree level. Part-time tuition and fees vary according to course load and degree level. *Required fees:* $5520 full-time. *Payment plan:* installment. *Waivers:* employees or children of employees.

Financial Aid Of all full-time matriculated undergraduates who enrolled in 2002, 520 applied for aid, 465 were judged to have need. *Average percent of need met:* 40%. *Average financial aid package:* $6100. *Average need-based loan:* $3100. *Average indebtedness upon graduation:* $14,000.

Applying *Options:* electronic application, deferred entrance. *Application fee:* $100. *Required:* high school transcript, 1 letter of recommendation. *Required for some:* essay or personal statement, 2 letters of recommendation. *Application deadline:* rolling (freshmen). *Notification:* continuous (freshmen).

Freshman Application Contact Musicians Institute, 1655 North McCadden Place, Hollywood, CA 90028. *Phone:* 323-860-4345. *Toll-free phone:* 800-255-PLAY. *Web site:* http://www.mi.edu/.

The National Hispanic University

San Jose, California

Director of Admissions Ms. Pamela Bustillo, Director of Office of Admissions/Registrar, The National Hispanic University, 14271 Story Road, San Jose, CA 95127-3823. *Phone:* 408-273-2772. *E-mail:* chernandez@nhu.edu. *Web site:* http://www.nhu.edu/.

National University

La Jolla, California

- **Independent** comprehensive, founded 1971, part of National University System
- **Urban** campus
- **Endowment** $342.5 million
- **Coed** 6,790 undergraduate students, 55% full-time, 61% women, 39% men
- **Minimally difficult** entrance level, 100% of applicants were admitted

Undergraduates 3,740 full-time, 3,050 part-time. Students come from 48 states and territories; 61 other countries; 10% are from out of state; 10% Black or African American, non-Hispanic/Latino; 21% Hispanic/Latino; 10% Asian, non-Hispanic/Latino; 2% Native Hawaiian or other Pacific Islander, non-Hispanic/Latino; 0.7% American Indian or Alaska Native, non-Hispanic/Latino; 2% Two or more races, non-Hispanic/Latino; 9% Race/ethnicity unknown; 2% international; 84% transferred in. *Retention:* 76% of full-time freshmen returned.

Freshmen *Admission:* 2,283 applied, 2,283 admitted, 757 enrolled.

Faculty *Total:* 2,949, 9% full-time, 26% with terminal degrees. *Student/faculty ratio:* 19:1.

Academics *Calendar:* continuous. *Degrees:* certificates, associate, bachelor's, master's, and postbachelor's certificates. *Special study options:* accelerated degree program, adult/continuing education programs, advanced placement credit, distance learning, double majors, English as a second language, independent study, internships, off-campus study, part-time degree program, services for LD students, summer session for credit. *ROTC:* Army (c), Air Force (c).

Computers on Campus 3,100 computers/terminals are available on campus for general student use. Students can access the following: computer help desk, online (class) grades, online (class) registration, online (class) schedules. Campuswide network is available. Wireless service is available via libraries.

Student Life *Housing:* college housing not available. *Activities and organizations:* student-run television station. *Campus security:* 24-hour emergency response devices and patrols, late-night transport/escort service.

Costs (2011–12) *Tuition:* $11,088 full-time, $308 per unit part-time. Full-time tuition and fees vary according to course load and location. Part-time tuition and fees vary according to course load and location. *Required fees:* $60 full-time. *Waivers:* employees or children of employees.

Financial Aid Of all full-time matriculated undergraduates who enrolled in 2008, 7,894 applied for aid, 7,562 were judged to have need, 64 had their need fully met. *Average percent of need met:* 89%. *Average financial aid package:* $6267. *Average need-based loan:* $4522. *Average need-based gift aid:* $3319.

Applying *Options:* electronic application, deferred entrance. *Application fee:* $60. *Required:* high school transcript, minimum 2 GPA, interview. *Required for some:* essay or personal statement. *Application deadlines:* rolling (freshmen), rolling (transfers). *Notification:* continuous (freshmen), continuous (transfers).

Freshman Application Contact National University, 11255 North Torrey Pines Road, La Jolla, CA 92037-1011. *Phone:* 858-628-8648 Ext. 7701. *Toll-free phone:* 800-NAT-UNIV. *Web site:* http://www.nu.edu/.

NewSchool of Architecture & Design
San Diego, California

Freshman Application Contact Ms. Lexi Rogers, Director of Admissions, NewSchool of Architecture & Design, 1249 F Street, San Diego, CA 92101-6634. *Phone:* 619-235-4100 Ext. 106. *Web site:* http://www.newschoolarch.edu/.

New York Film Academy
Los Angeles, California

Freshman Application Contact Admissions Office, New York Film Academy, 3801 Barham Boulevard, Los Angeles, CA 90068. *Phone:* 818-733-2600. *Fax:* 818-733-4074. *E-mail:* studios@nyfa.edu. *Web site:* http://www.nyfa.com/.

Northwestern Polytechnic University
Fremont, California

- **Independent** comprehensive, founded 1984
- **Urban** 3-acre campus with easy access to San Francisco and San Jose
- **Coed**
- 100% of applicants were admitted

Faculty *Student/faculty ratio:* 16:1.

Academics *Calendar:* trimesters. *Degrees:* bachelor's, master's, and doctoral-other.

Student Life *Campus security:* late-night transport/escort service.

Standardized Tests *Recommended:* SAT (for admission).

Costs (2010–11) *Tuition:* $7200 full-time, $300 per unit part-time. *Required fees:* $140 full-time. *Room only:* $4800.

Applying *Options:* electronic application, deferred entrance. *Application fee:* $60. *Required:* high school transcript, minimum 2 GPA. *Required for some:* essay or personal statement, interview.

Freshman Application Contact Mr. Michael Tang, Admission Officer, Northwestern Polytechnic University, 47671 Westinghouse Drive, Fremont, CA 94539. *Phone:* 510-592-9688 Ext. 15. *Fax:* 510-657-8975. *E-mail:* admission@npu.edu. *Web site:* http://www.npu.edu/.

Notre Dame de Namur University
Belmont, California

- **Independent Roman Catholic** comprehensive, founded 1851
- **Suburban** 50-acre campus with easy access to San Francisco
- **Endowment** $9.6 million
- **Coed** 1,002 undergraduate students, 64% full-time, 65% women, 35% men
- **Minimally difficult** entrance level, 73% of applicants were admitted

Undergraduates 638 full-time, 364 part-time. Students come from 24 states and territories; 22 other countries; 9% are from out of state; 8% Black or African American, non-Hispanic/Latino; 25% Hispanic/Latino; 10% Asian, non-Hispanic/Latino; 3% Native Hawaiian or other Pacific Islander, non-Hispanic/Latino; 0.9% American Indian or Alaska Native, non-Hispanic/Latino; 2% Two or more races, non-Hispanic/Latino; 15% Race/ethnicity unknown; 3%

international; 19% transferred in; 40% live on campus. *Retention:* 72% of full-time freshmen returned.

Freshmen *Admission:* 1,251 applied, 919 admitted, 146 enrolled. *Average high school GPA:* 2.91. *Test scores:* SAT critical reading scores over 500: 40%; SAT math scores over 500: 33%; SAT writing scores over 500: 41%; ACT scores over 18: 74%; SAT critical reading scores over 600: 4%; SAT math scores over 600: 9%; SAT writing scores over 600: 4%; ACT scores over 24: 6%.

Faculty *Total:* 192, 31% full-time. *Student/faculty ratio:* 12:1.

Academics *Calendar:* semesters. *Degrees:* bachelor's, master's, and post-bachelor's certificates. *Special study options:* academic remediation for entering students, accelerated degree program, adult/continuing education programs, advanced placement credit, cooperative education, double majors, English as a second language, independent study, internships, off-campus study, part-time degree program, services for LD students, student-designed majors, study abroad, summer session for credit.

Computers on Campus 80 computers/terminals and 10 ports are available on campus for general student use. Students can access the following: campus intranet, computer help desk, free student e-mail accounts, online (class) grades, online (class) registration, online (class) schedules. Campuswide network is available. Wireless service is available via classrooms, computer centers, computer labs, dorm rooms, learning centers, libraries, student centers.

Student Life *Housing:* on-campus residence required through sophomore year. *Options:* coed. Campus housing is university owned. Freshman campus housing is guaranteed. *Activities and organizations:* drama/theater group, student-run newspaper, choral group, Associated Students of Notre Dame de Namur University, BizCom, Rotaract, Students for Sustainability, International Club. *Campus security:* 24-hour emergency response devices and patrols, student patrols, late-night transport/escort service, controlled dormitory access. *Student services:* health clinic, personal/psychological counseling.

Athletics Member NCAA. All Division II. *Intercollegiate sports:* basketball M(s)/W(s), cross-country running M(s)/W(s), golf M(s), lacrosse M(s), soccer M(s)/W(s), softball W(s), tennis W(s), volleyball W(s).

Standardized Tests *Required:* SAT or ACT (for admission).

Costs (2011–12) *Comprehensive fee:* $41,660 includes full-time tuition ($29,610), mandatory fees ($370), and room and board ($11,680). Full-time tuition and fees vary according to degree level. Part-time tuition: $955 per unit. Part-time tuition and fees vary according to degree level and program. *Required fees:* $3 per unit part-time, $35 per term part-time. *College room only:* $7610. Room and board charges vary according to board plan and housing facility. *Payment plan:* installment. *Waivers:* senior citizens and employees or children of employees.

Financial Aid Of all full-time matriculated undergraduates who enrolled in 2009, 575 applied for aid, 548 were judged to have need, 19 had their need fully met. 90 Federal Work-Study jobs (averaging $1493). *Average percent of need met:* 57%. *Average financial aid package:* $21,607. *Average need-based loan:* $4839. *Average need-based gift aid:* $17,338. *Average indebtedness upon graduation:* $25,843.

Applying *Options:* electronic application, early admission, early action, deferred entrance. *Application fee:* $50. *Required:* essay or personal statement, high school transcript, audition is required for music programs. *Required for some:* interview. *Application deadlines:* rolling (freshmen), rolling (transfers). *Notification:* continuous (freshmen), continuous (transfers).

Freshman Application Contact Notre Dame de Namur University, 1500 Ralston Avenue, Belmont, CA 94002-1908. *Phone:* 650-508-3600. *Toll-free phone:* 800-263-0545. *Web site:* http://www.ndnu.edu/.

Occidental College
Los Angeles, California

- **Independent** comprehensive, founded 1887
- **Urban** 120-acre campus
- **Endowment** $273.8 million
- **Coed**
- **Very difficult** entrance level

Faculty *Student/faculty ratio:* 10:1.

Academics *Calendar:* semesters. *Degrees:* bachelor's and master's.

Student Life *Campus security:* 24-hour emergency response devices and patrols, late-night transport/escort service, controlled dormitory access, lighted pathways and sidewalks; whistle alert program.

Athletics Member NCAA. All Division III.

Standardized Tests *Required:* SAT or ACT (for admission). *Recommended:* SAT Subject Tests (for admission).

Costs (2010–11) *Comprehensive fee:* $52,299 includes full-time tuition ($39,870), mandatory fees ($1069), and room and board ($11,360). Part-time tuition: $1661 per credit. Part-time tuition and fees vary according to course load. *College room only:* $6460. Room and board charges vary according to board plan. *Payment plans:* tuition prepayment, installment.

Financial Aid *Of all full-time matriculated undergraduates who enrolled in 2009, 1,341 applied for aid, 1,169 were judged to have need, 1,162 had their need fully met. 789 Federal Work-Study jobs (averaging $2319). 168 state and other part-time jobs (averaging $3114). *In 2009,* 392 non-need-based awards were made. *Average percent of need met:* 100. *Average financial aid package:* $37,652. *Average need-based loan:* $6021. *Average need-based gift aid:* $30,766. *Average non-need-based aid:* $9772. *Average indebtedness upon graduation:* $25,549. *Financial aid deadline:* 2/1.

Applying *Options:* electronic application, early admission, early decision, deferred entrance. *Application fee:* $50. *Required:* essay or personal statement, high school transcript, 2 letters of recommendation. *Recommended:* interview.

Freshman Application Contact Mr. Vince Cuseo, Vice President of Admission and Financial Aid, Occidental College, 1600 Campus Road, Los Angeles, CA 90041. *Phone:* 323-259-2700. *Toll-free phone:* 800-825-5262. *Fax:* 323-341-4875. *E-mail:* admission@oxy.edu. *Web site:* http://www.oxy.edu/.

Otis College of Art and Design

Los Angeles, California

- **Independent** comprehensive, founded 1918
- **Urban** 5-acre campus
- **Coed** 1,158 undergraduate students, 99% full-time, 68% women, 32% men
- **Moderately difficult** entrance level, 50% of applicants were admitted

Undergraduates 1,145 full-time, 13 part-time. Students come from 24 states and territories; 8 other countries; 13% are from out of state; 4% Black or African American, non-Hispanic/Latino; 14% Hispanic/Latino; 32% Asian, non-Hispanic/Latino; 0.3% Native Hawaiian or other Pacific Islander, non-Hispanic/Latino; 0.7% American Indian or Alaska Native, non-Hispanic/Latino; 0.2% Two or more races, non-Hispanic/Latino; 10% Race/ethnicity unknown; 16% international; 13% transferred in; 9% live on campus. *Retention:* 87% of full-time freshmen returned.

Freshmen *Admission:* 1,554 applied, 777 admitted, 167 enrolled. *Average high school GPA:* 3.1. *Test scores:* ACT scores over 18: 86%; ACT scores over 24: 41%; ACT scores over 30: 1%.

Faculty *Total:* 326, 16% full-time, 18% with terminal degrees. *Student/faculty ratio:* 8:1.

Academics *Calendar:* semesters. *Degrees:* bachelor's and master's. *Special study options:* academic remediation for entering students, adult/continuing education programs, advanced placement credit, cooperative education, freshman honors college, honors programs, internships, off-campus study, study abroad, summer session for credit.

Computers on Campus 300 computers/terminals are available on campus for general student use. Students can access the following: campus intranet, computer help desk, free student e-mail accounts, online (class) grades, online (class) registration, online (class) schedules. Campuswide network is available. Wireless service is available via entire campus.

Student Life *Housing options:* Campus housing is provided by a third party. Freshman applicants given priority for college housing. *Activities and organizations:* Student Government Association, international students organization, Otis Students in Service (OASIS), Literary Magazine Club, Campus Crusade. *Campus security:* 24-hour patrols. *Student services:* personal/psychological counseling.

Athletics *Intramural sports:* skiing (downhill) W, soccer M.

Standardized Tests *Required:* SAT or ACT (for admission).

Costs (2011–12) *Tuition:* $34,454 full-time, $1149 per unit part-time. *Required fees:* $900 full-time. *Payment plan:* installment. *Waivers:* employees or children of employees.

Financial Aid Of all full-time matriculated undergraduates who enrolled in 2009, 923 applied for aid, 762 were judged to have need, 30 had their need fully met. 185 Federal Work-Study jobs (averaging $969). 12 state and other part-time jobs (averaging $608). In 2009, 159 non-need-based awards were made. *Average percent of need met:* 52%. *Average financial aid package:* $21,146. *Average need-based loan:* $4715. *Average need-based gift aid:* $15,903. *Average non-need-based aid:* $6432. *Average indebtedness upon graduation:* $27,903.

Applying *Options:* electronic application, early admission. *Application fee:* $50. *Required:* essay or personal statement, high school transcript, minimum 2.5 GPA, portfolio. *Recommended:* interview. *Application deadlines:* rolling (freshmen), rolling (transfers). *Notification:* continuous (freshmen), continuous (transfers).

Freshman Application Contact Otis College of Art and Design, 9045 Lincoln Boulevard, Los Angeles, CA 90045-9785. *Phone:* 310-665-6820. *Toll-free phone:* 800-527-OTIS. *Web site:* http://www.otis.edu/.

Pacific Oaks College

Pasadena, California

- **Independent** upper-level, founded 1945, part of The Chicago School Education System
- **Small-town** 2-acre campus with easy access to Los Angeles, San Gabriel Valley
- **Endowment** $7.3 million
- **Coed, primarily women** 257 undergraduate students, 7% full-time, 96% women, 4% men
- 77% of applicants were admitted

Undergraduates 17 full-time, 240 part-time. 21% transferred in.

Freshmen *Admission:* 339 applied, 262 admitted.

Faculty *Total:* 125, 22% full-time. *Student/faculty ratio:* 22:1.

Academics *Calendar:* semesters summer sessions and 2 intensive sessions. *Degrees:* certificates, bachelor's, master's, and post-master's certificates. *Special study options:* adult/continuing education programs, distance learning, independent study, internships, off-campus study, part-time degree program, summer session for credit.

Computers on Campus 25 computers/terminals are available on campus for general student use. Students can access the following: online class listings. Campuswide network is available.

Student Life *Housing:* college housing not available. *Activities and organizations:* Latina/o Support Group, Student Empowerment Group, Teacher Education Student Association, Marriage, Family Therapy Student Association.

Costs (2010–11) *Tuition:* $21,864 full-time, $911 per unit part-time. Full-time tuition and fees vary according to course load. Part-time tuition and fees vary according to course load. *Required fees:* $200 full-time, $100 per term part-time. *Payment plan:* installment. *Waivers:* employees or children of employees.

Financial Aid Of all full-time matriculated undergraduates who enrolled in 2006, 11 Federal Work-Study jobs (averaging $5000).

Applying *Options:* electronic application, deferred entrance. *Application fee:* $55. *Application deadline:* 6/1 (transfers). *Notification:* continuous until 9/1 (transfers).

Application Contact Ms. Augusta Pickens, Office of Admissions, Pacific Oaks College, 5 Westmoreland Place, Pasadena, CA 91103. *Phone:* 626-397-1349. *Toll-free phone:* 800-684-0900. *Fax:* 626-666-1220. *E-mail:* admissions@pacificoaks.edu. *Web site:* http://www.pacificoaks.edu/.

Pacific States University

Los Angeles, California

- **Independent** comprehensive, founded 1928
- **Urban** 1-acre campus
- **Coed** 50 undergraduate students, 100% full-time, 40% women, 60% men
- **Noncompetitive** entrance level, 67% of applicants were admitted

Undergraduates 50 full-time. Students come from 7 other countries; 78% are from out of state; 2% Black or African American, non-Hispanic/Latino; 14% Asian, non-Hispanic/Latino; 6% Race/ethnicity unknown; 78% international; 16% transferred in.

Freshmen *Admission:* 72 applied, 48 admitted, 2 enrolled.

Faculty *Total:* 31, 26% full-time, 42% with terminal degrees. *Student/faculty ratio:* 13:1.

Academics *Calendar:* quarters. *Degrees:* bachelor's, master's, doctoral-research/scholarship, and postbachelor's certificates. *Special study options:* academic remediation for entering students, accelerated degree program, adult/continuing education programs, distance learning, double majors, English as a second language, independent study.

Computers on Campus 50 computers/terminals are available on campus for general student use. Students can access the following: online (class) schedules. Campuswide network is available. 90% of college-owned or -operated housing units are wired for high-speed Internet access. Wireless service is available via classrooms, computer labs, dorm rooms, libraries, student centers.

Student Life *Housing options:* coed. Campus housing is university owned. *Campus security:* patrols by trained security personnel during campus hours.

Standardized Tests *Required for some:* TOEFL or IELTS. *Recommended:* SAT or ACT (for admission).

Costs (2011–12) *Tuition:* $14,055 full-time. Full-time tuition and fees vary according to course load. Part-time tuition and fees vary according to course load and program. No tuition increase for student's term of enrollment. *Required fees:* $600 full-time. *Room only:* $7200. Room and board charges vary according to housing facility. *Payment plan:* installment. *Waivers:* employees or children of employees.

Applying *Options:* electronic application, deferred entrance. *Application fee:* $100. *Required:* high school transcript, minimum 2.5 GPA, proof of English proficiency. *Application deadlines:* rolling (freshmen), rolling (out-of-state freshmen), rolling (transfers). *Notification:* continuous (freshmen), continuous (out-of-state freshmen), continuous (transfers).

Freshman Application Contact Miss Michelle Sinfuego, Student Service Advisor, Pacific States University, 3450 Wilshire Bjoulevard, #500, Los Angeles, CA 90010. *Phone:* 323-731-2383 Ext. 200. *Toll-free phone:* 888-200-0383. *Fax:* 323-731-7276. *E-mail:* info@psuca.edu. *Web site:* http://www.psuca.edu/.

Pacific Union College
Angwin, California

- **Independent Seventh-day Adventist** comprehensive, founded 1882
- **Rural** 200-acre campus with easy access to San Francisco Bay Area
- **Endowment** $19.3 million
- **Coed** 1,527 undergraduate students, 93% full-time, 56% women, 44% men
- **Moderately difficult** entrance level

Undergraduates 1,417 full-time, 110 part-time. Students come from 39 states and territories; 23 other countries; 14% are from out of state; 6% Black or African American, non-Hispanic/Latino; 22% Hispanic/Latino; 20% Asian, non-Hispanic/Latino; 0.7% Native Hawaiian or other Pacific Islander, non-Hispanic/Latino; 1% American Indian or Alaska Native, non-Hispanic/Latino; 5% Two or more races, non-Hispanic/Latino; 8% Race/ethnicity unknown; 5% international; 8% transferred in; 70% live on campus. *Retention:* 70% of full-time freshmen returned.

Freshmen *Admission:* 1,795 applied, 281 enrolled. *Average high school GPA:* 3.31. *Test scores:* SAT critical reading scores over 500: 57%; SAT math scores over 500: 55%; ACT scores over 18: 78%; SAT critical reading scores over 600: 20%; SAT math scores over 600: 22%; ACT scores over 24: 43%; SAT critical reading scores over 700: 3%; SAT math scores over 700: 4%; ACT scores over 30: 7%.

Faculty *Total:* 97, 89% full-time, 49% with terminal degrees. *Student/faculty ratio:* 16:1.

Academics *Calendar:* quarters. *Degrees:* associate, bachelor's, and master's. *Special study options:* academic remediation for entering students, adult/continuing education programs, advanced placement credit, cooperative education, distance learning, double majors, honors programs, independent study, internships, off-campus study, part-time degree program, services for LD students, study abroad, summer session for credit.

Computers on Campus 150 computers/terminals and 1,200 ports are available on campus for general student use. Students can access the following: campus intranet, computer help desk, free student e-mail accounts, online (class) grades, online (class) registration, online (class) schedules, student financial information. Campuswide network is available. 100% of college-owned or -operated housing units are wired for high-speed Internet access. Wireless service is available via computer centers, computer labs, learning centers, libraries, student centers.

Student Life *Housing:* on-campus residence required through senior year. *Options:* men-only, women-only. Campus housing is university owned. *Activities and organizations:* drama/theater group, student-run newspaper, choral group, Student Association, Business Club, Asian Student Association, Korean Adventist Student Association, Student Organization of Latinos. *Campus security:* 24-hour emergency response devices and patrols, late-night transport/escort service. *Student services:* health clinic, personal/psychological counseling.

Athletics Member NAIA. *Intercollegiate sports:* basketball M/W, cross-country running M/W, soccer M, volleyball W. *Intramural sports:* badminton M/W, baseball M/W, basketball M/W, cross-country running M/W, football M/W, golf M/W, soccer M/W, softball M/W, tennis M/W, volleyball M/W.

Standardized Tests *Required:* SAT or ACT (for admission).

Costs (2011–12) *Comprehensive fee:* $33,240 includes full-time tuition ($25,740), mandatory fees ($225), and room and board ($7275). Full-time tuition and fees vary according to course load. Part-time tuition: $725 per quarter hour. Part-time tuition and fees vary according to course load. No tuition increase for student's term of enrollment. *Required fees:* $75 per term part-time. *College room only:* $4260. *Payment plan:* installment. *Waivers:* senior citizens and employees or children of employees.

Financial Aid Of all full-time matriculated undergraduates who enrolled in 2009, 1,127 applied for aid, 841 were judged to have need, 17 had their need fully met. 158 Federal Work-Study jobs (averaging $2632). In 2009, 305 non-need-based awards were made. *Average percent of need met:* 44%. *Average financial aid package:* $20,000. *Average need-based loan:* $3834. *Average need-based gift aid:* $17,500. *Average non-need-based aid:* $3015. *Average indebtedness upon graduation:* $21,000.

Applying *Options:* electronic application, deferred entrance. *Application fee:* $30. *Required:* high school transcript, minimum 2.3 GPA, 3 letters of recommendation. *Application deadlines:* rolling (freshmen), rolling (transfers).

Freshman Application Contact Mr. Craig Philpott, Associate Director, Admissions, Pacific Union College, Enrollment Services, One Angwin Avenue, Angwin, CA 94508. *Phone:* 800-862-7080. *Toll-free phone:* 800-

862-7080. *Fax:* 707-965-6432. *E-mail:* enroll@puc.edu. *Web site:* http://www.puc.edu/.

Patten University
Oakland, California

- **Independent interdenominational** comprehensive, founded 1944
- **Urban** 5-acre campus with easy access to San Francisco
- **Endowment** $1.3 million
- **Coed**
- **Noncompetitive** entrance level

Faculty *Student/faculty ratio:* 17:1.

Academics *Calendar:* semesters. *Degrees:* certificates, associate, bachelor's, master's, and postbachelor's certificates.

Student Life *Campus security:* 24-hour emergency response devices, student patrols, late-night transport/escort service.

Athletics Member NAIA.

Standardized Tests *Required:* SAT or ACT (for admission).

Costs (2010–11) *Comprehensive fee:* $20,820 includes full-time tuition ($13,440) and room and board ($7380). Full-time tuition and fees vary according to course load. Part-time tuition: $560 per unit.

Applying *Options:* early admission, deferred entrance. *Application fee:* $30. *Required:* essay or personal statement, high school transcript, minimum 2.5 GPA, 2 letters of recommendation. *Recommended:* interview.

Freshman Application Contact Ms. Kim Guerra, Director of Admissions, Patten University, 2433 Coolidge Avenue, Oakland, CA 94601-2699. *Phone:* 510-261-8500 Ext. 7763. *Fax:* 510-534-4344. *Web site:* http://www.patten.edu/.

Pepperdine University
Malibu, California

- **Independent** university, founded 1937, affiliated with Church of Christ
- **Suburban** 830-acre campus with easy access to Los Angeles
- **Endowment** $551.9 million
- **Coed** 3,447 undergraduate students, 88% full-time, 54% women, 46% men
- **Very difficult** entrance level

Undergraduates 3,019 full-time, 428 part-time. Students come from 50 states and territories; 65 other countries; 40% are from out of state; 7% Black or African American, non-Hispanic/Latino; 13% Hispanic/Latino; 10% Asian, non-Hispanic/Latino; 1% Native Hawaiian or other Pacific Islander, non-Hispanic/Latino; 1% American Indian or Alaska Native, non-Hispanic/Latino; 2% Two or more races, non-Hispanic/Latino; 7% Race/ethnicity unknown; 6% international; 2% transferred in; 58% live on campus. *Retention:* 89% of full-time freshmen returned.

Freshmen *Admission:* 7,949 applied, 628 enrolled. *Average high school GPA:* 3.65. *Test scores:* SAT critical reading scores over 500: 92%; SAT math scores over 500: 92%; SAT writing scores over 500: 91%; ACT scores over 18: 100%; SAT critical reading scores over 600: 57%; SAT math scores over 600: 62%; SAT writing scores over 600: 56%; ACT scores over 24: 87%; SAT critical reading scores over 700: 16%; SAT math scores over 700: 19%; SAT writing scores over 700: 14%; ACT scores over 30: 29%.

Faculty *Total:* 690, 54% full-time, 77% with terminal degrees. *Student/faculty ratio:* 13:1.

Academics *Calendar:* semesters. *Degrees:* certificates, bachelor's, master's, doctoral-professional, and doctoral-research/scholarship. *Special study options:* advanced placement credit, double majors, honors programs, independent study, internships, student-designed majors, study abroad, summer session for credit. *ROTC:* Army (c), Air Force (c). *Unusual degree programs:* 3-2 business administration; engineering with University of Southern California, Washington University in St. Louis.

Computers on Campus 292 computers/terminals are available on campus for general student use. Students can access the following: campus intranet, computer help desk, free student e-mail accounts, online (class) grades, online (class) registration, online (class) schedules. Campuswide network is available. 100% of college-owned or -operated housing units are wired for high-speed Internet access. Wireless service is available via entire campus.

Student Life *Housing:* on-campus residence required through sophomore year. *Options:* men-only, women-only, disabled students. Campus housing is university owned. Freshman campus housing is guaranteed. *Activities and organizations:* drama/theater group, student-run newspaper, radio and television station, choral group, Latino Student Association, Black Student Union, Panhellenic Council, Interfraternity Council, International Justice Mission, national fraternities, national sororities. *Campus security:* 24-hour emergency response devices and patrols, student patrols, late-night transport/escort service, front gate security, 24-hour security in residence halls, controlled access, crime prevention programs. *Student services:* health clinic, personal/psychological counseling.

Athletics Member NCAA. All Division I. *Intercollegiate sports:* baseball M(s), basketball M(s)/W(s), cheerleading M/W, crew M(c)/W(c), cross-country running M(s)/W(s), field hockey W(c), golf M(s)/W(s), lacrosse M(c), rugby M(c), sailing M(c)/W(c), soccer M(c)/W(s), swimming and diving W(s), tennis M(s)/W(s), volleyball M(s)/W(s), water polo M(s)/W(c). *Intramural sports:* badminton M/W, basketball M/W, cross-country running M/W, football M/W, golf M/W, lacrosse M, soccer M/W, softball M/W, swimming and diving M/W, tennis M/W, volleyball M/W.

Standardized Tests *Required:* SAT or ACT (for admission).

Costs (2010–11) *Comprehensive fee:* $50,470 includes full-time tuition ($38,960), mandatory fees ($120), and room and board ($11,390). Part-time tuition: $1210 per credit hour. *College room only:* $8760. Room and board charges vary according to board plan and housing facility. *Payment plan:* installment. *Waivers:* employees or children of employees.

Financial Aid Of all full-time matriculated undergraduates who enrolled in 2009, 1,816 applied for aid, 1,481 were judged to have need, 337 had their need fully met. In 2009, 249 non-need-based awards were made. *Average percent of need met:* 75%. *Average financial aid package:* $33,248. *Average need-based loan:* $4437. *Average need-based gift aid:* $30,089. *Average non-need-based aid:* $20,522. *Average indebtedness upon graduation:* $35,747. *Financial aid deadline:* 2/15.

Applying *Options:* electronic application. *Application fee:* $65. *Required:* essay or personal statement, high school transcript, 2 letters of recommendation. *Application deadlines:* 1/15 (freshmen), 1/15 (out-of-state freshmen), 1/15 (transfers). *Notification:* 4/1 (freshmen), 4/1 (out-of-state freshmen), 4/1 (transfers).

Freshman Application Contact Mrs. Kristin Collins, Director of Admission, Admission, Enrollment Management, Seaver College, Pepperdine University, 24255 Pacific Coast Highway, Malibu, CA 90263. *Phone:* 310-506-4116. *E-mail:* kristy.collins@pepperdine.edu. *Web site:* http://www.pepperdine.edu/.

Perelandra College
La Mesa, California

- **Independent religious** comprehensive
- **Suburban** campus
- **Coed** 2 undergraduate students, 50% women, 50% men
- **Minimally difficult** entrance level

Undergraduates 2 part-time. Students come from 1 other country; 80% are from out of state; 100% Race/ethnicity unknown; 100% transferred in. *Retention:* 100% of full-time freshmen returned.

Freshmen *Admission:* 2 applied. *Average high school GPA:* 2.8.

Faculty *Total:* 11, 73% with terminal degrees. *Student/faculty ratio:* 3:1.

Academics *Degrees:* diplomas, bachelor's, and master's. *Special study options:* accelerated degree program, adult/continuing education programs, advanced placement credit, distance learning, external degree program, independent study, off-campus study, part-time degree program, services for LD students, summer session for credit.

Computers on Campus Students can access the following: computer help desk, free student e-mail accounts, online (class) grades, online (class) registration.

Student Life *Housing:* college housing not available. *Student services:* personal/psychological counseling.

Costs (2011–12) *Tuition:* $200 per credit part-time. No tuition increase for student's term of enrollment. *Payment plans:* tuition prepayment, installment. *Waivers:* employees or children of employees.

Applying *Options:* electronic application. *Application fee:* $50. *Required:* essay or personal statement, minimum 2.5 GPA, 2 letters of recommendation, letter of intent. *Required for some:* high school transcript. *Notification:* continuous (freshmen), continuous (out-of-state freshmen), continuous (transfers).

Freshman Application Contact Perelandra College, 8697-C La Mesa Boulevard, PMB 21, La Mesa, CA 91941. *Phone:* 619-335-0441. *Web site:* http://www.perelandra.edu/.

Pima Medical Institute
Chula Vista, California

- **Proprietary** primarily 2-year, founded 1998, administratively affiliated with Vocational Training Institutes, Inc.
- **Urban** campus
- **Coed** 813 undergraduate students
- **Minimally difficult** entrance level

Academics *Calendar:* modular. *Degrees:* certificates, associate, and bachelor's. *Special study options:* cooperative education, distance learning, internships.

Student Life *Housing:* college housing not available.

Standardized Tests *Required:* Wonderlic Scholastic Level Exam (for admission).

Applying *Required:* high school transcript, interview.

Freshman Application Contact Admissions Office, Pima Medical Institute, 780 Bay Boulevard, Suite 101, Chula Vista, CA 91910. *Phone:* 619-425-3200. *Toll-free phone:* 888-898-9048. *Web site:* http://www.pmi.edu/.

Pitzer College
Claremont, California

- **Independent** 4-year, founded 1963, part of The Claremont Colleges Consortium
- **Suburban** 35-acre campus with easy access to Los Angeles
- **Coed** 1,080 undergraduate students, 96% full-time, 60% women, 40% men
- **Moderately difficult** entrance level, 26% of applicants were admitted

Undergraduates 1,033 full-time, 47 part-time. 53% are from out of state; 6% Black or African American, non-Hispanic/Latino; 15% Hispanic/Latino; 9% Asian, non-Hispanic/Latino; 0.7% American Indian or Alaska Native, non-Hispanic/Latino; 26% Race/ethnicity unknown; 3% international; 1% transferred in; 74% live on campus. *Retention:* 94% of full-time freshmen returned.

Freshmen *Admission:* 3,812 applied, 978 admitted, 268 enrolled. *Average high school GPA:* 3.83.

Faculty *Total:* 105, 75% full-time, 98% with terminal degrees. *Student/faculty ratio:* 11:1.

Academics *Calendar:* semesters. *Degree:* bachelor's. *Special study options:* adult/continuing education programs, advanced placement credit, cooperative education, double majors, English as a second language, honors programs, independent study, internships, off-campus study, part-time degree program, services for LD students, student-designed majors, study abroad, summer session for credit. *ROTC:* Army (c), Air Force (c). *Unusual degree programs:* 3-2 business administration; public administration, mathematics, psychology with Claremont Graduate University.

Computers on Campus 100 computers/terminals are available on campus for general student use. Students can access the following: campus intranet, computer help desk, free student e-mail accounts, online (class) grades, online (class) registration, online (class) schedules. Campuswide network is available. 100% of college-owned or -operated housing units are wired for high-speed Internet access. Wireless service is available via entire campus.

Student Life *Housing:* on-campus residence required for freshman year. *Options:* coed, women-only, cooperative, disabled students. Campus housing is university owned. Freshman campus housing is guaranteed. *Activities and organizations:* drama/theater group, student-run newspaper, radio station, choral group, Student Senate, The Other Side, Without A Box, Residence Hall Association. *Campus security:* 24-hour emergency response devices and patrols, late-night transport/escort service, controlled dormitory access. *Student services:* health clinic, personal/psychological counseling, women's center.

Athletics Member NCAA. All Division III. *Intercollegiate sports:* baseball M, basketball M/W, cross-country running M/W, football M, golf M, lacrosse W, soccer M/W, softball W, swimming and diving M/W, tennis M/W, track and field M/W, volleyball M/W, water polo M/W. *Intramural sports:* badminton M/W, baseball M, basketball M/W, fencing M(c)/W(c), football M, lacrosse M(c)/W(c), rugby M(c), sailing M(c)/W(c), skiing (downhill) M(c)/W(c), soccer M/W, softball W, tennis M/W, track and field M/W, ultimate Frisbee M/W, volleyball M(c)/W, water polo M(c)/W(c).

Standardized Tests *Required for some:* SAT or ACT (for admission).

Costs (2011–12) *Comprehensive fee:* $53,080 includes full-time tuition ($37,520), mandatory fees ($3610), and room and board ($11,950). Full-time tuition and fees vary according to course load. Part-time tuition: $5108 per course. Part-time tuition and fees vary according to course load. *College room only:* $7540. Room and board charges vary according to board plan. *Payment plans:* installment, deferred payment. *Waivers:* employees or children of employees.

Financial Aid Of all full-time matriculated undergraduates who enrolled in 2009, 482 applied for aid, 418 were judged to have need, 418 had their need fully met. 368 Federal Work-Study jobs (averaging $2463). In 2009, 43 non-need-based awards were made. *Average percent of need met:* 100%. *Average financial aid package:* $38,235. *Average need-based loan:* $3916. *Average need-based gift aid:* $33,155. *Average non-need-based aid:* $4942. *Average indebtedness upon graduation:* $20,089. *Financial aid deadline:* 2/1.

Applying *Options:* electronic application, early decision, deferred entrance. *Application fee:* $60. *Required:* essay or personal statement, high school transcript, minimum 2 GPA, 3 letters of recommendation. *Recommended:* interview. *Application deadlines:* 1/1 (freshmen), 4/15 (transfers). *Early decision deadline:* 11/15. *Notification:* 4/1 (freshmen), 5/15 (transfers), 1/1 (early decision).

Freshman Application Contact Angel Perez, Director of Admission, Pitzer College, 1050 North Mills Avenue, Claremont, CA 91711-6101. *Phone:* 909-621-8129. *Toll-free phone:* 800-748-9371. *Fax:* 909-621-8770. *E-mail:* admission@pitzer.edu. *Web site:* http://www.pitzer.edu/.

See page 118 for Display. See page 1504 for the College Close-Up.

Platt College

Huntington Beach, California

Director of Admissions Ms. Lisa Rhodes, President, Platt College, 7755 Center Avenue, Suite 600, Huntington Beach, CA 92647. *Phone:* 949-833-2300 Ext. 222. *Toll-free phone:* 888-866-6697 Ext. 230. *Web site:* http://www.plattcollege.edu/.

Platt College

Ontario, California

Director of Admissions Ms. Jennifer Abandonato, Director of Admissions, Platt College, 3700 Inland Empire Boulevard, Suite 400, Ontario, CA 91764. *Phone:* 909-941-9410. *Toll-free phone:* 888-866-6697. *Web site:* http://www.plattcollege.edu/.

Platt College–Los Angeles

Alhambra, California

Director of Admissions Mr. Detroit Whiteside, Director of Admissions, Platt College–Los Angeles, 1000 South Fremont A9W, Alhambra, CA 91803. *Phone:* 323-258-8050. *Toll-free phone:* 888-866-6697. *Web site:* http://www.plattcollege.edu/.

Platt College San Diego

San Diego, California

- **Proprietary** 4-year, founded 1879
- **Suburban** 1-acre campus
- **Coed**

Faculty *Student/faculty ratio:* 21:1.

Academics *Calendar:* continuous. *Degrees:* certificates, diplomas, associate, and bachelor's.

Student Life *Campus security:* 24-hour emergency response devices, surveillance cameras, security guard for evening session.

Standardized Tests *Required:* Wonderlic aptitude test (for admission). *Recommended:* SAT or ACT (for admission), SAT and SAT Subject Tests or ACT (for admission), SAT Subject Tests (for admission).

Costs (2010–11) *One-time required fee:* $110. *Tuition:* $25,040 full-time.

Applying *Options:* early admission, deferred entrance. *Application fee:* $110. *Required:* essay or personal statement, high school transcript, interview.

Freshman Application Contact Mr. Steve Gallup, Admissions Representative, Platt College San Diego, 6250 El Cajon Boulevard, San Diego, CA 92115-3919. *Phone:* 619-265-0107. *Toll-free phone:* 866-752-8826. *Fax:* 619-265-8655. *E-mail:* sgallup@platt.edu. *Web site:* http://www.platt.edu/.

Point Loma Nazarene University

San Diego, California

- **Independent Nazarene** comprehensive, founded 1902
- **Suburban** 93-acre campus with easy access to San Diego
- **Coed**
- **Moderately difficult** entrance level

Academics *Calendar:* semesters. *Degrees:* bachelor's, master's, and post-master's certificates.

Student Life *Campus security:* 24-hour patrols, student patrols, late-night transport/escort service.

Athletics Member NAIA.

Standardized Tests *Required:* SAT or ACT (for admission). *Recommended:* SAT (for admission).

Costs (2010–11) *Comprehensive fee:* $36,100 includes full-time tuition ($26,500), mandatory fees ($600), and room and board ($9000). Full-time tuition and fees vary according to course load. Part-time tuition: $1105 per credit hour. Part-time tuition and fees vary according to course load. *College room only:* $5000. Room and board charges vary according to board plan.

Financial Aid *Of all full-time matriculated undergraduates who enrolled in 2009,* 1,478 applied for aid, 1,423 were judged to have need, 265 had their need fully met. *In 2009,* 412 non-need-based awards were made. *Average percent of need met:* 68. *Average financial aid package:* $18,695. *Average need-based loan:* $5785. *Average need-based gift aid:* $13,258. *Average non-need-based aid:* $6256. *Average indebtedness upon graduation:* $29,491.

Applying *Options:* electronic application, early action. *Application fee:* $50. *Required:* essay or personal statement, high school transcript, minimum 2.8 GPA, 2 letters of recommendation, interview.
Freshman Application Contact Eric Groves, Director of Admissions, Point Loma Nazarene University, 3900 Lomaland Drive, San Diego, CA 92106. *Phone:* 619-849-2273. *Toll-free phone:* 800-733-7770. *Fax:* 619-849-2601. *E-mail:* admissions@pointloma.edu. *Web site:* http://www.pointloma.edu/.

Pomona College
Claremont, California

- **Independent** 4-year, founded 1887
- **Suburban** 140-acre campus with easy access to Los Angeles
- **Endowment** $1.5 billion
- **Coed** 1,560 undergraduate students, 99% full-time, 51% women, 49% men
- **Most difficult** entrance level, 15% of applicants were admitted

Undergraduates 1,549 full-time, 11 part-time. Students come from 49 states and territories; 21 other countries; 68% are from out of state; 7% Black or African American, non-Hispanic/Latino; 12% Hispanic/Latino; 11% Asian, non-Hispanic/Latino; 0.1% American Indian or Alaska Native, non-Hispanic/Latino; 5% Two or more races, non-Hispanic/Latino; 15% Race/ethnicity unknown; 4% international; 0.6% transferred in; 98% live on campus. *Retention:* 97% of full-time freshmen returned.
Freshmen *Admission:* 6,764 applied, 997 admitted, 401 enrolled. *Test scores:* SAT critical reading scores over 500: 100%; SAT math scores over 500: 101%; SAT writing scores over 500: 100%; ACT scores over 18: 99%; SAT critical reading scores over 600: 94%; SAT math scores over 600: 96%; SAT writing scores over 600: 94%; ACT scores over 24: 98%; SAT critical reading scores over 700: 69%; SAT math scores over 700: 77%; SAT writing scores over 700: 69%; ACT scores over 30: 80%.
Faculty *Total:* 226, 85% full-time, 93% with terminal degrees. *Student/faculty ratio:* 7:1.
Academics *Calendar:* semesters. *Degree:* bachelor's. *Special study options:* advanced placement credit, double majors, independent study, internships, off-campus study, services for LD students, student-designed majors, study abroad. *ROTC:* Army (c), Air Force (c). *Unusual degree programs:* 3-2 engineering with California Institute of Technology, Washington University in St. Louis.
Computers on Campus 180 computers/terminals are available on campus for general student use. Students can access the following: computer help desk, free student e-mail accounts, online (class) grades, online (class) schedules. Campuswide network is available. 100% of college-owned or -operated housing units are wired for high-speed Internet access. Wireless service is available via entire campus.
Student Life *Housing:* on-campus residence required for freshman year. *Options:* coed. Campus housing is university owned. Freshman campus housing is guaranteed. *Activities and organizations:* drama/theater group, student-run newspaper, radio and television station, choral group, student government, music/choral organizations, service organizations, intramural sports, outdoor activities club. *Campus security:* 24-hour emergency response devices and patrols, late-night transport/escort service, controlled dormitory access. *Student services:* health clinic, personal/psychological counseling, women's center.
Athletics Member NCAA. All Division III. *Intercollegiate sports:* baseball M, basketball M/W, cross-country running M/W, football M, golf M/W, lacrosse W, soccer M/W, softball W, swimming and diving M/W, tennis M/W, track and field M/W, ultimate Frisbee M(c)/W(c), volleyball M(c)/W, water polo M/W. *Intramural sports:* badminton M(c)/W(c), basketball M/W, crew W(c), cross-country running M/W, equestrian sports M(c)/W(c), fencing M/W, field hockey M(c)/W(c), football M, golf M/W, lacrosse M(c), racquetball M/W, rock climbing M/W, skiing (cross-country) M(c)/W(c), skiing (downhill) M(c)/W(c), soccer M/W, softball M/W, squash M/W, swimming and diving M/W, tennis M/W, track and field M/W, ultimate Frisbee M, volleyball M/W, water polo M/W.
Standardized Tests *Required:* SAT and SAT Subject Tests or ACT (for admission).
Costs (2011–12) *Comprehensive fee:* $53,110 includes full-time tuition ($39,572), mandatory fees ($311), and room and board ($13,227). *Room and board:* Room and board charges vary according to board plan. *Payment plan:* installment. *Waivers:* employees or children of employees.
Financial Aid Of all full-time matriculated undergraduates who enrolled in 2009, 924 applied for aid, 837 were judged to have need, 837 had their need fully met. 210 Federal Work-Study jobs (averaging $1100). 612 state and other part-time jobs (averaging $1700). *Average percent of need met:* 100%. *Average financial aid package:* $37,621. *Average need-based gift aid:* $35,615. *Average indebtedness upon graduation:* $9700. *Financial aid deadline:* 2/1.
Applying *Options:* electronic application, early admission, early decision, deferred entrance. *Application fee:* $65. *Required:* essay or personal statement, high school transcript, 2 letters of recommendation. *Recommended:*

interview, Supplemental forms for visual and performing arts, athletics, and science research are available. *Application deadlines:* 1/2 (freshmen), 3/15 (transfers). *Early decision deadline:* 11/1 (for plan 1), 12/28 (for plan 2). *Notification:* 4/1 (freshmen), 5/15 (transfers), 12/15 (early decision plan 1), 2/15 (early decision plan 2).
Freshman Application Contact Mr. Art D. Rodriguez AIA, Acting Dean of Admissions, Pomona College, 333 North College Way, Claremont, CA 91711. *Phone:* 909-621-8134. *Fax:* 909-621-8952. *E-mail:* admissions@pomona.edu. *Web site:* http://www.pomona.edu/.

Saint Mary's College of California
Moraga, California

- **Independent Roman Catholic** comprehensive, founded 1863
- **Suburban** 420-acre campus with easy access to San Francisco
- **Endowment** $111.4 million
- **Coed** 2,799 undergraduate students, 91% full-time, 61% women, 39% men
- **Moderately difficult** entrance level, 78% of applicants were admitted

Undergraduates 2,561 full-time, 238 part-time. Students come from 39 states and territories; 27 other countries; 12% are from out of state; 5% Black or African American, non-Hispanic/Latino; 22% Hispanic/Latino; 10% Asian, non-Hispanic/Latino; 0.3% Native Hawaiian or other Pacific Islander, non-Hispanic/Latino; 1% American Indian or Alaska Native, non-Hispanic/Latino; 2% Two or more races, non-Hispanic/Latino; 11% Race/ethnicity unknown; 2% international; 8% transferred in; 59% live on campus. *Retention:* 86% of full-time freshmen returned.
Freshmen *Admission:* 3,730 applied, 2,928 admitted, 695 enrolled. *Average high school GPA:* 3.42. *Test scores:* SAT critical reading scores over 500: 69%; SAT math scores over 500: 73%; ACT scores over 18: 97%; SAT critical reading scores over 600: 25%; SAT math scores over 600: 27%; ACT scores over 24: 54%; SAT critical reading scores over 700: 4%; SAT math scores over 700: 4%; ACT scores over 30: 7%.
Faculty *Total:* 460, 41% full-time, 94% with terminal degrees. *Student/faculty ratio:* 13:1.
Academics *Calendar:* 4-1-4. *Degrees:* associate, bachelor's, master's, and doctoral-professional. *Special study options:* adult/continuing education programs, advanced placement credit, double majors, honors programs, independent study, internships, off-campus study, part-time degree program, services for LD students, student-designed majors, study abroad, summer session for credit. *ROTC:* Army (c), Air Force (c). *Unusual degree programs:* 3-2 engineering with Washington University in St. Louis, University of Southern California, Boston University.
Computers on Campus 325 computers/terminals and 1,800 ports are available on campus for general student use. Students can access the following: campus intranet, computer help desk, free student e-mail accounts, online (class) grades, online (class) registration, online (class) schedules, student accounts. Campuswide network is available. 100% of college-owned or -operated housing units are wired for high-speed Internet access. Wireless service is available via classrooms, computer centers, computer labs, learning centers, libraries, student centers.
Student Life *Housing:* on-campus residence required for freshman year. *Options:* coed, men-only, women-only, disabled students. Campus housing is university owned. Freshman campus housing is guaranteed. *Activities and organizations:* drama/theater group, student-run newspaper, radio and television station, choral group, Gael Force, Student Alumni Association, LASA-Latin American Student Association-Black Student Union, Inter-Varsity Christian Fellowship, Asian Pacific America Student Association. *Campus security:* 24-hour emergency response devices and patrols, late-night transport/escort service. *Student services:* health clinic, personal/psychological counseling, women's center.
Athletics Member NCAA. All Division I. *Intercollegiate sports:* baseball M(s), basketball M(s)/W(s), crew M(c)/W, cross-country running M(s)/W(s), golf M(s), lacrosse M(c)/W, rugby M(c)/W(c), soccer M(s)/W(s), softball W(s), tennis M(s)/W(s), volleyball M(c)/W(s), water polo M(c)/W(c). *Intramural sports:* badminton M/W, basketball M/W, bowling M/W, crew M, cross-country running M/W, football M/W, golf M/W, rock climbing M/W, skiing (cross-country) M/W, soccer M(c)/W, softball W, swimming and diving M/W, table tennis M/W, ultimate Frisbee M/W, volleyball M/W(c).
Standardized Tests *Required:* SAT or ACT (for admission).
Costs (2010–11) *Comprehensive fee:* $47,780 includes full-time tuition ($35,280), mandatory fees ($150), and room and board ($12,350). Part-time tuition: $4412 per course. Part-time tuition and fees vary according to program. *College room only:* $6770. Room and board charges vary according to board plan and housing facility. *Payment plan:* installment. *Waivers:* employees or children of employees.
Financial Aid Of all full-time matriculated undergraduates who enrolled in 2009, 1,921 applied for aid, 1,840 were judged to have need, 116 had their need fully met. 483 Federal Work-Study jobs (averaging $2771). In 2009, 104 non-need-based awards were made. *Average percent of need met:* 75%. *Aver-*

age financial aid package: $25,104. *Average need-based loan:* $4789. *Average need-based gift aid:* $21,692. *Average non-need-based aid:* $12,574. *Average indebtedness upon graduation:* $31,330.

Applying *Options:* electronic application, deferred entrance. *Application fee:* $55. *Required:* essay or personal statement, high school transcript, minimum 2 GPA, 1 letter of recommendation. *Required for some:* minimum 3 GPA, interview. *Recommended:* minimum 3 GPA. *Application deadlines:* 2/1 (freshmen), 7/1 (transfers). *Notification:* 3/15 (freshmen), continuous (transfers).

Freshman Application Contact Mr. Michael McKeon, Dean of Admissions, Saint Mary's College of California, PO Box 4800, Moraga, CA 94575-4800. *Phone:* 925-631-4224. *Toll-free phone:* 800-800-4SMC. *Fax:* 925-376-7193. *E-mail:* smcadmit@stmarys-ca.edu. *Web site:* http://www.stmarys-ca.edu/.

Samuel Merritt University

Oakland, California

- **Independent** upper-level, founded 1909
- **Urban** 1-acre campus with easy access to San Francisco
- **Endowment** $33.6 million
- **Coed, primarily women** 585 undergraduate students, 87% full-time, 84% women, 16% men
- **Moderately difficult** entrance level, 31% of applicants were admitted

Undergraduates 510 full-time, 75 part-time. Students come from 6 states and territories; 1% are from out of state; 43% transferred in.

Freshmen *Admission:* 336 applied, 103 admitted.

Faculty *Total:* 251, 44% full-time, 35% with terminal degrees. *Student/faculty ratio:* 11:1.

Academics *Calendar:* trimesters. *Degrees:* bachelor's, master's, and doctoral-professional (bachelor's degree offered jointly with Saint Mary's College of California). *Special study options:* academic remediation for entering students, accelerated degree program, advanced placement credit, cooperative education, distance learning, independent study, internships, off-campus study, part-time degree program, services for LD students, summer session for credit. *ROTC:* Army (c), Air Force (c).

Computers on Campus 92 computers/terminals are available on campus for general student use. Students can access the following: campus intranet, computer help desk, free student e-mail accounts, online (class) grades, online (class) registration, online (class) schedules. Campuswide network is available. Wireless service is available via entire campus.

Student Life *Housing:* college housing not available. *Activities and organizations:* student-run newspaper, Student Body Association, Green Team, International Health Club, Multicultural Group. *Campus security:* 24-hour emergency response devices and patrols, late-night transport/escort service, controlled dormitory access, 24-hour controlled access. *Student services:* health clinic, personal/psychological counseling.

Costs (2011–12) *One-time required fee:* $1335. *Tuition:* $37,648 full-time, $1587 per unit part-time. Full-time tuition and fees vary according to degree level and program. Part-time tuition and fees vary according to degree level and program. *Payment plan:* installment.

Financial Aid Of all full-time matriculated undergraduates who enrolled in 2009, 495 applied for aid, 448 were judged to have need, 20 had their need fully met. 120 Federal Work-Study jobs (averaging $1583). *Average percent of need met:* 69%. *Average financial aid package:* $32,000. *Average need-based loan:* $10,457. *Average need-based gift aid:* $20,000.

Applying *Options:* deferred entrance. *Application fee:* $50. *Application deadline:* 3/1 (transfers). *Notification:* continuous (transfers).

Application Contact Samuel Merritt University, 3100 Telegraph Avenue, Oakland, CA 94609-3108. *Phone:* 510-869-6610. *Toll-free phone:* 800-607-MERRITT. *Web site:* http://www.samuelmerritt.edu/.

San Diego Christian College

El Cajon, California

- **Independent nondenominational** 4-year, founded 1970
- **Suburban** 55-acre campus with easy access to San Diego
- **Endowment** $500,383
- **Coed** 471 undergraduate students, 88% full-time, 49% women, 51% men
- **Moderately difficult** entrance level, 48% of applicants were admitted

Undergraduates 415 full-time, 56 part-time. Students come from 26 states and territories; 7 other countries; 14% are from out of state; 10% Black or African American, non-Hispanic/Latino; 19% Hispanic/Latino; 3% Asian, non-Hispanic/Latino; 0.4% Native Hawaiian or other Pacific Islander, non-Hispanic/Latino; 2% American Indian or Alaska Native, non-Hispanic/Latino; 2% Two or more races, non-Hispanic/Latino; 14% Race/ethnicity unknown; 2% international; 19% transferred in; 32% live on campus. *Retention:* 49% of full-time freshmen returned.

Freshmen *Admission:* 389 applied, 186 admitted, 73 enrolled. *Average high school GPA:* 3.08. *Test scores:* SAT critical reading scores over 500: 31%; SAT math scores over 500: 34%; SAT writing scores over 500: 35%; ACT

scores over 18: 82%; SAT critical reading scores over 600: 8%; SAT math scores over 600: 2%; SAT writing scores over 600: 4%; ACT scores over 24: 27%; SAT critical reading scores over 700: 2%; SAT writing scores over 700: 2%.

Faculty *Total:* 75, 20% full-time, 16% with terminal degrees. *Student/faculty ratio:* 14:1.

Academics *Calendar:* semesters. *Degrees:* certificates, bachelor's, and post-bachelor's certificates. *Special study options:* academic remediation for entering students, accelerated degree program, adult/continuing education programs, advanced placement credit, distance learning, double majors, English as a second language, honors programs, independent study, internships, off-campus study, part-time degree program, student-designed majors, summer session for credit. *ROTC:* Army (c), Air Force (c).

Computers on Campus 187 computers/terminals and 69 ports are available on campus for general student use. Students can access the following: computer help desk, free student e-mail accounts, online (class) grades, online (class) schedules. Campuswide network is available. 100% of college-owned or -operated housing units are wired for high-speed Internet access. Wireless service is available via classrooms, computer centers, computer labs, learning centers, libraries, student centers.

Student Life *Housing:* on-campus residence required through sophomore year. *Options:* men-only, women-only. Campus housing is leased by the school. *Activities and organizations:* drama/theater group, student-run newspaper, choral group, Senate, Missions Club, Aviators Club, Women of Influence, Hope Ministries. *Campus security:* 24-hour emergency response devices and patrols. *Student services:* health clinic, personal/psychological counseling.

Athletics Member NAIA. *Intercollegiate sports:* baseball M(s), basketball M(s)/W(s), cross-country running M(s)/W(s), soccer M(s)/W(s), volleyball W(s). *Intramural sports:* basketball M/W, football M, golf M/W(c), soccer M/W, softball M/W, swimming and diving M/W, tennis M/W, ultimate Frisbee M/W, volleyball M/W, weight lifting M/W.

Standardized Tests *Required:* SAT or ACT (for admission).

Costs (2011–12) *One-time required fee:* $100. *Comprehensive fee:* $32,146 includes full-time tuition ($22,690), mandatory fees ($1134), and room and board ($8322). Full-time tuition and fees vary according to class time, course load, and program. Part-time tuition and fees vary according to class time, course load, and program. *Payment plan:* installment. *Waivers:* employees or children of employees.

Financial Aid Of all full-time matriculated undergraduates who enrolled in 2009, 386 applied for aid, 363 were judged to have need, 55 had their need fully met. 14 Federal Work-Study jobs (averaging $2396). 11 state and other part-time jobs (averaging $2182). In 2009, 39 non-need-based awards were made. *Average percent of need met:* 81%. *Average financial aid package:* $15,073. *Average need-based loan:* $3837. *Average need-based gift aid:* $7204. *Average non-need-based aid:* $4946. *Average indebtedness upon graduation:* $20,921. *Financial aid deadline:* 7/15.

Applying *Options:* electronic application, deferred entrance. *Application fee:* $25. *Required:* essay or personal statement, high school transcript, 2 letters of recommendation. *Recommended:* minimum 2.75 GPA, interview. *Application deadlines:* 7/1 (freshmen), 7/1 (transfers). *Notification:* continuous (freshmen), continuous (transfers).

Freshman Application Contact Candice Del Giudice, Director of Admissions, San Diego Christian College, 2100 Greenfield Drive, El Cajon, CA 92019-1157. *Phone:* 619-201-8741. *Toll-free phone:* 800-676-2242. *Fax:* 619-201-8749. *E-mail:* cdelgiudice@sdcc.edu. *Web site:* http://www.sdcc.edu/.

San Diego State University

San Diego, California

- **State-supported** university, founded 1897, part of California State University System
- **Urban** 300-acre campus
- **Endowment** $109.4 million
- **Coed** 24,590 undergraduate students, 88% full-time, 57% women, 43% men
- **Moderately difficult** entrance level, 30% of applicants were admitted

Undergraduates 21,573 full-time, 3,017 part-time. Students come from 54 states and territories; 70 other countries; 6% are from out of state; 4% Black or African American, non-Hispanic/Latino; 27% Hispanic/Latino; 7% Asian, non-Hispanic/Latino; 8% Native Hawaiian or other Pacific Islander, non-Hispanic/Latino; 0.4% American Indian or Alaska Native, non-Hispanic/Latino; 3% Two or more races, non-Hispanic/Latino; 8% Race/ethnicity unknown; 4% international; 10% transferred in; 13% live on campus. *Retention:* 86% of full-time freshmen returned.

Freshmen *Admission:* 44,848 applied, 13,450 admitted, 3,339 enrolled. *Average high school GPA:* 3.62. *Test scores:* SAT critical reading scores over 500: 67%; SAT math scores over 500: 77%; ACT scores over 18: 94%; SAT critical reading scores over 600: 21%; SAT math scores over 600: 32%; ACT scores

over 24: 53%; SAT critical reading scores over 700: 2%; SAT math scores over 700: 3%; ACT scores over 30: 5%.

Faculty *Total:* 1,467, 54% full-time, 51% with terminal degrees. *Student/faculty ratio:* 21:1.

Academics *Calendar:* semesters. *Degrees:* bachelor's, master's, doctoral-research/scholarship, and postbachelor's certificates. *Special study options:* academic remediation for entering students, advanced placement credit, distance learning, double majors, English as a second language, external degree program, honors programs, independent study, internships, off-campus study, part-time degree program, services for LD students, study abroad, summer session for credit. *ROTC:* Army (b), Navy (b), Air Force (b).

Computers on Campus 2,055 computers/terminals and 400 ports are available on campus for general student use. Students can access the following: computer help desk, free student e-mail accounts, online (class) grades, online (class) registration, online (class) schedules. Campuswide network is available. Wireless service is available via entire campus.

Student Life *Housing:* on-campus residence required for freshman year. *Options:* coed. Campus housing is university owned. Freshman applicants given priority for college housing. *Activities and organizations:* drama/theater group, student-run newspaper, radio and television station, choral group, marching band, AB Samahan, Asian Pacific Student Alliance, Enviro-Business Society, M.E.Ch.A de SDSU, Social fraternities and Sororities, including both general and culturally based organizations, national fraternities, national sororities. *Campus security:* 24-hour emergency response devices and patrols, student patrols, late-night transport/escort service. *Student services:* health clinic, personal/psychological counseling, women's center.

Athletics Member NCAA. All Division I. *Intercollegiate sports:* baseball M(s), basketball M(s)/W(s), crew W(s), cross-country running W(s), football M(s), golf M(s)/W(s), soccer M(s)/W(s), softball W(s), swimming and diving W(s), tennis M(s)/W(s), track and field W(s), volleyball W(s), water polo W(s). *Intramural sports:* basketball M/W, bowling M/W, cheerleading W(c), crew M(c), football M/W, golf M/W, ice hockey M(c), lacrosse M(c)/W(c), racquetball M/W, rugby M(c), skiing (downhill) M(c)/W(c), soccer M(c)/W(c), softball M/W, swimming and diving M/W, tennis M/W, ultimate Frisbee M(c)/W(c), volleyball M(c)/W(c), water polo M(c)/W(c).

Standardized Tests *Required:* SAT or ACT (for admission).

Costs (2011–12) *Tuition:* state resident $0 full-time; nonresident $11,160 full-time, $372 per unit part-time. Full-time tuition and fees vary according to degree level. Part-time tuition and fees vary according to course load and degree level. *Required fees:* $5206 full-time, $1715 per term part-time. *Room and board:* $11,485. Room and board charges vary according to board plan and housing facility. *Payment plan:* installment. *Waivers:* employees or children of employees.

Financial Aid Of all full-time matriculated undergraduates who enrolled in 2009, 17,400 applied for aid, 13,000 were judged to have need, 1,200 had their need fully met. 609 Federal Work-Study jobs (averaging $2200). In 2009, 1200 non-need-based awards were made. *Average percent of need met:* 73%. *Average financial aid package:* $10,000. *Average need-based loan:* $4100. *Average need-based gift aid:* $9200. *Average non-need-based aid:* $1700. *Average indebtedness upon graduation:* $15,500. *Financial aid deadline:* 3/2.

Applying *Options:* electronic application. *Application fee:* $55. *Required:* high school transcript, minimum 2 GPA, 2.5 GPA for non-California residents. *Application deadlines:* 11/30 (freshmen), 11/30 (transfers). *Notification:* 3/1 (freshmen), 3/1 (transfers).

Freshman Application Contact Ms. Beverly Arata, Director of Admissions, San Diego State University, 5500 Campanile Drive, San Diego, CA 92182-0771. *Phone:* 619-594-6336. *E-mail:* admissions@sdsu.edu. *Web site:* http://www.sdsu.edu/.

San Diego State University–Imperial Valley Campus

Calexico, California

Freshman Application Contact Aracely Bororquez, Admissions Department, San Diego State University–Imperial Valley Campus, 720 Heber Avenue, Calexico, CA 92231. *Phone:* 760-768-5506. *Fax:* 760-768-5589. *E-mail:* transfer@mail.sdsu.edu. *Web site:* http://www.ivcampus.sdsu.edu/.

San Francisco Art Institute

San Francisco, California

Freshman Application Contact Office of Admissions, San Francisco Art Institute, 800 Chestnut Street, San Francisco, CA 94133. *Phone:* 415-749-4500. *Toll-free phone:* 800-345-SFAI. *E-mail:* admissions@sfai.edu. *Web site:* http://www.sfai.edu/.

San Francisco Conservatory of Music

San Francisco, California

- **Independent** comprehensive, founded 1917
- **Urban** 2-acre campus
- **Endowment** $32.2 million
- **Coed** 207 undergraduate students, 97% full-time, 46% women, 54% men
- **Moderately difficult** entrance level, 40% of applicants were admitted

Undergraduates 201 full-time, 6 part-time. Students come from 25 states and territories; 22 other countries; 31% are from out of state; 10% transferred in; 33% live on campus. *Retention:* 76% of full-time freshmen returned.

Freshmen *Admission:* 286 applied, 114 admitted, 54 enrolled.

Faculty *Total:* 108, 31% full-time, 20% with terminal degrees. *Student/faculty ratio:* 7:1.

Academics *Calendar:* semesters. *Degrees:* diplomas, bachelor's, master's, and post-master's certificates. *Special study options:* academic remediation for entering students, advanced placement credit, independent study, internships, part-time degree program.

Computers on Campus 15 computers/terminals and 50 ports are available on campus for general student use. Students can access the following: campus intranet, computer help desk, free student e-mail accounts. Campuswide network is available. Wireless service is available via computer labs, libraries, student centers.

Student Life *Housing options:* Campus housing is leased by the school. *Activities and organizations:* drama/theater group, choral group, Coffee Talk, yoga group, Conservatory Formal Planning committee, DIG Process Group. *Campus security:* 24-hour patrols. *Student services:* personal/psychological counseling.

Standardized Tests *Recommended:* SAT or ACT (for admission).

Costs (2011–12) *Tuition:* $36,500 full-time. Part-time tuition and fees vary according to course load. *Payment plan:* installment. *Waivers:* employees or children of employees.

Financial Aid Of all full-time matriculated undergraduates who enrolled in 2009, 127 applied for aid, 112 were judged to have need, 16 had their need fully met. In 2009, 69 non-need-based awards were made. *Average percent of need met:* 66%. *Average financial aid package:* $22,952. *Average need-based loan:* $6127. *Average need-based gift aid:* $17,133. *Average non-need-based aid:* $12,389. *Average indebtedness upon graduation:* $15,454.

Applying *Options:* electronic application, deferred entrance. *Application fee:* $100. *Required:* essay or personal statement, high school transcript, minimum 2.5 GPA, 2 letters of recommendation, audition, pre-screen recording in select areas. *Application deadlines:* 12/1 (freshmen), 12/1 (out-of-state freshmen), 12/1 (transfers). *Notification:* 4/1 (freshmen), 4/1 (out-of-state freshmen), 4/1 (transfers).

Freshman Application Contact Mr. Alexander Brose, San Francisco Conservatory of Music, 50 Oak Street, San Francisco, CA 94102. *Phone:* 800-899-7326. *Fax:* 415-503-6299. *E-mail:* admit@sfcm.edu. *Web site:* http://www.sfcm.edu/.

San Francisco State University

San Francisco, California

- **State-supported** university, founded 1899, part of California State University System
- **Urban** 142-acre campus
- **Endowment** $49.0 million
- **Coed** 25,170 undergraduate students, 83% full-time, 58% women, 42% men
- **Moderately difficult** entrance level, 63% of applicants were admitted

Undergraduates 20,963 full-time, 4,207 part-time. Students come from 44 states and territories; 90 other countries; 0.7% are from out of state; 5% Black or African American, non-Hispanic/Latino; 19% Hispanic/Latino; 27% Asian, non-Hispanic/Latino; 0.7% Native Hawaiian or other Pacific Islander, non-Hispanic/Latino; 0.4% American Indian or Alaska Native, non-Hispanic/Latino; 4% Two or more races, non-Hispanic/Latino; 9% Race/ethnicity unknown; 7% international; 15% transferred in; 12% live on campus. *Retention:* 77% of full-time freshmen returned.

Freshmen *Admission:* 29,395 applied, 18,401 admitted, 3,659 enrolled. *Average high school GPA:* 3.12. *Test scores:* SAT critical reading scores over 500: 52%; SAT math scores over 500: 57%; ACT scores over 18: 86%; SAT critical reading scores over 600: 15%; SAT math scores over 600: 15%; ACT scores over 24: 31%; SAT critical reading scores over 700: 1%; SAT math scores over 700: 1%; ACT scores over 30: 2%.

Faculty *Total:* 1,580, 51% full-time, 54% with terminal degrees. *Student/faculty ratio:* 23:1.

Academics *Calendar:* semesters. *Degrees:* certificates, bachelor's, master's, doctoral-professional, doctoral-research/scholarship, and postbachelor's certificates. *Special study options:* academic remediation for entering students, adult/continuing education programs, advanced placement credit, cooperative education, distance learning, double majors, English as a second language, honors programs, independent study, internships, off-campus study, part-time degree program, services for LD students, student-designed majors, study abroad, summer session for credit. *ROTC:* Army (c), Air Force (c).

Computers on Campus 2,800 computers/terminals and 500 ports are available on campus for general student use. Students can access the following: campus intranet, computer help desk, free student e-mail accounts, online (class) grades, online (class) registration, online (class) schedules. Campuswide network is available. 100% of college-owned or -operated housing units are wired for high-speed Internet access. Wireless service is available via entire campus.

Student Life *Housing options:* coed, disabled students. Campus housing is university owned. Freshman applicants given priority for college housing. *Activities and organizations:* drama/theater group, student-run newspaper, radio and television station, choral group, Fraternity/Sorority Council, International Education Exchange Council, Laraza Student Organization, Pilipino American Collegial Endeavor, Black Student Union, national fraternities, national sororities. *Campus security:* 24-hour emergency response devices and patrols, student patrols, late-night transport/escort service, controlled dormitory access. *Student services:* health clinic, personal/psychological counseling, women's center, legal services.

Athletics Member NCAA. All Division II. *Intercollegiate sports:* baseball M(s), basketball M(s)/W(s), cross-country running M(s)/W(s), soccer M(s)/W(s), softball W(s), track and field W(s), volleyball W(s), wrestling M(s). *Intramural sports:* basketball M/W, cheerleading M(c)/W(c), rugby M(c)/W(c), soccer M/W, tennis M/W, volleyball M/W, water polo M(c)/W(c).

Standardized Tests *Required:* SAT or ACT (for admission).

Costs (2011–12) *Tuition:* state resident $0 full-time; nonresident $11,160 full-time, $372 per unit part-time. Full-time tuition and fees vary according to course load. Part-time tuition and fees vary according to course load. *Required fees:* $5668 full-time, $1808 per term part-time. *Room and board:* $11,408. Room and board charges vary according to board plan and housing facility. *Payment plan:* installment. *Waivers:* senior citizens and employees or children of employees.

Financial Aid Of all full-time matriculated undergraduates who enrolled in 2009, 13,807 applied for aid, 12,269 were judged to have need, 544 had their need fully met. In 2009, 85 non-need-based awards were made. *Average percent of need met:* 61%. *Average financial aid package:* $10,662. *Average need-based loan:* $3244. *Average need-based gift aid:* $9001. *Average non-need-based aid:* $2168. *Average indebtedness upon graduation:* $17,706.

Applying *Options:* electronic application. *Application fee:* $55. *Required:* high school transcript. *Application deadlines:* 11/30 (freshmen), 8/31 (transfers). *Notification:* 10/1 (freshmen).

Freshman Application Contact Admissions Officer, San Francisco State University, 1600 Holloway Avenue, San Francisco, CA 94132-1722. *Phone:* 415-338-1113. *Fax:* 415-338-7196. *E-mail:* ugadmit@sfsu.edu. *Web site:* http://www.sfsu.edu/.

San Jose State University

San Jose, California

- **State-supported** comprehensive, founded 1857, part of California State University System
- **Urban** 104-acre campus
- **Coed** 23,021 undergraduate students, 79% full-time, 51% women, 49% men
- **Very difficult** entrance level, 57% of applicants were admitted

Undergraduates 18,169 full-time, 4,852 part-time. 1% are from out of state; 4% Black or African American, non-Hispanic/Latino; 23% Hispanic/Latino; 32% Asian, non-Hispanic/Latino; 0.7% Native Hawaiian or other Pacific Islander, non-Hispanic/Latino; 0.3% American Indian or Alaska Native, non-Hispanic/Latino; 3% Two or more races, non-Hispanic/Latino; 6% Race/ethnicity unknown; 4% international; 12% transferred in; 12% live on campus. *Retention:* 85% of full-time freshmen returned.

Freshmen *Admission:* 23,002 applied, 13,013 admitted, 2,761 enrolled. *Average high school GPA:* 3.28. *Test scores:* SAT critical reading scores over 500: 50%; SAT math scores over 500: 66%; SAT writing scores over 500: 52%; ACT scores over 18: 86%; SAT critical reading scores over 600: 12%; SAT math scores over 600: 25%; SAT writing scores over 600: 11%; ACT scores over 24: 33%; SAT critical reading scores over 700: 1%; SAT math scores over 700: 3%; SAT writing scores over 700: 1%; ACT scores over 30: 3%.

Faculty *Total:* 1,593, 40% full-time. *Student/faculty ratio:* 25:1.

Academics *Calendar:* semesters. *Degrees:* bachelor's and master's. *Special study options:* academic remediation for entering students, adult/continuing education programs, advanced placement credit, distance learning, double majors, honors programs, independent study, internships, off-campus study, part-time degree program, services for LD students, student-designed majors, study abroad, summer session for credit. *ROTC:* Army (b), Air Force (b).

Computers on Campus Students can access the following: online (class) registration. Campuswide network is available. Wireless service is available via entire campus.

Student Life *Housing options:* coed, men-only, women-only, cooperative, disabled students. *Activities and organizations:* drama/theater group, student-run newspaper, radio and television station, choral group, marching band, national fraternities, national sororities. *Campus security:* 24-hour emergency response devices and patrols, student patrols, late-night transport/escort service. *Student services:* health clinic, personal/psychological counseling, women's center.

Athletics Member NCAA. All Division I except football (Division I-A). *Intercollegiate sports:* badminton M(c)/W(c), baseball M(s), basketball M(s)/W(s), bowling M(c)/W(c), cheerleading M(c)/W(c), cross-country running M(s)/W(s), golf M(s)/W(s), gymnastics W(s), ice hockey M(c)/W(c), rugby M(c), sailing M(c)/W(c), soccer M(s)/W(s), softball W, swimming and diving W(s), tennis W(s), volleyball M(c)/W(s), water polo W(s), wrestling M(c)/W(c). *Intramural sports:* archery M(c)/W(c), badminton M/W, baseball M, basketball M/W, bowling M/W, cross-country running M(c)/W(c), fencing M(c)/W(c), field hockey W(c), football M/W, ice hockey M(c), lacrosse M(c)/W(c), racquetball M/W, rugby W(c), soccer M/W, softball M/W, table tennis M(c)/W(c), tennis M/W, track and field M(c)/W(c), volleyball M(c)/W, water polo M/W, wrestling M(c)/W(c).

Standardized Tests *Required for some:* SAT or ACT (for admission).

Costs (2010–11) *Tuition:* state resident $0 full-time; nonresident $11,160 full-time, $372 per unit part-time. *Required fees:* $5475 full-time. *Room and board:* $10,733; room only: $6633.

Financial Aid Of all full-time matriculated undergraduates who enrolled in 2008, 11,937 applied for aid, 10,466 were judged to have need, 4,546 had their need fully met. 6,169 Federal Work-Study jobs (averaging $4680). In 2008, 109 non-need-based awards were made. *Average percent of need met:* 93%. *Average financial aid package:* $13,364. *Average need-based loan:* $4713. *Average need-based gift aid:* $7363. *Average non-need-based aid:* $2641. *Average indebtedness upon graduation:* $9483.

Applying *Options:* electronic application. *Application fee:* $55. *Required:* high school transcript. *Application deadlines:* 11/30 (freshmen), 11/30 (transfers). *Notification:* continuous (freshmen), continuous (transfers).

Freshman Application Contact Admissions Office, San Jose State University, One Washington Square, San Jose, CA 95192-0001. *Phone:* 408-283-7500. *Fax:* 408-924-2050. *E-mail:* admissions@sjsu.edu. *Web site:* http://www.sjsu.edu/.

Santa Clara University

Santa Clara, California

- **Independent Roman Catholic (Jesuit)** university, founded 1851
- **Suburban** 106-acre campus with easy access to San Francisco and San Jose
- **Endowment** $603.6 million
- **Coed** 5,107 undergraduate students, 98% full-time, 51% women, 49% men
- **Moderately difficult** entrance level, 58% of applicants were admitted

Undergraduates 5,016 full-time, 91 part-time. Students come from 48 states and territories; 38 other countries; 38% are from out of state; 4% Black or African American, non-Hispanic/Latino; 18% Hispanic/Latino; 14% Asian, non-Hispanic/Latino; 0.7% Native Hawaiian or other Pacific Islander, non-Hispanic/Latino; 0.2% American Indian or Alaska Native, non-Hispanic/Latino; 4% Two or more races, non-Hispanic/Latino; 14% Race/ethnicity unknown; 3% international; 4% transferred in; 30% live on campus. *Retention:* 93% of full-time freshmen returned.

Freshmen *Admission:* 11,787 applied, 6,830 admitted, 1,296 enrolled. *Average high school GPA:* 3.6. *Test scores:* SAT critical reading scores over 500: 93%; SAT math scores over 500: 95%; SAT writing scores over 500: 95%; ACT scores over 18: 100%; SAT critical reading scores over 600: 58%; SAT math scores over 600: 73%; SAT writing scores over 600: 62%; ACT scores over 24: 89%; SAT critical reading scores over 700: 12%; SAT math scores over 700: 21%; SAT writing scores over 700: 12%; ACT scores over 30: 31%.

Faculty *Total:* 840, 53% full-time, 76% with terminal degrees. *Student/faculty ratio:* 13:1.

Academics *Calendar:* quarters. *Degrees:* bachelor's, master's, doctoral-professional, doctoral-research/scholarship, post-master's, and postbachelor's certificates. *Special study options:* advanced placement credit, cooperative education, double majors, honors programs, independent study, internships, services for LD students, student-designed majors, study abroad, summer session for credit. *ROTC:* Army (b), Air Force (c).

Computers on Campus 782 computers/terminals are available on campus for general student use. Students can access the following: campus intranet, computer help desk, free student e-mail accounts, online (class) grades, online (class) registration, online (class) schedules. Campuswide network is available. 100% of college-owned or -operated housing units are wired for high-speed Internet access. Wireless service is available via entire campus.

Student Life *Housing options:* coed. Campus housing is university owned. Freshman applicants given priority for college housing. *Activities and organizations:* drama/theater group, student-run newspaper, radio and television station, choral group, Santa Clara Community Action Program, Associated Students, Ruff Riders, MECha El Frente, Accounting Association. *Campus security:* 24-hour emergency response devices and patrols, late-night transport/escort service, controlled dormitory access. *Student services:* health clinic, personal/psychological counseling, legal services.

Athletics Member NCAA. All Division I. *Intercollegiate sports:* baseball M(s), basketball M(s)/W(s), crew M/W, cross-country running M(s)/W(s), golf M(s)/W(s), soccer M(s)/W(s), softball W(s), tennis M(s)/W(s), track and field M(s)/W(s), volleyball W(s), water polo M(s)/W(s). *Intramural sports:* badminton M/W, basketball M/W, cheerleading W(c), equestrian sports M(c)/W(c), field hockey W(c), football M/W, ice hockey M(c), lacrosse M(c)/W(c), rugby M(c)/W(c), sailing M(c)/W(c), soccer M/W, softball M/W, swimming and diving M(c)/W(c), table tennis M/W, tennis M/W, volleyball M/W.

Standardized Tests *Required:* SAT or ACT (for admission).

Costs (2011–12) *Comprehensive fee:* $49,110 includes full-time tuition ($37,368) and room and board ($11,742). Part-time tuition: $1038 per unit. Part-time tuition and fees vary according to course load. *Room and board:* Room and board charges vary according to board plan, housing facility, and student level. *Payment plans:* installment, deferred payment. *Waivers:* employees or children of employees.

Financial Aid Of all full-time matriculated undergraduates who enrolled in 2009, 3,049 applied for aid, 2,329 were judged to have need, 770 had their need fully met. 473 Federal Work-Study jobs (averaging $3581). In 2009, 1326 non-need-based awards were made. *Average percent of need met:* 67%. *Average financial aid package:* $23,774. *Average need-based loan:* $4461. *Average need-based gift aid:* $18,666. *Average non-need-based aid:* $11,557. *Average indebtedness upon graduation:* $23,909.

Applying *Options:* electronic application, early action, deferred entrance. *Application fee:* $55. *Required:* essay or personal statement, high school transcript, 1 letter of recommendation. *Application deadlines:* 1/7 (freshmen), 5/1 (transfers), 11/1 (early action). *Notification:* 4/1 (freshmen), 6/1 (transfers), 12/31 (early action).

Freshman Application Contact Ms. Sandra Hayes, Dean of Undergraduate Admissions, Santa Clara University, 500 El Camino Real, Santa Clara, CA 95053. *Phone:* 408-554-4700. *Fax:* 408-554-5255. *E-mail:* ugadmissions@scu.edu. *Web site:* http://www.scu.edu/.

School of Urban Missions
Oakland, California

- **Independent interdenominational** primarily 2-year, founded 1991
- **Coed**
- **59%** of applicants were admitted

Faculty *Student/faculty ratio:* 11:1.

Academics *Calendar:* trimesters. *Degrees:* associate and bachelor's.

Costs (2010–11) *Tuition:* $7800 full-time, $260 per credit hour part-time. Full-time tuition and fees vary according to program. Part-time tuition and fees vary according to program. *Required fees:* $105 full-time. *Room only:* Room and board charges vary according to housing facility.

Applying *Options:* deferred entrance. *Application fee:* $25. *Required:* essay or personal statement, 2 letters of recommendation, interview, pastoral recommendation.

Freshman Application Contact Admissions, School of Urban Missions, 735 105th Avenue, Oakland, CA 94603. *Phone:* 510-567-6174. *Toll-free phone:* 800-385-6364. *Fax:* 510-568-1024. *Web site:* http://www.sum.edu/.

Scripps College
Claremont, California

- **Independent** 4-year, founded 1926, part of The Claremont Colleges Consortium
- **Suburban** 37-acre campus with easy access to Los Angeles
- **Endowment** $231.2 million
- **Women only** 956 undergraduate students, 98% full-time
- **Very difficult** entrance level, 39% of applicants were admitted

Undergraduates 941 full-time, 15 part-time. Students come from 46 states and territories; 15 other countries; 55% are from out of state; 4% Black or African American, non-Hispanic/Latino; 10% Hispanic/Latino; 9% Asian, non-Hispanic/Latino; 0.1% Native Hawaiian or other Pacific Islander, non-Hispanic/Latino; 0.1% American Indian or Alaska Native, non-Hispanic/Latino; 7% Two or more races, non-Hispanic/Latino; 6% Race/ethnicity unknown; 4% international; 2% transferred in; 91% live on campus. *Retention:* 96% of full-time freshmen returned.

Freshmen *Admission:* 2,097 applied, 820 admitted, 263 enrolled. *Average high school GPA:* 4.1. *Test scores:* SAT critical reading scores over 500: 100%; SAT math scores over 500: 100%; SAT writing scores over 500: 100%;

ACT scores over 18: 100%; SAT critical reading scores over 600: 91%; SAT math scores over 600: 89%; SAT writing scores over 600: 92%; ACT scores over 24: 96%; SAT critical reading scores over 700: 45%; SAT math scores over 700: 37%; SAT writing scores over 700: 50%; ACT scores over 30: 58%.

Faculty *Total:* 113, 75% full-time, 95% with terminal degrees. *Student/faculty ratio:* 10:1.

Academics *Calendar:* semesters. *Degrees:* certificates, bachelor's, and post-bachelor's certificates. *Special study options:* accelerated degree program, advanced placement credit, double majors, independent study, internships, off-campus study, part-time degree program, student-designed majors, study abroad. *ROTC:* Army (c), Air Force (c). *Unusual degree programs:* 3-2 business administration with Claremont Graduate University; engineering with Stanford University, University of Southern California, Harvey Mudd College, University of California, Berkeley, Washington University in St. Louis, Columbia University, Boston University; public policy, religion, government, international studies, economics, philosophy with Claremont Graduate University.

Computers on Campus 87 computers/terminals are available on campus for general student use. Students can access the following: campus intranet, computer help desk, free student e-mail accounts, online (class) grades, online (class) registration, online (class) schedules, 2 ports per dorm room. Campus-wide network is available. 100% of college-owned or -operated housing units are wired for high-speed Internet access. Wireless service is available via classrooms, computer centers, computer labs, dorm rooms, libraries, student centers.

Student Life *Housing:* on-campus residence required for freshman year. *Options:* women-only, disabled students. Campus housing is university owned. Freshman campus housing is guaranteed. *Activities and organizations:* drama/theater group, student-run newspaper, radio station, choral group, Scripps Associated Students, Asian/Black/Latina clubs, National Organization for Women, Sexual Assault Task Force. *Campus security:* 24-hour emergency response devices and patrols, late-night transport/escort service, controlled dormitory access. *Student services:* health clinic, personal/psychological counseling, women's center.

Athletics Member NCAA. All Division III. *Intercollegiate sports:* basketball W, cross-country running W, fencing W(c), golf W, lacrosse W, rock climbing W(c), rugby W(c), skiing (downhill) W(c), soccer W, softball W, swimming and diving W, tennis W, track and field W, ultimate Frisbee W(c), volleyball W, water polo W. *Intramural sports:* basketball W, cheerleading W, football W, soccer W, softball W, volleyball W, water polo W.

Standardized Tests *Required:* SAT or ACT (for admission).

Costs (2010–11) *Comprehensive fee:* $52,900 includes full-time tuition ($40,236), mandatory fees ($214), and room and board ($12,450). Full-time tuition and fees vary according to program. Part-time tuition: $5030 per course. Part-time tuition and fees vary according to program. *College room only:* $6720. Room and board charges vary according to board plan. *Payment plans:* tuition prepayment, installment. *Waivers:* employees or children of employees.

Financial Aid Of all full-time matriculated undergraduates who enrolled in 2009, 512 applied for aid, 425 were judged to have need, 425 had their need fully met. 319 Federal Work-Study jobs (averaging $1548). 37 state and other part-time jobs (averaging $1591). In 2009, 90 non-need-based awards were made. *Average percent of need met:* 100%. *Average financial aid package:* $36,614. *Average need-based loan:* $3271. *Average need-based gift aid:* $33,163. *Average non-need-based aid:* $22,102. *Average indebtedness upon graduation:* $9435. *Financial aid deadline:* 5/1.

Applying *Options:* early admission, early decision, deferred entrance. *Application fee:* $60. *Required:* essay or personal statement, high school transcript, 3 letters of recommendation, graded writing sample. *Recommended:* minimum 3 GPA, interview. *Application deadlines:* 1/1 (freshmen), 4/1 (transfers). *Early decision deadline:* 11/1 (for plan 1), 1/1 (for plan 2). *Notification:* 4/1 (freshmen), 5/1 (transfers), 12/15 (early decision plan 1), 2/15 (early decision plan 2).

Freshman Application Contact Ms. Laura Stratton, Director of Admissions, Scripps College, 1030 Columbia Avenue, Claremont, CA 91711. *Phone:* 909-621-8149. *Toll-free phone:* 800-770-1333. *Fax:* 909-607-7508. *E-mail:* admission@scrippscollege.edu. *Web site:* http://www.scrippscollege.edu/.

Shasta Bible College
Redding, California

- **Independent nondenominational** comprehensive, founded 1971
- **Small-town** 55-acre campus
- **Coed**
- **Noncompetitive** entrance level

Faculty *Student/faculty ratio:* 3:1.

Academics *Calendar:* semesters. *Degrees:* certificates, diplomas, associate, bachelor's, and master's.

Student Life *Campus security:* 24-hour emergency response devices, student patrols.

Costs (2010–11) *Tuition:* $9600 full-time, $300 per unit part-time. *Required fees:* $480 per year part-time. *Room only:* $2400.

Financial Aid *Of all full-time matriculated undergraduates who enrolled in 2007,* 40 applied for aid, 35 were judged to have need, 3 had their need fully met. 12 Federal Work-Study jobs (averaging $640). 4 state and other part-time jobs (averaging $1000). *In 2007,* 2 non-need-based awards were made. *Average percent of need met:* 60. *Average financial aid package:* $2582. *Average need-based gift aid:* $4050. *Average non-need-based aid:* $1000.

Applying *Options:* electronic application, early admission. *Application fee:* $50. *Required:* essay or personal statement, high school transcript, 4 letters of recommendation. *Required for some:* interview.

Freshman Application Contact Connie Barton, Registrar, Shasta Bible College, 2951 Goodwater Avenue, Redding, CA 96002. *Phone:* 530-221-4275 Ext. 26. *Toll-free phone:* 800-800-45BC (in-state); 800-800-6929 (out-of-state). *Fax:* 530-221-6929. *E-mail:* registrar@shasta.edu. *Web site:* http://www.shasta.edu/.

Silicon Valley University
San Jose, California

- **Proprietary** comprehensive
- **Suburban** 1-acre campus with easy access to San Jose
- **Coed** 1,090 students

Undergraduates *Retention:* 100% of full-time freshmen returned.

Faculty *Total:* 31, 3% full-time, 55% with terminal degrees. *Student/faculty ratio:* 24:1.

Academics *Calendar:* trimesters. *Degrees:* certificates, diplomas, bachelor's, and master's. *Special study options:* accelerated degree program, cooperative education, double majors, English as a second language, honors programs, independent study, internships, part-time degree program, summer session for credit.

Computers on Campus 24 computers/terminals and 20 ports are available on campus for general student use. Students can access the following: campus intranet, computer help desk, free student e-mail accounts, online (class) schedules. Campuswide network is available. Wireless service is available via entire campus.

Student Life *Housing options:* Campus housing is provided by a third party. *Activities and organizations:* Student Association Club. *Campus security:* 24-hour emergency response devices and patrols.

Standardized Tests *Required:* TOEFL for students whose first language is not English (for admission). *Recommended:* SAT (for admission), ACT (for admission), SAT or ACT (for admission).

Costs (2010–11) *Tuition:* $295 per unit part-time. Full-time tuition and fees vary according to course load, degree level, and program. Part-time tuition and fees vary according to course load, degree level, and program. *Required fees:* $185 per term part-time. *Payment plan:* installment.

Applying *Options:* electronic application, deferred entrance. *Application fee:* $50. *Required:* high school transcript, copy of diploma. *Required for some:* interview. *Recommended:* essay or personal statement.

Freshman Application Contact Admissions Office, Silicon Valley University, 2160 Lundy Avenue, Suite 110, San Jose, CA 95131. *Phone:* 408-435-8989 Ext. 109. *E-mail:* admission-office@svuca.edu. *Web site:* http://www.svuca.edu/.

Simpson University
Redding, California

- **Independent** comprehensive, founded 1921, affiliated with The Christian and Missionary Alliance
- **Suburban** 100-acre campus
- **Endowment** $3.8 million
- **Coed** 974 undergraduate students, 98% full-time, 65% women, 35% men
- **Moderately difficult** entrance level, 65% of applicants were admitted

Undergraduates 951 full-time, 23 part-time. Students come from 32 states and territories; 8 other countries; 14% are from out of state; 3% Black or African American, non-Hispanic/Latino; 8% Hispanic/Latino; 6% Asian, non-Hispanic/Latino; 0.7% Native Hawaiian or other Pacific Islander, non-Hispanic/Latino; 2% American Indian or Alaska Native, non-Hispanic/Latino; 1% Two or more races, non-Hispanic/Latino; 26% Race/ethnicity unknown; 0.1% international; 10% transferred in; 70% live on campus. *Retention:* 65% of full-time freshmen returned.

Freshmen *Admission:* 533 applied, 346 admitted, 158 enrolled. *Average high school GPA:* 3.36. *Test scores:* SAT critical reading scores over 500: 50%; SAT math scores over 500: 48%; SAT writing scores over 500: 39%; ACT scores over 18: 84%; SAT critical reading scores over 600: 9%; SAT math scores over 600: 10%; SAT writing scores over 600: 6%; ACT scores over 24: 37%; SAT critical reading scores over 700: 1%; ACT scores over 30: 5%.

Faculty *Total:* 125, 37% full-time, 42% with terminal degrees. *Student/faculty ratio:* 15:1.

Academics *Calendar:* semesters. *Degrees:* certificates, associate, bachelor's, and master's. *Special study options:* academic remediation for entering students, accelerated degree program, adult/continuing education programs, advanced placement credit, distance learning, double majors, honors programs, independent study, internships, off-campus study, part-time degree program, services for LD students, student-designed majors, study abroad, summer session for credit. *ROTC:* Army (b).

Computers on Campus 50 computers/terminals are available on campus for general student use. Students can access the following: campus intranet, computer help desk, free student e-mail accounts, online (class) grades, online (class) registration, online (class) schedules. Campuswide network is available. 100% of college-owned or -operated housing units are wired for high-speed Internet access. Wireless service is available via entire campus.

Student Life *Housing:* on-campus residence required through junior year. *Options:* men-only, women-only, disabled students. Campus housing is university owned. Freshman campus housing is guaranteed. *Activities and organizations:* drama/theater group, student-run newspaper, choral group, Summer Missions Trips, Social Action Committee, Asian Fellowship, Vida, Psychology Club. *Campus security:* 24-hour emergency response devices and patrols, student patrols, late-night transport/escort service, controlled dormitory access, emergency whistle program and monthly campus safety meetings. *Student services:* health clinic, personal/psychological counseling.

Athletics Member NAIA, NCCAA. *Intercollegiate sports:* baseball M(s), basketball M(s)/W(s), cross-country running M(s)/W(s), golf M(s)/W(s), soccer M(s)/W(s), softball W(s), volleyball W(s). *Intramural sports:* basketball M/W, volleyball M(c).

Standardized Tests *Required:* SAT or ACT (for admission). *Recommended:* SAT Subject Tests (for admission).

Costs (2011–12) *Comprehensive fee:* $28,900 includes full-time tuition ($21,600) and room and board ($7300). Full-time tuition and fees vary according to course load and program. Part-time tuition: $900 per unit. Part-time tuition and fees vary according to course load and program. *College room only:* $6300. Room and board charges vary according to board plan. *Payment plan:* deferred payment. *Waivers:* employees or children of employees.

Financial Aid Of all full-time matriculated undergraduates who enrolled in 2009, 663 applied for aid, 615 were judged to have need, 78 had their need fully met. 187 Federal Work-Study jobs (averaging $443). In 2009, 46 non-need-based awards were made. *Average percent of need met:* 75%. *Average financial aid package:* $19,509. *Average need-based loan:* $4357. *Average need-based gift aid:* $15,243. *Average non-need-based aid:* $6623. *Average indebtedness upon graduation:* $22,831.

Applying *Options:* electronic application, deferred entrance. *Application fee:* $20. *Required:* essay or personal statement, high school transcript, 2 letters of recommendation, Christian commitment. *Required for some:* interview. *Application deadlines:* rolling (freshmen), rolling (transfers). *Notification:* continuous (freshmen), continuous (transfers).

Freshman Application Contact Mrs. Kendell Kluttz, Director of Undergraduate Admissions, Simpson University, 2211 College View Drive, Redding, CA 96003-8606. *Phone:* 530-226-5600. *Toll-free phone:* 800-598-2493. *Fax:* 530-226-4861. *E-mail:* admissions@simpsonu.edu. *Web site:* http://www.simpsonu.edu/.

Soka University of America
Aliso Viejo, California

- **Independent** comprehensive, founded 2001
- **Suburban** 103-acre campus
- **Endowment** $563.0 million
- **Coed** 438 undergraduate students, 99% full-time, 64% women, 36% men
- **Moderately difficult** entrance level, 32% of applicants were admitted

Undergraduates 435 full-time, 3 part-time. Students come from 26 states and territories; 32 other countries; 45% are from out of state; 2% Black or African American, non-Hispanic/Latino; 10% Hispanic/Latino; 20% Asian, non-Hispanic/Latino; 0.2% Native Hawaiian or other Pacific Islander, non-Hispanic/Latino; 0.5% American Indian or Alaska Native, non-Hispanic/Latino; 5% Two or more races, non-Hispanic/Latino; 4% Race/ethnicity unknown; 42% international; 99% live on campus. *Retention:* 91% of full-time freshmen returned.

Freshmen *Admission:* 504 applied, 163 admitted, 103 enrolled. *Average high school GPA:* 3.61. *Test scores:* SAT critical reading scores over 500: 53%; SAT math scores over 500: 95%; SAT writing scores over 500: 69%; ACT scores over 18: 100%; SAT critical reading scores over 600: 27%; SAT math scores over 600: 75%; SAT writing scores over 600: 26%; ACT scores over 24: 56%; SAT critical reading scores over 700: 7%; SAT math scores over 700: 21%; SAT writing scores over 700: 6%.

Faculty *Total:* 55, 69% full-time, 82% with terminal degrees. *Student/faculty ratio:* 9:1.

Academics *Calendar:* semesters. *Degrees:* bachelor's and master's. *Special study options:* academic remediation for entering students, independent study, internships, services for LD students, study abroad.

Computers on Campus Students can access the following: campus intranet, computer help desk, free student e-mail accounts, online (class) grades, online (class) registration, online (class) schedules, Angel courseware/PeopleSoft Portal. Campuswide network is available. 100% of college-owned or -operated housing units are wired for high-speed Internet access. Wireless service is available via classrooms, computer centers, computer labs, learning centers, libraries, student centers.
Student Life *Housing:* on-campus residence required through senior year. *Options:* coed, disabled students. Campus housing is university owned. Freshman campus housing is guaranteed. *Activities and organizations:* student-run newspaper, choral group. *Campus security:* 24-hour emergency response devices and patrols, late-night transport/escort service, controlled dormitory access. *Student services:* health clinic, personal/psychological counseling.
Athletics Member NAIA. *Intercollegiate sports:* cross-country running M(s)/W(s), soccer M(s)/W(s), swimming and diving M(s)/W(s), track and field M(s)/W(s), water polo M/W. *Intramural sports:* badminton M/W, baseball M, basketball M/W, soccer W, table tennis M/W, tennis M/W, volleyball M/W.
Standardized Tests *Required:* SAT or ACT (for admission).
Costs (2010–11) *Comprehensive fee:* $35,842 includes full-time tuition ($25,344), mandatory fees ($858), and room and board ($9640). Full-time tuition and fees vary according to course load. *Payment plan:* installment.
Applying *Options:* electronic application, early admission, early action, deferred entrance. *Application fee:* $45. *Required:* essay or personal statement, high school transcript, 2 letters of recommendation. *Application deadlines:* 1/15 (freshmen), 10/15 (early action). *Notification:* 3/15 (freshmen), 12/1 (early action).
Freshman Application Contact Ms. Marilyn Grove, Director of Student Recruitment Programs, Soka University of America, Enrollment Services, 1 University Drive, Aliso Viejo, CA 92656. *Phone:* 949-480-4131. *Toll-free phone:* 888-600-SOKA. *Fax:* 949-480-4151. *E-mail:* admission@soka.edu. *Web site:* http://www.soka.edu/.

Sonoma State University
Rohnert Park, California

- **State-supported** comprehensive, founded 1960, part of California State University System
- **Small-town** 280-acre campus with easy access to San Francisco
- **Endowment** $28.0 million
- **Coed** 7,390 undergraduate students, 89% full-time, 61% women, 39% men
- **Moderately difficult** entrance level

Undergraduates 6,597 full-time, 793 part-time. Students come from 11 states and territories; 24 other countries; 1% are from out of state; 2% Black or African American, non-Hispanic/Latino; 13% Hispanic/Latino; 5% Asian, non-Hispanic/Latino; 0.7% Native Hawaiian or other Pacific Islander, non-Hispanic/Latino; 0.9% American Indian or Alaska Native, non-Hispanic/Latino; 6% Two or more races, non-Hispanic/Latino; 4% Race/ethnicity unknown; 1% international; 12% transferred in; 36% live on campus. *Retention:* 79% of full-time freshmen returned.
Freshmen *Admission:* 4,186 applied, 1,574 enrolled. *Average high school GPA:* 3.16. *Test scores:* SAT critical reading scores over 500: 59%; SAT math scores over 500: 59%; ACT scores over 18: 91%; SAT critical reading scores over 600: 23%; SAT math scores over 600: 22%; ACT scores over 24: 32%; SAT critical reading scores over 700: 2%; SAT math scores over 700: 1%; ACT scores over 30: 11%.
Faculty *Total:* 567, 46% full-time, 63% with terminal degrees. *Student/faculty ratio:* 23:1.
Academics *Calendar:* semesters. *Degrees:* bachelor's and master's. *Special study options:* academic remediation for entering students, accelerated degree program, adult/continuing education programs, advanced placement credit, cooperative education, distance learning, double majors, English as a second language, honors programs, independent study, internships, off-campus study, part-time degree program, services for LD students, student-designed majors, study abroad, summer session for credit. *ROTC:* Army (c), Air Force (c).
Computers on Campus 400 computers/terminals are available on campus for general student use. Students can access the following: computer help desk, free student e-mail accounts, online (class) grades, online (class) registration, online (class) schedules. Campuswide network is available. 100% of college-owned or -operated housing units are wired for high-speed Internet access. Wireless service is available via entire campus.
Student Life *Housing options:* coed, women-only, disabled students. Campus housing is university owned. Freshman applicants given priority for college housing. *Activities and organizations:* drama/theater group, student-run newspaper, radio station, choral group, Accounting Forum, Sonoma Earth Action, Re-Entry Student Association, Inter-Varsity Christian Fellowship, national fraternities, national sororities. *Campus security:* 24-hour emergency response devices and patrols, student patrols, late-night transport/escort service, controlled dormitory access. *Student services:* health clinic, personal/psychological counseling, women's center, legal services.

Athletics Member NCAA. All Division II. *Intercollegiate sports:* baseball M(s), basketball M(s)/W(s), cross-country running M(s), golf M/W, soccer M(s)/W(s), softball W(s), tennis M(s)/W(s), volleyball W(s), water polo W. *Intramural sports:* baseball M, basketball M/W, cheerleading M/W, crew M/W, cross-country running M, fencing M/W, lacrosse M/W, rock climbing M/W, soccer M/W, softball M/W, swimming and diving M/W, volleyball M/W.
Standardized Tests *Required:* SAT or ACT (for admission).
Costs (2010–11) *Tuition:* state resident $0 full-time; nonresident $10,416 full-time, $372 per unit part-time. Full-time tuition and fees vary according to course load and degree level. Part-time tuition and fees vary according to course load and degree level. *Required fees:* $5508 full-time, $1866 per term part-time. *Room and board:* $10,522; room only: $6774. Room and board charges vary according to housing facility. *Waivers:* employees or children of employees.
Financial Aid Of all full-time matriculated undergraduates who enrolled in 2009, 4,502 applied for aid, 3,616 were judged to have need, 378 had their need fully met. 211 Federal Work-Study jobs (averaging $2845). 620 state and other part-time jobs (averaging $2570). In 2009, 226 non-need-based awards were made. *Average percent of need met:* 83%. *Average financial aid package:* $9977. *Average need-based loan:* $4126. *Average need-based gift aid:* $8664. *Average non-need-based aid:* $1532. *Average indebtedness upon graduation:* $18,201.
Applying *Options:* electronic application, early admission. *Application fee:* $55. *Required:* high school transcript. *Application deadlines:* rolling (freshmen), rolling (transfers). *Notification:* continuous (freshmen), continuous (transfers).
Freshman Application Contact Mr. Gustavo Flores, Director of Admissions, Sonoma State University, 1801 East Cotati Avenue, Rohnert Park, CA 94928-3609. *Phone:* 707-664-2778. *E-mail:* gustavo.flores@sonoma.edu. *Web site:* http://www.sonoma.edu/.

Southern California Institute of Architecture
Los Angeles, California

- **Independent** comprehensive, founded 1972
- **Urban** campus with easy access to Los Angeles
- **Coed**
- **Moderately difficult** entrance level

Faculty *Student/faculty ratio:* 15:1.
Academics *Calendar:* semesters. *Degrees:* certificates, bachelor's, master's, and doctoral-professional.
Student Life *Campus security:* 24-hour emergency response devices and patrols.
Standardized Tests *Required:* SAT or ACT (for admission).
Costs (2011–12) *Tuition:* $30,250 full-time. *Required fees:* $400 full-time.
Financial Aid Of all full-time matriculated undergraduates who enrolled in 2005, 173 applied for aid, 147 were judged to have need. In 2005, 12 non-need-based awards were made. *Average percent of need met:* 19. *Average financial aid package:* $11,946. *Average need-based loan:* $4589. *Average need-based gift aid:* $4271. *Average non-need-based aid:* $2239. *Average indebtedness upon graduation:* $33,000.
Applying *Options:* deferred entrance. *Application fee:* $75. *Required:* essay or personal statement, high school transcript, minimum 2 GPA, 3 letters of recommendation, portfolio. *Required for some:* interview.
Freshman Application Contact Mr. J.J. Jackman, Admissions Director, Southern California Institute of Architecture, 960 East Third Street, Los Angeles, CA 90013. *Phone:* 213-613-2200 Ext. 321. *Toll-free phone:* 800-774-7242. *Fax:* 213-613-2260. *E-mail:* jj@sciarc.edu. *Web site:* http://www.sciarc.edu/.

Southern California Institute of Technology
Anaheim, California

- **Proprietary** 4-year, founded 1987
- **Urban** campus with easy access to Anaheim, Los Angeles
- **Coed** 604 undergraduate students, 100% full-time, 25% women, 75% men

Undergraduates 604 full-time. *Retention:* 47% of full-time freshmen returned.
Freshmen *Admission:* 604 enrolled.
Academics *Degrees:* diplomas, associate, and bachelor's. *Special study options:* accelerated degree program, double majors, English as a second language.
Computers on Campus 300 computers/terminals are available on campus for general student use. Students can access the following: campus intranet. Campuswide network is available. Wireless service is available via entire campus.

Student Life *Housing:* college housing not available.
Standardized Tests *Required:* Entrance Exam (for admission).
Financial Aid Of all full-time matriculated undergraduates who enrolled in 2009, 8 Federal Work-Study jobs (averaging $2800).
Applying *Application fee:* $100. *Required:* interview, Entrance Examination. *Required for some:* high school transcript.
Freshman Application Contact Director of Admissions, Southern California Institute of Technology, 222 South Harbor Boulevard, Suite 200, Anaheim, CA 92805. *Phone:* 714-300-0300. *Fax:* 714-300-0311. *E-mail:* admissions@ scitech.edu. *Web site:* http://www.scitech.edu.

Southern California Seminary
El Cajon, California

Freshman Application Contact Thomas Pittman, Director of Admissions, Southern California Seminary, 2075 East Madison Avenue, El Cajon, CA 92019. *Phone:* 888-389-7244. *E-mail:* thpittman@socalsem.edu. *Web site:* http://www.socalsem.edu/.

Stanford University
Stanford, California

- **Independent** university, founded 1891
- **Suburban** 8180-acre campus with easy access to San Francisco and San Jose
- **Endowment** $13.9 billion
- **Coed** 6,940 undergraduate students, 99% full-time, 49% women, 51% men
- **Most difficult** entrance level, 7% of applicants were admitted

Undergraduates 6,889 full-time, 51 part-time. Students come from 52 states and territories; 89 other countries; 53% are from out of state; 7% Black or African American, non-Hispanic/Latino; 16% Hispanic/Latino; 18% Asian, non-Hispanic/Latino; 0.3% Native Hawaiian or other Pacific Islander, non-Hispanic/Latino; 1% American Indian or Alaska Native, non-Hispanic/Latino; 8% Two or more races, non-Hispanic/Latino; 8% Race/ethnicity unknown; 7% international; 0.3% transferred in; 91% live on campus. *Retention:* 98% of full-time freshmen returned.
Freshmen *Admission:* 32,024 applied, 2,340 admitted, 1,672 enrolled. *Test scores:* SAT critical reading scores over 500: 100%; SAT math scores over 500: 100%; SAT writing scores over 500: 99%; ACT scores over 18: 100%; SAT critical reading scores over 600: 94%; SAT math scores over 600: 97%; SAT writing scores over 600: 96%; ACT scores over 24: 99%; SAT critical reading scores over 700: 62%; SAT math scores over 700: 73%; SAT writing scores over 700: 69%; ACT scores over 30: 84%.
Faculty *Total:* 1,014, 99% full-time, 98% with terminal degrees. *Student/faculty ratio:* 6:1.
Academics *Calendar:* quarters. *Degrees:* bachelor's, master's, doctoral-professional, and doctoral-research/scholarship. *Special study options:* advanced placement credit, double majors, honors programs, independent study, internships, off-campus study, services for LD students, student-designed majors, study abroad, summer session for credit. *ROTC:* Army (c), Navy (c), Air Force (c).
Computers on Campus 1,000 computers/terminals and 22,000 ports are available on campus for general student use. Students can access the following: campus intranet, computer help desk, free student e-mail accounts, online (class) grades, online (class) registration, online (class) schedules. Campuswide network is available. 100% of college-owned or -operated housing units are wired for high-speed Internet access. Wireless service is available via entire campus.
Student Life *Housing:* on-campus residence required for freshman year. *Options:* coed, women-only, cooperative, disabled students. Campus housing is university owned. Freshman campus housing is guaranteed. *Activities and organizations:* drama/theater group, student-run newspaper, radio and television station, choral group, marching band, Ram's Head (theatre club), Axe Committee (athletic support), Business Association of Engineering Students, Asian-American Student Association, Stanford Daily, national fraternities, national sororities. *Campus security:* 24-hour emergency response devices and patrols, late-night transport/escort service, controlled dormitory access. *Student services:* health clinic, personal/psychological counseling, women's center, legal services.
Athletics Member NCAA, NAIA. All NCAA Division I except football (Division I-A). *Intercollegiate sports:* archery M(c)/W(c), baseball M(s), basketball M(s)/W(s), cheerleading M(c)/W, crew M(s)/W(s), cross-country running M(s)/W(s), equestrian sports M(c)/W(c), fencing M(s)/W(s), field hockey W(s), golf M(s)/W(s), gymnastics M(s)/W(s), ice hockey M(c), lacrosse M(c)/W(s), racquetball M(c)/W(c), rugby M(c)/W(c), sailing M/W, skiing (downhill) M(c)/W(c), soccer M(s)/W(s), softball W(s), squash M(c)/W, swimming and diving M(s)/W(s), tennis M(s)/W(s), track and field M(s)/W(s), ultimate Frisbee M(c)/W(c), volleyball M(s)/W(s), water polo M(s)/W(s), wrestling

M(s). *Intramural sports:* badminton M/W, baseball M, basketball M/W, bowling M/W, cross-country running M/W, field hockey W, football M/W, golf M/W, lacrosse W(c), soccer M(c)/W(c), softball M/W, table tennis M(c)/W(c), tennis M(c)/W(c), track and field M/W, volleyball M/W, water polo M/W.
Standardized Tests *Required:* SAT or ACT (for admission). *Recommended:* SAT Subject Tests (for admission).
Costs (2011–12) *Comprehensive fee:* $53,297 includes full-time tuition ($40,500), mandatory fees ($506), and room and board ($12,291). *Room and board:* Room and board charges vary according to board plan and housing facility. *Waivers:* employees or children of employees.
Financial Aid Of all full-time matriculated undergraduates who enrolled in 2008, 3,933 applied for aid, 3,545 were judged to have need, 3,004 had their need fully met. 750 Federal Work-Study jobs (averaging $2618). 1,575 state and other part-time jobs (averaging $1933). In 2008, 837 non-need-based awards were made. *Average percent of need met:* 100%. *Average financial aid package:* $40,593. *Average need-based loan:* $2747. *Average need-based gift aid:* $37,930. *Average non-need-based aid:* $3329. *Average indebtedness upon graduation:* $14,058.
Applying *Options:* electronic application, early action, deferred entrance. *Application fee:* $90. *Required:* essay or personal statement, high school transcript, 2 letters of recommendation. *Application deadlines:* 1/1 (freshmen), 3/15 (transfers), 11/1 (early action). *Notification:* 4/1 (freshmen), 5/15 (transfers), 12/15 (early action).
Freshman Application Contact Rick Shaw, Dean of Undergraduate Admission and Financial Aid, Stanford University, Montag Hall, 355 Galvez Street, Stanford, CA 94305-3020. *Phone:* 650-723-2091. *Fax:* 650-725-2846. *E-mail:* admission@stanford.edu. *Web site:* http://www.stanford.edu/.

Thomas Aquinas College
Santa Paula, California

- **Independent Roman Catholic** 4-year, founded 1971
- **Rural** 131-acre campus with easy access to Los Angeles
- **Endowment** $11.1 million
- **Coed** 355 undergraduate students, 100% full-time, 54% women, 46% men
- **Very difficult** entrance level, 76% of applicants were admitted

Undergraduates 355 full-time. Students come from 45 states and territories; 7 other countries; 60% are from out of state; 11% Hispanic/Latino; 0.8% Asian, non-Hispanic/Latino; 2% Two or more races, non-Hispanic/Latino; 7% Race/ethnicity unknown; 6% international; 100% live on campus. *Retention:* 90% of full-time freshmen returned.
Freshmen *Admission:* 168 applied, 128 admitted, 87 enrolled. *Average high school GPA:* 3.79. *Test scores:* SAT critical reading scores over 500: 99%; SAT math scores over 500: 97%; SAT writing scores over 500: 100%; ACT scores over 18: 100%; SAT critical reading scores over 600: 86%; SAT math scores over 600: 66%; SAT writing scores over 600: 67%; ACT scores over 24: 100%; SAT critical reading scores over 700: 41%; SAT math scores over 700: 10%; SAT writing scores over 700: 14%; ACT scores over 30: 36%.
Faculty *Total:* 36, 83% full-time, 72% with terminal degrees. *Student/faculty ratio:* 11:1.
Academics *Calendar:* semesters. *Degree:* bachelor's. *Special study options:* cooperative education.
Computers on Campus 20 computers/terminals and 24 ports are available on campus for general student use. Students can access the following: free student e-mail accounts. Campuswide network is available.
Student Life *Housing:* on-campus residence required through senior year. *Options:* men-only, women-only. Campus housing is university owned. Freshman campus housing is guaranteed. *Activities and organizations:* drama/theater group, choral group, Musical Groups (Choir, Chamber Orchestra), Theatre Groups, Language Clubs, Pro-Life Ministry, religious groups. *Campus security:* 24-hour emergency response devices, Daily Security Daytime Patrol. *Student services:* health clinic, personal/psychological counseling.
Athletics *Intramural sports:* basketball M/W, football M, soccer M/W, softball M/W, table tennis M/W, tennis M/W, ultimate Frisbee M/W, volleyball M/W.
Standardized Tests *Required:* SAT or ACT (for admission).
Costs (2011–12) *Comprehensive fee:* $30,400 includes full-time tuition ($22,850) and room and board ($7550). *Payment plan:* installment.
Financial Aid Of all full-time matriculated undergraduates who enrolled in 2009, 285 applied for aid, 278 were judged to have need, 278 had their need fully met. 247 state and other part-time jobs (averaging $3825). *Average percent of need met:* 100%. *Average financial aid package:* $19,324. *Average need-based loan:* $3625. *Average need-based gift aid:* $14,550. *Average indebtedness upon graduation:* $16,311. *Financial aid deadline:* 3/2.
Applying *Options:* electronic application, deferred entrance. *Required:* essay or personal statement, high school transcript, 3 letters of recommendation. *Required for some:* interview. *Recommended:* minimum 3 GPA. *Application deadlines:* rolling (freshmen), rolling (out-of-state freshmen). *Notification:* continuous (freshmen), continuous (out-of-state freshmen).

Freshman Application Contact Mr. Jonathan P. Daly, Director of Admissions, Thomas Aquinas College, 10000 Ojai Road, Santa Paula, CA 93060-9621. *Phone:* 805-525-4417 Ext. 5901. *Toll-free phone:* 800-634-9797. *Fax:* 805-421-5905. *E-mail:* admissions@thomasaquinas.edu. *Web site:* http://www.thomasaquinas.edu/.

TUI University
Cypress, California

- **Independent** university
- **Urban** campus
- **Coed** 3,685 undergraduate students, 51% full-time, 32% women, 68% men
- **Minimally difficult** entrance level

Undergraduates 1,891 full-time, 1,794 part-time. Students come from 50 states and territories; 41 other countries; 88% are from out of state; 13% Black or African American, non-Hispanic/Latino; 6% Hispanic/Latino; 3% Asian, non-Hispanic/Latino; 0.4% Native Hawaiian or other Pacific Islander, non-Hispanic/Latino; 0.6% American Indian or Alaska Native, non-Hispanic/Latino; 57% Race/ethnicity unknown; 97% transferred in.
Faculty *Total:* 268, 16% full-time. *Student/faculty ratio:* 21:1.
Academics *Calendar:* four 12 week sessions per year. *Degrees:* certificates, diplomas, bachelor's, master's, doctoral-research/scholarship, post-master's, and postbachelor's certificates (offers only online degree programs). *Special study options:* adult/continuing education programs, distance learning, double majors, honors programs, part-time degree program, summer session for credit.
Computers on Campus Students can access the following: computer help desk, free student e-mail accounts, online (class) grades, online (class) registration, online (class) schedules. Campuswide network is available.
Student Life *Housing:* college housing not available.
Costs (2011–12) *Tuition:* $9440 full-time, $295 per semester hour part-time. Full-time tuition and fees vary according to course load, degree level, and program. Part-time tuition and fees vary according to course load, degree level, and program. *Payment plans:* installment, deferred payment. *Waivers:* employees or children of employees.
Financial Aid Of all full-time matriculated undergraduates who enrolled in 2008, 650 applied for aid, 650 were judged to have need, 552 had their need fully met. In 2008, 55 non-need-based awards were made. *Average percent of need met:* 98%. *Average financial aid package:* $4415. *Average need-based gift aid:* $3293. *Average non-need-based aid:* $5898. *Average indebtedness upon graduation:* $38,298.
Applying *Options:* electronic application. *Required:* high school transcript, minimum 3 GPA. *Required for some:* essay or personal statement. *Application deadlines:* rolling (freshmen), rolling (out-of-state freshmen), rolling (transfers). *Notification:* continuous (freshmen), continuous (out-of-state freshmen), continuous (transfers).
Freshman Application Contact TUI University, 5665 Plaza Drive, 3rd Floor, Cypress, CA 90630. *Phone:* 714-816-0366 Ext. 2015. *Web site:* http://www.tuiu.edu/.

United States University
National City, California

Freshman Application Contact Admissions, United States University, 140 West 16th Street, National City, CA 91950. *Phone:* 619-477-6310. *Toll-free phone:* 888-422-3381. *Fax:* 619-477-7340. *Web site:* http://www.usuniversity.edu/.

University of California, Berkeley
Berkeley, California

- **State-supported** university, founded 1868, part of University of California System
- **Urban** 1232-acre campus with easy access to San Francisco
- **Endowment** $2.6 billion
- **Coed** 25,540 undergraduate students
- **Very difficult** entrance level, 22% of applicants were admitted

Undergraduates 7% are from out of state; 3% Black or African American, non-Hispanic/Latino; 12% Hispanic/Latino; 40% Asian, non-Hispanic/Latino; 0.6% American Indian or Alaska Native, non-Hispanic/Latino; 7% Race/ethnicity unknown; 7% international; 35% live on campus. *Retention:* 97% of full-time freshmen returned.
Freshmen *Admission:* 50,393 applied, 10,844 admitted. *Average high school GPA:* 3.84. *Test scores:* SAT critical reading scores over 500: 94%; SAT math scores over 500: 97%; SAT writing scores over 500: 96%; ACT scores over 18: 99%; SAT critical reading scores over 600: 76%; SAT math scores over 600: 84%; SAT writing scores over 600: 80%; ACT scores over 24: 89%; SAT criti-

cal reading scores over 700: 34%; SAT math scores over 700: 56%; SAT writing scores over 700: 45%; ACT scores over 30: 59%.
Academics *Calendar:* semesters. *Degrees:* bachelor's, master's, doctoral-professional, doctoral-research/scholarship, and postbachelor's certificates. *Special study options:* accelerated degree program, adult/continuing education programs, advanced placement credit, double majors, English as a second language, honors programs, independent study, internships, off-campus study, services for LD students, student-designed majors, study abroad, summer session for credit. *ROTC:* Army (b), Navy (b), Air Force (b).
Computers on Campus Students can access the following: computer help desk, free student e-mail accounts, online (class) grades, online (class) registration, online (class) schedules. Campuswide network is available.
Student Life *Housing options:* coed, men-only, women-only, cooperative, disabled students. Campus housing is university owned and is provided by a third party. Freshman campus housing is guaranteed. *Activities and organizations:* drama/theater group, student-run newspaper, radio and television station, choral group, marching band, national fraternities, national sororities. *Campus security:* 24-hour emergency response devices and patrols, late-night transport/escort service, controlled dormitory access, Office of Emergency Preparedness. *Student services:* health clinic, personal/psychological counseling, women's center, legal services.
Athletics Member NCAA. All Division I. *Intercollegiate sports:* basketball M/W, crew M/W, cross-country running M/W, field hockey W, football M, golf M/W, gymnastics W, lacrosse W, rugby M, soccer M/W, softball W, swimming and diving M/W, tennis M/W, track and field M/W, volleyball W, water polo M/W. *Intramural sports:* basketball M/W, soccer M/W, softball M/W, tennis M/W, ultimate Frisbee M/W, volleyball M/W.
Standardized Tests *Required:* SAT and SAT Subject Tests or ACT (for admission).
Costs (2011–12) *Tuition:* state resident $10,152 full-time; nonresident $33,030 full-time. Full-time tuition and fees vary according to course load, degree level, and program. Part-time tuition and fees vary according to course load, degree level, and program. *Room and board:* Room and board charges vary according to board plan and housing facility. *Payment plan:* installment.
Financial Aid Of all full-time matriculated undergraduates who enrolled in 2009, 17,140 applied for aid, 14,530 were judged to have need, 3,301 had their need fully met. In 2009, 1192 non-need-based awards were made. *Average percent of need met:* 81%. *Average financial aid package:* $19,261. *Average need-based loan:* $5874. *Average need-based gift aid:* $15,863. *Average non-need-based aid:* $6472. *Average indebtedness upon graduation:* $16,056. *Financial aid deadline:* 3/2.
Applying *Options:* electronic application. *Application fee:* $60. *Required:* essay or personal statement, high school transcript. *Application deadlines:* 11/30 (freshmen), 11/30 (transfers). *Notification:* 3/31 (freshmen), 4/30 (transfers).
Freshman Application Contact University of California, Berkeley, Berkeley, CA 94720-1500. *Phone:* 510-642-2316. *Web site:* http://www.berkeley.edu/.

University of California, Davis
Davis, California

- **State-supported** university, founded 1905, part of University of California System
- **Suburban** 5993-acre campus with easy access to San Francisco
- **Coed** 24,737 undergraduate students, 99% full-time, 55% women, 45% men
- **Very difficult** entrance level, 46% of applicants were admitted

Undergraduates 24,425 full-time, 312 part-time. Students come from 49 states and territories; 105 other countries; 2% are from out of state; 3% Black or African American, non-Hispanic/Latino; 15% Hispanic/Latino; 38% Asian, non-Hispanic/Latino; 0.5% Native Hawaiian or other Pacific Islander, non-Hispanic/Latino; 0.6% American Indian or Alaska Native, non-Hispanic/Latino; 2% Two or more races, non-Hispanic/Latino; 5% Race/ethnicity unknown; 3% international; 11% transferred in; 19% live on campus. *Retention:* 92% of full-time freshmen returned.
Freshmen *Admission:* 43,306 applied, 20,043 admitted, 4,504 enrolled. *Average high school GPA:* 3.86. *Test scores:* SAT critical reading scores over 500: 85%; SAT math scores over 500: 92%; SAT writing scores over 500: 86%; ACT scores over 18: 99%; SAT critical reading scores over 600: 51%; SAT math scores over 600: 68%; SAT writing scores over 600: 53%; ACT scores over 24: 77%; SAT critical reading scores over 700: 11%; SAT math scores over 700: 22%; SAT writing scores over 700: 13%; ACT scores over 30: 26%.
Faculty *Total:* 1,620, 91% full-time, 98% with terminal degrees. *Student/faculty ratio:* 16:1.
Academics *Calendar:* quarters. *Degrees:* bachelor's, master's, doctoral-other, doctoral-professional, doctoral-research/scholarship, post-master's, and postbachelor's certificates. *Special study options:* academic remediation for entering students, adult/continuing education programs, advanced placement credit, double majors, English as a second language, freshman honors college, honors programs, independent study, internships, part-time degree program, services

for LD students, student-designed majors, study abroad, summer session for credit. *ROTC:* Army (b), Navy (c), Air Force (c).

Computers on Campus 1,500 computers/terminals and 550 ports are available on campus for general student use. Students can access the following: campus intranet, computer help desk, free student e-mail accounts, online (class) grades, online (class) registration, online (class) schedules, software packages. Campuswide network is available. 100% of college-owned or -operated housing units are wired for high-speed Internet access. Wireless service is available via classrooms, libraries.

Student Life *Housing options:* coed, women-only, cooperative, disabled students. Campus housing is university owned, leased by the school and is provided by a third party. Freshman campus housing is guaranteed. *Activities and organizations:* drama/theater group, student-run newspaper, radio and television station, choral group, marching band, Filipino Student Organization, Vietnamese Student Association, Jewish Student Union, Alpha Phi Omega, national fraternities, national sororities. *Campus security:* 24-hour emergency response devices and patrols, student patrols, late-night transport/escort service, controlled dormitory access, Rape prevention programs. *Student services:* health clinic, personal/psychological counseling, women's center, legal services.

Athletics Member NCAA. All Division I except football (Division I-AA). *Intercollegiate sports:* baseball M(s), basketball M(s)/W(s), cross-country running M(s)/W(s), field hockey W(s), golf M(s)/W(s), gymnastics W(s), lacrosse W(s), soccer M(s)/W(s), softball W(s), swimming and diving W(s), tennis M(s)/W(s), track and field M(s)/W(s), volleyball W(s), water polo M(s)/W(s). *Intramural sports:* archery M(c)/W(c), badminton M(c)/W(c), basketball M/W, crew M(c)/W(c), equestrian sports M(c)/W(c), fencing M(c)/W(c), football M/W, golf M/W, gymnastics M(c), ice hockey M(c)/W, lacrosse M(c)/W(c), racquetball M(c)/W(c), riflery M(c)/W(c), rugby M(c), sailing M(c)/W(c), skiing (cross-country) M(c)/W(c), skiing (downhill) M(c)/W(c), soccer M/W, softball M/W, swimming and diving W(c), table tennis M/W, tennis M/W, volleyball M(c)/W, water polo W(c).

Standardized Tests *Required:* SAT or ACT (for admission), SAT Subject Tests (for admission).

Costs (2011–12) *Tuition:* state resident $9402 full-time; nonresident $32,281 full-time. *Required fees:* $2582 full-time. *Room and board:* $12,498. Room and board charges vary according to board plan. *Payment plan:* deferred payment.

Financial Aid Of all full-time matriculated undergraduates who enrolled in 2009, 17,282 applied for aid, 15,066 were judged to have need, 2,971 had their need fully met. In 2009, 789 non-need-based awards were made. *Average percent of need met:* 81%. *Average financial aid package:* $18,136. *Average need-based loan:* $5386. *Average need-based gift aid:* $14,883. *Average non-need-based aid:* $5918. *Average indebtedness upon graduation:* $16,659.

Applying *Options:* electronic application. *Application fee:* $60. *Required:* essay or personal statement, high school transcript, minimum 2.8 GPA, high school subject requirements. *Application deadlines:* 11/30 (freshmen), 11/30 (transfers). *Notification:* 3/15 (freshmen), continuous until 3/15 (transfers).

Freshman Application Contact Frank Wada, Interim Deputy Director of Undergraduate Admissions, University of California, Davis, Undergraduate Admission and Outreach Services, 178 Mrak Hall, Davis, CA 95616. *Phone:* 530-752-1011. *Fax:* 530-752-1280. *E-mail:* undergraduateadmissions@ucdavis.edu. *Web site:* http://www.ucdavis.edu/.

University of California, Irvine
Irvine, California

- **State-supported** university, founded 1965, part of University of California System
- **Suburban** 1477-acre campus with easy access to Los Angeles
- **Coed** 21,976 undergraduate students, 98% full-time, 54% women, 46% men
- **Very difficult** entrance level, 45% of applicants were admitted

Undergraduates 21,522 full-time, 454 part-time. Students come from 38 states and territories; 87 other countries; 1% are from out of state; 2% Black or African American, non-Hispanic/Latino; 15% Hispanic/Latino; 51% Asian, non-Hispanic/Latino; 0.2% Native Hawaiian or other Pacific Islander, non-Hispanic/Latino; 0.3% American Indian or Alaska Native, non-Hispanic/Latino; 1% Two or more races, non-Hispanic/Latino; 6% Race/ethnicity unknown; 3% international; 8% transferred in; 41% live on campus. *Retention:* 95% of full-time freshmen returned.

Freshmen *Admission:* 45,742 applied, 20,678 admitted, 4,411 enrolled. *Average high school GPA:* 3.88. *Test scores:* SAT critical reading scores over 500: 83%; SAT math scores over 500: 92%; SAT writing scores over 500: 87%; SAT critical reading scores over 600: 43%; SAT math scores over 600: 65%; SAT writing scores over 600: 46%; SAT critical reading scores over 700: 10%; SAT math scores over 700: 22%; SAT writing scores over 700: 9%.

Faculty *Total:* 1,886, 76% full-time, 98% with terminal degrees. *Student/faculty ratio:* 19:1.

Academics *Calendar:* quarters. *Degrees:* bachelor's, master's, doctoral-professional, doctoral-research/scholarship, and postbachelor's certificates. *Special study options:* accelerated degree program, advanced placement credit, distance learning, double majors, English as a second language, honors programs, independent study, internships, off-campus study, services for LD students, study abroad, summer session for credit. *ROTC:* Army (c), Air Force (c). *Unusual degree programs:* 3-2 business administration.

Computers on Campus 1,500 computers/terminals are available on campus for general student use. Students can access the following: campus intranet, computer help desk, free student e-mail accounts, online (class) grades, online (class) registration, online (class) schedules. Campuswide network is available. Wireless service is available via entire campus.

Student Life *Housing options:* coed, men-only, women-only, disabled students. Campus housing is university owned and is provided by a third party. Freshman campus housing is guaranteed. *Activities and organizations:* drama/theater group, student-run newspaper, radio station, choral group, national fraternities, national sororities. *Campus security:* 24-hour emergency response devices and patrols, late-night transport/escort service, controlled dormitory access. *Student services:* health clinic, personal/psychological counseling.

Athletics Member NCAA. All Division I. *Intercollegiate sports:* baseball M(s), basketball M(s)/W(s), cross-country running M(s)/W(s), golf M(s)/W(s), soccer M(s)/W(s), tennis M(s)/W(s), track and field M(s)/W(s), volleyball M(s)/W(s), water polo M(s)/W(s). *Intramural sports:* archery M(c)/W(c), badminton M(c)/W(c), basketball M/W, bowling M/W, cheerleading M(c)/W(c), crew M(c)/W(c), equestrian sports M(c)/W(c), fencing M(c)/W(c), field hockey M(c)/W(c), golf M(c)/W(c), ice hockey M(c), lacrosse M(c), racquetball M/W, rugby M(c), sailing M(c)/W(c), skiing (downhill) M(c)/W(c), soccer M/W, softball W, swimming and diving M/W, table tennis M(c)/W(c), tennis M/W, track and field M/W, ultimate Frisbee M/W, volleyball M/W, water polo M/W, wrestling M/W.

Standardized Tests *Required:* SAT or ACT (for admission). *Recommended:* SAT Subject Tests (for admission).

Costs (2011–12) *Tuition:* state resident $9402 full-time; nonresident $32,281 full-time. *Required fees:* $2525 full-time. *Room and board:* $11,400. Room and board charges vary according to board plan and housing facility. *Payment plan:* installment.

Financial Aid Of all full-time matriculated undergraduates who enrolled in 2009, 15,791 applied for aid, 13,305 were judged to have need, 4,649 had their need fully met. 3,387 Federal Work-Study jobs (averaging $1545). In 2009, 595 non-need-based awards were made. *Average percent of need met:* 84%. *Average financial aid package:* $18,359. *Average need-based loan:* $6305. *Average need-based gift aid:* $14,919. *Average non-need-based aid:* $8633. *Average indebtedness upon graduation:* $16,878. *Financial aid deadline:* 5/1.

Applying *Options:* electronic application. *Application fee:* $60. *Required:* essay or personal statement, high school transcript. *Application deadlines:* 11/30 (freshmen), 11/30 (transfers). *Notification:* 3/31 (freshmen), 5/1 (transfers).

Freshman Application Contact University of California, Irvine, Irvine, CA 92697. *Phone:* 949-824-6703. *Web site:* http://www.uci.edu/.

University of California, Los Angeles
Los Angeles, California

- **State-supported** university, founded 1919, part of University of California System
- **Urban** 419-acre campus with easy access to Los Angeles
- **Coed** 26,162 undergraduate students, 97% full-time, 55% women, 45% men
- **Very difficult** entrance level, 23% of applicants were admitted

Undergraduates 25,417 full-time, 745 part-time. Students come from 54 states and territories; 71 other countries; 5% are from out of state; 4% Black or African American, non-Hispanic/Latino; 16% Hispanic/Latino; 36% Asian, non-Hispanic/Latino; 0.2% Native Hawaiian or other Pacific Islander, non-Hispanic/Latino; 0.4% American Indian or Alaska Native, non-Hispanic/Latino; 2% Two or more races, non-Hispanic/Latino; 4% Race/ethnicity unknown; 6% international; 12% transferred in; 36% live on campus. *Retention:* 97% of full-time freshmen returned.

Freshmen *Admission:* 57,670 applied, 13,088 admitted, 4,636 enrolled. *Average high school GPA:* 4.25. *Test scores:* SAT critical reading scores over 500: 91%; SAT math scores over 500: 94%; SAT writing scores over 500: 93%; ACT scores over 18: 98%; SAT critical reading scores over 600: 64%; SAT math scores over 600: 77%; SAT writing scores over 600: 70%; ACT scores over 24: 82%; SAT critical reading scores over 700: 20%; SAT math scores over 700: 42%; SAT writing scores over 700: 30%; ACT scores over 30: 44%.

Faculty *Total:* 2,595, 77% full-time, 98% with terminal degrees. *Student/faculty ratio:* 17:1.

Academics *Calendar:* quarters. *Degrees:* bachelor's, master's, doctoral-professional, and doctoral-research/scholarship. *Special study options:* accelerated degree program, advanced placement credit, distance learning, double majors, freshman honors college, honors programs, independent study, internships, off-campus study, services for LD students, student-designed majors,

study abroad, summer session for credit. *ROTC:* Army (b), Navy (b), Air Force (b).
Computers on Campus 3,930 computers/terminals are available on campus for general student use. Students can access the following: campus intranet, computer help desk, free student e-mail accounts, online (class) grades, online (class) registration, online (class) schedules. Campuswide network is available. 100% of college-owned or -operated housing units are wired for high-speed Internet access. Wireless service is available via entire campus.
Student Life *Housing options:* coed, disabled students. Campus housing is university owned. Freshman campus housing is guaranteed. *Activities and organizations:* drama/theater group, student-run newspaper, radio and television station, choral group, marching band, national fraternities, national sororities. *Campus security:* 24-hour emergency response devices and patrols, student patrols, late-night transport/escort service, controlled dormitory access. *Student services:* health clinic, personal/psychological counseling, women's center, legal services.
Athletics Member NCAA. All Division I except football (Division I-A). *Intercollegiate sports:* baseball M(s), basketball M(s)/W(s), crew W(s), cross-country running M(s)/W(s), golf M(s)/W(s), gymnastics W(s), soccer M(s)/W(s), softball W(s), swimming and diving W(s), tennis M(s)/W(s), track and field M(s)/W(s), volleyball M(s)/W(s), water polo M(s)/W(s). *Intramural sports:* archery M/W, badminton M/W, basketball M/W, bowling M/W, crew M/W, cross-country running M/W, fencing M/W, field hockey M/W, football M/W, golf M/W, gymnastics M/W, ice hockey M/W, lacrosse M/W, racquetball M/W, riflery M/W, rugby M/W, sailing M/W, skiing (cross-country) M/W, skiing (downhill) M/W, soccer M/W, softball M/W, squash M/W, swimming and diving M/W, table tennis M/W, tennis M/W, track and field M/W, ultimate Frisbee M/W, volleyball M/W, water polo M/W.
Standardized Tests *Required:* SAT or ACT (for admission).
Costs (2010–11) *Tuition:* state resident $0 full-time; nonresident $22,879 full-time. *Required fees:* $11,868 full-time. *Room and board:* $13,734. Room and board charges vary according to board plan and housing facility.
Financial Aid Of all full-time matriculated undergraduates who enrolled in 2009, 15,212 applied for aid, 13,948 were judged to have need, 3,458 had their need fully met. 2,848 Federal Work-Study jobs (averaging $1953). 776 state and other part-time jobs (averaging $1029). In 2009, 924 non-need-based awards were made. *Average percent of need met:* 82%. *Average financial aid package:* $18,896. *Average need-based loan:* $6471. *Average need-based gift aid:* $15,364. *Average non-need-based aid:* $5074. *Average indebtedness upon graduation:* $18,203.
Applying *Options:* electronic application. *Application fee:* $60. *Required:* essay or personal statement. *Application deadlines:* 11/30 (freshmen), 11/30 (transfers). *Notification:* 3/31 (freshmen), 4/30 (transfers).
Freshman Application Contact Dr. Vu T. Tran, Director of Undergraduate Admissions, University of California, Los Angeles, 405 Hilgard Avenue, Box 951436, Los Angeles, CA 90095-1436. *Phone:* 310-825-3101. *E-mail:* ugadm@saonet.ucla.edu. *Web site:* http://www.ucla.edu/.

University of California, Merced

Merced, California

- **State-supported** university, part of University of California System
- **Small-town** 815-acre campus with easy access to Fresno
- **Endowment** $22.8 million
- **Coed** 4,138 undergraduate students, 99% full-time, 50% women, 50% men
- **Moderately difficult** entrance level, 89% of applicants were admitted

Undergraduates 4,107 full-time, 31 part-time. Students come from 20 states and territories; 14 other countries; 1% are from out of state; 6% Black or African American, non-Hispanic/Latino; 35% Hispanic/Latino; 29% Asian, non-Hispanic/Latino; 0.7% Native Hawaiian or other Pacific Islander, non-Hispanic/Latino; 0.5% American Indian or Alaska Native, non-Hispanic/Latino; 2% Two or more races, non-Hispanic/Latino; 4% Race/ethnicity unknown; 1% international; 5% transferred in; 39% live on campus. *Retention:* 87% of full-time freshmen returned.
Freshmen *Admission:* 22,902 applied, 20,296 admitted, 1,341 enrolled. *Average high school GPA:* 3.45. *Test scores:* SAT critical reading scores over 500: 49%; SAT math scores over 500: 61%; SAT writing scores over 500: 51%; SAT critical reading scores over 600: 14%; SAT math scores over 600: 22%; SAT writing scores over 600: 11%; SAT critical reading scores over 700: 2%; SAT math scores over 700: 3%; SAT writing scores over 700: 1%.
Faculty *Total:* 242, 84% full-time, 74% with terminal degrees. *Student/faculty ratio:* 18:1.
Academics *Degrees:* bachelor's, master's, and doctoral-research/scholarship. *Special study options:* academic remediation for entering students, advanced placement credit, double majors, internships, off-campus study, part-time degree program, services for LD students, study abroad, summer session for credit.
Computers on Campus 157 computers/terminals are available on campus for general student use. Students can access the following: campus intranet, com-

puter help desk, free student e-mail accounts, online (class) grades, online (class) registration, online (class) schedules. Campuswide network is available. 100% of college-owned or -operated housing units are wired for high-speed Internet access. Wireless service is available via entire campus.
Student Life *Housing options:* coed, disabled students. Campus housing is university owned. Freshman campus housing is guaranteed. *Activities and organizations:* student-run newspaper, radio station, choral group, marching band, national fraternities, national sororities. *Campus security:* 24-hour emergency response devices. *Student services:* health clinic, personal/psychological counseling, women's center.
Athletics *Intramural sports:* badminton M/W, basketball M/W, soccer M/W, softball M/W, ultimate Frisbee M/W, volleyball M/W.
Standardized Tests *Required:* SAT or ACT (for admission), SAT Subject Tests (for admission).
Costs (2011–12) *Tuition:* state resident $9402 full-time, $4701 per year part-time; nonresident $32,280 full-time, $16,140 per year part-time. *Required fees:* $728 full-time. *Room and board:* $12,801.
Applying *Options:* electronic application. *Application fee:* $60. *Required:* essay or personal statement, high school transcript, minimum 3.0 high school GPA for California residents. *Application deadlines:* 1/1 (freshmen), 1/31 (transfers). *Notification:* 3/31 (freshmen), 4/30 (transfers).
Freshman Application Contact Susan Fauroat, Associate Director of Admissions and Outreach, University of California, Merced, 5200 North Lake Road, Merced, CA 95343. *Phone:* 209-228-4241. *E-mail:* admissions@ucmerced.edu. *Web site:* http://www.ucmerced.edu/.

University of California, Riverside

Riverside, California

- **State-supported** university, founded 1954, part of University of California System
- **Urban** 1200-acre campus with easy access to Los Angeles
- **Endowment** $120.5 million
- **Coed**
- **Very difficult** entrance level

Faculty *Student/faculty ratio:* 19:1.
Academics *Calendar:* quarters. *Degrees:* bachelor's, master's, doctoral-research/scholarship, and postbachelor's certificates.
Student Life *Campus security:* 24-hour emergency response devices and patrols, student patrols, late-night transport/escort service, controlled dormitory access.
Athletics Member NCAA. All Division I.
Standardized Tests *Required:* SAT or ACT (for admission), SAT Subject Tests (for admission).
Costs (2010–11) *Tuition:* state resident $0 full-time; nonresident $22,881 full-time. Full-time tuition and fees vary according to course load. Part-time tuition and fees vary according to course load. *Required fees:* $11,029 full-time. *Room and board:* $11,600. Room and board charges vary according to board plan and housing facility.
Financial Aid Of all full-time matriculated undergraduates who enrolled in 2009, 14,753 applied for aid, 13,381 were judged to have need, 4,575 had their need fully met. 3,839 Federal Work-Study jobs (averaging $2063). In 2009, 105 non-need-based awards were made. *Average percent of need met:* 85. *Average financial aid package:* $19,431. *Average need-based loan:* $6182. *Average need-based gift aid:* $15,329. *Average non-need-based aid:* $6901. *Average indebtedness upon graduation:* $18,094. *Financial aid deadline:* 3/2.
Applying *Options:* electronic application. *Application fee:* $60. *Required:* essay or personal statement, high school transcript, minimum 3 GPA.
Freshman Application Contact Emily Engelschall, Director, Undergraduate Recruitment, University of California, Riverside, 3221 Student Services, 900 University Avenue, Riverside, CA 92521. *Phone:* 951-827-3986. *Fax:* 951-827-6344. *E-mail:* discover@ucr.edu. *Web site:* http://www.ucr.edu/.

University of California, San Diego

La Jolla, California

- **State-supported** university, founded 1959, part of University of California System
- **Suburban** 1976-acre campus with easy access to San Diego
- **Coed**
- **Very difficult** entrance level

Faculty *Student/faculty ratio:* 19:1.
Academics *Calendar:* quarters. *Degrees:* bachelor's, master's, doctoral-professional, and doctoral-research/scholarship.
Student Life *Campus security:* 24-hour emergency response devices and patrols, student patrols, late-night transport/escort service, crime prevention programs.
Athletics Member NCAA. All Division II.

Standardized Tests *Required:* SAT or ACT (for admission), ACT Assessment with Writing or SAT Reasoning Test, plus two SAT Subject Tests (for admission).

Costs (2010–11) *Tuition:* state resident $0 full-time; nonresident $22,881 full-time. *Required fees:* $12,176 full-time. *Room and board:* $11,719. Room and board charges vary according to board plan and housing facility.

Financial Aid *Of all full-time matriculated undergraduates who enrolled in 2009,* 15,627 applied for aid, 13,651 were judged to have need, 4,901 had their need fully met. *In 2009,* 736 non-need-based awards were made. *Average percent of need met:* 86. *Average financial aid package:* $18,560. *Average need-based loan:* $5833. *Average need-based gift aid:* $13,983. *Average non-need-based aid:* $9419. *Average indebtedness upon graduation:* $17,679.

Applying *Options:* electronic application. *Application fee:* $60. *Required:* essay or personal statement, high school transcript, minimum 2.8 GPA. *Required for some:* minimum 3.4 GPA.

Freshman Application Contact Ms. Mae Brown, Assistant Vice Chancellor, Admissions and Relations with Schools, University of California, San Diego, 9500 Gilman Drive, 0021, La Jolla, CA 92093-0021. *Phone:* 858-534-4831. *E-mail:* admissionsreply@ucsd.edu. *Web site:* http://www.ucsd.edu/.

University of California, Santa Barbara

Santa Barbara, California

- **State-supported** university, founded 1909, part of University of California System
- **Suburban** 989-acre campus
- **Endowment** $98.9 million
- **Coed** 19,186 undergraduate students, 98% full-time, 53% women, 47% men
- **Very difficult** entrance level, 46% of applicants were admitted

Undergraduates 18,807 full-time, 379 part-time. Students come from 50 states and territories; 95 other countries; 3% are from out of state; 8% transferred in; 33% live on campus. *Retention:* 91% of full-time freshmen returned.

Freshmen *Admission:* 46,671 applied, 21,241 admitted, 3,716 enrolled. *Average high school GPA:* 3.92. *Test scores:* SAT critical reading scores over 500: 90%; SAT math scores over 500: 91%; SAT writing scores over 500: 89%; ACT scores over 18: 98%; SAT critical reading scores over 600: 52%; SAT math scores over 600: 62%; SAT writing scores over 600: 53%; ACT scores over 24: 82%; SAT critical reading scores over 700: 11%; SAT math scores over 700: 18%; SAT writing scores over 700: 12%; ACT scores over 30: 25%.

Faculty *Total:* 1,057, 86% full-time, 98% with terminal degrees. *Student/faculty ratio:* 17:1.

Academics *Calendar:* quarters plus 6-week summer term. *Degrees:* bachelor's, master's, doctoral-research/scholarship, post-master's, and postbachelor's certificates. *Special study options:* accelerated degree program, advanced placement credit, cooperative education, double majors, English as a second language, honors programs, independent study, internships, off-campus study, services for LD students, student-designed majors, study abroad, summer session for credit. *ROTC:* Army (b).

Computers on Campus 700 computers/terminals are available on campus for general student use. Students can access the following: computer help desk, free student e-mail accounts, online (class) grades, online (class) registration, online (class) schedules. Campuswide network is available. Wireless service is available via dorm rooms, libraries, student centers.

Student Life *Housing:* on-campus residence required for freshman year. *Options:* coed, cooperative. Campus housing is university owned and is provided by a third party. Freshman applicants given priority for college housing. *Activities and organizations:* drama/theater group, student-run newspaper, radio and television station, choral group, national fraternities, national sororities. *Campus security:* 24-hour emergency response devices, late-night transport/escort service. *Student services:* health clinic, personal/psychological counseling, women's center, legal services.

Athletics Member NCAA. All Division I. *Intercollegiate sports:* baseball M(s), basketball M(s)/W(s), bowling M(c)/W(c), crew M(c)/W(c), cross-country running M(s)/W(s), equestrian sports M(c)/W(c), fencing M(c)/W(c), field hockey W(c), golf M(s), gymnastics M(s)/W(s), lacrosse M(c)/W(c), rugby M(c), sailing M(c)/W(c), skiing (downhill) M(c)/W(c), soccer M(s)/W(s), softball W(s), swimming and diving M(s)/W(s), tennis M(s)/W(s), track and field M(s)/W(s), ultimate Frisbee M(c)/W(c), volleyball M(s)/W(s), water polo M(s)/W(s). *Intramural sports:* badminton M/W, basketball M/W, bowling M/W, cross-country running M/W, football M/W, golf M/W, gymnastics M/W, racquetball M/W, soccer M/W, softball M/W, squash M/W, tennis M/W, ultimate Frisbee M/W, volleyball M/W, water polo M/W.

Standardized Tests *Required:* SAT or ACT (for admission), SAT Subject Tests (for admission).

Costs (2010–11) *Tuition:* state resident $0 full-time; nonresident $22,879 full-time. *Required fees:* $11,686 full-time. *Room and board:* $13,109. Room and board charges vary according to board plan and housing facility. *Payment plan:* installment.

Financial Aid Of all full-time matriculated undergraduates who enrolled in 2009, 12,791 applied for aid, 10,275 were judged to have need, 2,885 had their need fully met. In 2009, 423 non-need-based awards were made. *Average percent of need met:* 82%. *Average financial aid package:* $17,380. *Average need-based loan:* $6264. *Average need-based gift aid:* $13,876. *Average non-need-based aid:* $6021. *Average indebtedness upon graduation:* $17,768.

Applying *Options:* electronic application. *Application fee:* $60. *Required:* essay or personal statement, high school transcript. *Required for some:* interview. *Application deadlines:* 11/30 (freshmen), 11/30 (transfers). *Notification:* 3/15 (freshmen), 5/1 (transfers).

Freshman Application Contact Office of Admissions, University of California, Santa Barbara, 1210 Cheadle Hall, Santa Barbara, CA 93106-2014. *Phone:* 805-893-2881. *Fax:* 805-893-2676. *E-mail:* admissions@sa.ucsb.edu. *Web site:* http://www.ucsb.edu/.

University of California, Santa Cruz

Santa Cruz, California

- **State-supported** university, founded 1965, part of University of California System
- **Small-town** 2000-acre campus with easy access to San Francisco and San Jose
- **Endowment** $200.3 million
- **Coed** 15,668 undergraduate students, 98% full-time, 53% women, 47% men
- **Very difficult** entrance level, 65% of applicants were admitted

Undergraduates 15,411 full-time, 257 part-time. Students come from 38 states and territories; 16 other countries; 2% are from out of state; 2% Black or African American, non-Hispanic/Latino; 20% Hispanic/Latino; 21% Asian, non-Hispanic/Latino; 0.2% Native Hawaiian or other Pacific Islander, non-Hispanic/Latino; 0.7% American Indian or Alaska Native, non-Hispanic/Latino; 4% Two or more races, non-Hispanic/Latino; 7% Race/ethnicity unknown; 0.5% international; 8% transferred in; 48% live on campus. *Retention:* 89% of full-time freshmen returned.

Freshmen *Admission:* 27,658 applied, 17,843 admitted, 3,291 enrolled. *Average high school GPA:* 3.61. *Test scores:* SAT critical reading scores over 500: 76%; SAT math scores over 500: 81%; SAT writing scores over 500: 78%; ACT scores over 18: 94%; SAT critical reading scores over 600: 38%; SAT math scores over 600: 45%; SAT writing scores over 600: 37%; ACT scores over 24: 61%; SAT critical reading scores over 700: 7%; SAT math scores over 700: 9%; SAT writing scores over 700: 6%; ACT scores over 30: 11%.

Faculty *Total:* 803, 70% full-time, 95% with terminal degrees. *Student/faculty ratio:* 18:1.

Academics *Calendar:* quarters. *Degrees:* bachelor's, master's, doctoral-research/scholarship, and postbachelor's certificates. *Special study options:* accelerated degree program, advanced placement credit, cooperative education, double majors, freshman honors college, honors programs, independent study, internships, off-campus study, services for LD students, student-designed majors, study abroad, summer session for credit. *ROTC:* Army (c), Navy (c), Air Force (c).

Computers on Campus Students can access the following: campus intranet, computer help desk, free student e-mail accounts, online (class) grades, online (class) registration, online (class) schedules. Campuswide network is available. 100% of college-owned or -operated housing units are wired for high-speed Internet access. Wireless service is available via entire campus.

Student Life *Housing options:* coed, men-only, women-only, cooperative. Campus housing is university owned. Freshman campus housing is guaranteed. *Activities and organizations:* drama/theater group, student-run newspaper, radio and television station, choral group, Filipino Student Association, Movimiento Estudiantil Chicano de Aztlan, CSA (Chinese Student Association), A/BSA (African/Black Student Alliance), SEC (Student Environmental Center), national fraternities, national sororities. *Campus security:* 24-hour emergency response devices and patrols, late-night transport/escort service, controlled dormitory access, evening main gate security, campus police force and fire station. *Student services:* health clinic, personal/psychological counseling, women's center.

Athletics Member NCAA. All Division III. *Intercollegiate sports:* badminton M(c)/W(c), baseball M(c)/W(c), basketball M/W, cheerleading M(c)/W(c), cross-country running M(c)/W, equestrian sports M(c)/W(c), fencing M(c)/W(c), golf W, lacrosse M(c), racquetball M(c)/W(c), rugby M(c)/W(c), soccer M/W, swimming and diving M/W, table tennis M(c)/W(c), tennis M/W, track and field M(c)/W(c), ultimate Frisbee M(c)/W(c), volleyball M/W, water polo M(c)/W(c). *Intramural sports:* basketball M/W, soccer M/W, softball M/W, ultimate Frisbee M/W, volleyball M/W, water polo M/W.

Standardized Tests *Required:* SAT or ACT (for admission), SAT and SAT Subject Tests or ACT (for admission), SAT Subject Tests required in two different areas: history/social science, English literature, mathematics, laboratory science, or language other than English (for admission).

Costs (2011–12) *Tuition:* state resident $0 full-time; nonresident $22,878 full-time. Part-time tuition and fees vary according to course load. *Required fees:* $12,447 full-time. *Room and board:* $14,610. Room and board charges vary according to board plan and housing facility. *Payment plans:* installment, deferred payment.

Financial Aid Of all full-time matriculated undergraduates who enrolled in 2009, 11,365 applied for aid, 9,443 were judged to have need, 3,743 had their need fully met. 6,709 Federal Work-Study jobs (averaging $1435). In 2009, 273 non-need-based awards were made. *Average percent of need met:* 88%. *Average financial aid package:* $20,442. *Average need-based loan:* $6188. *Average need-based gift aid:* $15,538. *Average non-need-based aid:* $9351. *Average indebtedness upon graduation:* $17,546. *Financial aid deadline:* 6/1.

Applying *Options:* electronic application. *Application fee:* $60. *Required:* essay or personal statement, high school transcript, minimum high school GPA of 3.0 for California residents, 3.4 for non-residents. *Application deadlines:* 11/30 (freshmen), 11/30 (transfers). *Notification:* 3/31 (freshmen), 4/30 (transfers).

Freshman Application Contact Michael McCawley, Associate Director, Admissions, University of California, Santa Cruz, 1156 High Street, Santa Cruz, CA 95064. *Phone:* 831-459-2374. *Fax:* 831-459-4163. *E-mail:* admissions@ucsc.edu. *Web site:* http://www.ucsc.edu/.

University of La Verne

La Verne, California

- **Independent** university, founded 1891
- **Suburban** 38-acre campus with easy access to Los Angeles
- **Coed** 1,896 undergraduate students, 95% full-time, 60% women, 40% men
- **Moderately difficult** entrance level, 59% of applicants were admitted

Undergraduates 1,807 full-time, 89 part-time. Students come from 12 states and territories; 6 other countries; 2% are from out of state; 6% Black or African American, non-Hispanic/Latino; 41% Hispanic/Latino; 6% Asian, non-Hispanic/Latino; 1% American Indian or Alaska Native, non-Hispanic/Latino; 19% Race/ethnicity unknown; 0.6% international; 12% transferred in; 29% live on campus. *Retention:* 83% of full-time freshmen returned.

Freshmen *Admission:* 3,012 applied, 1,785 admitted, 538 enrolled. *Average high school GPA:* 3.41. *Test scores:* SAT critical reading scores over 500: 49%; SAT math scores over 500: 54%; SAT writing scores over 500: 47%; ACT scores over 18: 83%; SAT critical reading scores over 600: 10%; SAT math scores over 600: 13%; SAT writing scores over 600: 6%; ACT scores over 24: 22%; SAT critical reading scores over 700: 1%; ACT scores over 30: 2%.

Faculty *Total:* 435, 48% full-time. *Student/faculty ratio:* 11:1.

Academics *Calendar:* 4-1-4. *Degrees:* certificates, associate, bachelor's, master's, doctoral-professional, doctoral-research/scholarship, and postbachelor's certificates (also offers continuing education program with significant enrollment not reflected in profile). *Special study options:* academic remediation for entering students, accelerated degree program, adult/continuing education programs, advanced placement credit, distance learning, double majors, English as a second language, freshman honors college, honors programs, independent study, internships, off-campus study, part-time degree program, services for LD students, student-designed majors, study abroad, summer session for credit. *ROTC:* Army (c).

Computers on Campus 250 computers/terminals and 250 ports are available on campus for general student use. Students can access the following: computer help desk, free student e-mail accounts, online (class) grades, online (class) registration, online (class) schedules, MyULV (online). Campuswide network is available. 100% of college-owned or -operated housing units are wired for high-speed Internet access. Wireless service is available via entire campus.

Student Life *Housing options:* coed, women-only, disabled students. Campus housing is university owned. Freshman campus housing is guaranteed. *Activities and organizations:* drama/theater group, student-run newspaper, radio and television station, choral group, Latino Student Forum, African-American Student Association, Associated Students Federation, Alpha Kappa Psi, national fraternities, national sororities. *Campus security:* 24-hour emergency response devices and patrols, late-night transport/escort service, controlled dormitory access. *Student services:* health clinic, personal/psychological counseling.

Athletics Member NCAA. All Division III. *Intercollegiate sports:* baseball M, basketball M/W, cross-country running M/W, football M, golf M, soccer M/W, softball W, swimming and diving M/W, tennis M/W, track and field M/W, volleyball W, water polo M/W.

Standardized Tests *Required:* SAT or ACT (for admission).

Costs (2011–12) *Comprehensive fee:* $42,580 includes full-time tuition ($31,300) and room and board ($11,280). Full-time tuition and fees vary according to location. Part-time tuition: $890 per unit. Part-time tuition and fees vary according to location. *College room only:* $5790. Room and board

charges vary according to board plan and housing facility. *Payment plans:* installment, deferred payment. *Waivers:* employees or children of employees.

Financial Aid Of all full-time matriculated undergraduates who enrolled in 2009, 1,608 applied for aid, 1,509 were judged to have need, 161 had their need fully met. In 2009, 209 non-need-based awards were made. *Average percent of need met:* 52%. *Average financial aid package:* $26,408. *Average need-based loan:* $2163. *Average need-based gift aid:* $12,068. *Average non-need-based aid:* $16,631. *Average indebtedness upon graduation:* $31,112.

Applying *Options:* electronic application, deferred entrance. *Application fee:* $50. *Required:* essay or personal statement, high school transcript, 2 letters of recommendation. *Recommended:* interview. *Application deadlines:* 2/1 (freshmen), 4/1 (transfers). *Notification:* continuous (freshmen), continuous (transfers).

Freshman Application Contact Ms. Ana Liza V. Zell, Associate Dean of Undergraduate Admissions, University of La Verne, 1950 Third Street, La Verne, CA 91750. *Phone:* 909-593-3511 Ext. 4035. *Toll-free phone:* 800-876-4858. *Fax:* 909-392-2714. *E-mail:* admissions@ulv.edu. *Web site:* http://www.laverne.edu/.

University of Phoenix–Bay Area Campus

Pleasanton, California

Freshman Application Contact Ms. Audra McQuarie, Registrar/Executive Director, University of Phoenix–Bay Area Campus, 4035 South Riverpoint Parkway, Mail Stop CF-L101, Phoenix, AZ 85040-1958. *Phone:* 480-557-6151. *Toll-free phone:* 877-4-STUDENT. *Fax:* 480-643-3068. *E-mail:* audra.mcquarie@phoenix.edu. *Web site:* http://www.phoenix.edu/.

University of Phoenix–Central Valley Campus

Fresno, California

Freshman Application Contact Ms. Audra McQuarie, Registrar/Executive Director, University of Phoenix–Central Valley Campus, 4035 South Riverpoint Parkway, Mail Stop CF-L101, Phoenix, AZ 85040. *Phone:* 480-557-6151. *Toll-free phone:* 888-776-4867 (in-state); 888-228-7240 (out-of-state). *Fax:* 480-643-3068. *E-mail:* audra.mcquarie@phoenix.edu. *Web site:* http://phoenix.edu/.

University of Phoenix–Sacramento Valley Campus

Sacramento, California

Freshman Application Contact Ms. Audra McQuarie, Registrar/Executive Director, University of Phoenix–Sacramento Valley Campus, 4035 South Riverpoint Parkway, Mail Stop CF-L101, Phoenix, AZ 85040. *Phone:* 480-557-6151. *Toll-free phone:* 800-776-4867 (in-state); 800-228-7240 (out-of-state). *Fax:* 480-643-3068. *E-mail:* audra.mcquarie@phoenix.edu. *Web site:* http://www.phoenix.edu/.

University of Phoenix–San Diego Campus

San Diego, California

Freshman Application Contact Ms. Audra McQuarie, Registrar/Executive Director, University of Phoenix–San Diego Campus, 4035 South Riverpoint Parkway, Mail Stop CF-L101, Phoenix, AZ 85040. *Phone:* 480-557-6151. *Toll-free phone:* 888-776-4867 (in-state); 888-228-7240 (out-of-state). *Fax:* 480-643-3068. *E-mail:* audra.mcquarie@phoenix.edu. *Web site:* http://www.phoenix.edu/.

University of Phoenix–Southern California Campus

Costa Mesa, California

Freshman Application Contact Ms. Audra McQuarie, Registrar/Executive Director, University of Phoenix–Southern California Campus, 4035 South Riverpoint Parkway, Mail Stop CF-L101, Phoenix, AZ 85040. *Phone:* 480-557-6151. *Toll-free phone:* 800-776-4867 (in-state); 800-228-7240 (out-of-state). *Fax:* 480-643-3068. *E-mail:* audra.mcquarie@phoenix.edu. *Web site:* http://www.phoenix.edu/.

University of Redlands

Redlands, California

- **Independent** comprehensive, founded 1907
- **Small-town** 140-acre campus with easy access to Los Angeles
- **Endowment** $89.6 million
- **Coed** 3,032 undergraduate students, 76% full-time, 56% women, 44% men
- **Moderately difficult** entrance level, 67% of applicants were admitted

Undergraduates 2,313 full-time, 719 part-time. Students come from 42 states and territories; 6 other countries; 23% are from out of state; 5% Black or African American, non-Hispanic/Latino; 19% Hispanic/Latino; 4% Asian, non-Hispanic/Latino; 0.8% Native Hawaiian or other Pacific Islander, non-Hispanic/Latino; 0.7% American Indian or Alaska Native, non-Hispanic/Latino; 1% Two or more races, non-Hispanic/Latino; 17% Race/ethnicity unknown; 0.2% international; 7% transferred in; 53% live on campus. *Retention:* 86% of full-time freshmen returned.

Freshmen *Admission:* 3,587 applied, 2,387 admitted, 646 enrolled. *Average high school GPA:* 3.54. *Test scores:* SAT critical reading scores over 500: 88%; SAT math scores over 500: 85%; ACT scores over 18: 99%; SAT critical reading scores over 600: 32%; SAT math scores over 600: 39%; ACT scores over 24: 59%; SAT critical reading scores over 700: 4%; SAT math scores over 700: 3%; ACT scores over 30: 6%.

Faculty *Total:* 479, 43% full-time. *Student/faculty ratio:* 15:1.

Academics *Calendar:* 4-4-1. *Degrees:* bachelor's, master's, doctoral-professional, post-master's, and postbachelor's certificates. *Special study options:* academic remediation for entering students, adult/continuing education programs, advanced placement credit, double majors, freshman honors college, honors programs, independent study, internships, off-campus study, part-time degree program, services for LD students, student-designed majors, study abroad. *ROTC:* Army (c), Air Force (c).

Computers on Campus 804 computers/terminals and 920 ports are available on campus for general student use. Students can access the following: campus intranet, computer help desk, free student e-mail accounts, online (class) grades, online (class) registration, online (class) schedules. Campuswide network is available. 100% of college-owned or -operated housing units are wired for high-speed Internet access. Wireless service is available via entire campus.

Student Life *Housing:* on-campus residence required through senior year. *Options:* coed, men-only, women-only, cooperative, disabled students. Campus housing is university owned. Freshman campus housing is guaranteed. *Activities and organizations:* drama/theater group, student-run newspaper, radio station, choral group, Associated Students, service organizations, cultural organizations, social awareness groups. *Campus security:* 24-hour emergency response devices and patrols, student patrols, late-night transport/escort service, controlled dormitory access. *Student services:* health clinic, personal/psychological counseling, women's center.

Athletics Member NCAA. All Division III. *Intercollegiate sports:* baseball M, basketball M/W, cross-country running M/W, football M, golf M/W, lacrosse M, soccer M/W, softball W, swimming and diving M/W, tennis M/W, track and field M/W, volleyball W, water polo M/W. *Intramural sports:* basketball M/W, cheerleading W, football M, racquetball M/W, soccer M/W, softball M/W, table tennis M/W, volleyball W, water polo M/W.

Standardized Tests *Required:* SAT or ACT (for admission).

Costs (2010–11) *Comprehensive fee:* $46,372 includes full-time tuition ($35,240), mandatory fees ($300), and room and board ($10,832). Full-time tuition and fees vary according to program. Part-time tuition: $1101 per credit hour. Part-time tuition and fees vary according to course load and program. *Required fees:* $150 per term part-time. *College room only:* $5988. Room and board charges vary according to board plan and housing facility. *Payment plan:* installment. *Waivers:* employees or children of employees.

Financial Aid Of all full-time matriculated undergraduates who enrolled in 2009, 2,120 applied for aid, 1,737 were judged to have need, 343 had their need fully met. In 2009, 355 non-need-based awards were made. *Average percent of need met:* 78%. *Average financial aid package:* $31,753. *Average need-based loan:* $5462. *Average need-based gift aid:* $24,970. *Average non-need-based aid:* $13,060. *Average indebtedness upon graduation:* $20,364.

Applying *Options:* electronic application, deferred entrance. *Application fee:* $30. *Required:* essay or personal statement, high school transcript, 2 letters of recommendation. *Recommended:* interview. *Application deadlines:* 3/1 (freshmen), 3/1 (transfers). *Notification:* continuous (freshmen), continuous (transfers).

Freshman Application Contact University of Redlands, 1200 East Colton Avenue, PO Box 3080, Redlands, CA 92373-0999. *Phone:* 909-748-8159. *Toll-free phone:* 800-455-5064. *Web site:* http://www.redlands.edu/.

See page 1730 for the College Close-Up.

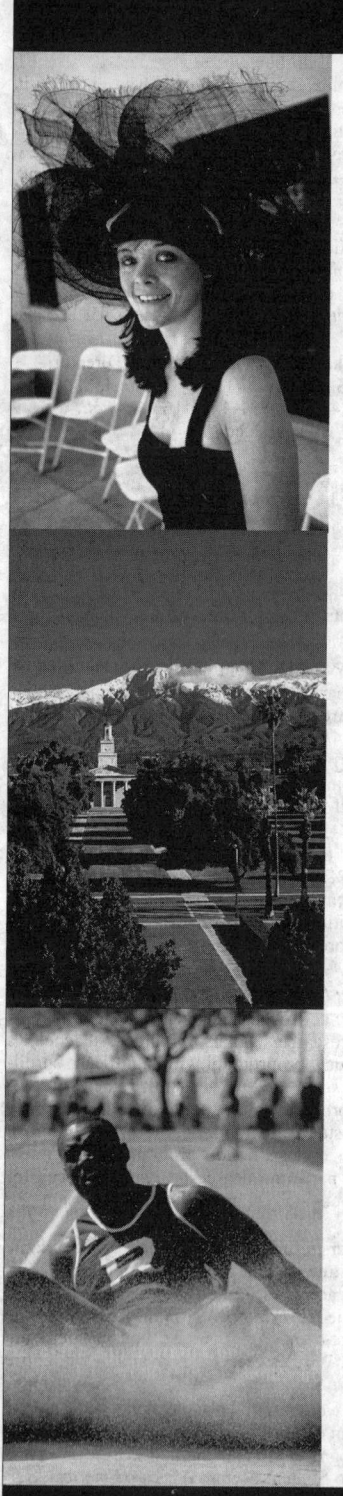

UR Unique
UR Connected
UR Bold

UR Home.

2,400 undergraduates, a 160-acre residential campus in Southern California, and an innovative curriculum make Redlands the place for you—who you are now, and who you will become.

UNIVERSITY OF REDLANDS
www.redlands.edu

University of San Diego
San Diego, California

- **Independent Roman Catholic** university, founded 1949
- **Urban** 180-acre campus with easy access to San Diego
- **Endowment** $260.0 million
- **Coed** 5,388 undergraduate students, 96% full-time, 55% women, 45% men
- **Very difficult** entrance level, 51% of applicants were admitted

Undergraduates 5,167 full-time, 221 part-time. Students come from 52 states and territories; 49 other countries; 38% are from out of state; 2% Black or African American, non-Hispanic/Latino; 16% Hispanic/Latino; 6% Asian, non-Hispanic/Latino; 0.3% Native Hawaiian or other Pacific Islander, non-Hispanic/Latino; 0.5% American Indian or Alaska Native, non-Hispanic/Latino; 6% Two or more races, non-Hispanic/Latino; 6% Race/ethnicity unknown; 5% international; 8% transferred in; 46% live on campus. *Retention:* 88% of full-time freshmen returned.

Freshmen *Admission:* 12,141 applied, 6,227 admitted, 1,150 enrolled. *Average high school GPA:* 3.81. *Test scores:* SAT critical reading scores over 500: 91%; SAT math scores over 500: 95%; SAT writing scores over 500: 92%; ACT scores over 18: 100%; SAT critical reading scores over 600: 49%; SAT math scores over 600: 59%; SAT writing scores over 600: 53%; ACT scores over 24: 87%; SAT critical reading scores over 700: 6%; SAT math scores over 700: 10%; SAT writing scores over 700: 8%; ACT scores over 30: 20%.

Faculty *Total:* 843, 47% full-time, 75% with terminal degrees. *Student/faculty ratio:* 15:1.

Academics *Calendar:* 4-1-4. *Degrees:* bachelor's, master's, doctoral-professional, doctoral-research/scholarship, post-master's, and postbachelor's certificates. *Special study options:* advanced placement credit, double majors, English as a second language, honors programs, independent study, internships, part-time degree program, services for LD students, study abroad, summer session for credit. *ROTC:* Army (c), Navy (b), Air Force (c).

Computers on Campus 1,283 computers/terminals and 4,250 ports are available on campus for general student use. Students can access the following: campus intranet, computer help desk, free student e-mail accounts, online (class) grades, online (class) registration, online (class) schedules. Campuswide network is available. 100% of college-owned or -operated housing units are wired for high-speed Internet access. Wireless service is available via entire campus.

Student Life *Housing:* on-campus residence required for freshman year. *Options:* coed, men-only, women-only, disabled students. Campus housing is university owned. Freshman campus housing is guaranteed. *Activities and organizations:* drama/theater group, student-run newspaper, radio and television station, choral group, Panhellenic Council, Interfraternity Council, Residence Hall Association, Gamma Phi Beta Sorority, Alpha Phi Sorority, national fraternities, national sororities. *Campus security:* 24-hour emergency response devices and patrols, student patrols, late-night transport/escort service, controlled dormitory access. *Student services:* health clinic, personal/psychological counseling, women's center, legal services.

Athletics Member NCAA. All Division I except football (Division I-AA). *Intercollegiate sports:* baseball M(s), basketball M(s)/W(s), crew M/W(s), cross-country running M(s)/W(s), equestrian sports W(c), golf M(s), lacrosse M(c)/W(c), rock climbing M(c), rugby M(c), soccer M(s)/W(s), softball W(s), swimming and diving W(s), tennis M(s)/W(s), track and field W(s), ultimate Frisbee M(c)/W(c), volleyball M(c)/W(s). *Intramural sports:* baseball M(c), basketball M/W, football M/W, golf M/W, soccer M(c)/W(c), softball M/W, tennis M/W, ultimate Frisbee M/W, volleyball M/W(c), water polo M(c).

Standardized Tests *Required:* SAT or ACT (for admission).

Costs (2011–12) *Comprehensive fee:* $50,330 includes full-time tuition ($38,150), mandatory fees ($428), and room and board ($11,752). Part-time tuition: $1315 per unit. Part-time tuition and fees vary according to course load. *Room and board:* Room and board charges vary according to board plan and housing facility. *Payment plan:* installment. *Waivers:* employees or children of employees.

Financial Aid Of all full-time matriculated undergraduates who enrolled in 2009, 3,051 applied for aid, 2,683 were judged to have need, 406 had their need fully met. 674 Federal Work-Study jobs (averaging $3009). In 2009, 738 non-need-based awards were made. *Average percent of need met:* 71%. *Average financial aid package:* $29,415. *Average need-based loan:* $7967. *Average need-based gift aid:* $22,077. *Average non-need-based aid:* $13,525. *Average indebtedness upon graduation:* $29,928.

Applying *Options:* electronic application, early action, deferred entrance. *Application fee:* $55. *Required:* essay or personal statement, high school transcript, 1 letter of recommendation. *Application deadlines:* 1/15 (freshmen), 3/1 (transfers), 11/15 (early action). *Notification:* 4/1 (freshmen), continuous until 7/15 (transfers), 1/31 (early action).

Freshman Application Contact Mr. Stephen Pultz, Director of Admission, University of San Diego, 5998 Alcala Park, San Diego, CA 92110. *Phone:*

619-260-4506. *Toll-free phone:* 800-248-4873. *Fax:* 619-260-6836. *E-mail:* admissions@sandiego.edu. *Web site:* http://www.sandiego.edu/.

See page 1736 for the College Close-Up.

University of San Francisco
San Francisco, California

- **Independent Roman Catholic (Jesuit)** university, founded 1855
- **Urban** 55-acre campus
- **Coed** 5,761 undergraduate students, 94% full-time, 64% women, 36% men
- **Moderately difficult** entrance level, 68% of applicants were admitted

Undergraduates 5,431 full-time, 330 part-time. Students come from 49 states and territories; 62 other countries; 26% are from out of state; 3% Black or African American, non-Hispanic/Latino; 17% Hispanic/Latino; 19% Asian, non-Hispanic/Latino; 0.5% Native Hawaiian or other Pacific Islander, non-Hispanic/Latino; 0.4% American Indian or Alaska Native, non-Hispanic/Latino; 7% Two or more races, non-Hispanic/Latino; 4% Race/ethnicity unknown; 11% international; 8% transferred in; 39% live on campus. *Retention:* 88% of full-time freshmen returned.
Freshmen *Admission:* 9,178 applied, 6,213 admitted, 1,176 enrolled. *Average high school GPA:* 3.52. *Test scores:* SAT critical reading scores over 500: 78%; SAT math scores over 500: 80%; SAT writing scores over 500: 80%; ACT scores over 18: 98%; SAT critical reading scores over 600: 30%; SAT math scores over 600: 34%; SAT writing scores over 600: 32%; ACT scores over 24: 61%; SAT critical reading scores over 700: 4%; SAT math scores over 700: 5%; SAT writing scores over 700: 5%; ACT scores over 30: 12%.
Faculty *Total:* 962, 41% full-time. *Student/faculty ratio:* 12:1.
Academics *Calendar:* 4-1-4. *Degrees:* certificates, bachelor's, master's, doctoral-other, doctoral-professional, and post-master's certificates. *Special study options:* academic remediation for entering students, adult/continuing education programs, advanced placement credit, cooperative education, distance learning, double majors, English as a second language, external degree program, honors programs, independent study, internships, off-campus study, part-time degree program, services for LD students, student-designed majors, study abroad, summer session for credit. *ROTC:* Army (b), Air Force (c). *Unusual degree programs:* 3-2 business administration; engineering with University of Southern California; physics.
Computers on Campus 350 computers/terminals are available on campus for general student use. Students can access the following: campus intranet, computer help desk, free student e-mail accounts, online (class) grades, online (class) registration, online (class) schedules. Campuswide network is available. 90% of college-owned or -operated housing units are wired for high-speed Internet access. Wireless service is available via classrooms, computer centers, computer labs, dorm rooms, learning centers, libraries, student centers.
Student Life *Housing:* on-campus residence required through sophomore year. *Options:* coed, women-only. Campus housing is university owned and leased by the school. Freshman campus housing is guaranteed. *Activities and organizations:* drama/theater group, student-run newspaper, radio and television station, choral group, student leadership, student media, College Players, national fraternities, national sororities. *Campus security:* 24-hour emergency response devices and patrols, late-night transport/escort service, controlled dormitory access. *Student services:* health clinic, personal/psychological counseling, women's center.
Athletics Member NCAA. All Division I. *Intercollegiate sports:* baseball M(s), basketball M(s)/W(s), cross-country running M(s)/W(s), golf M(s)/W(s), soccer M(s)/W(s), softball M(c)/W(c), tennis M(s)/W(s), track and field M/W(s), volleyball M(c)/W(c). *Intramural sports:* basketball M/W, bowling M/W, fencing M(c)/W(c), football M/W, golf M(c)/W(c), lacrosse M(c), racquetball M/W, rugby M(c)/W(c), skiing (cross-country) M(c)/W(c), soccer M/W, softball M/W, swimming and diving M/W, table tennis M/W, tennis M/W, volleyball M/W.
Standardized Tests *Required:* SAT or ACT (for admission), Sat Writing and Reading are used for Core Curriculum placement in the Foundation of Communication Core requirements (for admission).
Costs (2011–12) *Comprehensive fee:* $49,674 includes full-time tuition ($37,040), mandatory fees ($384), and room and board ($12,250). Full-time tuition and fees vary according to course load, degree level, program, and reciprocity agreements. Part-time tuition: $1315 per credit hour. Part-time tuition and fees vary according to course load, degree level, program, and reciprocity agreements. *College room only:* $8240. Room and board charges vary according to housing facility. *Payment plans:* installment, deferred payment. *Waivers:* employees or children of employees.
Financial Aid Of all full-time matriculated undergraduates who enrolled in 2008, 3,188 applied for aid, 2,896 were judged to have need, 182 had their need fully met. 856 Federal Work-Study jobs (averaging $3737). 535 state and other part-time jobs (averaging $3512). In 2008, 88 non-need-based awards were made. *Average percent of need met:* 65%. *Average financial aid package:* $26,830. *Average need-based loan:* $4795. *Average need-based gift aid:*

$21,762. *Average non-need-based aid:* $18,254. *Average indebtedness upon graduation:* $26,886.
Applying *Options:* electronic application, early action, deferred entrance. *Application fee:* $55. *Required:* essay or personal statement, high school transcript, 1 letter of recommendation. *Required for some:* interview. *Recommended:* minimum 3 GPA. *Application deadlines:* 1/15 (freshmen), rolling (transfers), 11/15 (early action). *Notification:* continuous until 8/15 (transfers), 1/16 (early action).
Freshman Application Contact Mr. Michael Hughes, Director, University of San Francisco, 2130 Fulton Street, San Francisco, CA 94117-1080. *Phone:* 415-422-6563. *Toll-free phone:* 800-CALLUSF. *Fax:* 415-422-2217. *E-mail:* admissions@usfca.edu. *Web site:* http://www.usfca.edu/.

See page 1738 for the College Close-Up.

University of Southern California
Los Angeles, California

- **Independent** university, founded 1880
- **Rural** 229-acre campus
- **Endowment** $2.9 billion
- **Coed** 17,380 undergraduate students, 96% full-time, 51% women, 49% men
- **Most difficult** entrance level, 24% of applicants were admitted

Undergraduates 16,688 full-time, 692 part-time. Students come from 55 states and territories; 129 other countries; 36% are from out of state; 4% Black or African American, non-Hispanic/Latino; 13% Hispanic/Latino; 22% Asian, non-Hispanic/Latino; 0.2% Native Hawaiian or other Pacific Islander, non-Hispanic/Latino; 0.2% American Indian or Alaska Native, non-Hispanic/Latino; 4% Two or more races, non-Hispanic/Latino; 1% Race/ethnicity unknown; 11% international; 9% transferred in; 41% live on campus. *Retention:* 97% of full-time freshmen returned.
Freshmen *Admission:* 35,794 applied, 8,715 admitted, 2,973 enrolled. *Average high school GPA:* 3.69. *Test scores:* SAT critical reading scores over 500: 99%; SAT math scores over 500: 99%; SAT writing scores over 500: 99%; ACT scores over 18: 100%; SAT critical reading scores over 600: 83%; SAT math scores over 600: 90%; SAT writing scores over 600: 89%; ACT scores over 24: 96%; SAT critical reading scores over 700: 32%; SAT math scores over 700: 54%; SAT writing scores over 700: 47%; ACT scores over 30: 67%.
Faculty *Total:* 2,964, 56% full-time, 79% with terminal degrees. *Student/faculty ratio:* 9:1.
Academics *Calendar:* semesters. *Degrees:* bachelor's, master's, doctoral-other, doctoral-professional, doctoral-research/scholarship, post-master's, and postbachelor's certificates. *Special study options:* accelerated degree program, advanced placement credit, cooperative education, distance learning, double majors, English as a second language, freshman honors college, honors programs, independent study, internships, off-campus study, part-time degree program, services for LD students, student-designed majors, study abroad, summer session for credit. *ROTC:* Army (b), Navy (b), Air Force (b). *Unusual degree programs:* 3-2 engineering with more than 20 liberal arts colleges nationwide.
Computers on Campus 2,500 computers/terminals and 6,000 ports are available on campus for general student use. Students can access the following: campus intranet, computer help desk, free student e-mail accounts, online (class) grades, online (class) registration, online (class) schedules, online degree progress, financial aid applications, document sharing, calendars, personal Web space, customizable Web portal, course management systems (including data and video). Campuswide network is available. 100% of college-owned or -operated housing units are wired for high-speed Internet access. Wireless service is available via entire campus.
Student Life *Housing options:* coed, disabled students. Campus housing is university owned and is provided by a third party. Freshman campus housing is guaranteed. *Activities and organizations:* drama/theater group, student-run newspaper, radio and television station, choral group, marching band, Troy Camp, USC Helenes, Alpha Phi Omega, Student Bar Association, USC Accounting Society, national fraternities, national sororities. *Campus security:* 24-hour emergency response devices and patrols, student patrols, late-night transport/escort service, controlled dormitory access. *Student services:* health clinic, personal/psychological counseling, women's center, legal services.
Athletics Member NCAA. All Division I except football (Division I-A). *Intercollegiate sports:* archery M(c)/W(c), badminton M(c)/W(c), baseball M(s), basketball M(s)/W(s), cheerleading M(c)/W(c), crew M(c)/W(s), cross-country running M(c)/W(s), equestrian sports M(c)/W(c), fencing M(c)/W(c), golf M(s)/W(s), ice hockey M(c)/W(c), lacrosse M(c)/W(c), racquetball M(c)/W(c), rock climbing M(c)/W(c), rugby M(c)/W(c), skiing (downhill) M(c)/W(c), soccer M(c)/W(s), softball W(c), squash M(c)/W(c), swimming and diving M(s)/W(s), table tennis M(c)/W(c), tennis M(s)/W(s), track and field M(s)/W(s), ultimate Frisbee M(c)/W(c), volleyball M(s)/W(s), water polo M(s)/W(s). *Intramural sports:* basketball M/W, football M/W, golf M/W, racquet-

ball M/W, soccer M/W, softball M/W, tennis M/W, track and field M/W, ultimate Frisbee M/W, volleyball M/W.

Standardized Tests *Required:* SAT or ACT (for admission).

Costs (2010–11) *One-time required fee:* $150. *Comprehensive fee:* $52,602 includes full-time tuition ($40,384), mandatory fees ($638), and room and board ($11,580). Full-time tuition and fees vary according to program. Part-time tuition: $1360 per unit. Part-time tuition and fees vary according to course load and program. *College room only:* $6680. Room and board charges vary according to board plan and housing facility. *Payment plans:* tuition prepayment, installment. *Waivers:* employees or children of employees.

Financial Aid Of all full-time matriculated undergraduates who enrolled in 2008, 8,671 applied for aid, 6,400 were judged to have need, 5,931 had their need fully met. 4,945 Federal Work-Study jobs (averaging $2681). In 2008, 2769 non-need-based awards were made. *Average percent of need met:* 100%. *Average financial aid package:* $35,906. *Average need-based loan:* $5873. *Average need-based gift aid:* $24,777. *Average non-need-based aid:* $15,639. *Average indebtedness upon graduation:* $30,090.

Applying *Options:* electronic application, deferred entrance. *Application fee:* $65. *Required:* essay or personal statement, high school transcript. *Application deadlines:* 1/10 (freshmen), 2/1 (transfers). *Notification:* 4/1 (freshmen), 6/1 (transfers).

Freshman Application Contact Timothy Brunold, Dean of Admission, University of Southern California, University Park Campus, Los Angeles, CA 90089. *Phone:* 213-740-1111. *Fax:* 213-821-0200. *E-mail:* admitusc@usc.edu. *Web site:* http://www.usc.edu/.

University of the Pacific

Stockton, California

- **Independent** university, founded 1851
- **Suburban** 175-acre campus with easy access to Sacramento
- **Coed** 3,757 undergraduate students, 97% full-time, 55% women, 45% men
- **Moderately difficult** entrance level, 38% of applicants were admitted

Undergraduates 3,661 full-time, 96 part-time. 11% are from out of state; 1% Black or African American, non-Hispanic/Latino; 3% Hispanic/Latino; 14% Asian, non-Hispanic/Latino; 36% Native Hawaiian or other Pacific Islander, non-Hispanic/Latino; 2% American Indian or Alaska Native, non-Hispanic/Latino; 4% Two or more races, non-Hispanic/Latino; 5% Race/ethnicity unknown; 3% international; 7% transferred in; 57% live on campus. *Retention:* 88% of full-time freshmen returned.

Freshmen *Admission:* 19,811 applied, 7,544 admitted, 1,010 enrolled. *Average high school GPA:* 3.49. *Test scores:* SAT critical reading scores over 500: 79%; SAT math scores over 500: 85%; SAT writing scores over 500: 79%; ACT scores over 18: 97%; SAT critical reading scores over 600: 36%; SAT math scores over 600: 50%; SAT writing scores over 600: 35%; ACT scores over 24: 65%; SAT critical reading scores over 700: 6%; SAT math scores over 700: 15%; SAT writing scores over 700: 8%; ACT scores over 30: 17%.

Faculty *Total:* 783, 56% full-time, 76% with terminal degrees. *Student/faculty ratio:* 14:1.

Academics *Calendar:* semesters. *Degrees:* bachelor's, master's, doctoral-professional, and doctoral-research/scholarship. *Special study options:* academic remediation for entering students, accelerated degree program, advanced placement credit, cooperative education, double majors, English as a second language, honors programs, independent study, internships, part-time degree program, services for LD students, student-designed majors, summer session for credit. *ROTC:* Air Force (c).

Computers on Campus Students can access the following: online (class) registration. Campuswide network is available. 100% of college-owned or -operated housing units are wired for high-speed Internet access. Wireless service is available via entire campus.

Student Life *Housing:* on-campus residence required through sophomore year. *Options:* coed. Campus housing is university owned. Freshman campus housing is guaranteed. *Activities and organizations:* drama/theater group, student-run newspaper, radio station, choral group, national fraternities, national sororities. *Campus security:* 24-hour emergency response devices and patrols, late-night transport/escort service, controlled dormitory access. *Student services:* health clinic, personal/psychological counseling, legal services.

Athletics Member NCAA. All Division I. *Intercollegiate sports:* baseball M(s), basketball M(s)/W(s), cross-country running W(s), field hockey W(s), golf M(s), soccer W(s), softball W(s), swimming and diving M(s)/W(s), tennis M(s)/W(s), volleyball M(s)/W(s), water polo M(s)/W(s). *Intramural sports:* badminton M(c)/W(c), basketball M/W, bowling M/W, football M/W, golf M,

lacrosse M(c)/W(c), rugby M(c), soccer M(c)/W(c), tennis M/W, volleyball M/W.

Standardized Tests *Required:* SAT or ACT (for admission). *Recommended:* SAT Subject Tests (for admission).

Costs (2010–11) *Comprehensive fee:* $45,242 includes full-time tuition ($33,600), mandatory fees ($500), and room and board ($11,142). Part-time tuition and fees vary according to course load. *Room and board:* Room and board charges vary according to board plan and housing facility. *Payment plan:* deferred payment. *Waivers:* employees or children of employees.

Financial Aid Of all full-time matriculated undergraduates who enrolled in 2009, 2,959 applied for aid, 2,724 were judged to have need, 438 had their need fully met. In 2009, 410 non-need-based awards were made. *Average financial aid package:* $30,458. *Average need-based loan:* $7702. *Average need-based gift aid:* $22,530. *Average non-need-based aid:* $9224.

Applying *Options:* electronic application, early action. *Application fee:* $60. *Required:* essay or personal statement, high school transcript, minimum 2.5 GPA, 1 letter of recommendation. *Required for some:* audition for music program. *Recommended:* minimum 3 GPA. *Application deadlines:* 1/15 (freshmen), 6/1 (transfers), 11/15 (early action). *Notification:* continuous (freshmen), continuous (transfers), 1/15 (early action).

Freshman Application Contact Mr. Rich Toledo, Director of Admissions, University of the Pacific, 3601 Pacific Avenue, Stockton, CA 95211-0197. *Phone:* 209-946-2211. *Toll-free phone:* 800-959-2867. *Fax:* 209-946-2413. *E-mail:* admissions@pacific.edu. *Web site:* http://www.pacific.edu/.

University of the West

Rosemead, California

- **Independent** comprehensive, founded 1991
- **Suburban** 10-acre campus
- **Coed** 71 undergraduate students, 76% full-time, 56% women, 44% men
- **Moderately difficult** entrance level, 85% of applicants were admitted

Undergraduates 54 full-time, 17 part-time. Students come from 5 states and territories; 14 other countries; 6% are from out of state; 35% live on campus.

Freshmen *Admission:* 235 applied, 200 admitted, 42 enrolled.

Faculty *Total:* 62, 16% full-time, 100% with terminal degrees. *Student/faculty ratio:* 9:1.

Academics *Calendar:* semesters. *Degrees:* certificates, diplomas, bachelor's, master's, doctoral-research/scholarship, post-master's, and postbachelor's certificates. *Special study options:* accelerated degree program, adult/continuing education programs, cooperative education, double majors, English as a second language, independent study, internships, part-time degree program, summer session for credit.

Computers on Campus 501 computers/terminals are available on campus for general student use. Students can access the following: computer help desk, free student e-mail accounts, online (class) grades, online (class) registration. Campuswide network is available. 100% of college-owned or -operated housing units are wired for high-speed Internet access. Wireless service is available via entire campus.

Student Life *Housing options:* coed, disabled students. Campus housing is university owned. Freshman campus housing is guaranteed. *Activities and organizations:* Buddhawest Club, music club, Explorer Club, Badminton Club, Chaplaincy Club. *Campus security:* 24-hour patrols. *Student services:* personal/psychological counseling.

Costs (2011–12) *One-time required fee:* $75. *Comprehensive fee:* $13,726 includes full-time tuition ($8040), mandatory fees ($250), and room and board ($5436). Full-time tuition and fees vary according to course level, course load, degree level, and program. Part-time tuition: $335 per unit. Part-time tuition and fees vary according to course level, course load, degree level, and program. *Required fees:* $250 per term part-time. *Room and board:* Room and board charges vary according to board plan and housing facility. *Payment plan:* installment. *Waivers:* employees or children of employees.

Financial Aid Of all full-time matriculated undergraduates who enrolled in 2003, 30 applied for aid, 18 were judged to have need. 20 state and other part-time jobs.

Applying *Options:* electronic application, deferred entrance. *Application fee:* $50. *Required:* essay or personal statement, high school transcript, minimum 2 GPA, 3 letters of recommendation. *Application deadlines:* 6/15 (freshmen), 6/15 (out-of-state freshmen), 6/15 (transfers). *Notification:* 7/15 (freshmen), 7/15 (out-of-state freshmen), 7/15 (transfers).

Freshman Application Contact University of the West, 1409 North Walnut Grove Avenue, Rosemead, CA 91770. *Phone:* 626-571-8811 Ext. 120. *Web site:* http://www.uwest.edu/.

See page 136 for Display. See page 1748 for the College Close-Up.

Vanguard University of Southern California
Costa Mesa, California

- **Independent** comprehensive, founded 1920, affiliated with Assemblies of God
- **Suburban** 38-acre campus with easy access to Los Angeles
- **Endowment** $5.0 million
- **Coed**
- **Moderately difficult** entrance level

Faculty *Student/faculty ratio:* 17:1.

Academics *Calendar:* semesters. *Degrees:* bachelor's and master's.

Student Life *Campus security:* 24-hour emergency response devices and patrols, student patrols, late-night transport/escort service.

Athletics Member NAIA.

Standardized Tests *Required:* SAT or ACT (for admission).

Costs (2010–11) *Comprehensive fee:* $34,616 includes full-time tuition ($26,342) and room and board ($8274). Full-time tuition and fees vary according to course load. Part-time tuition: $1098 per unit. Part-time tuition and fees vary according to course load. *College room only:* $4074. Room and board charges vary according to board plan and housing facility.

Financial Aid *Of all full-time matriculated undergraduates who enrolled in 2009,* 1,183 applied for aid, 1,110 were judged to have need, 135 had their need fully met. 94 Federal Work-Study jobs (averaging $2386). *In 2009,* 196 non-need-based awards were made. *Average percent of need met:* 67. *Average financial aid package:* $19,230. *Average need-based loan:* $4683. *Average need-based gift aid:* $8695. *Average non-need-based aid:* $12,957. *Average indebtedness upon graduation:* $28,256.

Applying *Options:* electronic application, early admission, early action, deferred entrance. *Application fee:* $45. *Required:* essay or personal statement, high school transcript, minimum 2.8 GPA, 2 letters of recommendation. *Required for some:* interview.

Freshman Application Contact Kristi Pruett, Undergraduate Inquiry Data Coordinator, Vanguard University of Southern California, 55 Fair Drive, Costa Mesa, CA 92626. *Phone:* 800-722-6279 Ext. 4107. *Toll-free phone:* 800-722-6279. *Fax:* 714-966-5471. *E-mail:* admissions@vanguard.edu. *Web site:* http://www.vanguard.edu/.

West Coast University
North Hollywood, California

Director of Admissions Mr. Roger A. Miller, Dean of Admissions and Registrar, West Coast University, 12215 Victory Boulevard, North Hollywood, CA 91606. *Phone:* 213-427-4400. *Toll-free phone:* 866-508-2684. *E-mail:* info@katz.wcula.edu. *Web site:* http://www.westcoastuniversity.edu/.

Westmont College
Santa Barbara, California

- **Independent nondenominational** 4-year, founded 1937
- **Suburban** 113-acre campus with easy access to Los Angeles
- **Endowment** $60.0 million
- **Coed** 1,378 undergraduate students, 99% full-time, 64% women, 36% men
- **Moderately difficult** entrance level, 75% of applicants were admitted

Undergraduates 1,369 full-time, 9 part-time. Students come from 37 states and territories; 10 other countries; 35% are from out of state; 4% transferred in; 80% live on campus. *Retention:* 87% of full-time freshmen returned.

Freshmen *Admission:* 1,877 applied, 1,417 admitted, 385 enrolled. *Average high school GPA:* 3.77. *Test scores:* SAT critical reading scores over 500: 91%; SAT math scores over 500: 87%; SAT writing scores over 500: 86%; ACT scores over 18: 99%; SAT critical reading scores over 600: 50%; SAT math scores over 600: 48%; SAT writing scores over 600: 46%; ACT scores over 24: 70%; SAT critical reading scores over 700: 13%; SAT math scores over 700: 8%; SAT writing scores over 700: 13%; ACT scores over 30: 18%.

Faculty *Total:* 151, 63% full-time, 68% with terminal degrees. *Student/faculty ratio:* 12:1.

Academics *Calendar:* semesters. *Degrees:* bachelor's and postbachelor's certificates. *Special study options:* academic remediation for entering students, accelerated degree program, advanced placement credit, double majors, honors programs, internships, off-campus study, services for LD students, student-designed majors, study abroad, summer session for credit. *ROTC:* Army (c), Air Force (c). *Unusual degree programs:* 3-2 engineering with Washington University in St. Louis; Boston University; University of Southern California; University of California, Berkeley; Los Angeles; Santa Barbara; California Polytechnic State University; Stanford University.

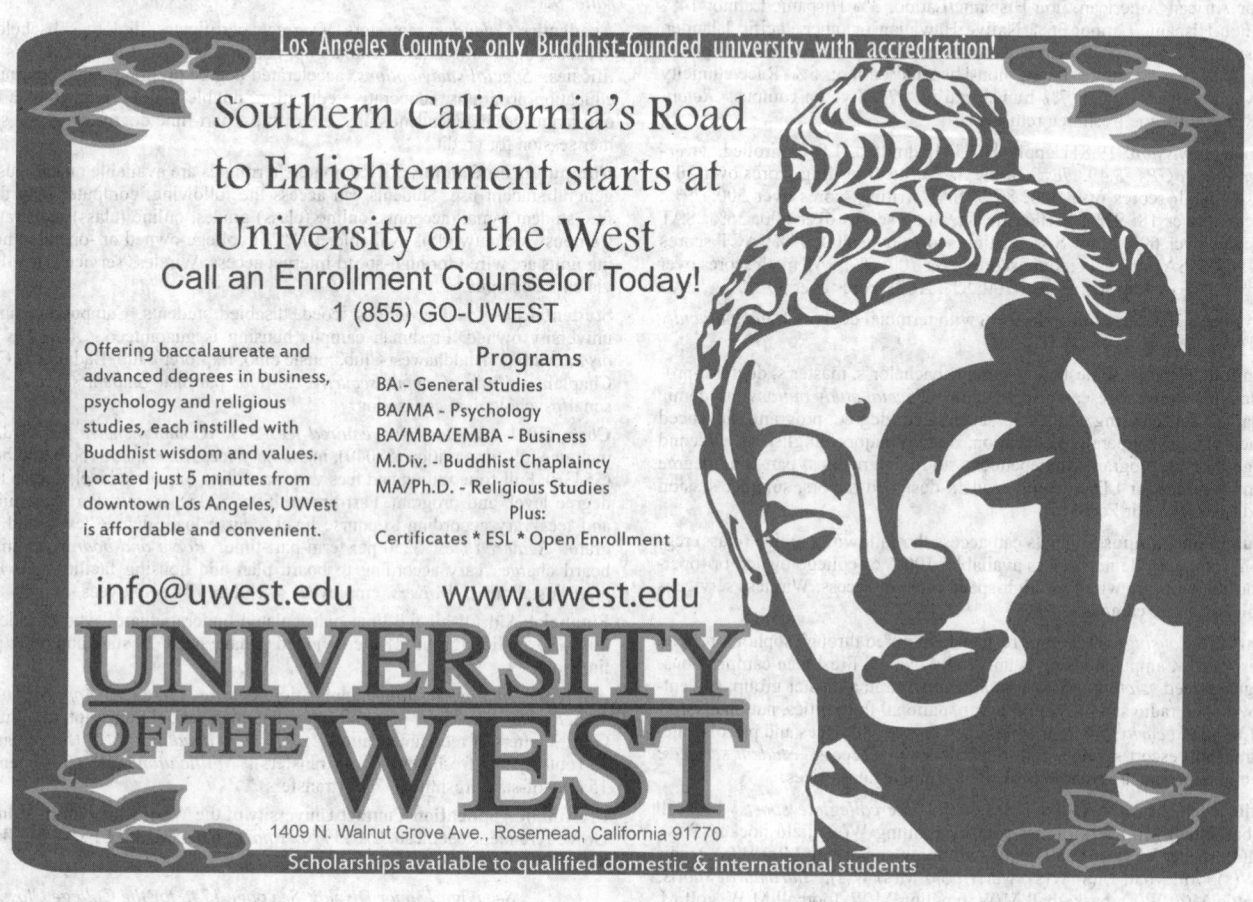

Computers on Campus 100 computers/terminals are available on campus for general student use. Students can access the following: campus intranet, computer help desk, free student e-mail accounts, online (class) schedules. Campuswide network is available. Wireless service is available via entire campus.

Student Life *Housing:* on-campus residence required for freshman year. *Options:* men-only, women-only. Campus housing is university owned. Freshman campus housing is guaranteed. *Activities and organizations:* drama/theater group, student-run newspaper, radio station, choral group, student ministries, student government, competitive athletics, music and theater ensembles, intramural athletics. *Campus security:* 24-hour emergency response devices and patrols, late-night transport/escort service, controlled dormitory access. *Student services:* health clinic, personal/psychological counseling, women's center.

Athletics Member NAIA. *Intercollegiate sports:* baseball M(s), basketball M(s)/W(s), cross-country running M(s)/W(s), equestrian sports M(c), rugby M(c), soccer M(s)/W(s), tennis M(s)/W(s), track and field M(s)/W(s), volleyball M(c)/W(s). *Intramural sports:* badminton M/W, basketball M/W, bowling M/W, cross-country running M/W, football M/W, golf M/W, racquetball M/W, soccer M(c)/W, softball M/W, table tennis M/W, tennis M/W, ultimate Frisbee M(c), volleyball M/W, water polo M/W.

Standardized Tests *Required:* SAT or ACT (for admission).

Costs (2011–12) *Comprehensive fee:* $45,420 includes full-time tuition ($33,400), mandatory fees ($1060), and room and board ($10,960). *College room only:* $6810. Room and board charges vary according to board plan. *Waivers:* employees or children of employees.

Financial Aid Of all full-time matriculated undergraduates who enrolled in 2009, 910 applied for aid, 805 were judged to have need, 77 had their need fully met. 143 Federal Work-Study jobs (averaging $946). In 2009, 353 non-need-based awards were made. *Average percent of need met:* 70%. *Average financial aid package:* $24,129. *Average need-based loan:* $5483. *Average need-based gift aid:* $19,229. *Average non-need-based aid:* $10,128. *Average indebtedness upon graduation:* $25,565.

Applying *Options:* electronic application, early action. *Application fee:* $25. *Required:* essay or personal statement, high school transcript, 1 letter of recommendation. *Required for some:* interview. *Recommended:* interview. *Application deadlines:* 2/20 (freshmen), 3/1 (transfers), 11/1 (early action). *Notification:* 4/1 (freshmen), 3/15 (transfers), 12/20 (early action).

Freshman Application Contact Mrs. Joyce Luy, Dean of Admission, Westmont College, 955 La Paz Road, Santa Barbara, CA 93108. *Phone:* 805-565-6200. *Toll-free phone:* 800-777-9011. *Fax:* 805-565-6234. *E-mail:* admissions@westmont.edu. *Web site:* http://www.westmont.edu/.

See page 1786 for the College Close-Up.

Westwood College–Anaheim

Anaheim, California

- **Proprietary** 4-year
- **Coed**

Academics *Calendar:* continuous. *Degrees:* associate and bachelor's.

Freshman Application Contact Westwood College–Anaheim, 1551 South Douglass Road, Anaheim, CA 92806. *Phone:* 714-704-2721. *Toll-free phone:* 877-650-6050. *Web site:* http://www.westwood.edu/.

Westwood College–Inland Empire

Upland, California

- **Proprietary** 4-year
- **Coed**

Academics *Calendar:* continuous. *Degrees:* associate and bachelor's.

Freshman Application Contact Westwood College–Inland Empire, 20 West 7th Street, Upland, CA 91786. *Phone:* 909-931-7599. *Toll-free phone:* 866-288-9488. *Web site:* http://www.westwood.edu/.

Westwood College–Los Angeles

Los Angeles, California

- **Proprietary** 4-year
- **Coed**

Academics *Calendar:* continuous. *Degrees:* associate and bachelor's.

Freshman Application Contact Westwood College–Los Angeles, 3250 Wilshire Boulevard, 4th Floor, Los Angeles, CA 90010. *Phone:* 213-382-2328. *Toll-free phone:* 877-377-4600. *Web site:* http://www.westwood.edu/.

Westwood College–South Bay Campus

Torrance, California

- **Proprietary** 4-year, founded 2002, part of Association of Independent Technological Universities (AITU)
- **Coed**

Academics *Calendar:* continuous. *Degrees:* associate and bachelor's.

Freshman Application Contact Westwood College–South Bay Campus, 19700 South Vermont Avenue, Suite 100, Torrance, CA 90502. *Phone:* 310-965-0877. *Toll-free phone:* 800-281-2978. *Web site:* http://www.westwood.edu/.

Whittier College

Whittier, California

- **Independent** comprehensive, founded 1887
- **Suburban** 95-acre campus with easy access to Los Angeles
- **Endowment** $55.0 million
- **Coed**
- **Moderately difficult** entrance level

Faculty *Student/faculty ratio:* 13:1.

Academics *Calendar:* 4-1-4. *Degrees:* bachelor's, master's, and doctoral-professional.

Student Life *Campus security:* 24-hour emergency response devices and patrols, late-night transport/escort service, controlled dormitory access.

Athletics Member NCAA. All Division III.

Standardized Tests *Required:* SAT or ACT (for admission). *Recommended:* SAT Subject Tests (for admission).

Costs (2010–11) *Comprehensive fee:* $45,768 includes full-time tuition ($35,222), mandatory fees ($520), and room and board ($10,026). Part-time tuition: $1490 per unit. *Room and board:* Room and board charges vary according to board plan.

Financial Aid Of all full-time matriculated undergraduates who enrolled in 2009, 1,233 applied for aid, 1,125 were judged to have need, 134 had their need fully met. In 2009, 272 non-need-based awards were made. *Average percent of need met:* 74. *Average financial aid package:* $30,711. *Average need-based loan:* $7038. *Average need-based gift aid:* $25,978. *Average non-need-based aid:* $16,559. *Average indebtedness upon graduation:* $24,687. *Financial aid deadline:* 6/30.

Applying *Options:* electronic application, early action, deferred entrance. *Application fee:* $50. *Required:* essay or personal statement, high school transcript, minimum 2 GPA, 2 letters of recommendation. *Required for some:* minimum 3.5 GPA. *Recommended:* minimum 2.5 GPA, interview.

Freshman Application Contact Mr. Kieron Miller, Director of Admission, Whittier College, Office of Admission, 13406 East Philadelphia Street, Whittier, CA 90608-0634. *Phone:* 562-907-4238. *Fax:* 562-907-4870. *E-mail:* admission@whittier.edu. *Web site:* http://www.whittier.edu/.

William Jessup University

Rocklin, California

- **Independent nondenominational** 4-year, founded 1939
- **Suburban** 126-acre campus with easy access to Sacramento
- **Coed** 700 undergraduate students, 81% full-time, 60% women, 40% men
- **Moderately difficult** entrance level, 64% of applicants were admitted

Undergraduates 568 full-time, 132 part-time. Students come from 13 states and territories; 6 other countries; 8% are from out of state; 6% Black or African American, non-Hispanic/Latino; 9% Hispanic/Latino; 3% Asian, non-Hispanic/Latino; 1% Native Hawaiian or other Pacific Islander, non-Hispanic/Latino; 2% American Indian or Alaska Native, non-Hispanic/Latino; 6% Two or more races, non-Hispanic/Latino; 3% Race/ethnicity unknown; 0.9% international; 16% transferred in; 63% live on campus. *Retention:* 77% of full-time freshmen returned.

Freshmen *Admission:* 360 applied, 230 admitted, 117 enrolled. *Average high school GPA:* 3.4. *Test scores:* SAT critical reading scores over 500: 61%; SAT math scores over 500: 65%; SAT writing scores over 500: 63%; ACT scores over 18: 90%; SAT critical reading scores over 600: 14%; SAT math scores over 600: 22%; SAT writing scores over 600: 13%; ACT scores over 24: 48%; SAT critical reading scores over 700: 1%; SAT math scores over 700: 2%; SAT writing scores over 700: 2%; ACT scores over 30: 3%.

Faculty *Total:* 97, 21% full-time, 33% with terminal degrees. *Student/faculty ratio:* 13:1.

Academics *Calendar:* semesters. *Degrees:* certificates, associate, bachelor's, and postbachelor's certificates. *Special study options:* adult/continuing education programs, advanced placement credit, double majors, independent study, internships, part-time degree program, services for LD students, study abroad, summer session for credit.

Computers on Campus 26 computers/terminals are available on campus for general student use. Students can access the following: campus intranet, computer help desk, free student e-mail accounts, online (class) grades, online (class) registration, online (class) schedules. Campuswide network is available. 100% of college-owned or -operated housing units are wired for high-speed Internet access. Wireless service is available via entire campus.

Student Life *Housing:* on-campus residence required through junior year. *Options:* men-only, women-only. Campus housing is university owned. Freshman campus housing is guaranteed. *Activities and organizations:* drama/theater group, student-run newspaper, choral group. *Campus security:* student patrols, late-night transport/escort service, controlled dormitory access, day and evening patrols by trained security personnel. *Student services:* personal/psychological counseling.

Athletics Member NAIA. *Intercollegiate sports:* basketball M(s)/W(s), cross-country running M(s)/W(s), golf M(s), soccer M(s)/W(s), softball W(s), track and field M(s)/W(s), volleyball W(s). *Intramural sports:* basketball M/W, softball M/W, table tennis M/W, volleyball M/W.

Standardized Tests *Required:* SAT or ACT (for admission).

Costs (2011–12) *Comprehensive fee:* $30,440 includes full-time tuition ($21,800) and room and board ($8640). Full-time tuition and fees vary according to course load. Part-time tuition: $930 per credit hour. Part-time tuition and fees vary according to course load. *Room and board:* Room and board charges vary according to housing facility. *Payment plan:* deferred payment. *Waivers:* employees or children of employees.

Financial Aid Of all full-time matriculated undergraduates who enrolled in 2009, 499 applied for aid, 462 were judged to have need, 56 had their need fully met. 14 Federal Work-Study jobs (averaging $2857). 39 state and other part-time jobs (averaging $2496). In 2009, 84 non-need-based awards were made. *Average percent of need met:* 71%. *Average financial aid package:* $18,279. *Average need-based loan:* $4422. *Average need-based gift aid:* $15,051. *Average non-need-based aid:* $6721. *Average indebtedness upon graduation:* $23,160.

Applying *Options:* electronic application. *Application fee:* $45. *Required:* essay or personal statement, high school transcript, minimum 2.5 GPA. *Required for some:* 1 letter of recommendation, interview. *Recommended:* 1 letter of recommendation. *Application deadlines:* 8/15 (freshmen), 8/15 (transfers). *Notification:* continuous (freshmen), continuous (transfers). **Freshman Application Contact** Mr. Vance Pascua, Director of Admission, William Jessup University, 333 Sunset Boulevard, Rocklin, CA 95765. *Phone:* 916-577-2222. *Toll-free phone:* 800-355-7522. *Fax:* 916-577-2220. *E-mail:* admissions@jessup.edu. *Web site:* http://www.jessup.edu/.

Woodbury University
Burbank, California

- **Independent** comprehensive, founded 1884
- **Suburban** 22-acre campus with easy access to Los Angeles
- **Endowment** $13.4 million
- **Coed** 1,282 undergraduate students, 82% full-time, 53% women, 47% men
- **Moderately difficult** entrance level, 68% of applicants were admitted

Undergraduates 1,048 full-time, 234 part-time. Students come from 32 other countries; 4% Black or African American, non-Hispanic/Latino; 32% Hispanic/Latino; 10% Asian, non-Hispanic/Latino; 0.1% American Indian or Alaska Native, non-Hispanic/Latino; 1% Race/ethnicity unknown; 13% international; 16% transferred in; 16% live on campus. *Retention:* 75% of full-time freshmen returned.

Freshmen *Admission:* 531 applied, 359 admitted, 271 enrolled. *Test scores:* SAT critical reading scores over 500: 44%; SAT math scores over 500: 49%; ACT scores over 18: 83%; SAT critical reading scores over 600: 10%; SAT math scores over 600: 17%; ACT scores over 24: 20%; SAT critical reading scores over 700: 3%; SAT math scores over 700: 2%; ACT scores over 30: 3%.

Faculty *Total:* 288, 23% full-time, 52% with terminal degrees. *Student/faculty ratio:* 11:1.

Academics *Calendar:* semesters. *Degrees:* bachelor's and master's. *Special study options:* academic remediation for entering students, accelerated degree program, adult/continuing education programs, advanced placement credit, double majors, English as a second language, independent study, internships, part-time degree program, services for LD students, student-designed majors, study abroad, summer session for credit.

Computers on Campus 169 computers/terminals are available on campus for general student use. Students can access the following: campus intranet, computer help desk, free student e-mail accounts, online (class) grades, online (class) registration, online (class) schedules. Campuswide network is available. 100% of college-owned or -operated housing units are wired for high-speed Internet access. Wireless service is available via classrooms, computer centers, computer labs, learning centers, libraries, student centers.

Student Life *Housing options:* coed. Campus housing is university owned and is provided by a third party. Freshman applicants given priority for college housing. *Activities and organizations:* Associated Student Government, Common Threads, American Institute of Architecture Students, Collegiate Entrepreneurs' Organization (CEO), American Institute of Graphic Arts (AIGA), national fraternities, national sororities. *Campus security:* 24-hour patrols, late-night transport/escort service, controlled dormitory access. *Student services:* health clinic, personal/psychological counseling.

Athletics *Intramural sports:* basketball M/W, soccer M/W.

Standardized Tests *Required:* SAT or ACT (for admission).

Costs (2010–11) *Comprehensive fee:* $38,148 includes full-time tuition ($28,465), mandatory fees ($390), and room and board ($9293). Full-time tuition and fees vary according to course load and degree level. Part-time tuition: $965 per credit hour. Part-time tuition and fees vary according to course load and degree level. *College room only:* $5788.

Financial Aid Of all full-time matriculated undergraduates who enrolled in 2009, 894 applied for aid, 859 were judged to have need, 14 had their need fully met. 127 Federal Work-Study jobs (averaging $1124). In 2009, 73 non-need-based awards were made. *Average percent of need met:* 53%. *Average financial aid package:* $19,861. *Average need-based loan:* $4488. *Average need-based gift aid:* $15,712. *Average non-need-based aid:* $7988. *Average indebtedness upon graduation:* $44,579.

Applying *Options:* electronic application, deferred entrance. *Application fee:* $50. *Required:* minimum 2 GPA. *Required for some:* high school transcript. *Recommended:* essay or personal statement, minimum 3 GPA, 2 letters of recommendation. *Application deadlines:* rolling (freshmen), rolling (transfers). *Notification:* continuous (freshmen), continuous (transfers). **Freshman Application Contact** Ms. Sabrina Taylor, Woodbury University, 7500 Glenoaks Boulevard, Burbank, CA 91510-7846. *Phone:* 800-784-9663. *Toll-free phone:* 800-784-WOOD. *Fax:* 818-767-0032. *E-mail:* admissions@woodbury.edu. *Web site:* http://www.woodbury.edu/.

Yeshiva Ohr Elchonon Chabad/West Coast Talmudical Seminary
Los Angeles, California

Director of Admissions Rabbi Ezra Binyomin Schochet, Dean, Yeshiva Ohr Elchonon Chabad/West Coast Talmudical Seminary, 7215 Waring Avenue, Los Angeles, CA 90046-7660. *Phone:* 323-937-3763. *E-mail:* roshyeshiva@yoec.edu. *Web site:* http://www.yoec.edu/.

COLORADO

Adams State College
Alamosa, Colorado

- **State-supported** comprehensive, founded 1921
- **Small-town** 90-acre campus with easy access to Pueblo
- **Endowment** $98,612
- **Coed** 2,455 undergraduate students, 83% full-time, 56% women, 44% men
- **Moderately difficult** entrance level, 55% of applicants were admitted

Undergraduates 2,027 full-time, 428 part-time. Students come from 47 states and territories; 7 other countries; 18% are from out of state; 6% Black or African American, non-Hispanic/Latino; 32% Hispanic/Latino; 2% Asian, non-Hispanic/Latino; 0.2% Native Hawaiian or other Pacific Islander, non-Hispanic/Latino; 1% American Indian or Alaska Native, non-Hispanic/Latino; 1% Two or more races, non-Hispanic/Latino; 6% Race/ethnicity unknown; 10% transferred in; 42% live on campus. *Retention:* 62% of full-time freshmen returned.

Freshmen *Admission:* 2,828 applied, 1,556 admitted, 577 enrolled. *Average high school GPA:* 2.98. *Test scores:* SAT critical reading scores over 500: 37%; SAT math scores over 500: 35%; SAT writing scores over 500: 32%; ACT scores over 18: 72%; SAT critical reading scores over 600: 5%; SAT math scores over 600: 6%; SAT writing scores over 600: 3%; ACT scores over 24: 16%; ACT scores over 30: 1%.

Faculty *Total:* 175, 62% full-time, 37% with terminal degrees. *Student/faculty ratio:* 18:1.

Academics *Calendar:* semesters. *Degrees:* associate, bachelor's, and master's. *Special study options:* academic remediation for entering students, accelerated degree program, adult/continuing education programs, advanced placement credit, distance learning, double majors, independent study, internships, off-campus study, part-time degree program, services for LD students, student-designed majors, study abroad, summer session for credit.

Computers on Campus 336 computers/terminals and 1,300 ports are available on campus for general student use. Students can access the following: campus intranet, computer help desk, free student e-mail accounts, online (class) grades, online (class) registration, online (class) schedules. Campuswide network is available. 100% of college-owned or -operated housing units are wired for high-speed Internet access. Wireless service is available via classrooms, computer centers, computer labs, dorm rooms, learning centers, libraries, student centers.

Student Life *Housing:* on-campus residence required through sophomore year. *Options:* coed, men-only, women-only. Campus housing is university owned. Freshman campus housing is guaranteed. *Activities and organizations:* drama/theater group, student-run newspaper, radio station, choral group, marching band, Student Programming Board, student government, Semillas de la Tierra, Newman Club (Psychology), Fellowship of Christian Athletes. *Campus security:* 24-hour emergency response devices and patrols, student patrols, late-night transport/escort service, controlled dormitory access. *Student services:* personal/psychological counseling.

Athletics Member NCAA. All Division II. *Intercollegiate sports:* basketball M(s)/W(s), cross-country running M(s)/W(s), football M(s), golf M(s)/W(s), lacrosse M(s)/W(s), soccer M(s)/W(s), softball W(s), swimming and diving M(s)/W(s), track and field M(s)/W(s), volleyball W(s), wrestling M(s). *Intramural sports:* basketball M/W, bowling M/W, cheerleading M(c)/W(c), football M/W, golf M(c)/W(c), racquetball M/W, rock climbing M/W, rugby M(c)/W(c), skiing (cross-country) M/W, skiing (downhill) M/W, soccer M/W, softball M/W, swimming and diving M/W, volleyball M/W, water polo M/W.

Standardized Tests *Required:* SAT or ACT (for admission).

Costs (2010–11) *Tuition:* state resident $2952 full-time, $123 per credit hour part-time; nonresident $12,912 full-time, $538 per credit hour part-time. Full-time tuition and fees vary according to course load. Part-time tuition and fees vary according to course load. *Required fees:* $2019 full-time, $84 per credit hour part-time. *Room and board:* $7060; room only: $3300. Room and board charges vary according to board plan and housing facility. *Payment plans:* installment, deferred payment. *Waivers:* senior citizens and employees or children of employees.

Financial Aid Of all full-time matriculated undergraduates who enrolled in 2008, 1,816 applied for aid, 1,573 were judged to have need, 10 had their need fully met. 279 Federal Work-Study jobs (averaging $1220). 333 state and other part-time jobs (averaging $1125). In 2008, 72 non-need-based awards were made. *Average percent of need met:* 51%. *Average financial aid package:* $9453. *Average need-based loan:* $3588. *Average need-based gift aid:* $5313. *Average non-need-based aid:* $2323. *Average indebtedness upon graduation:* $22,915.

Applying *Options:* electronic application, early admission, deferred entrance. *Application fee:* $30. *Required:* high school transcript, minimum 2 GPA. *Required for some:* essay or personal statement, interview, audition for music majors, portfolio for art majors. *Application deadlines:* 8/1 (freshmen), 8/1 (out-of-state freshmen), 8/1 (transfers). *Notification:* continuous (freshmen), continuous (out-of-state freshmen), continuous (transfers).

Freshman Application Contact Mr. Eric Carpio, Director of Admissions, Adams State College, 208 Edgemont Boulevard, Alamosa, CO 81102. *Phone:* 719-587-7712. *Toll-free phone:* 800-824-6494. *Fax:* 719-587-7522. *E-mail:* ascadmit@adams.edu. *Web site:* http://www.adams.edu/.

American Sentinel University
Aurora, Colorado

Director of Admissions Natalie Nixon, Vice President of Admission, American Sentinel University, 2260 South Xanadu Way, Suite 310, Aurora, CO 80014. *Phone:* 800-729-2427. *Toll-free phone:* 800-729-2427. *Fax:* 866-505-2450. *E-mail:* natalie.nixon@AmericanSentinel.edu. *Web site:* http://www.americansentinel.edu/.

Argosy University, Denver
Denver, Colorado

- **Proprietary** university
- **Coed**

Academics *Degrees:* bachelor's, master's, and doctoral-professional.

Costs (2010–11) *Tuition:* Tuition varies by program. Students should contact Argosy University for tuition information.

Freshman Application Contact Argosy University, Denver, 7600 East Eastman Avenue, Denver, CO 80231. *Phone:* 303-248-2700. *Toll-free phone:* 866-431-5981. *Web site:* http://www.argosy.edu/denver/.

See page 1002 for the College Close-Up.

The Art Institute of Colorado
Denver, Colorado

- **Proprietary** 4-year, founded 1952, part of Education Management Corporation
- **Urban** campus
- **Coed**

Academics *Calendar:* quarters. *Degrees:* diplomas, associate, and bachelor's.

Costs (2010–11) *Tuition:* Tuition cost varies by program. Prospective students should contact the school for current tuition costs. Other charges include a starting kit for all first-quarter students. Kits vary in price, depending on the program of study.

Freshman Application Contact The Art Institute of Colorado, 1200 Lincoln Street, Denver, CO 80203. *Phone:* 303-837-0825. *Toll-free phone:* 800-275-2420. *Web site:* http://www.artinstitutes.edu/denver/.

See page 1032 for the College Close-Up.

Aspen University
Denver, Colorado

Director of Admissions Admissions, Aspen University, 501 South Cherry Street, Suite 350, Denver, CO 80246. *Phone:* 303-333-4224. *Toll-free phone:* 800-441-4746. *Fax:* 303-336-1144. *E-mail:* admissions@aspen.edu. *Web site:* http://www.aspen.edu/.

CollegeAmerica–Colorado Springs
Colorado Springs, Colorado

Freshman Application Contact CollegeAmerica–Colorado Springs, 3645 Citadel Drive South, Colorado Springs, CO 80909. *Phone:* 719-637-0600. *Web site:* http://www.collegeamerica.edu/.

CollegeAmerica–Denver
Denver, Colorado

Freshman Application Contact Admissions Office, CollegeAmerica–Denver, 1385 South Colorado Boulevard, Denver, CO 80222. *Phone:* 303-300-8740. *Web site:* http://www.collegeamerica.com/.

CollegeAmerica–Fort Collins
Fort Collins, Colorado

Director of Admissions Ms. Anna DiTorrice-Mull, Director of Admissions, CollegeAmerica–Fort Collins, 4601 South Mason Street, Fort Collins, CO 80525-3740. *Phone:* 970-223-6060 Ext. 8002. *Toll-free phone:* 800-97-SKILLS. *Web site:* http://www.collegeamerica.edu/.

Colorado Christian University
Lakewood, Colorado

Freshman Application Contact Jo Leda Martin, Associate Director of Admissions, Colorado Christian University, 8787 W Alameda Avenue. *Phone:* 303-963-3000. *Toll-free phone:* 800-44-FAITH. *Fax:* 303-963-3201. *E-mail:* jomartin@ccu.edu. *Web site:* http://www.ccu.edu/.

The Colorado College
Colorado Springs, Colorado

- **Independent** comprehensive, founded 1874
- **Urban** 90-acre campus with easy access to Denver
- **Endowment** $431.0 million
- **Coed** 2,065 undergraduate students, 99% full-time, 54% women, 46% men
- **Very difficult** entrance level, 34% of applicants were admitted

Undergraduates 2,040 full-time, 25 part-time. Students come from 51 states and territories; 46 other countries; 78% are from out of state; 1% Black or African American, non-Hispanic/Latino; 7% Hispanic/Latino; 5% Asian, non-Hispanic/Latino; 0.5% American Indian or Alaska Native, non-Hispanic/Latino; 4% Two or more races, non-Hispanic/Latino; 1% Race/ethnicity unknown; 6% international; 2% transferred in; 75% live on campus. *Retention:* 96% of full-time freshmen returned.

Freshmen *Admission:* 4,466 applied, 1,499 admitted, 536 enrolled. *Test scores:* SAT critical reading scores over 500: 99%; SAT math scores over 500: 99%; SAT writing scores over 500: 99%; ACT scores over 18: 100%; SAT critical reading scores over 600: 81%; SAT math scores over 600: 82%; SAT writing scores over 600: 83%; ACT scores over 24: 94%; SAT critical reading scores over 700: 34%; SAT math scores over 700: 26%; SAT writing scores over 700: 28%; ACT scores over 30: 52%.

Faculty *Total:* 203, 83% full-time. *Student/faculty ratio:* 10:1.

Academics *Calendar:* modular. *Degrees:* bachelor's and master's (master's degree in education only). *Special study options:* advanced placement credit, double majors, English as a second language, independent study, internships, off-campus study, services for LD students, student-designed majors, study abroad, summer session for credit. *ROTC:* Army (c). *Unusual degree programs:* 3-2 engineering with Rensselaer Polytechnic Institute, Washington

University in St. Louis, University of Southern California, Columbia University.

Computers on Campus 396 computers/terminals are available on campus for general student use. Students can access the following: campus intranet, computer help desk, free student e-mail accounts, online (class) grades, online (class) registration, online (class) schedules. Campuswide network is available. 100% of college-owned or -operated housing units are wired for high-speed Internet access. Wireless service is available via entire campus.

Student Life *Housing:* on-campus residence required through junior year. *Options:* coed, men-only, women-only. Campus housing is university owned. Freshman campus housing is guaranteed. *Activities and organizations:* drama/theater group, student-run newspaper, choral group, national fraternities, national sororities. *Campus security:* 24-hour emergency response devices and patrols, late-night transport/escort service, controlled dormitory access, whistle program, student escort service, good campus lighting. *Student services:* health clinic, personal/psychological counseling, women's center.

Athletics Member NCAA. All Division III except ice hockey (Division I), soccer (Division I). *Intercollegiate sports:* baseball M(c), basketball M/W, cross-country running M/W, equestrian sports M(c)/W(c), field hockey M(c)/W(c), ice hockey M(s)/W(c), lacrosse M/W, rugby M(c)/W(c), skiing (downhill) M(c)/W(c), soccer M/W(s), swimming and diving M/W, tennis M/W, track and field M/W, ultimate Frisbee M(c)/W(c), volleyball W. *Intramural sports:* basketball M/W, football M/W, ice hockey M, racquetball M/W, soccer M/W, softball M/W, tennis M/W, ultimate Frisbee M/W, volleyball M/W, water polo M/W.

Standardized Tests *Required:* SAT or ACT (for admission), (for admission).

Costs (2010–11) *One-time required fee:* $150. *Comprehensive fee:* $48,364 includes full-time tuition ($38,748), mandatory fees ($200), and room and board ($9416). Part-time tuition: $6458 per course. Part-time tuition and fees vary according to course load. *College room only:* $5184. Room and board charges vary according to board plan and housing facility. *Payment plan:* installment. *Waivers:* employees or children of employees.

Financial Aid Of all full-time matriculated undergraduates who enrolled in 2009, 888 applied for aid, 750 were judged to have need, 469 had their need fully met. 225 Federal Work-Study jobs (averaging $1750). 128 state and other part-time jobs (averaging $1664). In 2009, 158 non-need-based awards were made. *Average percent of need met:* 92%. *Average financial aid package:* $33,298. *Average need-based loan:* $4355. *Average need-based gift aid:* $30,672. *Average non-need-based aid:* $13,573. *Average indebtedness upon graduation:* $18,349. *Financial aid deadline:* 2/15.

Applying *Options:* electronic application, early decision, early action, deferred entrance. *Application fee:* $50. *Required:* essay or personal statement, high school transcript, 2 letters of recommendation. *Recommended:* interview. *Application deadlines:* 1/15 (freshmen), 3/1 (transfers), 11/15 (early action). *Early decision deadline:* 11/15 (for plan 1), 1/1 (for plan 2). *Notification:* 4/1 (freshmen), 5/1 (transfers), 12/15 (early decision plan 1), 2/10 (early decision plan 2), 12/20 (early action).

Freshman Application Contact Mr. Matthew Bonser, Associate Director of Admission, The Colorado College, 14 East Cache La Poudre, Colorado Springs, CO 80903-3294. *Phone:* 719-389-6344. *Toll-free phone:* 800-542-7214. *Fax:* 719-389-6816. *E-mail:* admission@coloradocollege.edu. *Web site:* http://www.coloradocollege.edu/.

Colorado Heights University

Denver, Colorado

Director of Admissions Ashley Henderson, Admissions Coordinator, Colorado Heights University, 3001 South Federal Boulevard, Denver, CO 80236-2711. *Phone:* 303-937-4221. *E-mail:* admissions@tlhu.edu. *Web site:* http://www.chu.edu/.

Colorado School of Mines

Golden, Colorado

- **State-supported** university, founded 1874
- **Small-town** 373-acre campus with easy access to Denver
- **Coed** 3,795 undergraduate students, 94% full-time, 25% women, 75% men
- **Very difficult** entrance level, 46% of applicants were admitted

Undergraduates 3,579 full-time, 216 part-time. Students come from 49 states and territories; 42 other countries; 24% are from out of state; 1% Black or African American, non-Hispanic/Latino; 7% Hispanic/Latino; 5% Asian, non-Hispanic/Latino; 0.6% American Indian or Alaska Native, non-Hispanic/Latino; 0.6% Two or more races, non-Hispanic/Latino; 7% Race/ethnicity unknown; 6% international; 2% transferred in; 38% live on campus. *Retention:* 88% of full-time freshmen returned.

Freshmen *Admission:* 9,785 applied, 4,544 admitted, 875 enrolled. *Average high school GPA:* 3.76. *Test scores:* SAT critical reading scores over 500: 94%; SAT math scores over 500: 99%; SAT writing scores over 500: 87%;

ACT scores over 18: 100%; SAT critical reading scores over 600: 58%; SAT math scores over 600: 84%; SAT writing scores over 600: 46%; ACT scores over 24: 94%; SAT critical reading scores over 700: 10%; SAT math scores over 700: 32%; SAT writing scores over 700: 6%; ACT scores over 30: 41%.

Faculty *Total:* 331, 71% full-time, 69% with terminal degrees. *Student/faculty ratio:* 15:1.

Academics *Calendar:* semesters. *Degrees:* bachelor's, master's, doctoral-research/scholarship, and post-master's certificates. *Special study options:* accelerated degree program, advanced placement credit, cooperative education, double majors, honors programs, independent study, internships, services for LD students, study abroad, summer session for credit. *ROTC:* Army (b), Air Force (b).

Computers on Campus 400 computers/terminals are available on campus for general student use. Students can access the following: campus intranet, computer help desk, free student e-mail accounts, online (class) grades, online (class) registration, online (class) schedules. Campuswide network is available. 100% of college-owned or -operated housing units are wired for high-speed Internet access. Wireless service is available via entire campus.

Student Life *Housing:* on-campus residence required for freshman year. *Options:* coed. Campus housing is university owned and is provided by a third party. Freshman campus housing is guaranteed. *Activities and organizations:* drama/theater group, student-run newspaper, radio station, choral group, marching band, Society of Women Engineers, Residence Hall Association, Associated Students of Colorado School of Mines, Student Professional Societies, Campus Crusade for Christ/Fellowship for Christian Athletes, national fraternities, national sororities. *Campus security:* 24-hour emergency response devices and patrols, late-night transport/escort service, controlled dormitory access. *Student services:* health clinic, personal/psychological counseling, women's center.

Athletics Member NCAA. All Division II. *Intercollegiate sports:* baseball M(s), basketball M(s)/W(s), bowling M(c)/W(c), cross-country running M(s)/W(s), football M(s), golf M, ice hockey M(c)/W(c), lacrosse M(c), rugby M(c)/W(c), skiing (downhill) M(c)/W(c), soccer M(s)/W(s), softball W(s), swimming and diving M/W, track and field M(s)/W(s), ultimate Frisbee M(c)/W(c), volleyball M(c)/W(s), wrestling M(s). *Intramural sports:* badminton M/W, basketball M/W, bowling M/W, cross-country running M/W, field hockey M/W, football M/W, golf M/W, lacrosse M, racquetball M/W, soccer M/W, softball M/W, swimming and diving M/W, table tennis M/W, tennis M/W, track and field M/W, ultimate Frisbee M/W, volleyball M/W, wrestling M/W.

Standardized Tests *Required:* SAT or ACT (for admission).

Costs (2010–11) *Tuition:* state resident $11,550 full-time, $385 per credit hour part-time; nonresident $25,980 full-time, $866 per credit hour part-time. Part-time tuition and fees vary according to course load. *Required fees:* $1875 full-time. *Room and board:* $8596. Room and board charges vary according to board plan and housing facility. *Payment plan:* installment. *Waivers:* employees or children of employees.

Financial Aid Of all full-time matriculated undergraduates who enrolled in 2008, 2,342 applied for aid, 1,710 were judged to have need, 486 had their need fully met. In 2008, 674 non-need-based awards were made. *Average percent of need met:* 53%. *Average financial aid package:* $9004. *Average need-based loan:* $5490. *Average need-based gift aid:* $7677. *Average non-need-based aid:* $4411. *Average indebtedness upon graduation:* $28,126.

Applying *Options:* electronic application, deferred entrance. *Application fee:* $45. *Required:* high school transcript. *Required for some:* essay or personal statement, 2 letters of recommendation, interview. *Recommended:* minimum 3.7 GPA, rank in upper one-third of high school class. *Application deadlines:* 5/1 (freshmen), 5/1 (transfers). *Notification:* continuous until 10/1 (freshmen), continuous until 10/1 (transfers).

Freshman Application Contact Mrs. Joanne Lambert, Assistant Director of Enrollment Management, Colorado School of Mines, Student Center, 1600 Maple Street, Golden, CO 80401. *Phone:* 303-273-3220. *Toll-free phone:* 800-446-9488 Ext. 3220. *Fax:* 303-273-3509. *E-mail:* admit@mines.edu. *Web site:* http://www.mines.edu/.

Colorado State University

Fort Collins, Colorado

- **State-supported** university, founded 1870, part of Colorado State University System
- **Urban** 582-acre campus with easy access to Denver
- **Endowment** $176.6 million
- **Coed** 22,979 undergraduate students, 90% full-time, 51% women, 49% men
- **Moderately difficult** entrance level, 81% of applicants were admitted

Undergraduates 20,637 full-time, 2,342 part-time. Students come from 54 states and territories; 46 other countries; 16% are from out of state; 2% Black or African American, non-Hispanic/Latino; 7% Hispanic/Latino; 2% Asian, non-Hispanic/Latino; 0.2% Native Hawaiian or other Pacific Islander, non-Hispanic/Latino; 0.4% American Indian or Alaska Native, non-Hispanic/Latino; 3% Two or more races, non-Hispanic/Latino; 5% Race/ethnicity

unknown; 2% international; 6% transferred in; 26% live on campus. *Retention:* 84% of full-time freshmen returned.

Freshmen *Admission:* 14,680 applied, 11,822 admitted, 4,472 enrolled. *Average high school GPA:* 3.56. *Test scores:* SAT critical reading scores over 500: 80%; SAT math scores over 500: 82%; ACT scores over 18: 98%; SAT critical reading scores over 600: 35%; SAT math scores over 600: 40%; ACT scores over 24: 59%; SAT critical reading scores over 700: 5%; SAT math scores over 700: 5%; ACT scores over 30: 9%.

Faculty *Total:* 962, 96% full-time, 99% with terminal degrees. *Student/faculty ratio:* 17:1.

Academics *Calendar:* semesters. *Degrees:* bachelor's, master's, doctoral-professional, and doctoral-research/scholarship. *Special study options:* accelerated degree program, advanced placement credit, cooperative education, distance learning, double majors, English as a second language, external degree program, honors programs, independent study, internships, off-campus study, part-time degree program, services for LD students, study abroad, summer session for credit. *ROTC:* Army (b), Air Force (b). *Unusual degree programs:* 3-2 engineering.

Computers on Campus 2,500 computers/terminals and 3,200 ports are available on campus for general student use. Students can access the following: campus intranet, computer help desk, free student e-mail accounts, online (class) grades, online (class) registration, online (class) schedules, personalized portal services including transcripts and financials (billing, financial aid). Campuswide network is available. 100% of college-owned or -operated housing units are wired for high-speed Internet access. Wireless service is available via classrooms, computer centers, computer labs, dorm rooms, libraries, student centers.

Student Life *Housing:* on-campus residence required for freshman year. *Options:* coed, disabled students. Campus housing is university owned. Freshman campus housing is guaranteed. *Activities and organizations:* drama/theater group, student-run newspaper, radio and television station, choral group, marching band, Golden Key International Honor Society, Council of International Student Affairs, Campus Crusade for Christ, Associated Students of CSU (ASCSU Student Government), Snowriders, national fraternities, national sororities. *Campus security:* 24-hour emergency response devices and patrols, student patrols, late-night transport/escort service, controlled dormitory access. *Student services:* health clinic, personal/psychological counseling, women's center, legal services.

Athletics Member NCAA. All Division I except football (Division I-A). *Intercollegiate sports:* baseball M(c), basketball M(s)/W(s), crew M(c)/W(c), cross-country running M(s)/W(s), field hockey M(c)/W(c), golf M(s)/W(s), ice hockey M(c)/W(c), lacrosse M(c)/W(c), rugby M(c)/W(c), skiing (downhill) M(c)/W(c), soccer M(c)/W(c), softball W(s), swimming and diving W(s), tennis M(c)/W(s), track and field M(s)/W(s), ultimate Frisbee M(c)/W(c), volleyball W(s), water polo M(c)/W(c), wrestling M(c)/W(c). *Intramural sports:* basketball M/W, bowling M/W, golf M/W, racquetball M/W, soccer M/W, softball M/W, ultimate Frisbee M/W, volleyball M/W.

Standardized Tests *Required:* SAT or ACT (for admission).

Costs (2010–11) *Tuition:* state resident $5256 full-time, $263 per credit hour part-time; nonresident $21,366 full-time, $1068 per credit hour part-time. Full-time tuition and fees vary according to course load. Part-time tuition and fees vary according to course load. *Required fees:* $1729 full-time, $30 per credit hour part-time, $148 per term part-time. *Room and board:* $8744; room only: $4322. Room and board charges vary according to board plan and housing facility. *Waivers:* employees or children of employees.

Financial Aid Of all full-time matriculated undergraduates who enrolled in 2008, 13,383 applied for aid, 9,036 were judged to have need, 3,937 had their need fully met. 419 Federal Work-Study jobs (averaging $2063). 997 state and other part-time jobs (averaging $1823). In 2008, 1905 non-need-based awards were made. *Average percent of need met:* 77%. *Average financial aid package:* $11,085. *Average need-based loan:* $6906. *Average need-based gift aid:* $6626. *Average non-need-based aid:* $3539. *Average indebtedness upon graduation:* $21,224.

Applying *Options:* electronic application, deferred entrance. *Application fee:* $50. *Required:* essay or personal statement, high school transcript, 1 letter of recommendation. *Application deadlines:* 7/1 (freshmen), 7/1 (transfers). *Notification:* continuous (freshmen), continuous (transfers).

Freshman Application Contact Mr. Jim Rawlins, Executive Director of Admissions, Colorado State University, Spruce Hall, Fort Collins, CO 80523-0015. *Phone:* 970-491-6909. *Fax:* 970-491-7799. *E-mail:* admissions@colostate.edu. *Web site:* http://www.colostate.edu/.

Colorado State University–Pueblo
Pueblo, Colorado

- **State-supported** comprehensive, founded 1933, part of Colorado State University System
- **Small-town** 275-acre campus with easy access to Colorado Springs
- **Endowment** $7.3 million
- **Coed**
- **Moderately difficult** entrance level

Faculty *Student/faculty ratio:* 16:1.

Academics *Calendar:* semesters. *Degrees:* bachelor's and master's.

Student Life *Campus security:* 24-hour emergency response devices and patrols, late-night transport/escort service, controlled dormitory access.

Athletics Member NCAA. All Division II.

Standardized Tests *Required:* SAT or ACT (for admission).

Costs (2010–11) *Tuition:* state resident $4068 full-time, $162 per credit hour part-time; nonresident $14,141 full-time, $565 per credit hour part-time. Full-time tuition and fees vary according to course load. Part-time tuition and fees vary according to course load. *Required fees:* $1547 full-time, $52 per credit hour part-time. *Room and board:* $8660; room only: $5000. Room and board charges vary according to board plan. *Payment plans:* installment, deferred payment.

Financial Aid *Of all full-time matriculated undergraduates who enrolled in 2009,* 3,223 applied for aid, 2,739 were judged to have need, 142 had their need fully met. 215 Federal Work-Study jobs (averaging $2061). 281 state and other part-time jobs (averaging $2738). *In 2009,* 202 non-need-based awards were made. *Average percent of need met:* 56. *Average financial aid package:* $8828. *Average need-based loan:* $3555. *Average need-based gift aid:* $6344. *Average non-need-based aid:* $2482. *Average indebtedness upon graduation:* $20,141.

Applying *Options:* electronic application, deferred entrance. *Application fee:* $25. *Required:* minimum 2 GPA. *Required for some:* high school transcript.

Freshman Application Contact Mrs. Dana Trujillo, Director of Admissions, Colorado State University–Pueblo, 2200 Bonforte Boulevard, Pueblo, CO 81001-4901. *Phone:* 719-549-2391. *Fax:* 719-549-2419. *E-mail:* dana.trujillo@colostate-pueblo.edu. *Web site:* http://www.colostate-pueblo.edu/.

Colorado Technical University Colorado Springs
Colorado Springs, Colorado

Director of Admissions Beth Braaten, Vice President of Admissions, Colorado Technical University Colorado Springs, 4435 North Chestnut Street, Colorado Springs, CO 80907-3896. *Phone:* 888-404-7555. *E-mail:* bbraaten@coloradotech.edu. *Web site:* http://www.coloradotech.edu/.

Colorado Technical University Denver
Greenwood Village, Colorado

Director of Admissions Rosaland Giboney, Associate Director of Admissions, Colorado Technical University Denver, 5775 Denver Tech Center Boulevard, Greenwood Village, CO 80111. *Phone:* 888-404-7555. *E-mail:* rgiboney@coloradotech.edu. *Web site:* http://www.coloradotech.edu/.

Colorado Technical University Online
Colorado Springs, Colorado

Director of Admissions William Beckley, Chief Admission Officer, Colorado Technical University Online, 4435 North Chestnut Street, Suite E, Colorado Springs, CO 80907. *Phone:* 888-404-7555. *Web site:* http://www.coloradotech.edu/.

Denver School of Nursing
Denver, Colorado

Admissions Office Contact Denver School of Nursing, 1401 19th Street, Denver, CO 80202. *Toll-free phone:* 888-479-5550. *Web site:* http://www.denverschoolofnursing.edu/.

DeVry University
Colorado Springs, Colorado

Director of Admissions Admissions Office, DeVry University, 1175 Kelly Johnson Boulevard, Colorado Springs, CO 80920. *Toll-free phone:* 866-338-7934. *Web site:* http://www.devry.edu/.

DeVry University
Westminster, Colorado

- **Proprietary** comprehensive, founded 1945
- **Urban** 3-acre campus with easy access to Denver
- **Coed** 1,023 undergraduate students, 33% full-time, 38% women, 62% men
- **Noncompetitive** entrance level

Undergraduates 342 full-time, 681 part-time. 9% are from out of state; 5% Black or African American, non-Hispanic/Latino; 14% Hispanic/Latino; 4% Asian, non-Hispanic/Latino; 0.2% Native Hawaiian or other Pacific Islander, non-Hispanic/Latino; 1% American Indian or Alaska Native, non-Hispanic/Latino; 0.7% Two or more races, non-Hispanic/Latino; 23% Race/ethnicity unknown; 0.1% international; 26% transferred in.
Freshmen *Admission:* 144 enrolled.
Faculty *Total:* 67, 21% full-time. *Student/faculty ratio:* 19:1.
Academics *Calendar:* semesters. *Degrees:* associate, bachelor's, and master's. *Special study options:* academic remediation for entering students, accelerated degree program, adult/continuing education programs, distance learning, summer session for credit.
Computers on Campus Campuswide network is available.
Student Life *Housing:* college housing not available. *Campus security:* 24-hour patrols, late-night transport/escort service. *Student services:* personal/psychological counseling.
Costs (2010–11) *Tuition:* $14,766 full-time, $580 per credit hour part-time. Full-time tuition and fees vary according to course load. Part-time tuition and fees vary according to course load. *Required fees:* $60 full-time, $30 per term part-time. *Payment plans:* installment, deferred payment. *Waivers:* employees or children of employees.
Financial Aid Of all full-time matriculated undergraduates who enrolled in 2007, 148 applied for aid, 136 were judged to have need, 6 had their need fully met. In 2007, 17 non-need-based awards were made. *Average percent of need met:* 37%. *Average financial aid package:* $11,971. *Average need-based loan:* $8024. *Average need-based gift aid:* $6094. *Average non-need-based aid:* $13,350. *Average indebtedness upon graduation:* $11,071.
Applying *Options:* electronic application, deferred entrance. *Application fee:* $50. *Required:* high school transcript. *Required for some:* essay or personal statement, interview. *Application deadlines:* rolling (freshmen), rolling (transfers). *Notification:* continuous (freshmen), continuous (transfers).
Freshman Application Contact DeVry University, 1870 West 122nd Avenue, Westminster, CO 80234-2010. *Phone:* 303-280-7400. *Web site:* http://www.devry.edu/.

Fort Lewis College
Durango, Colorado

- **State-supported** 4-year, founded 1911
- **Small-town** 350-acre campus
- **Coed** 3,864 undergraduate students, 90% full-time, 49% women, 51% men
- **Moderately difficult** entrance level, 66% of applicants were admitted

Undergraduates 3,472 full-time, 392 part-time. 34% are from out of state; 10% transferred in; 34% live on campus. *Retention:* 63% of full-time freshmen returned.
Freshmen *Admission:* 3,059 applied, 2,004 admitted, 847 enrolled. *Average high school GPA:* 3.1. *Test scores:* ACT scores over 18: 94%; ACT scores over 24: 33%; ACT scores over 30: 3%.
Faculty *Total:* 257, 67% full-time, 68% with terminal degrees. *Student/faculty ratio:* 18:1.
Academics *Calendar:* modified trimesters. *Degree:* bachelor's. *Special study options:* academic remediation for entering students, accelerated degree program, adult/continuing education programs, advanced placement credit, cooperative education, distance learning, double majors, English as a second language, honors programs, independent study, internships, part-time degree program, services for LD students, student-designed majors, study abroad, summer session for credit. *Unusual degree programs:* 3-2 social work.
Computers on Campus Students can access the following: campus intranet, computer help desk, free student e-mail accounts, online (class) grades, online (class) registration, online (class) schedules. Campuswide network is available. Wireless service is available via entire campus.
Student Life *Housing:* on-campus residence required for freshman year. *Options:* coed. Campus housing is university owned. Freshman applicants given priority for college housing. *Activities and organizations:* drama/theater group, student-run newspaper, radio station, choral group, KDUR - Campus/community radio, Student Programming Council (SPC), Environmental Center (EC), Dance Co-motion, Engineers Without Borders. *Campus security:* 24-hour emergency response devices and patrols, late-night transport/escort service, controlled dormitory access. *Student services:* health clinic, personal/psychological counseling, legal services.

Athletics Member NCAA. All Division II. *Intercollegiate sports:* baseball M(c), basketball M(s)/W(s), cheerleading M(c)/W(c), cross-country running M(s)/W(s), fencing M(c)/W(c), football M(s), golf M(s), ice hockey M(c)/W(c), lacrosse M(c)/W(c), rock climbing M(c)/W(c), rugby M(c)/W(c), skiing (cross-country) M(c)/W(c), skiing (downhill) M(c)/W(c), soccer M(s)/W(s), softball W(s), ultimate Frisbee M(c)/W(c), volleyball W(s), wrestling M(c)/W(c). *Intramural sports:* badminton M/W, basketball M/W, football M/W, golf M/W, racquetball M/W, soccer M/W, softball M/W, ultimate Frisbee M/W, volleyball M/W.
Standardized Tests *Required:* SAT or ACT (for admission).
Costs (2011–12) *Tuition:* state resident $3380 full-time, $169 per credit hour part-time; nonresident $16,072 full-time, $803 per credit hour part-time. Full-time tuition and fees vary according to course load and reciprocity agreements. Part-time tuition and fees vary according to course load and reciprocity agreements. *Required fees:* $1544 full-time. *Room and board:* $7840; room only: $3940. Room and board charges vary according to board plan and housing facility. *Payment plan:* installment. *Waivers:* minority students and employees or children of employees.
Financial Aid Of all full-time matriculated undergraduates who enrolled in 2009, 2,213 applied for aid, 1,730 were judged to have need, 409 had their need fully met. In 2009, 412 non-need-based awards were made. *Average percent of need met:* 71%. *Average financial aid package:* $8042. *Average need-based loan:* $3835. *Average need-based gift aid:* $3660. *Average non-need-based aid:* $1241. *Average indebtedness upon graduation:* $15,962.
Applying *Options:* electronic application, deferred entrance. *Application fee:* $40. *Required:* high school transcript. *Required for some:* interview. *Recommended:* essay or personal statement, 2 letters of recommendation.
Freshman Application Contact Fort Lewis College, 1000 Rim Drive, Durango, CO 81301-3999. *Phone:* 970-247-7184. *Web site:* http://www.fortlewis.edu/.

ITT Technical Institute
Aurora, Colorado

- **Proprietary** primarily 2-year
- **Coed**
- **Minimally difficult** entrance level

Academics *Degrees:* associate and bachelor's.
Freshman Application Contact Director of Recruitment, ITT Technical Institute, 12500 East Iliff Avenue, Suite 100, Aurora, CO 80014. *Phone:* 303-695-6317. *Web site:* http://www.itt-tech.edu/.

ITT Technical Institute
Thornton, Colorado

- **Proprietary** primarily 2-year, founded 1984, part of ITT Educational Services, Inc.
- **Suburban** campus
- **Coed**
- **Minimally difficult** entrance level

Academics *Calendar:* quarters. *Degrees:* associate and bachelor's.
Student Life *Housing:* college housing not available.
Freshman Application Contact Director of Recruitment, ITT Technical Institute, 500 East 84th Avenue, Suite B12, Thornton, CO 80229. *Phone:* 303-288-4488. *Toll-free phone:* 800-395-4488. *Web site:* http://www.itt-tech.edu/.

Johnson & Wales University
Denver, Colorado

- **Independent** 4-year, founded 1993, administratively affiliated with Johnson & Wales University (RI)
- **Small-town** campus
- **Coed** 1,532 undergraduate students, 95% full-time, 57% women, 43% men
- **Moderately difficult** entrance level, 64% of applicants were admitted

Undergraduates 1,462 full-time, 70 part-time. 60% are from out of state; 3% Black or African American, non-Hispanic/Latino; 9% Hispanic/Latino; 2% Asian, non-Hispanic/Latino; 0.1% Native Hawaiian or other Pacific Islander, non-Hispanic/Latino; 0.9% American Indian or Alaska Native, non-Hispanic/Latino; 0.2% Two or more races, non-Hispanic/Latino; 49% Race/ethnicity unknown; 1% international; 11% transferred in; 38% live on campus. *Retention:* 67% of full-time freshmen returned.
Freshmen *Admission:* 3,019 applied, 1,920 admitted, 397 enrolled. *Average high school GPA:* 3.18.
Faculty *Total:* 87, 55% full-time. *Student/faculty ratio:* 24:1.
Academics *Calendar:* quarters. *Degrees:* associate and bachelor's. *Special study options:* academic remediation for entering students, accelerated degree program, adult/continuing education programs, advanced placement credit, cooperative education, English as a second language, honors programs, inde-

pendent study, internships, part-time degree program, services for LD students, study abroad, summer session for credit.

Computers on Campus Students can access the following: campus intranet, computer help desk, free student e-mail accounts, online (class) grades, online (class) registration, online (class) schedules. Campuswide network is available. Wireless service is available via entire campus.

Student Life *Housing:* on-campus residence required for freshman year. *Options:* coed. Campus housing is university owned. Freshman campus housing is guaranteed. *Activities and organizations:* drama/theater group, student-run newspaper. *Campus security:* 24-hour emergency response devices and patrols, student patrols, late-night transport/escort service.

Athletics Member NAIA. *Intercollegiate sports:* baseball M, basketball M/W, cheerleading M/W, golf M, soccer M, tennis M/W. *Intramural sports:* basketball M/W, football M/W, volleyball M/W.

Standardized Tests *Required for some:* SAT or ACT (for admission).

Costs (2011–12) *Comprehensive fee:* $34,668 includes full-time tuition ($23,955), mandatory fees ($1452), and room and board ($9261). Part-time tuition: $164 per credit hour. *Room and board:* Room and board charges vary according to board plan, housing facility, and location. *Payment plan:* installment. *Waivers:* employees or children of employees.

Financial Aid Of all full-time matriculated undergraduates who enrolled in 2009, 1,233 applied for aid, 1,070 were judged to have need, 150 had their need fully met. In 2009, 267 non-need-based awards were made. *Average percent of need met:* 69%. *Average financial aid package:* $15,792. *Average need-based loan:* $4987. *Average need-based gift aid:* $6502. *Average non-need-based aid:* $6141.

Applying *Options:* electronic application, early admission, deferred entrance. *Required:* high school transcript. *Required for some:* essay or personal statement, minimum 2.75 GPA, interview. *Recommended:* minimum 2 GPA. *Application deadlines:* rolling (freshmen), rolling (transfers). *Notification:* continuous (freshmen), continuous (transfers).

Freshman Application Contact Kim Ostrowski, Director of Admissions, Johnson & Wales University, 7150 Montview Boulevard, Denver, CO 80220. *Phone:* 303-256-9300. *Toll-free phone:* 877-598-3368. *Fax:* 303-598-3368. *E-mail:* den@admissions.jwu.edu. *Web site:* http://www.jwu.edu/.

Jones International University
Centennial, Colorado

- **Proprietary** university, founded 1995
- **Suburban** campus
- **Coed** 4,367 undergraduate students, 19% full-time, 60% women, 40% men
- **Noncompetitive** entrance level

Undergraduates 825 full-time, 3,542 part-time. Students come from 10 other countries; 93% are from out of state; 37% Black or African American, non-Hispanic/Latino; 5% Hispanic/Latino; 0.8% Asian, non-Hispanic/Latino; 0.5% Native Hawaiian or other Pacific Islander, non-Hispanic/Latino; 2% American Indian or Alaska Native, non-Hispanic/Latino; 6% Two or more races, non-Hispanic/Latino; 11% Race/ethnicity unknown. *Retention:* 78% of full-time freshmen returned.

Freshmen *Admission:* 2,147 enrolled.

Faculty *Total:* 131, 82% with terminal degrees.

Academics *Calendar:* continuous. *Degrees:* certificates, associate, bachelor's, master's, doctoral-other, and postbachelor's certificates (offers only online degree programs). *Special study options:* academic remediation for entering students, accelerated degree program, adult/continuing education programs, advanced placement credit, distance learning, double majors, external degree program, independent study, internships, part-time degree program, services for LD students, student-designed majors, summer session for credit. *Unusual degree programs:* 3-2 business administration.

Computers on Campus Students can access the following: computer help desk, free student e-mail accounts, online (class) grades, online (class) registration, online (class) schedules, we are entirely online.

Student Life *Housing:* college housing not available. *Campus security:* We are entirely online, therefore this does not apply.

Costs (2011–12) *Tuition:* $12,480 full-time, $520 per credit hour part-time. Full-time tuition and fees vary according to course level, course load, degree level, and program. Part-time tuition and fees vary according to course level, course load, degree level, and program. *Payment plan:* installment. *Waivers:* employees or children of employees.

Financial Aid Of all full-time matriculated undergraduates who enrolled in 2008, 469 applied for aid, 368 were judged to have need. *Average percent of need met:* 80%. *Average financial aid package:* $7020. *Average need-based loan:* $3450. *Average need-based gift aid:* $3570.

Applying *Options:* electronic application, early admission, deferred entrance. *Required:* high school transcript, minimum 2 GPA. *Required for some:* minimum 2.0 GPA for transfer applicants. *Application deadlines:* rolling (freshmen), rolling (out-of-state freshmen), rolling (transfers). *Notification:*

continuous (freshmen), continuous (out-of-state freshmen), continuous (transfers).

Freshman Application Contact Enrollment Center, Jones International University, 9697 East Mineral Avenue, Centennial, CO 80112. *Phone:* 800-811-5663. *Toll-free phone:* 800-811-5663. *Fax:* 303-799-0966. *E-mail:* registrar@international.edu. *Web site:* http://www.jiu.edu/.

Mesa State College
Grand Junction, Colorado

- **State-supported** comprehensive, founded 1925
- **Small-town** 78-acre campus
- **Coed** 8,046 undergraduate students, 75% full-time, 55% women, 45% men
- **Minimally difficult** entrance level, 80% of applicants were admitted

Undergraduates 6,008 full-time, 2,038 part-time. Students come from 43 states and territories; 14 other countries; 12% are from out of state; 2% Black or African American, non-Hispanic/Latino; 12% Hispanic/Latino; 1% Asian, non-Hispanic/Latino; 0.7% Native Hawaiian or other Pacific Islander, non-Hispanic/Latino; 1% American Indian or Alaska Native, non-Hispanic/Latino; 1% Two or more races, non-Hispanic/Latino; 6% Race/ethnicity unknown; 0.1% international; 7% transferred in; 22% live on campus. *Retention:* 66% of full-time freshmen returned.

Freshmen *Admission:* 5,457 applied, 4,371 admitted, 2,005 enrolled. *Average high school GPA:* 2.97. *Test scores:* SAT critical reading scores over 500: 43%; SAT math scores over 500: 52%; ACT scores over 18: 73%; SAT critical reading scores over 600: 9%; SAT math scores over 600: 16%; ACT scores over 24: 19%; SAT math scores over 700: 2%; ACT scores over 30: 1%.

Faculty *Total:* 454, 48% full-time. *Student/faculty ratio:* 22:1.

Academics *Calendar:* semesters. *Degrees:* certificates, associate, bachelor's, and master's. *Special study options:* academic remediation for entering students, accelerated degree program, adult/continuing education programs, advanced placement credit, distance learning, double majors, honors programs, independent study, internships, off-campus study, part-time degree program, services for LD students, study abroad, summer session for credit.

Computers on Campus 525 computers/terminals are available on campus for general student use. Students can access the following: campus intranet, computer help desk, free student e-mail accounts, online (class) grades, online (class) registration, online (class) schedules. Campuswide network is available. 100% of college-owned or -operated housing units are wired for high-speed Internet access. Wireless service is available via classrooms, computer centers, libraries, student centers.

Student Life *Housing:* on-campus residence required through sophomore year. *Options:* coed, women-only, disabled students. Campus housing is university owned. Freshman applicants given priority for college housing. *Activities and organizations:* drama/theater group, student-run newspaper, radio and television station, choral group, Environmental Club, Student Body Association, KMSA radio station, Rodeo Club, Campus Residents Association. *Campus security:* 24-hour emergency response devices and patrols, late-night transport/escort service, controlled dormitory access, Student Program to Escort other students after dark. *Student services:* health clinic, personal/psychological counseling, legal services.

Athletics Member NCAA. All Division II. *Intercollegiate sports:* baseball M(s), basketball M(s)/W(s), cross-country running M(s)/W(s), football M(s), golf M(s)/W(s), ice hockey M(c), rugby M(c)/W(c), skiing (cross-country) M(c)/W(c), skiing (downhill) M(c)/W(c), soccer M(s)/W(s), softball W(s), swimming and diving M(s)/W(s), tennis M(s)/W(s), track and field W(s), volleyball W(s), wrestling M(s). *Intramural sports:* basketball M/W, equestrian sports M/W, football M/W, racquetball M/W, soccer M/W, softball M/W, swimming and diving M/W, tennis M/W, track and field W, volleyball M/W, water polo M/W.

Standardized Tests *Required:* SAT or ACT (for admission).

Costs (2010–11) *Tuition:* state resident $5480 full-time, $183 per credit hour part-time; nonresident $15,658 full-time, $522 per credit hour part-time. Full-time tuition and fees vary according to course load. Part-time tuition and fees vary according to course load. *Required fees:* $768 full-time, $26 per credit hour part-time. *Room and board:* $8298. Room and board charges vary according to board plan and housing facility. *Payment plan:* installment. *Waivers:* employees or children of employees.

Financial Aid Of all full-time matriculated undergraduates who enrolled in 2008, 4,010 applied for aid, 3,204 were judged to have need, 822 had their need fully met. In 2008, 400 non-need-based awards were made. *Average percent of need met:* 75%. *Average financial aid package:* $10,678. *Average need-based loan:* $7804. *Average need-based gift aid:* $4938. *Average non-need-based aid:* $2135. *Average indebtedness upon graduation:* $18,966.

Applying *Options:* electronic application, deferred entrance. *Application fee:* $30. *Required:* high school transcript. *Recommended:* essay or personal statement, 2 letters of recommendation. *Application deadlines:* rolling (freshmen), rolling (transfers). *Notification:* continuous (freshmen), continuous (transfers).

Freshman Application Contact Admissions, Mesa State College, 1100 North Avenue, Grand Junction, CO 81501. *Phone:* 970-248-1875. *Toll-free phone:* 800-982-MESA. *Fax:* 970-248-1973. *E-mail:* rlarsen@mesastate.edu. *Web site:* http://www.mesastate.edu/.

Metropolitan State College of Denver
Denver, Colorado

- **State-supported** 4-year, founded 1963
- **Urban** 175-acre campus with easy access to Denver
- **Coed**
- **Minimally difficult** entrance level

Faculty *Student/faculty ratio:* 22:1.

Academics *Calendar:* semesters. *Degree:* bachelor's.

Student Life *Campus security:* 24-hour emergency response devices and patrols, late-night transport/escort service.

Athletics Member NCAA. All Division II.

Standardized Tests *Required:* SAT or ACT (for admission). *Required for some:* SAT (for admission), ACT (for admission).

Costs (2010–11) *Tuition:* state resident $3107 full-time, $129 per credit hour part-time; nonresident $13,454 full-time, $561 per credit hour part-time. Full-time tuition and fees vary according to course load and location. Part-time tuition and fees vary according to course load and location. *Required fees:* $986 full-time. *Payment plans:* installment, deferred payment.

Financial Aid *Of all full-time matriculated undergraduates who enrolled in 2009,* 9,892 applied for aid, 7,856 were judged to have need, 471 had their need fully met. 252 Federal Work-Study jobs (averaging $2733). 569 state and other part-time jobs (averaging $3503). *In 2009,* 1354 non-need-based awards were made. *Average percent of need met:* 63. *Average financial aid package:* $7724. *Average need-based loan:* $4059. *Average need-based gift aid:* $5551. *Average non-need-based aid:* $1919. *Average indebtedness upon graduation:* $25,774.

Applying *Options:* electronic application, deferred entrance. *Application fee:* $25. *Required:* high school transcript. *Recommended:* minimum 2 GPA.

Freshman Application Contact Ms. Michelle Brown, Associate Director of Admissions, Metropolitan State College of Denver, PO Box 173362, Denver, CO 80217-3362. *Phone:* 303-556-2615. *Web site:* http://www.mscd.edu/.

Naropa University
Boulder, Colorado

- **Independent** comprehensive, founded 1974
- **Urban** 12-acre campus with easy access to Denver
- **Endowment** $3.9 million
- **Coed** 454 undergraduate students, 88% full-time, 62% women, 38% men
- **Moderately difficult** entrance level, 90% of applicants were admitted

Undergraduates 400 full-time, 54 part-time. Students come from 41 states and territories; 9 other countries; 71% are from out of state; 0.4% Black or African American, non-Hispanic/Latino; 4% Hispanic/Latino; 2% Asian, non-Hispanic/Latino; 0.4% American Indian or Alaska Native, non-Hispanic/Latino; 5% Two or more races, non-Hispanic/Latino; 27% Race/ethnicity unknown; 1% international; 7% transferred in; 15% live on campus. *Retention:* 53% of full-time freshmen returned.

Freshmen *Admission:* 99 applied, 89 admitted, 45 enrolled. *Average high school GPA:* 3.03.

Faculty *Total:* 175, 27% full-time, 33% with terminal degrees. *Student/faculty ratio:* 7:1.

Academics *Calendar:* semesters. *Degrees:* certificates, bachelor's, and master's. *Special study options:* advanced placement credit, double majors, independent study, internships, part-time degree program, services for LD students, student-designed majors, summer session for credit.

Computers on Campus 77 computers/terminals and 80 ports are available on campus for general student use. Students can access the following: computer help desk, free student e-mail accounts, online (class) grades, online (class) registration, online (class) schedules. Campuswide network is available. 100% of college-owned or -operated housing units are wired for high-speed Internet access. Wireless service is available via entire campus.

Student Life *Housing:* on-campus residence required for freshman year. *Options:* coed. Campus housing is university owned. Freshman campus housing is guaranteed. *Activities and organizations:* drama/theater group, student-run newspaper, choral group, UN United Naropa-Student Government, Transition Naropa, Naropa Healers, Root Outdoor Organization, Students for Peace and Justice. *Campus security:* late-night transport/escort service, controlled dormitory access, foot and vehicle patrol 4:30 pm to midnight, 24 hour on-call Safety and Security Manager. *Student services:* personal/psychological counseling.

Costs (2011–12) *Comprehensive fee:* $35,072 includes full-time tuition ($26,200), mandatory fees ($160), and room and board ($8712). Full-time tuition and fees vary according to course load. Part-time tuition: $850 per

credit. Part-time tuition and fees vary according to course load. *Required fees:* $850 per credit part-time, $153 per term part-time. *College room only:* $5580. Room and board charges vary according to board plan. *Payment plan:* installment. *Waivers:* employees or children of employees.

Financial Aid Of all full-time matriculated undergraduates who enrolled in 2009, 310 applied for aid, 283 were judged to have need, 6 had their need fully met. *Average percent of need met:* 88%. *Average financial aid package:* $25,123. *Average need-based loan:* $9226. *Average need-based gift aid:* $15,279. *Average indebtedness upon graduation:* $23,717.

Applying *Options:* electronic application, deferred entrance. *Application fee:* $50. *Required:* essay or personal statement, high school transcript, 2 letters of recommendation. *Notification:* continuous (freshmen), continuous (out-of-state freshmen), continuous (transfers).

Freshman Application Contact Mr. Adam Shelffo, Associate Director of Admissions and Multicultural Recruitment Coordinator, Naropa University, 2130 Arapahoe Avenue, Boulder, CO 80302. *Phone:* 303-245-4693. *Toll-free phone:* 800-772-0410. *Fax:* 303-546-3583. *E-mail:* ashelffo@naropa.edu. *Web site:* http://www.naropa.edu/.

See page 1460 for the College Close-Up.

National American University
Colorado Springs, Colorado

Director of Admissions Director of Admissions, National American University, 5125 North Academy Boulevard, Colorado Springs, CO 80918. *Phone:* 719-590-8300. *E-mail:* csadmissions@national.edu. *Web site:* http://www.national.edu/.

National American University
Denver, Colorado

Freshman Application Contact National American University, 1325 South Colorado Blvd, Suite 100, Denver, CO 80222. *Phone:* 303-876-7112. *Web site:* http://www.national.edu/.

Nazarene Bible College
Colorado Springs, Colorado

- **Independent** 4-year, founded 1967, affiliated with Church of the Nazarene
- **Urban** 64-acre campus with easy access to Colorado Springs
- **Endowment** $2.3 million
- **Coed**
- **Noncompetitive** entrance level

Faculty *Student/faculty ratio:* 10:1.

Academics *Calendar:* quarters. *Degrees:* diplomas, associate, and bachelor's.

Student Life *Campus security:* student patrols.

Costs (2010–11) *Tuition:* $8505 full-time. *Required fees:* $540 full-time.

Financial Aid Of all full-time matriculated undergraduates who enrolled in 2008, 144 applied for aid, 144 were judged to have need. 6 Federal Work-Study jobs (averaging $3348). *Average percent of need met:* 50. *Average financial aid package:* $9210. *Average need-based gift aid:* $1500. *Average indebtedness upon graduation:* $31,211.

Applying *Options:* electronic application, deferred entrance. *Required:* essay or personal statement, high school transcript, 2 letters of recommendation.

Freshman Application Contact Dr. Laurel Matson, Director of Admissions/Public Relations, Nazarene Bible College, 1111 Academy Park Loop, Colorado Springs, CO 80910-3704. *Phone:* 719-884-5061. *Toll-free phone:* 800-873-3873. *Fax:* 719-884-5199. *Web site:* http://www.nbc.edu/.

Pima Medical Institute
Denver, Colorado

- **Proprietary** primarily 2-year, founded 1988, part of Vocational Training Institutes, Inc.
- **Urban** campus
- **Coed** 922 undergraduate students
- **Minimally difficult** entrance level

Academics *Calendar:* modular. *Degrees:* certificates, associate, and bachelor's. *Special study options:* academic remediation for entering students, cooperative education, distance learning, internships.

Computers on Campus Campuswide network is available.

Student Life *Housing:* college housing not available.

Standardized Tests *Required:* Wonderlic Scholastic Level Exam (for admission).

Applying *Required:* interview. *Required for some:* high school transcript.

Freshman Application Contact Admissions Office, Pima Medical Institute, 1701 West 72nd Avenue, Suite 130, Denver, CO 80221. *Phone:* 303-426-1800. *Toll-free phone:* 888-898-9048. *Web site:* http://www.pmi.edu/.

Platt College
Aurora, Colorado

Freshman Application Contact Admissions Office, Platt College, 3100 South Parker Road, Suite 200, Aurora, CO 80014-3141. *Phone:* 303-369-5151. *Web site:* http://www.plattcolorado.edu/.

Regis University
Denver, Colorado

- **Independent Roman Catholic (Jesuit)** comprehensive, founded 1877
- **Suburban** 90-acre campus with easy access to Denver
- **Endowment** $38.1 million
- **Coed** 5,594 undergraduate students, 45% full-time, 65% women, 35% men
- **Moderately difficult** entrance level, 87% of applicants were admitted

Undergraduates 2,503 full-time, 3,091 part-time. Students come from 52 states and territories; 10 other countries; 29% are from out of state; 6% Black or African American, non-Hispanic/Latino; 12% Hispanic/Latino; 4% Asian, non-Hispanic/Latino; 0.3% Two or more races, non-Hispanic/Latino; 11% Race/ethnicity unknown; 0.8% international; 17% transferred in; 50% live on campus. *Retention:* 79% of full-time freshmen returned.

Freshmen *Admission:* 3,701 applied, 3,214 admitted, 501 enrolled. *Average high school GPA:* 3.56. *Test scores:* SAT critical reading scores over 500: 64%; SAT math scores over 500: 61%; SAT writing scores over 500: 67%; ACT scores over 18: 96%; SAT critical reading scores over 600: 21%; SAT math scores over 600: 20%; SAT writing scores over 600: 21%; ACT scores over 24: 52%; SAT critical reading scores over 700: 4%; SAT math scores over 700: 2%; SAT writing scores over 700: 1%; ACT scores over 30: 4%.

Faculty *Total:* 2,222, 11% full-time, 22% with terminal degrees. *Student/faculty ratio:* 8:1.

Academics *Calendar:* semesters. *Degrees:* certificates, bachelor's, master's, doctoral-professional, post-master's, and postbachelor's certificates. *Special study options:* academic remediation for entering students, accelerated degree program, adult/continuing education programs, advanced placement credit, cooperative education, distance learning, double majors, external degree program, freshman honors college, honors programs, independent study, internships, off-campus study, part-time degree program, services for LD students, student-designed majors, study abroad, summer session for credit. *ROTC:* Army (c), Air Force (c). *Unusual degree programs:* 3-2 engineering with Washington University in St. Louis.

Computers on Campus 450 computers/terminals and 1,000 ports are available on campus for general student use. Students can access the following: campus intranet, computer help desk, free student e-mail accounts, online (class) grades, online (class) registration, online (class) schedules. Campus-wide network is available. 100% of college-owned or -operated housing units are wired for high-speed Internet access. Wireless service is available via entire campus.

Student Life *Housing:* on-campus residence required through sophomore year. *Options:* coed, disabled students. Campus housing is university owned. Freshman applicants given priority for college housing. *Activities and organizations:* drama/theater group, student-run newspaper, radio station, choral group, Musical Theater Club, student government, Club Sports, Outdoor Adventure, Black Student Association. *Campus security:* 24-hour emergency response devices and patrols, student patrols, late-night transport/escort service, controlled dormitory access. *Student services:* health clinic, personal/psychological counseling.

Athletics Member NCAA. All Division II. *Intercollegiate sports:* baseball M(s), basketball M(s)/W(s), cross-country running M(s)/W(s), golf M(s)/W(s), lacrosse W(s), soccer M(s)/W(s), softball W(s), volleyball W(s). *Intramural sports:* basketball M/W, bowling M/W, cheerleading M/W, football M/W, ice hockey M, lacrosse M, rugby M, soccer M/W, softball W, tennis M/W, ultimate Frisbee M/W, volleyball M/W.

Standardized Tests *Required:* SAT or ACT (for admission).

Costs (2011–12) *Comprehensive fee:* $32,982 includes full-time tuition ($23,482), mandatory fees ($400), and room and board ($9100). Full-time tuition and fees vary according to course load, location, program, and reciprocity agreements. Part-time tuition: $482 per credit hour. Part-time tuition and fees vary according to location, program, and reciprocity agreements. *Required fees:* $300 per term part-time. *College room only:* $5200. Room and board charges vary according to board plan and housing facility. *Payment plans:* installment, deferred payment. *Waivers:* employees or children of employees.

Financial Aid Of all full-time matriculated undergraduates who enrolled in 2008, 1,210 applied for aid, 765 were judged to have need, 432 had their need fully met. 231 Federal Work-Study jobs (averaging $1829). 443 state and other part-time jobs (averaging $1752). In 2008, 307 non-need-based awards were made. *Average percent of need met:* 54%. *Average financial aid package:* $15,333. *Average need-based loan:* $2226. *Average need-based gift aid:* $10,756. *Average non-need-based aid:* $10,411. *Average indebtedness upon graduation:* $25,558.

Applying *Options:* electronic application, deferred entrance. *Application fee:* $40. *Required:* essay or personal statement, high school transcript, minimum 2.5 GPA. *Required for some:* 1 letter of recommendation, interview. *Application deadlines:* rolling (freshmen), rolling (out-of-state freshmen), rolling (transfers). *Notification:* continuous (freshmen), continuous (transfers).

Freshman Application Contact Mr. Vic Davolt, Director of Admission, Regis University, 3333 Regis Boulevard, Denver, CO 80221-1099. *Phone:* 303-458-4905. *Toll-free phone:* 800-388-2366 Ext. 4900. *Fax:* 303-964-5534. *E-mail:* regisadm@regis.edu. *Web site:* http://www.regis.edu/.

Remington College–Colorado Springs Campus

Colorado Springs, Colorado

Freshman Application Contact Remington College–Colorado Springs Campus, 6050 Erin Park Drive, #250, Colorado Springs, CO 80918. *Phone:* 719-532-1234 Ext. 202. *Web site:* http://www.remingtoncollege.edu/.

Rocky Mountain College of Art + Design

Lakewood, Colorado

- **Proprietary** 4-year, founded 1963
- **Suburban** 23-acre campus
- **Coed** 684 undergraduate students, 89% full-time, 62% women, 38% men
- **Moderately difficult** entrance level, 100% of applicants were admitted

Undergraduates 612 full-time, 72 part-time. Students come from 42 states and territories; 27% are from out of state; 2% Black or African American, non-Hispanic/Latino; 11% Hispanic/Latino; 3% Asian, non-Hispanic/Latino; 1% American Indian or Alaska Native, non-Hispanic/Latino; 1% Two or more races, non-Hispanic/Latino; 8% Race/ethnicity unknown; 0.3% international; 14% transferred in. *Retention:* 62% of full-time freshmen returned.

Freshmen *Admission:* 502 applied, 502 admitted, 149 enrolled.

Faculty *Total:* 105, 38% full-time, 50% with terminal degrees. *Student/faculty ratio:* 10:1.

Academics *Calendar:* trimesters. *Degree:* bachelor's. *Special study options:* academic remediation for entering students, accelerated degree program, advanced placement credit, cooperative education, distance learning, double majors, honors programs, independent study, internships, part-time degree program, services for LD students, study abroad, summer session for credit.

Computers on Campus 330 computers/terminals are available on campus for general student use. Students can access the following: campus intranet, computer help desk, free student e-mail accounts, online (class) grades, online (class) registration, online (class) schedules, computer assistance, student web hosting. Campuswide network is available. Wireless service is available via entire campus.

Student Life *Housing:* college housing not available. *Activities and organizations:* student-run newspaper, The Sanatorium (student newspaper), The American Society of Interior Designers, The American Institute of Graphic Arts, Belly Dancing Club, writing club. *Campus security:* 24-hour emergency response devices, late-night transport/escort service. *Student services:* personal/psychological counseling.

Costs (2010–11) *Tuition:* $26,832 full-time, $1118 per credit hour part-time. Part-time tuition and fees vary according to course load. No tuition increase for student's term of enrollment. *Room only:* Room and board charges vary according to board plan and housing facility. *Payment plan:* installment. *Waivers:* employees or children of employees.

Financial Aid Of all full-time matriculated undergraduates who enrolled in 2009, 531 applied for aid, 447 were judged to have need, 20 had their need fully met. 30 Federal Work-Study jobs (averaging $2482). 46 state and other part-time jobs (averaging $2548). In 2009, 66 non-need-based awards were made. *Average percent of need met:* 66%. *Average financial aid package:* $18,770. *Average need-based loan:* $4688. *Average need-based gift aid:* $4764. *Average non-need-based aid:* $5145. *Average indebtedness upon graduation:* $26,247.

Applying *Options:* electronic application. *Application fee:* $50. *Required:* essay or personal statement, minimum 2 GPA, interview, portfolio. *Required for some:* high school transcript. *Application deadlines:* rolling (freshmen), rolling (transfers). *Notification:* continuous (freshmen), continuous (transfers).

Freshman Application Contact Mr. Joe Leonhardt, Vice President of Admissions, Rocky Mountain College of Art + Design, 1600 Pierce Street, Lakewood, CO 80214. *Phone:* 303-225-8567. *Toll-free phone:* 800-888-ARTS. *Fax:* 303-759-4970. *E-mail:* admit@rmcad.edu. *Web site:* http://www.rmcad.edu/.

United States Air Force Academy

Colorado Springs, Colorado

- **Federally supported** 4-year, founded 1954
- **Suburban** 18,000-acre campus with easy access to Colorado Springs and Denver
- **Coed, primarily men** 4,619 undergraduate students, 100% full-time, 21% women, 79% men
- **Most difficult** entrance level, 11% of applicants were admitted

Undergraduates 4,619 full-time. Students come from 52 states and territories; 17 other countries; 93% are from out of state; 6% Black or African American, non-Hispanic/Latino; 8% Hispanic/Latino; 8% Asian, non-Hispanic/Latino; 0.5% Native Hawaiian or other Pacific Islander, non-Hispanic/Latino; 0.8% American Indian or Alaska Native, non-Hispanic/Latino; 2% Race/ethnicity unknown; 1% international; 100% live on campus. *Retention:* 89% of full-time freshmen returned.

Freshmen *Admission:* 11,627 applied, 1,269 admitted, 1,245 enrolled. *Average high school GPA:* 3.86. *Test scores:* SAT critical reading scores over 500: 98%; SAT math scores over 500: 100%; SAT writing scores over 500: 97%; ACT scores over 18: 99%; SAT critical reading scores over 600: 75%; SAT math scores over 600: 90%; SAT writing scores over 600: 56%; ACT scores over 24: 99%; SAT critical reading scores over 700: 17%; SAT math scores over 700: 29%; SAT writing scores over 700: 10%; ACT scores over 30: 52%.

Faculty *Total:* 569, 95% full-time, 48% with terminal degrees. *Student/faculty ratio:* 8:1.

Academics *Calendar:* semesters. *Degree:* bachelor's. *Special study options:* academic remediation for entering students, advanced placement credit, double majors, English as a second language, honors programs, independent study, internships, off-campus study, student-designed majors, study abroad, summer session for credit.

Computers on Campus 125 computers/terminals are available on campus for general student use. Students can access the following: campus intranet, computer help desk, free student e-mail accounts, online (class) grades, online (class) registration, online (class) schedules. Campuswide network is available. Wireless service is available via classrooms, computer centers, computer labs, learning centers, libraries, student centers.

Student Life *Housing:* on-campus residence required through senior year. *Options:* coed. Campus housing is university owned. Freshman campus housing is guaranteed. *Activities and organizations:* drama/theater group, student-run radio station, choral group, marching band, Cadet Ski Club, Men's and Women's Rugby Club, Cadet Cycling Club, Aviation Club, Drum and Bugle Corps. *Campus security:* 24-hour emergency response devices and patrols, late-night transport/escort service, controlled dormitory access, self-defense education, well-lit campus. *Student services:* health clinic, personal/psychological counseling, legal services.

Athletics Member NCAA. All Division I except football (Division I-A). *Intercollegiate sports:* archery M(c)/W(c), baseball M, basketball M/W, cheerleading M/W, cross-country running M/W, equestrian sports M(c)/W(c), fencing M/W, golf M(c), gymnastics M/W, ice hockey M, lacrosse M/W(c), racquetball M(c)/W(c), riflery M/W, rock climbing M(c)/W(c), rugby M(c)/W(c), skiing (cross-country) M(c)/W(c), skiing (downhill) M(c)/W(c), soccer M/W, softball W(c), squash M(c)/W(c), swimming and diving M/W, track and field M/W, ultimate Frisbee M(c)/W(c), volleyball M(c)/W, water polo M/W(c), weight lifting M(c)/W(c), wrestling M. *Intramural sports:* basketball M/W, cross-country running M/W, racquetball M/W, rugby M/W, soccer M/W, softball M/W, ultimate Frisbee M/W, volleyball M/W, wrestling M.

Standardized Tests *Required:* SAT or ACT (for admission).

Costs (2010–11) *Comprehensive fee:* Tuition, room and board, and medical and dental care are provided by the U.S. government. Each cadet receives a salary from which to pay for uniforms, supplies, and personal expenses.

Applying *Options:* electronic application. *Required:* essay or personal statement, high school transcript, minimum 2 GPA, interview, authorized nomination. *Recommended:* 3 letters of recommendation. *Application deadlines:* 1/31 (freshmen), 1/31 (transfers). *Notification:* 10/15 (freshmen), 10/15 (transfers).

Freshman Application Contact Selections Division Admission Counselor, United States Air Force Academy, HQ USAFA/RR, 2304 Cadet Drive, Suite 2400, USAF Academy, CO 80840-5025. *Phone:* 800-443-9266. *Toll-free phone:* 800-443-9266. *Fax:* 719-333-3012. *Web site:* http://www.usafa.edu/.

See page 1676 for the College Close-Up.

University of Colorado at Colorado Springs
Colorado Springs, Colorado

- **State-supported** university, founded 1965, part of University of Colorado System
- **Suburban** 532-acre campus with easy access to Denver
- **Endowment** $20.0 million
- **Coed** 7,300 undergraduate students, 80% full-time, 54% women, 46% men
- **Moderately difficult** entrance level, 62% of applicants were admitted

Undergraduates 5,861 full-time, 1,439 part-time. Students come from 51 states and territories; 41 other countries; 9% are from out of state; 4% Black or African American, non-Hispanic/Latino; 12% Hispanic/Latino; 5% Asian, non-Hispanic/Latino; 0.9% American Indian or Alaska Native, non-Hispanic/Latino; 0.9% Two or more races, non-Hispanic/Latino; 5% Race/ethnicity unknown; 0.5% international; 13% transferred in; 13% live on campus. *Retention:* 68% of full-time freshmen returned.

Freshmen *Admission:* 4,853 applied, 3,022 admitted, 1,156 enrolled. *Average high school GPA:* 3.27. *Test scores:* SAT critical reading scores over 500: 70%; SAT math scores over 500: 70%; ACT scores over 18: 96%; SAT critical reading scores over 600: 28%; SAT math scores over 600: 31%; ACT scores over 24: 48%; SAT critical reading scores over 700: 4%; SAT math scores over 700: 3%; ACT scores over 30: 7%.

Faculty *Total:* 601, 54% full-time, 37% with terminal degrees. *Student/faculty ratio:* 21:1.

Academics *Calendar:* semesters. *Degrees:* certificates, bachelor's, master's, doctoral-professional, doctoral-research/scholarship, and postbachelor's certificates. *Special study options:* academic remediation for entering students, accelerated degree program, adult/continuing education programs, advanced placement credit, cooperative education, distance learning, double majors, English as a second language, honors programs, independent study, internships, off-campus study, part-time degree program, services for LD students, student-designed majors, study abroad, summer session for credit. *ROTC:* Army (b).

Computers on Campus 500 computers/terminals are available on campus for general student use. Students can access the following: campus intranet, computer help desk, free student e-mail accounts, online (class) grades, online (class) registration, online (class) schedules, student portal, learning management system (Blackboard). Campuswide network is available. 100% of college-owned or -operated housing units are wired for high-speed Internet access. Wireless service is available via entire campus.

Student Life *Housing options:* coed, men-only, women-only, disabled students. Campus housing is university owned. Freshman applicants given priority for college housing. *Activities and organizations:* drama/theater group, student-run newspaper, radio station, Fans Initiating Growth Honor and Tradition (spirit club), Pi Beta Phi, Sustainability Club, Campus Crusade for Christ, Navigators, national fraternities, national sororities. *Campus security:* 24-hour emergency response devices and patrols, student patrols, late-night transport/escort service, controlled dormitory access. *Student services:* health clinic, personal/psychological counseling.

Athletics Member NCAA. All Division II. *Intercollegiate sports:* baseball M(c), basketball M(s)/W(s), cross-country running M(s)/W(s), golf M(s), ice hockey M(c), lacrosse M(c), rock climbing M(c)/W(c), soccer M(s)/W(s), softball W(s), tennis M(c)/W(c), track and field M(s)/W(s), volleyball M(c)/W(s). *Intramural sports:* badminton M/W, basketball M/W, bowling M/W, soccer M/W, table tennis M/W, ultimate Frisbee M/W, volleyball M/W.

Standardized Tests *Required:* SAT or ACT (for admission).

Costs (2010–11) *One-time required fee:* $40. *Tuition:* state resident $6270 full-time, $271 per credit hour part-time; nonresident $15,920 full-time, $796 per credit hour part-time. Full-time tuition and fees vary according to course load, location, program, reciprocity agreements, and student level. Part-time tuition and fees vary according to course load, location, program, reciprocity agreements, and student level. *Required fees:* $1146 full-time, $27 per credit hour part-time, $209 per term part-time. *Room only:* $6778. Room and board charges vary according to board plan and housing facility. *Payment plan:* installment. *Waivers:* employees or children of employees.

Financial Aid Of all full-time matriculated undergraduates who enrolled in 2009, 4,762 applied for aid, 3,285 were judged to have need, 265 had their need fully met. 104 Federal Work-Study jobs (averaging $3673). 299 state and other part-time jobs (averaging $3795). In 2009, 214 non-need-based awards were made. *Average percent of need met:* 55%. *Average financial aid package:* $8648. *Average need-based loan:* $4285. *Average need-based gift aid:* $6470. *Average non-need-based aid:* $1551. *Average indebtedness upon graduation:* $21,551.

Applying *Options:* electronic application, deferred entrance. *Application fee:* $50. *Required:* high school transcript. *Application deadlines:* rolling (freshmen), rolling (out-of-state freshmen), rolling (transfers). *Notification:* continuous (freshmen), continuous (out-of-state freshmen), continuous (transfers).

Freshman Application Contact Mr. Chris Beiswanger, Director of Student Recruitment and Admissions Counseling, University of Colorado at Colorado Springs, 1420 Austin Bluffs Parkway, Colorado Springs, CO 80918. *Phone:* 719-255-3088. *Toll-free phone:* 800-990-8227 Ext. 3383. *E-mail:* cbeiswan@uccs.edu. *Web site:* http://www.uccs.edu/.

University of Colorado Boulder
Boulder, Colorado

- **State-supported** university, founded 1876, part of University of Colorado System
- **Suburban** 600-acre campus with easy access to Denver
- **Endowment** $330.6 million
- **Coed** 26,433 undergraduate students, 91% full-time, 47% women, 53% men
- **Moderately difficult** entrance level, 83% of applicants were admitted

Undergraduates 24,013 full-time, 2,420 part-time. Students come from 51 states and territories; 95 other countries; 33% are from out of state; 2% Black or African American, non-Hispanic/Latino; 7% Hispanic/Latino; 6% Asian, non-Hispanic/Latino; 0.6% American Indian or Alaska Native, non-Hispanic/Latino; 0.9% Two or more races, non-Hispanic/Latino; 4% Race/ethnicity unknown; 2% international; 4% transferred in; 24% live on campus. *Retention:* 85% of full-time freshmen returned.

Freshmen *Admission:* 20,995 applied, 17,427 admitted, 5,201 enrolled. *Average high school GPA:* 3.55. *Test scores:* SAT critical reading scores over 500: 85%; SAT math scores over 500: 90%; ACT scores over 18: 99%; SAT critical reading scores over 600: 41%; SAT math scores over 600: 53%; ACT scores over 24: 78%; SAT critical reading scores over 700: 7%; SAT math scores over 700: 10%; ACT scores over 30: 18%.

Faculty *Total:* 2,050, 68% full-time, 70% with terminal degrees. *Student/faculty ratio:* 18:1.

Academics *Calendar:* semesters. *Degrees:* bachelor's, master's, doctoral-professional, doctoral-research/scholarship, and post-master's certificates. *Special study options:* accelerated degree program, adult/continuing education programs, advanced placement credit, cooperative education, distance learning, double majors, English as a second language, freshman honors college, honors programs, independent study, internships, off-campus study, part-time degree program, services for LD students, student-designed majors, study abroad, summer session for credit. *ROTC:* Army (b), Navy (b), Air Force (b). *Unusual degree programs:* 3-2 nursing with University of Colorado at Denver and Health Sciences Center; child health associate, dental hygiene, medical technology, pharmacy at the University of Colorado at Denver and Health Sciences Center.

Computers on Campus 1,823 computers/terminals are available on campus for general student use. Students can access the following: campus intranet, computer help desk, free student e-mail accounts, online (class) grades, online (class) registration, online (class) schedules, standard and academic software, student government voting. Campuswide network is available. 100% of college-owned or -operated housing units are wired for high-speed Internet access. Wireless service is available via entire campus.

Student Life *Housing:* on-campus residence required for freshman year. *Options:* coed, disabled students. Campus housing is university owned and is provided by a third party. Freshman campus housing is guaranteed. *Activities and organizations:* drama/theater group, student-run newspaper, radio station, choral group, marching band, student government, Environmental Center, Ski and Snowboard Club, AIESEC (international leadership organization), Program Council, national fraternities, national sororities. *Campus security:* 24-hour emergency response devices and patrols, student patrols, late-night transport/escort service, controlled dormitory access, University police department. *Student services:* health clinic, personal/psychological counseling, women's center, legal services.

Athletics Member NCAA. All Division I except football (Division I-A). *Intercollegiate sports:* baseball M(c), basketball M(s)/W(s), crew M(c)/W(c), cross-country running M(s)/W(s), equestrian sports M(c)/W(c), fencing M(c)/W(c), field hockey M(c)/W(c), golf M(s)/W(s), ice hockey M(c)/W(c), lacrosse M(c)/W(c), racquetball M(c)/W(c), rugby M(c)/W(c), skiing (cross-country) M(s)/W(s), skiing (downhill) M(s)/W(s), soccer M(c)/W(s), softball W(c), swimming and diving M(c)/W(c), tennis M(c)/W(s), track and field M(s)/W(s), ultimate Frisbee M(c)/W(c), volleyball M(c)/W(s), water polo M(c)/W(c), wrestling M(c). *Intramural sports:* basketball M/W, ice hockey M/W, soccer M/W, tennis M/W, ultimate Frisbee M/W, volleyball M/W, water polo M/W.

Standardized Tests *Required:* SAT or ACT (for admission).

Costs (2010–11) *One-time required fee:* $182. *Tuition:* state resident $7018 full-time; nonresident $28,000 full-time. Full-time tuition and fees vary according to program. Part-time tuition and fees vary according to course load and program. *Required fees:* $1493 full-time. *Room and board:* $10,792. Room and board charges vary according to board plan, housing facility, and location. *Payment plan:* deferred payment. *Waivers:* senior citizens and employees or children of employees.

Financial Aid Of all full-time matriculated undergraduates who enrolled in 2008, 18,910 applied for aid, 8,983 were judged to have need, 5,027 had their need fully met. 1,271 Federal Work-Study jobs (averaging $1640). 867 state and other part-time jobs (averaging $2356). In 2008, 6582 non-need-based awards were made. *Average percent of need met:* 87%. *Average financial aid package:* $14,151. *Average need-based loan:* $6718. *Average need-based gift aid:* $7873. *Average non-need-based aid:* $6678. *Average indebtedness upon graduation:* $19,758.

Applying *Options:* electronic application, early action, deferred entrance. *Application fee:* $50. *Required:* essay or personal statement, high school transcript. *Required for some:* audition for music program. *Recommended:* minimum 3 GPA. *Application deadlines:* 1/15 (freshmen), 4/1 (transfers), 12/1 (early action). *Notification:* 4/1 (freshmen), continuous (transfers), 1/15 (early action).

Freshman Application Contact Admissions Office, University of Colorado Boulder, Regent Administrative Center 125, 552 UCB, Boulder, CO 80309. *Phone:* 303-492-6301. *Fax:* 303-492-7115. *E-mail:* apply@colorado.edu. *Web site:* http://www.colorado.edu/.

See page 1686 for the College Close-Up.

University of Colorado Denver
Denver, Colorado

- **State-supported** university, founded 1912, part of University of Colorado System
- **Urban** 171-acre campus
- **Endowment** $243.2 million
- **Coed** 13,337 undergraduate students, 57% full-time, 55% women, 45% men
- **Moderately difficult** entrance level, 60% of applicants were admitted

Undergraduates 7,594 full-time, 5,743 part-time. Students come from 50 states and territories; 72 other countries; 6% are from out of state; 6% Black or African American, non-Hispanic/Latino; 13% Hispanic/Latino; 11% Asian, non-Hispanic/Latino; 1% American Indian or Alaska Native, non-Hispanic/Latino; 0.3% Two or more races, non-Hispanic/Latino; 6% Race/ethnicity unknown; 6% international; 11% transferred in; 4% live on campus. *Retention:* 73% of full-time freshmen returned.

Freshmen *Admission:* 5,413 applied, 3,235 admitted, 1,111 enrolled. *Average high school GPA:* 3.29. *Test scores:* SAT critical reading scores over 500: 70%; SAT math scores over 500: 71%; ACT scores over 18: 94%; SAT critical reading scores over 600: 27%; SAT math scores over 600: 31%; ACT scores over 24: 42%; SAT critical reading scores over 700: 4%; SAT math scores over 700: 2%; ACT scores over 30: 3%.

Faculty *Total:* 3,158, 82% full-time, 72% with terminal degrees. *Student/faculty ratio:* 19:1.

Academics *Calendar:* semesters. *Degrees:* bachelor's, master's, doctoral-professional, doctoral-research/scholarship, and post-master's certificates. *Special study options:* accelerated degree program, adult/continuing education programs, advanced placement credit, cooperative education, distance learning, double majors, English as a second language, honors programs, independent study, internships, off-campus study, part-time degree program, services for LD students, student-designed majors, study abroad, summer session for credit. *ROTC:* Army (c), Air Force (c). *Unusual degree programs:* 3-2 School of Public Affairs: Criminal Justice Dual BACJ/MCJ.

Computers on Campus 750 computers/terminals are available on campus for general student use. Students can access the following: campus intranet, computer help desk, free student e-mail accounts, online (class) grades, online (class) registration, online (class) schedules. Campuswide network is available. 100% of college-owned or -operated housing units are wired for high-speed Internet access. Wireless service is available via entire campus.

Student Life *Housing:* on-campus residence required for freshman year. *Options:* coed. Campus housing is provided by a third party. Freshman applicants given priority for college housing. *Activities and organizations:* drama/theater group, student-run newspaper, choral group, Golden Key Honor Society (Academic), Minority Association for Pre-Health Students (Health), Intercultural Club Beijing (Cultural and Social), College of Arts and Media Records (Performing Arts), Veterans Student Organization (Service). *Campus security:* 24-hour emergency response devices and patrols, student patrols, late-night transport/escort service. *Student services:* health clinic, personal/psychological counseling.

Athletics *Intramural sports:* basketball M/W, football M, lacrosse M(c), rugby M(c), skiing (downhill) M(c)/W(c), tennis M/W, volleyball M/W, water polo M(c)/W(c).

Standardized Tests *Required:* SAT or ACT (for admission).

Costs (2011–12) *Tuition:* state resident $6216 full-time, $259 per credit hour part-time; nonresident $19,128 full-time, $797 per credit hour part-time. Full-time tuition and fees vary according to course level, course load, degree level, location, program, reciprocity agreements, and student level. Part-time tuition and fees vary according to course level, course load, degree level, location,

program, reciprocity agreements, and student level. *Required fees:* $998 full-time. *Room and board:* $9956; room only: $6702. Room and board charges vary according to board plan. *Payment plans:* installment, deferred payment. *Waivers:* employees or children of employees.

Financial Aid Of all full-time matriculated undergraduates who enrolled in 2008, 4,154 applied for aid, 3,509 were judged to have need, 242 had their need fully met. In 2008, 410 non-need-based awards were made. *Average percent of need met:* 55%. *Average financial aid package:* $8804. *Average need-based loan:* $4501. *Average need-based gift aid:* $5038. *Average non-need-based aid:* $4268. *Average indebtedness upon graduation:* $21,264.

Applying *Options:* electronic application, deferred entrance. *Application fee:* $50. *Required:* high school transcript, minimum 2.5 GPA. *Required for some:* essay or personal statement, minimum 3 GPA, audition, portfolio, entrance exam. *Application deadlines:* 7/22 (freshmen), 7/22 (transfers). *Notification:* continuous (freshmen), continuous (transfers).

Freshman Application Contact Office of Admissions, University of Colorado Denver, PO Box 173354, Campus Box 167, Denver, CO 80217. *Phone:* 303-556-2704. *E-mail:* admissions@ucdenver.edu. *Web site:* http://www.ucdenver.edu/.

University of Denver
Denver, Colorado

- **Independent** university, founded 1864
- **Urban** 125-acre campus with easy access to Denver
- **Endowment** $289.0 million
- **Coed** 5,455 undergraduate students, 91% full-time, 56% women, 44% men
- **Moderately difficult** entrance level, 72% of applicants were admitted

Undergraduates 4,951 full-time, 504 part-time. Students come from 52 states and territories; 63 other countries; 48% are from out of state; 3% Black or African American, non-Hispanic/Latino; 8% Hispanic/Latino; 4% Asian, non-Hispanic/Latino; 0.1% Native Hawaiian or other Pacific Islander, non-Hispanic/Latino; 0.7% American Indian or Alaska Native, non-Hispanic/Latino; 2% Two or more races, non-Hispanic/Latino; 5% Race/ethnicity unknown; 7% international; 4% transferred in; 43% live on campus. *Retention:* 88% of full-time freshmen returned.

Freshmen *Admission:* 9,337 applied, 6,683 admitted, 1,226 enrolled. *Average high school GPA:* 3.7. *Test scores:* SAT critical reading scores over 500: 90%; SAT math scores over 500: 93%; SAT writing scores over 500: 86%; ACT scores over 18: 100%; SAT critical reading scores over 600: 54%; SAT math scores over 600: 57%; SAT writing scores over 600: 44%; ACT scores over 24: 85%; SAT critical reading scores over 700: 11%; SAT math scores over 700: 12%; SAT writing scores over 700: 6%; ACT scores over 30: 27%.

Faculty *Total:* 1,244, 51% full-time, 46% with terminal degrees. *Student/faculty ratio:* 9:1.

Academics *Calendar:* quarters; semesters for law school. *Degrees:* certificates, bachelor's, master's, doctoral-professional, doctoral-research/scholarship, post-master's, and postbachelor's certificates. *Special study options:* accelerated degree program, adult/continuing education programs, advanced placement credit, cooperative education, distance learning, double majors, English as a second language, freshman honors college, honors programs, independent study, internships, off-campus study, part-time degree program, services for LD students, student-designed majors, study abroad, summer session for credit. *ROTC:* Army (c), Air Force (c). *Unusual degree programs:* 3-2 business administration; engineering; social work; art history; public policy; accounting; international studies; education; environmental science; and geography.

Computers on Campus 200 computers/terminals and 30,000 ports are available on campus for general student use. Students can access the following: campus intranet, computer help desk, free student e-mail accounts, online (class) grades, online (class) registration, online (class) schedules. Campuswide network is available. 95% of college-owned or -operated housing units are wired for high-speed Internet access. Wireless service is available via entire campus.

Student Life *Housing:* on-campus residence required through sophomore year. *Options:* coed, men-only, women-only, cooperative. Campus housing is university owned. Freshman campus housing is guaranteed. *Activities and organizations:* drama/theater group, student-run newspaper, radio station, choral group, Club Sports Council, Alpine Club, DU Programs Board, Greek Life Council, Residence Hall Association, national fraternities, national sororities. *Campus security:* 24-hour emergency response devices and patrols, late-night transport/escort service, controlled dormitory access, 24-hour locked residence hall entrances. *Student services:* health clinic, personal/psychological counseling, women's center.

Athletics Member NCAA. All Division I. *Intercollegiate sports:* baseball M(c), basketball M(s)/W(s), cross-country running M(c)/W(c), equestrian sports M(c)/W(c), golf M(s)/W(s), gymnastics W(s), ice hockey M(s)/W(c), lacrosse M(s)/W(s), racquetball M(c)/W(c), skiing (cross-country) M(s)/W(s), skiing (downhill) M(s)/W(s), soccer M(s)/W(s), softball W(c), swimming and diving M(s)/W(s), tennis M(s)/W(s), volleyball W(s), water polo M(c)/W(c). *Intramural sports:* basketball M/W, field hockey M(c)/W(c), football M/W, golf M(c)/W(c), ice hockey M(c), lacrosse M(c)/W(c), racquetball M(c)/W(c), rock climbing M(c)/W(c), rugby M(c), skiing (downhill) M(c)/W(c), soccer M(c)/W(c), softball M/W, tennis M(c)/W(c), ultimate Frisbee M(c)/W(c), volleyball M(c)/W(c).

Standardized Tests *Required:* SAT or ACT (for admission).

Costs (2011–12) *Comprehensive fee:* $48,017 includes full-time tuition ($36,936), mandatory fees ($897), and room and board ($10,184). Full-time tuition and fees vary according to class time, course load, and program. Part-time tuition and fees vary according to class time, course load, and program. *Room and board:* Room and board charges vary according to board plan and housing facility. *Payment plans:* installment, deferred payment. *Waivers:* senior citizens and employees or children of employees.

Financial Aid Of all full-time matriculated undergraduates who enrolled in 2009, 2,595 applied for aid, 2,117 were judged to have need, 503 had their need fully met. 377 Federal Work-Study jobs (averaging $2771). 274 state and other part-time jobs (averaging $2851). In 2009, 1800 non-need-based awards were made. *Average percent of need met:* 79%. *Average financial aid package:* $28,195. *Average need-based loan:* $4381. *Average need-based gift aid:* $22,351. *Average non-need-based aid:* $12,114. *Average indebtedness upon graduation:* $25,578. *Financial aid deadline:* 4/1.

Applying *Options:* electronic application, early admission, early action, deferred entrance. *Application fee:* $50. *Required:* essay or personal statement, high school transcript, 2 letters of recommendation. *Required for some:* minimum 2 GPA. *Recommended:* interview. *Application deadlines:* 1/15 (freshmen), rolling (transfers), 11/1 (early action). *Notification:* 3/15 (freshmen), continuous (transfers), 1/15 (early action).

Freshman Application Contact Mr. Todd R. Rinehart, Assistant Vice Chancellor for Enrollment, University of Denver, 2197 South University Boulevard, Denver, CO 80208. *Phone:* 303-871-3125. *Toll-free phone:* 800-525-9495. *Fax:* 303-871-3301. *E-mail:* admission@du.edu. *Web site:* http://www.du.edu/.

See page 1688 for the College Close-Up.

University of Northern Colorado
Greeley, Colorado

- **State-supported** university, founded 1890
- **Suburban** 240-acre campus with easy access to Denver
- **Endowment** $66.1 million
- **Coed** 10,090 undergraduate students, 91% full-time, 62% women, 38% men
- **Moderately difficult** entrance level, 88% of applicants were admitted

Undergraduates 9,189 full-time, 901 part-time. Students come from 50 states and territories; 23 other countries; 10% are from out of state; 4% Black or African American, non-Hispanic/Latino; 12% Hispanic/Latino; 2% Asian, non-Hispanic/Latino; 0.1% Native Hawaiian or other Pacific Islander, non-Hispanic/Latino; 0.6% American Indian or Alaska Native, non-Hispanic/Latino; 2% Two or more races, non-Hispanic/Latino; 9% Race/ethnicity unknown; 0.6% international; 8% transferred in; 29% live on campus. *Retention:* 70% of full-time freshmen returned.

Freshmen *Admission:* 6,410 applied, 5,645 admitted, 2,247 enrolled. *Average high school GPA:* 3.22. *Test scores:* SAT critical reading scores over 500: 65%; SAT math scores over 500: 63%; ACT scores over 18: 91%; SAT critical reading scores over 600: 21%; SAT math scores over 600: 21%; ACT scores over 24: 36%; SAT critical reading scores over 700: 4%; SAT math scores over 700: 1%; ACT scores over 30: 4%.

Faculty *Total:* 715, 70% full-time. *Student/faculty ratio:* 19:1.

Academics *Calendar:* semesters. *Degrees:* bachelor's, master's, doctoral-professional, doctoral-research/scholarship, post-master's, and postbachelor's certificates. *Special study options:* academic remediation for entering students, accelerated degree program, adult/continuing education programs, advanced placement credit, cooperative education, distance learning, double majors, English as a second language, external degree program, honors programs, independent study, internships, off-campus study, part-time degree program, services for LD students, student-designed majors, study abroad, summer session for credit. *ROTC:* Army (b), Air Force (b).

Computers on Campus 1,513 computers/terminals and 800 ports are available on campus for general student use. Students can access the following: computer help desk, free student e-mail accounts, online (class) grades, online (class) registration, online (class) schedules. Campuswide network is available. 100% of college-owned or -operated housing units are wired for high-speed Internet access. Wireless service is available via entire campus.

Student Life *Housing:* on-campus residence required for freshman year. *Options:* coed, women-only, disabled students. Campus housing is university owned. Freshman campus housing is guaranteed. *Activities and organizations:* drama/theater group, student-run newspaper, radio and television station, choral group, marching band, national fraternities, national sororities. *Campus*

security: 24-hour emergency response devices and patrols, student patrols, late-night transport/escort service, controlled dormitory access. *Student services:* health clinic, personal/psychological counseling, women's center, legal services.

Athletics Member NCAA. All Division I. *Intercollegiate sports:* baseball M(s), basketball M(s)/W(s), cross-country running W(s), football M(s), golf M(s)/W(s), ice hockey M(c), lacrosse M(c), rugby M(c)/W(c), soccer M(c)/W(s), softball W(s), swimming and diving W(s), tennis M(s)/W(s), track and field M(s)/W(s), volleyball W(s), wrestling M(s). *Intramural sports:* basketball M/W, football M/W, soccer M/W, softball M/W, volleyball M/W, water polo M/W.

Standardized Tests *Required:* SAT or ACT (for admission).

Costs (2010–11) *Tuition:* state resident $4680 full-time, $195 per credit hour part-time; nonresident $15,864 full-time, $661 per credit hour part-time. Full-time tuition and fees vary according to program. Part-time tuition and fees vary according to program. *Required fees:* $1317 full-time, $60 per credit hour part-time. *Room and board:* $8920; room only: $4188. Room and board charges vary according to board plan, housing facility, and student level. *Payment plan:* deferred payment. *Waivers:* employees or children of employees.

Financial Aid Of all full-time matriculated undergraduates who enrolled in 2008, 6,381 applied for aid, 4,156 were judged to have need, 2,049 had their need fully met. In 2008, 934 non-need-based awards were made. *Average percent of need met:* 99%. *Average financial aid package:* $14,255. *Average need-based loan:* $4245. *Average need-based gift aid:* $7007. *Average non-need-based aid:* $3993.

Applying *Options:* electronic application, deferred entrance. *Application fee:* $45. *Required:* high school transcript, minimum 2.9 GPA. *Application deadlines:* 8/1 (freshmen), 8/1 (out-of-state freshmen), rolling (transfers). *Notification:* continuous (freshmen), continuous (transfers).

Freshman Application Contact Mindy Marshall, Director of Admissions, University of Northern Colorado, Campus Box 10, Carter Hall 3006, Greeley, CO 80639. *Phone:* 970-351-2881. *Toll-free phone:* 888-700-4UNC. *Fax:* 970-351-2984. *E-mail:* admissions@unco.edu. *Web site:* http://www.unco.edu/.

University of Phoenix–Denver Campus
Lone Tree, Colorado

Freshman Application Contact Ms. Audra McQuarie, Registrar/Executive Director, University of Phoenix–Denver Campus, 4035 South Riverpoint Parkway, Mail Stop CF-L101, Phoenix, AZ 85040. *Phone:* 480-557-6151. *Toll-free phone:* 800-776-4867 (in-state); 800-228-7240 (out-of-state). *Fax:* 480-643-3068. *E-mail:* audra.mcquarie@phoenix.edu. *Web site:* http://www.phoenix.edu/.

University of Phoenix–Southern Colorado Campus
Colorado Springs, Colorado

Freshman Application Contact Ms. Audra McQuarie, Registrar/Executive Director, University of Phoenix–Southern Colorado Campus, 4035 South Riverpoint Parkway, Mail Stop CF-L101, Phoenix, AZ 85040. *Phone:* 480-557-6151. *Toll-free phone:* 800-776-4867 (in-state); 800-228-7240 (out-of-state). *Fax:* 480-643-3068. *E-mail:* audra.mcquarie@phoenix.edu. *Web site:* http://www.phoenix.edu/.

Western State College of Colorado
Gunnison, Colorado

- **State-supported** comprehensive, founded 1901
- **Rural** 381-acre campus
- **Coed** 2,169 undergraduate students, 92% full-time, 40% women, 60% men
- **Moderately difficult** entrance level, 66% of applicants were admitted

Undergraduates 1,991 full-time, 178 part-time. Students come from 49 states and territories; 8 other countries; 24% are from out of state; 2% Black or African American, non-Hispanic/Latino; 4% Hispanic/Latino; 1% Native Hawaiian or other Pacific Islander, non-Hispanic/Latino; 0.5% American Indian or Alaska Native, non-Hispanic/Latino; 14% Race/ethnicity unknown; 0.4% international; 7% transferred in. *Retention:* 60% of full-time freshmen returned.

Freshmen *Admission:* 1,928 applied, 1,280 admitted, 491 enrolled. *Average high school GPA:* 3. *Test scores:* SAT critical reading scores over 500: 59%; SAT math scores over 500: 51%; ACT scores over 18: 89%; SAT critical reading scores over 600: 11%; SAT math scores over 600: 11%; ACT scores over 24: 28%; ACT scores over 30: 1%.

Faculty *Total:* 161, 65% full-time, 65% with terminal degrees. *Student/faculty ratio:* 17:1.

Academics *Calendar:* semesters. *Degrees:* bachelor's and master's. *Special study options:* adult/continuing education programs, advanced placement credit, double majors, honors programs, independent study, internships, off-campus study, part-time degree program, services for LD students, study abroad, summer session for credit.

Computers on Campus 181 computers/terminals and 600 ports are available on campus for general student use. Students can access the following: computer help desk, free student e-mail accounts, online (class) grades, online (class) registration, online (class) schedules. Campuswide network is available. 100% of college-owned or -operated housing units are wired for high-speed Internet access. Wireless service is available via classrooms, computer centers, computer labs, dorm rooms, learning centers, libraries, student centers.

Student Life *Housing:* on-campus residence required for freshman year. *Options:* coed, men-only, women-only. Campus housing is university owned. Freshman campus housing is guaranteed. *Activities and organizations:* drama/theater group, student-run newspaper, radio and television station, choral group, Mountain Search and Rescue Team, Student Government Association, Rodeo Club, wilderness pursuits, Peak Productions, national fraternities, national sororities. *Campus security:* 24-hour emergency response devices and patrols, student patrols, late-night transport/escort service, controlled dormitory access. *Student services:* health clinic, personal/psychological counseling.

Athletics Member NCAA. All Division II. *Intercollegiate sports:* baseball M(c), basketball M(s)/W(s), cheerleading M(c)/W(c), cross-country running M(s)/W(s), football M(s), ice hockey M(c), lacrosse M(c)/W(c), rock climbing M(c)/W(c), rugby M(c)/W(c), skiing (cross-country) M(c)/W(c), skiing (downhill) M(c)/W(c), soccer M(s)/W(c), track and field M(s)/W(s), volleyball M(c)/W(s), wrestling M(s)/W(c). *Intramural sports:* basketball M/W, football M/W, golf M/W, soccer M/W, softball M/W, table tennis M/W, tennis M/W, ultimate Frisbee M/W, volleyball M/W.

Standardized Tests *Required:* SAT or ACT (for admission).

Costs (2011–12) *Tuition:* state resident $3422 full-time; nonresident $12,888 full-time. Full-time tuition and fees vary according to course load. Part-time tuition and fees vary according to course load. *Required fees:* $1353 full-time. *Room and board:* $8518; room only: $4420. Room and board charges vary according to board plan and housing facility. *Payment plans:* installment, deferred payment. *Waivers:* senior citizens.

Financial Aid Of all full-time matriculated undergraduates who enrolled in 2009, 1,467 applied for aid, 983 were judged to have need, 84 had their need fully met. 270 Federal Work-Study jobs (averaging $1120). 221 state and other part-time jobs (averaging $1115). In 2009, 482 non-need-based awards were made. *Average percent of need met:* 40%. *Average financial aid package:* $10,049. *Average need-based loan:* $5300. *Average need-based gift aid:* $2500. *Average non-need-based aid:* $1700. *Average indebtedness upon graduation:* $18,600.

Applying *Options:* electronic application, deferred entrance. *Application fee:* $30. *Required:* high school transcript. *Required for some:* essay or personal statement, interview. *Recommended:* minimum 2.5 GPA. *Application deadlines:* 7/1 (freshmen), 7/1 (out-of-state freshmen), 7/1 (transfers). *Notification:* continuous until 11/15 (freshmen), continuous until 11/15 (out-of-state freshmen), continuous (transfers).

Freshman Application Contact Mr. Timothy Albers, Director of Admissions, Western State College of Colorado, 600 North Adams Street, Gunnison, CO 81231. *Phone:* 970-943-2119. *Toll-free phone:* 800-876-5309. *Fax:* 970-943-2212. *E-mail:* admissions@western.edu. *Web site:* http://www.western.edu/.

Westwood College–Denver North
Denver, Colorado

- **Proprietary** 4-year, founded 1953
- **Suburban** campus
- **Coed**

Academics *Calendar:* 5 terms. *Degrees:* diplomas, associate, and bachelor's.
Freshman Application Contact Westwood College–Denver North, 7350 North Broadway, Denver, CO 80221-3653. *Phone:* 303-426-7000. *Toll-free phone:* 800-992-5050. *Web site:* http://www.westwood.edu/.

Westwood College–Denver South
Denver, Colorado

- **Proprietary** 4-year
- **Coed**

Academics *Calendar:* continuous. *Degrees:* associate and bachelor's.
Freshman Application Contact Westwood College–Denver South, 3150 South Sheridan Boulevard, Denver, CO 80227. *Phone:* 303-934-1122. *Toll-free phone:* 800-281-2978. *Web site:* http://www.westwood.edu/.

Westwood College–Online Campus
Broomfield, Colorado

- **Proprietary** comprehensive
- **Coed**

Academics *Degrees:* associate, bachelor's, and master's.
Freshman Application Contact Westwood College–Online Campus, 10249 Church Ranch Way, Broomfield, CO 80021. *Phone:* 720-887-8888. *Web site:* http://www.westwood.edu/.

Yeshiva Toras Chaim Talmudical Seminary
Denver, Colorado

Director of Admissions Rabbi Israel Kagan, Dean, Yeshiva Toras Chaim Talmudical Seminary, 1555 Stuart Street, Denver, CO 80204-1415. *Phone:* 303-629-8200. *Fax:* 303-623-5949.

Yorktown University
Denver, Colorado

Admissions Office Contact Yorktown University, 4340 East Kentucky Avenue, Suite 457, Denver, CO 80246. *Web site:* http://yorktownuniversity.edu/.

CONNECTICUT

Albertus Magnus College
New Haven, Connecticut

- **Independent Roman Catholic** comprehensive, founded 1925
- **Suburban** 55-acre campus
- **Endowment** $12.5 million
- **Coed** 1,571 undergraduate students, 84% full-time, 68% women, 32% men
- **Moderately difficult** entrance level, 82% of applicants were admitted

Undergraduates 1,320 full-time, 251 part-time. Students come from 6 states and territories; 1 other country; 18% Black or African American, non-Hispanic/Latino; 9% Hispanic/Latino; 1% Asian, non-Hispanic/Latino; 0.1% American Indian or Alaska Native, non-Hispanic/Latino; 2% Two or more races, non-Hispanic/Latino; 24% Race/ethnicity unknown; 0.2% international; 7% transferred in; 55% live on campus. *Retention:* 76% of full-time freshmen returned.

Freshmen *Admission:* 537 applied, 440 admitted, 167 enrolled. *Average high school GPA:* 2.81. *Test scores:* SAT critical reading scores over 500: 54%; SAT math scores over 500: 48%; SAT writing scores over 500: 48%; SAT critical reading scores over 600: 15%; SAT math scores over 600: 9%; SAT writing scores over 600: 8%; SAT critical reading scores over 700: 4%; SAT math scores over 700: 4%; SAT writing scores over 700: 2%.

Faculty *Total:* 65, 65% full-time, 63% with terminal degrees. *Student/faculty ratio:* 15:1.

Academics *Calendar:* semesters. *Degrees:* associate, bachelor's, and master's. *Special study options:* academic remediation for entering students, accelerated degree program, advanced placement credit, distance learning, double majors, English as a second language, freshman honors college, honors programs, independent study, internships, part-time degree program, services for LD students, student-designed majors, summer session for credit.

Computers on Campus 196 computers/terminals and 110 ports are available on campus for general student use. Students can access the following: computer help desk, free student e-mail accounts, online (class) grades, online (class) registration. Campuswide network is available. 100% of college-owned or -operated housing units are wired for high-speed Internet access. Wireless service is available via entire campus.

Student Life *Housing options:* coed, women-only. Campus housing is university owned. Freshman campus housing is guaranteed. *Activities and organizations:* drama/theater group, student-run newspaper, Student Government Association, College Drama, Minority Student Union. *Campus security:* 24-hour emergency response devices and patrols, late-night transport/escort service, controlled dormitory access. *Student services:* health clinic, personal/psychological counseling.

Athletics Member NCAA. All Division III. *Intercollegiate sports:* baseball M, basketball M/W, cross-country running M/W, lacrosse M/W, soccer M/W, softball W, tennis M/W, volleyball M/W. *Intramural sports:* basketball M/W, racquetball M/W, soccer M/W, squash M/W, table tennis M/W.

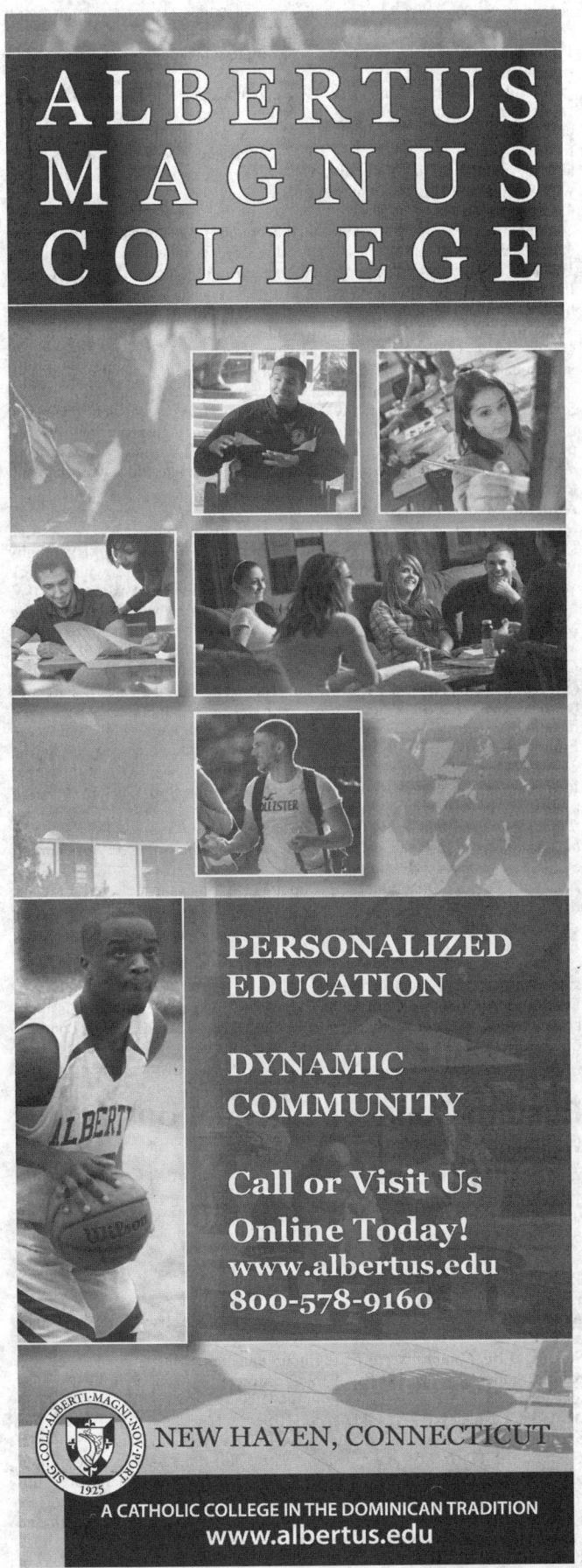

Standardized Tests *Required:* SAT or ACT (for admission). *Recommended:* SAT Subject Tests (for admission).

Costs (2010–11) *Comprehensive fee:* $34,834 includes full-time tuition ($23,904), mandatory fees ($470), and room and board ($10,460). Full-time tuition and fees vary according to program. Part-time tuition: $2390 per course. Part-time tuition and fees vary according to program. *Payment plan:* installment. *Waivers:* senior citizens and employees or children of employees.

Financial Aid Of all full-time matriculated undergraduates who enrolled in 2008, 1,442 applied for aid, 1,307 were judged to have need, 90 had their need fully met. 78 Federal Work-Study jobs (averaging $1583). 34 state and other part-time jobs (averaging $3400). In 2008, 32 non-need-based awards were made. *Average percent of need met:* 53%. *Average financial aid package:* $9074. *Average need-based loan:* $4398. *Average need-based gift aid:* $5739. *Average non-need-based aid:* $3537. *Average indebtedness upon graduation:* $26,404.

Applying *Options:* deferred entrance. *Application fee:* $35. *Required:* high school transcript, 1 letter of recommendation. *Required for some:* minimum 2.5 GPA. *Recommended:* essay or personal statement, minimum 2.5 GPA, interview. *Application deadlines:* 8/20 (freshmen), rolling (transfers). *Notification:* continuous (freshmen), continuous (transfers).

Freshman Application Contact Mr. Nilvio Perez, Dean of Admissions, Albertus Magnus College, 700 Prospect Street, New Haven, CT 06511-1189. *Phone:* 203-773-8501. *Toll-free phone:* 800-578-9160. *Fax:* 203-773-5248. *E-mail:* admissions@albertus.edu. *Web site:* http://www.albertus.edu/.

See page 988 for the College Close-Up.

Bais Binyomin Academy

Stamford, Connecticut

Director of Admissions Director of Admissions, Bais Binyomin Academy, 132 Prospect Street, Stamford, CT 06901-1202. *Phone:* 203-325-4351.

Central Connecticut State University

New Britain, Connecticut

- **State-supported** comprehensive, founded 1849, part of Connecticut State University System
- **Suburban** 294-acre campus
- **Endowment** $26.7 million
- **Coed** 10,085 undergraduate students, 79% full-time, 48% women, 52% men
- **Moderately difficult** entrance level, 60% of applicants were admitted

Undergraduates 7,925 full-time, 2,160 part-time. Students come from 29 states and territories; 41 other countries; 3% are from out of state; 9% Black or African American, non-Hispanic/Latino; 8% Hispanic/Latino; 3% Asian, non-Hispanic/Latino; 0.1% Native Hawaiian or other Pacific Islander, non-Hispanic/Latino; 0.1% American Indian or Alaska Native, non-Hispanic/Latino; 2% Two or more races, non-Hispanic/Latino; 2% Race/ethnicity unknown; 1% international; 7% transferred in; 23% live on campus. *Retention:* 81% of full-time freshmen returned.

Freshmen *Admission:* 6,837 applied, 4,113 admitted, 1,357 enrolled. *Average high school GPA:* 3.01. *Test scores:* SAT critical reading scores over 500: 54%; SAT math scores over 500: 60%; SAT writing scores over 500: 57%; SAT critical reading scores over 600: 9%; SAT math scores over 600: 13%; SAT writing scores over 600: 10%; SAT critical reading scores over 700: 1%; SAT writing scores over 700: 1%.

Faculty *Total:* 966, 46% full-time, 47% with terminal degrees. *Student/faculty ratio:* 16:1.

Academics *Calendar:* semesters. *Degrees:* bachelor's, master's, doctoral-professional, post-master's, and postbachelor's certificates. *Special study options:* academic remediation for entering students, adult/continuing education programs, advanced placement credit, cooperative education, distance learning, English as a second language, honors programs, independent study, internships, off-campus study, part-time degree program, services for LD students, student-designed majors, study abroad, summer session for credit. *ROTC:* Army (c), Air Force (c).

Computers on Campus 750 computers/terminals are available on campus for general student use. Students can access the following: campus intranet, computer help desk, free student e-mail accounts, online (class) grades, online (class) registration, online (class) schedules. Campuswide network is available. 97% of college-owned or -operated housing units are wired for high-speed Internet access. Wireless service is available via entire campus.

Student Life *Housing options:* coed, women-only. Campus housing is university owned. *Activities and organizations:* drama/theater group, student-run newspaper, radio and television station, choral group, Inter-Residence Council, student radio station, Program Council, Outing Club, NAACP, national fraternities, national sororities. *Campus security:* 24-hour emergency response devices and patrols, student patrols, late-night transport/escort service, controlled dormitory access. *Student services:* health clinic, personal/psychological counseling, women's center.

Athletics Member NCAA. All Division I except football (Division I-AA). *Intercollegiate sports:* baseball M(s), basketball M(s)/W(s), cross-country running M(s)/W(s), fencing M(c)/W(c), golf M(s)/W(s), lacrosse M(c)/W(s), soccer M(s)/W(s), softball W(s), swimming and diving W(s), track and field M(s)/W(s), volleyball W(s). *Intramural sports:* basketball M/W, field hockey W(c), football M, rugby M(c)/W(c), soccer M/W, softball M/W, volleyball M/W.

Standardized Tests *Required:* SAT (for admission).

Costs (2010–11) *Tuition:* state resident $4023 full-time, $168 per credit part-time; nonresident $13,020 full-time, $171 per credit part-time. Full-time tuition and fees vary according to course level, course load, program, and reciprocity agreements. Part-time tuition and fees vary according to course level, course load, and program. *Required fees:* $3838 full-time, $207 per credit part-time, $55 per term part-time. *Room and board:* $9576; room only: $5572. Room and board charges vary according to board plan. *Payment plan:* installment. *Waivers:* senior citizens and employees or children of employees.

Financial Aid Of all full-time matriculated undergraduates who enrolled in 2009, 6,898 applied for aid, 5,295 were judged to have need, 478 had their need fully met. In 2009, 147 non-need-based awards were made. *Average percent of need met:* 62%. *Average financial aid package:* $7759. *Average need-based loan:* $4181. *Average need-based gift aid:* $4007. *Average non-need-based aid:* $3615. *Average indebtedness upon graduation:* $19,086.

Applying *Options:* electronic application. *Application fee:* $50. *Required:* essay or personal statement, high school transcript, minimum 2 GPA. *Required for some:* interview. *Recommended:* minimum 3 GPA, 1 letter of recommendation. *Application deadlines:* 6/1 (freshmen), 6/1 (transfers). *Notification:* 12/1 (freshmen), continuous until 7/1 (transfers).

Freshman Application Contact Central Connecticut State University, 1615 Stanley Street, New Britain, CT 06050. *Phone:* 860-832-2285. *Toll-free phone:* 888-733-2278. *Fax:* 860-832-2522. *E-mail:* admissions@ccsu.edu. *Web site:* http://www.ccsu.edu/.

Charter Oak State College
New Britain, Connecticut

- **State-supported** 4-year, founded 1973
- **Small-town** campus
- **Endowment** $1.4 million
- **Coed**
- **Noncompetitive** entrance level

Faculty *Student/faculty ratio:* 11:1.

Academics *Calendar:* continuous. *Degrees:* associate and bachelor's (offers only external degree programs).

Costs (2010–11) *Tuition:* state resident $203 per credit hour part-time; nonresident $275 per credit hour part-time. *Required fees:* $45 per term part-time.

Financial Aid *Of all full-time matriculated undergraduates who enrolled in 2003,* 355 applied for aid, 226 were judged to have need, 25 had their need fully met. *Average percent of need met:* 75. *Average financial aid package:* $4464. *Average need-based loan:* $1800.

Applying *Options:* electronic application, deferred entrance. *Application fee:* $75.

Freshman Application Contact Ms. Lori Pendleton, Director of Admissions, Charter Oak State College, 55 Paul J. Manafort Drive, New Britain, CT 06053-2150. *Phone:* 860-832-3858. *Fax:* 860-832-3999. *E-mail:* info@charteroak.edu. *Web site:* http://www.charteroak.edu/.

Connecticut College
New London, Connecticut

- **Independent** comprehensive, founded 1911
- **Suburban** 702-acre campus
- **Endowment** $179.3 million
- **Coed** 1,880 undergraduate students, 97% full-time, 60% women, 40% men
- **Very difficult** entrance level, 32% of applicants were admitted

Undergraduates 1,832 full-time, 48 part-time. Students come from 46 states and territories; 74 other countries; 83% are from out of state; 4% Black or African American, non-Hispanic/Latino; 6% Hispanic/Latino; 3% Asian, non-Hispanic/Latino; 0.1% Native Hawaiian or other Pacific Islander, non-Hispanic/Latino; 0.1% American Indian or Alaska Native, non-Hispanic/Latino; 3% Two or more races, non-Hispanic/Latino; 4% Race/ethnicity unknown; 4% international; 0.6% transferred in; 99% live on campus. *Retention:* 89% of full-time freshmen returned.

Freshmen *Admission:* 5,301 applied, 1,678 admitted, 488 enrolled. *Test scores:* SAT critical reading scores over 500: 99%; SAT math scores over 500: 98%; SAT writing scores over 500: 99%; ACT scores over 18: 100%; SAT critical reading scores over 600: 90%; SAT math scores over 600: 86%; SAT writing scores over 600: 89%; ACT scores over 24: 92%; SAT critical reading

scores over 700: 33%; SAT math scores over 700: 22%; SAT writing scores over 700: 32%; ACT scores over 30: 45%.

Faculty *Total:* 241, 72% full-time, 74% with terminal degrees. *Student/faculty ratio:* 9:1.

Academics *Calendar:* semesters. *Degrees:* bachelor's and master's. *Special study options:* adult/continuing education programs, advanced placement credit, double majors, independent study, internships, off-campus study, part-time degree program, services for LD students, student-designed majors, study abroad, summer session for credit. *Unusual degree programs:* 3-2 engineering with Washington University in St. Louis.

Computers on Campus Students can access the following: campus intranet, computer help desk, free student e-mail accounts, online (class) grades, online (class) registration, online (class) schedules. Campuswide network is available. 100% of college-owned or -operated housing units are wired for high-speed Internet access. Wireless service is available via classrooms, dorm rooms, libraries, student centers.

Student Life *Housing:* on-campus residence required through senior year. *Options:* coed. Campus housing is university owned. Freshman campus housing is guaranteed. *Activities and organizations:* drama/theater group, student-run newspaper, radio station, choral group, Student Government Association, Student Activity Council, Unity House organizations, sports clubs, student radio station. *Campus security:* 24-hour emergency response devices and patrols, late-night transport/escort service, controlled dormitory access. *Student services:* health clinic, personal/psychological counseling, women's center.

Athletics Member NCAA. All Division III. *Intercollegiate sports:* baseball M(c), basketball M/W, crew M/W, cross-country running M/W, equestrian sports M(c)/W(c), field hockey W, ice hockey M/W, lacrosse M/W, rugby W(c), sailing M/W, skiing (cross-country) M(c)/W(c), skiing (downhill) M(c)/W(c), soccer M/W, squash M/W, swimming and diving M/W, tennis M/W, track and field M/W, ultimate Frisbee M(c)/W(c), volleyball M/W, water polo M/W. *Intramural sports:* basketball M/W, football M, golf M/W, ice hockey M/W, lacrosse M, soccer M/W, softball M/W, tennis M/W, volleyball M/W.

Costs (2010–11) *Comprehensive fee:* $53,110 includes full-time tuition ($43,780), mandatory fees ($210), and room and board ($9120). Part-time tuition: $1233 per credit hour. *College room only:* $4080. *Payment plan:* installment. *Waivers:* senior citizens and employees or children of employees.

Financial Aid Of all full-time matriculated undergraduates who enrolled in 2009, 997 applied for aid, 859 were judged to have need, 859 had their need fully met. 719 Federal Work-Study jobs (averaging $1386). 18 state and other part-time jobs (averaging $992). *Average percent of need met:* 100%. *Average financial aid package:* $31,101. *Average need-based loan:* $4389. *Average need-based gift aid:* $29,616. *Average indebtedness upon graduation:* $22,038. *Financial aid deadline:* 2/1.

Applying *Options:* electronic application, early decision, deferred entrance. *Application fee:* $60. *Required:* essay or personal statement, high school transcript, minimum 2 GPA. *Recommended:* interview. *Application deadlines:* 1/1 (freshmen), 4/1 (transfers). *Early decision deadline:* 11/15 (for plan 1), 1/1 (for plan 2). *Notification:* 3/31 (freshmen), 5/15 (transfers), 12/15 (early decision plan 1), 2/15 (early decision plan 2).

Freshman Application Contact Ms. Martha C. Merrill, Dean of Admissions and Financial Aid, Connecticut College, 270 Mohegan Avenue, New London, CT 06320-4196. *Phone:* 860-439-2200. *Fax:* 860-439-4301. *E-mail:* admission@conncoll.edu. *Web site:* http://www.connecticutcollege.edu/.

Eastern Connecticut State University
Willimantic, Connecticut

- **State-supported** comprehensive, founded 1889, part of Connecticut State University System
- **Small-town** 182-acre campus with easy access to Boston
- **Endowment** $6.9 million
- **Coed**
- **Moderately difficult** entrance level

Faculty *Student/faculty ratio:* 16:1.

Academics *Calendar:* semesters. *Degrees:* associate, bachelor's, and master's.

Student Life *Campus security:* 24-hour emergency response devices and patrols, student patrols, late-night transport/escort service, controlled dormitory access.

Athletics Member NCAA. All Division III.

Standardized Tests *Required:* SAT or ACT (for admission).

Costs (2010–11) *Tuition:* state resident $4023 full-time, $400 per credit hour part-time; nonresident $13,020 full-time, $400 per credit hour part-time. Full-time tuition and fees vary according to reciprocity agreements. *Required fees:* $4327 full-time. *Room and board:* $10,048; room only: $5674. Room and board charges vary according to board plan.

Financial Aid *Of all full-time matriculated undergraduates who enrolled in 2008,* 3,327 applied for aid, 2,574 were judged to have need, 207 had their need fully met. 61 Federal Work-Study jobs (averaging $1932). 44 state and other part-time jobs (averaging $2421). *In 2008,* 12 non-need-based awards were made. *Average percent of need met:* 56. *Average financial aid package:* $8018. *Average need-based loan:* $4116. *Average need-based gift aid:* $6226. *Average non-need-based aid:* $2520. *Average indebtedness upon graduation:* $24,427.

Applying *Options:* electronic application, early admission, deferred entrance. *Application fee:* $50. *Required:* high school transcript. *Required for some:* interview. *Recommended:* essay or personal statement, rank in upper 50% of high school class.

Freshman Application Contact Christopher Dorsey, Interim Director of Admissions and Enrollment Management, Eastern Connecticut State University, 83 Windham Street, Willimantic, CT 06226. *Phone:* 860-465-5286. *Toll-free phone:* 877-353-3278. *Fax:* 860-465-5544. *E-mail:* admissions@easternct.edu. *Web site:* http://www.easternct.edu/.

See page 1266 for the College Close-Up.

Fairfield University
Fairfield, Connecticut

- **Independent Roman Catholic (Jesuit)** comprehensive, founded 1942
- **Suburban** 200-acre campus with easy access to New York City
- **Endowment** $218.7 million
- **Coed** 3,923 undergraduate students, 86% full-time, 59% women, 41% men
- **Moderately difficult** entrance level, 72% of applicants were admitted

Undergraduates 3,388 full-time, 535 part-time. Students come from 28 states and territories; 56 other countries; 62% are from out of state; 2% Black or African American, non-Hispanic/Latino; 3% Hispanic/Latino; 1% Asian, non-Hispanic/Latino; 0.1% Native Hawaiian or other Pacific Islander, non-Hispanic/Latino; 0.5% Two or more races, non-Hispanic/Latino; 68% Race/ethnicity unknown; 1% international; 1% transferred in; 63% live on campus. *Retention:* 89% of full-time freshmen returned.

Freshmen *Admission:* 8,420 applied, 6,024 admitted, 922 enrolled. *Average high school GPA:* 3.34. *Test scores:* SAT critical reading scores over 500: 57%; SAT math scores over 500: 63%; SAT writing scores over 500: 63%; SAT critical reading scores over 600: 24%; SAT math scores over 600: 30%; SAT writing scores over 600: 30%; SAT critical reading scores over 700: 2%; SAT math scores over 700: 4%; SAT writing scores over 700: 4%.

Faculty *Total:* 527, 50% full-time, 48% with terminal degrees. *Student/faculty ratio:* 12:1.

Academics *Calendar:* semesters. *Degrees:* associate, bachelor's, master's, doctoral-professional, and post-master's certificates. *Special study options:* adult/continuing education programs, advanced placement credit, distance learning, double majors, English as a second language, honors programs, independent study, internships, part-time degree program, services for LD students, student-designed majors, study abroad, summer session for credit. *ROTC:* Army (c), Air Force (c). *Unusual degree programs:* 3-2 engineering with University of Connecticut, Rensselaer Polytechnic Institute, Columbia University, Stevens Institute of Technology, Fairfield University.

Computers on Campus 220 computers/terminals and 150 ports are available on campus for general student use. Students can access the following: campus intranet, computer help desk, free student e-mail accounts, online (class) grades, online (class) registration, online (class) schedules. Campuswide network is available. 100% of college-owned or -operated housing units are wired for high-speed Internet access. Wireless service is available via classrooms, dorm rooms, libraries, student centers.

Student Life *Housing:* on-campus residence required through senior year. *Options:* coed, disabled students. Campus housing is university owned. Freshman campus housing is guaranteed. *Activities and organizations:* drama/theater group, student-run newspaper, radio and television station, choral group, student government, Glee Club, Residence Hall Council, Stags in the Stands, Campus Ministry. *Campus security:* 24-hour emergency response devices and patrols, late-night transport/escort service, controlled dormitory access, bicycle patrols. *Student services:* health clinic, personal/psychological counseling, women's center.

Athletics Member NCAA. All Division I. *Intercollegiate sports:* baseball M(s), basketball M(s)/W(s), cheerleading M(c)/W(c), crew M(s)/W(s), cross-country running M(s)/W(s), equestrian sports M(c)/W(c), field hockey W(s), golf M(s)/W(s), ice hockey M(c)/W(c), lacrosse M(s)/W(s), rugby M(c)/W(c), sailing M(c)/W(c), skiing (downhill) M(c)/W(c), soccer M(s)/W(s), softball W(s), swimming and diving M(s)/W(s), tennis M(s)/W(s), track and field M(c)/W(c), volleyball M(c)/W(s). *Intramural sports:* basketball M/W, field hockey W, football M(c), golf M/W, lacrosse M/W, racquetball M/W, soccer M/W, softball M/W, table tennis M/W, tennis M/W, volleyball M/W.

Costs (2010–11) *One-time required fee:* $60. *Comprehensive fee:* $50,780 includes full-time tuition ($38,450), mandatory fees ($590), and room and

board ($11,740). Part-time tuition: $525 per credit hour. Part-time tuition and fees vary according to course load. *Required fees:* $25 per term part-time. *College room only:* $7010. Room and board charges vary according to board plan and housing facility. *Payment plan:* installment. *Waivers:* employees or children of employees.

Financial Aid Of all full-time matriculated undergraduates who enrolled in 2009, 2,179 applied for aid, 1,908 were judged to have need, 389 had their need fully met. 598 Federal Work-Study jobs (averaging $1251). In 2009, 312 non-need-based awards were made. *Average percent of need met:* 85%. *Average financial aid package:* $28,923. *Average need-based loan:* $4600. *Average need-based gift aid:* $22,147. *Average non-need-based aid:* $19,733. *Average indebtedness upon graduation:* $37,015. *Financial aid deadline:* 2/15.

Applying *Options:* electronic application, early admission, early action, deferred entrance. *Application fee:* $60. *Required:* essay or personal statement, high school transcript, 1 letter of recommendation. *Recommended:* interview. *Application deadlines:* 1/15 (freshmen), 5/1 (transfers), 12/15 (early action). *Notification:* 3/15 (freshmen), continuous (transfers), 1/15 (early action).

Freshman Application Contact Ms. Karen Pellegrino, Director of Admission, Fairfield University, 1073 North Benson Road, Fairfield, CT 06824-5195. *Phone:* 203-254-4100. *Fax:* 203-254-4199. *E-mail:* admis@fairfield.edu. *Web site:* http://www.fairfield.edu/.

Goodwin College
East Hartford, Connecticut

- **Proprietary** primarily 2-year, founded 1999
- **Urban** 660-acre campus with easy access to Hartford
- **Coed** 2,791 undergraduate students, 24% full-time, 84% women, 16% men
- **Minimally difficult** entrance level, 100% of applicants were admitted

Undergraduates 670 full-time, 2,121 part-time. 1% are from out of state; 26% Black or African American, non-Hispanic/Latino; 18% Hispanic/Latino; 2% Asian, non-Hispanic/Latino; 0.3% Native Hawaiian or other Pacific Islander, non-Hispanic/Latino; 0.4% American Indian or Alaska Native, non-Hispanic/Latino; 2% Two or more races, non-Hispanic/Latino; 0.6% Race/ethnicity unknown; 18% transferred in. *Retention:* 38% of full-time freshmen returned.

Freshmen *Admission:* 918 applied, 918 admitted, 455 enrolled.

Faculty *Total:* 225, 21% full-time, 18% with terminal degrees. *Student/faculty ratio:* 13:1.

Academics *Calendar:* semesters. *Degrees:* certificates, associate, and bachelor's. *Special study options:* academic remediation for entering students, adult/continuing education programs, advanced placement credit, distance learning, double majors, English as a second language, internships, off-campus study, part-time degree program, services for LD students, summer session for credit.

Computers on Campus 200 computers/terminals are available on campus for general student use. Students can access the following: campus intranet, computer help desk, free student e-mail accounts, online (class) grades, online (class) registration, online (class) schedules. Campuswide network is available. Wireless service is available via entire campus.

Student Life *Housing:* college housing not available. *Activities and organizations:* student-run newspaper, choral group. *Campus security:* 24-hour emergency response devices, evening security patrolman. *Student services:* personal/psychological counseling.

Costs (2010–11) *Tuition:* $18,000 full-time, $560 per credit hour part-time. Full-time tuition and fees vary according to course load and program. Part-time tuition and fees vary according to course load and program. *Required fees:* $500 full-time. *Payment plan:* installment. *Waivers:* employees or children of employees.

Financial Aid Of all full-time matriculated undergraduates who enrolled in 2009, 508 applied for aid, 506 were judged to have need. *Average percent of need met:* 31%. *Average financial aid package:* $9109. *Average need-based loan:* $3567. *Average need-based gift aid:* $4876.

Applying *Options:* electronic application, early admission, early decision, early action, deferred entrance. *Application fee:* $50. *Required:* essay or personal statement, high school transcript, minimum 2 GPA, medical exam. *Recommended:* 2 letters of recommendation, interview. *Application deadlines:* rolling (freshmen), rolling (transfers), 6/1 (early action). *Early decision deadline:* 3/1. *Notification:* continuous (freshmen), continuous (transfers), 3/15 (early decision), 6/15 (early action).

Freshman Application Contact Mr. Nicholas Lentino, Director of Admissions, Goodwin College, One Riverside Drive, East Hartford, CT 06118. *Phone:* 860-727-6765. *Toll-free phone:* 800-889-3282. *Fax:* 860-291-9550. *E-mail:* nlantino@goodwin.edu. *Web site:* http://www.goodwin.edu/.

Holy Apostles College and Seminary
Cromwell, Connecticut

- **Independent Roman Catholic** comprehensive, founded 1956
- **Suburban** 17-acre campus with easy access to Hartford and New Haven
- **Endowment** $657,367
- **Coed** 58 undergraduate students, 45% full-time, 55% women, 45% men
- **Noncompetitive** entrance level, 100% of applicants were admitted

Undergraduates 26 full-time, 32 part-time. 17% Hispanic/Latino; 11% international; 9% transferred in. *Retention:* 60% of full-time freshmen returned.
Freshmen *Admission:* 10 applied, 10 admitted, 3 enrolled.
Faculty *Total:* 30, 57% full-time, 67% with terminal degrees. *Student/faculty ratio:* 2:1.
Academics *Calendar:* semesters. *Degrees:* certificates, associate, bachelor's, master's, post-master's, and postbachelor's certificates. *Special study options:* academic remediation for entering students, adult/continuing education programs, English as a second language, external degree program, independent study, part-time degree program, services for LD students, summer session for credit.
Computers on Campus 10 computers/terminals are available on campus for general student use. Students can access the following: free student e-mail accounts. Campuswide network is available. 100% of college-owned or -operated housing units are wired for high-speed Internet access. Wireless service is available via libraries.
Student Life *Housing:* college housing not available. *Activities and organizations:* Toastmasters, Pro-Life Organization, Student Council, Schola Choir. *Student services:* personal/psychological counseling.
Standardized Tests *Recommended:* SAT (for admission).
Costs (2010–11) *Tuition:* $9600 full-time, $400 per credit part-time. Part-time tuition and fees vary according to course load. *Payment plan:* installment. *Waivers:* employees or children of employees.
Applying *Options:* deferred entrance. *Application fee:* $50. *Required:* high school transcript. *Required for some:* interview. *Application deadlines:* rolling (freshmen), rolling (out-of-state freshmen), rolling (transfers).
Freshman Application Contact Holy Apostles College and Seminary, 33 Prospect Hill Road, Cromwell, CT 06416-2005. *Phone:* 860-632-3010. *Toll-free phone:* 800-330-7272. *Web site:* http://www.holyapostles.edu/.

Lincoln College of New England
Southington, Connecticut

- **Proprietary** 4-year, founded 1966
- **Small-town** 32-acre campus with easy access to Boston and Hartford
- **Endowment** $27,595
- **Coed**
- **Minimally difficult** entrance level

Faculty *Student/faculty ratio:* 8:1.
Academics *Calendar:* semesters. *Degrees:* certificates, diplomas, associate, and bachelor's.
Student Life *Campus security:* 24-hour patrols, late-night transport/escort service.
Athletics Member NJCAA.
Costs (2010–11) *Tuition:* $18,400 full-time, $615 per credit hour part-time. Part-time tuition and fees vary according to course load. *Required fees:* $650 full-time, $150 per term part-time. *Room only:* $4600.
Financial Aid *Of all full-time matriculated undergraduates who enrolled in 2009,* 92 Federal Work-Study jobs (averaging $2000). 30 state and other part-time jobs.
Applying *Options:* electronic application. *Application fee:* $30. *Required:* high school transcript. *Required for some:* essay or personal statement, interview. *Recommended:* essay or personal statement.
Freshman Application Contact Anthony Reich, Vice President of Admissions, Lincoln College of New England, 2279 Mount Vernon Road, Southington, CT 06489. *Phone:* 860-628-4751 Ext. 40904. *Toll-free phone:* 800-952-2444. *Fax:* 860-628-6444. *E-mail:* areich@lincolncollegene.edu. *Web site:* http://www.lincolncollegene.edu/.

Lyme Academy College of Fine Arts
Old Lyme, Connecticut

- **Independent** 4-year, founded 1976
- **Rural** 47-acre campus with easy access to New Haven, Hartford
- **Endowment** $4.0 million
- **Coed** 83 undergraduate students, 80% full-time, 60% women, 40% men
- **Moderately difficult** entrance level, 68% of applicants were admitted

Undergraduates 66 full-time, 17 part-time. Students come from 21 states and territories; 2 other countries; 47% are from out of state; 7% transferred in. *Retention:* 89% of full-time freshmen returned.

Freshmen *Admission:* 82 applied, 56 admitted, 19 enrolled. *Average high school GPA:* 3.22.
Faculty *Total:* 24, 33% full-time, 13% with terminal degrees. *Student/faculty ratio:* 4:1.
Academics *Calendar:* semesters. *Degrees:* bachelor's and postbachelor's certificates. *Special study options:* adult/continuing education programs, advanced placement credit, independent study, part-time degree program.
Computers on Campus 24 computers/terminals are available on campus for general student use. Students can access the following: campus intranet. Campuswide network is available. Wireless service is available via entire campus.
Student Life *Housing:* college housing not available. *Options:* Campus housing is provided by a third party. *Activities and organizations:* Student Organization. *Campus security:* student patrols. *Student services:* personal/psychological counseling.
Athletics *Intramural sports:* volleyball M/W.
Standardized Tests *Required:* SAT or ACT (for admission).
Costs (2011–12) *Comprehensive fee:* $35,334 includes full-time tuition ($25,248), mandatory fees ($1536), and room and board ($8550). Part-time tuition: $974 per credit. Part-time tuition and fees vary according to course load. *Required fees:* $60 per credit part-time. *Room and board:* Room and board charges vary according to housing facility. *Payment plan:* installment. *Waivers:* employees or children of employees.
Financial Aid Of all full-time matriculated undergraduates who enrolled in 2009, 52 applied for aid, 48 were judged to have need. In 2009, 9 non-need-based awards were made. *Average financial aid package:* $16,870. *Average non-need-based aid:* $4055. *Average indebtedness upon graduation:* $24,578.
Applying *Options:* electronic application, deferred entrance. *Application fee:* $55. *Required:* essay or personal statement, high school transcript, minimum 3 GPA, 2 letters of recommendation. *Recommended:* interview. *Application deadlines:* rolling (freshmen), rolling (out-of-state freshmen), rolling (transfers). *Notification:* continuous (freshmen), continuous (out-of-state freshmen), continuous (transfers).
Freshman Application Contact Miss Jena Thomas, Admissions Representative, Lyme Academy College of Fine Arts, 84 Lyme Street, Old Lyme, CT 06371. *Phone:* 860-434-3571 Ext. 127. *Fax:* 860-434-8725. *E-mail:* jthomas@lymeacademy.edu. *Web site:* http://www.lymeacademy.edu/.

Mitchell College
New London, Connecticut

- **Independent** 4-year, founded 1938
- **Suburban** 67-acre campus with easy access to Hartford and Providence
- **Coed** 992 undergraduate students, 86% full-time, 45% women, 55% men
- **Moderately difficult** entrance level, 90% of applicants were admitted

Undergraduates 850 full-time, 142 part-time. 46% are from out of state; 12% Black or African American, non-Hispanic/Latino; 9% Hispanic/Latino; 1% Asian, non-Hispanic/Latino; 0.3% Native Hawaiian or other Pacific Islander, non-Hispanic/Latino; 0.9% American Indian or Alaska Native, non-Hispanic/Latino; 3% Two or more races, non-Hispanic/Latino; 0.9% Race/ethnicity unknown; 1% international; 7% transferred in; 59% live on campus. *Retention:* 61% of full-time freshmen returned.
Freshmen *Admission:* 908 applied, 818 admitted, 235 enrolled. *Average high school GPA:* 2.73.
Faculty *Total:* 106, 34% full-time, 28% with terminal degrees. *Student/faculty ratio:* 15:1.
Academics *Calendar:* semesters. *Degrees:* associate and bachelor's. *Special study options:* advanced placement credit, cooperative education, double majors, independent study, internships, part-time degree program, services for LD students, student-designed majors, study abroad, summer session for credit.
Computers on Campus 176 computers/terminals are available on campus for general student use. Students can access the following: campus intranet, computer help desk, free student e-mail accounts, online (class) grades, online (class) schedules. Campuswide network is available. 100% of college-owned or -operated housing units are wired for high-speed Internet access. Wireless service is available via classrooms, computer centers, computer labs, dorm rooms, learning centers, libraries, student centers.
Student Life *Housing:* on-campus residence required through senior year. *Options:* coed, men-only, women-only. Campus housing is university owned. Freshman applicants given priority for college housing. *Activities and organizations:* drama/theater group, student-run newspaper, radio station, choral group, Mitchell College Drama Society, Sigma Alpha Pi Leadership Society, Behavioral Science, Early Childhood, Gaming Club. *Campus security:* 24-hour emergency response devices and patrols, student patrols, late-night transport/escort service, controlled dormitory access. *Student services:* health clinic, personal/psychological counseling.
Athletics Member NCAA. All Division III. *Intercollegiate sports:* baseball M, basketball M/W, cross-country running M/W, golf M, lacrosse M, sailing M/W, soccer M/W, softball W, tennis M/W, volleyball W. *Intramural sports:*

basketball M/W, cheerleading M/W, rugby M/W, sailing M/W, soccer M/W, softball M/W, tennis M/W, volleyball M/W.

Costs (2010–11) *Comprehensive fee:* $39,034 includes full-time tuition ($25,237), mandatory fees ($1670), and room and board ($12,127). Full-time tuition and fees vary according to course load. Part-time tuition: $300 per credit hour. *Required fees:* $35 per term part-time. *College room only:* $6306. Room and board charges vary according to housing facility. *Payment plan:* deferred payment. *Waivers:* employees or children of employees.

Financial Aid Of all full-time matriculated undergraduates who enrolled in 2004, 491 applied for aid, 414 were judged to have need. 44 Federal Work-Study jobs (averaging $1000). In 2004, 70 non-need-based awards were made. *Average percent of need met:* 89%. *Average financial aid package:* $16,357. *Average need-based loan:* $2904. *Average need-based gift aid:* $8058. *Average non-need-based aid:* $2890.

Applying *Options:* electronic application, early admission, early decision, deferred entrance. *Application fee:* $30. *Required:* essay or personal statement, high school transcript, minimum 2 GPA, interview. *Application deadlines:* rolling (freshmen), rolling (transfers). *Early decision deadline:* 11/15. *Notification:* continuous until 12/15 (freshmen), continuous (transfers), 12/1 (early decision).

Freshman Application Contact Ms. Kimberly Hodges, Director of Admissions, Mitchell College, 437 Pequot Avenue, New London, CT 06320. *Phone:* 860-701-5038. *Toll-free phone:* 800-443-2811. *Fax:* 860-444-1209. *E-mail:* admissions@mitchell.edu. *Web site:* http://www.mitchell.edu/.

See page 1442 for the College Close-Up.

Paier College of Art, Inc.

Hamden, Connecticut

- **Proprietary** 4-year, founded 1946
- **Suburban** 3-acre campus with easy access to New York City
- **Coed** 223 undergraduate students, 74% full-time, 67% women, 33% men
- **Minimally difficult** entrance level, 84% of applicants were admitted

Undergraduates 166 full-time, 57 part-time. Students come from 4 states and territories; 8% transferred in. *Retention:* 82% of full-time freshmen returned.

Freshmen *Admission:* 50 applied, 42 admitted, 21 enrolled. *Average high school GPA:* 2.6. *Test scores:* SAT critical reading scores over 500: 38%; SAT math scores over 500: 33%; SAT critical reading scores over 600: 14%.

Faculty *Total:* 40, 25% full-time, 48% with terminal degrees. *Student/faculty ratio:* 6:1.

Academics *Calendar:* semesters plus 1 summer session. *Degrees:* certificates, diplomas, associate, and bachelor's. *Special study options:* academic remediation for entering students, advanced placement credit, independent study, part-time degree program, services for LD students, study abroad, summer session for credit.

Computers on Campus 40 computers/terminals are available on campus for general student use. Wireless service is available via entire campus.

Student Life *Housing:* college housing not available. *Activities and organizations:* Student Council. *Campus security:* evening patrols by security.

Standardized Tests *Required:* SAT or ACT (for admission).

Financial Aid Of all full-time matriculated undergraduates who enrolled in 1999, 102 applied for aid, 92 were judged to have need, 1 had their need fully met. *Average percent of need met:* 62%. *Average financial aid package:* $6717. *Average need-based loan:* $3446. *Average need-based gift aid:* $3460. *Average indebtedness upon graduation:* $13,536.

Applying *Options:* deferred entrance. *Application fee:* $25. *Required:* high school transcript, minimum 2 GPA, 2 letters of recommendation, interview, portfolio. *Recommended:* essay or personal statement. *Application deadlines:* rolling (freshmen), rolling (transfers). *Notification:* continuous (freshmen), continuous (transfers).

Freshman Application Contact Ms. Lynn Pascale, Secretary to Admissions, Paier College of Art, Inc., 20 Gorham Avenue, Hamden, CT 06514-3902. *Phone:* 203-287-3031. *Fax:* 203-287-3021. *E-mail:* paier.admission@ snet.net. *Web site:* http://www.paiercollegeofart.edu/.

Post University

Waterbury, Connecticut

- **Independent** comprehensive, founded 1890
- **Suburban** 70-acre campus with easy access to Hartford
- **Coed**
- **Minimally difficult** entrance level

Faculty *Student/faculty ratio:* 19:1.

Academics *Calendar:* semesters (modular courses offered in the evening). *Degrees:* certificates, associate, bachelor's, master's, and postbachelor's certificates.

Student Life *Campus security:* 24-hour emergency response devices and patrols, late-night transport/escort service, controlled dormitory access.

Athletics Member NCAA. All Division II.

Standardized Tests *Recommended:* SAT or ACT (for admission).

Costs (2010–11) *Comprehensive fee:* $34,750 includes full-time tuition ($24,000), mandatory fees ($1050), and room and board ($9700). Full-time tuition and fees vary according to degree level and program. Part-time tuition: $800 per credit hour. Part-time tuition and fees vary according to class time, course load, degree level, and program. *College room only:* $5335. Room and board charges vary according to housing facility.

Financial Aid *Of all full-time matriculated undergraduates who enrolled in 2008,* 940 applied for aid, 940 were judged to have need, 5 had their need fully met. 132 Federal Work-Study jobs (averaging $1833). 11 state and other part-time jobs (averaging $1727). *Average percent of need met:* 78. *Average financial aid package:* $13,550. *Average need-based loan:* $4391. *Average need-based gift aid:* $10,633. *Average indebtedness upon graduation:* $18,000.

Applying *Options:* electronic application, deferred entrance. *Application fee:* $40. *Required:* high school transcript, 1 letter of recommendation. *Recommended:* essay or personal statement, minimum 2 GPA, interview.

Freshman Application Contact Mr. Jay Murray, Director of Admissions, Post University, PO Box 2540, Waterbury, CT 06723. *Phone:* 203-596-4500. *Toll-free phone:* 800-345-2562. *Fax:* 203-756-5810. *E-mail:* admiss@post.edu. *Web site:* http://www.post.edu/.

See page 1506 for the College Close-Up.

Quinnipiac University
Hamden, Connecticut

- **Independent** comprehensive, founded 1929
- **Suburban** 600-acre campus with easy access to New Haven, Hartford
- **Endowment** $238.5 million
- **Coed** 6,118 undergraduate students, 96% full-time, 63% women, 37% men
- **Moderately difficult** entrance level, 72% of applicants were admitted

Undergraduates 5,859 full-time, 259 part-time. Students come from 28 states and territories; 20 other countries; 70% are from out of state; 4% Black or African American, non-Hispanic/Latino; 6% Hispanic/Latino; 3% Asian, non-Hispanic/Latino; 0.3% American Indian or Alaska Native, non-Hispanic/Latino; 0.5% Two or more races, non-Hispanic/Latino; 7% Race/ethnicity unknown; 1% international; 3% transferred in; 78% live on campus. *Retention:* 86% of full-time freshmen returned.

Freshmen *Admission:* 13,885 applied, 9,997 admitted, 1,640 enrolled. *Average high school GPA:* 3.4. *Test scores:* SAT critical reading scores over 500: 82%; SAT math scores over 500: 87%; ACT scores over 18: 100%; SAT critical reading scores over 600: 23%; SAT math scores over 600: 31%; ACT scores over 24: 71%; SAT critical reading scores over 700: 2%; SAT math scores over 700: 3%; ACT scores over 30: 10%.

Faculty *Total:* 837, 37% full-time, 67% with terminal degrees. *Student/faculty ratio:* 12:1.

Academics *Calendar:* semesters. *Degrees:* bachelor's, master's, doctoral-professional, post-master's, and postbachelor's certificates. *Special study options:* advanced placement credit, distance learning, double majors, honors programs, independent study, internships, part-time degree program, services for LD students, student-designed majors, study abroad, summer session for credit. *ROTC:* Army (c), Air Force (c).

Computers on Campus 600 computers/terminals and 2,500 ports are available on campus for general student use. Students can access the following: campus intranet, computer help desk, free student e-mail accounts, online (class) grades, online (class) registration, online (class) schedules, e-commerce 'Q' card for local merchants, food service, dorm card access. Campuswide network is available. 100% of college-owned or -operated housing units are wired for high-speed Internet access. Wireless service is available via entire campus.

Student Life *Housing options:* coed. Campus housing is university owned. Freshman campus housing is guaranteed. *Activities and organizations:* drama/theater group, student-run newspaper, radio and television station, choral group, student government, Social Programming Board, Drama Club, Chronicle (student newspaper), dance company, national fraternities, national sororities. *Campus security:* 24-hour emergency response devices and patrols, late-night transport/escort service, controlled dormitory access, text message emergency notification system. *Student services:* health clinic, personal/psychological counseling.

Athletics Member NCAA. All Division I. *Intercollegiate sports:* baseball M(s), basketball M(s)/W(s), cross-country running M(s)/W(s), field hockey W(s), golf W(s), gymnastics W(s), ice hockey M(s)/W(s), lacrosse M(s)/W(s), rugby W(s), soccer M(s)/W(s), softball W(s), tennis M(s)/W(s), track and field W(s), volleyball W(s). *Intramural sports:* baseball M, basketball M/W, bowling M/W, field hockey W, soccer M/W, softball W, tennis M/W, volleyball M/W.

Standardized Tests *Required:* SAT or ACT (for admission).

Costs (2011–12) *Comprehensive fee:* $49,560 includes full-time tuition ($34,710), mandatory fees ($1420), and room and board ($13,430). *Part-time tuition:* $835 per credit hour. Part-time tuition and fees vary according to class time and course load. *Required fees:* $35 per credit part-time. *Room and board:* Room and board charges vary according to housing facility. *Payment plans:* installment, deferred payment. *Waivers:* employees or children of employees.

Financial Aid Of all full-time matriculated undergraduates who enrolled in 2009, 4,330 applied for aid, 3,700 were judged to have need, 461 had their need fully met. 2,097 Federal Work-Study jobs (averaging $2031). 47 state and other part-time jobs (averaging $1634). In 2009, 765 non-need-based awards were made. *Average percent of need met:* 66%. *Average financial aid package:* $21,051. *Average need-based loan:* $4520. *Average need-based gift aid:* $15,458. *Average non-need-based aid:* $10,948. *Average indebtedness upon graduation:* $38,953.

Applying *Options:* electronic application, early action, deferred entrance. *Application fee:* $45. *Required:* essay or personal statement, high school transcript, 1 letter of recommendation. *Required for some:* minimum 3 GPA. *Recommended:* minimum 3 GPA, interview. *Application deadlines:* 2/1 (freshmen), 2/1 (out-of-state freshmen), 4/1 (transfers), 11/1 (early action). *Notification:* continuous (freshmen), continuous (out-of-state freshmen), continuous (transfers).

Freshman Application Contact Ms. Joan Isaac Mohr, Vice President and Dean of Admissions, Quinnipiac University, 275 Mount Carmel Avenue, Hamden, CT 06518. *Phone:* 203-582-8600. *Toll-free phone:* 800-462-1944. *Fax:* 203-582-8906. *E-mail:* admissions@quinnipiac.edu. *Web site:* http://www.quinnipiac.edu/.

See page 1518 for the College Close-Up.

Sacred Heart University
Fairfield, Connecticut

- **Independent Roman Catholic** comprehensive, founded 1963
- **Suburban** 69-acre campus with easy access to New York City
- **Endowment** $82.8 million
- **Coed** 4,198 undergraduate students, 84% full-time, 61% women, 39% men
- **Moderately difficult** entrance level, 64% of applicants were admitted

Undergraduates 3,511 full-time, 687 part-time. Students come from 38 states and territories; 21 other countries; 67% are from out of state; 4% Black or African American, non-Hispanic/Latino; 6% Hispanic/Latino; 1% Asian, non-Hispanic/Latino; 0.1% Native Hawaiian or other Pacific Islander, non-Hispanic/Latino; 0.3% American Indian or Alaska Native, non-Hispanic/Latino; 13% Race/ethnicity unknown; 2% international; 3% transferred in; 60% live on campus. *Retention:* 77% of full-time freshmen returned.

Freshmen *Admission:* 7,569 applied, 4,849 admitted, 974 enrolled. *Average high school GPA:* 3.2. *Test scores:* SAT critical reading scores over 500: 65%; SAT math scores over 500: 73%; SAT critical reading scores over 600: 11%; SAT math scores over 600: 20%; SAT critical reading scores over 700: 1%; SAT math scores over 700: 1%.

Faculty *Total:* 579, 37% full-time, 52% with terminal degrees. *Student/faculty ratio:* 13:1.

Academics *Calendar:* semesters. *Degrees:* certificates, associate, bachelor's, master's, doctoral-professional, and post-master's certificates (also offers part-time program with significant enrollment not reflected in profile). *Special study options:* academic remediation for entering students, accelerated degree program, adult/continuing education programs, advanced placement credit, cooperative education, distance learning, double majors, English as a second language, honors programs, independent study, internships, off-campus study, part-time degree program, services for LD students, study abroad, summer session for credit. *Unusual degree programs:* Combined undergraduate/graduate

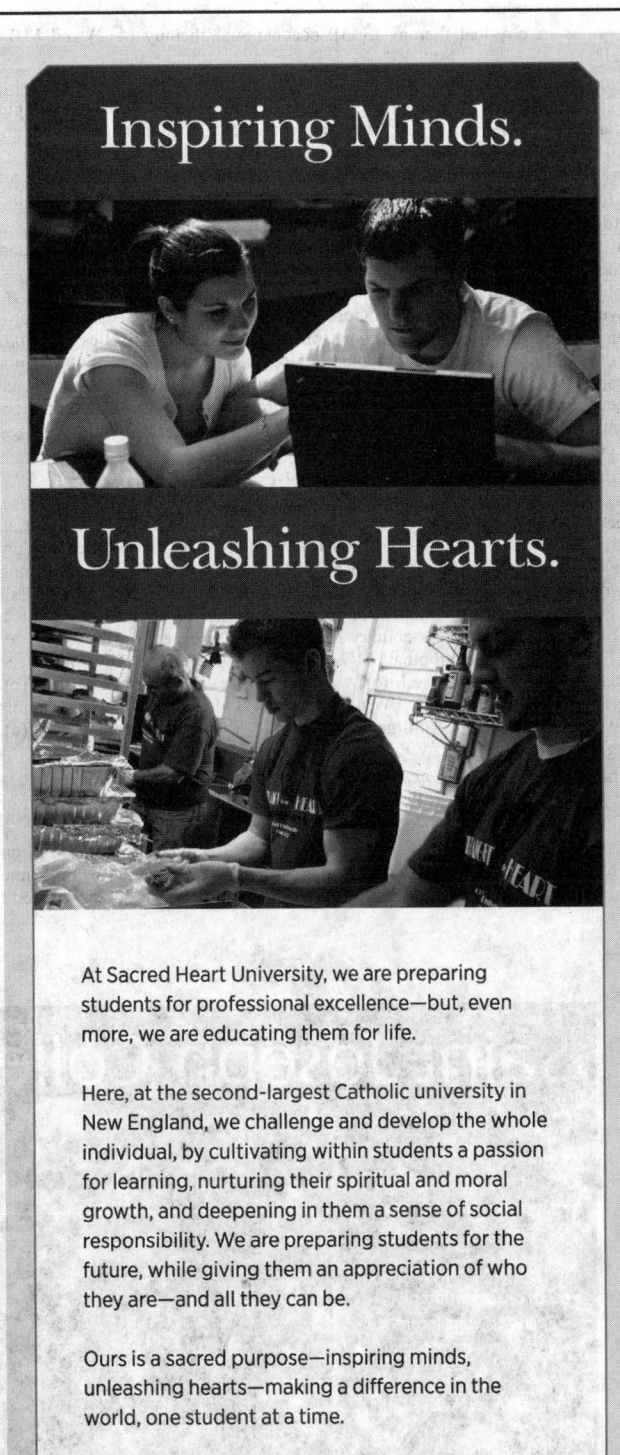

programs in physical therapy (3+3), occupational therapy (4+2) and MBA (4+1).

Computers on Campus 45 computers/terminals and 3,100 ports are available on campus for general student use. Students can access the following: campus intranet, computer help desk, free student e-mail accounts, online (class) grades, online (class) registration, online (class) schedules. Campuswide network is available. 100% of college-owned or -operated housing units are wired for high-speed Internet access. Wireless service is available via entire campus.

Student Life *Housing options:* coed, disabled students. Campus housing is university owned and leased by the school. Freshman campus housing is guaranteed. *Activities and organizations:* drama/theater group, student-run newspaper, radio and television station, choral group, marching band, Student Government Association, Club Sports, Marching/Pep Band, theatre arts program, Habitat for Humanity, national fraternities, national sororities. *Campus security:* 24-hour emergency response devices and patrols, late-night transport/escort service, controlled dormitory access, Campus Emergency Plan, Personal Safety Escort Program, Security Alarm Systems, Crime Prevention Announcements, Security Surveys. *Student services:* health clinic, personal/psychological counseling.

Athletics Member NCAA. All Division I except football (Division I-AA). *Intercollegiate sports:* baseball M(s), basketball M(s)/W(s), bowling W(s), cheerleading W(c), crew W, cross-country running M(s)/W(s), equestrian sports W, fencing M/W(s), field hockey W(s), golf M(s)/W(s), ice hockey M(s)/W(s), lacrosse M(s)/W(s), soccer M(s)/W(s), softball W(s), swimming and diving W(s), tennis M(s)/W(s), track and field M(s)/W(s), volleyball M(s)/W(s), wrestling M(s). *Intramural sports:* baseball M(c), basketball M(c)/W(c), bowling M(c), cross-country running M(c)/W(c), equestrian sports M/W, field hockey W(c), football M/W, golf M(c)/W(c), gymnastics W(c), ice hockey M(c)/W(c), lacrosse M(c)/W(c), rugby M(c)/W(c), sailing M(c)/W(c), soccer M(c)/W(c), softball M/W(c), swimming and diving M(c), table tennis M/W, tennis M(c)/W(c), ultimate Frisbee M(c)/W(c), volleyball M(c)/W(c), weight lifting M(c)/W(c).

Standardized Tests *Recommended:* Sacred Heart University adheres to a Test-Optional Admissions Policy. SAT/ACT scores are not a required part of the application but will be considered if submitted.

Costs (2010–11) *Comprehensive fee:* $43,780 includes full-time tuition ($31,224), mandatory fees ($216), and room and board ($12,340). Full-time tuition and fees vary according to program. Part-time tuition: $475 per credit hour. Part-time tuition and fees vary according to program. *Required fees:* $85 per term part-time. *College room only:* $8840. Room and board charges vary according to board plan and housing facility. *Payment plan:* installment. *Waivers:* employees or children of employees.

Financial Aid Of all full-time matriculated undergraduates who enrolled in 2009, 3,121 applied for aid, 2,585 were judged to have need, 247 had their need fully met. 1,284 Federal Work-Study jobs (averaging $1243). 565 state and other part-time jobs (averaging $1041). In 2009, 486 non-need-based awards were made. *Average percent of need met:* 60%. *Average financial aid package:* $18,135. *Average need-based loan:* $5103. *Average need-based gift aid:* $13,658. *Average non-need-based aid:* $5092. *Average indebtedness upon graduation:* $40,865.

Applying *Options:* electronic application, early admission, early decision, deferred entrance. *Application fee:* $50. *Required:* essay or personal statement, high school transcript, 1 letter of recommendation. *Required for some:* interview, Interview required for Early Decision candidates. *Recommended:* minimum 3.2 GPA, interview. *Early decision deadline:* 12/1. *Notification:* continuous (freshmen), continuous (transfers), 12/15 (early decision).

Freshman Application Contact Mr. Jamie P. Romeo, Associate Dean of Undergraduate Admissions, Sacred Heart University, 5151 Park Avenue, Fairfield, CT 06825-1000. *Phone:* 203-365-7560. *Fax:* 203-365-7607. *E-mail:* enroll@sacredheart.edu. *Web site:* http://www.sacredheart.edu/.

See page 1552 for the College Close-Up.

Saint Joseph College
West Hartford, Connecticut

- **Independent Roman Catholic** comprehensive, founded 1932
- **Suburban** 84-acre campus with easy access to Hartford
- **Endowment** $15.3 million
- **Undergraduate: women only; graduate: coed** 1,059 undergraduate students, 81% full-time, 99% women, 1% men
- 81% of applicants were admitted

Undergraduates 858 full-time, 201 part-time. 7% are from out of state; 8% Black or African American, non-Hispanic/Latino; 10% Hispanic/Latino; 2% Asian, non-Hispanic/Latino; 0.2% American Indian or Alaska Native, non-Hispanic/Latino; 0.8% Two or more races, non-Hispanic/Latino; 35% Race/

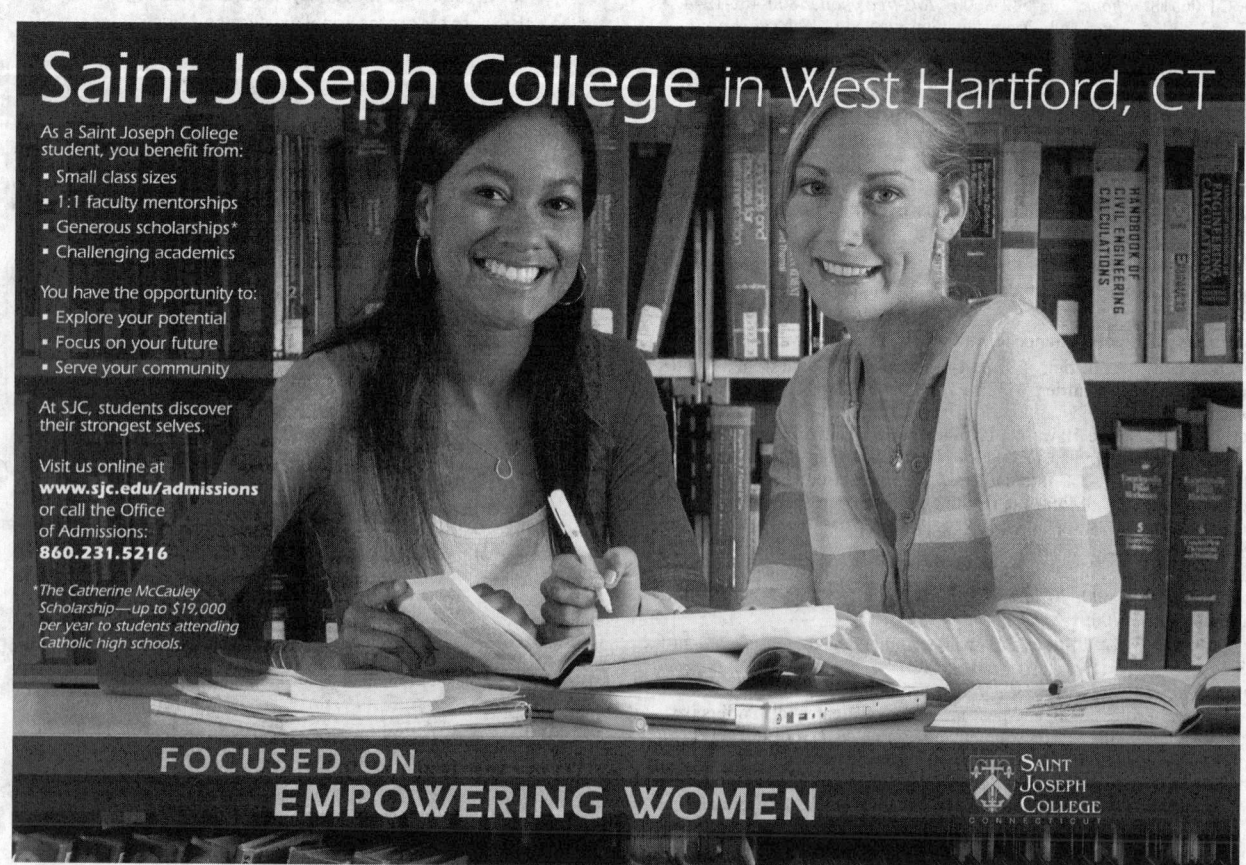

ethnicity unknown; 10% transferred in; 41% live on campus. *Retention:* 78% of full-time freshmen returned.

Freshmen *Admission:* 1,292 applied, 1,049 admitted, 232 enrolled. *Average high school GPA:* 3.2. *Test scores:* SAT critical reading scores over 500: 51%; SAT math scores over 500: 41%; SAT critical reading scores over 600: 11%; SAT math scores over 600: 7%.

Faculty *Total:* 247, 31% full-time. *Student/faculty ratio:* 13:1.

Academics *Calendar:* semesters. *Degrees:* certificates, bachelor's, master's, doctoral-professional, post-master's, and postbachelor's certificates. *Special study options:* accelerated degree program, adult/continuing education programs, advanced placement credit, distance learning, double majors, honors programs, independent study, internships, off-campus study, part-time degree program, services for LD students, student-designed majors, study abroad, summer session for credit.

Computers on Campus Students can access the following: campus intranet, computer help desk, free student e-mail accounts, online (class) grades, online (class) registration, online (class) schedules. Campuswide network is available. 100% of college-owned or -operated housing units are wired for high-speed Internet access.

Student Life *Housing options:* women-only, disabled students. Campus housing is university owned. *Activities and organizations:* drama/theater group, student-run newspaper, choral group. *Campus security:* 24-hour emergency response devices and patrols, late-night transport/escort service, controlled dormitory access. *Student services:* health clinic, personal/psychological counseling.

Athletics Member NCAA. All Division III. *Intercollegiate sports:* basketball W, cross-country running W, lacrosse W, soccer W, softball W, swimming and diving W, tennis W, volleyball W.

Standardized Tests *Required:* SAT or ACT (for admission). *Recommended:* SAT (for admission).

Costs (2010–11) *Comprehensive fee:* $41,470 includes full-time tuition ($27,580), mandatory fees ($950), and room and board ($12,940). Full-time tuition and fees vary according to course load, degree level, location, program, and student level. Part-time tuition: $625 per credit. Part-time tuition and fees vary according to course load, degree level, location, program, and student level. *Required fees:* $30 per quarter hour part-time. *College room only:* $5970. Room and board charges vary according to board plan and housing facility. *Payment plan:* installment. *Waivers:* employees or children of employees.

Applying *Options:* electronic application, deferred entrance. *Application fee:* $50. *Required:* high school transcript. *Recommended:* essay or personal statement, interview. *Application deadlines:* rolling (freshmen), rolling (out-of-state freshmen), rolling (transfers). *Notification:* continuous (freshmen), continuous (out-of-state freshmen), continuous (transfers).

Freshman Application Contact Office of Admissions, Saint Joseph College, 1678 Asylum Avenue, West Hartford, CT 06117. *Phone:* 866-442-8752. *Toll-free phone:* 866-442-8752. *Fax:* 860-231-5744. *E-mail:* admissions@sjc.edu. *Web site:* http://www.sjc.edu/.

See page 1564 for the College Close-Up.

Southern Connecticut State University
New Haven, Connecticut

- **State-supported** comprehensive, founded 1893, part of Connecticut State University System
- **Suburban** 168-acre campus with easy access to New York City
- **Endowment** $11.3 million
- **Coed** 8,776 undergraduate students, 85% full-time, 61% women, 39% men
- **Moderately difficult** entrance level, 70% of applicants were admitted

Undergraduates 7,494 full-time, 1,282 part-time. Students come from 34 states and territories; 11 other countries; 6% are from out of state; 14% Black or African American, non-Hispanic/Latino; 9% Hispanic/Latino; 3% Asian, non-Hispanic/Latino; 0.1% Native Hawaiian or other Pacific Islander, non-Hispanic/Latino; 0.3% American Indian or Alaska Native, non-Hispanic/Latino; 2% Two or more races, non-Hispanic/Latino; 3% Race/ethnicity unknown; 0.6% international; 11% transferred in; 32% live on campus. *Retention:* 78% of full-time freshmen returned.

Freshmen *Admission:* 5,744 applied, 4,046 admitted, 1,253 enrolled. *Average high school GPA:* 2.92. *Test scores:* SAT critical reading scores over 500: 39%; SAT math scores over 500: 39%; SAT writing scores over 500: 45%; ACT scores over 18: 79%; SAT critical reading scores over 600: 8%; SAT math scores over 600: 8%; SAT writing scores over 600: 8%; ACT scores over 24: 18%; SAT critical reading scores over 700: 1%; SAT math scores over 700: 1%; SAT writing scores over 700: 1%; ACT scores over 30: 1%.

Faculty *Total:* 1,132, 37% full-time, 49% with terminal degrees. *Student/faculty ratio:* 15:1.

Academics *Calendar:* semesters. *Degrees:* bachelor's, master's, doctoral-professional, post-master's, and postbachelor's certificates. *Special study options:* academic remediation for entering students, accelerated degree program, advanced placement credit, cooperative education, distance learning, double majors, freshman honors college, honors programs, independent study, internships, off-campus study, part-time degree program, services for LD students, student-designed majors, study abroad, summer session for credit. *ROTC:* Army (c), Air Force (c).

Computers on Campus 800 computers/terminals are available on campus for general student use. Students can access the following: computer help desk, free student e-mail accounts, online (class) grades, online (class) registration, online (class) schedules. Campuswide network is available. 100% of college-owned or -operated housing units are wired for high-speed Internet access. Wireless service is available via classrooms, computer centers, computer labs, learning centers, libraries, student centers.

Student Life *Housing options:* coed, disabled students. Campus housing is university owned. Freshman campus housing is guaranteed. *Activities and organizations:* drama/theater group, student-run newspaper, radio and television station, choral group, marching band, Student Government Association, Psychology Club, Habitat for Humanity, Crescent Players, Black Student Union, national fraternities, national sororities. *Campus security:* 24-hour emergency response devices and patrols, late-night transport/escort service, controlled dormitory access. *Student services:* health clinic, personal/psychological counseling, women's center.

Athletics Member NCAA. All Division II. *Intercollegiate sports:* baseball M(s), basketball M(s)/W(s), cheerleading M(c)/W(c), cross-country running M(s)/W(s), field hockey W(s), football M(s), gymnastics W(s), lacrosse W(s), rugby M(c)/W(c), soccer M(s)/W(s), softball W(s), swimming and diving M(s)/W(s), track and field M(s)/W(s), ultimate Frisbee M(c)/W(c), volleyball W(s). *Intramural sports:* badminton M/W, basketball M/W, football M/W, ice hockey M(c)/W(c), soccer M/W, softball M/W, tennis M/W, volleyball M/W.

Standardized Tests *Required:* SAT or ACT (for admission).

Costs (2011–12) *Tuition:* state resident $4023 full-time, $403 per credit part-time; nonresident $13,020 full-time, $416 per credit part-time. Full-time tuition and fees vary according to course load and reciprocity agreements. Part-time tuition and fees vary according to course load. *Required fees:* $4027 full-time, $55 per term part-time. *Room and board:* $9983; room only: $5541. Room and board charges vary according to board plan and housing facility. *Payment plans:* installment, deferred payment. *Waivers:* senior citizens and employees or children of employees.

Financial Aid Of all full-time matriculated undergraduates who enrolled in 2009, 6,307 applied for aid, 4,206 were judged to have need, 1,335 had their need fully met. 112 Federal Work-Study jobs (averaging $3777). In 2009, 270 non-need-based awards were made. *Average percent of need met:* 79%. *Average financial aid package:* $8355. *Average need-based loan:* $3731. *Average need-based gift aid:* $5784. *Average non-need-based aid:* $3677. *Average indebtedness upon graduation:* $17,374. *Financial aid deadline:* 3/9.

Applying *Options:* electronic application, deferred entrance. *Application fee:* $50. *Required:* essay or personal statement, high school transcript. *Application deadlines:* 4/1 (freshmen), 8/1 (transfers). *Notification:* continuous (freshmen), continuous (transfers).

Freshman Application Contact Ms. Paula Kennedy, Associate Director of Admissions, Southern Connecticut State University, Admissions House, 131 Farnham Avenue, New Haven, CT 06515-1202. *Phone:* 203-392-5651. *Fax:* 203-392-5727. *Web site:* http://www.southernct.edu/.

See page 1616 for the College Close-Up.

Trinity College
Hartford, Connecticut

- **Independent** comprehensive, founded 1823
- **Urban** 100-acre campus
- **Endowment** $370.8 million
- **Coed** 2,331 undergraduate students, 95% full-time, 50% women, 50% men
- **Most difficult** entrance level, 43% of applicants were admitted

Undergraduates 2,212 full-time, 119 part-time. Students come from 47 states and territories; 49 other countries; 83% are from out of state; 7% Black or African American, non-Hispanic/Latino; 7% Hispanic/Latino; 6% Asian, non-Hispanic/Latino; 0.1% American Indian or Alaska Native, non-Hispanic/Latino; 11% Race/ethnicity unknown; 6% international; 0.6% transferred in; 95% live on campus. *Retention:* 91% of full-time freshmen returned.

Freshmen *Admission:* 4,688 applied, 2,024 admitted, 591 enrolled. *Test scores:* SAT critical reading scores over 500: 97%; SAT math scores over 500: 97%; SAT writing scores over 500: 98%; ACT scores over 18: 100%; SAT critical reading scores over 600: 75%; SAT math scores over 600: 78%; SAT writing scores over 600: 79%; ACT scores over 24: 85%; SAT critical reading scores over 700: 17%; SAT math scores over 700: 22%; SAT writing scores over 700: 27%; ACT scores over 30: 20%.

Faculty *Total:* 239, 76% full-time, 85% with terminal degrees. *Student/faculty ratio:* 10:1.

Academics *Calendar:* semesters. *Degrees:* bachelor's and master's. *Special study options:* accelerated degree program, adult/continuing education programs, advanced placement credit, double majors, honors programs, independent study, internships, off-campus study, student-designed majors, study abroad, summer session for credit. *ROTC:* Army (c). *Unusual degree programs:* 3-2 engineering with Rensselaer Polytechnic Institute.

Computers on Campus 249 computers/terminals and 3,000 ports are available on campus for general student use. Students can access the following: campus intranet, computer help desk, free student e-mail accounts, online (class) grades, online (class) registration, online (class) schedules, Web pages. Campuswide network is available. 100% of college-owned or -operated housing units are wired for high-speed Internet access. Wireless service is available via classrooms, computer centers, computer labs, learning centers, libraries, student centers.

Student Life *Housing:* on-campus residence required for freshman year. *Options:* coed, disabled students. Campus housing is university owned. Freshman campus housing is guaranteed. *Activities and organizations:* drama/theater group, student-run newspaper, radio station, choral group, Friends Active in Community Engagement and Service (FACES), The Mill, Student Government Association, Relay for Life, Multi-Cultural Affairs Council, national fraternities, national sororities. *Campus security:* 24-hour emergency response devices and patrols, late-night transport/escort service, controlled dormitory access. *Student services:* health clinic, personal/psychological counseling, women's center.

Athletics Member NCAA. All Division III. *Intercollegiate sports:* baseball M, basketball M/W, crew M/W, cross-country running M/W, equestrian sports M(c)/W(c), fencing M(c)/W(c), football M, golf M, ice hockey M/W, lacrosse M/W, rugby M(c)/W(c), sailing M(c)/W(c), skiing (downhill) M(c)/W(c), soccer M/W, softball W, squash M/W, swimming and diving M/W, tennis M/W, track and field M/W, ultimate Frisbee M(c)/W(c), volleyball W, water polo M(c)/W(c), wrestling M. *Intramural sports:* badminton M/W, basketball M/W, soccer M/W, softball M/W, squash M/W, tennis M/W.

Standardized Tests *Required for some:* SAT or ACT (for admission), SAT Subject Tests (for admission).

Costs (2010–11) *One-time required fee:* $25. *Comprehensive fee:* $53,330 includes full-time tuition ($40,360), mandatory fees ($2010), and room and board ($10,960). Full-time tuition and fees vary according to course load and program. Part-time tuition: $4484 per course. Part-time tuition and fees vary according to course load and program. *College room only:* $7120. Room and board charges vary according to board plan. *Payment plan:* installment. *Waivers:* adult students and employees or children of employees.

Financial Aid Of all full-time matriculated undergraduates who enrolled in 2009, 1,023 applied for aid, 975 were judged to have need, 975 had their need fully met. 518 Federal Work-Study jobs (averaging $1748). In 2009, 31 non-need-based awards were made. *Average percent of need met:* 100%. *Average financial aid package:* $38,498. *Average need-based loan:* $4320. *Average need-based gift aid:* $36,812. *Average non-need-based aid:* $32,748. *Average indebtedness upon graduation:* $21,671. *Financial aid deadline:* 3/1.

Applying *Options:* electronic application, early admission, early decision, deferred entrance. *Application fee:* $60. *Required:* essay or personal statement, high school transcript, 3 letters of recommendation. *Recommended:* interview. *Application deadlines:* 1/1 (freshmen), 4/1 (transfers). *Early decision deadline:* 11/15 (for plan 1), 1/1 (for plan 2). *Notification:* 4/1 (freshmen), 6/10 (transfers), 12/15 (early decision plan 1), 2/15 (early decision plan 2).

Freshman Application Contact Trinity College, 300 Summit Street, Hartford, CT 06106-3100. *Phone:* 860-297-2180. *Web site:* http://www.trincoll.edu/.

See page 1670 for the College Close-Up.

United States Coast Guard Academy
New London, Connecticut

- **Federally supported** 4-year, founded 1876
- **Suburban** 110-acre campus with easy access to Providence and Hartford
- **Endowment** $1.3 million
- **Coed** 1,017 undergraduate students, 100% full-time, 29% women, 71% men
- **Very difficult** entrance level, 17% of applicants were admitted

Undergraduates 1,017 full-time. Students come from 49 states and territories; 16 other countries; 95% are from out of state; 3% Black or African American, non-Hispanic/Latino; 8% Hispanic/Latino; 4% Asian, non-Hispanic/Latino; 0.8% Native Hawaiian or other Pacific Islander, non-Hispanic/Latino; 0.3%

American Indian or Alaska Native, non-Hispanic/Latino; 1% Two or more races, non-Hispanic/Latino; 1% Race/ethnicity unknown; 2% international; 100% live on campus. *Retention:* 93% of full-time freshmen returned.
Freshmen *Admission:* 2,223 applied, 385 admitted, 279 enrolled. *Average high school GPA:* 3.77. *Test scores:* SAT critical reading scores over 500: 89%; SAT math scores over 500: 95%; SAT writing scores over 500: 85%; ACT scores over 18: 99%; SAT critical reading scores over 600: 55%; SAT math scores over 600: 77%; SAT writing scores over 600: 46%; ACT scores over 24: 72%; SAT critical reading scores over 700: 14%; SAT math scores over 700: 22%; SAT writing scores over 700: 9%; ACT scores over 30: 18%.
Faculty *Total:* 141, 82% full-time, 51% with terminal degrees. *Student/faculty ratio:* 8:1.
Academics *Calendar:* semesters. *Degree:* bachelor's. *Special study options:* academic remediation for entering students, double majors, honors programs, independent study, internships, off-campus study, summer session for credit.
Computers on Campus 325 computers/terminals are available on campus for general student use. Students can access the following: campus intranet, computer help desk, free student e-mail accounts, online (class) grades, online (class) registration, online (class) schedules. Campuswide network is available. 100% of college-owned or -operated housing units are wired for high-speed Internet access. Wireless service is available via classrooms, dorm rooms, libraries, student centers.
Student Life *Housing:* on-campus residence required through senior year. *Options:* coed. Campus housing is university owned. Freshman campus housing is guaranteed. *Activities and organizations:* drama/theater group, choral group, marching band, Companneros Club - Latino culture and traditions, Genesis Club - Multicultural awareness, Men's and Women's Lacrosse Club, Men's and Women's Rugby Club, Officers' Christian Fellowship. *Campus security:* 24-hour patrols, student patrols. *Student services:* health clinic, personal/psychological counseling, legal services.
Athletics Member NCAA. All Division III. *Intercollegiate sports:* baseball M, basketball M/W, bowling M(c)/W(c), crew M/W, cross-country running M/W, football M, golf M(c)/W(c), ice hockey M(c), lacrosse M(c)/W(c), riflery M/W, rugby M(c)/W(c), sailing M/W, soccer M/W, softball W, swimming and diving M/W, tennis M/W(c), track and field M/W, volleyball W, water polo M(c), wrestling M. *Intramural sports:* basketball M/W, bowling M/W, football M, golf M/W, racquetball M/W, sailing M/W, skiing (downhill) M(c)/W(c), soccer M/W, softball M/W, swimming and diving M/W, table tennis M/W, track and field M/W, ultimate Frisbee M/W, volleyball M/W, water polo M, wrestling M.
Standardized Tests *Required:* SAT or ACT (for admission).
Costs (2011–12) *Tuition:* Tuition, room and board, and medical and dental care are provided by the U.S. government. Each cadet receives a salary from which to pay for uniforms, supplies, and personal expenses. Entering freshmen are required to deposit $3000 to defray the initial cost of computer, uniforms, books and other items.
Applying *Options:* electronic application, early action. *Required:* essay or personal statement, high school transcript, 3 letters of recommendation, Medical examination, Physical Fitness Examination. *Recommended:* interview. *Application deadlines:* 2/1 (freshmen), 2/1 (out-of-state freshmen), 2/1 (transfers), 11/1 (early action). *Notification:* continuous until 4/15 (freshmen), continuous until 4/15 (out-of-state freshmen), continuous until 4/15 (transfers), 1/15 (early action).
Freshman Application Contact Capt. Stephan P. Finton, Director of Admissions, United States Coast Guard Academy, 31 Mohegan Avenue, New London, CT 06320-4195. *Phone:* 860-444-8500. *Toll-free phone:* 800-883-8724. *Fax:* 860-701-6700. *E-mail:* admissions@uscga.edu. *Web site:* http://www.uscga.edu/.

University of Bridgeport
Bridgeport, Connecticut

- **Independent** comprehensive, founded 1927
- **Urban** 86-acre campus with easy access to New York City
- **Endowment** $8.1 million
- **Coed** 2,534 undergraduate students, 68% full-time, 70% women, 30% men
- **Moderately difficult** entrance level, 57% of applicants were admitted

Undergraduates 1,718 full-time, 816 part-time. Students come from 46 states and territories; 55 other countries; 39% are from out of state; 38% Black or African American, non-Hispanic/Latino; 18% Hispanic/Latino; 4% Asian, non-Hispanic/Latino; 0.4% American Indian or Alaska Native, non-Hispanic/Latino; 4% Two or more races, non-Hispanic/Latino; 9% international; 7% transferred in; 53% live on campus. *Retention:* 52% of full-time freshmen returned.
Freshmen *Admission:* 6,369 applied, 3,659 admitted, 610 enrolled. *Average high school GPA:* 2.85. *Test scores:* SAT critical reading scores over 500: 22%; SAT math scores over 500: 23%; SAT writing scores over 500: 24%; ACT scores over 18: 48%; SAT critical reading scores over 600: 2%; SAT math scores over 600: 3%; SAT writing scores over 600: 2%; ACT scores over

24: 7%; SAT critical reading scores over 700: 1%; SAT writing scores over 700: 1%.
Faculty *Total:* 484, 25% full-time. *Student/faculty ratio:* 16:1.
Academics *Calendar:* semesters. *Degrees:* certificates, associate, bachelor's, master's, doctoral-professional, doctoral-research/scholarship, post-master's, and postbachelor's certificates. *Special study options:* academic remediation for entering students, accelerated degree program, adult/continuing education programs, advanced placement credit, cooperative education, distance learning, double majors, English as a second language, honors programs, independent study, internships, off-campus study, part-time degree program, services for LD students, student-designed majors, study abroad, summer session for credit. *ROTC:* Army (b).
Computers on Campus 100 computers/terminals and 100 ports are available on campus for general student use. Students can access the following: computer help desk, free student e-mail accounts, online (class) grades, online (class) registration, online (class) schedules. Campuswide network is available. 100% of college-owned or -operated housing units are wired for high-speed Internet access. Wireless service is available via classrooms, computer centers, computer labs, dorm rooms, learning centers, libraries, student centers.
Student Life *Housing:* on-campus residence required through sophomore year. *Options:* coed. Campus housing is university owned. Freshman campus housing is guaranteed. *Activities and organizations:* student-run newspaper, choral group, Student Congress, International Relations Club, Black Students Alliance, Latin America Club, Martial Arts Club, national fraternities, national sororities. *Campus security:* 24-hour emergency response devices and patrols, student patrols, late-night transport/escort service, controlled dormitory access. *Student services:* health clinic, personal/psychological counseling, women's center.
Athletics Member NCAA. All Division II. *Intercollegiate sports:* baseball M(s), basketball M(s)/W(s), cross-country running M(s)/W(s), gymnastics W(s), lacrosse W(s), soccer M(s)/W(s), softball W(s), swimming and diving M(s)/W(s), volleyball W(s). *Intramural sports:* basketball M/W, football M/W, golf M/W, racquetball M/W, soccer M/W, softball M/W, tennis M/W.
Standardized Tests *Required:* SAT or ACT (for admission).
Costs (2010–11) *Comprehensive fee:* $37,895 includes full-time tuition ($24,300), mandatory fees ($2195), and room and board ($11,400). Full-time tuition and fees vary according to course load and program. Part-time tuition: $810 per credit hour. Part-time tuition and fees vary according to course load and program. *Required fees:* $80 per year part-time. *Room and board:* Room and board charges vary according to board plan and student level. *Payment plans:* installment, deferred payment. *Waivers:* senior citizens and employees or children of employees.
Financial Aid Of all full-time matriculated undergraduates who enrolled in 2009, 1,444 applied for aid, 1,184 were judged to have need, 142 had their need fully met. 400 Federal Work-Study jobs (averaging $2000). In 2009, 320 non-need-based awards were made. *Average percent of need met:* 56%. *Average financial aid package:* $22,618. *Average need-based loan:* $5539. *Average need-based gift aid:* $8420. *Average non-need-based aid:* $15,194.
Applying *Options:* electronic application, early admission, deferred entrance. *Application fee:* $50. *Required:* essay or personal statement, high school transcript, minimum 2 GPA. *Required for some:* interview, portfolio, audition. *Recommended:* 1 letter of recommendation, interview. *Application deadlines:* rolling (freshmen), rolling (out-of-state freshmen), rolling (transfers). *Notification:* continuous (freshmen), continuous (out-of-state freshmen), continuous (transfers).
Freshman Application Contact University of Bridgeport, 126 Park Avenue, Bridgeport, CT 06604. *Phone:* 203-576-4552. *Toll-free phone:* 800-EXCEL-UB (in-state); 800-243-9496 (out-of-state). *Fax:* 203-576-4941. *E-mail:* admit@bridgeport.edu. *Web site:* http://www.bridgeport.edu/.

University of Connecticut
Storrs, Connecticut

- **State-supported** university, founded 1881
- **Rural** 4108-acre campus
- **Endowment** $247.0 million
- **Coed**
- **Moderately difficult** entrance level

Faculty *Student/faculty ratio:* 18:1.
Academics *Calendar:* semesters. *Degrees:* associate, bachelor's, master's, doctoral-professional, doctoral-research/scholarship, post-master's, and postbachelor's certificates.
Student Life *Campus security:* 24-hour emergency response devices, late-night transport/escort service.
Athletics Member NCAA. All Division I except football (Division I-A).
Standardized Tests *Required:* SAT or ACT (for admission).
Costs (2011–12) *Tuition:* state resident $8256 full-time, $344 per credit part-time; nonresident $25,152 full-time, $1048 per credit part-time. Part-time tuition and fees vary according to course load. *Required fees:* $2414 full-time. *Room and board:* $11,050; room only: $5918. Room and board charges vary

according to board plan and housing facility. *Payment plans:* installment, deferred payment.

Financial Aid *Of all full-time matriculated undergraduates who enrolled in 2009,* 11,967 applied for aid, 9,336 were judged to have need, 1,517 had their need fully met. 1,959 Federal Work-Study jobs (averaging $1931). 5,301 state and other part-time jobs (averaging $3095). *In 2009,* 1311 non-need-based awards were made. *Average percent of need met:* 66. *Average financial aid package:* $12,789. *Average need-based loan:* $4307. *Average need-based gift aid:* $8167. *Average non-need-based aid:* $6761. *Average indebtedness upon graduation:* $23,237.

Applying *Options:* electronic application, early action, deferred entrance. *Application fee:* $70. *Required:* essay or personal statement, high school transcript. *Recommended:* 1 letter of recommendation.

Freshman Application Contact Mr. Brian Usher, Interim Director of Admissions, University of Connecticut, 2131 Hillside Road, U-88, Storrs, CT 06269. *Phone:* 860-486-3137. *Fax:* 860-486-1476. *E-mail:* beahusky@ uconnvm.uconn.edu. *Web site:* http://www.uconn.edu/.

University of Hartford
West Hartford, Connecticut

- **Independent** comprehensive, founded 1877
- **Suburban** 320-acre campus with easy access to Hartford
- **Endowment** $107.4 million
- **Coed** 5,498 undergraduate students, 85% full-time, 52% women, 48% men
- **Moderately difficult** entrance level, 62% of applicants were admitted

Undergraduates 4,694 full-time, 804 part-time. Students come from 43 states and territories; 39 other countries; 54% are from out of state; 14% Black or African American, non-Hispanic/Latino; 7% Hispanic/Latino; 3% Asian, non-Hispanic/Latino; 0.1% Native Hawaiian or other Pacific Islander, non-Hispanic/Latino; 0.3% American Indian or Alaska Native, non-Hispanic/Latino; 0.4% Two or more races, non-Hispanic/Latino; 11% Race/ethnicity unknown; 2% international; 4% transferred in; 60% live on campus. *Retention:* 71% of full-time freshmen returned.

Freshmen *Admission:* 11,946 applied, 7,354 admitted, 1,376 enrolled. *Test scores:* SAT critical reading scores over 500: 55%; SAT math scores over 500: 55%; ACT scores over 18: 88%; SAT critical reading scores over 600: 16%; SAT math scores over 600: 17%; ACT scores over 24: 28%; SAT critical reading scores over 700: 3%; SAT math scores over 700: 2%; ACT scores over 30: 4%.

Faculty *Total:* 925, 38% full-time. *Student/faculty ratio:* 12:1.

Academics *Calendar:* semesters. *Degrees:* certificates, diplomas, associate, bachelor's, master's, doctoral-professional, doctoral-research/scholarship, post-master's, and postbachelor's certificates. *Special study options:* academic remediation for entering students, adult/continuing education programs, advanced placement credit, cooperative education, distance learning, double majors, English as a second language, honors programs, independent study, internships, off-campus study, part-time degree program, services for LD students, student-designed majors, study abroad, summer session for credit. *ROTC:* Army (c), Air Force (c).

Computers on Campus 400 computers/terminals are available on campus for general student use. Students can access the following: campus intranet, computer help desk, free student e-mail accounts, online (class) grades, online (class) registration, online (class) schedules, student Web pages. Campuswide network is available. 100% of college-owned or -operated housing units are wired for high-speed Internet access. Wireless service is available via classrooms, computer centers, computer labs, libraries, student centers.

Student Life *Housing options:* coed, women-only, disabled students. Campus housing is university owned and leased by the school. Freshman campus housing is guaranteed. *Activities and organizations:* drama/theater group, student-run newspaper, radio and television station, choral group, Program Council, Brothers and Sisters United, Hillel, Student Government Association, Residence Hall Association, national fraternities, national sororities. *Campus security:* 24-hour emergency response devices and patrols, late-night transport/ escort service, controlled dormitory access, bicycle patrols. *Student services:* health clinic, personal/psychological counseling, women's center, legal services.

Athletics Member NCAA. All Division I. *Intercollegiate sports:* badminton M(c)/W(c), baseball M(s), basketball M(s)/W(s), cross-country running M(s)/ W(s), golf M(s)/W(s), lacrosse M(s), racquetball M(c)/W(c), rugby M(c)/W(c), soccer M(s)/W(s), softball W(s), squash M(c)/W(c), tennis M(s)/W(s), track and field M/W, volleyball M(c)/W(s). *Intramural sports:* basketball M/W, football M/W, racquetball M/W, soccer M/W, softball M/W, tennis M/W, ultimate Frisbee M/W, volleyball M/W, water polo M/W.

Standardized Tests *Required:* SAT or ACT (for admission).

Costs (2011–12) *Comprehensive fee:* $42,674 includes full-time tuition ($29,440), mandatory fees ($1314), and room and board ($11,920). Full-time tuition and fees vary according to program. Part-time tuition: $440 per credit hour. Part-time tuition and fees vary according to course load and program.

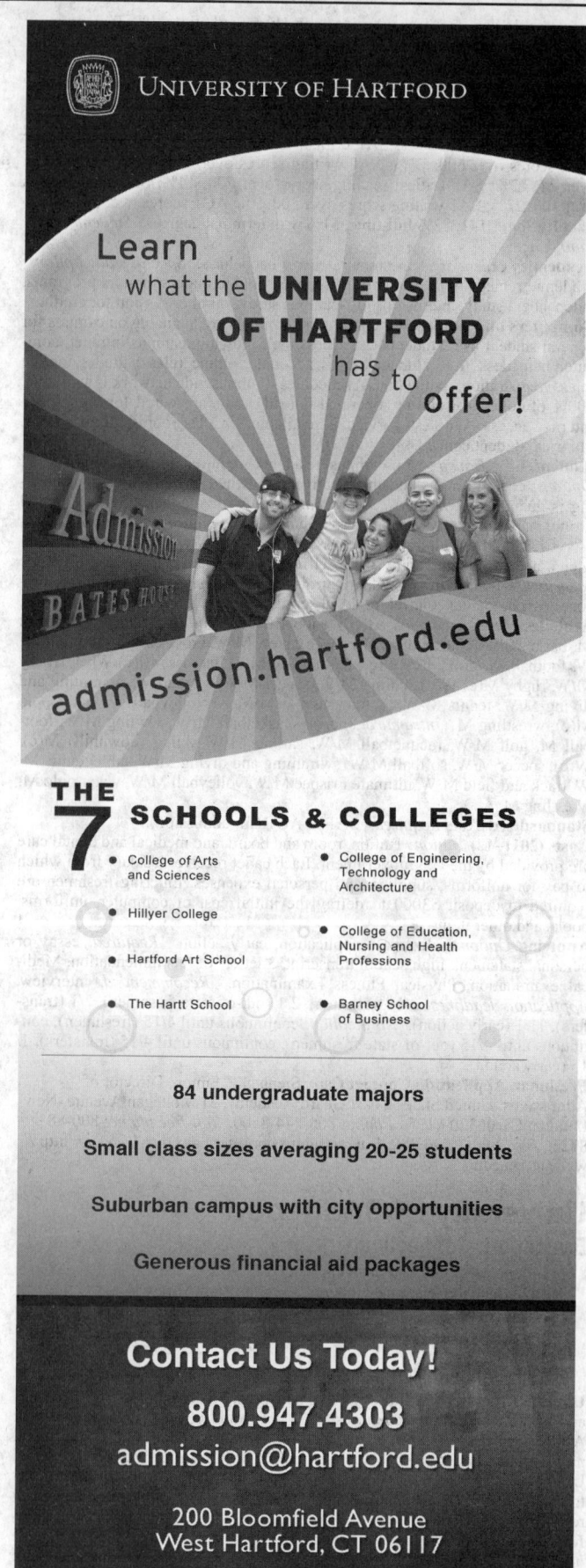

College room only: $7328. Room and board charges vary according to board plan and housing facility. *Payment plans:* tuition prepayment, installment. *Waivers:* senior citizens and employees or children of employees.

Financial Aid Of all full-time matriculated undergraduates who enrolled in 2009, 4,376 applied for aid, 3,698 were judged to have need, 925 had their need fully met. 723 Federal Work-Study jobs (averaging $6719). In 2009, 919 non-need-based awards were made. *Average percent of need met:* 80%. *Average financial aid package:* $5464. *Average need-based loan:* $9814. *Average need-based gift aid:* $4153. *Average non-need-based aid:* $3578. *Average indebtedness upon graduation:* $14,855.

Applying *Options:* electronic application, early admission, deferred entrance. *Application fee:* $35. *Required:* high school transcript. *Recommended:* essay or personal statement, 2 letters of recommendation, interview. *Application deadlines:* rolling (freshmen), rolling (transfers). *Notification:* continuous (freshmen), continuous (transfers).

Freshman Application Contact Mr. Richard Zeiser, Dean of Admissions, University of Hartford, 200 Bloomfield Avenue, West Hartford, CT 06117. *Phone:* 860-768-4296. *Toll-free phone:* 800-947-4303. *Fax:* 860-768-4961. *E-mail:* admissions@hartford.edu. *Web site:* http://www.hartford.edu/.

See page 1698 for the College Close-Up.

University of New Haven
West Haven, Connecticut

- **Independent** comprehensive, founded 1920
- **Suburban** 78-acre campus with easy access to Hartford and New Haven
- **Coed** 4,203 undergraduate students, 87% full-time, 50% women, 50% men
- **Moderately difficult** entrance level, 62% of applicants were admitted

Undergraduates 3,642 full-time, 561 part-time. Students come from 43 states and territories; 19 other countries; 47% are from out of state; 7% Black or African American, non-Hispanic/Latino; 6% Hispanic/Latino; 1% Asian, non-Hispanic/Latino; 0.3% American Indian or Alaska Native, non-Hispanic/Latino; 37% Race/ethnicity unknown; 7% international; 6% transferred in; 57% live on campus. *Retention:* 72% of full-time freshmen returned.

Freshmen *Admission:* 8,618 applied, 5,355 admitted, 1,021 enrolled. *Average high school GPA:* 3.3. *Test scores:* SAT critical reading scores over 500: 61%;

SAT math scores over 500: 67%; SAT writing scores over 500: 61%; ACT scores over 18: 92%; SAT critical reading scores over 600: 14%; SAT math scores over 600: 21%; SAT writing scores over 600: 16%; ACT scores over 24: 40%; SAT critical reading scores over 700: 1%; SAT math scores over 700: 2%; SAT writing scores over 700: 1%; ACT scores over 30: 2%.

Faculty *Total:* 535, 38% full-time, 46% with terminal degrees. *Student/faculty ratio:* 16:1.

Academics *Calendar:* 4-1-4. *Degrees:* certificates, associate, bachelor's, master's, post-master's, and postbachelor's certificates. *Special study options:* academic remediation for entering students, accelerated degree program, adult/continuing education programs, advanced placement credit, cooperative education, distance learning, double majors, English as a second language, honors programs, independent study, internships, off-campus study, part-time degree program, services for LD students, study abroad, summer session for credit. *ROTC:* Army (b), Air Force (c).

Computers on Campus 300 computers/terminals are available on campus for general student use. Students can access the following: computer help desk, free student e-mail accounts, online (class) grades, online (class) registration, online (class) schedules, computer repair services. Campuswide network is available. 100% of college-owned or -operated housing units are wired for high-speed Internet access. Wireless service is available via entire campus.

Student Life *Housing options:* coed, disabled students. Campus housing is university owned. *Activities and organizations:* drama/theater group, student-run newspaper, radio station, choral group, marching band, student government, Criminal Justice Club, Music Entertainment and Industry Association, Black Student Union, Fire Science Club, national fraternities. *Campus security:* 24-hour emergency response devices and patrols, late-night transport/escort service, escort service, vehicle, bicycle and foot patrols, crime prevention programs. *Student services:* health clinic, personal/psychological counseling.

Athletics Member NCAA. All Division II. *Intercollegiate sports:* baseball M(s), basketball M(s)/W(s), cheerleading M/W, cross-country running M(s)/W(s), football M(s), golf M(s), lacrosse W(s), soccer M(s)/W(s), softball W(s), tennis W(s), track and field M(s)/W(s), volleyball M(s)/W(s). *Intramural sports:* basketball M/W, bowling M/W, cross-country running M/W, football M, lacrosse M, racquetball M/W, soccer M/W, softball M/W, table tennis M/W, tennis M/W, ultimate Frisbee M/W, volleyball M/W, weight lifting M/W.

Standardized Tests *Required:* SAT or ACT (for admission).

Costs (2010–11) *One-time required fee:* $350. *Comprehensive fee:* $43,528 includes full-time tuition ($29,500), mandatory fees ($1250), and room and board ($12,778). Full-time tuition and fees vary according to course load and program. Part-time tuition: $495 per credit hour. Part-time tuition and fees vary according to class time, course load, and program. *Required fees:* $75 per term part-time. *College room only:* $8000. Room and board charges vary according to board plan and housing facility. *Payment plan:* installment. *Waivers:* senior citizens and employees or children of employees.

Financial Aid Of all full-time matriculated undergraduates who enrolled in 2009, 3,098 applied for aid, 2,809 were judged to have need, 441 had their need fully met. 157 Federal Work-Study jobs (averaging $1290). In 2009, 441 non-need-based awards were made. *Average percent of need met:* 65%. *Average financial aid package:* $19,495. *Average need-based loan:* $4129. *Average need-based gift aid:* $15,882. *Average non-need-based aid:* $9607. *Average indebtedness upon graduation:* $36,272. *Financial aid deadline:* 3/1.

Applying *Options:* electronic application, early action. *Application fee:* $75. *Required:* essay or personal statement, high school transcript, 1 letter of recommendation. *Recommended:* interview. *Application deadlines:* rolling (freshmen), rolling (transfers), 11/15 (early action). *Notification:* continuous (freshmen), continuous (transfers), 12/15 (early action).

Freshman Application Contact Mr. Kevin Phillips, Associate Vice Presidents of Undergraduate Admissions, University of New Haven, Bayer Hall, 300 Boston Post Road, West Haven, CT 06516. *Phone:* 203-932-7318. *Toll-free phone:* 800-DIAL-UNH. *Fax:* 203-931-6093. *E-mail:* adminfo@ newhaven.edu. *Web site:* http://www.newhaven.edu/.

See page 1716 for the College Close-Up.

Wesleyan University

Middletown, Connecticut

- **Independent** university, founded 1831
- **Small-town** 240-acre campus
- **Endowment** $513.0 million
- **Coed** 2,854 undergraduate students, 100% full-time, 52% women, 48% men
- **Most difficult** entrance level, 21% of applicants were admitted

Undergraduates 2,845 full-time, 9 part-time. 92% are from out of state; 6% Black or African American, non-Hispanic/Latino; 9% Hispanic/Latino; 7% Asian, non-Hispanic/Latino; 6% Two or more races, non-Hispanic/Latino; 9% Race/ethnicity unknown; 7% international; 2% transferred in; 98% live on campus. *Retention:* 98% of full-time freshmen returned.

Freshmen *Admission:* 10,657 applied, 2,190 admitted, 748 enrolled. *Average high school GPA:* 3.77. *Test scores:* SAT critical reading scores over 500: 99%; SAT math scores over 500: 99%; SAT writing scores over 500: 98%; ACT scores over 18: 100%; SAT critical reading scores over 600: 87%; SAT math scores over 600: 91%; SAT writing scores over 600: 88%; ACT scores over 24: 99%; SAT critical reading scores over 700: 52%; SAT math scores over 700: 56%; SAT writing scores over 700: 55%; ACT scores over 30: 81%.

Faculty *Total:* 372, 91% full-time, 89% with terminal degrees. *Student/faculty ratio:* 9:1.

Academics *Calendar:* semesters. *Degrees:* bachelor's, master's, doctoral-research/scholarship, and post-master's certificates. *Special study options:* adult/continuing education programs, advanced placement credit, double majors, honors programs, independent study, off-campus study, services for LD students, student-designed majors, study abroad, summer session for credit. *ROTC:* Air Force (c). *Unusual degree programs:* 3-2 engineering with Columbia University, California Institute of Technology.

Computers on Campus 1,600 computers/terminals are available on campus for general student use. Students can access the following: campus intranet, computer help desk, free student e-mail accounts, online (class) grades, online (class) registration, online (class) schedules, electronic portfolio, online course drop/add, Blackboard course management system. Campuswide network is available. 100% of college-owned or -operated housing units are wired for high-speed Internet access. Wireless service is available via entire campus.

Student Life *Housing:* on-campus residence required through senior year. *Options:* coed, disabled students. Campus housing is university owned. Freshman campus housing is guaranteed. *Activities and organizations:* drama/theater group, student-run newspaper, radio station, choral group, Environmental Organizers Network, WesDems, Ajuacampos (Latino affinity group), national fraternities, national sororities. *Campus security:* 24-hour emergency response devices and patrols, student patrols, late-night transport/escort service, controlled dormitory access. *Student services:* health clinic, personal/psychological counseling, women's center.

Athletics Member NCAA. All Division III. *Intercollegiate sports:* baseball M, basketball M/W, crew M/W, cross-country running M/W, equestrian sports M(c)/W(c), field hockey W, football M, ice hockey M/W, lacrosse M/W, rugby M(c)/W(c), sailing M(c)/W(c), skiing (cross-country) M(c)/W(c), skiing (downhill) M(c)/W(c), soccer M/W, softball W, squash M/W, swimming and diving M/W, tennis M/W, track and field M/W, volleyball

M(c)/W, water polo M(c), wrestling M. *Intramural sports:* basketball M/W, ice hockey M/W, soccer M/W, softball M/W, squash M/W, ultimate Frisbee M/W, water polo M/W.

Standardized Tests *Required:* SAT and SAT Subject Tests or ACT (for admission).

Costs (2010–11) *One-time required fee:* $300. *Comprehensive fee:* $53,676 includes full-time tuition ($41,814), mandatory fees ($270), and room and board ($11,592). *Room and board:* Room and board charges vary according to board plan and housing facility. *Payment plan:* installment.

Financial Aid Of all full-time matriculated undergraduates who enrolled in 2008, 1,401 applied for aid, 1,334 were judged to have need, 1,334 had their need fully met. 1,113 Federal Work-Study jobs (averaging $2332). 77 state and other part-time jobs (averaging $2357). In 2008, 47 non-need-based awards were made. *Average percent of need met:* 100%. *Average financial aid package:* $35,548. *Average need-based loan:* $5192. *Average need-based gift aid:* $32,789. *Average non-need-based aid:* $47,089. *Average indebtedness upon graduation:* $29,227. *Financial aid deadline:* 2/15.

Applying *Options:* electronic application, early admission, early decision, deferred entrance. *Application fee:* $55. *Required:* essay or personal statement, high school transcript, 2 letters of recommendation. *Required for some:* interview. *Recommended:* interview. *Application deadlines:* 1/1 (freshmen), 3/15 (transfers). *Early decision deadline:* 11/15 (for plan 1), 1/1 (for plan 2). *Notification:* 4/1 (freshmen), 5/15 (transfers), 12/15 (early decision plan 1), 2/15 (early decision plan 2).

Freshman Application Contact Ms. Nancy Meislahn, Dean of Admission and Financial Aid, Wesleyan University, Stewart M. Reid House, 70 Wyllys Avenue, Middletown, CT 06459-0265. *Phone:* 860-685-3000. *Fax:* 860-685-3001. *E-mail:* admissions@wesleyan.edu. *Web site:* http://www.wesleyan.edu/.

Western Connecticut State University

Danbury, Connecticut

- **State-supported** comprehensive, founded 1903, part of Connecticut State University System
- **Urban** 340-acre campus with easy access to New York City
- **Coed** 5,960 undergraduate students, 82% full-time, 54% women, 46% men
- **Moderately difficult** entrance level, 63% of applicants were admitted

Undergraduates 4,905 full-time, 1,055 part-time. 8% are from out of state; 6% Black or African American, non-Hispanic/Latino; 6% Hispanic/Latino; 2% Asian, non-Hispanic/Latino; 0.1% Native Hawaiian or other Pacific Islander, non-Hispanic/Latino; 5% Two or more races, non-Hispanic/Latino; 21% Race/ethnicity unknown; 0.3% international; 9% transferred in; 28% live on campus. *Retention:* 75% of full-time freshmen returned.

Freshmen *Admission:* 4,200 applied, 2,662 admitted, 986 enrolled. *Average high school GPA:* 3. *Test scores:* SAT critical reading scores over 500: 46%; SAT math scores over 500: 47%; SAT writing scores over 500: 46%; SAT critical reading scores over 600: 10%; SAT math scores over 600: 10%; SAT writing scores over 600: 8%; SAT critical reading scores over 700: 1%; SAT math scores over 700: 1%; SAT writing scores over 700: 1%.

Faculty *Total:* 579, 39% full-time. *Student/faculty ratio:* 16:1.

Academics *Calendar:* semesters. *Degrees:* associate, bachelor's, master's, and doctoral-professional. *Special study options:* academic remediation for entering students, advanced placement credit, cooperative education, distance learning, honors programs, independent study, internships, off-campus study, part-time degree program, services for LD students, student-designed majors, study abroad, summer session for credit. *ROTC:* Army (c), Air Force (c).

Computers on Campus Students can access the following: computer help desk, free student e-mail accounts, online (class) grades, online (class) registration, online (class) schedules. Campuswide network is available. Wireless service is available via classrooms, computer labs, libraries.

Student Life *Housing options:* coed, women-only. Campus housing is university owned. Freshman campus housing is guaranteed. *Activities and organizations:* drama/theater group, student-run newspaper, radio station, choral group, national fraternities, national sororities. *Campus security:* 24-hour emergency response devices and patrols, student patrols, late-night transport/escort service, controlled dormitory access. *Student services:* health clinic, personal/psychological counseling.

Athletics Member NCAA. All Division III. *Intercollegiate sports:* baseball M, basketball M/W, cheerleading W(c), field hockey W, football M, lacrosse M/W, soccer M/W, softball W, swimming and diving W, tennis M/W, volleyball W. *Intramural sports:* basketball M/W, football M, ice hockey M(c), rock climbing M(c)/W(c), softball M/W.

Standardized Tests *Required:* SAT or ACT (for admission).

Costs (2010–11) *Tuition:* state resident $4023 full-time, $168 per credit hour part-time; nonresident $13,020 full-time, $171 per credit hour part-time. Full-time tuition and fees vary according to program and reciprocity agreements. *Required fees:* $3886 full-time, $196 per credit hour part-time. *Room only:* $5698. Room and board charges vary according to board plan and housing facility. *Payment plan:* installment. *Waivers:* senior citizens and employees or children of employees.

Financial Aid Of all full-time matriculated undergraduates who enrolled in 2008, 3,814 applied for aid, 2,923 were judged to have need, 83 had their need fully met. 116 Federal Work-Study jobs (averaging $1501). 29 state and other part-time jobs (averaging $2138). In 2008, 35 non-need-based awards were made. *Average percent of need met:* 65%. *Average financial aid package:* $7368. *Average need-based loan:* $3973. *Average need-based gift aid:* $4468. *Average non-need-based aid:* $6883. *Average indebtedness upon graduation:* $23,487. *Financial aid deadline:* 4/15.

Applying *Options:* electronic application, early admission, deferred entrance. *Application fee:* $50. *Required:* high school transcript, 2 letters of recommendation, standardized test scores. *Required for some:* essay or personal statement, interview. *Application deadline:* rolling (transfers). *Notification:* continuous (freshmen), continuous (transfers).

Freshman Application Contact Office of University Admissions, Western Connecticut State University, 181 White Street, Danbury, CT 06810. *Phone:* 203-837-9000. *Toll-free phone:* 877-837-WCSU. *E-mail:* admissions@ wcsu.edu. *Web site:* http://www.wcsu.edu/.

See page 1778 for the College Close-Up.

Yale University
New Haven, Connecticut

- **Independent** university, founded 1701
- **Urban** 200-acre campus with easy access to New York City
- **Endowment** $16.5 billion
- **Coed** 5,294 undergraduate students, 100% full-time, 50% women, 50% men
- **Most difficult** entrance level, 8% of applicants were admitted

Undergraduates 5,279 full-time, 15 part-time. Students come from 52 states and territories; 71 other countries; 94% are from out of state; 91% transferred in; 88% live on campus. *Retention:* 99% of full-time freshmen returned.

Freshmen *Admission:* 25,876 applied, 2,009 admitted. *Test scores:* SAT critical reading scores over 500: 100%; SAT math scores over 500: 101%; SAT writing scores over 500: 99%; SAT critical reading scores over 600: 97%; SAT math scores over 600: 99%; SAT writing scores over 600: 97%; SAT critical reading scores over 700: 78%; SAT math scores over 700: 80%; SAT writing scores over 700: 78%.

Faculty *Total:* 1,653, 70% full-time, 85% with terminal degrees. *Student/faculty ratio:* 6:1.

Academics *Calendar:* semesters. *Degrees:* bachelor's, master's, doctoral-professional, doctoral-research/scholarship, and post-master's certificates. *Special study options:* accelerated degree program, advanced placement credit, double majors, English as a second language, honors programs, independent study, internships, part-time degree program, services for LD students, student-designed majors, study abroad, summer session for credit. *ROTC:* Army (c), Air Force (c).

Computers on Campus 350 computers/terminals are available on campus for general student use. Students can access the following: campus intranet, computer help desk, free student e-mail accounts, online (class) grades, online (class) registration, online (class) schedules. Campuswide network is available. 100% of college-owned or -operated housing units are wired for high-speed Internet access. Wireless service is available via classrooms, computer centers, computer labs, learning centers, libraries, student centers.

Student Life *Housing:* on-campus residence required through sophomore year. *Options:* coed, disabled students. Campus housing is university owned. Freshman campus housing is guaranteed. *Activities and organizations:* drama/theater group, student-run newspaper, radio and television station, choral group, marching band, community service, athletics, Various Performance Groups, Political and Social Activism, campus publications, national fraternities, national sororities. *Campus security:* 24-hour emergency response devices and patrols, late-night transport/escort service, controlled dormitory access. *Student services:* health clinic, personal/psychological counseling, women's center.

Athletics Member NCAA. All Division I except football (Division I-AA). *Intercollegiate sports:* archery M(c)/W(c), baseball M, basketball M/W, crew M/W, cross-country running M/W, equestrian sports M(c)/W(c), fencing M/W, field hockey W, golf M/W, gymnastics W, ice hockey M/W, lacrosse M/W, riflery M(c)/W(c), rock climbing M(c)/W(c), rugby M(c)/W(c), sailing M/W, skiing (cross-country) M(c)/W(c), skiing (downhill) M(c)/W(c), soccer M/W, softball W, squash M/W, swimming and diving M/W, table tennis M(c)/W(c), tennis M/W, track and field M/W, ultimate Frisbee M(c)/W(c), volleyball M(c)/W, water polo M(c)/W(c), wrestling M(c). *Intramural sports:* badminton M(c)/W(c), baseball M, basketball M/W, bowling M/W, cheerleading M(c)/W(c), cross-country running M/W, field hockey W, football M/W, golf M/W, ice hockey M/W, soccer M/W, softball M/W, squash M/W, swimming and diving M/W, table tennis M/W, tennis M/W, ultimate Frisbee M/W, volleyball M/W, water polo M/W.

Standardized Tests *Required:* SAT and SAT Subject Tests or ACT (for admission).

Costs (2010–11) *Comprehensive fee:* $49,800 includes full-time tuition ($38,300) and room and board ($11,500). *College room only:* $6300. Room and board charges vary according to board plan. *Payment plan:* installment.

Financial Aid Of all full-time matriculated undergraduates who enrolled in 2009, 2,958 applied for aid, 2,861 were judged to have need, 2,861 had their need fully met. 606 Federal Work-Study jobs (averaging $1895). 1,564 state and other part-time jobs (averaging $2070). *Average percent of need met:* 100%. *Average financial aid package:* $39,270. *Average need-based loan:* $2136. *Average need-based gift aid:* $37,639. *Average indebtedness upon graduation:* $10,717. *Financial aid deadline:* 3/1.

Applying *Options:* electronic application, early admission, early action, deferred entrance. *Application fee:* $75. *Required:* essay or personal statement, high school transcript, 3 letters of recommendation. *Recommended:* interview. *Application deadlines:* 12/31 (freshmen), 3/1 (transfers), 11/1 (early action). *Notification:* 4/1 (freshmen), 5/15 (transfers), 12/15 (early action).

Freshman Application Contact Admissions Director, Yale University, PO Box 208234, New Haven, CT 06520. *Phone:* 203-432-9300. *E-mail:* student.questions@yale.edu. *Web site:* http://www.yale.edu/.

DELAWARE

Delaware State University
Dover, Delaware

- **State-supported** university, founded 1891, part of Delaware Higher Education Commission
- **Small-town** 400-acre campus
- **Coed** 3,372 undergraduate students, 91% full-time, 62% women, 38% men
- **Moderately difficult** entrance level, 41% of applicants were admitted

Undergraduates 3,065 full-time, 307 part-time. Students come from 32 states and territories; 14 other countries; 54% are from out of state; 66% Black or African American, non-Hispanic/Latino; 3% Hispanic/Latino; 0.9% Asian, non-Hispanic/Latino; 0.1% American Indian or Alaska Native, non-Hispanic/Latino; 21% Race/ethnicity unknown; 0.8% international; 6% transferred in; 64% live on campus. *Retention:* 58% of full-time freshmen returned.

Freshmen *Admission:* 8,229 applied, 3,414 admitted, 906 enrolled. *Average high school GPA:* 2.99. *Test scores:* SAT critical reading scores over 500: 16%; SAT math scores over 500: 20%; ACT scores over 18: 49%; SAT critical reading scores over 600: 2%; SAT math scores over 600: 2%; ACT scores over 24: 7%.

Faculty *Total:* 343, 58% full-time. *Student/faculty ratio:* 14:1.

Academics *Calendar:* semesters. *Degrees:* bachelor's, master's, and doctoral-research/scholarship. *Special study options:* academic remediation for entering students, accelerated degree program, adult/continuing education programs, advanced placement credit, cooperative education, distance learning, double majors, English as a second language, honors programs, internships, off-campus study, part-time degree program, services for LD students, study abroad, summer session for credit. *ROTC:* Army (b), Air Force (c). *Unusual degree programs:* 3-2 engineering with University of Delaware.

Computers on Campus 641 computers/terminals are available on campus for general student use. Students can access the following: campus intranet, computer help desk, free student e-mail accounts, online (class) grades, online (class) registration, online (class) schedules. Campuswide network is available. 100% of college-owned or -operated housing units are wired for high-speed Internet access. Wireless service is available via classrooms, computer centers, computer labs, learning centers, libraries, student centers.

Student Life *Housing:* on-campus residence required for freshman year. *Options:* coed, men-only, women-only, disabled students. Campus housing is university owned. Freshman applicants given priority for college housing. *Activities and organizations:* drama/theater group, student-run newspaper, radio and television station, choral group, marching band, SGA, NPHC, Women's Senate, RHA, Men's Council, national fraternities, national sororities. *Campus security:* 24-hour emergency response devices and patrols, student patrols, late-night transport/escort service, controlled dormitory access. *Student services:* health clinic, personal/psychological counseling, women's center.

Athletics Member NCAA. All Division I except football (Division I-AA). *Intercollegiate sports:* baseball M(s), basketball M(s)/W(s), bowling W(s), cheerleading M(s)/W(s), cross-country running M(s)/W(s), equestrian sports W(s), soccer W(s), softball W(s), tennis W(s), track and field M(s)/W(s), volleyball W(s). *Intramural sports:* basketball M/W, football M(c)/W(c), soccer M/W, softball M/W, swimming and diving M/W, table tennis M/W, tennis M/W, track and field M/W, volleyball M/W.

Standardized Tests *Required:* SAT or ACT (for admission).

Costs (2010–11) *Tuition:* state resident $6731 full-time, $246 per credit hour part-time; nonresident $14,310 full-time, $562 per credit hour part-time. Full-time tuition and fees vary according to reciprocity agreements. Part-time tuition and fees vary according to reciprocity agreements. *Required fees:* $830 full-time, $50 per term part-time. *Room and board:* Room and board charges vary according to board plan and housing facility. *Payment plan:* deferred payment. *Waivers:* minority students, senior citizens, and employees or children of employees.

Financial Aid Of all full-time matriculated undergraduates who enrolled in 2004, 2,315 applied for aid, 2,056 were judged to have need, 761 had their need fully met. In 2004, 471 non-need-based awards were made. *Average percent of need met:* 73%. *Average financial aid package:* $8026. *Average need-based loan:* $4925. *Average need-based gift aid:* $2443. *Average non-need-based aid:* $5223.

Applying *Options:* electronic application, early admission. *Application fee:* $25. *Required:* high school transcript, minimum 2 GPA.

Freshman Application Contact Mrs. Lawita G. Scott-Cheatham, Executive Director for Admissions, Delaware State University, 1200 North DuPont Highway, Dover, DE 19901-2277. *Phone:* 302-857-6351. *Toll-free phone:* 800-845-2544. *Fax:* 302-857-6352. *E-mail:* gcheatha@desu.edu. *Web site:* http://www.desu.edu/.

Goldey-Beacom College
Wilmington, Delaware

- **Independent** comprehensive, founded 1886
- **Suburban** 24-acre campus with easy access to Philadelphia
- **Endowment** $35.1 million
- **Coed** 724 undergraduate students, 70% full-time, 55% women, 45% men
- **Moderately difficult** entrance level

Undergraduates 508 full-time, 216 part-time. Students come from 19 states and territories; 50 other countries; 40% are from out of state; 23% Black or African American, non-Hispanic/Latino; 7% Hispanic/Latino; 6% Asian, non-Hispanic/Latino; 0.1% American Indian or Alaska Native, non-Hispanic/Latino; 8% Race/ethnicity unknown; 0.1% international; 7% transferred in; 25% live on campus. *Retention:* 85% of full-time freshmen returned.

Freshmen *Admission:* 102 admitted, 105 enrolled. *Average high school GPA:* 2.9.

Faculty *Total:* 52, 38% full-time, 54% with terminal degrees. *Student/faculty ratio:* 24:1.

Academics *Calendar:* semesters. *Degrees:* associate, bachelor's, master's, and postbachelor's certificates. *Special study options:* academic remediation for entering students, accelerated degree program, advanced placement credit, cooperative education, double majors, honors programs, internships, part-time degree program, summer session for credit. *ROTC:* Air Force (c).

Computers on Campus 159 computers/terminals are available on campus for general student use. Students can access the following: campus intranet, computer help desk, free student e-mail accounts, online (class) grades, online (class) schedules, campus Web. Campuswide network is available. 100% of college-owned or -operated housing units are wired for high-speed Internet access. Wireless service is available via entire campus.

Student Life *Housing options:* coed. Campus housing is university owned. *Activities and organizations:* student-run newspaper, Student Athletic Advisory Committee, Alpha Chi, Resident Student Association, Student Ambassadors, International Student Association. *Campus security:* 24-hour emergency response devices and patrols, student patrols, late-night transport/escort service.

Athletics Member NCAA. All Division II. *Intercollegiate sports:* basketball M(s)/W(s), cross-country running M(s)/W(s), golf M(s)/W, soccer M(s)/W(s), softball W(s), tennis W(s), volleyball W(s).

Standardized Tests *Required:* SAT or ACT (for admission).

Costs (2011–12) *Tuition:* $19,560 full-time, $623 per credit hour part-time. Full-time tuition and fees vary according to course load. Part-time tuition and fees vary according to course load. *Required fees:* $300 full-time, $10 per credit hour part-time. *Room only:* $5172. Room and board charges vary according to housing facility. *Payment plans:* installment, deferred payment. *Waivers:* employees or children of employees.

Financial Aid Of all full-time matriculated undergraduates who enrolled in 2008, 358 applied for aid, 323 were judged to have need, 50 had their need fully met. In 2008, 162 non-need-based awards were made. *Average percent of need met:* 60%. *Average financial aid package:* $14,174. *Average need-based loan:* $4597. *Average need-based gift aid:* $10,285. *Average non-need-based aid:* $4857. *Average indebtedness upon graduation:* $26,045.

Applying *Options:* electronic application, early admission, deferred entrance. *Required:* high school transcript, minimum 2 GPA. *Required for some:* 1 letter of recommendation, interview. *Application deadlines:* rolling (freshmen), rolling (transfers). *Notification:* continuous until 8/15 (freshmen), continuous until 8/15 (transfers).

Freshman Application Contact Mr. Larry Eby, Director of Admissions, Goldey-Beacom College, 4701 Limestone Road, Wilmington, DE 19808.

Phone: 302-225-6289. *Toll-free phone:* 800-833-4877. *Fax:* 302-996-5408. *E-mail:* admissions@gbc.edu. *Web site:* http://www.gbc.edu/.

Strayer University - Christiana Campus
Newark, Delaware

- **Proprietary** comprehensive
- **Coed**

Academics *Degrees:* certificates, diplomas, associate, bachelor's, master's, and postbachelor's certificates.

Costs (2010–11) *Tuition:* $13,635 full-time, $1590 per course part-time.

Freshman Application Contact Strayer University - Christiana Campus, 240 Continental Drive, Suite 108, Newark, DE 19713. *Web site:* http://www.strayer.edu/christiana.

University of Delaware
Newark, Delaware

- **State-related** university, founded 1743
- **Small-town** 1000-acre campus with easy access to Philadelphia and Baltimore
- **Coed** 16,733 undergraduate students, 91% full-time, 57% women, 43% men
- **Moderately difficult** entrance level, 54% of applicants were admitted

Undergraduates 15,146 full-time, 1,587 part-time. 63% are from out of state; 5% Black or African American, non-Hispanic/Latino; 6% Hispanic/Latino; 4% Asian, non-Hispanic/Latino; 0.2% Native Hawaiian or other Pacific Islander, non-Hispanic/Latino; 0.1% American Indian or Alaska Native, non-Hispanic/Latino; 1% Two or more races, non-Hispanic/Latino; 3% Race/ethnicity unknown; 3% international; 3% transferred in. *Retention:* 92% of full-time freshmen returned.

Freshmen *Admission:* 23,510 applied, 12,752 admitted, 3,262 enrolled. *Average high school GPA:* 3.6. *Test scores:* SAT critical reading scores over 500: 88%; SAT math scores over 500: 92%; SAT writing scores over 500: 90%; ACT scores over 18: 99%; SAT critical reading scores over 600: 43%; SAT math scores over 600: 57%; SAT writing scores over 600: 51%; ACT scores over 24: 80%; SAT critical reading scores over 700: 8%; SAT math scores over 700: 12%; SAT writing scores over 700: 10%; ACT scores over 30: 19%.

Faculty *Total:* 1,466, 80% full-time, 77% with terminal degrees. *Student/faculty ratio:* 12:1.

Academics *Calendar:* 4-1-4. *Degrees:* associate, bachelor's, master's, and doctoral-research/scholarship. *Special study options:* academic remediation for entering students, accelerated degree program, adult/continuing education programs, advanced placement credit, cooperative education, distance learning, double majors, English as a second language, honors programs, independent study, internships, part-time degree program, services for LD students, student-designed majors, study abroad, summer session for credit. *ROTC:* Army (b), Air Force (b). *Unusual degree programs:* 3-2 engineering; leadership, public administration.

Computers on Campus Students can access the following: online (class) registration, e-mail, personal Web page. Campuswide network is available.

Student Life *Housing:* on-campus residence required for freshman year. *Options:* coed, women-only, disabled students. Campus housing is university owned. Freshman campus housing is guaranteed. *Activities and organizations:* drama/theater group, student-run newspaper, radio and television station, choral group, marching band, national fraternities, national sororities. *Campus security:* 24-hour emergency response devices and patrols, student patrols, late-night transport/escort service, controlled dormitory access. *Student services:* health clinic, personal/psychological counseling, women's center.

Athletics Member NCAA. All Division I except football (Division I-AA). *Intercollegiate sports:* baseball M(s), basketball M(s)/W(s), bowling M(c)/W(c), cheerleading M(s)/W(s), crew M(c)/W(s), cross-country running M/W, equestrian sports M(c)/W(c), field hockey W(s), golf M, ice hockey M(c), lacrosse M(s)/W(s), rugby W(c), sailing M(c)/W(c), soccer M(s)/W(s), softball W(s), swimming and diving M/W(s), tennis M/W, track and field M/W(s), volleyball M/W, wrestling M(c). *Intramural sports:* badminton M/W, field hockey W(c), football M/W, golf M/W, lacrosse M(c)/W(c), racquetball M/W, soccer M/W(c), softball M/W, squash M/W, table tennis M/W, tennis M/W, ultimate Frisbee M/W, volleyball M(c)/W(c), water polo M/W.

Standardized Tests *Required:* SAT or ACT (for admission). *Recommended:* SAT Subject Tests (for admission).

Costs (2010–11) *Tuition:* state resident $9040 full-time, $377 per credit hour part-time; nonresident $24,240 full-time, $1010 per credit hour part-time. *Required fees:* $1168 full-time. *Room and board:* $9636; room only: $5826. Room and board charges vary according to board plan, housing facility, and student level. *Payment plan:* installment. *Waivers:* senior citizens and employees or children of employees.

Financial Aid Of all full-time matriculated undergraduates who enrolled in 2009, 10,382 applied for aid, 7,167 were judged to have need, 3,326 had their need fully met. In 2009, 2163 non-need-based awards were made. *Average percent of need met:* 74%. *Average financial aid package:* $13,445. *Average need-based loan:* $7755. *Average need-based gift aid:* $6734. *Average non-need-based aid:* $6467. *Average indebtedness upon graduation:* $17,200. *Financial aid deadline:* 3/15.

Applying *Options:* electronic application, early admission, deferred entrance. *Application fee:* $75. *Required:* essay or personal statement, high school transcript, 1 letter of recommendation. *Application deadlines:* 1/15 (freshmen), 5/1 (transfers). *Notification:* 3/15 (freshmen), continuous (transfers).

Freshman Application Contact Mr. Lou Hirsh, Director of Admissions, University of Delaware, 116 Hullihen Hall, Newark, DE 19716. *Phone:* 302-831-8123. *Fax:* 302-831-6905. *E-mail:* admissions@udel.edu. *Web site:* http://www.udel.edu/.

Wesley College

Dover, Delaware

Freshman Application Contact Mr. Arthur Jacobs, Director of Undergraduate Admissions, Wesley College, 120 North State Street, Dover, DE 19901-3875. *Phone:* 302-736-2400. *Toll-free phone:* 800-937-5398 Ext. 2400. *Fax:* 302-736-2382. *E-mail:* admissions@wesley.edu. *Web site:* http://www.wesley.edu/.

See page 1774 for the College Close-Up.

Wilmington University

New Castle, Delaware

- **Independent** comprehensive, founded 1967
- **Suburban** 17-acre campus with easy access to Philadelphia
- **Endowment** $15.5 million
- **Coed** 6,628 undergraduate students, 51% full-time, 62% women, 38% men
- **Noncompetitive** entrance level, 97% of applicants were admitted

Undergraduates 3,386 full-time, 3,242 part-time. Students come from 29 states and territories; 22 other countries; 23% are from out of state; 19% transferred in. *Retention:* 56% of full-time freshmen returned.

Freshmen *Admission:* 1,458 applied, 1,410 admitted, 577 enrolled.

Faculty *Total:* 1,086, 8% full-time, 22% with terminal degrees. *Student/faculty ratio:* 17:1.

Academics *Calendar:* semesters. *Degrees:* certificates, associate, bachelor's, master's, doctoral-research/scholarship, post-master's, and postbachelor's certificates. *Special study options:* academic remediation for entering students, accelerated degree program, adult/continuing education programs, cooperative education, distance learning, double majors, external degree program, independent study, internships, part-time degree program, summer session for credit. *ROTC:* Army (c), Air Force (c).

Computers on Campus 600 computers/terminals are available on campus for general student use. Students can access the following: free student e-mail accounts, online (class) grades, online (class) registration, online (class) schedules. Campuswide network is available. Wireless service is available via entire campus.

Student Life *Housing:* college housing not available. *Campus security:* 24-hour emergency response devices and patrols, late-night transport/escort service.

Athletics Member NCAA. All Division II. *Intercollegiate sports:* baseball M(s), basketball M(s)/W(s), cross-country running M(s)/W(s), softball W(s), volleyball W(s).

Costs (2010–11) *Tuition:* $7224 full-time, $301 per credit hour part-time. Full-time tuition and fees vary according to location. Part-time tuition and fees vary according to location. *Required fees:* $50 full-time. *Payment plan:* installment. *Waivers:* employees or children of employees.

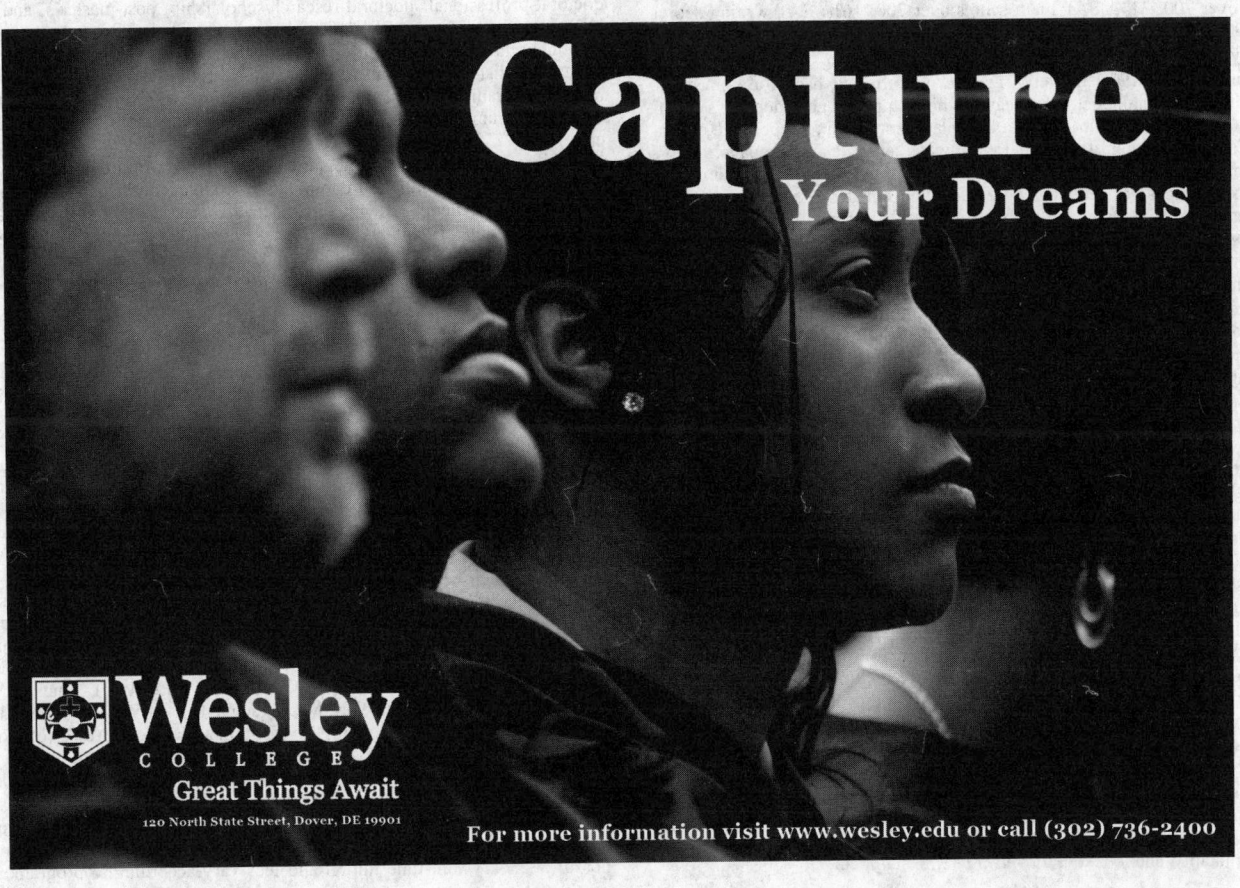

Financial Aid Of all full-time matriculated undergraduates who enrolled in 2004, 1,217 applied for aid, 900 were judged to have need. 25 Federal Work-Study jobs (averaging $2000). In 2004, 74 non-need-based awards were made. *Average percent of need met:* 48%. *Average financial aid package:* $5770. *Average need-based loan:* $3889. *Average need-based gift aid:* $2464. *Average non-need-based aid:* $1100. *Average indebtedness upon graduation:* $17,486.

Applying *Options:* early admission, deferred entrance. *Application fee:* $25. *Required:* high school transcript. *Recommended:* interview. *Application deadlines:* rolling (freshmen), rolling (transfers). *Notification:* continuous (freshmen), continuous (transfers).

Freshman Application Contact Ms. Laura Morris, Director of Admissions, Wilmington University, 320 North DuPont Highway, New Castle, DE 19720-6491. *Phone:* 302-295-1179. *Toll-free phone:* 877-967-5464. *E-mail:* undergradadmissions@wilmu.edu. *Web site:* http://www.wilmu.edu/.

DISTRICT OF COLUMBIA

American University
Washington, District of Columbia

- **Independent Methodist** university, founded 1893
- **Suburban** 84-acre campus
- **Coed** 7,070 undergraduate students, 96% full-time, 60% women, 40% men
- **Very difficult** entrance level, 43% of applicants were admitted

Undergraduates 6,813 full-time, 257 part-time. 83% are from out of state; 4% Black or African American, non-Hispanic/Latino; 6% Hispanic/Latino; 6% Asian, non-Hispanic/Latino; 0.1% Native Hawaiian or other Pacific Islander, non-Hispanic/Latino; 0.4% American Indian or Alaska Native, non-Hispanic/Latino; 3% Two or more races, non-Hispanic/Latino; 14% Race/ethnicity unknown; 7% international; 5% transferred in; 56% live on campus. *Retention:* 91% of full-time freshmen returned.

Freshmen *Admission:* 16,924 applied, 7,357 admitted, 1,502 enrolled. *Test scores:* SAT critical reading scores over 500: 96%; SAT math scores over 500: 94%; SAT writing scores over 500: 96%; ACT scores over 18: 100%; SAT critical reading scores over 600: 75%; SAT math scores over 600: 68%; SAT writing scores over 600: 70%; ACT scores over 24: 93%; SAT critical reading scores over 700: 31%; SAT math scores over 700: 16%; SAT writing scores over 700: 24%; ACT scores over 30: 41%.

Faculty *Total:* 1,221, 55% full-time. *Student/faculty ratio:* 13:1.

Academics *Calendar:* semesters. *Degrees:* certificates, bachelor's, master's, doctoral-professional, doctoral-research/scholarship, and postbachelor's certificates. *Special study options:* advanced placement credit, cooperative education, distance learning, double majors, English as a second language, honors programs, independent study, internships, off-campus study, part-time degree program, services for LD students, student-designed majors, study abroad, summer session for credit. *ROTC:* Army (c), Air Force (c). *Unusual degree programs:* 3-2 engineering with University of Maryland College Park.

Computers on Campus Students can access the following: campus intranet, computer help desk, free student e-mail accounts, online (class) grades, online (class) registration, online (class) schedules. Campuswide network is available. 100% of college-owned or -operated housing units are wired for high-speed Internet access. Wireless service is available via entire campus.

Student Life *Housing options:* coed, disabled students. Campus housing is university owned and leased by the school. Freshman campus housing is guaranteed. *Activities and organizations:* drama/theater group, student-run newspaper, radio and television station, choral group, national fraternities, national sororities. *Campus security:* 24-hour emergency response devices and patrols, late-night transport/escort service, controlled dormitory access. *Student services:* health clinic, personal/psychological counseling.

Athletics Member NCAA. All Division I. *Intercollegiate sports:* basketball M(s)/W(s), cross-country running M(s)/W(s), field hockey W(s), lacrosse W(s), soccer M(s)/W(s), swimming and diving M/W, track and field M(s)/W(s), volleyball W(s), wrestling M(s). *Intramural sports:* basketball M(c)/W, crew M(c)/W(c), equestrian sports M(c)/W(c), field hockey M(c)/W(c), football M/W, gymnastics M(c)/W(c), ice hockey M(c)/W(c), lacrosse M(c), rugby M(c)/W(c), sailing M(c)/W(c), soccer M(c)/W(c), softball M/W, tennis M(c)/W(c), ultimate Frisbee M(c)/W(c), volleyball M/W(c), weight lifting M.

Standardized Tests *Required:* SAT or ACT (for admission).

Costs (2010–11) *Comprehensive fee:* $50,165 includes full-time tuition ($36,180), mandatory fees ($517), and room and board ($13,468). Full-time tuition and fees vary according to degree level. Part-time tuition: $1205 per credit hour. Part-time tuition and fees vary according to course load. *College room only:* $9018. Room and board charges vary according to board plan, housing facility, and location. *Payment plan:* installment.

Financial Aid Of all full-time matriculated undergraduates who enrolled in 2009, 3,967 applied for aid, 3,376 were judged to have need, 665 had their need fully met. In 2009, 1075 non-need-based awards were made. *Average percent of need met:* 76%. *Average financial aid package:* $29,620. *Average need-based loan:* $5043. *Average need-based gift aid:* $14,487. *Average non-need-based aid:* $18,780. *Average indebtedness upon graduation:* $36,206. *Financial aid deadline:* 2/15.

Applying *Options:* electronic application, early decision, deferred entrance. *Application fee:* $65. *Required:* essay or personal statement, high school transcript, 2 letters of recommendation. *Application deadlines:* 1/15 (freshmen), 3/1 (transfers). *Early decision deadline:* 11/15. *Notification:* 4/1 (freshmen), continuous (transfers), 12/31 (early decision).

Freshman Application Contact Greg Grauman, Director of Admissions, American University, 4400 Massachusetts Avenue, NW, Washington, DC 20016-8001. *Phone:* 202-885-6000. *E-mail:* admissions@american.edu. *Web site:* http://www.american.edu/.

The Catholic University of America
Washington, District of Columbia

- **Independent** university, founded 1887, affiliated with Roman Catholic Church
- **Urban** 193-acre campus
- **Coed** 3,573 undergraduate students, 94% full-time, 55% women, 45% men
- **Moderately difficult** entrance level, 87% of applicants were admitted

Undergraduates 3,347 full-time, 226 part-time. Students come from 49 states and territories; 41 other countries; 96% are from out of state; 6% Black or African American, non-Hispanic/Latino; 7% Hispanic/Latino; 3% Asian, non-Hispanic/Latino; 0.2% Native Hawaiian or other Pacific Islander, non-Hispanic/Latino; 0.3% American Indian or Alaska Native, non-Hispanic/Latino; 18% Race/ethnicity unknown; 4% international; 3% transferred in; 62% live on campus. *Retention:* 80% of full-time freshmen returned.

Freshmen *Admission:* 6,207 applied, 5,386 admitted, 993 enrolled. *Average high school GPA:* 3.29. *Test scores:* SAT critical reading scores over 500: 76%; SAT math scores over 500: 78%; ACT scores over 18: 98%; SAT critical reading scores over 600: 30%; SAT math scores over 600: 31%; ACT scores over 24: 57%; SAT critical reading scores over 700: 5%; SAT math scores over 700: 3%; ACT scores over 30: 11%.

Faculty *Total:* 746, 52% full-time. *Student/faculty ratio:* 9:1.

Academics *Calendar:* semesters. *Degrees:* associate, bachelor's, master's, doctoral-professional, doctoral-research/scholarship, post-master's, and postbachelor's certificates. *Special study options:* accelerated degree program, adult/continuing education programs, advanced placement credit, cooperative education, distance learning, double majors, English as a second language, honors programs, independent study, internships, off-campus study, part-time degree program, services for LD students, study abroad, summer session for credit. *ROTC:* Army (c), Navy (c), Air Force (c). *Unusual degree programs:* 3-2 engineering; nursing; architecture, accounting, education, psychology.

Computers on Campus 500 computers/terminals and 50 ports are available on campus for general student use. Students can access the following: campus intranet, computer help desk, free student e-mail accounts, online (class) grades, online (class) registration, online (class) schedules, Internet 2, video streaming, online voting, pedagogical software. Campuswide network is available. 100% of college-owned or -operated housing units are wired for high-speed Internet access. Wireless service is available via computer centers, computer labs, dorm rooms, libraries, student centers.

Student Life *Housing:* on-campus residence required through sophomore year. *Options:* coed, men-only, women-only, disabled students. Campus housing is university owned. Freshman campus housing is guaranteed. *Activities and organizations:* drama/theater group, student-run newspaper, radio station, choral group, Habitat for Humanity, College Democrats, College Republicans, Students for Life, Centerstage Theatre Company, national fraternities, national sororities. *Campus security:* 24-hour emergency response devices and patrols, late-night transport/escort service, controlled dormitory access, controlled access of academic buildings. *Student services:* health clinic, personal/psychological counseling, legal services.

Athletics Member NCAA. All Division III. *Intercollegiate sports:* baseball M, basketball M/W, cross-country running M/W, field hockey W, football M, lacrosse M/W, soccer M/W, softball W, swimming and diving M/W, tennis M/W, track and field M/W, volleyball W. *Intramural sports:* badminton M/W, basketball M/W, cheerleading M(c)/W(c), crew M(c)/W(c), fencing M(c)/W(c), football M/W, ice hockey M(c), racquetball M/W, rugby M(c)/W(c), soccer M/W, softball M/W, tennis M/W, ultimate Frisbee M(c)/W(c), volleyball M/W.

Standardized Tests *Required:* SAT or ACT (for admission). *Recommended:* SAT Subject Tests (for admission).

Costs (2010–11) *One-time required fee:* $425. *Comprehensive fee:* $46,522 includes full-time tuition ($33,580), mandatory fees ($200), and room and board ($12,742). Full-time tuition and fees vary according to program. Part-time tuition: $1315 per credit hour. Part-time tuition and fees vary according to course load. *Required fees:* $100 per year part-time. *College room only:* $7744. Room and board charges vary according to board plan and housing facility. *Payment plan:* installment. *Waivers:* employees or children of employees.

Financial Aid Of all full-time matriculated undergraduates who enrolled in 2009, 2,292 applied for aid, 1,971 were judged to have need, 842 had their need fully met. 509 Federal Work-Study jobs (averaging $2557). In 2009, 979 non-need-based awards were made. *Average percent of need met:* 77%. *Average financial aid package:* $30,654. *Average need-based loan:* $4364. *Average need-based gift aid:* $16,212. *Average non-need-based aid:* $11,578. *Financial aid deadline:* 4/10.

Applying *Options:* electronic application, early action, deferred entrance. *Application fee:* $55. *Required:* essay or personal statement, high school transcript, 1 letter of recommendation. *Required for some:* interview. *Recommended:* minimum 3 GPA. *Application deadlines:* 2/15 (freshmen), 7/15 (transfers), 11/15 (early action). *Notification:* 3/15 (freshmen), 12/15 (early action).

Freshman Application Contact Ms. Christine Mica, Dean, University Admissions, The Catholic University of America, 102 McMahon Hall, 620 Michigan Avenue, NE, Washington, DC 20064. *Phone:* 202-319-5305. *Toll-free phone:* 800-673-2772. *Fax:* 202-319-6533. *E-mail:* cua-admissions@cua.edu. *Web site:* http://www.cua.edu/.

Corcoran College of Art and Design
Washington, District of Columbia

- **Independent** comprehensive, founded 1890
- **Urban** 7-acre campus
- **Endowment** $18.3 million
- **Coed** 406 undergraduate students, 79% full-time, 66% women, 34% men
- **Moderately difficult** entrance level, 43% of applicants were admitted

Undergraduates 319 full-time, 87 part-time. Students come from 30 states and territories; 26 other countries; 73% are from out of state; 9% Black or African American, non-Hispanic/Latino; 9% Hispanic/Latino; 8% Asian, non-Hispanic/Latino; 0.7% Native Hawaiian or other Pacific Islander, non-Hispanic/Latino; 0.5% American Indian or Alaska Native, non-Hispanic/Latino; 1% Two or more races, non-Hispanic/Latino; 7% Race/ethnicity unknown; 5% international; 12% transferred in; 21% live on campus. *Retention:* 79% of full-time freshmen returned.

Freshmen *Admission:* 576 applied, 247 admitted, 58 enrolled. *Average high school GPA:* 3.15. *Test scores:* SAT critical reading scores over 500: 60%; SAT math scores over 500: 42%; SAT writing scores over 500: 49%; ACT scores over 18: 92%; SAT critical reading scores over 600: 18%; SAT math scores over 600: 6%; SAT writing scores over 600: 9%; ACT scores over 24: 30%.

Faculty *Total:* 158, 16% full-time, 56% with terminal degrees. *Student/faculty ratio:* 10:1.

Academics *Calendar:* semesters. *Degrees:* certificates, associate, bachelor's, and master's. *Special study options:* academic remediation for entering students, adult/continuing education programs, advanced placement credit, independent study, internships, off-campus study, part-time degree program, study abroad, summer session for credit. *Unusual degree programs:* 3-2 BFA & MAT Art Education.

Computers on Campus 154 computers/terminals are available on campus for general student use. Students can access the following: campus intranet, computer help desk, free student e-mail accounts, online (class) grades, online (class) schedules. 100% of college-owned or -operated housing units are wired for high-speed Internet access. Wireless service is available via classrooms, computer centers, computer labs, dorm rooms, libraries.

Student Life *Housing options:* coed. Campus housing is leased by the school. Freshman applicants given priority for college housing. *Activities and organizations:* Student Activities Programming Board, American Society of Interior Designers, National Art Education Association, Corcoran Student Council, Society of Environmental Designers. *Campus security:* 24-hour emergency response devices and patrols, controlled dormitory access, ID check at all entrances. *Student services:* personal/psychological counseling.

Athletics *Intercollegiate sports:* ultimate Frisbee M(s)/W(s), volleyball M(s)/W(s). *Intramural sports:* ultimate Frisbee M/W, volleyball M/W.

Standardized Tests *Required:* SAT or ACT (for admission).

Costs (2011–12) *Comprehensive fee:* $42,610 includes full-time tuition ($29,940), mandatory fees ($200), and room and board ($12,470). Part-time tuition: $998 per credit hour. Part-time tuition and fees vary according to course load and degree level. *Required fees:* $998 per credit hour part-time, $200 per year part-time. *College room only:* $9970. *Payment plan:* installment. *Waivers:* employees or children of employees.

Financial Aid Of all full-time matriculated undergraduates who enrolled in 2009, 248 applied for aid, 248 were judged to have need. 48 Federal Work-Study jobs (averaging $1857). In 2009, 73 non-need-based awards were made.

Average percent of need met: 28%. *Average financial aid package:* $19,972. *Average need-based loan:* $4090. *Average need-based gift aid:* $9234. *Average non-need-based aid:* $6507. *Average indebtedness upon graduation:* $35,562.

Applying *Options:* electronic application, early admission, deferred entrance. *Application fee:* $45. *Required:* high school transcript, minimum 2.5 GPA, portfolio. *Required for some:* essay or personal statement, interview. *Recommended:* essay or personal statement, minimum 3 GPA, interview. *Application deadlines:* rolling (freshmen), rolling (transfers). *Notification:* continuous (freshmen), continuous (transfers).

Freshman Application Contact Corcoran College of Art and Design, 500 17th Street NW, Washington, DC 20006-4804. *Phone:* 202-639-1830. *Toll-free phone:* 888-CORCORAN. *Web site:* http://www.corcoran.edu/.

Gallaudet University
Washington, District of Columbia

- **Independent** university, founded 1864
- **Urban** 99-acre campus
- **Coed** 1,100 undergraduate students, 92% full-time, 55% women, 45% men
- **Moderately difficult** entrance level, 55% of applicants were admitted

Undergraduates 1,012 full-time, 88 part-time. Students come from 48 states and territories; 21 other countries; 96% are from out of state; 11% Black or African American, non-Hispanic/Latino; 10% Hispanic/Latino; 4% Asian, non-Hispanic/Latino; 0.1% Native Hawaiian or other Pacific Islander, non-Hispanic/Latino; 0.6% American Indian or Alaska Native, non-Hispanic/Latino; 2% Two or more races, non-Hispanic/Latino; 0.6% Race/ethnicity unknown; 5% international; 8% transferred in. *Retention:* 73% of full-time freshmen returned.

Freshmen *Admission:* 491 applied, 270 admitted, 198 enrolled. *Test scores:* ACT scores over 18: 43%; ACT scores over 24: 9%; ACT scores over 30: 2%.

Faculty *Student/faculty ratio:* 5:1.

Academics *Calendar:* semesters. *Degrees:* bachelor's, master's, doctoral-other, doctoral-research/scholarship, and postbachelor's certificates (undergraduate programs are open primarily to the hearing-impaired). *Special study options:* academic remediation for entering students, accelerated degree program, adult/continuing education programs, advanced placement credit, distance learning, double majors, English as a second language, honors programs, independent study, internships, off-campus study, part-time degree program, services for LD students, student-designed majors, study abroad, summer session for credit.

Computers on Campus Students can access the following: campus intranet, computer help desk, free student e-mail accounts, online (class) grades, online (class) registration, online (class) schedules. Campuswide network is available.

Student Life *Housing options:* coed, disabled students. Campus housing is university owned. *Activities and organizations:* drama/theater group, student-run newspaper, Student Body Government, Delta Epsilon, Rainbow Society, Black Deaf Student Union, national fraternities, national sororities. *Campus security:* 24-hour emergency response devices and patrols, late-night transport/escort service, controlled dormitory access. *Student services:* health clinic, personal/psychological counseling.

Athletics Member NCAA. All Division III. *Intercollegiate sports:* baseball M, basketball M/W, cross-country running M/W, football M(c), soccer M/W, softball W, swimming and diving M/W, tennis M, track and field M/W, volleyball W, wrestling M. *Intramural sports:* basketball M/W, football M/W, gymnastics M(c)/W(c), soccer M, softball W.

Standardized Tests *Required:* SAT or ACT (for admission). *Recommended:* ACT (for admission).

Costs (2010–11) *Comprehensive fee:* $20,886 includes full-time tuition ($10,850), mandatory fees ($376), and room and board ($9660). Full-time tuition and fees vary according to degree level. Part-time tuition: $543 per credit hour. Part-time tuition and fees vary according to degree level. *College room only:* $5460. Room and board charges vary according to board plan. *Waivers:* employees or children of employees.

Financial Aid Of all full-time matriculated undergraduates who enrolled in 2008, 900 applied for aid, 754 were judged to have need, 291 had their need fully met. In 2008, 42 non-need-based awards were made. *Average percent of need met:* 84%. *Average financial aid package:* $16,918. *Average need-based loan:* $3574. *Average need-based gift aid:* $15,364. *Average non-need-based aid:* $6967. *Average indebtedness upon graduation:* $13,484.

Applying *Options:* electronic application, deferred entrance. *Application fee:* $50. *Required:* essay or personal statement, high school transcript, 2 letters of recommendation, audiogram. *Required for some:* interview. *Application deadline:* rolling (freshmen). *Notification:* continuous (freshmen), continuous (transfers).

Freshman Application Contact Gallaudet University, 800 Florida Avenue, NE, Washington, DC 20002-3625. *Phone:* 202-651-5750. *Toll-free phone:* 800-995-0550. *Web site:* http://www.gallaudet.edu/.

Georgetown University
Washington, District of Columbia

- **Independent Roman Catholic (Jesuit)** university, founded 1789
- **Urban** 110-acre campus
- **Coed** 7,553 undergraduate students, 96% full-time, 55% women, 45% men
- **Most difficult** entrance level, 20% of applicants were admitted

Undergraduates 7,228 full-time, 325 part-time. Students come from 52 states and territories; 106 other countries; 98% are from out of state; 6% Black or African American, non-Hispanic/Latino; 6% Hispanic/Latino; 9% Asian, non-Hispanic/Latino; 0.1% Native Hawaiian or other Pacific Islander, non-Hispanic/Latino; 0.1% American Indian or Alaska Native, non-Hispanic/Latino; 3% Two or more races, non-Hispanic/Latino; 3% Race/ethnicity unknown; 10% international; 3% transferred in; 71% live on campus. *Retention:* 96% of full-time freshmen returned.

Freshmen *Admission:* 18,078 applied, 3,682 admitted, 1,570 enrolled. *Test scores:* SAT critical reading scores over 500: 99%; SAT math scores over 500: 99%; SAT critical reading scores over 600: 90%; SAT math scores over 600: 90%; SAT critical reading scores over 700: 50%; SAT math scores over 700: 43%.

Faculty *Total:* 1,749, 51% full-time, 74% with terminal degrees.

Academics *Calendar:* semesters. *Degrees:* certificates, bachelor's, master's, doctoral-professional, and doctoral-research/scholarship. *Special study options:* academic remediation for entering students, adult/continuing education programs, advanced placement credit, double majors, English as a second language, honors programs, independent study, internships, off-campus study, services for LD students, student-designed majors, study abroad, summer session for credit. *ROTC:* Army (b), Navy (c), Air Force (c). *Unusual degree programs:* 3-2 foreign service.

Computers on Campus Students can access the following: computer help desk, free student e-mail accounts, online (class) registration, online grade reports. Campuswide network is available. Wireless service is available via classrooms, computer centers, computer labs, dorm rooms, learning centers, libraries, student centers.

Student Life *Housing:* on-campus residence required through sophomore year. *Options:* coed, disabled students. Campus housing is university owned. Freshman campus housing is guaranteed. *Activities and organizations:* drama/theater group, student-run newspaper, radio and television station, choral group. *Campus security:* 24-hour emergency response devices and patrols, late-night transport/escort service, controlled dormitory access, student guards at residence halls and academic facilities. *Student services:* health clinic, personal/psychological counseling, women's center.

Athletics Member NCAA. All Division I except football (Division I-AA). *Intercollegiate sports:* baseball M(s), basketball M(s)/W(s), crew M/W, cross-country running M(s)/W(s), field hockey W, golf M(s), ice hockey M(c), lacrosse M(s)/W(s), rugby M(c)/W(c), sailing M/W, soccer M(s)/W(s), softball W(s), swimming and diving M/W, tennis M/W(s), track and field M(s)/W(s), ultimate Frisbee M(c)/W(c), volleyball M(c)/W(s), water polo M(c). *Intramural sports:* basketball M/W, cross-country running M/W, football M/W, golf M/W, racquetball M/W, soccer M/W, softball M/W, squash M/W, table tennis M/W, tennis M/W, track and field M/W, ultimate Frisbee M, volleyball M/W.

Standardized Tests *Required:* SAT or ACT (for admission). *Recommended:* SAT Subject Tests (for admission).

Costs (2010–11) *Comprehensive fee:* $52,443 includes full-time tuition ($39,768), mandatory fees ($435), and room and board ($12,240). Full-time tuition and fees vary according to course load and program. Part-time tuition: $1657 per credit hour. Part-time tuition and fees vary according to course load and program. *Required fees:* $435 per year part-time. *College room only:* $8770. Room and board charges vary according to board plan and housing facility. *Payment plan:* installment.

Financial Aid Of all full-time matriculated undergraduates who enrolled in 2009, 3,525 applied for aid, 3,054 were judged to have need, 3,054 had their need fully met. 1,925 Federal Work-Study jobs (averaging $2800). *Average percent of need met:* 100%. *Average financial aid package:* $33,784. *Average need-based loan:* $4716. *Average need-based gift aid:* $30,715. *Average indebtedness upon graduation:* $25,315. *Financial aid deadline:* 2/1.

Applying *Options:* electronic application, early action, deferred entrance. *Application fee:* $65. *Required:* essay or personal statement, high school transcript, 2 letters of recommendation, interview. *Application deadlines:* 1/10 (freshmen), 3/1 (transfers), 11/1 (early action). *Notification:* 4/1 (freshmen), 6/1 (transfers), 12/15 (early action).

Freshman Application Contact Mr. Charles A. Deacon, Dean of Undergraduate Admissions, Georgetown University, 37th and O Street, NW, Washington, DC 20057. *Phone:* 202-687-3600. *Fax:* 202-687-5084. *Web site:* http://www.georgetown.edu/.

The George Washington University
Washington, District of Columbia

- **Independent** university, founded 1821
- **Urban** 36-acre campus
- **Coed**
- **Very difficult** entrance level

Faculty *Student/faculty ratio:* 13:1.

Academics *Calendar:* semesters. *Degrees:* certificates, associate, bachelor's, master's, doctoral-professional, doctoral-research/scholarship, post-master's, and postbachelor's certificates.

Student Life *Campus security:* 24-hour emergency response devices and patrols, late-night transport/escort service, controlled dormitory access.

Athletics Member NCAA. All Division I.

Standardized Tests *Required:* SAT or ACT (for admission).

Costs (2010–11) *Comprehensive fee:* $53,025 includes full-time tuition ($42,860), mandatory fees ($45), and room and board ($10,120). Full-time tuition and fees vary according to student level. Part-time tuition: $1192 per credit hour. Part-time tuition and fees vary according to course load. No tuition increase for student's term of enrollment. *Required fees:* $2 per credit hour part-time, $23 per term part-time. *College room only:* $6720. Room and board charges vary according to housing facility.

Financial Aid *Of all full-time matriculated undergraduates who enrolled in 2008,* 4,663 applied for aid, 3,897 were judged to have need, 3,182 had their need fully met. *In 2008,* 2093 non-need-based awards were made. *Average percent of need met:* 93. *Average financial aid package:* $37,252. *Average need-based loan:* $6892. *Average need-based gift aid:* $24,075. *Average non-need-based aid:* $19,616. *Average indebtedness upon graduation:* $31,299. *Financial aid deadline:* 2/1.

Applying *Options:* electronic application, early admission, early decision, deferred entrance. *Application fee:* $65. *Required:* essay or personal statement, high school transcript, 2 letters of recommendation. *Recommended:* interview.

Freshman Application Contact The George Washington University, 2121 Eye Street, NW, Washington, DC 20052. *Phone:* 202-994-6040. *Toll-free phone:* 800-447-3765. *Web site:* http://www.gwu.edu/.

See page 1306 for the College Close-Up.

Howard University
Washington, District of Columbia

Director of Admissions Ms. Linda Sanders-Hawkins, Interim Director of Admissions, Howard University, 2400 Sixth Street, NW, Washington, DC 20059-0002. *Phone:* 202-806-2700. *Toll-free phone:* 800-HOWARD-U. *Fax:* 202-806-4467. *E-mail:* lsanders-hawkins@howard.edu. *Web site:* http://www.howard.edu/.

Potomac College
Washington, District of Columbia

- **Proprietary** 4-year, founded 1991
- **Urban** campus with easy access to Washington, D.C.
- **Coed**
- **Noncompetitive** entrance level

Faculty *Student/faculty ratio:* 15:1.

Academics *Calendar:* 6-week modules. *Degrees:* certificates, associate, and bachelor's.

Student Life *Campus security:* 24-hour emergency response devices.

Applying *Application fee:* $15. *Required:* high school transcript, interview.

Freshman Application Contact Asha Ellison, Assistant to the President, Potomac College, 4000 Chesapeake Street, NW, Washington, DC 20016. *Phone:* 202-686-0876 Ext. 203. *Toll-free phone:* 888-686-0876. *Fax:* 202-686-0818. *E-mail:* info@potomac.edu. *Web site:* http://www.potomac.edu/.

Strayer University - Takoma Park Campus
Washington, District of Columbia

- **Proprietary** comprehensive
- **Coed**

Academics *Degrees:* certificates, diplomas, associate, bachelor's, master's, and postbachelor's certificates.

Costs (2010–11) *Tuition:* $13,635 full-time, $1590 per course part-time.

Freshman Application Contact Strayer University - Takoma Park Campus, 6830 Laurel Street, NW, Washington, DC 20012. *Web site:* http://www.strayer.edu/takoma_park.

Strayer University - Washington Campus
Washington, District of Columbia
- **Proprietary** comprehensive
- **Coed**

Academics *Degrees:* certificates, diplomas, associate, bachelor's, master's, and postbachelor's certificates.
Costs (2010–11) *Tuition:* $13,635 full-time, $1590 per course part-time.
Freshman Application Contact Strayer University - Washington Campus, 1133 15th Street, NW, Washington, DC 200025. *Web site:* http://www.strayer.edu/washington_dc.

Trinity (Washington) University
Washington, District of Columbia
Director of Admissions Director of Admissions, Trinity (Washington) University, 125 Michigan Avenue, NE, Washington, DC 20017-1094. *Phone:* 800-492-6882. *Toll-free phone:* 800-IWANTTC. *E-mail:* admissions@trinitydc.edu. *Web site:* http://www.trinitydc.edu/.

University of Phoenix–Washington D.C. Campus
Washington, District of Columbia
Freshman Application Contact Ms. Audra McQuarie, Registrar/Executive Director, University of Phoenix–Washington D.C. Campus, 4035 South Riverpoint Parkway, Mail Stop CF-L101, Phoenix, AZ 85040. *Phone:* 480-557-6151. *Fax:* 480-643-3068. *E-mail:* audra.mcquarie@phoenix.edu. *Web site:* http://www.phoenix.edu/.

University of the District of Columbia
Washington, District of Columbia
- **District-supported** comprehensive, founded 1976
- **Urban** 28-acre campus
- **Endowment** $11.7 million
- **Coed** 5,311 undergraduate students, 44% full-time, 62% women, 38% men
- **Noncompetitive** entrance level, 63% of applicants were admitted

Undergraduates 2,314 full-time, 2,997 part-time. Students come from 42 states and territories; 93 other countries; 33% are from out of state; 49% Black or African American, non-Hispanic/Latino; 4% Hispanic/Latino; 2% Asian, non-Hispanic/Latino; 0.1% American Indian or Alaska Native, non-Hispanic/Latino; 42% Race/ethnicity unknown; 8% transferred in. *Retention:* 59% of full-time freshmen returned.
Freshmen *Admission:* 5,651 applied, 3,570 admitted, 1,024 enrolled. *Average high school GPA:* 2.
Faculty *Total:* 341, 68% full-time, 35% with terminal degrees. *Student/faculty ratio:* 13:1.
Academics *Calendar:* semesters. *Degrees:* associate, bachelor's, and master's. *Special study options:* academic remediation for entering students, accelerated degree program, adult/continuing education programs, cooperative education, English as a second language, external degree program, honors programs, internships, off-campus study, part-time degree program, services for LD students, summer session for credit. *ROTC:* Army (c), Air Force (c).
Computers on Campus 1,586 computers/terminals are available on campus for general student use. Students can access the following: campus intranet, computer help desk, free student e-mail accounts, online (class) grades, online (class) registration, online (class) schedules. Campuswide network is available. Wireless service is available via classrooms, computer labs, learning centers, libraries.
Student Life *Housing:* college housing not available. *Activities and organizations:* drama/theater group, student-run newspaper, choral group, marching band, Caribbean Student Association, Theater Arts Ensemble, National Association for the Advancement of Colored People, national fraternities, national sororities. *Campus security:* 24-hour emergency response devices and patrols. *Student services:* health clinic, personal/psychological counseling.
Athletics Member NCAA. All Division II. *Intercollegiate sports:* golf M(s), soccer M(s), tennis M(s)/W(s), track and field M(s)/W(s), volleyball W(s).
Standardized Tests *Recommended:* SAT (for admission).
Costs (2011–12) *Tuition:* district resident $6380 full-time, $266 per credit hour part-time; nonresident $13,380 full-time, $558 per credit part-time. Part-time tuition and fees vary according to course load. *Required fees:* $620 full-time, $30 per credit part-time. *Room and board:* $6660. *Payment plans:* installment, deferred payment. *Waivers:* senior citizens and employees or children of employees.

Financial Aid Of all full-time matriculated undergraduates who enrolled in 2009, 2,028 applied for aid, 1,833 were judged to have need, 750 had their need fully met. In 2009, 154 non-need-based awards were made. *Average percent of need met:* 93%. *Average financial aid package:* $5500. *Average need-based loan:* $2750. *Average need-based gift aid:* $3275. *Average non-need-based aid:* $2750. *Average indebtedness upon graduation:* $17,547.
Applying *Options:* deferred entrance. *Application fee:* $35. *Required:* high school transcript. *Required for some:* GED. *Application deadlines:* 8/1 (freshmen), 8/1 (transfers). *Notification:* continuous until 8/15 (freshmen), continuous until 8/15 (transfers).
Freshman Application Contact University of the District of Columbia, 4200 Connecticut Avenue, NW, Washington, DC 20008-1175. *Phone:* 202-274-6110. *Web site:* http://www.udc.edu/.

FLORIDA

American InterContinental University South Florida
Weston, Florida
Freshman Application Contact American InterContinental University South Florida, 2250 North Commerce Parkway, Suite 100, Weston, FL 33326. *Phone:* 877-564-6248. *Toll-free phone:* 888-603-4888. *Fax:* 877-564-6248. *Web site:* http://www.aiuniv.edu/.

Angley College
Deland, Florida
Freshman Application Contact Admissions Office, Angley College, 230 North Woodland Boulevard, Suite 310, Deland, FL 32720. *Phone:* 877-483-3635. *Toll-free phone:* 866-483-3635. *Fax:* 866-507-0524. *E-mail:* admissions@angley.edu. *Web site:* http://www.angley.edu/.

Argosy University, Sarasota
Sarasota, Florida
- **Proprietary** university, founded 1974, part of Education Management Corporation
- **Coed**

Academics *Calendar:* semesters. *Degrees:* bachelor's, master's, and doctoral-professional.
Costs (2010–11) *Tuition:* Tuition varies by program. Students should contact Argosy University for tuition information.
Freshman Application Contact Argosy University, Sarasota, 5250 17th Street, Sarasota, FL 34235. *Phone:* 941-379-0404. *Toll-free phone:* 800-331-5995. *Web site:* http://www.argosy.edu/sarasota/.
See page 1002 for the College Close-Up.

Argosy University, Tampa
Tampa, Florida
- **Proprietary** university, part of Education Management Corporation
- **Urban** campus
- **Coed**

Academics *Calendar:* semesters. *Degrees:* bachelor's, master's, and doctoral-professional.
Costs (2010–11) *Tuition:* Tuition varies by program. Students should contact Argosy University for tuition information.
Freshman Application Contact Argosy University, Tampa, 1403 North Howard Avenue, Tampa, FL 33607. *Phone:* 813-393-5290. *Toll-free phone:* 800-850-6488. *Web site:* http://www.argosy.edu/tampa/.
See page 1002 for the College Close-Up.

The Art Institute of Fort Lauderdale
Fort Lauderdale, Florida
- **Proprietary** 4-year, founded 1968, part of Education Management Corporation
- **Urban** campus with easy access to Miami
- **Coed**

Academics *Calendar:* quarters. *Degrees:* diplomas, associate, and bachelor's.
Costs (2010–11) *Tuition:* Tuition cost varies by program. Prospective students should contact the school for current tuition costs. Other charges include a

starting kit for all first-quarter students. Kits vary in price, depending on the program of study.

Freshman Application Contact The Art Institute of Fort Lauderdale, 1799 Southeast 17th Street, Fort Lauderdale, FL 33316. *Phone:* 954-463-3000. *Toll-free phone:* 800-275-7603. *Web site:* http://www.artinstitutes.edu/fortlauderdale/.

See page 1036 for the College Close-Up.

The Art Institute of Jacksonville
Jacksonville, Florida

- **Proprietary** 4-year, founded 2006, part of Education Management Corporation
- **Suburban** campus
- **Coed**

Academics *Degrees:* diplomas, associate, and bachelor's.

Costs (2010–11) *Tuition:* Tuition cost varies by program. Prospective students should contact the school for current tuition costs. Other charges include a starting kit for all first-quarter students. Kits vary in price, depending on the program of study.

Freshman Application Contact The Art Institute of Jacksonville, 8775 Baypine Road, Jacksonville, FL 32256. *Phone:* 904-486-3000. *Toll-free phone:* 800-924-1589. *Web site:* http://www.artinstitutes.edu/jacksonville/.

See page 1046 for the College Close-Up.

The Art Institute of Tampa
Tampa, Florida

- **Proprietary** 4-year, part of Education Management Corporation
- **Suburban** campus
- **Coed**

Academics *Calendar:* quarters. *Degrees:* diplomas, associate, and bachelor's.

Costs (2010–11) *Tuition:* Tuition cost varies by program. Prospective students should contact the school for current tuition costs. Other charges include a starting kit for all first-quarter students. Kits vary in price, depending on the program of study.

Freshman Application Contact The Art Institute of Tampa, Parkside at Tampa Bay Park, 4401 North Himes Avenue, Suite 150, Tampa, FL 33614. *Phone:* 813-873-2112. *Toll-free phone:* 866-703-3277. *Web site:* http://www.artinstitutes.edu/tampa/.

See page 1070 for the College Close-Up.

Ave Maria University
Ave Maria, Florida

Freshman Application Contact Ave Maria University, 5050 Ave Maria Boulevard, Ave Maria, FL 34142. *Phone:* 239-280-2487. *Toll-free phone:* 877-283-8648. *Fax:* 239-280-2559. *Web site:* http://www.avemaria.edu/.

See page 1096 for the College Close-Up.

The Baptist College of Florida
Graceville, Florida

- **Independent Southern Baptist** comprehensive, founded 1943
- **Small-town** 165-acre campus
- **Endowment** $5.4 million
- **Coed** 622 undergraduate students, 70% full-time, 38% women, 62% men
- **Noncompetitive** entrance level, 63% of applicants were admitted

Undergraduates 437 full-time, 185 part-time. Students come from 21 states and territories; 29% are from out of state; 5% Black or African American, non-Hispanic/Latino; 4% Hispanic/Latino; 0.5% Asian, non-Hispanic/Latino; 0.2% American Indian or Alaska Native, non-Hispanic/Latino; 1% Two or more races, non-Hispanic/Latino; 6% Race/ethnicity unknown; 13% transferred in; 44% live on campus. *Retention:* 65% of full-time freshmen returned.

Freshmen *Admission:* 173 applied, 109 admitted, 61 enrolled.

Faculty *Total:* 65, 34% full-time, 72% with terminal degrees. *Student/faculty ratio:* 14:1.

Academics *Calendar:* semesters. *Degrees:* certificates, associate, bachelor's, and master's. *Special study options:* academic remediation for entering students, advanced placement credit, distance learning, double majors, independent study, internships, part-time degree program, services for LD students, summer session for credit.

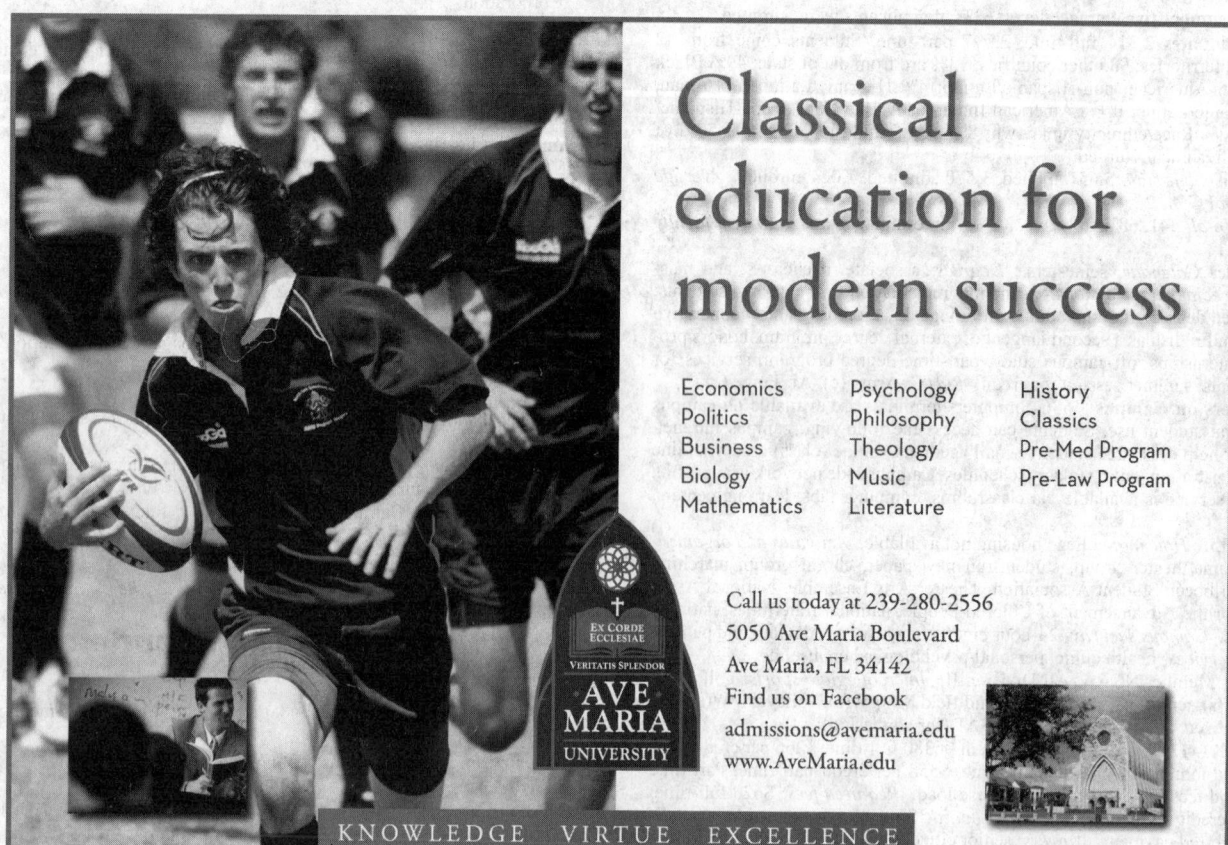

Computers on Campus 25 computers/terminals are available on campus for general student use. Students can access the following: free student e-mail accounts, online (class) grades, online (class) registration. Campuswide network is available. Wireless service is available via entire campus.

Student Life *Housing:* on-campus residence required through sophomore year. *Options:* men-only, women-only. Campus housing is university owned. Freshman campus housing is guaranteed. *Activities and organizations:* drama/theater group, student-run radio station, choral group, Baptist Collegiate Ministry, College Choir, AACC. *Campus security:* student patrols, patrols by police officers 11 pm to 7 am. *Student services:* personal/psychological counseling.

Athletics Member NCCAA. *Intercollegiate sports:* golf M, volleyball W. *Intramural sports:* basketball M/W, football M/W, soccer M/W, softball M/W, table tennis M/W, tennis M/W, ultimate Frisbee M/W, volleyball M/W.

Standardized Tests *Required:* SAT or ACT (for admission).

Costs (2010–11) *Comprehensive fee:* $12,866 includes full-time tuition ($8400), mandatory fees ($400), and room and board ($4066). Full-time tuition and fees vary according to course load and location. Part-time tuition: $280 per semester hour. Part-time tuition and fees vary according to course load and location. *Room and board:* Room and board charges vary according to board plan and housing facility. *Payment plan:* installment. *Waivers:* employees or children of employees.

Financial Aid Of all full-time matriculated undergraduates who enrolled in 2009, 496 applied for aid, 441 were judged to have need, 23 had their need fully met. 24 Federal Work-Study jobs (averaging $2035). In 2009, 14 non-need-based awards were made. *Average percent of need met:* 45%. *Average financial aid package:* $7348. *Average need-based loan:* $3325. *Average need-based gift aid:* $5145. *Average non-need-based aid:* $1428. *Average indebtedness upon graduation:* $7988. *Financial aid deadline:* 4/15.

Applying *Options:* electronic application, deferred entrance. *Application fee:* $25. *Required:* essay or personal statement, high school transcript, 2 letters of recommendation, Christian/Church Member for 1 year minimum. *Recommended:* interview. *Application deadlines:* 8/11 (freshmen), 8/11 (transfers). *Notification:* continuous (freshmen), continuous (transfers).

Freshman Application Contact The Baptist College of Florida, 5400 College Drive, Graceville, FL 32440-1898. *Phone:* 850-263-3261 Ext. 460. *Toll-free phone:* 800-328-2660 Ext. 460. *Web site:* http://www.baptistcollege.edu/.

Barry University
Miami Shores, Florida

- **Independent Roman Catholic** university, founded 1940
- **Suburban** 122-acre campus with easy access to Miami
- **Endowment** $25.1 million
- **Coed** 4,940 undergraduate students, 83% full-time, 68% women, 32% men
- **Moderately difficult** entrance level, 57% of applicants were admitted

Undergraduates 4,092 full-time, 848 part-time. 17% Black or African American, non-Hispanic/Latino; 18% Hispanic/Latino; 0.8% Asian, non-Hispanic/Latino; 0.2% American Indian or Alaska Native, non-Hispanic/Latino; 47% Race/ethnicity unknown; 6% international; 41% live on campus.

Freshmen *Admission:* 5,182 applied, 2,978 admitted, 627 enrolled. *Average high school GPA:* 2. *Test scores:* SAT critical reading scores over 500: 35%; SAT math scores over 500: 31%; ACT scores over 18: 73%; SAT critical reading scores over 600: 6%; SAT math scores over 600: 6%; ACT scores over 24: 17%.

Faculty *Total:* 861, 49% full-time. *Student/faculty ratio:* 20:1.

Academics *Calendar:* semesters. *Degrees:* certificates, bachelor's, master's, doctoral-other, doctoral-professional, doctoral-research/scholarship, post-master's, and postbachelor's certificates. *Special study options:* academic remediation for entering students, accelerated degree program, adult/continuing education programs, advanced placement credit, distance learning, double majors, English as a second language, honors programs, independent study, internships, off-campus study, part-time degree program, services for LD students, study abroad, summer session for credit. *ROTC:* Army (c), Air Force (c). *Unusual degree programs:* 3-2 engineering with University of Miami.

Computers on Campus 368 computers/terminals are available on campus for general student use. Students can access the following: campus intranet, computer help desk, free student e-mail accounts, online (class) grades, online (class) registration, online (class) schedules, Blackboard. Campuswide network is available. Wireless service is available via computer centers, computer labs, learning centers, student centers.

Student Life *Housing:* on-campus residence required for freshman year. *Options:* coed, men-only, women-only, disabled students. Campus housing is university owned. *Activities and organizations:* drama/theater group, student-run newspaper, radio and television station, choral group, Student Government

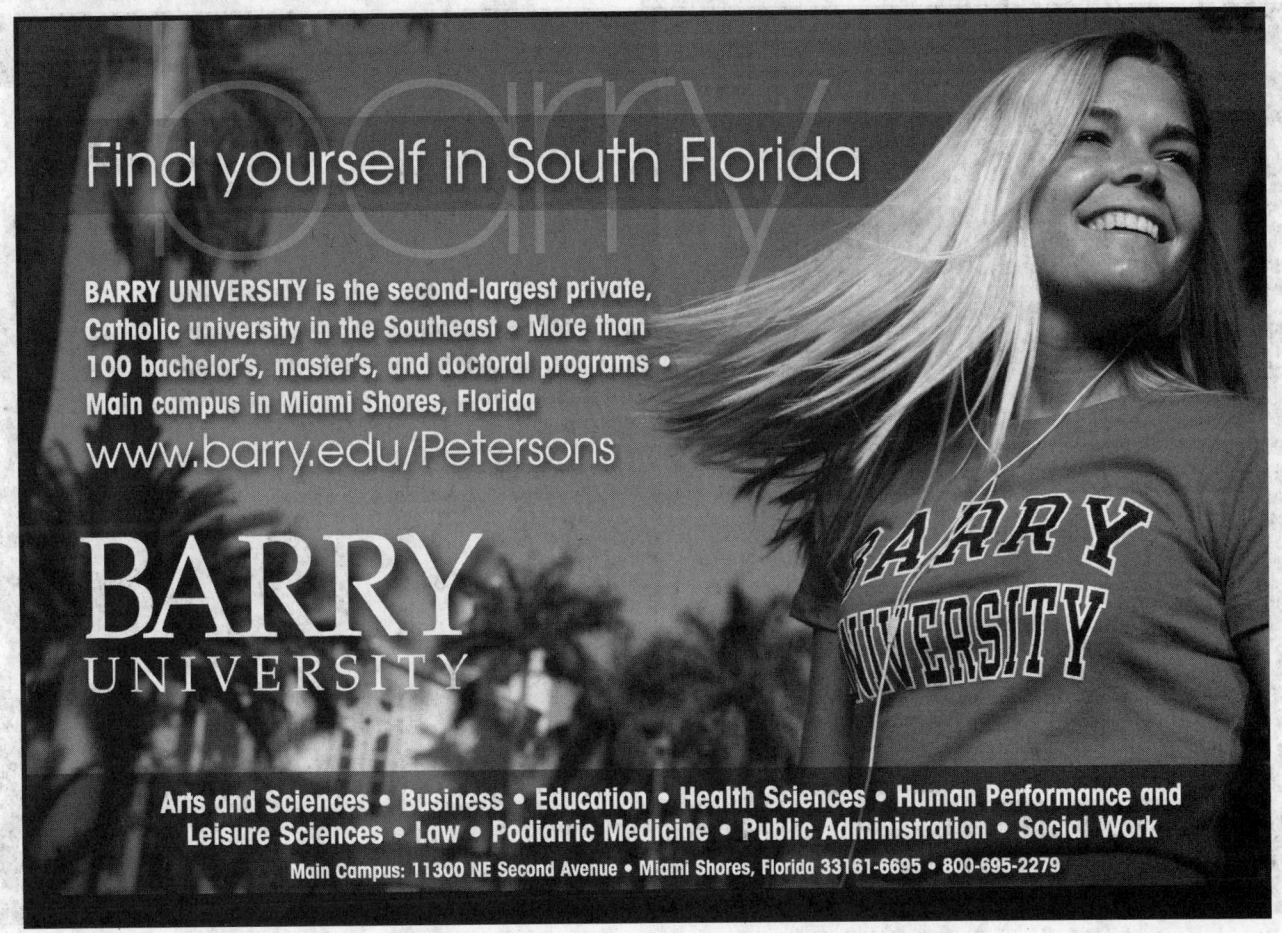

Association, Campus Activities Board, SCUBA Society, Caribbean Students Association, Jamaican Association, national fraternities, national sororities. *Campus security:* 24-hour emergency response devices and patrols, late-night transport/escort service. *Student services:* health clinic, personal/psychological counseling.

Athletics Member NCAA. All Division II. *Intercollegiate sports:* baseball M(s), basketball M(s)/W(s), crew W(s), golf M(s)/W(s), soccer M(s)/W(s), softball W(s), tennis M(s)/W(s), volleyball W(s). *Intramural sports:* basketball M/W, football M/W, golf M/W, soccer M/W, softball M/W, volleyball M/W.

Standardized Tests *Required:* SAT or ACT (for admission).

Costs (2011–12) *Tuition:* $845 per credit part-time. Full-time tuition and fees vary according to program. Part-time tuition and fees vary according to course load. *Room only:* Room and board charges vary according to board plan. *Payment plans:* tuition prepayment, installment, deferred payment. *Waivers:* employees or children of employees.

Financial Aid Of all full-time matriculated undergraduates who enrolled in 2008, 3,482 applied for aid, 3,370 were judged to have need, 128 had their need fully met. In 2008, 395 non-need-based awards were made. *Average percent of need met:* 53%. *Average financial aid package:* $20,365. *Average need-based loan:* $5212. *Average need-based gift aid:* $8596. *Average non-need-based aid:* $6786. *Average indebtedness upon graduation:* $35,880.

Applying *Options:* electronic application, early admission, deferred entrance. *Application fee:* $30. *Required:* high school transcript, minimum 2 GPA. *Required for some:* essay or personal statement. *Recommended:* interview. *Application deadlines:* rolling (freshmen), rolling (transfers). *Notification:* continuous (freshmen), continuous (transfers).

Freshman Application Contact Barry University, 11300 Northeast Second Avenue, Miami Shores, FL 33161-6695. *Phone:* 305-899-3100. *Toll-free phone:* 800-695-2279. *Web site:* http://www.barry.edu/.

See page 1106 for the College Close-Up.

Beacon College
Leesburg, Florida

- **Independent** 4-year, founded 1989
- **Small-town** 5-acre campus with easy access to Orlando
- **Coed** 139 undergraduate students, 100% full-time, 40% women, 60% men
- **Minimally difficult** entrance level, 73% of applicants were admitted

Undergraduates 139 full-time. Students come from 33 states and territories; 2 other countries; 65% are from out of state; 6% Black or African American, non-Hispanic/Latino; 7% Hispanic/Latino; 1% Asian, non-Hispanic/Latino; 2% Native Hawaiian or other Pacific Islander, non-Hispanic/Latino; 0.7% American Indian or Alaska Native, non-Hispanic/Latino; 0.7% international; 24% transferred in; 95% live on campus. *Retention:* 88% of full-time freshmen returned.

Freshmen *Admission:* 96 applied, 70 admitted, 33 enrolled. *Average high school GPA:* 3.3.

Faculty *Total:* 21, 95% full-time, 57% with terminal degrees. *Student/faculty ratio:* 6:1.

Academics *Calendar:* semesters. *Degrees:* associate and bachelor's. *Special study options:* academic remediation for entering students, adult/continuing education programs, double majors, independent study, internships, services for LD students, study abroad, summer session for credit.

Computers on Campus 44 computers/terminals are available on campus for general student use. Students can access the following: campus intranet, free student e-mail accounts. Campuswide network is available. 100% of college-owned or -operated housing units are wired for high-speed Internet access. Wireless service is available via classrooms, computer centers, computer labs, dorm rooms, learning centers, libraries, student centers.

Student Life *Housing options:* men-only, women-only. Campus housing is university owned. Freshman campus housing is guaranteed. *Activities and organizations:* drama/theater group, student-run newspaper, choral group, Bowling Club, Cooking Club, Student Government Association, national fraternities, national sororities. *Campus security:* 24-hour emergency response devices, student patrols, late-night transport/escort service. *Student services:* personal/psychological counseling.

Standardized Tests *Recommended:* SAT or ACT (for admission).

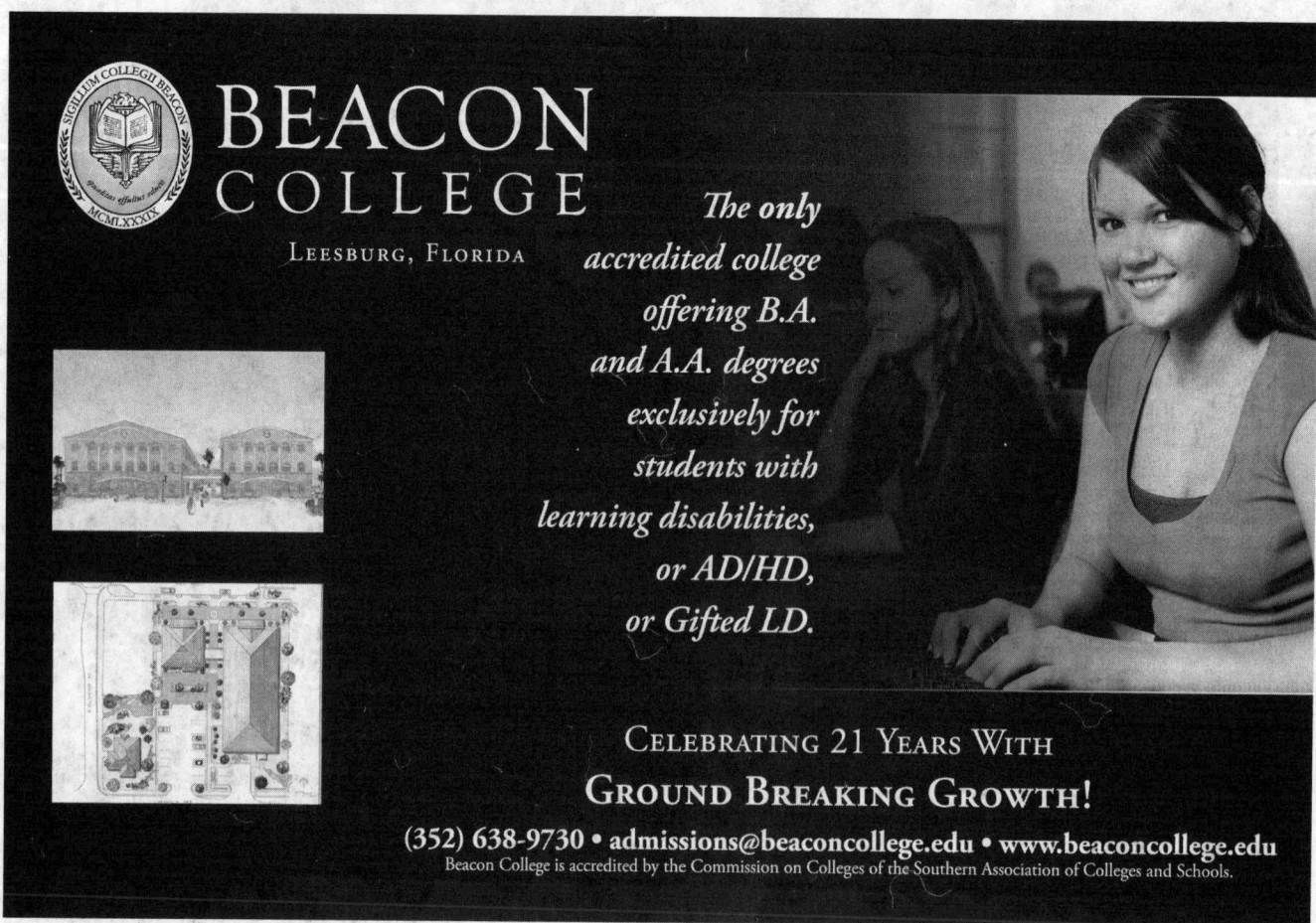

Costs (2011–12) *One-time required fee:* $400. *Comprehensive fee:* $37,900 includes full-time tuition ($28,650), mandatory fees ($900), and room and board ($8350). Part-time tuition: $610 per course. *College room only:* $5150. Room and board charges vary according to board plan and housing facility. *Payment plan:* installment.

Applying *Options:* early admission, early decision, deferred entrance. *Application fee:* $50. *Required:* essay or personal statement, high school transcript, 3 letters of recommendation, psycho-educational evaluation. *Recommended:* minimum 3 GPA, interview. *Application deadlines:* rolling (freshmen), rolling (transfers). *Notification:* 8/1 (freshmen), 8/1 (transfers).

Freshman Application Contact Mrs. Celia Corrad, Director of Admissions, Beacon College, 105 East Main Street, Leesburg, FL 34748. *Phone:* 352-787-7660. *Fax:* 352-787-0796. *E-mail:* ccorrad@beaconcollege.edu. *Web site:* http://www.beaconcollege.edu/.

See page 1114 for the College Close-Up.

Belhaven University
Orlando, Florida

Director of Admissions Jeremy Couch, Director of Admission, Belhaven University, 5200 Vineland Road, Suite 100, Orlando, FL 32811. *Phone:* 407-804-1424. *Toll-free phone:* 877-804-1424. *Fax:* 407-661-1732. *E-mail:* orlando@belhaven.edu. *Web site:* http://orlando.belhaven.edu/.

Bethune-Cookman University
Daytona Beach, Florida

- **Independent Methodist** comprehensive, founded 1904
- **Urban** 60-acre campus with easy access to Orlando
- **Endowment** $34.0 million
- **Coed** 3,545 undergraduate students, 96% full-time, 61% women, 39% men
- **Minimally difficult** entrance level, 70% of applicants were admitted

Undergraduates 3,405 full-time, 140 part-time. Students come from 39 states and territories; 18 other countries; 31% are from out of state; 92% Black or African American, non-Hispanic/Latino; 2% Hispanic/Latino; 0.2% Asian, non-Hispanic/Latino; 1% Native Hawaiian or other Pacific Islander, non-Hispanic/Latino; 0.8% Two or more races, non-Hispanic/Latino; 0.2% Race/ethnicity unknown; 2% international; 3% transferred in; 55% live on campus. *Retention:* 68% of full-time freshmen returned.

Freshmen *Admission:* 4,763 applied, 3,312 admitted, 928 enrolled. *Average high school GPA:* 2.9. *Test scores:* SAT critical reading scores over 500: 14%; SAT math scores over 500: 12%; SAT writing scores over 500: 14%; ACT scores over 18: 34%; SAT critical reading scores over 600: 1%; SAT math scores over 600: 2%; SAT writing scores over 600: 1%; ACT scores over 24: 3%; SAT math scores over 700: 1%; ACT scores over 30: 1%.

Faculty *Total:* 230, 88% full-time, 47% with terminal degrees. *Student/faculty ratio:* 17:1.

Academics *Calendar:* semesters. *Degrees:* bachelor's and master's. *Special study options:* academic remediation for entering students, accelerated degree program, adult/continuing education programs, advanced placement credit, cooperative education, distance learning, double majors, honors programs, independent study, internships, part-time degree program, study abroad, summer session for credit. *ROTC:* Army (c), Air Force (c). *Unusual degree programs:* 3-2 engineering with Tuskegee University, University of Florida, Florida Atlantic University, Florida Agricultural and Mechanical University, University of Central Florida.

Computers on Campus 451 computers/terminals are available on campus for general student use. Students can access the following: campus intranet, computer help desk, free student e-mail accounts, online (class) grades, online (class) registration, online (class) schedules. Campuswide network is available. 100% of college-owned or -operated housing units are wired for high-speed Internet access. Wireless service is available via entire campus.

Student Life *Housing:* on-campus residence required for freshman year. *Options:* men-only, women-only. Campus housing is university owned. Freshman campus housing is guaranteed. *Activities and organizations:* drama/theater group, student-run newspaper, radio station, choral group, marching band, Concert Chorale, marching band, Inspirational Gospel Choir, Student Government Association, national fraternities, national sororities. *Campus security:* 24-hour emergency response devices and patrols, student patrols, late-night transport/escort service. *Student services:* health clinic, personal/psychological counseling.

Athletics Member NCAA. All Division I except football (Division I-AA). *Intercollegiate sports:* baseball M(s), basketball M(s)/W(s), bowling W(s), cheerleading W, cross-country running M(s)/W(s), golf M(s)/W(s), softball W(s), tennis M(s)/W(s), track and field M(s)/W(s), volleyball W(s). *Intramural sports:* basketball M/W, bowling M/W, football M, racquetball W, soccer M/W, table tennis W.

Standardized Tests *Required:* SAT or ACT (for admission).

Costs (2010–11) *Comprehensive fee:* $21,552 includes full-time tuition ($13,572) and room and board ($7980). Full-time tuition and fees vary according to course load. Part-time tuition: $560 per credit hour. Part-time tuition and fees vary according to course load. *Payment plan:* installment. *Waivers:* employees or children of employees.

Financial Aid Of all full-time matriculated undergraduates who enrolled in 2009, 3,342 applied for aid, 3,216 were judged to have need, 181 had their need fully met. 230 Federal Work-Study jobs (averaging $2200). 120 state and other part-time jobs (averaging $2000). In 2009, 91 non-need-based awards were made. *Average percent of need met:* 52%. *Average financial aid package:* $13,046. *Average need-based loan:* $4659. *Average need-based gift aid:* $9245. *Average non-need-based aid:* $8636. *Average indebtedness upon graduation:* $27,103.

Applying *Options:* electronic application, early admission, deferred entrance. *Application fee:* $25. *Required:* high school transcript, minimum 2.25 GPA, 1 letter of recommendation, medical history. *Required for some:* interview. *Recommended:* essay or personal statement. *Application deadlines:* 6/30 (freshmen), 6/30 (transfers). *Notification:* continuous (freshmen), continuous (transfers).

Freshman Application Contact Mrs. Aixa Melendez, Director of Admissions, Bethune-Cookman University, 640 Dr. Mary McLeod Bethune Boulevard, Daytona Beach, FL 32114-3099. *Phone:* 386-481-2600. *Toll-free phone:* 800-448-0228. *Fax:* 386-481-2601. *E-mail:* admissions@cookman.edu. *Web site:* http://www.cookman.edu/.

Broward College
Fort Lauderdale, Florida

Freshman Application Contact Willie J. Alexander, Associate Vice President for Student Affairs/College Registrar, Broward College, 225 East Las Olas Boulevard, Fort Lauderdale, FL 33301. *Phone:* 954-201-7471. *Fax:* 954-201-7466. *E-mail:* walexand@broward.edu. *Web site:* http://www.broward.edu/.

Brown Mackie College–Miami
Miami, Florida

- **Proprietary** primarily 2-year, part of Education Management Corporation
- **Coed**

Academics *Degrees:* diplomas, associate, and bachelor's.

Costs (2010–11) *Tuition:* Tuition varies by program. Students should contact Brown Mackie College for tuition information.

Freshman Application Contact Brown Mackie College–Miami, One Herald Plaza, Miami, FL 33132. *Phone:* 305-341-6600. *Toll-free phone:* 866-505-0335. *Web site:* http://www.brownmackie.edu/miami/.

See page 1152 for the College Close-Up.

Carlos Albizu University, Miami Campus
Miami, Florida

- **Independent** comprehensive, founded 1980, part of Carlos Albizu University
- **Urban** 18-acre campus
- **Coed, primarily women** 431 undergraduate students, 60% full-time, 77% women, 23% men

Undergraduates 258 full-time, 173 part-time. 5% Black or African American, non-Hispanic/Latino; 87% Hispanic/Latino; 0.5% American Indian or Alaska Native, non-Hispanic/Latino; 3% Two or more races, non-Hispanic/Latino; 2% Race/ethnicity unknown; 2% international; 15% transferred in. *Retention:* 85% of full-time freshmen returned.

Freshmen *Admission:* 50 applied, 26 enrolled. *Average high school GPA:* 2.73.

Faculty *Total:* 56, 11% full-time, 43% with terminal degrees. *Student/faculty ratio:* 14:1.

Academics *Calendar:* trimesters. *Degrees:* certificates, diplomas, associate, bachelor's, master's, and doctoral-research/scholarship. *Special study options:* academic remediation for entering students, accelerated degree program, adult/continuing education programs, advanced placement credit, cooperative education, distance learning, double majors, English as a second language, external degree program, independent study, internships, part-time degree program, services for LD students, summer session for credit.

Computers on Campus 116 computers/terminals are available on campus for general student use. Students can access the following: computer help desk, free student e-mail accounts, online (class) grades, online (class) schedules. Campuswide network is available. Wireless service is available via entire campus.

Student Life *Housing:* college housing not available. *Activities and organizations:* student-run newspaper, Student Council, Psi Chi, Kappa Delta Pi, Nu Sigma Si, Future Educators of America. *Campus security:* 24-hour emergency response devices and patrols, late-night transport/escort service.

Costs (2010–11) *Tuition:* $11,304 full-time, $314 per credit part-time. Full-time tuition and fees vary according to course load, degree level, and program. Part-time tuition and fees vary according to course load, degree level, and program. *Required fees:* $744 full-time, $248 per term part-time. *Payment plan:* installment. *Waivers:* employees or children of employees.

Financial Aid Of all full-time matriculated undergraduates who enrolled in 2003, 121 applied for aid, 118 were judged to have need. 27 Federal Work-Study jobs (averaging $3059). *Average percent of need met:* 50%. *Average financial aid package:* $7925. *Average need-based loan:* $3549. *Average need-based gift aid:* $5300. *Average indebtedness upon graduation:* $23,000.

Applying *Options:* electronic application. *Application fee:* $25. *Required:* high school transcript, minimum 2 GPA. *Recommended:* essay or personal statement, interview. *Application deadlines:* rolling (freshmen), rolling (transfers). *Notification:* continuous (freshmen).

Freshman Application Contact Ms. Mildred Triana, Admissions Officer, Carlos Albizu University, Miami Campus, 2173 NW 99 Avenue, Miami, FL 33172. *Phone:* 305-593-1223 Ext. 259. *Toll-free phone:* 888-672-3246. *Fax:* 305-593-1854. *E-mail:* mtriana@albizu.edu. *Web site:* http://www.mia.albizu.edu/.

See page 1192 for the College Close-Up.

Chipola College
Marianna, Florida

- **State-supported** primarily 2-year, founded 1947
- **Rural** 105-acre campus
- **Coed** 2,434 undergraduate students, 44% full-time, 63% women, 37% men
- **Noncompetitive** entrance level

Undergraduates 1,073 full-time, 1,361 part-time. Students come from 11 states and territories; 3 other countries; 6% are from out of state; 17% Black or African American, non-Hispanic/Latino; 2% Hispanic/Latino; 0.7% Asian, non-Hispanic/Latino; 0.8% American Indian or Alaska Native, non-Hispanic/Latino; 4% transferred in.

Freshmen *Admission:* 269 enrolled. *Average high school GPA:* 2.5. *Test scores:* SAT critical reading scores over 500: 16%; SAT math scores over 500: 36%; ACT scores over 18: 81%; SAT critical reading scores over 600: 4%; SAT math scores over 600: 12%; ACT scores over 24: 25%; ACT scores over 30: 3%.

Faculty *Total:* 154, 28% full-time, 12% with terminal degrees. *Student/faculty ratio:* 24:1.

Academics *Calendar:* semesters. *Degrees:* certificates, associate, and bachelor's. *Special study options:* academic remediation for entering students, adult/continuing education programs, advanced placement credit, distance learning, honors programs, independent study, part-time degree program, services for LD students, summer session for credit.

Computers on Campus 80 computers/terminals are available on campus for general student use. Campuswide network is available.

Student Life *Housing:* college housing not available. *Activities and organizations:* drama/theater group, student-run newspaper, choral group, Drama/Theater Group. *Campus security:* night security personnel.

Athletics Member NJCAA. *Intercollegiate sports:* baseball M(s), basketball M(s)/W(s), softball W(s).

Costs (2011–12) *Tuition:* state resident $2790 full-time, $93 per semester hour part-time; nonresident $7950 full-time, $265 per semester hour part-time. Full-time tuition and fees vary according to degree level. Part-time tuition and fees vary according to degree level. *Required fees:* $40 full-time. *Waivers:* employees or children of employees.

Applying *Options:* early admission. *Required:* high school transcript. *Application deadlines:* rolling (freshmen), rolling (transfers). *Notification:* continuous (freshmen), continuous (transfers).

Freshman Application Contact Mrs. Kathy L. Rehberg, Registrar, Chipola College, 3094 Indian Circle, Marianna, FL 32446-3065. *Phone:* 850-718-2233. *Fax:* 850-718-2287. *E-mail:* rehbergk@chipola.edu. *Web site:* http://www.chipola.edu/.

City College
Casselberry, Florida

Director of Admissions Ms. Kimberly Bowden, Director of Admissions, City College, 853 Semoran Boulevard, Suite 200, Casselberry, FL 32707-5342.

Phone: 352-335-4000. *Fax:* 352-335-4303. *E-mail:* kbowden@ citycollege.edu. *Web site:* http://www.citycollegeorlando.edu/.

City College

Fort Lauderdale, Florida

Freshman Application Contact City College, 2000 West Commercial Boulevard, Suite 200, Fort Lauderdale, FL 33309. *Phone:* 954-492-5353. *Web site:* http://www.citycollege.edu/.

City College

Gainesville, Florida

Freshman Application Contact Admissions Office, City College, 7001 Northwest 4th Boulevard, Gainesville, FL 32607. *Phone:* 352-335-4000. *Web site:* http://www.citycollege.edu/.

City College

Miami, Florida

Freshman Application Contact Admissions Office, City College, 9300 South Dadeland Boulevard, Suite PH, Miami, FL 33156. *Phone:* 305-666-9242. *Fax:* 305-666-9243. *Web site:* http://www.citycollege.edu/.

Clearwater Christian College

Clearwater, Florida

- **Independent nondenominational** comprehensive, founded 1966
- **Suburban** 138-acre campus with easy access to Tampa-St. Petersburg
- **Endowment** $472,520
- **Coed** 570 undergraduate students, 97% full-time, 51% women, 49% men
- **Minimally difficult** entrance level, 74% of applicants were admitted

Undergraduates 554 full-time, 16 part-time. Students come from 42 states and territories; 3 other countries; 52% are from out of state; 4% Black or African American, non-Hispanic/Latino; 3% Hispanic/Latino; 1% Asian, non-Hispanic/Latino; 0.3% Native Hawaiian or other Pacific Islander, non-Hispanic/Latino; 0.2% American Indian or Alaska Native, non-Hispanic/Latino; 5% Race/ethnicity unknown; 0.5% international; 5% transferred in; 76% live on campus. *Retention:* 70% of full-time freshmen returned.

Freshmen *Admission:* 341 applied, 252 admitted, 142 enrolled. *Average high school GPA:* 3.32. *Test scores:* SAT critical reading scores over 500: 62%; SAT math scores over 500: 44%; ACT scores over 18: 94%; SAT critical reading scores over 600: 15%; SAT math scores over 600: 4%; ACT scores over 24: 38%; ACT scores over 30: 3%.

Faculty *Total:* 41, 68% full-time, 63% with terminal degrees. *Student/faculty ratio:* 18:1.

Academics *Calendar:* semesters. *Degrees:* certificates, associate, bachelor's, and master's. *Special study options:* academic remediation for entering students, advanced placement credit, distance learning, double majors, independent study, internships, off-campus study, part-time degree program, services for LD students, study abroad, summer session for credit. *ROTC:* Army (c), Navy (c), Air Force (c).

Computers on Campus 25 computers/terminals are available on campus for general student use. Students can access the following: campus intranet, computer help desk, free student e-mail accounts, online (class) grades, online (class) schedules. Campuswide network is available. 100% of college-owned or -operated housing units are wired for high-speed Internet access. Wireless service is available via entire campus.

Student Life *Housing:* on-campus residence required through senior year. *Options:* men-only, women-only. Campus housing is university owned. Freshman campus housing is guaranteed. *Activities and organizations:* drama/theater group, student-run newspaper, choral group, Drama Club, Alpha Chi, College Republicans, Science Club, Student Missionary Fellowship. *Campus security:* 24-hour emergency response devices and patrols. *Student services:* personal/psychological counseling.

Athletics Member NCCAA. *Intercollegiate sports:* baseball M, basketball M/W, golf M/W, soccer M/W, softball W, volleyball W. *Intramural sports:* basketball M/W, football M, table tennis M/W, tennis M/W, volleyball M/W.

Standardized Tests *Required:* SAT or ACT (for admission).

Costs (2011–12) *Comprehensive fee:* $23,720 includes full-time tuition ($16,250) and room and board ($7470). Part-time tuition: $635 per credit. No tuition increase for student's term of enrollment. *College room only:* $4600. Room and board charges vary according to board plan. *Payment plan:* installment. *Waivers:* employees or children of employees.

Financial Aid Of all full-time matriculated undergraduates who enrolled in 2009, 543 applied for aid, 433 were judged to have need, 65 had their need fully met. 50 Federal Work-Study jobs (averaging $670). 20 state and other part-time jobs (averaging $612). In 2009, 132 non-need-based awards were made. *Average percent of need met:* 60%. *Average financial aid package:* $10,353. *Average need-based loan:* $4324. *Average need-based gift aid:* $7918. *Average non-need-based aid:* $2848. *Average indebtedness upon graduation:* $18,000.

Applying *Options:* electronic application, early admission, deferred entrance. *Application fee:* $35. *Required:* essay or personal statement, high school transcript, minimum 2 GPA, 2 letters of recommendation, Christian testimony. *Recommended:* interview. *Application deadlines:* rolling (freshmen), rolling (transfers). *Notification:* continuous (freshmen), continuous (transfers).

Freshman Application Contact Miss Colleen Gumbert, Admissions Administrative Assistant, Clearwater Christian College, 3400 Gulf-to-Bay Boulevard, Clearwater, FL 33759-4595. *Phone:* 727-726-1153 Ext. 228. *Toll-free phone:* 800-348-4463. *Fax:* 813-726-8597. *E-mail:* admissions@ clearwater.edu. *Web site:* http://www.clearwater.edu/.

College of Central Florida

Ocala, Florida

- **State and locally supported** primarily 2-year, founded 1957, part of Florida Community College System
- **Small-town** 139-acre campus
- **Endowment** $40.1 million
- **Coed** 8,766 undergraduate students, 42% full-time, 62% women, 38% men
- **Noncompetitive** entrance level

Undergraduates 3,666 full-time, 5,100 part-time. 13% Black or African American, non-Hispanic/Latino; 10% Hispanic/Latino; 2% Asian, non-Hispanic/Latino; 0.3% American Indian or Alaska Native, non-Hispanic/Latino; 6% Race/ethnicity unknown; 1% international.

Freshmen *Admission:* 1,345 enrolled. *Test scores:* ACT scores over 18: 77%; ACT scores over 24: 29%; ACT scores over 30: 5%.

Faculty *Total:* 611, 21% full-time, 10% with terminal degrees. *Student/faculty ratio:* 18:1.

Academics *Calendar:* semesters. *Degrees:* certificates, diplomas, associate, and bachelor's. *Special study options:* academic remediation for entering students, adult/continuing education programs, advanced placement credit, cooperative education, distance learning, English as a second language, freshman honors college, honors programs, independent study, internships, part-time degree program, services for LD students, summer session for credit.

Computers on Campus 737 computers/terminals are available on campus for general student use. Students can access the following: online (class) registration. Campuswide network is available.

Student Life *Housing:* college housing not available. *Activities and organizations:* drama/theater group, student-run newspaper, choral group, Student Activities Board, African-American Student Union, ROC (Realizing Our Cause), Gay Straight Alliance, Musagettas. *Campus security:* 24-hour emergency response devices and patrols, student patrols, late-night transport/escort service. *Student services:* personal/psychological counseling.

Athletics Member NJCAA. *Intercollegiate sports:* baseball M(s), basketball M(s)/W(s), softball W(s), tennis W(s), volleyball W(s).

Standardized Tests *Recommended:* SAT (for admission), ACT (for admission), SAT or ACT (for admission), SAT and SAT Subject Tests or ACT (for admission), SAT Subject Tests (for admission).

Costs (2011–12) *Tuition:* $91 per credit hour part-time; state resident $2106 full-time, $91 per credit hour part-time; nonresident $9688 full-time, $344 per credit hour part-time. Full-time tuition and fees vary according to course level, degree level, and program. Part-time tuition and fees vary according to course level, degree level, and program. *Required fees:* $632 full-time, $21 per credit hour part-time. *Room and board:* $5796; room only: $3960. *Waivers:* employees or children of employees.

Financial Aid Of all full-time matriculated undergraduates who enrolled in 2009, 85 Federal Work-Study jobs (averaging $1505).

Applying *Options:* early admission. *Application fee:* $30. *Required:* high school transcript. *Application deadlines:* rolling (freshmen), rolling (transfers). *Notification:* continuous (freshmen), continuous (transfers).

Freshman Application Contact Ms. Devona Sewell, Registrar, Admission and Records, College of Central Florida, 3001 SW College Road, Ocala, FL 34474. *Phone:* 352-237-2111 Ext. 1398. *Fax:* 352-873-5882. *E-mail:* sewelld@cf.edu. *Web site:* http://www.cf.edu/.

Daytona State College

Daytona Beach, Florida

- **State-supported** primarily 2-year, founded 1958, part of Florida Community College System
- **Suburban** 100-acre campus with easy access to Orlando
- **Coed** 18,838 undergraduate students, 46% full-time, 61% women, 39% men
- **Noncompetitive** entrance level, 100% of applicants were admitted

Undergraduates 8,605 full-time, 10,233 part-time. Students come from 51 states and territories; 52 other countries; 9% are from out of state; 16% Black or African American, non-Hispanic/Latino; 10% Hispanic/Latino; 2% Asian, non-Hispanic/Latino; 0.5% American Indian or Alaska Native, non-Hispanic/Latino; 0.4% Two or more races, non-Hispanic/Latino; 1% Race/ethnicity unknown; 0.4% international; 3% transferred in. *Retention:* 81% of full-time freshmen returned.

Freshmen *Admission:* 2,015 applied, 2,015 admitted, 2,523 enrolled.

Faculty *Total:* 1,138, 30% full-time, 59% with terminal degrees. *Student/faculty ratio:* 22:1.

Academics *Calendar:* semesters. *Degrees:* certificates, diplomas, associate, bachelor's, and postbachelor's certificates. *Special study options:* academic remediation for entering students, adult/continuing education programs, advanced placement credit, cooperative education, distance learning, double majors, English as a second language, external degree program, freshman honors college, honors programs, independent study, internships, off-campus study, part-time degree program, services for LD students, study abroad, summer session for credit. *ROTC:* Army (c), Air Force (c).

Computers on Campus 2,942 computers/terminals are available on campus for general student use. Students can access the following: campus intranet, free student e-mail accounts, online (class) grades, online (class) registration, online (class) schedules. Campuswide network is available. Wireless service is available via entire campus.

Student Life *Housing:* college housing not available. *Activities and organizations:* drama/theater group, student-run newspaper, choral group, Florida Student Nursing Association, Phi Theta Kappa, Mu Rho Chapter, Student Government Association, Campus Crusade for Christ, Student Paralegal Association, national fraternities, national sororities. *Campus security:* 24-hour emergency response devices and patrols, late-night transport/escort service. *Student services:* personal/psychological counseling, women's center.

Athletics Member NJCAA. *Intercollegiate sports:* baseball M(s), basketball M(s)/W(s), golf W(s), softball W(s), swimming and diving M(s)/W(s). *Intramural sports:* basketball M/W, cheerleading M/W, football M/W, golf M/W, racquetball M/W, soccer M/W, table tennis M/W, tennis M/W, volleyball M/W.

Costs (2011–12) *Tuition:* state resident $2847 full-time, $95 per credit hour part-time; nonresident $10,737 full-time, $358 per credit hour part-time. Full-time tuition and fees vary according to course level, course load, degree level, and program. Part-time tuition and fees vary according to course level, course load, degree level, and program. *Required fees:* $60 full-time, $30 per term part-time. *Payment plan:* deferred payment. *Waivers:* employees or children of employees.

Financial Aid Of all full-time matriculated undergraduates who enrolled in 2009, 193 Federal Work-Study jobs (averaging $1542).

Applying *Options:* electronic application, early admission, deferred entrance. *Required:* high school transcript. *Application deadlines:* rolling (freshmen), rolling (transfers). *Notification:* continuous (freshmen), continuous (transfers).

Freshman Application Contact Mrs. Karen Sanders, Director of Admissions and Recruitment, Daytona State College, 1200 International Speedway Boulevard, Daytona Beach, FL 32114. *Phone:* 386-506-3050. *E-mail:* sanderk@daytonastate.edu. *Web site:* http://www.daytonastate.edu/.

DeVry University

Jacksonville, Florida

Admissions Office Contact DeVry University, 5200 Belfort Road, Jacksonville, FL 32256-6040. *Web site:* http://www.devry.edu/locations/campuses/loc_jacksonville.jsp.

DeVry University

Miami, Florida

Admissions Office Contact DeVry University, 8700 West Flagler Street, Suite 100, Miami, FL 33174-2535. *Web site:* http://www.devry.edu/.

DeVry University

Miramar, Florida

- **Proprietary** comprehensive, founded 2002, part of DeVry University
- **Coed** 1,320 undergraduate students, 40% full-time, 39% women, 61% men
- **Minimally difficult** entrance level

Undergraduates 528 full-time, 792 part-time. 4% are from out of state; 22% Black or African American, non-Hispanic/Latino; 41% Hispanic/Latino; 0.8% Asian, non-Hispanic/Latino; 0.1% American Indian or Alaska Native, non-Hispanic/Latino; 0.3% Two or more races, non-Hispanic/Latino; 14% Race/ethnicity unknown; 10% international; 24% transferred in.

Freshmen *Admission:* 164 enrolled.

Faculty *Total:* 67, 31% full-time. *Student/faculty ratio:* 25:1.

Academics *Calendar:* semesters. *Degrees:* associate, bachelor's, and master's. *Special study options:* academic remediation for entering students, accelerated degree program, advanced placement credit, distance learning, part-time degree program, services for LD students.

Student Life *Housing:* college housing not available.

Costs (2010–11) *Tuition:* $14,766 full-time, $580 per credit hour part-time. Full-time tuition and fees vary according to course load. Part-time tuition and fees vary according to course load. *Required fees:* $60 full-time, $30 per term part-time. *Payment plans:* installment, deferred payment. *Waivers:* employees or children of employees.

Financial Aid Of all full-time matriculated undergraduates who enrolled in 2007, 204 applied for aid, 197 were judged to have need, 2 had their need fully met. In 2007, 35 non-need-based awards were made. *Average percent of need met:* 38%. *Average financial aid package:* $12,172. *Average need-based loan:* $7414. *Average need-based gift aid:* $7044. *Average non-need-based aid:* $12,256. *Average indebtedness upon graduation:* $51,131.

Applying *Options:* electronic application, deferred entrance. *Application fee:* $50. *Required:* high school transcript, interview. *Application deadlines:* rolling (freshmen), rolling (transfers). *Notification:* continuous (freshmen), continuous (transfers).

Freshman Application Contact DeVry University, 2300 Southwest 145th Avenue, Miramar, FL 33027-4150. *Phone:* 954-499-9700. *Web site:* http://www.devry.edu/.

DeVry University

Orlando, Florida

- **Proprietary** comprehensive, founded 2000, part of DeVry University
- **Urban** 10-acre campus
- **Coed** 2,074 undergraduate students, 45% full-time, 36% women, 64% men
- **Minimally difficult** entrance level

Undergraduates 925 full-time, 1,149 part-time. 6% are from out of state; 19% Black or African American, non-Hispanic/Latino; 23% Hispanic/Latino; 2% Asian, non-Hispanic/Latino; 0.3% Native Hawaiian or other Pacific Islander, non-Hispanic/Latino; 0.6% American Indian or Alaska Native, non-Hispanic/Latino; 0.9% Two or more races, non-Hispanic/Latino; 19% Race/ethnicity unknown; 1% international; 28% transferred in.

Freshmen *Admission:* 279 enrolled.

Faculty *Total:* 170, 14% full-time. *Student/faculty ratio:* 20:1.

Academics *Calendar:* semesters. *Degrees:* associate, bachelor's, and master's. *Special study options:* academic remediation for entering students, accelerated degree program, adult/continuing education programs, advanced placement credit, distance learning, part-time degree program, services for LD students, summer session for credit.

Computers on Campus Students can access the following: online (class) registration. Campuswide network is available.

Student Life *Housing:* college housing not available. *Campus security:* 24-hour emergency response devices and patrols, late-night transport/escort service, lighted pathways/sidewalks.

Costs (2010–11) *Tuition:* $14,766 full-time, $580 per credit hour part-time. Full-time tuition and fees vary according to course load. Part-time tuition and fees vary according to course load. *Required fees:* $60 full-time, $30 per term part-time. *Payment plans:* installment, deferred payment. *Waivers:* employees or children of employees.

Financial Aid Of all full-time matriculated undergraduates who enrolled in 2007, 314 applied for aid, 294 were judged to have need, 2 had their need fully met. In 2007, 35 non-need-based awards were made. *Average percent of need met:* 33%. *Average financial aid package:* $10,774. *Average need-based loan:* $7062. *Average need-based gift aid:* $5608. *Average non-need-based aid:* $18,240. *Average indebtedness upon graduation:* $23,511.

Applying *Options:* electronic application, early admission, deferred entrance. *Application fee:* $50. *Required:* high school transcript, interview. *Application deadlines:* rolling (freshmen), rolling (transfers). *Notification:* continuous (freshmen), continuous (transfers).

Freshman Application Contact DeVry University, 4000 Millenia Boulevard, Orlando, FL 32839. *Phone:* 407-345-2800. *Web site:* http://www.devry.edu/.

DeVry University
Tampa, Florida

Admissions Office Contact DeVry University, 3030 North Rocky Point Drive West, Suite 100, Tampa, FL 33607-5901. *Web site:* http://www.devry.edu/.

Eckerd College
St. Petersburg, Florida

- **Independent Presbyterian** 4-year, founded 1958
- **Suburban** 188-acre campus with easy access to Tampa
- **Endowment** $37.8 million
- **Coed** 1,832 undergraduate students, 97% full-time, 58% women, 42% men
- **Moderately difficult** entrance level, 71% of applicants were admitted

Undergraduates 1,785 full-time, 47 part-time. Students come from 45 states and territories; 35 other countries; 73% are from out of state; 4% Black or African American, non-Hispanic/Latino; 6% Hispanic/Latino; 1% Asian, non-Hispanic/Latino; 0.1% Native Hawaiian or other Pacific Islander, non-Hispanic/Latino; 0.4% American Indian or Alaska Native, non-Hispanic/Latino; 3% Two or more races, non-Hispanic/Latino; 1% Race/ethnicity unknown; 4% international; 4% transferred in; 81% live on campus. *Retention:* 79% of full-time freshmen returned.

Freshmen *Admission:* 3,252 applied, 2,324 admitted, 500 enrolled. *Average high school GPA:* 3.3. *Test scores:* SAT critical reading scores over 500: 80%; SAT math scores over 500: 75%; SAT writing scores over 500: 75%; ACT scores over 18: 98%; SAT critical reading scores over 600: 35%; SAT math scores over 600: 35%; SAT writing scores over 600: 29%; ACT scores over 24: 63%; SAT critical reading scores over 700: 5%; SAT math scores over 700: 4%; SAT writing scores over 700: 3%; ACT scores over 30: 12%.

Faculty *Total:* 163, 67% full-time, 77% with terminal degrees. *Student/faculty ratio:* 13:1.

Academics *Calendar:* 4-1-4. *Degree:* bachelor's. *Special study options:* accelerated degree program, adult/continuing education programs, advanced placement credit, double majors, external degree program, honors programs, independent study, internships, off-campus study, part-time degree program, services for LD students, student-designed majors, study abroad, summer session for credit. *ROTC:* Army (c), Air Force (c). *Unusual degree programs:* 3-2 engineering with Columbia University, Washington University in St. Louis.

Computers on Campus 300 computers/terminals and 2,000 ports are available on campus for general student use. Students can access the following: campus intranet, computer help desk, free student e-mail accounts, online (class) grades, online (class) registration, online (class) schedules, free computer repair shop. Campuswide network is available. 100% of college-owned or -operated housing units are wired for high-speed Internet access. Wireless service is available via entire campus.

Student Life *Housing:* on-campus residence required for freshman year. *Options:* coed, women-only. Campus housing is university owned. Freshman campus housing is guaranteed. *Activities and organizations:* drama/theater group, student-run newspaper, radio and television station, choral group, Earth Society, Water Search and Rescue Team, The Current (student newspaper), College Choir, Organization of Students. *Campus security:* 24-hour emergency response devices and patrols, student patrols, late-night transport/escort service, controlled dormitory access. *Student services:* health clinic, personal/psychological counseling, women's center.

Athletics Member NCAA. All Division II. *Intercollegiate sports:* baseball M(s), basketball M(s)/W(s), golf M(s)/W, sailing M/W, soccer M(s)/W(s), softball W(s), tennis M(s)/W(s), volleyball W(s). *Intramural sports:* baseball M, basketball M/W, bowling M/W, cheerleading M(c)/W(c), equestrian sports M(c)/W(c), field hockey M(c)/W(c), football M(c)/W(c), golf M(c)/W(c), lacrosse M(c)/W(c), rugby M(c)/W(c), sailing M/W, soccer M(c)/W(c), softball M/W, swimming and diving M(c)/W(c), table tennis M/W, tennis M(c)/W(c), ultimate Frisbee M(c)/W(c), volleyball M/W.

Standardized Tests *Required:* SAT or ACT (for admission). *Recommended:* SAT Subject Tests (for admission).

Costs (2011–12) *Comprehensive fee:* $44,198 includes full-time tuition ($34,250), mandatory fees ($296), and room and board ($9652). Part-time tuition: $4110 per course. *College room only:* $4858. Room and board charges vary according to board plan and housing facility. *Payment plan:* installment. *Waivers:* employees or children of employees.

Financial Aid Of all full-time matriculated undergraduates who enrolled in 2009, 1,253 applied for aid, 1,048 were judged to have need, 246 had their need fully met. 600 Federal Work-Study jobs (averaging $2000). In 2009, 580 non-need-based awards were made. *Average percent of need met:* 87%. *Average financial aid package:* $27,743. *Average need-based loan:* $4807. Aver-

age *need-based gift aid:* $18,255. *Average non-need-based aid:* $10,777. *Average indebtedness upon graduation:* $30,494.

Applying *Options:* electronic application, deferred entrance. *Application fee:* $35. *Required:* essay or personal statement, high school transcript, 1 letter of recommendation. *Recommended:* minimum 3 GPA, interview. *Application deadlines:* rolling (freshmen), rolling (transfers). *Notification:* continuous (freshmen), continuous (transfers).

Freshman Application Contact Ms. Donna Grosso, Eckerd College, 4200 54th Avenue South, St. Petersburg, FL 33711. *Phone:* 727-864-8331. *Toll-free phone:* 800-456-9009. *Fax:* 727-866-2304. *E-mail:* admissions@eckerd.edu. *Web site:* http://www.eckerd.edu/.

Edison State College
Fort Myers, Florida

Freshman Application Contact Ms. Pat Armstrong, Admissions Specialist, Edison State College, 8099 College Parkway, Fort Myers, FL 33919. *Phone:* 239-489-9360 Ext. 1360. *Toll-free phone:* 800-749-2ECC. *E-mail:* registrar@edison.edu. *Web site:* http://www.edison.edu/.

Edward Waters College
Jacksonville, Florida

- **Independent African Methodist Episcopal** 4-year, founded 1866
- **Urban** 44-acre campus
- **Endowment** $2.0 million
- **Coed**
- **Noncompetitive** entrance level

Faculty *Student/faculty ratio:* 13:1.

Academics *Calendar:* semesters. *Degree:* bachelor's.

Student Life *Campus security:* 24-hour emergency response devices and patrols, student patrols, late-night transport/escort service, controlled dormitory access.

Athletics Member NAIA.

Costs (2010–11) *Comprehensive fee:* $16,944 includes full-time tuition ($10,470) and room and board ($6474). Part-time tuition: $436 per credit hour.

Financial Aid Of all full-time matriculated undergraduates who enrolled in 2001, 1,242 applied for aid, 1,242 were judged to have need, 11 had their need fully met. 318 Federal Work-Study jobs (averaging $851). In 2001, 262 non-need-based awards were made. *Average percent of need met:* 61. *Average financial aid package:* $4835. *Average need-based loan:* $2625. *Average need-based gift aid:* $4835. *Average non-need-based aid:* $1488. *Average indebtedness upon graduation:* $9000.

Applying *Application fee:* $25. *Required:* high school transcript, medical forms.

Freshman Application Contact Edward Waters College, 1658 Kings Road, Jacksonville, FL 32209-6199. *Phone:* 904-470-8202. *Toll-free phone:* 888-898-3191. *Web site:* http://www.ewc.edu/.

Embry-Riddle Aeronautical University–Daytona
Daytona Beach, Florida

- **Independent** comprehensive, founded 1926
- **Suburban** 178-acre campus with easy access to Orlando
- **Endowment** $63.9 million
- **Coed** 4,496 undergraduate students, 95% full-time, 15% women, 85% men
- **Moderately difficult** entrance level, 80% of applicants were admitted

Undergraduates 4,249 full-time, 247 part-time. Students come from 53 states and territories; 99 other countries; 65% are from out of state; 7% Black or African American, non-Hispanic/Latino; 9% Hispanic/Latino; 6% Asian, non-Hispanic/Latino; 0.1% Native Hawaiian or other Pacific Islander, non-Hispanic/Latino; 0.5% American Indian or Alaska Native, non-Hispanic/Latino; 1% Two or more races, non-Hispanic/Latino; 6% Race/ethnicity unknown; 14% international; 7% transferred in; 40% live on campus. *Retention:* 72% of full-time freshmen returned.

Freshmen *Admission:* 3,975 applied, 3,177 admitted, 953 enrolled. *Average high school GPA:* 3.26. *Test scores:* SAT critical reading scores over 500: 63%; SAT math scores over 500: 80%; ACT scores over 18: 93%; SAT critical reading scores over 600: 21%; SAT math scores over 600: 41%; ACT scores over 24: 55%; SAT critical reading scores over 700: 2%; SAT math scores over 700: 7%; ACT scores over 30: 12%.

Faculty *Total:* 341, 73% full-time, 52% with terminal degrees. *Student/faculty ratio:* 15:1.

Academics *Calendar:* semesters. *Degrees:* associate, bachelor's, master's, and doctoral-other. *Special study options:* academic remediation for entering students, accelerated degree program, adult/continuing education programs,

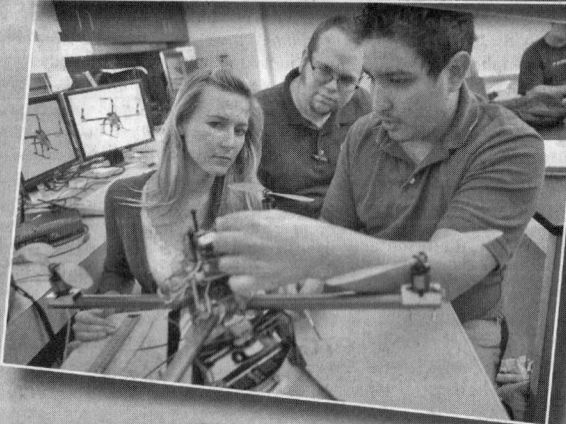

advanced placement credit, cooperative education, distance learning, double majors, English as a second language, honors programs, independent study, internships, part-time degree program, services for LD students, study abroad, summer session for credit. *ROTC:* Army (b), Navy (b), Air Force (b).

Computers on Campus 1,049 computers/terminals are available on campus for general student use. Students can access the following: campus intranet, computer help desk, free student e-mail accounts, online (class) grades, online (class) registration, online (class) schedules. Campuswide network is available. 100% of college-owned or -operated housing units are wired for high-speed Internet access. Wireless service is available via entire campus.

Student Life *Housing:* on-campus residence required for freshman year. *Options:* coed. Campus housing is university owned. Freshman campus housing is guaranteed. *Activities and organizations:* drama/theater group, student-run newspaper, radio station, choral group, Eagle Wing, Future Professional Pilots Association, African Student Association, Caribbean Student Association, Sigma Gamma Tau, national fraternities, national sororities. *Campus security:* 24-hour emergency response devices and patrols, student patrols, late-night transport/escort service, controlled dormitory access. *Student services:* health clinic, personal/psychological counseling, women's center.

Athletics Member NAIA. *Intercollegiate sports:* baseball M(s), basketball M(s), cheerleading M/W, cross-country running M(s)/W(s), golf M(s)/W(s), soccer M(s)/W(s), tennis M(s)/W(s), track and field M(s)/W(s), volleyball W(s). *Intramural sports:* basketball M/W, bowling M/W, football M/W, golf M/W, racquetball M/W, soccer M/W, softball M/W, table tennis M/W, tennis M/W, ultimate Frisbee M/W, volleyball M/W.

Standardized Tests *Required:* SAT or ACT (for admission).

Costs (2011–12) *Comprehensive fee:* $39,602 includes full-time tuition ($28,680), mandatory fees ($1172), and room and board ($9750). Part-time tuition: $1195 per credit hour. *College room only:* $5350. Room and board charges vary according to board plan and housing facility. *Payment plans:* installment, deferred payment. *Waivers:* employees or children of employees.

Financial Aid Of all full-time matriculated undergraduates who enrolled in 2009, 2,917 applied for aid, 2,557 were judged to have need. 193 Federal Work-Study jobs (averaging $1425). 1,133 state and other part-time jobs (averaging $1838). *Average financial aid package:* $15,246. *Average need-based loan:* $4672. *Average need-based gift aid:* $9085.

Applying *Options:* electronic application, deferred entrance. *Application fee:* $50. *Required:* high school transcript, minimum 2 GPA, 2 letters of recommendation. *Required for some:* minimum 3 GPA, medical examination for flight students. *Recommended:* essay or personal statement, interview. *Application deadlines:* rolling (freshmen), 6/1 (transfers). *Notification:* continuous (freshmen), continuous (transfers).

Freshman Application Contact Embry-Riddle Aeronautical University–Daytona, 600 South Clyde Morris Boulevard, Daytona Beach, FL 32114-3900. *Phone:* 386-226-6100. *Toll-free phone:* 800-862-2416. *Fax:* 386-226-7070. *E-mail:* dbadmit@erau.edu. *Web site:* http://www.embryriddle.edu/.

See page 1274 for the College Close-Up.

Embry-Riddle Aeronautical University– Worldwide
Daytona Beach, Florida

• **Independent** comprehensive, founded 1970
• **Endowment** $63.9 million
• **Coed** 11,191 undergraduate students, 22% full-time, 12% women, 88% men
• **Minimally difficult** entrance level

Undergraduates 2,504 full-time, 8,687 part-time.

Freshmen *Admission:* 479 enrolled.

Faculty *Total:* 2,531, 5% full-time, 21% with terminal degrees.

Academics *Calendar:* 5 9-week terms. *Degrees:* associate, bachelor's, master's, and doctoral-other (programs offered at 100 military bases worldwide). *Special study options:* adult/continuing education programs, advanced placement credit, cooperative education, external degree program, independent study, off-campus study, part-time degree program, services for LD students.

Student Life *Housing:* college housing not available.

Costs (2011–12) *Tuition:* $5580 full-time, $290 per credit hour part-time. Full-time tuition and fees vary according to program. Part-time tuition and fees vary according to program. *Payment plan:* deferred payment. *Waivers:* employees or children of employees.

Financial Aid Of all full-time matriculated undergraduates who enrolled in 2009, 631 applied for aid, 536 were judged to have need. *Average financial aid package:* $6753. *Average need-based loan:* $4304. *Average need-based gift aid:* $4469.

Applying *Options:* electronic application, deferred entrance. *Application fee:* $50. *Required for some:* essay or personal statement, college transcript, statement of good standing from prior institution. *Application deadlines:* rolling (freshmen), rolling (transfers). *Notification:* continuous (freshmen), continuous (transfers).

Freshman Application Contact Embry-Riddle Aeronautical University–Worldwide, 600 South Clyde Morris Boulevard, Daytona Beach, FL 32114-3900. *Phone:* 866-509-0743. *Toll-free phone:* 800-522-6787. *Fax:* 386-226-6984. *E-mail:* ecinfo@erau.edu. *Web site:* http://www.embryriddle.edu/.

Everest University

Clearwater, Florida

Freshman Application Contact Mr. Kevin Buskirk, Director of Admissions, Everest University, 2471 McMullen Road, Clearwater, FL 33759. *Phone:* 727-725-2688. *Toll-free phone:* 800-353-FMUS. *Fax:* 727-796-3406. *E-mail:* kbuskirk@cci.edu. *Web site:* http://www.everest.edu/.

Everest University

Jacksonville, Florida

Director of Admissions Mr. Robin Manning, Admissions Director, Everest University, 8226 Phillips Highway, Jacksonville, FL 32256. *Phone:* 904-731-4949. *Toll-free phone:* 888-741-4270. *E-mail:* rmanning@cci.edu. *Web site:* http://www.everest.edu/.

Everest University

Lakeland, Florida

- **Proprietary** comprehensive, founded 1890, part of Corinthian Colleges, Inc.
- **Suburban** 3-acre campus with easy access to Orlando and Tampa-St. Petersburg
- **Coed** 683 undergraduate students, 50% full-time, 79% women, 21% men
- **Minimally difficult** entrance level

Undergraduates 343 full-time, 340 part-time. Students come from 5 states and territories; 0.5% are from out of state; 1% transferred in. *Retention:* 3% of full-time freshmen returned.

Freshmen *Admission:* 302 enrolled.

Faculty *Total:* 36, 28% full-time, 100% with terminal degrees. *Student/faculty ratio:* 18:1.

Academics *Calendar:* quarters. *Degrees:* certificates, diplomas, associate, bachelor's, and master's (bachelor's degree in business administration only). *Special study options:* academic remediation for entering students, accelerated degree program, adult/continuing education programs, distance learning, external degree program, independent study, internships, part-time degree program, services for LD students, summer session for credit.

Computers on Campus 50 computers/terminals are available on campus for general student use.

Student Life *Housing:* college housing not available. *Activities and organizations:* C. J. Association, Paralegal Society, Club Med, Phi Beta Lambda. *Campus security:* 24-hour patrols.

Standardized Tests *Required:* CPAt (for admission). *Recommended:* SAT or ACT (for admission).

Financial Aid Of all full-time matriculated undergraduates who enrolled in 2002, 679 applied for aid, 646 were judged to have need, 10 had their need fully met. 6 Federal Work-Study jobs (averaging $4863). *Average percent of need met:* 76%. *Average financial aid package:* $3510. *Average need-based loan:* $3875. *Average need-based gift aid:* $1000. *Average indebtedness upon graduation:* $29,852.

Applying *Options:* early admission. *Application fee:* $25. *Required:* high school transcript, interview, Copy of original High School Diploma. *Recommended:* essay or personal statement, high school transcript.

Freshman Application Contact Ms. Patricia Sabol, Director of Student Services, Everest University, 995 East Memorial Boulevard, Suite 110, Lakeland, FL 33801. *Phone:* 863-686-1444. *Toll-free phone:* 877-225-0014. *Fax:* 863-688-9881. *E-mail:* psabol@cci.edu. *Web site:* http://www.everest.edu/.

Everest University

Melbourne, Florida

Director of Admissions Mr. Timothy Alexander, Director of Admissions, Everest University, 2401 North Harbor City Boulevard, Melbourne, FL 32935-6657. *Phone:* 321-253-2929 Ext. 121. *Web site:* http://www.everest.edu/.

Everest University

Orange Park, Florida

Freshman Application Contact Admissions Office, Everest University, 805 Wells Road, Orange Park, FL 32073. *Phone:* 904-264-9122. *Web site:* http://www.everest.edu/.

Everest University

Orlando, Florida

Freshman Application Contact Joann Derosa-Weber, Director of Admissions, Everest University, 5421 Diplomat Circle, Orlando, FL 32810-5674. *Phone:* 407-628-5870. *Toll-free phone:* 800-628-5870. *Fax:* 407-628-1344. *Web site:* http://www.everest.edu/.

Everest University

Orlando, Florida

Director of Admissions Ms. Annette Cloin, Director of Admissions, Everest University, 9200 South Park Center Loop, Orlando, FL 32819. *Phone:* 407-851-2525 Ext. 111. *Toll-free phone:* 407-851-2525 (in-state); 888-471-4270 (out-of-state). *Fax:* 407-354-7946. *Web site:* http://www.everest.edu/.

Everest University

Pompano Beach, Florida

Freshman Application Contact Martin Levert, Director of Admissions, Everest University, 225 North Federal Highway, Pompano Beach, FL 33062. *Phone:* 954-783-7339. *Fax:* 954-943-2571. *Web site:* http://www.everest.edu/.

Everest University

Tampa, Florida

- **Proprietary** comprehensive, founded 1890, part of Corinthian Colleges, Inc.
- **Urban** 4-acre campus
- **Coed** 3,386 undergraduate students, 81% full-time, 64% women, 36% men
- **Minimally difficult** entrance level, 74% of applicants were admitted

Undergraduates 2,750 full-time, 636 part-time. Students come from 15 states and territories; 3 other countries; 1% transferred in.

Freshmen *Admission:* 2,225 applied, 1,638 admitted, 1,618 enrolled.

Faculty *Total:* 61, 21% full-time. *Student/faculty ratio:* 20:1.

Academics *Calendar:* quarters. *Degrees:* diplomas, associate, bachelor's, and master's. *Special study options:* accelerated degree program, adult/continuing education programs, advanced placement credit, cooperative education, distance learning, double majors, English as a second language, external degree program, independent study, internships, part-time degree program, student-designed majors, summer session for credit.

Computers on Campus 113 computers/terminals are available on campus for general student use.

Student Life *Housing:* college housing not available. *Activities and organizations:* Legal Network, Phi Beta Lambda, Ambassadors Club. *Campus security:* 24-hour emergency response devices, evening and Saturday afternoon patrols by trained security personnel.

Standardized Tests *Required:* CPAt (for admission). *Required for some:* SAT (for admission), ACT (for admission).

Costs (2011–12) *Tuition:* $47,272 full-time. *Required fees:* $60 full-time. *Payment plans:* installment, deferred payment.

Financial Aid Of all full-time matriculated undergraduates who enrolled in 2006, 1,054 applied for aid, 1,054 were judged to have need, 850 had their need fully met. 25 Federal Work-Study jobs (averaging $4000). *Average percent of need met:* 83%. *Average financial aid package:* $6625. *Average need-based loan:* $2625. *Average need-based gift aid:* $1350. *Average indebtedness upon graduation:* $12,000.

Applying *Options:* deferred entrance. *Application fee:* $25. *Required:* high school transcript. *Application deadlines:* rolling (freshmen), rolling (transfers). *Notification:* continuous (freshmen), continuous (transfers).

Freshman Application Contact Everest University, 3319 West Hillsborough Avenue, Tampa, FL 33614-5899. *Phone:* 813-879-6000 Ext. 129. *Web site:* http://www.everest.edu/.

Everest University

Tampa, Florida

- **Proprietary** comprehensive, founded 1890, part of Corinthian Colleges, Inc.
- **Urban** 5-acre campus with easy access to Tampa
- **Coed** 12,523 undergraduate students, 18% full-time, 82% women, 18% men
- **Minimally difficult** entrance level

Undergraduates 2,196 full-time, 10,327 part-time. 31% Black or African American, non-Hispanic/Latino; 25% Hispanic/Latino; 1% Asian, non-Hispanic/Latino; 0.4% Native Hawaiian or other Pacific Islander, non-Hispanic/Latino; 0.4% American Indian or Alaska Native, non-Hispanic/Latino; 1% Two or more races, non-Hispanic/Latino; 3% Race/ethnicity unknown.

Faculty *Total:* 61, 41% full-time. *Student/faculty ratio:* 17:1.

Academics *Calendar:* quarters. *Degrees:* diplomas, associate, bachelor's, and master's. *Special study options:* academic remediation for entering students, accelerated degree program, adult/continuing education programs, cooperative education, distance learning, double majors, English as a second language, external degree program, part-time degree program, services for LD students, summer session for credit.

Computers on Campus 200 computers/terminals are available on campus for general student use. Students can access the following: online (class) grades. Campuswide network is available. Wireless service is available via entire campus.

Student Life *Housing:* college housing not available. *Activities and organizations:* Accounting Club, Medical Assistants Club, Paralegal Club, Criminal Justice Club, Surgical Technology Club. *Campus security:* 24-hour emergency response devices, On campus Security Guard on duty during business hours.

Costs (2011–12) *Tuition:* $16,272 full-time, $452 per credit hour part-time. Full-time tuition and fees vary according to degree level and program. Part-time tuition and fees vary according to degree level and program. *Required fees:* $180 full-time, $60 per term part-time. *Payment plans:* installment, deferred payment. *Waivers:* employees or children of employees.

Financial Aid Of all full-time matriculated undergraduates who enrolled in 2001, 1,000 applied for aid, 900 were judged to have need. 41 Federal Work-Study jobs (averaging $2500). In 2001, 200 non-need-based awards were made. *Average percent of need met:* 15%. *Average need-based loan:* $3500. *Average need-based gift aid:* $4000. *Average indebtedness upon graduation:* $15,000.

Applying *Options:* early admission, deferred entrance. *Application fee:* $25. *Required:* high school transcript, interview. *Application deadlines:* rolling (freshmen), rolling (transfers). *Notification:* continuous (freshmen), continuous (transfers).

Freshman Application Contact Everest University, 3924 Coconut Palm Drive, Tampa, FL 33619. *Phone:* 813-621-0041 Ext. 106. *Toll-free phone:* 877-338-0068. *Web site:* http://www.everest.edu/.

Everglades University

Altamonte Springs, Florida

Freshman Application Contact Everglades University, 887 East Altamonte Drive, Altamonte Springs, FL 32701. *Phone:* 407-277-0311. *Toll-free phone:* 866-289-1078. *Web site:* http://www.evergladesuniversity.edu/.

Everglades University

Boca Raton, Florida

Freshman Application Contact Everglades University, 5002 T-Rex Avenue, Suite 100, Boca Raton, FL 33431. *Phone:* 561-912-1211. *Toll-free phone:* 888-772-6077. *Web site:* http://www.evergladesuniversity.edu/.

Everglades University

Sarasota, Florida

Director of Admissions Director of Admissions, Everglades University, 6001 Lake Osprey Drive #110, Sarasota, FL 34240. *Phone:* 941-907-2262. *Toll-free phone:* 866-907-2262. *Fax:* 941-907-6634. *E-mail:* admissions-sar@evergladesuniversity.edu. *Web site:* http://www.evergladesuniversity.edu/.

Flagler College

St. Augustine, Florida

- **Independent** 4-year, founded 1968
- **Small-town** 42-acre campus with easy access to Jacksonville
- **Endowment** $27.8 million
- **Coed** 2,753 undergraduate students, 97% full-time, 58% women, 42% men
- **Moderately difficult** entrance level, 56% of applicants were admitted

Undergraduates 2,678 full-time, 75 part-time. Students come from 43 states and territories; 25 other countries; 32% are from out of state; 2% Black or African American, non-Hispanic/Latino; 7% Hispanic/Latino; 0.5% Asian, non-Hispanic/Latino; 0.2% Native Hawaiian or other Pacific Islander, non-Hispanic/Latino; 0.6% American Indian or Alaska Native, non-Hispanic/Latino; 3% Two or more races, non-Hispanic/Latino; 5% Race/ethnicity unknown; 2% international; 7% transferred in; 40% live on campus. *Retention:* 75% of full-time freshmen returned.

Freshmen *Admission:* 2,650 applied, 1,474 admitted, 615 enrolled. *Average high school GPA:* 3.37. *Test scores:* SAT critical reading scores over 500: 86%; SAT math scores over 500: 78%; SAT writing scores over 500: 75%; ACT scores over 18: 100%; SAT critical reading scores over 600: 24%; SAT math scores over 600: 18%; SAT writing scores over 600: 21%; ACT scores over 24: 38%; SAT critical reading scores over 700: 2%; SAT math scores over 700: 1%; SAT writing scores over 700: 3%; ACT scores over 30: 3%.

Faculty *Total:* 218, 44% full-time, 45% with terminal degrees. *Student/faculty ratio:* 18:1.

Academics *Calendar:* semesters. *Degree:* bachelor's. *Special study options:* academic remediation for entering students, advanced placement credit, double majors, independent study, internships, off-campus study, services for LD students, study abroad, summer session for credit.

Computers on Campus 250 computers/terminals are available on campus for general student use. Students can access the following: campus intranet, computer help desk, free student e-mail accounts, online (class) grades, online (class) registration, online (class) schedules. Campuswide network is available. 100% of college-owned or -operated housing units are wired for high-speed Internet access. Wireless service is available via entire campus.

Student Life *Housing:* on-campus residence required for freshman year. *Options:* men-only, women-only. Campus housing is university owned. Freshman campus housing is guaranteed. *Activities and organizations:* drama/theater group, student-run newspaper, radio station, choral group, Student Government Association, Inter-Varsity, Campus Crusade, Mu Epsilon Nu (men's service club), Phi Alpha Omega (women's service club). *Campus security:* 24-hour emergency response devices and patrols, late-night transport/escort service, controlled dormitory access. *Student services:* health clinic, personal/psychological counseling.

Athletics Member NCAA. All Division II. *Intercollegiate sports:* baseball M(s), basketball M(s)/W(s), cross-country running M(s)/W(s), golf M(s)/W(s), lacrosse M(c), soccer M(s)/W(s), softball W(s), tennis M(s)/W(s), volleyball M(c)/W(s). *Intramural sports:* badminton M/W, basketball M/W, bowling M/W, football M/W, soccer M/W, softball M/W, swimming and diving M/W, table tennis M/W, tennis M/W, volleyball M/W, weight lifting M/W.

Standardized Tests *Required:* SAT or ACT (for admission).

Costs (2010–11) *Comprehensive fee:* $21,450 includes full-time tuition ($13,860) and room and board ($7590). Part-time tuition: $465 per credit hour. *Room and board:* Room and board charges vary according to board plan. *Waivers:* employees or children of employees.

Financial Aid Of all full-time matriculated undergraduates who enrolled in 2009, 1,957 applied for aid, 1,540 were judged to have need, 279 had their need fully met. 240 Federal Work-Study jobs (averaging $1223). 65 state and other part-time jobs (averaging $1141). In 2009, 119 non-need-based awards were made. *Average percent of need met:* 90%. *Average financial aid package:* $13,820. *Average need-based loan:* $3583. *Average need-based gift aid:* $5072. *Average non-need-based aid:* $2073. *Average indebtedness upon graduation:* $20,895.

Applying *Options:* electronic application, early admission, early decision, deferred entrance. *Application fee:* $40. *Required:* essay or personal statement, high school transcript. *Recommended:* minimum 2 GPA, 1 letter of recommendation, interview, rank in upper 50% of high school class. *Application deadlines:* 3/1 (freshmen), 3/1 (transfers). *Early decision deadline:* 12/1. *Notification:* 3/30 (freshmen), 3/30 (transfers), 12/15 (early decision).

Freshman Application Contact Mr. Marc Williar, Director of Admissions, Flagler College, 74 King Street, St. Augustine, FL 32085. *Phone:* 904-819-6220. *Toll-free phone:* 800-304-4208. *Fax:* 904-819-6466. *E-mail:* admiss@flagler.edu. *Web site:* http://www.flagler.edu/.

Florida Agricultural and Mechanical University
Tallahassee, Florida

- **State-supported** university, founded 1887, part of State University System of Florida
- **Urban** 419-acre campus with easy access to Jacksonville
- **Endowment** $79.3 million
- **Coed** 11,289 undergraduate students, 92% full-time, 60% women, 40% men
- **Moderately difficult** entrance level, 61% of applicants were admitted

Undergraduates 10,336 full-time, 953 part-time. Students come from 43 states and territories; 63 other countries; 17% are from out of state; 95% Black or African American, non-Hispanic/Latino; 1% Hispanic/Latino; 0.9% Asian, non-Hispanic/Latino; 0.2% American Indian or Alaska Native, non-Hispanic/Latino; 0.5% international; 4% transferred in; 24% live on campus. *Retention:* 81% of full-time freshmen returned.
Freshmen *Admission:* 8,170 applied, 4,993 admitted, 2,742 enrolled. *Average high school GPA:* 2.93. *Test scores:* SAT critical reading scores over 500: 32%; SAT math scores over 500: 31%; SAT writing scores over 500: 25%; ACT scores over 18: 73%; SAT critical reading scores over 600: 7%; SAT math scores over 600: 7%; SAT writing scores over 600: 4%; ACT scores over 24: 10%; SAT critical reading scores over 700: 1%; SAT math scores over 700: 1%; ACT scores over 30: 1%.
Faculty *Total:* 746, 77% full-time, 58% with terminal degrees. *Student/faculty ratio:* 20:1.
Academics *Calendar:* semesters. *Degrees:* certificates, associate, bachelor's, master's, doctoral-professional, doctoral-research/scholarship, and post-master's certificates. *Special study options:* academic remediation for entering students, accelerated degree program, adult/continuing education programs, advanced placement credit, cooperative education, distance learning, double majors, honors programs, independent study, internships, off-campus study, part-time degree program, services for LD students, study abroad, summer session for credit. *ROTC:* Army (b), Navy (b), Air Force (c). *Unusual degree programs:* 3-2 business administration; pharmacy, architecture, occupational therapy.
Computers on Campus 4,000 computers/terminals and 5,400 ports are available on campus for general student use. Students can access the following: campus intranet, computer help desk, free student e-mail accounts, online (class) grades, online (class) registration, online (class) schedules. Campuswide network is available. 100% of college-owned or -operated housing units are wired for high-speed Internet access. Wireless service is available via classrooms, computer centers, computer labs, dorm rooms, learning centers, libraries, student centers.
Student Life *Housing:* on-campus residence required for freshman year. *Options:* coed, men-only, women-only, disabled students. Campus housing is university owned. Freshman applicants given priority for college housing. *Activities and organizations:* drama/theater group, student-run newspaper, radio and television station, choral group, marching band, National Council of Negro Women, FAMU Chapter, American Society of Mechanical Engineers, Psi Chi International Honor Society, Caribbean Student Association, Academy of Student Pharmacists/Student National Pharmaceutical Association, national fraternities, national sororities. *Campus security:* 24-hour emergency response devices and patrols, late-night transport/escort service, controlled dormitory access. *Student services:* health clinic, personal/psychological counseling.
Athletics Member NCAA. All Division I except football (Division I-AA). *Intercollegiate sports:* baseball M(s), basketball M(s)/W(s), bowling W(s), cheerleading M/W, cross-country running M(s)/W(s), golf M(s)/W(s), softball W(s), swimming and diving M(s)/W(s), tennis M(s)/W(s), track and field M(s)/W(s), volleyball W(s). *Intramural sports:* badminton M/W, basketball M/W, bowling M/W, cheerleading W, football M, golf M/W, gymnastics M/W, racquetball M/W, skiing (downhill) M/W, soccer M/W, softball M/W, swimming and diving M/W, table tennis M/W, tennis M/W, track and field M/W, ultimate Frisbee M/W, volleyball M/W, weight lifting M/W, wrestling M/W.
Standardized Tests *Required:* SAT or ACT (for admission).
Costs (2010–11) *Tuition:* state resident $3990 full-time, $133 per credit hour part-time; nonresident $15,933 full-time, $531 per credit hour part-time. *Required fees:* $258 full-time, $129 per term part-time. *Room and board:* $7856; room only: $4212. Room and board charges vary according to board plan and housing facility. *Waivers:* senior citizens and employees or children of employees.
Financial Aid Of all full-time matriculated undergraduates who enrolled in 2008, 7,329 applied for aid, 7,175 were judged to have need, 2,666 had their need fully met. 250 Federal Work-Study jobs (averaging $1734). In 2008, 215 non-need-based awards were made. *Average percent of need met:* 87%. *Average financial aid package:* $13,514. *Average need-based loan:* $3982. *Average need-based gift aid:* $4527. *Average non-need-based aid:* $8107. *Average indebtedness upon graduation:* $28,144.

Applying *Options:* electronic application, early admission. *Application fee:* $30. *Required:* essay or personal statement, high school transcript, minimum 2.5 GPA, 3 letters of recommendation. *Required for some:* interview, audition required of music major applicants. *Recommended:* minimum 3 GPA. *Application deadlines:* 5/15 (freshmen), 5/15 (out-of-state freshmen), 5/15 (transfers). *Notification:* continuous (freshmen), continuous (out-of-state freshmen), continuous (transfers).
Freshman Application Contact Ms. Barbara R. Cox, Director, Admissions, Florida Agricultural and Mechanical University, Office of Admissions, Florida A & M University, Tallahassee, FL 32307. *Phone:* 850-599-3796. *Fax:* 850-599-3069. *E-mail:* ugrdadmissions@famu.edu. *Web site:* http://www.famu.edu/.

Florida Atlantic University
Boca Raton, Florida

- **State-supported** university, founded 1961, part of State University System of Florida
- **Suburban** 850-acre campus with easy access to Miami, Fort Lauderdale, Palm Beach
- **Endowment** $182.3 million
- **Coed** 23,107 undergraduate students, 61% full-time, 57% women, 43% men
- **Moderately difficult** entrance level, 51% of applicants were admitted

Undergraduates 14,100 full-time, 9,007 part-time. Students come from 50 states and territories; 140 other countries; 5% are from out of state; 18% Black or African American, non-Hispanic/Latino; 22% Hispanic/Latino; 4% Asian, non-Hispanic/Latino; 0.1% Native Hawaiian or other Pacific Islander, non-Hispanic/Latino; 0.3% American Indian or Alaska Native, non-Hispanic/Latino; 1% Two or more races, non-Hispanic/Latino; 0.8% Race/ethnicity unknown; 2% international; 15% transferred in; 4% live on campus. *Retention:* 79% of full-time freshmen returned.
Freshmen *Admission:* 14,436 applied, 7,324 admitted, 2,773 enrolled. *Average high school GPA:* 3.3. *Test scores:* SAT critical reading scores over 500: 70%; SAT math scores over 500: 75%; SAT writing scores over 500: 63%; ACT scores over 18: 99%; SAT critical reading scores over 600: 17%; SAT math scores over 600: 21%; SAT writing scores over 600: 13%; ACT scores over 24: 37%; SAT critical reading scores over 700: 2%; SAT math scores over 700: 2%; SAT writing scores over 700: 1%; ACT scores over 30: 4%.
Faculty *Total:* 1,284, 62% full-time, 53% with terminal degrees. *Student/faculty ratio:* 21:1.
Academics *Calendar:* semesters. *Degrees:* certificates, associate, bachelor's, master's, doctoral-professional, doctoral-research/scholarship, and post-master's certificates. *Special study options:* accelerated degree program, adult/continuing education programs, advanced placement credit, cooperative education, distance learning, double majors, English as a second language, freshman honors college, honors programs, independent study, internships, off-campus study, part-time degree program, services for LD students, study abroad, summer session for credit. *ROTC:* Army (b), Air Force (c).
Computers on Campus 1,000 computers/terminals are available on campus for general student use. Students can access the following: campus intranet, computer help desk, free student e-mail accounts, online (class) grades, online (class) registration, online (class) schedules. Campuswide network is available. Wireless service is available via entire campus.
Student Life *Housing:* on-campus residence required for freshman year. *Options:* coed, women-only. Campus housing is university owned. Freshman campus housing is guaranteed. *Activities and organizations:* drama/theater group, student-run newspaper, radio and television station, choral group, marching band, American Society of Civil Engineers, Dive Club, Pre-Law Society, Submarine Club, American Criminal Justice Society, national fraternities, national sororities. *Campus security:* 24-hour emergency response devices and patrols, student patrols, late-night transport/escort service, controlled dormitory access. *Student services:* health clinic, personal/psychological counseling, women's center.
Athletics Member NCAA. All Division I. *Intercollegiate sports:* baseball M(s), basketball M(s)/W(s), cheerleading M/W, cross-country running M/W, football M(s), golf M(s)/W(s), soccer M/W, softball W(s), swimming and diving M/W, tennis M/W, track and field W, volleyball W(s). *Intramural sports:* baseball M/W, bowling M/W, football M, ice hockey M(c)/W(c), lacrosse M(c), rock climbing M(c)/W(c), rugby M(c)/W(c), sailing M(c)/W(c), soccer M/W, softball W, table tennis M/W, ultimate Frisbee M/W, volleyball M/W, weight lifting M(c), wrestling M(c).
Standardized Tests *Required:* SAT or ACT (for admission).
Costs (2010–11) *Tuition:* state resident $4797 full-time, $160 per credit hour part-time; nonresident $18,132 full-time, $604 per credit hour part-time. Full-time tuition and fees vary according to course load. Part-time tuition and fees vary according to course load. *Room and board:* $9690. Room and board charges vary according to board plan and housing facility. *Payment plans:* tuition prepayment, installment, deferred payment. *Waivers:* senior citizens and employees or children of employees.

Financial Aid Of all full-time matriculated undergraduates who enrolled in 2009, 9,606 applied for aid, 8,080 were judged to have need, 1,381 had their need fully met. 182 Federal Work-Study jobs (averaging $3210). 5 state and other part-time jobs (averaging $3000). In 2009, 167 non-need-based awards were made. *Average percent of need met:* 70%. *Average financial aid package:* $10,337. *Average need-based loan:* $5976. *Average need-based gift aid:* $6487. *Average non-need-based aid:* $2557. *Average indebtedness upon graduation:* $18,342.

Applying *Options:* electronic application, early admission, deferred entrance. *Application fee:* $30. *Required:* high school transcript. *Application deadline:* 5/1 (freshmen).

Freshman Application Contact Assistant Director, Florida Atlantic University, 777 Glades Road, PO Box 3091, Boca Raton, FL 33431-0991. *Phone:* 561-297-3040. *Toll-free phone:* 800-299-4FAU. *Fax:* 561-297-2758. *Web site:* http://www.fau.edu/.

See page 1290 for the College Close-Up.

Florida Christian College

Kissimmee, Florida

Director of Admissions Admissions Office, Florida Christian College, 1011 Bill Beck Boulevard, Kissimmee, FL 34744-5301. *Phone:* 407-569-1172. *Toll-free phone:* 888-GO-TO-FCC. *E-mail:* admissionsforms@fcc.edu. *Web site:* http://www.fcc.edu/.

Florida College

Temple Terrace, Florida

- **Independent** 4-year, founded 1944
- **Small-town** 95-acre campus with easy access to Tampa
- **Endowment** $10.4 million
- **Coed** 478 undergraduate students, 96% full-time, 53% women, 47% men
- **Moderately difficult** entrance level, 57% of applicants were admitted

Undergraduates 459 full-time, 19 part-time. Students come from 4 other countries; 66% are from out of state; 6% Black or African American, non-Hispanic/Latino; 4% Hispanic/Latino; 0.4% Asian, non-Hispanic/Latino; 0.6% Native Hawaiian or other Pacific Islander, non-Hispanic/Latino; 1% American Indian or Alaska Native, non-Hispanic/Latino; 3% Two or more races, non-Hispanic/Latino; 2% international; 4% transferred in; 78% live on campus.

Freshmen *Admission:* 380 applied, 217 admitted, 200 enrolled. *Test scores:* SAT critical reading scores over 500: 66%; SAT math scores over 500: 55%; SAT writing scores over 500: 51%; ACT scores over 18: 84%; SAT critical reading scores over 600: 23%; SAT math scores over 600: 20%; SAT writing scores over 600: 17%; ACT scores over 24: 38%; SAT critical reading scores over 700: 4%; SAT math scores over 700: 1%; SAT writing scores over 700: 3%; ACT scores over 30: 7%.

Faculty *Total:* 56, 66% full-time, 30% with terminal degrees. *Student/faculty ratio:* 11:1.

Academics *Calendar:* semesters. *Degrees:* associate and bachelor's. *Special study options:* academic remediation for entering students, advanced placement credit, independent study, summer session for credit. *ROTC:* Army (c), Air Force (c).

Computers on Campus 36 computers/terminals are available on campus for general student use. Students can access the following: campus intranet, computer help desk, free student e-mail accounts, online (class) grades, online (class) schedules. Campuswide network is available. 100% of college-owned or -operated housing units are wired for high-speed Internet access. Wireless service is available via classrooms, computer centers, computer labs, dorm rooms, libraries, student centers.

Student Life *Housing:* on-campus residence required through sophomore year. *Options:* men-only, women-only. Campus housing is university owned. Freshman campus housing is guaranteed. *Activities and organizations:* drama/theater group, choral group, Co-ed Societies, Circle K, CMENC, SBGA, Footlighters. *Campus security:* controlled dormitory access, evening patrols by trained security personnel. *Student services:* health clinic, personal/psychological counseling.

Athletics Member USCAA. *Intercollegiate sports:* basketball M(s), cheerleading W, cross-country running M(s)/W(s), volleyball W(s). *Intramural sports:* basketball M/W, football M/W, soccer M/W, softball M/W, ultimate Frisbee M/W, volleyball M/W.

Standardized Tests *Required:* SAT or ACT (for admission).

Costs (2010–11) *One-time required fee:* $150. *Comprehensive fee:* $19,390 includes full-time tuition ($11,600), mandatory fees ($750), and room and board ($7040). Part-time tuition: $485 per credit hour. Part-time tuition and fees vary according to course load. *Required fees:* $300 per term part-time.

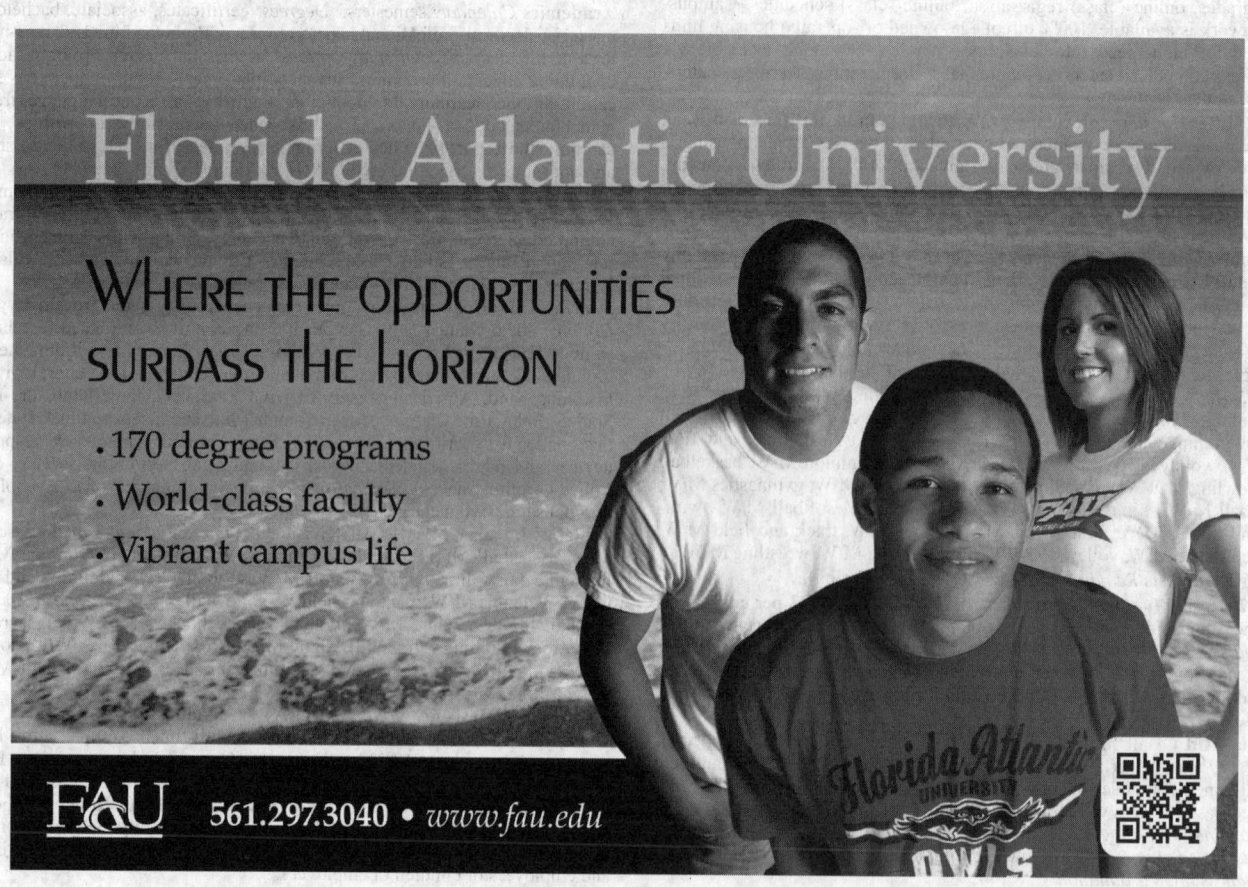

College room only: $3650. Room and board charges vary according to board plan and housing facility. *Payment plan:* installment. *Waivers:* employees or children of employees.

Financial Aid Of all full-time matriculated undergraduates who enrolled in 2008, 354 applied for aid, 280 were judged to have need, 32 had their need fully met. In 2008, 107 non-need-based awards were made. *Average percent of need met:* 57%. *Average financial aid package:* $12,478. *Average need-based loan:* $3973. *Average need-based gift aid:* $5859. *Average non-need-based aid:* $1907.

Applying *Options:* electronic application. *Application fee:* $30. *Required:* high school transcript, minimum 2 GPA, 2 letters of recommendation. *Required for some:* essay or personal statement, essay required for international students. *Application deadlines:* 8/1 (freshmen), 8/1 (transfers). *Notification:* continuous (freshmen), continuous (transfers).

Freshman Application Contact Mrs. Shay Angelo, Assistant Director of Admissions, Florida College, 119 North Glen Arven Avenue, Temple Terrace, FL 33617. *Phone:* 813-988-5131 Ext. 6716. *Toll-free phone:* 800-326-7655. *Fax:* 813-899-6772. *E-mail:* admissions@floridacollege.edu. *Web site:* http://www.floridacollege.edu/.

Florida Gateway College

Lake City, Florida

Freshman Application Contact Florida Gateway College, Lake City, FL 32025-8703. *Fax:* 386-755-1521. *E-mail:* admissions@mail.lakecity.cc.fl.us. *Web site:* http://www.fgc.edu/.

Florida Gulf Coast University

Fort Myers, Florida

- **State-supported** comprehensive, founded 1991, part of State University System of Florida
- **Suburban** 760-acre campus
- **Endowment** $51.8 million
- **Coed** 10,562 undergraduate students, 80% full-time, 55% women, 45% men
- **Moderately difficult** entrance level, 70% of applicants were admitted

Undergraduates 8,463 full-time, 2,099 part-time. Students come from 47 states and territories; 87 other countries; 8% are from out of state; 5% Black or African American, non-Hispanic/Latino; 16% Hispanic/Latino; 1% Asian, non-Hispanic/Latino; 0.3% Native Hawaiian or other Pacific Islander, non-Hispanic/Latino; 0.3% American Indian or Alaska Native, non-Hispanic/Latino; 2% Two or more races, non-Hispanic/Latino; 0.9% Race/ethnicity unknown; 2% international; 10% transferred in; 30% live on campus. *Retention:* 74% of full-time freshmen returned.

Freshmen *Admission:* 8,650 applied, 6,046 admitted, 2,241 enrolled. *Average high school GPA:* 3.35. *Test scores:* SAT critical reading scores over 500: 57%; SAT math scores over 500: 61%; SAT writing scores over 500: 49%; ACT scores over 18: 92%; SAT critical reading scores over 600: 12%; SAT math scores over 600: 14%; SAT writing scores over 600: 7%; ACT scores over 24: 25%; SAT critical reading scores over 700: 1%; SAT math scores over 700: 1%; ACT scores over 30: 1%.

Faculty *Total:* 589, 64% full-time. *Student/faculty ratio:* 17:1.

Academics *Calendar:* semesters. *Degrees:* certificates, associate, bachelor's, and master's. *Special study options:* academic remediation for entering students, accelerated degree program, advanced placement credit, cooperative education, distance learning, double majors, honors programs, independent study, internships, off-campus study, part-time degree program, services for LD students, study abroad, summer session for credit.

Computers on Campus 871 computers/terminals are available on campus for general student use. Students can access the following: online (class) registration, online admissions and advising. Campuswide network is available. 100% of college-owned or -operated housing units are wired for high-speed Internet access.

Student Life *Housing options:* coed. Campus housing is university owned. *Activities and organizations:* drama/theater group, student-run newspaper, student government, Ignite (Religious Organization), International Club, Martial Arts Club, Physical Therapy Association, national fraternities, national sororities. *Campus security:* 24-hour emergency response devices and patrols, late-night transport/escort service. *Student services:* health clinic, personal/psychological counseling.

Athletics Member NCAA. All Division I. *Intercollegiate sports:* baseball M(s), basketball M(s)/W(s), cheerleading W, cross-country running M(s)/W(s), golf M(s)/W(s), soccer M(s)/W(s), softball W(s), swimming and diving W(s), tennis M(s)/W(s), volleyball W(s). *Intramural sports:* basketball M/W, cross-country running M(c)/W(c), fencing M(c)/W(c), football M/W, ice hockey M(c), lacrosse M(c)/W(c), sailing M(c)/W(c), skiing (downhill) M(c)/W(c), soccer M/W, softball M/W, swimming and diving M(c)/W(c), table tennis M/W, tennis M(c)/W(c), ultimate Frisbee M/W, volleyball M/W, water polo M/W, weight lifting M(c)/W(c), wrestling M(c)/W(c).

Standardized Tests *Required:* SAT and SAT Subject Tests or ACT (for admission), SAT Subject Tests (for admission).

Costs (2010–11) *Tuition:* state resident $4991 full-time; nonresident $21,318 full-time. Full-time tuition and fees vary according to course load. Part-time tuition and fees vary according to course load. *Required fees:* $1737 full-time. *Room and board:* $8150. Room and board charges vary according to board plan. *Waivers:* senior citizens and employees or children of employees.

Financial Aid Of all full-time matriculated undergraduates who enrolled in 2008, 6,150 applied for aid, 2,834 were judged to have need, 238 had their need fully met. In 2008, 311 non-need-based awards were made. *Average percent of need met:* 60%. *Average financial aid package:* $7519. *Average need-based loan:* $5699. *Average need-based gift aid:* $5035. *Average non-need-based aid:* $3399. *Average indebtedness upon graduation:* $22,328. *Financial aid deadline:* 6/30.

Applying *Options:* electronic application, deferred entrance. *Application fee:* $30. *Required:* high school transcript, minimum 2 GPA. *Application deadlines:* 2/15 (freshmen), 7/1 (transfers). *Notification:* continuous (freshmen), continuous (transfers).

Freshman Application Contact Florida Gulf Coast University, 10501 FGCU Boulevard South, Fort Myers, FL 33965-6565. *Phone:* 239-590-7878. *Toll-free phone:* 888-889-1095. *Web site:* http://www.fgcu.edu/.

Florida Hospital College of Health Sciences

Orlando, Florida

Freshman Application Contact Florida Hospital College of Health Sciences, 671 Winyah Drive, Orlando, FL 32803. *Phone:* 407-303-7742. *Toll-free phone:* 800-500-7747. *Web site:* http://www.fhchs.edu/.

Florida Institute of Technology

Melbourne, Florida

- **Independent** university, founded 1958
- **Small-town** 130-acre campus with easy access to Orlando
- **Endowment** $40.3 million
- **Coed** 5,582 undergraduate students, 72% full-time, 51% women, 49% men
- **Moderately difficult** entrance level, 59% of applicants were admitted

Undergraduates 4,032 full-time, 1,550 part-time. Students come from 51 states and territories; 88 other countries; 54% are from out of state; 17% Black or African American, non-Hispanic/Latino; 6% Hispanic/Latino; 2% Asian, non-Hispanic/Latino; 0.3% Native Hawaiian or other Pacific Islander, non-Hispanic/Latino; 0.7% American Indian or Alaska Native, non-Hispanic/Latino; 0.6% Two or more races, non-Hispanic/Latino; 10% Race/ethnicity unknown; 13% international; 3% transferred in; 50% live on campus. *Retention:* 75% of full-time freshmen returned.

Freshmen *Admission:* 4,687 applied, 2,749 admitted, 490 enrolled. *Average high school GPA:* 3.6. *Test scores:* SAT critical reading scores over 500: 76%; SAT math scores over 500: 87%; ACT scores over 18: 99%; SAT critical reading scores over 600: 30%; SAT math scores over 600: 51%; ACT scores over 24: 71%; SAT critical reading scores over 700: 5%; SAT math scores over 700: 10%; ACT scores over 30: 17%.

Faculty *Total:* 664, 36% full-time, 66% with terminal degrees. *Student/faculty ratio:* 16:1.

Academics *Calendar:* semesters. *Degrees:* associate, bachelor's, master's, doctoral-research/scholarship, and post-master's certificates. *Special study options:* academic remediation for entering students, accelerated degree program, adult/continuing education programs, advanced placement credit, cooperative education, distance learning, double majors, English as a second language, independent study, internships, part-time degree program, services for LD students, student-designed majors, study abroad, summer session for credit. *ROTC:* Army (b).

Computers on Campus 415 computers/terminals and 75 ports are available on campus for general student use. Students can access the following: computer help desk, free student e-mail accounts, online (class) grades, online (class) registration, online (class) schedules. Campuswide network is available. 100% of college-owned or -operated housing units are wired for high-speed Internet access. Wireless service is available via classrooms, computer centers, computer labs, learning centers, libraries, student centers.

Student Life *Housing:* on-campus residence required through sophomore year. *Options:* coed. Campus housing is university owned. Freshman campus housing is guaranteed. *Activities and organizations:* drama/theater group, student-run newspaper, radio and television station, choral group, FITSSFF, College Players, Saudi Student House, Squamish, Phi Eta Sigma National Honor Society, national fraternities, national sororities. *Campus security:* 24-hour emergency response devices and patrols, late-night transport/escort service, controlled dormitory access. *Student services:* health clinic, personal/psychological counseling.

Athletics Member NCAA. All Division II. *Intercollegiate sports:* baseball M(s), basketball M(s)/W(s), crew W(s), cross-country running M(s)/W(s), football M(c)/W(c), golf M(s)/W(s), racquetball M(c)/W(c), soccer M(s)/W(s), softball W(s), tennis M(s)/W(s), ultimate Frisbee M(c)/W(c), volleyball W(s), water polo M(c)/W(c). *Intramural sports:* badminton M/W, baseball M(c)/W(c), basketball M/W, bowling M/W, cheerleading M(c)/W(c), crew M(c)/W(c), fencing M(c)/W(c), football M/W, golf M/W, ice hockey M(c)/W(c), racquetball M/W, sailing W(c), soccer M/W, softball M/W, tennis M/W, ultimate Frisbee M/W, volleyball M/W, water polo M/W, weight lifting M/W, wrestling M(c)/W(c).

Standardized Tests *Required:* SAT or ACT (for admission).

Costs (2010–11) *Comprehensive fee:* $43,504 includes full-time tuition ($31,734), mandatory fees ($560), and room and board ($11,210). Full-time tuition and fees vary according to course load and program. Part-time tuition: $950 per credit hour. *College room only:* $6670. Room and board charges vary according to board plan and housing facility. *Payment plan:* installment. *Waivers:* senior citizens and employees or children of employees.

Financial Aid Of all full-time matriculated undergraduates who enrolled in 2009, 1,613 applied for aid, 1,470 were judged to have need, 304 had their need fully met. 755 Federal Work-Study jobs (averaging $1282). 10 state and other part-time jobs (averaging $3327). In 2009, 541 non-need-based awards were made. *Average percent of need met:* 79%. *Average financial aid package:* $28,521. *Average need-based loan:* $4813. *Average need-based gift aid:* $19,809. *Average non-need-based aid:* $10,298. *Average indebtedness upon graduation:* $41,565.

Applying *Options:* electronic.application, early admission, deferred entrance. *Application fee:* $50. *Required:* essay or personal statement, high school transcript, minimum 2.6 GPA. *Recommended:* minimum 3.3 GPA. *Application deadlines:* rolling (freshmen), rolling (transfers). *Notification:* continuous (freshmen), continuous (transfers).

Freshman Application Contact Michael J. Perry, Director of Undergraduate Admission, Florida Institute of Technology, 150 West University Boulevard, Melbourne, FL 32901-6975. *Phone:* 321-674-8030. *Toll-free phone:* 800-888-4348. *Fax:* 321-723-9468. *E-mail:* admission@fit.edu. *Web site:* http://www.fit.edu/.

Florida International University
Miami, Florida

- **State-supported** university, founded 1965, part of State University System of Florida
- **Urban** 573-acre campus with easy access to Miami
- **Endowment** $95.3 million
- **Coed** 33,786 undergraduate students, 63% full-time, 55% women, 45% men
- **Moderately difficult** entrance level, 39% of applicants were admitted

Undergraduates 21,438 full-time, 12,348 part-time. Students come from 48 states and territories; 124 other countries; 3% are from out of state; 12% Black or African American, non-Hispanic/Latino; 65% Hispanic/Latino; 3% Asian, non-Hispanic/Latino; 0.1% Native Hawaiian or other Pacific Islander, non-Hispanic/Latino; 0.1% American Indian or Alaska Native, non-Hispanic/Latino; 0.7% Two or more races, non-Hispanic/Latino; 2% Race/ethnicity unknown; 5% international; 13% transferred in; 8% live on campus. *Retention:* 82% of full-time freshmen returned.

Freshmen *Admission:* 15,061 applied, 5,949 admitted, 3,693 enrolled. *Average high school GPA:* 3.7. *Test scores:* SAT critical reading scores over 500: 94%; SAT math scores over 500: 88%; SAT writing scores over 500: 89%; ACT scores over 18: 100%; SAT critical reading scores over 600: 32%; SAT math scores over 600: 30%; SAT writing scores over 600: 25%; ACT scores over 24: 82%; SAT critical reading scores over 700: 3%; SAT math scores over 700: 2%; SAT writing scores over 700: 2%; ACT scores over 30: 4%.

Faculty *Total:* 1,798, 50% full-time, 64% with terminal degrees. *Student/faculty ratio:* 28:1.

Academics *Calendar:* semesters. *Degrees:* bachelor's, master's, doctoral-professional, doctoral-research/scholarship, and postbachelor's certificates. *Special study options:* accelerated degree program, adult/continuing education programs, advanced placement credit, cooperative education, distance learning, double majors, freshman honors college, honors programs, independent study, internships, off-campus study, part-time degree program, services for LD students, study abroad, summer session for credit. *ROTC:* Army (b), Air Force (b). *Unusual degree programs:* 3-2 business administration; engineering.

Computers on Campus Students can access the following: computer help desk, free student e-mail accounts, online (class) grades, online (class) registration, online (class) schedules, online financial and cashier's information; class schedule, financial, campus maps information available on cell phones. Campuswide network is available. 100% of college-owned or -operated housing

units are wired for high-speed Internet access. Wireless service is available via entire campus.

Student Life *Housing options:* coed. Campus housing is university owned. *Activities and organizations:* drama/theater group, student-run newspaper, radio station, choral group, marching band, Students for Community Service, Black Student Leadership Council, Hospitality Management Student Club, Hispanic Students Association, Haitian Students Organization, national fraternities, national sororities. *Campus security:* 24-hour emergency response devices and patrols, late-night transport/escort service, controlled dormitory access. *Student services:* health clinic, personal/psychological counseling, women's center.

Athletics Member NCAA. All Division I. *Intercollegiate sports:* baseball M(s), basketball M(s)/W(s), cross-country running M(s)/W(s), football M(s), golf W(s), soccer M(s)/W(s), softball W(s), swimming and diving W(s), tennis W(s), track and field M(s)/W(s), volleyball W(s). *Intramural sports:* badminton M(c)/W(c), baseball M(c), cheerleading M(c)/W(c), ice hockey M(c)/W(c), lacrosse M(c)/W(c), rugby M(c)/W(c), water polo M(c).

Standardized Tests *Required:* SAT or ACT (for admission), TOEFL is required of all applicants whose native language is not English (for admission). *Recommended:* SAT Subject Tests (for admission).

Costs (2010–11) *Tuition:* state resident $4743 full-time, $158 per credit hour part-time; nonresident $17,142 full-time, $571 per credit hour part-time. Full-time tuition and fees vary according to course load. Part-time tuition and fees vary according to course load. *Required fees:* $348 full-time, $174 per term part-time. *Room and board:* $11,440. Room and board charges vary according to housing facility. *Payment plan:* installment. *Waivers:* senior citizens and employees or children of employees.

Financial Aid Of all full-time matriculated undergraduates who enrolled in 2009, 12,444 applied for aid, 12,242 were judged to have need, 2,069 had their need fully met. 529 Federal Work-Study jobs (averaging $2249). 9 state and other part-time jobs (averaging $5008). In 2009, 1131 non-need-based awards were made. *Average percent of need met:* 24%. *Average financial aid package:* $8514. *Average need-based loan:* $9151. *Average need-based gift aid:* $6452. *Average non-need-based aid:* $606. *Average indebtedness upon graduation:* $16,026. *Financial aid deadline:* 5/15.

Applying *Options:* electronic application. *Application fee:* $30. *Required:* high school transcript, minimum 3 GPA. *Required for some:* portfolio, audition. *Application deadlines:* rolling (freshmen), rolling (out-of-state freshmen), rolling (transfers). *Notification:* continuous (freshmen), continuous (out-of-state freshmen), continuous (transfers).

Freshman Application Contact Mr. Barry Taylor, Director of Admissions, Florida International University, 11200 SW Eighth Street, PC 140, Miami, FL 33199. *Phone:* 305-348-2363. *Fax:* 305-348-3648. *E-mail:* admiss@fiu.edu. *Web site:* http://www.fiu.edu/.

Florida Memorial University
Miami-Dade, Florida

Director of Admissions Mrs. Peggy Murray Martin, Director of Admissions and International Student Advisor, Florida Memorial University, 15800 NW 42nd Avenue, Miami-Dade, FL 33054. *Phone:* 305-626-3147. *Toll-free phone:* 800-822-1362. *Web site:* http://www.fmuniv.edu/.

Florida National College
Hialeah, Florida

- **Proprietary** 4-year, founded 1982
- **Urban** 4-acre campus with easy access to Miami
- **Coed** 2,819 undergraduate students, 72% full-time, 69% women, 31% men
- **Moderately difficult** entrance level, 87% of applicants were admitted

Undergraduates 2,019 full-time, 800 part-time. Students come from 16 states and territories; 14 other countries; 1% are from out of state; 5% Black or African American, non-Hispanic/Latino; 89% Hispanic/Latino; 0.5% Asian, non-Hispanic/Latino; 0.1% American Indian or Alaska Native, non-Hispanic/Latino; 0.4% Two or more races, non-Hispanic/Latino; 4% international; 5% transferred in.

Freshmen *Admission:* 764 applied, 668 admitted, 668 enrolled.

Faculty *Total:* 134, 60% full-time, 8% with terminal degrees. *Student/faculty ratio:* 25:1.

Academics *Calendar:* semesters. *Degrees:* certificates, diplomas, associate, and bachelor's. *Special study options:* academic remediation for entering students, accelerated degree program, adult/continuing education programs, advanced placement credit, cooperative education, distance learning, English as a second language, independent study, internships, part-time degree program, services for LD students, summer session for credit.

Computers on Campus 230 computers/terminals are available on campus for general student use. Students can access the following: computer help desk, online (class) grades, online (class) registration, online (class) schedules. Campuswide network is available.

Student Life *Housing:* college housing not available. *Activities and organizations:* student-run newspaper, Student Government Association, Bible Club, Salsa Club, W.I.C.S (Women Community Service), Criminal Justice Society. *Campus security:* 24-hour emergency response devices.

Standardized Tests *Required:* SAT or ACT (for admission).

Costs (2011–12) *Tuition:* $12,600 full-time, $525 per credit part-time. No tuition increase for student's term of enrollment. *Required fees:* $570 full-time. *Payment plans:* tuition prepayment, installment. *Waivers:* employees or children of employees.

Financial Aid Of all full-time matriculated undergraduates who enrolled in 2008, 1,344 applied for aid, 1,330 were judged to have need. 14 Federal Work-Study jobs (averaging $7253). *Average need-based gift aid:* $4650. *Average indebtedness upon graduation:* $8750.

Applying *Options:* electronic application, deferred entrance. *Required:* high school transcript, interview. *Application deadlines:* rolling (freshmen), rolling (transfers). *Notification:* continuous (freshmen), continuous (transfers).

Freshman Application Contact Mr. Guillermo Araya, Director of Admissions, Florida National College, 4425 West Dr. Jose Regueiro Avenue (20th), Hialeah, FL 33012. *Phone:* 305-821-3333 Ext. 1015. *Fax:* 305-362-0595. *E-mail:* garaya@mm.fnc.edu. *Web site:* http://www.fnc.edu/.

Florida Southern College

Lakeland, Florida

- **Independent** comprehensive, founded 1885, affiliated with United Methodist Church
- **Suburban** 100-acre campus with easy access to Tampa and Orlando
- **Endowment** $58.7 million
- **Coed** 1,984 undergraduate students, 98% full-time, 58% women, 42% men
- **Moderately difficult** entrance level, 67% of applicants were admitted

Undergraduates 1,938 full-time, 46 part-time. Students come from 41 states and territories; 43 other countries; 30% are from out of state; 7% Black or African American, non-Hispanic/Latino; 8% Hispanic/Latino; 2% Asian, non-Hispanic/Latino; 0.1% Native Hawaiian or other Pacific Islander, non-Hispanic/Latino; 0.6% American Indian or Alaska Native, non-Hispanic/Latino; 2%

Two or more races, non-Hispanic/Latino; 0.1% Race/ethnicity unknown; 4% international; 5% transferred in; 74% live on campus. *Retention:* 74% of full-time freshmen returned.

Freshmen *Admission:* 2,948 applied, 1,981 admitted, 605 enrolled. *Average high school GPA:* 3.4. *Test scores:* SAT critical reading scores over 500: 65%; SAT math scores over 500: 78%; SAT writing scores over 500: 58%; ACT scores over 18: 100%; SAT critical reading scores over 600: 18%; SAT math scores over 600: 23%; SAT writing scores over 600: 17%; ACT scores over 24: 49%; SAT critical reading scores over 700: 3%; SAT math scores over 700: 3%; SAT writing scores over 700: 2%; ACT scores over 30: 6%.

Faculty *Total:* 217, 50% full-time, 52% with terminal degrees. *Student/faculty ratio:* 14:1.

Academics *Calendar:* semesters. *Degrees:* bachelor's and master's. *Special study options:* adult/continuing education programs, advanced placement credit, double majors, honors programs, independent study, internships, off-campus study, part-time degree program, student-designed majors, study abroad, summer session for credit. *ROTC:* Army (b), Air Force (c). *Unusual degree programs:* 3-2 business administration with Students can now follow a focused enrollment track that includes summer enrollment to complete the BA in Business Administration in three years and proceed directly into the MBA. Students still must meet all MBA admission requirements.

Computers on Campus 450 computers/terminals and 50 ports are available on campus for general student use. Students can access the following: campus intranet, computer help desk, free student e-mail accounts, online (class) grades, online (class) registration, online (class) schedules, campus portal. Campuswide network is available. 100% of college-owned or -operated housing units are wired for high-speed Internet access. Wireless service is available via classrooms, dorm rooms, libraries, student centers.

Student Life *Housing:* on-campus residence required through senior year. *Options:* coed, men-only, women-only, disabled students. Campus housing is university owned. Freshman campus housing is guaranteed. *Activities and organizations:* drama/theater group, student-run newspaper, television station, choral group, Student Government Association, Toastmasters, Association of Campus Entertainment, Beyond (Campus Ministry), Fellowship of Christian Athletes, national fraternities, national sororities. *Campus security:* 24-hour emergency response devices and patrols, student patrols, late-night transport/escort service, controlled dormitory access. *Student services:* health clinic, personal/psychological counseling.

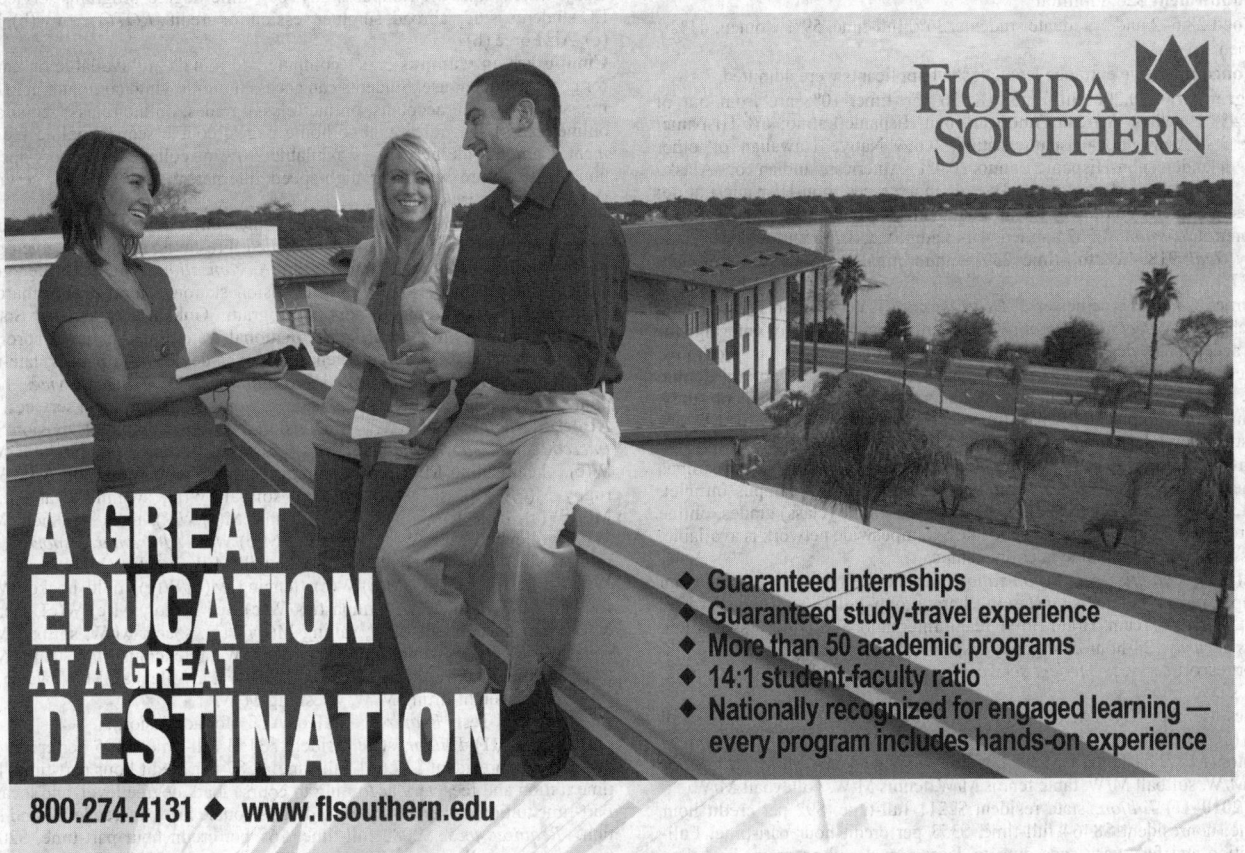

Athletics Member NCAA. All Division II. *Intercollegiate sports:* baseball M(s), basketball M(s)/W(s), cheerleading W(c), cross-country running M(s)/W(s), golf M(s)/W(s), lacrosse M(s)/W(s), soccer M(s)/W(s), softball W(s), swimming and diving M(s)/W(s), tennis M(s)/W(s), track and field M(s)/W(s), volleyball M(c)/W(s). *Intramural sports:* basketball M/W, bowling M/W, cross-country running M/W, football M/W, golf M/W, soccer M/W, softball M/W, swimming and diving M/W, table tennis M/W, tennis M/W, ultimate Frisbee M/W, volleyball M/W.

Standardized Tests *Required:* SAT or ACT (for admission).

Costs (2011–12) *Comprehensive fee:* $34,920 includes full-time tuition ($25,529), mandatory fees ($583), and room and board ($8808). Full-time tuition and fees vary according to student level. Part-time tuition: $750 per semester hour. Part-time tuition and fees vary according to class time. *College room only:* $4982. Room and board charges vary according to board plan and housing facility. *Payment plan:* installment. *Waivers:* children of alumni and employees or children of employees.

Financial Aid Of all full-time matriculated undergraduates who enrolled in 2009, 1,531 applied for aid, 1,395 were judged to have need, 294 had their need fully met. 244 Federal Work-Study jobs (averaging $1500). 501 state and other part-time jobs (averaging $1500). In 2009, 208 non-need-based awards were made. *Average percent of need met:* 76%. *Average financial aid package:* $21,825. *Average need-based loan:* $4213. *Average need-based gift aid:* $9236. *Average non-need-based aid:* $9656. *Average indebtedness upon graduation:* $28,294. *Financial aid deadline:* 7/1.

Applying *Options:* electronic application, early admission, early decision, deferred entrance. *Application fee:* $30. *Required:* essay or personal statement, high school transcript, 1 letter of recommendation. *Recommended:* minimum 2 GPA, interview. *Application deadlines:* 3/1 (freshmen), rolling (transfers). *Early decision deadline:* 12/1. *Notification:* continuous (freshmen), continuous (transfers), 12/15 (early decision).

Freshman Application Contact Florida Southern College, 111 Lake Hollingsworth Drive, Lakeland, FL 33801-5698. *Phone:* 863-680-4131. *Toll-free phone:* 800-274-4131. *Web site:* http://www.flsouthern.edu/.

See page 1292 for the College Close-Up.

Florida State College at Jacksonville

Jacksonville, Florida

- **State-supported** primarily 2-year, founded 1963, part of Florida Community College System
- **Urban** 825-acre campus
- **Endowment** $28.8 million
- **Coed** 28,642 undergraduate students, 36% full-time, 59% women, 41% men
- **Noncompetitive** entrance level, 48% of applicants were admitted

Undergraduates 10,206 full-time, 18,436 part-time. 10% are from out of state; 24% Black or African American, non-Hispanic/Latino; 6% Hispanic/Latino; 3% Asian, non-Hispanic/Latino; 0.6% Native Hawaiian or other Pacific Islander, non-Hispanic/Latino; 0.4% American Indian or Alaska Native, non-Hispanic/Latino; 1% Two or more races, non-Hispanic/Latino; 13% Race/ethnicity unknown; 7% international; 7% transferred in.

Freshmen *Admission:* 8,562 applied, 4,148 admitted, 3,233 enrolled.

Faculty *Total:* 918, 43% full-time, 23% with terminal degrees. *Student/faculty ratio:* 37:1.

Academics *Calendar:* semesters. *Degrees:* certificates, diplomas, associate, and bachelor's. *Special study options:* academic remediation for entering students, accelerated degree program, adult/continuing education programs, advanced placement credit, cooperative education, distance learning, double majors, English as a second language, honors programs, independent study, internships, off-campus study, part-time degree program, services for LD students, study abroad, summer session for credit. *ROTC:* Navy (c).

Computers on Campus 2,500 computers/terminals are available on campus for general student use. Students can access the following: campus intranet, computer help desk, free student e-mail accounts, online (class) grades, online (class) registration, online (class) schedules. Campuswide network is available. Wireless service is available via entire campus.

Student Life *Activities and organizations:* drama/theater group, student-run newspaper, radio and television station, choral group, Phi Theta Kappa, Troupe de Kent, Forensic Team, Brain Bowl Team, International Student Association. *Campus security:* 24-hour emergency response devices and patrols, late-night transport/escort service. *Student services:* personal/psychological counseling, women's center.

Athletics Member NJCAA. *Intercollegiate sports:* baseball M(s), basketball M(s)/W(s), softball W(s), tennis W(s), volleyball W(s). *Intramural sports:* badminton M/W, basketball M/W, bowling M/W, football M/W, golf M/W, soccer M/W, softball M/W, table tennis M/W, tennis M/W, volleyball M/W.

Costs (2010–11) *Tuition:* state resident $2211 full-time, $92 per credit hour part-time; nonresident $8464 full-time, $353 per credit hour part-time. Full-time tuition and fees vary according to degree level and program. Part-time

tuition and fees vary according to degree level and program. *Required fees:* $240 full-time. *Payment plan:* installment. *Waivers:* employees or children of employees.

Applying *Options:* electronic application, early admission, deferred entrance. *Application fee:* $25. *Required:* high school transcript. *Application deadlines:* rolling (freshmen), rolling (out-of-state freshmen), rolling (transfers).

Freshman Application Contact Dr. Peter Biegel, AVP, Enrollment Management, Florida State College at Jacksonville, 501 West State Street, Jacksonville, FL 32202. *Phone:* 904-632-3131. *Fax:* 904-632-5105. *E-mail:* pbiegel@fscj.edu. *Web site:* http://www.fscj.edu/.

Florida State University

Tallahassee, Florida

- **State-supported** university, founded 1851, part of State University System of Florida
- **Suburban** 451-acre campus
- **Endowment** $445.8 million
- **Coed** 31,418 undergraduate students, 93% full-time, 55% women, 45% men
- **Very difficult** entrance level, 60% of applicants were admitted

Undergraduates 29,069 full-time, 2,349 part-time. Students come from 52 states and territories; 130 other countries; 9% are from out of state; 10% Black or African American, non-Hispanic/Latino; 14% Hispanic/Latino; 3% Asian, non-Hispanic/Latino; 1% American Indian or Alaska Native, non-Hispanic/Latino; 1% Race/ethnicity unknown; 0.4% international; 7% transferred in; 20% live on campus. *Retention:* 92% of full-time freshmen returned.

Freshmen *Admission:* 26,037 applied, 15,498 admitted, 5,927 enrolled. *Average high school GPA:* 3.76. *Test scores:* SAT critical reading scores over 500: 97%; SAT math scores over 500: 97%; SAT writing scores over 500: 96%; ACT scores over 18: 100%; SAT critical reading scores over 600: 51%; SAT math scores over 600: 54%; SAT writing scores over 600: 46%; ACT scores over 24: 87%; SAT critical reading scores over 700: 8%; SAT math scores over 700: 7%; SAT writing scores over 700: 6%; ACT scores over 30: 13%.

Faculty *Total:* 1,614, 77% full-time, 92% with terminal degrees. *Student/faculty ratio:* 22:1.

Academics *Calendar:* semesters. *Degrees:* certificates, associate, bachelor's, master's, doctoral-professional, doctoral-research/scholarship, post-master's, and postbachelor's certificates. *Special study options:* accelerated degree program, advanced placement credit, cooperative education, distance learning, double majors, English as a second language, honors programs, independent study, internships, off-campus study, part-time degree program, services for LD students, study abroad, summer session for credit. *ROTC:* Army (b), Navy (c), Air Force (b).

Computers on Campus 3,821 computers/terminals are available on campus for general student use. Students can access the following: computer help desk, free student e-mail accounts, online (class) grades, online (class) registration, online (class) schedules, course home pages, course search, online fee payment. Campuswide network is available. 90% of college-owned or -operated housing units are wired for high-speed Internet access. Wireless service is available via entire campus.

Student Life *Housing options:* coed, women-only, cooperative, disabled students. Campus housing is university owned. Freshman applicants given priority for college housing. *Activities and organizations:* drama/theater group, student-run newspaper, radio and television station, choral group, marching band, student government, honors program, Golden Key Honor Society, Marching Chiefs, intramural sports, national fraternities, national sororities. *Campus security:* 24-hour emergency response devices and patrols, late-night transport/escort service, controlled dormitory access. *Student services:* health clinic, personal/psychological counseling, women's center, legal services.

Athletics Member NCAA. All Division I except football (Division I-A). *Intercollegiate sports:* baseball M(s), basketball M(s)/W(s), bowling M(c)/W(c), cheerleading M/W, cross-country running M(s)/W(s), golf M(s)/W(s), rugby M(c)/W(c), soccer M(c)/W(s), softball W(s), swimming and diving M(s)/W(s), table tennis M(c)/W(c), tennis M(s)/W(s), track and field M(s)/W(s), volleyball M(c)/W(s), wrestling M(c)/W(c). *Intramural sports:* badminton M(c)/W(c), baseball M(c), basketball M/W, bowling M/W, crew M(c)/W(c), equestrian sports M(c)/W(c), fencing M(c)/W(c), field hockey W(c), football M/W, golf M/W, gymnastics W(c), ice hockey M(c)/W(c), lacrosse M(c)/W(c), racquetball M/W, sailing M(c)/W(c), soccer M/W, softball M/W, squash M(c)/W(c), swimming and diving M/W, table tennis M/W, tennis M/W, track and field M/W, ultimate Frisbee M(c)/W(c), volleyball M/W, water polo M(c)/W(c), weight lifting M/W, wrestling M/W.

Standardized Tests *Required:* SAT or ACT (for admission).

Costs (2010–11) *Tuition:* state resident $3153 full-time, $105 per credit hour part-time; nonresident $17,691 full-time, $587 per credit hour part-time. Full-time tuition and fees vary according to course load, degree level, and location. Part-time tuition and fees vary according to course load, degree level, and location. *Required fees:* $2082 full-time, $68 per credit hour part-time, $20 per term part-time. *Room and board:* $9180; room only: $5280. Room and board charges vary according to board plan and housing facility. *Payment plans:* tuition prepayment, installment. *Waivers:* senior citizens and employees or children of employees.

Financial Aid Of all full-time matriculated undergraduates who enrolled in 2009, 18,080 applied for aid, 9,498 were judged to have need, 7,253 had their need fully met. 697 Federal Work-Study jobs (averaging $1100). 26 state and other part-time jobs (averaging $1100). In 2009, 1278 non-need-based awards were made. *Average percent of need met:* 75%. *Average financial aid package:* $10,709. *Average need-based loan:* $3703. *Average need-based gift aid:* $4390. *Average non-need-based aid:* $2302. *Average indebtedness upon graduation:* $20,993.

Applying *Options:* electronic application, early admission. *Application fee:* $30. *Required:* high school transcript. *Recommended:* essay or personal statement, minimum 3 GPA. *Application deadlines:* 1/25 (freshmen), 1/25 (out-of-state freshmen), 7/1 (transfers). *Notification:* 3/21 (freshmen), 3/21 (out-of-state freshmen), continuous (transfers).

Freshman Application Contact Florida State University, Tallahassee, FL 32306. *Phone:* 850-644-6200. *Web site:* http://www.fsu.edu/.

Full Sail University
Winter Park, Florida

- **Proprietary** comprehensive, founded 1979
- **Suburban** 190-acre campus with easy access to Orlando
- **Coed, primarily men**

Faculty *Student/faculty ratio:* 8:1.

Academics *Calendar:* modular. *Degrees:* associate, bachelor's, and master's.

Student Life *Campus security:* 24-hour patrols.

Financial Aid *Of all full-time matriculated undergraduates who enrolled in 2008,* 7,337 applied for aid, 6,925 were judged to have need. 475 Federal Work-Study jobs (averaging $1380). *In 2008,* 1291 non-need-based awards were made. *Average financial aid package:* $7921. *Average need-based gift aid:* $4212. *Average non-need-based aid:* $3572. *Average indebtedness upon graduation:* $63,978.

Applying *Options:* electronic application. *Application fee:* $150. *Required:* high school transcript. *Required for some:* minimum "A" average in Algebra II.

Freshman Application Contact Ms. Mary Beth Plank, Director of Admissions, Full Sail University, 3300 University Boulevard, Winter Park, FL 32792-7437. *Phone:* 407-679-6333. *Toll-free phone:* 800-226-7625. *E-mail:* admissions@fullsail.com. *Web site:* http://www.fullsail.edu/.

See page 1302 for the College Close-Up.

Gulf Coast Community College
Panama City, Florida

- **State-supported** primarily 2-year, founded 1957
- **Suburban** 80-acre campus
- **Coed** 7,207 undergraduate students
- **Noncompetitive** entrance level

Academics *Calendar:* semesters. *Degrees:* certificates, associate, and bachelor's. *Special study options:* academic remediation for entering students, accelerated degree program, adult/continuing education programs, advanced placement credit, cooperative education, distance learning, double majors, English as a second language, external degree program, honors programs, independent study, off-campus study, part-time degree program, services for LD students, summer session for credit.

Computers on Campus Campuswide network is available.

Student Life *Housing:* college housing not available. *Activities and organizations:* drama/theater group, student-run newspaper, radio station, choral group. *Campus security:* patrols by trained security personnel during campus hours. *Student services:* personal/psychological counseling.

Athletics Member NJCAA. *Intercollegiate sports:* baseball M(s), basketball M(s)/W(s), cheerleading M(s)/W(s), softball W(s), volleyball W(s). *Intramural sports:* basketball M/W, volleyball M/W.

Costs (2010–11) *Tuition:* state resident $2025 full-time, $68 per credit hour part-time; nonresident $8176 full-time, $273 per credit hour part-time. *Required fees:* $607 full-time, $20 per credit hour part-time.

Financial Aid Of all full-time matriculated undergraduates who enrolled in 2009, 145 Federal Work-Study jobs (averaging $3200). 60 state and other part-time jobs (averaging $2600).

Applying *Options:* electronic application, early admission, deferred entrance. *Required:* high school transcript. *Application deadlines:* rolling (freshmen), rolling (transfers). *Notification:* continuous (freshmen).

Freshman Application Contact Mrs. Jackie Kuczenski, Administrative Secretary of Admissions, Gulf Coast Community College, 5230 West Highway 98, Panama City, FL 32401-1058. *Phone:* 850-769-1551 Ext. 4892. *Toll-free phone:* 800-311-3628. *Fax:* 850-913-3308. *Web site:* http://www.gulfcoast.edu/.

Herzing University
Winter Park, Florida

Director of Admissions Tessie Uranga, Director of Admissions, Herzing University, 1595 South Semoran Boulevard, Winter Park, FL 32792. *Phone:* 407-478-0500. *Fax:* 407-380-0269. *Web site:* http://www.herzing.edu/.

Hobe Sound Bible College
Hobe Sound, Florida

Freshman Application Contact Director of Admissions, Hobe Sound Bible College, PO Box 1065, Hobe Sound, FL 33475-1065. *Phone:* 772-545-1400. *Toll-free phone:* 800-930-4722. *E-mail:* info@hsbc.edu. *Web site:* http://www.hsbc.edu/.

Hodges University
Naples, Florida

- **Independent** comprehensive, founded 1990
- **Suburban** campus with easy access to Miami
- **Endowment** $3.0 million
- **Coed**
- **Minimally difficult** entrance level

Faculty *Student/faculty ratio:* 23:1.

Academics *Calendar:* trimesters. *Degrees:* certificates, associate, bachelor's, and master's.

Student Life *Campus security:* late-night transport/escort service, building security.

Standardized Tests *Required for some:* CPAt. *Recommended:* SAT (for admission), ACT (for admission).

Costs (2010–11) *Tuition:* $16,560 full-time, $460 per semester hour part-time. *Required fees:* $380 full-time.

Financial Aid *Of all full-time matriculated undergraduates who enrolled in 2009,* 1,600 applied for aid, 1,325 were judged to have need, 270 had their need fully met. 45 Federal Work-Study jobs (averaging $4444). *In 2009,* 64 non-need-based awards were made. *Average percent of need met:* 74. *Average financial aid package:* $9200. *Average need-based loan:* $2800. *Average need-based gift aid:* $4600. *Average non-need-based aid:* $260. *Average indebtedness upon graduation:* $17,600.

Applying *Options:* electronic application, deferred entrance. *Application fee:* $20. *Required:* essay or personal statement, high school transcript, interview. *Required for some:* 2 letters of recommendation.

Freshman Application Contact Hodges University, 2655 Northbrooke Drive, Naples, FL 34119. *Phone:* 239-513-1122 Ext. 104. *Toll-free phone:* 800-466-8017. *Web site:* http://www.hodges.edu/.

Indian River State College
Fort Pierce, Florida

- **State-supported** primarily 2-year, founded 1960, part of Florida Community College System
- **Small-town** 133-acre campus
- **Coed** 17,511 undergraduate students, 36% full-time, 61% women, 39% men
- **Noncompetitive** entrance level, 100% of applicants were admitted

Undergraduates 6,233 full-time, 11,278 part-time. Students come from 31 states and territories; 127 other countries; 15% are from out of state; 17% Black or African American, non-Hispanic/Latino; 13% Hispanic/Latino; 2% Asian, non-Hispanic/Latino; 0.1% Native Hawaiian or other Pacific Islander, non-Hispanic/Latino; 0.3% American Indian or Alaska Native, non-Hispanic/Latino; 0.6% Two or more races, non-Hispanic/Latino; 3% Race/ethnicity unknown; 0.9% international; 119% transferred in.

Freshmen *Admission:* 1,794 applied, 1,794 admitted, 2,133 enrolled. *Average high school GPA:* 2.86.

Faculty *Total:* 843, 24% full-time, 14% with terminal degrees. *Student/faculty ratio:* 24:1.

Academics *Calendar:* semesters. *Degrees:* certificates, diplomas, associate, and bachelor's. *Special study options:* academic remediation for entering students, adult/continuing education programs, advanced placement credit, distance learning, English as a second language, independent study, part-time degree program, services for LD students, summer session for credit.

Computers on Campus 1,800 computers/terminals are available on campus for general student use. Students can access the following: computer help desk, free student e-mail accounts, online (class) grades, online (class) registration, online (class) schedules. Campuswide network is available. Wireless service is available via classrooms, computer centers, computer labs, learning centers, libraries, student centers.

Student Life *Housing:* college housing not available. *Activities and organizations:* drama/theater group, choral group. *Campus security:* 24-hour emergency response devices and patrols. *Student services:* health clinic, personal/psychological counseling, women's center.

Athletics Member NJCAA. *Intercollegiate sports:* baseball M(s), basketball M(s)/W(s), softball W(s), swimming and diving M(s)/W(s), volleyball W(s). *Intramural sports:* basketball M/W, racquetball M/W, soccer M, volleyball M/W.

Costs (2010–11) *Tuition:* state resident $2208 full-time, $92 per credit part-time; nonresident $8424 full-time, $351 per credit part-time. Full-time tuition and fees vary according to course load and degree level. Part-time tuition and fees vary according to course load and degree level. *Payment plans:* installment, deferred payment.

Financial Aid Of all full-time matriculated undergraduates who enrolled in 2009, 130 Federal Work-Study jobs (averaging $1500).

Applying *Options:* early admission, deferred entrance. *Required:* high school transcript. *Application deadlines:* rolling (freshmen), rolling (transfers). *Notification:* continuous (freshmen), continuous (transfers).

Freshman Application Contact Mr. Steven Payne, Dean of Educational Services, Indian River State College, 3209 Virginia Avenue, Fort Pierce, FL 34981-5596. *Phone:* 772-462-7805. *E-mail:* spayne@ircc.edu. *Web site:* http://www.irsc.edu/.

International Academy of Design & Technology
Tampa, Florida

- **Proprietary** 4-year, founded 1984, part of Career Education Corporation
- **Urban** 1-acre campus
- **Coed** 1,250 undergraduate students, 67% full-time, 50% women, 50% men
- **Noncompetitive** entrance level

Undergraduates 835 full-time, 415 part-time. 17% Black or African American, non-Hispanic/Latino; 16% Hispanic/Latino; 2% Asian, non-Hispanic/Latino; 0.4% Native Hawaiian or other Pacific Islander, non-Hispanic/Latino; 0.5% American Indian or Alaska Native, non-Hispanic/Latino; 4% Two or more races, non-Hispanic/Latino; 10% Race/ethnicity unknown.

Freshmen *Admission:* 203 enrolled.

Faculty *Total:* 115, 21% full-time. *Student/faculty ratio:* 19:1.

Academics *Calendar:* quarters. *Degrees:* associate and bachelor's. *Special study options:* academic remediation for entering students, accelerated degree program, advanced placement credit, cooperative education, distance learning, independent study, internships, part-time degree program, services for LD students, study abroad, summer session for credit.

Computers on Campus 485 computers/terminals are available on campus for general student use. Campuswide network is available.

Student Life *Housing:* college housing not available. *Options:* Campus housing is provided by a third party. *Activities and organizations:* Student Chapter ASID, IIDA, Emerging Greenbuilders, Computer Animation Club, American Advertising Federation. *Campus security:* 24-hour emergency response devices, late night patrols by trained security personnel.

Costs (2011–12) *Comprehensive fee:* $20,756 includes full-time tuition ($13,860), mandatory fees ($600), and room and board ($6296). Part-time tuition: $385 per credit hour. *College room only:* $3392. *Payment plans:* installment, deferred payment. *Waivers:* employees or children of employees.

Financial Aid *Average percent of need met:* 48%.

Applying *Options:* electronic application, early admission, deferred entrance. *Application fee:* $50. *Required:* interview. *Application deadlines:* rolling (freshmen), rolling (out-of-state freshmen), rolling (transfers). *Notification:* continuous (freshmen), continuous (out-of-state freshmen), continuous (transfers).

Freshman Application Contact International Academy of Design & Technology, 5104 Eisenhower Boulevard, Tampa, FL 33634-7350. *Phone:* 813-881-0007-. *Toll-free phone:* 800-ACADEMY. *Web site:* http://www.academy.edu/.

ITT Technical Institute
Fort Lauderdale, Florida

- **Proprietary** primarily 2-year, founded 1991, part of ITT Educational Services, Inc.
- **Suburban** campus
- **Coed**
- **Minimally difficult** entrance level

Academics *Calendar:* quarters. *Degrees:* associate and bachelor's.

Student Life *Housing:* college housing not available.

Freshman Application Contact Director of Recruitment, ITT Technical Institute, 3401 South University Drive, Fort Lauderdale, FL 33328-2021. *Phone:* 954-476-9300. *Toll-free phone:* 800-488-7797. *Web site:* http://www.itt-tech.edu/.

ITT Technical Institute
Fort Myers, Florida

- **Proprietary** primarily 2-year
- **Coed**
- **Minimally difficult** entrance level

Academics *Degrees:* associate and bachelor's.

Freshman Application Contact Director of Recruitment, ITT Technical Institute, 13500 Powers Court, Suite 100, Fort Myers, FL 33912. *Phone:* 239-603-8700. *Toll-free phone:* 877-485-5313. *Web site:* http://www.itt-tech.edu/.

ITT Technical Institute
Jacksonville, Florida

- **Proprietary** primarily 2-year, founded 1991, part of ITT Educational Services, Inc.
- **Urban** campus
- **Coed**
- **Minimally difficult** entrance level

Academics *Calendar:* quarters. *Degrees:* associate and bachelor's.

Student Life *Housing:* college housing not available.

Financial Aid Of all full-time matriculated undergraduates who enrolled in 2009, 5 Federal Work-Study jobs.

Freshman Application Contact Director of Recruitment, ITT Technical Institute, 7011 A.C. Skinner Parkway, Jacksonville, FL 32256. *Phone:* 904-573-9100. *Toll-free phone:* 800-318-1264. *Web site:* http://www.itt-tech.edu/.

ITT Technical Institute
Lake Mary, Florida

- **Proprietary** primarily 2-year, founded 1989, part of ITT Educational Services, Inc.
- **Suburban** campus
- **Coed**
- **Minimally difficult** entrance level

Academics *Calendar:* quarters. *Degrees:* associate and bachelor's.

Freshman Application Contact Director of Recruitment, ITT Technical Institute, 1400 South International Parkway, Lake Mary, FL 32746. *Phone:* 407-660-2900. *Toll-free phone:* 866-489-8441. *Fax:* 407-660-2566. *Web site:* http://www.itt-tech.edu/.

ITT Technical Institute
Miami, Florida

- **Proprietary** primarily 2-year, founded 1996, part of ITT Educational Services, Inc.
- **Coed**
- **Minimally difficult** entrance level

Academics *Calendar:* quarters. *Degrees:* associate and bachelor's.

Student Life *Housing:* college housing not available.

Freshman Application Contact Director of Recruitment, ITT Technical Institute, 7955 NW 12th Street, Suite 119, Miami, FL 33126. *Phone:* 305-477-3080. *Toll-free phone:* 877-216-8352. *Web site:* http://www.itt-tech.edu/.

ITT Technical Institute
Pinellas Park, Florida

- **Proprietary** primarily 2-year, part of ITT Educational Services, Inc.
- **Coed**
- **Minimally difficult** entrance level

Academics *Degrees:* associate and bachelor's.

Student Life *Housing:* college housing not available.

Freshman Application Contact Director of Recruitment, ITT Technical Institute, 877 Executive Center Drive W, Suite 100, Pinellas Park, FL 33781-2658. *Phone:* 727-209-4700. *Toll-free phone:* 866-488-5084. *Web site:* http://www.itt-tech.edu/.

ITT Technical Institute
Tallahassee, Florida

- **Proprietary** primarily 2-year
- **Coed**
- **Minimally difficult** entrance level

Academics *Degrees:* associate and bachelor's.

Freshman Application Contact Director of Recruitment, ITT Technical Institute, 2639 North Monroe Street, Building A, Suite 100, Tallahassee, FL

32303. *Phone:* 850-422-6300. *Toll-free phone:* 877-230-3559. *Web site:* http://www.itt-tech.edu/.

ITT Technical Institute

Tampa, Florida

- **Proprietary** primarily 2-year, founded 1981, part of ITT Educational Services, Inc.
- **Suburban** campus
- **Coed**
- **Minimally difficult** entrance level

Academics *Calendar:* quarters. *Degrees:* associate and bachelor's.

Student Life *Housing:* college housing not available.

Freshman Application Contact Director of Recruitment, ITT Technical Institute, 4809 Memorial Highway, Tampa, FL 33634-7151. *Phone:* 813-885-2244. *Toll-free phone:* 800-825-2831. *Web site:* http://www.itt-tech.edu/.

Jacksonville University

Jacksonville, Florida

- **Independent** comprehensive, founded 1934
- **Suburban** 198-acre campus
- **Coed**
- **Moderately difficult** entrance level

Faculty *Student/faculty ratio:* 14:1.

Academics *Calendar:* semesters. *Degrees:* bachelor's, master's, and doctoral-professional.

Student Life *Campus security:* 24-hour emergency response devices and patrols, student patrols, late-night transport/escort service, controlled dormitory access, code lock doors in residence halls, trained security patrols during evening hours.

Athletics Member NCAA. All Division I except football (Division I-AA).

Standardized Tests *Required:* SAT or ACT (for admission).

Costs (2010–11) *Comprehensive fee:* $35,920 includes full-time tuition ($26,600) and room and board ($9320). Part-time tuition: $883 per credit hour. *College room only:* $5560. Room and board charges vary according to board plan and housing facility.

Financial Aid *Of all full-time matriculated undergraduates who enrolled in 2009,* 1,714 applied for aid, 1,523 were judged to have need, 253 had their need fully met. *In 2009,* 538 non-need-based awards were made. *Average percent of need met:* 61. *Average financial aid package:* $19,580. *Average need-based loan:* $4433. *Average need-based gift aid:* $15,432. *Average non-need-based aid:* $8925.

Applying *Options:* electronic application, early admission, deferred entrance. *Required:* high school transcript, minimum 2 GPA. *Required for some:* essay or personal statement. *Recommended:* interview.

Freshman Application Contact Ms. Lisa Hannasch, Director of First Year Student Admission and Enrollment, Jacksonville University, 2800 University Boulevard North, Office of Admissions, Jacksonville, FL 32211. *Phone:* 904-256-7000. *Toll-free phone:* 800-225-2027. *Fax:* 904-256-7012. *E-mail:* admissions@ju.edu. *Web site:* http://www.ju.edu/.

Johnson & Wales University

North Miami, Florida

- **Independent** 4-year, founded 1992, administratively affiliated with Johnson & Wales University (RI)
- **Suburban** 8-acre campus with easy access to Miami
- **Coed** 2,098 undergraduate students, 96% full-time, 57% women, 43% men
- **Moderately difficult** entrance level, 58% of applicants were admitted

Undergraduates 2,008 full-time, 90 part-time. 44% are from out of state; 17% Black or African American, non-Hispanic/Latino; 18% Hispanic/Latino; 0.9% Asian, non-Hispanic/Latino; 0.3% American Indian or Alaska Native, non-Hispanic/Latino; 39% Race/ethnicity unknown; 8% international; 7% transferred in; 47% live on campus. *Retention:* 69% of full-time freshmen returned.

Freshmen *Admission:* 6,764 applied, 3,892 admitted, 591 enrolled. *Average high school GPA:* 3.06.

Faculty *Total:* 90, 69% full-time. *Student/faculty ratio:* 28:1.

Academics *Calendar:* quarters. *Degrees:* associate and bachelor's. *Special study options:* academic remediation for entering students, accelerated degree program, advanced placement credit, cooperative education, English as a second language, honors programs, independent study, internships, part-time

degree program, services for LD students, study abroad, summer session for credit.

Computers on Campus Campuswide network is available.

Student Life *Housing:* on-campus residence required for freshman year. *Options:* coed. Campus housing is university owned and leased by the school. Freshman campus housing is guaranteed. *Activities and organizations:* national fraternities, national sororities. *Campus security:* 24-hour emergency response devices and patrols, video camera surveillance throughout campus. *Student services:* personal/psychological counseling.

Athletics Member NAIA. *Intramural sports:* basketball M/W, football M, golf M/W, soccer M/W, softball M/W, table tennis M/W, tennis M/W, volleyball M/W.

Standardized Tests *Required for some:* SAT or ACT (for admission).

Costs (2011–12) *Comprehensive fee:* $34,668 includes full-time tuition ($23,955), mandatory fees ($1452), and room and board ($9261). *Room and board:* Room and board charges vary according to board plan and housing facility. *Payment plan:* installment. *Waivers:* employees or children of employees.

Financial Aid Of all full-time matriculated undergraduates who enrolled in 2009, 1,651 applied for aid, 1,559 were judged to have need, 170 had their need fully met. In 2009, 248 non-need-based awards were made. *Average percent of need met:* 70%. *Average financial aid package:* $18,270. *Average need-based loan:* $5378. *Average need-based gift aid:* $8337. *Average non-need-based aid:* $5009.

Applying *Options:* early admission, deferred entrance. *Required:* high school transcript. *Required for some:* essay or personal statement, interview. *Recommended:* minimum 2 GPA. *Application deadlines:* rolling (freshmen), rolling (transfers). *Notification:* continuous (freshmen), continuous (transfers).

Freshman Application Contact Jeff Greenip, Director of Admissions, Johnson & Wales University, 1701 Northeast 127th Street, North Miami, FL 33181. *Phone:* 305-892-7600. *Toll-free phone:* 800-232-2433. *Fax:* 305-892-7020. *E-mail:* mia@admissions.jwu.edu. *Web site:* http://www.jwu.edu/northmiami/.

Jones College

Jacksonville, Florida

- **Independent** 4-year, founded 1918
- **Urban** 5-acre campus
- **Coed** 748 undergraduate students, 33% full-time, 79% women, 21% men
- **Noncompetitive** entrance level

Undergraduates 249 full-time, 499 part-time. Students come from 25 states and territories; 2 other countries; 14% are from out of state; 70% Black or African American, non-Hispanic/Latino; 5% Hispanic/Latino; 0.4% Asian, non-Hispanic/Latino; 0.4% Native Hawaiian or other Pacific Islander, non-Hispanic/Latino; 0.4% American Indian or Alaska Native, non-Hispanic/Latino; 2% Two or more races, non-Hispanic/Latino; 0.5% Race/ethnicity unknown; 0.4% international; 9% transferred in. *Retention:* 55% of full-time freshmen returned.

Freshmen *Admission:* 27 admitted, 27 enrolled.

Faculty *Total:* 75, 4% full-time, 24% with terminal degrees. *Student/faculty ratio:* 15:1.

Academics *Calendar:* trimesters. *Degrees:* associate and bachelor's. *Special study options:* academic remediation for entering students, accelerated degree program, adult/continuing education programs, advanced placement credit, cooperative education, distance learning, double majors, independent study, internships, part-time degree program, student-designed majors, summer session for credit.

Computers on Campus 80 computers/terminals are available on campus for general student use. Students can access the following: campus intranet, computer help desk, free student e-mail accounts, online (class) registration, online (class) schedules. Campuswide network is available. Wireless service is available via classrooms, computer centers, computer labs.

Student Life *Housing:* college housing not available. *Campus security:* late-night transport/escort service.

Standardized Tests *Required for some:* CPAt.

Costs (2011–12) *Tuition:* $305 per credit part-time. *Required fees:* $45 per term part-time. *Payment plans:* installment, deferred payment. *Waivers:* children of alumni and employees or children of employees.

Applying *Options:* electronic application. *Required:* interview. *Required for some:* high school transcript. *Application deadline:* rolling (freshmen). *Notification:* continuous (transfers).

Freshman Application Contact Jones College, 555 Arlington Expressway, Jacksonville, FL 32211-5588. *Phone:* 904-743-1122 Ext. 141. *Web site:* http://www.jones.edu/.

Keiser University

Fort Lauderdale, Florida

- **Independent** comprehensive, founded 1977
- **Urban** campus with easy access to Miami
- **Coed**

Faculty *Student/faculty ratio:* 11:1.

Academics *Calendar:* 3 semesters per year. *Degrees:* associate, bachelor's, master's, and doctoral-professional (profile includes data from 13 campuses located in Daytona Beach, Melbourne, Sarasota, Kendall, Tallahassee, Jacksonville, Orlando, Miami, Tampa, West Palm Beach, Port St. Lucie, Miami Lakes, Pembroke Pines, and Lakeland campuses; all programs not offered at all locations, but many classes offered 100% online).

Student Life *Campus security:* 24-hour emergency response devices, Alert-Now Rapid Communications Service.

Standardized Tests *Required:* SAT, ACT, Wonderlic Test (for admission).

Applying *Application fee:* $50. *Required:* high school transcript, interview.

Freshman Application Contact Keiser University, 1500 NW 49th Street, Fort Lauderdale, FL 33309. *Phone:* 954-776-4456. *Toll-free phone:* 888-KEISER-9. *Web site:* http://www.keiseruniversity.edu/.

Lincoln College of Technology

West Palm Beach, Florida

Director of Admissions Mr. Kevin Cassidy, Director of Admissions, Lincoln College of Technology, 2410 Metro Centre Boulevard, West Palm Beach, FL 33407. *Phone:* 561-842-8324 Ext. 117. *Toll-free phone:* 800-826-9986. *Fax:* 561-842-9503. *Web site:* http://www.lincolnedu.com/.

Lincoln Culinary Institute

West Palm Beach, Florida

- **Proprietary** 4-year, administratively affiliated with Lincoln Educational Services
- **Urban** 14-acre campus with easy access to West Palm Beach, Fort Lauderdale, Miami
- **Coed**

Academics *Degrees:* diplomas, associate, and bachelor's (degree in science only (18 or 24 month program)).

Financial Aid *Of all full-time matriculated undergraduates who enrolled in 2009,* 28 Federal Work-Study jobs (averaging $4160).

Freshman Application Contact Lincoln Culinary Institute, 2410 Metrocentre Boulevard, West Palm Beach, FL 33407. *Phone:* 561-842-8324 Ext. 202. *Web site:* http://www.lincolnedu.com/campus/west-palm-beach-culinary-fl.

Lynn University

Boca Raton, Florida

- **Independent** comprehensive, founded 1962, administratively affiliated with American College Dublin
- **Suburban** 123-acre campus with easy access to Fort Lauderdale
- **Coed** 1,660 undergraduate students, 89% full-time, 47% women, 53% men
- **Moderately difficult** entrance level, 62% of applicants were admitted

Undergraduates 1,470 full-time, 190 part-time. Students come from 46 states and territories; 77 other countries; 45% are from out of state; 5% Black or African American, non-Hispanic/Latino; 10% Hispanic/Latino; 0.8% Asian, non-Hispanic/Latino; 0.1% Native Hawaiian or other Pacific Islander, non-Hispanic/Latino; 0.4% American Indian or Alaska Native, non-Hispanic/Latino; 0.7% Two or more races, non-Hispanic/Latino; 20% Race/ethnicity unknown; 17% international; 6% transferred in; 42% live on campus. *Retention:* 61% of full-time freshmen returned.

Freshmen *Admission:* 3,115 applied, 1,929 admitted, 355 enrolled. *Average high school GPA:* 2.78. *Test scores:* SAT critical reading scores over 500: 40%; SAT math scores over 500: 35%; ACT scores over 18: 68%; SAT critical reading scores over 600: 6%; SAT math scores over 600: 10%; ACT scores

over 24: 16%; SAT critical reading scores over 700: 1%; SAT math scores over 700: 1%; ACT scores over 30: 1%.

Faculty *Total:* 157, 60% full-time, 52% with terminal degrees. *Student/faculty ratio:* 16:1.

Academics *Calendar:* semesters plus 3 summer sessions. *Degrees:* certificates, bachelor's, master's, doctoral-research/scholarship, post-master's, and postbachelor's certificates. *Special study options:* academic remediation for entering students, accelerated degree program, adult/continuing education programs, advanced placement credit, cooperative education, distance learning, double majors, English as a second language, freshman honors college, honors programs, independent study, internships, part-time degree program, services for LD students, study abroad, summer session for credit. *ROTC:* Air Force (c).

Computers on Campus Students can access the following: campus intranet, computer help desk, free student e-mail accounts, online (class) grades, online (class) registration, online (class) schedules. Campuswide network is available. Wireless service is available via entire campus.

Student Life *Housing:* on-campus residence required for freshman year. *Options:* coed, women-only, disabled students. Campus housing is university owned. Freshman campus housing is guaranteed. *Activities and organizations:* drama/theater group, student-run newspaper, radio and television station, choral group, Knights of the Round Table, intramural groups, student newspaper, Residence Hall Council, Activities Board, national fraternities, national sororities. *Campus security:* 24-hour emergency response devices and patrols, late-night transport/escort service, video monitor at residence entrances. *Student services:* health clinic, personal/psychological counseling.

Athletics Member NCAA. All Division II. *Intercollegiate sports:* baseball M(s), basketball M(s)/W(s), golf M(s)/W(s), soccer M(s)/W(s), softball W(s), tennis M(s)/W(s), volleyball W(s).

Standardized Tests *Required:* SAT or ACT (for admission).

Costs (2011–12) *Comprehensive fee:* $42,850 includes full-time tuition ($29,400), mandatory fees ($1500), and room and board ($11,950). Part-time tuition: $850 per credit. Part-time tuition and fees vary according to class time and course load. *Required fees:* $30 per term part-time. *Room and board:* Room and board charges vary according to housing facility. *Payment plans:* installment, deferred payment. *Waivers:* employees or children of employees.

Financial Aid Of all full-time matriculated undergraduates who enrolled in 2009, 1,076 applied for aid, 666 were judged to have need, 653 had their need fully met. In 2009, 340 non-need-based awards were made. *Average percent of need met:* 60%. *Average financial aid package:* $20,853. *Average need-based loan:* $5643. *Average need-based gift aid:* $13,761. *Average non-need-based aid:* $11,381. *Average indebtedness upon graduation:* $34,075.

Applying *Options:* electronic application, early admission, deferred entrance. *Application fee:* $35. *Required:* essay or personal statement, high school transcript, minimum 2.5 GPA. *Recommended:* minimum 3 GPA, interview. *Application deadlines:* rolling (freshmen), rolling (transfers). *Notification:* continuous (freshmen), continuous (transfers).

Freshman Application Contact Juan Camilo Tamayo, Director of Undergraduate Admission, Lynn University, Admissions Office, 3601 North Military Trail, Boca Raton, FL 33431. *Phone:* 561-237-7900. *Toll-free phone:* 800-888-5966. *Fax:* 561-237-7100. *E-mail:* jtamayo@lynn.edu. *Web site:* http://www.lynn.edu/.

See page 1402 for the College Close-Up.

Miami Dade College
Miami, Florida

- **State and locally supported** primarily 2-year, founded 1960, part of Florida Community College System
- **Urban** campus
- **Endowment** $147.9 million
- **Coed** 61,674 undergraduate students, 40% full-time, 59% women, 41% men
- **Noncompetitive** entrance level, 100% of applicants were admitted

Undergraduates 24,875 full-time, 36,799 part-time. Students come from 41 states and territories; 189 other countries; 1% are from out of state; 17% Black or African American, non-Hispanic/Latino; 69% Hispanic/Latino; 1% Asian, non-Hispanic/Latino; 0.1% Native Hawaiian or other Pacific Islander, non-Hispanic/Latino; 0.1% American Indian or Alaska Native, non-Hispanic/Latino; 0.2% Two or more races, non-Hispanic/Latino; 2% Race/ethnicity unknown; 2% international; 2% transferred in.

Freshmen *Admission:* 12,501 applied, 12,501 admitted, 12,501 enrolled.

Faculty *Total:* 2,340, 28% full-time, 19% with terminal degrees. *Student/faculty ratio:* 31:1.

Academics *Calendar:* 16-16-6-6. *Degrees:* certificates, associate, and bachelor's. *Special study options:* academic remediation for entering students, accelerated degree program, adult/continuing education programs, advanced placement credit, cooperative education, distance learning, English as a second language, freshman honors college, honors programs, independent study,

internships, off-campus study, part-time degree program, services for LD students, study abroad, summer session for credit. *ROTC:* Army (c), Air Force (c).

Computers on Campus 9,655 computers/terminals and 1,500 ports are available on campus for general student use. Students can access the following: campus intranet, computer help desk, free student e-mail accounts, online (class) grades, online (class) registration, online (class) schedules, admissions; student feedback of faculty; financial aid; IRS Form 1098;. Campuswide network is available. Wireless service is available via computer centers, computer labs, learning centers, libraries, student centers.

Student Life *Housing:* college housing not available. *Activities and organizations:* drama/theater group, student-run newspaper, radio and television station, choral group, national fraternities. *Campus security:* 24-hour patrols. *Student services:* personal/psychological counseling.

Athletics Member NJCAA. *Intercollegiate sports:* baseball M(s), basketball M(s)/W(s), softball W(s), volleyball W(s). *Intramural sports:* basketball M/W, racquetball M/W, soccer M/W, softball M/W, tennis M/W, volleyball M/W, weight lifting M/W.

Costs (2010–11) *One-time required fee:* $20. *Tuition:* state resident $2190 full-time, $95 per credit hour part-time; nonresident $10,370 full-time, $346 per credit hour part-time. Full-time tuition and fees vary according to course load. Part-time tuition and fees vary according to course load. *Waivers:* employees or children of employees.

Financial Aid Of all full-time matriculated undergraduates who enrolled in 2009, 800 Federal Work-Study jobs (averaging $5000). 125 state and other part-time jobs (averaging $5000).

Applying *Options:* electronic application, early admission. *Application fee:* $30. *Required:* high school transcript. *Application deadlines:* rolling (freshmen), rolling (transfers). *Notification:* continuous (freshmen), continuous (out-of-state freshmen), continuous (transfers).

Freshman Application Contact Ms. Dulce Beltran, College Registrar, Miami Dade College, 11011 SW 104th Street, Miami, FL 33176. *Phone:* 305-237-2103. *Fax:* 305-237-2964. *E-mail:* dbeltran@mdc.edu. *Web site:* http://www.mdc.edu/.

Miami International University of Art & Design
Miami, Florida

- **Proprietary** comprehensive, founded 1965, part of Education Management Corporation
- **Urban** 4-acre campus
- **Coed**

Academics *Calendar:* quarters. *Degrees:* associate, bachelor's, and master's.

Costs (2010–11) *Tuition:* Tuition cost varies by program. Prospective students should contact the school for current tuition costs. Other charges include a starting kit for all first-quarter students. Kits vary in price, depending on the program of study.

Freshman Application Contact Miami International University of Art & Design, 1501 Biscayne Boulevard, Suite 100, Miami, FL 33132-1418. *Phone:* 305-428-5700. *Toll-free phone:* 800-225-9023. *Web site:* http://www.artinstitutes.edu/miami/.

See page 1426 for the College Close-Up.

New College of Florida
Sarasota, Florida

- **State-supported** 4-year, founded 1960, part of State University System of Florida
- **Suburban** 119-acre campus with easy access to Tampa-St. Petersburg
- **Endowment** $46.3 million
- **Coed** 801 undergraduate students, 100% full-time, 60% women, 40% men
- **Very difficult** entrance level, 53% of applicants were admitted

Undergraduates 801 full-time. Students come from 40 states and territories; 22 other countries; 20% are from out of state; 1% Black or African American, non-Hispanic/Latino; 13% Hispanic/Latino; 3% Asian, non-Hispanic/Latino; 0.1% Native Hawaiian or other Pacific Islander, non-Hispanic/Latino; 0.5% American Indian or Alaska Native, non-Hispanic/Latino; 3% Two or more races, non-Hispanic/Latino; 3% Race/ethnicity unknown; 0.1% international; 5% transferred in; 76% live on campus. *Retention:* 82% of full-time freshmen returned.

Freshmen *Admission:* 1,414 applied, 751 admitted, 183 enrolled. *Average high school GPA:* 4.03. *Test scores:* SAT critical reading scores over 500: 99%; SAT math scores over 500: 99%; SAT writing scores over 500: 99%; ACT scores over 18: 101%; SAT critical reading scores over 600: 91%; SAT math scores over 600: 71%; SAT writing scores over 600: 78%; ACT scores

over 24: 97%; SAT critical reading scores over 700: 43%; SAT math scores over 700: 17%; SAT writing scores over 700: 21%; ACT scores over 30: 47%.

Faculty *Total:* 99, 72% full-time, 92% with terminal degrees. *Student/faculty ratio:* 10:1.

Academics *Calendar:* 4-1-4. *Degree:* bachelor's. *Special study options:* cooperative education, double majors, honors programs, independent study, internships, off-campus study, services for LD students, student-designed majors, study abroad.

Computers on Campus 41 computers/terminals and 1,000 ports are available on campus for general student use. Students can access the following: campus intranet, computer help desk, free student e-mail accounts, online (class) grades, online (class) registration, online (class) schedules. Campuswide network is available. 100% of college-owned or -operated housing units are wired for high-speed Internet access. Wireless service is available via classrooms, dorm rooms, learning centers, libraries, student centers.

Student Life *Housing:* on-campus residence required through senior year. *Options:* coed, disabled students. Campus housing is university owned. Freshman campus housing is guaranteed. *Activities and organizations:* drama/theater group, student-run newspaper, radio station, choral group, PRIDE, Interfaith groups, New College Student Alliance, Feminist Majority Leadership Alliance, Sailing Club. *Campus security:* 24-hour emergency response devices and patrols, student patrols, late-night transport/escort service, controlled dormitory access, campus police are state certified police officers and available 24/7. *Student services:* health clinic, personal/psychological counseling, women's center.

Athletics *Intercollegiate sports:* sailing M/W. *Intramural sports:* archery M(c)/W(c), basketball M/W, fencing M/W, football M, racquetball M/W, sailing M(c)/W(c), soccer M(c)/W(c), softball M(c)/W(c), swimming and diving M(c)/W(c), table tennis M(c)/W(c), tennis M(c)/W(c), ultimate Frisbee M(c)/W(c), volleyball M/W, weight lifting M(c)/W(c), wrestling M/W.

Standardized Tests *Required:* SAT or ACT (for admission).

Costs (2011–12) *Tuition:* state resident $6302 full-time; nonresident $28,949 full-time. *Room and board:* $8472; room only: $5788. Room and board charges vary according to board plan and housing facility. *Payment plan:* installment.

Financial Aid Of all full-time matriculated undergraduates who enrolled in 2009, 572 applied for aid, 413 were judged to have need, 208 had their need fully met. 20 Federal Work-Study jobs (averaging $3321). 168 state and other part-time jobs (averaging $1031). In 2009, 134 non-need-based awards were made. *Average percent of need met:* 89%. *Average financial aid package:* $14,233. *Average need-based loan:* $4542. *Average need-based gift aid:* $10,142. *Average non-need-based aid:* $1621. *Average indebtedness upon graduation:* $11,458.

Applying *Options:* electronic application, early admission, deferred entrance. *Application fee:* $30. *Required:* essay or personal statement, high school transcript, 1 letter of recommendation. *Required for some:* interview. *Recommended:* minimum 3 GPA. *Application deadlines:* 4/15 (freshmen), 4/15 (out-of-state freshmen), 4/15 (transfers). *Notification:* 4/25 (freshmen), 4/25 (out-of-state freshmen), 4/25 (transfers).

Freshman Application Contact Office of Admissions, New College of Florida, 5800 Bay Shore Road, Sarasota, FL 34243-2109. *Phone:* 941-487-5000. *Fax:* 941-487-5010. *E-mail:* admissions@ncf.edu. *Web site:* http://www.ncf.edu/.

See page 1464 for the College Close-Up.

New World School of the Arts
Miami, Florida

Freshman Application Contact Lourdes Werner, Recruitment and Admissions Coordinator, New World School of the Arts, 300 NE Second Avenue, Miami, FL 33132. *Phone:* 305-237-7007. *Fax:* 305-237-3794. *E-mail:* nwsaadm@mdc.edu. *Web site:* http://www.mdc.edu/nwsa/.

Northwest Florida State College
Niceville, Florida

- **State and locally supported** primarily 2-year, founded 1963, part of Florida Community College System
- **Small-town** 264-acre campus
- **Endowment** $28.6 million
- **Coed**
- **Noncompetitive** entrance level

Faculty *Student/faculty ratio:* 15:1.

Academics *Calendar:* semesters plus summer sessions. *Degrees:* certificates, associate, and bachelor's.

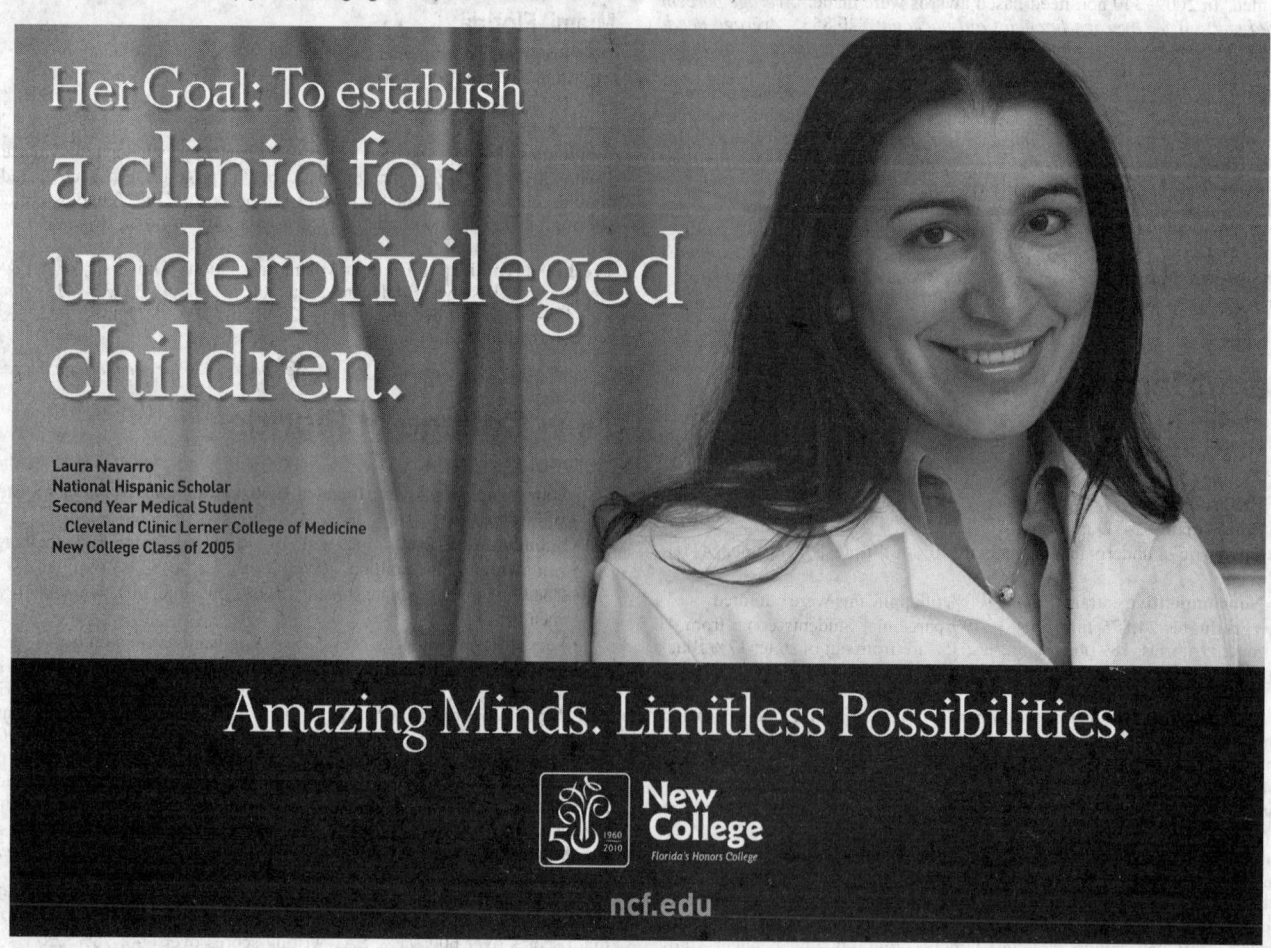

Student Life *Campus security:* 24-hour patrols.

Athletics Member NJCAA.

Standardized Tests *Required for some:* ACT, SAT I, ACT ASSET, MAPS, or Florida College Entry Placement Test are used for placement not admission.

Costs (2010–11) *Tuition:* state resident $2568 full-time, $85 per credit hour part-time; nonresident $11,511 full-time, $335 per credit hour part-time. Full-time tuition and fees vary according to course load, degree level, and reciprocity agreements. Part-time tuition and fees vary according to course load, degree level, and reciprocity agreements. *Required fees:* $15 per credit hour part-time. *Payment plans:* tuition prepayment, installment, deferred payment.

Financial Aid *Of all full-time matriculated undergraduates who enrolled in 2009,* 81 Federal Work-Study jobs (averaging $1500). 11 state and other part-time jobs (averaging $1460).

Applying *Options:* electronic application. *Required:* high school transcript.

Freshman Application Contact Ms. Christine Bishop, Registrar/Division Director Enrollment Services, Northwest Florida State College, 100 College Boulevard, Niceville, FL 32578. *Phone:* 850-729-5373. *Fax:* 850-729-5323. *E-mail:* registrar@nwfsc.edu. *Web site:* http://www.nwfsc.edu/.

Northwood University, Florida Campus

West Palm Beach, Florida

Freshman Application Contact Ms. Emily Mass, Associate Director of Admissions, Northwood University, Florida Campus, 2600 North Military Trail, West Palm Beach, FL 33409-2911. *Phone:* 800-622-9000. *Fax:* 561-681-7901. *E-mail:* fladmit@northwood.edu. *Web site:* http://www.northwood.edu/.

Nova Southeastern University

Fort Lauderdale, Florida

- **Independent** university, founded 1964
- **Suburban** 300-acre campus
- **Endowment** $54.2 million
- **Coed** 6,174 undergraduate students, 69% full-time, 71% women, 29% men
- **Moderately difficult** entrance level, 53% of applicants were admitted

Undergraduates 4,257 full-time, 1,917 part-time. 18% are from out of state; 25% Black or African American, non-Hispanic/Latino; 32% Hispanic/Latino; 5% Asian, non-Hispanic/Latino; 0.2% Native Hawaiian or other Pacific Islander, non-Hispanic/Latino; 0.3% American Indian or Alaska Native, non-Hispanic/Latino; 0.5% Two or more races, non-Hispanic/Latino; 5% Race/ethnicity unknown; 4% international; 20% transferred in; 9% live on campus. *Retention:* 69% of full-time freshmen returned.

Freshmen *Admission:* 4,586 applied, 2,444 admitted, 815 enrolled. *Average high school GPA:* 3.65. *Test scores:* SAT critical reading scores over 500: 58%; SAT math scores over 500: 62%; ACT scores over 18: 95%; SAT critical reading scores over 600: 17%; SAT math scores over 600: 23%; ACT scores over 24: 39%; SAT critical reading scores over 700: 1%; SAT math scores over 700: 4%; ACT scores over 30: 5%.

Faculty *Total:* 1,694, 43% full-time, 81% with terminal degrees. *Student/faculty ratio:* 22:1.

Academics *Calendar:* trimesters. *Degrees:* associate, bachelor's, master's, doctoral-other, doctoral-professional, doctoral-research/scholarship, and post-master's certificates. *Special study options:* academic remediation for entering students, adult/continuing education programs, advanced placement credit, distance learning, double majors, honors programs, independent study, internships, off-campus study, part-time degree program, services for LD students, study abroad, summer session for credit. *Unusual degree programs:* 3-2 business administration; marine biology, occupational therapy, criminal justice, psychology, mental health counseling, speech language pathology, computer science, education, physical therapy.

Computers on Campus 3,144 computers/terminals and 6,944 ports are available on campus for general student use. Students can access the following: computer help desk, free student e-mail accounts, online (class) registration. Campuswide network is available. 100% of college-owned or -operated housing units are wired for high-speed Internet access. Wireless service is available via entire campus.

Student Life *Housing:* on-campus residence required through sophomore year. *Options:* coed, disabled students. Campus housing is university owned. Freshman campus housing is guaranteed. *Activities and organizations:* drama/theater group, student-run newspaper, radio station, choral group, Pre-Pharmacy Society, Pre-Med Society, Kappa Sigma, Delta Phi Epsilon, PASA, national fraternities, national sororities. *Campus security:* 24-hour emergency response devices and patrols, late-night transport/escort service, controlled dormitory access, shuttle bus service. *Student services:* health clinic, personal/psychological counseling, women's center.

Athletics Member NCAA. All Division II. *Intercollegiate sports:* baseball M(s), basketball M(s)/W(s), cheerleading W, crew W(s), cross-country running M(s)/W(s), golf M(s)/W(s), soccer M(s)/W(s), softball W(s), swimming and diving M(s)/W(s), tennis W(s), track and field M(s)/W(s), volleyball W(s). *Intramural sports:* basketball M/W, football M/W, golf M/W, racquetball M/W, soccer M/W, softball M/W, ultimate Frisbee M/W, volleyball M/W.

Standardized Tests *Required:* SAT or ACT (for admission).

Costs (2011–12) *Comprehensive fee:* $31,836 includes full-time tuition ($22,200), mandatory fees ($550), and room and board ($9086). Full-time tuition and fees vary according to class time and program. Part-time tuition: $740 per credit hour. Part-time tuition and fees vary according to class time, course load, and program. *Room and board:* Room and board charges vary according to board plan and housing facility. *Payment plans:* installment, deferred payment. *Waivers:* employees or children of employees.

Financial Aid Of all full-time matriculated undergraduates who enrolled in 2009, 3,301 applied for aid, 2,943 were judged to have need, 204 had their need fully met. 278 Federal Work-Study jobs (averaging $2850), 1,511 state and other part-time jobs (averaging $3614). In 2009, 247 non-need-based awards were made. *Average percent of need met:* 67%. *Average financial aid package:* $16,863. *Average need-based loan:* $5568. *Average need-based gift aid:* $6287. *Average non-need-based aid:* $5631. *Average indebtedness upon graduation:* $36,908.

Applying *Options:* electronic application, deferred entrance. *Application fee:* $50. *Recommended:* minimum 2.6 GPA, essay and transcript of high school record recommended of some. *Application deadlines:* rolling (freshmen), rolling (out-of-state freshmen), rolling (transfers). *Notification:* continuous (freshmen), continuous (out-of-state freshmen), continuous (transfers).

Freshman Application Contact Ms. Maria Dillard, Director of Enrollment Management, Nova Southeastern University, Enrollment Processing Services, 3301 College Avenue, Ft. Lauderdale, FL 33329-9905. *Phone:* 954-262-8000. *Toll-free phone:* 800-541-NOVA. *Fax:* 954-262-3811. *E-mail:* nsuinfo@nova.edu. *Web site:* http://www.nova.edu/.

Palm Beach Atlantic University

West Palm Beach, Florida

- **Independent nondenominational** comprehensive, founded 1968
- **Urban** 27-acre campus with easy access to Orlando and the Caribbean
- **Endowment** $62.5 million
- **Coed** 2,841 undergraduate students, 80% full-time, 62% women, 38% men
- **Moderately difficult** entrance level, 85% of applicants were admitted

Undergraduates 2,284 full-time, 557 part-time. Students come from 47 states and territories; 45 other countries; 36% are from out of state; 17% Black or African American, non-Hispanic/Latino; 14% Hispanic/Latino; 1% Asian, non-Hispanic/Latino; 0.2% Native Hawaiian or other Pacific Islander, non-Hispanic/Latino; 0.5% American Indian or Alaska Native, non-Hispanic/Latino; 0.2% Two or more races, non-Hispanic/Latino; 9% Race/ethnicity unknown; 2% international; 11% transferred in; 54% live on campus. *Retention:* 64% of full-time freshmen returned.

Freshmen *Admission:* 1,246 applied, 1,061 admitted, 446 enrolled. *Test scores:* SAT critical reading scores over 500: 64%; SAT math scores over 500: 62%; SAT writing scores over 500: 56%; ACT scores over 18: 92%; SAT critical reading scores over 600: 18%; SAT math scores over 600: 18%; SAT writing scores over 600: 11%; ACT scores over 24: 40%; SAT critical reading scores over 700: 1%; SAT math scores over 700: 3%; SAT writing scores over 700: 1%; ACT scores over 30: 3%.

Faculty *Total:* 336, 46% full-time, 57% with terminal degrees. *Student/faculty ratio:* 13:1.

Academics *Calendar:* semesters. *Degrees:* associate, bachelor's, master's, and doctoral-professional. *Special study options:* academic remediation for entering students, accelerated degree program, adult/continuing education programs, advanced placement credit, distance learning, double majors, honors programs, independent study, internships, part-time degree program, services for LD students, student-designed majors, study abroad, summer session for credit. *ROTC:* Army (c).

Computers on Campus 465 computers/terminals and 500 ports are available on campus for general student use. Students can access the following: campus intranet, computer help desk, free student e-mail accounts, online (class) grades, online (class) registration, online (class) schedules. Campuswide network is available. 100% of college-owned or -operated housing units are wired for high-speed Internet access. Wireless service is available via classrooms, computer centers, computer labs, learning centers, libraries, student centers.

Student Life *Housing:* on-campus residence required through sophomore year. *Options:* coed, men-only, women-only. Campus housing is university owned. Freshman applicants given priority for college housing. *Activities and organizations:* drama/theater group, student-run newspaper, radio and television station, choral group, Christian Pharmacist Fellowship International, Caribbean Fellowship Club, Science Club, N.O.W. (Night of Worship), student government. *Campus security:* 24-hour emergency response devices and patrols,

late-night transport/escort service, controlled dormitory access. *Student services:* health clinic, personal/psychological counseling.
Athletics Member NCAA, NCCAA. All NCAA Division II. *Intercollegiate sports:* baseball M(s), basketball M(s)/W(s), cheerleading M(c)/W(c), cross-country running M(s)/W(s), fencing M(c)/W(c), lacrosse M(c)/W(c), soccer M(s)/W(s), tennis M(s)/W(s), volleyball W(s). *Intramural sports:* badminton M/W, basketball M/W, bowling M/W, golf M/W, racquetball M/W, soccer M/W, softball M/W, table tennis M/W, ultimate Frisbee M/W, volleyball M/W, water polo M/W.
Standardized Tests *Required:* SAT or ACT (for admission).
Costs (2010–11) *Comprehensive fee:* $31,620 includes full-time tuition ($23,100), mandatory fees ($300), and room and board ($8220). Full-time tuition and fees vary according to course load, degree level, location, program, and reciprocity agreements. Part-time tuition: $556 per credit hour. Part-time tuition and fees vary according to course load, degree level, location, program, and reciprocity agreements. *Required fees:* $99 per term part-time. *College room only:* $4570. Room and board charges vary according to board plan and housing facility. *Payment plan:* installment. *Waivers:* employees or children of employees.
Financial Aid Of all full-time matriculated undergraduates who enrolled in 2009, 1,897 applied for aid, 1,679 were judged to have need, 224 had their need fully met. 309 Federal Work-Study jobs (averaging $3154). 7 state and other part-time jobs (averaging $1932). In 2009, 445 non-need-based awards were made. *Average percent of need met:* 65%. *Average financial aid package:* $16,270. *Average need-based loan:* $4470. *Average need-based gift aid:* $12,075. *Average non-need-based aid:* $6561. *Average indebtedness upon graduation:* $22,150. *Financial aid deadline:* 8/1.
Applying *Options:* electronic application, early admission, deferred entrance. *Application fee:* $35. *Required:* essay or personal statement, high school transcript. *Recommended:* interview. *Application deadlines:* rolling (freshmen), rolling (transfers). *Notification:* continuous (freshmen), continuous (transfers).
Freshman Application Contact Palm Beach Atlantic University, 901 South Flagler Drive, PO Box 24708, West Palm Beach, FL 33416-4708. *Phone:* 561-803-2102. *Toll-free phone:* 800-238-3998. *Web site:* http://www.pba.edu/.

Palm Beach State College
Lake Worth, Florida

- **State-supported** primarily 2-year, founded 1933, part of Florida State College System
- **Urban** 150-acre campus with easy access to West Palm Beach
- **Endowment** $23.0 million
- **Coed** 29,534 undergraduate students, 37% full-time, 58% women, 42% men
- **Noncompetitive** entrance level, 100% of applicants were admitted

Undergraduates 10,913 full-time, 18,621 part-time. Students come from 49 states and territories; 146 other countries; 5% are from out of state; 24% Black or African American, non-Hispanic/Latino; 21% Hispanic/Latino; 3% Asian, non-Hispanic/Latino; 0.2% Native Hawaiian or other Pacific Islander, non-Hispanic/Latino; 0.3% American Indian or Alaska Native, non-Hispanic/Latino; 0.9% Two or more races, non-Hispanic/Latino; 4% Race/ethnicity unknown; 2% international; 5% transferred in.
Freshmen *Admission:* 5,127 applied, 5,127 admitted, 5,127 enrolled.
Faculty *Total:* 1,473, 19% full-time, 16% with terminal degrees. *Student/faculty ratio:* 43:1.
Academics *Calendar:* semesters. *Degrees:* certificates, diplomas, associate, and bachelor's. *Special study options:* academic remediation for entering students, adult/continuing education programs, advanced placement credit, cooperative education, distance learning, double majors, English as a second language, freshman honors college, honors programs, independent study, internships, off-campus study, part-time degree program, services for LD students, student-designed majors, study abroad, summer session for credit.
Computers on Campus 2,300 computers/terminals are available on campus for general student use. Students can access the following: computer help desk, free student e-mail accounts, online (class) registration. Campuswide network is available. Wireless service is available via entire campus.
Student Life *Housing:* college housing not available. *Activities and organizations:* drama/theater group, student-run newspaper, choral group, student government, Phi Theta Kappa, Students for International Understanding, Black Student Union, Drama Club, national fraternities. *Campus security:* 24-hour emergency response devices and patrols. *Student services:* health clinic, women's center.
Athletics Member NJCAA. *Intercollegiate sports:* baseball M(s), basketball M(s)/W(s), softball W(s), volleyball W(s).
Standardized Tests *Recommended:* SAT and SAT Subject Tests or ACT (for admission).
Costs (2010–11) *One-time required fee:* $20. *Tuition:* state resident $2138 full-time, $89 per credit hour part-time; nonresident $7752 full-time, $323 per credit hour part-time. Full-time tuition and fees vary according to course level,

course load, and student level. Part-time tuition and fees vary according to course level, course load, and student level. *Required fees:* $10 full-time, $10 per term part-time. *Room and board:* Room and board charges vary according to location. *Waivers:* employees or children of employees.
Applying *Options:* electronic application, early admission, deferred entrance. *Application fee:* $20. *Application deadlines:* 8/20 (freshmen), 8/20 (transfers). *Notification:* continuous until 8/20 (freshmen), continuous until 8/20 (transfers).
Freshman Application Contact Ms. Anne Guiler, Coordinator of Distance Learning, Palm Beach State College, Lake Worth, FL 33461. *Phone:* 561-868-3032. *Fax:* 561-868-3584. *E-mail:* enrollmt@palmbeachstate.edu. *Web site:* http://www.palmbeachstate.edu/.

Pensacola State College
Pensacola, Florida

- **State-supported** primarily 2-year, founded 1948, part of Florida Community College System
- **Urban** 160-acre campus
- **Coed** 11,676 undergraduate students, 39% full-time, 61% women, 39% men
- **Noncompetitive** entrance level

Undergraduates 4,600 full-time, 7,076 part-time. Students come from 25 states and territories; 1% are from out of state; 14% Black or African American, non-Hispanic/Latino; 5% Hispanic/Latino; 3% Asian, non-Hispanic/Latino; 0.2% Native Hawaiian or other Pacific Islander, non-Hispanic/Latino; 1% American Indian or Alaska Native, non-Hispanic/Latino; 3% Two or more races, non-Hispanic/Latino; 1% Race/ethnicity unknown; 0.5% international; 5% transferred in.
Freshmen *Admission:* 1,360 enrolled.
Faculty *Total:* 196, 100% full-time, 18% with terminal degrees. *Student/faculty ratio:* 25:1.
Academics *Calendar:* semesters. *Degrees:* certificates, diplomas, associate, and bachelor's. *Special study options:* academic remediation for entering students, adult/continuing education programs, advanced placement credit, cooperative education, distance learning, double majors, external degree program, honors programs, independent study, part-time degree program, services for LD students, summer session for credit. *ROTC:* Army (b).
Computers on Campus Campuswide network is available.
Student Life *Housing:* college housing not available. *Activities and organizations:* drama/theater group, student-run newspaper, choral group. *Campus security:* 24-hour emergency response devices and patrols, student patrols, late-night transport/escort service. *Student services:* health clinic, personal/psychological counseling.
Athletics Member NJCAA. *Intercollegiate sports:* baseball M(s), basketball M(s)/W(s), softball W(s), volleyball W. *Intramural sports:* archery M/W, badminton M/W, basketball M/W, bowling M/W, cross-country running M/W, gymnastics M/W, racquetball M/W, sailing M/W, swimming and diving M/W, tennis M/W, track and field M/W, volleyball M/W, weight lifting M/W, wrestling M.
Costs (2010–11) *One-time required fee:* $30. *Tuition:* state resident $2179 full-time; nonresident $8213 full-time. Full-time tuition and fees vary according to degree level. Part-time tuition and fees vary according to degree level. *Waivers:* senior citizens and employees or children of employees.
Financial Aid Of all full-time matriculated undergraduates who enrolled in 2009, 120 Federal Work-Study jobs (averaging $3000).
Applying *Options:* early admission. *Application fee:* $30. *Required:* high school transcript. *Application deadlines:* 8/30 (freshmen), 8/30 (transfers). *Notification:* continuous until 8/30 (freshmen), continuous until 8/30 (transfers).
Freshman Application Contact Ms. Martha Caughey, Registrar, Pensacola State College, 1000 College Boulevard, Pensacola, FL 32504-8998. *Phone:* 850-484-1600. *Fax:* 850-484-1829. *Web site:* http://www.pensacolastate.edu/.

Polk State College
Winter Haven, Florida

- **State-supported** primarily 2-year, founded 1964, part of Florida Community College System
- **Suburban** 98-acre campus with easy access to Orlando and Tampa
- **Endowment** $13.4 million
- **Coed** 10,589 undergraduate students, 35% full-time, 63% women, 37% men
- **Noncompetitive** entrance level

Undergraduates 3,739 full-time, 6,850 part-time. Students come from 15 states and territories; 63 other countries; 1% are from out of state; 17% Black or African American, non-Hispanic/Latino; 13% Hispanic/Latino; 3% Asian, non-Hispanic/Latino; 0.1% Native Hawaiian or other Pacific Islander, non-Hispanic/Latino; 0.3% American Indian or Alaska Native, non-Hispanic/

Latino; 1% Two or more races, non-Hispanic/Latino; 3% Race/ethnicity unknown; 0.7% international; 4% transferred in. *Retention:* 67% of full-time freshmen returned.

Freshmen *Admission:* 1,503 enrolled. *Test scores:* SAT math scores over 500: 53%; SAT math scores over 600: 5%; SAT math scores over 700: 1%.
Faculty *Total:* 721, 25% full-time, 10% with terminal degrees. *Student/faculty ratio:* 17:1.
Academics *Calendar:* semesters 16-16-6-6. *Degrees:* certificates, associate, and bachelor's. *Special study options:* academic remediation for entering students, accelerated degree program, adult/continuing education programs, advanced placement credit, cooperative education, distance learning, double majors, English as a second language, honors programs, independent study, off-campus study, part-time degree program, services for LD students, student-designed majors, study abroad, summer session for credit. *ROTC:* Army (c).
Computers on Campus 250 computers/terminals are available on campus for general student use. Students can access the following: computer help desk, free student e-mail accounts, online (class) grades, online (class) registration, online (class) schedules. Campuswide network is available. Wireless service is available via entire campus.
Student Life *Housing:* college housing not available. *Activities and organizations:* drama/theater group, choral group. *Campus security:* 24-hour emergency response devices and patrols. *Student services:* personal/psychological counseling.
Athletics Member NJCAA. *Intercollegiate sports:* baseball M(s), basketball M(s), soccer W(s), softball W(s), volleyball W(s). *Intramural sports:* basketball M/W, bowling M/W, football M/W, volleyball M/W.
Costs (2010–11) *Tuition:* state resident $2819 full-time, $94 per credit hour part-time; nonresident $10,443 full-time, $348 per credit hour part-time. Full-time tuition and fees vary according to course load and degree level. Part-time tuition and fees vary according to course load and degree level. Tuition for Upper Division in-state $3,184 full-time, $106.13 per credit hour part-time; nonresident $15,968 full-time, $532.26 per credit hour part-time. *Waivers:* employees or children of employees.
Financial Aid Of all full-time matriculated undergraduates who enrolled in 2009, 16 Federal Work-Study jobs (averaging $400).
Applying *Options:* electronic application, early admission, deferred entrance. *Required:* high school transcript. *Application deadlines:* rolling (freshmen), rolling (transfers). *Notification:* continuous (freshmen), continuous (transfers).
Freshman Application Contact Polk State College, 999 Avenue H, NE, Winter Haven, FL 33881-4299. *Phone:* 863-297-1010 Ext. 5016. *Web site:* http://www.polk.edu/.

Polytechnic University of Puerto Rico, Miami Campus
Miami, Florida

Director of Admissions Admissions Department, Polytechnic University of Puerto Rico, Miami Campus, 8180 Northwest 36th Street, Suite 401, Miami, FL 33166. *Phone:* 305-418-4220. *Toll-free phone:* 888-729-7659. *Fax:* 305-418-4325. *Web site:* http://www.pupr.edu/miami/.

Polytechnic University of Puerto Rico, Orlando Campus
Winter Park, Florida

Director of Admissions Teresa Cardona, Director of Recruitment and Admission, Polytechnic University of Puerto Rico, Orlando Campus, 4800 Howell Branch Road, Winter Park, FL 32792. *Phone:* 407-677-7000. *Toll-free phone:* 888-577-POLY. *Fax:* 407-677-5082. *Web site:* http://www.pupr.edu/orlando/.

Rasmussen College Fort Myers
Fort Myers, Florida

Director of Admissions Admissions Director, Rasmussen College Fort Myers, 9160 Forum Corporate Parkway, Suite 100, Fort Myers, FL 33905. *Phone:* 239-477-2100. *Toll-free phone:* 866-344-0229. *Fax:* 239-477-2101. *Web site:* http://www.rasmussen.edu/.

Rasmussen College Ocala
Ocala, Florida

Freshman Application Contact Admissions Office, Rasmussen College Ocala, 2221 Southwest 19th Avenue Road, Ocala, FL 34471. *Phone:* 352-629-1941. *Toll-free phone:* 877-593-2783. *Web site:* http://www.rasmussen.edu/.

Rasmussen College Pasco County
Holiday, Florida

Director of Admissions Ms. Claire L. Walker, Senior Admissions Representative, Rasmussen College Pasco County, 2127 Grand Boulevard, Holiday, FL 34690. *Phone:* 727-942-0069. *Toll-free phone:* 888-729-7247. *Web site:* http://www.rasmussen.edu/.

Remington College–Largo Campus
Largo, Florida

Director of Admissions Kathy McCabe, Director of Recruitment, Remington College–Largo Campus, 8550 Ulmerton Road, Largo, FL 33771. *Phone:* 727-532-1999. *Toll-free phone:* 888-900-2343. *Fax:* 727-530-7710. *E-mail:* kathy.mccabe@remingtoncollege.edu. *Web site:* http://www.remingtoncollege.edu/.

Remington College–Tampa Campus
Tampa, Florida

Freshman Application Contact Remington College–Tampa Campus, 2410 East Busch Boulevard, Tampa, FL 33612-8410. *Phone:* 813-932-0701. *Toll-free phone:* 800-992-4850. *Web site:* http://www.remingtoncollege.edu/.

Ringling College of Art and Design
Sarasota, Florida

- **Independent** 4-year, founded 1931
- **Small-town** 49-acre campus with easy access to Tampa-St. Petersburg
- **Endowment** $21.6 million
- **Coed** 1,368 undergraduate students, 96% full-time, 58% women, 42% men
- **Moderately difficult** entrance level, 74% of applicants were admitted

Undergraduates 1,317 full-time, 51 part-time. Students come from 49 states and territories; 45 other countries; 46% are from out of state; 4% Black or African American, non-Hispanic/Latino; 13% Hispanic/Latino; 6% Asian, non-Hispanic/Latino; 0.2% Native Hawaiian or other Pacific Islander, non-Hispanic/Latino; 0.6% American Indian or Alaska Native, non-Hispanic/Latino; 4% Two or more races, non-Hispanic/Latino; 7% international; 7% transferred in; 61% live on campus. *Retention:* 82% of full-time freshmen returned.
Freshmen *Admission:* 1,208 applied, 894 admitted, 317 enrolled. *Average high school GPA:* 3.17.
Faculty *Total:* 152, 58% full-time, 50% with terminal degrees. *Student/faculty ratio:* 12:1.
Academics *Calendar:* semesters. *Degree:* certificates and bachelor's. *Special study options:* academic remediation for entering students, advanced placement credit, independent study, internships, off-campus study, part-time degree program, services for LD students, study abroad.
Computers on Campus 800 computers/terminals are available on campus for general student use. Students can access the following: campus intranet, computer help desk, free student e-mail accounts, online (class) grades, online (class) registration, online (class) schedules, central file storage, high performance computing labs. Campuswide network is available. 100% of college-owned or -operated housing units are wired for high-speed Internet access. Wireless service is available via entire campus.
Student Life *Housing options:* coed, men-only, women-only. Campus housing is university owned. Freshman applicants given priority for college housing. *Activities and organizations:* drama/theater group, Student Government Association, Digital Painting Sketch Club, Gaming Club, Martial Arts Club, Quidditch Team. *Campus security:* 24-hour emergency response devices and patrols, late-night transport/escort service, controlled dormitory access, lighted campus. *Student services:* personal/psychological counseling.
Athletics *Intramural sports:* basketball M(c)/W(c), football M(c)/W(c), soccer M(c)/W(c), ultimate Frisbee M(c)/W(c), weight lifting M/W.
Costs (2010–11) *Comprehensive fee:* $41,620 includes full-time tuition ($29,800), mandatory fees ($930), and room and board ($10,890). Full-time tuition and fees vary according to course load, program, and student level. Part-time tuition: $1389 per semester hour. Part-time tuition and fees vary according to course load, program, and student level. *College room only:* $5740. Room and board charges vary according to board plan and housing facility. *Payment plan:* installment. *Waivers:* employees or children of employees.
Financial Aid Of all full-time matriculated undergraduates who enrolled in 2009, 1,033 applied for aid, 941 were judged to have need, 28 had their need fully met. In 2009, 90 non-need-based awards were made. *Average percent of need met:* 38%. *Average financial aid package:* $16,981. *Average need-based loan:* $8721. *Average need-based gift aid:* $9485. *Average non-need-based aid:* $12,150.

Applying *Options:* electronic application, deferred entrance. *Application fee:* $70. *Required:* essay or personal statement, high school transcript, minimum 2 GPA, 2 letters of recommendation, portfolio, resume. *Recommended:* interview. *Application deadlines:* rolling (freshmen), rolling (transfers). *Notification:* continuous (freshmen), continuous (transfers).
Freshman Application Contact Ms. Tracy Stephanski, Director of Admissions, Ringling College of Art and Design, 2700 North Tamiami Trail, Sarasota, FL 34234-5895. *Phone:* 941-359-7526. *Toll-free phone:* 800-255-7695. *Fax:* 941-359-7517. *E-mail:* admissions@ringling.edu. *Web site:* http://www.ringling.edu/.

Rollins College
Winter Park, Florida

- **Independent** comprehensive, founded 1885
- **Suburban** 70-acre campus with easy access to Orlando
- **Endowment** $282.2 million
- **Coed** 1,730 undergraduate students, 100% full-time, 59% women, 41% men
- **Very difficult** entrance level, 56% of applicants were admitted

Undergraduates 1,730 full-time. 43% are from out of state; 4% Black or African American, non-Hispanic/Latino; 10% Hispanic/Latino; 3% Asian, non-Hispanic/Latino; 0.1% Native Hawaiian or other Pacific Islander, non-Hispanic/Latino; 0.1% American Indian or Alaska Native, non-Hispanic/Latino; 2% Two or more races, non-Hispanic/Latino; 1% Race/ethnicity unknown; 5% international; 4% transferred in; 65% live on campus. *Retention:* 82% of full-time freshmen returned.
Freshmen *Admission:* 3,771 applied, 2,099 admitted, 469 enrolled. *Average high school GPA:* 3.6. *Test scores:* SAT critical reading scores over 500: 93%; SAT math scores over 500: 96%; SAT writing scores over 500: 93%; ACT scores over 18: 100%; SAT critical reading scores over 600: 58%; SAT math scores over 600: 56%; SAT writing scores over 600: 54%; ACT scores over 24: 78%; SAT critical reading scores over 700: 13%; SAT math scores over 700: 7%; SAT writing scores over 700: 13%; ACT scores over 30: 21%.
Faculty *Total:* 173, 100% full-time, 91% with terminal degrees. *Student/faculty ratio:* 10:1.
Academics *Calendar:* semesters. *Degrees:* bachelor's and master's. *Special study options:* academic remediation for entering students, accelerated degree program, adult/continuing education programs, advanced placement credit, double majors, honors programs, independent study, internships, off-campus study, part-time degree program, services for LD students, student-designed majors, study abroad, summer session for credit. *Unusual degree programs:* 3-2 business administration with Crummer Graduate School of Business, Rollins College; engineering with Columbia University, Washington University in St. Louis, or Auburn University; forestry with Duke University School of the Environment; Environmental Management with Duke University School of the Environment.
Computers on Campus 240 computers/terminals and 155 ports are available on campus for general student use. Students can access the following: campus intranet, computer help desk, free student e-mail accounts, online (class) grades, online (class) registration, online (class) schedules. Campuswide network is available. 100% of college-owned or -operated housing units are wired for high-speed Internet access. Wireless service is available via entire campus.
Student Life *Housing:* on-campus residence required through sophomore year. *Options:* coed, men-only, women-only, disabled students. Campus housing is university owned. Freshman campus housing is guaranteed. *Activities and organizations:* drama/theater group, student-run newspaper, radio and television station, choral group, Interfraternity Council, Panhellenic Association, Student Government Association, Off-Campus Student Association, National Society of Collegiate Scholars, national fraternities, national sororities. *Campus security:* 24-hour emergency response devices and patrols, late-night transport/escort service, controlled dormitory access. *Student services:* health clinic, personal/psychological counseling, women's center.
Athletics Member NCAA. All Division II. *Intercollegiate sports:* baseball M(s), basketball M(s)/W(s), crew M/W, cross-country running M/W, golf M(s)/W(s), lacrosse M/W, sailing M/W, skiing (downhill) M/W, soccer M(s)/W(s), softball W(s), swimming and diving M/W, tennis M(s)/W(s), volleyball W(s). *Intramural sports:* basketball M/W, bowling M/W, equestrian sports W, football M/W, ice hockey M, soccer M/W, softball M/W, table tennis M/W, tennis M/W, ultimate Frisbee M/W, volleyball W.
Standardized Tests *Required for some:* SAT or ACT (for admission), selection of Test Score Waived Option (TSWO) or official SAT/ACT scores (TSWO is not appropriate for applicants seeking academic merit scholarship, Honors Program, or 3/2 Accelerated Management Program consideration).
Costs (2010–11) *Comprehensive fee:* $49,400 includes full-time tuition ($37,640) and room and board ($11,760). *College room only:* $6920. Room and board charges vary according to housing facility. *Payment plan:* installment. *Waivers:* employees or children of employees.
Financial Aid Of all full-time matriculated undergraduates who enrolled in 2009, 940 applied for aid, 856 were judged to have need, 169 had their need

fully met. 375 Federal Work-Study jobs (averaging $2384). In 2009, 295 non-need-based awards were made. *Average percent of need met:* 90%. *Average financial aid package:* $35,180. *Average need-based loan:* $4433. *Average need-based gift aid:* $29,649. *Average non-need-based aid:* $16,999. *Average indebtedness upon graduation:* $25,294.
Applying *Options:* electronic application, early admission, early decision, deferred entrance. *Application fee:* $40. *Required:* essay or personal statement, high school transcript, 1 letter of recommendation. *Recommended:* minimum 2 GPA, interview. *Application deadlines:* 2/15 (freshmen), 4/15 (transfers). *Early decision deadline:* 11/15 (for plan 1), 1/5 (for plan 2). *Notification:* 4/1 (freshmen), continuous (transfers), 12/15 (early decision plan 1), 2/1 (early decision plan 2).
Freshman Application Contact Mr. David Erdmann, Dean of Admission and Enrollment, Rollins College, 1000 Holt Avenue, 2720, Winter Park, FL 32789. *Phone:* 407-646-2161. *Fax:* 407-646-1502. *E-mail:* admission@rollins.edu. *Web site:* http://www.rollins.edu/.

St. John Vianney College Seminary
Miami, Florida

Freshman Application Contact Br. Edward Van Merrienboer, Academic Dean, St. John Vianney College Seminary, 2900 Southwest 87th Avenue, Miami, FL 33165-3244. *Phone:* 305-223-4561 Ext. 13. *Web site:* http://www.sjvcs.edu/.

Saint Leo University
Saint Leo, Florida

- **Independent Roman Catholic** comprehensive, founded 1889
- **Rural** 186-acre campus with easy access to Tampa and Orlando
- **Endowment** $12.0 million
- **Coed** 1,862 undergraduate students, 97% full-time, 52% women, 48% men
- **Minimally difficult** entrance level, 78% of applicants were admitted

Undergraduates 1,801 full-time, 61 part-time. Students come from 41 states and territories; 44 other countries; 31% are from out of state; 10% Black or African American, non-Hispanic/Latino; 13% Hispanic/Latino; 1% Asian, non-Hispanic/Latino; 0.2% Native Hawaiian or other Pacific Islander, non-Hispanic/Latino; 0.4% American Indian or Alaska Native, non-Hispanic/Latino; 1% Two or more races, non-Hispanic/Latino; 13% Race/ethnicity unknown; 6% international; 8% transferred in; 66% live on campus. *Retention:* 70% of full-time freshmen returned.
Freshmen *Admission:* 2,241 applied, 1,738 admitted, 539 enrolled. *Average high school GPA:* 3.3. *Test scores:* SAT critical reading scores over 500: 46%; SAT math scores over 500: 52%; SAT writing scores over 500: 39%; ACT scores over 18: 95%; SAT critical reading scores over 600: 9%; SAT math scores over 600: 10%; SAT writing scores over 600: 5%; ACT scores over 24: 25%; SAT critical reading scores over 700: 2%; SAT math scores over 700: 1%.
Faculty *Total:* 164, 70% full-time, 70% with terminal degrees. *Student/faculty ratio:* 14:1.
Academics *Calendar:* semesters. *Degrees:* associate, bachelor's, master's, and postbachelor's certificates. *Special study options:* academic remediation for entering students, adult/continuing education programs, advanced placement credit, distance learning, double majors, honors programs, independent study, internships, part-time degree program, services for LD students, study abroad, summer session for credit. *ROTC:* Army (b), Air Force (c).
Computers on Campus 130 computers/terminals are available on campus for general student use. Students can access the following: campus intranet, computer help desk, free student e-mail accounts, online (class) grades, online (class) registration, online (class) schedules, campus residents are issued a laptop for their personal use. Campuswide network is available. 100% of college-owned or -operated housing units are wired for high-speed Internet access. Wireless service is available via classrooms, computer centers, computer labs, dorm rooms, learning centers, libraries, student centers.
Student Life *Housing:* on-campus residence required through junior year. *Options:* coed, men-only, women-only, disabled students. Campus housing is university owned. Freshman applicants given priority for college housing. *Activities and organizations:* drama/theater group, student-run newspaper, radio and television station, choral group, Student Government Union, Campus Activities Board, Caribbean Student Association, Samaritans, Intercultural Student Association, national fraternities, national sororities. *Campus security:* 24-hour emergency response devices and patrols, late-night transport/escort service, controlled dormitory access, Surveillance cameras in parking lots. *Student services:* health clinic, personal/psychological counseling.
Athletics Member NCAA. All Division II. *Intercollegiate sports:* baseball M(s), basketball M(s)/W(s), cross-country running M(s)/W(s), golf M(s)/W(s), lacrosse M(s)/W(s), soccer M(s)/W(s), softball W(s), swimming and diving M(s)/W(s), tennis M(s)/W(s), volleyball W(s). *Intramural sports:* basketball

M/W, football M/W, golf M/W, racquetball M/W, soccer M/W, softball M/W, table tennis M/W, tennis M/W, ultimate Frisbee M/W, volleyball M/W.

Standardized Tests *Required:* SAT or ACT (for admission).

Costs (2011–12) *Comprehensive fee:* $27,990 includes full-time tuition ($18,200), mandatory fees ($670), and room and board ($9120). *College room only:* $4720. Room and board charges vary according to board plan and housing facility. *Payment plan:* installment. *Waivers:* employees or children of employees.

Financial Aid Of all full-time matriculated undergraduates who enrolled in 2009, 1,617 applied for aid, 1,367 were judged to have need, 1,038 had their need fully met. 550 Federal Work-Study jobs (averaging $3223). In 2009, 22 non-need-based awards were made. *Average percent of need met:* 76%. *Average financial aid package:* $18,114. *Average need-based loan:* $4216. *Average need-based gift aid:* $12,653. *Average non-need-based aid:* $8624. *Average indebtedness upon graduation:* $26,780.

Applying *Options:* electronic application, early admission, deferred entrance. *Application fee:* $35. *Required:* high school transcript, minimum 2.3 GPA, 1 letter of recommendation. *Recommended:* minimum 3 GPA, interview. *Application deadlines:* 8/15 (freshmen), 8/1 (transfers). *Notification:* continuous (freshmen), continuous (transfers).

Freshman Application Contact Mr. Scott Rhodes, Associate Vice President of Enrollment, Saint Leo University, MC 2008, PO Box 6665, Saint Leo, FL 33574-6665. *Phone:* 352-588-8283. *Toll-free phone:* 800-334-5532. *Fax:* 352-588-8257. *E-mail:* admissions@saintleo.edu. *Web site:* http://www.saintleo.edu/.

See page 1572 for the College Close-Up.

St. Petersburg College
St. Petersburg, Florida

- **State and locally supported** 4-year, founded 1927
- **Suburban** 410-acre campus with easy access to Tampa
- **Endowment** $25.8 million
- **Coed** 31,793 undergraduate students, 32% full-time, 61% women, 39% men
- **Noncompetitive** entrance level

Undergraduates 10,297 full-time, 21,496 part-time. Students come from 23 states and territories; 120 other countries; 3% are from out of state; 72% transferred in.

Freshmen *Admission:* 3,708 enrolled.

Faculty *Total:* 1,731, 19% full-time, 7% with terminal degrees.

Academics *Calendar:* semesters. *Degrees:* certificates, diplomas, associate, and bachelor's. *Special study options:* academic remediation for entering students, accelerated degree program, adult/continuing education programs, advanced placement credit, cooperative education, distance learning, English as a second language, freshman honors college, honors programs, internships, off-campus study, part-time degree program, services for LD students, study abroad, summer session for credit.

Computers on Campus 4,555 computers/terminals are available on campus for general student use. Students can access the following: campus intranet, computer help desk, free student e-mail accounts, online (class) grades, online (class) registration, online (class) schedules. Campuswide network is available. Wireless service is available via entire campus.

Student Life *Housing:* college housing not available. *Activities and organizations:* drama/theater group, student-run newspaper, choral group. *Campus security:* late-night transport/escort service. *Student services:* women's center.

Athletics Member NJCAA. *Intercollegiate sports:* baseball M(s), basketball M(s)/W(s), softball W(s), tennis W(s), volleyball W(s).

Costs (2010–11) *Tuition:* state resident $2190 full-time, $73 per credit hour part-time; nonresident $8765 full-time, $292 per credit hour part-time. Full-time tuition and fees vary according to course level, degree level, and program. Part-time tuition and fees vary according to course level, degree level, and program. *Required fees:* $632 full-time, $21 per credit hour part-time. *Payment plan:* deferred payment. *Waivers:* senior citizens and employees or children of employees.

Financial Aid Of all full-time matriculated undergraduates who enrolled in 2009, 350 Federal Work-Study jobs (averaging $2500).

Applying *Options:* electronic application, early admission. *Application fee:* $40. *Required:* high school transcript. *Application deadline:* rolling (freshmen). *Notification:* continuous (freshmen).

Freshman Application Contact Ms. Susan Fell, Director of Admissions and Records, St. Petersburg College, PO Box 13489, St. Petersburg, FL 33733-3489. *Phone:* 727-341-3166. *E-mail:* information@spcollege.edu. *Web site:* http://www.spcollege.edu.

St. Thomas University
Miami Gardens, Florida

- **Independent Roman Catholic** comprehensive, founded 1961
- **Suburban** 140-acre campus
- **Coed** 1,149 undergraduate students, 93% full-time, 56% women, 44% men
- **Minimally difficult** entrance level, 63% of applicants were admitted

Undergraduates 1,067 full-time, 82 part-time. Students come from 19 states and territories; 27 other countries; 12% are from out of state; 26% Black or African American, non-Hispanic/Latino; 44% Hispanic/Latino; 0.4% Asian, non-Hispanic/Latino; 0.2% Native Hawaiian or other Pacific Islander, non-Hispanic/Latino; 1% Two or more races, non-Hispanic/Latino; 9% Race/ethnicity unknown; 10% international; 14% transferred in; 24% live on campus. *Retention:* 69% of full-time freshmen returned.

Freshmen *Admission:* 814 applied, 510 admitted, 270 enrolled. *Average high school GPA:* 2.96. *Test scores:* SAT critical reading scores over 500: 19%; SAT math scores over 500: 27%; SAT writing scores over 500: 20%; ACT scores over 18: 57%; SAT critical reading scores over 600: 4%; SAT math scores over 600: 2%; SAT writing scores over 600: 1%; ACT scores over 24: 8%.

Faculty *Total:* 242, 42% full-time, 54% with terminal degrees. *Student/faculty ratio:* 14:1.

Academics *Calendar:* semesters. *Degrees:* certificates, bachelor's, master's, doctoral-professional, doctoral-research/scholarship, post-master's, and post-bachelor's certificates. *Special study options:* academic remediation for entering students, adult/continuing education programs, advanced placement credit, distance learning, double majors, freshman honors college, honors programs, independent study, internships, part-time degree program, services for LD students, summer session for credit.

Computers on Campus 200 computers/terminals are available on campus for general student use. Students can access the following: campus intranet, free student e-mail accounts, online (class) grades, online (class) registration, online (class) schedules. Campuswide network is available. Wireless service is available via entire campus.

Student Life *Housing options:* men-only, women-only. Campus housing is university owned. *Activities and organizations:* student-run television station, choral group. *Campus security:* 24-hour emergency response devices and patrols, late-night transport/escort service, controlled dormitory access. *Student services:* health clinic, personal/psychological counseling.

Athletics Member NAIA. *Intercollegiate sports:* baseball M(s), cross-country running M(s)/W(s), golf M(s)/W(s), soccer M(s)/W(s), softball W(s), tennis M(s)/W(s), volleyball W(s). *Intramural sports:* baseball M, basketball M/W, cross-country running M/W, football M, golf M, soccer M/W, softball M/W, table tennis M/W, tennis M/W, volleyball M/W, water polo M/W, weight lifting M/W.

Standardized Tests *Required:* SAT or ACT (for admission).

Costs (2010–11) *Comprehensive fee:* $29,612 includes full-time tuition ($22,770) and room and board ($6842). Full-time tuition and fees vary according to program. Part-time tuition: $455 per credit hour. *Room and board:* Room and board charges vary according to board plan and housing facility. *Payment plan:* installment. *Waivers:* minority students, children of alumni, and employees or children of employees.

Financial Aid Of all full-time matriculated undergraduates who enrolled in 2009, 935 applied for aid, 792 were judged to have need, 71 had their need fully met. In 2009, 174 non-need-based awards were made. *Average need-based loan:* $4182. *Average need-based gift aid:* $2664. *Average non-need-based aid:* $8134.

Applying *Options:* electronic application, deferred entrance. *Application fee:* $40. *Required:* high school transcript, minimum 2 GPA. *Recommended:* essay or personal statement, 1 letter of recommendation, interview. *Application deadlines:* rolling (freshmen), rolling (transfers). *Notification:* continuous (freshmen), continuous (transfers).

Freshman Application Contact Mr. Andre Lightbourne, Director of Admissions, St. Thomas University, 16401 Northwest 37th Avenue, Miami Gardens, FL 33054-6459. *Phone:* 305-628-6712. *Toll-free phone:* 800-367-9010. *Fax:* 305-628-6591. *E-mail:* signup@stu.edu. *Web site:* http://www.stu.edu/.

See page 1586 for the College Close-Up.

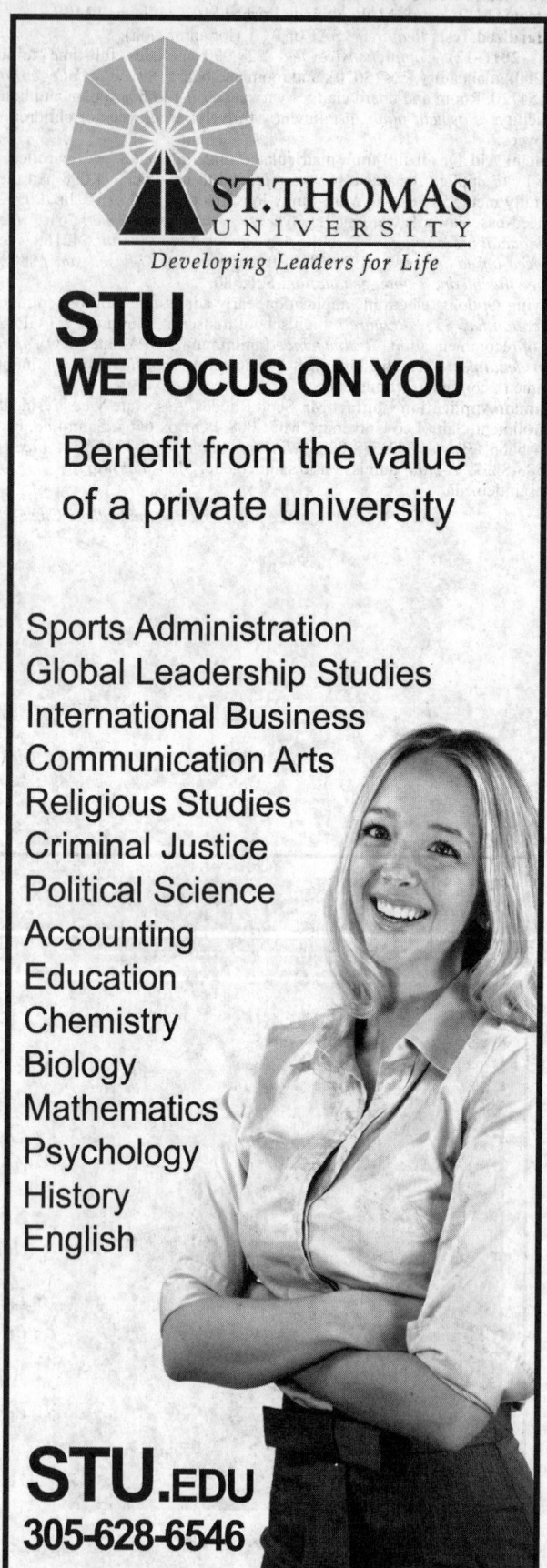

Santa Fe College

Gainesville, Florida

- **State and locally supported** 4-year, founded 1966, part of Florida College System
- **Suburban** 187-acre campus with easy access to Jacksonville
- **Coed** 15,745 undergraduate students, 43% full-time, 55% women, 45% men
- **Noncompetitive** entrance level

Undergraduates 6,777 full-time, 8,968 part-time. Students come from 28 states and territories; 61 other countries; 2% are from out of state; 16% Black or African American, non-Hispanic/Latino; 12% Hispanic/Latino; 2% Asian, non-Hispanic/Latino; 0.4% Native Hawaiian or other Pacific Islander, non-Hispanic/Latino; 0.5% American Indian or Alaska Native, non-Hispanic/Latino; 2% Two or more races, non-Hispanic/Latino; 8% Race/ethnicity unknown; 1% international; 11% transferred in.
Freshmen *Admission:* 3,076 enrolled.
Faculty *Total:* 829, 30% full-time, 19% with terminal degrees. *Student/faculty ratio:* 25:1.
Academics *Calendar:* semesters. *Degrees:* certificates, associate, and bachelor's (offers bachelor's degrees in conjunction with Saint Leo College). *Special study options:* academic remediation for entering students, adult/continuing education programs, advanced placement credit, cooperative education, distance learning, English as a second language, honors programs, independent study, internships, part-time degree program, services for LD students, study abroad, summer session for credit. *ROTC:* Army (c), Air Force (c).
Computers on Campus Students can access the following: computer help desk, free student e-mail accounts, online (class) grades, online (class) registration, online (class) schedules, apply for financial aid and view the status of awards, pay tuition, view and print unofficial transcripts, apply for graduation, view degree audits to check progress toward completion of their degree requirements. Campuswide network is available. Wireless service is available via classrooms, libraries, student centers.
Student Life *Housing:* college housing not available. *Activities and organizations:* drama/theater group, student-run newspaper, choral group. *Campus security:* 24-hour emergency response devices and patrols. *Student services:* health clinic, personal/psychological counseling, women's center, legal services.
Athletics Member NJCAA. *Intercollegiate sports:* baseball M(s), basketball M(s)/W(s), softball W(s). *Intramural sports:* badminton M(c)/W(c), basketball M/W, bowling M(c)/W(c), cheerleading M(c)/W(c), fencing M(c)/W(c), football M, racquetball M/W, soccer M/W, softball W, tennis M/W, track and field M(c)/W(c), ultimate Frisbee M/W, volleyball M/W, weight lifting M/W.
Costs (2010–11) *Tuition:* state resident $2168 full-time, $90 per credit hour part-time; nonresident $8170 full-time, $340 per credit hour part-time. Full-time tuition and fees vary according to degree level. Part-time tuition and fees vary according to degree level. *Room and board:* Room and board charges vary according to housing facility. *Waivers:* senior citizens and employees or children of employees.
Financial Aid Of all full-time matriculated undergraduates who enrolled in 2009, 190 Federal Work-Study jobs.
Applying *Options:* electronic application, early admission. *Required:* high school transcript. *Required for some:* essay or personal statement, high school transcript, interview. *Application deadlines:* rolling (freshmen), rolling (transfers). *Notification:* continuous (freshmen), continuous (transfers).
Freshman Application Contact Santa Fe College, 3000 Northwest 83rd Street, Gainesville, FL 32606. *Phone:* 352-395-4177. *Web site:* http://www.sfcollege.edu/.

Schiller International University

Largo, Florida

Freshman Application Contact Donald Trippe, Admissions Officer, Schiller International University, 300 East Bay Drive, Largo, FL 33770. *Phone:* 727-738-6365. *Toll-free phone:* 800-336-4133. *Fax:* 727-738-6376. *E-mail:* admissions@schiller.edu. *Web site:* http://www.schiller.edu/.

Seminole State College of Florida

Sanford, Florida

- **State and locally supported** primarily 2-year, founded 1966
- **Small-town** 200-acre campus with easy access to Orlando
- **Endowment** $6.2 million
- **Coed** 18,028 undergraduate students, 45% full-time, 59% women, 41% men
- **Noncompetitive** entrance level, 100% of applicants were admitted

Undergraduates 8,098 full-time, 9,930 part-time. Students come from 82 other countries; 0.2% are from out of state; 18% Black or African American, non-Hispanic/Latino; 19% Hispanic/Latino; 3% Asian, non-Hispanic/Latino; 0.2% Native Hawaiian or other Pacific Islander, non-Hispanic/Latino; 0.4% American Indian or Alaska Native, non-Hispanic/Latino; 1% Two or more races, non-Hispanic/Latino; 3% Race/ethnicity unknown; 2% international; 3% transferred in.
Freshmen *Admission:* 5,533 applied, 5,533 admitted, 3,010 enrolled.
Faculty *Total:* 784, 30% full-time, 12% with terminal degrees. *Student/faculty ratio:* 28:1.
Academics *Calendar:* semesters. *Degrees:* certificates, diplomas, associate, and bachelor's. *Special study options:* academic remediation for entering students, accelerated degree program, adult/continuing education programs, advanced placement credit, cooperative education, distance learning, double majors, English as a second language, external degree program, honors programs, independent study, internships, part-time degree program, services for LD students, study abroad, summer session for credit. *ROTC:* Army (b).
Computers on Campus 250 computers/terminals are available on campus for general student use. Students can access the following: online (class) registration, online (class) schedules. Campuswide network is available. Wireless service is available via entire campus.
Student Life *Housing:* college housing not available. *Activities and organizations:* drama/theater group, student-run newspaper, choral group, Phi Beta Lambda, Phi Theta Kappa, Student Government Association, Sigma Phi Gamma, Hispanic Student Association. *Campus security:* 24-hour emergency response devices and patrols. *Student services:* personal/psychological counseling.
Athletics Member NJCAA. *Intercollegiate sports:* baseball M(s), golf W(s), softball W(s).
Standardized Tests *Required:* CPT (for admission). *Recommended:* ACT (for admission).
Costs (2011–12) *Tuition:* state resident $2904 full-time, $97 per credit hour part-time; nonresident $10,607 full-time, $354 per credit hour part-time. Full-time tuition and fees vary according to degree level and program. Part-time tuition and fees vary according to degree level and program. *Required fees:* $714 full-time, $24 per credit hour part-time. *Payment plan:* deferred payment. *Waivers:* senior citizens and employees or children of employees.
Applying *Options:* electronic application, early admission, deferred entrance. *Required:* high school transcript, minimum 2 GPA. *Application deadlines:* rolling (freshmen), rolling (transfers). *Notification:* continuous (freshmen), continuous (transfers).
Freshman Application Contact Ms. Pamela Mennechey, Director of Admissions, Seminole State College of Florida, Sanford, FL 32773-6199. *Phone:* 407-708-2050. *Fax:* 407-708-2395. *E-mail:* admissions@scc-fl.edu. *Web site:* http://www.seminolestate.edu/.

Southeastern University

Lakeland, Florida

- **Independent** comprehensive, founded 1935, affiliated with Assemblies of God
- **Suburban** 87-acre campus with easy access to Tampa and Orlando
- **Endowment** $14.3 million
- **Coed** 2,510 undergraduate students, 89% full-time, 57% women, 43% men
- **Minimally difficult** entrance level, 75% of applicants were admitted

Undergraduates 2,223 full-time, 287 part-time. Students come from 48 states and territories; 40 other countries; 35% are from out of state; 9% Black or African American, non-Hispanic/Latino; 13% Hispanic/Latino; 0.8% Asian, non-Hispanic/Latino; 0.2% American Indian or Alaska Native, non-Hispanic/Latino; 0.1% Two or more races, non-Hispanic/Latino; 7% Race/ethnicity unknown; 1% international; 9% transferred in; 54% live on campus. *Retention:* 64% of full-time freshmen returned.
Freshmen *Admission:* 1,167 applied, 871 admitted, 519 enrolled. *Average high school GPA:* 3.35. *Test scores:* SAT critical reading scores over 500: 60%; SAT math scores over 500: 52%; SAT writing scores over 500: 55%; ACT scores over 18: 78%; SAT critical reading scores over 600: 20%; SAT math scores over 600: 14%; SAT writing scores over 600: 18%; ACT scores over 24: 33%; SAT critical reading scores over 700: 2%; SAT math scores over 700: 1%; SAT writing scores over 700: 1%; ACT scores over 30: 3%.
Faculty *Total:* 180, 56% full-time, 45% with terminal degrees. *Student/faculty ratio:* 19:1.
Academics *Calendar:* semesters. *Degrees:* bachelor's and master's. *Special study options:* academic remediation for entering students, adult/continuing education programs, advanced placement credit, distance learning, double majors, honors programs, independent study, internships, part-time degree program, services for LD students, study abroad, summer session for credit. *ROTC:* Army (c), Air Force (c).
Computers on Campus 145 computers/terminals are available on campus for general student use. Students can access the following: campus intranet, computer help desk, free student e-mail accounts, online (class) grades, online (class) registration, online (class) schedules, network programs. Campuswide

network is available. 100% of college-owned or -operated housing units are wired for high-speed Internet access. Wireless service is available via entire campus.

Student Life *Housing:* on-campus residence required through senior year. *Options:* men-only, women-only. Campus housing is university owned. Freshman campus housing is guaranteed. *Activities and organizations:* drama/theater group, student-run newspaper, radio and television station, choral group, intramurals, Students in Free Enterprise (SIFE), Destinations, Circle K, Light House Ministries. *Campus security:* 24-hour emergency response devices and patrols, late-night transport/escort service. *Student services:* health clinic, personal/psychological counseling.

Athletics Member NAIA, NCCAA. *Intercollegiate sports:* baseball M, basketball M/W, cheerleading M/W, golf M, soccer M/W, tennis W, volleyball W. *Intramural sports:* basketball M/W, football M/W, soccer M/W, softball M/W, ultimate Frisbee M/W, volleyball M/W.

Standardized Tests *Required:* SAT or ACT (for admission).

Costs (2010–11) *Comprehensive fee:* $24,330 includes full-time tuition ($15,830), mandatory fees ($600), and room and board ($7900). Full-time tuition and fees vary according to class time, degree level, and reciprocity agreements. Part-time tuition: $660 per credit. Part-time tuition and fees vary according to class time, course load, degree level, and reciprocity agreements. *Required fees:* $150 per term part-time. *Room and board:* Room and board charges vary according to board plan and housing facility. *Payment plan:* installment. *Waivers:* employees or children of employees.

Financial Aid Of all full-time matriculated undergraduates who enrolled in 2008, 2,253 applied for aid, 1,939 were judged to have need, 236 had their need fully met. In 2008, 308 non-need-based awards were made. *Average percent of need met:* 56%. *Average financial aid package:* $10,100. *Average need-based loan:* $3609. *Average need-based gift aid:* $7408. *Average non-need-based aid:* $2996. *Average indebtedness upon graduation:* $25,006.

Applying *Options:* electronic application, early admission, deferred entrance. *Application fee:* $40. *Required:* essay or personal statement, high school transcript, 2 letters of recommendation. *Required for some:* interview. *Application deadlines:* 7/1 (freshmen), 7/1 (transfers). *Notification:* 8/1 (freshmen), continuous until 8/1 (transfers).

Freshman Application Contact Southeastern University, 1000 Longfellow Boulevard, Lakeland, FL 33801-6099. *Phone:* 800-500-8760. *Toll-free phone:* 800-500-8760. *Web site:* http://www.seu.edu/.

South University
Royal Palm Beach, Florida

- **Proprietary** comprehensive, founded 1899, part of Education Management Corporation
- **Coed**

Academics *Calendar:* quarters. *Degrees:* associate, bachelor's, and master's.

Costs (2010–11) *Tuition:* Information about tuition and fees can be obtained by contacting the South University Admissions Office.

Freshman Application Contact South University, University Centre, 9801 Belvedere Road, Royal Palm Beach, FL 33411. *Phone:* 561-273-6500. *Toll-free phone:* 866-629-2902. *Web site:* http://www.southuniversity.edu/west-palm-beach/.

See page 1624 for the College Close-Up.

South University
Tampa, Florida

- **Proprietary** comprehensive, part of Education Management Corporation
- **Coed**

Academics *Degrees:* associate, bachelor's, and master's.

Costs (2010–11) *Tuition:* Information about tuition and fees can be obtained by contacting the South University Admissions Office.

Freshman Application Contact South University, 4401 North Himes Avenue, Suite 175, Tampa, FL 33614. *Phone:* 813-393-3800. *Toll-free phone:* 800-846-1472. *Web site:* http://www.southuniversity.edu/tampa/.

See page 1622 for the College Close-Up.

Southwest Florida College
Fort Myers, Florida

- **Independent** 4-year, founded 1940
- **Urban** campus
- **Coed**
- **Noncompetitive** entrance level

Academics *Calendar:* quarters. *Degrees:* diplomas, associate, and bachelor's.

Student Life *Campus security:* day and evening security guards.

Financial Aid *Of all full-time matriculated undergraduates who enrolled in 2009,* 10 Federal Work-Study jobs (averaging $5000).

Applying *Recommended:* high school transcript.

Freshman Application Contact Mr. Ken Reynolds, Director of Admissions, Southwest Florida College, 1685 Medical Lane, Fort Myers, FL 33907. *Phone:* 239-939-4766. *Toll-free phone:* 866-SWFC-NOW. *Fax:* 239-936-4040. *E-mail:* kreynolds@swfc.edu. *Web site:* http://www.swfc.edu/.

Southwest Florida College
Tampa, Florida

Director of Admissions Admissions, Southwest Florida College, 3910 Riga Boulevard, Tampa, FL 33619. *Phone:* 813-630-4401. *Toll-free phone:* 877-493-5147. *Web site:* http://www.swfc.edu/.

State College of Florida Manatee-Sarasota
Bradenton, Florida

- **State-supported** primarily 2-year, founded 1957, part of Florida Community College System
- **Suburban** 100-acre campus with easy access to Tampa-St. Petersburg
- **Coed**
- **Noncompetitive** entrance level

Academics *Calendar:* semesters. *Degrees:* certificates, associate, and bachelor's.

Student Life *Campus security:* 24-hour emergency response devices and patrols, late-night transport/escort service.

Athletics Member NJCAA.

Costs (2010–11) *Tuition:* state resident $2847 full-time, $95 per hour part-time; nonresident $10,737 full-time, $358 per hour part-time.

Financial Aid *Of all full-time matriculated undergraduates who enrolled in 2009,* 82 Federal Work-Study jobs (averaging $2800). *Financial aid deadline:* 8/15.

Applying *Options:* early admission. *Required:* high school transcript.

Freshman Application Contact Ms. MariLynn Lewy, AVP, Student Services, State College of Florida Manatee-Sarasota, Bradenton, FL 34206. *Phone:* 941-752-5384. *Fax:* 941-727-6380. *E-mail:* lewym@scf.edu. *Web site:* http://www.scf.edu/.

Stetson University
DeLand, Florida

- **Independent** comprehensive, founded 1883
- **Small-town** 175-acre campus with easy access to Orlando
- **Endowment** $123.0 million
- **Coed** 2,134 undergraduate students, 97% full-time, 57% women, 43% men
- **Moderately difficult** entrance level, 51% of applicants were admitted

Undergraduates 2,077 full-time, 57 part-time. Students come from 37 states and territories; 36 other countries; 17% are from out of state; 6% Black or African American, non-Hispanic/Latino; 12% Hispanic/Latino; 1% Asian, non-Hispanic/Latino; 0.2% Native Hawaiian or other Pacific Islander, non-Hispanic/Latino; 0.3% American Indian or Alaska Native, non-Hispanic/Latino; 2% Two or more races, non-Hispanic/Latino; 1% Race/ethnicity unknown; 4% international; 6% transferred in; 66% live on campus. *Retention:* 77% of full-time freshmen returned.

Freshmen *Admission:* 3,884 applied, 1,962 admitted, 547 enrolled. *Average high school GPA:* 3.73. *Test scores:* SAT critical reading scores over 500: 73%; SAT math scores over 500: 69%; SAT writing scores over 500: 64%; ACT scores over 18: 96%; SAT critical reading scores over 600: 31%; SAT math scores over 600: 30%; SAT writing scores over 600: 23%; ACT scores over 24: 44%; SAT critical reading scores over 700: 6%; SAT math scores over 700: 4%; SAT writing scores over 700: 3%; ACT scores over 30: 6%.

Faculty *Total:* 357, 64% full-time, 83% with terminal degrees. *Student/faculty ratio:* 11:1.

Academics *Calendar:* semesters. *Degrees:* bachelor's, master's, doctoral-professional, and post-master's certificates. *Special study options:* accelerated degree program, adult/continuing education programs, advanced placement credit, distance learning, double majors, honors programs, independent study, internships, off-campus study, part-time degree program, services for LD students, student-designed majors, study abroad, summer session for credit. *ROTC:* Army (c). *Unusual degree programs:* 3-2 engineering; forestry with Duke University; public administration with American University, J.D. with Stetson University College of Law.

Computers on Campus 487 computers/terminals are available on campus for general student use. Students can access the following: campus intranet, computer help desk, free student e-mail accounts, online (class) grades, online (class) registration, online (class) schedules. Campuswide network is available.

100% of college-owned or -operated housing units are wired for high-speed Internet access. Wireless service is available via entire campus.

Student Life *Housing:* on-campus residence required through junior year. *Options:* coed, men-only, women-only. Campus housing is university owned and leased by the school. Freshman campus housing is guaranteed. *Activities and organizations:* drama/theater group, student-run newspaper, radio station, choral group, Into the Streets, Multi-Cultural Student Council, Black Student Association, Habitat for Humanity, Hatter Harvest, national fraternities, national sororities. *Campus security:* 24-hour emergency response devices and patrols, late-night transport/escort service, controlled dormitory access. *Student services:* health clinic, personal/psychological counseling, women's center.

Athletics Member NCAA. All Division I. *Intercollegiate sports:* baseball M(s), basketball M(s)/W(s), crew M/W(s), cross-country running M(s)/W(s), golf M(s)/W(s), soccer M(s)/W(s), softball W(s), tennis M(s)/W(s), volleyball W(s). *Intramural sports:* baseball M, basketball M/W, bowling M/W, cross-country running M/W, equestrian sports M(c)/W(c), golf M/W, lacrosse M(c)/W(c), soccer M/W, softball M/W, swimming and diving M(c)/W(c), table tennis M(c)/W(c), tennis M(c)/W(c), ultimate Frisbee M(c)/W(c), volleyball M/W.

Standardized Tests *Required for some:* SAT or ACT (for admission).

Costs (2011–12) *Comprehensive fee:* $45,336 includes full-time tuition ($32,943), mandatory fees ($2138), and room and board ($10,255). Part-time tuition: $3465 per course. Part-time tuition and fees vary according to course load, location, and program. *Required fees:* $310 per term part-time. *College room only:* $5845. Room and board charges vary according to board plan and housing facility. *Payment plan:* installment. *Waivers:* employees or children of employees.

Financial Aid Of all full-time matriculated undergraduates who enrolled in 2009, 1,545 applied for aid, 1,388 were judged to have need, 281 had their need fully met. 957 Federal Work-Study jobs (averaging $2028). 206 state and other part-time jobs (averaging $3358). In 2009, 489 non-need-based awards were made. *Average percent of need met:* 80%. *Average financial aid package:* $29,689. *Average need-based loan:* $5117. *Average need-based gift aid:* $22,705. *Average non-need-based aid:* $13,171. *Average indebtedness upon graduation:* $33,817.

Applying *Options:* electronic application, early admission, early decision, deferred entrance. *Application fee:* $25. *Required:* essay or personal statement, high school transcript, 1 letter of recommendation. *Recommended:* interview. *Application deadlines:* 3/15 (freshmen), rolling (transfers). *Early decision deadline:* 11/1. *Notification:* 12/1 (freshmen), continuous (transfers), 11/15 (early decision).

Freshman Application Contact Ms. Rebecca Eckstein, Dean of Admissions, Stetson University, Unit 8378, Griffith Hall, DeLand, FL 32723. *Phone:* 386-822-7100. *Toll-free phone:* 800-688-0101. *Fax:* 386-822-7112. *E-mail:* admissions@stetson.edu. *Web site:* http://www.stetson.edu/.

Strayer University - Baymeadows Campus

Jacksonville, Florida

- **Proprietary** comprehensive
- **Coed**

Academics *Degrees:* certificates, diplomas, associate, bachelor's, master's, and postbachelor's certificates.

Costs (2010–11) *Tuition:* $13,635 full-time, $1590 per course part-time.

Freshman Application Contact Strayer University - Baymeadows Campus, 8375 Dix Ellis Trail, Suite 200, Jacksonville, FL 32256. *Web site:* http://www.strayer.edu/baymeadows/.

Strayer University - Brickell Campus

Miami, Florida

- **Proprietary** comprehensive
- **Coed**

Academics *Degrees:* certificates, diplomas, associate, bachelor's, master's, and postbachelor's certificates.

Costs (2010–11) *Tuition:* $13,635 full-time, $1590 per course part-time.

Freshman Application Contact Strayer University - Brickell Campus, 1201 Brickell Avenue, Suite 700, Miami, FL 33131. *Web site:* http://www.strayer.edu/brickell.

Strayer University - Coral Springs Campus

Coral Springs, Florida

- **Proprietary** comprehensive
- **Coed**

Academics *Degrees:* certificates, diplomas, associate, bachelor's, master's, and postbachelor's certificates.

Costs (2010–11) *Tuition:* $13,635 full-time, $1590 per course part-time.

Freshman Application Contact Strayer University - Coral Springs Campus, 5830 Coral Ridge Drive, Suite 300, Coral Springs, FL 33076. *Web site:* http://www.strayer.edu/coral_springs/.

Strayer University - Doral Campus

Miami, Florida

- **Proprietary** comprehensive
- **Coed**

Academics *Degrees:* certificates, diplomas, associate, bachelor's, master's, and postbachelor's certificates.

Costs (2010–11) *Tuition:* $13,635 full-time, $1590 per course part-time.

Freshman Application Contact Strayer University - Doral Campus, 11430 Northwest 20th Street, Suite 150, Miami, FL 33172. *Web site:* http://www.strayer.edu/doral.

Strayer University - Fort Lauderdale Campus

Fort Lauderdale, Florida

- **Proprietary** comprehensive
- **Coed**

Academics *Degrees:* certificates, diplomas, associate, bachelor's, master's, and postbachelor's certificates.

Costs (2010–11) *Tuition:* $13,635 full-time, $1590 per course part-time.

Freshman Application Contact Strayer University - Fort Lauderdale Campus, 2307 West Broward Boulevard, Suite 100, Fort Lauderdale, FL 33312. *Web site:* http://www.strayer.edu/fort_lauderdale/.

Strayer University - Maitland Campus

Maitland, Florida

- **Proprietary** comprehensive
- **Coed**

Academics *Degrees:* certificates, diplomas, associate, bachelor's, master's, and postbachelor's certificates.

Costs (2010–11) *Tuition:* $13,635 full-time, $1590 per course part-time.

Freshman Application Contact Strayer University - Maitland Campus, 850 Trafalgar Court, Suite 360, Maitland, FL 32751. *Web site:* http://www.strayer.edu/maitland/.

Strayer University - Miramar Campus

Miramar, Florida

- **Proprietary** comprehensive
- **Coed**

Academics *Degrees:* certificates, diplomas, associate, bachelor's, master's, and postbachelor's certificates.

Costs (2010–11) *Tuition:* $13,635 full-time, $1590 per course part-time.

Freshman Application Contact Strayer University - Miramar Campus, 15620 Southwest 29th Street, Miramar, FL 33027. *Web site:* http://www.strayer.edu/miramar.

Strayer University - Orlando East Campus

Orlando, Florida

- **Proprietary** comprehensive
- **Coed**

Academics *Degrees:* certificates, diplomas, associate, bachelor's, master's, and postbachelor's certificates.

Costs (2010–11) *Tuition:* $13,635 full-time, $1590 per course part-time.

Freshman Application Contact Strayer University - Orlando East Campus, 2200 North Alafaya Trail, Suite 500, Orlando, FL 32826. *Web site:* http://www.strayer.edu/orlando_east/.

Strayer University - Palm Beach Gardens Campus

Palm Beach Gardens, Florida

- **Proprietary** comprehensive
- **Coed**

Academics *Degrees:* certificates, diplomas, associate, bachelor's, master's, and postbachelor's certificates.

Costs (2010–11) *Tuition:* $13,635 full-time, $1590 per course part-time.

Freshman Application Contact Strayer University - Palm Beach Gardens Campus, 11025 RCA Center Drive, Suite 200, Palm Beach Gardens, FL 33410. *Web site:* http://www.strayer.edu/palm_beach_gardens.

Strayer University - Sand Lake Campus

Orlando, Florida

- **Proprietary** comprehensive
- **Coed**

Academics *Degrees:* certificates, diplomas, associate, bachelor's, master's, and postbachelor's certificates.

Costs (2010–11) *Tuition:* $13,635 full-time, $1590 per course part-time.

Freshman Application Contact Strayer University - Sand Lake Campus, 8541 South Park Circle, Building 900, Orlando, FL 32819. *Web site:* http://www.strayer.edu/sand_lake/.

Strayer University - Tampa East Campus

Tampa, Florida

- **Proprietary** comprehensive
- **Coed**

Academics *Degrees:* certificates, diplomas, associate, bachelor's, master's, and postbachelor's certificates.

Costs (2010–11) *Tuition:* $13,635 full-time, $1590 per course part-time.

Freshman Application Contact Strayer University - Tampa East Campus, 6302 East Martin Luther King Boulevard, Suite 450, Tampa, FL 33619. *Web site:* http://www.strayer.edu/tampa_east.

Strayer University - Tampa Westshore Campus

Tampa, Florida

- **Proprietary** comprehensive
- **Coed**

Academics *Degrees:* certificates, diplomas, associate, bachelor's, master's, and postbachelor's certificates.

Costs (2010–11) *Tuition:* $13,635 full-time, $1590 per course part-time.

Freshman Application Contact Strayer University - Tampa Westshore Campus, 4902 Eisenhower Boulevard, Suite 100, Tampa, FL 33634. *Web site:* http://www.strayer.edu/tampa_westshore.

Talmudic College of Florida

Miami Beach, Florida

Freshman Application Contact Rabbi Yeshaya Greenberg, Dean of Students, Talmudic College of Florida, 1910 Alton Road, Miami Beach, FL 33139. *Phone:* 305-534-7050. *Toll-free phone:* 888-825-6834. *Fax:* 305-534-8444. *E-mail:* yandtg@gmail.com. *Web site:* http://www.talmudicu.edu/.

Trinity Baptist College

Jacksonville, Florida

Freshman Application Contact Mr. Larry Appleby, Administrative Dean, Trinity Baptist College, 800 Hammond Boulevard, Jacksonville, FL 32221. *Phone:* 904-596-2538. *Toll-free phone:* 904-596-2400 (in-state); 800-786-2206 (out-of-state). *Fax:* 904-596-2531. *E-mail:* trinity@tbc.edu. *Web site:* http://www.tbc.edu/.

Trinity College of Florida

New Port Richey, Florida

- **Independent nondenominational** 4-year, founded 1932
- **Small-town** 40-acre campus with easy access to Tampa
- **Endowment** $1.9 million
- **Coed** 201 undergraduate students, 83% full-time, 40% women, 60% men
- **Minimally difficult** entrance level, 87% of applicants were admitted

Undergraduates 167 full-time, 34 part-time. Students come from 4 states and territories; 2 other countries; 2% are from out of state; 18% Black or African American, non-Hispanic/Latino; 12% Hispanic/Latino; 0.5% American Indian or Alaska Native, non-Hispanic/Latino; 2% Race/ethnicity unknown; 1% international; 24% transferred in; 33% live on campus. *Retention:* 41% of full-time freshmen returned.

Freshmen *Admission:* 136 applied, 118 admitted, 33 enrolled. *Average high school GPA:* 2.8. *Test scores:* SAT critical reading scores over 500: 72%; SAT math scores over 500: 61%; ACT scores over 18: 75%; SAT critical reading scores over 600: 16%; SAT math scores over 600: 22%; ACT scores over 24: 30%.

Faculty *Total:* 28, 25% full-time, 39% with terminal degrees. *Student/faculty ratio:* 11:1.

Academics *Calendar:* semesters. *Degrees:* certificates, associate, and bachelor's. *Special study options:* academic remediation for entering students, accelerated degree program, adult/continuing education programs, advanced placement credit, cooperative education, distance learning, double majors, external degree program, honors programs, independent study, internships, off-campus study, part-time degree program, services for LD students, student-designed majors, summer session for credit.

Computers on Campus 14 computers/terminals and 144 ports are available on campus for general student use. Students can access the following: campus intranet, computer help desk, free student e-mail accounts, online (class) grades, online (class) registration, online (class) schedules. Campuswide network is available. 100% of college-owned or -operated housing units are wired for high-speed Internet access. Wireless service is available via classrooms, computer labs, dorm rooms, libraries, student centers.

Student Life *Housing:* on-campus residence required through senior year. *Options:* men-only, women-only, disabled students. Campus housing is university owned and leased by the school. Freshman campus housing is guaranteed. *Activities and organizations:* drama/theater group, choral group, Great Commission Missionary Fellowship, Ad Honorem, Drama Team, student government, Dead to Sin Poets Society. *Campus security:* student patrols. *Student services:* personal/psychological counseling.

Athletics Member NCCAA. *Intercollegiate sports:* basketball M, volleyball W. *Intramural sports:* soccer M, softball M.

Standardized Tests *Required:* SAT or ACT (for admission).

Costs (2011–12) *Comprehensive fee:* $19,014 includes full-time tuition ($11,354), mandatory fees ($800), and room and board ($6860). Part-time tuition: $473 per credit hour. Part-time tuition and fees vary according to course load. *Required fees:* $400 per term part-time. *Payment plan:* installment. *Waivers:* senior citizens and employees or children of employees.

Financial Aid Of all full-time matriculated undergraduates who enrolled in 2008, 114 applied for aid, 102 were judged to have need, 28 had their need fully met. 22 Federal Work-Study jobs (averaging $1402). In 2008, 12 non-need-based awards were made. *Average percent of need met:* 84%. *Average financial aid package:* $4855. *Average need-based loan:* $2178. *Average need-based gift aid:* $3191. *Average non-need-based aid:* $619. *Average indebtedness upon graduation:* $15,233.

Applying *Options:* electronic application, early admission, deferred entrance. *Application fee:* $25. *Required:* essay or personal statement, high school transcript, 3 letters of recommendation, interview. *Recommended:* minimum 2.75 GPA. *Application deadlines:* 8/20 (freshmen), 8/20 (out-of-state freshmen), 8/20 (transfers). *Notification:* continuous until 8/20 (freshmen), continuous (out-of-state freshmen).

Freshman Application Contact Mark A. Sawyer, Director of Admissions, Trinity College of Florida, 24300 Welbilt Boulevard, Trinity, FL 34655. *Phone:* 727-376-6911 Ext. 309. *Toll-free phone:* 800-388-0869. *Fax:* 727-569-1410. *E-mail:* msawyer@trinitycollege.edu. *Web site:* http://www.trinitycollege.edu/.

Universidad FLET

Miami, Florida

Director of Admissions Dalia Sosa, Admissions Director, Universidad FLET, 14540 Southwest 136th Street, Suite 108, Miami, FL 33186. *Phone:* 305-378-8700. *Toll-free phone:* 888-376-3538. *Fax:* 305-232-5832. *E-mail:* admissiones@flet.edu. *Web site:* http://www.flet.edu/.

University of Central Florida
Orlando, Florida

- **State-supported** university, founded 1963, part of State University System of Florida
- **Suburban** 1415-acre campus with easy access to Orlando
- **Endowment** $102.1 million
- **Coed** 47,580 undergraduate students, 75% full-time, 54% women, 46% men
- **Moderately difficult** entrance level, 46% of applicants were admitted

Undergraduates 35,910 full-time, 11,670 part-time. Students come from 50 states and territories; 127 other countries; 5% are from out of state; 10% Black or African American, non-Hispanic/Latino; 17% Hispanic/Latino; 6% Asian, non-Hispanic/Latino; 0.1% Native Hawaiian or other Pacific Islander, non-Hispanic/Latino; 0.4% American Indian or Alaska Native, non-Hispanic/Latino; 0.8% Two or more races, non-Hispanic/Latino; 2% Race/ethnicity unknown; 1% international; 12% transferred in; 15% live on campus. *Retention:* 87% of full-time freshmen returned.

Freshmen *Admission:* 32,876 applied, 15,247 admitted, 6,153 enrolled. *Average high school GPA:* 3.72. *Test scores:* SAT critical reading scores over 500: 89%; SAT math scores over 500: 95%; SAT writing scores over 500: 80%; ACT scores over 18: 100%; SAT critical reading scores over 600: 39%; SAT math scores over 600: 53%; SAT writing scores over 600: 27%; ACT scores over 24: 75%; SAT critical reading scores over 700: 6%; SAT math scores over 700: 8%; SAT writing scores over 700: 3%; ACT scores over 30: 9%.

Faculty *Total:* 1,799, 72% full-time, 66% with terminal degrees. *Student/faculty ratio:* 31:1.

Academics *Calendar:* semesters. *Degrees:* certificates, associate, bachelor's, master's, doctoral-professional, doctoral-research/scholarship, and postbachelor's certificates. *Special study options:* accelerated degree program, adult/continuing education programs, advanced placement credit, cooperative education, distance learning, double majors, English as a second language, freshman honors college, honors programs, independent study, internships, off-campus study, part-time degree program, services for LD students, study abroad, summer session for credit. *ROTC:* Army (b), Air Force (b). *Unusual degree programs:* 3-2 engineering; nursing; history; communicative sciences and disorders; business economics; economics; computer science.

Computers on Campus 3,200 computers/terminals and 200 ports are available on campus for general student use. Students can access the following: campus intranet, computer help desk, free student e-mail accounts, online (class) grades, online (class) registration, online (class) schedules. Campuswide network is available. 100% of college-owned or -operated housing units are wired for high-speed Internet access. Wireless service is available via entire campus.

Student Life *Housing options:* coed, men-only, women-only. Campus housing is university owned and is provided by a third party. Freshman applicants given priority for college housing. *Activities and organizations:* drama/theater group, student-run newspaper, radio station, choral group, marching band, Volunteer UCF, Intramural Sports, Recreation and Wellness Center Group Exercise Programs, Multicultural Student Center and Organizations, Campus Religious Organizations, national fraternities, national sororities. *Campus security:* 24-hour emergency response devices and patrols, late-night transport/escort service, controlled dormitory access. *Student services:* health clinic, personal/psychological counseling, women's center, legal services.

Athletics Member NCAA. All Division I except football (Division I-A). *Intercollegiate sports:* baseball M(s), basketball M(s)/W(s), cheerleading M(s)/W(s), crew W, cross-country running W(s), golf M(s)/W(s), soccer M(s)/W(s), tennis M(s)/W(s), track and field W(s), volleyball W(s). *Intramural sports:* badminton M(c)/W(c), baseball M(c), basketball M/W, bowling M(c)/W(c), crew M(c)/W(c), equestrian sports M(c)/W(c), fencing M(c)/W(c), golf M/W, ice hockey M(c)/W(c), lacrosse M(c)/W(c), racquetball M/W, rock climbing M(c)/W(c), rugby M(c)/W(c), sailing M(c)/W(c), soccer M(c)/W(c), softball M/W, table tennis M(c)/W(c), tennis M(c)/W(c), ultimate Frisbee M(c)/W(c), volleyball M(c)/W(c), water polo M(c)/W(c), weight lifting M/W, wrestling M.

Standardized Tests *Required:* SAT or ACT (for admission).

Costs (2010–11) *Tuition:* state resident $5020 full-time, $167 per credit hour part-time; nonresident $20,500 full-time, $683 per credit hour part-time. Full-time tuition and fees vary according to course load. Part-time tuition and fees vary according to course load. *Room and board:* $8765; room only: $5150. Room and board charges vary according to board plan and housing facility. *Payment plans:* tuition prepayment, deferred payment. *Waivers:* senior citizens and employees or children of employees.

Financial Aid Of all full-time matriculated undergraduates who enrolled in 2008, 23,033 applied for aid, 20,297 were judged to have need, 2,536 had their need fully met. In 2008, 792 non-need-based awards were made. *Average percent of need met:* 62%. *Average financial aid package:* $7937. *Average need-based loan:* $4661. *Average need-based gift aid:* $5761. *Average non-need-based aid:* $2416. *Average indebtedness upon graduation:* $18,966. *Financial aid deadline:* 6/30.

Applying *Options:* electronic application, early admission. *Application fee:* $30. *Required:* high school transcript, minimum 2 GPA. *Recommended:* essay or personal statement. *Application deadlines:* 3/1 (freshmen), 5/1 (transfers). *Notification:* continuous (freshmen), continuous (transfers).

Freshman Application Contact Dr. Gordon Chavis Jr., Associate Vice President, Undergraduate Admissions, Student Financial Assistance and Outreach Programs, University of Central Florida, PO Box 160111, Orlando, FL 32816-0111. *Phone:* 407-823-3000. *Fax:* 407-823-5625. *E-mail:* admission@mail.ucf.edu. *Web site:* http://www.ucf.edu/.

University of Florida
Gainesville, Florida

- **State-supported** university, founded 1853, part of Board of Trustees
- **Suburban** 2000-acre campus with easy access to Jacksonville
- **Endowment** $1.1 billion
- **Coed** 32,660 undergraduate students, 93% full-time, 55% women, 45% men
- **Very difficult** entrance level, 43% of applicants were admitted

Undergraduates 30,475 full-time, 2,185 part-time. Students come from 49 states and territories; 133 other countries; 3% are from out of state; 10% Black or African American, non-Hispanic/Latino; 17% Hispanic/Latino; 8% Asian, non-Hispanic/Latino; 0.4% American Indian or Alaska Native, non-Hispanic/Latino; 4% Race/ethnicity unknown; 1% international; 4% transferred in; 22% live on campus.

Freshmen *Admission:* 26,513 applied, 11,460 admitted, 6,381 enrolled. *Test scores:* SAT critical reading scores over 500: 99%; SAT math scores over 500: 95%; ACT scores over 18: 100%; SAT critical reading scores over 600: 65%; SAT math scores over 600: 75%; ACT scores over 24: 96%; SAT critical reading scores over 700: 16%; SAT math scores over 700: 23%; ACT scores over 30: 37%.

Faculty *Total:* 3,643, 94% full-time, 75% with terminal degrees. *Student/faculty ratio:* 21:1.

Academics *Calendar:* semesters. *Degrees:* bachelor's, master's, doctoral-professional, and doctoral-research/scholarship. *Special study options:* accelerated degree program, adult/continuing education programs, advanced placement credit, cooperative education, distance learning, double majors, English as a second language, external degree program, honors programs, independent study, internships, off-campus study, part-time degree program, services for LD students, student-designed majors, study abroad, summer session for credit. *ROTC:* Army (b), Navy (b), Air Force (b). *Unusual degree programs:* 3-2 business administration.

Computers on Campus 2,200 computers/terminals and 1,000 ports are available on campus for general student use. Students can access the following: campus intranet, computer help desk, free student e-mail accounts, online (class) grades, online (class) registration, online (class) schedules, course management system. Campuswide network is available. 100% of college-owned or -operated housing units are wired for high-speed Internet access. Wireless service is available via classrooms, computer centers, computer labs, dorm rooms, learning centers, libraries, student centers.

Student Life *Housing options:* coed, disabled students. Campus housing is university owned. Freshman applicants given priority for college housing. *Activities and organizations:* drama/theater group, student-run newspaper, radio and television station, choral group, marching band, VISA - Volunteers for International Student Affairs, Fellowship of Christian Athletes, Black Student Union, Hispanic Student Association, Asian American Student Union, national fraternities, national sororities. *Campus security:* 24-hour emergency response devices and patrols, student patrols, late-night transport/escort service, controlled dormitory access, crime and rape prevention programs. *Student services:* health clinic, personal/psychological counseling, legal services.

Athletics Member NCAA. All Division I. *Intercollegiate sports:* baseball M(s), basketball M(s)/W(s), cheerleading M(s)/W(s), cross-country running M(s)/W(s), football M(s), golf M(s)/W(s), gymnastics W(s), lacrosse W(s), soccer W(s), softball W(s), swimming and diving M(s)/W(s), tennis M(s)/W(s), track and field M(s)/W(s), volleyball W(s). *Intramural sports:* basketball M/W, bowling M/W, golf M/W, racquetball M/W, soccer M/W, softball M/W, swimming and diving M/W, table tennis M/W, tennis M/W, track and field M/W, ultimate Frisbee M/W, volleyball M/W, weight lifting M/W, wrestling M/W.

Standardized Tests *Required:* SAT or ACT (for admission).

Costs (2010–11) *Tuition:* state resident $5044 full-time, $118 per credit hour part-time; nonresident $27,321 full-time, $825 per credit hour part-time. *Room and board:* $8640; room only: $5300. Room and board charges vary according to board plan and housing facility. *Waivers:* senior citizens.

Financial Aid Of all full-time matriculated undergraduates who enrolled in 2008, 19,148 applied for aid, 15,277 were judged to have need, 4,786 had their need fully met. 1,356 Federal Work-Study jobs (averaging $1846). 4,150 state and other part-time jobs (averaging $1988). In 2008, 2032 non-need-based awards were made. *Average percent of need met:* 83%. *Average financial aid package:* $13,387. *Average need-based loan:* $4248. *Average need-based gift*

aid: $7447. *Average non-need-based aid:* $2171. *Average indebtedness upon graduation:* $16,013.
Applying *Options:* electronic application, early admission. *Application fee:* $30. *Required:* essay or personal statement, high school transcript, SAT or ACT with writing section. *Application deadlines:* 11/1 (freshmen), rolling (transfers). *Notification:* 2/15 (freshmen), continuous (transfers).
Freshman Application Contact Office of Admissions, University of Florida, PO Box 114000, Gainesville, FL 32611-4000. *Phone:* 352-392-1365. *Web site:* http://www.ufl.edu/.

University of Miami
Coral Gables, Florida

- **Independent** university, founded 1925
- **Suburban** 230-acre campus with easy access to Miami
- **Coed** 10,368 undergraduate students, 93% full-time, 52% women, 48% men
- **Very difficult** entrance level, 39% of applicants were admitted

Undergraduates 9,640 full-time, 728 part-time. 50% are from out of state; 7% Black or African American, non-Hispanic/Latino; 25% Hispanic/Latino; 5% Asian, non-Hispanic/Latino; 0.1% Native Hawaiian or other Pacific Islander, non-Hispanic/Latino; 0.3% American Indian or Alaska Native, non-Hispanic/Latino; 1% Two or more races, non-Hispanic/Latino; 7% Race/ethnicity unknown; 9% international; 6% transferred in; 40% live on campus. *Retention:* 90% of full-time freshmen returned.
Freshmen *Admission:* 25,895 applied, 10,157 admitted, 2,132 enrolled. *Average high school GPA:* 4.2. *Test scores:* SAT critical reading scores over 500: 96%; SAT math scores over 500: 98%; SAT writing scores over 500: 97%; ACT scores over 18: 100%; SAT critical reading scores over 600: 74%; SAT math scores over 600: 83%; SAT writing scores over 600: 70%; ACT scores over 24: 97%; SAT critical reading scores over 700: 19%; SAT math scores over 700: 28%; SAT writing scores over 700: 18%; ACT scores over 30: 51%.
Faculty *Total:* 1,370, 71% full-time, 78% with terminal degrees. *Student/faculty ratio:* 11:1.
Academics *Calendar:* semesters. *Degrees:* certificates, bachelor's, master's, doctoral-professional, doctoral-research/scholarship, post-master's, and post-bachelor's certificates. *Special study options:* academic remediation for entering students, accelerated degree program, adult/continuing education programs, advanced placement credit, distance learning, double majors, English as a second language, honors programs, independent study, internships, part-time degree program, services for LD students, student-designed majors, study abroad, summer session for credit. *ROTC:* Army (b), Air Force (b). *Unusual degree programs:* 3-2 engineering; exercise physiology, Latin American studies, physical therapy, marine geology, medicine, law.
Computers on Campus Students can access the following: campus intranet, computer help desk, free student e-mail accounts, online (class) grades, online (class) registration, online (class) schedules, online student account information. Campuswide network is available. 100% of college-owned or -operated housing units are wired for high-speed Internet access. Wireless service is available via entire campus.
Student Life *Housing:* on-campus residence required for freshman year. *Options:* coed, disabled students. Campus housing is university owned. Freshman campus housing is guaranteed. *Activities and organizations:* drama/theater group, student-run newspaper, radio and television station, choral group, marching band, national fraternities, national sororities. *Campus security:* 24-hour emergency response devices and patrols, student patrols, late-night transport/escort service, controlled dormitory access, crime prevention and safety workshops, residential college crime watch. *Student services:* health clinic, personal/psychological counseling, women's center.
Athletics Member NCAA. All Division I except football (Division I-A). *Intercollegiate sports:* baseball M(s), basketball M(s)/W(s), cheerleading M/W, crew M(s), cross-country running M(s)/W(s), golf W(s), soccer W(s), swimming and diving W(s), tennis M(s)/W(s), track and field M(s)/W(s), volleyball W(s). *Intramural sports:* badminton M(c)/W(c), basketball M/W, bowling M(c)/W(c), equestrian sports M(c)/W(c), fencing M(c)/W(c), field hockey M(c)/W(c), golf M(c)/W(c), lacrosse M(c)/W(c), racquetball M(c)/W(c), rugby M(c)/W(c), sailing M(c)/W(c), soccer M(c)/W(c), softball M/W(c), swimming and diving M(c)/W(c), table tennis M(c)/W(c), tennis M(c)/W(c), ultimate Frisbee M(c)/W(c), volleyball M(c)/W(c), water polo M(c)/W(c), weight lifting M(c)/W(c).
Standardized Tests *Required:* SAT or ACT (for admission). *Required for some:* SAT Subject Tests (for admission).
Costs (2010–11) *Comprehensive fee:* $48,898 includes full-time tuition ($36,962), mandatory fees ($874), and room and board ($11,062). Part-time tuition: $1538 per credit hour. Part-time tuition and fees vary according to course load. *College room only:* $6448. Room and board charges vary according to board plan and housing facility. *Payment plans:* tuition prepayment, installment, deferred payment. *Waivers:* employees or children of employees.
Financial Aid Of all full-time matriculated undergraduates who enrolled in 2009, 5,433 applied for aid, 4,608 were judged to have need, 1,646 had their

need fully met. In 2009, 1754 non-need-based awards were made. *Average percent of need met:* 81%. *Average financial aid package:* $31,800. *Average need-based loan:* $5725. *Average need-based gift aid:* $23,552. *Average non-need-based aid:* $19,971. *Average indebtedness upon graduation:* $26,438.
Applying *Options:* electronic application, early admission, early decision, early action, deferred entrance. *Application fee:* $65. *Required:* essay or personal statement, high school transcript, counselor evaluation. *Application deadlines:* 1/15 (freshmen), 3/1 (transfers), 11/1 (early action). *Early decision deadline:* 11/1. *Notification:* 4/15 (freshmen), 4/15 (transfers), 12/15 (early decision), 2/1 (early action).
Freshman Application Contact University of Miami, University of Miami Branch, Coral Gables, FL 33124. *Phone:* 305-284-4323. *E-mail:* admission@miami.edu. *Web site:* http://www.miami.edu/.

University of North Florida
Jacksonville, Florida

- **State-supported** comprehensive, founded 1965, part of State University System of Florida
- **Urban** 1300-acre campus
- **Endowment** $69.7 million
- **Coed** 14,258 undergraduate students, 78% full-time, 56% women, 44% men
- **Very difficult** entrance level, 51% of applicants were admitted

Undergraduates 11,131 full-time, 3,127 part-time. Students come from 47 states and territories; 58 other countries; 3% are from out of state; 10% Black or African American, non-Hispanic/Latino; 7% Hispanic/Latino; 5% Asian, non-Hispanic/Latino; 0.1% Native Hawaiian or other Pacific Islander, non-Hispanic/Latino; 0.3% American Indian or Alaska Native, non-Hispanic/Latino; 2% Two or more races, non-Hispanic/Latino; 0.5% Race/ethnicity unknown; 1% international; 9% transferred in; 17% live on campus. *Retention:* 83% of full-time freshmen returned.
Freshmen *Admission:* 11,743 applied, 5,964 admitted, 1,997 enrolled. *Average high school GPA:* 3.64. *Test scores:* SAT critical reading scores over 500: 90%; SAT math scores over 500: 90%; ACT scores over 18: 100%; SAT critical reading scores over 600: 37%; SAT math scores over 600: 37%; ACT scores over 24: 44%; SAT critical reading scores over 700: 4%; SAT math scores over 700: 2%; ACT scores over 30: 2%.
Faculty *Total:* 821, 65% full-time, 61% with terminal degrees. *Student/faculty ratio:* 21:1.
Academics *Calendar:* semesters. *Degrees:* associate, bachelor's, master's, doctoral-professional, doctoral-research/scholarship, post-master's, and post-bachelor's certificates (doctoral degree in education only). *Special study options:* accelerated degree program, adult/continuing education programs, advanced placement credit, cooperative education, distance learning, double majors, English as a second language, honors programs, independent study, internships, off-campus study, part-time degree program, services for LD students, student-designed majors, study abroad, summer session for credit. *ROTC:* Army (b), Navy (c).
Computers on Campus 750 computers/terminals are available on campus for general student use. Students can access the following: campus intranet, computer help desk, free student e-mail accounts, online (class) grades, online (class) registration, online (class) schedules, applications software. Campuswide network is available. 100% of college-owned or -operated housing units are wired for high-speed Internet access. Wireless service is available via entire campus.
Student Life *Housing options:* coed, disabled students. Campus housing is university owned. Freshman applicants given priority for college housing. *Activities and organizations:* drama/theater group, student-run newspaper, radio and television station, choral group, Student Government Association, African Student Association, International Student Association, Filipino Student Association, National Education Association, national fraternities, national sororities. *Campus security:* 24-hour emergency response devices and patrols, student patrols, late-night transport/escort service, controlled dormitory access, electronic parking lot security. *Student services:* health clinic, personal/psychological counseling, women's center.
Athletics Member NCAA. All Division I. *Intercollegiate sports:* baseball M(s), basketball M(s)/W(s), cross-country running M(s)/W(s), golf M(s), soccer M(s)/W(s), softball W(s), swimming and diving W(s), tennis M(s)/W(s), track and field M(s)/W(s), volleyball W(s). *Intramural sports:* badminton M/W, basketball M/W, bowling M/W, fencing M(c)/W(c), football M/W, golf M/W, lacrosse M(c)/W(c), racquetball M(c)/W(c), rugby M(c), sailing M(c)/W(c), soccer M/W, swimming and diving M/W, table tennis M/W, track and field M/W, ultimate Frisbee M(c)/W(c), volleyball M(c)/W(c).
Standardized Tests *Required:* SAT or ACT (for admission).
Costs (2011–12) *Tuition:* state resident $3742 full-time, $182 per credit hour part-time; nonresident $18,002 full-time, $681 per credit hour part-time. Full-time tuition and fees vary according to course load. Part-time tuition and fees vary according to course load. *Required fees:* $1707 full-time. *Room and board:* $8452. Room and board charges vary according to board plan and hous-

ing facility. *Payment plan:* installment. *Waivers:* senior citizens and employees or children of employees.

Financial Aid Of all full-time matriculated undergraduates who enrolled in 2009, 6,770 applied for aid, 5,337 were judged to have need, 607 had their need fully met. 110 Federal Work-Study jobs (averaging $2944). In 2009, 1435 non-need-based awards were made. *Average percent of need met:* 89%. *Average financial aid package:* $8749. *Average need-based loan:* $1555. *Average need-based gift aid:* $1379. *Average non-need-based aid:* $1074. *Average indebtedness upon graduation:* $15,300.

Applying *Options:* electronic application, deferred entrance. *Application fee:* $30. *Required:* high school transcript, minimum 2.5 GPA, meet minimum test score requirements (460 SAT Critical Reading, 460 SAT Math, 440 SAT Writing; or 19 ACT Reading, 19 ACT Math, 18 ACT English/Writing. *Required for some:* essay or personal statement. *Recommended:* minimum 3 GPA. *Application deadlines:* rolling (freshmen), 5/6 (transfers). *Notification:* continuous until 1/11 (freshmen), continuous (transfers).

Freshman Application Contact Mr. John Yancey, Director of Admissions, University of North Florida, 1 UNF Drive, Jacksonville, FL 32224. *Phone:* 904-620-2624. *Fax:* 904-620-2014. *E-mail:* admissions@unf.edu. *Web site:* http://www.unf.edu/.

University of Phoenix–Central Florida Campus

Maitland, Florida

Freshman Application Contact Ms. Audra McQuarie, Registrar/Executive Director, University of Phoenix–Central Florida Campus, 4035 South Riverpoint Parkway, Mail Stop CF-L101, Phoenix, AZ 85040. *Phone:* 480-557-6151. *Toll-free phone:* 800-776-4867 (in-state); 800-228-7240 (out-of-state). *Fax:* 480-643-3068. *E-mail:* audra.mcquarie@phoenix.edu. *Web site:* http://www.phoenix.edu/.

University of Phoenix–North Florida Campus

Jacksonville, Florida

Freshman Application Contact Ms. Audra McQuarie, Registrar/Executive Director, University of Phoenix–North Florida Campus, 4035 South Riverpoint Parkway, Mail Stop CF-L101, Phoenix, AZ 85040. *Phone:* 480-557-6151. *Toll-free phone:* 800-776-4867 (in-state); 800-894-1758 (out-of-state). *Fax:* 480-643-3068. *E-mail:* audra.mcquarie@phoenix.edu. *Web site:* http://www.phoenix.edu/.

University of Phoenix–South Florida Campus

Fort Lauderdale, Florida

Freshman Application Contact Ms. Audra McQuarie, Registrar/Executive Director, University of Phoenix–South Florida Campus, 4035 South Riverpoint Parkway, Mail Stop CF-L101, Phoenix, AZ 85040. *Phone:* 480-557-6151. *Toll-free phone:* 800-228-7240. *Fax:* 480-643-3068. *E-mail:* audra.mcquarie@phoenix.edu. *Web site:* http://www.phoenix.edu/.

University of Phoenix–West Florida Campus

Temple Terrace, Florida

Freshman Application Contact Ms. Evelyn Gaskin, Registrar/Executive Director, University of Phoenix–West Florida Campus, 4615 East Elwood Street, Mail Stop AA-K101, Phoenix, AZ 85040-1958. *Phone:* 480-557-3303. *Toll-free phone:* 800-776-4867 (in-state); 800-228-7240 (out-of-state). *Fax:* 480-643-1020. *E-mail:* evelyn.gaskin@phoenix.edu. *Web site:* http://www.phoenix.edu/.

University of South Florida

Tampa, Florida

- **State-supported** university, founded 1956, part of State University System of Florida
- **Urban** 1561-acre campus
- **Coed** 30,914 undergraduate students, 76% full-time, 56% women, 44% men
- **Moderately difficult** entrance level, 45% of applicants were admitted

Undergraduates 23,428 full-time, 7,486 part-time. Students come from 51 states and territories; 154 other countries; 3% are from out of state; 12% Black or African American, non-Hispanic/Latino; 17% Hispanic/Latino; 6% Asian, non-Hispanic/Latino; 0.1% Native Hawaiian or other Pacific Islander, non-Hispanic/Latino; 0.4% American Indian or Alaska Native, non-Hispanic/Latino; 0.9% Two or more races, non-Hispanic/Latino; 2% Race/ethnicity unknown; 2% international; 10% transferred in; 18% live on campus. *Retention:* 88% of full-time freshmen returned.

Freshmen *Admission:* 29,179 applied, 13,003 admitted, 4,430 enrolled. *Average high school GPA:* 3.64. *Test scores:* SAT critical reading scores over 500: 82%; SAT math scores over 500: 86%; SAT writing scores over 500: 73%; ACT scores over 18: 100%; SAT critical reading scores over 600: 30%; SAT math scores over 600: 38%; SAT writing scores over 600: 20%; ACT scores over 24: 58%; SAT critical reading scores over 700: 4%; SAT math scores over 700: 5%; SAT writing scores over 700: 2%; ACT scores over 30: 9%.

Faculty *Total:* 1,235, 79% with terminal degrees. *Student/faculty ratio:* 28:1.

Academics *Calendar:* semesters. *Degrees:* associate, bachelor's, master's, doctoral-professional, and doctoral-research/scholarship. *Special study options:* academic remediation for entering students, accelerated degree program, adult/continuing education programs, advanced placement credit, cooperative education, distance learning, double majors, English as a second language, freshman honors college, honors programs, independent study, internships, off-campus study, part-time degree program, services for LD students, student-designed majors, study abroad, summer session for credit. *ROTC:* Army (b), Navy (b), Air Force (b).

Computers on Campus 500 computers/terminals are available on campus for general student use. Students can access the following: computer help desk, free student e-mail accounts, online (class) registration, online (class) schedules. Campuswide network is available. 100% of college-owned or -operated housing units are wired for high-speed Internet access. Wireless service is available via classrooms, computer centers, computer labs, dorm rooms, libraries, student centers.

Student Life *Housing:* on-campus residence required for freshman year. *Options:* coed, men-only, women-only, cooperative, disabled students. Campus housing is university owned. Freshman campus housing is guaranteed. *Activities and organizations:* drama/theater group, student-run newspaper, radio and television station, choral group, marching band, student government, Campus Activities Board, USF Ambassadors, Student Admissions Representatives, national fraternities, national sororities. *Campus security:* 24-hour emergency response devices and patrols, student patrols, late-night transport/escort service, controlled dormitory access, residence hall lobby personnel 8 pm to 6 am. *Student services:* health clinic, personal/psychological counseling, women's center, legal services.

Athletics Member NCAA. All Division I. *Intercollegiate sports:* baseball M(s), basketball M(s)/W(s), cross-country running M(s)/W(s), football M(s), golf M(s)/W(s), soccer M(s)/W(s), softball W(s), tennis M(s)/W(s), track and field M(s)/W(s), volleyball W(s). *Intramural sports:* badminton M/W, basketball M/W, bowling M/W, cross-country running M/W, football M, golf M/W, racquetball M/W, soccer M/W, softball M/W, swimming and diving M/W, table tennis M/W, tennis M/W, track and field M/W, volleyball M/W, wrestling M/W.

Standardized Tests *Required:* SAT or ACT (for admission).

Costs (2011–12) *Tuition:* state resident $5124 full-time, $171 per credit hour part-time; nonresident $15,933 full-time, $531 per credit hour part-time. Full-time tuition and fees vary according to course level, course load, and location. Part-time tuition and fees vary according to course level, course load, and location. *Required fees:* $74 full-time. *Room only:* $5380. Room and board charges vary according to board plan, housing facility, and location. *Payment plan:* installment. *Waivers:* senior citizens.

Financial Aid Of all full-time matriculated undergraduates who enrolled in 2007, 15,172 applied for aid, 12,526 were judged to have need, 604 had their need fully met. 924 Federal Work-Study jobs (averaging $3600). In 2007, 1871 non-need-based awards were made. *Average percent of need met:* 38%. *Average financial aid package:* $9666. *Average need-based loan:* $4633. *Average need-based gift aid:* $4786. *Average non-need-based aid:* $1997. *Average indebtedness upon graduation:* $18,568.

Applying *Options:* electronic application, early admission. *Application fee:* $30. *Required:* minimum 2 GPA. *Required for some:* high school transcript, 1 letter of recommendation. *Application deadlines:* 4/15 (freshmen), 4/15 (transfers). *Notification:* continuous (freshmen), continuous (transfers).

Freshman Application Contact Ms. Lisa Rycroft, Freshman Recruiter and Advisor, University of South Florida, Office of Undergraduate Admissions, 4202 East Fowler Avenue, Tampa, FL 33620-9951. *Phone:* 813-974-6431. *Fax:* 813-974-9689. *E-mail:* bullseye@admin.usf.edu. *Web site:* http://www.usf.edu/.

University of South Florida–Polytechnic

Lakeland, Florida

- **State-supported** upper-level, founded 1988, part of University of South Florida System
- **Coed**

Academics *Calendar:* semesters. *Degrees:* bachelor's, master's, and post-master's certificates.

Admissions Office Contact University of South Florida–Polytechnic, 3433 Winter Lake Road, Lakeland, FL 33803. *Web site:* http://www.poly.usf.edu/.

University of South Florida–St. Petersburg Campus

St. Petersburg, Florida

- **State-supported** comprehensive, founded 1965, part of University of South Florida System
- **Coed**

Academics *Calendar:* semesters. *Degrees:* certificates, bachelor's, master's, and post-master's certificates.

Admissions Office Contact University of South Florida–St. Petersburg Campus, 140 Seventh Ave S., St. Petersburg, FL 33701. *Web site:* http://www.stpt.usf.edu/.

University of South Florida Sarasota-Manatee

Sarasota, Florida

- **State-supported** upper-level, founded 1956, part of University of South Florida System
- **Coed**

Academics *Calendar:* semesters. *Degrees:* bachelor's, master's, and post-master's certificates.

Admissions Office Contact University of South Florida Sarasota-Manatee, 8350 N Tamiami Trail, Sarasota, FL 34243. *Web site:* http://www.sarasota.usf.edu/.

The University of Tampa

Tampa, Florida

- **Independent** comprehensive, founded 1931
- **Urban** 100-acre campus with easy access to Tampa-St. Petersburg, Clearwater
- **Coed** 5,687 undergraduate students, 94% full-time, 56% women, 44% men
- **Moderately difficult** entrance level, 57% of applicants were admitted

Undergraduates 5,339 full-time, 348 part-time. Students come from 50 states and territories; 114 other countries; 56% are from out of state; 8% transferred in; 59% live on campus. *Retention:* 69% of full-time freshmen returned.

Freshmen *Admission:* 11,112 applied, 6,372 admitted, 1,352 enrolled. *Average high school GPA:* 3.3. *Test scores:* SAT critical reading scores over 500: 70%; SAT math scores over 500: 75%; SAT writing scores over 500: 69%; ACT scores over 18: 98%; SAT critical reading scores over 600: 16%; SAT math scores over 600: 23%; SAT writing scores over 600: 18%; ACT scores over 24: 47%; SAT critical reading scores over 700: 1%; SAT math scores over 700: 1%; SAT writing scores over 700: 1%; ACT scores over 30: 3%.

Faculty *Total:* 534, 49% full-time, 60% with terminal degrees. *Student/faculty ratio:* 17:1.

Academics *Calendar:* semesters. *Degrees:* certificates, associate, bachelor's, master's, and post-master's certificates. *Special study options:* academic remediation for entering students, adult/continuing education programs, advanced placement credit, cooperative education, double majors, English as a second language, honors programs, independent study, internships, part-time degree program, services for LD students, study abroad, summer session for credit. *ROTC:* Army (b), Navy (c), Air Force (c). *Unusual degree programs:* 3-2 chemistry/MBA joint program.

Computers on Campus 800 computers/terminals and 8,000 ports are available on campus for general student use. Students can access the following: campus intranet, computer help desk, free student e-mail accounts, online

(class) grades, online (class) registration, online (class) schedules. Campus-wide network is available. 100% of college-owned or -operated housing units are wired for high-speed Internet access. Wireless service is available via entire campus.

Student Life *Housing options:* coed, disabled students. Campus housing is university owned. *Activities and organizations:* drama/theater group, student-run newspaper, radio and television station, choral group, Greek Life, student government, PEACE (volunteer organization), Student Productions, Minaret, national fraternities, national sororities. *Campus security:* 24-hour emergency response devices and patrols, student patrols, late-night transport/escort service, controlled dormitory access. *Student services:* health clinic, personal/psychological counseling, women's center.

Athletics Member NCAA. All Division II. *Intercollegiate sports:* baseball M(s), basketball M(s)/W(s), crew W(s), cross-country running M(s)/W(s), golf M(s), soccer M(s)/W(s), softball W(s), swimming and diving M(s)/W(s), tennis W(s), volleyball W(s). *Intramural sports:* basketball M/W, cheerleading W(c), crew M(c), field hockey W, football M/W, golf M/W, soccer M/W, softball M/W, swimming and diving M/W, table tennis W, tennis M/W, track and field M/W, ultimate Frisbee M/W, volleyball M/W.

Standardized Tests *Required:* SAT or ACT (for admission).

Costs (2010–11) *One-time required fee:* $85. *Comprehensive fee:* $31,808 includes full-time tuition ($22,116), mandatory fees ($1102), and room and board ($8590). Full-time tuition and fees vary according to class time. Part-time tuition: $470 per credit hour. Part-time tuition and fees vary according to class time. *Required fees:* $40 per term part-time. *College room only:* $4590. Room and board charges vary according to board plan and housing facility. *Payment plan:* installment. *Waivers:* employees or children of employees.

Financial Aid Of all full-time matriculated undergraduates who enrolled in 2009, 3,693 applied for aid, 3,112 were judged to have need, 631 had their need fully met. 276 Federal Work-Study jobs (averaging $2000). 3 state and other part-time jobs (averaging $2000). In 2009, 1749 non-need-based awards were made. *Average percent of need met:* 71%. *Average financial aid package:* $16,255. *Average need-based loan:* $4334. *Average need-based gift aid:* $12,002. *Average non-need-based aid:* $5694. *Average indebtedness upon graduation:* $29,264.

Applying *Options:* electronic application, early admission, early action, deferred entrance. *Application fee:* $40. *Required:* essay or personal statement, high school transcript, minimum 2 GPA. *Required for some:* 1 letter of recommendation, ACT/SAT test scores. *Recommended:* interview. *Application deadlines:* rolling (freshmen), rolling (out-of-state freshmen), rolling (transfers), 11/15 (early action). *Notification:* continuous (freshmen), continuous (out-of-state freshmen), continuous (transfers), 12/15 (early action).

Freshman Application Contact Dennis Nostrand, Vice President for Enrollment, The University of Tampa, 401 West Kennedy Boulevard, Tampa, FL 33606-1480. *Phone:* 813-257-1808. *Toll-free phone:* 888-646-2438 (in-state); 888-MINARET (out-of-state). *Fax:* 813-258-7398. *E-mail:* admissions@ut.edu. *Web site:* http://www.ut.edu/.

University of West Florida

Pensacola, Florida

- **State-supported** comprehensive, founded 1963, part of State University System of Florida
- **Suburban** 1600-acre campus
- **Endowment** $51.2 million
- **Coed** 9,554 undergraduate students, 72% full-time, 58% women, 42% men
- **Moderately difficult** entrance level, 66% of applicants were admitted

Undergraduates 6,865 full-time, 2,689 part-time. Students come from 49 states and territories; 85 other countries; 11% are from out of state; 10% Black or African American, non-Hispanic/Latino; 6% Hispanic/Latino; 4% Asian, non-Hispanic/Latino; 0.3% Native Hawaiian or other Pacific Islander, non-Hispanic/Latino; 0.9% American Indian or Alaska Native, non-Hispanic/Latino; 2% Two or more races, non-Hispanic/Latino; 0.2% Race/ethnicity unknown; 2% international; 12% transferred in; 15% live on campus. *Retention:* 73% of full-time freshmen returned.

Freshmen *Admission:* 5,349 applied, 3,533 admitted, 1,254 enrolled. *Average high school GPA:* 3.33. *Test scores:* SAT critical reading scores over 500: 66%; SAT math scores over 500: 62%; SAT writing scores over 500: 53%; ACT scores over 18: 98%; SAT critical reading scores over 600: 20%; SAT math scores over 600: 18%; SAT writing scores over 600: 11%; ACT scores over 24: 45%; SAT critical reading scores over 700: 4%; SAT math scores over 700: 2%; SAT writing scores over 700: 1%; ACT scores over 30: 4%.

Faculty *Total:* 542, 56% full-time, 60% with terminal degrees. *Student/faculty ratio:* 23:1.

Academics *Calendar:* semesters. *Degrees:* associate, bachelor's, master's, doctoral-other, and post-master's certificates. *Special study options:* advanced placement credit, cooperative education, distance learning, English as a second language, honors programs, independent study, internships, off-campus study, part-time degree program, services for LD students, study abroad, summer session for credit. *ROTC:* Army (b), Air Force (b). *Unusual degree programs:* 3-2 business administration.

Computers on Campus 1,064 computers/terminals and 100 ports are available on campus for general student use. Students can access the following: campus intranet, computer help desk, free student e-mail accounts, online (class) grades, online (class) registration, online (class) schedules. Campuswide network is available. 100% of college-owned or -operated housing units are wired for high-speed Internet access. Wireless service is available via entire campus.

Student Life *Housing options:* coed. Campus housing is university owned. *Activities and organizations:* drama/theater group, student-run newspaper, choral group, Marketing Association, Student Council for Exceptional Children, Inter-Varsity Christian Fellowship, Baptist Student Ministry, Golden Key Honor Society, national fraternities, national sororities. *Campus security:* 24-hour emergency response devices and patrols, student patrols, late-night transport/escort service, controlled dormitory access. *Student services:* health clinic, personal/psychological counseling.

Athletics Member NCAA. All Division II. *Intercollegiate sports:* baseball M(s), basketball M(s)/W(s), cross-country running M(s)/W(s), golf M(s), soccer M(s)/W(s), softball W(s), tennis M(s)/W(s), track and field W, volleyball W. *Intramural sports:* basketball M/W, bowling M/W, cheerleading W, fencing M/W, football M/W, sailing M/W, soccer M/W, swimming and diving M/W, tennis M/W, volleyball M/W.

Standardized Tests *Required:* SAT or ACT (for admission), SAT and SAT Subject Tests or ACT (for admission).

Costs (2010–11) *Tuition:* state resident $3254 full-time, $160 per semester hour part-time; nonresident $15,522 full-time, $589 per semester hour part-time. Full-time tuition and fees vary according to location and reciprocity agreements. Part-time tuition and fees vary according to location and reciprocity agreements. *Required fees:* $1540 full-time. *Room and board:* $7856. Room and board charges vary according to housing facility. *Payment plans:* tuition prepayment, deferred payment. *Waivers:* senior citizens and employees or children of employees.

Applying *Options:* electronic application, early admission, deferred entrance. *Application fee:* $30. *Required:* high school transcript, minimum 2 GPA. *Application deadlines:* 6/30 (freshmen), 6/30 (transfers). *Notification:* continuous (freshmen), continuous (transfers).

Freshman Application Contact Stephen McKellips, Director of Admissions, University of West Florida, Admissions, 11000 University Parkway, Pensacola, FL 32514. *Phone:* 850-474-2230. *Toll-free phone:* 800-263-1074. *Fax:* 850-474-3460. *E-mail:* admissions@uwf.edu. *Web site:* http://www.uwf.edu/.

Warner University

Lake Wales, Florida

Freshman Application Contact Mr. Jason Roe, Director of Admissions, Warner University, Warner Southern Center, 13895 Highway 27, Lake Wales, FL 33859. *Phone:* 863-638-7212 Ext. 7213. *Toll-free phone:* 800-949-7248. *Fax:* 863-638-1472. *E-mail:* admissions@warner.edu. *Web site:* http://www.warner.edu/.

Webber International University

Babson Park, Florida

- **Independent** comprehensive, founded 1927
- **Small-town** 110-acre campus with easy access to Orlando
- **Endowment** $4.4 million
- **Coed** 680 undergraduate students, 92% full-time, 36% women, 64% men
- **Moderately difficult** entrance level, 57% of applicants were admitted

Undergraduates 626 full-time, 54 part-time. Students come from 26 states and territories; 35 other countries; 8% are from out of state; 23% Black or African American, non-Hispanic/Latino; 8% Hispanic/Latino; 0.9% Asian, non-Hispanic/Latino; 0.4% American Indian or Alaska Native, non-Hispanic/Latino; 0.9% Two or more races, non-Hispanic/Latino; 23% international; 13% transferred in; 52% live on campus. *Retention:* 50% of full-time freshmen returned.

Freshmen *Admission:* 579 applied, 331 admitted, 179 enrolled. *Average high school GPA:* 3.19. *Test scores:* SAT critical reading scores over 500: 24%; SAT math scores over 500: 39%; ACT scores over 18: 72%; SAT math scores over 600: 3%; ACT scores over 24: 5%.

Faculty *Total:* 43, 44% full-time, 49% with terminal degrees. *Student/faculty ratio:* 24:1.

Academics *Calendar:* semesters. *Degrees:* associate, bachelor's, and master's. *Special study options:* academic remediation for entering students, accelerated degree program, adult/continuing education programs, advanced placement credit, cooperative education, distance learning, double majors, English as a second language, internships, part-time degree program, services for LD students, study abroad, summer session for credit.

Computers on Campus 89 computers/terminals are available on campus for general student use. Students can access the following: campus intranet, free student e-mail accounts, online (class) grades, online (class) schedules. Campuswide network is available. 100% of college-owned or -operated housing units are wired for high-speed Internet access. Wireless service is available via computer labs, libraries, student centers.

Student Life *Housing:* on-campus residence required for freshman year. *Options:* men-only, women-only. Campus housing is university owned and leased by the school. Freshman campus housing is guaranteed. *Activities and organizations:* student-run newspaper, marching band, Student Leadership Association, Phi Beta Lambda, Society of International Students, Fellowship of Christian Athletes, marketing club. *Campus security:* 24-hour emergency response devices and patrols, late-night transport/escort service, controlled dormitory access. *Student services:* health clinic, personal/psychological counseling.

Athletics Member NAIA. *Intercollegiate sports:* baseball M(s), basketball M(s)/W(s), bowling M(s)/W(s), cheerleading M(s)/W(s), cross-country running M(s)/W(s), football M(s), golf M(s)/W(s), soccer M(s)/W(s), softball W(s), tennis M(s)/W(s), track and field M(s)/W(s), volleyball W(s). *Intramural sports:* basketball M/W, football M/W, soccer M/W, softball W, table tennis M/W, tennis M/W, volleyball M(c)/W(c).

Standardized Tests *Required:* SAT or ACT (for admission).

Costs (2010–11) *Comprehensive fee:* $25,994 includes full-time tuition ($18,742) and room and board ($7252). Full-time tuition and fees vary according to class time and course load. Part-time tuition: $259 per credit hour. Part-time tuition and fees vary according to course load. *College room only:* $4656. Room and board charges vary according to board plan, gender, and housing facility. *Payment plan:* installment. *Waivers:* children of alumni, adult students, senior citizens, and employees or children of employees.

Financial Aid Of all full-time matriculated undergraduates who enrolled in 2009, 433 applied for aid, 397 were judged to have need, 9 had their need fully met. 21 Federal Work-Study jobs (averaging $1370). 38 state and other part-time jobs (averaging $985). In 2009, 170 non-need-based awards were made. *Average percent of need met:* 66%. *Average financial aid package:* $18,403. *Average need-based loan:* $4169. *Average need-based gift aid:* $14,062. *Average non-need-based aid:* $7933. *Average indebtedness upon graduation:* $28,655. *Financial aid deadline:* 8/1.

Applying *Options:* electronic application, early action. *Application fee:* $35. *Required:* high school transcript, minimum 2 GPA. *Required for some:* interview. *Recommended:* essay or personal statement. *Application deadlines:* 8/1 (freshmen), 8/1 (transfers), 4/1 (early action).

Freshman Application Contact Mr. Mike Mattison, Director of Admissions, Webber International University, PO Box 96, Babson Park, FL 33827. *Phone:* 863-638-2910. *Toll-free phone:* 800-741-1844. *Fax:* 863-638-1591. *E-mail:* admissions@webber.edu. *Web site:* http://www.webber.edu/.

Yeshiva Gedolah Rabbinical College

Miami Beach, Florida

Admissions Office Contact Yeshiva Gedolah Rabbinical College, 1140 Alton Road, Miami Beach, FL 33139.

GEORGIA

Abraham Baldwin Agricultural College

Tifton, Georgia

- **State-supported** 4-year, founded 1933, part of University System of Georgia
- **Small-town** 421-acre campus
- **Endowment** $7.5 million
- **Coed**
- **Noncompetitive** entrance level

Faculty *Student/faculty ratio:* 24:1.

Academics *Calendar:* semesters. *Degrees:* certificates, associate, and bachelor's.

Student Life *Campus security:* 24-hour emergency response devices and patrols, controlled dormitory access.

Athletics Member NJCAA.

Costs (2010–11) *Tuition:* state resident $2694 full-time; nonresident $10,176 full-time. Part-time tuition and fees vary according to course load. No tuition increase for student's term of enrollment. *Required fees:* $802 full-time. *Room and board:* $7220; room only: $4920. Room and board charges vary according to board plan and housing facility.

Financial Aid *Financial aid deadline:* 7/15.

Applying *Options:* electronic application, early admission, deferred entrance. *Application fee:* $20. *Required:* high school transcript. *Required for some:* minimum high school GPA of 2.0 for College Prep Diploma and 2.2 for Tech Prep Diploma.

Freshman Application Contact Mrs. Donna Webb, Director of Enrollment Services, Abraham Baldwin Agricultural College, Box 4, 2802 Moore Highway, Tifton, GA 31793-2601. *Phone:* 229-391-5004. *Toll-free phone:* 800-733-3653. *Fax:* 229-391-5002. *E-mail:* dwebb@abac.edu. *Web site:* http://www.abac.edu/.

Agnes Scott College

Decatur, Georgia

- **Independent** comprehensive, founded 1889, affiliated with Presbyterian Church (U.S.A.)
- **Urban** 100-acre campus with easy access to Atlanta
- **Endowment** $230.6 million
- **Undergraduate: women only; graduate: coed**
- **Very difficult** entrance level

Faculty *Student/faculty ratio:* 9:1.

Academics *Calendar:* semesters. *Degrees:* bachelor's, master's, and post-bachelor's certificates.

Student Life *Campus security:* 24-hour emergency response devices and patrols, late-night transport/escort service, controlled dormitory access, security systems in apartments, public safety facility, surveillance equipment, key required for residence hall entry.

Athletics Member NCAA. All Division III.

Standardized Tests *Required:* SAT or ACT scores or graded writing sample, home-schooled students must submit SAT or ACT (for admission). *Required for some:* SAT and SAT Subject Tests or ACT (for admission).

Costs (2010–11) *Comprehensive fee:* $41,133 includes full-time tuition ($31,068), mandatory fees ($215), and room and board ($9850). Full-time tuition and fees vary according to course load. Part-time tuition: $1295 per hour. Part-time tuition and fees vary according to course load. *College room only:* $4925. Room and board charges vary according to board plan and housing facility.

Financial Aid *Of all full-time matriculated undergraduates who enrolled in 2009,* 660 applied for aid, 599 were judged to have need, 209 had their need fully met. 498 Federal Work-Study jobs (averaging $2300). 116 state and other part-time jobs (averaging $2300). *In 2009,* 218 non-need-based awards were made. *Average percent of need met:* 92. *Average financial aid package:* $31,243. *Average need-based loan:* $3763. *Average need-based gift aid:* $24,148. *Average non-need-based aid:* $17,628. *Average indebtedness upon graduation:* $26,493. *Financial aid deadline:* 5/1.

Applying *Options:* electronic application, early admission, early action, deferred entrance. *Application fee:* $35. *Required:* essay or personal statement, high school transcript, 2 letters of recommendation. *Recommended:* interview.

Freshman Application Contact Agnes Scott College, 141 East College Avenue, Decatur, GA 30030-3797. *Phone:* 404-471-6285. *Toll-free phone:* 800-868-8602. *Web site:* http://www.agnesscott.edu/.

Albany State University

Albany, Georgia

- **State-supported** comprehensive, founded 1903, part of University System of Georgia
- **Urban** 232-acre campus
- **Coed** 4,166 undergraduate students, 86% full-time, 67% women, 33% men
- **Minimally difficult** entrance level, 55% of applicants were admitted

Undergraduates 3,581 full-time, 585 part-time. Students come from 33 states and territories; 19 other countries; 4% are from out of state; 6% transferred in; 41% live on campus. *Retention:* 72% of full-time freshmen returned.

Freshmen *Admission:* 4,388 applied, 2,422 admitted, 890 enrolled. *Average high school GPA:* 2.86. *Test scores:* SAT critical reading scores over 500: 11%; SAT math scores over 500: 8%; ACT scores over 18: 44%; SAT critical reading scores over 600: 1%; SAT math scores over 600: 1%; ACT scores over 24: 2%.

Faculty *Total:* 278, 54% full-time. *Student/faculty ratio:* 21:1.

Academics *Calendar:* semesters. *Degrees:* bachelor's, master's, and post-master's certificates. *Special study options:* academic remediation for entering students, advanced placement credit, cooperative education, distance learning, double majors, honors programs, independent study, internships, off-campus study, part-time degree program, services for LD students, study abroad, summer session for credit. *ROTC:* Army (b). *Unusual degree programs:* Engineering with Georgia Institute of Technology; Pre-Med, Pre-Med Technology, and Pre-Pharmacy study options.

Computers on Campus Students can access the following: campus intranet, computer help desk, free student e-mail accounts, online (class) grades, online (class) registration, online (class) schedules, academic advising tools, online payment, and campus one stop portal. Campuswide network is available. 100% of college-owned or -operated housing units are wired for high-speed Internet access. Wireless service is available via entire campus.

Student Life *Housing:* on-campus residence required for freshman year. *Options:* coed, men-only, women-only. Campus housing is university owned. Freshman applicants given priority for college housing. *Activities and organizations:* drama/theater group, student-run newspaper, radio and television station, choral group, marching band, Student Government Association, HEROS Mentoring Programs, SIFE, Peer Educators, ASU Anointed Gospel Choir, national fraternities, national sororities. *Campus security:* 24-hour emergency response devices and patrols, late-night transport/escort service, controlled dormitory access, Connect Ed.- Emergency E-mail, Emergency sirens, Active Shooter Team, Certified Police Officers. *Student services:* health clinic, personal/psychological counseling.

Athletics Member NCAA. All Division II. *Intercollegiate sports:* baseball M(s), basketball M(s)/W(s), cheerleading W, cross-country running M(s)/W(s), football M(s), softball W(s), tennis W(s), track and field M(s)/W(s), volleyball W(s). *Intramural sports:* basketball M/W, football M.

Standardized Tests *Required:* SAT or ACT (for admission).

Financial Aid Of all full-time matriculated undergraduates who enrolled in 2003, 2,524 applied for aid, 2,182 were judged to have need, 615 had their need fully met. 440 Federal Work-Study jobs (averaging $1050). 178 state and other part-time jobs (averaging $1655). In 2003, 164 non-need-based awards were made. *Average percent of need met:* 68%. *Average financial aid package:* $7057.

Applying *Options:* electronic application, early admission, deferred entrance. *Application fee:* $20. *Required:* high school transcript, minimum 2.22 GPA. *Application deadlines:* 6/1 (freshmen), 6/1 (out-of-state freshmen), 6/1 (transfers).

Freshman Application Contact Office of Recruitment and Admissions, Albany State University, 504 College Drive, Albany, GA 31705-2717. *Phone:* 229-430-4646. *Toll-free phone:* 800-822-RAMS. *Fax:* 229-430-4105. *E-mail:* admissions@asurams.edu. *Web site:* http://www.asurams.edu/.

American InterContinental University Atlanta

Atlanta, Georgia

Freshman Application Contact American InterContinental University Atlanta, 6600 Peachtree-Dunwoody Road, 500 Embassy Row, Atlanta, GA 30328. *Phone:* 877-564-6248. *Toll-free phone:* 800-353-1744. *Fax:* 877-564-6248. *Web site:* http://www.aiuniv.edu/.

Argosy University, Atlanta

Atlanta, Georgia

- **Proprietary** university, founded 1990, part of Education Management Corporation
- **Suburban** campus
- **Coed**

Academics *Calendar:* semesters. *Degrees:* bachelor's, master's, doctoral-professional, and post-master's certificates.

Costs (2010–11) *Tuition:* Tuition varies by program. Students should contact Argosy University for tuition information.

Freshman Application Contact Argosy University, Atlanta, 980 Hammond Drive, Suite 100, Atlanta, GA 30328. *Phone:* 770-671-1200. *Toll-free phone:* 888-671-4777. *Web site:* http://www.argosy.edu/atlanta/.

See page 1002 for the College Close-Up.

Armstrong Atlantic State University

Savannah, Georgia

- **State-supported** comprehensive, founded 1935, part of University System of Georgia
- **Suburban** 250-acre campus
- **Endowment** $7.1 million
- **Coed** 6,938 undergraduate students, 71% full-time, 64% women, 36% men
- **Minimally difficult** entrance level, 56% of applicants were admitted

Undergraduates 4,959 full-time, 1,979 part-time. Students come from 41 states and territories; 75 other countries; 12% are from out of state; 23% Black or African American, non-Hispanic/Latino; 4% Hispanic/Latino; 2% Asian, non-Hispanic/Latino; 0.2% Native Hawaiian or other Pacific Islander, non-Hispanic/Latino; 0.4% American Indian or Alaska Native, non-Hispanic/Latino; 4% Two or more races, non-Hispanic/Latino; 2% Race/ethnicity

unknown; 4% international; 9% transferred in; 13% live on campus. *Retention:* 66% of full-time freshmen returned.

Freshmen *Admission:* 3,729 applied, 2,096 admitted, 1,191 enrolled. *Average high school GPA:* 3.14. *Test scores:* SAT critical reading scores over 500: 54%; SAT math scores over 500: 48%; ACT scores over 18: 87%; SAT critical reading scores over 600: 14%; SAT math scores over 600: 13%; ACT scores over 24: 27%; SAT critical reading scores over 700: 1%; SAT math scores over 700: 2%; ACT scores over 30: 1%.

Faculty *Total:* 428, 59% full-time. *Student/faculty ratio:* 19:1.

Academics *Calendar:* semesters. *Degrees:* certificates, associate, bachelor's, master's, doctoral-professional, post-master's, and postbachelor's certificates. *Special study options:* academic remediation for entering students, adult/continuing education programs, advanced placement credit, cooperative education, distance learning, double majors, honors programs, independent study, internships, off-campus study, part-time degree program, services for LD students, study abroad, summer session for credit. *ROTC:* Army (b), Navy (c). *Unusual degree programs:* 3-2 engineering with Georgia Institute of Technology.

Computers on Campus 300 computers/terminals are available on campus for general student use. Students can access the following: campus intranet, computer help desk, free student e-mail accounts, online (class) grades, online (class) registration, online (class) schedules. Campuswide network is available. 100% of college-owned or -operated housing units are wired for high-speed Internet access. Wireless service is available via entire campus.

Student Life *Housing options:* coed. Campus housing is university owned. *Activities and organizations:* drama/theater group, student-run newspaper, choral group, Wesley Fellowship, Hispanic Student Society, Ebony Coalition, American Chemical Society, Phi Alpha Theta, national fraternities, national sororities. *Campus security:* 24-hour emergency response devices and patrols, student patrols, late-night transport/escort service. *Student services:* health clinic, personal/psychological counseling.

Athletics Member NCAA. All Division II. *Intercollegiate sports:* baseball M(s), basketball M(s)/W(s), cheerleading M/W, golf M(s)/W(s), softball W(s), tennis M(s)/W(s), volleyball W(s). *Intramural sports:* badminton M/W, basketball M/W, bowling M/W, football M/W, golf M/W, rugby M, soccer M/W, softball M/W, table tennis M/W, tennis M/W, ultimate Frisbee M/W, volleyball M/W.

Standardized Tests *Required:* SAT or ACT (for admission). *Required for some:* SAT Subject Tests (for admission).

Costs (2010–11) *Tuition:* state resident $3432 full-time, $143 per credit hour part-time; nonresident $12,720 full-time, $530 per credit hour part-time. Full-time tuition and fees vary according to location and program. Part-time tuition and fees vary according to location and program. *Required fees:* $1078 full-time, $539 per term part-time. *Room and board:* $8440; room only: $5590. Room and board charges vary according to board plan and housing facility. *Waivers:* senior citizens and employees or children of employees.

Financial Aid Of all full-time matriculated undergraduates who enrolled in 2008, 3,745 applied for aid, 2,471 were judged to have need, 660 had their need fully met. 96 Federal Work-Study jobs (averaging $5000). In 2008, 882 non-need-based awards were made. *Average percent of need met:* 82%. *Average financial aid package:* $7750. *Average need-based loan:* $4500. *Average need-based gift aid:* $4000. *Average non-need-based aid:* $3000. *Average indebtedness upon graduation:* $19,000.

Applying *Options:* electronic application, early admission, deferred entrance. *Application fee:* $25. *Required:* high school transcript, proof of immunization. *Application deadlines:* 8/1 (freshmen), 8/1 (transfers). *Notification:* continuous (freshmen), continuous (transfers).

Freshman Application Contact Armstrong Atlantic State University, 11935 Abercorn Street, Savannah, GA 31419-1997. *Phone:* 912-344-2503. *Toll-free phone:* 800-633-2349. *Web site:* http://www.armstrong.edu/.

The Art Institute of Atlanta
Atlanta, Georgia

- **Proprietary** comprehensive, founded 1949, part of Education Management Corporation
- **Suburban** 7-acre campus
- **Coed**

Academics *Calendar:* quarters. *Degrees:* diplomas, associate, and bachelor's.

Costs (2010–11) *Tuition:* Tuition cost varies by program. Prospective students should contact the school for current tuition costs. Other charges include a starting kit for all first-quarter students. Kits vary in price, depending on the program of study.

Freshman Application Contact The Art Institute of Atlanta, 6600 Peachtree Dunwoody Road, NE, 100 Embassy Row, Atlanta, GA 30328. *Phone:* 770-394-8300. *Toll-free phone:* 800-275-4242. *Web site:* http://www.artinstitutes.edu/atlanta/.

See page 1006 for the College Close-Up.

The Art Institute of Atlanta–Decatur
Decatur, Georgia

- **Proprietary** 4-year, founded 2007, part of Education Management Corporation
- **Coed**

Academics *Calendar:* quarters. *Degrees:* diplomas, associate, and bachelor's.

Costs (2010–11) *Tuition:* Tuition cost varies by program. Prospective students should contact the school for current tuition costs. Other charges include a starting kit for all first-quarter students. Kits vary in price, depending on the program of study.

Freshman Application Contact The Art Institute of Atlanta–Decatur, One West Court Square, Suite 110, Decatur, GA 30030. *Phone:* 404-942-1800. *Toll-free phone:* 866-856-6203. *Web site:* http://www.artinstitutes.edu/decatur/

See page 1008 for the College Close-Up.

Ashworth College
Norcross, Georgia

- **Proprietary** comprehensive, administratively affiliated with Professional Career Development, LLC
- **Suburban** campus with easy access to Atlanta
- **Coed** 9,706 undergraduate students
- **Noncompetitive** entrance level

Undergraduates Students come from 50 states and territories; 32 other countries; 90% are from out of state.

Academics *Calendar:* semesters. *Degrees:* certificates, diplomas, associate, bachelor's, master's, post-master's, and postbachelor's certificates. *Special study options:* accelerated degree program, adult/continuing education programs, advanced placement credit, distance learning, external degree program, independent study, off-campus study, part-time degree program, summer session for credit.

Computers on Campus Students can access the following: online (class) grades, online (class) registration, online (class) schedules.

Student Life *Housing:* college housing not available.

Costs (2011–12) *Tuition:* $1846 full-time. Full-time tuition and fees vary according to degree level. *Payment plan:* installment.

Applying *Options:* electronic application. *Required:* high school transcript. *Notification:* continuous (freshmen), continuous (out-of-state freshmen), continuous (transfers).

Freshman Application Contact Eric Ryall, Registrar, Ashworth College, 6625 The Corners Parkway, Suite 500, Norcross, GA 30092. *Phone:* 770-729-8400 Ext. 5297. *Toll-free phone:* 800-957-5412. *Web site:* http://www.ashworthcollege.edu/.

Atlanta Christian College
East Point, Georgia

- **Independent Christian** 4-year, founded 1937
- **Suburban** 52-acre campus with easy access to Atlanta
- **Endowment** $2.9 million
- **Coed** 1,023 undergraduate students, 96% full-time, 61% women, 39% men
- **Moderately difficult** entrance level, 48% of applicants were admitted

Undergraduates 979 full-time, 44 part-time. Students come from 9 states and territories; 4% are from out of state; 63% Black or African American, non-Hispanic/Latino; 4% Hispanic/Latino; 0.5% Asian, non-Hispanic/Latino; 0.1% American Indian or Alaska Native, non-Hispanic/Latino; 2% Race/ethnicity unknown; 50% live on campus. *Retention:* 69% of full-time freshmen returned.

Freshmen *Admission:* 338 applied, 163 admitted, 92 enrolled. *Average high school GPA:* 3.11. *Student/faculty ratio:* 11:1.

Faculty *Total:* 92, 20% full-time. *Student/faculty ratio:* 11:1.

Academics *Calendar:* semesters. *Degrees:* associate and bachelor's. *Special study options:* academic remediation for entering students, accelerated degree program, adult/continuing education programs, advanced placement credit, cooperative education, distance learning, double majors, independent study, internships, part-time degree program, services for LD students, summer session for credit.

Computers on Campus 28 computers/terminals and 10 ports are available on campus for general student use. Students can access the following: campus intranet, computer help desk, free student e-mail accounts, online (class) grades, online (class) registration, online (class) schedules. Campuswide network is available. 100% of college-owned or -operated housing units are wired for high-speed Internet access. Wireless service is available via entire campus.

Student Life *Housing:* on-campus residence required for freshman year. *Options:* men-only, women-only. Campus housing is university owned. Freshman campus housing is guaranteed. *Activities and organizations:* drama/theater group, student-run newspaper, choral group, Student Government Association, Global Mission Conference, Campus Life Ministers, Student Transition Team. *Campus security:* 24-hour patrols, student patrols, controlled dormitory access. *Student services:* health clinic, personal/psychological counseling.

Athletics Member NAIA, NCCAA. *Intercollegiate sports:* baseball M(s), basketball M(s)/W(s), cross-country running M(s), football M(s)(c), soccer M/W, softball W(s), volleyball W. *Intramural sports:* basketball W, table tennis M/W, ultimate Frisbee M/W, volleyball M/W, weight lifting M/W.

Standardized Tests *Required:* SAT or ACT (for admission).

Costs (2010–11) *Comprehensive fee:* $21,752 includes full-time tuition ($15,172), mandatory fees ($730), and room and board ($5850). Part-time tuition: $610 per credit hour. Part-time tuition and fees vary according to course load. *Required fees:* $365 per term part-time. *Waivers:* employees or children of employees.

Applying *Options:* electronic application, early admission, deferred entrance. *Application fee:* $25. *Required:* high school transcript, minimum 2 GPA, 1 letter of recommendation. *Required for some:* essay or personal statement, interview. *Application deadlines:* 8/1 (freshmen), 8/1 (out-of-state freshmen), 8/1 (transfers).

Freshman Application Contact Ms. Stacy Bartlett, Director of Admission, Atlanta Christian College, 2605 Ben Hill Road, East Point, GA 30344-1999. *Phone:* 404-669-4000. *Toll-free phone:* 800-776-1ACC. *Fax:* 404-460-2451. *E-mail:* admissions@acc.edu. *Web site:* http://www.acc.edu/.

Augusta State University

Augusta, Georgia

- **State-supported** comprehensive, founded 1925, part of University System of Georgia
- **Urban** 72-acre campus
- **Coed**
- **Minimally difficult** entrance level

Faculty *Student/faculty ratio:* 18:1.

Academics *Calendar:* semesters. *Degrees:* associate, bachelor's, master's, and post-master's certificates.

Student Life *Campus security:* 24-hour patrols, late-night transport/escort service.

Athletics Member NCAA, NAIA. All NCAA Division II.

Standardized Tests *Required:* SAT or ACT (for admission).

Costs (2010–11) *Tuition:* state resident $4274 full-time, $143 per credit hour part-time; nonresident $15,888 full-time, $530 per credit hour part-time. *Required fees:* $910 full-time, $455 per term part-time. *Room only:* $5250.

Financial Aid *Of all full-time matriculated undergraduates who enrolled in 2008,* 3,236 applied for aid, 2,449 were judged to have need, 248 had their need fully met. *In 2008,* 50 non-need-based awards were made. *Average financial aid package:* $3866. *Average need-based loan:* $2012. *Average need-based gift aid:* $2356. *Average non-need-based aid:* $843. *Average indebtedness upon graduation:* $7735. *Financial aid deadline:* 4/1.

Applying *Options:* electronic application, deferred entrance. *Application fee:* $30. *Required:* high school transcript, minimum 2 GPA.

Freshman Application Contact Ms. Jody Wilson, Coordinator of Publications and Marketing, Augusta State University, 2500 Walton Way, Augusta, GA 30904-2200. *Phone:* 706-737-1632. *Toll-free phone:* 800-341-4373. *Fax:* 706-667-4355. *E-mail:* admissions@aug.edu. *Web site:* http://www.aug.edu/.

Bauder College

Atlanta, Georgia

- **Proprietary** 4-year, founded 1964, administratively affiliated with Kaplan Higher Education
- **Urban** campus
- **Coed**

Academics *Calendar:* quarters. *Degrees:* certificates, diplomas, associate, and bachelor's.

Freshman Application Contact Bauder College, 384 Northyards Boulevard NW, Suites 190 and 400, Atlanta, GA 30313. *Phone:* 404-237-7573. *Toll-free phone:* 800-241-3797. *Web site:* http://www.bauder.edu/.

Berry College

Mount Berry, Georgia

- **Independent interdenominational** comprehensive, founded 1902
- **Suburban** 26,000-acre campus with easy access to Atlanta
- **Endowment** $600.5 million
- **Coed** 1,928 undergraduate students, 98% full-time, 67% women, 33% men
- **Moderately difficult** entrance level, 64% of applicants were admitted

Undergraduates 1,886 full-time, 42 part-time. Students come from 38 states and territories; 19 other countries; 23% are from out of state; 5% Black or African American, non-Hispanic/Latino; 4% Hispanic/Latino; 2% Asian, non-Hispanic/Latino; 0.2% American Indian or Alaska Native, non-Hispanic/Latino; 0.6% Two or more races, non-Hispanic/Latino; 3% Race/ethnicity unknown; 1% international; 2% transferred in; 86% live on campus. *Retention:* 78% of full-time freshmen returned.

Freshmen *Admission:* 2,926 applied, 1,870 admitted, 653 enrolled. *Average high school GPA:* 3.69. *Test scores:* SAT critical reading scores over 500: 88%; SAT math scores over 500: 86%; SAT writing scores over 500: 81%; ACT scores over 18: 100%; SAT critical reading scores over 600: 43%; SAT math scores over 600: 40%; SAT writing scores over 600: 32%; ACT scores over 24: 72%; SAT critical reading scores over 700: 10%; SAT math scores over 700: 4%; SAT writing scores over 700: 6%; ACT scores over 30: 16%.

Faculty *Total:* 218, 67% full-time, 72% with terminal degrees. *Student/faculty ratio:* 12:1.

Academics *Calendar:* semesters. *Degrees:* bachelor's, master's, and post-master's certificates. *Special study options:* adult/continuing education programs, advanced placement credit, cooperative education, double majors, honors programs, independent study, internships, part-time degree program, student-designed majors, study abroad, summer session for credit. *Unusual degree programs:* 3-2 engineering with Georgia Institute of Technology; nursing with Emory University.

Computers on Campus 140 computers/terminals and 80 ports are available on campus for general student use. Students can access the following: campus intranet, computer help desk, free student e-mail accounts, online (class) grades, online (class) registration, online (class) schedules. Campuswide network is available. 100% of college-owned or -operated housing units are wired for high-speed Internet access. Wireless service is available via classrooms, computer centers, computer labs, dorm rooms, learning centers, libraries, student centers.

Student Life *Housing:* on-campus residence required through senior year. *Options:* coed, men-only, women-only. Campus housing is university owned. Freshman campus housing is guaranteed. *Activities and organizations:* drama/theater group, student-run newspaper, choral group, Student Government Association, Pre-Vet Club, Campus Outreach, Athletes Bettering the Community, Viking Crew. *Campus security:* 24-hour emergency response devices and patrols, controlled dormitory access, lighted pathways, gated campus, mobile police patrols, identification of valuables, limited access to campus, on campus police officers. *Student services:* health clinic, personal/psychological counseling.

Athletics Member NCAA. All Division III. *Intercollegiate sports:* baseball M, basketball M/W, cross-country running M/W, equestrian sports W, golf M/W, lacrosse M/W, soccer M/W, softball W, swimming and diving M/W, tennis M/W, track and field M/W, volleyball W. *Intramural sports:* badminton M/W, basketball M/W, bowling M/W, cheerleading M(c)/W(c), crew M(c)/W(c), cross-country running M/W, football M/W, golf M/W, racquetball M/W, rock climbing M/W, soccer M/W, softball M/W, swimming and diving M/W, table tennis M/W, tennis M/W, ultimate Frisbee M/W, volleyball M/W, water polo M/W, weight lifting M/W.

Standardized Tests *Required:* SAT or ACT (for admission).

Costs (2010–11) *Comprehensive fee:* $33,344 includes full-time tuition ($24,420), mandatory fees ($200), and room and board ($8724). Part-time tuition: $814 per credit hour. *College room only:* $4894. Room and board charges vary according to board plan and housing facility. *Payment plan:* installment. *Waivers:* senior citizens and employees or children of employees.

Financial Aid Of all full-time matriculated undergraduates who enrolled in 2009, 1,622 applied for aid, 1,325 were judged to have need, 347 had their need fully met. 241 Federal Work-Study jobs (averaging $3880). 1,670 state and other part-time jobs (averaging $3840). In 2009, 512 non-need-based awards were made. *Average percent of need met:* 78%. *Average financial aid package:* $20,845. *Average need-based loan:* $4351. *Average need-based gift aid:* $16,699. *Average non-need-based aid:* $10,596. *Average indebtedness upon graduation:* $12,412.

Applying *Options:* electronic application, early admission, deferred entrance. *Application fee:* $50. *Required:* high school transcript. *Application deadlines:* 7/22 (freshmen), 7/22 (transfers). *Notification:* continuous (freshmen), continuous (transfers).

Freshman Application Contact Mr. Timothy Tarpley, Director of Operations, Enrollment Management, Berry College, PO Box 490159, 2277 Martha Berry Highway, NW, Mount Berry, GA 30149-0159. *Phone:* 706-236-2215. *Toll-*

free phone: 800-237-7942. *Fax:* 706-290-2178. *E-mail:* admissions@berry.edu. *Web site:* http://www.berry.edu/.

Beulah Heights University
Atlanta, Georgia

- **Independent Pentecostal** comprehensive, founded 1918
- **Urban** 10-acre campus
- **Coed** 631 undergraduate students, 55% full-time, 53% women, 47% men
- **Noncompetitive** entrance level, 100% of applicants were admitted

Undergraduates 348 full-time, 283 part-time. Students come from 22 states and territories; 12 other countries; 30% are from out of state; 8% transferred in; 10% live on campus. *Retention:* 42% of full-time freshmen returned.
Freshmen *Admission:* 175 applied, 175 admitted, 71 enrolled. *Average high school GPA:* 3.
Faculty *Total:* 64, 17% full-time, 56% with terminal degrees. *Student/faculty ratio:* 13:1.
Academics *Calendar:* semesters. *Degrees:* associate, bachelor's, and master's. *Special study options:* academic remediation for entering students, accelerated degree program, adult/continuing education programs, advanced placement credit, cooperative education, distance learning, double majors, independent study, internships, off-campus study, part-time degree program, services for LD students, summer session for credit. *Unusual degree programs:* Bachelor of Arts in Religious Studies, Leadership Studies, Master of Divinity, Master of Arts in Leadership and Religious Studies can be complete at the Griffin campus extension.
Computers on Campus 28 computers/terminals are available on campus for general student use. Students can access the following: campus intranet, computer help desk, free student e-mail accounts, online (class) registration, online (class) schedules. Campuswide network is available. 100% of college-owned or -operated housing units are wired for high-speed Internet access. Wireless service is available via entire campus.
Student Life *Housing options:* men-only, women-only. Campus housing is university owned. *Activities and organizations:* student-run newspaper, choral group, Chapel Choir, student government, Club Give. *Campus security:* 24-hour emergency response devices and patrols. *Student services:* personal/psychological counseling.
Athletics *Intercollegiate sports:* ultimate Frisbee M(s)/W(s), volleyball M(s)/W(s). *Intramural sports:* ultimate Frisbee M/W, volleyball M/W.
Standardized Tests *Required:* TOFEL (Required for international students) (for admission). *Recommended:* SAT or ACT (for admission).
Costs (2011–12) *Tuition:* $230 per credit hour part-time. Full-time tuition and fees vary according to course load. *Required fees:* $100 per term part-time. *Room only:* Room and board charges vary according to housing facility. *Payment plans:* installment, deferred payment. *Waivers:* employees or children of employees.
Financial Aid Of all full-time matriculated undergraduates who enrolled in 2006, 207 applied for aid, 207 were judged to have need. 14 Federal Work-Study jobs (averaging $2897). *Average percent of need met:* 85%. *Average financial aid package:* $7732. *Average need-based loan:* $4642. *Average need-based gift aid:* $3209. *Average indebtedness upon graduation:* $30,742.
Applying *Options:* electronic application, early admission. *Application fee:* $35. *Required:* essay or personal statement, high school transcript, minimum 2 GPA, 2 letters of recommendation, statement of faith. *Recommended:* interview. *Application deadlines:* rolling (freshmen), rolling (transfers). *Notification:* continuous (freshmen), continuous (transfers).
Freshman Application Contact John Dreher, Director of Admissions, Beulah Heights University, 892 Berne Street, SE, Atlanta, GA 30316. *Phone:* 404-627-2681 Ext. 117. *Toll-free phone:* 888-777-BHBC. *E-mail:* john.dreher@beulah.org. *Web site:* http://www.beulah.org/.

Brenau University
Gainesville, Georgia

- **Independent** comprehensive, founded 1878
- **Small-town** 57-acre campus with easy access to Atlanta
- **Endowment** $26.1 million
- **Women only** 830 undergraduate students, 90% full-time
- **Moderately difficult** entrance level, 36% of applicants were admitted

Undergraduates 748 full-time, 82 part-time. Students come from 18 states and territories; 20 other countries; 7% are from out of state; 21% Black or African American, non-Hispanic/Latino; 6% Hispanic/Latino; 1% Asian, non-Hispanic/Latino; 0.1% Native Hawaiian or other Pacific Islander, non-Hispanic/Latino; 0.4% American Indian or Alaska Native, non-Hispanic/Latino; 4% Two or more races, non-Hispanic/Latino; 11% Race/ethnicity unknown; 6% international; 16% transferred in; 54% live on campus. *Retention:* 72% of full-time freshmen returned.
Freshmen *Admission:* 3,819 applied, 1,362 admitted, 175 enrolled. *Test scores:* SAT critical reading scores over 500: 47%; SAT math scores over 500: 39%; SAT critical reading scores over 600: 9%; SAT math scores over 600: 8%; SAT critical reading scores over 700: 1%; SAT math scores over 700: 1%.
Faculty *Total:* 147, 56% full-time, 60% with terminal degrees. *Student/faculty ratio:* 8:1.
Academics *Calendar:* semesters. *Degrees:* associate, bachelor's, and master's (also offers coed evening and weekend programs with significant enrollment not reflected in profile). *Special study options:* academic remediation for entering students, advanced placement credit, distance learning, double majors, English as a second language, honors programs, independent study, internships, part-time degree program, services for LD students, student-designed majors, study abroad, summer session for credit.
Computers on Campus 130 computers/terminals and 200 ports are available on campus for general student use. Students can access the following: campus intranet, computer help desk, free student e-mail accounts, online (class) grades, online (class) registration, online (class) schedules, students can create own Web sites, videos and other things made possible by Google apps. Campuswide network is available. 100% of college-owned or -operated housing units are wired for high-speed Internet access. Wireless service is available via classrooms, computer centers, computer labs, dorm rooms, learning centers, libraries, student centers.
Student Life *Housing:* on-campus residence required through junior year. *Options:* women-only, disabled students. Campus housing is university owned. Freshman campus housing is guaranteed. *Activities and organizations:* drama/theater group, student-run newspaper, radio station, choral group, Sigma Alpha Pi Leadership Society, Student Government Association/Student Activities Board, Circle K, Silhouettes, International Club, national sororities. *Campus security:* 24-hour emergency response devices and patrols, late-night transport/escort service. *Student services:* health clinic, personal/psychological counseling.
Athletics Member NAIA. *Intercollegiate sports:* basketball W(s), crew W(c), cross-country running W(s), soccer W(s), softball W(s), swimming and diving W(s), tennis W(s), volleyball W(s).
Standardized Tests *Required:* SAT or ACT (for admission).
Costs (2011–12) *Comprehensive fee:* $31,490 includes full-time tuition ($20,864), mandatory fees ($260), and room and board ($10,366). Full-time tuition and fees vary according to location and program. Part-time tuition: $695 per credit hour. Part-time tuition and fees vary according to course load, location, and program. *Required fees:* $130 per term part-time. *Payment plan:* installment. *Waivers:* employees or children of employees.
Financial Aid Of all full-time matriculated undergraduates who enrolled in 2009, 634 applied for aid, 592 were judged to have need, 113 had their need fully met. 108 Federal Work-Study jobs (averaging $1944). In 2009, 141 non-need-based awards were made. *Average percent of need met:* 70%. *Average financial aid package:* $18,714. *Average need-based loan:* $4206. *Average need-based gift aid:* $14,609. *Average non-need-based aid:* $12,542. *Average indebtedness upon graduation:* $20,634.
Applying *Options:* electronic application, deferred entrance. *Application fee:* $35. *Required:* high school transcript, minimum 2.5 GPA. *Required for some:* interview. *Application deadlines:* rolling (freshmen), rolling (out-of-state freshmen), rolling (transfers). *Notification:* continuous (freshmen), continuous (out-of-state freshmen), continuous (transfers).
Freshman Application Contact Mr. Scott Briell, Senior Vice President, Enrollment Management and Student Services, Brenau University, Admissions, 500 Washington Street, SE, Gainesville, GA 30501. *Phone:* 770-538-4704. *Toll-free phone:* 800-252-5119. *Fax:* 770-538-4701. *E-mail:* admissions@brenau.edu. *Web site:* http://www.brenau.edu/.

Brewton-Parker College
Mt. Vernon, Georgia

- **Independent Southern Baptist** 4-year, founded 1904
- **Rural** 280-acre campus
- **Coed** 778 undergraduate students, 70% full-time, 55% women, 45% men
- **Minimally difficult** entrance level

Undergraduates 548 full-time, 230 part-time. Students come from 13 states and territories; 11 other countries; 15% are from out of state; 8% transferred in; 41% live on campus. *Retention:* 39% of full-time freshmen returned.
Freshmen *Admission:* 635 applied, 132 enrolled. *Test scores:* SAT critical reading scores over 500: 37%; SAT math scores over 500: 39%; SAT writing scores over 500: 42%; ACT scores over 18: 58%; SAT critical reading scores over 600: 5%; SAT math scores over 600: 5%; SAT writing scores over 600: 7%; ACT scores over 24: 9%; SAT critical reading scores over 700: 1%; ACT scores over 30: 1%.
Faculty *Total:* 89, 48% full-time. *Student/faculty ratio:* 11:1.
Academics *Calendar:* semesters. *Degrees:* associate and bachelor's. *Special study options:* academic remediation for entering students, accelerated degree program, advanced placement credit, cooperative education, honors programs, independent study, internships, part-time degree program, services for LD students, summer session for credit.

Computers on Campus 104 computers/terminals are available on campus for general student use. Students can access the following: computer help desk, free student e-mail accounts, online (class) grades, online (class) registration, online (class) schedules. Campuswide network is available. 100% of college-owned or -operated housing units are wired for high-speed Internet access. Wireless service is available via classrooms, computer centers, computer labs, libraries, student centers.

Student Life *Housing:* on-campus residence required through junior year. *Options:* men-only, women-only. Campus housing is university owned. Freshman campus housing is guaranteed. *Activities and organizations:* drama/theater group, student-run newspaper, Council of Intramural Activities, Student Activities Council, Rotaract, Circle K, Baptist Student Union. *Campus security:* 24-hour emergency response devices, controlled dormitory access, Campus security is provided from 6 pm to 6 am. *Student services:* health clinic, personal/psychological counseling.

Athletics Member NAIA. *Intercollegiate sports:* baseball M(s), basketball M(s)/W(s), cheerleading M(s)/W(s), cross-country running M/W, soccer M(s)/W(s), softball W(s), volleyball W(s). *Intramural sports:* basketball M/W, football M/W, softball M/W, table tennis M/W, tennis M/W, ultimate Frisbee M/W, volleyball M/W.

Standardized Tests *Required:* SAT or ACT (for admission).

Costs (2010–11) *One-time required fee:* $200. *Comprehensive fee:* $23,122 includes full-time tuition ($15,470), mandatory fees ($810), and room and board ($6842). Full-time tuition and fees vary according to course load, location, and program. Part-time tuition: $455 per credit hour. Part-time tuition and fees vary according to course load, location, and program. *College room only:* $2768. Room and board charges vary according to board plan and housing facility. *Payment plan:* installment. *Waivers:* senior citizens and employees or children of employees.

Financial Aid Of all full-time matriculated undergraduates who enrolled in 2009, 819 applied for aid, 736 were judged to have need, 118 had their need fully met. 170 Federal Work-Study jobs (averaging $676). 114 state and other part-time jobs (averaging $466). In 2009, 96 non-need-based awards were made. *Average percent of need met:* 71%. *Average financial aid package:* $11,736. *Average need-based loan:* $3436. *Average need-based gift aid:* $9011. *Average non-need-based aid:* $3915. *Average indebtedness upon graduation:* $28,231. *Financial aid deadline:* 5/1.

Applying *Options:* electronic application, early admission. *Application fee:* $25. *Required:* high school transcript, minimum 2 GPA. *Application deadlines:* rolling (freshmen), rolling (out-of-state freshmen), rolling (transfers). *Notification:* continuous (freshmen), continuous (out-of-state freshmen), continuous (transfers).

Freshman Application Contact Ms. Sandra Clay, Director of Admissions, Brewton-Parker College, PO Box 197, Mount Vernon, GA 30445. *Phone:* 912-583-3247. *Toll-free phone:* 800-342-1087 Ext. 245. *Fax:* 912-583-3598. *E-mail:* sclay@bpc.edu. *Web site:* http://www.bpc.edu/.

Carver Bible College
Atlanta, Georgia

Director of Admissions Miss Bertha Mack, Vice President of Admissions Affairs and Dean of Admissions, Carver Bible College, 437 Nelson Street, Atlanta, GA 30313. *Phone:* 404-527-4520. *E-mail:* info@carver.edu. *Web site:* http://www.carver.edu/.

Clark Atlanta University
Atlanta, Georgia

- **Independent United Methodist** university, founded 1865
- **Urban** 126-acre campus
- **Endowment** $45.6 million
- **Coed** 3,267 undergraduate students, 94% full-time, 72% women, 28% men
- **Moderately difficult** entrance level, 69% of applicants were admitted

Undergraduates 3,081 full-time, 186 part-time. Students come from 44 states and territories; 10 other countries; 63% are from out of state; 90% Black or African American, non-Hispanic/Latino; 0.4% Hispanic/Latino; 0.1% Asian, non-Hispanic/Latino; 0.1% American Indian or Alaska Native, non-Hispanic/Latino; 8% Race/ethnicity unknown; 0.8% international; 6% transferred in; 31% live on campus. *Retention:* 66% of full-time freshmen returned.

Freshmen *Admission:* 5,962 applied, 4,136 admitted, 852 enrolled. *Average high school GPA:* 2.98. *Test scores:* SAT critical reading scores over 500: 17%; SAT math scores over 500: 14%; ACT scores over 18: 81%; SAT critical reading scores over 600: 1%; SAT math scores over 600: 2%; ACT scores over 24: 14%.

Faculty *Total:* 279, 63% full-time, 64% with terminal degrees. *Student/faculty ratio:* 17:1.

Academics *Calendar:* semesters. *Degrees:* bachelor's, master's, doctoral-research/scholarship, post-master's, and postbachelor's certificates. *Special*

study options: academic remediation for entering students, accelerated degree program, adult/continuing education programs, advanced placement credit, cooperative education, double majors, honors programs, independent study, internships, off-campus study, part-time degree program, services for LD students, study abroad, summer session for credit. *ROTC:* Army (c), Navy (c). *Unusual degree programs:* 3-2 engineering with Georgia Institute of Technology, Boston University, North Carolina Agricultural and Technical State University.

Computers on Campus 700 computers/terminals and 2,000 ports are available on campus for general student use. Students can access the following: computer help desk, free student e-mail accounts, online (class) grades, online (class) registration, online (class) schedules. Campuswide network is available. 100% of college-owned or -operated housing units are wired for high-speed Internet access. Wireless service is available via entire campus.

Student Life *Housing:* on-campus residence required through sophomore year. *Options:* coed, men-only, women-only. Campus housing is university owned and is provided by a third party. Freshman applicants given priority for college housing. *Activities and organizations:* drama/theater group, student-run newspaper, radio and television station, choral group, marching band, Spirit Boosters, Pre-Alumni Council, Campus Activities Board, Orientation Guides, National Association for the Advancement of Colored People, national fraternities, national sororities. *Campus security:* 24-hour emergency response devices and patrols, late-night transport/escort service, controlled dormitory access. *Student services:* health clinic, personal/psychological counseling.

Athletics Member NCAA. All Division II. *Intercollegiate sports:* baseball M(s), basketball M(s)/W(s), cross-country running M(s)/W(s), football M(s), softball W(s), tennis W(s), track and field M(s)/W(s), volleyball W(s). *Intramural sports:* basketball M/W, football M, softball W, tennis W, track and field M/W, volleyball M/W.

Standardized Tests *Required:* SAT or ACT (for admission).

Costs (2011–12) *Comprehensive fee:* $26,078 includes full-time tuition ($17,244), mandatory fees ($710), and room and board ($8124). Part-time tuition: $719 per credit hour. *Required fees:* $355 per term part-time. *Room and board:* Room and board charges vary according to board plan and housing facility. *Payment plan:* installment. *Waivers:* employees or children of employees.

Financial Aid Of all full-time matriculated undergraduates who enrolled in 2005, 3,883 applied for aid, 3,712 were judged to have need, 1,567 had their need fully met. 229 Federal Work-Study jobs (averaging $1335). *Average percent of need met:* 8%. *Average financial aid package:* $10,935. *Average need-based loan:* $4526. *Average need-based gift aid:* $3818. *Average indebtedness upon graduation:* $17,751.

Applying *Options:* electronic application, early admission, deferred entrance. *Application fee:* $35. *Required:* essay or personal statement, high school transcript, minimum 2.5 GPA, 2 letters of recommendation. *Required for some:* interview. *Application deadlines:* 6/1 (freshmen), 6/1 (out-of-state freshmen), 6/1 (transfers). *Notification:* continuous (freshmen), continuous (out-of-state freshmen), continuous (transfers).

Freshman Application Contact Ms. Michelle Davis, Interim Director, Office of Admissions, Clark Atlanta University, 223 James P. Brawley Drive, SW, Atlanta, GA 30314. *Phone:* 404-880-8918. *Toll-free phone:* 800-688-3228. *Fax:* 404-880-6174. *E-mail:* cauadmissions@cau.edu. *Web site:* http://www.cau.edu/.

Clayton State University
Morrow, Georgia

- **State-supported** comprehensive, founded 1969, part of University System of Georgia
- **Suburban** 163-acre campus with easy access to Atlanta
- **Coed** 6,365 undergraduate students, 60% full-time, 71% women, 29% men
- **Minimally difficult** entrance level, 50% of applicants were admitted

Undergraduates 3,797 full-time, 2,568 part-time. Students come from 20 states and territories; 35 other countries; 2% are from out of state; 63% Black or African American, non-Hispanic/Latino; 2% Hispanic/Latino; 4% Asian, non-Hispanic/Latino; 0.3% American Indian or Alaska Native, non-Hispanic/Latino; 0.6% Two or more races, non-Hispanic/Latino; 3% Race/ethnicity unknown; 1% international; 12% transferred in; 7% live on campus. *Retention:* 61% of full-time freshmen returned.

Freshmen *Admission:* 5,478 applied, 2,727 admitted, 525 enrolled. *Average high school GPA:* 3.09. *Test scores:* SAT critical reading scores over 500: 33%; SAT math scores over 500: 42%; ACT scores over 18: 86%; SAT critical reading scores over 600: 6%; SAT math scores over 600: 17%; ACT scores over 24: 12%; SAT critical reading scores over 700: 1%; SAT math scores over 700: 11%; ACT scores over 30: 1%.

Faculty *Total:* 375, 57% full-time, 64% with terminal degrees. *Student/faculty ratio:* 18:1.

Academics *Calendar:* semesters. *Degrees:* certificates, associate, bachelor's, and master's. *Special study options:* academic remediation for entering students, adult/continuing education programs, advanced placement credit, cooperative education, distance learning, double majors, English as a second language, freshman honors college, honors programs, independent study, internships, off-campus study, part-time degree program, services for LD students, student-designed majors, study abroad, summer session for credit. *ROTC:* Army (c), Navy (c), Air Force (c).

Computers on Campus 3,500 computers/terminals are available on campus for general student use. Students can access the following: online (class) grades, online (class) registration, online (class) schedules. Campuswide network is available. 100% of college-owned or -operated housing units are wired for high-speed Internet access. Wireless service is available via entire campus.

Student Life *Housing:* on-campus residence required for freshman year. *Options:* coed. Campus housing is university owned. Freshman applicants given priority for college housing. *Activities and organizations:* drama/theater group, student-run newspaper, choral group, Accounting Club, International Awareness Club, Black Cultural Awareness Association, Student Government Association, music club, national fraternities, national sororities. *Campus security:* 24-hour emergency response devices and patrols, late-night transport/escort service, controlled dormitory access, lighted pathways. *Student services:* health clinic, personal/psychological counseling.

Athletics Member NCAA. All Division II. *Intercollegiate sports:* basketball M(s)/W(s), cheerleading W(s)(c), cross-country running M(s)/W(s), golf M(s), soccer M(s)/W(s), tennis M(s), track and field M/W(s). *Intramural sports:* bowling M/W, softball M/W, table tennis M/W, volleyball M/W.

Standardized Tests *Required:* SAT or ACT (for admission). *Required for some:* SAT Subject Tests (for admission).

Costs (2010–11) *Tuition:* state resident $3432 full-time; nonresident $12,720 full-time. Full-time tuition and fees vary according to course load. Part-time tuition and fees vary according to course load. No tuition increase for student's term of enrollment. *Required fees:* $1134 full-time, $143 per credit hour part-time, $567 per term part-time. *Room and board:* $8352; room only: $5254. *Waivers:* senior citizens and employees or children of employees.

Financial Aid Of all full-time matriculated undergraduates who enrolled in 2007, 2,633 applied for aid, 2,402 were judged to have need, 138 had their need fully met. In 2007, 144 non-need-based awards were made. *Average percent of need met:* 33%. *Average financial aid package:* $3855. *Average need-based loan:* $2133. *Average need-based gift aid:* $2126. *Average non-need-based aid:* $699.

Applying *Options:* electronic application, early admission, deferred entrance. *Application fee:* $40. *Required:* high school transcript, proof of immunization. *Application deadline:* 7/17 (freshmen). *Notification:* continuous (freshmen), continuous (transfers).

Freshman Application Contact Ms. Carol S. Montgomery, Admissions, Clayton State University, 2000 Clayton State Boulevard, Morrow, GA 30260-0285. *Phone:* 678-466-4115. *Fax:* 678-466-4149. *E-mail:* csc-info@clayton.edu. *Web site:* http://www.clayton.edu/.

College of Coastal Georgia

Brunswick, Georgia

- **State-supported** 4-year, founded 1961, part of University System of Georgia
- **Small-town** 193-acre campus with easy access to Jacksonville
- **Endowment** $5.5 million
- **Coed** 3,438 undergraduate students, 55% full-time, 69% women, 31% men
- **Minimally difficult** entrance level, 76% of applicants were admitted

Undergraduates 1,882 full-time, 1,556 part-time. Students come from 39 states and territories; 22 other countries; 8% are from out of state; 23% Black or African American, non-Hispanic/Latino; 3% Hispanic/Latino; 1% Native Hawaiian or other Pacific Islander, non-Hispanic/Latino; 2% Race/ethnicity unknown; 2% transferred in. *Retention:* 85% of full-time freshmen returned.

Freshmen *Admission:* 1,775 applied, 1,343 admitted, 827 enrolled. **Faculty** *Total:* 150, 56% full-time, 25% with terminal degrees. *Student/faculty ratio:* 23:1.

Academics *Calendar:* semesters. *Degrees:* associate and bachelor's. *Special study options:* academic remediation for entering students, adult/continuing education programs, advanced placement credit, distance learning, double majors, internships, part-time degree program, services for LD students, study abroad, summer session for credit.

Computers on Campus 300 computers/terminals and 300 ports are available on campus for general student use. Students can access the following: free student e-mail accounts, online (class) grades, online (class) registration, online (class) schedules. Campuswide network is available. Wireless service is available via entire campus.

Student Life *Housing:* college housing not available. *Activities and organizations:* student-run newspaper, Brunswick Association of Nursing Students, Minority Advisement and Social Development Association, Student Government Association, Programming Board, Phi Theta Kappa. *Campus security:*

24-hour emergency response devices and patrols, late-night transport/escort service. *Student services:* personal/psychological counseling.

Athletics Member NJCAA. *Intercollegiate sports:* basketball M(s), cross-country running M/W, golf M(s)/W(s), softball W(s), tennis M/W, volleyball W. *Intramural sports:* basketball M/W, tennis M/W, volleyball M/W.

Standardized Tests *Required:* SAT or ACT (for admission).

Costs (2010–11) *Tuition:* state resident $2160 full-time, $90 per credit hour part-time; nonresident $8160 full-time, $340 per credit hour part-time. Full-time tuition and fees vary according to student level. Part-time tuition and fees vary according to course load and student level. No tuition increase for student's term of enrollment. *Required fees:* $960 full-time, $378 per term part-time. *Waivers:* senior citizens and employees or children of employees.

Financial Aid Of all full-time matriculated undergraduates who enrolled in 2009, 80 Federal Work-Study jobs (averaging $1500).

Applying *Options:* electronic application, deferred entrance. *Application fee:* $20. *Required:* high school transcript, minimum 2 GPA, Application fee, ACT or SAT scores, immunization records, proof of residency. *Application deadlines:* 7/15 (freshmen), 7/15 (transfers). *Notification:* continuous (freshmen), continuous (transfers).

Freshman Application Contact Mr. Eric Felver, Director of Admissions and Orientation, College of Coastal Georgia, 3700 Altama Avenue, Brunswick, GA 31520. *Phone:* 912-279-5774. *Toll-free phone:* 800-675-7235. *Fax:* 912-262-3072. *E-mail:* admiss@ccga.edu. *Web site:* http://www.ccga.edu/.

Columbus State University

Columbus, Georgia

- **State-supported** comprehensive, founded 1958, part of University System of Georgia
- **Suburban** 132-acre campus with easy access to Atlanta
- **Endowment** $1.8 million
- **Coed** 7,069 undergraduate students, 71% full-time, 60% women, 40% men
- **Minimally difficult** entrance level, 60% of applicants were admitted

Undergraduates 4,995 full-time, 2,074 part-time. Students come from 40 states and territories; 41 other countries; 14% are from out of state; 35% Black or African American, non-Hispanic/Latino; 4% Hispanic/Latino; 2% Asian, non-Hispanic/Latino; 0.4% Native Hawaiian or other Pacific Islander, non-Hispanic/Latino; 0.7% American Indian or Alaska Native, non-Hispanic/Latino; 2% Two or more races, non-Hispanic/Latino; 1% international; 9% transferred in; 19% live on campus. *Retention:* 69% of full-time freshmen returned.

Freshmen *Admission:* 3,454 applied, 2,075 admitted, 1,240 enrolled. *Average high school GPA:* 2.96. *Test scores:* SAT critical reading scores over 500: 45%; SAT math scores over 500: 40%; SAT writing scores over 500: 38%; ACT scores over 18: 72%; SAT critical reading scores over 600: 12%; SAT math scores over 600: 9%; SAT writing scores over 600: 7%; ACT scores over 24: 14%; SAT critical reading scores over 700: 1%; SAT math scores over 700: 1%; ACT scores over 30: 1%.

Faculty *Total:* 473, 56% full-time, 53% with terminal degrees. *Student/faculty ratio:* 19:1.

Academics *Calendar:* semesters. *Degrees:* certificates, associate, bachelor's, master's, post-master's, and postbachelor's certificates. *Special study options:* academic remediation for entering students, adult/continuing education programs, advanced placement credit, cooperative education, distance learning, double majors, English as a second language, freshman honors college, honors programs, independent study, internships, off-campus study, part-time degree program, services for LD students, study abroad, summer session for credit. *ROTC:* Army (b). *Unusual degree programs:* 3-2 engineering with Georgia Institute of Technology.

Computers on Campus 1,135 computers/terminals are available on campus for general student use. Students can access the following: campus intranet, computer help desk, free student e-mail accounts, online (class) grades, online (class) registration, online (class) schedules. Campuswide network is available. 100% of college-owned or -operated housing units are wired for high-speed Internet access. Wireless service is available via entire campus.

Student Life *Housing:* on-campus residence required for freshman year. *Options:* coed, men-only, women-only, disabled students. Campus housing is university owned. Freshman applicants given priority for college housing. *Activities and organizations:* drama/theater group, student-run newspaper, choral group, Student Government Association, Student Activities Council, Campus Ministry Association, African Students Association, SABER Student Newspaper, national fraternities, national sororities. *Campus security:* 24-hour emergency response devices and patrols, late-night transport/escort service, controlled dormitory access. *Student services:* health clinic, personal/psychological counseling.

Athletics Member NCAA. All Division II except men's and women's riflery (Division I). *Intercollegiate sports:* baseball M(s), basketball M(s)/W(s), cross-country running M(s)/W(s), golf M(s)/W, riflery M/W, soccer W(s), softball W(s), tennis M(s)/W(s). *Intramural sports:* badminton M/W, basketball

M/W, bowling M/W, cross-country running M/W, football M/W, golf M/W, racquetball M/W, skiing (downhill) M/W, soccer M/W, softball M/W, table tennis M/W, tennis M/W, track and field M/W, volleyball M/W.

Standardized Tests *Required:* SAT or ACT (for admission).

Costs (2010–11) *Tuition:* state resident $4596 full-time, $154 per semester hour part-time; nonresident $16,572 full-time, $553 per credit hour part-time. *Required fees:* $1300 full-time. *Room and board:* $7296. Room and board charges vary according to board plan. *Waivers:* senior citizens and employees or children of employees.

Financial Aid Of all full-time matriculated undergraduates who enrolled in 2009, 4,019 applied for aid, 3,231 were judged to have need, 953 had their need fully met. 73 Federal Work-Study jobs (averaging $1953). In 2009, 129 non-need-based awards were made. *Average percent of need met:* 78%. *Average financial aid package:* $8501. *Average need-based loan:* $3912. *Average need-based gift aid:* $4862. *Average non-need-based aid:* $1681. *Average indebtedness upon graduation:* $21,486.

Applying *Options:* electronic application, early admission, deferred entrance. *Application fee:* $30. *Required:* high school transcript, minimum 2.3 GPA, proof of immunization. *Application deadlines:* 6/30 (freshmen), 6/30 (transfers). *Notification:* continuous (freshmen), continuous (transfers).

Freshman Application Contact Columbus State University, 4225 University Avenue, Columbus, GA 31907-5645. *Phone:* 706-507-8806. *Toll-free phone:* 866-264-2035. *Web site:* http://www.columbusstate.edu/.

Covenant College
Lookout Mountain, Georgia

- **Independent** comprehensive, founded 1955, affiliated with Presbyterian Church in America
- **Suburban** 350-acre campus
- **Endowment** $21.2 million
- **Coed** 986 undergraduate students, 97% full-time, 53% women, 47% men
- **Moderately difficult** entrance level, 60% of applicants were admitted

Undergraduates 959 full-time, 27 part-time. Students come from 43 states and territories; 20 other countries; 77% are from out of state; 3% Black or African American, non-Hispanic/Latino; 2% Hispanic/Latino; 2% Asian, non-Hispanic/Latino; 0.2% Native Hawaiian or other Pacific Islander, non-Hispanic/Latino; 0.5% American Indian or Alaska Native, non-Hispanic/Latino; 2% Two or more races, non-Hispanic/Latino; 2% international; 4% transferred in; 84% live on campus. *Retention:* 79% of full-time freshmen returned.

Freshmen *Admission:* 1,025 applied, 614 admitted, 269 enrolled. *Average high school GPA:* 3.6. *Test scores:* SAT critical reading scores over 500: 91%; SAT math scores over 500: 83%; SAT writing scores over 500: 88%; ACT scores over 18: 100%; SAT critical reading scores over 600: 54%; SAT math scores over 600: 39%; SAT writing scores over 600: 48%; ACT scores over 24: 74%; SAT critical reading scores over 700: 19%; SAT math scores over 700: 7%; SAT writing scores over 700: 10%; ACT scores over 30: 21%.

Faculty *Total:* 84, 74% full-time, 76% with terminal degrees. *Student/faculty ratio:* 14:1.

Academics *Calendar:* semesters. *Degrees:* associate, bachelor's, and master's (master's degree in education only). *Special study options:* academic remediation for entering students, adult/continuing education programs, advanced placement credit, double majors, independent study, internships, off-campus study, part-time degree program, services for LD students, student-designed majors, study abroad, summer session for credit.

Computers on Campus Students can access the following: computer help desk, free student e-mail accounts, online (class) registration, online student information system. Campuswide network is available. 100% of college-owned or -operated housing units are wired for high-speed Internet access. Wireless service is available via classrooms, computer labs, dorm rooms, libraries.

Student Life *Housing:* on-campus residence required through junior year. *Options:* men-only, women-only. Campus housing is university owned. Freshman campus housing is guaranteed. *Activities and organizations:* drama/theater group, student-run newspaper, radio station, choral group. *Campus security:* controlled dormitory access, night security guards. *Student services:* health clinic, personal/psychological counseling, women's center.

Athletics Member NCAA, NAIA, NCCAA. All NCAA Division III. *Intercollegiate sports:* baseball M, basketball M/W, cross-country running M/W, golf M/W, soccer M/W, softball W, tennis M/W, volleyball W. *Intramural sports:* badminton M/W, basketball M/W, football M, soccer M/W, volleyball M/W.

Standardized Tests *Required:* SAT or ACT (for admission).

Costs (2011–12) *Comprehensive fee:* $33,676 includes full-time tuition ($25,476), mandatory fees ($750), and room and board ($7450). Full-time tuition and fees vary according to course load. Part-time tuition and fees vary according to course load. *Payment plan:* installment. *Waivers:* senior citizens and employees or children of employees.

Financial Aid Of all full-time matriculated undergraduates who enrolled in 2008, 689 applied for aid, 587 were judged to have need, 168 had their need fully met. In 2008, 212 non-need-based awards were made. *Average percent*

of need met: 77%. *Average financial aid package:* $18,953. *Average need-based loan:* $4331. *Average need-based gift aid:* $14,127. *Average non-need-based aid:* $8392. *Average indebtedness upon graduation:* $20,519.

Applying *Options:* electronic application, early admission, deferred entrance. *Application fee:* $35. *Required:* essay or personal statement, high school transcript, minimum 2.5 GPA, 2 letters of recommendation, interview. *Application deadlines:* rolling (freshmen), rolling (transfers). *Notification:* continuous (freshmen).

Freshman Application Contact Mr. Philip Howlett, Assistant Director of Admissions, Covenant College, 14049 Scenic Highway, Lookout Mountain, GA 30750. *Phone:* 706-419-1145. *Toll-free phone:* 888-451-2683. *Fax:* 706-820-0893. *E-mail:* admissions@covenant.edu. *Web site:* http://www.covenant.edu/.

Dalton State College
Dalton, Georgia

- **State-supported** 4-year, founded 1963, part of University System of Georgia
- **Small-town** 141-acre campus
- **Coed** 5,988 undergraduate students, 61% full-time, 62% women, 38% men
- **Noncompetitive** entrance level, 51% of applicants were admitted

Undergraduates 3,665 full-time, 2,323 part-time. 3% are from out of state; 27% transferred in; 4% live on campus. *Retention:* 64% of full-time freshmen returned.

Freshmen *Admission:* 3,052 applied, 1,564 admitted, 1,215 enrolled. *Average high school GPA:* 3.05. *Test scores:* SAT critical reading scores over 500: 43%; SAT math scores over 500: 46%; ACT scores over 18: 82%; SAT critical reading scores over 600: 7%; SAT math scores over 600: 8%; ACT scores over 24: 19%; SAT critical reading scores over 700: 1%; SAT math scores over 700: 1%; ACT scores over 30: 1%.

Faculty *Total:* 249, 65% full-time, 45% with terminal degrees. *Student/faculty ratio:* 24:1.

Academics *Calendar:* semesters. *Degrees:* certificates, associate, and bachelor's. *Special study options:* academic remediation for entering students, adult/continuing education programs, advanced placement credit, cooperative education, double majors, English as a second language, internships, off-campus study, part-time degree program, services for LD students, study abroad, summer session for credit.

Computers on Campus Campuswide network is available. Wireless service is available via computer centers, computer labs, learning centers, libraries, student centers.

Student Life *Housing options:* coed, disabled students. Campus housing is university owned. *Activities and organizations:* student-run newspaper. *Campus security:* 24-hour emergency response devices and patrols.

Athletics *Intercollegiate sports:* basketball M(c)/W(c), golf W(c), softball M(c)/W(c), table tennis M(c)/W(c), tennis M(c)/W(c), volleyball M(c)/W(c). *Intramural sports:* badminton M/W, basketball M/W, football M/W, softball M/W, table tennis M/W, tennis M/W, volleyball M/W.

Costs (2010–11) *One-time required fee:* $300. *Tuition:* state resident $2160 full-time, $90 per credit hour part-time; nonresident $8160 full-time, $340 per credit hour part-time. *Required fees:* $376 full-time, $7 per credit hour part-time, $165 per term part-time. *Room and board:* $6750. *Waivers:* senior citizens.

Financial Aid Of all full-time matriculated undergraduates who enrolled in 2008, 2,064 applied for aid, 1,527 were judged to have need, 713 had their need fully met. In 2008, 31 non-need-based awards were made. *Average percent of need met:* 76%. *Average financial aid package:* $8985. *Average need-based loan:* $3476. *Average need-based gift aid:* $3636. *Average non-need-based aid:* $1345. *Average indebtedness upon graduation:* $11,953. *Financial aid deadline:* 7/1.

Applying *Options:* electronic application, deferred entrance. *Application fee:* $30. *Required:* high school transcript. *Application deadlines:* 7/15 (freshmen), 7/15 (transfers). *Notification:* continuous (freshmen).

Freshman Application Contact Director of Admissions, Dalton State College, 650 College Drive, Dalton, GA 30720-3797. *Phone:* 706-272-4476. *Toll-free phone:* 800-829-4436. *Fax:* 706-272-2530. *Web site:* http://www.daltonstate.edu/.

DeVry University
Alpharetta, Georgia

- **Proprietary** comprehensive, founded 1997, part of DeVry University
- **Suburban** 9-acre campus with easy access to Atlanta
- **Coed**
- **Minimally difficult** entrance level

Faculty *Student/faculty ratio:* 14:1.

Academics *Calendar:* semesters. *Degrees:* associate, bachelor's, and master's.

Student Life *Campus security:* 24-hour emergency response devices, late-night transport/escort service, lighted pathways, video recorder (CCTV).

Costs (2010–11) *Tuition:* $14,766 full-time, $580 per credit hour part-time. Full-time tuition and fees vary according to course load. Part-time tuition and fees vary according to course load. *Required fees:* $60 full-time, $30 per term part-time. *Payment plans:* installment, deferred payment.

Financial Aid *Of all full-time matriculated undergraduates who enrolled in 2007,* 171 applied for aid, 159 were judged to have need, 11 had their need fully met. In 2007, 17 non-need-based awards were made. *Average percent of need met:* 45. *Average financial aid package:* $13,554. *Average need-based loan:* $8238. *Average need-based gift aid:* $5898. *Average non-need-based aid:* $13,569. *Average indebtedness upon graduation:* $32,836.

Applying *Options:* electronic application, early admission, deferred entrance. *Application fee:* $50. *Required:* high school transcript, interview.

Freshman Application Contact DeVry University, 2555 Northwinds Parkway, Alpharetta, GA 30009. *Toll-free phone:* 800-346-5420. *Web site:* http://www.devry.edu/.

DeVry University
Decatur, Georgia

- **Proprietary** comprehensive, founded 1969, part of DeVry University
- **Suburban** 21-acre campus with easy access to Atlanta
- **Coed** 3,460 undergraduate students, 38% full-time, 52% women, 48% men
- **Minimally difficult** entrance level

Undergraduates 1,329 full-time, 2,131 part-time. 5% are from out of state; 50% Black or African American, non-Hispanic/Latino; 3% Hispanic/Latino; 1% Asian, non-Hispanic/Latino; 0.1% Native Hawaiian or other Pacific Islander, non-Hispanic/Latino; 0.2% American Indian or Alaska Native, non-Hispanic/Latino; 0.9% Two or more races, non-Hispanic/Latino; 27% Race/ethnicity unknown; 0.3% international; 28% transferred in.

Freshmen *Admission:* 499 enrolled.

Faculty *Total:* 150, 25% full-time. *Student/faculty ratio:* 30:1.

Academics *Calendar:* semesters. *Degrees:* associate, bachelor's, and master's. *Special study options:* academic remediation for entering students, accelerated degree program, adult/continuing education programs, advanced placement credit, distance learning, part-time degree program, services for LD students, summer session for credit.

Computers on Campus Students can access the following: online (class) registration. Campuswide network is available.

Student Life *Housing:* college housing not available. *Campus security:* 24-hour emergency response devices and patrols, late-night transport/escort service, lighted pathways/sidewalks.

Athletics *Intramural sports:* basketball M/W, football M/W, softball M/W, volleyball M/W.

Costs (2010–11) *Tuition:* $14,766 full-time, $580 per credit hour part-time. Full-time tuition and fees vary according to course load. Part-time tuition and fees vary according to course load. *Required fees:* $60 full-time, $30 per term part-time. *Payment plans:* installment, deferred payment. *Waivers:* employees or children of employees.

Financial Aid Of all full-time matriculated undergraduates who enrolled in 2007, 488 applied for aid, 477 were judged to have need, 14 had their need fully met. In 2007, 17 non-need-based awards were made. *Average percent of need met:* 43%. *Average financial aid package:* $14,044. *Average need-based loan:* $8002. *Average need-based gift aid:* $6480. *Average non-need-based aid:* $15,251. *Average indebtedness upon graduation:* $47,994.

Applying *Options:* electronic application, early admission, deferred entrance. *Application fee:* $50. *Required:* high school transcript, interview. *Application deadlines:* rolling (freshmen), rolling (transfers). *Notification:* continuous (freshmen), continuous (transfers).

Freshman Application Contact DeVry University, 1 West Court Square, Suite 100, Decatur, GA 30030-2556. *Phone:* 404-270-2700. *Web site:* http://www.devry.edu/.

DeVry University
Duluth, Georgia

Admissions Office Contact DeVry University, 3505 Koger Boulevard, Suite 170, Duluth, GA 30096-7671. *Web site:* http://www.devry.edu/.

Emmanuel College
Franklin Springs, Georgia

- **Independent** 4-year, founded 1919, affiliated with Pentecostal Holiness Church
- **Rural** 90-acre campus with easy access to Atlanta
- **Endowment** $2.7 million
- **Coed** 761 undergraduate students, 90% full-time, 51% women, 49% men
- **Minimally difficult** entrance level, 48% of applicants were admitted

Undergraduates 683 full-time, 78 part-time. Students come from 20 states and territories; 9 other countries; 22% are from out of state; 21% Black or African American, non-Hispanic/Latino; 5% Hispanic/Latino; 0.1% Asian, non-Hispanic/Latino; 0.3% American Indian or Alaska Native, non-Hispanic/Latino; 0.7% Two or more races, non-Hispanic/Latino; 3% international; 8% transferred in; 49% live on campus. *Retention:* 64% of full-time freshmen returned.

Freshmen *Admission:* 1,228 applied, 594 admitted, 196 enrolled. *Average high school GPA:* 3.05.

Faculty *Total:* 66, 65% full-time, 45% with terminal degrees. *Student/faculty ratio:* 14:1.

Academics *Calendar:* semesters. *Degrees:* associate and bachelor's. *Special study options:* academic remediation for entering students, accelerated degree program, advanced placement credit, distance learning, honors programs, independent study, internships, part-time degree program, services for LD students, study abroad, summer session for credit.

Computers on Campus 50 computers/terminals are available on campus for general student use. Students can access the following: campus intranet, computer help desk, free student e-mail accounts, online (class) grades, online (class) registration, online (class) schedules. Campuswide network is available. 100% of college-owned or -operated housing units are wired for high-speed Internet access. Wireless service is available via entire campus.

Student Life *Housing:* on-campus residence required through sophomore year. *Options:* men-only, women-only. Campus housing is university owned. Freshman campus housing is guaranteed. *Activities and organizations:* drama/theater group, choral group, Students in Free Enterprise (SIFE), FCA, SOS, BSU, International Students Club. *Campus security:* student patrols. *Student services:* personal/psychological counseling.

Athletics Member NAIA, NCCAA. *Intercollegiate sports:* baseball M(s), basketball M(s)/W(s), cross-country running M(s)/W(s), golf M(s)/W(s), soccer M(s)/W(s), softball W(s), tennis M(s)/W(s), track and field M(s)/W(s), volleyball W(s). *Intramural sports:* basketball M/W, football M/W, golf M/W, soccer M/W, tennis M/W, track and field M/W, volleyball M/W, weight lifting M/W.

Standardized Tests *Required:* SAT or ACT (for admission).

Costs (2011–12) *Comprehensive fee:* $20,650 includes full-time tuition ($14,550) and room and board ($6100). Part-time tuition: $600 per credit hour. *Payment plan:* installment. *Waivers:* senior citizens and employees or children of employees.

Financial Aid Of all full-time matriculated undergraduates who enrolled in 2009, 634 applied for aid, 589 were judged to have need, 55 had their need fully met. 286 Federal Work-Study jobs (averaging $1871). In 2009, 68 non-need-based awards were made. *Average percent of need met:* 66%. *Average financial aid package:* $12,455. *Average need-based loan:* $3512. *Average need-based gift aid:* $8768. *Average non-need-based aid:* $4658. *Average indebtedness upon graduation:* $28,298. *Financial aid deadline:* 6/15.

Applying *Options:* electronic application, early admission, deferred entrance. *Application fee:* $25. *Required:* high school transcript. *Application deadlines:* 8/1 (freshmen), 8/1 (transfers). *Notification:* 8/1 (freshmen), continuous until 8/1 (transfers).

Freshman Application Contact Ms. Amanda Strickland, Admissions Counselor, Emmanuel College, PO Box 129, 181 Spring Street, Franklin Springs, GA 30639-0129. *Phone:* 706-245-7226 Ext. 2907. *Toll-free phone:* 800-860-8800. *E-mail:* admissions@ec.edu. *Web site:* http://www.ec.edu/.

Emory University
Atlanta, Georgia

- **Independent Methodist** university, founded 1836
- **Suburban** 634-acre campus with easy access to Atlanta
- **Endowment** $5.3 billion
- **Coed**
- **Most difficult** entrance level

Faculty *Student/faculty ratio:* 7:1.

Academics *Calendar:* semesters. *Degrees:* associate, bachelor's, master's, doctoral-professional, doctoral-research/scholarship, and post-master's certificates (enrollment figures include Emory University, Oxford College; application data for main campus only).

Student Life *Campus security:* 24-hour emergency response devices and patrols, student patrols, late-night transport/escort service.

Athletics Member NCAA. All Division III.

Standardized Tests *Required:* SAT or ACT (for admission). *Recommended:* SAT Subject Tests (for admission).

Financial Aid *Of all full-time matriculated undergraduates who enrolled in 2009,* 3,680 applied for aid, 3,325 were judged to have need, 3,199 had their need fully met. *In 2009,* 497 non-need-based awards were made. *Average percent of need met:* 100. *Average financial aid package:* $34,853. *Average need-based loan:* $4147. *Average need-based gift aid:* $31,710. *Average non-need-based aid:* $20,859. *Average indebtedness upon graduation:* $26,311. *Financial aid deadline:* 3/1.

Applying *Options:* electronic application, early admission, early decision, deferred entrance. *Application fee:* $50. *Required:* essay or personal statement, high school transcript, 1 letter of recommendation. *Recommended:* minimum 3 GPA.

Freshman Application Contact Ms. Jean Jordan, Dean of Admission, Emory University, 200 Dowman Drive, Boisfeuillet Jones Center, Atlanta, GA 30322-1100. *Phone:* 404-727-6036. *Toll-free phone:* 800-727-6036. *Fax:* 404-727-4303. *E-mail:* admiss@emory.edu. *Web site:* http://www.emory.edu/.

Emory University, Oxford College
Oxford, Georgia

- **Independent Methodist** primarily 2-year, founded 1836, administratively affiliated with Emory University
- **Small-town** 150-acre campus with easy access to Atlanta
- **Endowment** $26.0 million
- **Coed**
- **Moderately difficult** entrance level

Faculty *Student/faculty ratio:* 10:1.

Academics *Calendar:* semesters. *Degrees:* associate and bachelor's.

Student Life *Campus security:* 24-hour emergency response devices and patrols, student patrols, late-night transport/escort service, controlled dormitory access.

Athletics Member NJCAA.

Standardized Tests *Required:* SAT or ACT (for admission). *Required for some:* SAT Subject Tests (for admission).

Costs (2010–11) *Comprehensive fee:* $42,734 includes full-time tuition ($32,800), mandatory fees ($462), and room and board ($9472). Full-time tuition and fees vary according to course load. Part-time tuition: $1000 per credit hour. Part-time tuition and fees vary according to course load. *College room only:* $6522. Room and board charges vary according to board plan.

Financial Aid *Of all full-time matriculated undergraduates who enrolled in 2009,* 225 Federal Work-Study jobs (averaging $1600).

Applying *Options:* electronic application, early admission, early action, deferred entrance. *Application fee:* $50. *Required:* essay or personal statement, high school transcript, 1 letter of recommendation. *Required for some:* interview. *Recommended:* minimum 3 GPA, 2 letters of recommendation.

Freshman Application Contact Emory University, Oxford College, 100 Hamill Street, PO Box 1328, Oxford, GA 30054. *Phone:* 770-784-8328. *Toll-free phone:* 800-723-8328. *Web site:* http://oxford.emory.edu/.

Fort Valley State University
Fort Valley, Georgia

- **State-supported** comprehensive, founded 1895, part of University System of Georgia
- **Small-town** 1365-acre campus
- **Coed**
- **Moderately difficult** entrance level

Faculty *Student/faculty ratio:* 19:1.

Academics *Calendar:* semesters. *Degrees:* associate, bachelor's, master's, doctoral-professional, and doctoral-research/scholarship.

Student Life *Campus security:* 24-hour emergency response devices and patrols, student patrols, late-night transport/escort service.

Athletics Member NCAA. All Division II.

Standardized Tests *Required:* SAT or ACT (for admission).

Costs (2010–11) *Tuition:* state resident $4274 full-time, $143 per credit hour part-time; nonresident $15,888 full-time, $530 per credit hour part-time. Full-time tuition and fees vary according to course load, degree level, and student level. Part-time tuition and fees vary according to course load, degree level, and student level. *Required fees:* $1288 full-time. *Room and board:* $7326; room only: $4456. Room and board charges vary according to board plan, housing facility, and student level.

Financial Aid *Of all full-time matriculated undergraduates who enrolled in 2009,* 2,671 applied for aid, 2,465 were judged to have need. *In 2009,* 7 non-need-based awards were made. *Average percent of need met:* 82. *Average financial aid package:* $4400. *Average need-based loan:* $1990. *Average need-based gift aid:* $3798. *Average non-need-based aid:* $1776. *Average indebtedness upon graduation:* $37,000. *Financial aid deadline:* 6/30.

Applying *Options:* electronic application, early admission, deferred entrance. *Application fee:* $30. *Required:* high school transcript.

Freshman Application Contact Mr. Donald Moore, Director of Admissions and Recruitment, Fort Valley State University, 1005 State University Drive, Fort Valley, GA 31030. *Phone:* 478-825-6307. *Toll-free phone:* 877-462-3878. *Fax:* 478-825-6169. *E-mail:* admissap@fvsu.edu. *Web site:* http://www.fvsu.edu/.

Gainesville State College
Oakwood, Georgia

- **State-supported** primarily 2-year, founded 1964, part of University System of Georgia
- **Small-town** 220-acre campus with easy access to Atlanta
- **Coed**
- **Noncompetitive** entrance level

Faculty *Student/faculty ratio:* 26:1.

Academics *Calendar:* semesters. *Degrees:* associate and bachelor's.

Student Life *Campus security:* 24-hour emergency response devices and patrols.

Standardized Tests *Recommended:* SAT or ACT (for admission).

Costs (2010–11) *Tuition:* state resident $2160 full-time, $90 per credit hour part-time; nonresident $8160 full-time, $340 per credit hour part-time. *Required fees:* $554 full-time, $484 per year part-time.

Applying *Options:* electronic application, early admission. *Application fee:* $35. *Required:* high school transcript.

Freshman Application Contact Mr. Mack Palmour, Director of Admissions, Gainesville State College, PO Box 1358, Gainesville, GA 30503. *Phone:* 678-717-3641. *Fax:* 678-717-3751. *E-mail:* admissions@gsc.edu. *Web site:* http://www.gsc.edu/.

Georgia College & State University
Milledgeville, Georgia

- **State-supported** comprehensive, founded 1889, part of University System of Georgia
- **Small-town** 590-acre campus
- **Endowment** $21.1 million
- **Coed** 5,715 undergraduate students, 91% full-time, 60% women, 40% men
- **Moderately difficult** entrance level, 62% of applicants were admitted

Undergraduates 5,186 full-time, 529 part-time. Students come from 29 states and territories; 46 other countries; 1% are from out of state; 7% transferred in; 37% live on campus. *Retention:* 85% of full-time freshmen returned.

Freshmen *Admission:* 4,122 applied, 2,576 admitted, 1,203 enrolled. *Average high school GPA:* 3.42. *Test scores:* SAT critical reading scores over 500: 90%; SAT math scores over 500: 89%; ACT scores over 18: 99%; SAT critical reading scores over 600: 33%; SAT math scores over 600: 36%; ACT scores over 24: 59%; SAT critical reading scores over 700: 2%; SAT math scores over 700: 2%; ACT scores over 30: 3%.

Faculty *Total:* 419, 75% full-time. *Student/faculty ratio:* 17:1.

Academics *Calendar:* semesters. *Degrees:* bachelor's, master's, and post-master's certificates. *Special study options:* accelerated degree program, advanced placement credit, distance learning, double majors, English as a second language, freshman honors college, honors programs, independent study, internships, part-time degree program, services for LD students, student-designed majors, study abroad, summer session for credit. *ROTC:* Army (c). *Unusual degree programs:* 3-2 engineering with Georgia Institute of Technology.

Computers on Campus 180 computers/terminals are available on campus for general student use. Students can access the following: campus intranet, computer help desk, free student e-mail accounts, online (class) grades, online (class) registration, online (class) schedules. Campuswide network is available. 100% of college-owned or -operated housing units are wired for high-speed Internet access. Wireless service is available via entire campus.

Student Life *Housing:* on-campus residence required for freshman year. *Options:* coed, disabled students. Campus housing is university owned and leased by the school. Freshman applicants given priority for college housing. *Activities and organizations:* drama/theater group, student-run newspaper, radio station, choral group, Eta Sigma Alpha, Delta Zeta, Alpha Delta Pi, Phi Mu, Zeta Tau Alpha, national fraternities, national sororities. *Campus security:* 24-hour emergency response devices and patrols, student patrols, late-night transport/escort service, controlled dormitory access. *Student services:* health clinic, personal/psychological counseling, women's center.

Athletics Member NCAA. All Division II. *Intercollegiate sports:* baseball M(s), basketball M(s)/W(s), cheerleading M/W, cross-country running M(s)/W(s), golf M(s), soccer W(s), softball W(s), tennis M(s)/W(s). *Intramural sports:* basketball M/W, football M/W, ice hockey M(c), lacrosse M(c)/W(c), rugby M(c), softball M/W, swimming and diving M(c)/W(c), ultimate Frisbee M/W, volleyball M(c)/W(c).

Standardized Tests *Required:* SAT or ACT (for admission). *Required for some:* SAT Subject Tests (for admission).

Costs (2010–11) *Tuition:* state resident $6284 full-time; nonresident $23,322 full-time. Full-time tuition and fees vary according to course load and location. Part-time tuition and fees vary according to course load and location. *Required fees:* $1568 full-time, $784 per term part-time. *Room and board:* $8414; room only: $4918. Room and board charges vary according to board plan and housing facility. *Payment plan:* installment. *Waivers:* senior citizens and employees or children of employees.

Financial Aid Of all full-time matriculated undergraduates who enrolled in 2009, 4,678 applied for aid, 2,273 were judged to have need, 1 had their need fully met. 75 Federal Work-Study jobs (averaging $2800). In 2009, 73 non-need-based awards were made. *Average percent of need met:* 37%. *Average financial aid package:* $7514. *Average need-based loan:* $4057. *Average need-based gift aid:* $4104. *Average non-need-based aid:* $1197. *Average indebtedness upon graduation:* $15,800.

Applying *Options:* electronic application, early admission, early action, deferred entrance. *Application fee:* $40. *Required:* essay or personal statement, proof of immunization. *Required for some:* interview. *Application deadlines:* 4/1 (freshmen), 7/1 (transfers), 11/1 (early action). *Notification:* continuous (freshmen), continuous (transfers), 12/1 (early action).

Freshman Application Contact Mr. Clayton Daniels, Director of Admissions, Georgia College & State University, CPO Box 023, Milledgeville, GA 31061. *Phone:* 478-445-6284. *Toll-free phone:* 800-342-0471. *Fax:* 478-445-3653. *E-mail:* admissions@gcsu.edu. *Web site:* http://www.gcsu.edu/.

Georgia Gwinnett College

Lawrenceville, Georgia

Freshman Application Contact Admissions Office, Georgia Gwinnett College, 1000 University Center Lane, Lawrenceville, GA 60043. *Phone:* 678-407-5313. *E-mail:* ggcadmissions@ggc.edu. *Web site:* http://www.ggc.usg.edu/.

Georgia Health Sciences University

Augusta, Georgia

- **State-supported** upper-level, founded 1828, part of University System of Georgia
- **Urban** 100-acre campus
- **Endowment** $6.6 million
- **Coed** 476 undergraduate students, 92% full-time, 88% women, 12% men
- 33% of applicants were admitted

Undergraduates 436 full-time, 40 part-time. Students come from 24 states and territories; 25 other countries; 12% are from out of state; 14% Black or African American, non-Hispanic/Latino; 3% Hispanic/Latino; 6% Asian, non-Hispanic/Latino; 0.6% Native Hawaiian or other Pacific Islander, non-Hispanic/Latino; 0.4% American Indian or Alaska Native, non-Hispanic/Latino; 3% Two or more races, non-Hispanic/Latino; 3% Race/ethnicity unknown; 0.8% international; 49% transferred in; 10% live on campus.

Freshmen *Admission:* 857 applied, 282 admitted.

Faculty *Total:* 824, 77% full-time.

Academics *Calendar:* semesters. *Degrees:* bachelor's, master's, doctoral-professional, post-master's, and postbachelor's certificates. *Special study options:* distance learning, off-campus study, summer session for credit.

Computers on Campus 250 computers/terminals and 250 ports are available on campus for general student use. Students can access the following: computer help desk, free student e-mail accounts, online (class) grades, online (class) registration, online (class) schedules. Campuswide network is available. 100% of college-owned or -operated housing units are wired for high-speed Internet access. Wireless service is available via classrooms, computer centers, computer labs, learning centers, libraries, student centers.

Student Life *Housing options:* coed. Campus housing is university owned. *Activities and organizations:* student-run newspaper, choral group, Student Government Association, Family Medicine Interest Group, Medical Campus Outreach, Surgery Interest Group, Project MCG. *Campus security:* 24-hour emergency response devices and patrols, late-night transport/escort service. *Student services:* health clinic, personal/psychological counseling.

Athletics *Intramural sports:* badminton M/W, basketball M/W, football M/W, golf M, racquetball M/W, soccer M/W, softball M/W, table tennis M/W, volleyball M/W.

Costs (2010–11) *Tuition:* state resident $7070 full-time, $236 per credit hour part-time; nonresident $25,280 full-time, $843 per credit hour part-time. Full-time tuition and fees vary according to course load, location, program, and reciprocity agreements. Part-time tuition and fees vary according to course load, location, program, and reciprocity agreements. *Required fees:* $1112 full-time.

Room and board: Room and board charges vary according to housing facility and location. *Waivers:* employees or children of employees.

Financial Aid Of all full-time matriculated undergraduates who enrolled in 2009, 403 applied for aid, 403 were judged to have need. 22 Federal Work-Study jobs (averaging $1561). *Average financial aid package:* $8594. *Average need-based loan:* $3747. *Average need-based gift aid:* $1897.

Applying *Options:* electronic application. *Application fee:* $30.

Application Contact Georgia Health Sciences University, 1120 15th Street, Augusta, GA 30912. *Phone:* 706-721-2725. *Toll-free phone:* 800-519-3388. *Web site:* http://www.georgiahealth.edu.

Georgia Institute of Technology

Atlanta, Georgia

- **State-supported** university, founded 1885, part of University System of Georgia
- **Urban** 400-acre campus
- **Endowment** $1.4 billion
- **Coed** 13,750 undergraduate students, 91% full-time, 31% women, 69% men
- **Very difficult** entrance level, 52% of applicants were admitted

Undergraduates 12,579 full-time, 1,171 part-time. Students come from 53 states and territories; 73 other countries; 26% are from out of state; 6% Black or African American, non-Hispanic/Latino; 5% Hispanic/Latino; 17% Asian, non-Hispanic/Latino; 0.1% Native Hawaiian or other Pacific Islander, non-Hispanic/Latino; 0.2% American Indian or Alaska Native, non-Hispanic/Latino; 2% Two or more races, non-Hispanic/Latino; 0.6% Race/ethnicity unknown; 7% international; 4% transferred in; 59% live on campus. *Retention:* 94% of full-time freshmen returned.

Freshmen *Admission:* 13,495 applied, 6,976 admitted, 2,712 enrolled. *Average high school GPA:* 3.87. *Test scores:* SAT critical reading scores over 500: 98%; SAT math scores over 500: 99%; SAT writing scores over 500: 97%; ACT scores over 18: 100%; SAT critical reading scores over 600: 74%; SAT math scores over 600: 92%; SAT writing scores over 600: 73%; ACT scores over 24: 96%; SAT critical reading scores over 700: 21%; SAT math scores over 700: 48%; SAT writing scores over 700: 21%; ACT scores over 30: 49%.

Faculty *Total:* 1,080, 85% full-time, 90% with terminal degrees. *Student/faculty ratio:* 20:1.

Academics *Calendar:* semesters. *Degrees:* bachelor's, master's, and doctoral-research/scholarship. *Special study options:* academic remediation for entering students, accelerated degree program, advanced placement credit, cooperative education, distance learning, double majors, English as a second language, honors programs, independent study, internships, off-campus study, part-time degree program, services for LD students, student-designed majors, study abroad, summer session for credit. *ROTC:* Army (b), Navy (b), Air Force (b). *Unusual degree programs:* 3-2 engineering with several universities and colleges in the University System of Georgia.

Computers on Campus 2,000 computers/terminals are available on campus for general student use. Students can access the following: campus intranet, computer help desk, free student e-mail accounts, online (class) grades, online (class) registration, online (class) schedules. Campuswide network is available. 100% of college-owned or -operated housing units are wired for high-speed Internet access. Wireless service is available via classrooms, computer centers, computer labs, dorm rooms, learning centers, libraries, student centers.

Student Life *Housing options:* coed, men-only, women-only, disabled students. Campus housing is university owned. Freshman campus housing is guaranteed. *Activities and organizations:* drama/theater group, student-run newspaper, radio and television station, choral group, marching band, India Club, Christian Campus Fellowship, Muslim Student Association, National Society of Black Engineers, national fraternities, national sororities. *Campus security:* 24-hour emergency response devices and patrols, late-night transport/escort service, controlled dormitory access, self defense education, lighted pathways and walks, video cameras, email and phone alerts of emergency situations. *Student services:* health clinic, personal/psychological counseling, women's center, legal services.

Athletics Member NCAA. All Division I except football (Division I-A). *Intercollegiate sports:* baseball M(s), basketball M(s)/W(s), cheerleading M(s)/W(s), cross-country running M(s)/W(s), golf M(s), ice hockey M(c), lacrosse M(c)/W(c), rugby M(c), soccer M(c)/W(c), softball W(s), swimming and diving M(s)/W(s), tennis M(s)/W(s), track and field M(s)/W(s), volleyball W(s), wrestling M(c). *Intramural sports:* archery M(c)/W(c), badminton M(c)/W(c), baseball M(c), basketball M/W, bowling M/W, crew M(c)/W(c), equestrian sports M(c)/W(c), fencing M(c)/W(c), field hockey M(c)/W(c), football M, golf M(c)/W(c), gymnastics M(c)/W(c), ice hockey M(c), lacrosse M(c)/W(c), racquetball M(c)/W(c), riflery M(c)/W(c), rugby M(c)/W(c), sailing M(c)/W(c), soccer M(c)/W(c), softball M/W, swimming and diving M(c)/W(c), table tennis M(c)/W(c), tennis M(c)/W(c), ultimate Frisbee M(c)/W(c), volleyball M(c)/W(c), water polo M(c)/W(c).

Standardized Tests *Required:* SAT or ACT (for admission).

Costs (2010–11) *Tuition:* state resident $7070 full-time, $350 per credit hour part-time; nonresident $25,280 full-time, $1250 per credit hour part-time. Full-time tuition and fees vary according to reciprocity agreements. Part-time tuition and fees vary according to course load and reciprocity agreements. *Required fees:* $1646 full-time, $373 per course part-time, $823 per term part-time. *Room and board:* $8746; room only: $5332. Room and board charges vary according to board plan and housing facility. *Waivers:* employees or children of employees.

Financial Aid Of all full-time matriculated undergraduates who enrolled in 2008, 7,646 applied for aid, 4,710 were judged to have need, 1,553 had their need fully met. 274 Federal Work-Study jobs (averaging $2345). In 2008, 975 non-need-based awards were made. *Average percent of need met:* 62%. *Average financial aid package:* $11,005. *Average need-based loan:* $3587. *Average need-based gift aid:* $9422. *Average non-need-based aid:* $3067. *Average indebtedness upon graduation:* $21,838. *Financial aid deadline:* 3/1.

Applying *Options:* electronic application, early admission, early action. *Application fee:* $65. *Required:* essay or personal statement, high school transcript. *Application deadlines:* 1/15 (freshmen), 2/1 (transfers). *Notification:* 3/15 (freshmen), continuous (transfers).

Freshman Application Contact Mr. Rick A. Clark Jr., Director of Undergraduate Admissions, Georgia Institute of Technology, Office of Undergraduate Admission, Atlanta, GA 30332-0320. *Phone:* 404-894-4154. *Fax:* 404-894-9511. *E-mail:* admission@gatech.edu. *Web site:* http://www.gatech.edu/.

Georgia Southern University
Statesboro, Georgia

- **State-supported** university, founded 1906, part of University System of Georgia
- **Small-town** 700-acre campus
- **Endowment** $33.8 million
- **Coed** 17,044 undergraduate students, 90% full-time, 49% women, 51% men
- **Moderately difficult** entrance level, 56% of applicants were admitted

Undergraduates 15,337 full-time, 1,707 part-time. Students come from 49 states and territories; 81 other countries; 3% are from out of state; 23% Black or African American, non-Hispanic/Latino; 4% Hispanic/Latino; 1% Asian, non-Hispanic/Latino; 0.2% Native Hawaiian or other Pacific Islander, non-Hispanic/Latino; 0.3% American Indian or Alaska Native, non-Hispanic/Latino; 2% Two or more races, non-Hispanic/Latino; 1% Race/ethnicity unknown; 1% international; 6% transferred in; 27% live on campus. *Retention:* 79% of full-time freshmen returned.

Freshmen *Admission:* 9,817 applied, 5,493 admitted, 3,622 enrolled. *Average high school GPA:* 3.2. *Test scores:* SAT critical reading scores over 500: 83%; SAT math scores over 500: 86%; SAT writing scores over 500: 66%; ACT scores over 18: 99%; SAT critical reading scores over 600: 20%; SAT math scores over 600: 27%; SAT writing scores over 600: 13%; ACT scores over 24: 37%; SAT critical reading scores over 700: 2%; SAT math scores over 700: 2%; SAT writing scores over 700: 1%; ACT scores over 30: 2%.

Faculty *Total:* 838, 87% full-time, 76% with terminal degrees. *Student/faculty ratio:* 23:1.

Academics *Calendar:* semesters. *Degrees:* bachelor's, master's, doctoral-research/scholarship, and post-master's certificates. *Special study options:* academic remediation for entering students, accelerated degree program, adult/continuing education programs, advanced placement credit, cooperative education, distance learning, double majors, English as a second language, honors programs, independent study, internships, off-campus study, part-time degree program, services for LD students, student-designed majors, study abroad, summer session for credit. *ROTC:* Army (b). *Unusual degree programs:* 3-2 engineering with Georgia Institute of Technology.

Computers on Campus 3,260 computers/terminals and 5,200 ports are available on campus for general student use. Students can access the following: campus intranet, computer help desk, free student e-mail accounts, online (class) grades, online (class) registration, online (class) schedules. Campus-wide network is available. 100% of college-owned or -operated housing units are wired for high-speed Internet access. Wireless service is available via classrooms, computer labs, dorm rooms, libraries, student centers.

Student Life *Housing:* on-campus residence required for freshman year. *Options:* coed, disabled students. Campus housing is university owned. Freshman applicants given priority for college housing. *Activities and organizations:* drama/theater group, student-run newspaper, radio and television station, choral group, marching band, Residence Hall Association, Campus Religious Ministries, Student Government Association, Black Student Association, Greek Life, national fraternities, national sororities. *Campus security:* 24-hour emergency response devices and patrols, student patrols, late-night transport/escort service, bike police and environmental safety services. *Student services:* health clinic, personal/psychological counseling, women's center, legal services.

Athletics Member NCAA. All Division I except football (Division I-AA). *Intercollegiate sports:* baseball M(s), basketball M(s)/W(s), bowling M(c)/W(c), cheerleading M/W, cross-country running W(s), equestrian sports M(c)/W(c), fencing M(c)/W(c), golf M(s), lacrosse M(c), rugby M(c)/W(c), soccer M(s)/W(s), softball W(s), swimming and diving W(s), tennis M(s)/W(s), track and field W(s), ultimate Frisbee M(c)/W(c), volleyball W(s), wrestling M(c)/W(c). *Intramural sports:* baseball M(c), basketball M/W, bowling M/W, football M/W, golf M/W, soccer M/W, softball M/W, tennis M/W, track and field M(c)/W(c), volleyball M/W.

Standardized Tests *Required:* SAT or ACT (for admission).

Costs (2010–11) *Tuition:* state resident $4596 full-time, $154 per credit hour part-time; nonresident $16,572 full-time, $553 per credit hour part-time. Full-time tuition and fees vary according to degree level, location, and program. Part-time tuition and fees vary according to course load, degree level, location, and program. *Required fees:* $1644 full-time, $822 per term part-time. *Room and board:* $8414; room only: $5364. Room and board charges vary according to board plan and housing facility. *Waivers:* senior citizens and employees or children of employees.

Financial Aid Of all full-time matriculated undergraduates who enrolled in 2008, 12,869 applied for aid, 8,840 were judged to have need, 864 had their need fully met. 245 Federal Work-Study jobs (averaging $1697). In 2008, 363 non-need-based awards were made. *Average percent of need met:* 55%. *Average financial aid package:* $8944. *Average need-based loan:* $4075. *Average need-based gift aid:* $6921. *Average non-need-based aid:* $1837. *Average indebtedness upon graduation:* $19,418.

Applying *Options:* electronic application, early admission, deferred entrance. *Application fee:* $30. *Required:* minimum 2 GPA, proof of immunization prior to enrollment. *Required for some:* high school transcript. *Application deadlines:* 5/1 (freshmen), 5/1 (out-of-state freshmen), 8/1 (transfers). *Notification:* continuous (freshmen), continuous (out-of-state freshmen), continuous (transfers).

Freshman Application Contact Mrs. Sarah Smith, Director, Georgia Southern University, PO Box 8024, Statesboro, GA 30460. *Phone:* 912-478-5391. *Fax:* 912-478-7240. *E-mail:* admissions@georgiasouthern.edu. *Web site:* http://www.georgiasouthern.edu/.

Georgia Southwestern State University
Americus, Georgia

Freshman Application Contact Mr. David Jenkins, Assistant Director of Admissions, Georgia Southwestern State University, 800 Wheatley Street, Americus, GA 31709. *Phone:* 229-928-1273. *Toll-free phone:* 800-338-0082. *Fax:* 229-931-2983. *E-mail:* gswapps@canes.gsw.edu. *Web site:* http://www.gsw.edu/.

Georgia State University
Atlanta, Georgia

- **State-supported** university, founded 1913, part of University System of Georgia
- **Urban** 55-acre campus with easy access to Atlanta
- **Endowment** $87.5 million
- **Coed** 23,486 undergraduate students, 75% full-time, 60% women, 40% men
- **Moderately difficult** entrance level, 52% of applicants were admitted

Undergraduates 17,547 full-time, 5,939 part-time. Students come from 55 states and territories; 151 other countries; 6% are from out of state; 36% Black or African American, non-Hispanic/Latino; 7% Hispanic/Latino; 11% Asian, non-Hispanic/Latino; 0.3% Native Hawaiian or other Pacific Islander, non-Hispanic/Latino; 0.2% American Indian or Alaska Native, non-Hispanic/Latino; 3% Two or more races, non-Hispanic/Latino; 1% Race/ethnicity unknown; 2% international; 11% transferred in; 14% live on campus. *Retention:* 84% of full-time freshmen returned.

Freshmen *Admission:* 12,626 applied, 6,555 admitted, 2,928 enrolled. *Average high school GPA:* 3.36. *Test scores:* SAT critical reading scores over 500: 77%; SAT math scores over 500: 79%; ACT scores over 18: 100%; SAT critical reading scores over 600: 24%; SAT math scores over 600: 26%; ACT scores over 24: 49%; SAT critical reading scores over 700: 2%; SAT math scores over 700: 4%; ACT scores over 30: 6%.

Faculty *Total:* 1,495, 75% full-time. *Student/faculty ratio:* 20:1.

Academics *Calendar:* semesters. *Degrees:* certificates, bachelor's, master's, doctoral-other, doctoral-professional, doctoral-research/scholarship, post-master's, and postbachelor's certificates. *Special study options:* academic remediation for entering students, accelerated degree program, advanced placement credit, cooperative education, distance learning, double majors, English as a second language, honors programs, independent study, internships, part-time degree program, services for LD students, study abroad, summer session for credit. *ROTC:* Army (b), Navy (c), Air Force (c). *Unusual degree programs:* 3-2 business administration.

Computers on Campus 727 computers/terminals and 24,000 ports are available on campus for general student use. Students can access the following: computer help desk, free student e-mail accounts, online (class) grades, online (class) registration, online (class) schedules. Campuswide network is available. 100% of college-owned or -operated housing units are wired for high-speed Internet access. Wireless service is available via entire campus.

Student Life *Housing options:* coed, disabled students. Campus housing is university owned and leased by the school. Freshman applicants given priority for college housing. *Activities and organizations:* drama/theater group, student-run newspaper, radio and television station, choral group, marching band, Spotlight Programs Board, Greek Organizations, International Student Associations Council, Academic Clubs, Sports Clubs, national fraternities, national sororities. *Campus security:* 24-hour emergency response devices and patrols, late-night transport/escort service, controlled dormitory access, Emergency Notification Center. *Student services:* health clinic, personal/psychological counseling.

Athletics Member NCAA. All Division I. *Intercollegiate sports:* baseball M(s), basketball M(s)/W(s), cross-country running M(s)/W(s), football M(s), golf M(s)/W(s), soccer M(s)/W(s), softball W(s), tennis M(s)/W(s), track and field M(s)/W(s), ultimate Frisbee M(c)/W(c), volleyball W(s). *Intramural sports:* basketball M/W, bowling M/W, crew M(c)/W(c), equestrian sports M(c)/W(c), football M/W, golf M/W, ice hockey M(c)/W(c), lacrosse M(c)/W(c), racquetball M/W, rock climbing M(c)/W(c), rugby M(c)/W(c), soccer M/W, softball M/W, swimming and diving M(c)/W(c), table tennis M(c)/W(c), ultimate Frisbee M/W, volleyball M/W, water polo M/W, weight lifting M/W.

Standardized Tests *Required:* SAT or ACT (for admission).

Costs (2010–11) *Tuition:* state resident $7070 full-time, $236 per credit hour part-time; nonresident $25,280 full-time, $843 per credit hour part-time. Part-time tuition and fees vary according to course load. *Required fees:* $1628 full-time, $108 per credit hour part-time. *Room and board:* $9325; room only: $7660. Room and board charges vary according to housing facility. *Waivers:* senior citizens and employees or children of employees.

Financial Aid Of all full-time matriculated undergraduates who enrolled in 2009, 15,687 applied for aid, 13,238 were judged to have need, 1,522 had their need fully met. 214 Federal Work-Study jobs (averaging $2369). In 2009, 2833 non-need-based awards were made. *Average percent of need met:* 30%. *Average financial aid package:* $9480. *Average need-based loan:* $3637. *Average need-based gift aid:* $3520. *Average non-need-based aid:* $3077. *Average indebtedness upon graduation:* $20,336. *Financial aid deadline:* 11/1.

Applying *Options:* electronic application, early action, deferred entrance. *Application fee:* $60. *Required:* high school transcript, minimum 2.8 GPA, college preparatory curriculum as specified by the University System of Georgia Board of Regents. Combined SAT of 900 or ACT composite of 19. *Application deadlines:* 3/1 (freshmen), 6/1 (transfers), 11/1 (early action). *Notification:* continuous until 4/1 (freshmen), 1/5 (early action).

Freshman Application Contact Daniel Niccum, Associate Director of Admissions, Georgia State University, PO Box 4009, Atlanta, GA 30302-4009. *Phone:* 404-413-2500. *Fax:* 404-413-2002. *E-mail:* dniccum@ gsu.edu. *Web site:* http://www.gsu.edu/.

Gordon College
Barnesville, Georgia

Freshman Application Contact Gordon College, 419 College Drive, Barnesville, GA 30204-1762. *Phone:* 678-359-5021. *Toll-free phone:* 800-282-6504. *Web site:* http://www.gdn.edu/.

Herzing University
Atlanta, Georgia

- **Proprietary** 4-year, founded 1949, part of Herzing, Inc.
- **Urban** campus with easy access to Atlanta
- **Coed** 609 undergraduate students, 70% full-time, 67% women, 33% men
- **Moderately difficult** entrance level, 75% of applicants were admitted

Undergraduates 426 full-time, 183 part-time. Students come from 5 states and territories; 10 other countries; 7% transferred in. *Retention:* 89% of full-time freshmen returned.

Freshmen *Admission:* 279 applied, 209 admitted, 93 enrolled.

Faculty *Total:* 25, 40% full-time, 28% with terminal degrees. *Student/faculty ratio:* 8:1.

Academics *Calendar:* semesters. *Degrees:* diplomas, associate, and bachelor's. *Special study options:* academic remediation for entering students, English as a second language, honors programs, internships.

Computers on Campus 125 computers/terminals are available on campus for general student use. Students can access the following: campus intranet, free

student e-mail accounts, online (class) grades, online (class) schedules. Campuswide network is available.

Student Life *Housing:* college housing not available. *Campus security:* 24-hour patrols. *Student services:* personal/psychological counseling, women's center.

Standardized Tests *Required:* Wonderlic aptitude test (for admission).

Costs (2011–12) *One-time required fee:* $100. *Tuition:* $10,200 full-time, $440 per credit part-time. Full-time tuition and fees vary according to class time and course load. Part-time tuition and fees vary according to class time and course load. *Payment plan:* installment. *Waivers:* employees or children of employees.

Applying *Application fee:* $25. *Required:* high school transcript, interview. *Application deadlines:* rolling (freshmen), rolling (transfers). *Notification:* continuous (freshmen), continuous (transfers).

Freshman Application Contact Miss Anissa Elder, Director of Admissions, Herzing University, 3393 Peachtree Road, NE, Suite 1003, Atlanta, GA 30326. *Phone:* 404-816-4533. *Toll-free phone:* 800-573-4533. *Fax:* 404-816-5576. *E-mail:* aelder@atl.herzing.edu. *Web site:* http://www.herzing.edu/atlanta/.

ITT Technical Institute
Atlanta, Georgia

- **Proprietary** primarily 2-year, part of ITT Educational Services, Inc.
- **Coed**
- **Minimally difficult** entrance level

Academics *Degrees:* associate and bachelor's.

Student Life *Housing:* college housing not available.

Freshman Application Contact Director of Recruitment, ITT Technical Institute, 485 Oak Place, Suite 800, Atlanta, GA 30349. *Phone:* 404-765-4600. *Toll-free phone:* 877-488-6102. *Web site:* http://www.itt-tech.edu/.

ITT Technical Institute
Duluth, Georgia

- **Proprietary** primarily 2-year, founded 2003, part of ITT Educational Services, Inc.
- **Coed**
- **Minimally difficult** entrance level

Academics *Calendar:* quarters. *Degrees:* associate and bachelor's.

Student Life *Housing:* college housing not available.

Freshman Application Contact Director of Recruitment, ITT Technical Institute, 10700 Abbotts Bridge Road, Duluth, GA 30097. *Phone:* 678-957-8510. *Toll-free phone:* 866-489-8818. *Web site:* http://www.itt-tech.edu/.

ITT Technical Institute
Kennesaw, Georgia

- **Proprietary** primarily 2-year, founded 2004, part of ITT Educational Services, Inc.
- **Coed**
- **Minimally difficult** entrance level

Academics *Calendar:* quarters. *Degrees:* associate and bachelor's.

Freshman Application Contact Director of Recruitment, ITT Technical Institute, 2065 ITT Tech Way, Kennesaw, GA 30144. *Phone:* 770-426-2300. *Toll-free phone:* 877-231-6415. *Web site:* http://www.itt-tech.edu/.

Kennesaw State University
Kennesaw, Georgia

- **State-supported** comprehensive, founded 1963, part of University System of Georgia
- **Suburban** 384-acre campus with easy access to Atlanta
- **Endowment** $24.0 million
- **Coed** 21,467 undergraduate students, 76% full-time, 59% women, 41% men
- **Moderately difficult** entrance level, 64% of applicants were admitted

Undergraduates 16,421 full-time, 5,046 part-time. 7% are from out of state; 13% Black or African American, non-Hispanic/Latino; 6% Hispanic/Latino; 3% Asian, non-Hispanic/Latino; 0.2% Native Hawaiian or other Pacific Islander, non-Hispanic/Latino; 0.3% American Indian or Alaska Native, non-Hispanic/Latino; 3% Two or more races, non-Hispanic/Latino; 8% Race/ethnicity unknown; 2% international; 9% transferred in; 14% live on campus. *Retention:* 77% of full-time freshmen returned.

Freshmen *Admission:* 8,652 applied, 5,530 admitted, 2,893 enrolled. *Average high school GPA:* 3.21. *Test scores:* SAT critical reading scores over 500: 77%; SAT math scores over 500: 76%; SAT writing scores over 500: 61%; ACT scores over 18: 98%; SAT critical reading scores over 600: 16%; SAT math scores over 600: 19%; SAT writing scores over 600: 12%; ACT scores

over 24: 33%; SAT critical reading scores over 700: 1%; SAT math scores over 700: 1%; SAT writing scores over 700: 1%; ACT scores over 30: 2%.

Faculty *Total:* 1,277, 58% full-time, 55% with terminal degrees. *Student/faculty ratio:* 20:1.

Academics *Calendar:* semesters. *Degrees:* bachelor's, master's, doctoral-research/scholarship, post-master's, and postbachelor's certificates. *Special study options:* adult/continuing education programs, advanced placement credit, cooperative education, distance learning, double majors, English as a second language, honors programs, internships, off-campus study, part-time degree program, services for LD students, study abroad, summer session for credit. *ROTC:* Army (c), Air Force (c).

Computers on Campus 1,650 computers/terminals and 12,000 ports are available on campus for general student use. Students can access the following: campus intranet, computer help desk, free student e-mail accounts, online (class) grades, online (class) registration, online (class) schedules. Campuswide network is available. 100% of college-owned or -operated housing units are wired for high-speed Internet access. Wireless service is available via classrooms, computer centers, computer labs, dorm rooms, learning centers, libraries, student centers.

Student Life *Housing options:* coed, disabled students. Campus housing is provided by a third party. Freshman applicants given priority for college housing. *Activities and organizations:* drama/theater group, student-run newspaper, radio station, choral group, Golden Key National Honor Society, Student Government Association, Kennesaw Activities Board, African-American Student Alliance, International Student Association, national fraternities, national sororities. *Campus security:* 24-hour emergency response devices and patrols, student patrols, late-night transport/escort service, controlled dormitory access. *Student services:* health clinic, personal/psychological counseling.

Athletics Member NCAA. All Division I. *Intercollegiate sports:* baseball M(s), basketball M(s)/W(s), cheerleading W(c), cross-country running M(s)/W(s), golf M(s)/W(s), soccer W(s), softball W(s), tennis M(s)/W(s), track and field M(s)/W(s), ultimate Frisbee M(c), volleyball M(c)/W(s). *Intramural sports:* baseball M, basketball M, bowling M/W, cross-country running M(c)/W(c), equestrian sports M(c)/W(c), football M/W, golf M/W, ice hockey M(c), lacrosse M(c)/W(c), rugby M(c)/W(c), soccer M/W, softball M/W, swimming and diving M(c)/W(c), table tennis M(c)/W(c), tennis M/W, ultimate Frisbee M/W, volleyball M/W, wrestling M(c).

Standardized Tests *Required:* SAT or ACT (for admission).

Costs (2010–11) *Tuition:* state resident $4596 full-time, $154 per credit hour part-time; nonresident $16,572 full-time, $553 per credit hour part-time. Part-time tuition and fees vary according to course load. *Required fees:* $1346 full-time. *Room and board:* $7298. Room and board charges vary according to board plan and housing facility. *Payment plan:* deferred payment. *Waivers:* senior citizens and employees or children of employees.

Financial Aid Of all full-time matriculated undergraduates who enrolled in 2009, 12,806 applied for aid, 10,470 were judged to have need, 1,922 had their need fully met. 230 Federal Work-Study jobs (averaging $2305). In 2009, 57 non-need-based awards were made. *Average percent of need met:* 73%. *Average financial aid package:* $7579. *Average need-based loan:* $3507. *Average need-based gift aid:* $5989. *Average non-need-based aid:* $1116. *Average indebtedness upon graduation:* $947.

Applying *Options:* electronic application, early admission, deferred entrance. *Application fee:* $40. *Required:* high school transcript, minimum 2.5 GPA, proof of immunization. *Application deadlines:* 5/14 (freshmen), 6/25 (transfers). *Notification:* continuous (freshmen), continuous (transfers).

Freshman Application Contact Admissions Office, Kennesaw State University, 1000 Chastain Road, Campus Box #0115, Kennesaw, GA 30144-5591. *Phone:* 770-423-6300. *Fax:* 770-420-4435. *E-mail:* ksuadmit@kennesaw.edu. *Web site:* http://www.kennesaw.edu/.

LaGrange College
LaGrange, Georgia

- **Independent United Methodist** comprehensive, founded 1831
- **Small-town** 120-acre campus with easy access to Atlanta
- **Endowment** $50.7 million
- **Coed** 834 undergraduate students, 90% full-time, 57% women, 43% men
- **Moderately difficult** entrance level, 58% of applicants were admitted

Undergraduates 753 full-time, 81 part-time. Students come from 19 states and territories; 11 other countries; 11% are from out of state; 9% transferred in; 68% live on campus. *Retention:* 61% of full-time freshmen returned.

Freshmen *Admission:* 1,024 applied, 593 admitted, 176 enrolled. *Average high school GPA:* 3.39. *Test scores:* SAT critical reading scores over 500: 53%; SAT math scores over 500: 64%; ACT scores over 18: 95%; SAT critical reading scores over 600: 16%; SAT math scores over 600: 21%; ACT scores over 24: 18%; SAT critical reading scores over 700: 4%.

Faculty *Total:* 141, 53% full-time, 43% with terminal degrees. *Student/faculty ratio:* 10:1.

Academics *Calendar:* 4-1-4. *Degrees:* bachelor's and master's. *Special study options:* accelerated degree program, adult/continuing education programs,

advanced placement credit, double majors, independent study, internships, part-time degree program, services for LD students, student-designed majors, study abroad, summer session for credit. *Unusual degree programs:* 3-2 engineering with Georgia Institute of Technology, Auburn University.

Computers on Campus 175 computers/terminals and 1,056 ports are available on campus for general student use. Students can access the following: campus intranet, free student e-mail accounts, online (class) grades, online (class) registration, online (class) schedules. Campuswide network is available. 100% of college-owned or -operated housing units are wired for high-speed Internet access. Wireless service is available via entire campus.

Student Life *Housing:* on-campus residence required through senior year. *Options:* coed, men-only, women-only. Campus housing is university owned. Freshman campus housing is guaranteed. *Activities and organizations:* drama/theater group, student-run newspaper, choral group, Greek Life, Student Government Association, Baptist Collegiate Ministries, Wesley Fellowship, Fellowship of Christian Athletes, national fraternities, national sororities. *Campus security:* 24-hour patrols, controlled dormitory access. *Student services:* health clinic, personal/psychological counseling.

Athletics Member NCAA. All Division III. *Intercollegiate sports:* baseball M, basketball M/W, cheerleading W, cross-country running M/W, football M, golf M, lacrosse W, soccer M/W, softball W, swimming and diving M/W, tennis M/W, volleyball W. *Intramural sports:* basketball M/W, softball M/W.

Standardized Tests *Required:* SAT or ACT (for admission).

Costs (2011–12) *Comprehensive fee:* $32,667 includes full-time tuition ($23,212) and room and board ($9455). Full-time tuition and fees vary according to class time, course load, degree level, and program. Part-time tuition: $956 per semester hour. Part-time tuition and fees vary according to class time, course load, degree level, and program. *Room and board:* Room and board charges vary according to board plan and housing facility. *Payment plan:* installment. *Waivers:* senior citizens and employees or children of employees.

Applying *Options:* electronic application, early admission, early action, deferred entrance. *Application fee:* $30. *Required:* essay or personal statement, high school transcript. *Required for some:* minimum 2.75 GPA, 1 letter of recommendation, interview. *Application deadlines:* rolling (freshmen), rolling (transfers), 12/31 (early action). *Notification:* continuous (freshmen), continuous (transfers).

Freshman Application Contact Mr. Dana Paul, Vice President of Enrollment Management, LaGrange College, 601 Broad Street, LaGrange, GA 30240-2999. *Phone:* 706-880-8253. *Toll-free phone:* 800-593-2885. *Fax:* 706-880-8010. *E-mail:* dpaul@lagrange.edu. *Web site:* http://www.lagrange.edu/.

Life University
Marietta, Georgia

- **Independent** comprehensive, founded 1974
- **Suburban** 96-acre campus
- **Coed** 792 undergraduate students, 71% full-time, 51% women, 49% men
- **Minimally difficult** entrance level, 67% of applicants were admitted

Undergraduates 561 full-time, 231 part-time. Students come from 52 states and territories; 14 other countries; 61% are from out of state; 23% Black or African American, non-Hispanic/Latino; 7% Hispanic/Latino; 5% Asian, non-Hispanic/Latino; 0.9% American Indian or Alaska Native, non-Hispanic/Latino; 8% Race/ethnicity unknown; 7% transferred in. *Retention:* 75% of full-time freshmen returned.

Freshmen *Admission:* 617 applied, 416 admitted, 53 enrolled. *Average high school GPA:* 3.01. *Test scores:* SAT critical reading scores over 500: 23%; SAT math scores over 500: 37%; SAT writing scores over 500: 35%; ACT scores over 18: 78%; SAT critical reading scores over 600: 7%; SAT math scores over 600: 15%; SAT writing scores over 600: 6%; ACT scores over 24: 20%.

Faculty *Total:* 139, 82% full-time, 91% with terminal degrees. *Student/faculty ratio:* 17:1.

Academics *Calendar:* quarters. *Degrees:* associate, bachelor's, master's, and doctoral-professional. *Special study options:* academic remediation for entering students, accelerated degree program, advanced placement credit, double majors, English as a second language, independent study, internships, off-campus study, services for LD students, summer session for credit.

Computers on Campus 200 computers/terminals are available on campus for general student use. Students can access the following: campus intranet, free student e-mail accounts, online (class) grades, online (class) registration. Campuswide network is available. 100% of college-owned or -operated housing units are wired for high-speed Internet access. Wireless service is available via classrooms, computer centers, computer labs, learning centers, libraries.

Student Life *Housing options:* Campus housing is university owned. *Activities and organizations:* student-run newspaper. *Campus security:* 24-hour emergency response devices and patrols, controlled dormitory access. *Student services:* health clinic.

Athletics Member NAIA. *Intramural sports:* basketball M/W, football M, rugby M, softball M/W, volleyball M/W.

Standardized Tests *Required:* SAT or ACT (for admission).

Costs (2010–11) *Comprehensive fee:* $21,849 includes full-time tuition ($8622), mandatory fees ($747), and room and board ($12,480). Full-time tuition and fees vary according to course load. Part-time tuition: $175 per credit hour. Part-time tuition and fees vary according to course load. *College room only:* $6300. *Payment plan:* installment. *Waivers:* employees or children of employees.

Financial Aid Of all full-time matriculated undergraduates who enrolled in 2009, 454 applied for aid, 439 were judged to have need, 3 had their need fully met. 221 Federal Work-Study jobs (averaging $1100). In 2009, 9 non-need-based awards were made. *Average financial aid package:* $9950. *Average need-based loan:* $4700. *Average need-based gift aid:* $5600. *Average non-need-based aid:* $2400. *Average indebtedness upon graduation:* $28,000.

Applying *Options:* electronic application. *Application fee:* $50. *Required:* high school transcript, minimum 2 GPA. *Application deadline:* 9/1 (freshmen). *Notification:* continuous (freshmen), continuous (transfers).

Freshman Application Contact Mr. Brian Gipson, Office of New Student Development, Life University, 1269 Barclay Circle, Marietta, GA 30060. *Phone:* 800-543-3202. *Toll-free phone:* 800-543-3202. *Fax:* 770-426-2895. *E-mail:* admissions@life.edu. *Web site:* http://www.life.edu/.

Luther Rice University

Lithonia, Georgia

Freshman Application Contact Mr. Steve Pray, Admissions Counselor, Luther Rice University, 3038 Evans Mill Road, Lithonia, GA 30038-2454. *Phone:* 770-484-1204. *Toll-free phone:* 800-442-1577. *E-mail:* admissions@lru.edu. *Web site:* http://www.lru.edu/.

Macon State College

Macon, Georgia

Freshman Application Contact Mr. Ryan Tucker, Admissions Representative, Macon State College, Macon, GA 31206. *Phone:* 478-471-2800. *Toll-free phone:* 800-272-7619 Ext. 2800. *Fax:* 478-471-5343. *E-mail:* mscinfo@mail.maconstate.edu. *Web site:* http://www.maconstate.edu/.

Mercer University

Macon, Georgia

- **Independent Baptist** university, founded 1833
- **Suburban** 150-acre campus with easy access to Atlanta
- **Endowment** $160.2 million
- **Coed** 2,344 undergraduate students, 97% full-time, 52% women, 48% men
- **Moderately difficult** entrance level, 64% of applicants were admitted

Undergraduates 2,276 full-time, 68 part-time. Students come from 43 states and territories; 37 other countries; 17% are from out of state; 19% Black or African American, non-Hispanic/Latino; 3% Hispanic/Latino; 7% Asian, non-Hispanic/Latino; 0.4% American Indian or Alaska Native, non-Hispanic/Latino; 1% Two or more races, non-Hispanic/Latino; 5% Race/ethnicity unknown; 3% international; 5% transferred in; 68% live on campus. *Retention:* 81% of full-time freshmen returned.

Freshmen *Admission:* 3,734 applied, 2,388 admitted, 595 enrolled. *Average high school GPA:* 3.62. *Test scores:* SAT critical reading scores over 500: 89%; SAT math scores over 500: 91%; SAT writing scores over 500: 81%; ACT scores over 18: 100%; SAT critical reading scores over 600: 40%; SAT math scores over 600: 50%; SAT writing scores over 600: 36%; ACT scores over 24: 73%; SAT critical reading scores over 700: 6%; SAT math scores over 700: 9%; SAT writing scores over 700: 6%; ACT scores over 30: 19%.

Faculty *Total:* 660, 59% full-time, 73% with terminal degrees. *Student/faculty ratio:* 13:1.

Academics *Calendar:* semesters. *Degrees:* bachelor's, master's, doctoral-other, doctoral-professional, doctoral-research/scholarship, and post-master's certificates. *Special study options:* accelerated degree program, adult/continuing education programs, advanced placement credit, cooperative education, double majors, English as a second language, honors programs, independent study, internships, off-campus study, part-time degree program, services for LD students, student-designed majors, study abroad, summer session for credit. *ROTC:* Army (b). *Unusual degree programs:* engineering; pharmacy.

Computers on Campus Students can access the following: campus intranet, computer help desk, free student e-mail accounts, online (class) grades, online (class) registration, online (class) schedules. Campuswide network is available. 100% of college-owned or -operated housing units are wired for high-speed Internet access. Wireless service is available via entire campus.

Student Life *Housing:* on-campus residence required through sophomore year. *Options:* coed, men-only, women-only, disabled students. Campus housing is university owned. Freshman campus housing is guaranteed. *Activities and organizations:* drama/theater group, student-run newspaper, radio and television station, choral group, national fraternities, national sororities. *Campus security:* 24-hour emergency response devices and patrols, student patrols, late-night transport/escort service, controlled dormitory access, patrols by police officers. *Student services:* health clinic, personal/psychological counseling.

Athletics Member NCAA. All Division I. *Intercollegiate sports:* baseball M(s), basketball M(s)/W(s), cross-country running M(s)/W(s), golf M(s)/W(s), lacrosse M/W(c), riflery M(s), soccer M(s)/W(s), softball W(s), tennis M(s)/W(s), volleyball W(s). *Intramural sports:* basketball M/W, bowling M/W, equestrian sports W(c), football M/W, golf M/W, soccer M/W, softball M/W, tennis M/W, ultimate Frisbee M/W, volleyball M/W, water polo M/W, wrestling M(c).

Standardized Tests *Required:* SAT or ACT (for admission).

Costs (2010–11) *Comprehensive fee:* $40,648 includes full-time tuition ($30,360), mandatory fees ($200), and room and board ($10,088). Full-time tuition and fees vary according to class time and location. Part-time tuition: $1012 per credit hour. Part-time tuition and fees vary according to class time, course load, and location. *Required fees:* $9 per credit hour part-time. *Room and board:* Room and board charges vary according to board plan, housing facility, and location. *Payment plan:* installment. *Waivers:* employees or children of employees.

Financial Aid Of all full-time matriculated undergraduates who enrolled in 2009, 1,840 applied for aid, 1,637 were judged to have need, 654 had their need fully met. In 2009, 613 non-need-based awards were made. *Average percent of need met:* 84%. *Average financial aid package:* $31,192. *Average need-based loan:* $8091. *Average need-based gift aid:* $21,295. *Average non-need-based aid:* $20,284. *Average indebtedness upon graduation:* $30,460.

Applying *Options:* electronic application, early admission, early action, deferred entrance. *Application fee:* $50. *Required:* high school transcript, minimum 3 GPA. *Required for some:* 2 letters of recommendation, interview. *Recommended:* interview, counselor's evaluation. *Application deadlines:* 7/1 (freshmen), rolling (transfers), 11/1 (early action). *Notification:* continuous (freshmen), continuous (transfers), 11/15 (early action).

Freshman Application Contact Mr. Emory Dunn, Director of Freshman Admissions, Mercer University, 1400 Coleman Avenue, Macon, GA 31207-0003. *Phone:* 478-301-2312. *Toll-free phone:* 800-840-8577. *E-mail:* dunn_e@mercer.edu. *Web site:* http://www.mercer.edu/.

Middle Georgia College

Cochran, Georgia

- **State-supported** primarily 2-year, founded 1884, part of University System of Georgia
- **Small-town** 165-acre campus
- **Endowment** $847,031
- **Coed**
- **Minimally difficult** entrance level

Faculty *Student/faculty ratio:* 22:1.

Academics *Calendar:* semesters. *Degrees:* certificates, associate, and bachelor's.

Student Life *Campus security:* 24-hour emergency response devices and patrols, late-night transport/escort service, controlled dormitory access, patrols by police officers.

Athletics Member NJCAA.

Standardized Tests *Required for some:* SAT or ACT (for admission). *Recommended:* SAT or ACT (for admission).

Costs (2010–11) *Tuition:* state resident $2694 full-time, $90 per credit hour part-time; nonresident $10,176 full-time, $340 per credit hour part-time. Full-time tuition and fees vary according to course load and program. Part-time tuition and fees vary according to course load and program. *Required fees:* $574 full-time. *Room and board:* $6980. Room and board charges vary according to board plan and housing facility.

Financial Aid Of all full-time matriculated undergraduates who enrolled in 2009, 91 Federal Work-Study jobs (averaging $692).

Applying *Options:* electronic application, early admission, deferred entrance. *Application fee:* $20. *Required:* high school transcript, minimum 2 GPA. *Required for some:* essay or personal statement, minimum 3.5 GPA, 3 letters of recommendation, interview.

Freshman Application Contact Ms. Jennifer Brannon, Director of Admissions, Middle Georgia College, 1100 2nd Street, Southeast, Cochran, GA 31014. *Phone:* 478-934-3103. *Fax:* 478-934-3403. *E-mail:* admissions@mgc.edu. *Web site:* http://www.mgc.edu/.

Morehouse College

Atlanta, Georgia

- **Independent** 4-year, founded 1867
- **Urban** 61-acre campus
- **Men only** 2,579 undergraduate students, 93% full-time
- **Moderately difficult** entrance level, 64% of applicants were admitted

Undergraduates 2,409 full-time, 170 part-time. Students come from 40 states and territories; 16 other countries; 67% are from out of state; 94% Black or African American, non-Hispanic/Latino; 0.4% Hispanic/Latino; 0.1% Asian, non-Hispanic/Latino; 0.1% American Indian or Alaska Native, non-Hispanic/Latino; 3% Race/ethnicity unknown; 2% international; 3% transferred in; 95% live on campus. *Retention:* 82% of full-time freshmen returned.

Freshmen *Admission:* 2,233 applied, 1,420 admitted, 530 enrolled. *Average high school GPA:* 3.2. *Test scores:* SAT critical reading scores over 500: 62%; SAT math scores over 500: 65%; SAT writing scores over 500: 55%; ACT scores over 18: 88%; SAT critical reading scores over 600: 19%; SAT math scores over 600: 23%; SAT writing scores over 600: 15%; ACT scores over 24: 26%; SAT critical reading scores over 700: 2%; SAT math scores over 700: 3%; SAT writing scores over 700: 2%; ACT scores over 30: 3%.

Faculty *Total:* 214, 77% full-time, 75% with terminal degrees. *Student/faculty ratio:* 14:1.

Academics *Calendar:* semesters. *Degree:* bachelor's. *Special study options:* academic remediation for entering students, advanced placement credit, cooperative education, double majors, honors programs, internships, off-campus study, part-time degree program, services for LD students, study abroad, summer session for credit. *ROTC:* Army (b), Navy (b), Air Force (b). *Unusual degree programs:* 3-2 engineering with Georgia Tech, Boston Univ., Auburn Univ., Rensselaer Polytechnic Univ., Rochester Institute of Technology, Columbia Univ., Dartmouth College, North Carolina A&T State Univ., Univ. of Florida, Univ. of Missouri-Rolla. Univ. of Michigan.

Computers on Campus 500 computers/terminals are available on campus for general student use. Students can access the following: campus intranet, computer help desk, free student e-mail accounts, online (class) grades, online (class) registration, online (class) schedules. Campuswide network is available. 100% of college-owned or -operated housing units are wired for high-speed Internet access. Wireless service is available via entire campus.

Student Life *Housing:* on-campus residence required for freshman year. *Options:* men-only. Campus housing is university owned. Freshman campus housing is guaranteed. *Activities and organizations:* drama/theater group, student-run newspaper, choral group, marching band, Morehouse College Glee Club, Morehouse Business Association, NAACP, Morehouse Public Health Association, Pre-Law Society, national fraternities. *Campus security:* 24-hour emergency response devices and patrols, late-night transport/escort service, controlled dormitory access. *Student services:* health clinic, personal/psychological counseling.

Athletics Member NCAA. All Division II. *Intercollegiate sports:* basketball M(s), cross-country running M(s), football M(s), tennis M(s), track and field M(s). *Intramural sports:* baseball M, basketball M, football M, golf M, soccer M, softball M, swimming and diving M, table tennis M, tennis M, weight lifting M.

Standardized Tests *Required:* SAT or ACT (for admission).

Costs (2010–11) *Comprehensive fee:* $33,938 includes full-time tuition ($20,394), mandatory fees ($2050), and room and board ($11,494). Full-time tuition and fees vary according to course load and student level. Part-time tuition: $850 per credit hour. Part-time tuition and fees vary according to course load. *Required fees:* $1025 per term part-time. *College room only:* $6550. Room and board charges vary according to board plan. *Waivers:* employees or children of employees.

Financial Aid Of all full-time matriculated undergraduates who enrolled in 2009, 2,393 applied for aid, 2,393 were judged to have need, 166 had their need fully met. *Average percent of need met:* 59%. *Average financial aid package:* $13,250. *Average need-based loan:* $5500. *Average need-based gift aid:* $10,000. *Financial aid deadline:* 4/1.

Applying *Options:* electronic application, early admission, early decision, early action, deferred entrance. *Application fee:* $45. *Required:* essay or personal statement, high school transcript, minimum 0 GPA. *Recommended:* minimum 3 GPA, interview. *Application deadlines:* 2/15 (freshmen), 2/15 (transfers), 11/1 (early action). *Early decision deadline:* 11/1. *Notification:* 4/1 (freshmen), 4/1 (transfers), 12/15 (early decision), 12/15 (early action).

Freshman Application Contact Morehouse College, 830 Westview Drive, SW, Atlanta, GA 30314. *Phone:* 404-215-2632. *Toll-free phone:* 800-851-1254. *Web site:* http://www.morehouse.edu/.

North Georgia College & State University

Dahlonega, Georgia

- **State-supported** comprehensive, founded 1873, part of University System of Georgia
- **Small-town** 140-acre campus with easy access to Atlanta
- **Endowment** $27.7 million
- **Coed** 5,353 undergraduate students, 84% full-time, 56% women, 44% men
- **Moderately difficult** entrance level, 56% of applicants were admitted

Undergraduates 4,515 full-time, 838 part-time. Students come from 36 states and territories; 44 other countries; 5% are from out of state; 3% Black or African American, non-Hispanic/Latino; 3% Hispanic/Latino; 1% Asian, non-Hispanic/Latino; 0.1% Native Hawaiian or other Pacific Islander, non-Hispanic/Latino; 0.4% American Indian or Alaska Native, non-Hispanic/Latino; 2% Two or more races, non-Hispanic/Latino; 3% Race/ethnicity unknown; 1% international; 11% transferred in; 35% live on campus. *Retention:* 81% of full-time freshmen returned.

Freshmen *Admission:* 3,737 applied, 2,092 admitted, 919 enrolled. *Average high school GPA:* 3.47. *Test scores:* SAT critical reading scores over 500: 85%; SAT math scores over 500: 79%; ACT scores over 18: 98%; SAT critical reading scores over 600: 25%; SAT math scores over 600: 23%; ACT scores over 24: 49%; SAT critical reading scores over 700: 3%; SAT math scores over 700: 2%; ACT scores over 30: 4%.

Faculty *Total:* 380, 63% full-time, 49% with terminal degrees. *Student/faculty ratio:* 18:1.

Academics *Calendar:* semesters. *Degrees:* certificates, associate, bachelor's, master's, doctoral-professional, post-master's, and postbachelor's certificates. *Special study options:* academic remediation for entering students, accelerated degree program, advanced placement credit, cooperative education, distance learning, double majors, external degree program, freshman honors college, honors programs, independent study, internships, part-time degree program, services for LD students, study abroad, summer session for credit. *ROTC:* Army (b). *Unusual degree programs:* 3-2 engineering with Georgia Institute of Technology, Clemson University; industrial management, computer science with Georgia Institute of Technology.

Computers on Campus 850 computers/terminals are available on campus for general student use. Students can access the following: computer help desk, free student e-mail accounts, online (class) grades, online (class) registration, online (class) schedules. Campuswide network is available. 100% of college-owned or -operated housing units are wired for high-speed Internet access. Wireless service is available via entire campus.

Student Life *Housing:* on-campus residence required through sophomore year. *Options:* coed, men-only, women-only. Campus housing is university owned. *Activities and organizations:* drama/theater group, student-run newspaper, choral group, Student Government Association, Commuter Council, Graduate Student Senate, Baptist Student Union, Greek organizations, national fraternities, national sororities. *Campus security:* 24-hour emergency response devices and patrols, late-night transport/escort service, controlled dormitory access. *Student services:* health clinic, personal/psychological counseling.

Athletics Member NCAA, NAIA. All NCAA Division II. *Intercollegiate sports:* baseball M(s), basketball M(s)/W(s), cheerleading M/W, cross-country running M(c)/W(c), equestrian sports W(c), golf M/W, lacrosse M(c)/W(c), riflery M(c)/W(c), rugby M(c)/W(c), soccer M(s)/W(s), softball W(s), tennis M(s)/W(s), track and field M/W, wrestling M(c). *Intramural sports:* basketball M/W, football M/W, golf M(c)/W(c), soccer M/W, softball M/W, table tennis M/W, ultimate Frisbee M/W, volleyball M/W, water polo M/W.

Standardized Tests *Required:* SAT or ACT (for admission). *Required for some:* SAT and SAT Subject Tests or ACT (for admission).

Costs (2010–11) *Tuition:* state resident $4596 full-time, $154 per credit hour part-time; nonresident $16,572 full-time, $553 per credit hour part-time. Part-time tuition and fees vary according to course load. *Required fees:* $1498 full-time. *Room and board:* $6166; room only: $2868. Room and board charges vary according to board plan and housing facility. *Waivers:* senior citizens and employees or children of employees.

Financial Aid Of all full-time matriculated undergraduates who enrolled in 2008, 3,806 applied for aid, 1,598 were judged to have need, 1,056 had their need fully met. In 2008, 175 non-need-based awards were made. *Average percent of need met:* 79%. *Average financial aid package:* $8400. *Average need-based loan:* $5500. *Average need-based gift aid:* $2000. *Average non-need-based aid:* $1500. *Average indebtedness upon graduation:* $9885.

Applying *Options:* electronic application, early admission. *Application fee:* $30. *Required:* high school transcript, minimum 2 GPA, proof of immunization. *Application deadlines:* 7/1 (freshmen), rolling (transfers). *Notification:* continuous (freshmen), continuous (transfers).

Freshman Application Contact Jennifer Chadwick, Director of Admissions, North Georgia College & State University, Admissions Center, Dahlonega, GA 30533. *Phone:* 706-864-1800. *Toll-free phone:* 800-498-9581. *Fax:* 706-864-

1478. *E-mail:* admissions@northgeorgia.edu. *Web site:* http://www.northgeorgia.edu/.

Oglethorpe University
Atlanta, Georgia

- **Independent** comprehensive, founded 1835
- **Suburban** 102-acre campus
- **Coed** 1,084 undergraduate students, 92% full-time, 60% women, 40% men
- **Very difficult** entrance level, 86% of applicants were admitted

Undergraduates 993 full-time, 91 part-time. 28% are from out of state; 24% Black or African American, non-Hispanic/Latino; 6% Hispanic/Latino; 4% Asian, non-Hispanic/Latino; 0.4% Native Hawaiian or other Pacific Islander, non-Hispanic/Latino; 0.5% American Indian or Alaska Native, non-Hispanic/Latino; 2% Two or more races, non-Hispanic/Latino; 16% Race/ethnicity unknown; 3% international; 5% transferred in; 62% live on campus. *Retention:* 78% of full-time freshmen returned.

Freshmen *Admission:* 2,443 applied, 2,111 admitted, 230 enrolled. *Average high school GPA:* 3.53. *Test scores:* SAT critical reading scores over 500: 86%; SAT math scores over 500: 80%; SAT writing scores over 500: 77%; ACT scores over 18: 97%; SAT critical reading scores over 600: 37%; SAT math scores over 600: 30%; SAT writing scores over 600: 27%; ACT scores over 24: 62%; SAT critical reading scores over 700: 8%; SAT math scores over 700: 2%; SAT writing scores over 700: 3%; ACT scores over 30: 13%.

Faculty *Total:* 111, 44% full-time, 86% with terminal degrees. *Student/faculty ratio:* 16:1.

Academics *Calendar:* semesters. *Degrees:* bachelor's and master's. *Special study options:* accelerated degree program, adult/continuing education programs, advanced placement credit, cooperative education, double majors, honors programs, independent study, internships, off-campus study, part-time degree program, services for LD students, student-designed majors, study abroad, summer session for credit. *ROTC:* Air Force (c). *Unusual degree programs:* 3-2 engineering with Auburn University, Georgia Institute of Technology, University of Florida, University of Southern California.

Computers on Campus Students can access the following: campus intranet, computer help desk, free student e-mail accounts, online (class) grades, online (class) registration, online (class) schedules. Campuswide network is available. 100% of college-owned or -operated housing units are wired for high-speed Internet access. Wireless service is available via classrooms, computer centers, computer labs, learning centers, libraries, student centers.

Student Life *Housing:* on-campus residence required through sophomore year. *Options:* coed. Campus housing is university owned. Freshman campus housing is guaranteed. *Activities and organizations:* drama/theater group, student-run newspaper, radio station, choral group, national fraternities, national sororities. *Campus security:* 24-hour emergency response devices and patrols, late-night transport/escort service, controlled dormitory access. *Student services:* health clinic, personal/psychological counseling.

Athletics Member NCAA. All Division III. *Intercollegiate sports:* baseball M, basketball M/W, cross-country running M/W, golf M/W, lacrosse M, soccer M/W, tennis M/W, track and field M/W, volleyball W. *Intramural sports:* badminton M/W, basketball M/W, football M/W, softball M/W, table tennis M/W, ultimate Frisbee M/W, volleyball M/W.

Standardized Tests *Required:* SAT or ACT (for admission).

Costs (2011–12) *Comprehensive fee:* $37,940 includes full-time tuition ($27,700), mandatory fees ($250), and room and board ($9990). Full-time tuition and fees vary according to degree level and program. Part-time tuition and fees vary according to course load, degree level, and program. *Room and board:* Room and board charges vary according to housing facility and location. *Payment plans:* tuition prepayment, installment. *Waivers:* employees or children of employees.

Financial Aid Of all full-time matriculated undergraduates who enrolled in 2009, 813 applied for aid, 731 were judged to have need, 111 had their need fully met. In 2009, 192 non-need-based awards were made. *Average percent of need met:* 75%. *Average financial aid package:* $23,960. *Average need-based loan:* $3318. *Average need-based gift aid:* $19,668. *Average non-need-based aid:* $13,384.

Applying *Options:* electronic application, early admission, early action, deferred entrance. *Application fee:* $35. *Required:* essay or personal statement, high school transcript, 1 letter of recommendation. *Required for some:* interview. *Recommended:* minimum 2.5 GPA, interview. *Application deadlines:* rolling (freshmen), rolling (transfers), 12/5 (early action). *Notification:* continuous (freshmen), continuous (transfers), 12/20 (early action).

Freshman Application Contact Ms. Lucy Leusch, Vice President for Enrollment and Financial Aid, Oglethorpe University, 4484 Peachtree Road,

NE, Atlanta, GA 30319. *Phone:* 404-364-8307. *Toll-free phone:* 800-428-4484. *Fax:* 404-364-8491. *E-mail:* admission@oglethorpe.edu. *Web site:* http://www.oglethorpe.edu/.

Paine College
Augusta, Georgia

- **Independent Methodist** 4-year, founded 1882
- **Urban** 65-acre campus with easy access to Atlanta
- **Endowment** $8.1 million
- **Coed** 925 undergraduate students, 94% full-time, 64% women, 36% men
- **Minimally difficult** entrance level, 41% of applicants were admitted

Undergraduates 874 full-time, 51 part-time. Students come from 32 states and territories; 5 other countries; 22% are from out of state; 96% Black or African American, non-Hispanic/Latino; 0.6% Hispanic/Latino; 0.1% Asian, non-Hispanic/Latino; 0.1% American Indian or Alaska Native, non-Hispanic/Latino; 2% Race/ethnicity unknown; 0.3% international; 5% transferred in; 58% live on campus. *Retention:* 65% of full-time freshmen returned.

Freshmen *Admission:* 3,475 applied, 1,422 admitted, 218 enrolled. *Average high school GPA:* 2.7. *Test scores:* SAT critical reading scores over 500: 7%; SAT math scores over 500: 5%; SAT writing scores over 500: 6%; ACT scores over 18: 20%; SAT critical reading scores over 600: 1%; SAT math scores over 600: 1%; SAT writing scores over 600: 1%; ACT scores over 24: 3%.

Faculty *Total:* 85, 74% full-time, 60% with terminal degrees. *Student/faculty ratio:* 12:1.

Academics *Calendar:* semesters. *Degree:* bachelor's. *Special study options:* academic remediation for entering students, accelerated degree program, advanced placement credit, cooperative education, distance learning, double majors, honors programs, independent study, internships, off-campus study, part-time degree program, study abroad, summer session for credit. *ROTC:* Army (c). *Unusual degree programs:* 3-2 engineering with Tennessee State University, Tuskegee University.

Computers on Campus 130 computers/terminals and 696 ports are available on campus for general student use. Students can access the following: campus intranet, computer help desk, free student e-mail accounts, online (class) grades, online (class) registration, online (class) schedules. Campuswide network is available. 100% of college-owned or -operated housing units are wired for high-speed Internet access. Wireless service is available via classrooms, computer centers, computer labs, learning centers, libraries.

Student Life *Housing options:* men-only, women-only. Campus housing is university owned. Freshman applicants given priority for college housing. *Activities and organizations:* drama/theater group, student-run newspaper, choral group, NAACP, Expressions, Pre-alumni council, Wesley Fellowship, International Student Association, national fraternities, national sororities. *Campus security:* 24-hour emergency response devices and patrols, late-night transport/escort service. *Student services:* health clinic, personal/psychological counseling.

Athletics Member NCAA. All Division II. *Intercollegiate sports:* baseball M(s), basketball M(s)/W(s), cross-country running M(s)/W(s), golf M(s), softball W(s), track and field M(s)/W(s), volleyball W(s). *Intramural sports:* baseball M, basketball M/W, cheerleading M/W, football M, soccer M/W, softball M/W, table tennis M/W, tennis M/W, track and field M/W, volleyball M/W, weight lifting M/W.

Standardized Tests *Required:* SAT or ACT (for admission).

Costs (2010–11) *Comprehensive fee:* $17,542 includes full-time tuition ($10,896), mandatory fees ($898), and room and board ($5748). Full-time tuition and fees vary according to course load, location, and reciprocity agreements. Part-time tuition: $454 per credit hour. Part-time tuition and fees vary according to course load, location, and reciprocity agreements. *Room and board:* Room and board charges vary according to gender and housing facility. *Payment plans:* installment, deferred payment. *Waivers:* children of alumni and employees or children of employees.

Financial Aid *Average indebtedness upon graduation:* $2304.

Applying *Options:* electronic application, early admission, deferred entrance. *Application fee:* $25. *Required:* essay or personal statement, high school transcript, minimum 2 GPA, 3 letters of recommendation. *Required for some:* score of 500 on each Georgia high school exit exam. *Application deadlines:* 8/1 (freshmen), 8/1 (out-of-state freshmen), 8/1 (transfers). *Notification:* continuous (freshmen), continuous (out-of-state freshmen), continuous (transfers).

Freshman Application Contact Mr. Joseph D. Tinsley, Director of Admissions, Paine College, 1235 15th Street, Augusta, GA 30901-3182. *Phone:* 706-821-8320. *Toll-free phone:* 800-476-7703. *Fax:* 706-821-8691. *E-mail:* jtinsley@paine.edu. *Web site:* http://www.paine.edu/.

Piedmont College

Demorest, Georgia

- **Independent** comprehensive, founded 1897, affiliated with United Church of Christ
- **Rural** 186-acre campus with easy access to Atlanta
- **Endowment** $43.3 million
- **Coed** 1,256 undergraduate students, 86% full-time, 69% women, 31% men
- **Moderately difficult** entrance level, 61% of applicants were admitted

Undergraduates 1,079 full-time, 177 part-time. Students come from 44 states and territories; 8 other countries; 3% are from out of state; 11% Black or African American, non-Hispanic/Latino; 2% Hispanic/Latino; 1% Asian, non-Hispanic/Latino; 0.6% American Indian or Alaska Native, non-Hispanic/Latino; 2% Race/ethnicity unknown; 0.3% international; 9% transferred in; 42% live on campus. *Retention:* 67% of full-time freshmen returned.

Freshmen *Admission:* 947 applied, 579 admitted, 323 enrolled. *Average high school GPA:* 3.41. *Test scores:* SAT critical reading scores over 500: 56%; SAT math scores over 500: 54%; ACT scores over 18: 91%; SAT critical reading scores over 600: 12%; SAT math scores over 600: 15%; ACT scores over 24: 27%; ACT scores over 30: 2%.

Faculty *Total:* 218, 51% full-time, 76% with terminal degrees. *Student/faculty ratio:* 14:1.

Academics *Calendar:* semesters. *Degrees:* bachelor's, master's, doctoral-professional, and post-master's certificates. *Special study options:* accelerated degree program, adult/continuing education programs, advanced placement credit, cooperative education, distance learning, double majors, honors programs, independent study, internships, off-campus study, part-time degree program, services for LD students, student-designed majors, study abroad, summer session for credit.

Computers on Campus 150 computers/terminals are available on campus for general student use. Students can access the following: free student e-mail accounts, online (class) grades, online (class) schedules. Campuswide network is available. Wireless service is available via classrooms, computer labs, learning centers, libraries, student centers.

Student Life *Housing:* on-campus residence required through sophomore year. *Options:* coed, men-only, women-only, disabled students. Campus housing is university owned. Freshman campus housing is guaranteed. *Activities and organizations:* drama/theater group, student-run newspaper, radio and television station, choral group, Campus Activity Board, Residence Hall Council, Outdoor Club, Team Piedmont, Alpha PSI Omega. *Campus security:* 24-hour emergency response devices and patrols, late-night transport/escort service. *Student services:* personal/psychological counseling.

Athletics Member NCAA. All Division III. *Intercollegiate sports:* baseball M, basketball M/W, cross-country running M/W, golf M/W, lacrosse M/W, soccer M/W, softball W, tennis M/W, volleyball W.

Standardized Tests *Required:* SAT or ACT (for admission).

Costs (2011–12) *Comprehensive fee:* $26,500 includes full-time tuition ($19,000) and room and board ($7500). Full-time tuition and fees vary according to course load, degree level, location, and program. Part-time tuition: $792 per semester hour. Part-time tuition and fees vary according to course load, degree level, location, and program. *Payment plan:* installment. *Waivers:* employees or children of employees.

Financial Aid Of all full-time matriculated undergraduates who enrolled in 2009, 955 applied for aid, 875 were judged to have need, 245 had their need fully met. 84 Federal Work-Study jobs (averaging $2404). 334 state and other part-time jobs (averaging $2389). In 2009, 179 non-need-based awards were made. *Average percent of need met:* 28%. *Average financial aid package:* $17,824. *Average need-based loan:* $1900. *Average need-based gift aid:* $5742. *Average non-need-based aid:* $10,532. *Average indebtedness upon graduation:* $18,402.

Applying *Options:* electronic application, early admission, deferred entrance. *Required:* high school transcript, minimum 2 GPA. *Required for some:* interview. *Recommended:* essay or personal statement. *Application deadlines:* 7/1 (freshmen), 7/1 (transfers).

Freshman Application Contact Ms. Cynthia L. Peterson, Director of Undergraduate Admissions, Piedmont College, PO Box 10, 165 Central Avenue, Demorest, GA 30535. *Phone:* 706-776-0103 Ext. 1188. *Toll-free phone:* 800-277-7020. *Fax:* 706-776-6635. *E-mail:* cpeterson@piedmont.edu. *Web site:* http://www.piedmont.edu/.

Reinhardt University

Waleska, Georgia

- **Independent** comprehensive, founded 1883, affiliated with United Methodist Church
- **Rural** 600-acre campus with easy access to Atlanta
- **Endowment** $34.6 million
- **Coed** 1,102 undergraduate students, 94% full-time, 57% women, 43% men
- **Moderately difficult** entrance level, 58% of applicants were admitted

Undergraduates 1,033 full-time, 69 part-time. Students come from 19 states and territories; 23 other countries; 4% are from out of state; 12% Black or African American, non-Hispanic/Latino; 3% Hispanic/Latino; 1% Asian, non-Hispanic/Latino; 0.5% American Indian or Alaska Native, non-Hispanic/Latino; 6% Race/ethnicity unknown; 0.1% international; 10% transferred in; 49% live on campus. *Retention:* 58% of full-time freshmen returned.

Freshmen *Admission:* 1,395 applied, 808 admitted, 245 enrolled. *Average high school GPA:* 2.94. *Test scores:* SAT critical reading scores over 500: 44%; SAT math scores over 500: 43%; SAT critical reading scores over 600: 14%; SAT math scores over 600: 7%; SAT critical reading scores over 700: 2%.

Faculty *Total:* 174, 36% full-time, 53% with terminal degrees. *Student/faculty ratio:* 12:1.

Academics *Calendar:* semesters. *Degrees:* associate, bachelor's, and master's. *Special study options:* academic remediation for entering students, adult/continuing education programs, advanced placement credit, cooperative education, distance learning, double majors, freshman honors college, honors programs, independent study, internships, off-campus study, part-time degree program, services for LD students, student-designed majors, study abroad, summer session for credit.

Computers on Campus 164 computers/terminals and 164 ports are available on campus for general student use. Students can access the following: campus intranet, computer help desk, free student e-mail accounts, online (class) grades, online (class) registration, online (class) schedules. Campuswide network is available. 100% of college-owned or -operated housing units are wired for high-speed Internet access. Wireless service is available via classrooms, computer centers, computer labs, dorm rooms, learning centers, libraries, student centers.

Student Life *Housing:* on-campus residence required for freshman year. *Options:* coed, men-only, women-only, disabled students. Campus housing is university owned. Freshman campus housing is guaranteed. *Activities and organizations:* drama/theater group, student-run newspaper, television station, choral group, Real Deal, International and Historical Film Society, Student Government Association, SOAR (Student Orientation Leaders), Communication Club. *Campus security:* 24-hour emergency response devices and patrols, late-night transport/escort service, controlled dormitory access. *Student services:* health clinic, personal/psychological counseling.

Athletics Member NAIA. *Intercollegiate sports:* baseball M(s), basketball M(s)/W(s), cross-country running M(s)/W(s), golf M(s), lacrosse M/W, soccer M(s)/W(s), softball W(s), tennis M(s)/W(s), volleyball W. *Intramural sports:* basketball M/W, cheerleading M/W, football M/W, soccer M/W, softball M/W, volleyball M/W.

Standardized Tests *Required:* SAT or ACT (for admission).

Costs (2011–12) *Comprehensive fee:* $24,420 includes full-time tuition ($17,500), mandatory fees ($340), and room and board ($6580). Full-time tuition and fees vary according to location and program. Part-time tuition: $592 per credit hour. Part-time tuition and fees vary according to course load, location, and program. *Room and board:* Room and board charges vary according to board plan and housing facility. *Payment plan:* installment. *Waivers:* senior citizens and employees or children of employees.

Financial Aid Of all full-time matriculated undergraduates who enrolled in 2009, 759 applied for aid, 674 were judged to have need, 56 had their need fully met. 97 Federal Work-Study jobs (averaging $574). 98 state and other part-time jobs (averaging $579). In 2009, 246 non-need-based awards were made. *Average percent of need met:* 27%. *Average financial aid package:* $9500. *Average need-based loan:* $3631. *Average need-based gift aid:* $7403. *Average non-need-based aid:* $5384. *Average indebtedness upon graduation:* $21,095.

Applying *Options:* electronic application, early admission, deferred entrance. *Application fee:* $25. *Required:* high school transcript, minimum 2 GPA. *Application deadlines:* rolling (freshmen), rolling (transfers). *Notification:* continuous (freshmen), continuous (transfers).

Freshman Application Contact Ms. Julie Fleming, Director of Admissions, Reinhardt University, 7300 Reinhardt College Circle, Waleska, GA 30183-0128. *Phone:* 770-720-5526. *Fax:* 770-720-5602. *E-mail:* admissions@mail.reinhardt.edu. *Web site:* http://www.reinhardt.edu/.

Savannah College of Art and Design

Savannah, Georgia

- **Independent** comprehensive, founded 1978
- **Urban** campus
- **Coed** 8,478 undergraduate students, 87% full-time, 62% women, 38% men
- **Moderately difficult** entrance level, 62% of applicants were admitted

Undergraduates 7,370 full-time, 1,108 part-time. Students come from 55 states and territories; 94 other countries; 76% are from out of state; 6% Black or African American, non-Hispanic/Latino; 3% Hispanic/Latino; 2% Asian, non-Hispanic/Latino; 0.1% Native Hawaiian or other Pacific Islander, non-Hispanic/Latino; 0.3% American Indian or Alaska Native, non-Hispanic/Latino; 0.3% Two or more races, non-Hispanic/Latino; 45% Race/ethnicity unknown; 9% international; 9% transferred in; 42% live on campus. *Retention:* 82% of full-time freshmen returned.

Freshmen *Admission:* 9,235 applied, 5,717 admitted, 1,690 enrolled. *Average high school GPA:* 3.42. *Test scores:* SAT critical reading scores over 500: 70%; SAT math scores over 500: 63%; SAT writing scores over 500: 64%; ACT scores over 18: 95%; SAT critical reading scores over 600: 29%; SAT math scores over 600: 21%; SAT writing scores over 600: 22%; ACT scores over 24: 47%; SAT critical reading scores over 700: 4%; SAT math scores over 700: 3%; SAT writing scores over 700: 3%; ACT scores over 30: 6%.

Faculty *Total:* 720, 72% full-time, 73% with terminal degrees. *Student/faculty ratio:* 16:1.

Academics *Calendar:* quarters. *Degrees:* certificates, bachelor's, master's, and postbachelor's certificates. *Special study options:* advanced placement credit, distance learning, double majors, English as a second language, independent study, internships, off-campus study, part-time degree program, services for LD students, study abroad, summer session for credit. *ROTC:* Army (c).

Computers on Campus 3,400 computers/terminals are available on campus for general student use. Students can access the following: campus intranet, computer help desk, free student e-mail accounts, online (class) grades, online (class) registration, online (class) schedules. Campuswide network is available. 100% of college-owned or -operated housing units are wired for high-speed Internet access. Wireless service is available via classrooms, computer centers, computer labs, dorm rooms, libraries, student centers.

Student Life *Housing options:* coed, women-only. Campus housing is university owned and leased by the school. Freshman applicants given priority for college housing. *Activities and organizations:* drama/theater group, student-run newspaper, radio station, choral group, Fashion Haus, Contemporary Animation Society, Christian Student Fellowship, SCAD Swing Club, Digital Media Club. *Campus security:* 24-hour emergency response devices and patrols, student patrols, late-night transport/escort service, controlled dormitory access, video camera surveillance. *Student services:* health clinic, personal/psychological counseling.

Athletics Member NCAA, NAIA. All NCAA Division I. *Intercollegiate sports:* baseball M(s), cheerleading M(c)/W(c), cross-country running M(s)/W(s), equestrian sports M(s)/W(s), fencing M(c)/W(c), golf M(s)/W(s), lacrosse W(s), soccer M(s)/W(s), softball W(s), swimming and diving M(s)/W(s), tennis M(s)/W(s), volleyball W(s). *Intramural sports:* basketball M/W, equestrian sports M(c)/W(c), lacrosse M(c), softball M/W, tennis M/W, ultimate Frisbee M/W, volleyball M/W.

Standardized Tests *Required:* SAT or ACT (for admission).

Costs (2011–12) *Comprehensive fee:* $43,265 includes full-time tuition ($30,510), mandatory fees ($500), and room and board ($12,255). Full-time tuition and fees vary according to course load, degree level, and location. Part-time tuition: $678 per quarter hour. Part-time tuition and fees vary according to course load, degree level, and location. *Room and board:* Room and board charges vary according to board plan, housing facility, and location. *Payment plan:* installment. *Waivers:* employees or children of employees.

Financial Aid Of all full-time matriculated undergraduates who enrolled in 2009, 4,796 applied for aid, 4,272 were judged to have need, 364 had their need fully met. In 2009, 1999 non-need-based awards were made. *Average percent of need met:* 21%. *Average financial aid package:* $20,926. *Average need-based loan:* $4181. *Average need-based gift aid:* $5228. *Average non-need-based aid:* $9535. *Average indebtedness upon graduation:* $39,066.

Applying *Options:* electronic application, early admission, deferred entrance. *Application fee:* $35. *Required:* high school transcript, 3 letters of recommendation. *Required for some:* essay or personal statement, high school transcript, portfolio/audition. *Recommended:* interview. *Application deadlines:* rolling (freshmen), rolling (transfers). *Notification:* continuous (freshmen), continuous (transfers).

Freshman Application Contact Ms. Ginger Hansen, Executive Director of Recruitment, Savannah College of Art and Design, 342 Bull Street, PO Box 3146, Savannah, GA 31402-3146. *Phone:* 912-525-5100. *Toll-free phone:* 800-869-7223. *Fax:* 912-525-5983. *E-mail:* admission@scad.edu. *Web site:* http://www.scad.edu/.

Savannah State University

Savannah, Georgia

- **State-supported** comprehensive, founded 1890, part of University System of Georgia
- **Suburban** 173-acre campus
- **Endowment** $3.7 million
- **Coed** 3,941 undergraduate students, 87% full-time, 55% women, 45% men
- **Minimally difficult** entrance level, 35% of applicants were admitted

Undergraduates 3,421 full-time, 520 part-time. Students come from 37 states and territories; 33 other countries; 8% are from out of state; 90% Black or African American, non-Hispanic/Latino; 0.7% Hispanic/Latino; 0.3% Asian, non-Hispanic/Latino; 0.1% American Indian or Alaska Native, non-Hispanic/Latino; 0.4% Two or more races, non-Hispanic/Latino; 3% Race/ethnicity unknown; 0.8% international; 5% transferred in. *Retention:* 72% of full-time freshmen returned.

Freshmen *Admission:* 5,680 applied, 1,981 admitted, 990 enrolled. *Average high school GPA:* 2.8.

Faculty *Total:* 200, 79% full-time. *Student/faculty ratio:* 23:1.

Academics *Calendar:* semesters. *Degrees:* bachelor's and master's. *Special study options:* academic remediation for entering students, accelerated degree program, adult/continuing education programs, advanced placement credit, cooperative education, double majors, honors programs, independent study, internships, off-campus study, part-time degree program, services for LD students, study abroad, summer session for credit. *ROTC:* Army (b), Navy (b). *Unusual degree programs:* 3-2 engineering with Georgia Institute of Technology.

Computers on Campus 420 computers/terminals are available on campus for general student use. Students can access the following: campus intranet, computer help desk, free student e-mail accounts, online (class) grades, online (class) registration, online (class) schedules. Campuswide network is available. 100% of college-owned or -operated housing units are wired for high-speed Internet access. Wireless service is available via entire campus.

Student Life *Housing options:* coed, men-only. Campus housing is university owned. *Activities and organizations:* drama/theater group, student-run newspaper, radio and television station, choral group, marching band, Marching band, Gospel Choir, Concert Choir, Student Orientation Leaders (SOL), Tiger Ambassadors, national fraternities, national sororities. *Campus security:* 24-hour emergency response devices and patrols, late-night transport/escort service, controlled dormitory access. *Student services:* health clinic, personal/psychological counseling.

Athletics Member NCAA. All Division I. *Intercollegiate sports:* baseball M(s), basketball M(s)/W(s), cheerleading M(s)/W(s), cross-country running M(s)/W(s), football M(s), golf M(s)/W(s), softball W(s), tennis W(s), track and field M(s)/W(s), volleyball W(s). *Intramural sports:* basketball M/W, football M/W, softball M/W, swimming and diving M/W, table tennis M/W, tennis M/W, volleyball M/W, weight lifting M/W.

Standardized Tests *Required:* SAT or ACT (for admission). *Required for some:* SAT Subject Tests (for admission). *Recommended:* SAT (for admission).

Costs (2010–11) *Tuition:* state resident $4274 full-time, $143 per credit hour part-time; nonresident $15,888 full-time, $530 per credit hour part-time. Full-time tuition and fees vary according to course load and program. Part-time tuition and fees vary according to course load and program. *Required fees:* $1350 full-time, $675 per term part-time. *Room and board:* $6288; room only: $2868. Room and board charges vary according to board plan and housing facility. *Waivers:* senior citizens.

Applying *Options:* electronic application, early admission, deferred entrance. *Application fee:* $20. *Required:* high school transcript, minimum 2.3 GPA. *Required for some:* essay or personal statement, interview. *Application deadlines:* 7/15 (freshmen), 6/15 (transfers). *Notification:* continuous (freshmen), continuous (transfers).

Freshman Application Contact Mrs. Carol Dolan, Assistant Director of Admissions for Operations, Savannah State University, PO Box 20209, Savannah, GA 31404. *Phone:* 912-358-4014. *Toll-free phone:* 800-788-0478. *Fax:* 912-358-4517. *E-mail:* dolanc@savannahstate.edu. *Web site:* http://www.savannahstate.edu/.

PROFILES

Shorter University

Rome, Georgia

- **Independent Baptist** comprehensive, founded 1873
- **Small-town** 155-acre campus with easy access to Atlanta
- **Endowment** $20.1 million
- **Coed** 1,542 undergraduate students, 93% full-time, 51% women, 49% men
- **Moderately difficult** entrance level, 62% of applicants were admitted

Undergraduates 1,432 full-time, 110 part-time. Students come from 34 states and territories; 22 other countries; 16% are from out of state; 15% Black or African American, non-Hispanic/Latino; 4% Hispanic/Latino; 1% Asian, non-Hispanic/Latino; 0.3% American Indian or Alaska Native, non-Hispanic/Latino; 0.8% Two or more races, non-Hispanic/Latino; 5% Race/ethnicity unknown; 3% international; 7% transferred in; 54% live on campus. *Retention:* 75% of full-time freshmen returned.

Freshmen *Admission:* 1,934 applied, 1,204 admitted, 448 enrolled. *Average high school GPA:* 3.33. *Test scores:* SAT critical reading scores over 500: 43%; SAT math scores over 500: 48%; SAT writing scores over 500: 35%; ACT scores over 18: 88%; SAT critical reading scores over 600: 13%; SAT math scores over 600: 12%; SAT writing scores over 600: 9%; ACT scores over 24: 31%; SAT critical reading scores over 700: 2%; SAT math scores over 700: 1%; ACT scores over 30: 13%.

Faculty *Total:* 174, 49% full-time, 44% with terminal degrees. *Student/faculty ratio:* 13:1.

Academics *Calendar:* semesters. *Degrees:* bachelor's and master's. *Special study options:* academic remediation for entering students, adult/continuing education programs, advanced placement credit, double majors, honors programs, independent study, internships, off-campus study, part-time degree program, services for LD students, student-designed majors, study abroad, summer session for credit.

Computers on Campus 100 computers/terminals are available on campus for general student use. Students can access the following: campus intranet, computer help desk, free student e-mail accounts, online (class) grades, online (class) registration, online (class) schedules. Campuswide network is available. 100% of college-owned or -operated housing units are wired for high-speed Internet access. Wireless service is available via classrooms, computer centers, computer labs, dorm rooms, learning centers, libraries, student centers.

Student Life *Housing options:* men-only, women-only. Campus housing is university owned. Freshman applicants given priority for college housing. *Activities and organizations:* drama/theater group, student-run newspaper, radio and television station, choral group, marching band, Baptist Collegiate Ministries, Student Government Association, Fellowship of Christian Athletes, Habitat for Humanity, SAVE (Students Advocating Volunteer Efforts), national fraternities, national sororities. *Campus security:* 24-hour emergency response devices and patrols. *Student services:* health clinic, personal/psychological counseling.

Athletics Member NAIA. *Intercollegiate sports:* baseball M(s), basketball M(s)/W(s), cheerleading M(s)/W(s), cross-country running M(s)/W(s), football M(s), golf M(s)/W(s), soccer M(s)/W(s), softball W(s), tennis M(s)/W(s), track and field M(s)/W(s), volleyball W(s). *Intramural sports:* basketball M/W, bowling M/W, soccer M/W, table tennis M/W, tennis M/W, ultimate Frisbee M/W, volleyball W.

Standardized Tests *Required:* SAT or ACT (for admission).

Costs (2011–12) *One-time required fee:* $99. *Comprehensive fee:* $25,270 includes full-time tuition ($16,700), mandatory fees ($370), and room and board ($8200). Full-time tuition and fees vary according to course load. Part-time tuition: $460 per credit hour. *College room only:* $4400. Room and board charges vary according to board plan and housing facility. *Payment plan:* installment. *Waivers:* senior citizens and employees or children of employees.

Financial Aid Of all full-time matriculated undergraduates who enrolled in 2009, 1,004 applied for aid, 857 were judged to have need, 238 had their need fully met. In 2009, 186 non-need-based awards were made. *Average percent of need met:* 71%. *Average financial aid package:* $15,152. *Average need-based loan:* $3939. *Average need-based gift aid:* $12,411. *Average non-need-based aid:* $4845. *Average indebtedness upon graduation:* $22,967.

Applying *Options:* electronic application, early admission, deferred entrance. *Application fee:* $25. *Required:* essay or personal statement, high school transcript. *Required for some:* interview, audition for music and theater programs. *Recommended:* minimum 2 GPA, 1 letter of recommendation, interview. *Application deadlines:* 8/25 (freshmen), 8/25 (transfers). *Notification:* continuous (freshmen), continuous (transfers).

Freshman Application Contact Shorter University, 315 Shorter Avenue, Rome, GA 30165. *Phone:* 706-233-7342. *Toll-free phone:* 800-868-6980. *Web site:* http://www.shorter.edu/.

See page 1604 for the College Close-Up.

Southern Polytechnic State University
Marietta, Georgia

- **State-supported** comprehensive, founded 1948, part of University System of Georgia
- **Suburban** 203-acre campus with easy access to Atlanta
- **Endowment** $2.7 million
- **Coed** 4,812 undergraduate students, 71% full-time, 20% women, 80% men
- **Moderately difficult** entrance level, 77% of applicants were admitted

Undergraduates 3,440 full-time, 1,372 part-time. Students come from 21 states and territories; 54 other countries; 2% are from out of state; 21% Black or African American, non-Hispanic/Latino; 6% Hispanic/Latino; 5% Asian, non-Hispanic/Latino; 0.1% Native Hawaiian or other Pacific Islander, non-Hispanic/Latino; 0.4% American Indian or Alaska Native, non-Hispanic/Latino; 3% Two or more races, non-Hispanic/Latino; 2% Race/ethnicity unknown; 6% international; 13% transferred in; 30% live on campus. *Retention:* 74% of full-time freshmen returned.

Freshmen *Admission:* 1,326 applied, 1,018 admitted, 611 enrolled. *Average high school GPA:* 3.24. *Test scores:* SAT critical reading scores over 500: 77%; SAT math scores over 500: 90%; SAT writing scores over 500: 56%; ACT scores over 18: 98%; SAT critical reading scores over 600: 24%; SAT math scores over 600: 42%; SAT writing scores over 600: 12%; ACT scores over 24: 39%; SAT critical reading scores over 700: 3%; SAT math scores over 700: 8%; ACT scores over 30: 6%.

Faculty *Total:* 287, 65% full-time, 59% with terminal degrees. *Student/faculty ratio:* 20:1.

Academics *Calendar:* semesters. *Degrees:* certificates, associate, bachelor's, master's, and postbachelor's certificates. *Special study options:* advanced placement credit, cooperative education, distance learning, double majors, honors programs, independent study, internships, off-campus study, part-time degree program, services for LD students, student-designed majors, study abroad, summer session for credit. *ROTC:* Army (c), Navy (c), Air Force (c).

Computers on Campus 1,400 computers/terminals and 50 ports are available on campus for general student use. Students can access the following: computer help desk, free student e-mail accounts, online (class) grades, online (class) registration, online (class) schedules. Campuswide network is available. 100% of college-owned or -operated housing units are wired for high-speed Internet access. Wireless service is available via classrooms, computer centers, computer labs, dorm rooms, learning centers, libraries, student centers.

Student Life *Housing options:* coed, cooperative, disabled students. Campus housing is university owned and is provided by a third party. Freshman applicants given priority for college housing. *Activities and organizations:* student-run newspaper, radio station, choral group, International Student Association, Campus Activities Board, National Society of Black Engineers, Baptist Collegiate Ministries, American Society of Civil Engineers, national fraternities, national sororities. *Campus security:* 24-hour emergency response devices and patrols, late-night transport/escort service, controlled dormitory access. *Student services:* health clinic, personal/psychological counseling.

Athletics Member NAIA. *Intercollegiate sports:* baseball M(s), basketball M(s)/W(s), cheerleading M/W, soccer M(s). *Intramural sports:* badminton M/W, basketball M/W, football M/W, golf M/W, racquetball M/W, soccer M/W, softball M/W, ultimate Frisbee M/W, volleyball M/W.

Standardized Tests *Required:* SAT or ACT (for admission).

Costs (2010–11) *Tuition:* state resident $4980 full-time, $166 per semester hour part-time; nonresident $18,120 full-time, $604 per semester hour part-time. Full-time tuition and fees vary according to course load. Part-time tuition and fees vary according to course load. *Required fees:* $1196 full-time, $598 per term part-time. *Room and board:* $6604; room only: $3650. Room and board charges vary according to housing facility. *Waivers:* senior citizens and employees or children of employees.

Financial Aid Of all full-time matriculated undergraduates who enrolled in 2009, 2,657 applied for aid, 2,145 were judged to have need, 457 had their need fully met. 215 Federal Work-Study jobs (averaging $4000). *Average percent of need met:* 72%. *Average financial aid package:* $3655. *Average need-based loan:* $4691. *Average need-based gift aid:* $3743. *Average indebtedness upon graduation:* $24,360.

Applying *Options:* electronic application, deferred entrance. *Application fee:* $20. *Required:* high school transcript, minimum 2.5 GPA, Proof of immunization, SAT/ACT Scores, International Students have additional requirements, 18 academic CPC units. *Application deadlines:* 7/1 (freshmen), 7/1 (out-of-state freshmen), 7/1 (transfers). *Notification:* continuous (freshmen), continuous (out-of-state freshmen), continuous (transfers).

Freshman Application Contact Mr. Gary Bush, Director of Admissions, Southern Polytechnic State University, 1100 South Marietta Parkway, Marietta, GA 30060. *Phone:* 678-915-7468. *Toll-free phone:* 800-635-3204. *Fax:* 678-915-7292. *E-mail:* gbush@spsu.edu. *Web site:* http://www.spsu.edu/.

South University
Savannah, Georgia

- **Proprietary** comprehensive, founded 1899, part of Education Management Corporation
- **Coed**

Academics *Calendar:* quarters. *Degrees:* associate, bachelor's, master's, and doctoral-research/scholarship.

Costs (2010–11) *Tuition:* Information about tuition and fees can be obtained by contacting the South University Admissions Office.

Freshman Application Contact South University, 709 Mall Boulevard, Savannah, GA 31406. *Phone:* 912-201-8000. *Toll-free phone:* 866-629-2901. *Web site:* http://www.southuniversity.edu/savannah/.

See page 1626 for the College Close-Up.

Spelman College
Atlanta, Georgia

- **Independent** 4-year, founded 1881
- **Urban** 32-acre campus with easy access to Atlanta
- **Women only** 2,177 undergraduate students, 96% full-time
- **Very difficult** entrance level, 39% of applicants were admitted

Undergraduates 2,080 full-time, 97 part-time. 71% are from out of state; 88% Black or African American, non-Hispanic/Latino; 0.1% Hispanic/Latino; 0.1% Asian, non-Hispanic/Latino; 0.1% American Indian or Alaska Native, non-Hispanic/Latino; 3% Two or more races, non-Hispanic/Latino; 9% Race/ethnicity unknown; 0.6% international; 2% transferred in; 40% live on campus. *Retention:* 88% of full-time freshmen returned.

Freshmen *Admission:* 5,129 applied, 2,010 admitted, 539 enrolled. *Average high school GPA:* 3.56. *Test scores:* SAT critical reading scores over 500: 67%; SAT math scores over 500: 54%; ACT scores over 18: 94%; SAT critical reading scores over 600: 16%; SAT math scores over 600: 9%; ACT scores over 24: 28%; SAT critical reading scores over 700: 2%; SAT math scores over 700: 1%; ACT scores over 30: 1%.

Faculty *Total:* 255, 72% full-time. *Student/faculty ratio:* 10:1.

Academics *Calendar:* semesters. *Degree:* bachelor's. *Special study options:* academic remediation for entering students, adult/continuing education programs, advanced placement credit, distance learning, double majors, honors programs, independent study, internships, off-campus study, part-time degree program, services for LD students, student-designed majors, study abroad. *ROTC:* Army (c), Navy (b), Air Force (c). *Unusual degree programs:* 3-2 engineering with North Carolina Agricultural and Technical State University, Rensselaer Polytechnic Institute, Georgia Institute of Technology, Boston University, The University of Alabama in Huntsville, Auburn University.

Computers on Campus Students can access the following: online (class) registration. Campuswide network is available.

Student Life *Housing:* on-campus residence required for freshman year. *Options:* women-only. Campus housing is university owned and leased by the school. Freshman applicants given priority for college housing. *Activities and organizations:* drama/theater group, student-run newspaper, choral group, national sororities. *Campus security:* 24-hour emergency response devices and patrols, late-night transport/escort service, controlled dormitory access. *Student services:* health clinic, personal/psychological counseling, women's center.

Athletics Member NCAA. *Intercollegiate sports:* basketball W, cross-country running W, golf W, soccer W, tennis W, track and field W, volleyball W. *Intramural sports:* softball W, swimming and diving W.

Standardized Tests *Required:* SAT or ACT (for admission).

Costs (2010–11) *One-time required fee:* $250. *Comprehensive fee:* $32,474 includes full-time tuition ($18,709), mandatory fees ($3301), and room and board ($10,464). Part-time tuition: $780 per credit hour. *College room only:* $6706. *Payment plan:* deferred payment. *Waivers:* employees or children of employees.

Financial Aid Of all full-time matriculated undergraduates who enrolled in 2007, 2,089 applied for aid, 1,618 were judged to have need, 388 had their need fully met. In 2007, 48 non-need-based awards were made. *Average financial aid package:* $12,691. *Average need-based loan:* $2645. *Average need-based gift aid:* $6073. *Average non-need-based aid:* $5288. *Average indebtedness upon graduation:* $17,500.

Applying *Options:* electronic application, early decision, early action. *Application fee:* $35. *Required:* essay or personal statement, high school transcript, minimum 2 GPA, 2 letters of recommendation. *Required for some:* interview. *Application deadlines:* 2/1 (freshmen), 4/1 (transfers), 11/15 (early action). *Early decision deadline:* 11/1. *Notification:* 4/1 (freshmen), 5/1 (transfers), 12/15 (early decision), 12/31 (early action).

Freshman Application Contact Ms. Arlene Cash, Vice President for Admissions and Orientation, Spelman College, 350 Spelman Lane, SW, Atlanta, GA 30314-4399. *Phone:* 404-681-3643. *Toll-free phone:* 800-982-

2411. *Fax:* 404-270-5201. *E-mail:* admiss@spelman.edu. *Web site:* http://www.spelman.edu/.

Strayer University - Augusta Campus
Augusta, Georgia

- **Proprietary** comprehensive
- **Coed**

Academics *Degrees:* certificates, diplomas, associate, bachelor's, master's, and postbachelor's certificates.
Costs (2010–11) *Tuition:* $13,635 full-time, $1590 per course part-time.
Freshman Application Contact Strayer University - Augusta Campus, 1330 Augusta West Parkway, Augusta, GA 30909. *Web site:* http://www.strayer.edu/augusta/.

Strayer University - Chamblee Campus
Atlanta, Georgia

- **Proprietary** comprehensive
- **Coed**

Academics *Degrees:* certificates, diplomas, associate, bachelor's, master's, and postbachelor's certificates.
Costs (2010–11) *Tuition:* $13,635 full-time, $1590 per course part-time.
Freshman Application Contact Strayer University - Chamblee Campus, 3355 Northeast Expressway, Suite 100, Atlanta, GA 30341. *Web site:* http://www.strayer.edu/chamblee/.

Strayer University - Cobb County Campus
Atlanta, Georgia

- **Proprietary** comprehensive
- **Coed**

Academics *Degrees:* certificates, diplomas, associate, bachelor's, master's, and postbachelor's certificates.
Costs (2010–11) *Tuition:* $13,635 full-time, $1590 per course part-time.
Freshman Application Contact Strayer University - Cobb County Campus, 3101 Towercreek Parkway, SE, Suite 700, Atlanta, GA 30339-3256. *Web site:* http://www.strayer.edu/cobb_county/.

Strayer University - Columbus Campus
Columbus, Georgia

- **Proprietary** comprehensive
- **Coed**

Academics *Degrees:* certificates, diplomas, associate, bachelor's, master's, and postbachelor's certificates.
Freshman Application Contact Strayer University - Columbus Campus, 6003 Veterans Parkway, Suite 100, Columbus, GA 31909. *Web site:* http://www.strayer.edu/columbus_ga/.

Strayer University - Douglasville Campus
Douglasville, Georgia

- **Proprietary** comprehensive
- **Coed**

Academics *Degrees:* certificates, diplomas, associate, bachelor's, master's, and postbachelor's certificates.
Costs (2010–11) *Tuition:* $13,635 full-time, $1590 per course part-time.
Freshman Application Contact Strayer University - Douglasville Campus, 4655 Timber Ridge Drive, Douglasville, GA 30135. *Web site:* http://www.strayer.edu/douglasville/.

Strayer University - Lithonia Campus
Lithonia, Georgia

- **Proprietary** comprehensive
- **Coed**

Academics *Degrees:* certificates, diplomas, associate, bachelor's, master's, and postbachelor's certificates.
Costs (2010–11) *Tuition:* $13,635 full-time, $1590 per course part-time.

Freshman Application Contact Strayer University - Lithonia Campus, 3120 Stonecrest Boulevard, Suite 200, Lithonia, GA 30038. *Web site:* http://www.strayer.edu/lithonia/.

Strayer University - Morrow Campus
Morrow, Georgia

- **Proprietary** comprehensive
- **Coed**

Academics *Degrees:* certificates, diplomas, associate, bachelor's, master's, and postbachelor's certificates.
Costs (2010–11) *Tuition:* $13,635 full-time, $1590 per course part-time.
Freshman Application Contact Strayer University - Morrow Campus, 3000 Corporate Center Drive, Suite 100, Morrow, GA 30260. *Web site:* http://www.strayer.edu/morrow.

Strayer University - Roswell Campus
Roswell, Georgia

- **Proprietary** comprehensive
- **Coed**

Academics *Degrees:* certificates, diplomas, associate, bachelor's, master's, and postbachelor's certificates.
Costs (2010–11) *Tuition:* $13,635 full-time, $1590 per course part-time.
Freshman Application Contact Strayer University - Roswell Campus, 100 Mansell Court East, Suite 100, Roswell, GA 30076. *Web site:* http://www.strayer.edu/roswell.

Strayer University - Savannah Campus
Savannah, Georgia

- **Proprietary** comprehensive
- **Coed**

Academics *Degrees:* certificates, diplomas, associate, bachelor's, master's, and postbachelor's certificates.
Costs (2010–11) *Tuition:* $13,635 full-time, $1590 per course part-time.
Freshman Application Contact Strayer University - Savannah Campus, 20 Martin Court, Savannah, GA 31419. *Web site:* http://www.strayer.edu/savannah/.

Thomas University
Thomasville, Georgia

- **Independent** comprehensive, founded 1950
- **Small-town** 24-acre campus
- **Endowment** $3.3 million
- **Coed** 849 undergraduate students, 52% full-time, 63% women, 37% men
- **Noncompetitive** entrance level

Undergraduates 445 full-time, 404 part-time. Students come from 8 states and territories; 13 other countries; 4% are from out of state; 12% transferred in; 9% live on campus. *Retention:* 50% of full-time freshmen returned.
Freshmen *Admission:* 71 applied, 42 enrolled.
Faculty *Total:* 49, 96% full-time, 57% with terminal degrees. *Student/faculty ratio:* 11:1.
Academics *Calendar:* semesters. *Degrees:* associate, bachelor's, master's, and postbachelor's certificates. *Special study options:* academic remediation for entering students, accelerated degree program, adult/continuing education programs, advanced placement credit, cooperative education, distance learning, double majors, independent study, internships, part-time degree program, services for LD students, study abroad, summer session for credit.
Computers on Campus 50 computers/terminals are available on campus for general student use. Students can access the following: free student e-mail accounts, online (class) schedules. Campuswide network is available.
Student Life *Housing options:* coed. Campus housing is university owned. Freshman applicants given priority for college housing. *Activities and organizations:* drama/theater group, student-run newspaper, choral group, Student Government Association, Professional Management Association, National Society for Leadership and Success. *Campus security:* late-night transport/escort service, controlled dormitory access, evening security guards. *Student services:* personal/psychological counseling.
Athletics Member NAIA. *Intercollegiate sports:* baseball M(s), golf M(s)/W, soccer M(s)/W(s), softball W(s). *Intramural sports:* football M/W, table tennis M/W, tennis M/W, volleyball M/W.
Standardized Tests *Recommended:* SAT (for admission), SAT and SAT Subject Tests or ACT (for admission).
Costs (2010–11) *Tuition:* $12,000 full-time, $475 per credit hour part-time. Full-time tuition and fees vary according to program. Part-time tuition and fees

vary according to course load and program. *Required fees:* $720 full-time, $150 per term part-time. *Room only:* $3150. *Payment plan:* installment. *Waivers:* employees or children of employees.

Financial Aid Of all full-time matriculated undergraduates who enrolled in 2009, 634 applied for aid, 634 were judged to have need, 279 had their need fully met. 29 Federal Work-Study jobs (averaging $2181). *Average percent of need met:* 48%. *Average financial aid package:* $5119. *Average need-based loan:* $3475. *Average need-based gift aid:* $2652. *Average indebtedness upon graduation:* $12,000.

Applying *Options:* electronic application, early admission, deferred entrance. *Application fee:* $25. *Required:* high school transcript. *Application deadlines:* rolling (freshmen), rolling (transfers). *Notification:* continuous (freshmen), continuous (transfers).

Freshman Application Contact Thomas University Office of Admission, Thomas University, 1501 Millpond Road, Thomasville, GA 31792. *Phone:* 229-226-1621 Ext. 214. *Toll-free phone:* 800-538-9784. *Fax:* 229-227-6919. *E-mail:* hmueller@thomasu.edu. *Web site:* http://www.thomasu.edu/.

Toccoa Falls College

Toccoa Falls, Georgia

Freshman Application Contact Toccoa Falls College, 107 North Chapel Drive, Toccoa Falls, GA 30598. *Phone:* 888-785-5624. *Web site:* http://www.tfc.edu/.

Truett-McConnell College

Cleveland, Georgia

- **Independent Baptist** 4-year, founded 1946
- **Rural** 310-acre campus with easy access to Atlanta
- **Coed** 755 undergraduate students, 61% full-time, 50% women, 50% men
- **Minimally difficult** entrance level, 77% of applicants were admitted

Undergraduates 464 full-time, 291 part-time. Students come from 14 states and territories; 5 other countries; 5% are from out of state; 9% Black or African American, non-Hispanic/Latino; 3% Hispanic/Latino; 0.6% American Indian or Alaska Native, non-Hispanic/Latino; 4% Race/ethnicity unknown; 3% international; 10% transferred in; 47% live on campus. *Retention:* 61% of full-time freshmen returned.

Freshmen *Admission:* 359 applied, 277 admitted, 173 enrolled. *Average high school GPA:* 3.16. *Test scores:* SAT critical reading scores over 500: 45%; SAT math scores over 500: 38%; SAT writing scores over 500: 36%; ACT scores over 18: 62%; SAT critical reading scores over 600: 8%; SAT math scores over 600: 7%; SAT writing scores over 600: 8%; ACT scores over 24: 9%; SAT critical reading scores over 700: 1%; SAT math scores over 700: 1%.

Faculty *Total:* 80, 36% full-time. *Student/faculty ratio:* 12:1.

Academics *Calendar:* semesters. *Degrees:* associate and bachelor's. *Special study options:* academic remediation for entering students, accelerated degree program, advanced placement credit, distance learning, double majors, services for LD students, summer session for credit.

Computers on Campus 45 computers/terminals are available on campus for general student use. Students can access the following: computer help desk, free student e-mail accounts, online (class) grades, online (class) registration, online (class) schedules. Campuswide network is available. 100% of college-owned or -operated housing units are wired for high-speed Internet access. Wireless service is available via classrooms, computer labs, dorm rooms, libraries, student centers.

Student Life *Housing:* on-campus residence required through senior year. *Options:* men-only, women-only. Campus housing is university owned. *Activities and organizations:* choral group, intramurals, Baptist Collegiate Ministries, College Choir, Student Government Association, Fellowship of Christian Athletes. *Campus security:* 24-hour weekday patrols, 10-hour weekend patrols by trained security personnel. *Student services:* health clinic.

Athletics Member NAIA, NCCAA. *Intercollegiate sports:* baseball M(s), basketball M(s)/W(s), cross-country running M(s)/W(s), golf M(s)/W(s), soccer M(s)/W(s), softball W(s). *Intramural sports:* basketball M/W, football M/W, ultimate Frisbee M/W, volleyball M/W.

Standardized Tests *Required:* SAT or ACT (for admission).

Costs (2010–11) *Comprehensive fee:* $20,440 includes full-time tuition ($14,040), mandatory fees ($500), and room and board ($5900). Full-time tuition and fees vary according to course load and location. Part-time tuition: $468 per semester hour. Part-time tuition and fees vary according to course load and location. *Required fees:* $250 per term part-time. *Room and board:* Room and board charges vary according to housing facility. *Payment plan:* installment. *Waivers:* employees or children of employees.

Financial Aid Of all full-time matriculated undergraduates who enrolled in 2009, 319 applied for aid, 283 were judged to have need, 42 had their need fully met. 18 Federal Work-Study jobs (averaging $1535). In 2009, 67 non-need-based awards were made. *Average percent of need met:* 70%. *Average financial aid package:* $12,784. *Average need-based loan:* $3398. *Average*

need-based gift aid: $10,351. *Average non-need-based aid:* $5114. *Average indebtedness upon graduation:* $16,742.

Applying *Options:* electronic application, early admission, deferred entrance. *Application fee:* $25. *Required:* essay or personal statement, high school transcript, minimum 2 GPA. *Required for some:* 1 letter of recommendation, interview. *Application deadlines:* 8/1 (freshmen), 8/1 (transfers). *Notification:* continuous (freshmen), continuous (transfers).

Freshman Application Contact Truett-McConnell College, 100 Alumni Drive, Cleveland, GA 30528. *Phone:* 706-865-2134 Ext. 210. *Toll-free phone:* 800-226-8621. *Web site:* http://www.truett.edu/.

University of Atlanta

Atlanta, Georgia

- **Independent** comprehensive
- **Coed**
- **Moderately difficult** entrance level

Faculty *Student/faculty ratio:* 6:1.

Academics *Degrees:* bachelor's, master's, doctoral-professional, and doctoral-research/scholarship.

Standardized Tests *Recommended:* SAT or ACT (for admission).

Costs (2010–11) *Tuition:* $3150 full-time, $350 per credit hour part-time. No tuition increase for student's term of enrollment. *Payment plans:* tuition prepayment, installment, deferred payment.

Applying *Options:* electronic application, early admission, deferred entrance. *Application fee:* $100. *Required:* essay or personal statement, high school transcript, minimum 3 GPA.

Freshman Application Contact Bill Kay, Vice President for Enrollment Management, University of Atlanta, 6685 Peachtree Industrial Boulevard, Atlanta, GA 30360. *Phone:* 404-424-8410 Ext. 5555. *Toll-free phone:* 800-533-3378. *Fax:* 678-736-8042. *E-mail:* bkay@uofa.edu. *Web site:* http://www.uofa.edu/.

University of Georgia

Athens, Georgia

- **State-supported** comprehensive, founded 1785, part of University System of Georgia
- **Suburban** 1508-acre campus with easy access to Atlanta
- **Coed** 25,947 undergraduate students, 94% full-time, 58% women, 42% men
- **Moderately difficult** entrance level, 59% of applicants were admitted

Undergraduates 24,408 full-time, 1,539 part-time. Students come from 53 states and territories; 126 other countries; 9% are from out of state; 7% Black or African American, non-Hispanic/Latino; 4% Hispanic/Latino; 7% Asian, non-Hispanic/Latino; 0.1% Native Hawaiian or other Pacific Islander, non-Hispanic/Latino; 0.2% American Indian or Alaska Native, non-Hispanic/Latino; 1% Two or more races, non-Hispanic/Latino; 3% Race/ethnicity unknown; 0.7% international; 4% transferred in; 28% live on campus. *Retention:* 94% of full-time freshmen returned.

Freshmen *Admission:* 17,408 applied, 10,318 admitted, 4,679 enrolled. *Average high school GPA:* 3.82. *Test scores:* SAT critical reading scores over 500: 93%; SAT math scores over 500: 95%; SAT writing scores over 500: 93%; ACT scores over 18: 99%; SAT critical reading scores over 600: 60%; SAT math scores over 600: 64%; SAT writing scores over 600: 57%; ACT scores over 24: 90%; SAT critical reading scores over 700: 13%; SAT math scores over 700: 14%; SAT writing scores over 700: 12%; ACT scores over 30: 34%.

Faculty *Total:* 2,086, 83% full-time, 90% with terminal degrees. *Student/faculty ratio:* 19:1.

Academics *Calendar:* semesters. *Degrees:* certificates, bachelor's, master's, doctoral-professional, doctoral-research/scholarship, post-master's, and post-bachelor's certificates. *Special study options:* academic remediation for entering students, accelerated degree program, adult/continuing education programs, advanced placement credit, cooperative education, distance learning, double majors, honors programs, independent study, internships, off-campus study, part-time degree program, services for LD students, student-designed majors, study abroad, summer session for credit. *ROTC:* Army (b), Air Force (b).

Computers on Campus 3,440 computers/terminals are available on campus for general student use. Students can access the following: campus intranet, computer help desk, free student e-mail accounts, online (class) grades, online (class) registration, online (class) schedules. Campuswide network is available. 100% of college-owned or -operated housing units are wired for high-speed Internet access. Wireless service is available via classrooms, computer centers, computer labs, dorm rooms, learning centers, libraries, student centers.

Student Life *Housing:* on-campus residence required for freshman year. *Options:* coed, women-only, disabled students. Campus housing is university owned. Freshman campus housing is guaranteed. *Activities and organizations:* drama/theater group, student-run newspaper, radio and television station, choral group, marching band, intramurals, Recreational sports program, Commu-niversity, University Union, Red Coat Band, national fraternities, national sororities. *Campus security:* 24-hour emergency response devices and patrols, late-night transport/escort service, controlled dormitory access. *Student services:* health clinic, personal/psychological counseling, women's center, legal services.

Athletics Member NCAA. All Division I except football (Division I-A). *Intercollegiate sports:* baseball M(s), basketball M(s)/W(s), cross-country running M(s)/W(s), equestrian sports W(s), golf M(s)/W(s), gymnastics W(s), soccer W(s), softball W(s), swimming and diving M(s)/W(s), tennis M(s)/W(s), track and field M(s)/W(s), volleyball W(s). *Intramural sports:* badminton M(c)/W(c), baseball M(c), basketball M/W, cheerleading M(c)/W(c), crew M(c)/W(c), cross-country running M(c)/W(c), equestrian sports M(c)/W(c), fencing M(c)/W(c), football M/W, golf M/W, gymnastics M(c)/W(c), ice hockey M(c), lacrosse M(c)/W(c), racquetball M/W, rugby M(c)/W(c), sailing M(c)/W(c), soccer M/W, softball M/W, squash M/W, swimming and diving M(c)/W(c), tennis M/W, track and field M/W, volleyball M/W, water polo M(c)/W(c), wrestling M(c).

Standardized Tests *Required:* SAT or ACT (for admission). *Recommended:* SAT Subject Tests (for admission).

Costs (2010–11) *Tuition:* state resident $7070 full-time; nonresident $25,280 full-time. Full-time tuition and fees vary according to course load, location, and program. Part-time tuition and fees vary according to course load, location, and program. No tuition increase for student's term of enrollment. *Required fees:* $1666 full-time, $833 per term part-time. *Room and board:* $8460; room only: $4772. Room and board charges vary according to board plan and housing facility. *Waivers:* senior citizens.

Financial Aid Of all full-time matriculated undergraduates who enrolled in 2009, 14,319 applied for aid, 9,387 were judged to have need, 2,845 had their need fully met. 389 Federal Work-Study jobs (averaging $2711). In 2009, 1242 non-need-based awards were made. *Average percent of need met:* 75%. *Average financial aid package:* $10,527. *Average need-based loan:* $3880. *Average need-based gift aid:* $8970. *Average non-need-based aid:* $1828. *Average indebtedness upon graduation:* $15,938.

Applying *Options:* electronic application, early admission, early action, deferred entrance. *Application fee:* $60. *Required:* high school transcript, counselor evaluation. *Recommended:* essay or personal statement, minimum 2 GPA. *Application deadlines:* 1/15 (freshmen), 4/1 (transfers), 10/15 (early action). *Notification:* 4/1 (freshmen), continuous (transfers), 12/15 (early action).

Freshman Application Contact Mr. Charles Carabello, Associate Director for Enrollment Management, University of Georgia, Terrell Hall, Athens, GA 30602. *Phone:* 706-542-8776. *Fax:* 706-542-1466. *E-mail:* undergrad@admissions.uga.edu. *Web site:* http://www.uga.edu/.

University of Phoenix–Atlanta Campus

Sandy Springs, Georgia

Freshman Application Contact Ms. Audra McQuarie, Registrar/Executive Director, University of Phoenix–Atlanta Campus, 4035 South Riverpoint Parkway, Mail Stop CF-L101, Phoenix, AZ 85040. *Phone:* 480-557-6151. *Toll-free phone:* 800-776-4867 (in-state); 800-228-7240 (out-of-state). *Fax:* 480-643-3068. *E-mail:* audra.mcquarie@phoenix.edu. *Web site:* http://www.phoenix.edu/.

University of Phoenix–Columbus Georgia Campus

Columbus, Georgia

Freshman Application Contact Ms. Audra McQuarie, Registrar/Executive Director, University of Phoenix–Columbus Georgia Campus, 4035 South Riverpoint Parkway, Mail Stop CF-L101, Phoenix, AZ 85040. *Phone:* 480-557-6151. *Toll-free phone:* 800-776-4867 (in-state); 800-228-7240 (out-of-state). *Fax:* 480-643-3068. *E-mail:* audra.mcquarie@phoenix.edu. *Web site:* http://www.phoenix.edu/.

University of West Georgia

Carrollton, Georgia

- **State-supported** comprehensive, founded 1933, part of University System of Georgia
- **Small-town** 645-acre campus with easy access to Atlanta
- **Endowment** $13.5 million
- **Coed** 9,707 undergraduate students, 84% full-time, 61% women, 39% men
- **Minimally difficult** entrance level, 54% of applicants were admitted

Undergraduates 8,123 full-time, 1,584 part-time. Students come from 43 states and territories; 64 other countries; 3% are from out of state; 18% Black or African American, non-Hispanic/Latino; 3% Hispanic/Latino; 0.7% Asian, non-Hispanic/Latino; 0.1% Native Hawaiian or other Pacific Islander, non-Hispanic/Latino; 0.2% American Indian or Alaska Native, non-Hispanic/Latino; 1% Two or more races, non-Hispanic/Latino; 39% Race/ethnicity unknown; 1% international; 6% transferred in; 28% live on campus. *Retention:* 73% of full-time freshmen returned.

Freshman *Admission:* 6,361 applied, 3,460 admitted, 1,903 enrolled. *Average high school GPA:* 2.95. *Test scores:* SAT critical reading scores over 500: 44%; SAT math scores over 500: 41%; SAT writing scores over 500: 36%; ACT scores over 18: 84%; SAT critical reading scores over 600: 7%; SAT math scores over 600: 9%; SAT writing scores over 600: 5%; ACT scores over 24: 14%.

Faculty *Total:* 577, 75% full-time, 65% with terminal degrees. *Student/faculty ratio:* 20:1.

Academics *Calendar:* semesters. *Degrees:* certificates, bachelor's, master's, doctoral-other, post-master's, and postbachelor's certificates. *Special study options:* academic remediation for entering students, accelerated degree program, adult/continuing education programs, advanced placement credit, cooperative education, distance learning, double majors, external degree program, honors programs, independent study, internships, off-campus study, part-time degree program, services for LD students, study abroad, summer session for credit. *ROTC:* Army (b). *Unusual degree programs:* 3-2 engineering with Georgia Institute of Technology, Auburn University, Mercer University, University of Georgia.

Computers on Campus 1,200 computers/terminals are available on campus for general student use. Students can access the following: campus intranet, computer help desk, free student e-mail accounts, online (class) grades, online (class) registration, online (class) schedules. Campuswide network is available. 100% of college-owned or -operated housing units are wired for high-speed Internet access. Wireless service is available via classrooms, computer centers, computer labs, dorm rooms, learning centers, libraries, student centers.

Student Life *Housing:* on-campus residence required for freshman year. *Options:* coed, women-only, disabled students. Campus housing is university owned. Freshman campus housing is guaranteed. *Activities and organizations:* drama/theater group, student-run newspaper, radio and television station, choral group, marching band, Black Student Alliance, Student Activities Council, Baptist Student Union, Campus Outreach, United Voices Gospel Choir, national fraternities, national sororities. *Campus security:* 24-hour emergency response devices and patrols, late-night transport/escort service, controlled dormitory access. *Student services:* health clinic, personal/psychological counseling.

Athletics Member NCAA. All Division II. *Intercollegiate sports:* baseball M(s), basketball M(s)/W(s), cheerleading M(s)/W(s), cross-country running M(s)/W(s), football M(s), golf M(s)/W(s), soccer W(s), softball W(s), tennis W(s), volleyball W(s). *Intramural sports:* basketball M/W, football M/W, golf M/W, soccer M/W, softball M/W, table tennis M/W, tennis M/W, track and field M/W, ultimate Frisbee M/W, volleyball M/W, water polo M/W, weight lifting M/W.

Standardized Tests *Required:* SAT or ACT (for admission).

Costs (2010–11) *Tuition:* state resident $4596 full-time, $154 per semester hour part-time; nonresident $16,572 full-time, $553 per semester hour part-time. Full-time tuition and fees vary according to course load and degree level. Part-time tuition and fees vary according to course load and degree level. *Required fees:* $1586 full-time, $44 per semester hour part-time, $397 per term part-time. *Room and board:* $6754; room only: $3700. Room and board charges vary according to board plan and housing facility. *Waivers:* senior citizens.

Financial Aid Of all full-time matriculated undergraduates who enrolled in 2009, 6,782 applied for aid, 5,631 were judged to have need, 660 had their need fully met. In 2009, 293 non-need-based awards were made. *Average percent of need met:* 57%. *Average financial aid package:* $8683. *Average need-based loan:* $4069. *Average need-based gift aid:* $6188. *Average non-need-based aid:* $1530. *Average indebtedness upon graduation:* $15,365.

Applying *Options:* electronic application, early admission, deferred entrance. *Application fee:* $30. *Required:* high school transcript, minimum 2.5 GPA, proof of immunization. *Application deadlines:* 6/1 (freshmen), 6/1 (out-of-state freshmen), 6/1 (transfers). *Notification:* continuous until 8/1 (freshmen), continuous until 8/1 (out-of-state freshmen), continuous (transfers).

Freshman Application Contact Mr. Justin Barlow, Assistant Director of Admissions, University of West Georgia, 1601 Maple Street, Carrollton, GA 30118. *Phone:* 678-839-4000. *Fax:* 678-839-4747. *E-mail:* admiss@ westga.edu. *Web site:* http://www.westga.edu/.

Valdosta State University
Valdosta, Georgia

- **State-supported** university, founded 1906, part of University System of Georgia
- **Small-town** 172-acre campus
- **Endowment** $24.8 million
- **Coed** 10,794 undergraduate students, 88% full-time, 59% women, 41% men
- **Moderately difficult** entrance level, 62% of applicants were admitted

Undergraduates 9,504 full-time, 1,290 part-time. Students come from 48 states and territories; 70 other countries; 4% are from out of state; 33% Black or African American, non-Hispanic/Latino; 3% Hispanic/Latino; 0.8% Asian, non-Hispanic/Latino; 0.2% Native Hawaiian or other Pacific Islander, non-Hispanic/Latino; 0.3% American Indian or Alaska Native, non-Hispanic/Latino; 3% Two or more races, non-Hispanic/Latino; 2% Race/ethnicity unknown; 2% international; 6% transferred in; 27% live on campus. *Retention:* 68% of full-time freshmen returned.
Freshmen *Admission:* 8,298 applied, 5,182 admitted, 2,522 enrolled. *Average high school GPA:* 3.08. *Test scores:* SAT critical reading scores over 500: 48%; SAT math scores over 500: 44%; SAT writing scores over 500: 39%; ACT scores over 18: 91%; SAT critical reading scores over 600: 9%; SAT math scores over 600: 8%; SAT writing scores over 600: 6%; ACT scores over 24: 15%; SAT critical reading scores over 700: 2%; SAT math scores over 700: 1%; ACT scores over 30: 1%.
Faculty *Total:* 623, 80% full-time, 62% with terminal degrees. *Student/faculty ratio:* 22:1.
Academics *Calendar:* semesters. *Degrees:* certificates, associate, bachelor's, master's, doctoral-research/scholarship, and post-master's certificates. *Special study options:* accelerated degree program, adult/continuing education programs, advanced placement credit, cooperative education, distance learning, double majors, English as a second language, external degree program, honors programs, independent study, internships, off-campus study, part-time degree program, services for LD students, study abroad, summer session for credit. *ROTC:* Air Force (b). *Unusual degree programs:* 3-2 engineering with Georgia Institute of Technology, Atlanta, GA.
Computers on Campus 1,225 computers/terminals are available on campus for general student use. Students can access the following: campus intranet, computer help desk, free student e-mail accounts, online (class) grades, online (class) registration, online (class) schedules. Campuswide network is available. 100% of college-owned or -operated housing units are wired for high-speed Internet access. Wireless service is available via entire campus.
Student Life *Housing:* on-campus residence required for freshman year. *Options:* coed, disabled students. Campus housing is university owned. Freshman applicants given priority for college housing. *Activities and organizations:* drama/theater group, student-run newspaper, radio station, choral group, marching band, Interfraternity Council, College Panhellenic Council, Black Student League, Residence Hall Association, Alpha Lambda Delta Freshmen Honor Society, national fraternities, national sororities. *Campus security:* 24-hour emergency response devices and patrols, late-night transport/escort service, controlled dormitory access, bicycle patrols, security cameras. *Student services:* health clinic, personal/psychological counseling.
Athletics Member NCAA. All Division II. *Intercollegiate sports:* baseball M(s), basketball M(s)/W(s), cross-country running M(s)/W(s), football M(s), golf M(s), soccer W, softball W(s), tennis M(s)/W(s), volleyball W(s). *Intramural sports:* badminton M/W, basketball M/W, bowling M/W, field hockey M/W, football M/W, golf M/W, racquetball M/W, soccer M/W, softball M/W, table tennis W, tennis M/W, ultimate Frisbee M/W, volleyball M/W.
Standardized Tests *Required:* SAT or ACT (for admission).
Costs (2010–11) *Tuition:* state resident $3262 full-time, $137 per credit hour part-time; nonresident $12,665 full-time, $528 per credit hour part-time. Full-time tuition and fees vary according to reciprocity agreements. Part-time tuition and fees vary according to course load and reciprocity agreements. Part-time mandatory fees per term: $253 for students enrolled in 3 credit hours or fewer, $855 for students enrolled in 4 credit hours or more. *Required fees:* $1710 full-time. *Room and board:* $6520; room only: $3290. Room and board charges vary according to board plan and housing facility. *Waivers:* senior citizens and employees or children of employees.
Financial Aid Of all full-time matriculated undergraduates who enrolled in 2009, 7,853 applied for aid, 6,088 were judged to have need, 792 had their need fully met. 168 Federal Work-Study jobs (averaging $2868). In 2009, 70 non-need-based awards were made. *Average percent of need met:* 63%. *Average financial aid package:* $9360. *Average need-based loan:* $4065. *Average need-based gift aid:* $6284. *Average non-need-based aid:* $1361. *Average indebtedness upon graduation:* $19,592.

Applying *Options:* electronic application, deferred entrance. *Application fee:* $40. *Required:* high school transcript, SAT and/or ACT scores. *Application deadlines:* 6/15 (freshmen), 6/15 (out-of-state freshmen), 6/15 (transfers). *Notification:* continuous (freshmen), continuous (transfers).
Freshman Application Contact Valdosta State University, 1500 North Patterson Street, Valdosta, GA 31698. *Phone:* 229-333-5791. *Toll-free phone:* 800-618-1878 Ext. 1. *Web site:* http://www.valdosta.edu/.

Wesleyan College
Macon, Georgia

- **Independent United Methodist** comprehensive, founded 1836
- **Suburban** 200-acre campus with easy access to Atlanta
- **Endowment** $46.7 million
- **Undergraduate: women only; graduate: coed** 630 undergraduate students, 64% full-time, 100% women
- **Moderately difficult** entrance level, 40% of applicants were admitted

Undergraduates 404 full-time, 226 part-time. Students come from 34 states and territories; 24 other countries; 4% are from out of state; 4% transferred in; 82% live on campus. *Retention:* 78% of full-time freshmen returned.
Freshmen *Admission:* 516 applied, 208 admitted, 106 enrolled. *Average high school GPA:* 3. *Test scores:* SAT critical reading scores over 500: 69%; SAT math scores over 500: 60%; SAT writing scores over 500: 69%; ACT scores over 18: 88%; SAT critical reading scores over 600: 23%; SAT math scores over 600: 36%; SAT writing scores over 600: 27%; ACT scores over 24: 16%; SAT critical reading scores over 700: 9%; SAT math scores over 700: 15%; SAT writing scores over 700: 3%; ACT scores over 30: 3%.
Faculty *Total:* 50, 96% full-time, 92% with terminal degrees. *Student/faculty ratio:* 8:1.
Academics *Calendar:* semesters. *Degrees:* bachelor's and master's. *Special study options:* adult/continuing education programs, advanced placement credit, cooperative education, double majors, external degree program, honors programs, independent study, internships, off-campus study, part-time degree program, services for LD students, student-designed majors, study abroad, summer session for credit. *Unusual degree programs:* 3-2 engineering with Georgia Tech, Auburn University and Mercer University.
Computers on Campus 22 computers/terminals are available on campus for general student use. Students can access the following: campus intranet, computer help desk, free student e-mail accounts, online (class) grades, online (class) registration, online (class) schedules, online payment. Campuswide network is available. 100% of college-owned or -operated housing units are wired for high-speed Internet access. Wireless service is available via classrooms, computer centers, computer labs, learning centers, libraries, student centers.
Student Life *Housing:* on-campus residence required through senior year. *Options:* women-only, disabled students. Campus housing is university owned. Freshman campus housing is guaranteed. *Activities and organizations:* drama/theater group, student-run newspaper, choral group, Student Recreation Council, Campus Activities Board, Student Government Association, Council on Religious Concerns, Christian Fellowship. *Campus security:* 24-hour emergency response devices and patrols, late-night transport/escort service, controlled dormitory access. *Student services:* health clinic, personal/psychological counseling, women's center.
Athletics Member NCAA. All Division III. *Intercollegiate sports:* basketball W, cross-country running W, equestrian sports W, soccer W, softball W, tennis W, volleyball W. *Intramural sports:* basketball W, cross-country running W, soccer W, softball W, tennis W, volleyball W.
Standardized Tests *Required:* SAT or ACT (for admission).
Costs (2010–11) *Comprehensive fee:* $26,100 includes full-time tuition ($18,000) and room and board ($8100). Full-time tuition and fees vary according to class time, course level, course load, degree level, and program. Part-time tuition: $425 per credit hour. Part-time tuition and fees vary according to class time, course level, course load, degree level, and program. *Room and board:* Room and board charges vary according to board plan and housing facility. *Waivers:* senior citizens and employees or children of employees.
Financial Aid Of all full-time matriculated undergraduates who enrolled in 2009, 276 applied for aid, 230 were judged to have need, 73 had their need fully met. 65 Federal Work-Study jobs (averaging $941). 79 state and other part-time jobs (averaging $1244). In 2009, 131 non-need-based awards were made. *Average percent of need met:* 81%. *Average financial aid package:* $16,418. *Average need-based loan:* $4925. *Average need-based gift aid:* $12,632. *Average non-need-based aid:* $18,887. *Average indebtedness upon graduation:* $20,896.
Applying *Options:* electronic application, early admission, early decision, early action, deferred entrance. *Application fee:* $30. *Required:* high school transcript, minimum 2 GPA, 1 letter of recommendation. *Required for some:* interview. *Recommended:* essay or personal statement, 2 letters of recommendation. *Application deadlines:* rolling (freshmen), rolling (transfers). *Early decision deadline:* 11/15. *Notification:* continuous (freshmen), continuous (transfers), 12/15 (early decision).

Freshman Application Contact Mr. Stephen Farr, Vice President for Enrollment Services, Wesleyan College, 4760 Forsyth Road, Macon, GA 31210-4462. *Phone:* 478-757-3700. *Toll-free phone:* 800-447-6610. *Fax:* 478-757-4030. *E-mail:* admissions@wesleyancollege.edu. *Web site:* http://www.wesleyancollege.edu/.

See page 1772 for the College Close-Up.

Westwood College–Atlanta Midtown
Atlanta, Georgia

- **Proprietary** 4-year, founded 2003
- **Coed**

Academics *Calendar:* continuous. *Degrees:* associate and bachelor's.
Freshman Application Contact Westwood College–Atlanta Midtown, 1100 Spring Street, Suite 102, Atlanta, GA 30309. *Phone:* 404-745-9862. *Toll-free phone:* 800-613-4595. *Web site:* http://www.westwood.edu/.

Westwood College–Atlanta Northlake
Atlanta, Georgia

- **Proprietary** 4-year, part of Alta College, Inc.
- **Coed**

Academics *Degrees:* diplomas, associate, and bachelor's.
Freshman Application Contact Westwood College–Atlanta Northlake, 2309 Parklake Drive, NE, Building 10, Atlanta, GA 30345. *Phone:* 404-962-2998. *Toll-free phone:* 866-821-6146. *Web site:* http://www.westwood.edu/.

Young Harris College
Young Harris, Georgia

- **Independent United Methodist** 4-year, founded 1886
- **Small-town** 800-acre campus
- **Endowment** $91.4 million
- **Coed** 820 undergraduate students, 96% full-time, 57% women, 43% men
- **Moderately difficult** entrance level, 54% of applicants were admitted

Undergraduates 791 full-time, 29 part-time. Students come from 14 states and territories; 23 other countries; 10% are from out of state; 6% Black or African American, non-Hispanic/Latino; 7% Hispanic/Latino; 0.7% Native Hawaiian or other Pacific Islander, non-Hispanic/Latino; 0.5% American Indian or Alaska Native, non-Hispanic/Latino; 0.7% Two or more races, non-Hispanic/Latino; 7% transferred in; 83% live on campus. *Retention:* 63% of full-time freshmen returned.
Freshmen *Admission:* 1,886 applied, 1,013 admitted, 337 enrolled. *Average high school GPA:* 3.19. *Test scores:* SAT critical reading scores over 500: 48%; SAT math scores over 500: 46%; SAT writing scores over 500: 30%; ACT scores over 18: 84%; SAT critical reading scores over 600: 11%; SAT math scores over 600: 7%; SAT writing scores over 600: 6%; ACT scores over 24: 20%; SAT critical reading scores over 700: 1%; ACT scores over 30: 2%.
Faculty *Total:* 86, 76% full-time, 51% with terminal degrees. *Student/faculty ratio:* 10:1.
Academics *Calendar:* semesters. *Degrees:* associate and bachelor's. *Special study options:* advanced placement credit, cooperative education, double majors, honors programs, internships, part-time degree program, services for LD students, study abroad, summer session for credit.
Computers on Campus 137 computers/terminals are available on campus for general student use. Students can access the following: campus intranet, computer help desk, free student e-mail accounts, online (class) grades, online (class) registration, online (class) schedules. Campuswide network is available. 100% of college-owned or -operated housing units are wired for high-speed Internet access. Wireless service is available via entire campus.
Student Life *Housing:* on-campus residence required through senior year. *Options:* coed, men-only, women-only, disabled students. Campus housing is university owned. *Activities and organizations:* drama/theater group, student-run newspaper, choral group, Greek life, religious organizations/Bible study, intramural sports, Student Government Association, Campus Activities Board. *Campus security:* 24-hour emergency response devices and patrols. *Student services:* health clinic, personal/psychological counseling.
Athletics *Intercollegiate sports:* baseball M(s), basketball M(s)/W(s), cheerleading W, cross-country running M(s)/W(s), golf M(s)/W(s), soccer M(s)/W(s), softball W(s), tennis M(s)/W(s). *Intramural sports:* basketball M/W, football M/W, softball M/W, ultimate Frisbee M/W, volleyball M/W, weight lifting M/W.
Standardized Tests *Required:* SAT or ACT (for admission).
Costs (2011–12) *Comprehensive fee:* $29,450 includes full-time tuition ($21,500), mandatory fees ($470), and room and board ($7480). Full-time tuition and fees vary according to course load. Part-time tuition: $650 per credit hour. Part-time tuition and fees vary according to course load. *Room and board:* Room and board charges vary according to housing facility. *Payment plan:* installment. *Waivers:* employees or children of employees.

Financial Aid Of all full-time matriculated undergraduates who enrolled in 2008, 592 applied for aid, 492 were judged to have need, 111 had their need fully met. In 2008, 209 non-need-based awards were made. *Average percent of need met:* 79%. *Average financial aid package:* $15,202. *Average need-based loan:* $3003. *Average need-based gift aid:* $13,075. *Average non-need-based aid:* $10,554.
Applying *Options:* electronic application. *Required:* high school transcript, SAT and/or ACT scores. *Application deadlines:* rolling (freshmen), rolling (out-of-state freshmen), rolling (transfers). *Notification:* continuous (freshmen), continuous (out-of-state freshmen), continuous (transfers).
Freshman Application Contact Mr. Clinton G. Hobbs, Vice President for Enrollment Management, Young Harris College, PO Box 116, Young Harris, GA 30582-0098. *Phone:* 706-379-3111. *Toll-free phone:* 800-241-3754. *Fax:* 706-379-3108. *E-mail:* admissions@yhc.edu. *Web site:* http://www.yhc.edu/.

HAWAII

Argosy University, Hawai`i
Honolulu, Hawaii

- **Proprietary** university, founded 1994, part of Education Management Corporation
- **Coed**

Academics *Calendar:* semesters. *Degrees:* bachelor's, master's, and doctoral-professional.
Costs (2010–11) *Tuition:* Tuition varies by program. Students should contact Argosy University for tuition information.
Freshman Application Contact Argosy University, Hawai`i, 400 ASB Tower, 1001 Bishop Street, Honolulu, HI 96813. *Phone:* 808-536-5555. *Toll-free phone:* 888-323-2777. *Web site:* http://www.argosy.edu/hawaii/.

See page 1002 for the College Close-Up.

Brigham Young University–Hawaii
Laie, Hawaii

- **Independent Latter-day Saints** 4-year, founded 1955, administratively affiliated with Brigham Young University
- **Small-town** 60-acre campus with easy access to Honolulu
- **Coed**
- **Moderately difficult** entrance level

Faculty *Student/faculty ratio:* 15:1.
Academics *Calendar:* semesters two semesters and three terms. *Degrees:* associate, bachelor's, and postbachelor's certificates.
Student Life *Campus security:* 24-hour patrols, late-night transport/escort service.
Athletics Member NCAA. All Division II.
Standardized Tests *Required:* SAT or ACT (for admission). *Recommended:* ACT (for admission).
Costs (2010–11) *Comprehensive fee:* $9086 includes full-time tuition ($4330) and room and board ($4756). Part-time tuition and fees vary according to course load. *Room and board:* Room and board charges vary according to board plan and housing facility.
Financial Aid *Of all full-time matriculated undergraduates who enrolled in 2006,* 2,230 applied for aid, 2,185 were judged to have need, 1,400 had their need fully met. *Average percent of need met:* 75. *Average financial aid package:* $11,000. *Average need-based loan:* $3700. *Average need-based gift aid:* $5200. *Average non-need-based aid:* $1400. *Average indebtedness upon graduation:* $12,418. *Financial aid deadline:* 3/31.
Applying *Options:* electronic application, early admission, deferred entrance. *Application fee:* $30. *Required:* essay or personal statement, high school transcript, minimum 3 GPA, resume of activities, ecclesiastical endorsement.
Freshman Application Contact Mr. Arapata P. Meha, Brigham Young University–Hawaii, 55-220 Kulanui Street, Laie, HI 96762-1294. *Phone:* 808-675-3731. *Fax:* 808-675-3741. *E-mail:* admissions@byuh.edu. *Web site:* http://www.byuh.edu/.

Chaminade University of Honolulu
Honolulu, Hawaii

- **Independent Roman Catholic** comprehensive, founded 1955
- **Urban** 62-acre campus with easy access to Honolulu
- **Endowment** $8.4 million
- **Coed**
- **Moderately difficult** entrance level

Faculty *Student/faculty ratio:* 12:1.

Academics *Calendar:* semesters. *Degrees:* associate, bachelor's, master's, and postbachelor's certificates.
Student Life *Campus security:* 24-hour emergency response devices and patrols, late-night transport/escort service, controlled dormitory access.
Athletics Member NCAA. All Division II.
Standardized Tests *Required:* SAT or ACT (for admission), TOEFL for international students (for admission).
Costs (2010–11) *Comprehensive fee:* $28,160 includes full-time tuition ($17,600), mandatory fees ($140), and room and board ($10,420). Full-time tuition and fees vary according to course load. Part-time tuition: $587 per credit hour. Part-time tuition and fees vary according to course load. *College room only:* $5170. Room and board charges vary according to board plan and housing facility.
Applying *Options:* electronic application, deferred entrance. *Application fee:* $50. *Required:* essay or personal statement, high school transcript, minimum 2.5 GPA. *Required for some:* minimum 2.75 GPA, 2 letters of recommendation, interview. *Recommended:* minimum 3 GPA, 2 letters of recommendation.
Freshman Application Contact Mr. Martin Motooka, Assistant Director of Admissions, Chaminade University of Honolulu, 3140 Waialae Avenue, Honolulu, HI 96816-1578. *Phone:* 808-735-4735. *Toll-free phone:* 800-735-3733. *Fax:* 808-739-4647. *E-mail:* admissions@chaminade.edu. *Web site:* http://www.chaminade.edu/.

Hawai`i Pacific University

Honolulu, Hawaii

- **Independent** comprehensive, founded 1965
- **Urban** 140-acre campus
- **Endowment** $65.8 million
- **Coed** 7,058 undergraduate students, 57% full-time, 56% women, 44% men
- **Moderately difficult** entrance level, 78% of applicants were admitted

Undergraduates 4,037 full-time, 3,021 part-time. Students come from 52 states and territories; 67 other countries; 29% are from out of state; 6% Black or African American, non-Hispanic/Latino; 10% Hispanic/Latino; 19% Asian, non-Hispanic/Latino; 4% Native Hawaiian or other Pacific Islander, non-Hispanic/Latino; 0.7% American Indian or Alaska Native, non-Hispanic/Latino; 16% Two or more races, non-Hispanic/Latino; 7% Race/ethnicity unknown; 9% international; 17% transferred in; 10% live on campus. *Retention:* 73% of full-time freshmen returned.
Freshmen *Admission:* 3,710 applied, 2,893 admitted, 644 enrolled. *Average high school GPA:* 3.33. *Test scores:* SAT critical reading scores over 500: 46%; SAT math scores over 500: 53%; SAT writing scores over 500: 43%; ACT scores over 18: 83%; SAT critical reading scores over 600: 11%; SAT math scores over 600: 12%; SAT writing scores over 600: 7%; ACT scores over 24: 31%; SAT critical reading scores over 700: 1%; SAT math scores over 700: 1%; ACT scores over 30: 3%.
Faculty *Total:* 639, 40% full-time, 52% with terminal degrees. *Student/faculty ratio:* 15:1.
Academics *Calendar:* semesters. *Degrees:* certificates, associate, bachelor's, master's, post-master's, and postbachelor's certificates. *Special study options:* academic remediation for entering students, accelerated degree program, adult/continuing education programs, advanced placement credit, cooperative education, distance learning, double majors, English as a second language, freshman honors college, honors programs, independent study, internships, off-campus study, part-time degree program, services for LD students, student-designed majors, study abroad, summer session for credit. *ROTC:* Army (c), Air Force (c). *Unusual degree programs:* 3-2 engineering with Washington University in St. Louis, University of Southern California.
Computers on Campus 590 computers/terminals are available on campus for general student use. Students can access the following: campus intranet, computer help desk, free student e-mail accounts, online (class) grades, online (class) registration, online (class) schedules. Campuswide network is available. Wireless service is available via entire campus.
Student Life *Housing options:* coed. Campus housing is university owned and is provided by a third party. Freshman applicants given priority for college housing. *Activities and organizations:* drama/theater group, student-run newspaper, choral group, Student Government Association, Swedish Student Association, President's Hosts, Akamai Advertising, Christian Fellowship. *Campus security:* 24-hour emergency response devices and patrols, student patrols, late-night transport/escort service, controlled dormitory access, Rave Alert System. *Student services:* personal/psychological counseling.
Athletics Member NCAA. All Division II. *Intercollegiate sports:* baseball M(s), basketball M(s)/W(s), cheerleading M(s)/W(s), cross-country running M(s)/W(s), golf M(s), soccer M(s)/W(s), softball W(s), tennis M(s)/W(s), volleyball W(s). *Intramural sports:* basketball M/W, football M/W, soccer M/W,

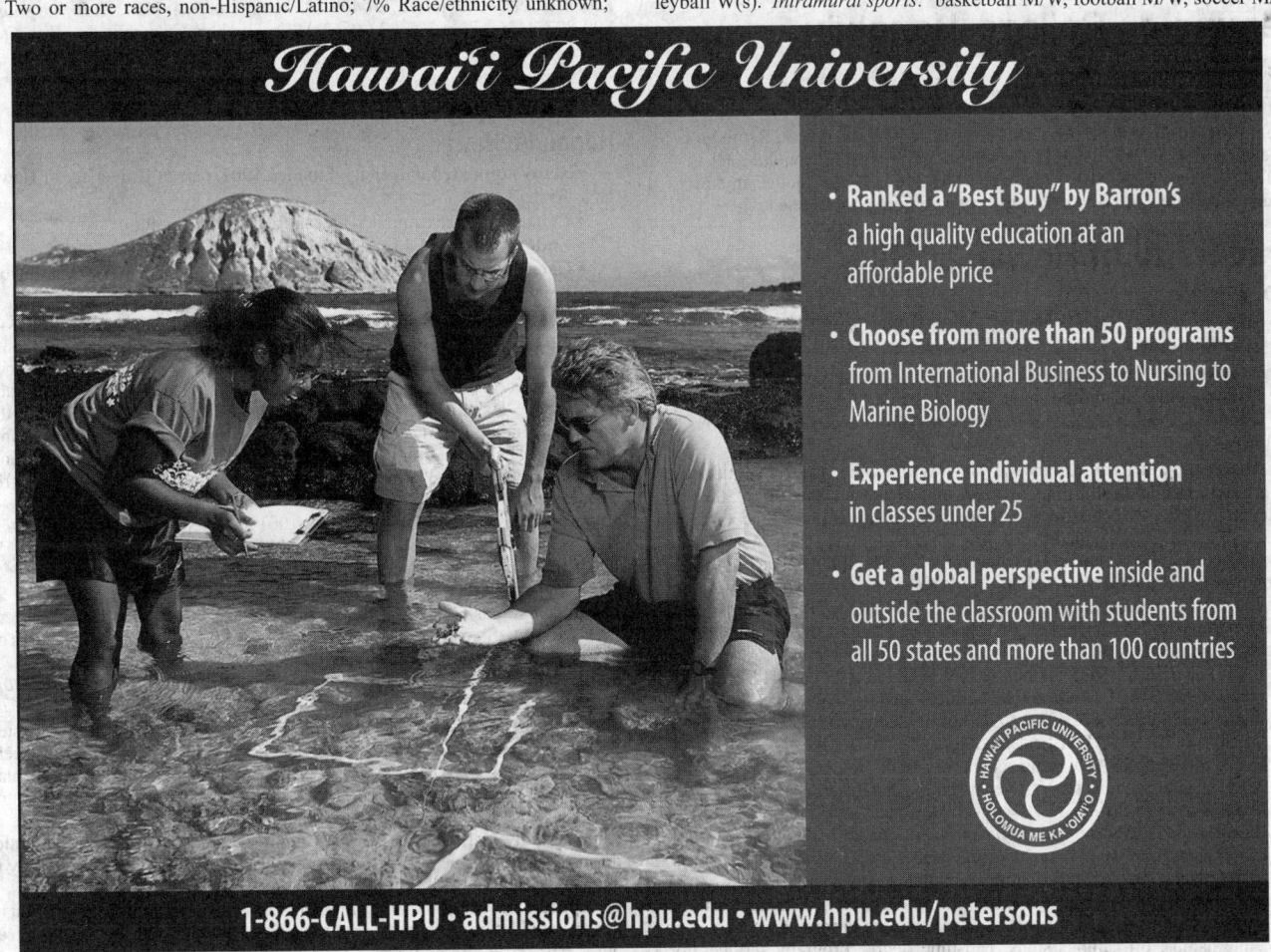

softball M/W, table tennis M/W, tennis M/W, ultimate Frisbee M/W, volleyball M/W.

Standardized Tests *Required:* SAT or ACT (for admission).

Costs (2010–11) *Comprehensive fee:* $27,468 includes full-time tuition ($15,720), mandatory fees ($100), and room and board ($11,648). Full-time tuition and fees vary according to course level, course load, program, and student level. Part-time tuition: $330 per credit hour. Part-time tuition and fees vary according to course level, course load, program, and student level. *Room and board:* Room and board charges vary according to housing facility. *Payment plan:* installment. *Waivers:* employees or children of employees.

Financial Aid Of all full-time matriculated undergraduates who enrolled in 2009, 3,031 applied for aid, 1,933 were judged to have need, 470 had their need fully met. 157 Federal Work-Study jobs (averaging $3000). In 2009, 182 non-need-based awards were made. *Average percent of need met:* 78%. *Average financial aid package:* $17,448. *Average need-based loan:* $6159. *Average need-based gift aid:* $2031. *Average non-need-based aid:* $2153. *Average indebtedness upon graduation:* $32,172.

Applying *Options:* electronic application, early admission, deferred entrance. *Application fee:* $50. *Required:* high school transcript, minimum 2.5 GPA. *Required for some:* interview. *Recommended:* essay or personal statement, 2 letters of recommendation. *Application deadlines:* rolling (freshmen), rolling (transfers). *Notification:* continuous (transfers).

Freshman Application Contact Mr. Scott Stensrud, Vice President, Enrollment Management, Hawai'i Pacific University, 1164 Bishop Street, Honolulu, HI 96813-2785. *Phone:* 808-544-0238. *Toll-free phone:* 866-225-5478. *Fax:* 808-544-1136. *E-mail:* admissions@hpu.edu. *Web site:* http://www.hpu.edu/.

See page 1324 for the College Close-Up.

Maui Community College
Kahului, Hawaii

Freshman Application Contact Mr. Stephen Kameda, Director of Admissions and Records, Maui Community College, 310 Kaahumanu Avenue, Kahului, HI 96732. *Phone:* 808-984-3267. *Toll-free phone:* 800-479-6692. *Fax:* 808-242-9618. *E-mail:* kameda@hawaii.edu. *Web site:* http://maui.hawaii.edu/.

Remington College–Honolulu Campus
Honolulu, Hawaii

Director of Admissions Louis LaMair, Director of Recruitment, Remington College–Honolulu Campus, 1111 Bishop Street, Suite 400, Honolulu, HI 96813. *Phone:* 808-942-1000. *Fax:* 808-533-3064. *E-mail:* louis.lamair@remingtoncollege.edu. *Web site:* http://www.remingtoncollege.edu/.

University of Hawaii at Hilo
Hilo, Hawaii

- **State-supported** comprehensive, founded 1970, part of University of Hawaii System
- **Small-town** 115-acre campus
- **Endowment** $2.8 million
- **Coed** 3,462 undergraduate students, 82% full-time, 60% women, 40% men
- **Moderately difficult** entrance level, 70% of applicants were admitted

Undergraduates 2,848 full-time, 614 part-time. Students come from 50 states and territories; 26 other countries; 24% are from out of state; 1% Black or African American, non-Hispanic/Latino; 9% Hispanic/Latino; 20% Asian, non-Hispanic/Latino; 14% Native Hawaiian or other Pacific Islander, non-Hispanic/Latino; 0.6% American Indian or Alaska Native, non-Hispanic/Latino; 26% Two or more races, non-Hispanic/Latino; 0.1% Race/ethnicity unknown; 5% international; 17% transferred in; 22% live on campus. *Retention:* 71% of full-time freshmen returned.

Freshmen *Admission:* 1,623 applied, 1,133 admitted, 403 enrolled. *Average high school GPA:* 3.5. *Test scores:* SAT critical reading scores over 500: 40%; SAT math scores over 500: 43%; SAT writing scores over 500: 30%; ACT scores over 18: 81%; SAT critical reading scores over 600: 9%; SAT math scores over 600: 12%; SAT writing scores over 600: 7%; ACT scores over 24: 27%; SAT critical reading scores over 700: 1%; SAT math scores over 700: 1%; ACT scores over 30: 1%.

Faculty *Total:* 347, 78% full-time. *Student/faculty ratio:* 17:1.

Academics *Calendar:* semesters. *Degrees:* certificates, bachelor's, master's, doctoral-professional, doctoral-research/scholarship, and postbachelor's certificates. *Special study options:* advanced placement credit, distance learning, double majors, English as a second language, honors programs, independent study, internships, off-campus study, part-time degree program, services for

LD students, student-designed majors, study abroad, summer session for credit.

Computers on Campus 600 computers/terminals are available on campus for general student use. Students can access the following: online (class) registration. Campuswide network is available.

Student Life *Housing options:* coed. Campus housing is university owned. *Activities and organizations:* drama/theater group, student-run newspaper, choral group, International Student Association, Hawaiian Leadership and Development, Delta Sigma Pi Business Fraternity, University Canoe Club, Samoan Club. *Campus security:* 24-hour emergency response devices and patrols, controlled dormitory access. *Student services:* health clinic, personal/psychological counseling, women's center.

Athletics Member NCAA. All Division II except baseball (Division I). *Intercollegiate sports:* baseball M(s), basketball M(s), cross-country running M(s)/W(s), golf M(s), softball W(s), tennis M(s)/W(s), volleyball W(s). *Intramural sports:* archery M/W, badminton M/W, basketball M/W, bowling M/W, golf M/W, soccer M/W, softball M/W, table tennis M/W, tennis M/W, volleyball M/W, weight lifting M/W.

Standardized Tests *Required:* SAT or ACT (for admission).

Costs (2011–12) *Tuition:* state resident $5112 full-time; nonresident $15,600 full-time. Full-time tuition and fees vary according to reciprocity agreements. Part-time tuition and fees vary according to course load. *Required fees:* $304 full-time. *Room and board:* $7134. Room and board charges vary according to board plan and housing facility.

Financial Aid Of all full-time matriculated undergraduates who enrolled in 2009, 2,191 applied for aid, 1,697 were judged to have need, 377 had their need fully met. 158 Federal Work-Study jobs (averaging $2065). 531 state and other part-time jobs (averaging $3993). In 2009, 12 non-need-based awards were made. *Average percent of need met:* 72%. *Average financial aid package:* $10,683. *Average need-based loan:* $4423. *Average need-based gift aid:* $4970. *Average non-need-based aid:* $1615. *Average indebtedness upon graduation:* $11,944.

Applying *Options:* electronic application, deferred entrance. *Application fee:* $50. *Required:* high school transcript. *Recommended:* minimum 3 GPA. *Application deadlines:* 7/1 (freshmen), 7/1 (transfers). *Notification:* 7/31 (freshmen), 7/31 (transfers).

Freshman Application Contact Mr. James Cromwell, Student Services Specialist/Director of Admissions, University of Hawaii at Hilo, 200 West Kawili Street, Hilo, HI 96720-4091. *Phone:* 808-974-7414. *Toll-free phone:* 800-897-4456. *Fax:* 808-933-0861. *E-mail:* uhhao@hawaii.edu. *Web site:* http://www.uhh.hawaii.edu/.

University of Hawaii at Manoa
Honolulu, Hawaii

- **State-supported** university, founded 1907, part of University of Hawaii System
- **Urban** 300-acre campus with easy access to Honolulu
- **Endowment** $134.4 million
- **Coed** 13,912 undergraduate students, 81% full-time, 54% women, 46% men
- **Moderately difficult** entrance level, 71% of applicants were admitted

Undergraduates 11,331 full-time, 2,581 part-time. Students come from 52 other countries; 22% are from out of state; 1% Black or African American, non-Hispanic/Latino; 2% Hispanic/Latino; 41% Asian, non-Hispanic/Latino; 17% Native Hawaiian or other Pacific Islander, non-Hispanic/Latino; 0.4% American Indian or Alaska Native, non-Hispanic/Latino; 13% Two or more races, non-Hispanic/Latino; 0.2% Race/ethnicity unknown; 4% international; 12% transferred in; 13% live on campus. *Retention:* 79% of full-time freshmen returned.

Freshmen *Admission:* 7,054 applied, 5,001 admitted, 1,863 enrolled. *Average high school GPA:* 3.43. *Test scores:* SAT critical reading scores over 500: 67%; SAT math scores over 500: 82%; SAT writing scores over 500: 65%; ACT scores over 18: 98%; SAT critical reading scores over 600: 20%; SAT math scores over 600: 31%; SAT writing scores over 600: 14%; ACT scores over 24: 42%; SAT critical reading scores over 700: 3%; SAT math scores over 700: 6%; SAT writing scores over 700: 2%; ACT scores over 30: 6%.

Faculty *Total:* 1,209, 94% full-time, 85% with terminal degrees. *Student/faculty ratio:* 14:1.

Academics *Calendar:* semesters. *Degrees:* certificates, bachelor's, master's, doctoral-professional, doctoral-research/scholarship, and postbachelor's certificates. *Special study options:* accelerated degree program, advanced placement credit, cooperative education, distance learning, double majors, English as a second language, honors programs, independent study, internships, off-campus study, part-time degree program, services for LD students, student-designed majors, study abroad, summer session for credit. *ROTC:* Army (b), Air Force (b).

Computers on Campus 400 computers/terminals are available on campus for general student use. Students can access the following: campus intranet, computer help desk, free student e-mail accounts, online (class) grades, online (class) registration, online (class) schedules. Campuswide network is available. 99% of college-owned or -operated housing units are wired for high-speed Internet access. Wireless service is available via entire campus.

Student Life *Housing options:* coed, disabled students. Campus housing is university owned. Freshman applicants given priority for college housing. *Activities and organizations:* drama/theater group, student-run newspaper, radio station, choral group, marching band, Associated Students of University of Hawaii, Campus Center Board, Broadcast Communication Authority, Board of Publications, Student Activities and Program Fee Board, national fraternities, national sororities. *Campus security:* 24-hour emergency response devices and patrols, student patrols, late-night transport/escort service, controlled dormitory access. *Student services:* health clinic, personal/psychological counseling, women's center.

Athletics Member NCAA. All Division I except football (Division I-A). *Intercollegiate sports:* archery M, baseball M(s), basketball M(s)/W(s), cheerleading M(s)/W(s), cross-country running W(s), golf M(s)/W(s), sailing M/W, soccer W(s), softball W(s), swimming and diving M(s)/W(s), tennis M(s)/W(s), track and field W(s), volleyball M(s)/W(s), water polo W(s). *Intramural sports:* badminton M/W, basketball M/W, crew M/W, cross-country running M/W, golf M/W, rugby M, sailing M/W, soccer M, softball M, swimming and diving M/W, table tennis M/W, tennis M/W, track and field M/W, ultimate Frisbee M/W, volleyball M/W, weight lifting M/W, wrestling M/W.

Standardized Tests *Required:* SAT or ACT (for admission).

Costs (2011–12) *Tuition:* state resident $8400 full-time, $350 per credit hour part-time; nonresident $23,232 full-time, $968 per credit hour part-time. Full-time tuition and fees vary according to class time, course level, course load, degree level, program, reciprocity agreements, and student level. Part-time tuition and fees vary according to class time, course level, course load, degree level, program, reciprocity agreements, and student level. *Required fees:* $511 full-time, $511 per term part-time. *Room and board:* $9410; room only: $5718. Room and board charges vary according to board plan and housing facility. *Payment plan:* installment. *Waivers:* minority students, adult students, senior citizens, and employees or children of employees.

Financial Aid Of all full-time matriculated undergraduates who enrolled in 2007, 6,777 applied for aid, 4,054 were judged to have need, 777 had their need fully met. In 2007, 2024 non-need-based awards were made. *Average percent of need met:* 61%. *Average financial aid package:* $7687. *Average need-based loan:* $4280. *Average need-based gift aid:* $5072. *Average non-need-based aid:* $5576. *Average indebtedness upon graduation:* $14,818.

Applying *Options:* electronic application. *Application fee:* $70. *Required:* high school transcript, minimum 2.8 GPA. *Application deadlines:* 5/1 (freshmen), 5/1 (transfers). *Notification:* continuous (freshmen), continuous (transfers).

Freshman Application Contact Ms. Lisa Buto, Student Services Specialist, University of Hawaii at Manoa, 2600 Campus Road, Room 001, Honolulu, HI 96822. *Phone:* 808-956-8975. *Toll-free phone:* 800-823-9771. *Fax:* 808-956-4148. *E-mail:* ar-info@hawaii.edu. *Web site:* http://manoa.hawaii.edu/.

University of Hawaii–West Oahu
Pearl City, Hawaii

- **State-supported** 4-year, founded 1976, part of University of Hawaii System
- **Small-town** campus with easy access to Honolulu
- **Coed** 1,471 undergraduate students, 33% full-time, 71% women, 29% men
- **Moderately difficult** entrance level, 71% of applicants were admitted

Undergraduates 483 full-time, 988 part-time. 3% are from out of state; 2% Black or African American, non-Hispanic/Latino; 1% Hispanic/Latino; 42% Asian, non-Hispanic/Latino; 25% Native Hawaiian or other Pacific Islander, non-Hispanic/Latino; 0.4% American Indian or Alaska Native, non-Hispanic/Latino; 11% Two or more races, non-Hispanic/Latino; 0.2% Race/ethnicity unknown; 3% international; 24% transferred in. *Retention:* 50% of full-time freshmen returned.

Freshmen *Admission:* 410 applied, 293 admitted, 108 enrolled. *Average high school GPA:* 3.17.

Faculty *Total:* 79, 56% full-time, 65% with terminal degrees. *Student/faculty ratio:* 15:1.

Academics *Calendar:* semesters. *Degree:* certificates and bachelor's. *Special study options:* academic remediation for entering students, advanced placement credit, distance learning, double majors, off-campus study, part-time degree program, services for LD students, summer session for credit. *ROTC:* Army (c), Air Force (c).

Computers on Campus Students can access the following: computer help desk, free student e-mail accounts, online (class) grades, online (class) registration, online (class) schedules. Campuswide network is available. Wireless service is available via classrooms.

Student Life *Housing:* college housing not available. *Campus security:* 24-hour emergency response devices and patrols, late-night transport/escort service. *Student services:* personal/psychological counseling.

Standardized Tests *Recommended:* SAT or ACT (for admission).

Costs (2011–12) *Tuition:* state resident $5136 full-time; nonresident $15,744 full-time, $656 per credit part-time. *Required fees:* $5 full-time. *Payment plan:* installment. *Waivers:* employees or children of employees.

Financial Aid Of all full-time matriculated undergraduates who enrolled in 2009, 215 applied for aid, 215 were judged to have need. In 2009, 2 non-need-based awards were made. *Average percent of need met:* 50%. *Average financial aid package:* $6197. *Average need-based loan:* $4190. *Average need-based gift aid:* $3956. *Average non-need-based aid:* $3058.

Applying *Options:* deferred entrance. *Application fee:* $50. *Required:* minimum 2.7 GPA. *Required for some:* high school transcript, 2 letters of recommendation, college transcripts. *Application deadlines:* 4/1 (freshmen), 4/1 (transfers). *Notification:* continuous (freshmen), continuous (transfers).

Freshman Application Contact Robyn Oshiro, University of Hawaii–West Oahu, 96-129 Ala Ike Street, Pearl City, HI 96782. *Phone:* 808-454-4700. *Toll-free phone:* 808-454-4700. *Fax:* 808-453-6075. *E-mail:* admissions@ hawaii.edu. *Web site:* http://www.uhwo.hawaii.edu/.

University of Phoenix–Hawaii Campus
Honolulu, Hawaii

Freshman Application Contact Ms. Audra McQuarie, Registrar/Executive Director, University of Phoenix–Hawaii Campus, 4035 South Riverpoint Parkway, Mail Stop CF-L101, Phoenix, AZ 85040. *Phone:* 480-557-6151. *Toll-free phone:* 800-776-4867 (in-state); 800-228-7240 (out-of-state). *Fax:* 480-643-3068. *E-mail:* audra.mcquarie@phoenix.edu. *Web site:* http:// www.phoenix.edu/.

IDAHO

Boise Bible College
Boise, Idaho

Freshman Application Contact Russell Grove, Director of Admissions, Boise Bible College, 8695 West Marigold Street, Boise, ID 83714-1220. *Phone:* 208-376-7731. *Toll-free phone:* 800-893-7755. *Fax:* 208-376-7743. *E-mail:* rgrove@boisebible.edu. *Web site:* http://www.boisebible.edu/.

Boise State University
Boise, Idaho

- **State-supported** university, founded 1932, part of Idaho System of Higher Education
- **Urban** 175-acre campus
- **Endowment** $63.9 million
- **Coed** 17,349 undergraduate students, 73% full-time, 54% women, 46% men
- **Moderately difficult** entrance level, 65% of applicants were admitted

Undergraduates 12,680 full-time, 4,669 part-time. Students come from 54 states and territories; 64 other countries; 12% are from out of state; 7% transferred in; 12% live on campus. *Retention:* 69% of full-time freshmen returned.

Freshmen *Admission:* 5,845 applied, 3,771 admitted, 2,429 enrolled. *Average high school GPA:* 3.31. *Test scores:* SAT critical reading scores over 500: 62%; SAT math scores over 500: 57%; SAT writing scores over 500: 51%; ACT scores over 18: 90%; SAT critical reading scores over 600: 20%; SAT math scores over 600: 17%; SAT writing scores over 600: 15%; ACT scores over 24: 38%; SAT critical reading scores over 700: 2%; SAT math scores over 700: 2%; SAT writing scores over 700: 1%; ACT scores over 30: 3%.

Faculty *Total:* 1,161, 46% full-time, 42% with terminal degrees. *Student/faculty ratio:* 21:1.

Academics *Calendar:* semesters. *Degrees:* associate, bachelor's, master's, doctoral-research/scholarship, and postbachelor's certificates. *Special study options:* academic remediation for entering students, adult/continuing education programs, advanced placement credit, cooperative education, distance learning, double majors, English as a second language, freshman honors college, honors programs, independent study, internships, off-campus study, part-time degree program, services for LD students, student-designed majors, study abroad, summer session for credit. *ROTC:* Army (b).

Computers on Campus 900 computers/terminals are available on campus for general student use. Students can access the following: online (class) registration. Campuswide network is available. 100% of college-owned or -operated housing units are wired for high-speed Internet access. Wireless service is available via classrooms, libraries, student centers.

Student Life *Housing options:* coed, men-only, women-only. Campus housing is university owned. Freshman applicants given priority for college housing. *Activities and organizations:* drama/theater group, student-run newspaper, choral group, marching band, Latter-Day Saints Student Association, Residence Hall Association, Organization of Student Social Workers, Marching Band Association, Teacher Education Association, national fraternities, national sororities. *Campus security:* 24-hour emergency response devices and patrols. *Student services:* health clinic, personal/psychological counseling, women's center, legal services.

Athletics Member NCAA. All Division I except football (Division I-A). *Intercollegiate sports:* basketball M(s)/W(s), cross-country running M(s)/W(s), golf M(s)/W(s), gymnastics W(s), soccer W, softball W, tennis M(s)/W(s), track and field M(s)/W(s), volleyball W(s), wrestling M(s). *Intramural sports:* basketball M/W, bowling M/W, lacrosse W(c), racquetball M/W, skiing (downhill) M(c)/W(c), soccer M/W, softball M/W, tennis M/W, volleyball M/W, weight lifting M/W.

Standardized Tests *Required for some:* SAT or ACT (for admission).

Costs (2010–11) *One-time required fee:* $75. *Tuition:* state resident $3555 full-time, $149 per credit hour part-time; nonresident $13,011 full-time, $233 per credit hour part-time. Full-time tuition and fees vary according to reciprocity agreements. *Required fees:* $1745 full-time, $83 per credit hour part-time. *Room and board:* $5610; room only: $2642. Room and board charges vary according to board plan and housing facility. *Payment plan:* installment. *Waivers:* senior citizens and employees or children of employees.

Financial Aid Of all full-time matriculated undergraduates who enrolled in 2009, 8,210 applied for aid, 8,193 were judged to have need, 1,078 had their need fully met. 986 Federal Work-Study jobs (averaging $3720). 834 state and other part-time jobs (averaging $3566). In 2009, 657 non-need-based awards were made. *Average percent of need met:* 23%. *Average financial aid package:* $8282. *Average need-based loan:* $6599. *Average need-based gift aid:* $4453. *Average non-need-based aid:* $1071. *Average indebtedness upon graduation:* $38,056. *Financial aid deadline:* 6/1.

Applying *Options:* electronic application. *Application fee:* $55. *Required for some:* high school transcript, minimum 2 GPA. *Recommended:* high school transcript. *Application deadlines:* 6/30 (freshmen), 6/30 (transfers). *Notification:* continuous (freshmen), continuous (transfers).

Freshman Application Contact Ms. Jenny Cerda, Dean of Admissions, Boise State University, Enrollment Services, 1910 University Drive, Boise, ID 83725. *Phone:* 208-426-1177. *Toll-free phone:* 800-632-6586 (in-state); 800-824-7017 (out-of-state). *E-mail:* bsuinfo@boisestate.edu. *Web site:* http://www.boisestate.edu/.

Brigham Young University–Idaho
Rexburg, Idaho

Freshman Application Contact Brigham Young University–Idaho, Rexburg, ID 83460. *Phone:* 208-496-1310. *Web site:* http://www.byui.edu/.

Broadview University-Boise
Meridian, Idaho

Director of Admissions Director of Admissions, Broadview University-Boise, 2750 East Gala Court, Meridian, ID 83642. *Phone:* 208-577-2900. *Toll-free phone:* 877-572-5757. *Fax:* 208-577-2901. *Web site:* http://www.broadviewuniversity.edu/.

Brown Mackie College–Boise
Boise, Idaho

- **Proprietary** primarily 2-year
- **Coed**

Academics *Degrees:* diplomas, associate, and bachelor's.

Costs (2010–11) *Tuition:* Tuition varies by program. Students should contact Brown Mackie College for tuition information.

Freshman Application Contact Brown Mackie College–Boise, 9050 West Overland Road, Suite 100, Boise, ID 83709. *Phone:* 208-321-8800. *Web site:* http://www.brownmackie.edu/boise/.

See page 1140 for the College Close-Up.

The College of Idaho
Caldwell, Idaho

- **Independent** comprehensive, founded 1891
- **Suburban** 50-acre campus
- **Endowment** $72.2 million
- **Coed**
- **Moderately difficult** entrance level

Faculty *Student/faculty ratio:* 12:1.

Academics *Calendar:* 12-6-12 week calendar. *Degrees:* bachelor's and master's.

Student Life *Campus security:* 24-hour emergency response devices and patrols, student patrols, late-night transport/escort service, controlled dormitory access.

Athletics Member NAIA.

Standardized Tests *Required:* SAT or ACT (for admission).

Costs (2010–11) *One-time required fee:* $330. *Comprehensive fee:* $28,750 includes full-time tuition ($20,600), mandatory fees ($450), and room and board ($7700). Part-time tuition: $850 per credit hour. Part-time tuition and fees vary according to course load. *College room only:* $3513. Room and board charges vary according to board plan and housing facility.

Financial Aid *Of all full-time matriculated undergraduates who enrolled in 2009,* 610 applied for aid, 610 were judged to have need, 105 had their need fully met. 182 Federal Work-Study jobs (averaging $720). 50 state and other part-time jobs (averaging $711). *In 2009,* 319 non-need-based awards were made. *Average percent of need met:* 83. *Average financial aid package:* $17,686. *Average need-based loan:* $4367. *Average need-based gift aid:* $6051. *Average non-need-based aid:* $11,036. *Average indebtedness upon graduation:* $19,976.

Applying *Options:* electronic application, early admission, early action, deferred entrance. *Required:* essay or personal statement, high school transcript, minimum 2 GPA, 1 letter of recommendation. *Recommended:* interview, class rank, extracurricular resume.

Freshman Application Contact Brian Bava, Interim Dean of Enrollment Management, The College of Idaho, 2112 Cleveland Boulevard, Caldwell, ID 83605-4432. *Phone:* 208-459-5319. *Toll-free phone:* 800-244-3246. *Fax:* 208-459-5757. *E-mail:* admission@collegeofidaho.edu. *Web site:* http://www.collegeofidaho.edu/.

Idaho State University
Pocatello, Idaho

- **State-supported** university, founded 1901
- **Urban** 1100-acre campus
- **Endowment** $30.9 million
- **Coed** 10,526 undergraduate students, 73% full-time, 54% women, 46% men
- **Minimally difficult** entrance level, 92% of applicants were admitted

Undergraduates 7,731 full-time, 2,795 part-time. Students come from 41 states and territories; 14 other countries; 3% are from out of state; 1% Black or African American, non-Hispanic/Latino; 6% Hispanic/Latino; 1% Asian, non-Hispanic/Latino; 0.1% Native Hawaiian or other Pacific Islander, non-Hispanic/Latino; 2% American Indian or Alaska Native, non-Hispanic/Latino; 20% Race/ethnicity unknown; 2% international; 5% transferred in; 8% live on campus.

Freshmen *Admission:* 2,809 applied, 2,596 admitted, 1,580 enrolled. *Average high school GPA:* 3.1. *Test scores:* SAT critical reading scores over 500: 63%; SAT math scores over 500: 64%; SAT writing scores over 500: 51%; ACT scores over 18: 78%; SAT critical reading scores over 600: 17%; SAT math scores over 600: 35%; SAT writing scores over 600: 15%; ACT scores over 24: 29%; SAT critical reading scores over 700: 1%; SAT math scores over 700: 6%; SAT writing scores over 700: 1%; ACT scores over 30: 3%.

Faculty *Total:* 772, 80% full-time, 39% with terminal degrees. *Student/faculty ratio:* 15:1.

Academics *Calendar:* semesters. *Degrees:* certificates, associate, bachelor's, master's, doctoral-professional, doctoral-research/scholarship, post-master's, and postbachelor's certificates. *Special study options:* academic remediation for entering students, adult/continuing education programs, advanced placement credit, distance learning, double majors, English as a second language, honors programs, independent study, internships, off-campus study, part-time degree program, services for LD students, student-designed majors, study abroad, summer session for credit. *ROTC:* Army (c).

Computers on Campus 697 computers/terminals are available on campus for general student use. Students can access the following: computer help desk, free student e-mail accounts, online (class) grades, online (class) registration, online (class) schedules. Campuswide network is available. 100% of college-owned or -operated housing units are wired for high-speed Internet access. Wireless service is available via classrooms, computer centers, computer labs, dorm rooms, learning centers, libraries, student centers.

Student Life *Housing options:* coed, men-only, women-only, disabled students. Campus housing is university owned. *Activities and organizations:* drama/theater group, student-run newspaper, radio and television station, choral group, marching band, Latter Day Saints Student Association, Greek Council, Academy of Students of Pharmacy, Skills USA - VICA, SHEPPARDS (Students of Health Education, Physical Education, Recreation and Dance), national fraternities, national sororities. *Campus security:* 24-hour emergency response devices and patrols, late-night transport/escort service, controlled dormitory access. *Student services:* health clinic, personal/psychological counseling, women's center.

Athletics Member NCAA. All Division I except football (Division I-AA). *Intercollegiate sports:* basketball M(s)/W(s), cross-country running M(s)/W(s), golf W(s), soccer W(s), softball W(s), tennis M(s)/W(s), track and field M(s)/W(s), volleyball W(s). *Intramural sports:* badminton M/W, basketball M/W, bowling M/W, cross-country running M/W, fencing M(c)/W(c), football M, golf M/W, racquetball M/W, skiing (cross-country) M/W, soccer M/W, softball M/W, table tennis M/W, tennis M/W, track and field M/W, ultimate Frisbee M/W, volleyball M/W, water polo M/W, wrestling M.

Standardized Tests *Required:* SAT or ACT (for admission). *Recommended:* ACT (for admission).

Costs (2011–12) *One-time required fee:* $40. *Tuition:* state resident $3800 full-time, $273 per credit part-time; nonresident $14,300 full-time, $423 per credit part-time. Full-time tuition and fees vary according to course load, program, and reciprocity agreements. Part-time tuition and fees vary according to course load and reciprocity agreements. *Required fees:* $1616 full-time. *Room and board:* $5274; room only: $2374. Room and board charges vary according to board plan and housing facility. *Payment plan:* deferred payment. *Waivers:* senior citizens and employees or children of employees.

Financial Aid *Financial aid deadline:* 3/1.

Applying *Options:* electronic application, early admission, deferred entrance. *Application fee:* $40. *Required:* high school transcript, minimum 2 GPA, ACT or SAT scores (Students 21 or older are exempt from submitting ACT/SAT scores). *Application deadlines:* 8/1 (freshmen), 3/1 (out-of-state freshmen), 8/1 (transfers). *Notification:* continuous (freshmen), continuous (out-of-state freshmen), continuous (transfers).

Freshman Application Contact Idaho State University, 921 South 7th, Stop 8270, Pocatello, ID 83209-8270. *Phone:* 208-282-2475. *Fax:* 208-282-4511. *E-mail:* info@isu.edu. *Web site:* http://www.isu.edu/.

ITT Technical Institute
Boise, Idaho

- **Proprietary** primarily 2-year, founded 1906, part of ITT Educational Services, Inc.
- **Urban** campus
- **Coed**
- **Minimally difficult** entrance level

Academics *Calendar:* quarters. *Degrees:* associate and bachelor's.

Student Life *Housing:* college housing not available.

Financial Aid Of all full-time matriculated undergraduates who enrolled in 2009, 9 Federal Work-Study jobs (averaging $5500).

Freshman Application Contact Director of Recruitment, ITT Technical Institute, 12302 West Explorer Drive, Boise, ID 83713. *Phone:* 208-322-8844. *Toll-free phone:* 800-666-4888. *Fax:* 208-322-0173. *Web site:* http://www.itt-tech.edu/.

Lewis-Clark State College
Lewiston, Idaho

- **State-supported** 4-year, founded 1893
- **Small-town** 44-acre campus
- **Coed** 4,542 undergraduate students, 60% full-time, 60% women, 40% men
- **Minimally difficult** entrance level

Undergraduates 2,733 full-time, 1,809 part-time. 18% are from out of state; 0.6% Black or African American, non-Hispanic/Latino; 5% Hispanic/Latino; 0.6% Asian, non-Hispanic/Latino; 0.3% Native Hawaiian or other Pacific Islander, non-Hispanic/Latino; 3% American Indian or Alaska Native, non-Hispanic/Latino; 3% Two or more races, non-Hispanic/Latino; 0.9% Race/ethnicity unknown; 2% international; 14% transferred in. *Retention:* 54% of full-time freshmen returned.

Freshmen *Admission:* 647 enrolled. *Average high school GPA:* 2.96. *Test scores:* SAT critical reading scores over 500: 46%; SAT math scores over 500: 46%; ACT scores over 18: 75%; SAT critical reading scores over 600: 11%; SAT math scores over 600: 14%; ACT scores over 24: 20%.

Faculty *Total:* 252, 63% full-time, 42% with terminal degrees. *Student/faculty ratio:* 18:1.

Academics *Calendar:* semesters. *Degrees:* certificates, associate, and bachelor's. *Special study options:* academic remediation for entering students, accelerated degree program, adult/continuing education programs, advanced placement credit, cooperative education, distance learning, English as a second language, independent study, internships, off-campus study, part-time degree program, services for LD students, study abroad, summer session for credit. *ROTC:* Army (c), Navy (c), Air Force (c).

Computers on Campus Students can access the following: online (class) registration. Campuswide network is available.

Student Life *Housing options:* coed. Campus housing is university owned, leased by the school and is provided by a third party. *Activities and organizations:* drama/theater group, student-run newspaper, radio station. *Campus*

security: 24-hour emergency response devices and patrols, student patrols, late-night transport/escort service. *Student services:* health clinic, personal/psychological counseling.

Athletics Member NAIA. *Intercollegiate sports:* baseball M(s), basketball M(s)/W(s), cross-country running M(s)/W(s), golf M(s)/W(s), tennis M(s)/W(s), volleyball W(s). *Intramural sports:* badminton M/W, baseball M/W, basketball M/W, bowling M/W, field hockey M/W, football M/W, golf M/W, lacrosse M/W, rock climbing M/W, rugby M/W, skiing (cross-country) M/W, skiing (downhill) M/W, soccer M/W, softball M/W, table tennis M/W, tennis M/W, track and field M/W, volleyball M/W, weight lifting M/W.

Standardized Tests *Required for some:* SAT or ACT (for admission), ACT COMPASS.

Costs (2010–11) *Tuition:* state resident $4998 full-time; nonresident $13,906 full-time. Full-time tuition and fees vary according to course load and reciprocity agreements. *Required fees:* $1232 full-time. *Room and board:* Room and board charges vary according to board plan and housing facility. *Payment plan:* deferred payment. *Waivers:* senior citizens and employees or children of employees.

Financial Aid Of all full-time matriculated undergraduates who enrolled in 2008, 2,006 applied for aid, 1,770 were judged to have need, 311 had their need fully met. 85 Federal Work-Study jobs (averaging $1502). 113 state and other part-time jobs (averaging $1300). In 2008, 217 non-need-based awards were made. *Average percent of need met:* 18%. *Average financial aid package:* $7956. *Average need-based loan:* $3856. *Average need-based gift aid:* $4449. *Average non-need-based aid:* $2618.

Applying *Options:* electronic application, deferred entrance. *Application fee:* $35. *Required:* high school transcript, minimum 2 GPA. *Required for some:* interview. *Application deadlines:* rolling (freshmen), rolling (transfers). *Notification:* continuous (freshmen), continuous (transfers).

Freshman Application Contact Soo Lee Bruce-Smith, Coordinator of New Student Recruitment, Lewis-Clark State College, 500 Eighth Avenue, Lewiston, ID 83501-2698. *Phone:* 208-792-2210. *Toll-free phone:* 800-933-5272. *Fax:* 208-792-2876. *E-mail:* admissions@lcsc.edu. *Web site:* http://www.lcsc.edu/.

New Saint Andrews College
Moscow, Idaho

- **Independent religious** comprehensive, founded 1993
- **Small-town** campus
- **Coed** 146 undergraduate students, 91% full-time, 51% women, 49% men
- **Moderately difficult** entrance level, 70% of applicants were admitted

Undergraduates 133 full-time, 13 part-time. Students come from 31 states and territories; 6 other countries; 84% are from out of state; 3% Hispanic/Latino; 0.7% American Indian or Alaska Native, non-Hispanic/Latino; 2% Two or more races, non-Hispanic/Latino; 22% Race/ethnicity unknown; 5% international; 5% transferred in. *Retention:* 79% of full-time freshmen returned.

Freshmen *Admission:* 106 applied, 74 admitted, 44 enrolled. *Test scores:* SAT critical reading scores over 500: 97%; SAT math scores over 500: 79%; SAT writing scores over 500: 97%; ACT scores over 18: 100%; SAT critical reading scores over 600: 68%; SAT math scores over 600: 36%; SAT writing scores over 600: 65%; ACT scores over 24: 72%; SAT critical reading scores over 700: 39%; SAT math scores over 700: 11%; SAT writing scores over 700: 22%; ACT scores over 30: 24%.

Faculty *Total:* 18, 56% full-time, 44% with terminal degrees. *Student/faculty ratio:* 11:1.

Academics *Calendar:* 4 8-week terms. *Degrees:* associate, bachelor's, master's, and postbachelor's certificates. *Special study options:* advanced placement credit, independent study, part-time degree program, summer session for credit.

Computers on Campus 4 computers/terminals and 4 ports are available on campus for general student use. Students can access the following: campus intranet, free student e-mail accounts, online (class) grades, online (class) registration, online (class) schedules. Campuswide network is available. Wireless service is available via entire campus.

Student Life *Housing:* college housing not available. *Activities and organizations:* choral group, Students for the Relief of the Oppressed, Nursing Home Visits and Elderly Assistance (snow and leaf removal), Blood Drives, Fall Carnival, St. Andrews Day Food Bank Drive. *Campus security:* 24-hour emergency response devices. *Student services:* personal/psychological counseling.

Standardized Tests *Required:* SAT or ACT (for admission).

Costs (2011–12) *Tuition:* $10,400 full-time. No tuition increase for student's term of enrollment. *Payment plan:* installment. *Waivers:* employees or children of employees.

Applying *Options:* electronic application, deferred entrance. *Application fee:* $40. *Required:* essay or personal statement, high school transcript, 2 letters of recommendation, SAT or ACT score. *Required for some:* interview. *Application deadlines:* 2/15 (freshmen), 2/15 (transfers). *Notification:* 3/15 (freshmen), 3/15 (transfers).

Freshman Application Contact Mr. John Sawyer, Manager of New Student Services, New Saint Andrews College, PO Box 9025, Moscow, ID 83843. *Phone:* 208-882-1566 Ext. 100. *Fax:* 208-882-4293. *E-mail:* info@nsa.edu. *Web site:* http://www.nsa.edu/.

Northwest Nazarene University
Nampa, Idaho

- **Independent** comprehensive, founded 1913, affiliated with Church of the Nazarene
- **Small-town** 85-acre campus with easy access to Boise, ID
- **Endowment** $21.9 million
- **Coed** 1,322 undergraduate students, 89% full-time, 60% women, 40% men
- **Moderately difficult** entrance level, 58% of applicants were admitted

Undergraduates 1,171 full-time, 151 part-time. 49% are from out of state; 6% transferred in. *Retention:* 96% of full-time freshmen returned.
Freshmen *Admission:* 1,783 applied, 1,027 admitted, 280 enrolled. *Average high school GPA:* 3.44. *Test scores:* SAT critical reading scores over 500: 64%; SAT math scores over 500: 62%; SAT writing scores over 500: 53%; ACT scores over 18: 91%; SAT critical reading scores over 600: 23%; SAT math scores over 600: 26%; SAT writing scores over 600: 19%; ACT scores over 24: 37%; SAT critical reading scores over 700: 3%; SAT math scores over 700: 4%; SAT writing scores over 700: 1%; ACT scores over 30: 8%.
Faculty *Total:* 112, 96% full-time, 70% with terminal degrees. *Student/faculty ratio:* 13:1.
Academics *Calendar:* semesters. *Degrees:* bachelor's and master's. *Special study options:* academic remediation for entering students, accelerated degree program, adult/continuing education programs, advanced placement credit, cooperative education, freshman honors college, honors programs, independent study, internships, off-campus study, part-time degree program, services for LD students, student-designed majors, study abroad, summer session for credit. *ROTC:* Army (b).
Computers on Campus 78 computers/terminals and 1,128 ports are available on campus for general student use. Students can access the following: campus intranet, computer help desk, free student e-mail accounts, online (class) grades, online (class) registration, online (class) schedules, various software packages. Campuswide network is available. 95% of college-owned or -operated housing units are wired for high-speed Internet access. Wireless service is available via entire campus.
Student Life *Housing:* on-campus residence required through sophomore year. *Options:* men-only, women-only, disabled students. Campus housing is university owned. Freshman campus housing is guaranteed. *Activities and organizations:* drama/theater group, student-run newspaper, choral group, Students in Free Enterprise (SIFE), Student Government Association, Fellowship of Christian Athletes, The Crusader newspaper, The Oasis yearbook. *Campus security:* 24-hour patrols, student patrols, late-night transport/escort service, controlled dormitory access, residence hall check-in system, on-campus police hub. *Student services:* health clinic, personal/psychological counseling.
Athletics Member NCAA. All Division II. *Intercollegiate sports:* baseball M(s), basketball M(s)/W(s), cheerleading W(c), cross-country running M(s)/W(s), golf M(s), soccer M/W(s), softball W(s), track and field M(s)/W(s), volleyball W(s). *Intramural sports:* basketball M/W, cross-country running M/W, football M/W, softball M/W, table tennis M/W, tennis M/W, ultimate Frisbee M/W, volleyball M/W.
Standardized Tests *Required:* SAT or ACT (for admission).
Costs (2011–12) *Comprehensive fee:* $30,250 includes full-time tuition ($23,730), mandatory fees ($300), and room and board ($6220). Full-time tuition and fees vary according to course load, degree level, program, and reciprocity agreements. Part-time tuition: $1028 per semester hour. *Room and board:* Room and board charges vary according to board plan. *Payment plans:* tuition prepayment, installment. *Waivers:* minority students, children of alumni, and employees or children of employees.
Financial Aid Of all full-time matriculated undergraduates who enrolled in 2008, 993 applied for aid, 881 were judged to have need, 166 had their need fully met. 145 Federal Work-Study jobs (averaging $996). In 2008, 273 non-need-based awards were made. *Average percent of need met:* 66%. *Average financial aid package:* $14,946. *Average need-based loan:* $8292. *Average need-based gift aid:* $16,314. *Average non-need-based aid:* $6577. *Average indebtedness upon graduation:* $26,752.
Applying *Options:* electronic application, early action, deferred entrance. *Application fee:* $25. *Required:* essay or personal statement, high school transcript, minimum 2.5 GPA, 2 letters of recommendation. *Required for some:* interview. *Application deadlines:* 8/15 (freshmen), 8/15 (transfers), 12/15 (early action). *Notification:* continuous (freshmen), continuous (transfers), 1/15 (early action).
Freshman Application Contact Northwest Nazarene University, 623 Holly Street, Nampa, ID 83686-5897. *Phone:* 208-467-8950. *Toll-free phone:* 877-668-4968. *Web site:* http://www.nnu.edu/.

Stevens-Henager College
Boise, Idaho

Director of Admissions David Breck, Director of Admission, Stevens-Henager College, 730 Americana Boulevard, Boise, ID 83702. *Phone:* 208-383-4540. *Toll-free phone:* 800-97SKILLS. *Fax:* 208-345-6999. *Web site:* http://www.stevenshenager.edu/.

University of Idaho
Moscow, Idaho

- **State-supported** university, founded 1889
- **Small-town** 1450-acre campus
- **Endowment** $164.8 million
- **Coed** 9,573 undergraduate students, 89% full-time, 46% women, 54% men
- **Moderately difficult** entrance level, 77% of applicants were admitted

Undergraduates 8,559 full-time, 1,014 part-time. Students come from 53 states and territories; 40 other countries; 32% are from out of state; 1% Black or African American, non-Hispanic/Latino; 7% Hispanic/Latino; 2% Asian, non-Hispanic/Latino; 0.3% Native Hawaiian or other Pacific Islander, non-Hispanic/Latino; 0.9% American Indian or Alaska Native, non-Hispanic/Latino; 2% Two or more races, non-Hispanic/Latino; 3% Race/ethnicity unknown; 2% international; 8% transferred in; 20% live on campus. *Retention:* 81% of full-time freshmen returned.
Freshmen *Admission:* 5,204 applied, 4,025 admitted, 1,757 enrolled. *Average high school GPA:* 3.35. *Test scores:* SAT critical reading scores over 500: 69%; SAT math scores over 500: 71%; SAT writing scores over 500: 58%; ACT scores over 18: 93%; SAT critical reading scores over 600: 26%; SAT math scores over 600: 29%; SAT writing scores over 600: 19%; ACT scores over 24: 45%; SAT critical reading scores over 700: 5%; SAT math scores over 700: 5%; SAT writing scores over 700: 2%; ACT scores over 30: 9%.
Faculty *Total:* 702, 76% full-time, 65% with terminal degrees. *Student/faculty ratio:* 18:1.
Academics *Calendar:* semesters. *Degrees:* certificates, bachelor's, master's, doctoral-professional, doctoral-research/scholarship, and post-master's certificates. *Special study options:* academic remediation for entering students, accelerated degree program, adult/continuing education programs, advanced placement credit, cooperative education, distance learning, double majors, English as a second language, honors programs, independent study, internships, off-campus study, part-time degree program, services for LD students, student-designed majors, study abroad, summer session for credit. *ROTC:* Army (b), Navy (b), Air Force (c).
Computers on Campus 495 computers/terminals are available on campus for general student use. Students can access the following: campus intranet, computer help desk, free student e-mail accounts, online (class) grades, online (class) registration, online (class) schedules. Campuswide network is available. 100% of college-owned or -operated housing units are wired for high-speed Internet access. Wireless service is available via entire campus.
Student Life *Housing:* on-campus residence required for freshman year. *Options:* coed, men-only, women-only, disabled students. Campus housing is university owned. Freshman campus housing is guaranteed. *Activities and organizations:* drama/theater group, student-run newspaper, radio and television station, choral group, marching band, ASUI - Associated Student of the University of Idaho, Student Alumni Relations Board, Multicultural Greek Council, Gay Straight Alliance, Campus Crusade for Christ, national fraternities, national sororities. *Campus security:* 24-hour emergency response devices, late-night transport/escort service, controlled dormitory access, contracted services with the city of Moscow police department. *Student services:* health clinic, personal/psychological counseling, women's center, legal services.
Athletics Member NCAA. All Division I except football (Division I-A). *Intercollegiate sports:* basketball M(s)/W(s), cross-country running M(s)/W(s), golf M(s)/W(s), soccer M(c)/W(s), swimming and diving W(s), tennis M(s)/W(s), track and field M(s)/W(s), volleyball W(s). *Intramural sports:* badminton M/W, baseball M, basketball M/W, equestrian sports M/W, football M/W, golf M/W, ice hockey M/W, lacrosse M/W, racquetball M/W, riflery M/W, rugby M/W, skiing (cross-country) M/W, skiing (downhill) M/W, soccer M/W, softball M/W, squash M/W, swimming and diving M/W, table tennis M/W, tennis M/W, track and field M/W, ultimate Frisbee M/W, volleyball M/W, water polo M, weight lifting M/W, wrestling M.
Standardized Tests *Required:* SAT or ACT (for admission).
Costs (2010–11) *Tuition:* state resident $0 full-time; nonresident $11,592 full-time, $580 per credit part-time. Full-time tuition and fees vary according to course load, degree level, program, and reciprocity agreements. Part-time tuition and fees vary according to course load, degree level, and program. *Required fees:* $5402 full-time, $270 per credit part-time. *Room and board:* $7194. Room and board charges vary according to board plan and housing facility. *Payment plans:* installment, deferred payment. *Waivers:* minority stu-

dents, children of alumni, senior citizens, and employees or children of employees.

Financial Aid Of all full-time matriculated undergraduates who enrolled in 2008, 6,193 applied for aid, 4,972 were judged to have need, 1,153 had their need fully met. 429 Federal Work-Study jobs (averaging $2000). 191 state and other part-time jobs (averaging $2000). In 2008, 1922 non-need-based awards were made. *Average percent of need met:* 74%. *Average financial aid package:* $11,751. *Average need-based loan:* $7106. *Average need-based gift aid:* $3825. *Average non-need-based aid:* $4652. *Average indebtedness upon graduation:* $21,702.

Applying *Options:* electronic application, deferred entrance. *Application fee:* $50. *Required:* high school transcript, minimum 2.2 GPA. *Required for some:* essay or personal statement. *Application deadlines:* 8/1 (freshmen), rolling (transfers). *Notification:* continuous (freshmen), continuous (transfers).

Freshman Application Contact Ms. Melissa Goodwin, Associate Director, Admissions, University of Idaho, PO Box 444264, Moscow, ID 83844-4264. *Phone:* 208-885-6326. *Toll-free phone:* 888-884-3246. *Fax:* 208-885-9119. *E-mail:* admissions@uidaho.edu. *Web site:* http://www.uidaho.edu/.

University of Phoenix–Idaho Campus
Meridian, Idaho

Freshman Application Contact Ms. Audra McQuarie, Registrar/Executive Director, University of Phoenix–Idaho Campus, 4305 South Riverpoint Parkway, Mail Stop CF-L101, Phoenix, AZ 85040. *Phone:* 480-557-6151. *Toll-free phone:* 800-776-4867 (in-state); 800-228-7240 (out-of-state). *Fax:* 480-643-3068. *E-mail:* audra.mcquarie@phoenix.edu. *Web site:* http://www.phoenix.edu/.

ILLINOIS

American Academy of Art
Chicago, Illinois

Freshman Application Contact Mr. Stuart Rosenbloom, Director of Admissions, American Academy of Art, 332 South Michigan Avenue, Suite 300, Chicago, IL 60604-4302. *Phone:* 312-461-0600 Ext. 159. *E-mail:* srosenbloom@aaart.edu. *Web site:* http://www.aaart.edu/.

American InterContinental University Online
Hoffman Estates, Illinois

Director of Admissions Jennifer Ziegenmier, Senior Vice President of Admissions and Marketing, American InterContinental University Online, 5550 Prairie Stone Parkway, Suite 400, Hoffman Estates, IL 60192. *Phone:* 877-564-6248. *Toll-free phone:* 877-701-3800. *E-mail:* jziegenmier@aiuonline.edu. *Web site:* http://www.aiuniv.edu/.

Argosy University, Chicago
Chicago, Illinois

- **Proprietary** university, founded 1976
- **Urban** campus
- **Coed**

Academics *Calendar:* semesters. *Degrees:* bachelor's, master's, and doctoral-professional.

Costs (2010–11) *Tuition:* Tuition varies by program. Students should contact Argosy University for tuition information.

Freshman Application Contact Argosy University, Chicago, 225 North Michigan Avenue, Suite 1300, Chicago, IL 60601. *Phone:* 312-777-7600. *Toll-free phone:* 800-626-4123. *Web site:* http://www.argosy.edu/chicago/.

See page 1002 for the College Close-Up.

Argosy University, Schaumburg
Schaumburg, Illinois

- **Proprietary** university, founded 1979
- **Coed**

Academics *Calendar:* semesters. *Degrees:* bachelor's, master's, doctoral-professional, and post-master's certificates.

Costs (2010–11) *Tuition:* Tuition varies by program. Students should contact Argosy University for tuition information.

Freshman Application Contact Argosy University, Schaumburg, 999 North Plaza Drive, Suite 111, Schaumburg, IL 60173-5403. *Phone:* 847-969-4900.

Toll-free phone: 866-290-2777. *Web site:* http://www.argosy.edu/schaumburg/

See page 1002 for the College Close-Up.

Augustana College
Rock Island, Illinois

- **Independent** 4-year, founded 1860, affiliated with Evangelical Lutheran Church in America
- **Suburban** 115-acre campus
- **Endowment** $99.3 million
- **Coed** 2,532 undergraduate students, 99% full-time, 58% women, 42% men
- **Moderately difficult** entrance level, 66% of applicants were admitted

Undergraduates 2,512 full-time, 20 part-time. Students come from 29 states and territories; 23 other countries; 13% are from out of state; 2% Black or African American, non-Hispanic/Latino; 3% Hispanic/Latino; 2% Asian, non-Hispanic/Latino; 0.4% Native Hawaiian or other Pacific Islander, non-Hispanic/Latino; 0.4% American Indian or Alaska Native, non-Hispanic/Latino; 1% Two or more races, non-Hispanic/Latino; 9% Race/ethnicity unknown; 1% international; 2% transferred in; 70% live on campus. *Retention:* 88% of full-time freshmen returned.

Freshmen *Admission:* 4,067 applied, 2,679 admitted, 744 enrolled. *Average high school GPA:* 3.27. *Test scores:* ACT scores over 18: 98%; ACT scores over 24: 68%; ACT scores over 30: 12%.

Faculty *Total:* 273, 67% full-time, 75% with terminal degrees. *Student/faculty ratio:* 12:1.

Academics *Calendar:* quarters. *Degree:* bachelor's. *Special study options:* advanced placement credit, double majors, honors programs, independent study, internships, part-time degree program, services for LD students, student-designed majors, study abroad, summer session for credit. *Unusual degree programs:* 3-2 engineering with Washington University in St. Louis, University of Illinois, Iowa State University of Science and Technology, Purdue University; forestry with Duke University; Occupational therapy with Washington University in St. Louis, landscape architecture with University of Illinois, environmental studies with Duke University.

Computers on Campus 600 computers/terminals and 1,800 ports are available on campus for general student use. Students can access the following: campus intranet, computer help desk, free student e-mail accounts, online (class) grades, online (class) registration, online (class) schedules. Campus-wide network is available. 100% of college-owned or -operated housing units are wired for high-speed Internet access. Wireless service is available via classrooms, computer centers, computer labs, libraries, student centers.

Student Life *Housing:* on-campus residence required through junior year. *Options:* coed, men-only, women-only. Campus housing is university owned. Freshman campus housing is guaranteed. *Activities and organizations:* drama/theater group, student-run newspaper, radio station, choral group, College Union Board of Managers, Student Government Association, student newspaper, student radio station, service organizations (APO, Dance Marathon committee). *Campus security:* 24-hour emergency response devices and patrols, late-night transport/escort service, controlled dormitory access. *Student services:* health clinic, personal/psychological counseling, women's center.

Athletics Member NCAA. All Division III. *Intercollegiate sports:* baseball M, basketball M/W, cheerleading M(c)/W(c), crew M(c)/W(c), cross-country running M/W, equestrian sports M(c)/W(c), fencing M(c)/W(c), football M, golf M/W, ice hockey M(c), lacrosse M(c)/W, soccer M/W, softball W, swimming and diving M/W, tennis M/W, track and field M/W, ultimate Frisbee M(c)/W(c), volleyball M(c)/W, wrestling M. *Intramural sports:* badminton M/W, basketball M/W, bowling M/W, cross-country running M/W, football M/W, golf M/W, racquetball M/W, rugby M, skiing (cross-country) M/W, skiing (downhill) M/W, soccer M/W, softball M/W, swimming and diving M/W, table tennis M/W, tennis M/W, track and field M/W, ultimate Frisbee M/W, volleyball M/W, wrestling M.

Standardized Tests *Required for some:* SAT or ACT (for admission). *Recommended:* SAT or ACT (for admission).

Costs (2011–12) *Comprehensive fee:* $41,829 includes full-time tuition ($33,363) and room and board ($8466). Full-time tuition and fees vary according to student level. Part-time tuition and fees vary according to course load. *Room and board:* Room and board charges vary according to board plan and housing facility. *Payment plans:* tuition prepayment, installment. *Waivers:* employees or children of employees.

Financial Aid Of all full-time matriculated undergraduates who enrolled in 2008, 2,006 applied for aid, 1,684 were judged to have need, 403 had their need fully met. 1,142 Federal Work-Study jobs (averaging $2043). In 2008, 703 non-need-based awards were made. *Average percent of need met:* 85%. *Average financial aid package:* $21,093. *Average need-based loan:* $4601. *Average need-based gift aid:* $15,619. *Average non-need-based aid:* $11,815. *Average indebtedness upon graduation:* $28,198.

Applying *Options:* electronic application, deferred entrance. *Application fee:* $35. *Required:* high school transcript. *Required for some:* essay or personal statement, interview. *Recommended:* essay or personal statement, 1 letter of recommendation, interview. *Application deadlines:* rolling (freshmen), rolling (transfers). *Notification:* continuous (freshmen), continuous (transfers).
Freshman Application Contact Kent Barnds, Director of Admissions, Augustana College, 639 38th Street, Rock Island, IL 61201-2296. *Phone:* 309-794-7341. *Toll-free phone:* 800-798-8100. *Fax:* 309-794-8797. *E-mail:* admissions@augustana.edu. *Web site:* http://www.augustana.edu/.

Aurora University
Aurora, Illinois

- **Independent** comprehensive, founded 1893
- **Suburban** 32-acre campus with easy access to Chicago
- **Endowment** $33.4 million
- **Coed**
- **Moderately difficult** entrance level

Faculty *Student/faculty ratio:* 14:1.
Academics *Calendar:* semesters. *Degrees:* bachelor's, master's, doctoral-research/scholarship, post-master's, and postbachelor's certificates.
Student Life *Campus security:* 24-hour emergency response devices and patrols, late-night transport/escort service, controlled dormitory access.
Athletics Member NCAA. All Division III.
Standardized Tests *Required:* SAT or ACT (for admission).
Costs (2010–11) *Comprehensive fee:* $27,500 includes full-time tuition ($18,600), mandatory fees ($100), and room and board ($8800). Full-time tuition and fees vary according to location. Part-time tuition: $550 per semester hour. Part-time tuition and fees vary according to course load, location, and program. *Room and board:* Room and board charges vary according to board plan, housing facility, and location. *Payment plans:* installment, deferred payment.
Financial Aid *Of all full-time matriculated undergraduates who enrolled in 2009,* 2,040 applied for aid, 1,843 were judged to have need, 569 had their need fully met. 1,032 Federal Work-Study jobs (averaging $1724). *In 2009,* 394 non-need-based awards were made. *Average percent of need met:* 86. *Average financial aid package:* $17,080. *Average need-based loan:* $4395. *Average need-based gift aid:* $7033. *Average non-need-based aid:* $7375. *Average indebtedness upon graduation:* $24,083.
Applying *Options:* electronic application, deferred entrance. *Application fee:* $25. *Required:* high school transcript, minimum 2 GPA. *Required for some:* 2 letters of recommendation, interview. *Recommended:* essay or personal statement, interview.
Freshman Application Contact Mr. James Lancaster, Director, Freshman Admission, Aurora University, 347 South Gladstone Avenue, Aurora, IL 60506-4892. *Phone:* 630-844-5533. *Toll-free phone:* 800-742-5281. *Fax:* 630-844-5535. *E-mail:* admission@aurora.edu. *Web site:* http://www.aurora.edu/.

See page 1092 for the College Close-Up.

Benedictine University
Lisle, Illinois

- **Independent Roman Catholic** comprehensive, founded 1887
- **Suburban** 108-acre campus with easy access to Chicago
- **Endowment** $24.9 million
- **Coed** 3,731 undergraduate students, 74% full-time, 60% women, 40% men
- **Moderately difficult** entrance level, 77% of applicants were admitted

Undergraduates 2,756 full-time, 975 part-time. Students come from 49 states and territories; 12 other countries; 6% are from out of state; 10% Black or African American, non-Hispanic/Latino; 7% Hispanic/Latino; 14% Asian, non-Hispanic/Latino; 0.3% Native Hawaiian or other Pacific Islander, non-Hispanic/Latino; 0.3% American Indian or Alaska Native, non-Hispanic/Latino; 0.1% Two or more races, non-Hispanic/Latino; 33% Race/ethnicity unknown; 1% international; 16% transferred in; 31% live on campus. *Retention:* 76% of full-time freshmen returned.
Freshmen *Admission:* 1,575 applied, 1,206 admitted, 561 enrolled. *Average high school GPA:* 3.29. *Test scores:* ACT scores over 18: 93%; ACT scores over 24: 41%; ACT scores over 30: 6%.
Faculty *Total:* 337, 26% full-time. *Student/faculty ratio:* 18:1.
Academics *Calendar:* semesters. *Degrees:* certificates, associate, bachelor's, master's, doctoral-professional, and postbachelor's certificates. *Special study options:* academic remediation for entering students, accelerated degree program, adult/continuing education programs, advanced placement credit, distance learning, double majors, English as a second language, honors programs, independent study, internships, off-campus study, part-time degree program, services for LD students, study abroad, summer session for credit. *ROTC:* Army (c). *Unusual degree programs:* 3-2 engineering with University of Illi-

nois at Urbana–Champaign, Illinois Institute of Technology, Purdue University.
Computers on Campus 200 computers/terminals are available on campus for general student use. Students can access the following: computer help desk, free student e-mail accounts, online (class) grades, online (class) registration, online (class) schedules. Campuswide network is available. 100% of college-owned or -operated housing units are wired for high-speed Internet access. Wireless service is available via computer centers, dorm rooms, libraries, student centers.
Student Life *Housing options:* coed, men-only, women-only. Campus housing is university owned and is provided by a third party. Freshman campus housing is guaranteed. *Activities and organizations:* drama/theater group, student-run newspaper, television station, choral group, Student Senate, MSA-Muslim Student Association, AMSA-American Medical Student Association, The Candor-Student Newspaper, SEWATE. *Campus security:* 24-hour emergency response devices and patrols, late-night transport/escort service, controlled dormitory access. *Student services:* health clinic, personal/psychological counseling.
Athletics Member NCAA. All Division III. *Intercollegiate sports:* baseball M, basketball M/W, cross-country running M/W, football M, golf M/W, soccer M/W, softball W, tennis W, track and field M/W, volleyball W. *Intramural sports:* basketball M/W, bowling M/W, cheerleading W(c), football M/W, lacrosse M(c), softball M/W, table tennis M/W, volleyball M/W.
Standardized Tests *Required:* SAT or ACT (for admission).
Costs (2011–12) *Comprehensive fee:* $31,250 includes full-time tuition ($22,950), mandatory fees ($800), and room and board ($7500). Full-time tuition and fees vary according to class time, degree level, and location. Part-time tuition and fees vary according to class time and degree level. *Room and board:* Room and board charges vary according to board plan, housing facility, and location. *Payment plans:* installment, deferred payment. *Waivers:* employees or children of employees.
Financial Aid Of all full-time matriculated undergraduates who enrolled in 2009, 1,850 applied for aid, 1,706 were judged to have need. 184 Federal Work-Study jobs (averaging $1239). 283 state and other part-time jobs (averaging $1771). In 2009, 267 non-need-based awards were made. *Average financial aid package:* $17,967. *Average need-based loan:* $3426. *Average need-based gift aid:* $7921. *Average non-need-based aid:* $8783. *Average indebtedness upon graduation:* $28,100.
Applying *Options:* electronic application, deferred entrance. *Application fee:* $40. *Required:* essay or personal statement, high school transcript. *Required for some:* interview. *Recommended:* rank in upper 50% of high school class. *Application deadlines:* rolling (freshmen), rolling (transfers). *Notification:* continuous (freshmen), continuous (transfers).
Freshman Application Contact Ms. Kari Gibbons, Dean of Enrollment, Benedictine University, 5700 College Road, Lisle, IL 60532-0900. *Phone:* 630-829-6300. *Toll-free phone:* 888-829-6363. *Fax:* 630-829-6301. *E-mail:* admissions@ben.edu. *Web site:* http://www.ben.edu/.

Blackburn College
Carlinville, Illinois

- **Independent Presbyterian** 4-year, founded 1837
- **Small-town** 80-acre campus with easy access to St. Louis
- **Endowment** $12.1 million
- **Coed** 598 undergraduate students, 96% full-time, 61% women, 39% men
- **Moderately difficult** entrance level, 56% of applicants were admitted

Undergraduates 573 full-time, 25 part-time. Students come from 19 states and territories; 1 other country; 8% are from out of state; 9% Black or African American, non-Hispanic/Latino; 0.7% Hispanic/Latino; 0.2% Asian, non-Hispanic/Latino; 0.5% American Indian or Alaska Native, non-Hispanic/Latino; 2% Two or more races, non-Hispanic/Latino; 0.3% Race/ethnicity unknown; 9% transferred in; 67% live on campus. *Retention:* 61% of full-time freshmen returned.
Freshmen *Admission:* 810 applied, 456 admitted, 151 enrolled. *Average high school GPA:* 3.3. *Test scores:* ACT scores over 18: 82%; ACT scores over 24: 25%; ACT scores over 30: 2%.
Faculty *Total:* 78, 46% full-time, 54% with terminal degrees. *Student/faculty ratio:* 12:1.
Academics *Calendar:* semesters. *Degree:* bachelor's. *Special study options:* advanced placement credit, cooperative education, double majors, honors programs, independent study, internships, off-campus study, services for LD students, student-designed majors, study abroad, summer session for credit. *Unusual degree programs:* 3-2 engineering with Washington University in St. Louis or University of Missouri, Kansas City.
Computers on Campus 202 computers/terminals are available on campus for general student use. Students can access the following: computer help desk, free student e-mail accounts, online (class) grades, online (class) registration, online (class) schedules. Campuswide network is available. 100% of college-owned or -operated housing units are wired for high-speed Internet access. Wireless service is available via libraries, student centers.

Student Life *Housing:* on-campus residence required through junior year. *Options:* coed, men-only, women-only. Campus housing is university owned. Freshman campus housing is guaranteed. *Activities and organizations:* drama/theater group, student-run newspaper, radio station, choral group, Cultural Expressions, Residence Hall Association, New Student Orientation Committee, choral groups, student government. *Campus security:* student patrols, late-night transport/escort service. *Student services:* personal/psychological counseling.

Athletics Member NCAA. All Division III. *Intercollegiate sports:* baseball M, basketball M/W, cross-country running M/W, golf M, soccer M/W, softball W, tennis W, volleyball W. *Intramural sports:* badminton M/W, basketball M/W, football M/W, golf M/W, racquetball M/W, soccer M/W, softball M/W, table tennis M/W, tennis M/W, ultimate Frisbee M/W, volleyball M/W.

Standardized Tests *Required:* SAT or ACT (for admission).

Costs (2010–11) *Comprehensive fee:* $19,786 includes full-time tuition ($14,886), mandatory fees ($110), and room and board ($4790). *College room only:* $2500. Room and board charges vary according to board plan and housing facility. *Payment plan:* installment. *Waivers:* employees or children of employees.

Financial Aid Of all full-time matriculated undergraduates who enrolled in 2009, 581 applied for aid, 502 were judged to have need, 194 had their need fully met. 388 Federal Work-Study jobs (averaging $2653). 113 state and other part-time jobs (averaging $2337). In 2009, 62 non-need-based awards were made. *Average percent of need met:* 80%. *Average financial aid package:* $13,873. *Average need-based loan:* $4107. *Average need-based gift aid:* $11,209. *Average non-need-based aid:* $5163. *Average indebtedness upon graduation:* $20,077.

Applying *Options:* electronic application, deferred entrance. *Required:* high school transcript, minimum 2 GPA. *Required for some:* essay or personal statement, 3 letters of recommendation, interview. *Recommended:* minimum 2.5 GPA. *Application deadlines:* rolling (freshmen), rolling (out-of-state freshmen), rolling (transfers). *Notification:* continuous (freshmen), continuous (out-of-state freshmen), continuous (transfers).

Freshman Application Contact Mr. John Malin, Director of Admission, Blackburn College, 700 College Avenue, Carlinville, IL 62626. *Phone:* 217-854-3231 Ext. 4252. *Toll-free phone:* 800-233-3550. *E-mail:* admit@mail.blackburn.edu. *Web site:* http://www.blackburn.edu/.

Blessing-Rieman College of Nursing

Quincy, Illinois

- **Independent** comprehensive, founded 1985
- **Small-town** 1-acre campus
- **Endowment** $7.0 million
- **Coed, primarily women**
- **Moderately difficult** entrance level

Faculty *Student/faculty ratio:* 12:1.

Academics *Calendar:* semesters. *Degrees:* bachelor's and master's.

Student Life *Campus security:* 24-hour patrols, late-night transport/escort service, controlled dormitory access.

Standardized Tests *Required:* SAT or ACT (for admission).

Costs (2010–11) *Comprehensive fee:* $30,955 includes full-time tuition ($22,245), mandatory fees ($530), and room and board ($8180). Full-time tuition and fees vary according to course load, location, and student level. Part-time tuition: $510 per credit hour. Part-time tuition and fees vary according to course load, location, and student level. *College room only:* $4115. Room and board charges vary according to board plan, location, and student level.

Financial Aid Of all full-time matriculated undergraduates who enrolled in 2009, 186 applied for aid, 186 were judged to have need, 186 had their need fully met. *Average percent of need met:* 100. *Average need-based loan:* $2394. *Average need-based gift aid:* $7902. *Average indebtedness upon graduation:* $20,000.

Applying *Options:* electronic application, deferred entrance. *Required:* high school transcript, minimum 3 GPA. *Recommended:* essay or personal statement, interview.

Freshman Application Contact Ms. Heather Mutter, Admissions Counselor, Blessing-Rieman College of Nursing, Broadway at 11th Street, POB 7005, Quincy, IL 62305-7005. *Phone:* 217-228-5520 Ext. 6979. *Toll-free phone:* 800-877-9140 Ext. 6964. *Fax:* 217-223-4661. *E-mail:* admissions@brcn.edu. *Web site:* http://www.brcn.edu/.

Bradley University

Peoria, Illinois

- **Independent** comprehensive, founded 1897
- **Suburban** 85-acre campus
- **Endowment** $187.1 million
- **Coed**
- **Minimally difficult** entrance level

Faculty *Student/faculty ratio:* 13:1.

Academics *Calendar:* semesters. *Degrees:* certificates, bachelor's, master's, and doctoral-other.

Student Life *Campus security:* 24-hour emergency response devices and patrols, late-night transport/escort service, controlled dormitory access, emergency text messaging, mass notification/emergency communication system in 20 academic buildings.

Athletics Member NCAA. All Division I.

Standardized Tests *Required:* SAT or ACT (for admission).

Costs (2010–11) *Comprehensive fee:* $33,374 includes full-time tuition ($25,150), mandatory fees ($274), and room and board ($7950). Full-time tuition and fees vary according to course load and program. Part-time tuition: $630 per credit hour. Part-time tuition and fees vary according to course load and program. *Room and board:* Room and board charges vary according to board plan.

Financial Aid Of all full-time matriculated undergraduates who enrolled in 2009, 4,050 applied for aid, 3,454 were judged to have need, 620 had their need fully met. 390 Federal Work-Study jobs (averaging $1790). In 2009, 1366 non-need-based awards were made. *Average percent of need met:* 69. *Average financial aid package:* $16,201. *Average need-based loan:* $4608. *Average need-based gift aid:* $12,618. *Average non-need-based aid:* $7764. *Average indebtedness upon graduation:* $17,067.

Applying *Options:* electronic application, early admission, deferred entrance. *Application fee:* $35. *Required:* essay or personal statement, high school transcript, 1 letter of recommendation. *Recommended:* interview.

Freshman Application Contact Rodney San Jose, Director of Admissions, Bradley University, 1501 West Bradley Avenue, Peoria, IL 61625-0002. *Phone:* 309-677-1000. *Toll-free phone:* 800-447-6460. *Fax:* 309-677-2797. *E-mail:* admissions@bradley.edu. *Web site:* http://www.bradley.edu/.

Chicago State University

Chicago, Illinois

Freshman Application Contact Ms. Addie Epps, Director of Admissions, Chicago State University, 95th Street at King Drive, ADM 200, Chicago, IL 60628. *Phone:* 773-995-2513. *Fax:* 773-995-3820. *E-mail:* ug-admissions@csu.edu. *Web site:* http://www.csu.edu/.

Christian Life College

Mount Prospect, Illinois

- **Independent religious** 4-year, founded 1950
- **Suburban** 5-acre campus with easy access to Chicago
- **Coed** 40 undergraduate students, 83% full-time, 45% women, 55% men
- **Noncompetitive** entrance level

Undergraduates 33 full-time, 7 part-time. Students come from 5 states and territories; 3 other countries; 10% are from out of state; 10% Black or African American, non-Hispanic/Latino; 15% Hispanic/Latino; 13% Asian, non-Hispanic/Latino; 5% Two or more races, non-Hispanic/Latino; 30% international; 13% transferred in.

Freshmen *Admission:* 6 enrolled. *Average high school GPA:* 3.61.

Faculty *Total:* 8, 25% full-time, 38% with terminal degrees. *Student/faculty ratio:* 4:1.

Academics *Degrees:* diplomas, associate, and bachelor's. *Special study options:* academic remediation for entering students, adult/continuing education programs, cooperative education, external degree program, independent study, internships, off-campus study, part-time degree program.

Computers on Campus 7 computers/terminals are available on campus for general student use. Students can access the following: free student e-mail accounts. 100% of college-owned or -operated housing units are wired for high-speed Internet access. Wireless service is available via entire campus.

Student Life *Housing options:* Campus housing is university owned. Freshman campus housing is guaranteed. *Campus security:* controlled dormitory access.

Standardized Tests *Required:* SAT or ACT (for admission).

Costs (2011–12) *Tuition:* $9440 full-time. *Required fees:* $1190 full-time. *Room only:* $3700.

Financial Aid Of all full-time matriculated undergraduates who enrolled in 2002, 33 applied for aid, 28 were judged to have need. 4 Federal Work-Study jobs (averaging $1646). In 2002, 6 non-need-based awards were made. *Average percent of need met:* 75%. *Average financial aid package:* $4464. *Aver-*

age need-based loan: $2393. *Average need-based gift aid:* $3160. *Average non-need-based aid:* $871.

Applying *Options:* early admission, deferred entrance. *Application fee:* $40. *Required:* high school transcript, minimum 2 GPA. *Required for some:* essay or personal statement, minimum 2.5 GPA, interview. *Recommended:* minimum 2.5 GPA. *Application deadlines:* rolling (freshmen), rolling (out-of-state freshmen), rolling (transfers). *Notification:* continuous (freshmen), continuous (out-of-state freshmen), continuous (transfers).

Freshman Application Contact Christian Life College, 400 East Gregory Street, Mount Prospect, IL 60056. *Phone:* 847-259-1840 Ext. 100. *Web site:* http://www.christianlifecollege.edu/.

Columbia College Chicago

Chicago, Illinois

- **Independent** comprehensive, founded 1890
- **Urban** campus with easy access to Chicago
- **Endowment** $96.4 million
- **Coed** 11,400 undergraduate students, 90% full-time, 53% women, 47% men
- **Moderately difficult** entrance level, 85% of applicants were admitted

Undergraduates 10,227 full-time, 1,173 part-time. Students come from 47 other countries; 34% are from out of state; 16% Black or African American, non-Hispanic/Latino; 12% Hispanic/Latino; 2% Asian, non-Hispanic/Latino; 0.3% Native Hawaiian or other Pacific Islander, non-Hispanic/Latino; 0.4% American Indian or Alaska Native, non-Hispanic/Latino; 3% Two or more races, non-Hispanic/Latino; 2% Race/ethnicity unknown; 1% international; 10% transferred in; 21% live on campus. *Retention:* 66% of full-time freshmen returned.

Freshmen *Admission:* 6,576 applied, 5,578 admitted, 2,252 enrolled. *Average high school GPA:* 3.09. *Test scores:* SAT critical reading scores over 500: 67%; SAT math scores over 500: 50%; ACT scores over 18: 84%; SAT critical reading scores over 600: 27%; SAT math scores over 600: 15%; ACT scores over 24: 35%; SAT critical reading scores over 700: 4%; SAT math scores over 700: 2%; ACT scores over 30: 5%.

Faculty *Total:* 2,108, 17% full-time. *Student/faculty ratio:* 12:1.

Academics *Calendar:* semesters. *Degrees:* certificates, diplomas, bachelor's, master's, and postbachelor's certificates. *Special study options:* academic remediation for entering students, adult/continuing education programs, advanced placement credit, cooperative education, distance learning, English as a second language, honors programs, independent study, internships, off-campus study, part-time degree program, services for LD students, student-designed majors, study abroad, summer session for credit.

Computers on Campus 851 computers/terminals are available on campus for general student use. Students can access the following: campus intranet, computer help desk, free student e-mail accounts, online (class) grades, online (class) registration, online (class) schedules. Campuswide network is available. 100% of college-owned or -operated housing units are wired for high-speed Internet access. Wireless service is available via entire campus.

Student Life *Housing options:* coed. Campus housing is university owned and leased by the school. Freshman applicants given priority for college housing. *Activities and organizations:* drama/theater group, student-run newspaper, radio and television station, choral group, Columbia Urban Music Association, International Student Organization, Acianza Latina, Marketing Club. *Campus security:* 24-hour emergency response devices and patrols, late-night transport/escort service, controlled dormitory access, escort upon request. *Student services:* health clinic, personal/psychological counseling.

Athletics *Intercollegiate sports:* baseball M(c), basketball M(c), lacrosse M(c). *Intramural sports:* cheerleading M/W, cross-country running M/W, fencing M/W, football M/W, rugby M/W, soccer M/W, softball W, swimming and diving M/W, tennis M/W, ultimate Frisbee M/W, volleyball M/W.

Standardized Tests *Recommended:* SAT or ACT (for admission).

Costs (2011–12) *Comprehensive fee:* $32,870 includes full-time tuition ($20,190) and room and board ($12,680). Full-time tuition and fees vary according to course load. Part-time tuition: $694 per credit hour. Part-time tuition and fees vary according to course load. *College room only:* $10,780. Room and board charges vary according to housing facility. *Payment plan:* installment. *Waivers:* employees or children of employees.

Financial Aid Of all full-time matriculated undergraduates who enrolled in 2009, 7,243 applied for aid, 6,428 were judged to have need, 5,780 had their need fully met. *Average percent of need met:* 29%. *Average financial aid package:* $8922. *Average need-based loan:* $4337. *Average need-based gift aid:* $2347.

Applying *Options:* electronic application, deferred entrance. *Application fee:* $35. *Required:* essay or personal statement, high school transcript, 1 letter of recommendation. *Recommended:* minimum 2 GPA, interview. *Application deadlines:* rolling (freshmen), rolling (out-of-state freshmen), rolling (trans-

fers). *Notification:* continuous (freshmen), continuous (out-of-state freshmen), continuous (transfers).

Freshman Application Contact Mr. Murphy Monroe, Executive Director of Admissions, Columbia College Chicago, 600 South Michigan Avenue, Chicago, IL 60605-1996. *Phone:* 312-369-7133. *Fax:* 312-344-8024. *E-mail:* admissions@colum.edu. *Web site:* http://www.colum.edu/.

Concordia University Chicago

River Forest, Illinois

- **Independent** comprehensive, founded 1864, affiliated with Lutheran Church–Missouri Synod, part of Concordia University System
- **Suburban** 40-acre campus with easy access to Chicago
- **Endowment** $13.5 million
- **Coed** 1,376 undergraduate students, 93% full-time, 57% women, 43% men
- **Moderately difficult** entrance level, 70% of applicants were admitted

Undergraduates 1,282 full-time, 94 part-time. Students come from 22 states and territories; 32% are from out of state; 13% Black or African American, non-Hispanic/Latino; 15% Hispanic/Latino; 1% Asian, non-Hispanic/Latino; 0.1% Native Hawaiian or other Pacific Islander, non-Hispanic/Latino; 0.1% American Indian or Alaska Native, non-Hispanic/Latino; 1% Two or more races, non-Hispanic/Latino; 6% Race/ethnicity unknown; 11% transferred in; 60% live on campus. *Retention:* 69% of full-time freshmen returned.

Freshmen *Admission:* 2,195 applied, 1,538 admitted, 303 enrolled. *Average high school GPA:* 3. *Test scores:* ACT scores over 18: 91%; ACT scores over 24: 30%; ACT scores over 30: 5%.

Faculty *Total:* 316, 45% full-time. *Student/faculty ratio:* 17:1.

Academics *Calendar:* semesters. *Degrees:* bachelor's, master's, doctoral-research/scholarship, post-master's, and postbachelor's certificates. *Special study options:* academic remediation for entering students, accelerated degree program, adult/continuing education programs, advanced placement credit, distance learning, double majors, honors programs, independent study, internships, off-campus study, part-time degree program, services for LD students, study abroad, summer session for credit.

Computers on Campus 85 computers/terminals are available on campus for general student use. Students can access the following: campus intranet, computer help desk, free student e-mail accounts, online (class) grades, online (class) registration, online (class) schedules. Campuswide network is available. 100% of college-owned or -operated housing units are wired for high-speed Internet access. Wireless service is available via libraries, student centers.

Student Life *Housing options:* coed, women-only. Campus housing is university owned. *Activities and organizations:* drama/theater group, student-run newspaper, radio station, choral group, Concordia Youth Ministries, Kappelle Choir, Wind Symphony, student government, intramural sports. *Campus security:* 24-hour emergency response devices and patrols, student patrols, late-night transport/escort service, controlled dormitory access, emergency call boxes. *Student services:* personal/psychological counseling, legal services.

Athletics Member NCAA. All Division III. *Intercollegiate sports:* baseball M, basketball M/W, cheerleading M/W, cross-country running M/W, football M, golf M, soccer M/W, softball W, tennis M/W, track and field M/W, volleyball W. *Intramural sports:* badminton M/W, basketball M/W, bowling M/W, football M, swimming and diving M/W, table tennis M/W, tennis M/W, volleyball M/W.

Standardized Tests *Required:* SAT or ACT (for admission).

Costs (2011–12) *Comprehensive fee:* $33,881 includes full-time tuition ($24,944), mandatory fees ($687), and room and board ($8250). Full-time tuition and fees vary according to program. Part-time tuition: $779 per semester hour. Part-time tuition and fees vary according to program. *Payment plan:* installment. *Waivers:* minority students, children of alumni, senior citizens, and employees or children of employees.

Financial Aid Of all full-time matriculated undergraduates who enrolled in 2008, 1,110 applied for aid, 992 were judged to have need, 387 had their need fully met. 116 Federal Work-Study jobs (averaging $1797). 321 state and other part-time jobs (averaging $2012). In 2008, 168 non-need-based awards were made. *Average percent of need met:* 86%. *Average financial aid package:* $21,388. *Average need-based loan:* $4076. *Average need-based gift aid:* $12,571. *Average non-need-based aid:* $9667. *Average indebtedness upon graduation:* $31,945. *Financial aid deadline:* 8/15.

Applying *Options:* electronic application, deferred entrance. *Required:* high school transcript, minimum 2 GPA, 1 letter of recommendation. *Required for some:* essay or personal statement, interview. *Application deadlines:* rolling (freshmen), rolling (transfers).

Freshman Application Contact Ms. Gwen Kanelos, Director of Admission, Concordia University Chicago, 7400 Augusta Street, River Forest, IL 60305. *Phone:* 708-209-3101. *Toll-free phone:* 800-285-2668. *Fax:* 708-209-3473. *E-mail:* gwen.kanelos@cuchicago.edu. *Web site:* http://www.cuchicago.edu/.

DePaul University

Chicago, Illinois

- **Independent Roman Catholic** university, founded 1898
- **Urban** 36-acre campus with easy access to Chicago
- **Endowment** $284.0 million
- **Coed** 16,052 undergraduate students, 83% full-time, 55% women, 45% men
- **Moderately difficult** entrance level, 69% of applicants were admitted

Undergraduates 13,250 full-time, 2,802 part-time. Students come from 55 states and territories; 101 other countries; 16% are from out of state; 9% Black or African American, non-Hispanic/Latino; 15% Hispanic/Latino; 8% Asian, non-Hispanic/Latino; 0.4% Native Hawaiian or other Pacific Islander, non-Hispanic/Latino; 0.2% American Indian or Alaska Native, non-Hispanic/Latino; 2% Two or more races, non-Hispanic/Latino; 9% Race/ethnicity unknown; 2% international; 10% transferred in; 16% live on campus. *Retention:* 87% of full-time freshmen returned.

Freshmen *Admission:* 12,031 applied, 8,281 admitted, 2,241 enrolled. *Average high school GPA:* 3.46. *Test scores:* SAT critical reading scores over 500: 88%; SAT math scores over 500: 82%; SAT writing scores over 500: 84%; ACT scores over 18: 99%; SAT critical reading scores over 600: 43%; SAT math scores over 600: 34%; SAT writing scores over 600: 42%; ACT scores over 24: 64%; SAT critical reading scores over 700: 9%; SAT math scores over 700: 6%; SAT writing scores over 700: 7%; ACT scores over 30: 11%.

Faculty *Total:* 1,862, 50% full-time, 53% with terminal degrees. *Student/faculty ratio:* 17:1.

Academics *Calendar:* quarters; semesters for law school. *Degrees:* certificates, bachelor's, master's, doctoral-professional, doctoral-research/scholarship, post-master's, and postbachelor's certificates. *Special study options:* academic remediation for entering students, accelerated degree program, adult/continuing education programs, advanced placement credit, cooperative education, distance learning, double majors, English as a second language, freshman honors college, honors programs, independent study, internships, part-time degree program, services for LD students, student-designed majors, study abroad, summer session for credit. *ROTC:* Army (b). *Unusual degree programs:* 3-2 engineering with Illinois Institute of Technology.

Computers on Campus 1,800 computers/terminals and 400 ports are available on campus for general student use. Students can access the following: campus intranet, computer help desk, free student e-mail accounts, online (class) grades, online (class) registration, online (class) schedules, tuition payments, degree progress, financial aid, transcript requests, housing services, student employment information. Campuswide network is available. 100% of college-owned or -operated housing units are wired for high-speed Internet access. Wireless service is available via entire campus.

Student Life *Housing options:* coed, disabled students. Campus housing is university owned, leased by the school and is provided by a third party. Freshman applicants given priority for college housing. *Activities and organizations:* drama/theater group, student-run newspaper, radio station, choral group, Panhellenic Association, DePaul Activities Board, Student Government Association, community service organizations, Catholic Campus Ministry, national fraternities, national sororities. *Campus security:* 24-hour emergency response devices and patrols, late-night transport/escort service, controlled dormitory access, security lighting, prevention/awareness programs, on-campus police officers, video cameras, smoke detectors in residence halls, etc. *Student services:* health clinic, personal/psychological counseling, women's center, legal services.

Athletics Member NCAA. All Division I. *Intercollegiate sports:* basketball M(s)/W(s), cross-country running M(s)/W(s), golf M(s), soccer M(s)/W(s), softball W(s), tennis M(s)/W(s), track and field M(s)/W(s), volleyball W(s). *Intramural sports:* badminton M/W, basketball M/W, football M/W, golf M(c)/W(c), ice hockey M(c)/W(c), lacrosse M(c)/W(c), racquetball M/W, rugby M(c)/W(c), skiing (downhill) M(c)/W(c), soccer M/W, softball M/W, table tennis M/W, tennis M/W, ultimate Frisbee M(c)/W(c), volleyball M/W, water polo M/W.

Standardized Tests *Required:* SAT or ACT (for admission).

Costs (2011–12) *Comprehensive fee:* $39,813 includes full-time tuition ($28,240), mandatory fees ($618), and room and board ($10,955). Full-time tuition and fees vary according to program. Part-time tuition: $490 per quarter hour. Part-time tuition and fees vary according to program. *College room only:* $8015. Room and board charges vary according to board plan, housing facility, and location. *Payment plans:* installment, deferred payment. *Waivers:* employees or children of employees.

Financial Aid Of all full-time matriculated undergraduates who enrolled in 2009, 10,763 applied for aid, 8,664 were judged to have need, 889 had their need fully met. In 2009, 486 non-need-based awards were made. *Average percent of need met:* 67%. *Average financial aid package:* $20,459. *Average need-based loan:* $4732. *Average need-based gift aid:* $14,428. *Average non-need-based aid:* $9128. *Average indebtedness upon graduation:* $19,072.

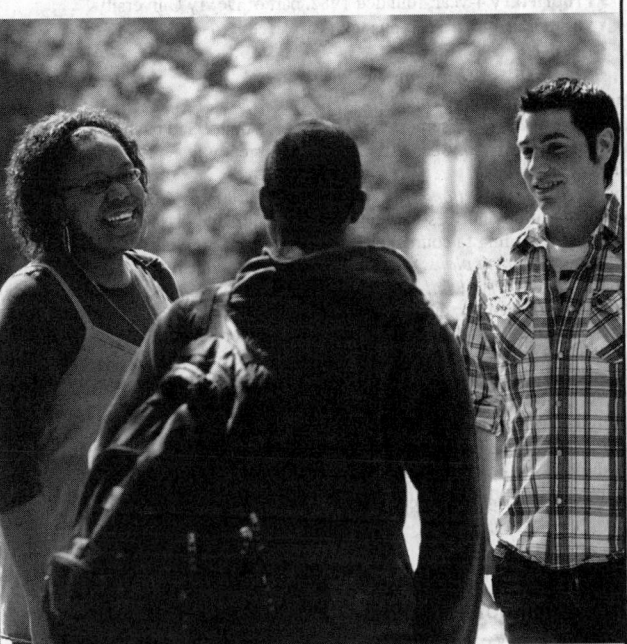

Founded in 1898, DePaul is the nation's largest Catholic university. DePaul's 25,000 students come to Chicago from across the nation and from around the globe. They're attracted by DePaul's proven record for preparing students to be leaders in their chosen fields and by the university's array of more than 150 undergraduate degree programs.

To learn more, visit **depaul.edu**

Applying *Options:* electronic application, early action, deferred entrance. *Application fee:* $40. *Required:* essay or personal statement, high school transcript, minimum 2 GPA. *Required for some:* minimum 3 GPA, Audition/Interviews are required for the School of Music and Theatre School applicants. *Recommended:* minimum 2.5 GPA. *Application deadlines:* 2/1 (freshmen), 2/1 (out-of-state freshmen), rolling (transfers), 11/15 (early action). *Notification:* 3/15 (freshmen), 3/15 (out-of-state freshmen), continuous (transfers), 1/15 (early action).
Freshman Application Contact Carlene Klaas-Kennelly, Dean of Undergraduate Admissions, DePaul University, 1 East Jackson Boulevard, Suite 9000, Chicago, IL 60604. *Phone:* 312-362-8300. *E-mail:* admission@depaul.edu. *Web site:* http://www.depaul.edu/.

See page 1254 for the College Close-Up.

DeVry University
Addison, Illinois

- **Proprietary** 4-year, founded 1982, part of DeVry University
- **Suburban** 14-acre campus with easy access to Chicago
- **Coed**
- **Minimally difficult** entrance level

Faculty *Student/faculty ratio:* 14:1.
Academics *Calendar:* semesters. *Degrees:* associate and bachelor's.
Student Life *Campus security:* 24-hour emergency response devices, lighted pathways/sidewalks.
Costs (2010–11) *Tuition:* $14,766 full-time, $580 per credit hour part-time. Full-time tuition and fees vary according to course load. Part-time tuition and fees vary according to course load. *Required fees:* $60 full-time, $30 per term part-time. *Payment plans:* installment, deferred payment.
Financial Aid *Of all full-time matriculated undergraduates who enrolled in 2007,* 481 applied for aid, 447 were judged to have need, 18 had their need fully met. *In 2007,* 57 non-need-based awards were made. *Average percent of need met:* 47. *Average financial aid package:* $13,134. *Average need-based loan:* $8478. *Average need-based gift aid:* $6727. *Average non-need-based aid:* $15,985. *Average indebtedness upon graduation:* $31,740.
Applying *Options:* electronic application, early admission, deferred entrance. *Application fee:* $50. *Required:* high school transcript, interview.
Freshman Application Contact DeVry University, 1221 North Swift Road, Addison, IL 60101-6106. *Toll-free phone:* 800-346-5420. *Web site:* http://www.devry.edu/.

DeVry University
Chicago, Illinois

- **Proprietary** comprehensive, founded 1931, part of DeVry University
- **Urban** 17-acre campus
- **Coed** 2,431 undergraduate students, 57% full-time, 44% women, 56% men
- **Minimally difficult** entrance level

Undergraduates 1,375 full-time, 1,056 part-time. 2% are from out of state; 30% Black or African American, non-Hispanic/Latino; 35% Hispanic/Latino; 4% Asian, non-Hispanic/Latino; 0.2% Native Hawaiian or other Pacific Islander, non-Hispanic/Latino; 0.3% American Indian or Alaska Native, non-Hispanic/Latino; 0.5% Two or more races, non-Hispanic/Latino; 15% Race/ethnicity unknown; 1% international; 16% transferred in.
Freshmen *Admission:* 380 enrolled.
Faculty *Total:* 182, 21% full-time. *Student/faculty ratio:* 18:1.
Academics *Calendar:* semesters. *Degrees:* associate, bachelor's, and master's. *Special study options:* academic remediation for entering students, accelerated degree program, adult/continuing education programs, advanced placement credit, distance learning, part-time degree program, services for LD students, summer session for credit.
Computers on Campus Students can access the following: online (class) registration. Campuswide network is available.
Student Life *Housing:* college housing not available. *Campus security:* 24-hour emergency response devices and patrols, late-night transport/escort service, lighted pathways/sidewalks.
Costs (2010–11) *Tuition:* $14,766 full-time, $580 per credit hour part-time. Full-time tuition and fees vary according to course load. Part-time tuition and fees vary according to course load. *Required fees:* $60 full-time, $30 per term part-time. *Payment plans:* installment, deferred payment. *Waivers:* employees or children of employees.
Financial Aid Of all full-time matriculated undergraduates who enrolled in 2007, 479 applied for aid, 467 were judged to have need, 5 had their need fully met. In 2007, 14 non-need-based awards were made. *Average percent of need met:* 48%. *Average financial aid package:* $16,145. *Average need-based loan:* $8033. *Average need-based gift aid:* $8371. *Average non-need-based aid:* $11,220. *Average indebtedness upon graduation:* $49,157.

Applying *Options:* electronic application, deferred entrance. *Application fee:* $50. *Required:* high school transcript, interview. *Application deadlines:* rolling (freshmen), rolling (transfers). *Notification:* continuous (freshmen), continuous (transfers).
Freshman Application Contact DeVry University, 3300 North Campbell Avenue, Chicago, IL 60618-5994. *Phone:* 773-929-8500. *Web site:* http://www.devry.edu/.

DeVry University
Downers Grove, Illinois

Admissions Office Contact DeVry University, 3005 Highland Parkway, Downers Grove, IL 60515. *Web site:* http://www.devry.edu/.

DeVry University
Elgin, Illinois

Admissions Office Contact DeVry University, Randall Point, 2250 Point Boulevard, Suite 250, Elgin, IL 60123. *Web site:* http://www.devry.edu/.

DeVry University
Gurnee, Illinois

Admissions Office Contact DeVry University, 1075 Tri-State Parkway, Suite 800, Gurnee, IL 60031-9126. *Toll-free phone:* 866-563-3879. *Web site:* http://www.devry.edu/.

DeVry University
Naperville, Illinois

Director of Admissions Admissions Office, DeVry University, 2056 Westings Avenue, Suite 40, Naperville, IL 60563-2361. *Toll-free phone:* 877-496-9050. *Web site:* http://www.devry.edu/.

DeVry University
Tinley Park, Illinois

- **Proprietary** comprehensive, founded 2000, part of DeVry University
- **Suburban** 12-acre campus
- **Coed**
- **Minimally difficult** entrance level

Faculty *Student/faculty ratio:* 19:1.
Academics *Calendar:* semesters. *Degrees:* associate, bachelor's, and master's.
Student Life *Campus security:* 24-hour emergency response devices, late-night transport/escort service, lighted pathways/sidewalks, security patrols.
Costs (2010–11) *Tuition:* $14,766 full-time, $580 per credit hour part-time. Full-time tuition and fees vary according to course load. Part-time tuition and fees vary according to course load. *Required fees:* $60 full-time, $30 per term part-time. *Payment plans:* installment, deferred payment.
Financial Aid *Of all full-time matriculated undergraduates who enrolled in 2007,* 379 applied for aid, 366 were judged to have need, 18 had their need fully met. *In 2007,* 24 non-need-based awards were made. *Average percent of need met:* 45. *Average financial aid package:* $12,346. *Average need-based loan:* $7379. *Average need-based gift aid:* $6916. *Average non-need-based aid:* $14,254. *Average indebtedness upon graduation:* $4375.
Applying *Options:* electronic application, deferred entrance. *Application fee:* $50. *Required:* high school transcript, interview.
Freshman Application Contact DeVry University, 18624 West Creek Drive, Tinley Park, IL 60477. *Web site:* http://www.devry.edu/.

DeVry University Online
Addison, Illinois

- **Proprietary** comprehensive, founded 2000
- **Coed** 24,289 undergraduate students, 25% full-time, 52% women, 48% men
- **Minimally difficult** entrance level

Undergraduates 6,101 full-time, 18,188 part-time. 88% are from out of state; 17% Black or African American, non-Hispanic/Latino; 8% Hispanic/Latino; 1% Asian, non-Hispanic/Latino; 0.3% Native Hawaiian or other Pacific Islander, non-Hispanic/Latino; 0.6% American Indian or Alaska Native, non-Hispanic/Latino; 0.7% Two or more races, non-Hispanic/Latino; 31% Race/ethnicity unknown; 0.1% international; 32% transferred in.
Freshmen *Admission:* 3,969 enrolled.
Faculty *Total:* 3,200, 0.3% full-time. *Student/faculty ratio:* 14:1.
Academics *Calendar:* semesters. *Degrees:* associate, bachelor's, and master's. *Special study options:* accelerated degree program, distance learning.

Costs (2010–11) *Tuition:* $14,766 full-time, $580 per credit hour part-time. Full-time tuition and fees vary according to course load. Part-time tuition and fees vary according to course load. *Required fees:* $60 full-time, $30 per term part-time. *Payment plans:* installment, deferred payment. *Waivers:* employees or children of employees.

Financial Aid Of all full-time matriculated undergraduates who enrolled in 2006, 810 applied for aid, 785 were judged to have need, 9 had their need fully met. In 2006, 146 non-need-based awards were made. *Average percent of need met:* 36%. *Average financial aid package:* $10,560. *Average need-based loan:* $6201. *Average need-based gift aid:* $7114. *Average non-need-based aid:* $10,591. *Average indebtedness upon graduation:* $35,423.

Applying *Options:* electronic application, deferred entrance. *Application fee:* $50. *Required:* high school transcript, interview. *Application deadlines:* rolling (freshmen), rolling (transfers). *Notification:* continuous (freshmen), continuous (transfers).

Freshman Application Contact DeVry University Online, 1221 North Swift Road, Addison, IL 60101-6106. *Phone:* 877-496-9050. *Web site:* http://www.devry.edu/.

Dominican University
River Forest, Illinois

- **Independent Roman Catholic** comprehensive, founded 1901
- **Suburban** 30-acre campus with easy access to Chicago
- **Endowment** $19.7 million
- **Coed** 1,939 undergraduate students, 91% full-time, 67% women, 33% men
- **Moderately difficult** entrance level, 81% of applicants were admitted

Undergraduates 1,774 full-time, 165 part-time. Students come from 27 states and territories; 21 other countries; 8% are from out of state; 7% Black or African American, non-Hispanic/Latino; 30% Hispanic/Latino; 3% Asian, non-Hispanic/Latino; 0.1% Native Hawaiian or other Pacific Islander, non-Hispanic/Latino; 0.3% American Indian or Alaska Native, non-Hispanic/Latino; 0.8% Two or more races, non-Hispanic/Latino; 3% Race/ethnicity unknown; 2% international; 6% transferred in; 37% live on campus. *Retention:* 81% of full-time freshmen returned.

Freshmen *Admission:* 1,916 applied, 1,545 admitted, 427 enrolled. *Average high school GPA:* 3.51. *Test scores:* SAT critical reading scores over 500: 55%; SAT math scores over 500: 50%; SAT writing scores over 500: 67%; ACT scores over 18: 97%; SAT critical reading scores over 600: 22%; SAT math scores over 600: 22%; SAT writing scores over 600: 28%; ACT scores over 24: 41%; SAT writing scores over 700: 6%; ACT scores over 30: 3%.

Faculty *Total:* 413, 39% full-time. *Student/faculty ratio:* 11:1.

Academics *Calendar:* semesters. *Degrees:* certificates, bachelor's, master's, doctoral-research/scholarship, post-master's, and postbachelor's certificates. *Special study options:* accelerated degree program, adult/continuing education programs, advanced placement credit, distance learning, double majors, English as a second language, honors programs, independent study, internships, off-campus study, part-time degree program, services for LD students, student-designed majors, study abroad, summer session for credit. *Unusual degree programs:* 3-2 business administration; engineering with Illinois Institute of Technology; nursing with Rush University; social work; library science, occupational therapy with Rush University, pharmacy with Midwestern University.

Computers on Campus 625 computers/terminals are available on campus for general student use. Students can access the following: campus intranet, computer help desk, free student e-mail accounts, online (class) grades, online (class) registration, online (class) schedules, online student account information, online financial aid information. Campuswide network is available. 100% of college-owned or -operated housing units are wired for high-speed Internet access. Wireless service is available via computer centers, learning centers, libraries, student centers.

Student Life *Housing options:* coed, men-only, women-only. Campus housing is university owned and leased by the school. Freshman applicants given priority for college housing. *Activities and organizations:* drama/theater group, student-run newspaper, choral group, student government, Student Theater, Commuter Student Association, Resident Student Association, International Club. *Campus security:* 24-hour emergency response devices and patrols, student patrols, late-night transport/escort service, controlled dormitory access, door alarms. *Student services:* health clinic, personal/psychological counseling.

Athletics Member NCAA. All Division III. *Intercollegiate sports:* baseball M, basketball M/W, cross-country running M/W, golf M, soccer M/W, softball W, tennis M/W, volleyball M(c)/W. *Intramural sports:* basketball M/W, bowling M/W, football M/W, racquetball M/W, soccer M/W, softball W, tennis M/W, volleyball W, water polo M/W.

Standardized Tests *Required:* SAT or ACT (for admission).

Costs (2010–11) *One-time required fee:* $150. *Comprehensive fee:* $33,710 includes full-time tuition ($25,560), mandatory fees ($150), and room and board ($8000). Full-time tuition and fees vary according to course load. Part-time tuition: $852 per semester hour. Part-time tuition and fees vary according

to course load. *Required fees:* $15 per course part-time. *Room and board:* Room and board charges vary according to board plan and housing facility. *Payment plan:* installment. *Waivers:* children of alumni and employees or children of employees.

Financial Aid Of all full-time matriculated undergraduates who enrolled in 2009, 1,521 applied for aid, 1,401 were judged to have need, 193 had their need fully met. 393 Federal Work-Study jobs (averaging $892,275). 125 state and other part-time jobs (averaging $302,654). In 2009, 194 non-need-based awards were made. *Average percent of need met:* 73%. *Average financial aid package:* $18,162. *Average need-based loan:* $4125. *Average need-based gift aid:* $14,312. *Average non-need-based aid:* $8039. *Average indebtedness upon graduation:* $22,605.

Applying *Options:* electronic application, deferred entrance. *Application fee:* $25. *Required:* essay or personal statement, high school transcript, minimum 2.75 GPA. *Required for some:* 2 letters of recommendation, interview. *Recommended:* interview. *Application deadlines:* rolling (freshmen), rolling (transfers). *Notification:* continuous (freshmen), continuous (transfers).

Freshman Application Contact Mr. Glenn Hamilton, Assistant Vice President, Enrollment Management, Dominican University, 7900 West Division Street, River Forest, IL 60305. *Phone:* 708-524-6800. *Toll-free phone:* 800-828-8475. *Fax:* 708-524-6864. *E-mail:* domadmis@dom.edu. *Web site:* http://www.dom.edu/.

Eastern Illinois University
Charleston, Illinois

- **State-supported** comprehensive, founded 1895
- **Small-town** 320-acre campus
- **Endowment** $42.4 million
- **Coed** 9,970 undergraduate students, 90% full-time, 58% women, 42% men
- **Moderately difficult** entrance level, 66% of applicants were admitted

Undergraduates 8,946 full-time, 1,024 part-time. Students come from 32 states and territories; 23 other countries; 2% are from out of state; 13% Black or African American, non-Hispanic/Latino; 3% Hispanic/Latino; 1% Asian, non-Hispanic/Latino; 0.1% Native Hawaiian or other Pacific Islander, non-Hispanic/Latino; 0.4% American Indian or Alaska Native, non-Hispanic/Latino; 0.7% Two or more races, non-Hispanic/Latino; 5% Race/ethnicity unknown; 0.6% international; 12% transferred in; 59% live on campus. *Retention:* 79% of full-time freshmen returned.

Freshmen *Admission:* 7,531 applied, 4,933 admitted, 1,464 enrolled. *Average high school GPA:* 3.1. *Test scores:* ACT scores over 18: 90%; ACT scores over 24: 24%; ACT scores over 30: 2%.

Faculty *Total:* 753, 81% full-time, 58% with terminal degrees. *Student/faculty ratio:* 16:1.

Academics *Calendar:* semesters. *Degrees:* bachelor's, master's, post-master's, and postbachelor's certificates. *Special study options:* academic remediation for entering students, adult/continuing education programs, advanced placement credit, cooperative education, distance learning, double majors, external degree program, freshman honors college, honors programs, independent study, internships, off-campus study, part-time degree program, services for LD students, study abroad, summer session for credit. *ROTC:* Army (b). *Unusual degree programs:* 3-2 engineering with University of Illinois at Urbana-Champaign and Southern Illinois University at Carbondale.

Computers on Campus 774 computers/terminals and 10,000 ports are available on campus for general student use. Students can access the following: computer help desk, free student e-mail accounts, online (class) grades, online (class) registration, online (class) schedules. Campuswide network is available. 100% of college-owned or -operated housing units are wired for high-speed Internet access. Wireless service is available via classrooms, computer centers, computer labs, dorm rooms, learning centers, libraries, student centers.

Student Life *Housing:* on-campus residence required for freshman year. *Options:* coed, men-only, women-only. Campus housing is university owned. Freshman campus housing is guaranteed. *Activities and organizations:* drama/theater group, student-run newspaper, radio and television station, choral group, marching band, Illinois Student Education Association, Math Energy at Eastern Illinois University, Black Student Union, Alpha Gamma, Alpha Phi, national fraternities, national sororities. *Campus security:* 24-hour emergency response devices and patrols, student patrols, late-night transport/escort service, AlertEIU & warning sirens. *Student services:* health clinic, personal/psychological counseling, women's center, legal services.

Athletics Member NCAA. All Division I except football (Division I-AA). *Intercollegiate sports:* badminton M(c)/W(c), baseball M(s), basketball M(s)/W(s), cross-country running M(s)/W(s), golf M(s)/W(s), racquetball M(c)/W(c), rugby M(c)/W(s), soccer M(s)/W(s), softball W(s), swimming and diving M(s)/W(s), tennis M(s)/W(s), track and field M(s)/W(s), ultimate Frisbee M(c)/W(c), volleyball M(c)/W(c), wrestling M(c)/W(c). *Intramural sports:* badminton M/W, basketball M/W, bowling M/W, lacrosse M(c)/W(c), racquetball M/W, soccer M/W, softball M/W, table tennis M/W, tennis M/W, volleyball M/W.

Standardized Tests *Required:* SAT or ACT (for admission).

Costs (2010–11) *Tuition:* state resident $7620 full-time, $254 per credit hour part-time; nonresident $22,860 full-time, $762 per credit hour part-time. Full-time tuition and fees vary according to course load and student level. Part-time tuition and fees vary according to course load and student level. No tuition increase for student's term of enrollment. *Required fees:* $2367 full-time, $85 per credit hour part-time. *Room and board:* $8584. Room and board charges vary according to board plan and housing facility. *Payment plan:* installment. *Waivers:* senior citizens and employees or children of employees.

Financial Aid Of all full-time matriculated undergraduates who enrolled in 2008, 7,407 applied for aid, 4,781 were judged to have need, 587 had their need fully met. 466 Federal Work-Study jobs (averaging $1056). 2,547 state and other part-time jobs (averaging $1221). In 2008, 414 non-need-based awards were made. *Average percent of need met:* 73%. *Average financial aid package:* $8727. *Average need-based loan:* $4070. *Average need-based gift aid:* $3220. *Average non-need-based aid:* $3523. *Average indebtedness upon graduation:* $14,233.

Applying *Options:* electronic application, deferred entrance. *Application fee:* $30. *Required:* high school transcript, minimum 2.25 GPA, audition for music program. *Required for some:* 3 letters of recommendation. *Recommended:* essay or personal statement, 2 letters of recommendation. *Application deadlines:* rolling (freshmen), rolling (out-of-state freshmen), rolling (transfers). *Notification:* continuous (freshmen), continuous (out-of-state freshmen), continuous (transfers).

Freshman Application Contact Brenda Major, Director of Admissions, Eastern Illinois University, 600 Lincoln Avenue, Charleston, IL 61920-3099. *Phone:* 217-581-2223. *Toll-free phone:* 800-252-5711. *Fax:* 217-581-7060. *E-mail:* admissions@eiu.edu. *Web site:* http://www.eiu.edu/.

East-West University

Chicago, Illinois

- **Independent** 4-year, founded 1978
- **Urban** 1-acre campus with easy access to Chicago
- **Endowment** $40.1 million
- **Coed**
- **Minimally difficult** entrance level

Faculty *Student/faculty ratio:* 15:1.

Academics *Calendar:* quarters. *Degrees:* certificates, associate, and bachelor's.

Standardized Tests *Required:* ACT (for admission).

Costs (2010–11) *One-time required fee:* $45. *Tuition:* $15,000 full-time, $500 per credit hour part-time. Full-time tuition and fees vary according to degree level and program. *Required fees:* $750 full-time.

Financial Aid *Of all full-time matriculated undergraduates who enrolled in 2009,* 53 Federal Work-Study jobs (averaging $4500). *Average indebtedness upon graduation:* $3500.

Applying *Options:* electronic application, early decision. *Application fee:* $40. *Required:* essay or personal statement, high school transcript, minimum 2 GPA, interview. *Required for some:* 1 letter of recommendation.

Freshman Application Contact Mr. Ho Chung, Director of Admissions, East-West University, 816 South Michigan Avenue, Chicago, IL 60605-2103. *Phone:* 312-939-0111 Ext. 1829. *Fax:* 312-939-0083. *E-mail:* ho@ eastwest.edu. *Web site:* http://www.eastwest.edu/.

Ellis University

Chicago, Illinois

Freshman Application Contact Office of Admissions, Ellis University, 111 North Canal Street, Suite 380, Chicago, IL 60606-7204. *Phone:* 312-669-5000. *Toll-free phone:* 877-355-4762. *E-mail:* admissions@ellis.edu. *Web site:* http://www.ellis.edu/.

Elmhurst College

Elmhurst, Illinois

- **Independent** comprehensive, founded 1871, affiliated with United Church of Christ
- **Suburban** 38-acre campus with easy access to Chicago
- **Endowment** $77.0 million
- **Coed** 3,145 undergraduate students, 92% full-time, 62% women, 38% men
- **Moderately difficult** entrance level, 73% of applicants were admitted

Undergraduates 2,904 full-time, 241 part-time. Students come from 19 states and territories; 38 other countries; 9% are from out of state; 3% Black or Afri-

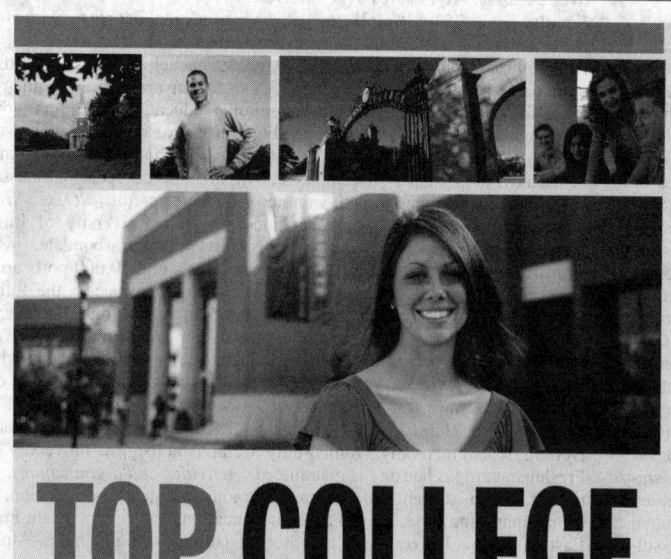

can American, non-Hispanic/Latino; 8% Hispanic/Latino; 4% Asian, non-Hispanic/Latino; 0.2% Native Hawaiian or other Pacific Islander, non-Hispanic/Latino; 0.5% American Indian or Alaska Native, non-Hispanic/Latino; 2% Two or more races, non-Hispanic/Latino; 4% Race/ethnicity unknown; 1% international; 10% transferred in; 40% live on campus. *Retention:* 77% of full-time freshmen returned.

Freshmen *Admission:* 2,555 applied, 1,870 admitted, 538 enrolled. *Average high school GPA:* 3.39. *Test scores:* SAT critical reading scores over 500: 59%; SAT math scores over 500: 85%; SAT writing scores over 500: 65%; ACT scores over 18: 99%; SAT critical reading scores over 600: 18%; SAT math scores over 600: 32%; SAT writing scores over 600: 27%; ACT scores over 24: 56%; SAT critical reading scores over 700: 6%; SAT math scores over 700: 3%; SAT writing scores over 700: 3%; ACT scores over 30: 9%.

Faculty *Total:* 375, 36% full-time, 28% with terminal degrees. *Student/faculty ratio:* 14:1.

Academics *Calendar:* 4-1-4. *Degrees:* bachelor's and master's. *Special study options:* academic remediation for entering students, accelerated degree program, adult/continuing education programs, advanced placement credit, cooperative education, double majors, honors programs, independent study, internships, off-campus study, part-time degree program, services for LD students, study abroad, summer session for credit. *ROTC:* Army (c), Air Force (c). *Unusual degree programs:* 3-2 engineering with University of Illinois at Urbana-Champaign, University of Southern California.

Computers on Campus 800 computers/terminals are available on campus for general student use. Students can access the following: campus intranet, computer help desk, free student e-mail accounts, online (class) grades, online (class) registration, online (class) schedules. Campuswide network is available. 100% of college-owned or -operated housing units are wired for high-speed Internet access. Wireless service is available via classrooms, computer labs, dorm rooms, libraries, student centers.

Student Life *Housing options:* coed. Campus housing is university owned, leased by the school and is provided by a third party. Freshman applicants given priority for college housing. *Activities and organizations:* drama/theater group, student-run newspaper, radio station, choral group, Programming Board and Student Government, theater and music groups, Black Student Union, residence life groups, Hablamos, national fraternities, national sororities. *Campus security:* 24-hour emergency response devices and patrols, late-night transport/escort service, controlled dormitory access. *Student services:* health clinic, personal/psychological counseling.

Athletics Member NCAA. All Division III. *Intercollegiate sports:* baseball M, basketball M/W, bowling W, cross-country running M/W, football M, golf M/W, soccer M/W, softball W, tennis M/W, track and field M/W, volleyball W, wrestling M. *Intramural sports:* basketball M/W, football M, golf M/W, racquetball M/W, soccer M/W, softball W, volleyball M/W.

Standardized Tests *Required:* SAT or ACT (for admission).

Costs (2011–12) *Comprehensive fee:* $38,578 includes full-time tuition ($29,994), mandatory fees ($60), and room and board ($8524). Part-time tuition: $854 per semester hour. Part-time tuition and fees vary according to course load. *College room only:* $5154. Room and board charges vary according to board plan and housing facility. *Payment plan:* installment. *Waivers:* senior citizens and employees or children of employees.

Financial Aid Of all full-time matriculated undergraduates who enrolled in 2009, 2,330 applied for aid, 2,147 were judged to have need, 572 had their need fully met. 409 Federal Work-Study jobs (averaging $1172). 302 state and other part-time jobs (averaging $1713). In 2009, 539 non-need-based awards were made. *Average percent of need met:* 69%. *Average financial aid package:* $20,180. *Average need-based loan:* $4439. *Average need-based gift aid:* $17,988. *Average non-need-based aid:* $11,386. *Average indebtedness upon graduation:* $23,912.

Applying *Options:* electronic application, deferred entrance. *Required:* high school transcript. *Required for some:* essay or personal statement, interview. *Recommended:* essay or personal statement, interview. *Application deadlines:* rolling (freshmen), rolling (transfers). *Notification:* continuous (freshmen), continuous (transfers).

Freshman Application Contact Mrs. Stephanie Levenson, Director of Admission, Elmhurst College, Elmhurst College, Admission Office, 190 South Prospect Avenue, Elmhurst, IL 60126-3296. *Phone:* 630-617-3400. *Toll-free phone:* 800-697-1871. *Fax:* 630-617-5501. *E-mail:* admit@elmhurst.edu. *Web site:* http://www.elmhurst.edu/.

See page 1270 for the College Close-Up.

Eureka College

Eureka, Illinois

Freshman Application Contact Dr. Brian Sajko, Dean of Admissions and Financial Aid, Eureka College, 300 East College Avenue, Eureka, IL 61530. *Phone:* 309-467-6350. *Toll-free phone:* 888-4-EUREKA. *Fax:* 309-467-6576. *E-mail:* admissions@eureka.edu. *Web site:* http://www.eureka.edu/.

Governors State University

University Park, Illinois

- **State-supported** upper-level, founded 1969
- **Suburban** 750-acre campus with easy access to Chicago
- **Coed** 2,995 undergraduate students, 38% full-time, 69% women, 31% men

Undergraduates 1,138 full-time, 1,857 part-time. 3% are from out of state; 38% Black or African American, non-Hispanic/Latino; 9% Hispanic/Latino; 1% Asian, non-Hispanic/Latino; 0.1% Native Hawaiian or other Pacific Islander, non-Hispanic/Latino; 0.4% American Indian or Alaska Native, non-Hispanic/Latino; 0.3% Two or more races, non-Hispanic/Latino; 4% Race/ethnicity unknown; 28% transferred in.

Faculty *Total:* 390, 55% full-time, 40% with terminal degrees. *Student/faculty ratio:* 13:1.

Academics *Calendar:* trimesters. *Degrees:* certificates, bachelor's, master's, doctoral-other, doctoral-professional, post-master's, and postbachelor's certificates. *Special study options:* adult/continuing education programs, advanced placement credit, distance learning, double majors, honors programs, independent study, internships, off-campus study, part-time degree program, services for LD students, student-designed majors, summer session for credit.

Computers on Campus Students can access the following: computer help desk, free student e-mail accounts, online (class) grades, online (class) registration, online (class) schedules, student portal. Campuswide network is available.

Student Life *Housing:* college housing not available. *Activities and organizations:* student-run newspaper, choral group. *Campus security:* 24-hour emergency response devices and patrols, late-night transport/escort service. *Student services:* personal/psychological counseling.

Athletics *Intramural sports:* badminton M/W, basketball M/W, racquetball M/W, skiing (cross-country) M/W, softball M/W, table tennis M/W, volleyball M/W.

Costs (2010–11) *Tuition:* state resident $7110 full-time, $237 per credit hour part-time; nonresident $14,220 full-time, $474 per credit hour part-time. Full-time tuition and fees vary according to reciprocity agreements and student level. Part-time tuition and fees vary according to reciprocity agreements and student level. No tuition increase for student's term of enrollment. *Required fees:* $1636 full-time, $63 per credit hour part-time, $126 per term part-time. *Payment plans:* installment, deferred payment. *Waivers:* senior citizens and employees or children of employees.

Applying *Options:* electronic application, deferred entrance. *Application deadline:* rolling (transfers).

Application Contact Ms. Sharon Evans, Director of Admissions, Governors State University, One University Parkway, University Park, IL 60466. *Phone:* 708-534-4490. *Fax:* 708-235-7455. *E-mail:* s-evans@govst.edu. *Web site:* http://www.govst.edu/.

Greenville College

Greenville, Illinois

- **Independent Free Methodist** comprehensive, founded 1892
- **Small-town** 12-acre campus with easy access to St. Louis
- **Endowment** $11.4 million
- **Coed** 1,365 undergraduate students, 95% full-time, 50% women, 50% men
- **Moderately difficult** entrance level, 77% of applicants were admitted

Undergraduates 1,293 full-time, 72 part-time. Students come from 40 states and territories; 10 other countries; 30% are from out of state; 9% Black or African American, non-Hispanic/Latino; 3% Hispanic/Latino; 0.9% Asian, non-Hispanic/Latino; 0.3% American Indian or Alaska Native, non-Hispanic/Latino; 0.2% Two or more races, non-Hispanic/Latino; 10% Race/ethnicity unknown; 1% international; 10% transferred in; 72% live on campus. *Retention:* 76% of full-time freshmen returned.

Freshmen *Admission:* 1,087 applied, 837 admitted, 283 enrolled. *Average high school GPA:* 3.32. *Test scores:* SAT critical reading scores over 500: 43%; SAT math scores over 500: 45%; SAT writing scores over 500: 33%; ACT scores over 18: 77%; SAT critical reading scores over 600: 13%; SAT math scores over 600: 15%; SAT writing scores over 600: 15%; ACT scores over 24: 35%; ACT scores over 30: 7%.

Faculty *Total:* 169, 36% full-time, 34% with terminal degrees. *Student/faculty ratio:* 14:1.

Academics *Calendar:* 4-1-4. *Degrees:* bachelor's and master's. *Special study options:* academic remediation for entering students, accelerated degree program, adult/continuing education programs, advanced placement credit, cooperative education, double majors, honors programs, independent study, internships, off-campus study, part-time degree program, student-designed majors, study abroad, summer session for credit. *Unusual degree programs:* 3-2 engineering with University of Illinois at Urbana-Champaign; Washington

University in St. Louis; nursing with St. John's College of Nursing; chiropractic at Logan College of Chiropractic.

Computers on Campus 65 computers/terminals are available on campus for general student use. Students can access the following: campus intranet, computer help desk, free student e-mail accounts, online (class) grades, online (class) registration, online (class) schedules. Campuswide network is available. 100% of college-owned or -operated housing units are wired for high-speed Internet access. Wireless service is available via entire campus.

Student Life *Housing:* on-campus residence required through senior year. *Options:* men-only, women-only. Campus housing is university owned. Freshman campus housing is guaranteed. *Activities and organizations:* drama/theater group, student-run newspaper, radio station, choral group, marching band, Campus Activity Board, Greenville Student Outreach, Fellowship of Christian Athletes, Greenville College Student Association, African American Student Union. *Campus security:* 24-hour emergency response devices, student patrols, late-night transport/escort service, controlled dormitory access. *Student services:* personal/psychological counseling.

Athletics Member NCAA, NCCAA. All NCAA Division III. *Intercollegiate sports:* baseball M, basketball M/W, cross-country running M/W, football M, soccer M/W, softball W, tennis M/W, track and field M/W, volleyball W. *Intramural sports:* basketball M/W, cheerleading W, football M/W, softball M/W, ultimate Frisbee M/W, volleyball M/W.

Standardized Tests *Required:* SAT or ACT (for admission).

Costs (2011–12) *Comprehensive fee:* $28,996 includes full-time tuition ($21,494), mandatory fees ($164), and room and board ($7338). Part-time tuition: $452 per credit hour. Part-time tuition and fees vary according to course load. *College room only:* $3550. Room and board charges vary according to housing facility. *Waivers:* senior citizens and employees or children of employees.

Financial Aid Of all full-time matriculated undergraduates who enrolled in 2009, 1,014 applied for aid, 941 were judged to have need, 87 had their need fully met. In 2009, 152 non-need-based awards were made. *Average percent of need met:* 71%. *Average financial aid package:* $17,718. *Average need-based loan:* $4138. *Average need-based gift aid:* $13,564. *Average non-need-based aid:* $6747. *Average indebtedness upon graduation:* $24,002.

Applying *Options:* electronic application, early admission, deferred entrance. *Application fee:* $30. *Required:* essay or personal statement, high school transcript, minimum 2.5 GPA, 2 letters of recommendation, agreement to code of conduct. *Required for some:* interview. *Application deadlines:* rolling (freshmen), rolling (transfers). *Notification:* continuous (freshmen), continuous (transfers).

Freshman Application Contact Mr. John R. Massena, Director of Undergraduate Admissions, Greenville College, 315 East College Avenue, Greenville, IL 62246. *Phone:* 618-664-7100. *Toll-free phone:* 800-345-4440. *Fax:* 618-664-9841. *E-mail:* admissions@greenville.edu. *Web site:* http://www.greenville.edu/.

Harrington College of Design

Chicago, Illinois

- **Proprietary** comprehensive, founded 1931, part of Career Education Corporation
- **Urban** campus with easy access to Chicago
- **Coed, primarily women**
- **Noncompetitive** entrance level

Faculty *Student/faculty ratio:* 10:1.

Academics *Calendar:* semesters. *Degrees:* certificates, diplomas, associate, bachelor's, and master's.

Student Life *Campus security:* 24-hour emergency response devices and patrols.

Costs (2010–11) *Tuition:* $17,550 full-time, $4550 per term part-time. Full-time tuition and fees vary according to course load, degree level, and program. Part-time tuition and fees vary according to course load, degree level, and program. *Required fees:* $1050 full-time, $410 per term part-time.

Financial Aid *Average percent of need met:* 30. *Average financial aid package:* $3500.

Applying *Options:* electronic application. *Application fee:* $60. *Required:* high school transcript, interview. *Recommended:* essay or personal statement, 1 letter of recommendation.

Freshman Application Contact Ms. Rian Hacker, Director of Admissions (HS Team), Harrington College of Design, 200 West Madison, Chicago, IL 60606. *Phone:* 312-697-8022. *Toll-free phone:* 877-939-4975. *E-mail:* rhacker@harringtoncollege.com. *Web site:* http://www.interiordesign.edu/.

Hebrew Theological College

Skokie, Illinois

Freshman Application Contact Rabbi Berish Cardash, Hebrew Theological College, 7135 North Carpenter Road, Skokie, IL 60077-3263. *Phone:* 847-982-2500. *Web site:* http://www.htc.edu/.

Illinois College

Jacksonville, Illinois

- **Independent interdenominational** 4-year, founded 1829
- **Small-town** 62-acre campus with easy access to St. Louis
- **Coed** 878 undergraduate students, 97% full-time, 49% women, 51% men
- **Moderately difficult** entrance level, 53% of applicants were admitted

Undergraduates 854 full-time, 24 part-time. 9% are from out of state; 6% Black or African American, non-Hispanic/Latino; 4% Hispanic/Latino; 0.2% Asian, non-Hispanic/Latino; 0.1% Native Hawaiian or other Pacific Islander, non-Hispanic/Latino; 0.2% American Indian or Alaska Native, non-Hispanic/Latino; 4% Two or more races, non-Hispanic/Latino; 1% Race/ethnicity unknown; 2% international; 5% transferred in; 80% live on campus. *Retention:* 86% of full-time freshmen returned.

Freshmen *Admission:* 1,493 applied, 789 admitted, 227 enrolled. *Average high school GPA:* 3.24. *Test scores:* ACT scores over 18: 89%; ACT scores over 24: 48%; ACT scores over 30: 6%.

Faculty *Total:* 85, 88% full-time, 78% with terminal degrees. *Student/faculty ratio:* 11:1.

Academics *Calendar:* semesters. *Degree:* bachelor's. *Special study options:* advanced placement credit, double majors, independent study, internships, student-designed majors, study abroad, summer session for credit. *Unusual degree programs:* 3-2 engineering with University of Illinois at Urbana-Champaign, Washington University in St. Louis; occupational therapy with Washington University in St. Louis.

Computers on Campus Students can access the following: computer help desk, free student e-mail accounts, online (class) grades, online (class) registration, online (class) schedules. Campuswide network is available. Wireless service is available via entire campus.

Student Life *Housing:* on-campus residence required through sophomore year. *Options:* coed, men-only, women-only. Campus housing is university owned. Freshman campus housing is guaranteed. *Activities and organizations:* drama/theater group, student-run newspaper, choral group. *Campus security:* 24-hour emergency response devices and patrols, late-night transport/escort service, controlled dormitory access. *Student services:* health clinic, personal/psychological counseling.

Athletics Member NCAA. All Division III. *Intercollegiate sports:* baseball M, cheerleading W, cross-country running M/W, football M, golf M/W, soccer M/W, softball W, swimming and diving M/W, tennis M/W, track and field M/W, volleyball W. *Intramural sports:* badminton M/W, basketball M/W, fencing M/W, football M, racquetball M/W, softball M/W, swimming and diving M/W, volleyball M/W, water polo M/W, weight lifting M/W.

Costs (2010–11) *Comprehensive fee:* $30,700 includes full-time tuition ($22,350), mandatory fees ($450), and room and board ($7900). Part-time tuition: $700 per semester hour. *Required fees:* $225 per year part-time. *College room only:* $4100. Room and board charges vary according to board plan and housing facility. *Payment plan:* installment. *Waivers:* employees or children of employees.

Financial Aid Of all full-time matriculated undergraduates who enrolled in 2009, 789 applied for aid, 700 were judged to have need, 203 had their need fully met. 427 Federal Work-Study jobs (averaging $1792). In 2009, 149 non-need-based awards were made. *Average percent of need met:* 89%. *Average financial aid package:* $18,014. *Average need-based loan:* $4660. *Average need-based gift aid:* $13,434. *Average non-need-based aid:* $8805. *Average indebtedness upon graduation:* $21,258.

Applying *Options:* electronic application, early admission, deferred entrance. *Required:* high school transcript, 1 letter of recommendation. *Required for some:* essay or personal statement. *Recommended:* essay or personal statement, minimum 2.5 GPA, interview. *Application deadline:* rolling (freshmen). *Notification:* continuous (freshmen).

Freshman Application Contact Mr. Rick Bystry, Associate Director of Admission, Illinois College, 1101 West College, Jacksonville, IL 62650. *Phone:* 217-245-3030. *Toll-free phone:* 866-464-5265. *Fax:* 217-245-3034. *E-mail:* admissions@ic.edu. *Web site:* http://www.ic.edu/.

The Illinois Institute of Art–Chicago
Chicago, Illinois

- **Proprietary** 4-year, founded 1916, part of Education Management Corporation
- **Urban** campus
- **Coed**

Academics *Calendar:* quarters. *Degrees:* certificates, associate, and bachelor's.
Costs (2010–11) *Tuition:* Tuition cost varies by program. Prospective students should contact the school for current tuition costs. Other charges include a starting kit for all first-quarter students. Kits vary in price, depending on the program of study.
Freshman Application Contact The Illinois Institute of Art–Chicago, 350 North Orleans Street, Chicago, IL 60654. *Phone:* 312-280-3500. *Toll-free phone:* 800-351-3450. *Web site:* http://www.artinstitutes.edu/chicago/.

See page 1340 for the College Close-Up.

The Illinois Institute of Art–Schaumburg
Schaumburg, Illinois

- **Proprietary** 4-year, part of Education Management Corporation
- **Suburban** campus
- **Coed**

Academics *Calendar:* quarters. *Degrees:* certificates, diplomas, associate, and bachelor's.
Costs (2010–11) *Tuition:* Tuition cost varies by program. Prospective students should contact the school for current tuition costs. Other charges include a starting kit for all first-quarter students. Kits vary in price, depending on the program of study.
Freshman Application Contact The Illinois Institute of Art–Schaumburg, 1000 North Plaza Drive, Suite 100, Schaumburg, IL 60173. *Phone:* 847-619-3450. *Toll-free phone:* 800-314-3450. *Web site:* http://www.artinstitutes.edu/schaumburg/.

See page 1342 for the College Close-Up.

The Illinois Institute of Art–Tinley Park
Tinley Park, Illinois

- **Proprietary** comprehensive
- **Coed**

Academics *Degrees:* associate and bachelor's.
Director of Admissions Director of Admissions, The Illinois Institute of Art–Tinley Park, 18670 Graphic Drive, Tinley Park, IL 60477. *Phone:* 708-781-4200. *Toll-free phone:* 877-342-3298. *Fax:* 708-781-4201. *Web site:* http://www.artinstitutes.edu/tinleypark.

See page 1344 for the College Close-Up.

Illinois Institute of Technology
Chicago, Illinois

- **Independent** comprehensive, founded 1890
- **Urban** 120-acre campus
- **Endowment** $180.0 million
- **Coed** 2,602 undergraduate students, 94% full-time, 30% women, 70% men
- **Very difficult** entrance level, 64% of applicants were admitted

Undergraduates 2,437 full-time, 165 part-time. Students come from 51 states and territories; 84 other countries; 28% are from out of state; 5% Black or African American, non-Hispanic/Latino; 9% Hispanic/Latino; 12% Asian, non-Hispanic/Latino; 0.9% Native Hawaiian or other Pacific Islander, non-Hispanic/Latino; 0.5% American Indian or Alaska Native, non-Hispanic/Latino; 0.5% Two or more races, non-Hispanic/Latino; 9% Race/ethnicity unknown; 20% international; 7% transferred in; 27% live on campus. *Retention:* 92% of full-time freshmen returned.
Freshmen *Admission:* 2,295 applied, 1,480 admitted, 403 enrolled. *Average high school GPA:* 3.92. *Test scores:* SAT critical reading scores over 500: 86%; SAT math scores over 500: 99%; SAT writing scores over 500: 78%; ACT scores over 18: 100%; SAT critical reading scores over 600: 54%; SAT math scores over 600: 80%; SAT writing scores over 600: 53%; ACT scores over 24: 83%; SAT critical reading scores over 700: 16%; SAT math scores over 700: 44%; SAT writing scores over 700: 11%; ACT scores over 30: 33%.
Faculty *Total:* 722, 53% full-time, 75% with terminal degrees. *Student/faculty ratio:* 10:1.

Academics *Calendar:* semesters. *Degrees:* bachelor's, master's, doctoral-professional, and doctoral-research/scholarship. *Special study options:* advanced placement credit, cooperative education, distance learning, double majors, English as a second language, independent study, internships, off-campus study, part-time degree program, services for LD students, study abroad, summer session for credit. *ROTC:* Army (b), Navy (b), Air Force (b). *Unusual degree programs:* 3-2 engineering with Joint Programs for earning two bachelor's degrees with Wheaton College, Benedictine University, Elmhurst College, Dominican University, DePaul University, and University of St. Francis; B.S. in Political Science/Master of Public Administration; B.S. in Psychology/M.S. in Personnel and Human Resources Development; B.S. in Psychology/M.S. in Rehabilitation Counseling Dual Degree Program.
Computers on Campus 500 computers/terminals are available on campus for general student use. Students can access the following: campus intranet, computer help desk, free student e-mail accounts, online (class) grades, online (class) registration, online (class) schedules. Campuswide network is available. 100% of college-owned or -operated housing units are wired for high-speed Internet access. Wireless service is available via classrooms, computer centers, computer labs, dorm rooms, learning centers, libraries, student centers.
Student Life *Housing:* on-campus residence required for freshman year. *Options:* coed. Campus housing is university owned and is provided by a third party. Freshman applicants given priority for college housing. *Activities and organizations:* drama/theater group, student-run newspaper, radio station, choral group, Union Board, International Students Association, Student Government Association, Greek Council, Commuter Student Associate, national fraternities, national sororities. *Campus security:* 24-hour emergency response devices and patrols, late-night transport/escort service, controlled dormitory access. *Student services:* health clinic, personal/psychological counseling, women's center, legal services.
Athletics Member NAIA. *Intercollegiate sports:* badminton M(c)/W(c), baseball M(s), bowling M(c)/W(c), cross-country running M(s)/W(s), lacrosse M(c)/W(c), rugby M(c)/W(c), soccer M(s)/W(s), swimming and diving M(s)/W(s), ultimate Frisbee M(c)/W(c), volleyball M(c)/W(s). *Intramural sports:* badminton M/W, basketball M/W, bowling M/W, field hockey M/W, football M/W, racquetball M/W, soccer M/W, softball M/W, squash M/W, table tennis M/W, tennis M(c)/W(c), track and field M(c)/W(c), ultimate Frisbee M/W, volleyball M/W.
Standardized Tests *Required for some:* SAT or ACT (for admission).
Costs (2011–12) *One-time required fee:* $165. *Comprehensive fee:* $45,218 includes full-time tuition ($33,800), mandatory fees ($1080), and room and board ($10,338). Full-time tuition and fees vary according to student level. Part-time tuition: $1032 per credit hour. Part-time tuition and fees vary according to course load and student level. *Required fees:* $25 per course part-time, $75 per term part-time. *College room only:* $5384. Room and board charges vary according to board plan and housing facility. *Payment plan:* installment. *Waivers:* employees or children of employees.
Financial Aid Of all full-time matriculated undergraduates who enrolled in 2009, 1,576 applied for aid, 1,487 were judged to have need, 223 had their need fully met. 741 Federal Work-Study jobs (averaging $2415). In 2009, 860 non-need-based awards were made. *Average percent of need met:* 77%. *Average financial aid package:* $27,639. *Average need-based loan:* $4829. *Average need-based gift aid:* $22,054. *Average non-need-based aid:* $14,481.
Applying *Options:* electronic application, early admission, early decision, early action, deferred entrance. *Required:* essay or personal statement, high school transcript, 1 letter of recommendation. *Recommended:* interview. *Application deadlines:* 6/11 (freshmen), 6/1 (transfers), 2/1 (early action). *Early decision deadline:* 11/1. *Notification:* continuous (freshmen), continuous (transfers), 1/1 (early decision), 3/1 (early action).
Freshman Application Contact Mr. Gerald Doyle, Vice Provost, Undergraduate Admissions and Financial Aid, Illinois Institute of Technology, Office of Undergraduate Admission, Perlstein 101, 10 West 33rd Street, Chicago, IL 60616. *Phone:* 312-567-3025. *Toll-free phone:* 800-448-2329. *Fax:* 312-567-6939. *E-mail:* admission@iit.edu. *Web site:* http://www.iit.edu/

Illinois State University
Normal, Illinois

- **State-supported** university, founded 1857
- **Urban** 850-acre campus
- **Endowment** $74.1 million
- **Coed** 18,314 undergraduate students, 94% full-time, 56% women, 44% men
- **Moderately difficult** entrance level, 67% of applicants were admitted

Undergraduates 17,279 full-time, 1,035 part-time. Students come from 45 states and territories; 32 other countries; 1% are from out of state; 6% Black or African American, non-Hispanic/Latino; 5% Hispanic/Latino; 2% Asian, non-Hispanic/Latino; 0.1% Native Hawaiian or other Pacific Islander, non-Hispanic/Latino; 0.4% American Indian or Alaska Native, non-Hispanic/Latino; 0.6% Two or more races, non-Hispanic/Latino; 3% Race/ethnicity unknown;

PROFILES

0.4% international; 10% transferred in; 33% live on campus. *Retention:* 85% of full-time freshmen returned.

Freshmen *Admission:* 13,671 applied, 9,141 admitted, 3,190 enrolled. *Average high school GPA:* 3.38. *Test scores:* ACT scores over 18: 99%; ACT scores over 24: 55%; ACT scores over 30: 4%.

Faculty *Total:* 1,184, 74% full-time, 69% with terminal degrees. *Student/faculty ratio:* 19:1.

Academics *Calendar:* semesters. *Degrees:* bachelor's, master's, doctoral-professional, doctoral-research/scholarship, post-master's, and postbachelor's certificates. *Special study options:* academic remediation for entering students, accelerated degree program, adult/continuing education programs, advanced placement credit, cooperative education, distance learning, double majors, English as a second language, honors programs, independent study, internships, off-campus study, part-time degree program, services for LD students, student-designed majors, study abroad, summer session for credit. *ROTC:* Army (b). *Unusual degree programs:* 3-2 engineering with University of Illinois.

Computers on Campus 2,204 computers/terminals and 2,204 ports are available on campus for general student use. Students can access the following: campus intranet, computer help desk, free student e-mail accounts, online (class) grades, online (class) registration, online (class) schedules. Campuswide network is available. 100% of college-owned or -operated housing units are wired for high-speed Internet access. Wireless service is available via classrooms, computer centers, computer labs, libraries, student centers.

Student Life *Housing:* on-campus residence required through sophomore year. *Options:* coed, women-only, disabled students. Campus housing is university owned. Freshman campus housing is guaranteed. *Activities and organizations:* drama/theater group, student-run newspaper, radio and television station, choral group, marching band, national fraternities, national sororities. *Campus security:* 24-hour emergency response devices and patrols, late-night transport/escort service, controlled dormitory access. *Student services:* health clinic, personal/psychological counseling, women's center, legal services.

Athletics Member NCAA. All Division I except football (Division I-AA). *Intercollegiate sports:* baseball M(s), basketball M(s)/W(s), cross-country running M(s)/W(s), golf M(s)/W(s), gymnastics W(s), soccer W(s), softball W(s), swimming and diving W(s), tennis M(s)/W(s), track and field M(s)/W(s), volleyball W(s). *Intramural sports:* badminton M/W, baseball M, basketball M/W, bowling M(c)/W(c), field hockey M/W, football M, golf M/W, gymnastics M(c), ice hockey M(c), lacrosse M(c), racquetball M/W, rugby M(c)/W(c), soccer M/W, softball M/W, tennis M/W, ultimate Frisbee M/W, volleyball M(c)/W.

Standardized Tests *Required:* SAT or ACT (for admission).

Costs (2010–11) *Tuition:* state resident $9030 full-time, $301 per credit hour part-time; nonresident $15,570 full-time, $519 per credit hour part-time. Full-time tuition and fees vary according to course load and degree level. Part-time tuition and fees vary according to course load and degree level. No tuition increase for student's term of enrollment. *Required fees:* $2387 full-time, $68 per credit hour part-time. *Room and board:* $8436; room only: $4326. Room and board charges vary according to board plan, housing facility, and location. *Payment plan:* installment. *Waivers:* minority students, senior citizens, and employees or children of employees.

Financial Aid Of all full-time matriculated undergraduates who enrolled in 2009, 12,609 applied for aid, 10,365 were judged to have need, 3,625 had their need fully met. 431 Federal Work-Study jobs (averaging $2480). 54 state and other part-time jobs (averaging $2046). In 2009, 253 non-need-based awards were made. *Average percent of need met:* 78%. *Average financial aid package:* $12,512. *Average need-based loan:* $7556. *Average need-based gift aid:* $9501. *Average non-need-based aid:* $4024. *Average indebtedness upon graduation:* $22,847.

Applying *Options:* electronic application. *Application fee:* $40. *Required:* essay or personal statement, high school transcript. *Application deadlines:* 3/1 (freshmen), rolling (transfers). *Notification:* continuous (freshmen), continuous (transfers).

Freshman Application Contact Ms. Doris Groves, Director of Admissions, Illinois State University, Campus Box 2200, Normal, IL 61790-2200. *Phone:* 309-438-2181. *Toll-free phone:* 800-366-2478. *Fax:* 309-438-3932. *E-mail:* admissions@ilstu.edu. *Web site:* http://www.illinoisstate.edu/.

Illinois Wesleyan University

Bloomington, Illinois

- **Independent** 4-year, founded 1850
- **Suburban** 79-acre campus
- **Coed** 2,094 undergraduate students, 100% full-time, 58% women, 42% men
- **Very difficult** entrance level, 62% of applicants were admitted

Undergraduates 2,088 full-time, 6 part-time. 12% are from out of state; 5% Black or African American, non-Hispanic/Latino; 3% Hispanic/Latino; 4% Asian, non-Hispanic/Latino; 0.3% American Indian or Alaska Native, non-Hispanic/Latino; 0.2% Two or more races, non-Hispanic/Latino; 8% Race/eth-

nicity unknown; 4% international; 1% transferred in; 75% live on campus. *Retention:* 91% of full-time freshmen returned.

Freshmen *Admission:* 3,395 applied, 2,100 admitted, 587 enrolled. *Average high school GPA:* 3.82. *Test scores:* SAT critical reading scores over 500: 96%; SAT math scores over 500: 94%; ACT scores over 18: 101%; SAT critical reading scores over 600: 61%; SAT math scores over 600: 69%; ACT scores over 24: 90%; SAT critical reading scores over 700: 25%; SAT math scores over 700: 25%; ACT scores over 30: 35%.

Faculty *Total:* 232, 69% full-time, 76% with terminal degrees. *Student/faculty ratio:* 11:1.

Academics *Calendar:* 4-4-1. *Degree:* bachelor's. *Special study options:* advanced placement credit, double majors, honors programs, independent study, internships, off-campus study, services for LD students, student-designed majors, study abroad. *ROTC:* Army (c). *Unusual degree programs:* 3-2 engineering with Case Western Reserve University, Northwestern University, Washington University in St. Louis, Dartmouth College, University of Illinois; forestry with Duke University; occupational therapy.

Computers on Campus Students can access the following: campus intranet, computer help desk, free student e-mail accounts, online (class) grades, online (class) registration, online (class) schedules. Campuswide network is available. Wireless service is available via entire campus.

Student Life *Housing:* on-campus residence required through sophomore year. *Options:* coed, disabled students. Campus housing is university owned. Freshman campus housing is guaranteed. *Activities and organizations:* drama/theater group, student-run newspaper, radio and television station, choral group, national fraternities, national sororities. *Campus security:* 24-hour emergency response devices and patrols, late-night transport/escort service, controlled dormitory access, emergency response team. *Student services:* health clinic, personal/psychological counseling.

Athletics Member NCAA. All Division III. *Intercollegiate sports:* baseball M, basketball M/W, cheerleading M(c)/W(c), cross-country running M/W, football M, golf M/W, lacrosse M(c), soccer M/W, softball W, swimming and diving M/W, tennis M/W, track and field M/W, ultimate Frisbee M(c)/W(c), volleyball M(c)/W, water polo M/W. *Intramural sports:* badminton M/W, basketball M/W, football M/W, golf M/W, racquetball M/W, soccer M/W, softball M/W, tennis M/W, volleyball M/W.

Standardized Tests *Required:* SAT or ACT (for admission).

Costs (2010–11) *Comprehensive fee:* $43,362 includes full-time tuition ($35,076), mandatory fees ($180), and room and board ($8106). Part-time tuition: $1096 per credit hour. *College room only:* $5040. Room and board charges vary according to board plan and housing facility.

Financial Aid Of all full-time matriculated undergraduates who enrolled in 2009, 1,593 applied for aid, 1,415 were judged to have need, 659 had their need fully met. In 2009, 551 non-need-based awards were made. *Average percent of need met:* 97%. *Average financial aid package:* $25,017. *Average need-based loan:* $5016. *Average need-based gift aid:* $19,513. *Average non-need-based aid:* $12,369. *Average indebtedness upon graduation:* $31,904. *Financial aid deadline:* 3/1.

Applying *Options:* electronic application, early admission, early action, deferred entrance. *Required:* essay or personal statement, high school transcript, minimum 2 GPA, 1 letter of recommendation. *Recommended:* minimum 3 GPA, 2 letters of recommendation, interview. *Application deadlines:* rolling (freshmen), 8/15 (transfers), 11/15 (early action). *Notification:* continuous (freshmen), continuous (transfers), 1/15 (early action).

Freshman Application Contact Mr. Tony Bankston, Dean of Admissions, Illinois Wesleyan University, PO Box 2900, Bloomington, IL 61702-2900. *Phone:* 309-556-3031. *Toll-free phone:* 800-332-2498. *Fax:* 309-556-3820. *E-mail:* iwuadmit@iwu.edu. *Web site:* http://www.iwu.edu/.

International Academy of Design & Technology

Chicago, Illinois

- **Proprietary** 4-year, founded 1977, part of Career Education Corporation
- **Urban** 1-acre campus
- **Coed**
- **Minimally difficult** entrance level

Faculty *Student/faculty ratio:* 27:1.

Academics *Calendar:* quarters. *Degrees:* associate and bachelor's.

Student Life *Campus security:* 24-hour emergency response devices, building security during hours of operation.

Costs (2010–11) *One-time required fee:* $150. *Tuition:* $14,580 full-time, $405 per credit hour part-time. Full-time tuition and fees vary according to course load and program. Part-time tuition and fees vary according to course load and program. *Required fees:* $450 full-time, $150 per term part-time. *Room only:* Room and board charges vary according to housing facility. *Payment plans:* tuition prepayment, installment, deferred payment.

Financial Aid *Of all full-time matriculated undergraduates who enrolled in 2002, 30 Federal Work-Study jobs.*

Applying *Options:* electronic application, early admission. *Application fee:* $20. *Required:* high school transcript, interview. *Required for some:* GED. *Recommended:* essay or personal statement, minimum 2 GPA.
Freshman Application Contact Ms. Suzanne Reichart, Director of Student Management, International Academy of Design & Technology, One North State Street, Suite 500, Chicago, IL 60602. *Phone:* 312-980-9200. *Toll-free phone:* 877-ACADEMY. *Fax:* 312-541-3929. *E-mail:* sreichart@ iadtchicago.edu. *Web site:* http://www.iadtchicago.edu/.

ITT Technical Institute
Burr Ridge, Illinois

- **Proprietary** primarily 2-year, founded 1998, part of ITT Educational Services, Inc.
- **Coed**
- **Minimally difficult** entrance level

Academics *Calendar:* quarters. *Degrees:* associate and bachelor's.
Student Life *Housing:* college housing not available.
Freshman Application Contact Director of Recruitment, ITT Technical Institute, 800 Jorie Boulevard, Suite 100, Burr Ridge, IL 60527. *Phone:* 630-472-7000. *Toll-free phone:* 877-488-0001. *Web site:* http://www.itt-tech.edu/.

ITT Technical Institute
Mount Prospect, Illinois

- **Proprietary** primarily 2-year, founded 1986, part of ITT Educational Services, Inc.
- **Suburban** campus
- **Coed**
- **Minimally difficult** entrance level

Academics *Calendar:* quarters. *Degrees:* associate and bachelor's.
Student Life *Housing:* college housing not available.
Freshman Application Contact Director of Recruitment, ITT Technical Institute, 1401 Feehanville Drive, Mount Prospect, IL 60056. *Phone:* 847-375-8800. *Web site:* http://www.itt-tech.edu/.

ITT Technical Institute
Orland Park, Illinois

- **Proprietary** primarily 2-year, founded 1993, part of ITT Educational Services, Inc.
- **Suburban** campus
- **Coed**
- **Minimally difficult** entrance level

Academics *Calendar:* quarters. *Degrees:* associate and bachelor's.
Student Life *Housing:* college housing not available.
Financial Aid Of all full-time matriculated undergraduates who enrolled in 2009, 6 Federal Work-Study jobs (averaging $4000).
Freshman Application Contact Director of Recruitment, ITT Technical Institute, 11551 184th Place, Orland Park, IL 60467. *Phone:* 708-326-3200. *Web site:* http://www.itt-tech.edu/.

Judson University
Elgin, Illinois

- **Independent Baptist** comprehensive, founded 1963
- **Suburban** 80-acre campus with easy access to Chicago
- **Endowment** $7.0 million
- **Coed**
- **Moderately difficult** entrance level

Faculty *Student/faculty ratio:* 14:1.
Academics *Calendar:* semesters. *Degrees:* bachelor's and master's.
Student Life *Campus security:* 24-hour emergency response devices and patrols, controlled dormitory access.
Athletics Member NAIA, NCCAA.
Standardized Tests *Required:* SAT or ACT (for admission).
Costs (2010–11) *Comprehensive fee:* $33,280 includes full-time tuition ($24,150), mandatory fees ($630), and room and board ($8500). Part-time tuition: $925 per credit hour. Part-time tuition and fees vary according to course load. *Room and board:* Room and board charges vary according to board plan.
Financial Aid *Of all full-time matriculated undergraduates who enrolled in 2005,* 689 applied for aid, 594 were judged to have need, 9 had their need fully met. *In 2005,* 55 non-need-based awards were made. *Average percent of need met:* 36. *Average financial aid package:* $12,036. *Average need-based loan:* $3777. *Average need-based gift aid:* $5954. *Average non-need-based aid:* $4405. *Average indebtedness upon graduation:* $21,960.

Applying *Options:* electronic application, early admission, deferred entrance. *Application fee:* $50. *Required:* high school transcript, minimum 2.3 GPA, lifestyle statement. *Required for some:* essay or personal statement, interview.
Freshman Application Contact Mr. William W. Dean, Director of Enrollment Management, Judson University, 1151 North State Street, Elgin, IL 60123-1498. *Phone:* 847-695-2522. *Toll-free phone:* 800-879-5376. *Fax:* 847-628-2526. *E-mail:* bdean@judsonu.edu. *Web site:* http:// www.judsonu.edu/.

Kendall College
Chicago, Illinois

- **Proprietary** 4-year, founded 1934, part of Laureate International Universities
- **Urban** campus with easy access to Chicago
- **Coed** 2,545 undergraduate students, 58% full-time, 74% women, 26% men
- **Minimally difficult** entrance level, 98% of applicants were admitted

Undergraduates 1,480 full-time, 1,065 part-time. Students come from 58 other countries; 23% are from out of state; 14% transferred in. *Retention:* 52% of full-time freshmen returned.
Freshmen *Admission:* 361 applied, 353 admitted, 163 enrolled. *Average high school GPA:* 2.75. *Test scores:* ACT scores over 18: 77%; ACT scores over 24: 31%; ACT scores over 30: 5%.
Faculty *Total:* 209, 22% full-time. *Student/faculty ratio:* 18:1.
Academics *Calendar:* quarters. *Degrees:* certificates, associate, and bachelor's. *Special study options:* academic remediation for entering students, accelerated degree program, distance learning, internships, part-time degree program, study abroad, summer session for credit.
Computers on Campus 45 ports are available on campus for general student use. Students can access the following: campus intranet, computer help desk, free student e-mail accounts. Campuswide network is available. Wireless service is available via entire campus.
Student Life *Housing options:* coed. Campus housing is leased by the school. *Campus security:* 24-hour emergency response devices and patrols, controlled dormitory access, late night security in dorms. *Student services:* personal/psychological counseling.
Standardized Tests *Required for some:* SAT or ACT (for admission).
Costs (2011–12) *Comprehensive fee:* $32,820 includes full-time tuition ($22,095), mandatory fees ($825), and room and board ($9900). Full-time tuition and fees vary according to program. Part-time tuition: $600 per credit. Part-time tuition and fees vary according to course load and program. *Required fees:* $275 per term part-time. *College room only:* $9450. Room and board charges vary according to housing facility. *Payment plan:* installment. *Waivers:* employees or children of employees.
Financial Aid Of all full-time matriculated undergraduates who enrolled in 2008, 30 Federal Work-Study jobs (averaging $1100). *Average indebtedness upon graduation:* $14,125.
Applying *Options:* electronic application, deferred entrance. *Application fee:* $50. *Required:* essay or personal statement, high school transcript, interview. *Recommended:* minimum 2 GPA. *Application deadlines:* rolling (freshmen), rolling (out-of-state freshmen), rolling (transfers). *Notification:* continuous (freshmen), continuous (out-of-state freshmen), continuous (transfers).
Freshman Application Contact Mr. Thomas Marigliano, Director of Enrollment, Kendall College, 900 North North Branch Street, Chicago, IL 60642. *Toll-free phone:* 866-667-3344 (in-state); 877-588-8860 (out-of-state). *E-mail:* admissions@kendall.edu. *Web site:* http://www.kendall.edu/.

See page 254 for Display. See page 1362 for the College Close-Up.

Knox College
Galesburg, Illinois

- **Independent** 4-year, founded 1837
- **Small-town** 82-acre campus with easy access to Peoria
- **Endowment** $67.4 million
- **Coed** 1,392 undergraduate students, 99% full-time, 59% women, 41% men
- **Moderately difficult** entrance level, 75% of applicants were admitted

Undergraduates 1,374 full-time, 18 part-time. Students come from 48 states and territories; 42 other countries; 47% are from out of state; 5% Black or African American, non-Hispanic/Latino; 6% Hispanic/Latino; 5% Asian, non-Hispanic/Latino; 0.1% American Indian or Alaska Native, non-Hispanic/Latino; 3% Two or more races, non-Hispanic/Latino; 9% Race/ethnicity unknown; 7% international; 3% transferred in; 85% live on campus. *Retention:* 88% of full-time freshmen returned.
Freshmen *Admission:* 2,395 applied, 1,806 admitted, 358 enrolled. *Average high school GPA:* 3.35. *Test scores:* SAT critical reading scores over 500: 94%; SAT math scores over 500: 93%; SAT writing scores over 500: 96%; SAT critical reading scores over 600: 74%; SAT math scores over 600: 62%;

SAT writing scores over 600: 75%; SAT critical reading scores over 700: 31%; SAT math scores over 700: 20%; SAT writing scores over 700: 24%.

Faculty *Total:* 120, 87% full-time, 89% with terminal degrees. *Student/faculty ratio:* 12:1.

Academics *Calendar:* trimesters. *Degree:* bachelor's. *Special study options:* advanced placement credit, double majors, honors programs, independent study, internships, off-campus study, part-time degree program, services for LD students, student-designed majors, study abroad. *Unusual degree programs:* 3-2 engineering with University of Illinois at Urbana, Washington University, Columbia University, Rensselaer Polytechnic Institute; forestry with Duke University; nursing with Rush University's College of Nursing.

Computers on Campus 335 computers/terminals are available on campus for general student use. Students can access the following: campus intranet, computer help desk, free student e-mail accounts, online (class) grades, online (class) registration, online (class) schedules. Campuswide network is available. 100% of college-owned or -operated housing units are wired for high-speed Internet access. Wireless service is available via entire campus.

Student Life *Housing:* on-campus residence required through sophomore year. *Options:* coed, men-only, women-only. Campus housing is university owned. Freshman campus housing is guaranteed. *Activities and organizations:* drama/theater group, student-run newspaper, radio station, choral group, Student-Run Radio Station, KARES (Recycling and Sustainability Club), Terpsichore (Dance Club), Circle K/APO (Service Organizations), LARP (Live-Action Role-Play Club), national fraternities, national sororities. *Campus security:* 24-hour emergency response devices and patrols, late-night transport/escort service. *Student services:* health clinic, personal/psychological counseling.

Athletics Member NCAA. All Division III. *Intercollegiate sports:* baseball M, basketball M/W, cross-country running M/W, football M, golf M/W, soccer M/W, softball W, swimming and diving M/W, tennis M/W, track and field M/W, volleyball W, wrestling M. *Intramural sports:* basketball M/W, fencing M(c)/W(c), lacrosse M(c)/W(c), rugby W(c), soccer M/W, softball M/W, ultimate Frisbee M(c)/W(c), volleyball M/W, water polo M(c)/W(c).

Costs (2011–12) *Comprehensive fee:* $41,952 includes full-time tuition ($34,110), mandatory fees ($354), and room and board ($7488). Part-time tuition and fees vary according to course load. *College room only:* $3750. Room and board charges vary according to board plan. *Payment plan:* installment. *Waivers:* employees or children of employees.

Financial Aid Of all full-time matriculated undergraduates who enrolled in 2009, 1,133 applied for aid, 998 were judged to have need, 264 had their need fully met. 679 Federal Work-Study jobs (averaging $2245). 86 state and other part-time jobs (averaging $2318). In 2009, 319 non-need-based awards were made. *Average percent of need met:* 89%. *Average financial aid package:* $26,585. *Average need-based loan:* $5021. *Average need-based gift aid:* $20,676. *Average non-need-based aid:* $11,097. *Average indebtedness upon graduation:* $26,506.

Applying *Options:* electronic application, early admission, early action, deferred entrance. *Application fee:* $40. *Required:* essay or personal statement, high school transcript, 2 letters of recommendation. *Recommended:* interview. *Application deadlines:* 2/1 (freshmen), 4/1 (transfers), 12/1 (early action). *Notification:* 3/31 (freshmen), 5/15 (transfers), 12/31 (early action).

Freshman Application Contact Mr. Paul Steenis, Dean of Admissions, Knox College, 2 East South Street K-148, Galesburg, IL 61401. *Phone:* 309-341-7100. *Toll-free phone:* 800-678-KNOX. *Fax:* 309-341-7070. *E-mail:* admission@knox.edu. *Web site:* http://www.knox.edu/.

Lake Forest College
Lake Forest, Illinois

- **Independent** comprehensive, founded 1857
- **Suburban** 107-acre campus with easy access to Chicago
- **Coed** 1,426 undergraduate students, 99% full-time, 60% women, 40% men
- **Very difficult** entrance level, 61% of applicants were admitted

Undergraduates 1,405 full-time, 21 part-time. Students come from 45 states and territories; 70 other countries; 55% are from out of state; 6% Black or African American, non-Hispanic/Latino; 9% Hispanic/Latino; 4% Asian, non-Hispanic/Latino; 0.1% Native Hawaiian or other Pacific Islander, non-Hispanic/Latino; 0.5% American Indian or Alaska Native, non-Hispanic/Latino; 2% Two or more races, non-Hispanic/Latino; 12% international; 80% live on campus. *Retention:* 83% of full-time freshmen returned.

Freshmen *Admission:* 2,398 applied, 1,452 admitted, 402 enrolled. *Average high school GPA:* 3.56.

Faculty *Total:* 158, 59% full-time, 76% with terminal degrees. *Student/faculty ratio:* 12:1.

Academics *Calendar:* semesters. *Degrees:* bachelor's and master's. *Special study options:* accelerated degree program, advanced placement credit, double majors, honors programs, independent study, internships, off-campus study, services for LD students, student-designed majors, study abroad, summer session for credit. *Unusual degree programs:* 3-2 engineering with Washington University in St. Louis; We have 3-3 programs in law and a 3-4 program in pharmacy.

Computers on Campus 130 computers/terminals and 1,200 ports are available on campus for general student use. Students can access the following: campus intranet, computer help desk, free student e-mail accounts, online (class) grades, online (class) registration, online (class) schedules, file storage. Campuswide network is available. 100% of college-owned or -operated housing units are wired for high-speed Internet access. Wireless service is available via classrooms, computer centers, computer labs, dorm rooms, learning centers, libraries, student centers.

Student Life *Housing options:* coed, women-only, disabled students. Campus housing is university owned and leased by the school. Freshman campus housing is guaranteed. *Activities and organizations:* drama/theater group, student-run newspaper, radio station, choral group, Athletic Council, United Black Association, Latinos Unidos, SNAP (Students for Non-Alcoholic Programming), e.Team, national fraternities, national sororities. *Campus security:* 24-hour emergency response devices and patrols, student patrols, late-night transport/escort service, controlled dormitory access. *Student services:* health clinic, personal/psychological counseling, women's center.

Athletics Member NCAA. All Division III. *Intercollegiate sports:* baseball M(c), basketball M/W, cheerleading M(c)/W(c), cross-country running M/W, fencing M(c)/W(c), football M, golf M(c)/W(c), ice hockey M/W, lacrosse M(c), rock climbing M(c)/W(c), rugby M(c)/W(c), sailing M(c)/W(c), soccer M/W, softball W, swimming and diving M/W, table tennis M(c)/W(c), tennis M/W, track and field M(c)/W(c), ultimate Frisbee M(c)/W(c), volleyball W, water polo M(c)/W(c). *Intramural sports:* basketball M/W, ice hockey M/W, racquetball M/W, soccer M/W, volleyball M/W.

Standardized Tests *Required for some:* SAT or ACT (for admission).

Costs (2010–11) *Comprehensive fee:* $43,852 includes full-time tuition ($34,885), mandatory fees ($640), and room and board ($8327). Full-time tuition and fees vary according to course load. Part-time tuition: $4360 per course. Part-time tuition and fees vary according to course load. *College room only:* $4105. Room and board charges vary according to board plan. *Payment plan:* installment. *Waivers:* employees or children of employees.

Financial Aid Of all full-time matriculated undergraduates who enrolled in 2009, 1,050 applied for aid, 1,050 were judged to have need, 1,050 had their need fully met. In 2009, 229 non-need-based awards were made. *Average percent of need met:* 80%. *Average financial aid package:* $26,500. *Average need-based loan:* $4900. *Average need-based gift aid:* $23,300. *Average non-need-based aid:* $12,400. *Average indebtedness upon graduation:* $29,279. *Financial aid deadline:* 5/1.

Applying *Options:* electronic application, early admission, early decision, early action, deferred entrance. *Required:* essay or personal statement, high school transcript, 2 letters of recommendation. *Recommended:* interview. *Application deadlines:* rolling (freshmen), rolling (transfers), 12/1 (early action). *Early decision deadline:* 12/1. *Notification:* 3/20 (freshmen), continuous (transfers), 12/20 (early decision), 1/20 (early action).

Freshman Application Contact Mr. William Motzer Jr., Vice President for Admissions and Career Services, Lake Forest College, 555 North Sheridan Road, Lake Forest, IL 60045-2338. *Phone:* 847-735-5000. *Toll-free phone:* 800-828-4751. *Fax:* 847-735-6271. *E-mail:* admissions@lakeforest.edu. *Web site:* http://www.lakeforest.edu/.

Lakeview College of Nursing

Danville, Illinois

- **Independent** upper-level, founded 1987
- **Small-town** 1-acre campus
- **Coed**
- **Moderately difficult** entrance level

Faculty *Student/faculty ratio:* 7:1.

Academics *Calendar:* semesters. *Degree:* bachelor's.

Student Life *Campus security:* 24-hour emergency response devices.

Costs (2010–11) *Tuition:* $11,840 full-time, $370 per credit hour part-time. *Required fees:* $1920 full-time, $60 per credit hour part-time.

Applying *Options:* early admission, early decision, deferred entrance. *Application fee:* $100.

Application Contact Admissions Office, Lakeview College of Nursing, 903 North Logan Avenue, Danville, IL 61832. *Phone:* 217-443-5238. *Fax:* 217-442-2279. *E-mail:* admission@lakeviewcol.edu. *Web site:* http://www.lakeviewcol.edu/.

Lewis University

Romeoville, Illinois

- **Independent** comprehensive, founded 1932, affiliated with Roman Catholic Church
- **Suburban** 376-acre campus with easy access to Chicago
- **Endowment** $34.8 million
- **Coed** 4,257 undergraduate students, 81% full-time, 57% women, 43% men
- **Moderately difficult** entrance level, 69% of applicants were admitted

Undergraduates 3,451 full-time, 806 part-time. Students come from 33 states and territories; 24 other countries; 5% are from out of state; 9% Black or African American, non-Hispanic/Latino; 13% Hispanic/Latino; 3% Asian, non-Hispanic/Latino; 0.1% Native Hawaiian or other Pacific Islander, non-Hispanic/Latino; 0.2% American Indian or Alaska Native, non-Hispanic/Latino; 0.5% Two or more races, non-Hispanic/Latino; 9% Race/ethnicity unknown; 1% international; 10% transferred in; 30% live on campus. *Retention:* 82% of full-time freshmen returned.

Freshmen *Admission:* 2,867 applied, 1,966 admitted, 636 enrolled. *Average high school GPA:* 3.2. *Test scores:* SAT critical reading scores over 500: 39%; SAT math scores over 500: 56%; SAT writing scores over 500: 11%; ACT scores over 18: 96%; SAT critical reading scores over 600: 6%; SAT math scores over 600: 22%; ACT scores over 24: 34%; ACT scores over 30: 3%.

Faculty *Total:* 625, 31% full-time, 31% with terminal degrees. *Student/faculty ratio:* 14:1.

Academics *Calendar:* semesters. *Degrees:* certificates, associate, bachelor's, master's, doctoral-research/scholarship, and post-master's certificates. *Special study options:* academic remediation for entering students, accelerated degree program, adult/continuing education programs, advanced placement credit, distance learning, double majors, English as a second language, honors programs, independent study, internships, off-campus study, part-time degree program, services for LD students, student-designed majors, study abroad, summer session for credit. *ROTC:* Army (c), Air Force (c).

Computers on Campus 267 computers/terminals are available on campus for general student use. Students can access the following: campus intranet, computer help desk, free student e-mail accounts, online (class) grades, online (class) registration, online (class) schedules, online help, online billing, online financial aid, online payments, online application for admission, online housing application, online application for graduation, Blackboard course management system. Campuswide network is available. 100% of college-owned or -operated housing units are wired for high-speed Internet access. Wireless service is available via entire campus.

Student Life *Housing options:* coed. Campus housing is university owned. Freshman campus housing is guaranteed. *Activities and organizations:* drama/theater group, student-run newspaper, radio and television station, choral group, Student Governing Board, The PULSE, Black Student Union, Delta Sigma Pi (business fraternity), Student Nursing Association, national fraternities, national sororities. *Campus security:* 24-hour emergency response devices and patrols, student patrols, late-night transport/escort service, controlled dormitory access. *Student services:* health clinic, personal/psychological counseling.

Athletics Member NCAA. All Division II. *Intercollegiate sports:* baseball M(s), basketball M(s)/W(s), cheerleading M(s)(c)/W(s)(c), cross-country running M(s)/W(s), golf M(s)/W(s), ice hockey M(c), rugby M(c), soccer M(s)/W(s), softball W(s), swimming and diving M(s)/W(s), tennis M(s)/W(s), track and field M(s)/W(s), volleyball M(s)/W(s). *Intramural sports:* badminton M/W, baseball M, basketball M/W, bowling M/W, cross-country running M/W, football M/W, golf M/W, racquetball M/W, soccer M/W, softball M/W, swimming and diving M/W, table tennis M/W, tennis M/W, track and field M/W, ultimate Frisbee M/W, volleyball M(c)/W.

Standardized Tests *Required:* SAT or ACT (for admission).

Costs (2011–12) *Comprehensive fee:* $33,670 includes full-time tuition ($24,770) and room and board ($8900). Full-time tuition and fees vary according to course load and program. Part-time tuition: $750 per semester hour. Part-time tuition and fees vary according to course load and program. *Room and board:* Room and board charges vary according to board plan and housing facility. *Payment plan:* installment. *Waivers:* children of alumni, adult students, and employees or children of employees.

Financial Aid Of all full-time matriculated undergraduates who enrolled in 2009, 2,763 applied for aid, 2,373 were judged to have need, 1,620 had their need fully met. 385 Federal Work-Study jobs (averaging $2800). 190 state and other part-time jobs (averaging $3600). In 2009, 299 non-need-based awards were made. *Average percent of need met:* 84%. *Average financial aid package:* $18,419. *Average need-based loan:* $4322. *Average need-based gift aid:* $8954. *Average non-need-based aid:* $7538. *Average indebtedness upon graduation:* $20,413.

Applying *Options:* electronic application, deferred entrance. *Application fee:* $40. *Required:* high school transcript, minimum 2 GPA. *Required for some:* interview. *Application deadlines:* 8/1 (freshmen), rolling (transfers). *Notification:* continuous (freshmen), continuous (transfers).

Freshman Application Contact Mr. Ryan Cockerill, Director of Admission, Lewis University, Box 297, One University Parkway, Romeoville, IL 60446. *Phone:* 815-836-5237. *Toll-free phone:* 800-897-9000. *Fax:* 815-836-5002. *E-mail:* admissions@lewisu.edu. *Web site:* http://www.lewisu.edu/.

Lexington College
Chicago, Illinois

- **Independent** 4-year, founded 1977
- **Urban** campus
- **Endowment** $29,600
- **Women only** 54 undergraduate students, 96% full-time
- **Noncompetitive** entrance level, 47% of applicants were admitted

Undergraduates 52 full-time, 2 part-time. Students come from 8 states and territories; 1 other country; 20% are from out of state; 11% transferred in. *Retention:* 71% of full-time freshmen returned.
Freshmen *Admission:* 62 applied, 29 admitted, 9 enrolled. *Average high school GPA:* 3.15.
Faculty *Total:* 19, 21% full-time, 26% with terminal degrees. *Student/faculty ratio:* 6:1.
Academics *Calendar:* semesters. *Degrees:* certificates, associate, and bachelor's. *Special study options:* academic remediation for entering students, advanced placement credit, cooperative education, independent study, internships, part-time degree program, study abroad.
Computers on Campus 30 computers/terminals are available on campus for general student use. Students can access the following: free student e-mail accounts, academic, coursework-supporting software. Campuswide network is available. Wireless service is available via entire campus.
Student Life *Housing:* college housing not available. *Activities and organizations:* student-run newspaper, student government, Dinner Club, student service program, Student Mentors, student tutoring. *Campus security:* 24-hour emergency response devices and patrols, patrols by municipal security personnel.
Standardized Tests *Required for some:* SAT or ACT (for admission).
Costs (2010–11) *One-time required fee:* $150. *Tuition:* $23,500 full-time, $783 per credit hour part-time. Full-time tuition and fees vary according to course load and program. Part-time tuition and fees vary according to course load and program. *Required fees:* $1000 full-time. *Payment plan:* installment. *Waivers:* employees or children of employees.
Financial Aid *Financial aid deadline:* 10/1.
Applying *Options:* electronic application. *Application fee:* $30. *Required:* essay or personal statement, high school transcript, minimum 2 GPA. *Recommended:* interview. *Application deadlines:* rolling (freshmen), rolling (transfers). *Notification:* continuous (freshmen), continuous (transfers).
Freshman Application Contact Mrs. Carmen Larios, Admissions Director, Lexington College, 310 South Peoria Street, Suite 512, Chicago, IL 60607-3534. *Phone:* 312-226-6294 Ext. 226. *Fax:* 312-226-6405. *E-mail:* admissions@lexingtoncollege.edu. *Web site:* http://www.lexingtoncollege.edu/.

Lincoln Christian University
Lincoln, Illinois

- **Independent** 4-year, founded 1944, affiliated with Christian Churches and Churches of Christ
- **Small-town** 227-acre campus
- **Coed** 666 undergraduate students, 83% full-time, 53% women, 47% men
- **Moderately difficult** entrance level, 63% of applicants were admitted

Undergraduates 555 full-time, 111 part-time. Students come from 25 states and territories; 5 other countries; 30% are from out of state; 6% Black or African American, non-Hispanic/Latino; 4% Hispanic/Latino; 0.8% Asian, non-Hispanic/Latino; 0.8% American Indian or Alaska Native, non-Hispanic/Latino; 0.5% Two or more races, non-Hispanic/Latino; 0.9% Race/ethnicity unknown; 0.8% international; 14% transferred in; 50% live on campus. *Retention:* 73% of full-time freshmen returned.
Freshmen *Admission:* 264 applied, 167 admitted, 97 enrolled. *Average high school GPA:* 3.2. *Test scores:* ACT scores over 18: 86%; ACT scores over 24: 27%; ACT scores over 30: 5%.
Faculty *Total:* 59, 49% full-time, 41% with terminal degrees. *Student/faculty ratio:* 13:1.
Academics *Calendar:* semesters. *Degrees:* certificates, associate, and bachelor's. *Special study options:* academic remediation for entering students, adult/continuing education programs, advanced placement credit, distance learning, double majors, English as a second language, external degree program, honors programs, independent study, internships, off-campus study, part-time degree program, services for LD students, summer session for credit. *Unusual degree programs:* 3-2 teacher education.
Computers on Campus 45 computers/terminals are available on campus for general student use. Students can access the following: campus intranet, com-

puter help desk, free student e-mail accounts, online (class) grades, online (class) registration, online (class) schedules. Campuswide network is available.
Student Life *Housing:* on-campus residence required through senior year. *Options:* men-only, women-only. Campus housing is university owned. Freshman campus housing is guaranteed. *Activities and organizations:* drama/theater group, choral group. *Campus security:* 24-hour emergency response devices, student patrols, controlled dormitory access. *Student services:* health clinic, personal/psychological counseling.
Athletics Member NCCAA. *Intercollegiate sports:* baseball M, basketball M/W, cheerleading M/W, cross-country running M/W, soccer M/W, volleyball W. *Intramural sports:* basketball M, tennis M/W, volleyball M/W, weight lifting M/W.
Standardized Tests *Required:* SAT or ACT (for admission).
Costs (2010–11) *Comprehensive fee:* $19,752 includes full-time tuition ($13,680) and room and board ($6072). Part-time tuition: $456 per semester hour. *Payment plans:* installment, deferred payment. *Waivers:* employees or children of employees.
Financial Aid Of all full-time matriculated undergraduates who enrolled in 2007, 716 applied for aid, 610 were judged to have need, 105 had their need fully met. 47 Federal Work-Study jobs (averaging $996). 149 state and other part-time jobs (averaging $1557). In 2007, 57 non-need-based awards were made. *Average percent of need met:* 64%. *Average financial aid package:* $8945. *Average need-based loan:* $3888. *Average need-based gift aid:* $3560. *Average non-need-based aid:* $4636. *Average indebtedness upon graduation:* $19,594.
Applying *Options:* electronic application, deferred entrance. *Application fee:* $20. *Required:* essay or personal statement, high school transcript, 3 letters of recommendation. *Required for some:* interview. *Application deadlines:* rolling (freshmen), rolling (out-of-state freshmen), rolling (transfers). *Notification:* continuous (freshmen), continuous (out-of-state freshmen), continuous (transfers).
Freshman Application Contact Mrs. Mary K. Davis, Assistant Director of Admissions, Lincoln Christian University, 100 Campus View Drive, Lincoln, IL 62656. *Phone:* 217-732-3168 Ext. 2251. *Toll-free phone:* 888-522-5228. *Fax:* 217-732-4199. *E-mail:* coladmis@lincolnchristian.edu. *Web site:* http://www.lincolnchristian.edu/.

Lincoln College–Normal
Normal, Illinois

- **Independent** 4-year, founded 1865
- **Suburban** 10-acre campus with easy access to Bloomington/Normal, Illinois
- **Coed**
- **Minimally difficult** entrance level

Faculty *Student/faculty ratio:* 14:1.
Academics *Calendar:* some programs are semester; some are continuous. *Degrees:* certificates, associate, and bachelor's.
Student Life *Campus security:* 24-hour emergency response devices and patrols, student patrols, late-night transport/escort service, controlled dormitory access.
Standardized Tests *Required for some:* SAT or ACT (for admission), ACT score required for some programs.
Costs (2010–11) *Tuition:* $21,000 full-time. Full-time tuition and fees vary according to location and program. Part-time tuition and fees vary according to location and program. *Room only:* $3500.
Applying *Options:* electronic application, deferred entrance. *Application fee:* $25. *Required:* high school transcript. *Required for some:* essay or personal statement, 1 letter of recommendation, interview. *Recommended:* minimum 2 GPA.
Freshman Application Contact Mr. Steve Puck, Director of Admissions, Lincoln College–Normal, 715 West Raab Road, Normal, IL 61761. *Phone:* 309-268-4314. *Toll-free phone:* 800-569-0558. *Fax:* 309-862-3352. *E-mail:* spuck@lincolncollege.edu. *Web site:* http://www.lincolncollege.edu/normal/.

Loyola University Chicago
Chicago, Illinois

- **Independent Roman Catholic (Jesuit)** university, founded 1870
- **Urban** 105-acre campus
- **Endowment** $315.3 million
- **Coed** 9,747 undergraduate students, 93% full-time, 64% women, 36% men
- **Moderately difficult** entrance level, 60% of applicants were admitted

Undergraduates 9,042 full-time, 705 part-time. Students come from 50 states and territories; 82 other countries; 34% are from out of state; 4% Black or African American, non-Hispanic/Latino; 11% Hispanic/Latino; 12% Asian, non-Hispanic/Latino; 0.1% Native Hawaiian or other Pacific Islander, non-Hispanic/Latino; 0.2% American Indian or Alaska Native, non-Hispanic/Latino;

2% Two or more races, non-Hispanic/Latino; 6% Race/ethnicity unknown; 1% international; 5% transferred in; 41% live on campus. *Retention:* 85% of full-time freshmen returned.

Freshmen *Admission:* 17,671 applied, 10,529 admitted, 2,063 enrolled. *Average high school GPA:* 3.7. *Test scores:* SAT critical reading scores over 500: 92%; SAT math scores over 500: 89%; SAT writing scores over 500: 91%; ACT scores over 18: 100%; SAT critical reading scores over 600: 49%; SAT math scores over 600: 50%; SAT writing scores over 600: 47%; ACT scores over 24: 84%; SAT critical reading scores over 700: 11%; SAT math scores over 700: 8%; SAT writing scores over 700: 10%; ACT scores over 30: 21%.

Faculty *Total:* 1,368, 48% full-time. *Student/faculty ratio:* 15:1.

Academics *Calendar:* semesters. *Degrees:* bachelor's, master's, doctoral-professional, doctoral-research/scholarship, post-master's, and postbachelor's certificates (also offers adult part-time program with significant enrollment not reflected in profile). *Special study options:* academic remediation for entering students, accelerated degree program, adult/continuing education programs, advanced placement credit, cooperative education, distance learning, double majors, English as a second language, freshman honors college, honors programs, independent study, internships, off-campus study, part-time degree program, services for LD students, study abroad, summer session for credit. *ROTC:* Army (c), Navy (c), Air Force (c). *Unusual degree programs:* 3-2 business administration; engineering with Washington University in St. Louis; Columbia University in NYC; social work; political science, sociology, psychology, mathematics, management, computer science, biology, education, accounting, information technology, criminal justice, environmental studies.

Computers on Campus 1,026 computers/terminals are available on campus for general student use. Students can access the following: campus intranet, computer help desk, free student e-mail accounts, online (class) grades, online (class) registration, online (class) schedules. Campuswide network is available. 100% of college-owned or -operated housing units are wired for high-speed Internet access. Wireless service is available via entire campus.

Student Life *Housing:* on-campus residence required through sophomore year. *Options:* coed, disabled students. Campus housing is university owned. Freshman campus housing is guaranteed. *Activities and organizations:* drama/theater group, student-run newspaper, radio station, Department of Programming, Panhellenic Sororities, American Medical Association, Habitat for Humanity, Intrafraternity Council, national fraternities, national sororities. *Campus security:* 24-hour emergency response devices and patrols, late-night transport/escort service, controlled dormitory access, Loyola Alert, a special service to provide personalized, time-sensitive alerts to students, faculty, staff & other personnel at Loyola. *Student services:* health clinic, personal/psychological counseling, women's center.

Athletics Member NCAA. All Division I. *Intercollegiate sports:* basketball M(s)/W(s), cheerleading M/W, cross-country running M(s)/W(s), golf M(s)/W(s), soccer M(s)/W(s), softball W(s), track and field M(s)/W(s), volleyball M(s)/W(s). *Intramural sports:* badminton M/W, baseball M(c), basketball M/W, cross-country running M(c)/W(c), fencing M(c)/W(c), football M/W, ice hockey M(c)/W(c), lacrosse M(c)/W(c), racquetball M/W, rugby M(c)/W(c), soccer M(c)/W(c), softball W(c), swimming and diving M(c)/W(c), table tennis M(c)/W(c), tennis M(c)/W(c), ultimate Frisbee M(c)/W(c), volleyball M(c)/W(c), water polo M(c)/W(c).

Standardized Tests *Required:* SAT or ACT (for admission).

Costs (2011–12) *Comprehensive fee:* $44,864 includes full-time tuition ($32,200), mandatory fees ($1094), and room and board ($11,570). Full-time tuition and fees vary according to location and program. Part-time tuition: $655 per credit. Part-time tuition and fees vary according to course load. *Required fees:* $145 per term part-time. *College room only:* $7590. Room and board charges vary according to board plan, housing facility, and location. *Payment plans:* installment, deferred payment. *Waivers:* senior citizens and employees or children of employees.

Financial Aid Of all full-time matriculated undergraduates who enrolled in 2009, 7,296 applied for aid, 6,599 were judged to have need, 640 had their need fully met. 5,284 Federal Work-Study jobs (averaging $2188). In 2009, 1509 non-need-based awards were made. *Average percent of need met:* 81%. *Average financial aid package:* $28,864. *Average need-based loan:* $5049. *Average need-based gift aid:* $17,598. *Average non-need-based aid:* $8203.

Applying *Options:* electronic application. *Required:* essay or personal statement, high school transcript, minimum 2 GPA. *Recommended:* interview. *Notification:* continuous (freshmen), continuous (out-of-state freshmen), continuous (transfers).

Freshman Application Contact Ms. Lori Greene, Director of Undergraduate Admissions, Loyola University Chicago, 1032 West Sheridan Road, Chicago, IL 60660. *Phone:* 773-508-3079. *Toll-free phone:* 800-262-2373. *E-mail:* admission@luc.edu. *Web site:* http://www.luc.edu/.

MacMurray College
Jacksonville, Illinois
- **Independent United Methodist** 4-year, founded 1846
- **Small-town** 60-acre campus
- **Endowment** $7.1 million
- **Coed** 528 undergraduate students, 82% full-time, 63% women, 38% men
- **Moderately difficult** entrance level, 77% of applicants were admitted

Undergraduates 435 full-time, 93 part-time. Students come from 21 states and territories; 1 other country; 12% are from out of state; 12% transferred in; 49% live on campus. *Retention:* 49% of full-time freshmen returned.

Freshmen *Admission:* 539 applied, 416 admitted, 90 enrolled. *Average high school GPA:* 2.77.

Faculty *Total:* 56, 59% full-time, 48% with terminal degrees. *Student/faculty ratio:* 11:1.

Academics *Calendar:* 4-1-4. *Degrees:* associate and bachelor's. *Special study options:* academic remediation for entering students, adult/continuing education programs, advanced placement credit, cooperative education, double majors, independent study, internships, off-campus study, part-time degree program, services for LD students, student-designed majors, study abroad, summer session for credit.

Computers on Campus 100 computers/terminals are available on campus for general student use. Students can access the following: computer help desk, free student e-mail accounts, various productivity software packages. 100% of college-owned or -operated housing units are wired for high-speed Internet access. Wireless service is available via classrooms, computer labs, learning centers, libraries, student centers.

Student Life *Housing:* on-campus residence required through junior year. *Options:* coed, women-only. Campus housing is university owned. Freshman campus housing is guaranteed. *Activities and organizations:* drama/theater group, choral group, Campus Activity Board, MacMurray Student Association, Sigma Tau Gamma, Alpha Phi Omega, Circle K, national fraternities. *Campus security:* 24-hour emergency response devices and patrols, late-night transport/escort service. *Student services:* health clinic, personal/psychological counseling.

Athletics Member NCAA. All Division III. *Intercollegiate sports:* baseball M, basketball M/W, football M, golf M/W, soccer M/W, softball W, volleyball W. *Intramural sports:* basketball M/W, cross-country running M/W, football M/W, soccer M/W, softball M/W, table tennis M/W, tennis M/W, volleyball M/W.

Standardized Tests *Recommended:* SAT or ACT (for admission).

Costs (2011–12) *Comprehensive fee:* $28,050 includes full-time tuition ($19,900), mandatory fees ($500), and room and board ($7650). Part-time tuition: $660 per credit hour. Part-time tuition and fees vary according to course load and program. *Required fees:* $30 per credit hour part-time. *Room and board:* Room and board charges vary according to board plan, housing facility, and student level. *Payment plan:* installment. *Waivers:* senior citizens and employees or children of employees.

Financial Aid Of all full-time matriculated undergraduates who enrolled in 2009, 463 applied for aid, 448 were judged to have need, 210 had their need fully met. 114 Federal Work-Study jobs (averaging $564). In 2009, 12 non-need-based awards were made. *Average percent of need met:* 93%. *Average financial aid package:* $24,166. *Average need-based loan:* $10,059. *Average need-based gift aid:* $14,107. *Average non-need-based aid:* $9212. *Average indebtedness upon graduation:* $27,524.

Applying *Options:* electronic application, early admission. *Required:* high school transcript. *Required for some:* essay or personal statement, minimum 2.5 GPA, 1 letter of recommendation, interview. *Application deadlines:* rolling (freshmen), rolling (transfers). *Notification:* continuous (freshmen), continuous (transfers).

Freshman Application Contact Ms. Alicia Zeone, Assistant Director of Admission, MacMurray College, MacMurray College, 447 East College Avenue, Jacksonville, IL 62650. *Phone:* 217-479-7059. *Toll-free phone:* 800-252-7485. *Fax:* 217-291-0702. *E-mail:* alicia.zeone@mac.edu. *Web site:* http://www.mac.edu/.

McKendree University
Lebanon, Illinois
- **Independent** comprehensive, founded 1828, affiliated with United Methodist Church
- **Small-town** 100-acre campus with easy access to St. Louis
- **Endowment** $23.1 million
- **Coed** 2,347 undergraduate students, 76% full-time, 56% women, 44% men
- **Moderately difficult** entrance level, 67% of applicants were admitted

Undergraduates 1,795 full-time, 552 part-time. Students come from 23 states and territories; 11 other countries; 25% are from out of state; 14% Black or African American, non-Hispanic/Latino; 2% Hispanic/Latino; 1% Asian, non-

PROFILES

Hispanic/Latino; 0.1% Native Hawaiian or other Pacific Islander, non-Hispanic/Latino; 0.3% American Indian or Alaska Native, non-Hispanic/Latino; 5% Race/ethnicity unknown; 2% international; 13% transferred in; 56% live on campus. *Retention:* 72% of full-time freshmen returned.

Freshmen *Admission:* 1,350 applied, 905 admitted, 341 enrolled. *Average high school GPA:* 3.5. *Test scores:* SAT critical reading scores over 500: 35%; SAT math scores over 500: 47%; SAT writing scores over 500: 24%; ACT scores over 18: 100%; SAT critical reading scores over 600: 6%; SAT math scores over 600: 18%; ACT scores over 24: 40%; ACT scores over 30: 10%.

Faculty *Total:* 323, 30% full-time. *Student/faculty ratio:* 13:1.

Academics *Calendar:* semesters. *Degrees:* bachelor's and master's. *Special study options:* academic remediation for entering students, accelerated degree program, advanced placement credit, double majors, honors programs, independent study, internships, off-campus study, part-time degree program, services for LD students, student-designed majors, study abroad, summer session for credit. *ROTC:* Army (c), Air Force (c). *Unusual degree programs:* 3-2 engineering with Program with University of Illinois- Urbana-Champaign; Occupational Therapy with Washington University in St. Louis.

Computers on Campus 140 computers/terminals are available on campus for general student use. Students can access the following: campus intranet, computer help desk, free student e-mail accounts, online (class) grades, online (class) registration, online (class) schedules. Campuswide network is available. 100% of college-owned or -operated housing units are wired for high-speed Internet access. Wireless service is available via entire campus.

Student Life *Housing:* on-campus residence required through junior year. *Options:* coed. Campus housing is university owned and leased by the school. Freshman campus housing is guaranteed. *Activities and organizations:* drama/theater group, student-run newspaper, choral group, marching band, Wonders of Wellness, Center for Public Service, Campus Ministries, Kappa Sigma Tau, Tri Sigma, national fraternities, national sororities. *Campus security:* 24-hour emergency response devices and patrols, student patrols, late-night transport/escort service, controlled dormitory access. *Student services:* health clinic, personal/psychological counseling.

Athletics Member NAIA. *Intercollegiate sports:* baseball M(s), basketball M(s)/W(s), bowling M(s)/W(s), cheerleading M(s)/W(s), cross-country running M(s)/W(s), football M(s), golf M(s)/W(s), ice hockey M, soccer M(s)/W(s), softball W(s), tennis M(s)/W(s), track and field M(s)/W(s), volleyball W(s), wrestling M(s). *Intramural sports:* basketball M/W, football M/W, softball M/W, table tennis M/W, ultimate Frisbee M/W, volleyball M/W.

Standardized Tests *Required:* SAT or ACT (for admission).

Costs (2011–12) *Comprehensive fee:* $33,590 includes full-time tuition ($24,190), mandatory fees ($900), and room and board ($8500). Full-time tuition and fees vary according to course load, degree level, and location. Part-time tuition and fees vary according to course load, degree level, and location. *College room only:* $4400. Room and board charges vary according to board plan and housing facility. *Payment plan:* installment. *Waivers:* employees or children of employees.

Financial Aid Of all full-time matriculated undergraduates who enrolled in 2009, 1,261 applied for aid, 1,171 were judged to have need, 216 had their need fully met. 859 Federal Work-Study jobs (averaging $1721). 95 state and other part-time jobs (averaging $1327). In 2009, 203 non-need-based awards were made. *Average percent of need met:* 77%. *Average financial aid package:* $19,185. *Average need-based loan:* $3777. *Average need-based gift aid:* $15,226. *Average non-need-based aid:* $7916. *Average indebtedness upon graduation:* $23,025.

Applying *Options:* electronic application, deferred entrance. *Required:* essay or personal statement, high school transcript, minimum 2.5 GPA, 1 letter of recommendation, rank in upper 50% of high school class, ACT score of 20 or higher. *Required for some:* interview. *Application deadlines:* rolling (freshmen), rolling (transfers). *Notification:* continuous (freshmen), continuous (transfers).

Freshman Application Contact Josie Blasdel, Director of Undergraduate Admission, McKendree University, 701 College Road, Lebanon, IL 62254. *Toll-free phone:* 800-232-7228 Ext. 6831. *Fax:* 618-537-6496. *E-mail:* inquiry@mckendree.edu. *Web site:* http://www.mckendree.edu/.

Midstate College

Peoria, Illinois

Freshman Application Contact Ms. Jessica Hancock, Director of Admissions, Midstate College, 411 West Northmoor Road, Peoria, IL 61614. *Phone:* 309-692-4092. *Fax:* 309-692-3893. *E-mail:* jhancock2@midstate.edu. *Web site:* http://www.midstate.edu/.

Millikin University

Decatur, Illinois

- **Independent** comprehensive, founded 1901, affiliated with Presbyterian Church (U.S.A.)
- **Suburban** 75-acre campus
- **Endowment** $89.2 million
- **Coed** 2,295 undergraduate students, 93% full-time, 61% women, 39% men
- **Moderately difficult** entrance level, 58% of applicants were admitted

Undergraduates 2,142 full-time, 153 part-time. Students come from 37 states and territories; 10 other countries; 12% are from out of state; 11% Black or African American, non-Hispanic/Latino; 5% Hispanic/Latino; 0.6% Asian, non-Hispanic/Latino; 0.2% Native Hawaiian or other Pacific Islander, non-Hispanic/Latino; 0.4% American Indian or Alaska Native, non-Hispanic/Latino; 2% Two or more races, non-Hispanic/Latino; 0.4% Race/ethnicity unknown; 0.8% international; 5% transferred in; 67% live on campus. *Retention:* 78% of full-time freshmen returned.

Freshmen *Admission:* 3,240 applied, 1,883 admitted, 498 enrolled. *Average high school GPA:* 3.38. *Test scores:* SAT critical reading scores over 500: 84%; SAT math scores over 500: 84%; SAT writing scores over 500: 80%; ACT scores over 18: 96%; SAT critical reading scores over 600: 24%; SAT math scores over 600: 16%; SAT writing scores over 600: 30%; ACT scores over 24: 43%; SAT critical reading scores over 700: 4%; SAT math scores over 700: 4%; ACT scores over 30: 7%.

Faculty *Total:* 289, 54% full-time, 53% with terminal degrees. *Student/faculty ratio:* 11:1.

Academics *Calendar:* semesters. *Degrees:* bachelor's and master's. *Special study options:* accelerated degree program, adult/continuing education programs, advanced placement credit, cooperative education, double majors, honors programs, independent study, internships, off-campus study, part-time degree program, services for LD students, student-designed majors, study abroad, summer session for credit. *Unusual degree programs:* 3-2 engineering with Washington University in St. Louis; occupational therapy with Washington University; pharmacy with Midwestern University.

Computers on Campus 280 computers/terminals and 318 ports are available on campus for general student use. Students can access the following: computer help desk, free student e-mail accounts, online (class) grades, online (class) registration, online (class) schedules, online degree audit; online financials (view and pay bills; view financial aid). Campuswide network is available. 100% of college-owned or -operated housing units are wired for high-speed Internet access. Wireless service is available via classrooms, computer centers, computer labs, dorm rooms, learning centers, libraries, student centers.

Student Life *Housing:* on-campus residence required through junior year. *Options:* coed, men-only, women-only, disabled students. Campus housing is university owned, leased by the school and is provided by a third party. Freshman campus housing is guaranteed. *Activities and organizations:* drama/theater group, student-run newspaper, radio station, choral group, University Center Board, Multicultural Student Council, Student Housing Council, Panhellenic Council, Interfraternity Council, national fraternities, national sororities. *Campus security:* 24-hour emergency response devices and patrols, late-night transport/escort service, controlled dormitory access. *Student services:* health clinic, personal/psychological counseling.

Athletics Member NCAA. All Division III. *Intercollegiate sports:* baseball M, basketball M/W, cheerleading M/W, cross-country running M/W, football M, golf M/W, soccer M/W, softball W, swimming and diving M/W, tennis W, track and field M/W, volleyball W. *Intramural sports:* basketball M/W, bowling M/W, football M, soccer M/W, softball M/W, volleyball M/W.

Standardized Tests *Required:* SAT or ACT (for admission).

Costs (2010–11) *Comprehensive fee:* $35,716 includes full-time tuition ($26,780), mandatory fees ($645), and room and board ($8291). Part-time tuition: $895 per credit hour. *Required fees:* $75 per term part-time. *College room only:* $4621. Room and board charges vary according to board plan and housing facility. *Payment plan:* installment. *Waivers:* employees or children of employees.

Financial Aid Of all full-time matriculated undergraduates who enrolled in 2008, 1,933 applied for aid, 1,683 were judged to have need, 909 had their need fully met. 519 Federal Work-Study jobs (averaging $1075). 259 state and other part-time jobs (averaging $830). In 2008, 214 non-need-based awards were made. *Average percent of need met:* 92%. *Average financial aid package:* $20,294. *Average need-based loan:* $4203. *Average need-based gift aid:* $8815. *Average non-need-based aid:* $9105. *Average indebtedness upon graduation:* $28,475.

Applying *Options:* electronic application, deferred entrance. *Required:* high school transcript, minimum 2 GPA, 2 letters of recommendation. *Required for some:* audition for music/theatre, art portfolio review. *Recommended:* interview. *Application deadlines:* rolling (freshmen), rolling (out-of-state freshmen), rolling (transfers). *Notification:* continuous (freshmen), continuous (out-of-state freshmen), continuous (transfers).

Freshman Application Contact Mr. Joe Havis, Assistant Director of Admission, Millikin University, 1184 West Main Street, Decatur, IL 62522-2084. *Phone:* 217-424-6210. *Toll-free phone:* 800-373-7733. *Fax:* 217-425-4669. *E-mail:* admis@millikin.edu. *Web site:* http://www.millikin.edu/.

Monmouth College
Monmouth, Illinois

- **Independent** 4-year, founded 1853, affiliated with Presbyterian Church
- **Small-town** 80-acre campus with easy access to Chicago
- **Endowment** $79.1 million
- **Coed** 1,347 undergraduate students, 98% full-time, 52% women, 48% men
- **Moderately difficult** entrance level, 68% of applicants were admitted

Undergraduates 1,324 full-time, 23 part-time. Students come from 22 states and territories; 11 other countries; 6% are from out of state; 9% Black or African American, non-Hispanic/Latino; 6% Hispanic/Latino; 0.3% Asian, non-Hispanic/Latino; 0.1% Native Hawaiian or other Pacific Islander, non-Hispanic/Latino; 0.7% American Indian or Alaska Native, non-Hispanic/Latino; 0.2% Two or more races, non-Hispanic/Latino; 1% Race/ethnicity unknown; 1% international; 4% transferred in; 94% live on campus. *Retention:* 75% of full-time freshmen returned.
Freshmen *Admission:* 1,980 applied, 1,342 admitted, 350 enrolled. *Average high school GPA:* 3.2. *Test scores:* ACT scores over 18: 94%; ACT scores over 24: 32%; ACT scores over 30: 3%.
Faculty *Total:* 118, 70% full-time, 62% with terminal degrees. *Student/faculty ratio:* 14:1.
Academics *Calendar:* semesters. *Degree:* bachelor's. *Special study options:* advanced placement credit, double majors, English as a second language, honors programs, independent study, internships, off-campus study, part-time degree program, services for LD students, student-designed majors, study abroad. *ROTC:* Army (b). *Unusual degree programs:* 3-2 engineering with Case Western Reserve University, Washington University in St. Louis, University of Southern California (joint five-year programs); nursing with Rush University College of Nursing; occupational therapy, medical technology with Rush University; architecture with Washington University - St. Louis, atmospheric science with Creighton University.
Computers on Campus 140 computers/terminals are available on campus for general student use. Students can access the following: campus intranet, computer help desk, free student e-mail accounts, online (class) grades, online (class) registration, online (class) schedules, 11 PC labs and 3 specialized Mac labs. Campuswide network is available. 100% of college-owned or -operated housing units are wired for high-speed Internet access. Wireless service is available via entire campus.
Student Life *Housing:* on-campus residence required through senior year. *Options:* coed, men-only, women-only, disabled students. Campus housing is university owned. Freshman campus housing is guaranteed. *Activities and organizations:* drama/theater group, student-run newspaper, radio and television station, choral group, marching band, Fighting Scots Marching Band and Jazz Band, Associated Students of Monmouth College, Crimson Masque (theatre), Alternative Spring Break, Coalition for Ethnic Awareness, national fraternities, national sororities. *Campus security:* 24-hour emergency response devices, late-night transport/escort service, night security. *Student services:* personal/psychological counseling.
Athletics Member NCAA. All Division III. *Intercollegiate sports:* baseball M, basketball M/W, cross-country running M/W, football M, golf M/W, soccer M/W, softball W, swimming and diving M/W, tennis M/W, track and field M/W, volleyball W. *Intramural sports:* archery M/W, badminton M/W, baseball M/W, basketball M/W, cheerleading M/W, cross-country running M/W, golf M/W, soccer M/W, softball M/W, swimming and diving M/W, table tennis M/W, tennis M/W, track and field M/W, ultimate Frisbee M/W, volleyball M/W, water polo M(c)/W(c), wrestling M.
Standardized Tests *Required:* SAT or ACT (for admission).
Costs (2011–12) *One-time required fee:* $150. *Comprehensive fee:* $35,950 includes full-time tuition ($28,650) and room and board ($7300). Full-time tuition and fees vary according to course load. *Room and board:* Room and board charges vary according to board plan and housing facility. *Payment plan:* installment. *Waivers:* employees or children of employees.
Financial Aid Of all full-time matriculated undergraduates who enrolled in 2009, 1,256 applied for aid, 1,165 were judged to have need, 265 had their need fully met. In 2009, 160 non-need-based awards were made. *Average percent of need met:* 88%. *Average financial aid package:* $24,186. *Average need-based loan:* $3982. *Average need-based gift aid:* $19,444. *Average non-need-based aid:* $10,758. *Average indebtedness upon graduation:* $25,909.
Applying *Options:* electronic application, deferred entrance. *Required:* high school transcript. *Required for some:* essay or personal statement, interview. *Recommended:* essay or personal statement, minimum 2.7 GPA, interview. *Application deadlines:* rolling (freshmen), rolling (transfers). *Notification:* continuous (freshmen), continuous (transfers).

Freshman Application Contact Mr. Omar Correa, Vice President for Enrollment Management, Monmouth College, 700 East Broadway, Monmouth, IL 61462-1988. *Phone:* 309-457-2210. *Toll-free phone:* 800-747-2687. *Fax:* 309-457-2141. *E-mail:* admit@monmouthcollege.edu. *Web site:* http://www.monm.edu/.

Moody Bible Institute
Chicago, Illinois

- **Independent nondenominational** comprehensive, founded 1886
- **Urban** 25-acre campus with easy access to Chicago
- **Endowment** $27.8 million
- **Coed**
- **Moderately difficult** entrance level

Faculty *Student/faculty ratio:* 15:1.
Academics *Calendar:* semesters. *Degrees:* bachelor's, master's, doctoral-professional, post-master's, and postbachelor's certificates.
Student Life *Campus security:* 24-hour emergency response devices and patrols, student patrols, late-night transport/escort service, controlled dormitory access.
Athletics Member NCCAA.
Standardized Tests *Required:* SAT and SAT Subject Tests or ACT (for admission).
Costs (2010–11) *Comprehensive fee:* $18,248 includes full-time tuition ($8000), mandatory fees ($2008), and room and board ($8240). Full-time tuition and fees vary according to course load, location, and program. Part-time tuition: $250 per credit hour. Part-time tuition and fees vary according to course load, location, and program. the college meets all of the tuition cost for each student. *Required fees:* $20 per credit hour part-time. *College room only:* $4810. Room and board charges vary according to board plan, housing facility, and location.
Applying *Options:* electronic application, early admission, early decision. *Required:* essay or personal statement, high school transcript, minimum 2 GPA, 4 letters of recommendation, Christian testimony. *Required for some:* interview.
Freshman Application Contact Ms. Jacqueline Holman, Admissions Office, Moody Bible Institute, 820 North LaSalle Boulevard, Chicago, IL 60610. *Phone:* 312-329-4307. *Toll-free phone:* 800-967-4MBI. *Fax:* 312-329-8987. *E-mail:* admissions@moody.edu. *Web site:* http://www.moody.edu/.

National-Louis University
Chicago, Illinois

- **Independent** university, founded 1886
- **Urban** 12-acre campus
- **Endowment** $25.1 million
- **Coed** 1,480 undergraduate students, 65% full-time, 74% women, 26% men
- **Minimally difficult** entrance level

Undergraduates 967 full-time, 513 part-time. 25% Black or African American, non-Hispanic/Latino; 13% Hispanic/Latino; 2% Asian, non-Hispanic/Latino; 0.3% Native Hawaiian or other Pacific Islander, non-Hispanic/Latino; 0.4% American Indian or Alaska Native, non-Hispanic/Latino; 1% Two or more races, non-Hispanic/Latino; 29% Race/ethnicity unknown; 0.2% international; 21% transferred in.
Freshmen *Admission:* 12 enrolled.
Faculty *Total:* 526, 48% full-time. *Student/faculty ratio:* 9:1.
Academics *Calendar:* quarters. *Degrees:* bachelor's, master's, doctoral-research/scholarship, post-master's, and postbachelor's certificates. *Special study options:* academic remediation for entering students, accelerated degree program, adult/continuing education programs, advanced placement credit, distance learning, English as a second language, external degree program, honors programs, independent study, internships, part-time degree program, services for LD students, summer session for credit.
Computers on Campus 165 computers/terminals are available on campus for general student use. Students can access the following: campus intranet, computer help desk, free student e-mail accounts, online (class) grades, online (class) registration, online (class) schedules. Campuswide network is available. Wireless service is available via classrooms, computer centers, computer labs, learning centers, libraries, student centers.
Student Life *Housing:* college housing not available. *Activities and organizations:* drama/theater group. *Campus security:* 24-hour emergency response devices and patrols. *Student services:* personal/psychological counseling.
Standardized Tests *Required for some:* SAT or ACT (for admission).
Costs (2010–11) *Tuition:* $18,315 full-time, $407 per quarter hour part-time. Full-time tuition and fees vary according to course level, course load, degree level, and program. Part-time tuition and fees vary according to course level, course load, degree level, and program. *Required fees:* $120 full-time. *Pay-*

ment plans: installment, deferred payment. *Waivers:* employees or children of employees.

Financial Aid Of all full-time matriculated undergraduates who enrolled in 2008, 922 applied for aid, 871 were judged to have need, 90 had their need fully met. 35 Federal Work-Study jobs (averaging $3430). In 2008, 37 non-need-based awards were made. *Average percent of need met: 54%. Average financial aid package:* $11,485. *Average need-based loan:* $4603. *Average need-based gift aid:* $7186. *Average non-need-based aid:* $1412. *Average indebtedness upon graduation:* $29,637.

Applying *Options:* electronic application, deferred entrance. *Application fee:* $40. *Required:* high school transcript, minimum 2 GPA. *Required for some:* 2 letters of recommendation. *Recommended:* interview. *Application deadlines:* rolling (freshmen), rolling (transfers). *Notification:* continuous (freshmen), continuous (transfers).

Freshman Application Contact National-Louis University, 1000 Capitol Drive, Wheeling, IL 60090. *Phone:* 888-NLU-TODAY. *Toll-free phone:* 888-NLU-TODAY (in-state); 800-443-5522 (out-of-state). *Web site:* http://www.nl.edu/.

North Central College
Naperville, Illinois

- **Independent United Methodist** comprehensive, founded 1861
- **Suburban** 59-acre campus with easy access to Chicago
- **Endowment** $79.0 million
- **Coed** 2,606 undergraduate students, 93% full-time, 55% women, 45% men
- **Moderately difficult** entrance level, 68% of applicants were admitted

Undergraduates 2,423 full-time, 183 part-time. Students come from 28 states and territories; 29 other countries; 8% are from out of state; 3% Black or African American, non-Hispanic/Latino; 6% Hispanic/Latino; 3% Asian, non-Hispanic/Latino; 0.2% American Indian or Alaska Native, non-Hispanic/Latino; 1% Two or more races, non-Hispanic/Latino; 8% Race/ethnicity unknown; 1% international; 11% transferred in; 55% live on campus. *Retention:* 81% of full-time freshmen returned.

Freshmen *Admission:* 2,900 applied, 1,985 admitted, 583 enrolled. *Average high school GPA:* 3.5. *Test scores:* ACT scores over 18: 98%; ACT scores over 24: 61%; ACT scores over 30: 9%.

Faculty *Total:* 238, 53% full-time, 66% with terminal degrees. *Student/faculty ratio:* 16:1.

Academics *Calendar:* quarters. *Degrees:* bachelor's, master's, and postbachelor's certificates. *Special study options:* academic remediation for entering students, accelerated degree program, advanced placement credit, double majors, English as a second language, honors programs, independent study, internships, off-campus study, part-time degree program, services for LD students, student-designed majors, study abroad, summer session for credit. *ROTC:* Army (c), Air Force (c). *Unusual degree programs:* 3-2 engineering with Washington University in St. Louis; University of Illinois at Urbana-Champaign; Marquette University; University of Minnesota, Twin Cities Campus.

Computers on Campus 351 computers/terminals and 31 ports are available on campus for general student use. Students can access the following: campus intranet, computer help desk, free student e-mail accounts, online (class) grades, online (class) registration, online (class) schedules, software packages. Campuswide network is available. 100% of college-owned or -operated housing units are wired for high-speed Internet access. Wireless service is available via computer centers, computer labs, dorm rooms, learning centers, libraries, student centers.

Student Life *Housing options:* coed, men-only, women-only, disabled students. Campus housing is university owned. Freshman applicants given priority for college housing. *Activities and organizations:* drama/theater group, student-run newspaper, radio station, choral group, College Union Activities Board, WONC (student radio station), Cardinals in Action (service group), Students in Free Enterprise (SIFE), Residence Hall Association. *Campus security:* 24-hour emergency response devices and patrols, late-night transport/escort service, controlled dormitory access. *Student services:* health clinic, personal/psychological counseling.

Athletics Member NCAA. All Division III. *Intercollegiate sports:* baseball M, basketball M/W, cheerleading W, cross-country running M/W, football M, golf M/W, lacrosse W, soccer M/W, softball W, swimming and diving M/W, tennis M/W, track and field M/W, volleyball W, wrestling M. *Intramural sports:* badminton M/W, basketball M/W, football M/W, golf M/W, racquetball M/W, soccer M/W, softball M/W, ultimate Frisbee M/W, volleyball M/W.

Standardized Tests *Required:* SAT or ACT (for admission). *Recommended:* ACT (for admission).

Costs (2010–11) *Comprehensive fee:* $36,687 includes full-time tuition ($27,984), mandatory fees ($240), and room and board ($8463). Part-time tuition: $676 per credit hour. Part-time tuition and fees vary according to course load. *Required fees:* $20 per term part-time. *Room and board:* Room

and board charges vary according to housing facility. *Payment plan:* installment. *Waivers:* senior citizens and employees or children of employees.

Financial Aid Of all full-time matriculated undergraduates who enrolled in 2009, 2,054 applied for aid, 1,868 were judged to have need, 388 had their need fully met. 1,211 Federal Work-Study jobs (averaging $162). In 2009, 465 non-need-based awards were made. *Average percent of need met: 75%. Average financial aid package:* $20,623. *Average need-based loan:* $4667. *Average need-based gift aid:* $15,813. *Average non-need-based aid:* $11,061. *Average indebtedness upon graduation:* $29,137.

Applying *Options:* electronic application, deferred entrance. *Application fee:* $25. *Required:* high school transcript, minimum 2.5 GPA. *Required for some:* interview. *Recommended:* essay or personal statement, 1 letter of recommendation. *Application deadlines:* rolling (freshmen), rolling (out-of-state freshmen), rolling (transfers). *Notification:* continuous (freshmen), continuous (out-of-state freshmen), continuous (transfers).

Freshman Application Contact Ms. Martha Stolze, Director of Freshman Admission, North Central College, 30 North Brainard Street, PO Box 3063, Naperville, IL 60566-7063. *Phone:* 630-637-5800. *Toll-free phone:* 800-411-1861. *Fax:* 630-637-5819. *E-mail:* admissions@noctrl.edu. *Web site:* http://www.northcentralcollege.edu/.

Northeastern Illinois University
Chicago, Illinois

- **State-supported** comprehensive, founded 1961
- **Urban** 67-acre campus
- **Endowment** $2.9 million
- **Coed** 9,498 undergraduate students, 59% full-time, 58% women, 42% men
- **Minimally difficult** entrance level, 65% of applicants were admitted

Undergraduates 5,623 full-time, 3,875 part-time. Students come from 20 states and territories; 104 other countries; 1% are from out of state; 10% Black or African American, non-Hispanic/Latino; 31% Hispanic/Latino; 10% Asian, non-Hispanic/Latino; 0.2% Native Hawaiian or other Pacific Islander, non-Hispanic/Latino; 0.2% American Indian or Alaska Native, non-Hispanic/Latino; 0.7% Two or more races, non-Hispanic/Latino; 4% Race/ethnicity unknown; 4% international; 15% transferred in. *Retention:* 67% of full-time freshmen returned.

Freshmen *Admission:* 5,104 applied, 3,341 admitted, 1,042 enrolled. *Average high school GPA:* 2.87. *Test scores:* ACT scores over 18: 62%; ACT scores over 24: 11%; ACT scores over 30: 1%.

Faculty *Total:* 718, 58% full-time, 52% with terminal degrees. *Student/faculty ratio:* 15:1.

Academics *Calendar:* semesters. *Degrees:* bachelor's and master's. *Special study options:* academic remediation for entering students, adult/continuing education programs, advanced placement credit, cooperative education, distance learning, double majors, English as a second language, external degree program, honors programs, independent study, internships, off-campus study, part-time degree program, services for LD students, study abroad, summer session for credit. *ROTC:* Army (c), Air Force (c).

Computers on Campus 520 computers/terminals are available on campus for general student use. Students can access the following: computer help desk, free student e-mail accounts, online (class) grades, online (class) registration, online (class) schedules, productivity software. Campuswide network is available. Wireless service is available via classrooms, computer centers, computer labs, learning centers, libraries, student centers.

Student Life *Housing:* college housing not available. *Activities and organizations:* student-run newspaper, radio station, choral group, Student Government Association, WZRD radio club, Anime Club, Future Health Professionals, Green Cycle Club, national fraternities, national sororities. *Campus security:* 24-hour emergency response devices and patrols, late-night transport/escort service. *Student services:* health clinic, personal/psychological counseling, women's center.

Athletics *Intramural sports:* baseball M(c), basketball M(c), rugby M(c), volleyball M(c)/W(c).

Standardized Tests *Required:* ACT (for admission).

Costs (2010–11) *Tuition:* state resident $7800 full-time, $260 per credit hour part-time; nonresident $15,600 full-time, $520 per credit hour part-time. Full-time tuition and fees vary according to location and student level. Part-time tuition and fees vary according to course load and location. No tuition increase for student's term of enrollment. *Required fees:* $1203 full-time, $52 per credit hour part-time, $3 per term part-time. *Payment plan:* deferred payment. *Waivers:* senior citizens and employees or children of employees.

Financial Aid Of all full-time matriculated undergraduates who enrolled in 2009, 3,911 applied for aid, 3,380 were judged to have need, 114 had their need fully met. In 2009, 161 non-need-based awards were made. *Average percent of need met: 48%. Average financial aid package:* $8362. *Average need-based loan:* $4477. *Average need-based gift aid:* $7038. *Average non-need-based aid:* $3063. *Average indebtedness upon graduation:* $10,903.

Applying *Options:* electronic application, deferred entrance. *Application fee:* $25. *Required:* high school transcript. *Application deadlines:* 7/1 (freshmen), 7/1 (transfers). *Notification:* 9/1 (freshmen), continuous (transfers).
Freshman Application Contact Ms. Zarrin Kerwell, Admissions Counselor, Northeastern Illinois University, 5500 North St. Louis Avenue, Chicago, IL 60625. *Phone:* 773-442-4026. *Fax:* 773-794-6243. *E-mail:* admrec@neiu.edu. *Web site:* http://www.neiu.edu/.

Northern Illinois University
De Kalb, Illinois

- **State-supported** university, founded 1895
- **Small-town** 650-acre campus with easy access to Chicago
- **Endowment** $2.7 million
- **Coed** 17,886 undergraduate students, 89% full-time, 51% women, 49% men
- **Moderately difficult** entrance level, 54% of applicants were admitted

Undergraduates 15,859 full-time, 2,027 part-time. Students come from 50 states and territories; 80 other countries; 3% are from out of state; 15% Black or African American, non-Hispanic/Latino; 9% Hispanic/Latino; 5% Asian, non-Hispanic/Latino; 0.2% Native Hawaiian or other Pacific Islander, non-Hispanic/Latino; 0.1% American Indian or Alaska Native, non-Hispanic/Latino; 1% Two or more races, non-Hispanic/Latino; 4% Race/ethnicity unknown; 1% international; 13% transferred in; 33% live on campus. *Retention:* 75% of full-time freshmen returned.
Freshmen *Admission:* 19,025 applied, 10,338 admitted, 2,705 enrolled. *Test scores:* ACT scores over 18: 85%; ACT scores over 24: 29%; ACT scores over 30: 3%.
Faculty *Total:* 1,173, 79% full-time, 73% with terminal degrees. *Student/faculty ratio:* 17:1.
Academics *Calendar:* semesters. *Degrees:* bachelor's, master's, doctoral-professional, and doctoral-research/scholarship. *Special study options:* accelerated degree program, adult/continuing education programs, advanced placement credit, cooperative education, double majors, honors programs, independent study, internships, off-campus study, part-time degree program, services for LD students, student-designed majors, study abroad, summer session for credit. *ROTC:* Army (b), Air Force (c). *Unusual degree programs:* 3-2 engineering with University of Illinois.
Computers on Campus 1,500 computers/terminals are available on campus for general student use. Students can access the following: computer help desk, free student e-mail accounts, online (class) registration. Campuswide network is available.
Student Life *Housing:* on-campus residence required for freshman year. *Options:* coed. Campus housing is university owned. Freshman applicants given priority for college housing. *Activities and organizations:* drama/theater group, student-run newspaper, radio station, choral group, marching band, American Marketing Association, Delta Sigma Pi, Pi Sigma Epsilon, Black Choir, Student Volunteer Choir, national fraternities, national sororities. *Campus security:* 24-hour emergency response devices and patrols, student patrols, late-night transport/escort service, controlled dormitory access. *Student services:* health clinic, personal/psychological counseling, women's center, legal services.
Athletics Member NCAA. All Division I except football (Division I-A). *Intercollegiate sports:* baseball M(s), basketball M(s)/W(s), cross-country running W, golf M(s)/W(s), gymnastics W(s), soccer M(s)/W(s), softball W(s), swimming and diving M(s)/W(s), tennis M(s)/W(s), volleyball W(s), wrestling M(s). *Intramural sports:* archery M(c)/W(c), badminton M/W, basketball M/W, bowling M(c)/W(c), cross-country running W, football M/W, golf M/W, ice hockey M(c)/W(c), lacrosse M(c)/W(c), racquetball M/W, rugby M(c)/W(c), skiing (downhill) M(c)/W(c), soccer M/W, softball M/W, table tennis M/W, tennis M/W, track and field M(c)/W(c), volleyball M/W, water polo M(c)/W(c), weight lifting M(c)/W(c).
Standardized Tests *Required:* SAT or ACT (for admission).
Costs (2010–11) *One-time required fee:* $500. *Tuition:* state resident $7950 full-time, $295 per credit hour part-time; nonresident $15,900 full-time, $589 per credit hour part-time. Full-time tuition and fees vary according to course load, location, and student level. Part-time tuition and fees vary according to course load, location, and student level. No tuition increase for student's term of enrollment. *Required fees:* $1904 full-time, $79 per credit hour part-time. *Room and board:* $10,366. Room and board charges vary according to board plan and housing facility. *Payment plan:* installment. *Waivers:* minority students, senior citizens, and employees or children of employees.
Financial Aid Of all full-time matriculated undergraduates who enrolled in 2008, 13,616 applied for aid, 11,366 were judged to have need, 1,489 had their need fully met. 7,239 Federal Work-Study jobs (averaging $3489). *Average percent of need met:* 67%. *Average financial aid package:* $11,108. *Average need-based loan:* $4236. *Average need-based gift aid:* $7391. *Average indebtedness upon graduation:* $27,101.
Applying *Options:* electronic application. *Application fee:* $40. *Required:* high school transcript, high school rank. *Application deadlines:* 8/1 (fresh-

men), 8/1 (transfers). *Notification:* continuous (freshmen), continuous (transfers).
Freshman Application Contact Dr. Brandon Lagana, Director of Admissions, Northern Illinois University, Office of Admissions, DeKalb, IL 60115-2857. *Phone:* 815-753-0446. *Toll-free phone:* 800-892-3050. *E-mail:* admission-info@niu.edu. *Web site:* http://www.niu.edu/.

North Park University
Chicago, Illinois

Freshman Application Contact Office of Admissions, North Park University, 3225 West Foster Avenue, Chicago, IL 60625-4895. *Phone:* 773-244-5500. *Toll-free phone:* 800-888-NPC8. *Fax:* 773-583-0858. *E-mail:* afao@northpark.edu. *Web site:* http://www.northpark.edu/.

Northwestern University
Evanston, Illinois

Freshman Application Contact Mr. Christopher Watson, Dean of Undergraduate Admission, Northwestern University, PO Box 3060, Evanston, IL 60204-3060. *Phone:* 847-491-7271. *E-mail:* ug-admission@northwestern.edu. *Web site:* http://www.northwestern.edu/.

Olivet Nazarene University
Bourbonnais, Illinois

Freshman Application Contact Olivet Nazarene University, One University Avenue, Bourbonnais, IL 60914. *Phone:* 815-939-5203. *Toll-free phone:* 800-648-1463. *Web site:* http://www.olivet.edu/.

See page 262 for Display. See page 1490 for the College Close-Up.

Principia College
Elsah, Illinois

- **Independent Christian Science** 4-year, founded 1910
- **Rural** 2600-acre campus with easy access to St. Louis
- **Endowment** $493.7 million
- **Coed** 542 undergraduate students, 99% full-time, 52% women, 48% men
- **Moderately difficult** entrance level, 61% of applicants were admitted

Undergraduates 536 full-time, 6 part-time. Students come from 38 states and territories; 24 other countries; 92% are from out of state; 3% transferred in; 100% live on campus. *Retention:* 78% of full-time freshmen returned.
Freshmen *Admission:* 242 applied, 148 admitted, 139 enrolled. *Average high school GPA:* 3.4. *Test scores:* SAT critical reading scores over 500: 81%; SAT math scores over 500: 73%; ACT scores over 18: 92%; SAT critical reading scores over 600: 51%; SAT math scores over 600: 33%; ACT scores over 24: 62%; SAT critical reading scores over 700: 12%; SAT math scores over 700: 6%; ACT scores over 30: 20%.
Faculty *Total:* 66, 83% full-time, 44% with terminal degrees. *Student/faculty ratio:* 8:1.
Academics *Calendar:* quarters. *Degree:* bachelor's. *Special study options:* accelerated degree program, advanced placement credit, double majors, English as a second language, honors programs, independent study, internships, off-campus study, student-designed majors, study abroad. *Unusual degree programs:* 3-2 engineering with Washington University in St. Louis, Southern Illinois University at Edwardsville, University of Southern California.
Computers on Campus 200 computers/terminals are available on campus for general student use. Students can access the following: online (class) registration. Campuswide network is available.
Student Life *Housing:* on-campus residence required through senior year. *Options:* men-only, women-only. Campus housing is university owned. Freshman campus housing is guaranteed. *Activities and organizations:* drama/theater group, student-run newspaper, radio and television station, choral group, Christian Science Organization, student newspaper, International Students Association, student radio station, student government. *Campus security:* 24-hour patrols. *Student services:* health clinic.
Athletics Member NCAA. All Division III. *Intercollegiate sports:* baseball M, basketball M/W, cross-country running M/W, soccer M/W, softball W, swimming and diving M/W, tennis M/W, track and field M/W, volleyball W. *Intramural sports:* basketball M/W, rugby M(c), soccer M/W, softball M/W.
Standardized Tests *Required:* SAT or ACT (for admission). *Recommended:* SAT Subject Tests (for admission).
Costs (2011–12) *Comprehensive fee:* $35,140 includes full-time tuition ($25,200), mandatory fees ($440), and room and board ($9500). Full-time tuition and fees vary according to course load. *College room only:* $4620. *Payment plan:* installment. *Waivers:* employees or children of employees.
Financial Aid Of all full-time matriculated undergraduates who enrolled in 2009, 361 applied for aid, 350 were judged to have need, 297 had their need

fully met. 142 state and other part-time jobs (averaging $1252). In 2009, 85 non-need-based awards were made. *Average percent of need met:* 85%. *Average financial aid package:* $24,175. *Average need-based loan:* $5342. *Average need-based gift aid:* $20,119. *Average non-need-based aid:* $16,727. *Average indebtedness upon graduation:* $14,963.

Applying *Options:* electronic application, deferred entrance. *Required:* essay or personal statement, high school transcript, minimum 2.3 GPA, 4 letters of recommendation, Christian Science commitment. *Required for some:* interview. *Recommended:* interview. *Application deadlines:* rolling (freshmen), rolling (transfers). *Notification:* continuous (freshmen), continuous (transfers). **Freshman Application Contact** Mr. Brian McCauley, Dean of Enrollment Management, Principia College, One Maybeck Place, Elsah, IL 62028-9799. *Phone:* 618-374-5180. *Toll-free phone:* 800-277-4648 Ext. 2802. *Web site:* http://www.principiacollege.edu.

Quincy University
Quincy, Illinois

- **Independent Roman Catholic** comprehensive, founded 1860
- **Small-town** 70-acre campus
- **Endowment** $12.7 million
- **Coed** 1,269 undergraduate students, 91% full-time, 58% women, 42% men
- **Moderately difficult** entrance level, 91% of applicants were admitted

Undergraduates 1,161 full-time, 108 part-time. Students come from 25 states and territories; 6 other countries; 27% are from out of state; 11% Black or African American, non-Hispanic/Latino; 3% Hispanic/Latino; 0.7% Asian, non-Hispanic/Latino; 0.1% Native Hawaiian or other Pacific Islander, non-Hispanic/Latino; 0.7% American Indian or Alaska Native, non-Hispanic/Latino; 0.8% Two or more races, non-Hispanic/Latino; 16% Race/ethnicity unknown; 0.7% international; 8% transferred in; 54% live on campus. *Retention:* 75% of full-time freshmen returned.

Freshmen *Admission:* 1,030 applied, 937 admitted, 274 enrolled. *Average high school GPA:* 3.24. *Test scores:* SAT critical reading scores over 500: 29%; SAT math scores over 500: 52%; ACT scores over 18: 88%; SAT critical reading scores over 600: 5%; SAT math scores over 600: 19%; ACT scores over 24: 30%; ACT scores over 30: 4%.

Faculty *Total:* 180, 32% full-time, 37% with terminal degrees. *Student/faculty ratio:* 14:1.

Academics *Calendar:* semesters. *Degrees:* associate, bachelor's, and master's. *Special study options:* academic remediation for entering students, accelerated degree program, adult/continuing education programs, advanced placement credit, distance learning, double majors, honors programs, independent study, internships, part-time degree program, student-designed majors, study abroad, summer session for credit. *Unusual degree programs:* 3-2 engineering with Washington University in St. Louis.

Computers on Campus 160 computers/terminals are available on campus for general student use. Students can access the following: campus intranet, computer help desk, free student e-mail accounts, online (class) grades, online (class) registration, online (class) schedules. Campuswide network is available. 100% of college-owned or -operated housing units are wired for high-speed Internet access. Wireless service is available via classrooms, computer centers, computer labs, dorm rooms, learning centers, libraries, student centers.

Student Life *Housing:* on-campus residence required through junior year. *Options:* coed, men-only, women-only, disabled students. Campus housing is university owned. Freshman campus housing is guaranteed. *Activities and organizations:* drama/theater group, student-run newspaper, choral group, marching band, Student Senate, Kappa Kappa Psi, Student Programming Board, Minority Student Association, Students in Free Enterprise (SIFE), national fraternities, national sororities. *Campus security:* 24-hour emergency response devices and patrols, student patrols, late-night transport/escort service, controlled dormitory access, self-defense education, shuttle buses, lighted pathways/sidewalks. *Student services:* health clinic, personal/psychological counseling.

Athletics Member NCAA, NAIA. All NCAA Division II except volleyball (Division I). *Intercollegiate sports:* baseball M(s), basketball M(s)/W(s), cheerleading M(c)/W(c), cross-country running M(s)/W(s), football M(s), golf M(s)/W(s), soccer M(s)/W(s), softball W(s), tennis M(s)/W(s), volleyball M(s)/W(s). *Intramural sports:* basketball M/W, bowling M/W, football M/W, racquetball M/W, soccer M/W, softball M/W, table tennis M/W, volleyball M/W.

Standardized Tests *Required:* SAT or ACT (for admission).

Costs (2011–12) *Comprehensive fee:* $33,560 includes full-time tuition ($23,340), mandatory fees ($800), and room and board ($9420). Part-time tuition: $565 per semester hour. Part-time tuition and fees vary according to

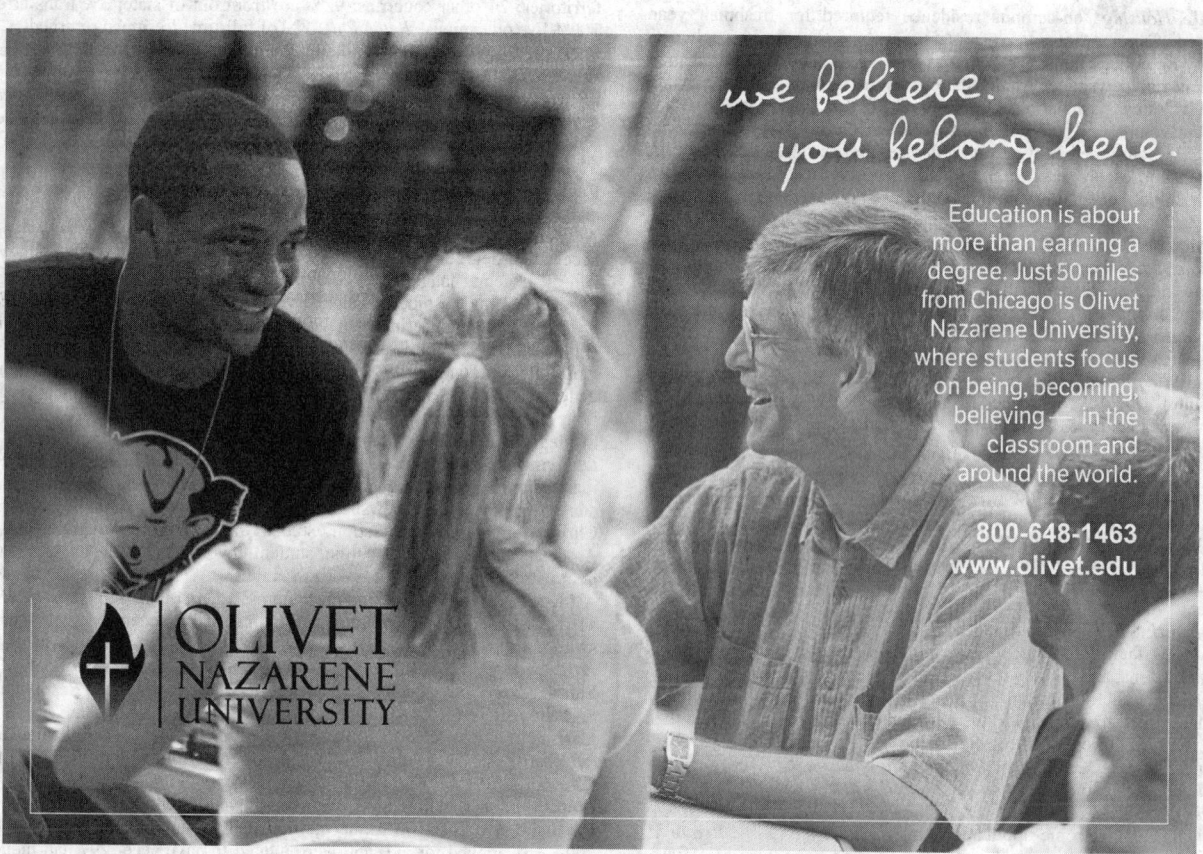

course load. *Required fees:* $15 per semester hour part-time. *College room only:* $5210. Room and board charges vary according to board plan and housing facility. *Payment plan:* installment. *Waivers:* senior citizens and employees or children of employees.

Financial Aid Of all full-time matriculated undergraduates who enrolled in 2009, 1,057 applied for aid, 975 were judged to have need, 219 had their need fully met. 345 Federal Work-Study jobs (averaging $2000). 23 state and other part-time jobs (averaging $3794). In 2009, 45 non-need-based awards were made. *Average percent of need met:* 80%. *Average financial aid package:* $21,853. *Average need-based loan:* $4378. *Average need-based gift aid:* $18,155. *Average non-need-based aid:* $10,477. *Average indebtedness upon graduation:* $23,711.

Applying *Options:* electronic application, deferred entrance. *Application fee:* $25. *Required:* essay or personal statement, high school transcript, minimum 2 GPA. *Required for some:* 1 letter of recommendation, interview, audition required of music majors, portfolio recommended for art majors. *Application deadlines:* rolling (freshmen), rolling (out-of-state freshmen), rolling (transfers). *Notification:* continuous (freshmen), continuous (out-of-state freshmen), continuous (transfers).

Freshman Application Contact Mrs. Syndi Peck, Vice President of Enrollment Management, Quincy University, Admissions Office, 1800 College Avenue, Quincy, IL 62301-2699. *Phone:* 217-228-5210. *Toll-free phone:* 800-688-4295. *E-mail:* admissions@quincy.edu. *Web site:* http://www.quincy.edu/.

Resurrection University
Oak Park, Illinois

- **Independent** upper-level, founded 1982
- **Suburban** 10-acre campus with easy access to Chicago
- **Coed, primarily women** 237 undergraduate students, 85% full-time, 86% women, 14% men
- **Moderately difficult** entrance level, 73% of applicants were admitted

Undergraduates 202 full-time, 35 part-time. Students come from 2 states and territories; 12% Black or African American, non-Hispanic/Latino; 16% Hispanic/Latino; 15% Asian, non-Hispanic/Latino; 2% Native Hawaiian or other Pacific Islander, non-Hispanic/Latino; 11% Two or more races, non-Hispanic/Latino; 2% Race/ethnicity unknown; 40% transferred in.

Freshmen *Admission:* 148 applied, 108 admitted.

Faculty *Total:* 25, 92% full-time, 16% with terminal degrees. *Student/faculty ratio:* 8:1.

Academics *Calendar:* semesters. *Degrees:* bachelor's and master's. *Special study options:* academic remediation for entering students, accelerated degree program, advanced placement credit, independent study, part-time degree program, summer session for credit.

Computers on Campus 27 computers/terminals are available on campus for general student use. Students can access the following: computer help desk, free student e-mail accounts, online (class) grades, online (class) registration, online (class) schedules. Campuswide network is available. Wireless service is available via entire campus.

Student Life *Housing:* college housing not available. *Campus security:* 24-hour emergency response devices and patrols, late-night transport/escort service.

Costs (2011–12) *Tuition:* $711 per credit hour part-time. Full-time tuition and fees vary according to program. Part-time tuition and fees vary according to course load and program. *Required fees:* $135 per term part-time. *Payment plan:* installment. *Waivers:* employees or children of employees.

Financial Aid Of all full-time matriculated undergraduates who enrolled in 2009, 198 applied for aid, 198 were judged to have need, 76 had their need fully met. 9 Federal Work-Study jobs (averaging $4800). *Average percent of need met:* 84%. *Average financial aid package:* $15,550. *Average need-based loan:* $5500. *Average need-based gift aid:* $3000.

Applying *Options:* electronic application, deferred entrance. *Application fee:* $30. *Application deadline:* 4/1 (transfers). *Notification:* 5/15 (transfers).

Application Contact Resurrection University, 3 Erie Court, Oak Park, IL 60302. *Phone:* 708-763-6530. *Web site:* http://www.resu.edu/.

Robert Morris University Illinois
Chicago, Illinois

- **Independent** comprehensive, founded 1913
- **Urban** campus with easy access to Chicago
- **Endowment** $44.2 million
- **Coed** 4,071 undergraduate students, 95% full-time, 58% women, 42% men
- **Minimally difficult** entrance level, 80% of applicants were admitted

Undergraduates 3,859 full-time, 212 part-time. Students come from 24 states and territories; 17 other countries; 6% are from out of state; 33% Black or African American, non-Hispanic/Latino; 24% Hispanic/Latino; 2% Asian, non-

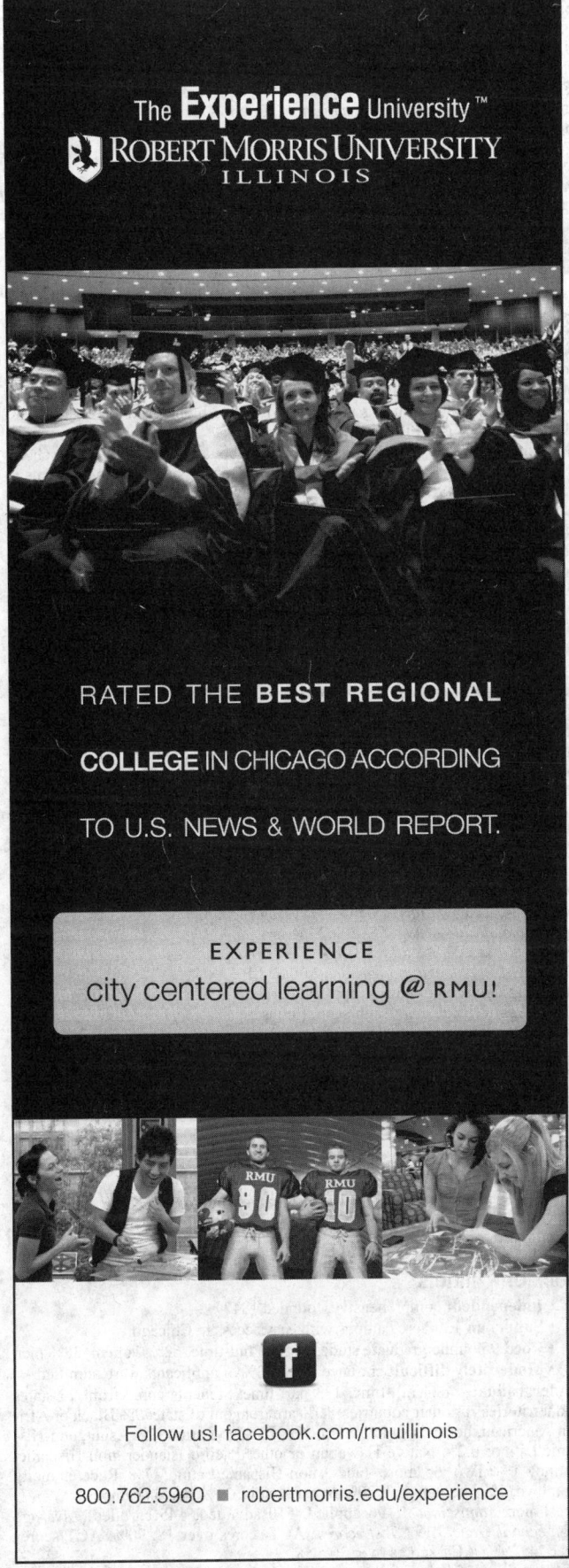

Hispanic/Latino; 0.4% Native Hawaiian or other Pacific Islander, non-Hispanic/Latino; 0.2% American Indian or Alaska Native, non-Hispanic/Latino; 0.8% Two or more races, non-Hispanic/Latino; 2% Race/ethnicity unknown; 0.7% international; 17% transferred in; 6% live on campus. *Retention:* 51% of full-time freshmen returned.

Freshmen *Admission:* 3,107 applied, 2,490 admitted, 938 enrolled. *Average high school GPA:* 2.62. *Test scores:* ACT scores over 18: 52%; ACT scores over 24: 9%.

Faculty *Total:* 317, 42% full-time, 23% with terminal degrees. *Student/faculty ratio:* 21:1.

Academics *Calendar:* 5 ten-week academic sessions per year. *Degrees:* diplomas, associate, bachelor's, and master's. *Special study options:* accelerated degree program, adult/continuing education programs, advanced placement credit, distance learning, honors programs, independent study, internships, part-time degree program, services for LD students, study abroad, summer session for credit. *ROTC:* Army (c).

Computers on Campus 1,830 computers/terminals are available on campus for general student use. Students can access the following: campus intranet, computer help desk, free student e-mail accounts, online (class) grades, online (class) schedules, online credentials, online payments, online student accounts, online degree audit. Campuswide network is available. 100% of college-owned or -operated housing units are wired for high-speed Internet access. Wireless service is available via entire campus.

Student Life *Housing options:* coed. Campus housing is leased by the school. *Activities and organizations:* student-run newspaper, choral group, Students in Free Enterprise (SIFE), Cooks for a Cause, Student Chapter of Society for Human Resource Management, Morris Men, Volunteer Club. *Campus security:* 24-hour emergency response devices, Surveillance camera system at each campus, viewable via the internet. *Student services:* personal/psychological counseling.

Athletics Member NAIA and USCAA. *Intercollegiate sports:* baseball M(s), basketball M(s)/W(s), bowling M(s)/W(s), cheerleading M(s)(c)/W(s)(c), crew W(s)(c), cross-country running M(s)/W(s), golf M(s)/W(s), ice hockey M/W, lacrosse W(s), sailing M(s)(c)/W(s)(c), soccer M(s)/W(s), softball W(s), swimming and diving W(s), tennis W(s), track and field W(s), volleyball M(s)/W(s).

Standardized Tests *Required for some:* SAT or ACT (for admission).

Costs (2011–12) *Comprehensive fee:* $31,926 includes full-time tuition ($21,600) and room and board ($10,326). Full-time tuition and fees vary according to location. Part-time tuition: $600 per credit hour. Part-time tuition and fees vary according to course load and location. *College room only:* $8100. Room and board charges vary according to housing facility and location. *Payment plans:* tuition prepayment, installment. *Waivers:* employees or children of employees.

Financial Aid Of all full-time matriculated undergraduates who enrolled in 2008, 5,485 applied for aid, 5,314 were judged to have need, 158 had their need fully met. 326 Federal Work-Study jobs (averaging $2056). In 2008, 119 non-need-based awards were made. *Average percent of need met:* 48%. *Average financial aid package:* $12,862. *Average need-based loan:* $4767. *Average need-based gift aid:* $10,127. *Average non-need-based aid:* $5320. *Average indebtedness upon graduation:* $28,103.

Applying *Options:* electronic application, deferred entrance. *Application fee:* $50. *Required for some:* high school transcript. *Recommended:* minimum 2 GPA, interview. *Application deadlines:* rolling (freshmen), rolling (out-of-state freshmen), rolling (transfers). *Notification:* continuous (freshmen), continuous (out-of-state freshmen), continuous (transfers).

Freshman Application Contact Ms. Connie Esparza, Vice President for Marketing, Robert Morris University Illinois, 401 South State Street, Chicago, IL 60605. *Phone:* 312-935-4141. *Toll-free phone:* 800-RMC-5960. *Fax:* 312-935-4440. *E-mail:* enroll@robertmorris.edu. *Web site:* http://www.robertmorris.edu/.

See page 1536 for the College Close-Up.

Rockford College
Rockford, Illinois

- **Independent** comprehensive, founded 1847
- **Suburban** 130-acre campus with easy access to Chicago
- **Coed** 957 undergraduate students, 86% full-time, 62% women, 38% men
- **Moderately difficult** entrance level, 43% of applicants were admitted

Undergraduates 824 full-time, 133 part-time. Students come from 25 states and territories; 11 other countries; 10% are from out of state; 9% Black or African American, non-Hispanic/Latino; 7% Hispanic/Latino; 2% Asian, non-Hispanic/Latino; 0.2% Native Hawaiian or other Pacific Islander, non-Hispanic/Latino; 1% Two or more races, non-Hispanic/Latino; 7% Race/ethnicity unknown; 1% international; 20% transferred in; 31% live on campus.

Freshmen *Admission:* 1,196 applied, 510 admitted, 145 enrolled. *Average high school GPA:* 3.19. *Test scores:* ACT scores over 18: 90%; ACT scores over 24: 29%; ACT scores over 30: 3%.

Faculty *Total:* 156, 46% full-time, 36% with terminal degrees. *Student/faculty ratio:* 11:1.

Academics *Calendar:* semesters. *Degrees:* bachelor's and master's. *Special study options:* academic remediation for entering students, accelerated degree program, adult/continuing education programs, advanced placement credit, double majors, English as a second language, honors programs, independent study, internships, off-campus study, part-time degree program, services for LD students, study abroad, summer session for credit. *ROTC:* Army (c).

Computers on Campus 75 computers/terminals are available on campus for general student use. Students can access the following: campus intranet, computer help desk, free student e-mail accounts, online (class) grades, online (class) registration, online (class) schedules, online bill payment. Campuswide network is available. 100% of college-owned or -operated housing units are wired for high-speed Internet access. Wireless service is available via entire campus.

Student Life *Housing options:* coed, disabled students. Campus housing is university owned. *Activities and organizations:* drama/theater group, choral group, student government, multicultural club, RAGE (Regent Athletics Getting Excited), Psychology Society, Nursing Student Organization. *Campus security:* 24-hour emergency response devices and patrols, late-night transport/escort service, controlled dormitory access. *Student services:* health clinic, personal/psychological counseling.

Athletics Member NCAA. All Division III. *Intercollegiate sports:* baseball M, basketball M/W, football M, golf M/W, soccer M/W, softball W, tennis M/W, volleyball M(c)/W. *Intramural sports:* basketball M/W, bowling M/W, cheerleading M(c)/W(c), football M/W, table tennis M/W, tennis M/W, volleyball M/W.

Standardized Tests *Required:* SAT or ACT (for admission).

Costs (2010–11) *Comprehensive fee:* $31,700 includes full-time tuition ($24,750) and room and board ($6950). Full-time tuition and fees vary according to course load. Part-time tuition: $675 per credit hour. Part-time tuition and fees vary according to course load. *Required fees:* $40 per term part-time. *College room only:* $3950. Room and board charges vary according to board plan and housing facility. *Payment plan:* installment. *Waivers:* employees or children of employees.

Financial Aid Of all full-time matriculated undergraduates who enrolled in 2009, 846 applied for aid, 799 were judged to have need, 88 had their need fully met. In 2009, 68 non-need-based awards were made. *Average percent of need met:* 68%. *Average financial aid package:* $17,513. *Average need-based loan:* $4755. *Average need-based gift aid:* $12,447. *Average non-need-based aid:* $8810. *Average indebtedness upon graduation:* $28,343.

Applying *Options:* electronic application, early admission, deferred entrance. *Required:* high school transcript. *Required for some:* essay or personal statement, minimum 2.65 GPA, 2 letters of recommendation. *Recommended:* minimum 2.65 GPA, interview, campus visit. *Application deadlines:* 8/15 (freshmen), 8/15 (out-of-state freshmen), 8/15 (transfers). *Notification:* continuous (freshmen), continuous (out-of-state freshmen), continuous (transfers).

Freshman Application Contact Rebecca Miziniak, Assistant Director of Admission, Rockford College, 5050 East State Street, Rockford, IL 61108-2393. *Phone:* 815-226-4050. *Toll-free phone:* 800-892-2984. *Fax:* 815-226-2822. *E-mail:* rcadmissions@rockford.edu. *Web site:* http://www.rockford.edu/.

Roosevelt University
Chicago, Illinois

- **Independent** comprehensive, founded 1945
- **Urban** campus with easy access to Chicago
- **Endowment** $69.0 million
- **Coed** 3,919 undergraduate students, 71% full-time, 66% women, 34% men
- **Moderately difficult** entrance level, 54% of applicants were admitted

Undergraduates 2,796 full-time, 1,123 part-time. Students come from 42 states and territories; 41 other countries; 13% are from out of state; 21% Black or African American, non-Hispanic/Latino; 15% Hispanic/Latino; 5% Asian, non-Hispanic/Latino; 0.1% Native Hawaiian or other Pacific Islander, non-Hispanic/Latino; 0.2% American Indian or Alaska Native, non-Hispanic/Latino; 4% Two or more races, non-Hispanic/Latino; 4% Race/ethnicity unknown; 3% international; 18% transferred in; 22% live on campus. *Retention:* 56% of full-time freshmen returned.

Freshmen *Admission:* 3,994 applied, 2,173 admitted, 502 enrolled. *Average high school GPA:* 3.14. *Test scores:* SAT critical reading scores over 500: 100%; SAT math scores over 500: 57%; SAT writing scores over 500: 61%; ACT scores over 18: 99%; SAT critical reading scores over 600: 33%; SAT math scores over 600: 21%; SAT writing scores over 600: 22%; ACT scores over 24: 34%; SAT math scores over 700: 1%; SAT writing scores over 700: 3%; ACT scores over 30: 3%.

Faculty *Total:* 727, 33% full-time.

Academics *Calendar:* semesters. *Degrees:* bachelor's, master's, doctoral-professional, doctoral-research/scholarship, and post-master's certificates. *Special study options:* academic remediation for entering students, accelerated degree program, adult/continuing education programs, advanced placement credit, distance learning, double majors, English as a second language, honors programs, independent study, internships, off-campus study, part-time degree program, services for LD students, student-designed majors, study abroad, summer session for credit.

Computers on Campus 345 computers/terminals are available on campus for general student use. Students can access the following: computer help desk, free student e-mail accounts, online (class) grades, online (class) registration, online (class) schedules. Campuswide network is available. 50% of college-owned or -operated housing units are wired for high-speed Internet access. Wireless service is available via classrooms, computer centers, computer labs, dorm rooms, libraries, student centers.

Student Life *Housing:* on-campus residence required through sophomore year. *Options:* coed. Campus housing is university owned, leased by the school and is provided by a third party. Freshman campus housing is guaranteed. *Activities and organizations:* student-run newspaper, radio station, International Student Union, RU Proud, Association of Latin Americans (ALAS), student government, Residence Hall Council, national fraternities, national sororities. *Campus security:* 24-hour emergency response devices and patrols, late-night transport/escort service, controlled dormitory access. *Student services:* personal/psychological counseling.

Athletics Member NAIA. *Intercollegiate sports:* baseball M, basketball M/W, cross-country running M/W, golf M, soccer M/W, softball W, tennis M/W, volleyball W.

Standardized Tests *Required:* SAT or ACT (for admission).

Costs (2011–12) *Tuition:* $25,000 full-time, $689 per hour part-time. Full-time tuition and fees vary according to course load and program. Part-time tuition and fees vary according to course load and program. *Room only:* Room and board charges vary according to board plan and housing facility. *Payment plans:* installment, deferred payment. *Waivers:* senior citizens and employees or children of employees.

Financial Aid Of all full-time matriculated undergraduates who enrolled in 2004, 1,471 applied for aid, 1,275 were judged to have need, 196 had their need fully met. In 2004, 119 non-need-based awards were made. *Average percent of need met:* 75%. *Average financial aid package:* $13,173. *Average need-based gift aid:* $5579. *Average non-need-based aid:* $5115.

Applying *Options:* electronic application, deferred entrance. *Application fee:* $25. *Required:* high school transcript, minimum 2.5 GPA, audition for music and theater programs. *Required for some:* essay or personal statement, interview. *Recommended:* essay or personal statement. *Application deadlines:* 8/1 (freshmen), rolling (transfers). *Notification:* continuous (freshmen), continuous (transfers).

Freshman Application Contact Ms. Beth Gierach, Assistant Vice President for Admission, Roosevelt University, 430 South Michigan Avenue, Chicago, IL 60605. *Phone:* 312-341-6733. *Toll-free phone:* 877-APPLYRU. *Fax:* 312-341-3523. *E-mail:* bgierach@roosevelt.edu. *Web site:* http://www.roosevelt.edu/.

Rush University
Chicago, Illinois

Application Contact Rush University, 600 South Paulina, Chicago, IL 60612-3832. *Phone:* 312-942-7100. *Web site:* http://www.rushu.rush.edu/.

Saint Anthony College of Nursing
Rockford, Illinois

Application Contact Ms. Nancy Sanders, Assistant Dean for Admissions and Student Affairs, Saint Anthony College of Nursing, 5658 East State Street, Rockford, IL 61108-2468. *Phone:* 815-395-5100. *Fax:* 815-395-2275. *E-mail:* info@sacn.edu. *Web site:* http://www.sacn.edu/.

St. Augustine College
Chicago, Illinois

- **Independent** 4-year, founded 1980
- **Urban** 4-acre campus
- **Endowment** $501,935
- **Coed**
- **Noncompetitive** entrance level

Faculty *Student/faculty ratio:* 20:1.

Academics *Calendar:* semesters. *Degrees:* certificates, associate, and bachelor's (offers bilingual Spanish/English degree programs).

Student Life *Campus security:* 24-hour patrols, late-night transport/escort service.

Costs (2010–11) *Tuition:* $8400 full-time, $350 per credit hour part-time.

Financial Aid *Of all full-time matriculated undergraduates who enrolled in 2003,* 2,025 applied for aid, 1,699 were judged to have need. 57 Federal Work-Study jobs (averaging $3080). *In 2003,* 83 non-need-based awards were made.

Average percent of need met: 75. *Average need-based gift aid:* $5762. *Average non-need-based aid:* $2233.

Freshman Application Contact Ms. Gloria Quiroz, Director of Admissions, St. Augustine College, 1333-1345 West Argyle, Chicago, IL 60640-3501. *Phone:* 773-878-3256. *Fax:* 773-878-0937. *E-mail:* info@staugustine.edu. *Web site:* http://www.staugustine.edu/.

Saint Francis Medical Center College of Nursing
Peoria, Illinois

- **Independent Roman Catholic** upper-level, founded 1986
- **Urban** campus
- **Coed, primarily women** 339 undergraduate students, 79% full-time, 90% women, 10% men
- 61% of applicants were admitted

Undergraduates 268 full-time, 71 part-time. Students come from 2 states and territories; 4 other countries; 1% are from out of state; 8% Black or African American, non-Hispanic/Latino; 2% Hispanic/Latino; 3% Asian, non-Hispanic/Latino; 0.6% American Indian or Alaska Native, non-Hispanic/Latino; 27% transferred in; 3% live on campus.

Freshmen *Admission:* 180 applied, 110 admitted.

Faculty *Total:* 47, 60% full-time, 26% with terminal degrees. *Student/faculty ratio:* 9:1.

Academics *Calendar:* semesters. *Degrees:* bachelor's, master's, doctoral-professional, and post-master's certificates. *Special study options:* advanced placement credit, distance learning, independent study, summer session for credit.

Computers on Campus 49 computers/terminals and 53 ports are available on campus for general student use. Students can access the following: campus intranet, computer help desk, free student e-mail accounts, online (class) grades, online (class) registration, online (class) schedules. Campuswide network is available. 100% of college-owned or -operated housing units are wired for high-speed Internet access. Wireless service is available via entire campus.

Student Life *Housing options:* coed. Campus housing is university owned. *Activities and organizations:* Student Senate, SNAI, Minority Student Association. *Campus security:* 24-hour emergency response devices, controlled dormitory access. *Student services:* health clinic, personal/psychological counseling.

Costs (2010–11) *Tuition:* $14,400 full-time, $480 per semester hour part-time. Full-time tuition and fees vary according to course load. Part-time tuition and fees vary according to course load. *Required fees:* $556 full-time, $130 per term part-time. *Room only:* $2400. *Payment plan:* installment. *Waivers:* employees or children of employees.

Financial Aid Of all full-time matriculated undergraduates who enrolled in 2009, 241 applied for aid, 200 were judged to have need, 16 had their need fully met. In 2009, 18 non-need-based awards were made. *Average percent of need met:* 73%. *Average financial aid package:* $13,483. *Average need-based loan:* $5156. *Average need-based gift aid:* $6870. *Average non-need-based aid:* $2877.

Applying *Options:* deferred entrance. *Application fee:* $50.

Application Contact Saint Francis Medical Center College of Nursing, 511 Northeast Greenleaf Street, Peoria, IL 61603-3783. *Phone:* 309-624-8980. *Web site:* http://www.sfmccon.edu/.

St. John's College
Springfield, Illinois

Application Contact St. John's College, 729 East Carpenter Street, Springfield, IL 62702. *Phone:* 217-525-5628. *Web site:* http://www.stjohnscollegespringfield.edu/.

Saint Xavier University
Chicago, Illinois

- **Independent Roman Catholic** comprehensive, founded 1847
- **Urban** 70-acre campus
- **Endowment** $10.0 million
- **Coed** 2,968 undergraduate students, 84% full-time, 69% women, 31% men
- **Moderately difficult** entrance level

Undergraduates 2,483 full-time, 485 part-time. 5% are from out of state; 17% Black or African American, non-Hispanic/Latino; 16% Hispanic/Latino; 3% Asian, non-Hispanic/Latino; 0.1% Native Hawaiian or other Pacific Islander, non-Hispanic/Latino; 0.5% American Indian or Alaska Native, non-Hispanic/Latino; 1% Two or more races, non-Hispanic/Latino; 6% Race/ethnicity unknown; 0.1% international; 13% transferred in; 29% live on campus. *Retention:* 71% of full-time freshmen returned.

Freshmen *Admission:* 8,039 applied, 491 enrolled. *Average high school GPA:* 3.4. *Test scores:* SAT critical reading scores over 500: 62%; SAT math scores over 500: 54%; SAT writing scores over 500: 61%; ACT scores over 18: 95%; SAT critical reading scores over 600: 31%; SAT math scores over 600: 23%; SAT writing scores over 600: 15%; ACT scores over 24: 36%; ACT scores over 30: 4%.

Faculty *Total:* 426, 42% full-time, 47% with terminal degrees. *Student/faculty ratio:* 14:1.

Academics *Calendar:* semesters. *Degrees:* certificates, bachelor's, master's, post-master's, and postbachelor's certificates. *Special study options:* academic remediation for entering students, accelerated degree program, adult/continuing education programs, advanced placement credit, cooperative education, double majors, English as a second language, honors programs, independent study, internships, part-time degree program, services for LD students, student-designed majors, study abroad, summer session for credit. *ROTC:* Air Force (c).

Computers on Campus 500 computers/terminals are available on campus for general student use. Students can access the following: campus intranet, computer help desk, free student e-mail accounts, online (class) grades, online (class) registration, online (class) schedules. Campuswide network is available. 100% of college-owned or -operated housing units are wired for high-speed Internet access. Wireless service is available via classrooms, computer centers, computer labs, dorm rooms, learning centers, libraries, student centers.

Student Life *Housing options:* coed. Campus housing is university owned. *Activities and organizations:* drama/theater group, student-run newspaper, radio station, choral group, marching band, Student Activities Board, Black Student Union, UNIDOS (Hispanic Organization), Student Nurses Association, Business Students Association. *Campus security:* 24-hour emergency response devices and patrols, late-night transport/escort service. *Student services:* health clinic, personal/psychological counseling, women's center.

Athletics Member NAIA. *Intercollegiate sports:* baseball M(s), basketball M(s), cross-country running W(s), football M(s), golf M(s), soccer M(s)/W(s), softball W(s), volleyball W(s). *Intramural sports:* basketball M, bowling M/W, volleyball M/W, weight lifting M.

Standardized Tests *Required:* SAT or ACT (for admission).

Costs (2010–11) *Comprehensive fee:* $34,212 includes full-time tuition ($24,790), mandatory fees ($730), and room and board ($8692). Part-time tuition: $830 per credit hour. *College room only:* $5142. Room and board charges vary according to board plan and housing facility. *Payment plan:* installment. *Waivers:* senior citizens and employees or children of employees.

Financial Aid Of all full-time matriculated undergraduates who enrolled in 2009, 2,167 applied for aid, 2,167 were judged to have need, 354 had their need fully met. 1,605 Federal Work-Study jobs (averaging $2644). 31 state and other part-time jobs (averaging $8237). In 2009, 275 non-need-based awards were made. *Average percent of need met:* 80%. *Average financial aid package:* $20,926. *Average need-based loan:* $4612. *Average need-based gift aid:* $15,152. *Average non-need-based aid:* $7946. *Average indebtedness upon graduation:* $29,326.

Applying *Options:* electronic application, deferred entrance. *Application fee:* $25. *Required:* high school transcript. *Required for some:* interview. *Recommended:* essay or personal statement, minimum 2.5 GPA, interview. *Application deadlines:* rolling (freshmen), rolling (transfers). *Notification:* continuous (freshmen), continuous (transfers).

Freshman Application Contact Dr. Kathleen Carlson, Vice President, Saint Xavier University, 3700 West 103rd Street, Chicago, IL 60655-3105. *Phone:* 773-298-3305. *Toll-free phone:* 800-462-9288. *E-mail:* carlson@sxu.edu. *Web site:* http://www.sxu.edu/.

School of the Art Institute of Chicago
Chicago, Illinois

- **Independent** comprehensive, founded 1866
- **Urban** 1-acre campus with easy access to Chicago
- **Endowment** $186.3 million
- **Coed**
- **Very difficult** entrance level

Faculty *Student/faculty ratio:* 8:1.

Academics *Calendar:* semesters. *Degrees:* certificates, bachelor's, master's, and postbachelor's certificates.

Student Life *Campus security:* 24-hour emergency response devices and patrols, late-night transport/escort service, controlled dormitory access.

Standardized Tests *Required:* SAT or ACT (for admission).

Costs (2010–11) *Tuition:* $35,550 full-time, $1185 per semester hour part-time. *Required fees:* $400 full-time. *Room only:* $9800.

Financial Aid *Of all full-time matriculated undergraduates who enrolled in 2008,* 1,334 applied for aid, 1,215 were judged to have need, 53 had their need fully met. *In 2008,* 602 non-need-based awards were made. *Average percent of need met:* 83. *Average financial aid package:* $27,348. *Average need-based loan:* $4692. *Average need-based gift aid:* $13,170. *Average non-need-based aid:* $5248. *Average indebtedness upon graduation:* $34,578.

Applying *Options:* electronic application, early action, deferred entrance. *Application fee:* $65. *Required:* essay or personal statement, high school transcript, 1 letter of recommendation, portfolio. *Recommended:* interview.

Freshman Application Contact Mr. Scott Ramon, Director, Undergraduate Admissions, School of the Art Institute of Chicago, 36 South Wabash, Chicago, IL 60603. *Phone:* 312-629-6100. *Toll-free phone:* 800-232-SAIC. *Fax:* 312-629-6101. *E-mail:* ugadmiss@saic.edu. *Web site:* http://www.saic.edu/.

See page 1592 for the College Close-Up.

Shimer College

Chicago, Illinois

- **Independent** 4-year, founded 1853
- **Urban** 3-acre campus with easy access to Chicago and Milwaukee
- **Coed** 112 undergraduate students, 82% full-time, 50% women, 50% men
- **Moderately difficult** entrance level, 36% of applicants were admitted

Undergraduates 92 full-time, 20 part-time. 54% are from out of state; 2% Black or African American, non-Hispanic/Latino; 5% Hispanic/Latino; 5% Asian, non-Hispanic/Latino; 0.9% American Indian or Alaska Native, non-Hispanic/Latino; 6% Two or more races, non-Hispanic/Latino; 4% Race/ethnicity unknown; 0.9% international; 15% transferred in. *Retention:* 70% of full-time freshmen returned.

Freshmen *Admission:* 200 applied, 72 admitted, 20 enrolled. *Average high school GPA:* 3.59. *Test scores:* SAT critical reading scores over 500: 100%; SAT math scores over 500: 86%; SAT writing scores over 500: 100%; ACT scores over 18: 100%; SAT critical reading scores over 600: 100%; SAT math scores over 600: 58%; SAT writing scores over 600: 100%; ACT scores over 24: 79%; SAT critical reading scores over 700: 43%; SAT math scores over 700: 29%; SAT writing scores over 700: 17%; ACT scores over 30: 14%.

Faculty *Total:* 14, 50% full-time, 71% with terminal degrees. *Student/faculty ratio:* 8:1.

Academics *Calendar:* semesters. *Degree:* bachelor's. *Special study options:* adult/continuing education programs, cooperative education, double majors, independent study, internships, off-campus study, part-time degree program, student-designed majors, study abroad, summer session for credit.

Computers on Campus Students can access the following: campus intranet, computer help desk, free student e-mail accounts, online (class) schedules. Campuswide network is available. 100% of college-owned or -operated housing units are wired for high-speed Internet access. Wireless service is available via entire campus.

Student Life *Housing options:* coed. Campus housing is university owned and leased by the school. Freshman campus housing is guaranteed. *Activities and organizations:* drama/theater group, student-run newspaper, radio station, choral group. *Campus security:* 24-hour emergency response devices, late-night transport/escort service. *Student services:* personal/psychological counseling.

Athletics *Intramural sports:* baseball M, basketball M/W, cross-country running M/W, soccer M/W, softball W, track and field M/W, volleyball M/W.

Costs (2010–11) *Comprehensive fee:* $40,660 includes full-time tuition ($26,510), mandatory fees ($1300), and room and board ($12,850). Full-time tuition and fees vary according to class time, course load, and program. Part-time tuition: $970 per credit hour. Part-time tuition and fees vary according to class time, course load, and program. *Required fees:* $400 per term part-time. *College room only:* $7526. Room and board charges vary according to housing facility. *Payment plan:* installment. *Waivers:* adult students, senior citizens, and employees or children of employees.

Financial Aid Of all full-time matriculated undergraduates who enrolled in 2008, 74 applied for aid, 65 were judged to have need. 25 Federal Work-Study jobs (averaging $1750). 5 state and other part-time jobs (averaging $1750). In 2008, 7 non-need-based awards were made. *Average financial aid package:* $11,993. *Average need-based loan:* $5159. *Average need-based gift aid:* $7971. *Average non-need-based aid:* $4000.

Applying *Options:* electronic application. *Application fee:* $25. *Required:* essay or personal statement, high school transcript, 1 letter of recommendation, interview. *Application deadlines:* 8/1 (freshmen), rolling (transfers). *Notification:* continuous (freshmen), continuous (transfers).

Freshman Application Contact Ms. Amy Pritts, Director of Admission, Shimer College, 3424 South State Street, Chicago, IL 60616. *Phone:* 312-235-3504. *Toll-free phone:* 800-215-7173. *Fax:* 888-808-3133. *E-mail:* admission@shimer.edu. *Web site:* http://www.shimer.edu/.

Southern Illinois University Carbondale

Carbondale, Illinois

- **State-supported** university, founded 1869, part of Southern Illinois University
- **Rural** 1136-acre campus with easy access to St. Louis
- **Endowment** $77.9 million
- **Coed** 15,551 undergraduate students, 88% full-time, 44% women, 56% men
- **Moderately difficult** entrance level, 69% of applicants were admitted

Undergraduates 13,619 full-time, 1,932 part-time. Students come from 50 states and territories; 92 other countries; 14% are from out of state; 14% transferred in; 25% live on campus. *Retention:* 67% of full-time freshmen returned.

Freshmen *Admission:* 11,509 applied, 7,900 admitted, 2,450 enrolled. *Test scores:* SAT math scores over 500: 40%; ACT scores over 18: 85%; SAT math scores over 600: 17%; ACT scores over 24: 30%; SAT math scores over 700: 3%; ACT scores over 30: 4%.

Faculty *Total:* 1,094, 88% full-time, 79% with terminal degrees. *Student/faculty ratio:* 16:1.

Academics *Calendar:* semesters plus 8-week summer session. *Degrees:* associate, bachelor's, master's, doctoral-professional, doctoral-research/scholarship, and postbachelor's certificates. *Special study options:* academic remediation for entering students, adult/continuing education programs, advanced placement credit, cooperative education, distance learning, double majors, English as a second language, honors programs, independent study, internships, off-campus study, part-time degree program, services for LD students, student-designed majors, study abroad, summer session for credit. *ROTC:* Army (b), Air Force (b).

Computers on Campus 1,820 computers/terminals are available on campus for general student use. Students can access the following: campus intranet, computer help desk, free student e-mail accounts, online (class) grades, online (class) registration, online (class) schedules. Campuswide network is available. 80% of college-owned or -operated housing units are wired for high-speed Internet access. Wireless service is available via classrooms, computer centers, computer labs, learning centers, libraries, student centers.

Student Life *Housing:* on-campus residence required for freshman year. *Options:* coed, men-only, women-only, disabled students. Campus housing is university owned. Freshman campus housing is guaranteed. *Activities and organizations:* drama/theater group, student-run newspaper, radio and television station, choral group, marching band, Inter-Greek Council, Black Affairs Council, International Student Council, Undergraduate Student government, Graduate and Professional Student Council, national fraternities, national sororities. *Campus security:* 24-hour emergency response devices and patrols, student patrols, late-night transport/escort service, controlled dormitory access, well-lit pathways, night safety vans, student transit system. *Student services:* health clinic, personal/psychological counseling, women's center, legal services.

Athletics Member NCAA. All Division I except football (Division I-AA). *Intercollegiate sports:* baseball M(s), basketball M(s)/W(s), cheerleading M/W, cross-country running M(s)/W(s), golf M(s)/W(s), racquetball M/W, softball W(s), swimming and diving M(s)/W(s), tennis M(s)/W(s), track and field M(s)/W(s), volleyball W(s). *Intramural sports:* archery M(c)/W(c), badminton M(c)/W(c), baseball M(c), basketball M/W, bowling M(c)/W(c), cross-country running M/W, equestrian sports M(c)/W(c), fencing M(c)/W(c), football M/W, golf M/W, gymnastics M(c)/W(c), lacrosse M(c)/W(c), racquetball M(c)/W(c), riflery M(c)/W(c), rock climbing M(c)/W(c), rugby M(c)/W(c), sailing M(c)/W(c), skiing (downhill) M(c)/W(c), soccer M(c)/W(c), softball M/W, swimming and diving M/W, table tennis M(c)/W(c), tennis M(c)/W(c), ultimate Frisbee M(c)/W(c), volleyball M(c)/W(c), water polo M(c)/W(c), weight lifting M(c)/W(c), wrestling M(c).

Standardized Tests *Required:* SAT or ACT (for admission).

Costs (2010–11) *Tuition:* state resident $7290 full-time, $243 per credit hour part-time; nonresident $18,225 full-time, $608 per credit hour part-time. Full-time tuition and fees vary according to course load. Part-time tuition and fees vary according to course load. No tuition increase for student's term of enrollment. *Required fees:* $3178 full-time, $293 per credit hour part-time. *Room and board:* $8292. Room and board charges vary according to board plan and housing facility. *Payment plan:* installment. *Waivers:* children of alumni, senior citizens, and employees or children of employees.

Financial Aid Of all full-time matriculated undergraduates who enrolled in 2008, 10,510 applied for aid, 8,884 were judged to have need, 7,441 had their need fully met. In 2008, 1278 non-need-based awards were made. *Average percent of need met:* 95%. *Average financial aid package:* $11,809. *Average need-based loan:* $4121. *Average need-based gift aid:* $6934. *Average non-need-based aid:* $6359. *Average indebtedness upon graduation:* $21,359.

Applying *Options:* electronic application, deferred entrance. *Application fee:* $30. *Required:* high school transcript. *Application deadlines:* rolling (freshmen), 7/1 (transfers). *Notification:* continuous (freshmen).

Freshman Application Contact Katharine Suski, Interim Director, Southern Illinois University Carbondale, Undergraduate Admissions, 425 Clocktower Drive, Carbondale, IL 62901. *Phone:* 618-536-4405. *Fax:* 618-453-4609. *E-mail:* joinsiuc@siu.edu. *Web site:* http://www.siuc.edu/.

Southern Illinois University Edwardsville

Edwardsville, Illinois

- **State-supported** comprehensive, founded 1957, part of Southern Illinois University
- **Suburban** 2660-acre campus with easy access to St. Louis
- **Endowment** $13.5 million
- **Coed** 11,305 undergraduate students, 85% full-time, 53% women, 47% men
- **Moderately difficult** entrance level, 82% of applicants were admitted

Undergraduates 9,620 full-time, 1,685 part-time. Students come from 47 states and territories; 53 other countries; 8% are from out of state; 12% Black or African American, non-Hispanic/Latino; 3% Hispanic/Latino; 2% Asian, non-Hispanic/Latino; 0.2% Native Hawaiian or other Pacific Islander, non-Hispanic/Latino; 0.4% American Indian or Alaska Native, non-Hispanic/Latino; 2% Two or more races, non-Hispanic/Latino; 3% Race/ethnicity unknown; 0.7% international; 11% transferred in; 30% live on campus. *Retention:* 72% of full-time freshmen returned.

Freshmen *Admission:* 7,354 applied, 6,052 admitted, 2,065 enrolled. *Test scores:* ACT scores over 18: 92%; ACT scores over 24: 37%; ACT scores over 30: 5%.

Faculty *Total:* 876, 72% full-time. *Student/faculty ratio:* 19:1.

Academics *Calendar:* semesters. *Degrees:* bachelor's, master's, doctoral-other, doctoral-professional, doctoral-research/scholarship, post-master's, and postbachelor's certificates. *Special study options:* academic remediation for entering students, accelerated degree program, advanced placement credit, cooperative education, distance learning, double majors, English as a second language, honors programs, independent study, internships, off-campus study, part-time degree program, services for LD students, student-designed majors, study abroad, summer session for credit. *ROTC:* Army (b), Air Force (b). *Unusual degree programs:* 3-2 engineering.

Computers on Campus 600 computers/terminals are available on campus for general student use. Students can access the following: campus intranet, computer help desk, free student e-mail accounts, online (class) grades, online (class) registration, online (class) schedules, online job finder. Campuswide network is available. 100% of college-owned or -operated housing units are wired for high-speed Internet access. Wireless service is available via entire campus.

Student Life *Housing options:* coed, disabled students. Campus housing is university owned. Freshman applicants given priority for college housing. *Activities and organizations:* drama/theater group, student-run newspaper, radio and television station, choral group, sorority and fraternity participation, Collegiate Entrepreneurs, Indi, International Student Council, Indian Student Association, national fraternities, national sororities. *Campus security:* 24-hour emergency response devices and patrols, student patrols, late-night transport/escort service, controlled dormitory access, 24-hour ID check at residence hall entrances, emergency call boxes located throughout campus. *Student services:* health clinic, personal/psychological counseling, legal services.

Athletics Member NCAA. All Division I. *Intercollegiate sports:* baseball M(s), basketball M(s)/W(s), cross-country running M(s)/W(s), golf M(s)/W(s), soccer M(s)/W(s), softball W(s), tennis M(s)/W(s), track and field M(s)/W(s), volleyball W(s), wrestling M(s). *Intramural sports:* badminton M/W, basketball M/W, bowling M/W, cheerleading M/W, fencing M/W, football M, ice hockey M, racquetball M/W, rock climbing M/W, rugby M, soccer M/W, softball M/W, table tennis M/W, tennis M/W, ultimate Frisbee M/W, volleyball M/W, water polo M/W, weight lifting M/W.

Standardized Tests *Required:* SAT or ACT (for admission).

Costs (2010–11) *Tuition:* state resident $6201 full-time, $207 per semester hour part-time; nonresident $15,503 full-time. Full-time tuition and fees vary according to course load. Part-time tuition and fees vary according to course load. No tuition increase for student's term of enrollment. *Required fees:* $2200 full-time, $251 per semester hour part-time. *Room and board:* $7821. Room and board charges vary according to board plan and housing facility. *Payment plan:* installment. *Waivers:* senior citizens and employees or children of employees.

Financial Aid Of all full-time matriculated undergraduates who enrolled in 2009, 7,411 applied for aid, 6,344 were judged to have need, 1,977 had their need fully met. In 2009, 407 non-need-based awards were made. *Average percent of need met:* 61%. *Average financial aid package:* $16,364. *Average*

need-based loan: $11,078. *Average need-based gift aid:* $9150. *Average non-need-based aid:* $7848. *Average indebtedness upon graduation:* $21,633.

Applying *Options:* electronic application, deferred entrance. *Application fee:* $30. *Required:* high school transcript. *Recommended:* minimum 2.5 GPA. *Application deadlines:* 5/1 (freshmen), 7/22 (transfers). *Notification:* continuous (freshmen), continuous (transfers).

Freshman Application Contact Mr. Todd Burrell, Director of Admissions, Southern Illinois University Edwardsville, Campus Box 1600, Rendleman Hall, Edwardsville, IL 62026-1600. *Phone:* 618-650-3705. *Toll-free phone:* 800-447-SIUE. *Fax:* 618-650-5013. *E-mail:* admissions@siue.edu. *Web site:* http://www.siue.edu/.

Telshe Yeshiva–Chicago

Chicago, Illinois

Freshman Application Contact Rosh Hayeshiva, Telshe Yeshiva–Chicago, 3535 West Foster Avenue, Chicago, IL 60625-5598. *Phone:* 773-463-7738.

Trinity Christian College

Palos Heights, Illinois

- **Independent Christian Reformed** 4-year, founded 1959
- **Suburban** 53-acre campus with easy access to Chicago
- **Endowment** $5.4 million
- **Coed**
- **Moderately difficult** entrance level

Faculty *Student/faculty ratio:* 12:1.

Academics *Calendar:* semesters plus 2 week interim term. *Degrees:* bachelor's and postbachelor's certificates.

Student Life *Campus security:* 24-hour emergency response devices, student patrols, late-night transport/escort service.

Athletics Member NAIA, NCCAA.

Standardized Tests *Required:* SAT or ACT (for admission). *Recommended:* ACT (for admission).

Costs (2010–11) *Comprehensive fee:* $29,472 includes full-time tuition ($21,398), mandatory fees ($110), and room and board ($7964). Full-time tuition and fees vary according to course load. Part-time tuition: $715 per semester hour. Part-time tuition and fees vary according to course load. *College room only:* $4272. Room and board charges vary according to board plan. *Payment plans:* installment, deferred payment.

Financial Aid *Of all full-time matriculated undergraduates who enrolled in 2009,* 1,002 applied for aid, 897 were judged to have need, 41 had their need fully met. 135 Federal Work-Study jobs (averaging $1500). *In 2009,* 107 non-need-based awards were made. *Average percent of need met:* 49. *Average financial aid package:* $12,219. *Average need-based loan:* $4447. *Average need-based gift aid:* $4120. *Average non-need-based aid:* $7024. *Average indebtedness upon graduation:* $26,571.

Applying *Options:* electronic application, deferred entrance. *Application fee:* $20. *Required:* essay or personal statement, high school transcript, minimum 2 GPA, interview. *Required for some:* 1 letter of recommendation.

Freshman Application Contact Mr. Jeremy Klyn, Director of Admissions, Trinity Christian College, 6601 West College Drive, Palos Heights, IL 60463. *Phone:* 708-239-4708. *Toll-free phone:* 800-748-0085. *Fax:* 708-239-4826. *E-mail:* admissions@trnty.edu. *Web site:* http://www.trnty.edu/.

Trinity College of Nursing and Health Sciences

Rock Island, Illinois

- **Independent** 4-year, founded 1994, administratively affiliated with Trinity Medical Center
- **Urban** 2-acre campus
- **Endowment** $1.8 million
- **Coed** 238 undergraduate students, 54% full-time, 84% women, 16% men
- **Moderately difficult** entrance level, 30% of applicants were admitted

Undergraduates 129 full-time, 109 part-time. 55% are from out of state; 84% transferred in. *Retention:* 100% of full-time freshmen returned.

Freshmen *Admission:* 10 applied, 3 admitted, 7 enrolled. *Average high school GPA:* 3.42. *Test scores:* ACT scores over 18: 82%; ACT scores over 24: 24%; ACT scores over 30: 1%.

Faculty *Total:* 28, 61% full-time, 18% with terminal degrees. *Student/faculty ratio:* 10:1.

Academics *Calendar:* semesters. *Degrees:* certificates, diplomas, associate, and bachelor's (general education requirements are taken off campus, usually at Black Hawk College, Eastern Iowa Community College District and Western Illinois University). *Special study options:* accelerated degree program, adult/continuing education programs, advanced placement credit, distance learning, honors programs, independent study, internships, off-campus study, part-time degree program, services for LD students, summer session for credit.

Computers on Campus 20 computers/terminals are available on campus for general student use. Students can access the following: computer help desk, free student e-mail accounts, online (class) grades, online (class) schedules. Campuswide network is available. Wireless service is available via entire campus.

Student Life *Housing:* college housing not available. *Activities and organizations:* Student Government Association, Phi Theta Kappa, BSN Honor Society, Association of Surgical Technologists Honor Society. *Campus security:* 24-hour emergency response devices. *Student services:* personal/psychological counseling.

Standardized Tests *Required for some:* SAT or ACT (for admission).

Costs (2011–12) *Tuition:* $11,472 full-time, $478 per credit part-time. Full-time tuition and fees vary according to course load, degree level, program, and student level. Part-time tuition and fees vary according to course load, degree level, program, and student level. *Required fees:* $1184 full-time, $529 per term part-time. *Payment plans:* installment, deferred payment.

Financial Aid Of all full-time matriculated undergraduates who enrolled in 2009, 110 applied for aid, 110 were judged to have need. *Average indebtedness upon graduation:* $9500.

Applying *Options:* electronic application, early admission, early decision. *Application fee:* $50. *Required:* minimum 2.5 GPA. *Required for some:* essay or personal statement, high school transcript, minimum 3 GPA, interview. *Application deadlines:* rolling (freshmen), rolling (out-of-state freshmen), rolling (transfers). *Early decision deadline:* 12/1. *Notification:* continuous until 2/1 (freshmen), continuous until 2/1 (out-of-state freshmen), continuous until 2/1 (transfers), 12/15 (early decision).

Freshman Application Contact Ms. Lori Perez, Admissions Representative, Trinity College of Nursing and Health Sciences, 2122 - 25th Avenue, Rock Island, IL 61201. *Phone:* 309-779-7700. *Toll-free phone:* 309-779-7700. *Fax:* 309-779-7748. *E-mail:* PerezLJ@ihs.org. *Web site:* http://www.trinitycollegeqc.edu/.

Trinity International University

Deerfield, Illinois

Freshman Application Contact Mr. Aaron Mahl, Director of Undergraduate Admissions, Trinity International University, 2065 Half Day Road, Deerfield, IL 60015-1284. *Phone:* 847-317-7000. *Toll-free phone:* 800-822-3225. *Fax:* 847-317-8097. *E-mail:* tcadmissions@tiu.edu. *Web site:* http://www.tiu.edu/.

University of Chicago

Chicago, Illinois

- **Independent** university, founded 1891
- **Urban** 211-acre campus
- **Endowment** $5.9 billion
- **Coed**
- **Most difficult** entrance level

Faculty *Student/faculty ratio:* 6:1.

Academics *Calendar:* quarters. *Degrees:* bachelor's, master's, doctoral-professional, and doctoral-research/scholarship.

Student Life *Campus security:* 24-hour emergency response devices and patrols, student patrols, late-night transport/escort service, controlled dormitory access.

Athletics Member NCAA. All Division III.

Standardized Tests *Required:* SAT or ACT (for admission).

Costs (2010–11) *Comprehensive fee:* $53,244 includes full-time tuition ($40,188), mandatory fees ($903), and room and board ($12,153). Part-time tuition and fees vary according to course load. *Room and board:* Room and board charges vary according to board plan and housing facility. *Payment plans:* tuition prepayment, installment.

Financial Aid *Of all full-time matriculated undergraduates who enrolled in 2009,* 3,278 applied for aid, 2,433 were judged to have need, 1,954 had their need fully met. In 2009, 535 non-need-based awards were made. *Average percent of need met:* 100. *Average financial aid package:* $36,915. *Average need-based loan:* $5074. *Average need-based gift aid:* $33,027. *Average non-need-based aid:* $13,208. *Average indebtedness upon graduation:* $24,238.

Applying *Options:* electronic application, early admission, early action, deferred entrance. *Application fee:* $65. *Required:* essay or personal statement, high school transcript, 3 letters of recommendation, 2 teacher recommendations and counselor recommendation required. *Recommended:* interview.

Freshman Application Contact Mr. James G. Nondorf, Vice President, Dean of College Admissions and Financial Aid, University of Chicago, Rosenwald Hall, 1101 East 58th Street, Suite 105, Chicago, IL 60637. *Phone:* 773-702-8650. *Fax:* 773-702-4199. *E-mail:* collegeadmissions@uchicago.edu. *Web site:* http://www.uchicago.edu/.

University of Illinois at Chicago

Chicago, Illinois

- **State-supported** university, founded 1946, part of University of Illinois System
- **Urban** 240-acre campus with easy access to Chicago
- **Endowment** $164.0 million
- **Coed** 16,806 undergraduate students, 92% full-time, 52% women, 48% men
- **Moderately difficult** entrance level, 63% of applicants were admitted

Undergraduates 15,514 full-time, 1,292 part-time. Students come from 44 states and territories; 49 other countries; 2% are from out of state; 8% Black or African American, non-Hispanic/Latino; 20% Hispanic/Latino; 21% Asian, non-Hispanic/Latino; 0.5% Native Hawaiian or other Pacific Islander, non-Hispanic/Latino; 0.1% American Indian or Alaska Native, non-Hispanic/Latino; 2% Two or more races, non-Hispanic/Latino; 2% Race/ethnicity unknown; 1% international; 10% transferred in; 19% live on campus. *Retention:* 82% of full-time freshmen returned.

Freshmen *Admission:* 14,889 applied, 9,411 admitted, 3,204 enrolled. *Test scores:* SAT critical reading scores over 500: 63%; SAT math scores over 500: 79%; ACT scores over 18: 99%; SAT critical reading scores over 600: 29%; SAT math scores over 600: 45%; ACT scores over 24: 49%; SAT critical reading scores over 700: 7%; SAT math scores over 700: 12%; ACT scores over 30: 7%.

Faculty *Total:* 1,540, 74% full-time, 66% with terminal degrees. *Student/faculty ratio:* 19:1.

Academics *Calendar:* semesters. *Degrees:* bachelor's, master's, doctoral-other, doctoral-professional, doctoral-research/scholarship, post-master's, and postbachelor's certificates. *Special study options:* academic remediation for entering students, accelerated degree program, advanced placement credit, cooperative education, distance learning, double majors, honors programs, independent study, internships, off-campus study, part-time degree program, services for LD students, student-designed majors, study abroad, summer session for credit. *ROTC:* Army (b), Navy (c), Air Force (c).

Computers on Campus 910 computers/terminals are available on campus for general student use. Students can access the following: campus intranet, computer help desk, free student e-mail accounts, online (class) grades, online (class) registration, online (class) schedules. Campuswide network is available. 100% of college-owned or -operated housing units are wired for high-speed Internet access. Wireless service is available via classrooms, computer centers, computer labs, dorm rooms, libraries, student centers.

Student Life *Housing options:* coed. Campus housing is university owned. *Activities and organizations:* drama/theater group, student-run newspaper, radio station, choral group, MBA Association, StudentsMuslim Student Association, Society of Automotive Engineers, Pakistani Student Organization, Society of Future Physicians, national fraternities, national sororities. *Campus security:* 24-hour emergency response devices and patrols, student patrols, late-night transport/escort service, controlled dormitory access, housing ID stickers, guest escort policy, 24-hour closed circuit videos for exits and entrances, security screen for first floor. *Student services:* health clinic, personal/psychological counseling, women's center, legal services.

Athletics Member NCAA. All Division I. *Intercollegiate sports:* baseball M(s), basketball M(s)/W(s), cross-country running M(s)/W(s), gymnastics M(s)/W(s), soccer M(s), softball W(s), swimming and diving M(s)/W(s), tennis M(s)/W(s), track and field M(s)/W(s), volleyball W(s). *Intramural sports:* badminton M/W, basketball M/W, bowling M/W, fencing M(c)/W(c), field hockey W, football M/W, golf M/W, racquetball M/W, rugby M(c)/W(c), soccer M/W, softball M/W, squash M/W, table tennis M/W, tennis M/W, volleyball M(c)/W, water polo M(c)/W(c), wrestling M.

Standardized Tests *Required:* SAT or ACT (for admission), SAT and SAT Subject Tests or ACT (for admission), SAT Subject Tests (for admission).

Costs (2010–11) *Tuition:* state resident $9134 full-time, $1522 per term part-time; nonresident $21,524 full-time, $3587 per term part-time. Full-time tuition and fees vary according to degree level and program. Part-time tuition and fees vary according to course load, degree level, and program. No tuition increase for student's term of enrollment. Fees do not include Health Insurance Fee which can be waived with proof of insurance and Student-to-Student fee which is refundable on request. *Required fees:* $2922 full-time, $909 per term part-time. *Room and board:* $9994; room only: $7174. Room and board charges vary according to board plan and housing facility. *Payment plan:* installment. *Waivers:* senior citizens and employees or children of employees.

Financial Aid Of all full-time matriculated undergraduates who enrolled in 2008, 11,718 applied for aid, 10,077 were judged to have need, 1,168 had their need fully met. 1,006 Federal Work-Study jobs (averaging $1904). 2,571 state and other part-time jobs (averaging $2577). In 2008, 626 non-need-based awards were made. *Average percent of need met:* 70%. *Average financial aid package:* $13,312. *Average need-based loan:* $4485. *Average need-based gift aid:* $11,769. *Average non-need-based aid:* $3677. *Average indebtedness upon graduation:* $18,526.

Applying *Options:* electronic application. *Application fee:* $50. *Required:* essay or personal statement, high school transcript, auditions required of music and theater majors. Portfolios required of art majors. *Application deadlines:* 1/15 (freshmen), 3/31 (transfers). *Notification:* continuous until 11/30 (freshmen), continuous (transfers).

Freshman Application Contact Mr. Thomas Glenn, Executive Director of Admissions, University of Illinois at Chicago, 1100 SSB, m/c 018, Chicago, IL 60607-7128. *Phone:* 312-996-5133. *Fax:* 312-996-2953. *E-mail:* uic.admit@uic.edu. *Web site:* http://www.uic.edu/.

University of Illinois at Springfield
Springfield, Illinois

- **State-supported** comprehensive, founded 1969, part of University of Illinois System
- **Suburban** 746-acre campus
- **Endowment** $8.8 million
- **Coed** 3,197 undergraduate students, 66% full-time, 53% women, 47% men
- **Moderately difficult** entrance level, 59% of applicants were admitted

Undergraduates 2,126 full-time, 1,071 part-time. Students come from 47 states and territories; 13 other countries; 8% are from out of state; 21% transferred in; 28% live on campus. *Retention:* 76% of full-time freshmen returned.
Freshmen *Admission:* 1,311 applied, 779 admitted, 294 enrolled. *Average high school GPA:* 3.35. *Test scores:* ACT scores over 18: 95%; ACT scores over 24: 39%; ACT scores over 30: 5%.
Faculty *Total:* 362, 53% full-time. *Student/faculty ratio:* 14:1.
Academics *Calendar:* semesters. *Degrees:* bachelor's, master's, doctoral-research/scholarship, post-master's, and postbachelor's certificates. *Special study options:* academic remediation for entering students, advanced placement credit, cooperative education, distance learning, double majors, English as a second language, honors programs, independent study, internships, off-campus study, part-time degree program, services for LD students, study abroad, summer session for credit.
Computers on Campus 353 computers/terminals and 27 ports are available on campus for general student use. Students can access the following: campus intranet, computer help desk, free student e-mail accounts, online (class) grades, online (class) registration, online (class) schedules. Campuswide network is available. 100% of college-owned or -operated housing units are wired for high-speed Internet access. Wireless service is available via entire campus.
Student Life *Housing:* on-campus residence required for freshman year. *Options:* coed, disabled students. Campus housing is university owned. Freshman campus housing is guaranteed. *Activities and organizations:* drama/theater group, student-run newspaper, radio station, choral group, Student Activities Committee, Christian Student Fellowship, Indian Student Organization, Black Student Union, DODGE - Dodge Ball Club. *Campus security:* 24-hour emergency response devices and patrols, late-night transport/escort service, controlled dormitory access. *Student services:* health clinic, personal/psychological counseling, women's center.
Athletics Member NCAA. All Division II. *Intercollegiate sports:* baseball M(s), basketball M(s)/W(s), golf M(s)/W(s), soccer M(s)/W(s), softball W(s), tennis M(s)/W(s), volleyball W(s). *Intramural sports:* badminton M/W, baseball M(c)/W(c), basketball M/W, football M/W, racquetball M/W, soccer M/W, softball M/W, squash M(c)/W(c), table tennis M/W, ultimate Frisbee M/W, volleyball M/W.
Standardized Tests *Required:* SAT or ACT (for admission).
Costs (2010–11) *Tuition:* state resident $8108 full-time, $270 per credit hour part-time; nonresident $17,258 full-time, $575 per credit hour part-time. Full-time tuition and fees vary according to course load. Part-time tuition and fees vary according to course load. No tuition increase for student's term of enrollment. *Required fees:* $2259 full-time, $15 per credit hour part-time, $772 per term part-time. *Room and board:* $9400; room only: $6400. Room and board charges vary according to board plan and housing facility. *Payment plan:* installment. *Waivers:* senior citizens and employees or children of employees.
Financial Aid Of all full-time matriculated undergraduates who enrolled in 2008, 1,396 applied for aid, 1,113 were judged to have need, 132 had their need fully met. In 2008, 257 non-need-based awards were made. *Average percent of need met:* 72%. *Average financial aid package:* $10,264. *Average need-based loan:* $4138. *Average need-based gift aid:* $7585. *Average non-need-based aid:* $3819. *Average indebtedness upon graduation:* $14,717. *Financial aid deadline:* 11/15.
Applying *Options:* electronic application, deferred entrance. *Application fee:* $50. *Required:* essay or personal statement, high school transcript. *Application deadlines:* rolling (freshmen), rolling (transfers). *Notification:* continuous (transfers).
Freshman Application Contact Dr. Lori Giordano, Interim Director of Student Services/ Admissions, University of Illinois at Springfield, Springfield, IL 62703. *Phone:* 217-206-4847. *Toll-free phone:* 888-977-4847. *E-mail:* admissions@uis.edu. *Web site:* http://www.uis.edu/.

University of Illinois at Urbana–Champaign
Champaign, Illinois

- **State-supported** university, founded 1867, part of University of Illinois System
- **Urban** 1470-acre campus
- **Coed**
- **Very difficult** entrance level

Faculty *Student/faculty ratio:* 16:1.
Academics *Calendar:* semesters. *Degrees:* certificates, bachelor's, master's, doctoral-professional, doctoral-research/scholarship, post-master's, and post-bachelor's certificates.
Student Life *Campus security:* 24-hour emergency response devices and patrols, student patrols, late-night transport/escort service, controlled dormitory access, safety training classes, ID cards with safety numbers.
Athletics Member NCAA. All Division I except football (Division I-A).
Standardized Tests *Required:* SAT or ACT (for admission).
Costs (2010–11) *Tuition:* state resident $10,386 full-time; nonresident $24,528 full-time. Full-time tuition and fees vary according to course load, program, and student level. No tuition increase for student's term of enrollment. *Required fees:* $3254 full-time. *Room and board:* $9714. Room and board charges vary according to board plan, housing facility, and location.
Financial Aid Of all full-time matriculated undergraduates who enrolled in 2008, 17,577 applied for aid, 13,187 were judged to have need, 5,833 had their need fully met. In 2008, 3866 non-need-based awards were made. *Average percent of need met:* 69. *Average financial aid package:* $12,076. *Average need-based loan:* $4425. *Average need-based gift aid:* $9868. *Average non-need-based aid:* $3046. *Average indebtedness upon graduation:* $19,378.
Applying *Options:* early admission, deferred entrance. *Application fee:* $40. *Required:* essay or personal statement, high school transcript. *Required for some:* audition, statement of professional interest.
Freshman Application Contact Mrs. Stacey Kostell, Director of Admissions, University of Illinois at Urbana–Champaign, 901 West Illinois, Urbana, IL 61801. *Phone:* 217-333-0302. *Fax:* 217-244-4614. *E-mail:* ugradadmissions@uiuc.edu. *Web site:* http://www.illinois.edu/.

University of Phoenix–Chicago Campus
Schaumburg, Illinois

Freshman Application Contact Ms. Audra McQuarie, Registrar/Executive Director, University of Phoenix–Chicago Campus, 4035 South Riverpoint Parkway, Mail Stop CF-L101, Phoenix, AZ 85040-1958. *Phone:* 480-557-6151. *Toll-free phone:* 800-776-4867 (in-state); 800-228-7240 (out-of-state). *Fax:* 480-643-3068. *E-mail:* audra.mcquarie@phoenix.edu. *Web site:* http://www.phoenix.edu/.

University of St. Francis
Joliet, Illinois

- **Independent Roman Catholic** comprehensive, founded 1920
- **Suburban** 24-acre campus with easy access to Chicago
- **Coed** 1,353 undergraduate students, 96% full-time, 68% women, 32% men
- **Moderately difficult** entrance level, 57% of applicants were admitted

Undergraduates 1,297 full-time, 56 part-time. Students come from 21 states and territories; 6% are from out of state; 7% Black or African American, non-Hispanic/Latino; 13% Hispanic/Latino; 3% Asian, non-Hispanic/Latino; 0.4% Native Hawaiian or other Pacific Islander, non-Hispanic/Latino; 0.1% American Indian or Alaska Native, non-Hispanic/Latino; 2% Two or more races, non-Hispanic/Latino; 0.1% Race/ethnicity unknown; 0.9% international; 16% transferred in; 27% live on campus. *Retention:* 83% of full-time freshmen returned.
Freshmen *Admission:* 1,120 applied, 633 admitted, 210 enrolled. *Average high school GPA:* 3.3. *Test scores:* SAT critical reading scores over 500: 62%; SAT math scores over 500: 69%; SAT writing scores over 500: 61%; ACT scores over 18: 97%; SAT critical reading scores over 600: 8%; SAT math scores over 600: 15%; SAT writing scores over 600: 15%; ACT scores over 24: 43%; ACT scores over 30: 3%.
Faculty *Total:* 223, 39% full-time, 43% with terminal degrees. *Student/faculty ratio:* 13:1.
Academics *Calendar:* semesters. *Degrees:* bachelor's, master's, doctoral-other, and post-master's certificates. *Special study options:* academic remediation for entering students, accelerated degree program, adult/continuing education programs, advanced placement credit, distance learning, double majors, external degree program, honors programs, independent study, internships, off-

campus study, part-time degree program, services for LD students, student-designed majors, study abroad, summer session for credit. *ROTC:* Army (c).

Computers on Campus 382 computers/terminals and 1,500 ports are available on campus for general student use. Students can access the following: campus intranet, computer help desk, free student e-mail accounts, online (class) grades, online (class) registration, online (class) schedules, billing/payment. Campuswide network is available. 100% of college-owned or -operated housing units are wired for high-speed Internet access. Wireless service is available via entire campus.

Student Life *Housing options:* coed. Campus housing is university owned. Freshman campus housing is guaranteed. *Activities and organizations:* drama/theater group, student-run newspaper, radio and television station, choral group, Student Activities Board, Student Nurses Association, Student Business Association, Ethnic Affairs Council, Justice League of USF. *Campus security:* 24-hour emergency response devices and patrols, student patrols, late-night transport/escort service, controlled dormitory access, First Response trained security personnel. *Student services:* personal/psychological counseling.

Athletics Member NAIA. *Intercollegiate sports:* baseball M(s), basketball M(s)/W(s), cheerleading W(s), cross-country running M(s)/W(s), football M(s), golf M(s)/W(s), soccer M(s)/W(s), softball W(s), tennis M(s)/W(s), track and field M(s)/W(s), volleyball W(s). *Intramural sports:* basketball M/W, bowling M/W, volleyball M/W.

Standardized Tests *Required:* SAT or ACT (for admission).

Costs (2010–11) *Comprehensive fee:* $32,918 includes full-time tuition ($24,292), mandatory fees ($450), and room and board ($8176). Part-time tuition: $790 per credit hour. *Room and board:* Room and board charges vary according to board plan and housing facility. *Payment plans:* installment, deferred payment. *Waivers:* children of alumni and employees or children of employees.

Financial Aid Of all full-time matriculated undergraduates who enrolled in 2009, 1,190 applied for aid, 1,084 were judged to have need, 539 had their need fully met. 174 Federal Work-Study jobs (averaging $1107). 241 state and other part-time jobs (averaging $1470). In 2009, 192 non-need-based awards were made. *Average percent of need met:* 67%. *Average financial aid package:* $19,955. *Average need-based loan:* $4457. *Average need-based gift aid:* $8409. *Average non-need-based aid:* $8266. *Average indebtedness upon graduation:* $27,088.

Applying *Options:* electronic application, deferred entrance. *Application fee:* $30. *Required:* high school transcript, minimum 2.5 GPA. *Required for some:* essay or personal statement, 2 letters of recommendation, interview. *Application deadline:* 8/1 (freshmen). *Notification:* continuous (freshmen), continuous (transfers).

Freshman Application Contact Ms. Julie Marlatt, Director of Undergraduate Admissions, University of St. Francis, 500 North Wilcox Street, Joliet, IL 60435-6188. *Phone:* 800-735-7500. *Toll-free phone:* 800-735-3500 (in-state); 800-735-7500 (out-of-state). *Fax:* 815-740-5032. *E-mail:* jmarlatt@stfrancis.edu. *Web site:* http://www.stfrancis.edu/.

VanderCook College of Music
Chicago, Illinois

- **Independent** comprehensive, founded 1909
- **Urban** 1-acre campus
- **Endowment** $3.4 million
- **Coed** 171 undergraduate students, 78% full-time, 52% women, 48% men
- **Moderately difficult** entrance level, 79% of applicants were admitted

Undergraduates 133 full-time, 38 part-time. Students come from 14 states and territories; 4 other countries; 27% are from out of state; 9% Black or African American, non-Hispanic/Latino; 11% Hispanic/Latino; 4% Asian, non-Hispanic/Latino; 1% Race/ethnicity unknown; 5% international; 3% transferred in; 23% live on campus. *Retention:* 84% of full-time freshmen returned.

Freshmen *Admission:* 63 applied, 50 admitted, 34 enrolled. *Average high school GPA:* 3.29. *Test scores:* SAT critical reading scores over 500: 51%; SAT math scores over 500: 50%; SAT writing scores over 500: 50%; ACT scores over 18: 100%; SAT critical reading scores over 600: 34%; SAT math scores over 600: 33%; SAT writing scores over 600: 17%; ACT scores over 24: 33%; SAT critical reading scores over 700: 17%.

Faculty *Total:* 33, 30% full-time, 27% with terminal degrees. *Student/faculty ratio:* 9:1.

Academics *Calendar:* semesters. *Degrees:* bachelor's and master's. *Special study options:* advanced placement credit, distance learning, independent study, internships, part-time degree program.

Computers on Campus 21 computers/terminals are available on campus for general student use. Students can access the following: campus intranet, free student e-mail accounts. Campuswide network is available.

Student Life *Housing options:* coed, disabled students. Campus housing is provided by a third party. *Activities and organizations:* choral group, MENC (Music Educators Natural Conference), ACDA (American Choral Directors Association), NBA (National Band Association), ASTA (American String Teachers Association), national fraternities, national sororities. *Campus secu-*

rity: 24-hour emergency response devices and patrols, late-night transport/escort service, controlled dormitory access.

Standardized Tests *Required for some:* SAT or ACT (for admission).

Costs (2010–11) *Comprehensive fee:* $32,608 includes full-time tuition ($21,060), mandatory fees ($1210), and room and board ($10,338). Full-time tuition and fees vary according to course level, course load, degree level, and program. Part-time tuition: $890 per semester hour. Part-time tuition and fees vary according to course level, course load, degree level, and program. *Required fees:* $480 per term part-time. *College room only:* $5384. Room and board charges vary according to board plan and housing facility. *Payment plan:* installment. *Waivers:* employees or children of employees.

Financial Aid Of all full-time matriculated undergraduates who enrolled in 2006, 7 Federal Work-Study jobs (averaging $500). 37 state and other part-time jobs (averaging $959).

Applying *Options:* deferred entrance. *Application fee:* $35. *Required:* essay or personal statement, high school transcript, 3 letters of recommendation, interview, audition. *Required for some:* minimum 3 GPA. *Recommended:* minimum 3 GPA. *Application deadlines:* rolling (freshmen), rolling (out-of-state freshmen), rolling (transfers). *Notification:* continuous (freshmen), continuous (out-of-state freshmen), continuous (transfers).

Freshman Application Contact Ms. Amy Lenting, Director of Admissions, VanderCook College of Music, 3140 South Federal Street, Chicago, IL 60616. *Phone:* 312-225-6288 Ext. 230. *Toll-free phone:* 800-448-2655. *Fax:* 312-225-5211. *E-mail:* admissions@vandercook.edu. *Web site:* http://www.vandercook.edu/.

Western Illinois University
Macomb, Illinois

- **State-supported** comprehensive, founded 1899
- **Small-town** 1050-acre campus
- **Endowment** $23.0 million
- **Coed** 10,474 undergraduate students, 91% full-time, 48% women, 52% men
- **Moderately difficult** entrance level, 65% of applicants were admitted

Undergraduates 9,496 full-time, 978 part-time. Students come from 38 states and territories; 65 other countries; 8% are from out of state; 11% Black or African American, non-Hispanic/Latino; 6% Hispanic/Latino; 0.9% Asian, non-Hispanic/Latino; 0.2% Native Hawaiian or other Pacific Islander, non-Hispanic/Latino; 0.2% American Indian or Alaska Native, non-Hispanic/Latino; 2% Two or more races, non-Hispanic/Latino; 4% Race/ethnicity unknown; 1% international; 13% transferred in; 43% live on campus. *Retention:* 73% of full-time freshmen returned.

Freshmen *Admission:* 8,398 applied, 5,423 admitted, 1,754 enrolled. *Average high school GPA:* 3. *Test scores:* ACT scores over 18: 85%; ACT scores over 24: 22%; ACT scores over 30: 2%.

Faculty *Total:* 731, 90% full-time, 68% with terminal degrees. *Student/faculty ratio:* 16:1.

Academics *Calendar:* semesters. *Degrees:* bachelor's, master's, doctoral-research/scholarship, and postbachelor's certificates. *Special study options:* academic remediation for entering students, adult/continuing education programs, advanced placement credit, distance learning, double majors, English as a second language, external degree program, freshman honors college, honors programs, independent study, internships, off-campus study, part-time degree program, services for LD students, student-designed majors, study abroad, summer session for credit. *ROTC:* Army (b).

Computers on Campus 1,000 computers/terminals are available on campus for general student use. Students can access the following: online (class) registration. Campuswide network is available. 100% of college-owned or -operated housing units are wired for high-speed Internet access. Wireless service is available via classrooms, computer labs, dorm rooms, libraries, student centers.

Student Life *Housing:* on-campus residence required through sophomore year. *Options:* coed, men-only, women-only. Campus housing is university owned. Freshman campus housing is guaranteed. *Activities and organizations:* drama/theater group, student-run newspaper, radio and television station, choral group, marching band, Student Government Association, Black Student Association, University Union Board, International Friendship Club, Bureau of Cultural Affairs, national fraternities, national sororities. *Campus security:* 24-hour emergency response devices and patrols, student patrols, late-night transport/escort service, controlled dormitory access. *Student services:* health clinic, personal/psychological counseling, women's center, legal services.

Athletics Member NCAA. All Division I except football (Division I-AA). *Intercollegiate sports:* baseball M(s), basketball M(s)/W(s), cross-country running M(s)/W(s), golf M(s)/W, soccer W(s), softball W(s), swimming and diving M(s)/W(s), tennis M(s)/W(s), track and field M(s)/W(s), volleyball W(s). *Intramural sports:* badminton M/W, basketball M/W, bowling M/W, cheerleading M/W, cross-country running M/W, football M/W, golf M/W, lacrosse M, racquetball M/W, rugby M/W, soccer M/W, softball M/W, swimming and diving M/W, table tennis M/W, tennis M/W, volleyball M/W, water polo M/W.

Standardized Tests *Required:* SAT or ACT (for admission).

Costs (2010–11) *Tuition:* state resident $7220 full-time, $241 per credit hour part-time; nonresident $10,829 full-time, $361 per credit hour part-time. Full-time tuition and fees vary according to course load and student level. Part-time tuition and fees vary according to course load and student level. No tuition increase for student's term of enrollment. *Required fees:* $2270 full-time, $76 per credit hour part-time. *Room and board:* $8138. Room and board charges vary according to board plan, housing facility, and student level. *Waivers:* senior citizens and employees or children of employees.

Financial Aid Of all full-time matriculated undergraduates who enrolled in 2009, 7,523 applied for aid, 6,419 were judged to have need, 2,405 had their need fully met. 212 Federal Work-Study jobs (averaging $2469). 1,506 state and other part-time jobs (averaging $1157). In 2009, 299 non-need-based awards were made. *Average percent of need met:* 62%. *Average financial aid package:* $9879. *Average need-based loan:* $4301. *Average need-based gift aid:* $7998. *Average non-need-based aid:* $3112. *Average indebtedness upon graduation:* $22,007.

Applying *Options:* electronic application, deferred entrance. *Application fee:* $30. *Required:* high school transcript, minimum 2.5 GPA. *Application deadlines:* 5/15 (freshmen), rolling (transfers). *Notification:* 8/3 (freshmen), continuous (transfers).

Freshman Application Contact Western Illinois University, 1 University Circle, Macomb, IL 61455-1390. *Phone:* 309-298-3157. *Toll-free phone:* 877-742-5948. *Web site:* http://www.wiu.edu/.

Westwood College–Chicago Du Page
Woodridge, Illinois

- **Proprietary** 4-year
- **Coed**

Academics *Calendar:* continuous. *Degrees:* diplomas, associate, and bachelor's.

Freshman Application Contact Westwood College–Chicago Du Page, 7155 Janes Avenue, Woodridge, IL 60517. *Phone:* 630-434-8250. *Toll-free phone:* 866-721-7646. *Web site:* http://www.westwood.edu/.

Westwood College–Chicago Loop Campus
Chicago, Illinois

- **Proprietary** 4-year, founded 2002
- **Coed**

Academics *Degrees:* associate and bachelor's.

Freshman Application Contact Westwood College–Chicago Loop Campus, 17 North State Street, Suite 300, Chicago, IL 60602. *Phone:* 312-739-0890. *Toll-free phone:* 800-693-5415. *Web site:* http://www.westwood.edu/.

Westwood College–Chicago O'Hare Airport
Chicago, Illinois

- **Proprietary** 4-year
- **Coed**

Academics *Calendar:* continuous. *Degrees:* diplomas, associate, and bachelor's.

Freshman Application Contact Westwood College–Chicago O'Hare Airport, 8501 West Higgins Road, Suite 100, Chicago, IL 60631. *Phone:* 773-380-6801. *Toll-free phone:* 877-877-8857. *Web site:* http://www.westwood.edu/.

Westwood College–Chicago River Oaks
Calumet City, Illinois

- **Proprietary** 4-year
- **Coed**

Academics *Calendar:* continuous. *Degrees:* diplomas, associate, and bachelor's.

Freshman Application Contact Westwood College–Chicago River Oaks, 80 River Oaks Drive, Suite 111, Calumet City, IL 60409. *Phone:* 708-832-9760. *Toll-free phone:* 888-549-6873. *Web site:* http://www.westwood.edu/.

Wheaton College
Wheaton, Illinois

- **Independent nondenominational** comprehensive, founded 1860
- **Suburban** 80-acre campus with easy access to Chicago
- **Endowment** $273.7 million
- **Coed** 2,434 undergraduate students, 97% full-time, 51% women, 49% men
- **Very difficult** entrance level, 66% of applicants were admitted

Undergraduates 2,362 full-time, 72 part-time. Students come from 51 states and territories; 26 other countries; 76% are from out of state; 3% Black or African American, non-Hispanic/Latino; 4% Hispanic/Latino; 8% Asian, non-Hispanic/Latino; 0.1% Native Hawaiian or other Pacific Islander, non-Hispanic/Latino; 0.1% American Indian or Alaska Native, non-Hispanic/Latino; 0.6% Two or more races, non-Hispanic/Latino; 1% Race/ethnicity unknown; 1% international; 3% transferred in; 90% live on campus. *Retention:* 96% of full-time freshmen returned.

Freshmen *Admission:* 2,010 applied, 1,326 admitted, 602 enrolled. *Average high school GPA:* 3.7. *Test scores:* SAT critical reading scores over 500: 97%; SAT math scores over 500: 97%; SAT writing scores over 500: 97%; ACT scores over 18: 100%; SAT critical reading scores over 600: 81%; SAT math scores over 600: 79%; SAT writing scores over 600: 75%; ACT scores over 24: 91%; SAT critical reading scores over 700: 36%; SAT math scores over 700: 28%; SAT writing scores over 700: 30%; ACT scores over 30: 47%.

Faculty *Total:* 291, 68% full-time, 79% with terminal degrees. *Student/faculty ratio:* 12:1.

Academics *Calendar:* semesters. *Degrees:* bachelor's, master's, doctoral-professional, doctoral-research/scholarship, and postbachelor's certificates. *Special study options:* advanced placement credit, double majors, independent study, internships, off-campus study, services for LD students, student-designed majors, study abroad, summer session for credit. *ROTC:* Army (b), Air Force (c). *Unusual degree programs:* 3-2 engineering with University of Illinois, Washington University in St. Louis, Illinois Institute of Technology, University of Minnesota; nursing with Emory University, Johns Hopkins University, Rush University, Vanderbilt University, Case Western Reserve University.

Computers on Campus 125 computers/terminals and 3,500 ports are available on campus for general student use. Students can access the following: campus intranet, computer help desk, free student e-mail accounts, online (class) grades, online (class) registration, online (class) schedules, financial information, degree requirements evaluation. Campuswide network is available. 100% of college-owned or -operated housing units are wired for high-speed Internet access. Wireless service is available via computer centers, computer labs, dorm rooms, learning centers, libraries, student centers.

Student Life *Housing:* on-campus residence required through senior year. *Options:* coed, men-only, women-only, cooperative, disabled students. Campus housing is university owned. Freshman campus housing is guaranteed. *Activities and organizations:* drama/theater group, student-run newspaper, choral group, Discipleship small groups, Christian Service Council, Orientation Committee, Resident Assistant Staff. *Campus security:* 24-hour emergency response devices and patrols, student patrols, late-night transport/escort service, controlled dormitory access. *Student services:* health clinic, personal/psychological counseling.

Athletics Member NCAA. All Division III. *Intercollegiate sports:* baseball M, basketball M/W, cheerleading W(c), crew M(c)/W(c), cross-country running M/W, football M, golf M/W, ice hockey M(c), lacrosse M(c)/W(c), soccer M/W, softball W, swimming and diving M/W, tennis M/W, track and field M/W, volleyball M(c)/W, water polo M(c)/W, wrestling M. *Intramural sports:* badminton M/W, basketball M/W, football M, golf M/W, soccer M/W, softball M, tennis M/W, ultimate Frisbee M/W, volleyball M/W, water polo M/W.

Standardized Tests *Required:* SAT or ACT (for admission).

Costs (2010–11) *Comprehensive fee:* $35,630 includes full-time tuition ($27,580) and room and board ($8050). Part-time tuition: $1149 per credit hour. Part-time tuition and fees vary according to course load. *College room only:* $4750. Room and board charges vary according to board plan and housing facility. *Payment plans:* installment, deferred payment.

Financial Aid Of all full-time matriculated undergraduates who enrolled in 2009, 1,531 applied for aid, 1,236 were judged to have need, 328 had their need fully met. 203 Federal Work-Study jobs (averaging $1324). In 2009, 283 non-need-based awards were made. *Average percent of need met:* 91%. *Average financial aid package:* $23,282. *Average need-based loan:* $4922. *Average need-based gift aid:* $16,029. *Average non-need-based aid:* $4564. *Average indebtedness upon graduation:* $21,241.

Applying *Options:* electronic application, early action. *Application fee:* $50. *Required:* essay or personal statement, high school transcript, 2 letters of recommendation. *Recommended:* interview. *Application deadlines:* 1/10 (freshmen), 3/1 (transfers), 11/1 (early action). *Notification:* 4/1 (freshmen), 4/1 (transfers), 12/31 (early action).

Freshman Application Contact Ms. Shawn Leftwich, Director of Admissions, Wheaton College, 501 College Avenue, Wheaton, IL 60187-

5593. *Phone:* 630-752-5011. *Toll-free phone:* 800-222-2419. *Fax:* 630-752-5285. *E-mail:* admissions@wheaton.edu. *Web site:* http://www.wheaton.edu/.

See page 1788 for the College Close-Up.

INDIANA

Anderson University
Anderson, Indiana

- **Independent** comprehensive, founded 1917, affiliated with Church of God
- **Suburban** 163-acre campus with easy access to Indianapolis
- **Endowment** $22.0 million
- **Coed** 2,022 undergraduate students, 91% full-time, 57% women, 43% men
- **Moderately difficult** entrance level, 79% of applicants were admitted

Undergraduates 1,840 full-time, 182 part-time. Students come from 35 states and territories; 26 other countries; 28% are from out of state; 7% Black or African American, non-Hispanic/Latino; 1% Hispanic/Latino; 0.8% Asian, non-Hispanic/Latino; 0.1% Native Hawaiian or other Pacific Islander, non-Hispanic/Latino; 0.2% American Indian or Alaska Native, non-Hispanic/Latino; 0.1% Two or more races, non-Hispanic/Latino; 4% Race/ethnicity unknown; 2% international; 5% transferred in; 62% live on campus. *Retention:* 70% of full-time freshmen returned.

Freshmen *Admission:* 1,830 applied, 1,451 admitted, 469 enrolled. *Average high school GPA:* 3.39. *Test scores:* SAT critical reading scores over 500: 59%; SAT math scores over 500: 64%; ACT scores over 18: 93%; SAT critical reading scores over 600: 20%; SAT math scores over 600: 25%; ACT scores over 24: 51%; SAT critical reading scores over 700: 3%; SAT math scores over 700: 2%; ACT scores over 30: 5%.

Faculty *Total:* 279, 49% full-time, 32% with terminal degrees. *Student/faculty ratio:* 11:1.

Academics *Calendar:* semesters. *Degrees:* associate, bachelor's, master's, and doctoral-research/scholarship. *Special study options:* academic remediation for entering students, accelerated degree program, adult/continuing educa-tion programs, advanced placement credit, distance learning, double majors, honors programs, independent study, internships, off-campus study, part-time degree program, services for LD students, student-designed majors, study abroad, summer session for credit. *Unusual degree programs:* 3-2 engineering with Purdue University.

Computers on Campus 250 computers/terminals are available on campus for general student use. Students can access the following: campus intranet, computer help desk, free student e-mail accounts, online (class) grades, online (class) registration, online (class) schedules, microcomputer software. Campuswide network is available. 100% of college-owned or -operated housing units are wired for high-speed Internet access. Wireless service is available via entire campus.

Student Life *Housing:* on-campus residence required through junior year. *Options:* men-only, women-only. Campus housing is university owned. Freshman campus housing is guaranteed. *Activities and organizations:* drama/theater group, student-run newspaper, radio station, choral group, Adult and Continuing Education Students Association, Multicultural Student Union, Campus Ministries. *Campus security:* 24-hour emergency response devices and patrols, student patrols, late-night transport/escort service, controlled dormitory access, 24-hour crime line. *Student services:* health clinic, personal/psychological counseling.

Athletics Member NCAA. All Division III. *Intercollegiate sports:* baseball M, basketball M/W, cross-country running M/W, football M, golf M/W, soccer M/W, softball W, tennis M/W, track and field M/W, volleyball W. *Intramural sports:* badminton M/W, basketball M/W, cheerleading M(c)/W(c), rugby M(c), soccer M/W, softball M/W, tennis M/W, volleyball M/W.

Standardized Tests *Required:* SAT or ACT (for admission).

Costs (2011–12) *Comprehensive fee:* $33,170 includes full-time tuition ($24,540), mandatory fees ($70), and room and board ($8560). Part-time tuition: $1023 per semester hour. Part-time tuition and fees vary according to course load. *College room only:* $5480. Room and board charges vary according to board plan and housing facility. *Payment plan:* installment. *Waivers:* employees or children of employees.

Financial Aid Of all full-time matriculated undergraduates who enrolled in 2008, 1,740 applied for aid, 1,572 were judged to have need, 346 had their need fully met. 1,500 Federal Work-Study jobs (averaging $2200). In 2008, 356 non-need-based awards were made. *Average percent of need met:* 93%. *Average financial aid package:* $20,553. *Average need-based loan:* $1651.

Average need-based gift aid: $13,414. *Average non-need-based aid:* $9500. *Average indebtedness upon graduation:* $25,401.

Applying *Options:* electronic application, deferred entrance. *Application fee:* $25. *Required:* high school transcript, minimum 2 GPA, 2 letters of recommendation, lifestyle statement. *Required for some:* interview. *Recommended:* essay or personal statement. *Application deadlines:* 7/1 (freshmen), rolling (transfers). *Notification:* 9/1 (freshmen), continuous until 9/1 (transfers).

Freshman Application Contact Mr. Joe Davis, Director of Admissions, Anderson University, 1100 East 5th Street, Anderson, IN 46012-3495. *Phone:* 765-641-4076. *Toll-free phone:* 800-421-3014 (in-state); 800-428-6414 (out-of-state). *Fax:* 765-641-3851. *E-mail:* info@anderson.edu. *Web site:* http://www.anderson.edu/.

The Art Institute of Indianapolis
Indianapolis, Indiana

- **Proprietary** 4-year, part of Education Management Corporation
- **Suburban** campus
- **Coed**

Academics *Degrees:* certificates, associate, and bachelor's.

Costs (2010–11) *Tuition:* Tuition cost varies by program. Prospective students should contact the school for current tuition costs. Other charges include a starting kit for all first-quarter students. Kits vary in price, depending on the program of study.

Freshman Application Contact The Art Institute of Indianapolis, 3500 Depauw Boulevard, Suite 1010, Indianapolis, IN 46268. *Phone:* 317-613-4800. *Toll-free phone:* 866-441-9031. *Web site:* http://www.artinstitutes.edu/indianapolis/.

See page 1044 for the College Close-Up.

Ball State University
Muncie, Indiana

- **State-supported** university, founded 1918
- **Suburban** 1140-acre campus with easy access to Indianapolis
- **Endowment** $141.0 million
- **Coed** 18,127 undergraduate students, 93% full-time, 53% women, 47% men
- **Moderately difficult** entrance level, 65% of applicants were admitted

Undergraduates 16,868 full-time, 1,259 part-time. Students come from 50 states and territories; 70 other countries; 11% are from out of state; 7% Black or African American, non-Hispanic/Latino; 2% Hispanic/Latino; 0.7% Asian, non-Hispanic/Latino; 0.1% Native Hawaiian or other Pacific Islander, non-Hispanic/Latino; 0.3% American Indian or Alaska Native, non-Hispanic/Latino; 2% Two or more races, non-Hispanic/Latino; 2% Race/ethnicity unknown; 2% international; 4% transferred in; 42% live on campus. *Retention:* 80% of full-time freshmen returned.

Freshman *Admission:* 17,481 applied, 11,298 admitted, 3,882 enrolled. *Average high school GPA:* 3.33. *Test scores:* SAT critical reading scores over 500: 69%; SAT math scores over 500: 70%; SAT writing scores over 500: 59%; ACT scores over 18: 98%; SAT critical reading scores over 600: 19%; SAT math scores over 600: 21%; SAT writing scores over 600: 15%; ACT scores over 24: 28%; SAT critical reading scores over 700: 2%; SAT math scores over 700: 2%; SAT writing scores over 700: 1%; ACT scores over 30: 3%.

Faculty *Total:* 1,207, 79% full-time, 65% with terminal degrees. *Student/faculty ratio:* 18:1.

Academics *Calendar:* semesters. *Degrees:* associate, bachelor's, master's, doctoral-other, doctoral-professional, doctoral-research/scholarship, post-master's, and postbachelor's certificates. *Special study options:* accelerated degree program, adult/continuing education programs, advanced placement credit, cooperative education, distance learning, double majors, English as a second language, external degree program, freshman honors college, honors programs, independent study, internships, off-campus study, part-time degree program, services for LD students, student-designed majors, study abroad, summer session for credit. *ROTC:* Army (b). *Unusual degree programs:* 3-2 engineering with Purdue University, Tri-State University.

Computers on Campus 865 computers/terminals and 28,303 ports are available on campus for general student use. Students can access the following: campus intranet, computer help desk, free student e-mail accounts, online (class) grades, online (class) registration, online (class) schedules, room reservations, testing and test results, manage and pay tuition, order/buy textbooks, request room repairs, order transcripts, manage meal plan, manage and prepay long distance service, undergraduate degree progress report. Campuswide network is available. 100% of college-owned or -operated housing units are wired for high-speed Internet access. Wireless service is available via entire campus.

Student Life *Housing:* on-campus residence required for freshman year. *Options:* coed, men-only, women-only, disabled students. Campus housing is university owned. Freshman campus housing is guaranteed. *Activities and organizations:* drama/theater group, student-run newspaper, radio and televi-

sion station, choral group, marching band, Epsilon Sigma Alpha International, Student Council for Exceptional Children, American Advertising Federation, Excellence in Leadership (EIL), Student Voluntary Services, national fraternities, national sororities. *Campus security:* 24-hour emergency response devices and patrols, late-night transport/escort service, controlled dormitory access. *Student services:* health clinic, personal/psychological counseling, women's center, legal services.

Athletics Member NCAA. All Division I except football (Division I-A). *Intercollegiate sports:* baseball M(s)/W(c), basketball M(s)/W(s), bowling M(c)/W(c), cheerleading M/W, cross-country running W(s), equestrian sports M(c)/W(c), fencing M(c)/W(c), field hockey W(s), golf M(s)/W(s), gymnastics W(s), lacrosse M(c)/W(c), racquetball M(c)/W(c), rock climbing M(c)/W(c), rugby M(c)/W(c), soccer M(c)/W(s), softball W(s), swimming and diving M(s)/W(s), tennis M(s)/W(s), track and field W(s), ultimate Frisbee M(c)/W(c), volleyball M(s)/W(s), water polo M(c)/W(c), wrestling M(c). *Intramural sports:* badminton M/W, basketball M/W, bowling M/W, golf M/W, racquetball M/W, soccer M/W, softball M/W, swimming and diving M/W, tennis M/W, track and field M/W, ultimate Frisbee M/W, volleyball M/W.

Standardized Tests *Required for some:* SAT or ACT (for admission).

Costs (2010–11) *Tuition:* state resident $7508 full-time, $289 per credit hour part-time; nonresident $20,960 full-time, $771 per credit hour part-time. Full-time tuition and fees vary according to course level, program, and reciprocity agreements. Part-time tuition and fees vary according to course level, course load, and reciprocity agreements. *Required fees:* $706 full-time. *Room and board:* $8208. Room and board charges vary according to board plan and housing facility. *Payment plan:* installment. *Waivers:* senior citizens and employees or children of employees.

Financial Aid Of all full-time matriculated undergraduates who enrolled in 2009, 13,860 applied for aid, 11,250 were judged to have need, 2,268 had their need fully met. 794 Federal Work-Study jobs (averaging $2235). In 2009, 1078 non-need-based awards were made. *Average percent of need met:* 56%. *Average financial aid package:* $9849. *Average need-based loan:* $4203. *Average need-based gift aid:* $6130. *Average non-need-based aid:* $6525. *Average indebtedness upon graduation:* $24,121.

Applying *Options:* electronic application, deferred entrance. *Application fee:* $50. *Required:* high school transcript. *Required for some:* essay or personal statement. *Application deadlines:* 8/15 (freshmen), rolling (transfers). *Notification:* continuous (freshmen), continuous (transfers).

Freshman Application Contact Ball State University, 2000 West University Avenue, Muncie, IN 47306-1099. *Phone:* 765-285-8300. *Toll-free phone:* 800-482-4BSU. *Web site:* http://www.bsu.edu/.

Bethel College
Mishawaka, Indiana

- **Independent** comprehensive, founded 1947, affiliated with Missionary Church
- **Suburban** 80-acre campus
- **Endowment** $7.5 million
- **Coed** 1,925 undergraduate students, 78% full-time, 66% women, 34% men
- **Minimally difficult** entrance level, 72% of applicants were admitted

Undergraduates 1,511 full-time, 414 part-time. Students come from 31 states and territories; 16 other countries; 25% are from out of state; 12% Black or African American, non-Hispanic/Latino; 3% Hispanic/Latino; 0.4% Asian, non-Hispanic/Latino; 0.3% Native Hawaiian or other Pacific Islander, non-Hispanic/Latino; 0.6% American Indian or Alaska Native, non-Hispanic/Latino; 1% Two or more races, non-Hispanic/Latino; 2% international; 13% transferred in; 44% live on campus. *Retention:* 79% of full-time freshmen returned.

Freshmen *Admission:* 1,010 applied, 732 admitted, 278 enrolled. *Average high school GPA:* 3.32. *Test scores:* SAT critical reading scores over 500: 56%; SAT math scores over 500: 58%; SAT writing scores over 500: 56%; ACT scores over 18: 87%; SAT critical reading scores over 600: 16%; SAT math scores over 600: 18%; SAT writing scores over 600: 21%; ACT scores over 24: 36%; SAT critical reading scores over 700: 2%; SAT math scores over 700: 2%; SAT writing scores over 700: 1%; ACT scores over 30: 4%.

Faculty *Total:* 222, 40% full-time, 27% with terminal degrees. *Student/faculty ratio:* 13:1.

Academics *Calendar:* semesters. *Degrees:* associate, bachelor's, and master's. *Special study options:* academic remediation for entering students, accelerated degree program, adult/continuing education programs, advanced placement credit, double majors, independent study, internships, off-campus study, part-time degree program, services for LD students, student-designed majors, study abroad, summer session for credit. *ROTC:* Army (c), Air Force (c). *Unusual degree programs:* 3-2 engineering with University of Notre Dame, Tri-State University.

Computers on Campus 160 computers/terminals are available on campus for general student use. Students can access the following: computer help desk, free student e-mail accounts, online (class) grades, online (class) registration, online (class) schedules. Campuswide network is available. 100% of college-owned or -operated housing units are wired for high-speed Internet access. Wireless service is available via entire campus.

Student Life *Housing:* on-campus residence required through sophomore year. *Options:* men-only, women-only. Campus housing is university owned. *Activities and organizations:* drama/theater group, student-run newspaper, radio station, choral group, Task Force Mission Teams, Student Council, Center for Community Service, Fellowship of Christian Athletes. *Campus security:* 24-hour emergency response devices and patrols, late-night transport/escort service, controlled dormitory access. *Student services:* health clinic, personal/psychological counseling.

Athletics Member NAIA, NCCAA. *Intercollegiate sports:* baseball M(s), basketball M(s)/W(s), cheerleading M(s)/W(s), cross-country running M(s)/W(s), golf M(s)/W(s), soccer M(s)/W(s), softball W(s), tennis M(s)/W(s), track and field M(s)/W(s), volleyball W(s). *Intramural sports:* badminton M/W, baseball M, basketball M/W, soccer M/W, softball M/W, table tennis M/W, tennis M/W, ultimate Frisbee M/W, volleyball M/W.

Standardized Tests *Required:* SAT or ACT (for admission).

Costs (2011–12) *One-time required fee:* $600. *Comprehensive fee:* $30,100 includes full-time tuition ($23,030) and room and board ($7070). Full-time tuition and fees vary according to program. Part-time tuition: $730 per hour. Part-time tuition and fees vary according to course load and program. *College room only:* $3560. Room and board charges vary according to board plan and housing facility. *Payment plan:* installment. *Waivers:* employees or children of employees.

Financial Aid Of all full-time matriculated undergraduates who enrolled in 2009, 1,347 applied for aid, 1,184 were judged to have need. 674 Federal Work-Study jobs (averaging $2160). 304 state and other part-time jobs (averaging $2200). In 2009, 174 non-need-based awards were made. *Average financial aid package:* $18,230. *Average need-based loan:* $5330. *Average need-based gift aid:* $8140. *Average non-need-based aid:* $6240. *Average indebtedness upon graduation:* $17,800.

Applying *Options:* electronic application, early admission, deferred entrance. *Application fee:* $25. *Required:* essay or personal statement, high school transcript, minimum 2 GPA, 1 letter of recommendation. *Recommended:* minimum 2.5 GPA, interview. *Application deadlines:* 8/15 (freshmen), 8/15 (transfers). *Notification:* continuous (freshmen), continuous (transfers).

Freshman Application Contact Ms. Krista Wong, Director of Admission, Bethel College, 1001 Bethel Circle, Mishwawaka, IN 46545. *Phone:* 574-807-7600. *Toll-free phone:* 800-422-4101. *Fax:* 574-807-7650. *E-mail:* admissions@bethelcollege.edu. *Web site:* http://www.bethelcollege.edu/.

Brown Mackie College–Fort Wayne

Fort Wayne, Indiana

- **Proprietary** primarily 2-year, part of Education Management Corporation
- **Coed**

Academics *Calendar:* quarters. *Degrees:* certificates, diplomas, associate, and bachelor's.

Costs (2010–11) *Tuition:* Tuition varies by program. Students should contact Brown Mackie College for tuition information.

Freshman Application Contact Brown Mackie College–Fort Wayne, 3000 East Coliseum Boulevard, Fort Wayne, IN 46805. *Phone:* 260-484-4400. *Toll-free phone:* 866-433-2289. *Web site:* http://www.brownmackie.edu/fortwayne/.

See page 1142 for the College Close-Up.

Brown Mackie College–Indianapolis

Indianapolis, Indiana

- **Proprietary** primarily 2-year, part of Education Management Corporation
- **Coed**

Academics *Degrees:* certificates, diplomas, associate, and bachelor's.

Costs (2010–11) *Tuition:* Tuition varies by program. Students should contact Brown Mackie College for tuition information.

Freshman Application Contact Brown Mackie College–Indianapolis, 1200 North Meridian Street, Suite 100, Indianapolis, IN 46204. *Phone:* 317-554-8301. *Toll-free phone:* 866-255-0279. *Web site:* http://www.brownmackie.edu/indianapolis/.

See page 1146 for the College Close-Up.

Brown Mackie College–Merrillville

Merrillville, Indiana

- **Proprietary** primarily 2-year, founded 1890, part of Education Management Corporation
- **Small-town** campus
- **Coed**

Academics *Calendar:* quarters. *Degrees:* certificates, diplomas, associate, and bachelor's.

Costs (2010–11) *Tuition:* Tuition varies by program. Students should contact Brown Mackie College for tuition information.

Freshman Application Contact Brown Mackie College–Merrillville, 1000 East 80th Place, Suite 205S, Merrillville, IN 46410. *Phone:* 219-769-3321. *Toll-free phone:* 800-258-3321. *Web site:* http://www.brownmackie.edu/merrillville/.

See page 1150 for the College Close-Up.

Brown Mackie College–Michigan City

Michigan City, Indiana

- **Proprietary** primarily 2-year, part of Education Management Corporation
- **Rural** campus
- **Coed**

Academics *Calendar:* quarters. *Degrees:* certificates, diplomas, associate, and bachelor's.

Costs (2010–11) *Tuition:* Tuition varies by program. Students should contact Brown Mackie College for tuition information.

Freshman Application Contact Brown Mackie College–Michigan City, 325 East US Highway 20, Michigan City, IN 46360. *Phone:* 219-877-3100. *Toll-free phone:* 800-519-2416. *Web site:* http://www.brownmackie.edu/michigancity/.

See page 1154 for the College Close-Up.

Brown Mackie College–South Bend

South Bend, Indiana

- **Proprietary** primarily 2-year, founded 1882, part of Education Management Corporation
- **Urban** campus
- **Coed, primarily women**

Academics *Calendar:* quarters. *Degrees:* certificates, associate, and bachelor's.

Costs (2010–11) *Tuition:* Tuition varies by program. Students should contact Brown Mackie College for tuition information.

Freshman Application Contact Brown Mackie College–South Bend, 3454 Douglas Road, South Bend, IN 46635. *Phone:* 574-237-0774. *Toll-free phone:* 800-743-2447. *Web site:* http://www.brownmackie.edu/southbend/.

See page 1164 for the College Close-Up.

Butler University

Indianapolis, Indiana

- **Independent** comprehensive, founded 1855
- **Urban** 290-acre campus
- **Endowment** $133.0 million
- **Coed** 3,861 undergraduate students, 99% full-time, 59% women, 41% men
- **Moderately difficult** entrance level, 73% of applicants were admitted

Undergraduates 3,815 full-time, 46 part-time. Students come from 46 states and territories; 44 other countries; 43% are from out of state; 4% Black or African American, non-Hispanic/Latino; 3% Hispanic/Latino; 2% Asian, non-Hispanic/Latino; 0.2% American Indian or Alaska Native, non-Hispanic/Latino; 0.9% Two or more races, non-Hispanic/Latino; 5% Race/ethnicity unknown; 2% international; 3% transferred in; 68% live on campus. *Retention:* 89% of full-time freshmen returned.

Freshmen *Admission:* 6,760 applied, 4,946 admitted, 1,049 enrolled. *Average high school GPA:* 3.69. *Test scores:* SAT critical reading scores over 500: 85%; SAT math scores over 500: 87%; SAT writing scores over 500: 80%; ACT scores over 18: 100%; SAT critical reading scores over 600: 38%; SAT math scores over 600: 46%; SAT writing scores over 600: 30%; ACT scores over 24: 84%; SAT critical reading scores over 700: 3%; SAT math scores over 700: 3%; ACT scores over 30: 25%.

Faculty *Total:* 479, 69% full-time, 61% with terminal degrees. *Student/faculty ratio:* 11:1.

Academics *Calendar:* semesters. *Degrees:* associate, bachelor's, master's, and doctoral-professional. *Special study options:* adult/continuing education programs, advanced placement credit, cooperative education, double majors, honors programs, independent study, internships, off-campus study, part-time degree program, services for LD students, student-designed majors, study abroad, summer session for credit. *ROTC:* Army (b), Air Force (c). *Unusual degree programs:* 3-2 engineering with Indiana University-Purdue University Indianapolis.

Computers on Campus 450 computers/terminals are available on campus for general student use. Students can access the following: campus intranet, computer help desk, free student e-mail accounts, online (class) grades, online (class) registration, online (class) schedules. Campuswide network is available. 100% of college-owned or -operated housing units are wired for high-speed Internet access. Wireless service is available via entire campus.

Student Life *Housing:* on-campus residence required through junior year. *Options:* coed, women-only. Campus housing is university owned. Freshman campus housing is guaranteed. *Activities and organizations:* drama/theater group, student-run newspaper, television station, choral group, marching band, University YMCA, Student Government Association, Academic Service Honoraries, Alpha Phi Omega, Mortar Board, national fraternities, national sororities. *Campus security:* 24-hour emergency response devices and patrols, late-night transport/escort service, controlled dormitory access. *Student services:* health clinic, personal/psychological counseling.

Athletics Member NCAA. All Division I except football (Division III). *Intercollegiate sports:* baseball M(s), basketball M(s)/W(s), crew M(c)/W(c), cross-country running M(s)/W(s), football M, golf M(s)/W(s), ice hockey M(c), rugby M(c), soccer M(s)/W(s), softball W(s), swimming and diving W, tennis M(s)/W(s), track and field M/W, volleyball W(s). *Intramural sports:* badminton M/W, baseball M, basketball M/W, bowling M/W, football M, soccer M/W, softball M/W, swimming and diving M/W, table tennis M/W, tennis M/W, track and field M/W, volleyball M/W, weight lifting M/W.

Standardized Tests *Required:* SAT or ACT (for admission).

Costs (2010–11) *Comprehensive fee:* $40,688 includes full-time tuition ($29,740), mandatory fees ($818), and room and board ($10,130). Full-time tuition and fees vary according to course load, degree level, and program. Part-time tuition: $1250 per credit hour. Part-time tuition and fees vary according to course load, degree level, and program. *College room only:* $4960. Room and board charges vary according to housing facility. *Payment plan:* installment. *Waivers:* employees or children of employees.

Financial Aid Of all full-time matriculated undergraduates who enrolled in 2009, 3,696 applied for aid, 2,761 were judged to have need, 369 had their need fully met. 331 Federal Work-Study jobs (averaging $759). In 2009, 831 non-need-based awards were made. *Average percent of need met:* 74%. *Average financial aid package:* $21,971. *Average need-based loan:* $5411. *Average need-based gift aid:* $16,943. *Average non-need-based aid:* $11,452. *Average indebtedness upon graduation:* $30,581.

Applying *Options:* electronic application, early action, deferred entrance. *Application fee:* $35. *Required:* essay or personal statement, high school transcript. *Required for some:* audition. *Application deadlines:* rolling (freshmen), 8/15 (transfers), 11/15 (early action). *Notification:* continuous (freshmen), continuous (transfers), 12/17 (early action).

Freshman Application Contact Mr. Scott Ham, Director of Admissions, Butler University, 4600 Sunset Avenue, Indianapolis, IN 46208-3485. *Phone:* 317-940-8100. *Toll-free phone:* 888-940-8100. *Fax:* 317-940-8150. *E-mail:* admission@butler.edu. *Web site:* http://www.butler.edu/.

See page 1174 for the College Close-Up.

Calumet College of Saint Joseph
Whiting, Indiana

- **Independent Roman Catholic** comprehensive, founded 1951
- **Urban** 25-acre campus with easy access to Chicago
- **Endowment** $3.8 million
- **Coed** 1,115 undergraduate students, 50% full-time, 48% women, 52% men
- **Noncompetitive** entrance level, 51% of applicants were admitted

Undergraduates 561 full-time, 554 part-time. Students come from 2 states and territories; 1% are from out of state; 11% transferred in. *Retention:* 69% of full-time freshmen returned.

Freshmen *Admission:* 470 applied, 240 admitted, 156 enrolled. *Average high school GPA:* 2.49. *Test scores:* SAT critical reading scores over 500: 8%; SAT math scores over 500: 19%; ACT scores over 18: 50%; SAT critical reading scores over 600: 1%; SAT math scores over 600: 1%; ACT scores over 24: 3%.

Faculty *Total:* 126, 26% full-time, 34% with terminal degrees. *Student/faculty ratio:* 12:1.

Academics *Calendar:* semesters. *Degrees:* certificates, associate, bachelor's, master's, and postbachelor's certificates. *Special study options:* academic remediation for entering students, accelerated degree program, adult/continuing education programs, advanced placement credit, cooperative education, distance learning, double majors, external degree program, independent study, internships, part-time degree program, services for LD students, summer session for credit.

Computers on Campus 132 computers/terminals are available on campus for general student use. Students can access the following: computer help desk, free student e-mail accounts, online (class) grades, online (class) registration, online (class) schedules. Campuswide network is available. Wireless service is available via libraries, student centers.

Student Life *Housing:* college housing not available. *Activities and organizations:* drama/theater group, student-run newspaper, student government, Los Amigos Hispanic Club, Criminal Justice Club, Drama Club, Black Student Union. *Campus security:* day and night security. *Student services:* personal/psychological counseling.

Athletics Member NAIA. *Intercollegiate sports:* baseball M, basketball M/W, bowling M/W, cross-country running M/W, golf M/W, soccer M/W, softball W, tennis M/W, track and field M/W, volleyball W.

Standardized Tests *Required for some:* ACT COMPASS. *Recommended:* SAT or ACT (for admission).

Costs (2010–11) *Tuition:* $14,000 full-time, $440 per credit hour part-time. Full-time tuition and fees vary according to course load, degree level, and program. Part-time tuition and fees vary according to course load, degree level, and program. *Required fees:* $200 full-time, $100 per term part-time. *Payment plan:* installment. *Waivers:* children of alumni, senior citizens, and employees or children of employees.

Financial Aid Of all full-time matriculated undergraduates who enrolled in 2009, 588 applied for aid, 492 were judged to have need, 21 had their need fully met. 16 Federal Work-Study jobs (averaging $1097). 1 state and other part-time job (averaging $1365). In 2009, 2 non-need-based awards were made. *Average percent of need met:* 72%. *Average financial aid package:* $11,510. *Average need-based loan:* $3591. *Average need-based gift aid:* $7300. *Average non-need-based aid:* $2400. *Average indebtedness upon graduation:* $22,534.

Applying *Options:* electronic application, deferred entrance. *Required:* high school transcript. *Required for some:* essay or personal statement, interview. *Recommended:* minimum 2 GPA, interview. *Application deadlines:* rolling (freshmen), rolling (out-of-state freshmen), rolling (transfers). *Notification:* continuous (transfers).

Freshman Application Contact Miss Rebecca Leevey, Assistant Director of Admissions, Calumet College of Saint Joseph, 2400 New York Avenue, Whiting, IN 46394. *Phone:* 219-473-4215 Ext. 218. *Toll-free phone:* 877-700-9100. *Fax:* 219-473-4259. *E-mail:* admissions@ccsj.edu. *Web site:* http://www.ccsj.edu/.

Crossroads Bible College

Indianapolis, Indiana

- **Independent Baptist** 4-year, founded 1980
- **Urban** 6-acre campus with easy access to Indianapolis
- **Coed** 254 undergraduate students, 56% full-time, 55% women, 45% men
- **Noncompetitive** entrance level, 95% of applicants were admitted

Undergraduates 141 full-time, 113 part-time. Students come from 9 states and territories; 8 other countries; 9% are from out of state; 90% transferred in. *Retention:* 45% of full-time freshmen returned.

Freshmen *Admission:* 42 applied, 40 admitted, 30 enrolled.

Faculty *Total:* 37, 22% full-time, 19% with terminal degrees. *Student/faculty ratio:* 7:1.

Academics *Calendar:* semesters. *Degrees:* certificates, associate, and bachelor's. *Special study options:* academic remediation for entering students, accelerated degree program, adult/continuing education programs, cooperative education, distance learning, double majors, external degree program, independent study, internships, part-time degree program, summer session for credit.

Computers on Campus 15 computers/terminals are available on campus for general student use. Students can access the following: free student e-mail accounts, online (class) registration. Campuswide network is available. Wireless service is available via classrooms, computer centers, computer labs, learning centers, libraries, student centers.

Student Life *Housing options:* men-only, women-only. Campus housing is leased by the school. Freshman campus housing is guaranteed. *Activities and organizations:* choral group. *Campus security:* 24-hour emergency response devices, student patrols, late-night transport/escort service. *Student services:* personal/psychological counseling.

Standardized Tests *Recommended:* SAT and SAT Subject Tests or ACT (for admission).

Costs (2011–12) *Tuition:* $9480 full-time. *Required fees:* $370 full-time. *Room only:* $3400. *Payment plan:* installment. *Waivers:* employees or children of employees.

Financial Aid *Financial aid deadline:* 6/30.

Applying *Options:* electronic application, deferred entrance. *Application fee:* $10. *Required:* essay or personal statement, high school transcript. *Required for some:* interview. *Application deadlines:* rolling (freshmen), rolling (out-of-state freshmen), rolling (transfers). *Notification:* continuous (freshmen), continuous (out-of-state freshmen), continuous (transfers).

Freshman Application Contact Michael Garrison, Admissions Counselor, Crossroads Bible College, 601 North Shortridge Road, Indianapolis, IN 46219. *Phone:* 317-352-8736 Ext. 232. *Toll-free phone:* 800-273-2224 Ext. 230. *E-mail:* admissions@crossroads.edu. *Web site:* http://www.crossroads.edu/.

DePauw University

Greencastle, Indiana

- **Independent** 4-year, founded 1837, affiliated with United Methodist Church
- **Small-town** 655-acre campus with easy access to Indianapolis
- **Coed** 2,390 undergraduate students, 99% full-time, 57% women, 43% men
- **Moderately difficult** entrance level

Undergraduates 2,372 full-time, 18 part-time. 57% are from out of state; 7% Black or African American, non-Hispanic/Latino; 4% Hispanic/Latino; 3% Asian, non-Hispanic/Latino; 0.2% American Indian or Alaska Native, non-Hispanic/Latino; 3% Two or more races, non-Hispanic/Latino; 0.8% Race/ethnicity unknown; 10% international; 0.6% transferred in; 98% live on campus. *Retention:* 90% of full-time freshmen returned.

Freshmen *Admission:* 609 enrolled. *Average high school GPA:* 3.56. *Test scores:* SAT critical reading scores over 500: 85%; SAT math scores over 500: 89%; SAT writing scores over 500: 86%; ACT scores over 18: 99%; SAT critical reading scores over 600: 40%; SAT math scores over 600: 51%; SAT writing scores over 600: 43%; ACT scores over 24: 78%; SAT critical reading scores over 700: 8%; SAT math scores over 700: 19%; SAT writing scores over 700: 9%; ACT scores over 30: 24%.

Faculty *Total:* 282, 79% full-time, 88% with terminal degrees. *Student/faculty ratio:* 10:1.

Academics *Calendar:* 4-1-4. *Degree:* bachelor's. *Special study options:* advanced placement credit, double majors, honors programs, independent study, internships, off-campus study, part-time degree program, services for LD students, student-designed majors, study abroad. *ROTC:* Army (c), Air Force (c). *Unusual degree programs:* 3-2 engineering with Columbia University, Washington University in St. Louis.

Computers on Campus Students can access the following: online (class) registration. Campuswide network is available.

Student Life *Housing:* on-campus residence required through senior year. *Options:* coed, disabled students. Campus housing is university owned. Freshman campus housing is guaranteed. *Activities and organizations:* drama/theater group, student-run newspaper, radio and television station, choral group, national fraternities, national sororities. *Campus security:* 24-hour emergency response devices and patrols, student patrols, late-night transport/escort service, controlled dormitory access. *Student services:* health clinic, personal/psychological counseling, women's center.

Athletics Member NCAA. All Division III. *Intercollegiate sports:* baseball M, basketball M/W, cheerleading M(c)/W(c), crew M(c)/W(c), cross-country running M/W, field hockey W, football M, golf M/W, rugby M(c), soccer M/W, softball W, swimming and diving M/W, tennis M/W, track and field M/W, volleyball W. *Intramural sports:* badminton M/W, basketball M/W, bowling M/W, football M/W, golf M, racquetball M/W, soccer M/W, softball M/W, table tennis M/W, tennis M/W, ultimate Frisbee M/W, volleyball M/W.

Standardized Tests *Required:* SAT or ACT (for admission).

Costs (2011–12) *Comprehensive fee:* $44,085 includes full-time tuition ($34,440), mandatory fees ($465), and room and board ($9180). Part-time tuition: $1076 per credit hour. *Room and board:* Room and board charges vary according to board plan. *Payment plan:* installment. *Waivers:* employees or children of employees.

Financial Aid Of all full-time matriculated undergraduates who enrolled in 2009, 1,541 applied for aid, 1,347 were judged to have need, 369 had their need fully met. In 2009, 977 non-need-based awards were made. *Average percent of need met:* 87%. *Average financial aid package:* $28,549. *Average need-based loan:* $4043. *Average need-based gift aid:* $24,625. *Average non-need-based aid:* $15,592. *Average indebtedness upon graduation:* $23,778.

Applying *Options:* electronic application, early admission, early decision, early action, deferred entrance. *Application fee:* $40. *Required:* essay or personal statement, high school transcript, 1 letter of recommendation. *Recommended:* interview. *Application deadlines:* 2/1 (freshmen), 3/1 (transfers), 12/1 (early action). *Early decision deadline:* 11/1. *Notification:* 4/1 (freshmen), 4/1 (transfers), 1/1 (early decision), 2/15 (early action).

Freshman Application Contact Earl Macam, Director of Admission, DePauw University, 313 South Locust Street, Greencastle, IN 46135. *Phone:* 765-658-4006. *Toll-free phone:* 800-447-2495. *Fax:* 765-658-4007. *E-mail:* emacam@depauw.edu. *Web site:* http://www.depauw.edu/.

DeVry University
Indianapolis, Indiana

- **Proprietary** comprehensive, part of DeVry University
- **Coed**
- **Minimally difficult** entrance level

Faculty *Student/faculty ratio:* 18:1.

Academics *Calendar:* semesters. *Degrees:* associate, bachelor's, and master's.

Costs (2010–11) *Tuition:* $14,766 full-time, $580 per credit hour part-time. Full-time tuition and fees vary according to course load. Part-time tuition and fees vary according to course load. *Required fees:* $60 full-time, $30 per term part-time. *Payment plans:* installment, deferred payment.

Financial Aid *Of all full-time matriculated undergraduates who enrolled in 2007,* 19 applied for aid, 19 were judged to have need. *In 2007,* 1 non-need-based awards were made. *Average percent of need met:* 42. *Average financial aid package:* $14,132. *Average need-based loan:* $10,993. *Average need-based gift aid:* $6728. *Average non-need-based aid:* $20,854.

Applying *Options:* electronic application, deferred entrance. *Application fee:* $50. *Required:* high school transcript, interview.

Freshman Application Contact DeVry University, 9100 Keystone Crossing, Suite 350, Indianapolis, IN 46240-2158. *Web site:* http://www.devry.edu/.

DeVry University
Merrillville, Indiana

Admissions Office Contact DeVry University, Twin Towers, 1000 East 80th Place, Suite 222 Mall, Merrillville, IN 46410-5673. *Web site:* http://www.devry.edu/.

Earlham College
Richmond, Indiana

- **Independent** comprehensive, founded 1847, affiliated with Society of Friends
- **Small-town** 800-acre campus with easy access to Cincinnati, Indianapolis, and Dayton
- **Endowment** $276.2 million
- **Coed** 1,181 undergraduate students, 99% full-time, 55% women, 45% men
- **Very difficult** entrance level, 74% of applicants were admitted

Undergraduates 1,172 full-time, 9 part-time. Students come from 42 states and territories; 81 other countries; 76% are from out of state; 8% Black or African American, non-Hispanic/Latino; 3% Hispanic/Latino; 3% Asian, non-Hispanic/Latino; 0.6% American Indian or Alaska Native, non-Hispanic/Latino; 8% Race/ethnicity unknown; 16% international; 1% transferred in; 95% live on campus. *Retention:* 83% of full-time freshmen returned.

Freshmen *Admission:* 1,804 applied, 1,334 admitted, 301 enrolled. *Average high school GPA:* 3.5. *Test scores:* SAT critical reading scores over 500: 82%; SAT math scores over 500: 82%; SAT writing scores over 500: 78%; ACT scores over 18: 97%; SAT critical reading scores over 600: 61%; SAT math scores over 600: 45%; SAT writing scores over 600: 52%; ACT scores over 24: 75%; SAT critical reading scores over 700: 22%; SAT math scores over 700: 10%; SAT writing scores over 700: 10%; ACT scores over 30: 29%.

Faculty *Total:* 101, 92% full-time, 92% with terminal degrees. *Student/faculty ratio:* 12:1.

Academics *Calendar:* semesters. *Degrees:* bachelor's, master's, and doctoral-professional. *Special study options:* accelerated degree program, advanced placement credit, double majors, English as a second language, independent study, internships, off-campus study, services for LD students, student-designed majors, study abroad. *Unusual degree programs:* 3-2 engineering with Columbia University, University of Michigan, Rensselaer Polytechnic Institute; forestry with Duke University; nursing with Case Western Reserve University, Washington University in St. Louis, Emory University, Columbia University.

Computers on Campus 175 computers/terminals and 30 ports are available on campus for general student use. Students can access the following: campus intranet, computer help desk, free student e-mail accounts, online (class) grades, online (class) registration, online (class) schedules. Campuswide network is available. 100% of college-owned or -operated housing units are wired for high-speed Internet access. Wireless service is available via classrooms, computer centers, computer labs, learning centers, libraries, student centers.

Student Life *Housing:* on-campus residence required through senior year. *Options:* coed, men-only, women-only, disabled students. Campus housing is university owned. Freshman campus housing is guaranteed. *Activities and organizations:* drama/theater group, student-run newspaper, radio station, choral group, Gospel Revelations Chorus, Dance Alloy, club sports, student government, Black Student Union. *Campus security:* 24-hour emergency response devices and patrols, student patrols, late-night transport/escort service, con-

trolled dormitory access. *Student services:* health clinic, personal/psychological counseling, women's center.

Athletics Member NCAA. All Division III. *Intercollegiate sports:* baseball M, basketball M/W, cheerleading W(c), cross-country running M/W, equestrian sports W(c), field hockey W, football M, lacrosse M(c)/W(c), rugby M(c)/W(c), soccer M/W, tennis M/W, track and field M/W, ultimate Frisbee M(c)/W(c), volleyball M(c)/W. *Intramural sports:* basketball M/W, bowling M/W, football M, racquetball M/W, soccer M/W.

Standardized Tests *Required:* SAT or ACT (for admission).

Costs (2010–11) *Comprehensive fee:* $44,094 includes full-time tuition ($35,920), mandatory fees ($774), and room and board ($7400). Part-time tuition: $1197 per credit. *College room only:* $3750. Room and board charges vary according to board plan. *Payment plans:* tuition prepayment, installment, deferred payment. *Waivers:* employees or children of employees.

Financial Aid Of all full-time matriculated undergraduates who enrolled in 2008, 719 applied for aid, 657 were judged to have need, 205 had their need fully met. 494 Federal Work-Study jobs (averaging $2034). 158 state and other part-time jobs (averaging $2176). In 2008, 193 non-need-based awards were made. *Average percent of need met:* 86%. *Average financial aid package:* $30,359. *Average need-based loan:* $4871. *Average need-based gift aid:* $19,965. *Average non-need-based aid:* $7555. *Average indebtedness upon graduation:* $17,573. *Financial aid deadline:* 3/1.

Applying *Options:* electronic application, early admission, early decision, early action, deferred entrance. *Required:* essay or personal statement, high school transcript, minimum 3 GPA, 2 letters of recommendation. *Recommended:* interview. *Application deadlines:* 2/15 (freshmen), 4/1 (transfers), 1/1 (early action). *Early decision deadline:* 12/1. *Notification:* 3/15 (freshmen), 4/15 (transfers), 12/15 (early decision), 2/1 (early action).

Freshman Application Contact Mr. Jeff Rickey, Dean of Admissions and Financial Aid, Earlham College, 801 National Road West, Richmond, IN 47374. *Phone:* 765-983-1600. *Toll-free phone:* 800-327-5426. *Fax:* 765-983-1560. *E-mail:* admission@earlham.edu. *Web site:* http://www.earlham.edu/.

Franklin College
Franklin, Indiana

- **Independent** 4-year, founded 1834, affiliated with American Baptist Churches in the U.S.A.
- **Small-town** 337-acre campus with easy access to Indianapolis
- **Endowment** $73.9 million
- **Coed** 1,106 undergraduate students, 96% full-time, 52% women, 48% men
- **Moderately difficult** entrance level, 56% of applicants were admitted

Undergraduates 1,060 full-time, 46 part-time. Students come from 13 states and territories; 3 other countries; 3% are from out of state; 7% Black or African American, non-Hispanic/Latino; 0.6% Hispanic/Latino; 0.1% Asian, non-Hispanic/Latino; 0.3% American Indian or Alaska Native, non-Hispanic/Latino; 0.4% Two or more races, non-Hispanic/Latino; 9% Race/ethnicity unknown; 2% transferred in; 69% live on campus. *Retention:* 76% of full-time freshmen returned.

Freshmen *Admission:* 2,130 applied, 1,201 admitted, 287 enrolled. *Average high school GPA:* 3.4. *Test scores:* SAT critical reading scores over 500: 50%; SAT math scores over 500: 60%; SAT writing scores over 500: 46%; ACT scores over 18: 91%; SAT critical reading scores over 600: 12%; SAT math scores over 600: 16%; SAT writing scores over 600: 8%; ACT scores over 24: 30%; ACT scores over 30: 3%.

Faculty *Total:* 105, 66% full-time, 61% with terminal degrees. *Student/faculty ratio:* 12:1.

Academics *Calendar:* 4-1-4. *Degree:* bachelor's. *Special study options:* academic remediation for entering students, advanced placement credit, cooperative education, double majors, independent study, internships, off-campus study, part-time degree program, services for LD students, study abroad, summer session for credit. *ROTC:* Army (c). *Unusual degree programs:* 3-2 engineering with Indiana University - Purdue University Indianapolis.

Computers on Campus 150 computers/terminals are available on campus for general student use. Students can access the following: online (class) registration. Campuswide network is available. Wireless service is available via classrooms, computer centers, computer labs, learning centers, libraries, student centers.

Student Life *Housing:* on-campus residence required through junior year. *Options:* coed. Campus housing is university owned. Freshman campus housing is guaranteed. *Activities and organizations:* drama/theater group, student-run newspaper, radio and television station, choral group, FLOW, FC Volunteers, Student Entertainment Board, Student Congress, national fraternities, national sororities. *Campus security:* 24-hour emergency response devices and patrols, late-night transport/escort service. *Student services:* health clinic, personal/psychological counseling.

Athletics Member NCAA. All Division III. *Intercollegiate sports:* baseball M, basketball M/W, cross-country running M/W, football M, golf M/W, soccer

M/W, softball W, tennis M/W, track and field M/W, volleyball W. *Intramural sports:* basketball M/W, softball W, volleyball W.

Standardized Tests *Required:* SAT or ACT (for admission).

Costs (2010–11) *Comprehensive fee:* $31,950 includes full-time tuition ($24,470), mandatory fees ($185), and room and board ($7295). Part-time tuition: $345 per credit hour. Part-time tuition and fees vary according to course load. *College room only:* $4330. Room and board charges vary according to board plan and housing facility. *Payment plan:* installment. *Waivers:* senior citizens and employees or children of employees.

Financial Aid Of all full-time matriculated undergraduates who enrolled in 2008, 1,034 applied for aid, 912 were judged to have need, 144 had their need fully met. 328 Federal Work-Study jobs (averaging $863). 31 state and other part-time jobs (averaging $637). In 2008, 158 non-need-based awards were made. *Average percent of need met:* 81%. *Average financial aid package:* $18,496. *Average need-based loan:* $5051. *Average need-based gift aid:* $14,213. *Average non-need-based aid:* $8197. *Average indebtedness upon graduation:* $29,387.

Applying *Options:* electronic application, deferred entrance. *Application fee:* $30. *Required:* essay or personal statement, high school transcript. *Required for some:* interview. *Application deadline:* rolling (freshmen). *Notification:* continuous (freshmen), continuous (transfers).

Freshman Application Contact Ms. Jacqueline Acosta, Director of Admissions, Franklin College, 101 Branigin Boulevard, Franklin, IN 46131-2623. *Phone:* 317-738-8062. *Toll-free phone:* 800-852-0232. *Fax:* 317-738-8274. *E-mail:* jacosta@franklincollege.edu. *Web site:* http://www.franklincollege.edu/.

See page 1298 for the College Close-Up.

Goshen College
Goshen, Indiana

- **Independent Mennonite** comprehensive, founded 1894
- **Small-town** 135-acre campus
- **Endowment** $72.1 million
- **Coed**
- **Moderately difficult** entrance level

Faculty *Student/faculty ratio:* 11:1.

Academics *Calendar:* semesters. *Degrees:* certificates, bachelor's, and master's.

Student Life *Campus security:* 24-hour emergency response devices and patrols, late-night transport/escort service.

Athletics Member NAIA.

Standardized Tests *Required:* SAT or ACT (for admission).

Costs (2010–11) *Comprehensive fee:* $32,800 includes full-time tuition ($24,500) and room and board ($8300). Full-time tuition and fees vary according to degree level. Part-time tuition: $1020 per credit hour. Part-time tuition and fees vary according to course load and degree level. *College room only:* $4350. Room and board charges vary according to board plan and housing facility.

Financial Aid *Of all full-time matriculated undergraduates who enrolled in 2009,* 744 applied for aid, 680 were judged to have need, 112 had their need fully met. 250 Federal Work-Study jobs (averaging $800). 50 state and other part-time jobs (averaging $1000). *In 2009,* 198 non-need-based awards were made. *Average percent of need met:* 81. *Average financial aid package:* $19,304. *Average need-based loan:* $4423. *Average need-based gift aid:* $15,731. *Average non-need-based aid:* $9879. *Average indebtedness upon graduation:* $19,819.

Applying *Options:* electronic application, deferred entrance. *Application fee:* $25. *Required:* essay or personal statement, high school transcript, minimum 2 GPA, 2 letters of recommendation. *Recommended:* minimum 2.6 GPA, interview, rank in upper 50% of high school class.

Freshman Application Contact Ms. Lynn Jackson, Vice President for Enrollment Management, Goshen College, 1700 South Main Street, Goshen, IN 46526-4794. *Phone:* 574-535-7535. *Toll-free phone:* 800-348-7422. *Fax:* 574-535-7609. *E-mail:* lynnj@goshen.edu. *Web site:* http://www.goshen.edu/

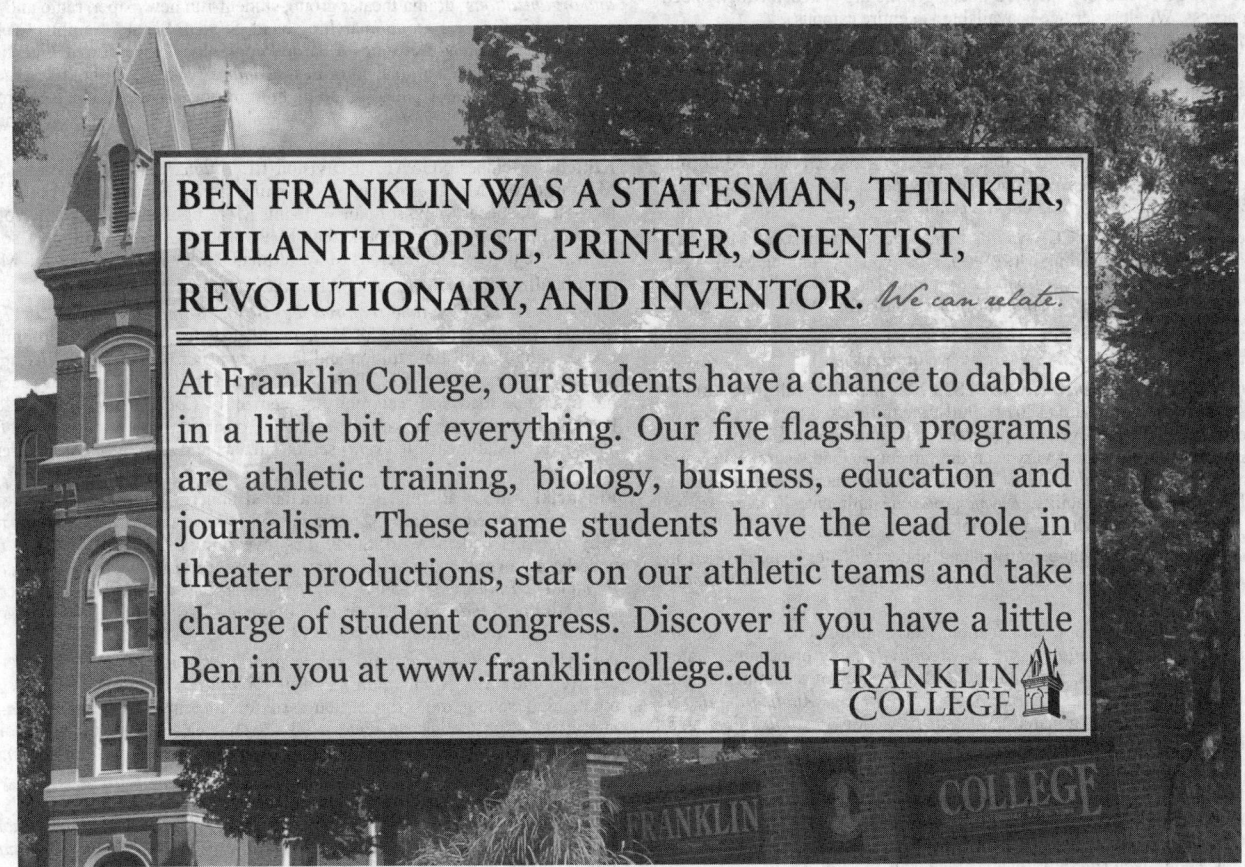

Grace College

Winona Lake, Indiana

- **Independent** comprehensive, founded 1948, affiliated with Fellowship of Grace Brethren Churches, administratively affiliated with Grace Theological Seminary
- **Small-town** 160-acre campus
- **Endowment** $8.1 million
- **Coed** 1,534 undergraduate students, 85% full-time, 44% women, 56% men
- **Moderately difficult** entrance level, 91% of applicants were admitted

Undergraduates 1,303 full-time, 231 part-time. Students come from 34 states and territories; 5 other countries; 42% are from out of state; 12% Black or African American, non-Hispanic/Latino; 3% Hispanic/Latino; 0.7% Asian, non-Hispanic/Latino; 0.8% American Indian or Alaska Native, non-Hispanic/Latino; 0.9% Two or more races, non-Hispanic/Latino; 0.8% Race/ethnicity unknown; 0.3% international; 3% transferred in; 63% live on campus. *Retention:* 78% of full-time freshmen returned.

Freshmen *Admission:* 1,514 applied, 1,385 admitted, 240 enrolled. *Average high school GPA:* 3.41. *Test scores:* SAT critical reading scores over 500: 56%; SAT math scores over 500: 57%; ACT scores over 18: 91%; SAT critical reading scores over 600: 20%; SAT math scores over 600: 20%; ACT scores over 24: 45%; SAT critical reading scores over 700: 5%; SAT math scores over 700: 3%; ACT scores over 30: 7%.

Faculty *Total:* 101, 37% full-time, 34% with terminal degrees. *Student/faculty ratio:* 26:1.

Academics *Calendar:* semesters. *Degrees:* certificates, diplomas, associate, bachelor's, master's, and doctoral-other. *Special study options:* academic remediation for entering students, accelerated degree program, adult/continuing education programs, advanced placement credit, cooperative education, distance learning, double majors, honors programs, independent study, internships, off-campus study, part-time degree program, services for LD students, study abroad, summer session for credit.

Computers on Campus 150 computers/terminals are available on campus for general student use. Students can access the following: campus intranet, computer help desk, free student e-mail accounts, online (class) grades, online (class) registration, online (class) schedules. Campuswide network is available. 100% of college-owned or -operated housing units are wired for high-speed Internet access. Wireless service is available via entire campus.

Student Life *Housing:* on-campus residence required through senior year. *Options:* men-only, women-only. Campus housing is university owned. Freshman campus housing is guaranteed. *Activities and organizations:* drama/theater group, student-run newspaper, choral group, Grace Ministries in Action, Student Activities Board, Funfest, women's ministries, Breakout. *Campus security:* student patrols, late-night transport/escort service, controlled dormitory access, evening patrols by trained security personnel. *Student services:* health clinic, personal/psychological counseling.

Athletics Member NAIA, NCCAA. *Intercollegiate sports:* baseball M(s), basketball M(s)/W(s), cheerleading M(s)/W(s), cross-country running M(s)/W(s), golf M(s), soccer M(s)/W(s), softball W(s), tennis M(s)/W(s), track and field M(s)/W(s), volleyball W(s). *Intramural sports:* basketball M/W, soccer M/W, volleyball M/W.

Standardized Tests *Required:* SAT or ACT (for admission).

Costs (2010–11) *Comprehensive fee:* $28,774 includes full-time tuition ($21,700) and room and board ($7074). Full-time tuition and fees vary according to course load, degree level, and program. Part-time tuition: $480 per credit hour. Part-time tuition and fees vary according to course load, degree level, and program. *College room only:* $3700. Room and board charges vary according to board plan and housing facility. *Payment plan:* installment. *Waivers:* senior citizens and employees or children of employees.

Financial Aid Of all full-time matriculated undergraduates who enrolled in 2008, 1,276 applied for aid, 1,273 were judged to have need. *Average financial aid package:* $11,338.

Applying *Options:* electronic application, early admission, early action, deferred entrance. *Application fee:* $30. *Required:* essay or personal statement, high school transcript, minimum 2.3 GPA, 2 letters of recommendation, personal statement of faith. *Required for some:* interview. *Application deadlines:* 8/1 (freshmen), 8/1 (transfers), 12/1 (early action). *Notification:* 8/15 (freshmen), continuous until 8/15 (transfers).

Freshman Application Contact Mrs. Jessica Hauck, Admissions Office, Grace College, 200 Seminary Drive, Winona Lake, IN 46590. *Phone:* 574-372-5100 Ext. 6008. *Toll-free phone:* 800-54-GRACE Ext. 6412 (in-state); 800-54 GRACE Ext. 6412 (out-of-state). *Fax:* 574-372-5120. *E-mail:* enroll@grace.edu. *Web site:* http://www.grace.edu/.

Hanover College

Hanover, Indiana

- **Independent Presbyterian** 4-year, founded 1827
- **Rural** 630-acre campus with easy access to Louisville
- **Endowment** $121.6 million
- **Coed** 1,006 undergraduate students, 100% full-time, 56% women, 44% men
- **Moderately difficult** entrance level, 67% of applicants were admitted

Undergraduates 1,005 full-time, 1 part-time. Students come from 30 states and territories; 9 other countries; 36% are from out of state; 4% Black or African American, non-Hispanic/Latino; 2% Hispanic/Latino; 0.9% Asian, non-Hispanic/Latino; 0.3% American Indian or Alaska Native, non-Hispanic/Latino; 2% Two or more races, non-Hispanic/Latino; 4% Race/ethnicity unknown; 3% international; 1% transferred in; 95% live on campus. *Retention:* 81% of full-time freshmen returned.

Freshmen *Admission:* 2,964 applied, 1,996 admitted, 320 enrolled. *Average high school GPA:* 3.64. *Test scores:* SAT critical reading scores over 500: 80%; SAT math scores over 500: 78%; SAT writing scores over 500: 65%; ACT scores over 18: 99%; SAT critical reading scores over 600: 31%; SAT math scores over 600: 28%; SAT writing scores over 600: 23%; ACT scores over 24: 60%; SAT critical reading scores over 700: 6%; SAT math scores over 700: 3%; SAT writing scores over 700: 1%; ACT scores over 30: 12%.

Faculty *Total:* 99, 94% full-time, 96% with terminal degrees. *Student/faculty ratio:* 11:1.

Academics *Calendar:* 4-4-1. *Degree:* bachelor's. *Special study options:* advanced placement credit, cooperative education, double majors, independent study, internships, off-campus study, services for LD students, student-designed majors, study abroad.

Computers on Campus 120 computers/terminals and 1,550 ports are available on campus for general student use. Students can access the following: campus intranet, computer help desk, free student e-mail accounts, online (class) grades, online (class) registration, online (class) schedules. Campuswide network is available. 100% of college-owned or -operated housing units are wired for high-speed Internet access. Wireless service is available via entire campus.

Student Life *Housing:* on-campus residence required through senior year. *Options:* coed, men-only, women-only. Campus housing is university owned and leased by the school. Freshman campus housing is guaranteed. *Activities and organizations:* drama/theater group, student-run newspaper, radio and television station, choral group, marching band, Student Senate, Campus Crusade for Christ, Campus Activities Board, People for Peace, Love Out Loud, national fraternities, national sororities. *Campus security:* 24-hour emergency response devices and patrols, late-night transport/escort service, controlled dormitory access. *Student services:* health clinic, personal/psychological counseling.

Athletics Member NCAA. All Division III. *Intercollegiate sports:* baseball M, basketball M/W, cross-country running M/W, football M, golf M/W, lacrosse M, soccer M/W, softball W, tennis M/W, track and field M/W, volleyball W. *Intramural sports:* basketball M/W, football M/W, rugby M(c), soccer M/W, softball M/W, table tennis M/W, ultimate Frisbee M(c), volleyball M/W.

Standardized Tests *Required:* SAT or ACT (for admission).

Costs (2011–12) *One-time required fee:* $250. *Comprehensive fee:* $37,500 includes full-time tuition ($28,250), mandatory fees ($600), and room and board ($8650). Full-time tuition and fees vary according to reciprocity agreements. Part-time tuition: $3150 per unit. Part-time tuition and fees vary according to course load and reciprocity agreements. *College room only:* $4300. Room and board charges vary according to housing facility and location. *Payment plan:* installment. *Waivers:* senior citizens and employees or children of employees.

Financial Aid Of all full-time matriculated undergraduates who enrolled in 2009, 896 applied for aid, 832 were judged to have need, 212 had their need fully met. 331 Federal Work-Study jobs (averaging $996). In 2009, 179 non-need-based awards were made. *Average percent of need met:* 86%. *Average financial aid package:* $25,098. *Average need-based loan:* $4885. *Average need-based gift aid:* $20,399. *Average non-need-based aid:* $13,064. *Average indebtedness upon graduation:* $26,714.

Applying *Options:* electronic application, early admission, early action, deferred entrance. *Application fee:* $40. *Required:* essay or personal statement, high school transcript, 1 letter of recommendation. *Recommended:* interview. *Application deadlines:* 3/1 (freshmen), rolling (transfers), 12/1 (early action). *Notification:* continuous (freshmen), continuous (transfers), 12/20 (early action).

Freshman Application Contact Mr. Christopher Gage, Director of Admission, Hanover College, PO Box 108, Hanover, IN 47243-0108. *Phone:* 812-866-7021. *Toll-free phone:* 800-213-2178. *Fax:* 812-866-7098. *E-mail:* admission@hanover.edu. *Web site:* http://www.hanover.edu/.

Harrison College
Elkhart, Indiana
- **Proprietary** primarily 2-year
- **Coed**
- **Moderately difficult** entrance level

Faculty *Student/faculty ratio:* 25:1.
Academics *Calendar:* quarters. *Degrees:* certificates, diplomas, associate, and bachelor's.
Standardized Tests *Required:* Wonderlic Scholastic Level Exam (SLE) (for admission).
Applying *Application fee:* $50. *Required:* high school transcript, interview.
Freshman Application Contact Matt Brady, Director of Admissions, Harrison College, 56075 Parkway Avenue, Elkhart, IN 46516. *Phone:* 574-522-0397. *Toll-free phone:* 888-544-4422. *E-mail:* matt.brady@harrison.edu. *Web site:* http://www.harrison.edu/.

Harrison College
Evansville, Indiana
- **Proprietary** primarily 2-year
- **Urban** campus
- **Coed**
- **Moderately difficult** entrance level

Faculty *Student/faculty ratio:* 15:1.
Academics *Calendar:* quarters. *Degrees:* certificates, diplomas, associate, and bachelor's.
Standardized Tests *Required:* Wonderlic Scholastic Level Exam (SLE) (for admission).
Applying *Options:* electronic application. *Application fee:* $50. *Required:* high school transcript, interview.
Freshman Application Contact Mr. Bryan Barber, Harrison College, 4601 Theater Drive, Evansville, IN 47715. *Phone:* 812-476-6000. *Toll-free phone:* 888-544-4422. *Fax:* 812-471-8576. *E-mail:* bryan.barber@harrison.edu. *Web site:* http://www.harrison.edu/.

Harrison College
Fort Wayne, Indiana
- **Proprietary** primarily 2-year
- **Urban** campus
- **Coed**
- **Moderately difficult** entrance level

Faculty *Student/faculty ratio:* 15:1.
Academics *Calendar:* quarters. *Degrees:* certificates, diplomas, associate, and bachelor's.
Standardized Tests *Required:* Wonderlic Scholastic Level Exam (SLE) (for admission).
Applying *Options:* electronic application. *Application fee:* $50. *Required:* high school transcript, interview.
Freshman Application Contact Mr. Matt Wallace, Associate Director of Admissions, Harrison College, 6413 North Clinton Street, Fort Wayne, IN 46825. *Phone:* 260-471-7667. *Toll-free phone:* 888-544-4422. *Fax:* 260-471-6918. *E-mail:* matt.wallace@harrison.edu. *Web site:* http://www.harrison.edu/.

Harrison College
Indianapolis, Indiana
- **Proprietary** primarily 2-year, founded 1902
- **Urban** 1-acre campus with easy access to Indianapolis
- **Coed** 2,668 undergraduate students, 65% full-time, 75% women, 25% men
- **Moderately difficult** entrance level, 78% of applicants were admitted

Undergraduates 1,740 full-time, 928 part-time. Students come from 32 states and territories; 1 other country; 17% Black or African American, non-Hispanic/Latino; 2% Hispanic/Latino; 0.5% Asian, non-Hispanic/Latino; 0.3% American Indian or Alaska Native, non-Hispanic/Latino; 0.6% Two or more races, non-Hispanic/Latino; 36% Race/ethnicity unknown; 12% transferred in. *Retention:* 44% of full-time freshmen returned.
Freshmen *Admission:* 622 applied, 484 admitted, 387 enrolled.
Faculty *Student/faculty ratio:* 16:1.
Academics *Calendar:* quarters. *Degrees:* certificates, diplomas, associate, and bachelor's. *Special study options:* adult/continuing education programs, cooperative education, distance learning, double majors, internships, part-time degree program, summer session for credit.

Computers on Campus Students can access the following: free student e-mail accounts, online (class) registration. Campuswide network is available.
Student Life *Housing:* college housing not available. *Activities and organizations:* Student Advisory Board, Student Ambassadors, Phi Beta Lambda. *Campus security:* 24-hour patrols.
Standardized Tests *Required:* Wonderlic Scholastic Level Exam (SLE) (for admission).
Applying *Options:* electronic application. *Application fee:* $50. *Required:* high school transcript, interview. *Application deadlines:* rolling (freshmen), rolling (transfers). *Notification:* continuous (freshmen), continuous (transfers).
Freshman Application Contact Mr. Ted Lukomski, Director of Admissions, Harrison College, 550 East Washington Street, Indianapolis, IN 46204. *Phone:* 317-264-5656. *Toll-free phone:* 888-544-4422. *Fax:* 317-264-5650. *E-mail:* ted.lukomski@ibcschools.edu. *Web site:* http://www.harrison.edu/.

Harrison College
Lafayette, Indiana
- **Proprietary** primarily 2-year
- **Small-town** campus
- **Coed** 350 undergraduate students, 82% full-time, 85% women, 15% men
- **Moderately difficult** entrance level, 100% of applicants were admitted

Undergraduates 286 full-time, 64 part-time. 5% Black or African American, non-Hispanic/Latino; 6% Hispanic/Latino; 0.6% Asian, non-Hispanic/Latino; 0.3% Native Hawaiian or other Pacific Islander, non-Hispanic/Latino; 0.3% American Indian or Alaska Native, non-Hispanic/Latino; 1% Two or more races, non-Hispanic/Latino; 17% transferred in. *Retention:* 45% of full-time freshmen returned.
Freshmen *Admission:* 32 applied, 32 admitted, 32 enrolled.
Faculty *Student/faculty ratio:* 15:1.
Academics *Calendar:* quarters. *Degrees:* certificates, diplomas, associate, and bachelor's. *Special study options:* adult/continuing education programs, cooperative education, distance learning, double majors, independent study, internships, part-time degree program.
Student Life *Housing:* college housing not available.
Standardized Tests *Required:* Wonderlic Scholastic Level Exam (SLE) (for admission).
Applying *Options:* electronic application. *Application fee:* $50. *Required:* high school transcript, interview. *Application deadlines:* rolling (freshmen), rolling (out-of-state freshmen), rolling (transfers). *Notification:* continuous (freshmen), continuous (out-of-state freshmen), continuous (transfers).
Freshman Application Contact Ms. Stacy Golleher, Associate Director of Admissions, Harrison College, 4705 Meijer Court, Lafayette, IN 47905. *Phone:* 765-447-9550. *Toll-free phone:* 888-544-4422. *Fax:* 765-447-0868. *E-mail:* stacy.golleher@harrison.edu. *Web site:* http://www.harrison.edu/.

Harrison College
Muncie, Indiana
- **Proprietary** primarily 2-year
- **Small-town** campus
- **Coed, primarily women** 229 undergraduate students, 82% full-time, 78% women, 22% men
- **Moderately difficult** entrance level, 78% of applicants were admitted

Undergraduates 187 full-time, 42 part-time. 12% Black or African American, non-Hispanic/Latino; 2% Two or more races, non-Hispanic/Latino. *Retention:* 52% of full-time freshmen returned.
Freshmen *Admission:* 67 applied, 52 admitted, 117 enrolled.
Faculty *Student/faculty ratio:* 16:1.
Academics *Calendar:* quarters. *Degrees:* certificates, diplomas, associate, and bachelor's. *Special study options:* adult/continuing education programs, cooperative education, distance learning, double majors, independent study, part-time degree program.
Computers on Campus Students can access the following: free student e-mail accounts.
Student Life *Housing:* college housing not available. *Activities and organizations:* Phi Beta Lambda.
Standardized Tests *Required:* Wonderlic Scholastic Level Exam (SLE) (for admission).
Applying *Options:* electronic application. *Application fee:* $50. *Required:* high school transcript, interview. *Application deadlines:* rolling (freshmen), rolling (transfers). *Notification:* continuous (freshmen), continuous (transfers).
Freshman Application Contact Mr. Jeremy Linder, Associate Director of Admissions, Harrison College, Muncie, IN 47303. *Phone:* 765-288-8681. *Toll-free phone:* 888-544-4422. *Fax:* 765-288-8797. *E-mail:* Jeremy.linder@harrison.edu. *Web site:* http://www.harrison.edu/.

PROFILES

Harrison College
Terre Haute, Indiana

- **Proprietary** primarily 2-year, founded 1902
- **Small-town** campus
- **Coed**
- **Moderately difficult** entrance level

Faculty *Student/faculty ratio:* 15:1.

Academics *Calendar:* quarters. *Degrees:* certificates, diplomas, associate, and bachelor's.

Standardized Tests *Required:* Wonderlic Scholastic Level Exam (SLE) (for admission).

Applying *Options:* electronic application. *Application fee:* $50. *Required:* high school transcript, interview.

Freshman Application Contact Sarah Stultz, Associate Director of Admissions, Harrison College, 1378 South State Road 46, Terre Haute, IN 47803. *Phone:* 812-877-2100. *Toll-free phone:* 888-544-4422. *Fax:* 812-877-4440. *E-mail:* sarah.stultz@harrison.edu. *Web site:* http://www.harrison.edu/.

Holy Cross College
Notre Dame, Indiana

- **Independent Roman Catholic** 4-year, founded 1966
- **Suburban** 150-acre campus with easy access to Chicago and Indianapolis
- **Coed** 459 undergraduate students, 95% full-time, 35% women, 65% men
- **Moderately difficult** entrance level

Undergraduates 436 full-time, 23 part-time. Students come from 31 states and territories; 7 other countries; 64% are from out of state; 6% Black or African American, non-Hispanic/Latino; 8% Hispanic/Latino; 1% Asian, non-Hispanic/Latino; 0.7% Two or more races, non-Hispanic/Latino; 3% Race/ethnicity unknown; 6% international; 7% transferred in; 54% live on campus. *Retention:* 55% of full-time freshmen returned.

Freshmen *Admission:* 550 applied, 144 enrolled. *Average high school GPA:* 3. *Test scores:* SAT critical reading scores over 500: 40%; SAT math scores over 500: 42%; SAT writing scores over 500: 37%; ACT scores over 18: 95%; SAT critical reading scores over 600: 15%; SAT math scores over 600: 11%; SAT writing scores over 600: 8%; ACT scores over 24: 36%; SAT critical reading scores over 700: 2%; SAT math scores over 700: 2%; ACT scores over 30: 2%.

Faculty *Total:* 70, 49% full-time, 20% with terminal degrees. *Student/faculty ratio:* 14:1.

Academics *Calendar:* semesters. *Degrees:* associate and bachelor's. *Special study options:* academic remediation for entering students, accelerated degree program, advanced placement credit, double majors, English as a second language, freshman honors college, honors programs, independent study, internships, off-campus study, student-designed majors, study abroad, summer session for credit. *ROTC:* Army (c), Air Force (c).

Computers on Campus 91 computers/terminals are available on campus for general student use. Students can access the following: campus intranet, free student e-mail accounts, online (class) registration, online (class) schedules. Campuswide network is available. 100% of college-owned or -operated housing units are wired for high-speed Internet access. Wireless service is available via entire campus.

Student Life *Housing options:* coed, men-only, women-only, cooperative, disabled students. Campus housing is university owned. Freshman campus housing is guaranteed. *Activities and organizations:* drama/theater group, student-run newspaper, choral group, marching band, Student Government Association, Campus Ministry, Volunteers in Support of Admissions, intramural athletics, Commuter Student Organization. *Campus security:* 24-hour emergency response devices and patrols, controlled dormitory access, 24-hour patrols by trained personnel on certain days. *Student services:* personal/psychological counseling.

Athletics Member NAIA. *Intercollegiate sports:* baseball M(s), basketball M(s), crew M, cross-country running M(s)/W(s), ice hockey M, lacrosse M, soccer M(s)/W(s), track and field M(s)/W(s). *Intramural sports:* basketball M/W, cheerleading M/W, football M/W, golf M/W, lacrosse M, rugby M, skiing (downhill) M(c)/W(c), soccer M, softball M/W, table tennis M/W, tennis M/W, ultimate Frisbee M/W, volleyball M/W, weight lifting M/W.

Standardized Tests *Required:* SAT or ACT (for admission).

Costs (2011–12) *Comprehensive fee:* $31,100 includes full-time tuition ($21,700), mandatory fees ($1000), and room and board ($8400). Part-time tuition: $725 per semester hour. No tuition increase for student's term of enrollment. *Room and board:* Room and board charges vary according to housing facility. *Payment plan:* installment. *Waivers:* employees or children of employees.

Applying *Options:* electronic application, deferred entrance. *Required:* essay or personal statement, high school transcript. *Recommended:* minimum 2.5

GPA, interview. *Application deadlines:* rolling (freshmen), rolling (out-of-state freshmen), rolling (transfers).

Freshman Application Contact Mr. Adam DeBeck, Office of Admissions, Holy Cross College, Notre Dame, IN 46556. *Phone:* 574-239-8400. *Fax:* 574-239-8323. *E-mail:* admissions@hcc-nd.edu. *Web site:* http://www.hcc-nd.edu/.

Huntington University
Huntington, Indiana

- **Independent** comprehensive, founded 1897, affiliated with Church of the United Brethren in Christ, administratively affiliated with Church of the United Brethren in Christ
- **Small-town** 170-acre campus with easy access to Fort Wayne
- **Coed** 1,170 undergraduate students, 91% full-time, 55% women, 45% men
- **Moderately difficult** entrance level, 80% of applicants were admitted

Undergraduates 1,066 full-time, 104 part-time. Students come from 36 states and territories; 20 other countries; 36% are from out of state; 1% Black or African American, non-Hispanic/Latino; 2% Hispanic/Latino; 0.3% Asian, non-Hispanic/Latino; 0.1% Native Hawaiian or other Pacific Islander, non-Hispanic/Latino; 0.3% American Indian or Alaska Native, non-Hispanic/Latino; 1% Two or more races, non-Hispanic/Latino; 3% international; 5% transferred in; 76% live on campus. *Retention:* 78% of full-time freshmen returned.

Freshmen *Admission:* 1,012 applied, 805 admitted, 264 enrolled. *Average high school GPA:* 3.45. *Test scores:* SAT critical reading scores over 500: 56%; SAT math scores over 500: 61%; ACT scores over 18: 93%; SAT critical reading scores over 600: 20%; SAT math scores over 600: 24%; ACT scores over 24: 41%; SAT critical reading scores over 700: 4%; SAT math scores over 700: 3%; ACT scores over 30: 10%.

Faculty *Total:* 186, 32% full-time, 41% with terminal degrees. *Student/faculty ratio:* 14:1.

Academics *Calendar:* 4-1-4. *Degrees:* associate, bachelor's, master's, and postbachelor's certificates. *Special study options:* academic remediation for entering students, accelerated degree program, adult/continuing education programs, advanced placement credit, distance learning, double majors, English as a second language, independent study, internships, off-campus study, part-time degree program, services for LD students, study abroad, summer session for credit.

Computers on Campus 270 computers/terminals and 2,954 ports are available on campus for general student use. Students can access the following: campus intranet, computer help desk, free student e-mail accounts, online (class) grades, online (class) registration, online (class) schedules. Campuswide network is available. 100% of college-owned or -operated housing units are wired for high-speed Internet access. Wireless service is available via classrooms, computer centers, computer labs, dorm rooms, learning centers, libraries, student centers.

Student Life *Housing:* on-campus residence required through junior year. *Options:* men-only, women-only, disabled students. Campus housing is university owned. Freshman campus housing is guaranteed. *Activities and organizations:* drama/theater group, student-run newspaper, radio and television station, choral group, Habitat for Humanity, Film Club, Global Vision, Amnesty International, Ultimate Frisbee Club. *Campus security:* 24-hour emergency response devices, late-night transport/escort service, campus police on duty from 6 pm to 6 am. *Student services:* health clinic, personal/psychological counseling.

Athletics Member NAIA, NCCAA. *Intercollegiate sports:* baseball M(s), basketball M(s)/W(s), cheerleading M/W, cross-country running M(s)/W(s), golf M(s), soccer M(s)/W(s), softball W(s), tennis M(s)/W(s), track and field M(s)/W(s), ultimate Frisbee M(c), volleyball W(s). *Intramural sports:* basketball M/W, football M, racquetball M/W, soccer M/W, table tennis M/W, volleyball M/W.

Standardized Tests *Required:* SAT or ACT (for admission).

Costs (2011–12) *Comprehensive fee:* $30,890 includes full-time tuition ($22,710), mandatory fees ($500), and room and board ($7680). Full-time tuition and fees vary according to course load, degree level, and program. Part-time tuition and fees vary according to course load, degree level, and program. *Room and board:* Room and board charges vary according to board plan. *Payment plan:* installment. *Waivers:* employees or children of employees.

Financial Aid Of all full-time matriculated undergraduates who enrolled in 2009, 936 applied for aid, 853 were judged to have need, 55 had their need fully met. 138 Federal Work-Study jobs (averaging $2106). In 2009, 161 non-need-based awards were made. *Average percent of need met:* 68%. *Average financial aid package:* $16,111. *Average need-based loan:* $4556. *Average need-based gift aid:* $13,243. *Average non-need-based aid:* $8716. *Average indebtedness upon graduation:* $30,885.

Applying *Options:* electronic application, deferred entrance. *Application fee:* $20. *Required:* essay or personal statement, high school transcript, minimum 2.3 GPA. *Recommended:* interview. *Application deadlines:* 8/1 (freshmen), rolling (transfers). *Notification:* 10/1 (freshmen), continuous (transfers).

Freshman Application Contact Huntington University, 2303 College Avenue, Huntington, IN 46750-1299. *Phone:* 260-356-6000 Ext. 4016. *Toll-free phone:* 800-642-6493. *Web site:* http://www.huntington.edu/.

Indiana State University

Terre Haute, Indiana

- **State-supported** university, founded 1865
- **Small-town** 91-acre campus with easy access to Indianapolis
- **Coed** 9,373 undergraduate students, 88% full-time, 51% women, 49% men
- **Moderately difficult** entrance level, 70% of applicants were admitted

Undergraduates 8,230 full-time, 1,143 part-time. Students come from 54 states and territories; 42 other countries; 14% are from out of state; 16% Black or African American, non-Hispanic/Latino; 1% Hispanic/Latino; 1% Asian, non-Hispanic/Latino; 0.3% American Indian or Alaska Native, non-Hispanic/Latino; 2% Two or more races, non-Hispanic/Latino; 7% Race/ethnicity unknown; 2% international; 8% transferred in; 36% live on campus. *Retention:* 64% of full-time freshmen returned.

Freshmen *Admission:* 12,183 applied, 8,500 admitted, 2,707 enrolled. *Average high school GPA:* 2.98. *Test scores:* SAT critical reading scores over 500: 31%; SAT math scores over 500: 35%; SAT writing scores over 500: 22%; ACT scores over 18: 62%; SAT critical reading scores over 600: 6%; SAT math scores over 600: 7%; SAT writing scores over 600: 3%; ACT scores over 24: 15%; SAT critical reading scores over 700: 1%; ACT scores over 30: 1%.

Faculty *Total:* 663, 63% full-time, 65% with terminal degrees. *Student/faculty ratio:* 20:1.

Academics *Calendar:* semesters. *Degrees:* certificates, associate, bachelor's, master's, doctoral-research/scholarship, post-master's, and postbachelor's certificates. *Special study options:* academic remediation for entering students, accelerated degree program, adult/continuing education programs, advanced placement credit, cooperative education, distance learning, double majors, English as a second language, freshman honors college, honors programs, independent study, internships, off-campus study, part-time degree program, services for LD students, study abroad, summer session for credit. *ROTC:* Army (b), Air Force (b).

Computers on Campus 395 computers/terminals are available on campus for general student use. Students can access the following: campus intranet, computer help desk, free student e-mail accounts, online (class) grades, online (class) registration, online (class) schedules. Campuswide network is available. 100% of college-owned or -operated housing units are wired for high-speed Internet access. Wireless service is available via entire campus.

Student Life *Housing:* on-campus residence required for freshman year. *Options:* coed, men-only, women-only, disabled students. Campus housing is university owned. Freshman campus housing is guaranteed. *Activities and organizations:* drama/theater group, student-run newspaper, radio station, choral group, marching band, Union Board, Student Government Association, Panhellenic Council (sororities), Interfraternity Council (fraternities), Pan-Hellenic Council (African American fraternities/sororities), national fraternities, national sororities. *Campus security:* 24-hour emergency response devices and patrols, student patrols, late-night transport/escort service. *Student services:* health clinic, personal/psychological counseling, women's center.

Athletics Member NCAA. All Division I except football (Division I-AA). *Intercollegiate sports:* baseball M(s), basketball M(s)/W(s), cross-country running M(s)/W(s), golf W(s), soccer W(s), softball W(s), track and field M(s)/W(s), volleyball W(s). *Intramural sports:* badminton M/W, basketball M/W, racquetball M/W, soccer M/W, softball M/W, swimming and diving M/W, track and field M/W, ultimate Frisbee M/W, volleyball M/W.

Standardized Tests *Required:* SAT or ACT (for admission).

Costs (2010–11) *Tuition:* state resident $7514 full-time, $272 per credit hour part-time; nonresident $16,426 full-time, $580 per credit hour part-time. Full-time tuition and fees vary according to reciprocity agreements. Part-time tuition and fees vary according to course load and reciprocity agreements. *Required fees:* $200 full-time, $100 per term part-time. *Room and board:* $7752; room only: $4488. Room and board charges vary according to board plan, housing facility, and student level. *Payment plans:* installment, deferred payment. *Waivers:* senior citizens and employees or children of employees.

Financial Aid Of all full-time matriculated undergraduates who enrolled in 2008, 6,167 applied for aid, 5,082 were judged to have need, 549 had their need fully met. 426 Federal Work-Study jobs (averaging $1387). In 2008, 725 non-need-based awards were made. *Average percent of need met:* 77%. *Average financial aid package:* $9054. *Average need-based loan:* $3814. *Average need-based gift aid:* $6211. *Average non-need-based aid:* $4782. *Average indebtedness upon graduation:* $22,124.

Applying *Options:* electronic application, deferred entrance. *Application fee:* $25. *Required:* high school transcript. *Required for some:* interview. *Application deadline:* 8/15 (freshmen). *Notification:* continuous (freshmen), continuous (transfers).

Freshman Application Contact Mr. Richard Toomey, Executive Director of Admissions, Indiana State University, 218 North Sixth Street, Erickson Hall, Terre Haute, IN 47809-9989. *Phone:* 812-237-2121. *Toll-free phone:* 800-742-0891. *Fax:* 812-237-8023. *E-mail:* admisu@isugw.indstate.edu. *Web site:* http://www.indstate.edu/.

Indiana Tech

Fort Wayne, Indiana

- **Independent** comprehensive, founded 1930
- **Urban** 42-acre campus
- **Endowment** $37.0 million
- **Coed** 4,010 undergraduate students, 68% full-time, 57% women, 43% men
- **Moderately difficult** entrance level, 69% of applicants were admitted

Undergraduates 2,733 full-time, 1,277 part-time. Students come from 47 states and territories; 7 other countries; 14% are from out of state; 2% Black or African American, non-Hispanic/Latino; 0.3% Hispanic/Latino; 0.1% American Indian or Alaska Native, non-Hispanic/Latino; 94% Race/ethnicity unknown; 0.9% international; 48% live on campus. *Retention:* 57% of full-time freshmen returned.

Freshmen *Admission:* 2,447 applied, 1,692 admitted, 444 enrolled. *Average high school GPA:* 2.83. *Test scores:* SAT critical reading scores over 500: 29%; SAT math scores over 500: 37%; SAT writing scores over 500: 23%; ACT scores over 18: 71%; SAT critical reading scores over 600: 4%; SAT math scores over 600: 11%; SAT writing scores over 600: 2%; ACT scores over 24: 17%; SAT math scores over 700: 1%; ACT scores over 30: 1%.

Faculty *Total:* 325, 12% full-time, 7% with terminal degrees. *Student/faculty ratio:* 19:1.

Academics *Calendar:* semesters. *Degrees:* associate, bachelor's, master's, and doctoral-research/scholarship. *Special study options:* academic remediation for entering students, accelerated degree program, adult/continuing education programs, advanced placement credit, cooperative education, distance learning, double majors, English as a second language, external degree program, honors programs, independent study, internships, part-time degree program, services for LD students, student-designed majors, summer session for credit. *ROTC:* Army (c).

Computers on Campus 360 computers/terminals and 20 ports are available on campus for general student use. Students can access the following: computer help desk, free student e-mail accounts, online (class) grades, online (class) registration, online (class) schedules. Campuswide network is available. 100% of college-owned or -operated housing units are wired for high-speed Internet access. Wireless service is available via entire campus.

Student Life *Housing:* on-campus residence required through sophomore year. *Options:* coed. Campus housing is university owned. Freshman campus housing is guaranteed. *Activities and organizations:* student-run newspaper, Student Board, Student Ambassadors, NSBE, SHRM, Sport Recreation and Leisure Society, national fraternities. *Campus security:* 24-hour emergency response devices and patrols, student patrols, controlled dormitory access.

Athletics Member NAIA. *Intercollegiate sports:* baseball M(s), basketball M(s)/W(s), bowling M(s)/W(s), cheerleading M(s)/W(s), cross-country running M(s)/W(s), golf M(s)/W(s), lacrosse M(s)/W(s), soccer M(s)/W(s), softball W(s), tennis M(s)/W(s), track and field M(s)/W(s), volleyball W(s), wrestling M(s). *Intramural sports:* badminton M/W, basketball M/W, bowling M/W, football M/W, golf M/W, soccer M/W, softball M/W, table tennis M/W, tennis M/W, ultimate Frisbee M/W, volleyball M/W.

Standardized Tests *Required:* SAT or ACT (for admission).

Costs (2011–12) *Comprehensive fee:* $32,220 includes full-time tuition ($23,050), mandatory fees ($380), and room and board ($8790). Full-time tuition and fees vary according to class time, course load, and program. Part-time tuition and fees vary according to class time, course load, and program. *Room and board:* Room and board charges vary according to housing facility. *Payment plan:* installment. *Waivers:* employees or children of employees.

Financial Aid *Average financial aid package:* $9125. *Average indebtedness upon graduation:* $16,500.

Applying *Options:* electronic application. *Application fee:* $50. *Required:* minimum 2 GPA. *Required for some:* high school transcript, minimum 3 GPA, 2 letters of recommendation, Interview with the Director of Software Engineering and college-level math courses for the Software Engineering program. *Recommended:* Interview with the Director of Software Engineering and college-level math courses for the Software Engineering program. *Application deadlines:* 8/15 (freshmen), 8/15 (transfers). *Notification:* 8/15 (freshmen), 8/15 (transfers).

Freshman Application Contact Ms. Monica Chamberlain, Associate Vice President of Enrollment Management, Indiana Tech, 1600 East Washington Boulevard, Fort Wayne, IN 46803. *Phone:* 260-422-5561 Ext. 2348. *Toll-free phone:* 800-937-2448 (in-state); 888-666-TECH (out-of-state). *Fax:* 260-422-7696. *E-mail:* admissions@indianatech.edu. *Web site:* http://www.indianatech.edu/.

Indiana University Bloomington
Bloomington, Indiana

- **State-supported** university, founded 1820, part of Indiana University System
- **Small-town** 1937-acre campus with easy access to Indianapolis
- **Endowment** $785.7 million
- **Coed** 32,367 undergraduate students, 96% full-time, 50% women, 50% men
- **Moderately difficult** entrance level, 69% of applicants were admitted

Undergraduates 30,957 full-time, 1,410 part-time. Students come from 51 states and territories; 137 other countries; 31% are from out of state; 4% Black or African American, non-Hispanic/Latino; 3% Hispanic/Latino; 4% Asian, non-Hispanic/Latino; 0.1% Native Hawaiian or other Pacific Islander, non-Hispanic/Latino; 0.2% American Indian or Alaska Native, non-Hispanic/Latino; 2% Two or more races, non-Hispanic/Latino; 1% Race/ethnicity unknown; 7% international; 3% transferred in; 36% live on campus. *Retention:* 90% of full-time freshmen returned.

Freshmen *Admission:* 36,719 applied, 25,391 admitted, 6,837 enrolled. *Average high school GPA:* 3.61. *Test scores:* SAT critical reading scores over 500: 84%; SAT math scores over 500: 90%; ACT scores over 18: 98%; SAT critical reading scores over 600: 40%; SAT math scores over 600: 50%; ACT scores over 24: 80%; SAT critical reading scores over 700: 8%; SAT math scores over 700: 11%; ACT scores over 30: 22%.

Faculty *Total:* 2,271, 85% full-time, 70% with terminal degrees. *Student/faculty ratio:* 19:1.

Academics *Calendar:* semesters plus 2 summer sessions. *Degrees:* certificates, bachelor's, master's, doctoral-professional, doctoral-research/scholarship, post-master's, and postbachelor's certificates. *Special study options:* academic remediation for entering students, accelerated degree program, adult/continuing education programs, advanced placement credit, cooperative education, distance learning, double majors, English as a second language, external degree program, freshman honors college, honors programs, independent study, internships, off-campus study, part-time degree program, services for LD students, student-designed majors, study abroad, summer session for credit. *ROTC:* Army (b), Air Force (b). *Unusual degree programs:* 3-2 accounting.

Computers on Campus Students can access the following: campus intranet, computer help desk, free student e-mail accounts, online (class) grades, online (class) registration, online (class) schedules, various software packages. Campuswide network is available. 100% of college-owned or -operated housing units are wired for high-speed Internet access. Wireless service is available via entire campus.

Student Life *Housing:* on-campus residence required for freshman year. *Options:* coed, men-only, women-only, cooperative, disabled students. Campus housing is university owned. Freshman applicants given priority for college housing. *Activities and organizations:* drama/theater group, student-run newspaper, radio and television station, choral group, marching band, Union Board, Student Association, Student Foundation, Habitat for Humanity, Student Athletic Board, national fraternities, national sororities. *Campus security:* 24-hour emergency response devices and patrols, late-night transport/escort service, safety seminars, lighted pathways, escort service, shuttle bus service, emergency telephones. *Student services:* health clinic, personal/psychological counseling, women's center, legal services.

Athletics Member NCAA. All Division I except football (Division I-A). *Intercollegiate sports:* baseball M(s), basketball M(s)/W(s), crew W(s), cross-country running M(s)/W(s), field hockey W(s), golf M(s)/W(s), soccer M(s)/W(s), softball W(s), swimming and diving M(s)/W(s), tennis M(s)/W(s), track and field M(s)/W(s), volleyball W(s), water polo W(s), wrestling M(s). *Intramural sports:* archery M/W, badminton M(c)/W(c), baseball M/W, basketball M/W, bowling M(c)/W(c), crew M(c)/W(c), cross-country running M/W, equestrian sports M(c)/W(c), fencing M(c)/W(c), field hockey W(c), golf M/W, gymnastics M/W, ice hockey M/W, lacrosse M(c)/W, racquetball M(c)/W(c), riflery M(c)/W(c), sailing M(c)/W(c), skiing (downhill) M(c)/W(c), soccer M/W(c), softball M/W, squash M/W, swimming and diving M/W, table tennis M/W, tennis M(c)/W, track and field M/W, volleyball M/W, water polo M(c)/W, weight lifting M(c)/W(c), wrestling M(c).

Standardized Tests *Required:* SAT or ACT (for admission). *Recommended:* SAT Subject Tests (for admission).

Costs (2010–11) *Tuition:* state resident $8124 full-time, $254 per credit hour part-time; nonresident $26,785 full-time, $837 per credit hour part-time. Full-time tuition and fees vary according to location and program. Part-time tuition and fees vary according to course load, location, and program. *Required fees:* $904 full-time. *Room and board:* $7918; room only: $5018. Room and board charges vary according to board plan and housing facility. *Payment plan:* deferred payment. *Waivers:* employees or children of employees.

Financial Aid Of all full-time matriculated undergraduates who enrolled in 2008, 18,782 applied for aid, 13,247 were judged to have need, 1,890 had their need fully met. In 2008, 6937 non-need-based awards were made. *Average percent of need met:* 89%. *Average financial aid package:* $10,480. *Average need-based loan:* $4318. *Average need-based gift aid:* $8655. *Average non-need-based aid:* $5699. *Average indebtedness upon graduation:* $27,752.

Applying *Options:* electronic application, deferred entrance. *Application fee:* $55. *Required:* high school transcript. *Recommended:* interview. *Application deadlines:* rolling (freshmen), rolling (transfers). *Notification:* continuous (freshmen), continuous (transfers).

Freshman Application Contact Ms. Mary Ellen Anderson, Director of Admissions, Indiana University Bloomington, 300 North Jordan Avenue, Bloomington, IN 47405-1106. *Phone:* 812-855-0661. *Fax:* 812-855-5102. *E-mail:* iuadmit@indiana.edu. *Web site:* http://www.iub.edu/.

Indiana University East
Richmond, Indiana

- **State-supported** comprehensive, founded 1971, part of Indiana University System
- **Small-town** 182-acre campus with easy access to Indianapolis
- **Endowment** $4.2 million
- **Coed** 3,285 undergraduate students, 53% full-time, 66% women, 34% men
- **Moderately difficult** entrance level, 60% of applicants were admitted

Undergraduates 1,746 full-time, 1,539 part-time. Students come from 28 states and territories; 20 other countries; 17% are from out of state; 4% Black or African American, non-Hispanic/Latino; 2% Hispanic/Latino; 0.6% Asian, non-Hispanic/Latino; 0.2% Native Hawaiian or other Pacific Islander, non-Hispanic/Latino; 0.2% American Indian or Alaska Native, non-Hispanic/Latino; 1% Two or more races, non-Hispanic/Latino; 2% Race/ethnicity unknown; 0.3% international; 9% transferred in. *Retention:* 64% of full-time freshmen returned.

Freshmen *Admission:* 1,122 applied, 678 admitted, 400 enrolled. *Average high school GPA:* 3.05. *Test scores:* SAT critical reading scores over 500: 29%; SAT math scores over 500: 34%; ACT scores over 18: 79%; SAT critical reading scores over 600: 4%; SAT math scores over 600: 6%; ACT scores over 24: 21%; ACT scores over 30: 2%.

Faculty *Total:* 228, 39% full-time, 30% with terminal degrees. *Student/faculty ratio:* 17:1.

Academics *Calendar:* semesters. *Degrees:* associate, bachelor's, master's, and postbachelor's certificates. *Special study options:* academic remediation for entering students, adult/continuing education programs, advanced placement credit, cooperative education, distance learning, double majors, external degree program, independent study, internships, off-campus study, part-time degree program, services for LD students, summer session for credit.

Computers on Campus Students can access the following: campus intranet, computer help desk, free student e-mail accounts, online (class) grades, online (class) registration, online (class) schedules. Campuswide network is available. Wireless service is available via entire campus.

Student Life *Housing:* college housing not available. *Activities and organizations:* drama/theater group, student-run newspaper, television station, Student Government Association, Phi Beta Lambda, Multicultural Awareness Association, Psychology Club, Sociology Club. *Campus security:* 24-hour emergency response devices, late-night transport/escort service, safety awareness, lighted pathways, 14-hour foot and vehicle patrol. *Student services:* personal/psychological counseling.

Athletics Member NAIA. *Intercollegiate sports:* basketball M, cheerleading W, cross-country running M/W, golf M/W, tennis M/W, track and field M/W, volleyball W. *Intramural sports:* basketball M(c)/W(c), softball M/W, volleyball M/W.

Standardized Tests *Required:* SAT or ACT (for admission).

Costs (2010–11) *Tuition:* state resident $5676 full-time, $189 per credit hour part-time; nonresident $15,912 full-time, $530 per credit hour part-time. Full-time tuition and fees vary according to course load, location, program, and reciprocity agreements. Part-time tuition and fees vary according to course load, location, program, and reciprocity agreements. *Required fees:* $393 full-time. *Payment plan:* deferred payment. *Waivers:* employees or children of employees.

Financial Aid Of all full-time matriculated undergraduates who enrolled in 2008, 1,382 applied for aid, 1,227 were judged to have need, 56 had their need fully met. In 2008, 56 non-need-based awards were made. *Average percent of need met:* 96%. *Average financial aid package:* $8044. *Average need-based loan:* $3684. *Average need-based gift aid:* $5786. *Average non-need-based aid:* $1412. *Average indebtedness upon graduation:* $27,069.

Applying *Options:* early admission, deferred entrance. *Application fee:* $35. *Required:* high school transcript. *Recommended:* minimum 2 GPA. *Application deadlines:* rolling (freshmen), rolling (transfers). *Notification:* continuous (freshmen), continuous (transfers).

Freshman Application Contact Ms. Molly Vanderpool, Admissions Counselor, Indiana University East, 2325 Chester Boulevard, WZ 116, Richmond, IN 47374-1289. *Phone:* 765-973-8415. *Toll-free phone:* 800-959-EAST. *Fax:* 765-973-8288. *Web site:* http://www.iue.edu/.

Indiana University Kokomo

Kokomo, Indiana

- **State-supported** comprehensive, founded 1945, part of Indiana University System
- **Small-town** 51-acre campus with easy access to Indianapolis
- **Endowment** $4.5 million
- **Coed** 2,978 undergraduate students, 57% full-time, 66% women, 34% men
- **Minimally difficult** entrance level, 76% of applicants were admitted

Undergraduates 1,706 full-time, 1,272 part-time. Students come from 11 states and territories; 19 other countries; 1% are from out of state; 5% Black or African American, non-Hispanic/Latino; 3% Hispanic/Latino; 0.9% Asian, non-Hispanic/Latino; 0.3% American Indian or Alaska Native, non-Hispanic/Latino; 0.7% Two or more races, non-Hispanic/Latino; 4% Race/ethnicity unknown; 9% transferred in. *Retention:* 61% of full-time freshmen returned.

Freshmen *Admission:* 932 applied, 709 admitted, 376 enrolled. *Average high school GPA:* 2.92. *Test scores:* SAT critical reading scores over 500: 35%; SAT math scores over 500: 43%; ACT scores over 18: 81%; SAT critical reading scores over 600: 6%; SAT math scores over 600: 7%; ACT scores over 24: 13%; ACT scores over 30: 2%.

Faculty *Total:* 177, 55% full-time, 39% with terminal degrees. *Student/faculty ratio:* 18:1.

Academics *Calendar:* semesters. *Degrees:* certificates, associate, bachelor's, master's, and postbachelor's certificates. *Special study options:* academic remediation for entering students, accelerated degree program, adult/continuing education programs, advanced placement credit, distance learning, double majors, external degree program, freshman honors college, honors programs, independent study, internships, part-time degree program, services for LD students, study abroad, summer session for credit. *ROTC:* Army (c).

Computers on Campus Students can access the following: campus intranet, computer help desk, free student e-mail accounts, online (class) grades, online (class) registration, online (class) schedules. Campuswide network is available. Wireless service is available via entire campus.

Student Life *Housing:* college housing not available. *Activities and organizations:* drama/theater group, student-run newspaper, choral group. *Campus security:* 24-hour patrols, late-night transport/escort service, campus police, lighted pathways. *Student services:* personal/psychological counseling.

Athletics *Intramural sports:* basketball M, soccer M/W, softball M/W, volleyball M/W.

Standardized Tests *Required:* SAT or ACT (for admission).

Costs (2010–11) *Tuition:* state resident $5663 full-time, $189 per credit hour part-time; nonresident $14,928 full-time, $498 per credit hour part-time. Full-time tuition and fees vary according to course load, location, and program. Part-time tuition and fees vary according to course load, location, and program. *Required fees:* $446 full-time. *Room and board:* Room and board charges vary according to board plan, housing facility, and location. *Payment plan:* deferred payment. *Waivers:* employees or children of employees.

Financial Aid Of all full-time matriculated undergraduates who enrolled in 2008, 1,351 applied for aid, 1,090 were judged to have need, 45 had their need fully met. In 2008, 52 non-need-based awards were made. *Average percent of need met:* 92%. *Average financial aid package:* $7744. *Average need-based loan:* $3669. *Average need-based gift aid:* $6212. *Average non-need-based aid:* $1501. *Average indebtedness upon graduation:* $23,454. *Financial aid deadline:* 3/1.

Applying *Options:* deferred entrance. *Application fee:* $45. *Required:* high school transcript. *Application deadline:* rolling (freshmen). *Notification:* continuous (freshmen), continuous (transfers).

Freshman Application Contact Indiana University Kokomo, Kelley Student Center, Room 230, 2300 South Washington Street, Kokomo, IN 46904-9003. *Phone:* 765-455-9217. *Toll-free phone:* 888-875-4485. *Fax:* 765-455-9537. *E-mail:* iuadmis@iuk.edu. *Web site:* http://www.iuk.edu/.

Indiana University Northwest

Gary, Indiana

- **State-supported** comprehensive, founded 1959, part of Indiana University System
- **Urban** 38-acre campus with easy access to Chicago
- **Endowment** $7.1 million
- **Coed** 5,307 undergraduate students, 64% full-time, 68% women, 32% men
- **Minimally difficult** entrance level, 77% of applicants were admitted

Undergraduates 3,416 full-time, 1,891 part-time. Students come from 7 states and territories; 39 other countries; 1% are from out of state; 22% Black or African American, non-Hispanic/Latino; 15% Hispanic/Latino; 2% Asian, non-Hispanic/Latino; 0.1% Native Hawaiian or other Pacific Islander, non-Hispanic/Latino; 0.3% American Indian or Alaska Native, non-Hispanic/Latino; 0.9% Two or more races, non-Hispanic/Latino; 4% Race/ethnicity unknown; 0.2% international; 8% transferred in. *Retention:* 68% of full-time freshmen returned.

Freshmen *Admission:* 1,912 applied, 1,481 admitted, 931 enrolled. *Average high school GPA:* 2.62. *Test scores:* SAT critical reading scores over 500: 27%; SAT math scores over 500: 27%; ACT scores over 18: 66%; SAT critical reading scores over 600: 5%; SAT math scores over 600: 6%; ACT scores over 24: 22%; ACT scores over 30: 1%.

Faculty *Total:* 390, 47% full-time, 42% with terminal degrees. *Student/faculty ratio:* 17:1.

Academics *Calendar:* semesters. *Degrees:* certificates, associate, bachelor's, master's, and postbachelor's certificates. *Special study options:* academic remediation for entering students, accelerated degree program, adult/continuing education programs, advanced placement credit, cooperative education, distance learning, double majors, external degree program, honors programs, independent study, internships, off-campus study, part-time degree program, services for LD students, student-designed majors, study abroad, summer session for credit. *ROTC:* Army (b).

Computers on Campus Students can access the following: campus intranet, computer help desk, free student e-mail accounts, online (class) grades, online (class) registration, online (class) schedules. Campuswide network is available. Wireless service is available via entire campus.

Student Life *Housing:* college housing not available. *Activities and organizations:* drama/theater group, student-run newspaper, choral group, Student Government Association, Student Guides Organization, Nursing Association, Dental Association, International Affairs Club, national fraternities, national sororities. *Campus security:* 24-hour emergency response devices and patrols, late-night transport/escort service, lighted pathways. *Student services:* personal/psychological counseling.

Athletics Member NAIA. *Intercollegiate sports:* basketball M/W, volleyball W. *Intramural sports:* basketball M(c), bowling M(c)/W(c), cheerleading W(c), fencing M(c)/W(c), soccer M(c), softball M(c)/W(c), table tennis M(c)/W(c), tennis M(c)/W(c), volleyball M(c)/W(c).

Standardized Tests *Required:* SAT or ACT (for admission).

Costs (2010–11) *Tuition:* state resident $5752 full-time, $192 per credit hour part-time; nonresident $15,940 full-time, $531 per credit hour part-time. Full-time tuition and fees vary according to course load, location, and program. Part-time tuition and fees vary according to course load, location, and program. *Required fees:* $441 full-time. *Payment plans:* installment, deferred payment. *Waivers:* employees or children of employees.

Financial Aid Of all full-time matriculated undergraduates who enrolled in 2008, 2,535 applied for aid, 2,141 were judged to have need, 58 had their need fully met. In 2008, 134 non-need-based awards were made. *Average percent of need met:* 91%. *Average financial aid package:* $8070. *Average need-based loan:* $3743. *Average need-based gift aid:* $6247. *Average non-need-based aid:* $3739. *Average indebtedness upon graduation:* $27,356.

Applying *Options:* early admission, deferred entrance. *Application fee:* $25. *Required:* high school transcript, minimum 2 GPA. *Application deadlines:* rolling (freshmen), rolling (transfers). *Notification:* continuous (freshmen), continuous (transfers).

Freshman Application Contact Dr. Linda B. Templeton, Director of Admissions, Indiana University Northwest, Hawthorn Hall 100, 3400 Broadway, Gary, IN 46408-1197. *Phone:* 219-980-6991. *Toll-free phone:* 800-968-7486. *Fax:* 219-981-4219. *E-mail:* admit@iun.edu. *Web site:* http://www.iun.edu/.

Indiana University–Purdue University Fort Wayne

Fort Wayne, Indiana

- **State-supported** comprehensive, founded 1917, part of Indiana University System and Purdue University System
- **Urban** 682-acre campus
- **Endowment** $33.8 million
- **Coed** 13,402 undergraduate students, 66% full-time, 55% women, 45% men
- **Minimally difficult** entrance level, 95% of applicants were admitted

Undergraduates 8,855 full-time, 4,547 part-time. Students come from 46 states and territories; 59 other countries; 5% are from out of state; 6% transferred in; 7% live on campus. *Retention:* 62% of full-time freshmen returned.

Freshmen *Admission:* 4,041 applied, 3,833 admitted, 2,297 enrolled. *Average high school GPA:* 3.01. *Test scores:* SAT critical reading scores over 500: 40%; SAT math scores over 500: 47%; SAT writing scores over 500: 31%; ACT scores over 18: 84%; SAT critical reading scores over 600: 10%; SAT math scores over 600: 13%; SAT writing scores over 600: 8%; ACT scores over 24: 34%; SAT critical reading scores over 700: 1%; SAT math scores over 700: 1%; SAT writing scores over 700: 1%; ACT scores over 30: 6%.

Faculty *Total:* 827, 52% full-time, 50% with terminal degrees. *Student/faculty ratio:* 19:1.

Academics *Calendar:* semesters. *Degrees:* certificates, associate, bachelor's, master's, and postbachelor's certificates. *Special study options:* academic remediation for entering students, accelerated degree program, adult/continuing education programs, advanced placement credit, cooperative education, distance learning, double majors, English as a second language, honors programs, independent study, internships, off-campus study, part-time degree program, services for LD students, student-designed majors, study abroad, summer session for credit. *ROTC:* Army (b).

Computers on Campus 642 computers/terminals are available on campus for general student use. Students can access the following: computer help desk, free student e-mail accounts, online (class) grades, online (class) registration, online (class) schedules, student academic records. Campuswide network is available. 100% of college-owned or -operated housing units are wired for high-speed Internet access. Wireless service is available via entire campus.

Student Life *Housing options:* coed. Campus housing is provided by a third party. *Activities and organizations:* drama/theater group, student-run newspaper, television station, choral group, Campus Ministry, Big Heart, Circle K, Anthropology, Club Seoul. *Campus security:* 24-hour emergency response devices and patrols, late-night transport/escort service, controlled dormitory access. *Student services:* health clinic, personal/psychological counseling, women's center.

Athletics Member NCAA. All Division I. *Intercollegiate sports:* baseball M(s), basketball M(s)/W(s), cross-country running M(s)/W(s), golf M(s)/W(s), soccer M(s)/W(s), softball W(s), tennis M(s)/W(s), track and field W(s), volleyball M(s)/W(s). *Intramural sports:* badminton M/W, basketball M/W, bowling M/W, golf M/W, racquetball M/W, soccer M/W, table tennis M/W, tennis M/W, ultimate Frisbee M/W, volleyball M/W.

Standardized Tests *Required:* SAT or ACT (for admission).

Costs (2010–11) *Tuition:* state resident $5712 full-time, $212 per credit hour part-time; nonresident $14,886 full-time, $551 per credit hour part-time. Full-time tuition and fees vary according to course load. Part-time tuition and fees vary according to course load. *Required fees:* $833 full-time, $31 per credit hour part-time. *Room only:* $5900. Room and board charges vary according to housing facility. *Payment plans:* installment, deferred payment. *Waivers:* senior citizens and employees or children of employees.

Financial Aid Of all full-time matriculated undergraduates who enrolled in 2008, 6,218 applied for aid, 5,067 were judged to have need, 36 had their need fully met. In 2008, 124 non-need-based awards were made. *Average percent of need met:* 53%. *Average financial aid package:* $8981. *Average need-based loan:* $3828. *Average need-based gift aid:* $5473. *Average non-need-based aid:* $2011. *Average indebtedness upon graduation:* $22,092.

Applying *Options:* electronic application, deferred entrance. *Application fee:* $50. *Required:* high school transcript. *Recommended:* rank in upper 50% of high school class. *Application deadlines:* 8/1 (freshmen), 8/1 (transfers). *Notification:* continuous (freshmen), continuous (transfers).

Freshman Application Contact Angela Morren, Undergraduate Applications Coordinator, Indiana University–Purdue University Fort Wayne, 2101 East Coliseum Boulevard, Fort Wayne, IN 46805-1499. *Phone:* 260-481-6142. *Toll-free phone:* 800-324-4739. *Fax:* 260-481-6880. *E-mail:* morrena@ipfw.edu. *Web site:* http://www.ipfw.edu/.

Indiana University–Purdue University Indianapolis

Indianapolis, Indiana

- **State-supported** university, founded 1969, part of Indiana University System
- **Urban** 509-acre campus
- **Endowment** $462.0 million
- **Coed** 22,245 undergraduate students, 72% full-time, 57% women, 43% men
- **Moderately difficult** entrance level, 63% of applicants were admitted

Undergraduates 16,015 full-time, 6,230 part-time. Students come from 51 states and territories; 136 other countries; 2% are from out of state; 10% Black or African American, non-Hispanic/Latino; 4% Hispanic/Latino; 3% Asian, non-Hispanic/Latino; 0.1% Native Hawaiian or other Pacific Islander, non-Hispanic/Latino; 0.2% American Indian or Alaska Native, non-Hispanic/Latino; 2% Two or more races, non-Hispanic/Latino; 2% Race/ethnicity unknown; 3% international; 7% transferred in; 5% live on campus. *Retention:* 73% of full-time freshmen returned.

Freshmen *Admission:* 11,765 applied, 7,452 admitted, 2,854 enrolled. *Average high school GPA:* 3.27. *Test scores:* SAT critical reading scores over 500: 47%; SAT math scores over 500: 54%; ACT scores over 18: 83%; SAT critical reading scores over 600: 12%; SAT math scores over 600: 17%; ACT scores over 24: 33%; SAT critical reading scores over 700: 1%; SAT math scores over 700: 2%; ACT scores over 30: 5%.

Faculty *Total:* 3,190, 68% full-time, 63% with terminal degrees. *Student/faculty ratio:* 16:1.

Academics *Calendar:* semesters. *Degrees:* certificates, associate, bachelor's, master's, doctoral-professional, doctoral-research/scholarship, and postbachelor's certificates. *Special study options:* academic remediation for entering students, accelerated degree program, adult/continuing education programs, advanced placement credit, cooperative education, distance learning, double majors, English as a second language, external degree program, honors programs, independent study, internships, off-campus study, part-time degree program, services for LD students, student-designed majors, study abroad, summer session for credit. *ROTC:* Army (b), Air Force (c).

Computers on Campus Students can access the following: campus intranet, computer help desk, free student e-mail accounts, online (class) grades, online (class) registration, online (class) schedules. Campuswide network is available. Wireless service is available via entire campus.

Student Life *Housing options:* coed. Campus housing is university owned. *Activities and organizations:* drama/theater group, student-run newspaper, choral group, Undergraduate Student Assembly, Black Student Union, Student Activities Programming Board, national fraternities, national sororities. *Campus security:* 24-hour emergency response devices and patrols, late-night transport/escort service, controlled dormitory access, lighted pathways, self-defense education. *Student services:* health clinic, personal/psychological counseling, women's center.

Athletics Member NCAA. All Division I. *Intercollegiate sports:* basketball M(s)/W(s), cross-country running M(s)/W(s), golf M(s)/W, soccer M(s)/W(s), softball W(s), swimming and diving M(s)/W(s), tennis M(s)/W(s), volleyball W(s). *Intramural sports:* badminton M/W, baseball M, basketball M/W, cross-country running M/W, football M, golf M/W, racquetball M/W, soccer M/W, softball M/W, swimming and diving M/W, table tennis M/W, tennis M/W, track and field M/W, volleyball M/W, water polo M/W.

Standardized Tests *Required:* SAT or ACT (for admission).

Costs (2010–11) *Tuition:* state resident $7255 full-time, $242 per credit hour part-time; nonresident $23,798 full-time, $793 per credit hour part-time. Full-time tuition and fees vary according to course load, location, and program. Part-time tuition and fees vary according to course load, location, and program. *Required fees:* $630 full-time. *Room and board:* $7944. Room and board charges vary according to housing facility. *Payment plans:* installment, deferred payment. *Waivers:* employees or children of employees.

Financial Aid Of all full-time matriculated undergraduates who enrolled in 2008, 12,522 applied for aid, 10,466 were judged to have need, 474 had their need fully met. In 2008, 1031 non-need-based awards were made. *Average percent of need met:* 89%. *Average financial aid package:* $9094. *Average need-based loan:* $4124. *Average need-based gift aid:* $7059. *Average non-need-based aid:* $3770. *Average indebtedness upon graduation:* $29,112.

Applying *Options:* electronic application, deferred entrance. *Application fee:* $50. *Required:* high school transcript. *Required for some:* interview. *Recommended:* portfolio for art program. *Application deadlines:* 6/1 (freshmen), rolling (transfers). *Notification:* continuous (freshmen), continuous (transfers).

Freshman Application Contact Mr. Chris J. Foley, Director of Admissions, Indiana University–Purdue University Indianapolis, Cavanaugh Hall 129, 425 University Boulevard, Indianapolis, IN 46202-5143. *Phone:* 317-274-4591. *Fax:* 317-278-1862. *E-mail:* apply@iupui.edu. *Web site:* http://www.iupui.edu/.

Indiana University South Bend

South Bend, Indiana

- **State-supported** comprehensive, founded 1922, part of Indiana University System
- **Suburban** 102-acre campus with easy access to Chicago
- **Endowment** $8.1 million
- **Coed** 7,790 undergraduate students, 58% full-time, 60% women, 40% men
- **Moderately difficult** entrance level, 69% of applicants were admitted

Undergraduates 4,504 full-time, 3,286 part-time. Students come from 27 states and territories; 84 other countries; 4% are from out of state; 8% Black or African American, non-Hispanic/Latino; 6% Hispanic/Latino; 1% Asian, non-Hispanic/Latino; 0.3% American Indian or Alaska Native, non-Hispanic/Latino; 1% Two or more races, non-Hispanic/Latino; 3% Race/ethnicity unknown; 2% international; 6% transferred in. *Retention:* 63% of full-time freshmen returned.

Freshmen *Admission:* 2,619 applied, 1,806 admitted, 1,048 enrolled. *Average high school GPA:* 2.91. *Test scores:* SAT critical reading scores over 500: 39%; SAT math scores over 500: 37%; ACT scores over 18: 77%; SAT critical reading scores over 600: 8%; SAT math scores over 600: 6%; ACT scores over 24: 21%; SAT critical reading scores over 700: 1%; SAT math scores over 700: 1%; ACT scores over 30: 1%.

Faculty *Total:* 559, 53% full-time, 40% with terminal degrees. *Student/faculty ratio:* 16:1.

Academics *Calendar:* semesters. *Degrees:* certificates, diplomas, associate, bachelor's, master's, and postbachelor's certificates. *Special study options:* accelerated degree program, adult/continuing education programs, distance learning, double majors, English as a second language, external degree program, honors programs, internships, off-campus study, part-time degree program, study abroad, summer session for credit. *ROTC:* Army (c), Navy (c), Air Force (c).

Computers on Campus Students can access the following: campus intranet, computer help desk, free student e-mail accounts, online (class) grades, online (class) registration, online (class) schedules. Campuswide network is available. Wireless service is available via entire campus.

Student Life *Activities and organizations:* drama/theater group, student-run newspaper, choral group, national fraternities. *Campus security:* 24-hour emergency response devices and patrols, late-night transport/escort service, safety seminars, lighted pathways. *Student services:* personal/psychological counseling, women's center.

Athletics Member NAIA. *Intercollegiate sports:* basketball M(s)/W(s), volleyball W. *Intramural sports:* badminton M/W, baseball M, basketball M/W, bowling M(c)/W(c), cheerleading W(c), cross-country running M/W, golf M/W, racquetball M/W, soccer M(c)/W(c), volleyball W(c).

Standardized Tests *Required:* SAT or ACT (for admission).

Costs (2010–11) *Tuition:* state resident $5843 full-time, $195 per credit hour part-time; nonresident $16,170 full-time, $539 per credit hour part-time. Full-time tuition and fees vary according to course load, location, and program. Part-time tuition and fees vary according to course load, location, and program. *Required fees:* $447 full-time. *Room only:* $5382. Room and board charges vary according to board plan, housing facility, and location. *Payment plan:* deferred payment. *Waivers:* employees or children of employees.

Financial Aid Of all full-time matriculated undergraduates who enrolled in 2008, 3,622 applied for aid, 3,054 were judged to have need, 95 had their need fully met. In 2008, 114 non-need-based awards were made. *Average percent of need met:* 93%. *Average financial aid package:* $7859. *Average need-based loan:* $3629. *Average need-based gift aid:* $6186. *Average non-need-based aid:* $4454. *Average indebtedness upon graduation:* $25,373. *Financial aid deadline:* 3/1.

Applying *Options:* deferred entrance. *Application fee:* $45. *Required:* high school transcript, minimum 2 GPA. *Required for some:* interview. *Application deadlines:* rolling (freshmen), rolling (transfers). *Notification:* continuous (freshmen), continuous (transfers).

Freshman Application Contact Mr. Michael Renfrow, Associate Director of Admissions, Indiana University South Bend, 1700 Mishawaka Avenue, PO Box 7111, South Bend, IN 46634-7111. *Phone:* 574-520-4839. *Toll-free phone:* 877-GO-2-IUSB. *Fax:* 574-520-4834. *E-mail:* admissio@iusb.edu. *Web site:* http://www.iusb.edu/.

Indiana University Southeast

New Albany, Indiana

- **State-supported** comprehensive, founded 1941, part of Indiana University System
- **Suburban** 178-acre campus with easy access to Louisville
- **Endowment** $10.5 million
- **Coed** 6,384 undergraduate students, 65% full-time, 59% women, 41% men
- **Minimally difficult** entrance level, 81% of applicants were admitted

Undergraduates 4,126 full-time, 2,258 part-time. Students come from 15 states and territories; 45 other countries; 29% are from out of state; 6% Black or African American, non-Hispanic/Latino; 2% Hispanic/Latino; 1% Asian, non-Hispanic/Latino; 0.1% Native Hawaiian or other Pacific Islander, non-Hispanic/Latino; 0.3% American Indian or Alaska Native, non-Hispanic/Latino; 2% Two or more races, non-Hispanic/Latino; 2% Race/ethnicity unknown; 0.4% international; 8% transferred in. *Retention:* 63% of full-time freshmen returned.

Freshmen *Admission:* 2,365 applied, 1,920 admitted, 1,052 enrolled. *Average high school GPA:* 2.96. *Test scores:* SAT critical reading scores over 500: 38%; SAT math scores over 500: 39%; ACT scores over 18: 74%; SAT critical reading scores over 600: 9%; SAT math scores over 600: 7%; ACT scores over 24: 17%; SAT critical reading scores over 700: 1%; ACT scores over 30: 1%.

Faculty *Total:* 479, 43% full-time, 39% with terminal degrees. *Student/faculty ratio:* 17:1.

Academics *Calendar:* semesters. *Degrees:* certificates, associate, bachelor's, master's, and postbachelor's certificates. *Special study options:* academic remediation for entering students, accelerated degree program, adult/continuing education programs, advanced placement credit, double majors, external degree program, independent study, internships, off-campus study, part-time degree program, services for LD students, student-designed majors, study abroad, summer session for credit. *ROTC:* Army (b).

Computers on Campus Students can access the following: campus intranet, computer help desk, free student e-mail accounts, online (class) grades, online (class) registration, online (class) schedules. Campuswide network is available. Wireless service is available via entire campus.

Student Life *Housing options:* coed. *Activities and organizations:* drama/theater group, student-run newspaper, choral group, national fraternities, national sororities. *Campus security:* 24-hour emergency response devices and patrols, self-defense education, lighted pathways, police department on campus. *Student services:* personal/psychological counseling.

Athletics Member NAIA. *Intercollegiate sports:* baseball M, basketball M(s)/W(s), cheerleading W, softball W, tennis M/W, volleyball W(s). *Intramural sports:* basketball M/W, bowling M/W, cross-country running M/W, softball M/W, tennis M/W, volleyball M/W.

Standardized Tests *Required:* SAT or ACT (for admission).

Costs (2010–11) *Tuition:* state resident $5672 full-time, $189 per credit hour part-time; nonresident $14,937 full-time, $498 per credit hour part-time. Full-time tuition and fees vary according to course load, location, program, and reciprocity agreements. Part-time tuition and fees vary according to course load, location, program, and reciprocity agreements. *Required fees:* $491 full-time. *Room only:* $5686. Room and board charges vary according to board plan and housing facility. *Payment plan:* deferred payment. *Waivers:* employees or children of employees.

Financial Aid Of all full-time matriculated undergraduates who enrolled in 2008, 3,133 applied for aid, 2,502 were judged to have need, 112 had their need fully met. In 2008, 136 non-need-based awards were made. *Average percent of need met:* 93%. *Average financial aid package:* $7667. *Average need-based loan:* $3783. *Average need-based gift aid:* $5948. *Average non-need-based aid:* $1855. *Average indebtedness upon graduation:* $21,456.

Applying *Options:* early admission, deferred entrance. *Application fee:* $30. *Required:* high school transcript. *Required for some:* interview. *Application deadlines:* rolling (freshmen), rolling (transfers). *Notification:* continuous (freshmen), continuous (transfers).

Freshman Application Contact Ms. Anne Skuce, Director of Admissions/Assistant Vice Chancellor for Enrollment Management, Indiana University Southeast, University Center Building, Room 102, 4201 Grant Line Road, New Albany, IN 47150. *Phone:* 812-941-2212. *Toll-free phone:* 800-852-8835. *Fax:* 812-941-2595. *E-mail:* admissions@ius.edu. *Web site:* http://www.ius.edu/.

Indiana Wesleyan University

Marion, Indiana

- **Independent Wesleyan** comprehensive, founded 1920
- **Small-town** 300-acre campus with easy access to Indianapolis
- **Endowment** $55.9 million
- **Coed** 3,201 undergraduate students, 95% full-time, 63% women, 37% men
- **Moderately difficult** entrance level, 67% of applicants were admitted

Undergraduates 3,025 full-time, 176 part-time. Students come from 45 states and territories; 55 other countries; 47% are from out of state; 1% Black or African American, non-Hispanic/Latino; 2% Hispanic/Latino; 0.6% Asian, non-Hispanic/Latino; 0.2% Native Hawaiian or other Pacific Islander, non-Hispanic/Latino; 0.1% American Indian or Alaska Native, non-Hispanic/Latino; 2% Two or more races, non-Hispanic/Latino; 0.5% Race/ethnicity unknown; 0.3% international; 5% transferred in; 82% live on campus. *Retention:* 77% of full-time freshmen returned.

Freshmen *Admission:* 2,835 applied, 1,908 admitted, 772 enrolled. *Average high school GPA:* 3.55. *Test scores:* SAT critical reading scores over 500: 65%; SAT math scores over 500: 65%; SAT writing scores over 500: 57%; ACT scores over 18: 94%; SAT critical reading scores over 600: 24%; SAT math scores over 600: 24%; SAT writing scores over 600: 20%; ACT scores over 24: 58%; SAT critical reading scores over 700: 4%; SAT math scores over 700: 4%; SAT writing scores over 700: 3%; ACT scores over 30: 10%.

Faculty *Total:* 284, 58% full-time, 37% with terminal degrees. *Student/faculty ratio:* 15:1.

Academics *Calendar:* semesters. *Degrees:* certificates, associate, bachelor's, master's, doctoral-other, post-master's, and postbachelor's certificates (also offers adult program with significant enrollment not reflected in profile). *Special study options:* academic remediation for entering students, advanced placement credit, distance learning, double majors, freshman honors college, honors programs, independent study, internships, off-campus study, part-time degree program, services for LD students, study abroad, summer session for credit. *ROTC:* Army (b).

Computers on Campus 691 computers/terminals are available on campus for general student use. Students can access the following: campus intranet, computer help desk, free student e-mail accounts, online (class) grades, online (class) registration, online (class) schedules. Campuswide network is available. 100% of college-owned or -operated housing units are wired for high-speed Internet access. Wireless service is available via entire campus.

Student Life *Housing:* on-campus residence required through junior year. *Options:* men-only, women-only. Campus housing is university owned. Freshman campus housing is guaranteed. *Activities and organizations:* drama/theater group, student-run newspaper, radio and television station, choral group, Student Government Organization, Student Activities Council, University Players, World Christian Fellowship, Sixth Man Club. *Campus security:* 24-hour emergency response devices and patrols, late-night transport/escort service, controlled dormitory access. *Student services:* health clinic, personal/psychological counseling.

Athletics Member NAIA, NCCAA. *Intercollegiate sports:* baseball M(s), basketball M(s)/W(s), cheerleading M(s)/W(s), cross-country running M(s)/W(s), golf M(s), soccer M(s)/W(s), softball W(s), tennis M(s)/W(s), track and field M(s)/W(s), volleyball W(s). *Intramural sports:* badminton M/W, basketball M/W, bowling M/W, football M/W, golf M/W, racquetball M/W, soccer M/W, softball M/W, swimming and diving M/W, table tennis M/W, tennis M/W, ultimate Frisbee M/W, volleyball M/W, weight lifting M/W.

Standardized Tests *Required:* SAT or ACT (for admission), TOEFL for non-English speaking, and some non-resident alien students (for admission).

Costs (2011–12) *Comprehensive fee:* $29,104 includes full-time tuition ($21,956) and room and board ($7148). Full-time tuition and fees vary according to course load. Part-time tuition: $785 per credit. Part-time tuition and fees vary according to course load. *College room only:* $3458. Room and board charges vary according to board plan. *Payment plan:* installment. *Waivers:* employees or children of employees.

Financial Aid Of all full-time matriculated undergraduates who enrolled in 2008, 2,833 applied for aid, 2,122 were judged to have need, 893 had their need fully met. 1,325 Federal Work-Study jobs (averaging $617). In 2008, 637 non-need-based awards were made. *Average percent of need met:* 87%. *Average financial aid package:* $21,291. *Average need-based loan:* $8904. *Average need-based gift aid:* $12,723. *Average non-need-based aid:* $7388. *Average indebtedness upon graduation:* $28,657.

Applying *Options:* electronic application, deferred entrance. *Application fee:* $25. *Required:* essay or personal statement, high school transcript, minimum 2 GPA, 2 letters of recommendation. *Application deadlines:* rolling (freshmen), rolling (out-of-state freshmen), rolling (transfers). *Notification:* continuous (freshmen), continuous (out-of-state freshmen), continuous (transfers).

Freshman Application Contact Mr. Daniel Solms, Director of Admissions, Indiana Wesleyan University, 4201 South Washington Street, Marion, IN 46953. *Phone:* 866-468-6498 Ext. 2138. *Toll-free phone:* 800-332-6901. *Fax:* 765-677-2333. *E-mail:* admissions@indwes.edu. *Web site:* http://www.indwes.edu/.

International Business College
Fort Wayne, Indiana

- **Private** 4-year, founded 1889
- **Suburban** campus
- **Coed** 656 undergraduate students
- 75% of applicants were admitted

Freshmen *Admission:* 979 applied, 739 admitted.
Academics *Calendar:* semesters. *Degrees:* diplomas, associate, and bachelor's. *Special study options:* accelerated degree program, internships.
Freshman Application Contact Admissions Office, International Business College, 5699 Coventry Lane, Fort Wayne, IN 46804. *Phone:* 260-459-4500. *Toll-free phone:* 800-589-6363. *Web site:* http://www.ibcfortwayne.edu/.

ITT Technical Institute
Fort Wayne, Indiana

- **Proprietary** primarily 2-year, founded 1967, part of ITT Educational Services, Inc.
- **Coed**
- **Minimally difficult** entrance level

Academics *Calendar:* quarters. *Degrees:* associate and bachelor's.
Student Life *Housing:* college housing not available.
Freshman Application Contact Director of Recruitment, ITT Technical Institute, 2810 Dupont Commerce Court, Fort Wayne, IN 46825. *Phone:* 260-497-6200. *Toll-free phone:* 800-866-4488. *Fax:* 260-497-6299. *Web site:* http://www.itt-tech.edu/.

ITT Technical Institute
Indianapolis, Indiana

- **Proprietary** founded 1966, part of ITT Educational Services, Inc.
- **Suburban** campus
- **Coed**
- **Minimally difficult** entrance level

Academics *Calendar:* quarters. *Degrees:* diplomas, associate, bachelor's, and master's.
Student Life *Housing:* college housing not available.

Freshman Application Contact Director of Recruitment, ITT Technical Institute, 9511 Angola Court, Indianapolis, IN 46268-1119. *Phone:* 317-875-8640. *Toll-free phone:* 800-937-4488. *Web site:* http://www.itt-tech.edu/.

ITT Technical Institute
Merrillville, Indiana

- **Proprietary** primarily 2-year
- **Coed**
- **Minimally difficult** entrance level

Academics *Degrees:* associate and bachelor's.
Freshman Application Contact Director of Recruitment, ITT Technical Institute, 8488 Georgia Street, Merrillville, IN 46410. *Phone:* 219-738-6100. *Toll-free phone:* 877-418-8134. *Web site:* http://www.itt-tech.edu/.

ITT Technical Institute
Newburgh, Indiana

- **Proprietary** primarily 2-year, founded 1966, part of ITT Educational Services, Inc.
- **Coed**
- **Minimally difficult** entrance level

Academics *Calendar:* quarters. *Degrees:* associate and bachelor's.
Student Life *Housing:* college housing not available.
Freshman Application Contact Director of Recruitment, ITT Technical Institute, 10999 Stahl Road, Newburgh, IN 47630-7430. *Phone:* 812-858-1600. *Toll-free phone:* 800-832-4488. *Web site:* http://www.itt-tech.edu/.

ITT Technical Institute
South Bend, Indiana

- **Proprietary** 4-year, part of ITT Educational Services, Inc.
- **Coed**
- **Minimally difficult** entrance level

Academics *Calendar:* quarters. *Degrees:* associate and bachelor's.
Student Life *Housing:* college housing not available.
Freshman Application Contact Director of Recruitment, ITT Technical Institute, 17390 Dugdale Drive, Suite 100, South Bend, IN 46635. *Phone:* 574-247-8300. *Toll-free phone:* 877-474-1926. *Web site:* http://www.itt-tech.edu/.

Manchester College
North Manchester, Indiana

- **Independent** comprehensive, founded 1889, affiliated with Church of the Brethren
- **Small-town** 125-acre campus
- **Endowment** $35.7 million
- **Coed** 1,274 undergraduate students, 97% full-time, 52% women, 48% men
- **Moderately difficult** entrance level, 64% of applicants were admitted

Undergraduates 1,240 full-time, 34 part-time. Students come from 22 states and territories; 20 other countries; 11% are from out of state; 3% Black or African American, non-Hispanic/Latino; 3% Hispanic/Latino; 0.8% Asian, non-Hispanic/Latino; 0.1% Native Hawaiian or other Pacific Islander, non-Hispanic/Latino; 0.7% American Indian or Alaska Native, non-Hispanic/Latino; 2% Two or more races, non-Hispanic/Latino; 0.6% Race/ethnicity unknown; 3% international; 3% transferred in; 75% live on campus. *Retention:* 67% of full-time freshmen returned.
Freshmen *Admission:* 3,473 applied, 2,234 admitted, 407 enrolled. *Average high school GPA:* 3.28. *Test scores:* SAT critical reading scores over 500: 47%; SAT math scores over 500: 58%; SAT writing scores over 500: 40%; ACT scores over 18: 95%; SAT critical reading scores over 600: 13%; SAT math scores over 600: 16%; SAT writing scores over 600: 9%; ACT scores over 24: 44%; SAT critical reading scores over 700: 1%; SAT math scores over 700: 1%; ACT scores over 30: 6%.
Faculty *Total:* 99, 72% full-time, 71% with terminal degrees. *Student/faculty ratio:* 16:1.
Academics *Calendar:* 4-1-4. *Degrees:* certificates, associate, bachelor's, and master's. *Special study options:* accelerated degree program, advanced placement credit, distance learning, double majors, honors programs, independent study, internships, off-campus study, part-time degree program, services for LD students, student-designed majors, study abroad, summer session for credit. *Unusual degree programs:* 3-2 engineering with Washington University in St. Louis; nursing with Goshen College; physical therapy, occupational therapy.
Computers on Campus 222 computers/terminals are available on campus for general student use. Students can access the following: campus intranet, com-

puter help desk, free student e-mail accounts, online (class) grades, online (class) registration, online (class) schedules. Campuswide network is available. 100% of college-owned or -operated housing units are wired for high-speed Internet access. Wireless service is available via computer centers, computer labs, dorm rooms, learning centers, libraries, student centers.

Student Life *Housing:* on-campus residence required through junior year. *Options:* coed, disabled students. Campus housing is university owned. Freshman campus housing is guaranteed. *Activities and organizations:* drama/theater group, student-run newspaper, radio station, choral group, A Cappella Choir, International Association, Accounting and Business Club, Habitat for Humanity, Student Education Association. *Campus security:* 24-hour emergency response devices and patrols, student patrols, late-night transport/escort service, alarm system, locked residence hall entrances. *Student services:* health clinic, personal/psychological counseling.

Athletics Member NCAA. All Division III. *Intercollegiate sports:* baseball M, basketball M/W, cheerleading W, cross-country running M/W, football M, golf M/W, soccer M/W, softball W, tennis M/W, track and field M/W, volleyball W, wrestling M. *Intramural sports:* badminton M/W, basketball M/W, football M/W, racquetball M/W, soccer M/W, softball M/W, table tennis M/W, tennis M/W, ultimate Frisbee M/W, volleyball M/W.

Standardized Tests *Required:* SAT or ACT (for admission).

Costs (2010–11) *One-time required fee:* $250. *Comprehensive fee:* $33,780 includes full-time tuition ($24,100), mandatory fees ($820), and room and board ($8860). Part-time tuition: $700 per credit hour. Part-time tuition and fees vary according to course load. *Required fees:* $24 per credit hour part-time. *College room only:* $5400. Room and board charges vary according to board plan and housing facility. *Payment plan:* installment. *Waivers:* employees or children of employees.

Financial Aid Of all full-time matriculated undergraduates who enrolled in 2009, 1,137 applied for aid, 1,070 were judged to have need, 203 had their need fully met. In 2009, 88 non-need-based awards were made. *Average percent of need met:* 83%. *Average financial aid package:* $23,512. *Average need-based loan:* $4172. *Average need-based gift aid:* $18,901. *Average non-need-based aid:* $14,058. *Average indebtedness upon graduation:* $21,305.

Applying *Options:* electronic application. *Application fee:* $25. *Required:* high school transcript, 1 letter of recommendation, rank in upper 50% of high school class. *Required for some:* essay or personal statement, minimum 3 GPA. *Recommended:* minimum 2.3 GPA. *Application deadlines:* rolling (freshmen), rolling (transfers). *Notification:* continuous (freshmen), continuous (transfers).

Freshman Application Contact Mr. Adam Hohman, Associate Director of Admissions, Manchester College, 604 East College Avenue, North Manchester, IN 46962-1225. *Phone:* 260-982-5055. *Toll-free phone:* 800-852-3648. *Fax:* 260-982-5239. *E-mail:* admitinfo@manchester.edu. *Web site:* http://www.manchester.edu/.

See page 1404 for the College Close-Up.

Marian University
Indianapolis, Indiana

- **Independent Roman Catholic** comprehensive, founded 1851
- **Suburban** 114-acre campus with easy access to Indianapolis
- **Endowment** $13.4 million
- **Coed**
- **Moderately difficult** entrance level

Faculty *Student/faculty ratio:* 14:1.

Academics *Calendar:* semesters. *Degrees:* associate, bachelor's, and master's.

Student Life *Campus security:* 24-hour patrols, student patrols, late-night transport/escort service, controlled dormitory access.

Athletics Member NAIA.

Standardized Tests *Required:* SAT or ACT (for admission).

Costs (2010–11) *Comprehensive fee:* $32,770 includes full-time tuition ($24,960) and room and board ($7810). Part-time tuition: $1090 per credit hour. *Room and board:* Room and board charges vary according to board plan and housing facility.

Financial Aid *Of all full-time matriculated undergraduates who enrolled in 2008,* 1,192 applied for aid, 1,068 were judged to have need, 231 had their need fully met. 200 Federal Work-Study jobs (averaging $1500). *In 2008,* 185 non-need-based awards were made. *Average percent of need met:* 75. *Average financial aid package:* $19,509. *Average need-based loan:* $4478. *Average need-based gift aid:* $11,188. *Average non-need-based aid:* $12,191. *Average indebtedness upon graduation:* $23,467.

Applying *Options:* electronic application, deferred entrance. *Application fee:* $35. *Required:* minimum 2.3 GPA, college transcripts. *Required for some:* essay or personal statement, high school transcript, interview.

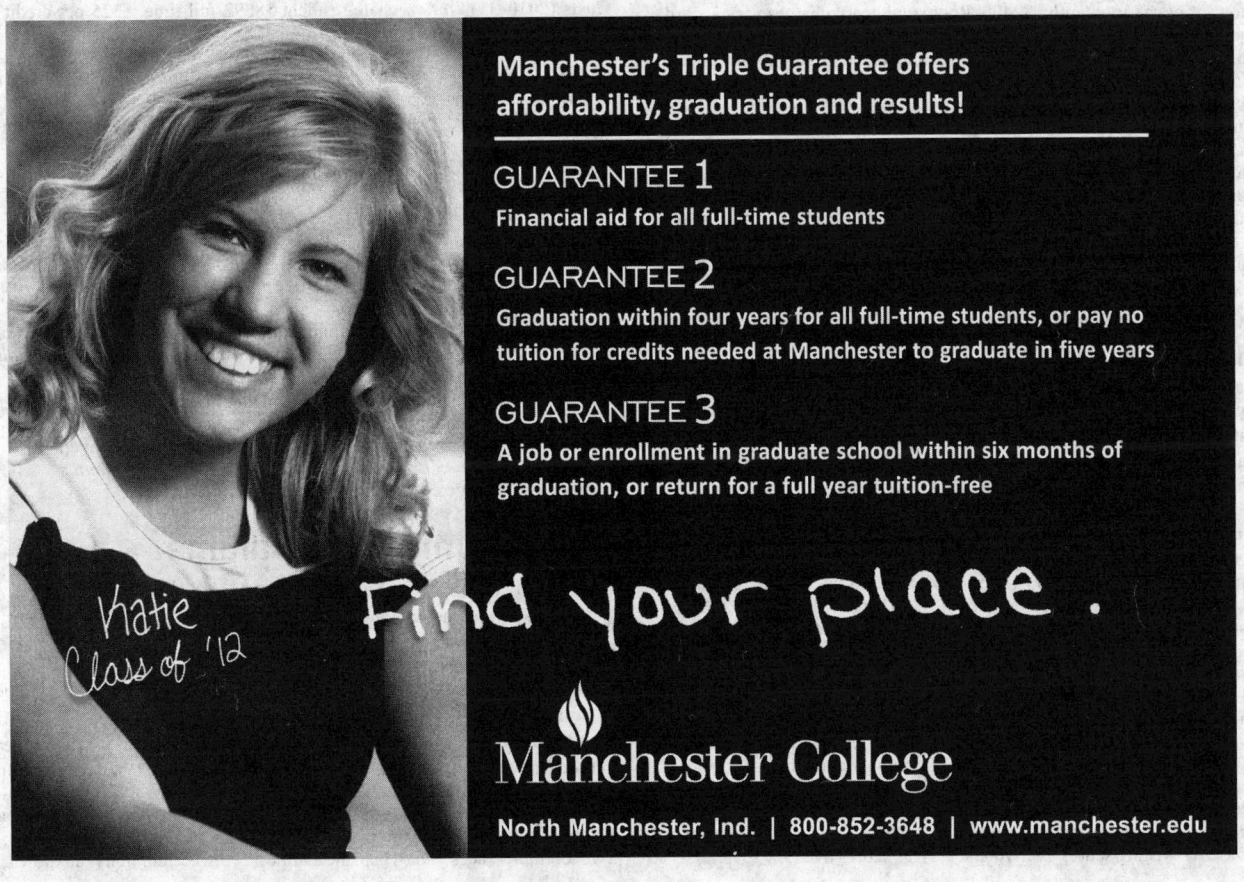

Freshman Application Contact Marian University, 3200 Cold Spring Road, Indianapolis, IN 46222-1997. *Phone:* 317-955-6300. *Toll-free phone:* 800-772-7264. *Fax:* 317-955-6401. *E-mail:* admissions@marian.edu. *Web site:* http://www.marian.edu/.

Martin University
Indianapolis, Indiana

Freshman Application Contact Ms. Brenda Shaheed, Director of Enrollment Management, Martin University, 2171 Avondale Place, PO Box 18567, Indianapolis, IN 46218-3867. *Phone:* 317-543-3237. *Fax:* 317-543-4790. *Web site:* http://www.martin.edu/.

Mid-America College of Funeral Service
Jeffersonville, Indiana

Freshman Application Contact Mr. Richard Nelson, Dean of Students, Mid-America College of Funeral Service, 3111 Hamburg Pike, Jeffersonville, IN 47130-9630. *Phone:* 812-288-8878. *Toll-free phone:* 800-221-6158. *Fax:* 812-288-5942. *E-mail:* macfs@mindspring.com. *Web site:* http://www.mid-america.edu/.

Oakland City University
Oakland City, Indiana

- **Independent General Baptist** comprehensive, founded 1885
- **Rural** 20-acre campus
- **Endowment** $3.2 million
- **Coed**
- **Minimally difficult** entrance level

Faculty *Student/faculty ratio:* 14:1.
Academics *Calendar:* semesters. *Degrees:* certificates, diplomas, associate, bachelor's, master's, and doctoral-professional.
Student Life *Campus security:* 24-hour patrols, student patrols.
Athletics Member NCAA, NCCAA. All NCAA Division II.
Standardized Tests *Required:* SAT or ACT (for admission).
Costs (2010–11) *Comprehensive fee:* $22,700 includes full-time tuition ($15,600), mandatory fees ($400), and room and board ($6700). Full-time tuition and fees vary according to degree level. Part-time tuition: $500 per credit hour. *College room only:* $2400. Room and board charges vary according to board plan and housing facility.
Financial Aid *Of all full-time matriculated undergraduates who enrolled in 2007,* 150 Federal Work-Study jobs (averaging $1600). 4 state and other part-time jobs (averaging $1500). *Average percent of need met:* 90.
Applying *Options:* electronic application, early admission, deferred entrance. *Application fee:* $35. *Required:* essay or personal statement, high school transcript, minimum 2 GPA. *Recommended:* interview.
Freshman Application Contact Ms. Kim Heldt, Director of Admissions, Oakland City University, 138 North Lucretia Street, Oakland City, IN 47660. *Phone:* 812-749-1222. *Toll-free phone:* 800-737-5125. *Web site:* http://www.oak.edu/.

Purdue University
West Lafayette, Indiana

- **State-supported** university, founded 1869, part of Purdue University System
- **Suburban** 2539-acre campus with easy access to Indianapolis
- **Endowment** $1.6 billion
- **Coed** 30,836 undergraduate students, 95% full-time, 42% women, 58% men
- **Moderately difficult** entrance level, 65% of applicants were admitted

Undergraduates 29,429 full-time, 1,407 part-time. Students come from 52 states and territories; 122 other countries; 33% are from out of state; 3% Black or African American, non-Hispanic/Latino; 3% Hispanic/Latino; 5% Asian, non-Hispanic/Latino; 0.3% American Indian or Alaska Native, non-Hispanic/Latino; 0.7% Two or more races, non-Hispanic/Latino; 2% Race/ethnicity unknown; 11% international; 3% transferred in; 38% live on campus. *Retention:* 89% of full-time freshmen returned.
Freshmen *Admission:* 30,707 applied, 19,993 admitted, 6,380 enrolled. *Average high school GPA:* 3.6. *Test scores:* SAT critical reading scores over 500: 75%; SAT math scores over 500: 90%; SAT writing scores over 500: 74%; ACT scores over 18: 99%; SAT critical reading scores over 600: 31%; SAT math scores over 600: 56%; SAT writing scores over 600: 29%; ACT scores over 24: 73%; SAT critical reading scores over 700: 5%; SAT math scores over 700: 18%; SAT writing scores over 700: 4%; ACT scores over 30: 23%.

Faculty *Total:* 2,464, 96% full-time, 87% with terminal degrees. *Student/faculty ratio:* 14:1.
Academics *Calendar:* semesters. *Degrees:* certificates, associate, bachelor's, master's, doctoral-other, doctoral-professional, doctoral-research/scholarship, post-master's, and postbachelor's certificates. *Special study options:* accelerated degree program, adult/continuing education programs, advanced placement credit, cooperative education, distance learning, double majors, freshman honors college, honors programs, independent study, internships, part-time degree program, services for LD students, study abroad, summer session for credit. *ROTC:* Army (b), Navy (b), Air Force (b). *Unusual degree programs:* 3-2 business administration; engineering; forestry; nursing; social work; pharmacy.
Computers on Campus 5,320 computers/terminals and 17,640 ports are available on campus for general student use. Students can access the following: campus intranet, computer help desk, free student e-mail accounts, online (class) grades, online (class) registration, online (class) schedules. Campus-wide network is available. 100% of college-owned or -operated housing units are wired for high-speed Internet access. Wireless service is available via entire campus.
Student Life *Housing options:* coed, men-only, women-only, cooperative, disabled students. Campus housing is university owned. Freshman applicants given priority for college housing. *Activities and organizations:* drama/theater group, student-run newspaper, radio and television station, choral group, marching band, student government, Golden Key National Honor Society, Society of Women Engineers, Purdue student union board, Krannert Graduate Student Association, national fraternities, national sororities. *Campus security:* 24-hour emergency response devices and patrols, student patrols, late-night transport/escort service, controlled dormitory access. *Student services:* health clinic, personal/psychological counseling, women's center.
Athletics Member NCAA. All Division I except football (Division I-A). *Intercollegiate sports:* baseball M(s), basketball M(s)/W(s), cross-country running M(s)/W(s), golf M(s)/W(s), soccer W(s), softball W(s), swimming and diving M(s)/W(s), tennis M(s)/W(s), track and field M(s)/W(s), volleyball W(s), wrestling M(s). *Intramural sports:* archery M(c)/W(c), badminton M(c)/W(c), bowling M(c)/W(c), crew M(c)/W(c), equestrian sports M(c)/W(c), fencing M(c)/W(c), golf M(c)/W(c), gymnastics M(c)/W(c), ice hockey M(c), lacrosse M(c)/W(c), racquetball M(c)/W(c), riflery M(c)/W(c), rock climbing M(c)/W(c), rugby M(c), sailing M(c)/W(c), skiing (downhill) M(c)/W(c), soccer M(c)/W(c), softball M(c)/W(c), swimming and diving M(c)/W(c), tennis M(c)/W(c), track and field M(c)/W(c), ultimate Frisbee M(c)/W(c), volleyball M(c)/W(c), water polo M(c)/W(c).
Standardized Tests *Required:* SAT or ACT (for admission).
Costs (2010–11) *Tuition:* state resident $8592 full-time, $325 per credit hour part-time; nonresident $26,144 full-time, $885 per credit hour part-time. Full-time tuition and fees vary according to course load and program. Part-time tuition and fees vary according to course load. *Required fees:* $477 full-time. *Room and board:* $9120; room only: $4319. Room and board charges vary according to board plan and housing facility. *Payment plan:* installment. *Waivers:* senior citizens and employees or children of employees.
Financial Aid Of all full-time matriculated undergraduates who enrolled in 2009, 19,161 applied for aid, 14,839 were judged to have need, 5,649 had their need fully met. 933 Federal Work-Study jobs (averaging $709). In 2009, 1975 non-need-based awards were made. *Average percent of need met:* 95%. *Average financial aid package:* $11,242. *Average need-based loan:* $4997. *Average need-based gift aid:* $8923. *Average non-need-based aid:* $6134. *Average indebtedness upon graduation:* $26,360.
Applying *Options:* electronic application, early admission, deferred entrance. *Application fee:* $50. *Required:* high school transcript. *Application deadlines:* 3/1 (freshmen), rolling (transfers). *Notification:* continuous (freshmen).
Freshman Application Contact Ms. Pamela T. Horne, Assistant Vice President for Enrollment Management and Dean of Admissions, Purdue University, 475 Stadium Mall Drive, Schleman Hall, West Lafayette, IN 47907-2050. *Phone:* 765-494-1776. *Fax:* 765-494-0544. *E-mail:* admissions@purdue.edu. *Web site:* http://www.purdue.edu/.

Purdue University Calumet
Hammond, Indiana

- **State-supported** comprehensive, founded 1951, part of Purdue University System
- **Urban** 167-acre campus with easy access to Chicago
- **Coed** 8,664 undergraduate students, 68% full-time, 55% women, 45% men
- **Moderately difficult** entrance level, 48% of applicants were admitted

Undergraduates 5,888 full-time, 2,776 part-time. 18% Black or African American, non-Hispanic/Latino; 17% Hispanic/Latino; 1% Asian, non-Hispanic/Latino; 0.1% Native Hawaiian or other Pacific Islander, non-Hispanic/Latino; 0.4% American Indian or Alaska Native, non-Hispanic/Latino; 1% Two or more races, non-Hispanic/Latino; 2% Race/ethnicity unknown; 4%

international; 5% transferred in; 7% live on campus. *Retention:* 69% of full-time freshmen returned.

Freshmen *Admission:* 4,200 applied, 2,019 admitted, 1,065 enrolled. *Average high school GPA:* 2.82. *Test scores:* SAT critical reading scores over 500: 39%; SAT math scores over 500: 39%; SAT critical reading scores over 600: 8%; SAT math scores over 600: 9%.

Academics *Calendar:* semesters. *Degrees:* certificates, associate, bachelor's, master's, post-master's, and postbachelor's certificates. *Special study options:* academic remediation for entering students, accelerated degree program, adult/continuing education programs, advanced placement credit, cooperative education, distance learning, double majors, English as a second language, freshman honors college, honors programs, independent study, internships, part-time degree program, services for LD students, study abroad, summer session for credit.

Computers on Campus Students can access the following: campus intranet, computer help desk, free student e-mail accounts, online (class) registration, student Web page publishing. Campuswide network is available. Wireless service is available via learning centers, libraries, student centers.

Student Life *Housing options:* Campus housing is university owned. *Activities and organizations:* drama/theater group, student-run newspaper, choral group, national fraternities, national sororities. *Campus security:* 24-hour emergency response devices and patrols, student patrols, late-night transport/escort service. *Student services:* health clinic, personal/psychological counseling.

Athletics Member NAIA. *Intercollegiate sports:* basketball M(s)/W(s). *Intramural sports:* bowling M/W, football M/W, golf M/W, racquetball M/W, sailing M/W, softball M/W, ultimate Frisbee M/W, volleyball M/W.

Standardized Tests *Required:* SAT or ACT (for admission).

Costs (2010–11) *Tuition:* state resident $6654 full-time, $221 per credit hour part-time; nonresident $14,306 full-time, $494 per credit hour part-time. Full-time tuition and fees vary according to course load and program. Part-time tuition and fees vary according to course load and program. *Required fees:* $22 per credit hour part-time. *Room and board:* $6924; room only: $4900. Room and board charges vary according to housing facility. *Payment plan:* deferred payment. *Waivers:* senior citizens and employees or children of employees.

Financial Aid Of all full-time matriculated undergraduates who enrolled in 2008, 5,259 applied for aid, 4,334 were judged to have need, 455 had their need fully met. 141 Federal Work-Study jobs (averaging $1909). In 2008, 250 non-need-based awards were made. *Average percent of need met:* 11%. *Average financial aid package:* $7408. *Average need-based loan:* $3421. *Average need-based gift aid:* $5698. *Average non-need-based aid:* $2879. *Average indebtedness upon graduation:* $22,106.

Applying *Options:* electronic application, deferred entrance. *Required:* high school transcript, minimum 2 GPA. *Application deadlines:* 8/1 (freshmen), rolling (transfers). *Notification:* continuous (freshmen), continuous (transfers). **Freshman Application Contact** Purdue University Calumet, 2200 169th Street, Hammond, IN 46323-2094. *Phone:* 219-989-2213. *Toll-free phone:* 800-447-8738. *Web site:* http://www.purduecal.edu/.

Purdue University North Central
Westville, Indiana

- **State-supported** comprehensive, founded 1967, part of Purdue University System
- **Rural** 305-acre campus with easy access to Chicago
- **Endowment** $2.9 million
- **Coed** 4,542 undergraduate students, 63% full-time, 56% women, 44% men
- **Minimally difficult** entrance level, 87% of applicants were admitted

Undergraduates 2,844 full-time, 1,698 part-time. Students come from 8 states and territories; 5 other countries; 1% are from out of state; 4% transferred in. *Retention:* 58% of full-time freshmen returned.

Freshmen *Admission:* 1,634 applied, 1,423 admitted, 882 enrolled. *Average high school GPA:* 2.83. *Test scores:* SAT critical reading scores over 500: 38%; SAT math scores over 500: 42%; SAT writing scores over 500: 29%; ACT scores over 18: 78%; SAT critical reading scores over 600: 7%; SAT math scores over 600: 11%; SAT writing scores over 600: 4%; ACT scores over 24: 14%; SAT math scores over 700: 1%; ACT scores over 30: 2%.

Faculty *Total:* 320, 39% full-time, 33% with terminal degrees. *Student/faculty ratio:* 18:1.

Academics *Calendar:* semesters. *Degrees:* certificates, associate, bachelor's, master's, and postbachelor's certificates. *Special study options:* academic remediation for entering students, advanced placement credit, distance learning, double majors, independent study, internships, off-campus study, part-time degree program, services for LD students, study abroad, summer session for credit.

Computers on Campus 450 computers/terminals and 65 ports are available on campus for general student use. Students can access the following: campus intranet, computer help desk, free student e-mail accounts, online (class)

grades, online (class) registration, online (class) schedules. Campuswide network is available. Wireless service is available via entire campus.

Student Life *Housing:* college housing not available. *Activities and organizations:* drama/theater group, student-run newspaper, choral group, Dean's Leadership Group, Society of Human Resource Management, PLAYCE (Early Childhood Education), Astronomy Club, PNC Veteran's. *Campus security:* 24-hour emergency response devices and patrols, late-night transport/escort service. *Student services:* personal/psychological counseling.

Athletics Member NAIA. *Intercollegiate sports:* cheerleading M/W.

Standardized Tests *Recommended:* SAT or ACT (for admission).

Costs (2010–11) *Tuition:* state resident $6128 full-time, $204 per credit hour part-time; nonresident $15,384 full-time, $513 per credit hour part-time. Full-time tuition and fees vary according to course load, location, program, and reciprocity agreements. Part-time tuition and fees vary according to course load, location, program, and reciprocity agreements. *Required fees:* $576 full-time, $19 per credit hour part-time. *Payment plans:* installment, deferred payment. *Waivers:* senior citizens and employees or children of employees.

Financial Aid Of all full-time matriculated undergraduates who enrolled in 2008, 2,219 applied for aid, 1,818 were judged to have need, 120 had their need fully met. 74 Federal Work-Study jobs (averaging $1671). In 2008, 24 non-need-based awards were made. *Average percent of need met:* 47%. *Average financial aid package:* $7804. *Average need-based loan:* $4158. *Average need-based gift aid:* $6576. *Average non-need-based aid:* $1856. *Average indebtedness upon graduation:* $22,137. *Financial aid deadline:* 6/30.

Applying *Options:* electronic application, deferred entrance. *Required:* high school transcript. *Required for some:* minimum 2 GPA, interview. *Application deadlines:* 8/15 (freshmen), 8/15 (transfers). *Notification:* continuous (freshmen), continuous (transfers).

Freshman Application Contact Ms. Janice Whisler, Interim Director Enrollment/Outreach Recruitment, Purdue University North Central, 1401 South U.S. Highway 421, Westville, IN 46391. *Phone:* 219-785-5415. *Toll-free phone:* 800-872-1231. *Fax:* 219-785-5538. *E-mail:* jwhisler@pnc.edu. *Web site:* http://www.pnc.edu/.

Rose-Hulman Institute of Technology
Terre Haute, Indiana

- **Independent** comprehensive, founded 1874
- **Suburban** 200-acre campus with easy access to Indianapolis
- **Endowment** $161.9 million
- **Coed, primarily men** 1,875 undergraduate students, 100% full-time, 20% women, 80% men
- **Very difficult** entrance level, 66% of applicants were admitted

Undergraduates 1,867 full-time, 8 part-time. Students come from 48 states and territories; 14 other countries; 59% are from out of state; 2% Black or African American, non-Hispanic/Latino; 3% Hispanic/Latino; 4% Asian, non-Hispanic/Latino; 0.2% Native Hawaiian or other Pacific Islander, non-Hispanic/Latino; 0.4% American Indian or Alaska Native, non-Hispanic/Latino; 3% Two or more races, non-Hispanic/Latino; 0.5% Race/ethnicity unknown; 4% international; 1% transferred in; 60% live on campus. *Retention:* 89% of full-time freshmen returned.

Freshmen *Admission:* 3,858 applied, 2,543 admitted, 552 enrolled. *Average high school GPA:* 3.89. *Test scores:* SAT critical reading scores over 500: 93%; SAT math scores over 500: 100%; SAT writing scores over 500: 90%; ACT scores over 18: 100%; SAT critical reading scores over 600: 64%; SAT math scores over 600: 87%; SAT writing scores over 600: 53%; ACT scores over 24: 94%; SAT critical reading scores over 700: 16%; SAT math scores over 700: 44%; SAT writing scores over 700: 9%; ACT scores over 30: 48%.

Faculty *Total:* 170, 93% full-time, 99% with terminal degrees. *Student/faculty ratio:* 12:1.

Academics *Calendar:* quarters. *Degrees:* bachelor's and master's. *Special study options:* accelerated degree program, adult/continuing education programs, advanced placement credit, cooperative education, double majors, independent study, internships, off-campus study, services for LD students, study abroad, summer session for credit. *ROTC:* Army (b), Air Force (b).

Computers on Campus 45 computers/terminals and 8,000 ports are available on campus for general student use. Students can access the following: campus intranet, computer help desk, free student e-mail accounts, online (class) grades, online (class) registration, online (class) schedules. Campuswide network is available. 100% of college-owned or -operated housing units are wired for high-speed Internet access. Wireless service is available via classrooms, computer centers, computer labs, learning centers, libraries, student centers.

Student Life *Housing:* on-campus residence required for freshman year. *Options:* coed, men-only. Campus housing is university owned. Freshman campus housing is guaranteed. *Activities and organizations:* drama/theater group, student-run newspaper, radio station, choral group, Drama Club, yoga club, Intervarsity Christian Fellowship, Chinese Culture Club, lacrosse club, national fraternities, national sororities. *Campus security:* 24-hour emergency response devices and patrols, late-night transport/escort service, controlled dormitory access. *Student services:* health clinic, personal/psychological counseling.

Athletics Member NCAA. All Division III. *Intercollegiate sports:* baseball M, basketball M/W, cross-country running M/W, football M, golf M/W, riflery M/W, soccer M/W, softball W, swimming and diving M/W, tennis M/W, track and field M/W, volleyball W. *Intramural sports:* archery M(c)/W(c), basketball M/W, bowling M/W, cross-country running M/W, fencing M(c)/W(c), football M/W, golf M/W, lacrosse M(c)/W(c), racquetball M/W, soccer M/W, softball M/W, swimming and diving M/W, table tennis M/W, tennis M/W, track and field M/W, ultimate Frisbee M/W, volleyball M/W, water polo M(c)/W(c).

Standardized Tests *Required:* SAT or ACT (for admission).

Costs (2010–11) *One-time required fee:* $2800. *Comprehensive fee:* $46,227 includes full-time tuition ($35,595), mandatory fees ($675), and room and board ($9957). Full-time tuition and fees vary according to course load. Part-time tuition: $1038 per credit hour. Part-time tuition and fees vary according to course load. *College room only:* $6084. Room and board charges vary according to board plan. *Payment plans:* tuition prepayment, installment. *Waivers:* employees or children of employees.

Financial Aid Of all full-time matriculated undergraduates who enrolled in 2009, 1,501 applied for aid, 1,340 were judged to have need, 241 had their need fully met. 485 Federal Work-Study jobs (averaging $1383). 660 state and other part-time jobs (averaging $1394). In 2009, 498 non-need-based awards were made. *Average percent of need met:* 79%. *Average financial aid package:* $24,442. *Average need-based loan:* $4871. *Average need-based gift aid:* $19,322. *Average non-need-based aid:* $10,125. *Average indebtedness upon graduation:* $40,619.

Applying *Options:* electronic application, deferred entrance. *Application fee:* $40. *Required:* high school transcript, 1 letter of recommendation, curricular. *Recommended:* essay or personal statement, interview. *Application deadline:* 3/1 (freshmen). *Notification:* continuous (freshmen), continuous (transfers).

Freshman Application Contact Mr. James Goecker, Vice President for Enrollment Management, Rose-Hulman Institute of Technology, 5500 Wabash Avenue, CM 1, Terre Haute, IN 47803-3920. *Phone:* 812-877-8894. *Toll-free phone:* 800-248-7448. *Fax:* 812-877-8941. *E-mail:* admissions@rose-hulman.edu. *Web site:* http://www.rose-hulman.edu/.

Saint Joseph's College
Rensselaer, Indiana

- **Independent Roman Catholic** comprehensive, founded 1889
- **Small-town** 180-acre campus
- **Endowment** $16.7 million
- **Coed** 1,033 undergraduate students, 94% full-time, 58% women, 42% men
- **Moderately difficult** entrance level, 61% of applicants were admitted

Undergraduates 967 full-time, 66 part-time. Students come from 21 states and territories; 6 other countries; 25% are from out of state; 11% Black or African American, non-Hispanic/Latino; 5% Hispanic/Latino; 0.9% Asian, non-Hispanic/Latino; 0.3% American Indian or Alaska Native, non-Hispanic/Latino; 2% Two or more races, non-Hispanic/Latino; 0.3% Race/ethnicity unknown; 0.6% international; 2% transferred in; 72% live on campus. *Retention:* 67% of full-time freshmen returned.

Freshmen *Admission:* 1,784 applied, 1,092 admitted, 259 enrolled. *Average high school GPA:* 3.12. *Test scores:* SAT critical reading scores over 500: 41%; SAT math scores over 500: 52%; ACT scores over 18: 85%; SAT critical reading scores over 600: 10%; SAT math scores over 600: 9%; ACT scores over 24: 36%; SAT critical reading scores over 700: 1%; ACT scores over 30: 6%.

Faculty *Total:* 101, 58% full-time, 50% with terminal degrees. *Student/faculty ratio:* 14:1.

Academics *Calendar:* semesters. *Degrees:* certificates, diplomas, associate, bachelor's, and master's. *Special study options:* academic remediation for entering students, accelerated degree program, advanced placement credit, double majors, honors programs, independent study, internships, part-time degree program, services for LD students, student-designed majors, study abroad, summer session for credit.

Computers on Campus 69 computers/terminals and 200 ports are available on campus for general student use. Students can access the following: campus intranet, computer help desk, free student e-mail accounts, online (class) grades, online (class) registration, online (class) schedules. Campuswide network is available. 100% of college-owned or -operated housing units are wired for high-speed Internet access. Wireless service is available via entire campus.

Student Life *Housing:* on-campus residence required through senior year. *Options:* coed, men-only, women-only, disabled students. Campus housing is university owned. Freshman campus housing is guaranteed. *Activities and organizations:* drama/theater group, student-run newspaper, radio and television station, choral group, marching band, Gallagher Charitable Society, Cup O' Joe, Habitat for Humanity, Science Club, Alpha Lambda Delta. *Campus security:* 24-hour emergency response devices and patrols, student patrols,

late-night transport/escort service. *Student services:* health clinic, personal/psychological counseling.

Athletics Member NCAA. All Division II. *Intercollegiate sports:* baseball M(s), basketball M(s)/W(s), cheerleading M(s)(c)/W(s)(c), cross-country running M(s)/W(s), football M(s), golf M(s)/W(s), soccer M(s)/W(s), softball W(s), tennis M(s)/W(s), track and field M(s)/W(s), volleyball W(s). *Intramural sports:* basketball M/W, lacrosse M(c)/W(c), rugby M(c), softball M/W, ultimate Frisbee M/W, volleyball M/W.

Standardized Tests *Required:* SAT or ACT (for admission).

Costs (2011–12) *Comprehensive fee:* $34,310 includes full-time tuition ($26,140), mandatory fees ($190), and room and board ($7980). Full-time tuition and fees vary according to reciprocity agreements. Part-time tuition: $870 per credit hour. Part-time tuition and fees vary according to course load and reciprocity agreements. *Room and board:* Room and board charges vary according to housing facility. *Payment plan:* installment. *Waivers:* minority students, children of alumni, and employees or children of employees.

Financial Aid Of all full-time matriculated undergraduates who enrolled in 2008, 752 applied for aid, 656 were judged to have need, 191 had their need fully met. 75 Federal Work-Study jobs (averaging $778). In 2008, 83 non-need-based awards were made. *Average percent of need met:* 80%. *Average financial aid package:* $21,891. *Average need-based loan:* $4382. *Average need-based gift aid:* $14,856. *Average non-need-based aid:* $12,711. *Average indebtedness upon graduation:* $28,135.

Applying *Options:* electronic application, deferred entrance. *Application fee:* $25. *Required:* high school transcript, minimum 2 GPA. *Required for some:* essay or personal statement. *Recommended:* interview. *Application deadlines:* rolling (freshmen), rolling (transfers). *Notification:* continuous (freshmen), continuous (transfers).

Freshman Application Contact Mr. John Wadell, Assistant Vice President for Enrollment Management, Saint Joseph's College, PO Box 815, Rensselaer, IN 47978-0850. *Phone:* 219-866-6170. *Toll-free phone:* 800-447-8781. *Fax:* 219-866-6122. *E-mail:* admissions@saintjoe.edu. *Web site:* http://www.saintjoe.edu/.

Saint Mary-of-the-Woods College
Saint Mary-of-the-Woods, Indiana

- **Independent Roman Catholic** comprehensive, founded 1840
- **Rural** 67-acre campus with easy access to Indianapolis
- **Endowment** $9.6 million
- **Coed, primarily women** 1,367 undergraduate students, 37% full-time, 94% women, 6% men
- **Moderately difficult** entrance level, 66% of applicants were admitted

Undergraduates 505 full-time, 862 part-time. Students come from 40 states and territories; 7 other countries; 23% are from out of state; 75% live on campus. *Retention:* 74% of full-time freshmen returned.

Freshmen *Admission:* 475 applied, 314 admitted, 157 enrolled. *Average high school GPA:* 3.2. *Test scores:* SAT critical reading scores over 500: 41%; SAT math scores over 500: 28%; SAT writing scores over 500: 37%; ACT scores over 18: 72%; SAT critical reading scores over 600: 12%; SAT math scores over 600: 12%; SAT writing scores over 600: 9%; ACT scores over 24: 28%; SAT critical reading scores over 700: 2%; ACT scores over 30: 7%.

Faculty *Total:* 178, 38% full-time, 22% with terminal degrees. *Student/faculty ratio:* 8:1.

Academics *Calendar:* semesters. *Degrees:* certificates, associate, bachelor's, master's, post-master's, and postbachelor's certificates (also offers external degree program with significant enrollment not reflected in profile). *Special study options:* academic remediation for entering students, accelerated degree program, adult/continuing education programs, advanced placement credit, distance learning, double majors, external degree program, honors programs, independent study, internships, off-campus study, part-time degree program, student-designed majors, study abroad, summer session for credit. *ROTC:* Army (c), Air Force (c).

Computers on Campus 85 computers/terminals and 150 ports are available on campus for general student use. Students can access the following: campus intranet, computer help desk, free student e-mail accounts, online (class) grades, online (class) registration, online (class) schedules. Campuswide network is available. 100% of college-owned or -operated housing units are wired for high-speed Internet access. Wireless service is available via entire campus.

Student Life *Housing:* on-campus residence required through senior year. *Options:* women-only. Campus housing is university owned. Freshman campus housing is guaranteed. *Activities and organizations:* drama/theater group, student-run newspaper, choral group, Student Activities Committee, Chorale, Student Senate, Woods Newspaper, Dance Team. *Campus security:* 24-hour emergency response devices and patrols, late-night transport/escort service. *Student services:* health clinic, personal/psychological counseling.

Athletics Member USCAA. *Intercollegiate sports:* basketball W(s), cross-country running W(s), equestrian sports W(s), golf W(s), soccer W(s), softball W(s).

Standardized Tests *Required:* SAT or ACT (for admission).

Costs (2010–11) *Comprehensive fee:* $33,390 includes full-time tuition ($23,750), mandatory fees ($750), and room and board ($8890). Full-time tuition and fees vary according to program. Part-time tuition: $450 per credit hour. Part-time tuition and fees vary according to program. *Required fees:* $200 per year part-time. *College room only:* $3470. *Payment plan:* installment. *Waivers:* employees or children of employees.

Financial Aid Of all full-time matriculated undergraduates who enrolled in 2008, 540 applied for aid, 513 were judged to have need, 184 had their need fully met. 104 Federal Work-Study jobs (averaging $883). In 2008, 11 non-need-based awards were made. *Average percent of need met:* 80%. *Average financial aid package:* $21,155. *Average need-based loan:* $2245. *Average need-based gift aid:* $8210. *Average non-need-based aid:* $6000. *Average indebtedness upon graduation:* $35,223.

Applying *Options:* electronic application, early admission, deferred entrance. *Application fee:* $30. *Required:* essay or personal statement, high school transcript, minimum 2.5 GPA, 1 letter of recommendation. *Recommended:* interview. *Application deadlines:* 8/1 (freshmen), 8/1 (transfers). *Notification:* 8/20 (freshmen), 8/20 (out-of-state freshmen), continuous until 8/20 (transfers).

Freshman Application Contact Mr. Aaron Kelley, Director of Admission, Saint Mary-of-the-Woods College, Rooney Library, SMWC, Saint Mary-of-the-Woods, IN 47876. *Phone:* 812-535-5107. *Toll-free phone:* 800-926-SMWC. *Fax:* 812-535-5010. *E-mail:* smwcadms@smwc.edu. *Web site:* http://www.smwc.edu/.

Saint Mary's College

Notre Dame, Indiana

- **Independent Roman Catholic** 4-year, founded 1844
- **Suburban** 275-acre campus with easy access to Chicago
- **Endowment** $108.7 million
- **Women only** 1,555 undergraduate students, 99% full-time
- **Moderately difficult** entrance level, 81% of applicants were admitted

Undergraduates 1,542 full-time, 13 part-time. Students come from 42 states and territories; 9 other countries; 71% are from out of state; 2% Black or African American, non-Hispanic/Latino; 8% Hispanic/Latino; 2% Asian, non-Hispanic/Latino; 0.1% Native Hawaiian or other Pacific Islander, non-Hispanic/Latino; 0.3% American Indian or Alaska Native, non-Hispanic/Latino; 1% Two or more races, non-Hispanic/Latino; 2% Race/ethnicity unknown; 0.7% international; 2% transferred in; 84% live on campus. *Retention:* 85% of full-time freshmen returned.

Freshmen *Admission:* 1,387 applied, 1,119 admitted, 333 enrolled. *Average high school GPA:* 3.67. *Test scores:* SAT critical reading scores over 500: 72%; SAT math scores over 500: 76%; SAT writing scores over 500: 73%; ACT scores over 18: 99%; SAT critical reading scores over 600: 26%; SAT math scores over 600: 26%; SAT writing scores over 600: 32%; ACT scores over 24: 67%; SAT critical reading scores over 700: 2%; SAT math scores over 700: 2%; SAT writing scores over 700: 5%; ACT scores over 30: 9%.

Faculty *Total:* 199, 64% full-time, 73% with terminal degrees. *Student/faculty ratio:* 10:1.

Academics *Calendar:* semesters. *Degree:* bachelor's. *Special study options:* academic remediation for entering students, accelerated degree program, advanced placement credit, cooperative education, double majors, independent study, internships, off-campus study, part-time degree program, services for LD students, student-designed majors, study abroad, summer session for credit. *ROTC:* Army (c), Navy (c), Air Force (c). *Unusual degree programs:* 3-2 engineering with University of Notre Dame.

Computers on Campus 261 computers/terminals and 1,456 ports are available on campus for general student use. Students can access the following: campus intranet, computer help desk, free student e-mail accounts, online (class) grades, online (class) registration, online (class) schedules. Campus-wide network is available. 100% of college-owned or -operated housing units are wired for high-speed Internet access. Wireless service is available via classrooms, computer centers, computer labs, dorm rooms, learning centers, libraries, student centers.

Student Life *Housing:* on-campus residence required through junior year. *Options:* women-only. Campus housing is university owned. Freshman campus housing is guaranteed. *Activities and organizations:* drama/theater group, student-run newspaper, radio and television station, choral group, marching band, Student Government Association, Dance Marathon, Class Boards, Residence Hall Association, Student Diversity Board. *Campus security:* 24-hour emergency response devices and patrols, late-night transport/escort service, controlled dormitory access. *Student services:* health clinic, personal/psychological counseling, women's center.

Athletics Member NCAA. All Division III. *Intercollegiate sports:* basketball W, cross-country running W, equestrian sports W(c), field hockey W(c), golf W, gymnastics W(c), skiing (downhill) W(c), soccer W, softball W, swimming and diving W, tennis W, ultimate Frisbee W(c), volleyball W, water polo W(c). *Intramural sports:* baseball W(c), basketball W, cheerleading W(c), lacrosse W(c), soccer W, volleyball W(c).

Standardized Tests *Required:* SAT or ACT (for admission).

Costs (2010–11) *Comprehensive fee:* $40,500 includes full-time tuition ($30,360), mandatory fees ($660), and room and board ($9480). Part-time tuition: $1200 per credit hour. *Required fees:* $330 per term part-time. *College room only:* $5840. Room and board charges vary according to board plan and housing facility. *Payment plan:* installment. *Waivers:* employees or children of employees.

Financial Aid Of all full-time matriculated undergraduates who enrolled in 2009, 1,168 applied for aid, 1,096 were judged to have need, 156 had their need fully met. In 2009, 350 non-need-based awards were made. *Average percent of need met:* 69%. *Average financial aid package:* $23,739. *Average need-based loan:* $4691. *Average need-based gift aid:* $18,255. *Average non-need-based aid:* $10,341. *Average indebtedness upon graduation:* $28,838. *Financial aid deadline:* 3/1.

Applying *Options:* electronic application, early admission, early decision, deferred entrance. *Application fee:* $30. *Required:* essay or personal statement, high school transcript, 1 letter of recommendation, 16 high school academic units; at least two years of study of the same foreign language. *Recommended:* interview. *Application deadlines:* 2/15 (freshmen), 4/15 (transfers). *Early decision deadline:* 11/15. *Notification:* continuous (freshmen), continuous (transfers), 12/15 (early decision).

Freshman Application Contact Ms. Kristin McAndrew, Director of Admission, Saint Mary's College, Notre Dame, IN 46556. *Phone:* 574-284-4587. *Toll-free phone:* 800-551-7621. *Fax:* 574-284-4841. *E-mail:* admission@saintmarys.edu. *Web site:* http://www.saintmarys.edu/.

See page 1576 for the College Close-Up.

Strayer University - North Indianapolis Campus

Indianapolis, Indiana

- **Proprietary** comprehensive
- **Coed**

Academics *Degrees:* bachelor's and master's.

Freshman Application Contact Strayer University - North Indianapolis Campus, 9025 N. River Road, Suite 400, Indianapolis, IN 46240. *Web site:* http://www.strayer.edu/northindianapolis.

Taylor University

Upland, Indiana

- **Independent interdenominational** comprehensive, founded 1846
- **Rural** 950-acre campus with easy access to Indianapolis
- **Endowment** $64.4 million
- **Coed** 2,444 undergraduate students, 76% full-time, 57% women, 43% men
- **Moderately difficult** entrance level, 83% of applicants were admitted

Undergraduates 1,847 full-time, 597 part-time. Students come from 45 states and territories; 25 other countries; 65% are from out of state; 2% Black or African American, non-Hispanic/Latino; 2% Hispanic/Latino; 2% Asian, non-Hispanic/Latino; 0.3% American Indian or Alaska Native, non-Hispanic/Latino; 1% Two or more races, non-Hispanic/Latino; 3% international; 2% transferred in; 82% live on campus. *Retention:* 88% of full-time freshmen returned.

Freshmen *Admission:* 1,771 applied, 1,476 admitted, 469 enrolled. *Average high school GPA:* 3.57. *Test scores:* SAT critical reading scores over 500: 74%; SAT math scores over 500: 74%; SAT writing scores over 500: 73%; ACT scores over 18: 99%; SAT critical reading scores over 600: 38%; SAT math scores over 600: 41%; SAT writing scores over 600: 33%; ACT scores over 24: 71%; SAT critical reading scores over 700: 11%; SAT math scores over 700: 8%; SAT writing scores over 700: 9%; ACT scores over 30: 27%.

Faculty *Total:* 252, 56% full-time, 56% with terminal degrees. *Student/faculty ratio:* 12:1.

Academics *Calendar:* 4-1-4. *Degrees:* certificates, diplomas, associate, bachelor's, and master's. *Special study options:* academic remediation for entering students, advanced placement credit, cooperative education, distance learning, double majors, English as a second language, honors programs, independent study, internships, off-campus study, part-time degree program, services for LD students, student-designed majors, study abroad, summer session for credit.

Computers on Campus 340 computers/terminals are available on campus for general student use. Students can access the following: campus intranet, computer help desk, free student e-mail accounts, online (class) grades, online (class) registration, online (class) schedules. Campuswide network is available. 100% of college-owned or -operated housing units are wired for high-speed Internet access. Wireless service is available via entire campus.

Student Life *Housing:* on-campus residence required through junior year. *Options:* men-only, women-only. Campus housing is university owned and is provided by a third party. Freshman campus housing is guaranteed. *Activities and organizations:* drama/theater group, student-run newspaper, radio and tele-

vision station, choral group, TWO (Taylor World Outreach), IFC (Integration of Faith and Culture), Spring Break Mission Trips, Community Outreach. *Campus security:* 24-hour patrols, student patrols, late-night transport/escort service. *Student services:* health clinic, personal/psychological counseling.

Athletics Member NAIA. *Intercollegiate sports:* baseball M(s), basketball M(s)/W(s), cross-country running M(s)/W(s), football M(s), golf M(s), soccer M(s)/W(s), softball W(s), tennis M(s)/W(s), track and field M(s)/W(s), volleyball W(s). *Intramural sports:* badminton M/W, basketball M/W, equestrian sports W(c), lacrosse M(c)/W(c), racquetball M/W, soccer M/W, softball M/W, tennis M/W, ultimate Frisbee M/W, volleyball M/W.

Standardized Tests *Required:* SAT or ACT (for admission).

Costs (2011–12) *Comprehensive fee:* $34,656 includes full-time tuition ($27,200), mandatory fees ($238), and room and board ($7218). Full-time tuition and fees vary according to course load. Part-time tuition and fees vary according to course load. *Room and board:* Room and board charges vary according to board plan and housing facility. *Payment plan:* installment. *Waivers:* senior citizens and employees or children of employees.

Financial Aid Of all full-time matriculated undergraduates who enrolled in 2009, 1,358 applied for aid, 1,154 were judged to have need, 243 had their need fully met. 860 Federal Work-Study jobs (averaging $630). In 2009, 421 non-need-based awards were made. *Average percent of need met:* 73%. *Average financial aid package:* $18,328. *Average need-based loan:* $4782. *Average need-based gift aid:* $14,416. *Average non-need-based aid:* $6632. *Average indebtedness upon graduation:* $21,302. *Financial aid deadline:* 3/10.

Applying *Options:* electronic application, early action, deferred entrance. *Application fee:* $25. *Required:* essay or personal statement, high school transcript, 2 letters of recommendation, interview. *Recommended:* minimum 2.8 GPA. *Application deadlines:* rolling (freshmen), rolling (transfers), 12/1 (early action). *Notification:* continuous (freshmen), continuous (transfers), 12/20 (early action).

Freshman Application Contact Ms. Laura Brocker, Manager of On-Campus Recruitment, Taylor University, 236 West Reade Avenue, Upland, IN 46989-1001. *Phone:* 800-882-3456. *Toll-free phone:* 800-882-3456. *Fax:* 765-998-4925. *E-mail:* admissions@taylor.edu. *Web site:* http://www.taylor.edu/.

Trine University

Angola, Indiana

- **Independent** comprehensive, founded 1884
- **Small-town** 400-acre campus
- **Endowment** $20.3 million
- **Coed** 1,779 undergraduate students, 89% full-time, 35% women, 65% men
- **Moderately difficult** entrance level, 75% of applicants were admitted

Undergraduates 1,583 full-time, 196 part-time. Students come from 30 states and territories; 10 other countries; 47% are from out of state; 5% Black or African American, non-Hispanic/Latino; 2% Hispanic/Latino; 0.8% Asian, non-Hispanic/Latino; 0.7% American Indian or Alaska Native, non-Hispanic/Latino; 12% Race/ethnicity unknown; 3% international; 3% transferred in; 85% live on campus. *Retention:* 77% of full-time freshmen returned.

Freshmen *Admission:* 2,808 applied, 2,093 admitted, 415 enrolled. *Average high school GPA:* 3.41. *Test scores:* SAT critical reading scores over 500: 62%; SAT math scores over 500: 76%; ACT scores over 18: 96%; SAT critical reading scores over 600: 19%; SAT math scores over 600: 36%; ACT scores over 24: 57%; SAT critical reading scores over 700: 1%; SAT math scores over 700: 6%; ACT scores over 30: 8%.

Faculty *Total:* 213, 35% full-time, 24% with terminal degrees. *Student/faculty ratio:* 18:1.

Academics *Calendar:* semesters. *Degrees:* associate, bachelor's, and master's. *Special study options:* academic remediation for entering students, adult/continuing education programs, advanced placement credit, cooperative education, distance learning, double majors, English as a second language, honors programs, internships, part-time degree program, student-designed majors, study abroad, summer session for credit. *ROTC:* Air Force (c). *Unusual degree programs:* 3-2 engineering.

Computers on Campus 150 computers/terminals are available on campus for general student use. Students can access the following: computer help desk, free student e-mail accounts, online (class) grades, online (class) registration, online (class) schedules, online campus billing accounts. Campuswide network is available. 100% of college-owned or -operated housing units are wired for high-speed Internet access. Wireless service is available via entire campus.

Student Life *Housing:* on-campus residence required through senior year. *Options:* coed, men-only, women-only. Campus housing is university owned and is provided by a third party. Freshman campus housing is guaranteed. *Activities and organizations:* drama/theater group, student-run newspaper, radio station, choral group, marching band, Campus Christian House, Drama Club, Habitat for Humanity, student newspaper, student radio station, national fraternities, national sororities. *Campus security:* 24-hour emergency response devices and patrols, late-night transport/escort service, controlled dormitory access. *Student services:* personal/psychological counseling.

Athletics Member NCAA. All Division III. *Intercollegiate sports:* baseball M, basketball M/W, cross-country running M/W, field hockey W, football M, golf M/W, lacrosse M/W, soccer M/W, softball W, tennis M/W, track and field M/W, volleyball W, wrestling M. *Intramural sports:* badminton M/W, basketball M/W, football M, golf M/W, racquetball M/W, softball M/W, table tennis M/W, volleyball M/W.

Standardized Tests *Required:* SAT or ACT (for admission).

Costs (2011–12) *Comprehensive fee:* $35,400 includes full-time tuition ($25,300), mandatory fees ($100), and room and board ($10,000). Full-time tuition and fees vary according to degree level and location. Part-time tuition and fees vary according to degree level and location. *Room and board:* Room and board charges vary according to board plan and housing facility. *Payment plan:* installment. *Waivers:* employees or children of employees.

Financial Aid Of all full-time matriculated undergraduates who enrolled in 2009, 1,533 applied for aid, 1,116 were judged to have need, 1,041 had their need fully met. In 2009, 59 non-need-based awards were made. *Average percent of need met:* 87%. *Average financial aid package:* $23,371. *Average need-based loan:* $3945. *Average need-based gift aid:* $4577. *Average non-need-based aid:* $10,970. *Average indebtedness upon graduation:* $26,050.

Applying *Options:* electronic application, deferred entrance. *Required:* high school transcript, minimum 2.5 GPA. *Recommended:* essay or personal statement, 2 letters of recommendation, interview. *Application deadlines:* 8/1 (freshmen), 8/1 (transfers). *Notification:* 8/15 (freshmen), continuous until 8/15 (transfers).

Freshman Application Contact Mr. Scott Goplin, Dean of Admission, Trine University, 1 University Avenue, Angola, IN 46703. *Phone:* 260-665-4365. *Toll-free phone:* 800-347-4TSU. *Fax:* 260-665-4578. *E-mail:* admit@trine.edu. *Web site:* http://www.trine.edu/.

See page 1668 for the College Close-Up.

University of Evansville
Evansville, Indiana

- **Independent** comprehensive, founded 1854, affiliated with United Methodist Church
- **Urban** 75-acre campus
- **Endowment** $68.5 million
- **Coed** 2,716 undergraduate students, 92% full-time, 59% women, 41% men
- **Moderately difficult** entrance level, 84% of applicants were admitted

Undergraduates 2,497 full-time, 219 part-time. Students come from 44 states and territories; 44 other countries; 40% are from out of state; 2% Black or African American, non-Hispanic/Latino; 2% Hispanic/Latino; 1% Asian, non-Hispanic/Latino; 0.1% Native Hawaiian or other Pacific Islander, non-Hispanic/Latino; 0.2% American Indian or Alaska Native, non-Hispanic/Latino; 2% Two or more races, non-Hispanic/Latino; 10% Race/ethnicity unknown; 5% international; 3% transferred in; 69% live on campus. *Retention:* 82% of full-time freshmen returned.

Freshmen *Admission:* 3,505 applied, 2,930 admitted, 683 enrolled. *Average high school GPA:* 3.74. *Test scores:* SAT critical reading scores over 500: 82%; SAT math scores over 500: 85%; SAT writing scores over 500: 71%; ACT scores over 18: 99%; SAT critical reading scores over 600: 34%; SAT math scores over 600: 38%; SAT writing scores over 600: 28%; ACT scores over 24: 73%; SAT critical reading scores over 700: 7%; SAT math scores over 700: 4%; SAT writing scores over 700: 5%; ACT scores over 30: 16%.

Faculty *Total:* 234, 74% full-time, 73% with terminal degrees. *Student/faculty ratio:* 14:1.

Academics *Calendar:* semesters. *Degrees:* associate, bachelor's, master's, and doctoral-professional. *Special study options:* accelerated degree program, adult/continuing education programs, advanced placement credit, cooperative education, double majors, English as a second language, external degree program, honors programs, independent study, internships, part-time degree program, services for LD students, student-designed majors, study abroad, summer session for credit. *ROTC:* Army (b).

Computers on Campus 385 computers/terminals and 3,000 ports are available on campus for general student use. Students can access the following: campus intranet, computer help desk, free student e-mail accounts, online (class) grades, online (class) registration, online (class) schedules. Campus-wide network is available. 100% of college-owned or -operated housing units are wired for high-speed Internet access. Wireless service is available via entire campus.

Student Life *Housing:* on-campus residence required for freshman year. *Options:* coed, men-only, women-only. Campus housing is university owned. Freshman campus housing is guaranteed. *Activities and organizations:* drama/theater group, student-run newspaper, radio station, choral group, Phi Eta Sigma, International Club, PT Club, Student Christian Fellowship, Alpha Omicron Pi, national fraternities, national sororities. *Campus security:* 24-hour

emergency response devices and patrols, student patrols, late-night transport/escort service, controlled dormitory access. *Student services:* health clinic, personal/psychological counseling.

Athletics Member NCAA. All Division I. *Intercollegiate sports:* baseball M(s), basketball M(s)/W(s), cross-country running M(s)/W(s), golf M(s)/W(s), soccer M(s)/W(s), softball W(s), swimming and diving M(s)/W(s), tennis W(s), volleyball W(s). *Intramural sports:* badminton M/W, basketball M/W, bowling M/W, cheerleading M(c)/W(c), cross-country running M/W, golf M/W, racquetball M/W, soccer M/W, softball M/W, swimming and diving M/W, table tennis M/W, tennis M/W, volleyball M/W.

Standardized Tests *Required:* SAT or ACT (for admission).

Costs (2010–11) *Comprehensive fee:* $37,186 includes full-time tuition ($27,310), mandatory fees ($766), and room and board ($9110). Part-time tuition: $760 per credit hour. Part-time tuition and fees vary according to course load. *Required fees:* $50 per term part-time. *College room only:* $4700. Room and board charges vary according to board plan and housing facility. *Payment plan:* installment. *Waivers:* minority students, children of alumni, adult students, senior citizens, and employees or children of employees.

Financial Aid Of all full-time matriculated undergraduates who enrolled in 2009, 2,148 applied for aid, 1,793 were judged to have need, 428 had their need fully met. 403 Federal Work-Study jobs (averaging $1414). 12 state and other part-time jobs (averaging $1257). In 2009, 521 non-need-based awards were made. *Average percent of need met:* 80%. *Average financial aid package:* $23,282. *Average need-based loan:* $4623. *Average need-based gift aid:* $20,114. *Average non-need-based aid:* $13,692. *Average indebtedness upon graduation:* $26,389.

Applying *Options:* electronic application, early action, deferred entrance. *Application fee:* $35. *Required:* high school transcript, 1 letter of recommendation. *Required for some:* essay or personal statement, interview. *Recommended:* minimum 3 GPA, interview. *Application deadlines:* 2/1 (freshmen), rolling (transfers), 12/1 (early action). *Notification:* 2/15 (freshmen), continuous (transfers), 12/15 (early action).

Freshman Application Contact Don Vos, Dean of Admission, University of Evansville, 1800 Lincoln Avenue, Evansville, IN 47722. *Phone:* 812-488-2468. *Toll-free phone:* 800-423-8633 Ext. 2468. *Fax:* 812-488-4076. *E-mail:* admission@evansville.edu. *Web site:* http://www.evansville.edu/.

University of Indianapolis
Indianapolis, Indiana

- **Independent** comprehensive, founded 1902, affiliated with United Methodist Church
- **Urban** 65-acre campus
- **Endowment** $61.2 million
- **Coed** 4,081 undergraduate students, 74% full-time, 68% women, 32% men
- **Moderately difficult** entrance level, 79% of applicants were admitted

Undergraduates 3,019 full-time, 1,062 part-time. 7% are from out of state; 12% Black or African American, non-Hispanic/Latino; 2% Hispanic/Latino; 0.8% Asian, non-Hispanic/Latino; 0.0% Native Hawaiian or other Pacific Islander, non-Hispanic/Latino; 0.2% American Indian or Alaska Native, non-Hispanic/Latino; 1% Two or more races, non-Hispanic/Latino; 5% Race/ethnicity unknown; 5% international; 5% transferred in; 36% live on campus. *Retention:* 77% of full-time freshmen returned.

Freshmen *Admission:* 5,255 applied, 4,160 admitted, 849 enrolled. *Average high school GPA:* 3.36. *Test scores:* SAT critical reading scores over 500: 48%; SAT math scores over 500: 53%; ACT scores over 18: 85%; SAT critical reading scores over 600: 11%; SAT math scores over 600: 14%; ACT scores over 24: 34%; SAT critical reading scores over 700: 1%; SAT math scores over 700: 1%; ACT scores over 30: 5%.

Faculty *Total:* 472, 45% full-time, 49% with terminal degrees. *Student/faculty ratio:* 14:1.

Academics *Calendar:* semesters. *Degrees:* associate, bachelor's, master's, doctoral-professional, and doctoral-research/scholarship. *Special study options:* academic remediation for entering students, accelerated degree program, adult/continuing education programs, advanced placement credit, cooperative education, distance learning, double majors, English as a second language, freshman honors college, honors programs, independent study, internships, off-campus study, part-time degree program, services for LD students, student-designed majors, study abroad, summer session for credit. *ROTC:* Army (c). *Unusual degree programs:* 3-2 business administration with BS/MBA (Accounting); engineering with Indiana University - Purdue University Indianapolis; physical therapy, occupational therapy.

Computers on Campus 222 computers/terminals are available on campus for general student use. Students can access the following: campus intranet, computer help desk, free student e-mail accounts, online (class) grades, online (class) schedules. Campuswide network is available. 100% of college-owned or -operated housing units are wired for high-speed Internet access. Wireless service is available via entire campus.

Student Life *Housing options:* coed, women-only. Campus housing is university owned. *Activities and organizations:* drama/theater group, student-run newspaper, radio and television station, choral group, Fellowship of Christian Athletes, Intercultural Association, Circle K, Indianapolis Student Government, Residence Hall Association. *Campus security:* 24-hour emergency response devices and patrols, student patrols, late-night transport/escort service, emergency call boxes. *Student services:* health clinic, personal/psychological counseling.

Athletics Member NCAA. All Division II. *Intercollegiate sports:* baseball M(s), basketball M(s)/W(s), cross-country running M(s)/W(s), football M(s), golf M(s)/W(s), soccer M(s)/W(s), softball W(s), swimming and diving M(s)/W(s), tennis M(s)/W(s), track and field M(s)/W(s), volleyball W(s), wrestling M(s). *Intramural sports:* badminton M/W, basketball M/W, cheerleading M/W, football M/W, racquetball M/W, softball M/W, table tennis M/W, tennis M/W, volleyball M/W.

Standardized Tests *Required:* SAT or ACT (for admission).

Costs (2010–11) *Comprehensive fee:* $30,680 includes full-time tuition ($22,020), mandatory fees ($220), and room and board ($8440). Part-time tuition: $917 per credit hour. Part-time tuition and fees vary according to course load. *College room only:* $4010. Room and board charges vary according to board plan and housing facility. *Waivers:* employees or children of employees.

Financial Aid Of all full-time matriculated undergraduates who enrolled in 2008, 3,258 applied for aid, 2,833 were judged to have need, 391 had their need fully met. In 2008, 684 non-need-based awards were made. *Average percent of need met:* 70%. *Average financial aid package:* $15,526. *Average need-based loan:* $4174. *Average need-based gift aid:* $8000. *Average non-need-based aid:* $6704. *Average indebtedness upon graduation:* $27,070.

Applying *Options:* electronic application, deferred entrance. *Application fee:* $25. *Required:* high school transcript, minimum 2 GPA. *Required for some:* interview. *Application deadlines:* rolling (freshmen), rolling (out-of-state freshmen), rolling (transfers). *Notification:* continuous (freshmen), continuous (out-of-state freshmen), continuous (transfers).

Freshman Application Contact Mr. Ronald Wilks, Director of Admissions, University of Indianapolis, 1400 East Hanna Avenue, Indianapolis, IN 46227-3697. *Phone:* 317-788-3216. *Toll-free phone:* 800-232-8634 Ext. 3216. *Fax:* 317-788-3300. *E-mail:* admissions@uindy.edu. *Web site:* http://www.uindy.edu/.

See page 1702 for the College Close-Up.

University of Notre Dame
Notre Dame, Indiana

- **Independent Roman Catholic** university, founded 1842
- **Suburban** 1250-acre campus
- **Coed** 8,442 undergraduate students, 100% full-time, 46% women, 54% men
- **Most difficult** entrance level, 29% of applicants were admitted

Undergraduates 8,419 full-time, 23 part-time. Students come from 53 states and territories; 42 other countries; 92% are from out of state; 3% Black or African American, non-Hispanic/Latino; 10% Hispanic/Latino; 6% Asian, non-Hispanic/Latino; 0.5% Native Hawaiian or other Pacific Islander, non-Hispanic/Latino; 2% Two or more races, non-Hispanic/Latino; 0.8% Race/ethnicity unknown; 3% international; 77% live on campus. *Retention:* 98% of full-time freshmen returned.

Freshmen *Admission:* 14,521 applied, 4,177 admitted, 2,068 enrolled.

Faculty *Total:* 1,085, 91% full-time. *Student/faculty ratio:* 12:1.

Academics *Calendar:* semesters. *Degrees:* bachelor's, master's, doctoral-professional, and doctoral-research/scholarship. *Special study options:* advanced placement credit, double majors, honors programs, independent study, internships, off-campus study, services for LD students, student-designed majors, study abroad, summer session for credit. *ROTC:* Army (b), Navy (b), Air Force (b).

Computers on Campus 261 computers/terminals are available on campus for general student use. Students can access the following: computer help desk, free student e-mail accounts, online (class) grades, online (class) registration, online (class) schedules. Campuswide network is available. Wireless service is available via entire campus.

Student Life *Housing:* on-campus residence required for freshman year. *Options:* men-only, women-only. Campus housing is university owned. Freshman campus housing is guaranteed. *Activities and organizations:* drama/theater group, student-run newspaper, radio station, choral group, marching band, marching band, Circle K, Finance Club, Notre Dame/St. Mary's Right to Life. *Campus security:* 24-hour emergency response devices and patrols, student patrols, late-night transport/escort service, controlled dormitory access, crime prevention and personal safety workshops, full-time trained police investigators, fire sprinklers in all residence halls. *Student services:* health clinic, personal/psychological counseling, women's center.

Athletics Member NCAA. All Division I except football (Division I-A). *Intercollegiate sports:* baseball M(s), basketball M(s)/W(s), crew W(s), cross-country running M(s)/W(s), fencing M(s)/W(s), golf M(s)/W(s), ice hockey M(s), lacrosse M(s)/W(s), soccer M(s)/W(s), softball W(s), swimming and diving M(s)/W(s), tennis M(s)/W(s), track and field M(s)/W(s), volleyball W(s). *Intramural sports:* badminton M/W, baseball M, basketball M/W, bowling M(c)/W(c), crew M(c), cross-country running M/W, equestrian sports M(c)/W(c), field hockey W(c), football M/W, golf M/W, gymnastics M(c)/W(c), ice hockey M/W(c), lacrosse M/W, racquetball M/W, rock climbing M(c)/W(c), rugby M(c), sailing M(c)/W(c), skiing (cross-country) M(c)/W(c), skiing (downhill) M(c)/W(c), soccer M/W, softball M/W, squash M(c)/W(c), table tennis M/W, tennis M/W, ultimate Frisbee M/W, volleyball M(c)/W(c), water polo M(c)/W(c).

Standardized Tests *Required:* SAT or ACT (for admission). *Required for some:* SAT Subject Tests (for admission).

Costs (2011–12) *Comprehensive fee:* $52,805 includes full-time tuition ($40,910), mandatory fees ($507), and room and board ($11,388). Part-time tuition: $1705 per credit hour. *Payment plan:* installment. *Waivers:* employees or children of employees.

Financial Aid Of all full-time matriculated undergraduates who enrolled in 2009, 5,181 applied for aid, 4,103 were judged to have need, 3,994 had their need fully met. 1,830 Federal Work-Study jobs (averaging $2323). 3,204 state and other part-time jobs (averaging $2907). In 2009, 289 non-need-based awards were made. *Average percent of need met:* 99%. *Average financial aid package:* $34,101. *Average need-based loan:* $4782. *Average need-based gift aid:* $26,847. *Average non-need-based aid:* $6106. *Average indebtedness upon graduation:* $28,371. *Financial aid deadline:* 2/15.

Applying *Options:* electronic application, early action, deferred entrance. *Application fee:* $65. *Required:* essay or personal statement, high school transcript, 1 letter of recommendation. *Application deadlines:* 12/31 (freshmen), 4/15 (transfers), 11/1 (early action). *Notification:* 4/10 (freshmen), 12/19 (early action).

Freshman Application Contact Office of Undergraduate Admissions, University of Notre Dame, 220 Main Building, Notre Dame, IN 46556-5612. *Phone:* 574-631-7505. *Fax:* 574-631-8865. *E-mail:* admissions@nd.edu. *Web site:* http://www.nd.edu/.

University of Phoenix–Indianapolis Campus
Indianapolis, Indiana

Freshman Application Contact Ms. Audra McQuarie, Registrar/Executive Director, University of Phoenix–Indianapolis Campus, 4035 South Riverpoint Parkway, Mail Stop CF-L101, Phoenix, AZ 85040. *Phone:* 480-557-6151. *Toll-free phone:* 800-776-4867 (in-state); 800-228-7240 (out-of-state). *Fax:* 480-643-3068. *E-mail:* audra.mcquarie@phoenix.edu. *Web site:* http://www.phoenix.edu/.

University of Saint Francis
Fort Wayne, Indiana

Freshman Application Contact Mr. Ron Schumacher, Vice President for Enrollment Management, University of Saint Francis, 2701 Spring Street, Fort Wayne, IN 46808. *Phone:* 260-434-3279. *Toll-free phone:* 800-729-4732. *E-mail:* admis@sf.edu. *Web site:* http://www.sf.edu/.

University of Southern Indiana
Evansville, Indiana

- **State-supported** comprehensive, founded 1965, part of Indiana Commission for Higher Education
- **Suburban** 330-acre campus
- **Coed** 9,846 undergraduate students, 83% full-time, 58% women, 42% men
- **Moderately difficult** entrance level, 74% of applicants were admitted

Undergraduates 8,211 full-time, 1,635 part-time. Students come from 43 states and territories; 44 other countries; 10% are from out of state; 5% Black or African American, non-Hispanic/Latino; 1% Hispanic/Latino; 0.9% Asian, non-Hispanic/Latino; 0.2% Native Hawaiian or other Pacific Islander, non-Hispanic/Latino; 0.4% American Indian or Alaska Native, non-Hispanic/Latino; 0.9% Race/ethnicity unknown; 3% international; 7% transferred in; 26% live on campus. *Retention:* 69% of full-time freshmen returned.

Freshmen *Admission:* 7,061 applied, 5,194 admitted, 2,098 enrolled. *Average high school GPA:* 3.02. *Test scores:* SAT critical reading scores over 500:

42%; SAT math scores over 500: 47%; SAT writing scores over 500: 32%; ACT scores over 18: 83%; SAT critical reading scores over 600: 9%; SAT math scores over 600: 11%; SAT writing scores over 600: 6%; ACT scores over 24: 24%; SAT critical reading scores over 700: 1%; SAT math scores over 700: 1%; ACT scores over 30: 2%.

Faculty *Total:* 656, 52% full-time, 43% with terminal degrees. *Student/faculty ratio:* 18:1.

Academics *Calendar:* semesters. *Degrees:* certificates, associate, bachelor's, master's, doctoral-other, and postbachelor's certificates. *Special study options:* academic remediation for entering students, adult/continuing education programs, advanced placement credit, cooperative education, distance learning, double majors, English as a second language, honors programs, independent study, internships, part-time degree program, services for LD students, study abroad, summer session for credit. *ROTC:* Army (b).

Computers on Campus 497 computers/terminals are available on campus for general student use. Students can access the following: computer help desk, free student e-mail accounts, online (class) grades, online (class) registration, online (class) schedules. Campuswide network is available. 100% of college-owned or -operated housing units are wired for high-speed Internet access. Wireless service is available via entire campus.

Student Life *Housing options:* coed. Campus housing is university owned. *Activities and organizations:* drama/theater group, student-run newspaper, radio station, choral group, student government, national fraternities, national sororities. *Campus security:* 24-hour emergency response devices and patrols, student patrols, late-night transport/escort service, controlled dormitory access. *Student services:* health clinic, personal/psychological counseling.

Athletics Member NCAA. All Division II. *Intercollegiate sports:* baseball M(s), basketball M(s)/W(s), cheerleading M/W, cross-country running M(s)/W(s), golf M(s)/W(s), ice hockey M(c), lacrosse M(c), rugby M(c)/W(c), soccer M(s)/W(s), softball W(s), tennis M(s)/W(s), volleyball W(s), wrestling M(c). *Intramural sports:* badminton M/W, basketball M/W, bowling M/W, football M/W, golf M/W, rock climbing M/W, skiing (downhill) M/W, soccer M/W, softball M/W, swimming and diving M/W, table tennis M/W, tennis M/W, volleyball M/W.

Standardized Tests *Required:* SAT or ACT (for admission).

Costs (2011–12) *Tuition:* state resident $5540 full-time, $185 per credit hour part-time; nonresident $13,186 full-time, $440 per credit hour part-time. Full-time tuition and fees vary according to course load and reciprocity agreements. Part-time tuition and fees vary according to course load and reciprocity agreements. *Required fees:* $200 full-time, $23 per term part-time. *Room and board:* $6920; room only: $3560. Room and board charges vary according to board plan and housing facility. *Payment plan:* installment. *Waivers:* employees or children of employees.

Financial Aid Of all full-time matriculated undergraduates who enrolled in 2009, 8,025 applied for aid, 5,323 were judged to have need, 682 had their need fully met. 115 Federal Work-Study jobs (averaging $1959). In 2009, 704 non-need-based awards were made. *Average percent of need met:* 80%. *Average financial aid package:* $8551. *Average need-based loan:* $3920. *Average need-based gift aid:* $6287. *Average non-need-based aid:* $2991. *Financial aid deadline:* 3/1.

Applying *Options:* electronic application. *Application fee:* $25. *Required:* high school transcript. *Required for some:* interview. *Recommended:* essay or personal statement, minimum 2 GPA. *Application deadline:* 8/15 (freshmen). *Notification:* 8/27 (freshmen), continuous (transfers).

Freshman Application Contact Mr. Eric Otto, Director of Admission, University of Southern Indiana, 8600 University Boulevard, Evansville, IN 47712-3590. *Phone:* 812-464-1765. *Toll-free phone:* 800-467-1965. *Fax:* 812-465-7154. *E-mail:* enroll@usi.edu. *Web site:* http://www.usi.edu/.

Valparaiso University
Valparaiso, Indiana

- **Independent** university, founded 1859, affiliated with Lutheran Church
- **Small-town** 320-acre campus with easy access to Chicago
- **Endowment** $140.4 million
- **Coed** 2,872 undergraduate students, 94% full-time, 53% women, 47% men
- **Moderately difficult** entrance level, 85% of applicants were admitted

Undergraduates 2,695 full-time, 177 part-time. Students come from 43 states and territories; 40 other countries; 60% are from out of state; 6% Black or African American, non-Hispanic/Latino; 5% Hispanic/Latino; 2% Asian, non-Hispanic/Latino; 0.3% Native Hawaiian or other Pacific Islander, non-Hispanic/Latino; 0.4% American Indian or Alaska Native, non-Hispanic/Latino; 0.5% Two or more races, non-Hispanic/Latino; 3% Race/ethnicity unknown; 4% international; 6% transferred in; 67% live on campus. *Retention:* 82% of full-time freshmen returned.

Freshmen *Admission:* 3,506 applied, 2,964 admitted, 692 enrolled. *Average high school GPA:* 3.52. *Test scores:* SAT critical reading scores over 500: 74%; SAT math scores over 500: 80%; SAT writing scores over 500: 68%; ACT scores over 18: 99%; SAT critical reading scores over 600: 26%; SAT math scores over 600: 34%; SAT writing scores over 600: 20%; ACT scores over 24: 70%; SAT critical reading scores over 700: 4%; SAT math scores over 700: 6%; SAT writing scores over 700: 4%; ACT scores over 30: 18%.

Faculty *Total:* 366, 69% full-time, 76% with terminal degrees. *Student/faculty ratio:* 13:1.

Academics *Calendar:* semesters. *Degrees:* certificates, associate, bachelor's, master's, doctoral-professional, doctoral-research/scholarship, post-master's, and postbachelor's certificates. *Special study options:* accelerated degree program, adult/continuing education programs, advanced placement credit, cooperative education, distance learning, double majors, English as a second language, freshman honors college, honors programs, independent study, internships, off-campus study, part-time degree program, services for LD students, student-designed majors, study abroad, summer session for credit. *ROTC:* Army (c), Air Force (c).

Computers on Campus 900 computers/terminals and 5,100 ports are available on campus for general student use. Students can access the following: campus intranet, computer help desk, free student e-mail accounts, online (class) grades, online (class) registration, online (class) schedules, Web academic information, degree audit. Campuswide network is available. 100% of college-owned or -operated housing units are wired for high-speed Internet access. Wireless service is available via classrooms, computer centers, computer labs, dorm rooms, learning centers, libraries, student centers.

Student Life *Housing:* on-campus residence required through junior year. *Options:* coed, women-only. Campus housing is university owned and leased by the school. Freshman campus housing is guaranteed. *Activities and organizations:* drama/theater group, student-run newspaper, radio station, choral group, Union Board, student government, student volunteer organization, chapel programs, national fraternities. *Campus security:* 24-hour emergency response devices and patrols, late-night transport/escort service, controlled dormitory access. *Student services:* health clinic, personal/psychological counseling, legal services.

Athletics Member NCAA. All Division I. *Intercollegiate sports:* baseball M(s), basketball M(s)/W(s), bowling W(s), cross-country running M(s)/W(s), football M, golf M(s)/W(s), soccer M(s)/W(s), softball W(s), swimming and diving M(s)/W(s), tennis M(s)/W(s), track and field M(s)/W(s), volleyball W(s). *Intramural sports:* badminton M(c)/W(c), basketball M/W, bowling M/W, football M/W, golf M/W, racquetball M/W, soccer M(c)/W(c), softball M/W, swimming and diving M/W, table tennis M/W, tennis M(c)/W(c), ultimate Frisbee M(c)/W(c), volleyball M/W.

Standardized Tests *Required:* SAT or ACT (for admission).

Costs (2011–12) *Comprehensive fee:* $39,796 includes full-time tuition ($30,000), mandatory fees ($1040), and room and board ($8756). Full-time tuition and fees vary according to course load. Part-time tuition: $1355 per credit hour. *College room only:* $5356. Room and board charges vary according to housing facility and student level. *Payment plan:* installment. *Waivers:* employees or children of employees.

Financial Aid Of all full-time matriculated undergraduates who enrolled in 2008, 2,324 applied for aid, 2,080 were judged to have need, 358 had their need fully met. 545 Federal Work-Study jobs (averaging $2000). 750 state and other part-time jobs (averaging $2000). In 2008, 557 non-need-based awards were made. *Average percent of need met:* 77%. *Average financial aid package:* $21,602. *Average need-based loan:* $5150. *Average need-based gift aid:* $17,177. *Average non-need-based aid:* $9427. *Average indebtedness upon graduation:* $33,024.

Applying *Options:* electronic application, deferred entrance. *Required:* essay or personal statement, high school transcript. *Required for some:* interview. *Recommended:* 2 letters of recommendation, interview. *Application deadlines:* rolling (freshmen), rolling (out-of-state freshmen), rolling (transfers). *Notification:* continuous (freshmen), continuous (out-of-state freshmen), continuous (transfers).

Freshman Application Contact Mr. T. Scott Henne, Director of Freshman Recruitment, Valparaiso University, Kretzmann Hall, 1700 Chapel Drive, Valparaiso, IN 46383-6493. *Phone:* 219-464-5011. *Toll-free phone:* 888-GO-VALPO. *Fax:* 219-464-6898. *E-mail:* Undergrad.Admission@valpo.edu. *Web site:* http://www.valpo.edu/.

Vincennes University

Vincennes, Indiana

Director of Admissions Christian Blome, Director of Admissions, Vincennes University, 1002 North First Street, Vincennes, IN 47591-5202. *Phone:* 800-742-9198. *Toll-free phone:* 800-742-9198. *E-mail:* cblome@vinu.edu. *Web site:* http://www.vinu.edu/.

Vincennes University Jasper Campus
Jasper, Indiana

- **State-supported** primarily 2-year, founded 1970, part of Vincennes University
- **Small-town** 140-acre campus
- **Coed** 915 undergraduate students
- **Noncompetitive** entrance level

Undergraduates Students come from 1 other state; 1 other country.
Faculty *Total:* 51, 39% full-time. *Student/faculty ratio:* 16:1.
Academics *Calendar:* semesters. *Degrees:* certificates, associate, and bachelor's. *Special study options:* academic remediation for entering students, adult/continuing education programs, advanced placement credit, distance learning, part-time degree program, summer session for credit.
Computers on Campus 140 computers/terminals are available on campus for general student use. Campuswide network is available.
Student Life *Housing:* college housing not available. *Activities and organizations:* student-run newspaper. *Student services:* personal/psychological counseling.
Costs (2010–11) *Tuition:* state resident $4326 full-time; nonresident $10,508 full-time. *Required fees:* $208 full-time. *Payment plan:* installment. *Waivers:* senior citizens and employees or children of employees.
Financial Aid Of all full-time matriculated undergraduates who enrolled in 2009, 3 Federal Work-Study jobs (averaging $3200).
Applying *Application fee:* $20. *Required:* high school transcript. *Application deadlines:* rolling (freshmen), rolling (transfers).
Freshman Application Contact Ms. Louann Gilbert, Admissions Director, Vincennes University Jasper Campus, 850 College Avenue, Jasper, IN 47546-9393. *Phone:* 812-482-3030. *Toll-free phone:* 800-809-VUJC. *Fax:* 812-481-5960. *E-mail:* lagilbert@vinu.edu. *Web site:* http://vujc.vinu.edu/.

Wabash College
Crawfordsville, Indiana

- **Independent** 4-year, founded 1832
- **Small-town** 60-acre campus with easy access to Indianapolis
- **Endowment** $282.0 million
- **Men only** 872 undergraduate students, 100% full-time
- **Moderately difficult** entrance level, 56% of applicants were admitted

Undergraduates 871 full-time, 1 part-time. Students come from 35 states and territories; 18 other countries; 25% are from out of state; 5% Black or African American, non-Hispanic/Latino; 5% Hispanic/Latino; 2% Asian, non-Hispanic/Latino; 0.3% Native Hawaiian or other Pacific Islander, non-Hispanic/Latino; 0.6% American Indian or Alaska Native, non-Hispanic/Latino; 1% Two or more races, non-Hispanic/Latino; 2% Race/ethnicity unknown; 6% international; 0.7% transferred in; 85% live on campus. *Retention:* 89% of full-time freshmen returned.
Freshmen *Admission:* 1,535 applied, 865 admitted, 247 enrolled. *Average high school GPA:* 3.58. *Test scores:* SAT critical reading scores over 500: 80%; SAT math scores over 500: 86%; SAT writing scores over 500: 72%; ACT scores over 18: 97%; SAT critical reading scores over 600: 35%; SAT math scores over 600: 50%; SAT writing scores over 600: 30%; ACT scores over 24: 68%; SAT critical reading scores over 700: 5%; SAT math scores over 700: 12%; SAT writing scores over 700: 4%; ACT scores over 30: 16%.
Faculty *Total:* 87, 92% full-time, 97% with terminal degrees. *Student/faculty ratio:* 11:1.
Academics *Calendar:* semesters. *Degree:* bachelor's. *Special study options:* advanced placement credit, double majors, independent study, internships, off-campus study, services for LD students, study abroad. *Unusual degree programs:* 3-2 engineering with Purdue University, Columbia University, Washington University in St. Louis; Law with Columbia University; Accounting with Indiana University.
Computers on Campus 350 computers/terminals are available on campus for general student use. Students can access the following: campus intranet, computer help desk, free student e-mail accounts, online (class) grades, online (class) schedules, online course management, degree audit, expenses. Campuswide network is available. 100% of college-owned or -operated housing units are wired for high-speed Internet access. Wireless service is available via entire campus.
Student Life *Housing:* on-campus residence required through sophomore year. *Options:* men-only. Campus housing is university owned. Freshman campus housing is guaranteed. *Activities and organizations:* drama/theater group, student-run newspaper, radio station, choral group, Sphinx Club, Alpha Phi Omega, The Bachelor, Malcolm X Institute of Black Studies, Wabash Christian Fellowship, national fraternities. *Campus security:* 24-hour emergency response devices and patrols, late-night transport/escort service. *Student services:* health clinic, personal/psychological counseling.
Athletics Member NCAA. All Division III. *Intercollegiate sports:* baseball M, basketball M, crew M(c), cross-country running M, football M, golf M,

lacrosse M(c), rugby M(c), sailing M(c), soccer M, swimming and diving M, tennis M, track and field M, water polo M(c), wrestling M. *Intramural sports:* badminton M, basketball M, bowling M, cross-country running M, football M, golf M, racquetball M, soccer M, softball M, swimming and diving M, table tennis M, tennis M, track and field M, volleyball M, weight lifting M, wrestling M.

Standardized Tests *Required:* SAT or ACT (for admission).

Costs (2010–11) *Comprehensive fee:* $39,350 includes full-time tuition ($30,400), mandatory fees ($650), and room and board ($8300). Full-time tuition and fees vary according to reciprocity agreements. Part-time tuition: $5067 per course. Part-time tuition and fees vary according to course load and reciprocity agreements. *Required fees:* $650 per year part-time. *College room only:* $3700. Room and board charges vary according to board plan and housing facility. *Payment plans:* tuition prepayment, installment. *Waivers:* employees or children of employees.

Financial Aid Of all full-time matriculated undergraduates who enrolled in 2009, 748 applied for aid, 691 were judged to have need, 585 had their need fully met. 763 state and other part-time jobs (averaging $2889). In 2009, 150 non-need-based awards were made. *Average percent of need met:* 97%. *Average financial aid package:* $27,618. *Average need-based loan:* $5074. *Average need-based gift aid:* $16,752. *Average non-need-based aid:* $16,797. *Average indebtedness upon graduation:* $29,897. *Financial aid deadline:* 3/1.

Applying *Options:* electronic application, early admission, early decision, early action, deferred entrance. *Application fee:* $40. *Required:* high school transcript. *Recommended:* essay or personal statement, 1 letter of recommendation, interview. *Application deadlines:* rolling (freshmen), 3/15 (transfers), 12/1 (early action). *Early decision deadline:* 11/15. *Notification:* continuous (freshmen), continuous until 4/1 (transfers), 12/1 (early decision), 12/22 (early action).

Freshman Application Contact Mr. Steven J. Klein, Dean of Admissions, Wabash College, PO Box 362, Crawfordsville, IN 47933-0352. *Phone:* 765-361-6225. *Toll-free phone:* 800-345-5385. *Fax:* 765-361-6437. *E-mail:* admissions@wabash.edu. *Web site:* http://www.wabash.edu/.

IOWA

AIB College of Business

Des Moines, Iowa

- **Independent** 4-year, founded 1921
- **Urban** 20-acre campus
- **Endowment** $5.7 million
- **Coed** 909 undergraduate students, 67% full-time, 67% women, 33% men
- **Minimally difficult** entrance level, 59% of applicants were admitted

Undergraduates 610 full-time, 299 part-time. Students come from 13 states and territories; 6% are from out of state; 3% Black or African American, non-Hispanic/Latino; 3% Hispanic/Latino; 2% Asian, non-Hispanic/Latino; 0.7% American Indian or Alaska Native, non-Hispanic/Latino; 1% Two or more races, non-Hispanic/Latino; 6% Race/ethnicity unknown; 0.1% international; 11% transferred in; 28% live on campus. *Retention:* 64% of full-time freshmen returned.

Freshmen *Admission:* 325 applied, 192 admitted, 113 enrolled. *Average high school GPA:* 3.11. *Test scores:* ACT scores over 18: 77%; ACT scores over 24: 20%.

Faculty *Total:* 74, 30% full-time. *Student/faculty ratio:* 18:1.

Academics *Calendar:* quarters. *Degrees:* associate and bachelor's. *Special study options:* academic remediation for entering students, advanced placement credit, cooperative education, distance learning, double majors, independent study, internships, part-time degree program, services for LD students, study abroad, summer session for credit.

Computers on Campus 372 computers/terminals are available on campus for general student use. Students can access the following: campus intranet, computer help desk, free student e-mail accounts, online (class) grades. Campus-wide network is available. 100% of college-owned or -operated housing units are wired for high-speed Internet access. Wireless service is available via entire campus.

Student Life *Housing options:* coed. Campus housing is university owned. *Activities and organizations:* Phi Theta Kappa, Business Management Association, Student Court Reporters and Captioners Association, Students in Free Enterprise (SIFE), Student Government Association, national sororities. *Campus security:* 24-hour emergency response devices and patrols, late-night transport/escort service, controlled dormitory access, video security. *Student services:* personal/psychological counseling.

Athletics Member NAIA. *Intercollegiate sports:* basketball M(s)/W(s), cheerleading M(s)/W(s), golf M(s)/W(s), volleyball W(s). *Intramural sports:* badminton M/W, basketball M/W, bowling M/W, football M/W, golf M/W, softball M/W, volleyball M(c)/W(c).

Standardized Tests *Required for some:* Nelson-Denny if no ACT score. *Recommended:* ACT (for admission).

Costs (2011–12) *Tuition:* $13,500 full-time, $1125 per course part-time. Full-time tuition and fees vary according to course load. Part-time tuition and fees vary according to course load. No tuition increase for student's term of enrollment. *Required fees:* $240 full-time, $80 per term part-time. *Room only:* $3318. Room and board charges vary according to housing facility. *Payment plans:* installment, deferred payment. *Waivers:* employees or children of employees.

Financial Aid Of all full-time matriculated undergraduates who enrolled in 2009, 104 Federal Work-Study jobs (averaging $1135). 1 state and other part-time job (averaging $457).

Applying *Options:* electronic application. *Required:* high school transcript, minimum 2 GPA. *Required for some:* Must take Nelson-Denny if no ACT score. *Recommended:* interview. *Application deadlines:* rolling (freshmen), rolling (out-of-state freshmen), rolling (transfers). *Notification:* continuous (freshmen), continuous (out-of-state freshmen), continuous (transfers).

Freshman Application Contact AIB College of Business, 2500 Fleur Drive, Des Moines, IA 50321-1799. *Phone:* 515-244-4221. *Toll-free phone:* 800-444-1921. *Web site:* http://www.aib.edu/.

Allen College

Waterloo, Iowa

- **Independent** comprehensive, founded 1989
- **Suburban** 20-acre campus
- **Endowment** $1.5 million
- **Coed, primarily women** 326 undergraduate students, 82% full-time, 94% women, 6% men
- **Moderately difficult** entrance level, 57% of applicants were admitted

Undergraduates 266 full-time, 60 part-time. Students come from 8 states and territories; 2 other countries; 5% are from out of state; 34% transferred in; 6% live on campus. *Retention:* 85% of full-time freshmen returned.

Freshmen *Admission:* 44 applied, 25 admitted, 5 enrolled. *Average high school GPA:* 3.81. *Test scores:* ACT scores over 18: 100%; ACT scores over 24: 40%.

Faculty *Total:* 39, 82% full-time, 23% with terminal degrees. *Student/faculty ratio:* 12:1.

Academics *Calendar:* semesters. *Degrees:* certificates, associate, bachelor's, master's, doctoral-professional, and post-master's certificates (liberal arts and general education courses offered at either University of North Iowa or Wartburg College). *Special study options:* accelerated degree program, advanced placement credit, cooperative education, distance learning, honors programs, independent study, internships, off-campus study, part-time degree program. *ROTC:* Army (c). *Unusual degree programs:* 3-2 nursing with Wartburg College, Loras College, Central College.

Computers on Campus 29 computers/terminals are available on campus for general student use. Students can access the following: campus intranet, computer help desk, free student e-mail accounts, online (class) grades, online (class) schedules. Campuswide network is available. 100% of college-owned or -operated housing units are wired for high-speed Internet access. Wireless service is available via entire campus.

Student Life *Housing options:* coed. Campus housing is university owned and is provided by a third party. *Activities and organizations:* choral group, Allen Student Nurses' Association, Nurses' Christian Fellowship. *Campus security:* 24-hour patrols, controlled dormitory access. *Student services:* health clinic, personal/psychological counseling.

Standardized Tests *Required for some:* SAT or ACT (for admission).

Costs (2010–11) *Comprehensive fee:* $22,152 includes full-time tuition ($13,458), mandatory fees ($1537), and room and board ($7157). Full-time tuition and fees vary according to course load and program. Part-time tuition: $500 per credit hour. Part-time tuition and fees vary according to course load and program. *Required fees:* $68 per credit hour part-time. *College room only:* $3578. Room and board charges vary according to housing facility. *Payment plan:* deferred payment. *Waivers:* employees or children of employees.

Financial Aid Of all full-time matriculated undergraduates who enrolled in 2008, 285 applied for aid, 253 were judged to have need, 10 had their need fully met. 15 Federal Work-Study jobs (averaging $2663). In 2008, 8 non-need-based awards were made. *Average percent of need met:* 49%. *Average financial aid package:* $9118. *Average need-based loan:* $4398. *Average need-based gift aid:* $5997. *Average non-need-based aid:* $1559. *Average indebtedness upon graduation:* $27,792.

Applying *Options:* electronic application. *Application fee:* $50. *Required for some:* essay or personal statement, high school transcript, 1 letter of recommendation, interview. *Recommended:* minimum 2.7 GPA. *Application deadlines:* 2/1 (freshmen), 2/1 (transfers). *Notification:* continuous until 3/1 (freshmen), continuous until 3/1 (transfers).

Freshman Application Contact Dina Dowden, Education Secretary, Student Services, Allen College, Barrett Forum, 1825 Logan Avenue, Waterloo, IA

50703. *Phone:* 319-226-2000. *Fax:* 319-226-2010. *E-mail:* allencollegeadmissions@ihs.org. *Web site:* http://www.allencollege.edu/.

Ashford University

Clinton, Iowa

Director of Admissions Ms. Waunita M. Sullivan, Director of Enrollment, Ashford University, 400 North Bluff Boulevard, PO Box 2967, Clinton, IA 52733-2967. *Phone:* 563-242-4023 Ext. 3401. *Toll-free phone:* 800-242-4153. *E-mail:* admissns@tfu.edu. *Web site:* http://www.ashford.edu/.

Briar Cliff University

Sioux City, Iowa

- **Independent Roman Catholic** comprehensive, founded 1930
- **Suburban** 75-acre campus
- **Endowment** $7.2 million
- **Coed** 1,066 undergraduate students, 82% full-time, 56% women, 44% men
- **Moderately difficult** entrance level, 58% of applicants were admitted

Undergraduates 869 full-time, 197 part-time. Students come from 29 states and territories; 11 other countries; 42% are from out of state; 3% transferred in. *Retention:* 68% of full-time freshmen returned.

Freshmen *Admission:* 1,774 applied, 1,035 admitted, 237 enrolled. *Average high school GPA:* 3.13. *Test scores:* ACT scores over 18: 89%; ACT scores over 24: 25%; ACT scores over 30: 3%.

Faculty *Total:* 107, 57% full-time, 49% with terminal degrees. *Student/faculty ratio:* 13:1.

Academics *Calendar:* (3 10-week terms plus 2 5-week summer sessions). *Degrees:* associate, bachelor's, and master's. *Special study options:* academic remediation for entering students, accelerated degree program, adult/continuing education programs, advanced placement credit, distance learning, double majors, honors programs, independent study, internships, off-campus study, part-time degree program, services for LD students, student-designed majors, study abroad, summer session for credit.

Computers on Campus 112 computers/terminals and 1,000 ports are available on campus for general student use. Students can access the following: campus intranet, computer help desk, free student e-mail accounts, online (class) grades, online (class) schedules. Campuswide network is available. Wireless service is available via classrooms, computer centers, computer labs, libraries, student centers.

Student Life *Housing:* on-campus residence required through junior year. *Options:* coed. Campus housing is university owned. Freshman campus housing is guaranteed. *Activities and organizations:* drama/theater group, student-run newspaper, radio station, choral group, Residence Hall Association, Briar Cliff Student Government, Choices, Blue Crew, Catholic Daughters. *Campus security:* 24-hour emergency response devices and patrols, student patrols, late-night transport/escort service, controlled dormitory access. *Student services:* health clinic, personal/psychological counseling.

Athletics Member NAIA. *Intercollegiate sports:* baseball M(s), basketball M(s)/W(s), cross-country running M(s)/W(s), football M(s), golf M(s)/W(s), soccer M(s)/W(s), softball W(s), tennis M(s)/W(s), track and field M(s)/W(s), volleyball W(s), wrestling M(s). *Intramural sports:* basketball M/W, football M, volleyball M/W.

Standardized Tests *Required:* SAT or ACT (for admission).

Costs (2011–12) *Comprehensive fee:* $30,708 includes full-time tuition ($22,719), mandatory fees ($699), and room and board ($7290). Part-time tuition: $759 per credit hour. *Required fees:* $23 per credit part-time. *Room and board:* Room and board charges vary according to board plan and housing facility. *Payment plans:* installment, deferred payment. *Waivers:* adult students, senior citizens, and employees or children of employees.

Financial Aid Of all full-time matriculated undergraduates who enrolled in 2009, 875 applied for aid, 625 were judged to have need, 428 had their need fully met. 240 Federal Work-Study jobs (averaging $1500). 115 state and other part-time jobs (averaging $1500). In 2009, 268 non-need-based awards were made. *Average percent of need met:* 78%. *Average financial aid package:* $6300. *Average need-based loan:* $4775. *Average need-based gift aid:* $6200. *Average non-need-based aid:* $11,550. *Average indebtedness upon graduation:* $31,853. *Financial aid deadline:* 3/15.

Applying *Options:* electronic application, early admission, deferred entrance. *Application fee:* $20. *Required:* high school transcript, minimum 2 GPA. *Required for some:* essay or personal statement, 3 letters of recommendation, interview. *Application deadlines:* rolling (freshmen), rolling (out-of-state freshmen), rolling (transfers). *Notification:* continuous (transfers).

Freshman Application Contact Brian Eben, Assistant Vice President for Enrollment Management, Briar Cliff University, 3303 Rebecca Street, Sioux

City, IA 51104-0100. *Phone:* 712-279-5200. *Toll-free phone:* 800-662-3303 Ext. 5200. *Fax:* 712-279-1632. *E-mail:* admissions@briarcliff.edu. *Web site:* http://www.briarcliff.edu/.

Buena Vista University

Storm Lake, Iowa

- **Independent** comprehensive, founded 1891, affiliated with Presbyterian Church (U.S.A.)
- **Small-town** 60-acre campus
- **Endowment** $100.5 million
- **Coed** 979 undergraduate students, 99% full-time, 52% women, 48% men
- **Moderately difficult** entrance level, 71% of applicants were admitted

Undergraduates 966 full-time, 13 part-time. Students come from 28 states and territories; 10 other countries; 24% are from out of state; 5% Black or African American, non-Hispanic/Latino; 7% Hispanic/Latino; 2% Asian, non-Hispanic/Latino; 0.1% Native Hawaiian or other Pacific Islander, non-Hispanic/Latino; 0.3% American Indian or Alaska Native, non-Hispanic/Latino; 0.8% Two or more races, non-Hispanic/Latino; 3% Race/ethnicity unknown; 5% international; 9% transferred in; 86% live on campus. *Retention:* 71% of full-time freshmen returned.

Freshmen *Admission:* 1,366 applied, 968 admitted, 265 enrolled. *Average high school GPA:* 3.38. *Test scores:* ACT scores over 18: 90%; ACT scores over 24: 45%; ACT scores over 30: 5%.

Faculty *Total:* 116, 73% full-time, 55% with terminal degrees. *Student/faculty ratio:* 10:1.

Academics *Calendar:* 4-1-4. *Degrees:* bachelor's and master's. *Special study options:* academic remediation for entering students, adult/continuing education programs, advanced placement credit, distance learning, double majors, English as a second language, external degree program, honors programs, independent study, internships, off-campus study, part-time degree program, services for LD students, student-designed majors, study abroad, summer session for credit. *ROTC:* Army (b). *Unusual degree programs:* 3-2 engineering with Washington University in St. Louis.

Computers on Campus 400 computers/terminals are available on campus for general student use. Students can access the following: computer help desk, free student e-mail accounts, online (class) grades, online (class) registration, online (class) schedules. Campuswide network is available. 100% of college-owned or -operated housing units are wired for high-speed Internet access. Wireless service is available via entire campus.

Student Life *Housing:* on-campus residence required through senior year. *Options:* coed, men-only, women-only. Campus housing is university owned. Freshman campus housing is guaranteed. *Activities and organizations:* drama/theater group, student-run newspaper, radio and television station, choral group, Student Activities Board, student orientation staff, Esprit De Corps, Student Senate, Marketing Association. *Campus security:* 24-hour emergency response devices, late-night transport/escort service, controlled dormitory access, night security patrols. *Student services:* health clinic, personal/psychological counseling.

Athletics Member NCAA. All Division III. *Intercollegiate sports:* baseball M, basketball M/W, cross-country running M/W, football M, golf M/W, soccer M/W, softball W, tennis M/W, track and field M/W, volleyball W, wrestling M. *Intramural sports:* basketball M/W, football M, racquetball M/W, softball M/W, ultimate Frisbee M/W, volleyball M/W.

Standardized Tests *Required:* SAT or ACT (for admission).

Costs (2010–11) *Comprehensive fee:* $33,888 includes full-time tuition ($26,306) and room and board ($7582). Full-time tuition and fees vary according to location. Part-time tuition: $884 per credit hour. Part-time tuition and fees vary according to location. No tuition increase for student's term of enrollment. *Room and board:* Room and board charges vary according to board plan. *Payment plan:* installment. *Waivers:* employees or children of employees.

Financial Aid Of all full-time matriculated undergraduates who enrolled in 2009, 871 applied for aid, 829 were judged to have need, 377 had their need fully met. In 2009, 68 non-need-based awards were made. *Average percent of need met:* 43%. *Average financial aid package:* $25,343. *Average need-based loan:* $4939. *Average need-based gift aid:* $8230. *Average non-need-based aid:* $14,341. *Average indebtedness upon graduation:* $37,502.

Applying *Options:* electronic application, deferred entrance. *Application fee:* $20. *Required:* high school transcript. *Required for some:* essay or personal statement, interview. *Recommended:* minimum 3 GPA. *Notification:* continuous (freshmen), continuous (transfers).

Freshman Application Contact Marcia Nance, Vice President for Enrollment Management, Buena Vista University, 610 West Fourth Street, Storm Lake, IA 50588. *Phone:* 712-749-2235. *Toll-free phone:* 800-383-9600. *E-mail:* admissions@bvu.edu. *Web site:* http://www.bvu.edu/.

Central College

Pella, Iowa

- **Independent** 4-year, founded 1853, affiliated with Reformed Church in America

- **Small-town** 169-acre campus with easy access to Des Moines

- **Coed** 1,648 undergraduate students, 97% full-time, 53% women, 47% men

- **Moderately difficult** entrance level, 73% of applicants were admitted

Undergraduates 1,606 full-time, 42 part-time. 22% are from out of state; 2% Black or African American, non-Hispanic/Latino; 3% Hispanic/Latino; 1% Asian, non-Hispanic/Latino; 0.2% Native Hawaiian or other Pacific Islander, non-Hispanic/Latino; 0.1% American Indian or Alaska Native, non-Hispanic/Latino; 1% Two or more races, non-Hispanic/Latino; 1% Race/ethnicity unknown; 0.5% international; 4% transferred in; 93% live on campus. *Retention:* 79% of full-time freshmen returned.

Freshmen *Admission:* 2,852 applied, 2,086 admitted, 402 enrolled. *Average high school GPA:* 3.48. *Test scores:* SAT critical reading scores over 500: 55%; SAT math scores over 500: 55%; ACT scores over 18: 97%; SAT critical reading scores over 600: 5%; SAT math scores over 600: 22%; ACT scores over 24: 48%; SAT math scores over 700: 5%; ACT scores over 30: 8%.

Faculty *Total:* 105, 85% full-time, 84% with terminal degrees. *Student/faculty ratio:* 16:1.

Academics *Calendar:* semesters. *Degree:* bachelor's. *Special study options:* cooperative education, double majors, honors programs, independent study, internships, off-campus study, part-time degree program, services for LD students, student-designed majors, study abroad, summer session for credit. *Unusual degree programs:* 3-2 engineering with Washington University in St. Louis, University of Iowa, and Iowa State University; nursing with Allen College; Palmer College of Chiropractic.

Computers on Campus Students can access the following: campus intranet, computer help desk, free student e-mail accounts, online (class) grades, online (class) registration, online (class) schedules. Campuswide network is available. 100% of college-owned or -operated housing units are wired for high-speed Internet access. Wireless service is available via entire campus.

Student Life *Housing:* on-campus residence required through senior year. *Options:* coed, men-only, women-only, disabled students. Campus housing is university owned. Freshman campus housing is guaranteed. *Activities and organizations:* drama/theater group, student-run newspaper, radio station, choral group. *Campus security:* 24-hour emergency response devices and patrols, late-night transport/escort service, controlled dormitory access. *Student services:* health clinic, personal/psychological counseling.

Athletics Member NCAA. All Division III. *Intercollegiate sports:* baseball M, basketball M/W, cross-country running M/W, football M, golf M/W, soccer M/W, softball W, tennis M/W, track and field M/W, volleyball W, wrestling M. *Intramural sports:* basketball M/W, football M, racquetball M/W, rugby M, soccer M/W, softball M/W, volleyball M/W.

Standardized Tests *Required:* SAT or ACT (for admission).

Costs (2010–11) *Comprehensive fee:* $34,944 includes full-time tuition ($25,862), mandatory fees ($380), and room and board ($8702). Part-time tuition: $898 per semester hour. Part-time tuition and fees vary according to course load. *College room only:* $4268. Room and board charges vary according to board plan. *Payment plan:* installment. *Waivers:* employees or children of employees.

Financial Aid Of all full-time matriculated undergraduates who enrolled in 2009, 1,508 applied for aid, 1,240 were judged to have need, 246 had their need fully met. 916 Federal Work-Study jobs (averaging $1365). 351 state and other part-time jobs (averaging $1316). In 2009, 266 non-need-based awards were made. *Average percent of need met:* 84%. *Average financial aid package:* $22,115. *Average need-based loan:* $4643. *Average need-based gift aid:* $16,141. *Average non-need-based aid:* $10,799. *Average indebtedness upon graduation:* $36,068.

Applying *Options:* electronic application, deferred entrance. *Application fee:* $25. *Required:* high school transcript. *Required for some:* essay or personal statement, 3 letters of recommendation, interview. *Recommended:* minimum 2.7 GPA, interview. *Application deadlines:* rolling (freshmen), rolling (transfers). *Notification:* continuous (freshmen), continuous (transfers).

Freshman Application Contact Central College, 812 University Street, Pella, IA 50219. *Phone:* 641-628-7600. *Toll-free phone:* 877-462-3687 (in-state); 877-462-3689 (out-of-state). *Web site:* http://www.central.edu/.

Clarke University

Dubuque, Iowa

- **Independent Roman Catholic** comprehensive, founded 1843
- **Urban** 55-acre campus
- **Endowment** $24.3 million
- **Coed** 993 undergraduate students, 84% full-time, 65% women, 35% men
- **Moderately difficult** entrance level, 81% of applicants were admitted

Undergraduates 834 full-time, 159 part-time. Students come from 29 states and territories; 12 other countries; 47% are from out of state; 2% Black or African American, non-Hispanic/Latino; 3% Hispanic/Latino; 0.9% Asian, non-Hispanic/Latino; 22% Race/ethnicity unknown; 2% international; 9% transferred in; 42% live on campus. *Retention:* 73% of full-time freshmen returned.

Freshmen *Admission:* 870 applied, 705 admitted, 176 enrolled. *Average high school GPA:* 3.33. *Test scores:* SAT critical reading scores over 500: 55%; SAT math scores over 500: 64%; ACT scores over 18: 98%; SAT critical reading scores over 600: 9%; ACT scores over 24: 39%; ACT scores over 30: 2%.

Faculty *Total:* 157, 50% full-time, 36% with terminal degrees. *Student/faculty ratio:* 10:1.

Academics *Calendar:* semesters. *Degrees:* associate, bachelor's, master's, and doctoral-professional. *Special study options:* accelerated degree program, adult/continuing education programs, advanced placement credit, cooperative education, distance learning, double majors, English as a second language, honors programs, independent study, internships, off-campus study, part-time degree program, student-designed majors, study abroad, summer session for credit. *ROTC:* Army (c).

Computers on Campus 237 computers/terminals are available on campus for general student use. Students can access the following: campus intranet, computer help desk, free student e-mail accounts, online (class) grades, online (class) registration, online (class) schedules. Campuswide network is available. Wireless service is available via classrooms, computer centers, computer labs, dorm rooms, learning centers, libraries, student centers.

Student Life *Housing:* on-campus residence required through sophomore year. *Options:* coed, men-only, women-only. Campus housing is university owned. Freshman campus housing is guaranteed. *Activities and organizations:* drama/theater group, student-run newspaper, radio station, choral group, Admissions Student Team, Student Multicultural Organization, concert choir, campus ministry, student government. *Campus security:* 24-hour emergency response devices and patrols, late-night transport/escort service, controlled dormitory access. *Student services:* health clinic, personal/psychological counseling.

Athletics Member NAIA. *Intercollegiate sports:* baseball M(s), basketball M(s)/W(s), bowling M(s)/W(s), cheerleading W, cross-country running M(s)/W(s), golf M(s)/W(s), soccer M(s)/W(s), softball W(s), tennis W(s), track and field M(s)/W(s), volleyball M(s)/W(s). *Intramural sports:* badminton M/W, basketball M/W, bowling M/W, football M/W, golf M/W, racquetball M/W, skiing (cross-country) M/W, skiing (downhill) M/W, softball M/W, table tennis M/W, tennis M/W, track and field M/W, volleyball M/W, water polo M/W, weight lifting M/W.

Standardized Tests *Required:* SAT or ACT (for admission).

Costs (2010–11) *Comprehensive fee:* $31,950 includes full-time tuition ($23,800), mandatory fees ($810), and room and board ($7340). Part-time tuition: $600 per credit hour. *College room only:* $3600. Room and board charges vary according to housing facility. *Payment plans:* installment, deferred payment. *Waivers:* children of alumni, adult students, senior citizens, and employees or children of employees.

Financial Aid Of all full-time matriculated undergraduates who enrolled in 2009, 772 applied for aid, 709 were judged to have need, 142 had their need fully met. 152 Federal Work-Study jobs (averaging $1300). In 2009, 84 non-need-based awards were made. *Average percent of need met:* 72%. *Average financial aid package:* $19,896. *Average need-based loan:* $4539. *Average need-based gift aid:* $15,907. *Average non-need-based aid:* $15,929. *Average indebtedness upon graduation:* $38,847.

Applying *Options:* electronic application, deferred entrance. *Application fee:* $25. *Required:* high school transcript, minimum 2 GPA. *Application deadlines:* rolling (freshmen), rolling (transfers). *Notification:* 7/15 (freshmen), continuous until 8/15 (transfers).

Freshman Application Contact Ms. Emily Kruse, Director of Admissions, Clarke University, 1550 Clarke Drive, Dubuque, IA 52001-3198. *Phone:* 563-588-6436. *Toll-free phone:* 800-383-2345. *E-mail:* admissions@clarke.edu. *Web site:* http://www.clarke.edu/.

Coe College

Cedar Rapids, Iowa

Freshman Application Contact Mr. John Grundig, Dean of Admission, Coe College, 1220 1st Avenue, NE, Cedar Rapids, IA 52402-5070. *Phone:* 319-399-8500. *Toll-free phone:* 877-225-5263. *Fax:* 319-399-8816. *E-mail:* admission@coe.edu. *Web site:* http://www.coe.edu/.

Cornell College

Mount Vernon, Iowa

- **Independent Methodist** 4-year, founded 1853
- **Small-town** 129-acre campus
- **Endowment** $60.2 million
- **Coed** 1,193 undergraduate students, 99% full-time, 54% women, 46% men
- **Moderately difficult** entrance level, 39% of applicants were admitted

Undergraduates 1,180 full-time, 13 part-time. Students come from 49 states and territories; 20 other countries; 77% are from out of state; 4% Black or African American, non-Hispanic/Latino; 6% Hispanic/Latino; 3% Asian, non-Hispanic/Latino; 1% American Indian or Alaska Native, non-Hispanic/Latino; 2% Two or more races, non-Hispanic/Latino; 3% Race/ethnicity unknown; 5% international; 3% transferred in; 90% live on campus. *Retention:* 81% of full-time freshmen returned.

Freshmen *Admission:* 3,791 applied, 1,491 admitted, 335 enrolled. *Average high school GPA:* 3.5. *Test scores:* SAT critical reading scores over 500: 91%; SAT math scores over 500: 87%; SAT writing scores over 500: 85%; ACT scores over 18: 100%; SAT critical reading scores over 600: 49%; SAT math scores over 600: 49%; SAT writing scores over 600: 41%; ACT scores over 24: 76%; SAT critical reading scores over 700: 20%; SAT math scores over 700: 18%; SAT writing scores over 700: 13%; ACT scores over 30: 25%.

Faculty *Total:* 88, 95% full-time, 94% with terminal degrees. *Student/faculty ratio:* 13:1.

Academics *Calendar:* 9 3&S1/&I2-week terms. *Degree:* bachelor's. *Special study options:* advanced placement credit, double majors, English as a second language, independent study, internships, off-campus study, services for LD students, student-designed majors, study abroad. *Unusual degree programs:* 3-2 engineering with University of Minnesota; forestry with Duke University; Environmental Management with Duke University; Architecture with Washington University–St. Louis.

Computers on Campus 190 computers/terminals are available on campus for general student use. Students can access the following: campus intranet, computer help desk, free student e-mail accounts, online (class) grades, online (class) registration, online (class) schedules. Campuswide network is available. 100% of college-owned or -operated housing units are wired for high-speed Internet access. Wireless service is available via classrooms, computer centers, computer labs, learning centers, libraries, student centers.

Student Life *Housing:* on-campus residence required through senior year. *Options:* coed, men-only, women-only. Campus housing is university owned. Freshman campus housing is guaranteed. *Activities and organizations:* drama/theater group, student-run newspaper, radio station, choral group, Student-initiated Living-learning Community, Lunch Buddies/Youth Mentoring, Chess and Games Club, PAAC (Performing Arts and Activities Council), Fellowship of Christian Athletes (FCA). *Campus security:* 24-hour emergency response devices and patrols, late-night transport/escort service, controlled dormitory access. *Student services:* health clinic, personal/psychological counseling, women's center.

Athletics Member NCAA. All Division III. *Intercollegiate sports:* baseball M, basketball M/W, cross-country running M/W, football M, golf M/W, lacrosse M(c)/W(c), soccer M/W, softball W, tennis M/W, track and field M/W, volleyball M(c)/W, wrestling M. *Intramural sports:* badminton M/W, basketball M/W, bowling M/W, cheerleading M/W, cross-country running M/W, equestrian sports M/W, fencing M/W, football M, golf M/W, ice hockey M/W, lacrosse M/W, racquetball M/W, riflery M/W, rock climbing M/W, skiing (downhill) M/W, soccer M/W, softball M/W, table tennis M/W, tennis M/W, track and field M/W, ultimate Frisbee M/W, volleyball M/W, weight lifting M/W, wrestling M/W.

Standardized Tests *Required:* SAT or ACT (for admission). *Recommended:* SAT Subject Tests (for admission).

Costs (2011–12) *Comprehensive fee:* $40,650 includes full-time tuition ($32,720), mandatory fees ($200), and room and board ($7730). Part-time tuition: $1022 per semester hour. Part-time tuition and fees vary according to course load and reciprocity agreements. *Room and board:* Room and board charges vary according to board plan and housing facility. *Payment plan:* installment. *Waivers:* employees or children of employees.

Financial Aid Of all full-time matriculated undergraduates who enrolled in 2009, 978 applied for aid, 881 were judged to have need, 309 had their need fully met. 618 Federal Work-Study jobs (averaging $1275). In 2009, 246 non-need-based awards were made. *Average percent of need met:* 92%. *Average financial aid package:* $31,400. *Average need-based loan:* $4443. *Average need-based gift aid:* $22,045. *Average non-need-based aid:* $12,565. *Average indebtedness upon graduation:* $22,455. *Financial aid deadline:* 3/1.

Applying *Options:* electronic application, early admission, early decision, early action, deferred entrance. *Application fee:* $30. *Required:* essay or personal statement, high school transcript, 1 letter of recommendation. *Recommended:* interview. *Application deadlines:* 2/1 (freshmen), 3/1 (transfers), 12/1 (early action). *Early decision deadline:* 11/1 (for plan 1), 2/1 (for plan 2).

Notification: 3/20 (freshmen), continuous (transfers), 11/15 (early decision plan 1), 3/15 (early decision plan 2), 2/1 (early action).

Freshman Application Contact Mr. Todd White, Director of Admission, Cornell College, 600 First Street SW, Mount Vernon, IA 52314-1098. *Phone:* 319-895-4167. *Toll-free phone:* 800-747-1112. *Fax:* 319-895-4451. *E-mail:* twhite@cornellcollege.edu. *Web site:* http://www.cornellcollege.edu/.

Divine Word College

Epworth, Iowa

- **Independent Roman Catholic** 4-year, founded 1912
- **Rural** 35-acre campus
- **Coed** 107 undergraduate students, 96% full-time, 31% women, 69% men

Undergraduates 103 full-time, 4 part-time.

Academics *Calendar:* semesters. *Degrees:* associate and bachelor's. *Special study options:* academic remediation for entering students, advanced placement credit, double majors, English as a second language, independent study, study abroad.

Computers on Campus Campuswide network is available.

Student Life *Housing:* on-campus residence required through senior year. *Options:* men-only, women-only. *Activities and organizations:* choral group. *Campus security:* controlled dormitory access. *Student services:* personal/psychological counseling.

Standardized Tests *Recommended:* SAT or ACT (for admission).

Costs (2011–12) *Comprehensive fee:* $14,850 includes full-time tuition ($11,600), mandatory fees ($100), and room and board ($3150). Part-time tuition: $387 per credit. *Payment plans:* installment, deferred payment. *Waivers:* senior citizens and employees or children of employees.

Applying *Options:* early admission. *Application fee:* $25. *Required:* essay or personal statement, high school transcript, 3 letters of recommendation, interview, medical history. *Application deadlines:* 7/15 (freshmen), 7/15 (transfers). *Notification:* continuous until 8/1 (freshmen), continuous until 8/1 (transfers).

Freshman Application Contact Divine Word College, 102 Jacoby Drive SW, Epworth, IA 52045-0380. *Phone:* 563-876-3353. *Toll-free phone:* 800-553-3321. *Web site:* http://www.dwci.edu/.

Dordt College

Sioux Center, Iowa

- **Independent Christian Reformed** comprehensive, founded 1955
- **Small-town** 110-acre campus
- **Endowment** $28.0 million
- **Coed** 1,368 undergraduate students, 98% full-time, 49% women, 51% men
- **Moderately difficult** entrance level, 84% of applicants were admitted

Undergraduates 1,335 full-time, 33 part-time. Students come from 34 states and territories; 16 other countries; 63% are from out of state; 1% Black or African American, non-Hispanic/Latino; 2% Hispanic/Latino; 2% Asian, non-Hispanic/Latino; 0.1% American Indian or Alaska Native, non-Hispanic/Latino; 0.7% Two or more races, non-Hispanic/Latino; 0.7% Race/ethnicity unknown; 5% transferred in; 90% live on campus. *Retention:* 79% of full-time freshmen returned.

Freshmen *Admission:* 1,111 applied, 933 admitted, 393 enrolled. *Average high school GPA:* 3.5. *Test scores:* SAT critical reading scores over 500: 60%; SAT math scores over 500: 66%; SAT writing scores over 500: 52%; ACT scores over 18: 97%; SAT critical reading scores over 600: 29%; SAT math scores over 600: 24%; SAT writing scores over 600: 22%; ACT scores over 24: 54%; SAT critical reading scores over 700: 6%; SAT math scores over 700: 5%; SAT writing scores over 700: 1%; ACT scores over 30: 13%.

Faculty *Total:* 142, 54% full-time, 42% with terminal degrees. *Student/faculty ratio:* 14:1.

Academics *Calendar:* semesters. *Degrees:* associate, bachelor's, and master's. *Special study options:* academic remediation for entering students, advanced placement credit, distance learning, double majors, English as a second language, freshman honors college, honors programs, independent study, internships, off-campus study, part-time degree program, services for LD students, student-designed majors, study abroad.

Computers on Campus 200 computers/terminals are available on campus for general student use. Students can access the following: campus intranet, computer help desk, free student e-mail accounts, online (class) grades, online (class) registration, online (class) schedules. Campuswide network is available. 100% of college-owned or -operated housing units are wired for high-speed Internet access. Wireless service is available via entire campus.

Student Life *Housing:* on-campus residence required through senior year. *Options:* men-only, women-only, disabled students. Campus housing is university owned. Freshman campus housing is guaranteed. *Activities and organizations:* drama/theater group, student-run newspaper, radio station, choral group, PLIA, Future Teachers, Ag Club, Lacrosse Club, Defenders of Life. *Campus* *security:* 24-hour emergency response devices, student patrols, late-night transport/escort service, controlled dormitory access. *Student services:* health clinic, personal/psychological counseling.

Athletics Member NAIA. *Intercollegiate sports:* baseball M(s), basketball M(s)/W(s), cross-country running M(s)/W(s), football M(s), golf M(s)/W(s), ice hockey M(s), lacrosse M, soccer M(s)/W(s), softball W(s), track and field M(s)/W(s), volleyball W(s). *Intramural sports:* basketball M/W, bowling M/W, field hockey M/W, gymnastics M/W, ice hockey M, lacrosse M, racquetball M/W, skiing (cross-country) M/W, soccer M/W, softball M/W, swimming and diving M/W, table tennis M/W, tennis M/W, track and field M/W, volleyball M/W, weight lifting M/W.

Standardized Tests *Required:* SAT or ACT (for admission).

Costs (2010–11) *Comprehensive fee:* $29,700 includes full-time tuition ($22,800), mandatory fees ($380), and room and board ($6520). Full-time tuition and fees vary according to course load. Part-time tuition: $930 per semester hour. *Required fees:* $190 per term part-time. *College room only:* $3330. Room and board charges vary according to board plan and housing facility. *Payment plan:* installment. *Waivers:* senior citizens and employees or children of employees.

Financial Aid Of all full-time matriculated undergraduates who enrolled in 2009, 1,113 applied for aid, 981 were judged to have need, 154 had their need fully met. 500 Federal Work-Study jobs (averaging $1500). 600 state and other part-time jobs (averaging $1500). In 2009, 235 non-need-based awards were made. *Average percent of need met:* 84%. *Average financial aid package:* $21,200. *Average need-based loan:* $5475. *Average need-based gift aid:* $11,807. *Average non-need-based aid:* $12,119. *Average indebtedness upon graduation:* $21,881.

Applying *Options:* electronic application, deferred entrance. *Application fee:* $25. *Required:* high school transcript, minimum 2.25 GPA. *Required for some:* essay or personal statement, interview. *Application deadlines:* 8/1 (freshmen), 8/1 (transfers). *Notification:* 8/1 (freshmen), continuous until 9/1 (transfers).

Freshman Application Contact Mr. Quentin Van Essen, Executive Director of Admissions, Dordt College, 498 4th Avenue, NE, Sioux Center, IA 51250-1697. *Phone:* 712-722-6080. *Toll-free phone:* 800-343-6738. *Fax:* 712-722-6035. *E-mail:* admissions@dordt.edu. *Web site:* http://www.dordt.edu/.

Drake University

Des Moines, Iowa

- **Independent** university, founded 1881
- **Suburban** 120-acre campus
- **Endowment** $135.0 million
- **Coed** 3,527 undergraduate students, 94% full-time, 57% women, 43% men
- **Moderately difficult** entrance level, 65% of applicants were admitted

Undergraduates 3,317 full-time, 210 part-time. Students come from 50 states and territories; 58 other countries; 61% are from out of state; 4% transferred in; 70% live on campus. *Retention:* 85% of full-time freshmen returned.

Freshmen *Admission:* 5,848 applied, 3,802 admitted, 864 enrolled. *Average high school GPA:* 3.69. *Test scores:* SAT critical reading scores over 500: 88%; SAT math scores over 500: 92%; ACT scores over 18: 100%; SAT critical reading scores over 600: 42%; SAT math scores over 600: 56%; ACT scores over 24: 83%; SAT critical reading scores over 700: 11%; SAT math scores over 700: 18%; ACT scores over 30: 26%.

Faculty *Total:* 435, 63% full-time, 62% with terminal degrees. *Student/faculty ratio:* 13:1.

Academics *Calendar:* semesters. *Degrees:* certificates, bachelor's, master's, doctoral-professional, doctoral-research/scholarship, post-master's, and post-bachelor's certificates. *Special study options:* accelerated degree program, advanced placement credit, cooperative education, distance learning, double majors, English as a second language, honors programs, independent study, internships, off-campus study, part-time degree program, services for LD students, student-designed majors, study abroad, summer session for credit. *ROTC:* Army (b), Air Force (c). *Unusual degree programs:* 3-2 journalism and law, arts and sciences and law, accounting.

Computers on Campus 1,000 computers/terminals are available on campus for general student use. Students can access the following: campus intranet, computer help desk, free student e-mail accounts, online (class) grades, online (class) registration, online (class) schedules. Campuswide network is available. 100% of college-owned or -operated housing units are wired for high-speed Internet access. Wireless service is available via classrooms, computer centers, computer labs, dorm rooms, libraries, student centers.

Student Life *Housing:* on-campus residence required through sophomore year. *Options:* coed, disabled students. Campus housing is university owned and is provided by a third party. Freshman campus housing is guaranteed. *Activities and organizations:* drama/theater group, student-run newspaper, radio and television station, choral group, marching band, Student Activities Board, Drake Magazine, Dog Pound Pep Squad, Alpha Phi Omega, Residence Hall Association, national fraternities, national sororities. *Campus security:* 24-hour emergency response devices and patrols, late-night transport/escort service, 24-hour desk attendants in residence halls. *Student services:* health clinic, personal/psychological counseling, legal services.

Athletics Member NCAA. All Division I except football (Division I-AA). *Intercollegiate sports:* basketball M(s)/W(s), cheerleading M(s)/W(s), crew W, cross-country running M(s)/W(s), golf M(s)/W, soccer M(s)/W(s), softball W(s), tennis M(s)/W(s), track and field M(s)/W(s), volleyball W(s). *Intramural sports:* badminton M/W, basketball M/W, football M/W, golf M/W, racquetball M/W, soccer M(c)/W, softball M/W, swimming and diving M/W, tennis M/W, volleyball M/W(c).

Standardized Tests *Required:* SAT or ACT (for admission).

Costs (2011–12) *Comprehensive fee:* $36,792 includes full-time tuition ($28,250), mandatory fees ($132), and room and board ($8410). Full-time tuition and fees vary according to course load, program, and student level. Part-time tuition: $573 per hour. Part-time tuition and fees vary according to class time and program. *College room only:* $4420. Room and board charges vary according to board plan. *Payment plan:* installment. *Waivers:* children of alumni, senior citizens, and employees or children of employees.

Financial Aid Of all full-time matriculated undergraduates who enrolled in 2009, 2,425 applied for aid, 1,973 were judged to have need, 560 had their need fully met. 1,676 Federal Work-Study jobs (averaging $1917). In 2009, 1107 non-need-based awards were made. *Average percent of need met:* 78%. *Average financial aid package:* $21,212. *Average need-based loan:* $4352. *Average need-based gift aid:* $14,579. *Average non-need-based aid:* $11,072. *Average indebtedness upon graduation:* $35,027.

Applying *Options:* electronic application, early admission, deferred entrance. *Application fee:* $25. *Required:* essay or personal statement, high school transcript. *Recommended:* interview. *Application deadlines:* 3/1 (freshmen), rolling (transfers). *Notification:* continuous (freshmen), continuous (transfers).

Freshman Application Contact Ms. Laura Linn, Director of Admission, Drake University, 2507 University Avenue, Des Moines, IA 50311. *Phone:* 515-271-3181 Ext. 3182. *Toll-free phone:* 800-44DRAKE Ext. 3181. *Fax:* 515-271-2831. *E-mail:* admission@drake.edu. *Web site:* http://www.drake.edu/.

Emmaus Bible College

Dubuque, Iowa

- **Independent nondenominational** 4-year, founded 1941
- **Small-town** 22-acre campus
- **Coed** 244 undergraduate students
- **Noncompetitive** entrance level

Academics *Calendar:* semesters. *Degrees:* certificates, associate, and bachelor's. *Special study options:* advanced placement credit, double majors, independent study, internships, off-campus study, part-time degree program.

Computers on Campus Campuswide network is available.

Student Life *Housing:* on-campus residence required through senior year. *Options:* men-only, women-only. Campus housing is university owned. Freshman campus housing is guaranteed. *Campus security:* 24-hour emergency response devices, student patrols, controlled dormitory access.

Athletics Member NCCAA. *Intercollegiate sports:* basketball M/W.

Costs (2010–11) *Comprehensive fee:* $18,416 includes full-time tuition ($11,904), mandatory fees ($700), and room and board ($5812). Full-time tuition and fees vary according to course load and program. Part-time tuition: $525 per credit hour. Part-time tuition and fees vary according to course load and program. *Required fees:* $700 per term part-time. *Payment plan:* installment. *Waivers:* employees or children of employees.

Financial Aid Of all full-time matriculated undergraduates who enrolled in 2005, 212 applied for aid, 145 were judged to have need. *Average percent of need met:* 74%. *Average financial aid package:* $5216. *Average need-based loan:* $3652. *Average need-based gift aid:* $2852.

Applying *Options:* electronic application, deferred entrance. *Application fee:* $25. *Required:* essay or personal statement, high school transcript, 3 letters of recommendation. *Application deadlines:* 6/1 (freshmen), 8/1 (transfers). *Notification:* continuous (freshmen), continuous (transfers).

Freshman Application Contact Emmaus Bible College, 2570 Asbury Road, Dubuque, IA 52001-3097. *Phone:* 563-588-8000 Ext. 1310. *Toll-free phone:* 800-397-2425. *Web site:* http://www.emmaus.edu/.

Faith Baptist Bible College and Theological Seminary

Ankeny, Iowa

- **Independent** comprehensive, founded 1921, affiliated with General Association of Regular Baptist Churches
- **Suburban** 52-acre campus
- **Endowment** $3.5 million
- **Coed** 325 undergraduate students, 90% full-time, 58% women, 42% men
- **Minimally difficult** entrance level, 74% of applicants were admitted

Undergraduates 294 full-time, 31 part-time. Students come from 27 states and territories; 12 other countries; 49% are from out of state; 7% transferred in; 77% live on campus. *Retention:* 79% of full-time freshmen returned.
Freshmen *Admission:* 202 applied, 149 admitted, 89 enrolled. *Average high school GPA:* 3.48. *Test scores:* SAT critical reading scores over 500: 50%; SAT math scores over 500: 50%; SAT writing scores over 500: 50%; ACT scores over 18: 80%; ACT scores over 24: 36%; ACT scores over 30: 7%.
Faculty *Total:* 34, 59% full-time, 50% with terminal degrees. *Student/faculty ratio:* 10:1.
Academics *Calendar:* semesters. *Degrees:* certificates, associate, bachelor's, master's, and doctoral-professional. *Special study options:* academic remediation for entering students, adult/continuing education programs, advanced placement credit, double majors, independent study, internships, part-time degree program, summer session for credit.
Computers on Campus 45 computers/terminals and 250 ports are available on campus for general student use. Students can access the following: free student e-mail accounts, online (class) registration. Campuswide network is available. 100% of college-owned or -operated housing units are wired for high-speed Internet access. Wireless service is available via entire campus.
Student Life *Housing:* on-campus residence required through senior year. *Options:* men-only, women-only, disabled students. Campus housing is university owned. Freshman campus housing is guaranteed. *Activities and organizations:* drama/theater group, student-run newspaper, choral group, Student Association, Student Missionary Fellowship, Intramural Sports, Photo Club, Chapel Orchestra. *Campus security:* 24-hour emergency response devices and patrols, late-night transport/escort service. *Student services:* personal/psychological counseling.
Athletics Member NCCAA. *Intercollegiate sports:* basketball M/W, cross-country running M/W, soccer M/W, track and field M/W, volleyball W. *Intramural sports:* basketball M/W, football M, ultimate Frisbee M/W, volleyball M/W.
Standardized Tests *Required:* SAT or ACT (for admission).
Costs (2010–11) *One-time required fee:* $50. *Comprehensive fee:* $19,354 includes full-time tuition ($13,414), mandatory fees ($400), and room and board ($5540). Full-time tuition and fees vary according to course load. Part-time tuition: $490 per credit hour. Part-time tuition and fees vary according to course load. *Required fees:* $200 per term part-time. *College room only:* $2510. *Payment plan:* installment. *Waivers:* employees or children of employees.
Financial Aid Of all full-time matriculated undergraduates who enrolled in 2004, 311 applied for aid, 290 were judged to have need, 5 had their need fully met. In 2004, 21 non-need-based awards were made. *Average percent of need met:* 48%. *Average financial aid package:* $7124. *Average need-based loan:* $3142. *Average need-based gift aid:* $6299. *Average non-need-based aid:* $2465. *Average indebtedness upon graduation:* $15,006.
Applying *Options:* electronic application, deferred entrance. *Required:* essay or personal statement, high school transcript, 2 letters of recommendation. *Required for some:* interview. *Recommended:* minimum 2 GPA. *Application deadlines:* 8/1 (freshmen), 8/1 (transfers). *Notification:* 9/1 (freshmen), continuous until 9/1 (transfers).
Freshman Application Contact Miss Carrie Johnson, Admissions Secretary, Faith Baptist Bible College and Theological Seminary, 1900 NW 4th Street, Ankeny, IA 50023. *Phone:* 515-964-0601. *Toll-free phone:* 888-FAITH 4U. *Fax:* 515-964-1638. *E-mail:* admissions@faith.edu. *Web site:* http://www.faith.edu/.

Graceland University

Lamoni, Iowa

- **Independent Community of Christ** comprehensive, founded 1895
- **Rural** 170-acre campus with easy access to Des Moines
- **Endowment** $34.6 million
- **Coed** 1,468 undergraduate students, 80% full-time, 60% women, 40% men
- **Moderately difficult** entrance level

Undergraduates 1,175 full-time, 293 part-time. Students come from 42 states and territories; 38 other countries; 63% are from out of state; 6% transferred in; 69% live on campus. *Retention:* 68% of full-time freshmen returned.

Freshmen *Admission:* 1,473 applied, 222 enrolled. *Average high school GPA:* 3.11. *Test scores:* SAT critical reading scores over 500: 25%; SAT math scores over 500: 29%; ACT scores over 18: 75%; SAT critical reading scores over 600: 7%; SAT math scores over 600: 9%; ACT scores over 24: 22%; SAT math scores over 700: 2%; ACT scores over 30: 5%.
Faculty *Total:* 122, 65% full-time, 56% with terminal degrees. *Student/faculty ratio:* 16:1.
Academics *Calendar:* 4-1-4. *Degrees:* associate, bachelor's, master's, and post-master's certificates. *Special study options:* academic remediation for entering students, accelerated degree program, adult/continuing education programs, advanced placement credit, cooperative education, distance learning, double majors, English as a second language, external degree program, freshman honors college, honors programs, independent study, internships, off-campus study, part-time degree program, services for LD students, student-designed majors, study abroad, summer session for credit.
Computers on Campus 139 computers/terminals and 1,046 ports are available on campus for general student use. Students can access the following: campus intranet, computer help desk, free student e-mail accounts, online (class) grades, online (class) registration, online (class) schedules. Campuswide network is available. 100% of college-owned or -operated housing units are wired for high-speed Internet access. Wireless service is available via classrooms, computer centers, computer labs, dorm rooms, learning centers, libraries, student centers.
Student Life *Housing:* on-campus residence required through sophomore year. *Options:* men-only, women-only. Campus housing is university owned. Freshman campus housing is guaranteed. *Activities and organizations:* drama/theater group, student-run newspaper, radio station, choral group, International Club, Student Athletic Trainers, Outreach International, Art Student Society, Students in Free Enterprise (SIFE). *Campus security:* 24-hour emergency response devices and patrols, late-night transport/escort service, controlled dormitory access. *Student services:* health clinic, personal/psychological counseling.
Athletics Member NAIA. *Intercollegiate sports:* baseball M(s), basketball M(s)/W(s), cheerleading M(s)/W(s), cross-country running M(s)/W(s), football M(s), golf M(s)/W(s), soccer M(s)/W(s), softball W(s), swimming and diving M(c)/W(c), tennis M(s)/W(s), track and field M(s)/W(s), ultimate Frisbee M(c)/W(c), volleyball M(s)/W(s). *Intramural sports:* basketball M/W, football M/W, golf M/W, ice hockey M/W, racquetball M/W, soccer M/W, softball M/W, swimming and diving M/W, table tennis M/W, ultimate Frisbee M/W, volleyball M/W.
Standardized Tests *Required:* SAT or ACT (for admission). *Required for some:* TOEFL for all students whose first language is not English.
Costs (2011–12) *Comprehensive fee:* $28,020 includes full-time tuition ($20,680), mandatory fees ($300), and room and board ($7040). Full-time tuition and fees vary according to course load. Part-time tuition: $650 per semester hour. *College room only:* $2810. Room and board charges vary according to board plan, housing facility, and location. *Payment plan:* installment. *Waivers:* senior citizens and employees or children of employees.
Financial Aid Of all full-time matriculated undergraduates who enrolled in 2009, 1,022 applied for aid, 942 were judged to have need, 135 had their need fully met. 252 Federal Work-Study jobs (averaging $1390). 273 state and other part-time jobs (averaging $1631). In 2009, 225 non-need-based awards were made. *Average percent of need met:* 73%. *Average financial aid package:* $18,364. *Average need-based loan:* $5164. *Average need-based gift aid:* $14,183. *Average non-need-based aid:* $10,059. *Average indebtedness upon graduation:* $31,404.
Applying *Options:* electronic application, deferred entrance. *Required:* high school transcript, minimum 2.5 GPA, ACT or SAT Scores are required. Class rank in top half of class is highly recommended. *Required for some:* essay or personal statement, 2 letters of recommendation, interview. *Recommended:* ACT or SAT Scores are required. Class rank in top half of class is highly recommended. *Application deadlines:* rolling (freshmen), rolling (out-of-state freshmen), rolling (transfers). *Notification:* continuous (freshmen), continuous (out-of-state freshmen), continuous (transfers).
Freshman Application Contact Mr. Kirk Bjorland, Director of Admissions, Graceland University, 1 University Place, Lamoni, IA 50140. *Phone:* 641-784-5145. *Toll-free phone:* 866-GRACELAND. *Fax:* 641-784-5480. *E-mail:* admissions@graceland.edu. *Web site:* http://www.graceland.edu/.

See page 1312 for the College Close-Up.

Grand View University

Des Moines, Iowa

- **Independent** comprehensive, founded 1896, affiliated with Evangelical Lutheran Church in America
- **Urban** 25-acre campus
- **Endowment** $13.0 million
- **Coed** 2,077 undergraduate students, 81% full-time, 60% women, 40% men
- **Minimally difficult** entrance level, 92% of applicants were admitted

Undergraduates 1,688 full-time, 389 part-time. Students come from 24 states and territories; 11 other countries; 10% are from out of state; 7% Black or African American, non-Hispanic/Latino; 3% Hispanic/Latino; 2% Asian, non-Hispanic/Latino; 0.3% Native Hawaiian or other Pacific Islander, non-Hispanic/Latino; 0.2% American Indian or Alaska Native, non-Hispanic/Latino; 1% Two or more races, non-Hispanic/Latino; 9% Race/ethnicity unknown; 1% international; 19% transferred in; 30% live on campus. *Retention:* 68% of full-time freshmen returned.

Freshmen *Admission:* 782 applied, 718 admitted, 300 enrolled. *Average high school GPA:* 3.17. *Test scores:* SAT critical reading scores over 500: 27%; SAT math scores over 500: 46%; SAT writing scores over 500: 16%; ACT scores over 18: 88%; SAT critical reading scores over 600: 3%; SAT math scores over 600: 14%; SAT writing scores over 600: 3%; ACT scores over 24: 19%; ACT scores over 30: 2%.

Faculty *Total:* 219, 40% full-time, 42% with terminal degrees. *Student/faculty ratio:* 14:1.

Academics *Calendar:* semesters. *Degrees:* certificates, associate, bachelor's, master's, and postbachelor's certificates. *Special study options:* academic remediation for entering students, accelerated degree program, adult/continuing education programs, advanced placement credit, cooperative education, distance learning, double majors, freshman honors college, honors programs, independent study, internships, off-campus study, part-time degree program, services for LD students, student-designed majors, study abroad, summer session for credit. *ROTC:* Army (c), Air Force (c). *Unusual degree programs:* 3-2 engineering with Iowa State University; hospital administration with The University of Iowa.

Computers on Campus 275 computers/terminals are available on campus for general student use. Students can access the following: campus intranet, computer help desk, free student e-mail accounts, online (class) grades, online (class) registration, online (class) schedules. Campuswide network is available. 100% of college-owned or -operated housing units are wired for high-speed Internet access. Wireless service is available via classrooms, computer labs, libraries, student centers.

Student Life *Housing:* on-campus residence required through sophomore year. *Options:* coed. Campus housing is university owned. Freshman applicants given priority for college housing. *Activities and organizations:* drama/theater group, student-run newspaper, radio and television station, choral group, Nursing Student Association, Art Club, Science Club, Education Club, Business Club. *Campus security:* 24-hour emergency response devices and patrols, late-night transport/escort service, controlled dormitory access, night security patrols. *Student services:* health clinic, personal/psychological counseling.

Athletics Member NAIA. *Intercollegiate sports:* baseball M(s), basketball M(s)/W(s), bowling M(s)/W(s), cheerleading W(s), cross-country running M(s)/W(s), football M(s), golf M(s)/W(s), soccer M(s)/W(s), softball W(s), tennis M(s)/W(s), track and field M(s)/W(s), volleyball M(s)/W(s), wrestling M(s). *Intramural sports:* basketball M/W, football M/W, soccer M/W, table tennis M/W, ultimate Frisbee M/W, volleyball M/W.

Standardized Tests *Required:* SAT or ACT (for admission).

Costs (2010–11) *Comprehensive fee:* $27,024 includes full-time tuition ($19,872), mandatory fees ($420), and room and board ($6732). Full-time tuition and fees vary according to class time and course load. Part-time tuition: $495 per credit hour. Part-time tuition and fees vary according to class time and course load. *Room and board:* Room and board charges vary according to board plan and housing facility. *Payment plan:* installment. *Waivers:* children of alumni, senior citizens, and employees or children of employees.

Financial Aid Of all full-time matriculated undergraduates who enrolled in 2009, 1,468 applied for aid, 1,312 were judged to have need, 266 had their need fully met. 426 Federal Work-Study jobs (averaging $1336). In 2009, 239 non-need-based awards were made. *Average percent of need met:* 75%. *Average financial aid package:* $14,309. *Average need-based loan:* $4029. *Average need-based gift aid:* $11,883. *Average non-need-based aid:* $5861. *Average indebtedness upon graduation:* $28,041.

Applying *Options:* electronic application. *Application fee:* $35. *Required:* high school transcript. *Recommended:* minimum 2 GPA. *Application deadlines:* 8/15 (freshmen), 8/15 (transfers). *Notification:* 9/15 (freshmen), continuous until 9/15 (transfers).

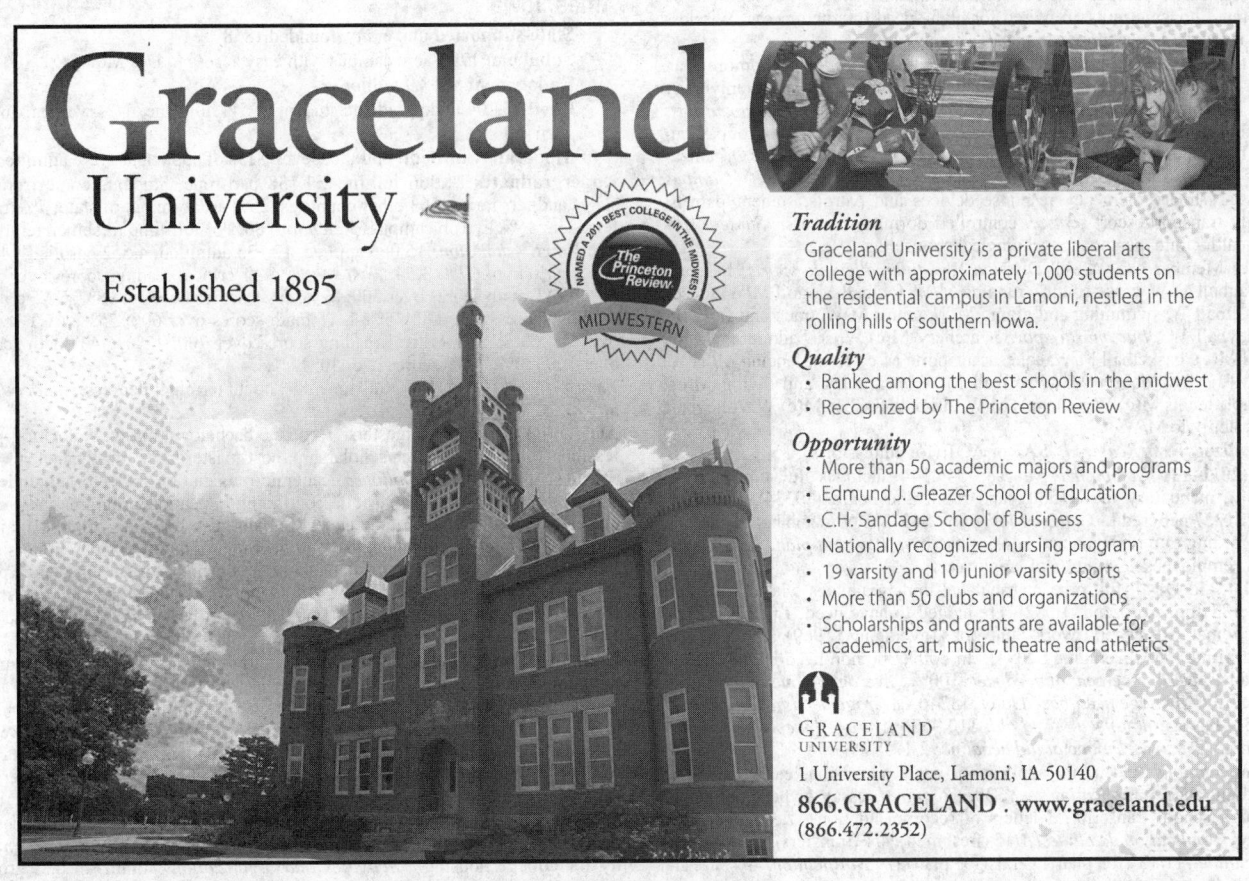

Freshman Application Contact Ms. Diane Schaefer, Director of Admissions, Grand View University, 1200 Grandview Avenue, Des Moines, IA 50316-1599. *Phone:* 515-263-2810. *Toll-free phone:* 800-444-6083 Ext. 2810. *Fax:* 515-263-2974. *E-mail:* admissions@grandview.edu. *Web site:* http://www.grandview.edu/.

See page 1314 for the College Close-Up.

Grinnell College

Grinnell, Iowa

- **Independent** 4-year, founded 1846
- **Small-town** 120-acre campus
- **Endowment** $1.2 billion
- **Coed** 1,655 undergraduate students, 97% full-time, 54% women, 46% men
- **Very difficult** entrance level, 43% of applicants were admitted

Undergraduates 1,609 full-time, 46 part-time. Students come from 50 states and territories; 54 other countries; 87% are from out of state; 5% Black or African American, non-Hispanic/Latino; 7% Hispanic/Latino; 6% Asian, non-Hispanic/Latino; 0.3% American Indian or Alaska Native, non-Hispanic/Latino; 4% Two or more races, non-Hispanic/Latino; 6% Race/ethnicity unknown; 12% international; 0.6% transferred in; 88% live on campus. *Retention:* 93% of full-time freshmen returned.

Freshmen *Admission:* 2,845 applied, 1,228 admitted, 415 enrolled. *Test scores:* SAT critical reading scores over 500: 96%; SAT math scores over 500: 94%; ACT scores over 18: 100%; SAT critical reading scores over 600: 80%; SAT math scores over 600: 79%; ACT scores over 24: 93%; SAT critical reading scores over 700: 44%; SAT math scores over 700: 43%; ACT scores over 30: 59%.

Faculty *Total:* 214, 75% full-time, 81% with terminal degrees. *Student/faculty ratio:* 9:1.

Academics *Calendar:* semesters. *Degree:* bachelor's. *Special study options:* accelerated degree program, advanced placement credit, double majors, independent study, internships, off-campus study, services for LD students, student-designed majors, study abroad. *Unusual degree programs:* 3-2 engineering with Columbia University, California Institute of Technology, Rensselaer Polytechnic Institute, Washington University in St. Louis; Architecture with Washington University in St. Louis, law at Columbia University.

Computers on Campus Students can access the following: campus intranet, computer help desk, free student e-mail accounts, online (class) grades, online (class) schedules. Campuswide network is available. 100% of college-owned or -operated housing units are wired for high-speed Internet access. Wireless service is available via entire campus.

Student Life *Housing:* on-campus residence required through sophomore year. *Options:* coed, cooperative, disabled students. Campus housing is university owned. Freshman campus housing is guaranteed. *Activities and organizations:* drama/theater group, student-run newspaper, radio station, choral group, Concerned Black Students, International Student Organization, Student Organization of Latinas/Latinos, Campus Democrats, Ultimate Frisbee. *Campus security:* 24-hour emergency response devices and patrols, student patrols, late-night transport/escort service, controlled dormitory access. *Student services:* health clinic, personal/psychological counseling.

Athletics Member NCAA. All Division III. *Intercollegiate sports:* baseball M, basketball M/W, cross-country running M/W, football M, golf M/W, soccer M/W, softball W, swimming and diving M/W, tennis M/W, track and field M/W, volleyball W. *Intramural sports:* archery M(c)/W(c), badminton M/W, baseball M(c), basketball M/W, equestrian sports M(c)/W(c), fencing M(c)/W, rugby M(c)/W(c), soccer M/W, softball M/W, swimming and diving M(c)/W(c), table tennis M(c)/W(c), tennis M/W, ultimate Frisbee M(c)/W(c), volleyball M/W, water polo M/W.

Standardized Tests *Required:* SAT or ACT (for admission).

Costs (2011–12) *Comprehensive fee:* $49,144 includes full-time tuition ($39,250), mandatory fees ($560), and room and board ($9334). Part-time tuition: $1227 per credit. *College room only:* $4372. Room and board charges vary according to board plan and housing facility. *Payment plan:* installment. *Waivers:* employees or children of employees.

Financial Aid Of all full-time matriculated undergraduates who enrolled in 2009, 1,185 applied for aid, 1,082 were judged to have need, 1,082 had their need fully met. 619 Federal Work-Study jobs (averaging $1969). 372 state and other part-time jobs (averaging $2094). In 2009, 300 non-need-based awards were made. *Average percent of need met:* 100%. *Average financial aid package:* $35,139. *Average need-based loan:* $3246. *Average need-based gift aid:* $30,085. *Average non-need-based aid:* $10,957. *Average indebtedness upon graduation:* $18,578. *Financial aid deadline:* 2/1.

Applying *Options:* electronic application, early admission, early decision, deferred entrance. *Application fee:* $30. *Required:* essay or personal statement, high school transcript, 3 letters of recommendation. *Recommended:* interview. *Application deadlines:* 1/15 (freshmen), 4/1 (transfers). *Early decision deadline:* 11/15 (for plan 1), 1/1 (for plan 2). *Notification:* 4/1 (fresh-

men), 5/20 (transfers), 12/15 (early decision plan 1), 2/1 (early decision plan 2).

Freshman Application Contact Mr. Seth Allen, Dean for Admission and Financial Aid, Grinnell College, 1103 Park Street, Grinnell, IA 50112. *Phone:* 641-269-3600. *Toll-free phone:* 800-247-0113. *Fax:* 641-269-4800. *E-mail:* askgrin@grinnell.edu. *Web site:* http://www.grinnell.edu/.

Hamilton Technical College

Davenport, Iowa

- **Proprietary** 4-year, founded 1969
- **Urban** campus
- **Coed**
- **Noncompetitive** entrance level

Freshmen *Admission:* 95 applied.

Faculty *Total:* 12, 92% full-time. *Student/faculty ratio:* 20:1.

Academics *Calendar:* continuous. *Degrees:* diplomas, associate, and bachelor's.

Student Life *Housing:* college housing not available. *Campus security:* 24-hour emergency response devices.

Costs (2010–11) *Tuition:* $8926 full-time. No tuition increase for student's term of enrollment. *Waivers:* employees or children of employees.

Applying *Options:* deferred entrance. *Application fee:* $25. *Required:* high school transcript, interview. *Application deadlines:* rolling (freshmen), rolling (transfers).

Freshman Application Contact Hamilton Technical College, 1011 East 53rd Street, Davenport, IA 52807-2653. *Phone:* 563-386-3570. *Web site:* http://www.hamiltontechcollege.com/.

INSTE Bible College

Ankeny, Iowa

Director of Admissions Admissions, INSTE Bible College, 2302 SW 3rd Street, Ankeny, IA 50023. *Phone:* 515-289-9200. *Fax:* 515-289-9201. *E-mail:* inste@inste.edu. *Web site:* http://www.inste.edu/.

Iowa State University of Science and Technology

Ames, Iowa

- **State-supported** university, founded 1858
- **Suburban** 1795-acre campus with easy access to Des Moines
- **Endowment** $508.9 million
- **Coed** 23,104 undergraduate students, 95% full-time, 44% women, 56% men
- **Moderately difficult** entrance level, 81% of applicants were admitted

Undergraduates 21,966 full-time, 1,138 part-time. Students come from 54 states and territories; 103 other countries; 25% are from out of state; 7% transferred in; 46% live on campus. *Retention:* 86% of full-time freshmen returned.

Freshmen *Admission:* 15,066 applied, 12,135 admitted, 4,552 enrolled. *Average high school GPA:* 3.54. *Test scores:* SAT critical reading scores over 500: 66%; SAT math scores over 500: 82%; ACT scores over 18: 98%; SAT critical reading scores over 600: 35%; SAT math scores over 600: 55%; ACT scores over 24: 63%; SAT critical reading scores over 700: 12%; SAT math scores over 700: 19%; ACT scores over 30: 14%.

Faculty *Total:* 1,646, 83% full-time, 89% with terminal degrees. *Student/faculty ratio:* 17:1.

Academics *Calendar:* semesters. *Degrees:* bachelor's, master's, doctoral-professional, doctoral-research/scholarship, post-master's, and postbachelor's certificates. *Special study options:* academic remediation for entering students, accelerated degree program, adult/continuing education programs, advanced placement credit, cooperative education, distance learning, double majors, English as a second language, external degree program, freshman honors college, honors programs, independent study, internships, off-campus study, part-time degree program, services for LD students, student-designed majors, study abroad, summer session for credit. *ROTC:* Army (b), Navy (b), Air Force (b). *Unusual degree programs:* 3-2 engineering with William Penn College.

Computers on Campus 2,410 computers/terminals are available on campus for general student use. Students can access the following: campus intranet, computer help desk, free student e-mail accounts, online (class) grades, online (class) registration, online (class) schedules, network services. Campuswide network is available. 100% of college-owned or -operated housing units are wired for high-speed Internet access. Wireless service is available via entire campus.

Student Life *Housing options:* coed, men-only, women-only, disabled students. Campus housing is university owned. Freshman applicants given priority for college housing. *Activities and organizations:* drama/theater group, student-run newspaper, radio and television station, choral group, marching band, student government, Student Alumni Association, Residence Hall Associations, national fraternities, national sororities. *Campus security:* 24-hour emergency response devices and patrols, student patrols, late-night transport/ escort service, controlled dormitory access, Crime prevention programs, threat assessment team, motor vehicle help van. *Student services:* health clinic, personal/psychological counseling, women's center, legal services.

Athletics Member NCAA. All Division I except football (Division I-A). *Intercollegiate sports:* basketball M(s)/W(s), cross-country running M(s)/ W(s), golf M(s)/W(s), gymnastics W(s), soccer W(s), softball W(s), swimming and diving M(s)/W(s), tennis W(s), track and field M(s)/W(s), volleyball W(s), wrestling M(s). *Intramural sports:* archery M(c)/W(c), badminton M(c)/ W(c), basketball M/W, bowling M(c)/W(c), cross-country running M/W, equestrian sports M(c)/W(c), fencing M(c)/W(c), football M/W, golf M/W, ice hockey M(c)/W(c), lacrosse M(c)/W(c), racquetball M(c)/W(c), riflery M(c)/ W(c), rugby M(c)/W(c), sailing M(c)/W(c), skiing (cross-country) M(c)/W(c), skiing (downhill) M(c)/W(c), soccer M(c)/W(c), softball M/W, squash M/W, swimming and diving M/W, table tennis M(c)/W(c), tennis M/W, volleyball M(c)/W(c), water polo M(c)/W(c), weight lifting M(c)/W(c), wrestling M/W.

Standardized Tests *Required:* SAT or ACT (for admission).

Costs (2010–11) *Tuition:* state resident $6102 full-time, $255 per semester hour part-time; nonresident $17,668 full-time, $736 per semester hour part-time. Full-time tuition and fees vary according to class time, degree level, and program. Part-time tuition and fees vary according to class time, course load, degree level, and program. *Required fees:* $895 full-time. *Room and board:* $7472; room only: $3882. Room and board charges vary according to board plan and housing facility. *Payment plans:* installment, deferred payment.

Financial Aid Of all full-time matriculated undergraduates who enrolled in 2009, 15,139 applied for aid, 10,755 were judged to have need, 4,245 had their need fully met. In 2009, 6347 non-need-based awards were made. *Average percent of need met:* 82%. *Average financial aid package:* $10,771. *Average need-based loan:* $4359. *Average need-based gift aid:* $5560. *Average non-need-based aid:* $2285. *Average indebtedness upon graduation:* $30,411.

Applying *Options:* electronic application, early admission, deferred entrance. *Application fee:* $40. *Required:* high school transcript, A Regent Admission Index (RAI) of at least 245, and meet minimum HS course requirements. *Application deadlines:* 7/1 (freshmen), 7/1 (transfers). *Notification:* continuous (freshmen), continuous (transfers).

Freshman Application Contact Mr. Phil Caffrey, Associate Director for Freshman Admissions, Iowa State University of Science and Technology, 100 Enrollment Services Center, Ames, IA 50011-2010. *Phone:* 515-294-5836. *Toll-free phone:* 800-262-3810. *Fax:* 515-294-2592. *E-mail:* admissions@ iastate.edu. *Web site:* http://www.iastate.edu/.

Iowa Wesleyan College
Mount Pleasant, Iowa

- **Independent United Methodist** 4-year, founded 1842
- **Small-town** 60-acre campus
- **Endowment** $9.5 million
- **Coed** 771 undergraduate students, 76% full-time, 60% women, 40% men
- **Moderately difficult** entrance level, 64% of applicants were admitted

Undergraduates 583 full-time, 188 part-time. Students come from 28 states and territories; 19 other countries; 41% are from out of state; 13% Black or African American, non-Hispanic/Latino; 8% Hispanic/Latino; 0.8% Asian, non-Hispanic/Latino; 0.5% Native Hawaiian or other Pacific Islander, non-Hispanic/Latino; 0.5% American Indian or Alaska Native, non-Hispanic/ Latino; 7% Race/ethnicity unknown; 8% international; 17% transferred in; 68% live on campus. *Retention:* 39% of full-time freshmen returned.

Freshmen *Admission:* 1,089 applied, 692 admitted, 104 enrolled. *Average high school GPA:* 2.89. *Test scores:* SAT critical reading scores over 500: 25%; SAT math scores over 500: 17%; ACT scores over 18: 80%; SAT critical reading scores over 600: 8%; ACT scores over 24: 16%.

Faculty *Total:* 105, 47% full-time, 32% with terminal degrees. *Student/faculty ratio:* 12:1.

Academics *Calendar:* semesters. *Degree:* bachelor's. *Special study options:* academic remediation for entering students, adult/continuing education programs, advanced placement credit, cooperative education, distance learning, double majors, independent study, internships, off-campus study, part-time degree program, services for LD students, student-designed majors, study abroad, summer session for credit. *Unusual degree programs:* 3-2 forestry with Iowa State University of Science and Technology, Duke University; Pre-Physical Therapy program with St. Ambrose University.

Computers on Campus 90 computers/terminals are available on campus for general student use. Students can access the following: campus intranet, computer help desk, free student e-mail accounts, online (class) grades, online (class) registration, online (class) schedules. Campuswide network is available. 100% of college-owned or -operated housing units are wired for high-speed Internet access. Wireless service is available via learning centers, libraries, student centers.

Student Life *Housing:* on-campus residence required through senior year. *Options:* coed, men-only, women-only. Campus housing is university owned. Freshman campus housing is guaranteed. *Activities and organizations:* student-run newspaper, radio station, choral group, Student Union Board, Student Senate, Commuter Club, choir, Student Ambassadors, national sororities. *Campus security:* late-night transport/escort service, controlled dormitory access, evening patrols by trained security personnel. *Student services:* health clinic, personal/psychological counseling.

Athletics Member NAIA. *Intercollegiate sports:* baseball M(s), basketball M(s)/W(s), cross-country running M(s)/W(s), football M(s), golf M(s)/W(s), soccer M(s)/W(s), softball W(s), track and field M(s)/W(s), volleyball W(s). *Intramural sports:* badminton M/W, basketball M/W, bowling M/W, cheerleading M/W, football M/W, soccer M/W, softball M/W, swimming and diving M/W, table tennis M/W, tennis M/W, track and field M/W, volleyball M/W, weight lifting M/W.

Standardized Tests *Required:* SAT or ACT (for admission).

Costs (2010–11) *Comprehensive fee:* $29,156 includes full-time tuition ($22,050) and room and board ($7106). Part-time tuition: $550 per credit hour. Part-time tuition and fees vary according to class time, course load, and location. *College room only:* $2846. Room and board charges vary according to board plan and housing facility. *Payment plans:* installment, deferred payment. *Waivers:* employees or children of employees.

Applying *Options:* electronic application, early admission, deferred entrance. *Application fee:* $20. *Required:* high school transcript, minimum 2.5 GPA, minimum ACT score of 19 or SAT of 890. *Required for some:* essay or personal statement, interview. *Application deadlines:* 8/15 (freshmen), 8/15 (transfers).

Freshman Application Contact Dean Mark T. Petty, Associate Vice President and Dean for Admissions, Iowa Wesleyan College, 601 N Main Street, Mount Pleasant, IA 52641. *Phone:* 319-385-6231. *Toll-free phone:* 800-582-2383 Ext. 6231. *Fax:* 319-385-6240. *E-mail:* mpetty@iwc.edu. *Web site:* http:// www.iwc.edu/.

ITT Technical Institute
Cedar Rapids, Iowa

- **Proprietary** primarily 2-year
- **Coed**
- **Minimally difficult** entrance level

Academics *Degrees:* associate and bachelor's.
Freshman Application Contact Director of Recruitment, ITT Technical Institute, 3735 Queen Court SW, Cedar Rapids, IA 52404. *Phone:* 319-297-3400. *Toll-free phone:* 877-320-4625. *Web site:* http://www.itt-tech.edu/.

ITT Technical Institute
Clive, Iowa

- **Proprietary** primarily 2-year, part of ITT Educational Services, Inc.
- **Coed**
- **Minimally difficult** entrance level

Academics *Degrees:* associate and bachelor's.
Student Life *Housing:* college housing not available.
Freshman Application Contact Director of Recruitment, ITT Technical Institute, 1860 Northwest 118th Street, Suite 110, Clive, IA 50325. *Phone:* 515-327-5500. *Toll-free phone:* 877-526-7312. *Web site:* http://www.itt-tech.edu/.

Kaplan University, Cedar Falls
Cedar Falls, Iowa

- **Proprietary** primarily 2-year, founded 2000
- **Coed**

Academics *Calendar:* quarters. *Degrees:* certificates, diplomas, associate, and bachelor's.
Freshman Application Contact Kaplan University, Cedar Falls, 7009 Nordic Drive, Cedar Falls, IA 50613. *Phone:* 319-277-0220. *Toll-free phone:* 800-728-1220. *Web site:* http://www.cedarfalls.kaplanuniversity.edu/.

Kaplan University, Cedar Rapids
Cedar Rapids, Iowa

- **Proprietary** primarily 2-year, founded 1900, administratively affiliated with Kaplan University - Davenport Campus
- **Suburban** campus
- **Coed**

Academics *Calendar:* quarters. *Degrees:* certificates, diplomas, associate, and bachelor's (branch locations in Des Moines, Mason City, and Cedar Falls with significant enrollment not reflected in profile).

Financial Aid *Of all full-time matriculated undergraduates who enrolled in 2009,* 10 Federal Work-Study jobs (averaging $889). 3 state and other part-time jobs (averaging $1885).
Freshman Application Contact Kaplan University, Cedar Rapids, 3165 Edgewood Parkway, SW, Cedar Rapids, IA 52404. *Phone:* 319-363-0481. *Toll-free phone:* 800-728-0481. *Web site:* http://www.cedarrapids.kaplanuniversity.edu/.

Kaplan University, Council Bluffs

Council Bluffs, Iowa

- **Proprietary** primarily 2-year, founded 2004
- **Coed**

Academics *Degrees:* certificates, associate, and bachelor's.
Standardized Tests *Required:* Wonderlic aptitude test (for admission).
Freshman Application Contact Kaplan University, Council Bluffs, 1751 Madison Avenue, Council Bluffs, IA 51503. *Phone:* 712-328-4212. *Toll-free phone:* 800-518-4212. *Web site:* http://www.councilbluffs.kaplanuniversity.edu/.

Kaplan University, Davenport Campus

Davenport, Iowa

- **Proprietary** comprehensive, founded 1937
- **Suburban** campus
- **Coed**

Academics *Calendar:* quarters. *Degrees:* certificates, diplomas, associate, bachelor's, and master's (profile includes both traditional and on-line students).
Freshman Application Contact Kaplan University, Davenport Campus, 1801 East Kimberly Road, Suite 1, Davenport, IA 52807-2095. *Phone:* 563-355-3500. *Toll-free phone:* 800-747-1035. *Web site:* http://www.davenport.kaplanuniversity.edu/.

Kaplan University, Des Moines

Urbandale, Iowa

- **Proprietary** primarily 2-year
- **Coed**

Academics *Degrees:* certificates, diplomas, associate, and bachelor's.
Freshman Application Contact Kaplan University, Des Moines, 4655 121st Street, Urbandale, IA 50323. *Phone:* 515-727-2100. *Web site:* http://www.desmoines.kaplanuniversity.edu/.

Kaplan University, Mason City Campus

Mason City, Iowa

- **Proprietary** 4-year, founded 1900
- **Coed**

Academics *Degrees:* certificates, diplomas, associate, and bachelor's.
Freshman Application Contact Kaplan University, Mason City Campus, 2570 4th Street, SW, Mason City, IA 50401. *Phone:* 641-423-2530. *Web site:* http://masoncity.kaplanuniversity.edu/Pages/Homepage.aspx.

Loras College

Dubuque, Iowa

- **Independent Roman Catholic** comprehensive, founded 1839
- **Suburban** 60-acre campus
- **Coed** 1,530 undergraduate students, 97% full-time, 49% women, 51% men
- **Moderately difficult** entrance level, 93% of applicants were admitted

Undergraduates 1,480 full-time, 50 part-time. Students come from 22 states and territories; 55% are from out of state; 1% Black or African American, non-Hispanic/Latino; 4% Hispanic/Latino; 0.7% Asian, non-Hispanic/Latino; 0.1% Native Hawaiian or other Pacific Islander, non-Hispanic/Latino; 0.3% American Indian or Alaska Native, non-Hispanic/Latino; 4% Race/ethnicity unknown; 4% international; 4% transferred in; 67% live on campus. *Retention:* 78% of full-time freshmen returned.
Freshmen *Admission:* 3,956 applied, 3,663 admitted, 416 enrolled. *Average high school GPA:* 3.36. *Test scores:* ACT scores over 18: 96%; ACT scores over 24: 40%; ACT scores over 30: 4%.
Faculty *Total:* 159, 72% full-time, 59% with terminal degrees. *Student/faculty ratio:* 12:1.
Academics *Calendar:* semesters. *Degrees:* associate, bachelor's, and master's. *Special study options:* academic remediation for entering students,

advanced placement credit, cooperative education, distance learning, double majors, honors programs, independent study, internships, off-campus study, part-time degree program, services for LD students, student-designed majors, summer session for credit. *ROTC:* Army (c). *Unusual degree programs:* 3-2 nursing.
Computers on Campus 20 computers/terminals are available on campus for general student use. Students can access the following: online (class) registration. Campuswide network is available.
Student Life *Housing:* on-campus residence required through junior year. *Options:* coed, men-only, women-only. Campus housing is university owned. Freshman campus housing is guaranteed. *Activities and organizations:* drama/theater group, student-run newspaper, radio and television station, choral group, Student Senate, Campus Ministry, College Activities Board, residence hall councils, national sororities. *Campus security:* 24-hour emergency response devices and patrols, late-night transport/escort service, controlled dormitory access. *Student services:* health clinic, personal/psychological counseling.
Athletics Member NCAA. All Division III. *Intercollegiate sports:* baseball M, basketball M/W, cross-country running M/W, football M, golf M/W, ice hockey M(c), rugby M(c), skiing (downhill) M(c), soccer M/W, softball W, swimming and diving M/W, tennis M/W, track and field M/W, volleyball M(c)/W, water polo M, wrestling M. *Intramural sports:* badminton M/W, baseball M, basketball M/W, cross-country running M/W, football M, golf M/W, ice hockey M/W, racquetball M/W, rugby M, skiing (cross-country) M/W, skiing (downhill) M/W, soccer M/W, softball M/W, swimming and diving M/W, table tennis M/W, tennis M/W, track and field M/W, volleyball M/W, water polo M/W, weight lifting M/W, wrestling M.
Standardized Tests *Required:* SAT or ACT (for admission).
Costs (2011–12) *Comprehensive fee:* $33,394 includes full-time tuition ($24,910), mandatory fees ($1178), and room and board ($7306). Full-time tuition and fees vary according to course load and degree level. Part-time tuition: $495 per credit hour. *Required fees:* $25 per credit hour part-time. *College room only:* $3695. Room and board charges vary according to board plan and housing facility. *Payment plan:* installment. *Waivers:* employees or children of employees.
Financial Aid Of all full-time matriculated undergraduates who enrolled in 2009, 1,300 applied for aid, 1,170 were judged to have need, 468 had their need fully met. 235 Federal Work-Study jobs (averaging $1567). 150 state and other part-time jobs (averaging $1320). In 2009, 360 non-need-based awards were made. *Average percent of need met:* 87%. *Average financial aid package:* $17,644. *Average need-based loan:* $3754. *Average need-based gift aid:* $11,754. *Average non-need-based aid:* $9027. *Average indebtedness upon graduation:* $30,790.
Applying *Options:* electronic application, deferred entrance. *Application fee:* $25. *Required:* high school transcript, minimum 2.5 GPA. *Required for some:* interview. *Recommended:* essay or personal statement, 1 letter of recommendation. *Application deadlines:* rolling (freshmen), rolling (transfers). *Notification:* continuous (freshmen), continuous (transfers).
Freshman Application Contact Ms. Sharon Lyons, Director of Admissions, Loras College, 1450 Alta Vista, Dubuque, IA 52004-0178. *Phone:* 563-588-7829. *Toll-free phone:* 800-245-6727. *Fax:* 563-588-7119. *E-mail:* adms@loras.edu. *Web site:* http://www.loras.edu/.

Luther College

Decorah, Iowa

- **Independent** 4-year, founded 1861, affiliated with Evangelical Lutheran Church in America
- **Small-town** 200-acre campus
- **Endowment** $99.8 million
- **Coed** 2,481 undergraduate students, 98% full-time, 57% women, 43% men
- **Moderately difficult** entrance level, 72% of applicants were admitted

Undergraduates 2,422 full-time, 59 part-time. Students come from 37 states and territories; 44 other countries; 67% are from out of state; 1% Black or African American, non-Hispanic/Latino; 3% Hispanic/Latino; 2% Asian, non-Hispanic/Latino; 1% Two or more races, non-Hispanic/Latino; 2% Race/ethnicity unknown; 5% international; 2% transferred in; 87% live on campus. *Retention:* 87% of full-time freshmen returned.
Freshmen *Admission:* 3,818 applied, 2,736 admitted, 612 enrolled. *Average high school GPA:* 3.62. *Test scores:* SAT critical reading scores over 500: 81%; SAT math scores over 500: 81%; SAT writing scores over 500: 79%; ACT scores over 18: 99%; SAT critical reading scores over 600: 56%; SAT math scores over 600: 49%; SAT writing scores over 600: 45%; ACT scores over 24: 76%; SAT critical reading scores over 700: 16%; SAT math scores over 700: 13%; SAT writing scores over 700: 11%; ACT scores over 30: 21%.
Faculty *Total:* 259, 69% full-time, 79% with terminal degrees. *Student/faculty ratio:* 12:1.
Academics *Calendar:* 4-1-4. *Degree:* bachelor's. *Special study options:* academic remediation for entering students, advanced placement credit, double

majors, honors programs, independent study, internships, off-campus study, part-time degree program, services for LD students, student-designed majors, study abroad, summer session for credit. *Unusual degree programs:* 3-2 engineering with Washington University in St. Louis; University of Minnesota, Twin Cities Campus; environmental management, resource management with Duke University.

Computers on Campus 500 computers/terminals are available on campus for general student use. Students can access the following: campus intranet, computer help desk, free student e-mail accounts, online (class) grades, online (class) registration, online (class) schedules. Campuswide network is available. 100% of college-owned or -operated housing units are wired for high-speed Internet access. Wireless service is available via entire campus.

Student Life *Housing:* on-campus residence required through senior year. *Options:* coed, disabled students. Campus housing is university owned. Freshman campus housing is guaranteed. *Activities and organizations:* drama/theater group, student-run newspaper, radio station, choral group, Alpha Phi Omega, Student Activities Council, intramural clubs and organizations, campus ministry groups, Diversity groups. *Campus security:* 24-hour emergency response devices and patrols, late-night transport/escort service, controlled dormitory access. *Student services:* health clinic, personal/psychological counseling, women's center.

Athletics Member NCAA. All Division III. *Intercollegiate sports:* baseball M, basketball M/W, cross-country running M/W, football M, golf M/W, soccer M/W, softball W, swimming and diving M/W, tennis M/W, track and field M/W, volleyball W, wrestling M. *Intramural sports:* archery M/W, badminton M/W, basketball M/W, bowling M/W, football M/W, golf M/W, racquetball M/W, rugby M(c)/W(c), soccer M/W, softball M/W, table tennis M/W, tennis M/W, track and field M/W, ultimate Frisbee M(c)/W(c), volleyball M/W.

Standardized Tests *Required:* SAT or ACT (for admission).

Costs (2011–12) *Comprehensive fee:* $40,735 includes full-time tuition ($34,735), mandatory fees ($150), and room and board ($5850). Full-time tuition and fees vary according to course load. Part-time tuition: $1240 per credit hour. Part-time tuition and fees vary according to course load. *College room only:* $2780. Room and board charges vary according to board plan and housing facility. *Payment plan:* installment. *Waivers:* employees or children of employees.

Financial Aid Of all full-time matriculated undergraduates who enrolled in 2009, 1,978 applied for aid, 1,682 were judged to have need, 451 had their need fully met. 984 Federal Work-Study jobs (averaging $2092). 1,108 state and other part-time jobs (averaging $2394). In 2009, 271 non-need-based awards were made. *Average percent of need met:* 87%. *Average financial aid package:* $25,802. *Average need-based loan:* $5057. *Average need-based gift aid:* $17,630. *Average non-need-based aid:* $12,741. *Average indebtedness upon graduation:* $33,492.

Applying *Options:* electronic application, deferred entrance. *Application fee:* $25. *Required:* essay or personal statement, high school transcript, 1 letter of recommendation. *Recommended:* interview. *Notification:* continuous (freshmen), continuous (transfers).

Freshman Application Contact Kirk Neubauer, Director of Recruiting Services, Luther College, 700 College Drive, Decorah, IA 52101. *Phone:* 563-387-1287. *Toll-free phone:* 800-458-8437. *Fax:* 563-387-2159. *E-mail:* admissions@luther.edu. *Web site:* http://www.luther.edu/.

See page 1396 for the College Close-Up.

Maharishi University of Management
Fairfield, Iowa

- **Independent** university, founded 1971
- **Small-town** 272-acre campus
- **Coed** 321 undergraduate students, 93% full-time, 49% women, 51% men
- **Moderately difficult** entrance level, 42% of applicants were admitted

Undergraduates 298 full-time, 23 part-time. 84% are from out of state; 9% Black or African American, non-Hispanic/Latino; 10% Hispanic/Latino; 2% Asian, non-Hispanic/Latino; 0.3% Native Hawaiian or other Pacific Islander, non-Hispanic/Latino; 0.3% American Indian or Alaska Native, non-Hispanic/Latino; 4% Two or more races, non-Hispanic/Latino; 0.9% Race/ethnicity unknown; 15% international; 52% live on campus. *Retention:* 72% of full-time freshmen returned.

Freshmen *Admission:* 379 applied, 159 admitted, 51 enrolled.

Faculty *Total:* 115, 57% full-time, 42% with terminal degrees. *Student/faculty ratio:* 10:1.

Academics *Calendar:* semesters. *Degrees:* bachelor's, master's, and doctoral-research/scholarship. *Special study options:* academic remediation for entering students, adult/continuing education programs, advanced placement credit, cooperative education, distance learning, double majors, honors programs, independent study, internships, services for LD students, student-designed majors, study abroad.

Computers on Campus Students can access the following: campus intranet, computer help desk, free student e-mail accounts, online (class) grades, online (class) schedules. Campuswide network is available. 100% of college-owned or -operated housing units are wired for high-speed Internet access.

Student Life *Housing:* on-campus residence required through senior year. *Options:* men-only, women-only, disabled students. Campus housing is university owned. Freshman campus housing is guaranteed. *Activities and organizations:* drama/theater group, student-run newspaper, radio station, choral group. *Campus security:* 24-hour emergency response devices and patrols, late-night transport/escort service, controlled dormitory access. *Student services:* health clinic, personal/psychological counseling, legal services.

Athletics *Intercollegiate sports:* soccer M(c)/W(c), ultimate Frisbee M(c)/W(c), volleyball M(c)/W(c). *Intramural sports:* archery M/W, badminton M/W, basketball M/W, football M/W, gymnastics M/W, rock climbing M/W, sailing M/W, soccer M/W, table tennis M/W, tennis M/W, ultimate Frisbee M/W, volleyball M/W.

Costs (2011–12) *Comprehensive fee:* $30,430 includes full-time tuition ($24,000), mandatory fees ($430), and room and board ($6000). Part-time tuition: $350 per credit. Part-time tuition and fees vary according to course load. *College room only:* $2800. *Payment plan:* installment.

Financial Aid Of all full-time matriculated undergraduates who enrolled in 2006, 150 applied for aid, 148 were judged to have need, 32 had their need fully met. 120 Federal Work-Study jobs (averaging $1422). 7 state and other part-time jobs (averaging $2729). In 2006, 5 non-need-based awards were made. *Average percent of need met:* 89%. *Average financial aid package:* $23,963. *Average need-based loan:* $8281. *Average need-based gift aid:* $14,082. *Average non-need-based aid:* $9300. *Average indebtedness upon graduation:* $22,691.

Applying *Options:* electronic application, early admission, deferred entrance. *Application fee:* $25. *Required:* essay or personal statement, high school transcript, minimum 2.5 GPA, 2 letters of recommendation. *Recommended:* interview. *Application deadlines:* 8/1 (freshmen), 8/1 (transfers). *Notification:* continuous until 8/15 (freshmen), continuous (transfers).

Freshman Application Contact Maharishi University of Management, Office of Admissions, Fairfield, IA 52557. *Phone:* 641-472-1110. *Toll-free phone:* 800-369-6480. *Fax:* 641-472-1179. *E-mail:* admissions@mum.edu. *Web site:* http://www.mum.edu/.

Mercy College of Health Sciences
Des Moines, Iowa

- **Independent** 4-year, founded 1995, affiliated with Roman Catholic Church, administratively affiliated with Catholic Health Initiatives, Mercy Medial Center
- **Urban** 5-acre campus
- **Endowment** $2.4 million
- **Coed, primarily women** 790 undergraduate students, 59% full-time, 84% women, 16% men
- 39% of applicants were admitted

Undergraduates 463 full-time, 327 part-time. Students come from 15 states and territories.

Freshmen *Admission:* 308 applied, 120 admitted.

Faculty *Total:* 49, 100% full-time, 6% with terminal degrees.

Academics *Calendar:* semesters. *Degrees:* certificates, associate, and bachelor's. *Special study options:* academic remediation for entering students, accelerated degree program, advanced placement credit, cooperative education, distance learning, double majors, English as a second language, off-campus study, part-time degree program, services for LD students, summer session for credit.

Computers on Campus 46 computers/terminals are available on campus for general student use. Students can access the following: campus intranet, computer help desk, free student e-mail accounts, online (class) grades, online (class) schedules. Campuswide network is available. Wireless service is available via entire campus.

Student Life *Housing:* college housing not available. *Activities and organizations:* Student senate. *Campus security:* 24-hour emergency response devices and patrols, late-night transport/escort service. *Student services:* personal/psychological counseling.

Standardized Tests *Required for some:* ACT (for admission).

Costs (2010–11) *Tuition:* $13,500 full-time, $460 per credit hour part-time. *Payment plan:* installment. *Waivers:* employees or children of employees.

Financial Aid Of all full-time matriculated undergraduates who enrolled in 2003, 331 applied for aid, 322 were judged to have need, 3 had their need fully met. 11 Federal Work-Study jobs (averaging $1964). In 2003, 9 non-need-based awards were made. *Average percent of need met:* 29%. *Average financial aid package:* $7670. *Average need-based loan:* $2492. *Average need-based gift aid:* $5132. *Average non-need-based aid:* $6697. *Average indebtedness upon graduation:* $17,567. *Financial aid deadline:* 7/1.

Applying *Options:* electronic application. *Application fee:* $30. *Required:* high school transcript, minimum 2.25 GPA. *Required for some:* interview. *Application deadlines:* rolling (freshmen), rolling (out-of-state freshmen), rolling (transfers). *Notification:* continuous (freshmen), continuous (out-of-state freshmen), continuous (transfers).

Freshman Application Contact Kara Scholten, Admissions Manager, Mercy College of Health Sciences, 928 Sixth Avenue, Des Moines, IA 50309-1239. *Phone:* 515-643-3180. *Toll-free phone:* 800-637-2994. *Fax:* 515-643-6698. *E-mail:* kscholten@mercydesmoines.org. *Web site:* http://www.mchs.edu/.

Morningside College
Sioux City, Iowa

- **Independent** comprehensive, founded 1894, affiliated with United Methodist Church
- **Suburban** 69-acre campus
- **Endowment** $32.2 million
- **Coed** 1,250 undergraduate students, 97% full-time, 53% women, 47% men
- **Moderately difficult** entrance level, 59% of applicants were admitted

Undergraduates 1,208 full-time, 42 part-time. Students come from 25 states and territories; 12 other countries; 33% are from out of state; 0.8% Black or African American, non-Hispanic/Latino; 4% Hispanic/Latino; 0.7% Asian, non-Hispanic/Latino; 0.2% Native Hawaiian or other Pacific Islander, non-Hispanic/Latino; 0.6% American Indian or Alaska Native, non-Hispanic/Latino; 1% Two or more races, non-Hispanic/Latino; 6% Race/ethnicity unknown; 2% international; 7% transferred in; 64% live on campus. *Retention:* 70% of full-time freshmen returned.

Freshmen *Admission:* 2,478 applied, 1,469 admitted, 343 enrolled. *Average high school GPA:* 3.4. *Test scores:* ACT scores over 18: 99%; ACT scores over 24: 39%; ACT scores over 30: 2%.

Faculty *Total:* 172, 44% full-time, 34% with terminal degrees. *Student/faculty ratio:* 13:1.

Academics *Calendar:* semesters. *Degrees:* bachelor's and master's. *Special study options:* academic remediation for entering students, adult/continuing education programs, advanced placement credit, distance learning, double majors, English as a second language, honors programs, independent study, internships, off-campus study, part-time degree program, services for LD students, student-designed majors, study abroad, summer session for credit. *ROTC:* Army (c).

Computers on Campus 150 computers/terminals are available on campus for general student use. Students can access the following: campus intranet, computer help desk, free student e-mail accounts, online (class) grades, online (class) registration, online (class) schedules, academic and financial records. Campuswide network is available. 100% of college-owned or -operated housing units are wired for high-speed Internet access. Wireless service is available via entire campus.

Student Life *Housing:* on-campus residence required through junior year. *Options:* coed. Campus housing is university owned. Freshman campus housing is guaranteed. *Activities and organizations:* drama/theater group, student-run newspaper, radio and television station, choral group, Student Government/Activities Council, Student Ambassadors, Homecoming Committee, national fraternities, national sororities. *Campus security:* 24-hour emergency response devices, student patrols, late-night transport/escort service, controlled dormitory access, 20-hour patrols by trained security personnel. *Student services:* health clinic, personal/psychological counseling, women's center.

Athletics Member NCAA, NAIA. All NCAA Division II. *Intercollegiate sports:* baseball M(s), basketball M(s)/W(s), cross-country running M(s)/W(s), football M(s), golf M(s)/W(s), soccer M(s)/W(s), softball W(s), swimming and diving M(s)/W(s), tennis M(s)/W(s), track and field M(s)/W(s), volleyball W(s), wrestling M(s). *Intramural sports:* basketball M/W, bowling M/W, ultimate Frisbee M/W, volleyball M/W.

Standardized Tests *Required:* SAT or ACT (for admission).

Costs (2011–12) *Comprehensive fee:* $31,348 includes full-time tuition ($22,814), mandatory fees ($1170), and room and board ($7364). Full-time tuition and fees vary according to degree level, program, and student level. Part-time tuition and fees vary according to course load and degree level. *College room only:* $3776. Room and board charges vary according to housing facility. *Payment plan:* installment. *Waivers:* children of alumni, senior citizens, and employees or children of employees.

Financial Aid Of all full-time matriculated undergraduates who enrolled in 2009, 1,124 applied for aid, 1,041 were judged to have need, 266 had their need fully met. 663 Federal Work-Study jobs (averaging $1350). 432 state and other part-time jobs (averaging $1446). In 2009, 146 non-need-based awards were made. *Average percent of need met:* 80%. *Average financial aid package:* $20,326. *Average need-based loan:* $4414. *Average need-based gift aid:* $6714. *Average non-need-based aid:* $9488. *Average indebtedness upon graduation:* $38,411.

Applying *Options:* electronic application, deferred entrance. *Required:* high school transcript, 20 ACT/1410 SAT and either rank in top half of class or 2.5

GPA required. *Recommended:* minimum 2.5 GPA, interview. *Application deadlines:* rolling (freshmen), rolling (out-of-state freshmen), rolling (transfers). *Notification:* continuous (freshmen), continuous (out-of-state freshmen), continuous (transfers).

Freshman Application Contact Ms. Amy Williams, Co-Director of Admissions, Morningside College, 1501 Morningside Avenue, Sioux City, IA 51106. *Phone:* 712-274-5111. *Toll-free phone:* 800-831-0806 Ext. 5111. *Fax:* 712-274-5101. *E-mail:* mscadm@morningside.edu. *Web site:* http://www.morningside.edu/.

See page 1450 for the College Close-Up.

Mount Mercy University
Cedar Rapids, Iowa

- **Independent Roman Catholic** comprehensive, founded 1928
- **Suburban** 40-acre campus
- **Endowment** $19.6 million
- **Coed** 1,441 undergraduate students, 62% full-time, 70% women, 30% men
- **Moderately difficult** entrance level, 70% of applicants were admitted

Undergraduates 900 full-time, 541 part-time. Students come from 16 states and territories; 10 other countries; 5% are from out of state; 3% Black or African American, non-Hispanic/Latino; 4% Hispanic/Latino; 2% Asian, non-Hispanic/Latino; 0.1% Native Hawaiian or other Pacific Islander, non-Hispanic/Latino; 0.1% American Indian or Alaska Native, non-Hispanic/Latino; 0.1% Two or more races, non-Hispanic/Latino; 8% Race/ethnicity unknown; 1% international; 18% transferred in; 35% live on campus. *Retention:* 82% of full-time freshmen returned.

Freshmen *Admission:* 376 applied, 264 admitted, 119 enrolled. *Average high school GPA:* 3.44. *Test scores:* ACT scores over 18: 96%; ACT scores over 24: 36%; ACT scores over 30: 3%.

Faculty *Total:* 148, 54% full-time, 39% with terminal degrees. *Student/faculty ratio:* 12:1.

Academics *Calendar:* 4-1-4. *Degrees:* bachelor's and master's. *Special study options:* academic remediation for entering students, accelerated degree program, adult/continuing education programs, advanced placement credit, double majors, honors programs, independent study, internships, off-campus study, part-time degree program, services for LD students, study abroad, summer session for credit.

Computers on Campus 120 computers/terminals and 200 ports are available on campus for general student use. Students can access the following: campus intranet, computer help desk, free student e-mail accounts, online (class) grades, online (class) registration, online (class) schedules. Campuswide network is available. 100% of college-owned or -operated housing units are wired for high-speed Internet access. Wireless service is available via entire campus.

Student Life *Housing:* on-campus residence required through sophomore year. *Options:* coed, men-only, women-only. Campus housing is university owned. Freshman campus housing is guaranteed. *Activities and organizations:* drama/theater group, student-run newspaper, choral group, Student Government Association, Students in Free Enterprise (SIFE), Mount Mercy University Association of Nursing Students, Student Ambassadors, Best Buddies. *Campus security:* 24-hour emergency response devices and patrols, student patrols, late-night transport/escort service, controlled dormitory access, The Mount Mercy University Department of Public Safety is operational 24 hours a day, seven days a week. *Student services:* health clinic, personal/psychological counseling.

Athletics Member NAIA. *Intercollegiate sports:* baseball M(s), basketball M(s)/W(s), cross-country running M(s)/W(s), golf M(s)/W(s), soccer M(s)/W(s), softball W(s), track and field M(s)/W(s), volleyball W(s). *Intramural sports:* baseball M, basketball M/W, bowling M/W, cheerleading W, football M/W, racquetball M/W, tennis M/W, volleyball M/W, weight lifting M/W.

Standardized Tests *Required:* SAT or ACT (for admission).

Costs (2011–12) *Comprehensive fee:* $31,830 includes full-time tuition ($24,360) and room and board ($7470). Full-time tuition and fees vary according to course load. Part-time tuition: $670 per credit hour. Part-time tuition and fees vary according to course load. *Required fees:* $670 per credit hour part-time. *Room and board:* Room and board charges vary according to board plan and housing facility. *Payment plan:* installment. *Waivers:* employees or children of employees.

Financial Aid Of all full-time matriculated undergraduates who enrolled in 2009, 901 applied for aid, 818 were judged to have need, 128 had their need fully met. 302 Federal Work-Study jobs (averaging $1997). 125 state and other part-time jobs (averaging $2000). In 2009, 137 non-need-based awards were made. *Average percent of need met:* 69%. *Average financial aid package:* $16,934. *Average need-based loan:* $4570. *Average need-based gift aid:* $12,357. *Average non-need-based aid:* $8354. *Average indebtedness upon graduation:* $23,373.

Applying *Options:* electronic application, deferred entrance. *Required:* high school transcript, minimum 2.5 GPA. *Required for some:* 1 letter of recom-

mendation. *Application deadlines:* 8/15 (freshmen), 8/15 (transfers). *Notification:* continuous (freshmen), continuous (transfers).
Freshman Application Contact Ms. Liz Metz, Assistant Director of Admissions, Mount Mercy University, 1330 Elmhurst Drive, NE, Cedar Rapids, IA 52402. *Phone:* 319-368-6460. *Toll-free phone:* 800-248-4504. *Fax:* 319-363-5270. *E-mail:* emetz@mtmercy.edu. *Web site:* http://www.mtmercy.edu/.

Northwestern College

Orange City, Iowa

- **Independent** 4-year, founded 1882, affiliated with Reformed Church in America
- **Rural** 100-acre campus
- **Endowment** $35.4 million
- **Coed** 1,206 undergraduate students, 97% full-time, 59% women, 41% men
- **Moderately difficult** entrance level, 70% of applicants were admitted

Undergraduates 1,164 full-time, 42 part-time. Students come from 20 states and territories; 30 other countries; 44% are from out of state; 3% transferred in; 89% live on campus. *Retention:* 78% of full-time freshmen returned.
Freshmen *Admission:* 1,487 applied, 1,047 admitted, 331 enrolled. *Average high school GPA:* 3.52. *Test scores:* ACT scores over 18: 97%; ACT scores over 24: 61%; ACT scores over 30: 10%.
Faculty *Total:* 134, 62% full-time, 49% with terminal degrees. *Student/faculty ratio:* 12:1.
Academics *Calendar:* semesters. *Degree:* bachelor's. *Special study options:* academic remediation for entering students, advanced placement credit, cooperative education, distance learning, double majors, English as a second language, honors programs, independent study, internships, off-campus study, services for LD students, student-designed majors, study abroad, summer session for credit.
Computers on Campus 250 computers/terminals are available on campus for general student use. Students can access the following: campus intranet, computer help desk, free student e-mail accounts, online (class) grades, online (class) registration, online (class) schedules, online degree audits. Campuswide network is available. Wireless service is available via classrooms, computer centers, computer labs, learning centers, libraries, student centers.
Student Life *Housing:* on-campus residence required through senior year. *Options:* men-only, women-only, disabled students. Campus housing is university owned. Freshman campus housing is guaranteed. *Activities and organizations:* drama/theater group, student-run newspaper, television station, choral group, Drama Ministries Ensemble, Acapella Choir, Psi Chi, Fellowship of Christian Athletes, International Club. *Campus security:* 24-hour emergency response devices, controlled dormitory access. *Student services:* health clinic, personal/psychological counseling.
Athletics Member NAIA. *Intercollegiate sports:* baseball M(s), basketball M(s)/W(s), cross-country running M(s)/W(s), football M(s), golf M(s)/W(s), soccer M(s)/W(s), softball W(s), tennis M(s)/W(s), track and field M(s)/W(s), volleyball W(s), wrestling M(s). *Intramural sports:* badminton M/W, basketball M/W, bowling M/W, cheerleading M/W, cross-country running M/W, football M/W, golf M/W, lacrosse M/W, racquetball M/W, softball M, table tennis M/W, tennis M/W, volleyball M/W.
Standardized Tests *Required:* SAT or ACT (for admission).
Costs (2011–12) *Comprehensive fee:* $30,420 includes full-time tuition ($23,330) and room and board ($7090). Full-time tuition and fees vary according to program. Part-time tuition and fees vary according to course load and program. *Room and board:* Room and board charges vary according to board plan and housing facility. *Payment plans:* tuition prepayment, installment. *Waivers:* employees or children of employees.
Financial Aid Of all full-time matriculated undergraduates who enrolled in 2007, 997 applied for aid, 997 were judged to have need, 418 had their need fully met. 354 Federal Work-Study jobs (averaging $1120). 412 state and other part-time jobs (averaging $1120). In 2007, 229 non-need-based awards were made. *Average percent of need met:* 87%. *Average financial aid package:* $16,330. *Average need-based loan:* $4453. *Average need-based gift aid:* $6289. *Average non-need-based aid:* $5562. *Average indebtedness upon graduation:* $23,817.
Applying *Options:* electronic application, early admission, deferred entrance. *Application fee:* $25. *Required:* essay or personal statement, high school transcript, minimum 2 GPA, 1 letter of recommendation. *Recommended:* minimum 2.5 GPA, interview. *Application deadlines:* rolling (freshmen), rolling (transfers). *Notification:* continuous (freshmen), continuous (transfers).
Freshman Application Contact Mr. Kenton Pauls, Dean of Enrollment Management, Northwestern College, 101 7th Street SW, Orange City, IA 51041-1996. *Phone:* 712-737-7130. *Toll-free phone:* 800-747-4757. *Fax:* 712-707-7164. *E-mail:* admissions@nwciowa.edu. *Web site:* http://www.nwciowa.edu/.

Palmer College of Chiropractic

Davenport, Iowa

- **Independent** comprehensive, founded 1897
- **Urban** 31-acre campus
- **Coed** 49 undergraduate students, 80% full-time, 51% women, 49% men
- **Noncompetitive** entrance level, 83% of applicants were admitted

Undergraduates 39 full-time, 10 part-time. Students come from 16 states and territories; 1 other country; 63% are from out of state; 2% Black or African American, non-Hispanic/Latino; 2% Hispanic/Latino; 2% Asian, non-Hispanic/Latino; 6% Race/ethnicity unknown; 59% transferred in. *Retention:* 50% of full-time freshmen returned.
Freshmen *Admission:* 24 applied, 20 admitted. *Average high school GPA:* 2.92.
Faculty *Total:* 15, 13% full-time. *Student/faculty ratio:* 3:1.
Academics *Calendar:* trimesters. *Degrees:* certificates, associate, incidental bachelor's, master's, and doctoral-professional. *Special study options:* academic remediation for entering students, internships, services for LD students, summer session for credit.
Computers on Campus 94 computers/terminals are available on campus for general student use. Students can access the following: computer help desk, free student e-mail accounts, online (class) grades, online (class) schedules. Campuswide network is available. Wireless service is available via libraries, student centers.
Student Life *Housing options:* Campus housing is university owned and is provided by a third party. *Activities and organizations:* student-run newspaper, Gonstead Club, intramural sports, campus guides, Student International Chiropractic Association, Palmer Student Alumni Foundation, national fraternities. *Campus security:* 24-hour emergency response devices and patrols, late-night transport/escort service. *Student services:* health clinic, personal/psychological counseling.
Athletics *Intercollegiate sports:* rugby M/W. *Intramural sports:* baseball M(c), basketball M(c)/W(c), field hockey M(c), golf M, ice hockey M(c), lacrosse M(c), soccer M/W, softball M/W, table tennis M/W, tennis M/W, volleyball M/W.
Costs (2010–11) *One-time required fee:* $100. *Tuition:* $186 per credit hour part-time. Full-time tuition and fees vary according to course load, degree level, and program. Part-time tuition and fees vary according to course load, degree level, and program. *Required fees:* $35 per term part-time. *Payment plans:* installment, deferred payment. *Waivers:* employees or children of employees.
Financial Aid Of all full-time matriculated undergraduates who enrolled in 2006, 4 Federal Work-Study jobs (averaging $2200). *Average indebtedness upon graduation:* $10,895.
Applying *Options:* electronic application, deferred entrance. *Application fee:* $50. *Required:* high school transcript, minimum 2 GPA, minimum 2.0 in math, science, and English courses. *Required for some:* essay or personal statement, interview. *Application deadlines:* rolling (freshmen), rolling (out-of-state freshmen), rolling (transfers). *Notification:* continuous (freshmen), continuous (out-of-state freshmen), continuous (transfers).
Freshman Application Contact Ms. Lisa Gisel, Undergraduate Admissions Representative, Palmer College of Chiropractic, 1000 Brady Street, Davenport, IA 52803-5287. *Phone:* 563-884-5743. *Toll-free phone:* 800-722-3648. *Fax:* 563-884-5226. *E-mail:* lisa.gisel@palmer.edu. *Web site:* http://www.palmer.edu/.

St. Ambrose University

Davenport, Iowa

- **Independent Roman Catholic** comprehensive, founded 1882
- **Urban** 118-acre campus
- **Endowment** $90.0 million
- **Coed** 2,813 undergraduate students, 86% full-time, 60% women, 40% men
- **Moderately difficult** entrance level, 84% of applicants were admitted

Undergraduates 2,411 full-time, 402 part-time. Students come from 33 states and territories; 7 other countries; 57% are from out of state; 3% Black or African American, non-Hispanic/Latino; 4% Hispanic/Latino; 1% Asian, non-Hispanic/Latino; 0.3% American Indian or Alaska Native, non-Hispanic/Latino; 0.7% Two or more races, non-Hispanic/Latino; 7% Race/ethnicity unknown; 0.2% international; 9% transferred in; 53% live on campus. *Retention:* 81% of full-time freshmen returned.
Freshmen *Admission:* 2,056 applied, 1,725 admitted, 520 enrolled. *Average high school GPA:* 3.19. *Test scores:* ACT scores over 18: 97%; ACT scores over 24: 39%; ACT scores over 30: 6%.
Faculty *Total:* 415, 47% full-time, 40% with terminal degrees. *Student/faculty ratio:* 10:1.
Academics *Calendar:* 4-1-4. *Degrees:* certificates, bachelor's, master's, doctoral-professional, doctoral-research/scholarship, post-master's, and postbach-

elor's certificates. *Special study options:* academic remediation for entering students, accelerated degree program, adult/continuing education programs, advanced placement credit, cooperative education, distance learning, double majors, external degree program, independent study, internships, off-campus study, part-time degree program, services for LD students, student-designed majors, study abroad, summer session for credit. *Unusual degree programs:* 3-2 physical therapy, occupational therapy, special education.

Computers on Campus 276 computers/terminals and 517 ports are available on campus for general student use. Students can access the following: campus intranet, computer help desk, free student e-mail accounts, online (class) grades, online (class) registration, online (class) schedules, online course syllabi, online class listings, and online payments. Campuswide network is available. 100% of college-owned or -operated housing units are wired for high-speed Internet access. Wireless service is available via classrooms, libraries, student centers.

Student Life *Housing:* on-campus residence required through sophomore year. *Options:* coed, men-only, women-only, disabled students. Campus housing is university owned. Freshman campus housing is guaranteed. *Activities and organizations:* drama/theater group, student-run newspaper, radio and television station, choral group, Up Till Dawn, SOTA, Ambrosinas for Obama, Amnesty International, SPTO. *Campus security:* 24-hour emergency response devices and patrols, late-night transport/escort service, controlled dormitory access, police officer on campus 10 pm to 6 am. *Student services:* health clinic, personal/psychological counseling, women's center.

Athletics Member NAIA. *Intercollegiate sports:* baseball M(s), basketball M(s)/W(s), bowling M(s)/W(s), cheerleading M(s)/W(s), cross-country running M(s)/W(s), football M(s), golf M(s)/W(s), soccer M(s)/W(s), softball W(s), tennis M(s)/W(s), track and field M(s)/W(s), volleyball M(s)/W(s). *Intramural sports:* badminton M/W, baseball M/W, basketball M/W, bowling M/W, football M/W, golf M/W, racquetball M/W, skiing (downhill) M/W, soccer M/W, softball M/W, table tennis M/W, tennis M/W, volleyball M/W.

Standardized Tests *Required:* SAT or ACT (for admission). *Recommended:* ACT (for admission).

Costs (2011–12) *Comprehensive fee:* $33,805 includes full-time tuition ($24,680), mandatory fees ($240), and room and board ($8885). Full-time tuition and fees vary according to course load, location, program, and reciprocity agreements. Part-time tuition: $770 per credit hour. Part-time tuition and fees vary according to course load and location. *Required fees:* $770 per credit hour part-time, $60 per term part-time. *Room and board:* Room and board charges vary according to board plan and housing facility. *Payment plan:* installment. *Waivers:* senior citizens and employees or children of employees.

Financial Aid Of all full-time matriculated undergraduates who enrolled in 2009, 2,400 applied for aid, 1,874 were judged to have need, 223 had their need fully met. 661 Federal Work-Study jobs (averaging $1852). 205 state and other part-time jobs (averaging $2828). In 2009, 513 non-need-based awards were made. *Average percent of need met:* 14%. *Average financial aid package:* $7207. *Average need-based loan:* $4369. *Average need-based gift aid:* $11,304. *Average non-need-based aid:* $8292. *Average indebtedness upon graduation:* $32,530.

Applying *Options:* electronic application, deferred entrance. *Application fee:* $25. *Required:* high school transcript, minimum 2.5 GPA, rank in upper 50% of high school class. *Required for some:* interview. *Recommended:* interview. *Application deadlines:* rolling (freshmen), rolling (transfers). *Notification:* 10/1 (freshmen), continuous (transfers).

Freshman Application Contact St. Ambrose University, 518 West Locust Street, Davenport, IA 52803-2898. *Phone:* 563-333-6300 Ext. 6311. *Toll-free phone:* 800-383-2627. *Web site:* http://www.sau.edu/.

Simpson College

Indianola, Iowa

- **Independent United Methodist** comprehensive, founded 1860
- **Suburban** 80-acre campus with easy access to Des Moines
- **Endowment** $63.6 million
- **Coed** 1,979 undergraduate students, 75% full-time, 56% women, 44% men
- **Moderately difficult** entrance level, 86% of applicants were admitted

Undergraduates 1,487 full-time, 492 part-time. Students come from 22 states and territories; 10 other countries; 11% are from out of state; 2% Black or African American, non-Hispanic/Latino; 2% Hispanic/Latino; 1% Asian, non-Hispanic/Latino; 0.3% American Indian or Alaska Native, non-Hispanic/Latino; 1% Two or more races, non-Hispanic/Latino; 2% Race/ethnicity unknown; 1% international; 4% transferred in; 83% live on campus. *Retention:* 80% of full-time freshmen returned.

Freshmen *Admission:* 1,350 applied, 1,164 admitted, 363 enrolled. *Test scores:* ACT scores over 18: 98%; ACT scores over 24: 52%; ACT scores over 30: 8%.

Faculty *Total:* 204, 48% full-time, 54% with terminal degrees. *Student/faculty ratio:* 14:1.

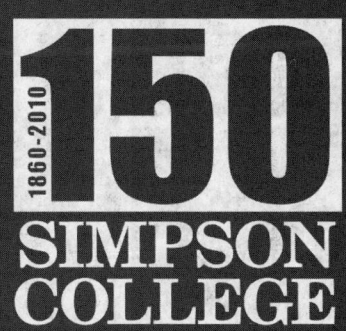

Academics *Calendar:* 4-4-1. *Degrees:* bachelor's, master's, and postbachelor's certificates. *Special study options:* accelerated degree program, adult/continuing education programs, advanced placement credit, cooperative education, double majors, honors programs, independent study, internships, off-campus study, part-time degree program, services for LD students, student-designed majors, study abroad, summer session for credit. *Unusual degree programs:* 3-2 engineering with Washington University in St. Louis, MO; Iowa State University in Ames, IA; Institute of Technology (University of Minnesota) in Minneapolis, MN.

Computers on Campus 362 computers/terminals are available on campus for general student use. Students can access the following: campus intranet, computer help desk, free student e-mail accounts, online (class) grades, online (class) registration, online (class) schedules, wireless campus. Campuswide network is available. 100% of college-owned or -operated housing units are wired for high-speed Internet access. Wireless service is available via entire campus.

Student Life *Housing:* on-campus residence required through junior year. *Options:* coed. Campus housing is university owned. Freshman campus housing is guaranteed. *Activities and organizations:* drama/theater group, student-run newspaper, radio station, choral group, Religious Life Community, Campus Activities Board, Student Government Association, Residence Hall Association, intramurals, national fraternities, national sororities. *Campus security:* 24-hour emergency response devices and patrols, student patrols, late-night transport/escort service, controlled dormitory access. *Student services:* health clinic, personal/psychological counseling, women's center.

Athletics Member NCAA. All Division III. *Intercollegiate sports:* baseball M, basketball M/W, cheerleading M/W, cross-country running M/W, football M, golf M/W, soccer M/W, softball W, swimming and diving M/W, tennis M/W, track and field M/W, volleyball W, wrestling M. *Intramural sports:* badminton M/W, basketball M/W, bowling M/W, football M/W, golf M/W, racquetball M/W, skiing (downhill) M/W, soccer M/W, softball M/W, swimming and diving M/W, table tennis M/W, tennis M/W, ultimate Frisbee M/W, volleyball M/W, weight lifting M/W.

Standardized Tests *Required:* SAT or ACT (for admission).

Costs (2011–12) *One-time required fee:* $200. *Comprehensive fee:* $36,086 includes full-time tuition ($27,568), mandatory fees ($555), and room and board ($7963). Full-time tuition and fees vary according to class time, course load, degree level, and program. Part-time tuition: $318 per credit. Part-time tuition and fees vary according to class time, course load, degree level, and program. *College room only:* $3860. Room and board charges vary according to board plan and housing facility. *Payment plan:* installment. *Waivers:* minority students, children of alumni, senior citizens, and employees or children of employees.

Financial Aid Of all full-time matriculated undergraduates who enrolled in 2009, 1,487 applied for aid, 1,301 were judged to have need, 353 had their need fully met. 376 Federal Work-Study jobs (averaging $1049). 399 state and other part-time jobs (averaging $1412). In 2009, 181 non-need-based awards were made. *Average percent of need met:* 88%. *Average financial aid package:* $28,858. *Average need-based loan:* $3742. *Average need-based gift aid:* $17,457. *Average non-need-based aid:* $13,237. *Average indebtedness upon graduation:* $34,214.

Applying *Options:* electronic application, deferred entrance. *Required:* high school transcript, online or paper application, guidance counselor recommendation form, ACT and/or SAT scores. *Recommended:* minimum 3 GPA, interview. *Application deadlines:* 8/15 (freshmen), 8/15 (transfers). *Notification:* continuous (freshmen), continuous (transfers).

Freshman Application Contact Deborah Tierney, Vice President for Enrollment, Simpson College, 701 North C Street, Indianola, IA 50125. *Phone:* 515-961-1624. *Toll-free phone:* 800-362-2454 (in-state); 800-362-2454 Ext. 1624 (out-of-state). *Fax:* 515-961-1870. *E-mail:* admiss@simpson.edu. *Web site:* http://www.simpson.edu/.

See page 1610 for the College Close-Up.

University of Dubuque
Dubuque, Iowa

- **Independent Presbyterian** comprehensive, founded 1852
- **Suburban** 77-acre campus
- **Endowment** $87.1 million
- **Coed** 1,548 undergraduate students, 93% full-time, 44% women, 56% men
- **Moderately difficult** entrance level, 76% of applicants were admitted

Undergraduates 1,438 full-time, 110 part-time. Students come from 41 states and territories; 8 other countries; 53% are from out of state; 12% Black or African American, non-Hispanic/Latino; 2% Hispanic/Latino; 2% Asian, non-His-

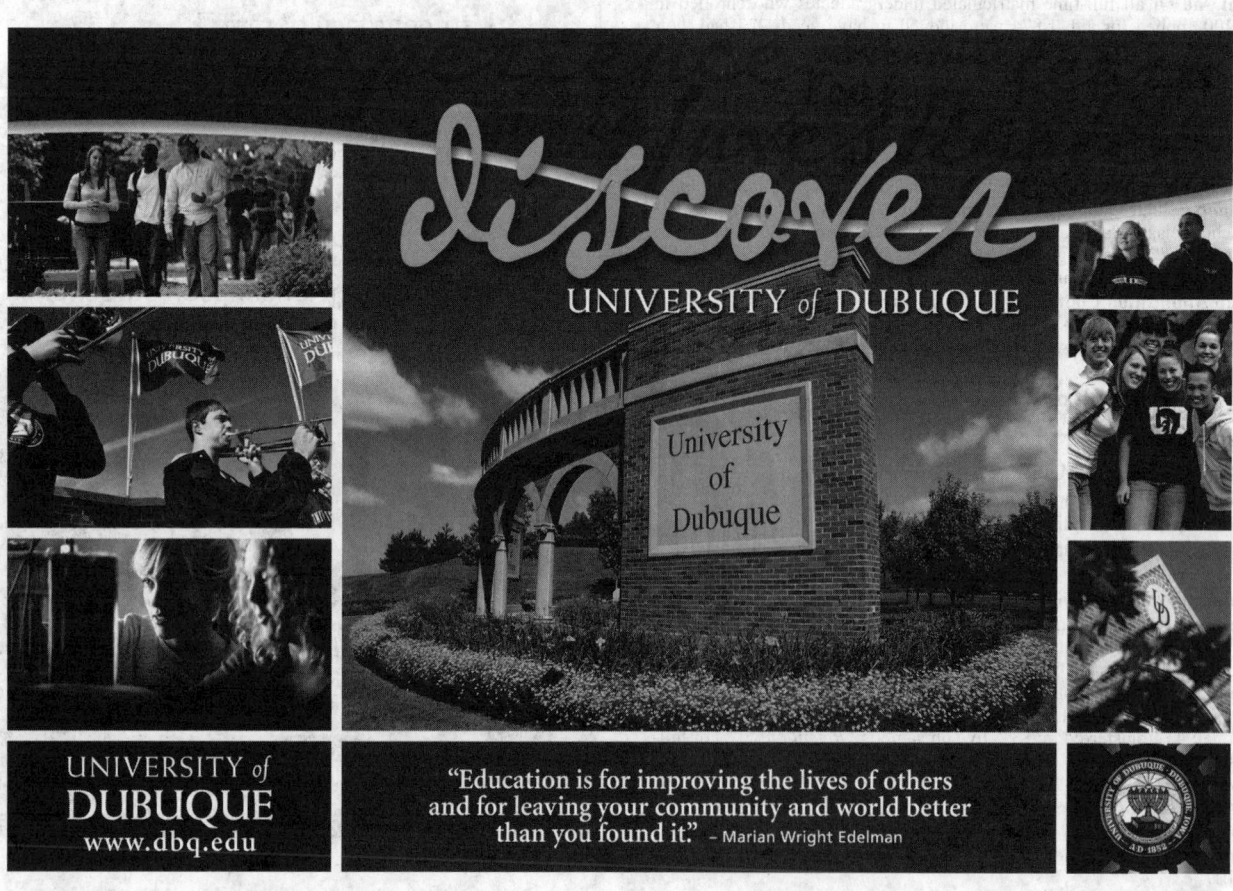

panic/Latino; 0.1% Native Hawaiian or other Pacific Islander, non-Hispanic/Latino; 1% American Indian or Alaska Native, non-Hispanic/Latino; 8% Race/ethnicity unknown; 10% international; 10% transferred in; 49% live on campus. *Retention:* 71% of full-time freshmen returned.

Freshmen *Admission:* 1,288 applied, 976 admitted, 341 enrolled. *Average high school GPA:* 3. *Test scores:* SAT critical reading scores over 500: 50%; SAT math scores over 500: 46%; ACT scores over 18: 79%; SAT critical reading scores over 600: 13%; SAT math scores over 600: 10%; ACT scores over 24: 21%; SAT critical reading scores over 700: 1%; SAT math scores over 700: 3%; ACT scores over 30: 1%.

Faculty *Total:* 153, 57% full-time, 32% with terminal degrees. *Student/faculty ratio:* 14:1.

Academics *Calendar:* semesters. *Degrees:* bachelor's, master's, and doctoral-professional. *Special study options:* academic remediation for entering students, accelerated degree program, adult/continuing education programs, advanced placement credit, distance learning, double majors, English as a second language, honors programs, independent study, internships, off-campus study, part-time degree program, services for LD students, student-designed majors, study abroad, summer session for credit. *ROTC:* Army (b). *Unusual degree programs:* 3-2 business administration; communications, theology.

Computers on Campus 220 computers/terminals are available on campus for general student use. Students can access the following: campus intranet, computer help desk, free student e-mail accounts, online (class) grades, online (class) registration, online (class) schedules. Campuswide network is available. 100% of college-owned or -operated housing units are wired for high-speed Internet access. Wireless service is available via libraries, student centers.

Student Life *Housing:* on-campus residence required through junior year. *Options:* coed, men-only, women-only. Campus housing is university owned. Freshman campus housing is guaranteed. *Activities and organizations:* drama/theater group, student-run newspaper, choral group, Black Student Union, Flight Team, Fellowship of Christian Athletes, Teacher Education Student Organization, Students in Free Enterprise (SIFE). *Campus security:* 24-hour patrols, late-night transport/escort service, controlled dormitory access. *Student services:* health clinic, personal/psychological counseling.

Athletics Member NCAA. All Division III. *Intercollegiate sports:* baseball M, basketball M/W, cross-country running M/W, football M, golf M/W, soccer M/W, softball W, tennis M/W, track and field M/W, volleyball W, wrestling M. *Intramural sports:* archery M/W, badminton M/W, baseball M, basketball M/W, bowling M/W, cheerleading M/W, football M, golf M/W, racquetball M/W, soccer M/W, softball M/W, table tennis M/W, tennis M/W, track and field M/W, ultimate Frisbee M/W, volleyball M/W, wrestling M.

Standardized Tests *Required:* SAT or ACT (for admission).

Costs (2011–12) *One-time required fee:* $60. *Comprehensive fee:* $28,960 includes full-time tuition ($21,000), mandatory fees ($590), and room and board ($7370). Part-time tuition: $490 per credit. *College room only:* $3550. Room and board charges vary according to board plan, housing facility, and location. *Payment plan:* installment. *Waivers:* employees or children of employees.

Financial Aid Of all full-time matriculated undergraduates who enrolled in 2008, 1,329 applied for aid, 1,230 were judged to have need, 324 had their need fully met. 175 Federal Work-Study jobs (averaging $1500). In 2008, 128 non-need-based awards were made. *Average percent of need met:* 76%. *Average financial aid package:* $18,863. *Average need-based loan:* $7135. *Average need-based gift aid:* $12,504. *Average non-need-based aid:* $6968. *Average indebtedness upon graduation:* $41,399.

Applying *Options:* electronic application. *Application fee:* $25. *Required:* essay or personal statement, high school transcript, minimum 2.5 GPA, 2 letters of recommendation. *Recommended:* interview. *Application deadlines:* rolling (freshmen), rolling (transfers). *Notification:* continuous (freshmen), continuous (transfers).

Freshman Application Contact Mr. Jesse James, Director of Admissions, University of Dubuque, 2000 University Avenue, Dubuque, IA 52001-5099. *Phone:* 563-589-3214. *Toll-free phone:* 800-722-5583. *Fax:* 563-589-3690. *E-mail:* admissns@dbq.edu. *Web site:* http://www.dbq.edu/.

See page 1690 for the College Close-Up.

The University of Iowa

Iowa City, Iowa

- **State-supported** university, founded 1847
- **Small-town** 1900-acre campus
- **Endowment** $928.4 million
- **Coed** 21,176 undergraduate students, 90% full-time, 52% women, 48% men
- **Moderately difficult** entrance level, 84% of applicants were admitted

Undergraduates 19,088 full-time, 2,088 part-time. Students come from 52 states and territories; 60 other countries; 37% are from out of state; 2% Black

or African American, non-Hispanic/Latino; 4% Hispanic/Latino; 3% Asian, non-Hispanic/Latino; 0.1% Native Hawaiian or other Pacific Islander, non-Hispanic/Latino; 0.4% American Indian or Alaska Native, non-Hispanic/Latino; 0.9% Two or more races, non-Hispanic/Latino; 4% Race/ethnicity unknown; 6% international; 5% transferred in; 30% live on campus. *Retention:* 86% of full-time freshmen returned.

Freshmen *Admission:* 17,220 applied, 14,434 admitted, 4,557 enrolled. *Average high school GPA:* 3.59. *Test scores:* SAT critical reading scores over 500: 65%; SAT math scores over 500: 90%; SAT writing scores over 500: 73%; ACT scores over 18: 98%; SAT critical reading scores over 600: 36%; SAT math scores over 600: 63%; SAT writing scores over 600: 38%; ACT scores over 24: 68%; SAT critical reading scores over 700: 10%; SAT math scores over 700: 27%; SAT writing scores over 700: 8%; ACT scores over 30: 14%.

Faculty *Student/faculty ratio:* 16:1.

Academics *Calendar:* semesters. *Degrees:* bachelor's, master's, doctoral-professional, doctoral-research/scholarship, post-master's, and postbachelor's certificates. *Special study options:* academic remediation for entering students, accelerated degree program, adult/continuing education programs, advanced placement credit, cooperative education, distance learning, double majors, English as a second language, external degree program, honors programs, independent study, internships, off-campus study, part-time degree program, services for LD students, student-designed majors, study abroad, summer session for credit. *ROTC:* Army (b), Air Force (b).

Computers on Campus 1,386 computers/terminals are available on campus for general student use. Students can access the following: computer help desk, free student e-mail accounts, online (class) grades, online (class) registration, online (class) schedules, online degree process, financial aid summary, university bill. Campuswide network is available. 100% of college-owned or -operated housing units are wired for high-speed Internet access. Wireless service is available via classrooms, computer centers, computer labs, dorm rooms, learning centers, libraries, student centers.

Student Life *Housing options:* coed, disabled students. Campus housing is university owned and leased by the school. *Activities and organizations:* drama/theater group, student-run newspaper, radio and television station, choral group, marching band, Association of Residence Halls, Graduate Student Senate, National Society of Collegiate Scholars, Organization for the Active Support of International Students (OASIS), Dance Marathon, national fraternities, national sororities. *Campus security:* 24-hour emergency response devices and patrols, late-night transport/escort service, controlled dormitory access. *Student services:* health clinic, personal/psychological counseling, women's center, legal services.

Athletics Member NCAA. All Division I except football (Division I-A). *Intercollegiate sports:* baseball M(s), basketball M(s)/W(s), crew M(c)/W(s), cross-country running M(s)/W(s), field hockey W(s), golf M(s)/W(s), gymnastics M(s)/W(s), ice hockey M(c), lacrosse M(c)/W(c), rugby M(c)/W(c), sailing M(c)/W(c), soccer M(c)/W(s), softball W(s), swimming and diving M(s)/W(s), table tennis M(c)/W(c), tennis M(s)/W(s), track and field M(s)/W(s), ultimate Frisbee M(c)/W(c), volleyball M(c)/W(s), wrestling M(s). *Intramural sports:* badminton M/W, basketball M/W, bowling M/W, fencing M(c)/W(c), football M/W, golf M/W, racquetball M/W, rugby M(c)/W(c), sailing M(c)/W(c), skiing (cross-country) M(c)/W(c), skiing (downhill) M(c)/W(c), soccer M/W, softball M/W, table tennis M/W, tennis M/W, track and field M/W, ultimate Frisbee M/W, volleyball M/W, water polo M(c)/W(c), wrestling M.

Standardized Tests *Required:* SAT or ACT (for admission).

Costs (2011–12) *Tuition:* state resident $6436 full-time, $268 per semester hour part-time; nonresident $23,770 full-time, $990 per semester hour part-time. Full-time tuition and fees vary according to course load, program, and student level. Part-time tuition and fees vary according to course load, program, and student level. *Required fees:* $1329 full-time. *Room and board:* $8750. Room and board charges vary according to board plan and housing facility. *Payment plan:* installment.

Financial Aid Of all full-time matriculated undergraduates who enrolled in 2008, 12,183 applied for aid, 8,400 were judged to have need, 2,700 had their need fully met. 1,516 Federal Work-Study jobs (averaging $2156). In 2008, 6125 non-need-based awards were made. *Average percent of need met:* 68%. *Average financial aid package:* $11,289. *Average need-based loan:* $5155. *Average need-based gift aid:* $6486. *Average non-need-based aid:* $4147. *Average indebtedness upon graduation:* $27,391.

Applying *Options:* electronic application, early admission, deferred entrance. *Application fee:* $40. *Required:* high school transcript, must meet Regent Admission Index (RAI) requirement: residents 245 or above; nonresidents 255 or above. *Application deadlines:* 4/1 (freshmen), 4/1 (transfers). *Notification:* continuous (freshmen), continuous (transfers).

Freshman Application Contact Mr. Michael Barron, Assistant Provost for Enrollment Management and Director of Admissions, The University of Iowa, 107 Calvin Hall, Iowa City, IA 52242. *Phone:* 319-335-3847. *Toll-free phone:* 800-553-4692. *Fax:* 319-335-1535. *E-mail:* admissions@uiowa.edu. *Web site:* http://www.uiowa.edu/.

University of Northern Iowa

Cedar Falls, Iowa

- **State-supported** comprehensive, founded 1876, part of Board of Regents, State of Iowa
- **Small-town** 916-acre campus
- **Endowment** $57.0 million
- **Coed** 11,391 undergraduate students, 91% full-time, 57% women, 43% men
- **Moderately difficult** entrance level, 83% of applicants were admitted

Undergraduates 10,378 full-time, 1,013 part-time. Students come from 36 states and territories; 45 other countries; 5% are from out of state; 3% Black or African American, non-Hispanic/Latino; 2% Hispanic/Latino; 0.9% Asian, non-Hispanic/Latino; 0.2% American Indian or Alaska Native, non-Hispanic/Latino; 0.9% Two or more races, non-Hispanic/Latino; 0.9% Race/ethnicity unknown; 3% international; 10% transferred in; 38% live on campus. *Retention:* 83% of full-time freshmen returned.

Freshmen *Admission:* 4,092 applied, 3,409 admitted, 1,978 enrolled. *Average high school GPA:* 3.45. *Test scores:* ACT scores over 18: 97%; ACT scores over 24: 42%; ACT scores over 30: 4%.

Faculty *Total:* 824, 76% full-time, 63% with terminal degrees. *Student/faculty ratio:* 17:1.

Academics *Calendar:* semesters. *Degrees:* bachelor's, master's, and doctoral-other. *Special study options:* academic remediation for entering students, accelerated degree program, adult/continuing education programs, advanced placement credit, cooperative education, distance learning, double majors, English as a second language, external degree program, honors programs, independent study, internships, off-campus study, part-time degree program, services for LD students, student-designed majors, study abroad, summer session for credit. *ROTC:* Army (b). *Unusual degree programs:* 3-2 nursing with University of Iowa; medical technology with St. Luke's Hospital/University of Iowa Medical School, cytotechnology with Mayo School of Health-Related Sciences, Wisconsin State Laboratory of Hygiene and Mercy School of Cytotechnology, chiropractic with Logan College of Chiropractic.

Computers on Campus 1,900 computers/terminals are available on campus for general student use. Students can access the following: campus intranet, computer help desk, free student e-mail accounts, online (class) grades, online (class) registration, online (class) schedules, course registration, student account, degree audit, program of study. Campuswide network is available. 100% of college-owned or -operated housing units are wired for high-speed Internet access. Wireless service is available via classrooms, computer centers, computer labs, learning centers, libraries, student centers.

Student Life *Housing options:* coed, women-only, disabled students. Campus housing is university owned. Freshman campus housing is guaranteed. *Activities and organizations:* drama/theater group, student-run newspaper, radio and television station, choral group, marching band, Catholic Student Association, National Society of Collegiate Scholars, Accounting Club, The River, Orchard Hill Church, national fraternities, national sororities. *Campus security:* 24-hour emergency response devices and patrols, student patrols, late-night transport/escort service, controlled dormitory access. *Student services:* health clinic, personal/psychological counseling.

Athletics Member NCAA. All Division I except football (Division I-AA). *Intercollegiate sports:* basketball M(s)/W(s), cross-country running M(s)/W(s), golf M(s)/W(s), soccer W(s), softball W(s), swimming and diving W(s), tennis W(s), track and field M(s)/W(s), volleyball W(s), wrestling M(s). *Intramural sports:* badminton M/W, baseball M(c), basketball M/W, bowling M(c)/W(c), cheerleading M/W, crew M(c)/W(c), cross-country running M(c)/W(c), football M(c), golf M(c)/W(c), ice hockey M(c), racquetball M(c)/W(c), rugby M(c)/W(c), skiing (cross-country) M(c)/W(c), skiing (downhill) M(c)/W(c), soccer M(c)/W(c), softball M(c)/W(c), swimming and diving M(c)/W(c), table tennis M/W, tennis M(c)/W(c), track and field M(c)/W(c), ultimate Frisbee M(c)/W(c), volleyball M/W(c), weight lifting M/W, wrestling M.

Standardized Tests *Required:* SAT or ACT (for admission). *Recommended:* SAT (for admission), ACT (for admission).

Costs (2010–11) *Tuition:* state resident $6102 full-time, $255 per hour part-time; nonresident $14,442 full-time, $602 per hour part-time. Full-time tuition and fees vary according to course load and program. Part-time tuition and fees vary according to course load and program. *Required fees:* $906 full-time. *Room and board:* $7140; room only: $3411. Room and board charges vary according to board plan and housing facility. *Payment plan:* installment.

Financial Aid Of all full-time matriculated undergraduates who enrolled in 2009, 8,431 applied for aid, 6,462 were judged to have need, 1,139 had their need fully met. 555 Federal Work-Study jobs (averaging $1884). In 2009, 1236 non-need-based awards were made. *Average percent of need met:* 65%. *Average financial aid package:* $7897. *Average need-based loan:* $4407. *Average need-based gift aid:* $4853. *Average non-need-based aid:* $2883. *Average indebtedness upon graduation:* $25,735.

Applying *Options:* electronic application, deferred entrance. *Application fee:* $40. *Required:* high school transcript, rank in upper 50% of high school class. *Required for some:* interview. *Application deadlines:* 8/15 (freshmen), 8/15 (transfers). *Notification:* 9/1 (freshmen), 9/1 (transfers).

Freshman Application Contact University of Northern Iowa, 1227 West 27th Street, Cedar Falls, IA 50614. *Phone:* 319-273-2281. *Toll-free phone:* 800-772-2037. *Web site:* http://www.uni.edu/.

Upper Iowa University

Fayette, Iowa

- **Independent** comprehensive, founded 1857
- **Rural** 80-acre campus with easy access to Minneapolis, Chicago
- **Endowment** $6.1 million
- **Coed** 5,242 undergraduate students, 50% full-time, 61% women, 39% men
- **Moderately difficult** entrance level, 61% of applicants were admitted

Undergraduates 2,621 full-time, 2,621 part-time. Students come from 52 states and territories; 20 other countries; 60% are from out of state; 18% Black or African American, non-Hispanic/Latino; 3% Hispanic/Latino; 2% Asian, non-Hispanic/Latino; 0.4% American Indian or Alaska Native, non-Hispanic/Latino; 1% Two or more races, non-Hispanic/Latino; 7% Race/ethnicity unknown; 2% international; 10% transferred in; 40% live on campus. *Retention:* 61% of full-time freshmen returned.

Freshmen *Admission:* 1,172 applied, 715 admitted, 218 enrolled. *Average high school GPA:* 2.94.

Faculty *Total:* 488, 15% full-time, 11% with terminal degrees. *Student/faculty ratio:* 22:1.

Academics *Calendar:* 4 8-week terms. *Degrees:* certificates, associate, bachelor's, and master's (enrollment figures include extended learning centers and online and distance education programs). *Special study options:* academic remediation for entering students, accelerated degree program, adult/continuing education programs, advanced placement credit, cooperative education, distance learning, double majors, English as a second language, external degree program, independent study, internships, off-campus study, part-time degree program, services for LD students, student-designed majors, study abroad, summer session for credit.

Computers on Campus 600 computers/terminals and 444 ports are available on campus for general student use. Students can access the following: campus intranet, computer help desk, free student e-mail accounts, online (class) grades, online (class) registration, online (class) schedules. Campuswide network is available. Wireless service is available via entire campus.

Student Life *Housing:* on-campus residence required through sophomore year. *Options:* coed, men-only, women-only. Campus housing is university owned. Freshman campus housing is guaranteed. *Activities and organizations:* drama/theater group, student-run newspaper, radio station, choral group, Beta Phi Omega, Student Activities Board, Greek Council, Student Government Association, International Student Association. *Campus security:* late-night transport/escort service, controlled dormitory access. *Student services:* health clinic, personal/psychological counseling.

Athletics Member NCAA. All Division II. *Intercollegiate sports:* baseball M(s), basketball M(s)/W(s), football M(s), golf M(s)/W(s), soccer M(s)/W(s), softball W(s), tennis M/W, volleyball W(s), wrestling M. *Intramural sports:* badminton M/W, basketball M/W, bowling M/W, cheerleading M(c)/W(c), football M, golf M/W, soccer M/W, softball M/W, table tennis M/W, ultimate Frisbee M/W, volleyball M/W.

Standardized Tests *Required:* SAT or ACT (for admission).

Costs (2011–12) *Comprehensive fee:* $30,426 includes full-time tuition ($23,356) and room and board ($7070). Full-time tuition and fees vary according to degree level, location, and program. Part-time tuition: $813 per credit hour. *College room only:* $2850. Room and board charges vary according to board plan, housing facility, and location. *Payment plan:* installment. *Waivers:* employees or children of employees.

Financial Aid *Average financial aid package:* $6000. *Average indebtedness upon graduation:* $17,125.

Applying *Options:* electronic application. *Application fee:* $50. *Required:* high school transcript, minimum 2 GPA. *Required for some:* essay or personal statement, interview. *Application deadlines:* rolling (freshmen), rolling (out-of-state freshmen), rolling (transfers).

Freshman Application Contact Ms. Jobyna A. Eastman Johnston, Vice President of Admissions and Financial Aid, Upper Iowa University, 605 Washington Street, Parker Fox Hall, Fayette, IA 52142. *Phone:* 563-425-5279. *Toll-free phone:* 800-553-4150 Ext. 2. *Fax:* 563-4255323. *E-mail:* admission@uiu.edu. *Web site:* http://www.uiu.edu/.

Vatterott College

Des Moines, Iowa

Freshman Application Contact Mr. Henry Franken, Co-Director, Vatterott College, 7000 Fleur Drive, Suite 290, Des Moines, IA 50321. *Phone:* 515-

309-9000. *Toll-free phone:* 800-353-7264. *Fax:* 515-309-0366. *Web site:* http://www.vatterott-college.edu/.

Waldorf College

Forest City, Iowa

- **Independent Lutheran** 4-year, founded 1903
- **Rural** 51-acre campus
- **Endowment** $4.1 million
- **Coed**
- **Moderately difficult** entrance level

Faculty *Student/faculty ratio:* 14:1.

Academics *Calendar:* semesters. *Degree:* bachelor's.

Student Life *Campus security:* late-night transport/escort service, controlled dormitory access, evening and night patrols by trained security personnel.

Athletics Member NAIA.

Standardized Tests *Required:* SAT or ACT (for admission).

Costs (2010–11) *Comprehensive fee:* $24,714 includes full-time tuition ($17,900), mandatory fees ($860), and room and board ($5954). Full-time tuition and fees vary according to class time, course load, and program. Part-time tuition: $244 per credit hour. *Room and board:* Room and board charges vary according to board plan and housing facility. *Payment plans:* installment, deferred payment.

Financial Aid *Of all full-time matriculated undergraduates who enrolled in 2009,* 502 applied for aid, 448 were judged to have need, 79 had their need fully met. 365 Federal Work-Study jobs (averaging $1419). 215 state and other part-time jobs (averaging $719). *In 2009,* 83 non-need-based awards were made. *Average percent of need met:* 80. *Average financial aid package:* $17,520. *Average need-based loan:* $4715. *Average need-based gift aid:* $12,934. *Average non-need-based aid:* $6221. *Average indebtedness upon graduation:* $30,348.

Applying *Options:* electronic application, early admission. *Required:* high school transcript. *Required for some:* interview. *Recommended:* minimum 2 GPA.

Freshman Application Contact Waldorf College, 106 South 6th Street, Forest City, IA 50436-1713. *Phone:* 641-585-8112. *Toll-free phone:* 800-292-1903. *E-mail:* admissions@waldorf.edu. *Web site:* http://www.waldorf.edu/.

Wartburg College

Waverly, Iowa

- **Independent Lutheran** 4-year, founded 1852
- **Small-town** 118-acre campus
- **Endowment** $40.2 million
- **Coed** 1,775 undergraduate students, 96% full-time, 53% women, 47% men
- **Moderately difficult** entrance level, 72% of applicants were admitted

Undergraduates 1,706 full-time, 69 part-time. Students come from 26 states and territories; 46 other countries; 26% are from out of state; 6% Black or African American, non-Hispanic/Latino; 2% Hispanic/Latino; 0.8% Asian, non-Hispanic/Latino; 0.1% Native Hawaiian or other Pacific Islander, non-Hispanic/Latino; 0.3% American Indian or Alaska Native, non-Hispanic/Latino; 2% Two or more races, non-Hispanic/Latino; 0.8% Race/ethnicity unknown; 6% international; 2% transferred in; 79% live on campus. *Retention:* 79% of full-time freshmen returned.

Freshmen *Admission:* 2,195 applied, 1,577 admitted, 484 enrolled. *Average high school GPA:* 3.45. *Test scores:* SAT critical reading scores over 500: 33%; SAT math scores over 500: 60%; SAT writing scores over 500: 36%; ACT scores over 18: 92%; SAT critical reading scores over 600: 18%; SAT math scores over 600: 24%; SAT writing scores over 600: 6%; ACT scores over 24: 50%; SAT math scores over 700: 3%; SAT writing scores over 700: 3%; ACT scores over 30: 10%.

Faculty *Total:* 166, 64% full-time, 55% with terminal degrees. *Student/faculty ratio:* 12:1.

Academics *Calendar:* 4-4-1. *Degree:* bachelor's. *Special study options:* academic remediation for entering students, accelerated degree program, advanced placement credit, double majors, honors programs, independent study, internships, off-campus study, part-time degree program, services for LD students, student-designed majors, study abroad, summer session for credit. *Unusual degree programs:* 3-2 nursing with Allen College.

Computers on Campus 250 computers/terminals are available on campus for general student use. Students can access the following: campus intranet, computer help desk, free student e-mail accounts, online (class) grades, online (class) registration, online (class) schedules. Campuswide network is available. 100% of college-owned or -operated housing units are wired for high-speed Internet access. Wireless service is available via classrooms, libraries, student centers.

Student Life *Housing:* on-campus residence required through senior year. *Options:* coed, men-only, women-only, disabled students. Campus housing is university owned. Freshman campus housing is guaranteed. *Activities and organizations:* drama/theater group, student-run newspaper, radio and television station, choral group, Entertainment To Knight, Student Senate, Campus Ministry, Symphonic Band, Wartburg Choir. *Campus security:* 24-hour emergency response devices and patrols, late-night transport/escort service, controlled dormitory access. *Student services:* health clinic, personal/psychological counseling.

Athletics Member NCAA. All Division III. *Intercollegiate sports:* baseball M, basketball M/W, cheerleading W, cross-country running M/W, football M, golf M/W, soccer M/W, softball W, tennis M/W, track and field M/W, volleyball W, wrestling M. *Intramural sports:* badminton M/W, basketball M/W, bowling M/W, golf M/W, racquetball M/W, rugby W(c), softball M/W, tennis M/W, ultimate Frisbee M/W, volleyball M/W.

Standardized Tests *Required:* SAT or ACT (for admission).

Costs (2011–12) *Comprehensive fee:* $39,110 includes full-time tuition ($30,110), mandatory fees ($850), and room and board ($8150). Part-time tuition: $1450 per course. *Required fees:* $90 per term part-time. *College room only:* $3905. Room and board charges vary according to board plan. *Payment plan:* installment. *Waivers:* children of alumni and employees or children of employees.

Financial Aid Of all full-time matriculated undergraduates who enrolled in 2008, 1,558 applied for aid, 1,369 were judged to have need, 545 had their need fully met. In 2008, 352 non-need-based awards were made. *Average percent of need met:* 83%. *Average financial aid package:* $21,639. *Average need-based loan:* $4637. *Average need-based gift aid:* $17,076. *Average non-need-based aid:* $13,202. *Average indebtedness upon graduation:* $29,867.

Applying *Options:* electronic application, early action, deferred entrance. *Required:* high school transcript, minimum 2 GPA. *Required for some:* interview. *Recommended:* secondary school report. *Application deadlines:* rolling (freshmen), rolling (transfers), 12/1 (early action). *Notification:* continuous (freshmen), continuous (transfers).

Freshman Application Contact Mr. Todd Coleman, Assistant Vice President for Admissions, Wartburg College, 100 Wartburg Boulevard, PO Box 1003, Waverly, IA 50677-0903. *Phone:* 319-352-8264. *Toll-free phone:* 800-772-2085. *Fax:* 319-352-8579. *E-mail:* admissions@wartburg.edu. *Web site:* http://www.wartburg.edu/.

William Penn University

Oskaloosa, Iowa

- **Independent** comprehensive, founded 1873, affiliated with Society of Friends
- **Rural** 60-acre campus with easy access to Des Moines
- **Endowment** $6.8 million
- **Coed**
- **Moderately difficult** entrance level

Faculty *Student/faculty ratio:* 15:1.

Academics *Calendar:* semesters. *Degrees:* associate, bachelor's, and master's.

Student Life *Campus security:* 24-hour emergency response devices and patrols, late-night transport/escort service, controlled dormitory access.

Athletics Member NAIA.

Standardized Tests *Required:* SAT or ACT (for admission).

Costs (2010–11) *Comprehensive fee:* $25,626 includes full-time tuition ($19,864), mandatory fees ($370), and room and board ($5392). Full-time tuition and fees vary according to location. Part-time tuition: $450 per credit hour. Part-time tuition and fees vary according to location.

Financial Aid *Of all full-time matriculated undergraduates who enrolled in 2005,* 808 applied for aid, 768 were judged to have need, 238 had their need fully met. 511 Federal Work-Study jobs (averaging $1287). 1 state and other part-time job (averaging $1103). *In 2005,* 2 non-need-based awards were made. *Average percent of need met:* 82. *Average financial aid package:* $17,782. *Average need-based loan:* $4600. *Average need-based gift aid:* $11,300. *Average non-need-based aid:* $4500. *Average indebtedness upon graduation:* $22,169.

Applying *Options:* electronic application, deferred entrance. *Application fee:* $20. *Required:* high school transcript, minimum 2 GPA. *Required for some:* essay or personal statement, interview.

Freshman Application Contact John Ottosson, Vice President for Enrollment Management, William Penn University, 201 Trueblood Avenue, Oskaloosa, IA 52577-1799. *Phone:* 641-673-1012. *Toll-free phone:* 800-779-7366. *Fax:* 641-673-2113. *E-mail:* admissions@wmpenn.edu. *Web site:* http://www.wmpenn.edu/.

KANSAS

The Art Institutes International–Kansas City

Lenexa, Kansas

- **Proprietary** 4-year, founded 2008, part of Education Management Corporation
- **Coed**

Academics *Degrees:* associate and bachelor's.

Costs (2010–11) *Tuition:* Tuition cost varies by program. Prospective students should contact the school for current tuition costs. Other charges include a starting kit for all first-quarter students. Kits vary in price, depending on the program of study.

Freshman Application Contact The Art Institutes International–Kansas City, 8208 Melrose Drive, Lenexa, KS 66214. *Phone:* 913-217-4600. *Toll-free phone:* 866-530-8508. *Web site:* http://www.artinstitutes.edu/kansascity/.

See page 1086 for the College Close-Up.

Baker University

Baldwin City, Kansas

- **Independent United Methodist** comprehensive, founded 1858
- **Small-town** 26-acre campus with easy access to Kansas City
- **Endowment** $30.3 million
- **Coed** 966 undergraduate students, 90% full-time, 51% women, 49% men
- **Moderately difficult** entrance level, 50% of applicants were admitted

Undergraduates 869 full-time, 97 part-time. Students come from 25 states and territories; 4 other countries; 26% are from out of state; 7% transferred in; 82% live on campus. *Retention:* 82% of full-time freshmen returned.

Freshmen *Admission:* 1,160 applied, 580 admitted, 185 enrolled. *Average high school GPA:* 3.42. *Test scores:* ACT scores over 18: 95%; ACT scores over 24: 44%; ACT scores over 30: 7%.

Faculty *Total:* 97, 59% full-time, 62% with terminal degrees. *Student/faculty ratio:* 12:1.

Academics *Calendar:* 4-1-4, semesters for nursing program. *Degrees:* bachelor's, master's, and doctoral-research/scholarship (profile includes information primarily for undergraduate residential campus in Baldwin City, KS). *Special study options:* advanced placement credit, double majors, honors programs, independent study, internships, services for LD students, student-designed majors, study abroad, summer session for credit. *ROTC:* Army (c), Air Force (c). *Unusual degree programs:* 3-2 engineering with Washington University in St. Louis, University of Kansas, University of Missouri Kansas City; forestry with Duke University.

Computers on Campus 222 computers/terminals are available on campus for general student use. Students can access the following: computer help desk, free student e-mail accounts, online (class) grades, online (class) registration, online (class) schedules. Campuswide network is available. 100% of college-owned or -operated housing units are wired for high-speed Internet access. Wireless service is available via classrooms, computer labs, libraries, student centers.

Student Life *Housing:* on-campus residence required through senior year. *Options:* coed, men-only, women-only, disabled students. Campus housing is university owned. Freshman campus housing is guaranteed. *Activities and organizations:* drama/theater group, student-run newspaper, radio and television station, choral group, Cardinal Key, Earth We Are, Mungano, Fellowship of Christian Athletes, Student Activities Council, national fraternities, national sororities. *Campus security:* 24-hour emergency response devices and patrols, student patrols, controlled dormitory access. *Student services:* health clinic, personal/psychological counseling.

Athletics Member NAIA. *Intercollegiate sports:* baseball M(s), basketball M(s)/W(s), bowling W(s), cheerleading M(s)/W(s), cross-country running M(s)/W(s), football M(s), golf M(s)/W(s), soccer M(s)/W(s), softball W(s), tennis M(s)/W(s), track and field M(s)/W(s), volleyball W(s), wrestling M(s). *Intramural sports:* basketball M/W, football M/W, softball M/W, table tennis M/W, volleyball M/W.

Standardized Tests *Required:* SAT or ACT (for admission).

Costs (2010–11) *One-time required fee:* $80. *Comprehensive fee:* $29,230 includes full-time tuition ($22,200) and room and board ($7030). Full-time tuition and fees vary according to course load, degree level, location, and program. Part-time tuition: $675 per credit hour. Part-time tuition and fees vary according to course load, degree level, location, and program. *College room only:* $3250. Room and board charges vary according to board plan and housing facility. *Payment plan:* installment. *Waivers:* senior citizens and employees or children of employees.

Financial Aid Of all full-time matriculated undergraduates who enrolled in 2008, 839 applied for aid, 713 were judged to have need, 268 had their need

fully met. In 2008, 180 non-need-based awards were made. *Average percent of need met:* 84%. *Average financial aid package:* $13,600. *Average need-based loan:* $5622. *Average need-based gift aid:* $6787. *Average non-need-based aid:* $9006. *Average indebtedness upon graduation:* $26,869.

Applying *Options:* electronic application, deferred entrance. *Required:* high school transcript, minimum 2.75 GPA, 1 letter of recommendation. *Required for some:* essay or personal statement, interview. *Application deadlines:* rolling (freshmen), rolling (transfers).

Freshman Application Contact Mr. Kevin Kropf, Director of Enrollment Management, Baker University, PO Box 65, Baldwin City, KS 66006-0065. *Phone:* 785-594-8327. *Toll-free phone:* 800-873-4282. *Fax:* 785-594-8353. *E-mail:* admissions@bakeru.edu. *Web site:* http://www.bakeru.edu/.

Barclay College

Haviland, Kansas

- **Independent** 4-year, founded 1917, affiliated with Society of Friends
- **Rural** 17-acre campus
- **Endowment** $700,000
- **Coed** 245 undergraduate students, 87% full-time, 50% women, 50% men
- **Minimally difficult** entrance level, 100% of applicants were admitted

Undergraduates 213 full-time, 32 part-time. Students come from 24 states and territories; 3 other countries; 64% are from out of state; 3% Black or African American, non-Hispanic/Latino; 5% Hispanic/Latino; 0.4% Asian, non-Hispanic/Latino; 1% American Indian or Alaska Native, non-Hispanic/Latino; 2% Race/ethnicity unknown; 1% international; 11% transferred in; 78% live on campus. *Retention:* 80% of full-time freshmen returned.

Freshmen *Admission:* 72 applied, 72 admitted, 49 enrolled. *Test scores:* SAT critical reading scores over 500: 75%; SAT math scores over 500: 25%; SAT writing scores over 500: 75%; ACT scores over 18: 66%; SAT critical reading scores over 600: 25%; SAT writing scores over 600: 25%; ACT scores over 24: 20%; SAT critical reading scores over 700: 25%; SAT writing scores over 700: 25%.

Faculty *Total:* 35, 43% full-time, 23% with terminal degrees. *Student/faculty ratio:* 11:1.

Academics *Calendar:* semesters. *Degrees:* certificates, associate, and bachelor's. *Special study options:* academic remediation for entering students, adult/continuing education programs, advanced placement credit, distance learning, double majors, external degree program, independent study, internships, part-time degree program. *Unusual degree programs:* 3-2 nursing with Pratt Community College.

Computers on Campus 28 computers/terminals are available on campus for general student use. Students can access the following: campus intranet, computer help desk, free student e-mail accounts, online (class) grades, online (class) registration, online (class) schedules. Campuswide network is available. 100% of college-owned or -operated housing units are wired for high-speed Internet access. Wireless service is available via entire campus.

Student Life *Housing:* on-campus residence required through senior year. *Options:* men-only, women-only. Campus housing is university owned. Freshman campus housing is guaranteed. *Activities and organizations:* drama/theater group, choral group, Pep Club, Drama Club, Missions Club. *Campus security:* student patrols. *Student services:* personal/psychological counseling.

Athletics *Intercollegiate sports:* basketball M/W, cheerleading M/W, soccer M, tennis M/W, volleyball W. *Intramural sports:* basketball M/W, volleyball M/W.

Standardized Tests *Required:* SAT or ACT (for admission).

Costs (2011–12) *Comprehensive fee:* $20,590 includes full-time tuition ($11,000), mandatory fees ($2790), and room and board ($6800). Part-time tuition: $250 per hour. Part-time tuition and fees vary according to course load. *Room and board:* Room and board charges vary according to board plan and housing facility. *Payment plan:* installment. *Waivers:* employees or children of employees.

Financial Aid Of all full-time matriculated undergraduates who enrolled in 2003, 163 applied for aid, 163 were judged to have need, 145 had their need fully met. 33 Federal Work-Study jobs (averaging $1200). 67 state and other part-time jobs (averaging $600). In 2003, 4 non-need-based awards were made. *Average percent of need met:* 85%. *Average financial aid package:* $6700. *Average need-based loan:* $3750. *Average need-based gift aid:* $1500. *Average non-need-based aid:* $1500. *Average indebtedness upon graduation:* $10,000.

Applying *Options:* electronic application, early admission, deferred entrance. *Application fee:* $15. *Required:* essay or personal statement, high school transcript, minimum 2.3 GPA, 2 letters of recommendation, interview. *Application deadlines:* 9/1 (freshmen), 9/1 (transfers). *Notification:* continuous (freshmen), continuous (transfers).

Freshman Application Contact Mr. Justin Kendall, Admissions Recruiter, Barclay College, 607 North Kingman, Haviland, KS 67059. *Phone:* 620-862-5252 Ext. 21. *Toll-free phone:* 800-862-0226. *Fax:* 620-862-5242. *E-mail:* jkendall@barclaycollege.edu. *Web site:* http://www.barclaycollege.edu/.

Benedictine College

Atchison, Kansas

- **Independent Roman Catholic** comprehensive, founded 1859
- **Small-town** 225-acre campus with easy access to Kansas City
- **Endowment** $15.8 million
- **Coed** 1,880 undergraduate students, 83% full-time, 57% women, 43% men
- **Moderately difficult** entrance level, 60% of applicants were admitted

Undergraduates 1,566 full-time, 314 part-time. Students come from 39 states and territories; 13 other countries; 70% are from out of state; 3% Black or African American, non-Hispanic/Latino; 6% Hispanic/Latino; 0.7% Asian, non-Hispanic/Latino; 0.5% Native Hawaiian or other Pacific Islander, non-Hispanic/Latino; 0.3% American Indian or Alaska Native, non-Hispanic/Latino; 2% Two or more races, non-Hispanic/Latino; 4% Race/ethnicity unknown; 2% international; 4% transferred in; 76% live on campus. *Retention:* 81% of full-time freshmen returned.

Freshmen *Admission:* 3,091 applied, 1,864 admitted, 388 enrolled. *Average high school GPA:* 3.4. *Test scores:* ACT scores over 18: 95%; ACT scores over 24: 49%; ACT scores over 30: 9%.

Faculty *Total:* 188, 48% full-time, 53% with terminal degrees. *Student/faculty ratio:* 14:1.

Academics *Calendar:* semesters. *Degrees:* associate, bachelor's, and master's. *Special study options:* academic remediation for entering students, advanced placement credit, cooperative education, double majors, English as a second language, independent study, internships, off-campus study, part-time degree program, services for LD students, student-designed majors, study abroad, summer session for credit. *ROTC:* Army (b). *Unusual degree programs:* 3-2 engineering with Kansas State University, University of Missouri–Columbia, South Dakota School of Mines and Technology; occupational therapy with Washington University in St. Louis.

Computers on Campus 100 computers/terminals are available on campus for general student use. Students can access the following: computer help desk, free student e-mail accounts, online (class) grades, online (class) registration, online (class) schedules. Campuswide network is available. 100% of college-owned or -operated housing units are wired for high-speed Internet access. Wireless service is available via entire campus.

Student Life *Housing:* on-campus residence required through senior year. *Options:* coed, men-only, women-only. Campus housing is university owned. Freshman campus housing is guaranteed. *Activities and organizations:* drama/theater group, student-run newspaper, choral group, marching band, student government, Students in Free Enterprise (SIFE), Knights of Columbus, Concert Chorale/Chamber Singers, Campus Activities Board. *Campus security:* 24-hour emergency response devices and patrols, late-night transport/escort service. *Student services:* health clinic, personal/psychological counseling.

Athletics Member NAIA. *Intercollegiate sports:* baseball M(s), basketball M(s)/W(s), cheerleading M(s)/W(s), cross-country running M(s)/W(s), football M(s), golf M(s)/W(s), soccer M(s)/W(s), softball W(s), track and field M(s)/W(s), volleyball W(s). *Intramural sports:* basketball M/W, football M/W, racquetball M/W, soccer M/W, softball M/W, table tennis M/W, volleyball M/W.

Standardized Tests *Required:* SAT or ACT (for admission).

Costs (2010–11) *Comprehensive fee:* $27,850 includes full-time tuition ($20,475) and room and board ($7375). Full-time tuition and fees vary according to course load and degree level. Part-time tuition: $600 per credit hour. Part-time tuition and fees vary according to course load and degree level. *College room only:* $4125. Room and board charges vary according to board plan and housing facility. *Payment plan:* installment. *Waivers:* senior citizens and employees or children of employees.

Financial Aid Of all full-time matriculated undergraduates who enrolled in 2009, 1,257 applied for aid, 1,127 were judged to have need, 172 had their need fully met. In 2009, 248 non-need-based awards were made. *Average percent of need met:* 66%. *Average financial aid package:* $24,117. *Average need-based loan:* $4650. *Average need-based gift aid:* $4168. *Average non-need-based aid:* $8608. *Average indebtedness upon graduation:* $28,887.

Applying *Options:* electronic application, deferred entrance. *Application fee:* $25. *Required:* high school transcript, minimum 2 GPA. *Required for some:* interview. *Notification:* continuous (freshmen), continuous (transfers).

Freshman Application Contact Benedictine College, 1020 North 2nd Street, Atchison, KS 66002-1499. *Phone:* 913-367-5340 Ext. 2476. *Toll-free phone:* 800-467-5340. *Web site:* http://www.benedictine.edu/.

Bethany College

Lindsborg, Kansas

- **Independent Lutheran** 4-year, founded 1881
- **Small-town** 80-acre campus
- **Endowment** $22.2 million
- **Coed** 610 undergraduate students, 96% full-time, 50% women, 50% men
- **Moderately difficult** entrance level, 64% of applicants were admitted

Undergraduates 588 full-time, 22 part-time. Students come from 30 states and territories; 14 other countries; 42% are from out of state; 9% Black or African American, non-Hispanic/Latino; 7% Hispanic/Latino; 0.5% Asian, non-Hispanic/Latino; 0.8% Native Hawaiian or other Pacific Islander, non-Hispanic/Latino; 0.8% American Indian or Alaska Native, non-Hispanic/Latino; 2% Two or more races, non-Hispanic/Latino; 2% Race/ethnicity unknown; 4% international; 9% transferred in; 72% live on campus. *Retention:* 61% of full-time freshmen returned.

Freshmen *Admission:* 804 applied, 514 admitted, 163 enrolled. *Average high school GPA:* 3.31. *Test scores:* SAT critical reading scores over 500: 41%; SAT math scores over 500: 54%; SAT writing scores over 500: 28%; ACT scores over 18: 86%; SAT critical reading scores over 600: 8%; SAT math scores over 600: 8%; SAT writing scores over 600: 8%; ACT scores over 24: 35%; ACT scores over 30: 1%.

Faculty *Total:* 77, 47% full-time, 49% with terminal degrees. *Student/faculty ratio:* 11:1.

Academics *Calendar:* 4-1-4. *Degree:* bachelor's. *Special study options:* academic remediation for entering students, accelerated degree program, advanced placement credit, double majors, honors programs, independent study, internships, off-campus study, services for LD students, student-designed majors, study abroad, summer session for credit. *Unusual degree programs:* 3-2 engineering with Wichita State University.

Computers on Campus 48 computers/terminals are available on campus for general student use. Students can access the following: campus intranet, computer help desk, free student e-mail accounts, online (class) grades, online (class) registration, online (class) schedules. Campuswide network is available. 99% of college-owned or -operated housing units are wired for high-speed Internet access. Wireless service is available via entire campus.

Student Life *Housing:* on-campus residence required through junior year. *Options:* coed, women-only. Campus housing is university owned. Freshman campus housing is guaranteed. *Activities and organizations:* drama/theater group, student-run newspaper, choral group, Von Neuman Society, Alpha Theta Chi, Alpha Sigma Nu, Fellowship of Christian Athletes, BC Bacchus. *Campus security:* 24-hour emergency response devices, late-night transport/escort service, controlled dormitory access, night patrols by security personnel. *Student services:* health clinic, personal/psychological counseling.

Athletics Member NAIA. *Intercollegiate sports:* baseball M(s), basketball M(s)/W(s), cross-country running M(s)/W(s), football M(s), golf M(s), soccer M(s)/W(s), softball W(s), tennis M(s)/W(s), track and field M(s)/W(s), volleyball W(s). *Intramural sports:* badminton M/W, basketball M/W, football M/W, racquetball M/W, soccer M/W, softball M/W, volleyball M/W.

Standardized Tests *Required:* SAT or ACT (for admission).

Costs (2011–12) *Comprehensive fee:* $27,482 includes full-time tuition ($20,368), mandatory fees ($600), and room and board ($6514). Part-time tuition: $425 per hour. Part-time tuition and fees vary according to course load. *College room only:* $3426. Room and board charges vary according to board plan and housing facility. *Payment plan:* installment. *Waivers:* employees or children of employees.

Financial Aid Of all full-time matriculated undergraduates who enrolled in 2009, 551 applied for aid, 448 were judged to have need, 188 had their need fully met. 97 Federal Work-Study jobs (averaging $1500). In 2009, 40 non-need-based awards were made. *Average percent of need met:* 94%. *Average financial aid package:* $20,638. *Average need-based loan:* $4784. *Average need-based gift aid:* $7389. *Average non-need-based aid:* $6948. *Average indebtedness upon graduation:* $22,699.

Applying *Options:* electronic application, deferred entrance. *Required:* high school transcript, minimum 2.5 GPA. *Required for some:* essay or personal statement, interview. *Application deadlines:* rolling (freshmen), rolling (out-of-state freshmen), rolling (transfers). *Notification:* continuous (freshmen), continuous (out-of-state freshmen), continuous (transfers).

Freshman Application Contact Richard Strange, Associate director of Admissions, Bethany College, 335 East Swensson Avenue, Lindsborg, KS 67456-1895. *Phone:* 785-227-3311 Ext. 8110. *Toll-free phone:* 800-826-2281. *Fax:* 785-227-8993. *E-mail:* stranger@bethanylb.edu. *Web site:* http://www.bethanylb.edu/.

Bethel College

North Newton, Kansas

- **Independent** 4-year, founded 1887, affiliated with Mennonite Church USA
- **Small-town** 60-acre campus with easy access to Wichita
- **Endowment** $12.9 million
- **Coed**
- **Moderately difficult** entrance level

Faculty *Student/faculty ratio:* 9:1.

Academics *Calendar:* 4-1-4. *Degree:* certificates and bachelor's.

Student Life *Campus security:* 24-hour emergency response devices, student patrols, controlled dormitory access, community police patrols.

Athletics Member NAIA.

Standardized Tests *Required:* SAT or ACT (for admission).

Costs (2010–11) *Comprehensive fee:* $27,680 includes full-time tuition ($20,700) and room and board ($6980). Full-time tuition and fees vary according to course load. Part-time tuition: $745 per semester hour. Part-time tuition and fees vary according to course load. *College room only:* $3730. Room and board charges vary according to board plan and housing facility. *Payment plans:* installment, deferred payment.

Financial Aid *Of all full-time matriculated undergraduates who enrolled in 2008,* 357 applied for aid, 338 were judged to have need, 160 had their need fully met. 194 Federal Work-Study jobs (averaging $1711). 193 state and other part-time jobs (averaging $1195). *In 2008,* 78 non-need-based awards were made. *Average percent of need met:* 94. *Average financial aid package:* $21,698. *Average need-based loan:* $6764. *Average need-based gift aid:* $5359. *Average non-need-based aid:* $8932. *Average indebtedness upon graduation:* $24,860.

Applying *Options:* deferred entrance. *Application fee:* $20. *Required:* high school transcript, minimum 2.5 GPA. *Required for some:* essay or personal statement, 2 letters of recommendation. *Recommended:* interview.

Freshman Application Contact Mr. Todd H. Moore, Vice President for Admissions, Bethel College, 300 East 27th Street, North Newton, KS 67117-0531. *Phone:* 316-284-5230. *Toll-free phone:* 800-522-1887 Ext. 230. *Fax:* 316-284-5870. *E-mail:* admissions@bethelks.edu. *Web site:* http://www.bethelks.edu/.

Central Christian College of Kansas

McPherson, Kansas

- **Independent Free Methodist** 4-year, founded 1884
- **Small-town** 16-acre campus
- **Endowment** $6.9 million
- **Coed**
- **Minimally difficult** entrance level

Faculty *Student/faculty ratio:* 14:1.

Academics *Calendar:* 4-1-4. *Degrees:* certificates, associate, and bachelor's.

Athletics Member NAIA, NCCAA.

Standardized Tests *Required:* SAT or ACT (for admission).

Costs (2010–11) *Comprehensive fee:* $23,900 includes full-time tuition ($17,800), mandatory fees ($200), and room and board ($5900). Full-time tuition and fees vary according to course load and program. Part-time tuition: $500 per credit hour. Part-time tuition and fees vary according to course load and program. *College room only:* $2700. Room and board charges vary according to board plan and gender.

Financial Aid *Of all full-time matriculated undergraduates who enrolled in 2007,* 267 applied for aid, 244 were judged to have need, 57 had their need fully met. 58 Federal Work-Study jobs (averaging $1000). *In 2007,* 53 non-need-based awards were made. *Average percent of need met:* 75. *Average financial aid package:* $13,423. *Average need-based loan:* $5024. *Average need-based gift aid:* $4383. *Average non-need-based aid:* $5284. *Average indebtedness upon graduation:* $20,000.

Applying *Options:* electronic application, deferred entrance. *Application fee:* $20. *Required:* high school transcript, minimum 2.5 GPA, 2 letters of recommendation. *Recommended:* essay or personal statement, interview.

Freshman Application Contact Central Christian College of Kansas, 1200 South Main, PO Box 1403, McPherson, KS 67460-5799. *Phone:* 620-241-0723 Ext. 380. *Toll-free phone:* 800-835-0078 Ext. 337. *Web site:* http://www.centralchristian.edu/.

Cleveland Chiropractic College–Kansas City Campus

Overland Park, Kansas

- **Independent** comprehensive, founded 1922, administratively affiliated with Cleveland Chiropractic College-Los Angeles Campus
- **Urban** 10-acre campus
- **Coed** 115 undergraduate students, 88% full-time, 37% women, 63% men
- **Noncompetitive** entrance level, 100% of applicants were admitted

Undergraduates 101 full-time, 14 part-time. Students come from 18 states and territories; 2 other countries; 78% are from out of state; 5% Black or African American, non-Hispanic/Latino; 6% Hispanic/Latino; 3% Asian, non-Hispanic/Latino; 3% American Indian or Alaska Native, non-Hispanic/Latino; 2% Two or more races, non-Hispanic/Latino; 23% Race/ethnicity unknown; 3% international; 43% transferred in.

Freshmen *Admission:* 5 applied, 5 admitted, 5 enrolled. *Average high school GPA:* 2.5. *Test scores:* ACT scores over 18: 100%; ACT scores over 24: 50%.

Faculty *Total:* 53, 81% full-time, 89% with terminal degrees. *Student/faculty ratio:* 11:1.

Academics *Calendar:* trimesters. *Degrees:* associate, bachelor's, and doctoral-professional. *Special study options:* academic remediation for entering students, accelerated degree program, advanced placement credit, cooperative education, internships, services for LD students, summer session for credit.

Computers on Campus 30 computers/terminals are available on campus for general student use. Students can access the following: computer help desk, free student e-mail accounts, online (class) grades, online (class) schedules, educational software. Campuswide network is available. Wireless service is available via entire campus.

Student Life *Housing:* college housing not available. *Student services:* health clinic, personal/psychological counseling.

Standardized Tests *Required for some:* SAT or ACT (for admission).

Costs (2011–12) *Tuition:* $6630 full-time, $221 per credit part-time. Full-time tuition and fees vary according to course load and program. Part-time tuition and fees vary according to course load and program. *Required fees:* $140 per term part-time. *Payment plan:* installment.

Applying *Options:* electronic application, deferred entrance. *Application fee:* $50. *Required:* high school transcript, minimum 2.5 GPA. *Required for some:* interview. *Application deadline:* 8/28 (freshmen). *Notification:* 1/28 (freshmen).

Freshman Application Contact Ms. Melissa Denton, Director of Admissions, Cleveland Chiropractic College–Kansas City Campus, 10850 Lowell Avenue, Overland Park, KS 66210. *Phone:* 913-234-0750. *Toll-free phone:* 800-467-2252. *Fax:* 913-234-0906. *E-mail:* kc.admissions@cleveland.edu. *Web site:* http://www.cleveland.edu/.

Donnelly College

Kansas City, Kansas

- **Independent Roman Catholic** primarily 2-year, founded 1949
- **Urban** 4-acre campus
- **Coed**
- **Noncompetitive** entrance level

Faculty *Student/faculty ratio:* 16:1.

Academics *Calendar:* semesters. *Degrees:* certificates, associate, and bachelor's.

Student Life *Campus security:* 24-hour emergency response devices.

Costs (2010–11) *Comprehensive fee:* $11,760 includes full-time tuition ($5910), mandatory fees ($40), and room and board ($5810). Full-time tuition and fees vary according to course level, course load, degree level, program, and student level. Part-time tuition and fees vary according to course level, degree level, program, and student level. *College room only:* $3680.

Applying *Options:* electronic application, early admission, deferred entrance. *Recommended:* high school transcript.

Freshman Application Contact Mr. Edward Marquez, Director of Admissions, Donnelly College, 608 North 18th Street, Kansas City, KS 66102. *Phone:* 913-621-8713. *Fax:* 913-621-8719. *E-mail:* admissions@donnelly.edu. *Web site:* http://www.donnelly.edu/.

Emporia State University
Emporia, Kansas

- **State-supported** comprehensive, founded 1863, part of Kansas State Board of Regents
- **Small-town** 207-acre campus with easy access to Wichita
- **Endowment** $66.3 million
- **Coed** 4,066 undergraduate students, 89% full-time, 61% women, 39% men
- **Noncompetitive** entrance level, 86% of applicants were admitted

Undergraduates 3,615 full-time, 451 part-time. Students come from 27 states and territories; 16 other countries; 8% are from out of state; 6% Black or African American, non-Hispanic/Latino; 5% Hispanic/Latino; 1% Asian, non-Hispanic/Latino; 0.2% Native Hawaiian or other Pacific Islander, non-Hispanic/Latino; 0.6% American Indian or Alaska Native, non-Hispanic/Latino; 3% Two or more races, non-Hispanic/Latino; 3% Race/ethnicity unknown; 7% international; 10% transferred in; 22% live on campus. *Retention:* 73% of full-time freshmen returned.
Freshmen *Admission:* 1,486 applied, 1,279 admitted, 641 enrolled. *Average high school GPA:* 3.26. *Test scores:* ACT scores over 18: 87%; ACT scores over 24: 29%; ACT scores over 30: 2%.
Faculty *Total:* 273, 94% full-time, 75% with terminal degrees. *Student/faculty ratio:* 18:1.
Academics *Calendar:* semesters. *Degrees:* bachelor's, master's, doctoral-research/scholarship, post-master's, and postbachelor's certificates. *Special study options:* academic remediation for entering students, accelerated degree program, adult/continuing education programs, advanced placement credit, cooperative education, distance learning, double majors, English as a second language, honors programs, independent study, internships, off-campus study, part-time degree program, services for LD students, study abroad, summer session for credit. *Unusual degree programs:* 3-2 engineering with Kansas State University, University of Kansas, Wichita State University.
Computers on Campus 410 computers/terminals are available on campus for general student use. Students can access the following: campus intranet, computer help desk, free student e-mail accounts, online (class) grades, online (class) registration, online (class) schedules, various software packages. Campuswide network is available. 100% of college-owned or -operated housing units are wired for high-speed Internet access. Wireless service is available via classrooms, computer centers, computer labs, libraries.
Student Life *Housing:* on-campus residence required for freshman year. *Options:* coed, men-only, women-only, disabled students. Campus housing is university owned. Freshman campus housing is guaranteed. *Activities and organizations:* drama/theater group, student-run newspaper, choral group, marching band, Union Activities Council, Associated Student Government, Black Student Union, national fraternities, national sororities. *Campus security:* 24-hour emergency response devices and patrols, student patrols, late-night transport/escort service, controlled dormitory access, 24-hour residence hall monitoring, safety and self-awareness programs. *Student services:* health clinic, personal/psychological counseling, women's center, legal services.
Athletics Member NCAA. All Division II. *Intercollegiate sports:* baseball M(s), basketball M(s)/W(s), cheerleading M(s)/W(s), cross-country running M(s)/W(s), football M(s), soccer W(s), softball W(s), tennis M(s)/W(s), track and field M(s)/W(s), volleyball W(s). *Intramural sports:* badminton M/W, basketball M/W, fencing M(c)/W(c), football M/W, rugby M(c), soccer M(c)/W(c), softball M/W, table tennis M/W, tennis M/W, volleyball M/W.
Standardized Tests *Required:* SAT or ACT (for admission).
Costs (2010–11) *Tuition:* state resident $3614 full-time, $120 per credit hour part-time; nonresident $13,324 full-time, $444 per credit hour part-time. Full-time tuition and fees vary according to course load, degree level, and location. Part-time tuition and fees vary according to course load, degree level, and location. *Required fees:* $1022 full-time, $62 per credit hour part-time. *Room and board:* $6230; room only: $3180. Room and board charges vary according to board plan and housing facility. *Payment plans:* installment, deferred payment. *Waivers:* senior citizens and employees or children of employees.
Financial Aid Of all full-time matriculated undergraduates who enrolled in 2009, 2,760 applied for aid, 2,264 were judged to have need, 240 had their need fully met. 125 Federal Work-Study jobs (averaging $1922). 15 state and other part-time jobs (averaging $1642). In 2009, 499 non-need-based awards were made. *Average percent of need met:* 72%. *Average financial aid package:* $5297. *Average need-based loan:* $5143. *Average need-based gift aid:* $5344. *Average non-need-based aid:* $1351. *Average indebtedness upon graduation:* $23,498.
Applying *Options:* electronic application, early admission, deferred entrance. *Application fee:* $30. *Required:* high school transcript. *Recommended:* minimum 2 GPA. *Application deadlines:* rolling (freshmen), rolling (transfers). *Notification:* continuous (freshmen), continuous (transfers).
Freshman Application Contact Ms. Laura Eddy, Director of Admissions, Emporia State University, 1200 Commercial Street, Campus Box 4034, Emporia, KS 66801-5087. *Phone:* 620-341-5465. *Toll-free phone:* 877-

GOTOESU (in-state); 877-468-6378 (out-of-state). *Fax:* 620-341-5599. *E-mail:* go2esu@emporia.edu. *Web site:* http://www.emporia.edu/.

Fort Hays State University
Hays, Kansas

- **State-supported** comprehensive, founded 1902, part of Kansas State Board of Education
- **Small-town** 200-acre campus
- **Coed**
- **Noncompetitive** entrance level

Faculty *Student/faculty ratio:* 17:1.
Academics *Calendar:* semesters. *Degrees:* certificates, associate, bachelor's, master's, and post-master's certificates.
Student Life *Campus security:* 24-hour emergency response devices.
Athletics Member NCAA. All Division II.
Standardized Tests *Required:* SAT or ACT (for admission).
Costs (2010–11) *Tuition:* state resident $2427 full-time, $101 per credit hour part-time; nonresident $9142 full-time, $381 per credit hour part-time. Full-time tuition and fees vary according to course load. Part-time tuition and fees vary according to course load. *Required fees:* $30 full-time. *Room and board:* $6625; room only: $3335. Room and board charges vary according to board plan and housing facility.
Financial Aid Of all full-time matriculated undergraduates who enrolled in 2007, 3,244 applied for aid, 2,653 were judged to have need, 483 had their need fully met. In 2007, 1162 non-need-based awards were made. *Average percent of need met:* 62. *Average financial aid package:* $5955. *Average need-based loan:* $3634. *Average need-based gift aid:* $3390. *Average non-need-based aid:* $3358. *Average indebtedness upon graduation:* $15,601.
Applying *Options:* deferred entrance. *Application fee:* $35. *Required:* high school transcript.
Freshman Application Contact Fort Hays State University, 600 Park Street, Hays, KS 67601-4099. *Phone:* 785-628-4091. *Toll-free phone:* 800-628-FHSU. *Web site:* http://www.fhsu.edu/.

Friends University
Wichita, Kansas

- **Independent religious** comprehensive, founded 1898
- **Urban** 45-acre campus
- **Endowment** $38.1 million
- **Coed** 1,962 undergraduate students, 78% full-time, 56% women, 44% men
- **Moderately difficult** entrance level, 61% of applicants were admitted

Undergraduates 1,530 full-time, 432 part-time. Students come from 29 states and territories; 12 other countries; 18% are from out of state; 10% Black or African American, non-Hispanic/Latino; 4% Hispanic/Latino; 2% Asian, non-Hispanic/Latino; 2% American Indian or Alaska Native, non-Hispanic/Latino; 0.9% Two or more races, non-Hispanic/Latino; 15% Race/ethnicity unknown; 16% transferred in; 36% live on campus. *Retention:* 65% of full-time freshmen returned.
Freshmen *Admission:* 707 applied, 430 admitted, 206 enrolled. *Average high school GPA:* 3.18. *Test scores:* SAT critical reading scores over 500: 15%; SAT math scores over 500: 39%; ACT scores over 18: 83%; ACT scores over 24: 36%; ACT scores over 30: 5%.
Faculty *Total:* 339, 22% full-time. *Student/faculty ratio:* 13:1.
Academics *Calendar:* semesters. *Degrees:* associate, bachelor's, and master's. *Special study options:* academic remediation for entering students, accelerated degree program, adult/continuing education programs, advanced placement credit, cooperative education, distance learning, double majors, honors programs, independent study, internships, off-campus study, part-time degree program, services for LD students, student-designed majors, study abroad, summer session for credit.
Computers on Campus 360 computers/terminals are available on campus for general student use. Students can access the following: campus intranet, computer help desk, free student e-mail accounts, online (class) grades, online (class) schedules. Campuswide network is available. 80% of college-owned or -operated housing units are wired for high-speed Internet access. Wireless service is available via classrooms, computer centers, computer labs, dorm rooms, libraries, student centers.
Student Life *Housing options:* coed. Campus housing is university owned. *Activities and organizations:* drama/theater group, student-run newspaper, choral group, Psychology Club, Sigma Delta Pi Spanish Club, FACE-Falcon Activities and Campus Events, Drama Club. *Campus security:* 24-hour patrols, late-night transport/escort service, controlled dormitory access. *Student services:* health clinic, personal/psychological counseling.
Athletics Member NAIA. *Intercollegiate sports:* baseball M(s), basketball M(s)/W(s), cheerleading M(s)/W(s), cross-country running M(s)/W(s), football M(s), golf M(s), soccer M(s)/W(s), softball W(s), tennis M(s)/W(s), track

and field M(s)/W(s), volleyball W(s). *Intramural sports:* basketball M/W, football M/W, racquetball M/W, soccer M/W, table tennis M/W, tennis M/W, ultimate Frisbee M/W, volleyball M/W.

Standardized Tests *Required:* SAT or ACT (for admission). *Required for some:* SAT or ACT (for admission).

Costs (2010–11) *Comprehensive fee:* $25,830 includes full-time tuition ($19,890), mandatory fees ($150), and room and board ($5790). Full-time tuition and fees vary according to course level, course load, degree level, and program. Part-time tuition: $663 per credit hour. Part-time tuition and fees vary according to course level, course load, degree level, and program. *Required fees:* $5 per credit hour part-time, $75 per term part-time. *College room only:* $2650. Room and board charges vary according to board plan and housing facility. *Payment plan:* installment. *Waivers:* senior citizens and employees or children of employees.

Financial Aid Of all full-time matriculated undergraduates who enrolled in 2006, 1,290 applied for aid, 1,160 were judged to have need, 279 had their need fully met. 239 Federal Work-Study jobs (averaging $1221). 185 state and other part-time jobs (averaging $1608). In 2006, 227 non-need-based awards were made. *Average percent of need met:* 66%. *Average financial aid package:* $11,219. *Average need-based loan:* $4098. *Average need-based gift aid:* $7092. *Average non-need-based aid:* $7792. *Average indebtedness upon graduation:* $17,750.

Applying *Options:* electronic application. *Application fee:* $35. *Required for some:* high school transcript, interview. *Application deadlines:* rolling (freshmen), rolling (out-of-state freshmen), rolling (transfers). *Notification:* continuous (freshmen), continuous (out-of-state freshmen), continuous (transfers).

Freshman Application Contact Ms. Erin Haneberg, Executive Director of Admissions, Friends University, 2100 West University Avenue, Wichita, KS 67213. *Phone:* 316-295-5100. *Toll-free phone:* 800-577-2233. *Fax:* 316-295-5101. *E-mail:* haneberg@friends.edu. *Web site:* http://www.friends.edu/.

Haskell Indian Nations University
Lawrence, Kansas

Freshman Application Contact Ms. Patty Grant, Recruitment Officer, Haskell Indian Nations University, 155 Indian Avenue, #5031, Lawrence, KS 66046-4800. *Phone:* 785-749-8437 Ext. 437. *Web site:* http://www.haskell.edu/.

ITT Technical Institute
Wichita, Kansas

- **Proprietary** 4-year, part of ITT Educational Services, Inc.
- **Coed**
- **Minimally difficult** entrance level

Academics *Calendar:* quarters. *Degrees:* associate and bachelor's.
Student Life *Housing:* college housing not available.
Freshman Application Contact Director of Recruitment, ITT Technical Institute, 8111 E. 32nd Street North, Suite 103, Wichita, KS 67208. *Phone:* 316-609-4100. *Toll-free phone:* 877-207-1047. *Web site:* http://www.itt-tech.edu/.

Kansas State University
Manhattan, Kansas

- **State-supported** university, founded 1863, part of Kansas Board of Regents
- **Suburban** 668-acre campus
- **Endowment** $277.6 million
- **Coed** 19,205 undergraduate students, 89% full-time, 48% women, 52% men
- **Noncompetitive** entrance level, 99% of applicants were admitted

Undergraduates 17,029 full-time, 2,176 part-time. Students come from 51 states and territories; 61 other countries; 15% are from out of state; 4% Black or African American, non-Hispanic/Latino; 5% Hispanic/Latino; 1% Asian, non-Hispanic/Latino; 0.2% Native Hawaiian or other Pacific Islander, non-Hispanic/Latino; 0.5% American Indian or Alaska Native, non-Hispanic/Latino; 2% Two or more races, non-Hispanic/Latino; 0.4% Race/ethnicity unknown; 5% international; 8% transferred in. *Retention:* 81% of full-time freshmen returned.

Freshmen *Admission:* 8,268 applied, 8,147 admitted, 3,561 enrolled. *Average high school GPA:* 3.45. *Test scores:* ACT scores over 18: 95%; ACT scores over 24: 55%; ACT scores over 30: 12%.

Faculty *Total:* 1,109, 86% full-time, 80% with terminal degrees. *Student/faculty ratio:* 21:1.

Academics *Calendar:* semesters. *Degrees:* certificates, associate, bachelor's, master's, doctoral-professional, doctoral-research/scholarship, and postbachelor's certificates. *Special study options:* academic remediation for entering students, accelerated degree program, adult/continuing education programs,

advanced placement credit, cooperative education, distance learning, double majors, English as a second language, freshman honors college, honors programs, independent study, internships, off-campus study, part-time degree program, services for LD students, study abroad, summer session for credit. *ROTC:* Army (b), Air Force (b). *Unusual degree programs:* 3-2 engineering; biology, kinesiology, horticulture, master of public health, biochemistry.

Computers on Campus Students can access the following: computer help desk, free student e-mail accounts, online (class) grades, online (class) registration, online (class) schedules. Campuswide network is available. Wireless service is available via entire campus.

Student Life *Housing options:* coed, men-only, women-only, cooperative. Campus housing is university owned. *Activities and organizations:* drama/theater group, student-run newspaper, radio and television station, choral group, marching band, athletic department groups, marching band, Union Governing Board, theater productions, debate team, national fraternities, national sororities. *Campus security:* 24-hour emergency response devices and patrols, late-night transport/escort service, controlled dormitory access. *Student services:* health clinic, personal/psychological counseling, women's center, legal services.

Athletics Member NCAA. All Division I except football (Division I-A). *Intercollegiate sports:* baseball M(s), basketball M(s)/W(s), crew W(s), cross-country running M(s)/W(s), golf M(s)/W(s), tennis W(s), track and field M(s)/W(s), volleyball W(s). *Intramural sports:* badminton M/W, basketball M/W, bowling M/W, crew M/W, cross-country running M/W, football M/W, golf M/W, ice hockey M, lacrosse M, racquetball M/W, soccer M/W, softball M/W, table tennis M/W, tennis M/W, track and field M/W, volleyball M/W, water polo M/W, weight lifting M/W, wrestling M.

Standardized Tests *Required for some:* SAT or ACT (for admission). *Recommended:* SAT or ACT (for admission).

Costs (2010–11) *Tuition:* state resident $6672 full-time; nonresident $17,700 full-time. Full-time tuition and fees vary according to course load, degree level, location, program, and reciprocity agreements. Part-time tuition and fees vary according to course load, degree level, location, program, and reciprocity agreements. *Required fees:* $704 full-time. *Room and board:* $6954. Room and board charges vary according to board plan, housing facility, and location. *Payment plans:* installment, deferred payment. *Waivers:* employees or children of employees.

Financial Aid Of all full-time matriculated undergraduates who enrolled in 2008, 11,299 applied for aid, 8,384 were judged to have need, 1,676 had their need fully met. In 2008, 1195 non-need-based awards were made. *Average percent of need met:* 83%. *Average financial aid package:* $10,607. *Average need-based loan:* $4185. *Average need-based gift aid:* $4179. *Average non-need-based aid:* $3014. *Average indebtedness upon graduation:* $22,633.

Applying *Options:* electronic application, early admission. *Application fee:* $30. *Required:* high school transcript, minimum 2 GPA. *Application deadlines:* rolling (freshmen), rolling (transfers). *Notification:* continuous (freshmen), continuous (transfers).

Freshman Application Contact Ms. Molly McGaughey, Associate Director of Admissions, Kansas State University, 119 Anderson Hall, Manhattan, KS 66506. *Phone:* 785-532-6250. *Toll-free phone:* 800-432-8270. *Fax:* 785-532-6393. *E-mail:* k-state@k-state.edu. *Web site:* http://www.k-state.edu/.

Kansas Wesleyan University
Salina, Kansas

Freshman Application Contact Kansas Wesleyan University, 100 East Claflin Avenue, Salina, KS 67401-6196. *Phone:* 785-827-5541 Ext. 1283. *Toll-free phone:* 800-874-1154 Ext. 1285. *Web site:* http://www.kwu.edu/.

Manhattan Christian College
Manhattan, Kansas

Director of Admissions Eric Ingmire, Director of Admissions, Manhattan Christian College, 1415 Anderson Avenue, Manhattan, KS 66502-4081. *Phone:* 785-539-3571 Ext. 324. *Toll-free phone:* 877-246-4622. *E-mail:* admit@mccks.edu. *Web site:* http://www.mccks.edu/.

McPherson College
McPherson, Kansas

- **Independent** 4-year, founded 1887, affiliated with Church of the Brethren
- **Small-town** 26-acre campus
- **Coed**
- **Moderately difficult** entrance level

Faculty *Student/faculty ratio:* 15:1.
Academics *Calendar:* 4-1-4. *Degrees:* associate and bachelor's.
Student Life *Campus security:* student patrols, controlled dormitory access.
Athletics Member NAIA.

Standardized Tests *Required:* SAT or ACT (for admission). *Recommended:* ACT (for admission).

Costs (2010–11) *Comprehensive fee:* $26,950 includes full-time tuition ($19,125), mandatory fees ($500), and room and board ($7325). Full-time tuition and fees vary according to course load and program. *College room only:* $2900.

Financial Aid *Of all full-time matriculated undergraduates who enrolled in 2009,* 504 applied for aid, 465 were judged to have need, 156 had their need fully met. 325 Federal Work-Study jobs (averaging $910). *In 2009,* 78 non-need-based awards were made. *Average percent of need met:* 88. *Average financial aid package:* $20,097. *Average need-based loan:* $5194. *Average need-based gift aid:* $6464. *Average non-need-based aid:* $9344. *Average indebtedness upon graduation:* $25,787.

Applying *Options:* electronic application, deferred entrance. *Application fee:* $25. *Required:* high school transcript, minimum 2 GPA.

Freshman Application Contact Mr. Matt Pfannenstiel, Director of Admissions, McPherson College, 1600 East Euclid, McPherson, KS 67460. *Phone:* 800-365-7402. *Toll-free phone:* 800-365-7402. *E-mail:* admiss@mcpherson.edu. *Web site:* http://www.mcpherson.edu/.

MidAmerica Nazarene University
Olathe, Kansas

- **Independent** comprehensive, founded 1966, affiliated with Church of the Nazarene
- **Suburban** 105-acre campus with easy access to Kansas City
- **Coed** 1,355 undergraduate students, 79% full-time, 57% women, 43% men
- **Moderately difficult** entrance level, 65% of applicants were admitted

Undergraduates 1,075 full-time, 280 part-time. 31% are from out of state; 11% Black or African American, non-Hispanic/Latino; 4% Hispanic/Latino; 0.8% Asian, non-Hispanic/Latino; 0.2% Native Hawaiian or other Pacific Islander, non-Hispanic/Latino; 0.5% American Indian or Alaska Native, non-Hispanic/Latino; 4% Two or more races, non-Hispanic/Latino; 2% Race/ethnicity unknown; 2% international; 7% transferred in; 44% live on campus. *Retention:* 76% of full-time freshmen returned.

Freshmen *Admission:* 617 applied, 398 admitted, 230 enrolled. *Average high school GPA:* 3.37. *Test scores:* SAT critical reading scores over 500: 47%;

SAT math scores over 500: 47%; ACT scores over 18: 88%; SAT critical reading scores over 600: 12%; SAT math scores over 600: 21%; ACT scores over 24: 36%; SAT critical reading scores over 700: 3%; SAT math scores over 700: 12%; ACT scores over 30: 9%.

Faculty *Total:* 247, 35% full-time, 30% with terminal degrees. *Student/faculty ratio:* 10:1.

Academics *Calendar:* semesters. *Degrees:* associate, bachelor's, master's, and post-master's certificates. *Special study options:* academic remediation for entering students, accelerated degree program, adult/continuing education programs, advanced placement credit, distance learning, double majors, independent study, internships, off-campus study, part-time degree program, services for LD students, student-designed majors, study abroad, summer session for credit. *ROTC:* Army (c), Air Force (c).

Computers on Campus Students can access the following: campus intranet, computer help desk, free student e-mail accounts, online (class) grades, online (class) registration, online (class) schedules. Campuswide network is available. Wireless service is available via entire campus.

Student Life *Housing:* on-campus residence required through senior year. *Options:* men-only, women-only, disabled students. Campus housing is university owned. Freshman campus housing is guaranteed. *Activities and organizations:* drama/theater group, student-run newspaper, radio and television station, choral group. *Campus security:* 24-hour emergency response devices and patrols, student patrols, late-night transport/escort service, controlled dormitory access. *Student services:* personal/psychological counseling.

Athletics Member NAIA. *Intercollegiate sports:* baseball M(s), basketball M(s)/W(s), cheerleading M(s)/W(s), football M(s), soccer M(s)/W(s), softball W(s), volleyball W(s). *Intramural sports:* basketball M/W, bowling M/W, football M/W, golf M/W, soccer M/W, softball M/W, table tennis M/W, tennis M/W, ultimate Frisbee M/W, volleyball M/W.

Standardized Tests *Required:* SAT or ACT (for admission).

Costs (2011–12) *Comprehensive fee:* $28,500 includes full-time tuition ($20,500), mandatory fees ($1000), and room and board ($7000). Full-time tuition and fees vary according to course load. Part-time tuition and fees vary according to course load. *Room and board:* Room and board charges vary according to board plan and housing facility. *Payment plan:* installment. *Waivers:* senior citizens and employees or children of employees.

Financial Aid Of all full-time matriculated undergraduates who enrolled in 2008, 796 applied for aid, 692 were judged to have need, 97 had their need

fully met. In 2008, 187 non-need-based awards were made. *Average percent of need met:* 65%. *Average financial aid package:* $13,686. *Average need-based loan:* $5638. *Average need-based gift aid:* $8989. *Average non-need-based aid:* $4891. *Average indebtedness upon graduation:* $28,859.

Applying *Options:* electronic application, deferred entrance. *Application fee:* $25. *Required:* high school transcript, minimum 2 GPA, 2 letters of recommendation. *Application deadlines:* 8/1 (freshmen), 8/1 (transfers). *Notification:* continuous (freshmen), continuous (transfers).

Freshman Application Contact Mr. Dennis Miller, Associate Director of Admissions, MidAmerica Nazarene University, 2030 East College Way, Olathe, KS 66062-1899. *Phone:* 913-971-3380. *Toll-free phone:* 800-800-8887. *Fax:* 913-971-3481. *E-mail:* admissions@mnu.edu. *Web site:* http://www.mnu.edu/.

See page 1430 for the College Close-Up.

Newman University

Wichita, Kansas

- **Independent Roman Catholic** comprehensive, founded 1933
- **Urban** 61-acre campus
- **Endowment** $15.9 million
- **Coed** 2,003 undergraduate students, 55% full-time, 63% women, 37% men
- **Minimally difficult** entrance level, 44% of applicants were admitted

Undergraduates 1,100 full-time, 903 part-time. Students come from 25 states and territories; 26 other countries; 14% are from out of state; 6% Black or African American, non-Hispanic/Latino; 10% Hispanic/Latino; 4% Asian, non-Hispanic/Latino; 0.1% Native Hawaiian or other Pacific Islander, non-Hispanic/Latino; 2% American Indian or Alaska Native, non-Hispanic/Latino; 1% Two or more races, non-Hispanic/Latino; 0.4% Race/ethnicity unknown; 5% international; 12% transferred in; 23% live on campus. *Retention:* 71% of full-time freshmen returned.

Freshmen *Admission:* 2,419 applied, 1,070 admitted, 198 enrolled. *Average high school GPA:* 3.47. *Test scores:* SAT critical reading scores over 500: 75%; SAT math scores over 500: 69%; SAT writing scores over 500: 50%; ACT scores over 18: 97%; SAT critical reading scores over 600: 12%; SAT math scores over 600: 19%; SAT writing scores over 600: 12%; ACT scores over 24: 44%; SAT critical reading scores over 700: 12%; ACT scores over 30: 11%.

Faculty *Total:* 183, 42% full-time. *Student/faculty ratio:* 16:1.

Academics *Calendar:* semesters. *Degrees:* associate, bachelor's, and master's. *Special study options:* academic remediation for entering students, accelerated degree program, adult/continuing education programs, advanced placement credit, cooperative education, distance learning, double majors, honors programs, independent study, internships, off-campus study, part-time degree program, services for LD students, student-designed majors, study abroad, summer session for credit. *Unusual degree programs:* 3-2 occupational therapy with Washington University in St. Louis.

Computers on Campus 90 computers/terminals and 300 ports are available on campus for general student use. Students can access the following: computer help desk, free student e-mail accounts, online (class) grades, online (class) registration, online (class) schedules. Campuswide network is available. 100% of college-owned or -operated housing units are wired for high-speed Internet access. Wireless service is available via computer centers, dorm rooms, learning centers, libraries.

Student Life *Housing:* on-campus residence required through sophomore year. *Options:* coed, men-only, women-only, cooperative, disabled students. Campus housing is university owned. Freshman campus housing is guaranteed. *Activities and organizations:* drama/theater group, student-run newspaper, choral group, Chemistry Club, Multicultural Leadership Organization, Pre-Med Club, Health Professions Club, Nursing Club. *Campus security:* 24-hour emergency response devices and patrols, student patrols, late-night transport/escort service, controlled dormitory access. *Student services:* personal/psychological counseling.

Athletics Member NCAA. All Division II. *Intercollegiate sports:* baseball M(s), basketball M(s)/W(s), bowling M(s)/W(s), cross-country running M(s)/W(s), golf M(s)/W(s), soccer M(s)/W(s), softball W(s), tennis M(s)/W(s), volleyball W(s), wrestling M(s). *Intramural sports:* baseball M, basketball M/W, bowling M/W, cheerleading M/W, football M/W, golf M/W, soccer M/W, softball M/W, table tennis M/W, volleyball M/W, weight lifting M/W.

Standardized Tests *Required:* SAT or ACT (for admission).

Costs (2011–12) *Comprehensive fee:* $28,476 includes full-time tuition ($20,866), mandatory fees ($900), and room and board ($6710). Full-time tuition and fees vary according to class time, course load, location, and program. Part-time tuition: $696 per credit hour. Part-time tuition and fees vary according to class time, course load, location, and program. *Required fees:* $15 per credit hour part-time. *College room only:* $3600. Room and board charges vary according to board plan and housing facility. *Payment plan:* installment. *Waivers:* employees or children of employees.

Financial Aid Of all full-time matriculated undergraduates who enrolled in 2009, 1,074 applied for aid, 919 were judged to have need, 146 had their need fully met. 66 Federal Work-Study jobs (averaging $1037). 80 state and other part-time jobs (averaging $994). In 2009, 43 non-need-based awards were made. *Average percent of need met:* 62%. *Average financial aid package:* $14,370. *Average need-based loan:* $4065. *Average need-based gift aid:* $4869. *Average non-need-based aid:* $5673. *Average indebtedness upon graduation:* $23,996.

Applying *Options:* electronic application, early admission, deferred entrance. *Application fee:* $20. *Required:* high school transcript, minimum 2 GPA. *Recommended:* interview. *Application deadlines:* rolling (freshmen), rolling (transfers). *Notification:* continuous (freshmen), continuous (transfers).

Freshman Application Contact Jann Reusser, Admissions Coordinator, Newman University, 3100 McCormick Avenue, Wichita, KS 67213. *Phone:* 316-942-4291 Ext. 2144. *Toll-free phone:* 877-NEWMANU Ext. 2144. *Fax:* 316-942-4483. *E-mail:* reusserj@newmanu.edu. *Web site:* http://www.newmanu.edu/.

Ottawa University

Ottawa, Kansas

- **Independent American Baptist Churches in the USA** comprehensive, founded 1865
- **Small-town** 64-acre campus with easy access to Kansas City
- **Endowment** $15.9 million
- **Coed**
- **Moderately difficult** entrance level

Faculty *Student/faculty ratio:* 18:1.

Academics *Calendar:* semesters. *Degrees:* certificates and bachelor's (also offers master's, adult, international and on-line education programs with significant enrollment not reflected in profile).

Student Life *Campus security:* 24-hour emergency response devices and patrols, controlled dormitory access, locked residence hall entrances.

Athletics Member NAIA.

Standardized Tests *Required:* SAT or ACT (for admission).

Costs (2010–11) *Comprehensive fee:* $27,414 includes full-time tuition ($20,000), mandatory fees ($400), and room and board ($7014). Full-time tuition and fees vary according to course load. Part-time tuition: $833 per credit hour. Part-time tuition and fees vary according to course load. *Required fees:* $17 per credit hour part-time. *Room and board:* Room and board charges vary according to board plan and housing facility.

Applying *Options:* electronic application. *Application fee:* $25. *Required:* high school transcript, minimum 2.5 GPA, rank in upper 50% of high school class. *Required for some:* essay or personal statement. *Recommended:* 2 letters of recommendation, interview.

Freshman Application Contact Ottawa University, 1001 South Cedar, Ottawa, KS 66067-3399. *Phone:* 785-229-1051. *Toll-free phone:* 800-755-5200 Ext. 5559. *Web site:* http://www.ottawa.edu/.

Pittsburg State University

Pittsburg, Kansas

- **State-supported** comprehensive, founded 1903, part of Kansas State Board of Regents
- **Small-town** 630-acre campus
- **Endowment** $48.1 million
- **Coed** 5,891 undergraduate students, 95% full-time, 46% women, 54% men
- **Minimally difficult** entrance level, 86% of applicants were admitted

Undergraduates 5,601 full-time, 290 part-time. Students come from 45 states and territories; 27 other countries; 31% are from out of state; 3% Black or African American, non-Hispanic/Latino; 3% Hispanic/Latino; 0.5% Asian, non-Hispanic/Latino; 0.1% Native Hawaiian or other Pacific Islander, non-Hispanic/Latino; 2% American Indian or Alaska Native, non-Hispanic/Latino; 3% Two or more races, non-Hispanic/Latino; 0.7% Race/ethnicity unknown; 4% international; 9% transferred in; 16% live on campus. *Retention:* 73% of full-time freshmen returned.

Freshmen *Admission:* 2,295 applied, 1,969 admitted, 1,087 enrolled. *Average high school GPA:* 3.25. *Test scores:* ACT scores over 18: 89%; ACT scores over 24: 30%; ACT scores over 30: 3%.

Faculty *Total:* 410, 76% full-time, 64% with terminal degrees. *Student/faculty ratio:* 19:1.

Academics *Calendar:* semesters. *Degrees:* certificates, associate, bachelor's, master's, and post-master's certificates. *Special study options:* academic remediation for entering students, adult/continuing education programs, advanced placement credit, cooperative education, distance learning, double majors, English as a second language, freshman honors college, honors programs, independent study, internships, off-campus study, part-time degree program, services for LD students, student-designed majors, study abroad, summer session for credit. *ROTC:* Army (b).

Computers on Campus 425 computers/terminals are available on campus for general student use. Students can access the following: campus intranet, computer help desk, free student e-mail accounts, online (class) grades, online (class) registration, online (class) schedules. Campuswide network is available. 100% of college-owned or -operated housing units are wired for high-speed Internet access. Wireless service is available via entire campus.

Student Life *Housing:* on-campus residence required for freshman year. *Options:* coed, disabled students. Campus housing is university owned. Freshman applicants given priority for college housing. *Activities and organizations:* drama/theater group, student-run newspaper, radio and television station, choral group, marching band, Student Government Association, student yearbook, student newspaper, Student Activities Council, Students in Free Enterprise (SIFE), national fraternities, national sororities. *Campus security:* 24-hour emergency response devices and patrols, controlled dormitory access. *Student services:* health clinic, personal/psychological counseling, legal services.

Athletics Member NCAA. All Division II. *Intercollegiate sports:* baseball M(s), basketball M(s)/W(s), cheerleading M(s)/W(s), cross-country running M(s)/W(s), football M(s), golf M(s), softball W(s), track and field M(s)/W(s), volleyball W(s). *Intramural sports:* badminton M/W, basketball M/W, fencing M(c)/W(c), football M/W, golf M(c)/W(c), lacrosse M(c), racquetball M/W, rugby M(c), soccer M(c)/W(c), softball M/W, table tennis M/W, tennis M/W, ultimate Frisbee M/W, volleyball M/W, wrestling M(c).

Standardized Tests *Required:* ACT (for admission).

Costs (2010–11) *Tuition:* state resident $3868 full-time, $129 per credit hour part-time; nonresident $12,608 full-time, $420 per credit hour part-time. Part-time tuition and fees vary according to course load. *Required fees:* $980 full-time, $44 per credit hour part-time. *Room and board:* $6016. Room and board charges vary according to board plan and housing facility. *Payment plan:* installment. *Waivers:* children of alumni and employees or children of employees.

Financial Aid Of all full-time matriculated undergraduates who enrolled in 2009, 4,141 applied for aid, 3,260 were judged to have need, 258 had their need fully met. In 2009, 430 non-need-based awards were made. *Average percent of need met:* 75%. *Average financial aid package:* $9900. *Average need-based loan:* $3889. *Average need-based gift aid:* $4525. *Average non-need-based aid:* $2450. *Average indebtedness upon graduation:* $18,516.

Applying *Options:* electronic application. *Application fee:* $30. *Required:* high school transcript. *Required for some:* minimum 2 GPA. *Application deadlines:* rolling (freshmen), rolling (transfers).

Freshman Application Contact Director of Admission, Pittsburg State University, 1701 South Broadway, Pittsburg, KS 66762. *Phone:* 620-235-4251. *Toll-free phone:* 800-854-7488 Ext. 1. *Fax:* 620-235-6003. *E-mail:* psuadmit@pittstate.edu. *Web site:* http://www.pittstate.edu/.

Southwestern College

Winfield, Kansas

- **Independent United Methodist** comprehensive, founded 1885
- **Small-town** 70-acre campus with easy access to Wichita
- **Endowment** $18.7 million
- **Coed** 1,524 undergraduate students, 40% full-time, 47% women, 53% men
- **Minimally difficult** entrance level, 92% of applicants were admitted

Undergraduates 614 full-time, 910 part-time. Students come from 20 states and territories; 11 other countries; 38% are from out of state; 10% Black or African American, non-Hispanic/Latino; 5% Hispanic/Latino; 1% Asian, non-Hispanic/Latino; 0.1% Native Hawaiian or other Pacific Islander, non-Hispanic/Latino; 1% American Indian or Alaska Native, non-Hispanic/Latino; 2% Two or more races, non-Hispanic/Latino; 17% Race/ethnicity unknown; 2% international; 4% transferred in; 70% live on campus. *Retention:* 64% of full-time freshmen returned.

Freshmen *Admission:* 323 applied, 296 admitted, 173 enrolled. *Average high school GPA:* 3.33. *Test scores:* SAT critical reading scores over 500: 14%; SAT math scores over 500: 29%; ACT scores over 18: 89%; SAT math scores over 600: 5%; ACT scores over 24: 28%; ACT scores over 30: 3%.

Faculty *Total:* 107, 46% full-time, 36% with terminal degrees. *Student/faculty ratio:* 9:1.

Academics *Calendar:* semesters. *Degrees:* certificates, bachelor's, master's, post-master's, and postbachelor's certificates. *Special study options:* accelerated degree program, adult/continuing education programs, advanced placement credit, distance learning, double majors, honors programs, independent study, internships, off-campus study, part-time degree program, student-designed majors, study abroad, summer session for credit.

Computers on Campus 30 computers/terminals and 100 ports are available on campus for general student use. Students can access the following: campus

intranet, computer help desk, free student e-mail accounts, online (class) grades, online (class) registration, online (class) schedules. Campuswide network is available. 100% of college-owned or -operated housing units are wired for high-speed Internet access. Wireless service is available via entire campus.

Student Life *Housing:* on-campus residence required through sophomore year. *Options:* coed, men-only, women-only. Campus housing is university owned. Freshman campus housing is guaranteed. *Activities and organizations:* drama/theater group, student-run newspaper, radio and television station, choral group, Discipleship SC, Leadership SC, A Cappella Choir, Concert Band, Southwestern Singers, national fraternities. *Campus security:* 24-hour emergency response devices and patrols, late-night transport/escort service, controlled dormitory access. *Student services:* health clinic, personal/psychological counseling.

Athletics Member NAIA. *Intercollegiate sports:* basketball M(s)/W(s), cross-country running M(s)/W(s), football M(s), golf M(s)/W(s), soccer M(s)/W(s), softball W(s), tennis M(s)/W(s), track and field M(s)/W(s), volleyball W(s). *Intramural sports:* badminton M(c)/W(c), basketball M/W, softball M/W, tennis M/W, ultimate Frisbee M(c)/W(c), volleyball M/W.

Standardized Tests *Required:* SAT or ACT (for admission).

Costs (2011–12) *Comprehensive fee:* $28,002 includes full-time tuition ($21,530), mandatory fees ($150), and room and board ($6322). Full-time tuition and fees vary according to class time, course load, degree level, location, and program. Part-time tuition: $897 per credit hour. Part-time tuition and fees vary according to class time, course load, degree level, location, and program. *College room only:* $2910. Room and board charges vary according to board plan and housing facility. *Payment plan:* installment. *Waivers:* senior citizens and employees or children of employees.

Financial Aid Of all full-time matriculated undergraduates who enrolled in 2008, 497 applied for aid, 460 were judged to have need, 76 had their need fully met. 173 Federal Work-Study jobs (averaging $1099). In 2008, 101 non-need-based awards were made. *Average percent of need met:* 86%. *Average financial aid package:* $17,210. *Average need-based loan:* $5253. *Average need-based gift aid:* $10,752. *Average non-need-based aid:* $8576. *Average indebtedness upon graduation:* $30,794. *Financial aid deadline:* 8/15.

Applying *Options:* electronic application. *Application fee:* $25. *Required:* high school transcript, minimum 2.5 GPA. *Required for some:* 2 letters of recommendation, interview. *Recommended:* essay or personal statement. *Application deadlines:* 8/15 (freshmen), 8/15 (out-of-state freshmen), 8/15 (transfers). *Notification:* continuous (freshmen), continuous (out-of-state freshmen), continuous (transfers).

Freshman Application Contact Southwestern College, 100 College Street, Winfield, KS 67156-2499. *Phone:* 620-229-6364. *Toll-free phone:* 800-846-1543. *Web site:* http://www.sckans.edu/.

Sterling College

Sterling, Kansas

- **Independent Presbyterian** 4-year, founded 1887
- **Rural** 46-acre campus
- **Endowment** $5.6 million
- **Coed**
- **Minimally difficult** entrance level

Faculty *Student/faculty ratio:* 14:1.

Academics *Calendar:* 4-1-4. *Degree:* bachelor's.

Student Life *Campus security:* controlled dormitory access, late night security patrol.

Athletics Member NAIA.

Standardized Tests *Required:* SAT or ACT (for admission).

Costs (2010–11) *One-time required fee:* $100. *Comprehensive fee:* $25,830 includes full-time tuition ($19,000) and room and board ($6830). Part-time tuition: $365 per credit hour. *Room and board:* Room and board charges vary according to board plan and housing facility.

Financial Aid *Of all full-time matriculated undergraduates who enrolled in 2004,* 449 applied for aid, 363 were judged to have need, 176 had their need fully met. 169 Federal Work-Study jobs (averaging $501). 196 state and other part-time jobs (averaging $808). *In 2004,* 77 non-need-based awards were made. *Average percent of need met:* 100. *Average financial aid package:* $15,375. *Average need-based loan:* $4214. *Average need-based gift aid:* $7863. *Average non-need-based aid:* $6817. *Average indebtedness upon graduation:* $9647.

Applying *Options:* electronic application, early action, deferred entrance. *Application fee:* $25. *Required:* high school transcript, minimum 2.2 GPA. *Required for some:* 2 letters of recommendation, audition required for fine arts majors. *Recommended:* essay or personal statement, interview.

Freshman Application Contact Marge Jones, Admissions Office Manager, Sterling College, 125 West Cooper, Sterling, KS 67579. *Phone:* 620-278-4275. *Toll-free phone:* 800-346-1017. *Fax:* 620-278-4416. *E-mail:* admissions@sterling.edu. *Web site:* http://www.sterling.edu/.

Tabor College

Hillsboro, Kansas

- **Independent Mennonite Brethren** comprehensive, founded 1908
- **Small-town** 26-acre campus with easy access to Wichita
- **Endowment** $4.7 million
- **Coed** 646 undergraduate students, 85% full-time, 47% women, 53% men
- **Moderately difficult** entrance level, 94% of applicants were admitted

Undergraduates 548 full-time, 98 part-time. Students come from 33 states and territories; 6 other countries; 46% are from out of state; 9% Black or African American, non-Hispanic/Latino; 9% Hispanic/Latino; 0.9% Asian, non-Hispanic/Latino; 0.3% Native Hawaiian or other Pacific Islander, non-Hispanic/Latino; 0.5% American Indian or Alaska Native, non-Hispanic/Latino; 2% Two or more races, non-Hispanic/Latino; 0.2% Race/ethnicity unknown; 1% international; 11% transferred in; 86% live on campus. *Retention:* 66% of full-time freshmen returned.

Freshmen *Admission:* 414 applied, 388 admitted, 153 enrolled. *Average high school GPA:* 3.25. *Test scores:* SAT critical reading scores over 500: 40%; SAT math scores over 500: 41%; ACT scores over 18: 90%; SAT critical reading scores over 600: 9%; SAT math scores over 600: 10%; ACT scores over 24: 40%; SAT critical reading scores over 700: 2%; ACT scores over 30: 10%.

Faculty *Total:* 80, 43% full-time, 36% with terminal degrees. *Student/faculty ratio:* 13:1.

Academics *Calendar:* 4-1-4. *Degrees:* associate, bachelor's, and master's. *Special study options:* academic remediation for entering students, accelerated degree program, adult/continuing education programs, advanced placement credit, cooperative education, distance learning, double majors, honors programs, independent study, internships, off-campus study, part-time degree program, services for LD students, student-designed majors, study abroad.

Computers on Campus 60 computers/terminals and 450 ports are available on campus for general student use. Students can access the following: campus intranet, computer help desk, free student e-mail accounts, online (class) grades, online (class) registration, online (class) schedules. Campuswide network is available. 100% of college-owned or -operated housing units are wired for high-speed Internet access. Wireless service is available via dorm rooms, learning centers, libraries, student centers.

Student Life *Housing:* on-campus residence required through junior year. *Options:* men-only, women-only, disabled students. Campus housing is university owned. Freshman campus housing is guaranteed. *Activities and organizations:* drama/theater group, student-run newspaper, choral group, Student Activities Board, Campus Ministries Council, Multi-Cultural Student Union, Science Club, Public Relations Student Society of America/ American Marketing Association. *Student services:* personal/psychological counseling.

Athletics Member NAIA. *Intercollegiate sports:* baseball M(s), basketball M(s)/W(s), cheerleading M(s)/W(s), cross-country running M(s)/W(s), football M(s)/W(s), golf M(s)/W(s), soccer M(s)/W(s), softball W(s), tennis M(s)/W(s), track and field M(s)/W(s), volleyball W(s). *Intramural sports:* basketball M/W, football M/W, golf M/W, racquetball M/W, soccer M/W, tennis M/W, track and field M/W, volleyball M/W.

Standardized Tests *Required:* SAT or ACT (for admission).

Costs (2010–11) *One-time required fee:* $175. *Comprehensive fee:* $27,790 includes full-time tuition ($20,170), mandatory fees ($460), and room and board ($7160). Full-time tuition and fees vary according to course load. Part-time tuition: $840 per credit hour. Part-time tuition and fees vary according to course load. *Required fees:* $10 per credit hour part-time. *College room only:* $2820. Room and board charges vary according to board plan, housing facility, and location. *Payment plan:* installment. *Waivers:* employees or children of employees.

Financial Aid Of all full-time matriculated undergraduates who enrolled in 2009, 558 applied for aid, 481 were judged to have need, 109 had their need fully met. 201 Federal Work-Study jobs (averaging $550). In 2009, 75 non-need-based awards were made. *Average percent of need met:* 81%. *Average financial aid package:* $18,977. *Average need-based loan:* $8219. *Average need-based gift aid:* $4241. *Average non-need-based aid:* $7449. *Average indebtedness upon graduation:* $20,500. *Financial aid deadline:* 8/15.

Applying *Options:* electronic application, early admission, deferred entrance. *Application fee:* $30. *Required:* essay or personal statement, high school transcript, minimum 2.5 GPA. *Recommended:* interview. *Application deadlines:* 8/1 (freshmen), 8/1 (out-of-state freshmen), 8/1 (transfers). *Notification:* 8/15 (freshmen), 8/15 (out-of-state freshmen), 8/15 (transfers).

Freshman Application Contact Dr. Linda Cantwell, Vice President of Enrollment Management, Tabor College, 400 South Jefferson, Hillsboro, KS 67063. *Phone:* 620-947-3121 Ext. 1727. *Toll-free phone:* 800-822-6799. *Fax:* 620-947-6276. *E-mail:* lindac@tabor.edu. *Web site:* http://www.tabor.edu/.

The University of Kansas

Lawrence, Kansas

- **State-supported** university, founded 1866, part of Kansas Board of Regents System
- **Suburban** 1000-acre campus with easy access to Kansas City
- **Endowment** $1.5 billion
- **Coed** 20,343 undergraduate students, 90% full-time, 49% women, 51% men
- **Moderately difficult** entrance level, 93% of applicants were admitted

Undergraduates 18,307 full-time, 2,036 part-time. Students come from 51 states and territories; 76 other countries; 21% are from out of state; 3% Black or African American, non-Hispanic/Latino; 5% Hispanic/Latino; 4% Asian, non-Hispanic/Latino; 0.1% Native Hawaiian or other Pacific Islander, non-Hispanic/Latino; 0.7% American Indian or Alaska Native, non-Hispanic/Latino; 0.9% Two or more races, non-Hispanic/Latino; 2% Race/ethnicity unknown; 5% international; 7% transferred in; 22% live on campus. *Retention:* 79% of full-time freshmen returned.

Freshmen *Admission:* 10,157 applied, 9,397 admitted, 3,702 enrolled. *Average high school GPA:* 3.5. *Test scores:* ACT scores over 18: 97%; ACT scores over 24: 62%; ACT scores over 30: 14%.

Faculty *Total:* 1,700, 77% full-time, 83% with terminal degrees. *Student/faculty ratio:* 20:1.

Academics *Calendar:* semesters. *Degrees:* bachelor's, master's, doctoral-professional, doctoral-research/scholarship, and post-master's certificates (University of Kansas is a single institution with academic programs and facilities at two primary locations: Lawrence and Kansas City). *Special study options:* academic remediation for entering students, accelerated degree program, advanced placement credit, cooperative education, distance learning, double majors, English as a second language, honors programs, independent study, internships, part-time degree program, services for LD students, study abroad, summer session for credit. *ROTC:* Army (b), Navy (b), Air Force (b).

Computers on Campus 1,500 computers/terminals are available on campus for general student use. Students can access the following: campus intranet, computer help desk, free student e-mail accounts, online (class) grades, online (class) registration, online (class) schedules. Campuswide network is available. 100% of college-owned or -operated housing units are wired for high-speed Internet access. Wireless service is available via entire campus.

Student Life *Housing options:* coed, women-only, cooperative. Campus housing is university owned. *Activities and organizations:* drama/theater group, student-run newspaper, radio and television station, choral group, marching band, Association of University Residence Halls, Hillel, Panhellenic Association, International Student Association, Interfraternity Council, national fraternities, national sororities. *Campus security:* 24-hour emergency response devices and patrols, late-night transport/escort service, controlled dormitory access, University police department. *Student services:* health clinic, personal/psychological counseling, women's center, legal services.

Athletics Member NCAA. All Division I except football (Division I-A). *Intercollegiate sports:* baseball M(s), basketball M(s)/W(s), crew W(s), cross-country running M(s)/W(s), golf M(s)/W(s), ice hockey M(c), rugby M(c), soccer W(s), softball W(s), swimming and diving W(s), tennis W(s), track and field M(s)/W(s), ultimate Frisbee M(c)/W(c), volleyball W(s). *Intramural sports:* baseball M(c), basketball M/W, bowling M/W, crew M(c)/W(c), equestrian sports M(c)/W(c), fencing M(c)/W(c), football M/W, golf M(c)/W(c), lacrosse M(c)/W(c), racquetball M(c)/W(c), rock climbing M(c)/W(c), rugby W(c), sailing M(c)/W(c), soccer M(c)/W(c), softball M/W, swimming and diving M(c)/W(c), table tennis M(c)/W(c), tennis M(c)/W(c), ultimate Frisbee M/W, volleyball M(c)/W(c), water polo M(c), wrestling M(c).

Standardized Tests *Required:* SAT or ACT (for admission).

Costs (2010–11) *Tuition:* state resident $7875 full-time, $263 per credit hour part-time; nonresident $20,680 full-time, $689 per credit hour part-time. Full-time tuition and fees vary according to program, reciprocity agreements, and student level. Part-time tuition and fees vary according to program, reciprocity agreements, and student level. No tuition increase for student's term of enrollment. *Required fees:* $858 full-time, $71 per credit hour part-time. *Room and board:* $6982; room only: $3642. Room and board charges vary according to board plan and housing facility. *Payment plan:* installment. *Waivers:* employees or children of employees.

Financial Aid Of all full-time matriculated undergraduates who enrolled in 2008, 14,388 applied for aid, 8,108 were judged to have need, 2,329 had their need fully met. 537 Federal Work-Study jobs (averaging $2647). 90 state and other part-time jobs (averaging $4360). In 2008, 1943 non-need-based awards were made. *Average percent of need met:* 54%. *Average financial aid package:* $11,520. *Average need-based loan:* $3554. *Average need-based gift aid:* $6181. *Average non-need-based aid:* $3377. *Average indebtedness upon graduation:* $23,319.

Applying *Options:* electronic application. *Application fee:* $30. *Required:* high school transcript, minimum 2 GPA, Kansas Board of Regents admissions criteria. *Required for some:* minimum 2.5 GPA. *Application deadlines:* 4/1 (freshmen), 5/1 (transfers). *Notification:* continuous (freshmen), continuous (transfers).

Freshman Application Contact Ms. Lisa Pinamonti Kress, Director of Admissions and Scholarships, The University of Kansas, KU Visitor Center, 1502 Iowa Street, Lawrence, KS 66045-7576. *Phone:* 785-864-3911. *Toll-free phone:* 888-686-7323. *Fax:* 785-864-5006. *E-mail:* adm@ku.edu. *Web site:* http://www.ku.edu/.

University of Phoenix–Wichita Campus
Wichita, Kansas

Freshman Application Contact Ms. Audra McQuarie, Registrar/Executive Director, University of Phoenix–Wichita Campus, 4035 South Riverpoint Parkway, Mail Stop CF-L101, Phoenix, AZ 85040. *Phone:* 480-557-6151. *Toll-free phone:* 800-776-4867 (in-state); 800-228-7240 (out-of-state). *Fax:* 480-643-3068. *E-mail:* audra.mcquarie@phoenix.edu. *Web site:* http://www.phoenix.edu/.

University of Saint Mary
Leavenworth, Kansas

- **Independent Roman Catholic** comprehensive, founded 1923
- **Small-town** 240-acre campus with easy access to Kansas City
- **Endowment** $12.8 million
- **Coed** 780 undergraduate students, 68% full-time, 62% women, 38% men
- **Moderately difficult** entrance level, 68% of applicants were admitted

Undergraduates 532 full-time, 248 part-time. Students come from 38 states and territories; 1 other country; 32% are from out of state; 12% Black or African American, non-Hispanic/Latino; 6% Hispanic/Latino; 1% Asian, non-Hispanic/Latino; 0.4% American Indian or Alaska Native, non-Hispanic/Latino; 13% Race/ethnicity unknown; 0.1% international; 11% transferred in; 42% live on campus. *Retention:* 56% of full-time freshmen returned.

Freshmen *Admission:* 731 applied, 495 admitted, 134 enrolled. *Average high school GPA:* 3.22. *Test scores:* SAT critical reading scores over 500: 26%; SAT math scores over 500: 47%; ACT scores over 18: 80%; SAT math scores over 600: 12%; ACT scores over 24: 29%; SAT math scores over 700: 3%; ACT scores over 30: 5%.

Faculty *Total:* 104, 40% full-time, 30% with terminal degrees. *Student/faculty ratio:* 10:1.

Academics *Calendar:* semesters. *Degrees:* certificates, associate, bachelor's, and master's. *Special study options:* adult/continuing education programs, advanced placement credit, cooperative education, distance learning, double majors, honors programs, independent study, internships, off-campus study, part-time degree program, services for LD students, student-designed majors, study abroad, summer session for credit. *ROTC:* Army (c), Air Force (c).

Computers on Campus 45 computers/terminals are available on campus for general student use. Students can access the following: campus intranet, computer help desk, free student e-mail accounts, online (class) grades, online (class) registration, online (class) schedules. Campuswide network is available. 100% of college-owned or -operated housing units are wired for high-speed Internet access. Wireless service is available via entire campus.

Student Life *Housing:* on-campus residence required through sophomore year. *Options:* coed. Campus housing is university owned. Freshman campus housing is guaranteed. *Activities and organizations:* drama/theater group, choral group, Student Government Association, BACCHUS, Theatrical Union, campus ministry, Amnesty International. *Campus security:* late-night transport/escort service, controlled dormitory access. *Student services:* health clinic, personal/psychological counseling.

Athletics Member NAIA. *Intercollegiate sports:* baseball M(s), basketball M(s)/W(s), football M(s), soccer M(s)/W(s), softball W(s), volleyball W(s). *Intramural sports:* badminton M/W, basketball M/W, bowling M/W, football M, racquetball M/W, soccer M/W, softball W, table tennis M/W, ultimate Frisbee M/W, volleyball M/W, weight lifting M/W.

Standardized Tests *Required:* SAT or ACT (for admission).

Costs (2011–12) *Comprehensive fee:* $27,840 includes full-time tuition ($20,300), mandatory fees ($470), and room and board ($7070). Full-time tuition and fees vary according to class time, course load, location, and program. Part-time tuition: $390 per credit. Part-time tuition and fees vary according to class time, course load, location, and program. *Required fees:* $110 per term part-time. *Room and board:* Room and board charges vary according to board plan and housing facility. *Payment plan:* installment. *Waivers:* senior citizens and employees or children of employees.

Financial Aid *Average percent of need met:* 82%.

Applying *Options:* electronic application. *Application fee:* $25. *Required:* high school transcript, minimum 2.5 GPA. *Recommended:* 1 letter of recom-

mendation, interview. *Application deadlines:* rolling (freshmen), rolling (transfers). *Notification:* continuous (freshmen), continuous (transfers).

Freshman Application Contact Mr. Ken Wuertzberger, Director of Admissions, University of Saint Mary, 4100 South Fourth Street, Leavenworth, KS 66048. *Phone:* 913-758-6118. *Toll-free phone:* 800-752-7043. *Fax:* 913-758-6140. *E-mail:* admiss@stmary.edu. *Web site:* http://www.stmary.edu/.

Washburn University
Topeka, Kansas

- **City-supported** comprehensive, founded 1865
- **Urban** 160-acre campus with easy access to Kansas City
- **Endowment** $139.0 million
- **Coed** 6,321 undergraduate students, 65% full-time, 60% women, 40% men
- **Noncompetitive** entrance level, 100% of applicants were admitted

Undergraduates 4,088 full-time, 2,233 part-time. Students come from 40 states and territories; 38 other countries; 7% are from out of state; 10% transferred in; 10% live on campus. *Retention:* 66% of full-time freshmen returned.

Freshmen *Admission:* 1,942 applied, 1,942 admitted, 915 enrolled. *Average high school GPA:* 3.3. *Test scores:* ACT scores over 18: 80%; ACT scores over 24: 24%; ACT scores over 30: 2%.

Faculty *Total:* 527, 49% full-time, 62% with terminal degrees. *Student/faculty ratio:* 16:1.

Academics *Calendar:* semesters. *Degrees:* certificates, associate, bachelor's, master's, doctoral-professional, and postbachelor's certificates. *Special study options:* academic remediation for entering students, adult/continuing education programs, advanced placement credit, cooperative education, distance learning, double majors, English as a second language, honors programs, independent study, internships, off-campus study, part-time degree program, services for LD students, student-designed majors, study abroad, summer session for credit. *ROTC:* Army (b), Navy (c), Air Force (c). *Unusual degree programs:* 3-2 engineering with University of Kansas, Kansas State University.

Computers on Campus 400 computers/terminals are available on campus for general student use. Students can access the following: campus intranet, computer help desk, free student e-mail accounts, online (class) grades, online (class) registration, online (class) schedules. Campuswide network is available. 100% of college-owned or -operated housing units are wired for high-speed Internet access. Wireless service is available via entire campus.

Student Life *Housing options:* coed. Campus housing is university owned. *Activities and organizations:* drama/theater group, student-run newspaper, television station, choral group, marching band, national fraternities, national sororities. *Campus security:* 24-hour emergency response devices and patrols, student patrols, late-night transport/escort service. *Student services:* health clinic, personal/psychological counseling, legal services.

Athletics Member NCAA. All Division II. *Intercollegiate sports:* baseball M(s), basketball M(s)/W(s), cheerleading M(s)/W(s), football M(s), golf M(s), soccer W(s), softball W(s), tennis M(s)/W(s), volleyball W(s). *Intramural sports:* badminton M/W, basketball M/W, crew M(c)/W(c), football M/W, golf M/W, rugby M(c), soccer M/W, softball M/W, table tennis M/W, tennis M/W, volleyball M/W.

Standardized Tests *Required:* ACT (for admission).

Costs (2010–11) *Tuition:* state resident $6210 full-time, $207 per credit hour part-time; nonresident $14,100 full-time, $470 per credit hour part-time. Full-time tuition and fees vary according to program. Part-time tuition and fees vary according to program. *Required fees:* $86 full-time, $21 per term part-time. *Room and board:* $5982; room only: $3332. Room and board charges vary according to board plan and housing facility. *Payment plan:* installment. *Waivers:* senior citizens and employees or children of employees.

Financial Aid Of all full-time matriculated undergraduates who enrolled in 2009, 3,612 applied for aid, 2,624 were judged to have need, 305 had their need fully met. 241 Federal Work-Study jobs (averaging $2698). 5 state and other part-time jobs (averaging $7877). In 2009, 582 non-need-based awards were made. *Average percent of need met:* 45%. *Average financial aid package:* $9078. *Average need-based loan:* $4298. *Average need-based gift aid:* $4938. *Average non-need-based aid:* $1861. *Average indebtedness upon graduation:* $17,017.

Applying *Options:* electronic application, early admission. *Application fee:* $20. *Required:* high school transcript. *Application deadlines:* 8/1 (freshmen), 8/1 (transfers). *Notification:* continuous (freshmen), continuous (transfers).

Freshman Application Contact Mr. Morgan Boyack, Director of Admissions, Washburn University, 1700 SW College, MO 114, Topeka, KS 66621. *Phone:* 785-670-1030. *Toll-free phone:* 800-332-0291. *Fax:* 785-670-1113. *E-mail:* admissions@washburn.edu. *Web site:* http://www.washburn.edu/.

Wichita State University
Wichita, Kansas

- **State-supported** university, founded 1895, part of Kansas State Board of Education
- **Urban** 335-acre campus
- **Endowment** $199.3 million
- **Coed** 11,763 undergraduate students, 69% full-time, 54% women, 46% men
- **Noncompetitive** entrance level, 90% of applicants were admitted

Undergraduates 8,174 full-time, 3,589 part-time. Students come from 46 states and territories; 111 other countries; 4% are from out of state; 7% Black or African American, non-Hispanic/Latino; 6% Hispanic/Latino; 6% Asian, non-Hispanic/Latino; 1% American Indian or Alaska Native, non-Hispanic/Latino; 1% Two or more races, non-Hispanic/Latino; 6% Race/ethnicity unknown; 6% international; 12% transferred in; 8% live on campus. *Retention:* 70% of full-time freshmen returned.

Freshmen *Admission:* 2,840 applied, 2,570 admitted, 1,305 enrolled. *Average high school GPA:* 3.34. *Test scores:* SAT critical reading scores over 500: 62%; SAT math scores over 500: 77%; ACT scores over 18: 92%; SAT critical reading scores over 600: 29%; SAT math scores over 600: 39%; ACT scores over 24: 47%; SAT critical reading scores over 700: 7%; SAT math scores over 700: 9%; ACT scores over 30: 7%.

Faculty *Total:* 487, 89% full-time, 73% with terminal degrees. *Student/faculty ratio:* 20:1.

Academics *Calendar:* semesters. *Degrees:* certificates, associate, bachelor's, master's, doctoral-professional, doctoral-research/scholarship, post-master's, and postbachelor's certificates. *Special study options:* academic remediation for entering students, accelerated degree program, advanced placement credit, cooperative education, distance learning, double majors, English as a second language, freshman honors college, honors programs, independent study, internships, off-campus study, part-time degree program, services for LD students, study abroad, summer session for credit. *Unusual degree programs:* 3-2 nursing; accounting.

Computers on Campus 1,500 computers/terminals are available on campus for general student use. Students can access the following: computer help desk, free student e-mail accounts, online (class) grades, online (class) registration, online (class) schedules, online Blackboard. Campuswide network is available. 100% of college-owned or -operated housing units are wired for high-speed Internet access. Wireless service is available via entire campus.

Student Life *Housing:* on-campus residence required for freshman year. *Options:* coed, disabled students. Campus housing is university owned. *Activities and organizations:* drama/theater group, student-run newspaper, radio and television station, choral group, Golden Key Honor Society, WSU Green Group, Criminal Justice Society, Future Health Care Professionals, Students in Free Enterprise (SIFE), national fraternities, national sororities. *Campus security:* 24-hour emergency response devices and patrols, student patrols, late-night transport/escort service, controlled dormitory access, bicycle patrols by campus security. *Student services:* health clinic, personal/psychological counseling, women's center, legal services.

Athletics Member NCAA. All Division I. *Intercollegiate sports:* baseball M(s), basketball M(s)/W(s), bowling M(s)/W(s), cheerleading M/W, cross-country running M(s)/W(s), golf M(s)/W(s), ice hockey M(c), rock climbing M(c)/W(c), soccer M(c), softball W(s), table tennis M(c)/W(c), tennis M(s)/W(s), track and field M(s)/W(s), volleyball M(c)/W(s), wrestling M(c)/W(c). *Intramural sports:* badminton M/W, basketball M/W, bowling M/W, crew M/W, football M/W, golf M/W, racquetball M/W, soccer M/W, softball M/W, swimming and diving M/W, table tennis M/W, tennis M/W, track and field M/W, volleyball M/W.

Standardized Tests *Required for some:* SAT or ACT (for admission). *Recommended:* SAT or ACT (for admission).

Costs (2010–11) *Tuition:* state resident $4722 full-time, $157 per credit hour part-time; nonresident $12,756 full-time, $425 per credit hour part-time. Full-time tuition and fees vary according to course load, degree level, and student level. Part-time tuition and fees vary according to course load, degree level, and student level. *Required fees:* $1168 full-time. *Room and board:* $6200. Room and board charges vary according to board plan and housing facility. *Payment plan:* installment. *Waivers:* senior citizens and employees or children of employees.

Financial Aid Of all full-time matriculated undergraduates who enrolled in 2008, 6,549 applied for aid, 3,562 were judged to have need, 2,447 had their need fully met. 236 Federal Work-Study jobs (averaging $1900). In 2008, 1380 non-need-based awards were made. *Average percent of need met:* 51%. *Average financial aid package:* $7674. *Average need-based loan:* $4733. *Average need-based gift aid:* $4632. *Average non-need-based aid:* $1830. *Average indebtedness upon graduation:* $15,847.

Applying *Options:* electronic application, deferred entrance. *Application fee:* $30. *Required for some:* minimum 2.5 GPA, rank in upper one-third of high school class or complete the pre-college curriculum with a minimum 2.0 GPA (2.5 GPA for nonresidents). *Recommended:* high school transcript. *Applica-*

tion deadlines: rolling (freshmen), rolling (transfers). *Notification:* continuous (freshmen), continuous (transfers).

Freshman Application Contact Wichita State University, 1845 North Fairmount, Wichita, KS 67260. *Phone:* 316-978-3085. *Toll-free phone:* 800-362-2594. *Web site:* http://www.wichita.edu/.

KENTUCKY

Alice Lloyd College
Pippa Passes, Kentucky

Freshman Application Contact Mr. Ronnie Collins, Director of Admissions, Alice Lloyd College, 100 Purpose Road, Pippa Passes, KY 41844. *Phone:* 606-368-6036. *Fax:* 606-368-6215. *E-mail:* ronniecollins@alc.edu. *Web site:* http://www.alc.edu/.

Asbury University
Wilmore, Kentucky

- **Independent nondenominational** comprehensive, founded 1890
- **Small-town** 400-acre campus with easy access to Lexington
- **Coed** 1,481 undergraduate students, 90% full-time, 62% women, 38% men
- **Moderately difficult** entrance level, 64% of applicants were admitted

Undergraduates 1,328 full-time, 153 part-time. Students come from 42 states and territories; 19 other countries; 52% are from out of state; 5% transferred in; 80% live on campus. *Retention:* 75% of full-time freshmen returned.

Freshmen *Admission:* 789 applied, 507 admitted, 285 enrolled. *Average high school GPA:* 3.65. *Test scores:* SAT critical reading scores over 500: 79%; SAT math scores over 500: 72%; ACT scores over 18: 96%; SAT critical reading scores over 600: 49%; SAT math scores over 600: 32%; ACT scores over 24: 54%; SAT critical reading scores over 700: 12%; SAT math scores over 700: 3%; ACT scores over 30: 13%.

Faculty *Total:* 156, 54% full-time, 55% with terminal degrees. *Student/faculty ratio:* 14:1.

Academics *Calendar:* semesters. *Degrees:* associate, bachelor's, and master's. *Special study options:* adult/continuing education programs, advanced placement credit, distance learning, double majors, off-campus study, study abroad, summer session for credit. *ROTC:* Army (c), Air Force (c). *Unusual degree programs:* 3-2 engineering with University of Kentucky.

Computers on Campus 200 computers/terminals are available on campus for general student use. Students can access the following: campus intranet, computer help desk, free student e-mail accounts, online (class) grades, online (class) registration, online (class) schedules. Campuswide network is available. 100% of college-owned or -operated housing units are wired for high-speed Internet access. Wireless service is available via classrooms, computer labs, libraries, student centers.

Student Life *Housing:* on-campus residence required through senior year. *Options:* men-only, women-only. Campus housing is university owned. Freshman campus housing is guaranteed. *Activities and organizations:* drama/theater group, student-run newspaper, radio and television station, choral group, Fellowship of Christian Athletes, Impact (community service), Christian Service Association, ministry teams, Student-Faculty Council. *Campus security:* 24-hour emergency response devices, late-night transport/escort service, controlled dormitory access, late night security personnel. *Student services:* health clinic, personal/psychological counseling.

Athletics Member NAIA, NCCAA. *Intercollegiate sports:* baseball M(s), basketball M(s)/W(s), cross-country running M(s)/W(s), golf M(s)/W(s), soccer M(s)/W(s), softball W(s), swimming and diving M(s)/W(s), tennis M(s)/W(s), volleyball W(s). *Intramural sports:* basketball M/W, football M/W, golf M/W, racquetball M/W, soccer M/W, softball M/W, ultimate Frisbee M/W, volleyball M/W.

Standardized Tests *Required:* SAT or ACT (for admission). *Required for some:* ACT (for admission).

Costs (2011–12) *Comprehensive fee:* $29,863 includes full-time tuition ($24,058), mandatory fees ($171), and room and board ($5634). Full-time tuition and fees vary according to course load and program. Part-time tuition: $925 per credit hour. Part-time tuition and fees vary according to course load and program. *College room only:* $3270. Room and board charges vary according to board plan, housing facility, and location. *Payment plan:* installment. *Waivers:* senior citizens and employees or children of employees.

Financial Aid Of all full-time matriculated undergraduates who enrolled in 2008, 1,061 applied for aid, 915 were judged to have need, 234 had their need fully met. In 2008, 131 non-need-based awards were made. *Average percent of need met:* 80%. *Average financial aid package:* $17,754. *Average need-based loan:* $3897. *Average need-based gift aid:* $11,667. *Average non-need-based aid:* $10,252. *Average indebtedness upon graduation:* $29,411.

Applying *Options:* electronic application, early admission, deferred entrance. *Required:* essay or personal statement, high school transcript, minimum 2.5 GPA, 1 letter of recommendation. *Required for some:* interview. *Application deadlines:* rolling (freshmen), rolling (transfers). *Notification:* continuous (freshmen), continuous (transfers).
Freshman Application Contact Mrs. Lisa D. Harper, Director of Admissions, Asbury University, One Macklem Drive, Wilmore, KY 40390. *Phone:* 800-888-1818. *Toll-free phone:* 800-888-1818. *E-mail:* admissions@asbury.edu. *Web site:* http://www.asbury.edu/.

Beckfield College
Florence, Kentucky
Freshman Application Contact Mrs. Leah Boerger, Director of Admissions, Beckfield College, 16 Spiral Drive, Florence, KY 41042. *Phone:* 859-371-9393. *E-mail:* lboerger@beckfield.edu. *Web site:* http://www.beckfield.edu/.

Bellarmine University
Louisville, Kentucky
- **Independent Roman Catholic** comprehensive, founded 1950
- **Suburban** 144-acre campus with easy access to Louisville
- **Endowment** $32.8 million
- **Coed** 2,612 undergraduate students, 86% full-time, 65% women, 35% men
- **Moderately difficult** entrance level, 51% of applicants were admitted

Undergraduates 2,241 full-time, 371 part-time. Students come from 31 states and territories; 30 other countries; 31% are from out of state; 0.3% Black or African American, non-Hispanic/Latino; 3% Hispanic/Latino; 3% Asian, non-Hispanic/Latino; 1% Native Hawaiian or other Pacific Islander, non-Hispanic/Latino; 0.1% American Indian or Alaska Native, non-Hispanic/Latino; 82% Two or more races, non-Hispanic/Latino; 7% Race/ethnicity unknown; 1% international; 3% transferred in; 44% live on campus. *Retention:* 83% of full-time freshmen returned.
Freshmen *Admission:* 6,816 applied, 3,507 admitted, 577 enrolled. *Average high school GPA:* 3.52. *Test scores:* SAT critical reading scores over 500: 72%; SAT math scores over 500: 76%; ACT scores over 18: 100%; SAT critical reading scores over 600: 26%; SAT math scores over 600: 28%; ACT scores over 24: 55%; SAT critical reading scores over 700: 1%; SAT math scores over 700: 4%; ACT scores over 30: 8%.
Faculty *Total:* 320, 43% full-time, 53% with terminal degrees. *Student/faculty ratio:* 13:1.
Academics *Calendar:* semesters. *Degrees:* bachelor's, master's, doctoral-professional, and postbachelor's certificates. *Special study options:* accelerated degree program, adult/continuing education programs, advanced placement credit, double majors, honors programs, independent study, internships, off-campus study, part-time degree program, services for LD students, student-designed majors, study abroad, summer session for credit. *ROTC:* Army (c), Air Force (c).
Computers on Campus 434 computers/terminals and 434 ports are available on campus for general student use. Students can access the following: campus intranet, computer help desk, free student e-mail accounts, online (class) grades, online (class) registration, online (class) schedules. Campuswide network is available. 100% of college-owned or -operated housing units are wired for high-speed Internet access. Wireless service is available via classrooms, computer centers, computer labs, dorm rooms, learning centers, libraries, student centers.
Student Life *Housing:* on-campus residence required through junior year. *Options:* coed, men-only, women-only, disabled students. Campus housing is university owned. Freshman campus housing is guaranteed. *Activities and organizations:* drama/theater group, student-run newspaper, radio station, choral group, student government, Bellarmine Activities Council, Knights Nation, Fellowship of Christian Athletes, Delta Sigma Pi Knights Nation, national fraternities, national sororities. *Campus security:* 24-hour emergency response devices and patrols, student patrols, late-night transport/escort service, controlled dormitory access, 24-hour locked residence hall entrances, security cameras. *Student services:* health clinic, personal/psychological counseling.
Athletics Member NCAA. All Division II except lacrosse (Division I). *Intercollegiate sports:* baseball M(s), basketball M(s)/W(s), bowling M/W(s), cross-country running M(s)/W(s), field hockey W(s), golf M(s)/W(s), lacrosse M(s), soccer M(s)/W(s), softball W(s), swimming and diving M(c)/W(c), tennis M(s)/W(s), track and field M(s)/W(s), volleyball W(s). *Intramural sports:* basketball M/W, bowling M/W, football M/W, golf M/W, soccer M/W, softball M/W, table tennis M/W, tennis M/W, ultimate Frisbee M/W, volleyball M/W, weight lifting M/W.
Standardized Tests *Required:* SAT or ACT (for admission).
Costs (2010–11) *One-time required fee:* $300. *Comprehensive fee:* $39,130 includes full-time tuition ($29,160), mandatory fees ($1150), and room and board ($8820). Part-time tuition: $690 per credit hour. *Required fees:* $45 per

course part-time. *College room only:* $5200. Room and board charges vary according to board plan and housing facility. *Payment plan:* installment. *Waivers:* senior citizens and employees or children of employees.
Financial Aid Of all full-time matriculated undergraduates who enrolled in 2009, 1,828 applied for aid, 1,699 were judged to have need, 225 had their need fully met. 241 Federal Work-Study jobs (averaging $1661). In 2009, 471 non-need-based awards were made. *Average percent of need met:* 63%. *Average financial aid package:* $22,192. *Average need-based loan:* $3428. *Average need-based gift aid:* $16,878. *Average non-need-based aid:* $17,265. *Average indebtedness upon graduation:* $23,925.
Applying *Options:* electronic application, early admission, early action, deferred entrance. *Application fee:* $25. *Required:* high school transcript, minimum 2.5 GPA, 1 letter of recommendation. *Required for some:* essay or personal statement. *Recommended:* interview. *Application deadlines:* 8/15 (freshmen), 11/1 (early action). *Notification:* continuous (freshmen), 11/15 (early action).
Freshman Application Contact Mr. Timothy A. Sturgeon, Dean of Admission, Bellarmine University, 2001 Newburg Road, Louisville, KY 40205-0671. *Phone:* 502-272-8131. *Toll-free phone:* 800-274-4723 Ext. 8131. *E-mail:* admissions@bellarmine.edu. *Web site:* http://www.bellarmine.edu/.

Berea College
Berea, Kentucky
- **Independent** 4-year, founded 1855
- **Small-town** 140-acre campus
- **Endowment** $843.7 million
- **Coed** 1,613 undergraduate students, 97% full-time, 58% women, 42% men
- **Moderately difficult** entrance level, 17% of applicants were admitted

Undergraduates 1,564 full-time, 49 part-time. Students come from 45 states and territories; 58 other countries; 56% are from out of state; 14% Black or African American, non-Hispanic/Latino; 2% Hispanic/Latino; 0.9% Asian, non-Hispanic/Latino; 0.1% Native Hawaiian or other Pacific Islander, non-Hispanic/Latino; 0.4% American Indian or Alaska Native, non-Hispanic/Latino; 5% Two or more races, non-Hispanic/Latino; 8% Race/ethnicity unknown; 7% international; 5% transferred in; 86% live on campus. *Retention:* 79% of full-time freshmen returned.
Freshmen *Admission:* 3,264 applied, 564 admitted, 429 enrolled. *Average high school GPA:* 3.42. *Test scores:* SAT critical reading scores over 500: 82%; SAT math scores over 500: 76%; SAT writing scores over 500: 72%; ACT scores over 18: 100%; SAT critical reading scores over 600: 54%; SAT math scores over 600: 31%; SAT writing scores over 600: 31%; ACT scores over 24: 57%; SAT critical reading scores over 700: 6%; SAT math scores over 700: 1%; SAT writing scores over 700: 4%; ACT scores over 30: 5%.
Faculty *Total:* 158, 75% full-time, 73% with terminal degrees. *Student/faculty ratio:* 11:1.
Academics *Calendar:* 4-1-4. *Degree:* bachelor's. *Special study options:* academic remediation for entering students, advanced placement credit, double majors, English as a second language, honors programs, independent study, internships, off-campus study, services for LD students, student-designed majors, study abroad, summer session for credit. *Unusual degree programs:* 3-2 engineering with Washington University in St. Louis, University of Kentucky.
Computers on Campus 7,000 ports are available on campus for general student use. Students can access the following: campus intranet, computer help desk, free student e-mail accounts, online (class) grades, online (class) registration, online (class) schedules. Campuswide network is available. 100% of college-owned or -operated housing units are wired for high-speed Internet access. Wireless service is available via classrooms, learning centers, libraries, student centers.
Student Life *Housing:* on-campus residence required through senior year. *Options:* men-only, women-only. Campus housing is university owned. Freshman campus housing is guaranteed. *Activities and organizations:* drama/theater group, student-run newspaper, choral group, Campus Activities Board, Cosmopolitan Club, CELTS (Center for Excellence in Learning through Service), Black Cultural Center, African Student Association. *Campus security:* 24-hour emergency response devices and patrols, late-night transport/escort service, controlled dormitory access, crime prevention programs. *Student services:* health clinic, personal/psychological counseling, women's center.
Athletics Member NAIA. *Intercollegiate sports:* baseball M, basketball M/W, cross-country running M/W, golf M, soccer M/W, softball W, swimming and diving M/W, tennis M/W, track and field M/W, volleyball W. *Intramural sports:* basketball M/W, football M/W, racquetball M/W, soccer M/W, softball M/W, ultimate Frisbee M/W, volleyball M/W.
Standardized Tests *Required:* SAT or ACT (for admission).
Costs (2010–11) *Comprehensive fee:* includes mandatory fees ($910) and room and board ($5574). financial aid is provided to all students for tuition costs.

Financial Aid Of all full-time matriculated undergraduates who enrolled in 2009, 1,495 applied for aid, 1,495 were judged to have need. *Average percent of need met:* 93%. *Average financial aid package:* $32,141. *Average need-based loan:* $213. *Average need-based gift aid:* $29,964. *Average indebtedness upon graduation:* $8133.
Applying *Options:* electronic application. *Required:* essay or personal statement, high school transcript, interview, financial aid application. *Recommended:* 2 letters of recommendation. *Application deadlines:* 4/30 (freshmen), rolling (transfers). *Notification:* continuous (freshmen), continuous (transfers).
Freshman Application Contact Mr. Luke Hodson, Director of Admissions/Operations, Berea College, CPO 2220, Berea, KY 40404. *Phone:* 859-985-3500. *Toll-free phone:* 800-326-5948. *Fax:* 859-985-3512. *E-mail:* admissions@berea.edu. *Web site:* http://www.berea.edu/.

Brescia University

Owensboro, Kentucky

- **Independent Roman Catholic** comprehensive, founded 1950
- **Urban** 9-acre campus
- **Endowment** $7.1 million
- **Coed**
- **Moderately difficult** entrance level

Faculty *Student/faculty ratio:* 11:1.
Academics *Calendar:* semesters. *Degrees:* certificates, associate, bachelor's, master's, and postbachelor's certificates.
Student Life *Campus security:* 24-hour emergency response devices, late-night transport/escort service, controlled dormitory access.
Athletics Member NAIA.
Standardized Tests *Required:* SAT or ACT (for admission).
Costs (2010–11) *One-time required fee:* $120. *Comprehensive fee:* $25,390 includes full-time tuition ($16,950), mandatory fees ($440), and room and board ($8000). Full-time tuition and fees vary according to class time and course load. Part-time tuition: $495 per credit hour. Part-time tuition and fees vary according to class time and course load. *Room and board:* Room and board charges vary according to board plan and housing facility.
Financial Aid *Of all full-time matriculated undergraduates who enrolled in 2009,* 609 applied for aid, 581 were judged to have need. 64 Federal Work-Study jobs (averaging $1200). 15 state and other part-time jobs (averaging $2500). *Average indebtedness upon graduation:* $18,638.
Applying *Options:* electronic application, deferred entrance. *Application fee:* $25. *Required:* high school transcript, GPA coincides with test scores. *Required for some:* essay or personal statement, 1 letter of recommendation, interview.
Freshman Application Contact Brescia University, 717 Frederica Street, Owensboro, KY 42301-3023. *Phone:* 270-686-4241 Ext. 241. *Toll-free phone:* 877-273-7242. *Web site:* http://www.brescia.edu/.

Brown Mackie College–Louisville

Louisville, Kentucky

- **Proprietary** primarily 2-year, founded 1972, part of Education Management Corporation
- **Suburban** campus
- **Coed**

Academics *Calendar:* quarters. *Degrees:* certificates, diplomas, associate, and bachelor's.
Costs (2010–11) *Tuition:* Tuition varies by program. Students should contact Brown Mackie College for tuition information.
Freshman Application Contact Brown Mackie College–Louisville, 3605 Fern Valley Road, Louisville, KY 40219. *Phone:* 502-968-7191. *Toll-free phone:* 800-999-7387. *Web site:* http://www.brownmackie.edu/louisville/.

See page 1148 for the College Close-Up.

Brown Mackie College–Northern Kentucky

Fort Mitchell, Kentucky

- **Proprietary** primarily 2-year, founded 1927, part of Education Management Corporation
- **Suburban** campus
- **Coed**

Academics *Calendar:* quarters. *Degrees:* certificates, diplomas, associate, and bachelor's.
Costs (2010–11) *Tuition:* Tuition varies by program. Students should contact Brown Mackie College for tuition information.

Freshman Application Contact Brown Mackie College–Northern Kentucky, 309 Buttermilk Pike, Fort Mitchell, KY 41017-2191. *Phone:* 859-341-5627. *Toll-free phone:* 800-888-1445. *Web site:* http://www.brownmackie.edu/northernkentucky/.

See page 1156 for the College Close-Up.

Campbellsville University

Campbellsville, Kentucky

- **Independent** comprehensive, founded 1906, affiliated with Kentucky Baptist Convention
- **Small-town** 90-acre campus
- **Endowment** $7.2 million
- **Coed** 2,978 undergraduate students, 61% full-time, 57% women, 43% men
- **Moderately difficult** entrance level, 65% of applicants were admitted

Undergraduates 1,829 full-time, 1,149 part-time. Students come from 31 states and territories; 37 other countries; 13% are from out of state; 8% transferred in; 57% live on campus. *Retention:* 68% of full-time freshmen returned.
Freshmen *Admission:* 2,146 applied, 1,389 admitted, 509 enrolled. *Average high school GPA:* 3.18. *Test scores:* SAT critical reading scores over 500: 26%; SAT math scores over 500: 27%; SAT writing scores over 500: 20%; ACT scores over 18: 77%; SAT critical reading scores over 600: 4%; SAT math scores over 600: 15%; SAT writing scores over 600: 8%; ACT scores over 24: 25%; ACT scores over 30: 2%.
Faculty *Total:* 310, 41% full-time, 22% with terminal degrees. *Student/faculty ratio:* 13:1.
Academics *Calendar:* semesters. *Degrees:* certificates, associate, bachelor's, master's, and postbachelor's certificates. *Special study options:* academic remediation for entering students, accelerated degree program, adult/continuing education programs, advanced placement credit, distance learning, double majors, English as a second language, honors programs, independent study, internships, off-campus study, part-time degree program, study abroad, summer session for credit. *ROTC:* Army (c). *Unusual degree programs:* 3-2 engineering with University of Kentucky.
Computers on Campus 175 computers/terminals are available on campus for general student use. Campuswide network is available.
Student Life *Housing:* on-campus residence required through sophomore year. *Options:* men-only, women-only. Campus housing is university owned. Freshman campus housing is guaranteed. *Activities and organizations:* drama/theater group, student-run newspaper, radio and television station, choral group, marching band, Student Government Association, Baptist Student Union, Phi Beta Lambda, African-American Leadership League, Fellowship of Christian Athletes. *Campus security:* 24-hour emergency response devices and patrols, student patrols, late-night transport/escort service, controlled dormitory access. *Student services:* health clinic, personal/psychological counseling.
Athletics Member NAIA. *Intercollegiate sports:* baseball M(s), basketball M(s)/W(s), bowling M(s)/W(s), cheerleading M(s)/W(s), cross-country running M(s)/W(s), football M(s), golf M(s)/W(s), soccer M(s)/W(s), softball W(s), swimming and diving W(s), tennis M(s)/W(s), track and field M(s)/W(s), volleyball W(s), wrestling M(s). *Intramural sports:* basketball M/W, bowling M/W, football M/W, racquetball M/W, soccer M/W, swimming and diving M/W, table tennis M/W, tennis M/W, volleyball M/W, weight lifting M/W.
Standardized Tests *Required:* SAT or ACT (for admission).
Costs (2011–12) *Comprehensive fee:* $27,720 includes full-time tuition ($20,290), mandatory fees ($450), and room and board ($6980). Part-time tuition: $846 per credit. *Room and board:* Room and board charges vary according to housing facility. *Payment plan:* installment. *Waivers:* adult students, senior citizens, and employees or children of employees.
Financial Aid Of all full-time matriculated undergraduates who enrolled in 2008, 1,557 applied for aid, 1,465 were judged to have need, 252 had their need fully met. 360 Federal Work-Study jobs (averaging $1695). 36 state and other part-time jobs (averaging $1950). In 2008, 92 non-need-based awards were made. *Average percent of need met:* 74%. *Average financial aid package:* $14,521. *Average need-based loan:* $3785. *Average need-based gift aid:* $11,351. *Average non-need-based aid:* $5340. *Average indebtedness upon graduation:* $18,100.
Applying *Options:* electronic application, deferred entrance. *Application fee:* $20. *Required:* high school transcript, minimum 2 GPA. *Recommended:* essay or personal statement, minimum 3 GPA, interview. *Application deadlines:* rolling (freshmen), rolling (transfers). *Notification:* continuous (freshmen), continuous (transfers).
Freshman Application Contact Mr. David Walters, Vice President for Admissions and Student Services, Campbellsville University, 1 University Drive, Campbellsville, KY 42718-2799. *Phone:* 270-789-5220 Ext. 5007. *Toll-free phone:* 800-264-6014. *Fax:* 270-789-5071. *E-mail:* admissions@campbellsville.edu. *Web site:* http://www.campbellsville.edu/.

Centre College

Danville, Kentucky

- **Independent** 4-year, founded 1819, affiliated with Presbyterian Church (U.S.A.)
- **Small-town** 100-acre campus
- **Endowment** $152.2 million
- **Coed** 1,242 undergraduate students, 100% full-time, 54% women, 46% men
- **Very difficult** entrance level, 74% of applicants were admitted

Undergraduates 1,241 full-time, 1 part-time. Students come from 37 states and territories; 14 other countries; 41% are from out of state; 4% Black or African American, non-Hispanic/Latino; 3% Hispanic/Latino; 3% Asian, non-Hispanic/Latino; 1% Two or more races, non-Hispanic/Latino; 2% international; 1% transferred in; 98% live on campus. *Retention:* 92% of full-time freshmen returned.

Freshmen *Admission:* 2,257 applied, 1,664 admitted, 356 enrolled. *Average high school GPA:* 3.6. *Test scores:* SAT critical reading scores over 500: 91%; SAT math scores over 500: 93%; SAT writing scores over 500: 86%; ACT scores over 18: 100%; SAT critical reading scores over 600: 64%; SAT math scores over 600: 71%; SAT writing scores over 600: 57%; ACT scores over 24: 96%; SAT critical reading scores over 700: 23%; SAT math scores over 700: 19%; SAT writing scores over 700: 12%; ACT scores over 30: 38%.

Faculty *Total:* 127, 83% full-time, 87% with terminal degrees. *Student/faculty ratio:* 11:1.

Academics *Calendar:* 4-1-4. *Degree:* bachelor's. *Special study options:* advanced placement credit, double majors, honors programs, independent study, internships, off-campus study, services for LD students, student-designed majors, study abroad. *ROTC:* Army (c), Air Force (c). *Unusual degree programs:* 3-2 engineering with Washington University in St. Louis, Columbia University, Vanderbilt University, University of Kentucky.

Computers on Campus 943 computers/terminals and 2,000 ports are available on campus for general student use. Students can access the following: campus intranet, computer help desk, free student e-mail accounts, online (class) grades, online (class) registration, online (class) schedules. Campuswide network is available. 100% of college-owned or -operated housing units are wired for high-speed Internet access. Wireless service is available via classrooms, computer centers, computer labs, dorm rooms, learning centers, libraries, student centers.

Student Life *Housing:* on-campus residence required through senior year. *Options:* coed, men-only, disabled students. Campus housing is university owned. Freshman campus housing is guaranteed. *Activities and organizations:* drama/theater group, student-run newspaper, radio and television station, choral group, Student Government Association, campus newspaper, admission tour guides and hosts, Christian fellowship group, Diversity Student Union, national fraternities, national sororities. *Campus security:* 24-hour emergency response devices and patrols, late-night transport/escort service, controlled dormitory access. *Student services:* health clinic, personal/psychological counseling.

Athletics Member NCAA. All Division III. *Intercollegiate sports:* baseball M, basketball M/W, cheerleading W, cross-country running M/W, field hockey W, football M, golf M/W, lacrosse M/W, soccer M/W, swimming and diving M/W, tennis M/W, track and field M/W, volleyball W. *Intramural sports:* badminton M/W, basketball M/W, bowling M/W, equestrian sports M/W, football M/W, golf M/W, racquetball M/W, soccer M/W, softball M/W, swimming and diving M/W, table tennis M/W, tennis M/W, track and field M/W, ultimate Frisbee M/W, volleyball M/W, weight lifting M/W, wrestling M.

Standardized Tests *Required:* SAT or ACT (for admission).

Costs (2011–12) *Comprehensive fee:* $42,500. *Payment plan:* installment. *Waivers:* employees or children of employees.

Financial Aid Of all full-time matriculated undergraduates who enrolled in 2009, 908 applied for aid, 764 were judged to have need, 234 had their need fully met. 331 Federal Work-Study jobs (averaging $1577). 5 state and other part-time jobs (averaging $1652). In 2009, 433 non-need-based awards were made. *Average percent of need met:* 85%. *Average financial aid package:* $25,713. *Average need-based loan:* $4436. *Average need-based gift aid:* $22,538. *Average non-need-based aid:* $15,287. *Average indebtedness upon graduation:* $19,820. *Financial aid deadline:* 3/1.

Applying *Options:* electronic application, early admission, early action, deferred entrance. *Application fee:* $40. *Required:* essay or personal statement, high school transcript, 1 letter of recommendation. *Recommended:* interview. *Application deadlines:* 2/1 (freshmen), rolling (transfers), 12/1 (early action). *Notification:* 3/15 (freshmen), 1/15 (early action).

Freshman Application Contact Mr. Bob Nesmith, Director of Admissions, Centre College, 600 West Walnut Street, Danville, KY 40422-1394. *Phone:* 859-238-5350. *Toll-free phone:* 800-423-6236. *Fax:* 859-238-5373. *E-mail:* admission@centre.edu. *Web site:* http://www.centre.edu/.

Clear Creek Baptist Bible College

Pineville, Kentucky

- **Independent Southern Baptist** 4-year, founded 1926
- **Rural** 700-acre campus
- **Coed, primarily men** 163 undergraduate students, 64% full-time, 27% women, 73% men
- **Noncompetitive** entrance level

Undergraduates 105 full-time, 58 part-time. *Retention:* 87% of full-time freshmen returned.

Freshmen *Admission:* 58 admitted.

Faculty *Total:* 16, 50% full-time. *Student/faculty ratio:* 13:1. .

Academics *Calendar:* semesters. *Degrees:* certificates, diplomas, associate, and bachelor's. *Special study options:* off-campus study, part-time degree program, summer session for credit.

Computers on Campus 15 computers/terminals are available on campus for general student use. Campuswide network is available.

Student Life *Housing options:* coed, men-only, women-only. Campus housing is university owned. *Activities and organizations:* choral group. *Campus security:* 24-hour emergency response devices, student patrols. *Student services:* health clinic, personal/psychological counseling.

Athletics *Intramural sports:* basketball M/W, table tennis M/W, tennis M/W, volleyball M/W.

Costs (2010–11) *Tuition:* $8700 full-time, $238 per credit hour part-time. *Room only:* Room and board charges vary according to housing facility. *Payment plan:* installment.

Financial Aid Of all full-time matriculated undergraduates who enrolled in 2009, 121 applied for aid, 107 were judged to have need, 7 had their need fully met. 23 Federal Work-Study jobs (averaging $1656). In 2009, 13 non-need-based awards were made. *Average percent of need met:* 69%. *Average financial aid package:* $6949. *Average need-based gift aid:* $6949. *Average non-need-based aid:* $407.

Applying *Options:* electronic application, deferred entrance. *Application fee:* $50. *Required:* essay or personal statement, 4 letters of recommendation. *Recommended:* high school transcript, interview. *Application deadlines:* 7/15 (freshmen), 7/15 (transfers). *Notification:* continuous (freshmen), continuous (transfers).

Freshman Application Contact Mr. Billy Howell, Director of Admissions, Clear Creek Baptist Bible College, 300 Clear Creek Road, Pineville, KY 40977. *Phone:* 606-337-3196 Ext. 103. *Fax:* 606-337-1631. *E-mail:* bhowell@ccbbc.edu. *Web site:* http://www.ccbbc.edu/.

DeVry University

Louisville, Kentucky

- **Proprietary** 4-year
- **Coed**

Faculty *Student/faculty ratio:* 9:1.

Academics *Degrees:* associate and bachelor's.

Costs (2010–11) *Tuition:* $14,766 full-time, $580 per credit hour part-time. Full-time tuition and fees vary according to course load. Part-time tuition and fees vary according to course load. *Required fees:* $60 full-time, $30 per term part-time. *Payment plans:* installment, deferred payment.

Applying *Options:* deferred entrance. *Application fee:* $50.

Freshman Application Contact DeVry University, 10172 Linn Station Road, Suite 300, Louisville, KY 40223. *Toll-free phone:* 866-906-9388. *Web site:* http://www.devry.edu/.

Eastern Kentucky University

Richmond, Kentucky

Freshman Application Contact Mr. Stephen Byrn, Director of Admissions, Eastern Kentucky University, SSB CPO 54, 521 Lancaster Avenue, Richmond, KY 40475-3102. *Phone:* 859-622-2106. *Toll-free phone:* 800-465-9191. *Fax:* 859-622-8024. *E-mail:* admissions@eku.edu. *Web site:* http://www.eku.edu/.

Georgetown College

Georgetown, Kentucky

- **Independent** comprehensive, founded 1829, affiliated with Baptist Church
- **Suburban** 110-acre campus with easy access to Cincinnati
- **Endowment** $35.8 million
- **Coed** 1,284 undergraduate students, 96% full-time, 55% women, 45% men
- **Moderately difficult** entrance level, 79% of applicants were admitted

Undergraduates 1,235 full-time, 49 part-time. Students come from 29 states and territories; 8 other countries; 16% are from out of state; 8% Black or African American, non-Hispanic/Latino; 2% Hispanic/Latino; 0.2% Asian, non-Hispanic/Latino; 0.7% Two or more races, non-Hispanic/Latino; 1% international; 3% transferred in; 88% live on campus. *Retention:* 82% of full-time freshmen returned.

Freshmen *Admission:* 1,784 applied, 1,404 admitted, 336 enrolled. *Average high school GPA:* 3.47. *Test scores:* SAT critical reading scores over 500: 56%; SAT math scores over 500: 72%; ACT scores over 18: 97%; SAT critical reading scores over 600: 16%; SAT math scores over 600: 16%; ACT scores over 24: 54%; SAT critical reading scores over 700: 4%; ACT scores over 30: 7%.

Faculty *Total:* 167, 68% full-time, 71% with terminal degrees. *Student/faculty ratio:* 11:1.

Academics *Calendar:* semesters. *Degrees:* bachelor's and master's. *Special study options:* advanced placement credit, cooperative education, distance learning, double majors, English as a second language, honors programs, independent study, internships, off-campus study, part-time degree program, student-designed majors, study abroad, summer session for credit. *ROTC:* Army (c), Air Force (c). *Unusual degree programs:* 3-2 engineering with University of Kentucky; nursing with University of Kentucky; University of Kentucky, Patterson School of Diplomacy.

Computers on Campus 175 computers/terminals are available on campus for general student use. Students can access the following: campus intranet, computer help desk, free student e-mail accounts, online (class) grades, online (class) registration, online (class) schedules. Campuswide network is available. 100% of college-owned or -operated housing units are wired for high-speed Internet access. Wireless service is available via classrooms, computer centers, computer labs, dorm rooms, learning centers, libraries, student centers.

Student Life *Housing:* on-campus residence required through senior year. *Options:* men-only, women-only. Campus housing is university owned. Freshman campus housing is guaranteed. *Activities and organizations:* drama/theater group, student-run newspaper, radio station, choral group, Campus Ministries, Association of Georgetown Students, Harper-Gatton Leadership Center, President's Ambassadors, Phi Beta Lambda, national fraternities, national sororities. *Campus security:* 24-hour patrols, late-night transport/escort service. *Student services:* health clinic, personal/psychological counseling.

Athletics Member NAIA. *Intercollegiate sports:* baseball M(s), basketball M(s)/W(s), cheerleading W(s), cross-country running M(s)/W(s), football M(s), golf M(s)/W(s), soccer M(s)/W(s), softball W(s), tennis M(s)/W(s), track and field M(s)/W(s), volleyball W(s). *Intramural sports:* basketball M/W, football M/W, golf M/W, racquetball M/W, soccer M/W, softball M/W, table tennis M/W, tennis M/W, ultimate Frisbee M/W, volleyball M/W.

Standardized Tests *Required:* SAT or ACT (for admission). *Recommended:* ACT (for admission).

Costs (2010–11) *Comprehensive fee:* $34,960 includes full-time tuition ($27,640) and room and board ($7320). Full-time tuition and fees vary according to course load and degree level. Part-time tuition: $1140 per credit hour. Part-time tuition and fees vary according to degree level. *College room only:* $3530. Room and board charges vary according to board plan and housing facility. *Payment plan:* installment. *Waivers:* senior citizens and employees or children of employees.

Financial Aid Of all full-time matriculated undergraduates who enrolled in 2009, 1,031 applied for aid, 970 were judged to have need, 285 had their need fully met. 589 Federal Work-Study jobs (averaging $1108). In 2009, 194 non-need-based awards were made. *Average percent of need met:* 84%. *Average financial aid package:* $25,683. *Average need-based loan:* $4629. *Average need-based gift aid:* $21,654. *Average non-need-based aid:* $14,123. *Average indebtedness upon graduation:* $23,612. *Financial aid deadline:* 3/15.

Applying *Options:* electronic application, early decision, early action, deferred entrance. *Application fee:* $30. *Required:* high school transcript, minimum 2.5 GPA. *Required for some:* essay or personal statement, interview. *Application deadlines:* 8/1 (freshmen), rolling (transfers). *Notification:* 10/1 (freshmen), continuous (out-of-state freshmen), continuous (transfers).

Freshman Application Contact Mr. Garvel Kindrick, Vice President for Enrollment Management, Georgetown College, 400 East College Street, Georgetown, KY 40324. *Phone:* 502-863-8015. *Toll-free phone:* 800-788-9985. *Fax:* 502-868-7733. *E-mail:* admissions@georgetowncollege.edu. *Web site:* http://www.georgetowncollege.edu/.

ITT Technical Institute

Lexington, Kentucky

- **Proprietary** 4-year, founded 2006, part of ITT Educational Services, Inc.
- **Coed**
- **Minimally difficult** entrance level

Academics *Degrees:* associate and bachelor's.

Student Life *Housing:* college housing not available.

Freshman Application Contact Director of Recruitment, ITT Technical Institute, 2473 Fortune Drive, Suite 180, Lexington, KY 40509. *Phone:* 859-246-3300. *Toll-free phone:* 800-519-8151. *Web site:* http://www.itt-tech.edu/.

ITT Technical Institute

Louisville, Kentucky

- **Proprietary** primarily 2-year, founded 1993, part of ITT Educational Services, Inc.
- **Suburban** campus
- **Coed**
- **Minimally difficult** entrance level

Academics *Calendar:* quarters. *Degrees:* associate and bachelor's.

Student Life *Housing:* college housing not available.

Freshman Application Contact Director of Recruitment, ITT Technical Institute, 9500 Ormsby Station Road, Suite 100, Louisville, KY 40223. *Phone:* 502-327-7424. *Toll-free phone:* 888-790-7427. *Web site:* http://www.itt-tech.edu/.

Kentucky Christian University

Grayson, Kentucky

Freshman Application Contact Ms. Kara Bomer, Director of Admissions, Kentucky Christian University, 100 Academic Parkway, Grayson, KY 41143. *Phone:* 606-474-3266. *Toll-free phone:* 800-522-3181. *Fax:* 606-474-3155. *E-mail:* kbomer@kcu.edu. *Web site:* http://www.kcu.edu/.

Kentucky Mountain Bible College

Vancleve, Kentucky

- **Independent interdenominational** 4-year, founded 1931
- **Rural** 400-acre campus with easy access to Lexington
- **Coed**

Faculty *Student/faculty ratio:* 6:1.

Academics *Calendar:* semesters. *Degrees:* associate and bachelor's.

Student Life *Campus security:* student patrols.

Standardized Tests *Required:* ACT (for admission).

Applying *Application fee:* $25. *Required:* essay or personal statement, high school transcript, minimum 2 GPA, testimony of religious life. *Recommended:* interview.

Freshman Application Contact Mr. David Lorimer, Director of Recruiting, Kentucky Mountain Bible College, PO Box 10, Vancleve, KY 41385. *Phone:* 606-693-5000 Ext. 138. *Toll-free phone:* 800-879-KMBC Ext. 130 (in-state); 800-879-KMBC Ext. 136 (out-of-state). *Fax:* 606-693-4884. *E-mail:* kmbc@kmbc.edu. *Web site:* http://www.kmbc.edu/.

Kentucky State University

Frankfort, Kentucky

- **State-related** comprehensive, founded 1886
- **Small-town** 915-acre campus with easy access to Louisville
- **Endowment** $8.8 million
- **Coed** 2,606 undergraduate students, 82% full-time, 60% women, 40% men
- **Minimally difficult** entrance level, 25% of applicants were admitted

Undergraduates 2,133 full-time, 473 part-time. Students come from 33 states and territories; 17 other countries; 47% are from out of state; 61% Black or African American, non-Hispanic/Latino; 1% Hispanic/Latino; 0.1% Asian, non-Hispanic/Latino; 0.1% Native Hawaiian or other Pacific Islander, non-Hispanic/Latino; 2% Two or more races, non-Hispanic/Latino; 14% Race/ethnicity unknown; 2% international; 6% transferred in; 38% live on campus. *Retention:* 54% of full-time freshmen returned.

Freshmen *Admission:* 12,271 applied, 3,116 admitted, 635 enrolled. *Average high school GPA:* 2.58. *Test scores:* SAT critical reading scores over 500: 16%; SAT math scores over 500: 16%; SAT writing scores over 500: 10%; ACT scores over 18: 40%; SAT critical reading scores over 600: 2%; SAT math scores over 600: 2%; SAT writing scores over 600: 2%; ACT scores over 24: 4%.

Faculty *Total:* 180, 72% full-time, 54% with terminal degrees. *Student/faculty ratio:* 17:1.

Academics *Calendar:* semesters. *Degrees:* associate, bachelor's, and master's. *Special study options:* academic remediation for entering students, adult/continuing education programs, advanced placement credit, cooperative education, distance learning, double majors, English as a second language, honors programs, independent study, internships, off-campus study, part-time degree program, services for LD students, student-designed majors, study abroad, summer session for credit. *ROTC:* Army (c), Air Force (c). *Unusual degree programs:* 3-2 engineering with University of Kentucky, University of Maryland at College Park, Vanderbilt University, Florida A&M University.
Computers on Campus 450 computers/terminals and 200 ports are available on campus for general student use. Students can access the following: campus intranet, computer help desk, free student e-mail accounts, online (class) grades, online (class) registration, online (class) schedules, accepting financial aid awards. Campuswide network is available. 100% of college-owned or -operated housing units are wired for high-speed Internet access. Wireless service is available via entire campus.
Student Life *Housing:* on-campus residence required through sophomore year. *Options:* coed, men-only, women-only. Campus housing is university owned. Freshman applicants given priority for college housing. *Activities and organizations:* drama/theater group, student-run newspaper, choral group, marching band, Student Government Association, NAACP, Apostolic Lighthouse Organization, Whitney Young Council, Kentucky Education Association, national fraternities, national sororities. *Campus security:* 24-hour emergency response devices and patrols, controlled dormitory access. *Student services:* health clinic, personal/psychological counseling.
Athletics Member NCAA. All Division II. *Intercollegiate sports:* baseball M(s), basketball M(s)/W(s), cheerleading W(s), cross-country running M(s)/W(s), football M(s), golf M(s), softball W(s), track and field M(s)/W(s), volleyball W(s).
Standardized Tests *Required:* SAT or ACT (for admission).
Costs (2010–11) *Tuition:* state resident $5460 full-time, $205 per credit hour part-time; nonresident $14,154 full-time, $527 per credit hour part-time. Full-time tuition and fees vary according to course load. Part-time tuition and fees vary according to course load. *Required fees:* $750 full-time, $25 per credit hour part-time. *Room and board:* $6480; room only: $3240. Room and board charges vary according to board plan and housing facility. *Payment plan:* installment. *Waivers:* senior citizens and employees or children of employees.
Financial Aid Of all full-time matriculated undergraduates who enrolled in 2009, 1,825 applied for aid, 1,818 were judged to have need, 247 had their need fully met. 490 Federal Work-Study jobs (averaging $1730). In 2009, 60 non-need-based awards were made. *Average percent of need met:* 55%. *Average financial aid package:* $11,028. *Average need-based loan:* $3988. *Average need-based gift aid:* $5920. *Average non-need-based aid:* $7140. *Average indebtedness upon graduation:* $33,320.
Applying *Options:* electronic application, early admission. *Application fee:* $30. *Required:* high school transcript. *Required for some:* essay or personal statement, 2 letters of recommendation, interview. *Recommended:* minimum 2 GPA. *Application deadlines:* rolling (freshmen), rolling (transfers).
Freshman Application Contact Mr. James Burrell, Director of Admission, Kentucky State University, 400 East Main Street, Academic Suite Building 312, Frankfort, KY 40601. *Phone:* 502-597-6813. *Toll-free phone:* 800-633-9415 (in-state); 800-325-1716 (out-of-state). *Fax:* 502-597-5814. *E-mail:* james.burrell@kysu.edu. *Web site:* http://www.kysu.edu/.

Kentucky Wesleyan College
Owensboro, Kentucky

- **Independent Methodist** 4-year, founded 1858
- **Suburban** 52-acre campus
- **Endowment** $25.2 million
- **Coed** 802 undergraduate students, 95% full-time, 48% women, 52% men
- **Moderately difficult** entrance level, 54% of applicants were admitted

Undergraduates 758 full-time, 44 part-time. Students come from 22 states and territories; 12 other countries; 30% are from out of state; 10% Black or African American, non-Hispanic/Latino; 1% Hispanic/Latino; 0.5% Asian, non-Hispanic/Latino; 0.4% American Indian or Alaska Native, non-Hispanic/Latino; 11% Race/ethnicity unknown; 2% international; 7% transferred in; 47% live on campus. *Retention:* 61% of full-time freshmen returned.
Freshmen *Admission:* 1,510 applied, 813 admitted, 205 enrolled. *Average high school GPA:* 3.23. *Test scores:* SAT critical reading scores over 500: 42%; SAT math scores over 500: 46%; SAT writing scores over 500: 39%; ACT scores over 18: 87%; SAT critical reading scores over 600: 6%; SAT math scores over 600: 9%; SAT writing scores over 600: 3%; ACT scores over 24: 32%; ACT scores over 30: 6%.
Faculty *Total:* 90, 48% full-time, 50% with terminal degrees. *Student/faculty ratio:* 13:1.
Academics *Calendar:* semesters. *Degree:* bachelor's. *Special study options:* academic remediation for entering students, accelerated degree program, adult/continuing education programs, advanced placement credit, cooperative education, distance learning, double majors, honors programs, independent study,

internships, off-campus study, part-time degree program, services for LD students, student-designed majors, study abroad, summer session for credit. *ROTC:* Army (c). *Unusual degree programs:* 3-2 engineering with Auburn University, University of Kentucky; nursing with University of Louisville.
Computers on Campus 125 computers/terminals are available on campus for general student use. Students can access the following: campus intranet, computer help desk, free student e-mail accounts, online (class) grades, online (class) registration, online (class) schedules. Campuswide network is available. 100% of college-owned or -operated housing units are wired for high-speed Internet access. Wireless service is available via entire campus.
Student Life *Housing:* on-campus residence required through junior year. *Options:* coed, men-only, women-only, disabled students. Campus housing is university owned. Freshman campus housing is guaranteed. *Activities and organizations:* drama/theater group, student-run newspaper, radio station, choral group, Student Government Association, Student Activities Programming Board, Campus Ministries, Pre-Professional Society, St Jude Up 'Til Dawn Executive Board, national fraternities, national sororities. *Campus security:* 24-hour emergency response devices, late-night transport/escort service, controlled dormitory access, 12-hour patrols by trained security personnel. *Student services:* health clinic, personal/psychological counseling, women's center.
Athletics Member NCAA. All Division II. *Intercollegiate sports:* baseball M(s), basketball M(s)/W(s), cheerleading M/W, cross-country running M(s)/W(s), football M(s), golf M(s)/W(s), soccer M(s)/W(s), softball W(s), tennis W, volleyball W(s). *Intramural sports:* basketball M/W, racquetball M/W, soccer M/W, softball M, table tennis M/W, volleyball M/W.
Standardized Tests *Required:* SAT or ACT (for admission).
Costs (2011–12) *Comprehensive fee:* $26,310 includes full-time tuition ($18,790), mandatory fees ($600), and room and board ($6920). Full-time tuition and fees vary according to course load. Part-time tuition and fees vary according to course load. *College room only:* $3100. Room and board charges vary according to board plan and housing facility. *Payment plans:* installment, deferred payment. *Waivers:* children of alumni, senior citizens, and employees or children of employees.
Financial Aid Of all full-time matriculated undergraduates who enrolled in 2008, 803 applied for aid, 727 were judged to have need, 173 had their need fully met. 135 Federal Work-Study jobs (averaging $1089). In 2008, 137 non-need-based awards were made. *Average percent of need met:* 73%. *Average financial aid package:* $14,942. *Average need-based loan:* $3699. *Average need-based gift aid:* $12,115. *Average non-need-based aid:* $8354. *Average indebtedness upon graduation:* $19,516. *Financial aid deadline:* 3/15.
Applying *Options:* electronic application, early admission, deferred entrance. *Required:* high school transcript. *Notification:* continuous (freshmen), continuous (transfers).
Freshman Application Contact Mrs. Lauren Lee, Director of Admissions, Kentucky Wesleyan College, 3000 Frederica Street, Owensboro, KY 42301. *Phone:* 270-852-3120. *Toll-free phone:* 800-999-0592 (in-state); 800-990-0592 (out-of-state). *Fax:* 270-852-3133. *Web site:* http://www.kwc.edu/.

Lindsey Wilson College
Columbia, Kentucky

- **Independent United Methodist** comprehensive, founded 1903
- **Rural** 225-acre campus
- **Coed** 2,164 undergraduate students, 96% full-time, 60% women, 40% men
- **Minimally difficult** entrance level, 78% of applicants were admitted

Undergraduates 2,083 full-time, 81 part-time. Students come from 33 states and territories; 27 other countries; 16% are from out of state; 11% Black or African American, non-Hispanic/Latino; 0.6% Hispanic/Latino; 0.3% Asian, non-Hispanic/Latino; 0.6% American Indian or Alaska Native, non-Hispanic/Latino; 1% Two or more races, non-Hispanic/Latino; 9% Race/ethnicity unknown; 15% transferred in; 48% live on campus. *Retention:* 59% of full-time freshmen returned.
Freshmen *Admission:* 2,718 applied, 2,129 admitted, 601 enrolled. *Average high school GPA:* 3.06. *Test scores:* ACT scores over 18: 75%; ACT scores over 24: 20%; ACT scores over 30: 1%.
Faculty *Total:* 223, 43% full-time. *Student/faculty ratio:* 15:1.
Academics *Calendar:* semesters. *Degrees:* associate, bachelor's, and master's. *Special study options:* academic remediation for entering students, accelerated degree program, adult/continuing education programs, advanced placement credit, cooperative education, double majors, English as a second language, independent study, internships, off-campus study, part-time degree program, services for LD students, student-designed majors, study abroad, summer session for credit.
Computers on Campus 120 computers/terminals are available on campus for general student use. Students can access the following: campus intranet, computer help desk, free student e-mail accounts, online (class) grades, online (class) registration, online (class) schedules. Campuswide network is available.

100% of college-owned or -operated housing units are wired for high-speed Internet access. Wireless service is available via entire campus.

Student Life *Housing:* on-campus residence required through senior year. *Options:* men-only, women-only. Campus housing is university owned. Freshman campus housing is guaranteed. *Activities and organizations:* drama/theater group, student-run newspaper, choral group, marching band. *Campus security:* 24-hour emergency response devices and patrols. *Student services:* health clinic, personal/psychological counseling, women's center.

Athletics Member NAIA. *Intercollegiate sports:* baseball M(s), basketball M(s)/W(s), bowling M(s)/W(s), cheerleading M(s)/W(s), cross-country running M(s)/W(s), football M(s)/W(s), golf M(s)/W(s), soccer M(s)/W(s), softball W(s), swimming and diving M(s)/W(s), tennis M(s)/W(s), track and field M(s)/W(s), volleyball W(s), wrestling M(s). *Intramural sports:* basketball M/W, football M/W, softball M/W, table tennis M/W, tennis M/W, volleyball M/W, weight lifting M/W.

Standardized Tests *Required for some:* SAT or ACT (for admission).

Costs (2010–11) *Comprehensive fee:* $26,595 includes full-time tuition ($18,720), mandatory fees ($230), and room and board ($7645). Full-time tuition and fees vary according to location. Part-time tuition: $780 per credit hour. Part-time tuition and fees vary according to location. *College room only:* $2820. *Payment plan:* installment. *Waivers:* senior citizens and employees or children of employees.

Financial Aid Of all full-time matriculated undergraduates who enrolled in 2009, 2,012 applied for aid, 1,894 were judged to have need, 697 had their need fully met. 195 Federal Work-Study jobs (averaging $1240). *Average financial aid package:* $15,082. *Average need-based loan:* $4233. *Average need-based gift aid:* $11,907. *Average indebtedness upon graduation:* $24,741.

Applying *Options:* electronic application. *Required:* high school transcript. *Recommended:* interview. *Application deadlines:* rolling (freshmen), rolling (transfers). *Notification:* continuous (freshmen), continuous (transfers).

Freshman Application Contact Mrs. Charity Ferguson, Assistant Director of Admissions, Lindsey Wilson College, 210 Lindsey Wilson Street, Columbia, KY 42728-1298. *Phone:* 270-384-8100. *Toll-free phone:* 800-264-0138. *Fax:* 270-384-8591. *Web site:* http://www.lindsey.edu/.

Mid-Continent University
Mayfield, Kentucky

- **Independent Southern Baptist** comprehensive, founded 1949
- **Small-town** 60-acre campus
- **Endowment** $3.0 million
- **Coed** 2,179 undergraduate students, 88% full-time, 62% women, 38% men
- **Minimally difficult** entrance level, 84% of applicants were admitted

Undergraduates 1,907 full-time, 272 part-time. Students come from 25 states and territories; 17 other countries; 19% are from out of state; 13% Black or African American, non-Hispanic/Latino; 2% Hispanic/Latino; 0.3% Asian, non-Hispanic/Latino; 0.5% American Indian or Alaska Native, non-Hispanic/Latino; 0.3% Two or more races, non-Hispanic/Latino; 4% Race/ethnicity unknown; 2% international; 25% transferred in; 6% live on campus. *Retention:* 66% of full-time freshmen returned.

Freshmen *Admission:* 487 applied, 408 admitted, 250 enrolled. *Average high school GPA:* 2.84. *Test scores:* ACT scores over 18: 57%; ACT scores over 24: 10%.

Faculty *Total:* 155, 22% full-time, 23% with terminal degrees. *Student/faculty ratio:* 27:1.

Academics *Calendar:* semesters. *Degrees:* certificates, associate, bachelor's, and master's. *Special study options:* academic remediation for entering students, accelerated degree program, advanced placement credit, distance learning, double majors, English as a second language, independent study, off-campus study, part-time degree program, student-designed majors, study abroad, summer session for credit.

Computers on Campus 43 computers/terminals are available on campus for general student use. Campuswide network is available. 100% of college-owned or -operated housing units are wired for high-speed Internet access. Wireless service is available via libraries, student centers.

Student Life *Housing:* on-campus residence required through sophomore year. *Options:* men-only, women-only. Campus housing is university owned. *Activities and organizations:* student-run newspaper, Student Government Association, Baptist Student Union, Psychology Club, International Club, Ministry Association. *Campus security:* student patrols. *Student services:* personal/psychological counseling.

Athletics Member NAIA, NCCAA. *Intercollegiate sports:* baseball M(s), basketball M(s)/W(s), soccer M(s), softball W(s), volleyball W(s). *Intramural sports:* cheerleading M/W.

Standardized Tests *Required:* SAT or ACT (for admission).

Costs (2010–11) *Comprehensive fee:* $19,900 includes full-time tuition ($12,100), mandatory fees ($1200), and room and board ($6600). Full-time tuition and fees vary according to course load and program. Part-time tuition:

$425 per credit hour. Part-time tuition and fees vary according to course load and program. *Room and board:* Room and board charges vary according to board plan and housing facility. *Payment plans:* installment, deferred payment. *Waivers:* employees or children of employees.

Financial Aid Of all full-time matriculated undergraduates who enrolled in 2008, 2,161 applied for aid, 2,117 were judged to have need, 58 had their need fully met. 72 Federal Work-Study jobs (averaging $2126). In 2008, 52 non-need-based awards were made. *Average percent of need met:* 35%. *Average financial aid package:* $8454. *Average need-based loan:* $3523. *Average need-based gift aid:* $6356. *Average non-need-based aid:* $8564. *Average indebtedness upon graduation:* $11,005.

Applying *Options:* electronic application, early admission. *Application fee:* $20. *Required:* essay or personal statement, high school transcript, minimum 2 GPA, 1 letter of recommendation. *Required for some:* interview. *Application deadlines:* rolling (freshmen), rolling (transfers). *Notification:* continuous (freshmen), continuous (transfers).

Freshman Application Contact Mr. Karl Hatton, Associate Dean for Student Life/Admissions/Orientation, Mid-Continent University, 99 Powell Road East, Mayfield, KY 42066. *Phone:* 270-247-8521 Ext. 312. *Fax:* 270-247-3115. *E-mail:* admissions@midcontinent.edu. *Web site:* http://www.midcontinent.edu/.

Midway College
Midway, Kentucky

- **Independent** comprehensive, founded 1847, affiliated with Christian Church (Disciples of Christ)
- **Small-town** 110-acre campus with easy access to Louisville and Lexington
- **Coed, primarily women** 1,513 undergraduate students, 68% full-time, 85% women, 15% men
- **Minimally difficult** entrance level

Undergraduates 1,022 full-time, 491 part-time. Students come from 27 states and territories; 2 other countries; 8% are from out of state; 9% Black or African American, non-Hispanic/Latino; 0.9% Hispanic/Latino; 0.5% Asian, non-Hispanic/Latino; 0.7% Native Hawaiian or other Pacific Islander, non-Hispanic/Latino; 0.7% American Indian or Alaska Native, non-Hispanic/Latino; 0.7% Two or more races, non-Hispanic/Latino; 4% Race/ethnicity unknown; 0.1% international; 15% transferred in; 14% live on campus. *Retention:* 75% of full-time freshmen returned.

Freshmen *Admission:* 1,572 applied, 447 enrolled. *Average high school GPA:* 3.19. *Test scores:* SAT critical reading scores over 500: 50%; SAT math scores over 500: 38%; ACT scores over 18: 72%; SAT critical reading scores over 600: 13%; SAT math scores over 600: 13%; ACT scores over 24: 20%; SAT critical reading scores over 700: 3%; SAT math scores over 700: 3%; ACT scores over 30: 2%.

Faculty *Total:* 118, 48% full-time, 31% with terminal degrees. *Student/faculty ratio:* 16:1.

Academics *Calendar:* semesters. *Degrees:* associate, bachelor's, master's, and doctoral-professional. *Special study options:* academic remediation for entering students, adult/continuing education programs, advanced placement credit, distance learning, external degree program, honors programs, independent study, internships, off-campus study, part-time degree program, services for LD students, study abroad, summer session for credit. *ROTC:* Army (c), Air Force (c).

Computers on Campus 50 computers/terminals are available on campus for general student use. Students can access the following: campus intranet, computer help desk, free student e-mail accounts, online (class) grades, online (class) registration, online (class) schedules. Campuswide network is available. 100% of college-owned or -operated housing units are wired for high-speed Internet access. Wireless service is available via classrooms, computer centers, computer labs, dorm rooms, learning centers, libraries, student centers.

Student Life *Housing:* on-campus residence required through sophomore year. *Options:* women-only. Campus housing is university owned. Freshman campus housing is guaranteed. *Activities and organizations:* choral group, student government, Midway Chorale, Midway Association of Nursing Students, Kentucky Education Association-Student Program, Midway Horse Women's Association. *Campus security:* 24-hour emergency response devices and patrols, late-night transport/escort service. *Student services:* health clinic, personal/psychological counseling, women's center.

Athletics Member NAIA. *Intercollegiate sports:* basketball W(s), equestrian sports W(s), soccer W(s), softball W(s), tennis W(s), track and field W(s), volleyball W(s).

Standardized Tests *Required:* SAT or ACT (for admission).

Costs (2010–11) *Comprehensive fee:* $26,180 includes full-time tuition ($18,900) and room and board ($7280). Full-time tuition and fees vary according to class time, location, and program. Part-time tuition: $630 per semester hour. Part-time tuition and fees vary according to class time, location, and program. *Room and board:* Room and board charges vary according to housing facility. *Payment plan:* deferred payment. *Waivers:* minority students and employees or children of employees.

Financial Aid Of all full-time matriculated undergraduates who enrolled in 2007, 771 applied for aid, 705 were judged to have need, 180 had their need fully met. 113 Federal Work-Study jobs (averaging $1372). In 2007, 8 non-need-based awards were made. *Average percent of need met:* 59%. *Average financial aid package:* $12,196. *Average need-based loan:* $3658. *Average need-based gift aid:* $5792. *Average non-need-based aid:* $3756. *Average indebtedness upon graduation:* $15,407.

Applying *Options:* electronic application, early admission, deferred entrance. *Application fee:* $25. *Required:* high school transcript. *Required for some:* essay or personal statement, interview. *Recommended:* minimum 2.2 GPA. *Application deadlines:* rolling (freshmen), rolling (transfers). *Notification:* continuous (freshmen), continuous (transfers).

Freshman Application Contact Midway College, 512 East Stephens Street, Midway, KY 40347-1120. *Phone:* 859-846-5799. *Toll-free phone:* 800-755-0031. *Web site:* http://www.midway.edu/.

Morehead State University
Morehead, Kentucky

- **State-supported** comprehensive, founded 1922
- **Small-town** 1016-acre campus
- **Coed** 7,399 undergraduate students, 73% full-time, 61% women, 39% men
- **Minimally difficult** entrance level, 89% of applicants were admitted

Undergraduates 5,430 full-time, 1,969 part-time. Students come from 49 states and territories; 32 other countries; 15% are from out of state; 3% Black or African American, non-Hispanic/Latino; 0.9% Hispanic/Latino; 0.4% Asian, non-Hispanic/Latino; 0.3% American Indian or Alaska Native, non-Hispanic/Latino; 0.2% Two or more races, non-Hispanic/Latino; 1% Race/ethnicity unknown; 0.6% international; 6% transferred in; 38% live on campus. *Retention:* 67% of full-time freshmen returned.

Freshmen *Admission:* 2,460 applied, 2,184 admitted, 1,180 enrolled. *Average high school GPA:* 3.31. *Test scores:* SAT critical reading scores over 500: 47%; SAT math scores over 500: 54%; ACT scores over 18: 88%; SAT critical reading scores over 600: 11%; SAT math scores over 600: 13%; ACT scores over 24: 29%; SAT critical reading scores over 700: 1%; SAT math scores over 700: 1%; ACT scores over 30: 3%.

Faculty *Total:* 469, 79% full-time, 53% with terminal degrees. *Student/faculty ratio:* 17:1.

Academics *Calendar:* semesters. *Degrees:* associate, bachelor's, master's, post-master's, and postbachelor's certificates. *Special study options:* academic remediation for entering students, accelerated degree program, adult/continuing education programs, advanced placement credit, cooperative education, distance learning, double majors, honors programs, independent study, internships, off-campus study, part-time degree program, services for LD students, student-designed majors, study abroad, summer session for credit. *ROTC:* Army (b). *Unusual degree programs:* 3-2 engineering with Chemical Engineering 3 + 2 Program: 3 years (96 hours) at Morehead State University, transfer to University of Kentucky to an approved engineering program.

Computers on Campus 1,000 computers/terminals and 1,820 ports are available on campus for general student use. Students can access the following: campus intranet, computer help desk, free student e-mail accounts, online (class) grades, online (class) registration, online (class) schedules. Campus-wide network is available. 100% of college-owned or -operated housing units are wired for high-speed Internet access. Wireless service is available via entire campus.

Student Life *Housing:* on-campus residence required through sophomore year. *Options:* coed, disabled students. Campus housing is university owned. Freshman applicants given priority for college housing. *Activities and organizations:* drama/theater group, student-run newspaper, radio and television station, choral group, marching band, national fraternities, national sororities. *Campus security:* 24-hour emergency response devices and patrols, student patrols, late-night transport/escort service, controlled dormitory access. *Student services:* health clinic, personal/psychological counseling.

Athletics Member NCAA. All Division I except football (Division I-AA). *Intercollegiate sports:* baseball M(s), basketball M(s)/W(s), bowling M(c)/W(c), cheerleading M/W, cross-country running M(s)/W(s), equestrian sports M(c)/W(c), golf M(s), riflery M(s)/W(s), soccer W(s), softball W(s), tennis M(s)/W(s), track and field M(s)/W(s), volleyball W(s). *Intramural sports:* archery M/W, badminton M/W, basketball M/W, bowling M/W, football M/W, golf M/W, racquetball M/W, soccer M(c)/W(c), softball M/W, swimming and diving M/W, table tennis M/W, tennis M/W, track and field M/W, volleyball M/W.

Standardized Tests *Required:* SAT or ACT (for admission).

Costs (2010–11) *Tuition:* state resident $6492 full-time, $246 per credit hour part-time; nonresident $16,236 full-time, $615 per credit hour part-time. Full-time tuition and fees vary according to course level, course load, location, reciprocity agreements, and student level. Part-time tuition and fees vary according to course level, course load, location, and student level. *Room and board:* $6582. Room and board charges vary according to board plan and housing facility. *Payment plan:* installment. *Waivers:* children of alumni, senior citizens, and employees or children of employees.

Financial Aid Of all full-time matriculated undergraduates who enrolled in 2009, 4,645 applied for aid, 4,085 were judged to have need, 1,184 had their need fully met. 381 Federal Work-Study jobs (averaging $2166). 716 state and other part-time jobs (averaging $2239). In 2009, 608 non-need-based awards were made. *Average percent of need met:* 68%. *Average financial aid package:* $9624. *Average need-based loan:* $3755. *Average need-based gift aid:* $5178. *Average non-need-based aid:* $6865. *Average indebtedness upon graduation:* $25,182.

Applying *Options:* electronic application, early admission, deferred entrance. *Application fee:* $30. *Required:* high school transcript. *Required for some:* essay or personal statement, 1 letter of recommendation, interview. *Application deadlines:* rolling (freshmen), rolling (transfers). *Notification:* continuous (freshmen), continuous (transfers).

Freshman Application Contact Mr. Jeffrey Liles, Assistant Vice President for Enrollment Services, Morehead State University, 100 Admissions Center, Morehead, KY 40351. *Phone:* 606-783-2000. *Toll-free phone:* 800-585-6781. *Fax:* 606-783-5038. *E-mail:* admissions@moreheadstate.edu. *Web site:* http://www.moreheadstate.edu/.

Murray State University
Murray, Kentucky

- **State-supported** comprehensive, founded 1922, part of Kentucky Council on Post Secondary Education
- **Small-town** 238-acre campus
- **Endowment** $47.5 million
- **Coed** 8,429 undergraduate students, 81% full-time, 59% women, 41% men
- **Moderately difficult** entrance level, 81% of applicants were admitted

Undergraduates 6,805 full-time, 1,624 part-time. Students come from 40 states and territories; 36 other countries; 29% are from out of state; 7% Black or African American, non-Hispanic/Latino; 1% Hispanic/Latino; 0.8% Asian, non-Hispanic/Latino; 0.1% Native Hawaiian or other Pacific Islander, non-Hispanic/Latino; 0.3% American Indian or Alaska Native, non-Hispanic/Latino; 0.6% Two or more races, non-Hispanic/Latino; 2% Race/ethnicity unknown; 2% international; 7% transferred in; 36% live on campus. *Retention:* 70% of full-time freshmen returned.

Freshmen *Admission:* 4,057 applied, 3,305 admitted, 1,390 enrolled. *Average high school GPA:* 3.3. *Test scores:* ACT scores over 18: 98%; ACT scores over 24: 43%; ACT scores over 30: 6%.

Faculty *Total:* 558, 72% full-time, 58% with terminal degrees. *Student/faculty ratio:* 15:1.

Academics *Calendar:* semesters. *Degrees:* certificates, associate, bachelor's, master's, and post-master's certificates. *Special study options:* academic remediation for entering students, adult/continuing education programs, advanced placement credit, cooperative education, distance learning, double majors, English as a second language, external degree program, freshman honors college, honors programs, independent study, internships, off-campus study, part-time degree program, services for LD students, study abroad, summer session for credit. *ROTC:* Army (b). *Unusual degree programs:* 3-2 biology, chemistry.

Computers on Campus 1,800 computers/terminals are available on campus for general student use. Students can access the following: campus intranet, computer help desk, free student e-mail accounts, online (class) grades, online (class) schedules, billing accounts. Campuswide network is available. 100% of college-owned or -operated housing units are wired for high-speed Internet access. Wireless service is available via entire campus.

Student Life *Housing:* on-campus residence required through sophomore year. *Options:* coed, women-only, disabled students. Campus housing is university owned. *Activities and organizations:* drama/theater group, student-run newspaper, radio and television station, choral group, marching band, student government, Baptist Student Union, Christ Ambassadors, Residential Colleges, Greek Organizations, national fraternities, national sororities. *Campus security:* 24-hour emergency response devices and patrols, student patrols, late-night transport/escort service, controlled dormitory access. *Student services:* health clinic, personal/psychological counseling, women's center, legal services.

Athletics Member NCAA. All Division I except football (Division I-AA). *Intercollegiate sports:* baseball M(s), basketball M(s)/W(s), cheerleading M/W, crew M(c)/W(c), cross-country running M(s)/W(s), equestrian sports M(s)(c)/W(s)(c), golf M(s)/W(s), riflery M(s)/W(s), soccer W(s), softball W(s), tennis M(s)/W(s), track and field W(s), volleyball W(s). *Intramural sports:* basketball M/W, bowling M/W, fencing M/W, field hockey M/W, football M/W, golf M/W, racquetball M/W, rugby M, sailing M/W, skiing (downhill) M/W, soccer M/W, softball M/W, swimming and diving M/W, track and field M/W, volleyball M/W, weight lifting M/W.

Standardized Tests *Required:* ACT (for admission).

Costs (2010–11) *Tuition:* state resident $5388 full-time, $225 per hour part-time; nonresident $16,164 full-time, $674 per hour part-time. Full-time tuition and fees vary according to reciprocity agreements. Part-time tuition and fees vary according to reciprocity agreements. *Required fees:* $876 full-time, $37 per hour part-time. *Room and board:* $6860; room only: $4006. Room and board charges vary according to board plan and housing facility. *Payment plan:* installment. *Waivers:* children of alumni, senior citizens, and employees or children of employees.

Financial Aid Of all full-time matriculated undergraduates who enrolled in 2009, 5,794 applied for aid, 4,035 were judged to have need, 3,792 had their need fully met. In 2009, 5167 non-need-based awards were made. *Average percent of need met:* 86%. *Average financial aid package:* $8023. *Average need-based loan:* $3209. *Average need-based gift aid:* $4493. *Average non-need-based aid:* $4181. *Average indebtedness upon graduation:* $26,100.

Applying *Options:* electronic application. *Application fee:* $30. *Required:* high school transcript, minimum 3 GPA. *Notification:* continuous until 8/1 (freshmen), continuous until 1/8 (out-of-state freshmen), continuous until 8/1 (transfers).

Freshman Application Contact Ms. Stacy Bell, Undergraduate Admissions Specialist, Murray State University, 113 Sparks Hall, Murray, KY 42701-0009. *Phone:* 270-809-3035. *Toll-free phone:* 800-272-4678. *Fax:* 270-809-3050. *E-mail:* admissions@murraystate.edu. *Web site:* http://www.murraystate.edu/.

National College

Lexington, Kentucky

Director of Admissions Kim Thomasson, Campus Director, National College, 2376 Sir Barton Way, Lexington, KY 40509. *Phone:* 859-253-0621. *Toll-free phone:* 800-664-1886. *Web site:* http://www.national-college.edu/.

National College

Louisville, Kentucky

Director of Admissions Vincent C. Tinebra, Campus Director, National College, 3950 Dixie Highway, Louisville, KY 40216. *Phone:* 502-447-7634. *Toll-free phone:* 800-664-1886. *Web site:* http://www.national-college.edu/.

Northern Kentucky University

Highland Heights, Kentucky

- **State-supported** comprehensive, founded 1968
- **Suburban** 398-acre campus with easy access to Cincinnati
- **Endowment** $56.5 million
- **Coed** 13,485 undergraduate students, 75% full-time, 56% women, 44% men
- **Moderately difficult** entrance level, 66% of applicants were admitted

Undergraduates 10,050 full-time, 3,435 part-time. Students come from 41 states and territories; 48 other countries; 32% are from out of state; 7% Black or African American, non-Hispanic/Latino; 2% Hispanic/Latino; 1% Asian, non-Hispanic/Latino; 0.3% American Indian or Alaska Native, non-Hispanic/Latino; 0.7% Two or more races, non-Hispanic/Latino; 4% Race/ethnicity unknown; 1% international; 5% transferred in; 14% live on campus. *Retention:* 68% of full-time freshmen returned.

Freshmen *Admission:* 7,202 applied, 4,772 admitted, 2,337 enrolled. *Average high school GPA:* 3.1. *Test scores:* SAT critical reading scores over 500: 44%; SAT math scores over 500: 47%; ACT scores over 18: 87%; SAT critical reading scores over 600: 13%; SAT math scores over 600: 10%; ACT scores over 24: 25%; SAT critical reading scores over 700: 3%; SAT math scores over 700: 1%; ACT scores over 30: 2%.

Faculty *Total:* 1,121, 47% full-time, 42% with terminal degrees. *Student/faculty ratio:* 17:1.

Academics *Calendar:* semesters. *Degrees:* certificates, associate, bachelor's, master's, doctoral-professional, doctoral-research/scholarship, post-master's, and postbachelor's certificates. *Special study options:* academic remediation for entering students, accelerated degree program, adult/continuing education programs, advanced placement credit, cooperative education, distance learning, double majors, English as a second language, honors programs, independent study, internships, off-campus study, part-time degree program, services for LD students, student-designed majors, study abroad, summer session for credit. *ROTC:* Army (c), Air Force (c).

Computers on Campus 250 computers/terminals are available on campus for general student use. Students can access the following: computer help desk, free student e-mail accounts, online (class) grades, online (class) registration, online (class) schedules. Campuswide network is available. 100% of college-

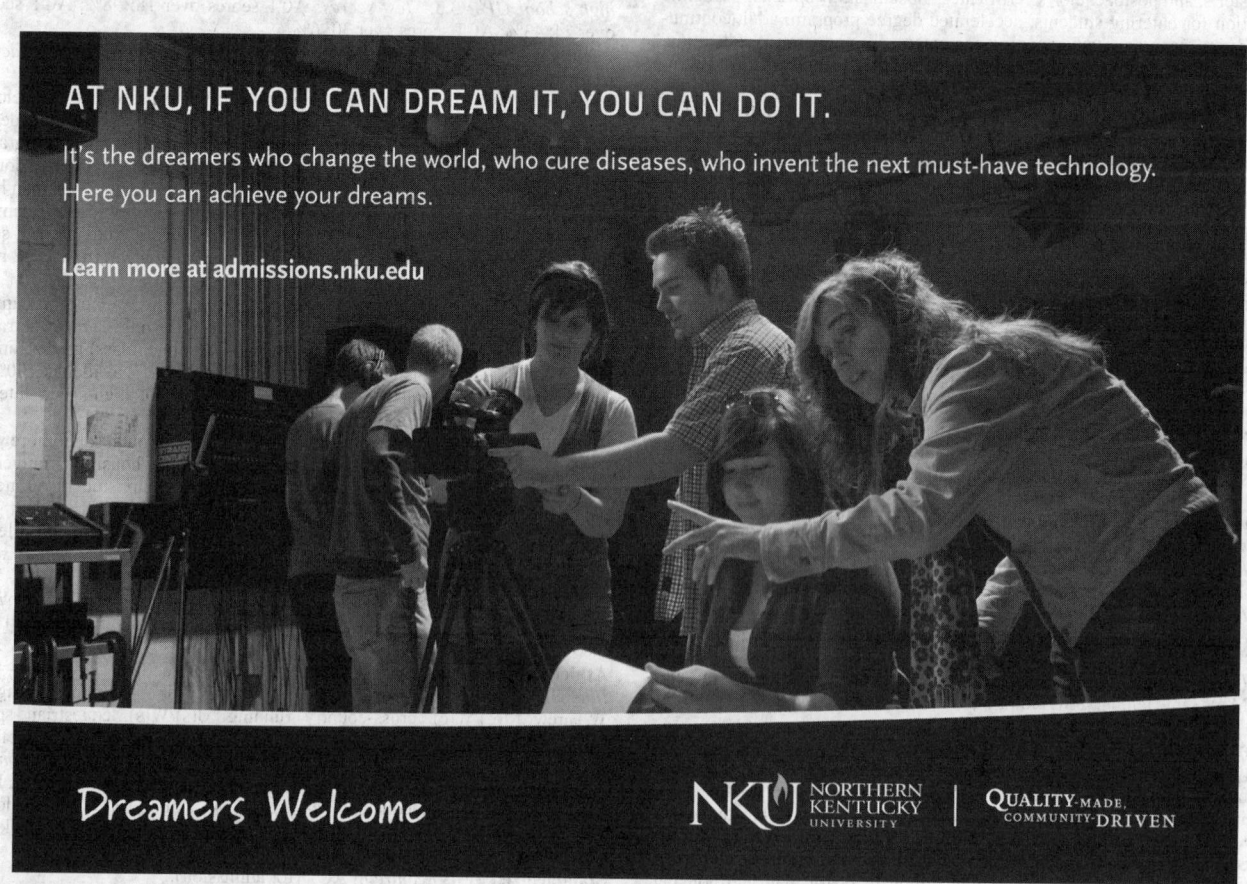

owned or -operated housing units are wired for high-speed Internet access. Wireless service is available via entire campus.

Student Life *Housing options:* coed, cooperative, disabled students. Campus housing is university owned. *Activities and organizations:* drama/theater group, student-run newspaper, radio and television station, choral group, Sororities, Fraternities, Freshmen Service Leadership Committee, Student Alumni Association, Activities Programming Board, national fraternities, national sororities. *Campus security:* 24-hour emergency response devices and patrols, late-night transport/escort service, controlled dormitory access. *Student services:* health clinic, personal/psychological counseling, women's center.

Athletics Member NCAA. All Division II. *Intercollegiate sports:* baseball M(s), basketball M(s)/W(s), cheerleading M/W, cross-country running M(s)/W(s), golf M(s)/W(s), soccer M(s)/W(s), softball W(s), tennis M(s)/W(s), volleyball W(s). *Intramural sports:* badminton M(c)/W(c), baseball M(c), basketball W, bowling M/W, equestrian sports M(c)/W(c), football M/W, ice hockey M(c), racquetball M/W, soccer M(c)/W(c), softball M(c)/W(c), tennis M/W, ultimate Frisbee M(c)/W(c), volleyball M(c)/W(c), water polo M/W, weight lifting M/W.

Standardized Tests *Required:* SAT or ACT (for admission).

Costs (2010–11) *Tuition:* state resident $7128 full-time, $297 per credit hour part-time; nonresident $13,896 full-time, $579 per credit hour part-time. Full-time tuition and fees vary according to course load and reciprocity agreements. Part-time tuition and fees vary according to course load and reciprocity agreements. *Room and board:* $6260; room only: $3420. Room and board charges vary according to board plan and housing facility. *Payment plan:* installment. *Waivers:* senior citizens and employees or children of employees.

Financial Aid Of all full-time matriculated undergraduates who enrolled in 2008, 7,451 applied for aid, 5,965 were judged to have need, 920 had their need fully met. In 2008, 765 non-need-based awards were made. *Average percent of need met:* 53%. *Average financial aid package:* $8482. *Average need-based loan:* $3874. *Average need-based gift aid:* $5801. *Average non-need-based aid:* $4438. *Average indebtedness upon graduation:* $21,535.

Applying *Options:* electronic application, early admission, early action, deferred entrance. *Application fee:* $40. *Required:* high school transcript. *Required for some:* some programs require separate applications. *Application deadlines:* 8/1 (freshmen), 8/1 (out-of-state freshmen), 8/1 (transfers), 1/15 (early action). *Notification:* continuous (freshmen), continuous (out-of-state freshmen), continuous (transfers).

Freshman Application Contact Office of Admissions, Northern Kentucky University, Lucas Administrative Center, 400 Nunn Drive, Highland Heights, KY 41099. *Phone:* 859-572-5220. *Toll-free phone:* 800-637-9948. *Fax:* 859-572-6665. *E-mail:* admitnku@nku.edu. *Web site:* http://www.nku.edu/.

See page 1478 for the College Close-Up.

Pikeville College
Pikeville, Kentucky

- **Independent** comprehensive, founded 1889, affiliated with Presbyterian Church (U.S.A.)
- **Small-town** 25-acre campus
- **Endowment** $14.9 million
- **Coed** 1,022 undergraduate students, 91% full-time, 46% women, 54% men
- **Noncompetitive** entrance level, 100% of applicants were admitted

Undergraduates 929 full-time, 93 part-time. Students come from 26 states and territories; 5 other countries; 23% are from out of state; 11% Black or African American, non-Hispanic/Latino; 1% Hispanic/Latino; 0.3% Asian, non-Hispanic/Latino; 0.2% American Indian or Alaska Native, non-Hispanic/Latino; 0.6% international; 12% transferred in; 51% live on campus. *Retention:* 54% of full-time freshmen returned.

Freshmen *Admission:* 1,219 applied, 1,219 admitted, 393 enrolled. *Average high school GPA:* 3.11. *Test scores:* ACT scores over 18: 68%; ACT scores over 24: 16%; ACT scores over 30: 1%.

Faculty *Total:* 82, 70% full-time, 44% with terminal degrees. *Student/faculty ratio:* 15:1.

Academics *Calendar:* semesters. *Degrees:* associate, bachelor's, doctoral-professional, and postbachelor's certificates. *Special study options:* academic remediation for entering students, advanced placement credit, double majors, independent study, internships, part-time degree program, services for LD students, student-designed majors, study abroad, summer session for credit. *ROTC:* Army (b).

Computers on Campus 166 computers/terminals are available on campus for general student use. Students can access the following: free student e-mail accounts, online (class) grades, online (class) registration, online (class) schedules. Campuswide network is available. 80% of college-owned or -operated housing units are wired for high-speed Internet access. Wireless service is available via classrooms, computer centers, computer labs, dorm rooms, libraries.

Student Life *Housing options:* coed, men-only, women-only. Campus housing is university owned. Freshman applicants given priority for college housing. *Activities and organizations:* student-run newspaper, choral group, student government, Phi Beta Lambda, Lambda Sigma, Concert Choir, Student Nurses at PC. *Campus security:* 24-hour emergency response devices and patrols, controlled dormitory access.

Athletics Member NAIA. *Intercollegiate sports:* baseball M(s), basketball M(s)/W(s), bowling M(s)/W(s), cheerleading M(s)/W(s), cross-country running M(s)/W(s), football M(s), golf M(s)/W(s), soccer M(s)/W(s), softball W(s), tennis M(s)/W(s), volleyball W(s).

Costs (2010–11) *Comprehensive fee:* $21,550 includes full-time tuition ($15,250) and room and board ($6300). Full-time tuition and fees vary according to course load. Part-time tuition: $635 per credit hour. Part-time tuition and fees vary according to course load. *Payment plan:* installment. *Waivers:* senior citizens and employees or children of employees.

Financial Aid Of all full-time matriculated undergraduates who enrolled in 2009, 891 applied for aid, 887 were judged to have need, 620 had their need fully met. 127 Federal Work-Study jobs (averaging $1542). *Average percent of need met:* 95%. *Average financial aid package:* $16,714. *Average need-based loan:* $3959. *Average need-based gift aid:* $13,834. *Average indebtedness upon graduation:* $21,250.

Applying *Options:* electronic application, deferred entrance. *Required:* high school transcript. *Application deadlines:* 8/15 (freshmen), 8/15 (transfers). *Notification:* continuous (freshmen), continuous (transfers).

Freshman Application Contact Mr. Gary Justice, Director of Admissions and Student Financial Aid, Pikeville College, 147 Sycamore Street, Pikeville, KY 41501. *Phone:* 606-218-5251. *Toll-free phone:* 866-232-7700. *Fax:* 606-218-5255. *E-mail:* wewantyou@pc.edu. *Web site:* http://www.pc.edu/.

Southern Baptist Theological Seminary
Louisville, Kentucky

Freshman Application Contact Dr. Daniel DeWitt, Southern Baptist Theological Seminary, 2825 Lexington Road, Louisville, KY 40280-0004. *Phone:* 502-897-4011 Ext. 4617. *Web site:* http://www.sbts.edu/.

Spalding University
Louisville, Kentucky

- **Independent** comprehensive, founded 1814, affiliated with Roman Catholic Church
- **Urban** 5-acre campus with easy access to Louisville
- **Endowment** $8.9 million
- **Coed** 1,306 undergraduate students, 74% full-time, 74% women, 26% men
- **Moderately difficult** entrance level, 21% of applicants were admitted

Undergraduates 961 full-time, 345 part-time. Students come from 5 states and territories; 10 other countries; 7% are from out of state; 29% Black or African American, non-Hispanic/Latino; 3% Hispanic/Latino; 0.8% Asian, non-Hispanic/Latino; 0.2% American Indian or Alaska Native, non-Hispanic/Latino; 3% Two or more races, non-Hispanic/Latino; 7% Race/ethnicity unknown; 0.6% international; 14% transferred in; 7% live on campus. *Retention:* 72% of full-time freshmen returned.

Freshmen *Admission:* 644 applied, 133 admitted, 140 enrolled. *Test scores:* SAT critical reading scores over 500: 30%; SAT math scores over 500: 20%; ACT scores over 18: 53%; SAT critical reading scores over 600: 10%; ACT scores over 24: 8%; SAT critical reading scores over 700: 10%.

Faculty *Total:* 168, 52% full-time, 58% with terminal degrees. *Student/faculty ratio:* 9:1.

Academics *Calendar:* other. *Degrees:* certificates, associate, bachelor's, master's, doctoral-research/scholarship, post-master's, and postbachelor's certificates. *Special study options:* academic remediation for entering students, accelerated degree program, adult/continuing education programs, advanced placement credit, cooperative education, distance learning, double majors, independent study, internships, off-campus study, part-time degree program, services for LD students, study abroad, summer session for credit. *ROTC:* Army (c), Air Force (c). *Unusual degree programs:* 3-2 Occupational Therapy.

Computers on Campus 250 computers/terminals are available on campus for general student use. Students can access the following: computer help desk, free student e-mail accounts, online (class) grades, online (class) registration, online (class) schedules. Campuswide network is available. 100% of college-owned or -operated housing units are wired for high-speed Internet access. Wireless service is available via entire campus.

Student Life *Housing options:* coed. Campus housing is university owned. *Activities and organizations:* student government, Nursing Society, Student Occupational Therapy Association, National Education Association, Psychology Student Organization. *Campus security:* 24-hour emergency response devices and patrols, late-night transport/escort service, controlled dormitory access. *Student services:* personal/psychological counseling.

Athletics Member USCAA and NCAA. All Division III. *Intercollegiate sports:* baseball M, basketball M/W, bowling W, cross-country running M/W, golf M/W, soccer M/W, softball W, track and field M/W, volleyball W.

Standardized Tests *Required:* SAT or ACT (for admission).

Costs (2010–11) *Comprehensive fee:* $23,836 includes full-time tuition ($17,550), mandatory fees ($600), and room and board ($5686). Full-time tuition and fees vary according to course load and program. Part-time tuition: $585 per credit hour. *College room only:* $2150. Room and board charges vary according to board plan. *Payment plans:* installment, deferred payment. *Waivers:* employees or children of employees.

Financial Aid *Average percent of need met:* 75%. *Average financial aid package:* $11,500.

Applying *Options:* electronic application, early action, deferred entrance. *Application fee:* $20. *Required:* high school transcript, minimum 2.5 GPA. *Required for some:* essay or personal statement. *Recommended:* interview. *Application deadlines:* rolling (freshmen), rolling (out-of-state freshmen), rolling (transfers). *Notification:* continuous (freshmen), continuous (out-of-state freshmen), continuous (transfers).

Freshman Application Contact Mr. Matt Elder, Assistant Director of Admissions, Spalding University, 845 South Third Street, Louisville, KY 40203. *Phone:* 502-585-9911 Ext. 2220. *Toll-free phone:* 800-896-8941 Ext. 2111. *Fax:* 502-992-2418. *E-mail:* admissions@spalding.edu. *Web site:* http://www.spalding.edu/.

Strayer University - Florence Campus
Florence, Kentucky
- **Proprietary** comprehensive
- **Coed**

Academics *Degrees:* certificates, diplomas, associate, bachelor's, master's, and postbachelor's certificates.

Costs (2010–11) *Tuition:* $13,635 full-time, $1590 per course part-time.

Freshman Application Contact Strayer University - Florence Campus, 7300 Turfway Road, Suite 250, Florence, KY 41042. *Web site:* http://strayer.edu/florence.

Strayer University - Lexington Campus
Lexington, Kentucky
- **Proprietary** comprehensive
- **Coed**

Academics *Degrees:* certificates, diplomas, associate, bachelor's, master's, and postbachelor's certificates.

Costs (2010–11) *Tuition:* $13,635 full-time, $1590 per course part-time.

Freshman Application Contact Strayer University - Lexington Campus, 220 Lexington Green Circle, Suite 550, Lexington, KY 40503. *Web site:* http://www.strayer.edu/lexington/.

Strayer University - Louisville Campus
Louisville, Kentucky
- **Proprietary** comprehensive
- **Coed**

Academics *Degrees:* certificates, diplomas, associate, bachelor's, master's, and postbachelor's certificates.

Costs (2010–11) *Tuition:* $13,635 full-time, $1590 per course part-time.

Freshman Application Contact Strayer University - Louisville Campus, 2650 Eastpoint Parkway, Suite 100, Louisville, KY 40223. *Web site:* http://www.strayer.edu/louisville/.

Sullivan College of Technology and Design
Louisville, Kentucky
- **Proprietary** primarily 2-year, founded 1961, part of The Sullivan University System, Inc.
- **Suburban** 10-acre campus with easy access to Louisville
- **Coed** 705 undergraduate students, 62% full-time, 30% women, 70% men
- **Moderately difficult** entrance level, 57% of applicants were admitted

Undergraduates 440 full-time, 265 part-time. Students come from 8 states and territories; 7 other countries; 11% are from out of state; 18% Black or African American, non-Hispanic/Latino; 3% Hispanic/Latino; 0.9% Asian, non-Hispanic/Latino; 0.3% Native Hawaiian or other Pacific Islander, non-Hispanic/Latino; 0.3% American Indian or Alaska Native, non-Hispanic/Latino; 6% Two or more races, non-Hispanic/Latino; 6% transferred in; 3% live on campus. *Retention:* 86% of full-time freshmen returned.

Freshmen *Admission:* 323 applied, 184 admitted, 181 enrolled.

Faculty *Total:* 82, 40% full-time. *Student/faculty ratio:* 11:1.

Academics *Calendar:* quarters. *Degrees:* certificates, diplomas, associate, and bachelor's. *Special study options:* academic remediation for entering students, accelerated degree program, adult/continuing education programs, advanced placement credit, double majors, independent study, internships, part-time degree program, services for LD students, summer session for credit.

Computers on Campus 250 computers/terminals and 16 ports are available on campus for general student use. Students can access the following: campus intranet, computer help desk, free student e-mail accounts, online (class) grades, online (class) schedules, Wireless Internet. Campuswide network is available. 50% of college-owned or -operated housing units are wired for high-speed Internet access. Wireless service is available via classrooms, computer centers, computer labs, dorm rooms, learning centers, libraries, student centers.

Student Life *Housing options:* coed. Campus housing is university owned and leased by the school. Freshman campus housing is guaranteed. *Activities and organizations:* ASID, IIDA, ADDA, ADFED, Skills USA. *Campus security:* late-night transport/escort service, controlled dormitory access, telephone alarm device during hours school is open; Patrols by trained security personnel while classes are in session.

Standardized Tests *Required:* Career Performance Assessment Test (CPAt) or ACT or SAT scores in place of CPAt results (for admission). *Recommended:* SAT or ACT (for admission).

Costs (2010–11) *One-time required fee:* $100. *Comprehensive fee:* $25,600 includes full-time tuition ($16,425), mandatory fees ($850), and room and board ($8325). Full-time tuition and fees vary according to course load, degree level, and program. Part-time tuition: $445 per credit hour. Part-time tuition and fees vary according to course load, degree level, and program. No tuition increase for student's term of enrollment. *Required fees:* $50 per course part-time. *College room only:* $5355. Room and board charges vary according to board plan and housing facility. *Payment plan:* installment. *Waivers:* employees or children of employees.

Applying *Options:* deferred entrance. *Application fee:* $100. *Required:* high school transcript, interview. *Recommended:* minimum 2 GPA. *Application deadlines:* rolling (freshmen), rolling (out-of-state freshmen), rolling (transfers). *Notification:* continuous (freshmen), continuous (out-of-state freshmen), continuous (transfers).

Freshman Application Contact Mr. Aamer Z. Chauhdri, Director of Admissions, Sullivan College of Technology and Design, 3901 Atkinson Square Drive, Louisville, KY 40218. *Phone:* 502-456-6509 Ext. 8220. *Toll-free phone:* 800-884-6528. *Fax:* 502-456-2341. *E-mail:* achauhdri@sctd.edu. *Web site:* http://www.sctd.edu/.

Sullivan University
Louisville, Kentucky
- **Proprietary** comprehensive, founded 1864, administratively affiliated with Sullivan University System
- **Suburban** 10-acre campus
- **Coed**
- **Minimally difficult** entrance level

Faculty *Student/faculty ratio:* 20:1.

Academics *Calendar:* quarters. *Degrees:* certificates, diplomas, associate, bachelor's, master's, post-master's, and postbachelor's certificates.

Student Life *Campus security:* 24-hour patrols.

Standardized Tests *Required:* ACT or CPAt (for admission).

Costs (2010–11) *Comprehensive fee:* $23,045 includes full-time tuition ($16,500), mandatory fees ($200), and room and board ($6345). Full-time tuition and fees vary according to class time, course level, course load, degree level, location, program, and student level. Part-time tuition: $275 per credit hour. Part-time tuition and fees vary according to class time, course level, course load, degree level, location, program, and student level. No tuition increase for student's term of enrollment. *Required fees:* $50 per course part-time. *Room and board:* Room and board charges vary according to board plan. *Payment plans:* installment, deferred payment.

Financial Aid *Of all full-time matriculated undergraduates who enrolled in 2002,* 6,028 applied for aid, 5,247 were judged to have need. 31 Federal Work-Study jobs (averaging $2065). *In 2002,* 374 non-need-based awards were made. *Average non-need-based aid:* $2000. *Average indebtedness upon graduation:* $15,000.

Applying *Application fee:* $100. *Required:* high school transcript, interview. *Required for some:* essay or personal statement.

Freshman Application Contact Ms. Terri Thomas, Director of Admissions, Sullivan University, 3101 Bardstown Road, Louisville, KY 40205. *Phone:* 502-456-6505 Ext. 370. *Toll-free phone:* 800-844-1354. *Fax:* 502-456-0040. *E-mail:* admissions@sullivan.edu. *Web site:* http://www.sullivan.edu/.

Thomas More College

Crestview Hills, Kentucky

- **Independent Roman Catholic** comprehensive, founded 1921
- **Suburban** 100-acre campus with easy access to Cincinnati
- **Endowment** $12.7 million
- **Coed** 1,732 undergraduate students, 79% full-time, 53% women, 47% men
- **Moderately difficult** entrance level, 86% of applicants were admitted

Undergraduates 1,365 full-time, 367 part-time. Students come from 15 states and territories; 3 other countries; 47% are from out of state; 4% transferred in; 30% live on campus. *Retention:* 70% of full-time freshmen returned.

Freshmen *Admission:* 885 applied, 763 admitted, 299 enrolled. *Average high school GPA:* 3.35. *Test scores:* SAT critical reading scores over 500: 47%; SAT math scores over 500: 61%; ACT scores over 18: 98%; SAT critical reading scores over 600: 19%; SAT math scores over 600: 18%; ACT scores over 24: 45%; SAT critical reading scores over 700: 5%; SAT math scores over 700: 1%; ACT scores over 30: 7%.

Faculty *Total:* 131, 56% full-time. *Student/faculty ratio:* 16:1.

Academics *Calendar:* semesters. *Degrees:* certificates, associate, bachelor's, and master's. *Special study options:* academic remediation for entering students, accelerated degree program, adult/continuing education programs, advanced placement credit, cooperative education, double majors, honors programs, independent study, internships, off-campus study, part-time degree program, services for LD students, student-designed majors, study abroad, summer session for credit. *ROTC:* Army (c), Air Force (c). *Unusual degree programs:* 3-2 engineering with Accredited institution of student's choice.

Computers on Campus 95 computers/terminals are available on campus for general student use. Students can access the following: campus intranet, computer help desk, free student e-mail accounts, online (class) grades, online (class) registration, online (class) schedules. Campuswide network is available. 100% of college-owned or -operated housing units are wired for high-speed Internet access. Wireless service is available via entire campus.

Student Life *Housing options:* coed, men-only, women-only, disabled students. Campus housing is university owned. *Activities and organizations:* drama/theater group, choral group, Student Government Association, Student Activities Board, More Ministry, Outdoors Adventure Club, International Student Society, national fraternities, national sororities. *Campus security:* 24-hour emergency response devices and patrols, late-night transport/escort service, controlled dormitory access. *Student services:* health clinic, personal/psychological counseling.

Athletics Member NCAA. All Division III. *Intercollegiate sports:* baseball M, basketball M/W, cross-country running M/W, football M, golf M/W, soccer M/W, softball W, tennis M/W, volleyball W. *Intramural sports:* basketball M/W, football M, soccer M/W, softball M/W, volleyball M/W.

Standardized Tests *Required:* SAT or ACT (for admission).

Costs (2010–11) *Comprehensive fee:* $31,510 includes full-time tuition ($24,000), mandatory fees ($720), and room and board ($6790). Full-time tuition and fees vary according to program and student level. Part-time tuition: $545 per credit hour. Part-time tuition and fees vary according to course load and program. *Required fees:* $30 per credit hour part-time, $15 per term part-time. *College room only:* $3200. Room and board charges vary according to board plan and housing facility. *Payment plans:* installment, deferred payment. *Waivers:* senior citizens and employees or children of employees.

Financial Aid Of all full-time matriculated undergraduates who enrolled in 2009, 828 applied for aid, 673 were judged to have need, 126 had their need fully met. 153 Federal Work-Study jobs (averaging $1337). 163 state and other part-time jobs (averaging $1056). In 2009, 171 non-need-based awards were made. *Average percent of need met:* 68%. *Average financial aid package:* $14,904. *Average need-based loan:* $4381. *Average need-based gift aid:* $12,187. *Average non-need-based aid:* $12,703. *Average indebtedness upon graduation:* $32,720.

Applying *Options:* electronic application, deferred entrance. *Application fee:* $25. *Required:* high school transcript, minimum 2.5 GPA. *Required for some:* 2 letters of recommendation. *Application deadlines:* 8/1 (freshmen), 8/1 (transfers). *Notification:* continuous (freshmen), continuous (transfers).

Freshman Application Contact Mr. Billy Sarge, Associate Director of Admissions, Thomas More College, 333 Thomas More Parkway, Crestview Hills, KY 41017-3495. *Phone:* 859-344-3332. *Toll-free phone:* 800-825-4557. *Fax:* 859-344-3444. *E-mail:* admissions@thomasmore.edu. *Web site:* http://www.thomasmore.edu/.

See page 1664 for the College Close-Up.

Transylvania University

Lexington, Kentucky

- **Independent** 4-year, founded 1780, affiliated with Christian Church (Disciples of Christ)
- **Urban** 40-acre campus with easy access to Cincinnati and Louisville
- **Endowment** $112.9 million
- **Coed** 1,110 undergraduate students, 99% full-time, 60% women, 40% men
- **Very difficult** entrance level, 84% of applicants were admitted

Undergraduates 1,099 full-time, 11 part-time. Students come from 28 states and territories; 5 other countries; 15% are from out of state; 4% Black or African American, non-Hispanic/Latino; 1% Hispanic/Latino; 0.6% Asian, non-Hispanic/Latino; 0.2% American Indian or Alaska Native, non-Hispanic/Latino; 1% Two or more races, non-Hispanic/Latino; 4% Race/ethnicity unknown; 0.7% international; 1% transferred in; 76% live on campus. *Retention:* 81% of full-time freshmen returned.

Freshmen *Admission:* 1,319 applied, 1,105 admitted, 303 enrolled. *Average high school GPA:* 3.79. *Test scores:* SAT critical reading scores over 500: 89%; SAT math scores over 500: 81%; ACT scores over 18: 100%; SAT critical reading scores over 600: 53%; SAT math scores over 600: 48%; ACT scores over 24: 79%; SAT critical reading scores over 700: 21%; SAT math scores over 700: 15%; ACT scores over 30: 21%.

Faculty *Total:* 103, 83% full-time, 80% with terminal degrees. *Student/faculty ratio:* 12:1.

Academics *Calendar:* 4-4-1. *Degree:* bachelor's. *Special study options:* advanced placement credit, double majors, independent study, internships, off-campus study, part-time degree program, student-designed majors, study abroad, summer session for credit. *ROTC:* Army (c), Air Force (c). *Unusual degree programs:* 3-2 engineering with University of Kentucky, Vanderbilt University.

Computers on Campus 200 computers/terminals and 200 ports are available on campus for general student use. Students can access the following: campus intranet, computer help desk, free student e-mail accounts, online (class) grades, online (class) registration, online (class) schedules. Campuswide network is available. 100% of college-owned or -operated housing units are wired for high-speed Internet access. Wireless service is available via classrooms, computer centers, computer labs, dorm rooms, learning centers, libraries, student centers.

Student Life *Housing:* on-campus residence required through junior year. *Options:* coed, men-only, women-only, disabled students. Campus housing is university owned. Freshman campus housing is guaranteed. *Activities and organizations:* drama/theater group, student-run newspaper, radio station, choral group, Student Alumni Association, Student Government Association, Student Activities Board, Crimson Crew, Transylvania Environmental Rights and Responsibility Alliance (TERRA), national fraternities, national sororities. *Campus security:* 24-hour emergency response devices and patrols, late-night transport/escort service, controlled dormitory access. *Student services:* health clinic, personal/psychological counseling.

Athletics Member NCAA. All Division III. *Intercollegiate sports:* baseball M, basketball M/W, cheerleading M/W, cross-country running M/W, field hockey W, golf M/W, soccer M/W, softball W, swimming and diving M/W, tennis M/W, track and field M/W, volleyball W. *Intramural sports:* badminton M/W, basketball M/W, cross-country running M/W, football M/W, golf M/W, racquetball M/W, soccer M/W, softball M/W, swimming and diving M/W, table tennis M/W, tennis M/W, track and field M/W, ultimate Frisbee M/W, volleyball M/W, weight lifting M/W.

Standardized Tests *Required:* SAT or ACT (for admission).

Costs (2010–11) *Comprehensive fee:* $34,830 includes full-time tuition ($25,650), mandatory fees ($1090), and room and board ($8090). Part-time tuition: $2845 per course. Part-time tuition and fees vary according to course load. *Room and board:* Room and board charges vary according to board plan and location. *Payment plan:* installment. *Waivers:* employees or children of employees.

Financial Aid Of all full-time matriculated undergraduates who enrolled in 2009, 841 applied for aid, 752 were judged to have need, 161 had their need fully met. 450 Federal Work-Study jobs (averaging $1727). 57 state and other part-time jobs (averaging $6178). In 2009, 325 non-need-based awards were made. *Average percent of need met:* 81%. *Average financial aid package:* $21,914. *Average need-based loan:* $4230. *Average need-based gift aid:* $17,573. *Average non-need-based aid:* $10,995. *Average indebtedness upon graduation:* $22,432.

Applying *Options:* electronic application, early admission, early action, deferred entrance. *Application fee:* $30. *Required:* essay or personal statement, high school transcript, minimum 2.75 GPA, 2 letters of recommendation. *Required for some:* interview. *Recommended:* interview. *Application deadlines:* 2/1 (freshmen), rolling (transfers), 12/1 (early action). *Notification:* 3/1 (freshmen), 1/15 (early action).

Freshman Application Contact Mr. Bradley Goan, Vice President for Enrollment and Dean of Admissions, Transylvania University, 300 North

Broadway, Lexington, KY 40508-1797. *Phone:* 859-233-4242. *Toll-free phone:* 800-872-6798. *Fax:* 859-281-3649. *E-mail:* admissions@transy.edu. *Web site:* http://www.transy.edu/.

See page 1666 for the College Close-Up.

Union College

Barbourville, Kentucky

- **Independent United Methodist** comprehensive, founded 1879
- **Small-town** 100-acre campus
- **Endowment** $16.7 million
- **Coed** 843 undergraduate students, 94% full-time, 46% women, 54% men
- **Moderately difficult** entrance level, 28% of applicants were admitted

Undergraduates 794 full-time, 49 part-time. Students come from 28 states and territories; 11 other countries; 25% are from out of state; 12% Black or African American, non-Hispanic/Latino; 0.9% Hispanic/Latino; 0.2% Asian, non-Hispanic/Latino; 0.4% American Indian or Alaska Native, non-Hispanic/Latino; 0.7% Race/ethnicity unknown; 3% international; 14% transferred in; 39% live on campus. *Retention:* 59% of full-time freshmen returned.

Freshmen *Admission:* 1,226 applied, 348 admitted, 198 enrolled. *Average high school GPA:* 2.9. *Test scores:* SAT critical reading scores over 500: 17%; SAT math scores over 500: 42%; ACT scores over 18: 66%; ACT scores over 24: 14%; ACT scores over 30: 1%.

Faculty *Total:* 109, 61% full-time, 51% with terminal degrees. *Student/faculty ratio:* 15:1.

Academics *Calendar:* semesters. *Degrees:* bachelor's, master's, post-master's, and postbachelor's certificates. *Special study options:* academic remediation for entering students, accelerated degree program, advanced placement credit, distance learning, double majors, honors programs, independent study, internships, off-campus study, part-time degree program, services for LD students, student-designed majors, study abroad, summer session for credit. *ROTC:* Army (b). *Unusual degree programs:* 3-2 engineering with University of Kentucky.

Computers on Campus 230 computers/terminals and 450 ports are available on campus for general student use. Students can access the following: campus intranet, computer help desk, free student e-mail accounts, online (class) grades, online (class) registration, online (class) schedules. Campuswide network is available. 100% of college-owned or -operated housing units are wired for high-speed Internet access. Wireless service is available via classrooms, computer centers, computer labs, dorm rooms, learning centers, libraries, student centers.

Student Life *Housing:* on-campus residence required through sophomore year. *Options:* men-only, women-only. Campus housing is university owned. Freshman campus housing is guaranteed. *Activities and organizations:* drama/theater group, choral group, Open Mic Night, Bingo Night, Movie Fest. *Campus security:* 24-hour emergency response devices and patrols, late-night transport/escort service, controlled dormitory access. *Student services:* health clinic, personal/psychological counseling.

Athletics Member NAIA. *Intercollegiate sports:* baseball M(s), basketball M(s)/W(s), bowling M(s)/W(s), cheerleading M(s)/W(s), cross-country running M(s)/W(s), football M(s), golf M(s)/W(s), soccer M(s)/W(s), softball W(s), swimming and diving M(s)/W(s), tennis M(s)/W(s), track and field M(s)/W(s), volleyball W(s). *Intramural sports:* basketball M/W, football M, soccer M/W, table tennis M/W, ultimate Frisbee M/W, volleyball M/W, water polo M/W.

Standardized Tests *Required:* SAT or ACT (for admission).

Costs (2011–12) *Comprehensive fee:* $26,204 includes full-time tuition ($19,174), mandatory fees ($830), and room and board ($6200). Full-time tuition and fees vary according to course load. Part-time tuition and fees vary according to course load. *College room only:* $2650. Room and board charges vary according to board plan and housing facility. *Payment plan:* installment. *Waivers:* senior citizens and employees or children of employees.

Financial Aid Of all full-time matriculated undergraduates who enrolled in 2009, 828 applied for aid, 733 were judged to have need, 75 had their need fully met. 166 Federal Work-Study jobs (averaging $1202). 84 state and other part-time jobs (averaging $1202). In 2009, 83 non-need-based awards were made. *Average percent of need met:* 66%. *Average financial aid package:* $17,700. *Average need-based loan:* $4229. *Average need-based gift aid:* $13,548. *Average non-need-based aid:* $10,965. *Average indebtedness upon graduation:* $15,272.

Applying *Options:* electronic application, deferred entrance. *Application fee:* $10. *Required:* high school transcript, minimum 2 GPA. *Required for some:* interview. *Notification:* continuous (freshmen), continuous (out-of-state freshmen), continuous (transfers).

Freshman Application Contact Mr. Jerry Jackson, Dean for Enrollment Management, Union College, 310 College Street, Barbourville, KY 40906. *Phone:* 606-546-1222. *Toll-free phone:* 800-489-8646. *Fax:* 606-546-1667. *E-mail:* enroll@unionky.edu. *Web site:* http://www.unionky.edu/.

University of Kentucky

Lexington, Kentucky

- **State-supported** university, founded 1865
- **Urban** 685-acre campus with easy access to Cincinnati and Louisville
- **Coed**
- **Moderately difficult** entrance level

Faculty *Student/faculty ratio:* 18:1.

Academics *Calendar:* semesters. *Degrees:* bachelor's, master's, doctoral-professional, doctoral-research/scholarship, and post-master's certificates.

Student Life *Campus security:* 24-hour emergency response devices and patrols, late-night transport/escort service, controlled dormitory access.

Athletics Member NCAA. All Division I except football (Division I-A).

Standardized Tests *Required:* SAT or ACT (for admission).

Costs (2010–11) *Tuition:* state resident $7656 full-time, $319 per credit hour part-time; nonresident $16,724 full-time, $697 per credit hour part-time. Full-time tuition and fees vary according to degree level, program, reciprocity agreements, and student level. Part-time tuition and fees vary according to degree level, program, reciprocity agreements, and student level. *Required fees:* $954 full-time, $24 per credit hour part-time. *Room and board:* $9439; room only: $4135. Room and board charges vary according to board plan and housing facility.

Financial Aid *Of all full-time matriculated undergraduates who enrolled in 2008,* 10,575 applied for aid, 7,994 were judged to have need, 1,493 had their need fully met. 430 Federal Work-Study jobs (averaging $1804). 91 state and other part-time jobs (averaging $3248). *In 2008,* 6312 non-need-based awards were made. *Average percent of need met:* 61. *Average financial aid package:* $8928. *Average need-based loan:* $4033. *Average need-based gift aid:* $5605. *Average non-need-based aid:* $5683. *Average indebtedness upon graduation:* $19,812.

Applying *Options:* electronic application, deferred entrance. *Application fee:* $50. *Required:* high school transcript, minimum 2 GPA.

Freshman Application Contact Ms. Michelle Nordin, Associate Director of Admissions, University of Kentucky, 100 W.D. Funkhouser Building, Lexington, KY 40506-0054. *Phone:* 859-257-2000. *Toll-free phone:* 800-432-0967. *E-mail:* admissio@uky.edu. *Web site:* http://www.uky.edu/.

University of Louisville

Louisville, Kentucky

- **State-supported** university, founded 1798
- **Urban** 345-acre campus with easy access to Louisville
- **Endowment** $669.0 million
- **Coed** 15,644 undergraduate students, 78% full-time, 51% women, 49% men
- **Moderately difficult** entrance level, 76% of applicants were admitted

Undergraduates 12,167 full-time, 3,477 part-time. Students come from 50 states and territories; 69 other countries; 16% are from out of state; 12% Black or African American, non-Hispanic/Latino; 3% Hispanic/Latino; 3% Asian, non-Hispanic/Latino; 0.1% Native Hawaiian or other Pacific Islander, non-Hispanic/Latino; 0.2% American Indian or Alaska Native, non-Hispanic/Latino; 2% Two or more races, non-Hispanic/Latino; 0.3% Race/ethnicity unknown; 1% international; 7% transferred in; 29% live on campus. *Retention:* 78% of full-time freshmen returned.

Freshmen *Admission:* 8,036 applied, 6,069 admitted, 2,562 enrolled. *Average high school GPA:* 3.46. *Test scores:* SAT critical reading scores over 500: 75%; SAT math scores over 500: 78%; ACT scores over 18: 99%; SAT critical reading scores over 600: 35%; SAT math scores over 600: 40%; ACT scores over 24: 55%; SAT critical reading scores over 700: 6%; SAT math scores over 700: 8%; ACT scores over 30: 13%.

Faculty *Total:* 1,388, 64% full-time, 70% with terminal degrees. *Student/faculty ratio:* 18:1.

Academics *Calendar:* semesters. *Degrees:* certificates, associate, bachelor's, master's, doctoral-other, doctoral-professional, doctoral-research/scholarship, post-master's, and postbachelor's certificates. *Special study options:* academic remediation for entering students, accelerated degree program, adult/continuing education programs, advanced placement credit, cooperative education, distance learning, double majors, English as a second language, honors programs, independent study, internships, off-campus study, part-time degree program, services for LD students, student-designed majors, study abroad, summer session for credit. *ROTC:* Army (b), Air Force (b). *Unusual degree programs:* 3-2 engineering with See: http://louisville.edu/speed/academics/degree-programs/master-of-engineering.html for details on the eight engineering degree options. Bachelor of Music and Bachelor of Music Education, Bachelor of Arts/Science and Master of Public Health.

Computers on Campus 400 computers/terminals are available on campus for general student use. Students can access the following: campus intranet, computer help desk, free student e-mail accounts, online (class) grades, online (class) registration, online (class) schedules. Campuswide network is available.

100% of college-owned or -operated housing units are wired for high-speed Internet access. Wireless service is available via classrooms, computer centers, libraries, student centers.

Student Life *Housing options:* coed, cooperative, disabled students. Campus housing is university owned and is provided by a third party. Freshman applicants given priority for college housing. *Activities and organizations:* drama/theater group, student-run newspaper, radio station, choral group, marching band, Baptist Campus Ministry, Society of Porter Scholars, Association of Black Students, commonGround, Phi Eta Sigma, national fraternities, national sororities. *Campus security:* 24-hour emergency response devices and patrols, late-night transport/escort service, controlled dormitory access, The University of Louisville Alert notification system. *Student services:* health clinic, personal/psychological counseling, women's center.

Athletics Member NCAA. All Division I except football (Division I-A). *Intercollegiate sports:* baseball M(s), basketball M(s)/W(s), cheerleading M(c)/W(c), crew W(s), cross-country running M(s)/W(s), field hockey W(s), golf M(s)/W(s), lacrosse W(s), soccer M(s)/W(s), softball W(s), swimming and diving M(s)/W(s), tennis M(s)/W(s), track and field M(s)/W(s), volleyball W(s). *Intramural sports:* badminton M/W, basketball M/W, bowling M/W, cross-country running M/W, equestrian sports W(c), fencing M/W, football M/W, golf M/W, gymnastics W(c), ice hockey M, lacrosse M(c)/W(c), racquetball M/W, rugby M(c), soccer M/W, softball W, swimming and diving M/W, table tennis M/W, tennis M/W, track and field M/W, ultimate Frisbee M/W, volleyball M/W.

Standardized Tests *Required:* SAT or ACT (for admission). *Required for some:* TOEFL for students whose primary language is not English.

Costs (2010–11) *Tuition:* state resident $8424 full-time, $351 per credit hour part-time; nonresident $20,424 full-time, $851 per credit hour part-time. Full-time tuition and fees vary according to reciprocity agreements. Part-time tuition and fees vary according to course load and reciprocity agreements. *Room and board:* $6602; room only: $4272. Room and board charges vary according to board plan and housing facility. *Payment plan:* installment. *Waivers:* senior citizens and employees or children of employees.

Financial Aid Of all full-time matriculated undergraduates who enrolled in 2009, 8,716 applied for aid, 7,299 were judged to have need, 1,398 had their need fully met. 536 Federal Work-Study jobs (averaging $2358). In 2009, 1504 non-need-based awards were made. *Average percent of need met:* 62%. *Average financial aid package:* $10,552. *Average need-based loan:* $4077. *Average need-based gift aid:* $7999. *Average non-need-based aid:* $7111. *Average indebtedness upon graduation:* $18,713.

Applying *Options:* electronic application, deferred entrance. *Application fee:* $40. *Required:* high school transcript, minimum 2.5 GPA. *Application deadlines:* 2/15 (freshmen), 7/1 (transfers). *Notification:* continuous (freshmen), continuous (transfers).

Freshman Application Contact Ms. Jenny L. Sawyer, Executive Director of Admissions, University of Louisville, 2301 South Third Street, Houchens Room 150, Louisville, KY 40292-0001. *Phone:* 502-852-6531. *Toll-free phone:* 800-334-8635. *Fax:* 502-852-4776. *E-mail:* admitme@louisville.edu. *Web site:* http://www.louisville.edu/.

University of the Cumberlands
Williamsburg, Kentucky

- **Independent Kentucky Baptist** comprehensive, founded 1889
- **Rural** 60-acre campus with easy access to Knoxville
- **Endowment** $61.6 million
- **Coed** 1,746 undergraduate students, 80% full-time, 51% women, 49% men
- **Moderately difficult** entrance level, 68% of applicants were admitted

Undergraduates 1,402 full-time, 344 part-time. Students come from 38 states and territories; 24 other countries; 35% are from out of state; 3% transferred in; 78% live on campus. *Retention:* 56% of full-time freshmen returned.

Freshmen *Admission:* 2,007 applied, 1,370 admitted, 448 enrolled. *Average high school GPA:* 3.4. *Test scores:* SAT critical reading scores over 500: 42%; SAT math scores over 500: 56%; ACT scores over 18: 94%; SAT critical reading scores over 600: 16%; SAT math scores over 600: 15%; ACT scores over 24: 35%; SAT critical reading scores over 700: 3%; SAT math scores over 700: 2%; ACT scores over 30: 4%.

Faculty *Total:* 163, 64% full-time, 71% with terminal degrees. *Student/faculty ratio:* 13:1.

Academics *Calendar:* semesters. *Degrees:* associate, bachelor's, master's, doctoral-other, post-master's, and postbachelor's certificates. *Special study options:* academic remediation for entering students, accelerated degree program, adult/continuing education programs, advanced placement credit, cooperative education, distance learning, double majors, English as a second language, honors programs, independent study, internships, part-time degree program, student-designed majors, study abroad, summer session for credit. *ROTC:* Army (b).

Computers on Campus 225 computers/terminals are available on campus for general student use. Students can access the following: computer help desk,

free student e-mail accounts, online (class) grades, online (class) registration, online (class) schedules. Campuswide network is available. 100% of college-owned or -operated housing units are wired for high-speed Internet access. Wireless service is available via entire campus.

Student Life *Housing:* on-campus residence required through senior year. *Options:* men-only, women-only. Campus housing is university owned. Freshman campus housing is guaranteed. *Activities and organizations:* drama/theater group, student-run newspaper, radio and television station, choral group, marching band, Baptist Student Union, Student Government Association, Campus Activity Board, Mountain Outreach, Fellowship of Christian Athletes. *Campus security:* 24-hour emergency response devices and patrols, student patrols, late-night transport/escort service, patrols by trained security personnel 11pm to 7am.

Athletics Member NAIA. *Intercollegiate sports:* baseball M(s), basketball M(s)/W(s), cheerleading M(s)/W(s), cross-country running M(s)/W(s), football M(s), golf M(s)/W(s), soccer M(s)/W(s), softball M/W(s), swimming and diving M(s)/W(s), tennis M(s)/W(s), track and field M(s)/W(s), volleyball W(s), wrestling M(s)/W(s). *Intramural sports:* basketball M/W, football M/W, golf M/W, soccer M/W, softball M/W, table tennis M/W, tennis M/W, volleyball M/W.

Standardized Tests *Required:* SAT or ACT (for admission).

Costs (2011–12) *Comprehensive fee:* $24,826 includes full-time tuition ($17,640), mandatory fees ($360), and room and board ($6826). Part-time tuition: $8820 per term. Part-time tuition and fees vary according to course load. *Required fees:* $570 per credit hour part-time. *Payment plan:* installment. *Waivers:* employees or children of employees.

Financial Aid Of all full-time matriculated undergraduates who enrolled in 2009, 1,273 applied for aid, 1,203 were judged to have need, 231 had their need fully met. 635 Federal Work-Study jobs (averaging $2267). 13 state and other part-time jobs (averaging $2104). In 2009, 172 non-need-based awards were made. *Average percent of need met:* 78%. *Average financial aid package:* $18,000. *Average need-based loan:* $3866. *Average need-based gift aid:* $13,987. *Average non-need-based aid:* $8521. *Average indebtedness upon graduation:* $15,221.

Applying *Options:* electronic application. *Application fee:* $30. *Required:* high school transcript, minimum 2 GPA. *Required for some:* essay or personal statement, interview. *Application deadline:* rolling (freshmen). *Notification:* continuous (freshmen), continuous (transfers).

Freshman Application Contact Mrs. Erica Harris, Director of Admissions, University of the Cumberlands, 6178 College Station Drive, Williamsburg, KY 40769. *Phone:* 606-539-4241. *Toll-free phone:* 800-343-1609. *Fax:* 606-539-4303. *E-mail:* admiss@ucumberlands.edu. *Web site:* http://www.ucumberlands.edu/.

See page 1744 for the College Close-Up.

Western Kentucky University
Bowling Green, Kentucky

- **State-supported** comprehensive, founded 1906
- **Suburban** 235-acre campus with easy access to Nashville
- **Endowment** $95.8 million
- **Coed** 17,821 undergraduate students, 79% full-time, 58% women, 42% men
- **Minimally difficult** entrance level, 92% of applicants were admitted

Undergraduates 14,070 full-time, 3,751 part-time. Students come from 46 states and territories; 41 other countries; 15% are from out of state; 11% Black or African American, non-Hispanic/Latino; 2% Hispanic/Latino; 0.9% Asian, non-Hispanic/Latino; 0.2% American Indian or Alaska Native, non-Hispanic/Latino; 1% Two or more races, non-Hispanic/Latino; 0.6% Race/ethnicity unknown; 2% international; 5% transferred in; 28% live on campus. *Retention:* 74% of full-time freshmen returned.

Freshmen *Admission:* 7,993 applied, 7,393 admitted, 3,377 enrolled. *Average high school GPA:* 3.16. *Test scores:* SAT critical reading scores over 500: 49%; SAT math scores over 500: 52%; ACT scores over 18: 80%; SAT critical reading scores over 600: 11%; SAT math scores over 600: 18%; ACT scores over 24: 31%; SAT critical reading scores over 700: 2%; SAT math scores over 700: 2%; ACT scores over 30: 5%.

Faculty *Total:* 1,120, 67% full-time, 53% with terminal degrees. *Student/faculty ratio:* 19:1.

Academics *Calendar:* semesters. *Degrees:* certificates, associate, bachelor's, master's, doctoral-research/scholarship, post-master's, and postbachelor's certificates. *Special study options:* academic remediation for entering students, accelerated degree program, adult/continuing education programs, advanced placement credit, cooperative education, distance learning, double majors, English as a second language, external degree program, freshman honors college, honors programs, independent study, internships, off-campus study, part-time degree program, services for LD students, student-designed majors, study abroad, summer session for credit. *ROTC:* Army (b), Air Force (c).

Computers on Campus 1,776 computers/terminals are available on campus for general student use. Students can access the following: campus intranet, computer help desk, free student e-mail accounts, online (class) grades, online (class) registration, online (class) schedules. Campuswide network is available. 100% of college-owned or -operated housing units are wired for high-speed Internet access. Wireless service is available via entire campus.

Student Life *Housing:* on-campus residence required through sophomore year. *Options:* coed, men-only, women-only, disabled students. Campus housing is university owned. Freshman applicants given priority for college housing. *Activities and organizations:* drama/theater group, student-run newspaper, radio and television station, choral group, marching band, Student Government Association, Campus Activities Board, Campus Crusade for Christ, campus ministries, Residence Hall Association, national fraternities, national sororities. *Campus security:* 24-hour emergency response devices and patrols, student patrols, late-night transport/escort service, controlled dormitory access. *Student services:* health clinic, personal/psychological counseling, women's center.

Athletics Member NCAA. All Division I except football (Division I-A). *Intercollegiate sports:* baseball M(s), basketball M(s)/W(s), cross-country running M(s)/W(s), golf M(s)/W(s), soccer W(s), softball W(s), swimming and diving M(s)/W(s), tennis M(s)/W(s), track and field M(s)/W(s), volleyball W(s). *Intramural sports:* badminton M/W, basketball M/W, bowling M(c)/W(c), fencing M(c)/W(c), field hockey M(c)/W(c), golf M/W, lacrosse M(c)/W(c), racquetball M/W, rugby M(c)/W(c), soccer M/W, softball M/W, swimming and diving M(c)/W(c), table tennis M/W, tennis M(c)/W(c), ultimate Frisbee M/W, volleyball M/W.

Standardized Tests *Required:* SAT or ACT (for admission).

Costs (2010–11) *Tuition:* state resident $7560 full-time, $315 per hour part-time; nonresident $18,840 full-time, $785 per hour part-time. Full-time tuition and fees vary according to course level, course load, location, program, and reciprocity agreements. Part-time tuition and fees vary according to course level, course load, location, program, and reciprocity agreements. *Room and board:* $6600; room only: $3810. Room and board charges vary according to board plan and housing facility. *Payment plan:* installment. *Waivers:* children of alumni, senior citizens, and employees or children of employees.

Financial Aid Of all full-time matriculated undergraduates who enrolled in 2008, 11,090 applied for aid, 8,833 were judged to have need, 2,530 had their need fully met. 690 Federal Work-Study jobs (averaging $2098). 1,887 state and other part-time jobs (averaging $2698). In 2008, 1173 non-need-based awards were made. *Average percent of need met:* 29%. *Average financial aid package:* $12,417. *Average need-based loan:* $3851. *Average need-based gift aid:* $5428. *Average non-need-based aid:* $5033. *Average indebtedness upon graduation:* $19,347.

Applying *Options:* electronic application. *Application fee:* $40. *Required:* high school transcript, minimum 2.5 GPA. *Required for some:* minimum 2 GPA. *Recommended:* minimum 2.5 GPA. *Application deadlines:* 8/1 (freshmen), 8/1 (transfers). *Notification:* continuous (freshmen), continuous (transfers).

Freshman Application Contact Western Kentucky University, 1906 College Heights Boulevard, Bowling Green, KY 42101. *Phone:* 270-745-2551. *Toll-free phone:* 800-495-8463. *Web site:* http://www.wku.edu/.

LOUISIANA

Centenary College of Louisiana
Shreveport, Louisiana

- **Independent United Methodist** comprehensive, founded 1825
- **Suburban** 65-acre campus
- **Coed** 812 undergraduate students, 99% full-time, 57% women, 43% men
- **Moderately difficult** entrance level, 60% of applicants were admitted

Undergraduates 800 full-time, 12 part-time. Students come from 33 states and territories; 12 other countries; 40% are from out of state; 5% transferred in; 68% live on campus. *Retention:* 75% of full-time freshmen returned.

Freshmen *Admission:* 1,659 applied, 995 admitted, 257 enrolled. *Test scores:* SAT critical reading scores over 500: 78%; SAT math scores over 500: 78%; ACT scores over 18: 100%; SAT critical reading scores over 600: 33%; SAT math scores over 600: 30%; ACT scores over 24: 62%; SAT critical reading scores over 700: 5%; SAT math scores over 700: 3%; ACT scores over 30: 11%.

Faculty *Total:* 80, 84% full-time, 88% with terminal degrees. *Student/faculty ratio:* 10:1.

Academics *Calendar:* 4-4-1. *Degrees:* bachelor's and master's. *Special study options:* adult/continuing education programs, advanced placement credit, double majors, honors programs, independent study, internships, off-campus study, part-time degree program, student-designed majors, study abroad, summer session for credit. *Unusual degree programs:* 3-2 engineering with

Columbia University, University of Southern California, Case Western Reserve University, Texas A&M University, Louisiana, Washington University in St. Louis; communication disorders with Louisiana State University Medical Center School of Medicine in Shreveport.

Computers on Campus 250 computers/terminals are available on campus for general student use. Students can access the following: online (class) registration. Campuswide network is available. Wireless service is available via classrooms, dorm rooms, libraries, student centers.

Student Life *Housing:* on-campus residence required through senior year. *Options:* coed, women-only. Campus housing is university owned. Freshman campus housing is guaranteed. *Activities and organizations:* drama/theater group, student-run newspaper, radio station, choral group, intramural sports, Student Activities Board, crew, Church Career/Campus Ministries, student media, national fraternities, national sororities. *Campus security:* 24-hour emergency response devices and patrols, late-night transport/escort service, controlled dormitory access. *Student services:* health clinic, personal/psychological counseling.

Athletics Member NCAA. All Division III. *Intercollegiate sports:* baseball M, basketball M/W, cheerleading M(c)/W(c), cross-country running M/W, golf M/W, gymnastics W, lacrosse M(c), soccer M/W, softball W, swimming and diving M/W, tennis M/W, volleyball W. *Intramural sports:* basketball M/W, cheerleading M/W, football M/W, golf M, lacrosse M, soccer M/W, softball M/W, table tennis M/W, tennis M/W, volleyball M/W.

Standardized Tests *Required:* SAT or ACT (for admission).

Costs (2010–11) *Comprehensive fee:* $31,220 includes full-time tuition ($22,080), mandatory fees ($1200), and room and board ($7940). Part-time tuition and fees vary according to course load and program. *College room only:* $4020. Room and board charges vary according to board plan and housing facility. *Payment plans:* installment, deferred payment. *Waivers:* employees or children of employees.

Financial Aid Of all full-time matriculated undergraduates who enrolled in 2009, 654 applied for aid, 543 were judged to have need, 141 had their need fully met. 190 Federal Work-Study jobs (averaging $2020). 51 state and other part-time jobs (averaging $1503). In 2009, 209 non-need-based awards were made. *Average percent of need met:* 83%. *Average financial aid package:* $21,547. *Average need-based loan:* $3959. *Average need-based gift aid:* $18,453. *Average non-need-based aid:* $9767. *Average indebtedness upon graduation:* $22,920.

Applying *Options:* electronic application, early admission, early action, deferred entrance. *Application fee:* $30. *Required:* essay or personal statement, high school transcript, minimum 2 GPA, 1 letter of recommendation. *Recommended:* interview, class rank. *Application deadlines:* 8/1 (freshmen), 8/1 (out-of-state freshmen), 8/15 (transfers), 1/15 (early action). *Notification:* continuous (freshmen), continuous (out-of-state freshmen), continuous (transfers), 2/1 (early action).

Freshman Application Contact Mr. Mickey Quinlan, Director of Admission, Centenary College of Louisiana, Office of Admission, 2911 Centenary Boulevard, Shreveport, LA 71134-1188. *Phone:* 318-869-5701. *Toll-free phone:* 800-234-4448. *Fax:* 318-869-5005. *E-mail:* mquinlan@ centenary.edu. *Web site:* http://www.centenary.edu/.

Dillard University
New Orleans, Louisiana

- **Independent interdenominational** 4-year, founded 1869
- **Urban** 55-acre campus
- **Endowment** $39.8 million
- **Coed** 1,187 undergraduate students, 93% full-time, 72% women, 28% men
- **Moderately difficult** entrance level, 48% of applicants were admitted

Undergraduates 1,101 full-time, 86 part-time. Students come from 29 states and territories; 10 other countries; 32% are from out of state; 92% Black or African American, non-Hispanic/Latino; 0.6% Hispanic/Latino; 0.1% Asian, non-Hispanic/Latino; 6% Race/ethnicity unknown; 1% international; 5% transferred in; 44% live on campus. *Retention:* 66% of full-time freshmen returned.

Freshmen *Admission:* 3,382 applied, 1,608 admitted, 446 enrolled. *Average high school GPA:* 3. *Test scores:* SAT critical reading scores over 500: 21%; SAT math scores over 500: 24%; SAT writing scores over 500: 23%; ACT scores over 18: 62%; SAT critical reading scores over 600: 5%; SAT math scores over 600: 4%; SAT writing scores over 600: 4%; ACT scores over 24: 7%.

Faculty *Total:* 127, 65% full-time, 44% with terminal degrees. *Student/faculty ratio:* 12:1.

Academics *Calendar:* semesters. *Degree:* bachelor's. *Special study options:* academic remediation for entering students, advanced placement credit, cooperative education, double majors, English as a second language, external degree program, honors programs, independent study, internships, part-time degree program, services for LD students, study abroad, summer session for credit. *ROTC:* Army (c), Air Force (c). *Unusual degree programs:* engineering with Columbia University, Tulane University, University of New Orleans, Georgia Institute of Technology; Biology: Boston University School of Medicine, Meharry Medical College School of Medicine, New York College of Podiatric Medicine and Ohio College of Medicine; Public Health: LSU Health Sciences Center School of Public Health and Tulane School of Public Healh and Tropical Medicine.

Computers on Campus 113 computers/terminals are available on campus for general student use. Students can access the following: free student e-mail accounts, online (class) grades, online (class) registration, online (class) schedules. Campuswide network is available. 100% of college-owned or -operated housing units are wired for high-speed Internet access. Wireless service is available via classrooms, computer centers, libraries.

Student Life *Housing options:* coed, men-only, women-only, disabled students. Campus housing is university owned and leased by the school. Freshman campus housing is guaranteed. *Activities and organizations:* drama/theater group, student-run newspaper, radio and television station, choral group, Student Government Association, Pre-Alumni Council, National Pan-Hellenic Council, Collegiate 100, Class Councils, national fraternities, national sororities. *Campus security:* 24-hour emergency response devices and patrols, late-night transport/escort service, controlled dormitory access. *Student services:* health clinic, personal/psychological counseling.

Athletics Member NAIA. *Intercollegiate sports:* basketball M(s)/W(s), cross-country running M(s)/W(s), softball W, track and field M(s)/W(s), volleyball W(s). *Intramural sports:* basketball M/W, football M/W, softball M/W, tennis M/W, volleyball M/W, weight lifting M/W.

Standardized Tests *Required:* SAT or ACT (for admission), minimum SAT score of 870 (math and verbal) or minimum ACT score of 18 (for admission).

Costs (2011–12) *Tuition:* $542 per credit hour part-time. Part-time tuition and fees vary according to course load. *Room only:* Room and board charges vary according to housing facility. *Payment plan:* installment. *Waivers:* employees or children of employees.

Financial Aid Of all full-time matriculated undergraduates who enrolled in 2009, 1,177 applied for aid, 1,135 were judged to have need, 276 had their need fully met. 291 Federal Work-Study jobs (averaging $1565). *Average percent of need met:* 69%. *Average financial aid package:* $18,745. *Average need-based loan:* $3563. *Average need-based gift aid:* $9469. *Average indebtedness upon graduation:* $26,250.

Applying *Options:* electronic application, early admission. *Application fee:* $30. *Required:* high school transcript, minimum 2.5 GPA, 2 letters of recommendation. *Required for some:* essay or personal statement, interview. *Application deadlines:* rolling (freshmen), rolling (out-of-state freshmen), rolling (transfers). *Notification:* continuous (freshmen), continuous (out-of-state freshmen), continuous (transfers).

Freshman Application Contact Ms. Monica White, Coordinator, Dillard University, 2601 Gentilly Boulevard, New Orleans, LA 70122-3097. *Phone:* 504-816-4374. *Toll-free phone:* 800-716-8353 (in-state); 800-216-6637 (out-of-state). *Fax:* 504-816-4895. *E-mail:* mwhite@dillard.edu. *Web site:* http://www.dillard.edu/.

Grambling State University
Grambling, Louisiana

- **State-supported** university, founded 1901, part of University of Louisiana System
- **Small-town** 383-acre campus with easy access to Shreveport
- **Endowment** $4.2 million
- **Coed**
- **Noncompetitive** entrance level

Faculty *Student/faculty ratio:* 19:1.

Academics *Calendar:* semesters. *Degrees:* associate, bachelor's, master's, doctoral-other, and post-master's certificates.

Student Life *Campus security:* 24-hour patrols, student patrols, controlled dormitory access.

Athletics Member NCAA. All Division I except football (Division I-AA).

Standardized Tests *Required:* SAT or ACT (for admission).

Costs (2010–11) *Tuition:* state resident $3018 full-time, $126 per credit hour part-time; nonresident $9492 full-time, $126 per credit hour part-time. Full-time tuition and fees vary according to course load. Part-time tuition and fees vary according to course load. *Required fees:* $1410 full-time, $126 per credit hour part-time, $440 per term part-time. *Room and board:* $8236; room only: $5442. Room and board charges vary according to housing facility.

Financial Aid *Of all full-time matriculated undergraduates who enrolled in 2007,* 4,191 applied for aid, 3,931 were judged to have need, 309 had their need fully met. 1,141 Federal Work-Study jobs (averaging $1310). 431 state and other part-time jobs (averaging $1487). *In 2007,* 200 non-need-based awards were made. *Average percent of need met:* 80. *Average financial aid package:* $6800. *Average need-based loan:* $3813. *Average need-based gift aid:* $2928. *Average non-need-based aid:* $2328. *Average indebtedness upon graduation:* $29,416. *Financial aid deadline:* 4/1.

Applying *Options:* electronic application, early admission. *Application fee:* $20. *Required:* high school transcript, minimum 2 GPA.

Freshman Application Contact Ms. Annie L. Moss, Director of Admissions and Recruitment, Grambling State University, GSU Box 4200, Grambling, LA 71270. *Phone:* 318-274-6183. *Fax:* 318-274-3292. *E-mail:* mossa@gram.edu. *Web site:* http://www.gram.edu/.

Herzing University
Kenner, Louisiana

Director of Admissions Genny Bordelon, Director of Admissions, Herzing University, 2500 Williams Boulevard, Kenner, LA 70062. *Phone:* 504-733-0074. *Fax:* 504-733-0020. *Web site:* http://www.herzing.edu/.

ITT Technical Institute
St. Rose, Louisiana

- **Proprietary** primarily 2-year, founded 1998, part of ITT Educational Services, Inc.
- **Coed**
- **Minimally difficult** entrance level

Academics *Calendar:* quarters. *Degrees:* associate and bachelor's.

Student Life *Housing:* college housing not available.

Freshman Application Contact Director of Recruitment, ITT Technical Institute, 140 James Drive East, St. Rose, LA 70087. *Phone:* 504-463-0338. *Toll-free phone:* 866-463-0338. *Web site:* http://www.itt-tech.edu/.

Louisiana College
Pineville, Louisiana

- **Independent Southern Baptist** comprehensive, founded 1906
- **Small-town** 81-acre campus
- **Endowment** $26.5 million
- **Coed** 1,071 undergraduate students, 93% full-time, 50% women, 50% men
- **Moderately difficult** entrance level, 51% of applicants were admitted

Undergraduates 992 full-time, 79 part-time. 18% Black or African American, non-Hispanic/Latino; 2% Hispanic/Latino; 2% Asian, non-Hispanic/Latino; 0.7% American Indian or Alaska Native, non-Hispanic/Latino; 1% Two or more races, non-Hispanic/Latino; 2% Race/ethnicity unknown; 0.7% international; 60% live on campus. *Retention:* 56% of full-time freshmen returned.

Freshmen *Admission:* 937 applied, 482 admitted, 290 enrolled. *Average high school GPA:* 3.17.

Faculty *Total:* 109, 63% full-time, 50% with terminal degrees. *Student/faculty ratio:* 17:1.

Academics *Calendar:* semesters. *Degrees:* associate, bachelor's, and master's. *Special study options:* academic remediation for entering students, accelerated degree program, adult/continuing education programs, advanced placement credit, distance learning, double majors, honors programs, independent study, internships, part-time degree program, services for LD students, student-designed majors, study abroad, summer session for credit. *ROTC:* Army (b).

Computers on Campus 247 computers/terminals are available on campus for general student use. Students can access the following: campus intranet, free student e-mail accounts, online (class) grades. Campuswide network is available. 100% of college-owned or -operated housing units are wired for high-speed Internet access.

Student Life *Housing:* on-campus residence required through senior year. *Options:* men-only, women-only. Campus housing is university owned. Freshman campus housing is guaranteed. *Activities and organizations:* drama/theater group, student-run newspaper, radio station, choral group, marching band, Baptist Student Union, Delta Xi Omega, Student Government Association, Union Board, Lambda Chi Beta. *Campus security:* 24-hour patrols, student patrols, late-night transport/escort service, controlled dormitory access. *Student services:* health clinic, personal/psychological counseling.

Athletics Member NCAA, NCCAA. All NCAA Division III. *Intercollegiate sports:* baseball M, basketball M/W, cheerleading M/W, cross-country running W, football M, golf M, soccer M/W, softball W, tennis W. *Intramural sports:* badminton M/W, basketball M/W, football M/W, racquetball M/W, soccer M/W, softball M/W, table tennis M/W, tennis M/W, ultimate Frisbee M/W, volleyball M/W, water polo M/W.

Standardized Tests *Required:* SAT or ACT (for admission).

Costs (2010–11) *Comprehensive fee:* $17,428 includes full-time tuition ($11,550), mandatory fees ($1430), and room and board ($4448). Full-time tuition and fees vary according to program. Part-time tuition: $385 per hour. Part-time tuition and fees vary according to program. *Room and board:* Room and board charges vary according to board plan and housing facility. *Payment plan:* installment. *Waivers:* employees or children of employees.

Financial Aid Of all full-time matriculated undergraduates who enrolled in 2009, 1,123 applied for aid, 895 were judged to have need, 286 had their need fully met. *Average percent of need met:* 39%. *Average financial aid package:* $7640. *Average need-based loan:* $4068. *Average need-based gift aid:* $2900.
Applying *Options:* electronic application, early admission. *Application fee:* $25. *Required:* high school transcript, minimum 2 GPA, class rank. *Required for some:* 3 letters of recommendation. *Recommended:* interview. *Application deadline:* 8/15 (freshmen). *Notification:* continuous (freshmen), continuous (transfers).
Freshman Application Contact Mr. Byron McGee, Director of Enrollment Management, Louisiana College, LC Box 566, Pineville, LA 71359. *Phone:* 318-487-7439. *Toll-free phone:* 800-487-1906. *Fax:* 318-487-7550. *E-mail:* admissions@lacollege.edu. *Web site:* http://www.lacollege.edu/.

Louisiana State University and Agricultural and Mechanical College
Baton Rouge, Louisiana

- **State-supported** university, founded 1860, part of Louisiana State University System
- **Urban** 2000-acre campus with easy access to New Orleans
- **Endowment** $311.7 million
- **Coed** 23,685 undergraduate students, 93% full-time, 51% women, 49% men
- **Moderately difficult** entrance level, 72% of applicants were admitted

Undergraduates 22,144 full-time, 1,541 part-time. Students come from 52 states and territories; 77 other countries; 19% are from out of state; 9% Black or African American, non-Hispanic/Latino; 4% Hispanic/Latino; 3% Asian, non-Hispanic/Latino; 0.4% American Indian or Alaska Native, non-Hispanic/Latino; 1% Two or more races, non-Hispanic/Latino; 2% Race/ethnicity unknown; 2% international; 4% transferred in; 24% live on campus. *Retention:* 84% of full-time freshmen returned.
Freshmen *Admission:* 18,214 applied, 13,148 admitted, 5,481 enrolled. *Average high school GPA:* 3.45. *Test scores:* SAT critical reading scores over 500: 79%; SAT math scores over 500: 88%; ACT scores over 18: 100%; SAT critical reading scores over 600: 39%; SAT math scores over 600: 49%; ACT scores over 24: 68%; SAT critical reading scores over 700: 9%; SAT math scores over 700: 10%; ACT scores over 30: 14%.
Faculty *Total:* 1,414, 88% full-time, 84% with terminal degrees. *Student/faculty ratio:* 22:1.
Academics *Calendar:* semesters. *Degrees:* bachelor's, master's, doctoral-professional, doctoral-research/scholarship, and post-master's certificates. *Special study options:* accelerated degree program, adult/continuing education programs, advanced placement credit, cooperative education, distance learning, double majors, English as a second language, freshman honors college, honors programs, independent study, internships, off-campus study, part-time degree program, services for LD students, student-designed majors, study abroad, summer session for credit. *ROTC:* Army (b), Navy (c), Air Force (b).
Computers on Campus 1,500 computers/terminals and 8,500 ports are available on campus for general student use. Students can access the following: computer help desk, free student e-mail accounts, online (class) grades, online (class) registration, online (class) schedules, free software for download, personal Web sites, storage, discounts on hardware, virtual computer lab. Campuswide network is available. 100% of college-owned or -operated housing units are wired for high-speed Internet access. Wireless service is available via entire campus.
Student Life *Housing options:* coed, men-only, women-only, disabled students. Campus housing is university owned. *Activities and organizations:* drama/theater group, student-run newspaper, radio and television station, choral group, marching band, intramural athletics, student political organizations, student professional organizations, religious organizations, national fraternities, national sororities. *Campus security:* 24-hour emergency response devices and patrols, late-night transport/escort service, controlled dormitory access, self-defense education, crime prevention programs. *Student services:* health clinic, personal/psychological counseling, women's center, legal services.
Athletics Member NCAA. All Division I except football (Division I-A). *Intercollegiate sports:* baseball M(s), basketball M(s)/W(s), cheerleading M/W, cross-country running M(s)/W(s), golf M(s)/W(s), gymnastics W(s), soccer W(s), softball W(s), swimming and diving M(s)/W(s), tennis M(s)/W(s), track and field M(s)/W(s), volleyball W(s). *Intramural sports:* badminton M/W, basketball M/W, bowling M(c)/W(c), crew M(c)/W(c), equestrian sports W(c), football M/W, golf M/W, ice hockey M(c), lacrosse M(c), racquetball M/W, rugby M(c), soccer M(c)/W(c), softball M/W, table tennis M/W, tennis M(c)/W(c), ultimate Frisbee M(c)/W, volleyball M(c)/W(c), weight lifting M(c)/W(c).
Standardized Tests *Required:* SAT or ACT (for admission).
Costs (2010–11) *Tuition:* state resident $3968 full-time; nonresident $14,753 full-time. Part-time tuition and fees vary according to course load. *Required*

fees: $1796 full-time. *Room and board:* $8210; room only: $4890. Room and board charges vary according to board plan and housing facility. *Payment plan:* deferred payment. *Waivers:* employees or children of employees.
Financial Aid Of all full-time matriculated undergraduates who enrolled in 2008, 10,778 applied for aid, 7,508 were judged to have need, 1,437 had their need fully met. 921 Federal Work-Study jobs (averaging $1400). 4,387 state and other part-time jobs (averaging $2500). In 2008, 3429 non-need-based awards were made. *Average percent of need met:* 68%. *Average financial aid package:* $11,241. *Average need-based loan:* $4373. *Average need-based gift aid:* $8378. *Average non-need-based aid:* $4875. *Average indebtedness upon graduation:* $19,242.
Applying *Options:* electronic application, early admission, deferred entrance. *Application fee:* $40. *Required:* high school transcript, minimum 3 GPA. *Required for some:* essay or personal statement. *Application deadlines:* 4/15 (freshmen), 4/15 (transfers). *Notification:* continuous (freshmen), continuous (transfers).
Freshman Application Contact Ms. Guadalupe Lamadrid, Associate Director, Undergraduate Admissions, Louisiana State University and Agricultural and Mechanical College, 1146 Pleasant Hall, Baton Rouge, LA 70803. *Phone:* 225-578-1175. *Fax:* 225-578-4433. *E-mail:* glamadrid@lsu.edu. *Web site:* http://www.lsu.edu/.

Louisiana State University at Alexandria
Alexandria, Louisiana

Freshman Application Contact Ms. Shelly Kieffer, Director of Admissions and Recruiting, Louisiana State University at Alexandria, 8100 Highway 71 South, Alexandria, LA 71302-9121. *Phone:* 318-473-6424. *Toll-free phone:* 888-473-6417. *Fax:* 318-473-6418. *E-mail:* admissions@lsua.edu. *Web site:* http://www.lsua.edu/.

Louisiana State University Health Sciences Center
New Orleans, Louisiana

- **State-supported** university, founded 1931, part of Louisiana State University System
- **Urban** 80-acre campus
- **Endowment** $68.5 million
- **Coed**

Academics *Calendar:* varies by academic program. *Degrees:* associate, bachelor's, master's, doctoral-professional, doctoral-research/scholarship, and post-master's certificates.
Student Life *Campus security:* 24-hour emergency response devices and patrols, late-night transport/escort service, controlled dormitory access.
Costs (2010–11) *Tuition:* state resident $3512 full-time, $174 per hour part-time; nonresident $5855 full-time, $291 per hour part-time. Full-time tuition and fees vary according to degree level, program, and reciprocity agreements. Part-time tuition and fees vary according to degree level, program, and reciprocity agreements. *Required fees:* $844 full-time, $39 per credit hour part-time. *Room only:* $6396. Room and board charges vary according to housing facility.
Applying *Application fee:* $50.
Freshman Application Contact Louisiana State University Health Sciences Center, 433 Bolivar Street, New Orleans, LA 70112-2223. *Phone:* 504-568-4829. *Web site:* http://www.lsuhsc.edu/.

Louisiana State University in Shreveport
Shreveport, Louisiana

- **State-supported** comprehensive, founded 1965, part of Louisiana State University System
- **Urban** 200-acre campus
- **Coed** 4,058 undergraduate students, 58% full-time, 61% women, 39% men
- **Moderately difficult** entrance level, 82% of applicants were admitted

Undergraduates 2,368 full-time, 1,690 part-time. Students come from 41 states and territories; 39 other countries; 9% are from out of state; 10% transferred in. *Retention:* 69% of full-time freshmen returned.
Freshmen *Admission:* 597 applied, 490 admitted, 340 enrolled. *Average high school GPA:* 3.15. *Test scores:* ACT scores over 18: 88%; ACT scores over 24: 30%; ACT scores over 30: 2%.
Faculty *Student/faculty ratio:* 22:1.

Academics *Calendar:* semesters plus 8-week and two 4-week summer terms. *Degrees:* bachelor's and master's. *Special study options:* academic remediation for entering students, accelerated degree program, adult/continuing education programs, advanced placement credit, cooperative education, distance learning, double majors, honors programs, independent study, internships, off-campus study, part-time degree program, services for LD students, student-designed majors, summer session for credit. *ROTC:* Army (b).

Computers on Campus Students can access the following: computer help desk, free student e-mail accounts, online (class) grades, online (class) registration, online (class) schedules. Campuswide network is available. Wireless service is available via entire campus.

Student Life *Housing options:* coed, men-only, women-only. Campus housing is university owned. *Activities and organizations:* drama/theater group, student-run newspaper, choral group, national fraternities, national sororities. *Campus security:* 24-hour emergency response devices and patrols, student patrols, controlled dormitory access. *Student services:* personal/psychological counseling.

Athletics Member NAIA. *Intercollegiate sports:* baseball M(s), basketball M/W, soccer W, tennis W. *Intramural sports:* archery M, basketball M/W, football M/W, lacrosse M, racquetball M/W, softball M/W, table tennis M/W, volleyball M/W.

Standardized Tests *Required for some:* SAT or ACT (for admission). *Recommended:* ACT (for admission).

Costs (2010–11) *Tuition:* state resident $3166 full-time, $126 per credit hour part-time; nonresident $8651 full-time, $354 per credit hour part-time. Full-time tuition and fees vary according to degree level. Part-time tuition and fees vary according to degree level. *Required fees:* $1151 full-time, $46 per credit hour part-time. *Waivers:* employees or children of employees.

Applying *Options:* early admission. *Application fee:* $10. *Required for some:* high school transcript, minimum 2 GPA. *Application deadline:* 8/1 (freshmen).

Freshman Application Contact Louisiana State University in Shreveport, 1 University Place, Shreveport, LA 71115-2399, *Phone:* 318-797-5063. *Toll-free phone:* 800-229-5957. *Web site:* http://www.lsus.edu/.

Louisiana Tech University

Ruston, Louisiana

- **State-supported** university, founded 1894, part of University of Louisiana System
- **Small-town** 247-acre campus
- **Coed**
- **Moderately difficult** entrance level

Faculty *Student/faculty ratio:* 21:1.

Academics *Calendar:* quarters. *Degrees:* associate, bachelor's, master's, doctoral-research/scholarship, and postbachelor's certificates.

Student Life *Campus security:* 24-hour emergency response devices and patrols, student patrols, late-night transport/escort service, controlled dormitory access.

Athletics Member NCAA. All Division I except football (Division I-A).

Standardized Tests *Required:* SAT or ACT (for admission). *Recommended:* ACT (for admission).

Costs (2010–11) *Tuition:* state resident $5643 full-time; nonresident $11,580 full-time. Full-time tuition and fees vary according to course load, location, and program. Part-time tuition and fees vary according to course load, location, and program. *Room and board:* $5160; room only: $2580. Room and board charges vary according to board plan and housing facility. *Payment plans:* installment, deferred payment.

Financial Aid *Of all full-time matriculated undergraduates who enrolled in 2009,* 4,909 applied for aid, 3,302 were judged to have need, 690 had their need fully met. 268 Federal Work-Study jobs (averaging $1815). 989 state and other part-time jobs (averaging $1969). *In 2009,* 1080 non-need-based awards were made. *Average percent of need met:* 65. *Average financial aid package:* $9446. *Average need-based loan:* $3745. *Average need-based gift aid:* $7171. *Average non-need-based aid:* $2370. *Average indebtedness upon graduation:* $12,408.

Applying *Options:* early admission. *Application fee:* $20. *Required:* high school transcript, minimum 2.2 GPA.

Freshman Application Contact Mrs. Jan B. Albritton, Director of Admissions, Louisiana Tech University, PO Box 3168, Ruston, LA 71272. *Phone:* 318-257-3036. *Toll-free phone:* 800-528-3241. *Fax:* 318-257-2499. *E-mail:* bulldog@latech.edu. *Web site:* http://www.latech.edu/.

Loyola University New Orleans

New Orleans, Louisiana

- **Independent Roman Catholic (Jesuit)** comprehensive, founded 1912
- **Suburban** 26-acre campus with easy access to New Orleans
- **Endowment** $237.0 million
- **Coed** 2,922 undergraduate students, 91% full-time, 58% women, 42% men
- **Moderately difficult** entrance level, 57% of applicants were admitted

Undergraduates 2,647 full-time, 275 part-time. Students come from 48 states and territories; 33 other countries; 50% are from out of state; 14% Black or African American, non-Hispanic/Latino; 12% Hispanic/Latino; 4% Asian, non-Hispanic/Latino; 0.6% American Indian or Alaska Native, non-Hispanic/Latino; 1% Two or more races, non-Hispanic/Latino; 7% Race/ethnicity unknown; 3% international; 5% transferred in; 49% live on campus. *Retention:* 82% of full-time freshmen returned.

Freshmen *Admission:* 5,399 applied, 3,058 admitted, 763 enrolled. *Average high school GPA:* 3.77. *Test scores:* SAT critical reading scores over 500: 99%; SAT math scores over 500: 94%; SAT writing scores over 500: 94%; ACT scores over 18: 100%; SAT critical reading scores over 600: 61%; SAT math scores over 600: 50%; SAT writing scores over 600: 61%; ACT scores over 24: 76%; SAT critical reading scores over 700: 16%; SAT math scores over 700: 7%; SAT writing scores over 700: 12%; ACT scores over 30: 19%.

Faculty *Total:* 457, 65% full-time, 75% with terminal degrees. *Student/faculty ratio:* 10:1.

Academics *Calendar:* semesters. *Degrees:* bachelor's, master's, doctoral-other, doctoral-professional, post-master's, and postbachelor's certificates. *Special study options:* accelerated degree program, adult/continuing education programs, advanced placement credit, distance learning, double majors, English as a second language, external degree program, honors programs, independent study, internships, off-campus study, part-time degree program, services for LD students, student-designed majors, study abroad, summer session for credit. *ROTC:* Army (c), Navy (c), Air Force (c). *Unusual degree programs:* 3-2 engineering with Tulane University.

Computers on Campus 525 computers/terminals and 2,500 ports are available on campus for general student use. Students can access the following: campus intranet, computer help desk, free student e-mail accounts, online (class) grades, online (class) registration, online (class) schedules. Campuswide network is available. 100% of college-owned or -operated housing units are wired for high-speed Internet access. Wireless service is available via entire campus.

Student Life *Housing:* on-campus residence required through sophomore year. *Options:* coed, disabled students. Campus housing is university owned. Freshman campus housing is guaranteed. *Activities and organizations:* drama/theater group, student-run newspaper, radio station, choral group, University Programming Board, Loyola Community Action Program, Black Student Union, Student Government Association, Loyola Society for Civic Engagement, national fraternities, national sororities. *Campus security:* 24-hour emergency response devices and patrols, student patrols, late-night transport/escort service, controlled dormitory access, self-defense education, bicycle patrols, closed circuit TV monitors, door alarms, crime prevention programs, card access control. *Student services:* health clinic, personal/psychological counseling, women's center.

Athletics Member NAIA. *Intercollegiate sports:* baseball M, basketball M(s)/W(s), cheerleading M(c)/W(c), cross-country running M/W, golf M(c)/W(c), ice hockey M(c)/W(c), lacrosse M(c), racquetball M/W, rugby M(c), sailing M(c)/W(c), soccer M(c)/W(c), swimming and diving M/W, tennis M(c)/W(c), track and field M/W, ultimate Frisbee M(c)/W(c), volleyball W, wrestling M(c). *Intramural sports:* basketball M/W, soccer M/W, softball M/W, swimming and diving M/W, volleyball M/W, weight lifting M/W.

Standardized Tests *Required:* SAT or ACT (for admission).

Costs (2011–12) *Comprehensive fee:* $44,292 includes full-time tuition ($32,266), mandatory fees ($1036), and room and board ($10,990). Part-time tuition: $920 per credit hour. *College room only:* $6526. Room and board charges vary according to board plan and housing facility. *Payment plan:* installment. *Waivers:* senior citizens and employees or children of employees.

Financial Aid Of all full-time matriculated undergraduates who enrolled in 2009, 1,975 applied for aid, 1,719 were judged to have need, 312 had their need fully met. In 2009, 833 non-need-based awards were made. *Average percent of need met:* 73%. *Average financial aid package:* $23,960. *Average need-based loan:* $4168. *Average need-based gift aid:* $20,219. *Average non-need-based aid:* $14,681. *Average indebtedness upon graduation:* $22,319. *Financial aid deadline:* 6/1.

Applying *Options:* electronic application, early admission. *Application fee:* $20. *Required:* essay or personal statement, high school transcript, 1 letter of recommendation. *Required for some:* interview. *Recommended:* interview. *Application deadlines:* rolling (freshmen), rolling (transfers). *Notification:* continuous (freshmen).

Freshman Application Contact Mr. Keith E. Gramling, Director, Admissions, Loyola University New Orleans, 6363 St. Charles Avenue,

Campus Box 18, New Orleans, LA 70118. *Phone:* 504-865-3240. *Toll-free phone:* 800-4-LOYOLA. *Fax:* 504-865-3383. *E-mail:* admit@loyno.edu. *Web site:* http://www.loyno.edu/.

McNeese State University
Lake Charles, Louisiana

- **State-supported** comprehensive, founded 1939, part of University of Louisiana System
- **Suburban** 766-acre campus
- **Coed**
- **Moderately difficult** entrance level

Faculty *Student/faculty ratio:* 21:1.

Academics *Calendar:* semesters. *Degrees:* associate, bachelor's, master's, post-master's, and postbachelor's certificates.

Student Life *Campus security:* 24-hour emergency response devices and patrols, late-night transport/escort service, controlled dormitory access.

Athletics Member NCAA. All Division I except football (Division I-AA).

Standardized Tests *Required:* SAT or ACT (for admission).

Costs (2010–11) *Tuition:* state resident $3600 full-time; nonresident $9800 full-time. Full-time tuition and fees vary according to course load. Part-time tuition and fees vary according to course load. *Room and board:* $6070. Room and board charges vary according to board plan and housing facility. *Payment plans:* installment, deferred payment.

Financial Aid *Of all full-time matriculated undergraduates who enrolled in 2007, 3,331 were judged to have need, 556 had their need fully met. In 2007, 1527 non-need-based awards were made. Average percent of need met: 64. Average financial aid package: $6705. Average need-based loan: $3899. Average need-based gift aid: $4085. Average non-need-based aid: $2847.*

Applying *Options:* electronic application, early admission. *Application fee:* $20. *Required:* high school transcript, minimum 2 GPA. *Recommended:* minimum 2.35 GPA.

Freshman Application Contact Ms. Kara Smith, Director of Admissions, McNeese State University, Box 91740, Lake Charles, LA 70609. *Phone:* 337-475-5504. *Toll-free phone:* 800-622-3352. *Fax:* 337-475-5978. *E-mail:* ksmith2@mcneese.edu. *Web site:* http://www.mcneese.edu/.

New Orleans Baptist Theological Seminary
New Orleans, Louisiana

Director of Admissions Dr. Paul E. Gregoire Jr., Registrar/Director of Admissions, New Orleans Baptist Theological Seminary, 3939 Gentilly Boulevard, New Orleans, LA 70126-4858. *Phone:* 504-282-4455 Ext. 3337. *Toll-free phone:* 800-662-8701. *Web site:* http://www.nobts.edu/.

Nicholls State University
Thibodaux, Louisiana

- **State-supported** comprehensive, founded 1948, part of University of Louisiana System
- **Small-town** 210-acre campus with easy access to New Orleans
- **Endowment** $13.5 million
- **Coed** 6,524 undergraduate students, 79% full-time, 62% women, 38% men
- **Noncompetitive** entrance level, 78% of applicants were admitted

Undergraduates 5,177 full-time, 1,347 part-time. Students come from 36 states and territories; 39 other countries; 4% are from out of state; 5% transferred in; 20% live on campus. *Retention:* 67% of full-time freshmen returned.

Freshmen *Admission:* 1,887 applied, 1,478 admitted, 1,247 enrolled. *Average high school GPA:* 3.15. *Test scores:* ACT scores over 18: 91%; ACT scores over 24: 24%; ACT scores over 30: 1%.

Faculty *Total:* 271, 98% full-time, 57% with terminal degrees. *Student/faculty ratio:* 22:1.

Academics *Calendar:* semesters. *Degrees:* associate, bachelor's, master's, and post-master's certificates. *Special study options:* academic remediation for entering students, accelerated degree program, adult/continuing education programs, advanced placement credit, cooperative education, distance learning, double majors, English as a second language, honors programs, independent study, internships, off-campus study, part-time degree program, services for LD students, study abroad, summer session for credit.

Computers on Campus 1,500 computers/terminals and 1,500 ports are available on campus for general student use. Students can access the following: campus intranet, free student e-mail accounts, online (class) grades, online (class) registration, online (class) schedules, course management system—Blackboard. Campuswide network is available. 100% of college-owned or -

operated housing units are wired for high-speed Internet access. Wireless service is available via entire campus.

Student Life *Housing options:* coed, men-only, women-only, disabled students. Campus housing is university owned. Freshman campus housing is guaranteed. *Activities and organizations:* drama/theater group, student-run newspaper, radio and television station, choral group, marching band, Student Government Association, Student Programming Association, Residence Hall Association, Food Advisory Association, national fraternities, national sororities. *Campus security:* 24-hour emergency response devices and patrols, student patrols, late-night transport/escort service. *Student services:* health clinic, personal/psychological counseling, women's center, legal services.

Athletics Member NCAA. All Division I except football (Division I-AA). *Intercollegiate sports:* baseball M(s), basketball M(s)/W(s), cross-country running M(s)/W(s), golf M(s)/W(s), soccer W(s), softball W(s), tennis M/W(s), track and field M(s)/W(s), volleyball W(s). *Intramural sports:* basketball M/W, football M/W, softball M/W, volleyball M/W.

Standardized Tests *Required:* SAT or ACT (for admission).

Costs (2010–11) *Tuition:* state resident $4292 full-time; nonresident $11,516 full-time. Part-time tuition and fees vary according to course load. *Room and board:* $7808; room only: $5200. Room and board charges vary according to board plan and housing facility. *Payment plans:* installment, deferred payment. *Waivers:* employees or children of employees.

Financial Aid Of all full-time matriculated undergraduates who enrolled in 2008, 4,084 applied for aid, 2,384 were judged to have need, 1,680 had their need fully met. In 2008, 317 non-need-based awards were made. *Average percent of need met:* 90%. *Average financial aid package:* $7415. *Average need-based loan:* $3532. *Average need-based gift aid:* $4482. *Average non-need-based aid:* $2811. *Average indebtedness upon graduation:* $18,822. *Financial aid deadline:* 6/30.

Applying *Options:* electronic application, early admission, deferred entrance. *Application fee:* $20. *Required:* high school transcript. *Application deadlines:* rolling (freshmen), rolling (transfers). *Notification:* 9/1 (freshmen), continuous until 8/28 (transfers).

Freshman Application Contact Mrs. Becky L. Durocher, Director of Admissions, Nicholls State University, PO Box 2004-NSU, Thibodaux, LA 70310. *Phone:* 985-448-4507. *Toll-free phone:* 877-NICHOLLS. *Fax:* 985-448-4929. *E-mail:* nicholls@nicholls.edu. *Web site:* http://www.nicholls.edu/.

Northwestern State University of Louisiana
Natchitoches, Louisiana

- **State-supported** comprehensive, founded 1884, part of University of Louisiana System
- **Small-town** 916-acre campus
- **Coed** 8,078 undergraduate students, 66% full-time, 68% women, 32% men
- **Moderately difficult** entrance level, 83% of applicants were admitted

Undergraduates 5,330 full-time, 2,748 part-time. Students come from 40 states and territories; 31 other countries; 9% are from out of state; 30% Black or African American, non-Hispanic/Latino; 3% Hispanic/Latino; 0.9% Asian, non-Hispanic/Latino; 0.1% Native Hawaiian or other Pacific Islander, non-Hispanic/Latino; 1% American Indian or Alaska Native, non-Hispanic/Latino; 3% Two or more races, non-Hispanic/Latino; 4% Race/ethnicity unknown; 0.7% international; 8% transferred in; 18% live on campus. *Retention:* 71% of full-time freshmen returned.

Freshmen *Admission:* 2,633 applied, 2,190 admitted, 1,125 enrolled. *Average high school GPA:* 3.16. *Test scores:* SAT critical reading scores over 500: 42%; SAT math scores over 500: 49%; ACT scores over 18: 87%; SAT critical reading scores over 600: 15%; SAT math scores over 600: 9%; ACT scores over 24: 22%; SAT critical reading scores over 700: 2%; ACT scores over 30: 2%.

Faculty *Total:* 515, 57% full-time, 45% with terminal degrees. *Student/faculty ratio:* 19:1.

Academics *Calendar:* semesters. *Degrees:* associate, bachelor's, master's, post-master's, and postbachelor's certificates. *Special study options:* academic remediation for entering students, adult/continuing education programs, advanced placement credit, cooperative education, distance learning, double majors, freshman honors college, honors programs, independent study, internships, part-time degree program, services for LD students, study abroad, summer session for credit. *ROTC:* Army (b), Air Force (c).

Computers on Campus Students can access the following: computer help desk, free student e-mail accounts, online (class) grades, online (class) registration, online (class) schedules. Campuswide network is available. Wireless service is available via classrooms, computer centers, computer labs, dorm rooms, learning centers, libraries, student centers.

Student Life *Housing:* on-campus residence required through junior year. *Options:* coed, disabled students. Campus housing is university owned and is provided by a third party. Freshman applicants given priority for college housing. *Activities and organizations:* drama/theater group, student-run newspaper, radio and television station, choral group, marching band, national fraternities, national sororities. *Campus security:* 24-hour emergency response devices and patrols, late-night transport/escort service, controlled dormitory access. *Student services:* health clinic, personal/psychological counseling.

Athletics Member NCAA. All Division I except football (Division I-AA). *Intercollegiate sports:* baseball M(s), basketball M(s)/W(s), cross-country running M(s)/W(s), soccer W(s), softball W(s), tennis W(s), track and field M(s)/W(s), volleyball W(s). *Intramural sports:* badminton M/W, basketball M/W, bowling M/W, cheerleading M(c)/W(c), crew M(c)/W(c), football M/W, golf M/W, racquetball M/W, soccer M/W, softball M/W, swimming and diving M/W, table tennis M/W, tennis M/W, volleyball M/W.

Standardized Tests *Required:* SAT or ACT (for admission).

Costs (2010–11) *Tuition:* state resident $3002 full-time; nonresident $10,744 full-time. Full-time tuition and fees vary according to course load and location. Part-time tuition and fees vary according to course load and location. *Required fees:* $1382 full-time. *Room and board:* $7070; room only: $4500. Room and board charges vary according to board plan, housing facility, and location. *Payment plan:* installment. *Waivers:* senior citizens and employees or children of employees.

Financial Aid Of all full-time matriculated undergraduates who enrolled in 2009, 4,114 applied for aid, 3,512 were judged to have need, 1,478 had their need fully met. 258 Federal Work-Study jobs (averaging $2098). 575 state and other part-time jobs (averaging $1421). In 2009, 1594 non-need-based awards were made. *Average percent of need met:* 59%. *Average financial aid package:* $6921. *Average need-based loan:* $6914. *Average need-based gift aid:* $4719. *Average non-need-based aid:* $4812. *Average indebtedness upon graduation:* $23,710.

Applying *Options:* electronic application, deferred entrance. *Application fee:* $20. *Required:* high school transcript, minimum 2 GPA, college preparatory curriculum. *Application deadlines:* 7/6 (freshmen), 7/6 (out-of-state freshmen), 7/6 (transfers). *Notification:* continuous (freshmen), continuous (out-of-state freshmen), continuous (transfers).

Freshman Application Contact Ms. Jana Lucky, Director of University Recruiting, Northwestern State University of Louisiana, South Hall, Natchitoches, LA 71497. *Phone:* 318-357-4503. *Toll-free phone:* 800-327-1903. *Fax:* 318-357-5567. *E-mail:* recruiting@nsula.edu. *Web site:* http://www.nsula.edu/.

Our Lady of Holy Cross College

New Orleans, Louisiana

Director of Admissions Donna Kennedy, Director of Admissions and Financial Aid, Our Lady of Holy Cross College, 4123 Woodland Drive, New Orleans, LA 70131-7399. *Phone:* 504-398-2175. *Toll-free phone:* 800-259-7744 Ext. 175. *E-mail:* dkennedy@olhcc.edu. *Web site:* http://www.olhcc.edu/.

Our Lady of the Lake College

Baton Rouge, Louisiana

- **Independent Roman Catholic** comprehensive, founded 1990
- **Suburban** 5-acre campus with easy access to New Orleans
- **Coed, primarily women** 1,745 undergraduate students, 33% full-time, 84% women, 16% men
- **Minimally difficult** entrance level, 22% of applicants were admitted

Undergraduates 571 full-time, 1,174 part-time. Students come from 10 states and territories; 1% are from out of state; 17% Black or African American, non-Hispanic/Latino; 1% Hispanic/Latino; 2% Asian, non-Hispanic/Latino; 0.4% Native Hawaiian or other Pacific Islander, non-Hispanic/Latino; 0.3% American Indian or Alaska Native, non-Hispanic/Latino; 34% Race/ethnicity unknown; 8% transferred in. *Retention:* 74% of full-time freshmen returned.

Freshmen *Admission:* 102 applied, 22 admitted, 99 enrolled. *Test scores:* ACT scores over 18: 91%; ACT scores over 24: 14%.

Faculty *Total:* 240, 40% full-time, 20% with terminal degrees. *Student/faculty ratio:* 19:1.

Academics *Calendar:* semesters. *Degrees:* certificates, diplomas, associate, bachelor's, master's, and postbachelor's certificates. *Special study options:* academic remediation for entering students, accelerated degree program, advanced placement credit, off-campus study, part-time degree program, services for LD students, summer session for credit. *ROTC:* Army (c), Air Force (c).

Computers on Campus 150 computers/terminals are available on campus for general student use. Students can access the following: campus intranet, computer help desk, free student e-mail accounts, online (class) grades, online

(class) registration, online (class) schedules. Campuswide network is available. Wireless service is available via entire campus.

Student Life *Housing:* college housing not available. *Activities and organizations:* Student Government Association, Cultural Arts Association, Christian Fellowship Association, Mathematics/Science Association. *Campus security:* 24-hour patrols. *Student services:* health clinic, personal/psychological counseling.

Standardized Tests *Required:* SAT or ACT (for admission), ACT ASSET (for admission).

Costs (2010–11) *Tuition:* $7920 full-time, $330 per credit hour part-time. Full-time tuition and fees vary according to course load and program. Part-time tuition and fees vary according to course load and program. *Required fees:* $744 full-time, $94 per credit hour part-time. *Payment plans:* installment, deferred payment. *Waivers:* employees or children of employees.

Financial Aid Of all full-time matriculated undergraduates who enrolled in 2008, 684 applied for aid, 546 were judged to have need, 10 had their need fully met. *Average financial aid package:* $5175. *Average need-based loan:* $3664. *Average need-based gift aid:* $2486. *Average indebtedness upon graduation:* $12,019.

Applying *Options:* electronic application, early admission, deferred entrance. *Application fee:* $35. *Required:* high school transcript, minimum 2 GPA. *Application deadlines:* 8/15 (freshmen), rolling (transfers). *Notification:* continuous (freshmen).

Freshman Application Contact Mrs. Rebecca Cannon, Director of Admissions, Our Lady of the Lake College, 7434 Perkins Road, Baton Rouge, LA 70808. *Phone:* 225-768-1718. *Toll-free phone:* 877-242-3509. *E-mail:* admissions@ololcollege.edu. *Web site:* http://www.ololcollege.edu/.

Saint Joseph Seminary College

Saint Benedict, Louisiana

- **Independent Roman Catholic** 4-year, founded 1891
- **Rural** 1300-acre campus with easy access to New Orleans
- **Endowment** $1.1 million
- **Coed, primarily men** 133 undergraduate students, 56% full-time, 16% women, 84% men
- **Minimally difficult** entrance level

Undergraduates 74 full-time, 59 part-time. Students come from 8 states and territories; 9 other countries; 53% are from out of state; 5% transferred in; 100% live on campus. *Retention:* 50% of full-time freshmen returned.

Freshmen *Admission:* 9 admitted, 9 enrolled. *Average high school GPA:* 3.25. *Test scores:* ACT scores over 18: 55%; ACT scores over 24: 22%.

Faculty *Total:* 24, 38% full-time, 42% with terminal degrees. *Student/faculty ratio:* 3:1.

Academics *Calendar:* semesters. *Degrees:* bachelor's (Religious Studies Institute is coed). *Special study options:* academic remediation for entering students, adult/continuing education programs, advanced placement credit, English as a second language, services for LD students.

Computers on Campus 14 computers/terminals and 90 ports are available on campus for general student use. Students can access the following: campus intranet, computer help desk, free student e-mail accounts. Campuswide network is available. 100% of college-owned or -operated housing units are wired for high-speed Internet access. Wireless service is available via entire campus.

Student Life *Housing:* on-campus residence required through senior year. *Options:* men-only. Campus housing is university owned. Freshman campus housing is guaranteed. *Activities and organizations:* drama/theater group, student-run newspaper, choral group, student government, yearbook. *Campus security:* 24-hour emergency response devices, controlled dormitory access, entrance gate. *Student services:* health clinic, personal/psychological counseling.

Athletics *Intramural sports:* football M, golf M.

Standardized Tests *Required:* ACT (for admission).

Costs (2010–11) *One-time required fee:* $150. *Comprehensive fee:* $25,435 includes full-time tuition ($12,250), mandatory fees ($1325), and room and board ($11,860). Part-time tuition: $175 per credit hour. *College room only:* $6230.

Financial Aid Of all full-time matriculated undergraduates who enrolled in 2009, 33 applied for aid, 33 were judged to have need, 33 had their need fully met. *Average percent of need met:* 100%. *Average financial aid package:* $4105. *Average need-based gift aid:* $4105. *Average indebtedness upon graduation:* $5000.

Applying *Options:* early admission, deferred entrance. *Required:* high school transcript, minimum 2 GPA. *Application deadlines:* rolling (freshmen), rolling (transfers). *Notification:* continuous (freshmen), continuous (transfers).

Freshman Application Contact Saint Joseph Seminary College, 75376 River Road, St. Benedict, LA 70457. *Phone:* 985-867-2273. *Fax:* 985-327-1085. *E-mail:* registrar@sjasc.edu. *Web site:* http://www.sjasc.edu/.

Southeastern Louisiana University
Hammond, Louisiana

- **State-supported** comprehensive, founded 1925, part of University of Louisiana System
- **Small-town** 375-acre campus with easy access to New Orleans
- **Endowment** $22.8 million
- **Coed** 13,950 undergraduate students, 79% full-time, 61% women, 39% men
- **Moderately difficult** entrance level, 81% of applicants were admitted

Undergraduates 11,005 full-time, 2,945 part-time. Students come from 40 states and territories; 44 other countries; 3% are from out of state; 17% Black or African American, non-Hispanic/Latino; 3% Hispanic/Latino; 0.9% Asian, non-Hispanic/Latino; 0.1% Native Hawaiian or other Pacific Islander, non-Hispanic/Latino; 0.5% American Indian or Alaska Native, non-Hispanic/Latino; 0.4% Two or more races, non-Hispanic/Latino; 2% Race/ethnicity unknown; 1% international; 6% transferred in; 18% live on campus. *Retention:* 67% of full-time freshmen returned.

Freshmen *Admission:* 3,795 applied, 3,087 admitted, 2,565 enrolled. *Average high school GPA:* 3.14. *Test scores:* ACT scores over 18: 95%; ACT scores over 24: 31%; ACT scores over 30: 2%.

Faculty *Total:* 613, 84% full-time, 61% with terminal degrees. *Student/faculty ratio:* 23:1.

Academics *Calendar:* semesters. *Degrees:* associate, bachelor's, master's, and doctoral-research/scholarship. *Special study options:* academic remediation for entering students, adult/continuing education programs, advanced placement credit, distance learning, double majors, English as a second language, honors programs, independent study, internships, off-campus study, part-time degree program, services for LD students, study abroad, summer session for credit. *ROTC:* Army (c).

Computers on Campus 1,440 computers/terminals and 568 ports are available on campus for general student use. Students can access the following: campus intranet, computer help desk, free student e-mail accounts, online (class) grades, online (class) registration, online (class) schedules, campus Webmail, student newspaper, transcripts, bookstore. Campuswide network is available. 100% of college-owned or -operated housing units are wired for high-speed Internet access. Wireless service is available via classrooms, computer centers, computer labs, dorm rooms, learning centers, libraries, student centers.

Student Life *Housing:* on-campus residence required through sophomore year. *Options:* coed, men-only, women-only. Campus housing is provided by a third party. Freshman applicants given priority for college housing. *Activities and organizations:* drama/theater group, student-run newspaper, radio and television station, choral group, marching band, IMPACT, Circle K International, NAACP, Campus Crusade for Christ, Catholic Student Association, national fraternities, national sororities. *Campus security:* 24-hour emergency response devices and patrols, student patrols, late-night transport/escort service, controlled dormitory access, video cameras, motorist assistance. *Student services:* health clinic, personal/psychological counseling.

Athletics Member NCAA. All Division I except football (Division I-AA). *Intercollegiate sports:* baseball M(s), basketball M(s)/W(s), cross-country running M(s)/W(s), golf M(s), soccer W(s), softball W(s), tennis M(s)/W(s), track and field M(s)/W(s), volleyball W(s). *Intramural sports:* baseball M/W, basketball M/W, football M/W, racquetball M/W, rugby M(c), soccer M(c)/W, softball M/W, volleyball M/W, weight lifting M/W.

Standardized Tests *Required:* SAT or ACT (for admission).

Costs (2010–11) *Tuition:* state resident $2993 full-time, $167 per credit hour part-time; nonresident $11,462 full-time, $520 per credit hour part-time. Full-time tuition and fees vary according to course load. Part-time tuition and fees vary according to course load. *Required fees:* $1007 full-time. *Room and board:* $6640; room only: $4140. Room and board charges vary according to board plan and housing facility. *Payment plans:* installment, deferred payment. *Waivers:* senior citizens and employees or children of employees.

Financial Aid Of all full-time matriculated undergraduates who enrolled in 2008, 317 Federal Work-Study jobs (averaging $3349). 1,216 state and other part-time jobs (averaging $2102). *Average indebtedness upon graduation:* $36,560.

Applying *Options:* electronic application, early admission, deferred entrance. *Application fee:* $20. *Required:* Proof of immunization for all applicants. Standardized test scores, College transcripts and Statement of good standing for some students. *Required for some:* high school transcript, minimum 2.5 GPA. *Application deadlines:* 8/1 (freshmen), 8/1 (out-of-state freshmen), 8/1 (transfers). *Notification:* continuous (freshmen), continuous (out-of-state freshmen), continuous (transfers).

Freshman Application Contact Ms. Lori Fairburn, Director, Enrollment Services, Southeastern Louisiana University, SLU 10752, Hammond, LA 70402. *Phone:* 985-549-5637. *Toll-free phone:* 800-222-7358. *Fax:* 985-549-5882. *E-mail:* admissions@selu.edu. *Web site:* http://www.selu.edu/.

Southern University and Agricultural and Mechanical College
Baton Rouge, Louisiana

- **State-supported** university, founded 1880, part of Southern University System
- **Suburban** 964-acre campus
- **Endowment** $9.7 million
- **Coed**
- **Moderately difficult** entrance level

Faculty *Student/faculty ratio:* 16:1.

Academics *Calendar:* semesters. *Degrees:* associate, bachelor's, master's, doctoral-research/scholarship, and post-master's certificates.

Student Life *Campus security:* 24-hour emergency response devices and patrols, late-night transport/escort service, controlled dormitory access.

Athletics Member NCAA. All Division I except football (Division I-AA).

Standardized Tests *Required:* SAT or ACT (for admission).

Costs (2010–11) *Tuition:* state resident $4581 full-time; nonresident $10,376 full-time. Full-time tuition and fees vary according to course load and location. Part-time tuition and fees vary according to course load and location. *Room and board:* $5580; room only: $3332. Room and board charges vary according to board plan, gender, and housing facility.

Financial Aid Of all full-time matriculated undergraduates who enrolled in 2006, 6,032 applied for aid, 5,642 were judged to have need, 85 had their need fully met. 900 Federal Work-Study jobs (averaging $1800). 300 state and other part-time jobs (averaging $2500). *Average percent of need met:* 85. *Average financial aid package:* $7444. *Average need-based loan:* $3738. *Average need-based gift aid:* $3436. *Average non-need-based aid:* $3151. *Average indebtedness upon graduation:* $23,000.

Applying *Options:* electronic application, early admission. *Application fee:* $20. *Required:* high school transcript, minimum 2 GPA, Louisiana Board of Regents Core curriculum of 16.5 units of selected courses.

Freshman Application Contact Ms. Velva Thomas, Director of Admissions, Southern University and Agricultural and Mechanical College, PO Box 9901, Baton Rouge, LA 70813. *Phone:* 225-771-2430. *Toll-free phone:* 800-256-1531. *Fax:* 225-771-2500. *E-mail:* velva_thomas@subr.edu. *Web site:* http://www.subr.edu/.

Southern University at New Orleans
New Orleans, Louisiana

- **State-supported** comprehensive, founded 1959, part of Southern University System
- **Urban** 66-acre campus with easy access to New Orleans
- **Endowment** $3.9 million
- **Coed, primarily women**
- **Noncompetitive** entrance level

Academics *Calendar:* semesters. *Degrees:* associate, bachelor's, and master's.

Student Life *Campus security:* 24-hour emergency response devices and patrols, late-night transport/escort service.

Athletics Member NAIA.

Standardized Tests *Required:* SAT or ACT (for admission). *Recommended:* ACT (for admission).

Costs (2010–11) *Tuition:* state resident $2326 full-time; nonresident $3738 full-time. Full-time tuition and fees vary according to course load. Part-time tuition and fees vary according to course load. *Required fees:* $1084 full-time. *Room and board:* $8236. Room and board charges vary according to housing facility. *Payment plans:* installment, deferred payment.

Applying *Options:* electronic application, early admission, early decision, early action, deferred entrance. *Application fee:* $20. *Required:* high school transcript, health forms.

Freshman Application Contact Southern University at New Orleans, 6400 Press Drive, New Orleans, LA 70126-1009. *Phone:* 504-286-5033. *Web site:* http://www.suno.edu/.

Southwest University
Kenner, Louisiana

- **Proprietary** comprehensive
- **Coed** 425 students

Academics *Degrees:* certificates, associate, bachelor's, and master's. *Special study options:* accelerated degree program, distance learning, double majors.

Costs (2010–11) *Tuition:* $190 per semester hour part-time.

Applying *Application fee:* $75. *Required:* high school transcript, resume.

Freshman Application Contact Admissions Office, Southwest University, 2200 Veterans Memorial Blvd., Kenner, LA 70062. *Phone:* 504-468-2900.

Toll-free phone: 800-433-5923. *Fax:* 504-468-3213. *E-mail:* admissions@ southwest.edu. *Web site:* http://www.southwest.edu/.

Strayer University - Metairie Campus
Metairie, Louisiana

- **Proprietary** comprehensive
- **Coed**

Academics *Degrees:* associate, bachelor's, master's, and postbachelor's certificates.

Costs (2010–11) *Tuition:* $13,635 full-time, $1590 per course part-time.

Freshman Application Contact Strayer University - Metairie Campus, 111 Veterans Memorial Boulevard, Suite 420, Metairie, LA 70005. *Web site:* http://www.strayer.edu/metairie.

Tulane University
New Orleans, Louisiana

- **Independent** university, founded 1834
- **Urban** 110-acre campus
- **Endowment** $1.1 billion
- **Coed** 7,803 undergraduate students, 77% full-time, 57% women, 43% men
- **Very difficult** entrance level, 26% of applicants were admitted

Undergraduates 5,993 full-time, 1,810 part-time. Students come from 53 states and territories; 79 other countries; 69% are from out of state; 8% Black or African American, non-Hispanic/Latino; 5% Hispanic/Latino; 4% Asian, non-Hispanic/Latino; 0.6% American Indian or Alaska Native, non-Hispanic/Latino; 2% Two or more races, non-Hispanic/Latino; 10% Race/ethnicity unknown; 3% international; 1% transferred in; 44% live on campus. *Retention:* 91% of full-time freshmen returned.

Freshmen *Admission:* 43,815 applied, 11,384 admitted, 1,625 enrolled. *Average high school GPA:* 3.55. *Test scores:* SAT critical reading scores over 500: 98%; SAT math scores over 500: 98%; SAT writing scores over 500: 98%; ACT scores over 18: 100%; SAT critical reading scores over 600: 82%; SAT math scores over 600: 85%; SAT writing scores over 600: 84%; ACT scores over 24: 97%; SAT critical reading scores over 700: 30%; SAT math scores over 700: 28%; SAT writing scores over 700: 34%; ACT scores over 30: 60%.

Faculty *Total:* 1,003, 59% full-time, 70% with terminal degrees. *Student/faculty ratio:* 11:1.

Academics *Calendar:* semesters plus 3 summer sessions. *Degrees:* certificates, associate, bachelor's, master's, doctoral-professional, doctoral-research/scholarship, and postbachelor's certificates. *Special study options:* accelerated degree program, adult/continuing education programs, advanced placement credit, cooperative education, distance learning, double majors, English as a second language, freshman honors college, honors programs, independent study, internships, off-campus study, part-time degree program, services for LD students, student-designed majors, study abroad, summer session for credit. *ROTC:* Army (b), Navy (b), Air Force (b). *Unusual degree programs:* 3-2 business administration; engineering; public health, tropical medicine.

Computers on Campus 556 computers/terminals are available on campus for general student use. Students can access the following: campus intranet, computer help desk, free student e-mail accounts, online (class) grades, online (class) registration, online (class) schedules. Campuswide network is available. 100% of college-owned or -operated housing units are wired for high-speed Internet access. Wireless service is available via entire campus.

Student Life *Housing:* on-campus residence required through sophomore year. *Options:* coed, women-only, disabled students. Campus housing is university owned. Freshman campus housing is guaranteed. *Activities and organizations:* drama/theater group, student-run newspaper, radio and television station, choral group, marching band, Community Action Council of Tulane Students (CACTUS), Associated Student Body, Tulane University Campus Programming (TUCP), Association of Club Sports (ACS), National Pan-Hellenic Council, national fraternities, national sororities. *Campus security:* 24-hour emergency response devices and patrols, student patrols, late-night transport/escort service, controlled dormitory access, on and off-campus shuttle service, crime prevention programs, lighted pathways. *Student services:* health clinic, personal/psychological counseling, women's center, legal services.

Athletics Member NCAA. All Division I except football (Division I-A). *Intercollegiate sports:* baseball M(s), basketball M(s)/W(s), crew M(c)/W(c), cross-country running M(s)/W(s), golf W(s), gymnastics M(c)/W(c), ice hockey M(c)/W(c), lacrosse M(c)/W(c), rugby M(c), sailing M(c)/W(c), soccer M(c)/W(c), swimming and diving M(c)/W(c), tennis M(s)/W(s), track and field M(c)/W(s), volleyball M(c)/W(c), water polo M(c)/W(c). *Intramural sports:* baseball M(c), cheerleading M(c)/W(c), crew M(c)/W(c), cross-country running M(c), fencing M(c)/W(c), field hockey M(c)/W(c), gymnastics M(c)/W(c), ice hockey M(c), lacrosse M(c)/W(c), racquetball M(c)/W(c), rock climbing M(c)/W(c), rugby M(c), sailing M(c)/W(c), soccer M(c)/W(c), swim-

ming and diving M(c)/W(c), tennis M(c)/W(c), track and field M(c)/W, ultimate Frisbee M(c)/W(c), volleyball M(c)/W(c), water polo M(c)/W(c).

Standardized Tests *Required:* SAT or ACT (for admission).

Costs (2010–11) *Comprehensive fee:* $51,708 includes full-time tuition ($38,300), mandatory fees ($3584), and room and board ($9824). *College room only:* $5774. Room and board charges vary according to board plan and housing facility. *Payment plans:* tuition prepayment, installment. *Waivers:* employees or children of employees.

Financial Aid Of all full-time matriculated undergraduates who enrolled in 2008, 2,940 applied for aid, 2,207 were judged to have need, 1,480 had their need fully met. 1,153 Federal Work-Study jobs (averaging $2343). In 2008, 2145 non-need-based awards were made. *Average percent of need met:* 92%. *Average financial aid package:* $35,543. *Average need-based loan:* $7054. *Average need-based gift aid:* $25,204. *Average non-need-based aid:* $21,316. *Average indebtedness upon graduation:* $27,510.

Applying *Options:* electronic application, early action, deferred entrance. *Required:* essay or personal statement, high school transcript, 1 letter of recommendation. *Application deadlines:* 1/15 (freshmen), 6/1 (transfers). *Notification:* 4/1 (freshmen), continuous (transfers).

Freshman Application Contact Earl Retif, Vice President for Enrollment Management and University Registrar, Tulane University, Office of Admissions, 210 Gibson Hall, New Orleans, LA 70118. *Phone:* 504-865-5731. *Toll-free phone:* 800-873-9283. *Fax:* 504-862-8715. *E-mail:* undergrad.admission@tulane.edu. *Web site:* http://www.tulane.edu/.

University of Louisiana at Lafayette
Lafayette, Louisiana

- **State-supported** university, founded 1898, part of University of Louisiana System
- **Urban** 1375-acre campus
- **Coed** 15,306 undergraduate students, 84% full-time, 58% women, 42% men
- **Moderately difficult** entrance level, 67% of applicants were admitted

Undergraduates 12,896 full-time, 2,410 part-time. Students come from 42 states and territories; 75 other countries; 4% are from out of state; 20% Black or African American, non-Hispanic/Latino; 2% Hispanic/Latino; 2% Asian, non-Hispanic/Latino; 0.5% American Indian or Alaska Native, non-Hispanic/Latino; 0.6% Two or more races, non-Hispanic/Latino; 1% Race/ethnicity unknown; 2% international; 4% transferred in; 12% live on campus. *Retention:* 74% of full-time freshmen returned.

Freshmen *Admission:* 8,426 applied, 5,635 admitted, 2,955 enrolled. *Average high school GPA:* 3.25. *Test scores:* SAT critical reading scores over 500: 79%; SAT math scores over 500: 59%; ACT scores over 18: 96%; SAT critical reading scores over 600: 28%; SAT math scores over 600: 23%; ACT scores over 24: 31%; SAT critical reading scores over 700: 8%; SAT math scores over 700: 6%; ACT scores over 30: 2%.

Faculty *Total:* 751, 80% full-time, 63% with terminal degrees. *Student/faculty ratio:* 23:1.

Academics *Calendar:* semesters. *Degrees:* bachelor's, master's, doctoral-research/scholarship, post-master's, and postbachelor's certificates. *Special study options:* academic remediation for entering students, accelerated degree program, adult/continuing education programs, advanced placement credit, cooperative education, distance learning, double majors, honors programs, independent study, internships, part-time degree program, services for LD students, student-designed majors, study abroad, summer session for credit. *ROTC:* Army (b).

Computers on Campus 600 computers/terminals and 855 ports are available on campus for general student use. Students can access the following: campus intranet, computer help desk, free student e-mail accounts, online (class) grades, online (class) registration, online (class) schedules. Campuswide network is available. 67% of college-owned or -operated housing units are wired for high-speed Internet access. Wireless service is available via libraries.

Student Life *Housing options:* men-only, women-only. Campus housing is university owned. Freshman campus housing is guaranteed. *Activities and organizations:* drama/theater group, student-run newspaper, radio station, choral group, marching band, Union Program Council, Chi Alpha, Student Government Association, Greek Council, Newman Club, national fraternities, national sororities. *Campus security:* 24-hour emergency response devices and patrols, late-night transport/escort service, controlled dormitory access. *Student services:* health clinic, personal/psychological counseling, women's center, legal services.

Athletics Member NCAA. All Division I except football (Division I-A). *Intercollegiate sports:* baseball M(s), basketball M(s)/W(s), cross-country running M(s)/W(s), golf M(s), soccer W, softball W(s), tennis M(s)/W(s), track and field M(s)/W(s), volleyball W(s). *Intramural sports:* badminton M/W, baseball M, basketball M/W, bowling M/W, cross-country running M/W, football M/W, golf M/W, ice hockey M, lacrosse M, racquetball M/W, rugby M/W, sailing M/W, soccer M/W, softball M/W, swimming and diving M/W, table tennis M/W, tennis M/W, track and field M/W, volleyball M/W, water polo M/W, weight lifting M/W.

Standardized Tests *Required:* SAT or ACT (for admission).

Costs (2010–11) *Tuition:* state resident $3002 full-time, $125 per credit hour part-time; nonresident $8572 full-time, $357 per credit hour part-time. Full-time tuition and fees vary according to course load. *Required fees:* $1424 full-time. *Room and board:* $4758. Room and board charges vary according to housing facility. *Payment plan:* deferred payment. *Waivers:* children of alumni, senior citizens, and employees or children of employees.

Financial Aid Of all full-time matriculated undergraduates who enrolled in 2008, 9,563 applied for aid, 6,125 were judged to have need, 606 had their need fully met. 480 Federal Work-Study jobs (averaging $1896). 253 state and other part-time jobs (averaging $1493). In 2008, 948 non-need-based awards were made. *Average percent of need met:* 59%. *Average financial aid package:* $7179. *Average need-based loan:* $3785. *Average need-based gift aid:* $5451. *Average non-need-based aid:* $1691.

Applying *Options:* electronic application, early admission, deferred entrance. *Application fee:* $25. *Required:* high school transcript, minimum 2 GPA, core requirements, no remedials. *Application deadlines:* rolling (freshmen), rolling (transfers).

Freshman Application Contact Mr. Leroy Broussard Jr., Admissions Director, University of Louisiana at Lafayette, PO Drawer 41210, Lafayette, LA 70504. *Phone:* 337-482-6473. *Toll-free phone:* 800-752-6553. *Fax:* 337-482-1317. *E-mail:* admissions@louisiana.edu. *Web site:* http://www.louisiana.edu/.

University of Louisiana at Monroe
Monroe, Louisiana

- **State-supported** university, founded 1931, part of University of Louisiana System
- **Urban** 238-acre campus
- **Coed** 7,513 undergraduate students, 76% full-time, 63% women, 37% men
- **Minimally difficult** entrance level, 70% of applicants were admitted

Undergraduates 5,695 full-time, 1,818 part-time. Students come from 37 states and territories; 31 other countries; 6% are from out of state; 7% transferred in; 22% live on campus. *Retention:* 72% of full-time freshmen returned.

Freshmen *Admission:* 2,492 applied, 1,743 admitted, 1,101 enrolled. *Average high school GPA:* 3.28. *Test scores:* SAT critical reading scores over 500: 30%; SAT math scores over 500: 51%; ACT scores over 18: 93%; SAT critical reading scores over 600: 4%; SAT math scores over 600: 12%; ACT scores over 24: 27%; ACT scores over 30: 3%.

Faculty *Total:* 361, 90% full-time. *Student/faculty ratio:* 18:1.

Academics *Calendar:* semesters. *Degrees:* associate, bachelor's, master's, doctoral-research/scholarship, post-master's, and postbachelor's certificates. *Special study options:* academic remediation for entering students, accelerated degree program, advanced placement credit, cooperative education, distance learning, double majors, English as a second language, honors programs, independent study, internships, off-campus study, part-time degree program, study abroad, summer session for credit. *ROTC:* Army (c).

Computers on Campus Students can access the following: campus intranet, computer help desk, free student e-mail accounts, online (class) grades, online (class) registration, online (class) schedules. Campuswide network is available. 100% of college-owned or -operated housing units are wired for high-speed Internet access. Wireless service is available via entire campus.

Student Life *Housing:* on-campus residence required through sophomore year. *Options:* coed, men-only, women-only. Campus housing is university owned and leased by the school. Freshman applicants given priority for college housing. *Activities and organizations:* drama/theater group, student-run newspaper, radio station, marching band, Maroon Platoon, Alpha Lambda Delta, Louisiana Pharmacist Alliance, Association for Students in Kinesiology, Pre-Pharmacy Organization/Sound of Today, national fraternities, national sororities. *Campus security:* 24-hour emergency response devices and patrols, student patrols, late-night transport/escort service. *Student services:* health clinic, personal/psychological counseling.

Athletics Member NCAA. All Division I except football (Division I-A). *Intercollegiate sports:* baseball M(s), basketball M(s)/W(s), cheerleading M(s)/W(s), cross-country running M(s)/W(s), golf M(s)/W, racquetball M/W, soccer M/W(s), softball W(s), swimming and diving M(s)/W(s), tennis M/W, track and field M(s)/W(s), volleyball M/W(s), weight lifting M/W. *Intramural sports:* archery M/W, badminton M/W, basketball M/W, bowling M/W, cross-country running M/W, football M/W, golf M/W, soccer M/W, softball M/W, swimming and diving M/W, table tennis M/W, tennis W, track and field M/W, volleyball W.

Standardized Tests *Required:* SAT or ACT (for admission).

Costs (2011–12) *Tuition:* state resident $4635 full-time; nonresident $10,925 full-time. Full-time tuition and fees vary according to course load and degree

level. Part-time tuition and fees vary according to course load and degree level. *Room and board:* $2992. Room and board charges vary according to board plan and housing facility. *Payment plan:* deferred payment. *Waivers:* children of alumni and employees or children of employees.

Applying *Options:* electronic application, early admission, deferred entrance. *Application fee:* $20. *Required:* high school transcript. *Application deadlines:* rolling (freshmen), rolling (out-of-state freshmen), rolling (transfers). *Notification:* continuous (freshmen), continuous (out-of-state freshmen), continuous (transfers).

Freshman Application Contact Ms. Frances Self, Assistant Director of Admissions, University of Louisiana at Monroe, Office of Recruitment and Admissions, Sandel Hall, 4020 Northeast Drive, Monroe, LA 71209. *Phone:* 318-342-5430. *Toll-free phone:* 800-372-5272 (in-state); 800-372-5127 (out-of-state). *Fax:* 318-342-1915. *E-mail:* admissions@ulm.edu. *Web site:* http://www.ulm.edu/.

University of New Orleans
New Orleans, Louisiana

- **State-supported** university, founded 1958, part of Louisiana State University System
- **Urban** 345-acre campus
- **Endowment** $15.6 million
- **Coed**
- **Moderately difficult** entrance level

Faculty *Student/faculty ratio:* 18:1.

Academics *Calendar:* semesters. *Degrees:* bachelor's, master's, doctoral-research/scholarship, and postbachelor's certificates.

Student Life *Campus security:* 24-hour emergency response devices and patrols, late-night transport/escort service, controlled dormitory access.

Athletics Member NCAA. All Division I.

Standardized Tests *Required:* SAT or ACT (for admission).

Costs (2010–11) *Tuition:* state resident $4152 full-time, $138 per credit hour part-time; nonresident $13,740 full-time, $458 per credit hour part-time. Full-time tuition and fees vary according to course load, location, and program. Part-time tuition and fees vary according to course load, location, and program. *Required fees:* $659 full-time. *Room and board:* $8127. Room and board charges vary according to board plan and housing facility. *Payment plans:* installment, deferred payment.

Financial Aid Of all full-time matriculated undergraduates who enrolled in 2009, 5,003 applied for aid, 4,335 were judged to have need, 299 had their need fully met. 184 Federal Work-Study jobs (averaging $2634). 397 state and other part-time jobs (averaging $1378). In 2009, 115 non-need-based awards were made. *Average percent of need met:* 51. *Average financial aid package:* $7929. *Average need-based loan:* $4262. *Average need-based gift aid:* $5837. *Average non-need-based aid:* $1666. *Average indebtedness upon graduation:* $16,427.

Applying *Options:* electronic application, early admission, deferred entrance. *Application fee:* $40. *Required:* high school transcript, Core Requirements (17.5 units). *Required for some:* minimum 2.5 GPA.

Freshman Application Contact University of New Orleans, 2000 Lakeshore Drive, New Orleans, LA 70148. *Phone:* 504-280-7013. *Toll-free phone:* 800-256-5866. *Web site:* http://www.uno.edu/.

See page 1718 for the College Close-Up.

University of Phoenix–Louisiana Campus
Metairie, Louisiana

Freshman Application Contact Ms. Audra McQuarie, Registrar/Executive Director, University of Phoenix–Louisiana Campus, 4035 South Riverpoint Parkway, Mail Stop CF-L101, Phoenix, AZ 85040. *Phone:* 480-557-6151. *Toll-free phone:* 800-776-4867 (in-state); 800-228-7240 (out-of-state). *Fax:* 480-643-3068. *E-mail:* audra.mcquarie@phoenix.edu. *Web site:* http://www.phoenix.edu/.

Xavier University of Louisiana
New Orleans, Louisiana

- **Independent Roman Catholic** comprehensive, founded 1925
- **Urban** 23-acre campus
- **Endowment** $117.3 million
- **Coed** 2,708 undergraduate students, 95% full-time, 71% women, 29% men
- **Moderately difficult** entrance level, 69% of applicants were admitted

Undergraduates 2,585 full-time, 123 part-time. Students come from 35 states and territories; 6 other countries; 38% are from out of state; 77% Black or African American, non-Hispanic/Latino; 2% Hispanic/Latino; 9% Asian, non-Hispanic/Latino; 0.1% American Indian or Alaska Native, non-Hispanic/Latino; 2% Two or more races, non-Hispanic/Latino; 3% Race/ethnicity unknown; 2% international; 6% transferred in; 47% live on campus. *Retention:* 66% of full-time freshmen returned.

Freshmen *Admission:* 3,397 applied, 2,337 admitted, 779 enrolled. *Average high school GPA:* 3.18. *Test scores:* SAT critical reading scores over 500: 40%; SAT math scores over 500: 38%; SAT writing scores over 500: 39%; ACT scores over 18: 82%; SAT critical reading scores over 600: 9%; SAT math scores over 600: 10%; SAT writing scores over 600: 8%; ACT scores over 24: 25%; SAT critical reading scores over 700: 1%; ACT scores over 30: 1%.

Faculty *Total:* 272, 89% full-time, 86% with terminal degrees. *Student/faculty ratio:* 13:1.

Academics *Calendar:* semesters. *Degrees:* bachelor's, master's, and doctoral-professional. *Special study options:* academic remediation for entering students, accelerated degree program, adult/continuing education programs, advanced placement credit, cooperative education, double majors, freshman honors college, honors programs, independent study, internships, off-campus study, part-time degree program, services for LD students, study abroad, summer session for credit. *ROTC:* Army (c), Navy (c), Air Force (c). *Unusual degree programs:* 3-2 business administration with Tulane University; engineering with Tulane University, University of Maryland, University of New Orleans, Georgia Institute of Technology, University of Wisconsin-Madison, Morgan State University, Southern University and Agricultural and Mechanical College; biostatistics with Louisiana State University Medical Center.

Computers on Campus 155 computers/terminals are available on campus for general student use. Students can access the following: computer help desk, free student e-mail accounts, online (class) grades, online (class) registration, online (class) schedules. Campuswide network is available. 100% of college-owned or -operated housing units are wired for high-speed Internet access. Wireless service is available via entire campus.

Student Life *Housing options:* coed, men-only, women-only, disabled students. Campus housing is university owned. Freshman applicants given priority for college housing. *Activities and organizations:* drama/theater group,

student-run newspaper, television station, choral group, Mobilization at Xavier, AWARE, NAACP, California Club, Beta Beta Beta (Biology Club), national fraternities, national sororities. *Campus security:* 24-hour emergency response devices and patrols, student patrols, bicycle patrols. *Student services:* health clinic, personal/psychological counseling.

Athletics Member NAIA. *Intercollegiate sports:* basketball M(s)/W(s), cross-country running M/W, tennis M(s)/W(s). *Intramural sports:* badminton M/W, basketball M/W, football M/W, golf M/W, softball M/W, swimming and diving M/W, table tennis M/W, tennis M/W, track and field M/W, volleyball M/W.

Standardized Tests *Required:* SAT or ACT (for admission).

Costs (2010–11) *One-time required fee:* $150. *Comprehensive fee:* $24,300 includes full-time tuition ($16,100), mandatory fees ($1000), and room and board ($7200). Part-time tuition: $725 per semester hour. Part-time tuition and fees vary according to course load. *Required fees:* $140 per semester hour part-time. *Room and board:* Room and board charges vary according to housing facility. *Payment plan:* installment. *Waivers:* employees or children of employees.

Financial Aid Of all full-time matriculated undergraduates who enrolled in 2008, 2,417 applied for aid, 2,224 were judged to have need, 29 had their need fully met. 286 Federal Work-Study jobs (averaging $973). In 2008, 75 non-need-based awards were made. *Average percent of need met:* 13%. *Average financial aid package:* $17,144. *Average need-based loan:* $4806. *Average need-based gift aid:* $6279. *Average non-need-based aid:* $8461. *Average indebtedness upon graduation:* $45,916.

Applying *Options:* electronic application, early action. *Application fee:* $25. *Required:* high school transcript, minimum 2 GPA, 1 letter of recommendation. *Required for some:* interview. *Application deadlines:* 7/1 (freshmen), 6/1 (transfers), 1/15 (early action). *Notification:* continuous (freshmen), continuous (transfers), 2/15 (early action).

Freshman Application Contact Mr. Winston Brown, Dean of Admissions, Xavier University of Louisiana, 7325 Palmetto Street, New Orleans, LA 70125. *Phone:* 504-520-7388. *Toll-free phone:* 877-XAVIERU. *Fax:* 504-520-7941. *E-mail:* apply@xula.edu. *Web site:* http://www.xula.edu/.

MAINE

Bates College
Lewiston, Maine

- **Independent** 4-year, founded 1855
- **Small-town** 109-acre campus
- **Endowment** $198.5 million
- **Coed** 1,725 undergraduate students, 100% full-time, 54% women, 46% men
- **Most difficult** entrance level, 32% of applicants were admitted

Undergraduates 1,725 full-time. Students come from 44 states and territories; 67 other countries; 90% are from out of state; 5% Black or African American, non-Hispanic/Latino; 5% Hispanic/Latino; 5% Asian, non-Hispanic/Latino; 0.1% Native Hawaiian or other Pacific Islander, non-Hispanic/Latino; 0.4% American Indian or Alaska Native, non-Hispanic/Latino; 3% Two or more races, non-Hispanic/Latino; 0.8% Race/ethnicity unknown; 6% international; 0.9% transferred in; 93% live on campus. *Retention:* 92% of full-time freshmen returned.

Freshmen *Admission:* 4,517 applied, 1,437 admitted, 495 enrolled. *Test scores:* SAT critical reading scores over 500: 100%; SAT math scores over 500: 99%; SAT writing scores over 500: 98%; ACT scores over 18: 100%; SAT critical reading scores over 600: 88%; SAT math scores over 600: 88%; SAT writing scores over 600: 88%; ACT scores over 24: 99%; SAT critical reading scores over 700: 29%; SAT math scores over 700: 29%; SAT writing scores over 700: 37%; ACT scores over 30: 65%.

Faculty *Total:* 183, 88% full-time, 90% with terminal degrees. *Student/faculty ratio:* 10:1.

Academics *Calendar:* 4-4-1. *Degree:* bachelor's. *Special study options:* accelerated degree program, advanced placement credit, cooperative education, double majors, honors programs, independent study, internships, off-campus study, services for LD students, student-designed majors, study abroad. *Unusual degree programs:* 3-2 engineering with Columbia University, Rensselaer Polytechnic Institute, Case Western Reserve University, Washington University in St. Louis, Dartmouth College.

Computers on Campus 521 computers/terminals and 2,075 ports are available on campus for general student use. Students can access the following: computer help desk, free student e-mail accounts, online (class) grades, online (class) registration, online (class) schedules, course web pages, course evaluation, financial records. Campuswide network is available. 100% of college-owned or -operated housing units are wired for high-speed Internet access. Wireless service is available via classrooms, computer labs, dorm rooms, learning centers, libraries, student centers.

Student Life *Housing:* on-campus residence required through senior year. *Options:* coed, men-only, women-only. Campus housing is university owned. Freshman campus housing is guaranteed. *Activities and organizations:* drama/theater group, student-run newspaper, radio station, choral group, Outing Club (outdoor recreation), International Club, Chase Hall Committee (student activities planning), Representative Assembly, WRBC (student radio station). *Campus security:* 24-hour emergency response devices and patrols, student patrols, late-night transport/escort service, controlled dormitory access. *Student services:* health clinic, personal/psychological counseling, women's center.

Athletics Member NCAA. All Division III. *Intercollegiate sports:* baseball M, basketball M/W, crew M/W, cross-country running M/W, equestrian sports M(c)/W(c), fencing M(c)/W(c), field hockey W, football M, golf M/W, ice hockey M(c)/W(c), lacrosse M/W, rugby M(c)/W(c), sailing M(c)/W(c), skiing (cross-country) M/W, skiing (downhill) M/W, soccer M/W, softball W, squash M/W, swimming and diving M/W, tennis M/W, track and field M/W, ultimate Frisbee M(c)/W(c), volleyball M(c)/W, water polo M(c)/W(c). *Intramural sports:* basketball M/W, bowling M/W, ice hockey M/W, racquetball M/W, soccer M/W, softball M/W, squash M/W, tennis M/W, ultimate Frisbee M/W, volleyball M/W.

Costs (2010–11) *Comprehensive fee:* $53,300. *Payment plans:* tuition prepayment, installment. *Waivers:* employees or children of employees.

Financial Aid Of all full-time matriculated undergraduates who enrolled in 2009, 850 applied for aid, 773 were judged to have need, 691 had their need fully met. 544 Federal Work-Study jobs (averaging $1713). 110 state and other part-time jobs (averaging $1729). *Average percent of need met:* 100%. *Average financial aid package:* $33,852. *Average need-based loan:* $4371. *Average need-based gift aid:* $31,083. *Average indebtedness upon graduation:* $17,945. *Financial aid deadline:* 2/1.

Applying *Options:* electronic application, early admission, early decision, deferred entrance. *Application fee:* $60. *Required:* essay or personal statement, high school transcript, 3 letters of recommendation. *Recommended:* interview. *Application deadline:* 1/1 (freshmen), 3/1 (transfers). *Early decision deadline:* 11/15 (for plan 1), 1/1 (for plan 2). *Notification:* 3/31 (freshmen), 4/15 (transfers), 12/20 (early decision plan 1), 2/14 (early decision plan 2).

Freshman Application Contact Mr. Wylie Mitchell, Dean of Admissions, Bates College, 2 Andrews Road, Bates College, Lewiston, ME 04240-6028. *Phone:* 207-786-6000. *Fax:* 207-786-6025. *E-mail:* admissions@bates.edu. *Web site:* http://www.bates.edu/.

Bowdoin College
Brunswick, Maine

- **Independent** 4-year, founded 1794
- **Small-town** 205-acre campus with easy access to Portland
- **Endowment** $753.5 million
- **Coed** 1,762 undergraduate students, 100% full-time, 51% women, 49% men
- **Most difficult** entrance level, 20% of applicants were admitted

Undergraduates 1,755 full-time, 7 part-time. Students come from 51 states and territories; 31 other countries; 87% are from out of state; 5% Black or African American, non-Hispanic/Latino; 12% Hispanic/Latino; 7% Asian, non-Hispanic/Latino; 0.2% Native Hawaiian or other Pacific Islander, non-Hispanic/Latino; 0.1% American Indian or Alaska Native, non-Hispanic/Latino; 6% Two or more races, non-Hispanic/Latino; 0.5% Race/ethnicity unknown; 3% international; 0.2% transferred in; 93% live on campus. *Retention:* 94% of full-time freshmen returned.

Freshmen *Admission:* 6,018 applied, 1,183 admitted, 507 enrolled. *Test scores:* SAT critical reading scores over 500: 100%; SAT math scores over 500: 100%; SAT writing scores over 500: 100%; ACT scores over 18: 100%; SAT critical reading scores over 600: 93%; SAT math scores over 600: 94%; SAT writing scores over 600: 92%; ACT scores over 24: 100%; SAT critical reading scores over 700: 59%; SAT math scores over 700: 56%; SAT writing scores over 700: 59%; ACT scores over 30: 76%.

Faculty *Total:* 216, 84% full-time, 98% with terminal degrees. *Student/faculty ratio:* 9:1.

Academics *Calendar:* semesters. *Degrees:* bachelor's (SAT or ACT considered if submitted. Test scores are required for home-schooled applicants). *Special study options:* accelerated degree program, advanced placement credit, double majors, independent study, off-campus study, services for LD students, student-designed majors, study abroad. *Unusual degree programs:* 3-2 engineering with California Institute of Technology, Columbia University, Dartmouth College, University of Maine Orono; Law Degree program with Columbia University.

Computers on Campus 450 computers/terminals and 5,500 ports are available on campus for general student use. Students can access the following: campus intranet, computer help desk, free student e-mail accounts, online (class) grades, online (class) schedules, training classes on variety of desktop and academic software. Campuswide network is available. 100% of college-owned or -operated housing units are wired for high-speed Internet access. Wireless service is available via entire campus.

Student Life *Housing:* on-campus residence required through sophomore year. *Options:* coed, disabled students. Campus housing is university owned. Freshman campus housing is guaranteed. *Activities and organizations:* drama/theater group, student-run newspaper, radio and television station, choral group, Outing Club, Crew/Rowing, Community Service Volunteer Programs, WBOR 91.1 FM, Bowdoin Student Government. *Campus security:* 24-hour emergency response devices and patrols, late-night transport/escort service, controlled dormitory access, self-defense education, whistle program, safe ride service. *Student services:* health clinic, personal/psychological counseling, women's center.

Athletics Member NCAA. All Division III except men's and women's sailing (Division I), men's and women's skiing (cross-country) (Division I), men's and women's squash (Division I). *Intercollegiate sports:* baseball M, basketball M/W, crew M(c)/W(c), cross-country running M/W, equestrian sports M(c)/W(c), fencing M(c)/W(c), field hockey W, football M, golf M/W, ice hockey M/W, lacrosse M/W, rugby M(c)/W, sailing M/W, skiing (cross-country) M/W, skiing (downhill) M(c)/W(c), soccer M/W, softball W, squash M/W, swimming and diving M/W, tennis M/W, track and field M/W, ultimate Frisbee M(c)/W(c), volleyball M(c)/W, water polo M(c)/W(c). *Intramural sports:* badminton M/W, basketball M/W, cheerleading M(c)/W(c), field hockey M/W, football M/W, ice hockey M/W, rock climbing M(c)/W(c), skiing (cross-country) M(c)/W(c), soccer M/W, softball M/W, tennis M/W, volleyball M/W, water polo M/W.

Costs (2010–11) *Comprehensive fee:* $52,880 includes full-time tuition ($41,150), mandatory fees ($415), and room and board ($11,315). *College room only:* $5295. Room and board charges vary according to board plan. *Payment plans:* installment, deferred payment. *Waivers:* employees or children of employees.

Financial Aid Of all full-time matriculated undergraduates who enrolled in 2009, 969 applied for aid, 800 were judged to have need, 800 had their need fully met. 279 Federal Work-Study jobs (averaging $1720). 369 state and other part-time jobs (averaging $1738). In 2009, 91 non-need-based awards were made. *Average percent of need met:* 100%. *Average financial aid package:* $39,484. *Average need-based gift aid:* $35,590. *Average non-need-based aid:*

$1000. *Average indebtedness upon graduation:* $18,229. *Financial aid deadline:* 2/15.

Applying *Options:* electronic application, early admission, early decision, deferred entrance. *Application fee:* $60. *Required:* essay or personal statement, high school transcript, 3 letters of recommendation. *Recommended:* interview. *Application deadlines:* 1/1 (freshmen), 1/1 (out-of-state freshmen), 3/1 (transfers). *Early decision deadline:* 11/15 (for plan 1), 1/1 (for plan 2). *Notification:* 4/5 (freshmen), 4/5 (out-of-state freshmen), 5/1 (transfers), 12/31 (early decision plan 1), 2/15 (early decision plan 2).

Freshman Application Contact Peter T. Wiley, Associate Dean of Admissions, Bowdoin College, 5000 College Station, Brunswick, ME 04011-8411. *Phone:* 207-725-3190. *Fax:* 207-725-3101. *E-mail:* admissions@ bowdoin.edu. *Web site:* http://www.bowdoin.edu/.

Colby College

Waterville, Maine

- **Independent** 4-year, founded 1813
- **Small-town** 714-acre campus
- **Endowment** $502.1 million
- **Coed** 1,825 undergraduate students, 100% full-time, 54% women, 46% men
- **Most difficult** entrance level, 34% of applicants were admitted

Undergraduates 1,825 full-time. Students come from 45 states and territories; 62 other countries; 86% are from out of state; 4% Black or African American, non-Hispanic/Latino; 4% Hispanic/Latino; 7% Asian, non-Hispanic/Latino; 0.1% Native Hawaiian or other Pacific Islander, non-Hispanic/Latino; 0.2% American Indian or Alaska Native, non-Hispanic/Latino; 2% Two or more races, non-Hispanic/Latino; 19% Race/ethnicity unknown; 5% international; 0.3% transferred in; 93% live on campus. *Retention:* 95% of full-time freshmen returned.

Freshmen *Admission:* 4,213 applied, 1,440 admitted, 484 enrolled. *Test scores:* SAT critical reading scores over 500: 98%; SAT math scores over 500: 99%; SAT writing scores over 500: 98%; ACT scores over 18: 100%; SAT critical reading scores over 600: 85%; SAT math scores over 600: 87%; SAT writing scores over 600: 84%; ACT scores over 24: 98%; SAT critical reading scores over 700: 32%; SAT math scores over 700: 40%; SAT writing scores over 700: 33%; ACT scores over 30: 53%.

Faculty *Total:* 214, 78% full-time, 90% with terminal degrees. *Student/faculty ratio:* 10:1.

Academics *Calendar:* 4-1-4. *Degree:* bachelor's. *Special study options:* advanced placement credit, double majors, honors programs, independent study, internships, off-campus study, services for LD students, student-designed majors, study abroad. *ROTC:* Army (c). *Unusual degree programs:* 3-2 engineering with Dartmouth College.

Computers on Campus 350 computers/terminals are available on campus for general student use. Students can access the following: campus intranet, computer help desk, free student e-mail accounts, online (class) grades, online (class) registration, online (class) schedules, portal. Campuswide network is available. 100% of college-owned or -operated housing units are wired for high-speed Internet access. Wireless service is available via classrooms, computer centers, computer labs, dorm rooms, learning centers, libraries, student centers.

Student Life *Housing:* on-campus residence required through senior year. *Options:* coed. Campus housing is university owned. Freshman campus housing is guaranteed. *Activities and organizations:* drama/theater group, student-run newspaper, radio station, choral group, Outing Club, volunteer center, WMHB-FM (College Radio Station), student government, Powder and Wig (theater). *Campus security:* 24-hour emergency response devices and patrols, late-night transport/escort service, controlled dormitory access, campus lighting, student emergency response team, self-defense class, property id program, party monitors. *Student services:* health clinic, personal/psychological counseling, women's center.

Athletics Member NCAA. All Division III except men's and women's skiing (downhill) (Division I). *Intercollegiate sports:* badminton M(c)/W(c), baseball M, basketball M/W, crew M/W, cross-country running M/W, equestrian sports M(c)/W(c), fencing M(c)/W(c), field hockey W, football M, golf M/W, ice hockey M/W, lacrosse M/W, rugby M(c)/W(c), skiing (downhill) M/W, soccer M/W, softball W, squash M/W, swimming and diving M/W, tennis M/W, track and field M/W, ultimate Frisbee M(c)/W(c), volleyball M(c)/W, water polo M(c)/W(c). *Intramural sports:* basketball M/W, football M, soccer M/W, softball M/W.

Standardized Tests *Required for some:* SAT or ACT (for admission), SAT Subject Tests (for admission).

Costs (2010–11) *Comprehensive fee:* $51,990. Full-time tuition and fees vary according to course load. Part-time tuition and fees vary according to course load. *Room and board:* Room and board charges vary according to housing facility. *Payment plan:* installment. *Waivers:* employees or children of employees.

Financial Aid Of all full-time matriculated undergraduates who enrolled in 2009, 900 applied for aid, 765 were judged to have need, 765 had their need fully met. 447 Federal Work-Study jobs (averaging $1636). 152 state and other part-time jobs (averaging $1683). In 2009, 45 non-need-based awards were made. *Average percent of need met:* 100%. *Average financial aid package:* $33,838. *Average need-based loan:* $1535. *Average need-based gift aid:* $32,609. *Average non-need-based aid:* $2970. *Average indebtedness upon graduation:* $24,600. *Financial aid deadline:* 2/1.

Applying *Options:* electronic application, early admission, early decision, deferred entrance. *Application fee:* $65. *Required:* essay or personal statement, high school transcript, 2 letters of recommendation. *Recommended:* interview. *Application deadlines:* 1/1 (freshmen), 3/1 (transfers). *Early decision deadline:* 11/15 (for plan 1), 1/1 (for plan 2). *Notification:* 4/1 (freshmen), 5/15 (transfers), 12/15 (early decision plan 1), 2/10 (early decision plan 2).

Freshman Application Contact Mr. Steve Thomas, Director of Admissions, Colby College, Mayflower Hill, Waterville, ME 04901-8840. *Phone:* 207-859-4800. *Toll-free phone:* 800-723-3032. *Fax:* 207-859-4828. *E-mail:* admissions@colby.edu. *Web site:* http://www.colby.edu/.

College of the Atlantic

Bar Harbor, Maine

- **Independent** comprehensive, founded 1969
- **Small-town** 35-acre campus
- **Endowment** $19.6 million
- **Coed** 364 undergraduate students, 92% full-time, 70% women, 30% men
- **Very difficult** entrance level, 64% of applicants were admitted

Undergraduates 335 full-time, 29 part-time. Students come from 36 states and territories; 34 other countries; 74% are from out of state; 0.8% Black or African American, non-Hispanic/Latino; 2% Hispanic/Latino; 0.8% Asian, non-Hispanic/Latino; 0.3% American Indian or Alaska Native, non-Hispanic/Latino; 3% Two or more races, non-Hispanic/Latino; 12% Race/ethnicity unknown; 16% international; 5% transferred in; 43% live on campus. *Retention:* 89% of full-time freshmen returned.

Freshmen *Admission:* 390 applied, 250 admitted, 85 enrolled. *Average high school GPA:* 3.56. *Test scores:* SAT critical reading scores over 500: 96%; SAT math scores over 500: 84%; SAT writing scores over 500: 98%; ACT scores over 18: 100%; SAT critical reading scores over 600: 64%; SAT math scores over 600: 40%; SAT writing scores over 600: 64%; ACT scores over 24: 87%; SAT critical reading scores over 700: 22%; SAT math scores over 700: 12%; SAT writing scores over 700: 12%; ACT scores over 30: 20%.

Faculty *Total:* 42, 64% full-time, 69% with terminal degrees. *Student/faculty ratio:* 11:1.

Academics *Calendar:* trimesters. *Degrees:* bachelor's and master's. *Special study options:* academic remediation for entering students, accelerated degree program, advanced placement credit, cooperative education, independent study, internships, off-campus study, part-time degree program, services for LD students, student-designed majors, study abroad.

Computers on Campus 38 computers/terminals and 50 ports are available on campus for general student use. Students can access the following: computer help desk, free student e-mail accounts, online (class) grades, online (class) registration, online (class) schedules. Campuswide network is available. 100% of college-owned or -operated housing units are wired for high-speed Internet access. Wireless service is available via entire campus.

Student Life *Housing:* on-campus residence required for freshman year. *Options:* coed. Campus housing is university owned. Freshman campus housing is guaranteed. *Activities and organizations:* drama/theater group, student-run newspaper, choral group, Sustain US, All College Meeting, Outdoor Program, Open Mic, Student Meeting. *Campus security:* 24-hour emergency response devices and patrols, late-night transport/escort service. *Student services:* health clinic, personal/psychological counseling.

Athletics *Intramural sports:* badminton M/W, basketball M, bowling M/W, ice hockey M/W, rock climbing M/W, sailing M/W, skiing (cross-country) M/W, soccer M/W, softball M/W, table tennis M/W, ultimate Frisbee M/W, volleyball M/W, water polo M/W.

Standardized Tests *Recommended:* SAT or ACT (for admission).

Costs (2011–12) *Comprehensive fee:* $44,883 includes full-time tuition ($35,532), mandatory fees ($531), and room and board ($8820). Part-time tuition: $3948 per credit. *Required fees:* $177 per term part-time. *College room only:* $5670. Room and board charges vary according to board plan. *Payment plan:* installment. *Waivers:* employees or children of employees.

Financial Aid Of all full-time matriculated undergraduates who enrolled in 2009, 296 applied for aid, 291 were judged to have need, 144 had their need fully met. 220 Federal Work-Study jobs (averaging $2356). 58 state and other part-time jobs (averaging $1831). *Average percent of need met:* 96%. *Average financial aid package:* $31,981. *Average need-based loan:* $4489. *Average need-based gift aid:* $27,548. *Average indebtedness upon graduation:* $20,125.

Applying *Options:* electronic application, early admission, early decision, deferred entrance. *Application fee:* $45. *Required:* essay or personal statement, high school transcript, 3 letters of recommendation. *Required for some:* interview. *Recommended:* minimum 3 GPA, interview. *Application deadlines:* 2/15 (freshmen), 4/1 (transfers). *Early decision deadline:* 12/1 (for plan 1), 1/10 (for plan 2). *Notification:* 4/1 (freshmen), 4/25 (transfers), 12/15 (early decision plan 1), 1/25 (early decision plan 2).

Freshman Application Contact Ms. Sarah Baker, Dean of Admission, College of the Atlantic, 105 Eden Street, Bar Harbor, ME 04609-1198. *Phone:* 207-801-5640. *Toll-free phone:* 800-528-0025. *Fax:* 207-288-4126. *E-mail:* inquiry@coa.edu. *Web site:* http://www.coa.edu/.

Husson University

Bangor, Maine

- **Independent** comprehensive, founded 1898
- **Suburban** 200-acre campus
- **Endowment** $6.2 million
- **Coed** 2,630 undergraduate students, 75% full-time, 57% women, 43% men
- **Moderately difficult** entrance level, 82% of applicants were admitted

Undergraduates 1,964 full-time, 666 part-time. Students come from 37 states and territories; 25 other countries; 15% are from out of state; 3% Black or African American, non-Hispanic/Latino; 1% Hispanic/Latino; 0.9% Asian, non-Hispanic/Latino; 0.4% American Indian or Alaska Native, non-Hispanic/Latino; 0.4% Two or more races, non-Hispanic/Latino; 6% Race/ethnicity unknown; 1% international; 5% transferred in; 37% live on campus. *Retention:* 68% of full-time freshmen returned.

Freshmen *Admission:* 1,284 applied, 1,047 admitted, 442 enrolled. *Average high school GPA:* 3.25. *Test scores:* SAT critical reading scores over 500: 32%; SAT math scores over 500: 35%; SAT writing scores over 500: 29%; ACT scores over 18: 77%; SAT critical reading scores over 600: 4%; SAT math scores over 600: 7%; SAT writing scores over 600: 4%; ACT scores over 24: 5%.

Faculty *Total:* 109, 83% full-time, 61% with terminal degrees. *Student/faculty ratio:* 27:1.

Academics *Calendar:* semesters. *Degrees:* certificates, associate, bachelor's, master's, doctoral-professional, post-master's, and postbachelor's certificates. *Special study options:* academic remediation for entering students, adult/continuing education programs, advanced placement credit, cooperative education, double majors, independent study, internships, part-time degree program, services for LD students, student-designed majors, summer session for credit. *ROTC:* Army (b), Navy (c). *Unusual degree programs:* 3-2 business administration; Occupational Therapy.

Computers on Campus 116 computers/terminals and 116 ports are available on campus for general student use. Students can access the following: campus intranet, computer help desk, free student e-mail accounts, online (class) grades, online (class) registration, online (class) schedules. Campuswide network is available. 100% of college-owned or -operated housing units are wired for high-speed Internet access. Wireless service is available via entire campus.

Student Life *Housing:* on-campus residence required through sophomore year. *Options:* coed. Campus housing is university owned and leased by the school. Freshman campus housing is guaranteed. *Activities and organizations:* drama/theater group, student-run newspaper, radio station, student government, Organization of Student Nurses, Organization of Physical Therapy Students, Accounting Society, Criminal Justice Club, national fraternities. *Campus security:* 24-hour emergency response devices and patrols, late-night transport/escort service, controlled dormitory access. *Student services:* health clinic, personal/psychological counseling.

Athletics Member NCAA. All Division III. *Intercollegiate sports:* baseball M, basketball M/W, cross-country running M/W, field hockey W, football M, golf M/W, lacrosse M/W, soccer M/W, softball W, swimming and diving W, volleyball W. *Intramural sports:* baseball M, basketball M/W, cheerleading M/W, football M, ice hockey M/W, lacrosse M, soccer M/W, softball M/W, swimming and diving M/W, tennis M/W, volleyball M/W, water polo M/W, wrestling M.

Standardized Tests *Required:* SAT or ACT (for admission).

Costs (2011–12) *Comprehensive fee:* $21,480 includes full-time tuition ($13,650), mandatory fees ($310), and room and board ($7520). Full-time tuition and fees vary according to class time. Part-time tuition: $455 per credit. Part-time tuition and fees vary according to class time and course load. *Payment plans:* tuition prepayment, installment. *Waivers:* senior citizens and employees or children of employees.

Financial Aid Of all full-time matriculated undergraduates who enrolled in 2009, 3,446 applied for aid, 2,451 were judged to have need, 103 had their need fully met. 1,001 Federal Work-Study jobs (averaging $1300). In 2009,

115 non-need-based awards were made. *Average percent of need met:* 57%. *Average financial aid package:* $9986. *Average need-based loan:* $4075. *Average need-based gift aid:* $7024. *Average non-need-based aid:* $3406. *Average indebtedness upon graduation:* $23,613.

Applying *Options:* electronic application, early admission, deferred entrance. *Application fee:* $40. *Required:* essay or personal statement, high school transcript, 1 letter of recommendation. *Recommended:* interview. *Application deadlines:* 8/1 (freshmen), 8/1 (transfers). *Notification:* continuous (freshmen), continuous until 9/1 (transfers).

Freshman Application Contact Ms. Carlena Bean, Director of Admissions, Husson University, 1 College Circle, Bangor, ME 04401-2999. *Phone:* 207-941-7067. *Toll-free phone:* 800-4-HUSSON. *Fax:* 207-941-7935. *E-mail:* beanc@husson.edu. *Web site:* http://www.husson.edu/.

Maine College of Art

Portland, Maine

- **Independent** comprehensive, founded 1882
- **Urban** campus with easy access to Boston
- **Endowment** $3.8 million
- **Coed** 318 undergraduate students, 97% full-time, 70% women, 30% men
- **Moderately difficult** entrance level, 94% of applicants were admitted

Undergraduates 308 full-time, 10 part-time. 0.9% Black or African American, non-Hispanic/Latino; 2% Hispanic/Latino; 0.6% Asian, non-Hispanic/Latino; 1% American Indian or Alaska Native, non-Hispanic/Latino; 0.9% Two or more races, non-Hispanic/Latino; 10% Race/ethnicity unknown; 34% live on campus.

Freshmen *Admission:* 341 applied, 322 admitted, 91 enrolled. *Average high school GPA:* 2.78.

Faculty *Total:* 62, 27% full-time. *Student/faculty ratio:* 10:1.

Academics *Calendar:* semesters. *Degrees:* bachelor's, master's, and post-bachelor's certificates. *Special study options:* advanced placement credit, cooperative education, double majors, internships, off-campus study, part-time degree program, services for LD students, study abroad.

Computers on Campus 86 computers/terminals are available on campus for general student use. Students can access the following: campus intranet, computer help desk, free student e-mail accounts, online (class) grades, online (class) registration, online (class) schedules. Campuswide network is available. 100% of college-owned or -operated housing units are wired for high-speed Internet access. Wireless service is available via classrooms, computer centers, computer labs, learning centers, libraries, student centers.

Student Life *Housing options:* coed. Campus housing is university owned. *Activities and organizations:* Student Senate, Community Action Group, Nontraditional and Transfer Group, running club, Green Group. *Campus security:* 24-hour emergency response devices and patrols, controlled dormitory access. *Student services:* personal/psychological counseling.

Costs (2010–11) *One-time required fee:* $50. *Comprehensive fee:* $38,640 includes full-time tuition ($27,965), mandatory fees ($680), and room and board ($9995). Part-time tuition: $1165 per credit hour. *Room and board:* Room and board charges vary according to board plan and housing facility. *Payment plan:* installment.

Financial Aid Of all full-time matriculated undergraduates who enrolled in 2008, 323 applied for aid, 292 were judged to have need, 29 had their need fully met. 54 Federal Work-Study jobs (averaging $2151). In 2008, 42 non-need-based awards were made. *Average percent of need met:* 56%. *Average financial aid package:* $13,894. *Average need-based loan:* $3965. *Average need-based gift aid:* $10,174. *Average non-need-based aid:* $6860. *Average indebtedness upon graduation:* $33,350.

Applying *Options:* electronic application, early admission, early action, deferred entrance. *Application fee:* $40. *Required:* essay or personal statement, high school transcript, 2 letters of recommendation, portfolio. *Recommended:* minimum 2 GPA, interview. *Application deadlines:* rolling (freshmen), rolling (transfers). *Notification:* continuous until 8/31 (freshmen), continuous until 8/31 (transfers).

Freshman Application Contact Stacy Howe, Admissions Operations Coordinator, Maine College of Art, 522 Congress Street, Portland, ME 04101-3987. *Phone:* 207-699-5026. *Toll-free phone:* 800-639-4808. *Fax:* 207-699-5080. *E-mail:* admissions@meca.edu. *Web site:* http://www.meca.edu/.

Maine Maritime Academy

Castine, Maine

Freshman Application Contact Maine Maritime Academy, Castine, ME 04420. *Phone:* 207-326-2215. *Toll-free phone:* 800-464-6565 (in-state); 800-227-8465 (out-of-state). *Web site:* http://www.mainemaritime.edu/.

New England School of Communications

Bangor, Maine

- **Independent** 4-year, founded 1981, administratively affiliated with Husson University
- **Small-town** 200-acre campus
- **Coed, primarily men**
- **Minimally difficult** entrance level

Faculty *Student/faculty ratio:* 14:1.

Academics *Calendar:* semesters. *Degree:* bachelor's.

Student Life *Campus security:* 24-hour emergency response devices and patrols, late-night transport/escort service.

Standardized Tests *Required:* Wonderlic aptitude test (for admission). *Recommended:* SAT or ACT (for admission).

Costs (2010–11) *Comprehensive fee:* $19,170 includes full-time tuition ($11,120), mandatory fees ($810), and room and board ($7240). Part-time tuition: $370 per credit. Part-time tuition and fees vary according to course load.

Financial Aid *Of all full-time matriculated undergraduates who enrolled in 2008,* 434 applied for aid, 379 were judged to have need, 21 had their need fully met. 51 Federal Work-Study jobs (averaging $1014). *In 2008,* 3 non-need-based awards were made. *Average need-based loan:* $3772. *Average need-based gift aid:* $1200. *Average non-need-based aid:* $4300. *Average indebtedness upon graduation:* $33,000.

Applying *Options:* electronic application, deferred entrance. *Application fee:* $25. *Required:* essay or personal statement, high school transcript, 2 letters of recommendation, interview. *Required for some:* placement test.

Freshman Application Contact Ms. Louise Grant, Director of Admissions, New England School of Communications, 1 College Circle, Bangor, ME 04401. *Phone:* 207-941-7176 Ext. 1093. *Toll-free phone:* 888-877-1876. *Fax:* 207-947-3987. *E-mail:* info@nescom.edu. *Web site:* http://www.nescom.edu/.

Saint Joseph's College of Maine

Standish, Maine

- **Independent** comprehensive, founded 1912, affiliated with Roman Catholic Church
- **Small-town** 350-acre campus
- **Endowment** $9.2 million
- **Coed** 1,050 undergraduate students, 97% full-time, 65% women, 35% men
- **Moderately difficult** entrance level, 82% of applicants were admitted

Undergraduates 1,015 full-time, 35 part-time. Students come from 15 states and territories; 1 other country; 45% are from out of state; 2% transferred in; 82% live on campus. *Retention:* 78% of full-time freshmen returned.

Freshmen *Admission:* 1,094 applied, 897 admitted, 364 enrolled. *Average high school GPA:* 3. *Test scores:* SAT critical reading scores over 500: 40%; SAT math scores over 500: 42%; SAT critical reading scores over 600: 7%; SAT math scores over 600: 9%; SAT critical reading scores over 700: 1%; SAT math scores over 700: 1%.

Faculty *Total:* 126, 54% full-time, 53% with terminal degrees. *Student/faculty ratio:* 15:1.

Academics *Calendar:* semesters. *Degrees:* certificates, bachelor's, master's, and post-master's certificates (profile does not include enrollment in distance learning master's program). *Special study options:* adult/continuing education programs, advanced placement credit, cooperative education, distance learning, double majors, honors programs, independent study, internships, off-campus study, part-time degree program, services for LD students, student-designed majors, study abroad, summer session for credit. *ROTC:* Army (c). *Unusual degree programs:* 3-2 engineering with Manhattan College; pharmacy with Massachusetts College of Pharmacy, optometry with Pennsylvania College of Optometry.

Computers on Campus 102 computers/terminals are available on campus for general student use. Students can access the following: campus intranet, computer help desk, free student e-mail accounts, online (class) grades, online (class) registration, online (class) schedules. Campuswide network is available. Wireless service is available via entire campus.

Student Life *Housing options:* coed, men-only, women-only. Campus housing is university owned. Freshman campus housing is guaranteed. *Activities and organizations:* drama/theater group, student-run newspaper, radio station, choral group, campus ministry, Superkids, Student Government Association and Senate, Business Club, Inter-Hall Council. *Campus security:* 24-hour emergency response devices and patrols, late-night transport/escort service, controlled dormitory access. *Student services:* health clinic, personal/psychological counseling.

Athletics Member NCAA. All Division III. *Intercollegiate sports:* baseball M, basketball M/W, cheerleading M(c)/W(c), cross-country running M/W, field hockey W, golf M, ice hockey M(c)/W(c), soccer M/W, softball W, volleyball W. *Intramural sports:* basketball M/W, lacrosse M(c)/W(c), rock climbing M(c)/W(c), soccer M/W, softball M/W, swimming and diving M(c)/W(c), volleyball M/W.

Standardized Tests *Required:* SAT or ACT (for admission).

Costs (2010–11) *Comprehensive fee:* $37,895 includes full-time tuition ($26,400), mandatory fees ($945), and room and board ($10,550). Part-time tuition: $475 per credit hour. Part-time tuition and fees vary according to course load. *Payment plan:* installment. *Waivers:* employees or children of employees.

Financial Aid Of all full-time matriculated undergraduates who enrolled in 2009, 946 applied for aid, 864 were judged to have need, 99 had their need fully met. 408 Federal Work-Study jobs (averaging $1382). In 2009, 172 non-need-based awards were made. *Average percent of need met:* 78%. *Average financial aid package:* $20,192. *Average need-based loan:* $6858. *Average need-based gift aid:* $13,447. *Average non-need-based aid:* $8155. *Average indebtedness upon graduation:* $36,071.

Applying *Options:* electronic application, early action, deferred entrance. *Application fee:* $50. *Required:* essay or personal statement, high school transcript, minimum 2 GPA, 2 letters of recommendation. *Recommended:* interview. *Application deadlines:* rolling (freshmen), rolling (transfers), 11/15 (early action). *Notification:* continuous (freshmen), continuous (transfers), 12/15 (early action).

Freshman Application Contact Mr. Vincent J. Kloskowski, Dean of Admission, Saint Joseph's College of Maine, 278 Whites Bridge Road, Standish, ME 04084-5263. *Phone:* 207-893-7746. *Toll-free phone:* 800-338-7057. *Fax:* 207-893-7862. *E-mail:* admission@sjcme.edu. *Web site:* http://www.sjcme.edu/.

Thomas College

Waterville, Maine

Freshman Application Contact Mr. James Love, Dean of Admissions, Thomas College, 180 West River Road, Waterville, ME 04901. *Phone:* 207-859-1101. *Toll-free phone:* 800-339-7001. *Fax:* 207-859-1114. *E-mail:* admiss@thomas.edu. *Web site:* http://www.thomas.edu/.

Unity College

Unity, Maine

Freshman Application Contact Mr. Gary Zane, Dean of Students, Unity College, 90 Quaker Hill Road, Unity, ME 04988. *Phone:* 207-948-3131. *Fax:* 207-948-6277. *E-mail:* gzane@unity.edu. *Web site:* http://www.unity.edu/.

University of Maine

Orono, Maine

- **State-supported** university, founded 1865, part of University of Maine System
- **Small-town** 3300-acre campus
- **Endowment** $159.6 million
- **Coed** 9,183 undergraduate students, 84% full-time, 49% women, 51% men
- **Moderately difficult** entrance level, 78% of applicants were admitted

Undergraduates 7,748 full-time, 1,435 part-time. 15% are from out of state; 1% Black or African American, non-Hispanic/Latino; 1% Hispanic/Latino; 1% Asian, non-Hispanic/Latino; 1% American Indian or Alaska Native, non-Hispanic/Latino; 1% Two or more races, non-Hispanic/Latino; 10% Race/ethnicity unknown; 2% international; 5% transferred in; 40% live on campus. *Retention:* 79% of full-time freshmen returned.

Freshmen *Admission:* 7,247 applied, 5,638 admitted, 1,754 enrolled. *Average high school GPA:* 3.25. *Test scores:* SAT critical reading scores over 500: 67%; SAT math scores over 500: 68%; SAT writing scores over 500: 62%; ACT scores over 18: 93%; SAT critical reading scores over 600: 23%; SAT math scores over 600: 26%; SAT writing scores over 600: 20%; ACT scores over 24: 50%; SAT critical reading scores over 700: 3%; SAT math scores over 700: 4%; SAT writing scores over 700: 2%; ACT scores over 30: 9%.

Faculty *Total:* 749, 74% full-time, 65% with terminal degrees. *Student/faculty ratio:* 15:1.

Academics *Calendar:* semesters. *Degrees:* bachelor's, master's, doctoral-research/scholarship, and post-master's certificates. *Special study options:* accelerated degree program, advanced placement credit, cooperative education, distance learning, double majors, English as a second language, freshman honors college, honors programs, independent study, internships, off-campus study, part-time degree program, services for LD students, student-designed majors, study abroad, summer session for credit. *ROTC:* Army (b), Navy (c).

Computers on Campus 500 computers/terminals are available on campus for general student use. Students can access the following: campus intranet, computer help desk, free student e-mail accounts, online (class) grades, online (class) registration, online (class) schedules, online housing and financial aid information. Campuswide network is available. 100% of college-owned or-operated housing units are wired for high-speed Internet access. Wireless service is available via classrooms, computer centers, computer labs, learning centers, libraries, student centers.

Student Life *Housing:* on-campus residence required for freshman year. *Options:* coed, disabled students. Campus housing is university owned. Freshman campus housing is guaranteed. *Activities and organizations:* drama/theater group, student-run newspaper, radio and television station, choral group, marching band, Alternative Spring Break, Circle K, Campus Crusade for Christ, Outing Club, Wilde Stein, national fraternities, national sororities. *Campus security:* 24-hour emergency response devices and patrols, late-night transport/escort service, controlled dormitory access, Area emergency text and email message system. *Student services:* health clinic, personal/psychological counseling, women's center, legal services.

Athletics Member NCAA. All Division I except football (Division I-AA). *Intercollegiate sports:* baseball M(s), basketball M(s)/W(s), cheerleading M/W, crew W(c), cross-country running M(s)/W(s), field hockey W(s), ice hockey M(s)/W(s), soccer W(s), softball W(s), swimming and diving M/W(s), tennis M(c)/W(c), track and field M(s)/W(s). *Intramural sports:* badminton M/W, basketball M/W, crew M(c)/W(c), cross-country running M/W, equestrian sports M(c)/W(c), fencing M(c)/W(c), field hockey M(c)/W(c), football M(c), golf M/W, ice hockey M(c)/W(c), lacrosse M(c)/W(c), racquetball M/W, rock climbing M(c)/W(c), rugby M(c)/W(c), skiing (cross-country) M/W, skiing (downhill) M(c)/W(c), soccer M/W, softball M/W, swimming and diving M/W, table tennis M/W, tennis M/W, track and field M/W, ultimate Frisbee M(c)/W(c), volleyball M(c)/W(c), water polo M/W, weight lifting M(c)/W(c), wrestling M(c).

Standardized Tests *Required:* SAT or ACT (for admission).

Costs (2010–11) *Tuition:* state resident $8010 full-time, $267 per credit hour part-time; nonresident $23,040 full-time, $768 per credit hour part-time. Full-time tuition and fees vary according to course load and program. Part-time tuition and fees vary according to course load and program. *Required fees:* $2158 full-time. *Room and board:* $8766. Room and board charges vary according to board plan and housing facility. *Payment plan:* installment. *Waivers:* senior citizens and employees or children of employees.

Financial Aid Of all full-time matriculated undergraduates who enrolled in 2009, 7,288 applied for aid, 6,166 were judged to have need, 1,977 had their need fully met. 800 Federal Work-Study jobs (averaging $2695). In 2009, 779 non-need-based awards were made. *Average percent of need met:* 74%. *Average financial aid package:* $10,588. *Average need-based loan:* $6392. *Average need-based gift aid:* $6826. *Average non-need-based aid:* $4115. *Average indebtedness upon graduation:* $30,824.

Applying *Options:* electronic application, early admission, early action, deferred entrance. *Application fee:* $40. *Required:* essay or personal statement, high school transcript, 1 letter of recommendation. *Required for some:* audition for music majors. *Application deadlines:* rolling (freshmen), rolling (out-of-state freshmen), rolling (transfers), 12/15 (early action). *Notification:* continuous (freshmen), continuous (out-of-state freshmen), continuous (transfers), 1/31 (early action).

Freshman Application Contact Ms. Sharon Oliver, Director of Admissions, University of Maine, 5713 Chadbourne Hall, Orono, ME 04469-5713. *Phone:* 207-581-1561. *Toll-free phone:* 877-486-2364. *Fax:* 207-581-1213. *E-mail:* um-admit@maine.edu. *Web site:* http://www.umaine.edu/.

See page 1704 for the College Close-Up.

University of Maine at Augusta
Augusta, Maine

- **State-supported** 4-year, founded 1965, part of University of Maine System
- **Small-town** 159-acre campus
- **Endowment** $4.3 million
- **Coed** 5,074 undergraduate students, 33% full-time, 72% women, 28% men
- **Noncompetitive** entrance level, 94% of applicants were admitted

Undergraduates 1,676 full-time, 3,398 part-time. Students come from 42 states and territories; 12 other countries; 2% are from out of state; 11% transferred in. *Retention:* 55% of full-time freshmen returned.

Freshmen *Admission:* 971 applied, 913 admitted, 552 enrolled.

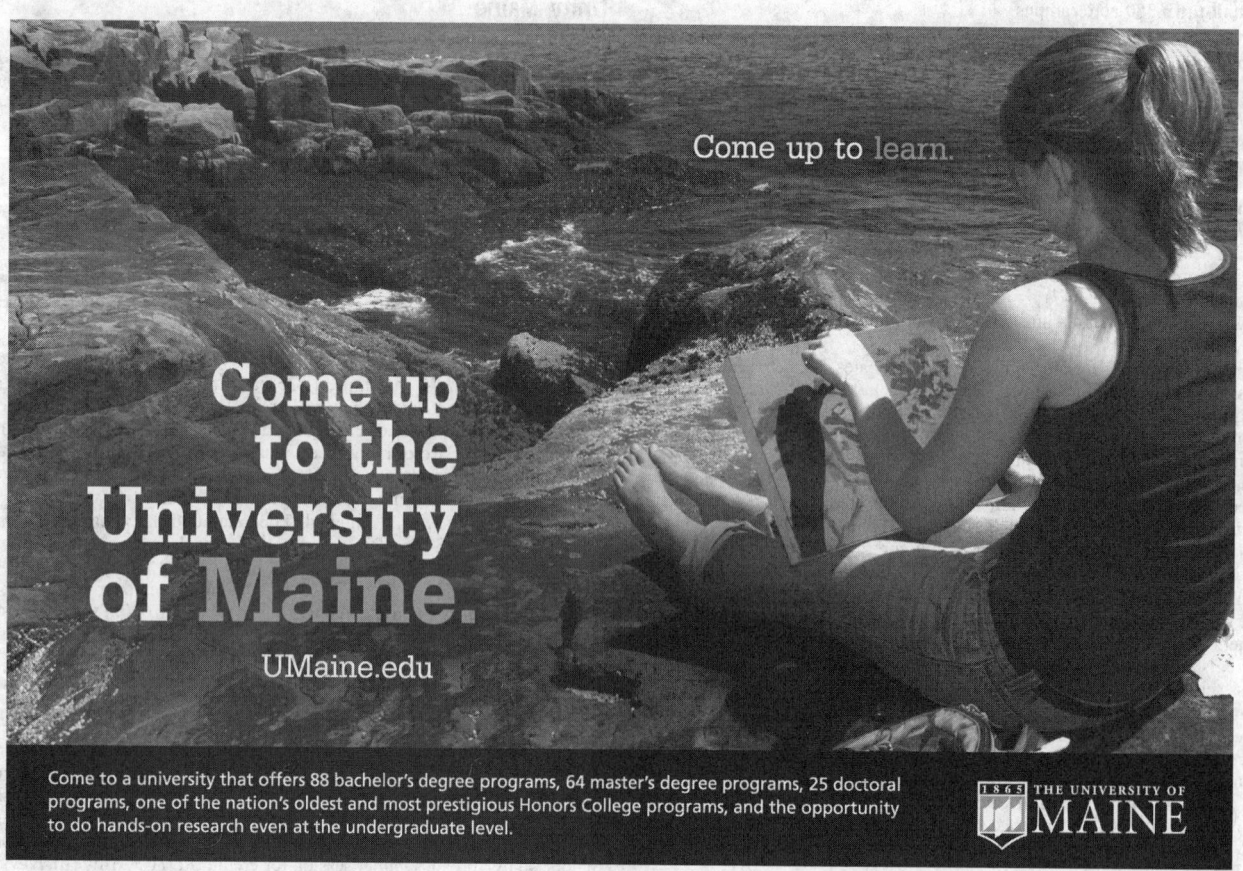

Come up to learn.

Come up to the University of Maine.

UMaine.edu

Come to a university that offers 88 bachelor's degree programs, 64 master's degree programs, 25 doctoral programs, one of the nation's oldest and most prestigious Honors College programs, and the opportunity to do hands-on research even at the undergraduate level.

1865 THE UNIVERSITY OF MAINE

Faculty *Total:* 274, 36% full-time, 24% with terminal degrees. *Student/faculty ratio:* 17:1.

Academics *Calendar:* semesters. *Degrees:* certificates, associate, bachelor's, and postbachelor's certificates (also offers some graduate courses and continuing education programs with significant enrollment not reflected in profile). *Special study options:* academic remediation for entering students, adult/continuing education programs, advanced placement credit, distance learning, double majors, honors programs, independent study, internships, off-campus study, part-time degree program, services for LD students, student-designed majors, study abroad, summer session for credit. *ROTC:* Army (c), Navy (c), Air Force (c).

Computers on Campus 142 computers/terminals are available on campus for general student use. Students can access the following: computer help desk, free student e-mail accounts, online (class) grades, online (class) registration, online (class) schedules. Campuswide network is available. Wireless service is available via entire campus.

Student Life *Housing:* college housing not available. *Activities and organizations:* drama/theater group, student-run newspaper, Honors Program Student Association, Arts and Architecture Students of UMA, Student Nurse Association, Student American Dental Hygiene Association, International Student Club. *Campus security:* 24-hour emergency response devices, late-night transport/escort service. *Student services:* personal/psychological counseling.

Athletics Member USCAA. *Intercollegiate sports:* basketball M(s)/W(s), bowling M/W, golf M/W, soccer W(s). *Intramural sports:* racquetball M/W, soccer M, softball M/W, tennis M/W, volleyball M/W.

Standardized Tests *Recommended:* SAT or ACT (for admission).

Costs (2010–11) *Tuition:* state resident $6240 full-time, $208 per credit hour part-time; nonresident $15,120 full-time, $504 per credit hour part-time. Full-time tuition and fees vary according to reciprocity agreements. Part-time tuition and fees vary according to reciprocity agreements. *Required fees:* $885 full-time, $30 per credit hour part-time. *Payment plan:* installment. *Waivers:* senior citizens and employees or children of employees.

Financial Aid Of all full-time matriculated undergraduates who enrolled in 2008, 1,604 applied for aid, 1,435 were judged to have need, 258 had their need fully met. 220 Federal Work-Study jobs (averaging $1500). In 2008, 135 non-need-based awards were made. *Average percent of need met:* 70%. *Average financial aid package:* $8467. *Average need-based loan:* $4063. *Average need-based gift aid:* $4828. *Average non-need-based aid:* $4862. *Average indebtedness upon graduation:* $15,842.

Applying *Options:* electronic application, early admission, deferred entrance. *Application fee:* $40. *Required:* high school transcript. *Required for some:* interview, music audition. *Recommended:* essay or personal statement. *Application deadlines:* rolling (freshmen), rolling (out-of-state freshmen), rolling (transfers). *Notification:* continuous (freshmen), continuous (out-of-state freshmen), continuous (transfers).

Freshman Application Contact Jonathan H. Henry, Director of Admissions/Dean of Enrollment, University of Maine at Augusta, 46 University Drive, Robinson Hall, Augusta, ME 04330. *Phone:* 207-621-3465. *Toll-free phone:* 877-862-1234 Ext. 3185. *Fax:* 207-621-3333. *E-mail:* umaadm@maine.edu. *Web site:* http://www.uma.maine.edu/.

University of Maine at Farmington
Farmington, Maine

- **State-supported** comprehensive, founded 1863, part of University of Maine System
- **Small-town** 50-acre campus
- **Coed** 2,339 undergraduate students, 89% full-time, 65% women, 35% men
- **Moderately difficult** entrance level, 58% of applicants were admitted

Undergraduates 2,075 full-time, 264 part-time. Students come from 27 states and territories; 7 other countries; 12% are from out of state; 0.9% Black or African American, non-Hispanic/Latino; 1% Hispanic/Latino; 0.5% Asian, non-Hispanic/Latino; 0.4% American Indian or Alaska Native, non-Hispanic/Latino; 1% Two or more races, non-Hispanic/Latino; 8% Race/ethnicity unknown; 0.1% international; 5% transferred in; 50% live on campus. *Retention:* 76% of full-time freshmen returned.

Freshmen *Admission:* 1,872 applied, 1,081 admitted, 556 enrolled. *Test scores:* SAT critical reading scores over 500: 54%; SAT math scores over 500: 42%; SAT critical reading scores over 600: 18%; SAT math scores over 600: 11%; SAT critical reading scores over 700: 3%.

Faculty *Total:* 168, 71% full-time, 75% with terminal degrees. *Student/faculty ratio:* 14:1.

Academics *Calendar:* semesters plus May term and 2 5-week summer terms. *Degrees:* certificates, bachelor's, and master's. *Special study options:* academic remediation for entering students, accelerated degree program, advanced placement credit, distance learning, double majors, honors programs, independent study, internships, off-campus study, part-time degree program, services for LD students, student-designed majors, study abroad, summer session for credit.

Computers on Campus 180 computers/terminals are available on campus for general student use. Students can access the following: campus intranet, computer help desk, free student e-mail accounts, online (class) grades, online (class) registration, online (class) schedules, laptop initiative. Campuswide network is available. 100% of college-owned or -operated housing units are wired for high-speed Internet access. Wireless service is available via entire campus.

Student Life *Housing options:* coed, women-only. Campus housing is university owned and is provided by a third party. Freshman campus housing is guaranteed. *Activities and organizations:* drama/theater group, student-run newspaper, radio station, choral group, Program Board, Intramural Board, Campus Residence Council, campus radio station, Commuter Council. *Campus security:* 24-hour emergency response devices and patrols, late-night transport/escort service, controlled dormitory access, safety whistles. *Student services:* health clinic, personal/psychological counseling.

Athletics Member NCAA, NAIA. All NCAA Division III. *Intercollegiate sports:* baseball M, basketball M/W, cross-country running M/W, field hockey W, golf M, ice hockey M(c), lacrosse M(c)/W(c), soccer M/W, softball W, tennis M(c)/W(c), ultimate Frisbee M(c)/W(c), volleyball W. *Intramural sports:* basketball M/W, cheerleading M(c)/W(c), football M/W, ice hockey M(c)/W(c), rugby M(c)/W(c), skiing (cross-country) M(c)/W(c), skiing (downhill) M(c)/W(c), soccer M/W, softball M/W, swimming and diving M/W, tennis M/W, ultimate Frisbee M/W, volleyball M/W.

Standardized Tests *Required for some:* SAT or ACT (for admission).

Costs (2010–11) *Tuition:* state resident $8032 full-time, $251 per credit hour part-time; nonresident $16,768 full-time, $524 per credit hour part-time. Full-time tuition and fees vary according to course load, reciprocity agreements, and student level. Part-time tuition and fees vary according to course load, reciprocity agreements, and student level. *Required fees:* $990 full-time. *Room and board:* $7854; room only: $4180. Room and board charges vary according to board plan and housing facility. *Payment plan:* installment. *Waivers:* minority students, senior citizens, and employees or children of employees.

Financial Aid Of all full-time matriculated undergraduates who enrolled in 2007, 1,709 applied for aid, 1,418 were judged to have need, 189 had their need fully met. 519 Federal Work-Study jobs (averaging $1448). 406 state and other part-time jobs (averaging $1719). In 2007, 65 non-need-based awards were made. *Average percent of need met:* 73%. *Average financial aid package:* $8719. *Average need-based loan:* $4300. *Average need-based gift aid:* $4210. *Average non-need-based aid:* $1770. *Average indebtedness upon graduation:* $19,490.

Applying *Options:* electronic application, early admission, early action, deferred entrance. *Application fee:* $40. *Required:* essay or personal statement, high school transcript, minimum 2 GPA, 1 letter of recommendation. *Required for some:* minimum 2.5 GPA. *Recommended:* interview. *Application deadlines:* rolling (freshmen), 12/1 (early action). *Notification:* continuous (freshmen), continuous (transfers), 1/8 (early action).

Freshman Application Contact Mr. James G. Collins, Associate Director of Admissions, University of Maine at Farmington, 246 Main Street, Farmington, ME 04938-1994. *Phone:* 207-778-7050. *Fax:* 207-778-8182. *E-mail:* umfadmit@maine.edu. *Web site:* http://www.umf.maine.edu/.

University of Maine at Fort Kent
Fort Kent, Maine

- **State-supported** 4-year, founded 1878, part of University of Maine System
- **Rural** 52-acre campus
- **Endowment** $1.9 million
- **Coed** 1,073 undergraduate students, 53% full-time, 67% women, 33% men
- **Minimally difficult** entrance level

Undergraduates 569 full-time, 504 part-time. Students come from 19 states and territories; 9 other countries; 13% are from out of state; 7% transferred in; 29% live on campus. *Retention:* 65% of full-time freshmen returned.

Freshmen *Admission:* 499 applied, 156 enrolled. *Average high school GPA:* 2.98. *Test scores:* SAT critical reading scores over 500: 23%; SAT math scores over 500: 29%; SAT writing scores over 500: 19%; SAT critical reading scores over 600: 3%; SAT math scores over 600: 3%; SAT writing scores over 600: 3%.

Faculty *Total:* 69, 51% full-time, 25% with terminal degrees. *Student/faculty ratio:* 16:1.

Academics *Calendar:* semesters. *Degrees:* associate and bachelor's. *Special study options:* academic remediation for entering students, accelerated degree program, advanced placement credit, cooperative education, distance learning, double majors, English as a second language, external degree program, honors programs, independent study, internships, part-time degree program, services for LD students, student-designed majors, summer session for credit.

Computers on Campus 100 computers/terminals are available on campus for general student use. Students can access the following: campus intranet, computer help desk, free student e-mail accounts, online (class) grades, online

PROFILES

(class) registration, online (class) schedules. Campuswide network is available. Wireless service is available via entire campus.

Student Life *Housing options:* coed. Campus housing is university owned. *Activities and organizations:* drama/theater group, choral group, Student Nurses Organization, Student Teachers Educational Professional Society, Student Senate, Performing Arts Club, Dorm Council, national fraternities, national sororities. *Campus security:* controlled dormitory access, 8-hour night patrols by security personnel 11pm-7am. *Student services:* health clinic, personal/psychological counseling.

Athletics Member USCAA. *Intercollegiate sports:* basketball M/W, soccer M/W, volleyball W. *Intramural sports:* basketball M/W, ice hockey M, racquetball M/W, soccer M/W, softball M/W, volleyball M/W.

Standardized Tests *Required for some:* SAT (for admission), SAT and SAT Subject Tests or ACT (for admission). *Recommended:* SAT and SAT Subject Tests or ACT (for admission).

Costs (2011–12) *Tuition:* state resident $6330 full-time, $211 per credit part-time; nonresident $15,930 full-time, $531 per credit part-time. *Required fees:* $833 full-time. *Room and board:* $7500; room only: $4000. Room and board charges vary according to board plan and housing facility.

Financial Aid Of all full-time matriculated undergraduates who enrolled in 2008, 525 applied for aid, 443 were judged to have need, 360 had their need fully met. In 2008, 35 non-need-based awards were made. *Average percent of need met:* 82%. *Average financial aid package:* $5400. *Average need-based loan:* $2400. *Average need-based gift aid:* $2800. *Average non-need-based aid:* $900.

Applying *Options:* electronic application, early admission, early decision, deferred entrance. *Application fee:* $40. *Required:* essay or personal statement, high school transcript. *Required for some:* interview. *Application deadlines:* rolling (freshmen), rolling (transfers). *Notification:* continuous (freshmen), continuous (transfers).

Freshman Application Contact University of Maine at Fort Kent, 23 University Drive, Fort Kent, ME 04743-1292. *Phone:* 207-834-7600. *Toll-free phone:* 888-TRY-UMFK. *Web site:* http://www.umfk.maine.edu/.

University of Maine at Machias

Machias, Maine

- **State-supported** 4-year, founded 1909, part of University of Maine System
- **Rural** 42-acre campus
- **Coed**
- **Moderately difficult** entrance level

Faculty *Student/faculty ratio:* 14:1.

Academics *Calendar:* semesters. *Degrees:* certificates, associate, and bachelor's.

Student Life *Campus security:* 24-hour emergency response devices, late-night transport/escort service, controlled dormitory access, night security guard until 3:00 am, day security.

Athletics Member NAIA.

Standardized Tests *Required:* SAT or ACT (for admission).

Costs (2010–11) *Tuition:* state resident $6330 full-time, $211 per credit part-time; nonresident $17,610 full-time, $587 per credit part-time. *Required fees:* $780 full-time. *Room and board:* $7282. Room and board charges vary according to housing facility. *Payment plans:* installment, deferred payment.

Financial Aid *Of all full-time matriculated undergraduates who enrolled in 2002,* 512 applied for aid, 419 were judged to have need, 108 had their need fully met. 140 Federal Work-Study jobs (averaging $1621). 83 state and other part-time jobs (averaging $1660). *In 2002,* 44 non-need-based awards were made. *Average percent of need met:* 83. *Average financial aid package:* $8182. *Average need-based loan:* $3356. *Average need-based gift aid:* $4847. *Average non-need-based aid:* $5051. *Average indebtedness upon graduation:* $14,873.

Applying *Options:* electronic application, early admission, early action, deferred entrance. *Application fee:* $40. *Required:* essay or personal statement, high school transcript, 1 letter of recommendation. *Required for some:* minimum 2 GPA, interview. *Recommended:* minimum 2.5 GPA, 2 letters of recommendation, interview.

Freshman Application Contact Mr. David Dollins, Director of Admissions, University of Maine at Machias, 9 O'Brien Avenue, Machias, ME 04654. *Phone:* 207-255-1318. *Toll-free phone:* 888-GOTOUMM (in-state); 888-468-6866 (out-of-state). *Fax:* 207-255-1363. *E-mail:* ummadmissions@maine.edu. *Web site:* http://umm.maine.edu/.

University of Maine at Presque Isle

Presque Isle, Maine

- **State-supported** 4-year, founded 1903, part of University of Maine System
- **Small-town** 150-acre campus
- **Endowment** $6.1 million
- **Coed** 1,434 undergraduate students, 66% full-time, 63% women, 37% men
- **Minimally difficult** entrance level, 87% of applicants were admitted

Undergraduates 941 full-time, 493 part-time. Students come from 27 states and territories; 5 other countries; 4% are from out of state; 20% transferred in; 92% live on campus. *Retention:* 77% of full-time freshmen returned.

Freshmen *Admission:* 480 applied, 417 admitted, 213 enrolled. *Average high school GPA:* 2.87. *Test scores:* SAT critical reading scores over 500: 35%; SAT math scores over 500: 31%; SAT critical reading scores over 600: 8%; SAT math scores over 600: 2%; SAT math scores over 700: 1%.

Faculty *Total:* 109, 45% full-time, 49% with terminal degrees. *Student/faculty ratio:* 20:1.

Academics *Calendar:* semesters. *Degrees:* certificates, associate, and bachelor's. *Special study options:* academic remediation for entering students, accelerated degree program, adult/continuing education programs, advanced placement credit, cooperative education, distance learning, double majors, honors programs, independent study, internships, off-campus study, part-time degree program, services for LD students, student-designed majors, summer session for credit.

Computers on Campus 82 computers/terminals are available on campus for general student use. Students can access the following: campus intranet, computer help desk, free student e-mail accounts, online (class) registration. Campuswide network is available. 98% of college-owned or -operated housing units are wired for high-speed Internet access. Wireless service is available via entire campus.

Student Life *Housing options:* coed. Campus housing is university owned and leased by the school. *Activities and organizations:* drama/theater group, student-run newspaper, radio station, Student Senate, OAPI-Outdoor Adventure Program International, Student Activities Board, Student Organization of Social Work, Campus Crusade for Christ, national fraternities, national sororities. *Campus security:* student patrols, late-night transport/escort service, crime prevention programs, lighted pathways. *Student services:* health clinic, personal/psychological counseling.

Athletics Member NAIA. *Intercollegiate sports:* baseball M, basketball M/W, cross-country running M/W, golf M, soccer M/W, softball W, volleyball W. *Intramural sports:* archery M/W, badminton M/W, basketball M/W, bowling M/W, cross-country running M/W, football M/W, ice hockey M/W, skiing (cross-country) M/W, skiing (downhill) M/W, soccer M/W, softball M/W, table tennis M/W, tennis M/W, track and field M/W, volleyball M/W, weight lifting M/W.

Costs (2011–12) *Tuition:* state resident $6330 full-time, $211 per credit part-time; nonresident $15,930 full-time, $531 per credit part-time. Full-time tuition and fees vary according to course load and reciprocity agreements. Part-time tuition and fees vary according to course load and reciprocity agreements. *Required fees:* $905 full-time, $18 per credit part-time. *Room and board:* $7046; room only: $3940. Room and board charges vary according to board plan and housing facility. *Payment plans:* installment, deferred payment. *Waivers:* minority students, senior citizens, and employees or children of employees.

Financial Aid Of all full-time matriculated undergraduates who enrolled in 2009, 730 applied for aid, 667 were judged to have need, 200 had their need fully met. *Average percent of need met:* 76%. *Average financial aid package:* $9876. *Average need-based loan:* $4685. *Average need-based gift aid:* $5002. *Average non-need-based aid:* $4054. *Average indebtedness upon graduation:* $18,272.

Applying *Options:* electronic application, early admission, early action, deferred entrance. *Application fee:* $40. *Required:* essay or personal statement, high school transcript, minimum 2 GPA. *Required for some:* 1 letter of recommendation, interview. *Application deadlines:* rolling (freshmen), 10/31 (early action). *Notification:* continuous (freshmen), continuous (transfers), 4/1 (early action).

Freshman Application Contact University of Maine at Presque Isle, 181 Main Street, Presque Isle, ME 04769-2888. *Phone:* 207-768-9453. *Web site:* http://www.umpi.edu/.

University of New England

Biddeford, Maine

- **Independent** comprehensive, founded 1831
- **Small-town** 540-acre campus
- **Coed** 2,692 undergraduate students, 79% full-time, 69% women, 31% men
- **Moderately difficult** entrance level, 85% of applicants were admitted

Undergraduates 2,124 full-time, 568 part-time. Students come from 49 states and territories; 13 other countries; 61% are from out of state; 1% Black or African American, non-Hispanic/Latino; 0.8% Hispanic/Latino; 2% Asian, non-Hispanic/Latino; 0.3% Native Hawaiian or other Pacific Islander, non-Hispanic/Latino; 0.3% American Indian or Alaska Native, non-Hispanic/Latino; 1% Two or more races, non-Hispanic/Latino; 13% Race/ethnicity unknown; 0.9% international; 4% transferred in; 53% live on campus. *Retention:* 80% of full-time freshmen returned.

Freshmen *Admission:* 3,180 applied, 2,697 admitted, 655 enrolled. *Average high school GPA:* 3.19. *Test scores:* SAT critical reading scores over 500: 60%; SAT math scores over 500: 66%; ACT scores over 18: 93%; SAT critical reading scores over 600: 12%; SAT math scores over 600: 21%; ACT scores over 24: 44%; SAT critical reading scores over 700: 1%; SAT math scores over 700: 1%; ACT scores over 30: 4%.

Faculty *Total:* 352, 55% full-time, 77% with terminal degrees. *Student/faculty ratio:* 13:1.

Academics *Calendar:* semesters. *Degrees:* associate, bachelor's, master's, doctoral-professional, post-master's, and postbachelor's certificates. *Special study options:* academic remediation for entering students, accelerated degree program, advanced placement credit, cooperative education, distance learning, double majors, independent study, internships, off-campus study, part-time degree program, services for LD students, study abroad, summer session for credit. *ROTC:* Army (c).

Computers on Campus 150 computers/terminals are available on campus for general student use. Students can access the following: campus intranet, computer help desk, free student e-mail accounts, online (class) grades, online (class) registration, online (class) schedules. Campuswide network is available. Wireless service is available via classrooms, computer centers, computer labs, learning centers, libraries, student centers.

Student Life *Housing:* on-campus residence required through junior year. *Options:* coed, women-only. Campus housing is university owned. *Activities and organizations:* student government, Outing Club, Campus Programming Board, Earth's Eco, Dance Team. *Campus security:* 24-hour emergency response devices and patrols, late-night transport/escort service, controlled dormitory access. *Student services:* health clinic, personal/psychological counseling.

Athletics Member NCAA. All Division III. *Intercollegiate sports:* basketball M/W, cross-country running M/W, field hockey W, golf M, lacrosse M/W, soccer M/W, softball W, swimming and diving W, volleyball W. *Intramural sports:* baseball M(c), basketball M/W, gymnastics M/W, racquetball M/W, soccer M/W, softball M/W, table tennis M/W, ultimate Frisbee M(c)/W(c), volleyball M(c)/W, water polo M/W.

Standardized Tests *Required:* SAT or ACT (for admission).

Costs (2010–11) *Comprehensive fee:* $40,740 includes full-time tuition ($28,300), mandatory fees ($1030), and room and board ($11,410). Part-time tuition: $1020 per credit hour. *Room and board:* Room and board charges vary according to board plan, housing facility, and location. *Payment plan:* installment. *Waivers:* children of alumni and employees or children of employees.

Financial Aid Of all full-time matriculated undergraduates who enrolled in 2008, 1,777 applied for aid, 1,648 were judged to have need, 306 had their need fully met. 850 Federal Work-Study jobs (averaging $1946). In 2008, 332 non-need-based awards were made. *Average percent of need met:* 83%. *Average financial aid package:* $23,956. *Average need-based loan:* $10,836. *Average need-based gift aid:* $12,857. *Average non-need-based aid:* $8424. *Average indebtedness upon graduation:* $44,325.

Applying *Options:* electronic application, deferred entrance. *Application fee:* $40. *Required:* high school transcript. *Recommended:* essay or personal statement, interview. *Application deadlines:* 2/15 (freshmen), rolling (transfers). *Notification:* continuous (freshmen), continuous (transfers).

Freshman Application Contact Mr. Robert J. Pecchia, Associate Dean of Admissions, University of New England, Hills Beach Road, Biddeford, ME 04005-9526. *Phone:* 207-283-0170 Ext. 2297. *Toll-free phone:* 800-477-4UNE. *Fax:* 207-602-5900. *E-mail:* admissions@une.edu. *Web site:* http://www.une.edu/.

See page 1712 for the College Close-Up.

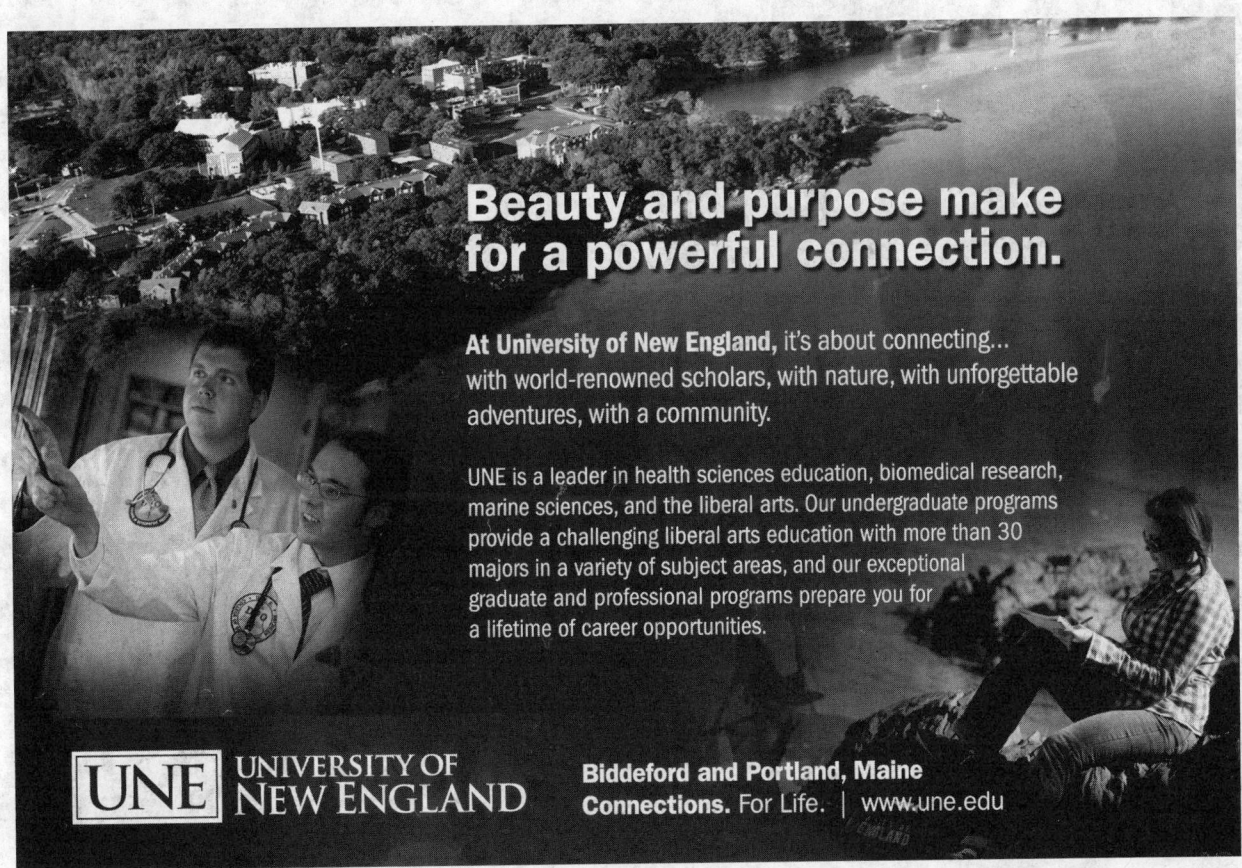

University of Southern Maine
Portland, Maine

- **State-supported** comprehensive, founded 1878, part of University of Maine System
- **Suburban** 144-acre campus
- **Coed** 7,561 undergraduate students, 64% full-time, 57% women, 43% men
- **Moderately difficult** entrance level, 78% of applicants were admitted

Undergraduates 4,845 full-time, 2,716 part-time. Students come from 30 states and territories; 7 other countries; 10% are from out of state; 2% Black or African American, non-Hispanic/Latino; 2% Hispanic/Latino; 2% Asian, non-Hispanic/Latino; 0.1% Native Hawaiian or other Pacific Islander, non-Hispanic/Latino; 1% American Indian or Alaska Native, non-Hispanic/Latino; 1% Two or more races, non-Hispanic/Latino; 8% Race/ethnicity unknown; 0.6% international; 11% transferred in; 15% live on campus. *Retention:* 70% of full-time freshmen returned.

Freshmen *Admission:* 4,320 applied, 3,378 admitted, 882 enrolled. *Average high school GPA:* 3.06. *Test scores:* SAT critical reading scores over 500: 52%; SAT math scores over 500: 48%; SAT writing scores over 500: 47%; ACT scores over 18: 87%; SAT critical reading scores over 600: 12%; SAT math scores over 600: 12%; SAT writing scores over 600: 10%; ACT scores over 24: 16%; SAT critical reading scores over 700: 2%; SAT math scores over 700: 1%; SAT writing scores over 700: 1%.

Faculty *Total:* 673, 56% full-time, 56% with terminal degrees. *Student/faculty ratio:* 15:1.

Academics *Calendar:* semesters. *Degrees:* associate, bachelor's, master's, doctoral-professional, doctoral-research/scholarship, and post-master's certificates. *Special study options:* academic remediation for entering students, accelerated degree program, adult/continuing education programs, advanced placement credit, cooperative education, distance learning, double majors, English as a second language, honors programs, independent study, internships, off-campus study, part-time degree program, services for LD students, student-designed majors, study abroad, summer session for credit. *ROTC:* Army (c), Air Force (c). *Unusual degree programs:* 3-2 business administration.

Computers on Campus 219 computers/terminals are available on campus for general student use. Students can access the following: campus intranet, computer help desk, free student e-mail accounts, online (class) grades, online (class) registration, online (class) schedules. Campuswide network is available. 100% of college-owned or -operated housing units are wired for high-speed Internet access. Wireless service is available via entire campus.

Student Life *Housing options:* coed. Campus housing is university owned. Freshman applicants given priority for college housing. *Activities and organizations:* drama/theater group, student-run newspaper, radio and television station, choral group, Outing and Ski Clubs, Gorham Events Board, Commuter Student Group, Circle K, national fraternities, national sororities. *Campus security:* 24-hour emergency response devices and patrols, student patrols, late-night transport/escort service, controlled dormitory access, security lighting, preventive programs within residence halls. *Student services:* health clinic, personal/psychological counseling, women's center, legal services.

Athletics Member NCAA. All Division III. *Intercollegiate sports:* baseball M, basketball M/W, cheerleading M/W, cross-country running M/W, field hockey W, golf M/W, ice hockey M/W, lacrosse M/W, sailing M/W, soccer M/W, softball W, tennis M/W, track and field M/W, volleyball W, wrestling M. *Intramural sports:* basketball M/W, cheerleading W, football M/W, ice hockey M/W, lacrosse M(c)/W(c), racquetball M/W, rugby M(c)/W(c), skiing (downhill) M(c)/W(c), soccer M/W, softball M/W, squash M/W, table tennis M/W, tennis M/W, ultimate Frisbee M/W, volleyball M/W, weight lifting M/W.

Standardized Tests *Required:* SAT or ACT (for admission).

Costs (2010–11) *Tuition:* state resident $7260 full-time, $244 per credit hour part-time; nonresident $19,620 full-time, $654 per credit hour part-time. Full-time tuition and fees vary according to course load, degree level, and reciprocity agreements. Part-time tuition and fees vary according to course load, degree level, and reciprocity agreements. *Required fees:* $1278 full-time, $27 per credit hour part-time. *Room and board:* $9394; room only: $4838. Room and board charges vary according to board plan, housing facility, and location. *Payment plan:* installment. *Waivers:* minority students, senior citizens, and employees or children of employees.

Financial Aid Of all full-time matriculated undergraduates who enrolled in 2009, 4,497 applied for aid, 3,958 were judged to have need, 2,361 had their need fully met. In 2009, 193 non-need-based awards were made. *Average percent of need met:* 69%. *Average financial aid package:* $13,618. *Average need-based loan:* $7613. *Average need-based gift aid:* $5518. *Average non-need-based aid:* $3474. *Average indebtedness upon graduation:* $25,892.

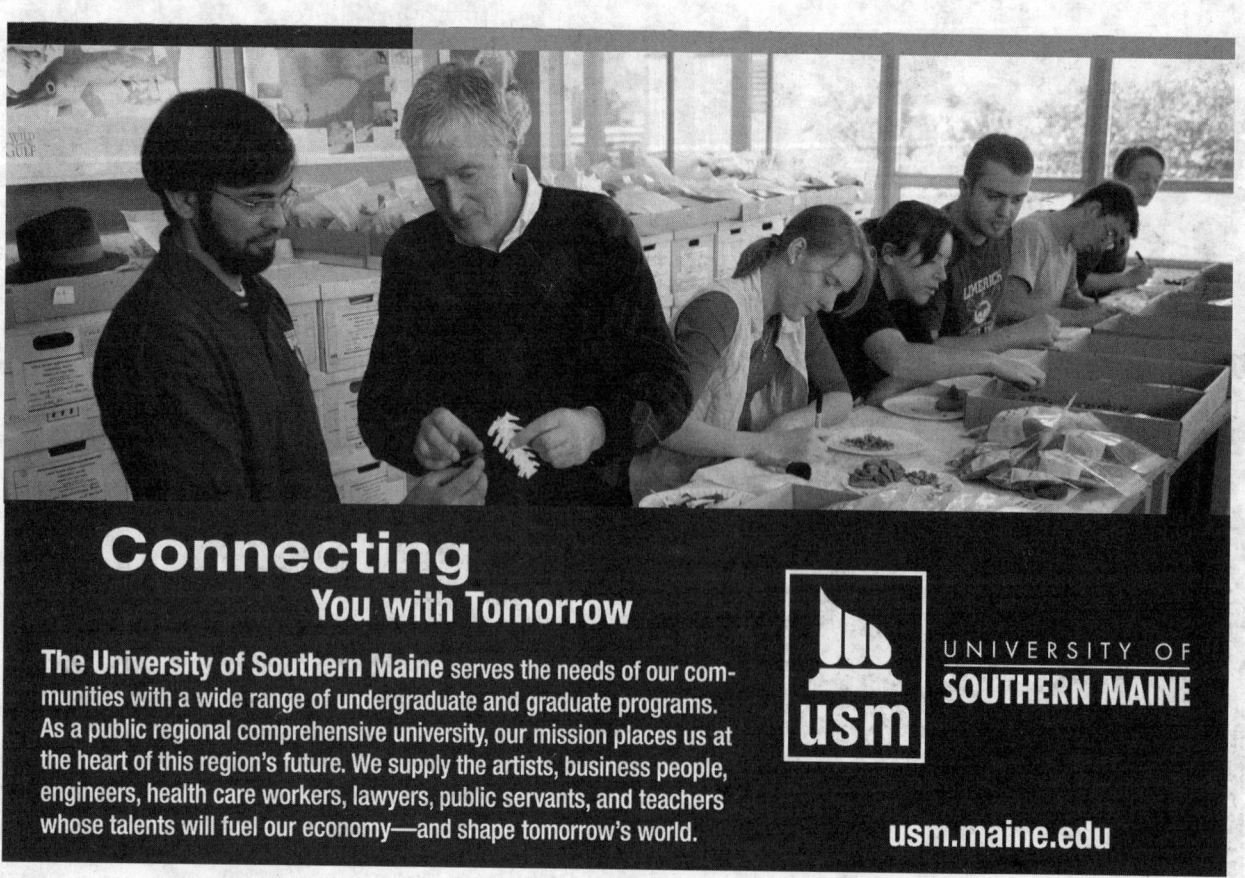

Applying *Options:* electronic application, early admission, deferred entrance. *Application fee:* $40. *Required:* essay or personal statement, high school transcript. *Required for some:* interview, auditions for music majors. *Recommended:* minimum 2.8 GPA, 1 letter of recommendation, interview. *Application deadlines:* 2/15 (freshmen), 2/15 (transfers). *Notification:* continuous (freshmen), continuous (transfers).
Freshman Application Contact Mr. Jonathan Barker, Director of Technology for Enrollment Management, University of Southern Maine, 96 Falmouth Street, PO Box 9300, Portland, ME 04104-9300. *Phone:* 207-780-5724. *Toll-free phone:* 800-800-4USM Ext. 5670. *Fax:* 207-780-5640. *E-mail:* usmadm@usm.maine.edu. *Web site:* http://www.usm.maine.edu/.

See page 1740 for the College Close-Up.

MARYLAND

Baltimore International College

Baltimore, Maryland

Freshman Application Contact Director of Admissions, Baltimore International College, Commerce Exchange, 17 Commerce Street, Baltimore, MD 21202-3230. *Phone:* 410-752-4710 Ext. 120. *Toll-free phone:* 800-624-9926 Ext. 120. *Fax:* 410-752-3730. *E-mail:* admissions@bic.edu. *Web site:* http://www.bic.edu/.

Bowie State University

Bowie, Maryland

- **State-supported** comprehensive, founded 1865, part of University System of Maryland
- **Small-town** 295-acre campus with easy access to Baltimore and Washington, D.C.
- **Endowment** $4.0 million
- **Coed** 4,401 undergraduate students, 84% full-time, 63% women, 37% men
- **Minimally difficult** entrance level, 21% of applicants were admitted

Undergraduates 3,709 full-time, 692 part-time. Students come from 31 states and territories; 14% are from out of state; 10% transferred in; 34% live on campus. *Retention:* 67% of full-time freshmen returned.
Freshmen *Admission:* 3,153 applied, 671 admitted, 530 enrolled. *Average high school GPA:* 2.73. *Test scores:* SAT critical reading scores over 500: 20%; SAT math scores over 500: 19%; SAT critical reading scores over 600: 2%; SAT math scores over 600: 3%.
Faculty *Total:* 400, 57% full-time, 60% with terminal degrees. *Student/faculty ratio:* 16:1.
Academics *Calendar:* semesters. *Degrees:* certificates, bachelor's, master's, doctoral-research/scholarship, and postbachelor's certificates. *Special study options:* academic remediation for entering students, adult/continuing education programs, advanced placement credit, cooperative education, distance learning, double majors, external degree program, honors programs, independent study, internships, off-campus study, part-time degree program, services for LD students, study abroad, summer session for credit. *Unusual degree programs:* 3-2 engineering with George Washington University, University of Maryland College Park, Howard University.
Computers on Campus 3,144 computers/terminals are available on campus for general student use. Students can access the following: online (class) registration. Campuswide network is available. Wireless service is available via entire campus.
Student Life *Housing options:* coed, men-only, women-only. Campus housing is university owned and is provided by a third party. Freshman applicants given priority for college housing. *Activities and organizations:* drama/theater group, student-run newspaper, radio and television station, choral group, marching band, NSAP Student Leadership Institute, Honda Campus All-Star

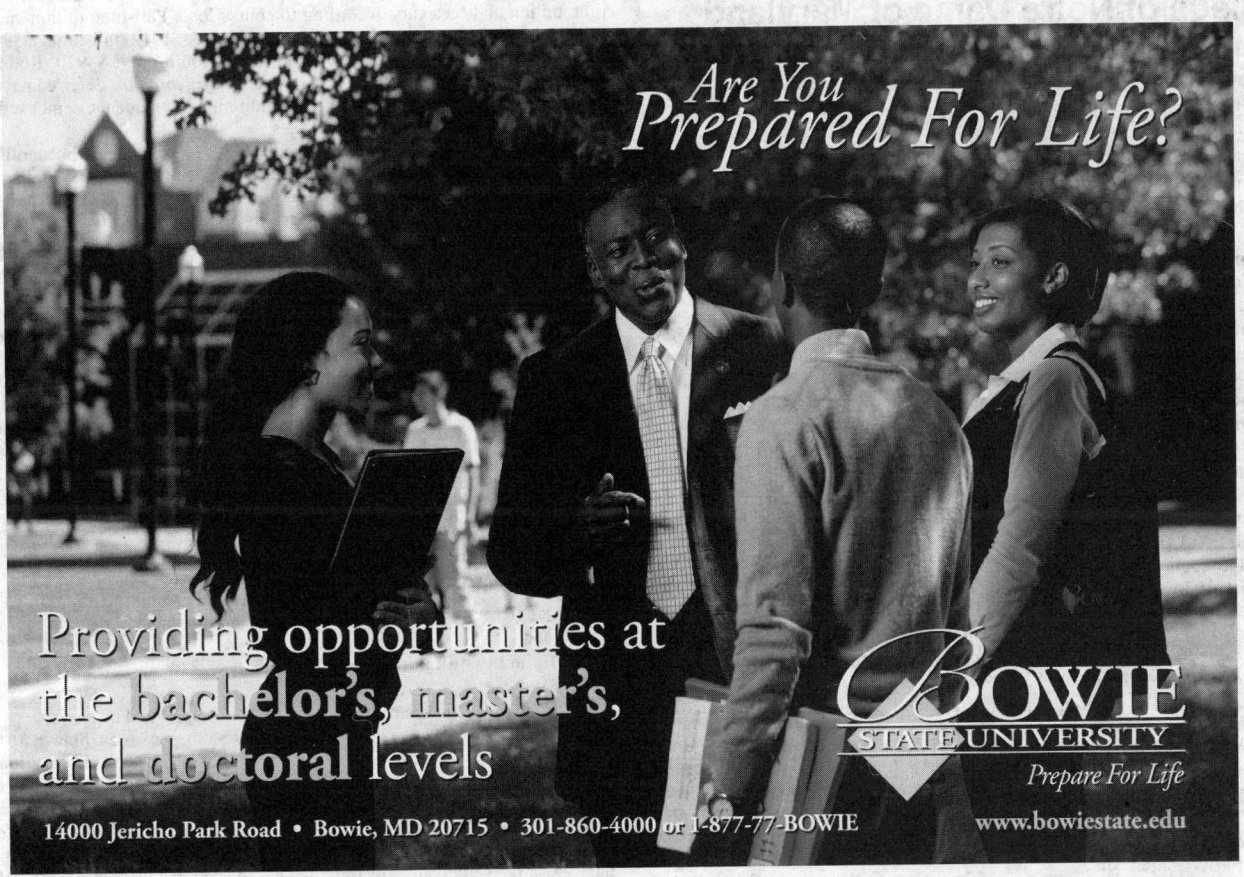

Challenge, national fraternities, national sororities. *Campus security:* 24-hour emergency response devices and patrols, student patrols, late-night transport/escort service, controlled dormitory access. *Student services:* health clinic, personal/psychological counseling.

Athletics Member NCAA. All Division II. *Intercollegiate sports:* basketball M(s)/W(s), bowling W, cross-country running M(s)/W(s), football M(s), softball W(s), tennis W(s), track and field M(s)/W(s), volleyball W(s).

Standardized Tests *Required:* SAT or ACT (for admission).

Costs (2010–11) *Tuition:* state resident $4415 full-time, $195 per credit hour part-time; nonresident $14,939 full-time, $629 per credit hour part-time. Part-time tuition and fees vary according to course load. *Required fees:* $1739 full-time, $87 per credit hour part-time. *Room and board:* $8570. Room and board charges vary according to board plan and housing facility. *Payment plans:* installment, deferred payment. *Waivers:* senior citizens and employees or children of employees.

Financial Aid Of all full-time matriculated undergraduates who enrolled in 2009, 2,664 applied for aid, 2,651 were judged to have need, 1,278 had their need fully met. 65 Federal Work-Study jobs (averaging $2627). In 2009, 55 non-need-based awards were made. *Average percent of need met:* 49%. *Average financial aid package:* $8376. *Average need-based loan:* $4110. *Average need-based gift aid:* $6466. *Average non-need-based aid:* $138. *Average indebtedness upon graduation:* $19,003.

Applying *Options:* electronic application. *Application fee:* $40. *Required:* high school transcript, minimum 2 GPA. *Application deadlines:* 4/1 (freshmen), 4/1 (transfers). *Notification:* continuous (freshmen), continuous (transfers).

Freshman Application Contact Don Kiah, Director of Admissions, Bowie State University, Administration Building, 1st Floor. *Phone:* 301-860-3415. *Toll-free phone:* 877-772-6943. *Fax:* 301-860-3438. *E-mail:* sholt@bowiestate.edu. *Web site:* http://www.bowiestate.edu/.

See page 1130 for the College Close-Up.

Capitol College
Laurel, Maryland

Director of Admissions Mr. George Walls, Director of Recruiting and Admissions, Capitol College, 11301 Springfield Road, Laurel, MD 20708-9759. *Phone:* 301-953-3200 Ext. 3033. *Toll-free phone:* 800-950-1992. *E-mail:* ghwalls@capitol-college.edu. *Web site:* http://www.capitol-college.edu/.

College of Notre Dame of Maryland
Baltimore, Maryland

- **Independent Roman Catholic** comprehensive, founded 1873
- **Urban** 58-acre campus with easy access to Baltimore and Washington, D.C.
- **Endowment** $26.3 million
- **Coed, primarily women**
- **Moderately difficult** entrance level

Faculty *Student/faculty ratio:* 12:1.

Academics *Calendar:* 4-1-4. *Degrees:* bachelor's, master's, doctoral-professional, doctoral-research/scholarship, post-master's, and postbachelor's certificates (offers coed undergraduate program for adult students).

Student Life *Campus security:* 24-hour emergency response devices and patrols, late-night transport/escort service, controlled dormitory access, emergency call boxes.

Athletics Member NCAA. All Division III.

Standardized Tests *Required:* SAT or ACT (for admission).

Costs (2010–11) *Comprehensive fee:* $37,850 includes full-time tuition ($27,600), mandatory fees ($750), and room and board ($9500). Part-time tuition: $425 per credit hour. *Room and board:* Room and board charges vary according to board plan.

Financial Aid *Of all full-time matriculated undergraduates who enrolled in 2009,* 445 applied for aid, 414 were judged to have need, 73 had their need fully met. 102 Federal Work-Study jobs (averaging $1026). *In 2009,* 44 non-need-based awards were made. *Average percent of need met:* 69. *Average financial aid package:* $19,708. *Average need-based loan:* $4079. *Average need-based gift aid:* $15,921. *Average non-need-based aid:* $14,732. *Average indebtedness upon graduation:* $33,882.

Applying *Options:* electronic application, early admission, early action, deferred entrance. *Application fee:* $45. *Required:* essay or personal statement, high school transcript, minimum 2 GPA, 2 letters of recommendation. *Recommended:* minimum 3 GPA, interview, resume.

Freshman Application Contact College of Notre Dame of Maryland, 4701 North Charles Street, Baltimore, MD 21210-2476. *Phone:* 410-532-5332. *Toll-free phone:* 800-435-0200 (in-state); 800-435-0300 (out-of-state). *Web site:* http://www.ndm.edu/.

Coppin State University
Baltimore, Maryland

- **State-supported** comprehensive, founded 1900, part of University System of Maryland
- **Urban** 33-acre campus
- **Coed** 3,298 undergraduate students, 79% full-time, 76% women, 24% men
- **Moderately difficult** entrance level, 54% of applicants were admitted

Undergraduates 2,599 full-time, 699 part-time. Students come from 25 states and territories; 7% are from out of state; 8% transferred in. *Retention:* 61% of full-time freshmen returned.

Freshmen *Admission:* 3,767 applied, 2,016 admitted, 547 enrolled. *Average high school GPA:* 2.62. *Test scores:* SAT critical reading scores over 500: 13%; SAT math scores over 500: 15%; SAT critical reading scores over 600: 1%; SAT math scores over 600: 2%; SAT math scores over 700: 1%.

Faculty *Total:* 312, 50% full-time, 40% with terminal degrees. *Student/faculty ratio:* 15:1.

Academics *Calendar:* semesters. *Degrees:* bachelor's, master's, and post-bachelor's certificates. *Special study options:* academic remediation for entering students, adult/continuing education programs, advanced placement credit, cooperative education, double majors, English as a second language, external degree program, freshman honors college, honors programs, internships, off-campus study, part-time degree program, services for LD students, summer session for credit. *ROTC:* Army (b). *Unusual degree programs:* 3-2 engineering with University of Maryland College Park; nursing; social work.

Computers on Campus Campuswide network is available.

Student Life *Housing options:* coed. Campus housing is university owned. *Activities and organizations:* drama/theater group, student-run newspaper, choral group, national fraternities, national sororities. *Campus security:* 24-hour emergency response devices and patrols, late-night transport/escort service, controlled dormitory access. *Student services:* health clinic, personal/psychological counseling.

Athletics Member NCAA. All Division I. *Intercollegiate sports:* baseball M(s), basketball M(s)/W(s), bowling W, cross-country running M(s)/W(s), rugby M(c), softball W, tennis M(s)/W(s), track and field M(s)/W(s), volleyball W(s). *Intramural sports:* basketball M/W, bowling M/W, softball W, tennis M/W, track and field M/W, volleyball W, weight lifting M/W, wrestling M.

Standardized Tests *Required:* SAT or ACT (for admission).

Costs (2010–11) *Tuition:* state resident $3633 full-time, $156 per credit hour part-time; nonresident $12,833 full-time, $441 per credit hour part-time. Full-time tuition and fees vary according to course load. Part-time tuition and fees vary according to course load. *Required fees:* $1912 full-time, $339 per semester part-time. *Room and board:* $8108; room only: $4920. Room and board charges vary according to board plan. *Payment plan:* deferred payment. *Waivers:* minority students, children of alumni, adult students, senior citizens, and employees or children of employees.

Financial Aid Of all full-time matriculated undergraduates who enrolled in 2009, 2,303 applied for aid, 2,182 were judged to have need, 417 had their need fully met. 165 Federal Work-Study jobs (averaging $3212). In 2009, 9 non-need-based awards were made. *Average percent of need met:* 74%. *Average financial aid package:* $8873. *Average need-based loan:* $4036. *Average need-based gift aid:* $5887. *Average non-need-based aid:* $1056. *Average indebtedness upon graduation:* $8559.

Applying *Options:* electronic application, early admission, deferred entrance. *Application fee:* $35. *Required:* high school transcript. *Required for some:* 2 letters of recommendation. *Recommended:* minimum 2.5 GPA, interview. *Application deadlines:* 7/15 (freshmen), 7/15 (transfers). *Notification:* continuous (freshmen), continuous (transfers).

Freshman Application Contact Ms. Michelle Gross, Director of Admissions, Coppin State University, 2500 West North Avenue, Baltimore, MD 21216-3698. *Phone:* 410-951-3600. *Toll-free phone:* 800-635-3674. *Fax:* 410-523-7351. *E-mail:* mgross@coppin.edu. *Web site:* http://www.coppin.edu/.

DeVry University
Bethesda, Maryland

- **Proprietary** comprehensive, part of DeVry University
- **Coed**
- **Minimally difficult** entrance level

Faculty *Student/faculty ratio:* 10:1.

Academics *Calendar:* semesters. *Degrees:* bachelor's and master's.

Costs (2010–11) *Tuition:* $14,766 full-time, $580 per credit hour part-time. Full-time tuition and fees vary according to course load. Part-time tuition and fees vary according to course load. *Required fees:* $60 full-time, $30 per term part-time. *Payment plans:* installment, deferred payment.

Financial Aid *Of all full-time matriculated undergraduates who enrolled in 2007,* 5 applied for aid, 4 were judged to have need. *In 2007,* 2 non-need-based awards were made. *Average percent of need met:* 24. *Average financial* *aid package:* $11,820. *Average need-based loan:* $9900. *Average need-based gift aid:* $5760. *Average non-need-based aid:* $22,795.

Applying *Options:* electronic application, deferred entrance. *Application fee:* $50. *Required:* high school transcript, interview.

Freshman Application Contact DeVry University, 4550 Montgomery Avenue, Suite 100 North, Bethesda, MD 20814-3304. *Web site:* http://www.devry.edu/.

Faith Theological Seminary

Baltimore, Maryland

Director of Admissions John Lepera, Admissions Director, Faith Theological Seminary, 529 Walker Avenue, Baltimore, MD 21212. *Phone:* 410-323-6211. *Fax:* 410-323-6331. *E-mail:* fts@faiththeological.org. *Web site:* http://www.faiththeological.org/.

Frostburg State University

Frostburg, Maryland

- **State-supported** comprehensive, founded 1898, part of University System of Maryland
- **Small-town** 260-acre campus with easy access to Baltimore and Washington, D.C.
- **Endowment** $10.9 million
- **Coed**
- **Moderately difficult** entrance level

Faculty *Student/faculty ratio:* 17:1.

Academics *Calendar:* semesters. *Degrees:* certificates, bachelor's, master's, post-master's, and postbachelor's certificates.

Student Life *Campus security:* 24-hour emergency response devices and patrols, student patrols, late-night transport/escort service, controlled dormitory access, bicycle patrols.

Athletics Member NCAA. All Division III.

Standardized Tests *Required:* SAT or ACT (for admission).

Costs (2010–11) *Tuition:* state resident $5150 full-time, $213 per credit hour part-time; nonresident $15,196 full-time, $427 per credit hour part-time. Full-time tuition and fees vary according to location. Part-time tuition and fees vary according to course load and location. *Required fees:* $1754 full-time, $86 per credit hour part-time, $12 per term part-time. *Room and board:* $7378; room only: $3510. Room and board charges vary according to board plan and housing facility. *Payment plans:* installment, deferred payment.

Financial Aid *Of all full-time matriculated undergraduates who enrolled in 2009,* 3,763 applied for aid, 2,779 were judged to have need, 539 had their need fully met. 145 Federal Work-Study jobs (averaging $614). *In 2009,* 341 non-need-based awards were made. *Average percent of need met:* 67. *Average financial aid package:* $8888. *Average need-based loan:* $3848. *Average need-based gift aid:* $6419. *Average non-need-based aid:* $3081. *Average indebtedness upon graduation:* $20,970.

Applying *Options:* electronic application, early admission. *Application fee:* $30. *Required:* high school transcript, minimum 2 GPA. *Required for some:* essay or personal statement. *Recommended:* interview.

Freshman Application Contact Frostburg State University, 101 Braddock Road, Frostburg, MD 21532-1099. *Phone:* 301-687-4201. *Web site:* http://www.frostburg.edu/.

Goucher College

Baltimore, Maryland

- **Independent** comprehensive, founded 1885
- **Suburban** 287-acre campus
- **Endowment** $158.4 million
- **Coed** 1,479 undergraduate students, 98% full-time, 69% women, 31% men
- **Moderately difficult** entrance level, 73% of applicants were admitted

Undergraduates 1,444 full-time, 35 part-time. Students come from 45 states and territories; 29 other countries; 74% are from out of state; 8% Black or African American, non-Hispanic/Latino; 6% Hispanic/Latino; 3% Asian, non-Hispanic/Latino; 0.7% American Indian or Alaska Native, non-Hispanic/Latino; 1% Two or more races, non-Hispanic/Latino; 14% Race/ethnicity unknown; 2% international; 3% transferred in; 81% live on campus. *Retention:* 83% of full-time freshmen returned.

Freshmen *Admission:* 3,587 applied, 2,611 admitted, 391 enrolled. *Average high school GPA:* 3.13. *Test scores:* SAT critical reading scores over 500: 83%; SAT math scores over 500: 77%; SAT writing scores over 500: 85%; ACT scores over 18: 96%; SAT critical reading scores over 600: 52%; SAT math scores over 600: 35%; SAT writing scores over 600: 50%; ACT scores over 24: 69%; SAT critical reading scores over 700: 11%; SAT math scores over 700: 3%; SAT writing scores over 700: 6%; ACT scores over 30: 17%.

Faculty *Total:* 215, 61% full-time, 88% with terminal degrees. *Student/faculty ratio:* 9:1.

Academics *Calendar:* semesters. *Degrees:* bachelor's, master's, and post-bachelor's certificates. *Special study options:* adult/continuing education programs, advanced placement credit, double majors, independent study, internships, off-campus study, part-time degree program, services for LD students, student-designed majors, study abroad. *ROTC:* Army (c), Air Force (c). *Unusual degree programs:* 3-2 engineering with Johns Hopkins University.

Computers on Campus 200 computers/terminals are available on campus for general student use. Students can access the following: campus intranet, computer help desk, free student e-mail accounts, online (class) grades, online (class) registration, online (class) schedules, transcripts, financial aid information, billing, ePortfolios, academic progress reports, study abroad plan. Campuswide network is available. 40% of college-owned or -operated housing units are wired for high-speed Internet access. Wireless service is available via entire campus.

Student Life *Housing:* on-campus residence required through senior year. *Options:* coed, men-only, women-only, disabled students. Campus housing is university owned and leased by the school. Freshman campus housing is guaranteed. *Activities and organizations:* drama/theater group, student-run newspaper, radio and television station, choral group, The Quindecim, Red Hot Blue (a co-ed acappella group), Umoja: The African Alliance, Hillel, Student Government Association. *Campus security:* 24-hour emergency response devices and patrols, late-night transport/escort service, controlled dormitory access. *Student services:* health clinic, personal/psychological counseling, women's center.

Athletics Member NCAA. All Division III. *Intercollegiate sports:* basketball M/W, cross-country running M/W, equestrian sports M/W, field hockey W, lacrosse M/W, soccer M/W, swimming and diving M/W, tennis M/W, track and field M/W, volleyball W. *Intramural sports:* basketball M/W, fencing M(c)/W(c), soccer M/W, tennis M/W, ultimate Frisbee M/W, volleyball M/W, water polo M/W, weight lifting M/W.

Costs (2011–12) *Comprehensive fee:* $47,122 includes full-time tuition ($36,011), mandatory fees ($542), and room and board ($10,569). *College room only:* $6404. Room and board charges vary according to board plan and housing facility. *Payment plans:* tuition prepayment, installment. *Waivers:* adult students, senior citizens, and employees or children of employees.

Financial Aid Of all full-time matriculated undergraduates who enrolled in 2009, 983 applied for aid, 865 were judged to have need, 149 had their need fully met. 358 Federal Work-Study jobs (averaging $1075). In 2009, 295 non-need-based awards were made. *Average percent of need met:* 77%. *Average financial aid package:* $26,377. *Average need-based loan:* $4128. *Average need-based gift aid:* $22,921. *Average non-need-based aid:* $11,942. *Average indebtedness upon graduation:* $20,900.

Applying *Options:* electronic application, early admission, early decision, early action, deferred entrance. *Application fee:* $55. *Required:* essay or personal statement, high school transcript. *Recommended:* 3 letters of recommendation, interview. *Application deadlines:* 2/1 (freshmen), 5/1 (transfers), 12/1 (early action). *Notification:* 4/1 (freshmen), 6/1 (transfers), 2/15 (early action).

Freshman Application Contact Goucher College, 1021 Dulaney Valley Road, Baltimore, MD 21204-2794. *Phone:* 410-337-6100. *Toll-free phone:* 800-468-2437. *Web site:* http://www.goucher.edu/.

Griggs University

Silver Spring, Maryland

- **Independent Seventh-day Adventist** 4-year, founded 1990, part of Seventh-day Adventist Parochial School System
- **Suburban** campus with easy access to Washington, D.C.
- **Coed**
- **Minimally difficult** entrance level

Academics *Calendar:* continuous. *Degrees:* associate and bachelor's (offers only external degree programs).

Costs (2010–11) *Tuition:* $7800 full-time, $325 per hour part-time. Full-time tuition and fees vary according to course load. Part-time tuition and fees vary according to course load. *Required fees:* $160 full-time.

Applying *Options:* early admission, deferred entrance. *Application fee:* $80. *Required:* essay or personal statement, high school transcript, minimum 2 GPA.

Freshman Application Contact Ms. Linda Lundberg, Enrollment Officer, Griggs University, PO Box 4437, Silver Spring, MD 20914-4437. *Phone:* 301-680-6590. *Toll-free phone:* 800-782-4769. *Fax:* 301-680-6577. *E-mail:* LLundberg@griggs.edu. *Web site:* http://www.griggs.edu/.

Hood College
Frederick, Maryland

- **Independent** comprehensive, founded 1893
- **Suburban** 50-acre campus with easy access to Baltimore and Washington, D.C.
- **Endowment** $51.6 million
- **Coed** 1,485 undergraduate students, 91% full-time, 67% women, 33% men
- **Moderately difficult** entrance level, 86% of applicants were admitted

Undergraduates 1,347 full-time, 138 part-time. Students come from 29 states and territories; 24 other countries; 19% are from out of state; 11% Black or African American, non-Hispanic/Latino; 6% Hispanic/Latino; 2% Asian, non-Hispanic/Latino; 0.1% Native Hawaiian or other Pacific Islander, non-Hispanic/Latino; 0.1% American Indian or Alaska Native, non-Hispanic/Latino; 3% Two or more races, non-Hispanic/Latino; 3% Race/ethnicity unknown; 3% international; 8% transferred in; 54% live on campus. *Retention:* 78% of full-time freshmen returned.

Freshmen *Admission:* 1,444 applied, 1,244 admitted, 327 enrolled. *Average high school GPA:* 3.53. *Test scores:* SAT critical reading scores over 500: 68%; SAT math scores over 500: 65%; SAT writing scores over 500: 64%; ACT scores over 18: 91%; SAT critical reading scores over 600: 25%; SAT math scores over 600: 27%; SAT writing scores over 600: 21%; ACT scores over 24: 33%; SAT critical reading scores over 700: 5%; SAT math scores over 700: 2%; SAT writing scores over 700: 2%; ACT scores over 30: 5%.

Faculty *Total:* 259, 32% full-time, 62% with terminal degrees. *Student/faculty ratio:* 12:1.

Academics *Calendar:* semesters. *Degrees:* certificates, bachelor's, master's, and postbachelor's certificates (also offers adult program with significant enrollment not reflected in profile). *Special study options:* academic remediation for entering students, advanced placement credit, double majors, English as a second language, honors programs, independent study, internships, off-campus study, part-time degree program, services for LD students, student-designed majors, study abroad, summer session for credit. *ROTC:* Army (b). *Unusual degree programs:* 3-2 engineering with George Washington University.

Computers on Campus 283 computers/terminals are available on campus for general student use. Students can access the following: campus intranet, computer help desk, free student e-mail accounts, online (class) grades, online (class) registration, online (class) schedules. Campuswide network is available. 100% of college-owned or -operated housing units are wired for high-speed Internet access. Wireless service is available via entire campus.

Student Life *Housing:* on-campus residence required through sophomore year. *Options:* coed, women-only. Campus housing is university owned and leased by the school. Freshman campus housing is guaranteed. *Activities and organizations:* drama/theater group, student-run newspaper, radio station, choral group, Education Club, Black Student Union, Campus Activities Board, International Club, Hood Today (newspaper). *Campus security:* 24-hour emergency response devices and patrols, late-night transport/escort service, controlled dormitory access. *Student services:* health clinic, personal/psychological counseling.

Athletics Member NCAA. All Division III. *Intercollegiate sports:* basketball M/W, cross-country running M/W, equestrian sports M(c)/W(c), field hockey W, golf M/W, lacrosse M/W, soccer M/W, softball W, swimming and diving M/W, tennis M/W, track and field M/W, volleyball W.

Standardized Tests *Required:* SAT or ACT (for admission).

Costs (2010–11) *Comprehensive fee:* $39,761 includes full-time tuition ($29,440), mandatory fees ($420), and room and board ($9901). Part-time tuition: $850 per credit hour. *Required fees:* $140 per term part-time. *College room only:* $5171. Room and board charges vary according to board plan. *Payment plan:* installment. *Waivers:* senior citizens and employees or children of employees.

Financial Aid Of all full-time matriculated undergraduates who enrolled in 2009, 1,272 applied for aid, 1,189 were judged to have need, 225 had their need fully met. In 2009, 134 non-need-based awards were made. *Average percent of need met:* 76%. *Average financial aid package:* $23,553. *Average need-based loan:* $4195. *Average need-based gift aid:* $20,186. *Average non-need-based aid:* $13,967. *Average indebtedness upon graduation:* $17,144.

Applying *Options:* electronic application, early decision, early action, deferred entrance. *Application fee:* $35. *Required:* high school transcript, minimum 2 GPA. *Required for some:* essay or personal statement. *Recommended:* essay or personal statement, interview. *Application deadlines:* 2/15 (freshmen), 2/15 (out-of-state freshmen), rolling (transfers), 12/1 (early action). *Early decision deadline:* 11/15 (for plan 1), 12/15 (for plan 2). *Notification:* 3/1 (freshmen), 3/1 (out-of-state freshmen), continuous (transfers), 12/1 (early decision plan 1), 1/1 (early decision plan 2), 12/15 (early action).

Freshman Application Contact Mr. David Adams, Director of Admissions, Hood College, 401 Rosemont Avenue, Frederick, MD 21701. *Phone:* 301-696-3400. *Toll-free phone:* 800-922-1599. *Fax:* 301-696-3819. *E-mail:* admissions@hood.edu. *Web site:* http://www.hood.edu/.

ITT Technical Institute
Owings Mills, Maryland

- **Proprietary** primarily 2-year, founded 2005
- **Coed**
- **Minimally difficult** entrance level

Academics *Calendar:* quarters. *Degrees:* associate and bachelor's.

Student Life *Housing:* college housing not available.

Freshman Application Contact Director of Recruitment, ITT Technical Institute, 11301 Red Run Boulevard, Owings Mills, MD 21117. *Phone:* 443-394-7115. *Toll-free phone:* 877-411-6782. *Web site:* http://www.itt-tech.edu/.

The Johns Hopkins University
Baltimore, Maryland

- **Independent** university, founded 1876
- **Urban** 140-acre campus with easy access to Washington, D.C.
- **Endowment** $2.2 billion
- **Coed** 4,997 undergraduate students, 100% full-time, 48% women, 52% men
- **Most difficult** entrance level, 21% of applicants were admitted

Undergraduates 4,974 full-time, 23 part-time. Students come from 55 states and territories; 60 other countries; 87% are from out of state; 5% Black or African American, non-Hispanic/Latino; 8% Hispanic/Latino; 21% Asian, non-Hispanic/Latino; 0.2% Native Hawaiian or other Pacific Islander, non-Hispanic/Latino; 0.2% American Indian or Alaska Native, non-Hispanic/Latino; 4% Two or more races, non-Hispanic/Latino; 2% Race/ethnicity unknown; 8% international; 0.7% transferred in; 55% live on campus. *Retention:* 97% of full-time freshmen returned.

Freshmen *Admission:* 18,459 applied, 3,799 admitted, 1,241 enrolled. *Average high school GPA:* 3.72. *Test scores:* SAT critical reading scores over 500: 99%; SAT math scores over 500: 100%; SAT writing scores over 500: 99%; ACT scores over 18: 100%; SAT critical reading scores over 600: 88%; SAT math scores over 600: 95%; SAT writing scores over 600: 88%; ACT scores over 24: 98%; SAT critical reading scores over 700: 43%; SAT math scores over 700: 60%; SAT writing scores over 700: 47%; ACT scores over 30: 72%.

Faculty *Total:* 592, 88% full-time, 84% with terminal degrees. *Student/faculty ratio:* 12:1.

Academics *Calendar:* 4-1-4. *Degrees:* certificates, diplomas, bachelor's, master's, doctoral-professional, doctoral-research/scholarship, post-master's, and postbachelor's certificates. *Special study options:* adult/continuing education programs, advanced placement credit, double majors, honors programs, independent study, internships, off-campus study, part-time degree program, services for LD students, student-designed majors, study abroad, summer session for credit. *ROTC:* Army (b), Air Force (c). *Unusual degree programs:* 3-2 engineering; international studies with Johns Hopkins University, School of Advanced International Studies (Washington, DC); biology; classics; German; history; neuroscience; public policy; mathematics; education.

Computers on Campus 140 computers/terminals and 1,000 ports are available on campus for general student use. Students can access the following: campus intranet, computer help desk, free student e-mail accounts, online (class) grades, online (class) registration, online (class) schedules. Campuswide network is available. 100% of college-owned or -operated housing units are wired for high-speed Internet access. Wireless service is available via classrooms, computer centers, computer labs, libraries.

Student Life *Housing:* on-campus residence required through sophomore year. *Options:* coed, men-only, women-only. Campus housing is university owned. Freshman campus housing is guaranteed. *Activities and organizations:* drama/theater group, student-run newspaper, radio station, choral group, The Outdoors Club, JHU Tutorial Project, The Barn Stormers (theater group), Inter-Asian Council, News-letter (student paper), national fraternities, national sororities. *Campus security:* 24-hour emergency response devices and patrols, student patrols, late-night transport/escort service, controlled dormitory access, CCTV monitoring of public areas. *Student services:* health clinic, personal/psychological counseling.

Athletics Member NCAA. All Division III except men's and women's lacrosse (Division I). *Intercollegiate sports:* baseball M, basketball M/W, cross-country running M/W, fencing M/W, field hockey W, football M, lacrosse M(s)/W(s), soccer M/W, swimming and diving M/W, tennis M/W, track and field M/W, volleyball W, water polo M, wrestling M. *Intramural sports:* badminton M/W, basketball M/W, cheerleading M/W, field hockey M/W, football M/W, ice hockey M/W, lacrosse M/W, rock climbing M/W, rugby M/W, sailing M/W, skiing (downhill) M/W, soccer M/W, softball M/W, table tennis M/W, tennis M/W, ultimate Frisbee M/W, volleyball M/W.

Standardized Tests *Required:* SAT or ACT (for admission). *Recommended:* SAT Subject Tests (for admission).

Costs (2010–11) *One-time required fee:* $500. *Comprehensive fee:* $53,190 includes full-time tuition ($40,680) and room and board ($12,510). Part-time tuition: $1355 per credit hour. *College room only:* $7150. Room and board

PROFILES

charges vary according to board plan and housing facility. *Payment plan:* installment. *Waivers:* employees or children of employees.

Financial Aid Of all full-time matriculated undergraduates who enrolled in 2009, 2,895 applied for aid, 2,358 were judged to have need, 2,346 had their need fully met. 1,840 Federal Work-Study jobs (averaging $2322). In 2009, 57 non-need-based awards were made. *Average percent of need met:* 99%. *Average financial aid package:* $33,142. *Average need-based loan:* $4486. *Average need-based gift aid:* $25,595. *Average non-need-based aid:* $27,491. *Average indebtedness upon graduation:* $24,307. *Financial aid deadline:* 3/1.

Applying *Options:* electronic application, early admission, early decision, deferred entrance. *Application fee:* $70. *Required:* essay or personal statement, high school transcript, 2 letters of recommendation. *Recommended:* 3 letters of recommendation, interview. *Application deadlines:* 1/1 (freshmen), 3/15 (transfers). *Early decision deadline:* 11/1. *Notification:* 4/1 (freshmen), 5/31 (transfers), 12/15 (early decision).

Freshman Application Contact Dr. John Latting, Dean of Undergraduate Admissions, The Johns Hopkins University, Mason Hall, 3400 North Charles Street, Baltimore, MD 21218-2699. *Phone:* 410-516-8341. *Fax:* 410-516-6025. *E-mail:* gotojhu@jhu.edu. *Web site:* http://www.jhu.edu/.

See Display ads below and on page 366.
See pages 1354 and 1356 for the College Close-Ups.

Kaplan University, Hagerstown Campus

Hagerstown, Maryland

- **Proprietary** primarily 2-year, founded 1938, administratively affiliated with Kaplan Higher Education
- **Small-town** 8-acre campus
- **Coed**

Academics *Calendar:* quarters. *Degrees:* certificates, diplomas, associate, and bachelor's.

Financial Aid *Of all full-time matriculated undergraduates who enrolled in 2009,* 21 Federal Work-Study jobs (averaging $1343).

Freshman Application Contact Kaplan University, Hagerstown Campus, 18618 Crestwood Drive, Hagerstown, MD 21742-2797. *Phone:* 301-739-2680

Ext. 217. *Toll-free phone:* 800-422-2670. *Web site:* http://www.ku-hagerstown.com/.

Loyola University Maryland

Baltimore, Maryland

- **Independent Roman Catholic (Jesuit)** university, founded 1852
- **Urban** 89-acre campus with easy access to Washington, D.C.
- **Endowment** $122.6 million
- **Coed** 3,807 undergraduate students, 99% full-time, 60% women, 40% men
- **Moderately difficult** entrance level, 55% of applicants were admitted

Undergraduates 3,764 full-time, 43 part-time. Students come from 40 states and territories; 60 other countries; 82% are from out of state; 4% Black or African American, non-Hispanic/Latino; 5% Hispanic/Latino; 3% Asian, non-Hispanic/Latino; 0.2% American Indian or Alaska Native, non-Hispanic/Latino; 2% Two or more races, non-Hispanic/Latino; 1% Race/ethnicity unknown; 1% international; 0.8% transferred in; 75% live on campus. *Retention:* 87% of full-time freshmen returned.

Freshmen *Admission:* 10,901 applied, 6,030 admitted, 1,019 enrolled. *Average high school GPA:* 3.48. *Test scores:* SAT critical reading scores over 500: 94%; SAT math scores over 500: 94%; ACT scores over 18: 99%; SAT critical reading scores over 600: 47%; SAT math scores over 600: 56%; ACT scores over 24: 84%; SAT critical reading scores over 700: 9%; SAT math scores over 700: 8%; ACT scores over 30: 18%.

Faculty *Total:* 525, 62% full-time, 56% with terminal degrees. *Student/faculty ratio:* 13:1.

Academics *Calendar:* semesters. *Degrees:* bachelor's, master's, doctoral-professional, doctoral-research/scholarship, post-master's, and postbachelor's certificates. *Special study options:* accelerated degree program, advanced placement credit, cooperative education, double majors, honors programs, independent study, internships, off-campus study, part-time degree program, services for LD students, study abroad, summer session for credit. *ROTC:* Army (b), Air Force (c). *Unusual degree programs:* nursing with Special agreement with the Johns Hopkins University School of Nursing, students at Loyola University may pursue a career in nursing. The Loyola-Hopkins dual-degree program allows students to earn two degrees in five years.

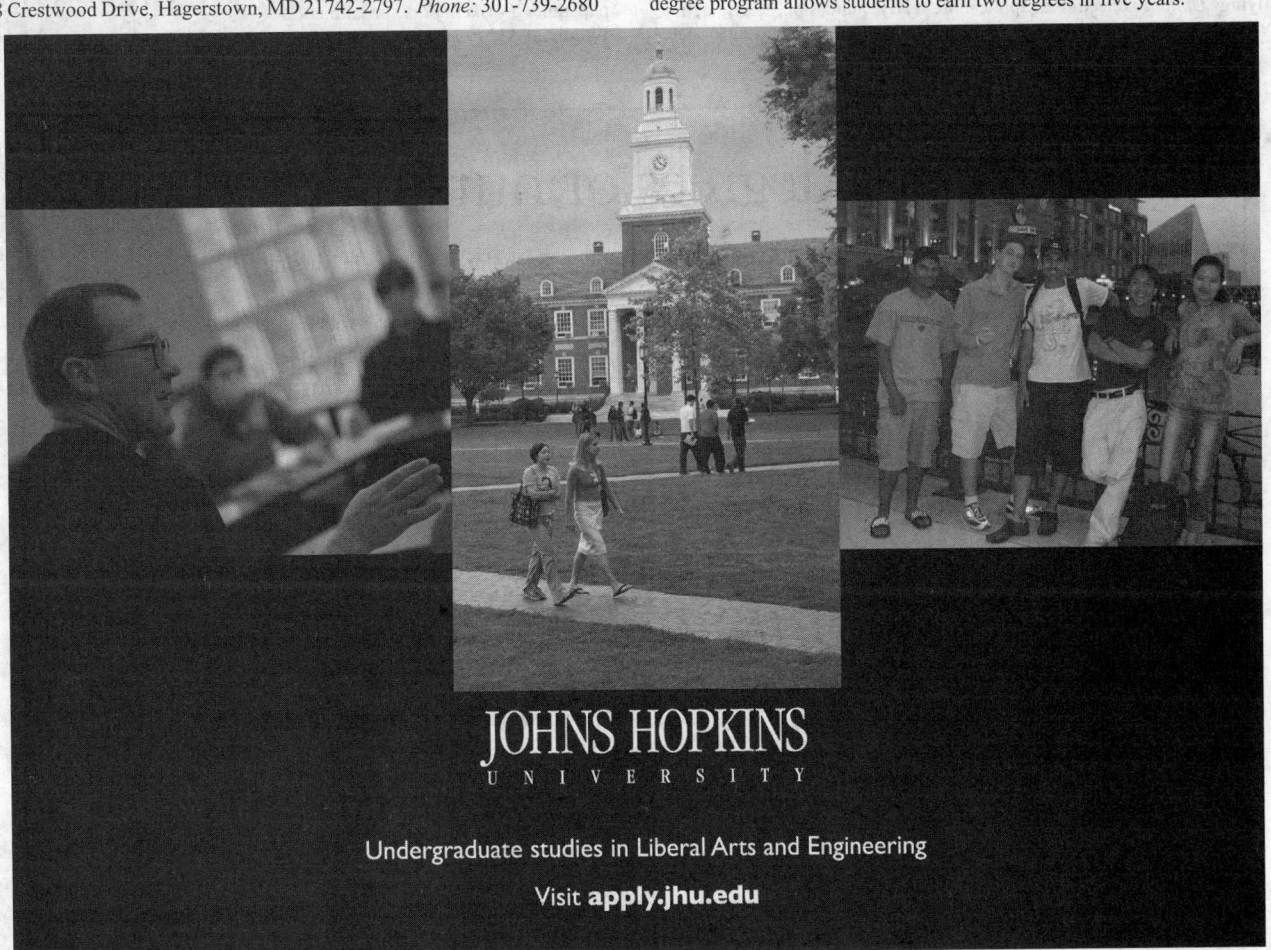

JOHNS HOPKINS
U N I V E R S I T Y

Undergraduate studies in Liberal Arts and Engineering

Visit **apply.jhu.edu**

Computers on Campus 775 computers/terminals and 775 ports are available on campus for general student use. Students can access the following: campus intranet, computer help desk, free student e-mail accounts, online (class) grades, online (class) registration, online (class) schedules. Campuswide network is available. 100% of college-owned or -operated housing units are wired for high-speed Internet access. Wireless service is available via entire campus.
Student Life *Housing options:* coed, cooperative. Campus housing is university owned. Freshman applicants given priority for college housing. *Activities and organizations:* drama/theater group, student-run newspaper, radio and television station, choral group, Student Government Association, Resident Affairs Council (RAC), Operation Smile, Relay for Life, Resident Assistants (RA)/Evergreen. *Campus security:* 24-hour emergency response devices and patrols, late-night transport/escort service, controlled dormitory access. *Student services:* health clinic, personal/psychological counseling, women's center.
Athletics Member NCAA. All Division I. *Intercollegiate sports:* basketball M(s)/W(s), crew M(s)/W(s), cross-country running M(s)/W(s), golf M(s), lacrosse M(s)/W(s), soccer M(s)/W(s), swimming and diving M(s)/W(s), tennis M(s)/W(s), track and field W(s), volleyball W(s). *Intramural sports:* badminton M(c)/W(c), baseball M(c), basketball M(c)/W(c), cheerleading M(c), field hockey W(c), riflery M(c)/W(c), rugby M(c), sailing M(c)/W(c), soccer M(c)/W(c), softball W(c), swimming and diving M(c)/W(c), ultimate Frisbee M(c), volleyball W(c), water polo M(c)/W(c), weight lifting M(c).
Costs (2010–11) *One-time required fee:* $165. *Comprehensive fee:* $51,080 includes full-time tuition ($37,950), mandatory fees ($1400), and room and board ($11,730). Full-time tuition and fees vary according to course load. Part-time tuition and fees vary according to course load. *College room only:* $9630. Room and board charges vary according to board plan, housing facility, and location. *Payment plan:* installment. *Waivers:* employees or children of employees.
Financial Aid Of all full-time matriculated undergraduates who enrolled in 2008, 2,363 applied for aid, 1,969 were judged to have need, 1,929 had their need fully met. 679 Federal Work-Study jobs (averaging $2627). 111 state and other part-time jobs (averaging $7610). In 2008, 423 non-need-based awards were made. *Average percent of need met:* 97%. *Average financial aid package:* $25,900. *Average need-based loan:* $5930. *Average need-based gift aid:* $17,910. *Average non-need-based aid:* $13,980. *Average indebtedness upon graduation:* $26,740. *Financial aid deadline:* 2/15.
Applying *Options:* electronic application, early admission, early action, deferred entrance. *Application fee:* $50. *Required:* essay or personal statement, high school transcript. *Application deadlines:* 1/15 (freshmen), 1/15 (out-of-state freshmen), 7/15 (transfers), 11/1 (early action). *Notification:* 4/1 (freshmen), 4/1 (out-of-state freshmen), continuous (transfers), 1/15 (early action).
Freshman Application Contact Loyola University Maryland, 4501 North Charles Street, Baltimore, MD 21210-2699. *Phone:* 410-617-2000. *Toll-free phone:* 800-221-9107. *Web site:* http://www.loyola.edu/.

See page 367 for the Display. See page 1394 for the College Close-Up.

Maple Springs Baptist Bible College and Seminary
Capitol Heights, Maryland

- **Independent Baptist** comprehensive, founded 1986
- **Suburban** 1-acre campus with easy access to Washington, D.C.
- **Coed** 92 undergraduate students, 5% full-time, 61% women, 39% men
- **Minimally difficult** entrance level

Undergraduates 5 full-time, 87 part-time. Students come from 3 states and territories; 21% are from out of state; 97% Black or African American, non-Hispanic/Latino; 3% Hispanic/Latino; 7% transferred in.
Freshmen *Admission:* 6 enrolled.
Faculty *Total:* 23, 13% full-time, 100% with terminal degrees.
Academics *Calendar:* semesters. *Degrees:* certificates, diplomas, associate, bachelor's, master's, and doctoral-other. *Special study options:* academic remediation for entering students, accelerated degree program, adult/continuing education programs, external degree program, independent study, internships, part-time degree program.
Student Life *Housing:* college housing not available. *Activities and organizations:* student-run newspaper. *Campus security:* 24-hour emergency response devices, part-time security personnel.
Standardized Tests *Required:* Math and English Placement examination for all new students who do not have college English and Math grades of C or above (for admission).
Costs (2011–12) *Comprehensive fee:* $13,671 includes full-time tuition ($4470), mandatory fees ($120), and room and board ($9081). Part-time tuition: $2230 per term. *Required fees:* $165 per credit part-time, $60 per term part-time. *Payment plan:* installment.
Financial Aid *Financial aid deadline:* 4/30.

Applying *Options:* deferred entrance. *Application fee:* $40. *Required:* essay or personal statement, high school transcript, 3 letters of recommendation, interview. *Application deadlines:* rolling (freshmen), rolling (transfers). *Notification:* continuous (freshmen), continuous (transfers).

Freshman Application Contact Ms. Jeannie Bowman, Assistant Director of Admissions and Records, Maple Springs Baptist Bible College and Seminary, 4130 Belt Road, Capitol Heights, MD 20743. *Phone:* 301-736-3631. *Fax:* 301-735-6507. *Web site:* http://www.msbbcs.edu/.

Maryland Institute College of Art

Baltimore, Maryland

- **Independent** comprehensive, founded 1826
- **Urban** 16-acre campus with easy access to Washington, D.C.
- **Endowment** $55.1 million
- **Coed** 1,737 undergraduate students, 99% full-time, 70% women, 30% men
- **Very difficult** entrance level, 51% of applicants were admitted

Undergraduates 1,720 full-time, 17 part-time. Students come from 45 states and territories; 45 other countries; 79% are from out of state; 4% Black or African American, non-Hispanic/Latino; 5% Hispanic/Latino; 10% Asian, non-Hispanic/Latino; 0.2% American Indian or Alaska Native, non-Hispanic/Latino; 6% Two or more races, non-Hispanic/Latino; 13% Race/ethnicity unknown; 5% international; 4% transferred in; 88% live on campus. *Retention:* 87% of full-time freshmen returned.

Freshmen *Admission:* 3,135 applied, 1,600 admitted, 430 enrolled. *Average high school GPA:* 3.5. *Test scores:* SAT critical reading scores over 500: 88%; SAT math scores over 500: 83%; SAT writing scores over 500: 84%; SAT critical reading scores over 600: 54%; SAT math scores over 600: 44%; SAT writing scores over 600: 46%; SAT critical reading scores over 700: 16%; SAT math scores over 700: 6%; SAT writing scores over 700: 12%.

Faculty *Total:* 327, 42% full-time, 82% with terminal degrees. *Student/faculty ratio:* 10:1.

Academics *Calendar:* semesters. *Degrees:* bachelor's, master's, and post-bachelor's certificates. *Special study options:* accelerated degree program, adult/continuing education programs, advanced placement credit, distance learning, double majors, English as a second language, independent study, internships, off-campus study, services for LD students, student-designed majors, study abroad, summer session for credit. *ROTC:* Army (c).

Computers on Campus 650 computers/terminals and 750 ports are available on campus for general student use. Students can access the following: campus intranet, computer help desk, free student e-mail accounts, online (class) grades, online (class) registration, online (class) schedules, campus Portal, online gallery space, network storage space, personal Web sites, online software training tutorials (Lynda.com), and Learning management system (Moodle). Campuswide network is available. 100% of college-owned or -operated housing units are wired for high-speed Internet access. Wireless service is available via classrooms, computer centers, computer labs, dorm rooms, learning centers, libraries, student centers.

Student Life *Housing options:* coed, disabled students. Campus housing is university owned. Freshman campus housing is guaranteed. *Activities and organizations:* drama/theater group, student-run radio station, choral group, Soccer Club, Volleyball Club, Black Student Union, Asian Student Alliance, MICAppella. *Campus security:* 24-hour emergency response devices and patrols, student patrols, late-night transport/escort service, controlled dormitory access, self-defense education, 24-hour building security, safety awareness programs, campus patrols by city police. *Student services:* health clinic, personal/psychological counseling.

Athletics *Intramural sports:* soccer M(c)/W(c), volleyball M(c)/W(c).

Standardized Tests *Required:* SAT or ACT (for admission).

Costs (2011–12) *One-time required fee:* $150. *Comprehensive fee:* $48,240 includes full-time tuition ($36,170), mandatory fees ($1300), and room and board ($10,770). Part-time tuition: $1506 per credit. *Required fees:* $650 per term part-time. *College room only:* $7790. Room and board charges vary according to board plan and housing facility. *Payment plan:* installment. *Waivers:* employees or children of employees.

Financial Aid *Average indebtedness upon graduation:* $17,472.

Applying *Options:* early admission, early decision, deferred entrance. *Application fee:* $60. *Required:* essay or personal statement, high school transcript, 3 letters of recommendation, art portfolio. *Recommended:* interview. *Application deadlines:* 2/15 (freshmen), 3/1 (transfers). *Early decision deadline:* 11/15. *Notification:* 3/11 (freshmen), 4/18 (transfers), 12/15 (early decision).

Freshman Application Contact Ms. Christine Seese, Director of Undergraduate Admission, Maryland Institute College of Art, 1300 Mount

Royal Avenue, Baltimore, MD 21217. *Phone:* 410-225-2222. *Fax:* 410-225-2337. *E-mail:* cgyland@mica.edu. *Web site:* http://www.mica.edu/.

McDaniel College
Westminster, Maryland

- **Independent** comprehensive, founded 1867
- **Suburban** 160-acre campus with easy access to Baltimore and Washington, D.C.
- **Endowment** $75.5 million
- **Coed** 1,635 undergraduate students, 98% full-time, 53% women, 47% men
- **Moderately difficult** entrance level, 74% of applicants were admitted

Undergraduates 1,599 full-time, 36 part-time. 36% are from out of state; 7% Black or African American, non-Hispanic/Latino; 4% Hispanic/Latino; 4% Asian, non-Hispanic/Latino; 0.1% Native Hawaiian or other Pacific Islander, non-Hispanic/Latino; 0.8% American Indian or Alaska Native, non-Hispanic/Latino; 3% Race/ethnicity unknown; 0.2% international; 3% transferred in; 81% live on campus. *Retention:* 85% of full-time freshmen returned.
Freshmen *Admission:* 2,867 applied, 2,114 admitted, 410 enrolled. *Average high school GPA:* 3.4. *Test scores:* SAT critical reading scores over 500: 81%; SAT math scores over 500: 78%; ACT scores over 18: 100%; SAT critical reading scores over 600: 31%; SAT math scores over 600: 33%; ACT scores over 24: 57%; SAT critical reading scores over 700: 7%; SAT math scores over 700: 7%; ACT scores over 30: 18%.
Faculty *Total:* 367, 28% full-time, 49% with terminal degrees. *Student/faculty ratio:* 12:1.
Academics *Calendar:* 4-1-4. *Degrees:* bachelor's, master's, and postbachelor's certificates. *Special study options:* academic remediation for entering students, adult/continuing education programs, advanced placement credit, distance learning, double majors, honors programs, independent study, internships, off-campus study, part-time degree program, services for LD students, student-designed majors, study abroad, summer session for credit. *ROTC:* Army (b). *Unusual degree programs:* 3-2 engineering with University of Maryland; Environmental Policy Science with Duke University.
Computers on Campus 315 computers/terminals and 1,228 ports are available on campus for general student use. Students can access the following: campus intranet, computer help desk, free student e-mail accounts, online (class) grades, online (class) registration, online (class) schedules, online billing summaries, financial aid letter, tax information. Campuswide network is available. 100% of college-owned or -operated housing units are wired for high-speed Internet access. Wireless service is available via entire campus.
Student Life *Housing:* on-campus residence required through junior year. *Options:* coed, men-only, women-only, disabled students. Campus housing is university owned. Freshman campus housing is guaranteed. *Activities and organizations:* drama/theater group, student-run newspaper, radio and television station, choral group, Student Government Association, Black Student Union, International Club, Maryland State Legislature, Up Till Dawn, national fraternities, national sororities. *Campus security:* 24-hour emergency response devices and patrols, late-night transport/escort service, About half patrol force sworn as campus police. All are certified to US DOT First Responder standards. *Student services:* health clinic, personal/psychological counseling.
Athletics Member NCAA. All Division III. *Intercollegiate sports:* baseball M, basketball M/W, cross-country running M/W, field hockey W, football M, golf M/W, lacrosse M/W, soccer M/W, softball W, swimming and diving M/W, tennis M/W, track and field M/W, volleyball W, wrestling M. *Intramural sports:* basketball M/W, cheerleading M(c)/W(c), football M, golf M/W, rugby M(c)/W(c), soccer M/W, softball M/W, tennis M/W, ultimate Frisbee M(c)/W(c), volleyball M/W.
Standardized Tests *Required:* SAT or ACT (for admission), SAT Optional Plan for students who are in the top 10% of their class if their HS ranks; otherwise, a cumulative GPA of a 3.5 or higher. SAT Subject Tests considered if submitted (for admission).
Costs (2010–11) *Comprehensive fee:* $40,340 includes full-time tuition ($33,280) and room and board ($7060). Part-time tuition: $1040 per credit hour. Part-time tuition and fees vary according to reciprocity agreements. *College room only:* $3800. Room and board charges vary according to board plan and housing facility. *Payment plans:* tuition prepayment, installment. *Waivers:* employees or children of employees.
Financial Aid Of all full-time matriculated undergraduates who enrolled in 2009, 1,253 applied for aid, 1,128 were judged to have need, 255 had their need fully met. 252 Federal Work-Study jobs (averaging $947). 238 state and other part-time jobs (averaging $913). In 2009, 327 non-need-based awards were made. *Average percent of need met:* 81%. *Average financial aid package:* $27,009. *Average need-based loan:* $4872. *Average need-based gift aid:* $22,231. *Average non-need-based aid:* $13,812. *Average indebtedness upon graduation:* $30,825.
Applying *Options:* electronic application, early admission, early action, deferred entrance. *Application fee:* $50. *Required:* essay or personal statement, high school transcript, minimum 2.5 GPA, 2 letters of recommendation.

Required for some: interview. *Recommended:* interview. *Application deadlines:* 2/15 (freshmen), 4/1 (transfers), 12/1 (early action). *Notification:* 3/1 (freshmen), 4/15 (transfers), 1/1 (early action).
Freshman Application Contact Ms. Florence Hines, Vice President for Enrollment Management and Dean of Admissions, McDaniel College, 2 College Hill, Westminster, MD 21157-4390. *Phone:* 410-857-2230. *Toll-free phone:* 800-638-5005. *Fax:* 410-857-2757. *E-mail:* admissions@mcdaniel.edu. *Web site:* http://www.mcdaniel.edu/.

Morgan State University
Baltimore, Maryland

Director of Admissions Ms. Shonda Gray, Acting Director of Admissions and Recruitment, Morgan State University, 1700 East Cold Spring Lane, Baltimore, MD 21251. *Phone:* 443-885-3000. *Toll-free phone:* 800-332-6674. *E-mail:* shantell.saunders@morgan.edu. *Web site:* http://www.morgan.edu/.

Mount St. Mary's University
Emmitsburg, Maryland

- **Independent Roman Catholic** comprehensive, founded 1808
- **Rural** 1400-acre campus with easy access to Baltimore and Washington, D.C.
- **Endowment** $38.0 million
- **Coed** 1,618 undergraduate students, 93% full-time, 56% women, 44% men
- **Moderately difficult** entrance level, 80% of applicants were admitted

Undergraduates 1,510 full-time, 108 part-time. Students come from 36 states and territories; 11 other countries; 48% are from out of state; 8% Black or African American, non-Hispanic/Latino; 7% Hispanic/Latino; 2% Asian, non-Hispanic/Latino; 0.5% American Indian or Alaska Native, non-Hispanic/Latino; 2% Two or more races, non-Hispanic/Latino; 2% Race/ethnicity unknown; 0.9% international; 3% transferred in; 84% live on campus. *Retention:* 80% of full-time freshmen returned.
Freshmen *Admission:* 3,476 applied, 2,796 admitted, 424 enrolled. *Average high school GPA:* 3.12. *Test scores:* SAT critical reading scores over 500: 72%; SAT math scores over 500: 71%; SAT writing scores over 500: 69%; ACT scores over 18: 83%; SAT critical reading scores over 600: 24%; SAT math scores over 600: 21%; SAT writing scores over 600: 23%; ACT scores over 24: 24%; SAT critical reading scores over 700: 3%; SAT math scores over 700: 1%; SAT writing scores over 700: 3%; ACT scores over 30: 2%.
Faculty *Total:* 186, 60% full-time, 63% with terminal degrees. *Student/faculty ratio:* 13:1.
Academics *Calendar:* semesters. *Degrees:* bachelor's, master's, doctoral-professional, post-master's, and postbachelor's certificates. *Special study options:* academic remediation for entering students, accelerated degree program, adult/continuing education programs, advanced placement credit, double majors, honors programs, independent study, internships, off-campus study, part-time degree program, services for LD students, student-designed majors, study abroad, summer session for credit. *ROTC:* Army (c). *Unusual degree programs:* 3-2 nursing with Johns Hopkins University; 3-3 with Sacred Heart (BS Bio, Ph.D. PT); 4-2 with Sacred Heart (BS Bio, MS OT).
Computers on Campus 100 computers/terminals are available on campus for general student use. Students can access the following: campus intranet, computer help desk, free student e-mail accounts, online (class) grades, online (class) registration, online (class) schedules, tuition payment, course management system. Campuswide network is available. 100% of college-owned or -operated housing units are wired for high-speed Internet access. Wireless service is available via entire campus.
Student Life *Housing:* on-campus residence required for freshman year. *Options:* coed, disabled students. Campus housing is university owned. Freshman campus housing is guaranteed. *Activities and organizations:* drama/theater group, student-run newspaper, radio and television station, choral group, Mount Students for Life, CRUX - Outdoor Adventures, Ice Hockey Club, Circle K, International Affairs Organization. *Campus security:* 24-hour emergency response devices and patrols, late-night transport/escort service, controlled dormitory access. *Student services:* health clinic, personal/psychological counseling.
Athletics Member NCAA. All Division I. *Intercollegiate sports:* baseball M(s), basketball M(s)/W(s), cheerleading W(c), cross-country running M(s)/W(s), equestrian sports M(c)/W(c), golf M(s)/W(s), ice hockey M(c), lacrosse M(s)/W(s), rugby M(c)/W(c), soccer M(s)/W(s), softball W(s), swimming and diving W(s), tennis M(s)/W(s), track and field M(s)/W(s). *Intramural sports:* basketball M/W, field hockey W, football M, racquetball M/W, skiing (downhill) M/W, soccer M/W, softball M/W, swimming and diving M/W, tennis M/W, volleyball M/W.
Standardized Tests *Required:* SAT or ACT (for admission).

Costs (2011–12) *Comprehensive fee:* $42,080 includes full-time tuition ($30,836), mandatory fees ($700), and room and board ($10,544). Full-time tuition and fees vary according to location. Part-time tuition: $1030 per credit hour. Part-time tuition and fees vary according to location. *College room only:* $5160. Room and board charges vary according to board plan. *Payment plan:* installment. *Waivers:* employees or children of employees.

Financial Aid Of all full-time matriculated undergraduates who enrolled in 2009, 1,190 applied for aid, 1,030 were judged to have need, 225 had their need fully met. 236 Federal Work-Study jobs (averaging $1032). 405 state and other part-time jobs (averaging $1059). In 2009, 423 non-need-based awards were made. *Average percent of need met:* 73%. *Average financial aid package:* $20,609. *Average need-based loan:* $4502. *Average need-based gift aid:* $16,501. *Average non-need-based aid:* $10,581. *Average indebtedness upon graduation:* $29,637. *Financial aid deadline:* 3/1.

Applying *Options:* electronic application, early action, deferred entrance. *Application fee:* $35. *Required:* high school transcript, minimum 2 GPA, 1 letter of recommendation. *Recommended:* essay or personal statement, minimum 3 GPA, interview. *Application deadlines:* rolling (freshmen), 6/1 (transfers), 12/1 (early action). *Notification:* continuous (freshmen), continuous (transfers), 12/15 (early action).

Freshman Application Contact Mr. Michael Post, Dean of Admissions and Enrollment Management, Mount St. Mary's University, 16300 Old Emmitsburg Road, Emmitsburg, MD 21727. *Phone:* 301-447-5214. *Toll-free phone:* 800-448-4347. *Fax:* 301-447-5860. *E-mail:* admissions@ msmary.edu. *Web site:* http://www.msmary.edu/.

National Labor College
Silver Spring, Maryland

Director of Admissions Carol Rodgers, Associate Provost for External Relations and Director of Admissions, National Labor College, 10000 New Hampshire Avenue, Silver Spring, MD 20903. *Phone:* 301-431-5440. *Toll-free phone:* 800-GMC-4CDP. *E-mail:* crodgers@nlc.edu. *Web site:* http://www.nlc.edu/.

Ner Israel Rabbinical College
Baltimore, Maryland

Freshman Application Contact Ner Israel Rabbinical College, 400 Mount Wilson Lane, Baltimore, MD 21208. *Phone:* 410-484-7200.

Peabody Conservatory of The Johns Hopkins University
Baltimore, Maryland

- **Independent** comprehensive, founded 1857, administratively affiliated with Johns Hopkins University
- **Urban** 1-acre campus with easy access to Washington, D.C.
- **Endowment** $75.4 million
- **Coed** 324 undergraduate students, 98% full-time, 44% women, 56% men
- **Very difficult** entrance level, 51% of applicants were admitted

Undergraduates 318 full-time, 6 part-time. Students come from 37 states and territories; 15 other countries; 77% are from out of state; 3% transferred in; 40% live on campus. *Retention:* 87% of full-time freshmen returned.

Freshmen *Admission:* 764 applied, 388 admitted, 85 enrolled.

Faculty *Total:* 165, 23% with terminal degrees. *Student/faculty ratio:* 4:1.

Academics *Calendar:* semesters. *Degrees:* certificates, diplomas, bachelor's, master's, doctoral-other, post-master's, and postbachelor's certificates. *Special study options:* academic remediation for entering students, accelerated degree program, advanced placement credit, double majors, English as a second language, honors programs, independent study, internships, off-campus study, services for LD students.

Computers on Campus 40 computers/terminals are available on campus for general student use. Students can access the following: campus intranet, computer help desk, free student e-mail accounts, online (class) grades, online (class) registration, online (class) schedules, word processing, music processing. Campuswide network is available. 100% of college-owned or -operated housing units are wired for high-speed Internet access. Wireless service is available via entire campus.

Student Life *Housing:* on-campus residence required through sophomore year. *Options:* coed. Campus housing is university owned. Freshman campus housing is guaranteed. *Activities and organizations:* choral group. *Campus security:* 24-hour emergency response devices and patrols, late-night transport/escort service, controlled dormitory access. *Student services:* health clinic, personal/psychological counseling.

Standardized Tests *Required for some:* SAT or ACT (for admission).

Costs (2011–12) *One-time required fee:* $700. *Comprehensive fee:* $49,625 includes full-time tuition ($37,000), mandatory fees ($425), and room and

board ($12,200). Full-time tuition and fees vary according to program. Part-time tuition: $1055 per semester hour. Part-time tuition and fees vary according to course load. *Room and board:* Room and board charges vary according to board plan. *Payment plan:* installment.

Financial Aid Of all full-time matriculated undergraduates who enrolled in 2009, 226 applied for aid, 200 were judged to have need, 43 had their need fully met. 108 Federal Work-Study jobs (averaging $2163). In 2009, 81 non-need-based awards were made. *Average percent of need met:* 72%. *Average financial aid package:* $15,694. *Average need-based loan:* $5014. *Average need-based gift aid:* $12,281. *Average non-need-based aid:* $14,314. *Average indebtedness upon graduation:* $38,034.

Applying *Application fee:* $100. *Required:* essay or personal statement, high school transcript, 3 letters of recommendation, interview, audition. *Recommended:* minimum 3 GPA. *Application deadlines:* 12/1 (freshmen), 12/1 (transfers). *Notification:* 4/1 (freshmen), 4/1 (transfers).

Freshman Application Contact Mr. David Lane, Director of Admissions, Peabody Conservatory of The Johns Hopkins University, Peabody Conservatory Admissions Office, One East Mount Vernon Place, Baltimore, MD 21202-2397. *Phone:* 410-234-4848. *Toll-free phone:* 800-368-2521. *Web site:* http://www.peabody.jhu.edu/.

St. John's College
Annapolis, Maryland

- **Independent** comprehensive, founded 1784
- **Small-town** 36-acre campus with easy access to Baltimore and Washington, D.C.
- **Coed** 463 undergraduate students, 100% full-time, 46% women, 54% men
- **Moderately difficult** entrance level, 81% of applicants were admitted

Undergraduates 462 full-time, 1 part-time. 79% are from out of state; 0.4% Black or African American, non-Hispanic/Latino; 4% Hispanic/Latino; 1% Asian, non-Hispanic/Latino; 0.6% American Indian or Alaska Native, non-Hispanic/Latino; 3% Two or more races, non-Hispanic/Latino; 4% Race/ethnicity unknown; 7% international; 70% live on campus. *Retention:* 82% of full-time freshmen returned.

Freshmen *Admission:* 357 applied, 289 admitted, 136 enrolled. *Test scores:* SAT critical reading scores over 500: 98%; SAT math scores over 500: 96%; ACT scores over 18: 100%; SAT critical reading scores over 600: 88%; SAT math scores over 600: 67%; ACT scores over 24: 88%; SAT critical reading scores over 700: 48%; SAT math scores over 700: 23%; ACT scores over 30: 42%.

Faculty *Total:* 78, 94% full-time, 5% with terminal degrees. *Student/faculty ratio:* 7:1.

Academics *Calendar:* semesters. *Degrees:* bachelor's and master's. *Special study options:* internships, off-campus study.

Computers on Campus Students can access the following: computer help desk, free student e-mail accounts. Campuswide network is available. 100% of college-owned or -operated housing units are wired for high-speed Internet access. Wireless service is available via computer labs, dorm rooms, libraries.

Student Life *Housing:* on-campus residence required for freshman year. *Options:* coed, disabled students. Campus housing is university owned. Freshman campus housing is guaranteed. *Activities and organizations:* drama/theater group, student-run newspaper, choral group. *Campus security:* 24-hour emergency response devices and patrols, late-night transport/escort service, controlled dormitory access. *Student services:* health clinic, personal/psychological counseling.

Athletics *Intercollegiate sports:* crew M(c)/W(c), fencing M(c)/W(c). *Intramural sports:* badminton M/W, basketball M/W, fencing M/W, football W, racquetball M/W, sailing M/W, soccer M/W, softball M/W, squash M/W, table tennis M/W, tennis M/W, track and field M/W, volleyball M/W, weight lifting M/W.

Standardized Tests *Required for some:* SAT or ACT (for admission). *Recommended:* SAT or ACT (for admission).

Costs (2010–11) *Comprehensive fee:* $52,176 includes full-time tuition ($41,792), mandatory fees ($400), and room and board ($9984). *Room and board:* Room and board charges vary according to board plan. *Payment plan:* installment. *Waivers:* employees or children of employees.

Financial Aid Of all full-time matriculated undergraduates who enrolled in 2008, 324 applied for aid, 304 were judged to have need, 300 had their need fully met. 128 Federal Work-Study jobs (averaging $1816). 163 state and other part-time jobs (averaging $1291). *Average percent of need met:* 98%. *Average financial aid package:* $34,236. *Average need-based loan:* $4788. *Average need-based gift aid:* $27,913. *Average indebtedness upon graduation:* $29,869.

Applying *Options:* electronic application, early admission, deferred entrance. *Required:* essay or personal statement, high school transcript, 2 letters of recommendation. *Recommended:* interview. *Application deadlines:* rolling (freshmen), rolling (transfers). *Notification:* continuous (freshmen), continuous (transfers).

PROFILES

Freshman Application Contact Mr. John Christensen, Director of Admissions, St. John's College, PO Box 2800, 60 College Avenue, Annapolis, MD 21404. *Phone:* 410-626-2522. *Toll-free phone:* 800-727-9238. *Fax:* 410-269-7916. *E-mail:* admissions@sjca.edu. *Web site:* http://www.stjohnscollege.edu/.

See page 1562 for the College Close-Up.

St. Mary's College of Maryland
St. Mary's City, Maryland

- **State-supported** comprehensive, founded 1840
- **Rural** 319-acre campus
- **Endowment** $28.0 million
- **Coed** 1,982 undergraduate students, 96% full-time, 59% women, 41% men
- **Very difficult** entrance level, 65% of applicants were admitted

Undergraduates 1,904 full-time, 78 part-time. Students come from 33 states and territories; 32 other countries; 17% are from out of state; 4% transferred in; 86% live on campus. *Retention:* 87% of full-time freshmen returned.

Freshmen *Admission:* 2,133 applied, 1,393 admitted, 443 enrolled. *Average high school GPA:* 3.58. *Test scores:* SAT critical reading scores over 500: 92%; SAT math scores over 500: 89%; ACT scores over 18: 99%; SAT critical reading scores over 600: 61%; SAT math scores over 600: 53%; ACT scores over 24: 77%; SAT critical reading scores over 700: 18%; SAT math scores over 700: 10%; ACT scores over 30: 23%.

Faculty *Total:* 227, 61% full-time, 77% with terminal degrees. *Student/faculty ratio:* 12:1.

Academics *Calendar:* semesters. *Degrees:* bachelor's and master's. *Special study options:* advanced placement credit, cooperative education, double majors, freshman honors college, honors programs, independent study, internships, off-campus study, part-time degree program, services for LD students, student-designed majors, study abroad, summer session for credit. *Unusual degree programs:* 3-2 engineering with University of Maryland, College Park.

Computers on Campus 390 computers/terminals and 500 ports are available on campus for general student use. Students can access the following: campus intranet, computer help desk, free student e-mail accounts, online (class) grades, online (class) registration, online (class) schedules, Blackboard. Campuswide network is available. 100% of college-owned or -operated housing units are wired for high-speed Internet access. Wireless service is available via classrooms, computer centers, computer labs, learning centers, libraries, student centers.

Student Life *Housing options:* coed, men-only, women-only, cooperative, disabled students. Campus housing is university owned. Freshman campus housing is guaranteed. *Activities and organizations:* drama/theater group, student-run newspaper, radio station, choral group, Crew, Acapella groups, SEAC (Student Environmental Action Coalition), Dance Club, rock climbing club. *Campus security:* 24-hour emergency response devices and patrols, late-night transport/escort service, controlled dormitory access. *Student services:* health clinic, personal/psychological counseling.

Athletics Member NCAA. All Division III. *Intercollegiate sports:* baseball M, basketball M/W, crew M(c)/W(c), cross-country running M(c)/W(c), equestrian sports M(c)/W(c), fencing M(c)/W(c), field hockey W, golf M(c)/W(c), lacrosse M/W, rock climbing M(c)/W(c), rugby M(c)/W(c), sailing M/W, soccer M/W, swimming and diving M/W, tennis M/W, ultimate Frisbee M(c)/W(c), volleyball W. *Intramural sports:* badminton M/W, basketball M/W, bowling M/W, football M/W, lacrosse M/W, soccer M/W, softball M/W, swimming and diving M/W, tennis M/W, volleyball M/W, water polo M/W.

Standardized Tests *Required:* SAT or ACT (for admission).

Costs (2010–11) *Tuition:* state resident $11,325 full-time, $185 per credit hour part-time; nonresident $22,718 full-time, $185 per credit hour part-time. Full-time tuition and fees vary according to course load. Part-time tuition and fees vary according to course load. *Required fees:* $2305 full-time. *Room and board:* $10,250; room only: $5745. Room and board charges vary according to board plan and housing facility. *Payment plan:* installment. *Waivers:* senior citizens and employees or children of employees.

Financial Aid Of all full-time matriculated undergraduates who enrolled in 2008, 1,341 applied for aid, 858 were judged to have need, 34 had their need fully met. 120 Federal Work-Study jobs (averaging $514). In 2008, 499 non-need-based awards were made. *Average percent of need met:* 49%. *Average financial aid package:* $13,093. *Average need-based loan:* $3001. *Average need-based gift aid:* $8664. *Average non-need-based aid:* $3579. *Average indebtedness upon graduation:* $17,505. *Financial aid deadline:* 2/28.

Applying *Options:* electronic application, early admission, early decision. *Application fee:* $50. *Required:* essay or personal statement, high school transcript, minimum 2 GPA, resume of co-curricular activities. *Recommended:* 2 letters of recommendation, interview. *Application deadlines:* 1/1 (freshmen), 2/1 (transfers). *Early decision deadline:* 11/1 (for plan 1), 12/1 (for plan 2). *Notification:* 4/1 (freshmen), 5/1 (transfers), 12/1 (early decision plan 1), 1/1 (early decision plan 2).

Freshman Application Contact Mr. Richard J. Edgar, Director of Admissions, St. Mary's College of Maryland, 18952 East Fisher Road, St. Mary's City, MD 20686-3001. *Phone:* 240-895-5000. *Toll-free phone:* 800-492-7181. *Fax:* 240-895-5001. *E-mail:* admissions@smcm.edu. *Web site:* http://www.smcm.edu/.

See page 1578 for the College Close-Up.

Salisbury University

Salisbury, Maryland

- **State-supported** comprehensive, founded 1925, part of University System of Maryland
- **Small-town** 154-acre campus
- **Endowment** $49.7 million
- **Coed** 7,706 undergraduate students, 92% full-time, 56% women, 44% men
- **Moderately difficult** entrance level, 53% of applicants were admitted

Undergraduates 7,103 full-time, 603 part-time. Students come from 26 states and territories; 52 other countries; 13% are from out of state; 11% Black or African American, non-Hispanic/Latino; 4% Hispanic/Latino; 2% Asian, non-Hispanic/Latino; 0.1% Native Hawaiian or other Pacific Islander, non-Hispanic/Latino; 0.4% American Indian or Alaska Native, non-Hispanic/Latino; 2% Two or more races, non-Hispanic/Latino; 0.5% Race/ethnicity unknown; 0.5% international; 12% transferred in; 35% live on campus. *Retention:* 81% of full-time freshmen returned.

Freshmen *Admission:* 7,739 applied, 4,129 admitted, 1,250 enrolled. *Average high school GPA:* 3.65. *Test scores:* SAT critical reading scores over 500: 89%; SAT math scores over 500: 90%; SAT writing scores over 500: 89%; ACT scores over 18: 96%; SAT critical reading scores over 600: 28%; SAT math scores over 600: 35%; SAT writing scores over 600: 28%; ACT scores over 24: 41%; SAT critical reading scores over 700: 2%; SAT math scores over 700: 3%; SAT writing scores over 700: 2%; ACT scores over 30: 2%.

Faculty *Total:* 597, 65% full-time, 59% with terminal degrees. *Student/faculty ratio:* 17:1.

Academics *Calendar:* 4-1-4. *Degrees:* bachelor's, master's, and postbachelor's certificates. *Special study options:* academic remediation for entering students, adult/continuing education programs, advanced placement credit, distance learning, double majors, English as a second language, honors programs, independent study, internships, off-campus study, part-time degree program, services for LD students, student-designed majors, study abroad, summer session for credit. *ROTC:* Army (b), Air Force (c). *Unusual degree programs:* 3-2 engineering with University of Maryland College Park, Old Dominion University, Widener University; social work with University of Maryland Eastern Shore; environmental marine science with University of Maryland Eastern Shore.

Computers on Campus 298 computers/terminals and 3,112 ports are available on campus for general student use. Students can access the following: computer help desk, free student e-mail accounts, online (class) grades, online (class) registration, online (class) schedules, accounts for all students. Campus-wide network is available. 99% of college-owned or -operated housing units are wired for high-speed Internet access. Wireless service is available via entire campus.

Student Life *Housing options:* coed, men-only, women-only. Campus housing is university owned. Freshman applicants given priority for college housing. *Activities and organizations:* drama/theater group, student-run newspaper, radio and television station, choral group, SOAP, Student Government Association, Panhellenic Council/Inter-Fraternity Council, Campus Crusade for Christ, UAS/Passion for Fashion/ASA, national fraternities, national sororities. *Campus security:* 24-hour emergency response devices and patrols, student patrols, late-night transport/escort service, controlled dormitory access. *Student services:* health clinic, personal/psychological counseling.

Athletics Member NCAA, NAIA. All NCAA Division III. *Intercollegiate sports:* baseball M, basketball M/W, cross-country running M/W, field hockey W, football M, lacrosse M/W, soccer M/W, softball W, swimming and diving M/W, tennis M/W, track and field M/W, volleyball W. *Intramural sports:* basketball M(c)/W(c), cheerleading M(c)/W(c), equestrian sports M(c)/W(c), fencing M/W, field hockey W(c), football M(c), golf M/W, ice hockey M(c), lacrosse M(c)/W(c), racquetball M/W, rock climbing M(c)/W(c), rugby M(c)/W(c), sailing M(c)/W(c), soccer M(c)/W(c), softball M(c)/W, ultimate Frisbee M(c)/W(c), volleyball M(c)/W, water polo M/W.

Standardized Tests *Required for some:* SAT or ACT (for admission).

Costs (2010–11) *Tuition:* state resident $4960 full-time, $206 per credit hour part-time; nonresident $13,456 full-time, $559 per credit hour part-time. Part-time tuition and fees vary according to course load. *Required fees:* $1948 full-time, $65 per credit hour part-time. *Room and board:* $8378; room only:

$4350. Room and board charges vary according to board plan and housing facility. *Payment plan:* installment. *Waivers:* senior citizens and employees or children of employees.

Financial Aid Of all full-time matriculated undergraduates who enrolled in 2008, 4,365 applied for aid, 2,778 were judged to have need, 560 had their need fully met. 70 Federal Work-Study jobs (averaging $1840). In 2008, 565 non-need-based awards were made. *Average percent of need met:* 60%. *Average financial aid package:* $7027. *Average need-based loan:* $3764. *Average need-based gift aid:* $5256. *Average non-need-based aid:* $2225. *Average indebtedness upon graduation:* $17,521.

Applying *Options:* electronic application, early admission, early action. *Application fee:* $45. *Required:* high school transcript, minimum 2 GPA. *Application deadlines:* 1/15 (freshmen), rolling (transfers), 12/1 (early action). *Notification:* 3/15 (freshmen), continuous (transfers), 1/15 (early action). **Freshman Application Contact** Mr. Aaron Basko, Director of Admissions, Salisbury University, Admissions House, 1101 Camden Avenue, Salisbury, MD 21801. *Phone:* 410-543-6161. *Toll-free phone:* 888-543-0148. *Fax:* 410-546-6016. *E-mail:* admissions@salisbury.edu. *Web site:* http://www.salisbury.edu/.

See page 1588 for the College Close-Up.

Sojourner-Douglass College
Baltimore, Maryland

Freshman Application Contact Sojourner-Douglass College, 500 North Caroline Street, Baltimore, MD 21205-1814. *Phone:* 410-276-0306 Ext. 251. *Web site:* http://sdc.edu/.

Stevenson University
Stevenson, Maryland

- **Independent** comprehensive, founded 1952
- **Suburban** 150-acre campus with easy access to Baltimore
- **Endowment** $44.5 million
- **Coed** 3,575 undergraduate students, 83% full-time, 67% women, 33% men
- **Moderately difficult** entrance level, 64% of applicants were admitted

Undergraduates 2,950 full-time, 625 part-time. 10% are from out of state; 22% Black or African American, non-Hispanic/Latino; 3% Hispanic/Latino; 3% Asian, non-Hispanic/Latino; 0.1% Native Hawaiian or other Pacific Islander, non-Hispanic/Latino; 0.6% American Indian or Alaska Native, non-Hispanic/Latino; 0.6% Two or more races, non-Hispanic/Latino; 6% Race/ethnicity unknown; 0.5% international; 8% transferred in; 43% live on campus. *Retention:* 76% of full-time freshmen returned.

Freshmen *Admission:* 4,428 applied, 2,826 admitted, 882 enrolled. *Average high school GPA:* 3.19. *Test scores:* SAT critical reading scores over 500: 42%; SAT math scores over 500: 44%; SAT writing scores over 500: 43%; ACT scores over 18: 75%; SAT critical reading scores over 600: 9%; SAT math scores over 600: 11%; SAT writing scores over 600: 8%; ACT scores over 24: 19%; SAT critical reading scores over 700: 1%; SAT writing scores over 700: 1%.

Faculty *Total:* 378, 29% full-time. *Student/faculty ratio:* 16:1.

Academics *Calendar:* semesters. *Degrees:* bachelor's and master's. *Special study options:* academic remediation for entering students, accelerated degree program, adult/continuing education programs, advanced placement credit, cooperative education, distance learning, double majors, honors programs, independent study, internships, off-campus study, part-time degree program, services for LD students, student-designed majors, study abroad, summer session for credit. *ROTC:* Army (c).

Computers on Campus 300 computers/terminals and 1,000 ports are available on campus for general student use. Students can access the following: campus intranet, computer help desk, free student e-mail accounts, online (class) grades, online (class) registration, online (class) schedules. Campuswide network is available. 100% of college-owned or -operated housing units are wired for high-speed Internet access. Wireless service is available via entire campus.

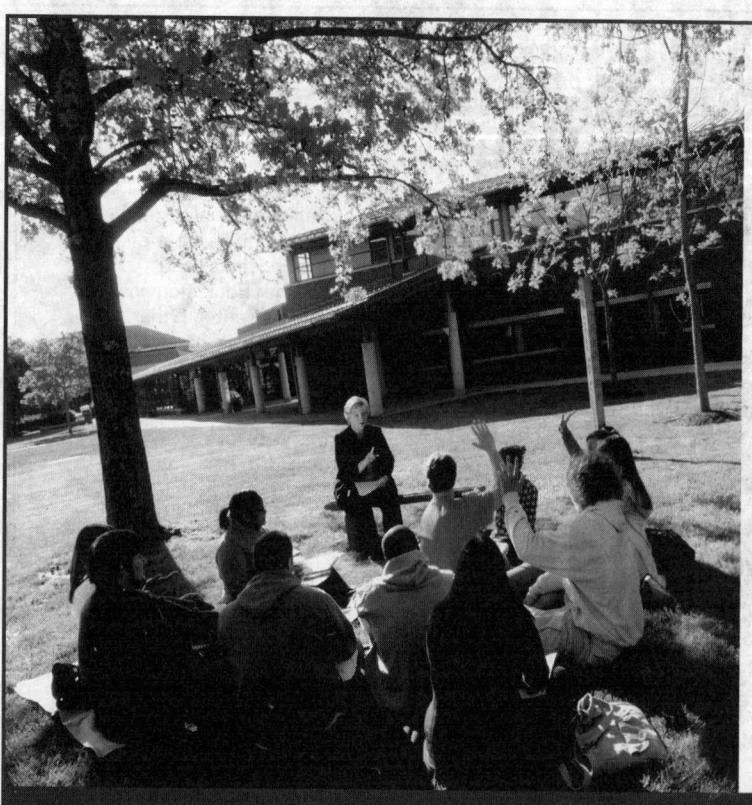

Student Life *Housing options:* coed, men-only, women-only, cooperative, disabled students. Campus housing is university owned. Freshman applicants given priority for college housing. *Activities and organizations:* drama/theater group, student-run newspaper, choral group, marching band, Student Government Association, Mustang Crew, Black Student Union, National Student Nurses Association, Phi Sigma, national sororities. *Campus security:* 24-hour emergency response devices and patrols, late-night transport/escort service, controlled dormitory access, patrols by trained security personnel during campus hours. *Student services:* health clinic, personal/psychological counseling.

Athletics Member NCAA. All Division III. *Intercollegiate sports:* baseball M, basketball M/W, cheerleading M/W, cross-country running M/W, field hockey W, football M, golf M/W, ice hockey W, lacrosse M/W, soccer M/W, softball W, tennis M/W, track and field M/W, volleyball M/W. *Intramural sports:* badminton M/W, baseball M, basketball M/W, fencing M(c)/W(c), field hockey W, football M/W, sailing M(c)/W(c), skiing (cross-country) M/W(c), skiing (downhill) M/W, softball W, table tennis M/W, tennis M/W, volleyball M.

Standardized Tests *Required:* SAT or ACT (for admission).

Costs (2010–11) *Comprehensive fee:* $32,916 includes full-time tuition ($20,580), mandatory fees ($1510), and room and board ($10,826). Full-time tuition and fees vary according to degree level. Part-time tuition: $521 per credit hour. Part-time tuition and fees vary according to course load and degree level. *Required fees:* $75 per term part-time. *College room only:* $7156. Room and board charges vary according to board plan and housing facility. *Payment plans:* installment, deferred payment. *Waivers:* employees or children of employees.

Financial Aid Of all full-time matriculated undergraduates who enrolled in 2009, 2,097 applied for aid, 1,806 were judged to have need, 530 had their need fully met. 225 Federal Work-Study jobs (averaging $2000). In 2009, 555 non-need-based awards were made. *Average percent of need met:* 63%. *Average financial aid package:* $14,124. *Average need-based loan:* $4095. *Average need-based gift aid:* $10,967. *Average non-need-based aid:* $6920. *Average indebtedness upon graduation:* $20,779.

Applying *Options:* electronic application, early admission, deferred entrance. *Application fee:* $40. *Required:* essay or personal statement, high school transcript, 2 letters of recommendation. *Recommended:* interview. *Application deadlines:* rolling (freshmen), rolling (transfers). *Notification:* continuous (freshmen), continuous (transfers).

Freshman Application Contact Mr. Mark Hergan, Vice President, Enrollment Management, Stevenson University, 1525 Greenspring Valley Road, Stevenson, MD 21153. *Phone:* 410-486-7001. *Toll-free phone:* 877-468-6852 (in-state); 877-468-3852 (out-of-state). *Fax:* 410-352-4440. *E-mail:* admissions@stevenson.edu. *Web site:* http://www.stevenson.edu/.

See page 1648 for the College Close-Up.

Strayer University - Anne Arundel Campus

Millersville, Maryland

- **Proprietary** comprehensive
- **Coed**

Academics *Degrees:* certificates, diplomas, associate, bachelor's, master's, and postbachelor's certificates.

Costs (2010–11) *Tuition:* $13,635 full-time, $1590 per course part-time.

Freshman Application Contact Strayer University - Anne Arundel Campus, 1520 Jabez Run, Millersville, MD 21108. *Web site:* http://www.strayer.edu/anne_arundel.

Strayer University - Owings Mills Campus

Owings Mills, Maryland

- **Proprietary** comprehensive
- **Coed**

Academics *Degrees:* certificates, diplomas, associate, bachelor's, master's, and postbachelor's certificates.

Costs (2010–11) *Tuition:* $13,635 full-time, $1590 per course part-time.

Freshman Application Contact Strayer University - Owings Mills Campus, 500 Redland Court, Suite 100, Owings Mills, MD 21117. *Web site:* http://www.strayer.edu/owings_mills.

Strayer University - Prince George's Campus

Suitland, Maryland

- **Proprietary** comprehensive
- **Coed**

Academics *Degrees:* certificates, diplomas, associate, bachelor's, master's, and postbachelor's certificates.

Costs (2010–11) *Tuition:* $13,635 full-time, $1590 per course part-time.

Freshman Application Contact Strayer University - Prince George's Campus, 4710 Auth Place, First Floor, Suitland, MD 20746. *Web site:* http://www.strayer.edu/prince_georges.

Strayer University - Rockville Campus

Rockville, Maryland

- **Proprietary** comprehensive
- **Coed**

Academics *Degrees:* certificates, diplomas, associate, bachelor's, master's, and postbachelor's certificates.

Costs (2010–11) *Tuition:* $13,635 full-time, $1590 per course part-time.

Freshman Application Contact Strayer University - Rockville Campus, 4 Research Place, Suite 100, Rockville, MD 20850. *Web site:* http://www.strayer.edu/rockville.

Strayer University - White Marsh Campus

Baltimore, Maryland

- **Proprietary** comprehensive, founded 1892
- **Coed**

Academics *Degrees:* certificates, diplomas, associate, bachelor's, master's, and postbachelor's certificates.

Costs (2010–11) *Tuition:* $13,635 full-time, $1590 per course part-time.

Freshman Application Contact Strayer University - White Marsh Campus, 9920 Franklin Square Drive, Suite 200, Baltimore, MD 21236. *Web site:* http://www.strayer.edu/white_marsh.

Towson University

Towson, Maryland

- **State-supported** university, founded 1866, part of University System of Maryland
- **Suburban** 321-acre campus with easy access to Baltimore and Washington, D.C.
- **Endowment** $4.0 million
- **Coed** 17,529 undergraduate students, 89% full-time, 60% women, 40% men
- **Moderately difficult** entrance level, 57% of applicants were admitted

Undergraduates 15,560 full-time, 1,969 part-time. Students come from 46 states and territories; 18% are from out of state; 12% Black or African American, non-Hispanic/Latino; 3% Hispanic/Latino; 4% Asian, non-Hispanic/Latino; 0.4% American Indian or Alaska Native, non-Hispanic/Latino; 1% Two or more races, non-Hispanic/Latino; 7% Race/ethnicity unknown; 3% international; 11% transferred in; 25% live on campus. *Retention:* 85% of full-time freshmen returned.

Freshmen *Admission:* 15,704 applied, 8,954 admitted, 2,431 enrolled. *Average high school GPA:* 3.52. *Test scores:* SAT critical reading scores over 500: 71%; SAT math scores over 500: 77%; SAT writing scores over 500: 77%; ACT scores over 18: 98%; SAT critical reading scores over 600: 17%; SAT math scores over 600: 23%; SAT writing scores over 600: 19%; ACT scores over 24: 42%; SAT critical reading scores over 700: 1%; SAT math scores over 700: 1%; SAT writing scores over 700: 1%; ACT scores over 30: 2%.

Faculty *Total:* 1,588, 52% full-time, 52% with terminal degrees. *Student/faculty ratio:* 17:1.

Academics *Calendar:* semesters. *Degrees:* bachelor's, master's, doctoral-professional, doctoral-research/scholarship, post-master's, and postbachelor's certificates. *Special study options:* academic remediation for entering students, accelerated degree program, adult/continuing education programs, advanced placement credit, cooperative education, distance learning, double majors, English as a second language, freshman honors college, honors programs, independent study, internships, off-campus study, part-time degree program, services for LD students, student-designed majors, study abroad, summer session for credit. *ROTC:* Army (c), Air Force (c). *Unusual degree programs:* 3-2 engineering with University of Maryland College Park; law with University of Baltimore.

Computers on Campus 1,200 computers/terminals are available on campus for general student use. Students can access the following: computer help desk, free student e-mail accounts, online (class) grades, online (class) registration, online (class) schedules. Campuswide network is available. 100% of college-owned or -operated housing units are wired for high-speed Internet access. Wireless service is available via entire campus.

Student Life *Housing options:* coed, disabled students. Campus housing is university owned and is provided by a third party. Freshman campus housing is guaranteed. *Activities and organizations:* drama/theater group, student-run newspaper, radio and television station, choral group, marching band, University Residence Government, Queer Student Union, Black Student Union, Hillel, African Diaspora Club, national fraternities, national sororities. *Campus security:* 24-hour emergency response devices and patrols, late-night transport/escort service, controlled dormitory access. *Student services:* health clinic, personal/psychological counseling, women's center.

Athletics Member NCAA. All Division I except football (Division I-AA). *Intercollegiate sports:* badminton M/W, baseball M(s), basketball M(s)/W(s), cheerleading M/W, cross-country running M(s)/W(s), equestrian sports M/W, field hockey W(s), golf M(s)/W(s), gymnastics W(s), lacrosse M(s)/W(s), rugby M/W, soccer M(s)/W(s), softball W(s), swimming and diving M(s)/W(s), tennis M(s)/W(s), track and field M(s)/W(s), ultimate Frisbee M/W, volleyball M/W, wrestling M. *Intramural sports:* basketball M/W, football M/W, golf M(c), ice hockey M, lacrosse M/W, racquetball M(c)/W(c), rock climbing M(c)/W(c), soccer M/W, softball M/W, tennis M/W, track and field M(c)/W(c).

Standardized Tests *Required:* SAT or ACT (for admission).

Costs (2010–11) *Tuition:* state resident $5336 full-time, $232 per credit part-time; nonresident $16,794 full-time, $641 per credit part-time. Full-time tuition and fees vary according to course load. No tuition increase for student's term of enrollment. *Required fees:* $2320 full-time, $96 per credit part-time. *Room and board:* $9614; room only: $5520. Room and board charges vary according to board plan and housing facility. *Payment plans:* tuition prepayment, installment. *Waivers:* senior citizens and employees or children of employees.

Financial Aid Of all full-time matriculated undergraduates who enrolled in 2009, 10,205 applied for aid, 7,769 were judged to have need, 1,188 had their need fully met. 511 Federal Work-Study jobs (averaging $1652). In 2009, 1190 non-need-based awards were made. *Average percent of need met:* 64%. *Average financial aid package:* $9275. *Average need-based loan:* $4229. *Average need-based gift aid:* $7601. *Average non-need-based aid:* $5170. *Average indebtedness upon graduation:* $14,055. *Financial aid deadline:* 2/10.

Applying *Options:* electronic application, early admission, deferred entrance. *Application fee:* $45. *Required:* high school transcript. *Required for some:* essay or personal statement, interview. *Recommended:* minimum 3 GPA, 2 letters of recommendation. *Application deadlines:* 2/15 (freshmen), 2/15 (transfers). *Notification:* continuous (freshmen), continuous (transfers).

Freshman Application Contact Mr. Brian Hazlett, Director of Admissions, Towson University, 8000 York Road, Towson, MD 21252. *Phone:* 410-704-2113. *Toll-free phone:* 888-4TOWSON. *Fax:* 410-704-3030. *E-mail:* admissions@towson.edu. *Web site:* http://www.towson.edu/.

United States Naval Academy
Annapolis, Maryland

- **Federally supported** 4-year, founded 1845
- **Small-town** 329-acre campus with easy access to Baltimore and Washington, D.C.
- **Coed, primarily men** 4,603 undergraduate students, 100% full-time, 20% women, 80% men
- **Very difficult** entrance level, 7% of applicants were admitted

Undergraduates 4,603 full-time. Students come from 54 states and territories; 26 other countries; 96% are from out of state; 6% Black or African American, non-Hispanic/Latino; 12% Hispanic/Latino; 4% Asian, non-Hispanic/Latino; 0.7% Native Hawaiian or other Pacific Islander, non-Hispanic/Latino; 0.3% American Indian or Alaska Native, non-Hispanic/Latino; 7% Two or more races, non-Hispanic/Latino; 0.9% Race/ethnicity unknown; 1% international; 100% live on campus. *Retention:* 98% of full-time freshmen returned.

Freshmen *Admission:* 17,419 applied, 1,245 admitted, 1,220 enrolled. *Test scores:* SAT critical reading scores over 500: 91%; SAT math scores over 500: 96%; SAT critical reading scores over 600: 56%; SAT math scores over 600: 72%; SAT critical reading scores over 700: 14%; SAT math scores over 700: 24%.

Faculty *Total:* 587, 89% full-time, 61% with terminal degrees. *Student/faculty ratio:* 9:1.

Academics *Calendar:* semesters. *Degree:* bachelor's. *Special study options:* academic remediation for entering students, advanced placement credit, double majors, honors programs, independent study, off-campus study, study abroad, summer session for credit.

Computers on Campus 6,100 computers/terminals are available on campus for general student use. Students can access the following: campus intranet, computer help desk, free student e-mail accounts, online (class) grades, online (class) registration, online (class) schedules. Campuswide network is available. 100% of college-owned or -operated housing units are wired for high-speed Internet access. Wireless service is available via classrooms, libraries.

Student Life *Housing:* on-campus residence required through senior year. *Options:* coed. Campus housing is university owned. Freshman campus housing is guaranteed. *Activities and organizations:* drama/theater group, student-run radio station, choral group, marching band, Mountaineering Club, Semper Fi, Black Studies Club, Midshipmen Action Club, Martial Arts Club. *Campus security:* 24-hour emergency response devices and patrols, campus gate security. *Student services:* health clinic, personal/psychological counseling, legal services.

Athletics Member NCAA. All Division I except football (Division I-A). *Intercollegiate sports:* baseball M, basketball M/W, cheerleading M(c)/W(c), crew M/W, cross-country running M/W, fencing M(c)/W(c), field hockey W(c), golf M, gymnastics M/W(c), ice hockey M(c), lacrosse M/W, riflery M/W, rugby M(c)/W(c), sailing M/W, skiing (downhill) M(c)/W(c), soccer M/W, softball W(c), squash M, swimming and diving M/W, tennis M/W, track and field M/W, volleyball M(c)/W, water polo M, weight lifting M(c)/W(c), wrestling M. *Intramural sports:* basketball M/W, cross-country running M/W, football M/W, lacrosse M(c), racquetball M/W, sailing M/W, soccer M/W, softball M/W, volleyball M/W, weight lifting M/W.

Standardized Tests *Required:* SAT or ACT (for admission).

Costs (2011–12) *Tuition:* Tuition, room and board, and medical and dental care are provided by the U.S. government. Each midshipman receives a salary from which to pay for uniforms, books, supplies, and personal expenses.

Applying *Options:* electronic application, early action. *Required:* essay or personal statement, high school transcript, 2 letters of recommendation, interview, age 17-22, medical exam, authorized nomination. *Application deadline:* 1/31 (freshmen). *Notification:* continuous until 4/15 (freshmen).

Freshman Application Contact Capt. Angela Cyrus, Director of Admissions, United States Naval Academy, 117 Decatur Road, Annapolis, MD 21402. *Phone:* 410-293-4361. *Fax:* 410-293-4348. *E-mail:* webmail@usna.edu. *Web site:* http://www.usna.edu/.

University of Baltimore
Baltimore, Maryland

- **State-supported** comprehensive, founded 1925, part of University System of Maryland
- **Urban** 49-acre campus
- **Coed** 3,226 undergraduate students, 60% full-time, 56% women, 44% men
- **Minimally difficult** entrance level, 60% of applicants were admitted

Undergraduates 1,924 full-time, 1,302 part-time. Students come from 14 states and territories; 62 other countries; 1% are from out of state; 42% Black or African American, non-Hispanic/Latino; 3% Hispanic/Latino; 4% Asian, non-Hispanic/Latino; 0.1% Native Hawaiian or other Pacific Islander, non-Hispanic/Latino; 0.4% American Indian or Alaska Native, non-Hispanic/Latino; 3% Two or more races, non-Hispanic/Latino; 11% Race/ethnicity unknown; 1% international; 25% transferred in. *Retention:* 78% of full-time freshmen returned.

Freshmen *Admission:* 806 applied, 482 admitted, 185 enrolled. *Average high school GPA:* 2.89. *Test scores:* SAT critical reading scores over 500: 41%; SAT math scores over 500: 32%; SAT writing scores over 500: 30%; SAT critical reading scores over 600: 11%; SAT math scores over 600: 11%; SAT writing scores over 600: 9%; SAT critical reading scores over 700: 1%; SAT math scores over 700: 3%.

Faculty *Total:* 404, 45% full-time, 68% with terminal degrees. *Student/faculty ratio:* 19:1.

Academics *Calendar:* semesters. *Degrees:* bachelor's, master's, doctoral-professional, doctoral-research/scholarship, and postbachelor's certificates. *Special study options:* academic remediation for entering students, accelerated degree program, adult/continuing education programs, advanced placement credit, cooperative education, distance learning, freshman honors college, honors programs, independent study, internships, off-campus study, part-time degree program, services for LD students, study abroad, summer session for credit. *ROTC:* Army (c), Air Force (c). *Unusual degree programs:* 3-2 business administration with MBA; Law.

Computers on Campus 135 computers/terminals are available on campus for general student use. Students can access the following: computer help desk, free student e-mail accounts, online (class) grades, online (class) registration, online (class) schedules. Campuswide network is available. Wireless service is available via entire campus.

Student Life *Housing:* college housing not available. *Options:* Campus housing is provided by a third party. *Activities and organizations:* drama/theater group, student-run newspaper, choral group, Psi Chi, APALSA, International Student Association, African Student Association, Forensics Student Association. *Campus security:* 24-hour emergency response devices and patrols, late-night transport/escort service. *Student services:* health clinic, personal/psychological counseling.

Athletics *Intramural sports:* basketball M/W, golf M/W, lacrosse M/W, racquetball M/W, soccer M/W, table tennis M/W, volleyball M/W, weight lifting M/W.

Standardized Tests *Required:* SAT or ACT (for admission).

Costs (2010–11) *Tuition:* state resident $5484 full-time, $250 per credit hour part-time; nonresident $15,000 full-time, $784 per credit hour part-time. Full-time tuition and fees vary according to course load. Part-time tuition and fees vary according to course load. *Required fees:* $1846 full-time, $75 per credit part-time, $25 per term part-time. *Payment plan:* installment. *Waivers:* employees or children of employees.

Financial Aid Of all full-time matriculated undergraduates who enrolled in 2007, 1,036 applied for aid, 912 were judged to have need, 113 had their need fully met. 93 Federal Work-Study jobs (averaging $4801). 48 state and other part-time jobs (averaging $6727). In 2007, 86 non-need-based awards were made. *Average percent of need met:* 55%. *Average financial aid package:* $9919. *Average need-based loan:* $4326. *Average need-based gift aid:* $2206. *Average non-need-based aid:* $4148.

Applying *Options:* electronic application, deferred entrance. *Application fee:* $30. *Required:* essay or personal statement, high school transcript. *Recommended:* minimum 3 GPA, 2 letters of recommendation, interview. *Application deadlines:* rolling (freshmen), 6/1 (transfers). *Notification:* continuous (freshmen), continuous (transfers).

Freshman Application Contact Ms. Brigid H. Lawler, Director, Freshman Admission, University of Baltimore, 1420 North Charles Street, Baltimore, MD 21201. *Phone:* 410-837-4777. *Toll-free phone:* 877-APPLYUB. *Fax:* 410-837-4793. *E-mail:* admissions@ubalt.edu. *Web site:* http://www.ubalt.edu/.

University of Maryland, Baltimore County
Baltimore, Maryland

- **State-supported** university, founded 1963, part of University System of Maryland
- **Suburban** 530-acre campus with easy access to Washington, D.C.
- **Endowment** $48.9 million
- **Coed** 10,210 undergraduate students, 86% full-time, 45% women, 55% men
- **Moderately difficult** entrance level, 63% of applicants were admitted

Undergraduates 8,830 full-time, 1,380 part-time. Students come from 41 states and territories; 81 other countries; 6% are from out of state; 16% Black or African American, non-Hispanic/Latino; 4% Hispanic/Latino; 21% Asian, non-Hispanic/Latino; 0.5% Native Hawaiian or other Pacific Islander, non-Hispanic/Latino; 0.4% American Indian or Alaska Native, non-Hispanic/Latino; 2% Two or more races, non-Hispanic/Latino; 2% Race/ethnicity unknown; 4% international; 12% transferred in; 37% live on campus. *Retention:* 85% of full-time freshmen returned.

Freshmen *Admission:* 6,987 applied, 4,406 admitted, 1,499 enrolled. *Average high school GPA:* 3.57. *Test scores:* SAT critical reading scores over 500: 89%; SAT math scores over 500: 95%; SAT writing scores over 500: 86%; ACT scores over 18: 99%; SAT critical reading scores over 600: 43%; SAT math scores over 600: 60%; SAT writing scores over 600: 41%; ACT scores over 24: 77%; SAT critical reading scores over 700: 8%; SAT math scores over 700: 16%; SAT writing scores over 700: 7%; ACT scores over 30: 18%.

Faculty *Total:* 724, 66% full-time, 67% with terminal degrees. *Student/faculty ratio:* 25:1.

Academics *Calendar:* 4-1-4. *Degrees:* bachelor's, master's, doctoral-research/scholarship, and postbachelor's certificates. *Special study options:* academic remediation for entering students, adult/continuing education programs, advanced placement credit, cooperative education, distance learning, double majors, English as a second language, external degree program, freshman honors college, honors programs, independent study, internships, off-campus study, part-time degree program, services for LD students, student-designed majors, study abroad, summer session for credit. *ROTC:* Army (c).

Computers on Campus 875 computers/terminals are available on campus for general student use. Students can access the following: campus intranet, computer help desk, free student e-mail accounts, online (class) grades, online (class) registration, online (class) schedules, student account information. Campuswide network is available. 100% of college-owned or -operated housing units are wired for high-speed Internet access. Wireless service is available via classrooms, computer centers, computer labs, libraries, student centers.

Student Life *Housing options:* coed, disabled students. Campus housing is university owned and is provided by a third party. Freshman campus housing is guaranteed. *Activities and organizations:* drama/theater group, student-run newspaper, radio station, choral group, Student Government Association, Student Events Board, Filipino American Student Association, Resident Student

Association, Pre-Med Society, national fraternities, national sororities. *Campus security:* 24-hour emergency response devices and patrols, late-night transport/escort service. *Student services:* health clinic, personal/psychological counseling, women's center, legal services.

Athletics Member NCAA. All Division I. *Intercollegiate sports:* badminton M(c)/W(c), baseball M(s), basketball M(s)/W(s), bowling M(c)/W(c), crew M(c)/W(c), cross-country running M(s)/W(s), fencing M(c)/W(c), field hockey W(c), ice hockey M(c), lacrosse M(s)/W(s), rugby M(c)/W(c), sailing M(c)/W(c), skiing (downhill) M(c)/W(c), soccer M(s)/W(s), softball W(s), swimming and diving M(s)/W(s), tennis M(s)/W(s), track and field M(s)/W(s), ultimate Frisbee M(c)/W(c), volleyball M(c)/W(c), wrestling M(c). *Intramural sports:* basketball M/W, football M/W, lacrosse M(c)/W(c), soccer M(c)/W(c), softball M/W, tennis M(c)/W(c), volleyball M/W(c).

Standardized Tests *Required:* SAT or ACT (for admission).

Costs (2011–12) *One-time required fee:* $100. *Tuition:* state resident $9171 full-time, $278 per credit hour part-time; nonresident $19,108 full-time, $691 per credit hour part-time. Full-time tuition and fees vary according to location and program. Part-time tuition and fees vary according to location and program. *Required fees:* $2492 full-time, $111 per credit hour part-time. *Room and board:* $9620; room only: $5860. Room and board charges vary according to board plan and housing facility. *Payment plan:* installment. *Waivers:* senior citizens and employees or children of employees.

Financial Aid Of all full-time matriculated undergraduates who enrolled in 2009, 5,655 applied for aid, 4,464 were judged to have need, 1,089 had their need fully met. In 2009, 2831 non-need-based awards were made. *Average percent of need met:* 60%. *Average financial aid package:* $10,615. *Average need-based loan:* $4271. *Average need-based gift aid:* $7758. *Average non-need-based aid:* $7755. *Average indebtedness upon graduation:* $19,594.

Applying *Options:* electronic application, early admission, early action, deferred entrance. *Application fee:* $50. *Required:* essay or personal statement, high school transcript. *Recommended:* minimum 3 GPA, 2 letters of recommendation. *Application deadlines:* 2/1 (freshmen), 5/31 (transfers), 11/1 (early action). *Notification:* continuous (freshmen), continuous (transfers), 12/15 (early action).

Freshman Application Contact Mr. Dale Bittinger, Director of Admissions, University of Maryland, Baltimore County, 1000 Hilltop Circle, Baltimore, MD 21250. *Phone:* 410-455-2291. *Toll-free phone:* 800-UMBC-4U2 (in-state); 800-862-2402 (out-of-state). *Fax:* 410-455-1094. *E-mail:* admissions@umbc.edu. *Web site:* http://www.umbc.edu/.

University of Maryland, College Park
College Park, Maryland

- **State-supported** university, founded 1856, part of University System of Maryland
- **Suburban** 1500-acre campus with easy access to Baltimore and Washington, D.C.
- **Endowment** $358.9 million
- **Coed** 26,876 undergraduate students, 92% full-time, 47% women, 53% men
- **Moderately difficult** entrance level, 44% of applicants were admitted

Undergraduates 24,814 full-time, 2,062 part-time. Students come from 49 states and territories; 137 other countries; 23% are from out of state; 12% Black or African American, non-Hispanic/Latino; 7% Hispanic/Latino; 15% Asian, non-Hispanic/Latino; 0.1% Native Hawaiian or other Pacific Islander, non-Hispanic/Latino; 0.2% American Indian or Alaska Native, non-Hispanic/Latino; 3% Two or more races, non-Hispanic/Latino; 3% Race/ethnicity unknown; 2% international; 7% transferred in; 42% live on campus. *Retention:* 95% of full-time freshmen returned.

Freshmen *Admission:* 26,358 applied, 11,624 admitted, 3,929 enrolled. *Average high school GPA:* 3.98. *Test scores:* SAT critical reading scores over 500: 96%; SAT math scores over 500: 97%; SAT critical reading scores over 600: 67%; SAT math scores over 600: 82%; SAT critical reading scores over 700: 18%; SAT math scores over 700: 32%.

Faculty *Total:* 2,284, 71% full-time, 80% with terminal degrees. *Student/faculty ratio:* 18:1.

Academics *Calendar:* semesters. *Degrees:* certificates, bachelor's, master's, doctoral-professional, doctoral-research/scholarship, post-master's, and postbachelor's certificates. *Special study options:* academic remediation for entering students, accelerated degree program, adult/continuing education programs, advanced placement credit, cooperative education, distance learning, double majors, English as a second language, external degree program, honors programs, independent study, internships, off-campus study, part-time degree program, services for LD students, student-designed majors, study abroad, summer session for credit. *ROTC:* Army (b), Navy (c), Air Force (b).

Computers on Campus 11,637 computers/terminals are available on campus for general student use. Students can access the following: campus intranet, computer help desk, free student e-mail accounts, online (class) grades, online (class) registration, online (class) schedules, student account information, financial aid summary. Campuswide network is available. 100% of college-owned or -operated housing units are wired for high-speed Internet access. Wireless service is available via entire campus.

Student Life *Housing options:* coed, women-only, cooperative, disabled students. Campus housing is university owned and is provided by a third party. Freshman campus housing is guaranteed. *Activities and organizations:* drama/theater group, student-run newspaper, radio and television station, choral group, marching band, Student Government Association, Residence Hall Association, Black Student Union, Asian-American Student Union/Jewish Student Union, Commuter Students Association, national fraternities, national sororities. *Campus security:* 24-hour emergency response devices and patrols, student patrols, late-night transport/escort service, controlled dormitory access, campus police, video camera surveillance. *Student services:* health clinic, personal/psychological counseling, women's center, legal services.

Athletics Member NCAA. All Division I except football (Division I-A). *Intercollegiate sports:* baseball M(s), basketball M(s)/W(s), cheerleading W(s), cross-country running M(s)/W(s), field hockey W(s), golf M(s)/W(s), gymnastics W(s), lacrosse M(s)/W(s), soccer M(s)/W(s), softball W(s), swimming and diving M(s)/W(s), tennis M(s)/W(s), track and field M(s)/W(s), volleyball W(s), water polo W(s), wrestling M(s). *Intramural sports:* badminton M(c)/W(c), baseball M(c), basketball M/W, crew M(c)/W(c), cross-country running M/W, equestrian sports M(c)/W(c), fencing M(c)/W(c), field hockey W(c), football M/W, golf M/W, ice hockey M(c)/W(c), lacrosse M(c)/W(c), racquetball M(c)/W(c), rock climbing M(c)/W(c), rugby M(c)/W(c), sailing M(c)/W(c), soccer M(c)/W(c), softball W, squash M(c)/W(c), swimming and diving M(c)/W(c), table tennis M/W, tennis M/W, track and field M/W, ultimate Frisbee M/W, volleyball M(c)/W(c), water polo M(c)/W(c), weight lifting M/W, wrestling M.

Standardized Tests *Required:* SAT or ACT (for admission).

Costs (2010–11) *Tuition:* state resident $6763 full-time, $282 per credit hour part-time; nonresident $23,178 full-time, $966 per credit hour part-time. Part-time tuition and fees vary according to course load. *Required fees:* $1653 full-time, $380 per term part-time. *Room and board:* $9599; room only: $5714. Room and board charges vary according to board plan. *Payment plans:* installment, deferred payment. *Waivers:* employees or children of employees.

Financial Aid Of all full-time matriculated undergraduates who enrolled in 2008, 14,294 applied for aid, 10,376 were judged to have need, 719 had their need fully met. 624 Federal Work-Study jobs (averaging $1300). In 2008, 2744 non-need-based awards were made. *Average percent of need met:* 58%. *Average financial aid package:* $9829. *Average need-based loan:* $4321. *Average need-based gift aid:* $6959. *Average non-need-based aid:* $6383. *Average indebtedness upon graduation:* $22,696.

Applying *Options:* electronic application, early admission, early action, deferred entrance. *Application fee:* $55. *Required:* essay or personal statement, high school transcript. *Required for some:* resume of activities, auditions. *Recommended:* 2 letters of recommendation. *Application deadlines:* 1/20 (freshmen), 6/1 (transfers), 11/1 (early action). *Notification:* 4/1 (freshmen), continuous (transfers), 2/15 (early action).

Freshman Application Contact Ms. Barbara Gill, Director of Undergraduate Admissions, University of Maryland, College Park, College Park, MD 20742. *Phone:* 301-314-8385. *Toll-free phone:* 800-422-5867. *Fax:* 301-314-9693. *Web site:* http://www.maryland.edu/.

University of Maryland Eastern Shore
Princess Anne, Maryland

- **State-supported** university, founded 1886, part of University System of Maryland
- **Rural** 700-acre campus
- **Coed**
- **Moderately difficult** entrance level

Faculty *Student/faculty ratio:* 20:1.

Academics *Calendar:* semesters. *Degrees:* bachelor's, master's, and doctoral-research/scholarship.

Student Life *Campus security:* 24-hour emergency response devices and patrols, student patrols, late-night transport/escort service, controlled dormitory access.

Athletics Member NCAA. All Division I.

Standardized Tests *Required:* SAT or ACT (for admission), ACCUPLACER (for admission).

Costs (2010–11) *Tuition:* state resident $4235 full-time, $176 per credit hour part-time; nonresident $11,676 full-time, $430 per credit hour part-time. Full-time tuition and fees vary according to course load. Part-time tuition and fees vary according to course load. *Required fees:* $2070 full-time, $43 per term part-time. *Room and board:* $7458; room only: $4008. Room and board charges vary according to board plan and housing facility. *Payment plans:* installment, deferred payment.

Financial Aid *Of all full-time matriculated undergraduates who enrolled in 2008,* 3,162 applied for aid, 2,846 were judged to have need, 1,579 had their need fully met. 156 Federal Work-Study jobs (averaging $1757). *In 2008,* 359 non-need-based awards were made. *Average percent of need met:* 84. *Average financial aid package:* $13,352. *Average need-based loan:* $4875. *Average need-based gift aid:* $7125. *Average non-need-based aid:* $2839. *Average indebtedness upon graduation:* $8500.

Applying *Options:* electronic application, early admission, early action, deferred entrance. *Application fee:* $25. *Required:* essay or personal statement, high school transcript, minimum 2.5 GPA, 2 letters of recommendation. *Recommended:* interview.

Freshman Application Contact University of Maryland Eastern Shore, Princess Anne, MD 21853-1299. *Phone:* 410-651-6410. *Web site:* http://www.umes.edu/.

University of Maryland University College
Adelphi, Maryland

- **State-supported** comprehensive, founded 1947, part of University System of Maryland
- **Suburban** campus with easy access to Washington, D.C.
- **Coed** 25,686 undergraduate students, 14% full-time, 55% women, 45% men
- **Noncompetitive** entrance level, 100% of applicants were admitted

Undergraduates 3,649 full-time, 22,037 part-time. Students come from 55 states and territories; 27 other countries; 39% are from out of state; 32% Black or African American, non-Hispanic/Latino; 7% Hispanic/Latino; 4% Asian, non-Hispanic/Latino; 0.2% Native Hawaiian or other Pacific Islander, non-Hispanic/Latino; 0.6% American Indian or Alaska Native, non-Hispanic/Latino; 1% Two or more races, non-Hispanic/Latino; 12% Race/ethnicity unknown; 1% international; 15% transferred in.

Freshmen *Admission:* 2,578 applied, 2,578 admitted, 1,027 enrolled.

Faculty *Total:* 2,193, 10% full-time, 69% with terminal degrees. *Student/faculty ratio:* 18:1.

Academics *Calendar:* semesters. *Degrees:* certificates, associate, bachelor's, master's, doctoral-professional, post-master's, and postbachelor's certificates (offers primarily part-time evening and weekend degree programs at more than 30 off-campus locations in Maryland and the Washington, DC area, and more than 180 military communities in Europe and Asia with military enrollment not reflected in this profile; associate of arts program available to military students only). *Special study options:* accelerated degree program, advanced placement credit, cooperative education, distance learning, double majors, external degree program, independent study, off-campus study, part-time degree program, services for LD students, summer session for credit.

Computers on Campus 281 computers/terminals are available on campus for general student use. Students can access the following: computer help desk, online (class) grades, online (class) registration, online (class) schedules. Campuswide network is available. Wireless service is available via entire campus.

Student Life *Housing:* college housing not available. *Campus security:* 24-hour emergency response devices and patrols, late-night transport/escort service.

Costs (2010–11) *Tuition:* state resident $5688 full-time, $237 per credit hour part-time; nonresident $11,976 full-time, $499 per credit hour part-time. *Required fees:* $312 full-time, $13 per credit hour part-time. *Payment plan:* installment. *Waivers:* senior citizens and employees or children of employees.

Financial Aid Of all full-time matriculated undergraduates who enrolled in 2008, 2,303 applied for aid, 2,180 were judged to have need, 20 had their need fully met. *Average percent of need met:* 28%. *Average financial aid package:* $7206. *Average need-based loan:* $4269. *Average need-based gift aid:* $4578.

Applying *Options:* electronic application, deferred entrance. *Application fee:* $50. *Required:* high school transcript. *Application deadlines:* rolling (freshmen), rolling (transfers). *Notification:* continuous (freshmen), continuous (transfers).

Freshman Application Contact University of Maryland University College, 3501 University Boulevard East, Adelphi, MD 20783. *Phone:* 800-888-UMUC (8682). *Toll-free phone:* 800-888-8682. *E-mail:* enroll@umuc.edu. *Web site:* http://www.umuc.edu/.

University of Phoenix–Maryland Campus
Columbia, Maryland

Freshman Application Contact Ms. Audra McQuarie, Registrar/Executive Director, University of Phoenix–Maryland Campus, 4035 South Riverpoint Parkway, Mail Stop CF-L101, Phoenix, AZ 85040. *Phone:* 480-557-6151. *Toll-free phone:* 800-776-4867 (in-state); 800-228-7240 (out-of-state). *Fax:* 480-643-3068. *E-mail:* audra.mcquarie@phoenix.edu. *Web site:* http://www.phoenix.edu/.

Washington Adventist University

Takoma Park, Maryland

- **Independent Seventh-day Adventist** comprehensive, founded 1904
- **Suburban** 19-acre campus with easy access to Washington, D.C.
- **Coed** 1,173 undergraduate students, 79% full-time, 68% women, 32% men
- **Moderately difficult** entrance level, 37% of applicants were admitted

Undergraduates 926 full-time, 247 part-time. 34% are from out of state; 44% Black or African American, non-Hispanic/Latino; 8% Hispanic/Latino; 4% Asian, non-Hispanic/Latino; 36% Race/ethnicity unknown. *Retention:* 69% of full-time freshmen returned.

Freshmen *Admission:* 1,039 applied, 389 admitted, 123 enrolled.

Faculty *Total:* 108, 44% full-time, 23% with terminal degrees. *Student/faculty ratio:* 15:1.

Academics *Calendar:* semesters. *Degrees:* associate, bachelor's, and master's. *Special study options:* academic remediation for entering students, accelerated degree program, adult/continuing education programs, advanced placement credit, cooperative education, distance learning, double majors, English as a second language, external degree program, honors programs, independent study, internships, off-campus study, part-time degree program, services for LD students, student-designed majors, study abroad, summer session for credit. *Unusual degree programs:* 3-2 engineering with University of Maryland College Park, Walla Walla College; social work with Andrews University.

Computers on Campus Students can access the following: campus intranet, free student e-mail accounts, online (class) grades. Campuswide network is available. Wireless service is available via entire campus.

Student Life *Housing options:* men-only, women-only. Campus housing is university owned. Freshman campus housing is guaranteed. *Activities and organizations:* student-run newspaper, radio station, choral group. *Campus security:* 24-hour emergency response devices and patrols, late-night transport/escort service. *Student services:* health clinic, personal/psychological counseling.

Athletics Member NCAA. All Division II. *Intercollegiate sports:* baseball M(s), basketball M(s)/W(s), cross-country running M(s)/W(s), soccer M(s)/W(s), softball W(s), track and field M(s)/W(s). *Intramural sports:* basketball M/W, cross-country running M/W, football M, golf M, gymnastics M/W, racquetball M/W, soccer M/W, track and field M/W.

Standardized Tests *Required:* SAT or ACT (for admission).

Costs (2010–11) *Comprehensive fee:* $27,710 includes full-time tuition ($18,900), mandatory fees ($1280), and room and board ($7530). Part-time tuition: $760 per credit hour. Part-time tuition and fees vary according to class time and course load. *Required fees:* $433 per term part-time. *Payment plan:* installment. *Waivers:* senior citizens and employees or children of employees.

Financial Aid *Average indebtedness upon graduation:* $16,225.

Applying *Options:* electronic application, early admission, deferred entrance. *Application fee:* $25. *Required:* essay or personal statement, high school transcript, minimum 2.5 GPA, 2 letters of recommendation. *Required for some:* interview. *Application deadlines:* 8/1 (freshmen), 8/1 (transfers). *Notification:* continuous (freshmen), continuous (transfers).

Freshman Application Contact Elaine Oliver, Associate Vice President, Enrollment Services, Washington Adventist University, 7600 Flower Avenue, Takoma Park, MD 20912. *Phone:* 301-891-4502. *Toll-free phone:* 800-835-4212. *Fax:* 301-971-4230. *E-mail:* enroll@cuc.edu. *Web site:* http://www.wau.edu/.

Washington Bible College

Lanham, Maryland

Freshman Application Contact Mr. Mark D. Johnson, Director of Admissions, Washington Bible College, 6511 Princess Garden Parkway, Lanham, MD 20706-3599. *Phone:* 877-793-7227. *Toll-free phone:* 877-793-7227 Ext. 1212. *Fax:* 301-552-2775. *E-mail:* admissions@bible.edu. *Web site:* http://www.bible.edu/.

Washington College

Chestertown, Maryland

- **Independent** comprehensive, founded 1782
- **Small-town** 140-acre campus with easy access to Baltimore and Washington, D.C.
- **Endowment** $144.4 million
- **Coed** 1,418 undergraduate students, 98% full-time, 58% women, 42% men
- **Moderately difficult** entrance level, 74% of applicants were admitted

Undergraduates 1,396 full-time, 22 part-time. Students come from 35 states and territories; 22 other countries; 47% are from out of state; 5% Black or Afri-

can American, non-Hispanic/Latino; 2% Hispanic/Latino; 2% Asian, non-Hispanic/Latino; 0.1% Native Hawaiian or other Pacific Islander, non-Hispanic/Latino; 0.3% American Indian or Alaska Native, non-Hispanic/Latino; 0.6% Two or more races, non-Hispanic/Latino; 3% Race/ethnicity unknown; 3% international; 2% transferred in; 86% live on campus. *Retention:* 85% of full-time freshmen returned.

Freshmen *Admission:* 3,980 applied, 2,961 admitted, 421 enrolled. *Average high school GPA:* 3.45. *Test scores:* SAT critical reading scores over 500: 91%; SAT math scores over 500: 90%; SAT writing scores over 500: 86%; ACT scores over 18: 100%; SAT critical reading scores over 600: 38%; SAT math scores over 600: 37%; SAT writing scores over 600: 36%; ACT scores over 24: 57%; SAT critical reading scores over 700: 7%; SAT math scores over 700: 5%; SAT writing scores over 700: 6%; ACT scores over 30: 6%.

Faculty *Total:* 155, 61% full-time, 69% with terminal degrees. *Student/faculty ratio:* 13:1.

Academics *Calendar:* semesters. *Degrees:* bachelor's and master's. *Special study options:* advanced placement credit, double majors, English as a second language, honors programs, independent study, internships, off-campus study, part-time degree program, services for LD students, student-designed majors, study abroad. *Unusual degree programs:* 3-2 engineering with University of Maryland, College Park; nursing with Johns Hopkins University.

Computers on Campus 100 computers/terminals and 225 ports are available on campus for general student use. Students can access the following: campus intranet, computer help desk, free student e-mail accounts, online (class) grades, online (class) registration, online (class) schedules, thousands of wireless addresses available for students. Campuswide network is available. 100% of college-owned or -operated housing units are wired for high-speed Internet access. Wireless service is available via entire campus.

Student Life *Housing:* on-campus residence required through sophomore year. *Options:* coed, men-only, women-only, disabled students. Campus housing is university owned. Freshman campus housing is guaranteed. *Activities and organizations:* drama/theater group, student-run newspaper, radio station, choral group, Writers Union, Student Government Association, Hands Out, Omicron Delta Kappa, Dale Adams Society, national fraternities, national sororities. *Campus security:* 24-hour emergency response devices and patrols, student patrols, late-night transport/escort service, controlled dormitory access. *Student services:* health clinic, personal/psychological counseling.

Athletics Member NCAA. All Division III. *Intercollegiate sports:* baseball M, basketball M/W, cheerleading W(c), crew M/W, equestrian sports M(c)/W(c), field hockey W, ice hockey M(c), lacrosse M/W, rugby M(c)/W(c), sailing M/W, soccer M/W, softball W, swimming and diving M/W, tennis M/W, volleyball W, water polo M(c)/W(c). *Intramural sports:* basketball M/W, football M/W, lacrosse M(c), racquetball M/W, rugby M/W, sailing M/W, soccer M/W, squash M/W, table tennis M/W, tennis M/W, ultimate Frisbee M/W.

Standardized Tests *Required:* SAT or ACT (for admission).

Costs (2010–11) *Comprehensive fee:* $44,572 includes full-time tuition ($36,078), mandatory fees ($660), and room and board ($7834). Part-time tuition: $6012 per course. Part-time tuition and fees vary according to course load. *College room only:* $3980. Room and board charges vary according to board plan, housing facility, and location. *Payment plan:* installment. *Waivers:* employees or children of employees.

Financial Aid Of all full-time matriculated undergraduates who enrolled in 2008, 785 applied for aid, 637 were judged to have need, 308 had their need fully met. 290 Federal Work-Study jobs (averaging $2000). In 2008, 366 non-need-based awards were made. *Average percent of need met:* 82%. *Average financial aid package:* $22,219. *Average need-based loan:* $3650. *Average need-based gift aid:* $17,417. *Average non-need-based aid:* $12,437. *Average indebtedness upon graduation:* $20,611.

Applying *Options:* electronic application, early admission, early decision, early action, deferred entrance. *Application fee:* $55. *Required:* essay or personal statement, high school transcript, 1 letter of recommendation. *Required for some:* interview. *Recommended:* interview. *Application deadlines:* 3/1 (freshmen), 7/15 (transfers), 11/15 (early action). *Early decision deadline:* 11/1. *Notification:* continuous (freshmen), continuous (transfers), 12/1 (early decision), 12/15 (early action).

Freshman Application Contact Mr. Kevin Coveney, Vice President for Admissions and Enrollment Management, Washington College, 300 Washington Avenue, Chesterton, MD 21620. *Phone:* 410-778-7700. *Toll-free phone:* 800-422-1782. *Fax:* 410-778-7287. *E-mail:* admissions_office@washcoll.edu. *Web site:* http://www.washcoll.edu/.

Yeshiva College of the Nation's Capital

Silver Spring, Maryland

Admissions Office Contact Yeshiva College of the Nation's Capital, 1216 Arcola Avenue, Silver Spring, MD 20902. *Web site:* http://www.yeshiva.edu/.

MASSACHUSETTS

American International College
Springfield, Massachusetts

- **Independent** comprehensive, founded 1885
- **Urban** 58-acre campus
- **Endowment** $5.3 million
- **Coed**
- **Moderately difficult** entrance level

Faculty *Student/faculty ratio:* 15:1.

Academics *Calendar:* semesters. *Degrees:* associate, bachelor's, master's, doctoral-professional, doctoral-research/scholarship, and post-master's certificates.

Student Life *Campus security:* 24-hour emergency response devices and patrols, student patrols, late-night transport/escort service, controlled dormitory access.

Athletics Member NCAA. All Division II except ice hockey (Division I).

Standardized Tests *Required:* SAT or ACT (for admission).

Costs (2010–11) *Comprehensive fee:* $38,465 includes full-time tuition ($26,700), mandatory fees ($835), and room and board ($10,930). *Room and board:* Room and board charges vary according to board plan. *Payment plans:* tuition prepayment, installment.

Financial Aid *Of all full-time matriculated undergraduates who enrolled in 2009,* 1,403 applied for aid, 1,344 were judged to have need, 158 had their need fully met. *In 2009,* 153 non-need-based awards were made. *Average percent of need met:* 68. *Average financial aid package:* $21,229. *Average need-based loan:* $4178. *Average need-based gift aid:* $17,033. *Average non-need-based aid:* $10,928. *Average indebtedness upon graduation:* $25,693.

Applying *Options:* electronic application, early admission, deferred entrance. *Application fee:* $25. *Required:* high school transcript, minimum 2.5 GPA, 1 letter of recommendation. *Required for some:* interview. *Recommended:* essay or personal statement, interview.

Freshman Application Contact Miss Kim LaBlanc, Director of Freshman Admissions, American International College, 1000 State Street, Springfield,

MA 01109-3189. *Phone:* 413-205-3275. *Fax:* 413-205-3051. *E-mail:* kim.lablanc@aic.edu. *Web site:* http://www.aic.edu/.

See page 992 for the College Close-Up.

Amherst College
Amherst, Massachusetts

- **Independent** 4-year, founded 1821
- **Small-town** 1020-acre campus
- **Endowment** $1.4 billion
- **Coed** 1,795 undergraduate students, 100% full-time, 51% women, 49% men
- **Most difficult** entrance level, 15% of applicants were admitted

Undergraduates 1,795 full-time. Students come from 34 states and territories; 23 other countries; 89% are from out of state; 12% Black or African American, non-Hispanic/Latino; 12% Hispanic/Latino; 11% Asian, non-Hispanic/Latino; 7% Two or more races, non-Hispanic/Latino; 7% Race/ethnicity unknown; 9% international; 1% transferred in; 97% live on campus. *Retention:* 94% of full-time freshmen returned.

Freshmen *Admission:* 8,099 applied, 1,240 admitted, 490 enrolled. *Test scores:* SAT critical reading scores over 500: 100%; SAT math scores over 500: 100%; SAT writing scores over 500: 100%; ACT scores over 18: 100%; SAT critical reading scores over 600: 95%; SAT math scores over 600: 94%; SAT writing scores over 600: 93%; ACT scores over 24: 100%; SAT critical reading scores over 700: 64%; SAT math scores over 700: 63%; SAT writing scores over 700: 68%; ACT scores over 30: 77%.

Faculty *Total:* 236, 83% full-time, 98% with terminal degrees. *Student/faculty ratio:* 8:1.

Academics *Calendar:* semesters. *Degree:* bachelor's. *Special study options:* double majors, honors programs, independent study, off-campus study, student-designed majors, study abroad. *ROTC:* Army (c), Air Force (c).

Computers on Campus 182 computers/terminals are available on campus for general student use. Students can access the following: campus intranet, computer help desk, free student e-mail accounts, online (class) grades, online (class) schedules. Campuswide network is available. 100% of college-owned or -operated housing units are wired for high-speed Internet access. Wireless service is available via entire campus.

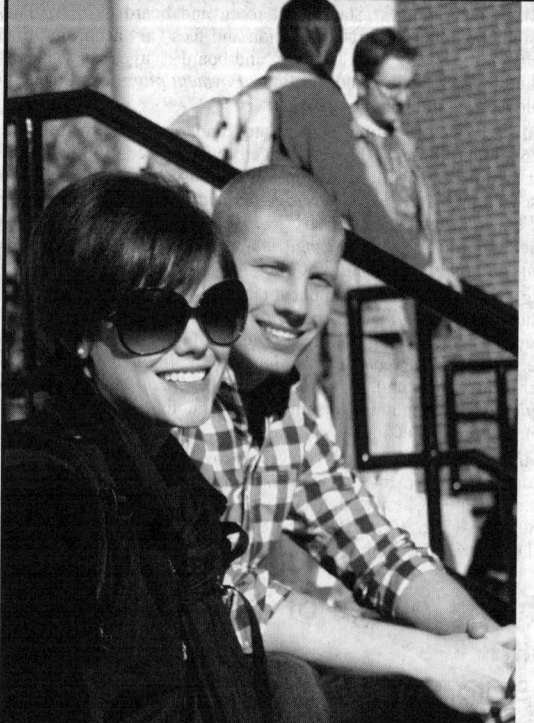

Student Life *Housing:* on-campus residence required for freshman year. *Options:* coed, cooperative, disabled students. Campus housing is university owned. Freshman campus housing is guaranteed. *Activities and organizations:* drama/theater group, student-run newspaper, radio station, choral group, choral groups, WAMH (campus radio station), OUTREACH (community service), literary magazines, The Amherst Student (school newspaper). *Campus security:* 24-hour emergency response devices and patrols, student patrols, late-night transport/escort service, controlled dormitory access. *Student services:* health clinic, personal/psychological counseling, women's center.

Athletics Member NCAA. All Division III. *Intercollegiate sports:* baseball M, basketball M/W, crew M(c)/W(c), cross-country running M/W, equestrian sports M(c)/W(c), fencing M(c)/W(c), field hockey W, football M, golf M/W, ice hockey M/W, lacrosse M/W, rugby M(c)/W(c), sailing M(c)/W(c), skiing (downhill) M(c)/W(c), soccer M/W, softball W, squash M/W, swimming and diving M/W, tennis M/W, track and field M/W, ultimate Frisbee M(c)/W(c), volleyball M(c)/W, water polo M(c)/W(c), wrestling M(c)/W(c). *Intramural sports:* badminton M/W, basketball M/W, golf M/W, ice hockey M/W, soccer M/W, softball M/W, squash M/W, table tennis M/W, tennis M/W, track and field M/W, volleyball M/W.

Standardized Tests *Required:* SAT and SAT Subject Tests or ACT (for admission).

Costs (2011–12) *Comprehensive fee:* $51,522 includes full-time tuition ($40,160), mandatory fees ($702), and room and board ($10,660). *College room only:* $5780. *Payment plans:* installment, deferred payment.

Financial Aid Of all full-time matriculated undergraduates who enrolled in 2009, 1,202 applied for aid, 1,081 were judged to have need, 1,081 had their need fully met. 590 Federal Work-Study jobs (averaging $1609). 262 state and other part-time jobs (averaging $1580). *Average percent of need met:* 100%. *Average financial aid package:* $40,087. *Average need-based loan:* $2977. *Average need-based gift aid:* $39,675. *Average indebtedness upon graduation:* $12,843.

Applying *Options:* electronic application, early admission, early decision, deferred entrance. *Application fee:* $60. *Required:* essay or personal statement, high school transcript, 3 letters of recommendation. *Application deadlines:* 1/1 (freshmen), 2/1 (transfers). *Early decision deadline:* 11/15. *Notification:* 4/5 (freshmen), 6/1 (transfers), 12/15 (early decision). **Freshman Application Contact** Mr. Thomas H. Parker, Dean of Admission and Financial Aid, Amherst College, PO Box 5000, Amherst, MA 01002-5000. *Phone:* 413-542-2328. *Fax:* 413-542-2040. *E-mail:* admission@amherst.edu. *Web site:* http://www.amherst.edu/.

Anna Maria College
Paxton, Massachusetts

- **Independent Roman Catholic** comprehensive, founded 1946
- **Rural** 180-acre campus with easy access to Boston
- **Endowment** $3.1 million
- **Coed** 1,100 undergraduate students, 81% full-time, 51% women, 49% men
- **Minimally difficult** entrance level, 63% of applicants were admitted

Undergraduates 888 full-time, 212 part-time. Students come from 15 states and territories; 17% are from out of state; 7% Black or African American, non-Hispanic/Latino; 8% Hispanic/Latino; 0.7% Asian, non-Hispanic/Latino; 0.5% American Indian or Alaska Native, non-Hispanic/Latino; 0.5% Two or more races, non-Hispanic/Latino; 15% Race/ethnicity unknown; 0.1% international; 6% transferred in; 48% live on campus. *Retention:* 54% of full-time freshmen returned.

Freshmen *Admission:* 2,672 applied, 1,695 admitted, 288 enrolled. *Average high school GPA:* 2.69. *Test scores:* SAT critical reading scores over 500: 25%; SAT math scores over 500: 26%; SAT writing scores over 500: 21%; ACT scores over 18: 50%; SAT critical reading scores over 600: 4%; SAT math scores over 600: 4%; SAT writing scores over 600: 5%; ACT scores over 24: 13%; ACT scores over 30: 3%.

Faculty *Total:* 221, 23% full-time, 28% with terminal degrees. *Student/faculty ratio:* 12:1.

Academics *Calendar:* semesters. *Degrees:* certificates, associate, bachelor's, master's, post-master's, and postbachelor's certificates. *Special study options:* academic remediation for entering students, accelerated degree program, adult/continuing education programs, advanced placement credit, cooperative education, distance learning, double majors, honors programs, independent study, internships, off-campus study, part-time degree program, services for LD students, student-designed majors, study abroad, summer session for credit. *ROTC:* Air Force (c).

Computers on Campus 94 computers/terminals are available on campus for general student use. Students can access the following: campus intranet, computer help desk, free student e-mail accounts, online (class) grades, online (class) registration, online (class) schedules, student account information. Campuswide network is available. 100% of college-owned or -operated hous-

ing units are wired for high-speed Internet access. Wireless service is available via entire campus.

Student Life *Housing options:* coed, disabled students. Campus housing is university owned. Freshman campus housing is guaranteed. *Activities and organizations:* drama/theater group, choral group, marching band, Habitat for Humanity, Social Action Group, Chorus Club, Alana, Programming Board - AMCAB. *Campus security:* 24-hour emergency response devices and patrols, late-night transport/escort service, controlled dormitory access. *Student services:* health clinic, personal/psychological counseling.

Athletics Member NCAA. All Division III. *Intercollegiate sports:* baseball M, basketball M/W, cross-country running M, field hockey W, football M, golf M, lacrosse M/W, soccer M/W, softball W, tennis M/W, volleyball W. *Intramural sports:* basketball M/W, football M, soccer M/W, softball M/W, volleyball M/W.

Standardized Tests *Required:* SAT or ACT (for admission).

Costs (2011–12) *Tuition:* $318 per credit hour part-time. Full-time tuition and fees vary according to course load and program. Part-time tuition and fees vary according to class time, course load, and program. *Required fees:* $100 per credit hour part-time. *Room only:* Room and board charges vary according to board plan and housing facility. *Payment plan:* installment. *Waivers:* senior citizens and employees or children of employees.

Financial Aid Of all full-time matriculated undergraduates who enrolled in 2008, 1,001 applied for aid, 932 were judged to have need, 106 had their need fully met. 215 Federal Work-Study jobs (averaging $454). In 2008, 59 non-need-based awards were made. *Average percent of need met:* 92%. *Average financial aid package:* $28,535. *Average need-based loan:* $4744. *Average need-based gift aid:* $5862. *Average non-need-based aid:* $7300. *Average indebtedness upon graduation:* $36,200.

Applying *Options:* electronic application, deferred entrance. *Application fee:* $40. *Required:* high school transcript, minimum 2 GPA. *Required for some:* essay or personal statement, audition for music programs, portfolio for art programs. *Recommended:* 1 letter of recommendation, interview. *Application deadlines:* rolling (freshmen), rolling (transfers). *Notification:* continuous (freshmen), continuous (transfers).

Freshman Application Contact Ms. Meghan McDonough, Director of Admissions, Anna Maria College, Box O, Sunset Lane, Paxton, MA 01612. *Phone:* 508-849-3586. *Toll-free phone:* 800-344-4586 Ext. 360. *Fax:* 508-849-3362. *E-mail:* admissions@annamaria.edu. *Web site:* http://www.annamaria.edu/.

The Art Institute of Boston at Lesley University
Boston, Massachusetts

- **Independent** comprehensive, founded 1912, administratively affiliated with Lesley University
- **Urban** 1-acre campus
- **Coed** 1,377 undergraduate students, 96% full-time, 76% women, 24% men
- **67% of applicants were admitted**

Undergraduates 1,327 full-time, 50 part-time. 44% are from out of state; 54% live on campus. *Retention:* 75% of full-time freshmen returned.

Freshmen *Admission:* 2,611 applied, 1,754 admitted. *Average high school GPA:* 2.9. *Test scores:* SAT critical reading scores over 500: 68%; SAT math scores over 500: 61%; SAT writing scores over 500: 66%; ACT scores over 18: 94%; SAT critical reading scores over 600: 26%; SAT math scores over 600: 20%; SAT writing scores over 600: 26%; ACT scores over 24: 41%; SAT critical reading scores over 700: 4%; SAT math scores over 700: 1%; SAT writing scores over 700: 3%; ACT scores over 30: 9%.

Faculty *Total:* 258, 28% full-time, 41% with terminal degrees. *Student/faculty ratio:* 10:1.

Academics *Calendar:* semesters. *Degrees:* associate, bachelor's, master's, doctoral-research/scholarship, post-master's, and postbachelor's certificates. *Special study options:* academic remediation for entering students, accelerated degree program, adult/continuing education programs, advanced placement credit, distance learning, double majors, English as a second language, external degree program, freshman honors college, honors programs, independent study, internships, off-campus study, part-time degree program, services for LD students, student-designed majors, study abroad, summer session for credit.

Computers on Campus Students can access the following: free student e-mail accounts, online (class) registration. Campuswide network is available. Wireless service is available via classrooms, student centers.

Student Life *Housing options:* coed, women-only. Campus housing is university owned and leased by the school. Freshman applicants given priority for college housing. *Activities and organizations:* drama/theater group, choral group. *Campus security:* 24-hour emergency response devices and patrols, late-night transport/escort service, controlled dormitory access. *Student services:* health clinic, personal/psychological counseling.

Athletics Member NCAA. All Division III. *Intercollegiate sports:* baseball M, basketball M/W, cross-country running M/W, soccer M/W, softball W, volleyball M/W. *Intramural sports:* swimming and diving M/W, tennis M.
Standardized Tests *Required:* SAT or ACT (for admission).
Costs (2010–11) *Comprehensive fee:* $40,400 includes full-time tuition ($26,850), mandatory fees ($750), and room and board ($12,800). *College room only:* $7950. Room and board charges vary according to housing facility. *Payment plan:* installment. *Waivers:* employees or children of employees.
Financial Aid Of all full-time matriculated undergraduates who enrolled in 2008, 1,070 applied for aid, 636 were judged to have need, 55 had their need fully met. 225 Federal Work-Study jobs (averaging $1800). 150 state and other part-time jobs (averaging $1500). In 2008, 234 non-need-based awards were made. *Average percent of need met:* 70%. *Average financial aid package:* $15,652. *Average need-based loan:* $3636. *Average need-based gift aid:* $13,218. *Average non-need-based aid:* $8439. *Average indebtedness upon graduation:* $17,000.
Applying *Options:* electronic application, early action, deferred entrance. *Application fee:* $40. *Required:* essay or personal statement, high school transcript. *Recommended:* interview. *Application deadlines:* rolling (freshmen), rolling (transfers). *Notification:* continuous (freshmen), continuous (transfers).
Freshman Application Contact The Art Institute of Boston at Lesley University, 700 Beacon Street, Boston, MA 02215-2598. *Phone:* 617-585-6710. *Toll-free phone:* 800-773-0494. *Web site:* http://www.aiboston.edu/.

Assumption College
Worcester, Massachusetts

- **Independent Roman Catholic** comprehensive, founded 1904
- **Suburban** 180-acre campus with easy access to Boston
- **Coed** 2,031 undergraduate students, 100% full-time, 59% women, 41% men
- **Moderately difficult** entrance level, 76% of applicants were admitted

Undergraduates 2,021 full-time, 10 part-time. 36% are from out of state; 3% Black or African American, non-Hispanic/Latino; 4% Hispanic/Latino; 2% Asian, non-Hispanic/Latino; 0.0% American Indian or Alaska Native, non-Hispanic/Latino; 0.8% Two or more races, non-Hispanic/Latino; 14% Race/ethnicity unknown; 0.7% international; 2% transferred in; 89% live on campus. *Retention:* 82% of full-time freshmen returned.
Freshmen *Admission:* 4,370 applied, 3,320 admitted, 590 enrolled. *Average high school GPA:* 3.51. *Test scores:* SAT critical reading scores over 500: 79%; SAT math scores over 500: 78%; ACT scores over 18: 97%; SAT critical reading scores over 600: 17%; SAT math scores over 600: 30%; ACT scores over 24: 44%; SAT critical reading scores over 700: 2%; SAT math scores over 700: 2%.
Faculty *Total:* 224, 69% full-time, 83% with terminal degrees. *Student/faculty ratio:* 11:1.
Academics *Calendar:* semesters. *Degrees:* bachelor's, master's, post-master's, and postbachelor's certificates. *Special study options:* advanced placement credit, double majors, honors programs, independent study, internships, off-campus study, part-time degree program, services for LD students, student-designed majors, study abroad, summer session for credit. *ROTC:* Army (c), Air Force (c). *Unusual degree programs:* 3-2 business administration; forestry with Duke University; nursing with Massachusetts College of Pharmacy and Health Sciences; special education, social rehabilitation counseling, school counseling; law with Duquesne Uni. School of Law; optometry with New England College of Optometry; osteopathic medicine with DesMoines Univ.; pharmacy and phys therapy with MA College of Pharmacy & Health Science; podiatry with Barry Univ.
Computers on Campus Students can access the following: campus intranet, computer help desk, free student e-mail accounts, online (class) grades, online (class) registration, online (class) schedules. Campuswide network is available. 100% of college-owned or -operated housing units are wired for high-speed Internet access. Wireless service is available via entire campus.
Student Life *Housing options:* coed, women-only, disabled students. Campus housing is university owned. Freshman campus housing is guaranteed. *Activities and organizations:* drama/theater group, student-run newspaper, television station, choral group. *Campus security:* 24-hour emergency response devices and patrols, student patrols, late-night transport/escort service, controlled dormitory access, front gate security, well-lit pathways. *Student services:* health clinic, personal/psychological counseling.
Athletics Member NCAA. All Division II. *Intercollegiate sports:* baseball M, basketball M(s)/W(s), crew W, cross-country running M/W, field hockey W, football M, golf M, ice hockey M, lacrosse M/W, soccer M/W, softball W, swimming and diving W, tennis M/W, track and field M/W, volleyball W. *Intramural sports:* basketball M/W, cheerleading M(c)/W(c), equestrian sports M(c)/W(c), football M, golf M/W, ice hockey M/W, racquetball M/W, soccer M/W, softball M/W, ultimate Frisbee M/W, volleyball M(c)/W(c).
Costs (2010–11) *Comprehensive fee:* $41,565 includes full-time tuition ($30,940), mandatory fees ($365), and room and board ($10,260). Full-time tuition and fees vary according to course load and reciprocity agreements. Part-

time tuition: $1031 per credit hour. Part-time tuition and fees vary according to course load. *Required fees:* $365 per year part-time. *College room only:* $6530. Room and board charges vary according to housing facility. *Waivers:* employees or children of employees.
Financial Aid Of all full-time matriculated undergraduates who enrolled in 2009, 1,846 applied for aid, 1,609 were judged to have need, 285 had their need fully met. 372 Federal Work-Study jobs (averaging $1663). In 2009, 400 non-need-based awards were made. *Average percent of need met:* 71%. *Average financial aid package:* $19,557. *Average need-based loan:* $4723. *Average need-based gift aid:* $15,334. *Average non-need-based aid:* $9517. *Average indebtedness upon graduation:* $24,382. *Financial aid deadline:* 2/15.
Applying *Options:* electronic application, early action, deferred entrance. *Application fee:* $50. *Required:* essay or personal statement, high school transcript, 1 letter of recommendation. *Recommended:* interview. *Application deadlines:* 2/15 (freshmen), 7/1 (transfers), 11/15 (early action). *Notification:* continuous until 5/1 (freshmen), continuous (transfers), 12/15 (early action).
Freshman Application Contact Ms. Kathleen Murphy, Dean of Enrollment, Assumption College, 500 Salisbury Street, Worcester, MA 01609-1296. *Phone:* 508-767-7110. *Toll-free phone:* 888-882-7786. *Fax:* 508-799-4412. *E-mail:* admiss@assumption.edu. *Web site:* http://www.assumption.edu/.

See page 1090 for the College Close-Up.

Atlantic Union College
South Lancaster, Massachusetts

- **Independent Seventh-day Adventist** comprehensive, founded 1882
- **Small-town** 314-acre campus with easy access to Boston
- **Coed** 490 undergraduate students, 84% full-time, 67% women, 33% men
- **Moderately difficult** entrance level, 49% of applicants were admitted

Undergraduates 411 full-time, 79 part-time. 13% transferred in; 53% live on campus.
Freshmen *Admission:* 244 applied, 119 admitted, 102 enrolled. *Average high school GPA:* 2.75. *Test scores:* SAT critical reading scores over 500: 11%; SAT math scores over 500: 19%; SAT writing scores over 500: 7%; ACT scores over 18: 50%.
Academics *Calendar:* semesters. *Degrees:* certificates, associate, bachelor's, master's, and postbachelor's certificates. *Special study options:* academic remediation for entering students, adult/continuing education programs, advanced placement credit, cooperative education, English as a second language, external degree program, freshman honors college, honors programs, internships, part-time degree program, student-designed majors, study abroad, summer session for credit.
Computers on Campus Students can access the following: free student e-mail accounts, online (class) grades, online (class) registration, online (class) schedules. Campuswide network is available.
Student Life *Housing:* on-campus residence required through senior year. *Options:* coed, men-only, women-only. Campus housing is university owned. Freshman campus housing is guaranteed. *Activities and organizations:* drama/theater group, student-run newspaper, choral group. *Campus security:* 24-hour patrols, late-night transport/escort service. *Student services:* health clinic, personal/psychological counseling.
Athletics *Intramural sports:* basketball M/W, football M/W, golf M/W, rock climbing M/W, skiing (downhill) M/W, soccer M/W, softball M/W, volleyball M/W.
Standardized Tests *Recommended:* SAT and SAT Subject Tests or ACT (for admission).
Costs (2011–12) *Comprehensive fee:* $23,140 includes full-time tuition ($16,180), mandatory fees ($1710), and room and board ($5250). Full-time tuition and fees vary according to course load and program. Part-time tuition and fees vary according to class time, course load, and program. No tuition increase for student's term of enrollment. *Room and board:* Room and board charges vary according to board plan and housing facility. *Waivers:* senior citizens and employees or children of employees.
Financial Aid Of all full-time matriculated undergraduates who enrolled in 2009, 407 applied for aid, 379 were judged to have need, 40 had their need fully met. 221 Federal Work-Study jobs (averaging $686). 240 state and other part-time jobs (averaging $1989). In 2009, 45 non-need-based awards were made. *Average percent of need met:* 64%. *Average financial aid package:* $12,049. *Average need-based loan:* $4384. *Average need-based gift aid:* $6876. *Average non-need-based aid:* $2963. *Average indebtedness upon graduation:* $39,013.
Applying *Options:* electronic application. *Application fee:* $25. *Required:* high school transcript, minimum 2.2 GPA, 2 letters of recommendation. *Required for some:* essay or personal statement, interview. *Application deadline:* 8/1 (freshmen).
Freshman Application Contact Dr. Bordes Henry-Saturne, Director for Admissions, Atlantic Union College, PO Box 1000, South Lancaster, MA 01561-1000. *Phone:* 978-368-2239. *Toll-free phone:* 800-282-2030. *Fax:*

978-368-2015. *E-mail:* bordes.henry-saturne@auc.edu. *Web site:* http://www.auc.edu/.

Babson College
Wellesley, Massachusetts

- **Independent** comprehensive, founded 1919
- **Suburban** 370-acre campus with easy access to Boston
- **Endowment** $171.0 million
- **Coed**
- **Very difficult** entrance level

Faculty *Student/faculty ratio:* 13:1.

Academics *Calendar:* semesters. *Degrees:* bachelor's, master's, and post-master's certificates.

Student Life *Campus security:* 24-hour emergency response devices and patrols, late-night transport/escort service, controlled dormitory access.

Athletics Member NCAA. All Division III.

Standardized Tests *Required:* SAT or ACT (for admission).

Costs (2010–11) *Comprehensive fee:* $51,916 includes full-time tuition ($39,040) and room and board ($12,876). *College room only:* $8308. Room and board charges vary according to board plan and housing facility.

Financial Aid *Of all full-time matriculated undergraduates who enrolled in 2009,* 946 applied for aid, 884 were judged to have need, 400 had their need fully met. 697 Federal Work-Study jobs (averaging $1982). 8 state and other part-time jobs (averaging $2200). *In 2009,* 102 non-need-based awards were made. *Average percent of need met:* 94. *Average financial aid package:* $32,105. *Average need-based loan:* $3948. *Average need-based gift aid:* $27,950. *Average non-need-based aid:* $20,000. *Average indebtedness upon graduation:* $30,357. *Financial aid deadline:* 2/15.

Applying *Options:* electronic application, early decision, early action, deferred entrance. *Application fee:* $65. *Required:* essay or personal statement, high school transcript, 2 letters of recommendation. *Recommended:* interview.

Freshman Application Contact Ms. Adrienne Ramsey, Senior Assistant Director of Undergraduate Admission, Babson College, Lunder Undergraduate Admission Center, Babson Park, MA 02457-0310. *Phone:* 781-239-5522.

Toll-free phone: 800-488-3696. *Fax:* 781-239-4135. *E-mail:* ugradadmission@babson.edu. *Web site:* http://www.babson.edu/.

See page 1098 for the College Close-Up.

Bard College at Simon's Rock
Great Barrington, Massachusetts

- **Independent** 4-year, founded 1964, administratively affiliated with Bard College
- **Small-town** 210-acre campus with easy access to Boston and New York City
- **Endowment** $17.3 million
- **Coed** 380 undergraduate students, 97% full-time, 64% women, 36% men
- **Moderately difficult** entrance level, 80% of applicants were admitted

Undergraduates 369 full-time, 11 part-time. Students come from 40 states and territories; 14 other countries; 91% are from out of state; 8% Black or African American, non-Hispanic/Latino; 4% Hispanic/Latino; 4% Asian, non-Hispanic/Latino; 10% Two or more races, non-Hispanic/Latino; 11% Race/ethnicity unknown; 3% international; 90% live on campus. *Retention:* 75% of full-time freshmen returned.

Freshmen *Admission:* 322 applied, 259 admitted, 135 enrolled.

Faculty *Total:* 68, 62% full-time, 79% with terminal degrees. *Student/faculty ratio:* 8:1.

Academics *Calendar:* semesters. *Degrees:* associate and bachelor's. *Special study options:* cooperative education, double majors, independent study, internships, off-campus study, services for LD students, student-designed majors, study abroad. *Unusual degree programs:* 3-2 engineering with Columbia University, Dartmouth College.

Computers on Campus 80 computers/terminals and 200 ports are available on campus for general student use. Students can access the following: campus intranet, computer help desk, free student e-mail accounts, online (class) schedules. Campuswide network is available. 100% of college-owned or -operated housing units are wired for high-speed Internet access. Wireless service is available via classrooms, computer centers, computer labs, libraries, student centers.

Student Life *Housing:* on-campus residence required through junior year. *Options:* coed, men-only, women-only. Campus housing is university owned.

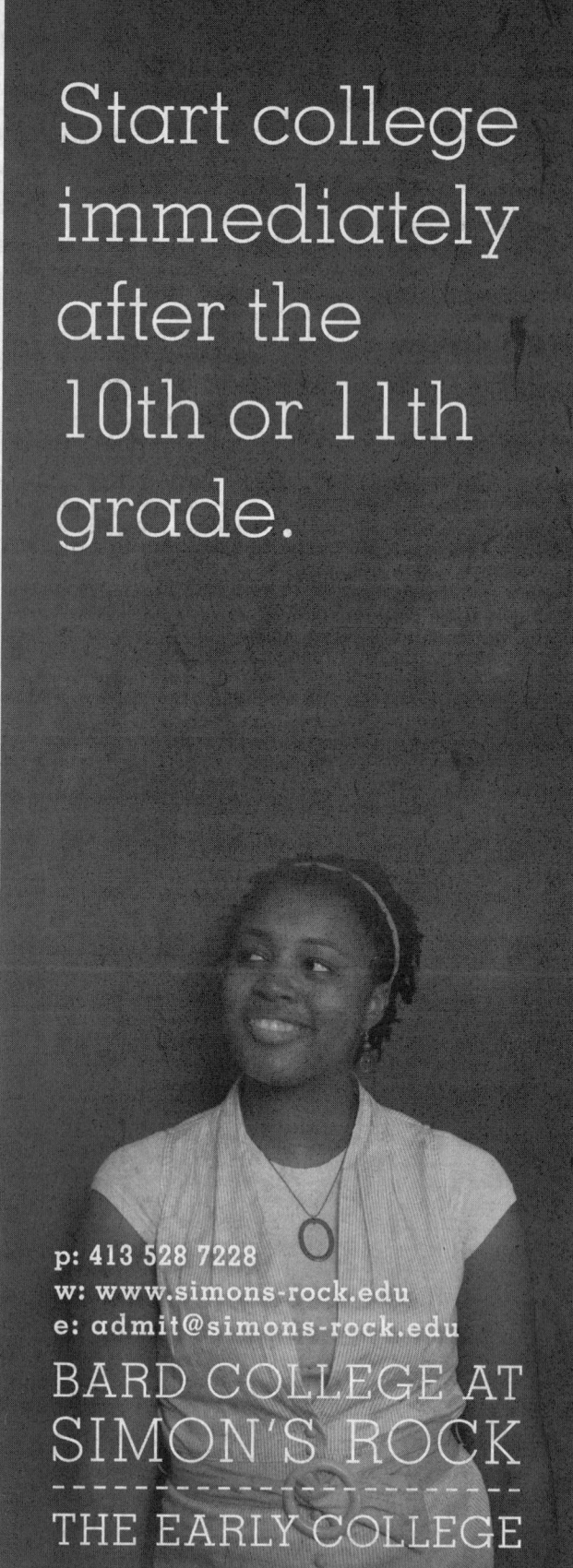

Freshman campus housing is guaranteed. *Activities and organizations:* drama/theater group, student-run newspaper, choral group, Black Student Union, QueerSA, Student Action Service Learning, U.S.O. (Untitled Student Organization), Boffing. *Campus security:* 24-hour patrols, controlled dormitory access. *Student services:* health clinic, personal/psychological counseling, women's center.

Athletics *Intercollegiate sports:* basketball M/W, soccer M/W, swimming and diving M/W. *Intramural sports:* archery M/W, racquetball M/W, rock climbing M/W, squash M/W, tennis M/W, ultimate Frisbee M/W, water polo M/W, weight lifting M/W.

Costs (2010–11) *One-time required fee:* $550. *Comprehensive fee:* $53,432 includes full-time tuition ($41,160), mandatory fees ($822), and room and board ($11,450). Full-time tuition and fees vary according to course load. Part-time tuition and fees vary according to course load. *Payment plan:* installment. *Waivers:* employees or children of employees.

Financial Aid Of all full-time matriculated undergraduates who enrolled in 2009, 301 applied for aid, 283 were judged to have need, 53 had their need fully met. 165 Federal Work-Study jobs (averaging $1000). In 2009, 69 non-need-based awards were made. *Average percent of need met:* 64%. *Average financial aid package:* $32,525. *Average need-based loan:* $4729. *Average need-based gift aid:* $17,947. *Average non-need-based aid:* $16,190. *Average indebtedness upon graduation:* $44,910.

Applying *Application fee:* $50. *Required:* essay or personal statement, high school transcript, 3 letters of recommendation, interview, school report, parent supplement. *Application deadlines:* rolling (freshmen), rolling (out-of-state freshmen), rolling (transfers). *Notification:* continuous (freshmen), continuous (transfers).

Freshman Application Contact Steven Coleman, Director of Admissions, Bard College at Simon's Rock, 84 Alford Road, Great Barrington, MA 01230-9702. *Phone:* 800-235-7186. *Toll-free phone:* 800-235-7186. *Fax:* 413-541-0081. *E-mail:* admit@simons-rock.edu. *Web site:* http://www.simons-rock.edu/.

See page 1102 for the College Close-Up.

Bay Path College
Longmeadow, Massachusetts

- **Independent** comprehensive, founded 1897
- **Suburban** 48-acre campus with easy access to Boston
- **Endowment** $18.7 million
- **Undergraduate: women only; graduate: coed**
- **Moderately difficult** entrance level

Faculty *Student/faculty ratio:* 15:1.

Academics *Calendar:* semesters. *Degrees:* certificates, bachelor's, master's, and postbachelor's certificates.

Student Life *Campus security:* 24-hour emergency response devices and patrols, late-night transport/escort service, controlled dormitory access.

Athletics Member NCAA. All Division III.

Standardized Tests *Required:* SAT or ACT (for admission).

Costs (2010–11) *Comprehensive fee:* $35,955 includes full-time tuition ($25,515) and room and board ($10,440). Part-time tuition: $470 per credit. *Room and board:* Room and board charges vary according to board plan.

Financial Aid *Of all full-time matriculated undergraduates who enrolled in 2004,* 858 applied for aid, 781 were judged to have need, 81 had their need fully met. 146 Federal Work-Study jobs (averaging $2000). *In 2004,* 119 non-need-based awards were made. *Average percent of need met:* 66. *Average financial aid package:* $11,453. *Average need-based loan:* $4045. *Average need-based gift aid:* $7465. *Average non-need-based aid:* $10,982. *Average indebtedness upon graduation:* $18,200.

Applying *Options:* electronic application, early admission, early action, deferred entrance. *Application fee:* $25. *Required:* high school transcript. *Required for some:* interview. *Recommended:* essay or personal statement, minimum 2.5 GPA, interview.

Freshman Application Contact Bay Path College, 588 Longmeadow Street, Longmeadow, MA 01106-2292. *Phone:* 413-565-1000 Ext. 1331. *Toll-free phone:* 800-782-7284 Ext. 1331. *Web site:* http://www.baypath.edu/.

Bay State College
Boston, Massachusetts

Freshman Application Contact Kim Olds, Director of Admissions, Bay State College, 122 Commonwealth Avenue, MA 02116. *Phone:* 617-217-9115. *Toll-free phone:* 800-81-LEARN. *Fax:* 617-536-1735. *E-mail:* admissions@baystate.edu. *Web site:* http://www.baystate.edu/.

See page 1112 for the College Close-Up.

Becker College
Worcester, Massachusetts

Freshman Application Contact Admissions Receptionist, Becker College, 61 Sever Street, Worcester, MA 01609. *Phone:* 508-373-9400. *Toll-free phone:* 877-5BECKER Ext. 245. *Fax:* 508-890-1500. *E-mail:* admissions@ beckercollege.edu. *Web site:* http://www.becker.edu/.

Benjamin Franklin Institute of Technology
Boston, Massachusetts

Freshman Application Contact Ms. Brittainy Johnson, Associate Director of Admissions, Benjamin Franklin Institute of Technology, Boston, MA 02116. *Phone:* 617-423-4630 Ext. 122. *Fax:* 617-482-3706. *E-mail:* bjohnson@ bfit.edu. *Web site:* http://www.bfit.edu/.

Bentley University
Waltham, Massachusetts

- **Independent** comprehensive, founded 1917
- **Suburban** 163-acre campus with easy access to Boston
- **Endowment** $173.6 million
- **Coed** 4,262 undergraduate students, 96% full-time, 41% women, 59% men
- **Very difficult** entrance level, 46% of applicants were admitted

Undergraduates 4,104 full-time, 158 part-time. Students come from 43 states and territories; 87 other countries; 52% are from out of state; 3% Black or African American, non-Hispanic/Latino; 6% Hispanic/Latino; 7% Asian, non-Hispanic/Latino; 1% Two or more races, non-Hispanic/Latino; 9% Race/ethnicity unknown; 11% international; 3% transferred in; 79% live on campus. *Retention:* 93% of full-time freshmen returned.

Freshmen *Admission:* 6,203 applied, 2,881 admitted, 962 enrolled. *Test scores:* SAT critical reading scores over 500: 90%; SAT math scores over 500: 97%; SAT writing scores over 500: 91%; ACT scores over 18: 100%; SAT critical reading scores over 600: 42%; SAT math scores over 600: 74%; SAT writing scores over 600: 45%; ACT scores over 24: 88%; SAT critical reading scores over 700: 4%; SAT math scores over 700: 15%; SAT writing scores over 700: 7%; ACT scores over 30: 12%.

Faculty *Total:* 471, 62% full-time, 65% with terminal degrees. *Student/faculty ratio:* 14:1.

Academics *Calendar:* semesters. *Degrees:* associate, bachelor's, master's, doctoral-research/scholarship, post-master's, and postbachelor's certificates. *Special study options:* accelerated degree program, adult/continuing education programs, advanced placement credit, double majors, honors programs, independent study, internships, off-campus study, part-time degree program, services for LD students, student-designed majors, study abroad, summer session for credit. *ROTC:* Army (c), Air Force (c).

Computers on Campus 4,523 computers/terminals and 10,752 ports are available on campus for general student use. Students can access the following: campus intranet, computer help desk, free student e-mail accounts, online (class) grades, online (class) registration, online (class) schedules, Grade checking, online admission, Blackboard, resume review, student employment, interlibrary loan, free software. Campuswide network is available. 100% of college-owned or -operated housing units are wired for high-speed Internet access. Wireless service is available via entire campus.

Student Life *Housing options:* coed, disabled students. Campus housing is university owned and leased by the school. Freshman campus housing is guaranteed. *Activities and organizations:* drama/theater group, student-run newspaper, radio and television station, choral group, Bentley Entrepreneurship Society, Campus Activities Board, Hall Council Advisory Board, Bentley Ultimate Society, National Association of Black Accountants, national fraternities, national sororities. *Campus security:* 24-hour emergency response devices and patrols, late-night transport/escort service, controlled dormitory access, Security cameras, Community Policing Team. *Student services:* health clinic, personal/psychological counseling, women's center.

Athletics Member NCAA. All Division II except ice hockey (Division I). *Intercollegiate sports:* baseball M, basketball M(s)/W(s), cross-country running M/W, field hockey W, football M, golf M, ice hockey M(s), lacrosse M(s)/W(s), soccer M/W, softball W, swimming and diving M/W, tennis M/W, track and field M/W, volleyball W. *Intramural sports:* basketball M/W, cheerleading W(c), football M, golf M(c)/W(c), racquetball M(c)/W(c), rugby M(c)/W(c), sailing M(c)/W(c), skiing (downhill) M(c)/W(c), soccer M/W, softball M/W, table tennis M(c)/W(c), ultimate Frisbee M/W, volleyball M/W, water polo M(c)/W(c), wrestling M(c).

Standardized Tests *Required:* SAT or ACT (for admission). *Required for some:* TOEFL or IELTS for students whose primary language is not English.

Costs (2011–12) *Comprehensive fee:* $50,848 includes full-time tuition ($36,840), mandatory fees ($1488), and room and board ($12,520). Part-time tuition: $1866 per course. Part-time tuition and fees vary according to class time and course load. *Required fees:* $45 per term part-time. *College room only:* $7530. Room and board charges vary according to board plan and housing facility. *Payment plan:* installment. *Waivers:* employees or children of employees.

Financial Aid Of all full-time matriculated undergraduates who enrolled in 2008, 2,619 applied for aid, 2,035 were judged to have need, 864 had their need fully met. 1,177 Federal Work-Study jobs (averaging $1458). 738 state and other part-time jobs (averaging $1918). In 2008, 601 non-need-based awards were made. *Average percent of need met:* 93%. *Average financial aid package:* $30,391. *Average need-based loan:* $5330. *Average need-based gift aid:* $23,502. *Average non-need-based aid:* $15,176. *Average indebtedness upon graduation:* $32,710. *Financial aid deadline:* 2/1.

Applying *Options:* electronic application, early admission, early decision, early action, deferred entrance. *Application fee:* $50. *Required:* essay or personal statement, high school transcript, 2 letters of recommendation. *Required for some:* interview. *Application deadlines:* 1/15 (freshmen), 1/15 (out-of-state freshmen), 11/15 (early action). *Early decision deadline:* 11/1. *Notification:* 4/1 (freshmen), 4/1 (out-of-state freshmen), 12/17 (early decision), 1/15 (early action).

Freshman Application Contact Admissions Office, Bentley University, 175 Forest Street, Waltham, MA 02452. *Phone:* 781-891-2244. *Toll-free phone:* 800-523-2354. *Fax:* 781-891-3414. *E-mail:* ugadmission@bentley.edu. *Web site:* http://www.bentley.edu/.

See page 1120 for the College Close-Up.

Berklee College of Music
Boston, Massachusetts

- **Independent** 4-year, founded 1945
- **Urban** campus
- **Coed**
- **Moderately difficult** entrance level

Faculty *Student/faculty ratio:* 12:1.

Academics *Calendar:* semesters. *Degree:* diplomas and bachelor's.

Student Life *Campus security:* 24-hour patrols.

Costs (2010–11) *Comprehensive fee:* $48,350 includes full-time tuition ($31,300), mandatory fees ($1220), and room and board ($15,830). Part-time tuition: $1100 per credit hour. *Payment plans:* tuition prepayment, deferred payment.

Financial Aid *Of all full-time matriculated undergraduates who enrolled in 2009,* 2,019 applied for aid, 1,779 were judged to have need, 119 had their need fully met. *In 2009,* 866 non-need-based awards were made. *Average percent of need met:* 36. *Average financial aid package:* $13,303. *Average need-based loan:* $5406. *Average need-based gift aid:* $5530. *Average non-need-based aid:* $10,667. *Financial aid deadline:* 5/1.

Applying *Options:* electronic application, early action, deferred entrance. *Application fee:* $150. *Required:* essay or personal statement, high school transcript, 2 letters of recommendation, interview, 2 years of formal music study and audition.

Freshman Application Contact Mr. Damien Bracken, Director of Admissions, Berklee College of Music, 1140 Boyleston Street, Boston, MA 02215-3693. *Phone:* 617-747-2222. *Toll-free phone:* 800-BERKLEE. *Fax:* 617-747-2047. *E-mail:* admissions@berklee.edu. *Web site:* http://www.berklee.edu/.

See page 1122 for the College Close-Up.

Boston Architectural College
Boston, Massachusetts

- **Independent** comprehensive, founded 1889
- **Urban** 1-acre campus
- **Endowment** $5.9 million
- **Coed** 615 undergraduate students, 98% full-time, 31% women, 69% men
- **Noncompetitive** entrance level, 100% of applicants were admitted

Undergraduates 600 full-time, 15 part-time. Students come from 35 states and territories; 4 other countries; 51% are from out of state; 7% Black or African American, non-Hispanic/Latino; 13% Hispanic/Latino; 6% Asian, non-Hispanic/Latino; 0.3% American Indian or Alaska Native, non-Hispanic/Latino; 2% Two or more races, non-Hispanic/Latino; 7% Race/ethnicity unknown; 31% transferred in. *Retention:* 49% of full-time freshmen returned.

Freshmen *Admission:* 100 applied, 100 admitted, 41 enrolled. *Average high school GPA:* 2.9.

Faculty *Total:* 229, 5% full-time, 26% with terminal degrees. *Student/faculty ratio:* 4:1.

Academics *Calendar:* semesters. *Degrees:* certificates, bachelor's, and master's. *Special study options:* adult/continuing education programs, advanced placement credit, distance learning, independent study, internships, off-campus study, summer session for credit.

Computers on Campus 63 computers/terminals are available on campus for general student use. Students can access the following: campus intranet, computer help desk, free student e-mail accounts, online (class) grades, online (class) registration, online (class) schedules. Campuswide network is available. Wireless service is available via entire campus.

Student Life *Activities and organizations:* Atelier, Student Government, American Institute of Architectural Students, BAC Interior Design Society (IIDA and ASID), National Organization of Minority Architecture Students (NOMAS), Student American Society of Landscape Architects (SASLA). *Campus security:* 24-hour emergency response devices and patrols, late-night transport/escort service, electronically operated building access and CCTV systems. *Student services:* personal/psychological counseling.

Costs (2010–11) *Tuition:* $16,128 full-time, $1344 per credit hour part-time. Full-time tuition and fees vary according to course load, degree level, program, and reciprocity agreements. Part-time tuition and fees vary according to course load, degree level, program, and reciprocity agreements. *Required fees:* $20 full-time, $10 per term part-time. *Payment plan:* installment. *Waivers:* employees or children of employees.

Financial Aid Of all full-time matriculated undergraduates who enrolled in 2009, 864 applied for aid, 794 were judged to have need, 17 had their need fully met. 45 Federal Work-Study jobs (averaging $3066). In 2009, 22 non-need-based awards were made. *Average percent of need met:* 26%. *Average financial aid package:* $9124. *Average need-based loan:* $4580. *Average need-based gift aid:* $5201. *Average non-need-based aid:* $3198. *Average indebtedness upon graduation:* $31,385.

Applying *Options:* electronic application. *Application fee:* $50. *Required:* essay or personal statement, high school transcript, resumes, creative exercise. *Recommended:* interview. *Application deadlines:* rolling (freshmen), rolling (out-of-state freshmen), rolling (transfers). *Notification:* continuous (freshmen), continuous (out-of-state freshmen), continuous (transfers).

Freshman Application Contact Richard Moyer, Director of Admission, Boston Architectural College, 320 Newbury Street, Boston, MA 02115-2795. *Phone:* 617-585-0256. *Toll-free phone:* 877-585-0100. *Fax:* 617-585-0121. *E-mail:* admissions@the-bac.edu. *Web site:* http://www.the-bac.edu/.

Boston Baptist College

Boston, Massachusetts

- **Independent Baptist** 4-year, founded 1976
- **Suburban** 8-acre campus with easy access to Boston and Providence
- **Coed** 110 undergraduate students, 92% full-time, 50% women, 50% men
- **Moderately difficult** entrance level, 47% of applicants were admitted

Undergraduates 101 full-time, 9 part-time. Students come from 21 states and territories; 3 other countries; 60% are from out of state; 8% transferred in; 65% live on campus. *Retention:* 77% of full-time freshmen returned.

Freshmen *Admission:* 108 applied, 51 admitted, 26 enrolled. *Average high school GPA:* 2.82.

Faculty *Total:* 21, 10% full-time, 38% with terminal degrees. *Student/faculty ratio:* 6:1.

Academics *Calendar:* semesters. *Degrees:* certificates, diplomas, associate, and bachelor's. *Special study options:* academic remediation for entering students, adult/continuing education programs, advanced placement credit, distance learning, honors programs, off-campus study, part-time degree program, summer session for credit.

Computers on Campus 10 computers/terminals and 10 ports are available on campus for general student use. Students can access the following: campus intranet, computer help desk, free student e-mail accounts, online (class) grades. Campuswide network is available. 100% of college-owned or -operated housing units are wired for high-speed Internet access. Wireless service is available via entire campus.

Student Life *Housing:* on-campus residence required through senior year. *Options:* men-only, women-only, disabled students. Campus housing is university owned. Freshman campus housing is guaranteed. *Activities and organizations:* choral group, Community Service Organization, Recruitment, Campus Life. *Campus security:* 24-hour emergency response devices, student patrols, late-night transport/escort service, controlled dormitory access. *Student services:* personal/psychological counseling.

Athletics *Intercollegiate sports:* basketball M.

Standardized Tests *Required:* SAT or ACT (for admission).

Costs (2011–12) *Comprehensive fee:* $18,760 includes full-time tuition ($9510), mandatory fees ($1500), and room and board ($7750). Part-time tuition: $391 per credit. *College room only:* $4600. Room and board charges vary according to board plan. *Payment plan:* installment.

Applying *Options:* electronic application, deferred entrance. *Application fee:* $50. *Required:* essay or personal statement, high school transcript, 1 letter of recommendation. *Recommended:* interview. *Application deadlines:* rolling

(freshmen), 3/15 (out-of-state freshmen), rolling (transfers). *Notification:* 4/15 (freshmen), 4/15 (out-of-state freshmen), 4/15 (transfers).

Freshman Application Contact Mrs. Karen Fox, Director of Admissions, Boston Baptist College, 950 Metropolitan Avenue, Boston, MA 02136. *Phone:* 617-364-3510 Ext. 217. *Toll-free phone:* 888-235-2014. *Fax:* 617-399-8220. *E-mail:* kfox@boston.edu. *Web site:* http://www.boston.edu/.

Boston College

Chestnut Hill, Massachusetts

- **Independent Roman Catholic (Jesuit)** university, founded 1863
- **Suburban** 328-acre campus with easy access to Boston
- **Endowment** $1.3 billion
- **Coed** 9,171 undergraduate students, 100% full-time, 52% women, 48% men
- **Very difficult** entrance level, 30% of applicants were admitted

Undergraduates 9,171 full-time. Students come from 54 states and territories; 60 other countries; 73% are from out of state; 5% Black or African American, non-Hispanic/Latino; 8% Hispanic/Latino; 10% Asian, non-Hispanic/Latino; 0.3% American Indian or Alaska Native, non-Hispanic/Latino; 6% Race/ethnicity unknown; 3% international; 2% transferred in; 80% live on campus. *Retention:* 95% of full-time freshmen returned.

Freshmen *Admission:* 29,289 applied, 8,804 admitted, 2,171 enrolled. *Test scores:* SAT critical reading scores over 500: 97%; SAT math scores over 500: 98%; SAT writing scores over 500: 97%; ACT scores over 18: 100%; SAT critical reading scores over 600: 82%; SAT math scores over 600: 87%; SAT writing scores over 600: 86%; ACT scores over 24: 96%; SAT critical reading scores over 700: 31%; SAT math scores over 700: 42%; SAT writing scores over 700: 39%; ACT scores over 30: 68%.

Faculty *Total:* 1,394, 52% full-time, 93% with terminal degrees. *Student/faculty ratio:* 13:1.

Academics *Calendar:* semesters. *Degrees:* bachelor's, master's, doctoral-other, doctoral-professional, doctoral-research/scholarship, and post-master's certificates (also offers continuing education program with significant enrollment not reflected in profile). *Special study options:* accelerated degree program, advanced placement credit, double majors, honors programs, independent study, internships, off-campus study, part-time degree program, services for LD students, student-designed majors, study abroad, summer session for credit. *ROTC:* Army (c), Navy (c), Air Force (c).

Computers on Campus 1,000 computers/terminals are available on campus for general student use. Students can access the following: campus intranet, computer help desk, free student e-mail accounts, online (class) grades, online (class) registration, online (class) schedules. Campuswide network is available. 100% of college-owned or -operated housing units are wired for high-speed Internet access. Wireless service is available via entire campus.

Student Life *Housing options:* coed, women-only. Campus housing is university owned. Freshman campus housing is guaranteed. *Activities and organizations:* drama/theater group, student-run newspaper, radio and television station, choral group, marching band, UGBC and individual School Senates, Asian Caucus, Appalachia Volunteers, Dance Marathon, 4Boston. *Campus security:* 24-hour emergency response devices and patrols, late-night transport/escort service, controlled dormitory access. *Student services:* health clinic, personal/psychological counseling, women's center.

Athletics Member NCAA. All Division I except football (Division I-A). *Intercollegiate sports:* baseball M(s), basketball M(s)/W(s), cheerleading M(c)/W(c), crew W(s), cross-country running M(s)/W(s), fencing M/W, field hockey W(s), golf M(s)/W(s), ice hockey M(s)/W(s), lacrosse W(s), sailing M/W, skiing (downhill) M/W, soccer M(s)/W(s), softball W(s), swimming and diving M(s)/W(s), tennis M(s)/W(s), track and field M(s)/W(s), volleyball W(s). *Intramural sports:* badminton M/W, basketball M(c)/W(c), crew M(c), cross-country running M(c)/W(c), equestrian sports M(c)/W(c), field hockey W(c), golf M(c)/W(c), ice hockey M/W, lacrosse M(c)/W(c), racquetball M/W, rugby M(c)/W(c), soccer M(c)/W(c), softball M/W, squash M/W, tennis M/W, track and field M(c)/W(c), ultimate Frisbee M(c)/W(c), volleyball M(c)/W, water polo M(c)/W(c).

Standardized Tests *Required:* SAT and SAT Subject Tests or ACT (for admission).

Costs (2010–11) *One-time required fee:* $430. *Comprehensive fee:* $52,624 includes full-time tuition ($39,880), mandatory fees ($662), and room and board ($12,082). *College room only:* $7450. Room and board charges vary according to housing facility. *Payment plan:* installment. *Waivers:* employees or children of employees.

Financial Aid Of all full-time matriculated undergraduates who enrolled in 2008, 4,421 applied for aid, 3,900 were judged to have need, 3,900 had their need fully met. 3,156 Federal Work-Study jobs (averaging $2143). In 2008, 184 non-need-based awards were made. *Average percent of need met:* 100%. *Average financial aid package:* $30,979. *Average need-based loan:* $4623. *Average need-based gift aid:* $26,556. *Average non-need-based aid:* $16,443. *Average indebtedness upon graduation:* $19,514.

Applying *Options:* electronic application, early admission, early action, deferred entrance. *Application fee:* $70. *Required:* essay or personal statement, high school transcript, 2 letters of recommendation. *Application deadlines:* 1/1 (freshmen), 3/15 (transfers), 11/1 (early action). *Notification:* 4/15 (freshmen), 6/1 (transfers), 12/25 (early action).
Freshman Application Contact Office of Undergraduate Admissions, Boston College, 140 Commonwealth Avenue, Devlin 208, Chestnut Hill, MA 02467-3809. *Phone:* 617-552-3100. *Toll-free phone:* 800-360-2522. *Fax:* 617-552-0798. *Web site:* http://www.bc.edu/.

See page 1126 for the College Close-Up.

The Boston Conservatory
Boston, Massachusetts

- **Independent** comprehensive, founded 1867
- **Urban** campus
- **Coed**
- **Moderately difficult** entrance level

Faculty *Student/faculty ratio:* 4:1.
Academics *Calendar:* semesters. *Degrees:* diplomas, bachelor's, master's, post-master's, and postbachelor's certificates.
Student Life *Campus security:* 24-hour emergency response devices and patrols, controlled dormitory access.
Standardized Tests *Required:* SAT or ACT (for admission).
Costs (2010–11) *Comprehensive fee:* $51,560 includes full-time tuition ($33,800), mandatory fees ($1710), and room and board ($16,050). Full-time tuition and fees vary according to course load, degree level, and program. Part-time tuition: $1400 per credit hour. Part-time tuition and fees vary according to course load, degree level, and program. *College room only:* $10,500. Room and board charges vary according to board plan and housing facility.
Financial Aid *Of all full-time matriculated undergraduates who enrolled in 2008,* 335 applied for aid, 293 were judged to have need, 23 had their need fully met. *In 2008,* 20 non-need-based awards were made. *Average percent of need met:* 0. *Average financial aid package:* $13,967. *Average need-based loan:* $4257. *Average need-based gift aid:* $12,772. *Average non-need-based aid:* $9235. *Average indebtedness upon graduation:* $34,931.
Applying *Options:* electronic application, deferred entrance. *Application fee:* $110. *Required:* essay or personal statement, high school transcript, minimum 2.7 GPA, 4 letters of recommendation, audition. *Required for some:* interview.
Freshman Application Contact The Boston Conservatory, 8 The Fenway, Boston, MA 02215. *Phone:* 617-912-9153. *Web site:* http://www.bostonconservatory.edu/.

Boston University
Boston, Massachusetts

- **Independent** university, founded 1839
- **Urban** 132-acre campus
- **Endowment** $1.0 billion
- **Coed** 18,714 undergraduate students, 92% full-time, 59% women, 41% men
- **Very difficult** entrance level, 58% of applicants were admitted

Undergraduates 17,266 full-time, 1,448 part-time. Students come from 52 states and territories; 104 other countries; 76% are from out of state; 3% Black or African American, non-Hispanic/Latino; 8% Hispanic/Latino; 15% Asian, non-Hispanic/Latino; 0.2% Native Hawaiian or other Pacific Islander, non-Hispanic/Latino; 0.2% American Indian or Alaska Native, non-Hispanic/Latino; 2% Two or more races, non-Hispanic/Latino; 9% Race/ethnicity unknown; 9% international; 1% transferred in; 66% live on campus. *Retention:* 91% of full-time freshmen returned.
Freshmen *Admission:* 38,275 applied, 22,187 admitted, 4,409 enrolled. *Average high school GPA:* 3.52. *Test scores:* SAT critical reading scores over 500: 96%; SAT math scores over 500: 99%; SAT writing scores over 500: 98%; ACT scores over 18: 100%; SAT critical reading scores over 600: 67%; SAT math scores over 600: 79%; SAT writing scores over 600: 74%; ACT scores over 24: 94%; SAT critical reading scores over 700: 14%; SAT math scores over 700: 26%; SAT writing scores over 700: 19%; ACT scores over 30: 32%.
Faculty *Total:* 2,630, 62% full-time. *Student/faculty ratio:* 13:1.
Academics *Calendar:* semesters. *Degrees:* bachelor's, master's, doctoral-professional, doctoral-research/scholarship, post-master's, and postbachelor's certificates. *Special study options:* accelerated degree program, adult/continuing education programs, advanced placement credit, cooperative education, distance learning, double majors, English as a second language, honors programs, independent study, internships, off-campus study, part-time degree program, services for LD students, student-designed majors, study abroad, summer session for credit. *ROTC:* Army (b), Navy (b), Air Force (b).
Computers on Campus 250 computers/terminals and 1,650 ports are available on campus for general student use. Students can access the following: campus intranet, computer help desk, free student e-mail accounts, online

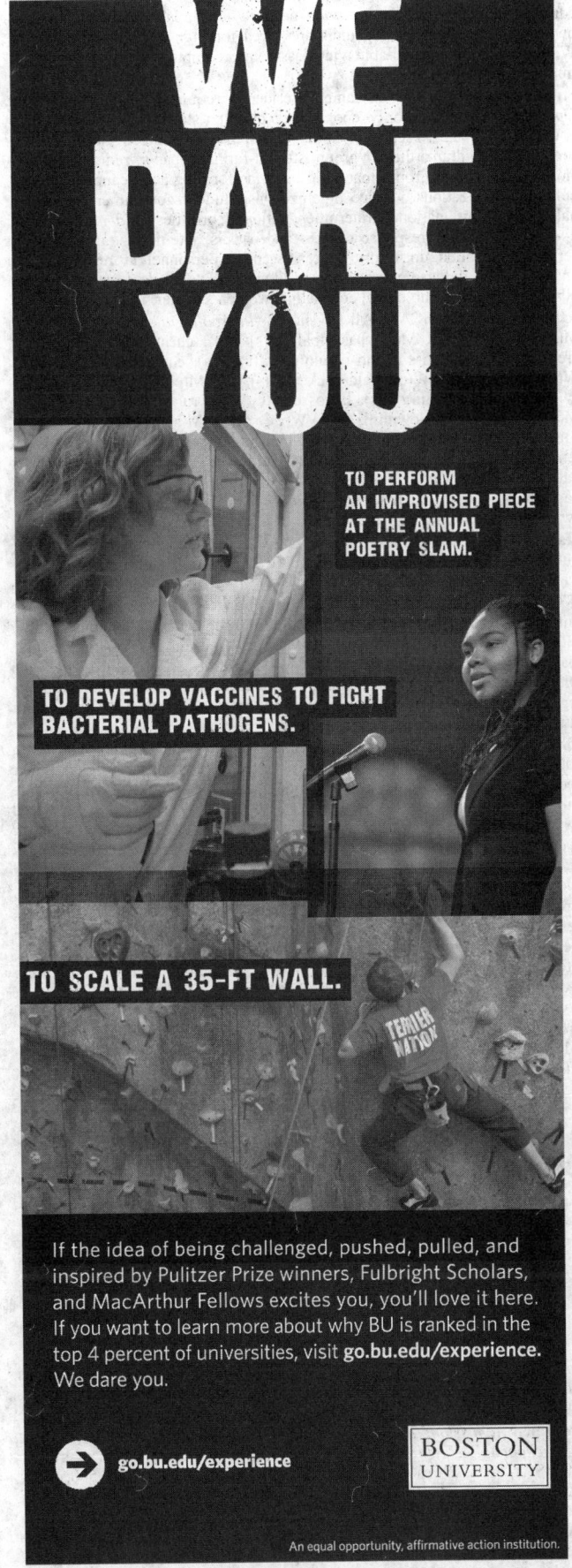

PROFILES

(class) grades, online (class) registration, online (class) schedules, research and educational networks. Campuswide network is available. 77% of college-owned or -operated housing units are wired for high-speed Internet access. Wireless service is available via classrooms, computer labs, dorm rooms, libraries, student centers.

Student Life *Housing:* on-campus residence required for freshman year. *Options:* coed, women-only, cooperative, disabled students. Campus housing is university owned. Freshman campus housing is guaranteed. *Activities and organizations:* drama/theater group, student-run newspaper, radio and television station, choral group, marching band, performing and acappella groups, cultural organizations, service organizations, student government, residence hall associations, national fraternities, national sororities. *Campus security:* 24-hour emergency response devices and patrols, late-night transport/escort service, controlled dormitory access, security personnel at residence hall entrances, self-defense education, well-lit sidewalks. *Student services:* health clinic, personal/psychological counseling, women's center.

Athletics Member NCAA. All Division I. *Intercollegiate sports:* badminton M(c)/W(c), baseball M(c), basketball M(s)/W(s), cheerleading M(c)/W(c), crew M(s)/W(s), cross-country running M(s)/W(s), equestrian sports M(c)/W(c), fencing M(c)/W(c), field hockey W(s), golf M(c)/W, gymnastics M(c)/W(c), ice hockey M(s)/W(s), lacrosse M(c)/W(s), rugby M(c)/W(c), sailing M(c)/W(c), skiing (downhill) M(c)/W(c), soccer M(s)/W(s), softball W(s), squash M(c)/W(c), swimming and diving M(s)/W(s), table tennis M(c)/W(c), tennis M/W(s), track and field M(s)/W(s), ultimate Frisbee M(c)/W(c), volleyball M(c)/W(c), water polo M(c)/W(c), wrestling M(s). *Intramural sports:* basketball M/W, football M/W, ice hockey M, soccer M/W, softball M/W, swimming and diving M/W, tennis M/W, volleyball M/W.

Standardized Tests *Required:* SAT or ACT (for admission), SAT and SAT Subject Tests or ACT (for admission), SAT Subject Tests (for admission).

Costs (2010–11) *Comprehensive fee:* $52,124 includes full-time tuition ($39,314), mandatory fees ($550), and room and board ($12,260). Full-time tuition and fees vary according to class time and degree level. Part-time tuition: $1228 per credit. Part-time tuition and fees vary according to class time, course load, and degree level. *Required fees:* $40 per term part-time. *College room only:* $7980. Room and board charges vary according to board plan and housing facility. *Payment plans:* tuition prepayment, installment. *Waivers:* senior citizens and employees or children of employees.

Financial Aid Of all full-time matriculated undergraduates who enrolled in 2009, 8,200 applied for aid, 7,498 were judged to have need, 3,613 had their need fully met. 3,483 Federal Work-Study jobs (averaging $2122). 115 state and other part-time jobs (averaging $11,339). In 2009, 1224 non-need-based awards were made. *Average percent of need met:* 89%. *Average financial aid package:* $35,198. *Average need-based loan:* $7185. *Average need-based gift aid:* $23,454. *Average non-need-based aid:* $19,843. *Average indebtedness upon graduation:* $31,809. *Financial aid deadline:* 2/15.

Applying *Options:* electronic application, early admission, early decision, deferred entrance. *Application fee:* $75. *Required:* essay or personal statement, high school transcript, 2 letters of recommendation. *Required for some:* interview, audition, portfolio. *Recommended:* minimum 3 GPA. *Application deadlines:* 1/1 (freshmen), 4/1 (transfers). *Early decision deadline:* 11/1. *Notification:* continuous until 4/15 (freshmen), 12/15 (early decision).

Freshman Application Contact Ms. Kelly Walter, Director of Undergraduate Admissions, Boston University, 121 Bay State Road, Boston, MA 02215. *Phone:* 617-353-2300. *Fax:* 617-353-9695. *E-mail:* admissions@bu.edu. *Web site:* http://www.bu.edu/.

See page 1128 for the College Close-Up.

Brandeis University
Waltham, Massachusetts

- **Independent** university, founded 1948
- **Suburban** 235-acre campus with easy access to Boston
- **Endowment** $620.2 million
- **Coed** 3,341 undergraduate students, 99% full-time, 56% women, 44% men
- **Most difficult** entrance level, 35% of applicants were admitted

Undergraduates 3,319 full-time, 22 part-time. Students come from 50 states and territories; 64 other countries; 72% are from out of state; 2% transferred in; 83% live on campus. *Retention:* 92% of full-time freshmen returned.

Freshmen *Admission:* 7,753 applied, 2,746 admitted, 690 enrolled. *Average high school GPA:* 3.77. *Test scores:* SAT critical reading scores over 500: 99%; SAT math scores over 500: 99%; SAT writing scores over 500: 99%; ACT scores over 18: 100%; SAT critical reading scores over 600: 88%; SAT math scores over 600: 90%; SAT writing scores over 600: 89%; ACT scores over 24: 94%; SAT critical reading scores over 700: 38%; SAT math scores over 700: 45%; SAT writing scores over 700: 40%; ACT scores over 30: 56%.

Faculty *Total:* 506, 72% full-time, 87% with terminal degrees. *Student/faculty ratio:* 9:1.

Academics *Calendar:* semesters. *Degrees:* bachelor's, master's, doctoral-research/scholarship, and postbachelor's certificates. *Special study options:* adult/continuing education programs, advanced placement credit, double majors, English as a second language, honors programs, independent study, internships, off-campus study, services for LD students, student-designed majors, study abroad, summer session for credit. *ROTC:* Army (c), Air Force (c). *Unusual degree programs:* engineering with Columbia University.

Computers on Campus 129 computers/terminals are available on campus for general student use. Students can access the following: computer help desk, free student e-mail accounts, online (class) grades, online (class) registration, online (class) schedules, educational software. Campuswide network is available. 100% of college-owned or -operated housing units are wired for high-speed Internet access. Wireless service is available via entire campus.

Student Life *Housing:* on-campus residence required for freshman year. *Options:* coed, men-only, women-only, disabled students. Campus housing is university owned. Freshman campus housing is guaranteed. *Activities and organizations:* drama/theater group, student-run newspaper, radio and television station, choral group, Waltham Group, Student Events (Student Programming Board), Student Union, Triskelion (GLBTQA group). *Campus security:* 24-hour emergency response devices and patrols, late-night transport/escort service, controlled dormitory access. *Student services:* health clinic, personal/psychological counseling.

Athletics Member NCAA. All Division III. *Intercollegiate sports:* baseball M, basketball M/W, crew M(c)/W(c), cross-country running M/W, fencing M/W, field hockey W(c), golf M(c), lacrosse M(c)/W(c), rugby M(c)/W(c), sailing M(c)/W(c), skiing (downhill) M(c)/W(c), soccer M/W, softball W, squash M(c), swimming and diving M(c)/W(c), tennis M/W, track and field M/W, ultimate Frisbee M(c)/W(c), volleyball W. *Intramural sports:* basketball M/W, cheerleading W, equestrian sports M/W, football M, ice hockey M, softball M/W, squash M/W, table tennis M/W, tennis M/W, volleyball M/W, water polo M/W, weight lifting M/W.

Standardized Tests *Required:* SAT or ACT (for admission).

Costs (2010–11) *Comprehensive fee:* $51,488 includes full-time tuition ($38,994), mandatory fees ($1280), and room and board ($11,214). Part-time tuition and fees vary according to course load. *Room and board:* Room and board charges vary according to board plan and housing facility. *Payment plans:* tuition prepayment, installment. *Waivers:* employees or children of employees.

Financial Aid Of all full-time matriculated undergraduates who enrolled in 2009, 1,686 applied for aid, 1,494 were judged to have need, 401 had their need fully met. In 2009, 453 non-need-based awards were made. *Average percent of need met:* 92%. *Average financial aid package:* $32,260. *Average need-based loan:* $4338. *Average need-based gift aid:* $27,772. *Average non-need-based aid:* $23,117. *Average indebtedness upon graduation:* $21,351. *Financial aid deadline:* 2/1.

Applying *Options:* electronic application, early decision, deferred entrance. *Application fee:* $55. *Required:* essay or personal statement, high school transcript, 2 letters of recommendation. *Recommended:* interview. *Application deadlines:* 1/15 (freshmen), 4/1 (transfers). *Early decision deadline:* 11/15 (for plan 1), 1/1 (for plan 2). *Notification:* 4/1 (freshmen), 6/1 (transfers), 12/15 (early decision plan 1), 2/1 (early decision plan 2).

Freshman Application Contact Mr. Mark Spencer, Dean of Admissions, Brandeis University, 415 South Street, PO Box 549110, Waltham, MA 02454-9110. *Phone:* 781-736-3500. *Toll-free phone:* 800-622-0622. *Fax:* 781-736-3536. *E-mail:* admissions@brandeis.edu. *Web site:* http://www.brandeis.edu/.

Bridgewater State University
Bridgewater, Massachusetts

- **State-supported** comprehensive, founded 1840, part of Massachusetts Public Higher Education System
- **Suburban** 235-acre campus with easy access to Boston
- **Endowment** $14.5 million
- **Coed** 9,328 undergraduate students, 84% full-time, 59% women, 41% men
- **Moderately difficult** entrance level, 66% of applicants were admitted

Undergraduates 7,789 full-time, 1,539 part-time. Students come from 27 states and territories; 20 other countries; 4% are from out of state; 6% transferred in; 30% live on campus. *Retention:* 81% of full-time freshmen returned.

Freshmen *Admission:* 6,998 applied, 4,596 admitted, 1,459 enrolled. *Average high school GPA:* 3.1. *Test scores:* SAT critical reading scores over 500: 55%; SAT math scores over 500: 61%; ACT scores over 18: 92%; SAT critical reading scores over 600: 12%; SAT math scores over 600: 13%; ACT scores over 24: 25%; SAT critical reading scores over 700: 1%; SAT math scores over 700: 1%; ACT scores over 30: 2%.

Faculty *Total:* 661, 47% full-time. *Student/faculty ratio:* 22:1.

Academics *Calendar:* semesters. *Degrees:* certificates, bachelor's, master's, post-master's, and postbachelor's certificates. *Special study options:* academic remediation for entering students, accelerated degree program, adult/continuing education programs, advanced placement credit, distance learning, double majors, English as a second language, honors programs, independent study, internships, off-campus study, part-time degree program, services for LD students, study abroad, summer session for credit. *ROTC:* Army (c), Air Force (c).

Computers on Campus Students can access the following: campus intranet, computer help desk, free student e-mail accounts, online (class) grades, online (class) registration, online (class) schedules, student account information, application software. Campuswide network is available. Wireless service is available via entire campus.

Student Life *Housing options:* coed, disabled students. Campus housing is university owned. Freshman applicants given priority for college housing. *Activities and organizations:* drama/theater group, student-run newspaper, radio station, choral group, marching band, Children's Developmental Clinic, Student Government Association, Afro-American/Latino Club, Program Committee, national fraternities, national sororities. *Campus security:* 24-hour emergency response devices and patrols, late-night transport/escort service, controlled dormitory access. *Student services:* health clinic, personal/psychological counseling, women's center.

Athletics Member NCAA. All Division III. *Intercollegiate sports:* baseball M, basketball M/W, cross-country running M/W, field hockey W, football M, lacrosse M(c)/W, soccer M/W, softball W, swimming and diving M/W, tennis M/W, track and field M/W, volleyball W, water polo M(c)/W(c), wrestling M. *Intramural sports:* basketball M/W, football M/W, soccer M/W, softball M/W, tennis M/W, volleyball M/W.

Standardized Tests *Required:* SAT or ACT (for admission).

Costs (2010–11) *Tuition:* state resident $910 full-time, $38 per credit hour part-time; nonresident $7050 full-time, $294 per credit hour part-time. *Required fees:* $6143 full-time, $251 per credit hour part-time. *Room and board:* $9670; room only: $6420. Room and board charges vary according to board plan and housing facility. *Payment plan:* installment. *Waivers:* employees or children of employees.

Financial Aid Of all full-time matriculated undergraduates who enrolled in 2008, 5,109 applied for aid, 3,991 were judged to have need. In 2008, 60 non-need-based awards were made. *Average percent of need met:* 75%. *Average financial aid package:* $7345. *Average need-based loan:* $3913. *Average need-based gift aid:* $3679. *Average non-need-based aid:* $5710. *Average indebtedness upon graduation:* $22,093.

Applying *Options:* electronic application, early admission, early action, deferred entrance. *Application fee:* $25. *Required:* essay or personal statement, high school transcript, minimum 3 GPA. *Application deadlines:* 2/15 (freshmen), 6/1 (transfers), 11/15 (early action). *Notification:* continuous (freshmen), 12/15 (early action).

Freshman Application Contact Mr. Gregg Meyer, Director of Admissions, Bridgewater State University, Bridgewater, MA 02325-0001. *Phone:* 508-531-1237. *E-mail:* admission@bridgew.edu. *Web site:* http://www.bridgew.edu/.

Cambridge College

Cambridge, Massachusetts

- **Independent** comprehensive, founded 1971
- **Urban** campus with easy access to Boston
- **Endowment** $9.8 million
- **Coed** 1,293 undergraduate students, 36% full-time, 69% women, 31% men
- **Noncompetitive** entrance level

Undergraduates 468 full-time, 825 part-time. Students come from 10 states and territories; 3% are from out of state; 13% transferred in. *Retention:* 35% of full-time freshmen returned.

Freshmen *Admission:* 20 enrolled.

Faculty *Total:* 530, 5% full-time, 62% with terminal degrees. *Student/faculty ratio:* 15:1.

Academics *Calendar:* trimesters. *Degrees:* certificates, bachelor's, master's, doctoral-research/scholarship, and post-master's certificates. *Special study options:* accelerated degree program, adult/continuing education programs, advanced placement credit, distance learning, independent study, internships, part-time degree program, services for LD students, summer session for credit.

Computers on Campus Students can access the following: computer help desk, free student e-mail accounts, online (class) grades, online (class) registration, online (class) schedules. Campuswide network is available. Wireless service is available via entire campus.

Student Life *Housing:* college housing not available.

Costs (2010–11) *Tuition:* $13,140 full-time, $365 per credit hour part-time. *Required fees:* $140 full-time. *Payment plan:* installment. *Waivers:* employees or children of employees.

Financial Aid Of all full-time matriculated undergraduates who enrolled in 2009, 230 applied for aid, 223 were judged to have need. *Average percent of need met:* 31%. *Average financial aid package:* $4328. *Average need-based loan:* $4328. *Average need-based gift aid:* $5277.

Applying *Options:* electronic application, deferred entrance. *Application fee:* $30. *Required:* essay or personal statement, high school transcript, 1 letter of recommendation, resume, health insurance, immunizations form, application form. *Recommended:* interview. *Application deadlines:* rolling (freshmen), rolling (out-of-state freshmen), rolling (transfers). *Notification:* continuous (freshmen), continuous (out-of-state freshmen), continuous (transfers).

Freshman Application Contact Kate Innes, Director of Admissions, Cambridge College, 1000 Massachusetts Avenue, Cambridge, MA 02138-5304. *Phone:* 800-877-4725. *Toll-free phone:* 800-877-4723. *Fax:* 617-349-3561. *E-mail:* kate.innes@cambridgecollege.edu. *Web site:* http://www.cambridgecollege.edu/.

Clark University

Worcester, Massachusetts

- **Independent** university, founded 1887
- **Urban** 50-acre campus with easy access to Boston
- **Endowment** $275.2 million
- **Coed** 2,317 undergraduate students, 96% full-time, 60% women, 40% men
- **Moderately difficult** entrance level, 69% of applicants were admitted

Undergraduates 2,217 full-time, 100 part-time. Students come from 46 states and territories; 73 other countries; 60% are from out of state; 3% Black or African American, non-Hispanic/Latino; 5% Hispanic/Latino; 4% Asian, non-Hispanic/Latino; 0.1% Native Hawaiian or other Pacific Islander, non-Hispanic/Latino; 0.2% American Indian or Alaska Native, non-Hispanic/Latino; 2% Two or more races, non-Hispanic/Latino; 8% Race/ethnicity unknown; 7% international; 2% transferred in; 70% live on campus. *Retention:* 90% of full-time freshmen returned.

Freshmen *Admission:* 4,038 applied, 2,790 admitted, 578 enrolled. *Average high school GPA:* 3.45. *Test scores:* SAT critical reading scores over 500: 91%; SAT math scores over 500: 89%; SAT writing scores over 500: 88%; ACT scores over 18: 99%; SAT critical reading scores over 600: 52%; SAT math scores over 600: 49%; SAT writing scores over 600: 54%; ACT scores over 24: 83%; SAT critical reading scores over 700: 15%; SAT math scores over 700: 8%; SAT writing scores over 700: 12%; ACT scores over 30: 26%.

Faculty *Total:* 270, 69% full-time. *Student/faculty ratio:* 10:1.

Academics *Calendar:* semesters. *Degrees:* bachelor's, master's, doctoral-research/scholarship, post-master's, and postbachelor's certificates. *Special study options:* academic remediation for entering students, accelerated degree program, adult/continuing education programs, advanced placement credit, double majors, English as a second language, honors programs, independent study, internships, off-campus study, part-time degree program, services for LD students, student-designed majors, study abroad, summer session for credit. *ROTC:* Army (c), Navy (c), Air Force (c). *Unusual degree programs:* 3-2 business administration; engineering with Columbia University, Washington University in St. Louis, Worcester Polytechnic Institute; environmental studies, international development, community planning, biology, biochemistry, chemistry, physics, economics, history, communication, public administration, geographic information systems.

Computers on Campus 115 computers/terminals and 4,000 ports are available on campus for general student use. Students can access the following: campus intranet, computer help desk, free student e-mail accounts, online (class) grades, online (class) registration, online (class) schedules, online course support. Campuswide network is available. 100% of college-owned or -operated housing units are wired for high-speed Internet access. Wireless service is available via entire campus.

Student Life *Housing:* on-campus residence required through sophomore year. *Options:* coed, women-only, disabled students. Campus housing is university owned. Freshman campus housing is guaranteed. *Activities and organizations:* drama/theater group, student-run newspaper, radio and television station, choral group, marching band, International Students Association, Outing Club, Science Fiction People of Clark, Ballroom Dance Team and Club, Hillel. *Campus security:* 24-hour emergency response devices and patrols, student patrols, late-night transport/escort service, controlled dormitory access. *Student services:* health clinic, personal/psychological counseling, women's center.

Athletics Member NCAA. All Division III. *Intercollegiate sports:* baseball M, basketball M/W, crew M/W, cross-country running M/W, field hockey W, lacrosse M, soccer M/W, softball W, swimming and diving M/W, tennis M/W, volleyball W. *Intramural sports:* basketball M/W, equestrian sports M(c)/W(c), football M/W, ice hockey M(c)/W(c), lacrosse W(c), racquetball M/W, soccer M/W, softball M/W, track and field M(c)/W(c), ultimate Frisbee M(c)/W(c), volleyball M(c)/W(c), water polo M/W.

Standardized Tests *Required:* SAT or ACT (for admission).

Costs (2011–12) *Comprehensive fee:* $44,450 includes full-time tuition ($37,000), mandatory fees ($350), and room and board ($7100). Part-time tuition: $1156 per course. *College room only:* $4000. Room and board charges vary according to board plan and housing facility. *Payment plans:* tuition prepayment, installment. *Waivers:* employees or children of employees.

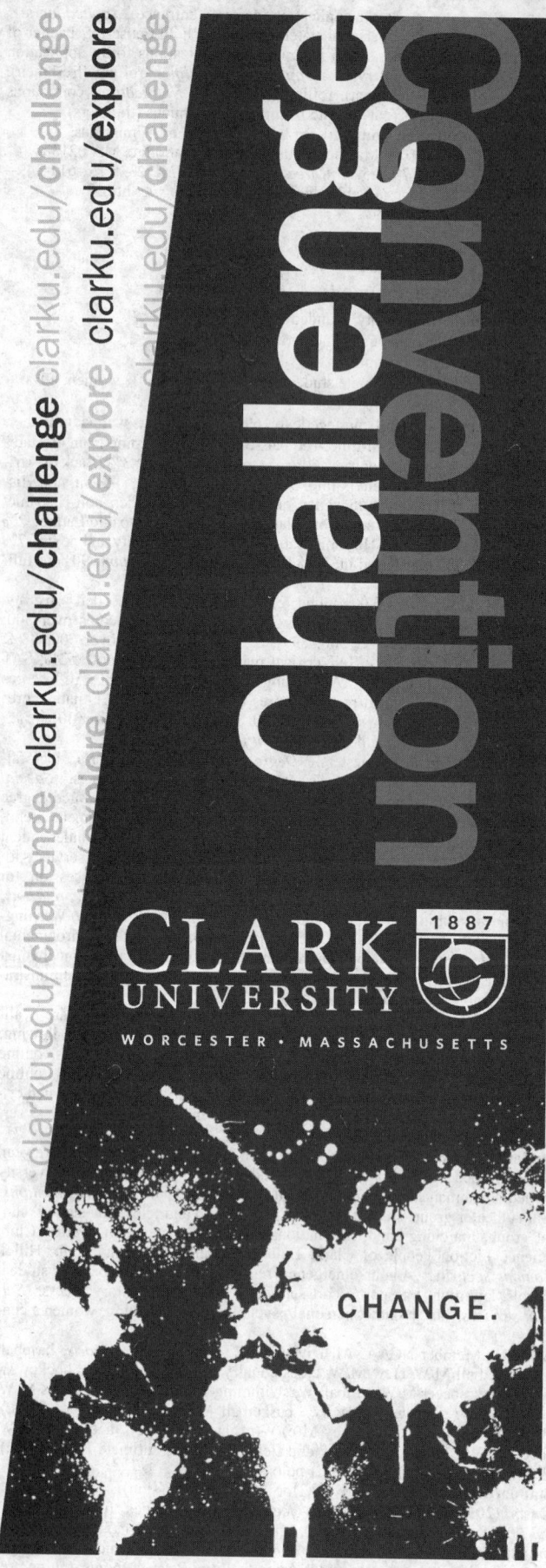

CHANGE.

Financial Aid Of all full-time matriculated undergraduates who enrolled in 2009, 1,772 applied for aid, 1,384 were judged to have need, 819 had their need fully met. 1,000 Federal Work-Study jobs (averaging $2000). In 2009, 596 non-need-based awards were made. *Average percent of need met:* 94%. *Average financial aid package:* $28,165. *Average need-based loan:* $3225. *Average need-based gift aid:* $23,789. *Average non-need-based aid:* $13,763. *Average indebtedness upon graduation:* $24,000. *Financial aid deadline:* 2/1.
Applying *Options:* electronic application, early admission, early action, deferred entrance. *Application fee:* $55. *Required:* essay or personal statement, high school transcript, 2 letters of recommendation. *Recommended:* interview. *Application deadlines:* 1/15 (freshmen), 4/15 (transfers), 11/15 (early action). *Notification:* 4/1 (freshmen), 6/1 (transfers), 12/23 (early action).
Freshman Application Contact Mr. Donald Honeman, Dean of Admissions, Clark University, Admissions House, 950 Main Street, Worcester, MA 01610. *Phone:* 508-793-7431. *Toll-free phone:* 800-GO-CLARK. *Fax:* 508-793-8821. *E-mail:* admissions@clarku.edu. *Web site:* http://www.clarku.edu/.

See page 1220 for the College Close-Up.

College of the Holy Cross
Worcester, Massachusetts

- **Independent Roman Catholic (Jesuit)** 4-year, founded 1843
- **Suburban** 174-acre campus with easy access to Boston
- **Endowment** $535.0 million
- **Coed** 2,899 undergraduate students, 99% full-time, 54% women, 46% men
- **Very difficult** entrance level, 35% of applicants were admitted

Undergraduates 2,862 full-time, 37 part-time. Students come from 45 states and territories; 19 other countries; 63% are from out of state; 5% Black or African American, non-Hispanic/Latino; 9% Hispanic/Latino; 5% Asian, non-Hispanic/Latino; 0.1% Native Hawaiian or other Pacific Islander, non-Hispanic/Latino; 0.3% American Indian or Alaska Native, non-Hispanic/Latino; 0.7% Two or more races, non-Hispanic/Latino; 13% Race/ethnicity unknown; 1% international; 0.6% transferred in; 89% live on campus. *Retention:* 94% of full-time freshmen returned.
Freshmen *Admission:* 6,911 applied, 2,451 admitted, 727 enrolled. *Average high school GPA:* 3.77. *Test scores:* SAT critical reading scores over 500: 96%; SAT math scores over 500: 97%; SAT writing scores over 500: 98%; ACT scores over 18: 100%; SAT critical reading scores over 600: 73%; SAT math scores over 600: 77%; SAT writing scores over 600: 75%; ACT scores over 24: 92%; SAT critical reading scores over 700: 19%; SAT math scores over 700: 23%; SAT writing scores over 700: 23%; ACT scores over 30: 41%.
Faculty *Total:* 315, 80% full-time, 89% with terminal degrees. *Student/faculty ratio:* 11:1.
Academics *Calendar:* semesters. *Degrees:* bachelor's (standardized tests are optional for admission to the College of Holy Cross). *Special study options:* accelerated degree program, advanced placement credit, double majors, honors programs, independent study, internships, off-campus study, services for LD students, student-designed majors, study abroad. *ROTC:* Army (c), Navy (b), Air Force (c). *Unusual degree programs:* 3-2 engineering with Columbia University and Dartmouth College.
Computers on Campus 485 computers/terminals are available on campus for general student use. Students can access the following: computer help desk, free student e-mail accounts, online (class) registration. Campuswide network is available. 100% of college-owned or -operated housing units are wired for high-speed Internet access. Wireless service is available via classrooms, computer centers, computer labs, dorm rooms, libraries, student centers.
Student Life *Housing:* on-campus residence required through sophomore year. *Options:* coed, disabled students. Campus housing is university owned. Freshman campus housing is guaranteed. *Activities and organizations:* drama/theater group, student-run newspaper, radio station, choral group, marching band, SPUD (community service organization), choral and music groups, Campus Activities Board, Student Government Association, Purple Key Society. *Campus security:* 24-hour emergency response devices and patrols, late-night transport/escort service, controlled dormitory access. *Student services:* health clinic, personal/psychological counseling.
Athletics Member NCAA. All Division I except football (Division I-AA). *Intercollegiate sports:* baseball M, basketball M(s)/W(s), crew M/W, cross-country running M/W, field hockey W(s), golf M/W, ice hockey M(s)/W, lacrosse M/W, soccer M(s)/W(s), softball W, swimming and diving M/W, tennis M/W, track and field M/W, volleyball W. *Intramural sports:* baseball M(c), basketball M/W, cross-country running M/W(c), equestrian sports M(c)/W(c), football M/W, ice hockey M(c), lacrosse M(c)/W(c), rugby M(c)/W(c), sailing M(c)/W(c), skiing (downhill) M(c)/W(c), soccer M(c)/W(c), softball M/W, tennis M(c)/W(c), ultimate Frisbee M(c)/W(c).
Costs (2011–12) *Comprehensive fee:* $52,758 includes full-time tuition ($40,910), mandatory fees ($578), and room and board ($11,270). *College room only:* $5970. Room and board charges vary according to board plan and

housing facility. *Payment plans:* tuition prepayment, installment. *Waivers:* employees or children of employees.

Financial Aid Of all full-time matriculated undergraduates who enrolled in 2009, 1,814 applied for aid, 1,674 were judged to have need, 1,587 had their need fully met. 1,035 Federal Work-Study jobs (averaging $1588). In 2009, 6 non-need-based awards were made. *Average percent of need met:* 100%. *Average financial aid package:* $29,917. *Average need-based loan:* $5313. *Average need-based gift aid:* $28,077. *Average non-need-based aid:* $31,389. *Average indebtedness upon graduation:* $23,662. *Financial aid deadline:* 2/1.

Applying *Options:* electronic application, early admission, early decision, deferred entrance. *Application fee:* $60. *Required:* essay or personal statement, high school transcript, 2 letters of recommendation. *Recommended:* interview. *Application deadlines:* 1/15 (freshmen), 3/1 (transfers). *Early decision deadline:* 12/15. *Notification:* 4/1 (freshmen), continuous (transfers), 1/15 (early decision).

Freshman Application Contact College of the Holy Cross, 1 College Street, Worcester, MA 01610-2395. *Phone:* 508-793-2443. *Toll-free phone:* 800-442-2421. *Web site:* http://www.holycross.edu/.

Curry College
Milton, Massachusetts

- **Independent** comprehensive, founded 1879
- **Suburban** 135-acre campus with easy access to Boston
- **Endowment** $49.6 million
- **Coed** 2,661 undergraduate students, 74% full-time, 60% women, 40% men
- **Moderately difficult** entrance level, 72% of applicants were admitted

Undergraduates 1,975 full-time, 686 part-time. Students come from 31 states and territories; 17 other countries; 24% are from out of state; 8% Black or African American, non-Hispanic/Latino; 4% Hispanic/Latino; 1% Asian, non-Hispanic/Latino; 0.3% American Indian or Alaska Native, non-Hispanic/Latino; 0.5% Two or more races, non-Hispanic/Latino; 19% Race/ethnicity unknown; 1% international; 3% transferred in; 70% live on campus. *Retention:* 66% of full-time freshmen returned.

Freshmen *Admission:* 4,791 applied, 3,447 admitted, 578 enrolled. *Average high school GPA:* 2.7. *Test scores:* SAT critical reading scores over 500: 29%; SAT math scores over 500: 33%; SAT writing scores over 500: 30%; ACT scores over 18: 82%; SAT critical reading scores over 600: 5%; SAT math scores over 600: 3%; SAT writing scores over 600: 4%; ACT scores over 24: 11%.

Faculty *Total:* 417, 28% full-time, 34% with terminal degrees. *Student/faculty ratio:* 10:1.

Academics *Calendar:* semesters. *Degrees:* certificates, bachelor's, and master's. *Special study options:* academic remediation for entering students, accelerated degree program, adult/continuing education programs, advanced placement credit, double majors, external degree program, honors programs, independent study, internships, off-campus study, part-time degree program, services for LD students, student-designed majors, study abroad, summer session for credit. *ROTC:* Army (c).

Computers on Campus 185 computers/terminals and 2,500 ports are available on campus for general student use. Students can access the following: campus intranet, computer help desk, free student e-mail accounts, online (class) grades, online (class) registration, online (class) schedules, library online catalog and research databases. Campuswide network is available. 100% of college-owned or -operated housing units are wired for high-speed Internet access. Wireless service is available via entire campus.

Student Life *Housing options:* coed, men-only, women-only. Campus housing is university owned. *Activities and organizations:* drama/theater group, student-run newspaper, radio and television station, choral group, student radio station, student government, Campus Activities Board, student newspaper, Drama Club. *Campus security:* 24-hour emergency response devices and patrols, late-night transport/escort service, controlled dormitory access. *Student services:* health clinic, personal/psychological counseling.

Athletics Member NCAA. All Division III. *Intercollegiate sports:* baseball M, basketball M/W, cross-country running W, football M, ice hockey M, lacrosse M/W, soccer M/W, softball W, tennis M/W. *Intramural sports:* basketball M/W, cheerleading M/W, equestrian sports W, rugby M/W, skiing (downhill) M/W, softball M/W, tennis M/W, ultimate Frisbee M/W, volleyball M/W.

Standardized Tests *Required for some:* SAT or ACT (for admission), TOEFL for international applicants.

Costs (2011–12) *One-time required fee:* $280. *Comprehensive fee:* $44,495 includes full-time tuition ($30,700), mandatory fees ($1510), and room and board ($12,285). Part-time tuition: $1023 per credit. Part-time tuition and fees vary according to course load. *College room only:* $6895. Room and board charges vary according to board plan and housing facility. *Payment plan:* installment. *Waivers:* children of alumni and employees or children of employees.

Financial Aid Of all full-time matriculated undergraduates who enrolled in 2009, 1,407 applied for aid, 1,406 were judged to have need, 27 had their need fully met. 835 Federal Work-Study jobs (averaging $1848). In 2009, 101 non-need-based awards were made. *Average percent of need met:* 59%. *Average financial aid package:* $17,600. *Average need-based loan:* $4263. *Average need-based gift aid:* $11,349. *Average non-need-based aid:* $5858. *Average indebtedness upon graduation:* $36,874.

Applying *Options:* electronic application, early admission, early action, deferred entrance. *Application fee:* $50. *Required:* essay or personal statement, high school transcript, minimum 2 GPA, 1 letter of recommendation, Supplemental form for Common Application subscribers and Program for Advancement of Learning. *Required for some:* interview. *Recommended:* interview. *Application deadlines:* 4/1 (freshmen), 7/1 (transfers), 12/1 (early action). *Notification:* continuous (freshmen), continuous (transfers), 12/15 (early action).

Freshman Application Contact Ms. Jane P. Fidler, Dean of Admission, Curry College, 1071 Blue Hill Avenue, Milton, MA 02186. *Phone:* 617-333-2210. *Toll-free phone:* 800-669-0686. *Fax:* 617-333-2114. *E-mail:* curryadm@curry.edu. *Web site:* http://www.curry.edu/.

See page 1246 for the College Close-Up.

Dean College
Franklin, Massachusetts

- **Independent** primarily 2-year, founded 1865
- **Small-town** 100-acre campus with easy access to Boston and Providence
- **Endowment** $22.8 million
- **Coed**
- **Minimally difficult** entrance level

Faculty *Student/faculty ratio:* 19:1.
Academics *Calendar:* semesters. *Degrees:* certificates, associate, and bachelor's.
Student Life *Campus security:* 24-hour emergency response devices and patrols, late-night transport/escort service, controlled dormitory access.
Athletics Member NJCAA.
Standardized Tests *Required:* SAT or ACT (for admission).
Costs (2010–11) *Comprehensive fee:* $41,582 includes full-time tuition ($29,140) and room and board ($12,442). Full-time tuition and fees vary according to program. Part-time tuition: $780 per course. Part-time tuition and fees vary according to program. *College room only:* $7868.
Applying *Options:* electronic application, deferred entrance. *Application fee:* $35. *Required:* essay or personal statement, high school transcript. *Recommended:* minimum 2 GPA, interview.
Freshman Application Contact Mr. James Fowler, Dean College, 99 Main Street, Franklin, MA 02038. *Phone:* 508-541-1547. *Toll-free phone:* 877-TRY-DEAN. *Fax:* 508-541-8726. *E-mail:* jfowler@dean.edu. *Web site:* http://www.dean.edu/.

Eastern Nazarene College
Quincy, Massachusetts

- **Independent** comprehensive, founded 1918, affiliated with Church of the Nazarene
- **Urban** 17-acre campus with easy access to Boston
- **Endowment** $11.7 million
- **Coed**
- **Moderately difficult** entrance level

Faculty *Student/faculty ratio:* 13:1.
Academics *Calendar:* semesters. *Degrees:* certificates, associate, bachelor's, and master's.
Student Life *Campus security:* 24-hour emergency response devices and patrols, student patrols, late-night transport/escort service, controlled dormitory access.
Athletics Member NCAA. All Division III.
Standardized Tests *Required:* SAT or ACT (for admission). *Recommended:* SAT and SAT Subject Tests or ACT (for admission), SAT Subject Tests (for admission).
Costs (2010–11) *Comprehensive fee:* $31,772 includes full-time tuition ($22,982), mandatory fees ($790), and room and board ($8000). Full-time tuition and fees vary according to course load, degree level, program, reciprocity agreements, and student level. Part-time tuition: $901 per credit hour. Part-time tuition and fees vary according to degree level, program, reciprocity agreements, and student level. *Required fees:* $102 per term part-time. *Room and board:* Room and board charges vary according to board plan and housing facility.
Financial Aid Of all full-time matriculated undergraduates who enrolled in 2008, 514 applied for aid, 434 were judged to have need, 133 had their need fully met. In 2008, 56 non-need-based awards were made. *Average percent of need met:* 71. *Average financial aid package:* $22,758. *Average need-based*

loan: $8559. *Average need-based gift aid:* $10,391. *Average non-need-based aid:* $9116. *Average indebtedness upon graduation:* $51,336.

Applying *Options:* electronic application, deferred entrance. *Application fee:* $25. *Required:* high school transcript, minimum 2 GPA, 1 letter of recommendation, interview. *Recommended:* essay or personal statement, minimum 3 GPA, 2 letters of recommendation.

Freshman Application Contact Mr. Andrew R. Wright, Director of Admissions, Eastern Nazarene College, 23 East Elm Avenue, Quincy, MA 02170. *Phone:* 617-745-3864. *Toll-free phone:* 800-88-ENC88. *Fax:* 617-745-3992. *E-mail:* andrew.wright@enc.edu. *Web site:* http://www.enc.edu/.

Elms College
Chicopee, Massachusetts

Freshman Application Contact Mr. Joseph Wagner, Director of Admissions, Elms College, Chicopee, MA 01013-2839. *Phone:* 413-592-3189 Ext. 350. *Toll-free phone:* 800-255-ELMS. *Fax:* 413-594-2781. *E-mail:* admissions@elms.edu. *Web site:* http://www.elms.edu/.

Emerson College
Boston, Massachusetts

- **Independent** comprehensive, founded 1880
- **Urban** campus
- **Endowment** $52.2 million
- **Coed**
- **Very difficult** entrance level

Faculty *Student/faculty ratio:* 13:1.

Academics *Calendar:* semesters. *Degrees:* certificates, bachelor's, master's, and doctoral-other.

Student Life *Campus security:* 24-hour emergency response devices and patrols, late-night transport/escort service, controlled dormitory access.

Athletics Member NCAA. All Division III.

Standardized Tests *Required:* SAT or ACT (for admission).

Costs (2010–11) *Comprehensive fee:* $44,153 includes full-time tuition ($30,752), mandatory fees ($520), and room and board ($12,881). Part-time tuition: $961 per credit hour. *Room and board:* Room and board charges vary according to board plan.

Financial Aid *Of all full-time matriculated undergraduates who enrolled in 2009,* 2,286 applied for aid, 1,965 were judged to have need, 939 had their need fully met. 427 Federal Work-Study jobs (averaging $2000). 60 state and other part-time jobs (averaging $12,071). *In 2009,* 205 non-need-based awards were made. *Average percent of need met:* 70. *Average financial aid package:* $17,981. *Average need-based loan:* $4490. *Average need-based gift aid:* $15,444. *Average non-need-based aid:* $12,713. *Average indebtedness upon graduation:* $17,459.

Applying *Options:* electronic application, early admission, early action, deferred entrance. *Application fee:* $65. *Required:* essay or personal statement, high school transcript, 1 letter of recommendation. *Required for some:* interview.

Freshman Application Contact Emerson College, 120 Boylston Street, Boston, MA 02116-4624. *Phone:* 617-824-8600. *Web site:* http://www.emerson.edu/.

See page 1276 for the College Close-Up.

Emmanuel College
Boston, Massachusetts

- **Independent Roman Catholic** comprehensive, founded 1919
- **Urban** 17-acre campus
- **Endowment** $56.8 million
- **Coed** 2,198 undergraduate students, 87% full-time, 76% women, 24% men
- **Moderately difficult** entrance level, 56% of applicants were admitted

Undergraduates 1,906 full-time, 292 part-time. Students come from 29 states and territories; 34 other countries; 38% are from out of state; 6% Black or African American, non-Hispanic/Latino; 5% Hispanic/Latino; 3% Asian, non-Hispanic/Latino; 0.1% American Indian or Alaska Native, non-Hispanic/Latino; 30% Race/ethnicity unknown; 1% international; 2% transferred in; 71% live on campus. *Retention:* 82% of full-time freshmen returned.

Freshmen *Admission:* 6,110 applied, 3,407 admitted, 528 enrolled. *Average high school GPA:* 3.44. *Test scores:* SAT critical reading scores over 500: 75%; SAT math scores over 500: 68%; SAT writing scores over 500: 76%; ACT scores over 18: 99%; SAT critical reading scores over 600: 26%; SAT math scores over 600: 19%; SAT writing scores over 600: 22%; ACT scores over 24: 42%; SAT critical reading scores over 700: 3%; SAT math scores over 700: 1%; SAT writing scores over 700: 2%; ACT scores over 30: 5%.

Faculty *Total:* 191, 43% full-time, 56% with terminal degrees. *Student/faculty ratio:* 16:1.

Academics *Calendar:* semesters. *Degrees:* bachelor's, master's, post-master's, and postbachelor's certificates. *Special study options:* academic remediation for entering students, accelerated degree program, adult/continuing education programs, advanced placement credit, distance learning, double majors, honors programs, independent study, internships, off-campus study, part-time degree program, services for LD students, student-designed majors, study abroad, summer session for credit. *ROTC:* Army (c).

Computers on Campus 239 computers/terminals are available on campus for general student use. Students can access the following: campus intranet, computer help desk, free student e-mail accounts, online (class) grades, online (class) registration, online (class) schedules, software applications. Campus-wide network is available. 100% of college-owned or -operated housing units are wired for high-speed Internet access. Wireless service is available via entire campus.

Student Life *Housing options:* coed, disabled students. Campus housing is university owned and leased by the school. Freshman campus housing is guaranteed. *Activities and organizations:* drama/theater group, student-run newspaper, radio station, choral group, HUELLAS (Latino Student Association), Student Government Association, Black Student Union, Theatre Guild, C.A.S.E. (Programming Board). *Campus security:* 24-hour emergency response devices and patrols, late-night transport/escort service, controlled dormitory access, 24-hour security personnel on duty at front desk in residence halls. *Student services:* health clinic, personal/psychological counseling.

Athletics Member NCAA. All Division III. *Intercollegiate sports:* basketball M/W, cross-country running M/W, golf M, lacrosse W, soccer M/W, softball W, tennis W, track and field M/W, volleyball M/W. *Intramural sports:* badminton M/W, baseball M(c), basketball M/W, bowling M/W, cheerleading W(c), field hockey W(c), lacrosse M(c), racquetball M/W, soccer M/W, softball M/W, tennis M/W, volleyball M/W.

Standardized Tests *Required:* SAT or ACT (for admission).

Costs (2010–11) *Comprehensive fee:* $43,190 includes full-time tuition ($30,600), mandatory fees ($290), and room and board ($12,300). Full-time tuition and fees vary according to course load, degree level, and program. Part-time tuition and fees vary according to program. *Room and board:* Room and board charges vary according to housing facility. *Payment plan:* installment. *Waivers:* employees or children of employees.

Financial Aid Of all full-time matriculated undergraduates who enrolled in 2009, 1,642 applied for aid, 1,476 were judged to have need, 782 had their need fully met. *Average percent of need met:* 72%. *Average financial aid package:* $22,286. *Average need-based loan:* $4835. *Average need-based gift aid:* $11,179.

Applying *Options:* electronic application, early admission, early decision, deferred entrance. *Application fee:* $40. *Required:* essay or personal statement, high school transcript, 2 letters of recommendation. *Application deadlines:* 3/1 (freshmen), 4/1 (transfers). *Early decision deadline:* 11/1. *Notification:* 12/1 (freshmen), 12/1 (transfers), 12/1 (early decision).

Freshman Application Contact Ms. Sandra Robbins, Dean for Enrollment, Emmanuel College, Admissions Office, 400 The Fenway, Boston, MA 02115. *Phone:* 617-735-9715. *Fax:* 617-735-9801. *E-mail:* enroll@emmanuel.edu. *Web site:* http://www.emmanuel.edu/.

Endicott College
Beverly, Massachusetts

- **Independent** comprehensive, founded 1939
- **Suburban** 231-acre campus with easy access to Boston
- **Endowment** $31.2 million
- **Coed** 2,228 undergraduate students, 97% full-time, 59% women, 41% men
- **Moderately difficult** entrance level, 59% of applicants were admitted

Undergraduates 2,158 full-time, 70 part-time. Students come from 28 states and territories; 28 other countries; 52% are from out of state; 2% Black or African American, non-Hispanic/Latino; 2% Hispanic/Latino; 0.6% Asian, non-Hispanic/Latino; 0.1% Native Hawaiian or other Pacific Islander, non-Hispanic/Latino; 0.4% American Indian or Alaska Native, non-Hispanic/Latino; 1% Two or more races, non-Hispanic/Latino; 13% Race/ethnicity unknown; 2% international; 2% transferred in; 83% live on campus. *Retention:* 80% of full-time freshmen returned.

Freshmen *Admission:* 3,711 applied, 2,190 admitted, 616 enrolled. *Average high school GPA:* 3.1. *Test scores:* SAT critical reading scores over 500: 69%; SAT math scores over 500: 79%; SAT writing scores over 500: 71%; ACT scores over 18: 97%; SAT critical reading scores over 600: 17%; SAT math scores over 600: 21%; SAT writing scores over 600: 21%; ACT scores over 24: 44%; SAT critical reading scores over 700: 2%; SAT math scores over 700: 1%; SAT writing scores over 700: 1%; ACT scores over 30: 2%.

Faculty *Total:* 288, 29% full-time, 43% with terminal degrees. *Student/faculty ratio:* 15:1.

Academics *Calendar:* semesters. *Degrees:* associate, bachelor's, master's, and postbachelor's certificates. *Special study options:* accelerated degree program, adult/continuing education programs, advanced placement credit, cooperative education, distance learning, honors programs, independent study, internships, off-campus study, part-time degree program, services for LD students, student-designed majors, study abroad, summer session for credit. *ROTC:* Army (c), Air Force (c).
Computers on Campus 158 computers/terminals are available on campus for general student use. Students can access the following: campus intranet, computer help desk, free student e-mail accounts, online (class) grades, online (class) registration, online (class) schedules. Campuswide network is available. 100% of college-owned or -operated housing units are wired for high-speed Internet access. Wireless service is available via classrooms, computer centers, computer labs, dorm rooms, learning centers, libraries, student centers.
Student Life *Housing options:* coed, women-only, disabled students. Campus housing is university owned. Freshman campus housing is guaranteed. *Activities and organizations:* drama/theater group, student-run newspaper, radio and television station, choral group, Campus Activities Board, Student Senate, intramurals, sailing club, Shipmates. *Campus security:* 24-hour emergency response devices and patrols, student patrols, late-night transport/escort service, controlled dormitory access, license plate recognition system, crime prevention programs, rape awareness defense, property identification, security cameras. *Student services:* health clinic, personal/psychological counseling.
Athletics Member NCAA. All Division III. *Intercollegiate sports:* baseball M, basketball M/W, cheerleading W(c), crew M(c)/W(c), cross-country running M/W, equestrian sports M/W, field hockey W, football M, golf M/W(c), ice hockey M(c)/W(c), lacrosse M/W, sailing M(c)/W(c), soccer M/W, softball W, tennis M/W, volleyball M/W. *Intramural sports:* basketball M/W, football M/W, racquetball M/W, soccer M/W, softball M/W, tennis M/W, volleyball M/W.
Standardized Tests *Required:* SAT or ACT (for admission).
Costs (2010–11) *Comprehensive fee:* $38,636 includes full-time tuition ($25,848), mandatory fees ($400), and room and board ($12,388). Part-time tuition: $793 per credit hour. *Required fees:* $150 per term part-time. *College room only:* $8578. Room and board charges vary according to board plan and housing facility. *Payment plan:* installment. *Waivers:* employees or children of employees.
Financial Aid Of all full-time matriculated undergraduates who enrolled in 2009, 1,852 applied for aid, 1,356 were judged to have need, 157 had their need fully met. 461 Federal Work-Study jobs (averaging $2000). In 2009, 379 non-need-based awards were made. *Average percent of need met:* 62%. *Average financial aid package:* $17,981. *Average need-based loan:* $4541. *Average need-based gift aid:* $9901. *Average non-need-based aid:* $7512. *Average indebtedness upon graduation:* $39,168.
Applying *Options:* electronic application. *Application fee:* $50. *Required:* essay or personal statement, high school transcript, minimum 2.5 GPA, 1 letter of recommendation. *Required for some:* interview. *Recommended:* interview. *Application deadlines:* 2/15 (freshmen), 3/15 (transfers). *Notification:* continuous (freshmen), continuous (transfers).
Freshman Application Contact Mr. Thomas J. Redman, Vice President of Admission and Financial Aid, Endicott College, 376 Hale Street, Beverly, MA 01915. *Phone:* 978-921-1000. *Toll-free phone:* 800-325-1114. *Fax:* 978-232-2520. *E-mail:* admissio@endicott.edu. *Web site:* http://www.endicott.edu/.

Fisher College
Boston, Massachusetts
- **Independent** 4-year, founded 1903
- **Urban** campus with easy access to Boston
- **Coed** 1,751 undergraduate students, 60% full-time, 75% women, 25% men
- **Minimally difficult** entrance level, 64% of applicants were admitted

Undergraduates 1,056 full-time, 695 part-time. 34% are from out of state; 12% Black or African American, non-Hispanic/Latino; 8% Hispanic/Latino; 2% Asian, non-Hispanic/Latino; 0.4% American Indian or Alaska Native, non-Hispanic/Latino; 3% Two or more races, non-Hispanic/Latino; 19% Race/ethnicity unknown; 8% international; 2% transferred in; 42% live on campus. *Retention:* 65% of full-time freshmen returned.
Freshmen *Admission:* 2,185 applied, 1,389 admitted, 349 enrolled. *Average high school GPA:* 2.31. *Test scores:* SAT critical reading scores over 500: 16%; SAT math scores over 500: 17%; ACT scores over 18: 50%; SAT critical reading scores over 600: 3%; SAT math scores over 600: 3%.
Faculty *Total:* 155, 19% full-time, 23% with terminal degrees. *Student/faculty ratio:* 18:1.
Academics *Calendar:* semesters. *Degrees:* certificates, associate, and bachelor's. *Special study options:* academic remediation for entering students, adult/continuing education programs, advanced placement credit, distance learning, English as a second language, honors programs, independent study, internships, off-campus study, part-time degree program, services for LD students, study abroad, summer session for credit. *ROTC:* Army (c).

Computers on Campus Students can access the following: campus intranet, computer help desk, free student e-mail accounts, online (class) grades, online (class) registration, online (class) schedules. Campuswide network is available. Wireless service is available via student centers.
Student Life *Housing options:* coed, women-only. Campus housing is university owned and leased by the school. *Activities and organizations:* drama/theater group, choral group. *Campus security:* 24-hour emergency response devices and patrols, controlled dormitory access. *Student services:* health clinic, personal/psychological counseling, women's center.
Athletics Member NAIA. *Intercollegiate sports:* baseball M, basketball M/W, soccer M/W, softball W.
Standardized Tests *Required for some:* SAT or ACT (for admission).
Costs (2011–12) *Comprehensive fee:* $39,564 includes full-time tuition ($24,783), mandatory fees ($995), and room and board ($13,786). Full-time tuition and fees vary according to class time, course level, course load, degree level, location, program, reciprocity agreements, and student level. Part-time tuition: $267 per credit. Part-time tuition and fees vary according to class time, course level, course load, degree level, location, program, reciprocity agreements, and student level. *Payment plan:* installment.
Applying *Options:* electronic application, deferred entrance. *Application fee:* $50. *Required:* high school transcript. *Required for some:* essay or personal statement, interview. *Recommended:* minimum 2 GPA. *Application deadlines:* rolling (freshmen), rolling (transfers). *Notification:* continuous (freshmen), continuous (transfers).
Freshman Application Contact Mr. Robert Melaragni, Dean of Admissions, Fisher College, Boston, MA 02116. *Phone:* 617-236-8818. *Toll-free phone:* 800-821-3050 (in-state); 800-446-1226 (out-of-state). *Fax:* 617-236-5473. *E-mail:* admissions@fisher.edu. *Web site:* http://www.fisher.edu/.

Fitchburg State University
Fitchburg, Massachusetts
- **State-supported** comprehensive, founded 1894, part of Massachusetts Public Higher Education System
- **Suburban** 78-acre campus with easy access to Boston
- **Endowment** $13.4 million
- **Coed** 4,274 undergraduate students, 83% full-time, 53% women, 47% men
- **Moderately difficult** entrance level, 68% of applicants were admitted

Undergraduates 3,549 full-time, 725 part-time. Students come from 21 states and territories; 6 other countries; 8% are from out of state; 4% Black or African American, non-Hispanic/Latino; 6% Hispanic/Latino; 2% Asian, non-Hispanic/Latino; 0.0% Native Hawaiian or other Pacific Islander, non-Hispanic/Latino; 0.2% American Indian or Alaska Native, non-Hispanic/Latino; 2% Two or more races, non-Hispanic/Latino; 6% Race/ethnicity unknown; 0.3% international; 8% transferred in; 35% live on campus. *Retention:* 78% of full-time freshmen returned.
Freshmen *Admission:* 3,492 applied, 2,388 admitted, 731 enrolled. *Average high school GPA:* 3.06. *Test scores:* SAT critical reading scores over 500: 53%; SAT math scores over 500: 58%; SAT writing scores over 500: 49%; SAT critical reading scores over 600: 12%; SAT math scores over 600: 10%; SAT writing scores over 600: 9%; SAT critical reading scores over 700: 2%; SAT math scores over 700: 1%; SAT writing scores over 700: 1%.
Faculty *Total:* 285, 62% full-time, 68% with terminal degrees. *Student/faculty ratio:* 17:1.
Academics *Calendar:* semesters. *Degrees:* certificates, bachelor's, master's, post-master's, and postbachelor's certificates. *Special study options:* academic remediation for entering students, accelerated degree program, adult/continuing education programs, advanced placement credit, distance learning, double majors, honors programs, independent study, internships, off-campus study, part-time degree program, services for LD students, student-designed majors, study abroad, summer session for credit. *ROTC:* Army (b).
Computers on Campus 500 computers/terminals are available on campus for general student use. Students can access the following: computer help desk, free student e-mail accounts, online (class) grades, online (class) registration, online (class) schedules. Campuswide network is available. 100% of college-owned or -operated housing units are wired for high-speed Internet access. Wireless service is available via entire campus.
Student Life *Housing options:* coed, disabled students. Campus housing is university owned. Freshman applicants given priority for college housing. *Activities and organizations:* drama/theater group, student-run newspaper, radio station, choral group, Student Government Association, Dance Club, Activities Board, Greek council, MassPirg, national fraternities, national sororities. *Campus security:* 24-hour emergency response devices and patrols, student patrols, late-night transport/escort service, controlled dormitory access. *Student services:* health clinic, personal/psychological counseling.
Athletics Member NCAA. All Division III. *Intercollegiate sports:* baseball M, basketball M/W, cross-country running M/W, field hockey W, football M, ice hockey M, lacrosse W, soccer M/W, softball W, track and field M/W. *Intramural sports:* basketball M/W, football M/W, racquetball M/W, soccer M/W,

softball M/W, swimming and diving M/W, table tennis M/W, ultimate Frisbee M/W, volleyball M/W, water polo M/W.

Standardized Tests *Required:* SAT or ACT (for admission).

Costs (2010–11) *Tuition:* state resident $970 full-time, $40 per credit part-time; nonresident $7050 full-time, $294 per credit part-time. Full-time tuition and fees vary according to class time and reciprocity agreements. Part-time tuition and fees vary according to class time and reciprocity agreements. *Required fees:* $6830 full-time, $285 per credit part-time. *Room and board:* $8106. Room and board charges vary according to board plan and housing facility. *Payment plan:* installment. *Waivers:* senior citizens and employees or children of employees.

Financial Aid Of all full-time matriculated undergraduates who enrolled in 2009, 3,132 applied for aid, 1,934 were judged to have need, 1,742 had their need fully met. 248 Federal Work-Study jobs (averaging $1076). In 2009, 76 non-need-based awards were made. *Average percent of need met:* 93%. *Average financial aid package:* $8645. *Average need-based loan:* $3679. *Average need-based gift aid:* $4336. *Average non-need-based aid:* $1292. *Average indebtedness upon graduation:* $19,902.

Applying *Options:* electronic application, deferred entrance. *Application fee:* $25. *Required:* essay or personal statement, high school transcript, minimum 2 GPA, 16 core courses. *Application deadlines:* rolling (freshmen), rolling (out-of-state freshmen), rolling (transfers). *Notification:* continuous (freshmen), continuous (out-of-state freshmen), continuous (transfers).

Freshman Application Contact Kay Reynolds, Director of Admissions, Fitchburg State University, 160 Pearl Street, Fitchburg, MA 01420-2697. *Phone:* 978-665-3144. *Toll-free phone:* 800-705-9692. *Fax:* 978-665-4540. *E-mail:* admissions@fitchburgstate.edu. *Web site:* http://www.fitchburgstate.edu/.

See page 1286 for the College Close-Up.

Framingham State University
Framingham, Massachusetts

- **State-supported** comprehensive, founded 1839, part of Massachusetts Public Higher Education System
- **Suburban** 50-acre campus with easy access to Boston
- **Endowment** $18.8 million
- **Coed** 3,858 undergraduate students, 83% full-time, 64% women, 36% men
- **Moderately difficult** entrance level, 66% of applicants were admitted

Undergraduates 3,188 full-time, 670 part-time. 5% are from out of state; 6% Black or African American, non-Hispanic/Latino; 5% Hispanic/Latino; 2% Asian, non-Hispanic/Latino; 0.1% Native Hawaiian or other Pacific Islander, non-Hispanic/Latino; 0.3% American Indian or Alaska Native, non-Hispanic/Latino; 0.4% Two or more races, non-Hispanic/Latino; 10% Race/ethnicity unknown; 0.9% international; 10% transferred in; 50% live on campus. *Retention:* 75% of full-time freshmen returned.

Freshmen *Admission:* 3,458 applied, 2,265 admitted, 722 enrolled. *Average high school GPA:* 3.11. *Test scores:* SAT critical reading scores over 500: 56%; SAT math scores over 500: 60%; SAT writing scores over 500: 53%; ACT scores over 18: 100%; SAT critical reading scores over 600: 11%; SAT math scores over 600: 11%; SAT writing scores over 600: 12%; ACT scores over 24: 40%; SAT critical reading scores over 700: 1%; ACT scores over 30: 10%.

Faculty *Total:* 251, 64% full-time, 52% with terminal degrees. *Student/faculty ratio:* 17:1.

Academics *Calendar:* semesters. *Degrees:* bachelor's, master's, and post-bachelor's certificates. *Special study options:* advanced placement credit, distance learning, double majors, English as a second language, honors programs, independent study, internships, off-campus study, part-time degree program, services for LD students, study abroad, summer session for credit.

Computers on Campus 232 computers/terminals and 3,500 ports are available on campus for general student use. Students can access the following: computer help desk, free student e-mail accounts, online (class) grades, online (class) registration, online (class) schedules. Campuswide network is available. Wireless service is available via entire campus.

Student Life *Housing options:* coed, women-only. Campus housing is university owned. *Activities and organizations:* drama/theater group, student-run

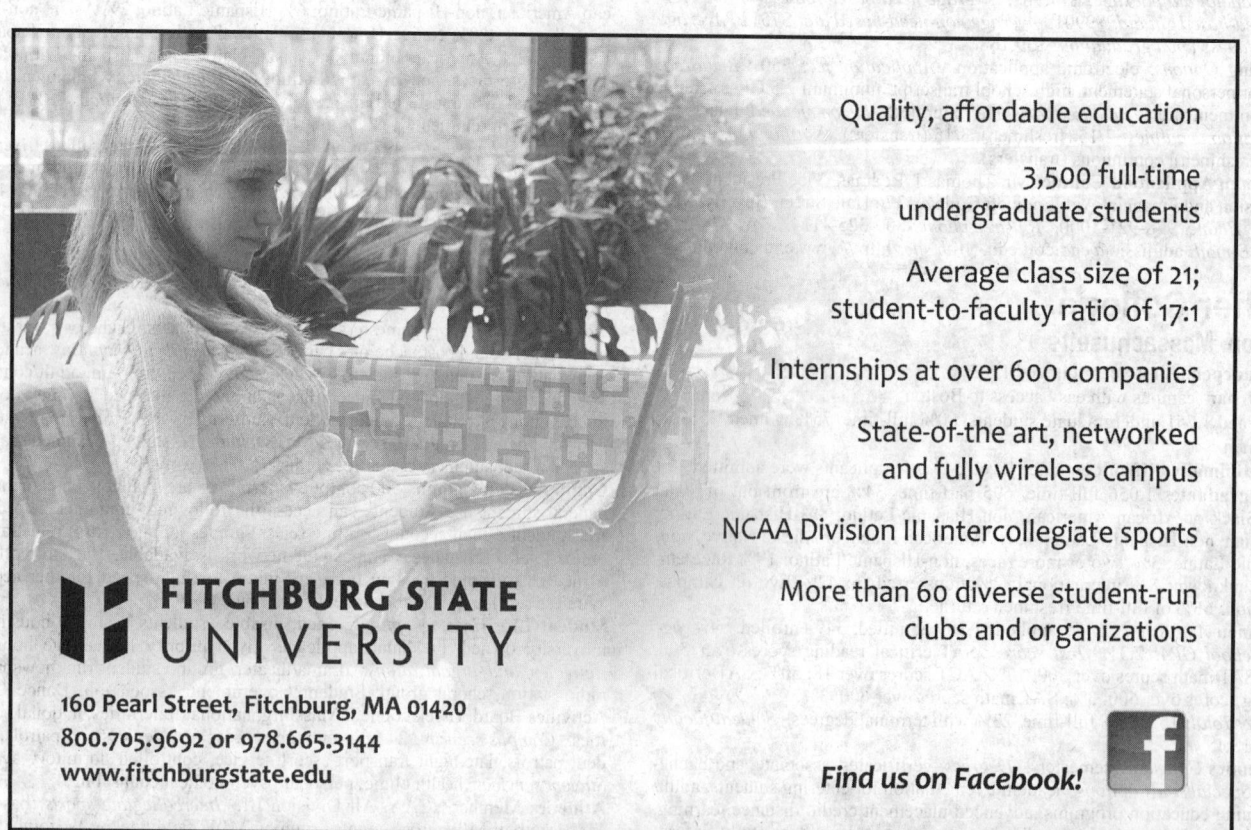

newspaper, radio station, choral group, Dance Club, Student Union Activities Board, Gatepost (student newspaper), Student Government Association, Hilltop Players (theater group). *Campus security:* 24-hour emergency response devices and patrols, student patrols, late-night transport/escort service, controlled dormitory access. *Student services:* health clinic, personal/psychological counseling.

Athletics Member NCAA. All Division III. *Intercollegiate sports:* baseball M, basketball M/W, cross-country running M/W, field hockey W, football M, ice hockey M, lacrosse W, soccer M/W, softball W, volleyball W. *Intramural sports:* badminton M(c)/W(c), basketball M/W, cheerleading M(c)/W(c), football M/W, golf M/W, rugby M(c)/W(c), skiing (downhill) M(c)/W(c), soccer M/W, tennis M/W, ultimate Frisbee M/W, volleyball M/W, weight lifting M/W.

Standardized Tests *Required:* SAT or ACT (for admission).

Costs (2010–11) *Tuition:* state resident $970 full-time, $162 per course part-time; nonresident $7050 full-time, $1175 per course part-time. Full-time tuition and fees vary according to class time. Part-time tuition and fees vary according to class time and course load. *Required fees:* $6095 full-time, $1081 per course part-time. *Room and board:* $7100; room only: $5600. Room and board charges vary according to board plan and housing facility. *Payment plans:* tuition prepayment, installment. *Waivers:* senior citizens and employees or children of employees.

Financial Aid Of all full-time matriculated undergraduates who enrolled in 2008, 2,151 applied for aid, 1,521 were judged to have need, 1,201 had their need fully met. In 2008, 85 non-need-based awards were made. *Average percent of need met:* 79%. *Average financial aid package:* $6934. *Average need-based loan:* $4988. *Average need-based gift aid:* $4142. *Average non-need-based aid:* $2278. *Average indebtedness upon graduation:* $19,000.

Applying *Options:* electronic application, early admission, early action, deferred entrance. *Application fee:* $45. *Required:* high school transcript, 1 letter of recommendation, minimum of 16 college preparatory courses in specified areas. *Recommended:* minimum 3 GPA. *Application deadlines:* 5/15 (freshmen), 5/1 (transfers), 11/15 (early action). *Notification:* continuous (freshmen), continuous (transfers), 12/15 (early action).

Freshman Application Contact Ms. Shayna Bailey, Assistant Dean of Admissions, Framingham State University, 100 State Street, PO Box 9101, Framingham, MA 01701-9101. *Phone:* 508-626-4500. *Fax:* 508-626-4017. *E-mail:* admiss@framingham.edu. *Web site:* http://www.framingham.edu/.

See page 1296 for the College Close-Up.

Franklin W. Olin College of Engineering
Needham, Massachusetts

- **Independent** 4-year, founded 2002
- **Suburban** 75-acre campus with easy access to Boston
- **Endowment** $333.6 million
- **Coed** 346 undergraduate students, 100% full-time, 45% women, 55% men
- **Most difficult** entrance level, 30% of applicants were admitted

Undergraduates 346 full-time. Students come from 44 states and territories; 15 other countries; 89% are from out of state; 0.6% Black or African American, non-Hispanic/Latino; 3% Hispanic/Latino; 17% Asian, non-Hispanic/Latino; 4% Two or more races, non-Hispanic/Latino; 9% Race/ethnicity unknown; 8% international; 100% live on campus. *Retention:* 100% of full-time freshmen returned.

Freshmen *Admission:* 567 applied, 171 admitted, 91 enrolled. *Average high school GPA:* 4. *Test scores:* SAT critical reading scores over 500: 100%; SAT math scores over 500: 100%; SAT writing scores over 500: 100%; ACT scores over 18: 100%; SAT critical reading scores over 600: 94%; SAT math scores over 600: 100%; SAT writing scores over 600: 95%; ACT scores over 24: 100%; SAT critical reading scores over 700: 58%; SAT math scores over 700: 85%; SAT writing scores over 700: 46%; ACT scores over 30: 95%.

Faculty *Total:* 44, 86% full-time, 95% with terminal degrees. *Student/faculty ratio:* 9:1.

Academics *Degree:* bachelor's. *Special study options:* independent study, internships, services for LD students, student-designed majors, study abroad.

Computers on Campus 15 computers/terminals and 5,500 ports are available on campus for general student use. Students can access the following: campus intranet, computer help desk, free student e-mail accounts, online (class) grades, online (class) registration, online (class) schedules. Campuswide network is available. 100% of college-owned or -operated housing units are wired for high-speed Internet access. Wireless service is available via entire campus.

Student Life *Housing:* on-campus residence required through senior year. *Options:* coed, disabled students. Campus housing is university owned. Freshman campus housing is guaranteed. *Activities and organizations:* drama/theater group, student-run newspaper, choral group, Greening Olin, Olin Fire Arts

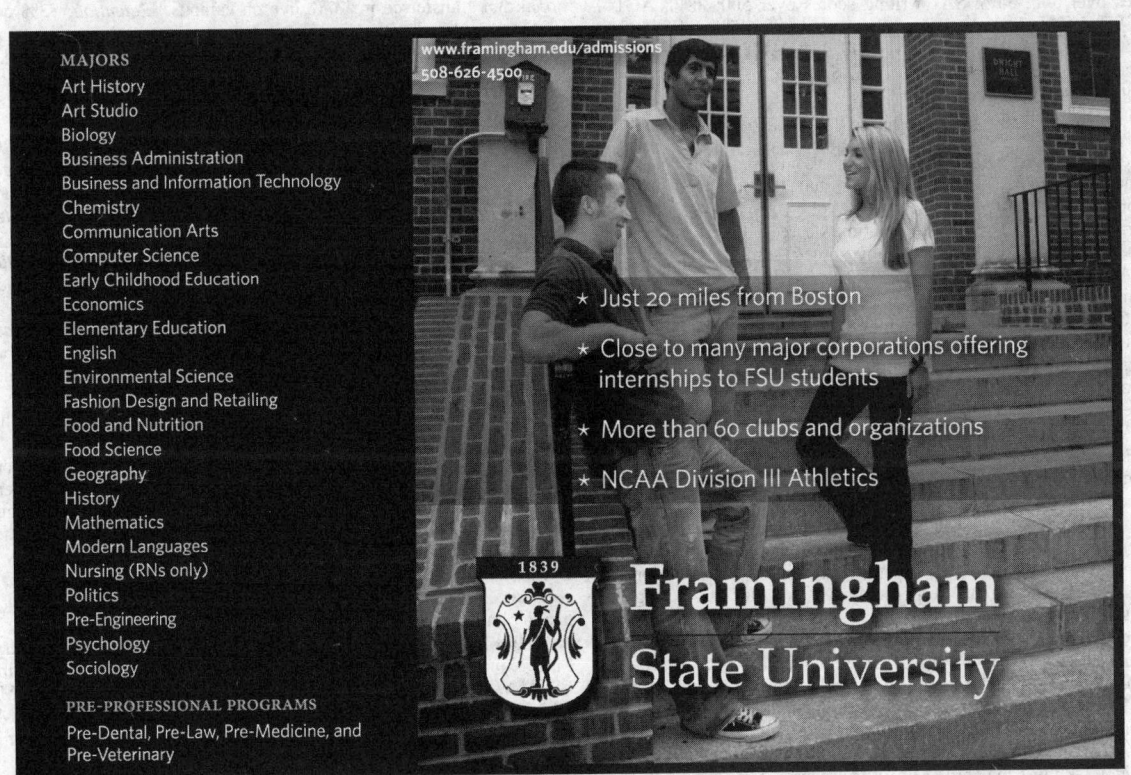

Club, Support, Encourage and Recognize Volunteerism (SERV), Olin Entrepreneurial Group, Open. *Campus security:* 24-hour emergency response devices and patrols, controlled dormitory access. *Student services:* health clinic, personal/psychological counseling.

Athletics *Intercollegiate sports:* soccer M(c)/W(c), ultimate Frisbee M(c)/W(c). *Intramural sports:* basketball M/W, softball M/W, volleyball M/W.

Standardized Tests *Required:* SAT or ACT (for admission), SAT Subject Tests (for admission).

Costs (2011–12) *Comprehensive fee:* $53,450 includes full-time tuition ($39,000), mandatory fees ($450), and room and board ($14,000). *College room only:* $8800. *Payment plan:* installment.

Financial Aid Of all full-time matriculated undergraduates who enrolled in 2009, 130 applied for aid, 115 were judged to have need, 115 had their need fully met. In 2009, 228 non-need-based awards were made. *Average percent of need met:* 100%. *Average financial aid package:* $34,439. *Average need-based loan:* $2805. *Average need-based gift aid:* $13,754. *Average non-need-based aid:* $35,310. *Average indebtedness upon graduation:* $13,200. *Financial aid deadline:* 2/15.

Applying *Options:* electronic application, deferred entrance. *Application fee:* $80. *Required:* essay or personal statement, high school transcript, 3 letters of recommendation, interview. *Application deadline:* 1/1 (freshmen). *Notification:* 3/21 (freshmen).

Freshman Application Contact Franklin W. Olin College of Engineering, Olin Way, Needham, MA 02492-1200. *Phone:* 781-292-2250. *Fax:* 781-292-2310. *E-mail:* info@olin.edu. *Web site:* http://www.olin.edu/.

Gordon College
Wenham, Massachusetts

- **Independent nondenominational** comprehensive, founded 1889
- **Suburban** 500-acre campus with easy access to Boston
- **Endowment** $22.3 million
- **Coed** 1,524 undergraduate students, 97% full-time, 61% women, 39% men
- **Moderately difficult** entrance level, 70% of applicants were admitted

Undergraduates 1,482 full-time, 42 part-time. Students come from 40 states and territories; 32 other countries; 68% are from out of state; 2% Black or African American, non-Hispanic/Latino; 4% Hispanic/Latino; 2% Asian, non-Hispanic/Latino; 3% Two or more races, non-Hispanic/Latino; 4% Race/ethnicity unknown; 4% international; 4% transferred in; 86% live on campus. *Retention:* 81% of full-time freshmen returned.

Freshmen *Admission:* 1,600 applied, 1,119 admitted, 350 enrolled. *Average high school GPA:* 3.6. *Test scores:* SAT critical reading scores over 500: 86%; SAT math scores over 500: 84%; SAT writing scores over 500: 88%; ACT scores over 18: 95%; SAT critical reading scores over 600: 45%; SAT math scores over 600: 36%; SAT writing scores over 600: 44%; ACT scores over 24: 80%; SAT critical reading scores over 700: 11%; SAT math scores over 700: 5%; SAT writing scores over 700: 8%; ACT scores over 30: 33%.

Faculty *Total:* 171, 57% full-time, 49% with terminal degrees. *Student/faculty ratio:* 12:1.

Academics *Calendar:* semesters. *Degrees:* bachelor's and master's. *Special study options:* academic remediation for entering students, advanced placement credit, cooperative education, double majors, honors programs, independent study, internships, off-campus study, part-time degree program, services for LD students, student-designed majors, study abroad, summer session for credit. *ROTC:* Army (c), Air Force (c). *Unusual degree programs:* 3-2 engineering with University of Southern California.

Computers on Campus 120 computers/terminals are available on campus for general student use. Students can access the following: campus intranet, computer help desk, free student e-mail accounts, online (class) grades, online (class) registration, online (class) schedules. Campuswide network is available. 100% of college-owned or -operated housing units are wired for high-speed Internet access. Wireless service is available via entire campus.

Student Life *Housing:* on-campus residence required through senior year. *Options:* coed, men-only, women-only, disabled students. Campus housing is university owned. Freshman campus housing is guaranteed. *Activities and organizations:* drama/theater group, student-run newspaper, radio station, choral group, Student Government Association, student ministries and volunteer programs, Diverse music ensembles, intramural sports, Short-term missions. *Campus security:* 24-hour emergency response devices and patrols, late-night transport/escort service, controlled dormitory access, Video cameras. *Student services:* health clinic, personal/psychological counseling.

Athletics Member NCAA. All Division III. *Intercollegiate sports:* baseball M, basketball M/W, cross-country running M/W, field hockey W, golf M(c)/W(c), lacrosse M/W, soccer M/W, softball W, swimming and diving M/W, tennis M/W, track and field M/W, volleyball W. *Intramural sports:* basketball M/W, cheerleading W(c), football M/W, ice hockey M(c)/W(c), racquetball M/W, rock climbing M/W, skiing (downhill) M(c)/W(c), soccer M/W, softball W, table tennis M/W, tennis M/W, track and field M/W, ultimate Frisbee M/W, volleyball M.

Standardized Tests *Required:* SAT or ACT (for admission). *Recommended:* SAT Subject Tests (for admission).

Costs (2011–12) *Comprehensive fee:* $39,040 includes full-time tuition ($29,310), mandatory fees ($1296), and room and board ($8434). Full-time tuition and fees vary according to course load. Part-time tuition: $1035 per credit. Part-time tuition and fees vary according to course load. *College room only:* $5628. Room and board charges vary according to board plan and housing facility. *Payment plan:* installment. *Waivers:* employees or children of employees.

Financial Aid Of all full-time matriculated undergraduates who enrolled in 2009, 1,192 applied for aid, 1,041 were judged to have need, 145 had their need fully met. 760 Federal Work-Study jobs (averaging $1468). In 2009, 355 non-need-based awards were made. *Average percent of need met:* 67%. *Average financial aid package:* $18,370. *Average need-based loan:* $4540. *Average need-based gift aid:* $13,765. *Average non-need-based aid:* $10,018. *Average indebtedness upon graduation:* $37,154.

Applying *Options:* electronic application, early admission, early decision, early action, deferred entrance. *Application fee:* $50. *Required:* high school transcript, 2 letters of recommendation, interview, Pastoral recommendation and statement of Christian faith. *Recommended:* essay or personal statement, minimum 3 GPA. *Application deadlines:* rolling (freshmen), rolling (transfers), 12/1 (early action). *Early decision deadline:* 11/15. *Notification:* continuous until 10/1 (freshmen), continuous (transfers), 12/15 (early decision), 1/1 (early action).

Freshman Application Contact Ms. June Budoni, Senior Admissions Director, Gordon College, 255 Grapevine Road, Wenham, MA 01984. *Phone:* 978-867-4218. *Toll-free phone:* 866-464-6736. *Fax:* 978-867-4682. *E-mail:* june.budoni@gordon.edu. *Web site:* http://www.gordon.edu/.

Hampshire College
Amherst, Massachusetts

- **Independent** 4-year, founded 1965
- **Small-town** 800-acre campus
- **Endowment** $36.5 million
- **Coed** 1,529 undergraduate students, 100% full-time, 60% women, 40% men
- **Moderately difficult** entrance level, 71% of applicants were admitted

Undergraduates 1,529 full-time. Students come from 46 states and territories; 24 other countries; 84% are from out of state; 3% Black or African American, non-Hispanic/Latino; 8% Hispanic/Latino; 3% Asian, non-Hispanic/Latino; 0.6% American Indian or Alaska Native, non-Hispanic/Latino; 3% Two or more races, non-Hispanic/Latino; 10% Race/ethnicity unknown; 5% international; 3% transferred in; 77% live on campus. *Retention:* 83% of full-time freshmen returned.

Freshmen *Admission:* 2,606 applied, 1,838 admitted, 418 enrolled. *Average high school GPA:* 3.68. *Test scores:* SAT critical reading scores over 500: 96%; SAT math scores over 500: 88%; SAT writing scores over 500: 96%; ACT scores over 18: 99%; SAT critical reading scores over 600: 76%; SAT math scores over 600: 55%; SAT writing scores over 600: 68%; ACT scores over 24: 84%; SAT critical reading scores over 700: 31%; SAT math scores over 700: 11%; SAT writing scores over 700: 18%; ACT scores over 30: 26%.

Faculty *Total:* 163, 55% full-time, 79% with terminal degrees. *Student/faculty ratio:* 13:1.

Academics *Calendar:* 4-1-4. *Degree:* bachelor's. *Special study options:* independent study, internships, off-campus study, services for LD students, student-designed majors, study abroad. *ROTC:* Army (c).

Computers on Campus 215 computers/terminals are available on campus for general student use. Students can access the following: campus intranet, computer help desk, free student e-mail accounts, online (class) grades, online (class) registration, online (class) schedules. Campuswide network is available. 100% of college-owned or -operated housing units are wired for high-speed Internet access. Wireless service is available via entire campus.

Student Life *Housing:* on-campus residence required through senior year. *Options:* coed, men-only, women-only, cooperative, disabled students. Campus housing is university owned. Freshman campus housing is guaranteed. *Activities and organizations:* drama/theater group, student-run newspaper, radio station, choral group, Red Scare Frisbee, Queer Community Alliance, Excalibur (fantasy/role playing), Sports Coop, Circus Folks Unite. *Campus security:* 24-hour emergency response devices and patrols. *Student services:* health clinic, personal/psychological counseling, women's center.

Athletics *Intercollegiate sports:* basketball M(c)/W(c), cross-country running M/W, equestrian sports M(c)/W(c), fencing M/W, soccer M/W, ultimate Frisbee M/W. *Intramural sports:* basketball M/W, equestrian sports M(c)/W(c), rock climbing M(c)/W(c), table tennis M(c)/W(c), ultimate Frisbee M/W.

Standardized Tests *Recommended:* SAT and SAT Subject Tests or ACT (for admission).

Costs (2011–12) *One-time required fee:* $110. *Comprehensive fee:* $54,080 includes full-time tuition ($41,900), mandatory fees ($1000), and room and board ($11,180). *College room only:* $7130. Room and board charges vary according to board plan. *Payment plan:* installment. *Waivers:* employees or children of employees.

Financial Aid Of all full-time matriculated undergraduates who enrolled in 2009, 951 applied for aid, 870 were judged to have need, 705 had their need fully met. 595 Federal Work-Study jobs (averaging $2200). 270 state and other part-time jobs (averaging $2245). In 2009, 239 non-need-based awards were made. *Average percent of need met:* 98%. *Average financial aid package:* $35,310. *Average need-based loan:* $4750. *Average need-based gift aid:* $28,085. *Average non-need-based aid:* $6220. *Average indebtedness upon graduation:* $20,669.

Applying *Options:* electronic application, early admission, early decision, early action, deferred entrance. *Application fee:* $60. *Required:* essay or personal statement, 1 letter of recommendation. *Required for some:* high school transcript, 2 letters of recommendation. *Recommended:* interview. *Application deadlines:* 1/1 (freshmen), 3/1 (transfers), 12/1 (early action). *Early decision deadline:* 11/15. *Notification:* 4/1 (freshmen), 4/15 (transfers), 12/15 (early decision), 2/1 (early action).

Freshman Application Contact Ms. Barbara Maryak, Director of Admissions, Hampshire College, Hampshire College, 893 West Street, Amherst, MA 01002. *Phone:* 413-559-5471. *Toll-free phone:* 877-937-4267. *Fax:* 413-559-5631. *E-mail:* admissions@hampshire.edu. *Web site:* http://www.hampshire.edu/.

Harvard University
Cambridge, Massachusetts

- **Independent** university, founded 1636
- **Urban** 380-acre campus with easy access to Boston
- **Endowment** $27.6 billion
- **Coed** 6,641 undergraduate students, 100% full-time, 50% women, 50% men
- **Most difficult** entrance level, 7% of applicants were admitted

Undergraduates 6,633 full-time, 8 part-time. Students come from 54 states and territories; 110 other countries; 74% are from out of state; 7% Black or African American, non-Hispanic/Latino; 8% Hispanic/Latino; 16% Asian, non-Hispanic/Latino; 0.1% Native Hawaiian or other Pacific Islander, non-Hispanic/Latino; 0.5% American Indian or Alaska Native, non-Hispanic/Latino; 3% Two or more races, non-Hispanic/Latino; 12% Race/ethnicity unknown; 10% international; 0.2% transferred in; 99% live on campus. *Retention:* 98% of full-time freshmen returned.

Freshmen *Admission:* 30,489 applied, 2,205 admitted, 1,663 enrolled.

Faculty *Total:* 2,189, 86% full-time, 98% with terminal degrees. *Student/faculty ratio:* 7:1.

Academics *Calendar:* semesters. *Degrees:* bachelor's, master's, and doctoral-research/scholarship. *Special study options:* accelerated degree program, advanced placement credit, double majors, honors programs, independent study, internships, off-campus study, services for LD students, student-designed majors, study abroad, summer session for credit. *ROTC:* Army (c), Navy (c), Air Force (c).

Computers on Campus 605 computers/terminals are available on campus for general student use. Students can access the following: computer help desk, free student e-mail accounts, online (class) grades, online (class) registration, online (class) schedules. Campuswide network is available. 100% of college-owned or -operated housing units are wired for high-speed Internet access. Wireless service is available via entire campus.

Student Life *Housing:* on-campus residence required for freshman year. *Options:* coed, cooperative, disabled students. Campus housing is university owned. Freshman campus housing is guaranteed. *Activities and organizations:* drama/theater group, student-run newspaper, radio and television station, choral group, marching band, Phillips Brooks House Association, Asian-American Association, International Relations Council, Harvard Crimson (newspaper), Harvard/Radcliffe Chorus. *Campus security:* 24-hour emergency response devices and patrols, late-night transport/escort service, controlled dormitory access, required and optional safety courses. *Student services:* health clinic, personal/psychological counseling, women's center.

Athletics Member NCAA. All Division I except football (Division I-AA). *Intercollegiate sports:* baseball M, basketball M/W, crew M/W, cross-country running M/W, fencing M/W, field hockey W, golf M/W, ice hockey M/W, lacrosse M/W, sailing M/W, skiing (cross-country) M/W, skiing (downhill) M/W, soccer M/W, softball W, squash M/W, swimming and diving M/W, tennis M/W, track and field M/W, volleyball M/W, water polo M/W, wrestling M. *Intramural sports:* archery M(c)/W(c), badminton M(c)/W(c), baseball M(c), basketball M/W, cheerleading M(c)/W(c), crew M/W, cross-country running M/W, fencing M/W, field hockey W(c), football M/W, ice hockey M/W, lacrosse M(c)/W(c), riflery M(c)/W(c), rugby M(c)/W(c), skiing (cross-country) M(c)/W(c), skiing (downhill) M(c)/W(c), soccer M/W, softball M/W, squash M/W, swimming and diving M/W, table tennis M/W, tennis M/W, ultimate Frisbee M/W, volleyball M/W, water polo M(c)/W(c), wrestling M(c)/W(c).

Standardized Tests *Required:* SAT or ACT (for admission), SAT Subject Tests (for admission).

Costs (2010–11) *Comprehensive fee:* $50,723 includes full-time tuition ($34,976), mandatory fees ($3439), and room and board ($12,308). *College room only:* $7525. *Payment plans:* tuition prepayment, installment.

Financial Aid Of all full-time matriculated undergraduates who enrolled in 2009, 4,439 applied for aid, 4,147 were judged to have need, 4,147 had their need fully met. 937 Federal Work-Study jobs (averaging $2553). 1,890 state and other part-time jobs (averaging $2602). *Average percent of need met:* 100%. *Average financial aid package:* $41,648. *Average need-based loan:* $3956. *Average need-based gift aid:* $39,156. *Average indebtedness upon graduation:* $10,102.

Applying *Options:* electronic application, deferred entrance. *Application fee:* $75. *Required:* essay or personal statement, high school transcript. *Recommended:* 2 letters of recommendation, interview. *Application deadlines:* 1/1 (freshmen), 3/1 (transfers). *Notification:* 4/1 (freshmen), 6/15 (transfers).

Freshman Application Contact Harvard University, Cambridge, MA 02138. *Phone:* 617-495-1551. *Web site:* http://www.harvard.edu/.

Hebrew College
Newton Centre, Massachusetts

- **Independent Jewish** comprehensive, founded 1921
- **Suburban** 3-acre campus with easy access to Boston
- **Coed** 6 undergraduate students, 17% women, 83% men
- **Minimally difficult** entrance level

Undergraduates 6 part-time. Students come from 3 states and territories; 1 other country; 1% are from out of state.

Faculty *Total:* 41, 49% full-time, 73% with terminal degrees.

Academics *Calendar:* semesters. *Degrees:* bachelor's, master's, and post-bachelor's certificates. *Special study options:* adult/continuing education programs, distance learning, double majors, independent study, off-campus study, part-time degree program, summer session for credit. *Unusual degree programs:* BA/MA combo for Jewish Studies or Jewish Education.

Computers on Campus 10 computers/terminals are available on campus for general student use.

Student Life *Housing:* college housing not available.

Standardized Tests *Required for some:* GRE. *Recommended:* SAT or ACT (for admission).

Costs (2010–11) *Tuition:* $22,500 full-time. Full-time tuition and fees vary according to program. Part-time tuition and fees vary according to course load and program. *Required fees:* $200 full-time. *Payment plan:* installment. *Waivers:* employees or children of employees.

Financial Aid Of all full-time matriculated undergraduates who enrolled in 2009, 2 applied for aid, 2 were judged to have need. In 2009, 2 non-need-based awards were made. *Average percent of need met:* 40%. *Average financial aid package:* $2900. *Average need-based gift aid:* $2900. *Average non-need-based aid:* $1200. *Average indebtedness upon graduation:* $8300.

Applying *Options:* early admission, early decision, deferred entrance. *Application fee:* $50. *Required:* essay or personal statement, high school transcript, 3 letters of recommendation, interview. *Required for some:* 60 credits of undergraduate transfer work for BA students. *Application deadlines:* rolling (freshmen), 4/15 (transfers). *Early decision deadline:* 12/15. *Notification:* continuous (freshmen), continuous until 8/1 (transfers).

Freshman Application Contact Director of Enrollment Management, Hebrew College, 160 Herreck Road, Newton Centre, MA 02459. *Phone:* 617-559-8610. *Toll-free phone:* 800-866-4814 Ext. 8619. *Fax:* 617-559-8601. *E-mail:* admissions@lhebrewcollege.edu. *Web site:* http://www.hebrewcollege.edu/.

Hellenic College
Brookline, Massachusetts

- **Independent Greek Orthodox** comprehensive, founded 1937
- **Suburban** 59-acre campus with easy access to Boston
- **Endowment** $22.6 million
- **Coed** 81 undergraduate students, 100% full-time, 46% women, 54% men
- **Minimally difficult** entrance level, 45% of applicants were admitted

Undergraduates 81 full-time. Students come from 30 states and territories; 7 other countries; 80% are from out of state; 1% Black or African American, non-Hispanic/Latino; 4% Hispanic/Latino; 1% Race/ethnicity unknown; 6% international; 14% transferred in; 95% live on campus. *Retention:* 94% of full-time freshmen returned.

Freshmen *Admission:* 58 applied, 26 admitted, 18 enrolled. *Average high school GPA:* 3. *Test scores:* SAT critical reading scores over 500: 70%; SAT math scores over 500: 60%; SAT writing scores over 500: 90%; SAT critical reading scores over 600: 45%; SAT math scores over 600: 15%; SAT writing scores over 600: 45%; SAT critical reading scores over 700: 20%; SAT writing scores over 700: 20%.

Faculty *Total:* 37, 32% full-time. *Student/faculty ratio:* 9:1.

Academics *Calendar:* semesters. *Degrees:* bachelor's and master's (also offers graduate degree programs through Holy Cross Greek Orthodox School of Theology). *Special study options:* academic remediation for entering students, advanced placement credit, double majors, independent study, internships, off-campus study, part-time degree program, summer session for credit.

Computers on Campus 35 computers/terminals and 100 ports are available on campus for general student use. Students can access the following: campus intranet, computer help desk, free student e-mail accounts, online (class) grades, online (class) registration, online (class) schedules. Campuswide network is available. 75% of college-owned or -operated housing units are wired for high-speed Internet access. Wireless service is available via dorm rooms, learning centers.

Student Life *Housing:* on-campus residence required through senior year. *Options:* coed. Campus housing is university owned. Freshman campus housing is guaranteed. *Activities and organizations:* student-run newspaper, choral group. *Campus security:* controlled dormitory access. *Student services:* health clinic, personal/psychological counseling.

Athletics *Intramural sports:* baseball M, basketball M/W, football M, golf M, soccer M, table tennis M/W, volleyball M/W.

Standardized Tests *Required:* SAT or ACT (for admission). *Required for some:* SAT Subject Tests (for admission).

Costs (2010–11) *Comprehensive fee:* $31,836 includes full-time tuition ($19,136), mandatory fees ($450), and room and board ($12,250). Part-time tuition: $797 per credit hour. *Room and board:* Room and board charges vary according to housing facility. *Payment plans:* installment, deferred payment. *Waivers:* children of alumni and employees or children of employees.

Financial Aid Of all full-time matriculated undergraduates who enrolled in 2008, 59 applied for aid, 57 were judged to have need. In 2008, 1 non-need-based awards were made. *Average percent of need met:* 80%. *Average financial aid package:* $9500. *Average need-based loan:* $5500. *Average non-need-based aid:* $5000. *Average indebtedness upon graduation:* $15,000.

Applying *Options:* electronic application, early action, deferred entrance. *Application fee:* $50. *Required:* essay or personal statement, high school transcript, minimum 2 GPA, interview, health certificate. *Application deadlines:* rolling (freshmen), rolling (transfers), 12/1 (early action). *Notification:* continuous (freshmen), continuous (transfers).

Freshman Application Contact Mr. Gregory Floor, Director of Admissions, Hellenic College, 50 Goddard Avenue, Brookline, MA 02445-7496. *Phone:* 617-850-1285. *Toll-free phone:* 866-424-2338. *Fax:* 617-850-1460. *E-mail:* admissions@hchc.edu. *Web site:* http://www.hchc.edu/.

ITT Technical Institute

Norwood, Massachusetts

- **Proprietary** primarily 2-year, founded 1990, part of ITT Educational Services, Inc.
- **Suburban** campus
- **Coed**
- **Minimally difficult** entrance level

Academics *Calendar:* quarters. *Degrees:* associate and bachelor's.

Student Life *Housing:* college housing not available.

Freshman Application Contact Director of Recruitment, ITT Technical Institute, 333 Providence Highway, Norwood, MA 02062. *Phone:* 781-278-7200. *Toll-free phone:* 800-879-8324. *Web site:* http://www.itt-tech.edu/.

ITT Technical Institute

Woburn, Massachusetts

- **Proprietary** primarily 2-year, founded 2000, part of ITT Educational Services, Inc.
- **Coed**
- **Minimally difficult** entrance level

Academics *Calendar:* quarters. *Degrees:* associate and bachelor's.

Student Life *Housing:* college housing not available.

Freshman Application Contact Director of Recruitment, ITT Technical Institute, 200 Ballardvale Stree, Suite 200, Woburn, MA 01801. *Phone:* 978-658-2636. *Toll-free phone:* 800-430-5097. *Web site:* http://www.itt-tech.edu/.

Lasell College

Newton, Massachusetts

- **Independent** comprehensive, founded 1851
- **Suburban** 50-acre campus with easy access to Boston
- **Coed** 1,630 undergraduate students, 98% full-time, 65% women, 35% men
- **Moderately difficult** entrance level, 68% of applicants were admitted

Undergraduates 1,603 full-time, 27 part-time. Students come from 26 states and territories; 15 other countries; 42% are from out of state; 4% transferred in; 81% live on campus. *Retention:* 73% of full-time freshmen returned.

Freshmen *Admission:* 3,398 applied, 2,295 admitted, 474 enrolled. *Average high school GPA:* 2.8. *Test scores:* SAT critical reading scores over 500: 51%; SAT math scores over 500: 51%; SAT writing scores over 500: 48%; ACT scores over 18: 97%; SAT critical reading scores over 600: 8%; SAT math scores over 600: 7%; SAT writing scores over 600: 8%; ACT scores over 24: 21%.

Faculty *Total:* 191, 36% full-time, 29% with terminal degrees. *Student/faculty ratio:* 15:1.

Academics *Calendar:* semesters. *Degrees:* bachelor's, master's, post-master's, and postbachelor's certificates. *Special study options:* advanced placement credit, cooperative education, double majors, English as a second language, honors programs, independent study, internships, part-time degree program, student-designed majors, study abroad.

Computers on Campus 150 computers/terminals are available on campus for general student use. Students can access the following: campus intranet, computer help desk, free student e-mail accounts, online (class) grades, online (class) registration, online (class) schedules. Campuswide network is available. 100% of college-owned or -operated housing units are wired for high-speed Internet access. Wireless service is available via computer centers, computer labs, dorm rooms, learning centers, libraries, student centers.

Student Life *Housing options:* coed, women-only, cooperative. Campus housing is university owned. Freshman campus housing is guaranteed. *Activities and organizations:* drama/theater group, student-run newspaper, radio station, choral group, Campus Activities Board, Tennis Club, Lasell College Radio Station, Students Advocating for Equality, Lasell Environmental Action Force. *Campus security:* 24-hour emergency response devices and patrols, late-night transport/escort service, controlled dormitory access. *Student services:* health clinic, personal/psychological counseling.

Athletics Member NCAA. All Division III. *Intercollegiate sports:* baseball M, basketball M/W, cross-country running M/W, field hockey W, lacrosse M/W, soccer M/W, softball W, track and field M/W, volleyball M/W. *Intramural sports:* basketball M/W, cheerleading M(c)/W(c), crew M(c)/W(c), rugby M(c), soccer M/W, tennis W(c), volleyball M/W.

Standardized Tests *Required:* SAT or ACT (for admission).

Costs (2011–12) *Comprehensive fee:* $39,800 includes full-time tuition ($26,500), mandatory fees ($1000), and room and board ($12,300). Full-time tuition and fees vary according to program. Part-time tuition: $900 per credit hour. Part-time tuition and fees vary according to program. *Required fees:* $270 per term part-time. *Room and board:* Room and board charges vary according to board plan. *Payment plan:* installment. *Waivers:* children of alumni and employees or children of employees.

Financial Aid Of all full-time matriculated undergraduates who enrolled in 2009, 1,308 applied for aid, 1,176 were judged to have need, 188 had their need fully met. 919 Federal Work-Study jobs (averaging $1900). In 2009, 128 non-need-based awards were made. *Average percent of need met:* 89%. *Average financial aid package:* $20,097. *Average need-based loan:* $7221. *Average need-based gift aid:* $14,766. *Average non-need-based aid:* $7742. *Average indebtedness upon graduation:* $38,428.

Applying *Options:* electronic application, deferred entrance. *Application fee:* $40. *Required:* essay or personal statement, high school transcript, 2 letters of recommendation, college preparatory program. *Recommended:* interview. *Application deadlines:* rolling (freshmen), rolling (transfers). *Notification:* continuous (freshmen), continuous (transfers).

Freshman Application Contact Lasell College, 1844 Commonwealth Avenue, Newton, MA 02466-2709. *Phone:* 617-243-2225. *Toll-free phone:* 888-LASELL-4. *Web site:* http://www.lasell.edu/.

Lesley University

Cambridge, Massachusetts

- **Independent** comprehensive, founded 1909
- **Urban** campus with easy access to Boston
- **Coed, primarily women** 1,377 undergraduate students, 96% full-time, 76% women, 24% men
- 67% of applicants were admitted

Undergraduates 1,327 full-time, 50 part-time. 44% are from out of state; 54% live on campus. *Retention:* 75% of full-time freshmen returned.

Freshmen *Admission:* 2,611 applied, 1,754 admitted. *Average high school GPA:* 2.9. *Test scores:* SAT critical reading scores over 500: 68%; SAT math scores over 500: 61%; SAT writing scores over 500: 66%; ACT scores over 18: 94%; SAT critical reading scores over 600: 26%; SAT math scores over 600: 20%; SAT writing scores over 600: 26%; ACT scores over 24: 41%; SAT critical reading scores over 700: 4%; SAT math scores over 700: 1%; SAT writing scores over 700: 3%; ACT scores over 30: 9%.

Faculty *Total:* 258, 28% full-time, 41% with terminal degrees. *Student/faculty ratio:* 10:1.

Academics *Calendar:* semesters. *Degrees:* associate, bachelor's, master's, doctoral-research/scholarship, post-master's, and postbachelor's certificates. *Special study options:* academic remediation for entering students, accelerated degree program, adult/continuing education programs, advanced placement credit, distance learning, double majors, external degree program, freshman honors college, honors programs, independent study, internships, off-campus study, part-time degree program, services for LD students, student-designed majors, study abroad, summer session for credit.

Computers on Campus Students can access the following: free student e-mail accounts, online (class) registration. Campuswide network is available. Wireless service is available via classrooms, student centers.

Student Life *Housing options:* coed, women-only. Campus housing is university owned and leased by the school. Freshman applicants given priority for college housing. *Activities and organizations:* drama/theater group, choral group. *Campus security:* 24-hour emergency response devices and patrols, late-night transport/escort service, controlled dormitory access. *Student services:* health clinic, personal/psychological counseling.

Athletics Member NCAA. All Division III except baseball (Division II). *Intercollegiate sports:* baseball M, basketball M/W, cross-country running M/W, soccer M/W, softball W, volleyball M/W. *Intramural sports:* swimming and diving M/W, tennis M.

Standardized Tests *Required:* SAT or ACT (for admission).

Costs (2010–11) *Comprehensive fee:* $42,200 includes full-time tuition ($29,150), mandatory fees ($250), and room and board ($12,800). *College room only:* $7950. Room and board charges vary according to housing facility. *Payment plan:* installment. *Waivers:* employees or children of employees.

Financial Aid Of all full-time matriculated undergraduates who enrolled in 2009, 1,337 applied for aid, 1,034 were judged to have need, 155 had their need fully met. In 2009, 224 non-need-based awards were made. *Average percent of need met:* 70%. *Average financial aid package:* $16,579. *Average need-based loan:* $4534. *Average need-based gift aid:* $14,563. *Average non-need-based aid:* $10,358. *Average indebtedness upon graduation:* $18,000.

Applying *Options:* electronic application, early action, deferred entrance. *Application fee:* $50. *Required:* essay or personal statement, high school transcript. *Recommended:* interview. *Application deadlines:* rolling (freshmen), rolling (transfers). *Notification:* continuous (freshmen), continuous (transfers).

Freshman Application Contact Lesley University, 29 Everett Street, Cambridge, MA 02138-2790. *Phone:* 617-349-8800. *Toll-free phone:* 800-999-1959 Ext. 8800. *Web site:* http://www.lesley.edu/.

Massachusetts College of Art and Design

Boston, Massachusetts

- **State-supported** comprehensive, founded 1873, part of Massachusetts Public Higher Education System
- **Urban** 5-acre campus
- **Endowment** $10.9 million
- **Coed** 2,259 undergraduate students, 73% full-time, 67% women, 33% men
- **Very difficult** entrance level, 59% of applicants were admitted

Undergraduates 1,649 full-time, 610 part-time. Students come from 26 states and territories; 49 other countries; 29% are from out of state; 3% Black or African American, non-Hispanic/Latino; 4% Hispanic/Latino; 6% Asian, non-Hispanic/Latino; 0.2% American Indian or Alaska Native, non-Hispanic/Latino; 4% Two or more races, non-Hispanic/Latino; 7% Race/ethnicity unknown; 2% international; 7% transferred in; 23% live on campus. *Retention:* 89% of full-time freshmen returned.

Freshmen *Admission:* 1,551 applied, 920 admitted, 340 enrolled. *Average high school GPA:* 3.27. *Test scores:* SAT critical reading scores over 500: 79%; SAT math scores over 500: 64%; SAT writing scores over 500: 71%; SAT critical reading scores over 600: 28%; SAT math scores over 600: 19%; SAT writing scores over 600: 27%; SAT critical reading scores over 700: 4%; SAT math scores over 700: 1%; SAT writing scores over 700: 3%.

Faculty *Total:* 252, 39% full-time. *Student/faculty ratio:* 10:1.

Academics *Calendar:* semesters. *Degrees:* certificates, bachelor's, master's, and postbachelor's certificates. *Special study options:* double majors, independent study, internships, off-campus study, part-time degree program, student-designed majors, study abroad, summer session for credit.

Computers on Campus 370 computers/terminals are available on campus for general student use. Students can access the following: campus intranet, computer help desk, free student e-mail accounts, online (class) schedules. Campuswide network is available. 100% of college-owned or -operated housing units are wired for high-speed Internet access. Wireless service is available via entire campus.

Student Life *Housing options:* coed. Campus housing is university owned. Freshman campus housing is guaranteed. *Activities and organizations:* drama/theater group, student-run newspaper, radio station, International Students' Club, Design Research Unit, Spectrum, film society, Event Works. *Campus security:* 24-hour emergency response devices and patrols, late-night transport/escort service, security lighting, self-defense workshops. *Student services:* health clinic, personal/psychological counseling, women's center.

Athletics *Intramural sports:* basketball M/W, ice hockey M, sailing M/W, softball M/W, table tennis M/W, volleyball M/W.

Standardized Tests *Required:* SAT or ACT (for admission).

Costs (2010–11) *Tuition:* state resident $9000 full-time; nonresident $25,400 full-time. Full-time tuition and fees vary according to course load and degree level. Part-time tuition and fees vary according to course load and degree level. *Room and board:* $11,750. Room and board charges vary according to board plan and housing facility. *Payment plan:* installment. *Waivers:* senior citizens and employees or children of employees.

Financial Aid Of all full-time matriculated undergraduates who enrolled in 2008, 1,126 applied for aid, 890 were judged to have need. 187 Federal Work-Study jobs (averaging $860). *Average financial aid package:* $8917. *Average need-based loan:* $4484. *Average need-based gift aid:* $5792.

Applying *Options:* electronic application, early admission, early action, deferred entrance. *Application fee:* $65. *Required:* essay or personal statement, high school transcript, minimum 3 GPA, 3 letters of recommendation, portfolio. *Application deadlines:* 2/1 (freshmen), 2/1 (transfers), 12/1 (early action). *Notification:* 1/5 (early action).

Freshman Application Contact Massachusetts College of Art and Design, 621 Huntington Avenue, Boston, MA 02115. *Phone:* 617-879-7230. *Fax:* 617-879-7250. *E-mail:* admissions@massart.edu. *Web site:* http://www.massart.edu/.

Massachusetts College of Liberal Arts

North Adams, Massachusetts

- **State-supported** comprehensive, founded 1894, part of Massachusetts State University System
- **Small-town** 105-acre campus
- **Endowment** $7.1 million
- **Coed** 1,721 undergraduate students, 88% full-time, 60% women, 40% men
- **Moderately difficult** entrance level, 70% of applicants were admitted

Undergraduates 1,507 full-time, 214 part-time. Students come from 16 states and territories; 24% are from out of state; 7% Black or African American, non-Hispanic/Latino; 6% Hispanic/Latino; 0.9% Asian, non-Hispanic/Latino; 0.2% Native Hawaiian or other Pacific Islander, non-Hispanic/Latino; 0.4% American Indian or Alaska Native, non-Hispanic/Latino; 0.2% Two or more races, non-Hispanic/Latino; 5% Race/ethnicity unknown; 0.1% international; 9% transferred in; 68% live on campus. *Retention:* 74% of full-time freshmen returned.

Freshmen *Admission:* 1,661 applied, 1,166 admitted, 353 enrolled. *Average high school GPA:* 3.04. *Test scores:* SAT critical reading scores over 500: 66%; SAT math scores over 500: 53%; SAT critical reading scores over 600: 20%; SAT math scores over 600: 10%; SAT critical reading scores over 700: 2%; SAT math scores over 700: 1%.

Faculty *Total:* 176, 51% full-time. *Student/faculty ratio:* 14:1.

Academics *Calendar:* semesters. *Degrees:* certificates, bachelor's, master's, and post-master's certificates. *Special study options:* academic remediation for entering students, accelerated degree program, advanced placement credit, cooperative education, distance learning, double majors, honors programs, independent study, internships, off-campus study, part-time degree program, services for LD students, student-designed majors, study abroad, summer session for credit. *Unusual degree programs:* 3-2 engineering with University of Massachusetts at Amherst; podiatric medicine with the New York School of Podiatric Medicine.

Computers on Campus 140 computers/terminals are available on campus for general student use. Students can access the following: campus intranet, computer help desk, free student e-mail accounts, online (class) grades, online (class) registration, online (class) schedules. Campuswide network is available. 100% of college-owned or -operated housing units are wired for high-speed Internet access. Wireless service is available via entire campus.

Student Life *Housing:* on-campus residence required through junior year. *Options:* coed, disabled students. Campus housing is university owned. Freshman applicants given priority for college housing. *Activities and organiza-*

tions: drama/theater group, student-run newspaper, radio and television station, choral group, Student Activities Council, Student Government Association, The Beacon (Student Newspaper), Harlequin-Musical Theatre Company, Dance Company, national fraternities, national sororities. *Campus security:* 24-hour emergency response devices and patrols, late-night transport/escort service, controlled dormitory access, escort service. *Student services:* health clinic, personal/psychological counseling, women's center.

Athletics Member NCAA. All Division III. *Intercollegiate sports:* baseball M, basketball M/W, cross-country running M/W, golf M, soccer M/W, softball W, tennis W. *Intramural sports:* basketball M/W, cross-country running M/W, equestrian sports M(c)/W(c), football M, golf M/W, lacrosse M(c)/W(c), racquetball M/W, rugby M(c)/W(c), skiing (cross-country) M(c)/W(c), skiing (downhill) M(c)/W(c), soccer M/W, softball M/W, squash M/W, swimming and diving M/W, tennis M/W, volleyball M/W, weight lifting M(c)/W(c), wrestling M(c)/W(c).

Standardized Tests *Required:* SAT or ACT (for admission).

Costs (2010–11) *One-time required fee:* $140. *Tuition:* state resident $1030 full-time, $43 per credit part-time; nonresident $9975 full-time, $416 per credit hour part-time. Part-time tuition and fees vary according to course load. *Required fees:* $6545 full-time, $221 per credit part-time. *Room and board:* $8246. Room and board charges vary according to board plan and housing facility. *Payment plan:* installment. *Waivers:* senior citizens and employees or children of employees.

Financial Aid Of all full-time matriculated undergraduates who enrolled in 2009, 1,309 applied for aid, 1,072 were judged to have need. 227 Federal Work-Study jobs (averaging $1508). In 2009, 72 non-need-based awards were made. *Average percent of need met:* 84%. *Average financial aid package:* $12,840. *Average need-based loan:* $3887. *Average need-based gift aid:* $5585. *Average non-need-based aid:* $2612. *Average indebtedness upon graduation:* $23,587.

Applying *Options:* electronic application, early admission, early action, deferred entrance. *Application fee:* $35. *Required:* essay or personal statement, high school transcript, minimum 3 GPA. *Required for some:* 3 letters of recommendation, interview, sliding scale applies (GPA and SAT) if below 3.0. *Application deadlines:* rolling (freshmen), rolling (transfers), 12/1 (early action). *Notification:* continuous (freshmen), continuous (transfers), 12/15 (early action).

Freshman Application Contact Ms. Gina Puc, Assistant Director of Freshman Admission, Massachusetts College of Liberal Arts, 375 Church Street, North Adams, MA 01247. *Phone:* 413-662-5428. *Toll-free phone:* 800-292-6632. *E-mail:* g.puc@mcla.edu. *Web site:* http://www.mcla.edu/.

Massachusetts College of Pharmacy and Health Sciences
Boston, Massachusetts

- **Independent** university, founded 1823
- **Urban** 3-acre campus
- **Endowment** $126.0 million
- **Coed**
- **55%** of applicants were admitted

Faculty *Student/faculty ratio:* 18:1.

Academics *Calendar:* semesters. *Degrees:* certificates, bachelor's, master's, doctoral-professional, doctoral-research/scholarship, and postbachelor's certificates.

Student Life *Campus security:* 24-hour emergency response devices and patrols, late-night transport/escort service, controlled dormitory access, electronically operated academic area entrances, security guards at entrance.

Standardized Tests *Required:* SAT or ACT (for admission).

Costs (2010–11) *Comprehensive fee:* $37,770 includes full-time tuition ($24,700), mandatory fees ($780), and room and board ($12,290). Full-time tuition and fees vary according to course load, degree level, location, program, and student level. Part-time tuition: $910 per credit. *Required fees:* $200 per term part-time. *Room and board:* Room and board charges vary according to board plan, housing facility, and location.

Financial Aid *Of all full-time matriculated undergraduates who enrolled in 2009,* 2,146 applied for aid, 1,953 were judged to have need, 953 had their need fully met. *In 2009,* 371 non-need-based awards were made. *Average percent of need met:* 41. *Average financial aid package:* $12,035. *Average need-based loan:* $5305. *Average need-based gift aid:* $8612. *Average non-need-based aid:* $11,269.

Applying *Options:* electronic application, early action, deferred entrance. *Application fee:* $70. *Required:* essay or personal statement, 2 letters of recommendation. *Required for some:* high school transcript, interview.

Freshman Application Contact Sandra Hernandez, Visit Concierge, Massachusetts College of Pharmacy and Health Sciences, 179 Longwood Avenue, Boston, MA 02115. *Phone:* 617-732-2850. *Toll-free phone:* 800-225-5506. *Fax:* 617-732-2118. *E-mail:* admissions@mcphs.edu. *Web site:* http://www.mcphs.edu/.

Massachusetts Institute of Technology
Cambridge, Massachusetts

- **Independent** university, founded 1861
- **Urban** 168-acre campus with easy access to Boston
- **Endowment** $8.3 billion
- **Coed** 4,299 undergraduate students, 99% full-time, 45% women, 55% men
- **Most difficult** entrance level, 10% of applicants were admitted

Undergraduates 4,252 full-time, 47 part-time. Students come from 54 states and territories; 92 other countries; 90% are from out of state; 8% Black or African American, non-Hispanic/Latino; 13% Hispanic/Latino; 24% Asian, non-Hispanic/Latino; 0.9% American Indian or Alaska Native, non-Hispanic/Latino; 2% Two or more races, non-Hispanic/Latino; 5% Race/ethnicity unknown; 9% international; 0.4% transferred in; 93% live on campus. *Retention:* 97% of full-time freshmen returned.

Freshmen *Admission:* 16,632 applied, 1,676 admitted, 1,067 enrolled. *Test scores:* SAT critical reading scores over 500: 99%; SAT math scores over 500: 100%; SAT writing scores over 500: 100%; ACT scores over 18: 100%; SAT critical reading scores over 600: 93%; SAT math scores over 600: 100%; SAT writing scores over 600: 95%; ACT scores over 24: 100%; SAT critical reading scores over 700: 62%; SAT math scores over 700: 93%; SAT writing scores over 700: 64%; ACT scores over 30: 93%.

Faculty *Total:* 1,411, 83% full-time, 86% with terminal degrees. *Student/faculty ratio:* 8:1.

Academics *Calendar:* 4-1-4. *Degrees:* bachelor's, master's, and doctoral-research/scholarship. *Special study options:* advanced placement credit, cooperative education, double majors, English as a second language, independent study, internships, off-campus study, services for LD students, study abroad. *ROTC:* Army (b), Navy (b), Air Force (b).

Computers on Campus 1,100 computers/terminals and 50,000 ports are available on campus for general student use. Students can access the following: campus intranet, computer help desk, free student e-mail accounts, online (class) grades, online (class) registration, online (class) schedules. Campus-wide network is available. 100% of college-owned or -operated housing units are wired for high-speed Internet access. Wireless service is available via entire campus.

Student Life *Housing:* on-campus residence required for freshman year. *Options:* coed, women-only, cooperative, disabled students. Campus housing is university owned. Freshman campus housing is guaranteed. *Activities and organizations:* drama/theater group, student-run newspaper, radio and television station, choral group, marching band, Tech Catholic Community, Outing Club, Society of Women Engineers, Hillel, South Asian-American Students, national fraternities, national sororities. *Campus security:* 24-hour emergency response devices and patrols, late-night transport/escort service, controlled dormitory access. *Student services:* health clinic, personal/psychological counseling.

Athletics Member NCAA. All Division III except crew (Division I). *Intercollegiate sports:* badminton M(c)/W(c), baseball M, basketball M/W, cheerleading M(c)/W(c), crew M/W, cross-country running M/W, fencing M/W, field hockey W, football M, golf M(c)/W(c), gymnastics M(c)/W(c), ice hockey M(c)/W(c), lacrosse M/W, riflery M/W, rugby M(c)/W(c), sailing M/W, soccer M/W, softball W, squash M, swimming and diving M/W, table tennis M(c)/W(c), tennis M/W, track and field M/W, ultimate Frisbee M(c)/W(c), volleyball M/W, water polo M/W(c), wrestling M(c). *Intramural sports:* archery M(c)/W(c), badminton M/W, basketball M/W, bowling M/W, cheerleading M(c)/W(c), crew M(c)/W(c), golf M(c)/W(c), gymnastics M(c)/W(c), ice hockey M/W, rugby M(c)/W(c), soccer M/W, softball M/W, table tennis M/W, tennis M/W, ultimate Frisbee M/W, volleyball M/W, water polo M/W.

Standardized Tests *Required:* SAT or ACT (for admission), SAT Subject Tests (for admission).

Costs (2010–11) *Comprehensive fee:* $50,446 includes full-time tuition ($38,940), mandatory fees ($272), and room and board ($11,234). Part-time tuition: $605 per unit. Part-time tuition and fees vary according to course load. *College room only:* $6884. Room and board charges vary according to board plan and housing facility. *Payment plan:* installment. *Waivers:* employees or children of employees.

Financial Aid Of all full-time matriculated undergraduates who enrolled in 2008, 3,186 applied for aid, 2,694 were judged to have need, 2,694 had their need fully met. 778 Federal Work-Study jobs (averaging $2542). 1,365 state and other part-time jobs (averaging $2229). *Average percent of need met:* 100%. *Average financial aid package:* $37,731. *Average need-based loan:* $3211. *Average need-based gift aid:* $35,504. *Average indebtedness upon graduation:* $15,228. *Financial aid deadline:* 2/15.

Applying *Options:* electronic application, early action, deferred entrance. *Application fee:* $75. *Required:* essay or personal statement, high school transcript, 2 letters of recommendation, Two SAT II Subject Tests: one in math and one in science. *Recommended:* interview. *Application deadlines:* 1/1 (fresh-

men), 3/15 (transfers), 11/1 (early action). *Notification:* 3/20 (freshmen), 5/1 (transfers), 12/20 (early action).
Freshman Application Contact Admissions Counselors, Massachusetts Institute of Technology, 77 Massachusetts Avenue, Building 3-108, Cambridge, MA 02139-4307. *Phone:* 617-253-3400. *Fax:* 617-258-8304. *E-mail:* admissions@mit.edu. *Web site:* http://web.mit.edu/.

Massachusetts Maritime Academy
Buzzards Bay, Massachusetts

- **State-supported** comprehensive, founded 1891, part of Massachusetts Public Higher Education University System
- **Small-town** 55-acre campus with easy access to Boston and Providence
- **Endowment** $7.0 million
- **Coed, primarily men** 1,200 undergraduate students, 95% full-time, 9% women, 91% men
- **Moderately difficult** entrance level, 52% of applicants were admitted

Undergraduates 1,138 full-time, 62 part-time. Students come from 25 states and territories; 3 other countries; 27% are from out of state; 1% Black or African American, non-Hispanic/Latino; 2% Hispanic/Latino; 1% Asian, non-Hispanic/Latino; 0.4% American Indian or Alaska Native, non-Hispanic/Latino; 0.5% international; 5% transferred in; 92% live on campus. *Retention:* 85% of full-time freshmen returned.
Freshmen *Admission:* 951 applied, 499 admitted, 282 enrolled. *Average high school GPA:* 2.7. *Test scores:* SAT critical reading scores over 500: 51%; SAT math scores over 500: 78%; SAT writing scores over 500: 52%; ACT scores over 18: 90%; SAT critical reading scores over 600: 10%; SAT math scores over 600: 28%; SAT writing scores over 600: 7%; ACT scores over 24: 30%; SAT critical reading scores over 700: 2%; SAT writing scores over 700: 1%.
Faculty *Total:* 100, 67% full-time, 34% with terminal degrees. *Student/faculty ratio:* 15:1.
Academics *Calendar:* semesters plus sea term. *Degrees:* certificates, bachelor's, and master's. *Special study options:* academic remediation for entering students, advanced placement credit, cooperative education, distance learning, double majors, internships, off-campus study, part-time degree program, services for LD students, study abroad, summer session for credit. *ROTC:* Army (c), Navy (b).
Computers on Campus 100 computers/terminals and 1,000 ports are available on campus for general student use. Students can access the following: campus intranet, computer help desk, free student e-mail accounts, online (class) grades, online (class) registration, online (class) schedules, course-supported e-learning, wireless available campus wide. Campuswide network is available. 100% of college-owned or -operated housing units are wired for high-speed Internet access. Wireless service is available via entire campus.
Student Life *Housing:* on-campus residence required for freshman year. *Options:* coed, disabled students. Campus housing is university owned. Freshman campus housing is guaranteed. *Activities and organizations:* drama/theater group, student-run newspaper, choral group, marching band, club hockey, water sports, sailing/crew, rugby club, scuba club. *Campus security:* 24-hour emergency response devices and patrols, late-night transport/escort service, controlled dormitory access. *Student services:* health clinic, personal/psychological counseling, women's center.
Athletics Member NCAA, NAIA. All NCAA Division III. *Intercollegiate sports:* baseball M, crew M/W, cross-country running M/W, football M, lacrosse M, riflery M/W, sailing M/W, soccer M, softball W, track and field M/W, volleyball W. *Intramural sports:* basketball M/W, golf M(c)/W(c), ice hockey M(c), racquetball M/W, rugby M(c), skiing (cross-country) M(c)/W(c), skiing (downhill) M(c)/W(c), soccer M, softball M/W, squash M/W, swimming and diving M/W, table tennis M/W, tennis M/W, ultimate Frisbee M/W, volleyball M/W, water polo M/W, weight lifting M(c)/W(c).
Standardized Tests *Required:* SAT and SAT Subject Tests or ACT (for admission). *Required for some:* SAT and SAT Subject Tests or ACT (for admission).
Costs (2011–12) *One-time required fee:* $2210. *Tuition:* area resident $1611 full-time, $296 per credit hour part-time; state resident $2617 full-time, $311 per credit hour part-time; nonresident $15,261 full-time, $838 per credit hour part-time. Full-time tuition and fees vary according to course load, program, reciprocity agreements, and student level. Part-time tuition and fees vary according to class time, course load, reciprocity agreements, and student level. No tuition increase for student's term of enrollment. *Required fees:* $10,311 full-time, $269 per credit part-time. *Room and board:* $9204; room only: $5126. Room and board charges vary according to board plan and student level. *Payment plans:* installment, deferred payment. *Waivers:* minority students, senior citizens, and employees or children of employees.
Financial Aid Of all full-time matriculated undergraduates who enrolled in 2008, 874 applied for aid, 527 were judged to have need. 118 Federal Work-Study jobs (averaging $1000). *Average percent of need met:* 54%. *Average financial aid package:* $7065. *Average need-based loan:* $3570. *Average need-based gift aid:* $3200. *Average indebtedness upon graduation:* $32,553.

Applying *Options:* electronic application, early admission, deferred entrance. *Application fee:* $50. *Required:* essay or personal statement, minimum 2 GPA, 2 letters of recommendation, for students transferring between 12 and 23 credits minimum college GPA 2.5, for less than 23 transferable credits minimum college GPA 2.0 and meet admission standards for freshman applicants, for more than 24 transferable credits minimum college GPA 2.0. *Required for some:* high school transcript. *Recommended:* interview. *Application deadlines:* rolling (freshmen), rolling (out-of-state freshmen), rolling (transfers). *Notification:* continuous (freshmen), continuous (out-of-state freshmen), continuous (transfers).
Freshman Application Contact John McLaughlin, Director of Admissions, Massachusetts Maritime Academy, 101 Academy Drive, Blinn Hall, Buzzards Bay, MA 02532. *Phone:* 508-830-5031. *Toll-free phone:* 800-544-3411. *Fax:* 508-830-5077. *E-mail:* jmclaughlin@maritime.edu. *Web site:* http://www.maritime.edu/.

Merrimack College
North Andover, Massachusetts

- **Independent Roman Catholic** comprehensive, founded 1947
- **Suburban** 220-acre campus with easy access to Boston
- **Endowment** $30.8 million
- **Coed** 2,091 undergraduate students, 91% full-time, 48% women, 52% men
- **Moderately difficult** entrance level, 78% of applicants were admitted

Undergraduates 1,910 full-time, 181 part-time. Students come from 23 states and territories; 20 other countries; 28% are from out of state; 3% Black or African American, non-Hispanic/Latino; 5% Hispanic/Latino; 2% Asian, non-Hispanic/Latino; 0.0% Native Hawaiian or other Pacific Islander, non-Hispanic/Latino; 0.1% American Indian or Alaska Native, non-Hispanic/Latino; 0.7% Two or more races, non-Hispanic/Latino; 11% Race/ethnicity unknown; 1% international; 4% transferred in; 75% live on campus. *Retention:* 81% of full-time freshmen returned.
Freshmen *Admission:* 3,908 applied, 3,053 admitted, 490 enrolled. *Average high school GPA:* 3.12.
Faculty *Total:* 227, 58% full-time. *Student/faculty ratio:* 12:1.
Academics *Calendar:* semesters. *Degrees:* certificates, associate, bachelor's, and master's. *Special study options:* academic remediation for entering students, adult/continuing education programs, advanced placement credit, cooperative education, double majors, English as a second language, honors programs, independent study, internships, off-campus study, part-time degree program, services for LD students, student-designed majors, study abroad, summer session for credit. *ROTC:* Air Force (c).
Computers on Campus Students can access the following: campus intranet, computer help desk, free student e-mail accounts, online (class) grades, online (class) registration, online (class) schedules. Campuswide network is available. 100% of college-owned or -operated housing units are wired for high-speed Internet access. Wireless service is available via classrooms, computer centers, libraries, student centers.
Student Life *Housing options:* coed, disabled students. Campus housing is university owned. Freshman applicants given priority for college housing. *Activities and organizations:* drama/theater group, student-run newspaper, television station, choral group, Programming Board, Student Government; Class Councils, Greek Life, national fraternities, national sororities. *Campus security:* 24-hour emergency response devices and patrols, student patrols, late-night transport/escort service, controlled dormitory access, 24-hour staffed dorm entrances (adult employees). *Student services:* health clinic, personal/psychological counseling.
Athletics Member NCAA. All Division II except ice hockey (Division I). *Intercollegiate sports:* baseball M(s), basketball M(s)/W(s), crew W(s), cross-country running M(s)/W(s), field hockey W(s), football M(s), golf W(s), ice hockey M(s), lacrosse M(s)/W(s), soccer M(s)/W(s), softball W(s), tennis M(s)/W(s), track and field M(s)/W(s), volleyball W(s). *Intramural sports:* baseball M(c), basketball M/W, cheerleading W(c), football M(c), ice hockey M/W, lacrosse M(c)/W(c), rugby M(c)/W(c), skiing (downhill) M(c)/W(c), soccer M/W, softball M/W, ultimate Frisbee M(c)/W(c), volleyball M/W, wrestling M(c).
Costs (2010–11) *Comprehensive fee:* $42,080 includes full-time tuition ($30,780), mandatory fees ($600), and room and board ($10,700). Part-time tuition: $1100 per credit hour. Part-time tuition and fees vary according to class time, course level, course load, and degree level. *Required fees:* $75 per term part-time. *College room only:* $6340. Room and board charges vary according to board plan and housing facility. *Payment plan:* installment. *Waivers:* senior citizens and employees or children of employees.
Financial Aid Of all full-time matriculated undergraduates who enrolled in 2009, 1,612 applied for aid, 1,545 were judged to have need, 417 had their need fully met. 204 Federal Work-Study jobs (averaging $1329). 359 state and other part-time jobs (averaging $1779). In 2009, 283 non-need-based awards were made. *Average percent of need met:* 60%. *Average financial aid package:* $18,124. *Average need-based loan:* $5144. *Average need-based gift aid:*

$12,510. *Average non-need-based aid:* $10,019. *Average indebtedness upon graduation:* $27,000. *Financial aid deadline:* 2/1.

Applying *Options:* electronic application, early admission, early action, deferred entrance. *Required:* essay or personal statement, high school transcript, 1 letter of recommendation, first quarter senior grades. *Required for some:* interview. *Recommended:* minimum 2.8 GPA, interview. *Application deadlines:* 2/1 (freshmen), 8/29 (transfers), 11/15 (early action). *Notification:* 4/15 (freshmen), continuous (transfers), 12/15 (early action).

Freshman Application Contact Director of Admissions, Merrimack College, Austin Hall, A22, North Andover, MA 01845. *Phone:* 978-837-5100. *Fax:* 978-837-5133. *E-mail:* admission@merrimack.edu. *Web site:* http://www.merrimack.edu/.

Montserrat College of Art
Beverly, Massachusetts

Freshman Application Contact Mr. Brian Bicknell, Dean of Students, Montserrat College of Art, 23 Essex Street, PO Box 26, Beverly, MA 01915. *Phone:* 978-921-4242 Ext. 1153. *Toll-free phone:* 800-836-0487. *Fax:* 978-921-4241. *E-mail:* bbicknell@montserrat.edu. *Web site:* http://www.montserrat.edu/.

Mount Holyoke College
South Hadley, Massachusetts

- **Independent** comprehensive, founded 1837
- **Small-town** 800-acre campus with easy access to Springfield
- **Endowment** $529.2 million
- **Women only** 2,333 undergraduate students, 98% full-time
- **Very difficult** entrance level, 52% of applicants were admitted

Undergraduates 2,286 full-time, 47 part-time. Students come from 50 states and territories; 74 other countries; 74% are from out of state; 4% Black or African American, non-Hispanic/Latino; 7% Hispanic/Latino; 7% Asian, non-Hispanic/Latino; 0.1% American Indian or Alaska Native, non-Hispanic/Latino; 5% Two or more races, non-Hispanic/Latino; 7% Race/ethnicity unknown; 21% international; 2% transferred in; 94% live on campus. *Retention:* 91% of full-time freshmen returned.

Freshmen *Admission:* 3,359 applied, 1,732 admitted, 540 enrolled. *Average high school GPA:* 3.7. *Test scores:* SAT critical reading scores over 500: 99%; SAT math scores over 500: 95%; SAT writing scores over 500: 98%; ACT scores over 18: 100%; SAT critical reading scores over 600: 81%; SAT math scores over 600: 71%; SAT writing scores over 600: 82%; ACT scores over 24: 90%; SAT critical reading scores over 700: 32%; SAT math scores over 700: 23%; SAT writing scores over 700: 31%; ACT scores over 30: 48%.

Faculty *Total:* 283, 80% full-time, 91% with terminal degrees. *Student/faculty ratio:* 9:1.

Academics *Calendar:* semesters. *Degrees:* bachelor's, master's, and post-bachelor's certificates. *Special study options:* adult/continuing education programs, advanced placement credit, cooperative education, double majors, independent study, internships, off-campus study, part-time degree program, services for LD students, student-designed majors, study abroad. *ROTC:* Army (c), Air Force (c). *Unusual degree programs:* 3-2 engineering with Dartmouth College, University of Massachusetts, California Institute of Technology.

Computers on Campus 422 computers/terminals and 800 ports are available on campus for general student use. Students can access the following: campus intranet, computer help desk, free student e-mail accounts, online (class) grades, online (class) registration, online (class) schedules, personal Web pages. Campuswide network is available. 100% of college-owned or -operated housing units are wired for high-speed Internet access. Wireless service is available via classrooms, computer centers, computer labs, dorm rooms, learning centers, libraries, student centers.

Student Life *Housing:* on-campus residence required through senior year. *Options:* women-only, disabled students. Campus housing is university owned. Freshman campus housing is guaranteed. *Activities and organizations:* drama/theater group, student-run newspaper, radio station, choral group, Student Government Association, Model UN, Mount Holyoke African and Caribbean Student Association (MHCASA), Rugby. *Campus security:* 24-hour emergency response devices and patrols, student patrols, late-night transport/escort service, controlled dormitory access, police officers on-campus. *Student services:* health clinic, personal/psychological counseling.

Athletics Member NCAA. All Division III. *Intercollegiate sports:* basketball W, crew W, cross-country running W, equestrian sports W, field hockey W, golf W, lacrosse W, soccer W, squash W, swimming and diving W, tennis W, track and field W, volleyball W. *Intramural sports:* cheerleading W(c), equestrian sports W(c), fencing W(c), ice hockey W(c), rugby W(c), sailing W(c), ultimate Frisbee W(c).

Standardized Tests *Required for some:* SAT Subject Tests (for admission).

Costs (2010–11) *Comprehensive fee:* $52,036 includes full-time tuition ($40,070), mandatory fees ($186), and room and board ($11,780). Part-time tuition: $1255 per credit hour. *College room only:* $5770. *Payment plans:* tuition prepayment, installment. *Waivers:* employees or children of employees.

Financial Aid Of all full-time matriculated undergraduates who enrolled in 2009, 1,826 applied for aid, 1,691 were judged to have need, 1,691 had their need fully met. 949 Federal Work-Study jobs (averaging $1996). 452 state and other part-time jobs (averaging $2019). In 2009, 213 non-need-based awards were made. *Average percent of need met:* 100%. *Average financial aid package:* $35,714. *Average need-based loan:* $4683. *Average need-based gift aid:* $30,538. *Average non-need-based aid:* $15,863. *Average indebtedness upon graduation:* $22,499. *Financial aid deadline:* 3/1.

Applying *Options:* electronic application, early admission, early decision, deferred entrance. *Application fee:* $60. *Required:* essay or personal statement, high school transcript, 2 letters of recommendation. *Recommended:* interview. *Application deadlines:* 1/15 (freshmen), 5/15 (transfers). *Early decision deadline:* 11/15 (for plan 1), 1/1 (for plan 2). *Notification:* 4/1 (freshmen), continuous (transfers), 1/1 (early decision plan 1), 2/1 (early decision plan 2).

Freshman Application Contact Ms. Diane Anci, Interim Vice President for Enrollment and College Relations/Dean of Admission, Mount Holyoke College, Office of Admission, Mount Holyoke College, South Hadley, MA 01075. *Phone:* 413-538-2023. *Fax:* 413-538-2409. *E-mail:* admission@mtholyoke.edu. *Web site:* http://www.mtholyoke.edu/.

Mount Ida College
Newton, Massachusetts

- **Independent** comprehensive, founded 1899
- **Suburban** 72-acre campus with easy access to Boston
- **Endowment** $10.0 million
- **Coed** 1,457 undergraduate students, 94% full-time, 66% women, 34% men
- **Moderately difficult** entrance level, 72% of applicants were admitted

Undergraduates 1,376 full-time, 81 part-time. Students come from 27 states and territories; 24 other countries; 42% are from out of state; 15% Black or African American, non-Hispanic/Latino; 8% Hispanic/Latino; 2% Asian, non-Hispanic/Latino; 0.1% Native Hawaiian or other Pacific Islander, non-Hispanic/Latino; 0.3% American Indian or Alaska Native, non-Hispanic/Latino; 14% Race/ethnicity unknown; 4% international; 8% transferred in; 68% live on campus. *Retention:* 64% of full-time freshmen returned.

Freshmen *Admission:* 1,965 applied, 1,405 admitted, 396 enrolled. *Average high school GPA:* 2.6. *Test scores:* SAT critical reading scores over 500: 21%; SAT math scores over 500: 24%; SAT writing scores over 500: 23%; ACT scores over 18: 41%; SAT critical reading scores over 600: 3%; SAT math scores over 600: 2%; SAT writing scores over 600: 2%; ACT scores over 24: 4%.

Faculty *Total:* 193, 34% full-time, 36% with terminal degrees. *Student/faculty ratio:* 13:1.

Academics *Calendar:* semesters. *Degrees:* certificates, associate, bachelor's, and master's. *Special study options:* academic remediation for entering students, advanced placement credit, cooperative education, distance learning, double majors, English as a second language, honors programs, independent study, internships, part-time degree program, services for LD students, study abroad, summer session for credit.

Computers on Campus 82 computers/terminals are available on campus for general student use. Students can access the following: computer help desk, free student e-mail accounts, online (class) grades, online (class) schedules. Campuswide network is available. 100% of college-owned or -operated housing units are wired for high-speed Internet access. Wireless service is available via computer labs, dorm rooms, student centers.

Student Life *Housing options:* coed, women-only, disabled students. Campus housing is university owned and is provided by a third party. Freshman campus housing is guaranteed. *Activities and organizations:* drama/theater group, student-run newspaper, radio station, choral group, Student Government Association, Campus Activities Team, Balfour Peer Leaders, Black Student Achievement Coalition, Alpha Chi. *Campus security:* 24-hour emergency response devices and patrols, student patrols, late-night transport/escort service, controlled dormitory access, secured campus entrance. *Student services:* health clinic, personal/psychological counseling.

Athletics Member NCAA. All Division III. *Intercollegiate sports:* baseball M(c), basketball M/W, cheerleading M/W, cross-country running M/W, equestrian sports W, football M, lacrosse M/W, soccer M/W, softball W, tennis W, volleyball M/W. *Intramural sports:* basketball M/W, soccer M/W, ultimate Frisbee M/W, volleyball M/W.

Standardized Tests *Required:* SAT or ACT (for admission).

Costs (2010–11) *Comprehensive fee:* $36,500 includes full-time tuition ($24,250), mandatory fees ($250), and room and board ($12,000). Part-time tuition: $655 per credit. Part-time tuition and fees vary according to course

load. *Payment plan:* installment. *Waivers:* employees or children of employees.
Financial Aid Of all full-time matriculated undergraduates who enrolled in 2009, 1,231 applied for aid, 1,111 were judged to have need, 77 had their need fully met. In 2009, 234 non-need-based awards were made. *Average percent of need met:* 58%. *Average financial aid package:* $15,105. *Average need-based loan:* $4063. *Average need-based gift aid:* $11,328. *Average indebtedness upon graduation:* $34,911.
Applying *Options:* electronic application, deferred entrance. *Application fee:* $45. *Required:* high school transcript, 1 letter of recommendation. *Required for some:* interview. *Recommended:* essay or personal statement, minimum 2 GPA. *Application deadlines:* rolling (freshmen), rolling (transfers). *Notification:* continuous (freshmen), continuous (transfers).
Freshman Application Contact Jay Titus, Dean of Admissions, Mount Ida College, 777 Dedham Street, Newton, MA 02459-3310. *Phone:* 617-928-4553. *E-mail:* admissions@mountida.edu. *Web site:* http://www.mountida.edu/.

Newbury College
Brookline, Massachusetts

- **Independent** 4-year, founded 1962
- **Suburban** 10-acre campus with easy access to Boston
- **Endowment** $1.6 million
- **Coed** 1,016 undergraduate students, 86% full-time, 60% women, 40% men
- **Minimally difficult** entrance level, 64% of applicants were admitted

Undergraduates 873 full-time, 143 part-time. Students come from 19 states and territories; 15 other countries; 26% are from out of state; 3% transferred in; 40% live on campus. *Retention:* 66% of full-time freshmen returned.
Freshmen *Admission:* 4,204 applied, 2,692 admitted, 329 enrolled. *Average high school GPA:* 2.51.
Faculty *Total:* 110, 30% full-time, 20% with terminal degrees. *Student/faculty ratio:* 16:1.
Academics *Calendar:* semesters. *Degrees:* certificates, associate, and bachelor's. *Special study options:* academic remediation for entering students, accelerated degree program, adult/continuing education programs, advanced placement credit, cooperative education, distance learning, double majors, honors programs, independent study, internships, off-campus study, part-time degree program, services for LD students, student-designed majors, study abroad, summer session for credit.
Computers on Campus 115 computers/terminals are available on campus for general student use. Students can access the following: campus intranet, computer help desk, free student e-mail accounts, online (class) grades, online (class) registration, online (class) schedules. Campuswide network is available. 100% of college-owned or -operated housing units are wired for high-speed Internet access. Wireless service is available via entire campus.
Student Life *Housing options:* coed, women-only. Campus housing is university owned and leased by the school. Freshman applicants given priority for college housing. *Activities and organizations:* student-run newspaper, radio and television station, choral group, student government, Newbury College Student Activities, Inn Keepers Club, Commuter Council, Resident Hall Council. *Campus security:* 24-hour emergency response devices and patrols, late-night transport/escort service, controlled dormitory access. *Student services:* personal/psychological counseling.
Athletics Member NCAA. All Division III. *Intercollegiate sports:* baseball M, basketball M/W, cross-country running M/W, golf M, soccer M/W, softball W, tennis M/W, volleyball M/W. *Intramural sports:* basketball M/W, lacrosse M(c)/W(c), softball W, volleyball M/W.
Costs (2010–11) *One-time required fee:* $150. *Comprehensive fee:* $36,850 includes full-time tuition ($24,000), mandatory fees ($1100), and room and board ($11,750). Full-time tuition and fees vary according to program and reciprocity agreements. Part-time tuition: $290 per credit. Part-time tuition and fees vary according to class time, course load, program, and reciprocity agreements. *Room and board:* Room and board charges vary according to housing facility. *Payment plan:* installment. *Waivers:* employees or children of employees.
Financial Aid Of all full-time matriculated undergraduates who enrolled in 2007, 678 applied for aid, 618 were judged to have need. 147 Federal Work-Study jobs (averaging $2000). *Average percent of need met:* 84%. *Average financial aid package:* $4250. *Average need-based loan:* $4500. *Average non-need-based aid:* $7695. *Average indebtedness upon graduation:* $8400.
Applying *Options:* electronic application. *Application fee:* $25. *Required:* essay or personal statement, high school transcript, 2 letters of recommendation. *Required for some:* interview. *Recommended:* minimum 2 GPA, interview. *Application deadlines:* 9/1 (freshmen), 9/1 (transfers). *Notification:* continuous (freshmen), continuous (transfers).
Freshman Application Contact Nora Harrington, Assistant Director of Admissions Operations, Newbury College, 129 Fisher Avenue, Brookline, MA 02445-5796. *Phone:* 617-730-7007. *Toll-free phone:* 800-NEWBURY. *Fax:*

617-731-9618. *E-mail:* admissions@newbury.edu. *Web site:* http://www.newbury.edu/.

New England College of Business and Finance
Boston, Massachusetts

- **Independent** comprehensive, founded 1909, part of Whitney International University
- **Urban** campus
- **Coed, primarily women**
- **Noncompetitive** entrance level

Faculty *Student/faculty ratio:* 38:1.
Academics *Calendar:* 8 week terms (6 per academic year). *Degrees:* certificates, associate, bachelor's, and master's (offers primarily part-time evening degree programs; bachelor's degree offered jointly with Bentley College, Assumption College, Providence College, University of Hartford, and University System College for Lifelong Learning).
Student Life *Campus security:* reception desk in lobby of building.
Costs (2010–11) *One-time required fee:* $50. *Tuition:* $9300 full-time, $258 per credit hour part-time. *Required fees:* $75 full-time.
Applying *Options:* electronic application. *Required:* essay or personal statement, high school transcript, interview.
Freshman Application Contact New England College of Business and Finance, 10 High Street, Suite 204, Boston, MA 02111-2645. *Phone:* 617-951-2350 Ext. 6912. *Toll-free phone:* 888-696-NECF. *Web site:* http://necb.edu/.

New England Conservatory of Music
Boston, Massachusetts

- **Independent** comprehensive, founded 1867
- **Urban** 2-acre campus
- **Endowment** $98.4 million
- **Coed** 413 undergraduate students, 92% full-time, 46% women, 54% men
- **Very difficult** entrance level, 30% of applicants were admitted

Undergraduates 381 full-time, 32 part-time. Students come from 31 states and territories; 10 other countries; 88% are from out of state; 5% Black or African American, non-Hispanic/Latino; 6% Hispanic/Latino; 9% Asian, non-Hispanic/Latino; 3% Two or more races, non-Hispanic/Latino; 4% Race/ethnicity unknown; 28% international; 2% transferred in; 30% live on campus. *Retention:* 90% of full-time freshmen returned.
Freshmen *Admission:* 1,192 applied, 360 admitted, 103 enrolled.
Faculty *Total:* 222, 43% full-time, 11% with terminal degrees. *Student/faculty ratio:* 6:1.
Academics *Calendar:* semesters. *Degrees:* certificates, diplomas, bachelor's, master's, doctoral-research/scholarship, post-master's, and postbachelor's certificates. *Special study options:* advanced placement credit, double majors, English as a second language, independent study, internships, off-campus study, services for LD students, study abroad, summer session for credit.
Computers on Campus 70 computers/terminals and 200 ports are available on campus for general student use. Students can access the following: campus intranet, computer help desk, free student e-mail accounts, online (class) grades, online (class) registration, online (class) schedules, online activity effective Fall 2010. Campuswide network is available. 100% of college-owned or -operated housing units are wired for high-speed Internet access. Wireless service is available via entire campus.
Student Life *Housing:* on-campus residence required for freshman year. *Options:* coed. Campus housing is university owned. Freshman campus housing is guaranteed. *Activities and organizations:* drama/theater group, student-run newspaper, choral group, Fellowship with Christ, Hillel, The Penguin (newspaper), Rockin' Rangers Theatre Improv. *Campus security:* 24-hour patrols, late-night transport/escort service. *Student services:* health clinic, personal/psychological counseling.
Costs (2010–11) *Comprehensive fee:* $47,050 includes full-time tuition ($34,500), mandatory fees ($450), and room and board ($12,100). Part-time tuition: $1100 per credit. *Room and board:* Room and board charges vary according to board plan. *Waivers:* employees or children of employees.
Financial Aid Of all full-time matriculated undergraduates who enrolled in 2009, 257 applied for aid, 217 were judged to have need, 32 had their need fully met. 182 Federal Work-Study jobs (averaging $2035). In 2009, 150 non-need-based awards were made. *Average percent of need met:* 62%. *Average financial aid package:* $24,091. *Average need-based loan:* $4955. *Average need-based gift aid:* $18,028. *Average non-need-based aid:* $14,801. *Average indebtedness upon graduation:* $26,373.
Applying *Options:* electronic application, deferred entrance. *Application fee:* $105. *Required:* essay or personal statement, high school transcript, minimum 2.75 GPA, 2 letters of recommendation, audition recording, repertoire list.

Application deadlines: 12/1 (freshmen), 12/1 (transfers). *Notification:* 4/1 (freshmen), 4/1 (transfers).

Freshman Application Contact New England Conservatory of Music, 290 Huntington Avenue, Boston, MA 02115-5000. *Phone:* 617-585-1103. *Web site:* http://necmusic.edu/.

The New England Institute of Art

Brookline, Massachusetts

- **Proprietary** 4-year, part of Education Management Corporation
- **Urban** campus with easy access to Boston
- **Coed**

Academics *Calendar:* semesters. *Degrees:* certificates, associate, and bachelor's.

Costs (2010–11) *Tuition:* Tuition cost varies by program. Prospective students should contact the school for current tuition costs. Other charges include a starting kit for all first-quarter students. Kits vary in price, depending on the program of study.

Freshman Application Contact The New England Institute of Art, 10 Brookline Place West, Brookline, MA 02445. *Phone:* 617-739-1700. *Toll-free phone:* 800-903-4425. *Web site:* http://www.artinstitutes.edu/boston/.

See page 1468 for the College Close-Up.

Nichols College

Dudley, Massachusetts

- **Independent** comprehensive, founded 1815
- **Suburban** 210-acre campus with easy access to Boston
- **Endowment** $11.9 million
- **Coed**
- **Moderately difficult** entrance level

Faculty *Student/faculty ratio:* 18:1.

Academics *Calendar:* semesters. *Degrees:* certificates, associate, bachelor's, and master's.

Student Life *Campus security:* 24-hour emergency response devices and patrols, student patrols, late-night transport/escort service.

Athletics Member NCAA. All Division III.

Standardized Tests *Required:* SAT or ACT (for admission).

Costs (2010–11) *Comprehensive fee:* $38,200 includes full-time tuition ($28,570), mandatory fees ($300), and room and board ($9330). Part-time tuition: $275 per credit hour. Part-time tuition and fees vary according to class time and course load. *College room only:* $4900. Room and board charges vary according to housing facility.

Financial Aid *Of all full-time matriculated undergraduates who enrolled in 2009,* 1,098 applied for aid, 1,078 were judged to have need, 61 had their need fully met. 327 Federal Work-Study jobs (averaging $1435). *In 2009,* 61 non-need-based awards were made. *Average percent of need met:* 78. *Average financial aid package:* $27,420. *Average need-based loan:* $3654. *Average need-based gift aid:* $17,542. *Average non-need-based aid:* $9983. *Average indebtedness upon graduation:* $27,715.

Applying *Options:* electronic application, deferred entrance. *Application fee:* $25. *Required:* essay or personal statement, high school transcript, 1 letter of recommendation. *Required for some:* interview.

Freshman Application Contact Ms. Marie Keegan, Admissions Assistant, Nichols College, 124 Center Road, Dudley, MA 01571. *Phone:* 508-213-2203. *Toll-free phone:* 800-470-3379. *Fax:* 508-943-9885. *E-mail:* admissions@nichols.edu. *Web site:* http://www.nichols.edu/.

Northeastern University

Boston, Massachusetts

- **Independent** university, founded 1898
- **Urban** 73-acre campus
- **Endowment** $521.2 million
- **Coed** 15,905 undergraduate students, 100% full-time, 51% women, 49% men
- **Very difficult** entrance level, 38% of applicants were admitted

Undergraduates 15,905 full-time. Students come from 52 states and territories; 119 other countries; 62% are from out of state; 4% Black or African American, non-Hispanic/Latino; 5% Hispanic/Latino; 8% Asian, non-Hispanic/Latino; 0.2% American Indian or Alaska Native, non-Hispanic/Latino; 2% Two or more races, non-Hispanic/Latino; 18% Race/ethnicity unknown; 10% international; 4% transferred in; 53% live on campus. *Retention:* 93% of full-time freshmen returned.

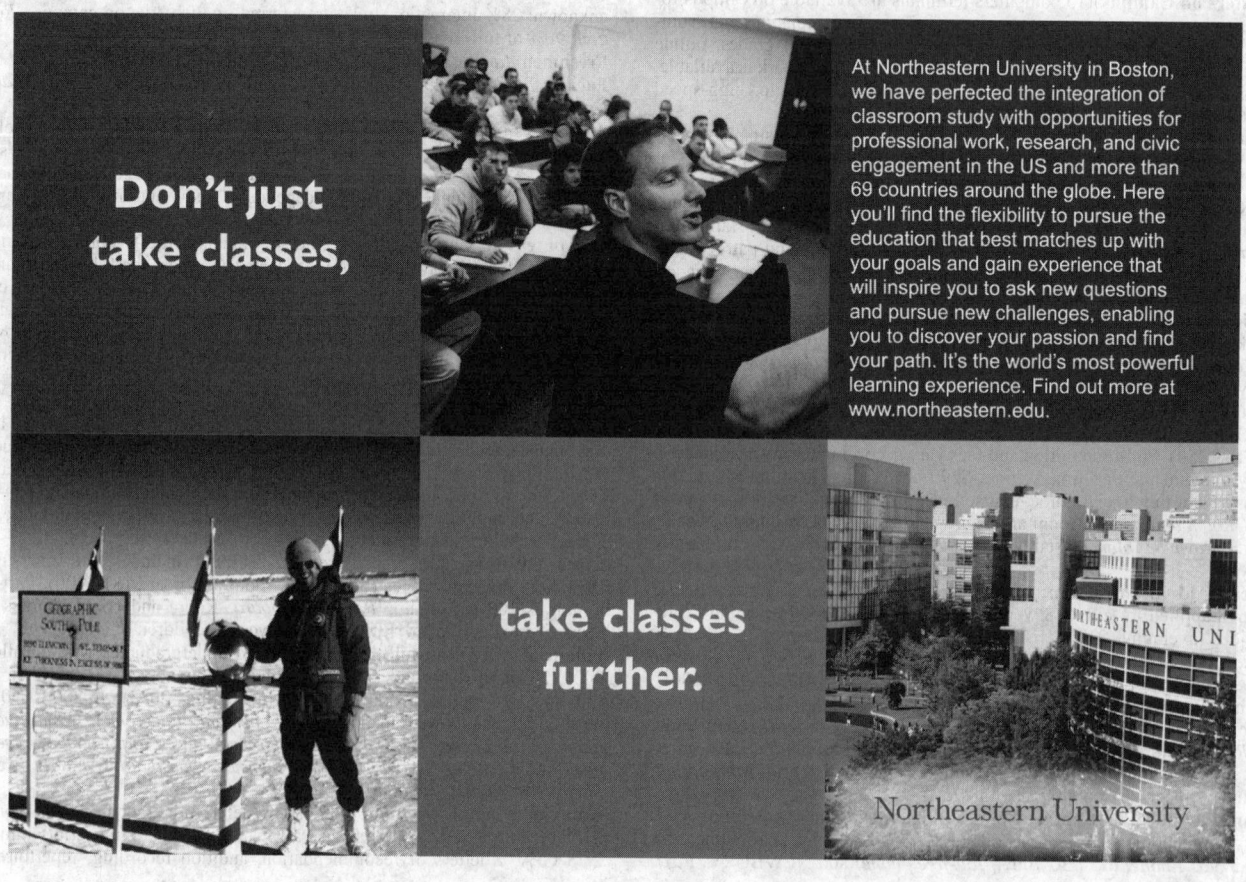

Don't just take classes, take classes further.

At Northeastern University in Boston, we have perfected the integration of classroom study with opportunities for professional work, research, and civic engagement in the US and more than 69 countries around the globe. Here you'll find the flexibility to pursue the education that best matches up with your goals and gain experience that will inspire you to ask new questions and pursue new challenges, enabling you to discover your passion and find your path. It's the world's most powerful learning experience. Find out more at www.northeastern.edu.

Northeastern University

Freshmen *Admission:* 37,688 applied, 14,291 admitted, 2,836 enrolled. *Test scores:* SAT critical reading scores over 500: 96%; SAT math scores over 500: 98%; SAT writing scores over 500: 96%; ACT scores over 18: 100%; SAT critical reading scores over 600: 76%; SAT math scores over 600: 88%; SAT writing scores over 600: 73%; ACT scores over 24: 97%; SAT critical reading scores over 700: 21%; SAT math scores over 700: 33%; SAT writing scores over 700: 19%; ACT scores over 30: 45%.

Faculty *Total:* 1,448, 71% full-time. *Student/faculty ratio:* 13:1.

Academics *Calendar:* semesters. *Degrees:* bachelor's, master's, doctoral-professional, doctoral-research/scholarship, and post-master's certificates. *Special study options:* academic remediation for entering students, accelerated degree program, adult/continuing education programs, advanced placement credit, cooperative education, distance learning, double majors, English as a second language, honors programs, independent study, internships, off-campus study, part-time degree program, services for LD students, student-designed majors, study abroad, summer session for credit. *ROTC:* Army (b), Navy (c), Air Force (c). *Unusual degree programs:* 3-2 engineering; nursing.

Computers on Campus 1,993 computers/terminals and 1,294 ports are available on campus for general student use. Students can access the following: campus intranet, computer help desk, free student e-mail accounts, online (class) grades, online (class) registration, online (class) schedules. Campuswide network is available. 100% of college-owned or -operated housing units are wired for high-speed Internet access. Wireless service is available via entire campus.

Student Life *Housing:* on-campus residence required for freshman year. *Options:* coed. Campus housing is university owned and leased by the school. Freshman campus housing is guaranteed. *Activities and organizations:* drama/theater group, student-run newspaper, radio and television station, choral group, Student Government Association, Council for University Programs, Resident Student Association, Society of Collegiate Scholars, No Limits Dance Crew, national fraternities, national sororities. *Campus security:* 24-hour emergency response devices and patrols, student patrols, late-night transport/escort service, controlled dormitory access, Public Safety web site. *Student services:* health clinic, personal/psychological counseling.

Athletics Member NCAA. All Division I. *Intercollegiate sports:* baseball M(s), basketball M(s)/W(s), cheerleading M(c)/W(c), crew M(s)/W(s), cross-country running M(s)/W(s), field hockey W(s), golf M(c)/W(c), ice hockey M(s)/W(s), lacrosse M(c)/W(c), racquetball M(c)/W(c), rugby M(c)/W(c), sailing M(c)/W(c), soccer M(s)/W(s), softball M(c)/W, swimming and diving W(s), table tennis M(c)/W(c), tennis M(c)/W, track and field M(s)/W(s), ultimate Frisbee M(c)/W, volleyball W(s), water polo M(c)/W(c), wrestling M(c). *Intramural sports:* basketball M/W, cheerleading M(c)/W(c), field hockey W(c), golf M(c)/W(c), racquetball M/W, skiing (cross-country) M(c)/W(c), skiing (downhill) M(c)/W(c), soccer M/W, squash M(c)/W(c), swimming and diving M(c)/W(c), volleyball M(c)/W(c), weight lifting M(c).

Standardized Tests *Required:* SAT or ACT (for admission). *Required for some:* SAT and SAT Subject Tests or ACT (for admission).

Costs (2010–11) *Comprehensive fee:* $49,552 includes full-time tuition ($36,380), mandatory fees ($412), and room and board ($12,760). *College room only:* $6760. Room and board charges vary according to board plan and housing facility. *Payment plan:* installment. *Waivers:* employees or children of employees.

Financial Aid Of all full-time matriculated undergraduates who enrolled in 2009, 9,944 applied for aid, 8,465 were judged to have need, 1,104 had their need fully met. 4,393 Federal Work-Study jobs (averaging $1820). In 2009, 3704 non-need-based awards were made. *Average percent of need met:* 59%. *Average financial aid package:* $20,131. *Average need-based loan:* $4895. *Average need-based gift aid:* $15,619. *Average non-need-based aid:* $9430.

Applying *Options:* electronic application, early admission, early action, deferred entrance. *Application fee:* $70. *Required:* essay or personal statement, high school transcript, 2 letters of recommendation. *Application deadlines:* 1/15 (freshmen), 5/1 (transfers), 11/1 (early action). *Notification:* continuous until 4/1 (freshmen), continuous (transfers), 12/31 (early action).

Freshman Application Contact David Hautanen, Associate Dean and Director of Admissions, Northeastern University, 360 Huntington Avenue, 150 Richards Hall, Boston, MA 02115. *Phone:* 617-373-2200. *Fax:* 617-373-8780. *E-mail:* admissions@neu.edu. *Web site:* http://www.northeastern.edu/.

See page 1476 for the College Close-Up.

Pine Manor College

Chestnut Hill, Massachusetts

Freshman Application Contact Mr. Robin Engel, Dean of Admissions and Financial Aid, Pine Manor College, 400 Heath Street, Chestnut Hill, MA 02467-2332. *Phone:* 617-731-7104. *Toll-free phone:* 800-762-1357. *Fax:* 617-731-7102. *E-mail:* admisson@pmc.edu. *Web site:* http://www.pmc.edu/.

Regis College

Weston, Massachusetts

- **Independent Roman Catholic** comprehensive, founded 1927
- **Small-town** 131-acre campus with easy access to Boston
- **Endowment** $14.2 million
- **Coed** 1,101 undergraduate students, 76% full-time, 79% women, 21% men
- **Moderately difficult** entrance level, 77% of applicants were admitted

Undergraduates 840 full-time, 261 part-time. Students come from 24 states and territories; 14 other countries; 9% are from out of state; 22% Black or African American, non-Hispanic/Latino; 11% Hispanic/Latino; 4% Asian, non-Hispanic/Latino; 0.2% Native Hawaiian or other Pacific Islander, non-Hispanic/Latino; 0.2% American Indian or Alaska Native, non-Hispanic/Latino; 0.3% Two or more races, non-Hispanic/Latino; 11% Race/ethnicity unknown; 1% international; 4% transferred in; 60% live on campus. *Retention:* 68% of full-time freshmen returned.

Freshmen *Admission:* 1,989 applied, 1,537 admitted, 287 enrolled. *Average high school GPA:* 2.83. *Test scores:* SAT critical reading scores over 500: 35%; SAT math scores over 500: 35%; SAT writing scores over 500: 35%; ACT scores over 18: 87%; SAT critical reading scores over 600: 6%; SAT math scores over 600: 8%; SAT writing scores over 600: 6%; ACT scores over 24: 16%; SAT math scores over 700: 1%.

Faculty *Total:* 130, 51% full-time, 59% with terminal degrees. *Student/faculty ratio:* 15:1.

Academics *Calendar:* semesters. *Degrees:* associate, bachelor's, master's, doctoral-professional, and post-master's certificates. *Special study options:* academic remediation for entering students, accelerated degree program, adult/continuing education programs, advanced placement credit, double majors, English as a second language, honors programs, independent study, internships, off-campus study, part-time degree program, services for LD students, student-designed majors, study abroad, summer session for credit. *ROTC:* Army (c). *Unusual degree programs:* 3-2 business administration; communication.

Computers on Campus 196 computers/terminals are available on campus for general student use. Students can access the following: campus intranet, computer help desk, free student e-mail accounts, online (class) grades, online (class) registration, online (class) schedules, online bills, financial aid award letters and check-in requirements. Campuswide network is available. 100% of college-owned or -operated housing units are wired for high-speed Internet access. Wireless service is available via computer labs, dorm rooms, learning centers, libraries, student centers.

Student Life *Housing options:* coed, women-only. Campus housing is university owned. Freshman campus housing is guaranteed. *Activities and organizations:* drama/theater group, student-run radio station, choral group, LASO-Latin American Student Organization (previously Amistades), AAA-Asian American Student Organization, SGA-Student Government Association, Nostalgia (Fashion Show), Glee Club. *Campus security:* 24-hour emergency response devices and patrols, late-night transport/escort service, controlled dormitory access. *Student services:* health clinic, personal/psychological counseling.

Athletics Member NCAA. All Division III. *Intercollegiate sports:* basketball M/W, cheerleading M(c)/W(c), field hockey W, lacrosse M/W, soccer M/W, softball W, swimming and diving M/W, tennis M/W, track and field M/W, volleyball M/W.

Standardized Tests *Required:* SAT or ACT (for admission).

Costs (2010–11) *One-time required fee:* $195. *Comprehensive fee:* $42,490 includes full-time tuition ($30,300) and room and board ($12,190). Full-time tuition and fees vary according to course load. Part-time tuition and fees vary according to class time. *College room only:* $6220. *Payment plan:* installment. *Waivers:* employees or children of employees.

Financial Aid Of all full-time matriculated undergraduates who enrolled in 2008, 695 applied for aid, 644 were judged to have need, 93 had their need fully met. 436 Federal Work-Study jobs (averaging $2000). 40 state and other part-time jobs (averaging $1500). In 2008, 66 non-need-based awards were made. *Average percent of need met:* 59%. *Average financial aid package:* $22,111. *Average need-based loan:* $4849. *Average need-based gift aid:* $12,529. *Average non-need-based aid:* $8231. *Average indebtedness upon graduation:* $24,178.

Applying *Options:* electronic application, deferred entrance. *Application fee:* $50. *Required:* essay or personal statement, high school transcript, minimum 2 GPA, 2 letters of recommendation. *Required for some:* interview. *Recommended:* minimum 3 GPA, interview, rank in upper 50% of high school class. *Application deadlines:* rolling (freshmen), rolling (transfers).

Freshman Application Contact Ms. Wanda Suriel, Director of Admission, Regis College, 235 Wellesley Street, Weston, MA 02493. *Phone:* 781-768-7100. *Toll-free phone:* 866-438-7344. *Fax:* 781-768-7071. *E-mail:* admission@regiscollege.edu. *Web site:* http://www.regiscollege.edu/.

Salem State University

Salem, Massachusetts

- **State-supported** comprehensive, founded 1854, part of Massachusetts Public Higher Education System

- **Urban** 62-acre campus with easy access to Boston

- **Endowment** $23.4 million

- **Coed** 7,839 undergraduate students, 77% full-time, 61% women, 39% men

- **Minimally difficult** entrance level, 57% of applicants were admitted

Undergraduates 6,008 full-time, 1,831 part-time. Students come from 28 states and territories; 3% are from out of state; 8% Black or African American, non-Hispanic/Latino; 7% Hispanic/Latino; 3% Asian, non-Hispanic/Latino; 0.3% American Indian or Alaska Native, non-Hispanic/Latino; 3% Race/ethnicity unknown; 4% international; 11% transferred in; 24% live on campus.

Freshmen *Admission:* 5,697 applied, 3,268 admitted, 998 enrolled. *Average high school GPA:* 2.94. *Test scores:* SAT critical reading scores over 500: 57%; SAT math scores over 500: 49%; SAT critical reading scores over 600: 10%; SAT math scores over 600: 10%; SAT critical reading scores over 700: 1%; SAT math scores over 700: 1%.

Faculty *Total:* 779, 43% full-time. *Student/faculty ratio:* 14:1.

Academics *Calendar:* semesters. *Degrees:* certificates, bachelor's, master's, and post-master's certificates. *Special study options:* academic remediation for entering students, accelerated degree program, adult/continuing education programs, advanced placement credit, distance learning, double majors, English as a second language, honors programs, independent study, internships, off-campus study, part-time degree program, services for LD students, student-designed majors, study abroad, summer session for credit. *ROTC:* Army (c), Air Force (c).

Computers on Campus 160 computers/terminals are available on campus for general student use. Students can access the following: campus intranet, computer help desk, free student e-mail accounts, online (class) grades, online (class) registration, online (class) schedules. Campuswide network is available. 100% of college-owned or -operated housing units are wired for high-speed Internet access. Wireless service is available via entire campus.

Student Life *Housing options:* coed. Campus housing is university owned. Freshman applicants given priority for college housing. *Activities and organizations:* drama/theater group, student-run newspaper, radio and television station, choral group, Student Government Association, Program Council, Residence Hall Association, Multicultural Student Association, Hispanic-American Society. *Campus security:* 24-hour emergency response devices and patrols, late-night transport/escort service, controlled dormitory access. *Student services:* health clinic, personal/psychological counseling, women's center, legal services.

Athletics Member NCAA. All Division III. *Intercollegiate sports:* baseball M, basketball M/W, cross-country running M/W, field hockey W, golf M, ice hockey M, lacrosse M, soccer M/W, softball W, tennis M/W, track and field M/W, volleyball W. *Intramural sports:* basketball M/W, cheerleading M/W, football M/W, ice hockey M/W, lacrosse W, soccer M/W, softball M/W, ultimate Frisbee M/W, volleyball M/W.

Standardized Tests *Required:* SAT or ACT (for admission).

Costs (2010–11) *Tuition:* state resident $910 full-time, $38 per credit part-time; nonresident $7050 full-time, $294 per credit part-time. Full-time tuition and fees vary according to class time and course load. Part-time tuition and fees vary according to class time and course load. *Required fees:* $6260 full-time, $261 per credit part-time. *Room only:* $7810. Room and board charges vary according to board plan and housing facility. *Payment plan:* installment. *Waivers:* senior citizens and employees or children of employees.

Financial Aid Of all full-time matriculated undergraduates who enrolled in 2009, 286 Federal Work-Study jobs (averaging $3000).

Applying *Options:* electronic application, early action, deferred entrance. *Application fee:* $75. *Required:* high school transcript, minimum 2 GPA. *Required for some:* interview. *Application deadlines:* 5/1 (freshmen), rolling (transfers). *Notification:* continuous (freshmen), continuous (transfers).

Freshman Application Contact Ms. Mary Dunn, Assistant Dean for Undergraduate Admissions, Salem State University, 352 Lafayette Street, Salem, MA 01970. *Phone:* 978-542-6202. *Fax:* 978-542-6893. *E-mail:* admissions@salemstate.edu. *Web site:* http://www.salemstate.edu/.

School of the Museum of Fine Arts, Boston

Boston, Massachusetts

- **Independent** comprehensive, founded 1876, administratively affiliated with Museum of Fine Arts, Boston; Northeastern and Tufts Universities

- **Urban** 14-acre campus with easy access to Boston

- **Endowment** $19.6 million

- **Coed** 640 undergraduate students, 83% full-time, 68% women, 32% men

- **Moderately difficult** entrance level, 92% of applicants were admitted

Undergraduates 529 full-time, 111 part-time. Students come from 33 states and territories; 39 other countries; 70% are from out of state; 2% Black or African American, non-Hispanic/Latino; 6% Hispanic/Latino; 4% Asian, non-Hispanic/Latino; 0.2% American Indian or Alaska Native, non-Hispanic/Latino; 5% Two or more races, non-Hispanic/Latino; 18% Race/ethnicity unknown; 8% international; 5% transferred in; 12% live on campus. *Retention:* 71% of full-time freshmen returned.

Freshmen *Admission:* 736 applied, 674 admitted, 99 enrolled. *Test scores:* SAT critical reading scores over 500: 83%; SAT math scores over 500: 67%; SAT writing scores over 500: 89%; ACT scores over 18: 100%; SAT critical reading scores over 600: 54%; SAT math scores over 600: 25%; SAT writing scores over 600: 42%; ACT scores over 24: 85%; SAT critical reading scores over 700: 14%; SAT math scores over 700: 2%; ACT scores over 30: 8%.

Faculty *Total:* 95, 51% full-time, 75% with terminal degrees. *Student/faculty ratio:* 10:1.

Academics *Calendar:* semesters. *Degrees:* certificates, diplomas, bachelor's, master's, and postbachelor's certificates. *Special study options:* adult/continuing education programs, double majors, independent study, internships, off-campus study, part-time degree program, services for LD students, student-designed majors, study abroad, summer session for credit. *Unusual degree programs:* 3-2 Fine Arts with Tufts University.

Computers on Campus 170 computers/terminals are available on campus for general student use. Students can access the following: free student e-mail accounts, online (class) grades, online (class) registration, online (class) schedules. Campuswide network is available. 100% of college-owned or -operated housing units are wired for high-speed Internet access. Wireless service is available via entire campus.

Student Life *Housing options:* coed. Campus housing is leased by the school. Freshman applicants given priority for college housing. *Activities and organizations:* Gay/Lesbian/Bisexual Alliance (Open Forum), Student Body, Inc, Metals Club, Kreep Attack Komics Kult, Bikes Are Really Fun (B.A.R.F.). *Campus security:* 24-hour emergency response devices and patrols, late night taxis service between buildings. *Student services:* personal/psychological counseling.

Standardized Tests *Recommended:* test scores are considered if submitted.

Costs (2010–11) *One-time required fee:* $125. *Tuition:* $33,000 full-time, $1240 per credit hour part-time. Full-time tuition and fees vary according to course load, degree level, program, and student level. Part-time tuition and fees vary according to class time, course load, program, and student level. *Required fees:* $1120 full-time. *Room only:* $13,200. Room and board charges vary according to housing facility. *Payment plan:* installment. *Waivers:* employees or children of employees.

Financial Aid Of all full-time matriculated undergraduates who enrolled in 2009, 426 applied for aid, 426 were judged to have need, 57 had their need fully met. In 2009, 38 non-need-based awards were made. *Average percent of need met:* 42%. *Average financial aid package:* $18,204. *Average need-based loan:* $4233. *Average need-based gift aid:* $14,091. *Average non-need-based aid:* $20,410. *Average indebtedness upon graduation:* $38,315.

Applying *Options:* electronic application, deferred entrance. *Application fee:* $65. *Required:* essay or personal statement, high school transcript, 2 letters of recommendation, portfolio. *Recommended:* interview. *Application deadlines:* rolling (freshmen), rolling (out-of-state freshmen), rolling (transfers). *Notification:* continuous (freshmen), continuous (out-of-state freshmen), continuous (transfers).

Freshman Application Contact Ms. Robyn Reed, Associate Dean of Admissions, School of the Museum of Fine Arts, Boston, 230 The Fenway, Boston, MA 02115. *Phone:* 617-369-3626. *Toll-free phone:* 800-643-6078. *Fax:* 617-369-4264. *E-mail:* admissions@smfa.edu. *Web site:* http://www.smfa.edu/.

Simmons College
Boston, Massachusetts

- **Independent** university, founded 1899
- **Urban** 12-acre campus with easy access to Boston
- **Undergraduate: women only; graduate: coed** 1,912 undergraduate students, 89% full-time, 100% women
- **Moderately difficult** entrance level, 54% of applicants were admitted

Undergraduates 1,704 full-time, 208 part-time. Students come from 36 states and territories; 53 other countries; 39% are from out of state; 8% Black or African American, non-Hispanic/Latino; 5% Hispanic/Latino; 7% Asian, non-Hispanic/Latino; 0.1% Native Hawaiian or other Pacific Islander, non-Hispanic/Latino; 0.3% American Indian or Alaska Native, non-Hispanic/Latino; 7% Race/ethnicity unknown; 3% international; 4% transferred in; 52% live on campus. *Retention:* 82% of full-time freshmen returned.

Freshmen *Admission:* 3,666 applied, 1,978 admitted, 380 enrolled. *Average high school GPA:* 3.2. *Test scores:* SAT critical reading scores over 500: 75%; SAT math scores over 500: 76%; SAT writing scores over 500: 80%; ACT scores over 18: 98%; SAT critical reading scores over 600: 26%; SAT math scores over 600: 21%; SAT writing scores over 600: 31%; ACT scores over 24: 51%; SAT critical reading scores over 700: 5%; SAT math scores over 700: 3%; SAT writing scores over 700: 3%; ACT scores over 30: 9%.

Faculty *Total:* 590, 35% full-time. *Student/faculty ratio:* 13:1.

Academics *Calendar:* semesters. *Degrees:* bachelor's, master's, doctoral-professional, doctoral-research/scholarship, post-master's, and postbachelor's certificates. *Special study options:* academic remediation for entering students, accelerated degree program, adult/continuing education programs, advanced placement credit, cooperative education, double majors, English as a second language, external degree program, honors programs, independent study, internships, off-campus study, part-time degree program, services for LD students, student-designed majors, study abroad, summer session for credit. *ROTC:* Army (c). *Unusual degree programs:* 3-2 business administration; nursing; social work; Teaching, Physician Assistant, Pharmacy with Massachusetts College of Pharmacy and Allied Health Sciences.

Computers on Campus 350 computers/terminals and 1,000 ports are available on campus for general student use. Students can access the following: campus intranet, computer help desk, free student e-mail accounts, online (class) grades, online (class) registration, online (class) schedules. Campus-wide network is available. 100% of college-owned or -operated housing units are wired for high-speed Internet access. Wireless service is available via classrooms, computer labs, learning centers, libraries, student centers.

Student Life *Housing options:* coed, women-only, disabled students. Campus housing is university owned and leased by the school. Freshman applicants given priority for college housing. *Activities and organizations:* drama/theater group, student-run newspaper, radio station, choral group, Student Government Association, Black Students Organization, Campus Activities Board, Asian Students Association, Simmons Voice. *Campus security:* 24-hour emergency response devices and patrols, late-night transport/escort service, controlled dormitory access. *Student services:* health clinic, personal/psychological counseling, women's center.

Athletics Member NCAA. All Division III. *Intercollegiate sports:* basketball W, crew W, cross-country running W(c), field hockey W, lacrosse W, soccer W, softball W, swimming and diving W, tennis W, volleyball W. *Intramural sports:* basketball W, rugby W, soccer W, ultimate Frisbee W, volleyball W.

Standardized Tests *Required:* SAT or ACT (for admission).

Costs (2010–11) *Comprehensive fee:* $44,700 includes full-time tuition ($31,280), mandatory fees ($950), and room and board ($12,470). Full-time tuition and fees vary according to course load and program. Part-time tuition: $978 per credit. Part-time tuition and fees vary according to course load and program. *Required fees:* $240 per term part-time. *Room and board:* Room and board charges vary according to board plan. *Payment plan:* installment. *Waivers:* employees or children of employees.

Financial Aid Of all full-time matriculated undergraduates who enrolled in 2009, 1,363 applied for aid, 1,252 were judged to have need, 100 had their need fully met. 1,040 Federal Work-Study jobs (averaging $2333). In 2009, 289 non-need-based awards were made. *Average percent of need met:* 64%. *Average financial aid package:* $22,495. *Average need-based loan:* $4800. *Average need-based gift aid:* $16,075. *Average non-need-based aid:* $8815.

Applying *Options:* electronic application, early admission, early action, deferred entrance. *Application fee:* $55. *Required:* essay or personal statement, high school transcript, 2 letters of recommendation. *Recommended:* minimum 3 GPA, interview. *Application deadlines:* 2/1 (freshmen), 2/1 (out-of-state freshmen), 4/1 (transfers), 12/1 (early action). *Notification:* 4/15 (freshmen), 4/15 (out-of-state freshmen), continuous (transfers), 1/20 (early action).

Freshman Application Contact Simmons College, 300 The Fenway, Boston, MA 02115. *Phone:* 617-521-2057. *Toll-free phone:* 800-345-8468. *Web site:* http://www.simmons.edu/.

See page 1608 for the College Close-Up.

Smith College

Northampton, Massachusetts

- **Independent** comprehensive, founded 1871
- **Small-town** 147-acre campus with easy access to Hartford
- **Endowment** $1.2 billion
- **Undergraduate: women only; graduate: coed** 2,588 undergraduate students, 99% full-time, 100% women
- **Very difficult** entrance level, 47% of applicants were admitted

Undergraduates 2,571 full-time, 17 part-time. Students come from 51 states and territories; 70 other countries; 78% are from out of state; 5% Black or African American, non-Hispanic/Latino; 7% Hispanic/Latino; 11% Asian, non-Hispanic/Latino; 0.2% Native Hawaiian or other Pacific Islander, non-Hispanic/Latino; 0.4% American Indian or Alaska Native, non-Hispanic/Latino; 3% Two or more races, non-Hispanic/Latino; 20% Race/ethnicity unknown; 9% international; 2% transferred in; 91% live on campus. *Retention:* 91% of full-time freshmen returned.

Freshmen *Admission:* 4,015 applied, 1,881 admitted, 631 enrolled. *Average high school GPA:* 3.87. *Test scores:* SAT critical reading scores over 500: 99%; SAT math scores over 500: 99%; SAT writing scores over 500: 98%; ACT scores over 18: 99%; SAT critical reading scores over 600: 78%; SAT math scores over 600: 73%; SAT writing scores over 600: 82%; ACT scores over 24: 86%; SAT critical reading scores over 700: 39%; SAT math scores over 700: 25%; SAT writing scores over 700: 37%; ACT scores over 30: 35%.

Faculty *Total:* 296, 92% full-time, 98% with terminal degrees. *Student/faculty ratio:* 9:1.

Academics *Calendar:* semesters. *Degrees:* bachelor's, master's, doctoral-research/scholarship, post-master's, and postbachelor's certificates. *Special study options:* accelerated degree program, adult/continuing education programs, advanced placement credit, double majors, honors programs, independent study, internships, off-campus study, part-time degree program, services for LD students, student-designed majors, study abroad. *ROTC:* Army (c), Air Force (c). *Unusual degree programs:* 3-2 engineering with Dartmouth College.

Computers on Campus 582 computers/terminals are available on campus for general student use. Students can access the following: campus intranet, computer help desk, free student e-mail accounts, online (class) grades, online (class) registration, online (class) schedules. Campuswide network is available. 100% of college-owned or -operated housing units are wired for high-speed Internet access. Wireless service is available via classrooms, computer centers, computer labs, dorm rooms, learning centers, libraries, student centers.

Student Life *Housing:* on-campus residence required through senior year. *Options:* women-only, cooperative. Campus housing is university owned. Freshman campus housing is guaranteed. *Activities and organizations:* drama/theater group, student-run newspaper, radio and television station, choral group, Student Activities Committee, Community Service Organization, Glee Club and Choir, Athletic Association, Black Student Alliance. *Campus security:* 24-hour emergency response devices and patrols, late-night transport/escort service, self-defense workshops, emergency telephones, programs in crime and sexual assault prevention. *Student services:* health clinic, personal/psychological counseling, women's center.

Athletics Member NCAA. All Division III. *Intercollegiate sports:* basketball W, crew W, cross-country running W, equestrian sports W, field hockey W, lacrosse W, skiing (downhill) W, soccer W, softball W, squash W, swimming and diving W, tennis W, track and field W, volleyball W. *Intramural sports:* badminton W(c), cheerleading W(c), crew W, equestrian sports W(c), fencing W(c), golf W(c), ice hockey W(c), rock climbing W, rugby W(c), soccer W, squash W, ultimate Frisbee W(c).

Costs (2010–11) *Comprehensive fee:* $51,898 includes full-time tuition ($38,640), mandatory fees ($258), and room and board ($13,000). Part-time tuition: $1210 per credit hour. *College room only:* $6500. *Payment plans:* tuition prepayment, installment. *Waivers:* employees or children of employees.

Financial Aid Of all full-time matriculated undergraduates who enrolled in 2009, 1,856 applied for aid, 1,646 were judged to have need, 1,646 had their need fully met. In 2009, 101 non-need-based awards were made. *Average percent of need met:* 100%. *Average financial aid package:* $36,156. *Average need-based loan:* $4576. *Average need-based gift aid:* $31,705. *Average non-need-based aid:* $13,588. *Average indebtedness upon graduation:* $20,989. *Financial aid deadline:* 2/15.

Applying *Options:* electronic application, early admission, early decision, deferred entrance. *Application fee:* $60. *Required:* essay or personal statement, high school transcript, 3 letters of recommendation. *Recommended:* interview. *Application deadlines:* 1/15 (freshmen), 5/15 (transfers). *Early*

decision deadline: 11/15 (for plan 1), 1/2 (for plan 2). *Notification:* 4/1 (freshmen), 6/1 (transfers), 12/15 (early decision plan 1), 2/2 (early decision plan 2).

Freshman Application Contact Ms. Debra Shaver, Director of Admissions, Smith College, 7 College Lane, Northampton, MA 01063. *Phone:* 413-585-2500. *Toll-free phone:* 800-383-3232. *Fax:* 413-585-2527. *E-mail:* admission@smith.edu. *Web site:* http://www.smith.edu/.

See page 1614 for the College Close-Up.

Springfield College
Springfield, Massachusetts

- **Independent** comprehensive, founded 1885
- **Suburban** 150-acre campus
- **Coed** 3,400 undergraduate students
- **Moderately difficult** entrance level

Faculty *Total:* 342. *Student/faculty ratio:* 13:1.

Academics *Calendar:* semesters. *Degrees:* bachelor's, master's, doctoral-professional, and postbachelor's certificates. *Special study options:* accelerated degree program, adult/continuing education programs, advanced placement credit, cooperative education, double majors, English as a second language, independent study, internships, off-campus study, part-time degree program, services for LD students, study abroad, summer session for credit. *ROTC:* Army (c), Air Force (c). *Unusual degree programs:* 3-2 physical therapy, physician assistant, occupational therapy.

Computers on Campus Campuswide network is available.

Student Life *Housing:* on-campus residence required through junior year. *Options:* coed, men-only, women-only. Campus housing is university owned. Freshman campus housing is guaranteed. *Activities and organizations:* drama/theater group, student-run newspaper, radio station, choral group. *Student services:* health clinic, personal/psychological counseling.

Athletics Member NCAA. All Division III. *Intercollegiate sports:* baseball M, basketball M/W, cross-country running M/W, field hockey W, football M, golf M, gymnastics M/W, lacrosse M/W, soccer M/W, softball W, swimming and diving M/W, tennis M/W, track and field M/W, volleyball M/W, wrestling M.

Standardized Tests *Required:* SAT or ACT (for admission).

Costs (2011–12) *Tuition:* $30,660 full-time. *Room only:* Room and board charges vary according to board plan and housing facility. *Payment plan:* installment. *Waivers:* employees or children of employees.

Financial Aid Of all full-time matriculated undergraduates who enrolled in 2003, 1,891 applied for aid, 1,636 were judged to have need, 316 had their need fully met. 1,080 Federal Work-Study jobs (averaging $1600). 80 state and other part-time jobs (averaging $1118). In 2003, 279 non-need-based awards were made. *Average percent of need met:* 83%. *Average financial aid package:* $15,258. *Average need-based loan:* $4227. *Average need-based gift aid:* $10,544. *Average non-need-based aid:* $12,209. *Average indebtedness upon graduation:* $20,869.

Applying *Options:* electronic application, early admission, early decision, deferred entrance. *Application fee:* $50. *Required:* high school transcript, 1 letter of recommendation. *Required for some:* portfolio. *Recommended:* interview. *Application deadlines:* 4/1 (freshmen), 8/1 (transfers). *Early decision deadline:* 12/1. *Notification:* continuous until 4/15 (freshmen), continuous until 8/15 (transfers), 2/1 (early decision).

Freshman Application Contact Richard K. Veres, Director of Undergraduate Admissions, Springfield College, 263 Alden Street, Springfield, MA 01109. *Phone:* 413-748-3136. *Toll-free phone:* 800-343-1257. *Fax:* 413-748-3694. *E-mail:* admissions@spfldcol.edu. *Web site:* http://www.spfldcol.edu/.

See page 1636 for the College Close-Up.

Stonehill College
Easton, Massachusetts

- **Independent Roman Catholic** 4-year, founded 1948
- **Suburban** 384-acre campus with easy access to Boston
- **Endowment** $127.3 million
- **Coed** 2,582 undergraduate students, 99% full-time, 62% women, 38% men
- **Very difficult** entrance level, 64% of applicants were admitted

Undergraduates 2,559 full-time, 23 part-time. Students come from 30 states and territories; 10 other countries; 47% are from out of state; 3% Black or African American, non-Hispanic/Latino; 3% Hispanic/Latino; 1% Asian, non-Hispanic/Latino; 1% Two or more races, non-Hispanic/Latino; 1% Race/ethnicity unknown; 0.5% international; 1% transferred in; 92% live on campus. *Retention:* 92% of full-time freshmen returned.

Freshmen *Admission:* 7,052 applied, 4,500 admitted, 728 enrolled. *Average high school GPA:* 3.4. *Test scores:* SAT critical reading scores over 500: 96%; SAT math scores over 500: 96%; ACT scores over 18: 100%; SAT critical reading scores over 600: 53%; SAT math scores over 600: 59%; ACT scores

over 24: 89%; SAT critical reading scores over 700: 6%; SAT math scores over 700: 7%; ACT scores over 30: 15%.

Faculty *Total:* 261, 60% full-time, 67% with terminal degrees. *Student/faculty ratio:* 13:1.

Academics *Calendar:* semesters. *Degree:* bachelor's. *Special study options:* advanced placement credit, double majors, honors programs, independent study, internships, off-campus study, part-time degree program, services for LD students, student-designed majors, study abroad, summer session for credit. *ROTC:* Army (b). *Unusual degree programs:* 3-2 engineering with University of Notre Dame.

Computers on Campus 370 computers/terminals and 300 ports are available on campus for general student use. Students can access the following: campus intranet, computer help desk, free student e-mail accounts, online (class) grades, online (class) registration, online (class) schedules. Campuswide network is available. 100% of college-owned or -operated housing units are wired for high-speed Internet access. Wireless service is available via classrooms, computer centers, computer labs, dorm rooms, learning centers, libraries, student centers.

Student Life *Housing options:* coed, women-only, disabled students. Campus housing is university owned. *Activities and organizations:* drama/theater group, student-run newspaper, radio station, choral group, Into the Streets, student radio station, student government, Summit (student newspaper), sports clubs. *Campus security:* 24-hour emergency response devices and patrols, late-night transport/escort service, controlled dormitory access. *Student services:* health clinic, personal/psychological counseling, women's center.

Athletics Member NCAA. All Division II. *Intercollegiate sports:* baseball M(s), basketball M(s)/W(s), bowling M(c)/W(c), cheerleading M(c)/W(c), cross-country running M(s)/W(s), equestrian sports W(s), field hockey W(s), football M(s), golf M(c)/W(c), ice hockey M, lacrosse M(c)/W(s), rugby M(c)/W(c), soccer M(s)/W(s), softball W(s), tennis M(s)/W(s), track and field M(s)/W(s), ultimate Frisbee M(c)/W(c), volleyball M(c)/W(s). *Intramural sports:* basketball M/W, field hockey M/W, soccer M/W, softball M/W, tennis M/W, volleyball M/W.

Costs (2010–11) *Comprehensive fee:* $45,230 includes full-time tuition ($32,620) and room and board ($12,610). Part-time tuition: $1087 per credit hour. Part-time tuition and fees vary according to course load. *College room only:* $7694. Room and board charges vary according to board plan. *Payment plans:* tuition prepayment, installment. *Waivers:* employees or children of employees.

Financial Aid Of all full-time matriculated undergraduates who enrolled in 2009, 2,368 applied for aid, 1,471 were judged to have need, 719 had their need fully met. In 2009, 652 non-need-based awards were made. *Average percent of need met:* 90%. *Average financial aid package:* $23,720. *Average need-based loan:* $5021. *Average need-based gift aid:* $17,448. *Average non-need-based aid:* $8857. *Average indebtedness upon graduation:* $30,435.

Applying *Options:* electronic application, early decision, early action, deferred entrance. *Application fee:* $60. *Required:* essay or personal statement, high school transcript, 2 letters of recommendation. *Required for some:* interview. *Recommended:* campus visit. *Application deadlines:* 1/15 (freshmen), 4/1 (transfers), 11/1 (early action). *Early decision deadline:* 11/1. *Notification:* 3/15 (freshmen), continuous until 5/31 (transfers), 12/25 (early decision), 1/15 (early action).

Freshman Application Contact Stonehill College, 320 Washington Street, Easton, MA 02357-5610. *Phone:* 508-565-1373. *Fax:* 508-565-1545. *E-mail:* admissions@stonehill.edu. *Web site:* http://www.stonehill.edu/.

See page 1650 for the College Close-Up.

Suffolk University
Boston, Massachusetts

- **Independent** comprehensive, founded 1906
- **Urban** 2-acre campus
- **Endowment** $99.2 million
- **Coed** 5,721 undergraduate students, 92% full-time, 55% women, 45% men
- **Moderately difficult** entrance level, 84% of applicants were admitted

Undergraduates 5,272 full-time, 449 part-time. Students come from 42 states and territories; 103 other countries; 30% are from out of state; 5% Black or African American, non-Hispanic/Latino; 0.8% Hispanic/Latino; 7% Asian, non-Hispanic/Latino; 0.3% American Indian or Alaska Native, non-Hispanic/Latino; 0.4% Two or more races, non-Hispanic/Latino; 17% Race/ethnicity unknown; 12% international; 7% transferred in; 23% live on campus. *Retention:* 72% of full-time freshmen returned.

Freshmen *Admission:* 9,145 applied, 7,718 admitted, 1,315 enrolled. *Average high school GPA:* 2.94. *Test scores:* SAT critical reading scores over 500: 53%; SAT math scores over 500: 61%; SAT writing scores over 500: 56%; ACT scores over 18: 95%; SAT critical reading scores over 600: 15%; SAT math scores over 600: 18%; SAT writing scores over 600: 14%; ACT scores

over 24: 41%; SAT critical reading scores over 700: 1%; SAT math scores over 700: 4%; SAT writing scores over 700: 2%; ACT scores over 30: 2%.

Faculty *Total:* 991, 43% full-time, 47% with terminal degrees. *Student/faculty ratio:* 12:1.

Academics *Calendar:* semesters. *Degrees:* certificates, diplomas, associate, bachelor's, master's, doctoral-professional, doctoral-research/scholarship, post-master's, and postbachelor's certificates (doctoral degree in law). *Special study options:* academic remediation for entering students, accelerated degree program, adult/continuing education programs, advanced placement credit, cooperative education, distance learning, double majors, English as a second language, freshman honors college, honors programs, independent study, internships, off-campus study, part-time degree program, services for LD students, study abroad, summer session for credit. *ROTC:* Army (c).

Computers on Campus 539 computers/terminals are available on campus for general student use. Students can access the following: campus intranet, computer help desk, free student e-mail accounts, online (class) grades, online (class) registration, online (class) schedules. Campuswide network is available. 100% of college-owned or -operated housing units are wired for high-speed Internet access. Wireless service is available via entire campus.

Student Life *Housing options:* coed. Campus housing is university owned. Freshman applicants given priority for college housing. *Activities and organizations:* drama/theater group, student-run newspaper, radio and television station, choral group, Student Government Association, Program Committee, Suffolk Free Radio, Black Student Union, Journey Leadership Program, national fraternities. *Campus security:* 24-hour emergency response devices, late-night transport/escort service, controlled dormitory access. *Student services:* health clinic, personal/psychological counseling, women's center.

Athletics Member NCAA. All Division III. *Intercollegiate sports:* baseball M, basketball M/W, cross-country running M/W, golf M, ice hockey M, soccer M, softball W, tennis M/W, volleyball W. *Intramural sports:* basketball M/W, soccer M/W, softball M/W, volleyball M/W.

Standardized Tests *Required:* SAT or ACT (for admission).

Costs (2010–11) *Comprehensive fee:* $43,150 includes full-time tuition ($28,414), mandatory fees ($112), and room and board ($14,624). Part-time tuition: $697 per credit hour. Part-time tuition and fees vary according to course load. *Required fees:* $10 per term part-time. *College room only:* $12,204. Room and board charges vary according to board plan and housing facility. *Payment plans:* installment, deferred payment. *Waivers:* senior citizens and employees or children of employees.

Financial Aid Of all full-time matriculated undergraduates who enrolled in 2009, 3,707 applied for aid, 3,275 were judged to have need, 321 had their need fully met. 2,163 Federal Work-Study jobs (averaging $2324). 371 state and other part-time jobs (averaging $3160). In 2009, 432 non-need-based awards were made. *Average percent of need met:* 37%. *Average financial aid package:* $20,408. *Average need-based loan:* $4582. *Average need-based gift aid:* $12,513. *Average non-need-based aid:* $8663. *Financial aid deadline:* 2/15.

Applying *Options:* electronic application, early action, deferred entrance. *Application fee:* $50. *Required:* essay or personal statement, high school transcript, 2 letters of recommendation. *Required for some:* interview. *Recommended:* minimum 2.5 GPA. *Application deadlines:* 2/15 (freshmen), 3/30 (transfers), 11/15 (early action). *Notification:* 2/5 (freshmen), continuous (transfers), 12/20 (early action).

Freshman Application Contact Mr. John Hamel, Vice President, Undergraduate Admissions, Suffolk University, 8 Ashburton Place, Boston, MA 02108. *Phone:* 617-573-8460. *Toll-free phone:* 800-6-SUFFOLK. *Fax:* 617-742-4291. *E-mail:* admission@suffolk.edu. *Web site:* http://www.suffolk.edu/.

Tufts University
Medford, Massachusetts

- **Independent** university, founded 1852
- **Suburban** 150-acre campus with easy access to Boston
- **Coed** 5,224 undergraduate students, 99% full-time, 51% women, 49% men
- **Most difficult** entrance level, 24% of applicants were admitted

Undergraduates 5,150 full-time, 74 part-time. Students come from 52 states and territories; 96 other countries; 75% are from out of state; 5% Black or African American, non-Hispanic/Latino; 6% Hispanic/Latino; 11% Asian, non-Hispanic/Latino; 0.1% Native Hawaiian or other Pacific Islander, non-Hispanic/Latino; 0.2% American Indian or Alaska Native, non-Hispanic/Latino; 2% Two or more races, non-Hispanic/Latino; 13% Race/ethnicity unknown; 6% international; 0.6% transferred in; 75% live on campus. *Retention:* 97% of full-time freshmen returned.

Freshmen *Admission:* 15,433 applied, 3,757 admitted, 1,313 enrolled. *Test scores:* SAT critical reading scores over 500: 100%; SAT math scores over 500: 101%; SAT writing scores over 500: 100%; ACT scores over 18: 100%; SAT critical reading scores over 600: 94%; SAT math scores over 600: 96%; SAT writing scores over 600: 96%; ACT scores over 24: 97%; SAT critical

reading scores over 700: 61%; SAT math scores over 700: 63%; SAT writing scores over 700: 65%; ACT scores over 30: 70%.

Faculty *Total:* 951, 70% full-time, 82% with terminal degrees. *Student/faculty ratio:* 9:1.

Academics *Calendar:* semesters. *Degrees:* bachelor's, master's, doctoral-professional, doctoral-research/scholarship, post-master's, and postbachelor's certificates. *Special study options:* adult/continuing education programs, advanced placement credit, double majors, honors programs, independent study, internships, off-campus study, services for LD students, student-designed majors, study abroad, summer session for credit. *ROTC:* Army (c), Navy (c), Air Force (c). *Unusual degree programs:* 3-2 New England Conservatory of Music, School of the Museum of Fine Arts.

Computers on Campus 300 computers/terminals are available on campus for general student use. Students can access the following: computer help desk, free student e-mail accounts, online (class) grades, online (class) registration, online (class) schedules. Campuswide network is available. 100% of college-owned or -operated housing units are wired for high-speed Internet access. Wireless service is available via classrooms, computer centers, computer labs, learning centers, libraries, student centers.

Student Life *Housing:* on-campus residence required through sophomore year. *Options:* coed, women-only, cooperative. Campus housing is university owned. Freshman campus housing is guaranteed. *Activities and organizations:* drama/theater group, student-run newspaper, radio and television station, choral group, marching band, Leonard Carmichael Society, Mountain Club, intramural sports, Tufts Daily (newspaper), Admissions Student Outreach, national fraternities, national sororities. *Campus security:* 24-hour emergency response devices and patrols, late-night transport/escort service, controlled dormitory access, security lighting, call boxes to campus police. *Student services:* health clinic, legal services.

Athletics Member NCAA. All Division III. *Intercollegiate sports:* baseball M, basketball M/W, crew M/W, cross-country running M/W, fencing W, field hockey W, football M, golf M, ice hockey M, lacrosse M/W, sailing M/W, soccer M/W, softball W, squash M/W, swimming and diving M/W, tennis M/W, track and field M/W, volleyball W. *Intramural sports:* basketball M/W, cheerleading M/W, cross-country running M/W, equestrian sports M/W, fencing M, football M, racquetball M/W, rugby M/W, skiing (downhill) M/W, soccer M/W, softball M/W, squash M/W, tennis M/W, track and field M/W, ultimate Frisbee M/W, volleyball M, water polo M.

Standardized Tests *Required:* SAT and SAT Subject Tests or ACT (for admission).

Costs (2010–11) *Comprehensive fee:* $53,800 includes full-time tuition ($41,598), mandatory fees ($934), and room and board ($11,268). *College room only:* $5982. Room and board charges vary according to board plan. *Payment plans:* tuition prepayment, installment. *Waivers:* employees or children of employees.

Financial Aid Of all full-time matriculated undergraduates who enrolled in 2009, 2,555 applied for aid, 2,228 were judged to have need, 2,187 had their need fully met. 1,721 Federal Work-Study jobs (averaging $1912). 85 state and other part-time jobs (averaging $1955). In 2009, 84 non-need-based awards were made. *Average percent of need met:* 100%. *Average financial aid package:* $32,696. *Average need-based loan:* $3554. *Average need-based gift aid:* $29,916. *Average non-need-based aid:* $500. *Average indebtedness upon graduation:* $27,443. *Financial aid deadline:* 2/15.

Applying *Options:* electronic application, early admission, early decision, deferred entrance. *Application fee:* $70. *Required:* essay or personal statement, high school transcript, 1 letter of recommendation. *Recommended:* interview. *Application deadlines:* 1/1 (freshmen), 3/1 (transfers). *Early decision deadline:* 11/1 (for plan 1), 1/1 (for plan 2). *Notification:* 4/1 (freshmen), 5/1 (transfers), 12/15 (early decision plan 1), 2/1 (early decision plan 2).

Freshman Application Contact Mr. Lee Coffin, Office of Undergraduate Admissions, Tufts University, Bendetson Hall, Medford, MA 02155. *Phone:* 617-627-3170. *Fax:* 617-627-3860. *E-mail:* admissions.inquiry@ase.tufts.edu. *Web site:* http://www.tufts.edu/.

University of Massachusetts Amherst
Amherst, Massachusetts

- **State-supported** university, founded 1863, part of University of Massachusetts
- **Small-town** 1463-acre campus with easy access to Hartford
- **Endowment** $181.5 million
- **Coed** 21,373 undergraduate students, 93% full-time, 50% women, 50% men
- **Moderately difficult** entrance level, 68% of applicants were admitted

Undergraduates 19,821 full-time, 1,552 part-time. Students come from 50 states and territories; 51 other countries; 17% are from out of state; 4% Black or African American, non-Hispanic/Latino; 5% Hispanic/Latino; 7% Asian, non-Hispanic/Latino; 0.1% Native Hawaiian or other Pacific Islander, non-Hispanic/Latino; 0.3% American Indian or Alaska Native, non-Hispanic/Latino; 2% Two or more races, non-Hispanic/Latino; 11% Race/ethnicity

unknown; 1% international; 5% transferred in; 60% live on campus. *Retention:* 89% of full-time freshmen returned.

Freshmen *Admission:* 30,853 applied, 20,858 admitted, 4,563 enrolled. *Average high school GPA:* 3.61. *Test scores:* SAT critical reading scores over 500: 85%; SAT math scores over 500: 91%; ACT scores over 18: 99%; SAT critical reading scores over 600: 36%; SAT math scores over 600: 50%; ACT scores over 24: 71%; SAT critical reading scores over 700: 5%; SAT math scores over 700: 9%; ACT scores over 30: 11%.

Faculty *Total:* 1,333, 87% full-time, 90% with terminal degrees. *Student/faculty ratio:* 19:1.

Academics *Calendar:* semesters. *Degrees:* certificates, associate, bachelor's, master's, doctoral-professional, doctoral-research/scholarship, post-master's, and postbachelor's certificates. *Special study options:* academic remediation for entering students, adult/continuing education programs, advanced placement credit, cooperative education, distance learning, double majors, English as a second language, freshman honors college, honors programs, independent study, internships, off-campus study, part-time degree program, services for LD students, student-designed majors, study abroad, summer session for credit. *ROTC:* Army (b), Air Force (b).

Computers on Campus 419 computers/terminals are available on campus for general student use. Students can access the following: computer help desk, free student e-mail accounts, online (class) grades, online (class) registration, online (class) schedules, online housing assignments, bill payment, Learning Management System, file storage, web hosting, blogs. Campuswide network is available. 100% of college-owned or -operated housing units are wired for high-speed Internet access. Wireless service is available via classrooms, computer centers, computer labs, learning centers, libraries, student centers.

Student Life *Housing:* on-campus residence required for freshman year. *Options:* coed, men-only, women-only, disabled students. Campus housing is university owned. Freshman campus housing is guaranteed. *Activities and organizations:* drama/theater group, student-run newspaper, radio and television station, choral group, marching band, Minutemen Marching Band, Theater Guild, Ski Club, Outing Club, student newspaper, national fraternities, national sororities. *Campus security:* 24-hour emergency response devices and patrols, student patrols, late-night transport/escort service, controlled dormitory access, residence halls locked nights and weekends. *Student services:* health clinic, personal/psychological counseling, women's center, legal services.

Athletics Member NCAA. All Division I except football (Division I-AA). *Intercollegiate sports:* baseball M(s), basketball M(s)/W(s), crew W(s), cross-country running M(s)/W(s), field hockey W(s), ice hockey M(s), lacrosse M(s)/W(s), soccer M(s)/W(s), softball W(s), swimming and diving M(s)/W(s), tennis W(s), track and field M(s)/W(s). *Intramural sports:* archery M(c)/W(c), baseball M(c), basketball M/W, crew M(c)/W(c), equestrian sports M(c)/W(c), fencing M(c)/W(c), field hockey W, football M/W, golf M(c)/W(c), ice hockey M/W, lacrosse M(c)/W(c), rugby M(c)/W(c), sailing M(c)/W(c), skiing (downhill) M(c)/W(c), soccer M/W, softball W, table tennis M(c)/W(c), tennis M/W, ultimate Frisbee M/W, volleyball M/W, water polo M(c), wrestling M(c)/W(c).

Standardized Tests *Required:* SAT or ACT (for admission).

Costs (2010–11) *One-time required fee:* $185. *Tuition:* state resident $1714 full-time, $72 per credit part-time; nonresident $9937 full-time, $414 per credit part-time. Full-time tuition and fees vary according to class time, course load, degree level, location, program, reciprocity agreements, and student level. Part-time tuition and fees vary according to class time, course load, degree level, location, program, reciprocity agreements, and student level. *Required fees:* $10,018 full-time. *Room and board:* $9339; room only: $4672. Room and board charges vary according to board plan and housing facility. *Payment plan:* installment. *Waivers:* senior citizens and employees or children of employees.

Financial Aid Of all full-time matriculated undergraduates who enrolled in 2008, 15,396 applied for aid, 11,051 were judged to have need, 2,976 had their need fully met. 5,636 Federal Work-Study jobs (averaging $1229). In 2008, 1042 non-need-based awards were made. *Average percent of need met:* 88%. *Average financial aid package:* $14,604. *Average need-based loan:* $4385. *Average need-based gift aid:* $8861. *Average non-need-based aid:* $2805. *Average indebtedness upon graduation:* $25,420.

Applying *Options:* electronic application, early action, deferred entrance. *Application fee:* $70. *Required:* essay or personal statement, high school transcript. *Recommended:* minimum 3 GPA. *Application deadlines:* 1/15 (freshmen), 4/15 (transfers), 11/1 (early action). *Notification:* continuous (freshmen), continuous (transfers), 12/15 (early action).

Freshman Application Contact Mr. Kevin Kelly, Director, Undergraduate Admissions, University of Massachusetts Amherst, 37 Mather Drive, Amherst, MA 01003. *Phone:* 413-545-0222. *Fax:* 413-545-4312. *E-mail:* mail@admissions.umass.edu. *Web site:* http://www.umass.edu/.

University of Massachusetts Boston
Boston, Massachusetts

- **State-supported** university, founded 1964, part of University of Massachusetts
- **Urban** 177-acre campus
- **Endowment** $42.0 million
- **Coed** 11,568 undergraduate students, 69% full-time, 57% women, 43% men
- **Moderately difficult** entrance level, 57% of applicants were admitted

Undergraduates 7,973 full-time, 3,595 part-time. Students come from 30 states and territories; 124 other countries; 5% are from out of state; 16% Black or African American, non-Hispanic/Latino; 9% Hispanic/Latino; 12% Asian, non-Hispanic/Latino; 0.3% American Indian or Alaska Native, non-Hispanic/Latino; 0.6% Two or more races, non-Hispanic/Latino; 10% Race/ethnicity unknown; 4% international; 14% transferred in. *Retention:* 75% of full-time freshmen returned.

Freshmen *Admission:* 6,748 applied, 3,850 admitted, 1,129 enrolled. *Average high school GPA:* 3. *Test scores:* SAT critical reading scores over 500: 56%; SAT math scores over 500: 65%; SAT critical reading scores over 600: 15%; SAT math scores over 600: 18%; SAT critical reading scores over 700: 1%; SAT math scores over 700: 3%.

Faculty *Total:* 1,038, 51% full-time, 59% with terminal degrees. *Student/faculty ratio:* 16:1.

Academics *Calendar:* semesters. *Degrees:* certificates, bachelor's, master's, doctoral-professional, doctoral-research/scholarship, post-master's, and postbachelor's certificates. *Special study options:* academic remediation for entering students, accelerated degree program, adult/continuing education programs, advanced placement credit, cooperative education, distance learning, double majors, English as a second language, freshman honors college, honors programs, independent study, internships, off-campus study, part-time degree program, services for LD students, student-designed majors, study abroad, summer session for credit. *ROTC:* Army (c), Navy (c), Air Force (c). *Unusual degree programs:* 3-2 engineering with University of Massachusetts Lowell, University of Massachusetts Amherst, Northeastern University.

Computers on Campus 350 computers/terminals are available on campus for general student use. Students can access the following: computer help desk, free student e-mail accounts, online (class) grades, online (class) registration, online (class) schedules. Campuswide network is available. Wireless service is available via entire campus.

Student Life *Housing:* college housing not available. *Activities and organizations:* drama/theater group, student-run newspaper, radio station, choral group, Student Arts & Events Council, Haitian Student Association, Golden Key Honor Society, Campus Kitchens, Mass Media. *Campus security:* 24-hour emergency response devices and patrols, late-night transport/escort service, crime prevention program, bicycle patrols. *Student services:* health clinic, personal/psychological counseling, women's center, legal services.

Athletics Member NCAA. All Division III. *Intercollegiate sports:* baseball M, basketball M/W, cross-country running M/W, ice hockey M, lacrosse M, soccer M/W, softball W, tennis M/W, track and field M/W, volleyball W. *Intramural sports:* badminton M/W, basketball M/W, golf M/W, ice hockey M/W, racquetball M/W, sailing M/W, soccer M/W, softball M/W, squash M/W, swimming and diving M/W, tennis M/W, volleyball M/W, weight lifting M/W.

Standardized Tests *Required:* SAT or ACT (for admission).

Costs (2010–11) *Tuition:* state resident $1714 full-time, $72 per credit hour part-time; nonresident $9758 full-time, $72 per credit hour part-time. Full-time tuition and fees vary according to class time, course load, program, reciprocity agreements, and student level. Part-time tuition and fees vary according to class time, course load, program, reciprocity agreements, and student level. *Required fees:* $8897 full-time, $370 per credit hour part-time. *Payment plan:* installment. *Waivers:* senior citizens and employees or children of employees.

Financial Aid Of all full-time matriculated undergraduates who enrolled in 2008, 5,073 applied for aid, 4,310 were judged to have need, 3,146 had their need fully met. 523 Federal Work-Study jobs (averaging $3061). In 2008, 261 non-need-based awards were made. *Average percent of need met:* 95%. *Average financial aid package:* $12,368. *Average need-based loan:* $5966. *Average need-based gift aid:* $6535. *Average non-need-based aid:* $3539. *Average indebtedness upon graduation:* $19,327.

Applying *Options:* electronic application, deferred entrance. *Application fee:* $40. *Required:* high school transcript, minimum 2.5 GPA. *Required for some:* essay or personal statement, minimum 2.75 GPA, interview. *Recommended:* essay or personal statement. *Application deadlines:* 6/1 (freshmen), 7/1 (transfers). *Notification:* continuous (freshmen), continuous (transfers).

Freshman Application Contact Mr. John Drew, Director of Undergraduate Admissions, University of Massachusetts Boston, 100 Morrissey Boulevard, Boston, MA 02125-3393. *Phone:* 617-287-6000. *Fax:* 617-287-5999. *E-mail:* enrollment.info@umb.edu. *Web site:* http://www.umb.edu/.

See page 410 for Display. See page 1706 for the College Close-Up.

University of Massachusetts Dartmouth

North Dartmouth, Massachusetts

- **State-supported** university, founded 1895, part of University of Massachusetts
- **Suburban** 710-acre campus with easy access to Boston and Providence
- **Endowment** $32.3 million
- **Coed** 7,749 undergraduate students, 88% full-time, 47% women, 53% men
- **Moderately difficult** entrance level, 71% of applicants were admitted

Undergraduates 6,838 full-time, 911 part-time. Students come from 24 states and territories; 16 other countries; 4% are from out of state; 10% Black or African American, non-Hispanic/Latino; 4% Hispanic/Latino; 3% Asian, non-Hispanic/Latino; 0.4% American Indian or Alaska Native, non-Hispanic/Latino; 1% Two or more races, non-Hispanic/Latino; 6% Race/ethnicity unknown; 0.3% international; 6% transferred in; 57% live on campus. *Retention:* 70% of full-time freshmen returned.

Freshmen *Admission:* 7,868 applied, 5,598 admitted, 1,707 enrolled. *Average high school GPA:* 3.13. *Test scores:* SAT critical reading scores over 500: 58%; SAT math scores over 500: 68%; ACT scores over 18: 87%; SAT critical reading scores over 600: 14%; SAT math scores over 600: 23%; ACT scores over 24: 34%; SAT critical reading scores over 700: 2%; SAT math scores over 700: 2%; ACT scores over 30: 2%.

Faculty *Total:* 653, 59% full-time, 51% with terminal degrees. *Student/faculty ratio:* 17:1.

Academics *Calendar:* semesters. *Degrees:* certificates, bachelor's, master's, doctoral-professional, doctoral-research/scholarship, post-master's, and post-bachelor's certificates. *Special study options:* academic remediation for entering students, advanced placement credit, cooperative education, distance learning, double majors, honors programs, independent study, internships, off-campus study, part-time degree program, services for LD students, student-designed majors, study abroad, summer session for credit. *ROTC:* Army (c).

Computers on Campus 368 computers/terminals are available on campus for general student use. Students can access the following: campus intranet, computer help desk, free student e-mail accounts, online (class) grades, online (class) registration, online (class) schedules. Campuswide network is available.

100% of college-owned or -operated housing units are wired for high-speed Internet access. Wireless service is available via entire campus.

Student Life *Housing options:* coed, disabled students. Campus housing is university owned. *Activities and organizations:* drama/theater group, student-run newspaper, radio station, choral group, Student Activities Board, Outing Club, Phi Sigma Sigma, Portuguese Language Club, United Brothers and Sisters, national fraternities, national sororities. *Campus security:* 24-hour emergency response devices and patrols, student patrols, late-night transport/escort service, controlled dormitory access. *Student services:* health clinic, personal/psychological counseling, women's center, legal services.

Athletics Member NCAA. All Division III. *Intercollegiate sports:* baseball M, basketball M/W, cheerleading W, cross-country running M/W, equestrian sports W(c), field hockey W, football M, golf M, ice hockey M, lacrosse M/W, rugby M(c)/W(c), soccer M/W, softball W, swimming and diving M/W, tennis M/W, track and field M/W, volleyball W. *Intramural sports:* badminton M/W, basketball M/W, field hockey W, rock climbing M(c)/W(c), sailing M/W, skiing (downhill) M(c)/W(c), soccer M/W, softball M/W, table tennis M/W, tennis M/W, ultimate Frisbee M/W, volleyball M/W.

Standardized Tests *Required:* SAT or ACT (for admission).

Costs (2010–11) *Tuition:* state resident $1417 full-time, $59 per credit part-time; nonresident $8099 full-time, $337 per credit part-time. Full-time tuition and fees vary according to class time, program, and reciprocity agreements. Part-time tuition and fees vary according to class time, course load, program, and reciprocity agreements. *Required fees:* $8941 full-time, $373 per credit part-time. *Room and board:* $9134; room only: $6317. Room and board charges vary according to board plan and housing facility. *Payment plan:* installment. *Waivers:* senior citizens and employees or children of employees.

Financial Aid Of all full-time matriculated undergraduates who enrolled in 2009, 5,497 applied for aid, 4,545 were judged to have need, 1,973 had their need fully met. In 2009, 357 non-need-based awards were made. *Average percent of need met:* 88%. *Average financial aid package:* $14,195. *Average need-based loan:* $7337. *Average need-based gift aid:* $7987. *Average non-need-based aid:* $3741. *Average indebtedness upon graduation:* $34,369.

Applying *Options:* electronic application, early admission, early action, deferred entrance. *Application fee:* $50. *Required:* essay or personal statement, high school transcript, minimum 3 GPA. *Application deadlines:* rolling (freshmen), rolling (transfers), 11/15 (early action). *Notification:* continuous (freshmen), continuous (transfers), 12/15 (early action).

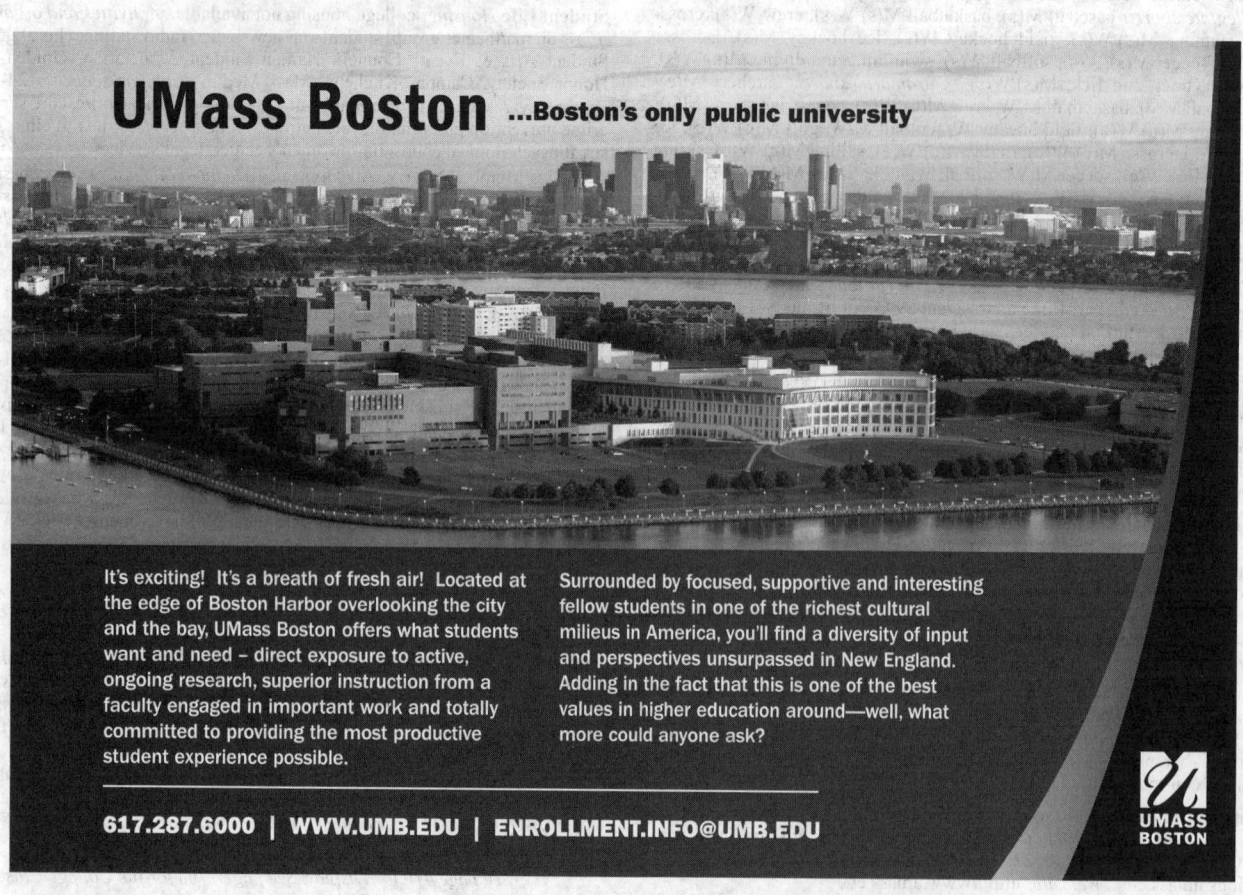

Freshman Application Contact University of Massachusetts Dartmouth, 285 Old Westport Road, North Dartmouth, MA 02747-2300. *Phone:* 508-999-8605. *Fax:* 508-999-8755. *E-mail:* admissions@umassd.edu. *Web site:* http://www.umassd.edu/.

University of Massachusetts Lowell
Lowell, Massachusetts

- **State-supported** university, founded 1894, part of University of Massachusetts
- **Urban** 100-acre campus with easy access to Boston
- **Endowment** $41.1 million
- **Coed** 11,276 undergraduate students, 72% full-time, 40% women, 60% men
- **Moderately difficult** entrance level, 74% of applicants were admitted

Undergraduates 8,133 full-time, 3,143 part-time. Students come from 55 states and territories; 25 other countries; 8% are from out of state; 6% Black or African American, non-Hispanic/Latino; 8% Hispanic/Latino; 8% Asian, non-Hispanic/Latino; 0.1% American Indian or Alaska Native, non-Hispanic/Latino; 2% Two or more races, non-Hispanic/Latino; 7% Race/ethnicity unknown; 0.6% international; 9% transferred in; 37% live on campus. *Retention:* 78% of full-time freshmen returned.

Freshmen *Admission:* 7,284 applied, 5,359 admitted, 1,636 enrolled. *Average high school GPA:* 3.19. *Test scores:* SAT critical reading scores over 500: 65%; SAT math scores over 500: 79%; SAT critical reading scores over 600: 20%; SAT math scores over 600: 31%; SAT critical reading scores over 700: 2%; SAT math scores over 700: 5%.

Faculty *Total:* 1,004, 43% full-time. *Student/faculty ratio:* 14:1.

Academics *Calendar:* semesters. *Degrees:* associate, bachelor's, master's, doctoral-professional, doctoral-research/scholarship, post-master's, and post-bachelor's certificates. *Special study options:* accelerated degree program, adult/continuing education programs, advanced placement credit, cooperative education, distance learning, double majors, honors programs, independent study, internships, off-campus study, part-time degree program, services for LD students, study abroad, summer session for credit. *ROTC:* Army (b), Air Force (b).

Computers on Campus 3,000 computers/terminals and 12,728 ports are available on campus for general student use. Students can access the following: campus intranet, computer help desk, free student e-mail accounts, online (class) grades, online (class) registration, online (class) schedules. Campus-wide network is available. 100% of college-owned or -operated housing units are wired for high-speed Internet access. Wireless service is available via classrooms, computer centers, computer labs, dorm rooms, learning centers, libraries, student centers.

Student Life *Housing options:* coed, men-only, women-only. Campus housing is university owned and leased by the school. *Activities and organizations:* drama/theater group, student-run newspaper, radio station, choral group, marching band, Student Government Association, Recreational Sports Club, Association of Students of African Origin, WUML (radio station), Campus Activities Programming Association. *Campus security:* 24-hour emergency response devices and patrols, late-night transport/escort service, controlled dormitory access. *Student services:* health clinic, personal/psychological counseling.

Athletics Member NCAA. All Division II except ice hockey (Division I). *Intercollegiate sports:* baseball M(s), basketball M(s)/W(s), crew M(c)/W, cross-country running M(s)/W(s), field hockey W(s), golf M, ice hockey M(s), soccer M(s)/W(s), softball W(s), track and field M(s)/W(s), volleyball W(s). *Intramural sports:* badminton M/W, basketball M/W, cheerleading M(c)/W(c), crew M(c), equestrian sports M(c)/W(c), fencing M(c)/W(c), football M/W, golf M/W, ice hockey M/W, lacrosse M(c)/W(c), racquetball M/W, rock climbing M/W, skiing (downhill) M/W, soccer M/W, softball M/W, squash M/W, swimming and diving M(c)/W(c), table tennis M/W, tennis M/W, ultimate Frisbee M(c)/W(c), volleyball M(c)/W(c), weight lifting M/W.

Standardized Tests *Required:* SAT or ACT (for admission).

Costs (2010–11) *Tuition:* state resident $1454 full-time, $61 per credit part-time; nonresident $13,893 full-time, $357 per credit part-time. Part-time tuition and fees vary according to course load. *Required fees:* $9052 full-time, $391 per credit part-time. *Room and board:* $9067; room only: $6044. Room and board charges vary according to board plan and housing facility. *Payment plan:* installment. *Waivers:* senior citizens and employees or children of employees.

Financial Aid Of all full-time matriculated undergraduates who enrolled in 2008, 6,036 applied for aid, 4,399 were judged to have need, 3,063 had their need fully met. 113 Federal Work-Study jobs (averaging $2099). 686 state and other part-time jobs (averaging $3098). In 2008, 1531 non-need-based awards were made. *Average percent of need met:* 95%. *Average financial aid package:* $12,035. *Average need-based loan:* $6252. *Average need-based gift aid:* $5982. *Average non-need-based aid:* $2190. *Average indebtedness upon graduation:* $24,087.

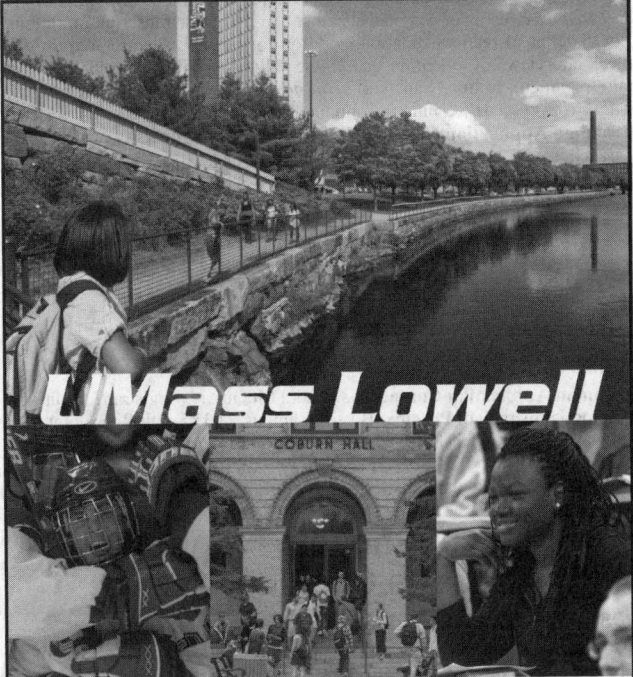

Host of the inaugural Innovative Cities Conference, Lowell is a recently restored mill city brimming with history and culture and within easy reach of Boston and New England's best recreational areas.

Applying *Options:* electronic application, deferred entrance. *Application fee:* $60. *Required:* essay or personal statement, high school transcript, minimum 3 GPA, 1 letter of recommendation, audition for music students. *Required for some:* interview. *Application deadlines:* rolling (freshmen), rolling (out-of-state freshmen), rolling (transfers). *Notification:* continuous (freshmen), continuous (out-of-state freshmen), continuous (transfers).

Freshman Application Contact Admissions Office, University of Massachusetts Lowell, 883 Broadway Street, Room 110, Lowell, MA 01854-5104. *Phone:* 978-934-3944. *Toll-free phone:* 800-410-4607. *Fax:* 978-934-3086. *E-mail:* admissions@uml.edu. *Web site:* http://www.uml.edu/.

See page 1708 for the College Close-Up.

University of Phoenix–Boston Campus
Braintree, Massachusetts

Freshman Application Contact Ms. Audra McQuarie, Registrar/Executive Director, University of Phoenix–Boston Campus, 4035 South Riverpoint Parkway, Mail Stop CF-L101, Phoenix, AZ 85040. *Phone:* 480-557-6151. *Toll-free phone:* 800-228-7240. *Fax:* 480-643-3068. *E-mail:* audra.mcquarie@phoenix.edu. *Web site:* http://www.phoenix.edu/.

University of Phoenix–Central Massachusetts Campus
Westborough, Massachusetts

Freshman Application Contact Ms. Audra McQuarie, Registrar/Executive Director, University of Phoenix–Central Massachusetts Campus, 4035 South Riverpoint Parkway, Mail Stop CF-L101, Phoenix, AZ 85040. *Phone:* 480-557-6151. *Toll-free phone:* 800-776-4867 (in-state); 800-228-7240 (out-of-state). *Fax:* 480-643-3068. *E-mail:* audra.mcquarie@phoenix.edu. *Web site:* http://www.phoenix.edu/.

Wellesley College
Wellesley, Massachusetts

- **Independent** 4-year, founded 1870
- **Suburban** 500-acre campus with easy access to Boston
- **Endowment** $1.3 billion
- **Women only** 2,411 undergraduate students, 95% full-time
- **Most difficult** entrance level, 34% of applicants were admitted

Undergraduates 2,294 full-time, 117 part-time. Students come from 52 states and territories; 73 other countries; 88% are from out of state; 6% Black or African American, non-Hispanic/Latino; 9% Hispanic/Latino; 22% Asian, non-Hispanic/Latino; 0.2% American Indian or Alaska Native, non-Hispanic/Latino; 4% Two or more races, non-Hispanic/Latino; 2% Race/ethnicity unknown; 10% international; 0.6% transferred in; 97% live on campus. *Retention:* 96% of full-time freshmen returned.

Freshmen *Admission:* 4,267 applied, 1,440 admitted, 633 enrolled. *Test scores:* SAT critical reading scores over 500: 99%; SAT math scores over 500: 99%; SAT writing scores over 500: 100%; ACT scores over 18: 100%; SAT critical reading scores over 600: 87%; SAT math scores over 600: 89%; SAT writing scores over 600: 92%; ACT scores over 24: 97%; SAT critical reading scores over 700: 46%; SAT math scores over 700: 45%; SAT writing scores over 700: 56%; ACT scores over 30: 61%.

Faculty *Total:* 323, 82% full-time, 94% with terminal degrees. *Student/faculty ratio:* 8:1.

Academics *Calendar:* semesters. *Degrees:* bachelor's (double bachelor's degree with Massachusetts Institute of Technology). *Special study options:* adult/continuing education programs, advanced placement credit, double majors, honors programs, independent study, internships, off-campus study, part-time degree program, services for LD students, student-designed majors, study abroad, summer session for credit. *ROTC:* Army (c), Air Force (c). *Unusual degree programs:* 3-2 engineering with Massachusetts Institute of Technology, Dartmouth College, Columbia University; architecture; aeronautics and astronautics; urban studies and planning with Massachusetts Institute of Technology; international economics and finance with Brandeis University.

Computers on Campus 200 computers/terminals and 200 ports are available on campus for general student use. Students can access the following: campus intranet, computer help desk, free student e-mail accounts, online (class) registration, online (class) schedules, electronic bulletin boards. Campuswide network is available. 100% of college-owned or -operated housing units are wired for high-speed Internet access. Wireless service is available via entire campus.

Student Life *Housing options:* women-only, cooperative. Campus housing is university owned. Freshman campus housing is guaranteed. *Activities and organizations:* drama/theater group, student-run newspaper, radio and television station, choral group, student government, radio station, cultural clubs, rugby club, theater groups. *Campus security:* 24-hour emergency response devices and patrols, late-night transport/escort service, controlled dormitory access. *Student services:* health clinic, personal/psychological counseling, women's center.

Athletics Member NCAA. All Division III. *Intercollegiate sports:* basketball W, crew W, cross-country running W, fencing W, field hockey W, golf W, lacrosse W, rugby W(c), sailing W(c), skiing (downhill) W(c), soccer W, softball W, squash W, swimming and diving W, tennis W, track and field W, ultimate Frisbee W(c), volleyball W. *Intramural sports:* archery W, badminton W(c), basketball W, cheerleading W(c), crew W, equestrian sports W(c), ice hockey W(c), racquetball W(c), sailing W(c), skiing (cross-country) W, soccer W, softball W, squash W(c), swimming and diving W, table tennis W(c), tennis W, volleyball W, water polo W, weight lifting W.

Standardized Tests *Required:* SAT and SAT Subject Tests or ACT (for admission).

Costs (2010–11) *Comprehensive fee:* $51,950 includes full-time tuition ($39,420), mandatory fees ($246), and room and board ($12,284). Part-time tuition: $1232 per credit hour. Part-time tuition and fees vary according to course load. *Required fees:* $31 per credit part-time. *College room only:* $6234. *Payment plans:* tuition prepayment, installment. *Waivers:* employees or children of employees.

Financial Aid Of all full-time matriculated undergraduates who enrolled in 2009, 1,613 applied for aid, 1,445 were judged to have need, 1,445 had their need fully met. 858 Federal Work-Study jobs (averaging $1190). 376 state and other part-time jobs (averaging $1315). *Average percent of need met:* 100%. *Average financial aid package:* $38,136. *Average need-based loan:* $3010. *Average need-based gift aid:* $36,299. *Average indebtedness upon graduation:* $12,495.

Applying *Options:* electronic application, early admission, early decision, deferred entrance. *Application fee:* $50. *Required:* essay or personal statement, high school transcript, 3 letters of recommendation, first senior marking period grades and mid-year report. *Required for some:* interview. *Recommended:* interview. *Application deadlines:* 1/15 (freshmen), 1/15 (out-of-state freshmen), 3/1 (transfers). *Early decision deadline:* 11/1. *Notification:* 4/1 (freshmen), 4/1 (out-of-state freshmen), 5/1 (transfers), 12/15 (early decision).

Freshman Application Contact Director of Admission, Wellesley College, 106 Central Street, Wellesley, MA 02481. *Phone:* 781-283-2270. *Fax:* 781-283-3678. *E-mail:* admission@wellesley.edu. *Web site:* http://www.wellesley.edu/.

Wentworth Institute of Technology
Boston, Massachusetts

- **Independent** comprehensive, founded 1904
- **Urban** 31-acre campus
- **Endowment** $66.8 million
- **Coed** 3,721 undergraduate students, 88% full-time, 19% women, 81% men
- **Moderately difficult** entrance level, 58% of applicants were admitted

Undergraduates 3,285 full-time, 436 part-time. Students come from 37 states and territories; 46 other countries; 42% are from out of state; 5% Black or African American, non-Hispanic/Latino; 3% Hispanic/Latino; 5% Asian, non-Hispanic/Latino; 0.2% American Indian or Alaska Native, non-Hispanic/Latino; 2% Two or more races, non-Hispanic/Latino; 14% Race/ethnicity unknown; 4% international; 6% transferred in; 45% live on campus. *Retention:* 80% of full-time freshmen returned.

Freshmen *Admission:* 4,757 applied, 2,777 admitted, 729 enrolled. *Average high school GPA:* 2.96. *Test scores:* SAT critical reading scores over 500: 63%; SAT math scores over 500: 87%; SAT writing scores over 500: 57%; ACT scores over 18: 99%; SAT critical reading scores over 600: 14%; SAT math scores over 600: 38%; SAT writing scores over 600: 12%; ACT scores over 24: 48%; SAT critical reading scores over 700: 1%; SAT math scores over 700: 2%; SAT writing scores over 700: 1%; ACT scores over 30: 6%.

Faculty *Total:* 282, 53% full-time, 27% with terminal degrees. *Student/faculty ratio:* 15:1.

Academics *Calendar:* semesters for freshmen and sophomores, trimesters for juniors and seniors. *Degrees:* associate, bachelor's, and master's. *Special study options:* academic remediation for entering students, advanced placement credit, cooperative education, internships, off-campus study, part-time degree program, services for LD students, study abroad, summer session for credit. *ROTC:* Army (c), Air Force (c).

Computers on Campus 120 computers/terminals and 200 ports are available on campus for general student use. Students can access the following: campus intranet, computer help desk, free student e-mail accounts, online (class) grades, online (class) registration, online (class) schedules. Campuswide network is available. 100% of college-owned or -operated housing units are wired for high-speed Internet access. Wireless service is available via entire campus.

Student Life *Housing:* on-campus residence required through sophomore year. *Options:* coed. Campus housing is university owned. Freshman campus housing is guaranteed. *Activities and organizations:* student-run radio station,

WENTWORTH
Institute of Technology

YOUR EDUCATIONAL EXPERIENCE AWAITS YOU IN BOSTON

- Our quality, hands-on, practical education prepares students for careers in architecture, computer science, construction management, engineering, engineering technology, management, and design

- Our full-time tuition is one of the lowest for private colleges in the Boston area, and includes a laptop for all students, customized with software for their specific major

- The average class size is 22

- Two semesters of cooperative education program (co-op) allows students to gain extensive real-world experience and develop valuable business contacts

- The average starting salary for the 2009 Wentworth graduate was $48,311

- Bachelor of Science in Engineering, Biomedical Engineering, Mechanical Engineering, and Electrical Engineering programs are being launched in Fall 2011

Wentworth Institute of Technology
550 Huntington Avenue
Boston, MA 02115-5998

Website: www.wit.edu
Telephone: 800-556-0610

intramural sports, Wentworth Events Board, Multicultural Student Association, Phi Sigma Pi, Major Particular Professional Student Associations. *Campus security:* 24-hour emergency response devices and patrols, student patrols, late-night transport/escort service, controlled dormitory access. *Student services:* health clinic, personal/psychological counseling, women's center.
Athletics Member NCAA. All Division III. *Intercollegiate sports:* baseball M, basketball M/W, crew M(c)/W(c), golf M, ice hockey M, lacrosse M/W(c), riflery M/W, rugby M(c)/W(c), soccer M/W, softball W, tennis M/W, ultimate Frisbee M(c)/W(c), volleyball M/W.
Standardized Tests *Required:* SAT or ACT (for admission).
Costs (2011–12) *Tuition:* $24,000 full-time, $750 per credit hour part-time. Full-time tuition and fees vary according to student level. Part-time tuition and fees vary according to class time, course load, and degree level. *Room only:* Room and board charges vary according to board plan and housing facility. *Payment plan:* installment. *Waivers:* employees or children of employees.
Financial Aid Of all full-time matriculated undergraduates who enrolled in 2009, 2,571 applied for aid, 2,338 were judged to have need, 60 had their need fully met. 2,026 Federal Work-Study jobs (averaging $1354). In 2009, 157 non-need-based awards were made. *Average financial aid package:* $14,453. *Average need-based loan:* $4674. *Average need-based gift aid:* $5568. *Average non-need-based aid:* $6766. *Average indebtedness upon graduation:* $20,208.
Applying *Options:* electronic application, deferred entrance. *Application fee:* $50. *Required:* essay or personal statement, high school transcript, 1 letter of recommendation. *Recommended:* minimum 2 GPA, interview. *Application deadlines:* 5/1 (freshmen), 5/1 (out-of-state freshmen), 5/1 (transfers). *Notification:* continuous (freshmen), continuous (transfers).
Freshman Application Contact Ms. Amy Dufour, Associate Director of Admissions, Wentworth Institute of Technology, 550 Huntington Avenue, Boston, MA 02115. *Phone:* 617-989-4116. *Toll-free phone:* 800-556-0610. *Fax:* 617-989-4010. *E-mail:* dufoura@wit.edu. *Web site:* http://www.wit.edu/
.

See page 1770 for the College Close-Up.

Western New England University
Springfield, Massachusetts

- **Independent** comprehensive, founded 1919
- **Suburban** 215-acre campus
- **Endowment** $34.1 million
- **Coed** 2,739 undergraduate students, 90% full-time, 40% women, 60% men
- **Moderately difficult** entrance level, 81% of applicants were admitted

Undergraduates 2,463 full-time, 276 part-time. Students come from 31 states and territories; 3 other countries; 61% are from out of state; 3% transferred in; 68% live on campus. *Retention:* 75% of full-time freshmen returned.
Freshmen *Admission:* 4,769 applied, 3,861 admitted, 689 enrolled. *Average high school GPA:* 3.16. *Test scores:* SAT critical reading scores over 500: 63%; SAT math scores over 500: 71%; ACT scores over 18: 94%; SAT critical reading scores over 600: 15%; SAT math scores over 600: 28%; ACT scores over 24: 38%; SAT critical reading scores over 700: 1%; SAT math scores over 700: 3%; ACT scores over 30: 1%.
Faculty *Total:* 301, 62% full-time. *Student/faculty ratio:* 15:1.
Academics *Calendar:* semesters. *Degrees:* associate, bachelor's, master's, doctoral-professional, and doctoral-research/scholarship. *Special study options:* accelerated degree program, adult/continuing education programs, advanced placement credit, distance learning, double majors, honors programs, independent study, internships, off-campus study, part-time degree program, services for LD students, student-designed majors, study abroad, summer session for credit. *ROTC:* Army (b), Air Force (c). *Unusual degree programs:* 3-2 business administration; engineering.
Computers on Campus 400 computers/terminals are available on campus for general student use. Students can access the following: computer help desk, free student e-mail accounts, online (class) grades, online (class) registration, online (class) schedules. Campuswide network is available. 100% of college-owned or -operated housing units are wired for high-speed Internet access.
Student Life *Housing options:* coed. Campus housing is university owned. Freshman campus housing is guaranteed. *Activities and organizations:* drama/theater group, student-run newspaper, radio station, choral group, Student Senate, Residence Hall Association, Campus Activities Board, student radio station, The Westerner (student newspaper). *Campus security:* 24-hour emergency response devices and patrols, student patrols, late-night transport/escort service, controlled dormitory access, security cameras. *Student services:* health clinic, personal/psychological counseling.
Athletics Member NCAA. All Division III. *Intercollegiate sports:* baseball M, basketball M/W, bowling M/W, cross-country running M/W, field hockey W, football M, golf M, ice hockey M, lacrosse M/W, soccer M/W, softball W, swimming and diving W, tennis M/W, volleyball W, wrestling M. *Intramural sports:* badminton M/W, basketball M/W, football M/W, rugby M/W, soccer

M/W, softball M/W, table tennis M/W, ultimate Frisbee M/W, volleyball M/W, water polo M/W.

Standardized Tests *Required:* SAT or ACT (for admission).

Costs (2010–11) *Comprehensive fee:* $41,148 includes full-time tuition ($27,762), mandatory fees ($2050), and room and board ($11,336). Full-time tuition and fees vary according to program. Part-time tuition: $523 per credit hour. Part-time tuition and fees vary according to location and program. *Room and board:* Room and board charges vary according to board plan and housing facility. *Payment plans:* tuition prepayment, installment. *Waivers:* senior citizens and employees or children of employees.

Financial Aid Of all full-time matriculated undergraduates who enrolled in 2009, 2,232 applied for aid, 1,979 were judged to have need, 288 had their need fully met. In 2009, 321 non-need-based awards were made. *Average percent of need met:* 69%. *Average financial aid package:* $19,699. *Average need-based loan:* $4728. *Average need-based gift aid:* $1455. *Average non-need-based aid:* $11,140.

Applying *Options:* electronic application. *Application fee:* $50. *Required:* high school transcript, 1 letter of recommendation. *Recommended:* essay or personal statement, interview. *Application deadlines:* rolling (freshmen), rolling (transfers). *Notification:* continuous (freshmen), continuous (transfers).

Freshman Application Contact Dr. Charles R. Pollock, Vice President of Enrollment Management, Western New England University, Springfield, MA 01119. *Phone:* 413-782-1321. *Toll-free phone:* 800-325-1122 Ext. 1321. *Fax:* 413-782-1777. *E-mail:* ugradmis@wnec.edu. *Web site:* http://www.wne.edu/.

Westfield State University
Westfield, Massachusetts

- **State-supported** comprehensive, founded 1838, part of Massachusetts Public Higher Education System
- **Small-town** 227-acre campus
- **Coed** 5,203 undergraduate students, 89% full-time, 52% women, 48% men
- **Moderately difficult** entrance level, 58% of applicants were admitted

Undergraduates 4,649 full-time, 554 part-time. Students come from 23 states and territories; 10 other countries; 7% are from out of state; 4% Black or African American, non-Hispanic/Latino; 5% Hispanic/Latino; 0.9% Asian, non-Hispanic/Latino; 0.1% Native Hawaiian or other Pacific Islander, non-Hispanic/Latino; 0.3% American Indian or Alaska Native, non-Hispanic/Latino; 1% Two or more races, non-Hispanic/Latino; 6% Race/ethnicity unknown; 0.3% international; 8% transferred in; 51% live on campus. *Retention:* 79% of full-time freshmen returned.

Freshmen *Admission:* 5,621 applied, 3,265 admitted, 1,139 enrolled. *Average high school GPA:* 2.99. *Test scores:* SAT critical reading scores over 500: 53%; SAT math scores over 500: 61%; ACT scores over 18: 90%; SAT critical reading scores over 600: 10%; SAT math scores over 600: 13%; ACT scores over 24: 33%; SAT critical reading scores over 700: 1%; ACT scores over 30: 1%.

Faculty *Total:* 468, 46% full-time, 51% with terminal degrees. *Student/faculty ratio:* 16:1.

Academics *Calendar:* semesters. *Degrees:* bachelor's, master's, post-master's, and postbachelor's certificates. *Special study options:* adult/continuing education programs, advanced placement credit, cooperative education, distance learning, double majors, honors programs, independent study, internships, off-campus study, part-time degree program, services for LD students, student-designed majors, study abroad, summer session for credit. *ROTC:* Army (c), Air Force (c).

Computers on Campus 275 computers/terminals are available on campus for general student use. Students can access the following: computer help desk, free student e-mail accounts, online (class) grades, online (class) registration, online (class) schedules, online transcripts and billing information. Campus-wide network is available. 100% of college-owned or -operated housing units are wired for high-speed Internet access. Wireless service is available via entire campus.

Student Life *Housing options:* coed, disabled students. Campus housing is university owned. Freshman applicants given priority for college housing. *Activities and organizations:* drama/theater group, student-run newspaper, radio and television station, choral group. *Campus security:* 24-hour emergency response devices and patrols, student patrols, late-night transport/escort service, controlled dormitory access. *Student services:* health clinic, personal/psychological counseling, legal services.

Athletics Member NCAA. All Division III. *Intercollegiate sports:* baseball M, basketball M/W, cheerleading W, cross-country running M/W, equestrian sports M(c)/W(c), field hockey W, football M, golf M/W, ice hockey M, lacrosse M(c)/W, soccer M/W, softball W, swimming and diving W, track and field M/W, volleyball W. *Intramural sports:* badminton M/W, basketball M/W, ice hockey M(c)/W(c), racquetball M/W, rock climbing M/W, rugby M(c), soccer M/W, softball M/W, table tennis M/W, ultimate Frisbee M/W, volleyball M/W, water polo M/W.

Standardized Tests *Required:* SAT or ACT (for admission).

Costs (2010–11) *Tuition:* state resident $970 full-time, $85 per credit hour part-time; nonresident $7050 full-time, $95 per credit hour part-time. Full-time tuition and fees vary according to reciprocity agreements. *Required fees:* $6461 full-time, $115 per credit hour part-time, $150 per term part-time. *Room and board:* $8525. Room and board charges vary according to board plan and housing facility. *Payment plan:* installment. *Waivers:* senior citizens and employees or children of employees.

Financial Aid Of all full-time matriculated undergraduates who enrolled in 2009, 4,033 applied for aid, 2,853 were judged to have need, 406 had their need fully met. 302 Federal Work-Study jobs (averaging $1613). In 2009, 55 non-need-based awards were made. *Average percent of need met:* 69%. *Average financial aid package:* $7666. *Average need-based loan:* $4081. *Average need-based gift aid:* $5090. *Average non-need-based aid:* $4258. *Average indebtedness upon graduation:* $21,182.

Applying *Options:* electronic application, deferred entrance. *Application fee:* $50. *Required:* high school transcript, minimum 2 GPA. *Required for some:* interview, audition for music major, portfolio for art major. *Application deadlines:* 3/1 (freshmen), 3/1 (out-of-state freshmen), 3/1 (transfers). *Notification:* continuous until 3/15 (freshmen), continuous until 3/15 (out-of-state freshmen), continuous until 3/15 (transfers).

Freshman Application Contact Dr. Kelly Hart, Director of Admissions, Westfield State University, 333 Western Avenue, Westfield, MA 01002. *Phone:* 413-572-5218. *Toll-free phone:* 800-322-8401. *Fax:* 413-572-0520. *E-mail:* admission@wsc.ma.edu. *Web site:* http://www.wsc.ma.edu/.

Wheaton College
Norton, Massachusetts

- **Independent** 4-year, founded 1834
- **Suburban** 400-acre campus with easy access to Boston
- **Endowment** $146.7 million
- **Coed** 1,635 undergraduate students, 100% full-time, 64% women, 36% men
- **Very difficult** entrance level, 62% of applicants were admitted

Undergraduates 1,630 full-time, 5 part-time. Students come from 42 states and territories; 40 other countries; 66% are from out of state; 5% Black or African American, non-Hispanic/Latino; 5% Hispanic/Latino; 2% Asian, non-Hispanic/Latino; 0.1% Native Hawaiian or other Pacific Islander, non-Hispanic/Latino; 0.2% American Indian or Alaska Native, non-Hispanic/Latino; 2% Two or more races, non-Hispanic/Latino; 5% Race/ethnicity unknown; 6% international; 1% transferred in; 93% live on campus. *Retention:* 87% of full-time freshmen returned.

Freshmen *Admission:* 3,272 applied, 2,014 admitted, 450 enrolled. *Average high school GPA:* 3.42.

Faculty *Total:* 188, 76% full-time, 77% with terminal degrees. *Student/faculty ratio:* 10:1.

Academics *Calendar:* semesters. *Degree:* bachelor's. *Special study options:* accelerated degree program, advanced placement credit, double majors, honors programs, independent study, internships, off-campus study, part-time degree program, student-designed majors, study abroad. *ROTC:* Army (c). *Unusual degree programs:* 3-2 business administration with University of Rochester; engineering with Dartmouth College, George Washington University; theology with Andover Newton Theological School, optometry with New England College of Optometry, integrated marketing communications studies with Emerson College, studio art with School of the Museum of Fine Arts.

Computers on Campus 356 computers/terminals and 2,100 ports are available on campus for general student use. Students can access the following: campus intranet, computer help desk, free student e-mail accounts, online (class) grades, online (class) registration, online (class) schedules. Campus-wide network is available. 100% of college-owned or -operated housing units are wired for high-speed Internet access. Wireless service is available via entire campus.

Student Life *Housing:* on-campus residence required through senior year. *Options:* coed, men-only, women-only, disabled students. Campus housing is university owned. Freshman campus housing is guaranteed. *Activities and organizations:* drama/theater group, student-run newspaper, radio station, choral group, Student Government Association, Community Service Network, Amnesty International, a cappella singing groups, Programming Council. *Campus security:* 24-hour emergency response devices and patrols, student patrols, late-night transport/escort service, controlled dormitory access. *Student services:* health clinic, personal/psychological counseling, women's center.

Athletics Member NCAA. All Division III. *Intercollegiate sports:* baseball M, basketball M/W, cross-country running M/W, field hockey W, lacrosse M/W, soccer M/W, softball W, swimming and diving M/W, tennis M/W, track and field M/W, volleyball W. *Intramural sports:* archery M(c)/W(c), badminton M/W, basketball M/W, equestrian sports M(c)/W(c), field hockey M(c)/W(c), golf M(c)/W(c), ice hockey M(c)/W(c), rugby M(c)/W(c), sailing M(c)/W(c), soccer M/W, softball M(c)/W(c), tennis M/W, ultimate Frisbee M(c)/W(c), volleyball M/W, wrestling M(c)/W(c).

Costs (2010–11) *One-time required fee:* $50. *Comprehensive fee:* $51,264 includes full-time tuition ($40,790), mandatory fees ($294), and room and board ($10,180). *College room only:* $5350. *Payment plans:* tuition prepayment, installment. *Waivers:* employees or children of employees.

Financial Aid Of all full-time matriculated undergraduates who enrolled in 2009, 1,085 applied for aid, 955 were judged to have need, 492 had their need fully met. 787 Federal Work-Study jobs (averaging $1799). 235 state and other part-time jobs (averaging $1646). In 2009, 225 non-need-based awards were made. *Average percent of need met:* 96%. *Average financial aid package:* $33,404. *Average need-based loan:* $4927. *Average need-based gift aid:* $28,511. *Average non-need-based aid:* $11,555. *Average indebtedness upon graduation:* $27,546. *Financial aid deadline:* 2/1.

Applying *Options:* electronic application, early admission, early decision, deferred entrance. *Application fee:* $55. *Required:* essay or personal statement, high school transcript, 2 letters of recommendation. *Recommended:* interview. *Application deadlines:* 1/15 (freshmen), 3/1 (transfers). *Early decision deadline:* 11/15 (for plan 1), 1/15 (for plan 2). *Notification:* 4/1 (freshmen), 5/15 (transfers), 12/15 (early decision plan 1), 2/15 (early decision plan 2).

Freshman Application Contact Gail Berson, Vice President for Enrollment and Dean of Admission and Student Aid, Wheaton College, 26 East Main Street, Norton, MA 02766. *Phone:* 508-286-8251. *Toll-free phone:* 800-394-6003. *Fax:* 508-286-8271. *E-mail:* admission@wheatoncollege.edu. *Web site:* http://www.wheatoncollege.edu/.

Wheelock College
Boston, Massachusetts

- **Independent** comprehensive, founded 1888
- **Urban** campus
- **Coed, primarily women** 830 undergraduate students, 97% full-time, 90% women, 10% men
- **Minimally difficult** entrance level, 70% of applicants were admitted

Undergraduates 804 full-time, 26 part-time. Students come from 15 states and territories; 8 other countries; 35% are from out of state; 12% Black or African American, non-Hispanic/Latino; 9% Hispanic/Latino; 2% Asian, non-Hispanic/Latino; 0.4% American Indian or Alaska Native, non-Hispanic/Latino; 4% Two or more races, non-Hispanic/Latino; 6% Race/ethnicity unknown; 0.6% international; 17% transferred in; 70% live on campus. *Retention:* 80% of full-time freshmen returned.

Freshmen *Admission:* 1,313 applied, 925 admitted, 237 enrolled. *Average high school GPA:* 3. *Test scores:* SAT critical reading scores over 500: 48%; SAT math scores over 500: 35%; SAT writing scores over 500: 47%; ACT scores over 18: 79%; SAT critical reading scores over 600: 13%; SAT math scores over 600: 5%; SAT writing scores over 600: 9%; ACT scores over 24: 24%; SAT critical reading scores over 700: 2%.

Faculty *Total:* 87, 77% full-time, 67% with terminal degrees. *Student/faculty ratio:* 11:1.

Academics *Calendar:* semesters. *Degrees:* bachelor's, master's, post-master's, and postbachelor's certificates. *Special study options:* advanced placement credit, double majors, freshman honors college, honors programs, independent study, internships, off-campus study, part-time degree program, services for LD students, study abroad, summer session for credit.

Computers on Campus Students can access the following: campus intranet, computer help desk, free student e-mail accounts, online (class) grades, online (class) registration, online (class) schedules. Campuswide network is available. Wireless service is available via classrooms, dorm rooms, libraries, student centers.

Student Life *Housing options:* coed, women-only, cooperative, disabled students. Campus housing is university owned. Freshman campus housing is guaranteed. *Activities and organizations:* drama/theater group, choral group. *Campus security:* 24-hour patrols, late-night transport/escort service, controlled dormitory access. *Student services:* health clinic, personal/psychological counseling, women's center.

Athletics Member NCAA. All Division III. *Intercollegiate sports:* basketball M/W, cross-country running M/W, field hockey W, lacrosse M/W, soccer M/W, softball W, tennis M. *Intramural sports:* basketball M/W, racquetball M/W, soccer M, softball M/W, squash M/W, table tennis M/W, ultimate Frisbee M/W, volleyball M/W, water polo M/W.

Standardized Tests *Required:* SAT or ACT (for admission).

Financial Aid Of all full-time matriculated undergraduates who enrolled in 2009, 729 applied for aid, 680 were judged to have need, 103 had their need fully met. 217 Federal Work-Study jobs (averaging $1800). In 2009, 91 non-need-based awards were made. *Average percent of need met:* 67%. *Average financial aid package:* $20,979. *Average need-based loan:* $4766. *Average need-based gift aid:* $16,442. *Average non-need-based aid:* $11,485. *Average indebtedness upon graduation:* $41,356.

Applying *Options:* electronic application, early admission, early action, deferred entrance. *Application fee:* $15. *Required:* essay or personal statement, high school transcript, minimum 2 GPA, 1 letter of recommendation. *Recommended:* interview. *Application deadlines:* 3/1 (freshmen), 6/1 (transfers), 12/1 (early action). *Notification:* continuous (freshmen), continuous (transfers).

Freshman Application Contact Ms. Kristen Harrington, Director of Undergraduate Admissions, Wheelock College, 200 The Riverway, Boston, MA 02215. *Phone:* 617-879-2206. *Toll-free phone:* 800-734-5212. *Fax:* 617-879-2449. *E-mail:* kharrington@wheelock.edu. *Web site:* http://www.wheelock.edu/.

Williams College
Williamstown, Massachusetts

- **Independent** comprehensive, founded 1793
- **Small-town** 450-acre campus with easy access to Albany, NY
- **Endowment** $1.5 billion
- **Coed** 2,029 undergraduate students, 98% full-time, 51% women, 49% men
- **Most difficult** entrance level, 19% of applicants were admitted

Undergraduates 1,996 full-time, 33 part-time. Students come from 50 states and territories; 57 other countries; 86% are from out of state; 8% Black or African American, non-Hispanic/Latino; 10% Hispanic/Latino; 11% Asian, non-Hispanic/Latino; 0.3% American Indian or Alaska Native, non-Hispanic/Latino; 4% Two or more races, non-Hispanic/Latino; 7% international; 0.3% transferred in; 94% live on campus. *Retention:* 97% of full-time freshmen returned.

Freshmen *Admission:* 6,631 applied, 1,241 admitted, 548 enrolled. *Test scores:* SAT critical reading scores over 500: 99%; SAT math scores over 500: 99%; ACT scores over 18: 100%; SAT critical reading scores over 600: 93%; SAT math scores over 600: 90%; ACT scores over 24: 99%; SAT critical reading scores over 700: 62%; SAT math scores over 700: 59%; ACT scores over 30: 76%.

Faculty *Total:* 304, 89% full-time, 94% with terminal degrees. *Student/faculty ratio:* 7:1.

Academics *Calendar:* 4-1-4. *Degrees:* bachelor's and master's. *Special study options:* advanced placement credit, double majors, independent study, internships, off-campus study, services for LD students, student-designed majors, study abroad. *ROTC:* Air Force (c). *Unusual degree programs:* 3-2 engineering with Columbia University, Washington University in St. Louis, Oxford-Style tutorials, Dartmouth College.

Computers on Campus 252 computers/terminals are available on campus for general student use. Students can access the following: computer help desk, free student e-mail accounts, online (class) grades, online (class) registration. Campuswide network is available. 100% of college-owned or -operated housing units are wired for high-speed Internet access. Wireless service is available via entire campus.

Student Life *Housing:* on-campus residence required for freshman year. *Options:* coed, cooperative. Campus housing is university owned. Freshman campus housing is guaranteed. *Activities and organizations:* drama/theater group, student-run newspaper, radio station, choral group. *Campus security:* 24-hour emergency response devices and patrols, student patrols, late-night transport/escort service, controlled dormitory access. *Student services:* health clinic, personal/psychological counseling, women's center.

Athletics Member NCAA. All Division III except men's and women's skiing (cross-country) (Division I), men's and women's skiing (downhill) (Division I). *Intercollegiate sports:* baseball M, basketball M/W, crew M/W, cross-country running M/W, equestrian sports M(c)/W(c), field hockey W, football M, golf M/W(c), ice hockey M/W, lacrosse M/W, rugby M(c)/W(c), sailing M(c)/W(c), skiing (cross-country) M/W, skiing (downhill) M/W, soccer M/W, softball W, squash M/W, swimming and diving M/W, tennis M/W, track and field M/W, volleyball M(c)/W, water polo M(c)/W(c), wrestling M. *Intramural sports:* badminton M/W, baseball M(c), basketball M/W, fencing M(c)/W(c), gymnastics M(c)/W(c), ice hockey M/W, skiing (cross-country) M/W, skiing (downhill) M/W, soccer M/W, softball M/W, ultimate Frisbee M(c)/W(c), volleyball M/W, water polo M/W.

Standardized Tests *Required:* SAT and SAT Subject Tests or ACT (for admission).

Costs (2010–11) *Comprehensive fee:* $52,340 includes full-time tuition ($41,190), mandatory fees ($244), and room and board ($10,906). *College room only:* $5542. Room and board charges vary according to board plan. *Payment plan:* installment.

Financial Aid Of all full-time matriculated undergraduates who enrolled in 2009, 1,275 applied for aid, 1,163 were judged to have need, 1,163 had their need fully met. 468 Federal Work-Study jobs (averaging $1846). 463 state and other part-time jobs (averaging $1886). *Average percent of need met:* 100%. *Average financial aid package:* $40,485. *Average need-based gift aid:* $38,035. *Average indebtedness upon graduation:* $8065. *Financial aid deadline:* 2/1.

Applying *Options:* electronic application, early admission, early decision, deferred entrance. *Application fee:* $60. *Required:* essay or personal statement, high school transcript, 2 letters of recommendation. *Application deadlines:* 1/1 (freshmen), 3/15 (transfers). *Early decision deadline:* 11/10. *Notification:* 4/1 (freshmen), 5/1 (transfers), 12/15 (early decision).
Freshman Application Contact Mr. Richard L. Nesbitt, Director of Admission, Williams College, 33 Stetson Court, Williamstown, MA 01267. *Phone:* 413-597-2211. *Fax:* 413-597-4052. *E-mail:* admission@williams.edu. *Web site:* http://www.williams.edu/.

Worcester Polytechnic Institute

Worcester, Massachusetts

- **Independent** university, founded 1865
- **Suburban** 80-acre campus with easy access to Boston
- **Endowment** $307.7 million
- **Coed** 3,649 undergraduate students, 95% full-time, 30% women, 70% men
- **Very difficult** entrance level, 59% of applicants were admitted

Undergraduates 3,470 full-time, 179 part-time. Students come from 44 states and territories; 62 other countries; 51% are from out of state; 3% Black or African American, non-Hispanic/Latino; 7% Hispanic/Latino; 6% Asian, non-Hispanic/Latino; 0.7% American Indian or Alaska Native, non-Hispanic/Latino; 2% Race/ethnicity unknown; 10% international; 1% transferred in; 50% live on campus. *Retention:* 95% of full-time freshmen returned.
Freshmen *Admission:* 6,660 applied, 3,933 admitted, 910 enrolled. *Average high school GPA:* 3.8. *Test scores:* SAT critical reading scores over 500: 92%; SAT math scores over 500: 100%; SAT writing scores over 500: 95%; ACT scores over 18: 100%; SAT critical reading scores over 600: 55%; SAT math scores over 600: 90%; SAT writing scores over 600: 62%; ACT scores over 24: 93%; SAT critical reading scores over 700: 12%; SAT math scores over 700: 38%; SAT writing scores over 700: 12%; ACT scores over 30: 39%.
Faculty *Total:* 396, 70% full-time, 79% with terminal degrees. *Student/faculty ratio:* 14:1.
Academics *Calendar:* 4 7-week terms. *Degrees:* bachelor's, master's, doctoral-research/scholarship, post-master's, and postbachelor's certificates. *Special study options:* accelerated degree program, advanced placement credit, cooperative education, distance learning, double majors, English as a second language, independent study, internships, off-campus study, part-time degree program, services for LD students, student-designed majors, study abroad, summer session for credit. *ROTC:* Army (b), Navy (c), Air Force (b). *Unusual degree programs:* 3-2 business administration; engineering.
Computers on Campus 500 computers/terminals and 775 ports are available on campus for general student use. Students can access the following: campus intranet, computer help desk, free student e-mail accounts, online (class) grades, online (class) registration, online (class) schedules, online course content. Campuswide network is available. 100% of college-owned or -operated housing units are wired for high-speed Internet access. Wireless service is available via entire campus.
Student Life *Housing options:* coed, men-only, women-only, disabled students. Campus housing is university owned. Freshman campus housing is guaranteed. *Activities and organizations:* drama/theater group, student-run newspaper, radio station, choral group, marching band, Student Government Association, Social Committee (Student Events Programming Board), Music Association (all music-performing groups), intramural and club sports, International Student Council, national fraternities, national sororities. *Campus security:* 24-hour emergency response devices and patrols, student patrols, late-night transport/escort service, controlled dormitory access. *Student services:* health clinic, personal/psychological counseling.
Athletics Member NCAA. All Division III. *Intercollegiate sports:* baseball M, basketball M/W, crew M/W, cross-country running M/W, field hockey W, football M, soccer M/W, softball W, swimming and diving M/W, track and field M/W, volleyball W, water polo M(c)/W(c), wrestling M. *Intramural sports:* baseball M/W, basketball M/W, bowling M/W, cheerleading M(c)/W(c), cross-country running M(c)/W(c), fencing M(c)/W(c), golf M(c)/W(c), ice hockey M(c)/W(c), lacrosse M(c)/W(c), racquetball M/W, rugby M(c)/W(c), sailing M(c)/W(c), skiing (cross-country) M(c)/W(c), skiing (downhill) M(c)/W(c), soccer M/W, softball M/W, squash M/W, swimming and diving M/W, table tennis M/W, tennis M(c)/W(c), track and field M/W, ultimate Frisbee M(c)/W(c), volleyball M(c)/W, water polo M(c)/W(c), wrestling M(c).
Standardized Tests *Required for some:* SAT or ACT (for admission), IELTS or TOEFL.
Costs (2011–12) *One-time required fee:* $200. *Comprehensive fee:* $51,964 includes full-time tuition ($39,450), mandatory fees ($580), and room and board ($11,934). Part-time tuition: $1060 per credit hour. Part-time tuition and fees vary according to course load. *College room only:* $6982. Room and

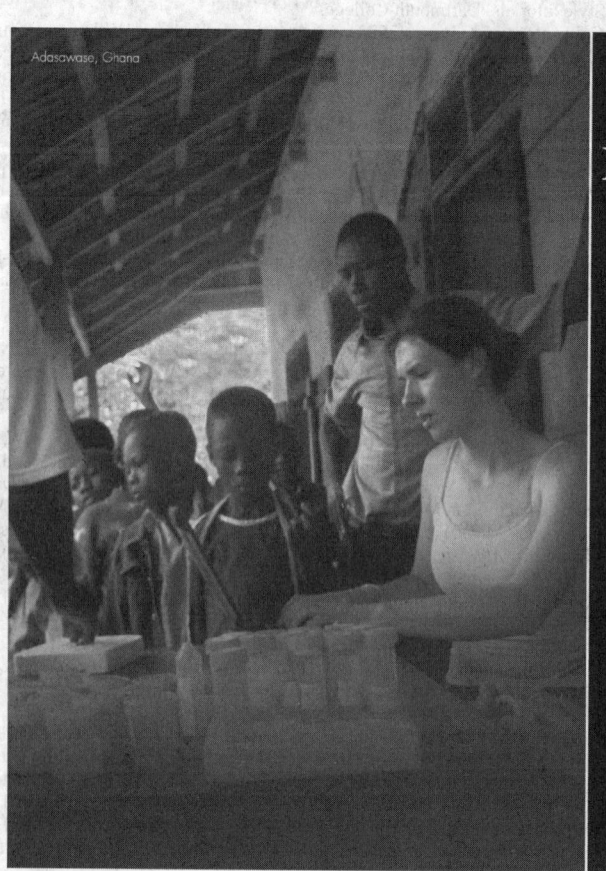

board charges vary according to board plan and housing facility. *Payment plans:* installment, deferred payment. *Waivers:* employees or children of employees.

Financial Aid Of all full-time matriculated undergraduates who enrolled in 2009, 2,740 applied for aid, 2,470 were judged to have need, 958 had their need fully met. 658 Federal Work-Study jobs (averaging $1129). In 2009, 928 non-need-based awards were made. *Average percent of need met:* 73%. *Average financial aid package:* $30,237. *Average need-based loan:* $2787. *Average need-based gift aid:* $18,707. *Average non-need-based aid:* $16,005. *Financial aid deadline:* 2/1.

Applying *Options:* electronic application, early admission, early action, deferred entrance. *Application fee:* $60. *Required:* essay or personal statement, high school transcript, 2 letters of recommendation. *Required for some:* interview. *Application deadlines:* 2/1 (freshmen), 4/15 (transfers), 11/10 (early action). *Notification:* 4/1 (freshmen), continuous (transfers), 12/20 (early action).

Freshman Application Contact Mr. Edward J. Connor, Dean of Admissions, Worcester Polytechnic Institute, 100 Institute Road, Worcester, MA 01609-2280. *Phone:* 508-831-5286. *Fax:* 508-831-5875. *E-mail:* admissions@wpi.edu. *Web site:* http://www.wpi.edu/.

See page 1796 for the College Close-Up.

Worcester State University
Worcester, Massachusetts

- **State-supported** comprehensive, founded 1874, part of Massachusetts Public Higher Education System
- **Urban** 58-acre campus with easy access to Boston
- **Endowment** $9.6 million
- **Coed** 4,830 undergraduate students, 75% full-time, 59% women, 41% men
- **Moderately difficult** entrance level, 65% of applicants were admitted

Undergraduates 3,627 full-time, 1,203 part-time. Students come from 17 states and territories; 22 other countries; 3% are from out of state; 5% Black or African American, non-Hispanic/Latino; 7% Hispanic/Latino; 3% Asian, non-Hispanic/Latino; 0.1% Native Hawaiian or other Pacific Islander, non-Hispanic/Latino; 0.5% American Indian or Alaska Native, non-Hispanic/Latino; 0.7% Two or more races, non-Hispanic/Latino; 4% Race/ethnicity unknown; 1% international; 10% transferred in; 27% live on campus. *Retention:* 75% of full-time freshmen returned.

Freshmen *Admission:* 3,916 applied, 2,534 admitted, 815 enrolled. *Average high school GPA:* 3.06. *Test scores:* SAT critical reading scores over 500: 51%; SAT math scores over 500: 61%; SAT writing scores over 500: 52%; ACT scores over 18: 93%; SAT critical reading scores over 600: 10%; SAT math scores over 600: 12%; SAT writing scores over 600: 10%; ACT scores over 24: 32%; SAT critical reading scores over 700: 1%.

Faculty *Total:* 412, 44% full-time, 35% with terminal degrees. *Student/faculty ratio:* 17:1.

Academics *Calendar:* semesters. *Degrees:* bachelor's, master's, post-master's, and postbachelor's certificates. *Special study options:* academic remediation for entering students, accelerated degree program, adult/continuing education programs, advanced placement credit, distance learning, double majors, English as a second language, honors programs, independent study, internships, off-campus study, part-time degree program, services for LD students, study abroad, summer session for credit. *ROTC:* Army (c), Navy (c), Air Force (c).

Computers on Campus 500 computers/terminals and 1,700 ports are available on campus for general student use. Students can access the following: campus intranet, computer help desk, free student e-mail accounts, online (class) grades, online (class) registration, online (class) schedules. Campus-wide network is available. 100% of college-owned or -operated housing units are wired for high-speed Internet access. Wireless service is available via entire campus.

Student Life *Housing options:* coed, men-only, women-only, disabled students. Campus housing is university owned. *Activities and organizations:* drama/theater group, student-run newspaper, radio and television station, choral group, Senate, SEC (Student Events Committee), TWA (Third World Alliance), WSCW (radio station), Dance Company/Club. *Campus security:* 24-hour emergency response devices and patrols, late-night transport/escort service, controlled dormitory access, Well-lit campus and limited access to campus at night. *Student services:* health clinic, personal/psychological counseling.

Athletics Member NCAA. All Division III. *Intercollegiate sports:* baseball M, basketball M/W, cross-country running M/W, field hockey W, football M, golf M, ice hockey M, lacrosse W, soccer M/W, softball W, tennis W, track and field M/W, volleyball W. *Intramural sports:* basketball M/W, cheerleading M/W, football M, skiing (downhill) M(c)/W(c), soccer M/W, softball M/W, ultimate Frisbee M/W, volleyball M(c)/W.

Standardized Tests *Required:* SAT or ACT (for admission).

Costs (2010–11) *Tuition:* state resident $970 full-time, $40 per credit part-time; nonresident $7050 full-time, $294 per credit part-time. Full-time tuition and fees vary according to class time, course load, degree level, and reciprocity agreements. Part-time tuition and fees vary according to class time, course load, degree level, and reciprocity agreements. *Required fees:* $6185 full-time, $258 per credit part-time. *Room and board:* $9658; room only: $6858. Room and board charges vary according to board plan and housing facility. *Payment plan:* installment. *Waivers:* senior citizens and employees or children of employees.

Financial Aid Of all full-time matriculated undergraduates who enrolled in 2008, 2,782 applied for aid, 1,851 were judged to have need, 871 had their need fully met. 286 Federal Work-Study jobs (averaging $1500). In 2008, 84 non-need-based awards were made. *Average percent of need met:* 85%. *Average financial aid package:* $10,538. *Average need-based loan:* $2587. *Average need-based gift aid:* $4939. *Average non-need-based aid:* $2451. *Average indebtedness upon graduation:* $20,851. *Financial aid deadline:* 5/1.

Applying *Options:* electronic application, deferred entrance. *Application fee:* $40. *Required:* high school transcript, minimum 2 GPA. *Required for some:* essay or personal statement. *Application deadlines:* 2/1 (freshmen), 6/1 (transfers). *Notification:* continuous (freshmen), continuous (transfers).

Freshman Application Contact Ms. Sarah Whitney, Clerk of Admissions, Worcester State University, 486 Chandler Street, Administration Building, Worcester, MA 01602-2597. *Phone:* 508-929-8040. *Toll-free phone:* 866-WSC-CALL. *Fax:* 508-929-8183. *E-mail:* admissions@worcester.edu. *Web site:* http://www.worcester.edu/.

Zion Bible College
Haverhill, Massachusetts

Director of Admissions Helen Brouillette, Admissions Director, Zion Bible College, 320 South Main Street, Haverhill, MA 01835. *Phone:* 800-356-4014. *Toll-free phone:* 800-356-4014. *E-mail:* admissions@zbc.edu. *Web site:* http://www.zbc.edu/.

MICHIGAN

Adrian College
Adrian, Michigan

Freshman Application Contact Ms. Carolyn Quinlan, Director of Admissions, Adrian College, 110 South Madison Street, Adrian, MI 49221. *Phone:* 800-877-2246. *Toll-free phone:* 800-877-2246. *Fax:* 517-264-3331. *E-mail:* admissions@adrian.edu. *Web site:* http://www.adrian.edu/.

Albion College
Albion, Michigan

- **Independent Methodist** 4-year, founded 1835
- **Small-town** 565-acre campus with easy access to Detroit
- **Endowment** $180.7 million
- **Coed** 1,860 undergraduate students, 99% full-time, 54% women, 46% men
- **Moderately difficult** entrance level, 83% of applicants were admitted

Undergraduates 1,842 full-time, 18 part-time. Students come from 28 states and territories; 18 other countries; 9% are from out of state; 1% transferred in; 90% live on campus. *Retention:* 86% of full-time freshmen returned.

Freshmen *Admission:* 1,958 applied, 1,630 admitted, 485 enrolled. *Average high school GPA:* 3.55. *Test scores:* SAT critical reading scores over 500: 82%; SAT math scores over 500: 82%; ACT scores over 18: 97%; SAT critical reading scores over 600: 49%; SAT math scores over 600: 45%; ACT scores over 24: 69%; SAT critical reading scores over 700: 14%; SAT math scores over 700: 8%; ACT scores over 30: 10%.

Faculty *Total:* 171, 81% full-time, 75% with terminal degrees. *Student/faculty ratio:* 12:1.

Academics *Calendar:* semesters. *Degree:* bachelor's. *Special study options:* advanced placement credit, double majors, honors programs, independent study, internships, off-campus study, part-time degree program, services for LD students, student-designed majors, study abroad, summer session for credit. *Unusual degree programs:* 3-2 engineering with Columbia University, University of Michigan, Case Western Reserve University, Michigan Technological University, Washington University in St. Louis; forestry with Duke University, Washington University in St. Louis; nursing with Case Western Reserve University; public policy studies with University of Michigan, fine arts with Bank Street College of Education.

Computers on Campus 435 computers/terminals and 25 ports are available on campus for general student use. Students can access the following: campus

intranet, computer help desk, free student e-mail accounts, online (class) grades, online (class) registration, online (class) schedules, online student account and financial aid. Campuswide network is available. 100% of college-owned or -operated housing units are wired for high-speed Internet access. Wireless service is available via classrooms, computer centers, computer labs, dorm rooms, learning centers, libraries, student centers.
Student Life *Housing:* on-campus residence required through senior year. *Options:* coed, men-only, women-only, cooperative, disabled students. Campus housing is university owned. Freshman campus housing is guaranteed. *Activities and organizations:* drama/theater group, student-run newspaper, radio station, choral group, marching band, Student Volunteer Bureau, Union Board, Inter-Varsity Christian Fellowship, Student Senate, Frisbee and Disc Club, national fraternities, national sororities. *Campus security:* 24-hour emergency response devices and patrols, student patrols, late-night transport/escort service, controlled dormitory access. *Student services:* health clinic, personal/psychological counseling, women's center.
Athletics Member NCAA. All Division III. *Intercollegiate sports:* baseball M, basketball M/W, cheerleading M/W, cross-country running M/W, equestrian sports M/W, football M, golf M/W, soccer M/W, softball W, swimming and diving M/W, tennis M/W, track and field M/W, volleyball M(c)/W. *Intramural sports:* badminton M/W, basketball M/W, equestrian sports M(c)/W(c), field hockey W, football M(c)/W(c), ice hockey M(c)/W(c), lacrosse M(c)/W(c), racquetball M/W, soccer M/W, softball M/W, swimming and diving M/W, tennis M/W, ultimate Frisbee M/W, volleyball M/W, water polo M(c)/W(c).
Standardized Tests *Required:* SAT or ACT (for admission).
Financial Aid Of all full-time matriculated undergraduates who enrolled in 2009, 1,206 applied for aid, 1,076 were judged to have need, 253 had their need fully met. 492 Federal Work-Study jobs (averaging $1242). In 2009, 485 non-need-based awards were made. *Average percent of need met:* 84%. *Average financial aid package:* $24,898. *Average need-based loan:* $5202. *Average need-based gift aid:* $19,847. *Average non-need-based aid:* $14,004. *Average indebtedness upon graduation:* $34,282.
Applying *Options:* electronic application, early action, deferred entrance. *Application fee:* $20. *Required:* essay or personal statement, high school transcript, 1 letter of recommendation. *Required for some:* interview. *Recommended:* minimum 3.2 GPA. *Application deadlines:* 5/1 (freshmen), 6/1 (transfers), 12/1 (early action). *Notification:* continuous (freshmen), 7/1 (transfers), 1/1 (early action).
Freshman Application Contact Albion College, 611 East Porter Street, Albion, MI 49224-1831. *Phone:* 517-629-0600. *Toll-free phone:* 800-858-6770. *Web site:* http://www.albion.edu/.

Alma College
Alma, Michigan

- **Independent Presbyterian** 4-year, founded 1886
- **Small-town** 125-acre campus
- **Endowment** $85.1 million
- **Coed** 1,422 undergraduate students, 97% full-time, 57% women, 43% men
- **Moderately difficult** entrance level, 75% of applicants were admitted

Undergraduates 1,383 full-time, 39 part-time. Students come from 25 states and territories; 15 other countries; 5% are from out of state; 2% Black or African American, non-Hispanic/Latino; 4% Hispanic/Latino; 1% Asian, non-Hispanic/Latino; 1% American Indian or Alaska Native, non-Hispanic/Latino; 0.3% Two or more races, non-Hispanic/Latino; 3% transferred in; 88% live on campus. *Retention:* 75% of full-time freshmen returned.
Freshmen *Admission:* 1,755 applied, 1,312 admitted, 362 enrolled. *Average high school GPA:* 3.53. *Test scores:* SAT critical reading scores over 500: 94%; SAT math scores over 500: 88%; SAT writing scores over 500: 77%; ACT scores over 18: 99%; SAT critical reading scores over 600: 47%; SAT math scores over 600: 35%; SAT writing scores over 600: 53%; ACT scores over 24: 57%; SAT critical reading scores over 700: 18%; SAT math scores over 700: 6%; SAT writing scores over 700: 18%; ACT scores over 30: 10%.
Faculty *Total:* 149, 59% full-time, 64% with terminal degrees. *Student/faculty ratio:* 13:1.
Academics *Calendar:* 4-4-1. *Degree:* bachelor's. *Special study options:* academic remediation for entering students, advanced placement credit, double majors, honors programs, independent study, internships, off-campus study, services for LD students, student-designed majors, study abroad, summer session for credit. *ROTC:* Army (c). *Unusual degree programs:* 3-2 engineering with University of Michigan, Michigan Technological University; occupational therapy with Washington University in St. Louis.
Computers on Campus 260 computers/terminals are available on campus for general student use. Students can access the following: campus intranet, computer help desk, free student e-mail accounts, online (class) grades, online (class) registration, online (class) schedules. Campuswide network is available. 100% of college-owned or -operated housing units are wired for high-speed Internet access. Wireless service is available via classrooms, dorm rooms, libraries, student centers.

Student Life *Housing:* on-campus residence required through senior year. *Options:* coed. Campus housing is university owned. Freshman campus housing is guaranteed. *Activities and organizations:* drama/theater group, student-run newspaper, radio station, choral group, marching band, Ambassadors, Alma College Union Board, New Life Campus Ministries, Student Congress, Alpha Phi Omega, national fraternities, national sororities. *Campus security:* 24-hour emergency response devices and patrols, controlled dormitory access. *Student services:* health clinic, personal/psychological counseling, women's center.
Athletics Member NCAA. All Division III. *Intercollegiate sports:* baseball M, basketball M/W, bowling W, cross-country running M/W, football M, golf M/W, lacrosse M/W, soccer M/W, softball W, swimming and diving M/W, tennis M/W, track and field M/W, volleyball W, wrestling M. *Intramural sports:* basketball M/W, cheerleading M(c)/W(c), lacrosse M(c)/W(c), skiing (downhill) M/W, softball M/W, ultimate Frisbee M/W, volleyball M/W.
Standardized Tests *Required:* SAT or ACT (for admission).
Costs (2011–12) *Comprehensive fee:* $38,070 includes full-time tuition ($28,980), mandatory fees ($250), and room and board ($8840). Part-time tuition: $1000 per credit hour. Part-time tuition and fees vary according to course load. *College room only:* $4420. Room and board charges vary according to board plan and housing facility. *Payment plans:* installment, deferred payment. *Waivers:* employees or children of employees.
Financial Aid Of all full-time matriculated undergraduates who enrolled in 2009, 1,275 applied for aid, 1,139 were judged to have need, 220 had their need fully met. 174 Federal Work-Study jobs (averaging $950). In 2009, 239 non-need-based awards were made. *Average percent of need met:* 81%. *Average financial aid package:* $23,877. *Average need-based loan:* $4905. *Average need-based gift aid:* $17,025. *Average non-need-based aid:* $13,913. *Average indebtedness upon graduation:* $28,734.
Applying *Options:* electronic application, deferred entrance. *Application fee:* $25. *Required:* high school transcript, minimum 3 GPA. *Required for some:* essay or personal statement, 3 letters of recommendation. *Recommended:* interview. *Application deadlines:* rolling (freshmen), rolling (out-of-state freshmen), rolling (transfers). *Notification:* continuous (freshmen), continuous (out-of-state freshmen), continuous (transfers).
Freshman Application Contact Mr. Bob Garcia, Director of Admissions, Alma College, Admissions Office, Alma, MI 48801-1599. *Phone:* 800-321-2562. *Toll-free phone:* 800-321-ALMA. *Fax:* 989-463-7057. *E-mail:* admissions@alma.edu. *Web site:* http://www.alma.edu/.

Andrews University
Berrien Springs, Michigan

- **Independent Seventh-day Adventist** university, founded 1874
- **Small-town** 1650-acre campus
- **Endowment** $30.3 million
- **Coed** 1,931 undergraduate students, 88% full-time, 55% women, 45% men
- **Moderately difficult** entrance level, 45% of applicants were admitted

Undergraduates 1,705 full-time, 226 part-time. Students come from 51 states and territories; 51 other countries; 60% are from out of state; 24% Black or African American, non-Hispanic/Latino; 16% Hispanic/Latino; 8% Asian, non-Hispanic/Latino; 0.6% Native Hawaiian or other Pacific Islander, non-Hispanic/Latino; 0.3% American Indian or Alaska Native, non-Hispanic/Latino; 3% Two or more races, non-Hispanic/Latino; 0.3% Race/ethnicity unknown; 12% international; 8% transferred in; 57% live on campus. *Retention:* 79% of full-time freshmen returned.
Freshmen *Admission:* 1,851 applied, 832 admitted, 365 enrolled. *Average high school GPA:* 3.44. *Test scores:* SAT critical reading scores over 500: 64%; SAT math scores over 500: 63%; SAT writing scores over 500: 62%; ACT scores over 18: 94%; SAT critical reading scores over 600: 22%; SAT math scores over 600: 24%; SAT writing scores over 600: 17%; ACT scores over 24: 44%; SAT critical reading scores over 700: 4%; SAT math scores over 700: 5%; SAT writing scores over 700: 2%; ACT scores over 30: 9%.
Faculty *Total:* 290, 78% full-time, 63% with terminal degrees. *Student/faculty ratio:* 10:1.
Academics *Calendar:* semesters. *Degrees:* associate, bachelor's, master's, doctoral-other, doctoral-research/scholarship, post-master's, and postbachelor's certificates. *Special study options:* academic remediation for entering students, accelerated degree program, adult/continuing education programs, advanced placement credit, cooperative education, distance learning, double majors, English as a second language, freshman honors college, honors programs, internships, off-campus study, part-time degree program, student-designed majors, study abroad, summer session for credit. *Unusual degree programs:* 3-2 physical therapy and architecture.
Computers on Campus 130 computers/terminals are available on campus for general student use. Students can access the following: campus intranet, computer help desk, free student e-mail accounts, online (class) grades, online (class) registration, online (class) schedules, degree audit. Campuswide network is available. 99% of college-owned or -operated housing units are wired

for high-speed Internet access. Wireless service is available via classrooms, computer centers, computer labs, learning centers, libraries, student centers. **Student Life** *Housing:* on-campus residence required through senior year. *Options:* men-only, women-only. Campus housing is university owned. Freshman campus housing is guaranteed. *Activities and organizations:* drama/theater group, student-run newspaper, radio station, choral group. *Campus security:* 24-hour emergency response devices and patrols, controlled dormitory access. *Student services:* health clinic, personal/psychological counseling. **Athletics** *Intramural sports:* basketball M/W, football M/W, golf M/W, gymnastics M/W, racquetball M/W, soccer M/W, softball M/W, volleyball M/W, water polo M/W.

Standardized Tests *Required:* SAT or ACT (for admission).

Costs (2010–11) *Comprehensive fee:* $29,382 includes full-time tuition ($21,550), mandatory fees ($692), and room and board ($7140). Full-time tuition and fees vary according to course load. Part-time tuition: $900 per credit hour. Part-time tuition and fees vary according to course load. *College room only:* $3670. Room and board charges vary according to board plan. *Payment plan:* installment. *Waivers:* senior citizens and employees or children of employees.

Financial Aid Of all full-time matriculated undergraduates who enrolled in 2009, 1,271 applied for aid, 1,159 were judged to have need, 131 had their need fully met. 632 Federal Work-Study jobs (averaging $902). 272 state and other part-time jobs (averaging $910). In 2009, 565 non-need-based awards were made. *Average percent of need met:* 85%. *Average financial aid package:* $25,030. *Average need-based loan:* $4681. *Average need-based gift aid:* $8686. *Average non-need-based aid:* $6861. *Average indebtedness upon graduation:* $34,200.

Applying *Options:* electronic application, deferred entrance. *Application fee:* $30. *Required:* high school transcript, minimum 2.25 GPA, 2 letters of recommendation. *Application deadlines:* rolling (freshmen), rolling (transfers). *Notification:* continuous (freshmen), continuous (transfers).

Freshman Application Contact Shanna Leak, Undergraduate Admissions Coordinator, Andrews University, Berrien Springs, MI 49104. *Phone:* 800-253-2874. *Toll-free phone:* 800-253-2874. *Fax:* 269-471-3228. *E-mail:* enroll@andrews.edu. *Web site:* http://www.andrews.edu/.

Aquinas College

Grand Rapids, Michigan

- **Independent Roman Catholic** comprehensive, founded 1886
- **Suburban** 107-acre campus with easy access to Detroit, Chicago, Grand Rapids
- **Endowment** $27.4 million
- **Coed** 1,953 undergraduate students, 85% full-time, 61% women, 39% men
- **Moderately difficult** entrance level, 79% of applicants were admitted

Undergraduates 1,653 full-time, 300 part-time. Students come from 26 states and territories; 6 other countries; 5% are from out of state; 4% Black or African American, non-Hispanic/Latino; 4% Hispanic/Latino; 1% Asian, non-Hispanic/Latino; 0.1% Native Hawaiian or other Pacific Islander, non-Hispanic/Latino; 0.5% American Indian or Alaska Native, non-Hispanic/Latino; 1% Two or more races, non-Hispanic/Latino; 1% Race/ethnicity unknown; 0.2% international; 4% transferred in; 47% live on campus. *Retention:* 74% of full-time freshmen returned.

Freshmen *Admission:* 2,266 applied, 1,792 admitted, 432 enrolled. *Average high school GPA:* 3.37. *Test scores:* ACT scores over 18: 98%; ACT scores over 24: 47%; ACT scores over 30: 4%.

Faculty *Total:* 244, 37% full-time, 39% with terminal degrees. *Student/faculty ratio:* 13:1.

Academics *Calendar:* semesters. *Degrees:* associate, bachelor's, and master's. *Special study options:* academic remediation for entering students, accelerated degree program, adult/continuing education programs, advanced placement credit, cooperative education, distance learning, double majors, external degree program, honors programs, independent study, internships, off-campus study, part-time degree program, services for LD students, student-designed majors, study abroad, summer session for credit.

Computers on Campus 175 computers/terminals are available on campus for general student use. Students can access the following: campus intranet, computer help desk, free student e-mail accounts, online (class) grades, online (class) registration, online (class) schedules. Campuswide network is available. 100% of college-owned or -operated housing units are wired for high-speed Internet access. Wireless service is available via classrooms, dorm rooms, learning centers, libraries, student centers.

Student Life *Housing:* on-campus residence required through sophomore year. *Options:* coed. Campus housing is university owned. Freshman applicants given priority for college housing. *Activities and organizations:* drama/theater group, student-run newspaper, radio station, choral group, Community Senate Programming Board, The Saint (newspaper), Insignis Honors Group, Community Action Volunteers of Aquinas (CAVA), RHC (Residence Heails Council). *Campus security:* 24-hour emergency response devices and patrols, student

PROFILES

patrols, late-night transport/escort service, controlled dormitory access. *Student services:* health clinic, personal/psychological counseling, women's center.

Athletics Member NAIA. *Intercollegiate sports:* baseball M(s), basketball M(s)/W(s), cross-country running M(s)/W(s), golf M(s)/W(s), lacrosse M(s)/W, soccer M(s)/W(s), softball W(s), tennis M(s)/W(s), track and field M(s)/W(s), volleyball W(s). *Intramural sports:* basketball M/W, football M/W, golf M, ice hockey M, skiing (cross-country) M/W, skiing (downhill) M/W, soccer M/W, softball M/W, tennis M/W, volleyball M/W.

Standardized Tests *Required:* SAT or ACT (for admission).

Costs (2010–11) *Comprehensive fee:* $30,432 includes full-time tuition ($23,206) and room and board ($7226). Full-time tuition and fees vary according to course load. Part-time tuition: $470 per credit hour. Part-time tuition and fees vary according to course load. *College room only:* $3320. Room and board charges vary according to board plan and housing facility. *Payment plans:* installment, deferred payment. *Waivers:* children of alumni and employees or children of employees.

Financial Aid Of all full-time matriculated undergraduates who enrolled in 2003, 1,181 applied for aid, 1,056 were judged to have need, 430 had their need fully met. 134 Federal Work-Study jobs (averaging $700). In 2003, 416 non-need-based awards were made. *Average percent of need met:* 92%. *Average financial aid package:* $15,461. *Average need-based loan:* $2800. *Average need-based gift aid:* $12,661. *Average non-need-based aid:* $8266. *Average indebtedness upon graduation:* $13,638. *Financial aid deadline:* 8/15.

Applying *Options:* electronic application, early admission, deferred entrance. *Required:* high school transcript, minimum 2.5 GPA. *Required for some:* essay or personal statement, interview. *Application deadlines:* rolling (freshmen), rolling (transfers).

Freshman Application Contact Ms. Ashley Hauch, Admissions Office Manager, Aquinas College, 1607 Robinson Road, SE, Grand Rapids, MI 49506-1799. *Phone:* 616-632-2900. *Toll-free phone:* 800-678-9593. *Fax:* 616-732-4469. *E-mail:* admissions@aquinas.edu. *Web site:* http://www.aquinas.edu/.

See page 998 for the College Close-Up.

The Art Institute of Michigan
Novi, Michigan

- **Proprietary** 4-year, part of Education Management Corporation
- **Coed**

Academics *Degrees:* certificates, diplomas, associate, and bachelor's.

Costs (2010–11) *Tuition:* Tuition cost varies by program. Prospective students should contact the school for current tuition costs. Other charges include a starting kit for all first-quarter students. Kits vary in price, depending on the program of study.

Freshman Application Contact The Art Institute of Michigan, 28125 Cabot Drive, Suite 120, Novi, MI 48377. *Phone:* 248-675-3800. *Toll-free phone:* 800-479-0087. *Web site:* http://www.artinstitutes.edu/detroit/.

See page 1050 for the College Close-Up.

Baker College of Allen Park
Allen Park, Michigan

- **Independent** 4-year, founded 2003, part of Baker College System
- **Suburban** 13-acre campus with easy access to Detroit
- **Coed, primarily women** 3,926 undergraduate students, 59% full-time, 72% women, 28% men
- **Minimally difficult** entrance level, 100% of applicants were admitted

Undergraduates 2,316 full-time, 1,610 part-time. Students come from 1 other state; 33% Black or African American, non-Hispanic/Latino; 5% Hispanic/Latino; 1% Asian, non-Hispanic/Latino; 0.5% American Indian or Alaska Native, non-Hispanic/Latino; 0.4% Race/ethnicity unknown.

Freshmen *Admission:* 1,518 applied, 1,518 admitted.

Faculty *Total:* 88, 2% full-time, 13% with terminal degrees. *Student/faculty ratio:* 34:1.

Academics *Calendar:* quarters. *Degrees:* certificates, diplomas, associate, and bachelor's. *Special study options:* academic remediation for entering students, accelerated degree program, advanced placement credit, cooperative education, distance learning, double majors, external degree program, independent study, internships, off-campus study, part-time degree program, services for LD students, summer session for credit.

Computers on Campus 150 computers/terminals are available on campus for general student use. Students can access the following: computer help desk, free student e-mail accounts, online (class) registration. Campuswide network is available. Wireless service is available via entire campus.

Student Life *Housing:* college housing not available. *Campus security:* 24-hour patrols. *Student services:* personal/psychological counseling.

Standardized Tests *Recommended:* SAT or ACT (for admission).

Costs (2011–12) *Tuition:* $7560 full-time, $210 per quarter hour part-time. Full-time tuition and fees vary according to program. Part-time tuition and fees vary according to program. *Room only:* Room and board charges vary according to location. *Waivers:* employees or children of employees.

Applying *Options:* electronic application, deferred entrance. *Required:* high school transcript, interview. *Application deadline:* 9/24 (freshmen). *Notification:* continuous (transfers).

Freshman Application Contact Mr. Steve Peterson, Vice President of Admissions, Baker College of Allen Park, 4500 Enterprise Drive, Allen Park, MI 48101. *Phone:* 313-425-3700. *Toll-free phone:* 800-767-4120. *E-mail:* steve.peterson@baker.edu. *Web site:* http://www.baker.edu/.

Baker College of Auburn Hills
Auburn Hills, Michigan

- **Independent** 4-year, founded 1911, part of Baker College System
- **Urban** 10-acre campus with easy access to Detroit
- **Coed** 4,179 undergraduate students, 49% full-time, 72% women, 28% men
- **Minimally difficult** entrance level, 100% of applicants were admitted

Undergraduates 2,048 full-time, 2,131 part-time. Students come from 1 other state; 20% Black or African American, non-Hispanic/Latino; 3% Hispanic/Latino; 2% Asian, non-Hispanic/Latino; 0.7% American Indian or Alaska Native, non-Hispanic/Latino.

Freshmen *Admission:* 1,627 applied, 1,627 admitted.

Faculty *Total:* 155, 7% full-time, 15% with terminal degrees. *Student/faculty ratio:* 41:1.

Academics *Calendar:* quarters. *Degrees:* certificates, diplomas, associate, bachelor's, and postbachelor's certificates. *Special study options:* academic remediation for entering students, accelerated degree program, advanced placement credit, cooperative education, distance learning, double majors, external degree program, independent study, internships, part-time degree program, services for LD students, summer session for credit.

Computers on Campus 110 computers/terminals are available on campus for general student use. Students can access the following: online (class) registration. Campuswide network is available.

Student Life *Housing:* college housing not available. *Activities and organizations:* Baker Business Club, Interior Design Society, Students Action in Engineering, Marketing Club. *Campus security:* 24-hour emergency response devices.

Standardized Tests *Recommended:* SAT or ACT (for admission).

Costs (2011–12) *Tuition:* $7560 full-time, $210 per quarter hour part-time. *Waivers:* employees or children of employees.

Applying *Options:* early admission, deferred entrance. *Application fee:* $20. *Required:* high school transcript. *Application deadlines:* rolling (freshmen), rolling (transfers).

Freshman Application Contact Ms. Jan Bohlen, Vice President for Admissions, Baker College of Auburn Hills, 1500 University Drive, Auburn Hills, MI 48326-1586. *Phone:* 248-340-0600. *Toll-free phone:* 888-429-0410. *Fax:* 248-340-0608. *E-mail:* jan.bohlen@baker.edu. *Web site:* http://www.baker.edu/.

Baker College of Cadillac
Cadillac, Michigan

- **Independent** 4-year, founded 1986, part of Baker College System
- **Small-town** 40-acre campus
- **Coed** 2,094 undergraduate students, 58% full-time, 70% women, 30% men
- **Minimally difficult** entrance level, 100% of applicants were admitted

Undergraduates 1,215 full-time, 879 part-time. Students come from 4 states and territories; 0.1% Black or African American, non-Hispanic/Latino; 0.1% Hispanic/Latino; 0.1% Asian, non-Hispanic/Latino; 2% Race/ethnicity unknown. *Retention:* 69% of full-time freshmen returned.

Freshmen *Admission:* 596 applied, 596 admitted.

Faculty *Total:* 105, 4% full-time, 5% with terminal degrees. *Student/faculty ratio:* 42:1.

Academics *Calendar:* quarters. *Degrees:* certificates, diplomas, associate, and bachelor's. *Special study options:* academic remediation for entering students, advanced placement credit, cooperative education, distance learning, double majors, external degree program, independent study, internships, part-time degree program, services for LD students, summer session for credit.

Computers on Campus 100 computers/terminals are available on campus for general student use. Students can access the following: online (class) registration. Campuswide network is available.

Student Life *Housing:* college housing not available. *Campus security:* 24-hour emergency response devices.

Standardized Tests *Recommended:* SAT or ACT (for admission).

Costs (2011–12) *Tuition:* $7560 full-time, $210 per quarter hour part-time. Full-time tuition and fees vary according to program. Part-time tuition and fees vary according to program. *Waivers:* employees or children of employees.
Applying *Options:* early admission, deferred entrance. *Application fee:* $20. *Required:* high school transcript. *Recommended:* interview. *Application deadlines:* 9/24 (freshmen), rolling (transfers).
Freshman Application Contact Ms. Audrey Charmoli, Admissions Advisor, Baker College of Cadillac, 9600 East 13th Street, Cadillac, MI 49601. *Phone:* 231-876-3100. *Toll-free phone:* 888-313-3463. *Fax:* 231-775-8505. *E-mail:* audrey.charmoli@baker.edu. *Web site:* http://www.baker.edu/.

Baker College of Clinton Township
Clinton Township, Michigan
- **Independent** 4-year, founded 1990, part of Baker College System
- **Urban** 30-acre campus with easy access to Detroit
- **Coed** 6,265 undergraduate students, 58% full-time, 68% women, 32% men
- **Minimally difficult** entrance level, 100% of applicants were admitted

Undergraduates 3,634 full-time, 2,631 part-time. Students come from 2 states and territories; 24% Black or African American, non-Hispanic/Latino; 2% Hispanic/Latino; 2% Asian, non-Hispanic/Latino; 0.8% American Indian or Alaska Native, non-Hispanic/Latino; 0.8% Race/ethnicity unknown.
Freshmen *Admission:* 2,593 applied, 2,593 admitted.
Faculty *Total:* 208, 8% full-time, 12% with terminal degrees. *Student/faculty ratio:* 45:1.
Academics *Calendar:* quarters. *Degrees:* certificates, diplomas, associate, and bachelor's. *Special study options:* academic remediation for entering students, advanced placement credit, cooperative education, external degree program, internships, part-time degree program, services for LD students, summer session for credit.
Computers on Campus 127 computers/terminals are available on campus for general student use. Campuswide network is available.
Student Life *Housing:* college housing not available. *Campus security:* 24-hour emergency response devices and patrols, evening security guard. *Student services:* personal/psychological counseling.
Standardized Tests *Required for some:* SAT or ACT (for admission).
Costs (2011–12) *Tuition:* $7560 full-time, $210 per quarter hour part-time. Full-time tuition and fees vary according to program. Part-time tuition and fees vary according to program. *Waivers:* employees or children of employees.
Applying *Options:* electronic application, early admission, deferred entrance. *Application fee:* $20. *Required:* high school transcript. *Application deadlines:* rolling (freshmen), rolling (transfers).
Freshman Application Contact Ms. Annette Looser, Vice President for Admissions, Baker College of Clinton Township, 34401 South Gratiot Avenue, Clinton Township, MI 48035. *Phone:* 586-791-3000. *Toll-free phone:* 888-272-2842. *Fax:* 586-791-6811. *E-mail:* annette.looser@baker.edu. *Web site:* http://www.baker.edu/.

Baker College of Flint
Flint, Michigan
- **Independent** 4-year, founded 1911, part of Baker College System
- **Urban** 53-acre campus with easy access to Detroit
- **Coed** 7,166 undergraduate students, 59% full-time, 67% women, 33% men
- **Minimally difficult** entrance level, 100% of applicants were admitted

Undergraduates 4,228 full-time, 2,938 part-time. Students come from 5 states and territories; 1% are from out of state; 23% Black or African American, non-Hispanic/Latino; 2% Hispanic/Latino; 0.2% Asian, non-Hispanic/Latino; 0.5% American Indian or Alaska Native, non-Hispanic/Latino; 0.6% Race/ethnicity unknown; 2% live on campus.
Freshmen *Admission:* 2,732 applied, 2,732 admitted.
Faculty *Total:* 315, 13% full-time, 12% with terminal degrees. *Student/faculty ratio:* 31:1.
Academics *Calendar:* quarters. *Degrees:* certificates, diplomas, associate, and bachelor's. *Special study options:* academic remediation for entering students, accelerated degree program, advanced placement credit, cooperative education, distance learning, double majors, external degree program, independent study, internships, part-time degree program, services for LD students, summer session for credit.
Computers on Campus 412 computers/terminals are available on campus for general student use. Campuswide network is available.
Student Life *Housing:* on-campus residence required for freshman year. *Options:* coed. Campus housing is university owned. *Activities and organizations:* Occupational Therapy Club, Interior Design Society, Medical Assistants Student Organization, Physical Therapist Assistant Club, Cyber Defense Team (2008 National Champions). *Campus security:* 24-hour patrols, late-night

transport/escort service, controlled dormitory access, video monitoring of high traffic areas. *Student services:* personal/psychological counseling.
Standardized Tests *Recommended:* SAT or ACT (for admission).
Costs (2011–12) *Tuition:* $7560 full-time, $210 per quarter hour part-time. Full-time tuition and fees vary according to program. Part-time tuition and fees vary according to program. *Room only:* $3000. Room and board charges vary according to housing facility. *Waivers:* employees or children of employees.
Applying *Options:* early admission, deferred entrance. *Application fee:* $20. *Required:* high school transcript. *Application deadlines:* 9/20 (freshmen), 9/20 (transfers).
Freshman Application Contact Ms. Jodi Cunez, Vice President for Admissions, Baker College of Flint, 1050 West Bristol Road, Flint, MI 48507-5508. *Phone:* 810-766-4008. *Toll-free phone:* 800-964-4299. *Fax:* 810-766-4049. *Web site:* http://www.baker.edu/.

Baker College of Jackson
Jackson, Michigan
- **Independent** 4-year, founded 1994, part of Baker College System
- **Suburban** 42-acre campus with easy access to Lansing
- **Coed** 2,917 undergraduate students, 58% full-time, 74% women, 26% men
- **Minimally difficult** entrance level, 100% of applicants were admitted

Undergraduates 1,692 full-time, 1,225 part-time. Students come from 2 states and territories; 1% are from out of state; 10% Black or African American, non-Hispanic/Latino; 2% Hispanic/Latino; 0.5% Asian, non-Hispanic/Latino; 0.4% American Indian or Alaska Native, non-Hispanic/Latino; 0.1% Race/ethnicity unknown.
Freshmen *Admission:* 925 applied, 925 admitted.
Faculty *Total:* 85, 6% full-time, 13% with terminal degrees. *Student/faculty ratio:* 36:1.
Academics *Calendar:* quarters. *Degrees:* certificates, diplomas, associate, and bachelor's. *Special study options:* academic remediation for entering students, accelerated degree program, advanced placement credit, cooperative education, distance learning, double majors, external degree program, independent study, internships, part-time degree program, services for LD students, summer session for credit.
Computers on Campus 150 computers/terminals are available on campus for general student use. Students can access the following: online (class) registration. Campuswide network is available.
Student Life *Housing:* college housing not available. *Campus security:* 24-hour emergency response devices. *Student services:* personal/psychological counseling.
Standardized Tests *Recommended:* SAT or ACT (for admission).
Costs (2011–12) *Tuition:* $7560 full-time, $210 per quarter hour part-time. Full-time tuition and fees vary according to program. Part-time tuition and fees vary according to program. *Required fees:* $20 full-time. *Waivers:* employees or children of employees.
Applying *Options:* electronic application, early admission, deferred entrance. *Application fee:* $20. *Required:* high school transcript. *Application deadlines:* 9/19 (freshmen), rolling (transfers). *Notification:* continuous (freshmen).
Freshman Application Contact Mr. Kevin Pnacek, Vice President for Admissions, Baker College of Jackson, 2800 Springport Road, Jackson, MI 49202. *Phone:* 517-788-7800. *Toll-free phone:* 888-343-3683. *Fax:* 517-789-7331. *E-mail:* kevin.pnacek@baker.edu. *Web site:* http://www.baker.edu/.

Baker College of Muskegon
Muskegon, Michigan
- **Independent** 4-year, founded 1888, part of Baker College System
- **Suburban** 45-acre campus with easy access to Grand Rapids
- **Coed** 5,810 undergraduate students, 63% full-time, 68% women, 32% men
- **Minimally difficult** entrance level, 100% of applicants were admitted

Undergraduates 3,660 full-time, 2,150 part-time. Students come from 13 states and territories; 1% are from out of state; 14% Black or African American, non-Hispanic/Latino; 5% Hispanic/Latino; 0.8% Asian, non-Hispanic/Latino; 0.8% American Indian or Alaska Native, non-Hispanic/Latino; 0.3% Race/ethnicity unknown; 11% live on campus.
Freshmen *Admission:* 2,309 applied, 2,309 admitted.
Faculty *Total:* 177, 10% full-time, 8% with terminal degrees. *Student/faculty ratio:* 55:1.
Academics *Calendar:* quarters. *Degrees:* certificates, diplomas, associate, and bachelor's. *Special study options:* academic remediation for entering students, accelerated degree program, adult/continuing education programs, advanced placement credit, cooperative education, distance learning, double majors, external degree program, independent study, internships, part-time degree program, services for LD students, summer session for credit.

Computers on Campus 165 computers/terminals are available on campus for general student use. Students can access the following: free student e-mail accounts. Campuswide network is available.
Student Life *Housing:* on-campus residence required for freshman year. *Options:* coed, disabled students. Campus housing is university owned. Freshman applicants given priority for college housing. *Activities and organizations:* Accounting Club, Rehab Club, Travel Club, Culinary Club. *Campus security:* 24-hour emergency response devices and patrols, late-night transport/escort service, controlled dormitory access, 24-hour security camera surveillance. *Student services:* personal/psychological counseling.
Standardized Tests *Recommended:* SAT or ACT (for admission).
Costs (2011–12) *Tuition:* $7560 full-time, $210 per quarter hour part-time. Full-time tuition and fees vary according to program. Part-time tuition and fees vary according to program. *Room only:* $3000. *Waivers:* employees or children of employees.
Applying *Options:* electronic application, early admission, deferred entrance. *Application fee:* $20. *Required:* high school transcript. *Application deadlines:* 9/24 (freshmen), rolling (transfers). *Notification:* continuous (freshmen).
Freshman Application Contact Ms. Kathy Jacobson, Vice President of Admissions, Baker College of Muskegon, 1903 Marquette Avenue, Muskegon, MI 49442-3497. *Phone:* 231-777-5207. *Toll-free phone:* 800-937-0337. *Fax:* 231-777-5201. *E-mail:* kathy.jacobson@baker.edu. *Web site:* http://www.baker.edu/.

Baker College of Owosso
Owosso, Michigan

- **Independent** 4-year, founded 1984, part of Baker College System
- **Small-town** 40-acre campus
- **Coed** 3,532 undergraduate students, 63% full-time, 63% women, 37% men
- **Minimally difficult** entrance level, 100% of applicants were admitted

Undergraduates 2,225 full-time, 1,307 part-time. Students come from 4 states and territories; 15% live on campus.
Freshmen *Admission:* 1,365 applied, 1,365 admitted.
Faculty *Total:* 144, 6% full-time, 15% with terminal degrees. *Student/faculty ratio:* 40:1.
Academics *Calendar:* quarters. *Degrees:* certificates, diplomas, associate, and bachelor's. *Special study options:* academic remediation for entering students, accelerated degree program, adult/continuing education programs, advanced placement credit, cooperative education, external degree program, internships, part-time degree program, services for LD students, summer session for credit.
Computers on Campus 210 computers/terminals are available on campus for general student use. Campuswide network is available.
Student Life *Housing options:* coed. *Activities and organizations:* student-run newspaper, Accounting Club, Travel Club, Management Club, Baker Health Information Management Club, RAD Club. *Campus security:* 24-hour emergency response devices and patrols, late-night transport/escort service, controlled dormitory access. *Student services:* personal/psychological counseling.
Standardized Tests *Recommended:* SAT or ACT (for admission).
Costs (2011–12) *Tuition:* $7560 full-time, $210 per quarter hour part-time. Full-time tuition and fees vary according to program. Part-time tuition and fees vary according to program. *Required fees:* $20 full-time. *Room only:* $2700. Room and board charges vary according to housing facility. *Waivers:* employees or children of employees.
Applying *Options:* early admission, deferred entrance. *Application fee:* $20. *Required:* high school transcript. *Application deadlines:* rolling (freshmen), rolling (transfers).
Freshman Application Contact Mr. Michael Konopacke, Vice President for Admissions, Baker College of Owosso, 1020 South Washington Street, Owosso, MI 48867-4400. *Phone:* 989-729-3350. *Toll-free phone:* 800-879-3797. *Fax:* 989-729-3441. *E-mail:* mike.konopacke@baker.edu. *Web site:* http://www.baker.edu/.

Baker College of Port Huron
Port Huron, Michigan

- **Independent** 4-year, founded 1990, part of Baker College System
- **Urban** 10-acre campus with easy access to Detroit
- **Coed** 1,776 undergraduate students, 69% full-time, 70% women, 30% men
- **Minimally difficult** entrance level, 100% of applicants were admitted

Undergraduates 1,225 full-time, 551 part-time. Students come from 1 other state; 3% Black or African American, non-Hispanic/Latino; 2% Hispanic/Latino; 0.2% Asian, non-Hispanic/Latino; 0.6% American Indian or Alaska Native, non-Hispanic/Latino; 2% Race/ethnicity unknown.
Freshmen *Admission:* 554 applied, 554 admitted.
Faculty *Total:* 126, 10% full-time, 7% with terminal degrees. *Student/faculty ratio:* 28:1.

Academics *Calendar:* quarters. *Degrees:* diplomas, associate, and bachelor's. *Special study options:* academic remediation for entering students, accelerated degree program, advanced placement credit, cooperative education, distance learning, double majors, external degree program, independent study, internships, part-time degree program, services for LD students, summer session for credit.
Computers on Campus 165 computers/terminals are available on campus for general student use. Students can access the following: online (class) registration, software. Campuswide network is available.
Student Life *Housing:* college housing not available. *Activities and organizations:* Travel Club, Student Association Dental Hygienists of America. *Campus security:* 24-hour emergency response devices, late-night transport/escort service. *Student services:* personal/psychological counseling.
Standardized Tests *Recommended:* SAT or ACT (for admission).
Costs (2011–12) *Tuition:* $7560 full-time, $210 per quarter hour part-time. Full-time tuition and fees vary according to program. Part-time tuition and fees vary according to program. *Waivers:* employees or children of employees.
Applying *Options:* early admission, deferred entrance. *Application fee:* $20. *Required:* high school transcript, interview. *Application deadlines:* 9/24 (freshmen), rolling (transfers). *Notification:* continuous (freshmen), continuous (transfers).
Freshman Application Contact Mr. Daniel Kenny, Vice President for Admissions, Baker College of Port Huron, 3403 Lapeer Road, Port Huron, MI 48060-2597. *Phone:* 810-985-7000. *Toll-free phone:* 888-262-2442. *Fax:* 810-985-7066. *E-mail:* kenny_d@porthuron.baker.edu. *Web site:* http://www.baker.edu/.

Calvin College
Grand Rapids, Michigan

- **Independent Christian Reformed** comprehensive, founded 1876
- **Suburban** 370-acre campus with easy access to Grand Rapids
- **Endowment** $89.0 million
- **Coed** 3,921 undergraduate students, 97% full-time, 53% women, 47% men
- **Moderately difficult** entrance level, 92% of applicants were admitted

Undergraduates 3,792 full-time, 129 part-time. Students come from 47 states and territories; 55 other countries; 44% are from out of state; 3% Black or African American, non-Hispanic/Latino; 2% Hispanic/Latino; 4% Asian, non-Hispanic/Latino; 0.4% American Indian or Alaska Native, non-Hispanic/Latino; 0.8% Two or more races, non-Hispanic/Latino; 3% Race/ethnicity unknown; 8% international; 3% transferred in; 60% live on campus. *Retention:* 87% of full-time freshmen returned.
Freshmen *Admission:* 2,566 applied, 2,368 admitted, 935 enrolled. *Average high school GPA:* 3.6. *Test scores:* SAT critical reading scores over 500: 80%; SAT math scores over 500: 89%; ACT scores over 18: 98%; SAT critical reading scores over 600: 42%; SAT math scores over 600: 50%; ACT scores over 24: 73%; SAT critical reading scores over 700: 15%; SAT math scores over 700: 14%; ACT scores over 30: 22%.
Faculty *Total:* 388, 82% full-time, 71% with terminal degrees. *Student/faculty ratio:* 11:1.
Academics *Calendar:* 4-1-4. *Degrees:* bachelor's and master's. *Special study options:* academic remediation for entering students, accelerated degree program, adult/continuing education programs, advanced placement credit, double majors, honors programs, independent study, internships, off-campus study, part-time degree program, services for LD students, student-designed majors, study abroad, summer session for credit. *ROTC:* Army (c). *Unusual degree programs:* 3-2 occupational therapy with Washington University in St. Louis.
Computers on Campus 1,004 computers/terminals and 2,656 ports are available on campus for general student use. Students can access the following: computer help desk, free student e-mail accounts, online (class) grades, online (class) registration, online (class) schedules. Campuswide network is available. 100% of college-owned or -operated housing units are wired for high-speed Internet access. Wireless service is available via classrooms, computer centers, computer labs, dorm rooms, libraries, student centers.
Student Life *Housing:* on-campus residence required through sophomore year. *Options:* men-only, women-only. Campus housing is university owned. Freshman campus housing is guaranteed. *Activities and organizations:* drama/theater group, student-run newspaper, television station, choral group, Social Justice Committee, Environmental Stewardship Coalition, Dance Guild, Chimes, Calvin Video Network. *Campus security:* 24-hour emergency response devices and patrols, student patrols, late-night transport/escort service, controlled dormitory access, crime prevention programs, crime alert bulletins. *Student services:* health clinic, personal/psychological counseling.
Athletics Member NCAA. All Division III. *Intercollegiate sports:* baseball M, basketball M/W, crew M(c)/W(c), cross-country running M/W, golf M/W, ice hockey M(c), lacrosse M(c)/W(c), rock climbing M(c)/W(c), rugby M(c), soccer M/W, softball W, swimming and diving M/W, tennis M/W, track and field M/W, ultimate Frisbee M(c)/W(c), volleyball M(c)/W. *Intramural sports:* badminton M/W, basketball M/W, cross-country running M/W, football M/W,

golf M/W, racquetball M/W, soccer M/W, softball M/W, swimming and diving M/W, tennis M/W, track and field M/W, volleyball M/W, water polo M/W.
Standardized Tests *Required:* SAT or ACT (for admission).
Costs (2010–11) *Comprehensive fee:* $33,395 includes full-time tuition ($24,645), mandatory fees ($225), and room and board ($8525). Full-time tuition and fees vary according to degree level and program. Part-time tuition: $590 per credit hour. Part-time tuition and fees vary according to course load and degree level. *Room and board:* Room and board charges vary according to board plan. *Payment plans:* tuition prepayment, installment. *Waivers:* employees or children of employees.
Financial Aid Of all full-time matriculated undergraduates who enrolled in 2009, 3,081 applied for aid, 2,498 were judged to have need, 384 had their need fully met. 1,190 Federal Work-Study jobs (averaging $1411). 963 state and other part-time jobs (averaging $1433). In 2009, 1097 non-need-based awards were made. *Average percent of need met:* 70%. *Average financial aid package:* $18,019. *Average need-based loan:* $6275. *Average need-based gift aid:* $11,775. *Average non-need-based aid:* $4888. *Average indebtedness upon graduation:* $27,700.
Applying *Options:* electronic application, deferred entrance. *Application fee:* $35. *Required:* essay or personal statement, high school transcript, minimum 2.5 GPA, 1 letter of recommendation. *Recommended:* interview. *Application deadlines:* 8/15 (freshmen), rolling (transfers). *Notification:* continuous (freshmen).
Freshman Application Contact Mr. Dale Kuiper, Director of Admissions and Financial Aid, Calvin College, 3201 Burton Street, SE, Grand Rapids, MI 49546. *Phone:* 616-526-6106. *Toll-free phone:* 800-688-0122. *Fax:* 616-526-6777. *E-mail:* admissions@calvin.edu. *Web site:* http://www.calvin.edu/.

See page 1184 for the College Close-Up.

Central Michigan University
Mount Pleasant, Michigan

- **State-supported** university, founded 1892
- **Small-town** 854-acre campus
- **Endowment** $65.9 million
- **Coed** 21,633 undergraduate students, 89% full-time, 55% women, 45% men
- **Moderately difficult** entrance level, 73% of applicants were admitted

Undergraduates 19,241 full-time, 2,392 part-time. Students come from 43 states and territories; 40 other countries; 2% are from out of state; 5% Black or African American, non-Hispanic/Latino; 2% Hispanic/Latino; 0.9% Asian, non-Hispanic/Latino; 0.6% American Indian or Alaska Native, non-Hispanic/Latino; 1% Two or more races, non-Hispanic/Latino; 7% Race/ethnicity unknown; 3% international; 6% transferred in; 34% live on campus. *Retention:* 80% of full-time freshmen returned.
Freshmen *Admission:* 18,051 applied, 13,092 admitted, 4,215 enrolled. *Average high school GPA:* 3.27. *Test scores:* SAT critical reading scores over 500: 62%; SAT math scores over 500: 63%; ACT scores over 18: 94%; SAT critical reading scores over 600: 19%; SAT math scores over 600: 29%; ACT scores over 24: 33%; SAT critical reading scores over 700: 12%; SAT math scores over 700: 4%; ACT scores over 30: 4%.
Faculty *Total:* 1,233, 61% full-time, 60% with terminal degrees. *Student/faculty ratio:* 22:1.
Academics *Calendar:* semesters. *Degrees:* bachelor's, master's, doctoral-other, doctoral-professional, doctoral-research/scholarship, post-master's, and postbachelor's certificates. *Special study options:* academic remediation for entering students, accelerated degree program, adult/continuing education programs, advanced placement credit, distance learning, double majors, English as a second language, freshman honors college, honors programs, independent study, internships, off-campus study, part-time degree program, student-designed majors, study abroad, summer session for credit. *ROTC:* Army (b). *Unusual degree programs:* 3-2 Apparel Product Development and Merchandising Technology; Computer Science; Economics; Experimental Psychology; Geographic Information Science; Human Development and Family Studies; Mathematics; Political Science.
Computers on Campus 3,000 computers/terminals and 10,000 ports are available on campus for general student use. Students can access the following:

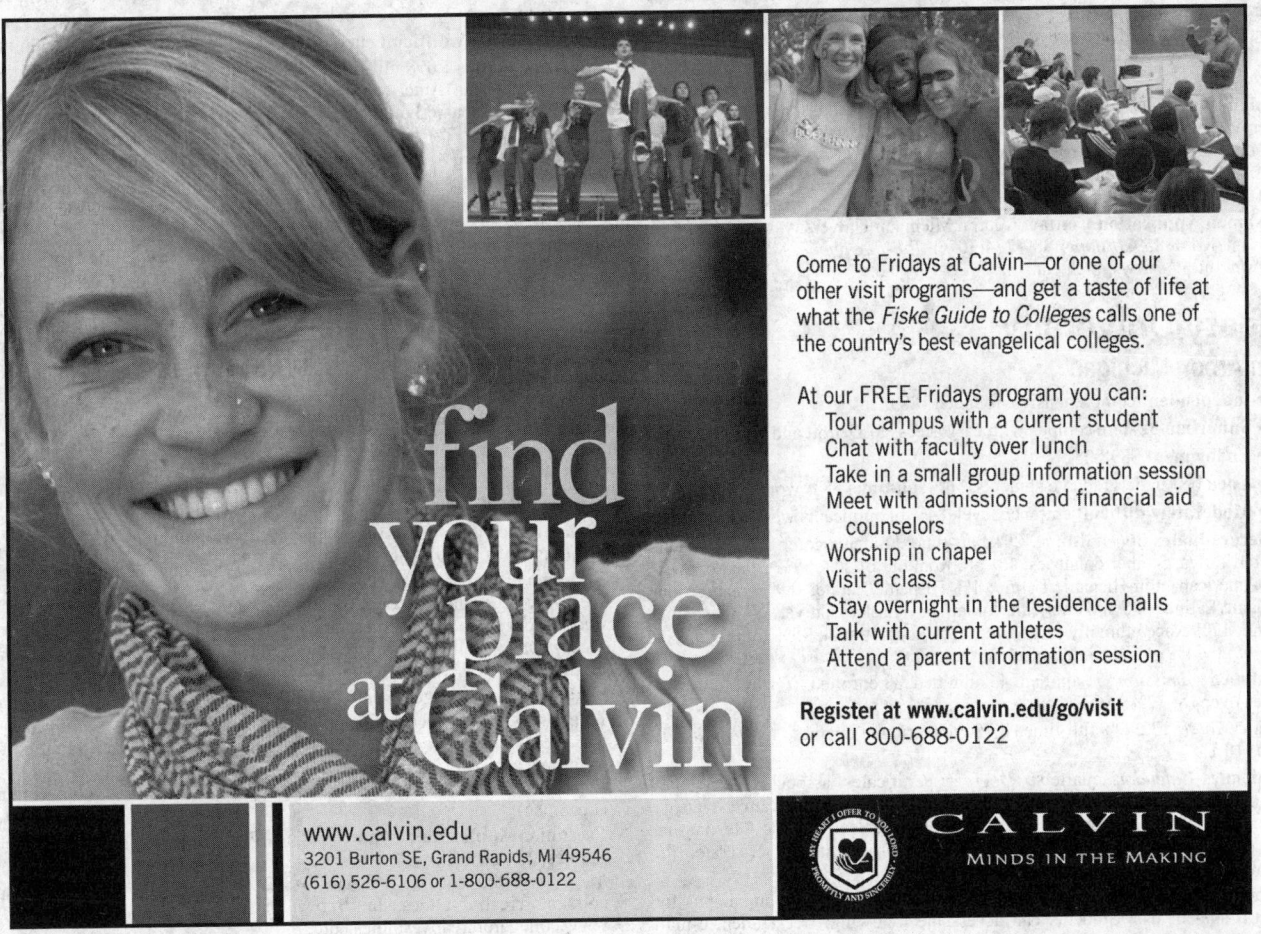

campus intranet, computer help desk, free student e-mail accounts, online (class) grades, online (class) registration, online (class) schedules, Blackboard. Campuswide network is available. 100% of college-owned or -operated housing units are wired for high-speed Internet access. Wireless service is available via entire campus.

Student Life *Housing:* on-campus residence required for freshman year. *Options:* coed, men-only, women-only, disabled students. Campus housing is university owned and is provided by a third party. Freshman campus housing is guaranteed. *Activities and organizations:* drama/theater group, student-run newspaper, radio and television station, choral group, marching band, Residence Hall Assembly, Student Government Association, High Adventure Club, Fellowship of Christian Athletes, College Republicans, national fraternities, national sororities. *Campus security:* 24-hour emergency response devices and patrols, student patrols, late-night transport/escort service, controlled dormitory access. *Student services:* health clinic, personal/psychological counseling, women's center.

Athletics Member NCAA. All Division I except football (Division I-A). *Intercollegiate sports:* baseball M(s), basketball M(s)/W(s), cross-country running M(s)/W(s), field hockey W(s), gymnastics W(s), soccer W(s), softball W(s), track and field M(s)/W(s), volleyball W(s), wrestling M(s). *Intramural sports:* archery M/W, baseball M(c), basketball M/W, bowling M/W, cheerleading M(c), cross-country running M/W, football M/W, golf M/W, ice hockey M(c), lacrosse M(c)/W(c), racquetball M/W, rugby M(c)/W(c), skiing (downhill) M/W, soccer M/W, softball M/W, swimming and diving M/W, table tennis M/W, tennis M/W, ultimate Frisbee M(c)/W(c), volleyball M(c)/W(c), water polo M/W, weight lifting M/W, wrestling M.

Standardized Tests *Required:* ACT (for admission).

Costs (2010–11) *Tuition:* state resident $10,380 full-time, $346 per credit hour part-time; nonresident $23,670 full-time, $789 per credit hour part-time. Full-time tuition and fees vary according to location and student level. Part-time tuition and fees vary according to location and student level. *Room and board:* $8092; room only: $4046. Room and board charges vary according to board plan, housing facility, location, and student level. *Payment plan:* installment. *Waivers:* children of alumni, senior citizens, and employees or children of employees.

Financial Aid Of all full-time matriculated undergraduates who enrolled in 2008, 14,260 applied for aid, 10,721 were judged to have need, 5,919 had their need fully met. 829 Federal Work-Study jobs (averaging $1731). 4,001 state and other part-time jobs (averaging $2269). In 2008, 1456 non-need-based awards were made. *Average percent of need met:* 84%. *Average financial aid package:* $11,764. *Average need-based loan:* $6696. *Average need-based gift aid:* $5344. *Average non-need-based aid:* $3930. *Average indebtedness upon graduation:* $28,142.

Applying *Options:* electronic application, early admission, early action, deferred entrance. *Application fee:* $35. *Required:* high school transcript. *Required for some:* essay or personal statement, interview. *Application deadlines:* rolling (freshmen), rolling (transfers). *Notification:* continuous (freshmen), continuous (transfers).

Freshman Application Contact Central Michigan University, Mount Pleasant, MI 48859. *Phone:* 989-774-3076. *Toll-free phone:* 888-292-5366. *Web site:* http://www.cmich.edu.

Cleary University

Ann Arbor, Michigan

- **Independent** comprehensive, founded 1883
- **Suburban** 32-acre campus with easy access to Detroit and Ann Arbor
- **Endowment** $898,082
- **Coed** 657 undergraduate students, 56% full-time, 58% women, 42% men
- **Moderately difficult** entrance level, 84% of applicants were admitted

Undergraduates 366 full-time, 291 part-time. Students come from 16 states and territories; 5 other countries; 1% are from out of state; 9% Black or African American, non-Hispanic/Latino; 1% Hispanic/Latino; 0.9% Asian, non-Hispanic/Latino; 0.5% American Indian or Alaska Native, non-Hispanic/Latino; 17% Race/ethnicity unknown; 0.3% international; 25% transferred in. *Retention:* 74% of full-time freshmen returned.

Freshmen *Admission:* 51 applied, 43 admitted, 33 enrolled. *Test scores:* ACT scores over 18: 77%; ACT scores over 24: 27%.

Faculty *Total:* 132, 5% full-time, 14% with terminal degrees. *Student/faculty ratio:* 10:1.

Academics *Calendar:* quarters. *Degrees:* certificates, associate, bachelor's, and master's. *Special study options:* accelerated degree program, advanced placement credit, cooperative education, distance learning, double majors, independent study, internships, part-time degree program, summer session for credit.

Computers on Campus 60 computers/terminals are available on campus for general student use. Students can access the following: free student e-mail

accounts, online (class) grades, online (class) schedules. Campuswide network is available. Wireless service is available via entire campus.

Student Life *Housing:* college housing not available. *Activities and organizations:* Cleary Professional Accounting Associates, Human Resources & Organizational Leadership Association, Event and Meeting Planning Student Association, Veterans Club, Accounting/Fraud Examiners Club. *Campus security:* 24-hour emergency response devices, Access to facilities limited to authorized persons. *Student services:* personal/psychological counseling.

Standardized Tests *Required:* SAT or ACT (for admission). *Required for some:* SAT Subject Tests (for admission).

Costs (2010–11) *Tuition:* $16,560 full-time, $345 per credit hour part-time. Full-time tuition and fees vary according to degree level. No tuition increase for student's term of enrollment. *Payment plans:* installment, deferred payment. *Waivers:* children of alumni, senior citizens, and employees or children of employees.

Financial Aid Of all full-time matriculated undergraduates who enrolled in 2008, 391 applied for aid, 391 were judged to have need, 13 had their need fully met. In 2008, 60 non-need-based awards were made. *Average percent of need met:* 42%. *Average financial aid package:* $12,759. *Average need-based loan:* $1193. *Average need-based gift aid:* $1265. *Average non-need-based aid:* $2258. *Average indebtedness upon graduation:* $20,830. *Financial aid deadline:* 7/1.

Applying *Options:* electronic application, early admission, deferred entrance. *Application fee:* $25. *Required:* high school transcript, minimum 2.5 GPA. *Required for some:* essay or personal statement, minimum high school GPA of 2.0 required for non-traditional and transfer students. *Recommended:* interview. *Application deadlines:* 8/15 (freshmen), rolling (transfers).

Freshman Application Contact Charlotte Paquette, Director of Recruiting, Cleary University, 3750 Cleary Drive, Howell, MI 48843. *Phone:* 888-525-3279. *Toll-free phone:* 888-5-CLEARY Ext. 2249. *Fax:* 517-338-3336. *E-mail:* admissions@cleary.edu. *Web site:* http://www.cleary.edu/.

College for Creative Studies

Detroit, Michigan

- **Independent** comprehensive, founded 1926
- **Urban** 11-acre campus
- **Coed** 1,328 undergraduate students, 83% full-time, 48% women, 52% men
- **Moderately difficult** entrance level, 36% of applicants were admitted

Undergraduates 1,098 full-time, 230 part-time. 18% are from out of state; 7% Black or African American, non-Hispanic/Latino; 5% Hispanic/Latino; 4% Asian, non-Hispanic/Latino; 0.6% American Indian or Alaska Native, non-Hispanic/Latino; 2% Two or more races, non-Hispanic/Latino; 10% Race/ethnicity unknown; 7% international; 10% transferred in; 30% live on campus.

Freshmen *Admission:* 1,398 applied, 508 admitted, 206 enrolled. *Average high school GPA:* 3.13. *Test scores:* ACT scores over 18: 79%; ACT scores over 24: 26%; ACT scores over 30: 1%.

Faculty *Total:* 249, 20% full-time. *Student/faculty ratio:* 11:1.

Academics *Calendar:* semesters. *Degrees:* bachelor's, master's, and post-bachelor's certificates. *Special study options:* academic remediation for entering students, advanced placement credit, cooperative education, double majors, English as a second language, independent study, internships, off-campus study, part-time degree program, services for LD students, study abroad, summer session for credit.

Computers on Campus Campuswide network is available.

Student Life *Housing options:* coed. Campus housing is university owned. *Activities and organizations:* student-run newspaper. *Campus security:* 24-hour patrols, late-night transport/escort service, controlled dormitory access. *Student services:* personal/psychological counseling.

Standardized Tests *Required:* SAT or ACT (for admission).

Costs (2011–12) *Tuition:* $31,440 full-time, $1048 per credit hour part-time. Full-time tuition and fees vary according to course load. Part-time tuition and fees vary according to course load. *Required fees:* $1345 full-time. *Room only:* Room and board charges vary according to board plan and location. *Payment plans:* installment, deferred payment. *Waivers:* employees or children of employees.

Financial Aid *Average indebtedness upon graduation:* $47,604.

Applying *Options:* electronic application, deferred entrance. *Application fee:* $35. *Required:* essay or personal statement, high school transcript, portfolio. *Required for some:* interview. *Recommended:* minimum 2.5 GPA. *Application deadlines:* 8/1 (freshmen), rolling (transfers). *Notification:* continuous (freshmen).

Freshman Application Contact Office of Admissions, College for Creative Studies, 201 East Kirby, Detroit, MI 48202-4034. *Phone:* 800-952-2787. *Toll-free phone:* 800-872-2739. *Fax:* 313-872-2739. *E-mail:* admissions@collegeforcreativestudies.edu. *Web site:* http://www.collegeforcreativestudies.edu/.

Concordia University
Ann Arbor, Michigan

Freshman Application Contact Amy Becher, Executive Director of Enrollment Services, Concordia University, 4090 Geddes Road, Ann Arbor, MI 48105-2797. *Phone:* 734-995-7450. *Toll-free phone:* 800-253-0680. *Fax:* 734-995-4610. *E-mail:* admissions@cuaa.edu. *Web site:* http://www.cuaa.edu/.

Cornerstone University
Grand Rapids, Michigan

- **Independent nondenominational** comprehensive, founded 1941
- **Suburban** 132-acre campus
- **Endowment** $4.6 million
- **Coed**
- **Minimally difficult** entrance level

Faculty *Student/faculty ratio:* 20:1.
Academics *Calendar:* semesters. *Degrees:* diplomas, associate, bachelor's, master's, and doctoral-professional.
Student Life *Campus security:* 24-hour emergency response devices and patrols, student patrols, late-night transport/escort service, controlled dormitory access.
Athletics Member NAIA.
Standardized Tests *Required:* SAT or ACT (for admission).
Costs (2010–11) *Comprehensive fee:* $27,964 includes full-time tuition ($20,808), mandatory fees ($370), and room and board ($6786). Full-time tuition and fees vary according to course load and reciprocity agreements. Part-time tuition: $798 per semester hour. Part-time tuition and fees vary according to course load. *Room and board:* Room and board charges vary according to board plan.
Financial Aid *Of all full-time matriculated undergraduates who enrolled in 2009,* 1,002 applied for aid, 915 were judged to have need, 127 had their need fully met. 237 Federal Work-Study jobs (averaging $825). *In 2009,* 174 non-need-based awards were made. *Average percent of need met:* 83. *Average financial aid package:* $19,772. *Average need-based loan:* $4365. *Average need-based gift aid:* $12,708. *Average non-need-based aid:* $6742. *Average indebtedness upon graduation:* $29,510.
Applying *Options:* electronic application, deferred entrance. *Application fee:* $25. *Required:* essay or personal statement, high school transcript, minimum 2.5 GPA, 1 letter of recommendation, pastoral letter. *Recommended:* interview.
Freshman Application Contact Office of Admissions, Cornerstone University, 1001 East Beltline Avenue, NE, Grand Rapids, MI 49525. *Phone:* 616-222-1426. *Toll-free phone:* 800-787-9778. *Fax:* 616-222-1400. *E-mail:* admissions@cornerstone.edu. *Web site:* http://www.cornerstone.edu/.

Davenport University
Grand Rapids, Michigan

- **Independent** comprehensive, founded 1866
- **Suburban** campus
- **Endowment** $11.1 million
- **Coed** 9,704 undergraduate students, 34% full-time, 65% women, 35% men
- **Minimally difficult** entrance level

Undergraduates 3,253 full-time, 6,451 part-time. Students come from 49 states and territories; 49 other countries; 2% are from out of state; 17% transferred in; 4% live on campus. *Retention:* 67% of full-time freshmen returned.
Freshmen *Admission:* 792 enrolled.
Faculty *Total:* 1,000, 16% full-time, 23% with terminal degrees. *Student/faculty ratio:* 15:1.
Academics *Calendar:* semesters. *Degrees:* diplomas, associate, bachelor's, master's, post-master's, and postbachelor's certificates. *Special study options:* academic remediation for entering students, accelerated degree program, adult/continuing education programs, advanced placement credit, cooperative education, distance learning, English as a second language, independent study, internships, part-time degree program, services for LD students, study abroad, summer session for credit.
Computers on Campus 3,098 computers/terminals are available on campus for general student use. Students can access the following: campus intranet, computer help desk, free student e-mail accounts, online (class) grades, online (class) registration, online (class) schedules. Campuswide network is available. 100% of college-owned or -operated housing units are wired for high-speed Internet access. Wireless service is available via entire campus.
Student Life *Housing options:* coed. Campus housing is university owned. Freshman applicants given priority for college housing. *Activities and organizations:* student-run newspaper, Business Professionals of America, Delta Epsilon Chi, Student government, Health Occupations Students of America,

Connect. *Campus security:* 24-hour emergency response devices and patrols, late-night transport/escort service, controlled dormitory access. *Student services:* personal/psychological counseling.
Athletics Member NAIA. *Intercollegiate sports:* baseball M(s), basketball M(s)/W(s), bowling M(s)/W(s), cheerleading W(s), cross-country running M(s)/W(s), golf M(s)/W(s), ice hockey M(s), lacrosse M(s)/W, rugby M(s), soccer M(s)/W(s), softball M/W(s), tennis M(s)/W(s), track and field M(s)/W(s), volleyball W(s).
Standardized Tests *Recommended:* SAT or ACT (for admission).
Costs (2010–11) *Comprehensive fee:* $20,206 includes full-time tuition ($11,544), mandatory fees ($250), and room and board ($8412). Full-time tuition and fees vary according to location and program. Part-time tuition: $481 per credit hour. Part-time tuition and fees vary according to location and program. *Room and board:* Room and board charges vary according to board plan and housing facility. *Payment plan:* installment. *Waivers:* employees or children of employees.
Applying *Options:* electronic application, deferred entrance. *Application fee:* $25. *Required:* high school transcript. *Recommended:* interview. *Application deadlines:* rolling (freshmen), rolling (out-of-state freshmen), rolling (transfers). *Notification:* continuous (freshmen), continuous (out-of-state freshmen), continuous (transfers).
Freshman Application Contact Ms. Heather Knechtel, Director of Admissions, Davenport University, 6191 Kraft Avenue, SE, Grand Rapids, MI 49512. *Phone:* 616-451-3511. *Toll-free phone:* 800-632-9569. *E-mail:* heather.knechtel@davenport.edu. *Web site:* http://www.davenport.edu/.

DeVry University
Southfield, Michigan

- **Proprietary** 4-year, founded 2008
- **Coed**

Faculty *Student/faculty ratio:* 10:1.
Academics *Calendar:* semesters. *Degrees:* associate and bachelor's.
Costs (2010–11) *Tuition:* $14,766 full-time, $580 per credit hour part-time. Full-time tuition and fees vary according to course load. Part-time tuition and fees vary according to course load. *Required fees:* $60 full-time, $30 per term part-time. *Payment plans:* installment, deferred payment.
Financial Aid *Of all full-time matriculated undergraduates who enrolled in 2007,* 2 applied for aid, 2 were judged to have need. *Average percent of need met:* 38. *Average financial aid package:* $8705. *Average need-based loan:* $5750. *Average need-based gift aid:* $5910.
Applying *Options:* deferred entrance. *Application fee:* $50.
Freshman Application Contact DeVry University, 26999 Central Park Boulevard, Suite 125, Southfield, MI 48076. *Web site:* http://www.devry.edu/.

Eastern Michigan University
Ypsilanti, Michigan

- **State-supported** comprehensive, founded 1849
- **Suburban** 460-acre campus with easy access to Detroit
- **Endowment** $40.7 million
- **Coed** 18,529 undergraduate students, 71% full-time, 57% women, 43% men
- **Moderately difficult** entrance level, 66% of applicants were admitted

Undergraduates 13,106 full-time, 5,423 part-time. Students come from 46 states and territories; 44 other countries; 7% are from out of state; 21% Black or African American, non-Hispanic/Latino; 2% Hispanic/Latino; 2% Asian, non-Hispanic/Latino; 0.1% Native Hawaiian or other Pacific Islander, non-Hispanic/Latino; 0.5% American Indian or Alaska Native, non-Hispanic/Latino; 0.7% Two or more races, non-Hispanic/Latino; 7% Race/ethnicity unknown; 2% international; 12% transferred in; 15% live on campus. *Retention:* 76% of full-time freshmen returned.
Freshmen *Admission:* 10,336 applied, 6,860 admitted, 2,039 enrolled. *Average high school GPA:* 3.08. *Test scores:* SAT critical reading scores over 500: 51%; SAT math scores over 500: 63%; SAT writing scores over 500: 51%; ACT scores over 18: 70%; SAT critical reading scores over 600: 20%; SAT math scores over 600: 21%; SAT writing scores over 600: 16%; ACT scores over 24: 26%; SAT critical reading scores over 700: 4%; SAT math scores over 700: 1%; SAT writing scores over 700: 5%; ACT scores over 30: 3%.
Faculty *Total:* 1,364, 56% full-time, 49% with terminal degrees. *Student/faculty ratio:* 18:1.
Academics *Calendar:* semesters. *Degrees:* bachelor's, master's, doctoral-research/scholarship, post-master's, and postbachelor's certificates. *Special study options:* academic remediation for entering students, accelerated degree program, advanced placement credit, cooperative education, distance learning, double majors, English as a second language, external degree program, honors programs, independent study, internships, part-time degree program, services for LD students, student-designed majors, study abroad, summer session for

credit. *ROTC:* Army (b), Navy (c), Air Force (c). *Unusual degree programs:* accounting, occupational therapy.

Computers on Campus 1,500 computers/terminals and 250 ports are available on campus for general student use. Students can access the following: campus intranet, computer help desk, free student e-mail accounts, online (class) grades, online (class) registration, online (class) schedules. Campuswide network is available. 100% of college-owned or -operated housing units are wired for high-speed Internet access. Wireless service is available via entire campus.

Student Life *Housing:* on-campus residence required through sophomore year. *Options:* coed, disabled students. Campus housing is university owned. *Activities and organizations:* drama/theater group, student-run newspaper, radio and television station, choral group, marching band, International Student Association, Golden Key International Honor Society, Psychology Club, Indian Student Association, GREEN (Gathering Resources to Educate about our Environment and Nature), national fraternities, national sororities. *Campus security:* 24-hour emergency response devices and patrols, student patrols, late-night transport/escort service, controlled dormitory access, bicycle patrols, local police in dormitories, self-defense education, lighted pathways, bike lock lease program. *Student services:* health clinic, personal/psychological counseling, women's center, legal services.

Athletics Member NCAA. All Division I except football (Division I-A). *Intercollegiate sports:* baseball M(s), basketball M(s)/W(s), crew W(s), cross-country running M(s)/W(s), golf M(s)/W(s), gymnastics W(s), soccer W(s), softball W(s), swimming and diving M(s)/W(s), tennis W(s), track and field M(s)/W(s), volleyball W(s), wrestling M(s). *Intramural sports:* badminton M/W, basketball M/W, bowling M/W, cross-country running M/W, golf M/W, ice hockey M(c), racquetball M/W, soccer M/W, softball M/W, swimming and diving M/W, table tennis M/W, tennis M/W, track and field M/W, ultimate Frisbee M(c)/W(c), volleyball M/W, weight lifting M(c)/W(c).

Standardized Tests *Required:* SAT or ACT (for admission).

Costs (2011–12) *One-time required fee:* $300. *Tuition:* state resident $7148 full-time, $238 per credit hour part-time; nonresident $21,053 full-time, $702 per credit hour part-time. Full-time tuition and fees vary according to course level and reciprocity agreements. Part-time tuition and fees vary according to course level and reciprocity agreements. *Required fees:* $1230 full-time, $38 per credit hour part-time, $45 per term part-time. *Room and board:* $7785; room only: $3656. Room and board charges vary according to board plan, housing facility, and location. *Payment plan:* installment. *Waivers:* employees or children of employees.

Financial Aid Of all full-time matriculated undergraduates who enrolled in 2008, 7,976 applied for aid, 6,864 were judged to have need, 85 had their need fully met. 908 Federal Work-Study jobs (averaging $1486). In 2008, 1090 non-need-based awards were made. *Average percent of need met:* 54%. *Average financial aid package:* $8767. *Average need-based loan:* $4437. *Average need-based gift aid:* $4960. *Average non-need-based aid:* $4183. *Average indebtedness upon graduation:* $23,669.

Applying *Options:* electronic application, deferred entrance. *Application fee:* $30. *Required:* high school transcript, minimum 2 GPA. *Required for some:* 1 letter of recommendation, interview. *Application deadlines:* rolling (freshmen), rolling (out-of-state freshmen), rolling (transfers). *Notification:* continuous (freshmen), continuous (out-of-state freshmen), continuous (transfers).

Freshman Application Contact Eastern Michigan University, Ypsilanti, MI 48197. *Phone:* 734-487-3060. *Toll-free phone:* 800-GO TO EMU. *Web site:* http://www.emich.edu/.

Ferris State University
Big Rapids, Michigan

- **State-supported** comprehensive, founded 1884
- **Small-town** 880-acre campus with easy access to Grand Rapids
- **Endowment** $28.9 million
- **Coed** 13,134 undergraduate students, 71% full-time, 50% women, 50% men
- **Minimally difficult** entrance level, 54% of applicants were admitted

Undergraduates 9,289 full-time, 3,845 part-time. Students come from 44 states and territories; 28 other countries; 4% are from out of state; 11% transferred in; 28% live on campus. *Retention:* 75% of full-time freshmen returned.

Freshmen *Admission:* 11,285 applied, 6,083 admitted, 2,017 enrolled. *Average high school GPA:* 3.21. *Test scores:* ACT scores over 18: 81%; ACT scores over 24: 28%; ACT scores over 30: 4%.

Faculty *Total:* 918, 61% full-time, 30% with terminal degrees. *Student/faculty ratio:* 16:1.

Academics *Calendar:* semesters. *Degrees:* certificates, associate, bachelor's, master's, doctoral-professional, and postbachelor's certificates (associate degree). *Special study options:* academic remediation for entering students, accelerated degree program, adult/continuing education programs, advanced placement credit, cooperative education, distance learning, double majors, external degree program, freshman honors college, honors programs, independent study, internships, off-campus study, part-time degree program, services

for LD students, student-designed majors, study abroad, summer session for credit. *ROTC:* Army (c).

Computers on Campus 1,950 computers/terminals are available on campus for general student use. Students can access the following: campus intranet, computer help desk, free student e-mail accounts, online (class) grades, online (class) registration, online (class) schedules. Campuswide network is available. 100% of college-owned or -operated housing units are wired for high-speed Internet access. Wireless service is available via entire campus.

Student Life *Housing:* on-campus residence required through sophomore year. *Options:* coed, disabled students. Campus housing is university owned. Freshman campus housing is guaranteed. *Activities and organizations:* drama/theater group, student-run newspaper, radio and television station, choral group, Student Government of Ferris State University, Intramural Sports Club, University theatre, Music Club, Forensics Club, national fraternities, national sororities. *Campus security:* 24-hour emergency response devices, student patrols, late-night transport/escort service, controlled dormitory access. *Student services:* health clinic, personal/psychological counseling.

Athletics Member NCAA. All Division II. *Intercollegiate sports:* basketball M(s)/W(s), cross-country running M(s)/W(s), football M(s), golf M(s)/W(s), ice hockey M(s), soccer W(s), softball W(s), tennis M(s)/W(s), track and field M(s)/W(s), volleyball W(s). *Intramural sports:* baseball M(c), basketball M/W, bowling M(c)/W(c), cheerleading M(c)/W(c), equestrian sports M(c)/W(c), football M/W, golf M/W, ice hockey M, lacrosse M(c), racquetball M/W, rugby M(c)/W(c), skiing (downhill) M(c)/W(c), soccer M(c)/W(c), softball M/W, swimming and diving M/W, table tennis M(c)/W(c), tennis M(c)/W(c), ultimate Frisbee M(c)/W(c), volleyball M(c)/W(c).

Standardized Tests *Required:* SAT or ACT (for admission).

Costs (2010–11) *One-time required fee:* $162. *Tuition:* state resident $9930 full-time, $331 per credit hour part-time; nonresident $15,900 full-time, $530 per credit hour part-time. Full-time tuition and fees vary according to location and program. Part-time tuition and fees vary according to location. *Room and board:* $9180. Room and board charges vary according to board plan and housing facility. *Payment plan:* deferred payment. *Waivers:* employees or children of employees.

Financial Aid Of all full-time matriculated undergraduates who enrolled in 2009, 6,538 applied for aid, 5,378 were judged to have need, 807 had their need fully met. 616 Federal Work-Study jobs (averaging $2150). In 2009, 662 non-need-based awards were made. *Average percent of need met:* 87%. *Average financial aid package:* $15,925. *Average need-based loan:* $4266. *Average need-based gift aid:* $5379. *Average non-need-based aid:* $4318. *Average indebtedness upon graduation:* $35,468.

Applying *Options:* electronic application. *Application fee:* $30. *Required:* high school transcript, minimum 2.5 GPA. *Application deadlines:* 8/1 (freshmen), 7/1 (transfers). *Notification:* continuous (freshmen), continuous (transfers).

Freshman Application Contact Mr. Troy Tissue, Associate Director of Admissions, Ferris State University, 1201 South State Street, CSS201, Big Rapids, MI 49307-2742. *Phone:* 231-591-2000. *Toll-free phone:* 800-433-7747. *Fax:* 231-591-3944. *E-mail:* admissions@ferris.edu. *Web site:* http://www.ferris.edu/.

Finlandia University
Hancock, Michigan

Freshman Application Contact Martin Kinard, Finlandia University, 601 Quincy Street, Hancock, MI 49930. *Phone:* 906-487-7352. *Toll-free phone:* 877-202-5491. *Fax:* 906-487-7383. *E-mail:* admissions@finlandia.edu. *Web site:* http://www.finlandia.edu/.

Grace Bible College
Grand Rapids, Michigan

- **Independent** 4-year, founded 1945, affiliated with Grace Gospel Fellowship
- **Suburban** 21-acre campus
- **Endowment** $319,000
- **Coed** 207 undergraduate students, 93% full-time, 43% women, 57% men
- **Minimally difficult** entrance level, 34% of applicants were admitted

Undergraduates 192 full-time, 15 part-time. Students come from 15 states and territories; 3 other countries; 19% are from out of state; 4% Black or African American, non-Hispanic/Latino; 2% Hispanic/Latino; 1% Asian, non-Hispanic/Latino; 0.5% Native Hawaiian or other Pacific Islander, non-Hispanic/Latino; 2% Two or more races, non-Hispanic/Latino; 0.5% international; 11% transferred in; 53% live on campus. *Retention:* 80% of full-time freshmen returned.

Freshmen *Admission:* 158 applied, 53 admitted, 53 enrolled. *Average high school GPA:* 3.03. *Test scores:* SAT critical reading scores over 500: 58%; SAT math scores over 500: 28%; SAT writing scores over 500: 43%; ACT scores over 18: 61%; SAT critical reading scores over 600: 29%; SAT math

scores over 600: 14%; SAT writing scores over 600: 14%; ACT scores over 24: 17%; ACT scores over 30: 2%.
Faculty *Total:* 21, 33% full-time, 29% with terminal degrees. *Student/faculty ratio:* 17:1.
Academics *Calendar:* semesters. *Degrees:* associate and bachelor's. *Special study options:* academic remediation for entering students, advanced placement credit, independent study, internships, off-campus study. *ROTC:* Army (c).
Computers on Campus 27 computers/terminals and 10 ports are available on campus for general student use. Students can access the following: computer help desk, free student e-mail accounts, library catalog search. Campuswide network is available. 70% of college-owned or -operated housing units are wired for high-speed Internet access. Wireless service is available via dorm rooms, learning centers, libraries, student centers.
Student Life *Housing options:* men-only, women-only. Campus housing is university owned. Freshman campus housing is guaranteed. *Activities and organizations:* choral group, Student Missionary Fellowship, Student Activities Committee, Student Council, Campus Ministry Team. *Campus security:* student patrols, controlled dormitory access. *Student services:* personal/psychological counseling.
Athletics Member NCCAA. *Intercollegiate sports:* basketball M/W, cross-country running M/W, soccer M/W, tennis M/W, volleyball W. *Intramural sports:* basketball M, football M, golf M, racquetball M/W, soccer M, volleyball M, weight lifting M/W.
Standardized Tests *Required:* SAT and SAT Subject Tests or ACT (for admission).
Costs (2011–12) *Comprehensive fee:* $21,100 includes full-time tuition ($14,850) and room and board ($6250). Part-time tuition: $495 per credit. Part-time tuition and fees vary according to course load. *College room only:* $3150. Room and board charges vary according to board plan and housing facility. *Payment plan:* installment. *Waivers:* employees or children of employees.
Financial Aid Of all full-time matriculated undergraduates who enrolled in 2008, 165 applied for aid, 156 were judged to have need, 5 had their need fully met. 45 Federal Work-Study jobs (averaging $497). In 2008, 20 non-need-based awards were made. *Average percent of need met:* 58%. *Average financial aid package:* $10,108. *Average need-based loan:* $4093. *Average need-based gift aid:* $4442. *Average non-need-based aid:* $2255. *Average indebtedness upon graduation:* $7957.
Applying *Options:* electronic application, early admission, deferred entrance. *Required:* high school transcript, 2 letters of recommendation. *Required for some:* interview. *Recommended:* minimum 2.5 GPA. *Application deadline:* 7/15 (freshmen). *Notification:* 8/1 (freshmen), continuous (transfers).
Freshman Application Contact Mr. Kevin Gilliam, Director of Enrollment, Grace Bible College, 1101 Aldon Street, SW, PO Box 910, Grand Rapids, MI 49509. *Phone:* 616-538-2330 Ext. 239. *Toll-free phone:* 800-968-1887. *Fax:* 616-538-0599. *E-mail:* gbc@gbcol.edu. *Web site:* http://www.gbcol.edu/.

Grand Valley State University
Allendale, Michigan
- **State-supported** comprehensive, founded 1960
- **Small-town** 1317-acre campus with easy access to Grand Rapids
- **Endowment** $61.2 million
- **Coed** 20,986 undergraduate students, 88% full-time, 58% women, 42% men
- **Moderately difficult** entrance level, 81% of applicants were admitted

Undergraduates 18,393 full-time, 2,593 part-time. Students come from 42 states and territories; 77 other countries; 4% are from out of state; 5% Black or African American, non-Hispanic/Latino; 4% Hispanic/Latino; 2% Asian, non-Hispanic/Latino; 0.5% American Indian or Alaska Native, non-Hispanic/Latino; 1% Two or more races, non-Hispanic/Latino; 1% Race/ethnicity unknown; 1% international; 8% transferred in; 28% live on campus. *Retention:* 84% of full-time freshmen returned.
Freshmen *Admission:* 12,351 applied, 9,974 admitted, 3,434 enrolled. *Average high school GPA:* 3.53. *Test scores:* ACT scores over 18: 97%; ACT scores over 24: 53%; ACT scores over 30: 8%.
Faculty *Total:* 1,618, 66% full-time, 50% with terminal degrees. *Student/faculty ratio:* 17:1.
Academics *Calendar:* semesters. *Degrees:* certificates, bachelor's, master's, doctoral-professional, post-master's, and postbachelor's certificates. *Special study options:* academic remediation for entering students, accelerated degree program, adult/continuing education programs, advanced placement credit, cooperative education, distance learning, double majors, English as a second language, freshman honors college, honors programs, independent study, internships, part-time degree program, services for LD students, study abroad, summer session for credit.
Computers on Campus 2,600 computers/terminals are available on campus for general student use. Students can access the following: campus intranet, computer help desk, free student e-mail accounts, online (class) grades, online (class) registration, online (class) schedules, transcript, degree audit, credit

card payments. Campuswide network is available. 63% of college-owned or -operated housing units are wired for high-speed Internet access. Wireless service is available via entire campus.
Student Life *Housing options:* coed. Campus housing is university owned. Freshman campus housing is guaranteed. *Activities and organizations:* drama/theater group, student-run radio and television station, choral group, marching band, Habitat for Humanity, Alternative Breaks, Hospitality and tourism Management Club, Dance Troupe, Colleges Against Cancer, national fraternities, national sororities. *Campus security:* 24-hour emergency response devices and patrols, student patrols, late-night transport/escort service, controlled dormitory access. *Student services:* health clinic, personal/psychological counseling, women's center.
Athletics Member NCAA. All Division II. *Intercollegiate sports:* baseball M(s), basketball M(s)/W(s), cheerleading M(c)/W(c), crew M(c)/W(c), cross-country running M(s)/W(s), football M(s), golf M(s)/W(s), ice hockey M(c), lacrosse M/W, rugby M(c)/W(c), sailing M(c)/W(c), skiing (downhill) M(c)/W(c), soccer M(c)/W(s), softball W(s), swimming and diving M(s)/W(s), tennis M(s)/W(s), track and field M(s)/W(s), volleyball M(c)/W(s), water polo M(c)/W(c), wrestling M(c). *Intramural sports:* archery M/W, badminton M/W, basketball M/W, bowling M/W, cheerleading M/W, crew M/W, cross-country running M/W, fencing M/W, field hockey M/W, football M/W, golf M/W, gymnastics M/W, lacrosse M(c)/W(c), racquetball M/W, skiing (cross-country) M/W, skiing (downhill) M/W, soccer M/W, softball M/W, squash M/W, swimming and diving M/W, tennis M/W, volleyball M/W, water polo M/W, weight lifting M/W, wrestling M.
Standardized Tests *Required:* SAT or ACT (for admission).
Costs (2010–11) *Tuition:* state resident $9088 full-time, $395 per credit hour part-time; nonresident $13,402 full-time, $571 per credit hour part-time. Full-time tuition and fees vary according to degree level, program, and student level. Part-time tuition and fees vary according to course load, degree level, program, and student level. *Room and board:* $7624; room only: $5344. Room and board charges vary according to board plan, housing facility, and location. *Payment plans:* installment, deferred payment. *Waivers:* employees or children of employees.
Financial Aid Of all full-time matriculated undergraduates who enrolled in 2009, 14,812 applied for aid, 11,368 were judged to have need, 1,135 had their need fully met. In 2009, 1532 non-need-based awards were made. *Average percent of need met:* 61%. *Average financial aid package:* $8485. *Average need-based loan:* $4542. *Average need-based gift aid:* $5572. *Average non-need-based aid:* $3384. *Average indebtedness upon graduation:* $24,030.
Applying *Options:* electronic application. *Application fee:* $30. *Required:* high school transcript. *Required for some:* essay or personal statement, interview. *Application deadlines:* 5/1 (freshmen), 7/24 (transfers). *Notification:* 5/1 (freshmen), continuous (transfers).
Freshman Application Contact Ms. Jodi Chycinski, Director of Admissions, Grand Valley State University, 1 Campus Drive, Allendale, MI 49401. *Phone:* 616-331-2025. *Toll-free phone:* 800-748-0246. *Fax:* 616-331-2000. *E-mail:* go2gvsu@gvsu.edu. *Web site:* http://www.gvsu.edu/.

Great Lakes Christian College
Lansing, Michigan
- **Independent** 4-year, founded 1949, affiliated with Christian Churches and Churches of Christ
- **Suburban** 47-acre campus
- **Endowment** $415,454
- **Coed** 238 undergraduate students, 74% full-time, 42% women, 58% men
- **Moderately difficult** entrance level

Undergraduates 177 full-time, 61 part-time. Students come from 4 states and territories; 3 other countries; 2% are from out of state. *Retention:* 70% of full-time freshmen returned.
Freshmen *Test scores:* ACT scores over 18: 79%; ACT scores over 24: 19%; ACT scores over 30: 2%.
Faculty *Total:* 23, 43% full-time, 30% with terminal degrees. *Student/faculty ratio:* 14:1.
Academics *Calendar:* semesters. *Degrees:* associate and bachelor's. *Special study options:* academic remediation for entering students, advanced placement credit, double majors, independent study, internships, off-campus study, part-time degree program, services for LD students.
Computers on Campus 24 computers/terminals and 190 ports are available on campus for general student use. Students can access the following: campus intranet, computer help desk, free student e-mail accounts, online (class) grades, online (class) schedules. Campuswide network is available. 100% of college-owned or -operated housing units are wired for high-speed Internet access. Wireless service is available via entire campus.
Student Life *Housing:* on-campus residence required through senior year. *Options:* men-only, women-only. Campus housing is university owned. *Activities and organizations:* drama/theater group, student-run newspaper, choral group. *Campus security:* controlled dormitory access, evening security patrols. *Student services:* personal/psychological counseling.

Athletics Member NCCAA. *Intercollegiate sports:* basketball M/W, soccer M, volleyball W.

Standardized Tests *Required:* SAT or ACT (for admission).

Costs (2011–12) *Comprehensive fee:* $21,712 includes full-time tuition ($12,672), mandatory fees ($1240), and room and board ($7800). Part-time tuition: $396 per credit. *Room and board:* Room and board charges vary according to board plan and housing facility. *Payment plan:* installment. *Waivers:* children of alumni and employees or children of employees.

Applying *Options:* electronic application. *Application fee:* $30. *Required:* essay or personal statement, high school transcript, minimum 2.25 GPA, 3 letters of recommendation. *Application deadlines:* 8/1 (freshmen), 8/1 (transfers). *Notification:* 8/15 (freshmen), continuing until 8/15 (transfers).

Freshman Application Contact Mrs. Judy Carter, Admissions Office Manager, Great Lakes Christian College, 6211 West Willow Highway, Lansing, MI 48917-1299. *Phone:* 517-321-0242 Ext. 221. *Toll-free phone:* 800-YES-GLCC. *Fax:* 517-321-5902. *E-mail:* jcarter@glcc.edu. *Web site:* http://www.glcc.edu/.

Hillsdale College

Hillsdale, Michigan

- **Independent** 4-year, founded 1844
- **Small-town** 200-acre campus
- **Endowment** $250.0 million
- **Coed** 1,391 undergraduate students, 98% full-time, 53% women, 47% men
- **Very difficult** entrance level, 57% of applicants were admitted

Undergraduates 1,358 full-time, 33 part-time. Students come from 48 states and territories; 7 other countries; 62% are from out of state; 3% transferred in; 75% live on campus. *Retention:* 96% of full-time freshmen returned.

Freshmen *Admission:* 1,865 applied, 1,067 admitted, 388 enrolled. *Average high school GPA:* 3.75. *Test scores:* SAT critical reading scores over 500: 100%; SAT math scores over 500: 99%; SAT writing scores over 500: 98%; ACT scores over 18: 100%; SAT critical reading scores over 600: 98%; SAT math scores over 600: 65%; SAT writing scores over 600: 78%; ACT scores over 24: 90%; SAT critical reading scores over 700: 44%; SAT math scores over 700: 24%; SAT writing scores over 700: 26%; ACT scores over 30: 38%.

Faculty *Total:* 161, 72% full-time, 88% with terminal degrees. *Student/faculty ratio:* 10:1.

Academics *Calendar:* semesters. *Degree:* bachelor's. *Special study options:* accelerated degree program, advanced placement credit, double majors, honors programs, independent study, internships, off-campus study, part-time degree program, study abroad, summer session for credit. *Unusual degree programs:* 3-2 engineering with Northwestern University, Tri-State University.

Computers on Campus 200 computers/terminals are available on campus for general student use. Students can access the following: computer help desk, free student e-mail accounts, online (class) grades, online (class) registration, online (class) schedules. Campuswide network is available. 100% of college-owned or -operated housing units are wired for high-speed Internet access. Wireless service is available via entire campus.

Student Life *Housing:* on-campus residence required through sophomore year. *Options:* men-only, women-only. Campus housing is university owned. Freshman campus housing is guaranteed. *Activities and organizations:* drama/theater group, student-run newspaper, choral group, Inter-Varsity Christian Fellowship, Varsity H-Club, Student Federation, Young Life, College Republicans, national fraternities, national sororities. *Campus security:* 24-hour emergency response devices and patrols, late-night transport/escort service, controlled dormitory access. *Student services:* health clinic, personal/psychological counseling.

Athletics Member NCAA. All Division II. *Intercollegiate sports:* baseball M(s), basketball M(s)/W(s), cheerleading M/W, cross-country running M(s)/W(s), equestrian sports W, football M(s), riflery M(s)/W(s), rugby M(c), soccer M/W, softball W(s), swimming and diving W(s), track and field M(s)/W(s), volleyball W(s). *Intramural sports:* basketball M/W, bowling M/W, equestrian sports W(c), football M/W, ice hockey M(c), lacrosse M(c), racquetball M/W, riflery M(c)/W(c), skiing (downhill) M(c)/W(c), soccer M(c)/W(c), softball M/W, squash M/W, swimming and diving W, table tennis M/W, tennis M/W, track and field M/W, ultimate Frisbee M/W, volleyball M/W.

Standardized Tests *Required:* SAT or ACT (for admission). *Recommended:* SAT Subject Tests (for admission).

Costs (2011–12) *Comprehensive fee:* $28,490 includes full-time tuition ($19,960), mandatory fees ($540), and room and board ($7990). Part-time tuition: $785 per credit. *College room only:* $3970. Room and board charges vary according to board plan. *Payment plans:* tuition prepayment, installment. *Waivers:* children of alumni and employees or children of employees.

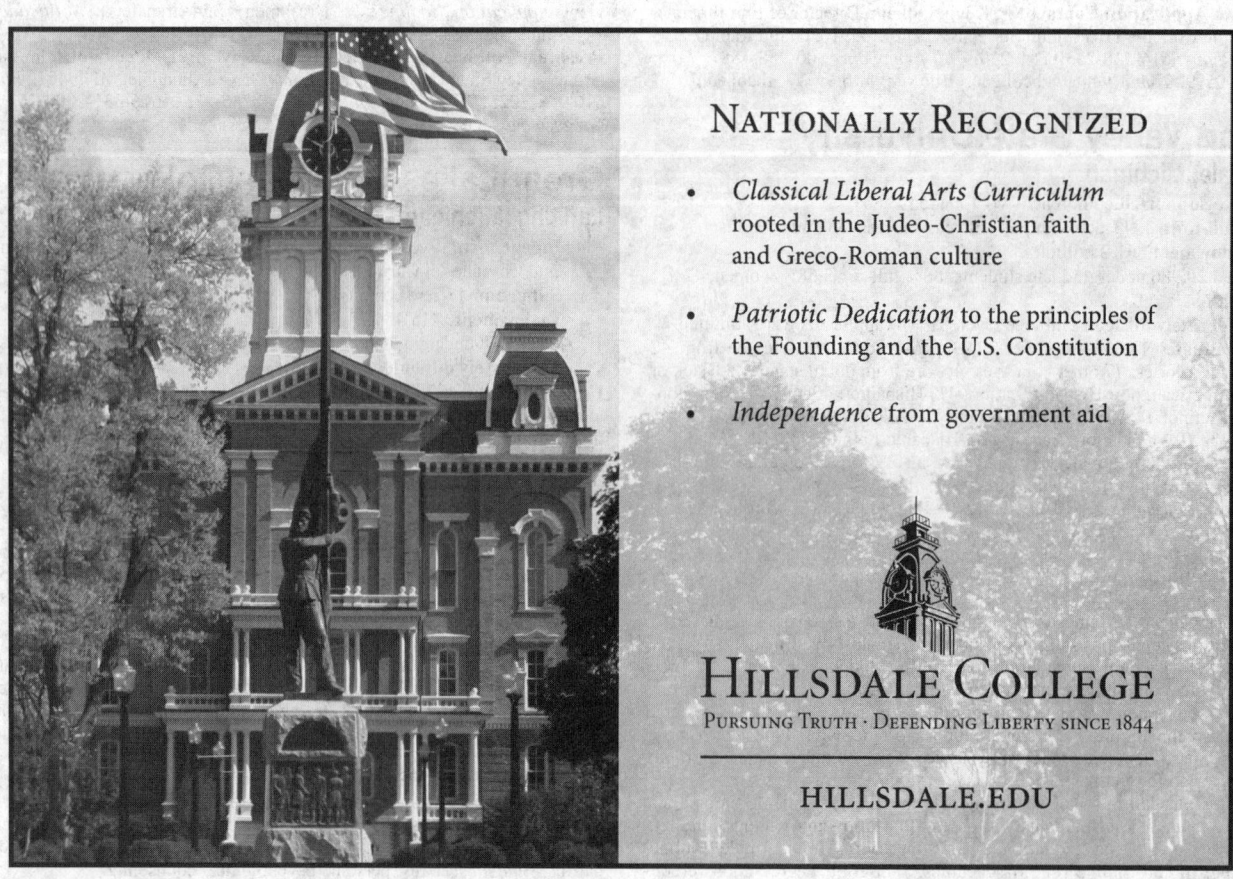

Financial Aid Of all full-time matriculated undergraduates who enrolled in 2008, 672 applied for aid, 601 were judged to have need, 235 had their need fully met. In 2008, 641 non-need-based awards were made. *Average percent of need met:* 72%. *Average financial aid package:* $16,760. *Average need-based loan:* $5900. *Average need-based gift aid:* $7350. *Average non-need-based aid:* $9740. *Average indebtedness upon graduation:* $16,500. *Financial aid deadline:* 4/1.

Applying *Options:* electronic application, early admission, early decision, early action, deferred entrance. *Required:* essay or personal statement, high school transcript, 2 letters of recommendation. *Required for some:* minimum 3.6 GPA, interview. *Recommended:* minimum 3.6 GPA, interview. *Application deadlines:* 2/15 (freshmen), 2/15 (out-of-state freshmen), 2/15 (transfers), 12/15 (early action). *Early decision deadline:* 11/15. *Notification:* 4/1 (freshmen), 4/1 (out-of-state freshmen), 4/1 (transfers), 12/1 (early decision), 2/15 (early action).

Freshman Application Contact Mr. Jeffrey S. Lantis, Director of Admissions, Hillsdale College, 33 East College Street, Hillsdale, MI 49242-1298. *Phone:* 517-607-2327. *Fax:* 517-607-2223. *E-mail:* admissions@hillsdale.edu. *Web site:* http://www.hillsdale.edu/.

See page 1328 for the College Close-Up.

Hope College
Holland, Michigan

- **Independent** 4-year, founded 1866, affiliated with Reformed Church in America
- **Suburban** 45-acre campus with easy access to Grand Rapids
- **Endowment** $125.3 million
- **Coed** 3,202 undergraduate students, 97% full-time, 60% women, 40% men
- **Moderately difficult** entrance level, 80% of applicants were admitted

Undergraduates 3,103 full-time, 99 part-time. Students come from 45 states and territories; 29 other countries; 30% are from out of state; 3% Black or African American, non-Hispanic/Latino; 4% Hispanic/Latino; 2% Asian, non-Hispanic/Latino; 0.2% American Indian or Alaska Native, non-Hispanic/Latino; 1% Two or more races, non-Hispanic/Latino; 2% international; 1% transferred in; 81% live on campus. *Retention:* 87% of full-time freshmen returned.

Freshmen *Admission:* 3,252 applied, 2,601 admitted, 781 enrolled. *Average high school GPA:* 3.78. *Test scores:* SAT critical reading scores over 500: 85%; SAT math scores over 500: 91%; ACT scores over 18: 100%; SAT critical reading scores over 600: 52%; SAT math scores over 600: 48%; ACT scores over 24: 77%; SAT critical reading scores over 700: 13%; SAT math scores over 700: 13%; ACT scores over 30: 23%.

Faculty *Total:* 342, 70% full-time, 65% with terminal degrees. *Student/faculty ratio:* 12:1.

Academics *Calendar:* semesters. *Degree:* bachelor's. *Special study options:* advanced placement credit, double majors, English as a second language, independent study, internships, off-campus study, part-time degree program, services for LD students, student-designed majors, study abroad, summer session for credit. *ROTC:* Army (c).

Computers on Campus 300 computers/terminals and 5,000 ports are available on campus for general student use. Students can access the following: campus intranet, computer help desk, free student e-mail accounts, online (class) grades, online (class) registration, online (class) schedules. Campus-wide network is available. 100% of college-owned or -operated housing units are wired for high-speed Internet access. Wireless service is available via entire campus.

Student Life *Housing:* on-campus residence required through junior year. *Options:* coed, men-only, women-only, disabled students. Campus housing is university owned and leased by the school. Freshman campus housing is guaranteed. *Activities and organizations:* drama/theater group, student-run newspaper, radio station, choral group, Social Activities Committee, Greek Life, Dance Marathon, Hockey Club, Relay for Life, national fraternities, national sororities. *Campus security:* 24-hour emergency response devices and patrols, late-night transport/escort service, controlled dormitory access. *Student services:* health clinic, personal/psychological counseling.

Athletics Member NCAA. All Division III. *Intercollegiate sports:* baseball M, basketball M/W, cheerleading M/W, cross-country running M/W, football M, golf M/W, ice hockey M(c), lacrosse M(c)/W(c), sailing M(c)/W(c), soccer M/W, softball W, swimming and diving M/W, tennis M/W, track and field M/W, volleyball W. *Intramural sports:* basketball M/W, bowling M/W, football M/W, racquetball M/W, soccer M/W, softball M/W, tennis M/W, ultimate Frisbee M/W, volleyball M/W, water polo M/W.

Standardized Tests *Required:* SAT or ACT (for admission).

Costs (2011–12) *Comprehensive fee:* $35,280 includes full-time tuition ($26,860), mandatory fees ($160), and room and board ($8260). Part-time tuition and fees vary according to course load. *College room only:* $3780. Room and board charges vary according to board plan. *Payment plan:* installment. *Waivers:* employees or children of employees.

Financial Aid Of all full-time matriculated undergraduates who enrolled in 2009, 2,273 applied for aid, 1,886 were judged to have need, 603 had their need fully met. 352 Federal Work-Study jobs (averaging $1246). 356 state and other part-time jobs (averaging $441). In 2009, 760 non-need-based awards were made. *Average percent of need met:* 82%. *Average financial aid package:* $22,917. *Average need-based loan:* $4765. *Average need-based gift aid:* $17,436. *Average non-need-based aid:* $7664. *Average indebtedness upon graduation:* $28,500.

Applying *Options:* electronic application, early admission, deferred entrance. *Application fee:* $50. *Required:* essay or personal statement, high school transcript. *Required for some:* 1 letter of recommendation. *Recommended:* interview. *Application deadlines:* rolling (freshmen), rolling (transfers). *Notification:* continuous (freshmen), continuous (transfers).

Freshman Application Contact Admissions Office, Hope College, 69 East 10th Street, PO Box 9000, Holland, MI 49422-9000. *Phone:* 616-395-7850. *Toll-free phone:* 800-968-7850. *E-mail:* admissions@hope.edu. *Web site:* http://www.hope.edu/.

See page 1336 for the College Close-Up.

ITT Technical Institute

Canton, Michigan

- **Proprietary** primarily 2-year, founded 2002, part of ITT Educational Services, Inc.
- **Coed**
- **Minimally difficult** entrance level

Academics *Calendar:* quarters. *Degrees:* associate and bachelor's.

Student Life *Housing:* college housing not available.

Freshman Application Contact Director of Recruitment, ITT Technical Institute, 1905 South Haggerty Road, Canton, MI 48188-2025. *Phone:* 784-397-7800. *Toll-free phone:* 800-247-4477. *Web site:* http://www.itt-tech.edu/.

ITT Technical Institute

Swartz Creek, Michigan

- **Proprietary** primarily 2-year, founded 2005, part of ITT Educational Services, Inc.
- **Coed**
- **Minimally difficult** entrance level

Academics *Calendar:* quarters. *Degrees:* associate and bachelor's.

Freshman Application Contact Director of Recruitment, ITT Technical Institute, 6359 Miller Road, Swartz Creek, MI 48473. *Phone:* 810-628-2500. *Toll-free phone:* 800-514-6564. *Web site:* http://www.itt-tech.edu/.

ITT Technical Institute

Troy, Michigan

- **Proprietary** primarily 2-year, founded 1987, part of ITT Educational Services, Inc.
- **Coed**
- **Minimally difficult** entrance level

Academics *Calendar:* quarters. *Degrees:* associate and bachelor's.

Student Life *Housing:* college housing not available.

Freshman Application Contact Director of Recruitment, ITT Technical Institute, 1522 East Big Beaver Road, Troy, MI 48083-1905. *Phone:* 248-524-1800. *Toll-free phone:* 800-832-6817. *Fax:* 248-524-1965. *Web site:* http://www.itt-tech.edu/.

ITT Technical Institute

Wyoming, Michigan

- **Proprietary** primarily 2-year, part of ITT Educational Services, Inc.
- **Coed**
- **Minimally difficult** entrance level

Academics *Calendar:* quarters. *Degrees:* associate and bachelor's.

Student Life *Housing:* college housing not available.

Freshman Application Contact Director of Recruitment, ITT Technical Institute, 1980 Metro Court SW, Wyoming, MI 49519. *Phone:* 616-406-1200. *Toll-free phone:* 800-632-4676. *Web site:* http://www.itt-tech.edu/.

Kalamazoo College

Kalamazoo, Michigan

- **Independent** 4-year, founded 1833, affiliated with American Baptist Churches in the U.S.A.
- **Suburban** 60-acre campus with easy access to Grand Rapids
- **Endowment** $172.0 million
- **Coed** 1,369 undergraduate students, 99% full-time, 57% women, 43% men
- **Very difficult** entrance level, 75% of applicants were admitted

Undergraduates 1,356 full-time, 13 part-time. Students come from 41 states and territories; 23 other countries; 34% are from out of state; 4% Black or African American, non-Hispanic/Latino; 6% Hispanic/Latino; 5% Asian, non-Hispanic/Latino; 0.8% American Indian or Alaska Native, non-Hispanic/Latino; 2% Two or more races, non-Hispanic/Latino; 6% Race/ethnicity unknown; 7% international; 0.5% transferred in; 70% live on campus. *Retention:* 91% of full-time freshmen returned.

Freshmen *Admission:* 1,945 applied, 1,451 admitted, 342 enrolled. *Average high school GPA:* 3.6. *Test scores:* SAT critical reading scores over 500: 88%; SAT math scores over 500: 92%; SAT writing scores over 500: 91%; ACT scores over 18: 100%; SAT critical reading scores over 600: 63%; SAT math scores over 600: 63%; SAT writing scores over 600: 60%; ACT scores over 24: 89%; SAT critical reading scores over 700: 22%; SAT math scores over 700: 15%; SAT writing scores over 700: 17%; ACT scores over 30: 35%.

Faculty *Total:* 112, 85% full-time, 84% with terminal degrees. *Student/faculty ratio:* 14:1.

Academics *Calendar:* quarters. *Degree:* bachelor's. *Special study options:* advanced placement credit, double majors, independent study, internships, off-campus study, services for LD students, student-designed majors, study abroad. *ROTC:* Army (c). *Unusual degree programs:* 3-2 engineering with University of Michigan, Washington University in St. Louis; architecture with Washington University in St. Louis education with Michigan State University, University of Michigan.

Computers on Campus 130 computers/terminals are available on campus for general student use. Students can access the following: campus intranet, computer help desk, free student e-mail accounts, online (class) grades, online (class) registration, online (class) schedules. Campuswide network is available. 100% of college-owned or -operated housing units are wired for high-speed Internet access. Wireless service is available via classrooms, computer centers, computer labs, dorm rooms, learning centers, libraries, student centers.

Student Life *Housing:* on-campus residence required through junior year. *Options:* coed. Campus housing is university owned. Freshman campus housing is guaranteed. *Activities and organizations:* drama/theater group, student-run newspaper, radio and television station, choral group, Student Activities Committee, Student Commission, Frelon Dance Company, Environmental Student Organization, volunteer organization. *Campus security:* 24-hour emergency response devices and patrols, late-night transport/escort service, controlled dormitory access. *Student services:* health clinic, personal/psychological counseling.

Athletics Member NCAA. All Division III. *Intercollegiate sports:* baseball M, basketball M/W, cross-country running M/W, football M, golf M/W, soccer M/W, softball W, swimming and diving M/W, tennis M/W, volleyball W. *Intramural sports:* badminton M/W, basketball M/W, cheerleading W, fencing M/W, gymnastics M/W, lacrosse W(c), racquetball M/W, soccer M/W, softball M/W, swimming and diving M/W, table tennis M/W, tennis M(c)/W, ultimate Frisbee M(c)/W(c), volleyball M/W, water polo M/W.

Standardized Tests *Required:* SAT or ACT (for admission).

Costs (2010–11) *One-time required fee:* $100. *Comprehensive fee:* $42,210 includes full-time tuition ($34,017), mandatory fees ($300), and room and board ($7893). *College room only:* $3849. Room and board charges vary according to board plan. *Payment plan:* installment. *Waivers:* employees or children of employees.

Applying *Options:* electronic application, early decision, early action, deferred entrance. *Application fee:* $40. *Required:* essay or personal statement, high school transcript, 2 letters of recommendation, Common Application Supplement. *Recommended:* minimum 3 GPA, interview. *Application deadlines:* 2/1 (freshmen), 5/1 (transfers), 11/20 (early action). *Early decision deadline:* 11/10. *Notification:* 4/1 (freshmen), 5/15 (transfers), 11/20 (early decision), 12/20 (early action).

Freshman Application Contact Mrs. Linda Wirgau, Records Manager, Kalamazoo College, Mandelle Hall, 1200 Academy Street, Kalamazoo, MI 49006-3295. *Phone:* 269-337-7166. *Toll-free phone:* 800-253-3602. *Fax:* 269-337-7390. *E-mail:* admission@kzoo.edu. *Web site:* http://www.kzoo.edu/.

Kettering University

Flint, Michigan

- **Independent** comprehensive, founded 1919
- **Urban** 85-acre campus with easy access to Detroit
- **Endowment** $54.0 million
- **Coed, primarily men** 1,844 undergraduate students, 99% full-time, 18% women, 82% men
- **Very difficult** entrance level, 64% of applicants were admitted

Undergraduates 1,817 full-time, 27 part-time. Students come from 46 states and territories; 26 other countries; 30% are from out of state; 4% Black or African American, non-Hispanic/Latino; 3% Hispanic/Latino; 3% Asian, non-Hispanic/Latino; 0.5% American Indian or Alaska Native, non-Hispanic/Latino; 0.8% Two or more races, non-Hispanic/Latino; 10% Race/ethnicity unknown; 5% international; 2% transferred in; 26% live on campus. *Retention:* 89% of full-time freshmen returned.

Freshmen *Admission:* 2,646 applied, 1,696 admitted, 277 enrolled. *Average high school GPA:* 3.2. *Test scores:* SAT critical reading scores over 500: 89%; SAT math scores over 500: 98%; ACT scores over 18: 100%; SAT critical reading scores over 600: 55%; SAT math scores over 600: 78%; ACT scores over 24: 85%; SAT critical reading scores over 700: 22%; SAT math scores over 700: 29%; ACT scores over 30: 26%.

Faculty *Total:* 154, 81% full-time, 77% with terminal degrees. *Student/faculty ratio:* 14:1.

Academics *Calendar:* semesters (11 weeks of full-time study plus 12 weeks of paid co-op experience per semester). *Degrees:* bachelor's and master's. *Special study options:* advanced placement credit, cooperative education, distance learning, double majors, independent study, internships, services for LD students, study abroad, summer session for credit.

Computers on Campus 450 computers/terminals and 800 ports are available on campus for general student use. Students can access the following: campus intranet, computer help desk, free student e-mail accounts, online (class) grades, online (class) registration, online (class) schedules. Campuswide network is available. 100% of college-owned or -operated housing units are wired for high-speed Internet access. Wireless service is available via classrooms, computer centers, computer labs, learning centers, libraries, student centers.

Student Life *Housing:* on-campus residence required for freshman year. *Options:* coed. Campus housing is university owned and is provided by a third party. Freshman campus housing is guaranteed. *Activities and organizations:* drama/theater group, student-run newspaper, radio station, choral group, student government, Society of Automotive Engineers, Firebirds, Outdoors Club, International Club, national fraternities, national sororities. *Campus security:* 24-hour emergency response devices and patrols, late-night transport/escort service, controlled dormitory access, security card access to all campus buildings after 5:00pm. *Student services:* health clinic, personal/psychological counseling, women's center.

Athletics *Intercollegiate sports:* ice hockey M(c). *Intramural sports:* baseball M(c)/W(c), basketball M/W, bowling M/W, football M/W, golf M/W(c), ice hockey M/W, lacrosse M(c)/W(c), racquetball M/W, riflery M(c)/W(c), soccer M(c)/W(c), softball M/W, squash M/W, swimming and diving M(c)/W(c), table tennis M(c)/W(c), tennis M/W, ultimate Frisbee M(c)/W(c), volleyball M/W, water polo M/W.

Standardized Tests *Required:* SAT or ACT (for admission).

Costs (2010–11) *One-time required fee:* $310. *Comprehensive fee:* $35,556 includes full-time tuition ($28,672), mandatory fees ($444), and room and board ($6440). Part-time tuition: $896 per credit hour. *College room only:* $4000. *Payment plan:* installment. *Waivers:* employees or children of employees.

Financial Aid Of all full-time matriculated undergraduates who enrolled in 2009, 1,327 applied for aid, 1,246 were judged to have need, 195 had their need fully met. 1,147 Federal Work-Study jobs (averaging $1165). In 2009, 598 non-need-based awards were made. *Average percent of need met:* 67%. *Average financial aid package:* $19,931. *Average need-based loan:* $4374. *Average need-based gift aid:* $15,347. *Average non-need-based aid:* $12,223. *Average indebtedness upon graduation:* $45,570.

Applying *Options:* electronic application, deferred entrance. *Application fee:* $35. *Required:* high school transcript. *Required for some:* essay or personal statement. *Recommended:* minimum 3 GPA, interview. *Application deadlines:* rolling (freshmen), rolling (transfers). *Notification:* continuous (freshmen), continuous (transfers).

Freshman Application Contact Ms. Karen Full, Director, International and Undergraduate Admissions, Kettering University, 1700 University Avenue, Flint, MI 48504-6214. *Phone:* 810-762-7496. *Toll-free phone:* 800-955-4464 Ext. 7865 (in-state); 800-955-4464 (out-of-state). *Fax:* 810-762-9837. *E-mail:* admissions@kettering.edu. *Web site:* http://www.kettering.edu/.

See page 1366 for the College Close-Up.

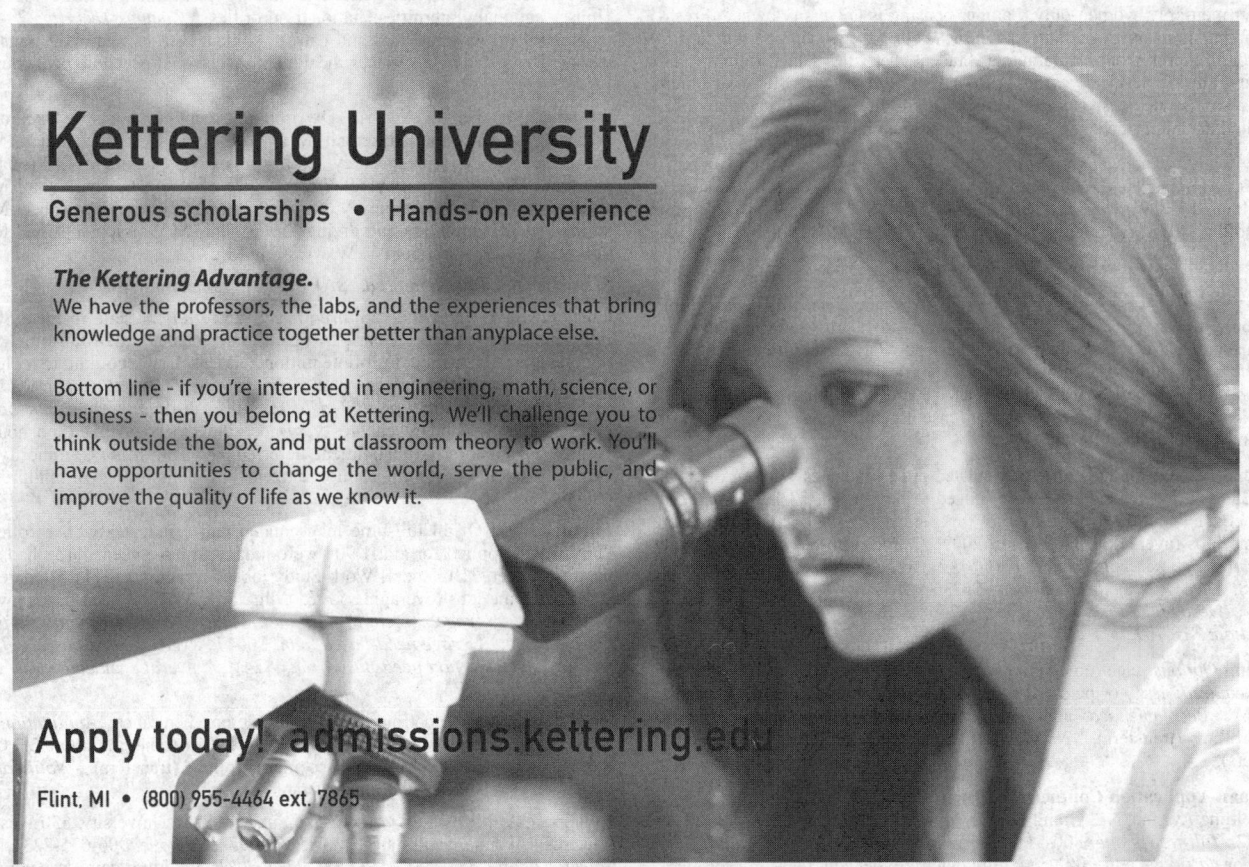

Kuyper College

Grand Rapids, Michigan

- **Independent religious** 4-year, founded 1939
- **Suburban** 34-acre campus with easy access to Grand Rapids
- **Endowment** $7.4 million
- **Coed** 344 undergraduate students, 85% full-time, 54% women, 46% men
- **Moderately difficult** entrance level, 88% of applicants were admitted

Undergraduates 294 full-time, 50 part-time. Students come from 17 states and territories; 12 other countries; 21% are from out of state; 3% Black or African American, non-Hispanic/Latino; 1% Hispanic/Latino; 2% Asian, non-Hispanic/Latino; 0.3% American Indian or Alaska Native, non-Hispanic/Latino; 3% Two or more races, non-Hispanic/Latino; 8% Race/ethnicity unknown; 4% international; 11% transferred in; 60% live on campus. *Retention:* 72% of full-time freshmen returned.

Freshmen *Admission:* 247 applied, 218 admitted, 52 enrolled. *Average high school GPA:* 3.21. *Test scores:* SAT critical reading scores over 500: 100%; SAT math scores over 500: 84%; SAT writing scores over 500: 80%; SAT critical reading scores over 600: 40%; SAT math scores over 600: 16%; SAT writing scores over 600: 20%.

Faculty *Total:* 43, 28% full-time, 23% with terminal degrees. *Student/faculty ratio:* 14:1.

Academics *Calendar:* semesters. *Degrees:* certificates, associate, bachelor's, and postbachelor's certificates. *Special study options:* academic remediation for entering students, advanced placement credit, cooperative education, distance learning, double majors, independent study, internships, off-campus study, part-time degree program, services for LD students, study abroad, summer session for credit. *ROTC:* Army (c).

Computers on Campus 70 computers/terminals and 70 ports are available on campus for general student use. Students can access the following: campus intranet, computer help desk, free student e-mail accounts, online (class) grades, online (class) registration, online (class) schedules. Campuswide network is available. 100% of college-owned or -operated housing units are wired for high-speed Internet access. Wireless service is available via entire campus.

Student Life *Housing:* on-campus residence required through sophomore year. *Options:* men-only, women-only. Campus housing is university owned. Freshman campus housing is guaranteed. *Activities and organizations:* drama/theater group, choral group, intramurals, Student Activities Club, Helping and Nurturing During Service, yearbook, Roots. *Campus security:* 24-hour emergency response devices, student patrols, late-night transport/escort service, controlled dormitory access. *Student services:* health clinic, personal/psychological counseling.

Athletics Member NCCAA. *Intercollegiate sports:* basketball M/W, soccer M, volleyball W. *Intramural sports:* basketball M/W, football M/W, soccer M/W, softball M/W, table tennis M/W, ultimate Frisbee M/W, volleyball M/W.

Standardized Tests *Required:* SAT or ACT (for admission).

Costs (2010–11) *Comprehensive fee:* $22,696 includes full-time tuition ($15,866), mandatory fees ($550), and room and board ($6280). Full-time tuition and fees vary according to course load. Part-time tuition: $760 per credit hour. Part-time tuition and fees vary according to course load. *Room and board:* Room and board charges vary according to board plan, housing facility, and student level. *Payment plan:* installment. *Waivers:* employees or children of employees.

Financial Aid Of all full-time matriculated undergraduates who enrolled in 2009, 284 applied for aid, 284 were judged to have need, 23 had their need fully met. 21 Federal Work-Study jobs (averaging $1192). 81 state and other part-time jobs (averaging $2000). In 2009, 27 non-need-based awards were made. *Average percent of need met:* 70%. *Average financial aid package:* $10,658. *Average need-based loan:* $6236. *Average need-based gift aid:* $5833. *Average non-need-based aid:* $2708. *Average indebtedness upon graduation:* $18,709.

Applying *Options:* electronic application, deferred entrance. *Application fee:* $30. *Required:* essay or personal statement, high school transcript, minimum 2.5 GPA. *Recommended:* interview. *Application deadlines:* rolling (freshmen), rolling (transfers). *Notification:* continuous (freshmen), continuous (transfers).

Freshman Application Contact Admissions Office, Kuyper College, 3333 East Beltline Avenue, NE, Grand Rapids, MI 49525. *Phone:* 616-222-3000 Ext. 632. *Toll-free phone:* 800-511-3749. *Fax:* 616-222-3045. *E-mail:* admissions@kuyper.edu. *Web site:* http://www.kuyper.edu/.

Lake Superior State University

Sault Sainte Marie, Michigan

- **State-supported** comprehensive, founded 1946
- **Small-town** 115-acre campus
- **Endowment** $12.8 million
- **Coed** 2,568 undergraduate students, 82% full-time, 51% women, 49% men
- **Moderately difficult** entrance level, 29% of applicants were admitted

Undergraduates 2,097 full-time, 471 part-time. Students come from 23 states and territories; 4 other countries; 14% are from out of state; 0.9% Black or African American, non-Hispanic/Latino; 1% Hispanic/Latino; 0.5% Asian, non-Hispanic/Latino; 9% American Indian or Alaska Native, non-Hispanic/Latino; 1% Race/ethnicity unknown; 9% international; 9% transferred in. *Retention:* 67% of full-time freshmen returned.

Freshmen *Admission:* 1,487 applied, 435 admitted, 424 enrolled. *Average high school GPA:* 3. *Test scores:* ACT scores over 18: 83%; ACT scores over 24: 30%; ACT scores over 30: 3%.

Faculty *Total:* 184, 63% full-time. *Student/faculty ratio:* 16:1.

Academics *Calendar:* semesters. *Degrees:* certificates, associate, bachelor's, master's, and postbachelor's certificates. *Special study options:* advanced placement credit, cooperative education, distance learning, double majors, freshman honors college, honors programs, independent study, internships, off-campus study, part-time degree program, services for LD students, student-designed majors, study abroad, summer session for credit.

Computers on Campus 350 computers/terminals are available on campus for general student use. Students can access the following: campus intranet, computer help desk, free student e-mail accounts, online (class) grades, online (class) registration, online (class) schedules. Campuswide network is available. 100% of college-owned or -operated housing units are wired for high-speed Internet access. Wireless service is available via entire campus.

Student Life *Housing:* on-campus residence required through sophomore year. *Options:* coed, men-only, women-only. Campus housing is university owned. Freshman campus housing is guaranteed. *Activities and organizations:* drama/theater group, student-run newspaper, radio station, choral group, Students in Free Enterprise (SIFE), SAILS - Student Alumni Involved in Lake State, Political Science Club, LSSNA-Lake State Nursing Association, Anchor House/His House, national fraternities, national sororities. *Campus security:* 24-hour emergency response devices and patrols, student patrols, late-night transport/escort service. *Student services:* health clinic, personal/psychological counseling.

Athletics Member NCAA. All Division II except ice hockey (Division I). *Intercollegiate sports:* basketball M(s)/W(s), cross-country running M(s)/W(s), golf M(s)/W(s), ice hockey M(s), softball W(s), tennis M(s)/W(s), track and field M(s)/W(s), volleyball W(s). *Intramural sports:* basketball M/W, cheerleading M/W, ice hockey M, racquetball M/W, riflery M/W, soccer M/W, softball M/W, swimming and diving M/W, tennis M/W, track and field M/W, volleyball M/W, water polo M/W, wrestling M(c).

Standardized Tests *Required:* SAT or ACT (for admission).

Costs (2010–11) *One-time required fee:* $125. *Tuition:* state resident $8664 full-time, $361 per credit hour part-time; nonresident $17,328 full-time, $722 per credit hour part-time. Full-time tuition and fees vary according to reciprocity agreements. Part-time tuition and fees vary according to course load and reciprocity agreements. *Required fees:* $100 full-time. *Room and board:* $8081. Room and board charges vary according to board plan and housing facility. *Payment plans:* installment, deferred payment. *Waivers:* minority students, children of alumni, senior citizens, and employees or children of employees.

Financial Aid Of all full-time matriculated undergraduates who enrolled in 2009, 1,904 applied for aid, 1,904 were judged to have need, 1,158 had their need fully met. 310 Federal Work-Study jobs (averaging $1411). 89 state and other part-time jobs (averaging $1161). In 2009, 231 non-need-based awards were made. *Average percent of need met:* 81%. *Average financial aid package:* $11,200. *Average need-based loan:* $6647. *Average need-based gift aid:* $5244. *Average non-need-based aid:* $2416. *Average indebtedness upon graduation:* $21,573.

Applying *Options:* electronic application, deferred entrance. *Application fee:* $35. *Required:* high school transcript. *Required for some:* minimum 2.2 GPA. *Application deadlines:* rolling (freshmen), rolling (transfers). *Notification:* continuous (freshmen), continuous (transfers).

Freshman Application Contact Lake Superior State University, 650 West Easterday Avenue, Sault Sainte Marie, MI 49783. *Phone:* 906-635-2231. *Toll-free phone:* 888-800-LSSU Ext. 2231. *Web site:* http://www.lssu.edu/.

Lawrence Technological University

Southfield, Michigan

- **Independent** university, founded 1932
- **Suburban** 102-acre campus with easy access to Detroit
- **Endowment** $35.0 million
- **Coed** 3,188 undergraduate students, 47% full-time, 25% women, 75% men
- **Moderately difficult** entrance level, 47% of applicants were admitted

Undergraduates 1,502 full-time, 1,686 part-time. Students come from 17 states and territories; 28 other countries; 2% are from out of state; 6% transferred in; 15% live on campus. *Retention:* 77% of full-time freshmen returned.

Freshmen *Admission:* 1,699 applied, 798 admitted, 274 enrolled. *Average high school GPA:* 3.36. *Test scores:* ACT scores over 18: 94%; ACT scores over 24: 51%; ACT scores over 30: 8%.

Faculty *Total:* 429, 28% full-time, 47% with terminal degrees. *Student/faculty ratio:* 11:1.

Academics *Calendar:* semesters. *Degrees:* certificates, associate, bachelor's, master's, doctoral-research/scholarship, and postbachelor's certificates. *Special study options:* academic remediation for entering students, accelerated degree program, adult/continuing education programs, advanced placement credit, cooperative education, distance learning, double majors, English as a second language, honors programs, independent study, internships, off-campus study, part-time degree program, services for LD students, study abroad, summer session for credit. *ROTC:* Air Force (c).

Computers on Campus 100 computers/terminals and 3,122 ports are available on campus for general student use. Students can access the following: campus intranet, computer help desk, free student e-mail accounts, online (class) grades, online (class) registration, online (class) schedules, degree audit, Blackboard, SCT Banner (student information). Campuswide network is available. 50% of college-owned or -operated housing units are wired for high-speed Internet access. Wireless service is available via entire campus.

Student Life *Housing:* on-campus residence required for freshman year. *Options:* coed, disabled students. Campus housing is university owned. Freshman applicants given priority for college housing. *Activities and organizations:* drama/theater group, student-run newspaper, American Institute of Architecture Students, American Society of Mechanical Engineers, Institute of Electric and Electronic Engineers, American Society of Civil Engineers, student government, national fraternities, national sororities. *Campus security:* 24-hour emergency response devices and patrols, late-night transport/escort service, controlled dormitory access. *Student services:* personal/psychological counseling.

Athletics *Intramural sports:* badminton M/W, basketball M/W, bowling M(c)/W(c), football M, golf M/W, ice hockey M(c), racquetball M/W, skiing (cross-country) M/W, skiing (downhill) M/W, soccer M(c)/W, softball M/W, table tennis M/W, tennis M/W, volleyball W(c), wrestling M.

Standardized Tests *Required:* ACT (preferred) (for admission).

Costs (2010–11) *Comprehensive fee:* $33,780 includes full-time tuition ($24,263), mandatory fees ($370), and room and board ($9147). Full-time tuition and fees vary according to course level, degree level, location, program, and student level. Part-time tuition: $809 per credit hour. Part-time tuition and fees vary according to course level, degree level, location, program, and student level. *Required fees:* $185 per term part-time. *College room only:* $5854. Room and board charges vary according to board plan and housing facility. *Payment plan:* installment. *Waivers:* employees or children of employees.

Financial Aid Of all full-time matriculated undergraduates who enrolled in 2008, 1,383 applied for aid, 1,098 were judged to have need, 92 had their need fully met. 102 Federal Work-Study jobs (averaging $1451). In 2008, 220 non-need-based awards were made. *Average percent of need met:* 62%. *Average financial aid package:* $19,256. *Average need-based loan:* $8129. *Average need-based gift aid:* $11,271. *Average non-need-based aid:* $9338. *Average indebtedness upon graduation:* $38,303.

Applying *Options:* electronic application, early admission, deferred entrance. *Application fee:* $30. *Required:* high school transcript, minimum 2.5 GPA. *Required for some:* essay or personal statement, minimum 2.75 GPA, 1 letter of recommendation, interview. *Application deadlines:* 8/15 (freshmen), 8/15 (transfers). *Notification:* continuous until 8/26 (freshmen), 8/26 (transfers).

Freshman Application Contact Jane Rohrback, Director of Admissions, Lawrence Technological University, 21000 West Ten Mile Road, Southfield, MI 48075. *Phone:* 248-204-3160. *Toll-free phone:* 800-225-5588. *Fax:* 248-204-2228. *E-mail:* admissions@ltu.edu. *Web site:* http://www.ltu.edu/.

See page 1374 for the College Close-Up.

Madonna University

Livonia, Michigan

- **Independent Roman Catholic** comprehensive, founded 1947
- **Suburban** 49-acre campus with easy access to Detroit
- **Endowment** $23.3 million
- **Coed** 3,252 undergraduate students, 54% full-time, 74% women, 26% men
- **Moderately difficult** entrance level

Undergraduates 1,755 full-time, 1,497 part-time. Students come from 9 states and territories; 22 other countries; 1% are from out of state; 14% transferred in; 6% live on campus. *Retention:* 81% of full-time freshmen returned.

Freshmen *Admission:* 806 applied, 199 enrolled. *Average high school GPA:* 3.26. *Test scores:* SAT critical reading scores over 500: 17%; SAT math scores over 500: 33%; SAT writing scores over 500: 17%; ACT scores over 18: 97%; SAT critical reading scores over 600: 17%; SAT math scores over 600: 17%; ACT scores over 24: 37%; ACT scores over 30: 3%.

Faculty *Total:* 396, 30% full-time, 97% with terminal degrees. *Student/faculty ratio:* 11:1.

Academics *Calendar:* semesters. *Degrees:* certificates, diplomas, associate, bachelor's, master's, doctoral-professional, post-master's, and postbachelor's certificates. *Special study options:* academic remediation for entering students, accelerated degree program, adult/continuing education programs, advanced placement credit, cooperative education, distance learning, double majors, English as a second language, independent study, internships, off-campus study, part-time degree program, services for LD students, student-designed majors, study abroad, summer session for credit. *ROTC:* Army (c).

Computers on Campus 104 computers/terminals and 104 ports are available on campus for general student use. Students can access the following: computer help desk, free student e-mail accounts, online (class) grades, online (class) registration, online (class) schedules, online payments, online statements, online Unofficial Transcripts. Campuswide network is available. 100% of college-owned or -operated housing units are wired for high-speed Internet access. Wireless service is available via classrooms, computer labs, dorm rooms, learning centers, libraries, student centers.

Student Life *Housing options:* men-only, women-only. Campus housing is university owned. Freshman campus housing is guaranteed. *Activities and organizations:* drama/theater group, student-run newspaper, radio station, choral group, Campus Ministry, Red Cross Club, Madonna University Nursing Student Association, Broadcast & Film Club, Society of Future Teachers. *Campus security:* 24-hour emergency response devices and patrols, late-night transport/escort service, controlled dormitory access. *Student services:* personal/psychological counseling.

Athletics Member NAIA. *Intercollegiate sports:* baseball M(s), basketball M(s)/W(s), cross-country running M(s)/W(s), golf M(s)/W(s), soccer M(s)/W(s), softball W(s), volleyball W(s). *Intramural sports:* basketball M/W, volleyball M/W.

Standardized Tests *Required:* SAT or ACT (for admission).

Costs (2010–11) *Comprehensive fee:* $20,960 includes full-time tuition ($13,740), mandatory fees ($100), and room and board ($7120). Full-time tuition and fees vary according to course load. Part-time tuition: $458 per credit hour. Part-time tuition and fees vary according to course load. *Required fees:* $50 per term part-time. *College room only:* $3200. Room and board charges vary according to board plan. *Payment plan:* deferred payment. *Waivers:* senior citizens and employees or children of employees.

Financial Aid Of all full-time matriculated undergraduates who enrolled in 2007, 862 applied for aid, 698 were judged to have need, 122 had their need fully met. In 2007, 172 non-need-based awards were made. *Average percent of need met:* 56%. *Average financial aid package:* $7396. *Average need-based loan:* $3862. *Average need-based gift aid:* $4508. *Average non-need-based aid:* $2427.

Applying *Options:* electronic application, early admission, deferred entrance. *Application fee:* $25. *Required:* essay or personal statement, high school transcript, minimum 2.75 GPA. *Required for some:* 2 letters of recommendation. *Recommended:* interview. *Application deadlines:* rolling (freshmen), rolling (transfers). *Notification:* continuous (freshmen), continuous (transfers).

Freshman Application Contact Mr. Mike Quattro, Director of Enrollment Management, Madonna University, 36600 Schoolcraft Road, Livonia, MI 48150-1173. *Phone:* 734-432-5341. *Toll-free phone:* 800-852-4951. *Fax:* 734-432-5393. *E-mail:* muinfo@madonna.edu. *Web site:* http://www.madonna.edu/.

Marygrove College

Detroit, Michigan

Freshman Application Contact Mr. John Ambrose, Director of Undergraduate Admissions, Marygrove College, Admissions Office, Detroit, MI 48221-2599. *Phone:* 313-927-1236. *Toll-free phone:* 866-313-1297. *Fax:* 313-927-1345. *E-mail:* info@marygrove.edu. *Web site:* http://www.marygrove.edu/.

www.facebook.com/find.colleges **433**

Michigan Jewish Institute
Oak Park, Michigan

Freshman Application Contact Mr. Dov Stein, Michigan Jewish Institute, 25401 Coolidge Highway, Oak Park, MI 48237. *Phone:* 248-414-6900 Ext. 103. *Fax:* 248-414-6907. *E-mail:* dstein@mji.edu. *Web site:* http://www.mji.edu/.

Michigan State University
East Lansing, Michigan

- **State-supported** university, founded 1855
- **Suburban** 5192-acre campus with easy access to Detroit
- **Endowment** $1.1 billion
- **Coed** 36,058 undergraduate students, 92% full-time, 52% women, 48% men
- **Moderately difficult** entrance level, 70% of applicants were admitted

Undergraduates 33,053 full-time, 3,005 part-time. Students come from 55 states and territories; 94 other countries; 9% are from out of state; 7% Black or African American, non-Hispanic/Latino; 3% Hispanic/Latino; 4% Asian, non-Hispanic/Latino; 0.1% Native Hawaiian or other Pacific Islander, non-Hispanic/Latino; 0.4% American Indian or Alaska Native, non-Hispanic/Latino; 2% Two or more races, non-Hispanic/Latino; 2% Race/ethnicity unknown; 8% international; 4% transferred in; 40% live on campus. *Retention:* 91% of full-time freshmen returned.

Freshmen *Admission:* 26,907 applied, 18,829 admitted, 7,375 enrolled. *Average high school GPA:* 3.6. *Test scores:* SAT critical reading scores over 500: 61%; SAT math scores over 500: 85%; SAT writing scores over 500: 65%; ACT scores over 18: 98%; SAT critical reading scores over 600: 29%; SAT math scores over 600: 52%; SAT writing scores over 600: 26%; ACT scores over 24: 71%; SAT critical reading scores over 700: 8%; SAT math scores over 700: 15%; SAT writing scores over 700: 6%; ACT scores over 30: 13%.

Faculty *Total:* 2,937, 86% full-time, 89% with terminal degrees. *Student/faculty ratio:* 16:1.

Academics *Calendar:* semesters. *Degrees:* certificates, bachelor's, master's, doctoral-research/scholarship, and post-master's certificates. *Special study options:* academic remediation for entering students, accelerated degree program, adult/continuing education programs, advanced placement credit, cooperative education, distance learning, double majors, English as a second language, freshman honors college, honors programs, independent study, internships, off-campus study, part-time degree program, services for LD students, student-designed majors, study abroad, summer session for credit. *ROTC:* Army (b), Air Force (b). *Unusual degree programs:* 3-2 engineering.

Computers on Campus 2,100 computers/terminals are available on campus for general student use. Students can access the following: campus intranet, computer help desk, free student e-mail accounts, online (class) grades, online (class) registration, online (class) schedules. Campuswide network is available. 100% of college-owned or -operated housing units are wired for high-speed Internet access. Wireless service is available via classrooms, computer centers, computer labs, dorm rooms, learning centers, libraries, student centers.

Student Life *Housing:* on-campus residence required for freshman year. *Options:* coed, women-only, cooperative, disabled students. Campus housing is university owned. Freshman campus housing is guaranteed. *Activities and organizations:* drama/theater group, student-run newspaper, radio and television station, choral group, marching band, national fraternities, national sororities. *Campus security:* 24-hour emergency response devices and patrols, late-night transport/escort service, controlled dormitory access, self-defense workshops. *Student services:* health clinic, personal/psychological counseling, women's center, legal services.

Athletics Member NCAA. All Division I except football (Division I-A). *Intercollegiate sports:* baseball M(s), basketball M(s)/W(s), cheerleading M/W, crew W(s), cross-country running M(s)/W(s), equestrian sports M(c)/W(c), field hockey W(s), golf M(s)/W(s), gymnastics W(s), ice hockey M(s)/W(s), lacrosse M(c)/W(c), racquetball M(c)/W(c), rugby M(c)/W(c), sailing M(c)/W(c), skiing (cross-country) M(c)/W(c), skiing (downhill) M(c)/W(c), soccer M(s)/W(s), softball W(s), swimming and diving M(s)/W(s), tennis M(s)/W(s), track and field M(s)/W(s), volleyball M(c)/W(c), water polo M(c)/W(c), wrestling M(s). *Intramural sports:* archery M/W, badminton M/W, baseball M, basketball M/W, bowling M/W, crew M/W, cross-country running M/W, fencing M/W, field hockey W, football M/W, golf M/W, gymnastics W, ice hockey M/W, lacrosse M/W, racquetball M/W, rugby M/W, sailing M/W, skiing (cross-country) M/W, skiing (downhill) M/W, soccer M/W, softball M/W, squash M/W, swimming and diving M/W, table tennis M/W, tennis M/W, track and field M/W, ultimate Frisbee M/W, volleyball M/W, water polo M/W, weight lifting M/W, wrestling M.

Standardized Tests *Required:* SAT or ACT (for admission).

Costs (2010–11) *Tuition:* state resident $11,153 full-time, $372 per credit hour part-time; nonresident $29,108 full-time, $970 per credit hour part-time. Full-time tuition and fees vary according to course load, degree level, program, and student level. Part-time tuition and fees vary according to course load, degree level, program, and student level. *Room and board:* $7770; room only: $3208. Room and board charges vary according to board plan and housing facility. *Payment plan:* deferred payment. *Waivers:* employees or children of employees.

Financial Aid Of all full-time matriculated undergraduates who enrolled in 2009, 21,550 applied for aid, 16,806 were judged to have need, 2,743 had their need fully met. 1,083 Federal Work-Study jobs (averaging $1570). In 2009, 1205 non-need-based awards were made. *Average percent of need met:* 47%. *Average financial aid package:* $9302. *Average need-based loan:* $4275. *Average need-based gift aid:* $8887. *Average non-need-based aid:* $7519. *Average indebtedness upon graduation:* $21,818.

Applying *Options:* electronic application, deferred entrance. *Application fee:* $50. *Required:* essay or personal statement, high school transcript. *Application deadlines:* rolling (freshmen), rolling (transfers). *Notification:* continuous (freshmen), continuous (transfers).

Freshman Application Contact James Cotter, Director of Admissions, Michigan State University, 250 Administration Building, East Lansing, MI 48824. *Phone:* 517-355-8332. *Fax:* 517-353-1647. *E-mail:* admis@msu.edu. *Web site:* http://www.msu.edu/.

Michigan Technological University
Houghton, Michigan

- **State-supported** university, founded 1885
- **Small-town** 925-acre campus
- **Coed**
- **Moderately difficult** entrance level

Faculty *Student/faculty ratio:* 15:1.

Academics *Calendar:* semesters. *Degrees:* certificates, associate, bachelor's, master's, doctoral-research/scholarship, and postbachelor's certificates.

Student Life *Campus security:* 24-hour emergency response devices and patrols, late-night transport/escort service, controlled dormitory access.

Athletics Member NCAA. All Division II except ice hockey (Division I).

Standardized Tests *Required:* SAT or ACT (for admission).

Costs (2010–11) *Tuition:* state resident $11,175 full-time, $373 per credit hour part-time; nonresident $23,685 full-time, $790 per credit hour part-time. Full-time tuition and fees vary according to course load and program. Part-time tuition and fees vary according to course load and program. *Required fees:* $842 full-time, $421 per term part-time. *Room and board:* $8462; room only: $4587. Room and board charges vary according to board plan and housing facility. *Payment plans:* installment, deferred payment.

Financial Aid *Of all full-time matriculated undergraduates who enrolled in 2009,* 4,308 applied for aid, 3,521 were judged to have need, 495 had their need fully met. *In 2009,* 1269 non-need-based awards were made. *Average percent of need met:* 70. *Average financial aid package:* $10,793. *Average need-based loan:* $4386. *Average need-based gift aid:* $5167. *Average non-need-based aid:* $4162. *Average indebtedness upon graduation:* $26,764.

Applying *Options:* electronic application, deferred entrance. *Required:* high school transcript. *Recommended:* minimum 2.75 GPA, interview.

Freshman Application Contact Ms. Allison Carter, Director of Admissions, Michigan Technological University, 1400 Townsend Drive, Houghton, MI 49931-1295. *Phone:* 906-487-2335. *Toll-free phone:* 888-MTU-1885. *Fax:* 906-487-2125. *E-mail:* mtu4u@mtu.edu. *Web site:* http://www.mtu.edu/.

See page 1428 for the College Close-Up.

Northern Michigan University
Marquette, Michigan

- **State-supported** comprehensive, founded 1899
- **Small-town** 300-acre campus
- **Endowment** $30.0 million
- **Coed** 8,578 undergraduate students, 91% full-time, 53% women, 47% men
- **Minimally difficult** entrance level, 73% of applicants were admitted

Undergraduates 7,794 full-time, 784 part-time. Students come from 45 states and territories; 17 other countries; 18% are from out of state; 6% transferred in; 35% live on campus. *Retention:* 73% of full-time freshmen returned.

Freshmen *Admission:* 5,955 applied, 4,338 admitted, 1,258 enrolled. *Average high school GPA:* 2.9. *Test scores:* ACT scores over 18: 95%; ACT scores over 24: 38%; ACT scores over 30: 5%.

Faculty *Total:* 462, 69% full-time, 55% with terminal degrees. *Student/faculty ratio:* 23:1.

Academics *Calendar:* semesters. *Degrees:* certificates, diplomas, associate, bachelor's, master's, post-master's, and postbachelor's certificates. *Special study options:* academic remediation for entering students, adult/continuing education programs, advanced placement credit, distance learning, double majors, honors programs, independent study, internships, off-campus study,

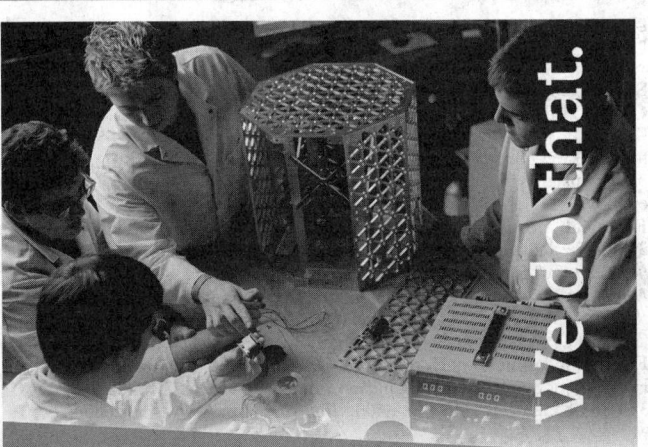

inspinnovation

(*n*, in-spin-uh-VAY-shun)

When inspiration meets innovation; like what you'll find at Michigan Tech. 130 innovative degree offerings, the Enterprise Program, and hundreds of internships and co-ops with some of the world's top companies, corporations, and organizations. *We do that.*

Michigan Tech enrolls more than 6,900 undergraduate and graduate students from across and nation and around the world. Our faculty explore the boundaries of knowledge while mentoring students to become citizens who will improve our world.

Tech students create the future in engineering; forest resources; computing; technology; business; economics; natural, physical, and environmental sciences; arts; humanities; and social sciences. Our students are in demand—in 2010, nearly 300 companies and organizations recruited on campus.

Great Education; Beautiful Location

We have our own ski hill, golf course, and on-campus forest and trails for cross country running, biking, hiking, and skiing. Lake Superior and many inland lakes and streams are nearby.

Campus traditions include Winter Carnival's massive snow statues; Parade of Nations, honoring 80 countries; and K-Day and Spring Fling student celebrations.

Michigan Tech
Create the Future

Michigan Technological University
Houghton, Michigan
mtu4u@mtu.edu
888-688-1885 • 906-487-2335

---

part-time degree program, services for LD students, student-designed majors, study abroad, summer session for credit. *ROTC:* Army (b).

Computers on Campus 9,500 computers/terminals are available on campus for general student use. Students can access the following: campus intranet, computer help desk, free student e-mail accounts, online (class) grades, online (class) registration, online (class) schedules. Campuswide network is available. 100% of college-owned or -operated housing units are wired for high-speed Internet access. Wireless service is available via entire campus.

Student Life *Housing:* on-campus residence required through sophomore year. *Options:* coed, disabled students. Campus housing is university owned. Freshman campus housing is guaranteed. *Activities and organizations:* drama/theater group, student-run newspaper, radio station, choral group, marching band, Superior Edge, Associated Students of Northern Michigan University, Skate and Snow Club, Campus Cinema, Northern Arts and Entertainment, national fraternities, national sororities. *Campus security:* 24-hour emergency response devices and patrols, student patrols, late-night transport/escort service. *Student services:* health clinic, personal/psychological counseling.

Athletics Member NCAA. All Division II except ice hockey (Division I). *Intercollegiate sports:* crew M(c)/W(c), cross-country running W(s), football M(s), golf M(s), ice hockey M(s)/W(c), lacrosse M(c), rugby M(c)/W(c), skiing (cross-country) M(s)/W(s), skiing (downhill) M(c)/W(c), soccer M(c)/W(s), track and field M(c)/W(s), ultimate Frisbee M/W, volleyball W(s). *Intramural sports:* badminton M/W, basketball M/W, cheerleading M/W, football M/W, ice hockey M/W, racquetball M/W, soccer M/W, softball M/W, table tennis M/W, ultimate Frisbee M/W, volleyball M/W, water polo M/W.

Standardized Tests *Required:* SAT or ACT (for admission).

Costs (2010–11) *One-time required fee:* $225. *Tuition:* state resident $7800 full-time, $302 per credit hour part-time; nonresident $12,216 full-time, $486 per credit hour part-time. Full-time tuition and fees vary according to program. Part-time tuition and fees vary according to program. *Required fees:* $616 full-time, $32 per term part-time. *Room and board:* $8026; room only: $3988. Room and board charges vary according to board plan and housing facility. *Payment plans:* installment, deferred payment. *Waivers:* senior citizens and employees or children of employees.

Financial Aid Of all full-time matriculated undergraduates who enrolled in 2008, 6,745 applied for aid, 4,730 were judged to have need, 618 had their need fully met. 486 Federal Work-Study jobs (averaging $1886). In 2008, 457 non-need-based awards were made. *Average percent of need met:* 63%. *Average financial aid package:* $8823. *Average need-based loan:* $3871. *Average need-based gift aid:* $5857. *Average non-need-based aid:* $2967. *Average indebtedness upon graduation:* $27,091.

Applying *Options:* electronic application, deferred entrance. *Application fee:* $30. *Required:* high school transcript. *Required for some:* minimum 2.25 GPA. *Application deadlines:* rolling (freshmen), rolling (transfers). *Notification:* continuous (freshmen), continuous (transfers).

Freshman Application Contact Ms. Gerri Daniels, Director of Admissions, Northern Michigan University, 1401 Preque Isle Avenue, Marquette, MI 49855. *Phone:* 906-227-2650. *Toll-free phone:* 800-682-9797. *Fax:* 906-227-1747. *E-mail:* admiss@nmu.edu. *Web site:* http://www.nmu.edu/.

Northwood University
Midland, Michigan

Freshman Application Contact Mr. Daniel F. Toland, Dean of Admission, Northwood University, 4000 Whiting Drive, Midland, MI 48640. *Phone:* 989-837-4273. *Toll-free phone:* 800-457-7878. *Fax:* 989-837-4490. *E-mail:* miadmit@northwood.edu. *Web site:* http://www.northwood.edu/.

Oakland University
Rochester, Michigan

- **State-supported** university, founded 1957
- **Suburban** 1444-acre campus with easy access to Detroit
- **Endowment** $50.9 million
- **Coed**
- **Moderately difficult** entrance level

Faculty *Student/faculty ratio:* 21:1.

Academics *Calendar:* semesters. *Degrees:* bachelor's, master's, doctoral-professional, doctoral-research/scholarship, post-master's, and postbachelor's certificates.

Student Life *Campus security:* 24-hour emergency response devices and patrols, student patrols, late-night transport/escort service, controlled dormitory access, security lighting, self-defense classes.

Athletics Member NCAA. All Division I.

Standardized Tests *Required for some:* ACT (for admission). *Recommended:* SAT or ACT (for admission).

Costs (2010–11) *Tuition:* state resident $9285 full-time, $310 per credit hour part-time; nonresident $21,675 full-time, $723 per credit hour part-time. Full-time tuition and fees vary according to program and student level. Part-time tuition and fees vary according to program and student level. *Room and board:* $7644. Room and board charges vary according to housing facility. *Payment plans:* installment, deferred payment.

Financial Aid *Of all full-time matriculated undergraduates who enrolled in 2008,* 8,356 applied for aid, 6,562 were judged to have need, 510 had their need fully met. *In 2008,* 1208 non-need-based awards were made. *Average percent of need met:* 65. *Average financial aid package:* $11,763. *Average need-based loan:* $8604. *Average need-based gift aid:* $4858. *Average non-need-based aid:* $2570. *Average indebtedness upon graduation:* $20,663.

Applying *Options:* electronic application, deferred entrance. *Required:* high school transcript, minimum 2.5 GPA. *Required for some:* minimum 3 GPA, interview, audition.

Freshman Application Contact Ms. Eleanor Reynolds, Interim Assistant Vice President, Student Affairs, Oakland University, Rochester, MI 48309-4401. *Phone:* 248-370-3364. *Toll-free phone:* 800-OAK-UNIV. *Fax:* 248-370-4462. *E-mail:* ouinfo@oakland.edu. *Web site:* http://www.oakland.edu/.

Olivet College
Olivet, Michigan

Freshman Application Contact Olivet College, 320 South Main Street, Olivet, MI 49076-9701. *Phone:* 269-749-7635. *Toll-free phone:* 800-456-7189. *Web site:* http://www.olivetcollege.edu/.

Rochester College
Rochester Hills, Michigan

- **Independent** comprehensive, founded 1959, affiliated with Church of Christ
- **Suburban** 83-acre campus with easy access to Detroit
- **Endowment** $1.5 million
- **Coed**
- **Minimally difficult** entrance level

Faculty *Student/faculty ratio:* 6:1.

Academics *Calendar:* semesters. *Degrees:* associate, bachelor's, and master's.

Student Life *Campus security:* 24-hour emergency response devices, late-night transport/escort service, controlled dormitory access, evening security guards.

Athletics Member NCCAA.

Standardized Tests *Required:* SAT or ACT (for admission).

Costs (2010–11) *Comprehensive fee:* $24,526 includes full-time tuition ($16,848), mandatory fees ($1632), and room and board ($6046). Full-time tuition and fees vary according to course load. Part-time tuition and fees vary according to course load. *Room and board:* Room and board charges vary according to housing facility.

Financial Aid *Of all full-time matriculated undergraduates who enrolled in 2007,* 130 Federal Work-Study jobs (averaging $1000). 71 state and other part-time jobs (averaging $2600).

Applying *Options:* electronic application, early admission, deferred entrance. *Application fee:* $25. *Required:* high school transcript, minimum 2.25 GPA. *Required for some:* interview. *Recommended:* essay or personal statement, 2 letters of recommendation.

Freshman Application Contact Mr. Larry Norman, Dean of Admissions, Rochester College, 800 West Avon Road, Rochester Hills, MI 48307-2764. *Phone:* 248-218-2190. *Toll-free phone:* 800-521-6010. *Fax:* 248-218-2035. *E-mail:* admissions@rc.edu. *Web site:* http://www.rc.edu/.

Sacred Heart Major Seminary
Detroit, Michigan

- **Independent Roman Catholic** comprehensive, founded 1919
- **Urban** 24-acre campus
- **Coed** 264 undergraduate students, 20% full-time, 41% women, 59% men
- **Moderately difficult** entrance level, 100% of applicants were admitted

Undergraduates 52 full-time, 212 part-time. 2% are from out of state; 3% Black or African American, non-Hispanic/Latino; 5% Hispanic/Latino; 3% Race/ethnicity unknown; 2% international; 8% transferred in; 16% live on campus. *Retention:* 83% of full-time freshmen returned.

Freshmen *Admission:* 1 applied, 1 admitted, 1 enrolled.

Faculty *Total:* 78, 36% full-time, 42% with terminal degrees. *Student/faculty ratio:* 5:1.

Academics *Calendar:* semesters. *Degrees:* diplomas, associate, bachelor's, master's, and postbachelor's certificates. *Special study options:* academic remediation for entering students, advanced placement credit, double majors, English as a second language, independent study, off-campus study, part-time degree program, services for LD students.

Student Life *Housing:* on-campus residence required through senior year. *Options:* Campus housing is university owned. Freshman campus housing is

guaranteed. *Activities and organizations:* choral group. *Campus security:* 24-hour emergency response devices, late-night transport/escort service. *Student services:* personal/psychological counseling.

Standardized Tests *Required:* SAT or ACT (for admission).

Costs (2010–11) *Comprehensive fee:* $23,538 includes full-time tuition ($15,170), mandatory fees ($100), and room and board ($8268). Part-time tuition: $355 per credit hour. *Required fees:* $50 per term part-time. *Payment plans:* installment, deferred payment. *Waivers:* employees or children of employees.

Financial Aid *Of all full-time matriculated undergraduates who enrolled in 2009,* 203 applied for aid, 203 were judged to have need. *Average percent of need met:* 70%. *Average financial aid package:* $2725.

Applying *Options:* early admission, deferred entrance. *Application fee:* $30. *Required:* essay or personal statement, high school transcript, minimum 2 GPA, 1 letter of recommendation, interview.

Freshman Application Contact Fr. Michael Byrnes, Vice Rector, Sacred Heart Major Seminary, 2701 Chicago Boulevard, Detroit, MI 48206. *Phone:* 313-883-8552. *Fax:* 313-868-6400. *Web site:* http://www.shms.edu/.

Saginaw Valley State University
University Center, Michigan

- **State-supported** comprehensive, founded 1963
- **Small-town** 782-acre campus
- **Endowment** $38.8 million
- **Coed** 9,116 undergraduate students, 84% full-time, 58% women, 42% men
- **Moderately difficult** entrance level, 81% of applicants were admitted

Undergraduates 7,629 full-time, 1,487 part-time. Students come from 22 states and territories; 26 other countries; 0.6% are from out of state; 7% transferred in; 29% live on campus. *Retention:* 68% of full-time freshmen returned.

Freshmen *Admission:* 6,173 applied, 5,009 admitted, 1,754 enrolled. *Average high school GPA:* 3.21. *Test scores:* ACT scores over 18: 84%; ACT scores over 24: 31%; ACT scores over 30: 3%.

Faculty *Total:* 597, 50% full-time. *Student/faculty ratio:* 22:1.

Academics *Calendar:* semesters plus summer session. *Degrees:* bachelor's, master's, and post-master's certificates. *Special study options:* academic remediation for entering students, accelerated degree program, adult/continuing education programs, advanced placement credit, cooperative education, distance learning, double majors, English as a second language, honors programs, independent study, internships, part-time degree program, services for LD students, student-designed majors, study abroad, summer session for credit.

Computers on Campus 1,033 computers/terminals are available on campus for general student use. Students can access the following: computer help desk, free student e-mail accounts, online (class) grades, online (class) registration, online (class) schedules. Campuswide network is available. Wireless service is available via dorm rooms, libraries, student centers.

Student Life *Housing options:* men-only, women-only, disabled students. Campus housing is university owned. Freshman campus housing is guaranteed. *Activities and organizations:* drama/theater group, student-run newspaper, choral group, marching band, His House Christian Fellowship, Criminal Justice Society, Delta Sigma Pi, Alpha Phi Omega, International Students Club, national fraternities, national sororities. *Campus security:* 24-hour emergency response devices and patrols, student patrols, late-night transport/escort service, controlled dormitory access, rape prevention program. *Student services:* health clinic, personal/psychological counseling.

Athletics Member NCAA. All Division II. *Intercollegiate sports:* baseball M(s), basketball M(s)/W(s), bowling M(s), cheerleading M/W, cross-country running M(s)/W(s), equestrian sports M(c)/W(c), football M(s), golf M(s), gymnastics M(c)/W, ice hockey M(c), lacrosse M(c)/W(c), rugby M(c)/W(c), soccer M(s)/W(s), softball W(s), tennis M(c)/W(s), track and field M(s)/W(s), ultimate Frisbee M(c)/W(c), volleyball W(s), wrestling M(c). *Intramural sports:* badminton M/W, basketball M/W, football M/W, golf M/W, soccer M/W, softball M/W, tennis M/W, volleyball M/W.

Standardized Tests *Required:* ACT (for admission).

Costs (2011–12) *Tuition:* state resident $6870 full-time, $229 per credit hour part-time; nonresident $16,719 full-time, $557 per credit hour part-time. Full-time tuition and fees vary according to course level, course load, location, and program. Part-time tuition and fees vary according to course level, course load, location, and program. *Required fees:* $438 full-time, $15 per credit hour part-time. *Room and board:* $7768; room only: $4815. Room and board charges vary according to board plan, housing facility, and student level. *Payment plan:* installment. *Waivers:* employees or children of employees.

Financial Aid *Of all full-time matriculated undergraduates who enrolled in 2008,* 6,168 applied for aid, 4,295 were judged to have need, 728 had their need fully met. 174 Federal Work-Study jobs (averaging $1938). 78 state and other part-time jobs (averaging $1895). *In 2008,* 705 non-need-based awards were made. *Average percent of need met:* 62%. *Average financial aid pack-*

age: $7086. *Average need-based loan:* $3816. *Average need-based gift aid:* $3432. *Average non-need-based aid:* $3745. *Average indebtedness upon graduation:* $23,555.

Applying *Options:* electronic application, deferred entrance. *Application fee:* $25. *Required:* high school transcript. *Recommended:* minimum 2.5 GPA. *Application deadlines:* rolling (freshmen), rolling (transfers). *Notification:* continuous (freshmen), continuous (transfers).

Freshman Application Contact Jennifer Pahl, Director of Admissions, Saginaw Valley State University, 7400 Bay Road, University Center, MI 48710-0001. *Phone:* 989-964-4200. *Toll-free phone:* 800-968-9500. *Fax:* 989-790-0180. *E-mail:* admissions@svsu.edu. *Web site:* http://www.svsu.edu/.

Siena Heights University

Adrian, Michigan

- **Independent Roman Catholic** comprehensive, founded 1919
- **Small-town** 140-acre campus with easy access to Detroit
- **Endowment** $7.7 million
- **Coed** 2,097 undergraduate students, 51% full-time, 58% women, 42% men
- **Moderately difficult** entrance level, 67% of applicants were admitted

Undergraduates 1,064 full-time, 1,033 part-time. Students come from 7 states and territories; 43 other countries; 5% are from out of state; 12% Black or African American, non-Hispanic/Latino; 4% Hispanic/Latino; 1% Asian, non-Hispanic/Latino; 0.1% Native Hawaiian or other Pacific Islander, non-Hispanic/Latino; 0.4% American Indian or Alaska Native, non-Hispanic/Latino; 1% Two or more races, non-Hispanic/Latino; 19% Race/ethnicity unknown; 1% international; 22% transferred in; 54% live on campus. *Retention:* 66% of full-time freshmen returned.

Freshmen *Admission:* 1,103 applied, 736 admitted, 201 enrolled. *Average high school GPA:* 3.12. *Test scores:* ACT scores over 18: 77%; ACT scores over 24: 19%; ACT scores over 30: 2%.

Faculty *Total:* 216, 31% full-time. *Student/faculty ratio:* 13:1.

Academics *Calendar:* semesters. *Degrees:* associate, bachelor's, and master's. *Special study options:* academic remediation for entering students, accelerated degree program, adult/continuing education programs, advanced placement credit, cooperative education, distance learning, double majors, English as a second language, independent study, internships, off-campus study, part-time degree program, services for LD students, student-designed majors, study abroad, summer session for credit.

Computers on Campus 75 computers/terminals are available on campus for general student use. Students can access the following: campus intranet, computer help desk, free student e-mail accounts, online (class) grades, online (class) registration, online (class) schedules. Campuswide network is available. 100% of college-owned or -operated housing units are wired for high-speed Internet access. Wireless service is available via entire campus.

Student Life *Housing:* on-campus residence required through sophomore year. *Options:* coed. Campus housing is university owned and is provided by a third party. Freshman campus housing is guaranteed. *Activities and organizations:* drama/theater group, student-run newspaper, choral group, International Club, Residence Hall Counsel, Student Senate, Sport Management Association, Gay Straight Alliance, national fraternities, national sororities. *Campus security:* 24-hour patrols, student patrols, late-night transport/escort service. *Student services:* health clinic, personal/psychological counseling.

Athletics Member NAIA. *Intercollegiate sports:* baseball M(s), basketball M(s)/W(s), bowling M(s)/W(s), cross-country running M(s)/W(s), football M(s), golf M(s)/W(s), lacrosse M(s)/W(s), soccer M(s)/W(s), softball W(s), track and field M(s)/W(s), volleyball M(s)/W(s). *Intramural sports:* basketball M/W, softball M/W, volleyball M/W.

Standardized Tests *Required:* SAT or ACT (for admission).

Costs (2011–12) *Comprehensive fee:* $27,997 includes full-time tuition ($19,937), mandatory fees ($620), and room and board ($7440). Full-time tuition and fees vary according to location. Part-time tuition and fees vary according to course load and location. *Room and board:* Room and board charges vary according to board plan, housing facility, and location. *Payment plans:* installment, deferred payment. *Waivers:* children of alumni, senior citizens, and employees or children of employees.

Financial Aid In 2002, 166 non-need-based awards were made. *Average percent of need met:* 66%. *Average financial aid package:* $12,200. *Average indebtedness upon graduation:* $13,500.

Applying *Options:* electronic application, deferred entrance. *Application fee:* $25. *Required:* high school transcript, transfer GPA 2.0. *Required for some:* essay or personal statement, interview. *Recommended:* minimum 2.5 GPA, interview. *Application deadlines:* rolling (freshmen), rolling (out-of-state freshmen), rolling (transfers).

Freshman Application Contact Ms. Sara Johnson, Director of Admissions, Siena Heights University, 1247 East Siena Heights Drive, Adrian, MI 49221. *Phone:* 517-264-7185. *Toll-free phone:* 800-521-0009. *Fax:* 517-264-7745. *E-mail:* sjohnson@sienaheights.edu. *Web site:* http://www.sienaheights.edu/.

South University

Novi, Michigan

- **Proprietary** comprehensive
- **Coed**

Academics *Degrees:* bachelor's and master's.

Director of Admissions Director of Admissions, South University, 41555 Twelve Mile Road, Novi, MI 48377. *Phone:* 248-675-0200. *Toll-free phone:* 877-693-2085. *Fax:* 248-675-0190.

See page 1628 for the College Close-Up.

Spring Arbor University

Spring Arbor, Michigan

- **Independent Free Methodist** comprehensive, founded 1873
- **Rural** 120-acre campus
- **Endowment** $9.1 million
- **Coed** 3,001 undergraduate students, 70% full-time, 68% women, 32% men
- **Moderately difficult** entrance level, 75% of applicants were admitted

Undergraduates 2,101 full-time, 900 part-time. Students come from 32 states and territories; 7 other countries; 13% are from out of state; 11% Black or African American, non-Hispanic/Latino; 3% Hispanic/Latino; 0.7% Asian, non-Hispanic/Latino; 0.4% American Indian or Alaska Native, non-Hispanic/Latino; 0.7% Two or more races, non-Hispanic/Latino; 0.6% Race/ethnicity unknown; 1% international; 4% transferred in; 72% live on campus. *Retention:* 71% of full-time freshmen returned.

Freshmen *Admission:* 2,550 applied, 1,914 admitted, 425 enrolled. *Average high school GPA:* 3.37. *Test scores:* SAT critical reading scores over 500: 62%; SAT math scores over 500: 77%; SAT writing scores over 500: 53%; ACT scores over 18: 89%; SAT critical reading scores over 600: 30%; SAT math scores over 600: 33%; SAT writing scores over 600: 21%; ACT scores over 24: 40%; SAT critical reading scores over 700: 6%; SAT math scores over 700: 9%; SAT writing scores over 700: 9%; ACT scores over 30: 6%.

Faculty *Total:* 139, 60% full-time, 47% with terminal degrees. *Student/faculty ratio:* 15:1.

Academics *Calendar:* 4-1-4. *Degrees:* associate, bachelor's, master's, and postbachelor's certificates. *Special study options:* academic remediation for entering students, accelerated degree program, adult/continuing education programs, advanced placement credit, distance learning, double majors, English as a second language, honors programs, independent study, internships, off-campus study, part-time degree program, services for LD students, student-designed majors, study abroad, summer session for credit. *ROTC:* Army (b), Air Force (c). *Unusual degree programs:* 3-2 engineering with University of Michigan, Michigan State University, Western Michigan University, Tri-State University.

Computers on Campus 251 computers/terminals and 1,193 ports are available on campus for general student use. Students can access the following: campus intranet, computer help desk, free student e-mail accounts, online (class) grades, online (class) registration, online (class) schedules. Campuswide network is available. 100% of college-owned or -operated housing units are wired for high-speed Internet access. Wireless service is available via entire campus.

Student Life *Housing:* on-campus residence required through senior year. *Options:* men-only, women-only, disabled students. Campus housing is university owned. Freshman campus housing is guaranteed. *Activities and organizations:* drama/theater group, student-run newspaper, radio and television station, choral group, Inter-faith Shelter Ministries, Band of Brothers, Action Jackson, Circle of Sisters, Heartside Homeless. *Campus security:* 24-hour emergency response devices and patrols, student patrols, late-night transport/escort service, controlled dormitory access. *Student services:* health clinic, personal/psychological counseling.

Athletics Member NAIA, NCCAA. *Intercollegiate sports:* baseball M(s), basketball M(s)/W(s), cross-country running M(s)/W(s), golf M(s), soccer M(s)/W(s), softball W(s), tennis M(s)/W(s), track and field M(s)/W(s), volleyball W(s). *Intramural sports:* basketball M/W, football M/W, soccer M/W, softball M/W, table tennis M/W, tennis M/W, ultimate Frisbee M/W, volleyball M/W.

Standardized Tests *Required:* SAT or ACT (for admission). *Recommended:* ACT (for admission).

Costs (2010–11) *Comprehensive fee:* $27,790 includes full-time tuition ($19,996), mandatory fees ($540), and room and board ($7254). Full-time tuition and fees vary according to course load, degree level, and program. Part-time tuition: $504 per credit hour. Part-time tuition and fees vary according to course load, degree level, program, and reciprocity agreements. *Required fees:* $225 per term part-time. *College room only:* $3400. Room and board charges vary according to board plan and housing facility. *Payment plan:* installment. *Waivers:* employees or children of employees.

Financial Aid Of all full-time matriculated undergraduates who enrolled in 2009, 1,351 applied for aid, 1,233 were judged to have need, 615 had their

need fully met. 384 Federal Work-Study jobs (averaging $794). 104 state and other part-time jobs (averaging $559). In 2009, 4 non-need-based awards were made. *Average percent of need met:* 91%. *Average financial aid package:* $22,445. *Average need-based loan:* $4394. *Average need-based gift aid:* $12,196. *Average non-need-based aid:* $6155. *Average indebtedness upon graduation:* $26,052.

Applying *Options:* electronic application, early admission, deferred entrance. *Application fee:* $30. *Required:* high school transcript. *Required for some:* essay or personal statement, interview. *Recommended:* minimum 2.6 GPA, Guidance counselor's form and ACT score of 20 or SAT score of 930 recommended. *Application deadlines:* 8/1 (freshmen), 8/1 (out-of-state freshmen), rolling (transfers). *Notification:* continuous (freshmen), continuous (out-of-state freshmen), continuous (transfers).

Freshman Application Contact Mr. Randy Comfort, Executive Director of Admissions, Spring Arbor University, 106 East Main Street, Spring Arbor, MI 49283-9799. *Phone:* 517-750-1200 Ext. 1468. *Toll-free phone:* 800-968-0011. *Fax:* 517-750-6620. *E-mail:* admissions@arbor.edu. *Web site:* http://www.arbor.edu/.

University of Detroit Mercy

Detroit, Michigan

Freshman Application Contact Office of Admissions, University of Detroit Mercy, 4001 West McNichols Road, Detroit, MI 48221-3038. *Phone:* 313-993-1245. *Toll-free phone:* 800-635-5020. *Fax:* 313-993-3326. *E-mail:* admissions@udmercy.edu. *Web site:* http://www.udmercy.edu/.

University of Michigan

Ann Arbor, Michigan

- **State-supported** university, founded 1817
- **Small-town** 3177-acre campus
- **Endowment** $6.8 billion
- **Coed** 27,027 undergraduate students, 97% full-time, 49% women, 51% men
- **Very difficult** entrance level, 51% of applicants were admitted

Undergraduates 26,185 full-time, 842 part-time. Students come from 56 states and territories; 86 other countries; 32% are from out of state; 4% Black or African American, non-Hispanic/Latino; 4% Hispanic/Latino; 12% Asian, non-Hispanic/Latino; 0.2% American Indian or Alaska Native, non-Hispanic/Latino; 3% Two or more races, non-Hispanic/Latino; 3% Race/ethnicity unknown; 6% international; 4% transferred in; 37% live on campus. *Retention:* 96% of full-time freshmen returned.

Freshmen *Admission:* 31,613 applied, 16,006 admitted, 6,481 enrolled. *Average high school GPA:* 3.76. *Test scores:* SAT critical reading scores over 500: 98%; SAT math scores over 500: 98%; SAT writing scores over 500: 97%; ACT scores over 18: 100%; SAT critical reading scores over 600: 75%; SAT math scores over 600: 88%; SAT writing scores over 600: 80%; ACT scores over 24: 94%; SAT critical reading scores over 700: 23%; SAT math scores over 700: 49%; SAT writing scores over 700: 31%; ACT scores over 30: 50%.

Faculty *Total:* 3,085, 81% full-time, 88% with terminal degrees. *Student/faculty ratio:* 15:1.

Academics *Calendar:* trimesters. *Degrees:* bachelor's, master's, doctoral-professional, doctoral-research/scholarship, post-master's, and postbachelor's certificates. *Special study options:* accelerated degree program, adult/continuing education programs, advanced placement credit, cooperative education, distance learning, double majors, honors programs, independent study, internships, off-campus study, part-time degree program, services for LD students, student-designed majors, study abroad, summer session for credit. *ROTC:* Army (b), Navy (b), Air Force (b). *Unusual degree programs:* 3-2 business administration; engineering; music; art and design.

Computers on Campus 2,529 computers/terminals are available on campus for general student use. Students can access the following: computer help desk, free student e-mail accounts, online (class) grades, online (class) registration, online (class) schedules, file storage. Campuswide network is available. 97% of college-owned or -operated housing units are wired for high-speed Internet access. Wireless service is available via entire campus.

Student Life *Housing options:* coed, women-only, cooperative. Campus housing is university owned. Freshman campus housing is guaranteed. *Activities and organizations:* drama/theater group, student-run newspaper, radio and television station, choral group, marching band, Hillel Society, K-Grams (Kids' Program), M-Powered Entrepreneurial Club, Dance Marathon, Alternative Spring Break, national fraternities, national sororities. *Campus security:* 24-hour emergency response devices and patrols, student patrols, late-night transport/escort service, controlled dormitory access, Safewalk, Night Owl ride service. *Student services:* health clinic, personal/psychological counseling, women's center, legal services.

Athletics Member NCAA. All Division I except football (Division I-A). *Intercollegiate sports:* baseball M(s), basketball M(s)/W(s), cheerleading M/

W, crew M(c), cross-country running M(s)/W(s), field hockey W(s), golf M(s), gymnastics M(s)/W(s), ice hockey M(s), soccer M(s)/W(s), softball W(s), swimming and diving M(s)/W(s), tennis M(s)/W(s), track and field M(s)/W(s), volleyball W(s), water polo W(s), wrestling M(s). *Intramural sports:* badminton M/W, baseball M(c)/W(c), basketball M/W, crew M(c)/W(c), fencing M(c)/W(c), field hockey M(c)/W(c), golf M/W, gymnastics W(c), ice hockey M(c)/W(c), lacrosse M(c)/W(c), racquetball M/W, riflery M(c)/W(c), rugby M(c)/W(c), sailing M(c)/W(c), soccer M(c)/W(c), softball M(c)/W(c), swimming and diving M(c)/W(c), table tennis M/W, tennis M(c)/W(c), track and field M/W, ultimate Frisbee M(c)/W(c), volleyball M/W, water polo M(c)/W(c), wrestling M(c).

Standardized Tests *Required:* SAT or ACT (for admission). *Required for some:* SAT Subject Tests (for admission).

Costs (2010–11) *Tuition:* state resident $12,590 full-time, $456 per credit hour part-time; nonresident $37,265 full-time, $1463 per credit hour part-time. Full-time tuition and fees vary according to course load, program, and student level. Part-time tuition and fees vary according to course load, program, and student level. *Required fees:* $189 full-time, $95 per term part-time. *Room and board:* $9192. Room and board charges vary according to board plan and housing facility. *Payment plan:* installment.

Financial Aid Of all full-time matriculated undergraduates who enrolled in 2008, 16,272 applied for aid, 12,061 were judged to have need, 10,855 had their need fully met. 3,037 Federal Work-Study jobs (averaging $1583). In 2008, 8300 non-need-based awards were made. *Average percent of need met:* 90%. *Average financial aid package:* $13,269. *Average need-based loan:* $4173. *Average need-based gift aid:* $10,783. *Average non-need-based aid:* $6036. *Average indebtedness upon graduation:* $27,828. *Financial aid deadline:* 5/31.

Applying *Options:* electronic application, early action, deferred entrance. *Application fee:* $65. *Required:* essay or personal statement, high school transcript. *Required for some:* interview, audition for School of Music, Theatre and Dance; portfolio for School of Art and Design. *Application deadlines:* 1/31 (freshmen), 1/31 (out-of-state freshmen), 1/31 (transfers), 11/1 (early action). *Notification:* continuous (freshmen), continuous (out-of-state freshmen), continuous (transfers), 12/22 (early action).

Freshman Application Contact University of Michigan, Ann Arbor, MI 48109. *Phone:* 734-764-7433. *Web site:* http://www.umich.edu/.

University of Michigan–Dearborn

Dearborn, Michigan

- **State-supported** comprehensive, founded 1959, part of University of Michigan System
- **Suburban** 210-acre campus with easy access to Detroit
- **Endowment** $25.0 million
- **Coed** 7,006 undergraduate students, 69% full-time, 52% women, 48% men
- **Moderately difficult** entrance level, 64% of applicants were admitted

Undergraduates 4,836 full-time, 2,170 part-time. 0.4% are from out of state; 11% Black or African American, non-Hispanic/Latino; 4% Hispanic/Latino; 5% Asian, non-Hispanic/Latino; 0.5% American Indian or Alaska Native, non-Hispanic/Latino; 2% Two or more races, non-Hispanic/Latino; 12% Race/ethnicity unknown; 0.7% international; 12% transferred in. *Retention:* 83% of full-time freshmen returned.

Freshmen *Admission:* 4,091 applied, 2,614 admitted, 911 enrolled. *Average high school GPA:* 3.55. *Test scores:* ACT scores over 18: 100%; ACT scores over 24: 53%; ACT scores over 30: 9%.

Faculty *Total:* 535, 57% full-time, 61% with terminal degrees. *Student/faculty ratio:* 16:1.

Academics *Calendar:* semesters. *Degrees:* bachelor's, master's, doctoral-research/scholarship, and postbachelor's certificates. *Special study options:* academic remediation for entering students, adult/continuing education programs, advanced placement credit, cooperative education, distance learning, double majors, honors programs, independent study, internships, off-campus study, part-time degree program, services for LD students, student-designed majors, study abroad, summer session for credit. *ROTC:* Army (c), Navy (c), Air Force (c).

Computers on Campus 695 computers/terminals are available on campus for general student use. Students can access the following: computer help desk, free student e-mail accounts, online (class) grades, online (class) registration, online (class) schedules, tuition and application payments accepted online. Campuswide network is available. Wireless service is available via entire campus.

Student Life *Housing:* college housing not available. *Activities and organizations:* drama/theater group, student-run newspaper, radio and television station, choral group, Dearborn Campus Engineers, student radio station, Volunteer Dearborn, Intervarsity Christian Fellowship, Muslim Students Association, national fraternities, national sororities. *Campus security:* 24-hour emergency response devices and patrols, late-night transport/escort service.

Student services: health clinic, personal/psychological counseling, women's center.

Athletics Member NAIA. *Intercollegiate sports:* basketball M(s)/W(s), bowling M(c)/W(c), cheerleading M(c)/W(c), cross-country running M(c)/W(c), ice hockey M(c), rugby M(c), soccer M(c)/W(c), softball W(s), ultimate Frisbee M(c), volleyball W(s). *Intramural sports:* basketball M/W, cross-country running M(c)/W(c), fencing M(c)/W(c), volleyball M/W.

Standardized Tests *Required:* SAT or ACT (for admission).

Costs (2010–11) *Tuition:* state resident $8908 full-time, $353 per credit hour part-time; nonresident $20,111 full-time, $800 per credit hour part-time. Full-time tuition and fees vary according to course level, course load, degree level, program, and student level. Part-time tuition and fees vary according to course level, course load, degree level, program, and student level. *Required fees:* $548 full-time, $222 per term part-time. *Payment plan:* installment. *Waivers:* senior citizens and employees or children of employees.

Financial Aid Of all full-time matriculated undergraduates who enrolled in 2008, 3,460 applied for aid, 2,700 were judged to have need, 1,293 had their need fully met. 199 Federal Work-Study jobs (averaging $1658). In 2008, 1201 non-need-based awards were made. *Average percent of need met:* 72%. *Average financial aid package:* $10,287. *Average need-based loan:* $4335. *Average need-based gift aid:* $5926. *Average non-need-based aid:* $4568. *Average indebtedness upon graduation:* $19,463.

Applying *Options:* electronic application, deferred entrance. *Application fee:* $30. *Required:* high school transcript, minimum 3 GPA. *Required for some:* interview. *Application deadlines:* rolling (freshmen), rolling (transfers). *Notification:* continuous (freshmen), continuous (transfers).

Freshman Application Contact Ms. Deb Peffer, Interim Director of Admissions, University of Michigan–Dearborn, 4901 Evergreen Road, Room 1145 UC, Dearborn, MI 48128-1491. *Phone:* 313-593-5100. *Fax:* 313-436-9167. *E-mail:* admissions@umd.umich.edu. *Web site:* http://www.umd.umich.edu/.

University of Michigan–Flint

Flint, Michigan

- **State-supported** comprehensive, founded 1956, part of University of Michigan System
- **Urban** 72-acre campus with easy access to Detroit, Lansing
- **Endowment** $67.4 million
- **Coed** 6,879 undergraduate students, 66% full-time, 60% women, 40% men
- **Moderately difficult** entrance level, 72% of applicants were admitted

Undergraduates 4,538 full-time, 2,341 part-time. Students come from 40 states and territories; 29 other countries; 2% are from out of state; 11% transferred in; 4% live on campus. *Retention:* 72% of full-time freshmen returned.

Freshmen *Admission:* 2,952 applied, 2,139 admitted, 781 enrolled. *Average high school GPA:* 3.23. *Test scores:* SAT critical reading scores over 500: 43%; SAT math scores over 500: 57%; SAT writing scores over 500: 57%; ACT scores over 18: 88%; SAT critical reading scores over 600: 7%; SAT math scores over 600: 29%; SAT writing scores over 600: 7%; ACT scores over 24: 33%; SAT math scores over 700: 7%; ACT scores over 30: 5%.

Faculty *Total:* 509, 53% full-time, 48% with terminal degrees. *Student/faculty ratio:* 17:1.

Academics *Calendar:* semesters. *Degrees:* bachelor's, master's, and doctoral-professional. *Special study options:* academic remediation for entering students, accelerated degree program, adult/continuing education programs, advanced placement credit, cooperative education, distance learning, double majors, English as a second language, honors programs, independent study, internships, off-campus study, part-time degree program, services for LD students, student-designed majors, study abroad, summer session for credit. *ROTC:* Army (c), Navy (c), Air Force (c). *Unusual degree programs:* 3-2 business administration.

Computers on Campus 770 computers/terminals are available on campus for general student use. Students can access the following: campus intranet, computer help desk, free student e-mail accounts, online (class) grades, online (class) registration, online (class) schedules. Campuswide network is available. 100% of college-owned or -operated housing units are wired for high-speed Internet access. Wireless service is available via entire campus.

Student Life *Housing options:* coed. Campus housing is university owned. *Activities and organizations:* drama/theater group, student-run newspaper, choral group, Students Moving the UCEN Forward (SMUF), International Student Organization, Muslim Student Association, Kappa Sigma Fraternity, Inter-Varsity Christian Fellowship, national fraternities, national sororities. *Campus security:* 24-hour emergency response devices and patrols, student patrols, late-night transport/escort service, controlled dormitory access. *Student services:* health clinic, personal/psychological counseling, women's center.

Athletics *Intramural sports:* basketball M/W, cheerleading M(c)/W(c), football M(c)/W(c), golf M(c)/W(c), ice hockey M(c)/W(c), racquetball M/W, soccer M/W, volleyball M(c)/W(c).

Standardized Tests *Required:* SAT or ACT (for admission).

Costs (2010–11) *One-time required fee:* $30. *Tuition:* state resident $8195 full-time, $323 per credit hour part-time; nonresident $15,993 full-time, $646 per credit hour part-time. Full-time tuition and fees vary according to course level, course load, degree level, program, and student level. Part-time tuition and fees vary according to course level, course load, degree level, program, and student level. *Required fees:* $406 full-time, $155 per term part-time. *Room and board:* $7212; room only: $4526. Room and board charges vary according to board plan. *Payment plan:* installment. *Waivers:* senior citizens.

Financial Aid Of all full-time matriculated undergraduates who enrolled in 2009, 3,644 applied for aid, 3,039 were judged to have need, 172 had their need fully met. In 2009, 224 non-need-based awards were made. *Average percent of need met:* 77%. *Average financial aid package:* $11,846. *Average need-based loan:* $4119. *Average need-based gift aid:* $6046. *Average non-need-based aid:* $2314. *Average indebtedness upon graduation:* $25,945.

Applying *Options:* electronic application, deferred entrance. *Application fee:* $30. *Required:* high school transcript. *Application deadline:* 8/19 (transfers). *Notification:* continuous (freshmen), continuous (out-of-state freshmen), continuous (transfers).

Freshman Application Contact University of Michigan–Flint, 303 East Kearsley Street, Flint, MI 48502-1950. *Phone:* 810-762-3300. *Toll-free phone:* 800-942-5636. *Web site:* http://www.umflint.edu/.

University of Phoenix–Metro Detroit Campus

Troy, Michigan

Freshman Application Contact Ms. Audra McQuarie, Registrar/Executive Director, University of Phoenix–Metro Detroit Campus, 4035 South Riverpoint Parkway, Mail Stop CF-L101, Phoenix, AZ 85040. *Phone:* 480-557-6151. *Toll-free phone:* 800-776-4867 (in-state); 800-228-7240 (out-of-state). *Fax:* 480-643-3068. *E-mail:* audra.mcquarie@phoenix.edu. *Web site:* http://www.phoenix.edu/.

University of Phoenix–West Michigan Campus

Walker, Michigan

Freshman Application Contact Ms. Audra McQuarie, Registrar/Executive Director, University of Phoenix–West Michigan Campus, 4035 South Riverpoint Parkway, Mail Stop CF-L101, Phoenix, AZ 85040. *Phone:* 480-557-6151. *Toll-free phone:* 800-776-4867 (in-state); 800-228-7240 (out-of-state). *Fax:* 480-643-3068. *E-mail:* audra.mcquarie@phoenix.edu. *Web site:* http://www.phoenix.edu/.

Walsh College of Accountancy and Business Administration

Troy, Michigan

Application Contact Walsh College of Accountancy and Business Administration, 3838 Livernois Road, PO Box 7006, Troy, MI 48007-7006. *Phone:* 248-823-1344. *Toll-free phone:* 800-925-7401. *Web site:* http://www.walshcollege.edu/.

Wayne State University

Detroit, Michigan

- **State-supported** university, founded 1868
- **Urban** 210-acre campus with easy access to Detroit
- **Endowment** $241.4 million
- **Coed** 20,837 undergraduate students, 65% full-time, 58% women, 42% men
- **Moderately difficult** entrance level, 86% of applicants were admitted

Undergraduates 13,561 full-time, 7,276 part-time. Students come from 42 states and territories; 44 other countries; 2% are from out of state; 30% Black or African American, non-Hispanic/Latino; 3% Hispanic/Latino; 7% Asian, non-Hispanic/Latino; 0.4% American Indian or Alaska Native, non-Hispanic/Latino; 0.5% Two or more races, non-Hispanic/Latino; 8% Race/ethnicity unknown; 3% international; 9% transferred in; 10% live on campus. *Retention:* 77% of full-time freshmen returned.

Freshmen *Admission:* 9,397 applied, 8,117 admitted, 2,683 enrolled. *Average high school GPA:* 3.17. *Test scores:* ACT scores over 18: 73%; ACT scores over 24: 29%; ACT scores over 30: 5%.

Faculty *Total:* 1,908, 54% full-time. *Student/faculty ratio:* 17:1.

Academics *Calendar:* semesters. *Degrees:* certificates, bachelor's, master's, doctoral-professional, doctoral-research/scholarship, post-master's, and post-bachelor's certificates. *Special study options:* academic remediation for entering students, accelerated degree program, adult/continuing education programs, advanced placement credit, cooperative education, distance learning, double majors, English as a second language, freshman honors college, honors programs, independent study, internships, off-campus study, part-time degree program, services for LD students, study abroad, summer session for credit. *ROTC:* Army (b), Air Force (c).

Computers on Campus 2,877 computers/terminals are available on campus for general student use. Students can access the following: computer help desk, free student e-mail accounts, online (class) grades, online (class) registration, online (class) schedules. Campuswide network is available. 100% of college-owned or -operated housing units are wired for high-speed Internet access. Wireless service is available via entire campus.

Student Life *Housing options:* coed, disabled students. Campus housing is university owned. Freshman applicants given priority for college housing. *Activities and organizations:* student-run newspaper, choral group, marching band, Muslim Students Association, Honors Students Association, Indian Students Association, American Medical Students Association-Pre-Med Chapter, national fraternities, national sororities. *Campus security:* 24-hour emergency response devices and patrols, late-night transport/escort service, controlled dormitory access. *Student services:* health clinic, personal/psychological counseling, legal services.

Athletics Member NCAA. All Division II except men's and women's fencing (Division I), ice hockey (Division I). *Intercollegiate sports:* baseball M(s), basketball M(s)/W(s), cross-country running W(s), fencing M(s)/W(s), football M(s), golf M(s), ice hockey W(s), softball W(s), swimming and diving M(s)/W(s), tennis M(s)/W(s), volleyball W(s). *Intramural sports:* badminton M/W, basketball M/W, bowling M/W, cheerleading M/W, field hockey M/W, football M/W, racquetball M/W, soccer M/W, softball M/W, table tennis M/W, tennis M/W, ultimate Frisbee M/W, volleyball M/W.

Standardized Tests *Required:* SAT or ACT (for admission).

Costs (2010–11) *Tuition:* state resident $7904 full-time, $263 per credit hour part-time; nonresident $18,104 full-time, $603 per credit hour part-time. Full-time tuition and fees vary according to course load, program, reciprocity agreements, and student level. Part-time tuition and fees vary according to course load, program, reciprocity agreements, and student level. *Required fees:* $1122 full-time, $25 per credit hour part-time, $188 per term part-time. *Room and board:* $7500; room only: $4750. Room and board charges vary according to board plan and housing facility. *Payment plan:* installment. *Waivers:* senior citizens and employees or children of employees.

Financial Aid Of all full-time matriculated undergraduates who enrolled in 2008, 10,224 applied for aid, 9,093 were judged to have need, 5,724 had their need fully met. 500 Federal Work-Study jobs (averaging $2521). In 2008, 1247 non-need-based awards were made. *Average percent of need met:* 72%. *Average financial aid package:* $19,836. *Average need-based loan:* $4473. *Average need-based gift aid:* $7192. *Average non-need-based aid:* $5782. *Average indebtedness upon graduation:* $20,250. *Financial aid deadline:* 4/30.

Applying *Options:* electronic application, deferred entrance. *Application fee:* $30. *Required:* high school transcript, minimum 2 GPA. *Required for some:* interview, portfolio. *Application deadlines:* 8/1 (freshmen), 8/1 (transfers). *Notification:* 8/1 (freshmen), continuous until 8/1 (transfers).

Freshman Application Contact Ms. La Joyce Brown, Associate Director, Recruitment and Outreach, Wayne State University, 42 West Warren, Undergraduate Admissions, Student Development and Campus Life, Detroit 48202. *Phone:* 313-577-4906. *Toll-free phone:* 877-WSU-INFO. *E-mail:* admissions@wayne.edu. *Web site:* http://www.wayne.edu/.

Western Michigan University
Kalamazoo, Michigan

- **State-supported** university, founded 1903
- **Urban** 1200-acre campus
- **Endowment** $153.8 million
- **Coed** 19,547 undergraduate students, 87% full-time, 49% women, 51% men
- **Moderately difficult** entrance level, 83% of applicants were admitted

Undergraduates 17,043 full-time, 2,504 part-time. Students come from 46 states and territories; 62 other countries; 6% are from out of state; 8% Black or African American, non-Hispanic/Latino; 4% Hispanic/Latino; 1% Asian, non-Hispanic/Latino; 0.1% Native Hawaiian or other Pacific Islander, non-Hispanic/Latino; 0.4% American Indian or Alaska Native, non-Hispanic/Latino; 3% Two or more races, non-Hispanic/Latino; 2% Race/ethnicity unknown; 3% international; 8% transferred in; 24% live on campus. *Retention:* 72% of full-time freshmen returned.

Freshmen *Admission:* 12,379 applied, 10,253 admitted, 3,193 enrolled. *Average high school GPA:* 3.24. *Test scores:* ACT scores over 18: 91%; ACT scores over 24: 33%; ACT scores over 30: 3%.

Faculty *Total:* 1,435, 63% full-time. *Student/faculty ratio:* 19:1.

Academics *Calendar:* semesters. *Degrees:* bachelor's, master's, doctoral-professional, doctoral-research/scholarship, post-master's, and postbachelor's certificates. *Special study options:* academic remediation for entering students, accelerated degree program, adult/continuing education programs, advanced placement credit, cooperative education, distance learning, double majors, English as a second language, freshman honors college, honors programs, independent study, internships, off-campus study, part-time degree program, services for LD students, student-designed majors, study abroad, summer session for credit. *ROTC:* Army (b).

Computers on Campus 2,000 computers/terminals are available on campus for general student use. Students can access the following: computer help desk, free student e-mail accounts, online (class) grades, online (class) registration, online (class) schedules. Campuswide network is available. 25% of college-owned or -operated housing units are wired for high-speed Internet access. Wireless service is available via entire campus.

Student Life *Housing options:* coed, men-only, women-only, disabled students. Campus housing is university owned. *Activities and organizations:* drama/theater group, student-run newspaper, radio station, choral group, marching band, Campus Activities Board, Western Student Association, Young Black Male Support Network, Drive Safe Kalamazoo, Alternative Spring Break, national fraternities, national sororities. *Campus security:* 24-hour emergency response devices and patrols, student patrols, late-night transport/escort service, controlled dormitory access. *Student services:* health clinic, personal/psychological counseling, women's center, legal services.

Athletics Member NCAA. All Division I except football (Division I-A). *Intercollegiate sports:* baseball M(s), basketball M(s)/W(s), golf W(s), gymnastics W(s), ice hockey M(s), soccer M(s)/W(s), softball W(s), tennis M(s)/W(s), track and field W(s), volleyball W(s). *Intramural sports:* badminton M/W, basketball M/W, bowling M/W, equestrian sports M(c)/W(c), fencing M(c)/W(c), football M/W, golf M, ice hockey M(c)/W(c), lacrosse M(c)/W(c), racquetball M/W, rugby M(c)/W(c), sailing M(c)/W(c), skiing (downhill) M(c)/W(c), soccer M/W, softball M/W, swimming and diving M/W, table tennis M/W, tennis M/W, ultimate Frisbee M/W, volleyball M/W.

Standardized Tests *Required:* SAT or ACT (for admission).

Costs (2010–11) *One-time required fee:* $300. *Tuition:* state resident $8182 full-time, $283 per credit hour part-time; nonresident $20,070 full-time, $694 per credit hour part-time. Full-time tuition and fees vary according to course load, location, program, and student level. Part-time tuition and fees vary according to course load, location, program, and student level. *Required fees:* $824 full-time, $223 per term part-time. *Room and board:* $8095; room only: $4167. Room and board charges vary according to board plan. *Payment plan:* installment. *Waivers:* senior citizens and employees or children of employees.

Financial Aid Of all full-time matriculated undergraduates who enrolled in 2007, 11,000 applied for aid, 9,000 were judged to have need, 4,000 had their need fully met. 691 Federal Work-Study jobs (averaging $2000). 218 state and other part-time jobs (averaging $2000). In 2007, 1600 non-need-based awards were made. *Average percent of need met:* 85%. *Average financial aid package:* $13,000. *Average need-based loan:* $4300. *Average need-based gift aid:* $5000. *Average non-need-based aid:* $2900. *Average indebtedness upon graduation:* $18,900.

Applying *Options:* electronic application, deferred entrance. *Application fee:* $35. *Required:* high school transcript. *Required for some:* interview. *Application deadlines:* rolling (freshmen), 8/1 (transfers). *Notification:* continuous (freshmen), continuous (transfers).

Freshman Application Contact Western Michigan University, 1903 West Michigan Avenue, Kalamazoo, MI 49008. *Phone:* 269-387-2000. *Web site:* http://www.wmich.edu/.

See page 1780 for the College Close-Up.

Yeshiva Gedolah of Greater Detroit
Oak Park, Michigan

Director of Admissions Rabbi P. Rushnawitz, Director, Yeshiva Gedolah of Greater Detroit, 24600 Greenfield, Oak Park, MI 48237-1544.

MINNESOTA

Academy College
Minneapolis, Minnesota

Freshman Application Contact Ms. Tracey Schantz, Director, Academy College, Bloomington, MN 55420. *Phone:* 952-851-0066. *Toll-free phone:* 800-292-9149. *Fax:* 952-851-0094. *E-mail:* admissions@academycollege.edu. *Web site:* http://www.academycollege.edu/.

Argosy University, Twin Cities

Eagan, Minnesota

- **Proprietary** university, founded 1961, part of Education Management Corporation
- **Suburban** campus
- **Coed**

Academics *Calendar:* semesters. *Degrees:* associate, bachelor's, master's, doctoral-professional, and post-master's certificates.

Costs (2010–11) *Tuition:* Tuition varies by program. Students should contact Argosy University for tuition information.

Freshman Application Contact Argosy University, Twin Cities, 1515 Central Parkway, Eagan, MN 55121. *Phone:* 651-846-2882. *Toll-free phone:* 888-844-2004. *Web site:* http://www.argosy.edu/twincities/.

See page 1004 for the College Close-Up.

The Art Institutes International Minnesota

Minneapolis, Minnesota

- **Proprietary** 4-year, founded 1964, part of Education Management Corporation
- **Urban** campus
- **Coed**

Academics *Calendar:* quarters. *Degrees:* certificates, associate, and bachelor's.

Costs (2010–11) *Tuition:* Tuition cost varies by program. Prospective students should contact the school for current tuition costs. Other charges include a starting kit for all first-quarter students. Kits vary in price, depending on the program of study.

Freshman Application Contact The Art Institutes International Minnesota, 15 South 9th Street, Minneapolis, MN 55402. *Phone:* 612-332-3361. *Toll-free phone:* 800-777-3643. *Web site:* http://www.artinstitutes.edu/minneapolis/.

See page 1088 for the College Close-Up.

Augsburg College

Minneapolis, Minnesota

- **Independent Lutheran** comprehensive, founded 1869
- **Urban** 23-acre campus with easy access to Minneapolis-St.Paul
- **Endowment** $28.2 million
- **Coed** 3,153 undergraduate students, 84% full-time, 55% women, 45% men
- **Moderately difficult** entrance level, 54% of applicants were admitted

Undergraduates 2,635 full-time, 518 part-time. Students come from 39 states and territories; 21 other countries; 14% are from out of state; 9% Black or African American, non-Hispanic/Latino; 3% Hispanic/Latino; 7% Asian, non-Hispanic/Latino; 0.2% Native Hawaiian or other Pacific Islander, non-Hispanic/Latino; 2% American Indian or Alaska Native, non-Hispanic/Latino; 2% Two or more races, non-Hispanic/Latino; 6% Race/ethnicity unknown; 2% international; 11% transferred in; 51% live on campus. *Retention:* 83% of full-time freshmen returned.

Freshmen *Admission:* 2,192 applied, 1,187 admitted, 417 enrolled. *Average high school GPA:* 3.04. *Test scores:* SAT critical reading scores over 500: 83%; SAT math scores over 500: 80%; ACT scores over 18: 89%; SAT critical reading scores over 600: 37%; SAT math scores over 600: 43%; ACT scores over 24: 40%; SAT critical reading scores over 700: 14%; SAT math scores over 700: 3%; ACT scores over 30: 3%.

Faculty *Total:* 403, 48% full-time, 68% with terminal degrees. *Student/faculty ratio:* 16:1.

Academics *Calendar:* semesters for undergraduate programs; trimesters for graduate programs and weekend college. *Degrees:* certificates, bachelor's, master's, doctoral-professional, post-master's, and postbachelor's certificates. *Special study options:* academic remediation for entering students, adult/continuing education programs, advanced placement credit, cooperative education, double majors, English as a second language, freshman honors college, honors programs, independent study, internships, off-campus study, part-time degree program, services for LD students, student-designed majors, study abroad, summer session for credit. *ROTC:* Army (c), Navy (c), Air Force (c). *Unusual degree programs:* 3-2 engineering with Michigan Technological University, University of Minnesota, Twin Cities Campus.

Computers on Campus 260 computers/terminals are available on campus for general student use. Students can access the following: campus intranet, computer help desk, free student e-mail accounts, online (class) grades, online (class) registration, online (class) schedules. Campuswide network is available. 100% of college-owned or -operated housing units are wired for high-speed Internet access. Wireless service is available via entire campus.

Student Life *Housing options:* coed, men-only, women-only, disabled students. Campus housing is university owned. Freshman applicants given prior-

ity for college housing. *Activities and organizations:* drama/theater group, student-run newspaper, radio station, choral group, Student Activities Council, student government, newspaper/yearbook, campus ministry, intramurals. *Campus security:* 24-hour emergency response devices and patrols, student patrols, late-night transport/escort service, controlled dormitory access. *Student services:* health clinic, personal/psychological counseling, women's center.

Athletics Member NCAA. All Division III. *Intercollegiate sports:* baseball M, basketball M/W, cross-country running M/W, football M, golf M/W, ice hockey M/W, soccer M/W, softball W, swimming and diving W, track and field M/W, volleyball W, wrestling M. *Intramural sports:* basketball M/W, football M, skiing (cross-country) M(c)/W(c), skiing (downhill) M(c)/W(c), softball M/W, volleyball M/W, wrestling M.

Standardized Tests *Recommended:* SAT or ACT (for admission).

Costs (2011–12) *Comprehensive fee:* $38,490 includes full-time tuition ($29,794), mandatory fees ($624), and room and board ($8072). Full-time tuition and fees vary according to location. Part-time tuition: $3599 per course. Part-time tuition and fees vary according to course load and location. *College room only:* $4116. Room and board charges vary according to board plan and housing facility. *Payment plan:* installment. *Waivers:* children of alumni, senior citizens, and employees or children of employees.

Financial Aid Of all full-time matriculated undergraduates who enrolled in 2009, 2,338 applied for aid, 2,033 were judged to have need, 233 had their need fully met. 363 Federal Work-Study jobs (averaging $2850). 818 state and other part-time jobs (averaging $2843). In 2009, 292 non-need-based awards were made. *Average percent of need met:* 67%. *Average financial aid package:* $20,143. *Average need-based loan:* $4902. *Average need-based gift aid:* $16,115. *Average non-need-based aid:* $8739. *Average indebtedness upon graduation:* $24,311. *Financial aid deadline:* 8/15.

Applying *Options:* electronic application, deferred entrance. *Application fee:* $25. *Required:* essay or personal statement, high school transcript, minimum 2.5 GPA, interview. *Required for some:* 2 letters of recommendation. *Application deadlines:* 8/15 (freshmen), 8/15 (transfers). *Notification:* continuous (freshmen), continuous (transfers).

Freshman Application Contact Ms. Carrie Carroll, Assistant Vice President for Admissions, Augsburg College, 2211 Riverside Avenue, Minneapolis, MN 55454-1351. *Phone:* 612-330-1001. *Toll-free phone:* 800-788-5678. *Fax:* 612-330-1590. *E-mail:* admissions@augsburg.edu. *Web site:* http://www.augsburg.edu/.

Bemidji State University

Bemidji, Minnesota

- **State-supported** comprehensive, founded 1919, part of Minnesota State Colleges and Universities System
- **Small-town** 89-acre campus
- **Endowment** $10.5 million
- **Coed** 4,932 undergraduate students, 77% full-time, 52% women, 48% men
- **Moderately difficult** entrance level, 78% of applicants were admitted

Undergraduates 3,788 full-time, 1,144 part-time. Students come from 36 states and territories; 40 other countries; 10% are from out of state; 1% Black or African American, non-Hispanic/Latino; 0.7% Hispanic/Latino; 0.8% Asian, non-Hispanic/Latino; 0.2% Native Hawaiian or other Pacific Islander, non-Hispanic/Latino; 4% American Indian or Alaska Native, non-Hispanic/Latino; 2% Race/ethnicity unknown; 3% international; 10% transferred in; 28% live on campus. *Retention:* 73% of full-time freshmen returned.

Freshmen *Admission:* 2,325 applied, 1,818 admitted, 875 enrolled. *Average high school GPA:* 3.14. *Test scores:* ACT scores over 18: 92%; ACT scores over 24: 28%; ACT scores over 30: 2%.

Faculty *Total:* 276, 66% full-time, 49% with terminal degrees. *Student/faculty ratio:* 20:1.

Academics *Calendar:* semesters. *Degrees:* associate, bachelor's, and master's. *Special study options:* academic remediation for entering students, adult/continuing education programs, advanced placement credit, cooperative education, distance learning, double majors, English as a second language, external degree program, honors programs, independent study, internships, off-campus study, part-time degree program, services for LD students, study abroad, summer session for credit.

Computers on Campus 1,200 computers/terminals are available on campus for general student use. Students can access the following: computer help desk, free student e-mail accounts, online (class) grades, online (class) registration, online (class) schedules. Campuswide network is available. Wireless service is available via entire campus.

Student Life *Housing options:* coed, disabled students. Campus housing is university owned. Freshman applicants given priority for college housing. *Activities and organizations:* drama/theater group, student-run newspaper, radio and television station, choral group, International Students Organization, Intervarsity Christian Fellowship, Madrigal Dinner Club, Student Senate, Council of Indian Students. *Campus security:* 24-hour emergency response

PROFILES

devices and patrols, late-night transport/escort service, controlled dormitory access. *Student services:* health clinic, personal/psychological counseling.

Athletics Member NCAA. All Division II except men's and women's ice hockey (Division I). *Intercollegiate sports:* baseball M(s), basketball M(s)/W(s), cross-country running W(s), football M(s), golf M(s)/W(s), ice hockey M(s)/W(s), soccer W(s), softball W(s), tennis W(s), track and field W(s), volleyball W(s). *Intramural sports:* basketball M/W, football M, ice hockey M/W, soccer M/W, softball M/W, volleyball M/W.

Standardized Tests *Required:* ACT (for admission), SAT or ACT (for admission).

Costs (2011–12) *Tuition:* state resident $6577 full-time, $230 per credit part-time; nonresident $6577 full-time, $230 per credit part-time. Full-time tuition and fees vary according to course load, location, program, and reciprocity agreements. Part-time tuition and fees vary according to course load, location, program, and reciprocity agreements. *Required fees:* $936 full-time, $93 per credit part-time. *Room and board:* $6480. Room and board charges vary according to board plan and housing facility. *Payment plan:* installment. *Waivers:* senior citizens and employees or children of employees.

Financial Aid Of all full-time matriculated undergraduates who enrolled in 2009, 3,053 applied for aid, 2,450 were judged to have need, 460 had their need fully met. 280 Federal Work-Study jobs (averaging $1286). 158 state and other part-time jobs (averaging $1185). In 2009, 582 non-need-based awards were made. *Average percent of need met:* 68%. *Average financial aid package:* $8995. *Average need-based loan:* $4020. *Average need-based gift aid:* $5403. *Average non-need-based aid:* $9246. *Average indebtedness upon graduation:* $26,799.

Applying *Options:* electronic application, deferred entrance. *Application fee:* $20. *Required:* high school transcript. *Required for some:* essay or personal statement, interview. *Application deadlines:* rolling (freshmen), rolling (transfers). *Notification:* continuous (freshmen), continuous (transfers).

Freshman Application Contact Bemidji State University, 1500 Birchmont Drive, NE, Bemidji, MN 56601-2699. *Phone:* 218-755-2602. *Toll-free phone:* 800-475-2001 (in-state); 800-652-9747 (out-of-state). *Web site:* http://www.bemidjistate.edu/.

Bethany Lutheran College

Mankato, Minnesota

- **Independent Lutheran** 4-year, founded 1927
- **Small-town** 50-acre campus
- **Endowment** $31.2 million
- **Coed** 607 undergraduate students, 96% full-time, 56% women, 44% men
- **Moderately difficult** entrance level, 83% of applicants were admitted

Undergraduates 583 full-time, 24 part-time. Students come from 23 states and territories; 8 other countries; 23% are from out of state; 2% Black or African American, non-Hispanic/Latino; 2% Hispanic/Latino; 1% Asian, non-Hispanic/Latino; 0.3% American Indian or Alaska Native, non-Hispanic/Latino; 2% Two or more races, non-Hispanic/Latino; 10% Race/ethnicity unknown; 1% international; 7% transferred in; 71% live on campus. *Retention:* 76% of full-time freshmen returned.

Freshmen *Admission:* 453 applied, 378 admitted, 165 enrolled. *Average high school GPA:* 3.35. *Test scores:* ACT scores over 18: 96%; ACT scores over 24: 46%; ACT scores over 30: 12%.

Faculty *Total:* 83, 51% full-time, 30% with terminal degrees. *Student/faculty ratio:* 12:1.

Academics *Calendar:* semesters. *Degree:* bachelor's. *Special study options:* academic remediation for entering students, advanced placement credit, double majors, independent study, internships, services for LD students, study abroad. *ROTC:* Army (c). *Unusual degree programs:* 3-2 engineering with University of Minnesota-Twin Cities.

Computers on Campus 100 computers/terminals are available on campus for general student use. Students can access the following: campus intranet, computer help desk, free student e-mail accounts, online (class) grades, online (class) registration, online (class) schedules. Campuswide network is available. 100% of college-owned or -operated housing units are wired for high-speed Internet access. Wireless service is available via entire campus.

Student Life *Housing:* on-campus residence required through sophomore year. *Options:* men-only, women-only. Campus housing is university owned. Freshman campus housing is guaranteed. *Activities and organizations:* drama/theater group, student-run newspaper, television station, choral group, Student Senate, Paul Ylvisaker Center, BLC Scholastic Leadership Society, Lambda Pi Eta, Bethany Activities Committee. *Campus security:* 24-hour emergency response devices and patrols, late-night transport/escort service, controlled dormitory access. *Student services:* personal/psychological counseling.

Athletics Member NCAA. All Division III. *Intercollegiate sports:* baseball M, basketball M/W, cross-country running M/W, equestrian sports M(c)/W(c), golf M/W, soccer M/W, softball W, tennis M/W, track and field M(c)/W(c), volleyball W. *Intramural sports:* basketball M/W, football M/W, racquetball M/W, table tennis M/W, ultimate Frisbee M/W, volleyball M/W.

Standardized Tests *Required:* SAT or ACT (for admission).

Costs (2010–11) *One-time required fee:* $130. *Comprehensive fee:* $27,450 includes full-time tuition ($20,650), mandatory fees ($300), and room and board ($6500). Part-time tuition: $870 per credit hour. *Required fees:* $150 per term part-time. *College room only:* $2890. Room and board charges vary according to board plan and housing facility. *Payment plan:* installment. *Waivers:* employees or children of employees.

Financial Aid Of all full-time matriculated undergraduates who enrolled in 2008, 583 applied for aid, 531 were judged to have need, 145 had their need fully met. 33 Federal Work-Study jobs (averaging $1217). 256 state and other part-time jobs (averaging $738). In 2008, 83 non-need-based awards were made. *Average percent of need met:* 85%. *Average financial aid package:* $16,769. *Average need-based loan:* $4778. *Average need-based gift aid:* $12,414. *Average non-need-based aid:* $5487. *Average indebtedness upon graduation:* $26,519.

Applying *Options:* electronic application. *Required:* essay or personal statement, high school transcript, minimum 2.4 GPA. *Required for some:* interview. *Recommended:* minimum 3.2 GPA, interview. *Application deadline:* 7/1 (freshmen). *Notification:* continuous (transfers).

Freshman Application Contact Mr. Don Westphal, Dean of Admissions, Bethany Lutheran College, 700 Luther Drive, Mankato, MN 56001. *Phone:* 507-344-7320. *Toll-free phone:* 800-944-3066 Ext. 331. *Fax:* 507-344-7376. *E-mail:* dwestpha@blc.edu. *Web site:* http://www.blc.edu/.

Bethel University

St. Paul, Minnesota

- **Independent** comprehensive, founded 1871, affiliated with Baptist General Conference
- **Suburban** 247-acre campus with easy access to Minneapolis-St. Paul
- **Endowment** $31.9 million
- **Coed** 3,388 undergraduate students, 81% full-time, 62% women, 38% men
- **Moderately difficult** entrance level, 80% of applicants were admitted

Undergraduates 2,733 full-time, 655 part-time. Students come from 40 states and territories; 9 other countries; 22% are from out of state; 3% Black or African American, non-Hispanic/Latino; 1% Hispanic/Latino; 2% Asian, non-Hispanic/Latino; 0.1% Native Hawaiian or other Pacific Islander, non-Hispanic/Latino; 0.1% American Indian or Alaska Native, non-Hispanic/Latino; 2% Two or more races, non-Hispanic/Latino; 13% Race/ethnicity unknown; 0.3% international; 2% transferred in; 69% live on campus. *Retention:* 86% of full-time freshmen returned.

Freshmen *Admission:* 2,065 applied, 1,655 admitted, 588 enrolled. *Average high school GPA:* 3.52. *Test scores:* ACT scores over 18: 99%; ACT scores over 24: 64%; ACT scores over 30: 16%.

Faculty *Total:* 303, 60% full-time, 60% with terminal degrees. *Student/faculty ratio:* 12:1.

Academics *Calendar:* 4-1-4. *Degrees:* associate, bachelor's, master's, doctoral-professional, doctoral-research/scholarship, post-master's, and postbachelor's certificates. *Special study options:* academic remediation for entering students, accelerated degree program, adult/continuing education programs, advanced placement credit, double majors, honors programs, independent study, internships, off-campus study, part-time degree program, services for LD students, student-designed majors, study abroad, summer session for credit. *ROTC:* Army (c), Air Force (c). *Unusual degree programs:* 3-2 engineering with University of Minnesota; other institutions by arrangement.

Computers on Campus 460 computers/terminals are available on campus for general student use. Students can access the following: campus intranet, computer help desk, free student e-mail accounts, online (class) grades, online (class) registration, online (class) schedules. Campuswide network is available. 100% of college-owned or -operated housing units are wired for high-speed Internet access. Wireless service is available via classrooms, computer centers, computer labs, dorm rooms, learning centers, libraries, student centers.

Student Life *Housing:* on-campus residence required through sophomore year. *Options:* coed, disabled students. Campus housing is university owned. Freshman campus housing is guaranteed. *Activities and organizations:* drama/theater group, student-run newspaper, radio station, choral group, Campus Ministries Small Groups, Pre-Medical Club, College Democrats/College Republicans, Student Activities, Tri Beta (Biology Honors Society). *Campus security:* 24-hour emergency response devices and patrols, student patrols, late-night transport/escort service, controlled dormitory access, video surveillance for residents halls, academic buildings, and parking lots. *Student services:* health clinic, personal/psychological counseling.

Athletics Member NCAA. All Division III. *Intercollegiate sports:* baseball M, basketball M/W, cross-country running M/W, football M, golf M/W, ice hockey M/W, soccer M/W, softball W, tennis M/W, track and field M/W, volleyball M(c)/W. *Intramural sports:* badminton M/W, basketball M/W, football M, ice hockey M(c), lacrosse M(c)/W(c), rugby M(c), softball M/W, volleyball M/W.

Standardized Tests *Required:* SAT or ACT (for admission).

Costs (2011–12) *Comprehensive fee:* $37,990 includes full-time tuition ($29,320), mandatory fees ($140), and room and board ($8530). Part-time tuition: $1225 per credit. Part-time tuition and fees vary according to course load. *College room only:* $4900. Room and board charges vary according to board plan. *Payment plans:* tuition prepayment, installment. *Waivers:* employees or children of employees.

Financial Aid Of all full-time matriculated undergraduates who enrolled in 2009, 2,247 applied for aid, 1,973 were judged to have need, 315 had their need fully met. 375 Federal Work-Study jobs (averaging $2200). 1,200 state and other part-time jobs (averaging $2000). In 2009, 547 non-need-based awards were made. *Average percent of need met:* 76%. *Average financial aid package:* $20,930. *Average need-based loan:* $4655. *Average need-based gift aid:* $14,941. *Average non-need-based aid:* $6877. *Average indebtedness upon graduation:* $32,698.

Applying *Options:* electronic application, early admission, deferred entrance. *Required:* essay or personal statement, high school transcript, rank in upper 50% of high school class. *Required for some:* 2 letters of recommendation. *Recommended:* minimum 2.5 GPA, interview. *Application deadlines:* rolling (freshmen), rolling (out-of-state freshmen), rolling (transfers). *Notification:* continuous (freshmen), continuous (out-of-state freshmen), continuous (transfers).

Freshman Application Contact Admissions Office, Bethel University, 3900 Bethel Drive, St. Paul, MN 55112. *Phone:* 651-638-6242. *Toll-free phone:* 800-255-8706 Ext. 6242. *Fax:* 651-635-1490. *E-mail:* buadmissions-cas@bethel.edu. *Web site:* http://www.bethel.edu/.

Brown College
Mendota Heights, Minnesota

Freshman Application Contact Mr. Mark Fredrichs, Registrar, Brown College, 1440 Northland Drive, Mendota Heights, MN 55120. *Phone:* 651-905-3400. *Toll-free phone:* 800-6BROWN6. *Fax:* 651-905-3550. *Web site:* http://www.browncollege.edu/.

Capella University
Minneapolis, Minnesota

- **Proprietary** upper-level, founded 1993
- **Urban** campus
- **Coed**
- **Minimally difficult** entrance level

Academics *Calendar:* quarters. *Degrees:* certificates, bachelor's, master's, doctoral-research/scholarship, post-master's, and postbachelor's certificates (offers only distance learning degree programs).

Costs (2010–11) *Tuition:* $10,980 full-time. Full-time tuition and fees vary according to degree level and program. Part-time tuition and fees vary according to degree level and program.

Financial Aid *Average percent of need met:* 90. *Average financial aid package:* $10,500. *Average indebtedness upon graduation:* $8000.

Applying *Options:* electronic application. *Application fee:* $75.

Application Contact Learner Support, Capella University, 225 South Sixth Street, Capella Tower, 9th Floor, Minneapolis, MN 55402. *Phone:* 888-277-3552. *Toll-free phone:* 888-CAPELLA. *Fax:* 612-977-5060. *E-mail:* info@capella.edu. *Web site:* http://www.capella.edu/.

Carleton College
Northfield, Minnesota

- **Independent** 4-year, founded 1866
- **Small-town** 955-acre campus with easy access to Minneapolis-St. Paul
- **Endowment** $563.4 million
- **Coed** 2,020 undergraduate students, 99% full-time, 52% women, 48% men
- **Very difficult** entrance level, 31% of applicants were admitted

Undergraduates 1,996 full-time, 24 part-time. Students come from 50 states and territories; 44 other countries; 70% are from out of state; 3% Black or African American, non-Hispanic/Latino; 6% Hispanic/Latino; 6% Asian, non-Hispanic/Latino; 0.1% Native Hawaiian or other Pacific Islander, non-Hispanic/Latino; 0.2% American Indian or Alaska Native, non-Hispanic/Latino; 5% Two or more races, non-Hispanic/Latino; 2% Race/ethnicity unknown; 8% international; 0.5% transferred in; 94% live on campus. *Retention:* 98% of full-time freshmen returned.

Freshmen *Admission:* 4,856 applied, 1,496 admitted, 512 enrolled. *Test scores:* SAT critical reading scores over 500: 99%; SAT math scores over 500: 100%; SAT writing scores over 500: 99%; ACT scores over 18: 100%; SAT critical reading scores over 600: 88%; SAT math scores over 600: 94%; SAT writing scores over 600: 88%; ACT scores over 24: 97%; SAT critical reading scores over 700: 54%; SAT math scores over 700: 52%; SAT writing scores over 700: 52%; ACT scores over 30: 80%.

Faculty *Total:* 235, 90% full-time, 94% with terminal degrees. *Student/faculty ratio:* 9:1.

Academics *Calendar:* three courses for each of three terms. *Degree:* bachelor's. *Special study options:* accelerated degree program, advanced placement credit, double majors, independent study, internships, off-campus study, services for LD students, student-designed majors, study abroad. *Unusual degree programs:* 3-2 engineering with Columbia University, Washington University in St. Louis; nursing with Rush University; elementary education with Bank Street College of Education.

Computers on Campus 300 computers/terminals and 220 ports are available on campus for general student use. Students can access the following: campus intranet, computer help desk, free student e-mail accounts, online (class) grades, online (class) registration, online (class) schedules. Campuswide network is available. 100% of college-owned or -operated housing units are wired for high-speed Internet access. Wireless service is available via classrooms, computer centers, computer labs, dorm rooms, learning centers, libraries, student centers.

Student Life *Housing:* on-campus residence required through senior year. *Options:* coed, disabled students. Campus housing is university owned. Freshman campus housing is guaranteed. *Activities and organizations:* drama/theater group, student-run newspaper, radio station, choral group, CANOE (Carleton Association of Nature and Outdoor Enthusiasts), Farm Club, Ebony II, WHIMS (Women in Math and Science), Amnesty International. *Campus security:* 24-hour emergency response devices and patrols, student patrols, late-night transport/escort service, controlled dormitory access, Emergency Notification Service (cell phone text and email alerts). *Student services:* health clinic, personal/psychological counseling, women's center.

Athletics Member NCAA. All Division III. *Intercollegiate sports:* badminton M(c)/W(c), baseball M, basketball M/W, crew M(c)/W(c), cross-country running M/W, equestrian sports M(c)/W(c), fencing M(c)/W(c), field hockey W(c), football M, golf M/W, gymnastics W(c), ice hockey M(c)/W(c), lacrosse M(c)/W(c), rugby M(c)/W(c), sailing M(c)/W(c), skiing (cross-country) M(c)/W(c), skiing (downhill) M(c)/W(c), soccer M/W, softball W, swimming and diving M/W, tennis M/W, track and field M/W, ultimate Frisbee M(c)/W(c), volleyball M(c)/W, water polo M(c)/W(c). *Intramural sports:* badminton M/W, basketball M/W, soccer M/W, softball M/W, table tennis M/W, tennis M/W, ultimate Frisbee M/W, volleyball M/W.

Standardized Tests *Required:* SAT or ACT (for admission). *Recommended:* SAT Subject Tests (for admission).

Costs (2011–12) *Comprehensive fee:* $54,180 includes full-time tuition ($42,690), mandatory fees ($252), and room and board ($11,238). *College room only:* $5904. Room and board charges vary according to board plan. *Payment plans:* tuition prepayment, installment. *Waivers:* employees or children of employees.

Financial Aid Of all full-time matriculated undergraduates who enrolled in 2008, 1,714 applied for aid, 1,103 were judged to have need, 1,103 had their need fully met. 364 Federal Work-Study jobs (averaging $2467). 1,306 state and other part-time jobs (averaging $2533). In 2008, 126 non-need-based awards were made. *Average percent of need met:* 100%. *Average financial aid package:* $35,456. *Average need-based loan:* $4452. *Average need-based gift aid:* $29,471. *Average non-need-based aid:* $2440. *Average indebtedness upon graduation:* $19,436. *Financial aid deadline:* 2/15.

Applying *Options:* electronic application, early admission, early decision, deferred entrance. *Application fee:* $30. *Required:* essay or personal statement, high school transcript, 2 letters of recommendation, common application supplement. *Recommended:* interview. *Application deadlines:* 1/15 (freshmen), 3/31 (transfers). *Early decision deadline:* 11/15 (for plan 1), 1/15 (for plan 2). *Notification:* 4/15 (freshmen), 5/15 (transfers), 12/15 (early decision plan 1), 2/15 (early decision plan 2).

Freshman Application Contact Carleton College, One North College Street, Northfield, MN 55057-4001. *Phone:* 507-222-4190. *Toll-free phone:* 800-995-2275. *Web site:* http://www.carleton.edu/.

See page 1190 for the College Close-Up.

College of Saint Benedict
Saint Joseph, Minnesota

- **Independent Roman Catholic** 4-year, founded 1887
- **Small-town** 800-acre campus with easy access to Minneapolis-St. Paul
- **Endowment** $37.3 million
- **Women only** 2,082 undergraduate students, 98% full-time
- **Moderately difficult** entrance level, 81% of applicants were admitted

Undergraduates 2,038 full-time, 44 part-time. Students come from 29 states and territories; 27 other countries; 14% are from out of state; 0.9% Black or African American, non-Hispanic/Latino; 3% Hispanic/Latino; 4% Asian, non-Hispanic/Latino; 0.5% American Indian or Alaska Native, non-Hispanic/Latino; 0.1% Two or more races, non-Hispanic/Latino; 0.3% Race/ethnicity unknown; 6% international; 1% transferred in; 80% live on campus. *Retention:* 89% of full-time freshmen returned.

Freshmen *Admission:* 1,707 applied, 1,382 admitted, 536 enrolled. *Average high school GPA:* 3.71. *Test scores:* SAT critical reading scores over 500: 75%; SAT math scores over 500: 82%; SAT writing scores over 500: 81%; ACT scores over 18: 99%; SAT critical reading scores over 600: 40%; SAT math scores over 600: 35%; SAT writing scores over 600: 34%; ACT scores over 24: 73%; SAT critical reading scores over 700: 9%; SAT math scores over 700: 6%; SAT writing scores over 700: 6%; ACT scores over 30: 18%.

Faculty *Total:* 196, 82% full-time, 77% with terminal degrees. *Student/faculty ratio:* 12:1.

Academics *Calendar:* semesters. *Degrees:* bachelor's (coordinate with Saint John's University for men). *Special study options:* advanced placement credit, double majors, English as a second language, honors programs, independent study, internships, off-campus study, services for LD students, student-designed majors, study abroad. *ROTC:* Army (c). *Unusual degree programs:* 3-2 engineering with 3-2 Program with University of Minnesota.

Computers on Campus 901 computers/terminals and 3,000 ports are available on campus for general student use. Students can access the following: campus intranet, computer help desk, free student e-mail accounts, online (class) grades, online (class) registration, online (class) schedules, online student accounts. Campuswide network is available. 100% of college-owned or -operated housing units are wired for high-speed Internet access. Wireless service is available via entire campus.

Student Life *Housing:* on-campus residence required through senior year. *Options:* women-only, disabled students. Campus housing is university owned. Freshman campus housing is guaranteed. *Activities and organizations:* drama/theater group, student-run newspaper, radio station, choral group, Asia Club, Outskirts Snow Club, Biology Club, Trapshooting Club, AKS Sorority. *Campus security:* 24-hour emergency response devices and patrols, student patrols, late-night transport/escort service, controlled dormitory access, well-lit pathways, closed circuit TV monitors. *Student services:* health clinic, personal/psychological counseling, women's center.

Athletics Member NCAA. All Division III. *Intercollegiate sports:* basketball W, crew W(c), cross-country running W, golf W, ice hockey W, lacrosse W(c), riflery W(c), rugby W(c), skiing (cross-country) W, soccer W, softball W, swimming and diving W, tennis W, track and field W, ultimate Frisbee W(c), volleyball W, water polo W(c). *Intramural sports:* badminton W, basketball W, football W, golf W(c), racquetball W, rock climbing W(c), skiing (cross-country) W(c), skiing (downhill) W(c), soccer W, softball W, table tennis W, tennis W, volleyball W.

Standardized Tests *Required:* SAT or ACT (for admission).

Costs (2010–11) *Comprehensive fee:* $40,898 includes full-time tuition ($31,416), mandatory fees ($830), and room and board ($8652). Part-time tuition: $1309 per credit hour. Part-time tuition and fees vary according to course load. *College room only:* $4166. Room and board charges vary according to board plan and housing facility. *Payment plan:* installment.

Financial Aid Of all full-time matriculated undergraduates who enrolled in 2009, 1,541 applied for aid, 1,346 were judged to have need, 524 had their need fully met. 600 Federal Work-Study jobs (averaging $2050). 300 state and other part-time jobs (averaging $2050). In 2009, 598 non-need-based awards were made. *Average percent of need met:* 88%. *Average financial aid package:* $23,152. *Average need-based loan:* $4405. *Average need-based gift aid:* $17,595. *Average non-need-based aid:* $10,821.

Applying *Options:* electronic application, early action, deferred entrance. *Required:* essay or personal statement, high school transcript, 1 letter of recommendation. *Recommended:* minimum 3 GPA, interview. *Application deadlines:* rolling (freshmen), rolling (transfers), 11/15 (early action). *Notification:* continuous (freshmen), continuous (transfers), 12/15 (early action).

Freshman Application Contact Ms. Karen Backes, Dean of Admissions, College of Saint Benedict, 37 South College Avenue, St. Joseph, MN 56374. *Phone:* 320-363-5055. *Toll-free phone:* 800-544-1489. *Fax:* 320-363-5650. *E-mail:* admissions@csbsju.edu. *Web site:* http://www.csbsju.edu/.

The College of St. Scholastica
Duluth, Minnesota

- **Independent** comprehensive, founded 1912, affiliated with Roman Catholic Church
- **Suburban** 186-acre campus
- **Endowment** $21.2 million
- **Coed** 2,856 undergraduate students, 89% full-time, 68% women, 32% men
- **Moderately difficult** entrance level, 80% of applicants were admitted

Undergraduates 2,556 full-time, 300 part-time. Students come from 30 states and territories; 38 other countries; 13% are from out of state; 2% Black or African American, non-Hispanic/Latino; 1% Hispanic/Latino; 1% Asian, non-Hispanic/Latino; 2% American Indian or Alaska Native, non-Hispanic/Latino; 1% Two or more races, non-Hispanic/Latino; 7% Race/ethnicity unknown; 4% international; 13% transferred in; 51% live on campus. *Retention:* 84% of full-time freshmen returned.

Freshmen *Admission:* 2,000 applied, 1,606 admitted, 596 enrolled. *Average high school GPA:* 3.46. *Test scores:* SAT critical reading scores over 500: 47%; SAT math scores over 500: 61%; SAT writing scores over 500: 41%; ACT scores over 18: 95%; SAT critical reading scores over 600: 22%; SAT math scores over 600: 18%; SAT writing scores over 600: 8%; ACT scores over 24: 49%; SAT critical reading scores over 700: 4%; SAT math scores over 700: 7%; SAT writing scores over 700: 4%; ACT scores over 30: 6%.

Faculty *Total:* 361, 48% full-time. *Student/faculty ratio:* 14:1.

Academics *Calendar:* semesters. *Degrees:* certificates, bachelor's, master's, doctoral-professional, post-master's, and postbachelor's certificates. *Special study options:* accelerated degree program, adult/continuing education programs, advanced placement credit, distance learning, double majors, external degree program, honors programs, independent study, internships, off-campus study, part-time degree program, services for LD students, student-designed majors, study abroad, summer session for credit. *ROTC:* Air Force (c). *Unusual degree programs:* 3-2 occupational therapy.

Computers on Campus 394 computers/terminals are available on campus for general student use. Students can access the following: campus intranet, computer help desk, free student e-mail accounts, online (class) grades, online (class) registration, online (class) schedules, student account information and transcripts online. Campuswide network is available. 100% of college-owned or -operated housing units are wired for high-speed Internet access. Wireless service is available via classrooms, computer centers, computer labs, dorm rooms, learning centers, libraries, student centers.

Student Life *Housing:* on-campus residence required through sophomore year. *Options:* coed, disabled students. Campus housing is university owned. Freshman campus housing is guaranteed. *Activities and organizations:* drama/theater group, student-run newspaper, television station, choral group, Campus Activity Board, Inter-Varsity, Habitat for Humanity, SHIMA, Volunteers Involved Through Action. *Campus security:* 24-hour emergency response devices and patrols, late-night transport/escort service, controlled dormitory access, student door monitor at night. *Student services:* health clinic, personal/psychological counseling.

Athletics Member NCAA. All Division III. *Intercollegiate sports:* baseball M, basketball M/W, cross-country running M/W, football M, ice hockey M/W, skiing (cross-country) M/W, soccer M/W, softball W, tennis M/W, track and field M/W, volleyball W. *Intramural sports:* basketball M/W, football M/W, ice hockey W(c), soccer M/W, tennis M/W, volleyball M/W.

Standardized Tests *Required:* SAT or ACT (for admission).

Costs (2011–12) *Comprehensive fee:* $37,222 includes full-time tuition ($29,328), mandatory fees ($178), and room and board ($7716). Full-time tuition and fees vary according to class time. Part-time tuition and fees vary according to class time and course load. *College room only:* $4376. Room and board charges vary according to board plan and housing facility. *Payment plan:* installment. *Waivers:* senior citizens and employees or children of employees.

Financial Aid Of all full-time matriculated undergraduates who enrolled in 2009, 2,233 applied for aid, 2,054 were judged to have need, 400 had their need fully met. In 2009, 156 non-need-based awards were made. *Average percent of need met:* 71%. *Average financial aid package:* $19,807. *Average need-based loan:* $4488. *Average need-based gift aid:* $6640. *Average non-need-based aid:* $10,918. *Average indebtedness upon graduation:* $40,816.

Applying *Options:* electronic application, early admission, deferred entrance. *Application fee:* $25. *Required:* high school transcript. *Required for some:* minimum 2 GPA, interview. *Recommended:* interview. *Application deadlines:* rolling (freshmen), rolling (transfers). *Notification:* continuous (freshmen), continuous (transfers).

Freshman Application Contact Mr. Eric Berg, Vice President for Enrollment Management, The College of St. Scholastica, 1200 Kenwood Avenue, Duluth, MN 55811-4199. *Phone:* 218-723-6053. *Toll-free phone:* 800-249-6412. *E-mail:* admissions@css.edu. *Web site:* http://www.css.edu/.

College of Visual Arts
St. Paul, Minnesota

- **Independent** 4-year, founded 1924
- **Urban** 2-acre campus with easy access to Minneapolis-St. Paul
- **Endowment** $540,238
- **Coed**
- **Moderately difficult** entrance level

Faculty *Student/faculty ratio:* 9:1.

Academics *Calendar:* semesters. *Degree:* bachelor's.

Student Life *Campus security:* 24-hour emergency response devices, late-night transport/escort service.

Standardized Tests *Required:* SAT or ACT (for admission).

Costs (2010–11) *Tuition:* $23,488 full-time, $1174 per credit part-time. Full-time tuition and fees vary according to course load. Part-time tuition and fees vary according to course load. *Required fees:* $500 full-time, $50 per course part-time.

Financial Aid *Of all full-time matriculated undergraduates who enrolled in 2009,* 166 applied for aid, 153 were judged to have need, 3 had their need fully met. 22 Federal Work-Study jobs (averaging $2000). 65 state and other part-time jobs (averaging $2000). *In 2009,* 13 non-need-based awards were made. *Average percent of need met:* 53. *Average financial aid package:* $14,826. *Average need-based loan:* $4488. *Average need-based gift aid:* $9863. *Average non-need-based aid:* $2431. *Average indebtedness upon graduation:* $38,402. *Financial aid deadline:* 6/1.

Applying *Options:* electronic application, deferred entrance. *Application fee:* $40. *Required:* essay or personal statement, high school transcript, portfolio. *Recommended:* minimum 3 GPA, 1 letter of recommendation, interview.

Freshman Application Contact Anne White, Director for Student Life, College of Visual Arts, 344 Summit Avenue, St. Paul, MN 55102-2124. *Phone:* 651-757-4049. *Toll-free phone:* 800-224-1536. *Fax:* 651-757-4010. *E-mail:* awhite@cva.edu. *Web site:* http://www.cva.edu/.

Concordia College

Moorhead, Minnesota

- **Independent** comprehensive, founded 1891, affiliated with Evangelical Lutheran Church in America
- **Suburban** 113-acre campus
- **Endowment** $74.3 million
- **Coed** 2,784 undergraduate students, 98% full-time, 61% women, 39% men
- **Moderately difficult** entrance level, 95% of applicants were admitted

Undergraduates 2,740 full-time, 44 part-time. Students come from 37 states and territories; 37 other countries; 31% are from out of state; 1% Black or African American, non-Hispanic/Latino; 1% Hispanic/Latino; 1% Asian, non-Hispanic/Latino; 0.2% American Indian or Alaska Native, non-Hispanic/Latino; 0.9% Two or more races, non-Hispanic/Latino; 5% Race/ethnicity unknown; 4% international; 2% transferred in; 62% live on campus. *Retention:* 84% of full-time freshmen returned.

Freshmen *Admission:* 2,094 applied, 1,980 admitted, 675 enrolled. *Average high school GPA:* 3.59. *Test scores:* SAT critical reading scores over 500: 73%; SAT math scores over 500: 73%; ACT scores over 18: 98%; SAT critical reading scores over 600: 29%; SAT math scores over 600: 36%; ACT scores over 24: 63%; SAT critical reading scores over 700: 7%; SAT math scores over 700: 2%; ACT scores over 30: 14%.

Faculty *Total:* 261, 74% full-time, 63% with terminal degrees. *Student/faculty ratio:* 13:1.

Academics *Calendar:* semesters. *Degrees:* bachelor's and master's. *Special study options:* adult/continuing education programs, advanced placement credit, cooperative education, distance learning, double majors, honors programs, independent study, internships, off-campus study, part-time degree program, services for LD students, student-designed majors, study abroad, summer session for credit. *ROTC:* Army (c), Air Force (c). *Unusual degree programs:* 3-2 engineering with Institute of Technology at the University of Minnesota.

Computers on Campus 570 computers/terminals and 87 ports are available on campus for general student use. Students can access the following: campus intranet, computer help desk, free student e-mail accounts, online (class) grades, online (class) registration, online (class) schedules, online degree audit. Campuswide network is available. 100% of college-owned or -operated housing units are wired for high-speed Internet access. Wireless service is available via entire campus.

Student Life *Housing:* on-campus residence required through sophomore year. *Options:* coed, men-only, women-only. Campus housing is university owned. Freshman applicants given priority for college housing. *Activities and organizations:* drama/theater group, student-run newspaper, radio and television station, choral group, Campus Service Commission, Habitat for Humanity, Lead Now, Colleges Against Cancer (Relay for Life), Campus Ministry Commission. *Campus security:* 24-hour emergency response devices and patrols, student patrols, late-night transport/escort service, controlled dormitory access, well-lighted campus. *Student services:* health clinic, personal/psychological counseling, women's center.

Athletics Member NCAA. All Division III. *Intercollegiate sports:* baseball M, basketball M/W, cheerleading W(c), cross-country running M/W, football M, golf M/W, ice hockey M/W, soccer M/W, softball W, swimming and diving W, tennis M/W, track and field M/W, volleyball M(c)/W, wrestling M. *Intramural sports:* badminton M(c)/W(c), basketball M/W, football M, ice hockey M(c), lacrosse M(c)/W(c), rugby M(c)/W(c), skiing (downhill) M(c)/W(c), tennis M(c)/W(c), ultimate Frisbee M(c)/W(c), volleyball M/W.

Standardized Tests *Required:* SAT or ACT (for admission).

Costs (2011–12) *Comprehensive fee:* $36,150 includes full-time tuition ($29,150), mandatory fees ($210), and room and board ($6790). Full-time tuition and fees vary according to course load and degree level. Part-time tuition: $1145 per credit hour. Part-time tuition and fees vary according to course load and degree level. *College room only:* $3000. Room and board

charges vary according to board plan and housing facility. *Payment plan:* installment. *Waivers:* employees or children of employees.

Financial Aid *Of all full-time matriculated undergraduates who enrolled in 2008,* 2,270 applied for aid, 1,960 were judged to have need, 287 had their need fully met. 695 Federal Work-Study jobs (averaging $1695). 1,840 state and other part-time jobs (averaging $1755). In 2008, 677 non-need-based awards were made. *Average percent of need met:* 89%. *Average financial aid package:* $21,679. *Average need-based loan:* $7655. *Average need-based gift aid:* $14,314. *Average non-need-based aid:* $9324. *Average indebtedness upon graduation:* $32,271.

Applying *Options:* electronic application, early admission, deferred entrance. *Application fee:* $20. *Required:* high school transcript, 2 letters of recommendation. *Application deadlines:* rolling (freshmen), rolling (transfers). *Notification:* continuous (freshmen), continuous (transfers).

Freshman Application Contact Mr. Scott D. Ellingson, Director of Admissions, Concordia College, 901 8th Street South, Moorhead, MN 56562. *Phone:* 218-299-3004. *Toll-free phone:* 800-699-9897. *Fax:* 218-299-4720. *E-mail:* admissions@cord.edu. *Web site:* http://www.concordiacollege.edu/.

Concordia University, St. Paul

St. Paul, Minnesota

- **Independent** comprehensive, founded 1893, affiliated with Lutheran Church–Missouri Synod
- **Urban** 37-acre campus
- **Endowment** $21.4 million
- **Coed** 1,742 undergraduate students, 80% full-time, 58% women, 42% men
- **Minimally difficult** entrance level, 97% of applicants were admitted

Undergraduates 1,386 full-time, 356 part-time. Students come from 40 states and territories; 4 other countries; 17% are from out of state; 5% transferred in; 28% live on campus. *Retention:* 66% of full-time freshmen returned.

Freshmen *Admission:* 584 applied, 566 admitted, 216 enrolled. *Average high school GPA:* 3.05. *Test scores:* ACT scores over 18: 78%; ACT scores over 24: 26%; ACT scores over 30: 3%.

Faculty *Total:* 344, 24% full-time, 38% with terminal degrees. *Student/faculty ratio:* 16:1.

Academics *Calendar:* semesters. *Degrees:* certificates, associate, bachelor's, master's, and postbachelor's certificates. *Special study options:* academic remediation for entering students, accelerated degree program, adult/continuing education programs, advanced placement credit, distance learning, double majors, honors programs, independent study, internships, off-campus study, part-time degree program, services for LD students, student-designed majors, study abroad, summer session for credit. *ROTC:* Army (c), Navy (c), Air Force (c).

Computers on Campus Students can access the following: campus intranet, computer help desk, free student e-mail accounts, online (class) grades, online (class) registration, online (class) schedules. Campuswide network is available. 100% of college-owned or -operated housing units are wired for high-speed Internet access. Wireless service is available via entire campus.

Student Life *Housing:* on-campus residence required for freshman year. *Options:* coed, men-only, women-only, disabled students. Campus housing is university owned. Freshman campus housing is guaranteed. *Activities and organizations:* drama/theater group, student-run newspaper, television station, choral group. *Campus security:* 24-hour emergency response devices and patrols, student patrols, late-night transport/escort service, controlled dormitory access. *Student services:* health clinic, personal/psychological counseling.

Athletics Member NCAA. All Division II. *Intercollegiate sports:* baseball M(s), basketball M(s)/W(s), cross-country running M(s)/W(s), football M(s), golf M(s)/W(s), soccer W(s), softball W(s), track and field M(s)/W(s), volleyball W(s). *Intramural sports:* basketball M/W, football M/W, lacrosse W, racquetball M/W, softball M/W, volleyball M/W.

Standardized Tests *Required:* ACT (for admission).

Costs (2011–12) *Comprehensive fee:* $36,000 includes full-time tuition ($28,500) and room and board ($7500). Full-time tuition and fees vary according to program. Part-time tuition: $600 per credit. Part-time tuition and fees vary according to course load and program. *Room and board:* Room and board charges vary according to housing facility. *Payment plan:* installment. *Waivers:* employees or children of employees.

Financial Aid *Of all full-time matriculated undergraduates who enrolled in 2009,* 1,175 applied for aid, 944 were judged to have need, 22 had their need fully met. 182 Federal Work-Study jobs (averaging $2197). 241 state and other part-time jobs (averaging $2254). In 2009, 162 non-need-based awards were made. *Average percent of need met:* 63%. *Average financial aid package:* $18,771. *Average need-based loan:* $4467. *Average need-based gift aid:* $7099. *Average non-need-based aid:* $8357. *Average indebtedness upon graduation:* $36,295.

Applying *Options:* electronic application, early admission, deferred entrance. *Application fee:* $30. *Required:* high school transcript, 2 letters of recommendation. *Required for some:* essay or personal statement. *Recommended:* minimum 2 GPA. *Application deadlines:* 8/1 (freshmen), 8/1 (transfers). *Notification:* continuous (freshmen), continuous (transfers).

Freshman Application Contact Kristin Schoon, Director of Undergraduate Admission, Concordia University, St. Paul, 275 Syndicate North, St. Paul, MN 55104-5494. *Phone:* 651-641-8230. *Toll-free phone:* 800-333-4705. *Fax:* 651-603-6320. *E-mail:* admission@csp.edu. *Web site:* http://www.csp.edu/.

Crossroads College
Rochester, Minnesota

Freshman Application Contact Mr. Scott Klaehn, Director of Admissions, Crossroads College, 920 Mayowood Road, SW, Rochester, MN 55902-2382. *Phone:* 507-288-4563 Ext. 304. *Toll-free phone:* 800-456-7651. *Fax:* 507-288-9046. *E-mail:* admissions@crossroadscollege.edu. *Web site:* http://www.crossroadscollege.edu/.

Crown College
St. Bonifacius, Minnesota

- **Independent** comprehensive, founded 1916, affiliated with The Christian and Missionary Alliance
- **Small-town** 215-acre campus with easy access to Minneapolis-St. Paul
- **Endowment** $6.2 million
- **Coed** 1,011 undergraduate students, 77% full-time, 57% women, 43% men
- **Minimally difficult** entrance level, 77% of applicants were admitted

Undergraduates 783 full-time, 228 part-time. Students come from 34 states and territories; 13 other countries; 34% are from out of state; 3% Black or African American, non-Hispanic/Latino; 3% Hispanic/Latino; 8% Asian, non-Hispanic/Latino; 0.5% American Indian or Alaska Native, non-Hispanic/Latino; 0.7% Two or more races, non-Hispanic/Latino; 8% Race/ethnicity unknown; 0.1% international; 5% transferred in; 79% live on campus. *Retention:* 72% of full-time freshmen returned.

Freshmen *Admission:* 384 applied, 295 admitted, 148 enrolled. *Average high school GPA:* 3.23. *Test scores:* SAT critical reading scores over 500: 76%; SAT math scores over 500: 57%; ACT scores over 18: 93%; SAT critical reading scores over 600: 38%; SAT math scores over 600: 33%; ACT scores over 24: 34%; SAT math scores over 700: 14%; ACT scores over 30: 1%.

Faculty *Total:* 113, 27% full-time, 19% with terminal degrees. *Student/faculty ratio:* 15:1.

Academics *Calendar:* semesters. *Degrees:* certificates, associate, bachelor's, master's, and postbachelor's certificates. *Special study options:* academic remediation for entering students, accelerated degree program, adult/continuing education programs, advanced placement credit, distance learning, double majors, English as a second language, external degree program, honors programs, independent study, internships, part-time degree program, services for LD students, study abroad, summer session for credit. *ROTC:* Army (c).

Computers on Campus 95 computers/terminals are available on campus for general student use. Students can access the following: campus intranet, computer help desk, free student e-mail accounts, online (class) registration. Campuswide network is available. 95% of college-owned or -operated housing units are wired for high-speed Internet access. Wireless service is available via classrooms, computer labs, dorm rooms, libraries, student centers.

Student Life *Housing:* on-campus residence required through senior year. *Options:* men-only, women-only. Campus housing is university owned. Freshman campus housing is guaranteed. *Activities and organizations:* drama/theater group, student-run newspaper, radio station, choral group, Hmong Student Fellowship, Global Impact Team, Student Activities Board, Student Senate, Storm Chaser Newspaper. *Campus security:* 24-hour emergency response devices, student patrols, late-night transport/escort service, controlled dormitory access. *Student services:* health clinic, personal/psychological counseling.

Athletics Member NCAA. All Division III. *Intercollegiate sports:* baseball M, basketball M/W, cross-country running M/W, football M, golf M, soccer M/W, softball W, volleyball W. *Intramural sports:* basketball M/W, track and field M(c)/W(c), volleyball M/W.

Standardized Tests *Required:* SAT or ACT (for admission).

Costs (2011–12) *Comprehensive fee:* $28,850 includes full-time tuition ($21,470) and room and board ($7380). Part-time tuition: $895 per credit. *College room only:* $3790. Room and board charges vary according to board plan and housing facility. *Payment plan:* installment. *Waivers:* minority students, children of alumni, and employees or children of employees.

Financial Aid Of all full-time matriculated undergraduates who enrolled in 2009, 596 applied for aid, 513 were judged to have need, 68 had their need fully met. In 2009, 72 non-need-based awards were made. *Average percent of need met:* 61%. *Average financial aid package:* $15,394. *Average need-based loan:* $4364. *Average need-based gift aid:* $6232. *Average non-need-based aid:* $7375. *Average indebtedness upon graduation:* $31,804. *Financial aid deadline:* 8/1.

Applying *Options:* electronic application, early admission, deferred entrance. *Application fee:* $35. *Required:* essay or personal statement, high school transcript, minimum 2 GPA. *Required for some:* interview. *Application deadlines:* rolling (freshmen), rolling (out-of-state freshmen), rolling (transfers). *Notification:* continuous (freshmen), continuous (out-of-state freshmen), continuous (transfers).

Freshman Application Contact Mr. Bret Hyder, Assistant Director of Admissions, Crown College, 8700 College View Drive, St. Bonifacius, MN 55375-9001. *Phone:* 952-446-4144. *Toll-free phone:* 800-68-CROWN. *Fax:* 952-446-4149. *E-mail:* info@crown.edu. *Web site:* http://www.crown.edu/.

DeVry University
Edina, Minnesota

- **Proprietary** comprehensive
- **Coed**

Academics *Degrees:* associate, bachelor's, and master's.

Costs (2010–11) *Tuition:* $14,766 full-time, $580 per credit hour part-time. Full-time tuition and fees vary according to course load. Part-time tuition and fees vary according to course load. *Required fees:* $60 full-time, $30 per term part-time. *Payment plans:* installment, deferred payment.

Financial Aid *Of all full-time matriculated undergraduates who enrolled in 2007,* 31 applied for aid, 29 were judged to have need. *In 2007,* 2 non-need-based awards were made. *Average percent of need met:* 38. *Average financial aid package:* $10,797. *Average need-based loan:* $8696. *Average need-based gift aid:* $5538. *Average non-need-based aid:* $10,606.

Applying *Options:* electronic application, deferred entrance. *Application fee:* $50. *Required:* high school transcript, interview.

Freshman Application Contact DeVry University, 7700 France Avenue South, Suite 575, Edina, MN 55435. *Web site:* http://www.devry.edu/.

Dunwoody College of Technology
Minneapolis, Minnesota

Freshman Application Contact Shaun Manning, Director of Admissions, Dunwoody College of Technology, 818 Dunwoody Boulevard, Minneapolis, MN 55403. *Phone:* 612-374-5800 Ext. 8110. *Toll-free phone:* 800-292-4625. *E-mail:* smanning@dunwoody.edu. *Web site:* http://www.dunwoody.edu/.

Globe University
Woodbury, Minnesota

Freshman Application Contact Director of Admissions, Globe University, 8089 Globe Drive, Woodbury, MN 55125. *Phone:* 651-730-5100. *Toll-free phone:* 800-231-0660. *Fax:* 651-730-5151. *Web site:* http://www.globeuniversity.edu/.

Gustavus Adolphus College
St. Peter, Minnesota

- **Independent** 4-year, founded 1862, affiliated with Evangelical Lutheran Church in America
- **Small-town** 340-acre campus with easy access to Minneapolis-St. Paul
- **Endowment** $85.9 million
- **Coed**
- **Very difficult** entrance level

Faculty *Student/faculty ratio:* 11:1.

Academics *Calendar:* 4-1-4. *Degree:* bachelor's.

Student Life *Campus security:* 24-hour emergency response devices and patrols, late-night transport/escort service, controlled dormitory access.

Athletics Member NCAA. All Division III.

Standardized Tests *Recommended:* SAT or ACT (for admission).

Costs (2010–11) *One-time required fee:* $400. *Comprehensive fee:* $41,800 includes full-time tuition ($33,100), mandatory fees ($300), and room and board ($8400). *College room only:* $5400.

Financial Aid *Of all full-time matriculated undergraduates who enrolled in 2009,* 1,911 applied for aid, 1,645 were judged to have need, 696 had their need fully met. In 2009, 811 non-need-based awards were made. *Average percent of need met:* 90. *Average financial aid package:* $23,652. *Average need-based loan:* $4812. *Average need-based gift aid:* $18,834. *Average non-need-based aid:* $7352. *Average indebtedness upon graduation:* $24,297. *Financial aid deadline:* 4/15.

Applying *Options:* electronic application, early admission, early action, deferred entrance. *Required:* essay or personal statement, high school transcript, 1 letter of recommendation. *Recommended:* interview.

Freshman Application Contact Mr. Mark Anderson, Vice President for Admission and Student Financial Aid, Gustavus Adolphus College, 800 West College Avenue, St. Peter, MN 56082-1498. *Phone:* 507-933-7676. *Toll-free* *phone:* 800-GUSTAVU(S). *Fax:* 507-933-7474. *E-mail:* admission@gac.edu. *Web site:* http://www.gustavus.edu/.

Hamline University
St. Paul, Minnesota

- **Independent** comprehensive, founded 1854, affiliated with United Methodist Church
- **Urban** 50-acre campus with easy access to Minneapolis-St. Paul
- **Endowment** $66.5 million
- **Coed** 1,982 undergraduate students, 95% full-time, 55% women, 45% men
- **Moderately difficult** entrance level, 77% of applicants were admitted

Undergraduates 1,873 full-time, 109 part-time. Students come from 36 states and territories; 64 other countries; 17% are from out of state; 7% Black or African American, non-Hispanic/Latino; 5% Hispanic/Latino; 5% Asian, non-Hispanic/Latino; 0.1% Native Hawaiian or other Pacific Islander, non-Hispanic/Latino; 0.6% American Indian or Alaska Native, non-Hispanic/Latino; 3% Two or more races, non-Hispanic/Latino; 6% Race/ethnicity unknown; 3% international; 7% transferred in; 39% live on campus. *Retention:* 80% of full-time freshmen returned.

Freshmen *Admission:* 2,155 applied, 1,662 admitted, 440 enrolled. *Average high school GPA:* 3.33. *Test scores:* SAT critical reading scores over 500: 64%; SAT math scores over 500: 67%; SAT writing scores over 500: 59%; ACT scores over 18: 94%; SAT critical reading scores over 600: 29%; SAT math scores over 600: 25%; SAT writing scores over 600: 24%; ACT scores over 24: 54%; SAT critical reading scores over 700: 7%; SAT math scores over 700: 7%; SAT writing scores over 700: 2%; ACT scores over 30: 10%.

Faculty *Total:* 512, 39% full-time, 48% with terminal degrees. *Student/faculty ratio:* 12:1.

Academics *Calendar:* 4-1-4. *Degrees:* bachelor's, master's, doctoral-professional, doctoral-research/scholarship, post-master's, and postbachelor's certificates. *Special study options:* adult/continuing education programs, advanced placement credit, double majors, English as a second language, honors programs, independent study, internships, off-campus study, part-time degree program, services for LD students, student-designed majors, study abroad, summer session for credit. *ROTC:* Army (c), Air Force (c). *Unusual degree programs:* 3-2 engineering with University of Minnesota, Washington University in St. Louis.

Computers on Campus 300 computers/terminals are available on campus for general student use. Students can access the following: campus intranet, computer help desk, free student e-mail accounts, online (class) grades, online (class) registration, online (class) schedules. Campuswide network is available. 99% of college-owned or -operated housing units are wired for high-speed Internet access. Wireless service is available via entire campus.

Student Life *Housing options:* coed, men-only, women-only, disabled students. Campus housing is university owned. Freshman campus housing is guaranteed. *Activities and organizations:* drama/theater group, student-run newspaper, radio and television station, choral group, Student Congress (HUSC), Hand in Hand (elementary school mentoring program), Residence Hall Association, PRIDE, Hamline Oracle (student newspaper), national fraternities. *Campus security:* 24-hour emergency response devices and patrols, late-night transport/escort service, controlled dormitory access. *Student services:* health clinic, personal/psychological counseling, women's center.

Athletics Member NCAA. All Division III. *Intercollegiate sports:* baseball M, basketball M/W, cheerleading W(c), cross-country running M/W, football M, gymnastics W, ice hockey M/W, lacrosse M(c)/W(c), soccer M/W, softball W, swimming and diving M/W, tennis M/W, track and field M/W, ultimate Frisbee M(c)/W(c), volleyball W. *Intramural sports:* basketball M/W, ice hockey M(c), rock climbing M(c)/W(c), soccer M/W, volleyball M/W.

Standardized Tests *Required:* SAT or ACT (for admission).

Costs (2011–12) *Comprehensive fee:* $40,306 includes full-time tuition ($31,652), mandatory fees ($150), and room and board ($8504). Full-time tuition and fees vary according to program. Part-time tuition: $990 per credit hour. Part-time tuition and fees vary according to course load and program. *College room only:* $4230. Room and board charges vary according to board plan and housing facility. *Payment plan:* installment. *Waivers:* employees or children of employees.

Financial Aid Of all full-time matriculated undergraduates who enrolled in 2009, 1,606 applied for aid, 1,472 were judged to have need, 232 had their need fully met. 522 Federal Work-Study jobs (averaging $2322). 1,016 state and other part-time jobs (averaging $2311). In 2009, 255 non-need-based awards were made. *Average percent of need met:* 78%. *Average financial aid package:* $23,853. *Average need-based loan:* $4874. *Average need-based gift aid:* $17,325. *Average non-need-based aid:* $10,337. *Average indebtedness upon graduation:* $36,339.

Applying *Options:* electronic application, early admission, early action, deferred entrance. *Required:* essay or personal statement, high school transcript, 1 letter of recommendation. *Recommended:* interview. *Application deadlines:* rolling (freshmen), rolling (out-of-state freshmen), rolling (transfers), 12/1 (early action). *Notification:* continuous (freshmen), continuous (out-of-state freshmen), continuous (transfers), 12/20 (early action).

Freshman Application Contact Mr. Milyon Trulove, Director of Admission, Hamline University, 1536 Hewitt Avenue, St. Paul, MN 55104. *Phone:* 651-523-2207. *Toll-free phone:* 800-753-9753. *Fax:* 651-523-2458. *E-mail:* admission@hamline.edu. *Web site:* http://www.hamline.edu/.

Herzing University
Minneapolis, Minnesota

Freshman Application Contact Ms. Shelly Larson, Director of Admissions, Herzing University, 5700 West Broadway, Minneapolis, MN 55428. *Phone:* 763-231-3155. *Fax:* 763-535-9205. *E-mail:* info@mpls.herzing.edu. *Web site:* http://www.herzing.edu/.

ITT Technical Institute
Eden Prairie, Minnesota

- **Proprietary** primarily 2-year, founded 2003, part of ITT Educational Services, Inc.
- **Coed**
- **Minimally difficult** entrance level

Academics *Calendar:* quarters. *Degrees:* associate and bachelor's.

Freshman Application Contact Director of Recruitment, ITT Technical Institute, 8911 Columbine Road, Eden Prairie, MN 55347. *Phone:* 952-914-5300. *Toll-free phone:* 888-488-9646. *Web site:* http://www.itt-tech.edu/.

Macalester College
St. Paul, Minnesota

- **Independent Presbyterian** 4-year, founded 1874
- **Urban** 53-acre campus
- **Endowment** $586.6 million
- **Coed** 2,033 undergraduate students, 98% full-time, 58% women, 42% men
- **Very difficult** entrance level, 43% of applicants were admitted

Undergraduates 1,987 full-time, 46 part-time. Students come from 50 states and territories; 94 other countries; 73% are from out of state; 4% Black or African American, non-Hispanic/Latino; 6% Hispanic/Latino; 6% Asian, non-Hispanic/Latino; 0.0% Native Hawaiian or other Pacific Islander, non-Hispanic/Latino; 0.5% American Indian or Alaska Native, non-Hispanic/Latino; 4% Two or more races, non-Hispanic/Latino; 11% international; 1% transferred in; 65% live on campus. *Retention:* 96% of full-time freshmen returned.

Freshmen *Admission:* 4,317 applied, 1,837 admitted, 515 enrolled. *Test scores:* SAT critical reading scores over 500: 97%; SAT math scores over 500: 100%; SAT writing scores over 500: 98%; ACT scores over 18: 100%; SAT critical reading scores over 600: 84%; SAT math scores over 600: 86%; SAT writing scores over 600: 87%; ACT scores over 24: 97%; SAT critical reading scores over 700: 50%; SAT math scores over 700: 35%; SAT writing scores over 700: 44%; ACT scores over 30: 62%.

Faculty *Total:* 231, 71% full-time, 85% with terminal degrees. *Student/faculty ratio:* 11:1.

Academics *Calendar:* semesters. *Degree:* bachelor's. *Special study options:* double majors, honors programs, independent study, internships, off-campus study, part-time degree program, student-designed majors, study abroad. *ROTC:* Army (c), Navy (c), Air Force (c). *Unusual degree programs:* 3-2 engineering with Washington University in St. Louis, University of Minnesota; Architecture with Washington University in St. Louis.

Computers on Campus 486 computers/terminals and 2,500 ports are available on campus for general student use. Students can access the following: campus intranet, computer help desk, free student e-mail accounts, online (class) grades, online (class) registration, online (class) schedules, Web space, online course management (LMS), shared calendars. Campuswide network is available. 100% of college-owned or -operated housing units are wired for high-speed Internet access. Wireless service is available via entire campus.

Student Life *Housing:* on-campus residence required through sophomore year. *Options:* coed, men-only, women-only, cooperative. Campus housing is university owned. Freshman campus housing is guaranteed. *Activities and organizations:* drama/theater group, student-run newspaper, radio station, choral group, Community Service Organization, Outing Club (outdoor recreation), Multicultural Organization, International Organization, campus publications. *Campus security:* 24-hour emergency response devices and patrols, late-night transport/escort service. *Student services:* health clinic, personal/psychological counseling.

Athletics Member NCAA. All Division III. *Intercollegiate sports:* baseball M, basketball M/W, crew M(c)/W(c), cross-country running M/W, fencing M(c)/W(c), football M, golf M/W, ice hockey M(c)/W(c), lacrosse W(c), rugby M(c)/W(c), skiing (cross-country) M(c)/W(c), soccer M/W, softball W, swimming and diving M/W, tennis M/W, track and field M/W, ultimate Frisbee

M(c)/W(c), volleyball M(c)/W, water polo M(c)/W. *Intramural sports:* basketball M/W, racquetball M/W, soccer M/W, softball M/W, table tennis M/W, ultimate Frisbee M/W.

Standardized Tests *Required:* SAT or ACT (for admission).

Costs (2011–12) *Comprehensive fee:* $51,417 includes full-time tuition ($41,800), mandatory fees ($221), and room and board ($9396). Full-time tuition and fees vary according to course load. Part-time tuition: $1306 per credit hour. Part-time tuition and fees vary according to course load. *College room only:* $5024. Room and board charges vary according to board plan and housing facility. *Payment plan:* installment. *Waivers:* employees or children of employees.

Financial Aid Of all full-time matriculated undergraduates who enrolled in 2009, 1,547 applied for aid, 1,398 were judged to have need, 1,398 had their need fully met. In 2009, 84 non-need-based awards were made. *Average percent of need met:* 100%. *Average financial aid package:* $33,773. *Average need-based loan:* $3909. *Average need-based gift aid:* $28,793. *Average non-need-based aid:* $7347. *Financial aid deadline:* 3/1.

Applying *Options:* electronic application, early admission, early decision, deferred entrance. *Application fee:* $40. *Required:* essay or personal statement, high school transcript, 2 letters of recommendation. *Recommended:* interview. *Application deadlines:* 1/15 (freshmen), 4/15 (transfers). *Early decision deadline:* 11/15 (for plan 1), 1/3 (for plan 2). *Notification:* 3/30 (freshmen), 5/15 (transfers), 12/15 (early decision plan 1), 2/7 (early decision plan 2).

Freshman Application Contact Mr. Lorne T. Robinson, Dean of Admissions and Financial Aid, Macalester College, 1600 Grand Avenue, St. Paul, MN 55105-1899. *Phone:* 651-696-6357. *Toll-free phone:* 800-231-7974. *Fax:* 651-696-6724. *E-mail:* admissions@macalester.edu. *Web site:* http://www.macalester.edu/.

Martin Luther College

New Ulm, Minnesota

- **Independent** comprehensive, founded 1995, affiliated with Wisconsin Evangelical Lutheran Synod
- **Small-town** 50-acre campus
- **Coed** 765 undergraduate students, 92% full-time, 48% women, 52% men
- **Moderately difficult** entrance level, 96% of applicants were admitted

Undergraduates 704 full-time, 61 part-time. 84% are from out of state; 0.4% Black or African American, non-Hispanic/Latino; 0.5% Hispanic/Latino; 0.1% Asian, non-Hispanic/Latino; 0.4% American Indian or Alaska Native, non-Hispanic/Latino; 0.4% Two or more races, non-Hispanic/Latino; 0.1% Race/ethnicity unknown; 1% international; 3% transferred in; 91% live on campus. *Retention:* 84% of full-time freshmen returned.

Freshmen *Admission:* 226 applied, 217 admitted, 166 enrolled. *Average high school GPA:* 3.39. *Test scores:* ACT scores over 18: 98%; ACT scores over 24: 54%; ACT scores over 30: 13%.

Faculty *Total:* 72, 67% full-time, 44% with terminal degrees. *Student/faculty ratio:* 13:1.

Academics *Calendar:* semesters. *Degrees:* certificates, diplomas, bachelor's, and master's. *Special study options:* academic remediation for entering students, advanced placement credit, distance learning, double majors, summer session for credit.

Computers on Campus Campuswide network is available.

Student Life *Housing:* on-campus residence required through junior year. *Options:* men-only, women-only. Campus housing is university owned. *Activities and organizations:* drama/theater group, choral group. *Campus security:* 24-hour emergency response devices, student patrols, controlled dormitory access. *Student services:* health clinic, personal/psychological counseling.

Athletics Member NCAA, NAIA. All NCAA Division III. *Intercollegiate sports:* baseball M, basketball M/W, cross-country running M/W, football M, golf M, soccer M/W, softball W, tennis M/W, track and field M/W, volleyball W. *Intramural sports:* badminton M/W, basketball M/W, bowling M/W, football M, soccer M/W, softball M/W, tennis M/W, volleyball M/W.

Standardized Tests *Required:* ACT (for admission).

Costs (2011–12) *Comprehensive fee:* $15,710 includes full-time tuition ($11,320) and room and board ($4390). *Payment plan:* installment.

Financial Aid Of all full-time matriculated undergraduates who enrolled in 2008, 650 applied for aid, 534 were judged to have need, 216 had their need fully met. In 2008, 73 non-need-based awards were made. *Average percent of need met:* 63%. *Average financial aid package:* $10,085. *Average need-based loan:* $3950. *Average need-based gift aid:* $4025. *Average non-need-based aid:* $1595. *Average indebtedness upon graduation:* $15,600. *Financial aid deadline:* 4/15.

Applying *Options:* deferred entrance. *Application fee:* $25. *Required:* high school transcript, minimum 2 GPA. *Application deadlines:* 4/15 (freshmen), 4/15 (transfers). *Notification:* continuous (freshmen), continuous (transfers).

Freshman Application Contact Prof. Ronald Brutlag, Director of Admissions, Martin Luther College, 1995 Luther Court, New Ulm, MN 56073.

Phone: 507-354-8221 Ext. 280. *E-mail:* brutlaro@mlc-wels.edu. *Web site:* http://www.mlc-wels.edu/.

McNally Smith College of Music

Saint Paul, Minnesota

- **Proprietary** comprehensive, founded 1985
- **Urban** 1-acre campus with easy access to Minneapolis-St. Paul
- **Coed** 680 undergraduate students, 90% full-time, 21% women, 79% men
- **Moderately difficult** entrance level

Undergraduates 611 full-time, 69 part-time. Students come from 36 states and territories; 12 other countries; 42% are from out of state; 16% transferred in; 15% live on campus. *Retention:* 76% of full-time freshmen returned.

Freshmen *Admission:* 133 enrolled.

Faculty *Total:* 112, 45% full-time. *Student/faculty ratio:* 9:1.

Academics *Calendar:* semesters. *Degrees:* diplomas, associate, bachelor's, and master's. *Special study options:* academic remediation for entering students, advanced placement credit, cooperative education, distance learning, double majors, independent study, internships, off-campus study, part-time degree program, services for LD students, study abroad, summer session for credit.

Computers on Campus 40 computers/terminals are available on campus for general student use. Students can access the following: campus intranet, computer help desk, free student e-mail accounts, online (class) grades, online (class) registration, online (class) schedules. Campuswide network is available. Wireless service is available via entire campus.

Student Life *Housing options:* coed. Campus housing is leased by the school. Freshman applicants given priority for college housing. *Activities and organizations:* student-run newspaper, choral group, Student Advisory Board, Audio Engineering Society, Minnesota Songwriters Association, Jazz Club, intramural sports. *Campus security:* 24-hour emergency response devices and patrols, late-night transport/escort service. *Student services:* personal/psychological counseling.

Standardized Tests *Required for some:* ACT (for admission). *Recommended:* ACT (for admission).

Costs (2011–12) *Tuition:* $22,620 full-time, $870 per credit part-time. Full-time tuition and fees vary according to course load. Part-time tuition and fees vary according to course load. No tuition increase for student's term of enrollment. *Required fees:* $3500 full-time, $450 per term part-time. *Room only:* Room and board charges vary according to board plan and housing facility. *Payment plans:* tuition prepayment, installment, deferred payment. *Waivers:* employees or children of employees.

Financial Aid Of all full-time matriculated undergraduates who enrolled in 2008, 40 Federal Work-Study jobs (averaging $1500). 19 state and other part-time jobs (averaging $1124). *Financial aid deadline:* 8/1.

Applying *Options:* electronic application. *Application fee:* $75. *Required:* essay or personal statement, high school transcript, minimum 2 GPA, 2 letters of recommendation, interview. *Required for some:* audition. *Recommended:* minimum 2.5 GPA. *Application deadline:* 8/1 (freshmen). *Notification:* 8/1 (freshmen).

Freshman Application Contact Mrs. Kathy Hawks, Director of Admissions, McNally Smith College of Music, 19 Exchange Street East, St. Paul, MN 55101. *Phone:* 651-361-3450. *Toll-free phone:* 800-594-9500. *Fax:* 651-291-0366. *E-mail:* kathy.hawks@mcnallysmith.edu. *Web site:* http://www.mcnallysmith.edu/.

Metropolitan State University

St. Paul, Minnesota

- **State-supported** comprehensive, founded 1971, part of Minnesota State Colleges and Universities System
- **Urban** campus with easy access to Minneapolis-St. Paul
- **Endowment** $2.6 million
- **Coed** 6,974 undergraduate students, 37% full-time, 57% women, 43% men
- **Minimally difficult** entrance level, 53% of applicants were admitted

Undergraduates 2,615 full-time, 4,359 part-time. Students come from 25 states and territories; 53 other countries; 2% are from out of state; 14% Black or African American, non-Hispanic/Latino; 5% Hispanic/Latino; 9% Asian, non-Hispanic/Latino; 0.1% Native Hawaiian or other Pacific Islander, non-Hispanic/Latino; 0.5% American Indian or Alaska Native, non-Hispanic/Latino; 6% Two or more races, non-Hispanic/Latino; 2% Race/ethnicity unknown; 1% international; 24% transferred in. *Retention:* 59% of full-time freshmen returned.

Freshmen *Admission:* 420 applied, 221 admitted, 39 enrolled. *Test scores:* ACT scores over 18: 65%; ACT scores over 24: 16%.

Faculty *Total:* 550, 22% full-time. *Student/faculty ratio:* 15:1.

Academics *Calendar:* semesters. *Degrees:* certificates, bachelor's, master's, doctoral-other, and postbachelor's certificates (offers primarily part-time evening degree programs). *Special study options:* adult/continuing education programs, advanced placement credit, distance learning, double majors, English as a second language, external degree program, independent study, internships, off-campus study, part-time degree program, student-designed majors, study abroad, summer session for credit.

Computers on Campus 375 computers/terminals are available on campus for general student use. Students can access the following: computer help desk, free student e-mail accounts, online (class) grades, online (class) registration, online (class) schedules. Campuswide network is available. Wireless service is available via entire campus.

Student Life *Housing:* college housing not available. *Activities and organizations:* drama/theater group, student-run newspaper, Psychology Club, Lavender Bridge, International Student Organization, Student Senate, African-American Student Association. *Campus security:* 24-hour emergency response devices, late-night transport/escort service. *Student services:* personal/psychological counseling.

Standardized Tests *Required for some:* SAT or ACT (for admission).

Costs (2010–11) *Tuition:* state resident $5610 full-time, $187 per credit hour part-time; nonresident $11,464 full-time, $382 per credit hour part-time. Full-time tuition and fees vary according to program and reciprocity agreements. Part-time tuition and fees vary according to course load, program, and reciprocity agreements. *Required fees:* $313 full-time, $10 per credit hour part-time. *Payment plan:* installment. *Waivers:* senior citizens and employees or children of employees.

Applying *Options:* electronic application, deferred entrance. *Application fee:* $20. *Required:* high school transcript, minimum 2 GPA. *Application deadlines:* 6/15 (freshmen), 6/15 (transfers).

Freshman Application Contact Mr. Daryl Johnson, Director, Metropolitan State University, 700 East 7th Street, St. Paul, MN 55106. *Phone:* 651-793-1227. *Fax:* 651-793-1546. *E-mail:* daryl.johnson@metrostate.edu. *Web site:* http://www.metrostate.edu/.

Minneapolis College of Art and Design

Minneapolis, Minnesota

- **Independent** comprehensive, founded 1886
- **Urban** 7-acre campus
- **Endowment** $25.9 million
- **Coed** 702 undergraduate students, 90% full-time, 60% women, 40% men
- **Moderately difficult** entrance level, 70% of applicants were admitted

Undergraduates 632 full-time, 70 part-time. Students come from 39 states and territories; 36% are from out of state; 2% Black or African American, non-Hispanic/Latino; 6% Hispanic/Latino; 5% Asian, non-Hispanic/Latino; 2% American Indian or Alaska Native, non-Hispanic/Latino; 16% Race/ethnicity unknown; 1% international; 9% transferred in; 45% live on campus. *Retention:* 70% of full-time freshmen returned.

Freshmen *Admission:* 427 applied, 301 admitted, 117 enrolled. *Average high school GPA:* 3.25. *Test scores:* SAT critical reading scores over 500: 82%; SAT math scores over 500: 69%; SAT writing scores over 500: 76%; ACT scores over 18: 95%; SAT critical reading scores over 600: 48%; SAT math scores over 600: 25%; SAT writing scores over 600: 31%; ACT scores over 24: 51%; SAT critical reading scores over 700: 10%; SAT math scores over 700: 7%; SAT writing scores over 700: 3%; ACT scores over 30: 5%.

Faculty *Total:* 111, 38% full-time. *Student/faculty ratio:* 13:1.

Academics *Calendar:* semesters. *Degrees:* bachelor's, master's, and post-bachelor's certificates. *Special study options:* adult/continuing education programs, advanced placement credit, cooperative education, distance learning, independent study, internships, off-campus study, part-time degree program, services for LD students, study abroad, summer session for credit.

Computers on Campus 110 computers/terminals are available on campus for general student use. Students can access the following: campus intranet, computer help desk, free student e-mail accounts, online (class) grades. Campuswide network is available. Wireless service is available via entire campus.

Student Life *Housing options:* coed. Campus housing is university owned, leased by the school and is provided by a third party. Freshman applicants given priority for college housing. *Activities and organizations:* student-run radio station. *Campus security:* 24-hour emergency response devices and patrols, late-night transport/escort service, controlled dormitory access. *Student services:* personal/psychological counseling.

Athletics *Intramural sports:* basketball M(c), soccer M(c)/W(c), softball M(c)/W(c).

Standardized Tests *Required:* SAT or ACT (for admission).

Costs (2011–12) *Tuition:* $30,385 full-time, $1266 per credit part-time. Part-time tuition and fees vary according to course load. *Required fees:* $200 full-time, $100 per term part-time. *Room only:* $4540. Room and board charges

vary according to housing facility. *Payment plan:* installment. *Waivers:* children of alumni and employees or children of employees.

Financial Aid Of all full-time matriculated undergraduates who enrolled in 2009, 613 applied for aid, 551 were judged to have need, 42 had their need fully met. 67 Federal Work-Study jobs (averaging $2082). 16 state and other part-time jobs (averaging $2078). In 2009, 57 non-need-based awards were made. *Average percent of need met:* 61%. *Average financial aid package:* $17,281. *Average need-based loan:* $4807. *Average need-based gift aid:* $12,448. *Average non-need-based aid:* $8490. *Average indebtedness upon graduation:* $46,293. *Financial aid deadline:* 4/1.

Applying *Options:* electronic application. *Application fee:* $50. *Required:* essay or personal statement, high school transcript, 1 letter of recommendation. *Required for some:* portfolio of visual artwork. *Recommended:* minimum 2.75 GPA, interview. *Application deadlines:* 5/1 (freshmen), 5/1 (out-of-state freshmen), 5/1 (transfers). *Notification:* continuous (freshmen), continuous (out-of-state freshmen), continuous (transfers).

Freshman Application Contact Minneapolis College of Art and Design, 2501 Stevens Avenue, Minneapolis, MN 55404-4347. *Phone:* 612-874-3762. *Toll-free phone:* 800-874-6223. *Web site:* http://www.mcad.edu/.

Minnesota School of Business–Blaine

Blaine, Minnesota

- **Proprietary** 4-year, part of Globe University/Minnesota School of Business
- **Suburban** campus
- **Coed, primarily women** 979 undergraduate students, 30% full-time, 73% women, 27% men
- **Moderately difficult** entrance level, 100% of applicants were admitted

Undergraduates 294 full-time, 685 part-time. Students come from 1 other state; 1 other country; 17% are from out of state; 2% Black or African American, non-Hispanic/Latino; 2% Hispanic/Latino; 3% Asian, non-Hispanic/Latino; 0.1% Native Hawaiian or other Pacific Islander, non-Hispanic/Latino; 1% American Indian or Alaska Native, non-Hispanic/Latino; 1% Two or more races, non-Hispanic/Latino; 22% transferred in. *Retention:* 80% of full-time freshmen returned.

Freshmen *Admission:* 375 applied, 375 admitted, 158 enrolled.

Faculty *Total:* 50, 24% full-time, 14% with terminal degrees. *Student/faculty ratio:* 19:1.

Academics *Degrees:* diplomas, associate, and bachelor's. *Special study options:* academic remediation for entering students, adult/continuing education programs, advanced placement credit, distance learning, external degree program, independent study, internships, part-time degree program, services for LD students.

Computers on Campus 65 computers/terminals and 20 ports are available on campus for general student use. Students can access the following: campus intranet, computer help desk, free student e-mail accounts, online (class) registration. Campuswide network is available.

Student Life *Housing:* college housing not available. *Activities and organizations:* student-run newspaper, Delta Epsilon Chi, SCNAVTA, Student Ambassadors. *Campus security:* 24-hour emergency response devices, student patrols, late-night transport/escort service.

Standardized Tests *Required for some:* SAT or ACT or ACCUPLACER.

Costs (2010–11) *Tuition:* $15,660 full-time, $435 per credit part-time. Full-time tuition and fees vary according to course load, program, and student level. Part-time tuition and fees vary according to course load, program, and student level. *Required fees:* $1100 full-time. *Payment plan:* installment. *Waivers:* senior citizens and employees or children of employees.

Applying *Options:* electronic application, early admission. *Application fee:* $50. *Required:* 1 letter of recommendation, interview. *Required for some:* high school transcript. *Application deadlines:* 10/5 (freshmen), 10/5 (transfers).

Freshman Application Contact Minnesota School of Business–Blaine, 3680 Pheasant Ridge Drive NE, Blaine, MN 55449. *Phone:* 763-225-8003. *Web site:* http://www.msbcollege.edu/oncampus/blaine/.

Minnesota School of Business–Brooklyn Center

Brooklyn Center, Minnesota

Freshman Application Contact Mr. Bruce Christman, Director of Admissions, Minnesota School of Business–Brooklyn Center, Brooklyn Center, MN 55430. *Phone:* 763-585-7777. *Fax:* 763-566-7030. *Web site:* http://www.msbcollege.edu/.

Minnesota School of Business–Plymouth

Minneapolis, Minnesota

Freshman Application Contact Minnesota School of Business–Plymouth, Plymouth, MN 55447. *Phone:* 763-476-2000. *Fax:* 763-476-1000. *Web site:* http://www.msbcollege.edu/.

Minnesota School of Business–Richfield

Richfield, Minnesota

Freshman Application Contact Ms. Patricia Murray, Director of Admissions, Minnesota School of Business–Richfield, Richfield, MN 55430. *Phone:* 612-861-2000 Ext. 720. *Toll-free phone:* 800-752-4223. *Fax:* 612-861-5548. *E-mail:* pmurray@msbcollege.com. *Web site:* http://www.msbcollege.edu/.

Minnesota School of Business–Rochester

Rochester, Minnesota

Freshman Application Contact Mr. Shan Pollitt, Director of Admissions, Minnesota School of Business–Rochester, 2521 Pennington Drive NW, Rochester, MN 55901. *Phone:* 507-536-9500. *Toll-free phone:* 888-662-8772. *Fax:* 507-535-8011. *Web site:* http://www.msbcollege.edu/.

Minnesota School of Business–St. Cloud

Waite Park, Minnesota

Freshman Application Contact Ms. Candi Janssen, Director of Admissions, Minnesota School of Business–St. Cloud, Waite Park, MN 56387. *Phone:* 320-257-2000. *Toll-free phone:* 866-403-3333. *Fax:* 320-257-0131. *E-mail:* cjanssen@msbcollege.edu. *Web site:* http://www.msbcollege.edu/.

Minnesota School of Business–Shakopee

Shakopee, Minnesota

Freshman Application Contact Ms. Gretchen Seifert, Director of Admissions, Minnesota School of Business–Shakopee, Shakopee, MN 55379. *Phone:* 952-516-7015. *Toll-free phone:* 866-766-1200. *Fax:* 952-345-1201. *Web site:* http://www.msbcollege.edu/.

Minnesota State University Mankato

Mankato, Minnesota

- **State-supported** university, founded 1868, part of Minnesota State Colleges and Universities System
- **Small-town** 303-acre campus with easy access to Minneapolis-St. Paul
- **Coed** 13,345 undergraduate students, 87% full-time, 51% women, 49% men
- **Moderately difficult** entrance level

Undergraduates 11,676 full-time, 1,669 part-time. Students come from 45 states and territories; 76 other countries; 13% are from out of state; 5% Black or African American, non-Hispanic/Latino; 2% Hispanic/Latino; 3% Asian, non-Hispanic/Latino; 3% Native Hawaiian or other Pacific Islander, non-Hispanic/Latino; 0.4% American Indian or Alaska Native, non-Hispanic/Latino; 4% Race/ethnicity unknown; 3% international; 7% transferred in; 25% live on campus. *Retention:* 77% of full-time freshmen returned.
Freshmen *Admission:* 2,425 enrolled. *Test scores:* ACT scores over 18: 91%; ACT scores over 24: 30%; ACT scores over 30: 2%.
Faculty *Total:* 761, 66% full-time, 56% with terminal degrees. *Student/faculty ratio:* 23:1.
Academics *Calendar:* semesters. *Degrees:* certificates, associate, bachelor's, master's, doctoral-other, and post-master's certificates. *Special study options:* academic remediation for entering students, accelerated degree program, adult/continuing education programs, advanced placement credit, cooperative education, distance learning, double majors, English as a second language, external degree program, honors programs, independent study, internships, off-campus study, part-time degree program, services for LD students, student-designed majors, study abroad, summer session for credit. *ROTC:* Army (b).
Computers on Campus 900 computers/terminals are available on campus for general student use. Students can access the following: campus intranet, computer help desk, free student e-mail accounts, online (class) grades, online (class) registration, online (class) schedules. Campuswide network is available. Wireless service is available via entire campus.
Student Life *Housing options:* coed. *Activities and organizations:* drama/theater group, student-run newspaper, radio station, choral group, national fraternities, national sororities. *Campus security:* 24-hour emergency response devices and patrols, student patrols, late-night transport/escort service, Night Owl security program in residence halls, closed circuit cameras in parking lots. *Student services:* health clinic, personal/psychological counseling, women's center, legal services.
Athletics Member NCAA. All Division II except men's and women's ice hockey (Division I). *Intercollegiate sports:* baseball M(s), basketball M(s)/W(s), bowling W, cheerleading M/W, cross-country running M(s)/W(s), football M(s), golf M(s)/W(s), ice hockey M(s)/W(s), soccer W(s), softball W(s), swimming and diving M(s)/W(s), tennis M(s)/W(s), track and field M(s)/W(s), volleyball W(s), wrestling M(s). *Intramural sports:* archery M/W, basketball M/W, bowling M/W, fencing M/W, football M, golf M/W, ice hockey M/W, lacrosse M/W, racquetball M/W, rock climbing M/W, rugby M/W, sailing M/W, skiing (downhill) M/W, soccer M/W, softball M/W, swimming and diving M/W, table tennis M/W, tennis M/W, track and field M/W, volleyball M/W, wrestling M.
Standardized Tests *Required:* SAT or ACT (for admission).
Costs (2010–11) *Tuition:* state resident $5927 full-time, $235 per credit hour part-time; nonresident $12,680 full-time, $505 per credit hour part-time. Full-time tuition and fees vary according to course load, location, and reciprocity agreements. Part-time tuition and fees vary according to course load, location, and reciprocity agreements. *Required fees:* $798 full-time. *Room and board:* $6730. Room and board charges vary according to board plan and housing facility. *Payment plan:* installment. *Waivers:* senior citizens and employees or children of employees.
Financial Aid Of all full-time matriculated undergraduates who enrolled in 2009, 9,221 applied for aid, 6,738 were judged to have need, 4,108 had their need fully met. 526 Federal Work-Study jobs (averaging $3558). 436 state and other part-time jobs (averaging $3434). In 2009, 202 non-need-based awards were made. *Average percent of need met:* 81%. *Average financial aid package:* $8423. *Average need-based loan:* $4343. *Average need-based gift aid:* $5216. *Average non-need-based aid:* $1522. *Average indebtedness upon graduation:* $27,086.
Applying *Options:* electronic application, early admission, deferred entrance. *Application fee:* $20. *Required:* high school transcript. *Required for some:* essay or personal statement, 3 letters of recommendation, personal statement. *Application deadlines:* rolling (freshmen), rolling (transfers). *Notification:* continuous (freshmen), continuous (transfers).
Freshman Application Contact Office of Admissions, Minnesota State University Mankato, 122 Taylor Center, Mankato, MN 56001. *Phone:* 507-389-1822. *Toll-free phone:* 800-722-0544. *Fax:* 507-389-1511. *E-mail:* admissions@mnsu.edu. *Web site:* http://www.mnsu.edu/.

Minnesota State University Moorhead

Moorhead, Minnesota

- **State-supported** comprehensive, founded 1885, part of Minnesota State Colleges and Universities System
- **Urban** 119-acre campus
- **Coed** 7,012 undergraduate students, 83% full-time, 57% women, 43% men
- **Moderately difficult** entrance level, 73% of applicants were admitted

Undergraduates 5,830 full-time, 1,182 part-time. Students come from 54 other countries; 3% Black or African American, non-Hispanic/Latino; 1% Hispanic/Latino; 1% Asian, non-Hispanic/Latino; 0.2% Native Hawaiian or other Pacific Islander, non-Hispanic/Latino; 1% American Indian or Alaska Native, non-Hispanic/Latino; 5% Race/ethnicity unknown; 6% international; 9% transferred in; 24% live on campus.
Freshmen *Admission:* 3,393 applied, 2,489 admitted, 1,217 enrolled. *Test scores:* SAT critical reading scores over 500: 57%; SAT math scores over 500: 78%; ACT scores over 18: 91%; SAT critical reading scores over 600: 23%; SAT math scores over 600: 26%; ACT scores over 24: 30%; SAT critical reading scores over 700: 3%; ACT scores over 30: 2%.
Faculty *Total:* 468, 61% full-time.
Academics *Calendar:* semesters. *Degrees:* certificates, associate, bachelor's, master's, doctoral-other, post-master's, and postbachelor's certificates. *Special study options:* academic remediation for entering students, adult/continuing education programs, advanced placement credit, distance learning, double majors, external degree program, freshman honors college, honors programs, independent study, internships, off-campus study, part-time degree program, services for LD students, student-designed majors, study abroad, summer session for credit. *ROTC:* Army (c), Air Force (c).
Computers on Campus 1,088 computers/terminals are available on campus for general student use. Students can access the following: computer help desk, free student e-mail accounts, online (class) grades, online (class) registration,

online (class) schedules. Campuswide network is available. 100% of college-owned or -operated housing units are wired for high-speed Internet access. Wireless service is available via classrooms, computer centers, computer labs, dorm rooms, libraries, student centers.

Student Life *Housing options:* coed, men-only, women-only, disabled students. Campus housing is university owned. *Activities and organizations:* drama/theater group, student-run newspaper, radio and television station, choral group, Student Senate, Sci-Fi Club, Pi Sigma Pi, Campus Crusade for Christ, Dragons 4 Wellness, national sororities. *Campus security:* 24-hour emergency response devices and patrols, student patrols, late-night transport/escort service, controlled dormitory access. *Student services:* health clinic, personal/psychological counseling, women's center.

Athletics Member NCAA. All Division II. *Intercollegiate sports:* basketball M(s)/W(s), cross-country running M/W, football M(s), golf M/W, soccer W(s), softball W(s), swimming and diving W, tennis W, track and field M(s)/W(s), volleyball W(s), wrestling M(s). *Intramural sports:* basketball M/W, football M, golf M/W, ice hockey M, racquetball M/W, soccer M/W, softball M/W, swimming and diving M/W, ultimate Frisbee M/W, volleyball W, water polo M/W.

Standardized Tests *Required:* SAT or ACT (for admission).

Costs (2010–11) *Tuition:* state resident $6140 full-time, $198 per credit hour part-time; nonresident $6140 full-time, $198 per credit hour part-time. Full-time tuition and fees vary according to program and reciprocity agreements. Part-time tuition and fees vary according to program and reciprocity agreements. *Required fees:* $783 full-time, $35 per credit hour part-time. *Room and board:* $6468; room only: $3986. Room and board charges vary according to board plan and housing facility. *Payment plan:* installment. *Waivers:* senior citizens and employees or children of employees.

Financial Aid Of all full-time matriculated undergraduates who enrolled in 2009, 5,139 applied for aid, 3,835 were judged to have need, 3,835 had their need fully met. 282 Federal Work-Study jobs (averaging $2307). 212 state and other part-time jobs (averaging $2446). *Average financial aid package:* $8172. *Average need-based loan:* $4307. *Average need-based gift aid:* $4001. *Average indebtedness upon graduation:* $27,918.

Applying *Options:* electronic application, early admission, deferred entrance. *Application fee:* $20. *Required:* high school transcript. *Application deadlines:* 8/1 (freshmen), 8/1 (out-of-state freshmen), 8/1 (transfers).

Freshman Application Contact Mr. Jeremy Johnson, Interim Director of Admissions, Minnesota State University Moorhead, Owens Hall, Moorhead, MN 56563-0002. *Phone:* 218-477-2161. *Toll-free phone:* 800-593-7246. *Fax:* 218-477-4374. *E-mail:* dragon@mnstate.edu. *Web site:* http://www.mnstate.edu/.

National American University
Roseville, Minnesota

Director of Admissions Mr. Steve Grunlan, Director of Admissions, National American University, 1500 West Highway 36, Roseville, MN 55113. *Phone:* 651-644-1265. *Web site:* http://www.national.edu/.

North Central University
Minneapolis, Minnesota

Freshman Application Contact Ms. Sigi Shawa, Assistant Director, North Central University, 910 Elliot Avenue, Minneapolis, MN 55404-1322. *Phone:* 612-343-4460. *Toll-free phone:* 800-289-6222. *Fax:* 612-343-4146. *E-mail:* admissions@northcentral.edu. *Web site:* http://www.northcentral.edu/.

Northwestern College
St. Paul, Minnesota

- **Independent nondenominational** comprehensive, founded 1902
- **Suburban** 107-acre campus with easy access to Minneapolis-St. Paul
- **Endowment** $11.6 million
- **Coed** 1,808 undergraduate students, 98% full-time, 57% women, 43% men
- **Moderately difficult** entrance level

Undergraduates 1,763 full-time, 45 part-time. Students come from 31 states and territories; 25 other countries; 30% are from out of state; 3% Black or African American, non-Hispanic/Latino; 3% Hispanic/Latino; 5% Asian, non-Hispanic/Latino; 0.4% American Indian or Alaska Native, non-Hispanic/Latino; 0.5% Two or more races, non-Hispanic/Latino; 0.9% Race/ethnicity unknown; 0.9% international; 7% transferred in; 67% live on campus. *Retention:* 80% of full-time freshmen returned.

Freshmen *Admission:* 1,388 applied, 450 enrolled. *Average high school GPA:* 3.46. *Test scores:* SAT critical reading scores over 500: 69%; SAT math scores over 500: 74%; ACT scores over 18: 94%; SAT critical reading scores over 600: 40%; SAT math scores over 600: 37%; ACT scores over 24: 55%; SAT

critical reading scores over 700: 9%; SAT math scores over 700: 11%; ACT scores over 30: 12%.

Faculty *Total:* 196, 51% full-time, 48% with terminal degrees. *Student/faculty ratio:* 14:1.

Academics *Calendar:* semesters. *Degrees:* certificates, associate, bachelor's, master's, and postbachelor's certificates. *Special study options:* academic remediation for entering students, adult/continuing education programs, advanced placement credit, distance learning, double majors, honors programs, independent study, internships, off-campus study, part-time degree program, services for LD students, student-designed majors, study abroad, summer session for credit. *ROTC:* Army (c), Air Force (c). *Unusual degree programs:* 3-2 engineering with University of Minnesota-Twin Cities.

Computers on Campus 194 computers/terminals and 1,350 ports are available on campus for general student use. Students can access the following: campus intranet, computer help desk, free student e-mail accounts, online (class) grades, online (class) registration, online (class) schedules, network file space, personal web site, integrated student portal, b/w and color printing, virtual labs. Campuswide network is available. 100% of college-owned or -operated housing units are wired for high-speed Internet access. Wireless service is available via classrooms, computer centers, computer labs, dorm rooms, learning centers, libraries, student centers.

Student Life *Housing:* on-campus residence required through junior year. *Options:* men-only, women-only, disabled students. Campus housing is university owned. Freshman campus housing is guaranteed. *Activities and organizations:* drama/theater group, student-run newspaper, radio and television station, choral group, Northwestern Student Association (student government), The Gathering (religious group), Student Missions Fellowship, Guardian Angels, Outreach Ministries. *Campus security:* 24-hour emergency response devices and patrols, late-night transport/escort service, controlled dormitory access, gated access to main campus, emergency notification system. *Student services:* health clinic, personal/psychological counseling.

Athletics Member NCAA, NCCAA. All NCAA Division III. *Intercollegiate sports:* baseball M, basketball M/W, cross-country running M/W, football M, golf M/W, ice hockey M(c), soccer M/W, softball W, tennis M/W, track and field M/W, volleyball M(c)/W. *Intramural sports:* basketball M/W, football M/W, softball M/W, table tennis M/W, tennis M/W, volleyball M/W.

Standardized Tests *Required:* SAT or ACT (for admission).

Costs (2011–12) *Comprehensive fee:* $33,700 includes full-time tuition ($25,490), mandatory fees ($210), and room and board ($8000). Full-time tuition and fees vary according to course load. Part-time tuition: $1090 per semester hour. Part-time tuition and fees vary according to course load. *Required fees:* $60 per term part-time. *College room only:* $4610. Room and board charges vary according to board plan. *Payment plan:* installment. *Waivers:* children of alumni and employees or children of employees.

Financial Aid Of all full-time matriculated undergraduates who enrolled in 2009, 1,637 applied for aid, 1,479 were judged to have need, 166 had their need fully met. 169 Federal Work-Study jobs (averaging $2139). 235 state and other part-time jobs (averaging $2080). In 2009, 253 non-need-based awards were made. *Average percent of need met:* 70%. *Average financial aid package:* $16,842. *Average need-based loan:* $4365. *Average need-based gift aid:* $12,088. *Average non-need-based aid:* $5383. *Average indebtedness upon graduation:* $26,259.

Applying *Options:* electronic application, early admission, deferred entrance. *Application fee:* $40. *Required:* essay or personal statement, high school transcript, minimum 2 GPA, 2 letters of recommendation, lifestyle agreement, statement of Christian faith. *Required for some:* interview. *Recommended:* minimum 3 GPA. *Application deadlines:* 8/1 (freshmen), 8/1 (out-of-state freshmen), 8/1 (transfers). *Notification:* continuous (freshmen), continuous (out-of-state freshmen), continuous (transfers).

Freshman Application Contact Mr. Kenneth K. Faffler, Director of Admissions, Northwestern College, Officer of Admissions, 3003 Snelling Avenue North, 212 Nazareth Hall, St. Paul, MN 55113-1598. *Phone:* 651-631-5111. *Toll-free phone:* 800-827-6827. *Fax:* 651-631-5680. *E-mail:* admissions@nwc.edu. *Web site:* http://www.nwc.edu/.

Oak Hills Christian College
Bemidji, Minnesota

- **Independent interdenominational** 4-year, founded 1946
- **Rural** 180-acre campus
- **Endowment** $371,108
- **Coed** 140 undergraduate students, 96% full-time, 52% women, 48% men
- **Minimally difficult** entrance level, 56% of applicants were admitted

Undergraduates 134 full-time, 6 part-time. Students come from 16 states and territories; 1 other country; 33% are from out of state; 4% Black or African American, non-Hispanic/Latino; 0.7% Hispanic/Latino; 1% Asian, non-Hispanic/Latino; 1% American Indian or Alaska Native, non-Hispanic/Latino; 0.7% international; 11% transferred in; 85% live on campus. *Retention:* 55% of full-time freshmen returned.

Freshmen *Admission:* 70 applied, 39 admitted, 33 enrolled. *Average high school GPA:* 3.07. *Test scores:* ACT scores over 18: 70%; ACT scores over 24: 8%.

Faculty *Total:* 19, 32% full-time, 47% with terminal degrees. *Student/faculty ratio:* 13:1.

Academics *Calendar:* semesters. *Degrees:* certificates, diplomas, associate, and bachelor's. *Special study options:* academic remediation for entering students, advanced placement credit, double majors, independent study, internships, off-campus study, part-time degree program, services for LD students.

Computers on Campus 8 computers/terminals are available on campus for general student use. Students can access the following: online (class) grades, online (class) registration, online (class) schedules. Campuswide network is available. 50% of college-owned or -operated housing units are wired for high-speed Internet access. Wireless service is available via entire campus.

Student Life *Housing:* on-campus residence required through sophomore year. *Options:* coed, men-only, women-only, disabled students. Campus housing is university owned. Freshman campus housing is guaranteed. *Activities and organizations:* choral group, Student Council (SALT), Students Older Than Average, Student Activity Team, Outreach Program. *Campus security:* controlled dormitory access, evening patrols by trained security personnel. *Student services:* health clinic, personal/psychological counseling.

Athletics *Intercollegiate sports:* basketball M, volleyball W. *Intramural sports:* basketball M/W, football M/W, golf M/W, soccer M/W, softball M/W, table tennis M/W, volleyball M/W, weight lifting M/W.

Standardized Tests *Required:* SAT or ACT (for admission).

Costs (2011–12) *Comprehensive fee:* $19,850 includes full-time tuition ($14,420), mandatory fees ($250), and room and board ($5180). Part-time tuition: $600 per credit. Part-time tuition and fees vary according to course load. No tuition increase for student's term of enrollment. *College room only:* $2072. Room and board charges vary according to board plan and housing facility. *Waivers:* employees or children of employees.

Financial Aid Of all full-time matriculated undergraduates who enrolled in 2002, 138 applied for aid, 131 were judged to have need, 9 had their need fully met. 22 Federal Work-Study jobs (averaging $1234). 54 state and other part-time jobs (averaging $2188). In 2002, 7 non-need-based awards were made. *Average percent of need met:* 73%. *Average financial aid package:* $9306. *Average need-based loan:* $3099. *Average need-based gift aid:* $6455. *Average non-need-based aid:* $2610. *Average indebtedness upon graduation:* $20,233.

Applying *Options:* electronic application, deferred entrance. *Application fee:* $25. *Required:* essay or personal statement, high school transcript, minimum 2 GPA, 2 letters of recommendation. *Required for some:* interview. *Application deadlines:* rolling (freshmen), rolling (out-of-state freshmen), rolling (transfers). *Notification:* continuous (freshmen), continuous (out-of-state freshmen), continuous (transfers).

Freshman Application Contact Shelly Fast, Assistant Director of Admissions, Oak Hills Christian College, 1600 Oak Hills Road SW, Bemidji, MN 56601. *Phone:* 218-751-8670 Ext. 1285. *Toll-free phone:* 888-751-8670 Ext. 285. *Fax:* 218-751-8825. *E-mail:* admissions@oakhills.edu. *Web site:* http://www.oakhills.edu/.

Rasmussen College Eagan

Eagan, Minnesota

Director of Admissions Ms. Jacinda Miller, Admissions Coordinator, Rasmussen College Eagan, 3500 Federal Drive, Eagan, MN 55122-1346. *Phone:* 651-687-9000. *Toll-free phone:* 800-852-6367. *Web site:* http://www.rasmussen.edu/.

Rasmussen College Eden Prairie

Eden Prairie, Minnesota

Freshman Application Contact Director of Admissions, Rasmussen College Eden Prairie, 7905 Golden Triangle Drive, Suite 100, Eden Prairie, MN 55344. *Phone:* 952-545-2000. *Toll-free phone:* 800-852-0929. *Fax:* 952-545-7038. *Web site:* http://www.rasmussen.edu/.

Rasmussen College Mankato

Mankato, Minnesota

Freshman Application Contact Ms. Kathy Clifford, Director of Admissions, Rasmussen College Mankato, 501 Holly Lane, Mankato, MN 56001-6803. *Phone:* 507-625-6556. *Toll-free phone:* 800-657-6767. *Fax:* 507-625-6557. *E-mail:* rascoll@ic.mankato.mn.us. *Web site:* http://www.rasmussen.edu/.

Rasmussen College Moorhead

Moorhead, Minnesota

Admissions Office Contact Rasmussen College Moorhead, 1250 29th Avenue South, Moorhead, MN 56560. *Toll-free phone:* 866-562-2758. *Web site:* http://www.rasmussen.edu/.

Rasmussen College St. Cloud

St. Cloud, Minnesota

Freshman Application Contact Ms. Andrea Peters, Director of Admissions, Rasmussen College St. Cloud, 226 Park Avenue South, St. Cloud, MN 56301-3713. *Phone:* 320-251-5600. *Toll-free phone:* 800-852-0460. *Fax:* 320-251-3702. *E-mail:* admstc@rasmussen.edu. *Web site:* http://www.rasmussen.edu/.

Rochester Community and Technical College

Rochester, Minnesota

Director of Admissions Mr. Troy Tynsky, Director of Admissions, Rochester Community and Technical College, 851 30th Avenue, SE, Rochester, MN 55904-4999. *Phone:* 507-280-3509. *Web site:* http://www.rctc.edu/.

St. Catherine University

St. Paul, Minnesota

- **Independent Roman Catholic** comprehensive, founded 1905
- **Urban** 110-acre campus with easy access to Minneapolis
- **Endowment** $44.7 million
- **Undergraduate: women only; graduate: coed** 3,830 undergraduate students, 67% full-time, 97% women, 3% men
- **Moderately difficult** entrance level, 61% of applicants were admitted

Undergraduates 2,573 full-time, 1,257 part-time. 9% are from out of state; 11% Black or African American, non-Hispanic/Latino; 3% Hispanic/Latino; 10% Asian, non-Hispanic/Latino; 1% American Indian or Alaska Native, non-Hispanic/Latino; 1% Two or more races, non-Hispanic/Latino; 3% Race/ethnicity unknown; 1% international; 20% transferred in; 41% live on campus. *Retention:* 84% of full-time freshmen returned.

Freshmen *Admission:* 2,441 applied, 1,494 admitted, 512 enrolled. *Average high school GPA:* 3.55. *Test scores:* ACT scores over 18: 99%; ACT scores over 24: 57%; ACT scores over 30: 9%.

Faculty *Total:* 458, 64% full-time, 46% with terminal degrees. *Student/faculty ratio:* 12:1.

Academics *Calendar:* 4-1-4. *Degrees:* certificates, associate, bachelor's, master's, doctoral-professional, post-master's, and postbachelor's certificates. *Special study options:* academic remediation for entering students, adult/continuing education programs, advanced placement credit, double majors, honors programs, independent study, internships, off-campus study, part-time degree program, services for LD students, student-designed majors, study abroad, summer session for credit. *ROTC:* Army (c), Air Force (c). *Unusual degree programs:* 3-2 engineering with Washington University in St. Louis, University of Minnesota, Twin Cities Campus; optometry with Illinois College of Optometry.

Computers on Campus 150 computers/terminals are available on campus for general student use. Students can access the following: campus intranet, computer help desk, free student e-mail accounts, online (class) grades, online (class) registration, online (class) schedules, transcript. Campuswide network is available. Wireless service is available via entire campus.

Student Life *Housing options:* women-only. Campus housing is university owned. Freshman campus housing is guaranteed. *Activities and organizations:* drama/theater group, student-run newspaper, radio station, choral group. *Campus security:* 24-hour emergency response devices and patrols, student patrols, late-night transport/escort service, controlled dormitory access. *Student services:* health clinic, personal/psychological counseling, women's center.

Athletics Member NCAA. All Division III. *Intercollegiate sports:* basketball W, cross-country running W, ice hockey W, soccer W, softball W, swimming and diving W, tennis W, track and field W, volleyball W. *Intramural sports:* basketball W, cheerleading W, cross-country running W, football W, golf W, lacrosse W, racquetball W, soccer W, softball W, swimming and diving W, tennis W, track and field W, volleyball W.

Standardized Tests *Required:* SAT or ACT (for admission).

Costs (2010–11) *One-time required fee:* $100. *Comprehensive fee:* $37,826 includes full-time tuition ($29,888), mandatory fees ($280), and room and board ($7658). Full-time tuition and fees vary according to class time and degree level. Part-time tuition: $934 per credit hour. Part-time tuition and fees vary according to class time and degree level. *Required fees:* $934 per credit hour part-time, $140 per term part-time. *College room only:* $4280. Room and board charges vary according to board plan and housing facility. *Payment* *plan:* installment. *Waivers:* senior citizens and employees or children of employees.

Financial Aid Of all full-time matriculated undergraduates who enrolled in 2009, 1,764 applied for aid, 1,649 were judged to have need, 185 had their need fully met. In 2009, 99 non-need-based awards were made. *Average percent of need met:* 84%. *Average financial aid package:* $25,790. *Average need-based loan:* $4620. *Average need-based gift aid:* $10,830. *Average non-need-based aid:* $8170. *Average indebtedness upon graduation:* $33,610.

Applying *Options:* deferred entrance. *Required:* high school transcript, 1 letter of recommendation. *Required for some:* essay or personal statement, interview. *Recommended:* interview. *Application deadlines:* rolling (freshmen), rolling (transfers). *Notification:* continuous (freshmen), continuous (transfers).

Freshman Application Contact Ms. Cory Piper-Hauswirth, Associate Director of Admission and Financial Aid, St. Catherine University, 2004 Randolph Avenue, St. Paul, MN 55105. *Phone:* 651-690-6047. *Toll-free phone:* 800-656-5283. *E-mail:* stkate@stkate.edu. *Web site:* http://www.stkate.edu/.

St. Cloud State University

St. Cloud, Minnesota

- **State-supported** comprehensive, founded 1869, part of Minnesota State Colleges and Universities System
- **Suburban** 922-acre campus with easy access to Minneapolis-St. Paul
- **Endowment** $15.6 million
- **Coed**
- **Moderately difficult** entrance level

Faculty *Student/faculty ratio:* 19:1.

Academics *Calendar:* semesters. *Degrees:* certificates, diplomas, associate, bachelor's, master's, doctoral-research/scholarship, post-master's, and post-bachelor's certificates.

Student Life *Campus security:* 24-hour emergency response devices and patrols, late-night transport/escort service.

Athletics Member NCAA. All Division II except men's and women's ice hockey (Division I).

Standardized Tests *Required:* SAT or ACT (for admission).

Costs (2010–11) *Tuition:* state resident $5985 full-time, $200 per credit part-time; nonresident $12,938 full-time, $431 per credit part-time. Full-time tuition and fees vary according to course load and reciprocity agreements. Part-time tuition and fees vary according to course load and reciprocity agreements. *Required fees:* $733 full-time, $32 per semester hour part-time. *Room and board:* $5984; room only: $3824. Room and board charges vary according to board plan and housing facility.

Financial Aid Of all full-time matriculated undergraduates who enrolled in 2008, 7,982 applied for aid, 5,885 were judged to have need, 3,268 had their need fully met. In 2008, 173 non-need-based awards were made. *Average percent of need met:* 56. *Average financial aid package:* $10,059. *Average need-based loan:* $4923. *Average need-based gift aid:* $4773. *Average non-need-based aid:* $1928. *Average indebtedness upon graduation:* $24,484.

Applying *Options:* electronic application, deferred entrance. *Application fee:* $20. *Required:* high school transcript.

Freshman Application Contact Mr. Richard Shearer, Director of Admissions, St. Cloud State University, 115 AS Building, 720 4th Avenue South, St. Cloud, MN 56301-4498. *Phone:* 320-308-2244. *Toll-free phone:* 877-654-7278. *Fax:* 320-308-2243. *E-mail:* scsu4u@stcloudstate.edu. *Web site:* http://www.stcloudstate.edu/.

Saint John's University

Collegeville, Minnesota

- **Independent Roman Catholic** comprehensive, founded 1857
- **Rural** 2500-acre campus with easy access to Minneapolis-St. Paul
- **Endowment** $121.6 million
- **Men only** 1,932 undergraduate students, 98% full-time
- **Moderately difficult** entrance level, 92% of applicants were admitted

Undergraduates 1,895 full-time, 37 part-time. Students come from 35 states and territories; 38 other countries; 14% are from out of state; 2% Black or African American, non-Hispanic/Latino; 2% Hispanic/Latino; 2% Asian, non-Hispanic/Latino; 0.2% Native Hawaiian or other Pacific Islander, non-Hispanic/Latino; 0.5% American Indian or Alaska Native, non-Hispanic/Latino; 0.2% Two or more races, non-Hispanic/Latino; 0.7% Race/ethnicity unknown; 7% international; 2% transferred in; 83% live on campus. *Retention:* 92% of full-time freshmen returned.

Freshmen *Admission:* 835 applied, 767 admitted, 503 enrolled. *Average high school GPA:* 3.52. *Test scores:* SAT critical reading scores over 500: 68%; SAT math scores over 500: 89%; SAT writing scores over 500: 68%; ACT scores over 18: 99%; SAT critical reading scores over 600: 34%; SAT math scores over 600: 52%; SAT writing scores over 600: 36%; ACT scores over 24:

73%; SAT critical reading scores over 700: 5%; SAT math scores over 700: 17%; SAT writing scores over 700: 8%; ACT scores over 30: 22%.

Faculty *Total:* 181, 82% full-time, 76% with terminal degrees. *Student/faculty ratio:* 12:1.

Academics *Calendar:* semesters. *Degrees:* bachelor's and master's (coordinate with College of Saint Benedict for women). *Special study options:* advanced placement credit, double majors, English as a second language, honors programs, independent study, internships, off-campus study, services for LD students, student-designed majors, study abroad. *ROTC:* Army (b). *Unusual degree programs:* 3-2 engineering with University of Minnesota.

Computers on Campus 901 computers/terminals and 3,000 ports are available on campus for general student use. Students can access the following: campus intranet, computer help desk, free student e-mail accounts, online (class) grades, online (class) registration, online (class) schedules, online student accounts. Campuswide network is available. 100% of college-owned or -operated housing units are wired for high-speed Internet access. Wireless service is available via entire campus.

Student Life *Housing:* on-campus residence required through senior year. *Options:* men-only, disabled students. Campus housing is university owned. Freshman campus housing is guaranteed. *Activities and organizations:* drama/theater group, student-run newspaper, radio station, choral group, Asia Club, Outskirts Snow Club, Biology Club, Trapshooting Club, Joints Events Council. *Campus security:* 24-hour emergency response devices and patrols, student patrols, late-night transport/escort service, controlled dormitory access, well-lit pathways, 911 center on campus, closed circuit TV monitors. *Student services:* health clinic, personal/psychological counseling.

Athletics Member NCAA. All Division III. *Intercollegiate sports:* baseball M, basketball M, crew M(c), cross-country running M, football M, golf M, ice hockey M, lacrosse M(c), riflery M(c), rugby M(c), skiing (cross-country) M, soccer M, swimming and diving M, tennis M, track and field M, ultimate Frisbee M(c), volleyball M(c), water polo M(c), wrestling M. *Intramural sports:* basketball M, football M, racquetball M, rock climbing M(c), skiing (cross-country) M(c), skiing (downhill) M(c), soccer M, softball M, table tennis M, ultimate Frisbee M, volleyball M.

Standardized Tests *Required:* SAT or ACT (for admission).

Costs (2010–11) *Comprehensive fee:* $39,620 includes full-time tuition ($31,006), mandatory fees ($570), and room and board ($8044). Part-time tuition: $1292 per credit hour. Part-time tuition and fees vary according to course load. *College room only:* $4040. Room and board charges vary according to board plan and housing facility. *Payment plan:* installment.

Financial Aid Of all full-time matriculated undergraduates who enrolled in 2009, 1,374 applied for aid, 1,171 were judged to have need, 487 had their need fully met. 308 Federal Work-Study jobs (averaging $2545). 818 state and other part-time jobs (averaging $2616). In 2009, 595 non-need-based awards were made. *Average percent of need met:* 87%. *Average financial aid package:* $22,605. *Average need-based loan:* $3980. *Average need-based gift aid:* $18,570. *Average non-need-based aid:* $11,430.

Applying *Options:* electronic application, early action, deferred entrance. *Required:* essay or personal statement, high school transcript, 1 letter of recommendation. *Recommended:* minimum 3 GPA, interview. *Application deadlines:* rolling (freshmen), rolling (transfers), 11/15 (early action). *Notification:* continuous (freshmen), continuous (transfers), 12/15 (early action).

Freshman Application Contact Mr. Matt Beirne, Director of Admission, Saint John's University, PO Box 7155, Collegeville, MN 56321-7155. *Phone:* 320-363-5055. *Toll-free phone:* 800-544-1489. *Fax:* 320-363-5650. *E-mail:* admissions@csbsju.edu. *Web site:* http://www.csbsju.edu/.

Saint Mary's University of Minnesota

Winona, Minnesota

- **Independent Roman Catholic** comprehensive, founded 1912
- **Small-town** 350-acre campus
- **Endowment** $37.1 million
- **Coed** 2,114 undergraduate students, 68% full-time, 53% women, 47% men
- **Moderately difficult** entrance level, 71% of applicants were admitted

Undergraduates 1,440 full-time, 674 part-time. Students come from 26 states and territories; 21 other countries; 36% are from out of state; 5% Black or African American, non-Hispanic/Latino; 3% Hispanic/Latino; 2% Asian, non-Hispanic/Latino; 0.0% Native Hawaiian or other Pacific Islander, non-Hispanic/Latino; 0.1% American Indian or Alaska Native, non-Hispanic/Latino; 24% Race/ethnicity unknown; 2% international; 8% transferred in; 83% live on campus. *Retention:* 75% of full-time freshmen returned.

Freshmen *Admission:* 1,507 applied, 1,076 admitted, 347 enrolled. *Average high school GPA:* 3.2. *Test scores:* SAT critical reading scores over 500: 78%; SAT math scores over 500: 64%; ACT scores over 18: 89%; SAT critical reading scores over 600: 23%; SAT math scores over 600: 9%; ACT scores over 24: 41%; SAT critical reading scores over 700: 5%; ACT scores over 30: 4%.

Faculty *Total:* 598, 17% full-time, 44% with terminal degrees. *Student/faculty ratio:* 13:1.

Academics *Calendar:* semesters. *Degrees:* certificates, diplomas, bachelor's, master's, doctoral-professional, doctoral-research/scholarship, post-master's, and postbachelor's certificates. *Special study options:* academic remediation for entering students, accelerated degree program, adult/continuing education programs, advanced placement credit, cooperative education, double majors, English as a second language, honors programs, independent study, internships, off-campus study, part-time degree program, services for LD students, student-designed majors, study abroad, summer session for credit. *ROTC:* Army (c).

Computers on Campus 200 computers/terminals and 50 ports are available on campus for general student use. Students can access the following: campus intranet, computer help desk, free student e-mail accounts, online (class) grades, online (class) registration, online (class) schedules. Campuswide network is available. 100% of college-owned or -operated housing units are wired for high-speed Internet access. Wireless service is available via computer centers, computer labs, dorm rooms, libraries, student centers.

Student Life *Housing:* on-campus residence required through sophomore year. *Options:* coed, men-only, women-only, disabled students. Campus housing is university owned. Freshman campus housing is guaranteed. *Activities and organizations:* drama/theater group, student-run newspaper, radio station, choral group, Student Activity Committee, Habitat for Humanity, Serving Others United in Love (Soul) - Mission Trips, Colleges Against Cancer, concert choir/chamber singers, national fraternities, national sororities. *Campus security:* 24-hour emergency response devices and patrols, late-night transport/escort service, controlled dormitory access. *Student services:* health clinic, personal/psychological counseling.

Athletics Member NCAA. All Division III. *Intercollegiate sports:* baseball M, basketball M/W, cross-country running M/W, golf M/W, ice hockey M/W, soccer M/W, softball W, swimming and diving M/W, tennis M/W, track and field M/W, volleyball W. *Intramural sports:* basketball M/W, cheerleading W(c), fencing M(c)/W(c), field hockey M/W, football M/W, ice hockey M, lacrosse M(c)/W(c), rugby M(c), skiing (downhill) M(c)/W(c), soccer M/W, softball M/W, tennis M/W, ultimate Frisbee M/W, volleyball M/W, water polo M(c)/W(c).

Standardized Tests *Required:* SAT or ACT (for admission).

Costs (2011–12) *Comprehensive fee:* $34,400 includes full-time tuition ($26,750), mandatory fees ($500), and room and board ($7150). Full-time tuition and fees vary according to course load, degree level, location, and program. Part-time tuition: $895 per credit. Part-time tuition and fees vary according to course load, degree level, location, and program. *Required fees:* $500 per year part-time. *College room only:* $4000. Room and board charges vary according to housing facility. *Payment plan:* installment. *Waivers:* employees or children of employees.

Financial Aid Of all full-time matriculated undergraduates who enrolled in 2009, 1,178 applied for aid, 1,082 were judged to have need, 192 had their need fully met. 185 Federal Work-Study jobs (averaging $1651). 347 state and other part-time jobs (averaging $1698). In 2009, 276 non-need-based awards were made. *Average percent of need met:* 74%. *Average financial aid package:* $19,789. *Average need-based loan:* $4573. *Average need-based gift aid:* $15,796. *Average non-need-based aid:* $10,244. *Average indebtedness upon graduation:* $30,237.

Applying *Options:* electronic application, early admission, deferred entrance. *Application fee:* $25. *Required:* essay or personal statement, high school transcript, minimum 2.5 GPA. *Required for some:* interview. *Recommended:* 2 letters of recommendation. *Application deadlines:* 5/1 (freshmen), rolling (transfers). *Notification:* continuous (freshmen), continuous (transfers).

Freshman Application Contact Mr. Anthony M. Piscitiello, Vice President for Admission, Saint Mary's University of Minnesota, 700 Terrace Heights, Winona, MN 55987-1399. *Phone:* 507-457-1700. *Toll-free phone:* 800-635-5987. *Fax:* 507-457-1722. *E-mail:* admission@smumn.edu. *Web site:* http://www.smumn.edu/.

St. Olaf College

Northfield, Minnesota

- **Independent Lutheran** 4-year, founded 1874
- **Small-town** 300-acre campus with easy access to Minneapolis-St. Paul
- **Endowment** $274.3 million
- **Coed** 3,156 undergraduate students, 98% full-time, 55% women, 45% men
- **Very difficult** entrance level, 57% of applicants were admitted

Undergraduates 3,105 full-time, 51 part-time. Students come from 47 states and territories; 39 other countries; 48% are from out of state; 2% Black or African American, non-Hispanic/Latino; 2% Hispanic/Latino; 5% Asian, non-Hispanic/Latino; 0.1% Native Hawaiian or other Pacific Islander, non-Hispanic/Latino; 0.3% American Indian or Alaska Native, non-Hispanic/Latino; 2% Two or more races, non-Hispanic/Latino; 2% Race/ethnicity unknown; 3% international; 1% transferred in; 92% live on campus. *Retention:* 93% of full-time freshmen returned.

Freshmen *Admission:* 4,024 applied, 2,303 admitted, 844 enrolled. *Average high school GPA:* 3.63. *Test scores:* SAT critical reading scores over 500: 95%; SAT math scores over 500: 96%; ACT scores over 18: 98%; SAT critical reading scores over 600: 75%; SAT math scores over 600: 76%; ACT scores over 24: 89%; SAT critical reading scores over 700: 34%; SAT math scores over 700: 30%; ACT scores over 30: 45%.

Faculty *Total:* 336, 63% full-time, 78% with terminal degrees. *Student/faculty ratio:* 12:1.

Academics *Calendar:* 4-1-4. *Degree:* bachelor's. *Special study options:* advanced placement credit, double majors, independent study, internships, off-campus study, part-time degree program, services for LD students, student-designed majors, study abroad, summer session for credit. *Unusual degree programs:* 3-2 engineering with Washington University in St. Louis and University of Minnesota in Minneapolis.

Computers on Campus 899 computers/terminals and 3,076 ports are available on campus for general student use. Students can access the following: campus intranet, computer help desk, free student e-mail accounts, online (class) grades, online (class) registration, online (class) schedules. Campuswide network is available. 100% of college-owned or -operated housing units are wired for high-speed Internet access. Wireless service is available via entire campus.

Student Life *Housing:* on-campus residence required through senior year. *Options:* coed, disabled students. Campus housing is university owned. Freshman campus housing is guaranteed. *Activities and organizations:* drama/theater group, student-run newspaper, radio and television station, choral group, Student Government Association, Ultimate Frisbee Teams, Ole Spring Relief, Taiko Drumming, SELAH. *Campus security:* 24-hour emergency response devices and patrols, late-night transport/escort service, controlled dormitory access, lighted pathways and sidewalks, first-year only dorms, quiet halls. *Student services:* health clinic, personal/psychological counseling.

Athletics Member NCAA. All Division III. *Intercollegiate sports:* baseball M, basketball M/W, cross-country running M/W, football M, golf M/W, ice hockey M/W, skiing (cross-country) M/W, skiing (downhill) M/W, soccer M/W, softball W, swimming and diving M/W, tennis M/W, track and field M/W, volleyball W, wrestling M. *Intramural sports:* badminton M(c)/W(c), basketball M/W, cheerleading M(c)/W(c), crew M(c)/W(c), equestrian sports M(c)/W(c), fencing M(c)/W(c), field hockey M, football M/W, golf M/W, ice hockey M(c), lacrosse M(c)/W(c), racquetball M/W, rugby M(c)/W(c), skiing (cross-country) M/W, skiing (downhill) M(c)/W(c), soccer M/W, softball M/W, swimming and diving M/W, table tennis M/W, tennis M/W, ultimate Frisbee M/W, volleyball M(c)/W, water polo M/W.

Standardized Tests *Required:* SAT or ACT (for admission).

Costs (2010–11) *Comprehensive fee:* $45,300 includes full-time tuition ($36,800) and room and board ($8500). Full-time tuition and fees vary according to course load. Part-time tuition: $1150 per credit hour. Part-time tuition and fees vary according to course load. *College room only:* $3950. Room and board charges vary according to board plan and housing facility. *Payment plan:* installment. *Waivers:* senior citizens and employees or children of employees.

Financial Aid Of all full-time matriculated undergraduates who enrolled in 2009, 2,391 applied for aid, 2,104 were judged to have need, 2,104 had their need fully met. 990 Federal Work-Study jobs (averaging $1996). 1,162 state and other part-time jobs (averaging $1750). In 2009, 521 non-need-based awards were made. *Average percent of need met:* 100%. *Average financial aid package:* $27,866. *Average need-based loan:* $4814. *Average need-based gift aid:* $23,711. *Average non-need-based aid:* $9951. *Average indebtedness upon graduation:* $26,115. *Financial aid deadline:* 3/1.

Applying *Options:* electronic application, early decision, deferred entrance. *Application fee:* $40. *Required:* essay or personal statement, high school transcript, 2 letters of recommendation. *Recommended:* minimum 3 GPA, interview. *Application deadlines:* 1/15 (freshmen), 3/1 (transfers). *Early decision deadline:* 11/15 (for plan 1), 1/15 (for plan 2). *Notification:* 3/20 (freshmen), 4/1 (transfers), 12/15 (early decision plan 1), 2/15 (early decision plan 2).

Freshman Application Contact Derek Gueldenzoph, Dean of Admissions, St. Olaf College, 1520 St. Olaf Avenue, Northfield, MN 55057. *Phone:* 507-786-3025. *Toll-free phone:* 800-800-3025. *Fax:* 507-786-3832. *E-mail:* admissions@stolaf.edu. *Web site:* http://www.stolaf.edu/.

Southwest Minnesota State University

Marshall, Minnesota

- **State-supported** comprehensive, founded 1963, part of Minnesota State Colleges and Universities System
- **Small-town** 216-acre campus
- **Endowment** $4.0 million
- **Coed**
- **Minimally difficult** entrance level

Faculty *Student/faculty ratio:* 20:1.

Academics *Calendar:* semesters. *Degrees:* associate, bachelor's, master's, and postbachelor's certificates.

Student Life *Campus security:* 24-hour emergency response devices and patrols, student patrols, late-night transport/escort service, controlled dormitory access.

Athletics Member NCAA. All Division II.

Standardized Tests *Required:* SAT or ACT (for admission). *Recommended:* ACT (for admission).

Financial Aid *Of all full-time matriculated undergraduates who enrolled in 2009,* 1,830 applied for aid, 1,472 were judged to have need, 263 had their need fully met. 101 Federal Work-Study jobs (averaging $2173). 205 state and other part-time jobs (averaging $2150). *In 2009,* 349 non-need-based awards were made. *Average percent of need met:* 57. *Average financial aid package:* $8541. *Average need-based loan:* $3946. *Average need-based gift aid:* $5128. *Average non-need-based aid:* $2643. *Average indebtedness upon graduation:* $18,830.

Applying *Options:* electronic application, early admission, deferred entrance. *Application fee:* $20. *Required:* high school transcript, minimum 3 GPA, top half of graduating class or 21 ACT. *Required for some:* interview.

Freshman Application Contact Ms. LeAnn Thooft, Director of Admissions (Interim), Southwest Minnesota State University, Southwest Minnesota State University, 1501 State Street, Marsahll, MN 56258. *Phone:* 507-537-6286. *Toll-free phone:* 800-642-0684. *Fax:* 507-537-7145. *E-mail:* leann.thooft@ smsu.edu. *Web site:* http://www.smsu.edu/.

University of Minnesota, Crookston

Crookston, Minnesota

- **State-supported** 4-year, founded 1966, part of University of Minnesota System
- **Rural** 237-acre campus
- **Endowment** $9.6 million
- **Coed** 2,528 undergraduate students, 51% full-time, 52% women, 48% men
- **Moderately difficult** entrance level, 78% of applicants were admitted

Undergraduates 1,282 full-time, 1,246 part-time. Students come from 41 states and territories; 29 other countries; 26% are from out of state; 7% transferred in; 41% live on campus. *Retention:* 67% of full-time freshmen returned.

Freshmen *Admission:* 787 applied, 615 admitted, 269 enrolled. *Average high school GPA:* 3.1. *Test scores:* SAT critical reading scores over 500: 37%; SAT math scores over 500: 41%; SAT writing scores over 500: 100%; ACT scores over 18: 91%; SAT critical reading scores over 600: 19%; SAT math scores over 600: 5%; SAT writing scores over 600: 50%; ACT scores over 24: 28%; SAT critical reading scores over 700: 5%; SAT math scores over 700: 5%; ACT scores over 30: 6%.

Faculty *Total:* 109, 52% full-time, 45% with terminal degrees. *Student/faculty ratio:* 20:1.

Academics *Calendar:* semesters. *Degree:* bachelor's. *Special study options:* academic remediation for entering students, advanced placement credit, distance learning, double majors, English as a second language, external degree program, honors programs, independent study, internships, off-campus study, part-time degree program, services for LD students, student-designed majors, study abroad, summer session for credit. *ROTC:* Air Force (c).

Computers on Campus 25 computers/terminals are available on campus for general student use. Students can access the following: campus intranet, computer help desk, free student e-mail accounts, online (class) grades, online (class) registration, online (class) schedules, personal Web pages. Campuswide network is available. 100% of college-owned or -operated housing units are wired for high-speed Internet access. Wireless service is available via entire campus.

Student Life *Housing options:* coed, disabled students. Campus housing is university owned. Freshman applicants given priority for college housing. *Activities and organizations:* drama/theater group, choral group, Students in Free Enterprise (SIFE), Natural Resources Club, Horseman's Association, Multicultural and International Club, Ag-Arama Planning Club, national fraternities, national sororities. *Campus security:* 24-hour emergency response devices, student patrols, controlled dormitory access. *Student services:* health clinic, personal/psychological counseling, women's center.

Athletics Member NCAA. All Division II. *Intercollegiate sports:* baseball M(s), basketball M(s)/W(s), equestrian sports W(s), football M(s), golf M(s)/ W(s), soccer W(s), softball W(s), tennis W(s), volleyball W(s). *Intramural sports:* basketball M/W, football M/W, golf M/W, ice hockey M(c), racquetball M/W, soccer M(c)/W, softball M/W, table tennis M/W, tennis M/W, volleyball M/W.

Standardized Tests *Required:* SAT or ACT (for admission). *Recommended:* ACT (for admission).

Costs (2010–11) *Tuition:* state resident $7932 full-time, $305 per semester hour part-time; nonresident $7932 full-time, $305 per semester hour part-time. Full-time tuition and fees vary according to course load and reciprocity agree-

ments. Part-time tuition and fees vary according to course load and reciprocity agreements. No tuition increase for student's term of enrollment. *Required fees:* $2691 full-time. *Room and board:* $6568; room only: $3088. Room and board charges vary according to board plan and housing facility. *Payment plan:* installment. *Waivers:* senior citizens.

Financial Aid Of all full-time matriculated undergraduates who enrolled in 2009, 970 applied for aid, 849 were judged to have need, 217 had their need fully met. 186 Federal Work-Study jobs (averaging $1000). 81 state and other part-time jobs (averaging $1000). In 2009, 84 non-need-based awards were made. *Average percent of need met:* 75%. *Average financial aid package:* $11,848. *Average need-based loan:* $4920. *Average need-based gift aid:* $7743. *Average non-need-based aid:* $2411. *Average indebtedness upon graduation:* $25,852.

Applying *Options:* electronic application, deferred entrance. *Application fee:* $30. *Required:* high school transcript, minimum 2 GPA, ACT composite 21 or SAT 980. *Application deadlines:* rolling (freshmen), rolling (out-of-state freshmen), rolling (transfers). *Notification:* continuous (freshmen), continuous (out-of-state freshmen), continuous (transfers).

Freshman Application Contact Ms. Amber Evans-Dailey, Director of Admissions, University of Minnesota, Crookston, 2900 University Avenue, Crookston, MN 56716-5001. *Phone:* 218-281-8569. *Toll-free phone:* 800-862-6466. *Fax:* 218-281-8575. *E-mail:* evan0331@umn.edu. *Web site:* http:/ /www.umcrookston.edu/.

University of Minnesota, Duluth

Duluth, Minnesota

- **State-supported** comprehensive, founded 1947, part of University of Minnesota System
- **Suburban** 250-acre campus
- **Endowment** $88.9 million
- **Coed** 10,628 undergraduate students, 89% full-time, 48% women, 52% men
- **Moderately difficult** entrance level, 76% of applicants were admitted

Undergraduates 9,458 full-time, 1,170 part-time. Students come from 38 states and territories; 45 other countries; 11% are from out of state; 1% Black or African American, non-Hispanic/Latino; 1% Hispanic/Latino; 3% Asian, non-Hispanic/Latino; 0.2% Native Hawaiian or other Pacific Islander, non-Hispanic/Latino; 1% American Indian or Alaska Native, non-Hispanic/Latino; 1% Race/ethnicity unknown; 1% international; 5% transferred in; 29% live on campus. *Retention:* 82% of full-time freshmen returned.

Freshmen *Admission:* 7,850 applied, 5,986 admitted, 2,344 enrolled. *Average high school GPA:* 3.41. *Test scores:* SAT critical reading scores over 500: 65%; SAT math scores over 500: 64%; SAT writing scores over 500: 55%; ACT scores over 18: 97%; SAT critical reading scores over 600: 23%; SAT math scores over 600: 41%; SAT writing scores over 600: 15%; ACT scores over 24: 50%; SAT critical reading scores over 700: 2%; SAT math scores over 700: 6%; SAT writing scores over 700: 2%; ACT scores over 30: 5%.

Faculty *Total:* 566, 78% full-time, 63% with terminal degrees. *Student/faculty ratio:* 20:1.

Academics *Calendar:* semesters. *Degrees:* bachelor's, master's, doctoral-professional, and postbachelor's certificates. *Special study options:* academic remediation for entering students, adult/continuing education programs, advanced placement credit, cooperative education, distance learning, double majors, English as a second language, external degree program, honors programs, independent study, internships, off-campus study, part-time degree program, services for LD students, student-designed majors, study abroad, summer session for credit. *ROTC:* Air Force (b).

Computers on Campus 465 computers/terminals are available on campus for general student use. Students can access the following: campus intranet, computer help desk, free student e-mail accounts, online (class) grades, online (class) registration, online (class) schedules. Campuswide network is available. 100% of college-owned or -operated housing units are wired for high-speed Internet access. Wireless service is available via entire campus.

Student Life *Housing options:* coed, men-only, women-only, disabled students. Campus housing is university owned. Freshman applicants given priority for college housing. *Activities and organizations:* drama/theater group, student-run newspaper, radio station, choral group, marching band, national fraternities, national sororities. *Campus security:* 24-hour emergency response devices and patrols, late-night transport/escort service. *Student services:* health clinic, personal/psychological counseling, women's center.

Athletics Member NCAA. All Division II except men's and women's ice hockey (Division I). *Intercollegiate sports:* baseball M(s), basketball M(s)/ W(s), cheerleading W(c), crew M(c)/W(c), cross-country running M(s)/W(s), football M(s), ice hockey M(s)/W(s), lacrosse M(s)(c)/W(c), rock climbing M(c)/W(c), rugby M(c)/W(c), skiing (cross-country) M(c)/W(c), skiing (downhill) M(c)/W(c), soccer M(c)/W(s), softball W(s), swimming and diving M(c)/W(s), tennis W(s), track and field M(s)/W(s), ultimate Frisbee M(c)/ W(c), volleyball M(c)/W(s). *Intramural sports:* badminton M/W, basketball M/W, bowling M/W, football M/W, golf M/W, ice hockey M/W, rugby M/W, sailing M/W, skiing (cross-country) M/W, skiing (downhill) M/W, soccer M/W, softball M/W, table tennis M/W, tennis M/W, ultimate Frisbee M/W, volleyball M/W, water polo M/W.

Standardized Tests *Required:* SAT or ACT (for admission).

Costs (2010–11) *Tuition:* state resident $9482 full-time, $365 per credit part-time; nonresident $11,482 full-time, $442 per credit part-time. Full-time tuition and fees vary according to course load and reciprocity agreements. Part-time tuition and fees vary according to course load and reciprocity agreements. *Required fees:* $2325 full-time, $65 per credit part-time. *Room and board:* $6422. Room and board charges vary according to board plan and housing facility. *Payment plan:* installment. *Waivers:* employees or children of employees.

Financial Aid Of all full-time matriculated undergraduates who enrolled in 2008, 7,447 applied for aid, 5,713 were judged to have need, 1,285 had their need fully met. In 2008, 873 non-need-based awards were made. *Average percent of need met:* 75%. *Average financial aid package:* $10,655. *Average need-based loan:* $4651. *Average need-based gift aid:* $6922. *Average non-need-based aid:* $3122. *Average indebtedness upon graduation:* $30,098.

Applying *Options:* electronic application. *Application fee:* $35. *Required:* high school transcript. *Application deadlines:* 12/15 (freshmen), 8/1 (transfers). *Notification:* continuous (freshmen), continuous (transfers).

Freshman Application Contact Office of Admissions, University of Minnesota, Duluth, 25 Solon Campus Center, 1117 University Drive, Duluth, MN 55812-3000. *Phone:* 218-726-7171. *Toll-free phone:* 800-232-1339. *Fax:* 218-726-7040. *E-mail:* umdadmis@d.umn.edu. *Web site:* http://www.d.umn.edu/.

University of Minnesota, Morris
Morris, Minnesota

Freshman Application Contact University of Minnesota, Morris, 600 East 4th Street, Morris, MN 56267-2134. *Phone:* 320-539-6035. *Toll-free phone:* 800-992-8863. *Fax:* 320-589-1673. *E-mail:* admissions@morris.umn.edu. *Web site:* http://www.mrs.umn.edu/.

University of Minnesota, Twin Cities Campus
Minneapolis, Minnesota

- **State-supported** comprehensive, founded 1851, part of University of Minnesota System
- **Urban** 2000-acre campus
- **Coed** 33,607 undergraduate students, 87% full-time, 52% women, 48% men
- **Moderately difficult** entrance level, 48% of applicants were admitted

Undergraduates 29,180 full-time, 4,427 part-time. Students come from 51 states and territories; 87 other countries; 25% are from out of state; 7% transferred in; 21% live on campus. *Retention:* 89% of full-time freshmen returned.

Freshmen *Admission:* 36,853 applied, 17,613 admitted, 5,323 enrolled. *Test scores:* SAT critical reading scores over 500: 84%; SAT math scores over 500: 96%; SAT writing scores over 500: 88%; ACT scores over 18: 99%; SAT critical reading scores over 600: 56%; SAT math scores over 600: 78%; SAT writing scores over 600: 54%; ACT scores over 24: 85%; SAT critical reading scores over 700: 21%; SAT math scores over 700: 35%; SAT writing scores over 700: 13%; ACT scores over 30: 27%.

Faculty *Total:* 2,706, 68% full-time, 69% with terminal degrees. *Student/faculty ratio:* 21:1.

Academics *Calendar:* semesters. *Degrees:* certificates, diplomas, bachelor's, master's, doctoral-professional, doctoral-research/scholarship, post-master's, and postbachelor's certificates. *Special study options:* academic remediation for entering students, accelerated degree program, adult/continuing education programs, advanced placement credit, cooperative education, distance learning, double majors, English as a second language, external degree program, freshman honors college, honors programs, independent study, internships, off-campus study, part-time degree program, services for LD students, student-designed majors, study abroad, summer session for credit. *ROTC:* Army (b), Navy (b), Air Force (b).

Computers on Campus Students can access the following: computer help desk, free student e-mail accounts, online (class) grades, online (class) registration, online (class) schedules. Campuswide network is available.

Student Life *Housing options:* coed, cooperative, disabled students. Campus housing is university owned. Freshman campus housing is guaranteed. *Activities and organizations:* drama/theater group, student-run newspaper, radio and television station, choral group, marching band, student government, national fraternities, national sororities. *Campus security:* 24-hour emergency response devices and patrols, student patrols, late-night transport/escort service, controlled dormitory access, safety/security orientation, security lighting. *Student*

services: health clinic, personal/psychological counseling, women's center, legal services.

Athletics Member NCAA. All Division I except football (Division I-A). *Intercollegiate sports:* baseball M(s), basketball M(s)/W(s), cross-country running M(s)/W(s), golf M(s)/W(s), gymnastics M(s)/W(s), ice hockey M(s)/W(s), soccer W(s), softball W(s), swimming and diving M(s)/W(s), tennis M(s)/W(s), track and field M(s)/W(s), volleyball W(s), wrestling M(s). *Intramural sports:* baseball M/W, basketball M/W, bowling M/W, crew M/W, football M/W, golf M/W, ice hockey M/W, rugby M/W, skiing (cross-country) M/W, skiing (downhill) M/W, soccer M/W, softball M/W, tennis M/W, volleyball M/W, water polo M/W, wrestling M/W.

Standardized Tests *Required:* SAT or ACT (for admission).

Costs (2010–11) *Tuition:* state resident $9794 full-time, $377 per credit part-time; nonresident $14,094 full-time, $542 per credit part-time. Full-time tuition and fees vary according to program and reciprocity agreements. Part-time tuition and fees vary according to course load, program, and reciprocity agreements. *Required fees:* $2409 full-time. *Room and board:* $7774; room only: $4348. Room and board charges vary according to board plan, housing facility, and location. *Payment plan:* installment. *Waivers:* senior citizens.

Financial Aid Of all full-time matriculated undergraduates who enrolled in 2009, 20,455 applied for aid, 15,663 were judged to have need, 4,629 had their need fully met. In 2009, 4051 non-need-based awards were made. *Average percent of need met:* 74%. *Average financial aid package:* $12,126. *Average need-based loan:* $5308. *Average need-based gift aid:* $7698. *Average non-need-based aid:* $4716. *Average indebtedness upon graduation:* $27,578.

Applying *Options:* electronic application, early admission, deferred entrance. *Application fee:* $45. *Required:* high school transcript. *Recommended:* minimum 2 GPA. *Application deadlines:* rolling (freshmen), rolling (transfers). *Notification:* continuous (freshmen), continuous (transfers).

Freshman Application Contact Rachelle Hernandez, Associate Director of Admissions, University of Minnesota, Twin Cities Campus, 240 Williamson, Minneapolis, MN 55455-0213. *Phone:* 612-625-2008. *Toll-free phone:* 800-752-1000. *Fax:* 612-626-1693. *E-mail:* admissions@tc.umn.edu. *Web site:* http://www.umn.edu/tc/.

University of St. Thomas
St. Paul, Minnesota

- **Independent Roman Catholic** university, founded 1885
- **Urban** 78-acre campus with easy access to Minneapolis
- **Coed** 6,270 undergraduate students, 95% full-time, 47% women, 53% men
- **Moderately difficult** entrance level, 85% of applicants were admitted

Undergraduates 5,958 full-time, 312 part-time. 16% are from out of state; 3% Black or African American, non-Hispanic/Latino; 4% Hispanic/Latino; 5% Asian, non-Hispanic/Latino; 0.1% American Indian or Alaska Native, non-Hispanic/Latino; 3% Two or more races, non-Hispanic/Latino; 3% Race/ethnicity unknown; 2% international; 4% transferred in; 27% live on campus. *Retention:* 89% of full-time freshmen returned.

Freshmen *Admission:* 5,120 applied, 4,348 admitted, 1,519 enrolled. *Average high school GPA:* 3.54. *Test scores:* SAT math scores over 500: 85%; SAT writing scores over 500: 84%; ACT scores over 18: 100%; SAT math scores over 600: 47%; SAT writing scores over 600: 46%; ACT scores over 24: 70%; SAT math scores over 700: 11%; SAT writing scores over 700: 13%; ACT scores over 30: 13%.

Faculty *Student/faculty ratio:* 15:1.

Academics *Calendar:* 4-1-4. *Degrees:* certificates, bachelor's, master's, doctoral-professional, doctoral-research/scholarship, post-master's, and postbachelor's certificates. *Special study options:* advanced placement credit, double majors, English as a second language, honors programs, independent study, internships, off-campus study, part-time degree program, services for LD students, student-designed majors, study abroad, summer session for credit. *ROTC:* Army (c), Navy (c), Air Force (b). *Unusual degree programs:* 3-2 engineering with University of Notre Dame, Washington University in St. Louis, University of Minnesota-Twin Cities, Kettering University.

Computers on Campus Students can access the following: online (class) registration. Campuswide network is available.

Student Life *Housing options:* men-only, women-only. Campus housing is university owned. Freshman applicants given priority for college housing. *Activities and organizations:* drama/theater group, student-run newspaper, radio and television station, choral group. *Campus security:* 24-hour emergency response devices and patrols, late-night transport/escort service, controlled dormitory access. *Student services:* health clinic, personal/psychological counseling, women's center, legal services.

Athletics Member NCAA. All Division III. *Intercollegiate sports:* baseball M, basketball M/W, crew M(c)/W(c), cross-country running M/W, football M, golf M/W, ice hockey M/W, lacrosse M(c)/W(c), skiing (downhill) M(c)/W(c), soccer M/W, softball W, swimming and diving M/W, tennis M/W, track and field M/W, volleyball W. *Intramural sports:* basketball M/W, golf M/W, racquetball M/W, soccer M/W, softball M/W, squash M/W, table tennis M/W, tennis M/W, volleyball M/W.

Standardized Tests *Required:* SAT or ACT (for admission).

Costs (2011–12) *Comprehensive fee:* $38,813 includes full-time tuition ($29,952), mandatory fees ($541), and room and board ($8320). Full-time tuition and fees vary according to course load, degree level, and program. Part-time tuition: $936 per credit hour. Part-time tuition and fees vary according to course load, degree level, and program. *College room only:* $5294. Room and board charges vary according to board plan and housing facility. *Waivers:* senior citizens and employees or children of employees.

Financial Aid Of all full-time matriculated undergraduates who enrolled in 2009, 4,407 applied for aid, 3,633 were judged to have need, 617 had their need fully met. 1,401 Federal Work-Study jobs (averaging $2770). 975 state and other part-time jobs (averaging $2712). In 2009, 613 non-need-based awards were made. *Average percent of need met:* 84%. *Average financial aid package:* $21,689. *Average need-based loan:* $7651. *Average need-based gift aid:* $15,632. *Average non-need-based aid:* $12,598. *Average indebtedness upon graduation:* $32,705.

Applying *Options:* electronic application, deferred entrance. *Required:* essay or personal statement, high school transcript. *Recommended:* interview. *Application deadlines:* rolling (freshmen), rolling (transfers). *Notification:* continuous (freshmen), continuous (transfers).

Freshman Application Contact University of St. Thomas, 2115 Summit Avenue, St. Paul, MN 55105-1096. *Phone:* 651-962-6150. *Toll-free phone:* 800-328-6819 Ext. 26150. *Web site:* http://www.stthomas.edu/.

Walden University

Minneapolis, Minnesota

- **Proprietary** upper-level, founded 1970, part of Laureate International Universities Network
- **Coed** 9,356 undergraduate students, 10% full-time, 74% women, 26% men
- 99% of applicants were admitted

Undergraduates 912 full-time, 8,444 part-time. Students come from 50 states and territories; 43 other countries; 99% are from out of state; 44% Black or African American, non-Hispanic/Latino; 4% Hispanic/Latino; 0.9% Asian, non-Hispanic/Latino; 0.1% Native Hawaiian or other Pacific Islander, non-Hispanic/Latino; 0.6% American Indian or Alaska Native, non-Hispanic/Latino; 2% Two or more races, non-Hispanic/Latino; 5% Race/ethnicity unknown; 10% international; 20% transferred in.

Freshmen *Admission:* 1,043 applied, 1,029 admitted.

Faculty *Total:* 2,362, 9% full-time, 86% with terminal degrees.

Academics *Calendar:* quarter/semester depending on program. *Degrees:* bachelor's, master's, doctoral-research/scholarship, post-master's, and post-bachelor's certificates. *Special study options:* academic remediation for entering students, advanced placement credit, distance learning, internships, part-time degree program, services for LD students, student-designed majors, study abroad, summer session for credit.

Computers on Campus Students can access the following: free student e-mail accounts, online (class) grades, online (class) registration, online (class) schedules.

Student Life *Student services:* personal/psychological counseling, legal services.

Costs (2010–11) *Tuition:* $9360 full-time, $260 per credit hour part-time. Full-time tuition and fees vary according to course level, course load, and program. Part-time tuition and fees vary according to course level, course load, and program. *Required fees:* $105 full-time, $35 per term part-time. *Payment plan:* installment. *Waivers:* employees or children of employees.

Financial Aid Of all full-time matriculated undergraduates who enrolled in 2008, 908 applied for aid, 878 were judged to have need, 7 had their need fully met. In 2008, 17 non-need-based awards were made. *Average percent of need met:* 26%. *Average financial aid package:* $6301. *Average need-based loan:* $3755. *Average need-based gift aid:* $3222. *Average non-need-based aid:* $1225.

Applying *Options:* electronic application. *Application fee:* $50. *Application deadline:* rolling (transfers). *Notification:* continuous (transfers).

Application Contact Walden University, 155 Fifth Avenue South, Minneapolis, MN 55401. *Phone:* 800-925-3368. *Toll-free phone:* 866-492-5336. *Web site:* http://www.waldenu.edu/.

Winona State University

Winona, Minnesota

- **State-supported** comprehensive, founded 1858, part of Minnesota State Colleges and Universities System
- **Small-town** 40-acre campus
- **Endowment** $15.0 million
- **Coed** 8,031 undergraduate students, 92% full-time, 60% women, 40% men
- **Moderately difficult** entrance level, 66% of applicants were admitted

Undergraduates 7,416 full-time, 615 part-time. 34% are from out of state; 2% Black or African American, non-Hispanic/Latino; 2% Hispanic/Latino; 2% Asian, non-Hispanic/Latino; 0.1% Native Hawaiian or other Pacific Islander, non-Hispanic/Latino; 0.2% American Indian or Alaska Native, non-Hispanic/Latino; 2% Two or more races, non-Hispanic/Latino; 2% Race/ethnicity unknown; 3% international; 7% transferred in; 92% live on campus. *Retention:* 75% of full-time freshmen returned.

Freshmen *Admission:* 6,609 applied, 4,380 admitted, 1,632 enrolled. *Average high school GPA:* 3.32. *Test scores:* SAT critical reading scores over 500: 90%; SAT math scores over 500: 90%; ACT scores over 18: 98%; SAT critical reading scores over 600: 30%; SAT math scores over 600: 20%; ACT scores over 24: 37%; ACT scores over 30: 3%.

Faculty *Total:* 605, 50% full-time, 44% with terminal degrees. *Student/faculty ratio:* 20:1.

Academics *Calendar:* semesters. *Degrees:* associate, bachelor's, master's, doctoral-other, post-master's, and postbachelor's certificates. *Special study options:* academic remediation for entering students, accelerated degree program, adult/continuing education programs, advanced placement credit, distance learning, double majors, English as a second language, external degree program, honors programs, independent study, internships, off-campus study, part-time degree program, services for LD students, student-designed majors, study abroad, summer session for credit. *ROTC:* Army (c).

Computers on Campus 1,400 computers/terminals and 15,000 ports are available on campus for general student use. Students can access the following: campus intranet, computer help desk, free student e-mail accounts, online (class) grades, online (class) registration, online (class) schedules, all students have a laptop. Campuswide network is available. 100% of college-owned or -operated housing units are wired for high-speed Internet access. Wireless service is available via entire campus.

Student Life *Housing options:* coed, men-only, women-only, disabled students. Campus housing is university owned and leased by the school. Freshman campus housing is guaranteed. *Activities and organizations:* drama/theater group, student-run newspaper, radio and television station, choral group, marching band, University Program Activities Committee, Student Senate, Residence Hall Association, Inter Varsity, national fraternities, national sororities. *Campus security:* 24-hour emergency response devices and patrols, student patrols, late-night transport/escort service, controlled dormitory access, security cameras. *Student services:* health clinic, personal/psychological counseling, women's center, legal services.

Athletics Member NCAA. All Division II. *Intercollegiate sports:* baseball M(s), basketball M(s)/W(s), bowling M(c)/W(c), cross-country running M/W(s), fencing M(c)/W(c), football M(s), golf M(s)/W(s), gymnastics W, rugby M(c)/W(c), skiing (downhill) M(c)/W(c), soccer M(c)/W(s), softball W(s), tennis W(s), track and field W(s), ultimate Frisbee M(c)/W(c), volleyball M(c)/W(s), wrestling M(c). *Intramural sports:* archery M/W, badminton M/W, baseball M, basketball M/W, bowling M/W, cross-country running M/W, fencing M/W, field hockey M/W, football M/W, golf M/W, ice hockey M/W, racquetball M/W, riflery M/W, rugby M/W, skiing (cross-country) M/W, skiing (downhill) M/W, soccer M/W, softball M/W, track and field W, volleyball M/W, weight lifting M/W, wrestling M.

Standardized Tests *Required:* SAT and SAT Subject Tests or ACT (for admission).

Costs (2011–12) *Tuition:* state resident $6240 full-time, $206 per credit part-time; nonresident $11,340 full-time, $374 per credit part-time. Full-time tuition and fees vary according to location and reciprocity agreements. Part-time tuition and fees vary according to location and reciprocity agreements. *Required fees:* $1960 full-time. *Room and board:* $7330. Room and board charges vary according to board plan, housing facility, and location. *Payment plan:* installment. *Waivers:* employees or children of employees.

Financial Aid Of all full-time matriculated undergraduates who enrolled in 2008, 5,247 applied for aid, 3,862 were judged to have need, 495 had their need fully met. 180 Federal Work-Study jobs (averaging $1815). 325 state and other part-time jobs (averaging $2004). In 2008, 868 non-need-based awards were made. *Average percent of need met:* 46%. *Average financial aid package:* $7112. *Average need-based loan:* $3908. *Average need-based gift aid:* $4968. *Average non-need-based aid:* $2601. *Average indebtedness upon graduation:* $29,123.

Applying *Options:* electronic application, early admission, early action, deferred entrance. *Application fee:* $20. *Required:* high school transcript, class rank. *Required for some:* essay or personal statement, minimum 3 GPA, interview. *Application deadlines:* 3/5 (freshmen), 7/15 (transfers). *Notification:* continuous (freshmen), continuous (transfers).

Freshman Application Contact Carl Stange, Director of Admissions, Winona State University, 170 West Sanborn, Winona, MN 55987. *Phone:* 507-457-5100. *Toll-free phone:* 800-DIAL WSU. *Fax:* 507-457-5620. *E-mail:* admissions@winona.edu. *Web site:* http://www.winona.edu/.

MISSISSIPPI

Alcorn State University
Alcorn State, Mississippi

- **State-supported** comprehensive, founded 1871, part of Mississippi Institutions of Higher Learning
- **Rural** 1756-acre campus
- **Endowment** $7.4 million
- **Coed** 2,980 undergraduate students, 92% full-time, 66% women, 34% men
- **Moderately difficult** entrance level, 34% of applicants were admitted

Undergraduates 2,749 full-time, 231 part-time. Students come from 34 states and territories; 14 other countries; 13% are from out of state; 93% Black or African American, non-Hispanic/Latino; 0.9% Hispanic/Latino; 0.1% Asian, non-Hispanic/Latino; 0.1% American Indian or Alaska Native, non-Hispanic/Latino; 0.2% Two or more races, non-Hispanic/Latino; 1% international; 11% transferred in; 49% live on campus. *Retention:* 69% of full-time freshmen returned.

Freshmen *Admission:* 4,358 applied, 1,486 admitted, 599 enrolled. *Average high school GPA:* 2.88. *Test scores:* SAT critical reading scores over 500: 18%; SAT math scores over 500: 18%; ACT scores over 18: 48%; SAT math scores over 600: 4%; ACT scores over 24: 7%.

Faculty *Total:* 210, 84% full-time, 61% with terminal degrees. *Student/faculty ratio:* 17:1.

Academics *Calendar:* semesters. *Degrees:* associate, bachelor's, master's, and post-master's certificates. *Special study options:* academic remediation for entering students, accelerated degree program, adult/continuing education programs, advanced placement credit, cooperative education, distance learning, double majors, honors programs, independent study, internships, off-campus study, part-time degree program, study abroad, summer session for credit. *ROTC:* Army (b).

Computers on Campus 500 computers/terminals are available on campus for general student use. Students can access the following: campus intranet, computer help desk, free student e-mail accounts, online (class) grades, online (class) registration, online (class) schedules. Campuswide network is available. 100% of college-owned or -operated housing units are wired for high-speed Internet access. Wireless service is available via classrooms, computer centers, computer labs, learning centers, libraries, student centers.

Student Life *Housing options:* men-only, women-only. Campus housing is university owned. Freshman campus housing is guaranteed. *Activities and organizations:* drama/theater group, student-run newspaper, radio and television station, choral group, marching band, marching band, Gospel Choir, interfaith choir, national fraternities, national sororities. *Campus security:* 24-hour emergency response devices and patrols, late-night transport/escort service. *Student services:* health clinic, personal/psychological counseling.

Athletics Member NCAA. All Division I. *Intercollegiate sports:* baseball M(s), basketball M(s)/W(s), cross-country running M(s)/W(s), football M(s), golf M(s)/W(s), soccer W(s), softball W(s), tennis M(s)/W(s), track and field M(s)/W(s), volleyball W(s). *Intramural sports:* basketball M/W, football M.

Standardized Tests *Required:* SAT or ACT (for admission).

Costs (2010–11) *Tuition:* state resident $4858 full-time, $202 per credit hour part-time; nonresident $11,950 full-time, $498 per credit hour part-time. Full-time tuition and fees vary according to course load. Part-time tuition and fees vary according to course load. *Room and board:* $7348. *Payment plan:* deferred payment. *Waivers:* employees or children of employees.

Financial Aid Of all full-time matriculated undergraduates who enrolled in 2008, 2,180 applied for aid, 2,180 were judged to have need, 1,905 had their need fully met. 213 Federal Work-Study jobs (averaging $964). *Average percent of need met:* 75%. *Average financial aid package:* $8670. *Average need-based loan:* $4563. *Average need-based gift aid:* $3856. *Average non-need-based aid:* $1476. *Average indebtedness upon graduation:* $18,123.

Applying *Options:* electronic application, early admission, deferred entrance. *Required:* high school transcript, minimum 2 GPA. *Application deadlines:* rolling (freshmen), rolling (transfers). *Notification:* continuous (freshmen), continuous (transfers).

Freshman Application Contact Mr. Emanuel Barnes, Director of Admissions, Alcorn State University, 1000 ASU Drive, #300, Alcorn State, MS 39096-7500. *Phone:* 601-877-6147. *Toll-free phone:* 800-222-6790.

Fax: 601-877-6347. *E-mail:* ebarnes@alcorn.edu. *Web site:* http://www.alcorn.edu/.

Belhaven University
Jackson, Mississippi

- **Independent Presbyterian** comprehensive, founded 1883
- **Urban** 42-acre campus
- **Endowment** $4.3 million
- **Coed** 2,467 undergraduate students, 93% full-time, 65% women, 35% men
- **Moderately difficult** entrance level, 46% of applicants were admitted

Undergraduates 2,283 full-time, 184 part-time. Students come from 33 states and territories; 21 other countries; 45% are from out of state; 24% Black or African American, non-Hispanic/Latino; 4% Hispanic/Latino; 2% Asian, non-Hispanic/Latino; 0.4% Native Hawaiian or other Pacific Islander, non-Hispanic/Latino; 0.6% American Indian or Alaska Native, non-Hispanic/Latino; 0.1% Two or more races, non-Hispanic/Latino; 7% Race/ethnicity unknown; 5% transferred in; 53% live on campus. *Retention:* 73% of full-time freshmen returned.

Freshmen *Admission:* 1,568 applied, 714 admitted, 187 enrolled. *Average high school GPA:* 3.2. *Test scores:* SAT critical reading scores over 500: 58%; SAT math scores over 500: 54%; ACT scores over 18: 98%; SAT critical reading scores over 600: 32%; SAT math scores over 600: 20%; ACT scores over 24: 40%; SAT critical reading scores over 700: 9%; ACT scores over 30: 7%.

Faculty *Total:* 123, 49% full-time, 43% with terminal degrees. *Student/faculty ratio:* 12:1.

Academics *Calendar:* semesters. *Degrees:* certificates, associate, bachelor's, and master's. *Special study options:* academic remediation for entering students, accelerated degree program, adult/continuing education programs, advanced placement credit, distance learning, double majors, English as a second language, honors programs, independent study, internships, off-campus study, part-time degree program, student-designed majors, study abroad, summer session for credit. *ROTC:* Army (c), Air Force (c). *Unusual degree programs:* 3-2 engineering with Mississippi State University.

Computers on Campus 36 computers/terminals are available on campus for general student use. Students can access the following: campus intranet, computer help desk, free student e-mail accounts, online (class) grades, online (class) registration, online (class) schedules. Campuswide network is available. 100% of college-owned or -operated housing units are wired for high-speed Internet access. Wireless service is available via classrooms, computer labs, dorm rooms, libraries, student centers.

Student Life *Housing:* on-campus residence required through sophomore year. *Options:* men-only, women-only. Campus housing is university owned. Freshman campus housing is guaranteed. *Activities and organizations:* drama/theater group, student-run newspaper, choral group, marching band, Belhaven Activities Team, intramurals, Reformed University Fellowship, Quartertone, Sports Medicine: Exercise Science Club. *Campus security:* 24-hour emergency response devices and patrols, late-night transport/escort service, controlled dormitory access. *Student services:* health clinic, personal/psychological counseling.

Athletics Member NAIA. *Intercollegiate sports:* baseball M(s), basketball M(s)/W(s), cross-country running M(s)/W(s), football M(s), golf M(s)/W(s), soccer M(s)/W(s), softball W(s), tennis M(s)/W(s), volleyball W(s). *Intramural sports:* basketball M/W, football M/W, soccer M/W, softball M/W, volleyball M/W.

Standardized Tests *Required:* SAT or ACT (for admission).

Costs (2010–11) *Comprehensive fee:* $24,200 includes full-time tuition ($17,700) and room and board ($6500). Part-time tuition: $350 per semester hour. *Payment plan:* installment. *Waivers:* employees or children of employees.

Financial Aid Of all full-time matriculated undergraduates who enrolled in 2009, 742 applied for aid, 667 were judged to have need, 81 had their need fully met. 148 Federal Work-Study jobs (averaging $1743). In 2009, 95 non-need-based awards were made. *Average percent of need met:* 61%. *Average financial aid package:* $14,653. *Average need-based loan:* $4342. *Average need-based gift aid:* $10,710. *Average non-need-based aid:* $6318. *Average indebtedness upon graduation:* $32,728.

Applying *Options:* electronic application, early admission, deferred entrance. *Application fee:* $25. *Required:* high school transcript, minimum 2 GPA, 1 letter of recommendation. *Required for some:* essay or personal statement, interview. *Application deadlines:* rolling (freshmen), rolling (out-of-state freshmen), rolling (transfers). *Notification:* continuous (freshmen), continuous (out-of-state freshmen), continuous (transfers).

Freshman Application Contact Ms. Suzanne T. Sullivan, Director of Admission, Belhaven University, 1500 Peachtree Street, Jackson, MS 39202. *Phone:* 601-968-5940. *Toll-free phone:* 800-960-5940. *Fax:* 601-968-8946. *E-mail:* admission@belhaven.edu. *Web site:* http://www.belhaven.edu/.

Blue Mountain College

Blue Mountain, Mississippi

- **Independent Southern Baptist** comprehensive, founded 1873
- **Rural** 44-acre campus with easy access to Memphis
- **Endowment** $8.4 million
- **Coed** 537 undergraduate students, 91% full-time, 61% women, 39% men
- **Moderately difficult** entrance level, 52% of applicants were admitted

Undergraduates 486 full-time, 51 part-time. Students come from 20 states and territories; 3 other countries; 16% are from out of state; 12% Black or African American, non-Hispanic/Latino; 1% Hispanic/Latino; 0.4% Asian, non-Hispanic/Latino; 0.6% international; 20% transferred in; 38% live on campus. *Retention:* 84% of full-time freshmen returned.

Freshmen *Admission:* 315 applied, 163 admitted, 88 enrolled. *Average high school GPA:* 3.33. *Test scores:* SAT critical reading scores over 500: 100%; SAT math scores over 500: 60%; SAT writing scores over 500: 80%; ACT scores over 18: 86%; SAT critical reading scores over 600: 60%; SAT math scores over 600: 20%; SAT writing scores over 600: 20%; ACT scores over 24: 22%; ACT scores over 30: 1%.

Faculty *Total:* 46, 54% full-time, 61% with terminal degrees. *Student/faculty ratio:* 16:1.

Academics *Calendar:* semesters. *Degrees:* bachelor's and master's. *Special study options:* academic remediation for entering students, accelerated degree program, advanced placement credit, distance learning, double majors, honors programs, internships, part-time degree program, summer session for credit. *Unusual degree programs:* 3-2 nursing with Union University.

Computers on Campus 41 computers/terminals are available on campus for general student use. Students can access the following: free student e-mail accounts, online (class) grades, online (class) registration, online (class) schedules. Campuswide network is available. 100% of college-owned or -operated housing units are wired for high-speed Internet access. Wireless service is available via classrooms, computer centers, computer labs, dorm rooms, learning centers, libraries, student centers.

Student Life *Housing options:* men-only, women-only. Campus housing is university owned. *Activities and organizations:* drama/theater group, choral group, Baptist Student Union, Student Body Association, Intramural Association, Ministerial Association, Mississippi Association of Educators/Student Program. *Campus security:* 24-hour patrols.

Athletics Member NAIA. *Intercollegiate sports:* baseball M(s), basketball M(s)/W(s), cross-country running M(s)/W(s), golf M(s)/W(s), softball W(s). *Intramural sports:* basketball M/W, football M, soccer M, softball M/W, swimming and diving W, table tennis M/W, tennis W, track and field M/W, ultimate Frisbee M, volleyball M/W.

Standardized Tests *Required:* SAT or ACT (for admission).

Costs (2010–11) *Comprehensive fee:* $12,820 includes full-time tuition ($7950), mandatory fees ($970), and room and board ($3900). Full-time tuition and fees vary according to course load and degree level. Part-time tuition and fees vary according to course load and degree level. *Room and board:* Room and board charges vary according to board plan. *Payment plan:* installment. *Waivers:* employees or children of employees.

Financial Aid Of all full-time matriculated undergraduates who enrolled in 2008, 431 applied for aid, 261 were judged to have need, 198 had their need fully met. In 2008, 261 non-need-based awards were made. *Average percent of need met:* 117%. *Average financial aid package:* $8899. *Average need-based loan:* $4488. *Average need-based gift aid:* $3551.

Applying *Options:* electronic application, deferred entrance. *Application fee:* $10. *Required:* high school transcript. *Recommended:* minimum 2 GPA. *Application deadlines:* rolling (freshmen), rolling (out-of-state freshmen), rolling (transfers). *Notification:* continuous (freshmen), continuous (out-of-state freshmen), continuous (transfers).

Freshman Application Contact Ms. Maria Teel, Director of Admissions, Blue Mountain College, PO Box 160, Blue Mountain, MS 38610-0160. *Phone:* 662-685-4771 Ext. 176. *Toll-free phone:* 800-235-0136. *Fax:* 662-685-4776. *E-mail:* mteel@bmc.edu. *Web site:* http://www.bmc.edu/.

Delta State University

Cleveland, Mississippi

- **State-supported** comprehensive, founded 1924, part of Mississippi Institutions of Higher Learning
- **Small-town** 332-acre campus
- **Endowment** $15.5 million
- **Coed** 2,948 undergraduate students, 81% full-time, 60% women, 40% men
- **Noncompetitive** entrance level, 73% of applicants were admitted

Undergraduates 2,390 full-time, 558 part-time. Students come from 49 states and territories; 22 other countries; 9% are from out of state; 39% Black or African American, non-Hispanic/Latino; 1% Hispanic/Latino; 1% Asian, non-Hispanic/Latino; 0.2% American Indian or Alaska Native, non-Hispanic/Latino; 0.1% Race/ethnicity unknown; 2% international; 14% transferred in; 31% live on campus. *Retention:* 59% of full-time freshmen returned.

Freshmen *Admission:* 715 applied, 522 admitted, 381 enrolled. *Average high school GPA:* 3.19. *Test scores:* ACT scores over 18: 77%; ACT scores over 24: 20%; ACT scores over 30: 1%.

Faculty *Total:* 254, 73% full-time, 62% with terminal degrees. *Student/faculty ratio:* 12:1.

Academics *Calendar:* semesters. *Degrees:* bachelor's, master's, doctoral-research/scholarship, and post-master's certificates. *Special study options:* academic remediation for entering students, adult/continuing education programs, advanced placement credit, cooperative education, distance learning, double majors, freshman honors college, honors programs, independent study, internships, part-time degree program, services for LD students, summer session for credit. *ROTC:* Army (c).

Computers on Campus 534 computers/terminals are available on campus for general student use. Students can access the following: campus intranet, computer help desk, free student e-mail accounts, online (class) grades, online (class) registration, online (class) schedules. Campuswide network is available. 100% of college-owned or -operated housing units are wired for high-speed Internet access. Wireless service is available via classrooms, computer centers, dorm rooms, libraries, student centers.

Student Life *Housing:* on-campus residence required for freshman year. *Options:* men-only, women-only, disabled students. Campus housing is university owned. Freshman campus housing is guaranteed. *Activities and organizations:* drama/theater group, student-run newspaper, choral group, marching band, Student Government Association, Student Alumni Association, Baptist Student Union, Union Program Council, Delta Volunteers, national fraternities, national sororities. *Campus security:* 24-hour emergency response devices and patrols, late-night transport/escort service, controlled dormitory access. *Student services:* health clinic, personal/psychological counseling.

Athletics Member NCAA. All Division II. *Intercollegiate sports:* baseball M(s), basketball M(s)/W(s), cheerleading M(s)/W(s), cross-country running W(s), football M(s), golf M(s), soccer M(s)/W(s), softball W(s), swimming and diving M(s)/W(s), tennis M(s)/W(s). *Intramural sports:* archery M/W, badminton M/W, basketball M/W, bowling M/W, cross-country running M/W, football M/W, golf M/W, racquetball M/W, soccer M/W, softball M/W, swimming and diving M/W, table tennis M/W, tennis M/W, ultimate Frisbee M/W, volleyball M/W.

Standardized Tests *Required:* ACT (for admission). *Recommended:* SAT or ACT (for admission).

Costs (2010–11) *Tuition:* state resident $4852 full-time, $202 per credit hour part-time; nonresident $12,558 full-time, $523 per credit hour part-time. Part-time tuition and fees vary according to course load. *Room and board:* $6166. Room and board charges vary according to housing facility. *Payment plan:* installment. *Waivers:* children of alumni, senior citizens, and employees or children of employees.

Financial Aid Of all full-time matriculated undergraduates who enrolled in 2008, 2,088 applied for aid, 1,786 were judged to have need. 274 Federal Work-Study jobs (averaging $1850). 145 state and other part-time jobs (averaging $1108). *Average financial aid package:* $8395. *Average need-based gift aid:* $4475. *Average indebtedness upon graduation:* $16,633.

Applying *Options:* electronic application, deferred entrance. *Application fee:* $25. *Required:* high school transcript, minimum 2 GPA. *Required for some:* interview for art, music majors. *Application deadlines:* rolling (freshmen), rolling (transfers). *Notification:* continuous (freshmen), continuous (transfers).

Freshman Application Contact Delta State University, Highway 8 West, Cleveland, MS 38733-0001. *Phone:* 662-846-4655. *Toll-free phone:* 800-468-6378. *Web site:* http://www.deltastate.edu/.

ITT Technical Institute

Madison, Mississippi

- **Proprietary** 4-year, part of ITT Educational Services, Inc.
- **Coed**
- **Minimally difficult** entrance level

Academics *Calendar:* quarters. *Degrees:* associate and bachelor's.

Student Life *Housing:* college housing not available.

Freshman Application Contact Director of Recruitment, ITT Technical Institute, 382 Galleria Parkway, Suite 100, Madison, MS 39110. *Phone:* 601-607-4500. *Toll-free phone:* 800-209-2521. *Web site:* http://www.itt-tech.edu/.

Jackson State University

Jackson, Mississippi

- **State-supported** university, founded 1877, part of Mississippi Institutions of Higher Learning
- **Urban** 250-acre campus
- **Coed**
- **Minimally difficult** entrance level

Faculty *Student/faculty ratio:* 16:1.

Academics *Calendar:* semesters. *Degrees:* bachelor's, master's, doctoral-research/scholarship, and post-master's certificates.

Student Life *Campus security:* 24-hour emergency response devices and patrols, late-night transport/escort service, controlled dormitory access.

Athletics Member NCAA. All Division I except football (Division I-AA).

Standardized Tests *Required:* SAT or ACT (for admission).

Costs (2010–11) *Tuition:* state resident $5050 full-time, $211 per credit hour part-time; nonresident $12,380 full-time, $517 per credit hour part-time. Full-time tuition and fees vary according to course load. Part-time tuition and fees vary according to course load. *Room and board:* $6244; room only: $3820. Room and board charges vary according to board plan and housing facility.

Applying *Options:* electronic application, early admission, deferred entrance. *Required:* high school transcript, minimum 2 GPA. *Required for some:* 3 letters of recommendation.

Freshman Application Contact Mrs. Linda Rush, Director, Marketing and Recruitment, Jackson State University, PO Box 17330, 1400 John R. Lynch Street, Jackson, MS 39217. *Phone:* 601-979-2911. *Toll-free phone:* 800-682-5390 (in-state); 800-848-6817 (out-of-state). *E-mail:* schatman@ccaix.jsums.edu. *Web site:* http://www.jsums.edu/.

Millsaps College

Jackson, Mississippi

- **Independent United Methodist** comprehensive, founded 1890
- **Urban** 100-acre campus
- **Endowment** $82.1 million
- **Coed** 965 undergraduate students, 98% full-time, 51% women, 49% men
- **Moderately difficult** entrance level, 77% of applicants were admitted

Undergraduates 945 full-time, 20 part-time. Students come from 28 states and territories; 23 other countries; 54% are from out of state; 9% Black or African American, non-Hispanic/Latino; 3% Hispanic/Latino; 5% Asian, non-Hispanic/Latino; 0.5% American Indian or Alaska Native, non-Hispanic/Latino; 0.5% Two or more races, non-Hispanic/Latino; 3% Race/ethnicity unknown; 3% international; 3% transferred in; 86% live on campus. *Retention:* 79% of full-time freshmen returned.

Freshmen *Admission:* 1,186 applied, 909 admitted, 214 enrolled. *Average high school GPA:* 3.61. *Test scores:* SAT critical reading scores over 500: 90%; SAT math scores over 500: 87%; ACT scores over 18: 100%; SAT critical reading scores over 600: 44%; SAT math scores over 600: 48%; ACT scores over 24: 78%; SAT critical reading scores over 700: 11%; SAT math scores over 700: 11%; ACT scores over 30: 18%.

Faculty *Total:* 121, 84% full-time, 83% with terminal degrees. *Student/faculty ratio:* 9:1.

Academics *Calendar:* semesters. *Degrees:* bachelor's and master's. *Special study options:* accelerated degree program, advanced placement credit, double majors, honors programs, independent study, internships, off-campus study, part-time degree program, services for LD students, student-designed majors, study abroad, summer session for credit. *ROTC:* Army (c), Air Force (c). *Unusual degree programs:* 3-2 engineering with Auburn University, Columbia University, Vanderbilt University, Washington University in St. Louis; nursing with University of Mississippi Medical Center School of Nursing, Vanderbilt University.

Computers on Campus 150 computers/terminals are available on campus for general student use. Students can access the following: campus intranet, computer help desk, free student e-mail accounts, online (class) grades, online (class) registration, online (class) schedules, online transcripts. Campuswide network is available. 100% of college-owned or -operated housing units are wired for high-speed Internet access. Wireless service is available via entire campus.

Student Life *Housing:* on-campus residence required through sophomore year. *Options:* coed, men-only, women-only, disabled students. Campus housing is university owned. Freshman campus housing is guaranteed. *Activities and organizations:* drama/theater group, student-run newspaper, choral group, Campus Ministry Team, Student Body Association, SAPS (Campus Programming Board), Inter-fraternity/Panhellenic Councils, intramural sports, national fraternities, national sororities. *Campus security:* 24-hour emergency response devices and patrols, student patrols, late-night transport/escort service, controlled dormitory access, self-defense education, lighted pathways. *Student services:* health clinic, personal/psychological counseling.

Athletics Member NCAA. All Division III. *Intercollegiate sports:* baseball M, basketball M/W, cross-country running M/W, football M, golf M/W, lacrosse M/W, soccer M/W, softball W, tennis M/W, track and field M/W, volleyball W. *Intramural sports:* basketball M/W, bowling M/W, cheerleading W(c), fencing M(c)/W(c), football M/W, golf M/W, lacrosse W(c), racquetball M/W, soccer M/W, softball M/W, table tennis M/W, tennis M/W, ultimate Frisbee M(c)/W(c), volleyball M/W.

Standardized Tests *Required:* SAT or ACT (for admission).

Costs (2011–12) *Comprehensive fee:* $39,794 includes full-time tuition ($27,650), mandatory fees ($1832), and room and board ($10,312). Part-time tuition: $864 per credit hour. Part-time tuition and fees vary according to course load. *Required fees:* $32 per credit hour part-time. *College room only:* $5820. Room and board charges vary according to housing facility. *Payment plan:* installment. *Waivers:* employees or children of employees.

Financial Aid Of all full-time matriculated undergraduates who enrolled in 2009, 707 applied for aid, 577 were judged to have need, 224 had their need fully met. In 2009, 386 non-need-based awards were made. *Average percent of need met:* 84%. *Average financial aid package:* $24,659. *Average need-based loan:* $4359. *Average need-based gift aid:* $18,969. *Average non-need-based aid:* $15,127. *Average indebtedness upon graduation:* $31,304.

Applying *Options:* electronic application, early admission, early decision, early action, deferred entrance. *Required:* essay or personal statement, high school transcript, minimum 2.5 GPA, 1 letter of recommendation, Secondary School Report. *Required for some:* interview. *Application deadlines:* 2/1 (freshmen), 2/1 (out-of-state freshmen), 7/1 (transfers), 12/1 (early action). *Early decision deadline:* 11/15. *Notification:* continuous until 10/15 (freshmen), continuous until 10/15 (out-of-state freshmen), continuous until 10/15 (transfers), 12/1 (early decision).

Freshman Application Contact Mr. Michael Thorp, Dean of Enrollment, Millsaps College, 1701 North State Street, Jackson, MS 39210-0001. *Phone:* 601-974-1050. *Toll-free phone:* 800-352-1050. *Fax:* 601-974-1059. *E-mail:* admissions@millsaps.edu. *Web site:* http://www.millsaps.edu/.

Mississippi College

Clinton, Mississippi

- **Independent Southern Baptist** comprehensive, founded 1826
- **Suburban** 320-acre campus with easy access to Jackson
- **Endowment** $50.8 million
- **Coed**
- **Moderately difficult** entrance level

Faculty *Student/faculty ratio:* 16:1.

Academics *Calendar:* semesters. *Degrees:* bachelor's, master's, doctoral-professional, doctoral-research/scholarship, post-master's, and postbachelor's certificates.

Student Life *Campus security:* 24-hour emergency response devices and patrols, late-night transport/escort service, controlled dormitory access.

Athletics Member NCAA. All Division III.

Standardized Tests *Required:* SAT or ACT (for admission).

Costs (2011–12) *Comprehensive fee:* $20,378 includes full-time tuition ($13,340), mandatory fees ($698), and room and board ($6340). Full-time tuition and fees vary according to class time, course load, location, and program. Part-time tuition: $418 per credit hour. Part-time tuition and fees vary according to class time, course load, location, and program. *Required fees:* $180 per term part-time. *Room and board:* Room and board charges vary according to housing facility. *Payment plans:* installment, deferred payment.

Financial Aid Of all full-time matriculated undergraduates who enrolled in 2009, 2,495 applied for aid, 1,579 were judged to have need, 521 had their need fully met. 229 Federal Work-Study jobs (averaging $1088). In 2009, 897 non-need-based awards were made. *Average percent of need met:* 78. *Average financial aid package:* $16,013. *Average need-based loan:* $7582. *Average need-based gift aid:* $9484. *Average non-need-based aid:* $10,104. *Average indebtedness upon graduation:* $26,323.

Applying *Options:* electronic application, early admission, early decision, deferred entrance. *Required:* high school transcript, 1 letter of recommendation. *Recommended:* minimum 2 GPA, interview.

Freshman Application Contact Mr. Chad Phillips, Director of Admissions, Mississippi College, PO Box 4026, 200 South Capitol Street, Clinton, MS 39058. *Phone:* 601-925-3800. *Toll-free phone:* 800-738-1236. *Fax:* 601-925-3804. *E-mail:* enrollment-services@mc.edu. *Web site:* http://www.mc.edu/.

Mississippi State University

Mississippi State, Mississippi

- **State-supported** university, founded 1878, part of Mississippi Institutions of Higher Learning
- **Small-town** 4200-acre campus
- **Endowment** $232.6 million
- **Coed** 15,543 undergraduate students, 91% full-time, 48% women, 52% men
- **Moderately difficult** entrance level, 66% of applicants were admitted

Undergraduates 14,079 full-time, 1,464 part-time. Students come from 52 states and territories; 55 other countries; 20% are from out of state; 22% Black or African American, non-Hispanic/Latino; 2% Hispanic/Latino; 1% Asian, non-Hispanic/Latino; 0.1% Native Hawaiian or other Pacific Islander, non-Hispanic/Latino; 0.4% American Indian or Alaska Native, non-Hispanic/Latino; 1% Two or more races, non-Hispanic/Latino; 2% Race/ethnicity unknown; 2% international; 11% transferred in; 26% live on campus. *Retention:* 82% of full-time freshmen returned.

Freshmen *Admission:* 9,300 applied, 6,162 admitted, 2,707 enrolled. *Average high school GPA:* 3.24. *Test scores:* SAT critical reading scores over 500: 66%; SAT math scores over 500: 73%; ACT scores over 18: 91%; SAT critical reading scores over 600: 29%; SAT math scores over 600: 36%; ACT scores over 24: 47%; SAT critical reading scores over 700: 6%; SAT math scores over 700: 7%; ACT scores over 30: 8%.

Faculty *Total:* 912, 88% full-time, 75% with terminal degrees. *Student/faculty ratio:* 20:1.

Academics *Calendar:* semesters. *Degrees:* bachelor's, master's, doctoral-professional, doctoral-research/scholarship, and post-master's certificates. *Special study options:* academic remediation for entering students, accelerated degree program, adult/continuing education programs, advanced placement credit, cooperative education, distance learning, double majors, English as a second language, freshman honors college, honors programs, independent study, internships, off-campus study, part-time degree program, services for LD students, student-designed majors, study abroad, summer session for credit. *ROTC:* Army (b), Air Force (b).

Computers on Campus 1,000 computers/terminals and 1,000 ports are available on campus for general student use. Students can access the following: campus intranet, computer help desk, free student e-mail accounts, online (class) grades, online (class) registration, online (class) schedules, campuswide wireless Internet access. Campuswide network is available. 100% of college-owned or -operated housing units are wired for high-speed Internet access. Wireless service is available via entire campus.

Student Life *Housing:* on-campus residence required for freshman year. *Options:* coed, men-only, women-only, disabled students. Campus housing is university owned. *Activities and organizations:* drama/theater group, student-run newspaper, radio and television station, choral group, marching band, Student Association, Black Student Alliance, Residence Hall Association, Fashion Board, Campus Activities Board, national fraternities, national sororities. *Campus security:* 24-hour emergency response devices and patrols, late-night transport/escort service, controlled dormitory access, bicycle patrols, crime prevention program, RAD program, general law enforcement services. *Student services:* health clinic, personal/psychological counseling.

Athletics Member NCAA. All Division I except football (Division I-A). *Intercollegiate sports:* baseball M(s), basketball M(s)/W(s), cheerleading M(s)/W(s), cross-country running M(s)/W(s), golf M(s)/W(s), soccer W(s), softball W(s), tennis M(s)/W(s), track and field M(s)/W(s), volleyball W(s). *Intramural sports:* badminton M(c)/W(c), basketball M/W, bowling M/W, cross-country running M(c)/W(c), fencing M(c)/W(c), football M/W, golf M/W, ice hockey M(c), lacrosse M(c), racquetball M/W, riflery M/W, rugby M(c)/W(c), soccer M(c)/W(c), softball M(c)/W(c), swimming and diving M(c)/W(c), table tennis M(c)/W(c), tennis M(c)/W(c), ultimate Frisbee M/W, volleyball M(c)/W(c), water polo M/W.

Standardized Tests *Required:* SAT or ACT (for admission).

Costs (2010–11) *Tuition:* state resident $5461 full-time, $228 per credit hour part-time; nonresident $13,801 full-time, $575 per credit hour part-time. Part-time tuition and fees vary according to course load. *Room and board:* $7729; room only: $4494. Room and board charges vary according to board plan, housing facility, and student level. *Payment plans:* tuition prepayment, installment. *Waivers:* children of alumni, senior citizens, and employees or children of employees.

Financial Aid Of all full-time matriculated undergraduates who enrolled in 2008, 8,951 applied for aid, 7,505 were judged to have need, 1,916 had their need fully met. 866 Federal Work-Study jobs (averaging $3393). In 2008, 2575 non-need-based awards were made. *Average percent of need met:* 67%. *Average financial aid package:* $11,371. *Average need-based loan:* $4107. *Average need-based gift aid:* $5836. *Average non-need-based aid:* $2848. *Average indebtedness upon graduation:* $25,261.

Applying *Options:* electronic application. *Application fee:* $40. *Required:* high school transcript, minimum 2 GPA. *Application deadlines:* 8/1 (freshmen), 8/1 (transfers). *Notification:* continuous (freshmen), continuous (transfers).

Freshman Application Contact Ms. Cheryl Dill, Associate Director of Admissions and Scholarships, Mississippi State University, PO Box 6334, Mississippi State, MS 39762. *Phone:* 662-325-2224. *Fax:* 662-325-1MSU. *E-mail:* admit@msstate.edu. *Web site:* http://www.msstate.edu/.

Mississippi University for Women

Columbus, Mississippi

- **State-supported** comprehensive, founded 1884, part of Mississippi Institutions of Higher Learning
- **Small-town** 110-acre campus
- **Endowment** $33.2 million
- **Coed, primarily women** 2,394 undergraduate students, 79% full-time, 82% women, 18% men
- **Moderately difficult** entrance level, 42% of applicants were admitted

Undergraduates 1,881 full-time, 513 part-time. Students come from 19 states and territories; 16 other countries; 9% are from out of state; 39% Black or African American, non-Hispanic/Latino; 0.8% Hispanic/Latino; 2% Asian, non-Hispanic/Latino; 0.5% American Indian or Alaska Native, non-Hispanic/Latino; 0.4% Race/ethnicity unknown; 1% international; 18% transferred in; 29% live on campus. *Retention:* 75% of full-time freshmen returned.

Freshmen *Admission:* 1,356 applied, 569 admitted, 199 enrolled. *Average high school GPA:* 3.39. *Test scores:* ACT scores over 18: 90%; ACT scores over 24: 33%; ACT scores over 30: 3%.

Faculty *Total:* 182, 71% full-time, 50% with terminal degrees. *Student/faculty ratio:* 15:1.

Academics *Calendar:* semesters. *Degrees:* associate, bachelor's, master's, and post-master's certificates. *Special study options:* academic remediation for entering students, adult/continuing education programs, advanced placement credit, distance learning, double majors, freshman honors college, honors programs, independent study, internships, off-campus study, part-time degree program, services for LD students, study abroad, summer session for credit. *ROTC:* Army (c), Air Force (c). *Unusual degree programs:* 3-2 engineering with Auburn University, Mississippi State University.

Computers on Campus 340 computers/terminals and 1,220 ports are available on campus for general student use. Students can access the following: campus intranet, computer help desk, free student e-mail accounts, online (class) grades, online (class) registration, online (class) schedules, various software packages. Campuswide network is available. 100% of college-owned or -operated housing units are wired for high-speed Internet access. Wireless service is available via entire campus.

Student Life *Housing options:* men-only, women-only, disabled students. Campus housing is university owned. Freshman campus housing is guaranteed. *Activities and organizations:* drama/theater group, student-run newspaper, radio station, choral group, Student Government Association, Residence Hall Association, Class Council, Modeling Squad, Student Programming Board, national fraternities, national sororities. *Campus security:* 24-hour emergency response devices and patrols, late-night transport/escort service, controlled dormitory access. *Student services:* health clinic, personal/psychological counseling, women's center.

Athletics *Intramural sports:* badminton M/W, basketball M/W, equestrian sports M/W, football M/W, golf M/W, racquetball M/W, soccer M/W, softball M/W, table tennis M/W, tennis M/W, ultimate Frisbee M/W, volleyball M/W.

Standardized Tests *Required for some:* SAT or ACT (for admission). *Recommended:* SAT or ACT (for admission).

Costs (2011–12) *Tuition:* state resident $4644 full-time, $194 per credit hour part-time; nonresident $12,653 full-time, $527 per credit hour part-time. Part-time tuition and fees vary according to course load. *Room and board:* $5483; room only: $3225. Room and board charges vary according to housing facility. *Payment plan:* installment. *Waivers:* employees or children of employees.

Financial Aid Of all full-time matriculated undergraduates who enrolled in 2008, 1,491 applied for aid, 1,305 were judged to have need, 874 had their need fully met. 93 Federal Work-Study jobs (averaging $1693). 194 state and other part-time jobs (averaging $1535). In 2008, 277 non-need-based awards were made. *Average percent of need met:* 63%. *Average financial aid package:* $8408. *Average need-based loan:* $4494. *Average need-based gift aid:* $5201. *Average non-need-based aid:* $4732. *Average indebtedness upon graduation:* $18,363.

Applying *Options:* electronic application, early admission. *Required:* high school transcript. *Required for some:* minimum 2 GPA, interview, rank in upper 50% of high school class. *Application deadlines:* rolling (freshmen), rolling (out-of-state freshmen), rolling (transfers). *Notification:* continuous (freshmen), continuous (out-of-state freshmen), continuous (transfers).

Freshman Application Contact Mississippi University for Women, 1100 College Street, MUW-1600, Columbus, MS 39701-9998. *Phone:* 662-329-7106. *Toll-free phone:* 877-GO 2 THE W. *Web site:* http://www.muw.edu/.

Mississippi Valley State University

Itta Bena, Mississippi

- **State-supported** comprehensive, founded 1946, part of Mississippi Institutions of Higher Learning
- **Small-town** 450-acre campus
- **Endowment** $1.2 million
- **Coed** 2,210 undergraduate students, 89% full-time, 62% women, 38% men
- **Minimally difficult** entrance level, 28% of applicants were admitted

Undergraduates 1,971 full-time, 239 part-time. Students come from 27 states and territories; 3 other countries; 12% are from out of state; 92% Black or African American, non-Hispanic/Latino; 0.8% Hispanic/Latino; 0.1% Asian, non-Hispanic/Latino; 3% Race/ethnicity unknown; 8% transferred in; 43% live on campus. *Retention:* 51% of full-time freshmen returned.

Freshmen *Admission:* 5,539 applied, 1,577 admitted, 394 enrolled. *Average high school GPA:* 2.73. *Test scores:* ACT scores over 18: 39%; ACT scores over 24: 2%; ACT scores over 30: 1%.

Faculty *Total:* 158, 80% full-time, 56% with terminal degrees. *Student/faculty ratio:* 17:1.

Academics *Calendar:* semesters. *Degrees:* bachelor's and master's. *Special study options:* academic remediation for entering students, cooperative education, distance learning, double majors, freshman honors college, honors programs, internships, part-time degree program, summer session for credit. *ROTC:* Army (b).

Computers on Campus 275 computers/terminals are available on campus for general student use. Students can access the following: computer help desk, free student e-mail accounts, online (class) registration. Campuswide network is available.

Student Life *Housing options:* men-only, women-only. Campus housing is university owned. *Activities and organizations:* drama/theater group, student-run newspaper, radio and television station, choral group, marching band, Student Government Association, Baptist Student Union, Black Student Fellowship, National Education Association, national fraternities, national sororities. *Campus security:* 24-hour emergency response devices and patrols, controlled dormitory access. *Student services:* health clinic, personal/psychological counseling.

Athletics Member NCAA. All Division I except football (Division I-AA). *Intercollegiate sports:* baseball M(s), basketball M(s)/W(s), bowling W, cross-country running M(s)/W(s), golf M(s)/W(s), softball W(s), tennis M(s)/W(s), track and field M(s)/W(s). *Intramural sports:* baseball M, basketball M/W, cross-country running M/W, football M, golf M/W, softball M/W, tennis M/W, track and field M/W.

Standardized Tests *Required:* SAT or ACT (for admission).

Costs (2011–12) *Tuition:* state resident $5184 full-time, $199 per credit hour part-time; nonresident $11,922 full-time, $497 per credit hour part-time. *Required fees:* $50 full-time. *Room and board:* $5537; room only: $3090. *Payment plan:* installment. *Waivers:* children of alumni and employees or children of employees.

Applying *Options:* deferred entrance. *Required:* high school transcript. *Required for some:* 2.5 letters of recommendation. *Recommended:* interview. *Application deadlines:* rolling (freshmen), rolling (transfers). *Notification:* continuous (freshmen), continuous (transfers).

Freshman Application Contact Mississippi Valley State University, 14000 Highway 82 West, Itta Bena, MS 38941-1400. *Toll-free phone:* 800-844-6885. *Web site:* http://www.mvsu.edu/.

Rust College

Holly Springs, Mississippi

- **Independent United Methodist** 4-year, founded 1866
- **Rural** 126-acre campus with easy access to Memphis
- **Coed** 960 undergraduate students, 83% full-time, 61% women, 39% men
- **Moderately difficult** entrance level

Undergraduates 795 full-time, 165 part-time. Students come from 27 states and territories; 52% are from out of state; 92% Black or African American, non-Hispanic/Latino; 0.2% Hispanic/Latino; 0.3% Asian, non-Hispanic/Latino; 0.1% American Indian or Alaska Native, non-Hispanic/Latino; 6% international; 5% transferred in.

Freshmen *Admission:* 238 enrolled. *Average high school GPA:* 2.69. *Test scores:* ACT scores over 18: 21%; ACT scores over 24: 1%.

Faculty *Total:* 50, 96% full-time. *Student/faculty ratio:* 17:1.

Academics *Calendar:* semesters. *Degrees:* associate and bachelor's. *Special study options:* academic remediation for entering students, adult/continuing education programs, advanced placement credit, distance learning, double majors, honors programs, independent study, internships, part-time degree program, study abroad, summer session for credit. *Unusual degree programs:* 3-2 Biology or chemistry and medicine with Meharry Medical College; Medical technology with Tennessee State University.

Computers on Campus 220 computers/terminals are available on campus for general student use. Students can access the following: campus intranet, computer help desk, free student e-mail accounts, online (class) grades. Campuswide network is available. Wireless service is available via computer centers, computer labs, dorm rooms, libraries, student centers.

Student Life *Housing:* on-campus residence required for freshman year. *Options:* men-only, women-only. Campus housing is university owned. Freshman campus housing is guaranteed. *Activities and organizations:* drama/theater group, student-run newspaper, radio and television station, choral group, marching band, Phi Beta Lambda, Phi Beta Sigma, Science Club, Track and Field, Zeta Phi Beta, national fraternities, national sororities. *Campus security:* 24-hour emergency response devices and patrols, late-night transport/escort service, controlled dormitory access. *Student services:* health clinic, personal/psychological counseling.

Athletics Member NCAA. All Division III. *Intercollegiate sports:* baseball M, basketball M/W, cheerleading M/W, cross-country running M/W, tennis M/W, track and field M/W. *Intramural sports:* badminton M/W, baseball M/W, basketball M/W, bowling M/W, cheerleading M/W, cross-country running M/W, football M/W, soccer M/W, softball M/W, swimming and diving M/W, table tennis M/W, tennis M/W, track and field M/W, volleyball M/W, weight lifting M/W.

Standardized Tests *Required:* ACT (for admission).

Costs (2011–12) *Comprehensive fee:* $10,940 includes full-time tuition ($7610), mandatory fees ($10), and room and board ($3320). Part-time tuition: $283 per credit hour. Part-time tuition and fees vary according to class time and course load. *College room only:* $1480. Room and board charges vary according to board plan. *Payment plan:* installment. *Waivers:* senior citizens and employees or children of employees.

Financial Aid Of all full-time matriculated undergraduates who enrolled in 2004, 806 applied for aid, 806 were judged to have need, 481 had their need fully met. 492 Federal Work-Study jobs (averaging $714). 189 state and other part-time jobs (averaging $546). In 2004, 112 non-need-based awards were made. *Average percent of need met:* 60%. *Average financial aid package:* $5067. *Average need-based loan:* $2158. *Average need-based gift aid:* $4281. *Average non-need-based aid:* $2795. *Average indebtedness upon graduation:* $9314.

Applying *Options:* deferred entrance. *Application fee:* $10. *Required:* high school transcript, minimum 2 GPA, 2 letters of recommendation. *Application deadlines:* 7/15 (freshmen), 7/15 (transfers). *Notification:* 7/15 (freshmen), 7/15 (transfers).

Freshman Application Contact Ms. JoAnn Scott, Director of Enrollment Services, Rust College, 150 Rust Avenue, Holly Springs, MS 38635-2328. *Phone:* 601-252-8000 Ext. 4065. *Toll-free phone:* 888-886-8492 Ext. 4065. *Fax:* 662-252-8895. *E-mail:* admissions@rustcollege.edu. *Web site:* http://www.rustcollege.edu/.

Southeastern Baptist College

Laurel, Mississippi

Freshman Application Contact Mrs. Emma Bond, Director of Admissions, Southeastern Baptist College, 4229 Highway 15 North, Laurel, MS 39440-1096. *Phone:* 601-426-6346.

Strayer University - Jackson Campus

Jackson, Mississippi

- **Proprietary** comprehensive
- **Coed**

Academics *Degrees:* certificates, diplomas, associate, bachelor's, and master's.

Costs (2010–11) *Tuition:* $13,635 full-time, $1590 per course part-time.

Freshman Application Contact Strayer University - Jackson Campus, 460 Briarwood Drive, Suite 200, Jackson, MS 39206. *Web site:* http://www.strayer.edu/jackson.

Tougaloo College

Tougaloo, Mississippi

Freshman Application Contact Ms. Juno Jacobs, Director of Admissions, Tougaloo College, 500 West County Line Road, Tougaloo, MS 39174. *Phone:* 601-977-7765. *Toll-free phone:* 888-42GALOO. *Fax:* 601-977-4501. *E-mail:* jjacobs@tougaloo.edu. *Web site:* http://www.tougaloo.edu/.

University of Mississippi

Oxford, Mississippi

- **State-supported** university, founded 1844, part of Mississippi Institutions of Higher Learning
- **Small-town** 2500-acre campus with easy access to Memphis
- **Endowment** $415.2 million
- **Coed** 14,159 undergraduate students, 93% full-time, 53% women, 47% men
- **Moderately difficult** entrance level, 78% of applicants were admitted

Undergraduates 13,119 full-time, 1,040 part-time. Students come from 49 states and territories; 59 other countries; 32% are from out of state; 16% Black or African American, non-Hispanic/Latino; 2% Hispanic/Latino; 1% Asian, non-Hispanic/Latino; 0.1% Native Hawaiian or other Pacific Islander, non-Hispanic/Latino; 0.4% American Indian or Alaska Native, non-Hispanic/Latino; 1% Two or more races, non-Hispanic/Latino; 0.2% Race/ethnicity unknown; 1% international; 10% transferred in. *Retention:* 83% of full-time freshmen returned.

Freshmen *Admission:* 10,908 applied, 8,479 admitted, 3,095 enrolled. *Average high school GPA:* 3.3. *Test scores:* SAT critical reading scores over 500: 64%; SAT math scores over 500: 64%; ACT scores over 18: 93%; SAT critical reading scores over 600: 23%; SAT math scores over 600: 25%; ACT scores over 24: 45%; SAT critical reading scores over 700: 5%; SAT math scores over 700: 4%; ACT scores over 30: 10%.

Faculty *Total:* 881, 83% full-time, 79% with terminal degrees. *Student/faculty ratio:* 18:1.

Academics *Calendar:* semesters. *Degrees:* bachelor's, master's, doctoral-professional, doctoral-research/scholarship, and post-master's certificates. *Special study options:* academic remediation for entering students, accelerated degree program, adult/continuing education programs, advanced placement credit, distance learning, double majors, English as a second language, freshman honors college, honors programs, independent study, internships, part-time degree program, services for LD students, study abroad, summer session for credit. *ROTC:* Army (b), Navy (b), Air Force (b).

Computers on Campus Students can access the following: campus intranet, computer help desk, free student e-mail accounts, online (class) grades, online (class) registration, online (class) schedules, application for admission, registration for orientation. Campuswide network is available. 100% of college-owned or -operated housing units are wired for high-speed Internet access. Wireless service is available via classrooms, computer centers, computer labs, learning centers, libraries, student centers.

Student Life *Housing:* on-campus residence required for freshman year. *Options:* men-only, women-only. Campus housing is university owned, leased by the school and is provided by a third party. Freshman campus housing is guaranteed. *Activities and organizations:* drama/theater group, student-run newspaper, radio and television station, choral group, marching band, Associated Student Body, Gospel Choir, sport clubs, Black Student Union, Student Programming Board, national fraternities, national sororities. *Campus security:* 24-hour emergency response devices and patrols, late-night transport/escort service, controlled dormitory access, crime prevention programs. *Student services:* health clinic, personal/psychological counseling, women's center, legal services.

Athletics Member NCAA. All Division I except football (Division I-A). *Intercollegiate sports:* baseball M(s), basketball M(s)/W(s), cheerleading M(s)/W(s), cross-country running M(s)/W(s), fencing M(c)/W(c), golf M(s)/W(s), ice hockey M, lacrosse M/W, riflery W(s), rugby M(c), soccer M(c)/W(s), softball W(s), tennis M(s)/W(s), track and field M(s)/W(s), volleyball M(c)/W(s). *Intramural sports:* badminton M/W, basketball M/W, bowling M/W, crew M(c)/W(c), football M/W, golf M/W, racquetball M/W, riflery M(c), soccer M/W, softball M/W, swimming and diving M/W, table tennis M(c)/W(c), tennis M/W, track and field M/W, ultimate Frisbee M/W, volleyball M/W, water polo M/W.

Standardized Tests *Required:* SAT or ACT (for admission).

Costs (2011–12) *Tuition:* state resident $5708 full-time; nonresident $14,584 full-time. Full-time tuition and fees vary according to course load and program. Part-time tuition and fees vary according to course load and program. *Room and board:* Room and board charges vary according to board plan, housing facility, and location. *Payment plan:* tuition prepayment. *Waivers:* children of alumni, senior citizens, and employees or children of employees.

Financial Aid Of all full-time matriculated undergraduates who enrolled in 2008, 7,715 applied for aid, 5,881 were judged to have need, 650 had their need fully met. 493 Federal Work-Study jobs (averaging $1411). In 2008, 2167 non-need-based awards were made. *Average percent of need met:* 74%. *Average financial aid package:* $7633. *Average need-based loan:* $4687. *Average need-based gift aid:* $6870. *Average non-need-based aid:* $4517. *Average indebtedness upon graduation:* $23,637.

Applying *Options:* electronic application, early admission, deferred entrance. *Application fee:* $50. *Required:* high school transcript, minimum 2 GPA. *Required for some:* essay or personal statement, interview. *Application dead-lines:* rolling (freshmen), rolling (out-of-state freshmen), rolling (transfers). *Notification:* 8/16 (freshmen), continuous until 8/16 (transfers).

Freshman Application Contact Mr. Jody Lowe, Associate Director of Enrollment Services, University of Mississippi, 145 Martindale Student Services Center, University, MS 38677. *Phone:* 662-915-7226. *Toll-free phone:* 800-653-6477. *Fax:* 662-915-5869. *E-mail:* admissions@olemiss.edu. *Web site:* http://www.olemiss.edu/.

University of Mississippi Medical Center

Jackson, Mississippi

Application Contact Ms. Barbara Westerfield, Director of Student Records and Registrar, University of Mississippi Medical Center, 2500 North State Street, Jackson, MS 39216-4505. *Phone:* 601-984-1080. *Fax:* 601-984-1079. *Web site:* http://www.umc.edu/.

University of Southern Mississippi

Hattiesburg, Mississippi

- **State-supported** university, founded 1910, part of Mississippi Institutions of Higher Learning
- **Suburban** 1090-acre campus with easy access to New Orleans
- **Coed** 12,826 undergraduate students, 86% full-time, 61% women, 39% men
- **Moderately difficult** entrance level, 60% of applicants were admitted

Undergraduates 11,021 full-time, 1,805 part-time. Students come from 48 states and territories; 63 other countries; 11% are from out of state; 30% Black or African American, non-Hispanic/Latino; 2% Hispanic/Latino; 1% Asian, non-Hispanic/Latino; 0.4% American Indian or Alaska Native, non-Hispanic/Latino; 0.6% Two or more races, non-Hispanic/Latino; 9% Race/ethnicity unknown; 0.5% international; 13% transferred in; 45% live on campus. *Retention:* 77% of full-time freshmen returned.

Freshmen *Admission:* 5,491 applied, 3,279 admitted, 1,591 enrolled. *Average high school GPA:* 3.08. *Test scores:* SAT critical reading scores over 500: 53%; SAT math scores over 500: 43%; ACT scores over 18: 86%; SAT critical reading scores over 600: 19%; SAT math scores over 600: 15%; ACT scores over 24: 28%; SAT critical reading scores over 700: 4%; SAT math scores over 700: 2%; ACT scores over 30: 4%.

Faculty *Total:* 884, 79% full-time, 68% with terminal degrees. *Student/faculty ratio:* 18:1.

Academics *Calendar:* semesters. *Degrees:* certificates, bachelor's, master's, doctoral-research/scholarship, and post-master's certificates. *Special study options:* academic remediation for entering students, accelerated degree program, advanced placement credit, cooperative education, distance learning, double majors, English as a second language, honors programs, independent study, internships, off-campus study, part-time degree program, services for LD students, study abroad, summer session for credit. *ROTC:* Army (b), Air Force (b).

Computers on Campus 600 computers/terminals are available on campus for general student use. Students can access the following: campus intranet, computer help desk, free student e-mail accounts, online (class) grades, online (class) registration, online (class) schedules. Campuswide network is available. 95% of college-owned or -operated housing units are wired for high-speed Internet access. Wireless service is available via entire campus.

Student Life *Housing options:* men-only, women-only, disabled students. Campus housing is university owned. *Activities and organizations:* drama/theater group, student-run newspaper, radio station, choral group, marching band, University Activities Council, residence halls associations, Student Government Association, Baptist Student Union, African American Student Organization, national fraternities, national sororities. *Campus security:* 24-hour emergency response devices and patrols, late-night transport/escort service, controlled dormitory access. *Student services:* health clinic, personal/psychological counseling, women's center, legal services.

Athletics Member NCAA. All Division I. *Intercollegiate sports:* baseball M(s), basketball M(s)/W(s), cheerleading M/W, cross-country running W(s), football M(s)/W(s), golf M(s)/W(s), soccer W(s), softball W(s), tennis M(s)/W(s), track and field M(s)/W(s), volleyball W(s). *Intramural sports:* badminton M/W, basketball M/W, bowling M/W, fencing M/W, racquetball M/W, riflery M/W, rugby M, soccer M/W, softball M/W, table tennis M/W, tennis M/W, track and field M/W, ultimate Frisbee M/W, volleyball M/W.

Standardized Tests *Required:* SAT or ACT (for admission).

Costs (2011–12) *Tuition:* state resident $5452 full-time, $228 per credit hour part-time; nonresident $13,408 full-time, $560 per credit hour part-time. Part-time tuition and fees vary according to course load and degree level. *Room and board:* $6634. Room and board charges vary according to board plan and housing facility. *Payment plan:* installment. *Waivers:* children of alumni, senior citizens, and employees or children of employees.

Financial Aid Of all full-time matriculated undergraduates who enrolled in 2008, 7,939 applied for aid, 6,794 were judged to have need, 1,754 had their need fully met. In 2008, 843 non-need-based awards were made. *Average percent of need met:* 82%. *Average financial aid package:* $9018. *Average need-based loan:* $4878. *Average need-based gift aid:* $3978. *Average non-need-based aid:* $3585. *Average indebtedness upon graduation:* $19,915.

Applying *Options:* electronic application, early admission. *Application fee:* $35. *Required:* high school transcript, minimum 2 GPA. *Application deadlines:* 7/1 (freshmen), 7/1 (transfers).

Freshman Application Contact Mr. Jason Beverly, Senior Admissions Counselor, University of Southern Mississippi, 118 College Drive, #5166, Hattiesburg, MS 39406-1000. *Phone:* 601-266-5000. *Fax:* 601-266-5148. *E-mail:* admissions@usm.edu. *Web site:* http://www.usm.edu/.

William Carey University
Hattiesburg, Mississippi

Freshman Application Contact Mr. William N. Curry, Dean of Enrollment Management, William Carey University, 498 Tuscan Avenue, Hattiesburg, MS 39401-5499. *Phone:* 601-318-6051. *Toll-free phone:* 800-962-5991. *Fax:* 601-318-6154. *E-mail:* admissions@wmcarey.edu. *Web site:* http://www.wmcarey.edu/.

MISSOURI

Avila University
Kansas City, Missouri

- **Independent Roman Catholic** comprehensive, founded 1916, administratively affiliated with The Sisters of Saint Joseph of Carondelet, St. Louis Province
- **Suburban** 50-acre campus
- **Endowment** $6.4 million
- **Coed** 1,222 undergraduate students, 81% full-time, 64% women, 36% men
- **Minimally difficult** entrance level, 49% of applicants were admitted

Undergraduates 984 full-time, 238 part-time. Students come from 22 states and territories; 17 other countries; 31% are from out of state; 18% Black or African American, non-Hispanic/Latino; 6% Hispanic/Latino; 1% Asian, non-Hispanic/Latino; 0.3% Native Hawaiian or other Pacific Islander, non-Hispanic/Latino; 1% American Indian or Alaska Native, non-Hispanic/Latino; 2% Two or more races, non-Hispanic/Latino; 2% Race/ethnicity unknown; 4% international; 10% transferred in; 28% live on campus. *Retention:* 71% of full-time freshmen returned.

Freshmen *Admission:* 1,052 applied, 513 admitted, 167 enrolled. *Average high school GPA:* 3.26. *Test scores:* SAT critical reading scores over 500: 53%; SAT math scores over 500: 53%; ACT scores over 18: 96%; SAT critical reading scores over 600: 12%; SAT math scores over 600: 12%; ACT scores over 24: 37%; ACT scores over 30: 5%.

Faculty *Total:* 200, 32% full-time, 41% with terminal degrees. *Student/faculty ratio:* 15:1.

Academics *Calendar:* semesters. *Degrees:* bachelor's, master's, and post-bachelor's certificates. *Special study options:* academic remediation for entering students, accelerated degree program, adult/continuing education programs, advanced placement credit, cooperative education, distance learning, double majors, English as a second language, independent study, internships, off-campus study, part-time degree program, services for LD students, study abroad, summer session for credit. *ROTC:* Army (c). *Unusual degree programs:* 3-2 occupational therapy, physical therapy, law with Rockhurst University, University of Missouri-Kansas City.

Computers on Campus 180 computers/terminals and 225 ports are available on campus for general student use. Students can access the following: campus intranet, computer help desk, free student e-mail accounts, online (class) grades, online (class) registration, online (class) schedules. Campuswide network is available. 100% of college-owned or -operated housing units are wired for high-speed Internet access. Wireless service is available via entire campus.

Student Life *Housing:* on-campus residence required through sophomore year. *Options:* coed, men-only, women-only. Campus housing is university owned. Freshman campus housing is guaranteed. *Activities and organizations:* drama/theater group, student-run newspaper, choral group, Avila Ambassadors, Avila Student Nurses Association, Campus Ministries, Saudi Arabian Student Association, Avila University Theatre Company. *Campus security:* 24-hour emergency response devices, student patrols, late-night transport/escort service, controlled dormitory access. *Student services:* health clinic, personal/psychological counseling.

Athletics Member NAIA. *Intercollegiate sports:* baseball M(s), basketball M(s)/W(s), cheerleading W(s), cross-country running M(s)/W(s), football M(s), golf M(s)/W(s), soccer M(s)/W(s), softball W(s), volleyball W(s). *Intramural sports:* bowling M/W, table tennis M/W.

Standardized Tests *Required:* SAT or ACT (for admission).

Costs (2010–11) *Comprehensive fee:* $28,250 includes full-time tuition ($21,050), mandatory fees ($850), and room and board ($6350). Full-time tuition and fees vary according to course load and program. Part-time tuition: $515 per credit hour. Part-time tuition and fees vary according to course load and program. No tuition increase for student's term of enrollment. *Required fees:* $24 per credit hour part-time. *College room only:* $3150. Room and board charges vary according to board plan and housing facility. *Payment plans:* installment, deferred payment. *Waivers:* children of alumni, senior citizens, and employees or children of employees.

Financial Aid Of all full-time matriculated undergraduates who enrolled in 2008, 1,927 applied for aid, 1,852 were judged to have need, 1,846 had their need fully met. 161 Federal Work-Study jobs (averaging $903). 55 state and other part-time jobs (averaging $885). In 2008, 60 non-need-based awards were made. *Average percent of need met:* 35%. *Average financial aid package:* $12,976. *Average need-based loan:* $5465. *Average need-based gift aid:* $7854. *Average non-need-based aid:* $9152. *Average indebtedness upon graduation:* $16,508.

Applying *Options:* electronic application, early admission. *Application fee:* $25. *Required:* high school transcript, minimum 2.5 GPA, secondary school report. *Required for some:* essay or personal statement. *Recommended:* interview. *Application deadlines:* 8/15 (freshmen), 8/15 (transfers). *Notification:* 8/15 (freshmen), 8/15 (transfers).

Freshman Application Contact Mr. Brandon Johnson, Director of Undergraduate Admission, Avila University, 11901 Wornall Road, Kansas City, MO 64145. *Phone:* 816-501-2400. *Toll-free phone:* 800-GO-AVILA. *Fax:* 816-501-2453. *E-mail:* brandon.johnson@avila.edu. *Web site:* http://www.avila.edu/.

Baptist Bible College
Springfield, Missouri

Freshman Application Contact Mr. Terry Allcorn, Director of Admissions, Baptist Bible College, 628 East Kearney Street, Springfield, MO 65803-3498. *Phone:* 417-268-6000. *Fax:* 417-268-6694. *Web site:* http://www.gobbc.edu/.

Brown Mackie College–St. Louis
Fenton, Missouri

- **Proprietary** primarily 2-year
- **Coed**

Academics *Degrees:* diplomas, associate, and bachelor's.

Costs (2010–11) *Tuition:* Tuition varies by program. Students should contact Brown Mackie College for tuition information.

Freshman Application Contact Brown Mackie College–St. Louis, #2 Soccer Park Road, Fenton, MO 63026. *Phone:* 636-651-3290. *Web site:* http://www.brownmackie.edu/st-louis/.

See page 1160 for the College Close-Up.

Calvary Bible College and Theological Seminary
Kansas City, Missouri

- **Independent nondenominational** comprehensive, founded 1932
- **Suburban** 55-acre campus
- **Endowment** $163,875
- **Coed** 282 undergraduate students, 65% full-time, 52% women, 48% men
- **Minimally difficult** entrance level, 60% of applicants were admitted

Undergraduates 182 full-time, 100 part-time. 10% Black or African American, non-Hispanic/Latino; 4% Hispanic/Latino; 0.4% Asian, non-Hispanic/Latino; 2% American Indian or Alaska Native, non-Hispanic/Latino; 1% Two or more races, non-Hispanic/Latino; 2% Race/ethnicity unknown; 1% international; 15% transferred in. *Retention:* 72% of full-time freshmen returned.

Freshmen *Admission:* 50 applied, 30 admitted, 30 enrolled. *Test scores:* SAT critical reading scores over 500: 100%; SAT math scores over 500: 100%; ACT scores over 18: 79%; SAT critical reading scores over 600: 50%; SAT math scores over 600: 50%; ACT scores over 24: 36%.

Faculty *Total:* 34, 53% full-time, 15% with terminal degrees. *Student/faculty ratio:* 11:1.

Academics *Calendar:* semesters. *Degrees:* certificates, diplomas, associate, bachelor's, and master's. *Special study options:* academic remediation for entering students, adult/continuing education programs, advanced placement credit, double majors, external degree program, independent study, internships, part-time degree program, student-designed majors, summer session for credit. *ROTC:* Army (c).

Computers on Campus 23 computers/terminals are available on campus for general student use. Students can access the following: campus intranet, computer help desk, free student e-mail accounts, online (class) grades, online (class) registration, online (class) schedules. Wireless service is available via entire campus.
Student Life *Housing:* on-campus residence required through senior year. *Options:* men-only, women-only. Campus housing is university owned. Freshman campus housing is guaranteed. *Activities and organizations:* drama/theater group, choral group, Missions Encounter, Masterworks (Fine Arts). *Campus security:* late-night transport/escort service, night patrols by trained security personnel. *Student services:* personal/psychological counseling.
Athletics Member NCCAA. *Intercollegiate sports:* basketball M/W, soccer M, volleyball W. *Intramural sports:* basketball M/W, golf M/W, racquetball M/W, tennis M/W, volleyball M/W, weight lifting M/W.
Standardized Tests *Required:* SAT or ACT (for admission).
Costs (2011–12) *Comprehensive fee:* $18,848 includes full-time tuition ($9280), mandatory fees ($768), and room and board ($8800). No tuition increase for student's term of enrollment. *Room and board:* Room and board charges vary according to housing facility. *Payment plan:* installment. *Waivers:* employees or children of employees.
Financial Aid *Financial aid deadline:* 4/1.
Applying *Application fee:* $25. *Required:* essay or personal statement, high school transcript, 2 letters of recommendation, statement of faith. *Application deadlines:* 7/15 (freshmen), 7/15 (transfers).
Freshman Application Contact Bob Crank, Director of Admissions, Calvary Bible College and Theological Seminary, 15800 Calvary Road, Kansas City, MO 64147-1341. *Phone:* 816-322-0110 Ext. 1321. *Toll-free phone:* 800-326-3960. *Fax:* 816-331-4474. *E-mail:* admissions@calvary.edu. *Web site:* http://www.calvary.edu/.

Central Bible College
Springfield, Missouri
Director of Admissions James Bell, Executive Director for Enrollment Services, Central Bible College, 3000 North Grant Avenue, Springfield, MO 65803-1096. *Phone:* 417-833-2551 Ext. 1290. *Toll-free phone:* 800-831-4222 Ext. 1184. *E-mail:* jbell@cbcag.edu. *Web site:* http://netcom.cbcag.edu/.

Central Christian College of the Bible
Moberly, Missouri
Freshman Application Contact Mr. Aaron Merritt, Director of Admissions, Central Christian College of the Bible, 911 Urbandale Drive East, Moberly, MO 65270-1997. *Phone:* 660-263-3900. *Toll-free phone:* 888-263-3900. *Fax:* 660-263-3936. *E-mail:* admissions@cccb.edu. *Web site:* http://www.cccb.edu/.

Central Methodist University
Fayette, Missouri
Freshman Application Contact Mr. Larry Anderson, Director of Admissions, Central Methodist University, 411 Central Methodist Square, Fayette, MO 65248-1198. *Phone:* 660-248-6247. *Toll-free phone:* 888-CMU-1854. *Fax:* 660-248-1872. *E-mail:* admissions@centralmethodist.edu. *Web site:* http://www.centralmethodist.edu/.

Chamberlain College of Nursing
St. Louis, Missouri
- **Proprietary** 4-year, founded 1889, part of DeVry Inc.
- **Urban** campus
- **Coed** 7,002 undergraduate students, 18% full-time, 93% women, 7% men
- **Moderately difficult** entrance level

Undergraduates 1,250 full-time, 5,752 part-time. 91% are from out of state; 10% Black or African American, non-Hispanic/Latino; 4% Hispanic/Latino; 2% Asian, non-Hispanic/Latino; 0.5% Native Hawaiian or other Pacific Islander, non-Hispanic/Latino; 0.3% American Indian or Alaska Native, non-Hispanic/Latino; 0.4% Two or more races, non-Hispanic/Latino; 41% Race/ethnicity unknown; 0.7% international.
Freshmen *Admission:* 93 enrolled.
Faculty *Total:* 219, 15% full-time. *Student/faculty ratio:* 34:1.
Academics *Calendar:* semesters. *Degree:* bachelor's. *Special study options:* academic remediation for entering students, advanced placement credit, English as a second language, off-campus study, part-time degree program, summer session for credit.
Student Life *Campus security:* 24-hour patrols, late-night transport/escort service, controlled dormitory access. *Student services:* personal/psychological counseling.
Standardized Tests *Required:* SAT or ACT (for admission).

Costs (2010–11) *Tuition:* $14,880 full-time, $620 per credit hour part-time. Full-time tuition and fees vary according to course load and program. Part-time tuition and fees vary according to course load and program. *Room only:* Room and board charges vary according to housing facility.
Applying *Options:* early admission, deferred entrance. *Application fee:* $95. *Required:* essay or personal statement, high school transcript. *Required for some:* interview. *Application deadlines:* rolling (freshmen), rolling (transfers). *Notification:* continuous (freshmen), continuous (transfers).
Freshman Application Contact Chamberlain College of Nursing, 6150 Oakland Avenue, St. Louis, MO 63139-3215. *Phone:* 630-953-3690. *Toll-free phone:* 800-942-4310. *Web site:* http://www.chamberlain.edu/.

City Vision College
Kansas City, Missouri
Director of Admissions Director of Admissions, City Vision College, PO Box 413188, Kansas City, MO 64141-3188. *Phone:* 816-960-2008. *Fax:* 816-569-0223. *E-mail:* info@cityvision.edu. *Web site:* http://www.cityvision.edu/.

College of the Ozarks
Point Lookout, Missouri
- **Independent Presbyterian** 4-year, founded 1906
- **Small-town** 1000-acre campus
- **Endowment** $277.4 million
- **Coed** 1,371 undergraduate students, 99% full-time, 57% women, 43% men
- **Moderately difficult** entrance level, 10% of applicants were admitted

Undergraduates 1,359 full-time, 12 part-time. Students come from 36 states and territories; 14 other countries; 20% are from out of state; 0.6% Black or African American, non-Hispanic/Latino; 2% Hispanic/Latino; 0.4% Asian, non-Hispanic/Latino; 0.1% Native Hawaiian or other Pacific Islander, non-Hispanic/Latino; 0.4% American Indian or Alaska Native, non-Hispanic/Latino; 2% Two or more races, non-Hispanic/Latino; 0.3% Race/ethnicity unknown; 1% international; 2% transferred in; 82% live on campus. *Retention:* 88% of full-time freshmen returned.
Freshmen *Admission:* 2,975 applied, 300 admitted, 271 enrolled. *Average high school GPA:* 3.53. *Test scores:* ACT scores over 18: 94%; ACT scores over 24: 36%; ACT scores over 30: 3%.
Faculty *Total:* 139, 61% full-time, 41% with terminal degrees. *Student/faculty ratio:* 13:1.
Academics *Calendar:* semesters. *Degree:* bachelor's. *Special study options:* academic remediation for entering students, advanced placement credit, double majors, independent study, internships, services for LD students, student-designed majors. *ROTC:* Army (b). *Unusual degree programs:* 3-2 engineering with Missouri University Science and Technology; law with University of Missouri, Medical Technology with Cox Medical Center.
Computers on Campus 164 computers/terminals and 1,097 ports are available on campus for general student use. Students can access the following: campus intranet, computer help desk, free student e-mail accounts, online (class) grades, online (class) registration, online (class) schedules. Campus-wide network is available. 100% of college-owned or -operated housing units are wired for high-speed Internet access. Wireless service is available via classrooms, dorm rooms, libraries, student centers.
Student Life *Housing:* on-campus residence required through senior year. *Options:* men-only, women-only. Campus housing is university owned. *Activities and organizations:* drama/theater group, student-run newspaper, radio station, choral group, Students in Free Enterprise (SIFE), Student Senate, Baptist Student Union, Aggie Club, Business Undergraduate Society. *Campus security:* 24-hour emergency response devices and patrols, controlled dormitory access, front gate closed 1 am to 6 am, gate security 5:30 pm to 1 am. *Student services:* health clinic, personal/psychological counseling.
Athletics Member NAIA. *Intercollegiate sports:* baseball M(s), basketball M(s)/W(s), cheerleading M/W, volleyball W(s). *Intramural sports:* basketball M/W, football M, racquetball M/W, softball M/W, tennis M/W, volleyball M/W.
Standardized Tests *Required:* SAT or ACT (for admission).
Costs (2011–12) *Comprehensive fee:* includes mandatory fees ($430) and room and board ($5600). Part-time tuition: $295 per credit hour. Part-time tuition and fees vary according to course load. The college guarantees to meet all of the tuition cost for each full-time student by using earnings from its endowment, operation of its own mandatory student work program, accepting student aid grants, gifts and other sources. In effect, each full-time student's Cost of Education (tuition) is met 100 percent by participating in the work program and a combination of private, institutional and federal/state student aid. *College room only:* $2750. *Payment plan:* installment.
Financial Aid Of all full-time matriculated undergraduates who enrolled in 2008, 1,432 applied for aid, 1,349 were judged to have need, 421 had their need fully met. 835 Federal Work-Study jobs (averaging $4379). 700 state and

other part-time jobs (averaging $3193). In 2008, 114 non-need-based awards were made. *Average percent of need met:* 82%. *Average financial aid package:* $15,783. *Average need-based gift aid:* $12,613. *Average non-need-based aid:* $10,299. *Average indebtedness upon graduation:* $6029.
Applying *Options:* electronic application. *Required:* high school transcript, 2 letters of recommendation, interview, medical history, financial statement. *Recommended:* minimum 3 GPA. *Application deadlines:* 2/15 (freshmen), 2/15 (transfers). *Notification:* continuous (freshmen), continuous (transfers).
Freshman Application Contact Mrs. Gayle Groves, Admissions Secretary, College of the Ozarks, PO Box 17, Point Lookout, MO 65726. *Phone:* 417-690-2637. *Toll-free phone:* 800-222-0525. *Fax:* 417-335-2618. *E-mail:* admiss4@cofo.edu. *Web site:* http://www.cofo.edu/.

Colorado Technical University North Kansas City
North Kansas City, Missouri

Director of Admissions Angela Vietti, Director of Admissions, Colorado Technical University North Kansas City, 520 East 19th Avenue, North Kansas City, MO 64116. *Phone:* 888-404-7555. *E-mail:* avietti@kc.coloradotech.edu. *Web site:* http://kc.coloradotech.edu/.

Columbia College
Columbia, Missouri

- **Independent** comprehensive, founded 1851, affiliated with Christian Church (Disciples of Christ)
- **Urban** 33-acre campus
- **Endowment** $59.0 million
- **Coed** 1,043 undergraduate students, 80% full-time, 58% women, 42% men
- **Moderately difficult** entrance level

Undergraduates 834 full-time, 209 part-time. Students come from 23 states and territories; 35 other countries; 7% are from out of state; 6% Black or African American, non-Hispanic/Latino; 2% Hispanic/Latino; 1% Asian, non-Hispanic/Latino; 0.1% Native Hawaiian or other Pacific Islander, non-Hispanic/Latino; 0.9% American Indian or Alaska Native, non-Hispanic/Latino; 0.5% Two or more races, non-Hispanic/Latino; 10% Race/ethnicity unknown; 10% international; 17% transferred in; 33% live on campus. *Retention:* 66% of full-time freshmen returned.
Freshmen *Admission:* 983 applied, 156 enrolled. *Average high school GPA:* 3.39. *Test scores:* SAT critical reading scores over 500: 40%; SAT math scores over 500: 60%; ACT scores over 18: 88%; SAT math scores over 600: 40%; ACT scores over 24: 46%; SAT math scores over 700: 20%; ACT scores over 30: 5%.
Faculty *Total:* 117, 57% full-time, 49% with terminal degrees. *Student/faculty ratio:* 12:1.
Academics *Calendar:* semesters. *Degrees:* bachelor's and master's (offers continuing education program with significant enrollment not reflected in profile). *Special study options:* adult/continuing education programs, advanced placement credit, distance learning, double majors, English as a second language, external degree program, honors programs, independent study, internships, off-campus study, part-time degree program, services for LD students, student-designed majors, study abroad, summer session for credit. *ROTC:* Army (c), Navy (c), Air Force (c).
Computers on Campus 83 computers/terminals are available on campus for general student use. Students can access the following: campus intranet, computer help desk, free student e-mail accounts, online (class) grades, online (class) registration, online (class) schedules. Campuswide network is available. 100% of college-owned or -operated housing units are wired for high-speed Internet access. Wireless service is available via entire campus.
Student Life *Housing:* on-campus residence required through sophomore year. *Options:* coed, women-only, disabled students. Campus housing is university owned. Freshman campus housing is guaranteed. *Activities and organizations:* drama/theater group, choral group, Elysium Players, Student Government Association, International Club, Chi Alpha Christian Fellowship, The Pride. *Campus security:* 24-hour emergency response devices and patrols, late-night transport/escort service, controlled dormitory access. *Student services:* health clinic, personal/psychological counseling.
Athletics Member NAIA. *Intercollegiate sports:* basketball M(s)/W(s), soccer M(s), softball W(s), volleyball W(s). *Intramural sports:* basketball M/W, football M/W, soccer M/W, softball M/W, volleyball M/W.
Standardized Tests *Required:* SAT or ACT (for admission).
Costs (2011–12) *Comprehensive fee:* $22,786 includes full-time tuition ($16,532) and room and board ($6254). Full-time tuition and fees vary according to class time and course load. Part-time tuition: $411 per credit hour. Part-time tuition and fees vary according to class time, course load, and location. *College room only:* $3892. Room and board charges vary according to board

plan. *Payment plans:* installment, deferred payment. *Waivers:* children of alumni, senior citizens, and employees or children of employees.
Financial Aid Of all full-time matriculated undergraduates who enrolled in 2008, 617 applied for aid, 552 were judged to have need. 139 Federal Work-Study jobs (averaging $1753). 218 state and other part-time jobs (averaging $1351). In 2008, 180 non-need-based awards were made. *Average percent of need met:* 31%. *Average financial aid package:* $13,965. *Average need-based loan:* $3981. *Average need-based gift aid:* $4609. *Average non-need-based aid:* $10,145. *Average indebtedness upon graduation:* $14,989.
Applying *Options:* electronic application, deferred entrance. *Application fee:* $35. *Required:* high school transcript, minimum 2.5 GPA. *Required for some:* essay or personal statement, interview. *Application deadlines:* 8/8 (freshmen), 8/8 (transfers). *Notification:* continuous (freshmen), continuous (transfers).
Freshman Application Contact Daniel Kruse, Admissions Counselor, Columbia College, 1001 Rogers Street, Columbia, MO 65216. *Phone:* 573-875-7358. *Toll-free phone:* 800-231-2391 Ext. 7366. *Fax:* 573-875-7506. *E-mail:* admissions@ccis.edu. *Web site:* http://www.ccis.edu/.

Conception Seminary College
Conception, Missouri

Freshman Application Contact Br. Etienne Huard OSB, Director of Recruitment and Admissions, Conception Seminary College, PO Box 502, Conception, MO 64433-0502. *Phone:* 660-944-2886. *Fax:* 660-944-2829. *E-mail:* vocations@conception.edu. *Web site:* http://www.conception.edu/.

Cox College
Springfield, Missouri

Freshman Application Contact Cox College, 1423 North Jefferson, Springfield, MO 65802. *Phone:* 417-269-3083. *Toll-free phone:* 866-898-5355. *Web site:* http://www.coxcollege.edu/.

Culver-Stockton College
Canton, Missouri

- **Independent** 4-year, founded 1853, affiliated with Christian Church (Disciples of Christ)
- **Rural** 143-acre campus
- **Endowment** $18.3 million
- **Coed** 771 undergraduate students, 96% full-time, 56% women, 44% men
- **Moderately difficult** entrance level, 61% of applicants were admitted

Undergraduates 740 full-time, 31 part-time. Students come from 22 states and territories; 15 other countries; 49% are from out of state; 10% Black or African American, non-Hispanic/Latino; 5% Hispanic/Latino; 0.4% Asian, non-Hispanic/Latino; 0.1% Native Hawaiian or other Pacific Islander, non-Hispanic/Latino; 1% American Indian or Alaska Native, non-Hispanic/Latino; 0.1% Race/ethnicity unknown; 2% international; 10% transferred in; 74% live on campus. *Retention:* 73% of full-time freshmen returned.
Freshmen *Admission:* 1,439 applied, 871 admitted, 212 enrolled. *Average high school GPA:* 3.17. *Test scores:* SAT critical reading scores over 500: 42%; SAT math scores over 500: 34%; ACT scores over 18: 96%; SAT critical reading scores over 600: 8%; ACT scores over 24: 25%; ACT scores over 30: 3%.
Faculty *Total:* 74, 64% full-time, 54% with terminal degrees. *Student/faculty ratio:* 14:1.
Academics *Calendar:* semesters. *Degree:* bachelor's. *Special study options:* academic remediation for entering students, adult/continuing education programs, advanced placement credit, distance learning, double majors, honors programs, independent study, internships, off-campus study, part-time degree program, services for LD students, student-designed majors, study abroad, summer session for credit. *Unusual degree programs:* 3-2 occupational therapy with Washington University in St. Louis.
Computers on Campus 75 computers/terminals and 50 ports are available on campus for general student use. Students can access the following: campus intranet, computer help desk, free student e-mail accounts, online (class) grades, online (class) registration, online (class) schedules. Campuswide network is available. 100% of college-owned or -operated housing units are wired for high-speed Internet access. Wireless service is available via entire campus.
Student Life *Housing:* on-campus residence required through senior year. *Options:* coed. Campus housing is university owned. Freshman campus housing is guaranteed. *Activities and organizations:* drama/theater group, student-run newspaper, radio station, choral group, Up 'Til Dawn (benefiting St. Judes Hospital), Interfraternity Council/Panhellenic Council, Student Government Association, Students in Free Enterprise (SIFE), Campus Programming Council, national fraternities, national sororities. *Campus security:* 24-hour emergency response devices and patrols, late-night transport/escort service, controlled dormitory access, lighted pathways/sidewalks; self defense educa-

tion is currently offered on campus. *Student services:* personal/psychological counseling.

Athletics Member NAIA. *Intercollegiate sports:* baseball M(s), basketball M(s)/W(s), cheerleading M(s)/W(s), cross-country running M(s)/W(s), football M(s), golf M(s)/W(s), soccer M(s)/W(s), softball W(s), track and field M(s)/W(s), volleyball W(s). *Intramural sports:* baseball M/W, basketball M/W, bowling M/W, football M/W, golf M/W, racquetball M/W, softball M/W, volleyball W.

Standardized Tests *Required:* SAT or ACT (for admission).

Costs (2011–12) *One-time required fee:* $200. *Comprehensive fee:* $30,150 includes full-time tuition ($22,250), mandatory fees ($300), and room and board ($7600). Part-time tuition: $515 per credit hour. *Required fees:* $13 per credit hour part-time. *College room only:* $3400. Room and board charges vary according to board plan. *Payment plan:* installment. *Waivers:* senior citizens and employees or children of employees.

Financial Aid Of all full-time matriculated undergraduates who enrolled in 2009, 647 applied for aid, 608 were judged to have need, 107 had their need fully met. 63 Federal Work-Study jobs (averaging $1168). 320 state and other part-time jobs (averaging $1031). In 2009, 81 non-need-based awards were made. *Average percent of need met:* 77%. *Average financial aid package:* $20,090. *Average need-based loan:* $4814. *Average need-based gift aid:* $15,772. *Average non-need-based aid:* $11,564. *Average indebtedness upon graduation:* $31,200. *Financial aid deadline:* 6/1.

Applying *Options:* electronic application, deferred entrance. *Required:* high school transcript, minimum 2 GPA. *Recommended:* essay or personal statement, 1 letter of recommendation, interview. *Application deadlines:* rolling (freshmen), rolling (transfers). *Notification:* continuous (freshmen), continuous (transfers).

Freshman Application Contact Misty McBee, Senior Associate Director of Admissions, Culver-Stockton College, One College Hill, Canton, MO 63435-1299. *Phone:* 573-288-6507. *Toll-free phone:* 800-537-1883. *Fax:* 573-288-6618. *E-mail:* admissions@culver.edu. *Web site:* http://www.culver.edu/.

DeVry University

Kansas City, Missouri

- **Proprietary** comprehensive, founded 1931, part of DeVry University
- **Urban** 12-acre campus
- **Coed** 1,215 undergraduate students, 47% full-time, 32% women, 68% men
- **Minimally difficult** entrance level

Undergraduates 573 full-time, 642 part-time. 36% are from out of state; 15% Black or African American, non-Hispanic/Latino; 5% Hispanic/Latino; 2% Asian, non-Hispanic/Latino; 0.2% Native Hawaiian or other Pacific Islander, non-Hispanic/Latino; 0.3% American Indian or Alaska Native, non-Hispanic/Latino; 0.9% Two or more races, non-Hispanic/Latino; 19% Race/ethnicity unknown; 0.3% international; 20% transferred in.

Freshmen *Admission:* 199 enrolled.

Faculty *Total:* 78, 36% full-time. *Student/faculty ratio:* 20:1.

Academics *Calendar:* semesters. *Degrees:* associate, bachelor's, and master's. *Special study options:* academic remediation for entering students, accelerated degree program, adult/continuing education programs, advanced placement credit, distance learning, part-time degree program, services for LD students, summer session for credit.

Computers on Campus Students can access the following: online (class) registration. Campuswide network is available.

Student Life *Housing:* college housing not available. *Campus security:* 24-hour emergency response devices and patrols, lighted pathways/sidewalks.

Costs (2010–11) *Tuition:* $14,766 full-time, $580 per credit hour part-time. Full-time tuition and fees vary according to course load. Part-time tuition and fees vary according to course load. *Required fees:* $60 full-time, $30 per term part-time. *Payment plans:* installment, deferred payment. *Waivers:* employees or children of employees.

Financial Aid Of all full-time matriculated undergraduates who enrolled in 2007, 294 applied for aid, 281 were judged to have need, 12 had their need fully met. In 2007, 30 non-need-based awards were made. *Average percent of need met:* 40%. *Average financial aid package:* $11,948. *Average need-based loan:* $8396. *Average need-based gift aid:* $5419. *Average non-need-based aid:* $13,609. *Average indebtedness upon graduation:* $8969.

Applying *Options:* electronic application, deferred entrance. *Application fee:* $50. *Required:* high school transcript, interview. *Application deadlines:* rolling (freshmen), rolling (transfers). *Notification:* continuous (freshmen), continuous (transfers).

Freshman Application Contact DeVry University, 11224 Holmes Road, Kansas City, MO 64131. *Phone:* 816-943-7300. *Web site:* http://www.devry.edu/.

DeVry University

Kansas City, Missouri

Admissions Office Contact DeVry University, City Center Square, 1100 Main Street, Suite 118, Kansas City, MO 64105-2112. *Web site:* http://www.devry.edu/.

DeVry University

St. Louis, Missouri

Admissions Office Contact DeVry University, 1801 Park 270 Drive, Suite 260, St. Louis, MO 63146-4020. *Web site:* http://www.devry.edu/.

Drury University

Springfield, Missouri

- **Independent** comprehensive, founded 1873
- **Urban** 80-acre campus
- **Endowment** $68.0 million
- **Coed** 1,631 undergraduate students, 98% full-time, 54% women, 46% men
- **Moderately difficult** entrance level, 68% of applicants were admitted

Undergraduates 1,599 full-time, 32 part-time. Students come from 30 states and territories; 29 other countries; 17% are from out of state; 2% Black or African American, non-Hispanic/Latino; 2% Hispanic/Latino; 2% Asian, non-Hispanic/Latino; 0.7% American Indian or Alaska Native, non-Hispanic/Latino; 6% international; 7% transferred in; 56% live on campus. *Retention:* 83% of full-time freshmen returned.

Freshmen *Admission:* 1,289 applied, 882 admitted, 406 enrolled. *Average high school GPA:* 3.78. *Test scores:* ACT scores over 18: 99%; ACT scores over 24: 69%; ACT scores over 30: 16%.

Faculty *Total:* 191, 71% full-time, 70% with terminal degrees. *Student/faculty ratio:* 12:1.

Academics *Calendar:* semesters. *Degrees:* bachelor's and master's (also offers evening program with significant enrollment not reflected in profile). *Special study options:* academic remediation for entering students, accelerated degree program, adult/continuing education programs, advanced placement credit, cooperative education, distance learning, double majors, English as a second language, honors programs, independent study, internships, off-campus study, part-time degree program, services for LD students, student-designed majors, study abroad, summer session for credit. *ROTC:* Army (c). *Unusual degree programs:* 3-2 engineering with Washington University in St. Louis; international management with American Graduate School of International Management, occupational therapy with Washington University in St. Louis.

Computers on Campus 389 computers/terminals are available on campus for general student use. Students can access the following: campus intranet, computer help desk, free student e-mail accounts, online (class) grades, online (class) registration, online (class) schedules, digital imaging lab, online bill payment/student information. Campuswide network is available. 100% of college-owned or -operated housing units are wired for high-speed Internet access. Wireless service is available via entire campus.

Student Life *Housing:* on-campus residence required through senior year. *Options:* coed. Campus housing is university owned and leased by the school. Freshman campus housing is guaranteed. *Activities and organizations:* drama/theater group, student-run newspaper, radio and television station, choral group, Drury Volunteer Corps (DVC), International Student Association, Lambda Chi Alpha, Zeta Tau Alpha, Kappa Delta, national fraternities, national sororities. *Campus security:* 24-hour emergency response devices and patrols, student patrols, late-night transport/escort service, controlled dormitory access, security cameras in parking areas. *Student services:* health clinic, personal/psychological counseling.

Athletics Member NCAA. All Division II. *Intercollegiate sports:* baseball M(s), basketball M(s)/W(s), cheerleading M(s)/W(s), cross-country running M(s)/W(s), golf M(s)/W(s), soccer M(s)/W(s), softball W(s), swimming and diving M(s)/W(s), tennis M(s)/W(s), track and field M(s)/W(s), volleyball W(s). *Intramural sports:* basketball M/W, cheerleading W, football M/W, ice hockey M(c), racquetball M/W, rugby M, soccer M/W, softball M/W, table tennis M/W, tennis M/W, ultimate Frisbee M/W, volleyball M/W.

Standardized Tests *Required:* SAT or ACT (for admission).

Costs (2011–12) *One-time required fee:* $145. *Comprehensive fee:* $28,509 includes full-time tuition ($20,500), mandatory fees ($543), and room and board ($7466). Full-time tuition and fees vary according to class time. Part-time tuition and fees vary according to class time. *Room and board:* Room and board charges vary according to board plan and housing facility. *Payment plans:* tuition prepayment, installment, deferred payment. *Waivers:* minority students, children of alumni, and employees or children of employees.

Financial Aid Of all full-time matriculated undergraduates who enrolled in 2009, 1,579 applied for aid, 1,542 were judged to have need, 1,291 had their need fully met. 824 Federal Work-Study jobs (averaging $3000). 187 state and other part-time jobs (averaging $2500). In 2009, 72 non-need-based awards were made. *Average percent of need met:* 86%. *Average financial aid package:* $7890. *Average need-based loan:* $6500. *Average need-based gift aid:* $6885. *Average non-need-based aid:* $415. *Average indebtedness upon graduation:* $20,500.

Applying *Options:* electronic application, deferred entrance. *Application fee:* $25. *Required:* essay or personal statement, high school transcript, minimum 2.7 GPA, 1 letter of recommendation. *Recommended:* interview. *Application deadlines:* 8/1 (freshmen), rolling (transfers). *Notification:* continuous (freshmen), continuous (transfers).

Freshman Application Contact Ms. Dawn Hiles, Dean of Admission, Drury University, 900 North Benton, Springfield, MO 65802. *Phone:* 417-873-7614. *Toll-free phone:* 800-922-2274. *Fax:* 417-866-3873. *E-mail:* druryad@drury.edu. *Web site:* http://www.drury.edu/.

Evangel University
Springfield, Missouri

- **Independent** comprehensive, founded 1955, affiliated with Assemblies of God
- **Urban** 80-acre campus
- **Coed** 1,770 undergraduate students, 90% full-time, 56% women, 44% men
- **Moderately difficult** entrance level, 68% of applicants were admitted

Undergraduates 1,594 full-time, 176 part-time. 4% Black or African American, non-Hispanic/Latino; 4% Hispanic/Latino; 2% Asian, non-Hispanic/Latino; 1% American Indian or Alaska Native, non-Hispanic/Latino; 1% Two or more races, non-Hispanic/Latino; 8% Race/ethnicity unknown; 0.6% international. *Retention:* 74% of full-time freshmen returned.

Freshmen *Admission:* 1,229 applied, 837 admitted, 400 enrolled. *Test scores:* SAT critical reading scores over 500: 54%; SAT math scores over 500: 55%; ACT scores over 18: 86%; SAT critical reading scores over 600: 22%; SAT math scores over 600: 14%; ACT scores over 24: 41%; SAT critical reading scores over 700: 5%; SAT math scores over 700: 3%; ACT scores over 30: 6%.

Faculty *Total:* 122, 66% full-time, 52% with terminal degrees. *Student/faculty ratio:* 19:1.

Academics *Calendar:* semesters. *Degrees:* associate, bachelor's, and master's. *Special study options:* academic remediation for entering students, accelerated degree program, advanced placement credit, independent study, internships, part-time degree program, services for LD students, study abroad, summer session for credit. *ROTC:* Army (c).

Computers on Campus Students can access the following: computer help desk, free student e-mail accounts, online (class) grades, online (class) registration, online (class) schedules, online payment. Campuswide network is available. Wireless service is available via classrooms, computer labs, learning centers, libraries, student centers.

Student Life *Housing:* on-campus residence required through senior year. *Options:* coed, men-only, women-only. Campus housing is university owned. *Activities and organizations:* drama/theater group, student-run newspaper, radio and television station, choral group. *Campus security:* 24-hour emergency response devices and patrols, student patrols, late-night transport/escort service, controlled dormitory access. *Student services:* health clinic, personal/psychological counseling.

Athletics Member NAIA. *Intercollegiate sports:* baseball M(s), basketball M(s)/W(s), cross-country running M(s)/W(s), football M(s), golf M(s)/W(s), softball W(s), tennis M(s)/W(s), track and field M(s)/W(s), volleyball W(s). *Intramural sports:* baseball M, basketball M/W, football M, golf M/W, soccer M/W, softball W, tennis M/W, volleyball M.

Standardized Tests *Required:* SAT or ACT (for admission).

Costs (2010–11) *Comprehensive fee:* $22,990 includes full-time tuition ($15,950), mandatory fees ($1040), and room and board ($6000). Full-time tuition and fees vary according to course load. Part-time tuition: $622 per credit hour. *College room only:* $3100. Room and board charges vary according to board plan. *Payment plan:* installment. *Waivers:* employees or children of employees.

Financial Aid Of all full-time matriculated undergraduates who enrolled in 2008, 1,572 applied for aid, 1,397 were judged to have need, 121 had their need fully met. 1,151 Federal Work-Study jobs (averaging $1493). 124 state and other part-time jobs (averaging $1564). In 2008, 151 non-need-based awards were made. *Average percent of need met:* 47%. *Average financial aid package:* $9851. *Average need-based loan:* $4131. *Average need-based gift aid:* $6201. *Average non-need-based aid:* $2549. *Average indebtedness upon graduation:* $30,449.

Applying *Options:* electronic application, deferred entrance. *Application fee:* $25. *Required:* essay or personal statement, high school transcript, interview. *Recommended:* minimum 2 GPA. *Application deadline:* rolling (freshmen). *Notification:* continuous (freshmen).

Freshman Application Contact Evangel University, 1111 North Glenstone, Springfield, MO 65802. *Phone:* 417-865-2811 Ext. 7205. *Toll-free phone:* 800-382-6435. *Fax:* 417-865-9599. *E-mail:* admissions@evangel.edu. *Web site:* http://www.evangel.edu/.

Everest College
Springfield, Missouri

Freshman Application Contact Admissions Office, Everest College, 1010 West Sunshine, Springfield, MO 65807-2488. *Phone:* 417-864-7220. *Fax:* 417-864-5697. *Web site:* http://www.everest.edu/campus/springfield/.

Fontbonne University
St. Louis, Missouri

- **Independent Roman Catholic** comprehensive, founded 1917
- **Suburban** 13-acre campus with easy access to St. Louis
- **Endowment** $17.4 million
- **Coed** 1,694 undergraduate students, 73% full-time, 69% women, 31% men
- **Moderately difficult** entrance level, 90% of applicants were admitted

Undergraduates 1,240 full-time, 454 part-time. Students come from 22 states and territories; 17 other countries; 14% are from out of state; 28% Black or African American, non-Hispanic/Latino; 1% Hispanic/Latino; 0.9% Asian, non-Hispanic/Latino; 0.1% American Indian or Alaska Native, non-Hispanic/Latino; 2% Race/ethnicity unknown; 4% international; 13% transferred in; 26% live on campus. *Retention:* 72% of full-time freshmen returned.

Freshmen *Admission:* 500 applied, 449 admitted, 165 enrolled. *Average high school GPA:* 3.21. *Test scores:* ACT scores over 18: 96%; ACT scores over 24: 38%; ACT scores over 30: 4%.

Faculty *Total:* 279, 29% full-time, 29% with terminal degrees. *Student/faculty ratio:* 13:1.

Academics *Calendar:* semesters. *Degrees:* certificates, bachelor's, master's, and postbachelor's certificates. *Special study options:* academic remediation for entering students, accelerated degree program, adult/continuing education programs, advanced placement credit, cooperative education, distance learning, double majors, English as a second language, honors programs, independent study, internships, off-campus study, part-time degree program, services for LD students, student-designed majors, study abroad, summer session for credit. *ROTC:* Army (c), Air Force (c). *Unusual degree programs:* 3-2 engineering with Washington University in St. Louis; social work with Washington University in St. Louis; Saint Louis University; occupational therapy with Washington University in St. Louis.

Computers on Campus 285 computers/terminals are available on campus for general student use. Students can access the following: campus intranet, computer help desk, free student e-mail accounts, online (class) grades, online (class) registration, online (class) schedules. Campuswide network is available. Wireless service is available via entire campus.

Student Life *Housing options:* coed, men-only, women-only, disabled students. Campus housing is university owned. Freshman campus housing is guaranteed. *Activities and organizations:* drama/theater group, student-run newspaper, choral group, Future Teachers Association, Students for the Enhancement of Black Awareness, Fontbonne Athletic Association, Fontbonne in Service and Humility, Student Government Association. *Campus security:* 24-hour patrols, late-night transport/escort service, controlled dormitory access. *Student services:* health clinic, personal/psychological counseling.

Athletics Member NCAA, NAIA. All NCAA Division III. *Intercollegiate sports:* baseball M, basketball M/W, bowling W, cheerleading W, cross-country running M/W, field hockey W, golf M/W, lacrosse M/W, soccer M/W, softball W, tennis M/W, track and field M/W, volleyball M/W. *Intramural sports:* basketball M/W, bowling M, soccer M, volleyball M/W.

Standardized Tests *Required:* SAT or ACT (for admission).

Costs (2010–11) *Comprehensive fee:* $28,180 includes full-time tuition ($20,060), mandatory fees ($320), and room and board ($7800). Full-time tuition and fees vary according to program. Part-time tuition: $537 per credit hour. Part-time tuition and fees vary according to program. *Required fees:* $16 per credit hour part-time. *College room only:* $4374. Room and board charges vary according to board plan and housing facility. *Payment plan:* installment. *Waivers:* employees or children of employees.

Financial Aid In 2003, 502 non-need-based awards were made. *Average percent of need met:* 86%. *Average financial aid package:* $15,600.

Applying *Options:* electronic application, early admission, deferred entrance. *Application fee:* $25. *Required:* high school transcript, minimum 2.5 GPA. *Required for some:* essay or personal statement. *Recommended:* 2 letters of recommendation, interview. *Application deadlines:* rolling (freshmen), rolling (transfers). *Notification:* continuous (freshmen), continuous (transfers).

Freshman Application Contact Dr. Greg Taylor, Executive Vice President, Fontbonne University, 6800 Wydown Boulevard, St. Louis, MO 63105. *Phone:* 314-889-1400. *Fax:* 314-889-1451. *E-mail:* gtaylor@fontbonne.edu. *Web site:* http://www.fontbonne.edu/.

Global University
Springfield, Missouri

- **Independent** comprehensive, founded 1948, affiliated with Assemblies of God
- **Small-town** campus
- **Coed**
- **Noncompetitive** entrance level

Faculty *Student/faculty ratio:* 11:1.

Academics *Calendar:* continuous. *Degrees:* certificates, diplomas, associate, bachelor's, master's, doctoral-professional, and postbachelor's certificates (offers only external degree programs).

Student Life *Campus security:* 24-hour emergency response devices.

Costs (2010–11) *One-time required fee:* $45. *Tuition:* $3520 full-time, $110 per credit hour part-time. Full-time tuition and fees vary according to course level, degree level, and location. Part-time tuition and fees vary according to course level, degree level, and location.

Applying *Application fee:* $40. *Required:* high school transcript. *Required for some:* 1 letter of recommendation. *Recommended:* essay or personal statement.

Freshman Application Contact Rev. Todd Waggoner, Enrollment and International Student Services Director, Global University, 1211 South Glenstone Avenue, Springfield, MO 65804. *Phone:* 417-862-9533 Ext. 2335. *Toll-free phone:* 800-443-1083. *Fax:* 417-863-9621. *E-mail:* twaggoner@ globaluniversity.edu. *Web site:* http://www.globaluniversity.edu/.

Goldfarb School of Nursing at Barnes-Jewish College
St. Louis, Missouri

- **Independent** comprehensive, founded 1902, administratively affiliated with Barnes Jewish Hospital
- **Urban** campus
- **Endowment** $18.4 million
- **Coed, primarily women** 523 undergraduate students, 93% full-time, 91% women, 9% men

Undergraduates 486 full-time, 37 part-time. Students come from 6 states and territories; 7 other countries; 22% are from out of state; 8% Black or African American, non-Hispanic/Latino; 2% Hispanic/Latino; 0.4% Asian, non-Hispanic/Latino; 3% Native Hawaiian or other Pacific Islander, non-Hispanic/Latino; 0.4% American Indian or Alaska Native, non-Hispanic/Latino; 0.4% Two or more races, non-Hispanic/Latino; 7% Race/ethnicity unknown; 0.2% international; 100% transferred in.

Faculty *Total:* 53, 68% full-time, 49% with terminal degrees. *Student/faculty ratio:* 10:1.

Academics *Calendar:* trimesters. *Degrees:* bachelor's, master's, doctoral-other, and post-master's certificates. *Special study options:* accelerated degree program, advanced placement credit, independent study, off-campus study, part-time degree program, services for LD students, summer session for credit.

Computers on Campus 110 computers/terminals are available on campus for general student use. Students can access the following: campus intranet, computer help desk, free student e-mail accounts, software, research databases. Campuswide network is available. Wireless service is available via entire campus.

Student Life *Housing:* college housing not available. *Activities and organizations:* student-run newspaper, Student Nurses Association. *Campus security:* 24-hour patrols, late-night transport/escort service. *Student services:* health clinic, personal/psychological counseling.

Costs (2011–12) *Tuition:* $17,250 full-time, $575 per credit part-time. Full-time tuition and fees vary according to course load and degree level. Part-time tuition and fees vary according to course load and degree level. *Required fees:* $1055 full-time. *Payment plan:* installment.

Financial Aid Of all full-time matriculated undergraduates who enrolled in 2003, 150 applied for aid, 150 were judged to have need, 21 had their need fully met. 10 Federal Work-Study jobs (averaging $3300). In 2003, 21 non-need-based awards were made. *Average financial aid package:* $16,000. *Average need-based loan:* $4000. *Average need-based gift aid:* $4000. *Average non-need-based aid:* $9000. *Average indebtedness upon graduation:* $10,000.

Applying *Options:* deferred entrance. *Application fee:* $50. *Required:* 2 letters of recommendation. *Application deadline:* rolling (transfers). *Notification:* continuous (transfers).

Freshman Application Contact Goldfarb School of Nursing at Barnes-Jewish College, 4483 Duncan Avenue, St. Louis, MO 63110. *Phone:* 314-362-9155. *Toll-free phone:* 800-832-9009. *Web site:* http:// www.barnesjewishcollege.edu/.

Graceland University
Independence, Missouri

- **Independent Community of Christ** comprehensive
- **Coed**

Academics *Calendar:* 4-1-4. *Degrees:* bachelor's, master's, and post-master's certificates.

Financial Aid *Of all full-time matriculated undergraduates who enrolled in 2009,* 1,000 applied for aid, 917 were judged to have need, 168 had their need fully met. 383 Federal Work-Study jobs (averaging $1382). 303 state and other part-time jobs (averaging $1708). *In 2009,* 230 non-need-based awards were made. *Average percent of need met:* 78. *Average financial aid package:* $18,566. *Average need-based loan:* $5397. *Average need-based gift aid:* $13,960. *Average non-need-based aid:* $10,029. *Average indebtedness upon graduation:* $29,934.

Freshman Application Contact Admissions, Graceland University, 1401 West Truman Road, Independence, MO 64050-3434. *Phone:* 816-833-0524. *E-mail:* gic@graceland.edu. *Web site:* http://www.graceland.edu/.

Grantham University
Kansas City, Missouri

- **Proprietary** comprehensive, founded 1951
- **Urban** campus with easy access to Kansas City
- **Coed**
- **Noncompetitive** entrance level

Academics *Calendar:* continuous. *Degrees:* associate, bachelor's, and master's (offers only external degree programs).

Costs (2010–11) *One-time required fee:* $30. *Tuition:* $7950 full-time, $265 per credit hour part-time. No tuition increase for student's term of enrollment. *Payment plans:* installment, deferred payment.

Applying *Options:* electronic application. *Application fee:* $30. *Required:* high school transcript.

Freshman Application Contact Mr. Matthew Hawes, Vice President of Enrollment Management, Grantham University, 7200 NW 86th Street, Kansas City, MO 64153. *Phone:* 800-955-2527. *Toll-free phone:* 800-955-2527. *Fax:* 816-595-5757. *E-mail:* admissions@grantham.edu. *Web site:* http:// www.grantham.edu/.

Hannibal-LaGrange University
Hannibal, Missouri

- **Independent Southern Baptist** comprehensive, founded 1858
- **Small-town** 110-acre campus
- **Endowment** $5.7 million
- **Coed** 1,176 undergraduate students, 75% full-time, 65% women, 35% men
- **Minimally difficult** entrance level

Undergraduates 886 full-time, 290 part-time. Students come from 25 states and territories; 25 other countries; 26% are from out of state; 16% transferred in; 56% live on campus. *Retention:* 58% of full-time freshmen returned.

Freshmen *Admission:* 697 applied, 170 enrolled.

Faculty *Total:* 146, 41% full-time, 14% with terminal degrees. *Student/faculty ratio:* 11:1.

Academics *Calendar:* semesters. *Degrees:* associate, bachelor's, and master's. *Special study options:* academic remediation for entering students, accelerated degree program, adult/continuing education programs, advanced placement credit, distance learning, double majors, English as a second language, honors programs, independent study, internships, off-campus study, part-time degree program, services for LD students, student-designed majors, study abroad, summer session for credit.

Computers on Campus 76 computers/terminals are available on campus for general student use. Students can access the following: online (class) grades, online (class) registration, online (class) schedules. Campuswide network is available. Wireless service is available via libraries, student centers.

Student Life *Housing:* on-campus residence required for freshman year. *Options:* men-only, women-only. Campus housing is university owned. Freshman campus housing is guaranteed. *Activities and organizations:* drama/theater group, student-run newspaper, choral group, Phi Beta Lambda, student government, Student Teachers Organization, Phi Beta Delta, Alpha Tau Beta, national fraternities, national sororities. *Campus security:* 24-hour emergency response devices and patrols, controlled dormitory access, Fletcher dorm only for electronic access.

Athletics Member NAIA. *Intercollegiate sports:* baseball M(s), basketball M(s)/W(s), cheerleading M(s)/W(s), cross-country running M(s)/W(s), golf M(s)/W(s), soccer M(s)/W(s), softball W(s), track and field M(s)/W(s), volleyball M(s)/W(s), wrestling M(s). *Intramural sports:* basketball M/W, racquetball M/W, table tennis M/W, ultimate Frisbee M/W, volleyball M/W.

Standardized Tests *Required:* SAT or ACT (for admission).

Costs (2011–12) *Comprehensive fee:* $23,090 includes full-time tuition ($16,170), mandatory fees ($720), and room and board ($6200). Full-time tuition and fees vary according to course load, degree level, program, and reciprocity agreements. *Part-time tuition:* $539 per credit. Part-time tuition and fees vary according to course load, degree level, program, and reciprocity agreements. *Room and board:* Room and board charges vary according to housing facility. *Payment plan:* installment. *Waivers:* employees or children of employees.

Financial Aid Of all full-time matriculated undergraduates who enrolled in 2009, 80 Federal Work-Study jobs (averaging $750).

Applying *Options:* electronic application, early admission, deferred entrance. *Application fee:* $25. *Required:* high school transcript, minimum 2 GPA. *Required for some:* GED. *Application deadlines:* 9/10 (freshmen), 8/10 (out-of-state freshmen), rolling (transfers). *Notification:* continuous until 9/10 (freshmen), 9/10 (out-of-state freshmen), continuous (transfers).

Freshman Application Contact Dr. Raymond Carty, Vice President for Enrollment Management, Hannibal-LaGrange University, 2800 Palmyra Road, Hannibal, MO 63401-1999. *Phone:* 573-629-2278. *Toll-free phone:* 800-HLG-1119. *E-mail:* admissio@hlg.edu. *Web site:* http://www.hlg.edu/.

Harris-Stowe State University

St. Louis, Missouri

- **State-supported** 4-year, founded 1857, part of Missouri Coordinating Board for Higher Education
- **Urban** 22-acre campus
- **Coed**
- **Noncompetitive** entrance level

Faculty *Student/faculty ratio:* 30:1.

Academics *Calendar:* semesters. *Degrees:* bachelor's and postbachelor's certificates.

Student Life *Campus security:* 24-hour emergency response devices and patrols, student patrols, late-night transport/escort service, controlled dormitory access, 16-hour patrols by trained security personnel Monday through Friday, 24-hour weekend and holiday patrols.

Athletics Member NAIA.

Standardized Tests *Required for some:* institutional placement test. *Recommended:* SAT or ACT (for admission).

Costs (2010–11) *Tuition:* state resident $4920 full-time, $164 per credit hour part-time; nonresident $9692 full-time, $323 per credit hour part-time. Full-time tuition and fees vary according to course load. Part-time tuition and fees vary according to course load. *Required fees:* $400 full-time, $200 per term part-time. *Room and board:* $8080. Room and board charges vary according to board plan.

Financial Aid *Of all full-time matriculated undergraduates who enrolled in 2008,* 990 applied for aid, 890 were judged to have need, 200 had their need fully met. 86 Federal Work-Study jobs (averaging $2000). 80 state and other part-time jobs (averaging $2000). *Average percent of need met:* 90. *Average financial aid package:* $9500. *Average need-based loan:* $5000. *Average need-based gift aid:* $4500. *Average non-need-based aid:* $3000. *Average indebtedness upon graduation:* $16,000.

Applying *Options:* early admission, deferred entrance. *Application fee:* $15. *Required:* high school transcript.

Freshman Application Contact Meghan Sprung, Assistant Director of Admissions, Harris-Stowe State University, 3026 Laclede Avenue, St. Louis, MO 63103. *Phone:* 314-340-3300. *Fax:* 314-340-3555. *E-mail:* admissions@hssu.edu. *Web site:* http://www.hssu.edu/.

Hickey College

St. Louis, Missouri

- **Private** 4-year, founded 1933
- **Suburban** 9-acre campus with easy access to St. Louis
- **Coed**
- 74% of applicants were admitted

Academics *Calendar:* semesters. *Degrees:* diplomas, associate, and bachelor's.

Student Life *Campus security:* 24-hour emergency response devices.

Applying *Options:* electronic application. *Required:* essay or personal statement, high school transcript, interview.

Freshman Application Contact Admissions Office, Hickey College, 940 West Port Plaza, Suite 101, St. Louis, MO 63146. *Phone:* 314-434-2212. *Toll-free phone:* 800-777-1544. *Web site:* http://www.hickeycollege.edu/.

ITT Technical Institute

Arnold, Missouri

- **Proprietary** primarily 2-year, founded 1997, part of ITT Educational Services, Inc.
- **Coed**
- **Minimally difficult** entrance level

Academics *Calendar:* quarters. *Degrees:* associate and bachelor's.

Student Life *Housing:* college housing not available.

Freshman Application Contact Director of Recruitment, ITT Technical Institute, 1930 Meyer Drury Drive, Arnold, MO 63010. *Phone:* 636-464-6600. *Toll-free phone:* 888-488-1082. *Web site:* http://www.itt-tech.edu/.

ITT Technical Institute

Earth City, Missouri

- **Proprietary** primarily 2-year, founded 1936, part of ITT Educational Services, Inc.
- **Suburban** campus
- **Coed**
- **Minimally difficult** entrance level

Academics *Calendar:* quarters. *Degrees:* associate and bachelor's.

Student Life *Housing:* college housing not available.

Freshman Application Contact Director of Recruitment, ITT Technical Institute, 3640 Corporate Trail Drive, Earth City, MO 63045. *Phone:* 314-298-7800. *Toll-free phone:* 800-235-5488. *Web site:* http://www.itt-tech.edu/.

ITT Technical Institute

Kansas City, Missouri

- **Proprietary** primarily 2-year, founded 2004, part of ITT Educational Services, Inc.
- **Coed**
- **Minimally difficult** entrance level

Academics *Calendar:* quarters. *Degrees:* associate and bachelor's.

Freshman Application Contact Director of Recruitment, ITT Technical Institute, 9150 East 41st Terrace, Kansas City, MO 64133. *Phone:* 816-276-1400. *Toll-free phone:* 877-488-1442. *Web site:* http://www.itt-tech.edu/.

ITT Technical Institute

Springfield, Missouri

- **Proprietary** 4-year, part of ITT Educational Services, Inc.
- **Coed**
- **Minimally difficult** entrance level

Academics *Calendar:* quarters. *Degrees:* associate and bachelor's.

Freshman Application Contact Director of Recruitment, ITT Technical Institute, 3216 South National Avenue, Springfield, MO 65807. *Phone:* 417-877-4800. *Toll-free phone:* 877-219-4387. *Web site:* http://www.itt-tech.edu/.

Kansas City Art Institute

Kansas City, Missouri

Freshman Application Contact Mr. Gerald Valet, Director of Admission Technology, Kansas City Art Institute, 4415 Warwick Boulevard, Kansas City, MO 64111-1874. *Phone:* 816-474-5224. *Toll-free phone:* 800-522-5224. *Fax:* 816-802-3309. *E-mail:* admiss@kcai.edu. *Web site:* http://www.kcai.edu/.

Lincoln University

Jefferson City, Missouri

- **State-supported** comprehensive, founded 1866, part of Missouri Coordinating Board for Higher Education
- **Small-town** 165-acre campus
- **Endowment** $1.6 million
- **Coed** 3,159 undergraduate students, 68% full-time, 60% women, 40% men
- **Noncompetitive** entrance level, 96% of applicants were admitted

Undergraduates 2,152 full-time, 1,007 part-time. Students come from 36 states and territories; 34 other countries; 18% are from out of state; 44% Black or African American, non-Hispanic/Latino; 2% Hispanic/Latino; 0.9% Asian, non-Hispanic/Latino; 0.1% Native Hawaiian or other Pacific Islander, non-Hispanic/Latino; 0.4% American Indian or Alaska Native, non-Hispanic/Latino; 2% Race/ethnicity unknown; 2% international; 5% transferred in; 26% live on campus. *Retention:* 49% of full-time freshmen returned.

Freshmen *Admission:* 1,578 applied, 1,507 admitted, 591 enrolled. *Average high school GPA:* 2.7. *Test scores:* SAT critical reading scores over 500: 19%; SAT math scores over 500: 35%; ACT scores over 18: 44%; SAT critical reading scores over 600: 8%; SAT math scores over 600: 8%; ACT scores over 24: 7%; SAT critical reading scores over 700: 8%; ACT scores over 30: 1%.

Faculty *Total:* 236, 60% full-time. *Student/faculty ratio:* 15:1.

Academics *Calendar:* semesters. *Degrees:* associate, bachelor's, master's, and post-master's certificates. *Special study options:* academic remediation for entering students, accelerated degree program, adult/continuing education programs, advanced placement credit, distance learning, double majors, honors programs, independent study, internships, off-campus study, part-time degree program, services for LD students, study abroad, summer session for credit. *ROTC:* Army (b), Navy (c), Air Force (c).

Computers on Campus 250 computers/terminals and 1,100 ports are available on campus for general student use. Students can access the following: campus intranet, computer help desk, free student e-mail accounts, online (class) grades, online (class) registration, online (class) schedules. Campus-wide network is available. 100% of college-owned or -operated housing units are wired for high-speed Internet access. Wireless service is available via entire campus.

Student Life *Housing:* on-campus residence required through sophomore year. *Options:* coed, men-only, women-only. Campus housing is university owned. *Activities and organizations:* drama/theater group, student-run newspaper, radio and television station, choral group, marching band, Student Government Association (SGA), Lincoln University Band, Alpha Kappa Mu, ROTC, Dedicated Individuals Vastly Affecting Society (DIVAS), national fraternities, national sororities. *Campus security:* 24-hour emergency response devices and patrols, student patrols, late-night transport/escort service, controlled dormitory access, Security-related training upon request, Operation I-dent (allows students to engrave belongings to prevent theft), and Timely Warnings. *Student services:* health clinic, personal/psychological counseling, women's center.

Athletics Member NCAA. All Division II. *Intercollegiate sports:* baseball M(s), basketball M(s)/W(s), cheerleading W(s), cross-country running W(s), football M(s), golf M(s)/W(s), softball W(s), tennis W(s), track and field M(s)/W(s). *Intramural sports:* basketball M/W, bowling M/W, volleyball M/W, weight lifting M/W.

Standardized Tests *Required:* SAT or ACT (for admission).

Costs (2011–12) *Tuition:* state resident $5685 full-time, $190 per credit hour part-time; nonresident $10,915 full-time, $364 per credit hour part-time. Full-time tuition and fees vary according to location and reciprocity agreements. Part-time tuition and fees vary according to location and reciprocity agreements. *Required fees:* $490 full-time, $15 per credit hour part-time, $20 per term part-time. *Room and board:* $5144; room only: $2500. Room and board charges vary according to board plan and housing facility. *Payment plans:* installment, deferred payment. *Waivers:* employees or children of employees.

Financial Aid Of all full-time matriculated undergraduates who enrolled in 2009, 1,836 applied for aid, 1,648 were judged to have need, 188 had their need fully met. 168 Federal Work-Study jobs (averaging $1253). 194 state and other part-time jobs (averaging $2999). In 2009, 5 non-need-based awards were made. *Average percent of need met:* 67%. *Average financial aid package:* $9333. *Average need-based loan:* $3992. *Average need-based gift aid:* $5232. *Average non-need-based aid:* $3958. *Average indebtedness upon graduation:* $25,950.

Applying *Application fee:* $20. *Required:* high school transcript. *Required for some:* minimum 2 GPA, audition for sacred music and music education. *Application deadlines:* 7/15 (freshmen), 7/15 (transfers). *Notification:* continuous (freshmen), continuous (transfers).

Freshman Application Contact Mr. Mike Kosher, Director of Admissions and Enrollment Management, Lincoln University, Office of Admissions, 820 Chestnut Street, B-7 Young Hall, Jefferson City, MO 65102-0029. *Phone:* 573-681-5599. *Toll-free phone:* 800-521-5052. *Fax:* 573-681-5889. *E-mail:* enroll@lincolnu.edu. *Web site:* http://www.lincolnu.edu/.

Lindenwood University
St. Charles, Missouri

- **Independent Presbyterian** comprehensive, founded 1827
- **Suburban** 500-acre campus with easy access to St. Louis
- **Endowment** $90.6 million
- **Coed** 7,596 undergraduate students, 91% full-time, 55% women, 45% men
- **Moderately difficult** entrance level, 56% of applicants were admitted

Undergraduates 6,896 full-time, 700 part-time. Students come from 44 states and territories; 86 other countries; 26% are from out of state; 15% Black or African American, non-Hispanic/Latino; 3% Hispanic/Latino; 0.6% Asian, non-Hispanic/Latino; 0.3% American Indian or Alaska Native, non-Hispanic/Latino; 19% Race/ethnicity unknown; 10% international; 6% transferred in; 54% live on campus. *Retention:* 73% of full-time freshmen returned.

Freshmen *Admission:* 3,736 applied, 2,085 admitted, 1,046 enrolled. *Average high school GPA:* 3.13. *Test scores:* SAT critical reading scores over 500: 98%; SAT math scores over 500: 50%; SAT writing scores over 500: 44%; ACT scores over 18: 99%; SAT critical reading scores over 600: 40%; SAT math scores over 600: 17%; SAT writing scores over 600: 13%; ACT scores over 24: 32%; SAT critical reading scores over 700: 6%; SAT math scores over 700: 4%; ACT scores over 30: 7%.

Faculty *Total:* 716, 32% full-time, 46% with terminal degrees. *Student/faculty ratio:* 18:1.

Academics *Calendar:* 4-1-4 for daytime programs; quarters and trimesters for evening programs. *Degrees:* bachelor's, master's, doctoral-research/scholarship, post-master's, and postbachelor's certificates. *Special study options:* academic remediation for entering students, accelerated degree program, adult/continuing education programs, advanced placement credit, distance learning, double majors, English as a second language, external degree program, freshman honors college, honors programs, independent study, internships, off-campus study, part-time degree program, services for LD students, student-designed majors, study abroad, summer session for credit. *ROTC:* Army (b). *Unusual degree programs:* 3-2 engineering with University of Missouri-Columbia.

Computers on Campus 150 computers/terminals are available on campus for general student use. Students can access the following: computer help desk, free student e-mail accounts, online (class) grades, online (class) registration, online (class) schedules, Blackboard. Campuswide network is available. 65% of college-owned or -operated housing units are wired for high-speed Internet access. Wireless service is available via classrooms, computer centers, computer labs, dorm rooms, learning centers, libraries, student centers.

Student Life *Housing options:* men-only, women-only. Campus housing is university owned. *Activities and organizations:* drama/theater group, student-run newspaper, radio and television station, choral group, marching band, A Cross Between Campus Ministry, American Humanics, Alpha Phi Omega, Campus YMCA, Campus Crusades for Christ, national fraternities, national sororities. *Campus security:* 24-hour emergency response devices and patrols, late-night transport/escort service, controlled dormitory access. *Student services:* health clinic, personal/psychological counseling.

Athletics Member NAIA. *Intercollegiate sports:* baseball M(s), basketball M(s)/W(s), bowling M(s)/W(s), cheerleading M(s)/W(s), cross-country running M(s)/W(s), field hockey W(s), football M(s), golf M(s)/W(s), ice hockey M(s)/W(s), lacrosse M(s)(c)/W(s)(c), riflery M(s)/W(s), soccer M(s)/W(s), softball W(s), swimming and diving M(s)/W(s), table tennis M(s)/W(s), tennis M(s)/W(s), track and field M(s)/W(s), volleyball M(s)/W(s), water polo M(s)/W(s), weight lifting M(s)/W(s), wrestling M(s)/W(s).

Standardized Tests *Required:* SAT or ACT (for admission).

Costs (2010–11) *Comprehensive fee:* $20,810 includes full-time tuition ($13,260), mandatory fees ($340), and room and board ($7210). Full-time tuition and fees vary according to program. Part-time tuition: $380 per credit hour. Part-time tuition and fees vary according to course load. *College room only:* $3980. *Payment plans:* installment, deferred payment. *Waivers:* senior citizens and employees or children of employees.

Financial Aid Of all full-time matriculated undergraduates who enrolled in 2009, 4,980 applied for aid, 4,587 were judged to have need, 2,880 had their need fully met. In 2009, 1007 non-need-based awards were made. *Average percent of need met:* 89%. *Average financial aid package:* $7024. *Average need-based loan:* $2649. *Average need-based gift aid:* $4461. *Average non-need-based aid:* $3868.

Applying *Options:* electronic application, deferred entrance. *Application fee:* $30. *Required:* high school transcript, minimum 2.5 GPA, resume and listing of activities. *Recommended:* essay or personal statement, 3 letters of recommendation, interview. *Application deadlines:* rolling (freshmen), rolling (transfers). *Notification:* continuous (freshmen), continuous (transfers).

Freshman Application Contact Lindenwood University, 209 South Kingshighway, St. Charles, MO 63301-1695. *Phone:* 636-949-4949. *Web site:* http://www.lindenwood.edu/.

See page 1388 for the College Close-Up.

Logan University–College of Chiropractic

Chesterfield, Missouri

- **Independent** upper-level, founded 1935
- **Suburban** 111-acre campus with easy access to St. Louis
- **Endowment** $12.4 million
- **Coed** 94 undergraduate students, 73% full-time, 41% women, 59% men
- **Moderately difficult** entrance level

Undergraduates 69 full-time, 25 part-time. 10% Black or African American, non-Hispanic/Latino; 1% Hispanic/Latino; 2% Asian, non-Hispanic/Latino;

1% Native Hawaiian or other Pacific Islander, non-Hispanic/Latino; 1% American Indian or Alaska Native, non-Hispanic/Latino; 1% Two or more races, non-Hispanic/Latino; 1% Race/ethnicity unknown; 1% international.

Faculty *Total:* 96, 55% full-time.

Academics *Calendar:* trimesters. *Degrees:* bachelor's, master's, and doctoral-professional. *Special study options:* adult/continuing education programs, advanced placement credit, distance learning, independent study, internships, part-time degree program, services for LD students.

Computers on Campus 95 computers/terminals are available on campus for general student use. Students can access the following: computer help desk, free student e-mail accounts, online (class) grades, online (class) registration, online (class) schedules, on-line classes, course homepages, wireless technologies, Academic Software Solutions for teaching and learning, library resources, academic records access. Campuswide network is available. Wireless service is available via classrooms, computer centers, computer labs, learning centers, libraries, student centers.

Student Life *Housing:* college housing not available. *Activities and organizations:* Pi Kappa Chi, Lambda Kappa Chi, Chiro Sigma, Student American Chiropractic Association, Omega Sigma Pi, national fraternities, national sororities. *Campus security:* 24-hour patrols, late-night transport/escort service. *Student services:* health clinic, personal/psychological counseling.

Athletics *Intercollegiate sports:* basketball M(c)/W(c), soccer M(c), tennis M(c). *Intramural sports:* basketball M/W, football M, ice hockey M, softball M/W, volleyball M/W.

Costs (2010–11) *Tuition:* $5400 full-time, $150 per credit hour part-time. *Required fees:* $390 full-time, $130 per term part-time.

Financial Aid Of all full-time matriculated undergraduates who enrolled in 1999, 160 applied for aid, 160 were judged to have need, 130 had their need fully met. 130 Federal Work-Study jobs (averaging $2693). *Average percent of need met:* 100%. *Average need-based loan:* $3500. *Average need-based gift aid:* $3000.

Applying *Options:* electronic application, deferred entrance. *Application fee:* $50. *Application deadline:* rolling (transfers). *Notification:* continuous (transfers).

Application Contact Logan University–College of Chiropractic, 1851 Schoettler Road, Chesterfield, MO 63006-1065. *Phone:* 636-227-2100. *Toll-free phone:* 800-533-9210. *Fax:* 636-207-2425. *E-mail:* loganadm@logan.edu. *Web site:* http://www.logan.edu/.

Maryville University of Saint Louis

St. Louis, Missouri

- **Independent** comprehensive, founded 1872
- **Suburban** 130-acre campus with easy access to St. Louis
- **Endowment** $31.3 million
- **Coed** 2,968 undergraduate students, 58% full-time, 75% women, 25% men
- **Moderately difficult** entrance level, 73% of applicants were admitted

Undergraduates 1,718 full-time, 1,250 part-time. Students come from 25 states and territories; 24 other countries; 13% are from out of state; 8% Black or African American, non-Hispanic/Latino; 2% Hispanic/Latino; 2% Asian, non-Hispanic/Latino; 0.1% Native Hawaiian or other Pacific Islander, non-Hispanic/Latino; 0.4% American Indian or Alaska Native, non-Hispanic/Latino; 0.6% Two or more races, non-Hispanic/Latino; 10% Race/ethnicity unknown; 1% international; 15% transferred in; 21% live on campus. *Retention:* 84% of full-time freshmen returned.

Freshmen *Admission:* 991 applied, 720 admitted, 372 enrolled. *Average high school GPA:* 3.63. *Test scores:* ACT scores over 18: 99%; ACT scores over 24: 70%; ACT scores over 30: 7%.

Faculty *Total:* 410, 28% full-time, 62% with terminal degrees. *Student/faculty ratio:* 12:1.

Academics *Calendar:* semesters. *Degrees:* bachelor's, master's, doctoral-research/scholarship, and postbachelor's certificates. *Special study options:* accelerated degree program, adult/continuing education programs, advanced placement credit, cooperative education, distance learning, double majors, honors programs, independent study, internships, off-campus study, part-time degree program, services for LD students, study abroad, summer session for credit. *ROTC:* Army (c). *Unusual degree programs:* 3-2 business administration; engineering with Washington University in St. Louis; social work with Saint Louis University; education.

Computers on Campus 450 computers/terminals are available on campus for general student use. Students can access the following: campus intranet, computer help desk, free student e-mail accounts, online (class) grades, online (class) registration, online (class) schedules, specialized software, university catalog. Campuswide network is available. 100% of college-owned or -operated housing units are wired for high-speed Internet access. Wireless service is available via entire campus.

Student Life *Housing options:* coed. Campus housing is university owned. *Activities and organizations:* drama/theater group, student-run newspaper, choral group, Campus Activities Board, Physical Therapy Club, Student Nurses

Association, Community Service Club, Campus Crusade for Christ. *Campus security:* 24-hour emergency response devices and patrols, late-night transport/escort service, controlled dormitory access, video security system in residence halls, self-defense and education programs. *Student services:* health clinic, personal/psychological counseling.

Athletics Member NCAA. All Division II. *Intercollegiate sports:* baseball M(s), basketball M(s)/W(s), cross-country running M(s)/W(s), golf M(s)/W(s), soccer M(s)/W(s), softball W(s), tennis M(s)/W(s), track and field M(s)/W(s), volleyball W(s). *Intramural sports:* basketball M/W, cheerleading M/W, football M/W, soccer M/W, softball W, volleyball M/W.

Standardized Tests *Required:* SAT or ACT (for admission).

Costs (2010–11) *Comprehensive fee:* $30,410 includes full-time tuition ($21,100), mandatory fees ($810), and room and board ($8500). Full-time tuition and fees vary according to course load. Part-time tuition: $634 per credit hour. Part-time tuition and fees vary according to class time. *Required fees:* $203 per term part-time. *Room and board:* Room and board charges vary according to housing facility. *Payment plans:* installment, deferred payment. *Waivers:* senior citizens and employees or children of employees.

Financial Aid Of all full-time matriculated undergraduates who enrolled in 2009, 1,476 applied for aid, 1,341 were judged to have need, 154 had their need fully met. 258 Federal Work-Study jobs (averaging $2055). 120 state and other part-time jobs (averaging $1941). In 2009, 170 non-need-based awards were made. *Average percent of need met:* 52%. *Average financial aid package:* $14,115. *Average need-based loan:* $4366. *Average need-based gift aid:* $10,798. *Average non-need-based aid:* $7051. *Average indebtedness upon graduation:* $22,636.

Applying *Options:* electronic application, deferred entrance. *Application fee:* $30. *Required:* high school transcript, minimum 2.5 GPA. *Required for some:* essay or personal statement, interview, audition, portfolio. *Application deadlines:* 8/15 (freshmen), rolling (transfers). *Notification:* continuous (freshmen), continuous (transfers).

Freshman Application Contact Ms. Shani Lenore-Jenkins, Assistant Vice President of Enrollment, Maryville University of Saint Louis, 650 Maryville University Drive, St. Louis, MO 63141-7299. *Phone:* 314-529-9350. *Toll-free phone:* 800-627-9855. *Fax:* 314-529-9927. *E-mail:* admissions@maryville.edu. *Web site:* http://www.maryville.edu/.

Messenger College
Joplin, Missouri

Freshman Application Contact Ron Cannon, Vice President of Academic Affairs, Messenger College, 300 East 50th Street, Joplin, MO 64804. *Phone:* 417-624-7070 Ext. 108. *Toll-free phone:* 800-385-8940. *Fax:* 417-624-5070. *E-mail:* info@messengercollege.edu. *Web site:* http://www.messengercollege.edu/.

Metro Business College
Cape Girardeau, Missouri

Director of Admissions Ms. Kyla Evans, Admissions Director, Metro Business College, 1732 North Kingshighway, Cape Girardeau, MO 63701. *Phone:* 573-334-9181. *Fax:* 573-334-0617. *Web site:* http://www.metrobusinesscollege.edu/.

Midwest University
Wentzville, Missouri

Director of Admissions Jeoung H. Ham, Registrar/Director of Admissions, Midwest University, PO Box 365, 851 Parr Road, Wentzville, MO 63385. *Phone:* 636-327-4645. *Fax:* 636-327-4715. *E-mail:* usa@midwest.edu. *Web site:* http://www.midwest.edu/.

Missouri Baptist University
St. Louis, Missouri

- **Independent Southern Baptist** comprehensive, founded 1964
- **Suburban** 65-acre campus
- **Endowment** $2.9 million
- **Coed** 3,688 undergraduate students, 39% full-time, 60% women, 40% men
- **Moderately difficult** entrance level, 61% of applicants were admitted

Undergraduates 1,437 full-time, 2,251 part-time. Students come from 26 states and territories; 15 other countries; 13% are from out of state; 9% Black or African American, non-Hispanic/Latino; 3% Hispanic/Latino; 0.2% Asian, non-Hispanic/Latino; 0.1% Native Hawaiian or other Pacific Islander, non-Hispanic/Latino; 0.7% American Indian or Alaska Native, non-Hispanic/Latino; 0.1% Two or more races, non-Hispanic/Latino; 12% Race/ethnicity unknown; 2% international; 9% transferred in; 14% live on campus. *Retention:* 64% of full-time freshmen returned.

Freshmen *Admission:* 872 applied, 533 admitted, 215 enrolled. *Test scores:* ACT scores over 18: 82%; ACT scores over 24: 22%; ACT scores over 30: 4%.

Faculty *Total:* 277, 27% full-time, 26% with terminal degrees. *Student/faculty ratio:* 20:1.

Academics *Calendar:* semesters. *Degrees:* certificates, associate, bachelor's, master's, doctoral-professional, post-master's, and postbachelor's certificates. *Special study options:* academic remediation for entering students, accelerated degree program, adult/continuing education programs, advanced placement credit, distance learning, double majors, independent study, internships, off-campus study, part-time degree program, services for LD students, student-designed majors, study abroad, summer session for credit. *ROTC:* Army (c). *Unusual degree programs:* 3-2 engineering with University of Missouri-Columbia.

Computers on Campus 122 computers/terminals are available on campus for general student use. Students can access the following: campus intranet, computer help desk, free student e-mail accounts, online (class) grades, online (class) schedules. Campuswide network is available. Wireless service is available via entire campus.

Student Life *Housing options:* men-only, women-only. Campus housing is university owned. *Activities and organizations:* drama/theater group, student-run radio station, choral group, Baptist Collegiate Ministry, Students in Free Enterprise (SIFE), Missouri State Teacher's Association, Fellowship of Christian Athletes, Ministerial Alliance. *Campus security:* 24-hour emergency response devices and patrols, late-night transport/escort service, controlled dormitory access, self-defense classes. *Student services:* personal/psychological counseling.

Athletics Member NAIA. *Intercollegiate sports:* baseball M(s), basketball M(s)/W(s), bowling M(s)(c)/W(c), cross-country running M(s)/W(s), golf M(s)/W, lacrosse M(s)(c)/W(s)(c), soccer M(s)/W(s), softball W(s), tennis M(s)/W(s), track and field M(s)/W(s), volleyball M(s)(c)/W(s), wrestling M(s). *Intramural sports:* basketball M/W, football M/W, soccer M/W, softball M/W, volleyball M/W.

Standardized Tests *Required for some:* SAT or ACT (for admission).

Costs (2010–11) *Comprehensive fee:* $26,140 includes full-time tuition ($17,820), mandatory fees ($880), and room and board ($7440). Full-time tuition and fees vary according to course load, degree level, and location. Part-time tuition: $615 per credit hour. Part-time tuition and fees vary according to course load, degree level, and location. *Required fees:* $15 per credit hour part-time, $30 per term part-time. *Room and board:* Room and board charges vary according to housing facility. *Payment plan:* installment. *Waivers:* children of alumni, senior citizens, and employees or children of employees.

Financial Aid Of all full-time matriculated undergraduates who enrolled in 2008, 65 state and other part-time jobs (averaging $4819). In 2008, 277 non-need-based awards were made. *Average financial aid package:* $13,290. *Average need-based loan:* $4442. *Average need-based gift aid:* $5411. *Average non-need-based aid:* $6718.

Applying *Options:* electronic application. *Application fee:* $30. *Required:* high school transcript, minimum 2 GPA, interview. *Application deadlines:* rolling (freshmen), rolling (transfers). *Notification:* continuous (freshmen), continuous (transfers).

Freshman Application Contact Mr. Aaron Black, Director of Admissions, Missouri Baptist University, One College Park Drive, St. Louis, MO 63141-8660. *Phone:* 877-434-1115. *Toll-free phone:* 877-434-1115 Ext. 2290. *Fax:* 314-434-7596. *E-mail:* admissions@mobap.edu. *Web site:* http://www.mobap.edu/.

Missouri College
St. Louis, Missouri

Director of Admissions Mr. Doug Brinker, Admissions Director, Missouri College, 10121 Manchester Road, St. Louis, MO 63122-1583. *Phone:* 314-821-7700. *Fax:* 314-821-0891. *Web site:* http://www.mocollege.com/.

Missouri Southern State University
Joplin, Missouri

- **State-supported** comprehensive, founded 1937
- **Small-town** 350-acre campus
- **Coed** 5,751 undergraduate students, 74% full-time, 58% women, 42% men
- **Moderately difficult** entrance level, 94% of applicants were admitted

Undergraduates 4,283 full-time, 1,468 part-time. 12% are from out of state; 8% transferred in; 27% live on campus. *Retention:* 61% of full-time freshmen returned.

Freshmen *Admission:* 1,788 applied, 1,687 admitted, 900 enrolled. *Average high school GPA:* 3.18. *Test scores:* ACT scores over 18: 73%; ACT scores over 24: 26%; ACT scores over 30: 3%.

Faculty *Total:* 312, 66% full-time, 50% with terminal degrees. *Student/faculty ratio:* 19:1.

Academics *Calendar:* semesters. *Degrees:* certificates, associate, bachelor's, and master's. *Special study options:* academic remediation for entering students, accelerated degree program, adult/continuing education programs, advanced placement credit, cooperative education, distance learning, double majors, English as a second language, honors programs, independent study, internships, off-campus study, part-time degree program, services for LD students, study abroad, summer session for credit.

Computers on Campus Students can access the following: campus intranet, computer help desk, free student e-mail accounts, online (class) grades, online (class) registration, online (class) schedules. Campuswide network is available. Wireless service is available via entire campus.

Student Life *Housing:* on-campus residence required for freshman year. *Options:* coed, men-only, women-only. Campus housing is university owned. Freshman campus housing is guaranteed. *Activities and organizations:* drama/theater group, student-run newspaper, radio and television station, choral group, marching band, national fraternities, national sororities. *Campus security:* 24-hour emergency response devices and patrols, late-night transport/escort service, controlled dormitory access, security at campus events, emergency vehicle assistance, safety awareness information to students. *Student services:* health clinic, personal/psychological counseling.

Athletics Member NCAA. All Division II. *Intercollegiate sports:* baseball M(s), basketball M(s)/W(s), cross-country running M(s)/W(s), football M(s), golf M(s), soccer M(s)/W(s), softball W(s), tennis W(s), track and field M(s)/W(s), volleyball W(s). *Intramural sports:* baseball M/W, basketball M/W, football M/W, golf M/W, racquetball M/W, soccer M/W, softball M/W, swimming and diving M/W, table tennis M/W, tennis M/W, ultimate Frisbee M/W, volleyball M/W.

Standardized Tests *Required:* SAT or ACT (for admission), SAT and SAT Subject Tests or ACT (for admission). *Required for some:* Michigan Test of English Language Proficiency. *Recommended:* ACT (for admission).

Costs (2011–12) *Tuition:* state resident $4290 full-time, $143 per credit hour part-time; nonresident $8580 full-time, $286 per credit hour part-time. Full-time tuition and fees vary according to course load. *Required fees:* $526 full-time. *Room and board:* $5500. Room and board charges vary according to board plan and housing facility. *Waivers:* senior citizens and employees or children of employees.

Financial Aid Of all full-time matriculated undergraduates who enrolled in 2009, 3,418 applied for aid, 2,646 were judged to have need, 146 had their need fully met. 94 Federal Work-Study jobs (averaging $2787). 424 state and other part-time jobs (averaging $2474). In 2009, 319 non-need-based awards were made. *Average percent of need met:* 55%. *Average financial aid package:* $14,602. *Average need-based loan:* $4283. *Average need-based gift aid:* $5953. *Average non-need-based aid:* $4122. *Average indebtedness upon graduation:* $10,006.

Applying *Options:* electronic application, deferred entrance. *Application fee:* $15. *Required:* high school transcript, class rank. *Required for some:* 2 letters of recommendation. *Application deadlines:* 8/1 (freshmen), 8/1 (transfers). *Notification:* continuous (freshmen), continuous (transfers).

Freshman Application Contact Mr. Derek Skaggs, Director of Enrollment Services, Missouri Southern State University, 3950 East Newman Road, Joplin, MO 64801-1595. *Phone:* 417-625-9537. *Toll-free phone:* 866-818-MSSU. *Fax:* 417-659-4429. *E-mail:* admissions@mssu.edu. *Web site:* http://www.mssu.edu/.

Missouri State University

Springfield, Missouri

- **State-supported** comprehensive, founded 1905
- **Suburban** 225-acre campus
- **Endowment** $48.7 million
- **Coed** 17,205 undergraduate students, 78% full-time, 56% women, 44% men
- **Moderately difficult** entrance level, 77% of applicants were admitted

Undergraduates 13,449 full-time, 3,756 part-time. Students come from 46 states and territories; 66 other countries; 9% are from out of state; 4% Black or African American, non-Hispanic/Latino; 3% Hispanic/Latino; 1% Asian, non-Hispanic/Latino; 0.2% Native Hawaiian or other Pacific Islander, non-Hispanic/Latino; 0.8% American Indian or Alaska Native, non-Hispanic/Latino; 2% Two or more races, non-Hispanic/Latino; 4% Race/ethnicity unknown; 4% international; 9% transferred in; 28% live on campus. *Retention:* 73% of full-time freshmen returned.

Freshmen *Admission:* 7,664 applied, 5,927 admitted, 2,676 enrolled. *Average high school GPA:* 3.58. *Test scores:* SAT critical reading scores over 500: 71%; SAT math scores over 500: 79%; ACT scores over 18: 97%; SAT critical reading scores over 600: 34%; SAT math scores over 600: 40%; ACT scores over 24: 51%; SAT critical reading scores over 700: 9%; SAT math scores over 700: 9%; ACT scores over 30: 9%.

Faculty *Total:* 1,013, 69% full-time, 62% with terminal degrees. *Student/faculty ratio:* 21:1.

Academics *Calendar:* semesters. *Degrees:* bachelor's, master's, doctoral-professional, post-master's, and postbachelor's certificates. *Special study options:* accelerated degree program, advanced placement credit, cooperative education, distance learning, double majors, English as a second language, freshman honors college, honors programs, independent study, internships, off-campus study, part-time degree program, services for LD students, student-designed majors, study abroad, summer session for credit. *ROTC:* Army (b).

Computers on Campus 1,800 computers/terminals and 3,082 ports are available on campus for general student use. Students can access the following: campus intranet, computer help desk, free student e-mail accounts, online (class) grades, online (class) registration, online (class) schedules. Campuswide network is available. 100% of college-owned or -operated housing units are wired for high-speed Internet access. Wireless service is available via classrooms, computer centers, computer labs, learning centers, libraries, student centers.

Student Life *Housing:* on-campus residence required for freshman year. *Options:* coed, disabled students. Campus housing is university owned. Freshman campus housing is guaranteed. *Activities and organizations:* drama/theater group, student-run newspaper, radio and television station, choral group, marching band, Residence Hall Association, Campus Ministries, Fraternity & Sorority Life, Student Government Association, Maroon Madness, national fraternities, national sororities. *Campus security:* 24-hour emergency response devices and patrols, late-night transport/escort service, controlled dormitory access, on-campus police substation. *Student services:* health clinic, personal/psychological counseling, legal services.

Athletics Member NCAA. All Division I except football (Division I-AA). *Intercollegiate sports:* baseball M(s), basketball M(s)/W(s), bowling M(c)/W(c), cross-country running W(s), equestrian sports M(c)/W(c), field hockey W(s), golf M(s)/W(s), ice hockey M(c), lacrosse M(c), racquetball M(c)/W(c), soccer M(s)/W(s), softball W(s), swimming and diving M(s)/W(s), track and field W(s), ultimate Frisbee M(c)/W(c), volleyball M(c)/W(s), wrestling M(c). *Intramural sports:* basketball M/W, bowling M/W, football M/W, golf M/W, racquetball M/W, soccer M/W, softball M/W, table tennis M/W, tennis M/W, track and field W, ultimate Frisbee M/W, volleyball M/W, weight lifting M/W.

Standardized Tests *Required:* SAT or ACT (for admission).

Costs (2010–11) *Tuition:* state resident $5580 full-time, $186 per credit hour part-time; nonresident $11,160 full-time, $372 per credit hour part-time. Full-time tuition and fees vary according to course level, location, and program. Part-time tuition and fees vary according to course level, course load, location, and program. *Required fees:* $696 full-time. *Room and board:* $6394. Room and board charges vary according to board plan and housing facility. *Payment plans:* tuition prepayment, installment, deferred payment. *Waivers:* children of alumni, senior citizens, and employees or children of employees.

Financial Aid Of all full-time matriculated undergraduates who enrolled in 2009, 10,126 applied for aid, 7,854 were judged to have need, 1,195 had their need fully met. In 2009, 1430 non-need-based awards were made. *Average percent of need met:* 66%. *Average financial aid package:* $8064. *Average need-based loan:* $4204. *Average need-based gift aid:* $5107. *Average non-need-based aid:* $4209. *Average indebtedness upon graduation:* $21,359.

Applying *Options:* electronic application, deferred entrance. *Application fee:* $35. *Required:* high school transcript. *Required for some:* essay or personal statement, interview. *Application deadlines:* 7/20 (freshmen), 7/20 (transfers). *Notification:* continuous (freshmen), continuous (transfers).

Freshman Application Contact Ms. Jill Duncan, Associate Director of Admissions and Recruitment, Missouri State University, 901 South National Avenue, Springfield, MO 65897. *Phone:* 417-836-5517. *Toll-free phone:* 800-492-7900. *Fax:* 417-836-5137. *E-mail:* info@missouristate.edu. *Web site:* http://www.missouristate.edu/.

Missouri Tech

St. Louis, Missouri

Freshman Application Contact Mr. Bob Honaker, Director of Admissions, Missouri Tech, 1167 Corporate Lake Drive, St. Louis, MO 63132. *Phone:* 314-569-3600. *Fax:* 314-569-1167. *Web site:* http://www.motech.edu/.

Missouri University of Science and Technology

Rolla, Missouri

- **State-supported** university, founded 1870, part of University of Missouri System
- **Small-town** 284-acre campus
- **Endowment** $106.6 million
- **Coed, primarily men** 5,504 undergraduate students, 91% full-time, 23% women, 77% men
- **Very difficult** entrance level, 91% of applicants were admitted

Undergraduates 4,995 full-time, 509 part-time. Students come from 47 states and territories; 28 other countries; 19% are from out of state; 5% Black or African American, non-Hispanic/Latino; 2% Hispanic/Latino; 2% Asian, non-Hispanic/Latino; 0.2% Native Hawaiian or other Pacific Islander, non-Hispanic/Latino; 0.6% American Indian or Alaska Native, non-Hispanic/Latino; 0.6% Two or more races, non-Hispanic/Latino; 4% Race/ethnicity unknown; 5% international; 6% transferred in; 51% live on campus. *Retention:* 88% of full-time freshmen returned.

Freshmen *Admission:* 2,756 applied, 2,514 admitted, 1,149 enrolled. *Average high school GPA:* 3.6. *Test scores:* SAT critical reading scores over 500: 91%; SAT math scores over 500: 96%; ACT scores over 18: 100%; SAT critical reading scores over 600: 52%; SAT math scores over 600: 75%; ACT scores over 24: 87%; SAT critical reading scores over 700: 20%; SAT math scores over 700: 30%; ACT scores over 30: 35%.

Faculty *Total:* 445, 79% full-time, 81% with terminal degrees. *Student/faculty ratio:* 17:1.

Academics *Calendar:* semesters. *Degrees:* certificates, bachelor's, master's, doctoral-research/scholarship, and postbachelor's certificates. *Special study options:* academic remediation for entering students, accelerated degree program, adult/continuing education programs, advanced placement credit, cooperative education, distance learning, double majors, English as a second language, freshman honors college, honors programs, independent study, internships, off-campus study, part-time degree program, services for LD students, study abroad, summer session for credit. *ROTC:* Army (b), Navy (c), Air Force (b).

Computers on Campus 980 computers/terminals and 4,500 ports are available on campus for general student use. Students can access the following: campus intranet, computer help desk, free student e-mail accounts, online (class) grades, online (class) registration, online (class) schedules. Campuswide network is available. 100% of college-owned or -operated housing units are wired for high-speed Internet access. Wireless service is available via entire campus.

Student Life *Housing:* on-campus residence required through sophomore year. *Options:* coed, men-only, women-only, cooperative, disabled students. Campus housing is university owned, leased by the school and is provided by a third party. Freshman campus housing is guaranteed. *Activities and organizations:* drama/theater group, student-run newspaper, radio station, choral group, marching band, student government, Student Union Board, Residence Hall Association, academic organizations, service organizations, national fraternities, national sororities. *Campus security:* 24-hour emergency response devices and patrols, student patrols, late-night transport/escort service, controlled dormitory access, crime prevention programs. *Student services:* health clinic, personal/psychological counseling.

Athletics Member NCAA. All Division II. *Intercollegiate sports:* baseball M(s), basketball M(s)/W(s), cross-country running M(s)/W(s), football M(s), soccer M(s)/W(s), softball W(s), swimming and diving M(s), track and field M(s)/W(s), volleyball W(s). *Intramural sports:* badminton M/W, basketball M/W, bowling M/W, cross-country running M/W, football M/W, golf M/W, racquetball M/W, soccer M/W, softball M/W, swimming and diving M/W, table tennis M/W, tennis M/W, track and field M/W, ultimate Frisbee M/W, volleyball M/W, weight lifting M/W.

Standardized Tests *Required:* SAT or ACT (for admission). *Recommended:* ACT (for admission).

Costs (2010–11) *Tuition:* state resident $7368 full-time, $246 per credit hour part-time; nonresident $19,383 full-time, $646 per credit hour part-time. Full-time tuition and fees vary according to course load, degree level, and program. Part-time tuition and fees vary according to course load, degree level, and program. *Required fees:* $1160 full-time, $246 per credit hour part-time. *Room and board:* $8290; room only: $5280. Room and board charges vary according to board plan, housing facility, and location. *Payment plan:* installment. *Waivers:* employees or children of employees.

Financial Aid Of all full-time matriculated undergraduates who enrolled in 2009, 4,603 applied for aid, 3,704 were judged to have need, 2,306 had their need fully met. 103 Federal Work-Study jobs (averaging $2519). In 2009, 542 non-need-based awards were made. *Average percent of need met:* 61%. *Average financial aid package:* $10,760. *Average need-based loan:* $3000. *Average need-based gift aid:* $6906. *Average non-need-based aid:* $4326. *Average indebtedness upon graduation:* $21,700.

Applying *Options:* electronic application, early admission, deferred entrance. *Application fee:* $45. *Required:* high school transcript. *Recommended:* essay or personal statement. *Application deadlines:* 7/1 (freshmen), 7/1 (transfers). *Notification:* continuous (freshmen), continuous (transfers).

Freshman Application Contact Admissions Office, Missouri University of Science and Technology, 300 West 13th Street, 106 Parker Hall, Rolla, MO 65401. *Phone:* 573-341-4165. *Toll-free phone:* 800-522-0938. *Fax:* 573-341-4082. *E-mail:* admissions@mst.edu. *Web site:* http://www.mst.edu/.

Missouri Valley College

Marshall, Missouri

Freshman Application Contact Ms. Debi Bultmann, Admissions Office Manager, Missouri Valley College, 500 East College, Marshall, MO 65340-3197. *Phone:* 660-831-4125. *Fax:* 660-831-4233. *E-mail:* admissions@moval.edu. *Web site:* http://www.moval.edu/.

Missouri Western State University

St. Joseph, Missouri

- **State-supported** comprehensive, founded 1915
- **Suburban** 744-acre campus with easy access to Kansas City
- **Endowment** $2.2 million
- **Coed**
- **Noncompetitive** entrance level

Faculty *Student/faculty ratio:* 19:1.

Academics *Calendar:* semesters. *Degrees:* certificates, associate, bachelor's, master's, and postbachelor's certificates.

Student Life *Campus security:* 24-hour emergency response devices and patrols, student patrols, late-night transport/escort service, controlled dormitory access.

Athletics Member NCAA. All Division II.

Costs (2010–11) *Tuition:* state resident $4992 full-time, $166 per credit hour part-time; nonresident $9605 full-time, $320 per credit hour part-time. *Required fees:* $568 full-time, $19 per credit hour part-time, $30 per term part-time. *Room and board:* $6600. Room and board charges vary according to board plan and housing facility.

Financial Aid *Of all full-time matriculated undergraduates who enrolled in 2008,* 3,449 applied for aid, 2,651 were judged to have need, 296 had their need fully met. 277 Federal Work-Study jobs (averaging $1447). 695 state and other part-time jobs (averaging $1688). *In 2008,* 381 non-need-based awards were made. *Average percent of need met:* 64. *Average financial aid package:* $7438. *Average need-based loan:* $3536. *Average need-based gift aid:* $5131. *Average non-need-based aid:* $3623.

Applying *Options:* electronic application, early admission. *Application fee:* $15. *Required:* high school transcript.

Freshman Application Contact Mr. Howard McCauley, Director of Admissions, Missouri Western State University, 4525 Downs Drive, St. Joseph, MO 64507-2294. *Phone:* 816-271-4267. *Toll-free phone:* 800-662-7041 Ext. 60. *Fax:* 816-271-5833. *E-mail:* admission@missouriwestern.edu. *Web site:* http://www.missouriwestern.edu/.

National American University

Kansas City, Missouri

Director of Admissions Admissions Office, National American University, 7490 Northwest 87th Street, Kansas City, MO 64153. *Phone:* 816-412-5500. *E-mail:* zradmissions@national.edu. *Web site:* http://www.national.edu/.

Northwest Missouri State University

Maryville, Missouri

- **State-supported** comprehensive, founded 1905, part of Missouri Coordinating Board for Higher Education
- **Small-town** 370-acre campus with easy access to Kansas City
- **Coed** 6,193 undergraduate students, 89% full-time, 56% women, 44% men
- **Moderately difficult** entrance level, 88% of applicants were admitted

Undergraduates 5,512 full-time, 681 part-time. Students come from 37 states and territories; 27 other countries; 28% are from out of state; 5% Black or African American, non-Hispanic/Latino; 2% Hispanic/Latino; 0.7% Asian, non-Hispanic/Latino; 0.1% Native Hawaiian or other Pacific Islander, non-Hispanic/Latino; 0.2% American Indian or Alaska Native, non-Hispanic/Latino; 2% Two or more races, non-Hispanic/Latino; 2% Race/ethnicity unknown; 2% international; 5% transferred in; 41% live on campus. *Retention:* 70% of full-time freshmen returned.

Freshmen *Admission:* 4,412 applied, 3,889 admitted, 1,462 enrolled. *Average high school GPA:* 3.3. *Test scores:* SAT critical reading scores over 500: 43%;

SAT math scores over 500: 50%; ACT scores over 18: 93%; SAT critical reading scores over 600: 21%; SAT math scores over 600: 21%; ACT scores over 24: 32%; SAT critical reading scores over 700: 7%; ACT scores over 30: 3%.

Faculty *Total:* 324, 82% full-time, 52% with terminal degrees. *Student/faculty ratio:* 22:1.

Academics *Calendar:* trimesters. *Degrees:* certificates, bachelor's, master's, post-master's, and postbachelor's certificates. *Special study options:* academic remediation for entering students, advanced placement credit, distance learning, double majors, English as a second language, honors programs, independent study, internships, off-campus study, part-time degree program, services for LD students, study abroad, summer session for credit. *ROTC:* Army (b).

Computers on Campus 7,550 computers/terminals and 12,608 ports are available on campus for general student use. Students can access the following: campus intranet, computer help desk, free student e-mail accounts, online (class) grades, online (class) registration, online (class) schedules, online courses with library and databases. Campuswide network is available. 100% of college-owned or -operated housing units are wired for high-speed Internet access. Wireless service is available via classrooms, computer centers, computer labs, dorm rooms, learning centers, libraries, student centers.

Student Life *Housing:* on-campus residence required for freshman year. *Options:* coed, disabled students. Campus housing is university owned. Freshman campus housing is guaranteed. *Activities and organizations:* drama/theater group, student-run newspaper, radio and television station, choral group, marching band, student government, Residence Hall Association, Greek Life, national fraternities, national sororities. *Campus security:* 24-hour emergency response devices and patrols, student patrols, late-night transport/escort service, controlled dormitory access, security personnel are all police officers. *Student services:* health clinic, personal/psychological counseling, women's center.

Athletics Member NCAA. All Division II. *Intercollegiate sports:* baseball M(s), basketball M(s)/W(s), cheerleading M(s)/W(s), cross-country running M(s)/W(s), football M(s), golf W(s), soccer W(s), softball W(s), tennis M(s)/W(s), track and field M(s)/W(s), volleyball W(s). *Intramural sports:* badminton M/W, basketball M/W, cross-country running M/W, football M/W, golf M/W, racquetball M/W, skiing (cross-country) M/W, soccer W(c), softball W, swimming and diving M/W, table tennis M/W, tennis M/W, track and field M/W, volleyball M/W, wrestling M(c).

Standardized Tests *Required:* SAT or ACT (for admission).

Costs (2010–11) *One-time required fee:* $140. *Tuition:* state resident $4722 full-time, $157 per credit hour part-time; nonresident $10,073 full-time, $336 per credit hour part-time. Full-time tuition and fees vary according to course load, location, and reciprocity agreements. Part-time tuition and fees vary according to course load and location. *Required fees:* $2325 full-time, $78 per credit hour part-time. *Room and board:* $7962; room only: $4996. Room and board charges vary according to board plan and housing facility. *Payment plans:* installment, deferred payment. *Waivers:* senior citizens and employees or children of employees.

Financial Aid Of all full-time matriculated undergraduates who enrolled in 2008, 4,663 applied for aid, 3,618 were judged to have need, 2,152 had their need fully met. 441 Federal Work-Study jobs (averaging $1092). 1,082 state and other part-time jobs (averaging $1372). In 2008, 562 non-need-based awards were made. *Average percent of need met:* 72%. *Average financial aid package:* $7657. *Average need-based loan:* $4016. *Average need-based gift aid:* $5827. *Average non-need-based aid:* $2228. *Average indebtedness upon graduation:* $21,230.

Applying *Options:* electronic application, deferred entrance. *Application fee:* $25. *Required:* high school transcript, minimum 2 GPA. *Required for some:* interview. *Application deadlines:* rolling (freshmen), rolling (out-of-state freshmen), rolling (transfers). *Notification:* continuous (freshmen), continuous (out-of-state freshmen), continuous (transfers).

Freshman Application Contact Ms. Tammi Grow, Associate Director of Admission, Northwest Missouri State University, 800 University Drive, Maryville, MO 64468-6001. *Phone:* 660-562-1146. *Toll-free phone:* 800-633-1175. *Fax:* 660-562-1146. *E-mail:* admissions@nwmissouri.edu. *Web site:* http://www.nwmissouri.edu/.

Ozark Christian College

Joplin, Missouri

Freshman Application Contact Mr. Troy B. Nelson, Executive Director of Admissions, Ozark Christian College, 1111 North Main Street, Joplin, MO 64801-4804. *Phone:* 417-624-2518. *Toll-free phone:* 800-299-4622. *Fax:* 417-624-0090. *E-mail:* occadmin@occ.edu. *Web site:* http://www.occ.edu/.

Park University

Parkville, Missouri

- **Independent** comprehensive, founded 1875
- **Suburban** 800-acre campus with easy access to Kansas City
- **Endowment** $44.8 million
- **Coed**
- **Moderately difficult** entrance level

Faculty *Student/faculty ratio:* 12:1.

Academics *Calendar:* semesters. *Degrees:* associate, bachelor's, master's, and postbachelor's certificates.

Student Life *Campus security:* 24-hour patrols, student patrols, late-night transport/escort service.

Athletics Member NAIA.

Standardized Tests *Required:* SAT or ACT (for admission).

Costs (2010–11) *Comprehensive fee:* $16,478 includes full-time tuition ($8848), mandatory fees ($50), and room and board ($7580). Full-time tuition and fees vary according to course load. Part-time tuition: $316 per credit hour. Part-time tuition and fees vary according to course load.

Financial Aid *Of all full-time matriculated undergraduates who enrolled in 2007,* 3,967 applied for aid, 2,767 were judged to have need, 3,171 had their need fully met. 209 Federal Work-Study jobs (averaging $2875). 103 state and other part-time jobs (averaging $2675). *In 2007,* 281 non-need-based awards were made. *Average percent of need met:* 84. *Average financial aid package:* $3811. *Average need-based loan:* $1478. *Average need-based gift aid:* $1713. *Average non-need-based aid:* $3690. *Average indebtedness upon graduation:* $12,800.

Applying *Options:* electronic application, early admission, deferred entrance. *Application fee:* $25. *Required:* high school transcript, minimum 2 GPA. *Required for some:* 2 letters of recommendation, interview. *Recommended:* essay or personal statement.

Freshman Application Contact Cathy Colapietro, Director of Admissions and Student Financial Services, Park University, 8700 NW River Park Drive, Campus Box 1, Parkville, MO 64152. *Phone:* 816-584-6728. *Toll-free phone:* 800-745-7275. *Fax:* 816-741-4462. *E-mail:* admissions@mail.park.edu. *Web site:* http://www.park.edu/.

Ranken Technical College

St. Louis, Missouri

Director of Admissions Ms. Elizabeth Keserauskis, Director of Admissions, Ranken Technical College, 4431 Finney Avenue, St. Louis, MO 63113. *Phone:* 314-371-0233 Ext. 4811. *Toll-free phone:* 866-4RANKEN. *Web site:* http://www.ranken.edu/.

Research College of Nursing

Kansas City, Missouri

- **Independent** comprehensive, founded 1980, part of Rockhurst University
- **Urban** 66-acre campus with easy access to Kansas City
- **Coed, primarily women** 320 undergraduate students, 99% full-time, 91% women, 9% men
- **Moderately difficult** entrance level, 68% of applicants were admitted

Undergraduates 318 full-time, 2 part-time. Students come from 7 states and territories; 3% transferred in.

Freshmen *Admission:* 244 applied, 165 admitted, 56 enrolled. *Average high school GPA:* 3.46.

Faculty *Total:* 29, 90% full-time, 14% with terminal degrees. *Student/faculty ratio:* 7:1.

Academics *Calendar:* semesters. *Degrees:* bachelor's and master's (bachelor's degree offered jointly with Rockhurst College). *Special study options:* accelerated degree program, advanced placement credit, double majors, honors programs, independent study, services for LD students, study abroad, summer session for credit. *ROTC:* Army (c).

Computers on Campus 125 computers/terminals are available on campus for general student use. Students can access the following: online (class) registration. Campuswide network is available.

Student Life *Housing options:* coed, men-only, women-only. Campus housing is university owned. Freshman campus housing is guaranteed. *Activities and organizations:* drama/theater group, student-run newspaper, radio station, choral group, national fraternities, national sororities. *Campus security:* 24-hour emergency response devices and patrols, late-night transport/escort service, controlled dormitory access. *Student services:* health clinic, personal/psychological counseling.

Athletics Member NCAA. All Division II. *Intercollegiate sports:* baseball M(s), basketball M(s)/W(s), golf M(s)/W(s), soccer M(s)/W(s), softball W(s), tennis M(s)/W(s), volleyball W(s). *Intramural sports:* badminton M/W, basketball M/W, cross-country running M/W, field hockey M/W, football M/W, golf M/W, lacrosse M/W, racquetball M/W, rugby M/W, soccer M/W, softball M/W, table tennis M/W, tennis M/W, volleyball M/W, weight lifting M.

Standardized Tests *Required:* SAT or ACT (for admission).

Costs (2010–11) *One-time required fee:* $500. *Comprehensive fee:* $35,080 includes full-time tuition ($26,450), mandatory fees ($740), and room and board ($7890). Part-time tuition: $882 per credit hour. Part-time tuition and fees vary according to class time. *College room only:* $4590. Room and board charges vary according to board plan, housing facility, and location. *Payment plans:* installment, deferred payment. *Waivers:* children of alumni, senior citizens, and employees or children of employees.

Financial Aid Of all full-time matriculated undergraduates who enrolled in 2004, 90 applied for aid, 81 were judged to have need, 19 had their need fully met. In 2004, 39 non-need-based awards were made. *Average percent of need met:* 60%. *Average financial aid package:* $21,196. *Average need-based loan:* $4580. *Average need-based gift aid:* $2000. *Average non-need-based aid:* $15,700. *Average indebtedness upon graduation:* $12,740.

Applying *Options:* electronic application, deferred entrance. *Application fee:* $20. *Required:* high school transcript, 1 letter of recommendation. *Recommended:* minimum 2.8 GPA, interview. *Application deadlines:* 6/30 (freshmen), 2/15 (transfers). *Notification:* 8/15 (freshmen), 3/15 (transfers).

Freshman Application Contact Research College of Nursing, 2252 East Meyer Boulevard, Kansas City, MO 64132. *Phone:* 816-995-2820. *Toll-free phone:* 800-842-6776. *Web site:* http://www.researchcollege.edu/.

Rockhurst University

Kansas City, Missouri

- **Independent Roman Catholic (Jesuit)** comprehensive, founded 1910
- **Urban** 35-acre campus
- **Endowment** $29.9 million
- **Coed** 2,107 undergraduate students, 65% full-time, 62% women, 38% men
- **Moderately difficult** entrance level, 78% of applicants were admitted

Undergraduates 1,377 full-time, 730 part-time. 29% are from out of state; 6% Black or African American, non-Hispanic/Latino; 6% Hispanic/Latino; 3% Asian, non-Hispanic/Latino; 0.1% Native Hawaiian or other Pacific Islander, non-Hispanic/Latino; 0.5% American Indian or Alaska Native, non-Hispanic/Latino; 6% Race/ethnicity unknown; 1% international; 3% transferred in; 54% live on campus. *Retention:* 82% of full-time freshmen returned.

Freshmen *Admission:* 2,083 applied, 1,622 admitted, 370 enrolled. *Test scores:* SAT critical reading scores over 500: 80%; SAT math scores over 500: 76%; ACT scores over 18: 98%; SAT critical reading scores over 600: 36%; SAT math scores over 600: 28%; ACT scores over 24: 63%; ACT scores over 30: 14%.

Faculty *Total:* 228, 56% full-time, 57% with terminal degrees. *Student/faculty ratio:* 11:1.

Academics *Calendar:* semesters. *Degrees:* certificates, bachelor's, master's, doctoral-other, and postbachelor's certificates. *Special study options:* academic remediation for entering students, accelerated degree program, advanced placement credit, cooperative education, distance learning, double majors, freshman honors college, honors programs, independent study, internships, off-campus study, part-time degree program, services for LD students, study abroad, summer session for credit. *ROTC:* Army (c).

Computers on Campus 1,200 computers/terminals are available on campus for general student use. Students can access the following: campus intranet, computer help desk, free student e-mail accounts, online (class) grades, online (class) registration, online (class) schedules. Campuswide network is available. 100% of college-owned or -operated housing units are wired for high-speed Internet access. Wireless service is available via entire campus.

Student Life *Housing:* on-campus residence required through sophomore year. *Options:* coed, women-only. Campus housing is university owned. Freshman campus housing is guaranteed. *Activities and organizations:* drama/theater group, student-run newspaper, choral group, Student Activities Board, Student Senate, Delta Sigma Pi Business Fraternity, Student Organization of Latinos, Rockhurst University Players (theatre troupe), national fraternities, national sororities. *Campus security:* 24-hour emergency response devices and patrols, late-night transport/escort service, controlled dormitory access, closed-circuit TV monitors. *Student services:* health clinic, personal/psychological counseling.

Athletics Member NCAA. All Division II. *Intercollegiate sports:* baseball M(s), basketball M(s)/W(s), golf M(s)/W(s), soccer M(s)/W(s), softball W(s), tennis M(s)/W(s), volleyball W(s). *Intramural sports:* basketball M/W, cheerleading M/W, field hockey W, football M/W, ice hockey M, lacrosse M, soccer M/W, softball M/W, tennis M/W, ultimate Frisbee M/W, volleyball M/W.

Standardized Tests *Required:* SAT or ACT (for admission).

Costs (2010–11) *Comprehensive fee:* $34,880 includes full-time tuition ($26,450), mandatory fees ($940), and room and board ($7490). Full-time tuition and fees vary according to class time and course load. Part-time tuition:

$882 per credit hour. Part-time tuition and fees vary according to class time and course load. *Required fees:* $25 per credit hour part-time. *College room only:* $4590. Room and board charges vary according to board plan and housing facility. *Payment plans:* installment, deferred payment. *Waivers:* senior citizens and employees or children of employees.

Financial Aid Of all full-time matriculated undergraduates who enrolled in 2009, 1,197 applied for aid, 1,197 were judged to have need, 327 had their need fully met. 531 Federal Work-Study jobs (averaging $1500). In 2009, 150 non-need-based awards were made. *Average percent of need met:* 89%. *Average financial aid package:* $26,223. *Average need-based loan:* $3731. *Average need-based gift aid:* $6962. *Average non-need-based aid:* $13,392. *Average indebtedness upon graduation:* $24,841.

Applying *Options:* electronic application, deferred entrance. *Application fee:* $25. *Required:* high school transcript, minimum 2 GPA, 1 letter of recommendation. *Required for some:* essay or personal statement, interview. *Application deadlines:* 6/30 (freshmen), rolling (transfers). *Notification:* continuous (freshmen), continuous (transfers).

Freshman Application Contact Mitch Nelson, Director of Freshman Admissions, Rockhurst University, 1100 Rockhurst Road, Kansas City, MO 64110-2561. *Phone:* 816-501-4100. *Toll-free phone:* 800-842-6776. *Fax:* 816-501-4142. *E-mail:* admission@rockhurst.edu. *Web site:* http://www.rockhurst.edu/.

St. Louis Christian College

Florissant, Missouri

- **Independent Christian** 4-year, founded 1956
- **Suburban** 20-acre campus with easy access to St. Louis
- **Endowment** $577,910
- **Coed** 338 undergraduate students, 83% full-time, 41% women, 59% men
- **Minimally difficult** entrance level, 61% of applicants were admitted

Undergraduates 281 full-time, 57 part-time. Students come from 20 states and territories; 1 other country; 39% are from out of state; 28% Black or African American, non-Hispanic/Latino; 4% Hispanic/Latino; 0.3% Asian, Non-Hispanic/Latino; 0.9% American Indian or Alaska Native, non-Hispanic/Latino; 0.9% Two or more races, non-Hispanic/Latino; 0.3% Race/ethnicity unknown; 2% international; ####% transferred in; 54% live on campus. *Retention:* 60% of full-time freshmen returned.

Freshmen *Admission:* 152 applied, 92 admitted. *Average high school GPA:* 2.99. *Test scores:* SAT critical reading scores over 500: 75%; SAT writing scores over 500: 50%; ACT scores over 18: 74%; SAT critical reading scores over 600: 25%; SAT writing scores over 600: 25%; ACT scores over 24: 28%; SAT critical reading scores over 700: 25%.

Faculty *Total:* 36, 33% full-time, 22% with terminal degrees. *Student/faculty ratio:* 15:1.

Academics *Calendar:* semesters. *Degrees:* associate and bachelor's. *Special study options:* academic remediation for entering students, accelerated degree program, adult/continuing education programs, advanced placement credit, double majors, English as a second language, internships, part-time degree program, services for LD students, study abroad, summer session for credit.

Computers on Campus 11 computers/terminals are available on campus for general student use. Students can access the following: free student e-mail accounts, online (class) schedules. Campuswide network is available. Wireless service is available via classrooms, computer labs, libraries, student centers.

Student Life *Housing options:* men-only, women-only. Campus housing is university owned. *Activities and organizations:* drama/theater group, choral group, World Christians Unlimited, Drama Club, pep band. *Campus security:* 24-hour emergency response devices and patrols, controlled dormitory access, night security. *Student services:* personal/psychological counseling.

Athletics Member NCCAA. *Intercollegiate sports:* baseball M, basketball M/W, cross-country running W, ultimate Frisbee M(s)/W(s), volleyball W(s). *Intramural sports:* basketball M/W, ultimate Frisbee M/W, volleyball M/W.

Standardized Tests *Required:* SAT or ACT (for admission).

Costs (2011–12) *Comprehensive fee:* $25,080 includes full-time tuition ($14,880), mandatory fees ($1300), and room and board ($8900). Part-time tuition: $480 per hour. *Required fees:* $325 per term part-time. *Room and board:* Room and board charges vary according to housing facility. *Waivers:* employees or children of employees.

Financial Aid *Average indebtedness upon graduation:* $11,654.

Applying *Options:* electronic application, early admission. *Application fee:* $25. *Required:* essay or personal statement, high school transcript, 1 letter of recommendation. *Required for some:* interview. *Recommended:* minimum 2 GPA. *Application deadlines:* 8/7 (freshmen), 8/7 (transfers). *Notification:* continuous (freshmen), continuous (transfers).

Freshman Application Contact Carrie Chapman, Admissions Director, St. Louis Christian College, 1360 Grandview Drive, Florissant, MO 63033. *Phone:* 314-837-6777 Ext. 1303. *Toll-free phone:* 800-887-SLCC. *E-mail:* cchapman@slcconline.edu. *Web site:* http://www.slcconline.edu/.

St. Louis College of Pharmacy

St. Louis, Missouri

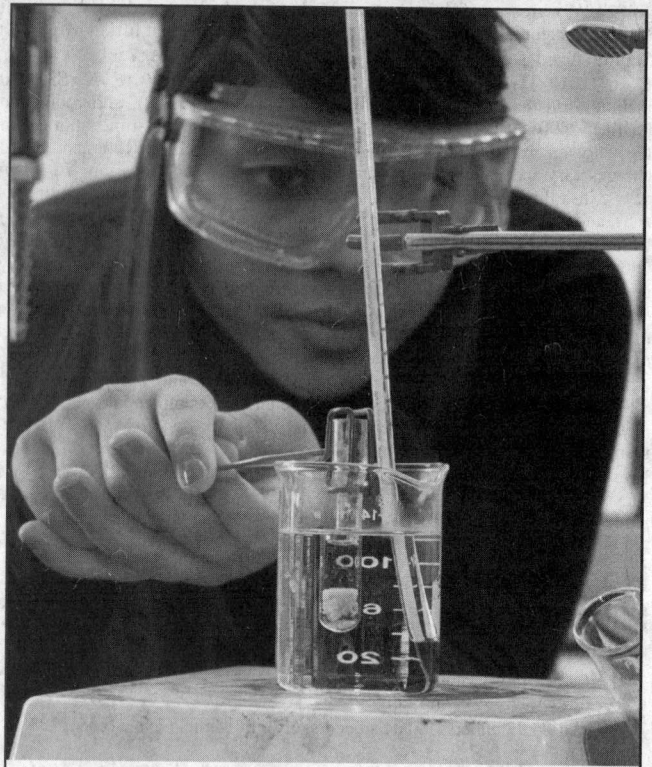

- **Independent** comprehensive, founded 1864
- **Urban** 5-acre campus with easy access to St. Louis
- **Endowment** $89.8 million
- **Coed** 660 undergraduate students, 100% full-time, 60% women, 40% men
- **Moderately difficult** entrance level, 47% of applicants were admitted

Undergraduates 659 full-time, 1 part-time. Students come from 27 states and territories; 1 other country; 54% are from out of state; 2% Black or African American, non-Hispanic/Latino; 1% Hispanic/Latino; 23% Asian, non-Hispanic/Latino; 0.2% Native Hawaiian or other Pacific Islander, non-Hispanic/Latino; 0.6% American Indian or Alaska Native, non-Hispanic/Latino; 0.3% Two or more races, non-Hispanic/Latino; 2% Race/ethnicity unknown; 0.9% international; 2% transferred in; 40% live on campus. *Retention:* 87% of full-time freshmen returned.

Freshmen *Admission:* 633 applied, 300 admitted, 234 enrolled. *Average high school GPA:* 3.8. *Test scores:* ACT scores over 18: 100%; ACT scores over 24: 100%; ACT scores over 30: 25%.

Faculty *Total:* 129, 60% full-time, 74% with terminal degrees. *Student/faculty ratio:* 20:1.

Academics *Calendar:* semesters. *Degree:* doctoral-professional. *Special study options:* academic remediation for entering students, advanced placement credit, internships, summer session for credit. *ROTC:* Army (c), Navy (c), Air Force (c).

Computers on Campus 6 computers/terminals and 2,200 ports are available on campus for general student use. Students can access the following: campus intranet, computer help desk, free student e-mail accounts, online (class) grades, online (class) registration, online (class) schedules. Campuswide network is available. 100% of college-owned or -operated housing units are wired for high-speed Internet access. Wireless service is available via entire campus.

Student Life *Housing options:* coed. Campus housing is university owned. Freshman applicants given priority for college housing. *Activities and organizations:* drama/theater group, student-run newspaper, choral group, Gateway Academy of Student Pharmacists, Student Council, International Student Council, student ambassadors, Student Alumni Association, national fraternities, national sororities. *Campus security:* 24-hour emergency response devices and patrols, late-night transport/escort service, controlled dormitory access. *Student services:* personal/psychological counseling.

Athletics Member NAIA. *Intercollegiate sports:* basketball M/W, cross-country running M/W, tennis M/W, track and field M/W, volleyball W. *Intramural sports:* basketball M/W, cheerleading W, cross-country running M/W, football M/W, golf M/W, soccer M/W, softball M/W, table tennis M/W, tennis M/W, volleyball M/W, weight lifting M/W.

Standardized Tests *Required:* SAT or ACT (for admission).

Costs (2011–12) *Comprehensive fee:* $32,525 includes full-time tuition ($23,520), mandatory fees ($250), and room and board ($8755). Full-time tuition and fees vary according to student level. Part-time tuition: $825 per credit. *College room only:* $5023. Room and board charges vary according to housing facility. *Payment plan:* installment. *Waivers:* employees or children of employees.

Financial Aid Of all full-time matriculated undergraduates who enrolled in 2009, 602 applied for aid, 517 were judged to have need, 40 had their need fully met. 285 Federal Work-Study jobs (averaging $992). In 2009, 135 non-need-based awards were made. *Average percent of need met:* 46%. *Average financial aid package:* $13,268. *Average need-based loan:* $5215. *Average need-based gift aid:* $9207. *Average non-need-based aid:* $5655. *Average indebtedness upon graduation:* $107,649.

Applying *Options:* electronic application, early decision. *Application fee:* $50. *Required:* essay or personal statement, high school transcript, minimum 3 GPA, 2 letters of recommendation, letter of reference from science teacher. *Required for some:* interview. *Application deadlines:* 2/1 (freshmen), 2/1 (transfers). *Early decision deadline:* 12/15. *Notification:* 3/1 (freshmen), 7/1 (transfers), 1/15 (early decision).

Freshman Application Contact Connie Horrall, Administrative Assistant, St. Louis College of Pharmacy, 4588 Parkview Place, St. Louis, MO 63110-1088. *Phone:* 314-446-8328. *Toll-free phone:* 800-278-5267. *Fax:* 314-446-8310. *E-mail:* chorrall@stlcop.edu. *Web site:* http://www.stlcop.edu/.

See page 1574 for the College Close-Up.

Saint Louis University

St. Louis, Missouri

- **Independent Roman Catholic (Jesuit)** university, founded 1818
- **Urban** 239-acre campus
- **Endowment** $708.3 million
- **Coed** 8,406 undergraduate students, 90% full-time, 59% women, 41% men
- **Moderately difficult** entrance level, 70% of applicants were admitted

Undergraduates 7,540 full-time, 866 part-time. Students come from 47 states and territories; 49 other countries; 59% are from out of state; 8% Black or African American, non-Hispanic/Latino; 4% Hispanic/Latino; 7% Asian, non-Hispanic/Latino; 0.3% American Indian or Alaska Native, non-Hispanic/Latino; 2% Two or more races, non-Hispanic/Latino; 5% Race/ethnicity unknown; 9% international; 5% transferred in; 53% live on campus. *Retention:* 84% of full-time freshmen returned.

Freshmen *Admission:* 10,962 applied, 7,663 admitted, 1,673 enrolled. *Average high school GPA:* 3.75. *Test scores:* SAT critical reading scores over 500: 88%; SAT math scores over 500: 90%; ACT scores over 18: 100%; SAT critical reading scores over 600: 53%; SAT math scores over 600: 60%; ACT scores over 24: 81%; SAT critical reading scores over 700: 14%; SAT math scores over 700: 20%; ACT scores over 30: 32%.

Faculty *Total:* 1,104, 63% full-time, 61% with terminal degrees. *Student/faculty ratio:* 13:1.

Academics *Calendar:* semesters. *Degrees:* certificates, bachelor's, master's, doctoral-other, doctoral-professional, doctoral-research/scholarship, post-master's, and postbachelor's certificates. *Special study options:* academic remediation for entering students, accelerated degree program, adult/continuing education programs, advanced placement credit, cooperative education, distance learning, double majors, English as a second language, freshman honors college, honors programs, independent study, internships, off-campus study, part-time degree program, services for LD students, student-designed majors, study abroad, summer session for credit. *ROTC:* Army (c), Air Force (b).

Computers on Campus 325 computers/terminals and 4,850 ports are available on campus for general student use. Students can access the following: campus intranet, computer help desk, free student e-mail accounts, online (class) grades, online (class) registration, online (class) schedules. Campuswide network is available. 100% of college-owned or -operated housing units are wired for high-speed Internet access. Wireless service is available via entire campus.

Student Life *Housing:* on-campus residence required through sophomore year. *Options:* coed, men-only, women-only, disabled students. Campus housing is university owned. Freshman campus housing is guaranteed. *Activities and organizations:* drama/theater group, student-run newspaper, radio and television station, choral group, Alpha Phi Omega, Oriflamme, Student Activities Board, Interfraternity Council, Panhellenic Council, national fraternities, national sororities. *Campus security:* 24-hour emergency response devices and patrols, late-night transport/escort service, controlled dormitory access, crime prevention program, bicycle patrols, pamphlets, posters, films, identification of valuables, video cameras. *Student services:* health clinic, personal/psychological counseling, women's center.

Athletics Member NCAA. All Division I. *Intercollegiate sports:* badminton M(c)/W(c), baseball M(s), basketball M(s)/W(s), bowling M(c)/W(c), crew M(c)/W(c), cross-country running M(s)/W(s), equestrian sports M(c)/W(c), fencing M(c)/W(c), field hockey W(s), golf M(c)/W(c), ice hockey M(c), lacrosse M(c)/W(c), racquetball M(c)/W(c), rugby M(c)/W(c), soccer M(s)/W(s), softball W(s), swimming and diving M(s)/W(s), table tennis M(c)/W(c), tennis M(s)/W(s), track and field M(s)/W(s), ultimate Frisbee M(c)/W(c), volleyball M(c)/W(s), water polo M(c). *Intramural sports:* badminton M/W, basketball M/W, bowling M/W, football M/W, golf M/W, racquetball M/W, soccer M/W, softball M/W, squash M/W, swimming and diving M/W, table tennis M/W, tennis M/W, ultimate Frisbee M/W, volleyball M/W.

Standardized Tests *Required:* SAT or ACT (for admission).

Costs (2010–11) *Comprehensive fee:* $41,826 includes full-time tuition ($32,180), mandatory fees ($476), and room and board ($9170). Full-time tuition and fees vary according to location and program. Part-time tuition: $1125 per credit hour. Part-time tuition and fees vary according to location and program. *Required fees:* $143 per term part-time. *College room only:* $5150. Room and board charges vary according to board plan, housing facility, and location. *Payment plan:* installment. *Waivers:* children of alumni and employees or children of employees.

Financial Aid Of all full-time matriculated undergraduates who enrolled in 2008, 4,625 applied for aid, 4,051 were judged to have need, 595 had their need fully met. 963 Federal Work-Study jobs (averaging $2137). 73 state and other part-time jobs (averaging $1772). In 2008, 2012 non-need-based awards were made. *Average percent of need met:* 65%. *Average financial aid package:* $22,188. *Average need-based loan:* $5186. *Average need-based gift aid:* $16,747. *Average non-need-based aid:* $10,227. *Average indebtedness upon graduation:* $33,734.

Applying *Options:* electronic application, deferred entrance. *Application fee:* $25. *Required:* essay or personal statement, high school transcript, minimum 2.5 GPA, secondary school report form. *Recommended:* 2 letters of recommendation, interview. *Application deadlines:* 8/1 (freshmen), 8/1 (out-of-state freshmen), 8/1 (transfers). *Notification:* 9/15 (freshmen), 9/15 (out-of-state freshmen), continuous until 9/15 (transfers).

Freshman Application Contact Jean M. Gilman, Dean of Undergraduate Admission, Saint Louis University, 221 North Grand Boulevard, DuBourg Hall, Room 100, St. Louis, MO 63103-2097. *Phone:* 314-977-2500. *Toll-free phone:* 800-758-3678. *Fax:* 314-977-7136. *E-mail:* admitme@slu.edu. *Web site:* http://www.slu.edu/.

Saint Luke's College of Health Sciences

Kansas City, Missouri

- **Independent Episcopal** upper-level, founded 1903, administratively affiliated with Saint Luke's Hospital
- **Urban** 3-acre campus
- **Endowment** $2.8 million
- **Coed, primarily women** 113 undergraduate students, 89% full-time, 90% women, 10% men
- **Very difficult** entrance level

Undergraduates 101 full-time, 12 part-time. Students come from 5 states and territories; 46% transferred in.

Faculty *Total:* 15, 100% full-time, 20% with terminal degrees. *Student/faculty ratio:* 8:1.

Academics *Calendar:* semesters. *Degree:* bachelor's. *Special study options:* cooperative education, part-time degree program, summer session for credit.

Computers on Campus 20 computers/terminals are available on campus for general student use. Students can access the following: free student e-mail accounts, online (class) grades, Evolve.

Student Life *Housing:* college housing not available. *Activities and organizations:* Saint Luke's Student Nurse Association. *Campus security:* 24-hour emergency response devices and patrols. *Student services:* health clinic, personal/psychological counseling.

Athletics *Intercollegiate sports:* ultimate Frisbee M(s)/W(s), volleyball M(s)/W(s). *Intramural sports:* ultimate Frisbee M/W, volleyball M/W.

Costs (2011–12) *Tuition:* $387 per credit part-time.

Financial Aid Of all full-time matriculated undergraduates who enrolled in 2009, 102 applied for aid, 96 were judged to have need, 4 had their need fully met. 2 Federal Work-Study jobs (averaging $1000). In 2009, 5 non-need-based awards were made. *Average percent of need met:* 70%. *Average financial aid package:* $13,000. *Average need-based loan:* $5500. *Average need-based gift aid:* $2000. *Average non-need-based aid:* $2000.

Applying *Options:* electronic application, early admission. *Application fee:* $35. *Application deadline:* 12/31 (transfers). *Notification:* continuous until 3/15 (transfers).

Application Contact Mrs. Jennifer Wright, Student Services Associate, Saint Luke's College of Health Sciences, 8320 Ward Parkway, Suite 300, Kansas City, MO 64114. *Phone:* 816-932-8629. *Fax:* 816-932-9064. *Web site:* http://www.saintlukescollege.edu/.

Sanford-Brown College

Fenton, Missouri

Director of Admissions Ms. Judy Wilga, Director of Admissions, Sanford-Brown College, 1203 Smizer Mill Road, Fenton, MO 63026. *Phone:* 636-349-4900 Ext. 102. *Toll-free phone:* 800-456-7222. *Fax:* 636-349-9170. *Web site:* http://www.sanford-brown.edu/.

Southeast Missouri State University

Cape Girardeau, Missouri

- **State-supported** comprehensive, founded 1873, part of Missouri Coordinating Board for Higher Education
- **Small-town** 400-acre campus
- **Endowment** $45.1 million
- **Coed** 10,035 undergraduate students, 78% full-time, 58% women, 42% men
- **Moderately difficult** entrance level, 97% of applicants were admitted

Undergraduates 7,837 full-time, 2,198 part-time. Students come from 39 states and territories; 36 other countries; 13% are from out of state; 8% Black or African American, non-Hispanic/Latino; 1% Hispanic/Latino; 0.8% Asian, non-Hispanic/Latino; 0.4% American Indian or Alaska Native, non-Hispanic/Latino; 0.1% Two or more races, non-Hispanic/Latino; 6% Race/ethnicity unknown; 4% international; 7% transferred in; 31% live on campus. *Retention:* 69% of full-time freshmen returned.

Freshmen *Admission:* 4,144 applied, 4,022 admitted, 1,928 enrolled. *Average high school GPA:* 3.33. *Test scores:* SAT critical reading scores over 500: 50%; SAT math scores over 500: 62%; ACT scores over 18: 97%; SAT critical reading scores over 600: 23%; SAT math scores over 600: 27%; ACT scores over 24: 40%; SAT math scores over 700: 8%; ACT scores over 30: 5%.
Faculty *Total:* 566, 73% full-time, 59% with terminal degrees. *Student/faculty ratio:* 20:1.
Academics *Calendar:* semesters. *Degrees:* certificates, associate, bachelor's, master's, post-master's, and postbachelor's certificates. *Special study options:* academic remediation for entering students, accelerated degree program, adult/continuing education programs, advanced placement credit, distance learning, double majors, English as a second language, honors programs, independent study, internships, part-time degree program, services for LD students, student-designed majors, study abroad, summer session for credit. *ROTC:* Air Force (b).
Computers on Campus 1,311 computers/terminals are available on campus for general student use. Students can access the following: campus intranet, computer help desk, free student e-mail accounts, online (class) grades, online (class) registration, online (class) schedules. Campuswide network is available. 100% of college-owned or -operated housing units are wired for high-speed Internet access. Wireless service is available via classrooms, computer centers, computer labs, learning centers, libraries, student centers.
Student Life *Housing:* on-campus residence required through junior year. *Options:* coed, men-only, women-only, disabled students. Campus housing is university owned. *Activities and organizations:* drama/theater group, student-run newspaper, radio station, choral group, marching band, Student Government, Panhellenic Council, Interfraternity Council, Residence Hall Association, Student Activities Council, national fraternities, national sororities. *Campus security:* 24-hour emergency response devices and patrols, late-night transport/escort service, controlled dormitory access. *Student services:* health clinic, personal/psychological counseling.
Athletics Member NCAA. All Division I. *Intercollegiate sports:* baseball M(s), basketball M(s)/W(s), cheerleading M(s)/W(s), cross-country running M(s)/W(s), football M(s), gymnastics W(s), soccer W(s), softball W(s), tennis W(s), track and field M(s)/W(s), volleyball W(s). *Intramural sports:* badminton M/W, baseball M(c), basketball M/W, bowling M/W, equestrian sports M(c)/W(c), fencing M(c)/W(c), football M/W, golf M/W, racquetball M/W, rock climbing M(c)/W(c), rugby M(c)/W(c), soccer M/W, softball M/W, swimming and diving M/W, table tennis M/W, tennis M/W, ultimate Frisbee M/W, volleyball W(c), wrestling M/W.
Standardized Tests *Required:* SAT or ACT (for admission).
Costs (2010–11) *Tuition:* state resident $5544 full-time, $185 per credit hour part-time; nonresident $10,479 full-time, $349 per credit hour part-time. Full-time tuition and fees vary according to course load and location. Part-time tuition and fees vary according to course load and location. *Required fees:* $711 full-time, $24 per credit hour part-time. *Room and board:* $7342; room only: $4872. Room and board charges vary according to board plan and housing facility. *Payment plans:* installment, deferred payment. *Waivers:* senior citizens and employees or children of employees.
Financial Aid Of all full-time matriculated undergraduates who enrolled in 2008, 5,609 applied for aid, 4,284 were judged to have need, 780 had their need fully met. 453 Federal Work-Study jobs (averaging $2955). 1,645 state and other part-time jobs (averaging $1890). In 2008, 1100 non-need-based awards were made. *Average percent of need met:* 68%. *Average financial aid package:* $8527. *Average need-based loan:* $3831. *Average need-based gift aid:* $5494. *Average non-need-based aid:* $4243. *Average indebtedness upon graduation:* $22,400.
Applying *Options:* electronic application. *Application fee:* $30. *Required:* high school transcript, minimum 2 GPA. *Application deadlines:* 7/1 (freshmen), 8/1 (transfers). *Notification:* continuous (freshmen), continuous (transfers).
Freshman Application Contact Southeast Missouri State University, One University Plaza, Cape Girardeau, MO 63701-4799. *Phone:* 573-651-2590. *Web site:* http://www.semo.edu/.

Southwest Baptist University
Bolivar, Missouri

- **Independent Southern Baptist** comprehensive, founded 1878
- **Small-town** 152-acre campus
- **Endowment** $16.0 million
- **Coed**
- **Moderately difficult** entrance level

Faculty *Student/faculty ratio:* 13:1.
Academics *Calendar:* 4-1-4. *Degrees:* certificates, associate, bachelor's, master's, doctoral-professional, and post-master's certificates.
Student Life *Campus security:* 24-hour emergency response devices and patrols, controlled dormitory access.
Athletics Member NCAA. All Division II.
Standardized Tests *Required:* SAT or ACT (for admission).

Costs (2010–11) *Comprehensive fee:* $23,000 includes full-time tuition ($16,500), mandatory fees ($780), and room and board ($5720). Full-time tuition and fees vary according to course load. Part-time tuition and fees vary according to course load and location. *College room only:* $2860. Room and board charges vary according to board plan and housing facility.
Financial Aid *Of all full-time matriculated undergraduates who enrolled in 2009,* 1,362 applied for aid, 1,205 were judged to have need, 315 had their need fully met. 334 Federal Work-Study jobs (averaging $1850). *In 2009,* 327 non-need-based awards were made. *Average percent of need met:* 77. *Average financial aid package:* $14,821. *Average need-based loan:* $4713. *Average need-based gift aid:* $5601. *Average non-need-based aid:* $7361.
Applying *Options:* electronic application. *Application fee:* $30. *Required:* high school transcript, minimum 2.5 GPA. *Required for some:* 3 letters of recommendation. *Recommended:* essay or personal statement, interview.
Freshman Application Contact Mr. Darren Crowder, Director of Admissions, Southwest Baptist University, 1600 University Avenue, Bolivar, MO 65613-2597. *Phone:* 417-328-1817. *Toll-free phone:* 800-526-5859. *Fax:* 417-328-1808. *E-mail:* dcrowder@sbuniv.edu. *Web site:* http://www.sbuniv.edu/.

Stephens College
Columbia, Missouri

- **Independent** comprehensive, founded 1833
- **Urban** 86-acre campus
- **Endowment** $24.5 million
- **Coed, primarily women** 863 undergraduate students, 80% full-time, 96% women, 4% men
- **Moderately difficult** entrance level, 69% of applicants were admitted

Undergraduates 694 full-time, 169 part-time. Students come from 43 states and territories; 2 other countries; 31% are from out of state; 15% Black or African American, non-Hispanic/Latino; 3% Hispanic/Latino; 0.9% Asian, non-Hispanic/Latino; 0.2% Native Hawaiian or other Pacific Islander, non-Hispanic/Latino; 1% American Indian or Alaska Native, non-Hispanic/Latino; 2% Two or more races, non-Hispanic/Latino; 0.5% Race/ethnicity unknown; 0.2% international; 6% transferred in; 66% live on campus. *Retention:* 65% of full-time freshmen returned.
Freshmen *Admission:* 649 applied, 448 admitted, 180 enrolled. *Average high school GPA:* 3.4. *Test scores:* SAT critical reading scores over 500: 67%; SAT math scores over 500: 57%; SAT writing scores over 500: 69%; SAT critical reading scores over 600: 27%; SAT math scores over 600: 19%; SAT writing scores over 600: 19%; SAT critical reading scores over 700: 7%; SAT writing scores over 700: 6%.
Faculty *Total:* 150, 37% full-time, 36% with terminal degrees. *Student/faculty ratio:* 10:1.
Academics *Calendar:* semesters. *Degrees:* associate, bachelor's, master's, and postbachelor's certificates. *Special study options:* academic remediation for entering students, accelerated degree program, adult/continuing education programs, advanced placement credit, cooperative education, distance learning, double majors, external degree program, freshman honors college, honors programs, independent study, internships, off-campus study, part-time degree program, services for LD students, student-designed majors, study abroad, summer session for credit. *ROTC:* Army (c), Navy (c), Air Force (c). *Unusual degree programs:* 3-2 occupational therapy with Washington University in St. Louis.
Computers on Campus 107 computers/terminals and 1 port are available on campus for general student use. Students can access the following: computer help desk, free student e-mail accounts, online (class) grades, online (class) schedules. Campuswide network is available. 100% of college-owned or -operated housing units are wired for high-speed Internet access. Wireless service is available via entire campus.
Student Life *Housing:* on-campus residence required through senior year. *Options:* women-only. Campus housing is university owned and is provided by a third party. Freshman campus housing is guaranteed. *Activities and organizations:* drama/theater group, student-run newspaper, radio station, choral group, IFA, Warehouse Theater, Student government, PRSSA, national sororities. *Campus security:* 24-hour emergency response devices and patrols, student patrols, late-night transport/escort service, controlled dormitory access. *Student services:* health clinic, personal/psychological counseling.
Athletics Member NAIA. *Intercollegiate sports:* basketball W(s), cross-country running W(s), golf W(s), softball W(s), tennis W(s), volleyball W(s). *Intramural sports:* equestrian sports W(c).
Standardized Tests *Required:* SAT or ACT (for admission).
Costs (2011–12) *One-time required fee:* $200. *Comprehensive fee:* $33,590 includes full-time tuition ($26,420) and room and board ($7170). Full-time tuition and fees vary according to course load, degree level, program, and reciprocity agreements. Part-time tuition: $734 per credit hour. Part-time tuition and fees vary according to course load, degree level, and program. *College room only:* $4770. Room and board charges vary according to board plan and

housing facility. *Payment plan:* installment. *Waivers:* employees or children of employees.

Financial Aid Of all full-time matriculated undergraduates who enrolled in 2009, 651 applied for aid, 582 were judged to have need, 118 had their need fully met. 99 Federal Work-Study jobs (averaging $1600). 140 state and other part-time jobs (averaging $1550). In 2009, 172 non-need-based awards were made. *Average percent of need met:* 78%. *Average financial aid package:* $20,787. *Average need-based loan:* $4334. *Average need-based gift aid:* $16,735. *Average non-need-based aid:* $8629. *Average indebtedness upon graduation:* $22,942.

Applying *Options:* electronic application, deferred entrance. *Application fee:* $25. *Required:* essay or personal statement, high school transcript, minimum 2 GPA. *Required for some:* 1 letter of recommendation, audition mandatory for dance, recommended for theater. *Recommended:* minimum 2.5 GPA, interview. *Notification:* continuous until 9/15 (freshmen), continuous until 9/15 (transfers).

Freshman Application Contact Mr. Chris Collier, Vice President of Enrollment Management, Stephens College, 1200 East Broadway, Box 2121, Columbia, MO 65215-0002. *Phone:* 573-876-7207. *Toll-free phone:* 800-876-7207. *Fax:* 573-876-7237. *E-mail:* apply@stephens.edu. *Web site:* http://www.stephens.edu/.

Stevens Institute of Business & Arts

St. Louis, Missouri

- **Proprietary** 4-year, founded 1947
- **Urban** campus
- **Coed, primarily women** 200 undergraduate students, 67% full-time, 90% women, 11% men
- **Moderately difficult** entrance level, 75% of applicants were admitted

Undergraduates 134 full-time, 66 part-time. Students come from 2 states and territories; 28% are from out of state. *Retention:* 100% of full-time freshmen returned.

Freshmen *Admission:* 24 applied, 18 admitted. *Average high school GPA:* 2.8.

Faculty *Total:* 22, 32% full-time, 14% with terminal degrees. *Student/faculty ratio:* 10:1.

Academics *Calendar:* quarters. *Degrees:* diplomas, associate, and bachelor's. *Special study options:* academic remediation for entering students, accelerated degree program, adult/continuing education programs, advanced placement credit, cooperative education, honors programs, independent study, internships, part-time degree program, summer session for credit.

Computers on Campus 42 computers/terminals are available on campus for general student use. Students can access the following: wireless Internet. Wireless service is available via entire campus.

Student Life *Housing:* college housing not available. *Campus security:* 24-hour emergency response devices and patrols. *Student services:* personal/psychological counseling.

Standardized Tests *Required for some:* SAT or ACT (for admission).

Costs (2011–12) *Tuition:* $225 per quarter hour part-time.

Applying *Options:* electronic application. *Application fee:* $15. *Required:* essay or personal statement, high school transcript, interview. *Required for some:* minimum 2.75 GPA. *Application deadlines:* rolling (freshmen), rolling (out-of-state freshmen), rolling (transfers). *Notification:* continuous (freshmen), continuous (out-of-state freshmen), continuous (transfers).

Freshman Application Contact Mr. John Willmon, Director of Admissions, Stevens Institute of Business & Arts, 1521 Washington Avenue, St. Louis, MO 63102. *Phone:* 314-421-0949. *Toll-free phone:* 800-871-0949. *Fax:* 314-421-0304. *E-mail:* admission@siba.edu. *Web site:* http://www.siba.edu/.

Truman State University

Kirksville, Missouri

- **State-supported** comprehensive, founded 1867
- **Small-town** 140-acre campus
- **Endowment** $19.7 million
- **Coed** 5,675 undergraduate students, 96% full-time, 59% women, 41% men
- **Moderately difficult** entrance level, 74% of applicants were admitted

Undergraduates 5,467 full-time, 208 part-time. Students come from 38 states and territories; 49 other countries; 21% are from out of state; 3% transferred in; 48% live on campus. *Retention:* 87% of full-time freshmen returned.

Freshmen *Admission:* 4,702 applied, 3,474 admitted, 1,417 enrolled. *Average high school GPA:* 3.76. *Test scores:* SAT critical reading scores over 500: 88%; SAT math scores over 500: 92%; ACT scores over 18: 100%; SAT critical reading scores over 600: 68%; SAT math scores over 600: 57%; ACT scores over 24: 85%; SAT critical reading scores over 700: 28%; SAT math scores over 700: 21%; ACT scores over 30: 28%.

Faculty *Total:* 382, 88% full-time, 78% with terminal degrees. *Student/faculty ratio:* 16:1.

Academics *Calendar:* semesters. *Degrees:* bachelor's and master's. *Special study options:* advanced placement credit, cooperative education, double majors, English as a second language, honors programs, independent study, internships, off-campus study, part-time degree program, services for LD students, student-designed majors, study abroad, summer session for credit. *ROTC:* Army (b). *Unusual degree programs:* 3-2 engineering with Missouri University of Science and Technology, University of Missouri-Columbia.

Computers on Campus 738 computers/terminals and 3,690 ports are available on campus for general student use. Students can access the following: campus intranet, computer help desk, free student e-mail accounts, online (class) grades, online (class) registration, online (class) schedules. Campus-wide network is available. 100% of college-owned or -operated housing units are wired for high-speed Internet access. Wireless service is available via entire campus.

Student Life *Housing:* on-campus residence required for freshman year. *Options:* coed, disabled students. Campus housing is university owned. Freshman campus housing is guaranteed. *Activities and organizations:* drama/theater group, student-run newspaper, radio and television station, choral group, marching band, Alpha Phi Omega (national coed service fraternity), Campus Christian Fellowship (CCF), Alpha Sigma Gamma (service sorority), Sigma Sigma Sigma (national social sorority) — 132, American Medical Student Association (AMSA), national fraternities, national sororities. *Campus security:* 24-hour emergency response devices and patrols, student patrols, late-night transport/escort service, controlled dormitory access, patrols by commissioned officers. *Student services:* health clinic, personal/psychological counseling, women's center.

Athletics Member NCAA. All Division II. *Intercollegiate sports:* baseball M(s), basketball M(s)/W(s), bowling M(c)/W(c), cheerleading M(c)/W(c), cross-country running M(s)/W(s), equestrian sports M(c)/W(c), football M(s), golf M(s)/W(s), lacrosse W(c), rugby M(c)/W(c), soccer M(s)/W(s), softball W(s), swimming and diving M(s)/W(s), tennis M(s)/W(s), track and field M(s)/W(s), ultimate Frisbee M(c)/W(c), volleyball M(c)/W(c), weight lifting M(c)/W(c), wrestling M(s). *Intramural sports:* badminton M/W, basketball M/W, cross-country running M/W, football M/W, rock climbing M/W, skiing (cross-country) M(c)/W(c), skiing (downhill) M(c)/W(c), soccer M/W, softball M/W, swimming and diving M/W, table tennis M/W, tennis M/W, track and field M/W, ultimate Frisbee M/W, volleyball M/W.

Standardized Tests *Required:* SAT or ACT (for admission).

Costs (2010–11) *One-time required fee:* $305. *Tuition:* state resident $6458 full-time, $269 per credit hour part-time; nonresident $11,856 full-time, $494 per credit hour part-time. Full-time tuition and fees vary according to course load, degree level, and program. Part-time tuition and fees vary according to course load, degree level, and program. *Required fees:* $234 full-time. *Room and board:* $7097. Room and board charges vary according to housing facility. *Payment plan:* installment. *Waivers:* senior citizens and employees or children of employees.

Financial Aid Of all full-time matriculated undergraduates who enrolled in 2008, 3,476 applied for aid, 2,245 were judged to have need, 1,524 had their need fully met. 239 Federal Work-Study jobs (averaging $1213). 837 state and other part-time jobs (averaging $1667). In 2008, 2410 non-need-based awards were made. *Average percent of need met:* 82%. *Average financial aid package:* $8425. *Average need-based loan:* $4312. *Average need-based gift aid:* $3607. *Average non-need-based aid:* $4884. *Average indebtedness upon graduation:* $21,858.

Applying *Options:* electronic application, deferred entrance. *Required:* essay or personal statement, high school transcript, Official college entrance exam scores required for all and activities list/resume recommended for all. *Recommended:* minimum 3 GPA, interview, Official college entrance exam scores required for all and activities list/resume recommended for all. *Application deadlines:* rolling (freshmen), rolling (out-of-state freshmen), rolling (transfers). *Notification:* continuous until 8/15 (freshmen), continuous until 8/15 (out-of-state freshmen), continuous (transfers).

Freshman Application Contact Melody Chambers, Director of Admissions, Truman State University, Ruth Towne Museum and Visitors Center, 100 East Normal Avenue, Kirksville, MO 63501-4221. *Phone:* 660-785-4114. *Toll-free phone:* 800-892-7792. *Fax:* 660-785-7456. *E-mail:* mchamber@truman.edu. *Web site:* http://www.truman.edu/.

University of Central Missouri

Warrensburg, Missouri

- **State-supported** comprehensive, founded 1871
- **Small-town** 1561-acre campus with easy access to Kansas City
- **Endowment** $24.7 million
- **Coed** 9,168 undergraduate students, 85% full-time, 54% women, 46% men
- **Moderately difficult** entrance level, 82% of applicants were admitted

Undergraduates 7,826 full-time, 1,342 part-time. Students come from 41 states and territories; 56 other countries; 8% are from out of state; 9% Black or African American, non-Hispanic/Latino; 2% Hispanic/Latino; 0.2% Asian, non-Hispanic/Latino; 0.1% Native Hawaiian or other Pacific Islander, non-Hispanic/Latino; 0.6% American Indian or Alaska Native, non-Hispanic/Latino; 1% Two or more races, non-Hispanic/Latino; 5% Race/ethnicity unknown; 3% international; 10% transferred in; 28% live on campus. *Retention:* 72% of full-time freshmen returned.

Freshmen *Admission:* 3,996 applied, 3,278 admitted, 1,570 enrolled. *Average high school GPA:* 3.25. *Test scores:* ACT scores over 18: 91%; ACT scores over 24: 31%; ACT scores over 30: 3%.

Faculty *Total:* 617, 73% full-time. *Student/faculty ratio:* 17:1.

Academics *Calendar:* semesters. *Degrees:* associate, bachelor's, master's, post-master's, and postbachelor's certificates. *Special study options:* academic remediation for entering students, adult/continuing education programs, advanced placement credit, cooperative education, distance learning, double majors, English as a second language, honors programs, internships, off-campus study, part-time degree program, services for LD students, student-designed majors, study abroad, summer session for credit. *ROTC:* Army (b), Air Force (c). *Unusual degree programs:* 3-2 engineering with University of Missouri-Columbia, University of Missouri-Rolla, University of Missouri-Kansas City; law, medical.

Computers on Campus 8,200 computers/terminals and 15,483 ports are available on campus for general student use. Students can access the following: campus intranet, computer help desk, free student e-mail accounts, online (class) grades, online (class) registration, online (class) schedules. Campuswide network is available. 100% of college-owned or -operated housing units are wired for high-speed Internet access. Wireless service is available via classrooms, computer centers, computer labs, dorm rooms, learning centers, libraries, student centers.

Student Life *Housing:* on-campus residence required for freshman year. *Options:* coed, women-only, disabled students. Campus housing is university owned. Freshman campus housing is guaranteed. *Activities and organizations:* drama/theater group, student-run newspaper, radio and television station, choral group, marching band, Roaring Red (Student Booster Club), Greek Organization, Campus Christian House, BSU (Baptist Student Union), International Student Organization, national fraternities, national sororities. *Campus security:* 24-hour emergency response devices and patrols, student patrols, late-night transport/escort service, controlled dormitory access, canine patrol. *Student services:* health clinic, personal/psychological counseling, women's center.

Athletics Member NCAA. All Division II. *Intercollegiate sports:* baseball M(s), basketball M(s)/W(s), bowling M(c)/W(c), cross-country running M(s)/W(s), football M(s), golf M(s), rock climbing M(c)/W(c), soccer M(c)/W(s), softball W(s), track and field M(s)/W(s), volleyball W(s), wrestling M(s). *Intramural sports:* archery M, badminton M/W, basketball M/W, bowling M/W, cheerleading M/W, cross-country running M/W, football M/W, golf M/W, racquetball M/W, riflery M/W, rock climbing M/W, soccer M/W, softball M/W, swimming and diving M/W, table tennis M/W, tennis M/W, track and field M/W, volleyball M/W, water polo M/W, weight lifting M, wrestling M.

Standardized Tests *Required:* ACT (for admission).

Costs (2010–11) *Tuition:* state resident $6585 full-time, $220 per credit hour part-time; nonresident $12,444 full-time, $415 per credit hour part-time. Full-time tuition and fees vary according to course load and location. Part-time tuition and fees vary according to course load and location. *Required fees:* $726 full-time, $24 per credit hour part-time. *Room and board:* $6320; room only: $4120. Room and board charges vary according to board plan and housing facility. *Payment plans:* installment, deferred payment. *Waivers:* children of alumni, senior citizens, and employees or children of employees.

Financial Aid Of all full-time matriculated undergraduates who enrolled in 2008, 862 applied for aid, 511 were judged to have need, 52 had their need fully met. 366 Federal Work-Study jobs (averaging $1460). 1,022 state and other part-time jobs (averaging $2068). In 2008, 877 non-need-based awards were made. *Average percent of need met:* 86%. *Average financial aid package:* $10,174. *Average need-based loan:* $3757. *Average need-based gift aid:* $4036. *Average non-need-based aid:* $9126. *Average indebtedness upon graduation:* $20,282.

Applying *Options:* electronic application, deferred entrance. *Application fee:* $30. *Required:* high school transcript, rank in upper two-thirds of high school class. *Application deadlines:* rolling (freshmen), rolling (transfers). *Notification:* continuous (freshmen), continuous (transfers).

Freshman Application Contact Ms. Ann Nordyke, Director of Admissions, University of Central Missouri, 1400 Ward Edwards, Warrensburg, MO 64093. *Phone:* 660-543-4170. *Toll-free phone:* 800-729-8266. *Fax:* 660-543-8517. *E-mail:* admit@ucmo.edu. *Web site:* http://www.ucmo.edu/.

University of Missouri
Columbia, Missouri

- **State-supported** university, founded 1839, part of University of Missouri System
- **Suburban** 1250-acre campus
- **Endowment** $514.0 million
- **Coed** 24,901 undergraduate students, 94% full-time, 52% women, 48% men
- **Moderately difficult** entrance level, 84% of applicants were admitted

Undergraduates 23,436 full-time, 1,465 part-time. Students come from 51 states and territories; 90 other countries; 18% are from out of state; 7% Black or African American, non-Hispanic/Latino; 3% Hispanic/Latino; 2% Asian, non-Hispanic/Latino; 0.4% American Indian or Alaska Native, non-Hispanic/Latino; 0.9% Two or more races, non-Hispanic/Latino; 2% Race/ethnicity unknown; 2% international; 5% transferred in; 28% live on campus. *Retention:* 84% of full-time freshmen returned.

Freshmen *Admission:* 17,465 applied, 14,596 admitted, 6,089 enrolled. *Test scores:* SAT critical reading scores over 500: 88%; SAT math scores over 500: 86%; ACT scores over 18: 99%; SAT critical reading scores over 600: 50%; SAT math scores over 600: 48%; ACT scores over 24: 70%; SAT critical reading scores over 700: 13%; SAT math scores over 700: 10%; ACT scores over 30: 16%.

Faculty *Total:* 1,396, 92% full-time, 93% with terminal degrees. *Student/faculty ratio:* 20:1.

Academics *Calendar:* semesters. *Degrees:* bachelor's, master's, doctoral-professional, doctoral-research/scholarship, and post-master's certificates. *Special study options:* accelerated degree program, adult/continuing education programs, advanced placement credit, cooperative education, distance learning, double majors, English as a second language, external degree program, freshman honors college, honors programs, independent study, internships, off-campus study, part-time degree program, services for LD students, student-designed majors, study abroad, summer session for credit. *ROTC:* Army (b), Navy (b), Air Force (b). *Unusual degree programs:* 3-2 accountancy, physical therapy, occupational therapy.

Computers on Campus 1,168 computers/terminals are available on campus for general student use. Students can access the following: computer help desk, free student e-mail accounts, online (class) grades, online (class) registration, online (class) schedules. Campuswide network is available. 90% of college-owned or -operated housing units are wired for high-speed Internet access. Wireless service is available via classrooms, computer centers, computer labs, learning centers, libraries, student centers.

Student Life *Housing:* on-campus residence required for freshman year. *Options:* coed, men-only, women-only, disabled students. Campus housing is university owned. Freshman campus housing is guaranteed. *Activities and organizations:* drama/theater group, student-run newspaper, radio and television station, choral group, marching band, Academic organizations, Greek organizations, religious organizations, sports clubs, Student Governance, national fraternities, national sororities. *Campus security:* 24-hour emergency response devices and patrols, late-night transport/escort service, controlled dormitory access. *Student services:* health clinic, personal/psychological counseling, women's center, legal services.

Athletics Member NCAA. All Division I except football (Division I-A). *Intercollegiate sports:* baseball M(s), basketball M(s)/W(s), cross-country running M(s)/W(s), golf M(s)/W(s), gymnastics W(s), soccer W(s), softball W(s), swimming and diving M(s)/W(s), tennis W(s), track and field M(s)/W(s), volleyball W(s), wrestling M(s). *Intramural sports:* archery M(c)/W(c), badminton W(c), baseball M(c), basketball M(c)/W(c), bowling M(c)/W(c), fencing M(c)/W(c), field hockey W(c), ice hockey M(c), lacrosse M(c)/W(c), racquetball M(c)/W(c), rugby M(c)/W(c), soccer M(c)/W(c), softball W(c), swimming and diving M(c)/W(c), table tennis M(c)/W(c), tennis M(c)/W(c), ultimate Frisbee M(c)/W(c), volleyball M(c)/W(c), water polo M(c)/W(c), weight lifting M(c)/W(c).

Standardized Tests *Required:* SAT or ACT (for admission). *Recommended:* ACT (for admission).

Costs (2010–11) *Tuition:* state resident $7368 full-time, $246 per credit hour part-time; nonresident $19,383 full-time, $646 per credit hour part-time. Full-time tuition and fees vary according to course load, program, and reciprocity agreements. Part-time tuition and fees vary according to course load, program, and reciprocity agreements. *Required fees:* $1133 full-time. *Room and board:* $8607. Room and board charges vary according to board plan and housing facility. *Payment plan:* installment. *Waivers:* senior citizens and employees or children of employees.

Financial Aid Of all full-time matriculated undergraduates who enrolled in 2009, 16,030 applied for aid, 11,757 were judged to have need, 1,770 had their need fully met. In 2009, 3790 non-need-based awards were made. *Average percent of need met:* 81%. *Average financial aid package:* $12,797. *Average need-based loan:* $4049. *Average need-based gift aid:* $7140. *Average non-need-based aid:* $3578. *Average indebtedness upon graduation:* $22,145.

Applying *Options:* electronic application, deferred entrance. *Application fee:* $50. *Required:* high school transcript, specific high school curriculum. *Application deadlines:* rolling (freshmen), rolling (transfers). *Notification:* continuous (freshmen), continuous (transfers).

Freshman Application Contact Ms. Barbara Rupp, Director of Admissions, University of Missouri, 230 Jesse Hall, Columbia, MO 65211. *Phone:* 573-882-7786. *Toll-free phone:* 800-225-6075. *Fax:* 573-882-7887. *E-mail:* mu4u@missouri.edu. *Web site:* http://www.missouri.edu/.

University of Missouri–Kansas City

Kansas City, Missouri

- **State-supported** university, founded 1929, part of University of Missouri System
- **Urban** 191-acre campus with easy access to Kansas City
- **Endowment** $209.1 million
- **Coed**
- **Moderately difficult** entrance level

Faculty *Student/faculty ratio:* 13:1.

Academics *Calendar:* semesters. *Degrees:* bachelor's, master's, doctoral-professional, doctoral-research/scholarship, and post-master's certificates.

Student Life *Campus security:* 24-hour emergency response devices and patrols, late-night transport/escort service, controlled dormitory access.

Athletics Member NCAA. All Division I.

Standardized Tests *Required:* SAT or ACT (for admission).

Costs (2010–11) *Tuition:* state resident $7368 full-time, $246 per credit hour part-time; nonresident $18,957 full-time, $632 per credit hour part-time. Full-time tuition and fees vary according to course load and program. Part-time tuition and fees vary according to course load and program. *Required fees:* $1234 full-time, $48 per credit hour part-time, $30 per term part-time. *Room and board:* $10,131. Room and board charges vary according to board plan and housing facility.

Financial Aid *Of all full-time matriculated undergraduates who enrolled in 2009,* 4,798 applied for aid, 4,222 were judged to have need, 296 had their need fully met. *In 2009,* 822 non-need-based awards were made. *Average percent of need met:* 51. *Average financial aid package:* $9704. *Average need-based loan:* $8436. *Average need-based gift aid:* $6675. *Average non-need-based aid:* $5101. *Average indebtedness upon graduation:* $20,512.

Applying *Options:* electronic application, deferred entrance. *Application fee:* $45. *Required:* high school transcript. *Required for some:* essay or personal statement, interview.

Freshman Application Contact Ms. Tammy Cloutier, Associate Director of Recruitment, University of Missouri–Kansas City, Office of Admissions, 5100 Rockhill Road, Kansas City, MO 64110-2499. *Phone:* 816-235-1111. *Toll-free phone:* 800-775-8652. *Fax:* 816-235-5544. *E-mail:* admit@umkc.edu. *Web site:* http://www.umkc.edu/.

University of Missouri–St. Louis

St. Louis, Missouri

- **State-supported** university, founded 1963, part of University of Missouri System
- **Suburban** 350-acre campus
- **Endowment** $44.9 million
- **Coed** 13,181 undergraduate students, 46% full-time, 59% women, 41% men
- **Moderately difficult** entrance level, 73% of applicants were admitted

Undergraduates 6,087 full-time, 7,094 part-time. Students come from 43 states and territories; 45 other countries; 10% are from out of state; 21% Black or African American, non-Hispanic/Latino; 2% Hispanic/Latino; 3% Asian, non-Hispanic/Latino; 0.3% American Indian or Alaska Native, non-Hispanic/Latino; 0.7% Two or more races, non-Hispanic/Latino; 9% Race/ethnicity unknown; 3% international; 13% transferred in; 8% live on campus. *Retention:* 74% of full-time freshmen returned.

Freshmen *Admission:* 1,798 applied, 1,306 admitted, 497 enrolled. *Test scores:* SAT math scores over 500: 57%; ACT scores over 18: 96%; SAT math scores over 600: 25%; ACT scores over 24: 50%; SAT math scores over 700: 7%; ACT scores over 30: 7%.

Faculty *Total:* 915, 53% full-time, 51% with terminal degrees. *Student/faculty ratio:* 17:1.

Academics *Calendar:* semesters. *Degrees:* bachelor's, master's, doctoral-professional, doctoral-research/scholarship, post-master's, and postbachelor's certificates. *Special study options:* accelerated degree program, adult/continuing education programs, advanced placement credit, cooperative education, distance learning, double majors, English as a second language, freshman honors college, honors programs, independent study, internships, off-campus study, part-time degree program, services for LD students, student-designed majors,

study abroad, summer session for credit. *ROTC:* Army (c), Air Force (c). *Unusual degree programs:* 3-2 engineering with Washington University; economics, history, philosophy, political science and sociology.

Computers on Campus 1,326 computers/terminals and 1,326 ports are available on campus for general student use. Students can access the following: campus intranet, computer help desk, free student e-mail accounts, online (class) grades, online (class) registration, online (class) schedules. Campus-wide network is available. 90% of college-owned or -operated housing units are wired for high-speed Internet access. Wireless service is available via classrooms, computer centers, computer labs, dorm rooms, learning centers, libraries, student centers.

Student Life *Housing options:* coed, women-only, disabled students. Campus housing is university owned and is provided by a third party. *Activities and organizations:* drama/theater group, student-run newspaper, radio station, choral group, Student Government Association, Associated Black Collegians, Pierre laclede Honors College Student Association, Residence Hall Association, UMSL Radio Station, national fraternities, national sororities. *Campus security:* 24-hour emergency response devices and patrols, late-night transport/escort service, controlled dormitory access. *Student services:* health clinic, personal/psychological counseling, women's center.

Athletics Member NCAA. All Division II. *Intercollegiate sports:* baseball M(s), basketball M(s)/W(s), cheerleading W, golf M(s)/W(s), ice hockey M(c), soccer M(s)/W(s), softball W(s), table tennis M(c)/W(c), tennis M(s)/W(s), volleyball W(s). *Intramural sports:* badminton M/W, basketball M/W, bowling M/W, football M/W, golf M/W, racquetball M/W, rock climbing M/W, skiing (downhill) M/W, soccer M/W, softball M/W, table tennis M/W, tennis M/W, volleyball M/W, weight lifting M/W.

Standardized Tests *Required:* SAT or ACT (for admission).

Costs (2011–12) *Tuition:* state resident $7737 full-time, $258 per credit hour part-time; nonresident $19,905 full-time, $664 per credit hour part-time. Full-time tuition and fees vary according to course load, program, and reciprocity agreements. Part-time tuition and fees vary according to course load, program, and reciprocity agreements. *Required fees:* $1301 full-time, $50 per credit hour part-time. *Room and board:* $8404; room only: $5044. Room and board charges vary according to board plan and housing facility. *Payment plan:* installment. *Waivers:* senior citizens and employees or children of employees.

Financial Aid Of all full-time matriculated undergraduates who enrolled in 2009, 4,593 applied for aid, 4,211 were judged to have need, 237 had their need fully met. 59 Federal Work-Study jobs (averaging $3375). In 2009, 448 non-need-based awards were made. *Average percent of need met:* 46%. *Average financial aid package:* $8700. *Average need-based loan:* $4588. *Average need-based gift aid:* $5702. *Average non-need-based aid:* $4583. *Average indebtedness upon graduation:* $27,334.

Applying *Options:* electronic application. *Application fee:* $35. *Required:* high school transcript, CBHE core requirements. *Required for some:* essay or personal statement, 2 letters of recommendation, interview. *Application deadlines:* 8/23 (freshmen), 8/23 (out-of-state freshmen), rolling (transfers). *Notification:* continuous until 10/1 (freshmen), continuous until 10/1 (out-of-state freshmen), continuous (transfers).

Freshman Application Contact Mr. Andrew L. Griffin, Associate Director of Admissions, University of Missouri–St. Louis, 351 Millennium Student Center, One University Boulevard, St. Louis, MO 63121-4400. *Phone:* 314-516-6941. *Toll-free phone:* 888-GO2-UMSL. *Fax:* 314-516-5310. *E-mail:* askdrew@umsl.edu. *Web site:* http://www.umsl.edu/.

University of Phoenix–Kansas City Campus

Kansas City, Missouri

Freshman Application Contact Ms. Audra McQuarie, Registrar/Executive Director, University of Phoenix–Kansas City Campus, 4035 South Riverpoint Parkway, Mail Stop CF-L101, Phoenix, AZ 85040. *Phone:* 480-557-6151. *Toll-free phone:* 800-776-4867 (in-state); 800-228-7240 (out-of-state). *Fax:* 480-643-3068. *E-mail:* audra.mcquarie@phoenix.edu. *Web site:* http://www.phoenix.edu/.

University of Phoenix–St. Louis Campus

St. Louis, Missouri

Freshman Application Contact Ms. Audra McQuarie, Registrar/Executive Director, University of Phoenix–St. Louis Campus, 4035 South Riverpoint Parkway, Mail Stop CF-L101, Phoenix, AZ 85040. *Phone:* 480-557-6151. *Toll-free phone:* 800-776-4867 (in-state); 800-228-7240 (out-of-state). *Fax:* 480-643-3068. *E-mail:* audra.mcquarie@phoenix.edu. *Web site:* http://www.phoenix.edu/.

University of Phoenix–Springfield Campus

Springfield, Missouri

Freshman Application Contact Ms. Audra McQuarie, Registrar/Executive Director, University of Phoenix–Springfield Campus, 4035 South Riverpoint Parkway, Mail Stop CF-L101, Phoenix, AZ 85040. *Phone:* 480-557-6151. *Toll-free phone:* 800-776-4867 (in-state); 800-228-7240 (out-of-state). *Fax:* 480-643-3068. *E-mail:* audra.mcquarie@phoenix.edu. *Web site:* http://www.phoenix.edu/.

Vatterott College

St. Ann, Missouri

Director of Admissions Ann Farajallah, Director of Admissions, Vatterott College, 3925 Industrial Drive, St. Ann, MO 63074-1807. *Phone:* 314-264-1020. *Toll-free phone:* 866-314-6454. *Web site:* http://www.vatterott-college.edu/.

Vatterott College

Sunset Hills, Missouri

Director of Admissions Director of Admission, Vatterott College, 12970 Maurer Industrial Drive, St. Louis, MO 63127. *Phone:* 314-843-4200. *Fax:* 314-843-1709. *Web site:* http://www.vatterott-college.edu/.

Washington University in St. Louis

St. Louis, Missouri

- **Independent** university, founded 1853
- **Suburban** 169-acre campus
- **Endowment** $4.6 billion
- **Coed** 7,138 undergraduate students, 88% full-time, 50% women, 50% men
- **Most difficult** entrance level, 21% of applicants were admitted

Undergraduates 6,285 full-time, 853 part-time. Students come from 54 states and territories; 60 other countries; 91% are from out of state; 6% Black or African American, non-Hispanic/Latino; 5% Hispanic/Latino; 15% Asian, non-Hispanic/Latino; 3% Two or more races, non-Hispanic/Latino; 8% Race/ethnicity unknown; 6% international; 0.8% transferred in; 79% live on campus. *Retention:* 97% of full-time freshmen returned.

Freshmen *Admission:* 24,939 applied, 5,285 admitted, 1,632 enrolled. *Test scores:* SAT critical reading scores over 500: 100%; SAT math scores over 500: 100%; ACT scores over 18: 100%; SAT critical reading scores over 600: 98%; SAT math scores over 600: 99%; ACT scores over 24: 100%; SAT critical reading scores over 700: 64%; SAT math scores over 700: 85%; ACT scores over 30: 94%.

Faculty *Total:* 1,085, 85% full-time, 84% with terminal degrees. *Student/faculty ratio:* 7:1.

Academics *Calendar:* semesters. *Degrees:* certificates, bachelor's, master's, doctoral-professional, doctoral-research/scholarship, post-master's, and post-bachelor's certificates. *Special study options:* accelerated degree program, adult/continuing education programs, advanced placement credit, cooperative education, double majors, English as a second language, independent study, internships, off-campus study, part-time degree program, services for LD students, student-designed majors, study abroad, summer session for credit. *ROTC:* Army (b), Air Force (c). *Unusual degree programs:* 3-2 business administration; engineering; social work; art, occupational therapy, physical therapy.

Computers on Campus 2,500 computers/terminals are available on campus for general student use. Students can access the following: campus intranet, computer help desk, free student e-mail accounts, online (class) grades, online (class) registration, online (class) schedules. Campuswide network is available. 90% of college-owned or -operated housing units are wired for high-speed Internet access. Wireless service is available via classrooms, computer centers, computer labs, dorm rooms, learning centers, libraries, student centers.

Student Life *Housing:* on-campus residence required for freshman year. *Options:* coed, men-only, women-only, cooperative. Campus housing is university owned. Freshman campus housing is guaranteed. *Activities and organizations:* drama/theater group, student-run newspaper, radio and television station, choral group, national fraternities, national sororities. *Campus security:* 24-hour emergency response devices and patrols, student patrols, late-night transport/escort service, controlled dormitory access. *Student services:* health clinic, personal/psychological counseling, women's center.

Athletics Member NCAA. All Division III. *Intercollegiate sports:* baseball M, basketball M/W, crew M(c)/W(c), cross-country running M/W, equestrian sports M(c)/W(c), fencing M(c)/W(c), field hockey W(c), football M, golf M(c)/W, gymnastics M(c)/W(c), ice hockey M(c), lacrosse M(c)/W(c), rugby M(c)/W(c), sailing M(c)/W(c), soccer M/W, softball W, swimming and diving M/W, table tennis M(c)/W(c), tennis M/W, track and field M/W, ultimate Frisbee M(c)/W(c), volleyball M(c)/W, water polo M(c)/W(c). *Intramural sports:* badminton M/W, basketball M/W, bowling M/W, cross-country running M/W, football M/W, golf M/W, racquetball M/W, soccer M(c)/W(c), softball M/W, swimming and diving M/W, table tennis M/W, tennis M/W, track and field M/W, ultimate Frisbee M/W, volleyball M/W, water polo M/W.

Standardized Tests *Required:* SAT or ACT (for admission).

Costs (2011–12) *Comprehensive fee:* $55,111 includes full-time tuition ($40,950), mandatory fees ($1042), and room and board ($13,119). *College room only:* $8819. Room and board charges vary according to board plan and housing facility. *Payment plans:* tuition prepayment, installment. *Waivers:* employees or children of employees.

Financial Aid Of all full-time matriculated undergraduates who enrolled in 2009, 4,313 applied for aid, 2,594 were judged to have need, 2,558 had their need fully met. 1,106 Federal Work-Study jobs (averaging $1944). In 2009, 920 non-need-based awards were made. *Average percent of need met:* 100%. *Average financial aid package:* $32,992. *Average need-based loan:* $6250. *Average need-based gift aid:* $29,457. *Average non-need-based aid:* $6893. *Financial aid deadline:* 2/1.

Applying *Options:* electronic application, early admission, early decision, deferred entrance. *Application fee:* $55. *Required:* essay or personal statement, high school transcript, 2 letters of recommendation. *Recommended:* minimum 3 GPA, portfolio for art and architecture programs. *Application deadlines:* 1/15 (freshmen), 4/15 (transfers). *Early decision deadline:* 11/15. *Notification:* 4/1 (freshmen), continuous (transfers), 12/15 (early decision).

Freshman Application Contact Ms. Julie Shimabukuro, Director of Admissions, Washington University in St. Louis, Campus Box 1089, One Brookings Drive, St. Louis, MO 63130-4899. *Phone:* 314-935-6000. *Toll-free phone:* 800-638-0700. *Fax:* 314-935-4290. *E-mail:* admissions@wustl.edu. *Web site:* http://www.wustl.edu/.

Webster University

St. Louis, Missouri

- **Independent** comprehensive, founded 1915
- **Suburban** 47-acre campus with easy access to St. Louis
- **Endowment** $70.3 million
- **Coed** 3,380 undergraduate students, 74% full-time, 57% women, 43% men
- **Moderately difficult** entrance level, 52% of applicants were admitted

Undergraduates 2,498 full-time, 882 part-time. Students come from 43 states and territories; 31 other countries; 21% are from out of state; 11% Black or African American, non-Hispanic/Latino; 3% Hispanic/Latino; 2% Asian, non-Hispanic/Latino; 0.4% American Indian or Alaska Native, non-Hispanic/Latino; 14% Race/ethnicity unknown; 2% international; 9% transferred in; 15% live on campus. *Retention:* 80% of full-time freshmen returned.

Freshmen *Admission:* 1,584 applied, 828 admitted, 424 enrolled. *Average high school GPA:* 3.23. *Test scores:* SAT critical reading scores over 500: 76%; SAT math scores over 500: 72%; ACT scores over 18: 94%; SAT critical reading scores over 600: 32%; SAT math scores over 600: 24%; ACT scores over 24: 52%; SAT critical reading scores over 700: 5%; SAT math scores over 700: 3%; ACT scores over 30: 7%.

Faculty *Total:* 783, 23% full-time. *Student/faculty ratio:* 13:1.

Academics *Calendar:* semesters. *Degrees:* certificates, bachelor's, master's, doctoral-professional, post-master's, and postbachelor's certificates. *Special study options:* academic remediation for entering students, accelerated degree program, adult/continuing education programs, advanced placement credit, cooperative education, distance learning, double majors, English as a second language, independent study, internships, off-campus study, part-time degree program, services for LD students, student-designed majors, study abroad, summer session for credit. *ROTC:* Army (c), Air Force (c). *Unusual degree programs:* 3-2 engineering with University of Missouri-Columbia, Washington University in St. Louis; architecture with Washington University in St. Louis.

Computers on Campus 450 computers/terminals and 100 ports are available on campus for general student use. Students can access the following: campus intranet, computer help desk, free student e-mail accounts, online (class) grades, online (class) registration, online (class) schedules. Campuswide network is available. 100% of college-owned or -operated housing units are wired for high-speed Internet access. Wireless service is available via classrooms, computer centers, computer labs, dorm rooms, learning centers, libraries, student centers.

Student Life *Housing options:* coed. Campus housing is university owned. Freshman applicants given priority for college housing. *Activities and organizations:* drama/theater group, student-run newspaper, radio and television station, choral group, Student Government Association, Habitat for Humanity, International Student Association, Marketing Communications Club, Residential Housing Association, national fraternities, national sororities. *Campus security:* 24-hour emergency response devices and patrols, student patrols,

late-night transport/escort service, controlled dormitory access. *Student services:* health clinic, personal/psychological counseling, women's center.
Athletics Member NCAA. All Division III. *Intercollegiate sports:* baseball M, basketball M/W, cross-country running M/W, golf M, soccer M/W, softball W, tennis M/W, track and field M/W, volleyball W. *Intramural sports:* bowling M(c)/W(c), cheerleading W(c), soccer M(c)/W(c), swimming and diving M(c)/W(c), table tennis M(c)/W(c), volleyball M(c).
Standardized Tests *Required:* SAT or ACT (for admission).
Costs (2010–11) *Comprehensive fee:* $30,978 includes full-time tuition ($21,688) and room and board ($9290). Full-time tuition and fees vary according to program. Part-time tuition: $570 per credit hour. Part-time tuition and fees vary according to location. *College room only:* $4970. Room and board charges vary according to board plan and housing facility. *Payment plan:* installment. *Waivers:* employees or children of employees.
Financial Aid Of all full-time matriculated undergraduates who enrolled in 2009, 2,131 applied for aid, 1,863 were judged to have need. 1,086 Federal Work-Study jobs (averaging $2166). 505 state and other part-time jobs (averaging $2145). In 2009, 460 non-need-based awards were made. *Average financial aid package:* $22,542. *Average need-based loan:* $4475. *Average need-based gift aid:* $7033. *Average non-need-based aid:* $8343. *Average indebtedness upon graduation:* $26,184.
Applying *Options:* electronic application, early admission, deferred entrance. *Application fee:* $35. *Required:* essay or personal statement, high school transcript, minimum 2.5 GPA, 1 letter of recommendation. *Required for some:* minimum 3 GPA, audition. *Recommended:* minimum 3 GPA, interview. *Application deadlines:* 6/1 (freshmen), 6/1 (out-of-state freshmen), 8/1 (transfers). *Notification:* continuous (freshmen), continuous (out-of-state freshmen), continuous (transfers).
Freshman Application Contact Mr. Andrew Laue, Associate Director of Undergraduate Admission, Webster University, 470 East Lockwood Avenue, St. Louis, MO 63119-3194. *Phone:* 314-961-2660. *Toll-free phone:* 800-75-ENROL. *Fax:* 314-968-7115. *E-mail:* admit@webster.edu. *Web site:* http://www.webster.edu/.

Westminster College

Fulton, Missouri

- **Independent** 4-year, founded 1851, affiliated with Presbyterian Church
- **Small-town** 80-acre campus
- **Endowment** $45.1 million
- **Coed** 1,151 undergraduate students, 99% full-time, 44% women, 56% men
- **Moderately difficult** entrance level, 78% of applicants were admitted

Undergraduates 1,135 full-time, 16 part-time. Students come from 25 states and territories; 65 other countries; 20% are from out of state; 7% Black or African American, non-Hispanic/Latino; 3% Hispanic/Latino; 1% Asian, non-Hispanic/Latino; 2% American Indian or Alaska Native, non-Hispanic/Latino; 1% Two or more races, non-Hispanic/Latino; 4% Race/ethnicity unknown; 13% international; 5% transferred in; 85% live on campus. *Retention:* 81% of full-time freshmen returned.
Freshmen *Admission:* 1,321 applied, 1,025 admitted, 322 enrolled. *Average high school GPA:* 3.44. *Test scores:* SAT critical reading scores over 500: 47%; SAT math scores over 500: 73%; SAT writing scores over 500: 55%; ACT scores over 18: 98%; SAT critical reading scores over 600: 22%; SAT math scores over 600: 18%; SAT writing scores over 600: 20%; ACT scores over 24: 63%; SAT critical reading scores over 700: 6%; ACT scores over 30: 16%.
Faculty *Total:* 95, 66% full-time, 63% with terminal degrees. *Student/faculty ratio:* 15:1.
Academics *Calendar:* semesters. *Degree:* bachelor's. *Special study options:* academic remediation for entering students, advanced placement credit, cooperative education, double majors, English as a second language, honors programs, independent study, internships, off-campus study, part-time degree program, services for LD students, student-designed majors, study abroad, summer session for credit. *ROTC:* Army (c), Air Force (c). *Unusual degree programs:* 3-2 engineering with Washington University in St. Louis, University of Missouri-Columbia.
Computers on Campus 188 computers/terminals are available on campus for general student use. Students can access the following: campus intranet, computer help desk, free student e-mail accounts, online (class) grades, online (class) registration, online (class) schedules. Campuswide network is available. 100% of college-owned or -operated housing units are wired for high-speed Internet access. Wireless service is available via entire campus.
Student Life *Housing:* on-campus residence required through junior year. *Options:* coed, men-only, women-only. Campus housing is university owned. Freshman campus housing is guaranteed. *Activities and organizations:* drama/theater group, student-run newspaper, choral group, Student Government Association, Environmentally Concerned Students, International Student Club, Habitat for Humanity, Little Brother/Little Sister, national fraternities, national sororities. *Campus security:* 24-hour emergency response devices and patrols,

late-night transport/escort service, controlled dormitory access, well-lit campus. *Student services:* health clinic, personal/psychological counseling, women's center.
Athletics Member NCAA. All Division III. *Intercollegiate sports:* baseball M, basketball M/W, cross-country running M/W, football M, golf M/W, soccer M/W, softball M/W, tennis M/W, track and field M/W, volleyball W. *Intramural sports:* basketball M/W, football M, table tennis M/W, volleyball M/W.
Standardized Tests *Required:* SAT or ACT (for admission).
Costs (2010–11) *Comprehensive fee:* $27,350 includes full-time tuition ($18,990), mandatory fees ($750), and room and board ($7610). Part-time tuition: $750 per credit hour. *College room only:* $3990. Room and board charges vary according to board plan and housing facility. *Payment plan:* installment. *Waivers:* children of alumni and employees or children of employees.
Financial Aid Of all full-time matriculated undergraduates who enrolled in 2009, 868 applied for aid, 711 were judged to have need, 488 had their need fully met. 292 Federal Work-Study jobs (averaging $2578). 191 state and other part-time jobs (averaging $2594). In 2009, 409 non-need-based awards were made. *Average percent of need met:* 75%. *Average financial aid package:* $17,846. *Average need-based loan:* $3897. *Average need-based gift aid:* $13,094. *Average non-need-based aid:* $8775. *Average indebtedness upon graduation:* $21,964.
Applying *Options:* electronic application, early admission, deferred entrance. *Required:* high school transcript, 1 letter of recommendation. *Required for some:* interview. *Recommended:* essay or personal statement, minimum 2.5 GPA. *Notification:* 8/1 (freshmen), continuous (transfers).
Freshman Application Contact Mr. George Wolf, Vice President and Dean of Enrollment Services, Westminster College, 501 Westminster Avenue, Fulton, MO 65251-1299. *Phone:* 573-592-5251. *Toll-free phone:* 800-475-3361. *Fax:* 573-592-5255. *E-mail:* admissions@westminster-mo.edu. *Web site:* http://www.westminster-mo.edu/.

William Jewell College

Liberty, Missouri

- **Independent** 4-year, founded 1849
- **Suburban** 200-acre campus with easy access to Kansas City
- **Endowment** $59.6 million
- **Coed** 1,060 undergraduate students, 96% full-time, 60% women, 40% men
- **Moderately difficult** entrance level, 50% of applicants were admitted

Undergraduates 1,018 full-time, 42 part-time. Students come from 34 states and territories; 14 other countries; 34% are from out of state; 3% Black or African American, non-Hispanic/Latino; 4% Hispanic/Latino; 1% Asian, non-Hispanic/Latino; 0.7% American Indian or Alaska Native, non-Hispanic/Latino; 2% Two or more races, non-Hispanic/Latino; 2% Race/ethnicity unknown; 3% international; 5% transferred in; 77% live on campus. *Retention:* 76% of full-time freshmen returned.
Freshmen *Admission:* 3,032 applied, 1,531 admitted, 271 enrolled. *Average high school GPA:* 3.69. *Test scores:* SAT critical reading scores over 500: 79%; SAT math scores over 500: 79%; ACT scores over 18: 99%; SAT critical reading scores over 600: 48%; SAT math scores over 600: 42%; ACT scores over 24: 70%; SAT critical reading scores over 700: 24%; SAT math scores over 700: 12%; ACT scores over 30: 17%.
Faculty *Total:* 125, 56% full-time, 56% with terminal degrees. *Student/faculty ratio:* 12:1.
Academics *Calendar:* semesters. *Degrees:* bachelor's (also offers evening program with significant enrollment not reflected in profile). *Special study options:* academic remediation for entering students, advanced placement credit, cooperative education, double majors, honors programs, independent study, internships, off-campus study, services for LD students, student-designed majors, study abroad, summer session for credit. *ROTC:* Army (c). *Unusual degree programs:* 3-2 engineering with Washington University in St. Louis, University of Kansas, Vanderbilt University; forestry with Duke University.
Computers on Campus 253 computers/terminals are available on campus for general student use. Students can access the following: campus intranet, computer help desk, free student e-mail accounts, online (class) grades, online (class) registration, online (class) schedules. Campuswide network is available. 100% of college-owned or -operated housing units are wired for high-speed Internet access. Wireless service is available via classrooms, dorm rooms, learning centers, libraries, student centers.
Student Life *Housing:* on-campus residence required through senior year. *Options:* coed, men-only, women-only, disabled students. Campus housing is university owned. Freshman campus housing is guaranteed. *Activities and organizations:* drama/theater group, student-run newspaper, radio station, choral group, College Union Activities, intramurals, Mosaic, Students in Free Enterprise (SIFE), American Humanics, national fraternities, national sororities. *Campus security:* 24-hour emergency response devices and patrols, late-

night transport/escort service, controlled dormitory access. *Student services:* health clinic, personal/psychological counseling.

Athletics Member NCAA, NAIA. All NCAA Division II. *Intercollegiate sports:* baseball M(s), basketball M(s)/W(s), cheerleading M(s)/W(s), cross-country running M(s)/W(s), football M(s), golf M(s)/W(s), soccer M(s)/W(s), softball W(s), swimming and diving M(s)/W(s), tennis M(s)/W(s), track and field M(s)/W(s), volleyball W(s). *Intramural sports:* racquetball M/W, soccer M/W, softball M/W, tennis M/W, ultimate Frisbee M/W, volleyball M/W.

Standardized Tests *Required:* SAT or ACT (for admission).

Costs (2011–12) Comprehensive fee: $37,460 includes full-time tuition ($29,600), mandatory fees ($300), and room and board ($7560). Full-time tuition and fees vary according to class time, course load, program, and student level. Part-time tuition: $850 per credit. *Room and board:* Room and board charges vary according to board plan and housing facility. *Payment plan:* installment. *Waivers:* children of alumni and employees or children of employees.

Financial Aid Of all full-time matriculated undergraduates who enrolled in 2009, 847 applied for aid, 762 were judged to have need, 110 had their need fully met. 519 Federal Work-Study jobs (averaging $2171). 150 state and other part-time jobs (averaging $754). In 2009, 126 non-need-based awards were made. *Average percent of need met:* 63%. *Average financial aid package:* $17,589. *Average need-based loan:* $5062. *Average need-based gift aid:* $13,688. *Average non-need-based aid:* $12,564. *Average indebtedness upon graduation:* $23,210.

Applying *Options:* electronic application, deferred entrance. *Application fee:* $25. *Required:* essay or personal statement, high school transcript. *Required for some:* interview. *Recommended:* interview. *Application deadlines:* 8/15 (freshmen), rolling (transfers). *Notification:* continuous (transfers).

Freshman Application Contact Mr. Clint Chapman, Dean of Admission, William Jewell College, 500 College Hill, Liberty, MO 64068-1843. *Phone:* 816-415-7872. *Toll-free phone:* 888-2JEWELL. *Fax:* 816-415-5040. *E-mail:* chapmanc@william.jewell.edu. *Web site:* http://www.jewell.edu/.

William Woods University
Fulton, Missouri

Freshman Application Contact Ms. Sharon Horn, Admissions Data Analyst, William Woods University, One University Avenue, Fulton, MO 65251. *Phone:* 573-592-4221. *Toll-free phone:* 800-995-3159 Ext. 4221. *Fax:* 573-592-1146. *E-mail:* admissions@williamwoods.edu. *Web site:* http://www.williamwoods.edu/.

MONTANA

Carroll College
Helena, Montana

Freshman Application Contact Ms. Cynthia Thornquist, Director of Admissions and Enrollment Operations, Carroll College, 1601 North Benton Avenue, Helena, MT 59625-0002. *Toll-free phone:* 800-992-3648. *Web site:* http://www.carroll.edu/.

See page 1198 for the College Close-Up.

Montana State University
Bozeman, Montana

- **State-supported** university, founded 1893, part of Montana University System
- **Small-town** 1781-acre campus
- **Endowment** $83.3 million
- **Coed** 11,579 undergraduate students, 82% full-time, 45% women, 55% men
- **Moderately difficult** entrance level, 61% of applicants were admitted

Undergraduates 9,515 full-time, 2,064 part-time. Students come from 50 states and territories; 72 other countries; 33% are from out of state; 0.6% Black or African American, non-Hispanic/Latino; 3% Hispanic/Latino; 0.9% Asian, non-Hispanic/Latino; 2% American Indian or Alaska Native, non-Hispanic/Latino; 3% Two or more races, non-Hispanic/Latino; 0.9% Race/ethnicity unknown; 3% international; 7% transferred in; 25% live on campus. *Retention:* 74% of full-time freshmen returned.

Freshmen *Admission:* 9,417 applied, 5,786 admitted, 2,623 enrolled. *Average high school GPA:* 3.28. *Test scores:* SAT critical reading scores over 500: 72%; SAT math scores over 500: 75%; SAT writing scores over 500: 68%; ACT scores over 18: 93%; SAT critical reading scores over 600: 33%; SAT math scores over 600: 36%; SAT writing scores over 600: 25%; ACT scores

over 24: 54%; SAT critical reading scores over 700: 6%; SAT math scores over 700: 7%; SAT writing scores over 700: 4%; ACT scores over 30: 12%.

Faculty *Total:* 847, 70% full-time, 65% with terminal degrees. *Student/faculty ratio:* 17:1.

Academics *Calendar:* semesters. *Degrees:* certificates, associate, bachelor's, master's, doctoral-other, and post-master's certificates. *Special study options:* academic remediation for entering students, adult/continuing education programs, advanced placement credit, distance learning, double majors, English as a second language, honors programs, independent study, internships, off-campus study, part-time degree program, services for LD students, student-designed majors, study abroad, summer session for credit. *ROTC:* Army (b), Air Force (b).

Computers on Campus 850 computers/terminals are available on campus for general student use. Students can access the following: computer help desk, free student e-mail accounts, online (class) registration, online (class) schedules. Campuswide network is available. 100% of college-owned or -operated housing units are wired for high-speed Internet access. Wireless service is available via entire campus.

Student Life *Housing:* on-campus residence required for freshman year. *Options:* coed, men-only, women-only. Campus housing is university owned. Freshman campus housing is guaranteed. *Activities and organizations:* drama/theater group, student-run newspaper, radio and television station, choral group, marching band, Spurs, Inter-Varsity Christian Fellowship, Campus Crusade for Christ, Fangs, Mortar Board, national fraternities, national sororities. *Campus security:* 24-hour emergency response devices and patrols, student patrols, late-night transport/escort service, 24-hour residence hall monitoring. *Student services:* health clinic, personal/psychological counseling, women's center, legal services.

Athletics Member NCAA. All Division I except football (Division I-AA). *Intercollegiate sports:* basketball M(s)/W(s), cheerleading M(s)/W(s), cross-country running M(s)/W(s), golf W(s), skiing (cross-country) M(s)/W(s), skiing (downhill) M(s)/W(s), tennis M(s)/W(s), track and field M(s)/W(s), volleyball W(s). *Intramural sports:* archery W, badminton M/W, baseball M, basketball M/W, bowling M/W, cross-country running M/W, fencing M/W, football M, golf M/W, gymnastics M/W, racquetball M/W, rugby M/W, skiing (cross-country) M/W, skiing (downhill) M/W, soccer M/W, softball M/W, swimming and diving M/W, table tennis M/W, tennis M/W, track and field M/W, ultimate Frisbee M/W, volleyball M/W, water polo M/W, weight lifting M/W, wrestling M.

Standardized Tests *Required:* SAT or ACT (for admission).

Costs (2010–11) *Tuition:* state resident $6168 full-time; nonresident $18,291 full-time. Full-time tuition and fees vary according to course load and degree level. Part-time tuition and fees vary according to course load and degree level. *Room and board:* $7900. Room and board charges vary according to board plan and housing facility. *Payment plans:* installment, deferred payment. *Waivers:* minority students, senior citizens, and employees or children of employees.

Financial Aid Of all full-time matriculated undergraduates who enrolled in 2008, 5,593 applied for aid, 4,425 were judged to have need, 160 had their need fully met. In 2008, 386 non-need-based awards were made. *Average percent of need met:* 72%. *Average financial aid package:* $10,268. *Average need-based loan:* $4422. *Average need-based gift aid:* $4530. *Average non-need-based aid:* $2039. *Average indebtedness upon graduation:* $21,571.

Applying *Options:* electronic application, early admission, deferred entrance. *Application fee:* $30. *Required:* high school transcript, minimum 2.5 GPA. *Application deadlines:* rolling (freshmen), rolling (out-of-state freshmen), rolling (transfers). *Notification:* continuous (freshmen), continuous (out-of-state freshmen), continuous (transfers).

Freshman Application Contact Ms. Ronda Russell, Director of New Student Services, Montana State University, PO Box 172190, Bozeman, MT 59717-2190. *Phone:* 406-994-2452. *Toll-free phone:* 888-MSU-CATS. *Fax:* 406-994-1923. *E-mail:* admissions@montana.edu. *Web site:* http://www.montana.edu/.

Montana State University Billings
Billings, Montana

- **State-supported** comprehensive, founded 1927, part of Montana University System
- **Urban** 92-acre campus
- **Endowment** $15.6 million
- **Coed** 4,789 undergraduate students, 73% full-time, 61% women, 39% men
- **Moderately difficult** entrance level, 97% of applicants were admitted

Undergraduates 3,473 full-time, 1,316 part-time. Students come from 45 states and territories; 12 other countries; 9% are from out of state; 0.8% Black or African American, non-Hispanic/Latino; 4% Hispanic/Latino; 1% Asian, non-Hispanic/Latino; 6% American Indian or Alaska Native, non-Hispanic/Latino; 4% Race/ethnicity unknown; 0.2% international; 10% transferred in; 13% live on campus. *Retention:* 56% of full-time freshmen returned.

Freshmen *Admission:* 1,712 applied, 1,661 admitted, 979 enrolled. *Average high school GPA:* 3.1. *Test scores:* SAT critical reading scores over 500: 50%; SAT math scores over 500: 54%; SAT critical reading scores over 600: 17%; SAT math scores over 600: 17%; SAT critical reading scores over 700: 4%.

Faculty *Total:* 290, 53% full-time. *Student/faculty ratio:* 20:1.

Academics *Calendar:* semesters. *Degrees:* certificates, associate, bachelor's, master's, and postbachelor's certificates. *Special study options:* academic remediation for entering students, accelerated degree program, adult/continuing education programs, advanced placement credit, cooperative education, distance learning, double majors, English as a second language, external degree program, honors programs, independent study, internships, off-campus study, part-time degree program, services for LD students, study abroad, summer session for credit. *ROTC:* Army (b).

Computers on Campus 1,500 computers/terminals and 1,500 ports are available on campus for general student use. Students can access the following: campus intranet, computer help desk, free student e-mail accounts, online (class) grades, online (class) registration, online (class) schedules, online degree programs. Campuswide network is available. 95% of college-owned or -operated housing units are wired for high-speed Internet access. Wireless service is available via classrooms, computer labs, dorm rooms, libraries, student centers.

Student Life *Housing:* on-campus residence required for freshman year. *Options:* coed, men-only, women-only, disabled students. Campus housing is university owned. Freshman applicants given priority for college housing. *Activities and organizations:* drama/theater group, student-run newspaper, radio station, choral group, Art Student League, Band Club, Inter-Varsity Christian Fellowship, Residence Hall Association, Student Council for Exceptional Children. *Campus security:* 24-hour emergency response devices and patrols, late-night transport/escort service, controlled dormitory access. *Student services:* health clinic, personal/psychological counseling, women's center, legal services.

Athletics Member NCAA. All Division II. *Intercollegiate sports:* baseball M, basketball M(s)/W(s), cross-country running M(s)/W(s), golf M/W, soccer M(s)/W(s), softball W, tennis M(s)/W(s), volleyball W(s). *Intramural sports:* baseball M/W, basketball M/W, bowling M/W, cheerleading M/W, cross-country running M/W, football M/W, golf M/W, racquetball M/W, skiing (cross-country) M/W, soccer M/W, softball M/W, swimming and diving M/W, table tennis M/W, tennis M/W, track and field M/W, volleyball M/W.

Standardized Tests *Required:* SAT or ACT (for admission).

Costs (2010–11) *Tuition:* state resident $3988 full-time, $146 per credit hour part-time; nonresident $15,235 full-time, $423 per credit hour part-time. Full-time tuition and fees vary according to course load, degree level, and location. Part-time tuition and fees vary according to course load, degree level, and location. *Required fees:* $1254 full-time. *Room and board:* $5620. Room and board charges vary according to board plan and housing facility. *Payment plan:* installment. *Waivers:* senior citizens and employees or children of employees.

Financial Aid Of all full-time matriculated undergraduates who enrolled in 2008, 2,447 applied for aid, 2,021 were judged to have need, 48 had their need fully met. 208 Federal Work-Study jobs (averaging $1340). 57 state and other part-time jobs (averaging $1136). In 2008, 89 non-need-based awards were made. *Average percent of need met:* 70%. *Average financial aid package:* $9529. *Average need-based loan:* $3465. *Average need-based gift aid:* $4935. *Average non-need-based aid:* $2122. *Average indebtedness upon graduation:* $24,026.

Applying *Options:* electronic application, early admission, deferred entrance. *Application fee:* $30. *Required:* high school transcript, minimum 2.5 GPA. *Application deadlines:* 7/1 (freshmen), rolling (transfers). *Notification:* continuous (freshmen), continuous (transfers).

Freshman Application Contact Ms. Shelly Andersen, Associate Director of Admissions, Montana State University Billings, 1500 University Drive, Billings, MT 59101. *Phone:* 406-657-2158. *Toll-free phone:* 800-565-6782. *Fax:* 406-657-2302. *E-mail:* sandersen@msubillings.edu. *Web site:* http://www.msubillings.edu/.

Montana State University–Northern

Havre, Montana

Director of Admissions Ms. Rosalie Spinler, Director of Admissions, Montana State University–Northern, PO Box 7751, Havre, MT 59501-7751. *Phone:* 406-265-3704. *Toll-free phone:* 800-662-6132. *Web site:* http://www.msun.edu/.

Montana Tech of The University of Montana

Butte, Montana

- **State-supported** comprehensive, founded 1895, part of Montana University System
- **Small-town** 56-acre campus
- **Endowment** $21.1 million
- **Coed** 2,713 undergraduate students, 83% full-time, 40% women, 60% men
- **Moderately difficult** entrance level, 90% of applicants were admitted

Undergraduates 2,245 full-time, 468 part-time. Students come from 34 states and territories; 11 other countries; 12% are from out of state; 0.6% Black or African American, non-Hispanic/Latino; 2% Hispanic/Latino; 0.9% Asian, non-Hispanic/Latino; 2% American Indian or Alaska Native, non-Hispanic/Latino; 10% Race/ethnicity unknown; 8% international; 7% transferred in; 11% live on campus. *Retention:* 66% of full-time freshmen returned.

Freshmen *Admission:* 831 applied, 745 admitted, 514 enrolled. *Average high school GPA:* 3.38. *Test scores:* SAT critical reading scores over 500: 65%; SAT math scores over 500: 83%; SAT writing scores over 500: 50%; ACT scores over 18: 95%; SAT critical reading scores over 600: 15%; SAT math scores over 600: 50%; SAT writing scores over 600: 15%; ACT scores over 24: 53%; SAT critical reading scores over 700: 1%; SAT math scores over 700: 5%; SAT writing scores over 700: 1%; ACT scores over 30: 9%.

Faculty *Total:* 214, 63% full-time. *Student/faculty ratio:* 15:1.

Academics *Calendar:* semesters. *Degrees:* certificates, diplomas, associate, bachelor's, master's, and postbachelor's certificates. *Special study options:* academic remediation for entering students, adult/continuing education programs, advanced placement credit, cooperative education, distance learning, double majors, external degree program, honors programs, independent study, internships, part-time degree program, services for LD students, student-designed majors, summer session for credit. *Unusual degree programs:* engineering.

Computers on Campus 522 computers/terminals are available on campus for general student use. Students can access the following: campus intranet, computer help desk, free student e-mail accounts, online (class) grades, online (class) registration, online (class) schedules. Campuswide network is available. 100% of college-owned or -operated housing units are wired for high-speed Internet access. Wireless service is available via entire campus.

Student Life *Housing:* on-campus residence required for freshman year. *Options:* coed, disabled students. Campus housing is university owned. Freshman campus housing is guaranteed. *Activities and organizations:* student-run newspaper, radio station, choral group, Health Physical Education Recreation Hooligans , Ski/Snowboard Club, Circle K, Mining Team, Gaming Club. *Campus security:* 24-hour patrols, controlled dormitory access. *Student services:* health clinic, personal/psychological counseling.

Athletics Member NAIA. *Intercollegiate sports:* basketball M(s)/W(s), football M(s), golf M(s)/W(s), volleyball W(s). *Intramural sports:* basketball M/W, cheerleading M(c)/W(c), football M/W, ice hockey M(c)/W(c), racquetball M/W, rugby M(c)/W(c), skiing (cross-country) M(c)/W(c), skiing (downhill) M(c)/W(c), softball M(c)/W(c), volleyball M/W.

Standardized Tests *Required:* SAT or ACT (for admission).

Costs (2010–11) *Tuition:* state resident $4696 full-time, $262 per credit part-time; nonresident $15,819 full-time, $725 per credit part-time. Full-time tuition and fees vary according to course load, degree level, location, program, and student level. Part-time tuition and fees vary according to course load, degree level, location, program, and student level. *Required fees:* $1466 full-time. *Room and board:* $6924; room only: $3084. Room and board charges vary according to board plan. *Payment plans:* installment, deferred payment. *Waivers:* employees or children of employees.

Financial Aid Of all full-time matriculated undergraduates who enrolled in 2008, 1,539 applied for aid, 1,213 were judged to have need, 342 had their need fully met. In 2008, 299 non-need-based awards were made. *Average percent of need met:* 81%. *Average financial aid package:* $9391. *Average need-based loan:* $3362. *Average need-based gift aid:* $4891. *Average non-need-based aid:* $2353. *Average indebtedness upon graduation:* $23,000.

Applying *Options:* electronic application, deferred entrance. *Application fee:* $30. *Required:* high school transcript, proof of immunization. *Required for some:* minimum 2.5 GPA. *Application deadlines:* rolling (freshmen), rolling (transfers). *Notification:* continuous (freshmen), continuous (transfers).

Freshman Application Contact Montana Tech of The University of Montana, 1300 West Park Street, Butte, MT 59701-8997. *Phone:* 406-496-4256. *Toll-free phone:* 800-445-TECH Ext. 1. *Web site:* http://www.mtech.edu/.

Rocky Mountain College
Billings, Montana

- **Independent interdenominational** comprehensive, founded 1878
- **Urban** 60-acre campus
- **Endowment** $17.7 million
- **Coed** 1,802 undergraduate students, 98% full-time, 50% women, 50% men
- **Moderately difficult** entrance level, 70% of applicants were admitted

Undergraduates 1,762 full-time, 40 part-time. Students come from 42 states and territories; 17 other countries; 42% are from out of state; 5% transferred in; 53% live on campus. *Retention:* 66% of full-time freshmen returned.
Freshmen *Admission:* 1,236 applied, 862 admitted, 286 enrolled. *Average high school GPA:* 3.33. *Test scores:* SAT critical reading scores over 500: 60%; SAT math scores over 500: 53%; SAT writing scores over 500: 48%; ACT scores over 18: 88%; SAT critical reading scores over 600: 20%; SAT math scores over 600: 14%; SAT writing scores over 600: 13%; ACT scores over 24: 39%; ACT scores over 30: 1%.
Faculty *Total:* 117, 54% full-time, 48% with terminal degrees. *Student/faculty ratio:* 12:1.
Academics *Calendar:* semesters. *Degrees:* associate, bachelor's, and master's. *Special study options:* academic remediation for entering students, accelerated degree program, adult/continuing education programs, advanced placement credit, distance learning, double majors, English as a second language, honors programs, independent study, internships, off-campus study, part-time degree program, services for LD students, student-designed majors, study abroad, summer session for credit. *ROTC:* Army (b). *Unusual degree programs:* 3-2 Athletic Training, Montana State University Billings.
Computers on Campus 129 computers/terminals are available on campus for general student use. Students can access the following: campus intranet, computer help desk, free student e-mail accounts, online (class) grades, online (class) registration, online (class) schedules. Campuswide network is available. 100% of college-owned or -operated housing units are wired for high-speed Internet access. Wireless service is available via entire campus.
Student Life *Housing:* on-campus residence required through sophomore year. *Options:* coed, disabled students. Campus housing is university owned. Freshman campus housing is guaranteed. *Activities and organizations:* drama/theater group, student-run newspaper, choral group, Outdoor Recreation/Climbing Club, Students in Free Enterprise (SIFE), Flight Team/Club, Residence Hall Association, OISTERS, Organization of Interested Students Toward Environmentally Responsible Solutions. *Campus security:* 24-hour emergency response devices, student patrols, controlled dormitory access, security cameras. *Student services:* health clinic, personal/psychological counseling.
Athletics Member NAIA. *Intercollegiate sports:* basketball M(s)/W(s), cheerleading W(s), cross-country running M(s)/W(s), equestrian sports M(c)/W(c), football M(s), golf M(s)/W(s), skiing (downhill) M(s)/W(s), soccer M(s)/W(s), volleyball W(s). *Intramural sports:* basketball M/W, football M, golf M/W, racquetball M/W, skiing (downhill) M/W, soccer M/W, softball M/W, tennis M/W, volleyball M/W.
Standardized Tests *Required:* SAT or ACT (for admission).
Costs (2011–12) *Comprehensive fee:* $29,030 includes full-time tuition ($21,684), mandatory fees ($450), and room and board ($6896). Full-time tuition and fees vary according to course load, degree level, and program. Part-time tuition: $904 per credit. Part-time tuition and fees vary according to course load, degree level, and program. *College room only:* $3264. Room and board charges vary according to board plan and housing facility. *Payment plan:* installment. *Waivers:* employees or children of employees.
Financial Aid Of all full-time matriculated undergraduates who enrolled in 2009, 740 applied for aid, 673 were judged to have need, 154 had their need fully met. 448 Federal Work-Study jobs (averaging $1872). 202 state and other part-time jobs (averaging $1923). In 2009, 149 non-need-based awards were made. *Average percent of need met:* 75%. *Average financial aid package:* $19,651. *Average need-based loan:* $4289. *Average need-based gift aid:* $15,667. *Average non-need-based aid:* $8134. *Average indebtedness upon graduation:* $20,122.
Applying *Options:* electronic application, early admission, early action, deferred entrance. *Application fee:* $35. *Required:* high school transcript, minimum 2.5 GPA. *Required for some:* essay or personal statement, 2 letters of recommendation, interview. *Application deadlines:* rolling (freshmen), rolling (transfers). *Notification:* continuous (freshmen), continuous (transfers).
Freshman Application Contact Mrs. Kelly Edwards, Director of Admissions, Rocky Mountain College, 1511 Poly Drive, Billings, MT 59102. *Phone:* 406-657-1026. *Toll-free phone:* 800-877-6259. *Fax:* 406-259-9751. *E-mail:* admissions@rocky.edu. *Web site:* http://www.rocky.edu/.

Salish Kootenai College
Pablo, Montana

Freshman Application Contact Ms. Jackie Moran, Admissions Officer, Salish Kootenai College, PO Box 70, Pablo, MT 59855-0117. *Phone:* 406-

275-4866. *Fax:* 406-275-4810. *E-mail:* jackie_moran@skc.edu. *Web site:* http://www.skc.edu/.

University of Great Falls
Great Falls, Montana

- **Independent Roman Catholic** comprehensive, founded 1932, administratively affiliated with Providence Services
- **Urban** 40-acre campus
- **Endowment** $7.0 million
- **Coed**
- **Noncompetitive** entrance level

Faculty *Student/faculty ratio:* 12:1.
Academics *Calendar:* semesters. *Degrees:* certificates, associate, bachelor's, and master's.
Student Life *Campus security:* 24-hour emergency response devices and patrols, late-night transport/escort service, controlled dormitory access.
Athletics Member NAIA.
Standardized Tests *Recommended:* SAT or ACT (for admission).
Costs (2010–11) *Comprehensive fee:* $25,568 includes full-time tuition ($17,856), mandatory fees ($1000), and room and board ($6712). Full-time tuition and fees vary according to course load. Part-time tuition: $566 per credit hour. Part-time tuition and fees vary according to course load, location, and program. *College room only:* $3512. Room and board charges vary according to housing facility.
Financial Aid Of all full-time matriculated undergraduates who enrolled in 2009, 428 applied for aid, 428 were judged to have need, 10 had their need fully met. In 2009, 26 non-need-based awards were made. *Average percent of need met:* 60. *Average financial aid package:* $15,294. *Average need-based loan:* $4364. *Average need-based gift aid:* $5238. *Average non-need-based aid:* $9542.
Applying *Options:* electronic application, early admission, deferred entrance. *Required:* high school transcript. *Recommended:* essay or personal statement, interview.
Freshman Application Contact Kelly Braun, Assistant Director of Admissions, University of Great Falls, 1301 20th Street South, Great Falls, MT 59405. *Phone:* 406-791-5202 Ext. 5211. *Toll-free phone:* 800-856-9544. *Fax:* 406-791-5209. *E-mail:* enroll@ugf.edu. *Web site:* http://www.ugf.edu/.

See page 1694 for the College Close-Up.

The University of Montana
Missoula, Montana

Freshman Application Contact Ms. Juana Alcala, Manager, Enrollment Services, The University of Montana, Missoula, MT 59812-0002. *Phone:* 406-243-6266. *Toll-free phone:* 800-462-8636. *Fax:* 406-243-5711. *E-mail:* admiss@umontana.edu. *Web site:* http://www.umt.edu/.

The University of Montana Western
Dillon, Montana

- **State-supported** 4-year, founded 1893
- **Small-town** 30-acre campus
- **Endowment** $3.3 million
- **Coed** 1,365 undergraduate students, 85% full-time, 56% women, 44% men
- **Minimally difficult** entrance level, 82% of applicants were admitted

Undergraduates 1,154 full-time, 211 part-time. Students come from 34 states and territories; 2 other countries; 22% are from out of state; 1% Black or African American, non-Hispanic/Latino; 1% Hispanic/Latino; 0.1% Asian, non-Hispanic/Latino; 3% Native Hawaiian or other Pacific Islander, non-Hispanic/Latino; 2% American Indian or Alaska Native, non-Hispanic/Latino; 3% Race/ethnicity unknown; 0.1% international; 36% transferred in; 25% live on campus. *Retention:* 68% of full-time freshmen returned.
Freshmen *Admission:* 517 applied, 424 admitted, 257 enrolled. *Average high school GPA:* 2.95. *Test scores:* SAT critical reading scores over 500: 28%; SAT math scores over 500: 32%; ACT scores over 18: 71%; SAT critical reading scores over 600: 5%; SAT math scores over 600: 3%; ACT scores over 24: 12%; ACT scores over 30: 1%.
Faculty *Total:* 82, 77% full-time, 66% with terminal degrees. *Student/faculty ratio:* 20:1.
Academics *Calendar:* semesters. *Degrees:* certificates, associate, bachelor's, and postbachelor's certificates. *Special study options:* academic remediation for entering students, adult/continuing education programs, advanced placement credit, cooperative education, distance learning, double majors, honors programs, independent study, internships, off-campus study, part-time degree program, services for LD students, summer session for credit.

Computers on Campus Students can access the following: computer help desk, free student e-mail accounts, online (class) grades, online (class) registration, online (class) schedules. Campuswide network is available. Wireless service is available via entire campus.

Student Life *Housing:* on-campus residence required for freshman year. *Options:* coed, men-only, women-only, disabled students. Campus housing is university owned. Freshman campus housing is guaranteed. *Activities and organizations:* drama/theater group, student-run radio station, choral group, Rodeo Club, Polynesian Club, Ambassadors Club, Humans in Performance, Campus Corp. *Campus security:* 24-hour emergency response devices and patrols, late-night transport/escort service. *Student services:* health clinic, personal/psychological counseling.

Athletics Member NAIA. *Intercollegiate sports:* basketball M(s)/W(s), equestrian sports M(s)/W(s), football M(s), volleyball W(s). *Intramural sports:* basketball M/W, equestrian sports M(c)/W(c), football M/W, racquetball M/W, rock climbing M(c)/W(c), rugby M(c)/W(c), skiing (downhill) M(c)/W(c), softball M/W, ultimate Frisbee M/W, volleyball M/W.

Standardized Tests *Required:* SAT or ACT (for admission).

Costs (2010–11) *Tuition:* state resident $2802 full-time, $117 per credit hour part-time; nonresident $12,098 full-time, $501 per credit hour part-time. Full-time tuition and fees vary according to program and student level. Part-time tuition and fees vary according to program and student level. *Required fees:* $924 full-time, $11 per credit hour part-time, $109 per term part-time. *Room and board:* $5620. Room and board charges vary according to housing facility. *Payment plan:* deferred payment. *Waivers:* senior citizens and employees or children of employees.

Financial Aid Of all full-time matriculated undergraduates who enrolled in 2008, 881 applied for aid, 741 were judged to have need, 20 had their need fully met. 79 Federal Work-Study jobs (averaging $2808). 126 state and other part-time jobs (averaging $2382). In 2008, 5 non-need-based awards were made. *Average percent of need met:* 17%. *Average financial aid package:* $2858. *Average need-based loan:* $3774. *Average need-based gift aid:* $2525. *Average non-need-based aid:* $1786. *Average indebtedness upon graduation:* $21,969.

Applying *Options:* electronic application, early admission, deferred entrance. *Required:* high school transcript. *Application deadlines:* rolling (freshmen), rolling (transfers). *Notification:* continuous (freshmen), continuous (transfers).

Freshman Application Contact Mrs. Janet Jones, Admissions Evaluator, The University of Montana Western, 710 South Atlantic, Dillon, MT 59725. *Phone:* 406-683-7331. *Toll-free phone:* 866-869-6668 (in-state); 877-683-7493 (out-of-state). *Fax:* 406-683-7493. *E-mail:* j_jones@umwestern.edu. *Web site:* http://www.umwestern.edu/.

NEBRASKA

Bellevue University
Bellevue, Nebraska

Freshman Application Contact Scott Kizzire, Director of Undergraduate Enrollment, Bellevue University, 1000 Galvin Road South, Bellevue, NE 68005-3098. *Phone:* 402-557-7235. *Toll-free phone:* 800-756-7920. *E-mail:* scott.kizzire@bellevue.edu. *Web site:* http://www.bellevue.edu/.

Chadron State College
Chadron, Nebraska

Freshman Application Contact Ms. Tena Cook, Director of Admissions, Chadron State College, 1000 Main Street, Chadron, NE 69337-2690. *Phone:* 308-432-6263. *Toll-free phone:* 800-242-3766. *Fax:* 308-432-6229. *E-mail:* inquire@csc.edu. *Web site:* http://www.csc.edu/.

Clarkson College
Omaha, Nebraska

- **Independent** comprehensive, founded 1888
- **Urban** 3-acre campus
- **Endowment** $937,115
- **Coed, primarily women** 658 undergraduate students, 100% full-time, 90% women, 10% men
- **Moderately difficult** entrance level, 55% of applicants were admitted

Undergraduates 658 full-time. Students come from 33 states and territories; 33% are from out of state; 438% transferred in; 14% live on campus. *Retention:* 85% of full-time freshmen returned.

Freshmen *Admission:* 87 applied, 48 admitted, 39 enrolled. *Test scores:* ACT scores over 18: 91%; ACT scores over 24: 30%.

Faculty *Total:* 101, 48% full-time. *Student/faculty ratio:* 8:1.

Academics *Calendar:* semesters. *Degrees:* certificates, associate, bachelor's, master's, and post-master's certificates. *Special study options:* accelerated degree program, adult/continuing education programs, advanced placement credit, cooperative education, distance learning, double majors, external degree program, independent study, internships, part-time degree program, study abroad, summer session for credit. *ROTC:* Army (c), Air Force (c).

Computers on Campus 40 computers/terminals are available on campus for general student use. Students can access the following: campus intranet, computer help desk, free student e-mail accounts, online (class) grades, online (class) registration, online (class) schedules. Campuswide network is available. 100% of college-owned or -operated housing units are wired for high-speed Internet access. Wireless service is available via entire campus.

Student Life *Housing options:* coed. Campus housing is university owned. *Activities and organizations:* student-run newspaper, Student Nurses Association, Radiology Student Association, Student Government Association, Student Ambassadors, Physical Therapist Assistant Student Association. *Campus security:* 24-hour emergency response devices and patrols, student patrols, late-night transport/escort service, controlled dormitory access. *Student services:* health clinic, personal/psychological counseling.

Athletics *Intramural sports:* bowling M/W, volleyball M/W.

Standardized Tests *Required for some:* SAT or ACT (for admission).

Costs (2010–11) *One-time required fee:* $100. *Tuition:* $10,920 full-time, $420 per credit hour part-time. Full-time tuition and fees vary according to course load and program. Part-time tuition and fees vary according to course load and program. *Required fees:* $910 full-time. *Room only:* $4400. *Payment plan:* installment. *Waivers:* employees or children of employees.

Financial Aid Of all full-time matriculated undergraduates who enrolled in 2001, 109 applied for aid, 94 were judged to have need, 22 had their need fully met. 40 Federal Work-Study jobs (averaging $2500). In 2001, 15 non-need-based awards were made. *Average percent of need met:* 71%. *Average financial aid package:* $8291. *Average need-based loan:* $3365. *Average need-based gift aid:* $5434. *Average non-need-based aid:* $4374. *Average indebtedness upon graduation:* $13,931.

Applying *Options:* electronic application, deferred entrance. *Application fee:* $35. *Required:* essay or personal statement, high school transcript, minimum 2.5 GPA. *Required for some:* minimum 3 GPA, 2 letters of recommendation. *Recommended:* minimum 3 GPA. *Application deadlines:* rolling (freshmen), rolling (out-of-state freshmen), rolling (transfers). *Notification:* continuous (freshmen), continuous (out-of-state freshmen), continuous (transfers).

Freshman Application Contact Clarkson College, 101 South 42nd Street, Omaha, NE 68131-2739. *Phone:* 402-552-3100. *Toll-free phone:* 800-647-5500. *Web site:* http://www.clarksoncollege.edu/.

College of Saint Mary
Omaha, Nebraska

- **Independent Roman Catholic** comprehensive, founded 1923
- **Urban** 25-acre campus
- **Endowment** $6.8 million
- **Women only** 814 undergraduate students, 81% full-time
- **Minimally difficult** entrance level, 45% of applicants were admitted

Undergraduates 658 full-time, 156 part-time. Students come from 24 states and territories; 11 other countries; 12% are from out of state; 10% Black or African American, non-Hispanic/Latino; 11% Hispanic/Latino; 1% Asian, non-Hispanic/Latino; 0.3% Native Hawaiian or other Pacific Islander, non-Hispanic/Latino; 0.9% American Indian or Alaska Native, non-Hispanic/Latino; 1% Two or more races, non-Hispanic/Latino; 0.1% Race/ethnicity unknown; 0.8% international; 19% transferred in; 30% live on campus. *Retention:* 63% of full-time freshmen returned.

Freshmen *Admission:* 419 applied, 190 admitted, 95 enrolled. *Average high school GPA:* 3.46. *Test scores:* ACT scores over 18: 94%; ACT scores over 24: 15%; ACT scores over 30: 1%.

Faculty *Total:* 188, 29% full-time, 31% with terminal degrees. *Student/faculty ratio:* 14:1.

Academics *Calendar:* semesters. *Degrees:* certificates, associate, bachelor's, master's, doctoral-research/scholarship, and postbachelor's certificates. *Special study options:* academic remediation for entering students, accelerated degree program, advanced placement credit, distance learning, double majors, honors programs, independent study, internships, part-time degree program, services for LD students, study abroad, summer session for credit. *ROTC:* Army (c), Air Force (c). *Unusual degree programs:* 3-2 engineering with University of Nebraska - Omaha.

Computers on Campus 170 computers/terminals and 300 ports are available on campus for general student use. Students can access the following: campus intranet, computer help desk, free student e-mail accounts, online (class) grades, online (class) registration, online (class) schedules. Campuswide network is available. 100% of college-owned or -operated housing units are wired for high-speed Internet access. Wireless service is available via entire campus.

Student Life *Housing:* on-campus residence required through sophomore year. *Options:* women-only. Campus housing is university owned. Freshman campus housing is guaranteed. *Activities and organizations:* drama/theater group, choral group, Students Against Violence (SAV), Campus Activities Board, Student Education Association of Nebraska, Student Occupational Therapy Club, Student Nurses Association. *Campus security:* 24-hour emergency response devices and patrols, late-night transport/escort service, controlled dormitory access, surveillance cameras at residence hall entrances; CSM Alert Text Message System. *Student services:* health clinic, personal/psychological counseling.

Athletics Member NAIA. *Intercollegiate sports:* basketball W(s), cross-country running W(s), golf W(s), soccer W(s), softball W(s), swimming and diving W(s), volleyball W(s). *Intramural sports:* basketball W, bowling W, volleyball W.

Standardized Tests *Required:* SAT or ACT (for admission).

Costs (2011–12) *Comprehensive fee:* $31,050 includes full-time tuition ($23,870), mandatory fees ($480), and room and board ($6700). Full-time tuition and fees vary according to location and program. Part-time tuition: $785 per credit. Part-time tuition and fees vary according to class time, course load, location, and program. *Required fees:* $16 per credit part-time. *Payment plans:* installment, deferred payment. *Waivers:* senior citizens and employees or children of employees.

Financial Aid Of all full-time matriculated undergraduates who enrolled in 2009, 710 applied for aid, 682 were judged to have need, 49 had their need fully met. 178 Federal Work-Study jobs (averaging $1200). 11 state and other part-time jobs (averaging $6400). In 2009, 23 non-need-based awards were made. *Average percent of need met:* 61%. *Average financial aid package:* $16,517. *Average need-based loan:* $5305. *Average need-based gift aid:* $11,538. *Average non-need-based aid:* $5596. *Average indebtedness upon graduation:* $30,325.

Applying *Options:* electronic application. *Application fee:* $30. *Required:* high school transcript, minimum 2 GPA, Students graduating high school within the past five years with less than 12 transfer credits are required to submit ACT scores. The minimum ACT score for admission is 18. *Required for some:* essay or personal statement, 2 letters of recommendation, interview. *Application deadlines:* rolling (freshmen), rolling (transfers). *Notification:* continuous (freshmen), continuous (transfers).

Freshman Application Contact Mr. Joe Szejk, Vice President for Enrollment Services and Marketing, College of Saint Mary, 7000 Mercy Road, Omaha, NE 68106. *Phone:* 402-399-2355. *Toll-free phone:* 800-926-5534. *Fax:* 402-399-2412. *E-mail:* enroll@csm.edu. *Web site:* http://www.csm.edu/.

Concordia University, Nebraska

Seward, Nebraska

- **Independent** comprehensive, founded 1894, affiliated with Lutheran Church–Missouri Synod
- **Small-town** 120-acre campus with easy access to Omaha
- **Endowment** $23.0 million
- **Coed**
- **Moderately difficult** entrance level

Faculty *Student/faculty ratio:* 13:1.

Academics *Calendar:* 4-4-1. *Degrees:* bachelor's, master's, and postbachelor's certificates.

Student Life *Campus security:* 24-hour emergency response devices and patrols, controlled dormitory access.

Athletics Member NAIA.

Standardized Tests *Required:* SAT or ACT (for admission).

Costs (2010–11) *Comprehensive fee:* $27,935 includes full-time tuition ($21,940), mandatory fees ($175), and room and board ($5820). Part-time tuition: $685 per credit hour. *College room only:* $2470. Room and board charges vary according to board plan and housing facility.

Financial Aid *Of all full-time matriculated undergraduates who enrolled in 2009,* 962 applied for aid, 821 were judged to have need, 234 had their need fully met. 116 Federal Work-Study jobs (averaging $960). *In 2009,* 116 non-need-based awards were made. *Average percent of need met:* 79. *Average financial aid package:* $17,208. *Average need-based loan:* $4374. *Average need-based gift aid:* $13,086. *Average non-need-based aid:* $8914. *Average indebtedness upon graduation:* $21,941.

Applying *Options:* deferred entrance. *Required:* high school transcript. *Recommended:* interview.

Freshman Application Contact Mr. Aaron W. Roberts, Director of Undergraduate Recruitment, Concordia University, Nebraska, 800 North Columbia Avenue, Seward, NE 68434-1556. *Phone:* 800-535-5494 Ext. 7233. *Toll-free phone:* 800-535-5494. *Fax:* 402-643-4073. *E-mail:* admiss@cune.edu. *Web site:* http://www.cune.edu/.

Creative Center

Omaha, Nebraska

- **Proprietary** primarily 2-year, founded 1993
- **Urban** 2-acre campus
- **Coed**

Faculty *Total:* 16, 25% full-time. *Student/faculty ratio:* 19:1.

Academics *Calendar:* semesters. *Degrees:* associate and bachelor's. *Special study options:* distance learning, part-time degree program, services for LD students.

Computers on Campus 8 computers/terminals are available on campus for general student use. Students can access the following: computer help desk. Wireless service is available via entire campus.

Student Life *Housing:* college housing not available.

Costs (2011–12) *Tuition:* $23,600 full-time. Full-time tuition and fees vary according to course load and student level. Part-time tuition and fees vary according to course load and student level.

Applying *Application fee:* $100. *Required:* essay or personal statement, high school transcript, 1 letter of recommendation, interview, portfolio. *Application deadlines:* rolling (freshmen), rolling (out-of-state freshmen), rolling (transfers). *Notification:* continuous (freshmen), continuous (out-of-state freshmen), continuous (transfers).

Freshman Application Contact Mr. Richard Caldwell, Director of Admissions, Creative Center, 10850 Emmet Street, Omaha, NE 68164. *Phone:* 402-898-1000 Ext. 216. *Toll-free phone:* 888-898-1789. *Fax:* 402-898-1301. *E-mail:* admission@creativecenter.edu. *Web site:* http://www.creativecenter.edu/.

Creighton University

Omaha, Nebraska

- **Independent Roman Catholic (Jesuit)** university, founded 1878
- **Urban** 130-acre campus with easy access to Omaha, NE
- **Endowment** $253.0 million
- **Coed** 4,206 undergraduate students, 93% full-time, 59% women, 41% men
- **Moderately difficult** entrance level, 78% of applicants were admitted

Undergraduates 3,929 full-time, 277 part-time. Students come from 53 states and territories; 42 other countries; 64% are from out of state; 3% Black or African American, non-Hispanic/Latino; 5% Hispanic/Latino; 9% Asian, non-Hispanic/Latino; 0.3% Native Hawaiian or other Pacific Islander, non-Hispanic/Latino; 0.7% American Indian or Alaska Native, non-Hispanic/Latino; 3% Two or more races, non-Hispanic/Latino; 0.8% Race/ethnicity unknown; 2% international; 1% transferred in; 61% live on campus. *Retention:* 88% of full-time freshmen returned.

Freshmen *Admission:* 5,064 applied, 3,965 admitted, 1,030 enrolled. *Average high school GPA:* 3.76. *Test scores:* SAT critical reading scores over 500: 84%; SAT math scores over 500: 92%; SAT writing scores over 500: 82%; ACT scores over 18: 100%; SAT critical reading scores over 600: 44%; SAT math scores over 600: 54%; SAT writing scores over 600: 39%; ACT scores over 24: 79%; SAT critical reading scores over 700: 8%; SAT math scores over 700: 12%; SAT writing scores over 700: 6%; ACT scores over 30: 24%.

Faculty *Total:* 740, 71% full-time, 74% with terminal degrees. *Student/faculty ratio:* 11:1.

Academics *Calendar:* semesters. *Degrees:* certificates, diplomas, associate, bachelor's, master's, doctoral-professional, and doctoral-research/scholarship. *Special study options:* academic remediation for entering students, accelerated degree program, adult/continuing education programs, advanced placement credit, distance learning, double majors, English as a second language, external degree program, freshman honors college, honors programs, independent study, internships, off-campus study, part-time degree program, services for LD students, study abroad, summer session for credit. *ROTC:* Army (b), Air Force (c). *Unusual degree programs:* 3-2 engineering with University of Detroit Mercy.

Computers on Campus 550 computers/terminals are available on campus for general student use. Students can access the following: campus intranet, computer help desk, free student e-mail accounts, online (class) grades, online (class) registration, online (class) schedules, financial aid information. Campuswide network is available. 100% of college-owned or -operated housing units are wired for high-speed Internet access. Wireless service is available via entire campus.

Student Life *Housing:* on-campus residence required through sophomore year. *Options:* coed, women-only, disabled students. Campus housing is university owned. Freshman campus housing is guaranteed. *Activities and organizations:* drama/theater group, student-run newspaper, choral group, Birdcage (Athletic Boosters), Pre-Medical Society, Student Nurses Association, Alpha Kappa Psi (business majors), Omicron Delta Kappa (Greek Leadership), national fraternities, national sororities. *Campus security:* 24-hour emergency response devices and patrols, student patrols, late-night transport/escort service, controlled dormitory access. *Student services:* health clinic, personal/psychological counseling, women's center.

Athletics Member NCAA. All Division I. *Intercollegiate sports:* baseball M(s), basketball M(s)/W(s), crew W(s), cross-country running M(s)/W(s), golf M(s)/W(s), soccer M(s)/W(s), softball W(s), tennis M(s)/W(s), volleyball W(s). *Intramural sports:* basketball M/W, crew M(c), football M/W, golf M/W, lacrosse M(c), racquetball M/W, rugby M(c), soccer M/W, tennis M/W, ultimate Frisbee M/W, volleyball M/W, weight lifting M(c)/W(c).

Standardized Tests *Required:* SAT or ACT (for admission).

Costs (2010–11) *Comprehensive fee:* $39,742 includes full-time tuition ($29,226), mandatory fees ($1352), and room and board ($9164). Full-time tuition and fees vary according to degree level. Part-time tuition: $913 per credit hour. Part-time tuition and fees vary according to degree level. *College room only:* $5220. Room and board charges vary according to board plan and housing facility. *Payment plan:* installment. *Waivers:* adult students and employees or children of employees.

Financial Aid Of all full-time matriculated undergraduates who enrolled in 2009, 2,761 applied for aid, 2,342 were judged to have need, 1,035 had their need fully met. 954 Federal Work-Study jobs (averaging $2022). In 2009, 1203 non-need-based awards were made. *Average percent of need met:* 90%. *Average financial aid package:* $25,122. *Average need-based loan:* $5902. *Average need-based gift aid:* $19,622. *Average non-need-based aid:* $12,524. *Average indebtedness upon graduation:* $32,152.

Applying *Options:* electronic application, deferred entrance. *Application fee:* $40. *Required:* essay or personal statement, high school transcript, minimum 2.75 GPA, 1 letter of recommendation. *Application deadlines:* 2/15 (freshmen), 8/1 (transfers). *Notification:* continuous (freshmen), continuous (transfers).

Freshman Application Contact Mr. William L. Pierce, Director of Admissions and Scholarships, Creighton University, 2500 California Plaza, Omaha, NE 68178-0001. *Phone:* 402-280-2703. *Toll-free phone:* 800-282-5835. *Fax:* 402-280-2685. *E-mail:* williampierce@creighton.edu. *Web site:* http://www.creighton.edu/.

Doane College
Crete, Nebraska

- **Independent** comprehensive, founded 1872, affiliated with United Church of Christ
- **Small-town** 300-acre campus with easy access to Omaha
- **Endowment** $71.2 million
- **Coed** 1,049 undergraduate students, 99% full-time, 51% women, 49% men
- **Moderately difficult** entrance level, 83% of applicants were admitted

Undergraduates 1,042 full-time, 7 part-time. Students come from 23 states and territories; 1 other country; 18% are from out of state; 3% Black or African American, non-Hispanic/Latino; 5% Hispanic/Latino; 1% Asian, non-Hispanic/Latino; 0.3% Native Hawaiian or other Pacific Islander, non-Hispanic/Latino; 0.6% American Indian or Alaska Native, non-Hispanic/Latino; 1% Two or more races, non-Hispanic/Latino; 3% Race/ethnicity unknown; 0.9% international; 4% transferred in; 82% live on campus. *Retention:* 77% of full-time freshmen returned.

Freshmen *Admission:* 1,479 applied, 1,221 admitted, 329 enrolled. *Average high school GPA:* 3.41. *Test scores:* ACT scores over 18: 95%; ACT scores over 24: 39%; ACT scores over 30: 9%.

Faculty *Total:* 123, 58% full-time, 65% with terminal degrees. *Student/faculty ratio:* 12:1.

Academics *Calendar:* 4-1-4. *Degrees:* bachelor's and master's (non-traditional undergraduate programs and graduate programs offered at Lincoln campus). *Special study options:* advanced placement credit, cooperative education, double majors, English as a second language, honors programs, independent study, internships, off-campus study, student-designed majors, study abroad, summer session for credit. *ROTC:* Army (c), Air Force (c). *Unusual degree programs:* 3-2 engineering with Columbia University, Washington University in St. Louis; forestry with Duke University; environmental studies with Duke University.

Computers on Campus 250 computers/terminals and 1,000 ports are available on campus for general student use. Students can access the following: campus intranet, computer help desk, free student e-mail accounts, online (class) grades, online (class) registration, online (class) schedules. Campuswide network is available. 100% of college-owned or -operated housing units are wired for high-speed Internet access. Wireless service is available via entire campus.

Student Life *Housing:* on-campus residence required through senior year. *Options:* coed, women-only. Campus housing is university owned. Freshman campus housing is guaranteed. *Activities and organizations:* drama/theater group, student-run newspaper, radio and television station, choral group, marching band, Student Activities Council, Hansen Leadership Program, band/

choir, Doane Ambassadors, Doane Art League. *Campus security:* 24-hour emergency response devices and patrols, student patrols, late-night transport/escort service, controlled dormitory access, evening patrols by trained security personnel. *Student services:* health clinic, personal/psychological counseling.

Athletics Member NAIA. *Intercollegiate sports:* baseball M(s), basketball M(s)/W(s), cross-country running M(s)/W(s), football M(s), golf M(s)/W(s), soccer M(s)/W(s), softball W(s), tennis M/W, track and field M(s)/W(s), volleyball W(s). *Intramural sports:* baseball M(c)/W(c), basketball M/W, bowling M/W, football M/W, golf M/W, ice hockey M, racquetball M(c)/W(c), softball M/W, swimming and diving M/W, table tennis M(c)/W(c), tennis M/W, volleyball M/W, water polo M/W.

Standardized Tests *Required:* SAT or ACT (for admission).

Costs (2010–11) *Comprehensive fee:* $28,630 includes full-time tuition ($21,570), mandatory fees ($600), and room and board ($6460). Full-time tuition and fees vary according to location. Part-time tuition: $720 per credit hour. Part-time tuition and fees vary according to course load and location. *College room only:* $2650. Room and board charges vary according to board plan, housing facility, and location. *Payment plan:* installment. *Waivers:* senior citizens and employees or children of employees.

Financial Aid Of all full-time matriculated undergraduates who enrolled in 2009, 947 applied for aid, 833 were judged to have need, 283 had their need fully met. In 2009, 71 non-need-based awards were made. *Average percent of need met:* 86%. *Average financial aid package:* $18,025. *Average need-based loan:* $4375. *Average need-based gift aid:* $13,741. *Average non-need-based aid:* $11,016. *Average indebtedness upon graduation:* $20,748.

Applying *Options:* electronic application, early admission, deferred entrance. *Required:* high school transcript, 2 letters of recommendation. *Required for some:* interview. *Recommended:* minimum 2 GPA. *Application deadlines:* rolling (freshmen), rolling (transfers). *Notification:* continuous (freshmen), continuous (transfers).

Freshman Application Contact Doane College, 1014 Boswell Avenue, Crete, NE 68333-2430. *Phone:* 800-333-6263. *Toll-free phone:* 800-333-6263. *Web site:* http://www.doane.edu/.

Grace University
Omaha, Nebraska

Freshman Application Contact Angela Wayman, Director of Admissions, Grace University, 1311 South Ninth Street, Omaha, NE 68108. *Phone:* 402-449-2831. *Toll-free phone:* 800-383-1422. *Fax:* 402-341-9587. *E-mail:* admissions@graceuniversity.com. *Web site:* http://www.graceuniversity.edu/.

Hastings College
Hastings, Nebraska

Freshman Application Contact Ms. Mary Molliconi, Director of Admissions, Hastings College, 710 North Turner Avenue, Hastings, NE 68901-7621. *Phone:* 402-461-7320. *Toll-free phone:* 800-532-7642. *Fax:* 402-461-7490. *E-mail:* mmolliconi@hastings.edu. *Web site:* http://www.hastings.edu/.

ITT Technical Institute
Omaha, Nebraska

- **Proprietary** primarily 2-year, founded 1991, part of ITT Educational Services, Inc.
- **Urban** campus
- **Coed**
- **Minimally difficult** entrance level

Academics *Calendar:* quarters. *Degrees:* associate and bachelor's.

Student Life *Housing:* college housing not available.

Freshman Application Contact Director of Recruitment, ITT Technical Institute, 9814 M Street, Omaha, NE 68127-2056. *Phone:* 402-331-2900. *Toll-free phone:* 800-677-9260. *Web site:* http://www.itt-tech.edu/.

Kaplan University, Lincoln
Lincoln, Nebraska

- **Proprietary** primarily 2-year, founded 1884
- **Urban** campus
- **Coed**

Academics *Calendar:* quarters. *Degrees:* certificates, diplomas, associate, and bachelor's.

Freshman Application Contact Kaplan University, Lincoln, 1821 K Street, Lincoln, NE 68501-2826. *Phone:* 402-474-5315. *Web site:* http://www.lincoln.kaplanuniversity.edu/.

Kaplan University, Omaha

Omaha, Nebraska

- **Proprietary** primarily 2-year, founded 1891
- **Urban** campus
- **Coed**

Academics *Calendar:* quarters. *Degrees:* certificates, diplomas, associate, and bachelor's.
Freshman Application Contact Kaplan University, Omaha, 5425 North 103rd Street, Omaha, NE 68134. *Phone:* 402-572-8500. *Toll-free phone:* 800-642-1456. *Web site:* http://www.omaha.kaplanuniversity.edu/.

Midland Lutheran College

Fremont, Nebraska

Freshman Application Contact Mr. Todd Hansen, Associate Director of Admissions, Midland Lutheran College, Fremont, NE 68025-4200. *Phone:* 402-941-6504. *Toll-free phone:* 800-642-8382 Ext. 6501. *Fax:* 402-941-6513. *E-mail:* admissions@mlc.edu. *Web site:* http://www.mlc.edu/.

Nebraska Christian College

Papillion, Nebraska

Freshman Application Contact Ms. Alisha Livengood, Associate Director of Admissions, Nebraska Christian College, 12550 South 114th Steet, Papillion, NE 68046. *Phone:* 402-935-9407. *Web site:* http://www.nechristian.edu/.

Nebraska Methodist College

Omaha, Nebraska

- **Independent** comprehensive, founded 1891, affiliated with United Methodist Church
- **Urban** 5-acre campus
- **Coed, primarily women**
- **Moderately difficult** entrance level

Faculty *Student/faculty ratio:* 9:1.
Academics *Calendar:* semesters. *Degrees:* certificates, associate, bachelor's, master's, and post-master's certificates.
Student Life *Campus security:* 24-hour emergency response devices, late-night transport/escort service, controlled dormitory access.
Standardized Tests *Required:* SAT or ACT (for admission).
Costs (2010–11) *One-time required fee:* $60. *Tuition:* $11,160 full-time, $465 per credit hour part-time. Full-time tuition and fees vary according to degree level and program. Part-time tuition and fees vary according to degree level and program. *Required fees:* $610 full-time, $20 per credit hour part-time. *Room only:* $5770. Room and board charges vary according to housing facility.
Financial Aid *Of all full-time matriculated undergraduates who enrolled in 2009,* 382 applied for aid, 314 were judged to have need, 32 had their need fully met. 17 Federal Work-Study jobs (averaging $1890). *In 2009,* 41 non-need-based awards were made. *Average percent of need met:* 51. *Average financial aid package:* $8382. *Average need-based loan:* $3913. *Average need-based gift aid:* $6010. *Average non-need-based aid:* $3518. *Average indebtedness upon graduation:* $29,132.
Applying *Options:* electronic application, deferred entrance. *Application fee:* $25. *Required:* essay or personal statement, high school transcript, minimum 2.5 GPA.
Freshman Application Contact Sara Bonney, Director of Enrollment Services, Nebraska Methodist College, 720 North 87th Street, Omaha, NE 68114. *Phone:* 402-354-7111. *Toll-free phone:* 800-335-5510. *Fax:* 402-354-7020. *E-mail:* sara.bonney@methodistcollege.edu. *Web site:* http://www.methodistcollege.edu/.

Nebraska Wesleyan University

Lincoln, Nebraska

- **Independent United Methodist** comprehensive, founded 1887
- **Suburban** 50-acre campus with easy access to Omaha
- **Endowment** $41.2 million
- **Coed** 1,903 undergraduate students, 88% full-time, 60% women, 40% men
- **Moderately difficult** entrance level, 78% of applicants were admitted

Undergraduates 1,670 full-time, 233 part-time. Students come from 25 states and territories; 14 other countries; 12% are from out of state; 2% Black or African American, non-Hispanic/Latino; 1% Hispanic/Latino; 2% Asian, non-Hispanic/Latino; 0.3% Native Hawaiian or other Pacific Islander, non-Hispanic/Latino; 0.5% American Indian or Alaska Native, non-Hispanic/Latino; 2% Two or more races, non-Hispanic/Latino; 7% Race/ethnicity unknown; 3%

transferred in; 65% live on campus. *Retention:* 79% of full-time freshmen returned.
Freshmen *Admission:* 1,665 applied, 1,303 admitted, 430 enrolled. *Average high school GPA:* 3.64. *Test scores:* ACT scores over 18: 100%; ACT scores over 24: 63%; ACT scores over 30: 10%.
Faculty *Total:* 175, 60% full-time, 63% with terminal degrees. *Student/faculty ratio:* 13:1.
Academics *Calendar:* semesters. *Degrees:* certificates, bachelor's, master's, post-master's, and postbachelor's certificates. *Special study options:* accelerated degree program, adult/continuing education programs, advanced placement credit, double majors, independent study, internships, off-campus study, part-time degree program, services for LD students, study abroad, summer session for credit. *ROTC:* Army (c), Air Force (c). *Unusual degree programs:* 3-2 engineering with Washington University in St. Louis, Columbia University, University of Nebraska-Lincoln.
Computers on Campus 360 computers/terminals are available on campus for general student use. Students can access the following: computer help desk, free student e-mail accounts, online (class) grades, online (class) registration, online (class) schedules. Campuswide network is available. Wireless service is available via classrooms, computer centers, computer labs, learning centers, libraries, student centers.
Student Life *Housing:* on-campus residence required through junior year. *Options:* coed, women-only. Campus housing is university owned. Freshman campus housing is guaranteed. *Activities and organizations:* drama/theater group, student-run newspaper, choral group, national fraternities, national sororities. *Campus security:* 24-hour emergency response devices, late-night transport/escort service, controlled dormitory access. *Student services:* health clinic, personal/psychological counseling, women's center.
Athletics Member NCAA, NAIA. All NCAA Division III. *Intercollegiate sports:* baseball M, basketball M/W, cheerleading W, cross-country running M/W, football M, golf M/W, soccer M/W, softball W, tennis M/W, track and field M/W, volleyball W. *Intramural sports:* basketball M/W, bowling M/W, football M/W, racquetball M/W, soccer M/W, softball M/W, tennis M/W, ultimate Frisbee M/W, volleyball M/W, weight lifting M/W.
Standardized Tests *Required:* SAT or ACT (for admission).
Costs (2010–11) *One-time required fee:* $120. *Comprehensive fee:* $29,774 includes full-time tuition ($23,124), mandatory fees ($350), and room and board ($6300). Part-time tuition: $869 per credit hour. *Required fees:* $175 per credit hour part-time. *College room only:* $3580. Room and board charges vary according to board plan and housing facility. *Payment plan:* installment. *Waivers:* senior citizens and employees or children of employees.
Financial Aid Of all full-time matriculated undergraduates who enrolled in 2009, 1,318 applied for aid, 1,155 were judged to have need, 222 had their need fully met. 146 Federal Work-Study jobs (averaging $780). 428 state and other part-time jobs (averaging $1625). In 2009, 432 non-need-based awards were made. *Average percent of need met:* 69%. *Average financial aid package:* $16,859. *Average need-based loan:* $4498. *Average need-based gift aid:* $12,131. *Average non-need-based aid:* $8197. *Average indebtedness upon graduation:* $24,873.
Applying *Options:* electronic application, early action, deferred entrance. *Application fee:* $20. *Required:* high school transcript. *Required for some:* essay or personal statement. *Recommended:* interview. *Application deadlines:* 8/15 (freshmen), 8/15 (transfers), 11/15 (early action). *Notification:* continuous (freshmen), 12/15 (early action).
Freshman Application Contact Mr. David Duzik, Director of Admissions, Nebraska Wesleyan University, 5000 Saint Paul Avenue, Lincoln, NE 68504. *Phone:* 402-465-2144. *Toll-free phone:* 800-541-3818. *Fax:* 402-465-2177. *E-mail:* admissions@nebrwesleyan.edu. *Web site:* http://www.nebrwesleyan.edu/.

Peru State College

Peru, Nebraska

- **State-supported** comprehensive, founded 1867, part of Nebraska State College System
- **Rural** 104-acre campus
- **Coed**
- **Noncompetitive** entrance level

Faculty *Student/faculty ratio:* 20:1.
Academics *Calendar:* semesters. *Degrees:* certificates, bachelor's, and master's.
Student Life *Campus security:* 24-hour patrols.
Athletics Member NAIA.
Standardized Tests *Required for some:* SAT or ACT (for admission).
Costs (2010–11) *Tuition:* state resident $3863 full-time, $129 per credit hour part-time; nonresident $3893 full-time, $130 per credit hour part-time. Full-time tuition and fees vary according to course level, course load, and location. Part-time tuition and fees vary according to course level, course load, and location. *Required fees:* $1103 full-time. *Room and board:* $5208; room only:

$2868. Room and board charges vary according to board plan and housing facility.

Applying *Options:* electronic application. *Required:* high school transcript.

Freshman Application Contact Ms. Micki Willis, Vice President for Enrollment Management and Student Affairs, Peru State College, PO Box 10, Peru, NE 68421. *Phone:* 402-872-2221. *Toll-free phone:* 800-742-4412. *Fax:* 402-872-2296. *E-mail:* mwillis@peru.edu. *Web site:* http://www.peru.edu/.

St. Gregory the Great Seminary

Seward, Nebraska

- **Independent religious** 4-year
- **Small-town** 60-acre campus
- **Men only** 44 undergraduate students, 100% full-time
- 100% of applicants were admitted

Undergraduates 44 full-time. Students come from 6 states and territories; 4 other countries; 45% are from out of state; 9% Hispanic/Latino; 5% international; 18% transferred in; 100% live on campus. *Retention:* 88% of full-time freshmen returned.

Freshmen *Admission:* 6 applied, 6 admitted, 6 enrolled.

Faculty *Total:* 13, 54% full-time, 46% with terminal degrees.

Academics *Degrees:* bachelor's and postbachelor's certificates.

Computers on Campus Students can access the following: computer help desk, free student e-mail accounts. Campuswide network is available.

Student Life *Housing:* on-campus residence required through senior year. *Options:* Campus housing is university owned. Freshman campus housing is guaranteed.

Standardized Tests *Required:* SAT or ACT (for admission).

Costs (2011–12) *Comprehensive fee:* $13,500 includes full-time tuition ($7800) and room and board ($5700).

Applying *Required:* essay or personal statement, high school transcript, 3 letters of recommendation, interview, Church documents, letter of sponsorship from diocese.

Freshman Application Contact Rev. Peter M. Mitchell, Dean of Men, St. Gregory the Great Seminary, 800 Fletcher Road, Seward, NE 68434. *Phone:* 402-643-4052. *Fax:* 402-643-6964. *E-mail:* sggs@stgregoryseminary.edu. *Web site:* http://www.stgregoryseminary.edu/.

Union College

Lincoln, Nebraska

- **Independent Seventh-day Adventist** comprehensive, founded 1891
- **Suburban** 26-acre campus with easy access to Omaha
- **Coed** 829 undergraduate students, 83% full-time, 59% women, 41% men
- **Moderately difficult** entrance level, 61% of applicants were admitted

Undergraduates 690 full-time, 139 part-time. 5% Black or African American, non-Hispanic/Latino; 11% Hispanic/Latino; 2% Asian, non-Hispanic/Latino; 0.6% Native Hawaiian or other Pacific Islander, non-Hispanic/Latino; 0.8% American Indian or Alaska Native, non-Hispanic/Latino; 2% Two or more races, non-Hispanic/Latino; 3% Race/ethnicity unknown; 7% international; 8% transferred in; 56% live on campus. *Retention:* 66% of full-time freshmen returned.

Freshmen *Admission:* 833 applied, 509 admitted, 168 enrolled. *Average high school GPA:* 3.33. *Test scores:* SAT critical reading scores over 500: 50%; SAT math scores over 500: 38%; SAT writing scores over 500: 47%; ACT scores over 18: 81%; SAT critical reading scores over 600: 28%; SAT math scores over 600: 16%; SAT writing scores over 600: 19%; ACT scores over 24: 36%; SAT critical reading scores over 700: 9%; SAT writing scores over 700: 6%; ACT scores over 30: 6%.

Faculty *Total:* 97, 57% full-time, 28% with terminal degrees. *Student/faculty ratio:* 11:1.

Academics *Calendar:* semesters. *Degrees:* associate, bachelor's, and master's. *Special study options:* accelerated degree program, adult/continuing education programs, advanced placement credit, cooperative education, double majors, English as a second language, honors programs, independent study, internships, off-campus study, part-time degree program, services for LD students, student-designed majors, study abroad, summer session for credit.

Computers on Campus 520 computers/terminals are available on campus for general student use. Students can access the following: free student e-mail accounts, online (class) grades, online (class) registration, online (class) schedules. Campuswide network is available.

Student Life *Housing:* on-campus residence required through junior year. *Options:* men-only, women-only. Campus housing is university owned. Freshman campus housing is guaranteed. *Activities and organizations:* drama/theater group, student-run newspaper, choral group. *Campus security:* 24-hour emergency response devices, student patrols, late-night transport/escort service. *Student services:* health clinic, personal/psychological counseling.

Athletics *Intercollegiate sports:* basketball M/W, golf M, volleyball W. *Intramural sports:* badminton M/W, basketball M/W, football M/W, golf M/W,

gymnastics M(c)/W(c), soccer M(c)/W(c), softball M/W, tennis M/W, ultimate Frisbee M/W, volleyball M/W.

Standardized Tests *Required:* SAT or ACT (for admission).

Costs (2011–12) *Comprehensive fee:* $24,800 includes full-time tuition ($18,120), mandatory fees ($660), and room and board ($6020). Full-time tuition and fees vary according to course load and degree level. Part-time tuition: $755 per credit hour. *College room only:* $3420. Room and board charges vary according to housing facility. *Payment plan:* installment. *Waivers:* employees or children of employees.

Financial Aid Of all full-time matriculated undergraduates who enrolled in 2005, 172 Federal Work-Study jobs (averaging $1663). *Average percent of need met:* 71%. *Average financial aid package:* $12,234. *Average need-based loan:* $4442. *Average need-based gift aid:* $7056. *Average non-need-based aid:* $3699. *Average indebtedness upon graduation:* $23,379.

Applying *Options:* electronic application. *Required:* high school transcript, minimum 2.5 GPA, 3 letters of recommendation. *Required for some:* essay or personal statement, interview. *Application deadlines:* rolling (freshmen), rolling (transfers). *Notification:* continuous (freshmen), continuous (transfers).

Freshman Application Contact Jennifer Enos, Admissions Assistant Director, Union College, 3800 South 48th Street, Lincoln, NE 68506. *Phone:* 402-486-2600 Ext. 2052. *Toll-free phone:* 800-228-4600. *Fax:* 402-486-2895. *E-mail:* ucenroll@ucollege.edu. *Web site:* http://www.ucollege.edu/.

University of Nebraska at Kearney

Kearney, Nebraska

- **State-supported** comprehensive, founded 1903, part of University of Nebraska System
- **Small-town** 235-acre campus
- **Coed**
- **Moderately difficult** entrance level

Faculty *Student/faculty ratio:* 16:1.

Academics *Calendar:* semesters. *Degrees:* bachelor's, master's, and postmaster's certificates.

Student Life *Campus security:* 24-hour emergency response devices and patrols, late-night transport/escort service.

Athletics Member NCAA. All Division II.

Standardized Tests *Required:* SAT and SAT Subject Tests or ACT (for admission).

Costs (2010–11) *Tuition:* state resident $4808 full-time, $160 per credit hour part-time; nonresident $9855 full-time, $329 per credit hour part-time. Full-time tuition and fees vary according to course level, course load, degree level, and location. Part-time tuition and fees vary according to course level, course load, degree level, and location. *Required fees:* $1151 full-time, $24 per credit hour part-time, $76 per term part-time. *Room and board:* $7206; room only: $3640. Room and board charges vary according to board plan and housing facility.

Financial Aid *Of all full-time matriculated undergraduates who enrolled in 2009,* 3,323 applied for aid, 2,753 were judged to have need, 813 had their need fully met. *In 2009,* 557 non-need-based awards were made. *Average percent of need met:* 80. *Average financial aid package:* $9443. *Average need-based loan:* $3512. *Average need-based gift aid:* $5582. *Average non-need-based aid:* $2200. *Average indebtedness upon graduation:* $19,160.

Applying *Options:* electronic application. *Application fee:* $45. *Required:* high school transcript, rank in upper 50% of high school class.

Freshman Application Contact Mr. Dusty Newton, Director of Admissions, University of Nebraska at Kearney, 905 West 25th Street, Kearney, NE 68849-0001. *Phone:* 308-865-8702. *Toll-free phone:* 800-532-7639. *Fax:* 308-865-8987. *E-mail:* admissionsug@unk.edu. *Web site:* http://www.unk.edu/.

University of Nebraska at Omaha

Omaha, Nebraska

- **State-supported** university, founded 1908, part of University of Nebraska System
- **Urban** 503-acre campus
- **Coed** 11,833 undergraduate students, 79% full-time, 51% women, 49% men
- **Minimally difficult** entrance level, 76% of applicants were admitted

Undergraduates 9,356 full-time, 2,477 part-time. Students come from 43 states and territories; 75 other countries; 7% are from out of state; 6% Black or African American, non-Hispanic/Latino; 5% Hispanic/Latino; 2% Asian, non-Hispanic/Latino; 0.1% Native Hawaiian or other Pacific Islander, non-Hispanic/Latino; 0.6% American Indian or Alaska Native, non-Hispanic/Latino; 0.9% Two or more races, non-Hispanic/Latino; 4% Race/ethnicity unknown; 3% international; 11% transferred in; 11% live on campus. *Retention:* 73% of full-time freshmen returned.

Freshmen *Admission:* 4,562 applied, 3,445 admitted, 1,788 enrolled. *Average high school GPA:* 3.6. *Test scores:* ACT scores over 18: 90%; ACT scores over 24: 40%; ACT scores over 30: 9%.

Faculty *Total:* 857, 54% full-time, 58% with terminal degrees. *Student/faculty ratio:* 19:1.

Academics *Calendar:* semesters. *Degrees:* bachelor's, master's, doctoral-other, post-master's, and postbachelor's certificates. *Special study options:* adult/continuing education programs, advanced placement credit, cooperative education, distance learning, double majors, English as a second language, honors programs, independent study, internships, off-campus study, part-time degree program, services for LD students, student-designed majors, study abroad, summer session for credit. *ROTC:* Army (c), Air Force (b).

Computers on Campus 2,000 computers/terminals are available on campus for general student use. Students can access the following: computer help desk, free student e-mail accounts, online (class) grades, online (class) registration, online (class) schedules. Campuswide network is available. 100% of college-owned or -operated housing units are wired for high-speed Internet access. Wireless service is available via classrooms, computer centers, computer labs, dorm rooms, learning centers, libraries, student centers.

Student Life *Housing options:* coed. Campus housing is university owned and leased by the school. *Activities and organizations:* drama/theater group, student-run newspaper, radio and television station, choral group, marching band, Student Programming Board-Maverick Productions, student government, Greek Life, Emerging Leaders, PRSSA - Public Relations student society of America, national fraternities, national sororities. *Campus security:* 24-hour emergency response devices and patrols, late-night transport/escort service, controlled dormitory access. *Student services:* health clinic, personal/psychological counseling, women's center, legal services.

Athletics Member NCAA. All Division II except ice hockey (Division I). *Intercollegiate sports:* baseball M(s), basketball M(s)/W(s), cross-country running W(s), football M(s), golf W(s), ice hockey M(s), soccer W, softball W(s), swimming and diving W, tennis M/W, volleyball W(s), wrestling M(s). *Intramural sports:* badminton M/W, baseball M/W, basketball M/W, bowling M/W, field hockey M/W, football M/W, golf M/W, gymnastics M/W, racquetball M/W, soccer M/W, softball M/W, squash M/W, swimming and diving M/W, tennis M/W, track and field M/W, ultimate Frisbee M/W, volleyball M/W, wrestling M/W.

Standardized Tests *Required:* SAT or ACT (for admission).

Costs (2010–11) *Tuition:* state resident $5423 full-time, $181 per credit hour part-time; nonresident $15,983 full-time, $533 per credit hour part-time. Full-time tuition and fees vary according to course load and reciprocity agreements. Part-time tuition and fees vary according to course load and reciprocity agreements. *Required fees:* $1203 full-time. *Room and board:* $7750. Room and board charges vary according to board plan and housing facility. *Payment plans:* installment, deferred payment. *Waivers:* children of alumni, senior citizens, and employees or children of employees.

Financial Aid Of all full-time matriculated undergraduates who enrolled in 2009, 6,200 applied for aid, 4,561 were judged to have need. 477 Federal Work-Study jobs (averaging $2134). In 2009, 477 non-need-based awards were made. *Average financial aid package:* $2714. *Average need-based loan:* $3348. *Average need-based gift aid:* $2440. *Average non-need-based aid:* $2134. *Average indebtedness upon graduation:* $20,000.

Applying *Options:* electronic application, deferred entrance. *Application fee:* $45. *Required:* high school transcript. *Application deadlines:* 8/1 (freshmen), 8/1 (transfers). *Notification:* continuous (freshmen), continuous (transfers).

Freshman Application Contact University of Nebraska at Omaha, 6001 Dodge Street, Omaha, NE 68182. *Phone:* 402-554-2416. *Toll-free phone:* 800-858-8648. *Web site:* http://www.unomaha.edu/.

University of Nebraska–Lincoln
Lincoln, Nebraska

- **State-supported** university, founded 1869, part of University of Nebraska System
- **Urban** 624-acre campus with easy access to Omaha
- **Endowment** $1.1 billion
- **Coed** 19,383 undergraduate students, 94% full-time, 46% women, 54% men
- **Moderately difficult** entrance level, 62% of applicants were admitted

Undergraduates 18,129 full-time, 1,254 part-time. Students come from 53 states and territories; 87 other countries; 17% are from out of state; 2% Black or African American, non-Hispanic/Latino; 4% Hispanic/Latino; 2% Asian, non-Hispanic/Latino; 0.1% Native Hawaiian or other Pacific Islander, non-Hispanic/Latino; 0.3% American Indian or Alaska Native, non-Hispanic/Latino; 1% Two or more races, non-Hispanic/Latino; 3% Race/ethnicity unknown; 4% international; 5% transferred in; 40% live on campus. *Retention:* 84% of full-time freshmen returned.

Freshmen *Admission:* 9,768 applied, 6,089 admitted, 4,075 enrolled. *Test scores:* SAT critical reading scores over 500: 76%; SAT math scores over 500: 84%; ACT scores over 18: 99%; SAT critical reading scores over 600: 43%;

SAT math scores over 600: 52%; ACT scores over 24: 63%; SAT critical reading scores over 700: 14%; SAT math scores over 700: 16%; ACT scores over 30: 18%.

Faculty *Total:* 1,126, 98% full-time, 96% with terminal degrees. *Student/faculty ratio:* 20:1.

Academics *Calendar:* semesters. *Degrees:* associate, bachelor's, master's, doctoral-professional, doctoral-research/scholarship, post-master's, and post-bachelor's certificates. *Special study options:* accelerated degree program, adult/continuing education programs, advanced placement credit, cooperative education, distance learning, double majors, English as a second language, honors programs, independent study, internships, off-campus study, part-time degree program, services for LD students, student-designed majors, study abroad, summer session for credit. *ROTC:* Army (b), Navy (b), Air Force (b).

Computers on Campus 600 computers/terminals are available on campus for general student use. Students can access the following: campus intranet, computer help desk, free student e-mail accounts, online (class) grades, online (class) registration, online (class) schedules. Campuswide network is available. 100% of college-owned or -operated housing units are wired for high-speed Internet access. Wireless service is available via entire campus.

Student Life *Housing:* on-campus residence required for freshman year. *Options:* coed, women-only, cooperative, disabled students. Campus housing is university owned. Freshman campus housing is guaranteed. *Activities and organizations:* drama/theater group, student-run newspaper, radio station, choral group, marching band, Student Alumni Association, University Ambassadors, University Program Council, Golden Key Honor Society, national fraternities, national sororities. *Campus security:* 24-hour emergency response devices and patrols, late-night transport/escort service, controlled dormitory access. *Student services:* health clinic, personal/psychological counseling, women's center, legal services.

Athletics Member NCAA. All Division I except football (Division I-A). *Intercollegiate sports:* baseball M(s), basketball M(s)/W(s), bowling W(s), cross-country running M(s)/W(s), golf M(s)/W(s), gymnastics M(s)/W(s), riflery W(s), soccer W(s), softball W(s), swimming and diving W(s), tennis M(s)/W(s), track and field M(s)/W(s), volleyball W(s), wrestling M(s). *Intramural sports:* archery M/W, badminton M/W, baseball M(c), basketball M/W, bowling M(c)/W, crew M(c)/W(c), cross-country running M/W, football M/W, golf M/W, ice hockey M(c)/W(c), lacrosse M(c)/W(c), racquetball M/W, riflery M(c)/W(c), rock climbing M(c)/W(c), rugby M(c)/W(c), skiing (downhill) M(c)/W(c), soccer M/W, softball M/W(c), swimming and diving M(c)/W(c), table tennis M(c)/W(c), tennis M(c)/W(c), track and field M/W, ultimate Frisbee M(c)/W(c), volleyball M(c)/W(c), water polo M(c)/W(c), weight lifting M/W, wrestling M/W.

Standardized Tests *Required:* SAT or ACT (for admission). *Recommended:* ACT (for admission).

Costs (2010–11) *Tuition:* state resident $5948 full-time, $198 per semester hour part-time; nonresident $17,648 full-time, $588 per semester hour part-time. Full-time tuition and fees vary according to course load, program, and reciprocity agreements. Part-time tuition and fees vary according to course load, program, and reciprocity agreements. *Required fees:* $1276 full-time, $10 per semester hour part-time, $287 per term part-time. *Room and board:* $7660; room only: $4039. Room and board charges vary according to board plan and housing facility. *Payment plan:* installment. *Waivers:* employees or children of employees.

Financial Aid Of all full-time matriculated undergraduates who enrolled in 2008, 11,789 applied for aid, 8,525 were judged to have need, 687 had their need fully met. 1,196 Federal Work-Study jobs (averaging $2468). In 2008, 1398 non-need-based awards were made. *Average percent of need met:* 85%. *Average financial aid package:* $10,926. *Average need-based loan:* $4048. *Average need-based gift aid:* $7304. *Average non-need-based aid:* $5494. *Average indebtedness upon graduation:* $16,664.

Applying *Options:* electronic application. *Application fee:* $45. *Required:* high school transcript. *Required for some:* rank in upper 50% of high school class. *Application deadlines:* 5/1 (freshmen), 5/1 (transfers). *Notification:* continuous (freshmen), continuous (transfers).

Freshman Application Contact Mr. Pat McBride, Director, New Student Enrollment, University of Nebraska–Lincoln, 1410 Q Street, Lincoln, NE 68588-0417. *Phone:* 402-472-2023. *Toll-free phone:* 800-742-8800. *Fax:* 402-472-0670. *E-mail:* admissions@unl.edu. *Web site:* http://www.unl.edu/.

University of Nebraska Medical Center
Omaha, Nebraska

- **State-supported** upper-level, founded 1869, part of University of Nebraska System
- **Urban** 51-acre campus
- **Endowment** $8.9 million
- **Coed**

Faculty *Student/faculty ratio:* 3:1.

Academics *Calendar:* semesters. *Degrees:* bachelor's, master's, doctoral-other, doctoral-professional, doctoral-research/scholarship, post-master's, and postbachelor's certificates.

Student Life *Campus security:* 24-hour emergency response devices and patrols, late-night transport/escort service.

Costs (2010–11) *Tuition:* state resident $7530 full-time, $251 per semester hour part-time; nonresident $22,050 full-time, $794 per semester hour part-time. Full-time tuition and fees vary according to location and program. Part-time tuition and fees vary according to location and program. *Required fees:* $500 full-time, $320 per year part-time.

Financial Aid *Of all full-time matriculated undergraduates who enrolled in 2008,* 863 applied for aid, 729 were judged to have need, 103 had their need fully met. 53 Federal Work-Study jobs (averaging $663). *In 2008,* 181 non-need-based awards were made. *Average percent of need met:* 56. *Average financial aid package:* $8239. *Average need-based loan:* $4871. *Average need-based gift aid:* $4760. *Average non-need-based aid:* $8607. *Average indebtedness upon graduation:* $29,188.

Applying *Options:* electronic application, deferred entrance. *Application fee:* $45.

Application Contact University of Nebraska Medical Center, Nebraska Medical Center, Omaha, NE 68198. *Phone:* 402-559-6468. *Toll-free phone:* 800-626-8431 Ext. 6468. *Web site:* http://www.unmc.edu/.

Wayne State College

Wayne, Nebraska

- **State-supported** comprehensive, founded 1910, part of Nebraska State College System
- **Small-town** 128-acre campus
- **Endowment** $10.2 million
- **Coed** 2,938 undergraduate students, 93% full-time, 55% women, 45% men
- **Noncompetitive** entrance level, 100% of applicants were admitted

Undergraduates 2,721 full-time, 217 part-time. Students come from 32 states and territories; 20 other countries; 14% are from out of state; 3% Black or African American, non-Hispanic/Latino; 3% Hispanic/Latino; 0.4% Asian, non-Hispanic/Latino; 0.1% Native Hawaiian or other Pacific Islander, non-Hispanic/Latino; 0.6% American Indian or Alaska Native, non-Hispanic/Latino; 0.9% Two or more races, non-Hispanic/Latino; 8% Race/ethnicity unknown; 0.5% international; 8% transferred in; 47% live on campus. *Retention:* 68% of full-time freshmen returned.

Freshmen *Admission:* 2,061 applied, 2,061 admitted, 681 enrolled. *Average high school GPA:* 3.2. *Test scores:* ACT scores over 18: 80%; ACT scores over 24: 35%; ACT scores over 30: 5%.

Faculty *Total:* 222, 56% full-time, 50% with terminal degrees. *Student/faculty ratio:* 19:1.

Academics *Calendar:* semesters. *Degrees:* bachelor's, master's, and post-master's certificates. *Special study options:* adult/continuing education programs, advanced placement credit, cooperative education, distance learning, double majors, honors programs, independent study, internships, off-campus study, part-time degree program, services for LD students, student-designed majors, study abroad, summer session for credit. *ROTC:* Army (b).

Computers on Campus 365 computers/terminals are available on campus for general student use. Students can access the following: campus intranet, computer help desk, free student e-mail accounts, online (class) grades, online (class) registration, online (class) schedules. Campuswide network is available. 100% of college-owned or -operated housing units are wired for high-speed Internet access. Wireless service is available via classrooms, computer centers, computer labs, learning centers, libraries, student centers.

Student Life *Housing:* on-campus residence required for freshman year. *Options:* coed. Campus housing is university owned. Freshman campus housing is guaranteed. *Activities and organizations:* drama/theater group, student-run newspaper, radio and television station, choral group, marching band, national fraternities, national sororities. *Campus security:* 24-hour emergency response devices and patrols, student patrols, late-night transport/escort service, controlled dormitory access. *Student services:* health clinic, personal/psychological counseling.

Athletics Member NCAA. All Division II. *Intercollegiate sports:* baseball M(s), basketball M(s)/W(s), cheerleading M(c)/W(c), cross-country running M(s)/W(s), football M(s), golf M(s)/W(s), rugby M(c)/W(c), soccer M(c)/W(s), softball W(s), track and field M(s)/W(s), volleyball W(s), wrestling M(c). *Intramural sports:* archery M/W, badminton M/W, basketball M/W, bowling M/W, football M/W, golf M/W, racquetball M/W, softball M/W, swimming and diving M/W, table tennis M/W, tennis M/W, track and field M/W, volleyball M/W, weight lifting M/W, wrestling M.

Costs (2010–11) *Tuition:* state resident $3863 full-time, $129 per credit hour part-time; nonresident $7725 full-time, $258 per credit hour part-time. Full-time tuition and fees vary according to course level and course load. Part-time

tuition and fees vary according to course level and course load. *Required fees:* $1208 full-time, $48 per credit hour part-time. *Room and board:* $5540; room only: $2660. Room and board charges vary according to board plan and housing facility. *Payment plan:* installment. *Waivers:* employees or children of employees.

Financial Aid Of all full-time matriculated undergraduates who enrolled in 2009, 2,312 applied for aid, 1,868 were judged to have need, 516 had their need fully met. In 2009, 74 non-need-based awards were made. *Average percent of need met:* 63%. *Average financial aid package:* $7744. *Average need-based loan:* $3769. *Average need-based gift aid:* $4029. *Average non-need-based aid:* $2715.

Applying *Options:* electronic application, deferred entrance. *Application fee:* $30. *Required:* high school transcript. *Application deadlines:* rolling (freshmen), rolling (out-of-state freshmen), rolling (transfers). *Notification:* continuous (freshmen), continuous (out-of-state freshmen), continuous (transfers).

Freshman Application Contact Mr. Kevin Halle, Director of Admissions, Wayne State College, 1111 Main Street, Wayne, NE 68787. *Phone:* 402-375-7234. *Toll-free phone:* 800-228-9972. *Fax:* 402-375-7204. *E-mail:* admit1@wsc.edu. *Web site:* http://www.wsc.edu/.

York College

York, Nebraska

- **Independent** 4-year, founded 1890, affiliated with Church of Christ
- **Small-town** 44-acre campus
- **Endowment** $5.9 million
- **Coed**
- **Moderately difficult** entrance level

Faculty *Student/faculty ratio:* 11:1.

Academics *Calendar:* semesters. *Degrees:* associate and bachelor's.

Student Life *Campus security:* 24-hour patrols, student patrols, controlled dormitory access.

Athletics Member NAIA, NCCAA.

Standardized Tests *Required:* SAT or ACT (for admission).

Costs (2010–11) *Comprehensive fee:* $20,678 includes full-time tuition ($13,198), mandatory fees ($1800), and room and board ($5680). Full-time tuition and fees vary according to course load. Part-time tuition: $460 per credit hour. Part-time tuition and fees vary according to course load. *Required fees:* $220 per credit hour part-time. *Room and board:* Room and board charges vary according to board plan and housing facility.

Financial Aid *Of all full-time matriculated undergraduates who enrolled in 2009,* 414 applied for aid, 371 were judged to have need, 64 had their need fully met. 64 Federal Work-Study jobs (averaging $1160). 112 state and other part-time jobs (averaging $1287). *In 2009,* 29 non-need-based awards were made. *Average percent of need met:* 77. *Average financial aid package:* $13,765. *Average need-based loan:* $4352. *Average need-based gift aid:* $9266. *Average non-need-based aid:* $4207. *Average indebtedness upon graduation:* $22,020.

Applying *Options:* electronic application, early admission, deferred entrance. *Application fee:* $20. *Required:* high school transcript, minimum 2 GPA. *Required for some:* 1 letter of recommendation.

Freshman Application Contact Ms. Janae Parsons, York College, 1125 East 8th Street, York, NE 68467-2699. *Phone:* 402-363-5627. *Toll-free phone:* 800-950-9675. *Fax:* 402-363-5623. *E-mail:* enroll@york.edu. *Web site:* http://www.york.edu/.

NEVADA

The Art Institute of Las Vegas

Henderson, Nevada

- **Proprietary** 4-year, founded 2002, part of Education Management Corporation
- **Suburban** campus
- **Coed**

Academics *Calendar:* quarters. *Degrees:* certificates, diplomas, associate, and bachelor's.

Costs (2010–11) *Tuition:* Tuition cost varies by program. Prospective students should contact the school for current tuition costs. Other charges include a starting kit for all first-quarter students. Kits vary in price, depending on the program of study.

Freshman Application Contact The Art Institute of Las Vegas, 2350 Corporate Circle Drive, Henderson, NV 89074. *Phone:* 702-369-9944. *Toll-free phone:* 800-833-2678. *Web site:* http://www.artinstitutes.edu/lasvegas/.

See page 1048 for the College Close-Up.

College of Southern Nevada
North Las Vegas, Nevada

Freshman Application Contact Admissions and Records, College of Southern Nevada, 3200 East Cheyenne Avenue, North Las Vegas, NV 89030-4296. *Phone:* 702-651-4060. *Web site:* http://www.csn.edu/.

DeVry University
Henderson, Nevada

- **Proprietary** comprehensive, part of DeVry University
- **Coed**
- **Minimally difficult** entrance level

Faculty *Student/faculty ratio:* 20:1.

Academics *Calendar:* semesters. *Degrees:* associate, bachelor's, and master's.

Costs (2010–11) *Tuition:* $14,766 full-time, $580 per credit hour part-time. Full-time tuition and fees vary according to course load. Part-time tuition and fees vary according to course load. *Required fees:* $60 full-time, $30 per term part-time. *Payment plans:* installment, deferred payment.

Financial Aid *Of all full-time matriculated undergraduates who enrolled in 2007,* 32 applied for aid, 32 were judged to have need, 1 had their need fully met. *Average percent of need met:* 36. *Average financial aid package:* $10,877. *Average need-based loan:* $8938. *Average need-based gift aid:* $5641. *Average indebtedness upon graduation:* $62,400.

Applying *Options:* electronic application, deferred entrance. *Application fee:* $50. *Required:* high school transcript, interview.

Freshman Application Contact DeVry University, 2490 Paseo Verde Parkway, Henderson, NV 89074-7120. *Web site:* http://www.devry.edu/.

Great Basin College
Elko, Nevada

- **State-supported** primarily 2-year, founded 1967, part of University and Community College System of Nevada
- **Small-town** 45-acre campus
- **Endowment** $187,761
- **Coed** 3,691 undergraduate students, 31% full-time, 66% women, 34% men
- **Noncompetitive** entrance level

Undergraduates 1,141 full-time, 2,550 part-time. Students come from 13 states and territories; 3% are from out of state; 2% Black or African American, non-Hispanic/Latino; 14% Hispanic/Latino; 1% Asian, non-Hispanic/Latino; 0.4% Native Hawaiian or other Pacific Islander, non-Hispanic/Latino; 3% American Indian or Alaska Native, non-Hispanic/Latino; 1% Two or more races, non-Hispanic/Latino; 3% Race/ethnicity unknown; 0.3% international; 5% live on campus. *Retention:* 77% of full-time freshmen returned.

Freshmen *Admission:* 558 admitted, 558 enrolled.

Faculty *Total:* 244, 26% full-time. *Student/faculty ratio:* 15:1.

Academics *Calendar:* semesters. *Degrees:* certificates, associate, bachelor's, and postbachelor's certificates. *Special study options:* academic remediation for entering students, accelerated degree program, adult/continuing education programs, cooperative education, distance learning, double majors, English as a second language, external degree program, independent study, part-time degree program, services for LD students, summer session for credit.

Computers on Campus 95 computers/terminals are available on campus for general student use. Students can access the following: online (class) registration. Campuswide network is available. 100% of college-owned or -operated housing units are wired for high-speed Internet access. Wireless service is available via classrooms, computer centers, computer labs, learning centers, libraries, student centers.

Student Life *Housing options:* coed, disabled students. Campus housing is university owned. *Activities and organizations:* Student Nurses Organization, Housing Central, Skills USA, Agriculture Student Organization, Colleges Against Cancer. *Campus security:* late-night transport/escort service, evening patrols by trained security personnel. *Student services:* personal/psychological counseling.

Athletics *Intramural sports:* badminton M/W, basketball M/W, rock climbing M/W, volleyball M/W, weight lifting M/W.

Costs (2011–12) *Tuition:* state resident $2243 full-time, $69 per credit hour part-time; nonresident $8590 full-time, $227 per credit hour part-time. Full-time tuition and fees vary according to course level. Part-time tuition and fees vary according to course level. *Required fees:* $165 full-time, $6 per credit hour part-time. *Room only:* $2299. Room and board charges vary according to housing facility. *Payment plan:* deferred payment. *Waivers:* senior citizens and employees or children of employees.

Financial Aid Of all full-time matriculated undergraduates who enrolled in 2009, 35 Federal Work-Study jobs (averaging $1000). 50 state and other part-time jobs (averaging $1800).

Applying *Options:* electronic application, early admission, deferred entrance. *Application fee:* $10. *Application deadlines:* rolling (freshmen), rolling (out-of-state freshmen), rolling (transfers). *Notification:* continuous (freshmen), continuous (out-of-state freshmen), continuous (transfers).

Freshman Application Contact Ms. Janice King, Director of Admissions and Registrar, Great Basin College, 1500 College Parkway, Elko, NV 89801-3348. *Phone:* 775-753-2361. *Fax:* 775-753-2311. *E-mail:* janicek@gwmail.gbcnv.edu. *Web site:* http://www.gbcnv.edu/.

ITT Technical Institute
Henderson, Nevada

- **Proprietary** primarily 2-year, founded 1997, part of ITT Educational Services, Inc.
- **Coed**
- **Minimally difficult** entrance level

Academics *Degrees:* associate and bachelor's.

Student Life *Housing:* college housing not available.

Financial Aid Of all full-time matriculated undergraduates who enrolled in 2009, 6 Federal Work-Study jobs (averaging $5000).

Freshman Application Contact Director of Recruitment, ITT Technical Institute, 168 North Gibson Road, Henderson, NV 89014. *Phone:* 702-558-5404. *Toll-free phone:* 800-488-8459. *Web site:* http://www.itt-tech.edu/.

Morrison University
Reno, Nevada

Freshman Application Contact Mr. Charles Timinsky, Director of Enrollment, Morrison University, 10315 Professional Circle, Suite 201, Reno, NV 89521. *Phone:* 775-850-0700 Ext. 101. *Toll-free phone:* 800-369-6144. *Fax:* 775-850-0711. *E-mail:* ctiminsky@morrison.neumont.edu. *Web site:* http://www.morrison.neumont.edu/.

Nevada State College at Henderson
Henderson, Nevada

- **State-supported** 4-year, founded 2002, part of Nevada System of Higher Education
- **Suburban** 520-acre campus with easy access to Las Vegas
- **Coed** 2,988 undergraduate students, 38% full-time, 75% women, 25% men
- **Minimally difficult** entrance level, 82% of applicants were admitted

Undergraduates 1,131 full-time, 1,857 part-time. Students come from 14 states and territories; 1 other country; 7% are from out of state; 12% Black or African American, non-Hispanic/Latino; 20% Hispanic/Latino; 11% Asian, non-Hispanic/Latino; 2% Native Hawaiian or other Pacific Islander, non-Hispanic/Latino; 1% American Indian or Alaska Native, non-Hispanic/Latino; 4% Two or more races, non-Hispanic/Latino; 1% Race/ethnicity unknown; 0.3% international; 19% transferred in. *Retention:* 65% of full-time freshmen returned.

Freshmen *Admission:* 652 applied, 535 admitted, 273 enrolled. *Average high school GPA:* 2.86. *Test scores:* SAT critical reading scores over 500: 41%; SAT math scores over 500: 36%; SAT writing scores over 500: 24%; ACT scores over 18: 67%; SAT critical reading scores over 600: 13%; SAT math scores over 600: 3%; SAT writing scores over 600: 5%; ACT scores over 24: 14%; SAT critical reading scores over 700: 3%; SAT writing scores over 700: 2%; ACT scores over 30: 2%.

Faculty *Total:* 94, 49% full-time, 36% with terminal degrees. *Student/faculty ratio:* 28:1.

Academics *Calendar:* semesters. *Degree:* bachelor's. *Special study options:* academic remediation for entering students, accelerated degree program, adult/continuing education programs, advanced placement credit, cooperative education, distance learning, double majors, independent study, internships, part-time degree program, services for LD students, student-designed majors, summer session for credit. *ROTC:* Army (c). *Unusual degree programs:* 3-2 nursing with Touro University.

Computers on Campus 136 computers/terminals are available on campus for general student use. Students can access the following: computer help desk, online (class) grades, online (class) registration, online (class) schedules. Campuswide network is available. Wireless service is available via entire campus.

Student Life *Housing:* college housing not available. *Activities and organizations:* student-run newspaper, Nevada State Student Alliance (Student Government), Pre-Professional Club, American Sign Language Club, Student Nurses Association, Circle K International. *Campus security:* private contracted security patrols.

Costs (2010–11) *One-time required fee:* $20. *Tuition:* state resident $3563 full-time, $113 per credit hour part-time; nonresident $13,381 full-time. Full-time tuition and fees vary according to course load and reciprocity agreements. Part-time tuition and fees vary according to course load and reciprocity agreements. *Payment plans:* tuition prepayment, deferred payment. *Waivers:* senior citizens and employees or children of employees.

Applying *Options:* electronic application. *Application fee:* $30. *Required:* high school transcript, minimum 2 GPA. *Application deadlines:* rolling (freshmen), rolling (transfers). *Notification:* continuous (freshmen), continuous (transfers).

Freshman Application Contact Ms. Patricia Ring, Registrar, Nevada State College at Henderson, Office of Admissions and Records, 1125 Nevada State Drive, Henderson, NV 89002. *Phone:* 702-992-2114. *Fax:* 702-992-2111. *E-mail:* admissions@nsc.nevada.edu. *Web site:* http://www.nsc.nevada.edu/.

Pima Medical Institute

Las Vegas, Nevada

- **Proprietary** primarily 2-year, founded 2003, part of Vocational Training Institutes, Inc.
- **Urban** campus
- **Coed** 820 undergraduate students
- **Moderately difficult** entrance level

Academics *Calendar:* modular. *Degrees:* certificates, associate, and bachelor's. *Special study options:* advanced placement credit, distance learning, internships.

Student Life *Housing:* college housing not available.

Standardized Tests *Required:* Wonderlic Scholastic Level Exam (for admission).

Applying *Required:* interview. *Required for some:* essay or personal statement, high school transcript.

Freshman Application Contact Admissions Office, Pima Medical Institute, 3333 East Flamingo Road, Las Vegas, NV 89121. *Phone:* 702-458-9650 Ext. 202. *Toll-free phone:* 800-477-PIMA. *Web site:* http://www.pmi.edu/.

Sierra Nevada College

Incline Village, Nevada

- **Independent** comprehensive, founded 1969
- **Small-town** 20-acre campus with easy access to Reno
- **Endowment** $3.6 million
- **Coed** 443 undergraduate students, 98% full-time, 42% women, 58% men
- **Moderately difficult** entrance level, 69% of applicants were admitted

Undergraduates 433 full-time, 10 part-time. Students come from 30 states and territories; 12 other countries; 81% are from out of state; 0.9% Black or African American, non-Hispanic/Latino; 6% Hispanic/Latino; 2% Asian, non-Hispanic/Latino; 1% Native Hawaiian or other Pacific Islander, non-Hispanic/Latino; 3% American Indian or Alaska Native, non-Hispanic/Latino; 12% Race/ethnicity unknown; 2% international; 17% transferred in; 28% live on campus. *Retention:* 67% of full-time freshmen returned.

Freshmen *Admission:* 423 applied, 293 admitted, 84 enrolled. *Average high school GPA:* 3.05.

Faculty *Total:* 123, 20% full-time, 61% with terminal degrees. *Student/faculty ratio:* 9:1.

Academics *Calendar:* semesters. *Degrees:* bachelor's and master's. *Special study options:* academic remediation for entering students, accelerated degree program, adult/continuing education programs, advanced placement credit, cooperative education, double majors, English as a second language, honors programs, independent study, internships, part-time degree program, services for LD students, student-designed majors, study abroad, summer session for credit. *Unusual degree programs:* 3-2 Master of Teaching, Elementary or Secondary Education.

Computers on Campus 50 computers/terminals are available on campus for general student use. Students can access the following: computer help desk, free student e-mail accounts, online (class) grades, online (class) schedules. Campuswide network is available. 100% of college-owned or -operated housing units are wired for high-speed Internet access. Wireless service is available via entire campus.

Student Life *Housing:* on-campus residence required for freshman year. *Options:* coed. Campus housing is university owned. Freshman campus housing is guaranteed. *Activities and organizations:* drama/theater group, student-run newspaper, choral group, Film Club, International Club, Sustainability Club, Rock Climbing Club, First Generation Club. *Campus security:* 24-hour emergency response devices and patrols, controlled dormitory access. *Student services:* health clinic, personal/psychological counseling.

Athletics *Intercollegiate sports:* rock climbing M/W, skiing (downhill) M(s)/W(s). *Intramural sports:* rock climbing M/W, skiing (downhill) M/W, soccer M/W, softball M/W, volleyball M/W.

Standardized Tests *Required:* SAT or ACT (for admission).

Costs (2011–12) *Comprehensive fee:* $34,985 includes full-time tuition ($24,720), mandatory fees ($515), and room and board ($9750). Full-time tuition and fees vary according to course load, degree level, location, and program. Part-time tuition: $1030 per credit hour. Part-time tuition and fees vary

according to course load, degree level, location, and program. *Required fees:* $165 per term part-time. *Room and board:* Room and board charges vary according to board plan. *Payment plan:* installment. *Waivers:* employees or children of employees.

Financial Aid Of all full-time matriculated undergraduates who enrolled in 2003, 203 applied for aid, 203 were judged to have need. 63 Federal Work-Study jobs (averaging $2000). 2 state and other part-time jobs (averaging $2500). In 2003, 36 non-need-based awards were made. *Average percent of need met:* 60%. *Average financial aid package:* $14,000. *Average need-based gift aid:* $6000. *Average non-need-based aid:* $8000. *Average indebtedness upon graduation:* $18,000.

Applying *Options:* electronic application, early admission, deferred entrance. *Required:* essay or personal statement, high school transcript, minimum 2.6 GPA. *Recommended:* interview. *Application deadlines:* rolling (freshmen), rolling (transfers). *Notification:* continuous (freshmen), continuous (transfers).

Freshman Application Contact Sierra Nevada College, 999 Tahoe Boulevard, Incline Village, NV 89451. *Phone:* 866-412-4636. *Fax:* 775-831-6223. *E-mail:* admissions@sierranevada.edu. *Web site:* http://www.sierranevada.edu/.

University of Nevada, Las Vegas

Las Vegas, Nevada

- **State-supported** university, founded 1957, part of Nevada System of Higher Education
- **Urban** 358-acre campus
- **Coed** 22,538 undergraduate students, 73% full-time, 55% women, 45% men
- **Moderately difficult** entrance level, 81% of applicants were admitted

Undergraduates 16,523 full-time, 6,015 part-time. 15% are from out of state; 8% Black or African American, non-Hispanic/Latino; 18% Hispanic/Latino; 15% Asian, non-Hispanic/Latino; 2% Native Hawaiian or other Pacific Islander, non-Hispanic/Latino; 0.7% American Indian or Alaska Native, non-Hispanic/Latino; 5% Two or more races, non-Hispanic/Latino; 2% Race/ethnicity unknown; 4% international; 10% transferred in; 5% live on campus. *Retention:* 78% of full-time freshmen returned.

Freshmen *Admission:* 6,438 applied, 5,222 admitted, 3,053 enrolled. *Average high school GPA:* 3.23. *Test scores:* SAT critical reading scores over 500: 53%; SAT math scores over 500: 60%; SAT writing scores over 500: 42%; ACT scores over 18: 86%; SAT critical reading scores over 600: 14%; SAT math scores over 600: 20%; SAT writing scores over 600: 9%; ACT scores over 24: 32%; SAT critical reading scores over 700: 2%; SAT math scores over 700: 3%; SAT writing scores over 700: 1%; ACT scores over 30: 3%.

Faculty *Total:* 1,274, 66% full-time. *Student/faculty ratio:* 22:1.

Academics *Calendar:* semesters. *Degrees:* certificates, bachelor's, master's, doctoral-professional, doctoral-research/scholarship, post-master's, post-bachelor's certificates. *Special study options:* academic remediation for entering students, accelerated degree program, adult/continuing education programs, advanced placement credit, cooperative education, distance learning, double majors, English as a second language, honors programs, independent study, internships, off-campus study, part-time degree program, services for LD students, student-designed majors, study abroad, summer session for credit. *ROTC:* Army (b), Air Force (b).

Computers on Campus Students can access the following: computer help desk, free student e-mail accounts, online (class) grades, online (class) registration, online (class) schedules. Campuswide network is available. 100% of college-owned or -operated housing units are wired for high-speed Internet access. Wireless service is available via entire campus.

Student Life *Housing options:* coed, disabled students. Campus housing is university owned. Freshman applicants given priority for college housing. *Activities and organizations:* drama/theater group, student-run newspaper, radio and television station, choral group, marching band, national fraternities, national sororities. *Campus security:* 24-hour emergency response devices and patrols, late-night transport/escort service, controlled dormitory access. *Student services:* health clinic, personal/psychological counseling, women's center.

Athletics Member NCAA. All Division I except football (Division I-A). *Intercollegiate sports:* baseball M(s), basketball M(s)/W(s), cheerleading M(s)/W(s), cross-country running W(s), golf M(s), soccer M(s)/W(s), softball W(s), swimming and diving M(s)/W(s), tennis M(s)/W(s), track and field W(s), volleyball W(s). *Intramural sports:* badminton M/W, basketball M/W, bowling M/W, football M/W, golf M/W, racquetball M/W, soccer M/W, softball M/W, swimming and diving M/W, tennis M/W, volleyball M/W.

Standardized Tests *Recommended:* SAT or ACT (for admission).

Costs (2010–11) *Tuition:* state resident $4913 full-time, $157 per credit hour part-time; nonresident $18,203 full-time, $314 per credit hour part-time. Full-time tuition and fees vary according to course level and reciprocity agreements. Part-time tuition and fees vary according to course level and reciprocity agreements. *Required fees:* $776 full-time. *Room and board:* $10,454; room only: $6544. Room and board charges vary according to board plan. *Payment* *plan:* deferred payment. *Waivers:* children of alumni, senior citizens, and employees or children of employees.

Financial Aid Of all full-time matriculated undergraduates who enrolled in 2009, 9,610 applied for aid, 8,002 were judged to have need, 1,373 had their need fully met. 208 Federal Work-Study jobs (averaging $4221). 473 state and other part-time jobs (averaging $3967). In 2009, 378 non-need-based awards were made. *Average percent of need met:* 56%. *Average financial aid package:* $9706. *Average need-based loan:* $4146. *Average need-based gift aid:* $5123. *Average non-need-based aid:* $3194. *Average indebtedness upon graduation:* $17,256.

Applying *Options:* electronic application, early admission, deferred entrance. *Application fee:* $60. *Required:* high school transcript, minimum 3 GPA. *Required for some:* 2 letters of recommendation. *Application deadlines:* rolling (freshmen), rolling (transfers). *Notification:* continuous (freshmen), continuous (transfers).

Freshman Application Contact Director of Admissions, University of Nevada, Las Vegas, 4505 Maryland Parkway, Box 451021, Las Vegas, NV 89154-1021. *Phone:* 702-774-8658. *Fax:* 702-774-8008. *E-mail:* admissions@unlv.edu. *Web site:* http://www.unlv.edu/.

University of Nevada, Reno

Reno, Nevada

- **State-supported** university, founded 1874, part of Nevada System of Higher Education
- **Urban** 200-acre campus
- **Endowment** $190.9 million
- **Coed** 14,185 undergraduate students, 81% full-time, 53% women, 47% men
- **Moderately difficult** entrance level, 91% of applicants were admitted

Undergraduates 11,435 full-time, 2,750 part-time. Students come from 46 states and territories; 44 other countries; 17% are from out of state; 3% Black or African American, non-Hispanic/Latino; 12% Hispanic/Latino; 6% Asian, non-Hispanic/Latino; 0.8% Native Hawaiian or other Pacific Islander, non-Hispanic/Latino; 1% American Indian or Alaska Native, non-Hispanic/Latino; 3% Two or more races, non-Hispanic/Latino; 1% Race/ethnicity unknown; 2% international; 8% transferred in; 14% live on campus. *Retention:* 79% of full-time freshmen returned.

Freshmen *Admission:* 5,808 applied, 5,312 admitted, 2,764 enrolled. *Average high school GPA:* 3.33. *Test scores:* SAT critical reading scores over 500: 62%; SAT math scores over 500: 65%; SAT writing scores over 500: 49%; ACT scores over 18: 91%; SAT critical reading scores over 600: 17%; SAT math scores over 600: 23%; SAT writing scores over 600: 12%; ACT scores over 24: 42%; SAT critical reading scores over 700: 2%; SAT math scores over 700: 2%; SAT writing scores over 700: 1%; ACT scores over 30: 6%.

Faculty *Total:* 567, 95% full-time, 89% with terminal degrees. *Student/faculty ratio:* 27:1.

Academics *Calendar:* semesters. *Degrees:* associate, bachelor's, master's, doctoral-professional, doctoral-research/scholarship, post-master's, and post-bachelor's certificates. *Special study options:* academic remediation for entering students, adult/continuing education programs, advanced placement credit, distance learning, double majors, English as a second language, honors programs, independent study, internships, off-campus study, part-time degree program, services for LD students, study abroad, summer session for credit. *ROTC:* Army (b). *Unusual degree programs:* 3-2 biotechnology.

Computers on Campus Students can access the following: computer help desk, free student e-mail accounts, online (class) registration, online (class) schedules. Campuswide network is available. Wireless service is available via entire campus.

Student Life *Housing options:* coed, men-only, women-only, disabled students. Campus housing is university owned. Freshman applicants given priority for college housing. *Activities and organizations:* drama/theater group, student-run newspaper, radio station, choral group, marching band, Intervarsity Christian Fellowship, Student Ambassadors, Young Democrats, Asian American Association, Blue Crew, national fraternities, national sororities. *Campus security:* 24-hour emergency response devices and patrols, late-night transport/escort service, controlled dormitory access. *Student services:* health clinic, personal/psychological counseling, women's center, legal services.

Athletics Member NCAA. All Division I except football (Division I-A). *Intercollegiate sports:* baseball M(s), basketball M(s)/W(s), cheerleading M(c)/W(c), cross-country running W(s), golf M(s)/W(s), riflery M(s)/W(s), soccer W(s), softball W(s), swimming and diving W(s), tennis M(s)/W(s), track and field W(s), volleyball W(s). *Intramural sports:* basketball M/W, bowling M/W, cross-country running M/W, equestrian sports M/W, football M, golf M/W, racquetball M/W, rock climbing M/W, rugby M/W, skiing (cross-country) M/W, skiing (downhill) M/W, soccer M/W, softball M/W, swimming and diving M/W, table tennis M/W, tennis M/W, track and field M/W, ultimate Frisbee M/W, volleyball M/W, water polo M/W.

Standardized Tests *Required for some:* SAT or ACT (for admission).

Costs (2011–12) *One-time required fee:* $110. *Tuition:* state resident $4193 full-time, $164 per credit part-time; nonresident $18,508 full-time. Full-time tuition and fees vary according to course load. Part-time tuition and fees vary according to course load. *Required fees:* $648 full-time. *Room and board:* $9518. Room and board charges vary according to board plan and housing facility. *Payment plan:* deferred payment. *Waivers:* children of alumni, senior citizens, and employees or children of employees.

Financial Aid Of all full-time matriculated undergraduates who enrolled in 2008, 5,025 applied for aid, 3,764 were judged to have need, 411 had their need fully met. In 2008, 4494 non-need-based awards were made. *Average percent of need met:* 57%. *Average financial aid package:* $7375. *Average need-based loan:* $4389. *Average need-based gift aid:* $5738. *Average non-need-based aid:* $2702. *Average indebtedness upon graduation:* $15,854.

Applying *Options:* electronic application, early admission, deferred entrance. *Application fee:* $60. *Required:* high school transcript, minimum 3 GPA. *Application deadlines:* rolling (freshmen), rolling (transfers). *Notification:* continuous (freshmen), continuous (transfers).

Freshman Application Contact Dr. Steve Maples, Director of Undergraduate Admissions, University of Nevada, Reno, Mail Stop 120, Reno, NV 89557. *Phone:* 775-784-4700. *Toll-free phone:* 866-263-8232. *Fax:* 775-784-4283. *E-mail:* asknevada@unr.edu. *Web site:* http://www.unr.edu/.

University of Phoenix–Las Vegas Campus

Las Vegas, Nevada

Freshman Application Contact Ms. Audra McQuarie, Registrar/Executive Director, University of Phoenix–Las Vegas Campus, 4305 South Riverpoint Parkway, Mail Stop CF-L101, Phoenix, AZ 85040. *Phone:* 480-557-6151. *Toll-free phone:* 800-776-4867 (in-state); 800-228-7240 (out-of-state). *Fax:* 480-643-3068. *E-mail:* audra.mcquarie@phoenix.edu. *Web site:* http://www.phoenix.edu/.

University of Phoenix–Northern Nevada Campus

Reno, Nevada

Freshman Application Contact Ms. Audra McQuarie, Registrar/Executive Director, University of Phoenix–Northern Nevada Campus, 4035 South Riverpoint Parkway, Mail Stop CF-L101, Phoenix, AZ 85040. *Phone:* 480-557-6151. *Fax:* 480-643-3068. *E-mail:* audra.mcquarie@phoenix.edu. *Web site:* http://www.phoenix.edu/.

Western Nevada College

Carson City, Nevada

Freshman Application Contact Admissions and Records, Western Nevada College, 2201 West College Parkway, Carson City, NV 89703. *Phone:* 775-445-2377. *Fax:* 775-445-3147. *E-mail:* wncc_aro@wncc.edu. *Web site:* http://www.wnc.edu/.

NEW HAMPSHIRE

Chester College of New England

Chester, New Hampshire

Freshman Application Contact Michael Hayes, Director of Admissions, Chester College of New England, 40 Chester Street, Chester, NH 03036. *Phone:* 603-887-7400. *Toll-free phone:* 800-974-6372. *Fax:* 603-887-1777. *E-mail:* admissions@chestercollege.edu. *Web site:* http://www.chestercollege.edu/.

Colby-Sawyer College

New London, New Hampshire

Freshman Application Contact Director of Admissions and Financial Aid, Colby-Sawyer College, 541 Main Street, New London, NH 03257-4648. *Phone:* 603-526-3700. *Toll-free phone:* 800-272-1015. *Fax:* 603-526-3452. *E-mail:* admissions@colby-sawyer.edu. *Web site:* http://www.colby-sawyer.edu/.

See page 1226 for the College Close-Up.

PROFILES

Daniel Webster College

Nashua, New Hampshire

- **Independent** comprehensive, founded 1965
- **Suburban** 59-acre campus
- **Coed** 693 undergraduate students, 94% full-time, 23% women, 77% men

Undergraduates 652 full-time, 41 part-time. Students come from 25 states and territories; 14 other countries; 62% are from out of state; 4% Black or African American, non-Hispanic/Latino; 2% Hispanic/Latino; 0.4% Asian, non-Hispanic/Latino; 2% Native Hawaiian or other Pacific Islander, non-Hispanic/Latino; 27% Race/ethnicity unknown; 0.1% international; 6% transferred in; 61% live on campus. *Retention:* 72% of full-time freshmen returned.

Freshmen *Admission:* 107 enrolled.

Faculty *Total:* 80, 35% full-time, 18% with terminal degrees. *Student/faculty ratio:* 16:1.

Academics *Calendar:* semesters. *Degrees:* diplomas, bachelor's, and master's. *Special study options:* academic remediation for entering students, advanced placement credit, distance learning, double majors, independent study, internships, part-time degree program, services for LD students, summer session for credit. *ROTC:* Army (c), Air Force (c).

Computers on Campus 46 computers/terminals and 519 ports are available on campus for general student use. Students can access the following: campus intranet, computer help desk, free student e-mail accounts, online (class) grades, online (class) schedules. Campuswide network is available. 100% of college-owned or -operated housing units are wired for high-speed Internet access. Wireless service is available via entire campus.

Student Life *Housing:* on-campus residence required through sophomore year. *Options:* coed, men-only, women-only, disabled students. Campus housing is university owned. Freshman campus housing is guaranteed. *Activities and organizations:* Student Activity Board, Gaming Guild, Silver Wings (a national organization affiliated with Arnold Air Society), AIAA (American Institute of Aeronautics and Astronautics), Culinary Club. *Campus security:* 24-hour emergency response devices and patrols, controlled dormitory access. *Student services:* health clinic, personal/psychological counseling.

Athletics Member NCAA. All Division III. *Intercollegiate sports:* baseball M, basketball M/W, cross-country running M/W, field hockey W, golf M, ice hockey M(c), lacrosse M/W, soccer M/W, softball W, volleyball M/W. *Intra-*

mural sports: basketball M/W, football M/W, ultimate Frisbee M/W, volleyball M/W.

Standardized Tests *Required:* SAT or ACT (for admission).

Costs (2011–12) *Comprehensive fee:* $25,385 includes full-time tuition ($14,370), mandatory fees ($725), and room and board ($10,290). Part-time tuition: $479 per credit. *Required fees:* $479 per credit part-time. *College room only:* $5050. Room and board charges vary according to board plan and housing facility. *Payment plan:* installment. *Waivers:* employees or children of employees.

Financial Aid Of all full-time matriculated undergraduates who enrolled in 2006, 567 applied for aid, 566 were judged to have need. 369 Federal Work-Study jobs (averaging $2000). In 2006, 31 non-need-based awards were made. *Average percent of need met:* 72%. *Average financial aid package:* $15,371. *Average need-based loan:* $4257. *Average need-based gift aid:* $6114. *Average non-need-based aid:* $8287. *Average indebtedness upon graduation:* $45,000.

Applying *Options:* electronic application, deferred entrance. *Required:* high school transcript. *Recommended:* interview. *Application deadlines:* rolling (freshmen), rolling (out-of-state freshmen), rolling (transfers). *Notification:* continuous (freshmen), continuous (out-of-state freshmen), continuous (transfers).

Freshman Application Contact Admissions Office, Daniel Webster College, 20 University Drive, Nashua, NH 03063-1300. *Phone:* 800-794-6188. *Toll-free phone:* 800-325-6876. *Web site:* http://www.dwc.edu/.

Daniel Webster College–Portsmouth Campus

Portsmouth, New Hampshire

- **Independent** comprehensive, founded 1999
- **Suburban** 59-acre campus
- **Coed** 693 undergraduate students, 94% full-time, 23% women, 77% men

Undergraduates 652 full-time, 41 part-time. Students come from 25 states and territories; 14 other countries; 62% are from out of state; 4% Black or African American, non-Hispanic/Latino; 2% Hispanic/Latino; 0.4% Asian, non-Hispanic/Latino; 2% Native Hawaiian or other Pacific Islander, non-Hispanic/

Latino; 27% Race/ethnicity unknown; 0.1% international; 6% transferred in; 61% live on campus. *Retention:* 72% of full-time freshmen returned. **Freshmen** *Admission:* 107 enrolled.

Faculty *Total:* 80, 35% full-time, 18% with terminal degrees. *Student/faculty ratio:* 16:1.

Academics *Special study options:* academic remediation for entering students, advanced placement credit, distance learning, double majors, independent study, internships, part-time degree program, services for LD students, summer session for credit. *ROTC:* Air Force (c).

Computers on Campus 46 computers/terminals and 519 ports are available on campus for general student use. Students can access the following: campus intranet, computer help desk, free student e-mail accounts, online (class) grades, online (class) schedules. Campuswide network is available. 100% of college-owned or -operated housing units are wired for high-speed Internet access. Wireless service is available via entire campus.

Student Life *Housing:* on-campus residence required through sophomore year. *Options:* coed, men-only, women-only, disabled students. Campus housing is university owned. Freshman campus housing is guaranteed. *Activities and organizations:* Student Activity Board, Gaming Guild, Silver Wings (a national organization that works with Arnold Air Society), AIAA (American Institute of Aeronautics and Astronautics), Culinary Club. *Campus security:* 24-hour emergency response devices and patrols, controlled dormitory access. *Student services:* health clinic, personal/psychological counseling.

Athletics *Intercollegiate sports:* baseball M, basketball M/W, cross-country running M/W, field hockey W, golf M, ice hockey M(c), lacrosse M/W, soccer M/W, softball W, volleyball M/W. *Intramural sports:* basketball M/W, football M/W, ultimate Frisbee M/W, volleyball M/W.

Standardized Tests *Required:* SAT or ACT (for admission).

Costs (2011–12) *Comprehensive fee:* $25,385 includes full-time tuition ($14,370), mandatory fees ($725), and room and board ($10,290). Part-time tuition: $479 per credit. *Required fees:* $479 per credit part-time. *College room only:* $5050. Room and board charges vary according to board plan and housing facility. *Payment plan:* installment. *Waivers:* employees or children of employees.

Applying *Required:* high school transcript. *Recommended:* interview.

Freshman Application Contact Admissions Office, Daniel Webster College–Portsmouth Campus, 119 International Drive, Pease International Tradeport, Portsmouth, NH 03801. *Phone:* 800-794-6188. *Toll-free phone:* 800-794-6188. *Web site:* http://www.dwc.edu/gcde/portsmouth/.

Dartmouth College
Hanover, New Hampshire

- **Independent** university, founded 1769
- **Small-town** 265-acre campus
- **Endowment** $3.0 billion
- **Coed** 4,248 undergraduate students, 99% full-time, 50% women, 50% men
- **Most difficult** entrance level, 12% of applicants were admitted

Undergraduates 4,187 full-time, 61 part-time. Students come from 54 states and territories; 60 other countries; 95% are from out of state; 8% Black or African American, non-Hispanic/Latino; 8% Hispanic/Latino; 14% Asian, non-Hispanic/Latino; 0.2% Native Hawaiian or other Pacific Islander, non-Hispanic/Latino; 3% American Indian or Alaska Native, non-Hispanic/Latino; 2% Two or more races, non-Hispanic/Latino; 8% Race/ethnicity unknown; 8% international; 0.4% transferred in; 85% live on campus. *Retention:* 97% of full-time freshmen returned.

Freshmen *Admission:* 18,778 applied, 2,193 admitted, 1,136 enrolled. *Test scores:* SAT critical reading scores over 500: 99%; SAT math scores over 500: 100%; SAT writing scores over 500: 100%; SAT critical reading scores over 600: 93%; SAT math scores over 600: 96%; SAT writing scores over 600: 95%; SAT critical reading scores over 700: 67%; SAT math scores over 700: 73%; SAT writing scores over 700: 72%.

Faculty *Total:* 1,004, 80% full-time. *Student/faculty ratio:* 8:1.

Academics *Calendar:* quarters. *Degrees:* bachelor's, master's, doctoral-professional, and doctoral-research/scholarship. *Special study options:* advanced placement credit, double majors, honors programs, independent study, internships, off-campus study, services for LD students, student-designed majors, study abroad, summer session for credit. *ROTC:* Army (c). *Unusual degree programs:* 3-2 engineering.

Computers on Campus 200 computers/terminals are available on campus for general student use. Students can access the following: campus intranet, computer help desk, free student e-mail accounts, online (class) grades, online (class) registration, online (class) schedules. Campuswide network is available. 100% of college-owned or -operated housing units are wired for high-speed Internet access. Wireless service is available via entire campus.

Student Life *Housing:* on-campus residence required for freshman year. *Options:* coed, cooperative. Campus housing is university owned. Freshman campus housing is guaranteed. *Activities and organizations:* drama/theater group, student-run newspaper, radio and television station, choral group,

marching band, Dartmouth Student Assembly, Dartmouth Outing Club, national fraternities, national sororities. *Campus security:* 24-hour emergency response devices and patrols, student patrols, late-night transport/escort service, controlled dormitory access. *Student services:* health clinic, personal/psychological counseling, women's center.

Athletics Member NCAA. All Division I except football (Division I-AA). *Intercollegiate sports:* badminton M(c)/W(c), baseball M, basketball M/W, cheerleading M(c)/W(c), crew M/W, cross-country running M/W, equestrian sports M/W, fencing M(c)/W(c), field hockey W, golf M/W, gymnastics M(c)/W(c), ice hockey M/W, lacrosse M/W, rugby M(c)/W(c), sailing M/W, skiing (cross-country) M/W, skiing (downhill) M/W, soccer M/W, softball W, squash M/W, swimming and diving M/W, table tennis M(c)/W(c), tennis M/W, track and field M/W, ultimate Frisbee M(c)/W(c), volleyball M(c)/W, water polo M(c)/W(c), wrestling M(c). *Intramural sports:* baseball M, basketball M/W, cross-country running M/W, football M/W, golf M/W, ice hockey M/W, lacrosse M/W, racquetball M/W, riflery M/W, rugby M/W, skiing (cross-country) M/W, skiing (downhill) M/W, soccer M/W, softball M/W, squash M/W, swimming and diving M/W, table tennis M/W, tennis M/W, track and field M/W, volleyball M/W, water polo M/W, weight lifting M/W, wrestling M.

Standardized Tests *Required:* SAT or ACT (for admission), SAT Subject Tests (for admission).

Costs (2010–11) *Comprehensive fee:* $52,275 includes full-time tuition ($39,978), mandatory fees ($459), and room and board ($11,838). *College room only:* $7077. Room and board charges vary according to board plan. *Payment plans:* tuition prepayment, installment.

Financial Aid Of all full-time matriculated undergraduates who enrolled in 2009, 2,599 applied for aid, 2,278 were judged to have need, 2,278 had their need fully met. 1,386 Federal Work-Study jobs (averaging $2196). 475 state and other part-time jobs (averaging $1760). *Average percent of need met:* 100%. *Average financial aid package:* $39,203. *Average need-based loan:* $3537. *Average need-based gift aid:* $36,373. *Average indebtedness upon graduation:* $18,712. *Financial aid deadline:* 2/1.

Applying *Options:* electronic application, early admission, early decision, deferred entrance. *Application fee:* $75. *Required:* essay or personal statement, high school transcript, 2 letters of recommendation, peer evaluation. *Recommended:* interview. *Application deadlines:* 1/1 (freshmen), 3/1 (transfers). *Early decision deadline:* 11/1. *Notification:* 4/5 (freshmen), 4/25 (transfers), 12/15 (early decision).

Freshman Application Contact Maria Laskaris, Dean of Admissions and Financial Aid, Dartmouth College, 6016 McNutt Hall, Hanover, NH 03755. *Phone:* 603-646-2875. *E-mail:* admissions.office@dartmouth.edu. *Web site:* http://www.dartmouth.edu/.

Franklin Pierce University
Rindge, New Hampshire

- **Independent** university, founded 1962
- **Rural** 1000-acre campus
- **Endowment** $7.7 million
- **Coed** 1,809 undergraduate students, 85% full-time, 52% women, 48% men
- **Minimally difficult** entrance level, 93% of applicants were admitted

Undergraduates 1,535 full-time, 274 part-time. Students come from 28 states and territories; 16 other countries; 78% are from out of state; 3% Black or African American, non-Hispanic/Latino; 3% Hispanic/Latino; 0.6% Asian, non-Hispanic/Latino; 0.1% Native Hawaiian or other Pacific Islander, non-Hispanic/Latino; 0.3% American Indian or Alaska Native, non-Hispanic/Latino; 0.2% Two or more races, non-Hispanic/Latino; 13% Race/ethnicity unknown; 2% international; 3% transferred in; 84% live on campus. *Retention:* 69% of full-time freshmen returned.

Freshmen *Admission:* 2,401 applied, 2,239 admitted, 399 enrolled. *Average high school GPA:* 2.72. *Test scores:* SAT critical reading scores over 500: 38%; SAT math scores over 500: 44%; SAT writing scores over 500: 38%; ACT scores over 18: 83%; SAT critical reading scores over 600: 6%; SAT math scores over 600: 8%; SAT writing scores over 600: 6%; ACT scores over 24: 31%; SAT critical reading scores over 700: 1%; SAT writing scores over 700: 1%; ACT scores over 30: 2%.

Faculty *Total:* 316, 31% full-time, 38% with terminal degrees. *Student/faculty ratio:* 14:1.

Academics *Calendar:* differs by branch and program. *Degrees:* certificates, associate, bachelor's, master's, doctoral-other, doctoral-professional, and post-master's certificates (profile does not reflect significant enrollment at 6 continuing education sites; master's degree is only offered at these sites). *Special study options:* academic remediation for entering students, accelerated degree program, adult/continuing education programs, advanced placement credit, distance learning, double majors, English as a second language, external degree program, freshman honors college, honors programs, independent study, internships, off-campus study, part-time degree program, services for LD students, student-designed majors, study abroad, summer session for credit. *ROTC:* Army (c), Air Force (c). *Unusual degree programs:* business administration.

Computers on Campus 60 computers/terminals and 200 ports are available on campus for general student use. Students can access the following: campus intranet, computer help desk, free student e-mail accounts, online (class) grades, online (class) registration, online (class) schedules. Campuswide network is available. 100% of college-owned or -operated housing units are wired for high-speed Internet access. Wireless service is available via classrooms, computer labs, libraries, student centers.

Student Life *Housing:* on-campus residence required through senior year. *Options:* coed. Campus housing is university owned. Freshman campus housing is guaranteed. *Activities and organizations:* drama/theater group, student-run newspaper, radio and television station, choral group, Outing Club, WFPR Radio, Student Senate, Law Club, Business Club. *Campus security:* 24-hour emergency response devices and patrols, student patrols, late-night transport/escort service, controlled dormitory access. *Student services:* health clinic, personal/psychological counseling.

Athletics Member NCAA. All Division II. *Intercollegiate sports:* baseball M(s), basketball M(s)/W(s), crew M/W, cross-country running M/W, field hockey W(s), golf M, ice hockey M, lacrosse M/W, soccer M(s)/W(s), softball W(s), tennis M(s)/W(s), volleyball W(s). *Intramural sports:* baseball M, basketball M/W, cheerleading W(c), cross-country running M/W, fencing M(c)/W(c), field hockey W, football M, golf M, ice hockey M, lacrosse M/W, rugby M/W, soccer M/W, softball W, tennis M/W, volleyball M/W.

Standardized Tests *Required:* SAT or ACT (for admission).

Costs (2010–11) *Comprehensive fee:* $38,900 includes full-time tuition ($27,700), mandatory fees ($1100), and room and board ($10,100). Full-time tuition and fees vary according to course load, degree level, and location. Part-time tuition and fees vary according to course load, degree level, and location. *College room only:* $5800. Room and board charges vary according to board plan, housing facility, and student level. *Payment plan:* installment. *Waivers:* senior citizens and employees or children of employees.

Financial Aid Of all full-time matriculated undergraduates who enrolled in 2008, 1,310 applied for aid, 1,168 were judged to have need, 194 had their need fully met. In 2008, 284 non-need-based awards were made. *Average percent of need met:* 66%. *Average financial aid package:* $18,733. *Average need-based loan:* $4921. *Average need-based gift aid:* $14,047. *Average non-need-based aid:* $8615. *Average indebtedness upon graduation:* $38,148.

Applying *Options:* electronic application, early admission, deferred entrance. *Application fee:* $40. *Required:* essay or personal statement, high school transcript, 1 letter of recommendation. *Required for some:* minimum 2 GPA. *Recommended:* minimum 2.2 GPA, interview. *Application deadlines:* rolling (freshmen), rolling (out-of-state freshmen), rolling (transfers). *Notification:* continuous (freshmen), continuous (out-of-state freshmen), continuous (transfers).

Freshman Application Contact Office of Admissions, Franklin Pierce University, 40 University Drive, Rindge, NH 03461. *Phone:* 603-899-4050. *Toll-free phone:* 800-437-0048. *Fax:* 603-899-4394. *E-mail:* admissions@franklinpierce.edu. *Web site:* http://www.franklinpierce.edu/.

Granite State College

Concord, New Hampshire

- **State and locally supported** 4-year, founded 1972, part of University System of New Hampshire
- **Suburban** campus
- **Coed** 1,590 undergraduate students, 47% full-time, 71% women, 29% men
- **Noncompetitive** entrance level, 100% of applicants were admitted

Undergraduates 740 full-time, 850 part-time. Students come from 23 states and territories; 10% are from out of state; 9% transferred in. *Retention:* 81% of full-time freshmen returned.

Freshmen *Admission:* 116 applied, 116 admitted, 61 enrolled.

Faculty *Total:* 185, 25% with terminal degrees. *Student/faculty ratio:* 10:1.

Academics *Calendar:* trimesters. *Degrees:* associate, bachelor's, and post-bachelor's certificates (offers primarily part-time degree programs; courses offered at 50 locations in New Hampshire). *Special study options:* academic remediation for entering students, accelerated degree program, adult/continuing education programs, advanced placement credit, cooperative education, distance learning, double majors, independent study, internships, off-campus study, part-time degree program, services for LD students, student-designed majors, summer session for credit. *ROTC:* Army (c).

Computers on Campus 139 computers/terminals are available on campus for general student use. Students can access the following: campus intranet, computer help desk, free student e-mail accounts, online (class) grades, online

(class) registration, online (class) schedules. Campuswide network is available. Wireless service is available via entire campus.

Student Life *Housing:* college housing not available. *Activities and organizations:* Alumni Learner Association, The Green Team. *Campus security:* UNH Alert, a system that provides emergency notifications via text and voice messages.

Costs (2010–11) *Tuition:* state resident $6240 full-time, $260 per credit part-time; nonresident $6600 full-time, $275 per credit part-time. *Required fees:* $195 full-time, $65 per term part-time. *Payment plan:* deferred payment. *Waivers:* senior citizens and employees or children of employees.

Applying *Options:* electronic application. *Application fee:* $45. *Required:* self-certify high school graduate or GED. *Application deadlines:* rolling (freshmen), rolling (transfers). *Notification:* continuous (freshmen), continuous (transfers).

Freshman Application Contact Dr. Elaine Millen, Dean of Center Operations, Granite State College, 53 Technology Lane, Ste 150, Conway, NH 03818. *Phone:* 603-447-3970. *Toll-free phone:* 800-582-7248 Ext. 313. *Fax:* 603-447-2740. *E-mail:* elaine.millen@granite.edu. *Web site:* http://www.granite.edu/.

Hesser College, Concord

Concord, New Hampshire

- **Proprietary** primarily 2-year
- **Coed**

Academics *Degrees:* certificates, diplomas, associate, and bachelor's.

Freshman Application Contact Hesser College, Concord, 25 Hall Street, Suite 104, Concord, NH 03301. *Phone:* 603-225-9200. *Web site:* http://www.concord.hesser.edu/.

Hesser College, Manchester

Manchester, New Hampshire

- **Proprietary** primarily 2-year, founded 1900
- **Urban** campus
- **Coed**

Academics *Calendar:* semesters. *Degrees:* certificates, diplomas, associate, and bachelor's.

Financial Aid Of all full-time matriculated undergraduates who enrolled in 2009, 700 Federal Work-Study jobs (averaging $1000).

Freshman Application Contact Hesser College, Manchester, 3 Sundial Avenue, Manchester, NH 03103. *Phone:* 603-668-6660. *Web site:* http://www.manchester.hesser.edu/.

Hesser College, Nashua

Nashua, New Hampshire

- **Proprietary** primarily 2-year
- **Coed**

Academics *Degrees:* certificates, diplomas, associate, and bachelor's.

Freshman Application Contact Hesser College, Nashua, 410 Amherst Street, Nashua, NH 03063. *Phone:* 603-883-0404. *Web site:* http://www.nashua.hesser.edu/.

Hesser College, Portsmouth

Portsmouth, New Hampshire

- **Proprietary** primarily 2-year
- **Coed**

Academics *Degrees:* certificates, diplomas, associate, and bachelor's.

Freshman Application Contact Hesser College, Portsmouth, 170 Commerce Way, Portsmouth, NH 03801. *Phone:* 603-436-5300. *Web site:* http://www.portsmouth.hesser.edu/.

Hesser College, Salem

Salem, New Hampshire

- **Proprietary** primarily 2-year
- **Coed**

Academics *Degrees:* certificates, diplomas, associate, and bachelor's.

Freshman Application Contact Hesser College, Salem, 11 Manor Parkway, Salem, NH 03079. *Phone:* 603-898-3480. *Web site:* http://www.salem.hesser.edu/.

Keene State College
Keene, New Hampshire

- **State-supported** comprehensive, founded 1909, part of University System of New Hampshire
- **Small-town** 160-acre campus
- **Coed** 5,206 undergraduate students, 94% full-time, 56% women, 44% men
- 70% of applicants were admitted

Undergraduates 4,904 full-time, 302 part-time. Students come from 23 states and territories; 3 other countries; 48% are from out of state; 0.6% Black or African American, non-Hispanic/Latino; 2% Hispanic/Latino; 0.6% Asian, non-Hispanic/Latino; 0.3% American Indian or Alaska Native, non-Hispanic/Latino; 0.9% Two or more races, non-Hispanic/Latino; 5% Race/ethnicity unknown; 0.1% international; 4% transferred in; 54% live on campus. *Retention:* 77% of full-time freshmen returned.

Freshmen *Admission:* 6,671 applied, 4,689 admitted, 1,205 enrolled. *Average high school GPA:* 3.05. *Test scores:* SAT critical reading scores over 500: 50%; SAT math scores over 500: 51%; SAT writing scores over 500: 51%; SAT critical reading scores over 600: 11%; SAT math scores over 600: 12%; SAT writing scores over 600: 10%; SAT critical reading scores over 700: 1%.

Faculty *Total:* 455, 43% full-time, 35% with terminal degrees. *Student/faculty ratio:* 18:1.

Academics *Calendar:* semesters. *Degrees:* certificates, bachelor's, master's, post-master's, and postbachelor's certificates. *Special study options:* advanced placement credit, cooperative education, double majors, English as a second language, freshman honors college, honors programs, independent study, internships, off-campus study, part-time degree program, services for LD students, student-designed majors, study abroad, summer session for credit. *ROTC:* Air Force (c). *Unusual degree programs:* 3-2 engineering with Clarkson University, University of New Hampshire.

Computers on Campus 500 computers/terminals are available on campus for general student use. Students can access the following: campus intranet, computer help desk, free student e-mail accounts, online (class) grades, online (class) registration, online (class) schedules, personal Web pages. Campuswide network is available. 100% of college-owned or -operated housing units are wired for high-speed Internet access. Wireless service is available via classrooms, computer centers, computer labs, learning centers, libraries, student centers.

Student Life *Housing options:* coed, women-only, disabled students. Campus housing is university owned. Freshman campus housing is guaranteed. *Activities and organizations:* drama/theater group, student-run newspaper, radio and television station, choral group, Social Activities Council, Concerned Students Coalition, Pride, Habitat for Humanity, sports clubs, national fraternities, national sororities. *Campus security:* 24-hour emergency response devices and patrols, late-night transport/escort service, controlled dormitory access. *Student services:* health clinic, personal/psychological counseling, women's center.

Athletics Member NCAA. All Division III. *Intercollegiate sports:* baseball M, basketball M/W, cross-country running M/W, field hockey W, lacrosse M/W, rock climbing M(c)/W(c), skiing (downhill) M(c)/W(c), soccer M/W, softball W, swimming and diving M/W, track and field M/W, volleyball W. *Intramural sports:* badminton M/W, basketball M/W, cheerleading M/W, fencing M(c), football M/W, racquetball M/W, soccer W, softball M/W, squash M/W, tennis M/W, volleyball M/W, water polo M/W.

Standardized Tests *Required:* SAT or ACT (for admission).

Costs (2010–11) *Tuition:* state resident $7650 full-time, $320 per credit part-time; nonresident $15,820 full-time, $660 per credit part-time. Part-time tuition and fees vary according to course load. *Required fees:* $2490 full-time, $99 per credit part-time. *Room and board:* $8670; room only: $5630. Room and board charges vary according to board plan and housing facility. *Payment plan:* installment. *Waivers:* senior citizens and employees or children of employees.

Financial Aid Of all full-time matriculated undergraduates who enrolled in 2008, 3,882 applied for aid, 2,828 were judged to have need, 522 had their need fully met. 784 Federal Work-Study jobs (averaging $1004). 644 state and other part-time jobs (averaging $1063). In 2008, 309 non-need-based awards were made. *Average percent of need met:* 70%. *Average financial aid package:* $9656. *Average need-based loan:* $4201. *Average need-based gift aid:* $6025. *Average non-need-based aid:* $2818. *Average indebtedness upon graduation:* $28,986. *Financial aid deadline:* 3/1.

Applying *Options:* electronic application, deferred entrance. *Application fee:* $40. *Required:* essay or personal statement, high school transcript, 1 letter of recommendation. *Application deadlines:* 4/1 (freshmen), rolling (transfers). *Notification:* continuous (freshmen), continuous (transfers).

Freshman Application Contact Ms. Margaret Richmond, Director of Admissions, Keene State College, 229 Main Street, Keene, NH 03435-2604. *Phone:* 603-358-2273. *Toll-free phone:* 800-KSC-1909. *Fax:* 603-358-2767. *E-mail:* admissions@keene.edu. *Web site:* http://www.keene.edu/.

Magdalen College
Warner, New Hampshire

Freshman Application Contact Admissions Director, Magdalen College, 511 Kearsarge Mountain Road, Warner, NH 03278. *Phone:* 603-456-2656. *Toll-free phone:* 877-498-1723. *Fax:* 603-456-2660. *E-mail:* admissions@magdalen.edu. *Web site:* http://www.magdalen.edu/.

New England College
Henniker, New Hampshire

- **Independent** comprehensive, founded 1946
- **Small-town** 225-acre campus with easy access to Boston
- **Endowment** $6.8 million
- **Coed** 984 undergraduate students, 94% full-time, 47% women, 53% men
- **Minimally difficult** entrance level, 80% of applicants were admitted

Undergraduates 923 full-time, 61 part-time. Students come from 28 states and territories; 22 other countries; 62% are from out of state; 7% Black or African American, non-Hispanic/Latino; 3% Hispanic/Latino; 2% Asian, non-Hispanic/Latino; 0.2% American Indian or Alaska Native, non-Hispanic/Latino; 0.1% Race/ethnicity unknown; 6% international; 8% transferred in; 62% live on campus. *Retention:* 59% of full-time freshmen returned.

Freshmen *Admission:* 1,893 applied, 1,512 admitted, 270 enrolled. *Average high school GPA:* 2.62. *Test scores:* SAT critical reading scores over 500: 30%; SAT math scores over 500: 35%; SAT writing scores over 500: 22%; ACT scores over 18: 66%; SAT critical reading scores over 600: 3%; SAT math scores over 600: 4%; SAT writing scores over 600: 2%; SAT critical reading scores over 700: 1%.

Faculty *Total:* 150, 43% full-time, 42% with terminal degrees. *Student/faculty ratio:* 12:1.

Academics *Calendar:* semesters. *Degrees:* associate, bachelor's, and master's. *Special study options:* academic remediation for entering students, accelerated degree program, adult/continuing education programs, advanced placement credit, distance learning, double majors, English as a second language, external degree program, honors programs, independent study, internships, off-campus study, part-time degree program, services for LD students, student-designed majors, study abroad, summer session for credit. *ROTC:* Army (c), Air Force (c). *Unusual degree programs:* 3-2 engineering with Clarkson University; nursing with Mass College of Pharmacy.

Computers on Campus 171 computers/terminals and 350 ports are available on campus for general student use. Students can access the following: campus intranet, computer help desk, free student e-mail accounts, online (class) grades, online (class) registration, online (class) schedules. Campuswide network is available. 100% of college-owned or -operated housing units are wired for high-speed Internet access. Wireless service is available via entire campus.

Student Life *Housing:* on-campus residence required through sophomore year. *Options:* coed. Campus housing is university owned. Freshman campus housing is guaranteed. *Activities and organizations:* drama/theater group, student-run newspaper, radio station, choral group, Student Senate, Campus Activities Board, Role Playing Association, International Student Association, Political Science Club, national fraternities, national sororities. *Campus security:* 24-hour emergency response devices and patrols, student patrols, late-night transport/escort service, controlled dormitory access, Emergency Text System. *Student services:* health clinic, personal/psychological counseling, women's center.

Athletics Member NCAA. All Division III. *Intercollegiate sports:* baseball M, basketball M/W, cross-country running M/W, field hockey W, ice hockey M/W, lacrosse M/W, soccer M/W, softball W. *Intramural sports:* basketball M/W, cheerleading M/W, golf M/W, ice hockey M/W, lacrosse M/W, rugby M/W, soccer M/W, softball W, table tennis M/W, tennis M/W, ultimate Frisbee M/W, volleyball M/W.

Costs (2011–12) *Comprehensive fee:* $41,163 includes full-time tuition ($30,215), mandatory fees ($280), and room and board ($10,668). Full-time tuition and fees vary according to class time, course load, degree level, location, program, and reciprocity agreements. Part-time tuition: $353 per semester hour. Part-time tuition and fees vary according to class time, course load, degree level, location, and program. *College room only:* $5549. Room and board charges vary according to board plan and housing facility. *Payment plan:* installment. *Waivers:* children of alumni, adult students, senior citizens, and employees or children of employees.

Financial Aid Of all full-time matriculated undergraduates who enrolled in 2009, 681 applied for aid, 667 were judged to have need, 47 had their need fully met. 239 Federal Work-Study jobs (averaging $1862). 33 state and other part-time jobs (averaging $1125). In 2009, 259 non-need-based awards were made. *Average percent of need met:* 73%. *Average financial aid package:* $22,947. *Average need-based loan:* $6812. *Average need-based gift aid:* $17,252. *Average non-need-based aid:* $11,075. *Average indebtedness upon graduation:* $36,203.

Applying *Options:* electronic application, deferred entrance. *Application fee:* $30. *Required:* essay or personal statement, high school transcript, 3 letters of recommendation. *Recommended:* interview. *Application deadlines:* 9/7 (freshmen), 8/7 (out-of-state freshmen), 8/7 (transfers). *Notification:* continuous (freshmen), continuous (out-of-state freshmen), continuous (transfers). **Freshman Application Contact** Valerie Salyer, Associate Director of Undergraduate Admissions, New England College, 98 Bridge Street, Henniker, NH 03242. *Phone:* 603-428 2223. *Toll-free phone:* 800-521-7642. *Fax:* 603-428 3155. *E-mail:* vsalyer@nec.edu. *Web site:* http://www.nec.edu/.

See page 1466 for the College Close-Up.

New Hampshire Institute of Art
Manchester, New Hampshire

- **Proprietary** 4-year, founded 1898
- **Urban** campus with easy access to Boston
- **Endowment** $220.1 million
- **Coed** 566 undergraduate students, 90% full-time, 69% women, 31% men
- **Moderately difficult** entrance level, 52% of applicants were admitted

Undergraduates 510 full-time, 56 part-time. Students come from 16 states and territories; 28% are from out of state; 0.5% Black or African American, non-Hispanic/Latino; 4% Hispanic/Latino; 1% Asian, non-Hispanic/Latino; 0.7% American Indian or Alaska Native, non-Hispanic/Latino; 10% Race/ethnicity unknown; 2% transferred in; 53% live on campus. *Retention:* 74% of full-time freshmen returned.
Freshmen *Admission:* 775 applied, 406 admitted, 196 enrolled. *Average high school GPA:* 2.97. *Test scores:* SAT critical reading scores over 500: 43%; SAT math scores over 500: 56%; SAT writing scores over 500: 46%; SAT critical reading scores over 600: 5%; SAT math scores over 600: 14%; SAT writing scores over 600: 12%; SAT math scores over 700: 1%.
Faculty *Total:* 79, 22% full-time, 44% with terminal degrees. *Student/faculty ratio:* 12:1.
Academics *Calendar:* semesters. *Degrees:* certificates, bachelor's, and post-bachelor's certificates. *Special study options:* adult/continuing education programs, advanced placement credit, cooperative education, double majors, independent study, part-time degree program, study abroad, summer session for credit.
Computers on Campus 100 computers/terminals are available on campus for general student use. Students can access the following: campus intranet, computer help desk, free student e-mail accounts, online (class) grades, online (class) registration, online (class) schedules. Campuswide network is available. 100% of college-owned or -operated housing units are wired for high-speed Internet access. Wireless service is available via entire campus.
Student Life *Housing options:* coed, women-only. Campus housing is university owned and leased by the school. *Activities and organizations:* choral group, Student Council, Comic Club, Neo-Victorian Club, Crit Club, Gay/Straight Alliance. *Campus security:* late-night transport/escort service, controlled dormitory access. *Student services:* personal/psychological counseling.
Standardized Tests *Recommended:* SAT and SAT Subject Tests or ACT (for admission).
Costs (2011–12) *Tuition:* $18,610 full-time, $1779 per course part-time. Part-time tuition and fees vary according to course load. *Required fees:* $1935 full-time, $245 per course part-time, $205 per term part-time. *Room only:* $7550. Room and board charges vary according to housing facility. *Payment plan:* installment. *Waivers:* employees or children of employees.
Applying *Options:* electronic application, early action, deferred entrance. *Application fee:* $25. *Required:* essay or personal statement, high school transcript, 2 letters of recommendation, interview, portfolio review. *Recommended:* interview. *Application deadlines:* rolling (freshmen), rolling (out-of-state freshmen), rolling (transfers), 12/6 (early action). *Notification:* continuous (freshmen), continuous (out-of-state freshmen), continuous (transfers), 12/23 (early action).
Freshman Application Contact Ms. Amanda Abbott, Assistant Director of Enrollment, New Hampshire Institute of Art, 148 Concord Street, Manchester, NH 03104-4158. *Phone:* 866-241-4918 Ext. 576. *Toll-free phone:* 866-241-4918. *Fax:* 603-647-0658. *E-mail:* aabbott@nhia.edu. *Web site:* http://www.nhia.edu/.

Plymouth State University
Plymouth, New Hampshire

- **State-supported** comprehensive, founded 1871, part of University System of New Hampshire
- **Small-town** 170-acre campus
- **Endowment** $6.4 million
- **Coed**
- **Moderately difficult** entrance level

Faculty *Student/faculty ratio:* 16:1.

Academics *Calendar:* semesters. *Degrees:* bachelor's, master's, doctoral-research/scholarship, post-master's, and postbachelor's certificates.

Student Life *Campus security:* 24-hour emergency response devices and patrols, student patrols, late-night transport/escort service, controlled dormitory access, shuttle bus service, crime prevention programs, self-defense education.

Athletics Member NCAA. All Division III.

Standardized Tests *Required:* SAT or ACT (for admission).

Costs (2010–11) *Tuition:* state resident $7650 full-time, $320 per credit hour part-time; nonresident $15,820 full-time, $660 per credit hour part-time. Full-time tuition and fees vary according to reciprocity agreements. Part-time tuition and fees vary according to course load and reciprocity agreements. *Required fees:* $2256 full-time, $97 per credit hour part-time. *Room and board:* $8840; room only: $6160. Room and board charges vary according to board plan and housing facility.

Financial Aid *Of all full-time matriculated undergraduates who enrolled in 2009,* 3,335 applied for aid, 2,421 were judged to have need, 440 had their need fully met. 1,737 Federal Work-Study jobs (averaging $2044). *In 2009,* 305 non-need-based awards were made. *Average percent of need met:* 62. *Average financial aid package:* $9403. *Average need-based loan:* $4225. *Average need-based gift aid:* $5042. *Average non-need-based aid:* $2567. *Average indebtedness upon graduation:* $29,709.

Applying *Options:* electronic application, deferred entrance. *Application fee:* $40. *Required:* essay or personal statement, high school transcript, 1 letter of recommendation. *Required for some:* interview.

Freshman Application Contact Mr. Eugene Fahey, Senior Associate Director of Admission, Plymouth State University, 17 High Street, MSC #52, Plymouth, NH 03264-1595. *Toll-free phone:* 800-842-6900. *Fax:* 603-535-2714. *E-mail:* plymouthadmit@plymouth.edu. *Web site:* http://www.plymouth.edu/.

Rivier College
Nashua, New Hampshire

- **Independent Roman Catholic** comprehensive, founded 1933
- **Suburban** 68-acre campus with easy access to Boston
- **Endowment** $25.4 million
- **Coed** 1,482 undergraduate students, 65% full-time, 83% women, 17% men
- **Moderately difficult** entrance level, 80% of applicants were admitted

Undergraduates 969 full-time, 513 part-time. Students come from 14 states and territories; 2 other countries; 38% are from out of state; 2% Black or African American, non-Hispanic/Latino; 5% Hispanic/Latino; 2% Asian, non-Hispanic/Latino; 0.7% American Indian or Alaska Native, non-Hispanic/Latino; 12% Race/ethnicity unknown; 0.1% international; 8% transferred in; 43% live on campus. *Retention:* 78% of full-time freshmen returned.

Freshmen *Admission:* 802 applied, 642 admitted, 263 enrolled. *Average high school GPA:* 2.87. *Test scores:* SAT critical reading scores over 500: 32%; SAT math scores over 500: 40%; SAT writing scores over 500: 37%; ACT scores over 18: 78%; SAT critical reading scores over 600: 4%; SAT math scores over 600: 5%; SAT writing scores over 600: 5%; ACT scores over 24: 14%.

Faculty *Total:* 194, 38% full-time, 36% with terminal degrees. *Student/faculty ratio:* 15:1.

Academics *Calendar:* semesters. *Degrees:* certificates, associate, bachelor's, master's, doctoral-research/scholarship, post-master's, and postbachelor's certificates. *Special study options:* accelerated degree program, advanced placement credit, double majors, English as a second language, honors programs, independent study, internships, off-campus study, part-time degree program, services for LD students. *ROTC:* Air Force (c).

Computers on Campus 189 computers/terminals are available on campus for general student use. Students can access the following: computer help desk, free student e-mail accounts, online (class) grades, online (class) registration, online (class) schedules. Campuswide network is available. Wireless service is available via entire campus.

Student Life *Housing options:* coed. Campus housing is university owned. Freshman campus housing is guaranteed. *Activities and organizations:* drama/theater group, student-run newspaper, choral group, Student Government Association, Student Program Board, Rivier Theater Company, Student Nurses

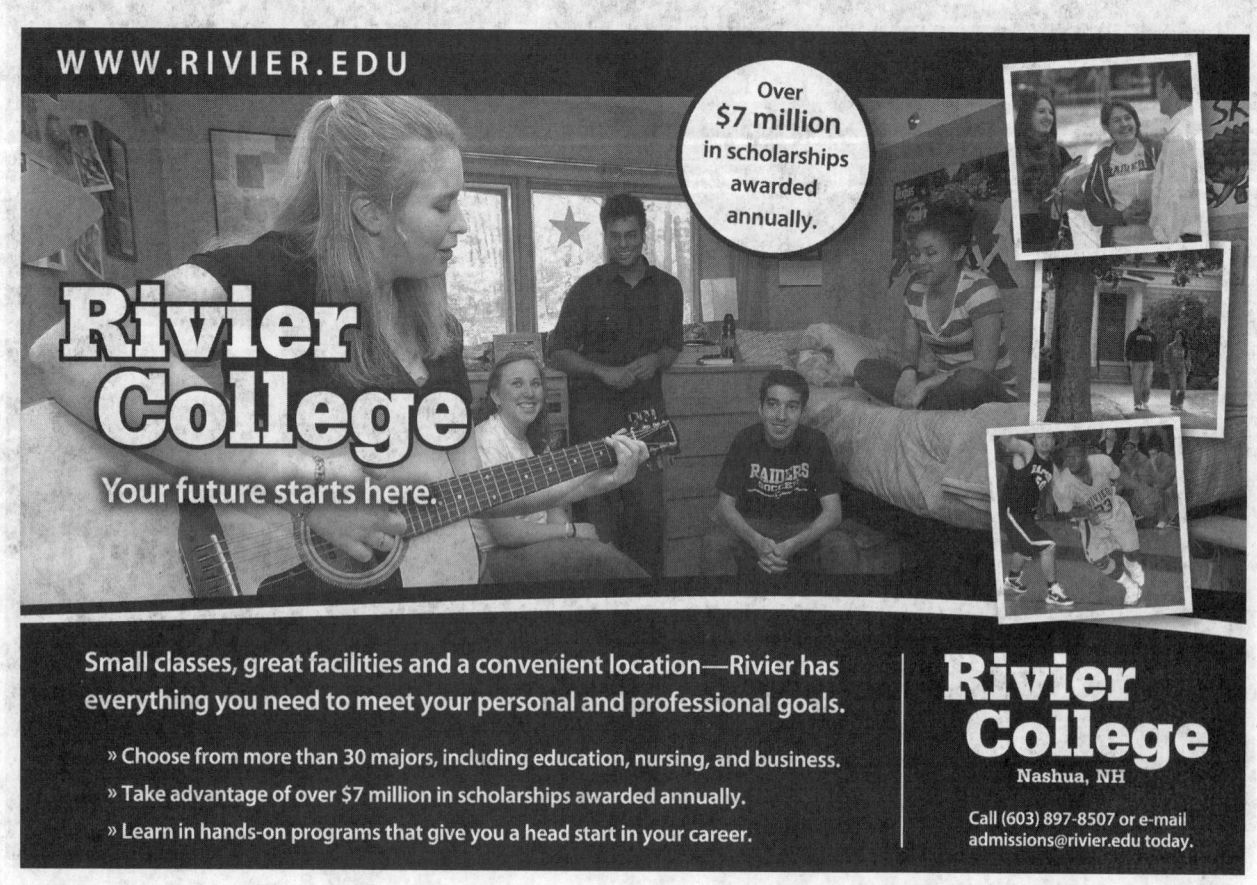

Association, Student Business Association. *Campus security:* 24-hour emergency response devices and patrols, late-night transport/escort service, controlled dormitory access. *Student services:* health clinic, personal/psychological counseling.

Athletics Member NCAA. All Division III. *Intercollegiate sports:* baseball M, basketball M/W, cross-country running M/W, field hockey W, lacrosse M/W, soccer M/W, softball W, volleyball M/W. *Intramural sports:* basketball M/W, soccer M/W, ultimate Frisbee M/W, volleyball M/W, weight lifting M/W.

Standardized Tests *Required:* SAT or ACT (for admission). *Required for some:* nursing exam.

Costs (2010–11) *One-time required fee:* $175. *Comprehensive fee:* $34,542 includes full-time tuition ($24,420), mandatory fees ($600), and room and board ($9522). Full-time tuition and fees vary according to program. Part-time tuition: $814 per credit. Part-time tuition and fees vary according to class time, course level, course load, and program. *Required fees:* $25 per year part-time. *Room and board:* Room and board charges vary according to board plan and housing facility. *Payment plans:* installment, deferred payment. *Waivers:* senior citizens and employees or children of employees.

Financial Aid Of all full-time matriculated undergraduates who enrolled in 2009, 888 applied for aid, 822 were judged to have need, 70 had their need fully met. In 2009, 105 non-need-based awards were made. *Average percent of need met:* 59%. *Average financial aid package:* $14,850. *Average need-based loan:* $4378. *Average need-based gift aid:* $10,806. *Average non-need-based aid:* $5066. *Average indebtedness upon graduation:* $43,189.

Applying *Options:* early action, deferred entrance. *Application fee:* $25. *Required:* essay or personal statement, high school transcript, 1 letter of recommendation. *Required for some:* interview. *Recommended:* minimum 2.3 GPA, interview. *Application deadlines:* rolling (freshmen), rolling (transfers), 11/15 (early action). *Notification:* continuous (freshmen), continuous (transfers), 12/1 (early action).

Freshman Application Contact David Boisvert, Vice President of Enrollment, Rivier College, 420 South Main Street, Nashua, NH 03060. *Phone:* 603-897-8507. *Toll-free phone:* 800-44RIVIER. *Fax:* 603-891-1799. *E-mail:* rivadmit@rivier.edu. *Web site:* http://www.rivier.edu/.

See page 1534 for the College Close-Up.

Saint Anselm College
Manchester, New Hampshire

- **Independent Roman Catholic** 4-year, founded 1889
- **Suburban** 450-acre campus with easy access to Boston
- **Endowment** $78.0 million
- **Coed** 1,896 undergraduate students, 98% full-time, 56% women, 44% men
- **Moderately difficult** entrance level, 77% of applicants were admitted

Undergraduates 1,857 full-time, 39 part-time. Students come from 29 states and territories; 5 other countries; 78% are from out of state; 1% Black or African American, non-Hispanic/Latino; 2% Hispanic/Latino; 1% Asian, non-Hispanic/Latino; 0.4% American Indian or Alaska Native, non-Hispanic/Latino; 0.6% Two or more races, non-Hispanic/Latino; 6% Race/ethnicity unknown; 0.4% international; 1% transferred in; 91% live on campus. *Retention:* 84% of full-time freshmen returned.

Freshmen *Admission:* 3,646 applied, 2,814 admitted, 536 enrolled. *Average high school GPA:* 3.11. *Test scores:* SAT critical reading scores over 500: 72%; SAT math scores over 500: 76%; SAT writing scores over 500: 73%; ACT scores over 18: 96%; SAT critical reading scores over 600: 23%; SAT math scores over 600: 24%; SAT writing scores over 600: 22%; ACT scores over 24: 39%; SAT critical reading scores over 700: 2%; SAT math scores over 700: 2%; SAT writing scores over 700: 1%; ACT scores over 30: 9%.

Faculty *Total:* 196, 72% full-time, 76% with terminal degrees. *Student/faculty ratio:* 12:1.

Academics *Calendar:* semesters. *Degree:* bachelor's. *Special study options:* advanced placement credit, honors programs, independent study, internships, off-campus study, part-time degree program, services for LD students, study abroad, summer session for credit. *ROTC:* Army (c), Air Force (c). *Unusual degree programs:* 3-2 engineering with University of Massachusetts Lowell, Catholic University of America, University of Notre Dame, Manhattan College.

Computers on Campus 400 computers/terminals are available on campus for general student use. Students can access the following: campus intranet, computer help desk, free student e-mail accounts, online (class) registration. Campuswide network is available. Wireless service is available via classrooms, computer centers, computer labs, dorm rooms, learning centers, libraries, student centers.

Student Life *Housing:* on-campus residence required for freshman year. *Options:* coed, men-only, women-only. Campus housing is university owned. Freshman campus housing is guaranteed. *Activities and organizations:* drama/theater group, student-run newspaper, radio station, choral group, Center for Volunteers, Anselmian Abbey Players, Knights of Columbus, spring break alternative, International Relations Club. *Campus security:* 24-hour emergency response devices and patrols, late-night transport/escort service, controlled dormitory access. *Student services:* health clinic, personal/psychological counseling.

Athletics Member NCAA. All Division II. *Intercollegiate sports:* baseball M, basketball M(s)/W(s), cheerleading W(c), cross-country running M/W, field hockey W, football M, golf M, ice hockey M/W, lacrosse M/W, skiing (downhill) M/W, soccer M/W, softball W, tennis M/W, volleyball W. *Intramural sports:* basketball M/W, football M/W, ice hockey M/W, racquetball M/W, rugby M(c)/W(c), skiing (cross-country) M/W, soccer M/W, softball M/W, swimming and diving M(c)/W(c), tennis M/W, track and field M(c)/W(c), ultimate Frisbee M/W, volleyball M/W, weight lifting M/W.

Standardized Tests *Required for some:* SAT or ACT (for admission).

Costs (2010–11) *Comprehensive fee:* $43,205 includes full-time tuition ($30,760), mandatory fees ($795), and room and board ($11,650). Part-time tuition: $3070 per course. *Room and board:* Room and board charges vary according to housing facility. *Payment plan:* installment. *Waivers:* employees or children of employees.

Financial Aid Of all full-time matriculated undergraduates who enrolled in 2009, 1,581 applied for aid, 1,384 were judged to have need, 216 had their need fully met. 1,184 Federal Work-Study jobs (averaging $1486). 7 state and other part-time jobs (averaging $2000). In 2009, 295 non-need-based awards were made. *Average percent of need met:* 81%. *Average financial aid package:* $23,864. *Average need-based loan:* $5529. *Average need-based gift aid:* $17,779. *Average non-need-based aid:* $9307. *Average indebtedness upon graduation:* $38,858. *Financial aid deadline:* 3/15.

Applying *Options:* electronic application, early action, deferred entrance. *Application fee:* $55. *Required:* essay or personal statement, high school transcript, 2 letters of recommendation. *Recommended:* interview. *Application deadlines:* 3/1 (freshmen), rolling (transfers), 11/15 (early action). *Notification:* continuous (freshmen), continuous (transfers), 1/15 (early action).

Freshman Application Contact Saint Anselm College, 100 Saint Anselm Drive, Manchester, NH 03102-1310. *Phone:* 603-641-7500. *Toll-free phone:* 888-4ANSELM. *Web site:* http://www.anselm.edu/.

See page 1554 for the College Close-Up.

Southern New Hampshire University
Manchester, New Hampshire

- **Independent** comprehensive, founded 1932
- **Suburban** 288-acre campus with easy access to Boston
- **Endowment** $19.1 million
- **Coed**
- **Moderately difficult** entrance level

Faculty *Student/faculty ratio:* 16:1.

Academics *Calendar:* semesters. *Degrees:* certificates, associate, bachelor's, master's, doctoral-research/scholarship, and postbachelor's certificates.

Student Life *Campus security:* 24-hour emergency response devices and patrols, student patrols, late-night transport/escort service, controlled dormitory access.

Athletics Member NCAA. All Division II.

Standardized Tests *Required:* SAT or ACT (for admission).

Costs (2010–11) *Comprehensive fee:* $36,618 includes full-time tuition ($26,112), mandatory fees ($330), and room and board ($10,176). Full-time tuition and fees vary according to class time. Part-time tuition: $1088 per credit. Part-time tuition and fees vary according to class time. *College room only:* $7276. Room and board charges vary according to board plan and housing facility.

Financial Aid Of all full-time matriculated undergraduates who enrolled in 2007, 1,560 applied for aid, 1,392 were judged to have need, 173 had their need fully met. In 2007, 330 non-need-based awards were made. *Average percent of need met:* 69. *Average financial aid package:* $15,514. *Average need-based loan:* $5174. *Average need-based gift aid:* $10,223. *Average non-need-based aid:* $3599.

Applying *Options:* electronic application, early action, deferred entrance. *Application fee:* $40. *Required:* essay or personal statement, high school transcript, minimum 2 GPA, 1 letter of recommendation. *Required for some:* 2 letters of recommendation. *Recommended:* interview.

Freshman Application Contact Mr. Steve Soba, Director of Admission, Southern New Hampshire University, 2500 North River Road, Manchester, NH 03106-1045. *Phone:* 603-645-9611. *Toll-free phone:* 800-642-4968. *Fax:* 603-645-9693. *E-mail:* admission@snhu.edu. *Web site:* http://www.snhu.edu/ .

See page 1618 for the College Close-Up.

Thomas More College of Liberal Arts
Merrimack, New Hampshire

- **Independent** 4-year, founded 1978, affiliated with Roman Catholic Church
- **Small-town** 14-acre campus with easy access to Boston
- **Coed** 99 undergraduate students, 100% full-time, 49% women, 51% men
- **Moderately difficult** entrance level, 70% of applicants were admitted

Undergraduates 99 full-time. Students come from 24 states and territories; 4 other countries; 84% are from out of state; 9% transferred in; 97% live on campus. *Retention:* 85% of full-time freshmen returned.
Freshmen *Admission:* 100 applied, 70 admitted, 24 enrolled. *Average high school GPA:* 3.33. *Test scores:* SAT critical reading scores over 500: 95%; SAT math scores over 500: 73%; ACT scores over 18: 100%; SAT critical reading scores over 600: 64%; SAT math scores over 600: 27%; ACT scores over 24: 100%; SAT critical reading scores over 700: 23%.
Faculty *Total:* 13. *Student/faculty ratio:* 12:1.
Academics *Calendar:* semesters. *Degree:* bachelor's. *Special study options:* independent study, study abroad.
Computers on Campus 6 computers/terminals are available on campus for general student use.
Student Life *Housing:* on-campus residence required through senior year. *Options:* men-only, women-only. Campus housing is university owned. Freshman campus housing is guaranteed. *Activities and organizations:* drama/theater group, choral group. *Campus security:* student patrols, late-night transport/escort service. *Student services:* personal/psychological counseling.
Standardized Tests *Recommended:* SAT or ACT (for admission).
Costs (2010–11) *Comprehensive fee:* $25,200 includes full-time tuition ($16,100) and room and board ($9100). *Payment plan:* installment. *Waivers:* employees or children of employees.
Financial Aid Of all full-time matriculated undergraduates who enrolled in 2009, 69 applied for aid, 64 were judged to have need, 11 had their need fully met. In 2009, 5 non-need-based awards were made. *Average percent of need met:* 77%. *Average financial aid package:* $15,632. *Average need-based loan:* $4129. *Average need-based gift aid:* $9775. *Average non-need-based aid:* $7620. *Average indebtedness upon graduation:* $28,194.
Applying *Options:* electronic application. *Required:* essay or personal statement, high school transcript, 2 letters of recommendation. *Required for some:* interview. *Application deadlines:* rolling (freshmen), rolling (transfers). *Notification:* continuous (freshmen), continuous (transfers).
Freshman Application Contact Teddy Sifert, Director of Admissions, Thomas More College of Liberal Arts, 6 Manchester Street, Merrimack, NH 03054-4818. *Toll-free phone:* 800-880-8308. *Fax:* 603-880-9280. *E-mail:* admissions@thomasmorecollege.edu. *Web site:* http://www.thomasmorecollege.edu/.

University of New Hampshire
Durham, New Hampshire

- **State-supported** university, founded 1866, part of University System of New Hampshire
- **Small-town** 2600-acre campus with easy access to Boston
- **Endowment** $195.6 million
- **Coed** 12,485 undergraduate students, 96% full-time, 55% women, 45% men
- **Moderately difficult** entrance level, 73% of applicants were admitted

Undergraduates 11,960 full-time, 525 part-time. Students come from 41 states and territories; 27 other countries; 40% are from out of state; 1% Black or African American, non-Hispanic/Latino; 3% Hispanic/Latino; 2% Asian, non-Hispanic/Latino; 0.2% American Indian or Alaska Native, non-Hispanic/Latino; 2% Two or more races, non-Hispanic/Latino; 5% Race/ethnicity unknown; 2% international; 5% transferred in; 59% live on campus. *Retention:* 89% of full-time freshmen returned.
Freshmen *Admission:* 16,545 applied, 12,140 admitted, 2,850 enrolled. *Test scores:* SAT critical reading scores over 500: 73%; SAT math scores over 500: 81%; ACT scores over 18: 98%; SAT critical reading scores over 600: 23%; SAT math scores over 600: 33%; ACT scores over 24: 65%; SAT critical reading scores over 700: 3%; SAT math scores over 700: 4%; ACT scores over 30: 10%.
Faculty *Total:* 1,008, 62% full-time, 59% with terminal degrees. *Student/faculty ratio:* 18:1.

Academics *Calendar:* semesters. *Degrees:* associate, bachelor's, master's, doctoral-research/scholarship, post-master's, and postbachelor's certificates. *Special study options:* accelerated degree program, advanced placement credit, cooperative education, distance learning, double majors, English as a second language, honors programs, independent study, internships, off-campus study, part-time degree program, services for LD students, student-designed majors, study abroad, summer session for credit. *ROTC:* Army (b), Air Force (b). *Unusual degree programs:* 3-2 business administration; social work; accounting, biochemistry, occupational therapy.
Computers on Campus 448 computers/terminals are available on campus for general student use. Students can access the following: campus intranet, computer help desk, free student e-mail accounts, online (class) grades, online (class) registration, online (class) schedules. Campuswide network is available. 100% of college-owned or -operated housing units are wired for high-speed Internet access. Wireless service is available via classrooms, computer centers, computer labs, dorm rooms, libraries, student centers.
Student Life *Housing options:* coed, disabled students. Campus housing is university owned. Freshman campus housing is guaranteed. *Activities and organizations:* drama/theater group, student-run newspaper, radio station, choral group, marching band, Campus Activity Board, The Outing Club, SCOPE (Student Committee on Popular Entertainment), Best Buddies, Memorial Union Student Organization, national fraternities, national sororities. *Campus security:* 24-hour emergency response devices and patrols, student patrols, late-night transport/escort service, controlled dormitory access, lighted pathways and sidewalks. *Student services:* health clinic, personal/psychological counseling, women's center, legal services.
Athletics Member NCAA. All Division I except football (Division I-AA). *Intercollegiate sports:* archery M(c)/W(c), badminton M(c)/W(c), baseball M(c), basketball M(s)/W(s), crew M(c)/W(c), cross-country running M(s)/W(s), fencing M(c)/W(c), field hockey W(s), golf M(c)/W(c), gymnastics W(s), ice hockey M(s)/W(s), lacrosse M(c)/W(s), riflery M(c)/W(c), rock climbing M(c)/W(c), rugby M(c)/W(c), sailing M(c)/W(c), skiing (cross-country) M(s)/W(s), skiing (downhill) M(s)/W(s), soccer M(s)/W(s), softball W(c), swimming and diving W(s), tennis M(c)/W(c), track and field M(s)/W(s), ultimate Frisbee M(c)/W(c), volleyball M(c)/W(c), wrestling M(c). *Intramural sports:* baseball M/W, basketball M/W, field hockey W, football M/W, ice hockey M/W, racquetball M/W, soccer M/W, softball M/W, swimming and diving M/W, table tennis M/W, tennis M/W, volleyball M/W, water polo M/W.
Standardized Tests *Required:* SAT or ACT (for admission).
Costs (2010–11) *Tuition:* state resident $10,730 full-time, $447 per credit hour part-time; nonresident $24,700 full-time, $1029 per credit hour part-time. Full-time tuition and fees vary according to degree level and program. Part-time tuition and fees vary according to course load, degree level, and program. *Required fees:* $2942 full-time, $736 per term part-time. *Room and board:* $9053; room only: $5528. Room and board charges vary according to board plan and housing facility. *Payment plan:* installment. *Waivers:* employees or children of employees.
Financial Aid Of all full-time matriculated undergraduates who enrolled in 2008, 9,112 applied for aid, 7,288 were judged to have need, 1,486 had their need fully met. 4,675 Federal Work-Study jobs (averaging $2486). 2,709 state and other part-time jobs (averaging $1850). In 2008, 2287 non-need-based awards were made. *Average percent of need met:* 81%. *Average financial aid package:* $20,195. *Average need-based loan:* $3323. *Average need-based gift aid:* $3679. *Average non-need-based aid:* $8289. *Average indebtedness upon graduation:* $32,323.
Applying *Options:* electronic application, early action, deferred entrance. *Application fee:* $50. *Required:* essay or personal statement, high school transcript, 1 letter of recommendation. *Recommended:* minimum 3 GPA. *Application deadlines:* 2/1 (freshmen), 2/1 (out-of-state freshmen), 3/1 (transfers), 11/15 (early action). *Notification:* 4/15 (freshmen), 4/15 (out-of-state freshmen), 4/15 (transfers), 1/15 (early action).
Freshman Application Contact Admissions Office, University of New Hampshire, 4 Garrison Avenue, Durham, NH 03824. *Phone:* 603-862-0077. *E-mail:* admissions@unh.edu. *Web site:* http://www.unh.edu/.

See page 1714 for the College Close-Up.

University of New Hampshire at Manchester
Manchester, New Hampshire

- **State-supported** comprehensive, founded 1967, part of University System of New Hampshire
- **Urban** campus with easy access to Boston
- **Coed** 1,003 undergraduate students, 68% full-time, 52% women, 48% men
- **Moderately difficult** entrance level, 80% of applicants were admitted

Undergraduates 685 full-time, 318 part-time. Students come from 4 states and territories; 5 other countries; 2% are from out of state; 2% Black or African American, non-Hispanic/Latino; 4% Hispanic/Latino; 2% Asian, non-Hispanic/Latino; 0.1% Native Hawaiian or other Pacific Islander, non-Hispanic/ Latino; 1% Two or more races, non-Hispanic/Latino; 13% Race/ethnicity unknown; 0.1% international; 12% transferred in. *Retention:* 56% of full-time freshmen returned.

Freshmen *Admission:* 257 applied, 206 admitted, 111 enrolled. *Test scores:* SAT critical reading scores over 500: 49%; SAT math scores over 500: 55%; SAT writing scores over 500: 39%; SAT critical reading scores over 600: 14%; SAT math scores over 600: 11%; SAT writing scores over 600: 7%; SAT critical reading scores over 700: 3%.

Faculty *Total:* 98, 37% full-time, 76% with terminal degrees. *Student/faculty ratio:* 12:1.

Academics *Calendar:* semesters. *Degrees:* certificates, associate, bachelor's, and master's. *Special study options:* academic remediation for entering students, adult/continuing education programs, advanced placement credit, double majors, independent study, internships, off-campus study, part-time degree program, services for LD students, student-designed majors, study abroad, summer session for credit. *ROTC:* Army (c), Air Force (c). *Unusual degree programs:* 3-2 pharmacy program with Massachusetts College of Pharmacy and Health Sciences.

Computers on Campus 47 computers/terminals are available on campus for general student use. Students can access the following: online (class) registration. Campuswide network is available. Wireless service is available via entire campus.

Student Life *Housing:* college housing not available. *Activities and organizations:* student-run radio station, Student Council. *Campus security:* 24-hour emergency response devices, late-night transport/escort service.

Standardized Tests *Required:* SAT or ACT (for admission).

Costs (2010–11) *Tuition:* state resident $10,650 full-time, $444 per credit hour part-time; nonresident $24,700 full-time, $1029 per credit hour part-time. Full-time tuition and fees vary according to course load and program. Part-time tuition and fees vary according to course load and program. *Required fees:* $576 full-time. *Payment plan:* installment. *Waivers:* senior citizens and employees or children of employees.

Financial Aid Of all full-time matriculated undergraduates who enrolled in 2008, 625 applied for aid, 477 were judged to have need, 57 had their need fully met. 164 Federal Work-Study jobs (averaging $2165). In 2008, 6 non-need-based awards were made. *Average percent of need met:* 66%. *Average financial aid package:* $11,739. *Average need-based loan:* $3683. *Average need-based gift aid:* $1924. *Average non-need-based aid:* $583. *Average indebtedness upon graduation:* $23,685.

Applying *Options:* electronic application, deferred entrance. *Application fee:* $45. *Required:* essay or personal statement, high school transcript, 1 letter of recommendation. *Recommended:* interview. *Application deadlines:* 6/15 (freshmen), 6/15 (transfers). *Notification:* continuous (freshmen), continuous (transfers).

Freshman Application Contact Ms. Donna Lukasiak, Senior Assistant Director Admissions, University of New Hampshire at Manchester, 400 Commercial Street, Manchester, NH 03101. *Phone:* 603-641-4150. *Fax:* 603-641-4342. *E-mail:* unhm@unh.edu. *Web site:* http://www.unhm.unh.edu/.

NEW JERSEY

Berkeley College

Woodland Park, New Jersey

Freshman Application Contact Berkeley College, 44 Rifle Camp Road, Woodland Park, NJ 07424-3353. *Phone:* 973-278-5400. *Toll-free phone:* 800-446-5400. *Web site:* http://www.berkeleycollege.edu/.

Beth Medrash Govoha

Lakewood, New Jersey

Director of Admissions Director of Admissions, Beth Medrash Govoha, 617 Sixth Street, Lakewood, NJ 08701-2797. *Phone:* 908-367-1060 Ext. 4224.

Bloomfield College

Bloomfield, New Jersey

- **Independent** comprehensive, founded 1868, affiliated with Presbyterian Church (U.S.A.)
- **Suburban** 12-acre campus with easy access to New York City
- **Endowment** $8.5 million
- **Coed** 2,168 undergraduate students, 85% full-time, 64% women, 36% men
- **Moderately difficult** entrance level, 49% of applicants were admitted

Undergraduates 1,852 full-time, 316 part-time. Students come from 19 states and territories; 37 other countries; 6% are from out of state; 54% Black or African American, non-Hispanic/Latino; 18% Hispanic/Latino; 3% Asian, non-Hispanic/Latino; 0.1% American Indian or Alaska Native, non-Hispanic/Latino; 0.1% Two or more races, non-Hispanic/Latino; 10% Race/ethnicity unknown; 2% international; 11% transferred in; 25% live on campus. *Retention:* 74% of full-time freshmen returned.

Freshmen *Admission:* 3,120 applied, 1,524 admitted, 423 enrolled. *Average high school GPA:* 2.61. *Test scores:* SAT critical reading scores over 500: 11%; SAT math scores over 500: 16%; SAT critical reading scores over 600: 1%; SAT math scores over 600: 2%.

Faculty *Total:* 220, 30% full-time, 33% with terminal degrees. *Student/faculty ratio:* 17:1.

Academics *Calendar:* semesters. *Degrees:* certificates, bachelor's, master's, and postbachelor's certificates. *Special study options:* academic remediation for entering students, accelerated degree program, advanced placement credit, cooperative education, distance learning, double majors, English as a second language, honors programs, independent study, internships, off-campus study, part-time degree program, services for LD students, student-designed majors, study abroad, summer session for credit. *ROTC:* Army (c).

Computers on Campus 300 computers/terminals and 50 ports are available on campus for general student use. Students can access the following: computer help desk, free student e-mail accounts, online (class) grades, online (class) schedules. Campuswide network is available. 100% of college-owned or -operated housing units are wired for high-speed Internet access. Wireless service is available via classrooms, computer centers, dorm rooms, learning centers, libraries, student centers.

Student Life *Housing options:* coed. Campus housing is university owned and is provided by a third party. *Activities and organizations:* drama/theater group, student-run newspaper, radio station, Greek Council, Team Infinite, Total Residential Undergraduate Education, Bloomfield College Student Government, Gentlemen's Club, national fraternities, national sororities. *Campus security:* 24-hour emergency response devices and patrols, late-night transport/escort service, security cameras in high-traffic areas. *Student services:* health clinic, personal/psychological counseling.

Athletics Member NCAA. All Division II. *Intercollegiate sports:* baseball M(s), basketball M(s)/W(s), cross-country running M(s)/W(s), soccer M(s)/W(s), softball W(s), tennis M(s), volleyball W(s). *Intramural sports:* basketball M/W, volleyball M/W.

Standardized Tests *Required:* SAT or ACT (for admission).

Costs (2010–11) *Comprehensive fee:* $33,000 includes full-time tuition ($21,200), mandatory fees ($1200), and room and board ($10,600). Part-time tuition: $2230 per course. Part-time tuition and fees vary according to course load. *College room only:* $5300. Room and board charges vary according to housing facility. *Payment plans:* installment, deferred payment. *Waivers:* senior citizens and employees or children of employees.

Financial Aid Of all full-time matriculated undergraduates who enrolled in 2009, 1,693 applied for aid, 1,574 were judged to have need, 178 had their need fully met. 478 Federal Work-Study jobs (averaging $2211). In 2009, 86 non-need-based awards were made. *Average percent of need met:* 74%. *Average financial aid package:* $23,758. *Average need-based loan:* $4044. *Average need-based gift aid:* $14,334. *Average non-need-based aid:* $12,986. *Average indebtedness upon graduation:* $30,515. *Financial aid deadline:* 6/1.

Applying *Options:* electronic application, early action, deferred entrance. *Application fee:* $40. *Required:* essay or personal statement, high school transcript, minimum 2.5 GPA, 2 letters of recommendation, graded essay/term paper or personal essay. *Required for some:* interview. *Application deadlines:* 8/1 (freshmen), 8/1 (out-of-state freshmen), 8/1 (transfers), 12/1 (early action). *Notification:* continuous (freshmen), continuous (out-of-state freshmen), continuous (transfers), 12/23 (early action).

Freshman Application Contact Mr. Adam Castro, Director of Admissions, Bloomfield College, Office of Enrollment Management and Admission, Bloomfield, NJ 07003-9981. *Phone:* 973-748-9000 Ext. 219. *Toll-free phone:* 800-848-4555 Ext. 230. *Fax:* 973-748-0916. *E-mail:* admission@bloomfield.edu. *Web site:* http://www.bloomfield.edu/.

Caldwell College

Caldwell, New Jersey

Freshman Application Contact Mr. Stephen Quinn, Director of Undergraduate Admissions, Caldwell College, 120 Bloomfield Avenue, Caldwell, NJ 07006. *Phone:* 973-618-3320. *Fax:* 973-618-3600. *E-mail:* admissions@caldwell.edu. *Web site:* http://www.caldwell.edu/.

Centenary College

Hackettstown, New Jersey

- **Independent** comprehensive, founded 1867, affiliated with United Methodist Church
- **Suburban** campus
- **Endowment** $2.4 million
- **Coed** 1,993 undergraduate students, 92% full-time, 63% women, 37% men
- **Moderately difficult** entrance level, 89% of applicants were admitted

Undergraduates 1,840 full-time, 153 part-time. Students come from 21 states and territories; 8 other countries; 12% are from out of state; 9% Black or African American, non-Hispanic/Latino; 7% Hispanic/Latino; 2% Asian, non-Hispanic/Latino; 0.1% American Indian or Alaska Native, non-Hispanic/Latino; 0.9% Two or more races, non-Hispanic/Latino; 14% Race/ethnicity unknown; 1% international; 9% transferred in; 54% live on campus. *Retention:* 75% of full-time freshmen returned.

Freshmen *Admission:* 826 applied, 732 admitted, 270 enrolled. *Average high school GPA:* 2.7. *Test scores:* SAT critical reading scores over 500: 33%; SAT math scores over 500: 35%; ACT scores over 18: 71%; SAT critical reading scores over 600: 8%; SAT math scores over 600: 5%; ACT scores over 24: 28%; SAT critical reading scores over 700: 1%; ACT scores over 30: 14%.

Faculty *Total:* 207, 35% full-time. *Student/faculty ratio:* 15:1.

Academics *Calendar:* semesters. *Degrees:* associate, bachelor's, master's, and postbachelor's certificates. *Special study options:* academic remediation for entering students, accelerated degree program, adult/continuing education programs, advanced placement credit, distance learning, double majors, English as a second language, honors programs, independent study, internships, off-campus study, part-time degree program, services for LD students, student-designed majors, study abroad, summer session for credit.

Computers on Campus 750 computers/terminals are available on campus for general student use. Students can access the following: campus intranet, computer help desk, free student e-mail accounts, online (class) grades, online (class) registration, online (class) schedules. Campuswide network is available. Wireless service is available via entire campus.

Student Life *Housing options:* coed, women-only. Campus housing is university owned. Freshman applicants given priority for college housing. *Activities and organizations:* drama/theater group, student-run newspaper, radio and television station, Student Government Association, First Year Leaders, Students in Free Enterprise (SIFE), Becca's Closet, International Student Organization. *Campus security:* 24-hour emergency response devices and patrols, late-night transport/escort service, controlled dormitory access. *Student services:* health clinic, personal/psychological counseling, women's center.

Athletics Member NCAA. All Division III. *Intercollegiate sports:* baseball M, basketball M/W, cheerleading W(c), cross-country running M/W, equestrian sports M(c)/W(c), golf M, lacrosse M/W, soccer M/W, softball W, volleyball W, wrestling M.

Standardized Tests *Required:* SAT or ACT (for admission).

Costs (2011–12) *Comprehensive fee:* $38,610 includes full-time tuition ($27,660), mandatory fees ($1230), and room and board ($9720). Full-time tuition and fees vary according to program. Part-time tuition: $535 per credit. Part-time tuition and fees vary according to program. *Required fees:* $30 per term part-time. *Room and board:* Room and board charges vary according to board plan. *Payment plan:* installment.

Financial Aid Of all full-time matriculated undergraduates who enrolled in 2008, 1,165 applied for aid, 1,025 were judged to have need, 191 had their need fully met. 239 Federal Work-Study jobs (averaging $645). 276 state and other part-time jobs (averaging $480). In 2008, 389 non-need-based awards were made. *Average percent of need met:* 67%. *Average financial aid package:* $17,741. *Average need-based loan:* $5625. *Average need-based gift aid:* $13,066. *Average non-need-based aid:* $7453. *Average indebtedness upon graduation:* $20,649.

Applying *Options:* electronic application, early action, deferred entrance. *Application fee:* $30. *Required:* essay or personal statement, high school transcript. *Required for some:* interview. *Recommended:* interview. *Application deadlines:* rolling (freshmen), rolling (transfers). *Notification:* continuous (freshmen), continuous (transfers).

Freshman Application Contact Centenary College, 400 Jefferson Street, Hackettstown, NJ 07840-2100. *Phone:* 908-852-1400. *Toll-free phone:* 800-236-8679. *Web site:* http://www.centenarycollege.edu/.

The College of New Jersey

Ewing, New Jersey

- **State-supported** comprehensive, founded 1855
- **Suburban** 255-acre campus with easy access to Philadelphia
- **Endowment** $18.5 million
- **Coed** 6,460 undergraduate students, 97% full-time, 57% women, 43% men
- **Very difficult** entrance level, 47% of applicants were admitted

Undergraduates 6,295 full-time, 165 part-time. Students come from 26 states and territories; 4 other countries; 6% are from out of state; 6% Black or African American, non-Hispanic/Latino; 9% Hispanic/Latino; 6% Asian, non-Hispanic/Latino; 0.5% Native Hawaiian or other Pacific Islander, non-Hispanic/Latino; 0.1% American Indian or Alaska Native, non-Hispanic/Latino; 2% Two or more races, non-Hispanic/Latino; 10% Race/ethnicity unknown; 0.6% international; 5% transferred in; 62% live on campus. *Retention:* 94% of full-time freshmen returned.

Freshmen *Admission:* 9,956 applied, 4,708 admitted, 1,421 enrolled. *Test scores:* SAT critical reading scores over 500: 92%; SAT math scores over 500: 96%; SAT writing scores over 500: 93%; SAT critical reading scores over 600: 59%; SAT math scores over 600: 72%; SAT writing scores over 600: 62%; SAT critical reading scores over 700: 12%; SAT math scores over 700: 19%; SAT writing scores over 700: 15%.

Faculty *Total:* 733, 47% full-time, 54% with terminal degrees. *Student/faculty ratio:* 13:1.

Academics *Calendar:* semesters. *Degrees:* bachelor's, master's, post-master's, and postbachelor's certificates. *Special study options:* academic remediation for entering students, accelerated degree program, advanced placement credit, double majors, honors programs, independent study, internships, off-campus study, part-time degree program, services for LD students, student-designed majors, study abroad, summer session for credit. *ROTC:* Army (c), Air Force (c). *Unusual degree programs:* 3-2 education of the deaf and hard of hearing and elementary education; special education and liberal arts.

Computers on Campus 631 computers/terminals are available on campus for general student use. Students can access the following: campus intranet, computer help desk, free student e-mail accounts, online (class) grades, online (class) registration, online (class) schedules. Campuswide network is available. 100% of college-owned or -operated housing units are wired for high-speed Internet access. Wireless service is available via classrooms, computer labs, learning centers, libraries, student centers.

Student Life *Housing:* on-campus residence required for freshman year. *Options:* coed, disabled students. Campus housing is university owned. Freshman campus housing is guaranteed. *Activities and organizations:* drama/theater group, student-run newspaper, radio and television station, choral group, Student Government Association, College Union Board, Inter-Greek Council, The Signal, national fraternities, national sororities. *Campus security:* 24-hour emergency response devices and patrols, student patrols, late-night transport/escort service, controlled dormitory access. *Student services:* health clinic, personal/psychological counseling, women's center, legal services.

Athletics Member NCAA. All Division III. *Intercollegiate sports:* baseball M, basketball M/W, cross-country running M/W, field hockey W, football M, lacrosse W, soccer M/W, softball W, swimming and diving M/W, tennis M/W, track and field M/W, wrestling M. *Intramural sports:* baseball M(c), basketball M(c)/W, bowling M(c)/W(c), cheerleading M(c)/W(c), crew M(c)/W(c), fencing M(c)/W(c), field hockey M/W, football M/W, golf M(c)/W(c), ice hockey M(c), lacrosse M(c)/W(c), racquetball M/W, rugby M(c)/W(c), skiing (cross-country) M(c)/W(c), skiing (downhill) M(c)/W(c), soccer M(c)/W(c), softball M/W(c), swimming and diving M(c)/W(c), table tennis M(c)/W(c), tennis M(c)/W(c), ultimate Frisbee M(c)/W(c), volleyball M(c)/W(c), water polo M(c)/W(c).

Standardized Tests *Required:* SAT or ACT (for admission).

Costs (2010–11) *Tuition:* state resident $9340 full-time, $331 per credit hour part-time; nonresident $18,726 full-time, $663 per credit hour part-time. Part-time tuition and fees vary according to course load. *Required fees:* $3933 full-time, $157 per credit hour part-time. *Room and board:* $10,358; room only: $7510. Room and board charges vary according to board plan. *Payment plan:* installment. *Waivers:* senior citizens and employees or children of employees.

Financial Aid Of all full-time matriculated undergraduates who enrolled in 2009, 4,544 applied for aid, 3,195 were judged to have need, 507 had their need fully met. 182 Federal Work-Study jobs (averaging $1426). In 2009, 775 non-need-based awards were made. *Average percent of need met:* 49%. *Average financial aid package:* $9775. *Average need-based loan:* $4520. *Average need-based gift aid:* $9690. *Average non-need-based aid:* $4242. *Average indebtedness upon graduation:* $27,057.

Applying *Options:* electronic application, early admission, early decision, deferred entrance. *Application fee:* $75. *Required:* essay or personal statement, high school transcript. *Required for some:* interview, art portfolio or music audition. *Recommended:* minimum 2.5 GPA, 3 letters of recommendation. *Application deadlines:* 1/15 (freshmen), 1/15 (transfers). *Early decision* *deadline:* 11/15. *Notification:* continuous (freshmen), continuous (transfers), 12/15 (early decision).

Freshman Application Contact Ms. Lisa Angeloni, Dean of Admissions, The College of New Jersey, PO Box 7718, Ewing, NJ 08628. *Phone:* 609-771-2131. *Toll-free phone:* 800-624-0967. *Fax:* 609-637-5174. *E-mail:* admiss@tcnj.edu. *Web site:* http://www.tcnj.edu/.

See page 1230 for the College Close-Up.

College of Saint Elizabeth

Morristown, New Jersey

- **Independent Roman Catholic** comprehensive, founded 1899
- **Suburban** 188-acre campus with easy access to New York City
- **Endowment** $18.3 million
- **Coed, primarily women** 1,256 undergraduate students, 48% full-time, 91% women, 9% men
- **Moderately difficult** entrance level, 80% of applicants were admitted

Undergraduates 603 full-time, 653 part-time. Students come from 10 states and territories; 47 other countries; 3% are from out of state; 17% Black or African American, non-Hispanic/Latino; 16% Hispanic/Latino; 5% Asian, non-Hispanic/Latino; 14% Race/ethnicity unknown; 6% international; 2% transferred in; 67% live on campus. *Retention:* 71% of full-time freshmen returned.

Freshmen *Admission:* 448 applied, 357 admitted, 118 enrolled. *Test scores:* SAT critical reading scores over 500: 25%; SAT math scores over 500: 22%; SAT writing scores over 500: 27%; SAT critical reading scores over 600: 5%; SAT math scores over 600: 5%; SAT writing scores over 600: 6%; SAT critical reading scores over 700: 1%; SAT math scores over 700: 1%; SAT writing scores over 700: 1%.

Faculty *Total:* 250, 28% full-time. *Student/faculty ratio:* 10:1.

Academics *Calendar:* semesters. *Degrees:* certificates, bachelor's, master's, doctoral-research/scholarship, and postbachelor's certificates (also offers coed adult undergraduate degree program and coed graduate programs). *Special study options:* academic remediation for entering students, accelerated degree program, advanced placement credit, distance learning, double majors, English as a second language, honors programs, independent study, internships, off-campus study, part-time degree program, services for LD students, student-

designed majors, study abroad, summer session for credit. *Unusual degree programs:* 3-2 business administration; counseling psychology.

Computers on Campus 127 computers/terminals and 20 ports are available on campus for general student use. Students can access the following: campus intranet, computer help desk, free student e-mail accounts, online (class) grades. Campuswide network is available. 100% of college-owned or -operated housing units are wired for high-speed Internet access. Wireless service is available via classrooms, computer labs, dorm rooms, libraries.

Student Life *Housing options:* women-only. Campus housing is university owned. Freshman campus housing is guaranteed. *Activities and organizations:* drama/theater group, student-run newspaper, choral group, Student Government Association, Students Take Action Committee, International/Intercultural Club, College Activities Board, Campus Ministry. *Campus security:* 24-hour emergency response devices and patrols, late-night transport/escort service, controlled dormitory access. *Student services:* health clinic, personal/psychological counseling.

Athletics Member NCAA. All Division III. *Intercollegiate sports:* basketball W, equestrian sports W, soccer W, softball W, swimming and diving W, tennis W, volleyball W. *Intramural sports:* volleyball W.

Standardized Tests *Required:* SAT or ACT (for admission).

Costs (2010–11) *Comprehensive fee:* $38,227 includes full-time tuition ($25,180), mandatory fees ($1707), and room and board ($11,340). Full-time tuition and fees vary according to degree level. Part-time tuition: $670 per credit hour. Part-time tuition and fees vary according to course load, degree level, location, and reciprocity agreements. *Required fees:* $70 per credit hour part-time. *Payment plan:* installment. *Waivers:* children of alumni, senior citizens, and employees or children of employees.

Financial Aid Of all full-time matriculated undergraduates who enrolled in 2008, 631 applied for aid, 507 were judged to have need. In 2008, 110 non-need-based awards were made. *Average need-based loan:* $5315. *Average need-based gift aid:* $14,148. *Average non-need-based aid:* $12,471.

Applying *Options:* electronic application, early admission, deferred entrance. *Application fee:* $35. *Required:* high school transcript, minimum 2 GPA, 2 letters of recommendation. *Recommended:* essay or personal statement, interview. *Application deadlines:* 8/15 (freshmen), rolling (transfers). *Notification:* 11/15 (freshmen), continuous (transfers).

Freshman Application Contact Ms. Donna Tatarka, Dean of Admissions, College of Saint Elizabeth, 2 Convent Road, Morristown, NJ 07960-6989.

Phone: 973-290-4700. *Toll-free phone:* 800-210-7900. *Fax:* 973-290-4710. *E-mail:* apply@csa.edu. *Web site:* http://www.cse.edu/.

See page 1232 for the College Close-Up.

DeVry University
North Brunswick, New Jersey

- **Proprietary** comprehensive, founded 1969, part of DeVry University
- **Urban** 10-acre campus with easy access to New York City
- **Coed** 1,773 undergraduate students, 47% full-time, 29% women, 71% men
- **Minimally difficult** entrance level

Undergraduates 827 full-time, 946 part-time. 6% are from out of state; 19% Black or African American, non-Hispanic/Latino; 21% Hispanic/Latino; 6% Asian, non-Hispanic/Latino; 0.5% Native Hawaiian or other Pacific Islander, non-Hispanic/Latino; 0.4% American Indian or Alaska Native, non-Hispanic/Latino; 0.3% Two or more races, non-Hispanic/Latino; 21% Race/ethnicity unknown; 1% international; 15% transferred in.
Freshmen *Admission:* 489 enrolled.
Faculty *Total:* 158, 23% full-time. *Student/faculty ratio:* 16:1.
Academics *Calendar:* semesters. *Degrees:* associate, bachelor's, and master's. *Special study options:* academic remediation for entering students, accelerated degree program, adult/continuing education programs, advanced placement credit, distance learning, part-time degree program, services for LD students, summer session for credit.
Computers on Campus Students can access the following: online (class) registration. Campuswide network is available.
Student Life *Housing:* college housing not available. *Campus security:* 24-hour emergency response devices and patrols, late-night transport/escort service.
Costs (2010–11) *Tuition:* $14,766 full-time, $580 per credit hour part-time. Full-time tuition and fees vary according to course load. Part-time tuition and fees vary according to course load. *Required fees:* $60 full-time, $30 per term part-time. *Payment plans:* installment, deferred payment. *Waivers:* employees or children of employees.
Financial Aid Of all full-time matriculated undergraduates who enrolled in 2007, 449 applied for aid, 430 were judged to have need, 9 had their need fully met. In 2007, 50 non-need-based awards were made. *Average percent of need* met: 34%. *Average financial aid package:* $12,399. *Average need-based loan:* $6629. *Average need-based gift aid:* $8242. *Average non-need-based aid:* $11,630. *Average indebtedness upon graduation:* $24,045.
Applying *Options:* electronic application, deferred entrance. *Application fee:* $50. *Required:* high school transcript, interview. *Application deadlines:* rolling (freshmen), rolling (transfers). *Notification:* continuous (freshmen), continuous (transfers).
Freshman Application Contact DeVry University, 630 US Highway 1, North Brunswick, NJ 08902-3362. *Phone:* 732-729-3532. *Web site:* http://www.devry.edu/.

DeVry University
Paramus, New Jersey

Admissions Office Contact DeVry University, 35 Plaza; 81 East State Route 4, Suite 102, Paramus, NJ 07652. *Web site:* http://www.devry.edu/.

Drew University
Madison, New Jersey

- **Independent** university, founded 1867, affiliated with United Methodist Church
- **Suburban** 186-acre campus with easy access to New York City
- **Coed** 1,787 undergraduate students, 96% full-time, 59% women, 41% men
- **Moderately difficult** entrance level, 80% of applicants were admitted

Undergraduates 1,713 full-time, 74 part-time. Students come from 39 states and territories; 21 other countries; 40% are from out of state; 9% Black or African American, non-Hispanic/Latino; 13% Hispanic/Latino; 5% Asian, non-Hispanic/Latino; 0.2% American Indian or Alaska Native, non-Hispanic/Latino; 2% Two or more races, non-Hispanic/Latino; 15% Race/ethnicity unknown; 2% international; 3% transferred in; 78% live on campus. *Retention:* 86% of full-time freshmen returned.
Freshmen *Admission:* 5,531 applied, 4,442 admitted, 495 enrolled. *Average high school GPA:* 3.34. *Test scores:* SAT critical reading scores over 500: 79%; SAT math scores over 500: 73%; SAT writing scores over 500: 78%; ACT scores over 18: 99%; SAT critical reading scores over 600: 38%; SAT

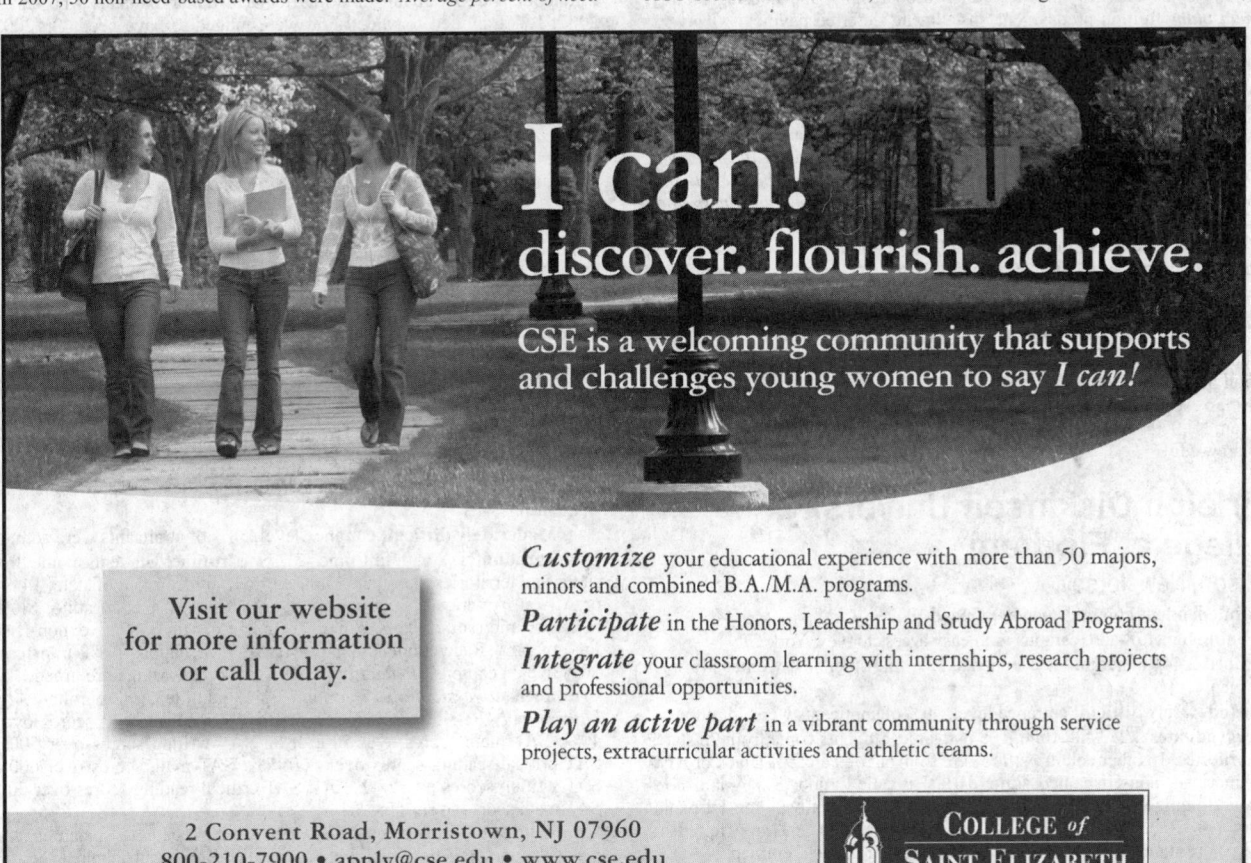

math scores over 600: 29%; SAT writing scores over 600: 37%; ACT scores over 24: 59%; SAT critical reading scores over 700: 7%; SAT math scores over 700: 4%; SAT writing scores over 700: 7%; ACT scores over 30: 13%.

Faculty *Total:* 256, 63% full-time. *Student/faculty ratio:* 11:1.

Academics *Calendar:* semesters. *Degrees:* bachelor's, master's, doctoral-professional, doctoral-research/scholarship, post-master's, and postbachelor's certificates. *Special study options:* academic remediation for entering students, accelerated degree program, adult/continuing education programs, advanced placement credit, double majors, external degree program, honors programs, independent study, internships, off-campus study, part-time degree program, services for LD students, student-designed majors, study abroad, summer session for credit. *Unusual degree programs:* 3-2 engineering with Columbia University, Washington University, Stevens Institute of Technology.

Computers on Campus 200 computers/terminals are available on campus for general student use. Students can access the following: campus intranet, computer help desk, free student e-mail accounts, online (class) grades, online (class) registration, online (class) schedules. Campuswide network is available. 100% of college-owned or -operated housing units are wired for high-speed Internet access. Wireless service is available via entire campus.

Student Life *Housing options:* coed, disabled students. Campus housing is university owned. Freshman campus housing is guaranteed. *Activities and organizations:* drama/theater group, student-run newspaper, radio and television station, choral group, The Acorn (student newspaper), Student Government Association, D.U.D.S.-Drew University Dramatic Society, University Program Board, Kuumba Pan African Student Association. *Campus security:* 24-hour emergency response devices and patrols, late-night transport/escort service, controlled dormitory access. *Student services:* health clinic, personal/psychological counseling.

Athletics Member NCAA. All Division III. *Intercollegiate sports:* baseball M, basketball M/W, cross-country running M/W, equestrian sports M/W, fencing M/W, field hockey W, lacrosse M/W, rugby M(c)/W(c), soccer M/W, softball W, swimming and diving M/W, tennis M/W. *Intramural sports:* basketball M/W, football M/W, racquetball M/W, soccer M/W, softball M/W, squash M/W, table tennis M/W, ultimate Frisbee M/W, volleyball M/W.

Costs (2010–11) *One-time required fee:* $325. *Comprehensive fee:* $50,322 includes full-time tuition ($38,765), mandatory fees ($785), and room and board ($10,772). Full-time tuition and fees vary according to course load. Part-time tuition and fees vary according to course load. *College room only:* $6964. Room and board charges vary according to board plan and housing facility. *Payment plans:* tuition prepayment, installment, deferred payment. *Waivers:* senior citizens and employees or children of employees.

Financial Aid Of all full-time matriculated undergraduates who enrolled in 2008, 1,186 applied for aid, 973 were judged to have need, 217 had their need fully met. 288 Federal Work-Study jobs (averaging $1261). 42 state and other part-time jobs (averaging $9854). In 2008, 605 non-need-based awards were made. *Average percent of need met:* 79%. *Average financial aid package:* $30,018. *Average need-based loan:* $5007. *Average need-based gift aid:* $24,363. *Average non-need-based aid:* $11,578. *Average indebtedness upon graduation:* $19,634. *Financial aid deadline:* 2/15.

Applying *Options:* electronic application, early admission, early decision, deferred entrance. *Application fee:* $50. *Required:* essay or personal statement, high school transcript, 1 letter of recommendation. *Recommended:* interview. *Application deadlines:* 2/15 (freshmen), 8/1 (transfers). *Early decision deadline:* 12/1 (for plan 1), 1/15 (for plan 2). *Notification:* 3/15 (freshmen), continuous until 4/1 (transfers), 12/24 (early decision plan 1), 2/15 (early decision plan 2).

Freshman Application Contact Drew University, 36 Madison Avenue, Madison, NJ 07940-1493. *Phone:* 973-408-3250. *Web site:* http://www.drew.edu/.

Fairleigh Dickinson University, College at Florham

Madison, New Jersey

- **Independent** comprehensive, founded 1942
- **Suburban** 178-acre campus with easy access to New York City
- **Coed** 2,441 undergraduate students, 93% full-time, 54% women, 46% men
- **Moderately difficult** entrance level, 70% of applicants were admitted

Undergraduates 2,273 full-time, 168 part-time. Students come from 28 states and territories; 16 other countries; 15% are from out of state; 9% Black or African American, non-Hispanic/Latino; 10% Hispanic/Latino; 3% Asian, non-Hispanic/Latino; 0.8% American Indian or Alaska Native, non-Hispanic/Latino; 11% Race/ethnicity unknown; 0.9% international; 6% transferred in; 61% live on campus. *Retention:* 71% of full-time freshmen returned.

Freshmen *Admission:* 4,220 applied, 2,943 admitted, 654 enrolled. *Average high school GPA:* 3.11. *Test scores:* SAT critical reading scores over 500: 49%; SAT math scores over 500: 57%; SAT writing scores over 500: 51%; SAT critical reading scores over 600: 12%; SAT math scores over 600: 12%;

SAT writing scores over 600: 13%; SAT critical reading scores over 700: 1%; SAT math scores over 700: 1%; SAT writing scores over 700: 1%.

Academics *Calendar:* semesters. *Degrees:* bachelor's, master's, post-master's, and postbachelor's certificates. *Special study options:* academic remediation for entering students, accelerated degree program, adult/continuing education programs, advanced placement credit, cooperative education, distance learning, double majors, honors programs, independent study, internships, off-campus study, part-time degree program, services for LD students, study abroad, summer session for credit. *ROTC:* Army (c), Air Force (c).

Computers on Campus 120 computers/terminals are available on campus for general student use. Students can access the following: computer help desk, free student e-mail accounts, online (class) grades, online (class) registration, online (class) schedules. Campuswide network is available. 100% of college-owned or -operated housing units are wired for high-speed Internet access. Wireless service is available via classrooms, computer centers, computer labs, learning centers, libraries, student centers.

Student Life *Housing options:* coed, disabled students. Campus housing is university owned. Freshman applicants given priority for college housing. *Activities and organizations:* drama/theater group, student-run newspaper, radio station, choral group, Student Government Association, Florham Programming Committee, Green Club, Association of Black Collegians, Latin American Student Organization, national fraternities, national sororities. *Campus security:* 24-hour emergency response devices and patrols, late-night transport/escort service, controlled dormitory access, trained law enforcement personnel on staff. *Student services:* health clinic, personal/psychological counseling.

Athletics Member NCAA. All Division III. *Intercollegiate sports:* baseball M, basketball M/W, cheerleading W, cross-country running M/W, field hockey W, football M, golf M/W, lacrosse M/W, soccer M/W, softball W, swimming and diving M/W, tennis M/W, volleyball W. *Intramural sports:* basketball M/W, football M, golf M/W, soccer M/W, softball M/W, volleyball M/W.

Standardized Tests *Required:* SAT or ACT (for admission).

Costs (2010–11) *Comprehensive fee:* $44,988 includes full-time tuition ($32,490), mandatory fees ($920), and room and board ($11,578). Part-time tuition: $866 per credit. *College room only:* $7342. Room and board charges vary according to board plan and housing facility. *Payment plans:* installment, deferred payment. *Waivers:* senior citizens and employees or children of employees.

Financial Aid Of all full-time matriculated undergraduates who enrolled in 2007, 1,788 applied for aid, 1,568 were judged to have need. In 2007, 213 non-need-based awards were made. *Average financial aid package:* $17,400. *Average need-based loan:* $4001. *Average need-based gift aid:* $9956. *Average non-need-based aid:* $6501.

Applying *Options:* electronic application, early admission, deferred entrance. *Application fee:* $40. *Required:* high school transcript, 2 letters of recommendation. *Required for some:* interview. *Application deadlines:* rolling (freshmen), rolling (transfers). *Notification:* continuous (freshmen), continuous (transfers).

Freshman Application Contact Fairleigh Dickinson University, College at Florham, 285 Madison Avenue, Madison, NJ 07940-1099. *Toll-free phone:* 800-338-8803. *Web site:* http://www.fdu.edu/.

Fairleigh Dickinson University, Metropolitan Campus

Teaneck, New Jersey

- **Independent** comprehensive, founded 1942
- **Suburban** 88-acre campus with easy access to New York City
- **Coed** 6,459 undergraduate students, 41% full-time, 58% women, 42% men
- **Moderately difficult** entrance level, 58% of applicants were admitted

Undergraduates 2,680 full-time, 3,779 part-time. Students come from 33 states and territories; 65 other countries; 15% are from out of state; 14% Black or African American, non-Hispanic/Latino; 30% Hispanic/Latino; 6% Asian, non-Hispanic/Latino; 0.2% American Indian or Alaska Native, non-Hispanic/Latino; 12% Race/ethnicity unknown; 7% international; 8% transferred in; 20% live on campus. *Retention:* 73% of full-time freshmen returned.

Freshmen *Admission:* 5,947 applied, 3,463 admitted, 782 enrolled. *Average high school GPA:* 3.65. *Test scores:* SAT critical reading scores over 500: 40%; SAT math scores over 500: 48%; SAT writing scores over 500: 41%; SAT critical reading scores over 600: 7%; SAT math scores over 600: 12%; SAT writing scores over 600: 10%; SAT critical reading scores over 700: 1%; SAT math scores over 700: 1%.

Academics *Calendar:* semesters. *Degrees:* certificates, associate, bachelor's, master's, doctoral-professional, post-master's, and postbachelor's certificates. *Special study options:* academic remediation for entering students, accelerated degree program, adult/continuing education programs, advanced placement credit, cooperative education, distance learning, double majors, English as a second language, honors programs, independent study, internships, off-campus study, part-time degree program, services for LD students, student-designed majors, study abroad, summer session for credit. *ROTC:* Army (c), Air Force (c).

Computers on Campus 200 computers/terminals are available on campus for general student use. Students can access the following: computer help desk, free student e-mail accounts, online (class) grades, online (class) registration, online (class) schedules. Campuswide network is available. 100% of college-owned or -operated housing units are wired for high-speed Internet access. Wireless service is available via classrooms, computer centers, computer labs, learning centers, libraries, student centers.

Student Life *Housing options:* coed. Campus housing is university owned. *Activities and organizations:* drama/theater group, student-run newspaper, radio station, choral group, Indian Cultural Experience, Student Program Board, International Student Association, Equinox Newspaper, Business Leaders of Tomorrow, national fraternities, national sororities. *Campus security:* 24-hour emergency response devices and patrols, late-night transport/escort service, controlled dormitory access, trained law enforcement personnel on staff. *Student services:* health clinic, personal/psychological counseling, women's center.

Athletics Member NCAA. All Division I. *Intercollegiate sports:* baseball M(s), basketball M(s)/W(s), bowling W(s), cross-country running M(s)/W(s), fencing W(s), golf M(s)/W(s), soccer M(s)/W(s), softball W(s), tennis M(s)/W(s), track and field M(s)/W(s), volleyball W(s). *Intramural sports:* badminton M/W, baseball M, basketball M/W, bowling M(c)/W(c), cheerleading M(c)/W(c), crew W(c), fencing W(c), football M/W, rugby M(c), soccer M/W, tennis M/W, volleyball M/W.

Standardized Tests *Required:* SAT or ACT (for admission).

Costs (2010–11) *Comprehensive fee:* $42,966 includes full-time tuition ($30,140), mandatory fees ($920), and room and board ($11,906). Part-time tuition: $866 per credit. *College room only:* $7670. Room and board charges vary according to board plan and housing facility. *Payment plans:* installment, deferred payment. *Waivers:* senior citizens and employees or children of employees.

Financial Aid Of all full-time matriculated undergraduates who enrolled in 2007, 1,671 applied for aid, 1,549 were judged to have need. In 2007, 117 non-need-based awards were made. *Average financial aid package:* $18,283. *Average need-based loan:* $3808. *Average need-based gift aid:* $8702. *Average non-need-based aid:* $6403.

Applying *Options:* electronic application, early admission, deferred entrance. *Application fee:* $40. *Required:* high school transcript, 2 letters of recommendation. *Required for some:* interview. *Application deadlines:* rolling (freshmen), rolling (transfers). *Notification:* continuous (freshmen), continuous (transfers).

Freshman Application Contact Fairleigh Dickinson University, Metropolitan Campus, 1000 River Road, Teaneck, NJ 07666-1914. *Toll-free phone:* 800-338-8803. *Web site:* http://www.fdu.edu/.

Felician College

Lodi, New Jersey

- **Independent Roman Catholic** comprehensive, founded 1942
- **Suburban** 37-acre campus with easy access to New York City
- **Endowment** $4.2 million
- **Coed** 1,790 undergraduate students, 81% full-time, 75% women, 25% men
- **Moderately difficult** entrance level, 88% of applicants were admitted

Undergraduates 1,441 full-time, 349 part-time. Students come from 12 states and territories; 21 other countries; 5% are from out of state; 11% Black or African American, non-Hispanic/Latino; 19% Hispanic/Latino; 8% Asian, non-Hispanic/Latino; 0.4% Native Hawaiian or other Pacific Islander, non-Hispanic/Latino; 0.2% American Indian or Alaska Native, non-Hispanic/Latino; 0.2% Two or more races, non-Hispanic/Latino; 29% Race/ethnicity unknown; 0.6% international; 9% transferred in. *Retention:* 63% of full-time freshmen returned.

Freshmen *Admission:* 2,148 applied, 1,885 admitted, 326 enrolled. *Average high school GPA:* 2.98. *Test scores:* SAT critical reading scores over 500: 21%; SAT math scores over 500: 26%; SAT writing scores over 500: 22%; ACT scores over 18: 74%; SAT critical reading scores over 600: 5%; SAT math scores over 600: 6%; SAT writing scores over 600: 3%; ACT scores over 24: 27%; SAT critical reading scores over 700: 1%; SAT math scores over 700: 1%; ACT scores over 30: 3%.

Faculty *Total:* 233, 49% full-time. *Student/faculty ratio:* 11:1.

Academics *Calendar:* semesters. *Degrees:* certificates, associate, bachelor's, master's, post-master's, and postbachelor's certificates. *Special study options:* academic remediation for entering students, accelerated degree program, adult/continuing education programs, advanced placement credit, cooperative education, distance learning, double majors, English as a second language, honors programs, independent study, internships, off-campus study, part-time degree program, services for LD students, student-designed majors, summer session for credit.

Computers on Campus 100 computers/terminals are available on campus for general student use. Students can access the following: computer help desk, free student e-mail accounts, online (class) grades, online (class) registration, online (class) schedules. Campuswide network is available. Wireless service is available via dorm rooms, learning centers, libraries, student centers.

Student Life *Housing options:* coed, men-only, women-only, disabled students. Campus housing is university owned. Freshman applicants given priority for college housing. *Activities and organizations:* drama/theater group, student-run radio station, choral group, Student Nurses Association, Zeta Alpha Zeta teaching sorority, Campus Activity Board, Students In Free Enterprise (SIFE), Student Government Association. *Campus security:* 24-hour patrols, student patrols, late-night transport/escort service. *Student services:* health clinic, personal/psychological counseling.

Athletics Member NCAA, NAIA. All NCAA Division II. *Intercollegiate sports:* baseball M(s), basketball M(s)/W(s), cross-country running M(s)/W(s), golf M(s), soccer M(s)/W(s), softball W(s), volleyball W(s). *Intramural sports:* soccer M/W, softball W, volleyball M/W, weight lifting M/W.

Standardized Tests *Required:* SAT or ACT (for admission). *Required for some:* ACT (for admission), SAT Subject Tests (for admission).

Costs (2011–12) *Comprehensive fee:* $38,675 includes full-time tuition ($26,350), mandatory fees ($1575), and room and board ($10,750). Part-time tuition: $865 per credit hour. *Room and board:* Room and board charges vary according to housing facility. *Payment plan:* installment.

Financial Aid Of all full-time matriculated undergraduates who enrolled in 2009, 1,169 applied for aid, 980 were judged to have need, 85 had their need fully met. 88 Federal Work-Study jobs (averaging $1352). 90 state and other part-time jobs (averaging $2652). In 2009, 73 non-need-based awards were made. *Average need-based loan:* $5217. *Average need-based gift aid:* $12,249. *Average non-need-based aid:* $18,968. *Average indebtedness upon graduation:* $22,963.

Applying *Options:* deferred entrance. *Application fee:* $30. *Required:* high school transcript, minimum 2 GPA. *Required for some:* essay or personal statement, interview. *Application deadlines:* rolling (freshmen), rolling (transfers). *Notification:* continuous (freshmen), continuous (transfers).

Freshman Application Contact College Admissions Office, Felician College, 262 South Main Street, Lodi, NJ 07644-2117. *Phone:* 201-559-6131. *Fax:* 201-559-6138. *E-mail:* admissions@felician.edu. *Web site:* http://www.felician.edu/.

See page 1284 for the College Close-Up.

Georgian Court University
Lakewood, New Jersey

- **Independent Roman Catholic** comprehensive, founded 1908
- **Suburban** 156-acre campus with easy access to New York City and Philadelphia
- **Endowment** $39.8 million
- **Coed, primarily women** 1,969 undergraduate students, 75% full-time, 89% women, 11% men
- **Moderately difficult** entrance level, 66% of applicants were admitted

Undergraduates 1,472 full-time, 497 part-time. Students come from 15 states and territories; 7 other countries; 4% are from out of state; 11% transferred in; 25% live on campus. *Retention:* 75% of full-time freshmen returned.

Freshmen *Admission:* 910 applied, 601 admitted, 224 enrolled. *Average high school GPA:* 2.9.

Faculty *Total:* 288, 36% full-time, 46% with terminal degrees. *Student/faculty ratio:* 14:1.

Academics *Calendar:* semesters. *Degrees:* certificates, bachelor's, master's, post-master's, and postbachelor's certificates. *Special study options:* academic remediation for entering students, accelerated degree program, adult/continuing education programs, advanced placement credit, distance learning, double majors, English as a second language, honors programs, independent study, internships, off-campus study, part-time degree program, services for LD students, study abroad, summer session for credit. *Unusual degree programs:* business administration.

Computers on Campus 197 computers/terminals are available on campus for general student use. Students can access the following: campus intranet, computer help desk, free student e-mail accounts, online (class) grades, online (class) registration, online (class) schedules. Campuswide network is available. 100% of college-owned or -operated housing units are wired for high-speed Internet access. Wireless service is available via classrooms, computer centers, computer labs, dorm rooms, learning centers, libraries, student centers.

Student Life *Housing options:* women-only. Campus housing is university owned. Freshman campus housing is guaranteed. *Activities and organizations:* student-run newspaper, choral group, Women in Leadership Development, Student Government Association, Latin American Student Organization, Social Work Club, Golden Z. *Campus security:* 24-hour emergency response devices and patrols, late-night transport/escort service, controlled dormitory access. *Student services:* health clinic, personal/psychological counseling.
Athletics Member NCAA. All Division II. *Intercollegiate sports:* basketball W(s), cross-country running W(s), lacrosse W(s), soccer W(s), softball W(s), tennis W(s), track and field W(s), volleyball W(s).
Standardized Tests *Recommended:* SAT or ACT (for admission).
Costs (2010–11) *Comprehensive fee:* $36,032 includes full-time tuition ($24,932), mandatory fees ($1244), and room and board ($9856). Part-time tuition: $570 per credit hour. Part-time tuition and fees vary according to location. *Required fees:* $622 per year part-time. *Payment plan:* installment. *Waivers:* employees or children of employees.
Financial Aid Of all full-time matriculated undergraduates who enrolled in 2009, 1,345 applied for aid, 1,208 were judged to have need, 400 had their need fully met. 199 Federal Work-Study jobs (averaging $1478). 30 state and other part-time jobs (averaging $1425). In 2009, 125 non-need-based awards were made. *Average percent of need met:* 86%. *Average financial aid package:* $21,915. *Average need-based loan:* $7133. *Average need-based gift aid:* $13,565. *Average non-need-based aid:* $7132. *Average indebtedness upon graduation:* $35,632. *Financial aid deadline:* 8/1.
Applying *Options:* electronic application, early action, deferred entrance. *Application fee:* $40. *Required:* high school transcript, minimum 2.5 GPA, 2 letters of recommendation. *Recommended:* essay or personal statement, interview. *Application deadlines:* 8/1 (freshmen), 8/1 (transfers), 11/15 (early action). *Notification:* continuous (freshmen), 12/30 (early action).
Freshman Application Contact Ms. Maria Colon, Assistant Director of Undergraduate Admissions, Georgian Court University, 900 Lakewood Avenue. *Phone:* 732-987-2760. *Toll-free phone:* 800-458-8422. *Fax:* 732-987-2000. *E-mail:* admissions@georgian.edu. *Web site:* http://www.georgian.edu/.

See page 1308 for the College Close-Up.

Kean University
Union, New Jersey

- **State-supported** comprehensive, founded 1855, part of New Jersey State College System
- **Suburban** 186-acre campus with easy access to New York City
- **Endowment** $10.9 million
- **Coed** 13,052 undergraduate students, 78% full-time, 61% women, 39% men
- **Moderately difficult** entrance level, 70% of applicants were admitted

Undergraduates 10,178 full-time, 2,874 part-time. Students come from 22 states and territories; 56 other countries; 2% are from out of state; 19% Black or African American, non-Hispanic/Latino; 22% Hispanic/Latino; 6% Asian, non-Hispanic/Latino; 0.2% Native Hawaiian or other Pacific Islander, non-Hispanic/Latino; 0.2% American Indian or Alaska Native, non-Hispanic/Latino; 0.8% Two or more races, non-Hispanic/Latino; 3% Race/ethnicity unknown; 2% international; 15% transferred in; 15% live on campus. *Retention:* 81% of full-time freshmen returned.
Freshmen *Admission:* 6,030 applied, 4,227 admitted, 1,765 enrolled. *Average high school GPA:* 3.
Faculty *Total:* 1,365, 25% full-time. *Student/faculty ratio:* 19:1.
Academics *Calendar:* semesters. *Degrees:* bachelor's, master's, doctoral-research/scholarship, and post-master's certificates. *Special study options:* academic remediation for entering students, accelerated degree program, adult/continuing education programs, advanced placement credit, cooperative education, distance learning, double majors, English as a second language, honors programs, independent study, internships, off-campus study, part-time degree program, services for LD students, study abroad, summer session for credit. *ROTC:* Army (c), Air Force (c). *Unusual degree programs:* 3-2 public administration; occupational therapy; science & technology; instruction & curriculum; biology/physician's assistant; health information management or psychology/psychiatric rehabilitation; DPT: UMDNJ; MD: Drexel University; DPM: NewYork College of Podiatric Medicine.
Computers on Campus 1,700 computers/terminals and 2,000 ports are available on campus for general student use. Students can access the following: free student e-mail accounts, online (class) grades, online (class) registration, online (class) schedules. Campuswide network is available. 100% of college-owned or -operated housing units are wired for high-speed Internet access. Wireless service is available via entire campus.
Student Life *Housing options:* coed, disabled students. Campus housing is university owned. Freshman applicants given priority for college housing. *Activities and organizations:* drama/theater group, student-run newspaper, radio station, choral group, Student Organization of Kean University, Graduate

and Part-time Student Council, Educators of Tomorrow, Delta Phi Epsilon, Kean Dance Theatre, national fraternities, national sororities. *Campus security:* 24-hour emergency response devices and patrols, student patrols, late-night transport/escort service, controlled dormitory access, 24-hour patrols by campus police. *Student services:* health clinic, personal/psychological counseling.
Athletics Member NCAA. All Division III. *Intercollegiate sports:* baseball M, basketball M/W, field hockey W, football M, lacrosse M/W, soccer M/W, softball W, tennis W, volleyball M/W. *Intramural sports:* basketball M/W, soccer M/W, softball M/W, tennis M/W, volleyball M/W, weight lifting M/W.
Standardized Tests *Required:* SAT or ACT (for admission).
Costs (2010–11) *Tuition:* state resident $6411 full-time, $230 per credit hour part-time; nonresident $12,000 full-time, $400 per credit hour part-time. Part-time tuition and fees vary according to course load. *Required fees:* $3404 full-time, $125 per credit hour part-time. *Room and board:* $12,950; room only: $10,000. Room and board charges vary according to board plan and housing facility. *Payment plan:* installment. *Waivers:* senior citizens and employees or children of employees.
Financial Aid Of all full-time matriculated undergraduates who enrolled in 2009, 8,056 applied for aid, 6,910 were judged to have need, 741 had their need fully met. 334 Federal Work-Study jobs (averaging $2154). In 2009, 66 non-need-based awards were made. *Average percent of need met:* 58%. *Average financial aid package:* $9431. *Average need-based loan:* $4436. *Average need-based gift aid:* $7044. *Average non-need-based aid:* $3808. *Average indebtedness upon graduation:* $20,668.
Applying *Options:* electronic application. *Application fee:* $75. *Required:* essay or personal statement, high school transcript, minimum 2.8 GPA. *Required for some:* interview. *Recommended:* 2 letters of recommendation. *Application deadlines:* 5/31 (freshmen), 7/6 (transfers). *Notification:* continuous (freshmen), continuous (transfers).
Freshman Application Contact Ms. Valerie Winslow, Director of Undergraduate Admissions, Kean University, 1000 Morris Avenue, Union, NJ 07083. *Phone:* 908-737-7100. *Fax:* 908-737-7105. *E-mail:* admitme@kean.edu. *Web site:* http://www.kean.edu/.

Monmouth University
West Long Branch, New Jersey

- **Independent** comprehensive, founded 1933
- **Suburban** 156-acre campus with easy access to New York City and Philadelphia
- **Endowment** $51.2 million
- **Coed** 4,669 undergraduate students, 92% full-time, 58% women, 42% men
- **Moderately difficult** entrance level, 60% of applicants were admitted

Undergraduates 4,285 full-time, 384 part-time. Students come from 22 states and territories; 17 other countries; 13% are from out of state; 4% Black or African American, non-Hispanic/Latino; 7% Hispanic/Latino; 2% Asian, non-Hispanic/Latino; 0.1% Native Hawaiian or other Pacific Islander, non-Hispanic/Latino; 0.1% American Indian or Alaska Native, non-Hispanic/Latino; 1% Two or more races, non-Hispanic/Latino; 6% Race/ethnicity unknown; 0.5% international; 7% transferred in; 47% live on campus. *Retention:* 80% of full-time freshmen returned.
Freshmen *Admission:* 6,561 applied, 3,934 admitted, 966 enrolled. *Average high school GPA:* 3.37. *Test scores:* SAT critical reading scores over 500: 71%; SAT math scores over 500: 79%; SAT writing scores over 500: 74%; ACT scores over 18: 100%; SAT critical reading scores over 600: 14%; SAT math scores over 600: 23%; SAT writing scores over 600: 20%; ACT scores over 24: 53%; SAT critical reading scores over 700: 1%; SAT math scores over 700: 2%; SAT writing scores over 700: 1%; ACT scores over 30: 1%.
Faculty *Total:* 603, 42% full-time, 48% with terminal degrees. *Student/faculty ratio:* 15:1.
Academics *Calendar:* semesters. *Degrees:* certificates, associate, bachelor's, master's, doctoral-professional, post-master's, and postbachelor's certificates. *Special study options:* academic remediation for entering students, accelerated degree program, advanced placement credit, cooperative education, distance learning, double majors, honors programs, independent study, internships, part-time degree program, services for LD students, student-designed majors, study abroad, summer session for credit. *ROTC:* Army (c), Air Force (c).
Computers on Campus 467 computers/terminals are available on campus for general student use. Students can access the following: computer help desk, free student e-mail accounts, online (class) grades, online (class) registration, online (class) schedules. Campuswide network is available. 85% of college-owned or -operated housing units are wired for high-speed Internet access. Wireless service is available via classrooms, computer centers, computer labs, dorm rooms, learning centers, libraries, student centers.
Student Life *Housing options:* coed. Campus housing is university owned and leased by the school. Freshman campus housing is guaranteed. *Activities and organizations:* drama/theater group, student-run newspaper, radio and television station, choral group, radio station WMCX 88.9 FM, Student Government

Association, student newspaper (Outlook), Student Activities Board, Shadows (yearbook), national fraternities, national sororities. *Campus security:* 24-hour emergency response devices and patrols, late-night transport/escort service, controlled dormitory access. *Student services:* health clinic, personal/psychological counseling, women's center, legal services.

Athletics Member NCAA. All Division I except football (Division I-AA). *Intercollegiate sports:* baseball M(s), basketball M(s)/W(s), bowling M(c)/W(s), cross-country running M(s)/W(s), field hockey W(s), golf M(s)/W(s), ice hockey M(c), lacrosse W(s), sailing M(c)/W(c), soccer M(s)/W(s), softball W(s), tennis M(s)/W(s), track and field M(s)/W(s). *Intramural sports:* badminton M/W, basketball M/W, cheerleading M(c)/W(c), field hockey W(c), football W, soccer M/W, softball M/W, volleyball M/W.

Standardized Tests *Required:* SAT or ACT (for admission).

Costs (2011–12) *One-time required fee:* $200. *Comprehensive fee:* $38,680 includes full-time tuition ($27,372), mandatory fees ($628), and room and board ($10,680). Part-time tuition: $793 per credit. *Required fees:* $157 per term part-time. *College room only:* $5932. Room and board charges vary according to board plan and housing facility. *Payment plan:* installment. *Waivers:* senior citizens and employees or children of employees.

Financial Aid Of all full-time matriculated undergraduates who enrolled in 2009, 3,480 applied for aid, 2,981 were judged to have need, 182 had their need fully met. 895 Federal Work-Study jobs (averaging $1976). In 2009, 1168 non-need-based awards were made. *Average percent of need met:* 69%. *Average financial aid package:* $19,984. *Average need-based loan:* $4794. *Average need-based gift aid:* $11,670. *Average non-need-based aid:* $7666. *Average indebtedness upon graduation:* $29,921.

Applying *Options:* electronic application, early action, deferred entrance. *Application fee:* $50. *Required:* high school transcript. *Required for some:* essay or personal statement, 2 letters of recommendation, interview. *Recommended:* resume of activities including community involvement and leadership positions. *Application deadlines:* 3/1 (freshmen), 7/15 (transfers), 12/1 (early action). *Notification:* 4/1 (freshmen), continuous (transfers), 1/15 (early action).

Freshman Application Contact Ms. Victoria Bobik, Director of Undergraduate Admission, Monmouth University, 400 Cedar Avenue, West Long Branch, NJ 07764-1898. *Phone:* 732-571-3456. *Toll-free phone:* 800-543-9671. *Fax:* 732-263-5166. *E-mail:* admission@monmouth.edu. *Web site:* http://www.monmouth.edu/.

See page 1446 for the College Close-Up.

Montclair State University
Montclair, New Jersey

- **State-supported** comprehensive, founded 1908
- **Suburban** 275-acre campus with easy access to New York City
- **Coed** 14,139 undergraduate students, 86% full-time, 61% women, 39% men
- **Moderately difficult** entrance level, 47% of applicants were admitted

Undergraduates 12,113 full-time, 2,026 part-time. Students come from 79 other countries; 3% are from out of state; 9% transferred in; 26% live on campus. *Retention:* 82% of full-time freshmen returned.

Freshmen *Admission:* 13,469 applied, 6,332 admitted, 2,114 enrolled. *Test scores:* SAT critical reading scores over 500: 46%; SAT math scores over 500: 53%; SAT writing scores over 500: 50%; SAT critical reading scores over 600: 10%; SAT math scores over 600: 11%; SAT writing scores over 600: 11%; SAT critical reading scores over 700: 1%; SAT math scores over 700: 1%; SAT writing scores over 700: 1%.

Faculty *Total:* 1,489, 37% full-time, 38% with terminal degrees. *Student/faculty ratio:* 17:1.

Academics *Calendar:* semesters. *Degrees:* bachelor's, master's, doctoral-research/scholarship, and postbachelor's certificates. *Special study options:* academic remediation for entering students, accelerated degree program, adult/continuing education programs, advanced placement credit, cooperative education, double majors, English as a second language, freshman honors college, honors programs, independent study, internships, off-campus study, part-time degree program, services for LD students, study abroad, summer session for credit. *ROTC:* Army (b), Navy (b), Air Force (b).

Computers on Campus 218 computers/terminals are available on campus for general student use. Students can access the following: campus intranet, computer help desk, free student e-mail accounts, online (class) grades, online (class) registration, online (class) schedules. Campuswide network is available. 20% of college-owned or -operated housing units are wired for high-speed Internet access. Wireless service is available via entire campus.

Student Life *Housing options:* coed, women-only. Campus housing is university owned and is provided by a third party. Freshman applicants given priority for college housing. *Activities and organizations:* drama/theater group, student-run newspaper, radio station, choral group, Latin American Student Organization, Campus Recreation, MSU Gamers, Unified Asian American Student Organization, Human Relations and Leadership Association, national fraterni-

ties, national sororities. *Campus security:* 24-hour emergency response devices and patrols, late-night transport/escort service, controlled dormitory access, video surveillance, student escorts. *Student services:* health clinic, personal/psychological counseling, women's center.

Athletics Member NCAA. All Division III. *Intercollegiate sports:* baseball M, basketball M/W, field hockey W, football M, golf M/W, lacrosse M/W, soccer M/W, softball W, swimming and diving M/W, track and field M/W, volleyball W. *Intramural sports:* badminton M(c)/W(c), baseball M, basketball M/W, bowling M/W, football M, ice hockey M(c), rugby M(c), softball M/W, volleyball M/W.

Standardized Tests *Required:* SAT or ACT (for admission).

Costs (2010–11) *Tuition:* state resident $7324 full-time, $244 per credit part-time; nonresident $15,656 full-time, $522 per credit part-time. *Required fees:* $155 per credit part-time. *Room and board:* $10,712; room only: $7442. Room and board charges vary according to board plan and housing facility. *Payment plan:* installment. *Waivers:* senior citizens and employees or children of employees.

Financial Aid Of all full-time matriculated undergraduates who enrolled in 2009, 8,878 applied for aid, 7,610 were judged to have need, 1,860 had their need fully met. 555 Federal Work-Study jobs (averaging $1383). 1,485 state and other part-time jobs (averaging $1940). In 2009, 179 non-need-based awards were made. *Average percent of need met:* 60%. *Average financial aid package:* $9153. *Average need-based loan:* $4154. *Average need-based gift aid:* $3573. *Average non-need-based aid:* $6473. *Average indebtedness upon graduation:* $24,226.

Applying *Options:* electronic application, deferred entrance. *Application fee:* $60. *Required:* essay or personal statement, high school transcript. *Required for some:* interview. *Application deadlines:* 3/1 (freshmen), 6/15 (transfers). *Notification:* continuous (freshmen), continuous (transfers).

Freshman Application Contact Jason Langdon, Director of Admissions, Montclair State University, One Normal Avenue, Montclair, NJ 07043-1624. *Phone:* 973-655-5116. *Toll-free phone:* 800-331-9205. *Fax:* 973-655-7700. *E-mail:* undergraduate.admissions@montclair.edu. *Web site:* http://www.montclair.edu/.

See page 1448 for the College Close-Up.

New Jersey City University
Jersey City, New Jersey

- **State-supported** comprehensive, founded 1927
- **Urban** 51-acre campus with easy access to New York City
- **Endowment** $3.3 million
- **Coed** 6,588 undergraduate students, 75% full-time, 61% women, 39% men
- **Moderately difficult** entrance level, 43% of applicants were admitted

Undergraduates 4,929 full-time, 1,659 part-time. Students come from 16 states and territories; 15 other countries; 1% are from out of state; 20% Black or African American, non-Hispanic/Latino; 36% Hispanic/Latino; 7% Asian, non-Hispanic/Latino; 0.1% American Indian or Alaska Native, non-Hispanic/Latino; 0.2% Two or more races, non-Hispanic/Latino; 10% Race/ethnicity unknown; 0.9% international; 13% transferred in; 4% live on campus. *Retention:* 73% of full-time freshmen returned.

Freshmen *Admission:* 4,439 applied, 1,921 admitted, 790 enrolled. *Test scores:* SAT critical reading scores over 500: 25%; SAT math scores over 500: 30%; SAT critical reading scores over 600: 3%; SAT math scores over 600: 5%; SAT math scores over 700: 1%.

Faculty *Total:* 738, 33% full-time, 28% with terminal degrees. *Student/faculty ratio:* 21:1.

Academics *Calendar:* semesters. *Degrees:* certificates, bachelor's, master's, post-master's, and postbachelor's certificates. *Special study options:* academic remediation for entering students, accelerated degree program, adult/continuing education programs, advanced placement credit, cooperative education, distance learning, double majors, English as a second language, honors programs, independent study, internships, off-campus study, part-time degree program, services for LD students, study abroad, summer session for credit.

Computers on Campus 704 computers/terminals are available on campus for general student use. Students can access the following: free student e-mail accounts, online (class) grades, online (class) registration, online (class) schedules. Campuswide network is available. Wireless service is available via learning centers, student centers.

Student Life *Housing options:* coed. Campus housing is university owned. *Activities and organizations:* drama/theater group, student-run newspaper, radio station, choral group, International Student Association, Black Freedom Society, Latin Power Association, national fraternities. *Campus security:* 24-hour emergency response devices and patrols, late-night transport/escort service. *Student services:* health clinic, personal/psychological counseling, women's center, legal services.

Athletics Member NCAA. All Division III. *Intercollegiate sports:* baseball M, basketball M/W, bowling W, cross-country running W, soccer M/W, softball W, track and field M/W, volleyball M/W. *Intramural sports:* basketball M/W, bowling W, soccer M/W, softball M/W, swimming and diving M/W, table tennis M/W, tennis M/W, volleyball M/W, weight lifting M/W.

Standardized Tests *Required:* SAT or ACT (for admission).

Costs (2010–11) *Tuition:* state resident $6804 full-time, $227 per credit hour part-time; nonresident $14,373 full-time, $479 per credit hour part-time. Full-time tuition and fees vary according to program. *Required fees:* $2544 full-time, $83 per credit hour part-time. *Room and board:* $9364; room only: $6079. *Payment plan:* deferred payment. *Waivers:* senior citizens and employees or children of employees.

Financial Aid Of all full-time matriculated undergraduates who enrolled in 2008, 3,611 applied for aid, 3,384 were judged to have need, 243 had their need fully met. In 2008, 63 non-need-based awards were made. *Average percent of need met:* 59%. *Average financial aid package:* $8440. *Average need-based loan:* $4280. *Average need-based gift aid:* $6727. *Average non-need-based aid:* $4982. *Average indebtedness upon graduation:* $11,337.

Applying *Options:* electronic application, early admission, deferred entrance. *Application fee:* $50. *Required:* essay or personal statement, high school transcript, minimum 2 GPA. *Required for some:* interview. *Recommended:* 1 letter of recommendation. *Application deadlines:* 4/1 (freshmen), rolling (transfers). *Notification:* continuous (freshmen).

Freshman Application Contact Mr. Jose Balda, Director of Admissions, New Jersey City University, 2039 Kennedy Boulevard, Jersey City, NJ 07305. *Phone:* 201-200-3234. *Toll-free phone:* 888-441-NJCU. *E-mail:* admissions@nicu.edu. *Web site:* http://www.njcu.edu/.

New Jersey Institute of Technology
Newark, New Jersey

- **State-supported** university, founded 1881
- **Urban** 48-acre campus with easy access to New York City
- **Endowment** $67.5 million
- **Coed** 6,103 undergraduate students, 82% full-time, 22% women, 78% men
- **Moderately difficult** entrance level, 67% of applicants were admitted

Undergraduates 4,979 full-time, 1,124 part-time. Students come from 29 states and territories; 64 other countries; 6% are from out of state; 10% Black or African American, non-Hispanic/Latino; 8% Hispanic/Latino; 15% Asian, non-Hispanic/Latino; 0.9% American Indian or Alaska Native, non-Hispanic/Latino; 11% Race/ethnicity unknown; 19% international; 8% transferred in; 25% live on campus. *Retention:* 81% of full-time freshmen returned.

Freshmen *Admission:* 4,398 applied, 2,949 admitted, 948 enrolled. *Test scores:* SAT critical reading scores over 500: 60%; SAT math scores over 500: 91%; SAT writing scores over 500: 80%; SAT critical reading scores over 600: 22%; SAT math scores over 600: 47%; SAT writing scores over 600: 40%; SAT critical reading scores over 700: 4%; SAT math scores over 700: 10%; SAT writing scores over 700: 23%.

Faculty *Total:* 654, 62% full-time, 97% with terminal degrees. *Student/faculty ratio:* 15:1.

Academics *Calendar:* semesters. *Degrees:* bachelor's, master's, doctoral-research/scholarship, and postbachelor's certificates. *Special study options:* academic remediation for entering students, accelerated degree program, adult/continuing education programs, advanced placement credit, cooperative education, distance learning, double majors, English as a second language, freshman honors college, honors programs, independent study, internships, off-campus study, part-time degree program, services for LD students, study abroad, summer session for credit. *ROTC:* Army (c), Air Force (b). *Unusual degree programs:* 3-2 business administration; engineering.

Computers on Campus 1,938 computers/terminals are available on campus for general student use. Students can access the following: campus intranet, computer help desk, free student e-mail accounts, online (class) grades, online (class) registration, online (class) schedules. Campuswide network is available. 100% of college-owned or -operated housing units are wired for high-speed Internet access. Wireless service is available via entire campus.

Student Life *Housing options:* coed. Campus housing is university owned. *Activities and organizations:* drama/theater group, student-run newspaper, radio station, marching band, Student Senate, Student Activities Council, Vector, Institute of Industrial Engineers, WJTB Geek Radio, national fraternities, national sororities. *Campus security:* 24-hour emergency response devices and patrols, late-night transport/escort service, controlled dormitory access, bicycle patrols. *Student services:* health clinic, personal/psychological counseling, women's center.

Athletics Member NCAA. All Division I. *Intercollegiate sports:* baseball M(s), basketball M(s)/W(s), bowling M(c), cross-country running M(s)/W(s), fencing M(s)/W(s), ice hockey M(c), soccer M(s)/W(s), swimming and diving M(s)/W(s), tennis M(s)/W(s), track and field M/W, volleyball M(s)/W(s). *Intramural sports:* basketball M/W, bowling M/W, cheerleading M/W, ice hockey M, racquetball M/W, soccer M/W, softball M, swimming and diving M/W, tennis M/W, track and field M/W, ultimate Frisbee M/W, volleyball M/W, water polo M/W.

Standardized Tests *Required:* SAT or ACT (for admission).

Financial Aid Of all full-time matriculated undergraduates who enrolled in 2009, 3,309 applied for aid, 3,156 were judged to have need, 226 had their need fully met. 422 Federal Work-Study jobs (averaging $1216). 331 state and other part-time jobs (averaging $1398). In 2009, 405 non-need-based awards were made. *Average percent of need met:* 55%. *Average financial aid package:* $12,400. *Average need-based loan:* $4241. *Average need-based gift aid:* $10,577. *Average non-need-based aid:* $13,886. *Average indebtedness upon graduation:* $34,760. *Financial aid deadline:* 5/5.

Applying *Options:* electronic application, early admission, deferred entrance. *Application fee:* $70. *Required:* high school transcript. *Required for some:* essay or personal statement, interview. *Recommended:* 1 letter of recommendation. *Application deadlines:* 4/1 (freshmen), 6/1 (transfers). *Notification:* continuous (freshmen), continuous (transfers).

Freshman Application Contact Mr. Stephen M. Eck, Director of University Admissions, New Jersey Institute of Technology, University Heights, Newark, NJ 07102. *Phone:* 973-596-3306. *Toll-free phone:* 800-925-NJIT. *Fax:* 973-596-3461. *E-mail:* admissions@njit.edu. *Web site:* http://www.njit.edu/.

Princeton University
Princeton, New Jersey

- **Independent** university, founded 1746
- **Suburban** 600-acre campus with easy access to New York City and Philadelphia
- **Endowment** $13.8 billion
- **Coed** 5,220 undergraduate students, 99% full-time, 49% women, 51% men
- **Most difficult** entrance level, 9% of applicants were admitted

Undergraduates 5,149 full-time, 71 part-time. Students come from 53 states and territories; 98 other countries; 85% are from out of state; 8% Black or African American, non-Hispanic/Latino; 8% Hispanic/Latino; 17% Asian, non-Hispanic/Latino; 0.1% Native Hawaiian or other Pacific Islander, non-Hispanic/Latino; 0.3% American Indian or Alaska Native, non-Hispanic/Latino; 5% Two or more races, non-Hispanic/Latino; 3% Race/ethnicity unknown; 11% international; 97% live on campus. *Retention:* 98% of full-time freshmen returned.

Freshmen *Admission:* 26,247 applied, 2,311 admitted, 1,312 enrolled. *Average high school GPA:* 3.89. *Test scores:* SAT critical reading scores over 500: 100%; SAT math scores over 500: 100%; SAT writing scores over 500: 100%; ACT scores over 18: 100%; SAT critical reading scores over 600: 97%; SAT math scores over 600: 99%; SAT writing scores over 600: 98%; ACT scores over 24: 100%; SAT critical reading scores over 700: 74%; SAT math scores over 700: 79%; SAT writing scores over 700: 79%; ACT scores over 30: 89%.

Faculty *Total:* 1,070, 79% full-time, 87% with terminal degrees. *Student/faculty ratio:* 6:1.

Academics *Calendar:* semesters. *Degrees:* bachelor's, master's, and doctoral-research/scholarship. *Special study options:* adult/continuing education programs, advanced placement credit, independent study, off-campus study, services for LD students, student-designed majors, study abroad. *ROTC:* Army (b), Navy (c).

Computers on Campus 500 computers/terminals and 17,000 ports are available on campus for general student use. Students can access the following: campus intranet, computer help desk, free student e-mail accounts, online (class) grades, online (class) registration, online (class) schedules, academic applications and courseware, printing, network file space, Web site hosting, media lab, broadcast center. Campuswide network is available. 100% of college-owned or -operated housing units are wired for high-speed Internet access. Wireless service is available via entire campus.

Student Life *Housing:* on-campus residence required through sophomore year. *Options:* coed, men-only, women-only, disabled students. Campus housing is university owned. Freshman campus housing is guaranteed. *Activities and organizations:* drama/theater group, student-run newspaper, radio station, choral group, marching band. *Campus security:* 24-hour emergency response devices and patrols, student patrols, late-night transport/escort service, controlled dormitory access. *Student services:* health clinic, personal/psychological counseling, women's center, legal services.

Athletics Member NCAA. All Division I except football (Division I-AA). *Intercollegiate sports:* baseball M, basketball M/W, crew M/W, cross-country running M/W, fencing M/W, field hockey W, golf M/W, ice hockey M/W, lacrosse M/W, soccer M/W, softball W, squash M/W, swimming and diving M/W, tennis M/W, track and field M/W, volleyball M/W, water polo M/W, wrestling M. *Intramural sports:* badminton M(c)/W(c), baseball M(c), basketball M(c)/W(c), cheerleading M(c)/W(c), cross-country running M(c)/W(c), equestrian sports M(c)/W(c), fencing M(c)/W(c), field hockey W(c), ice hockey M(c)/W(c), lacrosse M(c)/W(c), riflery M(c)/W(c), rugby M(c)/W(c), sailing M(c)/W(c), skiing (downhill) M(c)/W(c), soccer M(c)/W(c), softball W(c), squash M(c)/W(c), swimming and diving M(c)/W(c), table tennis M(c)/W(c), tennis M(c)/W(c), ultimate Frisbee M(c)/W(c), volleyball M(c)/W(c).

Standardized Tests *Required:* SAT or ACT (for admission). *Recommended:* SAT Subject Tests (for admission).

Costs (2011–12) *Comprehensive fee:* $49,069 includes full-time tuition ($37,000) and room and board ($12,069). *College room only:* $6596. Room and board charges vary according to board plan. *Payment plans:* installment, deferred payment. *Waivers:* employees or children of employees.

Financial Aid Of all full-time matriculated undergraduates who enrolled in 2008, 3,183 applied for aid, 2,953 were judged to have need, 2,953 had their need fully met. 883 Federal Work-Study jobs (averaging $901). 1,185 state and other part-time jobs (averaging $1545). *Average percent of need met:* 100%. *Average financial aid package:* $36,411. *Average need-based gift aid:* $34,719. *Average indebtedness upon graduation:* $5225.

Applying *Options:* electronic application, deferred entrance. *Application fee:* $65. *Required:* essay or personal statement, high school transcript, 3 letters of recommendation. *Recommended:* interview. *Application deadline:* 1/1 (freshmen). *Notification:* 4/1 (freshmen).

Freshman Application Contact Ms. Janet Rapelye, Dean of Admission, Princeton University, PO Box 430, Princeton, NJ 08542-0430. *Phone:* 609-258-3060. *Fax:* 609-258-6743. *E-mail:* uaoffice@princeton.edu. *Web site:* http://www.princeton.edu/.

Rabbi Jacob Joseph School

Edison, New Jersey

Admissions Office Contact Rabbi Jacob Joseph School, One Plainfield Ave, Edison, NJ 08817.

Rabbinical College of America

Morristown, New Jersey

Director of Admissions Sharon Miller, Registrar, Rabbinical College of America, 226 Sussex Avenue, PO Box 1996, Morristown, NJ 07962-1996. *Phone:* 973-267-9404. *E-mail:* rca079@aol.com.

Ramapo College of New Jersey

Mahwah, New Jersey

- **State-supported** comprehensive, founded 1969, part of New Jersey State College System
- **Suburban** 300-acre campus with easy access to New York City
- **Endowment** $9.1 million
- **Coed** 5,796 undergraduate students, 91% full-time, 59% women, 41% men
- **Moderately difficult** entrance level, 48% of applicants were admitted

Undergraduates 5,270 full-time, 526 part-time. Students come from 19 states and territories; 27 other countries; 4% are from out of state; 4% Black or African American, non-Hispanic/Latino; 10% Hispanic/Latino; 4% Asian, non-Hispanic/Latino; 0.4% Native Hawaiian or other Pacific Islander, non-Hispanic/Latino; 0.2% American Indian or Alaska Native, non-Hispanic/Latino; 1% Two or more races, non-Hispanic/Latino; 2% Race/ethnicity unknown; 1% international; 10% transferred in; 55% live on campus. *Retention:* 88% of full-time freshmen returned.

Freshmen *Admission:* 5,161 applied, 2,483 admitted, 897 enrolled. *Average high school GPA:* 3.4. *Test scores:* SAT critical reading scores over 500: 91%; SAT math scores over 500: 97%; SAT writing scores over 500: 88%; SAT critical reading scores over 600: 34%; SAT math scores over 600: 45%; SAT writing scores over 600: 36%; SAT critical reading scores over 700: 5%; SAT math scores over 700: 5%; SAT writing scores over 700: 5%.

Faculty *Total:* 452, 48% full-time. *Student/faculty ratio:* 18:1.

Academics *Calendar:* semesters. *Degrees:* certificates, bachelor's, and master's. *Special study options:* academic remediation for entering students, accelerated degree program, adult/continuing education programs, advanced placement credit, cooperative education, distance learning, double majors, external degree program, freshman honors college, honors programs, independent study, internships, off-campus study, part-time degree program, services for LD students, student-designed majors, study abroad, summer session for credit. *ROTC:* Air Force (c). *Unusual degree programs:* 3-2 biology, and chemistry with Rutgers, The State University of New Jersey; NY University College of Dentistry; SUNY State College of Optometry. RCNJ confers BSN & MSN degrees here on campus (with clinical internships at Valley Hospital, Englewood Hospital & Medical Center, and other state hospitals).

Computers on Campus 1,058 computers/terminals and 1,500 ports are available on campus for general student use. Students can access the following: campus intranet, computer help desk, free student e-mail accounts, online (class) grades, online (class) registration, online (class) schedules. Campus-wide network is available. 100% of college-owned or -operated housing units are wired for high-speed Internet access. Wireless service is available via classrooms, computer centers, computer labs, learning centers, libraries, student centers.

Student Life *Housing options:* coed, disabled students. Campus housing is university owned. Freshman campus housing is guaranteed. *Activities and organizations:* drama/theater group, student-run newspaper, radio and television station, choral group, WRPR, Accounting Club, Nursing Students organization, Student Government Association, Black Students union, national fraternities, national sororities. *Campus security:* 24-hour emergency response devices and patrols, late-night transport/escort service, controlled dormitory access, surveillance cameras, patrols by trained security personnel. *Student services:* health clinic, personal/psychological counseling, women's center.

Athletics Member NCAA. All Division III. *Intercollegiate sports:* baseball M, basketball M/W, cross-country running M/W, field hockey W, lacrosse W, soccer M/W, softball W, swimming and diving M/W, tennis M/W, track and field M/W, volleyball M/W. *Intramural sports:* basketball M/W, bowling M/W, football M/W, rock climbing M/W, soccer M/W, softball M/W, table tennis M/W, ultimate Frisbee M/W, volleyball M/W.

Standardized Tests *Required:* SAT (for admission). *Required for some:* ACT (for admission).

Costs (2010–11) *Tuition:* state resident $7805 full-time, $244 per credit part-time; nonresident $15,610 full-time, $488 per credit part-time. Full-time tuition and fees vary according to degree level and reciprocity agreements. Part-time tuition and fees vary according to degree level and reciprocity agreements. *Required fees:* $4069 full-time, $127 per credit part-time. *Room and board:* $10,250; room only: $7700. Room and board charges vary according to board plan and housing facility. *Payment plan:* installment. *Waivers:* senior citizens and employees or children of employees.

Financial Aid Of all full-time matriculated undergraduates who enrolled in 2009, 3,366 applied for aid, 2,586 were judged to have need, 121 had their need fully met. 125 Federal Work-Study jobs (averaging $2022). 760 state and other part-time jobs (averaging $2294). In 2009, 276 non-need-based awards were made. *Average percent of need met:* 54%. *Average financial aid package:* $11,723. *Average need-based loan:* $4612. *Average need-based gift aid:* $10,035. *Average non-need-based aid:* $11,462. *Average indebtedness upon graduation:* $26,187.

Applying *Options:* electronic application, early admission, early action, deferred entrance. *Application fee:* $60. *Required:* essay or personal statement, high school transcript. *Recommended:* minimum 3 GPA. *Application deadlines:* 3/1 (freshmen), 5/1 (transfers). *Notification:* continuous until 3/15 (freshmen), continuous until 7/1 (transfers).

Freshman Application Contact Michael DiBartolomeo, Associate Director for Freshmen Admissions, Ramapo College of New Jersey, Office of Admissions, 505 Ramapo Valley Road, Mahwah, NJ 07430-1680. *Phone:* 201-684-7300. *Toll-free phone:* 800-9RAMAPO. *Fax:* 201-684-7964. *E-mail:* admissions@ramapo.edu. *Web site:* http://www.ramapo.edu/.

See page 1520 for the College Close-Up.

The Richard Stockton College of New Jersey
Pomona, New Jersey

- **State-supported** comprehensive, founded 1969, part of New Jersey State College System
- **Suburban** 2000-acre campus with easy access to Philadelphia
- **Endowment** $9.9 million
- **Coed** 7,062 undergraduate students, 89% full-time, 58% women, 42% men
- **Very difficult** entrance level, 69% of applicants were admitted

Undergraduates 6,284 full-time, 778 part-time. Students come from 14 states and territories; 7 other countries; 1% are from out of state; 7% Black or African American, non-Hispanic/Latino; 8% Hispanic/Latino; 5% Asian, non-Hispanic/Latino; 0.1% Native Hawaiian or other Pacific Islander, non-Hispanic/Latino; 0.2% American Indian or Alaska Native, non-Hispanic/Latino; 2% Two or more races, non-Hispanic/Latino; 1% Race/ethnicity unknown; 0.2% international; 15% transferred in; 37% live on campus. *Retention:* 87% of full-time freshmen returned.

Freshmen *Admission:* 4,207 applied, 2,896 admitted, 862 enrolled. *Test scores:* SAT critical reading scores over 500: 61%; SAT math scores over 500: 70%; SAT writing scores over 500: 61%; ACT scores over 18: 66%; SAT critical reading scores over 600: 18%; SAT math scores over 600: 26%; SAT writing scores over 600: 17%; ACT scores over 24: 25%; SAT critical reading scores over 700: 2%; SAT math scores over 700: 3%; SAT writing scores over 700: 1%; ACT scores over 30: 1%.

Faculty *Total:* 546, 50% full-time, 66% with terminal degrees. *Student/faculty ratio:* 18:1.

Academics *Calendar:* semesters. *Degrees:* certificates, bachelor's, master's, doctoral-professional, and postbachelor's certificates. *Special study options:* academic remediation for entering students, accelerated degree program, adult/continuing education programs, advanced placement credit, distance learning, double majors, freshman honors college, honors programs, independent study, internships, off-campus study, part-time degree program, services for LD students, study abroad, summer session for credit. *Unusual degree programs:* 3-2 engineering with New Jersey Institute of Technology; Rutgers, The State University of New Jersey; dentistry, osteopathic medicine, podiatry, medicine with the University of Medicine and Dentistry of New Jersey.

Computers on Campus 865 computers/terminals and 2,400 ports are available on campus for general student use. Students can access the following: campus intranet, computer help desk, free student e-mail accounts, online (class) grades, online (class) registration, online (class) schedules. Campuswide network is available. 100% of college-owned or -operated housing units are wired for high-speed Internet access. Wireless service is available via entire campus.

Student Life *Housing options:* coed. Campus housing is university owned. Freshman campus housing is guaranteed. *Activities and organizations:* drama/theater group, student-run newspaper, radio and television station, choral group, Multi-Cultural Connection, Stockton Entertainment Team, Los Latinos Unidos, Unified Black Student Society, Stockton Action Volunteers for the Environment, national fraternities, national sororities. *Campus security:* 24-hour emergency response devices and patrols, late-night transport/escort service, controlled dormitory access, on-campus sworn/commissioned police force. *Student services:* health clinic, personal/psychological counseling, women's center.

Athletics Member NCAA. All Division III. *Intercollegiate sports:* baseball M, basketball M/W, cheerleading M/W, crew W, cross-country running M/W, field hockey W, lacrosse M, soccer M/W, softball W, tennis W, track and field M/W, volleyball W. *Intramural sports:* basketball M/W, bowling M(c)/W(c), crew M(c), fencing M(c)/W(c), football M/W, golf M(c)/W(c), ice hockey M(c), soccer M/W, softball M/W, table tennis M/W, tennis M/W, ultimate Frisbee M(c), volleyball M(c).

Standardized Tests *Required:* SAT or ACT (for admission).

Costs (2010–11) *Tuition:* state resident $7349 full-time, $262 per credit hour part-time; nonresident $13,260 full-time, $474 per credit hour part-time. Full-time tuition and fees vary according to degree level. Part-time tuition and fees vary according to course load and degree level. *Required fees:* $4044 full-time, $144 per credit hour part-time, $70 per term part-time. *Room and board:* $10,281; room only: $7165. Room and board charges vary according to board plan and housing facility. *Payment plans:* installment, deferred payment. *Waivers:* senior citizens and employees or children of employees.

Financial Aid Of all full-time matriculated undergraduates who enrolled in 2009, 5,102 applied for aid, 4,455 were judged to have need, 1,149 had their need fully met. 160 Federal Work-Study jobs (averaging $1703). 721 state and other part-time jobs (averaging $1513). In 2009, 1319 non-need-based awards were made. *Average percent of need met:* 67%. *Average financial aid package:* $15,555. *Average need-based loan:* $4599. *Average need-based gift aid:* $7940. *Average non-need-based aid:* $6318. *Average indebtedness upon graduation:* $30,843.

Applying *Options:* electronic application, early admission. *Application fee:* $50. *Required:* high school transcript, minimum 2 GPA. *Recommended:* essay or personal statement, minimum 3 GPA, 3 letters of recommendation. *Application deadlines:* 5/1 (freshmen), 6/1 (transfers). *Notification:* 5/15 (freshmen), continuous until 6/15 (transfers).

Freshman Application Contact The Richard Stockton College of New Jersey, PO Box 195, Jimmie Leeds Road, Pomona, NJ 08240-0195. *Phone:* 609-652-4261. *Web site:* http://www.stockton.edu/.

See page 1526 for the College Close-Up.

Rider University

Lawrenceville, New Jersey

- **Independent** comprehensive, founded 1865
- **Suburban** 280-acre campus with easy access to New York City and Philadelphia
- **Endowment** $46.8 million
- **Coed** 4,743 undergraduate students, 84% full-time, 60% women, 40% men
- **Moderately difficult** entrance level, 71% of applicants were admitted

Undergraduates 3,994 full-time, 749 part-time. Students come from 36 states and territories; 61 other countries; 22% are from out of state; 9% Black or Afri-

can American, non-Hispanic/Latino; 7% Hispanic/Latino; 4% Asian, non-Hispanic/Latino; 0.5% American Indian or Alaska Native, non-Hispanic/Latino; 2% Two or more races, non-Hispanic/Latino; 8% Race/ethnicity unknown; 4% international; 5% transferred in; 56% live on campus. *Retention:* 79% of full-time freshmen returned.

Freshmen *Admission:* 8,200 applied, 5,794 admitted, 1,010 enrolled. *Average high school GPA:* 3.29. *Test scores:* SAT critical reading scores over 500: 61%; SAT math scores over 500: 69%; SAT writing scores over 500: 62%; ACT scores over 18: 92%; SAT critical reading scores over 600: 16%; SAT math scores over 600: 23%; SAT writing scores over 600: 20%; ACT scores over 24: 38%; SAT critical reading scores over 700: 2%; SAT math scores over 700: 2%; SAT writing scores over 700: 3%; ACT scores over 30: 4%.

Faculty *Total:* 622, 40% full-time, 65% with terminal degrees. *Student/faculty ratio:* 12:1.

Academics *Calendar:* semesters. *Degrees:* certificates, associate, bachelor's, master's, and post-master's certificates. *Special study options:* academic remediation for entering students, adult/continuing education programs, advanced placement credit, cooperative education, distance learning, double majors, English as a second language, honors programs, independent study, internships, part-time degree program, services for LD students, study abroad, summer session for credit. *ROTC:* Army (c).

Computers on Campus 300 computers/terminals are available on campus for general student use. Students can access the following: computer help desk, free student e-mail accounts, online (class) grades, online (class) registration, online (class) schedules. Campuswide network is available. 100% of college-owned or -operated housing units are wired for high-speed Internet access. Wireless service is available via entire campus.

Student Life *Housing options:* coed, women-only, disabled students. Campus housing is university owned. Freshman applicants given priority for college housing. *Activities and organizations:* drama/theater group, student-run newspaper, radio and television station, choral group, Student Government Association, Greek Council, Association of Commuter Students, Black Student Union, Residence Hall Association, national fraternities, national sororities. *Campus security:* 24-hour emergency response devices and patrols, student patrols, late-night transport/escort service, controlled dormitory access. *Student services:* health clinic, personal/psychological counseling.

Athletics Member NCAA. All Division I. *Intercollegiate sports:* baseball M(s), basketball M(s)/W(s), cheerleading M/W, cross-country running M(s)/W(s), field hockey W(s), golf M(s), soccer M(s)/W(s), softball W(s), swimming and diving M(s)/W(s), tennis M(s)/W(s), track and field M(s)/W(s), volleyball W(s), wrestling M(s). *Intramural sports:* basketball M/W, cheerleading M/W, equestrian sports W(c), golf M, ice hockey M(c), lacrosse M(c)/W, soccer M/W, softball M/W, track and field M/W, volleyball M/W, water polo M/W.

Standardized Tests *Required:* SAT or ACT (for admission).

Costs (2010–11) *Comprehensive fee:* $41,670 includes full-time tuition ($29,870), mandatory fees ($600), and room and board ($11,200). Full-time tuition and fees vary according to course load and program. Part-time tuition: $540 per credit. Part-time tuition and fees vary according to course load and program. *Required fees:* $35 per course part-time. *College room only:* $6820. Room and board charges vary according to board plan, housing facility, and location. *Payment plan:* installment. *Waivers:* employees or children of employees.

Financial Aid Of all full-time matriculated undergraduates who enrolled in 2009, 3,253 applied for aid, 2,909 were judged to have need, 522 had their need fully met. In 2009, 803 non-need-based awards were made. *Average percent of need met:* 71%. *Average financial aid package:* $21,498. *Average need-based loan:* $4231. *Average need-based gift aid:* $15,912. *Average non-need-based aid:* $11,346. *Average indebtedness upon graduation:* $35,404.

Applying *Options:* electronic application, early admission, early action, deferred entrance. *Application fee:* $50. *Required:* essay or personal statement, high school transcript, 2 letters of recommendation. *Required for some:* interview. *Application deadlines:* rolling (freshmen), rolling (transfers), 11/15 (early action). *Notification:* continuous (freshmen), continuous (transfers), 12/15 (early action).

Freshman Application Contact Mr. William Larrousse, Director of Admissions, Rider University, 2083 Lawrenceville Road, Lawrenceville, NJ 08648. *Phone:* 609-896-5177. *Toll-free phone:* 800-257-9026. *Fax:* 609-895-6645. *E-mail:* wlarrousse@rider.edu. *Web site:* http://www.rider.edu/.

See page 1530 for the College Close-Up.

Rowan University

Glassboro, New Jersey

- **State-supported** comprehensive, founded 1923, part of New Jersey State College System
- **Suburban** 800-acre campus with easy access to Philadelphia
- **Endowment** $129.7 million
- **Coed** 9,918 undergraduate students, 86% full-time, 52% women, 48% men
- **Moderately difficult** entrance level, 56% of applicants were admitted

Undergraduates 8,540 full-time, 1,378 part-time. Students come from 21 states and territories; 8 other countries; 2% are from out of state; 9% Black or African American, non-Hispanic/Latino; 8% Hispanic/Latino; 4% Asian, non-Hispanic/Latino; 0.2% American Indian or Alaska Native, non-Hispanic/Latino; 18% Race/ethnicity unknown; 0.6% international; 11% transferred in; 35% live on campus. *Retention:* 84% of full-time freshmen returned.

Freshmen *Admission:* 8,607 applied, 4,832 admitted, 1,476 enrolled. *Average high school GPA:* 3.48. *Test scores:* SAT critical reading scores over 500: 69%; SAT math scores over 500: 78%; SAT writing scores over 500: 64%; SAT critical reading scores over 600: 19%; SAT math scores over 600: 32%; SAT writing scores over 600: 17%; SAT critical reading scores over 700: 2%; SAT math scores over 700: 4%; SAT writing scores over 700: 1%.

Faculty *Total:* 1,041, 38% full-time, 43% with terminal degrees. *Student/faculty ratio:* 16:1.

Academics *Calendar:* semesters. *Degrees:* certificates, bachelor's, master's, doctoral-professional, and postbachelor's certificates. *Special study options:* academic remediation for entering students, adult/continuing education programs, advanced placement credit, cooperative education, distance learning, double majors, English as a second language, freshman honors college, honors programs, independent study, internships, off-campus study, part-time degree program, services for LD students, study abroad, summer session for credit. *ROTC:* Army (c). *Unusual degree programs:* 3-2 mathematics and computer science.

Computers on Campus 1,200 computers/terminals and 2,500 ports are available on campus for general student use. Students can access the following: campus intranet, computer help desk, free student e-mail accounts, online (class) grades, online (class) registration, online (class) schedules, online

library. Campuswide network is available. 100% of college-owned or -operated housing units are wired for high-speed Internet access. Wireless service is available via entire campus.

Student Life *Housing:* on-campus residence required through sophomore year. *Options:* coed, men-only, women-only, disabled students. Campus housing is university owned and leased by the school. Freshman campus housing is guaranteed. *Activities and organizations:* drama/theater group, student-run newspaper, radio and television station, choral group, Kappa Delta Pi, Public Relations Student Society of America, Student University Programmes, Rowan Television Network, Elementary Education Club, national fraternities, national sororities. *Campus security:* 24-hour emergency response devices and patrols, student patrols, late-night transport/escort service, controlled dormitory access. *Student services:* health clinic, personal/psychological counseling, legal services.

Athletics Member NCAA. All Division III. *Intercollegiate sports:* baseball M, basketball M/W, cross-country running M/W, field hockey W, football M, lacrosse W, soccer M/W, softball W, swimming and diving M/W, tennis M/W, track and field M/W, volleyball W. *Intramural sports:* basketball M/W, bowling M/W, cheerleading W(c), field hockey W(c), golf M/W, ice hockey M(c), lacrosse M(c), racquetball M/W, rock climbing M(c), skiing (downhill) M(c)/W(c), soccer M/W, softball M/W, table tennis M/W, tennis M(c)/W(c), ultimate Frisbee W, volleyball M/W, wrestling M(c).

Standardized Tests *Required:* SAT or ACT (for admission).

Costs (2011–12) *Tuition:* state resident $8396 full-time, $323 per credit part-time; nonresident $15,754 full-time, $607 per credit part-time. Full-time tuition and fees vary according to course load, degree level, and program. Part-time tuition and fees vary according to course load, degree level, and program. *Required fees:* $3280 full-time, $140 per credit part-time. *Room and board:* $10,348; room only: $6248. Room and board charges vary according to board plan and housing facility. *Payment plan:* deferred payment. *Waivers:* employees or children of employees.

Financial Aid Of all full-time matriculated undergraduates who enrolled in 2008, 6,737 applied for aid, 5,159 were judged to have need, 871 had their need fully met. 592 Federal Work-Study jobs (averaging $1197). 816 state and other part-time jobs (averaging $1710). In 2008, 466 non-need-based awards were made. *Average percent of need met:* 83%. *Average financial aid package:* $9483. *Average need-based loan:* $4262. *Average need-based gift aid:*

$9285. *Average non-need-based aid:* $5219. *Average indebtedness upon graduation:* $29,073.

Applying *Options:* electronic application, early admission, deferred entrance. *Application fee:* $65. *Required:* high school transcript. *Required for some:* interview. *Recommended:* minimum 3 GPA. *Application deadlines:* 3/1 (freshmen), 3/1 (transfers). *Notification:* continuous (freshmen), continuous (transfers).

Freshman Application Contact Mr. Albert Betts, Director of Admissions, Rowan University, 201 Mullica Hill Road, Glassboro, NJ 08028. *Phone:* 856-256-4200. *Toll-free phone:* 800-447-1165. *Fax:* 856-256-4430. *E-mail:* admissions@rowan.edu. *Web site:* http://www.rowan.edu/.

See page 1548 for the College Close-Up.

Rutgers, The State University of New Jersey, Camden

Camden, New Jersey

- **State-supported** university, founded 1927, part of Rutgers, The State University of New Jersey
- **Urban** 34-acre campus with easy access to Philadelphia
- **Endowment** $508.8 million
- **Coed** 4,497 undergraduate students, 81% full-time, 54% women, 46% men
- **Moderately difficult** entrance level, 55% of applicants were admitted

Undergraduates 3,629 full-time, 868 part-time. Students come from 18 states and territories; 11 other countries; 3% are from out of state; 12% transferred in; 11% live on campus. *Retention:* 80% of full-time freshmen returned.

Freshmen *Admission:* 5,567 applied, 3,089 admitted, 500 enrolled. *Test scores:* SAT critical reading scores over 500: 72%; SAT math scores over 500: 81%; SAT writing scores over 500: 70%; SAT critical reading scores over 600: 22%; SAT math scores over 600: 24%; SAT writing scores over 600: 22%; SAT critical reading scores over 700: 2%; SAT math scores over 700: 2%; SAT writing scores over 700: 2%.

Faculty *Total:* 500, 51% full-time, 99% with terminal degrees. *Student/faculty ratio:* 12:1.

Academics *Calendar:* semesters. *Degrees:* bachelor's, master's, and doctoral-professional. *Special study options:* academic remediation for entering students, accelerated degree program, advanced placement credit, cooperative education, distance learning, double majors, English as a second language, freshman honors college, honors programs, independent study, internships, part-time degree program, services for LD students, student-designed majors, study abroad, summer session for credit. *ROTC:* Army (c), Air Force (c). *Unusual degree programs:* 3-2 business administration; engineering; medical technology with approved hospital; African-American studies, general science, childhood studies, English, history, liberal studies, psychology; biology, chemistry and mathematics with the Graduate School-Camden.

Computers on Campus 184 computers/terminals are available on campus for general student use. Students can access the following: campus intranet, computer help desk, free student e-mail accounts, online (class) grades, online (class) registration, online (class) schedules, online grade reports. Campuswide network is available. 100% of college-owned or -operated housing units are wired for high-speed Internet access. Wireless service is available via classrooms, computer centers, computer labs, dorm rooms, learning centers, libraries, student centers.

Student Life *Housing options:* coed, disabled students. Campus housing is university owned. *Activities and organizations:* drama/theater group, student-run radio station. *Campus security:* 24-hour emergency response devices and patrols, student patrols, late-night transport/escort service, controlled dormitory access.

Athletics Member NCAA. All Division III. *Intercollegiate sports:* baseball M, basketball M/W, crew M/W, cross-country running W, golf M, lacrosse W, soccer M/W, softball W, track and field M/W, volleyball W. *Intramural sports:* baseball M, basketball M/W, cheerleading W, crew M, golf M, ice hockey M, lacrosse M, racquetball M, soccer M, tennis M, track and field M, ultimate Frisbee M/W, volleyball M/W.

Standardized Tests *Required:* SAT or ACT (for admission).

Costs (2010–11) *Tuition:* state resident $9926 full-time, $319 per credit hour part-time; nonresident $20,985 full-time, $699 per credit hour part-time. Part-time tuition and fees vary according to course load. *Required fees:* $2438 full-time. *Room and board:* $10,362; room only: $7482. Room and board charges vary according to board plan and housing facility. *Payment plan:* installment. *Waivers:* employees or children of employees.

Financial Aid Of all full-time matriculated undergraduates who enrolled in 2009, 3,460 applied for aid, 2,992 were judged to have need, 484 had their need fully met. 150 Federal Work-Study jobs (averaging $1956). 400 state and other part-time jobs (averaging $2313). In 2009, 67 non-need-based awards were made. *Average percent of need met:* 58%. *Average financial aid package:* $10,884. *Average need-based loan:* $4418. *Average need-based gift aid:*

$8191. *Average non-need-based aid:* $5960. *Average indebtedness upon graduation:* $21,330.
Applying *Options:* electronic application. *Application fee:* $65. *Required:* high school transcript. *Application deadlines:* 12/1 (freshmen), 1/15 (transfers). *Notification:* 2/28 (freshmen), 5/15 (transfers).
Freshman Application Contact Rutgers, The State University of New Jersey, Camden, 406 Penn Street, Camden, NJ 08102-1401. *Phone:* 856-225-6104. *Web site:* http://www.rutgers.edu/.

Rutgers, The State University of New Jersey, Newark

Newark, New Jersey

- **State-supported** university, founded 1892, part of Rutgers, The State University of New Jersey
- **Urban** 38-acre campus
- **Endowment** $508.8 million
- **Coed** 7,479 undergraduate students, 79% full-time, 53% women, 47% men
- **Moderately difficult** entrance level, 60% of applicants were admitted

Undergraduates 5,880 full-time, 1,599 part-time. 19% Black or African American, non-Hispanic/Latino; 22% Hispanic/Latino; 23% Asian, non-Hispanic/Latino; 0.7% Native Hawaiian or other Pacific Islander, non-Hispanic/Latino; 0.1% American Indian or Alaska Native, non-Hispanic/Latino; 2% Two or more races, non-Hispanic/Latino; 3% Race/ethnicity unknown; 2% international; 17% live on campus. *Retention:* 86% of full-time freshmen returned.
Freshmen *Admission:* 12,462 applied, 7,430 admitted, 943 enrolled. *Test scores:* SAT critical reading scores over 500: 60%; SAT math scores over 500: 80%; SAT writing scores over 500: 68%; SAT critical reading scores over 600: 17%; SAT math scores over 600: 32%; SAT writing scores over 600: 20%; SAT critical reading scores over 700: 2%; SAT math scores over 700: 4%; SAT writing scores over 700: 3%.
Faculty *Total:* 704, 63% full-time, 99% with terminal degrees. *Student/faculty ratio:* 12:1.
Academics *Calendar:* semesters. *Degrees:* bachelor's, master's, doctoral-professional, and doctoral-research/scholarship. *Special study options:* academic remediation for entering students, accelerated degree program, adult/continuing education programs, advanced placement credit, cooperative education, distance learning, double majors, English as a second language, freshman honors college, honors programs, independent study, internships, off-campus study, part-time degree program, services for LD students, student-designed majors, study abroad, summer session for credit. *ROTC:* Army (b), Air Force (b). *Unusual degree programs:* 3-2 business administration; engineering; nursing.
Computers on Campus 708 computers/terminals are available on campus for general student use. Students can access the following: computer help desk, free student e-mail accounts, online (class) grades, online (class) schedules, online grade reports. Campuswide network is available. Wireless service is available via classrooms, computer centers, computer labs, dorm rooms, learning centers, libraries, student centers.
Student Life *Housing options:* coed. Campus housing is university owned. *Activities and organizations:* drama/theater group, student-run newspaper, radio station, choral group. *Campus security:* 24-hour emergency response devices and patrols, student patrols, late-night transport/escort service, controlled dormitory access.
Athletics Member NCAA. All Division III except volleyball (Division I). *Intercollegiate sports:* baseball M, basketball M/W, cross-country running M/W, soccer M/W, tennis M/W, track and field M, volleyball M/W. *Intramural sports:* baseball M/W, basketball M/W, racquetball M/W, rock climbing M/W, soccer M/W, swimming and diving M/W, weight lifting M/W.
Standardized Tests *Required:* SAT or ACT (for admission).
Costs (2010–11) *Tuition:* state resident $9926 full-time, $319 per credit hour part-time; nonresident $21,388 full-time, $693 per credit hour part-time. Part-time tuition and fees vary according to course load. *Required fees:* $2143 full-time. *Room and board:* $11,653; room only: $7295. Room and board charges vary according to board plan and housing facility. *Payment plan:* installment. *Waivers:* employees or children of employees.
Financial Aid Of all full-time matriculated undergraduates who enrolled in 2009, 4,975 applied for aid, 4,570 were judged to have need, 361 had their need fully met. 268 Federal Work-Study jobs (averaging $1939). 816 state and other part-time jobs (averaging $1795). In 2009, 65 non-need-based awards were made. *Average percent of need met:* 58%. *Average financial aid package:* $12,383. *Average need-based loan:* $5322. *Average need-based gift aid:* $9636. *Average non-need-based aid:* $7834. *Average indebtedness upon graduation:* $17,373.
Applying *Options:* electronic application. *Application fee:* $65. *Required:* high school transcript. *Application deadlines:* 12/1 (freshmen), 1/15 (transfers). *Notification:* 2/28 (freshmen), 5/15 (transfers).

Freshman Application Contact Mr. Jason Hand, Director of Admissions, Rutgers, The State University of New Jersey, Newark, 249 University Avenue, Newark, NJ 07102. *Phone:* 973-353-5205. *Fax:* 973-353-1440. *E-mail:* admissions@ugadm.rutgers.edu. *Web site:* http://www.rutgers.edu/.

Rutgers, The State University of New Jersey, New Brunswick

Piscataway, New Jersey

- **State-supported** university, founded 1766, part of Rutgers, The State University of New Jersey
- **Urban** 2683-acre campus with easy access to New York City
- **Endowment** $508.8 million
- **Coed** 30,351 undergraduate students, 95% full-time, 48% women, 52% men
- **Moderately difficult** entrance level, 59% of applicants were admitted

Undergraduates 28,904 full-time, 1,447 part-time. Students come from 47 states and territories; 6% are from out of state; 8% Black or African American, non-Hispanic/Latino; 11% Hispanic/Latino; 24% Asian, non-Hispanic/Latino; 0.4% Native Hawaiian or other Pacific Islander, non-Hispanic/Latino; 0.1% American Indian or Alaska Native, non-Hispanic/Latino; 3% Two or more races, non-Hispanic/Latino; 2% Race/ethnicity unknown; 2% international; 6% transferred in; 44% live on campus. *Retention:* 92% of full-time freshmen returned.
Freshmen *Admission:* 29,532 applied, 17,448 admitted, 6,033 enrolled. *Test scores:* SAT critical reading scores over 500: 86%; SAT math scores over 500: 93%; SAT writing scores over 500: 90%; SAT critical reading scores over 600: 39%; SAT math scores over 600: 60%; SAT writing scores over 600: 46%; SAT critical reading scores over 700: 8%; SAT math scores over 700: 18%; SAT writing scores over 700: 11%.
Faculty *Total:* 2,521, 66% full-time, 99% with terminal degrees. *Student/faculty ratio:* 15:1.
Academics *Calendar:* semesters. *Degrees:* bachelor's, master's, doctoral-professional, doctoral-research/scholarship, and post-master's certificates. *Special study options:* academic remediation for entering students, accelerated degree program, advanced placement credit, cooperative education, distance learning, double majors, English as a second language, honors programs, independent study, internships, part-time degree program, student-designed majors, study abroad. *ROTC:* Army (b), Air Force (b). *Unusual degree programs:* 3-2 business administration; engineering; University of Medicine and Dentistry of New Jersey, Robert Wood Johnson Medical School.
Computers on Campus 1,450 computers/terminals are available on campus for general student use. Students can access the following: online grade reports. Campuswide network is available.
Student Life *Housing options:* coed, men-only, women-only, cooperative. Campus housing is university owned. *Activities and organizations:* drama/theater group, student-run newspaper, radio and television station, choral group, marching band, national fraternities, national sororities. *Campus security:* 24-hour emergency response devices and patrols, student patrols, late-night transport/escort service, controlled dormitory access. *Student services:* health clinic.
Athletics Member NCAA. All Division I except football (Division I-A). *Intercollegiate sports:* baseball M, basketball M/W, crew M/W, cross-country running M/W, fencing M/W, golf M/W, gymnastics W, lacrosse M/W, soccer M/W, softball W, swimming and diving M/W, tennis M/W, track and field M/W, volleyball W, wrestling M. *Intramural sports:* badminton M/W, baseball M(c), basketball M/W, bowling M/W, cross-country running M/W, equestrian sports M(c)/W(c), field hockey W(c), football M, golf M/W, ice hockey M(c), lacrosse M/W, racquetball M/W, rugby M(c)/W(c), sailing M(c)/W(c), skiing (cross-country) M(c)/W(c), skiing (downhill) M(c)/W(c), soccer M/W, softball M/W, squash M(c)/W(c), swimming and diving M/W, table tennis M(c)/W(c), tennis M/W, track and field M/W, volleyball M/W, water polo M/W, wrestling M.
Standardized Tests *Required:* SAT or ACT (for admission).
Costs (2010–11) *Tuition:* state resident $9926 full-time, $319 per credit hour part-time; nonresident $21,388 full-time, $693 per credit hour part-time. *Required fees:* $2656 full-time. *Room and board:* $11,216; room only: $6836. Room and board charges vary according to board plan and housing facility. *Payment plan:* installment. *Waivers:* employees or children of employees.
Financial Aid Of all full-time matriculated undergraduates who enrolled in 2009, 20,078 applied for aid, 17,077 were judged to have need, 382 had their need fully met. 1,749 Federal Work-Study jobs (averaging $1746). 6,710 state and other part-time jobs (averaging $1862). In 2009, 493 non-need-based awards were made. *Average percent of need met:* 56%. *Average financial aid package:* $13,638. *Average need-based loan:* $4482. *Average need-based gift aid:* $9937. *Average non-need-based aid:* $7277. *Average indebtedness upon graduation:* $16,766.
Applying *Options:* electronic application. *Application fee:* $65. *Required:* high school transcript. *Required for some:* interview. *Recommended:* essay or

personal statement. *Application deadlines:* 12/1 (freshmen), 1/15 (transfers). *Notification:* 2/28 (freshmen), 5/15 (transfers).
Freshman Application Contact Rutgers, The State University of New Jersey, New Brunswick, 65 Davidson Road, Room 202, Piscataway, NJ 08854-8097. *Phone:* 732-445-4636. *Web site:* http://www.rutgers.edu/.

Saint Peter's College
Jersey City, New Jersey

Freshman Application Contact Saint Peter's College, 2641 Kennedy Boulevard, Jersey City, NJ 07306-5997. *Phone:* 201-761-7106. *Toll-free phone:* 888-SPC-9933. *Web site:* http://www.spc.edu/.

Seton Hall University
South Orange, New Jersey

- **Independent Roman Catholic** university, founded 1856
- **Suburban** 58-acre campus with easy access to New York City
- **Endowment** $178.7 million
- **Coed**
- **Moderately difficult** entrance level

Faculty *Student/faculty ratio:* 14:1.
Academics *Calendar:* semesters. *Degrees:* bachelor's, master's, doctoral-professional, doctoral-research/scholarship, and post-master's certificates.
Student Life *Campus security:* 24-hour emergency response devices and patrols, late-night transport/escort service, controlled dormitory access.
Athletics Member NCAA. All Division I.
Standardized Tests *Required:* SAT or ACT (for admission).
Costs (2010–11) *One-time required fee:* $300. *Comprehensive fee:* $43,940 includes full-time tuition ($29,940), mandatory fees ($1950), and room and board ($12,050). Full-time tuition and fees vary according to course load. Part-time tuition: $912 per credit hour. Part-time tuition and fees vary according to course load. *Required fees:* $185 per term part-time. *College room only:* $7774. Room and board charges vary according to board plan and housing facility. *Payment plans:* installment, deferred payment.
Financial Aid *Of all full-time matriculated undergraduates who enrolled in 2004, 3,604 applied for aid, 3,103 were judged to have need, 591 had their need fully met. 807 Federal Work-Study jobs (averaging $1930). 1,116 state and other part-time jobs (averaging $1289). In 2004, 751 non-need-based awards were made. Average percent of need met: 68. Average financial aid package: $14,664. Average need-based loan: $3198. Average need-based gift aid: $4651. Average non-need-based aid: $11,243. Average indebtedness upon graduation: $29,108.*
Applying *Options:* electronic application, early action, deferred entrance. *Application fee:* $55. *Required:* essay or personal statement, high school transcript, counselor report. *Required for some:* minimum 3 GPA, interview. *Recommended:* minimum 3 GPA, interview.
Freshman Application Contact Mr. Peter Nacy, Assistant Vice President for Admissions, Seton Hall University, Enrollment Management, South Orange, NJ 07079-2697. *Phone:* 973-275-2498. *Toll-free phone:* 800-THE HALL. *Fax:* 973-275-2040. *E-mail:* thehall@shu.edu. *Web site:* http://www.shu.edu/.

See page 1598 for the College Close-Up.

Somerset Christian College
Zarephath, New Jersey

- **Independent Pillar of Fire International** 4-year, founded 1908
- **Rural** campus with easy access to New York City
- **Coed**
- **Minimally difficult** entrance level

Faculty *Student/faculty ratio:* 15:1.
Academics *Calendar:* semesters plus "FastTrack" semesters. *Degrees:* certificates, associate, and bachelor's.
Standardized Tests *Required for some:* SAT or ACT (for admission).
Costs (2010–11) *Tuition:* $13,080 full-time, $545 per credit hour part-time. Full-time tuition and fees vary according to course load and program. Part-time tuition and fees vary according to course load and program. *Required fees:* $400 full-time, $200 per term part-time.
Financial Aid *Financial aid deadline:* 8/1.
Applying *Options:* electronic application, deferred entrance. *Application fee:* $35. *Required:* essay or personal statement. *Required for some:* high school transcript, minimum 2.5 GPA, interview.
Freshman Application Contact Ms. Linda Aarni, Senior Admissions Counselor, Somerset Christian College, 10 College Way, PO Box 9035, Zarephath, NJ 08890-9035. *Phone:* 732-356-1595. *Toll-free phone:* 800-234-

9305. *Fax:* 732-356-4846. *E-mail:* info@somerset.edu. *Web site:* http://www.somerset.edu/.

Stevens Institute of Technology
Hoboken, New Jersey

- **Independent** university, founded 1870
- **Urban** 55-acre campus with easy access to New York City
- **Endowment** $154.8 million
- **Coed**
- **Very difficult** entrance level

Faculty *Student/faculty ratio:* 7:1.
Academics *Calendar:* semesters. *Degrees:* bachelor's, master's, doctoral-research/scholarship, and postbachelor's certificates.
Student Life *Campus security:* 24-hour emergency response devices and patrols, late-night transport/escort service, controlled dormitory access.
Athletics Member NCAA. All Division III.
Standardized Tests *Required:* SAT or ACT (for admission). *Required for some:* SAT Subject Tests (for admission).
Costs (2010–11) *Comprehensive fee:* $52,310 includes full-time tuition ($38,400), mandatory fees ($1410), and room and board ($12,500). Part-time tuition: $1280 per credit. *Required fees:* $600 per term part-time. *Room and board:* Room and board charges vary according to board plan and housing facility.
Financial Aid *Of all full-time matriculated undergraduates who enrolled in 2005, 1,645 applied for aid, 1,431 were judged to have need, 245 had their need fully met. 818 Federal Work-Study jobs (averaging $1269). In 2005, 296 non-need-based awards were made. Average percent of need met: 85. Average financial aid package: $21,139. Average need-based loan: $4203. Average need-based gift aid: $12,871. Average non-need-based aid: $9973. Average indebtedness upon graduation: $14,113.*
Applying *Options:* electronic application, early admission, early decision, deferred entrance. *Application fee:* $55. *Required:* essay or personal statement, high school transcript, 2 letters of recommendation, interview.
Freshman Application Contact Mr. Daniel Gallagher, Dean of University Admissions, Stevens Institute of Technology, Castle Point on Hudson, Hoboken, NJ 07030. *Phone:* 201-216-5197. *Toll-free phone:* 800-458-5323. *E-mail:* admissions@stevens.edu. *Web site:* http://www.stevens.edu/.

Strayer University - Cherry Hill Campus
Cherry Hill, New Jersey

- **Proprietary** comprehensive
- **Coed**

Academics *Degrees:* bachelor's and master's.
Costs (2010–11) *Tuition:* $13,635 full-time, $1590 per course part-time.
Freshman Application Contact Strayer University - Cherry Hill Campus, 2201 Route 38, Suite 100, Cherry Hill, NJ 08002. *Web site:* http://www.strayer.edu/cherry_hill/.

Strayer University - Lawrenceville Campus
Lawrenceville, New Jersey

- **Proprietary** comprehensive
- **Coed**

Academics *Degrees:* bachelor's and master's.
Costs (2010–11) *Tuition:* $13,635 full-time, $1590 per course part-time.
Freshman Application Contact Strayer University - Lawrenceville Campus, 3150 Brunswick Pike, Suite 100, Lawrenceville, NJ 08648. *Web site:* http://www.strayer.edu/lawrenceville.

Strayer University - Piscataway Campus
Piscataway, New Jersey

- **Proprietary** comprehensive
- **Coed**

Academics *Degrees:* bachelor's and master's.
Costs (2010–11) *Tuition:* $13,635 full-time, $1590 per course part-time.
Freshman Application Contact Strayer University - Piscataway Campus, 242 Old New Brunswick Road, Suite 220, Piscataway, NJ 08854. *Web site:* http://www.strayer.edu/piscataway.

Strayer University - Willingboro Campus

Willingboro, New Jersey

- **Proprietary** comprehensive
- **Coed**

Academics *Degrees:* bachelor's and master's.

Costs (2010–11) *Tuition:* $13,635 full-time, $1590 per course part-time.

Freshman Application Contact Strayer University - Willingboro Campus, 300 Willingboro Parkway, Willingboro Town Center, Suite 125, Willingboro, NJ 08046. *Web site:* http://www.strayer.edu/willingboro.

Talmudical Academy of New Jersey

Adelphia, New Jersey

Director of Admissions Director of Admissions, Talmudical Academy of New Jersey, 868 Route 524, Adelphia, NJ 07710. *Phone:* 201-431-1600.

Thomas Edison State College

Trenton, New Jersey

- **State-supported** comprehensive, founded 1972
- **Urban** 2-acre campus with easy access to Philadelphia
- **Coed** 17,722 undergraduate students, 39% women, 61% men
- **Noncompetitive** entrance level

Undergraduates 17,722 part-time. Students come from 56 states and territories; 71 other countries; 66% are from out of state; 17% Black or African American, non-Hispanic/Latino; 10% Hispanic/Latino; 3% Asian, non-Hispanic/Latino; 0.5% Native Hawaiian or other Pacific Islander, non-Hispanic/Latino; 0.8% American Indian or Alaska Native, non-Hispanic/Latino; 9% Race/ethnicity unknown; 1% international.

Academics *Calendar:* continuous. *Degrees:* certificates, associate, bachelor's, master's, post-master's, and postbachelor's certificates (offers only distance learning degree programs). *Special study options:* adult/continuing education programs, advanced placement credit, distance learning, double majors, external degree program, independent study, part-time degree program, services for LD students, student-designed majors, summer session for credit.

Computers on Campus Students can access the following: online (class) grades, online (class) registration, online (class) schedules, undergraduate and Nursing students are able to schedule appointments online with their advisors. Campuswide network is available. Wireless service is available via entire campus.

Student Life *Housing:* college housing not available. *Campus security:* 24-hour emergency response devices and patrols, late-night transport/escort service, security officer from 7 am to 11 pm, local police patrol.

Costs (2010–11) *Tuition:* state resident $4883 full-time, $141 per quarter hour part-time; nonresident $7190 full-time, $193 per credit hour part-time. Part-time tuition and fees vary according to program and student level. Students may choose either the Comprehensive Tuition Plan: $4,883 per year (state residents and military personnel), $7,190 (out-of-state), which covers up to 36 credits per year for all credit-earning options, or the Enrolled Options Plan: $1,446 per year (state residents and military personnel), $2,696 (out-of-state) and $3,784 (international) for annual enrollment and a $107 technology services fee. Tests, portfolios, courses and other fees at additional cost. *Required fees:* $107 per year part-time. *Waivers:* employees or children of employees.

Applying *Options:* electronic application. *Application fee:* $75. *Required:* age 21 or older and a high school graduate. *Application deadlines:* rolling (freshmen), rolling (out-of-state freshmen), rolling (transfers).

Freshman Application Contact Mr. David Hoftiezer, Director of Admissions, Thomas Edison State College, 101 West State Street, Trenton, NJ 08608. *Phone:* 888-442-8372. *Toll-free phone:* 888-442-8372. *Fax:* 609-984-8447. *E-mail:* admissions@tesc.edu. *Web site:* http://www.tesc.edu/.

University of Medicine and Dentistry of New Jersey

Newark, New Jersey

Freshman Application Contact Student Contact, University of Medicine and Dentistry of New Jersey, 65 Bergen Street, PO Box 1709, Newark, NJ 07107-1709. *Phone:* 973-972-5000. *Web site:* http://www.umdnj.edu/.

William Paterson University of New Jersey

Wayne, New Jersey

- **State-supported** comprehensive, founded 1855, part of New Jersey State College System
- **Suburban** 370-acre campus with easy access to New York City
- **Endowment** $8.5 million
- **Coed** 9,860 undergraduate students, 85% full-time, 54% women, 46% men
- **Moderately difficult** entrance level, 65% of applicants were admitted

Undergraduates 8,333 full-time, 1,527 part-time. Students come from 44 states and territories; 48 other countries; 2% are from out of state; 14% Black or African American, non-Hispanic/Latino; 20% Hispanic/Latino; 7% Asian, non-Hispanic/Latino; 0.2% American Indian or Alaska Native, non-Hispanic/Latino; 0.4% Two or more races, non-Hispanic/Latino; 7% Race/ethnicity unknown; 0.7% international; 12% transferred in; 23% live on campus. *Retention:* 79% of full-time freshmen returned.

Freshmen *Admission:* 6,969 applied, 4,552 admitted, 1,543 enrolled. *Test scores:* SAT critical reading scores over 500: 44%; SAT math scores over 500: 50%; SAT critical reading scores over 600: 8%; SAT math scores over 600: 10%; SAT critical reading scores over 700: 1%; SAT math scores over 700: 1%.

Faculty *Total:* 942, 39% full-time. *Student/faculty ratio:* 15:1.

Academics *Calendar:* semesters. *Degrees:* bachelor's, master's, doctoral-professional, post-master's, and postbachelor's certificates. *Special study options:* academic remediation for entering students, accelerated degree program, adult/continuing education programs, advanced placement credit, distance learning, double majors, English as a second language, freshman honors college, honors programs, independent study, internships, off-campus study, part-time degree program, services for LD students, study abroad, summer session for credit. *ROTC:* Air Force (c).

Computers on Campus 700 computers/terminals are available on campus for general student use. Students can access the following: online (class) registration. Campuswide network is available. 100% of college-owned or -operated housing units are wired for high-speed Internet access. Wireless service is available via entire campus.

Student Life *Housing options:* coed, disabled students. Campus housing is university owned, leased by the school and is provided by a third party. *Activities and organizations:* drama/theater group, student-run newspaper, radio and television station, choral group, 720 Modeling Group, Organization of Latin American Students (OLAS), Young Democratic Socialists, WPBN (TV Club), Honors College Club, national fraternities, national sororities. *Campus security:* 24-hour emergency response devices and patrols, controlled dormitory access. *Student services:* health clinic, personal/psychological counseling, women's center, legal services.

Athletics Member NCAA. All Division III. *Intercollegiate sports:* baseball M, basketball M/W, bowling M(c)/W(c), field hockey W, football M, golf M, ice hockey M(c), skiing (downhill) M(c)/W(c), soccer M/W, softball W, swimming and diving M/W, volleyball W. *Intramural sports:* basketball M, equestrian sports M/W, football M, golf M, racquetball M/W, softball M/W, tennis M(c)/W(c), volleyball M/W, wrestling M.

Standardized Tests *Required:* SAT or ACT (for admission).

Costs (2010–11) *Tuition:* state resident $6830 full-time, $219 per credit hour part-time; nonresident $13,854 full-time, $449 per credit hour part-time. Full-time tuition and fees vary according to program. Part-time tuition and fees vary according to course load and program. *Required fees:* $4408 full-time, $142 per credit hour part-time. *Room and board:* $10,380; room only: $6800. Room and board charges vary according to board plan and housing facility. *Payment plan:* installment. *Waivers:* senior citizens and employees or children of employees.

Financial Aid Of all full-time matriculated undergraduates who enrolled in 2009, 6,969 applied for aid, 5,777 were judged to have need, 1,732 had their need fully met. In 2009, 380 non-need-based awards were made. *Average financial aid package:* $9711. *Average need-based loan:* $4389. *Average need-based gift aid:* $8043. *Average non-need-based aid:* $5831. *Average indebtedness upon graduation:* $28,537.

Applying *Options:* electronic application, early admission, early decision, deferred entrance. *Application fee:* $50. *Required:* high school transcript. *Required for some:* essay or personal statement, interview, portfolio for art, audition for music. *Recommended:* minimum 2.5 GPA. *Application deadlines:* 5/1 (freshmen), 6/1 (transfers). *Notification:* continuous (freshmen), continuous (transfers).

Freshman Application Contact Mr. Anthony Leckey, Associate Director of Admissions, William Paterson University of New Jersey, 300 Pompton Road, Wayne, NJ 07470-8420. *Phone:* 973-720-2903. *Toll-free phone:* 877-WPU-EXCEL. *Fax:* 973-720-2910. *E-mail:* admissions@wpunj.edu. *Web site:* http://www.wpunj.edu/.

See page 1794 for the College Close-Up.

NEW MEXICO

Brookline College
Albuquerque, New Mexico

- **Proprietary** 4-year
- **Urban** campus with easy access to Albuquerque
- **Coed** 522 undergraduate students, 100% full-time, 77% women, 23% men
- **Noncompetitive** entrance level

Undergraduates 522 full-time.

Faculty *Total:* 28, 46% full-time. *Student/faculty ratio:* 18:1.

Academics *Calendar:* continuous. *Degree:* diplomas and associate. *Special study options:* accelerated degree program, part-time degree program.

Computers on Campus 20 computers/terminals are available on campus for general student use. Students can access the following: campus intranet, computer help desk. Campuswide network is available.

Student Life *Campus security:* 24-hour emergency response devices.

Costs (2011–12) *Tuition:* $13,000 full-time. Full-time tuition and fees vary according to degree level and program. No tuition increase for student's term of enrollment. *Payment plan:* installment.

Applying *Options:* electronic application. *Required:* interview. *Application deadlines:* rolling (freshmen), rolling (out-of-state freshmen), rolling (transfers). *Notification:* continuous (freshmen), continuous (out-of-state freshmen), continuous (transfers).

Freshman Application Contact Mr. Andrew Webb, Campus Director, Brookline College, 4201 Central Avenue NW, Suite J, Albuquerque, NM 87105. *Phone:* 505-880-2877. *Toll-free phone:* 888-660-2428. *Fax:* 505-352-0199. *E-mail:* awebb@brooklinecollege.edu. *Web site:* http://brooklinecollege.edu/.

Brown Mackie College–Albuquerque
Albuquerque, New Mexico

- **Proprietary** primarily 2-year
- **Coed**

Academics *Degrees:* associate and bachelor's.

Costs (2010–11) *Tuition:* Tuition varies by program. Students should contact Brown Mackie College for tuition information.

Freshman Application Contact Brown Mackie College–Albuquerque, 10500 Cooper Avenue NE, Albuquerque, NM 87123. *Phone:* 505-559-5200. *Toll-free phone:* 877-271-3488. *Web site:* http://www.brownmackie.edu/.

See page 1136 for the College Close-Up.

Eastern New Mexico University
Portales, New Mexico

- **State-supported** comprehensive, founded 1934, part of Eastern New Mexico University System
- **Rural** 400-acre campus
- **Endowment** $7.9 million
- **Coed** 4,090 undergraduate students, 66% full-time, 56% women, 44% men
- **Minimally difficult** entrance level, 60% of applicants were admitted

Undergraduates 2,680 full-time, 1,410 part-time. Students come from 45 states and territories; 20 other countries; 23% are from out of state; 12% transferred in; 26% live on campus. *Retention:* 62% of full-time freshmen returned.

Freshmen *Admission:* 2,164 applied, 1,293 admitted, 615 enrolled. *Average high school GPA:* 3.21. *Test scores:* SAT critical reading scores over 500: 38%; SAT math scores over 500: 40%; ACT scores over 18: 75%; SAT critical reading scores over 600: 11%; SAT math scores over 600: 8%; ACT scores over 24: 19%; SAT critical reading scores over 700: 1%; SAT math scores over 700: 1%; ACT scores over 30: 1%.

Faculty *Total:* 336, 43% full-time, 40% with terminal degrees. *Student/faculty ratio:* 17:1.

Academics *Calendar:* semesters. *Degrees:* associate, bachelor's, and master's. *Special study options:* academic remediation for entering students, accelerated degree program, adult/continuing education programs, advanced placement credit, cooperative education, distance learning, double majors, English as a second language, independent study, internships, part-time degree program, services for LD students, student-designed majors, summer session for credit. *Unusual degree programs:* 3-2 Chemistry - qualified undergraduate students entering the chemistry program will be allowed to apply to the Graduate School during the last semester of the junior year to take a limited number of graduate courses for credit at the 500 level leading to a B.S. and an M.S. in 5-5.5 years total.

Computers on Campus 446 computers/terminals are available on campus for general student use. Students can access the following: campus intranet, computer help desk, free student e-mail accounts, online (class) grades, online (class) registration, online (class) schedules, Wifi in most student buildings. Campuswide network is available. 90% of college-owned or -operated housing units are wired for high-speed Internet access. Wireless service is available via classrooms, computer centers, computer labs, dorm rooms, libraries, student centers.

Student Life *Housing:* on-campus residence required for freshman year. *Options:* coed, women-only, disabled students. Campus housing is university owned. Freshman campus housing is guaranteed. *Activities and organizations:* drama/theater group, student-run newspaper, radio and television station, choral group, marching band, Student Government Association, Student Activities Board, Residence Hall Association, IFC (Inter Fraternity Council), Graduate Student Association, national fraternities, national sororities. *Campus security:* 24-hour emergency response devices and patrols, late-night transport/escort service, controlled dormitory access, University Emergency Notification System. *Student services:* health clinic, personal/psychological counseling.

Athletics Member NCAA. All Division II. *Intercollegiate sports:* baseball M(s), basketball M(s)/W(s), cross-country running M(s)/W(s), football M(s), soccer M(s)/W(s), softball W(s), track and field M(s)/W(s), volleyball W(s). *Intramural sports:* badminton M/W, basketball M/W, cross-country running M/W, football M/W, racquetball M/W, soccer M/W, softball M/W, volleyball M/W, water polo M/W.

Standardized Tests *Required:* SAT or ACT (for admission).

Costs (2010–11) *Tuition:* state resident $2688 full-time, $112 per credit hour part-time; nonresident $8220 full-time, $343 per credit hour part-time. Full-time tuition and fees vary according to course load and reciprocity agreements. Part-time tuition and fees vary according to course load. *Required fees:* $1212 full-time, $51 per credit hour part-time. *Room and board:* $5612; room only: $2694. Room and board charges vary according to gender, housing facility, location, and student level. *Payment plan:* installment. *Waivers:* senior citizens and employees or children of employees.

Financial Aid Of all full-time matriculated undergraduates who enrolled in 2009, 1,540 applied for aid, 1,540 were judged to have need, 1,540 had their need fully met. In 2009, 8 non-need-based awards were made. *Average percent of need met:* 47%. *Average financial aid package:* $8869. *Average need-based loan:* $4082. *Average need-based gift aid:* $4442. *Average non-need-based aid:* $2293. *Average indebtedness upon graduation:* $11,769.

Applying *Options:* electronic application, early admission, deferred entrance. *Required:* high school transcript, minimum 2 GPA, official transcripts from any post-secondary institution attended. *Application deadlines:* 8/24 (freshmen), 8/24 (out-of-state freshmen), 8/24 (transfers).

Freshman Application Contact Mr. Cody Spitz, Director, Enrollment Services, Eastern New Mexico University, Station #7 ENMU, Portales, NM 88130. *Phone:* 575-562-2178. *Toll-free phone:* 800-367-3668. *Fax:* 575-562-2118. *E-mail:* cody.spitz@enmu.edu. *Web site:* http://www.enmu.edu/.

Institute of American Indian Arts
Santa Fe, New Mexico

Director of Admissions Myra Garro, Manager of Enrollment and Admissions, Institute of American Indian Arts, 83 Avan Nu Po Road, Santa Fe, NM 87508. *Phone:* 505-424-2328. *Web site:* http://www.iaia.edu/.

ITT Technical Institute
Albuquerque, New Mexico

- **Proprietary** primarily 2-year, founded 1989, part of ITT Educational Services, Inc.
- **Coed**
- **Minimally difficult** entrance level

Academics *Calendar:* quarters. *Degrees:* associate and bachelor's.

Student Life *Housing:* college housing not available.

Freshman Application Contact Director of Recruitment, ITT Technical Institute, 5100 Masthead Street, NE, Albuquerque, NM 87109. *Phone:* 505-828-1114. *Toll-free phone:* 800-636-1114. *Web site:* http://www.itt-tech.edu/.

National American University
Albuquerque, New Mexico

Freshman Application Contact National American University, 4775 Indian School, NE, Suite 200, Albuquerque, NM 87110. *Phone:* 505-265-7517. *Toll-free phone:* 800-843-8892. *Web site:* http://www.national.edu/.

National College of Midwifery

Taos, New Mexico

Director of Admissions Ms. Beth Enson, Dean of Students, National College of Midwifery, 209 State Road 240, Taos, NM 87571. *Phone:* 505-758-8914. *E-mail:* info@midwiferycollege.org. *Web site:* http://www.midwiferycollege.org/.

New Mexico Highlands University

Las Vegas, New Mexico

- **State-supported** comprehensive, founded 1893
- **Small-town** campus
- **Endowment** $1.8 million
- **Coed** 2,201 undergraduate students, 73% full-time, 61% women, 39% men
- **Minimally difficult** entrance level, 55% of applicants were admitted

Undergraduates 1,607 full-time, 594 part-time. Students come from 38 states and territories; 23 other countries; 19% are from out of state; 14% transferred in; 16% live on campus. *Retention:* 46% of full-time freshmen returned.

Freshmen *Admission:* 3,409 applied, 1,871 admitted, 331 enrolled. *Average high school GPA:* 2.97. *Test scores:* ACT scores over 18: 52%; ACT scores over 24: 5%.

Faculty *Total:* 274, 53% full-time. *Student/faculty ratio:* 15:1.

Academics *Calendar:* semesters. *Degrees:* associate, bachelor's, and master's. *Special study options:* academic remediation for entering students, accelerated degree program, advanced placement credit, cooperative education, distance learning, double majors, honors programs, independent study, internships, off-campus study, part-time degree program, services for LD students, summer session for credit.

Computers on Campus 500 computers/terminals are available on campus for general student use. Students can access the following: online (class) registration. Campuswide network is available.

Student Life *Housing options:* coed, disabled students. Campus housing is university owned. *Activities and organizations:* drama/theater group, student-run newspaper, radio station, choral group, marching band, NMHU Rugby Club, Rotaract, Highlands University Geological Society, ASL Club, Native American Club, national fraternities. *Campus security:* 24-hour emergency response devices and patrols, late-night transport/escort service, controlled dormitory access. *Student services:* health clinic, personal/psychological counseling.

Athletics Member NCAA. All Division II. *Intercollegiate sports:* baseball M(s), basketball M(s)/W(s), cross-country running M(s)/W(s), football M(s), soccer W(s), softball W(s), track and field M/W, volleyball W(s). *Intramural sports:* badminton M/W, basketball M/W, football M, golf M/W, racquetball M/W, rugby M, skiing (cross-country) M/W, skiing (downhill) M/W, softball W, swimming and diving M/W, table tennis M/W, tennis M/W, volleyball M/W, weight lifting M/W.

Standardized Tests *Recommended:* SAT or ACT (for admission), COMPASS.

Costs (2010–11) *Tuition:* state resident $2952 full-time, $123 per credit hour part-time; nonresident $4632 full-time, $193 per credit hour part-time. Full-time tuition and fees vary according to course load and location. Part-time tuition and fees vary according to course load and location. *Room and board:* $6098; room only: $2743. Room and board charges vary according to board plan and housing facility. *Payment plan:* installment. *Waivers:* senior citizens and employees or children of employees.

Financial Aid Of all full-time matriculated undergraduates who enrolled in 2009, 1,131 applied for aid, 1,010 were judged to have need, 92 had their need fully met. 270 Federal Work-Study jobs (averaging $2628). 108 state and other part-time jobs (averaging $2791). In 2009, 83 non-need-based awards were made. *Average percent of need met:* 67%. *Average financial aid package:* $8183. *Average need-based loan:* $2867. *Average need-based gift aid:* $4588. *Average non-need-based aid:* $2015. *Average indebtedness upon graduation:* $12,147.

Applying *Options:* electronic application, early admission, deferred entrance. *Application fee:* $15. *Required:* high school transcript, minimum 2 GPA. *Required for some:* 2 letters of recommendation, interview. *Application deadlines:* rolling (freshmen), rolling (out-of-state freshmen), rolling (transfers). *Notification:* continuous (freshmen), continuous (out-of-state freshmen), continuous (transfers).

Freshman Application Contact Ms. Judy Cordova, Vice President for Student Affairs, New Mexico Highlands University, Box 9000, Las Vegas, NM 87701. *Phone:* 505-454-3566. *Toll-free phone:* 800-338-6648. *E-mail:* judycordova@nmhu.edu. *Web site:* http://www.nmhu.edu/.

New Mexico Institute of Mining and Technology

Socorro, New Mexico

- **State-supported** university, founded 1889
- **Small-town** 320-acre campus with easy access to Albuquerque
- **Endowment** $23.1 million
- **Coed** 1,385 undergraduate students, 85% full-time, 32% women, 68% men
- **Moderately difficult** entrance level

Undergraduates 1,184 full-time, 201 part-time. 16% are from out of state; 6% transferred in; 49% live on campus. *Retention:* 73% of full-time freshmen returned.

Freshmen *Admission:* 1,178 applied, 347 enrolled. *Average high school GPA:* 3.63. *Test scores:* SAT critical reading scores over 500: 87%; SAT math scores over 500: 91%; ACT scores over 18: 100%; SAT critical reading scores over 600: 53%; SAT math scores over 600: 65%; ACT scores over 24: 76%; SAT critical reading scores over 700: 17%; SAT math scores over 700: 19%; ACT scores over 30: 20%.

Faculty *Total:* 167, 72% full-time, 77% with terminal degrees. *Student/faculty ratio:* 11:1.

Academics *Calendar:* semesters. *Degrees:* associate, bachelor's, master's, and doctoral-research/scholarship. *Special study options:* accelerated degree program, advanced placement credit, cooperative education, distance learning, double majors, independent study, internships, services for LD students, student-designed majors, summer session for credit. *Unusual degree programs:* 3-2 engineering; Earth Sciences.

Computers on Campus 225 computers/terminals are available on campus for general student use. Students can access the following: computer help desk, free student e-mail accounts, online (class) registration, online (class) schedules. Campuswide network is available. Wireless service is available via computer centers, learning centers, student centers.

Student Life *Housing options:* coed, men-only, women-only. Campus housing is university owned. *Activities and organizations:* drama/theater group, student-run newspaper, radio station, choral group, Search and Rescue, Society for Creative Anachronism, Amateur Astronomers, Ski Club. *Campus security:* 24-hour emergency response devices and patrols, late-night transport/escort service. *Student services:* health clinic, personal/psychological counseling.

Athletics *Intercollegiate sports:* golf M(c)/W(c), rugby M(c)/W(c), soccer M(c)/W(c). *Intramural sports:* badminton M/W, basketball M/W, softball M/W, volleyball M/W.

Standardized Tests *Required:* SAT or ACT (for admission). *Recommended:* ACT (for admission).

Costs (2010–11) *Tuition:* state resident $4299 full-time, $179 per credit hour part-time; nonresident $13,977 full-time, $582 per credit hour part-time. Full-time tuition and fees vary according to reciprocity agreements. Part-time tuition and fees vary according to course load. *Required fees:* $643 full-time. *Room and board:* $5874. Room and board charges vary according to board plan and housing facility. *Waivers:* employees or children of employees.

Financial Aid Of all full-time matriculated undergraduates who enrolled in 2009, 1,067 applied for aid, 536 were judged to have need, 226 had their need fully met. 207 Federal Work-Study jobs (averaging $2659). 59 state and other part-time jobs (averaging $1949). In 2009, 474 non-need-based awards were made. *Average percent of need met:* 91%. *Average financial aid package:* $11,874. *Average need-based loan:* $3904. *Average need-based gift aid:* $6704. *Average non-need-based aid:* $6193. *Average indebtedness upon graduation:* $15,974.

Applying *Options:* electronic application, deferred entrance. *Application fee:* $15. *Required:* high school transcript, minimum 2.5 GPA, SAT or ACT Scores. *Required for some:* 2 letters of recommendation. *Recommended:* interview. *Application deadlines:* 8/1 (freshmen), 8/1 (transfers). *Notification:* continuous (freshmen), continuous (transfers).

Freshman Application Contact Mr. Mike Kloeppel, Director of Admissions, New Mexico Institute of Mining and Technology, 801 Leroy Place, Socorro, NM 87801. *Phone:* 575-835-5424. *Toll-free phone:* 800-428-TECH. *Fax:* 575-835-5989. *E-mail:* admission@admin.nmt.edu. *Web site:* http://www.nmt.edu/.

New Mexico State University
Las Cruces, New Mexico

- **State-supported** university, founded 1888, part of New Mexico State University System
- **Suburban** 900-acre campus with easy access to El Paso
- **Endowment** $68.6 million
- **Coed** 14,799 undergraduate students, 85% full-time, 55% women, 45% men
- **Moderately difficult** entrance level, 95% of applicants were admitted

Undergraduates 12,610 full-time, 2,189 part-time. Students come from 50 states and territories; 22% are from out of state; 3% Black or African American, non-Hispanic/Latino; 48% Hispanic/Latino; 2% Asian, non-Hispanic/Latino; 0.1% Native Hawaiian or other Pacific Islander, non-Hispanic/Latino; 3% American Indian or Alaska Native, non-Hispanic/Latino; 0.5% Two or more races, non-Hispanic/Latino; 7% Race/ethnicity unknown; 3% international; 5% transferred in; 18% live on campus. *Retention:* 75% of full-time freshmen returned.
Freshmen *Admission:* 5,942 applied, 5,621 admitted, 2,344 enrolled. *Average high school GPA:* 3.28. *Test scores:* SAT critical reading scores over 500: 35%; SAT math scores over 500: 42%; SAT writing scores over 500: 34%; ACT scores over 18: 75%; SAT critical reading scores over 600: 10%; SAT math scores over 600: 10%; SAT writing scores over 600: 7%; ACT scores over 24: 24%; SAT critical reading scores over 700: 1%; SAT writing scores over 700: 1%; ACT scores over 30: 2%.
Faculty *Total:* 976, 70% full-time, 63% with terminal degrees. *Student/faculty ratio:* 20:1.
Academics *Calendar:* semesters. *Degrees:* associate, bachelor's, master's, doctoral-research/scholarship, post-master's, and postbachelor's certificates. *Special study options:* academic remediation for entering students, accelerated degree program, adult/continuing education programs, advanced placement credit, cooperative education, distance learning, double majors, honors programs, independent study, internships, off-campus study, part-time degree program, services for LD students, student-designed majors, study abroad, summer session for credit. *ROTC:* Army (b), Air Force (b).
Computers on Campus 740 computers/terminals are available on campus for general student use. Students can access the following: campus intranet, computer help desk, free student e-mail accounts, online (class) grades, online (class) registration, online (class) schedules, online financial aid, wireless is available in many areas. Campuswide network is available. 100% of college-owned or -operated housing units are wired for high-speed Internet access. Wireless service is available via entire campus.
Student Life *Housing options:* coed, disabled students. Campus housing is university owned. *Activities and organizations:* drama/theater group, student-run newspaper, radio and television station, choral group, marching band, Pride Marching Band, Kappa Sigma (Social Fraternity), Alpha Chi (Honorary), American Society of Civil Engineers, Aggies for Christ, national fraternities, national sororities. *Campus security:* 24-hour emergency response devices and patrols, late-night transport/escort service, controlled dormitory access. *Student services:* health clinic, personal/psychological counseling, legal services.
Athletics Member NCAA. All Division I except football (Division I-A). *Intercollegiate sports:* baseball M(s), basketball M(s)/W(s), cross-country running M(s)/W(s), equestrian sports M/W, golf M(s)/W(s), softball W(s), swimming and diving W(s), tennis M(s)/W(s), track and field W(s), volleyball W(s). *Intramural sports:* archery M/W, badminton M/W, baseball M, basketball M/W, bowling M(c)/W(c), cheerleading M/W, football M/W, golf M/W, racquetball M/W, rock climbing M(c)/W(c), rugby M(c)/W(c), skiing (downhill) M(c)/W(c), soccer M(c)/W(c), softball M/W, tennis M/W, ultimate Frisbee M(c)/W(c), volleyball M(c)/W(c), water polo M/W, weight lifting M(c)/W(c), wrestling M.
Standardized Tests *Required:* SAT or ACT (for admission).
Costs (2010–11) *Tuition:* state resident $4128 full-time, $225 per credit hour part-time; nonresident $15,408 full-time, $695 per credit hour part-time. *Required fees:* $1272 full-time. *Room and board:* $6526; room only: $3736. Room and board charges vary according to board plan and housing facility. *Payment plans:* installment, deferred payment. *Waivers:* senior citizens and employees or children of employees.
Financial Aid Of all full-time matriculated undergraduates who enrolled in 2008, 8,508 applied for aid, 7,456 were judged to have need, 385 had their need fully met. 322 Federal Work-Study jobs (averaging $2803). 378 state and other part-time jobs (averaging $2800). In 2008, 1424 non-need-based awards were made. *Average percent of need met:* 55%. *Average financial aid package:* $8547. *Average need-based loan:* $11,385. *Average need-based gift aid:* $6383. *Average non-need-based aid:* $1992. *Average indebtedness upon graduation:* $16,619.
Applying *Options:* electronic application, early admission, deferred entrance. *Application fee:* $20. *Required:* high school transcript, minimum 2 GPA. *Application deadlines:* 8/19 (freshmen), 8/14 (transfers). *Notification:* continuous (freshmen), continuous (transfers).

Freshman Application Contact Valerie Pickett, Director of Admissions, New Mexico State University, Box 30001, MSC 3A, Las Cruces, NM 88003-8001. *Phone:* 575-646-3121. *Toll-free phone:* 800-662-6678. *Fax:* 575-646-6330. *E-mail:* admssions@nmsu.edu. *Web site:* http://www.nmsu.edu/.

Northern New Mexico College
Espa|fnola, New Mexico

Freshman Application Contact Mr. Mike L. Costello, Registrar, Northern New Mexico College, 921 Paseo de O|fnate, Espa|fnola, NM 87532. *Phone:* 505-747-2193. *Fax:* 505-747-2191. *E-mail:* dms@nnmc.edu. *Web site:* http://www.nnmc.edu/.

Pima Medical Institute
Albuquerque, New Mexico

- **Proprietary** primarily 2-year, founded 1985, part of Vocational Training Institutes, Inc.
- **Urban** campus
- **Coed** 716 undergraduate students
- **Minimally difficult** entrance level

Academics *Calendar:* modular. *Degrees:* certificates, associate, and bachelor's. *Special study options:* academic remediation for entering students, cooperative education, distance learning, internships, services for LD students.
Computers on Campus Campuswide network is available.
Student Life *Housing:* college housing not available.
Standardized Tests *Required:* Wonderlic Scholastic Level Exam (for admission).
Financial Aid Of all full-time matriculated undergraduates who enrolled in 2009, 6 Federal Work-Study jobs.
Applying *Options:* early admission. *Required:* interview. *Required for some:* high school transcript.
Freshman Application Contact Admissions Office, Pima Medical Institute, 2201 San Pedro NE, Building 3, Suite 100, Albuquerque, NM 87110. *Phone:* 505-881-1234. *Toll-free phone:* 888-898-9048. *Fax:* 505-881-5329. *Web site:* http://www.pmi.edu/.

St. John's College
Santa Fe, New Mexico

- **Independent** comprehensive, founded 1964, administratively affiliated with St. John's College (MD)
- **Suburban** 250-acre campus with easy access to Albuquerque
- **Endowment** $135.2 million
- **Coed** 409 undergraduate students, 100% full-time, 41% women, 59% men
- **Very difficult** entrance level, 86% of applicants were admitted

Undergraduates 407 full-time, 2 part-time. Students come from 24 other countries; 85% are from out of state; 0.5% Black or African American, non-Hispanic/Latino; 6% Hispanic/Latino; 1% Asian, non-Hispanic/Latino; 0.2% American Indian or Alaska Native, non-Hispanic/Latino; 5% Two or more races, non-Hispanic/Latino; 3% Race/ethnicity unknown; 9% international; 6% transferred in; 75% live on campus. *Retention:* 77% of full-time freshmen returned.
Freshmen *Admission:* 269 applied, 231 admitted, 119 enrolled. *Test scores:* SAT critical reading scores over 500: 96%; SAT math scores over 500: 80%; ACT scores over 18: 100%; SAT critical reading scores over 600: 77%; SAT math scores over 600: 59%; ACT scores over 24: 88%; SAT critical reading scores over 700: 48%; SAT math scores over 700: 19%; ACT scores over 30: 35%.
Faculty *Total:* 66, 98% full-time, 80% with terminal degrees. *Student/faculty ratio:* 8:1.
Academics *Calendar:* semesters. *Degrees:* bachelor's and master's. *Special study options:* internships, off-campus study, summer session for credit.
Computers on Campus 25 computers/terminals and 375 ports are available on campus for general student use. Students can access the following: computer help desk, free student e-mail accounts. Campuswide network is available. 100% of college-owned or -operated housing units are wired for high-speed Internet access. Wireless service is available via classrooms, computer labs, learning centers, student centers.
Student Life *Housing:* on-campus residence required for freshman year. *Options:* coed, men-only, women-only, disabled students. Campus housing is university owned. Freshman campus housing is guaranteed. *Activities and organizations:* drama/theater group, student-run newspaper, choral group, student government, Film Society, Search and Rescue Team, student newspaper, theatre group. *Campus security:* 24-hour emergency response devices and patrols, student patrols, late-night transport/escort service. *Student services:* health clinic, personal/psychological counseling.

Athletics *Intercollegiate sports:* fencing M/W, ultimate Frisbee M/W. *Intramural sports:* basketball M/W, cross-country running M/W, fencing M/W, ice hockey M/W, racquetball M/W, rock climbing M/W, skiing (cross-country) M/W, skiing (downhill) M/W, soccer M/W, softball M/W, squash M/W, table tennis M/W, tennis M/W, ultimate Frisbee M/W, volleyball M/W.
Standardized Tests *Required for some:* SAT (for admission).
Costs (2010–11) *Comprehensive fee:* $52,176 includes full-time tuition ($41,792), mandatory fees ($400), and room and board ($9984). *College room only:* $5054. Room and board charges vary according to board plan. *Payment plan:* installment. *Waivers:* employees or children of employees.
Financial Aid Of all full-time matriculated undergraduates who enrolled in 2008, 330 applied for aid, 292 were judged to have need, 302 had their need fully met. *Average percent of need met:* 94%. *Average financial aid package:* $27,902. *Average need-based loan:* $5047. *Average need-based gift aid:* $19,210. *Average indebtedness upon graduation:* $27,235. *Financial aid deadline:* 2/15.
Applying *Options:* electronic application, early admission, deferred entrance. *Required:* essay or personal statement, high school transcript, 2 letters of recommendation. *Required for some:* interview. *Recommended:* 3 letters of recommendation, interview. *Application deadlines:* rolling (freshmen), rolling (transfers). *Notification:* continuous (freshmen), continuous (transfers).
Freshman Application Contact Mr. Larry Clendenin, Director of Admissions, St. John's College, 1160 Camino Cruz Blanca, Santa Fe, NM 87505. *Phone:* 505-984-6060. *Toll-free phone:* 800-331-5232. *Fax:* 505-984-6162. *E-mail:* admissions@sjcsf.edu. *Web site:* http://www.stjohnscollege.edu/.

Santa Fe University of Art and Design
Santa Fe, New Mexico

- **Independent** university, founded 1947
- **Suburban** 100-acre campus with easy access to Albuquerque
- **Coed**
- **Moderately difficult** entrance level

Faculty *Student/faculty ratio:* 12:1.
Academics *Calendar:* semesters. *Degrees:* bachelor's and master's.
Student Life *Campus security:* 24-hour patrols, late-night transport/escort service.
Standardized Tests *Required:* SAT or ACT (for admission).
Costs (2010–11) *Comprehensive fee:* $37,604 includes full-time tuition ($27,996), mandatory fees ($1270), and room and board ($8338). *Room and board:* Room and board charges vary according to board plan and housing facility. *Payment plans:* tuition prepayment, installment.
Applying *Options:* electronic application, early admission, early decision, deferred entrance. *Application fee:* $35. *Required:* essay or personal statement, high school transcript, 2 letters of recommendation, interview. *Required for some:* portfolio or audition for visual and performing arts programs. *Recommended:* minimum 3 GPA.
Freshman Application Contact Ms. Jackie Donohoe, Santa Fe University of Art and Design, 1600 Saint Michael's Drive, Santa Fe, NM 87505-7634. *Phone:* 505-473-6133. *Toll-free phone:* 800-456-2673. *Fax:* 505-473-6129. *E-mail:* admissions@csf.edu. *Web site:* http://www.santafeuniversity.edu/.

University of New Mexico
Albuquerque, New Mexico

- **State-supported** university, founded 1889
- **Urban** 769-acre campus with easy access to Albuquerque
- **Endowment** $267.7 million
- **Coed**
- **Moderately difficult** entrance level

Faculty *Student/faculty ratio:* 19:1.
Academics *Calendar:* semesters. *Degrees:* certificates, associate, bachelor's, master's, doctoral-professional, doctoral-research/scholarship, and post-master's certificates.
Student Life *Campus security:* 24-hour emergency response devices and patrols, student patrols, late-night transport/escort service, controlled dormitory access.
Athletics Member NCAA. All Division I except football (Division I-A).
Standardized Tests *Required:* SAT or ACT (for admission).
Costs (2010–11) *Tuition:* state resident $5506 full-time, $229 per credit hour part-time; nonresident $18,691 full-time, $779 per credit hour part-time. Part-time tuition and fees vary according to course load. *Room and board:* $7948. Room and board charges vary according to board plan and housing facility.
Financial Aid *Of all full-time matriculated undergraduates who enrolled in 2001,* 7,598 applied for aid, 6,570 were judged to have need, 1,051 had their need fully met. 1,521 Federal Work-Study jobs, 865 state and other part-time jobs. *In 2001,* 4124 non-need-based awards were made. *Average percent of need met:* 75. *Average financial aid package:* $7829. *Average need-based*

loan: $3261. *Average need-based gift aid:* $4796. *Average non-need-based aid:* $3173. *Average indebtedness upon graduation:* $16,595.
Applying *Options:* electronic application, early admission, deferred entrance. *Application fee:* $20. *Required:* high school transcript, minimum 2.25 GPA. *Required for some:* essay or personal statement.
Freshman Application Contact Ms. Kathleen Roberts, Coordinator of Freshmen Admissions, University of New Mexico, Office of Admissions, PO Box 4895, Albuquerque, NM 87196-4895. *Phone:* 505-277-8900. *Toll-free phone:* 800-CALLUNM. *Fax:* 505-277-6686. *E-mail:* apply@unm.edu. *Web site:* http://www.unm.edu/.

University of New Mexico–Gallup
Gallup, New Mexico

Director of Admissions Ms. Pearl A. Morris, Admissions Representative, University of New Mexico–Gallup, 200 College Road, Gallup, NM 87301-5603. *Phone:* 505-863-7576. *Toll-free phone:* 505-863-7576. *Web site:* http://www.gallup.unm.edu/.

University of Phoenix–New Mexico Campus
Albuquerque, New Mexico

Freshman Application Contact Ms. Audra McQuarie, Registrar/Executive Director, University of Phoenix–New Mexico Campus, 4035 South Riverpoint Parkway, Mail Stop CF-L101, Phoenix, AZ 85040. *Phone:* 480-557-6151. *Toll-free phone:* 800-776-4867 (in-state); 800-228-7240 (out-of-state). *Fax:* 480-643-3068. *E-mail:* audra.mcquarie@phoenix.edu. *Web site:* http://www.phoenix.edu/.

University of the Southwest
Hobbs, New Mexico

- **Independent religious** comprehensive, founded 1962
- **Small-town** 162-acre campus
- **Endowment** $486,583
- **Coed** 310 undergraduate students, 87% full-time, 45% women, 55% men
- **Moderately difficult** entrance level

Undergraduates 271 full-time, 39 part-time. Students come from 14 states and territories; 6 other countries; 21% are from out of state; 13% Black or African American, non-Hispanic/Latino; 45% Hispanic/Latino; 0.6% Asian, non-Hispanic/Latino; 1% American Indian or Alaska Native, non-Hispanic/Latino; 0.6% Race/ethnicity unknown; 1% international; 23% transferred in; 48% live on campus. *Retention:* 38% of full-time freshmen returned.
Freshmen *Admission:* 213 applied, 57 enrolled. *Average high school GPA:* 2.93. *Test scores:* SAT critical reading scores over 500: 13%; SAT math scores over 500: 54%; SAT writing scores over 500: 46%; ACT scores over 18: 58%; SAT math scores over 600: 20%; SAT writing scores over 600: 6%; ACT scores over 24: 17%.
Faculty *Total:* 52, 27% full-time, 23% with terminal degrees. *Student/faculty ratio:* 10:1.
Academics *Calendar:* semesters. *Degrees:* bachelor's and master's. *Special study options:* advanced placement credit, distance learning, double majors, internships, part-time degree program, services for LD students, summer session for credit.
Computers on Campus 35 computers/terminals are available on campus for general student use. Students can access the following: campus intranet, computer help desk, free student e-mail accounts, online (class) grades, online (class) registration, online (class) schedules. Campuswide network is available. 100% of college-owned or -operated housing units are wired for high-speed Internet access. Wireless service is available via computer centers, computer labs, dorm rooms, learning centers, libraries, student centers.
Student Life *Housing:* on-campus residence required through sophomore year. *Options:* coed. Campus housing is university owned. Freshman applicants given priority for college housing. *Activities and organizations:* student-run newspaper, student government, Students in Free Enterprise (SIFE), Southwest Association of Future Educators, Fellowship of Christian Athletes, BEST. *Campus security:* student patrols, controlled dormitory access, night security. *Student services:* personal/psychological counseling.
Athletics Member NAIA. *Intercollegiate sports:* baseball M(s), basketball M(s)/W(s), cross-country running M(s)/W(s), golf M(s)/W(s), soccer M(s)/W(s), softball W(s), tennis M(s)/W(s), track and field M(s)/W(s). *Intramural sports:* badminton M/W, basketball M/W, golf M/W, soccer M/W, table tennis M/W, volleyball M/W.
Standardized Tests *Required:* SAT or ACT (for admission).
Costs (2011–12) *One-time required fee:* $300. *Comprehensive fee:* $18,219 includes full-time tuition ($11,664), mandatory fees ($25), and room and board ($6530). Full-time tuition and fees vary according to course load. Part-time

tuition: $486 per semester hour. Part-time tuition and fees vary according to course load. *College room only:* $3370. Room and board charges vary according to housing facility. *Payment plan:* deferred payment. *Waivers:* employees or children of employees.

Financial Aid Of all full-time matriculated undergraduates who enrolled in 2009, 306 applied for aid, 266 were judged to have need, 41 had their need fully met. 26 Federal Work-Study jobs (averaging $1035). 12 state and other part-time jobs (averaging $3008). In 2009, 17 non-need-based awards were made. *Average percent of need met:* 70%. *Average financial aid package:* $5460. *Average need-based loan:* $4140. *Average need-based gift aid:* $4557. *Average non-need-based aid:* $1240. *Average indebtedness upon graduation:* $19,645.

Applying *Options:* electronic application, early admission, deferred entrance. *Application fee:* $25. *Required:* high school transcript, minimum 2 GPA. *Application deadlines:* rolling (freshmen), rolling (transfers). *Notification:* continuous (freshmen), continuous (transfers).

Freshman Application Contact Ashley Taylor, Admissions Coordinator, University of the Southwest, 6610 Lovington Highway, Hobbs, NM 88240-9129. *Phone:* 575-492-2121 Ext. 2121. *Toll-free phone:* 800-530-4400. *Fax:* 575-392-6006. *E-mail:* ataylor@usw.edu. *Web site:* http://www.usw.edu/.

Western New Mexico University

Silver City, New Mexico

Freshman Application Contact Mr. Dan Tressler, Director of Admissions, Western New Mexico University, PO Box 680, Silver City, NM 88062-0680. *Phone:* 505-538-6106. *Toll-free phone:* 800-872-WNMU. *Fax:* 505-538-6127. *E-mail:* tresslerd@wnmu.edu. *Web site:* http://www.wnmu.edu/.

NEW YORK

Adelphi University

Garden City, New York

- **Independent** university, founded 1896
- **Suburban** 75-acre campus with easy access to New York City
- **Endowment** $101.4 million
- **Coed** 4,939 undergraduate students, 88% full-time, 70% women, 30% men
- **Moderately difficult** entrance level, 70% of applicants were admitted

Undergraduates 4,335 full-time, 604 part-time. Students come from 41 states and territories; 48 other countries; 7% are from out of state; 12% Black or African American, non-Hispanic/Latino; 9% Hispanic/Latino; 6% Asian, non-Hispanic/Latino; 0.4% Native Hawaiian or other Pacific Islander, non-Hispanic/Latino; 0.2% American Indian or Alaska Native, non-Hispanic/Latino; 2% Two or more races, non-Hispanic/Latino; 13% Race/ethnicity unknown; 3% international; 10% transferred in; 23% live on campus. *Retention:* 82% of full-time freshmen returned.

Freshmen *Admission:* 7,931 applied, 5,519 admitted, 921 enrolled. *Average high school GPA:* 3.36. *Test scores:* SAT critical reading scores over 500: 69%; SAT math scores over 500: 74%; SAT writing scores over 500: 74%; ACT scores over 18: 97%; SAT critical reading scores over 600: 21%; SAT math scores over 600: 24%; SAT writing scores over 600: 26%; ACT scores over 24: 47%; SAT critical reading scores over 700: 3%; SAT math scores over 700: 3%; SAT writing scores over 700: 5%; ACT scores over 30: 6%.

Faculty *Total:* 967, 32% full-time. *Student/faculty ratio:* 13:1.

Academics *Calendar:* semesters. *Degrees:* associate, bachelor's, master's, doctoral-professional, doctoral-research/scholarship, post-master's, and post-bachelor's certificates. *Special study options:* accelerated degree program, advanced placement credit, distance learning, double majors, English as a second language, freshman honors college, honors programs, independent study, internships, part-time degree program, services for LD students, student-designed majors, study abroad, summer session for credit. *ROTC:* Army (c), Air Force (c). *Unusual degree programs:* 3-2 engineering with Columbia University, Rensselaer Polytechnic University, Stevens Institute of Technology; physical therapy with New York Medical College; Tufts University; New York University College of Dentistry; New York Law School; SUNY College of Optometry; Columbia University; osteopathic with Touro College; New York College of Podiatric Medicine.

Computers on Campus 880 computers/terminals are available on campus for general student use. Students can access the following: computer help desk, free student e-mail accounts, online (class) grades, online (class) registration, online (class) schedules, payment, drop/add classes, check application status. Campuswide network is available. 100% of college-owned or -operated housing units are wired for high-speed Internet access. Wireless service is available via entire campus.

Student Life *Housing options:* coed, disabled students. Campus housing is university owned. Freshman applicants given priority for college housing. *Activities and organizations:* drama/theater group, student-run newspaper, radio station, choral group, Student Activities Board, C. A. L. I. B. E. R. (Cause to Achieve Leadership, Intelligence, Brotherhood, Excellence, and Respect), Circle K International, Future Teachers Association, Adelphi Christian Fellowship, national fraternities, national sororities. *Campus security:* 24-hour emergency response devices and patrols, late-night transport/escort service, controlled dormitory access. *Student services:* health clinic, personal/psychological counseling.

Athletics Member NCAA. All Division II except soccer (Division I). *Intercollegiate sports:* baseball M(s), basketball M(s)/W(s), bowling W(s), cross-country running M(s)/W(s), field hockey W(s), golf M(s), lacrosse M(s)/W(s), soccer M(s)/W(s), softball W(s), swimming and diving M(s)/W(s), tennis M(s)/W(s), track and field M(s)/W(s), volleyball W(s). *Intramural sports:* badminton M/W, basketball M/W, cheerleading W, fencing M(c)/W(c), football M/W, soccer M/W, ultimate Frisbee M(c)/W(c), volleyball M/W, water polo M/W.

Standardized Tests *Required for some:* SAT or ACT (for admission).

Costs (2010–11) *Comprehensive fee:* $37,915 includes full-time tuition ($25,465), mandatory fees ($1450), and room and board ($11,000). Full-time tuition and fees vary according to course level, location, and program. Part-time tuition: $820 per credit hour. Part-time tuition and fees vary according to course level, location, and program. *Required fees:* $365 per term part-time. *Room and board:* Room and board charges vary according to board plan and housing facility. *Payment plans:* installment, deferred payment. *Waivers:* employees or children of employees.

Financial Aid Of all full-time matriculated undergraduates who enrolled in 2009, 3,536 applied for aid, 3,111 were judged to have need, 19 had their need fully met. In 2009, 780 non-need-based awards were made. *Average percent of need met:* 37%. *Average financial aid package:* $18,475. *Average need-based loan:* $4679. *Average need-based gift aid:* $6722. *Average non-need-based aid:* $10,351. *Average indebtedness upon graduation:* $31,096.

Applying *Options:* electronic application, early action, deferred entrance. *Application fee:* $40. *Required:* essay or personal statement, high school transcript. *Required for some:* 2 letters of recommendation, interview, auditions/portfolios for performing and fine arts. *Recommended:* minimum 3.36 GPA, interview. *Application deadlines:* rolling (freshmen), rolling (transfers), 12/1 (early action). *Notification:* continuous (freshmen), continuous (transfers), 12/31 (early action).

Freshman Application Contact Ms. Christine Murphy, Director of Admissions, Adelphi University, Levermore Hall 110, 1 South Avenue, PO Box 701, Garden City, NY 11530-0701. *Phone:* 516-877-3050. *Toll-free phone:* 800-ADELPHI. *Fax:* 516-877-3039. *E-mail:* admissions@adelphi.edu. *Web site:* http://www.adelphi.edu/.

See page 986 for the College Close-Up.

Albany College of Pharmacy and Health Sciences

Albany, New York

- **Independent** comprehensive, founded 1881
- **Urban** 20-acre campus
- **Coed** 1,128 undergraduate students, 98% full-time, 60% women, 40% men
- **Very difficult** entrance level, 70% of applicants were admitted

Undergraduates 1,106 full-time, 22 part-time. Students come from 27 states and territories; 17 other countries; 34% are from out of state; 3% Black or African American, non-Hispanic/Latino; 3% Hispanic/Latino; 14% Asian, non-Hispanic/Latino; 0.3% Native Hawaiian or other Pacific Islander, non-Hispanic/Latino; 0.2% American Indian or Alaska Native, non-Hispanic/Latino; 2% Two or more races, non-Hispanic/Latino; 3% Race/ethnicity unknown; 8% international; 13% transferred in; 65% live on campus. *Retention:* 72% of full-time freshmen returned.

Freshmen *Admission:* 1,037 applied, 722 admitted, 220 enrolled. *Average high school GPA:* 3.7. *Test scores:* SAT critical reading scores over 500: 83%; SAT math scores over 500: 97%; SAT writing scores over 500: 83%; ACT scores over 18: 100%; SAT critical reading scores over 600: 29%; SAT math scores over 600: 60%; SAT writing scores over 600: 25%; ACT scores over 24: 68%; SAT critical reading scores over 700: 1%; SAT math scores over 700: 8%; SAT writing scores over 700: 1%; ACT scores over 30: 9%.

Faculty *Total:* 141, 72% full-time, 70% with terminal degrees. *Student/faculty ratio:* 14:1.

Academics *Calendar:* semesters. *Degrees:* bachelor's, master's, and doctoral-professional. *Special study options:* advanced placement credit, independent study, off-campus study, services for LD students, summer session for credit. *ROTC:* Army (c), Navy (c), Air Force (c).

Computers on Campus 30 computers/terminals are available on campus for general student use. Students can access the following: campus intranet, computer help desk, free student e-mail accounts, online (class) grades, online (class) registration, online (class) schedules. Campuswide network is available. 100% of college-owned or -operated housing units are wired for high-speed Internet access. Wireless service is available via entire campus.

Student Life *Housing:* on-campus residence required through sophomore year. *Options:* coed. Campus housing is university owned and is provided by a third party. Freshman campus housing is guaranteed. *Activities and organizations:* student-run newspaper, choral group, American Pharmacy Association-Student Chapter, Orthodox Christian Student Association, Student Government Association, Colleges Against Cancer, national fraternities, national sororities. *Campus security:* 24-hour emergency response devices and patrols, controlled dormitory access. *Student services:* health clinic, personal/psychological counseling.

Athletics *Intercollegiate sports:* basketball M/W, cross-country running M/W, soccer M/W. *Intramural sports:* basketball M/W, football M/W, golf M(c)/W(c), lacrosse M(c), tennis M(c)/W(c), ultimate Frisbee M/W, volleyball M/W.

Standardized Tests *Required:* SAT or ACT (for admission).

Costs (2010–11) *Comprehensive fee:* $34,520 includes full-time tuition ($24,500), mandatory fees ($620), and room and board ($9400). Full-time tuition and fees vary according to program. Part-time tuition: $815 per credit hour. Part-time tuition and fees vary according to course load and program. *College room only:* $6200. Room and board charges vary according to board plan, housing facility, and location. *Payment plan:* installment. *Waivers:* employees or children of employees.

Financial Aid Of all full-time matriculated undergraduates who enrolled in 2002, 567 applied for aid, 498 were judged to have need, 186 had their need fully met. 202 Federal Work-Study jobs (averaging $450). 12 state and other part-time jobs (averaging $432). In 2002, 74 non-need-based awards were made. *Average percent of need met:* 78%. *Average financial aid package:* $12,320. *Average need-based loan:* $8238. *Average need-based gift aid:* $5247. *Average non-need-based aid:* $8933. *Average indebtedness upon graduation:* $9397.

Applying *Options:* electronic application, early decision. *Application fee:* $75. *Required:* essay or personal statement, high school transcript, 2 letters of recommendation. *Required for some:* interview. *Recommended:* minimum 3 GPA. *Application deadlines:* 2/1 (freshmen), 2/1 (transfers). *Early decision deadline:* 11/1. *Notification:* 3/15 (freshmen), 3/15 (transfers), 12/15 (early decision).

Freshman Application Contact Mr. Matthew Stever, Director of Admissions, Albany College of Pharmacy and Health Sciences, 106 New Scotland Avenue, Albany, NY 12208. *Phone:* 518-694-7221. *Toll-free phone:* 888-203-8010. *Fax:* 518-694-7322. *E-mail:* admissions@acphs.edu. *Web site:* http://www.acphs.edu/.

Alfred University
Alfred, New York

- **Independent** university, founded 1836
- **Rural** 232-acre campus with easy access to Rochester
- **Coed** 1,905 undergraduate students, 98% full-time, 50% women, 50% men
- **Moderately difficult** entrance level, 70% of applicants were admitted

Undergraduates 1,860 full-time, 45 part-time. 30% are from out of state; 15% transferred in; 77% live on campus. *Retention:* 77% of full-time freshmen returned.

Freshmen *Admission:* 2,825 applied, 1,968 admitted, 528 enrolled. *Average high school GPA:* 3.19. *Test scores:* SAT critical reading scores over 500: 71%; SAT math scores over 500: 80%; SAT writing scores over 500: 61%; ACT scores over 18: 99%; SAT critical reading scores over 600: 22%; SAT math scores over 600: 31%; SAT writing scores over 600: 18%; ACT scores over 24: 52%; SAT critical reading scores over 700: 3%; SAT math scores over 700: 4%; SAT writing scores over 700: 2%; ACT scores over 30: 5%.

Faculty *Total:* 196, 80% full-time. *Student/faculty ratio:* 12:1.

Academics *Calendar:* semesters. *Degrees:* bachelor's, master's, doctoral-research/scholarship, and post-master's certificates. *Special study options:* academic remediation for entering students, accelerated degree program, advanced placement credit, cooperative education, double majors, honors programs, independent study, internships, off-campus study, part-time degree program, services for LD students, student-designed majors, study abroad, summer session for credit. *ROTC:* Army (c). *Unusual degree programs:* 3-2 engineering with Columbia University; forestry with Duke University; dentistry with New York University.

Computers on Campus Students can access the following: computer help desk, free student e-mail accounts, online (class) grades, online (class) registration, online (class) schedules, online bill pay. Campuswide network is available. 100% of college-owned or -operated housing units are wired for high-speed Internet access. Wireless service is available via classrooms, computer labs, dorm rooms, libraries, student centers.

Student Life *Housing:* on-campus residence required through junior year. *Options:* coed. Campus housing is university owned. Freshman campus housing is guaranteed. *Activities and organizations:* drama/theater group, student-run newspaper, radio and television station, choral group. *Campus security:* 24-hour emergency response devices, student patrols, late-night transport/escort service, all dormitories are key-only access, but not electronic. *Student services:* health clinic, personal/psychological counseling, women's center.

Athletics Member NCAA. All Division III. *Intercollegiate sports:* basketball M/W, cross-country running M/W, equestrian sports M/W, football M, lacrosse M/W, skiing (downhill) M/W, soccer M/W, softball W, swimming and diving M/W, tennis M/W, track and field M/W, volleyball W. *Intramural sports:* baseball M(c), basketball M/W, cheerleading W(c), football M/W, golf M/W, ice hockey M(c), lacrosse M/W, racquetball M/W, rugby M(c)/W(c), skiing (cross-country) M/W, soccer M/W, softball M/W, squash M/W, tennis M/W, ultimate Frisbee M(c)/W(c), volleyball M/W.

Standardized Tests *Required:* SAT or ACT (for admission).

Costs (2010–11) *Comprehensive fee:* $37,340 includes full-time tuition ($25,096), mandatory fees ($880), and room and board ($11,364). Full-time tuition and fees vary according to program. Part-time tuition: $814 per credit hour. Part-time tuition and fees vary according to course load. *Required fees:* $72 per term part-time. *College room only:* $5766. Room and board charges vary according to board plan and housing facility. *Payment plans:* tuition prepayment, installment, deferred payment. *Waivers:* employees or children of employees.

Financial Aid Of all full-time matriculated undergraduates who enrolled in 2009, 1,606 applied for aid, 1,414 were judged to have need, 256 had their need fully met. In 2009, 122 non-need-based awards were made. *Average percent of need met:* 85%. *Average financial aid package:* $22,557. *Average need-based loan:* $5563. *Average need-based gift aid:* $16,137. *Average non-need-based aid:* $8976. *Average indebtedness upon graduation:* $30,731. *Financial aid deadline:* 3/15.

Applying *Options:* electronic application, early admission, early decision, deferred entrance. *Application fee:* $50. *Required:* essay or personal statement, high school transcript, 1 letter of recommendation. *Required for some:* interview, portfolio. *Recommended:* interview. *Application deadlines:* 2/1 (freshmen), 8/1 (transfers). *Early decision deadline:* 12/1. *Notification:* continuous (freshmen), continuous (transfers), 12/15 (early decision).

Freshman Application Contact Mr. Jeremy C. Spencer, Director of Admissions, Alfred University, Alumni Hall, Alfred, NY 14802-1205. *Phone:* 607-871-2115. *Toll-free phone:* 800-541-9229. *Fax:* 607-871-2198. *E-mail:* admissions@alfred.edu. *Web site:* http://www.alfred.edu/.

Bard College
Annandale-on-Hudson, New York

- **Independent** comprehensive, founded 1860
- **Rural** 600-acre campus
- **Coed** 1,958 undergraduate students, 97% full-time, 57% women, 43% men
- **Very difficult** entrance level, 35% of applicants were admitted

Undergraduates 1,892 full-time, 66 part-time. Students come from 49 states and territories; 65 other countries; 67% are from out of state; 3% Black or African American, non-Hispanic/Latino; 2% Hispanic/Latino; 3% Asian, non-Hispanic/Latino; 0.5% American Indian or Alaska Native, non-Hispanic/Latino; 22% Race/ethnicity unknown; 12% international; 3% transferred in; 74% live on campus. *Retention:* 90% of full-time freshmen returned.

Freshmen *Admission:* 5,570 applied, 1,961 admitted, 497 enrolled. *Average high school GPA:* 3.5.

Faculty *Total:* 241, 65% full-time, 92% with terminal degrees. *Student/faculty ratio:* 10:1.

Academics *Calendar:* semesters. *Degrees:* associate, bachelor's, master's, and doctoral-research/scholarship. *Special study options:* adult/continuing education programs, advanced placement credit, double majors, independent study, internships, off-campus study, part-time degree program, services for LD students, student-designed majors, study abroad, summer session for credit. *Unusual degree programs:* 3-2 business administration; engineering with Columbia University, Washington University in St. Louis, Dartmouth College; forestry with Duke University; social work; teaching.

Computers on Campus 425 computers/terminals are available on campus for general student use. Students can access the following: campus intranet, computer help desk, free student e-mail accounts, online (class) grades, online (class) registration, online (class) schedules. Campuswide network is available. 100% of college-owned or -operated housing units are wired for high-speed Internet access. Wireless service is available via classrooms, computer centers, computer labs, dorm rooms, libraries, student centers.

Student Life *Housing:* on-campus residence required through sophomore year. *Options:* coed, women-only, cooperative. Campus housing is university owned. Freshman campus housing is guaranteed. *Activities and organizations:* drama/theater group, student-run newspaper, radio station, choral group, student government, Model United Nations, Queer-Straight Alliance, International Student Organization/Black Student Organization, Bard Step Team. *Campus security:* 24-hour emergency response devices and patrols, student patrols, late-night transport/escort service, controlled dormitory access. *Student services:* health clinic, personal/psychological counseling, legal services.

Athletics Member NCAA, NAIA. All NCAA Division III. *Intercollegiate sports:* basketball M/W, cross-country running M/W, soccer M/W, squash M, tennis M/W, track and field M/W, volleyball M/W. *Intramural sports:* badminton M/W, baseball M(c), basketball M/W, bowling M/W, equestrian sports M(c)/W(c), fencing M(c)/W(c), golf M/W, rugby M(c)/W(c), soccer M/W, softball M/W, squash M/W, swimming and diving M(c)/W(c), table tennis M/W, tennis M/W, ultimate Frisbee M(c)/W(c), volleyball M/W.   •

Costs (2010–11) *One-time required fee:* $800. *Comprehensive fee:* $53,480 includes full-time tuition ($40,840), mandatory fees ($830), and room and board ($11,810). Part-time tuition: $1277 per credit. *Room and board:* Room and board charges vary according to housing facility. *Payment plans:* tuition prepayment, installment. *Waivers:* employees or children of employees.

Financial Aid Of all full-time matriculated undergraduates who enrolled in 2009, 1,277 applied for aid, 1,204 were judged to have need, 614 had their need fully met. 716 Federal Work-Study jobs (averaging $1595). 88 state and other part-time jobs (averaging $1660). In 2009, 30 non-need-based awards were made. *Average percent of need met:* 94%. *Average financial aid package:* $38,530. *Average need-based loan:* $4942. *Average need-based gift aid:* $31,136. *Average non-need-based aid:* $17,841. *Average indebtedness upon graduation:* $24,311. *Financial aid deadline:* 2/15.

Applying *Options:* electronic application, early admission, early action, deferred entrance. *Application fee:* $50. *Required:* essay or personal statement, high school transcript, minimum 3 GPA, 3 letters of recommendation. *Required for some:* interview. *Recommended:* interview. *Application deadlines:* 1/1 (freshmen), 3/15 (transfers), 11/1 (early action). *Notification:* 4/1 (freshmen), 5/15 (transfers), 1/1 (early action).

Freshman Application Contact Ms. Mary Backlund, Director of Admissions, Bard College, PO Box 5000, 51 Ravine Road, Annandale-on-Hudson, NY 12504-5000. *Phone:* 845-758-7472. *Fax:* 845-758-5208. *E-mail:* admission@bard.edu. *Web site:* http://www.bard.edu/.

Barnard College
New York, New York
- **Independent** 4-year, founded 1889, part of Columbia University
- **Urban** 4-acre campus
- **Endowment** $184.0 million
- **Women only** 2,456 undergraduate students, 97% full-time
- **Most difficult** entrance level, 28% of applicants were admitted

Undergraduates 2,390 full-time, 66 part-time. Students come from 48 states and territories; 39 other countries; 68% are from out of state; 4% Black or African American, non-Hispanic/Latino; 9% Hispanic/Latino; 16% Asian, non-Hispanic/Latino; 0.2% Native Hawaiian or other Pacific Islander, non-Hispanic/Latino; 0.2% American Indian or Alaska Native, non-Hispanic/Latino; 0.4% Race/ethnicity unknown; 5% international; 3% transferred in; 90% live on campus. *Retention:* 94% of full-time freshmen returned.

Freshmen *Admission:* 4,618 applied, 1,285 admitted, 580 enrolled. *Average high school GPA:* 3.83. *Test scores:* SAT critical reading scores over 500: 99%; SAT math scores over 500: 99%; SAT writing scores over 500: 99%; ACT scores over 18: 100%; SAT critical reading scores over 600: 86%; SAT math scores over 600: 85%; SAT writing scores over 600: 90%; ACT scores over 24: 93%; SAT critical reading scores over 700: 40%; SAT math scores over 700: 33%; SAT writing scores over 700: 50%; ACT scores over 30: 60%.

Faculty *Total:* 361, 58% full-time, 89% with terminal degrees. *Student/faculty ratio:* 9:1.

Academics *Calendar:* semesters. *Degree:* bachelor's. *Special study options:* accelerated degree program, advanced placement credit, double majors, independent study, internships, off-campus study, services for LD students, student-designed majors, study abroad. *Unusual degree programs:* 3-2 engineering with Columbia University, The Fu Foundation School of Engineering and Applied Science; joint degrees with Columbia University, School of International and Public Affairs; School of Law; School of Dentistry; double degree programs with Julliard School; double degree and exchange program with the Jewish Theological Seminar; exchange program with the Manhattan School of Music.

Computers on Campus 164 computers/terminals are available on campus for general student use. Students can access the following: campus intranet, computer help desk, free student e-mail accounts, online (class) grades, online (class) registration, online (class) schedules. Campuswide network is available.

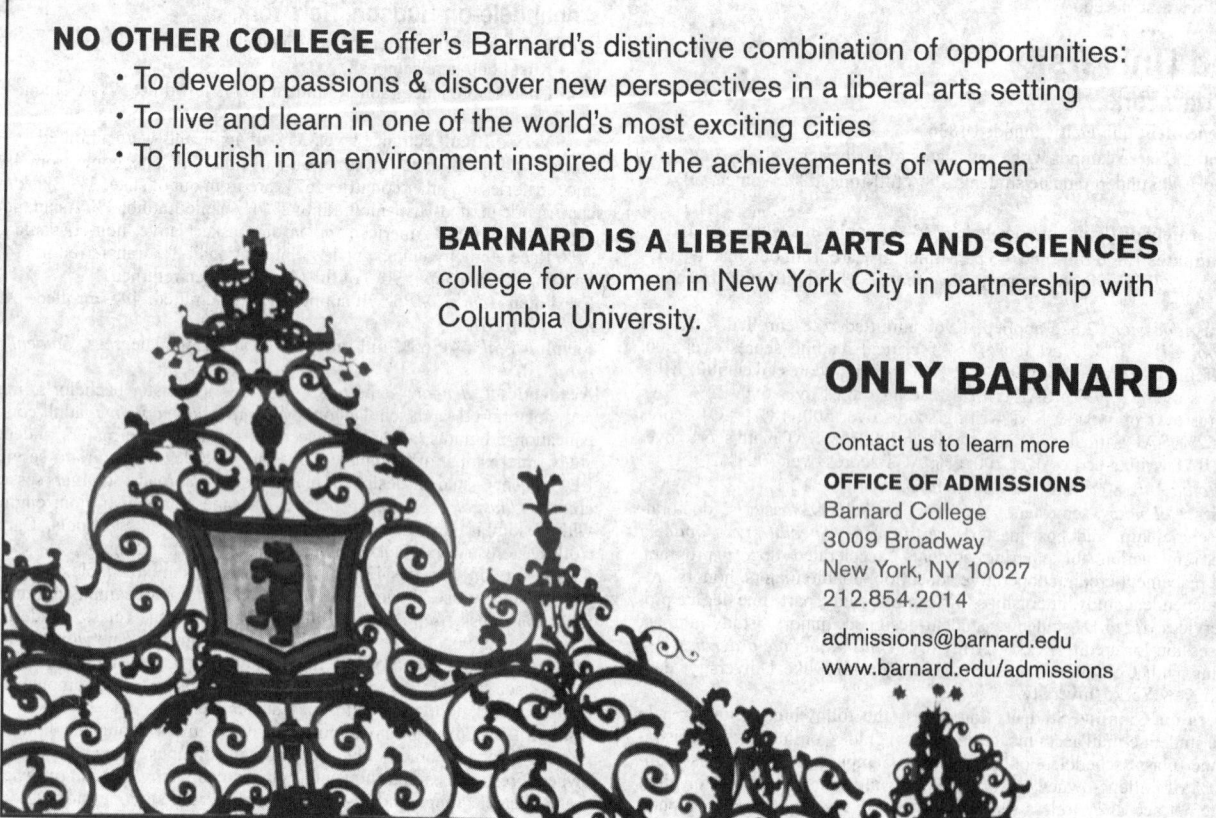

100% of college-owned or -operated housing units are wired for high-speed Internet access. Wireless service is available via computer centers, computer labs, dorm rooms, libraries, student centers.

Student Life *Housing options:* women-only, disabled students. Campus housing is university owned and leased by the school. Freshman campus housing is guaranteed. *Activities and organizations:* drama/theater group, student-run newspaper, radio and television station, choral group, marching band, Community Impact (community service), Student Government Association, Take Back the Night, Student Activities Council, College Democrats. *Campus security:* 24-hour emergency response devices and patrols, late-night transport/escort service, gated campus with permanent security posts. *Student services:* health clinic, personal/psychological counseling, women's center.

Athletics Member NCAA. All Division I. *Intercollegiate sports:* archery W, basketball W, crew W, cross-country running W, equestrian sports W(c), fencing W, field hockey W, golf W, ice hockey W(c), lacrosse W, rugby W(c), sailing W(c), skiing (downhill) W(c), soccer W, softball W, squash W(c), swimming and diving W, tennis W, track and field W, volleyball W. *Intramural sports:* archery W, badminton W, basketball W, equestrian sports W, ice hockey W, rugby W, sailing W, soccer W, squash W, tennis W, volleyball W, water polo W.

Standardized Tests *Required:* SAT with writing and two subject tests or ACT with writing (for admission).

Costs (2010–11) *Comprehensive fee:* $53,496 includes full-time tuition ($38,868), mandatory fees ($1678), and room and board ($12,950). Part-time tuition: $1295 per credit. *College room only:* $7750. Room and board charges vary according to board plan and housing facility. *Payment plans:* tuition prepayment, installment, deferred payment. *Waivers:* employees or children of employees.

Financial Aid Of all full-time matriculated undergraduates who enrolled in 2009, 1,167 applied for aid, 995 were judged to have need, 995 had their need fully met. 390 Federal Work-Study jobs (averaging $1789). 321 state and other part-time jobs (averaging $1811). *Average percent of need met:* 100%. *Average financial aid package:* $38,073. *Average need-based loan:* $4647. *Average need-based gift aid:* $33,617. *Average indebtedness upon graduation:* $14,617. *Financial aid deadline:* 2/1.

Applying *Options:* early admission, early decision, deferred entrance. *Application fee:* $55. *Required:* essay or personal statement, high school transcript, 3 letters of recommendation, Common Application with Barnard supplement. *Recommended:* interview. *Application deadlines:* 1/1 (freshmen), 4/1 (transfers). *Early decision deadline:* 11/15. *Notification:* 4/1 (freshmen), 5/15 (transfers), 12/15 (early decision).

Freshman Application Contact Ms. Jennifer Gill Fondiller, Dean of Admissions, Barnard College, 3009 Broadway, New York, NY 10027-6598. *Phone:* 212-854-2014. *Fax:* 212-854-6220. *E-mail:* admissions@barnard.edu. *Web site:* http://www.barnard.edu/.

See page 1104 for the College Close-Up.

Beis Medrash Heichal Dovid

Far Rockaway, New York

Admissions Office Contact Beis Medrash Heichal Dovid, 257 Beach 17th Street, Far Rockaway, NY 11691.

Berkeley College–New York City Campus

New York, New York

Freshman Application Contact Berkeley College–New York City Campus, 3 East 43rd Street, New York, NY 10017-4604. *Phone:* 212-986-4343. *Toll-free phone:* 800-446-5400. *Web site:* http://www.berkeleycollege.edu/.

Berkeley College–Westchester Campus

White Plains, New York

Freshman Application Contact Director of Admissions, Berkeley College–Westchester Campus, White Plains, NY 10601. *Phone:* 914-694-1122. *Toll-free phone:* 800-446-5400. *Fax:* 914-328-9469. *E-mail:* info@berkeleycollege.edu. *Web site:* http://www.berkeleycollege.edu/.

Bernard M. Baruch College of the City University of New York

New York, New York

- **State and locally supported** comprehensive, founded 1919, part of City University of New York System
- **Urban** campus
- **Endowment** $87.3 million
- **Coed**
- **Very difficult** entrance level

Faculty *Student/faculty ratio:* 17:1.

Academics *Calendar:* semesters. *Degrees:* bachelor's, master's, and post-master's certificates.

Student Life *Campus security:* 24-hour emergency response devices and patrols, late-night transport/escort service, controlled access by ID card.

Athletics Member NCAA. All Division III.

Standardized Tests *Required:* SAT or ACT (for admission).

Costs (2010–11) *Tuition:* state resident $4600 full-time, $195 per credit hour part-time; nonresident $12,450 full-time, $415 per credit hour part-time. Full-time tuition and fees vary according to course load. Part-time tuition and fees vary according to course load. *Required fees:* $420 full-time, $120 per term part-time. *Room only:* $9975. *Payment plans:* installment, deferred payment.

Financial Aid Of all full-time matriculated undergraduates who enrolled in 2009, 8,812 applied for aid, 8,012 were judged to have need, 1,179 had their need fully met. 675 Federal Work-Study jobs (averaging $800). 755 state and other part-time jobs (averaging $1200). *In 2009,* 80 non-need-based awards were made. *Average percent of need met:* 76. *Average financial aid package:* $6598. *Average need-based loan:* $5000. *Average need-based gift aid:* $4958. *Average non-need-based aid:* $4600. *Average indebtedness upon graduation:* $14,265.

Applying *Options:* electronic application, early admission, early decision, deferred entrance. *Application fee:* $65. *Required:* high school transcript, minimum 2.5 GPA, 16 academic units. *Required for some:* interview.

Freshman Application Contact Bernard M. Baruch College of the City University of New York, 1 Bernard Baruch Way, New York, NY 10010-5585. *Phone:* 646-312-1400. *Web site:* http://www.baruch.cuny.edu/.

Beth HaMedrash Shaarei Yosher Institute

Brooklyn, New York

Director of Admissions Director of Admissions, Beth HaMedrash Shaarei Yosher Institute, 4102-10 Sixteenth Avenue, Brooklyn, NY 11204. *Phone:* 718-854-2290.

Beth Hatalmud Rabbinical College

Brooklyn, New York

Director of Admissions Rabbi Osina, Director of Admissions, Beth Hatalmud Rabbinical College, 2127 Eighty-second Street, Brooklyn, NY 11214. *Phone:* 718-259-2525.

Boricua College

New York, New York

Freshman Application Contact Mrs. Miriam Pfeffer, Director of Student Services, Boricua College, 186 North 6th Street, Brooklyn, NY 11211. *Phone:* 718-782-2200. *Fax:* 718-782-2025. *E-mail:* mpfeffer@boricuacollege.edu. *Web site:* http://www.boricuacollege.edu/.

Briarcliffe College

Bethpage, New York

Freshman Application Contact Admissions Office, Briarcliffe College, 1055 Stewart Avenue, Bethpage, NY 11714. *Phone:* 516-918-3600. *Toll-free phone:* 888-349-4999. *Fax:* 516-470-6020. *Web site:* http://www.briarcliffe.edu/.

Brooklyn College of the City University of New York

Brooklyn, New York

- **State and locally supported** comprehensive, founded 1930, part of City University of New York System
- **Urban** 26-acre campus with easy access to Manhattan
- **Coed**
- **Moderately difficult** entrance level

Faculty *Student/faculty ratio:* 15:1.

Academics *Calendar:* semesters. *Degrees:* certificates, bachelor's, master's, doctoral-professional, post-master's, and postbachelor's certificates.

Student Life *Campus security:* 24-hour emergency response devices and patrols, late-night transport/escort service.

Athletics Member NCAA. All Division III.

Standardized Tests *Required:* SAT or ACT (for admission).

Costs (2010–11) *Tuition:* state resident $4830 full-time, $205 per credit part-time; nonresident $13,050 full-time, $435 per credit part-time. *Required fees:* $454 full-time, $177 per term part-time.

Financial Aid *Of all full-time matriculated undergraduates who enrolled in 2009,* 7,131 applied for aid, 6,743 were judged to have need, 6,709 had their need fully met. 1,570 Federal Work-Study jobs (averaging $1250). *In 2009,* 1000 non-need-based awards were made. *Average percent of need met:* 99. *Average financial aid package:* $7550. *Average need-based loan:* $2720. *Average need-based gift aid:* $3300. *Average non-need-based aid:* $4000. *Average indebtedness upon graduation:* $16,500. *Financial aid deadline:* 5/1.

Applying *Options:* early admission. *Application fee:* $65. *Required:* high school transcript, minimum 3.1 GPA, combined SAT or ACT scores of 1000.

Freshman Application Contact Office of Admissions, Brooklyn College of the City University of New York, 2900 Bedford Avenue, West Quad Building, Room 222, Brooklyn, NY 11210-2889. *Phone:* 718-951-5001. *Fax:* 718-951-4506. *E-mail:* adminqry@brooklyn.cuny.edu. *Web site:* http://www.brooklyn.cuny.edu/.

See page 1134 for the College Close-Up.

Bryant & Stratton College - Amherst Campus

Clarence, New York

- **Proprietary** primarily 2-year, founded 1977
- **Suburban** 5-acre campus with easy access to Buffalo
- **Coed**

Academics *Calendar:* trimesters. *Degrees:* associate and bachelor's.

Standardized Tests *Required:* TABE, CPAt or ACCUPLACER (for admission). *Recommended:* SAT or ACT (for admission).

Applying *Options:* electronic application, early admission. *Required:* high school transcript, interview, entrance evaluation and placement evaluation. *Required for some:* essay or personal statement.

Freshman Application Contact Mr. Brian K. Dioguardi, Director of Admissions, Bryant & Stratton College - Amherst Campus, Audubon Business Center, 40 Hazelwood Drive, Amherst, NY 14228. *Phone:* 716-691-0012. *Fax:* 716-691-0012. *E-mail:* bkdioguardi@bryantstratton.edu. *Web site:* http://www.bryantstratton.edu/.

Bryant & Stratton College - Buffalo Campus

Buffalo, New York

- **Proprietary** primarily 2-year, founded 1854
- **Urban** campus
- **Coed**
- 75% of applicants were admitted

Academics *Calendar:* trimesters. *Degrees:* associate and bachelor's.

Standardized Tests *Required:* TABE, CPAt or ACCUPLACER (for admission). *Recommended:* SAT or ACT (for admission).

Applying *Options:* electronic application, early admission. *Required:* high school transcript, interview, entrance and placement evaluation. *Required for some:* essay or personal statement.

Freshman Application Contact Mr. Philip J. Struebel, Director of Admissions, Bryant & Stratton College - Buffalo Campus, 465 Main Street, Suite 400, Buffalo, NY 14203. *Phone:* 716-884-9120. *Fax:* 716-884-0091. *E-mail:* pjstruebel@bryantstratton.edu. *Web site:* http://www.bryantstratton.edu/.

Bryant & Stratton College - Southtowns Campus

Orchard Park, New York

- **Proprietary** primarily 2-year, founded 1989
- **Suburban** campus with easy access to Buffalo
- **Coed**

Academics *Calendar:* trimesters. *Degrees:* associate and bachelor's.

Standardized Tests *Required:* TABE, CPAt or ACCUPLACER (for admission). *Recommended:* SAT or ACT (for admission).

Applying *Options:* electronic application, early admission. *Required:* high school transcript, interview, entrance and placement evaluations. *Required for some:* essay or personal statement.

Freshman Application Contact Bryant & Stratton College - Southtowns Campus, 200 Redtail, Orchard Park, NY 14127. *Phone:* 716-677-9500. *Web site:* http://www.bryantstratton.edu/.

Buffalo State College, State University of New York

Buffalo, New York

- **State-supported** comprehensive, founded 1867, part of State University of New York System
- **Urban** 115-acre campus
- **Endowment** $14.5 million
- **Coed**
- **Moderately difficult** entrance level

Faculty *Student/faculty ratio:* 17:1.

Academics *Calendar:* semesters. *Degrees:* bachelor's, master's, and post-master's certificates.

Student Life *Campus security:* 24-hour emergency response devices and patrols, student patrols, late-night transport/escort service, controlled dormitory access.

Athletics Member NCAA. All Division III.

Standardized Tests *Required:* SAT and SAT Subject Tests or ACT (for admission). *Recommended:* SAT (for admission).

Costs (2010–11) *Tuition:* state resident $4970 full-time, $207 per credit hour part-time; nonresident $13,380 full-time, $558 per credit hour part-time. Part-time tuition and fees vary according to course load. *Required fees:* $1083 full-time, $45 per credit hour part-time. *Room and board:* $9748; room only: $5770. Room and board charges vary according to board plan, housing facility, and student level.

Financial Aid *Of all full-time matriculated undergraduates who enrolled in 2009,* 386 Federal Work-Study jobs (averaging $1902). *Financial aid deadline:* 5/1.

Applying *Options:* electronic application, early admission, early decision, deferred entrance. *Application fee:* $40. *Required:* high school transcript, minimum 3 GPA. *Required for some:* essay or personal statement, interview.

Freshman Application Contact Ms. Carmella Thompson, Director of Admissions, Buffalo State College, State University of New York, 110 Moot Hall, Buffalo, NY 14222. *Phone:* 716-878-4017. *Fax:* 716-878-6100. *E-mail:* admissions@buffalostate.edu. *Web site:* http://www.buffalostate.edu/.

Canisius College

Buffalo, New York

- **Independent Roman Catholic (Jesuit)** comprehensive, founded 1870
- **Urban** 36-acre campus
- **Endowment** $74.4 million
- **Coed** 3,369 undergraduate students, 89% full-time, 49% women, 51% men
- **Moderately difficult** entrance level, 78% of applicants were admitted

Undergraduates 3,011 full-time, 358 part-time. Students come from 32 states and territories; 30 other countries; 7% are from out of state; 6% Black or African American, non-Hispanic/Latino; 2% Hispanic/Latino; 2% Asian, non-Hispanic/Latino; 0.5% American Indian or Alaska Native, non-Hispanic/Latino; 0.3% Two or more races, non-Hispanic/Latino; 9% Race/ethnicity unknown; 4% international; 5% transferred in; 42% live on campus. *Retention:* 84% of full-time freshmen returned.

Freshmen *Admission:* 3,852 applied, 2,993 admitted, 709 enrolled. *Average high school GPA:* 3.5. *Test scores:* SAT critical reading scores over 500: 70%; SAT math scores over 500: 75%; ACT scores over 18: 100%; SAT critical reading scores over 600: 28%; SAT math scores over 600: 31%; ACT scores over 24: 63%; SAT critical reading scores over 700: 4%; SAT math scores over 700: 4%; ACT scores over 30: 10%.

Faculty *Total:* 499, 45% full-time, 54% with terminal degrees. *Student/faculty ratio:* 12:1.

Academics *Calendar:* semesters. *Degrees:* associate, bachelor's, master's, and post-master's certificates. *Special study options:* academic remediation for entering students, adult/continuing education programs, advanced placement credit, cooperative education, distance learning, double majors, English as a second language, honors programs, independent study, internships, off-campus study, part-time degree program, services for LD students, study abroad, summer session for credit. *ROTC:* Army (b). *Unusual degree programs:* 3-2 business administration with B.A./B.S. M.B.A. program enables a qualified student in most majors to earn an undergraduate degree and an M.B.A. within a five-year period; engineering with The 3+2 Dual Degree Physics Engineering programs in conjunction with SUNY Buffalo (UB).

Computers on Campus 700 computers/terminals are available on campus for general student use. Students can access the following: computer help desk, free student e-mail accounts, online (class) grades, online (class) registration, online (class) schedules, online accounts. Campuswide network is available. 100% of college-owned or -operated housing units are wired for high-speed Internet access. Wireless service is available via entire campus.

Student Life *Housing:* on-campus residence required through sophomore year. *Options:* coed, disabled students. Campus housing is university owned. Freshman applicants given priority for college housing. *Activities and organizations:* drama/theater group, student-run newspaper, radio and television station, choral group, Campus Programming Board, Undergraduate Student Association, Afro-American Society, Residence Hall Association, Student Association, national fraternities, national sororities. *Campus security:* 24-hour emergency response devices and patrols, late-night transport/escort service, controlled dormitory access, crime prevention programs, closed-circuit television monitors, emergency call boxes across campus. *Student services:* health clinic, personal/psychological counseling.

Athletics Member NCAA. All Division I. *Intercollegiate sports:* baseball M(s), basketball M(s)/W(s), cross-country running M(s)/W(s), golf M(s), ice hockey M(s), lacrosse M(s)/W(s), rugby M(c), soccer M(s)/W(s), softball W(s), swimming and diving M(s)/W(s), volleyball M(c)/W(s). *Intramural sports:* basketball M/W, cheerleading M(c)/W(c), crew M(c)/W(c), field hockey W, racquetball M/W, riflery M(c)/W(c), soccer M/W, softball M(c)/W(c), tennis M/W, volleyball M/W.

Standardized Tests *Required:* SAT or ACT (for admission).

Costs (2010–11) *Comprehensive fee:* $41,057 includes full-time tuition ($29,020), mandatory fees ($1057), and room and board ($10,980). Full-time tuition and fees vary according to course load. Part-time tuition: $828 per credit hour. Part-time tuition and fees vary according to course load. *Required fees:* $21 per credit hour part-time, $33 per term part-time. *College room only:* $6480. Room and board charges vary according to board plan and housing facility. *Payment plans:* installment, deferred payment. *Waivers:* employees or children of employees.

Financial Aid Of all full-time matriculated undergraduates who enrolled in 2009, 2,501 applied for aid, 2,358 were judged to have need, 551 had their need fully met. 556 Federal Work-Study jobs (averaging $1739). In 2009, 544 non-need-based awards were made. *Average percent of need met:* 81%. *Average financial aid package:* $25,536. *Average need-based loan:* $4297. *Average need-based gift aid:* $19,366. *Average non-need-based aid:* $14,220. *Average indebtedness upon graduation:* $33,918.

Applying *Options:* electronic application, early admission, deferred entrance. *Application fee:* $40. *Required:* high school transcript, minimum 2 GPA. *Required for some:* interview. *Recommended:* essay or personal statement, 1 letter of recommendation, interview. *Application deadlines:* 5/1 (freshmen), rolling (transfers). *Notification:* continuous (freshmen), continuous (transfers).

Freshman Application Contact Ms. Molly Strasser, Director of Admissions, Canisius College, 2001 Main Street, Buffalo, NY 14208-1098. *Phone:* 716-888-2200. *Toll-free phone:* 800-843-1517. *Fax:* 716-888-3230. *E-mail:* admissions@canisius.edu. *Web site:* http://www.canisius.edu/.

See page 1186 for the College Close-Up.

Cazenovia College
Cazenovia, New York

- **Independent** 4-year, founded 1824
- **Small-town** 40-acre campus with easy access to Syracuse
- **Endowment** $30.0 million
- **Coed**
- **Minimally difficult** entrance level

Faculty *Student/faculty ratio:* 12:1.

Academics *Calendar:* semesters. *Degrees:* associate and bachelor's.

Student Life *Campus security:* 24-hour emergency response devices and patrols, late-night transport/escort service, controlled dormitory access.

Athletics Member NCAA. All Division III.

Standardized Tests *Recommended:* SAT or ACT (for admission).

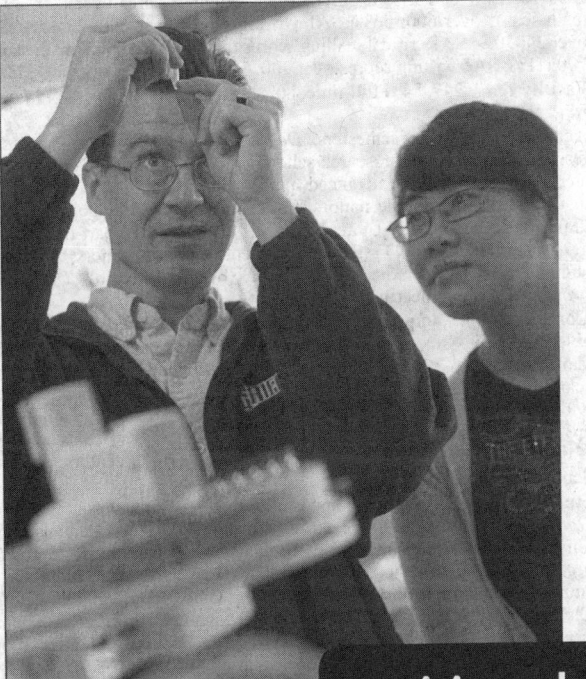

Costs (2010–11) *Comprehensive fee:* $36,306 includes full-time tuition ($25,060), mandatory fees ($422), and room and board ($10,824). Full-time tuition and fees vary according to class time, course load, and program. Part-time tuition: $532 per credit hour. Part-time tuition and fees vary according to class time and course load. *Room and board:* Room and board charges vary according to board plan and housing facility.

Financial Aid *Of all full-time matriculated undergraduates who enrolled in 2009,* 892 applied for aid, 819 were judged to have need, 144 had their need fully met. *In 2009,* 111 non-need-based awards were made. *Average percent of need met:* 77. *Average financial aid package:* $20,838. *Average need-based loan:* $4068. *Average need-based gift aid:* $16,422. *Average non-need-based aid:* $11,444.

Applying *Options:* electronic application, deferred entrance. *Application fee:* $30. *Required:* high school transcript, 1 letter of recommendation. *Recommended:* essay or personal statement, minimum 2 GPA, interview, portfolio for art and design students.

Freshman Application Contact Office of Admission and Enrollment Services, Cazenovia College, 3 Sullivan Street, Cazenovia, NY 13035. *Phone:* 315-655-7208. *Toll-free phone:* 800-654-3210. *Fax:* 315-655-4860. *E-mail:* admission@cazenovia.edu. *Web site:* http://www.cazenovia.edu/.

Central Yeshiva Tomchei Tmimim-Lubavitch

Brooklyn, New York

Director of Admissions Director of Admissions, Central Yeshiva Tomchei Tmimim-Lubavitch, 841-853 Ocean Parkway, Brooklyn, NY 11230. *Phone:* 718-859-7600.

City College of the City University of New York

New York, New York

- **State and locally supported** comprehensive, founded 1847, part of City University of New York System
- **Urban** 35-acre campus with easy access to New York City
- **Coed** 15,378 undergraduate students, 77% full-time, 51% women, 49% men
- **Moderately difficult** entrance level, 33% of applicants were admitted

Undergraduates 11,917 full-time, 3,461 part-time. Students come from 130 other countries; 4% are from out of state; 21% Black or African American, non-Hispanic/Latino; 32% Hispanic/Latino; 19% Asian, non-Hispanic/Latino; 0.2% American Indian or Alaska Native, non-Hispanic/Latino; 9% international; 6% transferred in; 1% live on campus. *Retention:* 83% of full-time freshmen returned.

Freshmen *Admission:* 22,856 applied, 7,545 admitted, 1,389 enrolled. *Average high school GPA:* 85.8. *Test scores:* SAT critical reading scores over 500: 49%; SAT math scores over 500: 76%; SAT critical reading scores over 600: 16%; SAT math scores over 600: 34%; SAT critical reading scores over 700: 4%; SAT math scores over 700: 7%.

Faculty *Total:* 1,536, 38% full-time, 46% with terminal degrees. *Student/faculty ratio:* 11:1.

Academics *Calendar:* semesters. *Degrees:* bachelor's, master's, doctoral-professional, and post-master's certificates. *Special study options:* academic remediation for entering students, accelerated degree program, adult/continuing education programs, advanced placement credit, cooperative education, English as a second language, freshman honors college, honors programs, independent study, internships, off-campus study, part-time degree program, services for LD students, student-designed majors, study abroad, summer session for credit. *ROTC:* Army (c), Air Force (c). *Unusual degree programs:* 3-2 optometry with State University of New York Optometry.

Computers on Campus 2,500 computers/terminals are available on campus for general student use. Students can access the following: campus intranet, computer help desk, free student e-mail accounts, online (class) grades, online (class) registration, online (class) schedules. Campuswide network is available. 100% of college-owned or -operated housing units are wired for high-speed Internet access. Wireless service is available via entire campus.

Student Life *Housing options:* coed. Campus housing is provided by a third party. *Activities and organizations:* drama/theater group, student-run newspaper, radio station, choral group, LAESA-SHPE, NSBE, BSA, Salsa-Mambo, IVCF, national fraternities. *Campus security:* 24-hour patrols, late-night transport/escort service, controlled dormitory access. *Student services:* health clinic, personal/psychological counseling.

Athletics Member NCAA. All Division III. *Intercollegiate sports:* baseball M, basketball M/W, cross-country running M/W, fencing W, lacrosse M, soccer M/W, softball W, tennis M/W, track and field M/W, volleyball W. *Intramural sports:* basketball M/W, fencing W, soccer M, softball W, tennis M/W, track and field M/W, volleyball W.

Standardized Tests *Required:* SAT or ACT (for admission).

Costs (2011–12) *Tuition:* state resident $4830 full-time, $205 per credit hour part-time; nonresident $10,440 full-time, $435 per credit hour part-time. Full-time tuition and fees vary according to course load and program. Part-time tuition and fees vary according to course load and program. *Room and board:* Room and board charges vary according to housing facility. *Payment plan:* deferred payment. *Waivers:* senior citizens.

Financial Aid Of all full-time matriculated undergraduates who enrolled in 2009, 8,932 applied for aid, 8,674 were judged to have need, 6,900 had their need fully met. In 2009, 1030 non-need-based awards were made. *Average percent of need met:* 80%. *Average financial aid package:* $9002. *Average need-based loan:* $3907. *Average need-based gift aid:* $6725. *Average non-need-based aid:* $2524. *Average indebtedness upon graduation:* $15,900.

Applying *Options:* early admission, deferred entrance. *Application fee:* $65. *Required:* high school transcript. *Required for some:* essay or personal statement, creative challenge for Architecture, supplemental application for Engineering. *Application deadlines:* 2/1 (freshmen), 2/1 (transfers). *Notification:* continuous until 2/1 (freshmen), continuous until 3/1 (transfers).

Freshman Application Contact City College of the City University of New York, 160 Convent Avenue, New York, NY 10031-9198. *Phone:* 212-650-6977. *Web site:* http://www.ccny.cuny.edu/.

Clarkson University

Potsdam, New York

- **Independent** university, founded 1896
- **Small-town** 640-acre campus
- **Endowment** $140.2 million
- **Coed** 2,848 undergraduate students, 99% full-time, 28% women, 72% men
- **Very difficult** entrance level, 80% of applicants were admitted

Undergraduates 2,824 full-time, 24 part-time. Students come from 40 states and territories; 46 other countries; 27% are from out of state; 3% Black or African American, non-Hispanic/Latino; 4% Hispanic/Latino; 3% Asian, non-Hispanic/Latino; 0.4% American Indian or Alaska Native, non-Hispanic/Latino; 2% Two or more races, non-Hispanic/Latino; 0.4% Race/ethnicity unknown; 4% international; 4% transferred in; 82% live on campus. *Retention:* 87% of full-time freshmen returned.

Freshmen *Admission:* 4,241 applied, 3,376 admitted, 712 enrolled. *Average high school GPA:* 3.47. *Test scores:* SAT critical reading scores over 500: 78%; SAT math scores over 500: 93%; SAT writing scores over 500: 69%; ACT scores over 18: 99%; SAT critical reading scores over 600: 30%; SAT math scores over 600: 56%; SAT writing scores over 600: 23%; ACT scores over 24: 70%; SAT critical reading scores over 700: 5%; SAT math scores over 700: 11%; SAT writing scores over 700: 1%; ACT scores over 30: 21%.

Faculty *Total:* 247, 84% full-time, 80% with terminal degrees. *Student/faculty ratio:* 15:1.

Academics *Calendar:* semesters. *Degrees:* bachelor's, master's, doctoral-professional, and doctoral-research/scholarship. *Special study options:* accelerated degree program, advanced placement credit, cooperative education, distance learning, double majors, English as a second language, honors programs, independent study, internships, off-campus study, part-time degree program, services for LD students, student-designed majors, study abroad, summer session for credit. *ROTC:* Army (b), Air Force (b). *Unusual degree programs:* 3-2 engineering.

Computers on Campus 350 computers/terminals and 10,000 ports are available on campus for general student use. Students can access the following: campus intranet, computer help desk, free student e-mail accounts, online (class) grades, online (class) registration, online (class) schedules. Campus-wide network is available. 100% of college-owned or -operated housing units are wired for high-speed Internet access. Wireless service is available via classrooms, computer centers, computer labs, learning centers, libraries, student centers.

Student Life *Housing:* on-campus residence required through senior year. *Options:* coed, men-only, women-only, disabled students. Campus housing is university owned. Freshman campus housing is guaranteed. *Activities and organizations:* drama/theater group, student-run newspaper, radio and television station, choral group, Ski Club, Outing Club, Pep Band, Ultimate Frisbee Club, Sports Car Club, national fraternities, national sororities. *Campus security:* 24-hour emergency response devices and patrols, late-night transport/escort service, controlled dormitory access. *Student services:* health clinic, personal/psychological counseling, legal services.

Athletics Member NCAA. All Division III except men's and women's ice hockey (Division I). *Intercollegiate sports:* baseball M, basketball M/W, cross-country running M/W, golf M, ice hockey M(s)/W(s), lacrosse M/W, skiing (cross-country) M/W, skiing (downhill) M/W, soccer M/W, swimming and diving M/W, volleyball W. *Intramural sports:* basketball M/W, bowling M(c)/W(c), crew M(c)/W(c), football M/W, golf M(c), ice hockey M/W, lacrosse M(c)/W(c), racquetball M(c)/W(c), rugby M(c)/W(c), skiing (cross-country)

M(c)/W(c), skiing (downhill) M(c)/W(c), soccer M/W, softball M/W, ultimate Frisbee M(c)/W(c), volleyball M/W.

Standardized Tests *Required:* SAT or ACT (for admission). *Recommended:* SAT Subject Tests (for admission).

Costs (2011–12) *Comprehensive fee:* $48,830 includes full-time tuition ($35,940), mandatory fees ($840), and room and board ($12,050). Full-time tuition and fees vary according to course load. Part-time tuition: $1198 per credit. Part-time tuition and fees vary according to course load. *College room only:* $6384. Room and board charges vary according to board plan and housing facility. *Payment plans:* tuition prepayment, installment. *Waivers:* employees or children of employees.

Financial Aid Of all full-time matriculated undergraduates who enrolled in 2009, 2,492 applied for aid, 2,366 were judged to have need, 428 had their need fully met. 1,521 Federal Work-Study jobs (averaging $2000). 78 state and other part-time jobs (averaging $4920). In 2009, 386 non-need-based awards were made. *Average percent of need met:* 88%. *Average financial aid package:* $32,857. *Average need-based loan:* $4417. *Average need-based gift aid:* $23,124. *Average non-need-based aid:* $13,981. *Average indebtedness upon graduation:* $36,142. *Financial aid deadline:* 3/1.

Applying *Options:* electronic application, early admission, early decision, deferred entrance. *Application fee:* $50. *Required:* essay or personal statement, high school transcript, 2 letters of recommendation. *Recommended:* interview. *Application deadline:* 1/15 (freshmen). *Early decision deadline:* 12/1. *Notification:* continuous (freshmen), continuous (transfers), 1/1 (early decision).

Freshman Application Contact Mr. Brian T. Grant, Dean of Admissions, Clarkson University, Holcroft House, PO Box 5605, Potsdam, NY 13699. *Phone:* 315-268-6480. *Toll-free phone:* 800-527-6577. *Fax:* 315-268-7647. *E-mail:* admission@clarkson.edu. *Web site:* http://www.clarkson.edu/.

See page 1218 for the College Close-Up.

Colgate University

Hamilton, New York

- **Independent** comprehensive, founded 1819
- **Rural** 515-acre campus
- **Coed** 2,884 undergraduate students, 99% full-time, 53% women, 47% men
- **Most difficult** entrance level, 33% of applicants were admitted

Undergraduates 2,868 full-time, 16 part-time. Students come from 48 states and territories; 36 other countries; 75% are from out of state; 4% Black or African American, non-Hispanic/Latino; 7% Hispanic/Latino; 4% Asian, non-Hispanic/Latino; 0.1% Native Hawaiian or other Pacific Islander, non-Hispanic/Latino; 0.4% American Indian or Alaska Native, non-Hispanic/Latino; 3% Two or more races, non-Hispanic/Latino; 4% Race/ethnicity unknown; 6% international; 0.4% transferred in; 91% live on campus. *Retention:* 93% of full-time freshmen returned.

Freshmen *Admission:* 7,872 applied, 2,597 admitted, 850 enrolled. *Average high school GPA:* 3.6. *Test scores:* SAT critical reading scores over 500: 97%; SAT math scores over 500: 98%; ACT scores over 18: 100%; SAT critical reading scores over 600: 84%; SAT math scores over 600: 88%; ACT scores over 24: 95%; SAT critical reading scores over 700: 36%; SAT math scores over 700: 44%; ACT scores over 30: 70%.

Faculty *Total:* 332, 83% full-time, 92% with terminal degrees. *Student/faculty ratio:* 10:1.

Academics *Calendar:* semesters. *Degrees:* bachelor's and master's. *Special study options:* advanced placement credit, double majors, honors programs, independent study, internships, off-campus study, services for LD students, student-designed majors, study abroad. *ROTC:* Army (c). *Unusual degree programs:* 3-2 engineering with Rensselaer Polytechnic Institute, Columbia University, Washington University in St. Louis.

Computers on Campus Students can access the following: campus intranet, computer help desk, free student e-mail accounts, online (class) registration, online (class) schedules, software applications. Campuswide network is available. 100% of college-owned or -operated housing units are wired for high-speed Internet access. Wireless service is available via entire campus.

Student Life *Housing:* on-campus residence required through junior year. *Options:* coed, men-only, women-only, cooperative. Campus housing is university owned. Freshman campus housing is guaranteed. *Activities and orga-*

nizations: drama/theater group, student-run newspaper, radio and television station, choral group, COVE, student government, cultural/ethnic interest groups, student publications, Outdoor Education, national fraternities, national sororities. *Campus security:* 24-hour emergency response devices and patrols, student patrols, late-night transport/escort service, controlled dormitory access. *Student services:* health clinic, personal/psychological counseling, women's center, legal services.

Athletics Member NCAA. All Division I except football (Division I-AA). *Intercollegiate sports:* baseball M(c), basketball M(s)/W(s), cheerleading M(c)/W(c), crew M/W, cross-country running M/W, equestrian sports M(c)/W(c), fencing M(c)/W(c), field hockey W(s), golf M/W(c), ice hockey M(s)/W(s), lacrosse M(s)/W(s), rugby M(c)/W(c), sailing M(c)/W(c), skiing (downhill) M(c)/W(c), soccer M(s)/W(s), softball W(s), squash M(c)/W(c), swimming and diving M/W, table tennis M(c)/W(c), tennis M/W, track and field M/W, volleyball M(c)/W(s), water polo M(c)/W(c), wrestling M(c)/W(c). *Intramural sports:* basketball M/W, bowling M/W, football M/W, golf M/W, ice hockey M/W, racquetball M/W, riflery M/W, soccer M/W, softball M/W, squash M/W, tennis M/W, ultimate Frisbee M/W, volleyball M/W.

Standardized Tests *Required:* SAT or ACT (for admission).

Costs (2010–11) *One-time required fee:* $50. *Comprehensive fee:* $52,060 includes full-time tuition ($41,585), mandatory fees ($285), and room and board ($10,190). Full-time tuition and fees vary according to course load. Part-time tuition: $5198 per course. Part-time tuition and fees vary according to course load. *College room only:* $4920. Room and board charges vary according to board plan and housing facility. *Payment plans:* tuition prepayment, installment, deferred payment. *Waivers:* employees or children of employees.

Financial Aid Of all full-time matriculated undergraduates who enrolled in 2009, 1,047 applied for aid, 979 were judged to have need, 979 had their need fully met. 489 Federal Work-Study jobs (averaging $2066). 307 state and other part-time jobs (averaging $1961). *Average percent of need met:* 100%. *Average financial aid package:* $38,568. *Average need-based loan:* $3123. *Average need-based gift aid:* $35,264. *Average indebtedness upon graduation:* $18,629. *Financial aid deadline:* 1/15.

Applying *Options:* electronic application, early decision, deferred entrance. *Application fee:* $60. *Required:* essay or personal statement, high school transcript, 3 letters of recommendation. *Application deadlines:* 1/15 (freshmen), 3/15 (transfers). *Early decision deadline:* 11/15 (for plan 1), 1/15 (for plan 2). *Notification:* 4/1 (freshmen), 5/1 (transfers), 12/15 (early decision plan 1), rolling (early decision plan 2).

Freshman Application Contact Mr. Gary L. Ross, Dean of Admission, Colgate University, 13 Oak Drive, Hamilton, NY 13346-1383. *Phone:* 315-228-7401. *Fax:* 315-228-7544. *E-mail:* admission@colgate.edu. *Web site:* http://www.colgate.edu/.

The College at Brockport, State University of New York

Brockport, New York

- **State-supported** comprehensive, founded 1867, part of State University of New York System
- **Small-town** 454-acre campus with easy access to Rochester
- **Endowment** $4.9 million
- **Coed**
- **Moderately difficult** entrance level

Faculty *Student/faculty ratio:* 18:1.

Academics *Calendar:* semesters. *Degrees:* bachelor's, master's, post-master's, and postbachelor's certificates.

Student Life *Campus security:* 24-hour emergency response devices and patrols, student patrols, late-night transport/escort service, controlled dormitory access.

Athletics Member NCAA. All Division III.

Standardized Tests *Required:* SAT or ACT (for admission).

Costs (2011–12) *Tuition:* state resident $4970 full-time; nonresident $13,380 full-time. Part-time tuition and fees vary according to course load. *Required fees:* $1206 full-time. *Room and board:* $9780; room only: $6400. Room and board charges vary according to board plan and housing facility. *Payment plans:* installment, deferred payment.

Financial Aid Of all full-time matriculated undergraduates who enrolled in 2009, 4,958 applied for aid, 4,065 were judged to have need, 611 had their need fully met. 654 Federal Work-Study jobs (averaging $1799). 1,664 state and other part-time jobs (averaging $1356). *In 2009,* 150 non-need-based awards were made. *Average percent of need met:* 71. *Average financial aid package:* $9529. *Average need-based loan:* $4705. *Average need-based gift aid:* $5275. *Average non-need-based aid:* $3891. *Average indebtedness upon graduation:* $25,733.

Applying *Options:* electronic application, deferred entrance. *Application fee:* $40. *Required:* essay or personal statement, high school transcript. *Required for some:* interview. *Recommended:* minimum 3.1 GPA.

Freshman Application Contact The College at Brockport, State University of New York, 350 New Campus Drive, Brockport, NY 14420-2997. *Phone:* 585-395-2751. *Web site:* http://www.brockport.edu/.

College of Mount Saint Vincent

Riverdale, New York

- **Independent** comprehensive, founded 1911
- **Suburban** 70-acre campus with easy access to New York City
- **Endowment** $5.9 million
- **Coed**
- **Moderately difficult** entrance level

Faculty *Student/faculty ratio:* 12:1.

Academics *Calendar:* semesters. *Degrees:* associate, bachelor's, master's, and post-master's certificates.

Student Life *Campus security:* 24-hour emergency response devices and patrols, late-night transport/escort service, controlled dormitory access, emergency call boxes.

Athletics Member NCAA. All Division III.

Standardized Tests *Required:* SAT or ACT (for admission).

Costs (2010–11) *Comprehensive fee:* $37,290 includes full-time tuition ($25,600), mandatory fees ($1310), and room and board ($10,380). Part-time tuition: $760 per credit. *Required fees:* $500 per term part-time. *Room and board:* Room and board charges vary according to housing facility.

Financial Aid Of all full-time matriculated undergraduates who enrolled in 2004, 1,019 applied for aid, 881 were judged to have need. *Average percent of need met:* 74. *Average financial aid package:* $17,000. *Average need-based loan:* $4100. *Average need-based gift aid:* $7500. *Average indebtedness upon graduation:* $17,000.

Applying *Options:* electronic application, early admission, early action, deferred entrance. *Application fee:* $35. *Required:* essay or personal statement, high school transcript, minimum 2 GPA. *Required for some:* interview. *Recommended:* 2 letters of recommendation, interview.

Freshman Application Contact Mr. Roland Pinzon, Director of Admissions, College of Mount Saint Vincent, 6301 Riverdale Avenue, Riverdale, NY 10471-1093. *Phone:* 718-405-3268. *Toll-free phone:* 800-665-CMSV. *Fax:* 718-549-7945. *E-mail:* roland.pinzon@mountsaintvincent.edu. *Web site:* http://www.mountsaintvincent.edu/.

The College of New Rochelle

New Rochelle, New York

- **Independent** comprehensive, founded 1904
- **Suburban** 20-acre campus with easy access to New York City
- **Coed, primarily women**
- **Moderately difficult** entrance level

Faculty *Student/faculty ratio:* 11:1.

Academics *Calendar:* semesters. *Degrees:* bachelor's, master's, post-master's, and postbachelor's certificates (also offers a non-traditional adult program with significant enrollment not reflected in profile).

Student Life *Campus security:* 24-hour emergency response devices and patrols, late-night transport/escort service, controlled dormitory access, 24-hour monitored security cameras at residence hall entrances.

Athletics Member NCAA. All Division III.

Standardized Tests *Required:* SAT or ACT (for admission).

Costs (2010–11) *Comprehensive fee:* $38,186 includes full-time tuition ($27,110), mandatory fees ($900), and room and board ($10,176). Full-time tuition and fees vary according to course load and program. Part-time tuition: $861 per credit. Part-time tuition and fees vary according to course load and program. *Required fees:* $250 per term part-time. *Room and board:* Room and board charges vary according to housing facility.

Financial Aid Of all full-time matriculated undergraduates who enrolled in 2008, 495 applied for aid, 473 were judged to have need, 16 had their need fully met. 383 Federal Work-Study jobs (averaging $2758). *In 2008,* 31 non-need-based awards were made. *Average percent of need met:* 57. *Average financial aid package:* $20,339. *Average need-based loan:* $5470. *Average need-based gift aid:* $11,070. *Average non-need-based aid:* $11,888. *Average indebtedness upon graduation:* $28,462.

Applying *Options:* early admission, early decision, deferred entrance. *Application fee:* $20. *Required:* high school transcript. *Recommended:* essay or personal statement, 1 letter of recommendation, interview.

Freshman Application Contact Ms. Bridget Kennedy, Assistant Director, Enrollment Management, The College of New Rochelle, 29 Castle Place, New Rochelle, NY 10805-2339. *Phone:* 914-654-5452. *Toll-free phone:* 800-933-5923. *Fax:* 914-654-5464. *E-mail:* admission@cnr.edu. *Web site:* http://www.cnr.edu/.

The College of Saint Rose

Albany, New York

- **Independent** comprehensive, founded 1920
- **Urban** 46-acre campus
- **Endowment** $26.8 million
- **Coed** 3,048 undergraduate students, 93% full-time, 69% women, 31% men
- **Moderately difficult** entrance level, 64% of applicants were admitted

Undergraduates 2,846 full-time, 202 part-time. Students come from 28 states and territories; 25 other countries; 7% are from out of state; 5% Black or African American, non-Hispanic/Latino; 4% Hispanic/Latino; 1% Asian, non-Hispanic/Latino; 0.1% Native Hawaiian or other Pacific Islander, non-Hispanic/Latino; 0.4% American Indian or Alaska Native, non-Hispanic/Latino; 1% Two or more races, non-Hispanic/Latino; 11% Race/ethnicity unknown; 1% international; 9% transferred in; 38% live on campus. *Retention:* 80% of full-time freshmen returned.

Freshmen *Admission:* 4,840 applied, 3,102 admitted, 640 enrolled. *Average high school GPA:* 3.4. *Test scores:* SAT critical reading scores over 500: 59%; SAT math scores over 500: 59%; ACT scores over 18: 94%; SAT critical reading scores over 600: 15%; SAT math scores over 600: 15%; ACT scores over 24: 40%; SAT critical reading scores over 700: 1%; SAT math scores over 700: 2%; ACT scores over 30: 2%.

Faculty *Total:* 460, 45% full-time. *Student/faculty ratio:* 14:1.

Academics *Calendar:* semesters. *Degrees:* bachelor's, master's, post-master's, and postbachelor's certificates. *Special study options:* academic remediation for entering students, accelerated degree program, advanced placement credit, double majors, external degree program, independent study, internships, off-campus study, part-time degree program, services for LD students, student-designed majors, study abroad, summer session for credit. *ROTC:* Army (c), Navy (c), Air Force (c). *Unusual degree programs:* 3-2 engineering with Alfred University, Clarkson University, Union College (NY), Rensselaer Polytechnic Institute.

Computers on Campus 634 computers/terminals and 3,968 ports are available on campus for general student use. Students can access the following: computer help desk, free student e-mail accounts, online (class) grades, online (class) registration, online (class) schedules. Campuswide network is available.

100% of college-owned or -operated housing units are wired for high-speed Internet access. Wireless service is available via entire campus.

Student Life *Housing options:* coed, men-only, women-only. Campus housing is university owned. Freshman applicants given priority for college housing. *Activities and organizations:* drama/theater group, student-run newspaper, radio and television station, choral group, Student Association, Student Events Board, Spectrum-ALANA Student Union, Environmental Club, Music & Entertainment Industry Student Association. *Campus security:* 24-hour emergency response devices and patrols, late-night transport/escort service, controlled dormitory access. *Student services:* health clinic, personal/psychological counseling.

Athletics Member NCAA. All Division II. *Intercollegiate sports:* baseball M(s), basketball M(s)/W(s), cross-country running M/W, golf M, lacrosse M(s), soccer M(s)/W(s), softball W(s), swimming and diving M(s)/W(s), tennis W, track and field M(s)/W(s), volleyball W(s). *Intramural sports:* basketball M/W, cheerleading M(c)/W(c), soccer M/W, softball M/W, ultimate Frisbee M/W, volleyball M/W.

Standardized Tests *Required:* SAT or ACT (for admission).

Costs (2011–12) *Comprehensive fee:* $35,998 includes full-time tuition ($24,614), mandatory fees ($850), and room and board ($10,534). Full-time tuition and fees vary according to class time and course load. Part-time tuition: $819 per credit. Part-time tuition and fees vary according to class time and course load. *Required fees:* $25 per credit part-time, $68 per year part-time. *Room and board:* Room and board charges vary according to board plan and housing facility. *Payment plan:* installment. *Waivers:* employees or children of employees.

Financial Aid Of all full-time matriculated undergraduates who enrolled in 2008, 2,808 applied for aid, 2,785 were judged to have need, 54 had their need fully met. 405 Federal Work-Study jobs (averaging $760). 8 state and other part-time jobs (averaging $796). In 2008, 251 non-need-based awards were made. *Average percent of need met:* 8%. *Average financial aid package:* $8897. *Average need-based loan:* $2346. *Average need-based gift aid:* $3453. *Average non-need-based aid:* $2104. *Average indebtedness upon graduation:* $29,391.

Applying *Options:* electronic application, early admission, early action, deferred entrance. *Application fee:* $40. *Required:* high school transcript, 1 letter of recommendation. *Required for some:* interview. *Recommended:* minimum 3 GPA, interview. *Application deadlines:* 5/1 (freshmen), 5/1 (transfers), 12/1 (early action). *Notification:* continuous (freshmen), continuous (transfers), 12/15 (early action).

Freshman Application Contact Mr. Jeremy Bogan, Assistant Vice President of Undergraduate Admissions, The College of Saint Rose, 1001 Madison Avenue, Albany, NY 12203. *Phone:* 518-454-5154. *Toll-free phone:* 800-637-8556. *Fax:* 518-454-2013. *E-mail:* admit@strose.edu. *Web site:* http://www.strose.edu/.

See page 1234 for the College Close-Up.

College of Staten Island of the City University of New York

Staten Island, New York

- **State and locally supported** comprehensive, founded 1955, part of City University of New York
- **Urban** 204-acre campus with easy access to New York City
- **Endowment** $4.9 million
- **Coed** 12,829 undergraduate students, 74% full-time, 57% women, 43% men
- **Moderately difficult** entrance level

Undergraduates 9,502 full-time, 3,327 part-time. Students come from 12 states and territories; 102 other countries; 0.5% are from out of state; 7% transferred in. *Retention:* 83% of full-time freshmen returned.

Faculty *Total:* 1,202, 28% full-time, 52% with terminal degrees. *Student/faculty ratio:* 18:1.

Academics *Calendar:* semesters. *Degrees:* certificates, associate, bachelor's, master's, doctoral-research/scholarship, and post-master's certificates. *Special study options:* academic remediation for entering students, accelerated degree program, adult/continuing education programs, advanced placement credit, cooperative education, distance learning, double majors, English as a second language, freshman honors college, honors programs, independent study, internships, off-campus study, part-time degree program, services for LD students, student-designed majors, study abroad, summer session for credit.

Computers on Campus 1,254 computers/terminals and 1,254 ports are available on campus for general student use. Students can access the following: campus intranet, computer help desk, free student e-mail accounts, online (class) grades, online (class) registration, online (class) schedules. Campus-wide network is available. 100% of college-owned or -operated housing units are wired for high-speed Internet access. Wireless service is available via entire campus.

Student Life *Activities and organizations:* drama/theater group, student-run newspaper, radio station, choral group, NYPIRG, Hillel, Gay/Straight Alliance, International Cultural Dance Club. *Campus security:* 24-hour emergency response devices and patrols, late-night transport/escort service, emergency call boxes, blue light system, bicycle patrols, radar-controlled traffic monitoring, lighted pathways. *Student services:* health clinic, personal/psychological counseling, women's center.

Athletics Member NCAA. All Division III. *Intercollegiate sports:* baseball M, basketball M/W, cheerleading M(c)/W(c), cross-country running M/W, soccer M/W, softball W, swimming and diving M/W, tennis M/W, track and field M(c)/W(c), volleyball W. *Intramural sports:* basketball M/W, racquetball M/W, tennis M/W, volleyball M/W.

Standardized Tests *Recommended:* SAT or ACT (for admission).

Costs (2010–11) *Tuition:* state resident $4600 full-time, $195 per credit part-time; nonresident $9960 full-time, $415 per credit part-time. Full-time tuition and fees vary according to course load. Part-time tuition and fees vary according to course load. *Required fees:* $378 full-time, $113 per term part-time. *Payment plan:* installment. *Waivers:* senior citizens and employees or children of employees.

Financial Aid Of all full-time matriculated undergraduates who enrolled in 2009, 2,113 applied for aid, 3,515 were judged to have need, 214 had their need fully met. 740 Federal Work-Study jobs (averaging $1400). In 2009, 450 non-need-based awards were made. *Average percent of need met:* 58%. *Average financial aid package:* $11,735. *Average need-based loan:* $4345. *Average need-based gift aid:* $6800. *Average non-need-based aid:* $450. *Average indebtedness upon graduation:* $7423.

Applying *Options:* electronic application, deferred entrance. *Application fee:* $65. *Required:* high school transcript, minimum 2 GPA. *Required for some:* essay or personal statement, interview. *Application deadlines:* 2/1 (freshmen), 2/1 (out-of-state freshmen), rolling (transfers). *Notification:* continuous (freshmen), continuous (transfers).

Freshman Application Contact Mr. Emmanuel Esperance Jr., Director of Recruitment and Admissions, College of Staten Island of the City University of New York, 2800 Victory Boulevard, Building 2A Room 103, Staten Island, NY 10314. *Phone:* 718-982-2010. *Fax:* 718-982-2500. *E-mail:* admissions@cuny.csi.edu. *Web site:* http://www.csi.cuny.edu/.

See page 1236 for the College Close-Up.

Columbia University

New York, New York

- **Independent** university, founded 1754
- **Urban** campus
- **Endowment** $5.9 billion
- **Coed**
- **Most difficult** entrance level

Faculty *Student/faculty ratio:* 6:1.

Academics *Calendar:* semesters. *Degrees:* bachelor's, master's, and doctoral-research/scholarship.

Athletics Member NCAA. All Division I except football (Division I-AA).

Standardized Tests *Required:* SAT and SAT Subject Tests or ACT (for admission).

Costs (2010–11) *Comprehensive fee:* $51,730 includes full-time tuition ($41,160) and room and board ($10,570).

Financial Aid *Of all full-time matriculated undergraduates who enrolled in 2009,* 3,367 applied for aid, 3,035 were judged to have need, 3,035 had their need fully met. *Average percent of need met:* 100. *Average financial aid package:* $40,937. *Average need-based loan:* $796. *Average need-based gift aid:* $38,356. *Financial aid deadline:* 3/1.

Applying *Options:* electronic application, early admission, early decision, deferred entrance. *Application fee:* $75. *Required:* essay or personal statement, high school transcript, 3 letters of recommendation.

Freshman Application Contact Columbia University, 116th Street and Broadway, New York, NY 10027. *Phone:* 212-854-1222. *Web site:* http://www.columbia.edu/.

See page 1240 for the College Close-Up.

Columbia University, School of General Studies

New York, New York

- **Independent** 4-year, founded 1754, part of Columbia University
- **Urban** 36-acre campus
- **Endowment** $6.5 billion
- **Coed** 1,464 undergraduate students, 63% full-time, 47% women, 53% men
- **Most difficult** entrance level, 23% of applicants were admitted

Undergraduates 921 full-time, 543 part-time. Students come from 80 other countries; 33% are from out of state; 7% Black or African American, non-Hispanic/Latino; 9% Hispanic/Latino; 8% Asian, non-Hispanic/Latino; 1% American Indian or Alaska Native, non-Hispanic/Latino; 6% Race/ethnicity unknown; 15% international; 27% transferred in; 24% live on campus.

Freshmen *Admission:* 396 applied, 90 admitted, 53 enrolled.

Faculty *Total:* 1,048, 77% full-time, 100% with terminal degrees. *Student/faculty ratio:* 8:1.

Academics *Calendar:* semesters. *Degrees:* bachelor's and postbachelor's certificates. *Special study options:* adult/continuing education programs, advanced placement credit, double majors, independent study, internships, off-campus study, part-time degree program, services for LD students, student-designed majors, study abroad, summer session for credit. *ROTC:* Army (c), Air Force (c). *Unusual degree programs:* 3-2 business administration with Columbia University, Graduate School of Business; engineering with Columbia University, School of Engineering and Applied Science; social work with Columbia University, School of Social Work; international affairs, public policy and administration with Columbia University, School of International and Public Affairs; public health with Columbia University, School of Public Health.

Computers on Campus 250 computers/terminals are available on campus for general student use. Students can access the following: campus intranet, computer help desk, free student e-mail accounts, online (class) grades, online (class) registration, online (class) schedules. Campuswide network is available. 80% of college-owned or -operated housing units are wired for high-speed Internet access. Wireless service is available via entire campus.

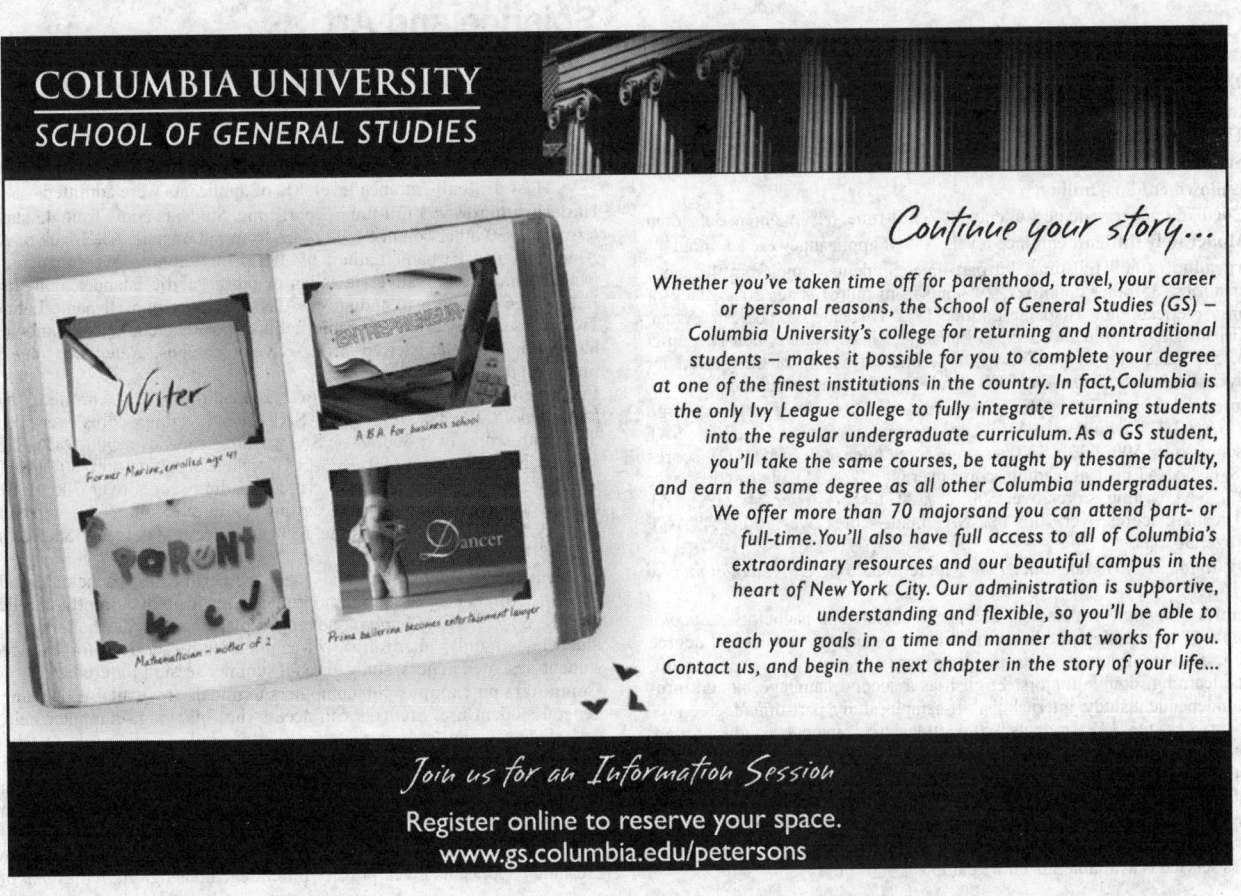

Student Life *Housing options:* coed, cooperative. Campus housing is university owned, leased by the school and is provided by a third party. *Activities and organizations:* drama/theater group, student-run newspaper, radio and television station, choral group, marching band, Columbia Dramatists, writers club, General Studies Student Council, The Observer, national fraternities, national sororities. *Campus security:* 24-hour emergency response devices and patrols, late-night transport/escort service. *Student services:* health clinic, personal/psychological counseling, women's center.

Athletics Member NCAA. All Division I except football (Division I-AA). *Intercollegiate sports:* archery W, badminton M(c)/W(c), baseball M, basketball M/W, crew M/W, cross-country running M/W, equestrian sports W(c), fencing M/W, field hockey W(c), golf M, gymnastics W, ice hockey M(c)/W(c), lacrosse M(c), racquetball M(c)/W(c), rugby M(c)/W(c), sailing M(c)/W(c), skiing (downhill) M(c)/W(c), soccer M/W, squash M(c)/W(c), swimming and diving M/W, table tennis M(c)/W(c), tennis M/W, track and field M/W, volleyball W, water polo M(c)/W(c), wrestling M. *Intramural sports:* football M/W, soccer M/W, volleyball M/W.

Standardized Tests *Required:* SAT or ACT (for admission), If the applicant's SAT scores are more than eight years old, they make take the General Studies Admissions Exam in place of taking the SAT or ACT (for admission). *Recommended:* SAT and SAT Subject Tests or ACT (for admission).

Costs (2010–11) *One-time required fee:* $230. *Comprehensive fee:* $52,860 includes full-time tuition ($39,900) and room and board ($12,960). Full-time tuition and fees vary according to course load, program, and student level. Part-time tuition: $1330 per credit hour. Part-time tuition and fees vary according to course load, program, and student level. *College room only:* $8775. Room and board charges vary according to board plan and housing facility. *Payment plans:* tuition prepayment, installment. *Waivers:* employees or children of employees.

Financial Aid *Financial aid deadline:* 6/1.

Applying *Options:* electronic application, early action, deferred entrance. *Application fee:* $75. *Required:* essay or personal statement, high school transcript, 2 letters of recommendation. *Required for some:* interview. *Application deadlines:* 6/1 (freshmen), 6/1 (transfers), 3/1 (early action). *Notification:* continuous (freshmen), continuous (transfers), 5/1 (early action).

Freshman Application Contact Mr. Curtis M. Rodgers, Dean of Enrollment Management, Columbia University, School of General Studies, 2970 Broadway, 408 Lewisohn Hall, MC 4101, New York, NY 10027. *Phone:* 212-854-2772. *Toll-free phone:* 800-895-1169. *Fax:* 212-854-6316. *E-mail:* gsdegree@columbia.edu. *Web site:* http://www.gs.columbia.edu/.

See page 1242 for the College Close-Up.

Concordia College–New York
Bronxville, New York

- **Independent Lutheran** 4-year, founded 1881, part of Concordia University System
- **Suburban** 33-acre campus with easy access to New York City
- **Endowment** $6.4 million
- **Coed** 759 undergraduate students, 88% full-time, 64% women, 36% men
- **Moderately difficult** entrance level, 71% of applicants were admitted

Undergraduates 669 full-time, 90 part-time. Students come from 46 states and territories; 35 other countries; 29% are from out of state; 20% Black or African American, non-Hispanic/Latino; 13% Hispanic/Latino; 2% Asian, non-Hispanic/Latino; 0.6% American Indian or Alaska Native, non-Hispanic/Latino; 5% Race/ethnicity unknown; 11% international; 6% transferred in; 68% live on campus. *Retention:* 73% of full-time freshmen returned.

Freshmen *Admission:* 842 applied, 594 admitted, 138 enrolled. *Average high school GPA:* 2.7. *Test scores:* SAT critical reading scores over 500: 36%; SAT math scores over 500: 40%; SAT writing scores over 500: 35%; ACT scores over 18: 66%; SAT critical reading scores over 600: 8%; SAT math scores over 600: 9%; SAT writing scores over 600: 6%; ACT scores over 24: 21%; SAT critical reading scores over 700: 1%; SAT math scores over 700: 1%; ACT scores over 30: 3%.

Faculty *Total:* 77, 43% full-time, 79% with terminal degrees. *Student/faculty ratio:* 16:1.

Academics *Calendar:* semesters. *Degrees:* associate and bachelor's. *Special study options:* academic remediation for entering students, accelerated degree program, adult/continuing education programs, advanced placement credit, distance learning, double majors, English as a second language, honors programs, independent study, internships, off-campus study, part-time degree program, services for LD students, student-designed majors, study abroad. *ROTC:* Army (c), Air Force (c).

Computers on Campus 50 computers/terminals are available on campus for general student use. Students can access the following: campus intranet, computer help desk, free student e-mail accounts, online (class) grades, online (class) registration, online (class) schedules. Campuswide network is available. Wireless service is available via entire campus.

Student Life *Housing options:* men-only, women-only. Campus housing is university owned. Freshman campus housing is guaranteed. *Activities and organizations:* drama/theater group, student-run newspaper, choral group, Campus Christian Ministries, Drama Club, Student Government Association, International and Afro/Latin American Club, Yearbook and newspaper, national fraternities, national sororities. *Campus security:* 24-hour emergency response devices and patrols, late-night transport/escort service, controlled dormitory access. *Student services:* health clinic, personal/psychological counseling.

Athletics Member NCAA. All Division II. *Intercollegiate sports:* baseball M(s), basketball M(s)/W(s), cross-country running M(s)/W(s), soccer M(s)/W(s), softball W(s), tennis M(s)/W(s), volleyball W(s). *Intramural sports:* basketball M/W, cheerleading W, equestrian sports W, racquetball M/W, squash M/W, table tennis M/W, tennis M/W, volleyball W.

Standardized Tests *Required:* SAT or ACT (for admission).

Costs (2010–11) *Comprehensive fee:* $35,050 includes full-time tuition ($24,670), mandatory fees ($900), and room and board ($9480). Full-time tuition and fees vary according to course load and program. Part-time tuition: $690 per credit hour. Part-time tuition and fees vary according to course load and program. *College room only:* $5100. Room and board charges vary according to board plan and housing facility. *Payment plan:* installment. *Waivers:* senior citizens and employees or children of employees.

Financial Aid Of all full-time matriculated undergraduates who enrolled in 2008, 533 applied for aid, 448 were judged to have need, 89 had their need fully met. In 2008, 100 non-need-based awards were made. *Average percent of need met:* 71%. *Average financial aid package:* $22,309. *Average need-based loan:* $4133. *Average need-based gift aid:* $11,129. *Average non-need-based aid:* $6170. *Average indebtedness upon graduation:* $24,153.

Applying *Options:* electronic application, early admission, early action, deferred entrance. *Application fee:* $50. *Required:* essay or personal statement, high school transcript, 1 letter of recommendation, Common Application Supplement. *Required for some:* interview. *Recommended:* minimum 2.7 GPA. *Application deadlines:* 3/15 (freshmen), 7/15 (transfers), 11/15 (early action). *Notification:* continuous until 4/15 (freshmen), continuous until 8/15 (transfers), 12/1 (early action).

Freshman Application Contact Ms. Donna J. Hoyt, Dean of Enrollment, Concordia College–New York, Bronxville, NY 10708. *Phone:* 914-337-9300 Ext. 2149. *Toll-free phone:* 800-YES-COLLEGE. *Fax:* 914-395-4636. *E-mail:* admission@concordia-ny.edu. *Web site:* http://www.concordia-ny.edu/.

Cooper Union for the Advancement of Science and Art
New York, New York

- **Independent** comprehensive, founded 1859
- **Urban** campus
- **Endowment** $579.2 million
- **Coed** 910 undergraduate students, 99% full-time, 39% women, 61% men
- **Most difficult** entrance level, 8% of applicants were admitted

Undergraduates 903 full-time, 7 part-time. Students come from 43 states and territories; 30 other countries; 42% are from out of state; 6% Black or African American, non-Hispanic/Latino; 9% Hispanic/Latino; 18% Asian, non-Hispanic/Latino; 0.1% Native Hawaiian or other Pacific Islander, non-Hispanic/Latino; 0.6% American Indian or Alaska Native, non-Hispanic/Latino; 6% Two or more races, non-Hispanic/Latino; 7% Race/ethnicity unknown; 16% international; 4% transferred in; 20% live on campus. *Retention:* 94% of full-time freshmen returned.

Freshmen *Admission:* 3,354 applied, 281 admitted, 214 enrolled. *Average high school GPA:* 3.6. *Test scores:* SAT critical reading scores over 500: 97%; SAT math scores over 500: 94%; SAT writing scores over 500: 98%; SAT critical reading scores over 600: 78%; SAT math scores over 600: 80%; SAT writing scores over 600: 79%; SAT critical reading scores over 700: 35%; SAT math scores over 700: 63%; SAT writing scores over 700: 36%.

Faculty *Total:* 226, 24% full-time, 63% with terminal degrees. *Student/faculty ratio:* 8:1.

Academics *Calendar:* semesters. *Degrees:* certificates, bachelor's, and master's (also offers master's program primarily made up of currently-enrolled students). *Special study options:* advanced placement credit, honors programs, independent study, internships, off-campus study, services for LD students, student-designed majors, study abroad, summer session for credit.

Computers on Campus 400 computers/terminals are available on campus for general student use. Students can access the following: computer help desk, free student e-mail accounts, online (class) grades, online (class) schedules. Campuswide network is available. 100% of college-owned or -operated housing units are wired for high-speed Internet access. Wireless service is available via classrooms, computer centers, computer labs, learning centers, student centers.

Student Life *Housing options:* coed. Campus housing is university owned. Freshman applicants given priority for college housing. *Activities and organi-*

zations: drama/theater group, student-run newspaper, choral group, South Asian Society, Pro Musica, Chinese Student Association, Drama Society, Outdoors Club; Intervarsity Christian Fellowship, national fraternities, national sororities. *Campus security:* 24-hour emergency response devices and patrols, controlled dormitory access, security guards. *Student services:* personal/psychological counseling.

Athletics *Intercollegiate sports:* badminton M/W, basketball M/W(c), cross-country running M/W, soccer M/W, tennis M/W, volleyball M/W. *Intramural sports:* basketball M/W, bowling M/W, fencing M(c)/W(c), golf M/W, sailing M/W, skiing (downhill) M/W, soccer M(c)/W(c), softball M/W, swimming and diving M/W, table tennis M(c)/W(c), tennis M/W, ultimate Frisbee M(c)/W(c), volleyball M/W.

Standardized Tests *Required:* SAT or ACT (for admission). *Required for some:* SAT Subject Tests (for admission).

Financial Aid Of all full-time matriculated undergraduates who enrolled in 2008, 407 applied for aid, 280 were judged to have need, 131 had their need fully met. 46 Federal Work-Study jobs (averaging $796). 529 state and other part-time jobs (averaging $1248). In 2008, 617 non-need-based awards were made. *Average percent of need met:* 93%. *Average financial aid package:* $35,000. *Average need-based loan:* $3164. *Average need-based gift aid:* $5034. *Average non-need-based aid:* $35,000. *Average indebtedness upon graduation:* $10,390. *Financial aid deadline:* 6/1.

Applying *Options:* electronic application, early admission, early decision, deferred entrance. *Application fee:* $65. *Required:* essay or personal statement, high school transcript, minimum 2 GPA. *Required for some:* minimum 3.5 GPA, 3 letters of recommendation, interview, portfolio, home examination for art and architecture applicants. *Recommended:* minimum 3 GPA. *Application deadlines:* 1/1 (freshmen), 1/1 (transfers). *Early decision deadline:* 12/1 (for plan 1), 12/1 (for plan 2). *Notification:* 4/1 (freshmen), 5/1 (transfers), 12/24 (early decision plan 1), 2/1 (early decision plan 2).

Freshman Application Contact Mr. Mitchell L. Lipton, Dean of Admissions and Records and Registrar, Cooper Union for the Advancement of Science and Art, 30 Cooper Square, New York, NY 10003. *Phone:* 212-353-4120. *Fax:* 212-353-4342. *E-mail:* admissions@cooper.edu. *Web site:* http://www.cooper.edu/.

Cornell University
Ithaca, New York

- **Independent** university, founded 1865
- **Small-town** 745-acre campus with easy access to Syracuse
- **Endowment** $4.4 billion
- **Coed** 13,935 undergraduate students, 100% full-time, 50% women, 50% men
- **Most difficult** entrance level, 18% of applicants were admitted

Undergraduates 13,935 full-time. Students come from 54 states and territories; 83 other countries; 64% are from out of state; 5% Black or African American, non-Hispanic/Latino; 8% Hispanic/Latino; 16% Asian, non-Hispanic/Latino; 0.1% Native Hawaiian or other Pacific Islander, non-Hispanic/Latino; 0.4% American Indian or Alaska Native, non-Hispanic/Latino; 3% Two or more races, non-Hispanic/Latino; 12% Race/ethnicity unknown; 9% international; 4% transferred in; 57% live on campus. *Retention:* 96% of full-time freshmen returned.

Freshmen *Admission:* 36,338 applied, 6,673 admitted, 3,179 enrolled. *Test scores:* SAT critical reading scores over 500: 96%; SAT math scores over 500: 98%; ACT scores over 18: 99%; SAT critical reading scores over 600: 78%; SAT math scores over 600: 89%; ACT scores over 24: 94%; SAT critical reading scores over 700: 34%; SAT math scores over 700: 58%; ACT scores over 30: 64%.

Faculty *Total:* 1,802, 91% full-time, 91% with terminal degrees. *Student/faculty ratio:* 9:1.

Academics *Calendar:* semesters. *Degrees:* bachelor's, master's, doctoral-professional, and doctoral-research/scholarship. *Special study options:* academic remediation for entering students, accelerated degree program, advanced placement credit, cooperative education, distance learning, double majors, English as a second language, honors programs, independent study, internships, off-campus study, services for LD students, student-designed majors, study abroad, summer session for credit. *ROTC:* Army (b), Navy (b), Air Force (b).

Computers on Campus 2,650 computers/terminals and 1,000 ports are available on campus for general student use. Students can access the following: campus intranet, computer help desk, free student e-mail accounts, online (class) grades, online (class) registration. Campuswide network is available. 100% of college-owned or -operated housing units are wired for high-speed Internet access. Wireless service is available via entire campus.

Student Life *Housing options:* coed, men-only, women-only, cooperative, disabled students. Campus housing is university owned. Freshman campus housing is guaranteed. *Activities and organizations:* drama/theater group, student-run newspaper, radio and television station, choral group, marching band, Student Assembly, Residence Hall Association, Catholic Community, Hillel, Con-

cert Commission, national fraternities, national sororities. *Campus security:* 24-hour emergency response devices and patrols, late-night transport/escort service, controlled dormitory access, Indoor and outdoor emergency phones. *Student services:* health clinic, personal/psychological counseling, women's center.

Athletics Member NCAA. All Division I except football (Division I-AA). *Intercollegiate sports:* baseball M, basketball M/W, crew M/W, cross-country running M/W, equestrian sports W, fencing W, field hockey W, golf M, gymnastics W, ice hockey M/W, lacrosse M/W, soccer M/W, softball W, squash M/W, swimming and diving M/W, table tennis M(c)/W(c), tennis M/W, track and field M/W, ultimate Frisbee M(c)/W(c), volleyball M(c)/W(c), water polo M(c)/W(c), wrestling M. *Intramural sports:* archery M(c)/W(c), badminton M/W, baseball M(c), basketball M/W, bowling M/W, cheerleading M(c)/W(c), cross-country running M(c)/W(c), equestrian sports M(c)/W(c), fencing M(c)/W(c), field hockey W(c), football M/W, golf M/W, gymnastics M(c)/W(c), ice hockey M/W, lacrosse W(c), rugby M(c)/W(c), sailing M(c)/W(c), skiing (cross-country) M(c)/W(c), skiing (downhill) M(c)/W(c), soccer M/W, softball M/W, squash M/W, table tennis M/W, tennis M/W, ultimate Frisbee M/W, volleyball M/W, water polo M(c)/W(c), wrestling M(c)/W(c).

Standardized Tests *Required:* SAT or ACT (for admission). *Required for some:* SAT Subject Tests (for admission).

Costs (2010–11) *Comprehensive fee:* $52,316 includes full-time tuition ($39,450), mandatory fees ($216), and room and board ($12,650). Full-time tuition and fees vary according to degree level. *College room only:* $7500. Room and board charges vary according to board plan and housing facility. *Payment plan:* installment. *Waivers:* employees or children of employees.

Financial Aid Of all full-time matriculated undergraduates who enrolled in 2009, 7,824 applied for aid, 6,852 were judged to have need, 6,852 had their need fully met. 4,852 Federal Work-Study jobs (averaging $1728). 1,357 state and other part-time jobs (averaging $1516). *Average percent of need met:* 100%. *Average financial aid package:* $37,425. *Average need-based loan:* $3378. *Average need-based gift aid:* $32,511. *Average indebtedness upon graduation:* $20,648. *Financial aid deadline:* 1/2.

Applying *Options:* electronic application, early admission, early decision, deferred entrance. *Application fee:* $70. *Required:* essay or personal statement, high school transcript, 2 letters of recommendation. *Required for some:* interview. *Application deadlines:* 1/3 (freshmen), 3/1 (transfers). *Early decision deadline:* 11/1. *Notification:* 3/31 (freshmen), continuous until 6/15 (transfers), 12/15 (early decision).

Freshman Application Contact Mr. Jason C. Locke, Director of Undergraduate Admissions, Cornell University, Ithaca, NY 14853-0001. *Phone:* 607-255-1446. *Fax:* 607-255-0659. *E-mail:* admissions@cornell.edu. *Web site:* http://www.cornell.edu/.

The Culinary Institute of America
Hyde Park, New York

- **Independent** 4-year, founded 1946
- **Suburban** 170-acre campus
- **Coed** 2,785 undergraduate students, 100% full-time, 45% women, 55% men
- **Moderately difficult** entrance level, 81% of applicants were admitted

Undergraduates 2,785 full-time. Students come from 55 states and territories; 39 other countries; 5% Black or African American, non-Hispanic/Latino; 9% Hispanic/Latino; 9% Asian, non-Hispanic/Latino; 0.4% Native Hawaiian or other Pacific Islander, non-Hispanic/Latino; 0.3% American Indian or Alaska Native, non-Hispanic/Latino; 2% Two or more races, non-Hispanic/Latino; 7% Race/ethnicity unknown; 84% live on campus. *Retention:* 79% of full-time freshmen returned.

Freshmen *Admission:* 1,151 applied, 936 admitted, 681 enrolled. *Average high school GPA:* 3.1.

Faculty *Total:* 189, 79% full-time. *Student/faculty ratio:* 17:1.

Academics *Calendar:* semesters plus 18 or 21 week externship program. *Degrees:* certificates, associate, and bachelor's. *Special study options:* academic remediation for entering students, honors programs, internships, services for LD students.

Computers on Campus 218 computers/terminals are available on campus for general student use. Students can access the following: campus intranet, computer help desk, free student e-mail accounts, online course guides. Campus-wide network is available. 100% of college-owned or -operated housing units are wired for high-speed Internet access. Wireless service is available via entire campus.

Student Life *Housing options:* coed. Campus housing is university owned. Freshman campus housing is guaranteed. *Activities and organizations:* student-run newspaper, choral group, Alliance, Baking and Pastry Society, Global Culinary Society, Eta Sigma Delta Honor Society, Chips Supporting Agriculture. *Campus security:* 24-hour emergency response devices and patrols, late-night transport/escort service, controlled dormitory access. *Student services:* health clinic, personal/psychological counseling.

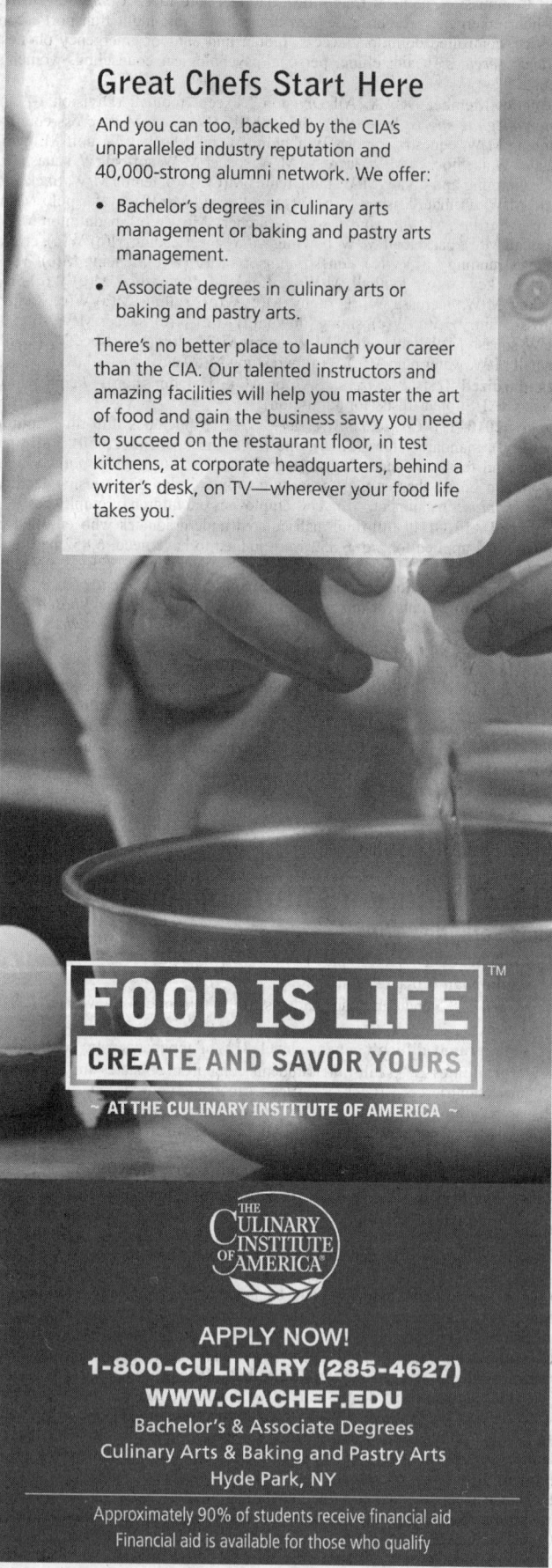

Athletics *Intercollegiate sports:* basketball M/W, cross-country running M/W, soccer M/W, tennis M/W, volleyball M/W. *Intramural sports:* basketball M/W, cross-country running M/W, football M/W, soccer M/W, softball M/W, swimming and diving M/W, tennis M/W, volleyball M/W.

Standardized Tests *Recommended:* SAT or ACT (for admission).

Costs (2010–11) *Comprehensive fee:* $33,980 includes full-time tuition ($24,360), mandatory fees ($1200), and room and board ($8420). Full-time tuition and fees vary according to degree level. *College room only:* $5900. Room and board charges vary according to board plan and housing facility. *Payment plan:* installment. *Waivers:* employees or children of employees.

Financial Aid Of all full-time matriculated undergraduates who enrolled in 2008, 2,600 applied for aid, 2,340 were judged to have need, 134 had their need fully met. 900 Federal Work-Study jobs (averaging $435). In 2008, 238 non-need-based awards were made. *Average percent of need met:* 44%. *Average financial aid package:* $13,805. *Average need-based loan:* $4032. *Average need-based gift aid:* $3500. *Average non-need-based aid:* $2500. *Average indebtedness upon graduation:* $29,351. *Financial aid deadline:* 2/15.

Applying *Options:* electronic application, deferred entrance. *Application fee:* $50. *Required:* essay or personal statement, high school transcript, 1 letter of recommendation. *Required for some:* an Affidavit of Support. *Application deadline:* rolling (freshmen). *Notification:* continuous (transfers).

Freshman Application Contact Ms. Rachel Birchwood, Director of Admissions, The Culinary Institute of America, 1946 Campus Drive, Hudson Hall, Hyde Park, NY 12538. *Phone:* 845-451-1459. *Toll-free phone:* 800-CULINARY. *Fax:* 845-451-1068. *E-mail:* admissions@culinary.edu. *Web site:* http://www.ciachef.edu/.

See page 1244 for the College Close-Up.

Daemen College
Amherst, New York

- **Independent** comprehensive, founded 1947
- **Suburban** 35-acre campus with easy access to Buffalo
- **Endowment** $5.1 million
- **Coed**
- **Moderately difficult** entrance level

Faculty *Student/faculty ratio:* 15:1.

Academics *Calendar:* semesters. *Degrees:* certificates, bachelor's, master's, doctoral-professional, and post-master's certificates.

Student Life *Campus security:* 24-hour emergency response devices and patrols, late-night transport/escort service, 24-hour security cameras.

Athletics Member NAIA.

Standardized Tests *Recommended:* SAT or ACT (for admission).

Costs (2010–11) *Comprehensive fee:* $31,310 includes full-time tuition ($20,950), mandatory fees ($510), and room and board ($9850). Full-time tuition and fees vary according to course load and reciprocity agreements. Part-time tuition: $695 per credit hour. Part-time tuition and fees vary according to course load and reciprocity agreements. *Required fees:* $6 per credit hour part-time, $70 per term part-time. *Room and board:* Room and board charges vary according to board plan and housing facility. *Payment plans:* installment, deferred payment.

Financial Aid *Of all full-time matriculated undergraduates who enrolled in 2008,* 1,302 applied for aid, 1,272 were judged to have need. 256 Federal Work-Study jobs (averaging $1328). 242 state and other part-time jobs (averaging $1059). *In 2008,* 217 non-need-based awards were made. *Average financial aid package:* $14,529. *Average need-based loan:* $4370. *Average need-based gift aid:* $6229. *Average non-need-based aid:* $5805. *Average indebtedness upon graduation:* $18,910.

Applying *Options:* electronic application, early admission, deferred entrance. *Application fee:* $25. *Required:* essay or personal statement, high school transcript, minimum 2 GPA, 1 letter of recommendation. *Required for some:* 3 letters of recommendation, interview, high school transcript, class rank, writing sample-test opt.

Freshman Application Contact Mr. Frank Williams, Director of Undergraduate Admissions, Daemen College, Amherst, NY 14226-3592. *Phone:* 716-839-8225. *Toll-free phone:* 800-462-7652. *Fax:* 716-839-8229. *E-mail:* admissions@daemen.edu. *Web site:* http://www.daemen.edu/.

See page 1248 for the College Close-Up.

Darkei Noam Rabbinical College
Brooklyn, New York

Director of Admissions Rabbi Pinchas Horowitz, Director of Admissions, Darkei Noam Rabbinical College, 2822 Avenue J, Brooklyn, NY 11210. *Phone:* 718-338-6464.

Davis College
Johnson City, New York

- **Independent nondenominational** 4-year, founded 1900
- **Suburban** 22-acre campus with easy access to Syracuse
- **Coed**
- **Minimally difficult** entrance level

Faculty *Student/faculty ratio:* 14:1.

Academics *Calendar:* semesters. *Degrees:* certificates, diplomas, associate, and bachelor's.

Student Life *Campus security:* 24-hour emergency response devices and patrols, student patrols, late-night transport/escort service.

Athletics Member NCCAA.

Standardized Tests *Required:* SAT or ACT (for admission).

Costs (2010–11) *Comprehensive fee:* $18,450 includes full-time tuition ($12,150) and room and board ($6300). Full-time tuition and fees vary according to course load. Part-time tuition: $420 per credit hour. Part-time tuition and fees vary according to course load. *Room and board:* Room and board charges vary according to housing facility.

Financial Aid *Of all full-time matriculated undergraduates who enrolled in 2007,* 182 applied for aid, 175 were judged to have need, 27 had their need fully met. 77 Federal Work-Study jobs (averaging $898). *In 2007,* 10 non-need-based awards were made. *Average percent of need met:* 37. *Average financial aid package:* $5120. *Average need-based loan:* $4893. *Average need-based gift aid:* $4360. *Average non-need-based aid:* $610. *Average indebtedness upon graduation:* $5360.

Applying *Options:* electronic application, deferred entrance. *Application fee:* $45. *Required:* high school transcript, 2 letters of recommendation, references. *Required for some:* essay or personal statement. *Recommended:* minimum 2 GPA, interview.

Freshman Application Contact Admissions Coordinator, Davis College, 400 Riverside Drive, Johnson City, NY 13790. *Phone:* 607-729-1581 Ext. 406. *Toll-free phone:* 800-331-4137 Ext. 406. *Fax:* 607-798-7754. *E-mail:* admissions@davisny.edu. *Web site:* http://www.davisny.edu/.

DeVry College of New York
Long Island City, New York

- **Proprietary** comprehensive, founded 1998, part of DeVry University
- **Urban** campus
- **Coed** 1,486 undergraduate students, 64% full-time, 27% women, 73% men
- **Minimally difficult** entrance level

Undergraduates 956 full-time, 530 part-time. 5% are from out of state; 27% Black or African American, non-Hispanic/Latino; 33% Hispanic/Latino; 8% Asian, non-Hispanic/Latino; 0.3% Native Hawaiian or other Pacific Islander, non-Hispanic/Latino; 0.5% American Indian or Alaska Native, non-Hispanic/Latino; 0.4% Two or more races, non-Hispanic/Latino; 19% Race/ethnicity unknown; 2% international; 20% transferred in.

Freshmen *Admission:* 345 enrolled.

Faculty *Total:* 64, 56% full-time. *Student/faculty ratio:* 28:1.

Academics *Calendar:* semesters. *Degrees:* associate, bachelor's, and master's. *Special study options:* academic remediation for entering students, accelerated degree program, adult/continuing education programs, advanced placement credit, distance learning, part-time degree program, summer session for credit.

Computers on Campus Students can access the following: online (class) registration. Campuswide network is available.

Student Life *Housing:* college housing not available. *Campus security:* 24-hour emergency response devices and patrols, student patrols, late-night transport/escort service.

Costs (2010–11) *Tuition:* $14,766 full-time, $580 per credit hour part-time. Full-time tuition and fees vary according to course load. Part-time tuition and fees vary according to course load. *Required fees:* $60 full-time, $30 per term part-time. *Payment plans:* installment, deferred payment. *Waivers:* employees or children of employees.

Financial Aid Of all full-time matriculated undergraduates who enrolled in 2007, 387 applied for aid, 371 were judged to have need, 8 had their need fully met. In 2007, 19 non-need-based awards were made. *Average percent of need met:* 5%. *Average financial aid package:* $15,942. *Average need-based loan:* $8712. *Average need-based gift aid:* $7343. *Average non-need-based aid:* $11,806. *Average indebtedness upon graduation:* $29,136.

Applying *Options:* electronic application, deferred entrance. *Application fee:* $50. *Required:* high school transcript, interview. *Application deadlines:* rolling (freshmen), rolling (transfers). *Notification:* continuous (freshmen), continuous (transfers).

Freshman Application Contact DeVry College of New York, 180 Madison Avenue, Suite 900, Long Island City, NY 11101. *Phone:* 888-713.3879. *Web site:* http://www.devry.edu/.

Dominican College

Orangeburg, New York

- **Independent** comprehensive, founded 1952
- **Suburban** 70-acre campus with easy access to New York City
- **Endowment** $892,984
- **Coed** 1,684 undergraduate students, 82% full-time, 68% women, 32% men
- **Noncompetitive** entrance level, 72% of applicants were admitted

Undergraduates 1,373 full-time, 311 part-time. Students come from 24 states and territories; 13 other countries; 27% are from out of state; 17% Black or African American, non-Hispanic/Latino; 21% Hispanic/Latino; 10% Asian, non-Hispanic/Latino; 0.2% American Indian or Alaska Native, non-Hispanic/Latino; 3% Two or more races, non-Hispanic/Latino; 6% Race/ethnicity unknown; 13% transferred in; 42% live on campus. *Retention:* 74% of full-time freshmen returned.

Freshmen *Admission:* 1,522 applied, 1,099 admitted, 322 enrolled. *Average high school GPA:* 2.71. *Test scores:* SAT critical reading scores over 500: 21%; SAT math scores over 500: 26%; SAT writing scores over 500: 23%; ACT scores over 18: 91%; SAT critical reading scores over 600: 1%; SAT math scores over 600: 5%; SAT writing scores over 600: 5%; ACT scores over 24: 29%; ACT scores over 30: 10%.

Faculty *Total:* 232, 31% full-time, 32% with terminal degrees. *Student/faculty ratio:* 15:1.

Academics *Calendar:* semesters. *Degrees:* certificates, associate, bachelor's, master's, and doctoral-professional. *Special study options:* academic remediation for entering students, accelerated degree program, adult/continuing education programs, advanced placement credit, cooperative education, distance learning, double majors, freshman honors college, honors programs, independent study, internships, off-campus study, part-time degree program, services for LD students, summer session for credit. *Unusual degree programs:* 3-2 occupational therapy.

Computers on Campus 150 computers/terminals are available on campus for general student use. Students can access the following: campus intranet, free student e-mail accounts, online (class) schedules, Web portal, Black Board. Campuswide network is available. 100% of college-owned or -operated housing units are wired for high-speed Internet access. Wireless service is available via entire campus.

Student Life *Housing options:* coed. Campus housing is university owned. Freshman campus housing is guaranteed. *Activities and organizations:* drama/theater group, student-run newspaper, radio station, choral group, Student Government Association, Business Club, Aquin Players, school newspaper, Nursing Association. *Campus security:* 24-hour emergency response devices and patrols, student patrols, late-night transport/escort service, controlled dormitory access. *Student services:* health clinic, personal/psychological counseling.

Athletics Member NCAA, NAIA. All NCAA Division II. *Intercollegiate sports:* baseball M(s), basketball M(s)/W(s), cross-country running W(s), golf M(s), lacrosse M(s)/W(s), soccer M(s)/W(s), softball W(s), track and field W(s), volleyball W(s). *Intramural sports:* basketball M/W, crew M(c)/W(c), volleyball M/W.

Standardized Tests *Required:* SAT or ACT (for admission).

Costs (2010–11) *One-time required fee:* $35. *Comprehensive fee:* $32,550 includes full-time tuition ($21,250), mandatory fees ($740), and room and board ($10,560). Full-time tuition and fees vary according to degree level. Part-time tuition: $640 per credit hour. Part-time tuition and fees vary according to degree level and program. *Room and board:* Room and board charges vary according to board plan and housing facility. *Payment plans:* installment, deferred payment. *Waivers:* senior citizens and employees or children of employees.

Financial Aid Of all full-time matriculated undergraduates who enrolled in 2008, 1,343 applied for aid, 1,232 were judged to have need, 132 had their need fully met. 217 Federal Work-Study jobs (averaging $1200). 73 state and other part-time jobs (averaging $3000). In 2008, 108 non-need-based awards were made. *Average percent of need met:* 59%. *Average financial aid package:* $15,385. *Average need-based loan:* $4270. *Average need-based gift aid:* $12,101. *Average non-need-based aid:* $6662. *Average indebtedness upon graduation:* $18,398.

Applying *Options:* electronic application, deferred entrance. *Application fee:* $35. *Required:* high school transcript. *Required for some:* essay or personal statement, interview. *Recommended:* interview. *Application deadlines:* rolling (freshmen), rolling (transfers). *Notification:* continuous (freshmen), continuous (transfers).

Freshman Application Contact Ms. Joyce Elbe, Director of Admissions, Dominican College, 470 Western Highway, Orangeburg, NY 10962-1210.

Phone: 845-359-7901. *Toll-free phone:* 866-432-4636. *Fax:* 845-365-3150. *E-mail:* admissions@dc.edu. *Web site:* http://www.dc.edu/.

Dowling College

Oakdale, New York

- **Independent** comprehensive, founded 1955
- **Suburban** 157-acre campus with easy access to New York City
- **Coed** 3,252 undergraduate students, 65% full-time, 54% women, 46% men
- **Moderately difficult** entrance level, 80% of applicants were admitted

Undergraduates 2,114 full-time, 1,138 part-time. 6% are from out of state; 10% Black or African American, non-Hispanic/Latino; 10% Hispanic/Latino; 1% Asian, non-Hispanic/Latino; 0.1% American Indian or Alaska Native, non-Hispanic/Latino; 23% Race/ethnicity unknown; 4% international; 8% transferred in. *Retention:* 62% of full-time freshmen returned.

Freshmen *Admission:* 2,490 applied, 2,003 admitted, 472 enrolled.

Faculty *Total:* 457, 26% full-time, 44% with terminal degrees. *Student/faculty ratio:* 16:1.

Academics *Calendar:* semesters. *Degrees:* bachelor's, master's, doctoral-other, post-master's, and postbachelor's certificates. *Special study options:* academic remediation for entering students, accelerated degree program, advanced placement credit, cooperative education, distance learning, double majors, English as a second language, honors programs, independent study, internships, off-campus study, part-time degree program, services for LD students, student-designed majors, study abroad, summer session for credit. *ROTC:* Army (c), Air Force (c).

Computers on Campus 253 computers/terminals and 73 ports are available on campus for general student use. Students can access the following: campus intranet, computer help desk, free student e-mail accounts, online (class) grades, online (class) registration, online (class) schedules. Campuswide network is available. 100% of college-owned or -operated housing units are wired for high-speed Internet access. Wireless service is available via classrooms, computer centers, computer labs, learning centers, libraries, student centers.

Student Life *Housing options:* coed. Campus housing is university owned. *Activities and organizations:* drama/theater group, student-run newspaper, choral group, Student Government Association, Dormitory Councils, Aviation Organization. *Campus security:* 24-hour emergency response devices and patrols, late-night transport/escort service. *Student services:* health clinic, personal/psychological counseling.

Athletics Member NCAA. All Division II. *Intercollegiate sports:* baseball M(s), basketball M(s)/W(s), crew M(s)(c)/W(s), cross-country running M(s)/W(s), equestrian sports M(c)/W(c), golf M(s), lacrosse M(s)/W(s), soccer M(s)/W(s), softball W(s), tennis M(s)/W(s), volleyball W(s). *Intramural sports:* bowling M(c)/W(c), weight lifting M/W.

Standardized Tests *Recommended:* SAT or ACT (for admission).

Costs (2010–11) *Comprehensive fee:* $35,400 includes full-time tuition ($22,860), mandatory fees ($1770), and room and board ($10,770). Full-time tuition and fees vary according to course load, degree level, and program. Part-time tuition: $767 per credit. Part-time tuition and fees vary according to course load, degree level, and program. *Required fees:* $566 per term part-time. *Room and board:* Room and board charges vary according to housing facility and location. *Payment plans:* installment, deferred payment. *Waivers:* minority students, children of alumni, adult students, senior citizens, and employees or children of employees.

Financial Aid Of all full-time matriculated undergraduates who enrolled in 2008, 1,543 applied for aid, 1,543 were judged to have need, 168 had their need fully met. 311 Federal Work-Study jobs (averaging $1674). 131 state and other part-time jobs (averaging $2076). In 2008, 239 non-need-based awards were made. *Average percent of need met:* 94%. *Average financial aid package:* $15,570. *Average need-based loan:* $4200. *Average need-based gift aid:* $8270. *Average non-need-based aid:* $5770. *Average indebtedness upon graduation:* $22,177.

Applying *Options:* electronic application, early action, deferred entrance. *Application fee:* $35. *Required:* essay or personal statement, high school transcript, minimum 2 GPA, 1 letter of recommendation. *Recommended:* minimum 2.5 GPA. *Application deadlines:* rolling (freshmen), rolling (out-of-state freshmen), rolling (transfers), 12/31 (early action). *Notification:* continuous (freshmen), continuous (out-of-state freshmen), continuous (transfers), 1/31 (early action).

Freshman Application Contact Ms. Ronnie Lee Macdonald, Vice President for Enrollment and Student Services, Dowling College, 150 Idle Hour Boulevard, Oakdale, NY 11769. *Phone:* 631-244-3480. *Toll-free phone:* 800-DOWLING. *Fax:* 631-244-1059. *Web site:* http://www.dowling.edu/.

D'Youville College

Buffalo, New York

- **Independent** comprehensive, founded 1908
- **Urban** 7-acre campus
- **Endowment** $25.2 million
- **Coed**
- **Moderately difficult** entrance level

Faculty *Student/faculty ratio:* 12:1.

Academics *Calendar:* semesters plus summer session. *Degrees:* bachelor's, master's, doctoral-professional, doctoral-research/scholarship, post-master's, and postbachelor's certificates.

Student Life *Campus security:* 24-hour emergency response devices and patrols, late-night transport/escort service, controlled dormitory access.

Athletics Member NCAA. All Division III.

Standardized Tests *Required:* SAT or ACT (for admission).

Costs (2010–11) *Comprehensive fee:* $30,860 includes full-time tuition ($20,800), mandatory fees ($260), and room and board ($9800). Full-time tuition and fees vary according to course load, degree level, and program. Part-time tuition: $640 per credit hour. Part-time tuition and fees vary according to course load, degree level, and program. No tuition increase for student's term of enrollment. *Required fees:* $2 per credit hour part-time, $40 per term part-time. *Room and board:* Room and board charges vary according to board plan and housing facility. *Payment plans:* installment, deferred payment.

Financial Aid *Of all full-time matriculated undergraduates who enrolled in 2009,* 1,332 applied for aid, 1,218 were judged to have need, 219 had their need fully met. 269 Federal Work-Study jobs (averaging $1115). 90 state and other part-time jobs (averaging $1467). *In 2009,* 141 non-need-based awards were made. *Average percent of need met:* 64. *Average financial aid package:* $14,972. *Average need-based loan:* $5784. *Average need-based gift aid:* $9957. *Average non-need-based aid:* $5731.

Applying *Options:* electronic application, deferred entrance. *Application fee:* $25. *Required:* high school transcript, minimum 2 GPA. *Required for some:* essay or personal statement, minimum 3 GPA, interview.

Freshman Application Contact D'Youville College, 320 Porter Avenue, Buffalo, NY 14201-1084. *Phone:* 716-829-7600. *Toll-free phone:* 800-777-3921. *Web site:* http://www.dyc.edu/.

See page 548 for Display. See page 1264 for the College Close-Up.

Elmira College

Elmira, New York

- **Independent** comprehensive, founded 1855
- **Suburban** 42-acre campus
- **Coed** 1,534 undergraduate students, 80% full-time, 73% women, 27% men
- **Moderately difficult** entrance level, 82% of applicants were admitted

Undergraduates 1,221 full-time, 313 part-time. Students come from 35 states and territories; 31 other countries; 52% are from out of state; 3% Black or African American, non-Hispanic/Latino; 2% Hispanic/Latino; 1% Asian, non-Hispanic/Latino; 0.1% American Indian or Alaska Native, non-Hispanic/Latino; 19% Race/ethnicity unknown; 5% international; 4% transferred in; 94% live on campus. *Retention:* 71% of full-time freshmen returned.

Freshmen *Admission:* 2,465 applied, 2,016 admitted, 428 enrolled. *Average high school GPA:* 3.37. *Test scores:* SAT critical reading scores over 500: 64%; SAT math scores over 500: 65%; ACT scores over 18: 100%; SAT critical reading scores over 600: 23%; SAT math scores over 600: 19%; ACT scores over 24: 54%; SAT critical reading scores over 700: 5%; SAT math scores over 700: 3%; ACT scores over 30: 2%.

Faculty *Total:* 212, 41% full-time. *Student/faculty ratio:* 10:1.

Academics *Calendar:* 4-4-1. *Degrees:* associate, bachelor's, and master's. *Special study options:* accelerated degree program, adult/continuing education programs, advanced placement credit, distance learning, double majors, English as a second language, independent study, internships, off-campus study, part-time degree program, services for LD students, student-designed majors, study abroad, summer session for credit. *ROTC:* Army (b), Air Force (c). *Unusual degree programs:* 3-2 chemical engineering with Clarkson University.

Computers on Campus 145 computers/terminals are available on campus for general student use. Students can access the following: campus intranet, computer help desk, free student e-mail accounts, online (class) grades, online (class) schedules. Campuswide network is available. 100% of college-owned

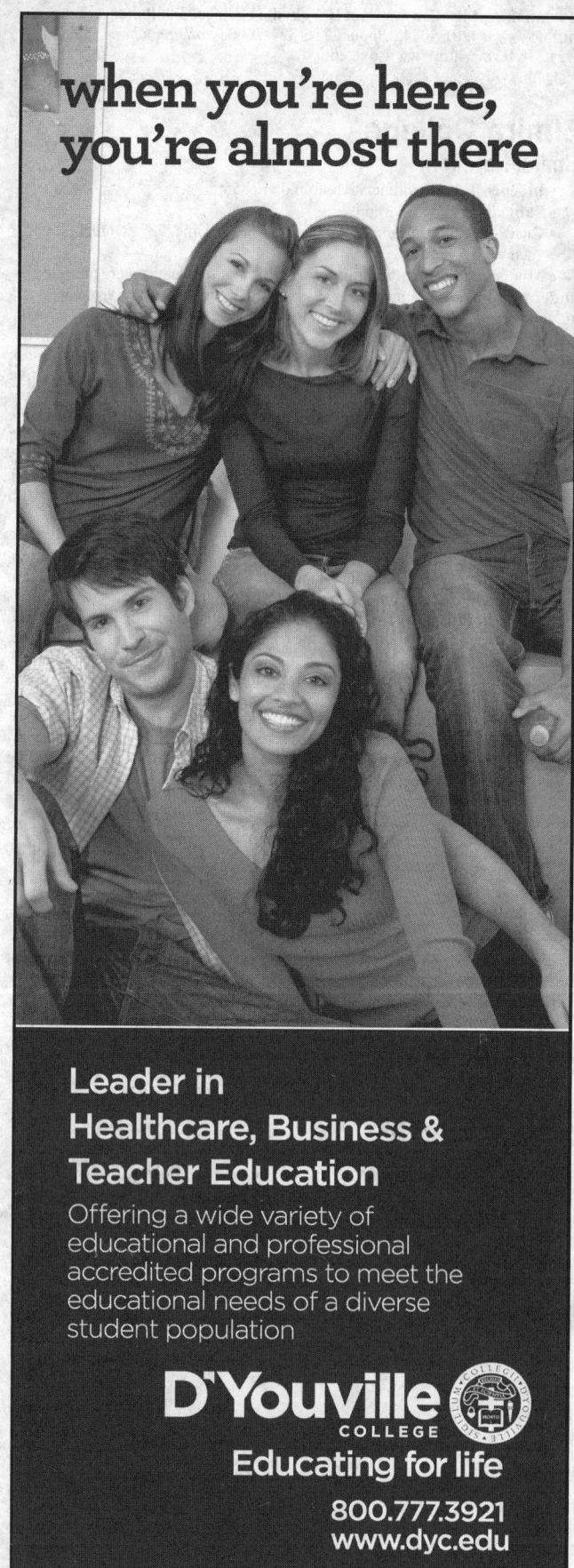

or -operated housing units are wired for high-speed Internet access. Wireless service is available via computer centers, computer labs, libraries, student centers. **Student Life** *Housing:* on-campus residence required through senior year. *Options:* coed, women-only, cooperative, disabled students. Campus housing is university owned. Freshman campus housing is guaranteed. *Activities and organizations:* drama/theater group, student-run newspaper, radio station, choral group, student radio station, Student Activities Board, College Republicans and Democrats, Ski Club, Habitat for Humanity. *Campus security:* 24-hour patrols, late-night transport/escort service, 24-hour locked residence hall entrances. *Student services:* health clinic, personal/psychological counseling. **Athletics** Member NCAA. All Division III. *Intercollegiate sports:* basketball M/W, cheerleading W, field hockey W, golf M/W, ice hockey M/W, lacrosse M/W, soccer M/W, softball W, tennis M/W, volleyball M/W. *Intramural sports:* badminton M/W, basketball M/W, equestrian sports M/W, football M/W, ice hockey M/W, lacrosse M/W, racquetball M/W, rock climbing M/W, skiing (cross-country) M/W, skiing (downhill) M/W, soccer M/W, softball M/W, swimming and diving M/W, table tennis M/W, tennis M/W, ultimate Frisbee M/W, volleyball M/W.

Standardized Tests *Required:* SAT or ACT (for admission).

Costs (2010–11) *Comprehensive fee:* $47,050 includes full-time tuition ($34,500), mandatory fees ($1400), and room and board ($11,150). Part-time tuition: $305 per credit hour. Part-time tuition and fees vary according to course load and degree level. *Room and board:* Room and board charges vary according to housing facility. *Payment plans:* tuition prepayment, installment. *Waivers:* employees or children of employees.

Financial Aid Of all full-time matriculated undergraduates who enrolled in 2009, 1,035 applied for aid, 962 were judged to have need, 160 had their need fully met. 376 Federal Work-Study jobs (averaging $1000). 220 state and other part-time jobs (averaging $1300). In 2009, 235 non-need-based awards were made. *Average percent of need met:* 80%. *Average financial aid package:* $26,953. *Average need-based loan:* $4148. *Average need-based gift aid:* $23,024. *Average non-need-based aid:* $19,232. *Average indebtedness upon graduation:* $25,438.

Applying *Options:* electronic application, early decision, deferred entrance. *Application fee:* $50. *Required:* essay or personal statement, high school transcript, minimum 2 GPA, 1 letter of recommendation. *Required for some:* interview. *Recommended:* interview. *Application deadlines:* 3/31 (freshmen), rolling (transfers). *Early decision deadline:* 11/15 (for plan 1), 1/15 (for plan 2). *Notification:* 4/30 (freshmen), continuous (transfers), 12/15 (early decision plan 1), 1/31 (early decision plan 2).

Freshman Application Contact Mr. Brett Moore, Director of Admissions, Elmira College, One Park Place, Elmira, NY 14901. *Phone:* 607-735-1724. *Toll-free phone:* 800-935-6472. *Fax:* 607-735-1718. *E-mail:* admissions@elmira.edu. *Web site:* http://www.elmira.edu/.

See page 1272 for the College Close-Up.

Eugene Lang College The New School for Liberal Arts

New York, New York

- **Independent** 4-year, founded 1978, part of The New School
- **Urban** 5-acre campus with easy access to New York City
- **Coed** 1,511 undergraduate students, 94% full-time, 67% women, 33% men
- **Very difficult** entrance level, 73% of applicants were admitted

Undergraduates 1,423 full-time, 88 part-time. 71% are from out of state; 5% Black or African American, non-Hispanic/Latino; 11% Hispanic/Latino; 5% Asian, non-Hispanic/Latino; 0.2% Native Hawaiian or other Pacific Islander, non-Hispanic/Latino; 0.5% American Indian or Alaska Native, non-Hispanic/Latino; 3% Two or more races, non-Hispanic/Latino; 14% Race/ethnicity unknown; 5% international; 11% transferred in; 27% live on campus. *Retention:* 75% of full-time freshmen returned.

Freshmen *Admission:* 1,661 applied, 1,211 admitted, 300 enrolled. *Average high school GPA:* 3.35. *Test scores:* SAT critical reading scores over 500: 87%; SAT math scores over 500: 67%; SAT writing scores over 500: 83%; ACT scores over 18: 98%; SAT critical reading scores over 600: 48%; SAT math scores over 600: 28%; SAT writing scores over 600: 47%; ACT scores over 24: 77%; SAT critical reading scores over 700: 13%; SAT math scores over 700: 4%; SAT writing scores over 700: 10%; ACT scores over 30: 6%.

Faculty *Total:* 157, 46% full-time, 34% with terminal degrees. *Student/faculty ratio:* 14:1.

Academics *Calendar:* semesters. *Degree:* bachelor's. *Special study options:* accelerated degree program, advanced placement credit, distance learning, double majors, English as a second language, independent study, internships, off-campus study, services for LD students, student-designed majors, study abroad, summer session for credit.

Computers on Campus Students can access the following: campus intranet, computer help desk, free student e-mail accounts, online (class) grades, online (class) registration, online (class) schedules, online portal. Campuswide network is available. 100% of college-owned or -operated housing units are wired for high-speed Internet access. Wireless service is available via entire campus. **Student Life** *Housing options:* coed, disabled students. Campus housing is university owned and leased by the school. Freshman applicants given priority for college housing. *Activities and organizations:* drama/theater group, student-run newspaper, radio station, choral group. *Campus security:* 24-hour emergency response devices, controlled dormitory access, 24-hour desk attendants in residence halls. *Student services:* health clinic, personal/psychological counseling.

Costs (2010–11) *Comprehensive fee:* $51,350 includes full-time tuition ($35,330), mandatory fees ($760), and room and board ($15,260). Part-time tuition: $1200 per credit. Part-time tuition and fees vary according to course load. *College room only:* $12,260. Room and board charges vary according to board plan and housing facility. *Payment plan:* installment. *Waivers:* employees or children of employees.

Financial Aid Of all full-time matriculated undergraduates who enrolled in 2009, 1,061 applied for aid, 842 were judged to have need, 121 had their need fully met. In 2009, 39 non-need-based awards were made. *Average percent of need met:* 80%. *Average financial aid package:* $34,210. *Average need-based loan:* $8390. *Average need-based gift aid:* $22,555. *Average non-need-based aid:* $2925. *Average indebtedness upon graduation:* $30,830.

Applying *Options:* electronic application, early decision, deferred entrance. *Application fee:* $50. *Required:* essay or personal statement, high school transcript, interview, counselor evaluation, teacher evaluation. *Recommended:* minimum 3 GPA. *Application deadlines:* 1/5 (freshmen), 4/1 (transfers). *Early decision deadline:* 11/1. *Notification:* 4/1 (freshmen), 5/1 (transfers), 12/1 (early decision).

Freshman Application Contact Eugene Lang College The New School for Liberal Arts, 65 West 11th Street, New York, NY 10011-8601. *Phone:* 212-229-5665. *Toll-free phone:* 877-528-3321. *Web site:* http://www.newschool.edu/lang.

See page 1280 for the College Close-Up.

Excelsior College

Albany, New York

- **Independent** comprehensive, founded 1970
- **Suburban** campus with easy access to Albany, NY
- **Coed**
- **Noncompetitive** entrance level

Faculty *Student/faculty ratio:* 79:1.

Academics *Calendar:* continuous. *Degrees:* certificates, associate, bachelor's, master's, post-master's, and postbachelor's certificates (offers only external degree programs).

Costs (2010–11) *Tuition:* $335 per credit hour part-time. *Required fees:* $440 per year part-time.

Applying *Options:* electronic application. *Application fee:* $75. *Required for some:* college transcripts.

Freshman Application Contact Admissions, Excelsior College, 7 Columbia Circle, Albany, NY 12203-5159. *Phone:* 518-464-8500. *Toll-free phone:* 888-647-2388. *Fax:* 518-464-8777. *E-mail:* admissions@excelsior.edu. *Web site:* http://www.excelsior.edu/.

Farmingdale State College

Farmingdale, New York

- **State-supported** 4-year, founded 1912, part of State University of New York System
- **Small-town** 380-acre campus with easy access to New York City
- **Endowment** $3.7 million
- **Coed**
- **Moderately difficult** entrance level

Faculty *Student/faculty ratio:* 18:1.

Academics *Calendar:* semesters. *Degrees:* certificates, associate, and bachelor's.

Student Life *Campus security:* 24-hour emergency response devices and patrols, controlled dormitory access.

Athletics Member NCAA. All Division III except basketball (Division II), lacrosse (Division II), volleyball (Division II).

Standardized Tests *Required:* SAT or ACT (for admission).

Costs (2010–11) *Tuition:* state resident $4970 full-time, $207 per credit part-time; nonresident $12,870 full-time, $562 per credit part-time. Part-time tuition and fees vary according to course load. *Required fees:* $1123 full-time, $44 per credit part-time. *Room and board:* $11,780. Room and board charges vary according to board plan and location.

Financial Aid *Of all full-time matriculated undergraduates who enrolled in 2000, 1,872 applied for aid, 1,480 were judged to have need, 257 had their* need fully met. 134 Federal Work-Study jobs, 78 state and other part-time jobs. *In 2000,* 213 non-need-based awards were made. *Average percent of need met:* 63. *Average financial aid package:* $5127. *Average need-based gift aid:* $3786. *Average non-need-based aid:* $3198.

Applying *Options:* electronic application, early admission. *Application fee:* $40. *Required:* high school transcript, minimum 2 GPA. *Required for some:* interview, portfolio for graphic arts / advertising.

Freshman Application Contact Farmingdale State College, 2350 Broadhollow Road, Farmingdale, NY 11735. *Phone:* 631-420-2457. *Toll-free phone:* 877-4-FARMINGDALE. *Web site:* http://www.farmingdale.edu/.

Fashion Institute of Technology

New York, New York

- **State and locally supported** comprehensive, founded 1944, part of State University of New York System
- **Urban** 5-acre campus
- **Endowment** $24.3 million
- **Coed, primarily women** 10,166 undergraduate students, 71% full-time, 85% women, 15% men
- **Moderately difficult** entrance level, 39% of applicants were admitted

Undergraduates 7,210 full-time, 2,956 part-time. Students come from 48 states and territories; 68 other countries; 29% are from out of state; 8% transferred in; 26% live on campus. *Retention:* 87% of full-time freshmen returned.

Freshmen *Admission:* 4,263 applied, 1,669 admitted, 1,070 enrolled. *Average high school GPA:* 3.4.

Faculty *Total:* 1,016, 25% full-time. *Student/faculty ratio:* 17:1.

Academics *Calendar:* semesters. *Degrees:* certificates, associate, bachelor's, and master's. *Special study options:* academic remediation for entering students, adult/continuing education programs, advanced placement credit, distance learning, English as a second language, honors programs, internships, part-time degree program, services for LD students, study abroad, summer session for credit.

Computers on Campus 1,300 computers/terminals are available on campus for general student use. Students can access the following: campus intranet, computer help desk, free student e-mail accounts, online (class) grades, online (class) registration, online (class) schedules. Campuswide network is available. 100% of college-owned or -operated housing units are wired for high-speed Internet access. Wireless service is available via classrooms, computer centers, computer labs, dorm rooms, learning centers, libraries, student centers.

Student Life *Housing options:* coed, women-only. Campus housing is university owned and is provided by a third party. Freshman applicants given priority for college housing. *Activities and organizations:* drama/theater group, student-run newspaper, radio and television station, choral group, FITSA/Student Government, Merchandising Society/Style Shop, Delta Epilson Chi: Promoting Leadership in Marketing, Merchandising, and Advertising, PRSSA: Public Relations Student Society of America, Student Ambassadors. *Campus security:* 24-hour emergency response devices and patrols, late-night transport/escort service, controlled dormitory access. *Student services:* health clinic, personal/psychological counseling.

Athletics Member NJCAA. *Intercollegiate sports:* basketball M, cheerleading W, cross-country running M/W, swimming and diving M/W, table tennis M/W, tennis W, volleyball W. *Intramural sports:* basketball M/W, table tennis M/W, tennis M/W, volleyball M/W.

Costs (2010–11) *Tuition:* state resident $5168 full-time, $215 per credit hour part-time; nonresident $13,550 full-time, $564 per credit hour part-time. Full-time tuition and fees vary according to degree level. Part-time tuition and fees vary according to degree level. *Required fees:* $500 full-time. *Room and board:* $11,700. Room and board charges vary according to board plan and housing facility. *Payment plan:* installment. *Waivers:* employees or children of employees.

Financial Aid Of all full-time matriculated undergraduates who enrolled in 2008, 4,507 applied for aid, 3,512 were judged to have need, 459 had their need fully met. 553 Federal Work-Study jobs (averaging $1479). In 2008, 170 non-need-based awards were made. *Average percent of need met:* 63%. *Average financial aid package:* $11,305. *Average need-based loan:* $4298. *Average need-based gift aid:* $5355. *Average non-need-based aid:* $1676. *Average indebtedness upon graduation:* $24,143.

Applying *Options:* electronic application. *Application fee:* $40. *Required:* essay or personal statement, high school transcript. *Required for some:* portfolio for art and design programs. *Application deadlines:* 2/1 (freshmen), 2/1 (transfers). *Notification:* continuous (freshmen), continuous (transfers).

Freshman Application Contact Ms. Laura Arbrogast, Director of Admissions, Fashion Institute of Technology, Seventh Avenue at 27th Street, New York, NY 10001-5992. *Phone:* 212-217-3760. *Toll-free phone:* 800-GOTOFIT. *Fax:* 212-217-3761. *E-mail:* fitinfo@fitnyc.edu. *Web site:* http://www.fitnyc.edu/.

See page 550 for Display. See page 1282 for the College Close-Up.

Five Towns College

Dix Hills, New York

- **Independent** comprehensive, founded 1972
- **Suburban** 40-acre campus with easy access to New York City
- **Coed** 1,262 undergraduate students, 97% full-time, 36% women, 64% men
- **Moderately difficult** entrance level, 44% of applicants were admitted

Undergraduates 1,230 full-time, 32 part-time. Students come from 12 states and territories; 5 other countries; 14% are from out of state; 8% transferred in; 20% live on campus. *Retention:* 67% of full-time freshmen returned.

Freshmen *Admission:* 958 applied, 425 admitted, 265 enrolled. *Average high school GPA:* 2.7.

Faculty *Total:* 133, 21% full-time. *Student/faculty ratio:* 13:1.

Academics *Calendar:* semesters. *Degrees:* associate, bachelor's, master's, and doctoral-professional. *Special study options:* academic remediation for entering students, adult/continuing education programs, advanced placement credit, cooperative education, independent study, internships, off-campus study, part-time degree program, services for LD students, summer session for credit.

Computers on Campus 110 computers/terminals are available on campus for general student use. Students can access the following: campus intranet, computer help desk, free student e-mail accounts, online (class) grades, online (class) registration, online (class) schedules. Campuswide network is available. 100% of college-owned or -operated housing units are wired for high-speed Internet access. Wireless service is available via entire campus.

Student Life *Housing options:* coed. Campus housing is university owned. Freshman applicants given priority for college housing. *Activities and organizations:* drama/theater group, student-run newspaper, radio station, choral group, Film Video Club, Audio Club, Music Business Club, Hip Hop Club, yearbook. *Campus security:* 24-hour emergency response devices and patrols, late-night transport/escort service, controlled dormitory access. *Student services:* personal/psychological counseling.

Standardized Tests *Required:* SAT or ACT (for admission).

Costs (2010–11) *Comprehensive fee:* $31,810 includes full-time tuition ($18,400), mandatory fees ($350), and room and board ($13,060). Full-time tuition and fees vary according to course level, degree level, program, and student level. Part-time tuition: $765 per credit hour. Part-time tuition and fees vary according to course level, course load, degree level, program, and student level. *Required fees:* $60 per term part-time. *College room only:* $8060. Room and board charges vary according to board plan. *Payment plan:* installment. *Waivers:* employees or children of employees.

Financial Aid Of all full-time matriculated undergraduates who enrolled in 2009, 939 applied for aid, 791 were judged to have need, 466 had their need fully met. 95 Federal Work-Study jobs (averaging $1387). In 2009, 69 non-need-based awards were made. *Average percent of need met:* 48%. *Average financial aid package:* $8100. *Average need-based loan:* $3700. *Average need-based gift aid:* $5500. *Average non-need-based aid:* $2400. *Average indebtedness upon graduation:* $19,000.

Applying *Options:* early decision, deferred entrance. *Application fee:* $35. *Required:* essay or personal statement, high school transcript, minimum 2.3 GPA, 2 letters of recommendation, immunization records and an audition for Music or Theatre students. *Required for some:* interview. *Application deadlines:* rolling (freshmen), rolling (transfers). *Early decision deadline:* 12/1. *Notification:* continuous (freshmen), continuous (transfers), rolling (early decision).

Freshman Application Contact Mr. Jerry Cohen, Dean of Enrollment, Five Towns College, 305 North Service Road, Dix Hills, NY 11746-6055. *Phone:* 631-424-7000 Ext. 2110. *Fax:* 631-656-2172. *E-mail:* jcohen@ftc.edu. *Web site:* http://www.ftc.edu/.

See page 1288 for the College Close-Up.

Fordham University

New York, New York

- **Independent Roman Catholic (Jesuit)** university, founded 1841
- **Urban** 85-acre campus with easy access to New York City
- **Endowment** $357.3 million
- **Coed**
- **Very difficult** entrance level

Faculty *Student/faculty ratio:* 13:1.

Academics *Calendar:* semesters. *Degrees:* bachelor's, master's, doctoral-professional, doctoral-research/scholarship, and post-master's certificates (branch locations at Rose Hill and Lincoln Center).

Student Life *Campus security:* 24-hour emergency response devices and patrols, student patrols, late-night transport/escort service, controlled dormitory access, security at each campus entrance and at residence halls.
Athletics Member NCAA. All Division I except football (Division I-AA).
Standardized Tests *Required:* SAT or ACT (for admission). *Recommended:* SAT Subject Tests (for admission).
Costs (2010–11) *Comprehensive fee:* $51,167 includes full-time tuition ($37,545), mandatory fees ($732), and room and board ($12,890). Full-time tuition and fees vary according to student level. Part-time tuition: $1250 per credit. Part-time tuition and fees vary according to course load. *College room only:* $7245. Room and board charges vary according to board plan and location.
Financial Aid *Of all full-time matriculated undergraduates who enrolled in 2008,* 6,253 applied for aid, 4,773 were judged to have need, 1,236 had their need fully met. 1,189 Federal Work-Study jobs (averaging $2752). *In 2008,* 1301 non-need-based awards were made. *Average percent of need met:* 75. *Average financial aid package:* $26,057. *Average need-based loan:* $8964. *Average need-based gift aid:* $18,140. *Average non-need-based aid:* $10,264. *Average indebtedness upon graduation:* $33,365. *Financial aid deadline:* 2/1.
Applying *Options:* electronic application, early admission, early action, deferred entrance. *Application fee:* $50. *Required:* essay or personal statement, high school transcript, 1 letter of recommendation.
Freshman Application Contact Mr. Peter Farrell, Director of Admission, Fordham University, 441 East Fordham Road, New York, NY 10458. *Phone:* 718-817-4000. *Toll-free phone:* 800-FORDHAM. *Fax:* 718-367-9404. *E-mail:* enroll@fordham.edu. *Web site:* http://www.fordham.edu/.

See page 1294 for the College Close-Up.

Global College of Long Island University
Brooklyn, New York

Freshman Application Contact Global College of Long Island University, 9 Hanover Place, 4th Floor, Brooklyn, NY 11201. *Phone:* 718-780-4320. *Web site:* http://www.liu.edu/globalcollege/.

Globe Institute of Technology
New York, New York

- **Proprietary** 4-year
- **Urban** campus with easy access to New York City
- **Coed**
- **Minimally difficult** entrance level

Academics *Calendar:* semesters. *Degrees:* associate and bachelor's.
Athletics Member NJCAA.
Standardized Tests *Recommended:* SAT or ACT (for admission).
Costs (2010–11) *Comprehensive fee:* $17,553 includes full-time tuition ($10,950), mandatory fees ($170), and room and board ($6433). Full-time tuition and fees vary according to program. Part-time tuition: $1425 per course. Part-time tuition and fees vary according to course load and program. *Required fees:* $475 per credit part-time, $60 per term part-time.
Applying *Options:* electronic application. *Application fee:* $50. *Required:* high school transcript, interview.
Freshman Application Contact Mr. Michael Scalice, Admissions Director, Globe Institute of Technology, 500 7th Avenue, New York, NY 10018. *Phone:* 212-349-4330 Ext. 1624. *Toll-free phone:* 877-394-5623. *Fax:* 212-227-5920. *E-mail:* admissions@globe.edu. *Web site:* http://www.globe.edu/.

Hamilton College
Clinton, New York

- **Independent** 4-year, founded 1812
- **Small-town** 1300-acre campus
- **Endowment** $552.8 million
- **Coed** 1,861 undergraduate students, 99% full-time, 53% women, 47% men
- **Very difficult** entrance level, 29% of applicants were admitted

Undergraduates 1,844 full-time, 17 part-time. Students come from 50 states and territories; 36 other countries; 67% are from out of state; 4% Black or African American, non-Hispanic/Latino; 5% Hispanic/Latino; 8% Asian, non-Hispanic/Latino; 0.5% American Indian or Alaska Native, non-Hispanic/Latino; 2% Two or more races, non-Hispanic/Latino; 10% Race/ethnicity unknown; 5% international; 0.9% transferred in; 98% live on campus. *Retention:* 95% of full-time freshmen returned.
Freshmen *Admission:* 4,857 applied, 1,430 admitted, 467 enrolled. *Test scores:* SAT critical reading scores over 500: 99%; SAT math scores over 500: 99%; SAT writing scores over 500: 99%; ACT scores over 18: 100%; SAT critical reading scores over 600: 89%; SAT math scores over 600: 91%; SAT writ-

ing scores over 600: 88%; ACT scores over 24: 90%; SAT critical reading scores over 700: 50%; SAT math scores over 700: 47%; SAT writing scores over 700: 49%; ACT scores over 30: 49%.
Faculty *Total:* 221, 83% full-time, 87% with terminal degrees. *Student/faculty ratio:* 9:1.
Academics *Calendar:* semesters. *Degree:* bachelor's. *Special study options:* accelerated degree program, adult/continuing education programs, advanced placement credit, double majors, English as a second language, independent study, internships, off-campus study, part-time degree program, services for LD students, student-designed majors, study abroad. *ROTC:* Army (c), Air Force (c). *Unusual degree programs:* 3-2 engineering with Columbia University, Dartmouth College, Rensselaer Polytechnic Institute, Washington University in St. Louis; Law with Columbia University (3-3 Degree Program).
Computers on Campus 878 computers/terminals and 3,000 ports are available on campus for general student use. Students can access the following: campus intranet, computer help desk, free student e-mail accounts, online (class) grades, online (class) registration, online (class) schedules. Campus-wide network is available. 100% of college-owned or -operated housing units are wired for high-speed Internet access. Wireless service is available via entire campus.
Student Life *Housing:* on-campus residence required through senior year. *Options:* coed, cooperative, disabled students. Campus housing is university owned. Freshman campus housing is guaranteed. *Activities and organizations:* drama/theater group, student-run newspaper, radio station, choral group, WHCL (Hamilton College Radio), People Who Like To Do Fun Things, College Democrats, Paintball, Hogwarts at Hamilton, national fraternities, national sororities. *Campus security:* 24-hour emergency response devices and patrols, late-night transport/escort service, controlled dormitory access, student safety program. *Student services:* health clinic, personal/psychological counseling, women's center.
Athletics Member NCAA. All Division III. *Intercollegiate sports:* baseball M, basketball M/W, crew M/W, cross-country running M/W, field hockey W, football M, golf M/W(c), ice hockey M/W, lacrosse M/W, soccer M/W, softball W, squash M/W, swimming and diving M/W, tennis M/W, track and field M/W, volleyball M(c)/W, water polo M(c)/W(c). *Intramural sports:* badminton M/W, basketball M/W, equestrian sports M(c)/W(c), fencing M(c)/W(c), football M/W, golf M/W, ice hockey M/W, racquetball M/W, rugby M(c)/W(c), sailing M(c)/W(c), skiing (cross-country) M/W, skiing (downhill) M(c)/W(c), soccer M/W, softball M/W, squash M/W, tennis M/W, ultimate Frisbee M(c)/W(c), volleyball M/W, water polo M.
Standardized Tests *Required:* SAT and SAT Subject Tests or ACT (for admission).
Costs (2010–11) *Comprehensive fee:* $51,760 includes full-time tuition ($40,870), mandatory fees ($410), and room and board ($10,480). Part-time tuition: $5109 per course. *College room only:* $5730. Room and board charges vary according to board plan. *Payment plan:* installment. *Waivers:* employees or children of employees.
Financial Aid Of all full-time matriculated undergraduates who enrolled in 2009, 897 applied for aid, 778 were judged to have need, 778 had their need fully met. 509 Federal Work-Study jobs (averaging $1602). 62 state and other part-time jobs (averaging $1882). In 2009, 32 non-need-based awards were made. *Average percent of need met:* 100%. *Average financial aid package:* $37,737. *Average need-based loan:* $3880. *Average need-based gift aid:* $33,381. *Average non-need-based aid:* $31,497. *Average indebtedness upon graduation:* $16,982. *Financial aid deadline:* 2/8.
Applying *Options:* electronic application, early decision, deferred entrance. *Application fee:* $60. *Required:* essay or personal statement, high school transcript, 1 letter of recommendation. *Recommended:* interview. *Application deadlines:* 1/1 (freshmen), 4/15 (transfers). *Early decision deadline:* 11/15 (for plan 1), 1/1 (for plan 2). *Notification:* 4/1 (freshmen), 6/1 (transfers), 12/15 (early decision plan 1), 2/15 (early decision plan 2).
Freshman Application Contact Ms. Monica Inzer, Vice President and Dean of Admission and Financial Aid, Hamilton College, 198 College Hill Road, Clinton, NY 13323. *Phone:* 800-843-2655. *Toll-free phone:* 800-843-2655. *Fax:* 315-859-4457. *E-mail:* admission@hamilton.edu. *Web site:* http://www.hamilton.edu/.

Hartwick College
Oneonta, New York

- **Independent** 4-year, founded 1797
- **Small-town** 425-acre campus with easy access to Albany, NY
- **Endowment** $52.3 million
- **Coed** 1,531 undergraduate students, 97% full-time, 59% women, 41% men
- **Moderately difficult** entrance level, 76% of applicants were admitted

Undergraduates 1,487 full-time, 44 part-time. Students come from 30 states and territories; 22 other countries; 28% are from out of state; 4% Black or African American, non-Hispanic/Latino; 5% Hispanic/Latino; 2% Asian, non-Hispanic/Latino; 0.1% Native Hawaiian or other Pacific Islander, non-Hispanic/

Latino; 0.5% American Indian or Alaska Native, non-Hispanic/Latino; 22% Race/ethnicity unknown; 3% international; 3% transferred in; 82% live on campus. *Retention:* 73% of full-time freshmen returned.
Freshmen *Admission:* 3,535 applied, 2,669 admitted, 488 enrolled. *Average high school GPA:* 3.2. *Test scores:* SAT critical reading scores over 500: 70%; SAT math scores over 500: 73%; SAT writing scores over 500: 65%; ACT scores over 18: 99%; SAT critical reading scores over 600: 25%; SAT math scores over 600: 30%; SAT writing scores over 600: 22%; ACT scores over 24: 57%; SAT critical reading scores over 700: 4%; SAT math scores over 700: 2%; SAT writing scores over 700: 2%; ACT scores over 30: 8%.
Faculty *Total:* 187, 56% full-time, 43% with terminal degrees. *Student/faculty ratio:* 11:1.
Academics *Calendar:* 4-1-4. *Degree:* bachelor's. *Special study options:* accelerated degree program, advanced placement credit, double majors, honors programs, independent study, internships, off-campus study, part-time degree program, services for LD students, student-designed majors, study abroad, summer session for credit. *Unusual degree programs:* 3-2 engineering with Clarkson University, Columbia University.
Computers on Campus 80 computers/terminals are available on campus for general student use. Students can access the following: computer help desk, free student e-mail accounts, online (class) grades, online (class) registration, online (class) schedules. Campuswide network is available. 100% of college-owned or -operated housing units are wired for high-speed Internet access. Wireless service is available via entire campus.
Student Life *Housing:* on-campus residence required through junior year. *Options:* coed. Campus housing is university owned. Freshman campus housing is guaranteed. *Activities and organizations:* drama/theater group, student-run newspaper, radio station, choral group, Student Union, student radio station, Student Senate, Hilltops campus newspaper, Cardboard Alley Players, national fraternities, national sororities. *Campus security:* 24-hour emergency response devices and patrols, late-night transport/escort service, controlled dormitory access. *Student services:* health clinic, personal/psychological counseling, women's center.
Athletics Member NCAA. All Division III except soccer (Division I), water polo (Division I). *Intercollegiate sports:* basketball M/W, cheerleading W, cross-country running M/W, equestrian sports W, field hockey W, football M, ice hockey M(c), lacrosse M/W, rugby M(c), soccer M(s)/W, swimming and diving M/W, tennis M/W, volleyball W, water polo M(c)/W(s). *Intramural sports:* basketball M/W, cross-country running M/W, football M, golf M/W, racquetball M/W, soccer M/W, squash M/W, swimming and diving M/W, table tennis M/W, tennis M/W, track and field M/W, volleyball M/W, water polo M/W.
Standardized Tests *Required for some:* SAT or ACT (for admission).
Costs (2010–11) *One-time required fee:* $300. *Comprehensive fee:* $43,975 includes full-time tuition ($33,850), mandatory fees ($780), and room and board ($9345). Part-time tuition: $1070 per credit hour. *College room only:* $4840. Room and board charges vary according to board plan and housing facility. *Payment plan:* installment. *Waivers:* employees or children of employees.
Applying *Options:* electronic application, early admission, early decision, deferred entrance. *Application fee:* $35. *Required:* high school transcript, audition for music program; portfolio for Art majors; SAT scores required of Nursing majors. *Recommended:* minimum 3 GPA, 2 letters of recommendation, interview. *Application deadlines:* rolling (freshmen), 8/1 (transfers). *Early decision deadline:* 11/15 (for plan 1), 1/15 (for plan 2). *Notification:* continuous (freshmen), continuous (transfers).
Freshman Application Contact Jonathan Kent, Director of Admissions, Hartwick College, PO Box 4022, Oneonta, NY 13820-4022. *Phone:* 607-431-4150. *Toll-free phone:* 888-HARTWICK. *Fax:* 607-431-4102. *E-mail:* admissions@hartwick.edu. *Web site:* http://www.hartwick.edu/.

Hilbert College
Hamburg, New York

- **Independent** 4-year, founded 1957
- **Small-town** 40-acre campus with easy access to Buffalo
- **Endowment** $2.9 million
- **Coed**
- **Minimally difficult** entrance level

Faculty *Student/faculty ratio:* 12:1.
Academics *Calendar:* semesters. *Degrees:* associate and bachelor's.
Student Life *Campus security:* 24-hour emergency response devices and patrols, student patrols, late-night transport/escort service, controlled dormitory access.
Athletics Member NCAA. All Division III.
Standardized Tests *Recommended:* SAT or ACT (for admission).
Costs (2010–11) *Comprehensive fee:* $26,480 includes full-time tuition ($17,890), mandatory fees ($600), and room and board ($7990). Full-time tuition and fees vary according to course load. Part-time tuition: $450 per credit hour. Part-time tuition and fees vary according to course load. *College*

room only: $4050. Room and board charges vary according to board plan and housing facility.
Financial Aid *Of all full-time matriculated undergraduates who enrolled in 2007,* 797 applied for aid, 707 were judged to have need, 192 had their need fully met. 67 Federal Work-Study jobs (averaging $1547). *In 2007,* 103 non-need-based awards were made. *Average percent of need met:* 74. *Average financial aid package:* $11,096. *Average need-based loan:* $4947. *Average need-based gift aid:* $6690. *Average non-need-based aid:* $10,870. *Average indebtedness upon graduation:* $24,444. *Financial aid deadline:* 5/1.
Applying *Options:* electronic application, early admission, deferred entrance. *Application fee:* $20. *Required:* high school transcript. *Required for some:* interview. *Recommended:* essay or personal statement, interview.
Freshman Application Contact Mr. Timothy Lee, Director of Admissions, Hilbert College, 5200 South Park Avenue, Hamburg, NY 14075-1597. *Phone:* 716-649-7900. *Fax:* 716-649-0702. *E-mail:* tlee@hilbert.edu. *Web site:* http://www.hilbert.edu/.

Hobart and William Smith Colleges
Geneva, New York

- **Independent** comprehensive, founded 1822
- **Small-town** 200-acre campus with easy access to Rochester and Syracuse
- **Endowment** $165.9 million
- **Coed** 2,165 undergraduate students, 100% full-time, 55% women, 45% men
- **Very difficult** entrance level, 62% of applicants were admitted

Undergraduates 2,161 full-time, 4 part-time. Students come from 45 states and territories; 17 other countries; 56% are from out of state; 4% Black or African American, non-Hispanic/Latino; 4% Hispanic/Latino; 2% Asian, non-Hispanic/Latino; 0.5% American Indian or Alaska Native, non-Hispanic/Latino; 23% Race/ethnicity unknown; 4% international; 0.7% transferred in; 90% live on campus. *Retention:* 89% of full-time freshmen returned.
Freshmen *Admission:* 4,682 applied, 2,909 admitted, 618 enrolled. *Average high school GPA:* 3.37. *Test scores:* SAT critical reading scores over 500: 97%; SAT math scores over 500: 98%; SAT critical reading scores over 600: 52%; SAT math scores over 600: 56%; SAT critical reading scores over 700: 10%; SAT math scores over 700: 6%.
Faculty *Total:* 203, 91% full-time, 95% with terminal degrees. *Student/faculty ratio:* 11:1.
Academics *Calendar:* semesters. *Degrees:* bachelor's, master's, and post-bachelor's certificates. *Special study options:* accelerated degree program, adult/continuing education programs, advanced placement credit, double majors, English as a second language, honors programs, independent study, internships, off-campus study, services for LD students, student-designed majors, study abroad. *Unusual degree programs:* 3-2 business administration with Clarkson University, Rochester Institute of Technology; engineering with Columbia University, Rensselaer Polytechnic Institute, Dartmouth College; architecture with Washington University in St. Louis.
Computers on Campus 250 computers/terminals are available on campus for general student use. Students can access the following: campus intranet, computer help desk, free student e-mail accounts, online (class) grades, online (class) registration, online (class) schedules. Campuswide network is available. 100% of college-owned or -operated housing units are wired for high-speed Internet access. Wireless service is available via entire campus.
Student Life *Housing:* on-campus residence required through junior year. *Options:* coed, men-only, women-only, cooperative. Campus housing is university owned. Freshman campus housing is guaranteed. *Activities and organizations:* drama/theater group, student-run newspaper, radio station, choral group, Student Life and Leadership, student government, campus publications, Service Network, sports clubs, national fraternities. *Campus security:* 24-hour emergency response devices and patrols, late-night transport/escort service, controlled dormitory access. *Student services:* health clinic, personal/psychological counseling, women's center, legal services.
Athletics Member NCAA. All Division III except lacrosse (Division I). *Intercollegiate sports:* basketball M/W, crew M/W, cross-country running M/W, equestrian sports M(c)/W(c), field hockey W, football M, golf M/W, ice hockey M/W(c), lacrosse M/W, rock climbing M(c)/W(c), rugby M(c)/W(c), sailing M/W, skiing (downhill) M(c)/W(c), soccer M/W, squash M/W, swimming and diving W, tennis M/W, ultimate Frisbee M(c)/W(c). *Intramural sports:* badminton M/W, baseball M, basketball M/W, fencing M/W, football M, golf M/W, ice hockey M/W, lacrosse M/W, racquetball M/W, skiing (cross-country) M/W, skiing (downhill) M/W, soccer M/W, softball M/W, squash M/W, swimming and diving M/W, table tennis M/W, tennis M/W, track and field M/W, ultimate Frisbee M/W, volleyball M/W, water polo M/W, weight lifting M/W.
Standardized Tests *Required for some:* SAT or ACT (for admission).
Costs (2010–11) *Comprehensive fee:* $52,258 includes full-time tuition ($40,592), mandatory fees ($1118), and room and board ($10,548). *Room and board:* Room and board charges vary according to board plan. *Payment plans:*

tuition prepayment, installment. *Waivers:* employees or children of employees.

Financial Aid Of all full-time matriculated undergraduates who enrolled in 2008, 1,581 applied for aid, 1,329 were judged to have need, 1,106 had their need fully met. 901 Federal Work-Study jobs (averaging $1752). 423 state and other part-time jobs (averaging $1896). In 2008, 396 non-need-based awards were made. *Average percent of need met:* 78%. *Average financial aid package:* $29,446. *Average need-based loan:* $4211. *Average need-based gift aid:* $25,001. *Average non-need-based aid:* $14,182. *Average indebtedness upon graduation:* $29,932. *Financial aid deadline:* 3/15.

Applying *Options:* electronic application, early admission, early decision, deferred entrance. *Application fee:* $45. *Required:* essay or personal statement, high school transcript, 1 letter of recommendation. *Recommended:* interview. *Application deadlines:* 2/1 (freshmen), 7/1 (transfers). *Early decision deadline:* 11/15 (for plan 1), 1/1 (for plan 2). *Notification:* 4/1 (freshmen), continuous (transfers), 12/15 (early decision plan 1), 2/1 (early decision plan 2).

Freshman Application Contact Hobart and William Smith Colleges, Geneva, NY 14456-3397. *Phone:* 315-781-3622. *Toll-free phone:* 800-245-0100. *Web site:* http://www.hws.edu/.

Hofstra University

Hempstead, New York

- **Independent** university, founded 1935
- **Suburban** 240-acre campus with easy access to New York City
- **Endowment** $231.0 million
- **Coed** 7,389 undergraduate students, 92% full-time, 53% women, 47% men
- **Moderately difficult** entrance level, 59% of applicants were admitted

Undergraduates 6,804 full-time, 585 part-time. Students come from 44 states and territories; 55 other countries; 36% are from out of state; 9% Black or African American, non-Hispanic/Latino; 9% Hispanic/Latino; 5% Asian, non-Hispanic/Latino; 0.1% Native Hawaiian or other Pacific Islander, non-Hispanic/Latino; 0.3% American Indian or Alaska Native, non-Hispanic/Latino; 2% Two or more races, non-Hispanic/Latino; 7% Race/ethnicity unknown; 2% international; 7% transferred in; 48% live on campus. *Retention:* 77% of full-time freshmen returned.

Freshmen *Admission:* 18,909 applied, 11,104 admitted, 1,450 enrolled. *Average high school GPA:* 3.46. *Test scores:* SAT critical reading scores over 500: 91%; SAT math scores over 500: 95%; ACT scores over 18: 100%; SAT critical reading scores over 600: 39%; SAT math scores over 600: 46%; ACT scores over 24: 76%; SAT critical reading scores over 700: 6%; SAT math scores over 700: 5%; ACT scores over 30: 7%.

Faculty *Total:* 1,165, 46% full-time, 64% with terminal degrees. *Student/faculty ratio:* 14:1.

Academics *Calendar:* 4-1-4. *Degrees:* certificates, bachelor's, master's, doctoral-professional, doctoral-research/scholarship, post-master's, and postbachelor's certificates. *Special study options:* accelerated degree program, advanced placement credit, distance learning, double majors, English as a second language, external degree program, freshman honors college, honors programs, independent study, internships, part-time degree program, services for LD students, student-designed majors, study abroad, summer session for credit. *ROTC:* Army (b). *Unusual degree programs:* 3-2 business administration.

Computers on Campus 1,628 computers/terminals and 1,900 ports are available on campus for general student use. Students can access the following: campus intranet, computer help desk, free student e-mail accounts, online (class) grades, online (class) registration, online (class) schedules, Gmail/Google Apps for students; Emergency Notification System; Online course management system; online card services balance update; online e-portfolio. Campuswide network is available. 100% of college-owned or -operated housing units are wired for high-speed Internet access. Wireless service is available via entire campus.

Student Life *Housing options:* coed, disabled students. Campus housing is university owned. Freshman applicants given priority for college housing. *Activities and organizations:* drama/theater group, student-run newspaper, radio and television station, choral group, Hofstra Entertainment Access Television, Hofstra Filmmakers Club, Inter Fraternal and Sororal Council, Masquerade Musical Theater Company, Spectrum Players, national fraternities, national sororities. *Campus security:* 24-hour emergency response devices and patrols, student patrols, late-night transport/escort service, controlled dormitory access, self-defense education; emergency notification system; security booths and cameras at each residence hall entrance. *Student services:* health clinic, personal/psychological counseling.

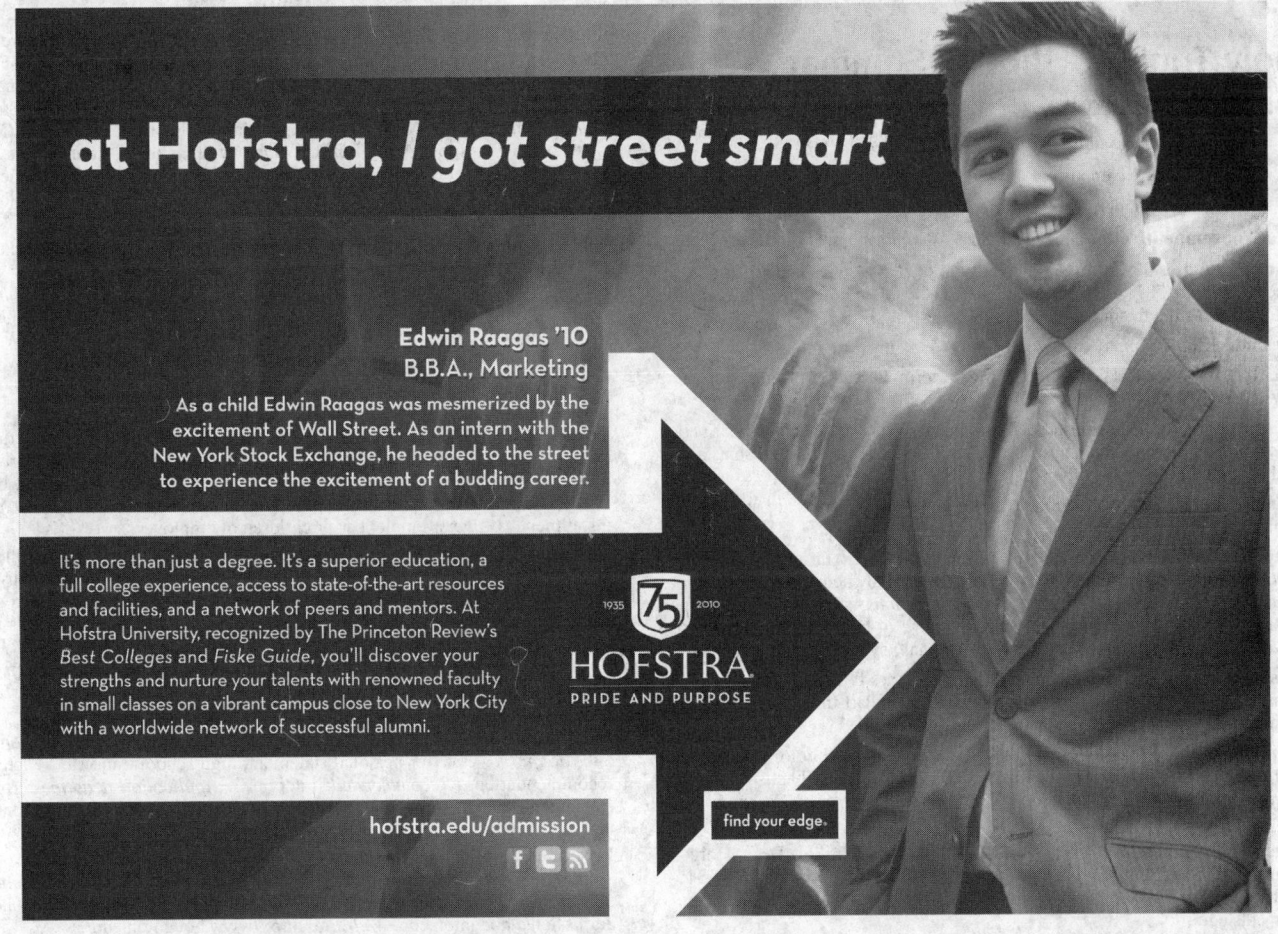

Athletics Member NCAA. All Division I. *Intercollegiate sports:* baseball M(s), basketball M(s)/W(s), cross-country running M(s)/W(s), field hockey W(s), golf M(s)/W(s), lacrosse M(s)/W(s), soccer M(s)/W(s), softball W(s), tennis M(s)/W(s), volleyball W(s), wrestling M(s). *Intramural sports:* badminton M/W, baseball M(c), basketball M/W, crew M(c)/W(c), cross-country running W(c), equestrian sports M(c)/W(c), ice hockey M(c), lacrosse M(c)/W(c), rugby M(c)/W(c), soccer M/W, softball M/W, table tennis M/W, tennis M/W, track and field W(c), ultimate Frisbee M/W, volleyball M/W, wrestling M(c).

Standardized Tests *Required for some:* SAT or ACT (for admission). *Recommended:* SAT Subject Tests (for admission).

Costs (2010–11) *Comprehensive fee:* $43,510 includes full-time tuition ($30,750), mandatory fees ($1050), and room and board ($11,710). Full-time tuition and fees vary according to course load and program. Part-time tuition: $940 per term. Part-time tuition and fees vary according to course load and program. *Required fees:* $155 per term part-time. *College room only:* $7830. Room and board charges vary according to board plan and housing facility. *Payment plans:* installment, deferred payment. *Waivers:* senior citizens and employees or children of employees.

Financial Aid Of all full-time matriculated undergraduates who enrolled in 2009, 5,150 applied for aid, 4,327 were judged to have need, 784 had their need fully met. 1,095 Federal Work-Study jobs (averaging $3009). 1,641 state and other part-time jobs (averaging $2840). In 2009, 1353 non-need-based awards were made. *Average percent of need met:* 58%. *Average financial aid package:* $20,000. *Average need-based loan:* $5000. *Average need-based gift aid:* $12,000. *Average non-need-based aid:* $10,000.

Applying *Options:* electronic application, early admission, early action, deferred entrance. *Application fee:* $70. *Required:* essay or personal statement, high school transcript, minimum 2.5 GPA, 2 letters of recommendation, proof of degree required for all; TOEFL required for international students. *Required for some:* interview. *Application deadlines:* rolling (freshmen), 12/15 (early action). *Notification:* 2/1 (freshmen), continuous (transfers), 1/15 (early action).

Freshman Application Contact Sunil Samuel, Director of Admissions, Hofstra University, 100 Hofstra University, Hempstead, NY 11549. *Phone:* 516-463-6700. *Toll-free phone:* 800-HOFSTRA. *Fax:* 516-463-5100. *E-mail:* admission@hofstra.edu. *Web site:* http://www.hofstra.edu/.

See page 1330 for the College Close-Up.

Holy Trinity Orthodox Seminary

Jordanville, New York

- **Independent Russian Orthodox** 5-year, founded 1948
- **Rural** 900-acre campus
- **Men only** 30 undergraduate students, 100% full-time
- **Noncompetitive** entrance level, 80% of applicants were admitted

Undergraduates 30 full-time. Students come from 8 states and territories; 12 other countries; 78% are from out of state; 100% live on campus. *Retention:* 100% of full-time freshmen returned.

Freshmen *Admission:* 10 applied, 8 admitted, 3 enrolled.

Faculty *Total:* 15, 67% full-time, 7% with terminal degrees. *Student/faculty ratio:* 2:1.

Academics *Calendar:* semesters. *Degree:* certificates and bachelor's. *Special study options:* accelerated degree program, distance learning, English as a second language.

Computers on Campus 8 computers/terminals and 12 ports are available on campus for general student use.

Student Life *Housing:* on-campus residence required through senior year. *Options:* men-only. Campus housing is university owned. Freshman campus housing is guaranteed. *Activities and organizations:* student-run newspaper, choral group, Student Union. *Campus security:* 24-hour emergency response devices. *Student services:* health clinic, personal/psychological counseling.

Costs (2010–11) *Comprehensive fee:* $5525 includes full-time tuition ($3000), mandatory fees ($25), and room and board ($2500). Part-time tuition: $300 per course.

Applying *Required:* essay or personal statement, high school transcript, special examination, proficiency in Russian, Eastern Orthodox baptism. *Recommended:* minimum 3 GPA. *Application deadlines:* 5/1 (freshmen), 5/1 (transfers).

Freshman Application Contact Very Rev. Vladimir Tsurikov, Dean, Holy Trinity Orthodox Seminary, PO Box 36, Jordanville, NY 13361. *Phone:* 315-858-0945. *Fax:* 315-858-0945. *E-mail:* vtsurikov@hts.edu. *Web site:* http://www.hts.edu/.

Houghton College

Houghton, New York

- **Independent Wesleyan** comprehensive, founded 1883
- **Rural** 1300-acre campus with easy access to Buffalo and Rochester
- **Endowment** $33.6 million
- **Coed** 1,256 undergraduate students, 95% full-time, 65% women, 35% men
- **Moderately difficult** entrance level, 83% of applicants were admitted

Undergraduates 1,196 full-time, 60 part-time. Students come from 40 states and territories; 32 other countries; 39% are from out of state; 3% Black or African American, non-Hispanic/Latino; 2% Hispanic/Latino; 1% Asian, non-Hispanic/Latino; 0.2% Native Hawaiian or other Pacific Islander, non-Hispanic/Latino; 0.6% American Indian or Alaska Native, non-Hispanic/Latino; 0.6% Two or more races, non-Hispanic/Latino; 0.6% Race/ethnicity unknown; 5% international; 3% transferred in; 88% live on campus. *Retention:* 84% of full-time freshmen returned.

Freshmen *Admission:* 890 applied, 740 admitted, 254 enrolled. *Average high school GPA:* 3.59. *Test scores:* SAT critical reading scores over 500: 84%; SAT math scores over 500: 81%; SAT writing scores over 500: 81%; ACT scores over 18: 98%; SAT critical reading scores over 600: 43%; SAT math scores over 600: 43%; SAT writing scores over 600: 42%; ACT scores over 24: 79%; SAT critical reading scores over 700: 8%; SAT math scores over 700: 8%; SAT writing scores over 700: 9%; ACT scores over 30: 22%.

Faculty *Total:* 128, 67% full-time, 67% with terminal degrees. *Student/faculty ratio:* 12:1.

Academics *Calendar:* semesters. *Degrees:* associate, bachelor's, and master's. *Special study options:* accelerated degree program, adult/continuing education programs, advanced placement credit, distance learning, double majors, honors programs, independent study, internships, off-campus study, services for LD students, study abroad, summer session for credit. *ROTC:* Army (c). *Unusual degree programs:* 3-2 engineering with Clarkson University.

Computers on Campus 30 computers/terminals and 820 ports are available on campus for general student use. Students can access the following: computer help desk, free student e-mail accounts, online (class) grades, online (class) registration, online (class) schedules. Campuswide network is available. 100% of college-owned or -operated housing units are wired for high-speed Internet access. Wireless service is available via entire campus.

Student Life *Housing:* on-campus residence required through sophomore year. *Options:* men-only, women-only. Campus housing is university owned. Freshman campus housing is guaranteed. *Activities and organizations:* drama/theater group, student-run newspaper, choral group, International Student Association, Gospel Choir, Global Christian Fellowship, American Choral Directors Association, Army ROTC. *Campus security:* 24-hour patrols, late-night transport/escort service, controlled dormitory access, phone connection to security patrols. *Student services:* health clinic, personal/psychological counseling.

Athletics Member NAIA. *Intercollegiate sports:* baseball M(s), basketball M(s)/W(s), cross-country running M(s)/W(s), field hockey W(s), soccer M(s)/W(s), softball W(s), track and field M(s)/W(s), volleyball W(s). *Intramural sports:* baseball M, basketball M/W, equestrian sports M/W, racquetball M/W, rock climbing M/W, skiing (cross-country) M/W, skiing (downhill) M/W, soccer M/W, softball M/W, swimming and diving M/W, table tennis M/W, ultimate Frisbee M/W, volleyball M/W, water polo M/W.

Standardized Tests *Required:* SAT or ACT (for admission).

Costs (2010–11) *Comprehensive fee:* $32,790 includes full-time tuition ($25,360), mandatory fees ($100), and room and board ($7330). Part-time tuition: $1065 per credit hour. *College room only:* $3932. Room and board charges vary according to board plan and housing facility. *Payment plan:* installment. *Waivers:* employees or children of employees.

Financial Aid Of all full-time matriculated undergraduates who enrolled in 2009, 1,054 applied for aid, 993 were judged to have need, 176 had their need fully met. 744 Federal Work-Study jobs (averaging $2127). 1 state and other part-time job (averaging $2250). In 2009, 169 non-need-based awards were made. *Average percent of need met:* 79%. *Average financial aid package:* $21,540. *Average need-based loan:* $5350. *Average need-based gift aid:* $15,315. *Average non-need-based aid:* $9743. *Average indebtedness upon graduation:* $23,010.

Applying *Options:* electronic application, deferred entrance. *Application fee:* $40. *Required:* essay or personal statement, high school transcript, 1 letter of recommendation. *Recommended:* interview. *Application deadlines:* rolling (freshmen), rolling (transfers). *Notification:* continuous (freshmen), continuous (transfers).

Freshman Application Contact Mr. Matthew Reitnour, Director of Admission, Houghton College, PO Box 128, Houghton, NY 14744. *Phone:* 585-567-9353. *Toll-free phone:* 800-777-2556. *Fax:* 585-567-9522. *E-mail:* admission@houghton.edu. *Web site:* http://www.houghton.edu/.

Hunter College of the City University of New York

New York, New York

- **State and locally supported** comprehensive, founded 1870, part of City University of New York System
- **Urban** campus
- **Endowment** $37.7 million
- **Coed** 15,787 undergraduate students, 70% full-time, 67% women, 33% men
- **Moderately difficult** entrance level, 25% of applicants were admitted

Undergraduates 11,023 full-time, 4,764 part-time. Students come from 38 states and territories; 147 other countries; 3% are from out of state; 11% Black or African American, non-Hispanic/Latino; 19% Hispanic/Latino; 22% Asian, non-Hispanic/Latino; 0.3% American Indian or Alaska Native, non-Hispanic/Latino; 8% international; 11% transferred in; 1% live on campus. *Retention:* 85% of full-time freshmen returned.

Freshmen *Admission:* 30,256 applied, 7,604 admitted, 1,788 enrolled. *Average high school GPA:* 3. *Test scores:* SAT critical reading scores over 500: 87%; SAT math scores over 500: 90%; SAT critical reading scores over 600: 34%; SAT math scores over 600: 40%; SAT critical reading scores over 700: 7%; SAT math scores over 700: 9%.

Faculty *Total:* 1,880, 38% full-time, 43% with terminal degrees. *Student/faculty ratio:* 14:1.

Academics *Calendar:* semesters. *Degrees:* bachelor's, master's, and post-master's certificates. *Special study options:* advanced placement credit, distance learning, double majors, English as a second language, freshman honors college, honors programs, independent study, internships, off-campus study, part-time degree program, services for LD students, student-designed majors, study abroad, summer session for credit. *Unusual degree programs:* 3-2 anthropology, economics, English, history, mathematics, music, physics, sociology.

Computers on Campus 1,280 computers/terminals are available on campus for general student use. Students can access the following: computer help desk, free student e-mail accounts, online (class) registration, online (class) schedules. Campuswide network is available.

Student Life *Housing options:* coed. *Activities and organizations:* drama/theater group, student-run newspaper, radio and television station, choral group. *Campus security:* 24-hour emergency response devices and patrols. *Student services:* personal/psychological counseling, women's center.

Athletics Member NCAA. All Division III. *Intercollegiate sports:* basketball M/W, cross-country running M/W, fencing M/W, gymnastics W, soccer M, swimming and diving W, tennis M/W, track and field M/W, volleyball M/W, wrestling M. *Intramural sports:* basketball M/W, cross-country running M/W, gymnastics M/W, racquetball M/W, rugby M, soccer M/W, swimming and diving M/W, tennis M/W, volleyball M/W.

Standardized Tests *Required:* SAT or ACT (for admission).

Costs (2011–12) *Tuition:* state resident $4830 full-time, $205 per term part-time; nonresident $13,050 full-time, $435 per term part-time. Full-time tuition and fees vary according to degree level and program. Part-time tuition and fees vary according to degree level and program. *Required fees:* $399 full-time, $184 per term part-time. *Room only:* $5500. *Payment plan:* installment.

Financial Aid Of all full-time matriculated undergraduates who enrolled in 2008, 7,634 applied for aid, 6,291 were judged to have need, 1,015 had their need fully met. In 2008, 750 non-need-based awards were made. *Average percent of need met:* 78%. *Average financial aid package:* $5092. *Average need-based loan:* $3179. *Average need-based gift aid:* $4141. *Average non-need-based aid:* $2368. *Average indebtedness upon graduation:* $7500.

Applying *Options:* early admission. *Application fee:* $65. *Required:* high school transcript. *Application deadlines:* 3/15 (freshmen), 3/15 (transfers). *Notification:* continuous (freshmen), continuous (transfers).

Freshman Application Contact Mr. William Zlata, Director of Admissions, Hunter College of the City University of New York, 695 Park Avenue, New York, NY 10065-5085. *Phone:* 212-772-4490. *Fax:* 212-650-3472. *E-mail:* bill.zlata@hunter.cuny.edu. *Web site:* http://www.hunter.cuny.edu/.

See page 1338 for the College Close-Up.

Iona College

New Rochelle, New York

- **Independent** comprehensive, founded 1940, affiliated with Roman Catholic Church
- **Suburban** 35-acre campus with easy access to New York City
- **Endowment** $21.5 million
- **Coed**
- **Moderately difficult** entrance level

Faculty *Student/faculty ratio:* 13:1.

Academics *Calendar:* semesters. *Degrees:* certificates, bachelor's, master's, post-master's, and postbachelor's certificates.

Student Life *Campus security:* 24-hour emergency response devices and patrols, controlled dormitory access.

Athletics Member NCAA. All Division I.

Standardized Tests *Required:* SAT or ACT (for admission). *Recommended:* SAT Subject Tests (for admission).

Costs (2010–11) *Comprehensive fee:* $40,650 includes full-time tuition ($26,850), mandatory fees ($2000), and room and board ($11,800). Full-time tuition and fees vary according to class time. Part-time tuition: $892 per credit. Part-time tuition and fees vary according to class time and course load. *Required fees:* $500 per term part-time. *Room and board:* Room and board charges vary according to housing facility. *Payment plans:* installment, deferred payment.

Financial Aid *Of all full-time matriculated undergraduates who enrolled in 2009,* 3,152 applied for aid, 2,439 were judged to have need, 574 had their need fully met. 613 Federal Work-Study jobs (averaging $1300). 251 state and other part-time jobs (averaging $871). *In 2009,* 672 non-need-based awards were made. *Average percent of need met:* 29. *Average financial aid package:* $18,067. *Average need-based loan:* $2964. *Average need-based gift aid:* $5153. *Average non-need-based aid:* $11,070. *Average indebtedness upon graduation:* $24,213. *Financial aid deadline:* 4/15.

Applying *Options:* electronic application, early action, deferred entrance. *Application fee:* $50. *Required:* essay or personal statement, high school transcript. *Recommended:* minimum 2.5 GPA, interview.

Freshman Application Contact Mr. Kevin Cavanagh, Assistant Vice President for College Admissions, Iona College, Admissions, 715 North Avenue, New Rochelle, NY 10801. *Phone:* 914-633-2502. *Toll-free phone:* 800-231-IONA. *Fax:* 914-637-2778. *E-mail:* icad@iona.edu. *Web site:* http://www.iona.edu/.

See page 1348 for the College Close-Up.

Ithaca College
Ithaca, New York

- **Independent** comprehensive, founded 1892
- **Small-town** 669-acre campus with easy access to Syracuse
- **Endowment** $175.3 million
- **Coed** 6,442 undergraduate students, 98% full-time, 56% women, 44% men
- **Moderately difficult** entrance level, 69% of applicants were admitted

Undergraduates 6,333 full-time, 109 part-time. Students come from 53 states and territories; 74 other countries; 56% are from out of state; 3% Black or African American, non-Hispanic/Latino; 5% Hispanic/Latino; 3% Asian, non-Hispanic/Latino; 0.1% Native Hawaiian or other Pacific Islander, non-Hispanic/Latino; 0.2% American Indian or Alaska Native, non-Hispanic/Latino; 3% Two or more races, non-Hispanic/Latino; 11% Race/ethnicity unknown; 2% international; 2% transferred in; 69% live on campus. *Retention:* 86% of full-time freshmen returned.

Freshmen *Admission:* 13,191 applied, 9,096 admitted, 1,619 enrolled. *Test scores:* SAT critical reading scores over 500: 87%; SAT math scores over 500: 88%; SAT writing scores over 500: 87%; SAT critical reading scores over 600: 43%; SAT math scores over 600: 46%; SAT writing scores over 600: 41%; SAT critical reading scores over 700: 9%; SAT math scores over 700: 7%; SAT writing scores over 700: 7%.

Faculty *Total:* 724, 65% full-time, 86% with terminal degrees. *Student/faculty ratio:* 12:1.

Academics *Calendar:* semesters. *Degrees:* certificates, bachelor's, master's, and doctoral-professional. *Special study options:* accelerated degree program, adult/continuing education programs, advanced placement credit, distance learning, double majors, freshman honors college, honors programs, independent study, internships, off-campus study, part-time degree program, services for LD students, student-designed majors, study abroad, summer session for credit. *ROTC:* Army (c), Air Force (c). *Unusual degree programs:* 3-2 engineering with Cornell University, Rensselaer Polytechnic Institute, Clarkson University, State University of New York at Binghamton.

Computers on Campus 640 computers/terminals and 20 ports are available on campus for general student use. Students can access the following: campus intranet, computer help desk, free student e-mail accounts, online (class) grades, online (class) registration, online (class) schedules. Campuswide network is available. 100% of college-owned or -operated housing units are wired for high-speed Internet access. Wireless service is available via entire campus. **Student Life** *Housing:* on-campus residence required through junior year. *Options:* coed, women-only, disabled students. Campus housing is university owned and leased by the school. Freshman campus housing is guaranteed. *Activities and organizations:* drama/theater group, student-run newspaper, radio and television station, choral group, Student Government Association, African-Latino Society, Residence Hall Association, Habitat for Humanity, Senior Class, national fraternities, national sororities. *Campus security:* 24-hour emergency response devices and patrols, student patrols, late-night transport/escort service, controlled dormitory access. *Student services:* health clinic, personal/psychological counseling.

Athletics Member NCAA. All Division III. *Intercollegiate sports:* baseball M, basketball M/W, crew M/W, cross-country running M/W, field hockey W, football M, golf W, gymnastics W, lacrosse M/W, soccer M/W, softball W, swimming and diving M/W, tennis M/W, track and field M/W, volleyball W, wrestling M. *Intramural sports:* basketball M/W, crew M(c)/W(c), equestrian sports M(c)/W(c), football M, golf M/W, ice hockey M(c), lacrosse M(c)/W(c), rugby W(c), skiing (downhill) M(c)/W(c), soccer M/W, softball M/W, squash M(c)/W(c), tennis M/W, ultimate Frisbee M(c)/W(c), volleyball M/W.

Standardized Tests *Required:* SAT or ACT (for admission).

Costs (2010–11) *Comprehensive fee:* $45,944 includes full-time tuition ($33,630) and room and board ($12,314). Part-time tuition: $1121 per credit hour. *College room only:* $6550. Room and board charges vary according to board plan and housing facility. *Payment plan:* installment. *Waivers:* children of alumni and employees or children of employees.

Financial Aid Of all full-time matriculated undergraduates who enrolled in 2009, 4,954 applied for aid, 4,369 were judged to have need, 2,119 had their need fully met. 3,317 Federal Work-Study jobs (averaging $2400). 1,646 state and other part-time jobs (averaging $2400). In 2009, 1218 non-need-based awards were made. *Average percent of need met:* 88%. *Average financial aid package:* $28,737. *Average need-based loan:* $6299. *Average need-based gift aid:* $19,199. *Average non-need-based aid:* $9716.

Applying *Options:* electronic application, early admission, early decision, deferred entrance. *Application fee:* $60. *Required:* essay or personal statement, high school transcript, 1 letter of recommendation. *Required for some:* audition for some programs. *Recommended:* minimum 3 GPA. *Application deadlines:* 2/1 (freshmen), 3/1 (transfers). *Early decision deadline:* 11/1. *Notification:* 4/15 (freshmen), continuous (transfers), 12/15 (early decision). **Freshman Application Contact** Mr. Gerard Turbide, Director of Admission, Ithaca College, 953 Danby Road, Ithaca, NY 14850-7002. *Phone:* 607-274-3124. *Toll-free phone:* 800-429-4274. *Fax:* 607-274-1900. *E-mail:* admission@ithaca.edu. *Web site:* http://www.ithaca.edu/.

Jamestown Business College

Jamestown, New York

- **Proprietary** primarily 2-year, founded 1886
- **Small-town** 1-acre campus
- **Coed** 386 undergraduate students, 97% full-time, 73% women, 27% men
- **Minimally difficult** entrance level, 89% of applicants were admitted

Undergraduates 375 full-time, 11 part-time. Students come from 2 states and territories; 9% are from out of state; 13% transferred in.

Freshmen *Admission:* 113 applied, 101 admitted, 78 enrolled. *Average high school GPA:* 82.

Faculty *Total:* 25, 32% full-time. *Student/faculty ratio:* 28:1.

Academics *Calendar:* quarters. *Degrees:* certificates, associate, and bachelor's. *Special study options:* academic remediation for entering students, advanced placement credit, double majors, internships, part-time degree program, summer session for credit.

Computers on Campus 106 computers/terminals are available on campus for general student use. Campuswide network is available.

Student Life *Housing:* college housing not available. *Campus security:* 24-hour emergency response devices.

Athletics *Intramural sports:* basketball M(c)/W(c), bowling M(c)/W(c), racquetball M(c)/W(c), skiing (cross-country) M(c)/W(c), skiing (downhill) M(c)/W(c), softball M(c)/W(c), swimming and diving M(c)/W(c), table tennis M(c)/W(c), volleyball M(c)/W(c), weight lifting M(c)/W(c).

Costs (2011–12) *One-time required fee:* $25. *Tuition:* $10,200 full-time, $283 per credit hour part-time. *Required fees:* $900 full-time, $150 per term part-time.

Applying *Application fee:* $25. *Required:* essay or personal statement, high school transcript, interview. *Application deadlines:* rolling (freshmen), rolling (transfers).

Freshman Application Contact Mrs. Brenda Salemme, Director of Admissions and Placement, Jamestown Business College, 7 Fairmount Avenue, Box 429, Jamestown, NY 14702-0429. *Phone:* 716-664-5100. *Fax:* 716-664-3144. *E-mail:* admissions@jbcny.org. *Web site:* http://www.jbcny.org/.

The Jewish Theological Seminary

New York, New York

Freshman Application Contact Mr. Sergio Lineberge, List College Admissions Coordinator, The Jewish Theological Seminary, 3080 Broadway, New York, NY 10027. *Phone:* 212-678-8820. *E-mail:* lcadmissions@jtsa.edu. *Web site:* http://www.jtsa.edu/.

John Jay College of Criminal Justice of the City University of New York

New York, New York

- **State and locally supported** comprehensive, founded 1964, part of City University of New York System
- **Urban** campus with easy access to New York City
- **Coed** 13,278 undergraduate students, 76% full-time, 57% women, 43% men
- **Moderately difficult** entrance level, 47% of applicants were admitted

Undergraduates 10,035 full-time, 3,243 part-time. Students come from 26 states and territories; 139 other countries; 4% are from out of state; 22% Black or African American, non-Hispanic/Latino; 40% Hispanic/Latino; 9% Asian, non-Hispanic/Latino; 0.3% American Indian or Alaska Native, non-Hispanic/Latino; 3% international; 9% transferred in. *Retention:* 77% of full-time freshmen returned.

Freshmen *Admission:* 12,911 applied, 6,132 admitted, 2,015 enrolled. *Average high school GPA:* 2.55. *Test scores:* SAT critical reading scores over 500: 25%; SAT math scores over 500: 31%; SAT writing scores over 500: 22%; SAT critical reading scores over 600: 3%; SAT math scores over 600: 5%; SAT writing scores over 600: 2%; SAT math scores over 700: 1%.

Faculty *Total:* 964, 40% full-time. *Student/faculty ratio:* 19:1.

Academics *Calendar:* semesters. *Degrees:* certificates, associate, bachelor's, and master's. *Special study options:* academic remediation for entering students, advanced placement credit, cooperative education, distance learning, double majors, English as a second language, honors programs, independent study, internships, off-campus study, part-time degree program, services for LD students, student-designed majors, study abroad, summer session for credit. *ROTC:* Air Force (c). *Unusual degree programs:* 3-2 public management, law enforcement.

Computers on Campus 1,900 computers/terminals are available on campus for general student use. Students can access the following: campus intranet, computer help desk, free student e-mail accounts, online (class) grades, online (class) registration, online (class) schedules. Campuswide network is available. Wireless service is available via classrooms, computer centers, computer labs, learning centers, libraries, student centers.

Student Life *Housing:* college housing not available. *Activities and organizations:* drama/theater group, student-run newspaper, radio station, choral group, JJC Debate Team, Universal Image Dance Group, Environmental Club, Justice in Action Club, Artist United. *Campus security:* 24-hour emergency response devices and patrols. *Student services:* health clinic, personal/psychological counseling, women's center, legal services.

Athletics Member NCAA. All Division III. *Intercollegiate sports:* baseball M, basketball M/W, cross-country running M/W, soccer M/W, softball W, swimming and diving W, tennis M/W, volleyball W. *Intramural sports:* baseball M, basketball M/W, cross-country running M/W, riflery M/W, soccer M/W, softball M/W, swimming and diving M/W, tennis M/W, track and field M/W, volleyball M/W, weight lifting M/W.

Standardized Tests *Required:* SAT or ACT (for admission).

Costs (2010–11) *Tuition:* state resident $4600 full-time, $195 per credit part-time; nonresident $12,450 full-time, $415 per credit part-time. Full-time tuition and fees vary according to course load and program. Part-time tuition and fees vary according to course load and program. *Required fees:* $330 full-time, $140 per course part-time. *Payment plan:* installment. *Waivers:* senior citizens.

Financial Aid Of all full-time matriculated undergraduates who enrolled in 2008, 9,114 applied for aid, 8,552 were judged to have need. *Average percent of need met:* 85%. *Average financial aid package:* $10,150. *Average need-based loan:* $3500. *Average need-based gift aid:* $3175. *Average indebtedness upon graduation:* $47,250.

Applying *Application fee:* $65. *Required:* high school transcript, minimum 2 GPA, high school diploma and minimum SAT score of 1100. *Application deadlines:* 5/31 (freshmen), rolling (transfers). *Notification:* continuous until 1/15 (freshmen), continuous (transfers).

Freshman Application Contact John Jay College of Criminal Justice of the City University of New York, 899 Tenth Avenue, New York, NY 10019-1093. *Phone:* 212-237-8878. *Toll-free phone:* 877-JOHNJAY. *Web site:* http://www.jjay.cuny.edu/.

The Juilliard School
New York, New York

- **Independent** comprehensive, founded 1905
- **Urban** campus
- **Coed** 649 undergraduate students, 79% full-time, 47% women, 53% men
- **Most difficult** entrance level, 8% of applicants were admitted

Undergraduates 510 full-time, 139 part-time. 84% are from out of state; 6% Black or African American, non-Hispanic/Latino; 5% Hispanic/Latino; 14% Asian, non-Hispanic/Latino; 7% Two or more races, non-Hispanic/Latino; 3% Race/ethnicity unknown; 22% international; 3% transferred in; 56% live on campus.

Freshmen *Admission:* 2,416 applied, 183 admitted, 131 enrolled.

Faculty *Total:* 299, 40% full-time. *Student/faculty ratio:* 5:1.

Academics *Calendar:* semesters. *Degrees:* diplomas, bachelor's, master's, doctoral-other, and post-master's certificates. *Special study options:* adult/continuing education programs, off-campus study. *Unusual degree programs:* 3-2 music/liberal arts with Columbia University.

Computers on Campus Campuswide network is available.

Student Life *Housing:* on-campus residence required for freshman year. *Options:* coed. Campus housing is university owned. Freshman campus housing is guaranteed. *Campus security:* 24-hour emergency response devices and patrols, controlled dormitory access, electronically operated main building entrances. *Student services:* health clinic, personal/psychological counseling, legal services.

Costs (2010–11) *Comprehensive fee:* $44,460 includes full-time tuition ($32,180) and room and board ($12,280). *Room and board:* Room and board charges vary according to housing facility. *Payment plan:* installment. *Waivers:* employees or children of employees.

Financial Aid Of all full-time matriculated undergraduates who enrolled in 2009, 449 applied for aid, 395 were judged to have need, 95 had their need fully met. In 2009, 27 non-need-based awards were made. *Average percent of need met:* 77%. *Average financial aid package:* $24,344. *Average need-based loan:* $4780. *Average need-based gift aid:* $23,290. *Average non-need-based aid:* $14,500. *Average indebtedness upon graduation:* $26,780. *Financial aid deadline:* 3/1.

Applying *Options:* electronic application. *Application fee:* $100. *Required:* essay or personal statement, high school transcript, audition. *Application deadlines:* 12/1 (freshmen), 12/1 (transfers). *Notification:* 4/1 (freshmen), 4/1 (transfers).

Freshman Application Contact Ms. Lee Cioppa, Associate Dean for Admissions, The Juilliard School, 60 Lincoln Center Plaza, New York, NY 10023-6588. *Phone:* 212-799-5000. *Fax:* 212-724-0263. *E-mail:* admissions@juilliard.edu. *Web site:* http://www.juilliard.edu/.

Kehilath Yakov Rabbinical Seminary
Ossining, New York

Director of Admissions Admissions Officer, Kehilath Yakov Rabbinical Seminary, 340 Illington Road, Ossining, NY 10562. *Phone:* 718-963-1212.

Keuka College
Keuka Park, New York

- **Independent** comprehensive, founded 1890, affiliated with American Baptist Churches in the U.S.A.
- **Rural** 173-acre campus with easy access to Rochester
- **Endowment** $5.8 million
- **Coed** 1,627 undergraduate students, 81% full-time, 76% women, 24% men
- **Moderately difficult** entrance level, 74% of applicants were admitted

Undergraduates 1,318 full-time, 309 part-time. Students come from 22 states and territories; 4 other countries; 6% are from out of state; 7% Black or African American, non-Hispanic/Latino; 3% Hispanic/Latino; 0.7% Asian, non-Hispanic/Latino; 0.7% American Indian or Alaska Native, non-Hispanic/Latino; 0.3% Two or more races, non-Hispanic/Latino; 9% Race/ethnicity unknown; 2% international; 5% transferred in; 81% live on campus. *Retention:* 68% of full-time freshmen returned.

Freshmen *Admission:* 791 applied, 586 admitted, 268 enrolled. *Average high school GPA:* 3.1. *Test scores:* SAT critical reading scores over 500: 31%; SAT math scores over 500: 40%; SAT writing scores over 500: 30%; ACT scores over 18: 72%; SAT critical reading scores over 600: 6%; SAT math scores over 600: 7%; SAT writing scores over 600: 5%; ACT scores over 24: 24%; SAT critical reading scores over 700: 1%; ACT scores over 30: 1%.

Faculty *Total:* 223, 35% full-time, 46% with terminal degrees. *Student/faculty ratio:* 14:1.

Academics *Calendar:* 4-1-4. *Degrees:* bachelor's and master's. *Special study options:* academic remediation for entering students, accelerated degree program, adult/continuing education programs, advanced placement credit, coop-erative education, double majors, independent study, internships, off-campus study, part-time degree program, services for LD students, student-designed majors, study abroad, summer session for credit. *Unusual degree programs:* 3-2 occupational therapy.

Computers on Campus 256 computers/terminals are available on campus for general student use. Campuswide network is available.

Student Life *Housing options:* coed, women-only, cooperative. Campus housing is university owned. Freshman campus housing is guaranteed. *Activities and organizations:* drama/theater group, student-run newspaper, radio station, choral group, Student Senate, Campus Activities Board, OTTERS (occupational therapy club), Education Club, BAKU. *Campus security:* 24-hour emergency response devices and patrols, late-night transport/escort service. *Student services:* health clinic, personal/psychological counseling.

Athletics Member NCAA. All Division III. *Intercollegiate sports:* baseball M, basketball M/W, cross-country running M/W, golf W, lacrosse M, soccer M/W, softball W, swimming and diving W, track and field M, volleyball W. *Intramural sports:* badminton M/W, basketball M/W, cheerleading M/W, crew M/W, lacrosse W, skiing (cross-country) M/W, skiing (downhill) M/W, soccer M/W, softball M/W, table tennis M/W, tennis M/W, volleyball W, water polo M/W.

Standardized Tests *Recommended:* SAT or ACT (for admission).

Costs (2010–11) *Comprehensive fee:* $33,270 includes full-time tuition ($23,130), mandatory fees ($640), and room and board ($9500). Full-time tuition and fees vary according to program. Part-time tuition: $770 per credit hour. Part-time tuition and fees vary according to program. *College room only:* $4510. Room and board charges vary according to board plan and housing facility. *Payment plan:* installment. *Waivers:* employees or children of employees.

Financial Aid Of all full-time matriculated undergraduates who enrolled in 2009, 1,351 applied for aid, 1,246 were judged to have need, 141 had their need fully met. In 2009, 74 non-need-based awards were made. *Average percent of need met:* 70%. *Average financial aid package:* $15,766. *Average need-based loan:* $5383. *Average need-based gift aid:* $11,695. *Average non-need-based aid:* $10,087. *Average indebtedness upon graduation:* $13,874.

Applying *Options:* electronic application, early admission, deferred entrance. *Application fee:* $30. *Required:* essay or personal statement, high school transcript, 1 letter of recommendation. *Required for some:* interview. *Recommended:* minimum 2.75 GPA, interview. *Application deadlines:* rolling (freshmen), rolling (transfers).

Freshman Application Contact Fred Hoyle, Associate Vice President of Admissions, Keuka College, Wagner House, Keuka Park, NY 14478. *Phone:* 315-279-5254. *Toll-free phone:* 800-33-KEUKA. *Fax:* 315-279-5386. *E-mail:* admissions@mail.keuka.edu. *Web site:* http://www.keuka.edu/.

The King's College
New York, New York

- **Independent** nondenominational 4-year, founded 1939
- **Urban** campus
- **Endowment** $689,657
- **Coed** 384 undergraduate students, 99% full-time, 62% women, 38% men
- **Moderately difficult** entrance level, 67% of applicants were admitted

Undergraduates 379 full-time, 5 part-time. Students come from 42 states and territories; 7 other countries; 90% are from out of state; 4% Black or African American, non-Hispanic/Latino; 6% Hispanic/Latino; 3% Asian, non-Hispanic/Latino; 7% Two or more races, non-Hispanic/Latino; 5% Race/ethnicity unknown; 2% international; 13% transferred in; 93% live on campus. *Retention:* 61% of full-time freshmen returned.

Freshmen *Admission:* 1,719 applied, 1,144 admitted, 155 enrolled. *Average high school GPA:* 3.66. *Test scores:* SAT critical reading scores over 500: 97%; SAT math scores over 500: 82%; SAT writing scores over 500: 95%; ACT scores over 18: 100%; SAT critical reading scores over 600: 66%; SAT math scores over 600: 38%; SAT writing scores over 600: 58%; ACT scores over 24: 87%; SAT critical reading scores over 700: 22%; SAT math scores over 700: 8%; SAT writing scores over 700: 15%; ACT scores over 30: 27%.

Faculty *Total:* 37, 57% full-time, 70% with terminal degrees. *Student/faculty ratio:* 14:1.

Academics *Calendar:* semesters. *Degree:* bachelor's. *Special study options:* advanced placement credit, distance learning, independent study, internships, summer session for credit.

Computers on Campus 20 computers/terminals are available on campus for general student use. Students can access the following: computer help desk, free student e-mail accounts, online (class) grades, online (class) registration, online (class) schedules. Campuswide network is available. 100% of college-owned or -operated housing units are wired for high-speed Internet access. Wireless service is available via entire campus.

Student Life *Housing options:* men-only, women-only. Campus housing is leased by the school. *Activities and organizations:* drama/theater group, student-run newspaper, choral group, King's Debate Society, King's Theater,

PROFILES

sports clubs, King's Dancers, The Tent. *Campus security:* 24-hour emergency response devices. *Student services:* personal/psychological counseling.
Athletics *Intercollegiate sports:* baseball M(c), basketball M(c)/W(c), cross-country running M(c)/W(c), soccer M(c)/W(c), volleyball W(c). *Intramural sports:* basketball M/W, softball M/W, ultimate Frisbee M/W.
Standardized Tests *Required:* SAT or ACT (for admission).
Costs (2011–12) *Tuition:* $28,890 full-time, $1204 per credit hour part-time. Full-time tuition and fees vary according to course load. Part-time tuition and fees vary according to course load. *Required fees:* $350 full-time, $350 per year part-time. *Room only:* $11,050. *Payment plans:* installment, deferred payment. *Waivers:* employees or children of employees.
Financial Aid Of all full-time matriculated undergraduates who enrolled in 2009, 236 applied for aid, 203 were judged to have need, 33 had their need fully met. 14 Federal Work-Study jobs (averaging $750). In 2009, 83 non-need-based awards were made. *Average percent of need met:* 71%. *Average financial aid package:* $20,902. *Average need-based loan:* $4269. *Average need-based gift aid:* $17,159. *Average non-need-based aid:* $11,993. *Average indebtedness upon graduation:* $15,434.
Applying *Options:* electronic application, early action, deferred entrance. *Application fee:* $30. *Required:* high school transcript. *Recommended:* high school transcript, minimum 3 GPA, interview. *Application deadlines:* rolling (freshmen), rolling (out-of-state freshmen), rolling (transfers), 11/15 (early action). *Notification:* continuous (freshmen), continuous (out-of-state freshmen), continuous (transfers), 12/15 (early action).
Freshman Application Contact The King's College, 350 Fifth Avenue, 15th Floor Empire State Building, New York, NY 10118. *Phone:* 212-659-7217. *Toll-free phone:* 888-969-7200 Ext. 3610. *Web site:* http://www.tkc.edu/.

Kol Yaakov Torah Center

Monsey, New York

Freshman Application Contact Assistant Director of Admissions, Kol Yaakov Torah Center, 29 West Maple Avenue, Monsey, NY 10952-2954. *Phone:* 914-425-3871. *E-mail:* horizonss@aol.com. *Web site:* http://horizons.edu/.

Lehman College of the City University of New York

Bronx, New York

- **State and locally supported** comprehensive, founded 1931, part of City University of New York System
- **Urban** 37-acre campus
- **Endowment** $7.6 million
- **Coed** 9,841 undergraduate students, 59% full-time, 69% women, 31% men
- **Moderately difficult** entrance level, 24% of applicants were admitted

Undergraduates 5,841 full-time, 4,000 part-time. Students come from 5 states and territories; 130 other countries; 1% are from out of state; 29% Black or African American, non-Hispanic/Latino; 52% Hispanic/Latino; 6% Asian, non-Hispanic/Latino; 4% international; 12% transferred in. *Retention:* 80% of full-time freshmen returned.
Freshmen *Admission:* 14,934 applied, 3,578 admitted, 641 enrolled. *Test scores:* SAT critical reading scores over 500: 47%; SAT math scores over 500: 62%; SAT writing scores over 500: 46%; SAT critical reading scores over 600: 10%; SAT math scores over 600: 9%; SAT writing scores over 600: 9%; SAT critical reading scores over 700: 1%.
Faculty *Total:* 900, 43% full-time, 41% with terminal degrees. *Student/faculty ratio:* 13:1.
Academics *Calendar:* semesters. *Degrees:* certificates, bachelor's, master's, and post-master's certificates. *Special study options:* adult/continuing education programs, advanced placement credit, cooperative education, distance learning, double majors, English as a second language, freshman honors college, honors programs, independent study, internships, off-campus study, part-time degree program, services for LD students, student-designed majors, study abroad, summer session for credit. *ROTC:* Army (c). *Unusual degree programs:* 3-2 mathematics.
Computers on Campus 800 computers/terminals are available on campus for general student use. Students can access the following: campus intranet, computer help desk, free student e-mail accounts, online (class) grades, online (class) registration, online (class) schedules. Campuswide network is available. Wireless service is available via entire campus.
Student Life *Housing options:* Campus housing is university owned. *Activities and organizations:* drama/theater group, student-run newspaper, radio and television station, choral group, Club Mac, African Students Association, Dominican Student Association, The Sociology Club, Club Live. *Campus security:* 24-hour emergency response devices and patrols, student patrols, late-night transport/escort service. *Student services:* health clinic, personal/psychological counseling, women's center.

Athletics Member NCAA. All Division III. *Intercollegiate sports:* baseball M, basketball M/W, cross-country running M/W, racquetball M/W, soccer M/W, softball M/W, swimming and diving M/W, table tennis M/W, tennis M/W, track and field M/W, volleyball M/W, water polo M, wrestling M. *Intramural sports:* badminton M/W, baseball M/W, basketball M/W, cross-country running M/W, racquetball M/W, soccer M, softball M/W, swimming and diving M/W, tennis M/W, volleyball M/W, wrestling M.
Standardized Tests *Required:* SAT or ACT (for admission).
Costs (2011–12) *Tuition:* state resident $4830 full-time, $205 per credit part-time; nonresident $13,050 full-time, $435 per credit part-time. *Required fees:* $378 full-time.
Financial Aid Of all full-time matriculated undergraduates who enrolled in 2008, 4,993 applied for aid, 4,993 were judged to have need, 118 had their need fully met. 1,796 Federal Work-Study jobs (averaging $1394). In 2008, 173 non-need-based awards were made. *Average percent of need met:* 65%. *Average financial aid package:* $4118. *Average need-based loan:* $1875. *Average need-based gift aid:* $1860. *Average non-need-based aid:* $1329. *Average indebtedness upon graduation:* $13,700.
Applying *Options:* deferred entrance. *Application fee:* $65. *Required:* high school transcript, minimum 3 GPA. *Required for some:* essay or personal statement, interview. *Application deadlines:* rolling (freshmen), rolling (transfers). *Notification:* continuous (freshmen), continuous (transfers).
Freshman Application Contact Ms. Laurie Austin, Director of Admissions, Lehman College of the City University of New York, 250 Bedford Park Boulevard West, Bronx, NY 10468. *Phone:* 718-960-8706. *Toll-free phone:* 877-Lehman1. *Fax:* 718-960-8712. *E-mail:* enroll@lehman.cuny.edu. *Web site:* http://www.lehman.cuny.edu/.

Le Moyne College

Syracuse, New York

- **Independent Roman Catholic (Jesuit)** comprehensive, founded 1946
- **Suburban** 161-acre campus
- **Endowment** $97.8 million
- **Coed** 2,786 undergraduate students, 85% full-time, 62% women, 38% men
- **Moderately difficult** entrance level, 64% of applicants were admitted

Undergraduates 2,361 full-time, 425 part-time. Students come from 29 states and territories; 30 other countries; 6% are from out of state; 4% Black or African American, non-Hispanic/Latino; 5% Hispanic/Latino; 2% Asian, non-Hispanic/Latino; 0.6% American Indian or Alaska Native, non-Hispanic/Latino; 0.9% Two or more races, non-Hispanic/Latino; 4% Race/ethnicity unknown; 0.5% international; 6% transferred in; 57% live on campus. *Retention:* 82% of full-time freshmen returned.
Freshmen *Admission:* 4,851 applied, 3,102 admitted, 618 enrolled. *Average high school GPA:* 3.38. *Test scores:* SAT critical reading scores over 500: 71%; SAT math scores over 500: 78%; ACT scores over 18: 96%; SAT critical reading scores over 600: 23%; SAT math scores over 600: 27%; ACT scores over 24: 39%; SAT critical reading scores over 700: 3%; SAT math scores over 700: 2%; ACT scores over 30: 5%.
Faculty *Total:* 353, 44% full-time, 60% with terminal degrees. *Student/faculty ratio:* 13:1.
Academics *Calendar:* semesters. *Degrees:* bachelor's, master's, and post-master's certificates. *Special study options:* academic remediation for entering students, accelerated degree program, adult/continuing education programs, advanced placement credit, double majors, honors programs, independent study, internships, off-campus study, part-time degree program, services for LD students, study abroad, summer session for credit. *ROTC:* Army (c), Air Force (c). *Unusual degree programs:* 3-2 engineering with Manhattan College, Clarkson University, University of Detroit Mercy, Syracuse University.
Computers on Campus 350 computers/terminals and 350 ports are available on campus for general student use. Students can access the following: campus intranet, computer help desk, free student e-mail accounts, online (class) grades, online (class) registration, online (class) schedules, ECHO (campus-wide portal). Campuswide network is available. 100% of college-owned or -operated housing units are wired for high-speed Internet access. Wireless service is available via classrooms, computer centers, computer labs, dorm rooms, learning centers, libraries, student centers.
Student Life *Housing:* on-campus residence required through senior year. *Options:* coed, men-only, women-only, disabled students. Campus housing is university owned. Freshman campus housing is guaranteed. *Activities and organizations:* drama/theater group, student-run newspaper, radio and television station, choral group, Student Programming Board, Outing Club, performing arts groups, Student Dancers, New Student Orientation Committee. *Campus security:* 24-hour emergency response devices and patrols, late-night transport/escort service, controlled dormitory access, lighted pathways, closed-circuit security cameras, and emergency code blue phones. *Student services:* health clinic, personal/psychological counseling.
Athletics Member NCAA. All Division II except baseball (Division I). *Intercollegiate sports:* baseball M(s), basketball M(s)/W(s), cross-country running

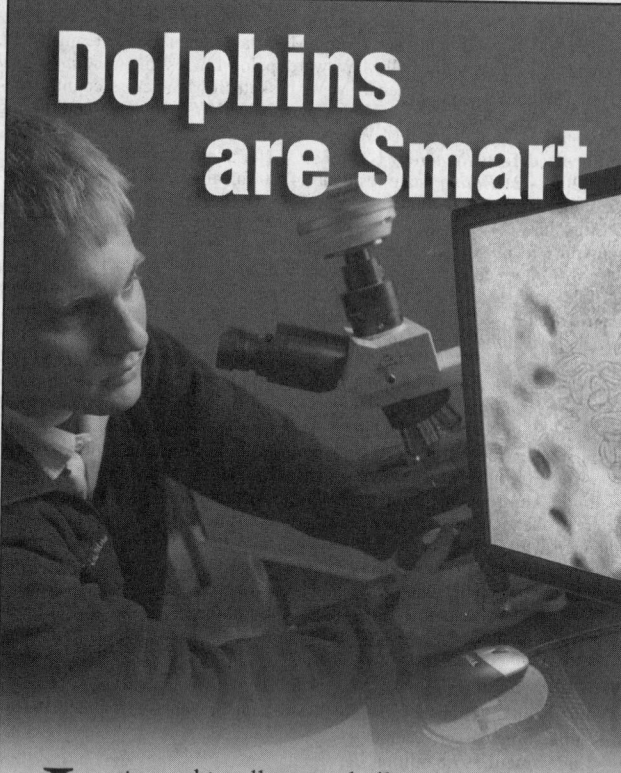

Dolphins are Smart

Inquiry and intelligence, hallmarks of Jesuit education, are traits embodied by Le Moyne College students. With incredible new facilities, top-notch faculty and a close-knit campus community, Le Moyne seeks to develop the whole person by supporting living and learning together, centered around a commitment to make our world a better place.

Le Moyne is nationally acclaimed as one of the best colleges in America, including ranking in the top 1 percent of the nation's masters universities by *Washington Monthly* Magazine and 19 consecutive years of recognition for academic quality and value by *U.S.News & World Report*.

This is the most exciting time in Le Moyne's history — and our best is yet to come.

LE MOYNE

SPIRIT. INQUIRY. LEADERSHIP. *JESUIT*.

To arrange for a campus visit, contact us at (800) 333-4733 or admission@lemoyne.edu.

M(s)/W(s), golf M(s)/W(s), lacrosse M(s)/W(s), soccer M(s)/W(s), softball W(s), swimming and diving M/W, tennis M(s)/W(s), volleyball W(s). *Intramural sports:* basketball M/W, field hockey W(c), football M, ice hockey M(c), racquetball M/W, rugby M(c)/W(c), soccer M/W, softball M/W, volleyball M/W.

Standardized Tests *Required:* SAT or ACT (for admission).

Costs (2011–12) *Comprehensive fee:* $39,270 includes full-time tuition ($27,390), mandatory fees ($990), and room and board ($10,890). Part-time tuition: $574 per credit hour. Part-time tuition and fees vary according to class time. *College room only:* $6910. Room and board charges vary according to board plan and housing facility. *Payment plans:* installment, deferred payment. *Waivers:* employees or children of employees.

Financial Aid Of all full-time matriculated undergraduates who enrolled in 2008, 2,134 applied for aid, 1,983 were judged to have need, 501 had their need fully met. 357 Federal Work-Study jobs (averaging $995). 512 state and other part-time jobs (averaging $985). In 2008, 195 non-need-based awards were made. *Average percent of need met:* 76%. *Average financial aid package:* $20,065. *Average need-based loan:* $4499. *Average need-based gift aid:* $15,652. *Average non-need-based aid:* $5414. *Average indebtedness upon graduation:* $25,587.

Applying *Options:* electronic application, early admission, deferred entrance. *Application fee:* $35. *Required:* essay or personal statement, high school transcript, 2 letters of recommendation. *Recommended:* interview. *Application deadlines:* 2/1 (freshmen), 6/1 (transfers). *Notification:* continuous until 12/1 (freshmen), continuous (transfers).

Freshman Application Contact Mr. Dennis J. Nicholson, Dean of Admission, Le Moyne College, 1419 Salt Springs Road, Syracuse, NY 13214-1301. *Phone:* 315-445-4300. *Toll-free phone:* 800-333-4733. *Fax:* 315-445-4711. *E-mail:* admission@lemoyne.edu. *Web site:* http://www.lemoyne.edu/.

See page 1378 for the College Close-Up.

LIM College
New York, New York

- **Proprietary** comprehensive, founded 1939
- **Urban** campus with easy access to New York City
- **Coed, primarily women**
- **Moderately difficult** entrance level

Faculty *Student/faculty ratio:* 18:1.

Academics *Calendar:* semesters. *Degrees:* associate, bachelor's, and master's.

Student Life *Campus security:* controlled dormitory access.

Standardized Tests *Required:* SAT or ACT (for admission).

Costs (2010–11) *Comprehensive fee:* $41,350 includes full-time tuition ($20,900), mandatory fees ($575), and room and board ($19,875). Part-time tuition: $695 per credit hour. *Required fees:* $138 per term part-time. *College room only:* $15,875. Room and board charges vary according to board plan.

Financial Aid Of all full-time matriculated undergraduates who enrolled in 2006, 798 applied for aid, 597 were judged to have need. 40 Federal Work-Study jobs (averaging $1640). In 2006, 98 non-need-based awards were made. *Average financial aid package:* $7326. *Average need-based loan:* $3666. *Average need-based gift aid:* $5182. *Average non-need-based aid:* $2746. *Average indebtedness upon graduation:* $19,593.

Applying *Options:* electronic application, early action, deferred entrance. *Application fee:* $40. *Required:* essay or personal statement, high school transcript, 2 letters of recommendation, interview. *Recommended:* minimum 2.5 GPA.

Freshman Application Contact Ms. Kristina Ortiz, Assistant Dean of Admissions, LIM College, 12 East 53rd Street, New York, NY 10022. *Phone:* 212-752-1530 Ext. 217. *Toll-free phone:* 800-677-1323. *Fax:* 212-317-8602. *E-mail:* admissions@limcollege.edu. *Web site:* http://www.limcollege.edu/.

See page 1384 for the College Close-Up.

Long Island University, Brentwood Campus
Brentwood, New York

- **Independent** upper-level, founded 1959, part of Long Island University
- **Suburban** 172-acre campus with easy access to Manhattan
- **Coed** 29 undergraduate students, 41% full-time, 52% women, 48% men

Undergraduates 12 full-time, 17 part-time. Students come from 1 other state; 21% Black or African American, non-Hispanic/Latino; 10% Hispanic/Latino; 10% Race/ethnicity unknown; 17% transferred in.

Faculty *Total:* 75, 27% full-time, 91% with terminal degrees. *Student/faculty ratio:* 6:1.

Academics *Calendar:* semesters. *Degrees:* bachelor's, master's, and post-master's certificates. *Special study options:* advanced placement credit, independent study, internships, part-time degree program, services for LD students, summer session for credit.

Computers on Campus 50 computers/terminals and 80 ports are available on campus for general student use. Students can access the following: campus intranet, computer help desk, free student e-mail accounts, online (class) grades, online (class) registration, online (class) schedules. Campuswide network is available. Wireless service is available via entire campus.

Student Life *Housing:* college housing not available. *Campus security:* evening security guards.

Costs (2011–12) *Tuition:* $30,002 full-time, $936 per credit part-time. Full-time tuition and fees vary according to course load. Part-time tuition and fees vary according to course load. *Required fees:* $1500 full-time, $375 per term part-time. *Payment plan:* installment. *Waivers:* senior citizens and employees or children of employees.

Applying *Options:* electronic application. *Application fee:* $30. *Application deadline:* rolling (transfers). *Notification:* continuous (transfers).

Application Contact Long Island University, Brentwood Campus, 100 Second Avenue, Brentwood, NY 11717. *Phone:* 631-273-5112 Ext. 202. *Web site:* http://www.liu.edu/.

Long Island University, Brooklyn Campus

Brooklyn, New York

- **Independent** university, founded 1926, part of Long Island University
- **Urban** 10-acre campus
- **Coed** 5,126 undergraduate students, 84% full-time, 72% women, 28% men
- **Minimally difficult** entrance level, 72% of applicants were admitted

Undergraduates 4,287 full-time, 839 part-time. Students come from 42 states and territories; 20% are from out of state; 12% transferred in; 25% live on campus. *Retention:* 64% of full-time freshmen returned.

Freshmen *Admission:* 4,420 applied, 3,189 admitted, 935 enrolled. *Average high school GPA:* 2.8. *Test scores:* SAT critical reading scores over 500: 23%; SAT math scores over 500: 35%; SAT critical reading scores over 600: 3%; SAT math scores over 600: 12%; SAT critical reading scores over 700: 1%; SAT math scores over 700: 1%.

Faculty *Total:* 816, 38% full-time. *Student/faculty ratio:* 14:1.

Academics *Calendar:* semesters. *Degrees:* associate, bachelor's, master's, doctoral-other, doctoral-professional, doctoral-research/scholarship, post-master's, and postbachelor's certificates. *Special study options:* academic remediation for entering students, accelerated degree program, advanced placement credit, cooperative education, double majors, English as a second language, honors programs, independent study, internships, services for LD students, student-designed majors, study abroad, summer session for credit. *Unusual degree programs:* 3-2 physical therapy, pharmacy.

Computers on Campus Students can access the following: campus intranet, computer help desk, free student e-mail accounts, online (class) grades, online (class) registration, online (class) schedules. Campuswide network is available. 100% of college-owned or -operated housing units are wired for high-speed Internet access. Wireless service is available via entire campus.

Student Life *Housing options:* coed, disabled students. Campus housing is university owned. Freshman applicants given priority for college housing. *Activities and organizations:* drama/theater group, student-run newspaper, radio and television station, choral group, The Student Government Association, The American Pharmacists Association - Academy of Student Pharmacists, Hillel Jewish Students Organization, Student Activities Board, The Society of Health Systems Pharmacists, national fraternities, national sororities. *Campus security:* 24-hour emergency response devices and patrols. *Student services:* health clinic, personal/psychological counseling.

Athletics Member NCAA. All Division I. *Intercollegiate sports:* baseball M(s), basketball M(s)/W(s), cross-country running M(s)/W(s), golf M(s)/W(s), lacrosse W(s), soccer M(s)/W(s), softball W(s), tennis W(s), track and field M(s)/W(s), volleyball W(s).

Standardized Tests *Required for some:* SAT or ACT (for admission).

Costs (2011–12) *Tuition:* $896 per credit part-time. Full-time tuition and fees vary according to program. Part-time tuition and fees vary according to program. *Room only:* Room and board charges vary according to board plan, gender, and housing facility. *Payment plans:* installment, deferred payment. *Waivers:* employees or children of employees.

Financial Aid Of all full-time matriculated undergraduates who enrolled in 2009, 3,893 applied for aid, 3,659 were judged to have need, 1,584 had their need fully met. In 2009, 210 non-need-based awards were made. *Average percent of need met:* 45%. *Average financial aid package:* $15,300. *Average need-based loan:* $4700. *Average need-based gift aid:* $11,300. *Average non-need-based aid:* $22,100. *Average indebtedness upon graduation:* $41,000.

Applying *Options:* electronic application, deferred entrance. *Application fee:* $30. *Required:* high school transcript, minimum 2 GPA. *Required for some:*

essay or personal statement, minimum 3 GPA, interview. *Recommended:* minimum 2.5 GPA. *Application deadlines:* rolling (freshmen), rolling (transfers).

Freshman Application Contact Elizabeth Storinge, Dean of Admissions, Long Island University, Brooklyn Campus, 1 University Plaza, Brooklyn, NY 11201. *Phone:* 718-488-1011. *Toll-free phone:* 800-LIU-PLAN. *E-mail:* admissions@brooklyn.liu.edu. *Web site:* http://www.liu.edu/.

Long Island University, C.W. Post Campus

Brookville, New York

- **Independent** comprehensive, founded 1954, part of Long Island University
- **Suburban** 308-acre campus with easy access to New York City
- **Coed** 7,957 undergraduate students, 51% full-time, 70% women, 30% men
- **Moderately difficult** entrance level, 82% of applicants were admitted

Undergraduates 4,053 full-time, 3,904 part-time. Students come from 50 states and territories; 10 other countries; 7% are from out of state; 7% transferred in; 20% live on campus. *Retention:* 76% of full-time freshmen returned.

Freshmen *Admission:* 6,555 applied, 5,385 admitted, 894 enrolled. *Average high school GPA:* 2.9. *Test scores:* SAT critical reading scores over 500: 43%; SAT math scores over 500: 51%; ACT scores over 18: 87%; SAT critical reading scores over 600: 8%; SAT math scores over 600: 12%; ACT scores over 24: 24%; SAT critical reading scores over 700: 1%; SAT math scores over 700: 1%; ACT scores over 30: 1%.

Faculty *Total:* 822, 37% full-time. *Student/faculty ratio:* 13:1.

Academics *Calendar:* semesters. *Degrees:* associate, bachelor's, master's, doctoral-other, doctoral-professional, post-master's, and postbachelor's certificates. *Special study options:* academic remediation for entering students, accelerated degree program, advanced placement credit, cooperative education, double majors, English as a second language, honors programs, independent study, internships, off-campus study, part-time degree program, services for LD students, student-designed majors, study abroad, summer session for credit. *ROTC:* Army (c), Air Force (c). *Unusual degree programs:* 3-2 respiratory therapy and pharmacy with Long Island University, Brooklyn Campus.

Computers on Campus 357 computers/terminals are available on campus for general student use. Students can access the following: campus intranet, computer help desk, free student e-mail accounts, online (class) grades, online (class) registration, online (class) schedules. Campuswide network is available. 100% of college-owned or -operated housing units are wired for high-speed Internet access. Wireless service is available via entire campus.

Student Life *Housing options:* coed. Campus housing is university owned. Freshman campus housing is guaranteed. *Activities and organizations:* drama/theater group, student-run newspaper, radio and television station, choral group, Student Government Association, Association for Campus Programming, African People's Organization, Resident Student Association, Post TV and Newman, national fraternities, national sororities. *Campus security:* 24-hour emergency response devices and patrols, late-night transport/escort service, controlled dormitory access. *Student services:* health clinic, personal/psychological counseling.

Athletics Member NCAA. All Division II. *Intercollegiate sports:* baseball M(s), basketball M(s)/W(s), crew M(c)/W(c), cross-country running M(s)/W(s), equestrian sports M(c)/W(c), field hockey W(s), football M(s), lacrosse M(s)/W(s), soccer M(s)/W(s), softball W(s), swimming and diving W(s), tennis W(s), volleyball W(s).

Standardized Tests *Required:* SAT or ACT (for admission).

Costs (2010–11) *Comprehensive fee:* $41,190 includes full-time tuition ($28,710), mandatory fees ($1500), and room and board ($10,980). Part-time tuition: $896 per credit. *Required fees:* $405 per term part-time. *College room only:* $7180. Room and board charges vary according to board plan and housing facility. *Payment plans:* installment, deferred payment. *Waivers:* employees or children of employees.

Financial Aid Of all full-time matriculated undergraduates who enrolled in 2009, 3,347 applied for aid, 2,744 were judged to have need, 399 had their need fully met. In 2009, 565 non-need-based awards were made. *Average percent of need met:* 75%. *Average financial aid package:* $14,500. *Average need-based loan:* $5350. *Average need-based gift aid:* $5800. *Average non-need-based aid:* $6950. *Financial aid deadline:* 3/1.

Applying *Options:* deferred entrance. *Application fee:* $30. *Required:* essay or personal statement, high school transcript, minimum 2.5 GPA. *Required for some:* interview. *Application deadlines:* rolling (freshmen), rolling (transfers). *Notification:* continuous (freshmen), continuous (transfers).

Freshman Application Contact Ms. Joanne Graziano, Executive Director of Admissions and Recruitment, Long Island University, C.W. Post Campus, 720 Northern Boulevard, Brookville, NY 11548-1300. *Phone:* 516-299-2900. *Toll-free phone:* 800-LIU-PLAN. *Fax:* 516-299-2137. *E-mail:* enroll@cwpost.liu.edu. *Web site:* http://www.liu.edu/.

Machzikei Hadath Rabbinical College
Brooklyn, New York

Director of Admissions Rabbi Abraham M. Lezerowitz, Director of Admissions, Machzikei Hadath Rabbinical College, 5407 Sixteenth Avenue, Brooklyn, NY 11204-1805. *Phone:* 718-854-8777.

Manhattan College
Riverdale, New York

- **Independent** comprehensive, founded 1853, affiliated with Roman Catholic Church
- **Urban** 31-acre campus with easy access to New York City
- **Endowment** $55.4 million
- **Coed** 3,002 undergraduate students, 97% full-time, 46% women, 54% men
- **Moderately difficult** entrance level, 63% of applicants were admitted

Undergraduates 2,913 full-time, 89 part-time. Students come from 35 states and territories; 22 other countries; 27% are from out of state; 3% Black or African American, non-Hispanic/Latino; 12% Hispanic/Latino; 3% Asian, non-Hispanic/Latino; 2% Two or more races, non-Hispanic/Latino; 10% Race/ethnicity unknown; 2% international; 5% transferred in; 60% live on campus. *Retention:* 83% of full-time freshmen returned.

Freshmen *Admission:* 5,766 applied, 3,645 admitted, 660 enrolled. *Average high school GPA:* 3.3. *Test scores:* SAT critical reading scores over 500: 70%; SAT math scores over 500: 80%; ACT scores over 18: 96%; SAT critical reading scores over 600: 18%; SAT math scores over 600: 31%; ACT scores over 24: 53%; SAT critical reading scores over 700: 2%; SAT math scores over 700: 3%; ACT scores over 30: 4%.

Faculty *Total:* 383, 52% full-time, 70% with terminal degrees. *Student/faculty ratio:* 12:1.

Academics *Calendar:* semesters. *Degrees:* bachelor's, master's, and post-master's certificates. *Special study options:* accelerated degree program, adult/continuing education programs, advanced placement credit, cooperative education, distance learning, double majors, English as a second language, honors programs, independent study, internships, off-campus study, part-time degree program, services for LD students, student-designed majors, study abroad, summer session for credit. *ROTC:* Army (c), Air Force (b). *Unusual degree programs:* business administration; engineering; Education.

Computers on Campus 350 computers/terminals and 600 ports are available on campus for general student use. Students can access the following: campus intranet, computer help desk, free student e-mail accounts, online (class) grades, online (class) registration, online (class) schedules, course management system. Campuswide network is available. 100% of college-owned or -operated housing units are wired for high-speed Internet access. Wireless service is available via entire campus.

Student Life *Housing options:* coed, disabled students. Campus housing is university owned. Freshman campus housing is guaranteed. *Activities and organizations:* drama/theater group, student-run newspaper, radio station, choral group, marching band, Society of Hispanic Professional Engineers, Gaelic Society, Student Government, LaSallian Collegians (Community Service Group), Manhattan College Players (Theater/Drama group_, national fraternities, national sororities. *Campus security:* 24-hour emergency response devices and patrols, late-night transport/escort service, controlled dormitory access. *Student services:* health clinic, personal/psychological counseling.

Athletics Member NCAA. All Division I. *Intercollegiate sports:* baseball M(s), basketball M(s)/W(s), cheerleading M/W, crew M(c)/W(c), cross-country running M(s)/W(s), golf M(s), lacrosse M(s)/W(s), rugby M(c), soccer M(s)/W(s), softball W(s), swimming and diving M(s)/W(s), tennis W(s), track and field M(s)/W(s), volleyball W(s). *Intramural sports:* baseball M, basketball M/W, cross-country running M/W, equestrian sports M/W, soccer M/W, softball M/W, swimming and diving W, track and field M/W, volleyball M/W.

Standardized Tests *Required:* SAT or ACT (for admission).

Costs (2011–12) *Comprehensive fee:* $41,220 includes full-time tuition ($27,600), mandatory fees ($2200), and room and board ($11,420). Full-time tuition and fees vary according to course load, program, and student level. Part-time tuition: $780 per credit. Part-time tuition and fees vary according to course load. *Room and board:* Room and board charges vary according to board plan. *Payment plans:* installment, deferred payment. *Waivers:* employees or children of employees.

Financial Aid Of all full-time matriculated undergraduates who enrolled in 2009, 2,342 applied for aid, 2,021 were judged to have need, 311 had their need fully met. In 2009, 330 non-need-based awards were made. *Average percent of need met:* 67%. *Average financial aid package:* $17,995. *Average*

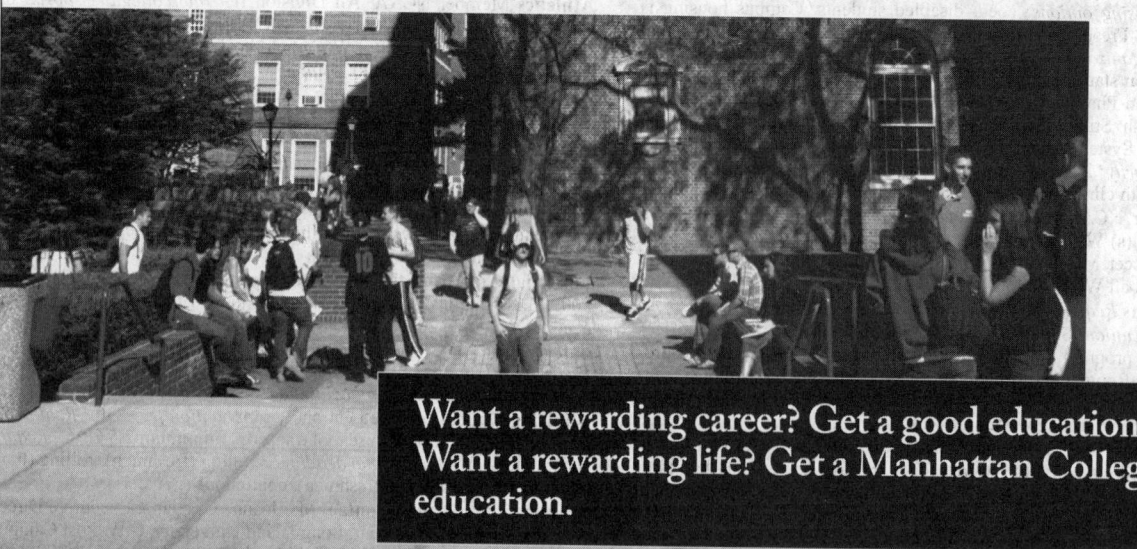

need-based loan: $8052. *Average need-based gift aid:* $9217. *Average non-need-based aid:* $8515. *Average indebtedness upon graduation:* $31,912.
Applying *Options:* electronic application, early admission, early decision, deferred entrance. *Application fee:* $60. *Required:* essay or personal statement, high school transcript, minimum 3 GPA, 1 letter of recommendation. *Required for some:* interview. *Recommended:* minimum 3 GPA. *Application deadlines:* 4/15 (freshmen), 7/1 (transfers). *Early decision deadline:* 11/15. *Notification:* continuous until 4/15 (freshmen), continuous until 8/15 (transfers), 12/1 (early decision).
Freshman Application Contact Mr. William Bisset, Vice President for Enrollment Management, Manhattan College, 4513 Manhattan College Parkway, Riverdale, NY 10471. *Phone:* 718-862-7200. *Toll-free phone:* 800-622-9235. *Fax:* 718-862-8019. *E-mail:* admit@manhattan.edu. *Web site:* http://www.manhattan.edu/.

See page 1406 for the College Close-Up.

Manhattan School of Music
New York, New York
- **Independent** comprehensive, founded 1917
- **Urban** 1-acre campus
- **Endowment** $15.5 million
- **Coed**
- **Very difficult** entrance level

Faculty *Student/faculty ratio:* 6:1.
Academics *Calendar:* semesters. *Degrees:* diplomas, bachelor's, master's, doctoral-other, post-master's, and postbachelor's certificates.
Student Life *Campus security:* 24-hour patrols, controlled dormitory access.
Standardized Tests *Recommended:* SAT or ACT (for admission).
Costs (2010–11) *Comprehensive fee:* $48,950 includes full-time tuition ($32,340), mandatory fees ($2800), and room and board ($13,810). Full-time tuition and fees vary according to course load. Part-time tuition and fees vary according to course load. *College room only:* $9150. Room and board charges vary according to board plan and housing facility. *Payment plans:* installment, deferred payment.
Financial Aid *Of all full-time matriculated undergraduates who enrolled in 2008,* 293 applied for aid, 273 were judged to have need, 23 had their need fully met. 70 Federal Work-Study jobs (averaging $942). 7 state and other part-time jobs (averaging $11,950). *In 2008,* 58 non-need-based awards were made. *Average percent of need met:* 48. *Average financial aid package:* $16,311. *Average need-based loan:* $5481. *Average need-based gift aid:* $17,098. *Average non-need-based aid:* $8226. *Average indebtedness upon graduation:* $23,508. *Financial aid deadline:* 3/1.
Applying *Options:* electronic application, deferred entrance. *Application fee:* $100. *Required:* essay or personal statement, high school transcript, minimum 2.8 GPA, 1 letter of recommendation, audition. *Recommended:* minimum 3 GPA, interview.
Freshman Application Contact Amy Anderson, Associate Dean for Enrollment Management, Manhattan School of Music, 120 Claremont Avenue, New York, NY 10027-4698. *Phone:* 917-493-4501. *Fax:* 212-749-3025. *E-mail:* admission@msmnyc.edu. *Web site:* http://www.msmnyc.edu/.

Manhattanville College
Purchase, New York
- **Independent** comprehensive, founded 1841
- **Suburban** 100-acre campus with easy access to New York City
- **Endowment** $10.4 million
- **Coed** 1,723 undergraduate students, 94% full-time, 66% women, 34% men
- **Moderately difficult** entrance level, 60% of applicants were admitted

Undergraduates 1,626 full-time, 97 part-time. Students come from 39 states and territories; 53 other countries; 39% are from out of state; 8% Black or African American, non-Hispanic/Latino; 17% Hispanic/Latino; 2% Asian, non-Hispanic/Latino; 0.3% American Indian or Alaska Native, non-Hispanic/Latino; 15% Race/ethnicity unknown; 12% international; 3% transferred in; 80% live on campus. *Retention:* 76% of full-time freshmen returned.
Freshmen *Admission:* 4,099 applied, 2,466 admitted, 430 enrolled. *Average high school GPA:* 3. *Test scores:* SAT critical reading scores over 500: 73%; SAT math scores over 500: 71%; ACT scores over 18: 100%; SAT critical reading scores over 600: 26%; SAT math scores over 600: 21%; ACT scores over 24: 40%; SAT critical reading scores over 700: 5%; SAT math scores over 700: 3%.
Faculty *Total:* 379, 27% full-time. *Student/faculty ratio:* 11:1.
Academics *Calendar:* semesters. *Degrees:* bachelor's, master's, doctoral-other, post-master's, and postbachelor's certificates. *Special study options:*

academic remediation for entering students, accelerated degree program, adult/continuing education programs, advanced placement credit, distance learning, double majors, English as a second language, honors programs, independent study, internships, off-campus study, part-time degree program, services for LD students, student-designed majors, study abroad, summer session for credit. *Unusual degree programs:* 3-2 business administration; Education.

Computers on Campus 240 computers/terminals are available on campus for general student use. Students can access the following: computer help desk, free student e-mail accounts, online (class) grades, online (class) registration, online (class) schedules. Campuswide network is available. 100% of college-owned or -operated housing units are wired for high-speed Internet access. Wireless service is available via classrooms, computer centers, computer labs, libraries, student centers.

Student Life *Housing options:* coed, disabled students. Campus housing is university owned. Freshman campus housing is guaranteed. *Activities and organizations:* drama/theater group, student-run newspaper, radio and television station, choral group, Latin American Student Organization, International Student Organization, Black Student Union, WMVL (radio station), Connie Hogarth Center. *Campus security:* 24-hour emergency response devices and patrols, late-night transport/escort service, controlled dormitory access. *Student services:* health clinic, personal/psychological counseling, women's center.

Athletics Member NCAA. All Division III. *Intercollegiate sports:* baseball M, basketball M/W, field hockey W, golf M, ice hockey M/W, lacrosse M/W, soccer M/W, softball W, swimming and diving W, tennis M/W, volleyball W. *Intramural sports:* basketball M/W, cheerleading M/W.

Standardized Tests *Required for some:* SAT or ACT (for admission).

Costs (2010–11) *Comprehensive fee:* $48,270 includes full-time tuition ($33,030), mandatory fees ($1320), and room and board ($13,920). Part-time tuition: $765 per credit. Part-time tuition and fees vary according to program. *Required fees:* $60 per term part-time. *College room only:* $8250. Room and board charges vary according to board plan. *Payment plans:* installment, deferred payment. *Waivers:* senior citizens and employees or children of employees.

Financial Aid Of all full-time matriculated undergraduates who enrolled in 2008, 1,234 applied for aid, 1,131 were judged to have need, 111 had their need fully met. 275 Federal Work-Study jobs (averaging $1300). 265 state and other part-time jobs (averaging $1300). In 2008, 480 non-need-based awards were made. *Average percent of need met:* 96%. *Average financial aid package:* $26,779. *Average need-based loan:* $4523. *Average need-based gift aid:* $17,427. *Average non-need-based aid:* $18,753.

Applying *Options:* electronic application, early admission, early decision, deferred entrance. *Application fee:* $75. *Required:* essay or personal statement, high school transcript, minimum 2 GPA, 2 letters of recommendation. *Recommended:* minimum 3 GPA, interview. *Application deadlines:* 3/1 (freshmen), 3/1 (transfers). *Notification:* continuous (freshmen), continuous (transfers).

Freshman Application Contact Ms. Kathy Fitzgerald, Director of Admissions, Manhattanville College, 2900 Purchase Street, Purchase, NY 10577. *Phone:* 914-323-5124. *Toll-free phone:* 800-328-4553. *Fax:* 914-694-1732. *E-mail:* admissions@mville.edu. *Web site:* http://www.manhattanville.edu/.

See page 1408 for the College Close-Up.

Mannes College The New School for Music

New York, New York

- **Independent** comprehensive, founded 1916, part of The New School
- **Urban** campus with easy access to Manhattan
- **Coed** 196 undergraduate students, 90% full-time, 53% women, 47% men
- **Very difficult** entrance level, 32% of applicants were admitted

Undergraduates 177 full-time, 19 part-time. 64% are from out of state; 2% Black or African American, non-Hispanic/Latino; 4% Hispanic/Latino; 11% Asian, non-Hispanic/Latino; 1% Two or more races, non-Hispanic/Latino; 10% Race/ethnicity unknown; 39% international; 8% transferred in; 14% live on campus. *Retention:* 90% of full-time freshmen returned.

Freshmen *Admission:* 493 applied, 156 admitted, 48 enrolled. *Average high school GPA:* 3.55.

Faculty *Total:* 156, 9% full-time, 0.6% with terminal degrees. *Student/faculty ratio:* 6:1.

Academics *Calendar:* semesters. *Degrees:* diplomas, bachelor's, master's, post-master's, and postbachelor's certificates. *Special study options:* academic remediation for entering students, advanced placement credit, English as a second language, independent study, internships, services for LD students, summer session for credit.

Computers on Campus Students can access the following: campus intranet, computer help desk, free student e-mail accounts, online (class) grades, online (class) registration, online (class) schedules, online portal. Campuswide network is available. 100% of college-owned or -operated housing units are wired for high-speed Internet access. Wireless service is available via entire campus.

Student Life *Housing options:* coed, disabled students. Campus housing is university owned and leased by the school. Freshman applicants given priority for college housing. *Activities and organizations:* drama/theater group, student-run newspaper, radio station, choral group. *Campus security:* 24-hour emergency response devices, controlled dormitory access. *Student services:* health clinic, personal/psychological counseling.

Costs (2010–11) *Comprehensive fee:* $50,360 includes full-time tuition ($34,340), mandatory fees ($760), and room and board ($15,260). Part-time tuition: $1125 per credit. Part-time tuition and fees vary according to course load. *College room only:* $12,260. Room and board charges vary according to board plan and housing facility. *Payment plan:* installment. *Waivers:* employees or children of employees.

Financial Aid Of all full-time matriculated undergraduates who enrolled in 2009, 52 applied for aid, 48 were judged to have need, 6 had their need fully met. In 2009, 3 non-need-based awards were made. *Average percent of need met:* 53%. *Average financial aid package:* $20,135. *Average need-based loan:* $8695. *Average need-based gift aid:* $14,825. *Average non-need-based aid:* $12,910. *Average indebtedness upon graduation:* $33,060.

Applying *Options:* electronic application. *Application fee:* $100. *Required:* essay or personal statement, high school transcript, 1 letter of recommendation, interview, audition, written test. *Application deadlines:* 12/1 (freshmen), 4/1 (transfers). *Notification:* 4/1 (freshmen).

Freshman Application Contact Mannes College The New School for Music, 150 West 85th Street, New York, NY 10024-4402. *Phone:* 212-580-0210 Ext. 4862. *Toll-free phone:* 800-292-3040. *Web site:* http://www.mannes.edu/.

See page 1410 for the College Close-Up.

Maria College

Albany, New York

- **Independent** 4-year, founded 1958
- **Urban** 9-acre campus
- **Coed** 866 undergraduate students, 27% full-time, 88% women, 12% men
- **Minimally difficult** entrance level, 28% of applicants were admitted

Undergraduates 236 full-time, 630 part-time. Students come from 6 states and territories; 1 other country; 6% are from out of state; 17% Black or African American, non-Hispanic/Latino; 2% Hispanic/Latino; 4% Asian, non-Hispanic/Latino; 0.1% Native Hawaiian or other Pacific Islander, non-Hispanic/Latino; 0.9% American Indian or Alaska Native, non-Hispanic/Latino; 0.3% Two or more races, non-Hispanic/Latino; 1% Race/ethnicity unknown; 0.1% international.

Freshmen *Admission:* 424 applied, 118 admitted, 52 enrolled.

Faculty *Total:* 60, 48% full-time, 18% with terminal degrees. *Student/faculty ratio:* 22:1.

Academics *Calendar:* semesters. *Degrees:* certificates, associate, and bachelor's. *Special study options:* academic remediation for entering students, adult/continuing education programs, advanced placement credit, distance learning, independent study, off-campus study, part-time degree program, services for LD students, summer session for credit. *ROTC:* Air Force (c).

Computers on Campus 78 computers/terminals are available on campus for general student use. Students can access the following: campus intranet, online (class) grades, online (class) registration, online (class) schedules. Campuswide network is available. Wireless service is available via entire campus.

Student Life *Housing:* college housing not available. *Campus security:* late-night transport/escort service. *Student services:* personal/psychological counseling.

Standardized Tests *Required:* SAT or ACT (for admission).

Costs (2010–11) *Tuition:* $9400 full-time, $390 per credit hour part-time. Full-time tuition and fees vary according to degree level and program. Part-time tuition and fees vary according to degree level and program. *Required fees:* $320 full-time, $80 per credit hour part-time. *Payment plan:* installment. *Waivers:* senior citizens and employees or children of employees.

Financial Aid Of all full-time matriculated undergraduates who enrolled in 2009, 25 Federal Work-Study jobs (averaging $1000).

Applying *Options:* electronic application, early admission. *Application fee:* $35. *Required:* essay or personal statement, high school transcript, minimum 2 GPA, 1 letter of recommendation, interview. *Application deadlines:* 8/25 (freshmen), 8/25 (transfers).

Freshman Application Contact Ms. Laurie A. Gilmore, Director of Admissions, Maria College, 700 New Scotland Avenue, Albany, NY 12208-1798. *Phone:* 518-438-3111. *Fax:* 518-453-1366. *E-mail:* admissions@mariacollege.edu. *Web site:* http://www.mariacollege.edu/.

Marist College
Poughkeepsie, New York

- **Independent** comprehensive, founded 1929
- **Suburban** 180-acre campus with easy access to Albany and New York City
- **Endowment** $118.6 million
- **Coed** 5,189 undergraduate students, 87% full-time, 57% women, 43% men
- **Very difficult** entrance level, 40% of applicants were admitted

Undergraduates 4,532 full-time, 657 part-time. Students come from 42 states and territories; 16 other countries; 44% are from out of state; 3% Black or African American, non-Hispanic/Latino; 7% Hispanic/Latino; 2% Asian, non-Hispanic/Latino; 0.1% Native Hawaiian or other Pacific Islander, non-Hispanic/Latino; 0.2% American Indian or Alaska Native, non-Hispanic/Latino; 0.3% Two or more races, non-Hispanic/Latino; 22% Race/ethnicity unknown; 0.5% international; 6% transferred in; 67% live on campus. *Retention:* 89% of full-time freshmen returned.
Freshmen *Admission:* 9,547 applied, 3,773 admitted, 1,088 enrolled. *Average high school GPA:* 3.3. *Test scores:* SAT critical reading scores over 500: 89%; SAT math scores over 500: 91%; SAT writing scores over 500: 89%; ACT scores over 18: 99%; SAT critical reading scores over 600: 38%; SAT math scores over 600: 48%; SAT writing scores over 600: 45%; ACT scores over 24: 73%; SAT critical reading scores over 700: 5%; SAT math scores over 700: 4%; SAT writing scores over 700: 6%; ACT scores over 30: 8%.
Faculty *Total:* 586, 39% full-time, 29% with terminal degrees. *Student/faculty ratio:* 15:1.
Academics *Calendar:* semesters. *Degrees:* certificates, bachelor's, master's, and postbachelor's certificates. *Special study options:* academic remediation for entering students, accelerated degree program, adult/continuing education programs, advanced placement credit, cooperative education, distance learning, double majors, English as a second language, honors programs, independent study, internships, off-campus study, part-time degree program, services for LD students, study abroad, summer session for credit. *ROTC:* Army (b).
Computers on Campus 761 computers/terminals and 1,000 ports are available on campus for general student use. Students can access the following: campus intranet, computer help desk, free student e-mail accounts, online (class) grades, online (class) registration, online (class) schedules, admissions application, billing, transcript, degree audit, online financial aid summary. Campuswide network is available. 100% of college-owned or -operated housing units are wired for high-speed Internet access. Wireless service is available via entire campus.
Student Life *Housing options:* coed, disabled students. Campus housing is university owned. Freshman campus housing is guaranteed. *Activities and organizations:* drama/theater group, student-run newspaper, radio and television station, choral group, marching band, Marist Singers, Dance Club, student government, Theater Club, Community Service and Campus Ministry, national fraternities. *Campus security:* 24-hour emergency response devices and patrols, student patrols, late-night transport/escort service, controlled dormitory access, night residence hall monitors. *Student services:* health clinic, personal/psychological counseling.
Athletics Member NCAA. All Division I except football (Division I-AA). *Intercollegiate sports:* baseball M(s), basketball M(s)/W(s), cheerleading M(c)/W(c), crew M/W(s), cross-country running M(s)/W(s), equestrian sports M(c)/W(c), fencing M(c)/W(c), ice hockey M(c), lacrosse M(s)/W(s), rugby M(c)/W(c), skiing (downhill) M(c)/W(c), soccer M(s)/W(s), softball W(s), swimming and diving M(s)/W(s), tennis M(s)/W(s), track and field M(s)/W(s), volleyball M(c)/W(s), water polo W(s). *Intramural sports:* basketball M/W, bowling M/W, soccer M/W, softball M/W, ultimate Frisbee M(c)/W(c), volleyball M/W.
Costs (2010–11) *One-time required fee:* $90. *Comprehensive fee:* $40,000 includes full-time tuition ($27,150), mandatory fees ($500), and room and board ($12,350). Part-time tuition: $634 per credit. *Required fees:* $40 per term part-time. *College room only:* $8775. Room and board charges vary according to board plan and housing facility. *Payment plan:* installment. *Waivers:* employees or children of employees.
Financial Aid Of all full-time matriculated undergraduates who enrolled in 2009, 3,424 applied for aid, 2,796 were judged to have need, 513 had their need fully met. In 2009, 1029 non-need-based awards were made. *Average percent of need met:* 69%. *Average financial aid package:* $17,712. *Average need-based loan:* $4619. *Average need-based gift aid:* $16,909. *Average non-need-based aid:* $7180. *Average indebtedness upon graduation:* $25,135. *Financial aid deadline:* 5/1.
Applying *Options:* electronic application, early admission, early decision, early action, deferred entrance. *Application fee:* $50. *Required:* essay or personal statement, high school transcript, 2 letters of recommendation. *Application deadlines:* 2/15 (freshmen), 6/1 (transfers), 12/1 (early action). *Early decision deadline:* 11/15. *Notification:* 3/15 (freshmen), continuous (transfers), 12/15 (early decision), 1/30 (early action).

Freshman Application Contact Mr. Kenton Rinehart, Dean of Undergraduate Admissions, Marist College, 3399 North Road, Poughkeepsie, NY 12601. *Phone:* 845-575-3226. *Toll-free phone:* 800-436-5483. *Fax:* 845-575-3215. *E-mail:* admission@marist.edu. *Web site:* http://www.marist.edu/.

Marymount Manhattan College
New York, New York

- **Independent** 4-year, founded 1936
- **Urban** 3-acre campus
- **Coed**
- **Moderately difficult** entrance level

Faculty *Student/faculty ratio:* 11:1.
Academics *Calendar:* semesters plus summer and January mini-semesters. *Degrees:* certificates, associate, and bachelor's.
Student Life *Campus security:* 24-hour emergency response devices and patrols, student patrols, 24-hour security in residence halls.
Standardized Tests *Required:* SAT or ACT (for admission).
Financial Aid Of all full-time matriculated undergraduates who enrolled in 2009, 1,303 applied for aid, 1,073 were judged to have need, 32 had their need fully met. In 2009, 294 non-need-based awards were made. *Average percent of need met:* 47. *Average financial aid package:* $13,251. *Average need-based loan:* $4236. *Average need-based gift aid:* $9454. *Average non-need-based aid:* $5119. *Average indebtedness upon graduation:* $15,988.
Applying *Options:* electronic application, deferred entrance. *Application fee:* $60. *Required:* essay or personal statement, high school transcript, minimum 2 GPA, 2 letters of recommendation. *Required for some:* audition for dance and theater programs. *Recommended:* interview.
Freshman Application Contact Mr. James Rogers, Dean of Admissions, Marymount Manhattan College, 221 East 71st Street, New York, NY 10021. *Phone:* 212-517-0430. *Toll-free phone:* 800-MARYMOUNT. *Fax:* 212-517-0448. *E-mail:* admissions@mmm.edu. *Web site:* http://www.mmm.edu/.

See page 1414 for the College Close-Up.

Medaille College
Buffalo, New York

- **Independent** comprehensive, founded 1875
- **Urban** 13-acre campus
- **Coed** 1,845 undergraduate students, 92% full-time, 65% women, 35% men
- **Moderately difficult** entrance level, 69% of applicants were admitted

Undergraduates 1,694 full-time, 151 part-time. Students come from 14 states and territories; 2 other countries; 6% are from out of state; 11% Black or African American, non-Hispanic/Latino; 1% Hispanic/Latino; 3% Asian, non-Hispanic/Latino; 2% Native Hawaiian or other Pacific Islander, non-Hispanic/Latino; 0.8% American Indian or Alaska Native, non-Hispanic/Latino; 17% Race/ethnicity unknown; 1% international; 7% transferred in; 23% live on campus. *Retention:* 68% of full-time freshmen returned.
Freshmen *Admission:* 1,433 applied, 987 admitted, 634 enrolled. *Test scores:* SAT critical reading scores over 500: 26%; SAT math scores over 500: 34%; SAT critical reading scores over 600: 1%; SAT math scores over 600: 5%.
Faculty *Total:* 231, 33% full-time, 23% with terminal degrees. *Student/faculty ratio:* 19:1.
Academics *Calendar:* semesters (modular courses available for evening studies and weekend college program). *Degrees:* certificates, associate, bachelor's, master's, and post-master's certificates. *Special study options:* academic remediation for entering students, accelerated degree program, adult/continuing education programs, advanced placement credit, double majors, honors programs, independent study, internships, off-campus study, part-time degree program, services for LD students, student-designed majors, summer session for credit. *ROTC:* Army (c). *Unusual degree programs:* 3-2 business administration; sport management.
Computers on Campus 120 computers/terminals are available on campus for general student use. Students can access the following: campus intranet, computer help desk, free student e-mail accounts, online (class) grades, online (class) registration, online (class) schedules. Campuswide network is available. 100% of college-owned or -operated housing units are wired for high-speed Internet access. Wireless service is available via entire campus.
Student Life *Housing options:* coed, men-only, women-only, disabled students. Campus housing is university owned. *Activities and organizations:* drama/theater group, student-run newspaper, radio and television station, student government, Club Green, Dance Team, WMCB The Lizard (college radio station), ice hockey club. *Campus security:* 24-hour emergency response devices and patrols, late-night transport/escort service, controlled dormitory access. *Student services:* health clinic, personal/psychological counseling.
Athletics Member NCAA. All Division III. *Intercollegiate sports:* baseball M, basketball M/W, bowling W, cross-country running M/W, golf M, lacrosse M/W, soccer M/W, softball W, volleyball M/W. *Intramural sports:* basketball

M/W, soccer M/W, softball M/W, table tennis M/W, tennis M/W, volleyball M/W, weight lifting M/W.

Standardized Tests *Required:* SAT or ACT (for admission). *Recommended:* SAT (for admission).

Costs (2010–11) *Comprehensive fee:* $30,330 includes full-time tuition ($20,580) and room and board ($9750). Full-time tuition and fees vary according to location. Part-time tuition: $725 per credit hour. Part-time tuition and fees vary according to course load. *Room and board:* Room and board charges vary according to housing facility. *Payment plan:* installment. *Waivers:* adult students, senior citizens, and employees or children of employees.

Financial Aid Of all full-time matriculated undergraduates who enrolled in 2008, 1,328 applied for aid, 1,328 were judged to have need, 20 had their need fully met. 150 Federal Work-Study jobs (averaging $1500). In 2008, 25 non-need-based awards were made. *Average percent of need met:* 70%. *Average financial aid package:* $15,800. *Average need-based loan:* $5000. *Average need-based gift aid:* $8000. *Average non-need-based aid:* $7500. *Average indebtedness upon graduation:* $22,000.

Applying *Options:* electronic application, early admission, deferred entrance. *Application fee:* $25. *Required:* high school transcript, interview. *Required for some:* essay or personal statement, 2.5 high school GPA for veterinary technology and elementary teacher education majors. *Recommended:* essay or personal statement, minimum 2 GPA, 1 letter of recommendation. *Application deadlines:* 8/1 (freshmen), rolling (transfers). *Notification:* continuous (freshmen), continuous (transfers).

Freshman Application Contact Mr. Greg Florczak, Director of Undergraduate Admissions, Medaille College, Office of Admissions, Buffalo, NY 14214. *Phone:* 716-880-2200. *Toll-free phone:* 800-292-1582. *Fax:* 716-880-2007. *E-mail:* admissionsug@medaille.edu. *Web site:* http://www.medaille.edu/.

Medgar Evers College of the City University of New York

Brooklyn, New York

- **State and locally supported** 4-year, founded 1969, part of City University of New York System
- **Urban** 8-acre campus
- **Coed** 6,921 undergraduate students, 66% full-time, 75% women, 25% men
- **Noncompetitive** entrance level, 100% of applicants were admitted

Undergraduates 4,542 full-time, 2,379 part-time. Students come from 7 states and territories; 75 other countries; 1% are from out of state; 87% Black or African American, non-Hispanic/Latino; 7% Hispanic/Latino; 1% Asian, non-Hispanic/Latino; 1% Two or more races, non-Hispanic/Latino; 0.9% Race/ethnicity unknown; 1% international; 6% transferred in. *Retention:* 53% of full-time freshmen returned.

Freshmen *Admission:* 7,494 applied, 7,494 admitted, 1,188 enrolled. *Average high school GPA:* 2.13.

Faculty *Total:* 518, 36% full-time. *Student/faculty ratio:* 18:1.

Academics *Calendar:* semesters. *Degrees:* certificates, associate, and bachelor's. *Special study options:* academic remediation for entering students, adult/continuing education programs, advanced placement credit, cooperative education, double majors, English as a second language, external degree program, honors programs, independent study, internships, off-campus study, part-time degree program, services for LD students, study abroad, summer session for credit.

Computers on Campus 120 computers/terminals are available on campus for general student use. Students can access the following: free student e-mail accounts, online (class) grades, online (class) registration, online (class) schedules. Campuswide network is available. Wireless service is available via entire campus.

Student Life *Housing:* college housing not available. *Activities and organizations:* drama/theater group, student-run newspaper, radio and television station, choral group, American Marketing Association, Drama Students Association, Rising Stars, Medgar Evers College Society of Public Administrators, National Society of Black Accountants. *Campus security:* 24-hour patrols. *Student services:* women's center, legal services.

Athletics Member NCAA. All Division III. *Intercollegiate sports:* basketball M/W, cross-country running M/W, soccer M/W, tennis W, track and field M/W, volleyball M/W. *Intramural sports:* basketball M/W, tennis W.

Standardized Tests *Recommended:* SAT and SAT Subject Tests or ACT (for admission).

Costs (2011–12) *Tuition:* state resident $4830 full-time, $205 per credit hour part-time; nonresident $13,050 full-time, $435 per credit hour part-time. Full-time tuition and fees vary according to course load. Part-time tuition and fees vary according to course load. *Required fees:* $302 full-time, $101 per term part-time. *Payment plans:* installment, deferred payment.

Financial Aid Of all full-time matriculated undergraduates who enrolled in 2008, 289 Federal Work-Study jobs (averaging $309,546). *Average financial*

aid package: $3835. *Average need-based loan:* $1758. *Average need-based gift aid:* $3572.

Applying *Options:* electronic application, deferred entrance. *Application fee:* $65. *Required:* high school transcript. *Application deadlines:* rolling (freshmen), rolling (transfers). *Notification:* continuous (freshmen), continuous (transfers).

Freshman Application Contact Ms. Julie M. Augustin, Director of Admissions, Medgar Evers College of the City University of New York, 1650 Bedford Avenue, Brooklyn, NY 11225. *Phone:* 718-270-6021. *Fax:* 718-270-6411. *E-mail:* jaugustin@mec.cuny.edu. *Web site:* http://www.mec.cuny.edu/.

Mercy College

Dobbs Ferry, New York

- **Independent** comprehensive, founded 1951
- **Suburban** 45-acre campus with easy access to New York City
- **Endowment** $20.4 million
- **Coed**
- **Moderately difficult** entrance level

Faculty *Student/faculty ratio:* 17:1.

Academics *Calendar:* semesters. *Degrees:* certificates, associate, bachelor's, master's, doctoral-other, post-master's, and postbachelor's certificates.

Student Life *Campus security:* 24-hour emergency response devices and patrols, late-night transport/escort service, controlled dormitory access.

Athletics Member NCAA. All Division II.

Standardized Tests *Recommended:* SAT or ACT (for admission), SAT and SAT Subject Tests or ACT (for admission), SAT Subject Tests (for admission).

Costs (2010–11) *Comprehensive fee:* $28,150 includes full-time tuition ($16,490), mandatory fees ($520), and room and board ($11,140). Full-time tuition and fees vary according to program and reciprocity agreements. Part-time tuition: $692 per credit hour. Part-time tuition and fees vary according to program and reciprocity agreements. *Required fees:* $130 per term part-time. *College room only:* $7890. Room and board charges vary according to board plan and housing facility.

Applying *Options:* electronic application, deferred entrance. *Application fee:* $40. *Required:* high school transcript, minimum 2 GPA. *Required for some:* essay or personal statement, interview.

Freshman Application Contact Mrs. Tara Fay-Reilly, Senior Director of Admissions, Mercy College, 555 Broadway, Dobbs Ferry, NY 10522-1189. *Phone:* 914-674-7762 Ext. 7762. *Toll-free phone:* 800-MERCY-NY. *Fax:* 914-674-7608. *E-mail:* admissions@mercy.edu. *Web site:* http://www.mercy.edu/.

Mesivta of Eastern Parkway–Yeshiva Zichron Meilech

Brooklyn, New York

Director of Admissions Rabbi Joseph Halberstadt, Dean, Mesivta of Eastern Parkway–Yeshiva Zichron Meilech, 510 Dahill Road, Brooklyn, NY 11218-5559. *Phone:* 718-438-1002.

Mesivta Tifereth Jerusalem of America

New York, New York

Director of Admissions Rabbi Fishellis, Director of Admissions, Mesivta Tifereth Jerusalem of America, 145 East Broadway, New York, NY 10002-6301. *Phone:* 212-964-2830.

Mesivta Torah Vodaath Rabbinical Seminary

Brooklyn, New York

Director of Admissions Rabbi Issac Braun, Administrator, Mesivta Torah Vodaath Rabbinical Seminary, 425 East Ninth Street, Brooklyn, NY 11218-5299. *Phone:* 718-941-8000.

Metropolitan College of New York

New York, New York

- **Independent** comprehensive, founded 1964
- **Urban** campus
- **Endowment** $9.0 million
- **Coed, primarily women**
- **Moderately difficult** entrance level

Faculty *Student/faculty ratio:* 11:1.

Academics *Calendar:* 3 15-week semesters. *Degrees:* certificates, associate, bachelor's, and master's.

Student Life *Campus security:* 24-hour patrols.

Standardized Tests *Required for some:* ACCUPLACER. *Recommended:* SAT or ACT (for admission).

Costs (2010–11) *Tuition:* $16,320 full-time, $544 per credit hour part-time. Full-time tuition and fees vary according to degree level and program. Part-time tuition and fees vary according to degree level and program. No tuition increase for student's term of enrollment. *Required fees:* $400 full-time. *Payment plans:* installment, deferred payment.

Financial Aid *Of all full-time matriculated undergraduates who enrolled in 2000,* 1,066 applied for aid, 1,062 were judged to have need. 52 Federal Work-Study jobs (averaging $1969). 30 state and other part-time jobs (averaging $1920). *Average financial aid package:* $6337. *Average need-based loan:* $3377. *Average need-based gift aid:* $3650. *Average indebtedness upon graduation:* $20,130.

Applying *Options:* electronic application, deferred entrance. *Application fee:* $30. *Required:* essay or personal statement, high school transcript, 2 letters of recommendation, interview. *Recommended:* minimum 3 GPA.

Freshman Application Contact Metropolitan College of New York, 431 Canal Street, New York, NY 10013. *Phone:* 212-343-1234 Ext. 2700. *Toll-free phone:* 800-33-THINK Ext. 5001. *Fax:* 212-343-8470. *Web site:* http://www.metropolitan.edu/.

Mirrer Yeshiva

Brooklyn, New York

Director of Admissions Director of Admissions, Mirrer Yeshiva, 1795 Ocean Parkway, Brooklyn, NY 11223-2010. *Phone:* 718-645-0536.

Molloy College

Rockville Centre, New York

- **Independent** comprehensive, founded 1955
- **Suburban** 30-acre campus with easy access to New York City
- **Endowment** $21.6 million
- **Coed** 3,175 undergraduate students, 79% full-time, 76% women, 24% men
- **Moderately difficult** entrance level, 74% of applicants were admitted

Undergraduates 2,511 full-time, 664 part-time. Students come from 10 states and territories; 15% transferred in. *Retention:* 89% of full-time freshmen returned.

Freshmen *Admission:* 1,963 applied, 1,451 admitted, 395 enrolled. *Average high school GPA:* 3.5. *Test scores:* SAT critical reading scores over 500: 55%; SAT math scores over 500: 68%; SAT writing scores over 500: 62%; ACT scores over 18: 67%; SAT critical reading scores over 600: 10%; SAT math scores over 600: 22%; SAT writing scores over 600: 17%; ACT scores over 24: 63%; SAT math scores over 700: 2%; SAT writing scores over 700: 1%; ACT scores over 30: 14%.

Faculty *Total:* 577, 30% full-time, 33% with terminal degrees. *Student/faculty ratio:* 10:1.

Academics *Calendar:* 4-1-4. *Degrees:* associate, bachelor's, master's, doctoral-research/scholarship, and post-master's certificates. *Special study options:* academic remediation for entering students, adult/continuing education programs, advanced placement credit, cooperative education, double majors, English as a second language, honors programs, internships, part-time degree program, services for LD students, study abroad, summer session for credit. *ROTC:* Army (c), Navy (c), Air Force (c).

Computers on Campus 328 computers/terminals are available on campus for general student use. Students can access the following: computer help desk, free student e-mail accounts, online (class) grades, online (class) registration, online (class) schedules. Campuswide network is available. Wireless service is available via entire campus.

Student Life *Housing:* college housing not available. *Activities and organizations:* drama/theater group, student-run newspaper, choral group, Nursing Student Association, African-American Caribbean Organization, Gaelic Society, Education Club, International Society. *Campus security:* 24-hour emergency

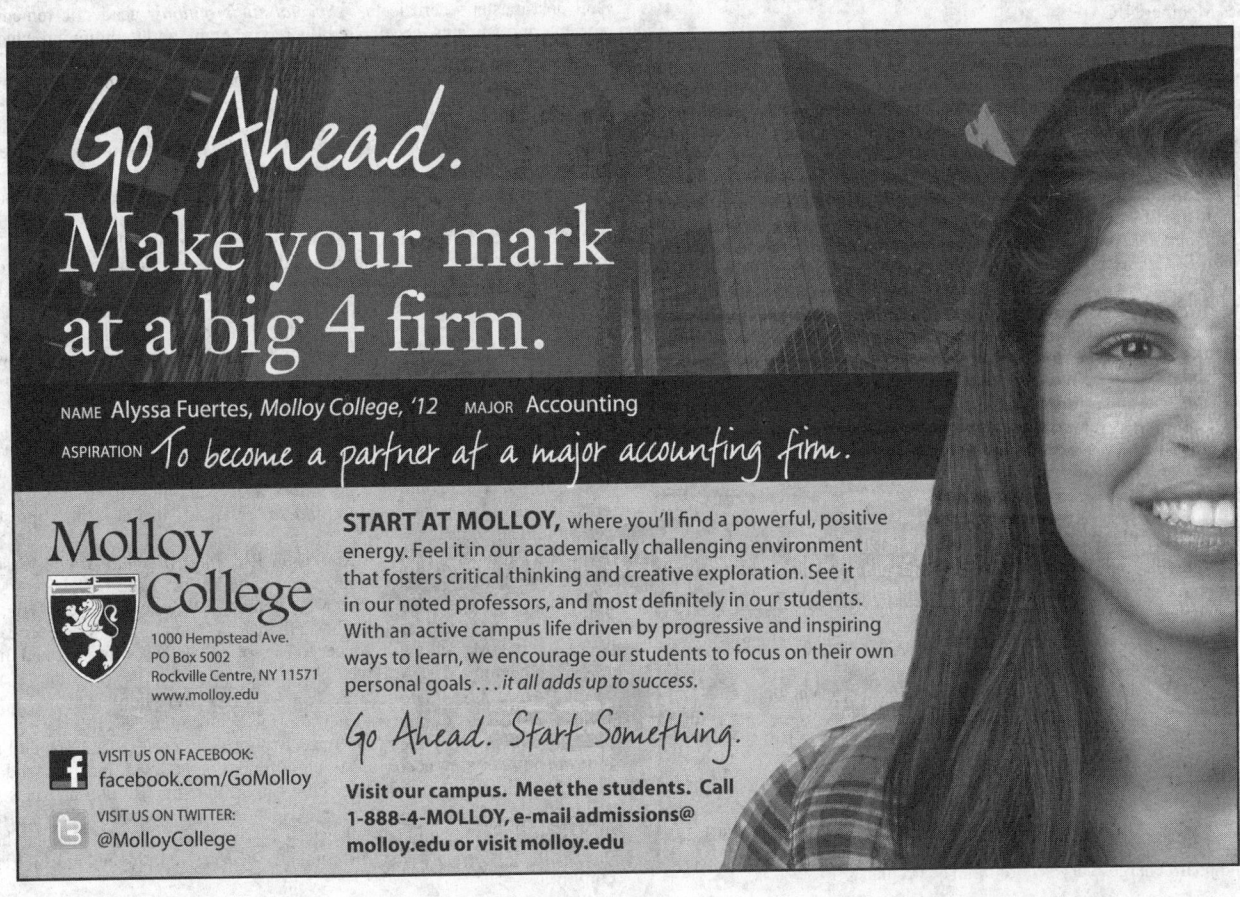

response devices and patrols, late-night transport/escort service. *Student services:* health clinic, personal/psychological counseling, women's center.

Athletics Member NCAA. All Division II. *Intercollegiate sports:* baseball M(s), basketball M(s)/W(s), cross-country running M(s)/W(s), equestrian sports W, lacrosse M(s)/W(s), rugby M/W, soccer M(s)/W(s), softball W(s), tennis W(s), track and field M(s)/W(s), volleyball W(s). *Intramural sports:* cheerleading W, rugby M/W, ultimate Frisbee M/W.

Standardized Tests *Required:* SAT or ACT (for admission).

Costs (2010–11) *One-time required fee:* $150. *Tuition:* $21,170 full-time, $700 per credit part-time. *Required fees:* $960 full-time. *Payment plan:* installment. *Waivers:* employees or children of employees.

Financial Aid Of all full-time matriculated undergraduates who enrolled in 2009, 2,075 applied for aid, 1,796 were judged to have need, 194 had their need fully met. 403 Federal Work-Study jobs (averaging $2244). In 2009, 179 non-need-based awards were made. *Average percent of need met:* 53%. *Average financial aid package:* $13,218. *Average need-based loan:* $5794. *Average need-based gift aid:* $9169. *Average non-need-based aid:* $6399. *Average indebtedness upon graduation:* $29,823. *Financial aid deadline:* 5/1.

Applying *Options:* electronic application, early admission, early action, deferred entrance. *Application fee:* $30. *Required for some:* essay or personal statement, high school transcript, 1 letter of recommendation. *Recommended:* interview. *Application deadlines:* rolling (freshmen), rolling (transfers). *Notification:* continuous (freshmen), continuous (transfers).

Freshman Application Contact Ms. Marguerite Lane, Director of Admissions, Molloy College, 1000 Hempstead Avenue, PO Box 5002, Rockville Centre, NY 11571-5002. *Phone:* 516-678-5000 Ext. 6240. *Toll-free phone:* 888-4MOLLOY. *Fax:* 516-256-2247. *E-mail:* admissions@molloy.edu. *Web site:* http://www.molloy.edu/.

See page 1444 for the College Close-Up.

Monroe College

Bronx, New York

- **Proprietary** comprehensive, founded 1933
- **Urban** campus
- **Coed**
- **Moderately difficult** entrance level

Faculty *Student/faculty ratio:* 32:1.

Academics *Calendar:* trimesters. *Degrees:* certificates, associate, bachelor's, and master's.

Student Life *Campus security:* late-night transport/escort service.

Athletics Member NJCAA.

Standardized Tests *Recommended:* SAT or ACT (for admission).

Costs (2010–11) *Comprehensive fee:* $19,550 includes full-time tuition ($11,400) and room and board ($8150). Full-time tuition and fees vary according to degree level and program. Part-time tuition and fees vary according to degree level and program. *Room and board:* Room and board charges vary according to board plan.

Financial Aid *Of all full-time matriculated undergraduates who enrolled in 2007,* 4,453 applied for aid, 4,405 were judged to have need, 983 had their need fully met. 276 Federal Work-Study jobs (averaging $2980). *Average percent of need met:* 90. *Average financial aid package:* $10,700. *Average need-based loan:* $4450. *Average need-based gift aid:* $6870. *Average indebtedness upon graduation:* $21,825.

Applying *Options:* electronic application, early admission, early decision, early action, deferred entrance. *Application fee:* $35. *Required:* essay or personal statement, high school transcript, interview. *Required for some:* 2 letters of recommendation.

Freshman Application Contact Monroe College, Monroe College Way, Bronx, NY 10468-5407. *Phone:* 718-933-6700 Ext. 8246. *Toll-free phone:* 800-55MONROE. *Web site:* http://www.monroecollege.edu/.

Monroe College

New Rochelle, New York

- **Proprietary** comprehensive, founded 1983
- **Suburban** campus with easy access to New York City
- **Coed**
- **Moderately difficult** entrance level

Faculty *Student/faculty ratio:* 38:1.

Academics *Calendar:* trimesters. *Degrees:* associate, bachelor's, and master's.

Student Life *Campus security:* late-night transport/escort service.

Athletics Member NJCAA.

Costs (2010–11) *Comprehensive fee:* $19,550 includes full-time tuition ($11,400) and room and board ($8150). Full-time tuition and fees vary according to degree level and program. Part-time tuition: $475 per credit. Part-time tuition and fees vary according to degree level and program. *Room and board:* Room and board charges vary according to board plan.

Financial Aid Of all full-time matriculated undergraduates who enrolled in 2008, 1,838 applied for aid, 1,819 were judged to have need, 1,112 had their need fully met. 47 Federal Work-Study jobs (averaging $2206). *Average percent of need met:* 89. *Average financial aid package:* $11,343. *Average need-based loan:* $4725. *Average need-based gift aid:* $6315. *Average indebtedness upon graduation:* $25,913.

Applying *Options:* electronic application, early admission, deferred entrance. *Application fee:* $35. *Required:* high school transcript, interview.

Freshman Application Contact Ms. Lisa Scorca, High School Admissions, Monroe College, 434 Main Street, New Rochelle, NY 10801. *Phone:* 914-654-3200. *Toll-free phone:* 800-55MONROE. *E-mail:* lscorca@monroecollege.edu. *Web site:* http://www.monroecollege.edu/.

Mount Saint Mary College

Newburgh, New York

- **Independent** comprehensive, founded 1960
- **Suburban** 72-acre campus with easy access to New York City
- **Endowment** $6.3 million
- **Coed** 2,299 undergraduate students, 83% full-time, 74% women, 26% men
- **Moderately difficult** entrance level, 77% of applicants were admitted

Undergraduates 1,899 full-time, 400 part-time. Students come from 11 states and territories; 26 other countries; 12% are from out of state; 7% Black or African American, non-Hispanic/Latino; 11% Hispanic/Latino; 2% Asian, non-Hispanic/Latino; 0.1% Native Hawaiian or other Pacific Islander, non-Hispanic/Latino; 0.4% American Indian or Alaska Native, non-Hispanic/Latino; 0.9% Two or more races, non-Hispanic/Latino; 3% Race/ethnicity unknown; 0.1% international; 11% transferred in; 41% live on campus. *Retention:* 73% of full-time freshmen returned.

Freshmen *Admission:* 2,278 applied, 1,748 admitted, 446 enrolled. *Average high school GPA:* 3.1. *Test scores:* SAT critical reading scores over 500: 46%; SAT math scores over 500: 52%; SAT writing scores over 500: 44%; ACT scores over 18: 85%; SAT critical reading scores over 600: 10%; SAT math scores over 600: 11%; SAT writing scores over 600: 8%; ACT scores over 24: 26%; SAT critical reading scores over 700: 1%; SAT math scores over 700: 1%; ACT scores over 30: 1%.

Faculty *Total:* 265, 32% full-time, 38% with terminal degrees. *Student/faculty ratio:* 15:1.

Academics *Calendar:* semesters. *Degrees:* certificates, bachelor's, master's, and post-master's certificates. *Special study options:* academic remediation for entering students, accelerated degree program, adult/continuing education programs, advanced placement credit, cooperative education, distance learning, double majors, freshman honors college, honors programs, independent study, internships, off-campus study, part-time degree program, services for LD students, student-designed majors, study abroad, summer session for credit. *Unusual degree programs:* 3-2 social work with Fordham University; publishing, counseling with Pace University.

Computers on Campus 586 computers/terminals are available on campus for general student use. Students can access the following: campus intranet, computer help desk, free student e-mail accounts, online (class) grades, online (class) registration, online (class) schedules, Intranet. Campuswide network is available. 100% of college-owned or -operated housing units are wired for high-speed Internet access. Wireless service is available via entire campus.

Student Life *Housing:* on-campus residence required through sophomore year. *Options:* coed, men-only, women-only. Campus housing is university owned. Freshman applicants given priority for college housing. *Activities and organizations:* drama/theater group, student-run radio station, choral group, Student Government Association, Delta Leadership Society, Big Brothers/Big Sisters, Black and Latin Student Unions, Habitat for Humanity. *Campus security:* 24-hour emergency response devices and patrols, student patrols, late-night transport/escort service, controlled dormitory access, monitored surveillance cameras in all residence halls. *Student services:* health clinic, personal/psychological counseling.

Athletics Member NCAA. All Division III. *Intercollegiate sports:* baseball M, basketball M/W, cross-country running M/W, lacrosse M/W, soccer M/W, softball W, swimming and diving M/W, tennis M/W, track and field M/W, volleyball W. *Intramural sports:* basketball M/W, bowling M/W, cheerleading W(c), football M, golf M/W, soccer M/W, softball M/W, swimming and diving M/W, table tennis M/W, volleyball M/W.

Standardized Tests *Required:* SAT or ACT (for admission).

Costs (2011–12) *Comprehensive fee:* $36,730 includes full-time tuition ($23,460), mandatory fees ($950), and room and board ($12,320). Full-time tuition and fees vary according to class time, degree level, location, and program. Part-time tuition: $782 per credit hour. Part-time tuition and fees vary according to class time, degree level, location, and program. *College room only:* $7140. Room and board charges vary according to board plan and housing facility. *Payment plan:* installment. *Waivers:* employees or children of employees.

Financial Aid Of all full-time matriculated undergraduates who enrolled in 2009, 1,729 applied for aid, 1,543 were judged to have need, 241 had their need fully met. 390 Federal Work-Study jobs (averaging $1369). In 2009, 220 non-need-based awards were made. *Average percent of need met: 60%. Average financial aid package:* $14,790. *Average need-based loan:* $4246. *Average need-based gift aid:* $11,045. *Average non-need-based aid:* $7471. *Average indebtedness upon graduation:* $37,273. *Financial aid deadline:* 3/1.

Applying *Options:* electronic application, early admission, deferred entrance. *Application fee:* $45. *Required:* essay or personal statement, high school transcript. *Required for some:* 2 letters of recommendation, interview. *Recommended:* minimum 3 GPA, 2 letters of recommendation, interview. *Application deadline:* 8/15 (freshmen). *Notification:* continuous (freshmen).

Freshman Application Contact Ms. Michelle Taylor, Director of Admissions, Mount Saint Mary College, 330 Powell Avenue, Newburgh, NY 12550-3494. *Phone:* 845-569-3248. *Toll-free phone:* 888-937-6762. *Fax:* 845-562-6762. *E-mail:* admissions@msmc.edu. *Web site:* http://www.msmc.edu/.

Nazareth College of Rochester

Rochester, New York

- **Independent** comprehensive, founded 1924
- **Suburban** 150-acre campus
- **Endowment** $48.1 million
- **Coed** 2,231 undergraduate students, 92% full-time, 76% women, 24% men
- **Moderately difficult** entrance level, 73% of applicants were admitted

Undergraduates 2,058 full-time, 173 part-time. Students come from 22 states and territories; 21 other countries; 8% are from out of state; 5% Black or African American, non-Hispanic/Latino; 4% Hispanic/Latino; 2% Asian, non-Hispanic/Latino; 0.4% American Indian or Alaska Native, non-Hispanic/Latino; 0.4% Two or more races, non-Hispanic/Latino; 11% Race/ethnicity unknown; 2% international; 7% transferred in; 55% live on campus. *Retention:* 81% of full-time freshmen returned.

Freshmen *Admission:* 2,518 applied, 1,842 admitted, 468 enrolled. *Average high school GPA:* 3.3. *Test scores:* SAT critical reading scores over 500: 78%; SAT math scores over 500: 82%; ACT scores over 18: 99%; SAT critical reading scores over 600: 29%; SAT math scores over 600: 32%; ACT scores over 24: 75%; SAT critical reading scores over 700: 4%; SAT math scores over 700: 3%; ACT scores over 30: 7%.

Faculty *Total:* 429, 38% full-time, 51% with terminal degrees. *Student/faculty ratio:* 11:1.

Academics *Calendar:* semesters. *Degrees:* bachelor's, master's, doctoral-professional, and post-master's certificates. *Special study options:* academic remediation for entering students, adult/continuing education programs, advanced placement credit, cooperative education, double majors, English as a second language, honors programs, independent study, internships, off-campus study, part-time degree program, services for LD students, study abroad, summer session for credit. *ROTC:* Army (c), Air Force (c).

Computers on Campus 240 computers/terminals are available on campus for general student use. Students can access the following: computer help desk, free student e-mail accounts, online (class) grades, online (class) registration, online (class) schedules. Campuswide network is available. 100% of college-owned or -operated housing units are wired for high-speed Internet access. Wireless service is available via classrooms, libraries, student centers.

Student Life *Housing:* on-campus residence required through sophomore year. *Options:* coed, disabled students. Campus housing is university owned. Freshman campus housing is guaranteed. *Activities and organizations:* drama/theater group, student-run newspaper, radio station, choral group, Student Activities Council, intramurals and recreation, Theater League, Center for Spirituality Council, NAZ Ultimate Frisbee. *Campus security:* 24-hour emergency response devices and patrols, student patrols, late-night transport/escort service, controlled dormitory access, alarm system, security beeper, lighted pathways. *Student services:* health clinic, personal/psychological counseling, women's center.

Athletics Member NCAA. All Division III. *Intercollegiate sports:* basketball M/W, cross-country running M/W, equestrian sports M/W, field hockey W, golf M/W, lacrosse M/W, soccer M/W, softball W, swimming and diving M/W, tennis M/W, track and field M/W, volleyball M/W. *Intramural sports:* basketball M/W, crew W(c), racquetball M/W, soccer M/W, ultimate Frisbee M/W, volleyball M/W.

Costs (2010–11) *Comprehensive fee:* $36,900 includes full-time tuition ($25,046), mandatory fees ($1138), and room and board ($10,716). Full-time tuition and fees vary according to course load and program. Part-time tuition: $597 per credit hour. *College room only:* $5962. Room and board charges vary

according to board plan and housing facility. *Payment plans:* installment, deferred payment. *Waivers:* minority students, children of alumni, and employees or children of employees.

Financial Aid Of all full-time matriculated undergraduates who enrolled in 2009, 1,822 applied for aid, 1,649 were judged to have need, 303 had their need fully met. 1,045 Federal Work-Study jobs (averaging $1996). In 2009, 336 non-need-based awards were made. *Average percent of need met:* 71%. *Average financial aid package:* $19,548. *Average need-based loan:* $4916. *Average need-based gift aid:* $14,146. *Average non-need-based aid:* $15,470. *Average indebtedness upon graduation:* $38,545.

Applying *Options:* electronic application, early admission, early decision, early action, deferred entrance. *Application fee:* $40. *Required:* essay or personal statement, high school transcript, 1 letter of recommendation. *Required for some:* audition/portfolio review. *Recommended:* interview. *Application deadlines:* 2/15 (freshmen), 5/15 (transfers), 12/15 (early action). *Early decision deadline:* 11/15. *Notification:* continuous until 3/1 (freshmen), continuous until 2/15 (transfers), 12/15 (early decision), 1/15 (early action).

Freshman Application Contact Mr. Thomas DaRin, Vice President for Enrollment Management, Nazareth College of Rochester, 4245 East Avenue, Rochester, NY 14618-3790. *Phone:* 585-389-2860. *Toll-free phone:* 800-462-3944. *Fax:* 585-389-2826. *E-mail:* admissions@naz.edu. *Web site:* http://www.naz.edu/.

The New School for General Studies

New York, New York

- **Independent** upper-level, founded 1919, part of The New School
- **Urban** campus with easy access to Manhattan
- **Coed** 671 undergraduate students, 53% full-time, 62% women, 38% men
- **Moderately difficult** entrance level, 94% of applicants were admitted

Undergraduates 354 full-time, 317 part-time. 34% are from out of state; 8% Black or African American, non-Hispanic/Latino; 10% Hispanic/Latino; 3% Asian, non-Hispanic/Latino; 0.6% American Indian or Alaska Native, non-Hispanic/Latino; 3% Two or more races, non-Hispanic/Latino; 12% Race/ethnicity unknown; 8% international; 27% transferred in.

Freshmen *Admission:* 18 applied, 17 admitted.

Faculty *Total:* 385, 17% full-time.

Academics *Calendar:* semesters. *Degrees:* certificates, bachelor's, master's, and postbachelor's certificates. *Special study options:* adult/continuing education programs, advanced placement credit, distance learning, English as a second language, independent study, internships, part-time degree program, services for LD students, student-designed majors, study abroad, summer session for credit.

Computers on Campus Students can access the following: campus intranet, computer help desk, free student e-mail accounts, online (class) grades, online (class) registration, online (class) schedules, online portal, unlimited wireless. Campuswide network is available. 100% of college-owned or -operated housing units are wired for high-speed Internet access. Wireless service is available via entire campus.

Student Life *Housing options:* coed, disabled students. Campus housing is university owned and leased by the school. *Activities and organizations:* drama/theater group, student-run newspaper, radio station, choral group. *Campus security:* 24-hour emergency response devices, controlled dormitory access, trained security personnel in central buildings. *Student services:* health clinic, personal/psychological counseling.

Costs (2010–11) *Comprehensive fee:* $40,580 includes full-time tuition ($25,320) and room and board ($15,260). Part-time tuition: $1055 per credit. Part-time tuition and fees vary according to course load. *College room only:* $12,260. Room and board charges vary according to board plan and housing facility. *Payment plan:* installment. *Waivers:* employees or children of employees.

Financial Aid Of all full-time matriculated undergraduates who enrolled in 2009, 264 applied for aid, 246 were judged to have need, 8 had their need fully met. In 2009, 4 non-need-based awards were made. *Average percent of need met:* 67%. *Average financial aid package:* $23,660. *Average need-based loan:* $11,430. *Average need-based gift aid:* $10,805. *Average non-need-based aid:* $6625.

Applying *Options:* electronic application, deferred entrance. *Application fee:* $50. *Application deadline:* 6/1 (transfers). *Notification:* continuous (transfers).

Application Contact Ms. Cory Meyers, Assistant Director of Admissions, The New School for General Studies, 72 Fifth Avenue, Room 304, New York, NY 10011. *Phone:* 212-229-5630. *Toll-free phone:* 800-862-5039. *Fax:* 212-627-2695. *E-mail:* nsadmissions@newschool.edu. *Web site:* http://www.newschool.edu/generalstudies/.

The New School for Jazz and Contemporary Music

New York, New York

- **Independent** 4-year, founded 1986, part of The New School
- **Urban** campus with easy access to Manhattan
- **Coed** 239 undergraduate students, 94% full-time, 17% women, 83% men
- **Very difficult** entrance level, 62% of applicants were admitted

Undergraduates 225 full-time, 14 part-time. 74% are from out of state; 10% Black or African American, non-Hispanic/Latino; 6% Hispanic/Latino; 3% Asian, non-Hispanic/Latino; 1% Two or more races, non-Hispanic/Latino; 9% Race/ethnicity unknown; 30% international; 14% transferred in; 27% live on campus. *Retention:* 73% of full-time freshmen returned.

Freshmen *Admission:* 263 applied, 164 admitted, 43 enrolled. *Average high school GPA:* 3.34.

Faculty *Total:* 59, 5% full-time. *Student/faculty ratio:* 11:1.

Academics *Calendar:* semesters. *Degree:* bachelor's. *Special study options:* academic remediation for entering students, advanced placement credit, double majors, English as a second language, independent study, internships, services for LD students.

Computers on Campus Students can access the following: campus intranet, computer help desk, free student e-mail accounts, online (class) grades, online (class) registration, online (class) schedules, online portal. Campuswide network is available. 100% of college-owned or -operated housing units are wired for high-speed Internet access. Wireless service is available via entire campus.

Student Life *Housing options:* coed, disabled students. Campus housing is university owned and leased by the school. Freshman applicants given priority for college housing. *Activities and organizations:* drama/theater group, student-run newspaper, radio station, choral group. *Campus security:* 24-hour emergency response devices, controlled dormitory access. *Student services:* health clinic, personal/psychological counseling.

Costs (2010–11) *Comprehensive fee:* $50,360 includes full-time tuition ($34,340), mandatory fees ($760), and room and board ($15,260). Part-time tuition: $1125 per credit. Part-time tuition and fees vary according to course load and program. *College room only:* $12,260. Room and board charges vary according to board plan and housing facility. *Payment plan:* installment. *Waivers:* employees or children of employees.

Financial Aid Of all full-time matriculated undergraduates who enrolled in 2009, 109 applied for aid, 99 were judged to have need, 13 had their need fully met. In 2009, 4 non-need-based awards were made. *Average percent of need met:* 70%. *Average financial aid package:* $24,691. *Average need-based loan:* $10,169. *Average need-based gift aid:* $17,942. *Average non-need-based aid:* $14,735. *Average indebtedness upon graduation:* $25,735.

Applying *Options:* electronic application, deferred entrance. *Application fee:* $100. *Required:* essay or personal statement, high school transcript, 1 letter of recommendation, audition, pre-screen tape/CD. *Application deadlines:* 1/1 (freshmen), 1/1 (transfers). *Notification:* continuous (freshmen), 4/1 (transfers).

Freshman Application Contact Ms. Terri Lucas, Jazz Admissions, The New School for Jazz and Contemporary Music, 55 West 13th Street, 5th Floor, New York, NY 10011. *Phone:* 212-229-5896. *Fax:* 212-229-8936. *E-mail:* jazzadm@newschool.edu. *Web site:* http://www.jazz.newschool.edu/.

See page 1470 for the College Close-Up.

New York City College of Technology of the City University of New York

Brooklyn, New York

- **State and locally supported** 4-year, founded 1946, part of City University of New York System
- **Urban** campus
- **Coed** 15,366 undergraduate students, 61% full-time, 47% women, 53% men
- **Noncompetitive** entrance level, 77% of applicants were admitted

Undergraduates 9,297 full-time, 6,069 part-time. Students come from 10 states and territories; 138 other countries; 38% Black or African American, non-Hispanic/Latino; 26% Hispanic/Latino; 16% Asian, non-Hispanic/Latino; 0.3% American Indian or Alaska Native, non-Hispanic/Latino; 5% international; 7% transferred in. *Retention:* 74% of full-time freshmen returned.

Freshmen *Admission:* 15,324 applied, 11,827 admitted, 2,930 enrolled.

Faculty *Total:* 1,211, 35% full-time, 35% with terminal degrees. *Student/faculty ratio:* 17:1.

Academics *Calendar:* semesters. *Degrees:* certificates, associate, and bachelor's. *Special study options:* academic remediation for entering students, accelerated degree program, adult/continuing education programs, advanced placement credit, distance learning, English as a second language, freshman honors college, honors programs, independent study, internships, off-campus

study, part-time degree program, services for LD students, student-designed majors, study abroad, summer session for credit.

Computers on Campus 367 computers/terminals are available on campus for general student use. Students can access the following: campus intranet, computer help desk, free student e-mail accounts, online (class) grades, online (class) registration, online (class) schedules. Campuswide network is available. Wireless service is available via classrooms, computer centers, computer labs, learning centers, libraries, student centers.

Student Life *Housing:* college housing not available. *Activities and organizations:* drama/theater group, student-run newspaper, choral group, International Business Organization (IBO), NYCCT - Mock Trial Club, Chess Club, Women in Islam, ASCE-Student Chapter of American Society of Civil Engineering. *Campus security:* 24-hour emergency response devices and patrols. *Student services:* health clinic, personal/psychological counseling, women's center.

Athletics Member NCAA. All Division III. *Intercollegiate sports:* basketball M/W, cross-country running M/W, soccer M, softball W, tennis M/W, track and field M/W, volleyball M/W. *Intramural sports:* basketball M/W, soccer M/W, table tennis M/W, volleyball M/W, weight lifting M/W.

Standardized Tests *Required for some:* SAT or ACT (for admission).

Costs (2011–12) *Tuition:* state resident $4600 full-time, $195 per credit part-time; nonresident $12,450 full-time, $415 per credit part-time. *Required fees:* $339 full-time, $85 per term part-time. *Payment plan:* installment. *Waivers:* employees or children of employees.

Financial Aid Of all full-time matriculated undergraduates who enrolled in 2009, 7,929 applied for aid, 7,514 were judged to have need, 203 had their need fully met. In 2009, 45 non-need-based awards were made. *Average percent of need met:* 60%. *Average financial aid package:* $7608. *Average need-based loan:* $3923. *Average need-based gift aid:* $7422. *Average non-need-based aid:* $511. *Financial aid deadline:* 4/30.

Applying *Options:* electronic application. *Application fee:* $65. *Required:* high school transcript. *Application deadlines:* 2/1 (freshmen), 2/1 (transfers). *Notification:* continuous until 2/1 (freshmen).

Freshman Application Contact Alexis Chaconis, Director of Admissions, New York City College of Technology of the City University of New York, 300 Jay Street, Brooklyn, NY 11201-2983. *Phone:* 718-260-5500. *E-mail:* achaconis@citytech.cuny.edu. *Web site:* http://www.citytech.cuny.edu/.

New York College of Health Professions

Syosset, New York

Director of Admissions Ms. Mary Rodas, Associate Director of Admissions, New York College of Health Professions, 6801 Jericho Turnpike, Syosset, NY 11791-4413. *Toll-free phone:* 800-922-7337 Ext. 351. *E-mail:* rdodas@nycollege.edu. *Web site:* http://www.nycollege.edu/.

New York Institute of Technology

Old Westbury, New York

- **Independent** university, founded 1955
- **Suburban** 1050-acre campus with easy access to New York City
- **Endowment** $46.8 million
- **Coed** 7,421 undergraduate students, 82% full-time, 36% women, 64% men
- **Moderately difficult** entrance level, 75% of applicants were admitted

Undergraduates 6,092 full-time, 1,329 part-time. Students come from 28 states and territories; 75 other countries; 10% are from out of state; 7% Black or African American, non-Hispanic/Latino; 8% Hispanic/Latino; 9% Asian, non-Hispanic/Latino; 0.1% Native Hawaiian or other Pacific Islander, non-Hispanic/Latino; 0.2% American Indian or Alaska Native, non-Hispanic/Latino; 0.3% Two or more races, non-Hispanic/Latino; 48% Race/ethnicity unknown; 9% international; 7% transferred in; 9% live on campus. *Retention:* 72% of full-time freshmen returned.

Freshmen *Admission:* 4,973 applied, 3,708 admitted, 1,306 enrolled. *Average high school GPA:* 3.4. *Test scores:* SAT critical reading scores over 500: 64%; SAT math scores over 500: 89%; ACT scores over 18: 99%; SAT critical reading scores over 600: 16%; SAT math scores over 600: 45%; ACT scores over 24: 66%; SAT critical reading scores over 700: 2%; SAT math scores over 700: 9%; ACT scores over 30: 10%.

Faculty *Total:* 1,106, 25% full-time. *Student/faculty ratio:* 13:1.

Academics *Calendar:* semesters. *Degrees:* certificates, associate, bachelor's, master's, doctoral-professional, post-master's, and postbachelor's certificates. *Special study options:* academic remediation for entering students, accelerated degree program, adult/continuing education programs, advanced placement credit, cooperative education, distance learning, double majors, English as a second language, external degree program, honors programs, independent study, internships, off-campus study, part-time degree program, services for LD students, student-designed majors, study abroad, summer session for credit. *ROTC:* Army (b), Air Force (b). *Unusual degree programs:* 3-2 occupational therapy, physical therapy, communication arts, architectural technology/energy management, architectural technology/MBA, mechanical engineering/energy management.

Computers on Campus 1,250 computers/terminals are available on campus for general student use. Students can access the following: e-mail. Campuswide network is available. 100% of college-owned or -operated housing units are wired for high-speed Internet access. Wireless service is available via classrooms, computer centers, computer labs, libraries.

Student Life *Housing options:* coed. Campus housing is university owned and is provided by a third party. Freshman campus housing is guaranteed. *Activities and organizations:* drama/theater group, student-run newspaper, radio and television station, choral group, national fraternities, national sororities. *Campus security:* 24-hour emergency response devices and patrols, late-night transport/escort service, controlled dormitory access. *Student services:* health clinic, personal/psychological counseling, women's center.

Athletics Member NCAA. All Division II except baseball (Division I). *Intercollegiate sports:* baseball M(s), basketball M(s)/W(s), cross-country running M(s)/W(s), lacrosse M(s), soccer M(s)/W(s), softball W(s), volleyball W(s). *Intramural sports:* basketball M/W, soccer M/W, softball W, volleyball W.

Standardized Tests *Required:* SAT or ACT (for admission).

Costs (2010–11) *Comprehensive fee:* $36,570 includes full-time tuition ($24,670), mandatory fees ($800), and room and board ($11,100). Full-time tuition and fees vary according to course load and program. Part-time tuition: $835 per credit hour. Part-time tuition and fees vary according to course load. *Required fees:* $330 per term part-time. *Room and board:* Room and board charges vary according to board plan, housing facility, and location. *Payment plan:* installment. *Waivers:* senior citizens and employees or children of employees.

Financial Aid Of all full-time matriculated undergraduates who enrolled in 2008, 3,307 applied for aid, 2,920 were judged to have need. In 2008, 573 non-need-based awards were made. *Average financial aid package:* $20,439. *Average need-based loan:* $6226. *Average need-based gift aid:* $6796. *Average non-need-based aid:* $11,506.

Applying *Options:* electronic application, deferred entrance. *Application fee:* $50. *Required:* essay or personal statement. *Required for some:* high school transcript, interview. *Application deadlines:* rolling (freshmen), rolling (transfers). *Notification:* continuous (freshmen), continuous (transfers).

Freshman Application Contact Ms. Doreen Meyer, Director of Financial Aid, New York Institute of Technology, PO Box 8000, Old Westbury, NY 11568. *Phone:* 516-686-1083. *Toll-free phone:* 800-345-NYIT. *Fax:* 516-686-7613. *E-mail:* admissions@nyit.edu. *Web site:* http://www.nyit.edu/.

New York School of Interior Design
New York, New York

- **Independent** comprehensive, founded 1916
- **Urban** 1-acre campus
- **Endowment** $2.9 million
- **Coed, primarily women** 656 undergraduate students, 30% full-time, 90% women, 10% men
- **Moderately difficult** entrance level, 48% of applicants were admitted

Undergraduates 200 full-time, 456 part-time. Students come from 31 states and territories; 28 other countries; 38% are from out of state; 4% Black or African American, non-Hispanic/Latino; 10% Hispanic/Latino; 14% Asian, non-Hispanic/Latino; 10% Race/ethnicity unknown; 1% international; 15% transferred in; 4% live on campus. *Retention:* 90% of full-time freshmen returned.

Freshmen *Admission:* 176 applied, 84 admitted, 39 enrolled. *Average high school GPA:* 3.44. *Test scores:* SAT critical reading scores over 500: 41%; SAT math scores over 500: 54%; SAT writing scores over 500: 26%; SAT critical reading scores over 600: 12%; SAT math scores over 600: 21%; SAT writing scores over 600: 9%; SAT critical reading scores over 700: 4%; SAT math scores over 700: 8%.

Faculty *Total:* 93, 8% full-time, 52% with terminal degrees. *Student/faculty ratio:* 8:1.

Academics *Calendar:* semesters. *Degrees:* certificates, associate, bachelor's, and master's. *Special study options:* adult/continuing education programs, advanced placement credit, English as a second language, external degree program, independent study, internships, part-time degree program, services for LD students, summer session for credit.

Computers on Campus 135 computers/terminals are available on campus for general student use. Students can access the following: free student e-mail accounts, online (class) grades, online (class) registration, online (class) schedules. Campuswide network is available. Wireless service is available via classrooms, libraries.

Student Life *Housing options:* coed. Campus housing is leased by the school and is provided by a third party. *Activities and organizations:* American Society of Interior Designers, Contract Club, Student Council. *Campus security:* security during school hours.

Standardized Tests *Required for some:* SAT or ACT (for admission).

Costs (2011–12) *Tuition:* $23,521 full-time, $796 per credit part-time. Full-time tuition and fees vary according to course load. Part-time tuition and fees vary according to course load. *Required fees:* $335 full-time, $335 per term part-time. *Room only:* $15,200. *Payment plan:* installment. *Waivers:* employees or children of employees.
Financial Aid Of all full-time matriculated undergraduates who enrolled in 2008, 403 applied for aid, 374 were judged to have need, 5 had their need fully met. 20 Federal Work-Study jobs (averaging $2212). In 2008, 4 non-need-based awards were made. *Average percent of need met:* 1%. *Average financial aid package:* $7890. *Average need-based loan:* $3775. *Average need-based gift aid:* $5907. *Average non-need-based aid:* $5750. *Average indebtedness upon graduation:* $13,327.
Applying *Options:* electronic application, deferred entrance. *Application fee:* $55. *Required:* essay or personal statement, high school transcript, minimum 2.8 GPA, 2 letters of recommendation, portfolio. *Application deadlines:* 2/1 (freshmen), 2/1 (transfers). *Notification:* 4/1 (freshmen), 4/1 (transfers).
Freshman Application Contact Sarah Morgan, Admissions Associate, New York School of Interior Design, 170 East 70th Street, New York, NY 10021-5110. *Phone:* 212-472-1500 Ext. 204. *Toll-free phone:* 800-336-9743 Ext. 204. *Fax:* 212-472-1867. *E-mail:* admissions@nysid.edu. *Web site:* http://www.nysid.edu/.

See page 1472 for the College Close-Up.

New York University
New York, New York

- **Independent** university, founded 1831
- **Urban** campus
- **Endowment** $2.5 billion
- **Coed** 22,097 undergraduate students, 94% full-time, 61% women, 39% men
- **Most difficult** entrance level, 38% of applicants were admitted

Undergraduates 20,815 full-time, 1,282 part-time. Students come from 57 states and territories; 129 other countries; 65% are from out of state; 4% Black or African American, non-Hispanic/Latino; 8% Hispanic/Latino; 20% Asian, non-Hispanic/Latino; 0.3% American Indian or Alaska Native, non-Hispanic/Latino; 1% Two or more races, non-Hispanic/Latino; 13% Race/ethnicity unknown; 9% international; 5% transferred in; 48% live on campus. *Retention:* 92% of full-time freshmen returned.
Freshmen *Admission:* 37,464 applied, 14,275 admitted, 5,012 enrolled. *Average high school GPA:* 3.6. *Test scores:* SAT critical reading scores over 500: 99%; SAT math scores over 500: 100%; SAT writing scores over 500: 99%; ACT scores over 18: 100%; SAT critical reading scores over 600: 83%; SAT math scores over 600: 88%; SAT writing scores over 600: 87%; ACT scores over 24: 98%; SAT critical reading scores over 700: 32%; SAT math scores over 700: 42%; SAT writing scores over 700: 37%; ACT scores over 30: 48%.
Faculty *Total:* 5,344, 45% full-time, 73% with terminal degrees. *Student/faculty ratio:* 11:1.
Academics *Calendar:* semesters. *Degrees:* certificates, associate, bachelor's, master's, doctoral-other, doctoral-professional, doctoral-research/scholarship, post-master's, and postbachelor's certificates. *Special study options:* adult/continuing education programs, advanced placement credit, double majors, honors programs, independent study, internships, off-campus study, part-time degree program, services for LD students, student-designed majors, study abroad, summer session for credit. *ROTC:* Army (c), Air Force (c). *Unusual degree programs:* 3-2 engineering with NYU-Polytechnic.
Computers on Campus 4,500 computers/terminals are available on campus for general student use. Students can access the following: computer help desk, free student e-mail accounts, online (class) grades, online (class) registration, online (class) schedules. Campuswide network is available. 100% of college-owned or -operated housing units are wired for high-speed Internet access. Wireless service is available via classrooms, computer labs, learning centers, libraries, student centers.
Student Life *Housing options:* coed, disabled students. Campus housing is university owned and leased by the school. Freshman campus housing is guaranteed. *Activities and organizations:* drama/theater group, student-run newspaper, radio and television station, choral group, Inter-Varsity Christian Fellowship, Asian Cultural Union, Hillel, Latinos Unidos Con Honor y Amistad (LUCHA), South Asian Student Association (SHRUTI), national fraternities, national sororities. *Campus security:* 24-hour emergency response devices and patrols, student patrols, late-night transport/escort service, controlled dormitory access, 24-hour security in residence halls. *Student services:* health clinic, personal/psychological counseling, women's center.
Athletics Member NCAA. All Division III. *Intercollegiate sports:* baseball M(c), basketball M/W, cheerleading M/W, crew M(c)/W(c), cross-country running M/W, equestrian sports M(c)/W(c), fencing M/W, golf M/W, ice hockey M(c), lacrosse M(c)/W(c), soccer M/W, softball W(c), swimming and diving M/W, tennis M/W, track and field M/W, ultimate Frisbee M(c)/W(c), volleyball M/W, wrestling M. *Intramural sports:* badminton M(c)/W(c), basketball

M/W, bowling M/W, ice hockey M(c), lacrosse M(c)/W(c), racquetball M/W, soccer M/W, softball M(c)/W(c), squash M/W, table tennis M(c)/W(c), tennis M/W, volleyball M/W, water polo M/W(c).
Standardized Tests *Required:* Applicants are able to submit the SAT and two SAT Subject Tests OR the ACT with Writing OR the SAT and two Advanced Placement Exam scores OR three SAT Subject Tests scores (one in literature or the humanities) one in math/science, and one in any non-language area OR three AP exam scores (one in lit). *Recommended:* SAT and SAT Subject Tests or ACT (for admission).
Costs (2010–11) *Comprehensive fee:* $53,592 includes full-time tuition ($37,866), mandatory fees ($2216), and room and board ($13,510). Full-time tuition and fees vary according to course load and program. Part-time tuition: $1179 per credit. Part-time tuition and fees vary according to program. No tuition increase for student's term of enrollment. *Required fees:* $60 per credit part-time, $409 per term part-time. *Room and board:* Room and board charges vary according to board plan and housing facility. *Payment plans:* tuition prepayment, installment, deferred payment. *Waivers:* employees or children of employees.
Financial Aid Of all full-time matriculated undergraduates who enrolled in 2008, 12,459 applied for aid, 10,817 were judged to have need. 2,960 Federal Work-Study jobs (averaging $2185). In 2008, 1387 non-need-based awards were made. *Average percent of need met:* 61%. *Average financial aid package:* $24,999. *Average need-based loan:* $5016. *Average need-based gift aid:* $18,459. *Average non-need-based aid:* $6920. *Average indebtedness upon graduation:* $41,300.
Applying *Options:* electronic application, early decision, deferred entrance. *Application fee:* $70. *Required:* essay or personal statement, high school transcript, 1 letter of recommendation. *Required for some:* audition, portfolio. *Application deadlines:* 1/1 (freshmen), 4/1 (transfers). *Early decision deadline:* 11/1 (for plan 1), 1/1 (for plan 2). *Notification:* 4/1 (freshmen), 12/15 (early decision plan 1), 2/20 (early decision plan 2).
Freshman Application Contact Undergraduate Admissions Processing Center, New York University, 665 Broadway, 11th Floor, New York, NY 10011. *Phone:* 212-998-4500. *Fax:* 212-995-4902. *E-mail:* nyuadmit@uccvm.nyu.edu. *Web site:* http://www.nyu.edu/.

Niagara University
Niagara Falls, New York

- **Independent** comprehensive, founded 1856, affiliated with Roman Catholic Church
- **Suburban** 160-acre campus with easy access to Buffalo and Toronto
- **Endowment** $74.8 million
- **Coed** 3,308 undergraduate students, 89% full-time, 61% women, 39% men
- **Moderately difficult** entrance level, 76% of applicants were admitted

Undergraduates 2,941 full-time, 367 part-time. Students come from 31 states and territories; 12 other countries; 7% are from out of state; 4% Black or African American, non-Hispanic/Latino; 2% Hispanic/Latino; 1% Asian, non-Hispanic/Latino; 0.8% American Indian or Alaska Native, non-Hispanic/Latino; 19% Race/ethnicity unknown; 10% international; 6% transferred in; 51% live on campus. *Retention:* 77% of full-time freshmen returned.
Freshmen *Admission:* 3,068 applied, 2,341 admitted, 671 enrolled. *Average high school GPA:* 3.3. *Test scores:* SAT critical reading scores over 500: 52%; SAT math scores over 500: 61%; ACT scores over 18: 90%; SAT critical reading scores over 600: 12%; SAT math scores over 600: 16%; ACT scores over 24: 39%; SAT critical reading scores over 700: 1%; SAT math scores over 700: 1%; ACT scores over 30: 4%.
Faculty *Total:* 351, 44% full-time, 41% with terminal degrees. *Student/faculty ratio:* 12:1.
Academics *Calendar:* semesters. *Degrees:* associate, bachelor's, master's, post-master's, and postbachelor's certificates. *Special study options:* academic remediation for entering students, accelerated degree program, advanced placement credit, cooperative education, double majors, English as a second language, freshman honors college, honors programs, internships, off-campus study, part-time degree program, services for LD students, study abroad, summer session for credit. *ROTC:* Army (b).
Computers on Campus 175 computers/terminals are available on campus for general student use. Students can access the following: campus intranet, computer help desk, free student e-mail accounts, online (class) grades, online (class) registration, online (class) schedules. Campuswide network is available. 100% of college-owned or -operated housing units are wired for high-speed Internet access. Wireless service is available via classrooms, computer centers, computer labs, libraries, student centers.
Student Life *Housing:* on-campus residence required through sophomore year. *Options:* coed, women-only. Campus housing is university owned. Freshman campus housing is guaranteed. *Activities and organizations:* drama/theater group, student-run newspaper, radio station, choral group, Niagara University Community Action Program, student government, Programming Board, national fraternities. *Campus security:* 24-hour emergency response devices

and patrols, late-night transport/escort service, controlled dormitory access, 24-hour escort service. *Student services:* health clinic, personal/psychological counseling.

Athletics Member NCAA. All Division I. *Intercollegiate sports:* baseball M(s), basketball M(s)/W(s), cross-country running M(s)/W(s), golf M(s)/W(s), ice hockey M(s)/W(s), lacrosse M/W(s), soccer M(s)/W(s), softball W(s), swimming and diving M(s)/W(s), tennis M(s)/W(s), volleyball W(s). *Intramural sports:* basketball M/W, ice hockey M/W, lacrosse M/W, racquetball M/W, rugby M(c)/W(c), skiing (downhill) M(c)/W(c), soccer M/W, softball M/W, volleyball M/W, water polo M/W.

Standardized Tests *Required:* SAT or ACT (for admission).

Costs (2010–11) *Comprehensive fee:* $36,300 includes full-time tuition ($24,600), mandatory fees ($1050), and room and board ($10,650). Part-time tuition: $820 per credit hour. *Payment plans:* installment, deferred payment. *Waivers:* senior citizens and employees or children of employees.

Financial Aid Of all full-time matriculated undergraduates who enrolled in 2009, 2,328 applied for aid, 2,143 were judged to have need, 1,080 had their need fully met. 381 Federal Work-Study jobs (averaging $3167). 35 state and other part-time jobs (averaging $4162). In 2009, 457 non-need-based awards were made. *Average percent of need met:* 82%. *Average financial aid package:* $20,370. *Average need-based loan:* $4598. *Average need-based gift aid:* $16,130. *Average non-need-based aid:* $10,208. *Average indebtedness upon graduation:* $27,813.

Applying *Options:* electronic application, early admission, deferred entrance. *Application fee:* $30. *Required:* high school transcript. *Recommended:* minimum 3 GPA, 3 letters of recommendation, interview. *Application deadlines:* 8/1 (freshmen), 8/15 (transfers).

Freshman Application Contact Ms. Christine M. McDermott, Associate Director of Admissions, Niagara University, Niagara University, NY 14109. *Phone:* 716-286-8700 Ext. 8715. *Toll-free phone:* 800-462-2111. *Fax:* 716-286-8733. *E-mail:* admissions@niagara.edu. *Web site:* http://www.niagara.edu/.

See page 1474 for the College Close-Up.

Nyack College
Nyack, New York

- **Independent** comprehensive, founded 1882, affiliated with The Christian and Missionary Alliance
- **Suburban** 125-acre campus with easy access to New York City
- **Coed** 2,150 undergraduate students, 86% full-time, 58% women, 42% men
- 100% of applicants were admitted

Undergraduates 1,848 full-time, 302 part-time. Students come from 35 states and territories; 54 other countries; 31% are from out of state; 35% Black or African American, non-Hispanic/Latino; 24% Hispanic/Latino; 7% Asian, non-Hispanic/Latino; 0.2% American Indian or Alaska Native, non-Hispanic/Latino; 3% Two or more races, non-Hispanic/Latino; 2% Race/ethnicity unknown; 5% international; 11% transferred in. *Retention:* 76% of full-time freshmen returned.

Freshmen *Admission:* 615 applied, 613 admitted, 325 enrolled. *Average high school GPA:* 2.72. *Test scores:* SAT critical reading scores over 500: 29%; SAT math scores over 500: 31%; ACT scores over 18: 68%; SAT critical reading scores over 600: 8%; SAT math scores over 600: 9%; ACT scores over 24: 13%; SAT critical reading scores over 700: 1%.

Faculty *Total:* 290, 38% full-time, 35% with terminal degrees. *Student/faculty ratio:* 14:1.

Academics *Calendar:* semesters. *Degrees:* certificates, associate, bachelor's, master's, and doctoral-professional. *Special study options:* academic remediation for entering students, accelerated degree program, adult/continuing education programs, advanced placement credit, distance learning, double majors, English as a second language, honors programs, independent study, internships, off-campus study, part-time degree program, services for LD students, study abroad, summer session for credit. *Unusual degree programs:* 3-2 Education (Childhood Special Education) - B.S./M.S.

Computers on Campus 124 computers/terminals are available on campus for general student use. Students can access the following: campus intranet, computer help desk, free student e-mail accounts, online (class) grades, online (class) registration, online (class) schedules. Campuswide network is available. 98% of college-owned or -operated housing units are wired for high-speed Internet access. Wireless service is available via entire campus.

Student Life *Housing:* on-campus residence required through sophomore year. *Options:* men-only, women-only, disabled students. Campus housing is university owned. Freshman campus housing is guaranteed. *Activities and organizations:* drama/theater group, student-run newspaper, radio station, choral group. *Campus security:* 24-hour emergency response devices and patrols, student patrols, late-night transport/escort service. *Student services:* health clinic, personal/psychological counseling.

Athletics Member NCAA, NCCAA. All NCAA Division II. *Intercollegiate sports:* baseball M(s), basketball M(s)/W(s), cheerleading M(s)/W(s), cross-country running M(s)/W(s), golf M(s), soccer M(s)/W(s), softball W(s), volleyball W(s).

Standardized Tests *Required:* SAT or ACT (for admission).

Costs (2011–12) *One-time required fee:* $100. *Comprehensive fee:* $29,750 includes full-time tuition ($20,500), mandatory fees ($1000), and room and board ($8250). Full-time tuition and fees vary according to course load, location, and program. Part-time tuition: $855 per credit hour. Part-time tuition and fees vary according to course load, location, and program. *Required fees:* $150 per term part-time. *Room and board:* Room and board charges vary according to board plan, housing facility, and location. *Payment plan:* installment. *Waivers:* employees or children of employees.

Financial Aid Of all full-time matriculated undergraduates who enrolled in 2008, 1,559 applied for aid, 1,482 were judged to have need, 141 had their need fully met. 213 Federal Work-Study jobs (averaging $1310). 61 state and other part-time jobs (averaging $1627). In 2008, 193 non-need-based awards were made. *Average percent of need met:* 63%. *Average financial aid package:* $16,846. *Average need-based loan:* $4534. *Average need-based gift aid:* $11,472. *Average non-need-based aid:* $6247. *Average indebtedness upon graduation:* $35,879.

Applying *Options:* electronic application, deferred entrance. *Application fee:* $25. *Required:* essay or personal statement, high school transcript, minimum 2 GPA, 1 letter of recommendation, Signed statement of faith and community life form. *Required for some:* interview. *Application deadlines:* rolling (freshmen), rolling (out-of-state freshmen), rolling (transfers). *Notification:* continuous (freshmen), continuous (out-of-state freshmen), continuous (transfers).

Freshman Application Contact Dinesh Mahtani, Director of Admissions, Nyack College, 1 South Boulevard, Nyack, NY 10960-3698. *Phone:* 845-675-4401. *Toll-free phone:* 800-33-NYACK. *Fax:* 845-358-3047. *E-mail:* admissions@nyack.edu. *Web site:* http://www.nyack.edu/.

Ohr Hameir Theological Seminary
Cortlandt Manor, New York

Director of Admissions Director of Admissions, Ohr Hameir Theological Seminary, 141 Furnace Woods Road, Cortlandt Manor, NY 10567. *Phone:* 914-736-1500.

Ohr Somayach/Joseph Tanenbaum Educational Center
Monsey, New York

- **Independent Jewish** comprehensive, founded 1979
- **Small-town** 7-acre campus with easy access to New York City
- **Men only**
- **Moderately difficult** entrance level

Academics *Calendar:* semesters. *Degrees:* bachelor's and doctoral-professional.

Student Life *Campus security:* 24-hour emergency response devices and patrols, controlled dormitory access.

Applying *Options:* early admission. *Required:* interview. *Required for some:* essay or personal statement. *Recommended:* high school transcript.

Freshman Application Contact Ohr Somayach/Joseph Tanenbaum Educational Center, PO Box 334, 244 Route 306, Monsey, NY 10952-0334. *Phone:* 845-425-1370 Ext. 22. *Web site:* http://ohr.edu/.

Pace University
New York, New York

- **Independent** university, founded 1906
- **Urban** campus with easy access to New York City
- **Endowment** $104.6 million
- **Coed** 8,126 undergraduate students, 84% full-time, 59% women, 41% men
- **Moderately difficult** entrance level, 79% of applicants were admitted

Undergraduates 6,814 full-time, 1,312 part-time. Students come from 49 states and territories; 80 other countries; 29% are from out of state; 10% Black or African American, non-Hispanic/Latino; 13% Hispanic/Latino; 8% Asian, non-Hispanic/Latino; 0.3% American Indian or Alaska Native, non-Hispanic/Latino; 0.6% Two or more races, non-Hispanic/Latino; 26% Race/ethnicity unknown; 5% international; 6% transferred in; 51% live on campus. *Retention:* 77% of full-time freshmen returned.

Freshmen *Admission:* 10,623 applied, 8,356 admitted, 1,787 enrolled. *Average high school GPA:* 3.2. *Test scores:* SAT critical reading scores over 500: 73%; SAT math scores over 500: 77%; ACT scores over 18: 100%; SAT criti-

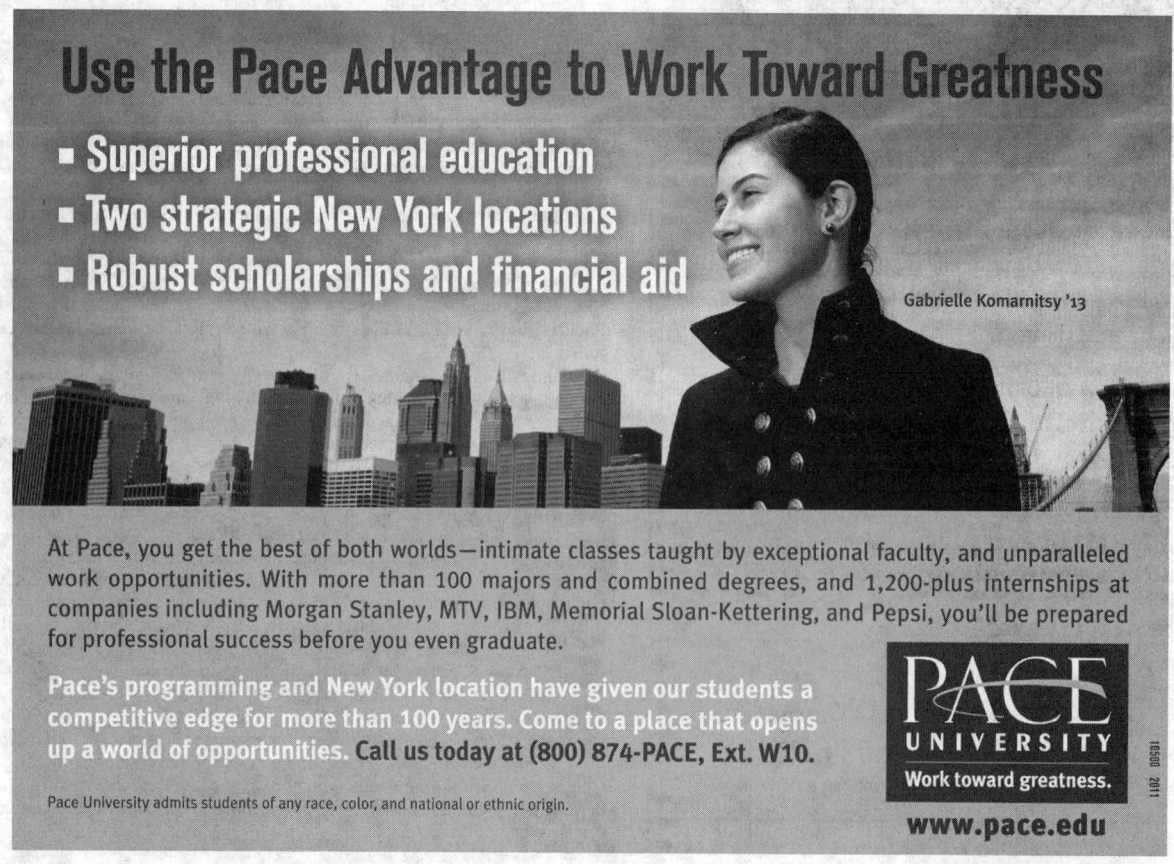

cal reading scores over 600: 22%; SAT math scores over 600: 24%; ACT scores over 24: 63%; SAT critical reading scores over 700: 2%; SAT math scores over 700: 2%; ACT scores over 30: 4%.

Faculty *Total:* 1,208, 37% full-time, 47% with terminal degrees. *Student/faculty ratio:* 14:1.

Academics *Calendar:* semesters. *Degrees:* certificates, diplomas, associate, bachelor's, master's, doctoral-professional, doctoral-research/scholarship, post-master's, and postbachelor's certificates. *Special study options:* academic remediation for entering students, accelerated degree program, adult/continuing education programs, advanced placement credit, cooperative education, distance learning, double majors, English as a second language, freshman honors college, honors programs, independent study, internships, part-time degree program, study abroad, summer session for credit. *ROTC:* Army (c), Air Force (c). *Unusual degree programs:* 3-2 engineering with Manhattan College, Rensselaer Polytechnic Institute; occupational therapy with Columbia University College of Physicians and Surgeons, physical therapy with New York Medical College, podiatry with the New York College of Podiatric Medicine.

Computers on Campus 279 computers/terminals are available on campus for general student use. Students can access the following: computer help desk, free student e-mail accounts, online (class) registration, online (class) schedules. Campuswide network is available. 100% of college-owned or -operated housing units are wired for high-speed Internet access. Wireless service is available via classrooms, computer centers, computer labs, libraries, student centers.

Student Life *Housing options:* coed. Campus housing is university owned and leased by the school. *Activities and organizations:* drama/theater group, student-run newspaper, radio and television station, choral group, Black Student Union, Beta Alpha Psi, OLAS (Organization of Latin American Students), Pace Board, Lubin Business Association, national fraternities, national sororities. *Campus security:* 24-hour emergency response devices and patrols, late-night transport/escort service, controlled dormitory access. *Student services:* health clinic, personal/psychological counseling.

Athletics Member NCAA. All Division II. *Intercollegiate sports:* baseball M(s), basketball M(s)/W(s), cross-country running M(s)/W(s), equestrian sports W, football M, golf M(s), lacrosse M(s), soccer W(s), softball W(s), swimming and diving M/W, tennis M(s)/W(s), track and field M(s)/W(s), volleyball W(s). *Intramural sports:* soccer M/W, softball M/W, volleyball M/W.

Standardized Tests *Required:* SAT or ACT (for admission).

Costs (2010–11) *Comprehensive fee:* $47,502 includes full-time tuition ($32,656), mandatory fees ($1046), and room and board ($13,800). Part-time tuition: $937 per credit hour. Part-time tuition and fees vary according to course load. *Room and board:* Room and board charges vary according to board plan, housing facility, and location. *Payment plan:* installment. *Waivers:* senior citizens and employees or children of employees.

Financial Aid Of all full-time matriculated undergraduates who enrolled in 2009, 5,544 applied for aid, 5,215 were judged to have need, 471 had their need fully met. 1,225 Federal Work-Study jobs (averaging $3491). In 2009, 1202 non-need-based awards were made. *Average percent of need met:* 71%. *Average financial aid package:* $26,579. *Average need-based loan:* $4641. *Average need-based gift aid:* $21,828. *Average non-need-based aid:* $10,785. *Average indebtedness upon graduation:* $38,035.

Applying *Options:* electronic application, early action, deferred entrance. *Application fee:* $50. *Required:* essay or personal statement, high school transcript, 2 letters of recommendation. *Recommended:* minimum 3 GPA, interview. *Application deadlines:* 2/15 (freshmen), rolling (transfers), 11/30 (early action). *Notification:* continuous (freshmen), continuous (transfers), 1/1 (early action).

Freshman Application Contact Ms. Donna J. Hoyt, Dean of Admissions, Pace University, One Pace Plaza, 163 William Street, New York, NY 10038. *Phone:* 212-346-1794. *Toll-free phone:* 800-874-7223. *Fax:* 212-346-1821. *E-mail:* dhoyt@pace.edu. *Web site:* http://www.pace.edu/.

See page 1494 for the College Close-Up.

Parsons The New School for Design

New York, New York

- **Independent** comprehensive, founded 1896, part of The New School
- **Urban** 2-acre campus with easy access to Manhattan
- **Coed** 4,191 undergraduate students, 89% full-time, 79% women, 21% men
- **Very difficult** entrance level, 63% of applicants were admitted

Undergraduates 3,745 full-time, 446 part-time. 72% are from out of state; 4% Black or African American, non-Hispanic/Latino; 9% Hispanic/Latino; 16% Asian, non-Hispanic/Latino; 0.3% Native Hawaiian or other Pacific Islander, non-Hispanic/Latino; 0.3% American Indian or Alaska Native, non-Hispanic/Latino; 1% Two or more races, non-Hispanic/Latino; 6% Race/ethnicity unknown; 34% international; 16% transferred in; 23% live on campus. *Retention:* 83% of full-time freshmen returned.

Freshmen *Admission:* 2,866 applied, 1,796 admitted, 784 enrolled. *Average high school GPA:* 3.27. *Test scores:* SAT critical reading scores over 500: 69%; SAT math scores over 500: 73%; SAT writing scores over 500: 73%; ACT scores over 18: 95%; SAT critical reading scores over 600: 26%; SAT math scores over 600: 36%; SAT writing scores over 600: 29%; ACT scores over 24: 50%; SAT critical reading scores over 700: 4%; SAT math scores over 700: 7%; SAT writing scores over 700: 5%; ACT scores over 30: 5%.

Faculty *Total:* 1,104, 14% full-time, 7% with terminal degrees. *Student/faculty ratio:* 9:1.

Academics *Calendar:* semesters. *Degrees:* certificates, associate, bachelor's, and master's. *Special study options:* advanced placement credit, cooperative education, distance learning, English as a second language, independent study, internships, off-campus study, services for LD students, student-designed majors, study abroad, summer session for credit.

Computers on Campus Students can access the following: campus intranet, computer help desk, free student e-mail accounts, online (class) grades, online (class) registration, online (class) schedules, online portal. Campuswide network is available. 100% of college-owned or -operated housing units are wired for high-speed Internet access. Wireless service is available via entire campus.

Student Life *Housing options:* coed, disabled students. Campus housing is university owned and leased by the school. Freshman applicants given priority for college housing. *Activities and organizations:* drama/theater group, student-run newspaper, radio station, choral group. *Campus security:* 24-hour emergency response devices, controlled dormitory access. *Student services:* health clinic, personal/psychological counseling.

Standardized Tests *Required:* SAT or ACT (for admission).

Costs (2010–11) *Comprehensive fee:* $52,870 includes full-time tuition ($36,800), mandatory fees ($810), and room and board ($15,260). Part-time tuition: $1255 per credit. Part-time tuition and fees vary according to course load. *College room only:* $12,260. Room and board charges vary according to board plan and housing facility. *Payment plan:* installment. *Waivers:* employees or children of employees.

Financial Aid Of all full-time matriculated undergraduates who enrolled in 2009, 2,078 applied for aid, 1,940 were judged to have need, 193 had their need fully met. In 2009, 96 non-need-based awards were made. *Average percent of need met:* 63%. *Average financial aid package:* $27,120. *Average need-based loan:* $10,395. *Average need-based gift aid:* $17,805. *Average non-need-based aid:* $4150. *Average indebtedness upon graduation:* $38,290.

Applying *Options:* electronic application, early action, deferred entrance. *Application fee:* $50. *Required:* high school transcript, portfolio, home examination. *Required for some:* essay or personal statement, interview. *Recommended:* minimum 3 GPA. *Application deadlines:* rolling (freshmen), 4/1 (transfers). *Notification:* continuous (freshmen), continuous (transfers).

Freshman Application Contact Director of Admissions, Parsons The New School for Design, 65 Fifth Avenue, New York, NY 10011-8878. *Phone:* 212-229-8989. *Toll-free phone:* 877-528-3321. *Fax:* 212-229-8975. *E-mail:* thinkparsons@newschool.edu. *Web site:* http://www.parsons.edu/.

See page 1498 for the College Close-Up.

Paul Smith's College

Paul Smiths, New York

Freshman Application Contact Admissions Office, Paul Smith's College, Routes 86 and 30, PO Box 265, Paul Smiths, NY 12970. *Phone:* 518-327-6227. *Toll-free phone:* 800-421-2605. *Fax:* 518-327-6016. *E-mail:* admissions@paulsmiths.edu. *Web site:* http://www.paulsmiths.edu/.

Plaza College

Jackson Heights, New York

- **Proprietary** primarily 2-year, founded 1916
- **Urban** campus with easy access to New York City
- **Coed**
- **Moderately difficult** entrance level

Academics *Calendar:* semesters. *Degrees:* associate and bachelor's.

Student Life *Campus security:* 24-hour emergency response devices.

Standardized Tests *Required:* CPAt (for admission).

Costs (2010–11) *One-time required fee:* $100. *Tuition:* $9900 full-time. Full-time tuition and fees vary according to program. Part-time tuition and fees vary according to course load and program. *Required fees:* $1450 full-time.

Applying *Options:* electronic application. *Application fee:* $100. *Required:* essay or personal statement, interview, placement test.

Freshman Application Contact Dean Rose Ann Black, Dean of Administration, Plaza College, 74-09 37th Avenue, Jackson Heights, NY 11372. *Phone:* 718-779-1430. *Toll-free phone:* 877-752-9233. *E-mail:* info@plazacollege.edu. *Web site:* http://www.plazacollege.edu/.

Polytechnic Institute of NYU

Brooklyn, New York

- **Independent** university, founded 1854, administratively affiliated with New York University
- **Urban** 3-acre campus
- **Endowment** $97.1 million
- **Coed** 1,768 undergraduate students, 96% full-time, 19% women, 81% men
- **Very difficult** entrance level, 64% of applicants were admitted

Undergraduates 1,695 full-time, 73 part-time. Students come from 26 states and territories; 34 other countries; 14% are from out of state; 8% Black or African American, non-Hispanic/Latino; 11% Hispanic/Latino; 32% Asian, non-Hispanic/Latino; 0.2% American Indian or Alaska Native, non-Hispanic/Latino; 9% Race/ethnicity unknown; 11% international; 5% transferred in; 25% live on campus. *Retention:* 86% of full-time freshmen returned.

Freshmen *Admission:* 2,537 applied, 1,627 admitted, 306 enrolled. *Average high school GPA:* 3.5. *Test scores:* SAT critical reading scores over 500: 91%; SAT math scores over 500: 100%; SAT writing scores over 500: 87%; ACT scores over 18: 100%; SAT critical reading scores over 600: 49%; SAT math scores over 600: 92%; SAT writing scores over 600: 45%; ACT scores over 24: 100%; SAT critical reading scores over 700: 6%; SAT math scores over 700: 38%; SAT writing scores over 700: 9%; ACT scores over 30: 17%.

Faculty *Total:* 370, 44% full-time, 73% with terminal degrees. *Student/faculty ratio:* 13:1.

Academics *Calendar:* semesters. *Degrees:* bachelor's, master's, doctoral-research/scholarship, and postbachelor's certificates. *Special study options:* academic remediation for entering students, accelerated degree program, advanced placement credit, cooperative education, double majors, English as a second language, honors programs, internships, part-time degree program, study abroad, summer session for credit. *ROTC:* Army (c), Air Force (c).

Computers on Campus 1,334 computers/terminals are available on campus for general student use. Students can access the following: campus intranet, computer help desk, free student e-mail accounts, online (class) grades, online (class) registration, online (class) schedules. Campuswide network is available. 100% of college-owned or -operated housing units are wired for high-speed Internet access. Wireless service is available via entire campus.

Student Life *Housing options:* coed. Campus housing is university owned. Freshman applicants given priority for college housing. *Activities and organizations:* student-run newspaper, National Society of Black Engineers, Society of Hispanic Professional Engineers, Association for Computing Machinery, Alpha Phi Omega, Chinese Student Society, national fraternities, national sororities. *Campus security:* 24-hour patrols, controlled dormitory access. *Student services:* health clinic, personal/psychological counseling, women's center.

Athletics Member NCAA. All Division III. *Intercollegiate sports:* baseball M, basketball M/W, cross-country running M/W, soccer M/W, softball W, tennis M/W, track and field M/W, volleyball M/W. *Intramural sports:* badminton M/W, basketball M/W, bowling M/W, football M/W, golf M(c)/W(c), soccer M/W, table tennis M(c)/W(c), track and field M(c)/W(c), volleyball M/W, weight lifting M(c)/W(c).

Standardized Tests *Required:* SAT or ACT (for admission). *Recommended:* SAT Subject Tests (for admission).

Costs (2010–11) *Comprehensive fee:* $46,364 includes full-time tuition ($35,104), mandatory fees ($1180), and room and board ($10,080). Full-time tuition and fees vary according to course load. Part-time tuition: $1116 per credit hour. Part-time tuition and fees vary according to course load. No tuition increase for student's term of enrollment. *Required fees:* $215 per term part-time. *College room only:* $7950. Room and board charges vary according to housing facility. *Payment plans:* tuition prepayment, installment, deferred payment. *Waivers:* employees or children of employees.

Financial Aid Of all full-time matriculated undergraduates who enrolled in 2008, 1,575 applied for aid, 1,204 were judged to have need, 659 had their need fully met. 221 Federal Work-Study jobs (averaging $3030). In 2008, 348 non-need-based awards were made. *Average percent of need met:* 89%. *Average financial aid package:* $26,211. *Average need-based loan:* $4683. *Average need-based gift aid:* $12,353. *Average non-need-based aid:* $18,428. *Average indebtedness upon graduation:* $31,035.

Applying *Options:* electronic application, early admission, deferred entrance. *Application fee:* $50. *Required:* essay or personal statement, high school transcript, 2 letters of recommendation. *Recommended:* interview. *Application deadlines:* 2/1 (freshmen), rolling (transfers).

Freshman Application Contact Joy Colelli, Dean of Admissions and New Students, Polytechnic Institute of NYU, Six Metrotech Center, Brooklyn, NY 11201-2990. *Phone:* 718-260-5917. *Toll-free phone:* 800-POLYTECH. *Fax:* 718-260-3446. *E-mail:* uadmit@poly.edu. *Web site:* http://www.poly.edu/.

Pratt Institute

Brooklyn, New York

- **Independent** comprehensive, founded 1887
- **Urban** 25-acre campus
- **Coed** 3,008 undergraduate students, 95% full-time, 63% women, 37% men
- **Very difficult** entrance level, 65% of applicants were admitted

Undergraduates 2,845 full-time, 163 part-time. 57% are from out of state; 4% Black or African American, non-Hispanic/Latino; 9% Hispanic/Latino; 17% Asian, non-Hispanic/Latino; 0.1% Native Hawaiian or other Pacific Islander, non-Hispanic/Latino; 0.3% American Indian or Alaska Native, non-Hispanic/Latino; 2% Two or more races, non-Hispanic/Latino; 4% Race/ethnicity unknown; 15% international; 5% transferred in; 52% live on campus. *Retention:* 85% of full-time freshmen returned.

Freshmen *Admission:* 3,987 applied, 2,609 admitted, 699 enrolled. *Average high school GPA:* 3.57. *Test scores:* SAT critical reading scores over 500: 79%; SAT math scores over 500: 85%; SAT writing scores over 500: 78%; ACT scores over 18: 99%; SAT critical reading scores over 600: 39%; SAT math scores over 600: 45%; SAT writing scores over 600: 44%; ACT scores over 24: 72%; SAT critical reading scores over 700: 8%; SAT math scores over 700: 10%; SAT writing scores over 700: 6%; ACT scores over 30: 15%.

Faculty *Total:* 1,032, 12% full-time. *Student/faculty ratio:* 10:1.

Academics *Calendar:* semesters plus optional May term and summer session. *Degrees:* associate, bachelor's, master's, and post-master's certificates. *Special study options:* advanced placement credit, English as a second language, independent study, internships, off-campus study, part-time degree program, services for LD students, study abroad, summer session for credit.

Computers on Campus Students can access the following: online (class) registration. Campuswide network is available.

Student Life *Housing options:* coed, disabled students. Campus housing is university owned. Freshman campus housing is guaranteed. *Activities and organizations:* student-run newspaper, radio and television station, national fraternities. *Campus security:* 24-hour emergency response devices and patrols, late-night transport/escort service. *Student services:* health clinic, personal/psychological counseling.

Athletics Member NCAA. All Division III. *Intercollegiate sports:* basketball M, cross-country running M/W, soccer M/W, tennis M/W, track and field M/W, volleyball W. *Intramural sports:* badminton M/W, basketball M, field hockey M, football M, golf M, lacrosse M/W, volleyball M, weight lifting M/W.

Standardized Tests *Required:* SAT or ACT (for admission). *Required for some:* SAT Subject Tests (for admission).

Costs (2011–12) *Comprehensive fee:* $49,520 includes full-time tuition ($37,500), mandatory fees ($1810), and room and board ($10,210). Part-time tuition: $1210 per credit. *College room only:* $6530. Room and board charges vary according to board plan and housing facility.

Financial Aid Of all full-time matriculated undergraduates who enrolled in 2009, 2,185 applied for aid, 1,937 were judged to have need. In 2009, 347 non-need-based awards were made. *Average percent of need met:* 64%. *Average financial aid package:* $13,039. *Average need-based loan:* $6956. *Average need-based gift aid:* $10,896. *Average non-need-based aid:* $7432. *Financial aid deadline:* 2/1.

Applying *Options:* electronic application, early action, deferred entrance. *Application fee:* $50. *Required:* essay or personal statement, high school transcript, 1 letter of recommendation. *Required for some:* portfolio. *Recommended:* minimum 3 GPA. *Application deadlines:* 1/5 (freshmen), 2/1 (transfers), 11/1 (early action). *Notification:* 4/1 (freshmen), 4/1 (transfers), 12/22 (early action).

Freshman Application Contact Ms. Olga Burger, Visit Coordinator, Pratt Institute, 200 Willoughby Avenue, DeKalb Hall, Brooklyn, NY 11205. *Phone:* 718-636-3779. *Toll-free phone:* 800-331-0834. *Fax:* 718-636-3670. *E-mail:* visit@pratt.edu. *Web site:* http://www.pratt.edu/.

See page 579 for Display. See page 1508 for the College Close-Up.

Purchase College, State University of New York

Purchase, New York

- **State-supported** comprehensive, founded 1967, part of State University of New York System
- **Small-town** 500-acre campus with easy access to New York City
- **Coed** 4,052 undergraduate students, 91% full-time, 57% women, 43% men
- **Moderately difficult** entrance level, 31% of applicants were admitted

Undergraduates 3,683 full-time, 369 part-time. Students come from 43 states and territories; 33 other countries; 18% are from out of state; 6% Black or African American, non-Hispanic/Latino; 12% Hispanic/Latino; 2% Asian, non-

Hispanic/Latino; 0.1% American Indian or Alaska Native, non-Hispanic/Latino; 5% Two or more races, non-Hispanic/Latino; 29% Race/ethnicity unknown; 2% international; 10% transferred in; 67% live on campus. *Retention:* 80% of full-time freshmen returned.

Freshmen *Admission:* 9,163 applied, 2,835 admitted, 672 enrolled. *Average high school GPA:* 3.2. *Test scores:* SAT critical reading scores over 500: 80%; SAT math scores over 500: 67%; SAT writing scores over 500: 76%; ACT scores over 18: 97%; SAT critical reading scores over 600: 33%; SAT math scores over 600: 19%; SAT writing scores over 600: 28%; ACT scores over 24: 56%; SAT critical reading scores over 700: 5%; SAT math scores over 700: 2%; SAT writing scores over 700: 3%; ACT scores over 30: 8%.

Faculty *Total:* 376, 42% full-time, 56% with terminal degrees. *Student/faculty ratio:* 17:1.

Academics *Calendar:* semesters. *Degrees:* certificates, bachelor's, master's, and post-master's certificates. *Special study options:* academic remediation for entering students, adult/continuing education programs, advanced placement credit, double majors, English as a second language, independent study, internships, off-campus study, part-time degree program, services for LD students, student-designed majors, study abroad, summer session for credit.

Computers on Campus 600 computers/terminals and 3,500 ports are available on campus for general student use. Students can access the following: campus intranet, computer help desk, free student e-mail accounts, online (class) grades, online (class) registration, online (class) schedules. Campuswide network is available. 100% of college-owned or -operated housing units are wired for high-speed Internet access. Wireless service is available via classrooms, computer centers, computer labs, learning centers, libraries, student centers.

Student Life *Housing options:* coed. Campus housing is university owned. *Activities and organizations:* drama/theater group, student-run newspaper, radio and television station, choral group, Student Union, WPUR radio station, Latinos Unidos, Gay/Lesbian/Bisexual/Transgender Union, Organization of African People in America. *Campus security:* 24-hour emergency response devices and patrols, late-night transport/escort service, controlled dormitory access, 24-hour patrols by police officers. *Student services:* health clinic, personal/psychological counseling, women's center, legal services.

Athletics Member NCAA. All Division III except golf (Division I), swimming and diving (Division I). *Intercollegiate sports:* baseball M, basketball M/W, cross-country running M/W, golf M, soccer M/W, softball W, swimming and diving M/W, tennis M/W, volleyball M/W. *Intramural sports:* badminton M/W, basketball M/W, bowling M/W, cross-country running M/W, fencing M/W, football M/W, golf M/W, racquetball M/W, skiing (cross-country) M/W, skiing (downhill) M/W, soccer M/W, softball M/W, squash M/W, swimming and diving M/W, table tennis M/W, tennis M/W, volleyball M/W, water polo M/W, weight lifting M/W.

Standardized Tests *Required:* SAT or ACT (for admission). *Recommended:* SAT (for admission).

Costs (2011–12) *One-time required fee:* $200. *Tuition:* state resident $4970 full-time, $207 per credit part-time; nonresident $13,380 full-time, $558 per credit part-time. Full-time tuition and fees vary according to program. Part-time tuition and fees vary according to course load and program. *Required fees:* $1534 full-time, $1 per credit hour part-time. *Room and board:* $10,646. Room and board charges vary according to board plan and housing facility. *Payment plan:* installment. *Waivers:* employees or children of employees.

Financial Aid Of all full-time matriculated undergraduates who enrolled in 2009, 2,694 applied for aid, 2,130 were judged to have need, 75 had their need fully met. In 2009, 101 non-need-based awards were made. *Average percent of need met:* 58%. *Average financial aid package:* $9829. *Average need-based loan:* $4688. *Average need-based gift aid:* $6070. *Average non-need-based aid:* $1688. *Average indebtedness upon graduation:* $33,125.

Applying *Options:* electronic application, early admission, early decision, deferred entrance. *Application fee:* $40. *Required:* high school transcript, minimum 3 GPA. *Required for some:* essay or personal statement, 1 letter of recommendation, interview, audition, portfolio. *Application deadlines:* 7/15 (freshmen), rolling (transfers). *Early decision deadline:* 11/1. *Notification:* continuous until 5/1 (freshmen), continuous (transfers), 12/5 (early decision).

Freshman Application Contact Stephanie McCaine, Director of Admissions, Purchase College, State University of New York, 735 Anderson Hill Road, Purchase, NY 10577-1400. *Phone:* 914-251-6300. *Fax:* 914-251-6314. *E-mail:* admission@purchase.edu. *Web site:* http://www.purchase.edu/.

See page 1514 for the College Close-Up.

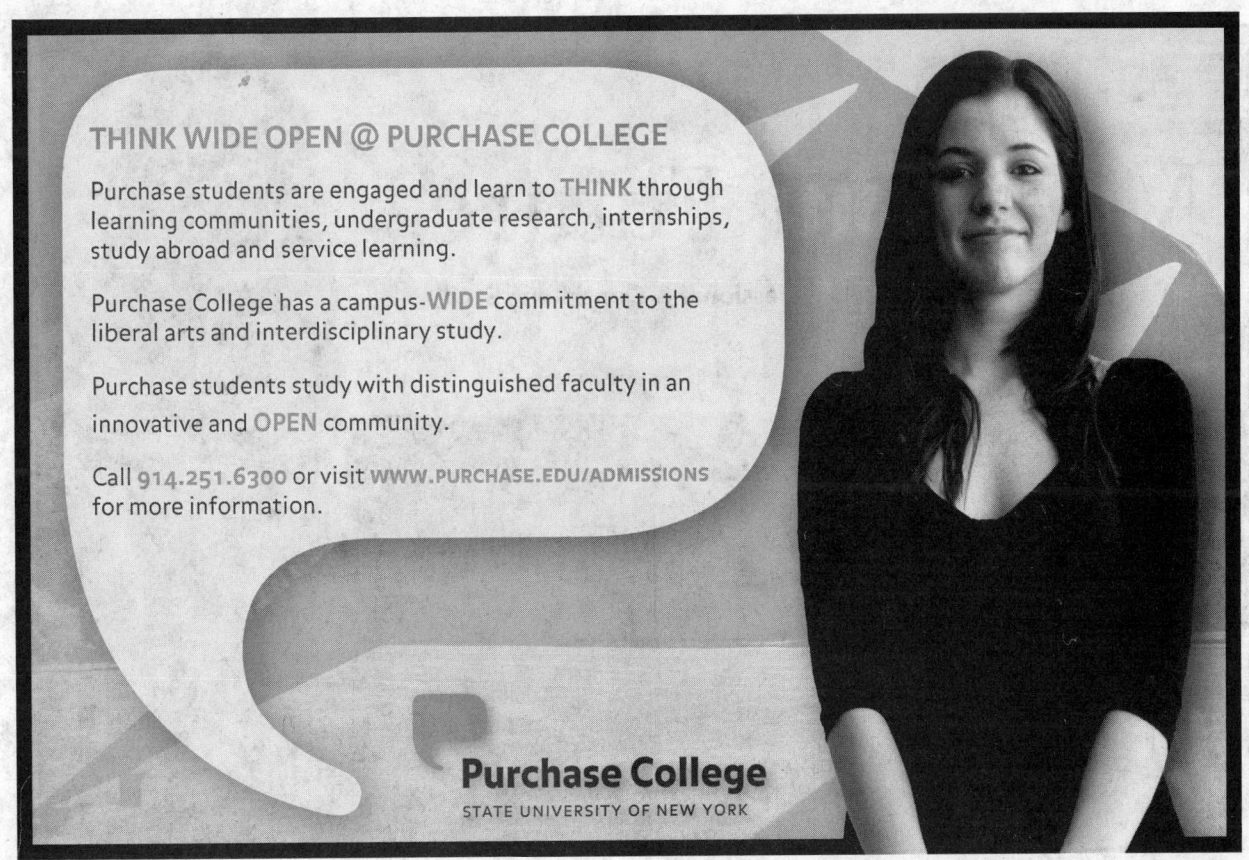

Queens College of the City University of New York

Flushing, New York

- **State and locally supported** comprehensive, founded 1937, part of City University of New York System
- **Urban** 77-acre campus with easy access to New York City
- **Coed** 16,195 undergraduate students, 73% full-time, 59% women, 41% men
- **Very difficult** entrance level, 30% of applicants were admitted

Undergraduates 11,866 full-time, 4,329 part-time. Students come from 15 states and territories; 140 other countries; 1% are from out of state; 8% Black or African American, non-Hispanic/Latino; 18% Hispanic/Latino; 24% Asian, non-Hispanic/Latino; 0.2% American Indian or Alaska Native, non-Hispanic/Latino; 5% international; 14% transferred in; 3% live on campus. *Retention:* 88% of full-time freshmen returned.

Freshmen *Admission:* 18,453 applied, 5,572 admitted, 1,491 enrolled. *Average high school GPA:* 3.7. *Test scores:* SAT critical reading scores over 500: 73%; SAT math scores over 500: 91%; SAT critical reading scores over 600: 20%; SAT math scores over 600: 32%; SAT critical reading scores over 700: 3%; SAT math scores over 700: 4%.

Faculty *Total:* 1,536, 42% full-time. *Student/faculty ratio:* 16:1.

Academics *Calendar:* semesters. *Degrees:* bachelor's, master's, post-master's, and postbachelor's certificates. *Special study options:* accelerated degree program, adult/continuing education programs, advanced placement credit, double majors, English as a second language, honors programs, independent study, internships, off-campus study, part-time degree program, services for LD students, student-designed majors, study abroad, summer session for credit. *ROTC:* Army (c), Navy (c). *Unusual degree programs:* chemistry, biochemistry, computer science, physics, political science, music, philosophy.

Computers on Campus 2,500 computers/terminals are available on campus for general student use. Students can access the following: campus intranet, computer help desk, free student e-mail accounts, online (class) grades, online (class) registration, online (class) schedules. Campuswide network is available. Wireless service is available via entire campus.

Student Life *Housing options:* coed. Campus housing is university owned. *Activities and organizations:* drama/theater group, student-run newspaper, radio station, choral group, Alliance of Latin American Students, Black Student Union, Caribbean Student Association, Hillel-Jewish Student Organization, India Cultural Exchange, national fraternities, national sororities. *Campus security:* 24-hour emergency response devices and patrols. *Student services:* health clinic, personal/psychological counseling.

Athletics Member NCAA. All Division II. *Intercollegiate sports:* baseball M(s), basketball M(s)/W(s), cross-country running M(s)/W(s), fencing W(s), lacrosse W(s), soccer M(s)/W(s), softball W(s), swimming and diving M(s)/W(s), table tennis W, tennis M(s)/W(s), track and field M(s)/W(s), volleyball W(s), water polo M(s). *Intramural sports:* basketball M/W, cross-country running M/W, football M/W, soccer M/W, softball M/W, table tennis M/W, tennis M/W, track and field M/W, volleyball M/W.

Standardized Tests *Required:* SAT or ACT (for admission). *Required for some:* SAT Subject Tests (for admission). *Recommended:* SAT Subject Tests (for admission).

Costs (2010–11) *Tuition:* state resident $4600 full-time, $195 per credit part-time; nonresident $9960 full-time, $415 per credit part-time. *Required fees:* $447 full-time, $141 per term part-time. *Room and board:* $11,125; room only: $8825. Room and board charges vary according to housing facility. *Payment plan:* installment. *Waivers:* senior citizens.

Financial Aid Of all full-time matriculated undergraduates who enrolled in 2009, 10,450 applied for aid, 9,146 were judged to have need. In 2009, 165 non-need-based awards were made. *Average percent of need met:* 95%. *Average financial aid package:* $7500. *Average need-based loan:* $4900. *Average need-based gift aid:* $4800. *Average non-need-based aid:* $8300. *Average indebtedness upon graduation:* $14,000.

Applying *Options:* electronic application, deferred entrance. *Application fee:* $100. *Required:* high school transcript, minimum 3 GPA. *Application deadline:* 5/15 (freshmen). *Notification:* 5/30 (freshmen).

Freshman Application Contact Queens College of the City University of New York, 65-30 Kissena Boulevard, Flushing, NY 11367-1597. *Phone:* 718-997-5600. *Web site:* http://www.qc.cuny.edu/.

See page 1516 for the College Close-Up.

Rabbinical Academy Mesivta Rabbi Chaim Berlin

Brooklyn, New York

Director of Admissions Executive Administrator, Rabbinical Academy Mesivta Rabbi Chaim Berlin, 1605 Coney Island Avenue, Brooklyn, NY 11230-4715. *Phone:* 718-377-0777. *Fax:* 718-338-5578.

Rabbinical College Beth Shraga

Monsey, New York

Director of Admissions Rabbi Sydney Schiff, Director of Admissions, Rabbinical College Beth Shraga, 28 Saddle River Road, Monsey, NY 10952-3035.

Rabbinical College Bobover Yeshiva B'nei Zion

Brooklyn, New York

Director of Admissions Director of Admissions, Rabbinical College Bobover Yeshiva B'nei Zion, 1577 Forty-eighth Street, Brooklyn, NY 11219. *Phone:* 718-438-2018.

Rabbinical College Ch'san Sofer

Brooklyn, New York

Director of Admissions Director of Admissions, Rabbinical College Ch'san Sofer, 1876 Fiftieth Street, Brooklyn, NY 11204. *Phone:* 718-236-1171.

Rabbinical College of Long Island

Long Beach, New York

Director of Admissions Director of Admissions, Rabbinical College of Long Island, 205 West Beech Street, Long Beach, NY 11561-3305. *Phone:* 516-431-7414.

Rabbinical College of Ohr Shimon Yisroel

Brooklyn, New York

Admissions Office Contact Rabbinical College of Ohr Shimon Yisroel, 215-217 Hewes Street, Brooklyn, NY 11211.

Rabbinical Seminary Adas Yereim

Brooklyn, New York

Director of Admissions Director of Admissions, Rabbinical Seminary Adas Yereim, 185 Wilson Street, Brooklyn, NY 11211-7206. *Phone:* 718-388-1751.

Rabbinical Seminary M'kor Chaim

Brooklyn, New York

Director of Admissions Director of Admissions, Rabbinical Seminary M'kor Chaim, 1571 Fifty-fifth Street, Brooklyn, NY 11219. *Phone:* 718-851-0183.

Rabbinical Seminary of America

Flushing, New York

Director of Admissions Rabbi Abraham Semmel, Director of Admissions, Rabbinical Seminary of America, 76-01 147th Street, Flushing, NY 11367. *Phone:* 718-268-4700.

Rensselaer Polytechnic Institute

Troy, New York

- **Independent** university, founded 1824
- **Suburban** 284-acre campus with easy access to Albany, NY
- **Endowment** $629.7 million
- **Coed** 5,431 undergraduate students, 100% full-time, 29% women, 71% men
- **Very difficult** entrance level, 40% of applicants were admitted

Undergraduates 5,407 full-time, 24 part-time. Students come from 54 states and territories; 28 other countries; 62% are from out of state; 3% Black or African American, non-Hispanic/Latino; 5% Hispanic/Latino; 10% Asian, non-

Hispanic/Latino; 0.1% Native Hawaiian or other Pacific Islander, non-Hispanic/Latino; 0.2% American Indian or Alaska Native, non-Hispanic/Latino; 4% Two or more races, non-Hispanic/Latino; 1% Race/ethnicity unknown; 3% international; 2% transferred in; 63% live on campus. *Retention:* 91% of full-time freshmen returned.

Freshmen *Admission:* 13,465 applied, 5,381 admitted, 1,154 enrolled. *Test scores:* SAT critical reading scores over 500: 98%; SAT math scores over 500: 100%; SAT writing scores over 500: 97%; ACT scores over 18: 100%; SAT critical reading scores over 600: 80%; SAT math scores over 600: 94%; SAT writing scores over 600: 70%; ACT scores over 24: 91%; SAT critical reading scores over 700: 30%; SAT math scores over 700: 48%; SAT writing scores over 700: 20%; ACT scores over 30: 35%.

Faculty *Total:* 484, 79% full-time, 81% with terminal degrees. *Student/faculty ratio:* 16:1.

Academics *Calendar:* semesters. *Degrees:* bachelor's, master's, and doctoral-research/scholarship. *Special study options:* accelerated degree program, adult/continuing education programs, advanced placement credit, cooperative education, distance learning, double majors, English as a second language, honors programs, independent study, internships, off-campus study, part-time degree program, services for LD students, student-designed majors, study abroad, summer session for credit. *ROTC:* Army (c), Navy (b), Air Force (b). *Unusual degree programs:* 3-2 engineering.

Computers on Campus Students can access the following: campus intranet, computer help desk, free student e-mail accounts, online (class) grades, online (class) registration, online (class) schedules, billing, downloadable software, web pages. Campuswide network is available. 100% of college-owned or -operated housing units are wired for high-speed Internet access. Wireless service is available via entire campus.

Student Life *Housing:* on-campus residence required through sophomore year. *Options:* coed, disabled students. Campus housing is university owned. Freshman campus housing is guaranteed. *Activities and organizations:* drama/theater group, student-run newspaper, radio and television station, choral group, Red Army Spirit Club, Outing Club, Indian Student Association, Chinese American Student Association, pep band, national fraternities, national sororities. *Campus security:* 24-hour emergency response devices and patrols, late-night transport/escort service, controlled dormitory access, campus foot patrols at night. *Student services:* health clinic, personal/psychological counseling, women's center, legal services.

Athletics Member NCAA. All Division III except men's and women's ice hockey (Division I). *Intercollegiate sports:* archery M(c)/W(c), badminton M(c)/W(c), baseball M/W(c), basketball M/W, crew M(c)/W(c), cross-country running M/W, equestrian sports M(c)/W(c), fencing M(c)/W(c), field hockey W, golf M, ice hockey M(s)/W(s), lacrosse M/W, racquetball M(c)/W(c), riflery M(c)/W(c), rugby M(c)/W(c), sailing M(c)/W(c), skiing (cross-country) M(c)/W(c), soccer M/W, softball W, squash M(c)/W(c), swimming and diving M/W, table tennis M(c)/W(c), tennis M/W, track and field M/W, ultimate Frisbee M(c)/W(c), volleyball M(c)/W(c), water polo M(c)/W(c), weight lifting M(c)/W(c). *Intramural sports:* basketball M/W, bowling M(c)/W(c), cheerleading M(c)/W(c), ice hockey M/W, lacrosse M(c), racquetball M/W, rock climbing M(c)/W(c), soccer M/W, softball M/W, swimming and diving M(c)/W(c), table tennis M/W, tennis M(c)/W(c), ultimate Frisbee M/W, volleyball M/W, wrestling M.

Standardized Tests *Required:* SAT or ACT (for admission). *Required for some:* SAT and SAT Subject Tests or ACT (for admission).

Costs (2010–11) *Comprehensive fee:* $52,145 includes full-time tuition ($39,600), mandatory fees ($1080), and room and board ($11,465). Part-time tuition: $1238 per credit hour. *College room only:* $6550. Room and board charges vary according to board plan and location. *Payment plan:* installment. *Waivers:* employees or children of employees.

Financial Aid Of all full-time matriculated undergraduates who enrolled in 2009, 3,916 applied for aid, 3,516 were judged to have need, 1,158 had their need fully met. 1,259 Federal Work-Study jobs (averaging $1994). In 2009, 1636 non-need-based awards were made. *Average percent of need met:* 83%. *Average financial aid package:* $33,165. *Average need-based loan:* $5100. *Average need-based gift aid:* $22,831. *Average non-need-based aid:* $12,958. *Average indebtedness upon graduation:* $30,125.

Applying *Options:* electronic application, early admission, early decision, deferred entrance. *Application fee:* $70. *Required:* high school transcript. *Required for some:* essay or personal statement, interview, portfolio for Electronic Arts. *Recommended:* 1 letter of recommendation. *Application deadline:* 1/15 (freshmen). *Early decision deadline:* 11/1 (for plan 1), 12/15 (for plan 2). *Notification:* 3/12 (freshmen), continuous (transfers), 12/10 (early decision plan 1), 1/14 (early decision plan 2).

Freshman Application Contact Mr. Paul Marthers, Vice President for Enrollment, Rensselaer Polytechnic Institute, 110 8th Street, Troy, NY 12180. *Phone:* 518-276-6216. *Toll-free phone:* 800-448-6562. *Fax:* 518-276-4072. *E-mail:* admissions@rpi.edu. *Web site:* http://www.rpi.edu/.

Roberts Wesleyan College
Rochester, New York

- **Independent** comprehensive, founded 1866, affiliated with Free Methodist Church of North America
- **Suburban** 75-acre campus
- **Endowment** $12.8 million
- **Coed**
- **Moderately difficult** entrance level

Faculty *Student/faculty ratio:* 11:1.

Academics *Calendar:* semesters. *Degrees:* associate, bachelor's, and master's.

Student Life *Campus security:* 24-hour emergency response devices and patrols, late-night transport/escort service, controlled dormitory access, 24-hour Resident Life staff on-call.

Athletics Member NAIA, NCCAA.

Standardized Tests *Required:* SAT or ACT (for admission).

Costs (2010–11) *One-time required fee:* $247. *Comprehensive fee:* $33,186 includes full-time tuition ($23,460), mandatory fees ($900), and room and board ($8826). Part-time tuition and fees vary according to course load. *College room only:* $5932. Room and board charges vary according to board plan and housing facility.

Financial Aid Of all full-time matriculated undergraduates who enrolled in 2009, 1,339 applied for aid, 1,272 were judged to have need, 118 had their need fully met. 843 Federal Work-Study jobs (averaging $1750). 15 state and other part-time jobs (averaging $1767). In 2009, 132 non-need-based awards were made. *Average percent of need met:* 69. *Average financial aid package:* $17,513. *Average need-based loan:* $5450. *Average need-based gift aid:* $11,890. *Average non-need-based aid:* $4707. *Average indebtedness upon graduation:* $30,329.

Applying *Options:* electronic application, early admission, deferred entrance. *Application fee:* $35. *Required:* essay or personal statement, high school transcript, 2 letters of recommendation. *Recommended:* minimum 2.5 GPA, interview.

Freshman Application Contact Ms. Linda Kurtz Hoffman, Admissions and Marketing Specialist, Roberts Wesleyan College, 2301 Westside Drive, Rochester, NY 14624-1997. *Phone:* 585-594-6400. *Toll-free phone:* 800-777-4RWC. *Fax:* 585-594-6371. *E-mail:* admissions@roberts.edu. *Web site:* http://www.roberts.edu/.

See page 1540 for the College Close-Up.

Rochester Institute of Technology
Rochester, New York

- **Independent** comprehensive, founded 1829
- **Suburban** 1300-acre campus with easy access to Buffalo
- **Endowment** $530.4 million
- **Coed**
- **Moderately difficult** entrance level

Faculty *Student/faculty ratio:* 13:1.

Academics *Calendar:* quarters. *Degrees:* certificates, associate, bachelor's, master's, doctoral-research/scholarship, post-master's, and postbachelor's certificates.

Student Life *Campus security:* 24-hour emergency response devices and patrols, student patrols, late-night transport/escort service.

Athletics Member NCAA. All Division III except ice hockey (Division I).

Standardized Tests *Required:* SAT or ACT (for admission).

Costs (2010–11) *Comprehensive fee:* $40,761 includes full-time tuition ($30,282), mandatory fees ($435), and room and board ($10,044). Full-time tuition and fees vary according to course load. Part-time tuition: $673 per quarter hour. Part-time tuition and fees vary according to class time and course load. *Required fees:* $37 per term part-time. *College room only:* $5862. Room and board charges vary according to board plan and housing facility. *Payment plans:* tuition prepayment, installment, deferred payment.

Financial Aid Of all full-time matriculated undergraduates who enrolled in 2009, 9,068 applied for aid, 8,134 were judged to have need, 7,050 had their need fully met. 2,000 Federal Work-Study jobs (averaging $2400). 5,000 state and other part-time jobs (averaging $2400). In 2009, 1200 non-need-based awards were made. *Average percent of need met:* 88. *Average financial aid package:* $22,500. *Average need-based loan:* $5500. *Average need-based gift aid:* $16,000. *Average non-need-based aid:* $8000.

Applying *Options:* electronic application, early admission, early decision, deferred entrance. *Application fee:* $50. *Required:* essay or personal statement, high school transcript. *Required for some:* portfolio of original artwork required. *Recommended:* minimum 3 GPA, 1 letter of recommendation, interview.

Freshman Application Contact Dr. Daniel Shelley, Assistant Vice President, Rochester Institute of Technology, 60 Lomb Memorial Drive, Rochester, NY

14623-5604. *Phone:* 585-475-6631. *Fax:* 585-475-7424. *E-mail:* admissions@rit.edu. *Web site:* http://www.rit.edu/.

See page 582 for Display. See page 1542 for the College Close-Up.

Russell Sage College
Troy, New York

- **Independent** 4-year, founded 1916, part of The Sage Colleges
- **Urban** 8-acre campus
- **Endowment** $26.7 million
- **Women only** 746 undergraduate students, 94% full-time
- **Moderately difficult** entrance level, 74% of applicants were admitted

Undergraduates 701 full-time, 45 part-time. Students come from 13 states and territories; 1 other country; 9% are from out of state; 7% Black or African American, non-Hispanic/Latino; 4% Hispanic/Latino; 2% Asian, non-Hispanic/Latino; 0.3% American Indian or Alaska Native, non-Hispanic/Latino; 0.4% Two or more races, non-Hispanic/Latino; 11% Race/ethnicity unknown; 1% international; 12% transferred in; 53% live on campus. *Retention:* 84% of full-time freshmen returned.

Freshmen *Admission:* 469 applied, 345 admitted, 122 enrolled. *Average high school GPA:* 3.33. *Test scores:* SAT critical reading scores over 500: 58%; SAT math scores over 500: 56%; ACT scores over 18: 97%; SAT critical reading scores over 600: 10%; SAT math scores over 600: 13%; ACT scores over 24: 30%; SAT critical reading scores over 700: 3%.

Faculty *Total:* 88, 70% full-time, 81% with terminal degrees. *Student/faculty ratio:* 10:1.

Academics *Calendar:* semesters. *Degree:* bachelor's. *Special study options:* academic remediation for entering students, accelerated degree program, advanced placement credit, cooperative education, distance learning, double majors, honors programs, independent study, internships, services for LD students, student-designed majors, study abroad, summer session for credit. *ROTC:* Army (c), Air Force (c). *Unusual degree programs:* 3-2 business administration with Sage Graduate School; engineering with Rensselaer Polytechnic Institute; nursing with Sage Graduate School; occupational therapy, physical therapy.

Computers on Campus 164 computers/terminals are available on campus for general student use. Students can access the following: campus intranet, computer help desk, free student e-mail accounts, online (class) grades, online (class) registration, online (class) schedules. Campuswide network is available. 100% of college-owned or -operated housing units are wired for high-speed Internet access. Wireless service is available via classrooms, computer labs, learning centers, libraries.

Student Life *Housing options:* women-only. Campus housing is university owned. Freshman campus housing is guaranteed. *Activities and organizations:* drama/theater group, student-run newspaper, choral group, student government, Sage Recreation Association, Physical Therapy Club, Crew Club, Black-Latin Student Alliance. *Campus security:* 24-hour emergency response devices and patrols, late-night transport/escort service, controlled dormitory access. *Student services:* health clinic, personal/psychological counseling, women's center.

Athletics Member NCAA. All Division III. *Intercollegiate sports:* basketball W, lacrosse W, soccer W, softball W, tennis W, volleyball W. *Intramural sports:* cheerleading W(c), crew W(c), ice hockey W, track and field W(c).

Standardized Tests *Required for some:* SAT or ACT (for admission).

Costs (2010–11) *Comprehensive fee:* $38,000 includes full-time tuition ($27,000), mandatory fees ($850), and room and board ($10,150). Part-time tuition: $900 per credit hour. *College room only:* $5350. Room and board charges vary according to board plan. *Payment plans:* installment, deferred payment. *Waivers:* senior citizens and employees or children of employees.

Financial Aid Of all full-time matriculated undergraduates who enrolled in 2009, 678 applied for aid, 608 were judged to have need, 218 had their need fully met. 380 Federal Work-Study jobs (averaging $2000), 135 state and other part-time jobs (averaging $1800). In 2009, 19 non-need-based awards were made. *Average financial aid package:* $31,600. *Average need-based loan:* $4976. *Average need-based gift aid:* $9845. *Average non-need-based aid:* $13,100. *Average indebtedness upon graduation:* $28,300.

Applying *Options:* electronic application, early admission, early action, deferred entrance. *Application fee:* $30. *Required:* high school transcript, minimum 2.5 GPA, 2 letters of recommendation. *Recommended:* essay or personal statement, interview. *Application deadlines:* rolling (freshmen), rolling (transfers). *Notification:* continuous (freshmen), continuous (transfers).

Freshman Application Contact Mr. Andrew Palumbo, Director of Undergraduate Admission, Russell Sage College, 140 New Scotland Avenue, Albany, NY 12208. *Phone:* 518-292-1926. *Toll-free phone:* 888-VERY-SAGE (in-state); 888-VERY SAGE (out-of-state). *Fax:* 518-292-1912. *E-mail:* paluma@sage.edu. *Web site:* http://www.sage.edu/rsc/.

Sage College of Albany

Albany, New York

- **Independent** 4-year, founded 1957, part of The Sage Colleges
- **Urban** 15-acre campus
- **Endowment** $26.7 million
- **Coed** 918 undergraduate students, 67% full-time, 63% women, 37% men
- **Minimally difficult** entrance level, 64% of applicants were admitted

Undergraduates 612 full-time, 306 part-time. Students come from 12 states and territories; 1 other country; 6% are from out of state; 12% Black or African American, non-Hispanic/Latino; 6% Hispanic/Latino; 2% Asian, non-Hispanic/Latino; 0.2% American Indian or Alaska Native, non-Hispanic/Latino; 1% Two or more races, non-Hispanic/Latino; 13% Race/ethnicity unknown; 0.1% international; 20% transferred in; 43% live on campus. *Retention:* 66% of full-time freshmen returned.

Freshmen *Admission:* 678 applied, 436 admitted, 130 enrolled. *Average high school GPA:* 3.08. *Test scores:* SAT critical reading scores over 500: 46%; SAT math scores over 500: 46%; ACT scores over 18: 70%; SAT critical reading scores over 600: 11%; SAT math scores over 600: 12%; ACT scores over 24: 26%; SAT critical reading scores over 700: 1%; SAT math scores over 700: 1%; ACT scores over 30: 4%.

Faculty *Total:* 98, 38% full-time, 59% with terminal degrees. *Student/faculty ratio:* 13:1.

Academics *Calendar:* semesters. *Degree:* bachelor's. *Special study options:* academic remediation for entering students, accelerated degree program, adult/continuing education programs, advanced placement credit, cooperative education, distance learning, honors programs, independent study, internships, off-campus study, part-time degree program, services for LD students, student-designed majors, study abroad, summer session for credit. *ROTC:* Army (c), Air Force (c). *Unusual degree programs:* 3-2 business administration with With Sage Graduate School; clinical biology and cytotechnology with Albany College of Pharmacy.

Computers on Campus 196 computers/terminals are available on campus for general student use. Students can access the following: campus intranet, computer help desk, free student e-mail accounts, online (class) grades, online (class) registration. Campuswide network is available. 100% of college-owned or -operated housing units are wired for high-speed Internet access. Wireless service is available via classrooms, computer labs, learning centers, libraries, student centers.

Student Life *Housing options:* coed, women-only. Campus housing is university owned. Freshman applicants given priority for college housing. *Activities and organizations:* student government, Phi Theta Kappa, Psychology Club, Ski Club, Vernacular (art and literary publication). *Campus security:* 24-hour emergency response devices and patrols, late-night transport/escort service, controlled dormitory access, 24-hour security cameras. *Student services:* health clinic, personal/psychological counseling.

Athletics Member NCAA. All Division III. *Intercollegiate sports:* basketball M/W, cross-country running M, golf M, lacrosse W, soccer M/W, softball W, tennis M/W, volleyball M/W. *Intramural sports:* badminton M/W, cheerleading W(c), crew M(c)/W(c), football M/W, ice hockey M(c)/W(c), skiing (cross-country) M(c).

Standardized Tests *Required for some:* SAT or ACT (for admission).

Costs (2010–11) *Comprehensive fee:* $38,800 includes full-time tuition ($27,000), mandatory fees ($850), and room and board ($10,950). Part-time tuition: $900 per credit hour. *College room only:* $5350. Room and board charges vary according to board plan. *Payment plans:* installment, deferred payment. *Waivers:* employees or children of employees.

Financial Aid Of all full-time matriculated undergraduates who enrolled in 2009, 550 applied for aid, 523 were judged to have need, 146 had their need fully met. 176 Federal Work-Study jobs (averaging $2000). 36 state and other part-time jobs (averaging $1500). In 2009, 27 non-need-based awards were made. *Average financial aid package:* $30,400. *Average need-based loan:* $5390. *Average need-based gift aid:* $10,136. *Average non-need-based aid:* $8650. *Average indebtedness upon graduation:* $26,400.

Applying *Options:* electronic application, deferred entrance. *Application fee:* $30. *Required:* essay or personal statement, high school transcript, minimum 2.5 GPA, 2 letters of recommendation, portfolio for fine arts program. *Recommended:* interview. *Application deadlines:* rolling (freshmen), 8/1 (transfers). *Notification:* 8/15 (freshmen), continuous until 8/15 (transfers).

Freshman Application Contact Mr. Andrew Palumbo, Director of Undergraduate Admission, Sage College of Albany, 140 New Scotland Avenue, Albany, NY 12208. *Phone:* 518-292-1730. *Toll-free phone:* 888-VERY-SAGE. *Fax:* 518-292-1912. *E-mail:* scaadm@sage.edu. *Web site:* http://www.sage.edu/.

St. Bonaventure University

St. Bonaventure, New York

- **Independent** comprehensive, founded 1858, affiliated with Roman Catholic Church
- **Small-town** 500-acre campus
- **Endowment** $42.4 million
- **Coed** 1,996 undergraduate students, 97% full-time, 52% women, 48% men
- **Moderately difficult** entrance level, 78% of applicants were admitted

Undergraduates 1,937 full-time, 59 part-time. Students come from 28 states and territories; 33 other countries; 24% are from out of state; 5% Black or African American, non-Hispanic/Latino; 4% Hispanic/Latino; 2% Asian, non-Hispanic/Latino; 1% Native Hawaiian or other Pacific Islander, non-Hispanic/Latino; 0.6% American Indian or Alaska Native, non-Hispanic/Latino; 0.1% Two or more races, non-Hispanic/Latino; 13% Race/ethnicity unknown; 2% international; 5% transferred in; 78% live on campus. *Retention:* 80% of full-time freshmen returned.

Freshmen *Admission:* 2,303 applied, 1,794 admitted, 494 enrolled. *Average high school GPA:* 3.21. *Test scores:* SAT critical reading scores over 500: 55%; SAT math scores over 500: 62%; SAT writing scores over 500: 52%; ACT scores over 18: 89%; SAT critical reading scores over 600: 19%; SAT math scores over 600: 20%; SAT writing scores over 600: 14%; ACT scores over 24: 41%; SAT critical reading scores over 700: 3%; SAT math scores over 700: 3%; SAT writing scores over 700: 3%; ACT scores over 30: 9%.

Faculty *Total:* 238, 66% full-time, 55% with terminal degrees. *Student/faculty ratio:* 13:1.

Academics *Calendar:* semesters. *Degrees:* bachelor's, master's, post-master's, and postbachelor's certificates. *Special study options:* accelerated degree program, advanced placement credit, distance learning, double majors, honors programs, independent study, internships, off-campus study, part-time degree program, services for LD students, student-designed majors, study abroad, summer session for credit. *ROTC:* Army (b).

Computers on Campus 180 computers/terminals are available on campus for general student use. Students can access the following: campus intranet, computer help desk, free student e-mail accounts, online (class) grades, online (class) registration, online (class) schedules. Campuswide network is available. 100% of college-owned or -operated housing units are wired for high-speed Internet access. Wireless service is available via entire campus.

Student Life *Housing:* on-campus residence required for freshman year. *Options:* coed, disabled students. Campus housing is university owned. Freshman campus housing is guaranteed. *Activities and organizations:* drama/theater group, student-run newspaper, radio and television station, choral group, Student Government Association, Bona Responds, BV newspaper, Students for the Mountain, Student Ambassadors. *Campus security:* 24-hour emergency response devices and patrols, late-night transport/escort service, controlled dormitory access. *Student services:* health clinic, personal/psychological counseling.

Athletics Member NCAA. All Division I. *Intercollegiate sports:* baseball M(s), basketball M(s)/W(s), cross-country running M(s)/W(s), field hockey W(c), golf M(s), lacrosse M(c)/W(s), rugby M(c)/W(c), soccer M(s)/W(s), softball W(s), swimming and diving M(s)/W(s), tennis M(s)/W(s). *Intramural sports:* basketball M/W, football M/W, golf M/W, ice hockey M(c), racquetball M/W, soccer M(c)/W(c), softball M/W, table tennis M/W, tennis M/W, volleyball M/W.

Standardized Tests *Required:* SAT or ACT (for admission). *Required for some:* SAT Subject Tests (for admission).

Costs (2010–11) *Comprehensive fee:* $35,966 includes full-time tuition ($25,930), mandatory fees ($965), and room and board ($9071). Part-time tuition: $775 per credit hour. Part-time tuition and fees vary according to course load. *College room only:* $4441. Room and board charges vary according to board plan and housing facility. *Waivers:* senior citizens and employees or children of employees.

Financial Aid Of all full-time matriculated undergraduates who enrolled in 2008, 1,577 applied for aid, 1,392 were judged to have need, 323 had their need fully met. 478 Federal Work-Study jobs (averaging $1025). 100 state and other part-time jobs (averaging $1000). In 2008, 382 non-need-based awards were made. *Average percent of need met:* 78%. *Average financial aid package:* $25,672. *Average need-based loan:* $4377. *Average need-based gift aid:* $19,178. *Average non-need-based aid:* $9512. *Average indebtedness upon graduation:* $36,940.

Applying *Options:* electronic application, deferred entrance. *Application fee:* $30. *Required:* high school transcript, 1 letter of recommendation. *Required for some:* essay or personal statement. *Recommended:* essay or personal statement, minimum 3 GPA, 3 letters of recommendation, interview. *Application deadlines:* 7/1 (freshmen), 8/15 (transfers). *Notification:* continuous until 10/15 (freshmen), continuous until 10/1 (transfers).

Freshman Application Contact Monica Emery, Director of Admissions, St. Bonaventure University, 3261 West State Road, St. Bonaventure, NY 14778.

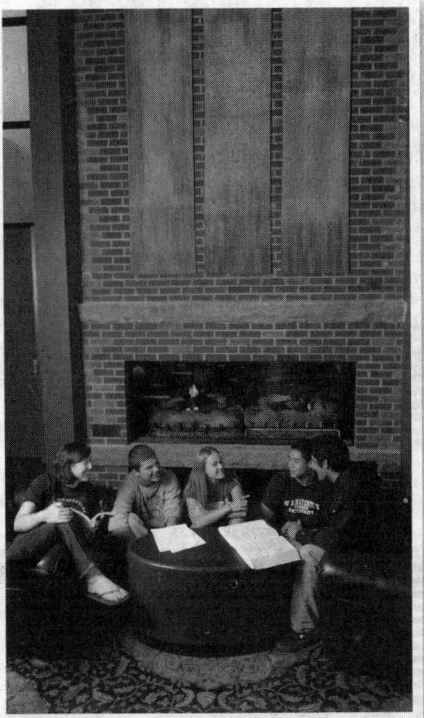

Phone: 716-375-2400. *Toll-free phone:* 800-462-5050. *Fax:* 716-375-4005. *E-mail:* memery@sbu.edu. *Web site:* http://www.sbu.edu/.

See page 1556 for the College Close-Up.

St. Francis College

Brooklyn Heights, New York

- **Independent Roman Catholic** comprehensive, founded 1884
- **Urban** 1-acre campus with easy access to New York City
- **Coed**
- **Moderately difficult** entrance level

Faculty *Student/faculty ratio:* 18:1.

Academics *Calendar:* semesters. *Degrees:* associate, bachelor's, and master's.

Student Life *Campus security:* ID checks, crime awareness workshops, pamphlets, posters, films, emergency notification system.

Athletics Member NCAA. All Division I.

Standardized Tests *Required:* SAT (for admission).

Costs (2010–11) *Tuition:* $16,720 full-time. Full-time tuition and fees vary according to course level, course load, and degree level. Part-time tuition and fees vary according to course level, course load, and degree level. *Required fees:* $560 full-time. *Payment plans:* installment, deferred payment.

Financial Aid *Of all full-time matriculated undergraduates who enrolled in 2006,* 1,747 applied for aid, 1,683 were judged to have need, 443 had their need fully met. 161 Federal Work-Study jobs (averaging $2200). *Average percent of need met:* 64. *Average financial aid package:* $9300. *Average need-based loan:* $7700. *Average need-based gift aid:* $6640.

Applying *Options:* electronic application, deferred entrance. *Application fee:* $35. *Required:* essay or personal statement, high school transcript, minimum 2 GPA, 1 letter of recommendation. *Recommended:* interview.

Freshman Application Contact Ms. Monica Michalski, Assistant Dean of Freshman Studies and Academic Enhancement, St. Francis College, 180 Remsen Street, Brooklyn Heights, NY 11201-4398. *Phone:* 718-489-5226. *Fax:* 718-522-1274. *E-mail:* mmichalski@stfranciscollege.edu. *Web site:* http://www.stfranciscollege.edu/.

St. John Fisher College

Rochester, New York

- **Independent** comprehensive, founded 1948, affiliated with Roman Catholic Church
- **Suburban** 154-acre campus
- **Endowment** $40.0 million
- **Coed** 2,888 undergraduate students, 93% full-time, 58% women, 42% men
- **Moderately difficult** entrance level, 65% of applicants were admitted

Undergraduates 2,688 full-time, 200 part-time. Students come from 21 states and territories; 9 other countries; 2% are from out of state; 4% Black or African American, non-Hispanic/Latino; 3% Hispanic/Latino; 2% Asian, non-Hispanic/Latino; 0.5% American Indian or Alaska Native, non-Hispanic/Latino; 0.5% Two or more races, non-Hispanic/Latino; 3% Race/ethnicity unknown; 0.2% international; 10% transferred in; 54% live on campus. *Retention:* 81% of full-time freshmen returned.

Freshmen *Admission:* 3,643 applied, 2,382 admitted, 623 enrolled. *Average high school GPA:* 3.5. *Test scores:* SAT critical reading scores over 500: 68%; SAT math scores over 500: 80%; SAT writing scores over 500: 59%; ACT scores over 18: 98%; SAT critical reading scores over 600: 16%; SAT math scores over 600: 30%; SAT writing scores over 600: 11%; ACT scores over 24: 59%; SAT critical reading scores over 700: 1%; SAT math scores over 700: 2%; SAT writing scores over 700: 1%; ACT scores over 30: 5%.

Faculty *Total:* 413, 52% full-time, 46% with terminal degrees. *Student/faculty ratio:* 13:1.

Academics *Calendar:* semesters. *Degrees:* bachelor's, master's, doctoral-professional, doctoral-research/scholarship, post-master's, and postbachelor's certificates. *Special study options:* academic remediation for entering students, accelerated degree program, adult/continuing education programs, advanced placement credit, distance learning, double majors, honors programs, independent study, internships, off-campus study, part-time degree program, services for LD students, student-designed majors, study abroad, summer session for credit. *ROTC:* Army (c), Navy (c), Air Force (c). *Unusual degree programs:* 3-2 engineering with Clarkson University, Manhattan College, Rensselaer Polytechnic Institute, Columbia University, University of Detroit Mercy, University of Rochester, S.U.N.Y. at Buffalo.

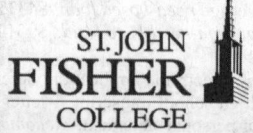
PROFILES

Computers on Campus 550 computers/terminals and 1,875 ports are available on campus for general student use. Students can access the following: campus intranet, computer help desk, free student e-mail accounts, online (class) grades, online (class) registration, online (class) schedules. Campuswide network is available. 100% of college-owned or -operated housing units are wired for high-speed Internet access. Wireless service is available via computer centers, computer labs, learning centers, libraries, student centers.

Student Life *Housing options:* coed, women-only, disabled students. Campus housing is university owned. Freshman campus housing is guaranteed. *Activities and organizations:* drama/theater group, student-run newspaper, television station, choral group, student government, Student Activities Board, Commuter Council, Resident Student Association, Teddi Dance for Love. *Campus security:* 24-hour emergency response devices and patrols, late-night transport/escort service, controlled dormitory access. *Student services:* health clinic, personal/psychological counseling.

Athletics Member NCAA. All Division III. *Intercollegiate sports:* baseball M, basketball M/W, cross-country running M/W, field hockey W, football M, golf M/W, lacrosse M/W, soccer M/W, softball W, tennis M/W, track and field M/W, volleyball W. *Intramural sports:* basketball M/W, cheerleading W(c), equestrian sports M(c)/W(c), ice hockey M(c)/W(c), rugby M(c)/W(c), soccer M/W, volleyball M.

Standardized Tests *Required:* SAT or ACT (for admission).

Costs (2010–11) *Comprehensive fee:* $35,560 includes full-time tuition ($24,800), mandatory fees ($470), and room and board ($10,290). Part-time tuition: $675 per credit hour. Part-time tuition and fees vary according to course load. *Required fees:* $25 per term part-time. *College room only:* $6680. Room and board charges vary according to board plan. *Payment plans:* installment, deferred payment. *Waivers:* employees or children of employees.

Financial Aid Of all full-time matriculated undergraduates who enrolled in 2009, 2,478 applied for aid, 2,260 were judged to have need, 510 had their need fully met. 1,345 Federal Work-Study jobs (averaging $1373). In 2009, 376 non-need-based awards were made. *Average percent of need met:* 81%. *Average financial aid package:* $18,929. *Average need-based loan:* $4192. *Average need-based gift aid:* $14,011. *Average non-need-based aid:* $8959. *Average indebtedness upon graduation:* $32,975.

Applying *Options:* electronic application, early decision, deferred entrance. *Application fee:* $30. *Required:* essay or personal statement, high school transcript, minimum 3 GPA, 1 letter of recommendation. *Recommended:* interview. *Application deadlines:* rolling (freshmen), rolling (transfers). *Early decision deadline:* 12/1. *Notification:* continuous until 12/1 (freshmen), continuous until 9/1 (transfers), 12/15 (early decision).

Freshman Application Contact Mrs. Stacy A. Ledermann, Director of Freshmen Admissions, St. John Fisher College, 3690 East Avenue, Rochester, NY 14618. *Phone:* 585-385-8064. *Toll-free phone:* 800-444-4640. *Fax:* 585-385-8386. *E-mail:* admissions@sjfc.edu. *Web site:* http://www.sjfc.edu/.

See page 1560 for the College Close-Up.

St. John's University

Queens, New York

- **Independent** university, founded 1870, affiliated with Roman Catholic Church
- **Urban** 98-acre campus with easy access to New York City
- **Endowment** $303.1 million
- **Coed** 15,720 undergraduate students, 75% full-time, 56% women, 44% men
- **Moderately difficult** entrance level, 46% of applicants were admitted

Undergraduates 11,803 full-time, 3,917 part-time. Students come from 46 states and territories; 90 other countries; 25% are from out of state; 4% transferred in; 30% live on campus. *Retention:* 78% of full-time freshmen returned.

Freshmen *Admission:* 54,871 applied, 24,993 admitted, 3,117 enrolled. *Average high school GPA:* 3.2. *Test scores:* SAT critical reading scores over 500: 67%; SAT math scores over 500: 72%; SAT critical reading scores over 600: 22%; SAT math scores over 600: 33%; SAT critical reading scores over 700: 2%; SAT math scores over 700: 9%.

Faculty *Total:* 1,418, 44% full-time, 61% with terminal degrees. *Student/faculty ratio:* 19:1.

Academics *Calendar:* semesters. *Degrees:* certificates, diplomas, associate, bachelor's, master's, doctoral-professional, doctoral-research/scholarship, post-master's, and postbachelor's certificates. *Special study options:* accelerated degree program, adult/continuing education programs, advanced placement credit, distance learning, double majors, English as a second language, honors programs, independent study, internships, off-campus study, part-time degree program, services for LD students, study abroad, summer session for credit. *ROTC:* Army (b). *Unusual degree programs:* 3-2 engineering with Manhattan College.

Computers on Campus 12,959 computers/terminals and 302 ports are available on campus for general student use. Students can access the following: campus intranet, computer help desk, free student e-mail accounts, online

(class) grades, online (class) registration, online (class) schedules, various software packages. Campuswide network is available. 100% of college-owned or -operated housing units are wired for high-speed Internet access. Wireless service is available via entire campus.

Student Life *Housing options:* coed. Campus housing is university owned and leased by the school. Freshman applicants given priority for college housing. *Activities and organizations:* drama/theater group, student-run newspaper, radio and television station, choral group, Student Government, Incorporated, Student Programming Board, Haraya (Pan-African Students Coalition), American Pharmaceutical Association, Latin American Student Organization, Muslim Student Organization, national fraternities, national sororities. *Campus security:* 24-hour emergency response devices and patrols, student patrols, late-night transport/escort service, controlled dormitory access, Emergency Notification System. *Student services:* health clinic, personal/psychological counseling.

Athletics Member NCAA. All Division I. *Intercollegiate sports:* baseball M(s), basketball M(s)/W(s), cross-country running W(s), fencing M(s)/W(s), golf M(s)/W(s), lacrosse M(s), soccer M(s)/W(s), softball W(s), tennis M(s)/W(s), track and field W(s), volleyball W(s). *Intramural sports:* badminton M/W, basketball M/W, bowling M(c)/W(c), cheerleading M/W, fencing M/W, football M/W, racquetball M/W, soccer M/W, softball M/W, table tennis M/W, tennis M/W, ultimate Frisbee M/W, volleyball M(c)/W(c), weight lifting M/W.

Standardized Tests *Required:* SAT or ACT (for admission).

Costs (2010–11) *Comprehensive fee:* $45,880 includes full-time tuition ($31,250), mandatory fees ($730), and room and board ($13,900). Full-time tuition and fees vary according to course load, program, and student level. Part-time tuition: $1042 per credit. Part-time tuition and fees vary according to course load, program, and student level. *Required fees:* $268 per term part-time. *College room only:* $8750. Room and board charges vary according to board plan, housing facility, and location. *Payment plan:* installment. *Waivers:* senior citizens and employees or children of employees.

Financial Aid Of all full-time matriculated undergraduates who enrolled in 2008, 10,302 applied for aid, 9,704 were judged to have need, 619 had their need fully met. 982 Federal Work-Study jobs (averaging $3479). In 2008, 461 non-need-based awards were made. *Average percent of need met:* 63%. *Average financial aid package:* $24,777. *Average need-based loan:* $5077. *Average need-based gift aid:* $12,118. *Average non-need-based aid:* $13,772. *Average indebtedness upon graduation:* $32,886.

Applying *Options:* electronic application, early admission, deferred entrance. *Application fee:* $50. *Required:* high school transcript. *Required for some:* essay or personal statement, 2 letters of recommendation, interview. *Recommended:* essay or personal statement, minimum 3 GPA. *Application deadlines:* rolling (freshmen), rolling (out-of-state freshmen), rolling (transfers). *Notification:* continuous (freshmen), continuous (out-of-state freshmen), continuous (transfers).

Freshman Application Contact Mrs. Karen Vahey, Admission Director, St. John's University, 8000 Utopia Parkway, Queens, NY 11439. *Phone:* 718-990-2000. *Toll-free phone:* 888-9STJOHNS. *Fax:* 718-990-2096. *E-mail:* admhelp@stjohns.edu. *Web site:* http://www.stjohns.edu/.

St. Joseph's College, Long Island Campus

Patchogue, New York

- **Independent** comprehensive, founded 1916
- **Suburban** 28-acre campus with easy access to New York City
- **Endowment** $31.1 million
- **Coed** 3,875 undergraduate students, 81% full-time, 71% women, 29% men
- **Moderately difficult** entrance level, 70% of applicants were admitted

Undergraduates 3,130 full-time, 745 part-time. Students come from 11 states and territories; 4 other countries; 1% are from out of state; 4% Black or African American, non-Hispanic/Latino; 8% Hispanic/Latino; 1% Asian, non-Hispanic/Latino; 0.1% Native Hawaiian or other Pacific Islander, non-Hispanic/Latino; 0.3% American Indian or Alaska Native, non-Hispanic/Latino; 1% Two or more races, non-Hispanic/Latino; 15% Race/ethnicity unknown; 13% transferred in. *Retention:* 85% of full-time freshmen returned.

Freshmen *Admission:* 1,515 applied, 1,067 admitted, 472 enrolled. *Average high school GPA:* 3.45. *Test scores:* SAT critical reading scores over 500: 76%; SAT math scores over 500: 75%; ACT scores over 18: 95%; SAT critical reading scores over 600: 23%; SAT math scores over 600: 15%; ACT scores over 24: 43%; SAT critical reading scores over 700: 2%; ACT scores over 30: 2%.

Faculty *Total:* 422, 28% full-time. *Student/faculty ratio:* 15:1.

Academics *Calendar:* 4-1-4. *Degrees:* certificates, bachelor's, and master's. *Special study options:* adult/continuing education programs, advanced placement credit, cooperative education, distance learning, double majors, honors programs, independent study, internships, off-campus study, part-time degree program, services for LD students, study abroad, summer session for credit. *Unusual degree programs:* 3-2 business administration; Math Education.

Computers on Campus 245 computers/terminals are available on campus for general student use. Students can access the following: campus intranet, computer help desk, free student e-mail accounts, online (class) grades, online (class) registration, online (class) schedules. Campuswide network is available. Wireless service is available via classrooms, computer centers, computer labs, libraries, student centers.

Student Life *Activities and organizations:* drama/theater group, student-run newspaper, choral group, Admissions Club, Science Club, Dramatics, Shild Study Club, Dance Team. *Campus security:* 24-hour emergency response devices and patrols, late-night transport/escort service. *Student services:* health clinic, personal/psychological counseling.

Athletics Member NCAA. All Division III. *Intercollegiate sports:* baseball M, basketball M/W, cross-country running M/W, equestrian sports W, golf M, soccer M/W, softball W, tennis M/W, track and field M/W, volleyball M/W. *Intramural sports:* basketball M/W, bowling M/W, field hockey M/W, football M/W, golf M/W, lacrosse M/W, soccer M/W, table tennis M/W, ultimate Frisbee M/W, volleyball M/W.

Standardized Tests *Required:* SAT or ACT (for admission).

Costs (2011–12) *Tuition:* $17,000 full-time. Full-time tuition and fees vary according to course load, degree level, and program. Part-time tuition and fees vary according to course load, degree level, and program. *Required fees:* $565 full-time. *Payment plans:* installment, deferred payment. *Waivers:* senior citizens and employees or children of employees.

Financial Aid Of all full-time matriculated undergraduates who enrolled in 2009, 2,872 applied for aid, 2,226 were judged to have need, 499 had their need fully met. 73 Federal Work-Study jobs (averaging $3087), 104 state and other part-time jobs (averaging $4147). In 2009, 441 non-need-based awards were made. *Average percent of need met:* 66%. *Average financial aid package:* $10,606. *Average need-based loan:* $4448. *Average need-based gift aid:* $6998. *Average non-need-based aid:* $7569. *Average indebtedness upon graduation:* $23,031.

Applying *Options:* electronic application, early admission, deferred entrance. *Application fee:* $25. *Required:* high school transcript, minimum 2.5 GPA. *Required for some:* essay or personal statement, interview. *Recommended:* 2 letters of recommendation. *Application deadlines:* 8/15 (freshmen), 8/15

(transfers). *Notification:* continuous until 11/1 (freshmen), continuous until 11/1 (transfers).

Freshman Application Contact Ms. Gigi Lamens, Associate Vice President for Enrollment Management, St. Joseph's College, Long Island Campus, 155 West Roe Boulevard, Patchogue, NY 11772-2399. *Phone:* 631-687-4500. *Toll-free phone:* 866-AT ST JOE. *E-mail:* glamens@sjcny.edu. *Web site:* http://www.sjcny.edu/.

St. Joseph's College, New York
Brooklyn, New York

- **Independent** comprehensive, founded 1916
- **Urban** campus
- **Endowment** $9.3 million
- **Coed** 1,260 undergraduate students, 72% full-time, 75% women, 25% men
- **Moderately difficult** entrance level, 75% of applicants were admitted

Undergraduates 903 full-time, 357 part-time. Students come from 4 states and territories; 18 other countries; 1% are from out of state; 34% Black or African American, non-Hispanic/Latino; 17% Hispanic/Latino; 5% Asian, non-Hispanic/Latino; 0.1% Native Hawaiian or other Pacific Islander, non-Hispanic/Latino; 0.3% American Indian or Alaska Native, non-Hispanic/Latino; 1% Two or more races, non-Hispanic/Latino; 5% Race/ethnicity unknown; 0.1% international; 11% transferred in; 1% live on campus. *Retention:* 82% of full-time freshmen returned.

Freshmen *Admission:* 988 applied, 741 admitted, 240 enrolled. *Average high school GPA:* 3.15. *Test scores:* SAT critical reading scores over 500: 45%; SAT math scores over 500: 45%; ACT scores over 18: 88%; SAT critical reading scores over 600: 10%; SAT math scores over 600: 8%; ACT scores over 24: 18%; SAT math scores over 700: 1%; ACT scores over 30: 2%.

Faculty *Total:* 176, 31% full-time. *Student/faculty ratio:* 12:1.

Academics *Calendar:* semesters. *Degrees:* certificates, bachelor's, and master's. *Special study options:* adult/continuing education programs, advanced placement credit, cooperative education, distance learning, double majors, honors programs, independent study, internships, part-time degree program, study abroad, summer session for credit. *Unusual degree programs:* 3-2 business administration.

Computers on Campus 205 computers/terminals are available on campus for general student use. Students can access the following: campus intranet, computer help desk, free student e-mail accounts, online (class) grades, online (class) registration, online (class) schedules. Campuswide network is available. Wireless service is available via classrooms, computer centers, computer labs, learning centers, libraries, student centers.

Student Life *Housing options:* coed. Campus housing is leased by the school. *Activities and organizations:* drama/theater group, student-run newspaper, choral group, Admissions Club, Science Club, dramatics, Child Study Club, Dance Team. *Campus security:* 24-hour emergency response devices and patrols, late-night transport/escort service, Emergency Notification System via Cell Phones. *Student services:* health clinic, personal/psychological counseling.

Athletics Member USCAA and NCAA. All Division III. *Intercollegiate sports:* baseball M, basketball M/W, cross-country running M/W, softball W, swimming and diving W, tennis M/W, volleyball M/W. *Intramural sports:* basketball M/W, bowling M/W, golf M, soccer M/W, table tennis M/W, volleyball M/W.

Standardized Tests *Required:* SAT or ACT (for admission).

Costs (2011–12) *Tuition:* $17,000 full-time. Full-time tuition and fees vary according to course load, degree level, and program. Part-time tuition and fees vary according to course load, degree level, and program. *Required fees:* $565 full-time. *Payment plans:* installment, deferred payment. *Waivers:* senior citizens and employees or children of employees.

Financial Aid Of all full-time matriculated undergraduates who enrolled in 2009, 849 applied for aid, 726 were judged to have need, 111 had their need fully met. 85 Federal Work-Study jobs (averaging $1437). 18 state and other part-time jobs (averaging $1212). In 2009, 111 non-need-based awards were made. *Average percent of need met:* 68%. *Average financial aid package:* $13,446. *Average need-based loan:* $4284. *Average need-based gift aid:* $9017. *Average non-need-based aid:* $8162. *Average indebtedness upon graduation:* $22,825.

Applying *Options:* electronic application, early admission, deferred entrance. *Application fee:* $25. *Required:* high school transcript, minimum 2.5 GPA. *Required for some:* interview. *Recommended:* essay or personal statement, 2 letters of recommendation. *Application deadlines:* 8/15 (freshmen), 8/15 (transfers).

Freshman Application Contact Mr. Michael Learmond, Director of Admissions Operation, St. Joseph's College, New York, 245 Clinton Avenue, Brooklyn, NY 11205-3688. *Phone:* 718-940-5828. *E-mail:* mlearmond@sjcny.edu. *Web site:* http://www.sjcny.edu/.

See page 1566 for the College Close-Up.

St. Lawrence University

Canton, New York

- **Independent** comprehensive, founded 1856
- **Small-town** 1000-acre campus
- **Endowment** $204.4 million
- **Coed** 2,327 undergraduate students, 99% full-time, 55% women, 45% men
- **Very difficult** entrance level, 39% of applicants were admitted

Undergraduates 2,300 full-time, 27 part-time. Students come from 41 states and territories; 45 other countries; 57% are from out of state; 3% Black or African American, non-Hispanic/Latino; 4% Hispanic/Latino; 1% Asian, non-Hispanic/Latino; 0.2% Native Hawaiian or other Pacific Islander, non-Hispanic/Latino; 0.3% American Indian or Alaska Native, non-Hispanic/Latino; 2% Two or more races, non-Hispanic/Latino; 2% Race/ethnicity unknown; 6% international; 0.8% transferred in; 97% live on campus. *Retention:* 92% of full-time freshmen returned.

Freshmen *Admission:* 4,900 applied, 1,887 admitted, 609 enrolled. *Average high school GPA:* 3.55. *Test scores:* SAT critical reading scores over 500: 93%; SAT math scores over 500: 94%; SAT writing scores over 500: 94%; ACT scores over 18: 99%; SAT critical reading scores over 600: 57%; SAT math scores over 600: 64%; SAT writing scores over 600: 55%; ACT scores over 24: 84%; SAT critical reading scores over 700: 11%; SAT math scores over 700: 10%; SAT writing scores over 700: 11%; ACT scores over 30: 23%.

Faculty *Total:* 192, 89% full-time, 93% with terminal degrees. *Student/faculty ratio:* 12:1.

Academics *Calendar:* semesters. *Degrees:* bachelor's, master's, and post-master's certificates. *Special study options:* advanced placement credit, double majors, independent study, internships, off-campus study, part-time degree program, services for LD students, student-designed majors, study abroad, summer session for credit. *ROTC:* Army (c), Air Force (c). *Unusual degree programs:* 3-2 business administration with Clarkson University, Union College, Rochester Institute of Technology; engineering with Columbia University, Clarkson University, Rensselaer Polytechnic Institute, University of Rochester, University of Southern California.

Computers on Campus 681 computers/terminals are available on campus for general student use. Students can access the following: computer help desk, free student e-mail accounts, online (class) grades, online (class) registration, online (class) schedules. Campuswide network is available. 100% of college-owned or -operated housing units are wired for high-speed Internet access. Wireless service is available via entire campus.

Student Life *Housing:* on-campus residence required through senior year. *Options:* coed, women-only, disabled students. Campus housing is university owned. Freshman campus housing is guaranteed. *Activities and organizations:* drama/theater group, student-run newspaper, radio station, choral group, Outing Club, student newspaper, student government, Circle K, Habitat for Humanity, national fraternities, national sororities. *Campus security:* 24-hour emergency response devices and patrols, student patrols, late-night transport/escort service, controlled dormitory access. *Student services:* health clinic, personal/psychological counseling, women's center.

Athletics Member NCAA. All Division III except men's and women's ice hockey (Division I). *Intercollegiate sports:* baseball M, basketball M/W, crew M/W, cross-country running M/W, equestrian sports M/W, field hockey W, football M, golf M/W, ice hockey M(s)/W(s), lacrosse M/W, skiing (cross-country) M/W, skiing (downhill) M/W, soccer M/W, softball W, squash M/W, swimming and diving M/W, tennis M/W, track and field M/W, volleyball W. *Intramural sports:* basketball M/W, football M, ice hockey M/W, skiing (cross-country) M/W, soccer M/W, softball W, ultimate Frisbee M/W, volleyball M/W.

Costs (2010–11) *Comprehensive fee:* $51,770 includes full-time tuition ($40,905), mandatory fees ($250), and room and board ($10,615). *College room only:* $5715. Room and board charges vary according to board plan. *Payment plan:* installment. *Waivers:* employees or children of employees.

Financial Aid Of all full-time matriculated undergraduates who enrolled in 2009, 1,640 applied for aid, 1,490 were judged to have need, 540 had their need fully met. 835 Federal Work-Study jobs (averaging $1572). 307 state and other part-time jobs (averaging $1548). In 2009, 372 non-need-based awards were made. *Average percent of need met:* 89%. *Average financial aid package:* $36,851. *Average need-based loan:* $4199. *Average need-based gift aid:* $27,839. *Average non-need-based aid:* $12,672. *Average indebtedness upon graduation:* $29,489. *Financial aid deadline:* 2/1.

Applying *Options:* electronic application, early admission, early decision, deferred entrance. *Application fee:* $60. *Required:* essay or personal statement, high school transcript, 2 letters of recommendation. *Recommended:* minimum 2 GPA, interview. *Application deadlines:* 2/1 (freshmen), 4/1 (transfers). *Early decision deadline:* 11/15 (for plan 1), 1/15 (for plan 2). *Notification:* 3/31 (freshmen), 5/1 (transfers), 12/15 (early decision plan 1), 2/15 (early decision plan 2).

Freshman Application Contact Ms. Terry Cowdrey, Vice President and Dean of Admissions and Financial Aid, St. Lawrence University, 23 Romoda Drive, Canton, NY 13617-1455. *Phone:* 315-229-5261. *Toll-free phone:* 800-285-1856. *Fax:* 315-229-5818. *E-mail:* tcowdrey@stlawu.edu. *Web site:* http://www.stlawu.edu/.

See page 1570 for the College Close-Up.

St. Thomas Aquinas College

Sparkill, New York

- **Independent** comprehensive, founded 1952
- **Suburban** 46-acre campus with easy access to New York City
- **Endowment** $23.1 million
- **Coed** 1,852 undergraduate students, 70% full-time, 55% women, 45% men
- **Moderately difficult** entrance level, 79% of applicants were admitted

Undergraduates 1,288 full-time, 564 part-time. Students come from 9 states and territories; 7 other countries; 21% are from out of state; 6% Black or African American, non-Hispanic/Latino; 16% Hispanic/Latino; 3% Asian, non-Hispanic/Latino; 0.1% Native Hawaiian or other Pacific Islander, non-Hispanic/Latino; 0.4% American Indian or Alaska Native, non-Hispanic/Latino; 0.4% Two or more races, non-Hispanic/Latino; 6% Race/ethnicity unknown; 0.7% international; 5% transferred in; 30% live on campus. *Retention:* 75% of full-time freshmen returned.

Freshmen *Admission:* 1,697 applied, 1,348 admitted, 291 enrolled. *Average high school GPA:* 2.99. *Test scores:* SAT critical reading scores over 500: 34%; SAT math scores over 500: 42%; SAT writing scores over 500: 33%; ACT scores over 18: 76%; SAT critical reading scores over 600: 9%; SAT math scores over 600: 11%; SAT writing scores over 600: 9%; ACT scores over 24: 32%; SAT critical reading scores over 700: 1%; SAT math scores over 700: 1%; SAT writing scores over 700: 1%; ACT scores over 30: 4%.

Faculty *Total:* 161, 38% full-time, 42% with terminal degrees. *Student/faculty ratio:* 19:1.

Academics *Calendar:* semesters. *Degrees:* associate, bachelor's, master's, post-master's, and postbachelor's certificates. *Special study options:* academic remediation for entering students, accelerated degree program, adult/continuing education programs, advanced placement credit, double majors, freshman honors college, honors programs, independent study, internships, off-campus study, part-time degree program, services for LD students, study abroad, summer session for credit. *ROTC:* Air Force (c). *Unusual degree programs:* 3-2 engineering with George Washington University, Manhattan College; social work with NYU School of Social Work; physical therapy with New York Medical College.

Computers on Campus 200 computers/terminals are available on campus for general student use. Students can access the following: campus intranet, computer help desk, free student e-mail accounts, online (class) grades, online (class) registration, online (class) schedules. Campuswide network is available. 100% of college-owned or -operated housing units are wired for high-speed Internet access. Wireless service is available via entire campus.

Student Life *Housing options:* men-only, women-only, disabled students. Campus housing is university owned. Freshman campus housing is guaranteed. *Activities and organizations:* drama/theater group, student-run newspaper, radio station, choral group, Spartan Volunteers, Campus Activities Board, WSTK campus radio, Bowling Club, Laetare Players, national fraternities. *Campus security:* 24-hour emergency response devices and patrols, student patrols, late-night transport/escort service, controlled dormitory access. *Student services:* health clinic, personal/psychological counseling.

Athletics Member NCAA, NAIA. All NCAA Division II. *Intercollegiate sports:* baseball M(s), basketball M(s)/W(s), cross-country running M(s)/W(s), golf M/W, lacrosse W, soccer M(s)/W(s), softball W(s), tennis M/W, volleyball W(s). *Intramural sports:* basketball M/W, volleyball M/W.

Standardized Tests *Required:* SAT or ACT (for admission).

Costs (2010–11) *Comprehensive fee:* $32,710 includes full-time tuition ($21,910), mandatory fees ($500), and room and board ($10,300). Part-time tuition: $705 per credit hour. *Required fees:* $125 per term part-time. *Room and board:* Room and board charges vary according to board plan and housing facility. *Payment plan:* installment. *Waivers:* employees or children of employees.

Applying *Options:* electronic application, early decision, early action, deferred entrance. *Application fee:* $30. *Required:* high school transcript, minimum 2 GPA. *Required for some:* 3 letters of recommendation. *Recommended:* essay or personal statement, 2 letters of recommendation, interview. *Application deadlines:* rolling (freshmen), rolling (transfers), 12/15 (early action). *Early*

decision deadline: 12/1. *Notification:* 10/1 (freshmen), continuous (transfers), 1/15 (early decision), 1/15 (early action).

Freshman Application Contact Ms. Danielle Mac Kay, Director of Admissions, St. Thomas Aquinas College, 125 Route 340, Sparkill, NY 10976. *Phone:* 845-398-4100. *Toll-free phone:* 800-999-STAC. *Fax:* 845-398-4114. *E-mail:* dmackay@stac.edu. *Web site:* http://www.stac.edu/.

See page 1584 for the College Close-Up.

Sarah Lawrence College

Bronxville, New York

- **Independent** comprehensive, founded 1926
- **Suburban** 44-acre campus with easy access to New York City
- **Endowment** $60.0 million
- **Coed** 1,328 undergraduate students, 97% full-time, 71% women, 29% men
- **Very difficult** entrance level, 62% of applicants were admitted

Undergraduates 1,288 full-time, 40 part-time. Students come from 47 states and territories; 38 other countries; 73% are from out of state; 3% Black or African American, non-Hispanic/Latino; 8% Hispanic/Latino; 5% Asian, non-Hispanic/Latino; 0.1% Native Hawaiian or other Pacific Islander, non-Hispanic/Latino; 0.2% American Indian or Alaska Native, non-Hispanic/Latino; 5% Two or more races, non-Hispanic/Latino; 7% Race/ethnicity unknown; 5% international; 84% live on campus. *Retention:* 86% of full-time freshmen returned.

Freshmen *Admission:* 1,927 applied, 1,202 admitted, 338 enrolled. *Average high school GPA:* 3.6.

Faculty *Total:* 309, 33% full-time. *Student/faculty ratio:* 9:1.

Academics *Calendar:* semesters. *Degrees:* bachelor's and master's. *Special study options:* adult/continuing education programs, advanced placement credit, double majors, independent study, internships, off-campus study, part-time degree program, services for LD students, student-designed majors, study abroad. *Unusual degree programs:* 3-2 engineering with Columbia University; education, women's history with Sarah Lawrence College.

Computers on Campus 110 computers/terminals and 30 ports are available on campus for general student use. Students can access the following: campus intranet, computer help desk, free student e-mail accounts. Campuswide network is available. 100% of college-owned or -operated housing units are wired for high-speed Internet access. Wireless service is available via classrooms, computer centers, computer labs, dorm rooms, libraries, student centers.

Student Life *Housing:* on-campus residence required for freshman year. *Options:* coed, men-only, women-only, cooperative. Campus housing is university owned. Freshman campus housing is guaranteed. *Activities and organizations:* drama/theater group, student-run newspaper, radio station, choral group, Queer Voice Coalition, New Kids on the Block (transfer student group), Harambe (African Americans), Midnight Cabaret, Hillel. *Campus security:* 24-hour emergency response devices and patrols, late-night transport/escort service, controlled dormitory access. *Student services:* health clinic, personal/psychological counseling.

Athletics *Intercollegiate sports:* basketball M, crew M/W, cross-country running M/W, equestrian sports M/W, soccer M, softball W, swimming and diving W, tennis M/W, volleyball W. *Intramural sports:* basketball W, cross-country running M(c)/W(c), fencing M(c)/W(c), soccer W(c), squash M(c)/W(c), swimming and diving M(c), ultimate Frisbee M/W.

Costs (2011–12) *Comprehensive fee:* $58,716 includes full-time tuition ($44,220), mandatory fees ($992), and room and board ($13,504). Full-time tuition and fees vary according to course load. Part-time tuition: $1420 per unit. Part-time tuition and fees vary according to course load. *Required fees:* $482 per term part-time. *College room only:* $9110. Room and board charges vary according to board plan. *Payment plan:* installment. *Waivers:* employees or children of employees.

Financial Aid Of all full-time matriculated undergraduates who enrolled in 2009, 847 applied for aid, 746 were judged to have need, 419 had their need fully met. 651 Federal Work-Study jobs (averaging $1660). 35 state and other part-time jobs (averaging $1625). In 2009, 5 non-need-based awards were made. *Average percent of need met:* 94%. *Average financial aid package:* $38,115. *Average need-based loan:* $3576. *Average need-based gift aid:* $30,919. *Average non-need-based aid:* $12,000. *Average indebtedness upon graduation:* $21,590. *Financial aid deadline:* 2/1.

Applying *Options:* electronic application, early admission, early decision, deferred entrance. *Application fee:* $60. *Required:* essay or personal statement, high school transcript, 3 letters of recommendation. *Recommended:* minimum 3 GPA, interview. *Application deadlines:* 1/1 (freshmen), 3/1 (transfers). *Early decision deadline:* 11/1 (for plan 1), 1/1 (for plan 2). *Notification:* 4/1 (freshmen), 5/1 (transfers), 12/15 (early decision plan 1), 2/15 (early decision plan 2).

Freshman Application Contact Mr. Stephen M. Schierloh, Director of Admission, Sarah Lawrence College, 1 Mead Way, Bronxville, NY 10708-5999. *Phone:* 914-395-2510. *Toll-free phone:* 800-888-2858. *Fax:* 914-395-2515. *E-mail:* slcadmit@sarahlawrence.edu. *Web site:* http://www.sarahlawrence.edu/.

School of Visual Arts
New York, New York

- **Proprietary** comprehensive, founded 1947
- **Urban** 1-acre campus
- **Coed** 3,650 undergraduate students, 93% full-time, 59% women, 41% men
- **Moderately difficult** entrance level, 74% of applicants were admitted

Undergraduates 3,394 full-time, 256 part-time. 55% are from out of state; 4% Black or African American, non-Hispanic/Latino; 11% Hispanic/Latino; 13% Asian, non-Hispanic/Latino; 0.5% American Indian or Alaska Native, non-Hispanic/Latino; 7% Race/ethnicity unknown; 19% international; 9% transferred in; 29% live on campus. *Retention:* 84% of full-time freshmen returned.

Freshmen *Admission:* 3,219 applied, 2,373 admitted, 669 enrolled. *Average high school GPA:* 3.09. *Test scores:* SAT critical reading scores over 500: 57%; SAT math scores over 500: 56%; SAT writing scores over 500: 53%; ACT scores over 18: 86%; SAT critical reading scores over 600: 20%; SAT math scores over 600: 20%; SAT writing scores over 600: 18%; ACT scores over 24: 61%; SAT critical reading scores over 700: 3%; SAT math scores over 700: 2%; SAT writing scores over 700: 2%; ACT scores over 30: 6%.

Faculty *Total:* 929, 15% full-time, 9% with terminal degrees. *Student/faculty ratio:* 10:1.

Academics *Calendar:* semesters. *Degrees:* bachelor's and master's. *Special study options:* academic remediation for entering students, adult/continuing education programs, advanced placement credit, English as a second language, freshman honors college, honors programs, independent study, internships, services for LD students, study abroad, summer session for credit.

Computers on Campus Students can access the following: campus intranet, computer help desk, free student e-mail accounts, online (class) grades, online (class) schedules. Campuswide network is available. Wireless service is available via classrooms, computer centers, computer labs, dorm rooms, libraries, student centers.

Student Life *Housing options:* coed, women-only. Campus housing is university owned, leased by the school and is provided by a third party. Freshman

applicants given priority for college housing. *Activities and organizations:* student-run newspaper, radio station. *Campus security:* 24-hour patrols. *Student services:* health clinic, personal/psychological counseling.

Athletics *Intramural sports:* baseball M/W, softball M/W.

Standardized Tests *Required:* SAT or ACT (for admission).

Costs (2010–11) *Comprehensive fee:* $43,640 includes full-time tuition ($28,140) and room and board ($15,500). Full-time tuition and fees vary according to degree level and program. Part-time tuition: $940 per credit hour. Part-time tuition and fees vary according to degree level. *College room only:* $12,500. Room and board charges vary according to board plan, gender, housing facility, and location. *Payment plan:* installment. *Waivers:* employees or children of employees.

Financial Aid Of all full-time matriculated undergraduates who enrolled in 2009, 2,060 applied for aid, 1,877 were judged to have need, 14 had their need fully met. In 2009, 240 non-need-based awards were made. *Average percent of need met:* 38%. *Average financial aid package:* $13,361. *Average need-based loan:* $4593. *Average need-based gift aid:* $9468. *Average non-need-based aid:* $7545. *Average indebtedness upon graduation:* $41,495. *Financial aid deadline:* 3/1.

Applying *Options:* electronic application, deferred entrance. *Application fee:* $50. *Required:* essay or personal statement, high school transcript, minimum 2.5 GPA, portfolio. *Recommended:* interview. *Application deadlines:* rolling (freshmen), rolling (transfers). *Notification:* continuous (freshmen), continuous (transfers).

Freshman Application Contact Admissions Office, School of Visual Arts, 209 East 23rd Street, New York, NY 10010. *Phone:* 212-592-2100. *Toll-free phone:* 800-436-4204. *Fax:* 212-592-2116. *E-mail:* admissions@sva.edu. *Web site:* http://www.sva.edu/.

Sh'or Yoshuv Rabbinical College
Lawrence, New York

Director of Admissions Rabbi Moshe Rubin, Registrar, Sh'or Yoshuv Rabbinical College, 1 Cedarlawn Avenue, Lawrence, NY 11559-1714. *Phone:* 516-239-9002 Ext. 124. *Fax:* 516-977-1282. *E-mail:* mrubin@shoryoshuv.org. *Web site:* http://www.shoryoshuv.org/.

Siena College
Loudonville, New York

- **Independent Roman Catholic** comprehensive, founded 1937
- **Suburban** 164-acre campus
- **Endowment** $112.7 million
- **Coed** 3,390 undergraduate students, 95% full-time, 54% women, 46% men
- **Moderately difficult** entrance level, 60% of applicants were admitted

Undergraduates 3,207 full-time, 183 part-time. Students come from 32 states and territories; 9 other countries; 17% are from out of state; 3% Black or African American, non-Hispanic/Latino; 5% Hispanic/Latino; 3% Asian, non-Hispanic/Latino; 0.3% American Indian or Alaska Native, non-Hispanic/Latino; 2% Two or more races, non-Hispanic/Latino; 1% Race/ethnicity unknown; 0.8% international; 4% transferred in; 76% live on campus. *Retention:* 87% of full-time freshmen returned.

Freshmen *Admission:* 7,079 applied, 4,260 admitted, 769 enrolled. *Average high school GPA:* 3.5. *Test scores:* SAT critical reading scores over 500: 81%; SAT math scores over 500: 87%; SAT writing scores over 500: 76%; ACT scores over 18: 99%; SAT critical reading scores over 600: 31%; SAT math scores over 600: 45%; SAT writing scores over 600: 28%; ACT scores over 24: 64%; SAT critical reading scores over 700: 3%; SAT math scores over 700: 4%; SAT writing scores over 700: 3%; ACT scores over 30: 7%.

Faculty *Total:* 330, 57% full-time, 69% with terminal degrees. *Student/faculty ratio:* 14:1.

Academics *Calendar:* semesters. *Degrees:* certificates, bachelor's, and master's. *Special study options:* accelerated degree program, advanced placement credit, double majors, English as a second language, honors programs, independent study, internships, off-campus study, part-time degree program, services for LD students, study abroad, summer session for credit. *ROTC:* Army (b), Navy (c), Air Force (c). *Unusual degree programs:* 3-2 engineering with Clarkson University, Manhattan College, Catholic University of America, Western New England College, Rensselaer Polytechnic Institute, State University of New York at Binghamton.

Computers on Campus 432 computers/terminals are available on campus for general student use. Students can access the following: campus intranet, computer help desk, free student e-mail accounts, online (class) grades, online (class) registration, online (class) schedules. Campuswide network is available. 100% of college-owned or -operated housing units are wired for high-speed Internet access. Wireless service is available via classrooms, computer centers, computer labs, dorm rooms, learning centers, libraries, student centers.

Student Life *Housing:* on-campus residence required through senior year. *Options:* coed, disabled students. Campus housing is university owned. Freshman applicants given priority for college housing. *Activities and organizations:* drama/theater group, student-run newspaper, television station, choral group, Dog Pound, Mentoring Program, Outing Club, Student Events Board, Student Senate. *Campus security:* 24-hour emergency response devices and patrols, late-night transport/escort service, controlled dormitory access, call boxes in parking lots and on roadways. *Student services:* health clinic, personal/psychological counseling, women's center.

Athletics Member NCAA. All Division I. *Intercollegiate sports:* baseball M(s), basketball M(s)/W(s), cheerleading W(c), cross-country running M(s)/W(s), equestrian sports M(c)/W(c), field hockey W(s), golf M(s)/W(s), ice hockey M(c), lacrosse M(s)/W(s), rugby M(c)/W(c), soccer M(s)/W(s), softball W(s), swimming and diving W(s), tennis M(s)/W(s), track and field M(c)/W(c), volleyball M(c)/W(s), water polo W(s). *Intramural sports:* basketball M/W, cheerleading W, golf M, soccer M/W, softball M/W, volleyball M/W.

Standardized Tests *Required:* SAT or ACT (for admission).

Costs (2011–12) *One-time required fee:* $340. *Comprehensive fee:* $40,419 includes full-time tuition ($28,660), mandatory fees ($325), and room and board ($11,434). Full-time tuition and fees vary according to program. Part-time tuition: $500 per credit. Part-time tuition and fees vary according to program. *Required fees:* $60 per term part-time. *College room only:* $6730. Room and board charges vary according to board plan and housing facility. *Payment plan:* installment. *Waivers:* senior citizens and employees or children of employees.

Financial Aid Of all full-time matriculated undergraduates who enrolled in 2008, 2,523 applied for aid, 2,077 were judged to have need, 319 had their need fully met. 500 Federal Work-Study jobs (averaging $644). In 2008, 411 non-need-based awards were made. *Average percent of need met:* 74%. *Average financial aid package:* $16,796. *Average need-based loan:* $4411. *Average need-based gift aid:* $12,865. *Average non-need-based aid:* $8685. *Average indebtedness upon graduation:* $28,200.

Applying *Options:* electronic application, early admission, early decision, early action, deferred entrance. *Application fee:* $50. *Required:* essay or personal statement, high school transcript, 1 letter of recommendation. *Required for some:* interview. *Recommended:* interview. *Application deadlines:* 2/15 (freshmen), 8/15 (transfers), 12/1 (early action). *Early decision deadline:* 12/

1. *Notification:* 3/15 (freshmen), continuous (transfers), 12/15 (early decision), 1/1 (early action).

Freshman Application Contact Ms. Heather Renault, Director of Admissions, Siena College, 515 Loudon Road, Loudonville, NY 12211-1462. *Phone:* 518-783-2426. *Toll-free phone:* 888-AT-SIENA. *Fax:* 518-783-2436. *E-mail:* admit@siena.edu. *Web site:* http://www.siena.edu/.

See page 1606 for the College Close-Up.

Skidmore College
Saratoga Springs, New York

- **Independent** comprehensive, founded 1903
- **Small-town** 800-acre campus with easy access to Albany, NY
- **Endowment** $271.0 million
- **Coed** 2,734 undergraduate students, 98% full-time, 62% women, 38% men
- **Very difficult** entrance level, 47% of applicants were admitted

Undergraduates 2,690 full-time, 44 part-time. Students come from 48 states and territories; 80 other countries; 67% are from out of state; 3% Black or African American, non-Hispanic/Latino; 7% Hispanic/Latino; 6% Asian, non-Hispanic/Latino; 0.3% Native Hawaiian or other Pacific Islander, non-Hispanic/Latino; 0.1% American Indian or Alaska Native, non-Hispanic/Latino; 5% Two or more races, non-Hispanic/Latino; 8% Race/ethnicity unknown; 3% international; 1% transferred in; 83% live on campus. *Retention:* 94% of full-time freshmen returned.

Freshmen *Admission:* 6,011 applied, 2,813 admitted, 768 enrolled. *Test scores:* SAT critical reading scores over 500: 92%; SAT math scores over 500: 95%; SAT writing scores over 500: 95%; ACT scores over 18: 100%; SAT critical reading scores over 600: 65%; SAT math scores over 600: 65%; SAT writing scores over 600: 71%; ACT scores over 24: 89%; SAT critical reading scores over 700: 19%; SAT math scores over 700: 13%; SAT writing scores over 700: 22%; ACT scores over 30: 29%.

Faculty *Total:* 343, 72% full-time, 71% with terminal degrees. *Student/faculty ratio:* 9:1.

Academics *Calendar:* semesters plus optional 6-week internship period. *Degrees:* bachelor's and master's. *Special study options:* accelerated degree program, adult/continuing education programs, advanced placement credit, double majors, honors programs, independent study, internships, off-campus study, services for LD students, student-designed majors, study abroad, summer session for credit. *ROTC:* Army (c), Air Force (c). *Unusual degree programs:* 3-2 business administration with Clarkson University; engineering with Dartmouth College, Clarkson University; nursing with NYU.

Computers on Campus Students can access the following: campus intranet, computer help desk, free student e-mail accounts, online (class) grades, online (class) registration, online (class) schedules. Campuswide network is available. Wireless service is available via classrooms, computer centers, computer labs, learning centers, libraries, student centers.

Student Life *Housing:* on-campus residence required through sophomore year. *Options:* coed, women-only, disabled students. Campus housing is university owned. Freshman campus housing is guaranteed. *Activities and organizations:* drama/theater group, student-run newspaper, radio and television station, choral group, Student Government Association, student radio station, Student Volunteer Bureau, Outing Club, Skidmore News. *Campus security:* 24-hour emergency response devices and patrols, late-night transport/escort service, controlled dormitory access, well-lit campus. *Student services:* health clinic, personal/psychological counseling.

Athletics Member NCAA. All Division III. *Intercollegiate sports:* baseball M, basketball M/W, crew M/W, equestrian sports W, field hockey W, golf M, ice hockey M, lacrosse M/W, soccer M/W, softball W, swimming and diving M/W, tennis M/W, volleyball W. *Intramural sports:* basketball M/W, football M, ice hockey M(c)/W(c), racquetball M/W, skiing (downhill) M(c)/W(c), soccer M/W, tennis M/W, ultimate Frisbee M(c)/W(c), volleyball M/W.

Standardized Tests *Required:* SAT or ACT (for admission). *Recommended:* SAT Subject Tests (for admission).

Costs (2010–11) *Comprehensive fee:* $52,170 includes full-time tuition ($40,350), mandatory fees ($834), and room and board ($10,986). Full-time tuition and fees vary according to course load. Part-time tuition: $1345 per credit hour. Part-time tuition and fees vary according to course load. *Required fees:* $25 per term part-time. *College room only:* $6496. Room and board charges vary according to board plan and housing facility. *Payment plans:* tuition prepayment, installment. *Waivers:* senior citizens and employees or children of employees.

Financial Aid Of all full-time matriculated undergraduates who enrolled in 2009, 1,264 applied for aid, 1,135 were judged to have need, 1,135 had their need fully met. 732 Federal Work-Study jobs (averaging $2000). 305 state and other part-time jobs (averaging $2000). In 2009, 8 non-need-based awards were made. *Average percent of need met:* 87%. *Average financial aid package:* $34,104. *Average need-based loan:* $3878. *Average need-based gift aid:* $28,524. *Average non-need-based aid:* $10,000. *Average indebtedness upon graduation:* $18,303. *Financial aid deadline:* 2/1.

Applying *Options:* electronic application, early admission, early decision, deferred entrance. *Application fee:* $60. *Required:* essay or personal statement, high school transcript, 2 letters of recommendation. *Recommended:* interview. *Application deadlines:* 1/15 (freshmen), 4/1 (transfers). *Early decision deadline:* 11/15 (for plan 1), 1/15 (for plan 2). *Notification:* 4/1 (freshmen), 12/15 (early decision plan 1), 2/15 (early decision plan 2).

Freshman Application Contact Ms. Mary Lou Bates, Dean of Admissions and Financial Aid, Skidmore College, 815 North Broadway, Saratoga Springs, NY 12866-1632. *Phone:* 518-580-5570. *Toll-free phone:* 800-867-6007. *Fax:* 518-580-5584. *E-mail:* admissions@skidmore.edu. *Web site:* http://www.skidmore.edu/.

See page 1612 for the College Close-Up.

State University of New York at Binghamton
Binghamton, New York

- **State-supported** university, founded 1946, part of State University of New York System
- **Suburban** 930-acre campus
- **Endowment** $63.1 million
- **Coed** 11,787 undergraduate students, 97% full-time, 47% women, 53% men
- **Very difficult** entrance level, 40% of applicants were admitted

Undergraduates 11,381 full-time, 406 part-time. Students come from 41 states and territories; 97 other countries; 11% are from out of state; 5% Black or African American, non-Hispanic/Latino; 8% Hispanic/Latino; 12% Asian, non-Hispanic/Latino; 0.2% American Indian or Alaska Native, non-Hispanic/Latino; 0.9% Two or more races, non-Hispanic/Latino; 15% Race/ethnicity unknown; 10% international; 9% transferred in; 59% live on campus. *Retention:* 91% of full-time freshmen returned.

Freshmen *Admission:* 27,248 applied, 10,918 admitted, 2,321 enrolled. *Average high school GPA:* 3.6. *Test scores:* SAT critical reading scores over 500: 97%; SAT math scores over 500: 100%; SAT writing scores over 500: 98%; ACT scores over 18: 100%; SAT critical reading scores over 600: 68%; SAT math scores over 600: 86%; SAT writing scores over 600: 74%; ACT scores

---

SKIDMORE
C O L L E G E

"Creative Thought Matters *actually* has *sentimental* value to *me*. I asked my *Mother* if she remembered THE SLOGAN from SKIDMORE, Creative Thought Matters. She answered as if it was the **stupidest** question I'd ever asked, 'Of course! It's why you went to Skidmore.'"

2008 Skidmore graduate

"Creative Thought Matters is *more* than just a theme for me. It really **captures** what makes SKIDMORE *unique*.... SKIDMORE understands that learning does not (and should not) exist in neat little **silos,** which I think helps GRADUATES thrive in a **complex,** *INTERCONNECTED* WORLD."

2007 Skidmore graduate

Skidmore College Office of Admissions
Saratoga Springs, New York
www.skidmore.edu

Creative Thought Matters

PROFILES

over 24: 98%; SAT critical reading scores over 700: 13%; SAT math scores over 700: 29%; SAT writing scores over 700: 20%; ACT scores over 30: 34%.

Faculty *Total:* 845, 67% full-time. *Student/faculty ratio:* 21:1.

Academics *Calendar:* semesters. *Degrees:* bachelor's, master's, doctoral-professional, doctoral-research/scholarship, and post-master's certificates. *Special study options:* academic remediation for entering students, accelerated degree program, adult/continuing education programs, advanced placement credit, distance learning, double majors, English as a second language, honors programs, independent study, internships, off-campus study, part-time degree program, services for LD students, student-designed majors, study abroad, summer session for credit. *ROTC:* Army (c), Air Force (c). *Unusual degree programs:* 3-2 business administration; engineering; anthropology; art history; Asian & Asian American studies; biology; chemistry; computer science; economics; education; French; geography; geology; Italian; mathematics; materials science; philosophy, politics, & law; physics; political science; public administration; Spanish; systems science; theatre.

Computers on Campus 1,116 computers/terminals and 40,000 ports are available on campus for general student use. Students can access the following: campus intranet, computer help desk, free student e-mail accounts, online (class) grades, online (class) registration, online (class) schedules, course management system, personal Web space, wiki, virtual desktop. Campuswide network is available. 100% of college-owned or -operated housing units are wired for high-speed Internet access. Wireless service is available via entire campus.

Student Life *Housing:* on-campus residence required for freshman year. *Options:* coed, disabled students. Campus housing is university owned and is provided by a third party. Freshman campus housing is guaranteed. *Activities and organizations:* drama/theater group, student-run newspaper, radio and television station, choral group, intramurals, club sports, Student Association, cultural organizations, Peer Counseling/Mentoring/Volunteering Program, national fraternities, national sororities. *Campus security:* 24-hour emergency response devices and patrols, student patrols, late-night transport/escort service, controlled dormitory access, safety programs, well-lit campus, self-defense education, secured campus entrance 12 am-5 am, emergency phones, emergency text messages. *Student services:* health clinic, personal/psychological counseling, women's center, legal services.

Athletics Member NCAA. All Division I. *Intercollegiate sports:* baseball M(s), basketball M(s)/W(s), cross-country running M(s)/W(s), golf M(s), lacrosse M(s)/W(s), soccer M(s)/W(s), softball W(s), swimming and diving M(s)/W(s), tennis M(s)/W(s), track and field M(s)/W(s), volleyball W(s), wrestling M(s). *Intramural sports:* badminton M(c)/W(c), baseball M(c), basketball M/W, bowling M/W, cheerleading M/W, crew M(c)/W(c), cross-country running M(c)/W(c), equestrian sports M(c)/W(c), fencing M(c)/W(c), field hockey M(c)/W(c), golf M(c)/W(c), gymnastics M(c)/W(c), ice hockey M(c)/W(c), lacrosse M(c)/W(c), racquetball M/W, rugby M(c)/W(c), skiing (downhill) M(c)/W(c), soccer M/W, softball M/W, swimming and diving M(c)/W(c), table tennis M/W, tennis M/W, ultimate Frisbee M(c)/W(c), volleyball M/W, water polo M(c)/W(c).

Standardized Tests *Required:* SAT or ACT (for admission).

Costs (2010–11) *Tuition:* state resident $4970 full-time, $207 per credit hour part-time; nonresident $13,380 full-time, $558 per credit hour part-time. Part-time tuition and fees vary according to course load. *Required fees:* $1911 full-time, $69 per credit hour part-time, $118 per term part-time. *Room and board:* $11,244; room only: $7036. Room and board charges vary according to board plan and housing facility.

Financial Aid Of all full-time matriculated undergraduates who enrolled in 2009, 7,694 applied for aid, 5,533 were judged to have need, 398 had their need fully met. 408 Federal Work-Study jobs (averaging $1425). In 2009, 84 non-need-based awards were made. *Average percent of need met:* 69%. *Average financial aid package:* $10,414. *Average need-based loan:* $4649. *Average need-based gift aid:* $6716. *Average non-need-based aid:* $5966. *Average indebtedness upon graduation:* $21,110.

Applying *Options:* electronic application, early admission, early action, deferred entrance. *Application fee:* $50. *Required:* essay or personal statement, high school transcript, 1 letter of recommendation. *Required for some:* portfolio, audition. *Application deadlines:* 1/15 (freshmen), 1/15 (out-of-state freshmen), rolling (transfers), 11/15 (early action). *Notification:* 4/1 (freshmen), 4/1 (out-of-state freshmen), continuous (transfers), 1/15 (early action).

Freshman Application Contact Sandra Starke, Vice Provost for Enrollment Management, State University of New York at Binghamton, Binghamton University, PO Box 6001, Binghamton, NY 13902-6001. *Phone:* 607-777-2171. *Fax:* 607-777-4445. *E-mail:* admit@binghamton.edu. *Web site:* http://www.binghamton.edu/.

State University of New York at Fredonia

Fredonia, New York

- **State-supported** comprehensive, founded 1826, part of State University of New York System
- **Small-town** 249-acre campus with easy access to Buffalo
- **Endowment** $17.7 million
- **Coed** 5,388 undergraduate students, 97% full-time, 56% women, 44% men
- **Moderately difficult** entrance level, 50% of applicants were admitted

Undergraduates 5,240 full-time, 148 part-time. Students come from 29 states and territories; 16 other countries; 2% are from out of state; 3% Black or African American, non-Hispanic/Latino; 3% Hispanic/Latino; 1% Asian, non-Hispanic/Latino; 0.1% Native Hawaiian or other Pacific Islander, non-Hispanic/Latino; 0.5% American Indian or Alaska Native, non-Hispanic/Latino; 1% Two or more races, non-Hispanic/Latino; 5% Race/ethnicity unknown; 1% international; 9% transferred in; 53% live on campus. *Retention:* 86% of full-time freshmen returned.

Freshmen *Admission:* 6,696 applied, 3,319 admitted, 1,070 enrolled. *Average high school GPA:* 3.4. *Test scores:* SAT critical reading scores over 500: 65%; SAT math scores over 500: 71%; ACT scores over 18: 97%; SAT critical reading scores over 600: 19%; SAT math scores over 600: 22%; ACT scores over 24: 53%; SAT critical reading scores over 700: 1%; SAT math scores over 700: 1%; ACT scores over 30: 6%.

Faculty *Total:* 474, 53% full-time, 55% with terminal degrees. *Student/faculty ratio:* 17:1.

Academics *Calendar:* semesters. *Degrees:* bachelor's, master's, and post-master's certificates. *Special study options:* accelerated degree program, adult/continuing education programs, advanced placement credit, distance learning, double majors, honors programs, independent study, internships, off-campus study, part-time degree program, services for LD students, student-designed majors, study abroad, summer session for credit. *ROTC:* Army (c). *Unusual degree programs:* 3-2 business administration with Clarkson University, State University of New York at Buffalo, University of Pittsburgh; engineering with Clarkson University, State University of New York at Buffalo, Case Western Reserve, Columbia University, Cornell University, Louisiana Technical University, New York State College of Ceramics at Alfred, Ohio State University.

Computers on Campus 500 computers/terminals are available on campus for general student use. Students can access the following: campus intranet, computer help desk, free student e-mail accounts, online (class) grades, online (class) registration, online (class) schedules. Campuswide network is available. 100% of college-owned or -operated housing units are wired for high-speed Internet access. Wireless service is available via entire campus.

Student Life *Housing:* on-campus residence required through sophomore year. *Options:* coed, men-only, women-only. Campus housing is university owned. Freshman campus housing is guaranteed. *Activities and organizations:* drama/theater group, student-run newspaper, radio and television station, choral group, Student Association, Undergraduate Alumni Council, Communication Club, ethnic organizations, spectrum entertainment board, national fraternities, national sororities. *Campus security:* 24-hour emergency response devices and patrols, late-night transport/escort service, controlled dormitory access. *Student services:* health clinic, personal/psychological counseling, legal services.

Athletics Member NCAA. All Division III. *Intercollegiate sports:* baseball M, basketball M/W, cheerleading M/W, cross-country running M/W, field hockey M(c)/W(c), ice hockey M, lacrosse W, soccer M/W, softball W, swimming and diving M/W, tennis M/W, track and field M/W, volleyball M/W. *Intramural sports:* basketball M/W, cross-country running M/W, field hockey W, football M, golf M, ice hockey M(c), lacrosse M, racquetball M/W, rock climbing M/W, rugby M(c)/W(c), skiing (cross-country) M/W, skiing (downhill) M/W, soccer M/W, softball M/W, squash M/W, table tennis M/W, tennis M/W, ultimate Frisbee M/W, volleyball M(c)/W, water polo M/W.

Standardized Tests *Required:* SAT or ACT (for admission).

Costs (2011–12) *Tuition:* state resident $4970 full-time, $207 per credit hour part-time; nonresident $13,380 full-time, $558 per credit hour part-time. Full-time tuition and fees vary according to program. Part-time tuition and fees vary according to program. *Required fees:* $1363 full-time, $57 per credit hour part-time. *Room and board:* $10,110; room only: $5950. Room and board charges vary according to board plan and housing facility. *Payment plan:* installment.

Financial Aid Of all full-time matriculated undergraduates who enrolled in 2009, 4,439 applied for aid, 3,562 were judged to have need, 388 had their need fully met. 298 Federal Work-Study jobs (averaging $1287). In 2009, 284 non-need-based awards were made. *Average percent of need met:* 64%. *Average financial aid package:* $9239. *Average need-based loan:* $4774. *Average need-based gift aid:* $4337. *Average non-need-based aid:* $2161. *Average indebtedness upon graduation:* $27,110.

Applying *Options:* electronic application, early admission, early decision, deferred entrance. *Application fee:* $50. *Required:* essay or personal state-

ment, high school transcript, minimum 2.5 GPA, 1 letter of recommendation. *Required for some:* interview, audition for music and theater programs, portfolio for art and media arts program. *Application deadlines:* rolling (freshmen), rolling (transfers). *Early decision deadline:* 11/1. *Notification:* continuous (freshmen), continuous (transfers), 12/1 (early decision).
Freshman Application Contact Office of Admissions, State University of New York at Fredonia, 178 Central Avenue, Fredonia, NY 14063. *Phone:* 716-673-3251. *Toll-free phone:* 800-252-1212. *Fax:* 716-673-3249. *E-mail:* admissions@fredonia.edu. *Web site:* http://www.fredonia.edu/.

State University of New York at New Paltz

New Paltz, New York

- **State-supported** comprehensive, founded 1828, part of State University of New York System
- **Small-town** 216-acre campus
- **Endowment** $9.2 million
- **Coed** 6,582 undergraduate students, 92% full-time, 64% women, 36% men
- **Very difficult** entrance level, 37% of applicants were admitted

Undergraduates 6,073 full-time, 509 part-time. 4% are from out of state; 5% Black or African American, non-Hispanic/Latino; 11% Hispanic/Latino; 4% Asian, non-Hispanic/Latino; 0.1% Native Hawaiian or other Pacific Islander, non-Hispanic/Latino; 0.1% American Indian or Alaska Native, non-Hispanic/Latino; 2% Two or more races, non-Hispanic/Latino; 9% Race/ethnicity unknown; 4% international; 9% transferred in. *Retention:* 87% of full-time freshmen returned.
Freshmen *Admission:* 15,204 applied, 5,688 admitted, 1,100 enrolled. *Average high school GPA:* 3.5. *Test scores:* SAT critical reading scores over 500: 83%; SAT math scores over 500: 86%; SAT writing scores over 500: 76%; ACT scores over 18: 99%; SAT critical reading scores over 600: 33%; SAT math scores over 600: 31%; SAT writing scores over 600: 26%; ACT scores over 24: 70%; SAT critical reading scores over 700: 3%; SAT math scores over 700: 2%; SAT writing scores over 700: 3%; ACT scores over 30: 4%.
Faculty *Total:* 650, 50% full-time, 55% with terminal degrees. *Student/faculty ratio:* 16:1.
Academics *Calendar:* semesters. *Degrees:* bachelor's, master's, and post-master's certificates. *Special study options:* academic remediation for entering students, adult/continuing education programs, advanced placement credit, cooperative education, distance learning, double majors, English as a second language, honors programs, independent study, internships, off-campus study, part-time degree program, services for LD students, student-designed majors, study abroad, summer session for credit. *Unusual degree programs:* 3-2 forestry with State University of New York College of Environmental Science and Forestry.
Computers on Campus 950 computers/terminals are available on campus for general student use. Students can access the following: campus intranet, computer help desk, free student e-mail accounts, online (class) grades, online (class) registration, online (class) schedules. Campuswide network is available. 100% of college-owned or -operated housing units are wired for high-speed Internet access. Wireless service is available via classrooms, dorm rooms, libraries, student centers.
Student Life *Housing:* on-campus residence required for freshman year. *Options:* coed, men-only, women-only, disabled students. Campus housing is university owned. Freshman campus housing is guaranteed. *Activities and organizations:* drama/theater group, student-run newspaper, radio and television station, choral group, Student Association, Residence Hall Student Association, intramurals and club sports, Outing Club, national fraternities, national sororities. *Campus security:* 24-hour emergency response devices and patrols, late-night transport/escort service, controlled dormitory access, safety seminars, RAD Women's Self Defense. *Student services:* health clinic, personal/psychological counseling, legal services.
Athletics Member NCAA. All Division III. *Intercollegiate sports:* baseball M, basketball M/W, cross-country running M/W, equestrian sports W(c), fencing M(c)/W(c), field hockey W, ice hockey M(c), lacrosse M(c)/W, racquetball M(c)/W(c), rugby M(c)/W(c), skiing (cross-country) M/W, soccer M/W, softball W, squash W, swimming and diving M/W, tennis M/W, track and field M(c)/W(c), ultimate Frisbee M(c)/W(c), volleyball M/W. *Intramural sports:* badminton M/W, basketball M/W, cheerleading M(c)/W(c), golf M/W, racquetball M/W, soccer M/W, softball M/W, swimming and diving M(c)/W(c), tennis M/W, volleyball M/W.
Standardized Tests *Required:* SAT or ACT (for admission).
Costs (2010–11) *Tuition:* state resident $4970 full-time, $207 per credit part-time; nonresident $13,380 full-time, $558 per credit part-time. *Required fees:* $1165 full-time, $34 per credit part-time, $175 per term part-time. *Room and board:* $9786; room only: $6364. Room and board charges vary according to board plan. *Payment plan:* installment.

Financial Aid Of all full-time matriculated undergraduates who enrolled in 2009, 4,547 applied for aid, 3,307 were judged to have need, 301 had their need fully met. 1,200 Federal Work-Study jobs (averaging $1000). 774 state and other part-time jobs (averaging $925). In 2009, 26 non-need-based awards were made. *Average percent of need met:* 57%. *Average financial aid package:* $9230. *Average need-based loan:* $4432. *Average need-based gift aid:* $4813. *Average non-need-based aid:* $1733. *Average indebtedness upon graduation:* $25,732.
Applying *Options:* electronic application, early admission, early action. *Application fee:* $40. *Required:* essay or personal statement, high school transcript, 1 letter of recommendation. *Required for some:* portfolio for art program, audition for music and theater programs. *Recommended:* minimum 3.4 GPA. *Application deadlines:* 4/1 (freshmen), 4/1 (transfers), 11/15 (early action). *Notification:* continuous (freshmen), continuous (transfers), 12/15 (early action).
Freshman Application Contact Ms. Kimberly A. Strano, Director of Freshman Admissions, State University of New York at New Paltz, 1 Hawk Drive, New Paltz, NY 12561-2499. *Phone:* 845-257-3200. *Fax:* 845-257-3209. *E-mail:* admissions@newpaltz.edu. *Web site:* http://www.newpaltz.edu/.

State University of New York at Oswego

Oswego, New York

- **State-supported** comprehensive, founded 1861, part of State University of New York System
- **Small-town** 696-acre campus with easy access to Syracuse
- **Endowment** $9.3 million
- **Coed** 7,377 undergraduate students, 95% full-time, 52% women, 48% men
- **Moderately difficult** entrance level, 47% of applicants were admitted

Undergraduates 6,983 full-time, 394 part-time. Students come from 31 states and territories; 11 other countries; 2% are from out of state; 4% Black or African American, non-Hispanic/Latino; 6% Hispanic/Latino; 2% Asian, non-Hispanic/Latino; 0.1% Native Hawaiian or other Pacific Islander, non-Hispanic/Latino; 0.3% American Indian or Alaska Native, non-Hispanic/Latino; 2% Two or more races, non-Hispanic/Latino; 3% Race/ethnicity unknown; 0.9% international; 11% transferred in; 57% live on campus. *Retention:* 82% of full-time freshmen returned.
Freshmen *Admission:* 10,594 applied, 5,021 admitted, 1,391 enrolled. *Average high school GPA:* 3.5. *Test scores:* SAT critical reading scores over 500: 81%; SAT math scores over 500: 83%; ACT scores over 18: 100%; SAT critical reading scores over 600: 21%; SAT math scores over 600: 21%; ACT scores over 24: 46%; SAT critical reading scores over 700: 2%; SAT math scores over 700: 1%; ACT scores over 30: 2%.
Faculty *Total:* 532, 60% full-time, 62% with terminal degrees. *Student/faculty ratio:* 19:1.
Academics *Calendar:* semesters. *Degrees:* bachelor's, master's, and post-master's certificates. *Special study options:* accelerated degree program, adult/continuing education programs, advanced placement credit, cooperative education, distance learning, double majors, English as a second language, freshman honors college, honors programs, independent study, internships, off-campus study, part-time degree program, services for LD students, student-designed majors, study abroad, summer session for credit. *ROTC:* Army (c). *Unusual degree programs:* 3-2 engineering with Clarkson University, Case Western Reserve University, State University of New York at Binghamton.
Computers on Campus 750 computers/terminals are available on campus for general student use. Students can access the following: campus intranet, computer help desk, free student e-mail accounts, online (class) grades, online (class) registration, online (class) schedules. Campuswide network is available. 100% of college-owned or -operated housing units are wired for high-speed Internet access. Wireless service is available via classrooms, computer centers, computer labs, learning centers, libraries, student centers.
Student Life *Housing:* on-campus residence required through sophomore year. *Options:* coed, disabled students. Campus housing is university owned. Freshman campus housing is guaranteed. *Activities and organizations:* drama/theater group, student-run newspaper, radio and television station, choral group, club/intramural sports, student radio/television stations (WNYO and WTOP), Outing/Recreation Club, Dance Organization (Del Sarte), Financial Management Association, national fraternities, national sororities. *Campus security:* 24-hour emergency response devices and patrols, controlled dormitory access. *Student services:* health clinic, personal/psychological counseling, women's center, legal services.
Athletics Member NCAA. All Division III. *Intercollegiate sports:* baseball M, basketball M/W, crew M(c)/W(c), cross-country running M/W, field hockey W, golf M, ice hockey M/W, lacrosse M/W, soccer M/W, softball W, swimming and diving M/W, tennis M/W, track and field M/W, volleyball W, wrestling M. *Intramural sports:* badminton M/W, basketball M/W, cheerlead-

ing W(c), equestrian sports M(c)/W(c), fencing M(c)/W(c), field hockey W(c), football M/W, golf M/W, gymnastics M(c)/W(c), ice hockey M(c)/W(c), racquetball M/W, rock climbing M(c)/W(c), rugby M(c)/W(c), skiing (cross-country) M(c)/W(c), skiing (downhill) M(c)/W(c), soccer M/W, softball M/W, swimming and diving M(c)/W(c), table tennis M/W, tennis M/W, ultimate Frisbee M(c)/W(c), volleyball M(c)/W, water polo M/W.

Standardized Tests *Required:* SAT or ACT (for admission).

Costs (2011–12) *Tuition:* state resident $4970 full-time, $207 per credit hour part-time; nonresident $13,380 full-time, $558 per credit hour part-time. Full-time tuition and fees vary according to degree level. Part-time tuition and fees vary according to course load and degree level. *Required fees:* $1216 full-time, $50 per credit hour part-time. *Room and board:* $11,610; room only: $7390. Room and board charges vary according to board plan and housing facility. *Payment plan:* installment.

Financial Aid Of all full-time matriculated undergraduates who enrolled in 2009, 5,906 applied for aid, 4,467 were judged to have need, 940 had their need fully met. 424 Federal Work-Study jobs (averaging $1132). 1,458 state and other part-time jobs (averaging $1639). In 2009, 590 non-need-based awards were made. *Average percent of need met:* 86%. *Average financial aid package:* $7248. *Average need-based loan:* $4239. *Average need-based gift aid:* $5701. *Average non-need-based aid:* $2923. *Average indebtedness upon graduation:* $25,931.

Applying *Options:* electronic application, early admission, early decision, deferred entrance. *Application fee:* $50. *Required:* high school transcript. *Recommended:* essay or personal statement, interview. *Application deadlines:* rolling (freshmen), rolling (transfers). *Early decision deadline:* 11/15. *Notification:* 1/15 (freshmen), 1/15 (transfers), 12/15 (early decision).

Freshman Application Contact Dr. Joseph Grant, Vice President for Student Affairs and Enrollment, State University of New York at Oswego, 7060 State Route 104, Oswego, NY 13126. *Phone:* 315-312-2250. *Fax:* 315-312-3260. *E-mail:* admiss@oswego.edu. *Web site:* http://www.oswego.edu/.

See page 1638 for the College Close-Up.

State University of New York at Plattsburgh

Plattsburgh, New York

- **State-supported** comprehensive, founded 1889, part of State University of New York System
- **Small-town** 265-acre campus with easy access to Montreal
- **Endowment** $11.1 million
- **Coed** 5,859 undergraduate students, 94% full-time, 54% women, 46% men
- **Moderately difficult** entrance level, 45% of applicants were admitted

Undergraduates 5,529 full-time, 330 part-time. Students come from 31 states and territories; 67 other countries; 5% are from out of state; 5% Black or African American, non-Hispanic/Latino; 5% Hispanic/Latino; 2% Asian, non-Hispanic/Latino; 0.4% American Indian or Alaska Native, non-Hispanic/Latino; 1% Two or more races, non-Hispanic/Latino; 6% Race/ethnicity unknown; 7% international; 11% transferred in; 47% live on campus. *Retention:* 81% of full-time freshmen returned.

Freshmen *Admission:* 7,617 applied, 3,451 admitted, 997 enrolled. *Average high school GPA:* 3.19. *Test scores:* SAT critical reading scores over 500: 69%; SAT math scores over 500: 74%; ACT scores over 18: 97%; SAT critical reading scores over 600: 19%; SAT math scores over 600: 19%; ACT scores over 24: 36%; SAT critical reading scores over 700: 3%; SAT math scores over 700: 1%; ACT scores over 30: 2%.

Faculty *Total:* 536, 53% full-time, 53% with terminal degrees. *Student/faculty ratio:* 16:1.

Academics *Calendar:* semesters plus 2 5-week summer sessions and 1 winter session. *Degrees:* certificates, bachelor's, master's, and post-master's certificates. *Special study options:* academic remediation for entering students, accelerated degree program, adult/continuing education programs, advanced placement credit, cooperative education, distance learning, double majors, English as a second language, honors programs, independent study, internships, off-campus study, part-time degree program, services for LD students, student-designed majors, study abroad, summer session for credit. *ROTC:* Army (b).

Computers on Campus 343 computers/terminals and 8 ports are available on campus for general student use. Students can access the following: campus

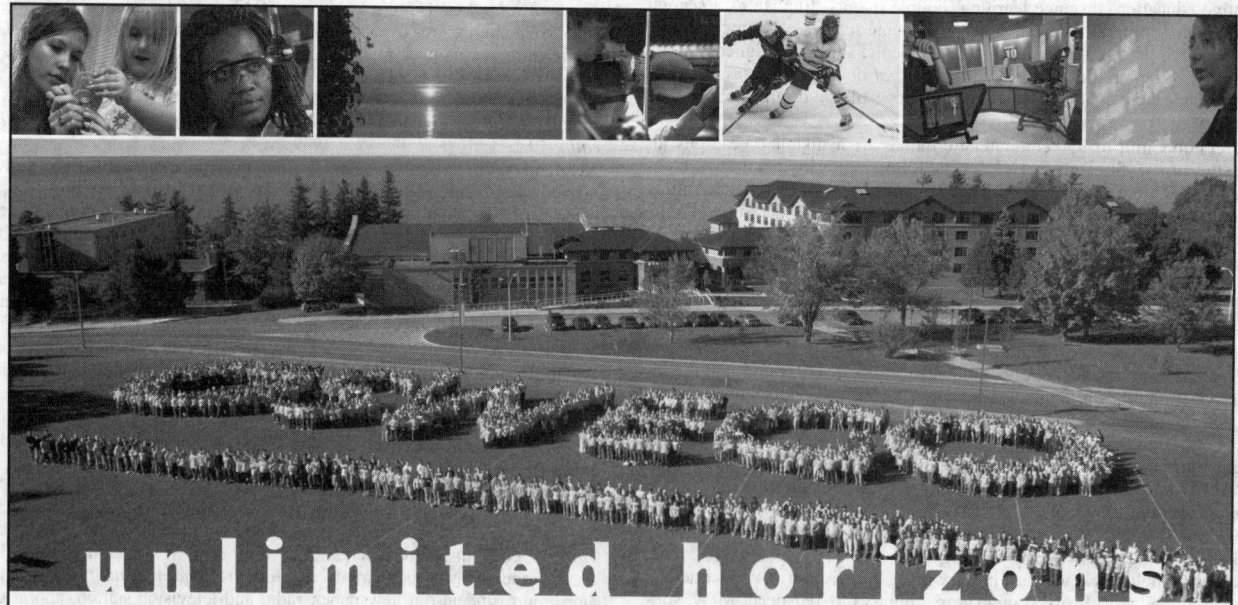

intranet, computer help desk, free student e-mail accounts, online (class) grades, online (class) registration, online (class) schedules. Campuswide network is available. Wireless service is available via classrooms, computer labs, dorm rooms, learning centers, libraries, student centers.

Student Life *Housing:* on-campus residence required through sophomore year. *Options:* coed, disabled students. Campus housing is university owned. Freshman campus housing is guaranteed. *Activities and organizations:* drama/theater group, student-run newspaper, radio and television station, choral group, Student Association, Honor Societies, Student Media Organizations, service/leadership organizations, intramural and recreational sports, national fraternities, national sororities. *Campus security:* 24-hour emergency response devices and patrols, late-night transport/escort service, controlled dormitory access. *Student services:* health clinic, personal/psychological counseling, women's center, legal services.

Athletics Member NCAA. All Division III. *Intercollegiate sports:* baseball M, basketball M/W, cross-country running M/W, ice hockey M/W, lacrosse M, soccer M/W, softball W, tennis W, track and field M/W, volleyball W. *Intramural sports:* basketball M/W, cheerleading M(c)/W(c), field hockey M/W, football M, ice hockey M(c)/W(c), racquetball M/W, rock climbing M(c)/W(c), rugby M(c)/W(c), soccer M/W, softball M/W, tennis M/W, ultimate Frisbee M/W, volleyball M/W.

Standardized Tests *Required:* SAT or ACT (for admission).

Costs (2010–11) *Tuition:* state resident $4970 full-time, $207 per credit hour part-time; nonresident $13,380 full-time, $558 per credit hour part-time. Part-time tuition and fees vary according to course load. *Required fees:* $1173 full-time, $47 per credit hour part-time. *Room and board:* $9000. Room and board charges vary according to board plan. *Payment plans:* installment, deferred payment. *Waivers:* employees or children of employees.

Financial Aid Of all full-time matriculated undergraduates who enrolled in 2009, 4,475 applied for aid, 3,500 were judged to have need, 938 had their need fully met. 770 Federal Work-Study jobs (averaging $2084). 825 state and other part-time jobs (averaging $2100). In 2009, 1372 non-need-based awards were made. *Average percent of need met:* 87%. *Average financial aid package:* $11,429. *Average need-based loan:* $7122. *Average need-based gift aid:* $5821. *Average non-need-based aid:* $6101. *Average indebtedness upon graduation:* $25,326.

Applying *Options:* electronic application, early admission, early decision, deferred entrance. *Application fee:* $50. *Required:* essay or personal statement, high school transcript, minimum 2.5 GPA, 1 letter of recommendation. *Required for some:* minimum 3.4 GPA. *Recommended:* minimum 3 GPA, interview. *Application deadline:* rolling (transfers). *Notification:* continuous (freshmen), continuous (transfers).

Freshman Application Contact Mrs. Carrie Woodward, Assistant Director for Freshman Admissions, State University of New York at Plattsburgh, 101 Broad Street, Plattsburgh, NY 12901. *Phone:* 888-673-0012. *Toll-free phone:* 888-673-0012. *Fax:* 518-564-2045. *E-mail:* carrie.woodward@plattsburgh.edu. *Web site:* http://www.plattsburgh.edu/.

State University of New York College at Cortland

Cortland, New York

- **State-supported** comprehensive, founded 1868, part of State University of New York System
- **Small-town** 191-acre campus with easy access to Syracuse
- **Coed**
- **Moderately difficult** entrance level

Faculty *Student/faculty ratio:* 16:1.

Academics *Calendar:* semesters. *Degrees:* bachelor's, master's, post-master's, and postbachelor's certificates.

Student Life *Campus security:* 24-hour emergency response devices and patrols, late-night transport/escort service.

Athletics Member NCAA. All Division III.

Standardized Tests *Required:* SAT or ACT (for admission).

Costs (2010–11) *Tuition:* state resident $4970 full-time, $207 per credit hour part-time; nonresident $12,870 full-time, $536 per credit hour part-time. Full-time tuition and fees vary according to course load and degree level. Part-time tuition and fees vary according to course load and degree level. *Required fees:* $1245 full-time, $56 per credit hour part-time. *Room and board:* $10,490; room only: $6260. Room and board charges vary according to board plan and housing facility.

Financial Aid *Of all full-time matriculated undergraduates who enrolled in 2008,* 5,088 applied for aid, 3,689 were judged to have need, 616 had their need fully met. *In 2008,* 109 non-need-based awards were made. *Average percent of need met:* 71. *Average financial aid package:* $12,245. *Average need-based loan:* $4195. *Average need-based gift aid:* $5010. *Average non-need-based aid:* $2275.

Applying *Options:* electronic application, early admission, early decision, deferred entrance. *Application fee:* $40. *Required:* essay or personal state-

ment, high school transcript, minimum 2.3 GPA, 1 letter of recommendation. *Recommended:* minimum 3 GPA, 3 letters of recommendation, interview.

Freshman Application Contact Mr. Mark Yacavone, Director of Admission, State University of New York College at Cortland, PO Box 2000, Cortland, NY 13045. *Phone:* 607-753-4711. *Fax:* 607-753-5998. *E-mail:* admissions@cortland.edu. *Web site:* http://www.cortland.edu/.

State University of New York College at Geneseo

Geneseo, New York

- **State-supported** comprehensive, founded 1871, part of State University of New York system
- **Small-town** 220-acre campus with easy access to Rochester
- **Endowment** $12.4 million
- **Coed** 5,485 undergraduate students, 98% full-time, 57% women, 43% men
- **Very difficult** entrance level, 38% of applicants were admitted

Undergraduates 5,378 full-time, 107 part-time. Students come from 26 states and territories; 39 other countries; 2% are from out of state; 2% Black or African American, non-Hispanic/Latino; 5% Hispanic/Latino; 6% Asian, non-Hispanic/Latino; 0.1% Native Hawaiian or other Pacific Islander, non-Hispanic/Latino; 0.2% American Indian or Alaska Native, non-Hispanic/Latino; 2% Two or more races, non-Hispanic/Latino; 6% Race/ethnicity unknown; 2% international; 18% transferred in; 53% live on campus. *Retention:* 92% of full-time freshmen returned.

Freshmen *Admission:* 9,885 applied, 3,711 admitted, 1,008 enrolled. *Test scores:* SAT critical reading scores over 500: 93%; SAT math scores over 500: 95%; ACT scores over 18: 100%; SAT critical reading scores over 600: 77%; SAT math scores over 600: 82%; ACT scores over 24: 97%; SAT critical reading scores over 700: 24%; SAT math scores over 700: 26%; ACT scores over 30: 31%.

Faculty *Total:* 339, 71% full-time, 68% with terminal degrees. *Student/faculty ratio:* 20:1.

Academics *Calendar:* semesters. *Degrees:* bachelor's and master's. *Special study options:* advanced placement credit, double majors, English as a second language, honors programs, independent study, internships, off-campus study, part-time degree program, services for LD students, study abroad, summer session for credit. *ROTC:* Army (c), Air Force (c). *Unusual degree programs:* 3-2 business administration with Syracuse University, State University of New York at Buffalo, State University of New York at Binghamton, Rochester Institute of Technology, Clarkson University, Alfred University, Union College; engineering with Columbia University, Case Western Reserve University, Alfred University, Clarkson University, Syracuse University, The Pennsylvania State University, University of Rochester, SUNY Binghamton, SUNY Buffalo, Rochester Institute of Technology; nursing with Johns Hopkins School of Nursing; optometry with State University of New York College of Optometry; dental with State University of New York at Buffalo.

Computers on Campus 640 computers/terminals and 96 ports are available on campus for general student use. Students can access the following: campus intranet, computer help desk, free student e-mail accounts, online (class) grades, online (class) registration, online (class) schedules. Campuswide network is available. 100% of college-owned or -operated housing units are wired for high-speed Internet access. Wireless service is available via entire campus.

Student Life *Housing:* on-campus residence required through sophomore year. *Options:* coed, disabled students. Campus housing is university owned. Freshman campus housing is guaranteed. *Activities and organizations:* drama/theater group, student-run newspaper, radio and television station, choral group, Big Brother Big Sister, Colleges Against Cancer, Inter Residence Council, Activities Commission, Council for Exceptional Children, national fraternities, national sororities. *Campus security:* 24-hour emergency response devices and patrols, student patrols, late-night transport/escort service, controlled dormitory access. *Student services:* health clinic, personal/psychological counseling, women's center, legal services.

Athletics Member NCAA. All Division III. *Intercollegiate sports:* baseball M(c)/W(c), basketball M/W, cheerleading M(c)/W(c), crew M(c)/W(c), cross-country running M/W, equestrian sports W, fencing M(c)/W(c), field hockey W, ice hockey M/W(c), lacrosse M/W, rugby M(c)/W(c), skiing (downhill) M(c)/W(c), soccer M/W, softball W, swimming and diving M/W, tennis M(c)/W, track and field M/W, ultimate Frisbee M(c)/W(c), volleyball M(c)/W, water polo M(c)/W(c). *Intramural sports:* badminton M/W, basketball M/W, football M/W, racquetball M/W, skiing (downhill) M/W, soccer M/W, softball M/W, squash M/W, table tennis M/W, tennis M/W, ultimate Frisbee M/W, volleyball M/W.

Standardized Tests *Required:* SAT or ACT (for admission).

Costs (2010–11) *Tuition:* state resident $4970 full-time, $207 per credit hour part-time; nonresident $13,380 full-time, $558 per credit hour part-time. Part-time tuition and fees vary according to course load. *Required fees:* $1431 full-time, $59 per credit hour part-time. *Room and board:* $10,042. Room and board charges vary according to board plan and housing facility. *Payment plans:* installment, deferred payment.

Financial Aid Of all full-time matriculated undergraduates who enrolled in 2009, 3,800 applied for aid, 2,358 were judged to have need, 1,698 had their need fully met. 395 Federal Work-Study jobs (averaging $1395). In 2009, 515 non-need-based awards were made. *Average percent of need met:* 73%. *Average financial aid package:* $8041. *Average need-based loan:* $4466. *Average need-based gift aid:* $4018. *Average non-need-based aid:* $2068. *Average indebtedness upon graduation:* $21,000. *Financial aid deadline:* 2/15.

Applying *Options:* electronic application, early admission, early decision, deferred entrance. *Application fee:* $40. *Required:* essay or personal statement, high school transcript. *Recommended:* minimum 3.5 GPA, 1 letter of recommendation, interview. *Application deadlines:* 1/1 (freshmen), 2/15 (transfers). *Early decision deadline:* 11/15. *Notification:* 3/1 (freshmen), 2/15 (transfers), 12/15 (early decision).

Freshman Application Contact Kris Shay, Director of Admissions, State University of New York College at Geneseo, 1 College Circle, Geneseo, NY 14454-1401. *Phone:* 585-245-5571. *Toll-free phone:* 866-245-5211. *Fax:* 585-245-5550. *E-mail:* admissions@geneseo.edu. *Web site:* http://www.geneseo.edu/.

State University of New York College at Old Westbury
Old Westbury, New York

- **State-supported** comprehensive, founded 1965, part of State University of New York System
- **Suburban** 604-acre campus with easy access to New York City
- **Coed** 4,194 undergraduate students, 84% full-time, 58% women, 42% men
- **Moderately difficult** entrance level, 49% of applicants were admitted

Undergraduates 3,512 full-time, 682 part-time. Students come from 19 states and territories; 60 other countries; 2% are from out of state; 34% Black or African American, non-Hispanic/Latino; 16% Hispanic/Latino; 8% Asian, non-Hispanic/Latino; 0.1% Native Hawaiian or other Pacific Islander, non-Hispanic/Latino; 0.6% American Indian or Alaska Native, non-Hispanic/Latino; 3% Race/ethnicity unknown; 2% international; 19% transferred in; 24% live on campus. *Retention:* 75% of full-time freshmen returned.

Freshmen *Admission:* 3,753 applied, 1,843 admitted, 397 enrolled. *Average high school GPA:* 3. *Test scores:* SAT critical reading scores over 500: 39%; SAT math scores over 500: 55%; SAT writing scores over 500: 36%; ACT scores over 18: 95%; SAT critical reading scores over 600: 4%; SAT math scores over 600: 11%; SAT writing scores over 600: 4%; ACT scores over 24: 21%.

Faculty *Total:* 285, 47% full-time, 55% with terminal degrees. *Student/faculty ratio:* 20:1.

Academics *Calendar:* semesters. *Degrees:* certificates, bachelor's, master's, and post-master's certificates. *Special study options:* academic remediation for entering students, advanced placement credit, distance learning, double majors, English as a second language, freshman honors college, honors programs, independent study, internships, off-campus study, part-time degree program, services for LD students, study abroad, summer session for credit. *ROTC:* Army (c), Air Force (c). *Unusual degree programs:* 3-2 engineering with State University of New York at Stony Brook; biological sciences/Doctor of Osteopathic Medicine with NY College of Osteopathic Medicine.

Computers on Campus 450 computers/terminals and 700 ports are available on campus for general student use. Students can access the following: campus intranet, free student e-mail accounts, online (class) grades, online (class) registration, financial aid, billing information, grades. Campuswide network is available. 100% of college-owned or -operated housing units are wired for high-speed Internet access. Wireless service is available via entire campus.

Student Life *Housing options:* coed. Campus housing is university owned. Freshman campus housing is guaranteed. *Activities and organizations:* drama/theater group, student-run newspaper, radio station, choral group, Student Government Association, Alianza Latina, PRIDE, Step Tunes, Anime Magna Games Club, national fraternities, national sororities. *Campus security:* 24-hour emergency response devices and patrols, student patrols, late-night transport/escort service, controlled dormitory access. *Student services:* health clinic, personal/psychological counseling, women's center.

Athletics Member NCAA. All Division III. *Intercollegiate sports:* baseball M, basketball M/W, cross-country running M/W, golf M, soccer M/W, softball W, swimming and diving M/W, volleyball W. *Intramural sports:* badminton M/W, basketball M/W, cheerleading M(c)/W(c), equestrian sports M(c)/W(c), football M/W, racquetball M/W, soccer M/W, softball W, squash M/W, ultimate Frisbee M/W, weight lifting M/W.

Standardized Tests *Required:* SAT or ACT (for admission).

Costs (2010–11) *Tuition:* state resident $4970 full-time, $207 per credit part-time; nonresident $12,870 full-time, $536 per credit part-time. Part-time tuition and fees vary according to course load. *Required fees:* $996 full-time,

---

$44 per credit part-time, $106 per term part-time. *Room and board:* $9700; room only: $6600. Room and board charges vary according to board plan and housing facility. *Payment plan:* installment. *Waivers:* senior citizens.

Financial Aid Of all full-time matriculated undergraduates who enrolled in 2009, 2,510 applied for aid, 2,119 were judged to have need, 1,951 had their need fully met. 210 Federal Work-Study jobs (averaging $819). *Average percent of need met:* 44%. *Average financial aid package:* $7115. *Average need-based loan:* $2561. *Average need-based gift aid:* $5785. *Average indebtedness upon graduation:* $17,104.

Applying *Options:* electronic application, early admission, early decision, deferred entrance. *Application fee:* $50. *Required:* essay or personal statement, high school transcript. *Required for some:* 2 letters of recommendation, interview. *Application deadlines:* rolling (freshmen), 12/15 (transfers). *Early decision deadline:* 11/1. *Notification:* continuous (freshmen), continuous (transfers), 12/15 (early decision).

Freshman Application Contact State University of New York College at Old Westbury, PO Box 307, Old Westbury, NY 11568. *Phone:* 516-876-3073. *Fax:* 516-876-3307. *E-mail:* enroll@oldwestbury.edu. *Web site:* http://www.oldwestbury.edu/.

State University of New York College at Oneonta
Oneonta, New York

- **State-supported** comprehensive, founded 1889, part of State University of New York System
- **Small-town** 250-acre campus
- **Endowment** $30.1 million
- **Coed** 5,847 undergraduate students, 98% full-time, 58% women, 42% men
- **Very difficult** entrance level, 41% of applicants were admitted

Undergraduates 5,716 full-time, 131 part-time. Students come from 15 states and territories; 26 other countries; 2% are from out of state; 3% Black or African American, non-Hispanic/Latino; 4% Hispanic/Latino; 1% Asian, non-Hispanic/Latino; 0.2% American Indian or Alaska Native, non-Hispanic/Latino; 7% Race/ethnicity unknown; 2% international; 9% transferred in; 58% live on campus. *Retention:* 86% of full-time freshmen returned.

Freshmen *Admission:* 12,819 applied, 5,257 admitted, 1,132 enrolled. *Average high school GPA:* 3.6. *Test scores:* SAT critical reading scores over 500: 88%; SAT math scores over 500: 96%; ACT scores over 18: 100%; SAT critical reading scores over 600: 22%; SAT math scores over 600: 33%; ACT scores over 24: 72%; SAT critical reading scores over 700: 1%; SAT math scores over 700: 2%; ACT scores over 30: 5%.

Faculty *Total:* 499, 52% full-time, 51% with terminal degrees. *Student/faculty ratio:* 17:1.

Academics *Calendar:* semesters. *Degrees:* bachelor's, master's, post-master's, and postbachelor's certificates. *Special study options:* academic remediation for entering students, adult/continuing education programs, advanced placement credit, distance learning, double majors, English as a second language, honors programs, independent study, internships, off-campus study, part-time degree program, services for LD students, study abroad, summer session for credit. *Unusual degree programs:* 3-2 business administration with State University of New York at Binghamton, Clarkson University, Rochester Institute of Technology, Union College; engineering with University at Buffalo, the State University of New York; Alfred University; Clarkson University; Rensselaer Polytechnic Institute; Syracuse University; accounting at State University of New York at Binghamton, fashion with Fashion Institute of Technology, American Intercontinental University in London.

Computers on Campus 700 computers/terminals are available on campus for general student use. Students can access the following: campus intranet, computer help desk, free student e-mail accounts, online (class) grades, online (class) registration, online (class) schedules. Campuswide network is available. 100% of college-owned or -operated housing units are wired for high-speed Internet access. Wireless service is available via entire campus.

Student Life *Housing:* on-campus residence required through sophomore year. *Options:* coed. Campus housing is university owned. Freshman campus housing is guaranteed. *Activities and organizations:* drama/theater group, student-run newspaper, radio and television station, choral group, Center for Social Responsibility and Community, Mask and Hammer, Terpsichorean, student government, WONY radio station, national fraternities, national sororities. *Campus security:* 24-hour emergency response devices and patrols, late-night transport/escort service, controlled dormitory access. *Student services:* health clinic, personal/psychological counseling, women's center.

Athletics Member NCAA. All Division III. *Intercollegiate sports:* baseball M, basketball M/W, cheerleading W(c), cross-country running M/W, fencing M(c)/W(c), field hockey W, ice hockey M(c), lacrosse M/W, rugby W(c), soccer M/W, softball W, swimming and diving M/W, tennis M/W, track and field M/W, volleyball W, wrestling M. *Intramural sports:* badminton M(c)/W(c), basketball M/W, equestrian sports W(c), football M, lacrosse M, racquetball

M(c)/W(c), skiing (downhill) M(c)/W(c), soccer M/W, softball M/W, ultimate Frisbee M/W, volleyball M/W.

Standardized Tests *Required:* SAT or ACT (for admission).

Costs (2011–12) *Tuition:* state resident $4970 full-time, $207 per semester hour part-time; nonresident $12,870 full-time, $536 per semester hour part-time. Part-time tuition and fees vary according to course load. *Required fees:* $1280 full-time, $47 per semester hour part-time. *Room and board:* $9284; room only: $5534. Room and board charges vary according to board plan and housing facility. *Payment plan:* installment. *Waivers:* employees or children of employees.

Financial Aid Of all full-time matriculated undergraduates who enrolled in 2009, 4,570 applied for aid, 4,559 were judged to have need, 608 had their need fully met. 350 Federal Work-Study jobs (averaging $1000). In 2009, 1068 non-need-based awards were made. *Average percent of need met:* 63%. *Average financial aid package:* $14,968. *Average need-based loan:* $3600. *Average need-based gift aid:* $5311. *Average non-need-based aid:* $1616. *Average indebtedness upon graduation:* $17,564.

Applying *Options:* electronic application, early admission, early action, deferred entrance. *Application fee:* $50. *Required:* essay or personal statement, high school transcript. *Recommended:* minimum 3 GPA, 3 letters of recommendation. *Application deadlines:* rolling (freshmen), rolling (transfers), 11/15 (early action). *Notification:* continuous (freshmen), continuous (transfers), 12/15 (early action).

Freshman Application Contact Ms. Karen Brown, Director of Admissions, State University of New York College at Oneonta, Alumni Hall 116, Oneonta, NY 13820-4015. *Phone:* 607-436-2524. *Toll-free phone:* 800-SUNY-123. *Fax:* 607-436-3074. *E-mail:* admissions@oneonta.edu. *Web site:* http://www.oneonta.edu/.

State University of New York College at Potsdam

Potsdam, New York

- **State-supported** comprehensive, founded 1816, part of State University of New York System
- **Small-town** 240-acre campus
- **Endowment** $15.2 million
- **Coed** 3,902 undergraduate students, 97% full-time, 58% women, 42% men
- **Moderately difficult** entrance level, 62% of applicants were admitted

Undergraduates 3,779 full-time, 123 part-time. Students come from 30 states and territories; 22 other countries; 3% are from out of state; 4% Black or African American, non-Hispanic/Latino; 3% Hispanic/Latino; 2% Asian, non-Hispanic/Latino; 0.1% Native Hawaiian or other Pacific Islander, non-Hispanic/Latino; 1% American Indian or Alaska Native, non-Hispanic/Latino; 1% Two or more races, non-Hispanic/Latino; 11% Race/ethnicity unknown; 8% transferred in; 40% live on campus. *Retention:* 77% of full-time freshmen returned.

Freshmen *Admission:* 5,028 applied, 3,123 admitted, 905 enrolled. *Average high school GPA:* 3.2.

Faculty *Total:* 333, 77% full-time, 63% with terminal degrees. *Student/faculty ratio:* 16:1.

Academics *Calendar:* semesters. *Degrees:* bachelor's and master's. *Special study options:* advanced placement credit, distance learning, double majors, honors programs, independent study, internships, off-campus study, part-time degree program, services for LD students, student-designed majors, study abroad, summer session for credit. *ROTC:* Army (c), Air Force (c). *Unusual degree programs:* 3-2 engineering with Clarkson University, State University of New York at Binghamton; management, accounting with State University of New York Institute of Technology at Utica/Rome; mathematics with Clarkson University.

Computers on Campus 690 computers/terminals and 80 ports are available on campus for general student use. Students can access the following: campus intranet, computer help desk, free student e-mail accounts, online (class) grades, online (class) registration, online (class) schedules, online access to financial aid status, unofficial transcripts, billing, meal plan and housing sign ups. Campuswide network is available. 100% of college-owned or -operated housing units are wired for high-speed Internet access. Wireless service is available via classrooms, computer centers, computer labs, dorm rooms, learning centers, libraries, student centers.

Student Life *Housing:* on-campus residence required through sophomore year. *Options:* coed, disabled students. Campus housing is university owned. Freshman campus housing is guaranteed. *Activities and organizations:* drama/theater group, student-run newspaper, radio station, choral group, Student Government Association, Crane Student Association, Student Entertainment Services (Programming Board), Black Student Alliance, The Racquette Student Newspaper, national fraternities, national sororities. *Campus security:* 24-hour emergency response devices and patrols, late-night transport/escort service, controlled dormitory access, Educational programs, campus rescue squad, portable jump start packets, vehicle lock outs and parking management.

Student services: health clinic, personal/psychological counseling, women's center, legal services.

Athletics Member NCAA. All Division III. *Intercollegiate sports:* basketball M/W, cross-country running M/W, equestrian sports M/W, golf M, ice hockey M/W, lacrosse M/W, rugby W(c), soccer M/W, softball W, swimming and diving M/W, tennis W, track and field M(c)/W(c), volleyball W. *Intramural sports:* archery M(c)/W(c), basketball M/W, cheerleading M(c)/W(c), football M/W, racquetball M/W, soccer M/W, softball M/W, volleyball M/W, water polo M/W, weight lifting M/W.

Costs (2010–11) *Tuition:* state resident $4970 full-time, $207 per credit hour part-time; nonresident $12,870 full-time, $536 per credit hour part-time. *Required fees:* $1213 full-time, $55 per credit hour part-time. *Room and board:* $9630; room only: $5570. Room and board charges vary according to board plan and housing facility. *Payment plan:* installment. *Waivers:* employees or children of employees.

Financial Aid Of all full-time matriculated undergraduates who enrolled in 2009, 3,100 applied for aid, 2,400 were judged to have need, 1,685 had their need fully met. 254 Federal Work-Study jobs (averaging $1200). In 2009, 224 non-need-based awards were made. *Average percent of need met:* 71%. *Average financial aid package:* $14,073. *Average need-based loan:* $4360. *Average need-based gift aid:* $5956. *Average non-need-based aid:* $11,677. *Average indebtedness upon graduation:* $19,220.

Applying *Options:* electronic application, early admission, deferred entrance. *Application fee:* $50. *Required:* high school transcript, minimum 2.5 GPA, audition for music program. *Required for some:* essay or personal statement, minimum 2 GPA, interview. *Application deadlines:* rolling (freshmen), rolling (transfers). *Notification:* continuous (freshmen), continuous (transfers).

Freshman Application Contact Mr. Thomas Nesbitt, Director of Admissions, State University of New York College at Potsdam, 44 Pierrepont Avenue, Potsdam, NY 13676. *Phone:* 315-267-2180. *Toll-free phone:* 877-POTSDAM. *Fax:* 315-267-2163. *E-mail:* admissions@potsdam.edu. *Web site:* http://www.potsdam.edu/.

State University of New York College of Agriculture and Technology at Cobleskill

Cobleskill, New York

Freshman Application Contact State University of New York College of Agriculture and Technology at Cobleskill, Cobleskill, NY 12043. *Phone:* 518-255-5525. *Toll-free phone:* 800-295-8988. *Web site:* http://www.cobleskill.edu/.

State University of New York College of Agriculture and Technology at Morrisville

Morrisville, New York

Director of Admissions Mr. Thomas VerDow, Director of Admissions, State University of New York College of Agriculture and Technology at Morrisville, PO Box 901, Morrisville, NY 13408-0901. *Phone:* 800-258-0111. *Toll-free phone:* 800-258-0111. *Fax:* 315-684-6427. *E-mail:* admissions@morrisville.edu. *Web site:* http://www.morrisville.edu/.

State University of New York College of Environmental Science and Forestry

Syracuse, New York

- **State-supported** university, founded 1911, part of State University of New York System
- **Urban** 12-acre campus
- **Endowment** $18.3 million
- **Coed** 1,725 undergraduate students, 92% full-time, 42% women, 58% men
- **Moderately difficult** entrance level, 46% of applicants were admitted

Undergraduates 1,584 full-time, 141 part-time. Students come from 33 states and territories; 9 other countries; 17% are from out of state; 1% Black or African American, non-Hispanic/Latino; 3% Hispanic/Latino; 4% Asian, non-Hispanic/Latino; 0.6% American Indian or Alaska Native, non-Hispanic/Latino; 0.9% international; 14% transferred in; 40% live on campus. *Retention:* 88% of full-time freshmen returned.

Freshmen *Admission:* 1,706 applied, 791 admitted, 262 enrolled. *Average high school GPA:* 3.8. *Test scores:* SAT critical reading scores over 500: 87%;

A Welcoming Atmosphere:
Approximately 500 new students attend ESF each year.

Hands-on Experience:
90 percent of undergraduate students participate in research, field studies and internships in science, design, engineering and management of natural resources and the environment.

More Choices:
- ESF offers more than 300 courses.

- 19 bachelor degree programs are available at the Syracuse campus.

- Three associate degree programs are available at The Ranger School, ESF's campus in the Adirondacks. Students can choose among forest technology, land surveying technology and a new program in environmental and natural resources conservation.

Lots of Opportunity:
- ESF's long-standing partnership with Syracuse University provides opportunities for ESF students to take SU classes, use library and computing facilities and join student organizations (all located right next to our ESF campus).

- 95 percent of ESF graduates get jobs or are admitted to graduate school within six months of degree completion.

- Centennial Hall, ESF's new 452–bed residence hall, opens in August 2011.

SUNY-ESF
Improve Your World
www.esf.edu

315-470-6600

State University of New York College of Environmental Science and Forestry
Syracuse, New York

SAT math scores over 500: 94%; ACT scores over 18: 100%; SAT critical reading scores over 600: 41%; SAT math scores over 600: 49%; ACT scores over 24: 77%; SAT critical reading scores over 700: 8%; SAT math scores over 700: 4%; ACT scores over 30: 12%.

Faculty *Total:* 172, 85% full-time, 91% with terminal degrees. *Student/faculty ratio:* 13:1.

Academics *Calendar:* semesters. *Degrees:* associate, bachelor's, master's, doctoral-research/scholarship, and postbachelor's certificates. *Special study options:* academic remediation for entering students, accelerated degree program, adult/continuing education programs, advanced placement credit, cooperative education, distance learning, double majors, English as a second language, freshman honors college, honors programs, independent study, internships, off-campus study, part-time degree program, services for LD students, study abroad, summer session for credit. *ROTC:* Army (c), Air Force (c). *Unusual degree programs:* 3-2 landscape architecture.

Computers on Campus 150 computers/terminals are available on campus for general student use. Students can access the following: campus intranet, computer help desk, free student e-mail accounts, online (class) grades, online (class) registration, online (class) schedules. Campuswide network is available. 100% of college-owned or -operated housing units are wired for high-speed Internet access. Wireless service is available via classrooms, computer centers, computer labs, dorm rooms, libraries, student centers.

Student Life *Housing:* on-campus residence required for freshman year. *Options:* coed, men-only, women-only, disabled students. Campus housing is university owned and is provided by a third party. Freshman campus housing is guaranteed. *Activities and organizations:* drama/theater group, student-run newspaper, radio station, choral group, marching band, Bob Marshall/Outing Club, Forestry Club, Student Environmental Action Coalition, Student Green Campus Initiative, Recycling Club, national fraternities, national sororities. *Campus security:* 24-hour emergency response devices and patrols, late-night transport/escort service, controlled dormitory access. *Student services:* health clinic, personal/psychological counseling, women's center, legal services.

Athletics Member NCAA, NAIA, and USCAA. All NCAA Division III. *Intercollegiate sports:* basketball M(c), cross-country running M/W, golf M/W, soccer M/W. *Intramural sports:* archery M/W, badminton M/W, baseball M/W, basketball M/W, bowling M/W, crew M/W, cross-country running M/W, equestrian sports M/W, fencing M/W, field hockey W, football M, gymnastics M/W, ice hockey M/W, lacrosse M/W, racquetball M/W, riflery M, rugby M/W, sailing M/W, skiing (cross-country) M/W, skiing (downhill) M/W, soccer M/W, softball M/W, squash M/W, swimming and diving M/W, table tennis M/W, tennis M/W, track and field M/W, ultimate Frisbee M/W, volleyball M/W, weight lifting M/W.

Standardized Tests *Required:* SAT or ACT (for admission).

Costs (2011–12) *Tuition:* state resident $4970 full-time, $207 per credit hour part-time; nonresident $13,380 full-time, $558 per credit hour part-time. Full-time tuition and fees vary according to location. Part-time tuition and fees vary according to course load and location. *Required fees:* $971 full-time, $41 per credit hour part-time. *Room and board:* $14,032. Room and board charges vary according to board plan, housing facility, and location. *Payment plans:* installment, deferred payment.

Financial Aid Of all full-time matriculated undergraduates who enrolled in 2009, 1,168 applied for aid, 1,079 were judged to have need, 1,020 had their need fully met. 220 Federal Work-Study jobs (averaging $1500). 195 state and other part-time jobs (averaging $1200). In 2009, 70 non-need-based awards were made. *Average percent of need met:* 90%. *Average financial aid package:* $13,000. *Average need-based loan:* $5500. *Average need-based gift aid:* $5000. *Average non-need-based aid:* $2420. *Average indebtedness upon graduation:* $27,000.

Applying *Options:* electronic application, early admission, early action, deferred entrance. *Application fee:* $50. *Required:* essay or personal statement, high school transcript, minimum 3.3 GPA, supplemental application. *Recommended:* 3 letters of recommendation, interview. *Application deadlines:* rolling (freshmen), rolling (out-of-state freshmen), rolling (transfers), 11/15 (early action). *Notification:* continuous (freshmen), continuous (out-of-state freshmen), continuous (transfers), 1/15 (early action).

Freshman Application Contact Ms. Susan Sanford, Director of Admissions, State University of New York College of Environmental Science and Forestry, Office of Undergraduate Admissions, 106 Bray Hall, 1 Forestry Lane, Syracuse, NY 13210-2779. *Phone:* 315-470-6600. *Toll-free phone:* 800-777-7373. *Fax:* 315-470-6933. *E-mail:* esfinfo@esf.edu. *Web site:* http://www.esf.edu/.

See page 1640 for the College Close-Up.

State University of New York College of Technology at Alfred

Alfred, New York

- **State-supported** primarily 2-year, founded 1908, part of The State University of New York System
- **Rural** 1084-acre campus
- **Endowment** $3.1 million
- **Coed** 3,717 undergraduate students, 90% full-time, 37% women, 63% men
- **Moderately difficult** entrance level, 53% of applicants were admitted

Undergraduates 3,359 full-time, 358 part-time. Students come from 35 states and territories; 19 other countries; 9% Black or African American, non-Hispanic/Latino; 5% Hispanic/Latino; 3% Asian, non-Hispanic/Latino; 0.1% Native Hawaiian or other Pacific Islander, non-Hispanic/Latino; 0.2% American Indian or Alaska Native, non-Hispanic/Latino; 2% Two or more races, non-Hispanic/Latino; 0.7% Race/ethnicity unknown; 8% transferred in; 74% live on campus. *Retention:* 85% of full-time freshmen returned.

Freshmen *Admission:* 5,386 applied, 2,852 admitted, 1,285 enrolled. *Average high school GPA:* 2.8.

Faculty *Total:* 206, 77% full-time. *Student/faculty ratio:* 20:1.

Academics *Calendar:* semesters. *Degrees:* certificates, associate, and bachelor's. *Special study options:* academic remediation for entering students, adult/continuing education programs, advanced placement credit, cooperative education, distance learning, double majors, English as a second language, honors programs, independent study, internships, off-campus study, part-time degree program, services for LD students, student-designed majors, study abroad, summer session for credit. *ROTC:* Army (c).

Computers on Campus 100 computers/terminals are available on campus for general student use. Students can access the following: computer help desk, free student e-mail accounts, online (class) grades, online (class) registration, online (class) schedules. Campuswide network is available. 100% of college-owned or -operated housing units are wired for high-speed Internet access. Wireless service is available via entire campus.

Student Life *Housing options:* coed, men-only, women-only, disabled students. Campus housing is university owned. Freshman campus housing is guaranteed. *Activities and organizations:* drama/theater group, student-run newspaper, radio station, choral group, Outdoor Recreation Club, International Club, intramural sports, Sustainability Club, Student Senate, national fraternities, national sororities. *Campus security:* 24-hour emergency response devices and patrols, late-night transport/escort service, controlled dormitory access, residence hall entrance guards. *Student services:* health clinic, personal/psychological counseling.

Athletics Member NJCAA. *Intercollegiate sports:* baseball M, basketball M/W, cross-country running M/W, football M(s), lacrosse M, soccer M/W, softball W, swimming and diving M/W, track and field M/W, volleyball W, wrestling M. *Intramural sports:* basketball M/W, football M/W, golf M/W, ice hockey M(c), rock climbing M/W, soccer M/W, softball M/W, tennis M/W, ultimate Frisbee M/W, volleyball M/W.

Standardized Tests *Required for some:* SAT or ACT (for admission). *Recommended:* SAT or ACT (for admission).

Costs (2011–12) *Tuition:* state resident $4970 full-time, $207 per credit part-time; nonresident $9100 full-time, $379 per credit part-time. Full-time tuition and fees vary according to course load and degree level. Part-time tuition and fees vary according to course load and degree level. *Required fees:* $1248 full-time, $121 per credit hour part-time, $5 per term part-time. *Room and board:* $9690; room only: $5600. Room and board charges vary according to board plan and housing facility. *Payment plan:* installment. *Waivers:* employees or children of employees.

Financial Aid Of all full-time matriculated undergraduates who enrolled in 2009, 3,097 applied for aid, 2,727 were judged to have need, 230 had their need fully met. 283 Federal Work-Study jobs (averaging $1210). In 2009, 470 non-need-based awards were made. *Average percent of need met:* 72%. *Average financial aid package:* $12,584. *Average need-based loan:* $6226. *Average need-based gift aid:* $4515. *Average non-need-based aid:* $1886. *Average indebtedness upon graduation:* $29,741.

Applying *Options:* electronic application. *Application fee:* $40. *Required:* high school transcript, minimum 2 GPA. *Recommended:* essay or personal statement, interview. *Application deadlines:* rolling (freshmen), rolling (out-of-state freshmen), rolling (transfers). *Notification:* continuous (freshmen), continuous (out-of-state freshmen), continuous (transfers).

Freshman Application Contact Mrs. Deborah Goodrich, Associate Vice President for Enrollment Management, State University of New York College of Technology at Alfred, Huntington Administration Building, 10 Upper College Drive, Alfred, NY 14802. *Phone:* 607-587-4215. *Toll-free phone:* 800-4-ALFRED. *Fax:* 607-587-4299. *E-mail:* admissions@alfredstate.edu. *Web site:* http://www.alfredstate.edu/.

State University of New York College of Technology at Canton

Canton, New York

- **State-supported** 4-year, founded 1906, part of State University of New York System
- **Small-town** 555-acre campus
- **Endowment** $5.3 million
- **Coed**
- **Minimally difficult** entrance level

Faculty *Student/faculty ratio:* 19:1.

Academics *Calendar:* semesters. *Degrees:* certificates, associate, and bachelor's.

Student Life *Campus security:* 24-hour emergency response devices and patrols, late-night transport/escort service, controlled dormitory access.

Athletics Member NAIA.

Standardized Tests *Required for some:* SAT or ACT (for admission).

Costs (2010–11) *One-time required fee:* $90. *Tuition:* state resident $4970 full-time, $207 per credit hour part-time; nonresident $8750 full-time, $536 per credit hour part-time. Full-time tuition and fees vary according to degree level, location, and program. Part-time tuition and fees vary according to degree level, location, and program. *Required fees:* $1337 full-time, $49 per credit hour part-time, $5 per term part-time. *Room and board:* $9790; room only: $5800. Room and board charges vary according to housing facility. *Payment plans:* installment, deferred payment.

Applying *Options:* electronic application, early admission, deferred entrance. *Application fee:* $40. *Required:* high school transcript. *Required for some:* essay or personal statement, interview. *Recommended:* minimum 2 GPA.

Freshman Application Contact Mr. Randy B. Sieminski, Assistant Vice President for Advancement, State University of New York College of Technology at Canton, Cornell Drive, Canton, NY 13617. *Phone:* 315-386-7123. *Toll-free phone:* 800-388-7123. *Fax:* 315-386-7929. *E-mail:* admissions@canton.edu. *Web site:* http://www.canton.edu/.

State University of New York College of Technology at Delhi

Delhi, New York

- **State-supported** 4-year, founded 1913, part of State University of New York System
- **Rural** 405-acre campus
- **Endowment** $2.9 million
- **Coed** 3,357 undergraduate students, 80% full-time, 49% women, 51% men
- **Moderately difficult** entrance level, 55% of applicants were admitted

Undergraduates 2,684 full-time, 673 part-time. Students come from 21 states and territories; 15 other countries; 2% are from out of state; 12% Black or African American, non-Hispanic/Latino; 9% Hispanic/Latino; 2% Asian, non-Hispanic/Latino; 0.5% American Indian or Alaska Native, non-Hispanic/Latino; 4% Race/ethnicity unknown; 1% international; 7% transferred in; 70% live on campus. *Retention:* 65% of full-time freshmen returned.

Freshmen *Admission:* 4,946 applied, 2,720 admitted, 966 enrolled. *Test scores:* SAT critical reading scores over 500: 24%; SAT math scores over 500: 7%; SAT critical reading scores over 600: 3%; SAT math scores over 600: 2%.

Faculty *Total:* 214, 59% full-time, 19% with terminal degrees. *Student/faculty ratio:* 18:1.

Academics *Calendar:* semesters. *Degrees:* certificates, associate, and bachelor's. *Special study options:* academic remediation for entering students, advanced placement credit, distance learning, English as a second language, honors programs, internships, part-time degree program, services for LD students, student-designed majors, summer session for credit.

Computers on Campus 350 computers/terminals are available on campus for general student use. Students can access the following: campus intranet, computer help desk, free student e-mail accounts, online (class) grades, online (class) registration, online (class) schedules. Campuswide network is available. 100% of college-owned or -operated housing units are wired for high-speed Internet access. Wireless service is available via entire campus.

Student Life *Housing:* on-campus residence required through sophomore year. *Options:* coed, women-only. Campus housing is university owned and is provided by a third party. *Activities and organizations:* drama/theater group, student-run newspaper, radio station, choral group, Latin American Student Organization, Hotel Sales Management Association, student radio station, Phi Theta Kappa, Student Programming Board, national fraternities. *Campus security:* 24-hour emergency response devices and patrols, controlled dormitory access. *Student services:* health clinic, personal/psychological counseling, legal services.

Athletics Member NAIA, NJCAA. *Intercollegiate sports:* basketball M/W, cross-country running M/W, golf M/W, lacrosse M, soccer M/W, softball W, swimming and diving M/W, tennis M/W, track and field M/W, volleyball W. *Intramural sports:* basketball M/W, bowling M/W, cross-country running M/W, football M/W, golf M/W, racquetball M/W, skiing (cross-country) M/W, skiing (downhill) M/W, swimming and diving M/W, tennis M/W, volleyball M/W, weight lifting M/W.

Standardized Tests *Required for some:* SAT or ACT (for admission).

Costs (2010–11) *Tuition:* state resident $4970 full-time, $207 per credit hour part-time; nonresident $13,380 full-time, $558 per credit hour part-time. Full-time tuition and fees vary according to degree level. Part-time tuition and fees vary according to degree level. *Required fees:* $1475 full-time, $79 per credit hour part-time, $738 per term part-time. *Room and board:* $9720; room only: $5620. Room and board charges vary according to board plan and location. *Payment plan:* installment.

Financial Aid Of all full-time matriculated undergraduates who enrolled in 2009, 2,386 applied for aid. 126 Federal Work-Study jobs (averaging $1158).

Applying *Options:* electronic application, early admission, deferred entrance. *Application fee:* $50. *Required:* high school transcript. *Required for some:* minimum 2 GPA. *Application deadlines:* rolling (freshmen), rolling (transfers). *Notification:* continuous (freshmen), continuous (transfers).

Freshman Application Contact Mr. Robert Mazzei, State University of New York College of Technology at Delhi, 2 Main St - Stop 2, Delhi, NY 13753. *Phone:* 607-746-4550. *Toll-free phone:* 800-96-DELHI. *Fax:* 607-746-4104. *E-mail:* mazzeirw@delhi.edu. *Web site:* http://www.delhi.edu/.

State University of New York Downstate Medical Center

Brooklyn, New York

- **State-supported** upper-level, founded 1858, part of State University of New York System
- **Urban** campus
- **Coed** 343 undergraduate students, 56% full-time, 83% women, 17% men
- **Moderately difficult** entrance level, 14% of applicants were admitted

Undergraduates 193 full-time, 150 part-time. 1% are from out of state; 39% Black or African American, non-Hispanic/Latino; 6% Hispanic/Latino; 14% Asian, non-Hispanic/Latino; 3% Race/ethnicity unknown; 1% international.

Freshmen *Admission:* 1,005 applied, 137 admitted.

Faculty *Total:* 981, 85% full-time.

Academics *Calendar:* semesters. *Degrees:* bachelor's, master's, doctoral-professional, doctoral-research/scholarship, post-master's, and postbachelor's certificates. *Special study options:* accelerated degree program, advanced placement credit, independent study, internships, off-campus study, part-time degree program, services for LD students, summer session for credit.

Computers on Campus 183 computers/terminals are available on campus for general student use. Campuswide network is available.

Student Life *Housing options:* coed. Campus housing is university owned. *Campus security:* late-night transport/escort service. *Student services:* health clinic, personal/psychological counseling.

Costs (2010–11) *Tuition:* state resident $4790 full-time, $207 per credit hour part-time; nonresident $13,380 full-time, $558 per credit hour part-time. Full-time tuition and fees vary according to course load, degree level, and program. Part-time tuition and fees vary according to course load, degree level, and program. *Required fees:* $502 full-time, $21 per credit hour part-time, $251 per term part-time. *Room only:* $12,044. Room and board charges vary according to housing facility. *Payment plan:* installment. *Waivers:* minority students and employees or children of employees.

Financial Aid Of all full-time matriculated undergraduates who enrolled in 2005, 302 applied for aid, 302 were judged to have need. 40 Federal Work-Study jobs (averaging $1000). *Average percent of need met:* 50%. *Average financial aid package:* $12,500. *Average need-based loan:* $4186. *Average need-based gift aid:* $2729.

Applying *Application fee:* $30. *Application deadline:* 5/1 (transfers). *Notification:* continuous until 8/31 (transfers).

Application Contact Admissions Office, State University of New York Downstate Medical Center, 450 Clarkson Avenue, Brooklyn, NY 11203-2446. *Phone:* 718-270-2446. *Fax:* 718-270-7592. *E-mail:* admissions@downstate.edu. *Web site:* http://www.downstate.edu/.

State University of New York Empire State College

Saratoga Springs, New York

- **State-supported** comprehensive, founded 1971, part of State University of New York System
- **Small-town** campus
- **Endowment** $11.9 million
- **Coed** 11,118 undergraduate students, 38% full-time, 61% women, 39% men
- **Minimally difficult** entrance level, 83% of applicants were admitted

Undergraduates 4,247 full-time, 6,871 part-time. Students come from 50 states and territories; 55 other countries; 9% are from out of state; 17% transferred in.

Freshmen *Admission:* 1,339 applied, 1,105 admitted, 468 enrolled.

Faculty *Total:* 1,318, 15% full-time. *Student/faculty ratio:* 10:1.

Academics *Calendar:* continuous. *Degrees:* associate, bachelor's, and master's (branch locations at 7 regional centers with 35 auxiliary units). *Special study options:* adult/continuing education programs, advanced placement credit, cooperative education, distance learning, external degree program, independent study, off-campus study, part-time degree program, services for LD students, student-designed majors, summer session for credit.

Computers on Campus 100 computers/terminals are available on campus for general student use. Students can access the following: online (class) registration. Campuswide network is available.

Student Life *Housing:* college housing not available.

Costs (2010–11) *One-time required fee:* $350. *Tuition:* state resident $4970 full-time, $207 per credit hour part-time; nonresident $13,380 full-time, $558 per credit hour part-time. Full-time tuition and fees vary according to course level, location, and program. Part-time tuition and fees vary according to course level, location, and program. *Required fees:* $225 full-time, $7 per credit hour part-time, $75 per term part-time. *Payment plan:* installment. *Waivers:* adult students.

Applying *Options:* electronic application, early admission. *Required:* essay or personal statement, high school transcript. *Required for some:* interview. *Application deadlines:* rolling (freshmen), rolling (transfers). *Notification:* continuous (transfers).

Freshman Application Contact Ms. Jennifer D'Agostino, Director of Admissions, State University of New York Empire State College, Two Union Avenue, Saratoga Springs, NY 12866. *Phone:* 518-587-2100 Ext. 2214. *Toll-free phone:* 800-847-3000. *Fax:* 518-587-9759. *E-mail:* Jennifer.D'Agostino@esc.edu. *Web site:* http://www.esc.edu/.

State University of New York Institute of Technology

Utica, New York

Freshman Application Contact Amy Stokes, State University of New York Institute of Technology, PO Box 3050, Utica, NY 13504-3050. *Phone:* 315-792-7500. *Toll-free phone:* 800-SUNYTEC. *Fax:* 315-792-7837. *E-mail:* admissions@sunyit.edu. *Web site:* http://www.sunyit.edu/.

See page 602 for Display. See page 1642 for the College Close-Up.

State University of New York Maritime College

Throggs Neck, New York

- **State-supported** comprehensive, founded 1874, part of State University of New York System
- **Suburban** 56-acre campus with easy access to New York City
- **Coed, primarily men** 1,679 undergraduate students, 95% full-time, 10% women, 90% men
- **Very difficult** entrance level, 46% of applicants were admitted

Undergraduates 1,589 full-time, 90 part-time. Students come from 33 states and territories; 20 other countries; 27% are from out of state; 5% Black or African American, non-Hispanic/Latino; 8% Hispanic/Latino; 4% Asian, non-Hispanic/Latino; 0.4% American Indian or Alaska Native, non-Hispanic/Latino; 8% Race/ethnicity unknown; 6% international; 6% transferred in; 80% live on campus. *Retention:* 79% of full-time freshmen returned.

Freshmen *Admission:* 1,889 applied, 862 admitted, 331 enrolled. *Test scores:* SAT critical reading scores over 500: 62%; SAT math scores over 500: 78%; ACT scores over 18: 95%; SAT critical reading scores over 600: 15%; SAT math scores over 600: 26%; ACT scores over 24: 41%; SAT critical reading scores over 700: 2%; SAT math scores over 700: 2%; ACT scores over 30: 5%.

Faculty *Total:* 154, 57% full-time, 32% with terminal degrees. *Student/faculty ratio:* 15:1.

Academics *Calendar:* semesters plus 2-month summer sea term. *Degrees:* associate, bachelor's, and master's. *Special study options:* academic remediation for entering students, accelerated degree program, adult/continuing education programs, advanced placement credit, cooperative education, distance learning, double majors, English as a second language, honors programs, independent study, internships, services for LD students, summer session for credit. *ROTC:* Army (c), Navy (b).

Computers on Campus 110 computers/terminals are available on campus for general student use. Students can access the following: computer help desk, free student e-mail accounts, online (class) grades, online (class) registration, online (class) schedules. Campuswide network is available. Wireless service is available via classrooms, computer centers, dorm rooms, libraries.

Student Life *Housing:* on-campus residence required through senior year. *Options:* coed. Campus housing is university owned. *Activities and organizations:* choral group, marching band, student government, Maritime Activities and Programs, Campus Crusade for Christ, The Propeller Club, Chorale. *Campus security:* 24-hour emergency response devices and patrols, student patrols, late-night transport/escort service, controlled dormitory access. *Student services:* health clinic, personal/psychological counseling.

Athletics Member NCAA. All Division III. *Intercollegiate sports:* baseball M, basketball M/W, crew W, cross-country running M/W, football M, ice hockey M, lacrosse M/W, riflery M/W, soccer M/W, softball W, swimming and diving M/W, volleyball W. *Intramural sports:* basketball M/W, cross-country running M/W, football M, rugby M, sailing M/W, soccer M/W, softball M/W, volleyball M/W.

Standardized Tests *Required:* SAT or ACT (for admission).

Costs (2010–11) *Tuition:* $310 per credit hour part-time; state resident $4970 full-time, $207 per credit hour part-time; nonresident $13,380 full-time, $558 per credit hour part-time. Full-time tuition and fees vary according to degree level and program. Part-time tuition and fees vary according to course load, degree level, and program. *Required fees:* $1187 full-time, $49 per credit hour part-time. *Room and board:* $10,090; room only: $6340. Room and board charges vary according to board plan and housing facility. *Payment plan:* installment. *Waivers:* employees or children of employees.

Financial Aid Of all full-time matriculated undergraduates who enrolled in 2008, 714 applied for aid, 709 were judged to have need, 63 had their need fully met. *Average percent of need met:* 53%. *Average financial aid package:* $9735. *Average need-based loan:* $4576. *Average need-based gift aid:* $4526. *Financial aid deadline:* 7/15.

Applying *Options:* electronic application, deferred entrance. *Application fee:* $40. *Required for some:* interview. *Recommended:* essay or personal statement, high school transcript, minimum 3 GPA, 1 letter of recommendation. *Application deadlines:* rolling (freshmen), rolling (transfers). *Notification:* continuous (freshmen), continuous (transfers).

Freshman Application Contact Mr. Jonathan White, Dean of Admissions, State University of New York Maritime College, 6 Pennyfield Avenue, Throggs Neck, NY 10465. *Phone:* 718-409-7222. *Toll-free phone:* 800-654-1874 (in-state); 800-642-1874 (out-of-state). *Fax:* 718-409-7465. *E-mail:* jwhite@sunymaritime.edu. *Web site:* http://www.sunymaritime.edu/.

See page 1644 for the College Close-Up.

State University of New York Upstate Medical University

Syracuse, New York

- **State-supported** upper-level, founded 1950, part of State University of New York System
- **Urban** 25-acre campus
- **Coed** 335 undergraduate students, 63% full-time, 75% women, 25% men
- **Moderately difficult** entrance level, 32% of applicants were admitted

Undergraduates 212 full-time, 123 part-time. Students come from 6 states and territories; 4 other countries; 2% are from out of state; 7% Black or African American, non-Hispanic/Latino; 1% Hispanic/Latino; 5% Asian, non-Hispanic/Latino; 0.3% Native Hawaiian or other Pacific Islander, non-Hispanic/Latino; 0.3% American Indian or Alaska Native, non-Hispanic/Latino; 4% Two or more races, non-Hispanic/Latino; 11% Race/ethnicity unknown; 98% transferred in; 50% live on campus.

Freshmen *Admission:* 547 applied, 176 admitted.

Faculty *Total:* 108, 40% full-time, 48% with terminal degrees.

Academics *Calendar:* semesters. *Degrees:* bachelor's, master's, doctoral-other, doctoral-professional, doctoral-research/scholarship, and post-master's certificates. *Special study options:* distance learning, internships, off-campus

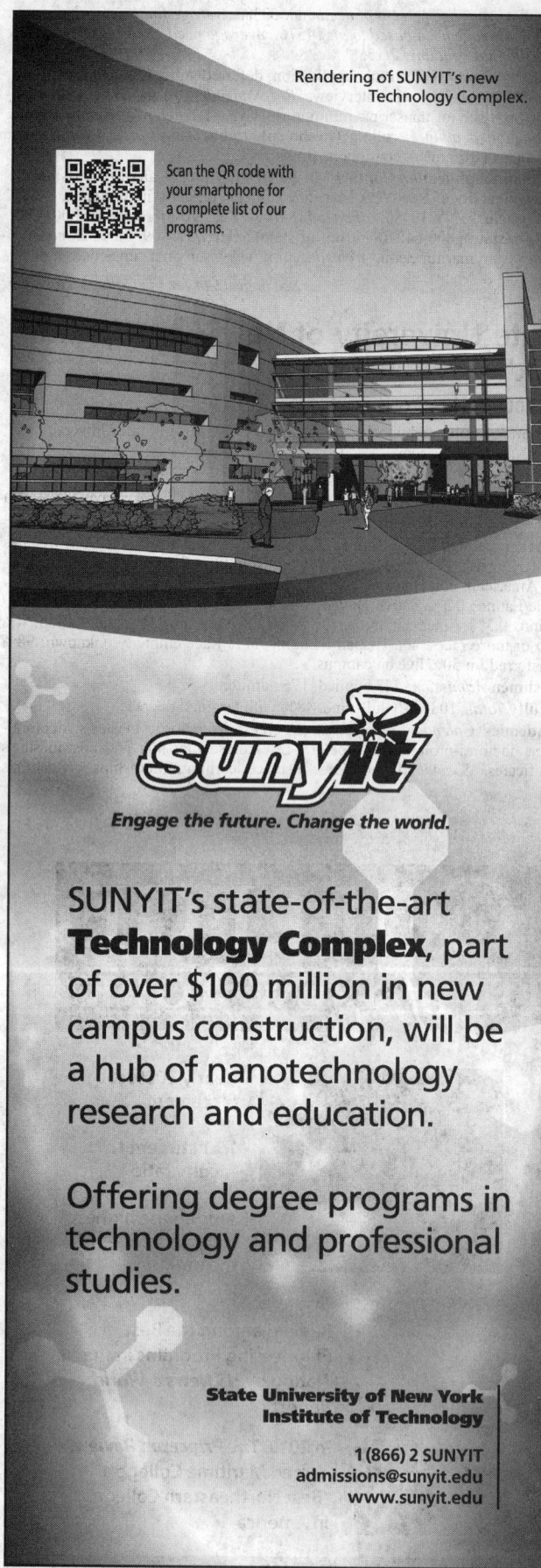

study, part-time degree program, services for LD students, summer session for credit. *ROTC:* Army (c).

Computers on Campus 150 computers/terminals are available on campus for general student use. Students can access the following: campus intranet, computer help desk, free student e-mail accounts, online (class) grades, online (class) registration, online (class) schedules. Campuswide network is available. 100% of college-owned or -operated housing units are wired for high-speed Internet access. Wireless service is available via classrooms, dorm rooms, libraries, student centers.

Student Life *Housing options:* coed. Campus housing is university owned. *Activities and organizations:* choral group, Upstate Student Government, Campus Activities Governing Board. *Campus security:* 24-hour emergency response devices and patrols, late-night transport/escort service, controlled dormitory access. *Student services:* health clinic, personal/psychological counseling.

Athletics *Intramural sports:* basketball M/W, racquetball M/W, soccer M/W, tennis M/W, volleyball M/W.

Costs (2011–12) *Tuition:* state resident $4970 full-time, $207 per credit part-time; nonresident $12,870 full-time, $558 per credit part-time. Full-time tuition and fees vary according to course load and program. Part-time tuition and fees vary according to course load and program. *Required fees:* $580 full-time, $20 per credit hour part-time. *Room and board:* $10,422; room only: $6525. Room and board charges vary according to housing facility. *Payment plan:* installment.

Financial Aid Of all full-time matriculated undergraduates who enrolled in 2009, 227 applied for aid, 227 were judged to have need. *Average percent of need met:* 86%. *Average financial aid package:* $11,847. *Average need-based loan:* $11,128. *Average need-based gift aid:* $1608.

Applying *Options:* electronic application, early admission, deferred entrance. *Application fee:* $50. *Application deadline:* rolling (transfers).

Application Contact Mrs. Donna L. Vavonese, Associate Director of Admissions, State University of New York Upstate Medical University, Weiskotten Hall, 766 Irving Avenue, Syracuse, NY 13210. *Phone:* 315-464-4570. *Toll-free phone:* 800-736-2171. *Fax:* 315-464-8867. *E-mail:* admiss@upstate.edu. *Web site:* http://www.upstate.edu/.

Stony Brook University, State University of New York
Stony Brook, New York

- **State-supported** university, founded 1957, part of State University of New York System
- **Small-town** 1450-acre campus with easy access to New York City
- **Endowment** $101.1 million
- **Coed** 16,342 undergraduate students, 92% full-time, 48% women, 52% men
- **Very difficult** entrance level, 41% of applicants were admitted

Undergraduates 15,014 full-time, 1,328 part-time. Students come from 48 states and territories; 111 other countries; 7% are from out of state; 6% Black or African American, non-Hispanic/Latino; 9% Hispanic/Latino; 23% Asian, non-Hispanic/Latino; 0.1% Native Hawaiian or other Pacific Islander, non-Hispanic/Latino; 0.2% American Indian or Alaska Native, non-Hispanic/Latino; 1% Two or more races, non-Hispanic/Latino; 15% Race/ethnicity unknown; 7% international; 8% transferred in; 59% live on campus. *Retention:* 89% of full-time freshmen returned.

Freshmen *Admission:* 27,822 applied, 11,395 admitted, 2,742 enrolled. *Average high school GPA:* 3.6. *Test scores:* SAT critical reading scores over 500: 85%; SAT math scores over 500: 96%; SAT writing scores over 500: 84%; ACT scores over 18: 99%; SAT critical reading scores over 600: 40%; SAT math scores over 600: 69%; SAT writing scores over 600: 41%; ACT scores over 24: 86%; SAT critical reading scores over 700: 6%; SAT math scores over 700: 20%; SAT writing scores over 700: 7%; ACT scores over 30: 18%.

Faculty *Total:* 1,482, 66% full-time. *Student/faculty ratio:* 19:1.

Academics *Calendar:* semesters. *Degrees:* bachelor's, master's, doctoral-professional, doctoral-research/scholarship, post-master's, and postbachelor's certificates. *Special study options:* academic remediation for entering students, adult/continuing education programs, advanced placement credit, distance learning, double majors, English as a second language, freshman honors college, honors programs, independent study, internships, off-campus study, part-time degree program, services for LD students, student-designed majors, study abroad, summer session for credit. *ROTC:* Army (c), Air Force (c).

Computers on Campus 2,600 computers/terminals are available on campus for general student use. Students can access the following: campus intranet, computer help desk, free student e-mail accounts, online (class) grades, online (class) registration, online (class) schedules. Campuswide network is available. Wireless service is available via computer labs, dorm rooms, libraries, student centers.

Student Life *Housing options:* coed. Campus housing is university owned. Freshman campus housing is guaranteed. *Activities and organizations:* drama/

theater group, student-run newspaper, radio and television station, choral group, marching band, Inter Fraternity and Sorority Council, Residence Hall Association, Commuter Student Association, Student Activities Board, Chinese Association at Stony Brook, national fraternities, national sororities. *Campus security:* 24-hour emergency response devices and patrols, late-night transport/escort service, controlled dormitory access. *Student services:* health clinic, personal/psychological counseling, women's center, legal services.

Athletics Member NCAA. All Division I. *Intercollegiate sports:* baseball M(s), basketball M(s)/W(s), cross-country running M(s)/W(s), football M(s), lacrosse M(s)/W(s), soccer M(s)/W(s), softball W(s), swimming and diving M(s)/W(s), tennis M(s)/W(s), track and field M(s)/W(s), volleyball W(s). *Intramural sports:* badminton M(c)/W(c), basketball M/W, bowling M/W, cheerleading W, crew M(c)/W(c), equestrian sports M(c)/W(c), fencing M(c)/W(c), golf M, ice hockey M(c), racquetball M/W, rugby M(c)/W(c), soccer M/W, softball M/W, squash M(c)/W(c), table tennis M(c)/W(c), tennis M(c)/W(c), ultimate Frisbee M(c)/W(c), volleyball M/W.

Standardized Tests *Required:* SAT or ACT (for admission).

Costs (2011–12) *Tuition:* state resident $4970 full-time; nonresident $13,380 full-time. *Required fees:* $1610 full-time. *Room and board:* $10,142; room only: $6442. Room and board charges vary according to board plan and housing facility. *Payment plan:* installment.

Financial Aid Of all full-time matriculated undergraduates who enrolled in 2009, 10,620 applied for aid, 8,518 were judged to have need, 1,179 had their need fully met. 466 Federal Work-Study jobs (averaging $2038). 1,748 state and other part-time jobs (averaging $2074). In 2009, 1031 non-need-based awards were made. *Average percent of need met:* 69%. *Average financial aid package:* $11,483. *Average need-based loan:* $4565. *Average need-based gift aid:* $7275. *Average non-need-based aid:* $3729. *Average indebtedness upon graduation:* $19,807.

Applying *Options:* electronic application, early action, deferred entrance. *Application fee:* $50. *Required:* essay or personal statement, high school transcript, minimum 3 GPA, 1 letter of recommendation. *Required for some:* audition. *Recommended:* interview. *Application deadlines:* 1/15 (freshmen), 3/1 (transfers). *Notification:* 4/1 (freshmen), continuous (transfers).

Freshman Application Contact Ms. Judith Burke-Berhanan, Stony Brook University, State University of New York, Admissions Office, 118 Administration Building, Stony Brook, NY 11794-1901. *Phone:* 631-632-6868. *Toll-free phone:* 800-872-7869. *Fax:* 631-632-9898. *E-mail:* enroll@stonybrook.edu. *Web site:* http://www.sunysb.edu/.

Swedish Institute, College of Health Sciences
New York, New York

Freshman Application Contact Admissions Advisor, Swedish Institute, College of Health Sciences, 226 West 26th Street, New York, NY 10001. *Phone:* 212-914-5900 Ext. 125. *E-mail:* admissions@swedishinstitute.edu. *Web site:* http://www.swedishinstitute.org/.

Syracuse University
Syracuse, New York

- **Independent** university, founded 1870
- **Urban** 200-acre campus with easy access to Syracuse
- **Endowment** $849.2 million
- **Coed** 14,201 undergraduate students, 95% full-time, 56% women, 44% men
- **Moderately difficult** entrance level, 60% of applicants were admitted

Undergraduates 13,504 full-time, 697 part-time. Students come from 50 states and territories; 71 other countries; 53% are from out of state; 8% Black or African American, non-Hispanic/Latino; 8% Hispanic/Latino; 9% Asian, non-Hispanic/Latino; 0.1% Native Hawaiian or other Pacific Islander, non-Hispanic/Latino; 0.8% American Indian or Alaska Native, non-Hispanic/Latino; 1% Two or more races, non-Hispanic/Latino; 8% Race/ethnicity unknown; 7% international; 2% transferred in; 75% live on campus. *Retention:* 91% of full-time freshmen returned.

Freshmen *Admission:* 22,935 applied, 13,704 admitted, 3,471 enrolled. *Average high school GPA:* 3.6. *Test scores:* SAT critical reading scores over 500: 82%; SAT math scores over 500: 89%; SAT writing scores over 500: 84%; ACT scores over 18: 98%; SAT critical reading scores over 600: 36%; SAT math scores over 600: 51%; SAT writing scores over 600: 41%; ACT scores over 24: 71%; SAT critical reading scores over 700: 5%; SAT math scores over 700: 10%; SAT writing scores over 700: 6%; ACT scores over 30: 13%.

Faculty *Total:* 1,513, 65% full-time. *Student/faculty ratio:* 16:1.

Academics *Calendar:* semesters. *Degrees:* certificates, associate, bachelor's, master's, doctoral-professional, doctoral-research/scholarship, post-master's, and postbachelor's certificates. *Special study options:* academic remediation for entering students, accelerated degree program, adult/continuing education programs, advanced placement credit, cooperative education, distance learning, double majors, English as a second language, freshman honors college, honors programs, independent study, internships, off-campus study, part-time degree program, services for LD students, student-designed majors, study abroad, summer session for credit. *ROTC:* Army (b), Air Force (b).

Computers on Campus 3,427 computers/terminals and 678 ports are available on campus for general student use. Students can access the following: campus intranet, computer help desk, free student e-mail accounts, online (class) grades, online (class) registration, online (class) schedules, online services, networked client and server computing. Campuswide network is available. 100% of college-owned or -operated housing units are wired for high-speed Internet access. Wireless service is available via classrooms, computer centers, computer labs, dorm rooms, learning centers, libraries, student centers.

Student Life *Housing:* on-campus residence required through sophomore year. *Options:* coed, disabled students. Campus housing is university owned. Freshman campus housing is guaranteed. *Activities and organizations:* drama/theater group, student-run newspaper, radio and television station, choral group, marching band, University Union, Citrus TV, Danceworks, Habitat for Humanity, Student Association, national fraternities, national sororities. *Campus security:* 24-hour emergency response devices and patrols, late-night transport/escort service, controlled dormitory access, crisis alert notification system, outdoor emergency sirens, off-campus patrols in student rental neighborhoods. *Student services:* health clinic, personal/psychological counseling, women's center, legal services.

Athletics Member NCAA. All Division I except football (Division I-A). *Intercollegiate sports:* badminton M(c)/W(c), baseball M(c)/W(c), basketball M(s)/W(s), bowling M(c)/W(c), cheerleading M/W, crew M(s)/W(s), cross-country running M(s)/W(s), equestrian sports M(c)/W(c), fencing M(c)/W(c), field hockey W(s), gymnastics M(c)/W(c), ice hockey M(c)/W(s), lacrosse M(s)/W(s), riflery M(c)/W(c), rugby M(c)/W(c), sailing M(c)/W(c), skiing (downhill) M(c)/W(c), soccer M(s)/W(s), softball M(c)/W(s), swimming and diving M(s)/W(s), table tennis M(c)/W(c), tennis M(s)/W(s), track and field M(s)/W(s), volleyball M(c)/W(s), water polo M(c)/W(c), wrestling M(c). *Intramural sports:* basketball M/W, field hockey M(c)/W(c), football M/W, golf M(c)/W(c), lacrosse M(c)/W(c), racquetball M/W, soccer M/W, softball M/W, swimming and diving M/W, tennis M/W, ultimate Frisbee M(c)/W(c), volleyball M/W.

Standardized Tests *Required:* SAT or ACT (for admission).

Costs (2010–11) *Comprehensive fee:* $49,152 includes full-time tuition ($34,970), mandatory fees ($1332), and room and board ($12,850). Part-time tuition: $1522 per credit hour. *College room only:* $6800. Room and board charges vary according to board plan and housing facility. *Payment plan:* installment. *Waivers:* employees or children of employees.

Financial Aid Of all full-time matriculated undergraduates who enrolled in 2009, 9,123 applied for aid, 7,853 were judged to have need, 5,100 had their need fully met. In 2009, 1596 non-need-based awards were made. *Average percent of need met:* 87%. *Average financial aid package:* $30,640. *Average need-based loan:* $7200. *Average need-based gift aid:* $22,250. *Average non-need-based aid:* $9100. *Average indebtedness upon graduation:* $30,813. *Financial aid deadline:* 2/1.

Applying *Options:* electronic application, early admission, early decision, deferred entrance. *Application fee:* $70. *Required:* essay or personal statement, high school transcript, 2 letters of recommendation. *Application deadlines:* 1/1 (freshmen), rolling (transfers). *Early decision deadline:* 11/15. *Notification:* 3/18 (freshmen), continuous (transfers), 12/31 (early decision).

Freshman Application Contact Office of Admissions, Syracuse University, 100 Crouse-Hinds Hall, 900 South Crouse Avenue, Syracuse, NY 13244-2130. *Phone:* 315-443-3611. *E-mail:* orange@syr.edu. *Web site:* http://www.syr.edu.

See page 1658 for the College Close-Up.

Talmudical Institute of Upstate New York

Rochester, New York

Director of Admissions Rabbi Menachem Davidowitz, Director of Admissions, Talmudical Institute of Upstate New York, 769 Park Avenue, Rochester, NY 14607-3046. *Phone:* 716-473-2810. *E-mail:* yeshiva@tiuny.org. *Web site:* http://www.tiuny.org/.

Talmudical Seminary Oholei Torah

Brooklyn, New York

Director of Admissions Rabbi Yisroel Friedman, Director of Academic Affairs, Talmudical Seminary Oholei Torah, 667 Eastern Parkway, Brooklyn, NY 11213-3310. *Phone:* 718-363-2034. *E-mail:* info@oholeitorah.com.

Torah Temimah Talmudical Seminary

Brooklyn, New York

Director of Admissions Principal, Torah Temimah Talmudical Seminary, 507 Ocean Parkway, Brooklyn, NY 11218-5913. *Phone:* 718-853-8500.

Touro College

New York, New York

Director of Admissions Mr. Andre Baron, Director of Admissions, Touro College, 27-33 West 23rd Street, New York, NY 10010. *Phone:* 212-463-0400 Ext. 665. *Web site:* http://www.touro.edu/.

Union College

Schenectady, New York

- **Independent** 4-year, founded 1795
- **Urban** 100-acre campus
- **Endowment** $297.1 million
- **Coed** 2,197 undergraduate students, 99% full-time, 49% women, 51% men
- **Very difficult** entrance level, 42% of applicants were admitted

Undergraduates 2,170 full-time, 27 part-time. Students come from 38 states and territories; 38 other countries; 57% are from out of state; 5% Black or African American, non-Hispanic/Latino; 5% Hispanic/Latino; 6% Asian, non-Hispanic/Latino; 0.3% American Indian or Alaska Native, non-Hispanic/Latino; 0.6% Two or more races, non-Hispanic/Latino; 0.8% Race/ethnicity unknown; 4% international; 1% transferred in; 85% live on campus. *Retention:* 93% of full-time freshmen returned.

Freshmen *Admission:* 4,946 applied, 2,094 admitted, 554 enrolled. *Average high school GPA:* 3.52. *Test scores:* SAT critical reading scores over 500: 98%; SAT math scores over 500: 99%; SAT writing scores over 500: 97%; ACT scores over 18: 100%; SAT critical reading scores over 600: 71%; SAT math scores over 600: 83%; SAT writing scores over 600: 66%; ACT scores over 24: 96%; SAT critical reading scores over 700: 13%; SAT math scores over 700: 27%; SAT writing scores over 700: 18%; ACT scores over 30: 33%. **Faculty** *Total:* 236, 83% full-time, 88% with terminal degrees. *Student/faculty ratio:* 10:1.

Academics *Calendar:* trimesters. *Degree:* bachelor's. *Special study options:* accelerated degree program, advanced placement credit, double majors, honors programs, independent study, internships, off-campus study, student-designed majors, study abroad, summer session for credit. *ROTC:* Army (c), Navy (c), Air Force (c).

Computers on Campus 491 computers/terminals and 3,032 ports are available on campus for general student use. Students can access the following: campus intranet, computer help desk, free student e-mail accounts, online (class) grades, online (class) registration, online (class) schedules, multimedia lab. Campuswide network is available. 100% of college-owned or -operated housing units are wired for high-speed Internet access. Wireless service is available via classrooms, computer centers, computer labs, learning centers, libraries, student centers.

Student Life *Housing:* on-campus residence required through senior year. *Options:* coed. Campus housing is university owned. Freshman campus housing is guaranteed. *Activities and organizations:* drama/theater group, student-run newspaper, radio and television station, choral group, U-Program (Programming Board), speaker's forum, student newspaper, Concert Committee, ski club, national fraternities, national sororities. *Campus security:* 24-hour emergency response devices and patrols, late-night transport/escort service, controlled dormitory access, awareness programs, bicycle patrol, shuttle service. *Student services:* health clinic, personal/psychological counseling, women's center.

Athletics Member NCAA. All Division III except men's and women's ice hockey (Division I). *Intercollegiate sports:* baseball M, basketball M/W, cheerleading M(c)/W(c), crew M/W, cross-country running M/W, fencing M(c)/W(c), field hockey W, football M, golf M(c)/W(c), ice hockey M/W, lacrosse M/W, rugby M(c)/W(c), soccer M/W, softball W, swimming and diving M/W, tennis M/W, track and field M/W, ultimate Frisbee M(c)/W(c), volleyball W. *Intramural sports:* basketball M/W, football M/W, ice hockey M(c), lacrosse M(c)/W, racquetball M/W, rock climbing M(c)/W(c), skiing (downhill) M(c)/W(c), soccer M/W, softball M/W, squash M/W, tennis M/W, volleyball M/W, water polo M/W.

Standardized Tests *Required for some:* SAT or ACT (for admission), SAT and SAT Subject Tests or ACT (for admission).

Costs (2010–11) *Comprehensive fee:* $52,329. *Payment plan:* installment. *Waivers:* senior citizens and employees or children of employees.

Financial Aid Of all full-time matriculated undergraduates who enrolled in 2009, 1,307 applied for aid, 1,113 were judged to have need, 1,078 had their need fully met. 515 Federal Work-Study jobs (averaging $1628). 225 state and other part-time jobs (averaging $1770). In 2009, 335 non-need-based awards were made. *Average percent of need met:* 97%. *Average financial aid package:* $34,600. *Average need-based loan:* $4167. *Average need-based gift aid:* $29,907. *Average non-need-based aid:* $10,538. *Average indebtedness upon graduation:* $25,621. *Financial aid deadline:* 2/1.

Applying *Options:* electronic application, early admission, early decision, deferred entrance. *Application fee:* $50. *Required:* essay or personal statement, high school transcript, 2 letters of recommendation. *Recommended:* interview. *Application deadlines:* 1/15 (freshmen), 5/1 (transfers). *Early decision deadline:* 11/15 (for plan 1), 1/15 (for plan 2). *Notification:* 4/1 (freshmen), continuous (transfers), 12/15 (early decision plan 1), 2/1 (early decision plan 2).

Freshman Application Contact Union College, Grant Hall, 807 Union Street, Schenectady, NY 12308. *Phone:* 518-388-6112. *Toll-free phone:* 888-843-6688. *Fax:* 518-388-6986. *E-mail:* admissions@union.edu. *Web site:* http://www.union.edu/.

See page 1672 for the College Close-Up.

United States Merchant Marine Academy

Kings Point, New York

- **Federally supported** comprehensive, founded 1943
- **Suburban** 82-acre campus with easy access to New York City
- **Coed** 1,117 undergraduate students, 100% full-time, 12% women, 88% men
- **Very difficult** entrance level, 17% of applicants were admitted

Undergraduates 1,117 full-time. Students come from 52 states and territories; 6 other countries; 87% are from out of state; 100% live on campus. *Retention:* 92% of full-time freshmen returned.

Freshmen *Admission:* 2,006 applied, 342 admitted, 342 enrolled. *Average high school GPA:* 3.6. *Test scores:* SAT critical reading scores over 500: 98%; SAT math scores over 500: 100%; ACT scores over 18: 100%; SAT critical reading scores over 600: 37%; SAT math scores over 600: 74%; ACT scores over 24: 98%; SAT critical reading scores over 700: 6%; SAT math scores over 700: 11%; ACT scores over 30: 9%.

Faculty *Total:* 95. *Student/faculty ratio:* 11:1.

Academics *Calendar:* trimesters. *Degrees:* bachelor's and master's. *Special study options:* honors programs, internships.

Computers on Campus 1,200 computers/terminals are available on campus for general student use. Students can access the following: campus intranet, computer help desk, free student e-mail accounts, engineering and economics software. Campuswide network is available.

Student Life *Housing:* on-campus residence required through senior year. *Options:* coed. Campus housing is university owned. Freshman campus housing is guaranteed. *Activities and organizations:* drama/theater group, student-run newspaper, choral group, marching band, Regimental Band, CFC, Neuman Club, Honor Guard. *Campus security:* 24-hour patrols. *Student services:* health clinic, personal/psychological counseling.

Athletics Member NCAA. All Division III. *Intercollegiate sports:* baseball M, basketball M/W, crew M/W, cross-country running M/W, football M, golf M/W, ice hockey M(c), lacrosse M, rugby M(c), sailing M/W, soccer M, softball W, swimming and diving M/W, tennis M/W, track and field M/W, volleyball W, wrestling M. *Intramural sports:* basketball M/W, bowling M/W, crew M/W, cross-country running M/W, football M, golf M/W, lacrosse M, racquetball M/W, riflery M/W, rugby M, sailing M/W, skiing (cross-country) M/W, skiing (downhill) M/W, soccer M/W, softball M/W, swimming and diving M/W, tennis M/W, track and field M/W, volleyball M/W, water polo M, wrestling M.

Standardized Tests *Required:* SAT or ACT (for admission).

Costs (2010–11) *Tuition:* Full-time tuition and fees vary according to student level. Tuition, room and board, and medical and dental care are provided by the U.S. government. Each midshipman receives a monthly stipend while assigned aboard ship for training. Entering freshmen are required to pay fees for laptop, equipment, and activity fees. *Required fees:* $2530 full-time.

Applying *Options:* electronic application. *Required:* essay or personal statement, high school transcript, 3 letters of recommendation. *Recommended:*

interview. *Application deadlines:* 3/1 (freshmen), 3/1 (transfers). *Notification:* continuous until 4/1 (freshmen), continuous until 4/1 (transfers).

Freshman Application Contact Capt. Robert E. Johnson, Director of Admissions and Financial Aid, United States Merchant Marine Academy, 300 Steamboat Road, Kings Point, NY 11024-1699. *Phone:* 516-773-5391. *Toll-free phone:* 866-546-4778. *Fax:* 516-773-5390. *E-mail:* admissions@ usmma.edu. *Web site:* http://www.usmma.edu/.

See page 1678 for the College Close-Up.

United States Military Academy
West Point, New York

- **Federally supported** 4-year, founded 1802
- **Small-town** 16,080-acre campus with easy access to New York City
- **Endowment** $155.9 million
- **Coed** 4,686 undergraduate students, 100% full-time, 16% women, 84% men
- **Most difficult** entrance level, 13% of applicants were admitted

Undergraduates 4,686 full-time. Students come from 55 states and territories; 35 other countries; 93% are from out of state; 6% Black or African American, non-Hispanic/Latino; 9% Hispanic/Latino; 5% Asian, non-Hispanic/Latino; 0.3% Native Hawaiian or other Pacific Islander, non-Hispanic/Latino; 0.8% American Indian or Alaska Native, non-Hispanic/Latino; 4% Two or more races, non-Hispanic/Latino; 1% Race/ethnicity unknown; 1% international; 100% live on campus. *Retention:* 95% of full-time freshmen returned.

Freshmen *Admission:* 12,264 applied, 1,601 admitted, 1,312 enrolled. *Average high school GPA:* 3.8. *Test scores:* SAT critical reading scores over 500: 94%; SAT math scores over 500: 96%; SAT writing scores over 500: 91%; ACT scores over 18: 100%; SAT critical reading scores over 600: 64%; SAT math scores over 600: 71%; SAT writing scores over 600: 52%; ACT scores over 24: 86%; SAT critical reading scores over 700: 16%; SAT math scores over 700: 21%; SAT writing scores over 700: 11%; ACT scores over 30: 30%.

Faculty *Total:* 615, 100% full-time, 44% with terminal degrees. *Student/faculty ratio:* 8:1.

Academics *Calendar:* semesters. *Degree:* bachelor's. *Special study options:* academic remediation for entering students, advanced placement credit, double majors, honors programs, independent study, off-campus study, study abroad, summer session for credit.

Computers on Campus 900 computers/terminals are available on campus for general student use. Students can access the following: computer help desk, free student e-mail accounts, online (class) grades, online (class) registration, online (class) schedules. Campuswide network is available. 100% of college-owned or -operated housing units are wired for high-speed Internet access. Wireless service is available via entire campus.

Student Life *Housing:* on-campus residence required through senior year. *Options:* coed. Campus housing is university owned. Freshman campus housing is guaranteed. *Activities and organizations:* drama/theater group, student-run radio station, choral group, Asian-Pacific Club, Officers' Christian Fellowship, Spirit Support Group, Fellowship of Christian Athletes, Philosophy Forum. *Campus security:* 24-hour emergency response devices and patrols, late-night transport/escort service. *Student services:* health clinic, personal/psychological counseling, legal services.

Athletics Member NCAA. All Division I except football (Division I-A). *Intercollegiate sports:* baseball M, basketball M/W, cheerleading M/W, crew M(c)/W(c), cross-country running M/W, equestrian sports M(c)/W(c), fencing M(c)/W(c), golf M, gymnastics M, ice hockey M, lacrosse M/W(c), riflery M/ W, rock climbing M(c)/W(c), rugby M(c)/W(c), sailing M(c)/W(c), skiing (cross-country) M(c)/W(c), skiing (downhill) M(c)/W(c), soccer M/W, softball W, swimming and diving M/W, tennis M/W, track and field M/W, volleyball M(c)/W, water polo M(c), weight lifting M(c)/W(c), wrestling M. *Intramural sports:* basketball M/W, bowling M(c)/W(c), football M, rugby M/W, soccer M/W, swimming and diving M/W, ultimate Frisbee M/W, wrestling M.

Standardized Tests *Required:* SAT or ACT (for admission).

Applying *Options:* electronic application. *Required:* essay or personal statement, high school transcript, 4 letters of recommendation, Obtain nominations from an approved source, pass a Department of Defense qualifying medical examination, must be at least 17 but not yet 23 years of age by July 1 of year of entry, and be an unmarried U.S. citizen (foreign nationals with approval) with no parental obligations. *Recommended:* interview. *Application deadline:* 2/28 (freshmen). *Notification:* 5/1 (freshmen).

Freshman Application Contact Col. Deborah J. McDonald, Director of Admissions, United States Military Academy, 600 Thayer Road, West Point, NY 10996. *Phone:* 845-938-4041. *E-mail:* 8dad@sunams.usma.army.mil. *Web site:* http://www.usma.edu/.

United Talmudical Seminary
Brooklyn, New York

Director of Admissions Director of Admissions, United Talmudical Seminary, 191 Rodney Street, Brooklyn, NY 11211. *Phone:* 718-963-9770.

University at Albany, State University of New York
Albany, New York

- **State-supported** university, founded 1844, part of State University of New York System
- **Suburban** 560-acre campus
- **Endowment** $27.7 million
- **Coed**
- **Very difficult** entrance level

Faculty *Student/faculty ratio:* 19:1.

Academics *Calendar:* semesters. *Degrees:* bachelor's, master's, doctoral-research/scholarship, post-master's, and postbachelor's certificates.

Student Life *Campus security:* 24-hour emergency response devices and patrols, late-night transport/escort service, controlled dormitory access, Five Quad Ambulance Service; On-Campus Dead Car Battery Assistance.

Athletics Member NCAA. All Division I.

Standardized Tests *Required:* SAT or ACT (for admission).

Costs (2010–11) *Tuition:* state resident $4970 full-time, $207 per credit part-time; nonresident $12,870 full-time, $536 per credit part-time. Part-time tuition and fees vary according to course load. *Required fees:* $1860 full-time, $45 per credit part-time. *Room and board:* $10,633; room only: $6577. Room and board charges vary according to board plan and housing facility.

Financial Aid *Of all full-time matriculated undergraduates who enrolled in 2009,* 9,556 applied for aid, 7,237 were judged to have need, 807 had their need fully met. 1,034 Federal Work-Study jobs (averaging $1566). 221 state and other part-time jobs (averaging $6115). *In 2009,* 560 non-need-based awards were made. *Average percent of need met:* 68. *Average financial aid package:* $9649. *Average need-based loan:* $4408. *Average need-based gift aid:* $6398. *Average non-need-based aid:* $3528. *Average indebtedness upon graduation:* $22,092.

Applying *Options:* electronic application, early admission, early action, deferred entrance. *Application fee:* $50. *Required:* essay or personal statement, high school transcript, 1 letter of recommendation. *Required for some:* portfolio, audition.

Freshman Application Contact University at Albany, State University of New York, 1400 Washington Avenue, Albany, NY 12222-0001. *Phone:* 518-442-5435. *Toll-free phone:* 800-293-7869. *Web site:* http://www.albany.edu/.

University at Buffalo, the State University of New York
Buffalo, New York

- **State-supported** university, founded 1846, part of State University of New York System
- **Suburban** 1350-acre campus
- **Endowment** $428.9 million
- **Coed** 19,395 undergraduate students, 93% full-time, 46% women, 54% men
- **Moderately difficult** entrance level, 51% of applicants were admitted

Undergraduates 17,980 full-time, 1,415 part-time. Students come from 46 states and territories; 91 other countries; 4% are from out of state; 7% Black or African American, non-Hispanic/Latino; 4% Hispanic/Latino; 10% Asian, non-Hispanic/Latino; 0.6% American Indian or Alaska Native, non-Hispanic/Latino; 7% Race/ethnicity unknown; 15% international; 10% transferred in; 34% live on campus. *Retention:* 88% of full-time freshmen returned.

Freshmen *Admission:* 21,985 applied, 11,298 admitted, 3,388 enrolled. *Average high school GPA:* 3.3. *Test scores:* SAT critical reading scores over 500: 77%; SAT math scores over 500: 92%; ACT scores over 18: 99%; SAT critical reading scores over 600: 29%; SAT math scores over 600: 52%; ACT scores over 24: 72%; SAT critical reading scores over 700: 4%; SAT math scores over 700: 10%; ACT scores over 30: 14%.

Faculty *Total:* 1,740, 69% full-time, 90% with terminal degrees. *Student/faculty ratio:* 16:1.

Academics *Calendar:* semesters. *Degrees:* bachelor's, master's, doctoral-professional, doctoral-research/scholarship, and post-master's certificates. *Special study options:* academic remediation for entering students, accelerated degree program, advanced placement credit, cooperative education, distance learning, double majors, English as a second language, freshman honors college, honors programs, independent study, internships, off-campus study, part-time degree program, services for LD students, student-designed majors, study abroad, summer session for credit. *ROTC:* Army (c). *Unusual degree programs:* 3-2 business administration; engineering; nursing; social work; law.

Computers on Campus 2,300 computers/terminals are available on campus for general student use. Students can access the following: campus intranet, computer help desk, free student e-mail accounts, online (class) grades, online (class) registration, online (class) schedules. Campuswide network is available. 100% of college-owned or -operated housing units are wired for high-speed Internet access. Wireless service is available via entire campus.

Student Life *Housing options:* coed, disabled students. Campus housing is university owned. Freshman campus housing is guaranteed. *Activities and organizations:* drama/theater group, student-run newspaper, radio and television station, choral group, marching band, national fraternities, national sororities. *Campus security:* 24-hour emergency response devices and patrols, student patrols, late-night transport/escort service, controlled dormitory access, self-defense and awareness programs, security cameras. *Student services:* health clinic, personal/psychological counseling, legal services.

Athletics Member NCAA. All Division I except football (Division I-A). *Intercollegiate sports:* baseball M(s), basketball M(s)/W(s), crew W(s), cross-country running M(s)/W(s), soccer M(s)/W(s), softball W(s), swimming and diving M(s)/W(s), tennis M(s)/W(s), track and field M(s)/W(s), volleyball W(s), wrestling M(s). *Intramural sports:* badminton M(c)/W(c), baseball M(c), basketball M/W, crew M(c), cross-country running M(c)/W(c), equestrian sports M(c)/W(c), field hockey W(c), gymnastics M(c)/W(c), ice hockey M(c)/W(c), lacrosse M(c)/W(c), racquetball M/W, rock climbing M(c)/W(c), rugby M(c)/W(c), skiing (cross-country) M(c)/W(c), skiing (downhill) M(c)/W(c), soccer M(c)/W(c), softball M/W, tennis M(c)/W(c), track and field M(c)/W(c), ultimate Frisbee M(c)/W(c), volleyball M(c)/W(c), wrestling M(c).

Standardized Tests *Required:* SAT or ACT (for admission).

Costs (2010–11) *Tuition:* state resident $4970 full-time, $207 per credit hour part-time; nonresident $13,380 full-time, $558 per credit hour part-time. Part-time tuition and fees vary according to course load. *Required fees:* $2166 full-time, $95 per credit hour part-time. *Room and board:* $10,028; room only: $5928. Room and board charges vary according to board plan and housing facility. *Payment plan:* installment. *Waivers:* minority students.

Financial Aid Of all full-time matriculated undergraduates who enrolled in 2009, 12,637 applied for aid, 9,622 were judged to have need, 5,709 had their need fully met. 1,146 Federal Work-Study jobs (averaging $1489). 2,301 state and other part-time jobs (averaging $3547). In 2009, 1456 non-need-based awards were made. *Average percent of need met:* 61%. *Average financial aid package:* $7189. *Average need-based loan:* $4334. *Average need-based gift aid:* $5646. *Average non-need-based aid:* $5529. *Average indebtedness upon graduation:* $17,425.

Applying *Options:* electronic application, early admission, early decision. *Application fee:* $50. *Required:* essay or personal statement, high school transcript, 1 letter of recommendation. *Required for some:* Architecture requires a portfolio and Dance, Music Theatre, Theatre and Music require an audition. *Early decision deadline:* 11/1. *Notification:* continuous (freshmen), continuous (transfers), 12/15 (early decision).

Freshman Application Contact Ms. Patricia Armstrong, Director of Admissions, University at Buffalo, the State University of New York, 12 Capen Hall, North Campus, Buffalo, NY 14260-1660. *Phone:* 716-645-6900. *Toll-free phone:* 888-UB-ADMIT. *Fax:* 716-645-6411. *E-mail:* ub-admissions@buffalo.edu. *Web site:* http://www.buffalo.edu/.

See page 1680 for the College Close-Up.

University of Rochester
Rochester, New York

- **Independent** university, founded 1850
- **Suburban** 655-acre campus
- **Endowment** $1.4 billion
- **Coed** 5,601 undergraduate students, 95% full-time, 52% women, 48% men
- **Very difficult** entrance level, 38% of applicants were admitted

Undergraduates 5,330 full-time, 271 part-time. Students come from 52 states and territories; 75 other countries; 60% are from out of state; 1% transferred in; 83% live on campus. *Retention:* 96% of full-time freshmen returned.

Freshmen *Admission:* 12,805 applied, 4,925 admitted, 1,308 enrolled. *Average high school GPA:* 3.8. *Test scores:* SAT critical reading scores over 500: 97%; SAT math scores over 500: 99%; SAT writing scores over 500: 98%; ACT scores over 18: 101%; SAT critical reading scores over 600: 75%; SAT math scores over 600: 86%; SAT writing scores over 600: 78%; ACT scores over 24: 98%; SAT critical reading scores over 700: 24%; SAT math scores over 700: 40%; SAT writing scores over 700: 26%; ACT scores over 30: 64%.

Faculty *Total:* 804, 65% full-time. *Student/faculty ratio:* 9:1.

Academics *Calendar:* semesters plus optional summer term. *Degrees:* bachelor's, master's, doctoral-professional, doctoral-research/scholarship, post-master's, and postbachelor's certificates. *Special study options:* accelerated degree program, advanced placement credit, cooperative education, double majors, English as a second language, honors programs, independent study, internships, off-campus study, part-time degree program, services for LD students, student-designed majors, study abroad, summer session for credit. *ROTC:* Army (c), Navy (b), Air Force (c). *Unusual degree programs:* 3-2 business administration; engineering; nursing; public health, optics, human development, neuroscience, medical physics, and physics & astronomy.

Computers on Campus 450 computers/terminals and 4,000 ports are available on campus for general student use. Students can access the following: computer help desk, free student e-mail accounts, online (class) grades, online (class) registration, online (class) schedules. Campuswide network is available. 100% of college-owned or -operated housing units are wired for high-speed Internet access. Wireless service is available via classrooms, computer centers, computer labs, learning centers, libraries, student centers.

Student Life *Housing:* on-campus residence required through sophomore year. *Options:* coed. Campus housing is university owned and leased by the school. Freshman campus housing is guaranteed. *Activities and organizations:* drama/theater group, student-run newspaper, radio and television station, choral group, marching band, Campus Activities Board, Black Students' Union, Grassroots (environmental group), Women's Caucus, American Sign Language Club, national fraternities, national sororities. *Campus security:* 24-hour emergency response devices and patrols, student patrols, late-night transport/escort service, controlled dormitory access. *Student services:* health clinic, personal/psychological counseling, women's center, legal services.

Athletics Member NCAA. All Division III except squash (Division I). *Intercollegiate sports:* badminton M(c)/W(c), baseball M, basketball M/W, crew M(c)/W, cross-country running M/W, equestrian sports M(c)/W(c), field hockey W, football M, golf M, ice hockey M(c)/W(c), lacrosse M(c)/W, rugby M(c)/W(c), skiing (downhill) M(c)/W(c), soccer M/W, softball W, squash M, swimming and diving M/W, tennis M/W, track and field M/W, ultimate Frisbee M(c)/W(c), volleyball M(c)/W, water polo M(c)/W(c). *Intramural sports:* archery M(c)/W(c), basketball M/W, cheerleading M(c)/W(c), fencing M(c)/W(c), football M/W, gymnastics M(c)/W(c), sailing M(c)/W(c), soccer M/W, softball M/W, tennis M/W, ultimate Frisbee M/W, volleyball M/W.

Standardized Tests *Required:* SAT or ACT (for admission). *Required for some:* SAT and SAT Subject Tests or ACT (for admission). *Recommended:* SAT Subject Tests (for admission).

Costs (2010–11) *Comprehensive fee:* $51,922 includes full-time tuition ($39,480), mandatory fees ($802), and room and board ($11,640). Part-time tuition: $1234 per credit hour. Part-time tuition and fees vary according to course load. *College room only:* $7050. Room and board charges vary according to board plan. *Payment plans:* tuition prepayment, installment. *Waivers:* employees or children of employees.

Financial Aid Of all full-time matriculated undergraduates who enrolled in 2009, 2,968 applied for aid, 2,621 were judged to have need, 2,502 had their need fully met. 1,664 Federal Work-Study jobs (averaging $1974). In 2009, 1370 non-need-based awards were made. *Average percent of need met:* 96%. *Average financial aid package:* $33,607. *Average need-based loan:* $4904. *Average need-based gift aid:* $28,429. *Average non-need-based aid:* $10,258. *Average indebtedness upon graduation:* $28,100.

Applying *Options:* electronic application, early admission, early decision, deferred entrance. *Application fee:* $60. *Required:* essay or personal statement, high school transcript. *Required for some:* audition is required for music programs at Eastman School of Music. *Recommended:* 2 letters of recommendation, interview. *Application deadlines:* 1/1 (freshmen), 1/1 (out-of-state freshmen), 6/1 (transfers). *Early decision deadline:* 11/1. *Notification:* 4/1 (freshmen), 4/1 (out-of-state freshmen), 7/1 (transfers), 12/15 (early decision).

Freshman Application Contact Office of Admissions, University of Rochester, PO Box 270251, 300 Wilson Boulevard, Rochester, NY 14627-0251. *Phone:* 585-275-3221. *Toll-free phone:* 888-822-2256. *Fax:* 585-461-4595. *E-mail:* admit@admissions.rochester.edu. *Web site:* http://www.rochester.edu/.

See page 1734 for the College Close-Up.

U.T.A. Mesivta of Kiryas Joel

Monroe, New York

Admissions Office Contact U.T.A. Mesivta of Kiryas Joel, 9 Nickelsburg Road, Unit 312, Monroe, NY 10950.

Utica College
Utica, New York

- **Independent** comprehensive, founded 1946
- **Suburban** 128-acre campus
- **Endowment** $16.4 million
- **Coed**
- **Moderately difficult** entrance level

Faculty *Student/faculty ratio:* 11:1.

Academics *Calendar:* semesters. *Degrees:* certificates, bachelor's, master's, doctoral-professional, and postbachelor's certificates.

Student Life *Campus security:* 24-hour emergency response devices and patrols, late-night transport/escort service, controlled dormitory access.

Athletics Member NCAA. All Division III.

Standardized Tests *Required for some:* SAT or ACT (for admission).

Costs (2010–11) *Comprehensive fee:* $40,210 includes full-time tuition ($28,100), mandatory fees ($520), and room and board ($11,590). Full-time tuition and fees vary according to class time and course load. Part-time tuition: $950 per credit hour. Part-time tuition and fees vary according to class time and course load. *Room and board:* Room and board charges vary according to board plan and housing facility. *Payment plans:* installment, deferred payment.

Financial Aid Of all full-time matriculated undergraduates who enrolled in 2009, 1,994 applied for aid, 1,903 were judged to have need, 176 had their need fully met. In 2009, 108 non-need-based awards were made. *Average percent of need met:* 68. *Average financial aid package:* $22,059. *Average need-based loan:* $4298. *Average need-based gift aid:* $6938. *Average non-need-based aid:* $10,557. *Average indebtedness upon graduation:* $39,371.

Applying *Options:* electronic application, early admission, deferred entrance. *Application fee:* $40. *Required:* essay or personal statement, high school transcript, minimum 2 GPA, 1 letter of recommendation. *Required for some:* minimum 3 GPA. *Recommended:* interview.

Freshman Application Contact Utica College, 1600 Burrstone Road, Utica, NY 13502-4892. *Phone:* 315-792-3006. *Toll-free phone:* 800-782-8884. *Web site:* http://www.utica.edu/.

See page 1756 for the College Close-Up.

Vassar College
Poughkeepsie, New York

- **Independent** comprehensive, founded 1861
- **Suburban** 1000-acre campus with easy access to New York City
- **Endowment** $699.5 million
- **Coed** 2,446 undergraduate students, 98% full-time, 58% women, 42% men
- **Very difficult** entrance level, 24% of applicants were admitted

Undergraduates 2,401 full-time, 45 part-time. Students come from 51 states and territories; 58 other countries; 73% are from out of state; 5% Black or African American, non-Hispanic/Latino; 9% Hispanic/Latino; 9% Asian, non-Hispanic/Latino; 0.2% American Indian or Alaska Native, non-Hispanic/Latino; 4% Two or more races, non-Hispanic/Latino; 0.2% Race/ethnicity unknown; 6% international; 0.4% transferred in; 95% live on campus. *Retention:* 96% of full-time freshmen returned.

Freshmen *Admission:* 7,822 applied, 1,847 admitted, 666 enrolled. *Average high school GPA:* 3.77. *Test scores:* SAT critical reading scores over 500: 100%; SAT math scores over 500: 100%; SAT writing scores over 500: 99%; ACT scores over 18: 100%; SAT critical reading scores over 600: 96%; SAT math scores over 600: 93%; SAT writing scores over 600: 91%; ACT scores over 24: 100%; SAT critical reading scores over 700: 56%; SAT math scores over 700: 37%; SAT writing scores over 700: 52%; ACT scores over 30: 76%.

Faculty *Total:* 328, 85% full-time, 84% with terminal degrees. *Student/faculty ratio:* 8:1.

Academics *Calendar:* semesters. *Degrees:* bachelor's and master's. *Special study options:* advanced placement credit, cooperative education, double majors, independent study, internships, off-campus study, part-time degree program, services for LD students, student-designed majors, study abroad. *Unusual degree programs:* 3-2 engineering with Dartmouth College.

Computers on Campus 300 computers/terminals are available on campus for general student use. Students can access the following: campus intranet, computer help desk, free student e-mail accounts, online (class) grades, online (class) registration, online (class) schedules, Ethernet. Campuswide network is available. 100% of college-owned or -operated housing units are wired for high-speed Internet access. Wireless service is available via entire campus.

Student Life *Housing:* on-campus residence required through senior year. *Options:* coed, women-only, cooperative. Campus housing is university owned. Freshman campus housing is guaranteed. *Activities and organizations:* drama/theater group, student-run newspaper, radio and television station, choral group, Student Association, WVKR radio station, VICE (programming social events), Vassar Greens, Ultimate Frisbee. *Campus security:* 24-hour emergency response devices and patrols, student patrols, late-night transport/escort service, controlled dormitory access. *Student services:* health clinic, personal/psychological counseling, women's center.

Athletics Member NCAA. All Division III. *Intercollegiate sports:* baseball M, basketball M/W, crew M/W, cross-country running M/W, fencing M/W, field hockey W, golf W, lacrosse M/W, rugby M(c)/W(c), soccer M/W, squash M/W, swimming and diving M/W, tennis M/W, track and field M(c)/W(c), ultimate Frisbee M(c)/W(c), volleyball M/W. *Intramural sports:* badminton M(c)/W(c), basketball M/W, bowling M/W, equestrian sports M(c)/W(c), golf M/W, sailing M(c)/W(c), skiing (cross-country) M(c)/W(c), skiing (downhill) M(c)/W(c), soccer M/W, softball M/W, squash M/W, tennis M/W, volleyball M/W, water polo M/W.

Standardized Tests *Required:* SAT and SAT Subject Tests or ACT (for admission).

Costs (2010–11) *Comprehensive fee:* $53,090 includes full-time tuition ($42,560), mandatory fees ($630), and room and board ($9900). Part-time tuition: $5040 per unit. Part-time tuition and fees vary according to course load. *College room only:* $5470. Room and board charges vary according to board plan and housing facility. *Payment plan:* installment. *Waivers:* employees or children of employees.

Financial Aid Of all full-time matriculated undergraduates who enrolled in 2009, 1,722 applied for aid, 1,536 were judged to have need, 1,536 had their need fully met. *Average percent of need met:* 100%. *Average financial aid package:* $40,631. *Average need-based loan:* $2656. *Average need-based gift aid:* $36,353. *Average indebtedness upon graduation:* $18,153. *Financial aid deadline:* 2/15.

Applying *Options:* electronic application, early decision, deferred entrance. *Application fee:* $60. *Required:* essay or personal statement, high school transcript, 2 letters of recommendation. *Application deadlines:* 1/1 (freshmen), 4/1 (transfers). *Early decision deadline:* 11/15. *Notification:* 4/1 (freshmen), 5/10 (transfers), 12/15 (early decision).

Freshman Application Contact Dr. David M. Borus, Dean of Admission and Financial Aid, Vassar College, 124 Raymond Avenue, Poughkeepsie, NY 12604. *Phone:* 845-437-7300. *Toll-free phone:* 800-827-7270. *Fax:* 845-437-7063. *E-mail:* admissions@vassar.edu. *Web site:* http://www.vassar.edu/.

Vaughn College of Aeronautics and Technology

Flushing, New York

- **Independent** comprehensive, founded 1932
- **Urban** 6-acre campus with easy access to New York City
- **Endowment** $17.9 million
- **Coed, primarily men** 1,530 undergraduate students, 73% full-time, 13% women, 87% men
- **Moderately difficult** entrance level, 82% of applicants were admitted

Undergraduates 1,114 full-time, 416 part-time. Students come from 22 states and territories; 8 other countries; 14% are from out of state; 20% Black or African American, non-Hispanic/Latino; 38% Hispanic/Latino; 11% Asian, non-Hispanic/Latino; 0.1% Native Hawaiian or other Pacific Islander, non-Hispanic/Latino; 0.6% American Indian or Alaska Native, non-Hispanic/Latino; 11% Race/ethnicity unknown; 2% international; 12% transferred in; 9% live on campus. *Retention:* 92% of full-time freshmen returned.

Freshmen *Admission:* 556 applied, 454 admitted, 251 enrolled. *Average high school GPA:* 3.2. *Test scores:* SAT critical reading scores over 500: 40%; SAT math scores over 500: 87%; ACT scores over 18: 100%; SAT critical reading scores over 600: 3%; SAT math scores over 600: 26%.

Faculty *Total:* 156, 23% full-time, 16% with terminal degrees. *Student/faculty ratio:* 17:1.

Academics *Calendar:* semesters. *Degrees:* certificates, associate, bachelor's, and master's. *Special study options:* academic remediation for entering students, advanced placement credit, cooperative education, distance learning, double majors, independent study, internships, part-time degree program, summer session for credit. *ROTC:* Army (c), Air Force (c).

Computers on Campus 199 computers/terminals are available on campus for general student use. Students can access the following: campus intranet, free student e-mail accounts, online (class) grades, online (class) schedules. Campuswide network is available. 100% of college-owned or -operated housing units are wired for high-speed Internet access. Wireless service is available via entire campus.

Student Life *Housing options:* coed, disabled students. Campus housing is university owned. Freshman applicants given priority for college housing. *Activities and organizations:* American Association of Airport Executives, Women in Aviation-International, Institute of Electrical and Electronics Engineers, Robotics Club, Red Tail Pilots Club. *Campus security:* 24-hour emergency response devices and patrols, controlled dormitory access.

Athletics *Intercollegiate sports:* basketball M, soccer M, tennis W, track and field M/W. *Intramural sports:* basketball M, soccer M, tennis W.

Standardized Tests *Required for some:* SAT and SAT Subject Tests or ACT (for admission).

Costs (2011–12) *One-time required fee:* $160. *Comprehensive fee:* $29,545 includes full-time tuition ($17,960), mandatory fees ($560), and room and board ($11,025). Full-time tuition and fees vary according to course load, location, and program. Part-time tuition: $605 per credit. Part-time tuition and fees vary according to course load, location, and program. *Required fees:* $200 per term part-time. *College room only:* $8610. Room and board charges vary according to board plan. *Payment plan:* installment. *Waivers:* employees or children of employees.

Financial Aid Of all full-time matriculated undergraduates who enrolled in 2008, 704 applied for aid, 704 were judged to have need, 476 had their need fully met. 25 Federal Work-Study jobs (averaging $3000). In 2008, 145 non-need-based awards were made. *Average percent of need met:* 82%. *Average financial aid package:* $18,030. *Average need-based loan:* $1770. *Average need-based gift aid:* $2950. *Average non-need-based aid:* $2000. *Average indebtedness upon graduation:* $17,125.

Applying *Options:* electronic application. *Application fee:* $40. *Required:* high school transcript. *Recommended:* essay or personal statement, 2 letters of recommendation, interview. *Application deadlines:* rolling (freshmen), rolling (out-of-state freshmen), rolling (transfers). *Notification:* continuous (freshmen), continuous (out-of-state freshmen), continuous (transfers).

Freshman Application Contact Mr. Celso Alvarez, Director of Admissions, Vaughn College of Aeronautics and Technology, Vaughn College, 8601 23rd Avenue, Flushing, NY 11369. *Phone:* 718-429.6600 Ext. 117. *Toll-free phone:* 800-776-2376 Ext. 145. *Fax:* 718-779.2231. *E-mail:* celso.alvarez@vaughn.edu. *Web site:* http://www.vaughn.edu/.

Villa Maria College of Buffalo

Buffalo, New York

- **Independent** 4-year, founded 1960, affiliated with Roman Catholic Church
- **Suburban** 9-acre campus
- **Endowment** $749,675
- **Coed** 507 undergraduate students, 79% full-time, 64% women, 36% men
- **Minimally difficult** entrance level, 78% of applicants were admitted

Undergraduates 399 full-time, 108 part-time. Students come from 7 states and territories; 1 other country; 1% are from out of state; 20% Black or African American, non-Hispanic/Latino; 3% Hispanic/Latino; 0.6% Asian, non-Hispanic/Latino; 1% American Indian or Alaska Native, non-Hispanic/Latino; 2% Two or more races, non-Hispanic/Latino; 1% Race/ethnicity unknown; 14% transferred in. *Retention:* 56% of full-time freshmen returned.

Freshmen *Admission:* 426 applied, 333 admitted, 114 enrolled. *Average high school GPA:* 2.56. *Test scores:* SAT critical reading scores over 500: 27%; SAT math scores over 500: 20%; ACT scores over 18: 45%; SAT critical reading scores over 600: 8%; SAT math scores over 600: 8%; ACT scores over 24: 9%.

Faculty *Total:* 84, 37% full-time, 42% with terminal degrees. *Student/faculty ratio:* 9:1.

Academics *Calendar:* semesters. *Degrees:* associate and bachelor's. *Special study options:* academic remediation for entering students, advanced placement credit, cooperative education, independent study, internships, off-campus study, part-time degree program, services for LD students, study abroad, summer session for credit.

Computers on Campus 250 computers/terminals are available on campus for general student use. Students can access the following: computer help desk, free student e-mail accounts, online (class) grades, online (class) registration, online (class) schedules. Campuswide network is available. Wireless service is available via libraries, student centers.

Student Life *Housing:* college housing not available. *Options:* Campus housing is provided by a third party. *Activities and organizations:* choral group, Design and Beyond, Teachers Love Children, Multicultural Club, Phi Theta Kappa, Helping Adults New Dreams Succeed. *Campus security:* late-night transport/escort service. *Student services:* health clinic, personal/psychological counseling.

Costs (2011–12) *Tuition:* $15,100 full-time, $500 per credit part-time. Full-time tuition and fees vary according to degree level and program. Part-time tuition and fees vary according to course load, degree level, and program. *Required fees:* $819 full-time. *Payment plan:* installment. *Waivers:* senior citizens and employees or children of employees.

Financial Aid Of all full-time matriculated undergraduates who enrolled in 2008, 408 applied for aid, 307 were judged to have need, 11 had their need fully met. 65 Federal Work-Study jobs (averaging $430). In 2008, 15 non-need-based awards were made. *Average percent of need met:* 50%. *Average financial aid package:* $7320. *Average need-based loan:* $4195. *Average need-based gift aid:* $4971. *Average non-need-based aid:* $1333. *Average indebtedness upon graduation:* $26,304.

Applying *Options:* electronic application, deferred entrance. *Required:* essay or personal statement, high school transcript, interview, writing sample, portfolio review. *Required for some:* writing sample, portfolio review. *Application deadlines:* rolling (freshmen), rolling (out-of-state freshmen), rolling (transfers). *Notification:* continuous (freshmen), continuous (out-of-state freshmen), continuous (transfers).

Freshman Application Contact Mr. Kevin Donovan, Director of Admissions, Villa Maria College of Buffalo, Buffalo, NY 14211. *Phone:* 716-896-0700 Ext. 1802. *Fax:* 716-896-0705. *E-mail:* admissions@villa.edu. *Web site:* http://www.villa.edu/.

Wagner College
Staten Island, New York

- **Independent** comprehensive, founded 1883
- **Urban** 105-acre campus with easy access to New York City
- **Endowment** $41.6 million
- **Coed** 1,839 undergraduate students, 95% full-time, 64% women, 36% men
- **Moderately difficult** entrance level, 65% of applicants were admitted

Undergraduates 1,740 full-time, 99 part-time. Students come from 43 states and territories; 21 other countries; 49% are from out of state; 6% Black or African American, non-Hispanic/Latino; 7% Hispanic/Latino; 2% Asian, non-Hispanic/Latino; 0.3% Native Hawaiian or other Pacific Islander, non-Hispanic/Latino; 0.1% American Indian or Alaska Native, non-Hispanic/Latino; 1% Two or more races, non-Hispanic/Latino; 7% Race/ethnicity unknown; 1% international; 4% transferred in; 68% live on campus. *Retention:* 78% of full-time freshmen returned.

Freshmen *Admission:* 2,581 applied, 1,687 admitted, 483 enrolled. *Average high school GPA:* 3.6. *Test scores:* SAT critical reading scores over 500: 90%; SAT math scores over 500: 92%; SAT writing scores over 500: 89%; ACT scores over 18: 100%; SAT critical reading scores over 600: 46%; SAT math scores over 600: 49%; SAT writing scores over 600: 49%; ACT scores over 24: 87%; SAT critical reading scores over 700: 5%; SAT math scores over 700: 7%; SAT writing scores over 700: 7%; ACT scores over 30: 7%.

Faculty *Total:* 266, 35% full-time. *Student/faculty ratio:* 14:1.

Academics *Calendar:* semesters. *Degrees:* bachelor's, master's, and post-master's certificates. *Special study options:* adult/continuing education programs, double majors, honors programs, independent study, internships, off-campus study, part-time degree program, services for LD students, student-designed majors, study abroad, summer session for credit. *ROTC:* Army (c). *Unusual degree programs:* 3-2 accounting.

Computers on Campus 230 computers/terminals are available on campus for general student use. Students can access the following: campus intranet, computer help desk, free student e-mail accounts, online (class) grades, online (class) registration, online (class) schedules. Campuswide network is available. 100% of college-owned or -operated housing units are wired for high-speed Internet access. Wireless service is available via entire campus.

Student Life *Housing options:* coed. Campus housing is university owned and leased by the school. Freshman campus housing is guaranteed. *Activities and organizations:* drama/theater group, student-run newspaper, radio station, choral group, Student Government Association, Student Activities Board, Wagner College Theatre, Wagner College Choir, student newspaper, national fraternities, national sororities. *Campus security:* 24-hour emergency response devices and patrols, late-night transport/escort service, controlled dormitory access. *Student services:* health clinic, personal/psychological counseling.

Athletics Member NCAA. All Division I except football (Division I-AA). *Intercollegiate sports:* baseball M(s), basketball M(s)/W(s), cross-country running M(s)/W(s), golf M(s)/W(s), ice hockey M(c), lacrosse M(s)/W(s), soccer W(s), softball W(s), swimming and diving W(s), tennis M(s)/W(s), track and field M(s)/W(s), water polo W(s). *Intramural sports:* basketball M/W, bowling M/W, football M, rugby M, soccer M/W, softball M/W, table tennis M/W, tennis M/W, ultimate Frisbee M/W, volleyball M/W.

Standardized Tests *Required for some:* SAT or ACT (for admission), SAT Subject Tests (for admission).

Costs (2011–12) *Comprehensive fee:* $46,500 includes full-time tuition ($35,620), mandatory fees ($200), and room and board ($10,680). Full-time tuition and fees vary according to course load. Part-time tuition: $4453 per unit. Part-time tuition and fees vary according to course load. *Waivers:* employees or children of employees.

Financial Aid Of all full-time matriculated undergraduates who enrolled in 2009, 1,292 applied for aid, 1,099 were judged to have need, 258 had their need fully met. 687 Federal Work-Study jobs (averaging $1576). In 2009, 449 non-need-based awards were made. *Average percent of need met:* 73%. *Average financial aid package:* $22,354. *Average need-based loan:* $4688. *Average need-based gift aid:* $17,672. *Average non-need-based aid:* $11,880. *Average indebtedness upon graduation:* $36,988.

Applying *Options:* electronic application, early decision, deferred entrance. *Application fee:* $50. *Required:* essay or personal statement, high school transcript, minimum 2.5 GPA, 2 letters of recommendation. *Required for some:* interview. *Recommended:* minimum 3 GPA, interview. *Application deadlines:* 2/15 (freshmen), 2/15 (out-of-state freshmen), 5/1 (transfers). *Early decision*

deadline: 12/1. *Notification:* 3/1 (freshmen), 3/1 (out-of-state freshmen), 5/15 (transfers), 12/15 (early decision).

Freshman Application Contact Ms. Leigh-Ann Nowicki, Dean of Admissions, Wagner College, One Campus Road, Pape Admissions Building, Staten Island, NY 10301. *Phone:* 718-420-4242. *Toll-free phone:* 800-221-1010. *Fax:* 718-390-3105. *E-mail:* leigh-ann.nowicki@wagner.edu. *Web site:* http://www.wagner.edu/.

Webb Institute
Glen Cove, New York

- **Independent** 4-year, founded 1889
- **Suburban** 26-acre campus with easy access to New York City
- **Endowment** $40.3 million
- **Coed**
- **Most difficult** entrance level

Faculty *Student/faculty ratio:* 7:1.

Academics *Calendar:* semesters. *Degree:* bachelor's.

Student Life *Campus security:* 24-hour emergency response devices and patrols, controlled dormitory access.

Standardized Tests *Required:* SAT (for admission), SAT Subject Tests (for admission).

Costs (2010–11) *Comprehensive fee:* includes room and board ($12,000). all students are awarded full tuition scholarships.

Financial Aid *Of all full-time matriculated undergraduates who enrolled in 2009,* 19 applied for aid, 19 were judged to have need, 19 had their need fully met. *Average percent of need met:* 53. *Average financial aid package:* $5200. *Average need-based loan:* $5200. *Average need-based gift aid:* $2710. *Average indebtedness upon graduation:* $8545.

Applying *Options:* early decision. *Application fee:* $25. *Required:* high school transcript, minimum 3.5 GPA, 2 letters of recommendation, interview, proof of U.S. citizenship or permanent residency status.

Freshman Application Contact Webb Institute, Crescent Beach Road, Glen Cove, NY 11542-1398. *Phone:* 516-671-2213. *Fax:* 516-674-9838. *E-mail:* admissions@webb-institute.edu. *Web site:* http://www.webb-institute.edu/.

See page 1766 for the College Close-Up.

Wells College
Aurora, New York

- **Independent** 4-year, founded 1868
- **Rural** 365-acre campus with easy access to Syracuse
- **Endowment** $27.9 million
- **Coed, primarily women** 570 undergraduate students, 98% full-time, 71% women, 29% men
- **Moderately difficult** entrance level, 71% of applicants were admitted

Undergraduates 561 full-time, 9 part-time. Students come from 31 states and territories; 8 other countries; 27% are from out of state; 7% Black or African American, non-Hispanic/Latino; 6% Hispanic/Latino; 2% Asian, non-Hispanic/Latino; 0.5% American Indian or Alaska Native, non-Hispanic/Latino; 2% Two or more races, non-Hispanic/Latino; 14% Race/ethnicity unknown; 2% international; 6% transferred in; 84% live on campus. *Retention:* 72% of full-time freshmen returned.

Freshmen *Admission:* 1,961 applied, 1,385 admitted, 166 enrolled. *Average high school GPA:* 3.5. *Test scores:* SAT critical reading scores over 500: 71%; SAT math scores over 500: 55%; SAT writing scores over 500: 66%; ACT scores over 18: 91%; SAT critical reading scores over 600: 24%; SAT math scores over 600: 15%; SAT writing scores over 600: 20%; ACT scores over 24: 46%; SAT critical reading scores over 700: 3%; SAT math scores over 700: 2%; SAT writing scores over 700: 2%; ACT scores over 30: 4%.

Faculty *Total:* 74, 61% full-time, 81% with terminal degrees. *Student/faculty ratio:* 10:1.

Academics *Calendar:* semesters. *Degree:* bachelor's. *Special study options:* accelerated degree program, adult/continuing education programs, advanced placement credit, double majors, English as a second language, independent study, internships, off-campus study, part-time degree program, services for LD students, student-designed majors, study abroad. *ROTC:* Army (c), Air Force (c). *Unusual degree programs:* 3-2 engineering with Columbia University, Clarkson University, and Cornell University; community health with University of Rochester, education with University of Rochester.

Computers on Campus 96 computers/terminals and 1,224 ports are available on campus for general student use. Students can access the following: campus intranet, computer help desk, free student e-mail accounts, online (class) grades, online (class) registration, online (class) schedules. Campuswide network is available. 100% of college-owned or -operated housing units are wired for high-speed Internet access. Wireless service is available via classrooms, dorm rooms, learning centers, libraries, student centers.

Student Life *Housing:* on-campus residence required through senior year. *Options:* coed, women-only. Campus housing is university owned. Freshman campus housing is guaranteed. *Activities and organizations:* drama/theater group, student-run newspaper, choral group, Programming Board, POWER, SAGA, choral groups, SIFE. *Campus security:* 24-hour emergency response devices and patrols, late-night transport/escort service, controlled dormitory access. *Student services:* health clinic, personal/psychological counseling, women's center.

Athletics Member NCAA. All Division III. *Intercollegiate sports:* basketball M/W, cross-country running M/W, field hockey W, golf M/W, lacrosse M/W, soccer M/W, softball W, swimming and diving M/W, tennis W. *Intramural sports:* basketball M/W, field hockey W, football W, golf M/W, sailing M/W, skiing (cross-country) M/W, skiing (downhill) M/W, soccer M/W, swimming and diving M/W, tennis W, ultimate Frisbee M/W, volleyball W.

Standardized Tests *Required:* SAT or ACT (for admission).

Costs (2011–12) *Comprehensive fee:* $43,180 includes full-time tuition ($30,680), mandatory fees ($1500), and room and board ($11,000). *Payment plan:* installment. *Waivers:* senior citizens and employees or children of employees.

Financial Aid Of all full-time matriculated undergraduates who enrolled in 2009, 493 applied for aid, 471 were judged to have need, 69 had their need fully met. 90 Federal Work-Study jobs (averaging $1100). 355 state and other part-time jobs (averaging $1100). In 2009, 55 non-need-based awards were made. *Average percent of need met:* 78%. *Average financial aid package:* $25,360. *Average need-based loan:* $4660. *Average need-based gift aid:* $20,230. *Average non-need-based aid:* $10,655. *Average indebtedness upon graduation:* $26,207.

Applying *Options:* electronic application, early admission, early decision, early action, deferred entrance. *Application fee:* $40. *Required:* essay or personal statement, high school transcript, 2 letters of recommendation. *Recommended:* interview. *Application deadlines:* 3/1 (freshmen), rolling (transfers), 12/15 (early action). *Early decision deadline:* 12/15. *Notification:* 4/1 (freshmen), continuous (transfers), 1/15 (early decision), 2/1 (early action).

Freshman Application Contact Ms. Susan Raith Sloan, Director of Admission, Wells College, 170 Main Street, Aurora, NY 13026. *Phone:* 315-364-3264. *Toll-free phone:* 800-952-9355. *Fax:* 315-364-3227. *E-mail:* admissions@wells.edu. *Web site:* http://www.wells.edu/.

See page 1768 for the College Close-Up.

Yeshiva and Kolel Bais Medrash Elyon

Monsey, New York

Admissions Office Contact Yeshiva and Kolel Bais Medrash Elyon, 73 Main Street, Monsey, NY 10952.

Yeshiva and Kollel Harbotzas Torah

Brooklyn, New York

Admissions Office Contact Yeshiva and Kollel Harbotzas Torah, 1049 East 15th Street, Brooklyn, NY 11230.

Yeshiva Derech Chaim

Brooklyn, New York

Director of Admissions Administrator, Yeshiva Derech Chaim, 1573 39th Street, Brooklyn, NY 11218. *Phone:* 718-438-5476.

Yeshiva D'Monsey Rabbinical College

Monsey, New York

Admissions Office Contact Yeshiva D'Monsey Rabbinical College, 2 Roman Boulevard, Monsey, NY 10952.

Yeshiva Gedolah Imrei Yosef D'Spinka

Brooklyn, New York

Admissions Office Contact Yeshiva Gedolah Imrei Yosef D'Spinka, 1466 56th Street, Brooklyn, NY 11219.

WEBB INSTITUTE

For more information, contact:

William G. Murray, Director of Enrollment Management
Office of Admissions
298 Crescent Beach Road
Glen Cove, New York 11542
E-mail: admissions@webb-institute.edu

Web site: www.webb-institute.edu

Yeshiva Karlin Stolin Rabbinical Institute
Brooklyn, New York

Director of Admissions Director of Admissions, Yeshiva Karlin Stolin Rabbinical Institute, 1818 Fifty-fourth Street, Brooklyn, NY 11204. *Phone:* 718-232-7800 Ext. 26.

Yeshiva of Nitra Rabbinical College
Mount Kisco, New York

Director of Admissions Administrator, Yeshiva of Nitra Rabbinical College, Pines Bridge Road, Mount Kisco, NY 10549. *Phone:* 718-384-5460. *Fax:* 718-387-9400.

Yeshiva of the Telshe Alumni
Riverdale, New York

Admissions Office Contact Yeshiva of the Telshe Alumni, 4904 Independence Avenue, Riverdale, NY 10471.

Yeshiva Shaarei Torah of Rockland
Suffern, New York

Admissions Office Contact Yeshiva Shaarei Torah of Rockland, 91 West Carlton Road, Suffern, NY 10901.

Yeshiva Shaar Hatorah Talmudic Research Institute
Kew Gardens, New York

Director of Admissions Assistant Dean, Yeshiva Shaar Hatorah Talmudic Research Institute, 117-06 84th Avenue, Kew Gardens, NY 11418-1469. *Phone:* 718-846-1940.

Yeshivas Novominsk
Brooklyn, New York

Admissions Office Contact Yeshivas Novominsk, 1569 47th Street, Brooklyn, NY 11219.

Yeshivath Viznitz
Monsey, New York

Director of Admissions Registrar, Yeshivath Viznitz, 25 Phyllis Terrace, Monsey, NY 10952. *Phone:* 914-356-1010.

Yeshivath Zichron Moshe
South Fallsburg, New York

Director of Admissions Rabbi Abba Gorelick, Dean, Yeshivath Zichron Moshe, Laurel Park Road, South Fallsburg, NY 12779. *Phone:* 914-434-5240.

Yeshivat Mikdash Melech
Brooklyn, New York

Director of Admissions Rabbi S. Beyda, Director of Admissions, Yeshivat Mikdash Melech, 1326 Ocean Parkway, Brooklyn, NY 11230-5601. *Phone:* 718-339-1090. *E-mail:* mikdashmelech@verizon.net. *Web site:* http://mikdashmelech.com/.

Yeshiva University
New York, New York

- **Independent** university, founded 1886
- **Urban** campus
- **Coed**
- **Moderately difficult** entrance level

Faculty *Student/faculty ratio:* 7:1.
Academics *Calendar:* semesters. *Degrees:* associate, bachelor's, master's, doctoral-professional, doctoral-research/scholarship, post-master's, and post-bachelor's certificates (Yeshiva College and Stern College for Women are coordinate undergraduate colleges of arts and sciences for men and women, respectively. Sy Syms School of Business offers programs at both campuses).

Student Life *Campus security:* 24-hour emergency response devices and patrols, late-night transport/escort service.
Athletics Member NCAA. All Division III.
Standardized Tests *Required:* SAT or ACT (for admission).
Costs (2010–11) *Comprehensive fee:* $42,474 includes full-time tuition ($31,594), mandatory fees ($500), and room and board ($10,380). Full-time tuition and fees vary according to student level. Part-time tuition: $1075 per credit. *College room only:* $7510.
Financial Aid *Of all full-time matriculated undergraduates who enrolled in 2001,* 1,606 applied for aid, 1,228 were judged to have need, 168 had their need fully met. *In 2001,* 183 non-need-based awards were made. *Average percent of need met:* 73. *Average financial aid package:* $14,088. *Average need-based loan:* $4757. *Average need-based gift aid:* $11,682. *Average non-need-based aid:* $4712. *Average indebtedness upon graduation:* $16,156.
Applying *Options:* early admission, deferred entrance. *Application fee:* $65. *Required:* essay or personal statement, high school transcript, 2 letters of recommendation, interview.
Freshman Application Contact Yeshiva University, 500 West 185th Street, New York, NY 10033-3201. *Phone:* 212-960-5277. *Web site:* http://www.yu.edu/.

York College of the City University of New York
Jamaica, New York

- **State and locally supported** comprehensive, founded 1967, part of City University of New York System
- **Urban** 50-acre campus with easy access to New York City
- **Coed** 7,784 undergraduate students, 63% full-time, 65% women, 35% men
- **Moderately difficult** entrance level

Undergraduates 4,885 full-time, 2,899 part-time. Students come from 7 states and territories; 120 other countries; 0.3% are from out of state; 27% Black or African American, non-Hispanic/Latino; 10% Hispanic/Latino; 7% Asian, non-Hispanic/Latino; 0.2% American Indian or Alaska Native, non-Hispanic/Latino; 54% Race/ethnicity unknown; 8% transferred in. *Retention:* 74% of full-time freshmen returned.
Freshmen *Admission:* 1,103 enrolled. *Average high school GPA:* 81.9. *Test scores:* SAT critical reading scores over 500: 16%; SAT math scores over 500: 27%; SAT critical reading scores over 600: 2%; SAT math scores over 600: 4%.
Faculty *Total:* 548, 43% full-time. *Student/faculty ratio:* 17:1.
Academics *Calendar:* semesters. *Degrees:* bachelor's and master's. *Special study options:* adult/continuing education programs, advanced placement credit, cooperative education, double majors, English as a second language, honors programs, independent study, internships, off-campus study, part-time degree program, services for LD students, summer session for credit. *ROTC:* Army (c), Air Force (c). *Unusual degree programs:* 3-2 occupational therapy.
Computers on Campus 650 computers/terminals and 844 ports are available on campus for general student use. Students can access the following: computer help desk, free student e-mail accounts, online (class) registration, online (class) schedules. Campuswide network is available. Wireless service is available via entire campus.
Student Life *Housing:* college housing not available. *Activities and organizations:* drama/theater group, student-run newspaper, television station, choral group, Haitian Students Association, Caribbean Students Association, Haitian Cultural Association, Latin Caucus, Muslim Student Association. *Campus security:* 24-hour emergency response devices and patrols, late-night transport/escort service. *Student services:* health clinic, personal/psychological counseling, women's center.
Athletics Member NCAA. All Division III. *Intercollegiate sports:* baseball M/W, basketball M/W, cross-country running M/W, soccer M, softball W, swimming and diving M/W, tennis M, track and field M/W, volleyball M/W. *Intramural sports:* basketball M/W, cross-country running M/W, soccer M, softball W, swimming and diving M/W, table tennis M/W, tennis M, track and field M/W, volleyball M/W.
Standardized Tests *Required:* SAT or ACT (for admission).
Costs (2011–12) *Tuition:* state resident $4830 full-time, $205 per credit part-time; nonresident $10,440 full-time, $435 per credit part-time. No tuition increase for student's term of enrollment. *Required fees:* $312 full-time. *Payment plan:* installment. *Waivers:* senior citizens and employees or children of employees.
Financial Aid Of all full-time matriculated undergraduates who enrolled in 2008, 3,376 applied for aid, 3,108 were judged to have need, 300 had their need fully met. 1,022 Federal Work-Study jobs (averaging $1517). In 2008, 13 non-need-based awards were made. *Average percent of need met:* 24%. *Average financial aid package:* $3795. *Average need-based loan:* $2078. *Average need-based gift aid:* $1608. *Average non-need-based aid:* $635. *Average indebtedness upon graduation:* $9351.

Applying *Options:* electronic application, early admission, deferred entrance. *Application fee:* $65. *Required:* high school transcript, minimum 2.5 GPA. *Required for some:* minimum 2.8 GPA. *Recommended:* minimum 3 GPA. *Application deadlines:* rolling (freshmen), rolling (out-of-state freshmen), rolling (transfers). *Notification:* continuous (freshmen), continuous (out-of-state freshmen), continuous (transfers).
Freshman Application Contact Ms. Diane Warmsley, Director of Admissions, York College of the City University of New York, 94-20 Guy R. Brewer Boulevard, Jamaica, NY 11451. *Phone:* 718-262-2188. *Fax:* 718-262-2601. *E-mail:* warmsley@york.cuny.edu. *Web site:* http://www.york.cuny.edu/.

NORTH CAROLINA

Apex School of Theology
Durham, North Carolina

- **Independent interdenominational** comprehensive, founded 1995
- **Suburban** campus
- **Coed** 187 undergraduate students, 89% full-time, 55% women, 45% men

Undergraduates 166 full-time, 21 part-time. Students come from 1 other state. *Retention:* 100% of full-time freshmen returned.
Freshmen *Admission:* 275 applied.
Faculty *Total:* 15, 20% full-time, 47% with terminal degrees.
Academics *Calendar:* semesters. *Degrees:* associate, bachelor's, master's, and doctoral-research/scholarship.
Student Life *Housing:* college housing not available. *Activities and organizations:* student-run newspaper, choral group.
Costs (2010–11) *Tuition:* $4800 full-time, $192 per credit hour part-time. No tuition increase for student's term of enrollment. *Payment plan:* installment.
Applying *Options:* electronic application. *Required:* essay or personal statement, high school transcript.
Freshman Application Contact Dr. Henry D. Wells Jr., Registrar, Apex School of Theology, 2945 South Miami Boulevard, Suite 114, Durham, NC 27703. *Phone:* 919-572-1625. *Fax:* 919-572-1762. *E-mail:* registrar@apexsot.edu. *Web site:* http://www.apexsot.edu/.

Appalachian State University
Boone, North Carolina

- **State-supported** comprehensive, founded 1899, part of University of North Carolina System
- **Small-town** 411-acre campus
- **Endowment** $56.1 million
- **Coed** 15,137 undergraduate students, 94% full-time, 52% women, 48% men
- **Moderately difficult** entrance level, 68% of applicants were admitted

Undergraduates 14,297 full-time, 840 part-time. Students come from 46 states and territories; 54 other countries; 8% are from out of state; 3% Black or African American, non-Hispanic/Latino; 3% Hispanic/Latino; 1% Asian, non-Hispanic/Latino; 0.4% American Indian or Alaska Native, non-Hispanic/Latino; 1% Two or more races, non-Hispanic/Latino; 3% Race/ethnicity unknown; 0.5% international; 7% transferred in; 34% live on campus. *Retention:* 87% of full-time freshmen returned.
Freshmen *Admission:* 12,434 applied, 8,418 admitted, 2,829 enrolled. *Average high school GPA:* 3.92. *Test scores:* SAT critical reading scores over 500: 83%; SAT math scores over 500: 90%; SAT writing scores over 500: 74%; ACT scores over 18: 98%; SAT critical reading scores over 600: 32%; SAT math scores over 600: 37%; SAT writing scores over 600: 23%; ACT scores over 24: 56%; SAT critical reading scores over 700: 4%; SAT math scores over 700: 3%; SAT writing scores over 700: 2%; ACT scores over 30: 7%.
Faculty *Total:* 1,216, 71% full-time, 94% with terminal degrees. *Student/faculty ratio:* 16:1.
Academics *Calendar:* semesters. *Degrees:* bachelor's, master's, doctoral-research/scholarship, post-master's, and postbachelor's certificates. *Special study options:* academic remediation for entering students, adult/continuing education programs, advanced placement credit, distance learning, double majors, English as a second language, honors programs, independent study, internships, off-campus study, part-time degree program, services for LD students, student-designed majors, study abroad, summer session for credit. *ROTC:* Army (b). *Unusual degree programs:* 3-2 engineering with Auburn University, Clemson University.
Computers on Campus 1,800 computers/terminals are available on campus for general student use. Students can access the following: campus intranet, computer help desk, free student e-mail accounts, online (class) grades, online (class) registration, online (class) schedules. Campuswide network is available.

100% of college-owned or -operated housing units are wired for high-speed Internet access. Wireless service is available via entire campus.
Student Life *Housing:* on-campus residence required for freshman year. *Options:* coed, men-only, women-only. Campus housing is university owned. Freshman campus housing is guaranteed. *Activities and organizations:* drama/theater group, student-run newspaper, radio station, choral group, marching band, national fraternities, national sororities. *Campus security:* 24-hour emergency response devices and patrols, late-night transport/escort service, controlled dormitory access. *Student services:* health clinic, personal/psychological counseling, women's center, legal services.
Athletics Member NCAA, NAIA. All NCAA Division I except football (Division I-AA). *Intercollegiate sports:* baseball M(s), basketball M(s)/W(s), cross-country running M(s)/W(s), field hockey W(s), golf M(s)/W(s), soccer M(s)/W(s), softball W(s), tennis M(s)/W(s), track and field M(s)/W(s), volleyball W(s), wrestling M(s). *Intramural sports:* badminton M/W, baseball M(c), basketball M/W, bowling M/W, cross-country running M/W, equestrian sports M(c)/W(c), fencing M(c)/W(c), football M/W, golf M/W, ice hockey M(c)/W(c), lacrosse M(c)/W(c), racquetball M/W, rugby M(c)/W(c), skiing (downhill) M(c)/W(c), soccer M/W, softball M/W, swimming and diving M(c)/W(c), table tennis M/W, tennis M/W, ultimate Frisbee M(c)/W(c), volleyball M/W.
Standardized Tests *Required:* SAT or ACT (for admission).
Costs (2011–12) *Tuition:* state resident $2961 full-time, $100 per semester hour part-time; nonresident $14,273 full-time, $482 per semester hour part-time. Part-time tuition and fees vary according to course load. *Required fees:* $2214 full-time, $12 per semester hour part-time. *Room and board:* $6600; room only: $3700. Room and board charges vary according to board plan and housing facility. *Payment plan:* installment. *Waivers:* employees or children of employees.
Financial Aid Of all full-time matriculated undergraduates who enrolled in 2009, 6,948 applied for aid, 6,834 were judged to have need, 2,735 had their need fully met. 289 Federal Work-Study jobs (averaging $1619). In 2009, 463 non-need-based awards were made. *Average percent of need met:* 79%. *Average financial aid package:* $9127. *Average need-based loan:* $4001. *Average need-based gift aid:* $6935. *Average non-need-based aid:* $2352. *Average indebtedness upon graduation:* $16,130.
Applying *Options:* electronic application, deferred entrance. *Application fee:* $50. *Required:* high school transcript. *Application deadline:* rolling (transfers). *Notification:* continuous (transfers).
Freshman Application Contact Mr. Lloyd Scott, Director of Admissions, Appalachian State University, ASU Box 32004, Boone, NC 28608. *Phone:* 828-262-2120. *Fax:* 828-262-3296. *E-mail:* admissions@appstate.edu. *Web site:* http://www.appstate.edu/.

The Art Institute of Charlotte
Charlotte, North Carolina

- **Proprietary** 4-year, founded 1973, part of Education Management Corporation
- **Suburban** campus
- **Coed**

Academics *Calendar:* quarters. *Degrees:* certificates, associate, and bachelor's.
Costs (2010–11) *Tuition:* Tuition cost varies by program. Prospective students should contact the school for current tuition costs. Other charges include a starting kit for all first-quarter students. Kits vary in price, depending on the program of study.
Freshman Application Contact The Art Institute of Charlotte, Three LakePointe Plaza, 2110 Water Ridge Parkway, Charlotte, NC 28217. *Phone:* 704-357-8020. *Toll-free phone:* 800-872-4417. *Web site:* http://www.artinstitutes.edu/charlotte/.

See page 1030 for the College Close-Up.

The Art Institute of Raleigh-Durham
Durham, North Carolina

- **Proprietary** 4-year, founded 2008, part of Education Management Corporation
- **Coed**

Academics *Degrees:* associate and bachelor's.
Costs (2010–11) *Tuition:* Tuition cost varies by program. Prospective students should contact the school for current tuition costs. Other charges include a starting kit for all first-quarter students. Kits vary in price, depending on the program of study.
Freshman Application Contact The Art Institute of Raleigh-Durham, 410 Blackwell Street, Suite 200, Durham, NC 27701. *Phone:* 919-317-3050. *Toll-free phone:* 888-245-9593. *Web site:* http://www.artinstitutes.edu/raleigh-durham.

See page 1062 for the College Close-Up.

Barton College

Wilson, North Carolina

- **Independent** comprehensive, founded 1902, affiliated with Christian Church (Disciples of Christ)
- **Small-town** 76-acre campus with easy access to Raleigh-Durham
- **Coed** 1,163 undergraduate students, 75% full-time, 72% women, 28% men
- **Minimally difficult** entrance level, 49% of applicants were admitted

Undergraduates 873 full-time, 290 part-time. Students come from 26 states and territories; 9 other countries; 14% are from out of state; 27% Black or African American, non-Hispanic/Latino; 2% Hispanic/Latino; 1% Asian, non-Hispanic/Latino; 0.3% Native Hawaiian or other Pacific Islander, non-Hispanic/Latino; 0.5% American Indian or Alaska Native, non-Hispanic/Latino; 3% Two or more races, non-Hispanic/Latino; 6% Race/ethnicity unknown; 1% international; 12% transferred in; 53% live on campus. *Retention:* 61% of full-time freshmen returned.

Freshmen *Admission:* 2,746 applied, 1,346 admitted, 232 enrolled. *Average high school GPA:* 3.02. *Test scores:* SAT critical reading scores over 500: 35%; SAT math scores over 500: 42%; ACT scores over 18: 72%; SAT critical reading scores over 600: 8%; SAT math scores over 600: 11%; ACT scores over 24: 13%; SAT critical reading scores over 700: 1%; SAT math scores over 700: 1%; ACT scores over 30: 2%.

Faculty *Total:* 119, 60% full-time, 45% with terminal degrees. *Student/faculty ratio:* 11:1.

Academics *Calendar:* 4-1-4. *Degrees:* bachelor's and master's. *Special study options:* academic remediation for entering students, adult/continuing education programs, advanced placement credit, cooperative education, double majors, English as a second language, honors programs, independent study, internships, part-time degree program, services for LD students, summer session for credit.

Computers on Campus 125 computers/terminals are available on campus for general student use. Students can access the following: campus intranet, computer help desk, free student e-mail accounts, student picture directory. Campuswide network is available. 100% of college-owned or -operated housing units are wired for high-speed Internet access. Wireless service is available via computer centers, computer labs, learning centers, libraries, student centers.

Student Life *Housing:* on-campus residence required through sophomore year. *Options:* coed, women-only. Campus housing is university owned. Freshman campus housing is guaranteed. *Activities and organizations:* drama/theater group, student-run newspaper, television station, choral group, Barton College Association of Nurses, Students in Free Enterprise (SIFE), Stage and Script, Campus Activities Board, College Habitat for Humanity, national fraternities, national sororities. *Campus security:* 24-hour emergency response devices, late-night transport/escort service, controlled dormitory access, city police substation on campus. *Student services:* health clinic, personal/psychological counseling.

Athletics Member NCAA. All Division II. *Intercollegiate sports:* baseball M(s), basketball M(s)/W(s), cross-country running M(s)/W(s), golf M(s)/W(s), soccer M(s)/W(s), softball W(s), tennis M(s)/W(s), track and field M(s)/W(s), volleyball M(s)/W(s). *Intramural sports:* archery M/W, badminton M/W, baseball M/W, basketball M/W, cheerleading M/W, football M/W, golf M/W, soccer M/W, softball M/W, swimming and diving M/W, table tennis M/W, tennis M/W, volleyball M/W, weight lifting M/W.

Standardized Tests *Required:* SAT or ACT (for admission).

Costs (2010–11) *Comprehensive fee:* $29,100 includes full-time tuition ($20,150), mandatory fees ($1634), and room and board ($7316). Full-time tuition and fees vary according to class time, course load, and program. Part-time tuition: $850 per credit hour. Part-time tuition and fees vary according to class time, course load, and program. *College room only:* $3344. Room and board charges vary according to housing facility. *Payment plan:* installment. *Waivers:* children of alumni, adult students, senior citizens, and employees or children of employees.

Financial Aid Of all full-time matriculated undergraduates who enrolled in 2009, 791 applied for aid, 740 were judged to have need, 74 had their need fully met. In 2009, 116 non-need-based awards were made. *Average percent of need met:* 67%. *Average financial aid package:* $19,289. *Average need-based loan:* $5318. *Average need-based gift aid:* $6134. *Average non-need-based aid:* $4837. *Average indebtedness upon graduation:* $28,343.

Applying *Options:* electronic application, deferred entrance. *Application fee:* $25. *Required:* high school transcript. *Recommended:* minimum 2.3 GPA, interview. *Application deadlines:* rolling (freshmen), rolling (transfers). *Notification:* continuous (freshmen), continuous (transfers).

Freshman Application Contact Barton College, PO Box 5000, Wilson, NC 27893-7000. *Phone:* 800-345-4973. *Toll-free phone:* 800-345-4973. *Web site:* http://www.barton.edu/.

See page 1108 for the College Close-Up.

Belmont Abbey College

Belmont, North Carolina

- **Independent Roman Catholic** 4-year, founded 1876
- **Small-town** 650-acre campus with easy access to Charlotte
- **Endowment** $5.8 million
- **Coed** 1,734 undergraduate students, 93% full-time, 60% women, 40% men
- **Moderately difficult** entrance level, 72% of applicants were admitted

Undergraduates 1,613 full-time, 121 part-time. Students come from 33 states and territories; 14 other countries; 28% are from out of state; 28% Black or African American, non-Hispanic/Latino; 4% Hispanic/Latino; 1% Asian, non-Hispanic/Latino; 0.3% Native Hawaiian or other Pacific Islander, non-Hispanic/Latino; 0.2% American Indian or Alaska Native, non-Hispanic/Latino; 23% Race/ethnicity unknown; 3% international; 11% transferred in; 48% live on campus. *Retention:* 69% of full-time freshmen returned.

Freshmen *Admission:* 1,744 applied, 1,247 admitted, 315 enrolled. *Average high school GPA:* 3.08. *Test scores:* SAT critical reading scores over 500: 50%; SAT math scores over 500: 50%; SAT critical reading scores over 600: 13%; SAT math scores over 600: 11%; SAT critical reading scores over 700: 4%; SAT math scores over 700: 1%.

Faculty *Total:* 154, 48% full-time. *Student/faculty ratio:* 17:1.

Academics *Calendar:* semesters. *Degree:* bachelor's. *Special study options:* accelerated degree program, adult/continuing education programs, advanced placement credit, cooperative education, double majors, external degree program, freshman honors college, honors programs, independent study, internships, off-campus study, part-time degree program, services for LD students, study abroad, summer session for credit. *ROTC:* Army (c), Air Force (c).

Computers on Campus 125 computers/terminals are available on campus for general student use. Students can access the following: computer help desk, free student e-mail accounts, online (class) grades, online (class) registration, online (class) schedules. Campuswide network is available. 100% of college-owned or -operated housing units are wired for high-speed Internet access. Wireless service is available via classrooms, computer labs, libraries, student centers.

Student Life *Housing:* on-campus residence required through senior year. *Options:* coed, men-only, women-only. Campus housing is university owned and leased by the school. Freshman campus housing is guaranteed. *Activities and organizations:* drama/theater group, student-run newspaper, radio station, choral group, Abbey Ambassadors, Abbey Players, The Crusader, Greek Life (fraternities and sororities), national fraternities, national sororities. *Campus security:* 24-hour emergency response devices and patrols, late-night transport/escort service. *Student services:* health clinic, personal/psychological counseling.

Athletics Member NCAA. All Division II. *Intercollegiate sports:* baseball M(s), basketball M(s)/W(s), cheerleading M/W, cross-country running M(s)/W(s), golf M(s)/W(s), lacrosse M(s)/W(s), soccer M(s)/W(s), softball W(s), tennis M(s)/W(s), track and field M/W, volleyball W, wrestling M. *Intramural sports:* badminton M/W, basketball M/W, crew M/W, cross-country running M/W, football M/W, rugby M(c), soccer M/W, softball M/W, table tennis M/W, tennis M/W, ultimate Frisbee M/W, volleyball M/W, weight lifting M, wrestling M.

Standardized Tests *Required for some:* SAT or ACT (for admission).

Costs (2010–11) *One-time required fee:* $400. *Comprehensive fee:* $34,856 includes full-time tuition ($24,584) and room and board ($10,272). Full-time tuition and fees vary according to class time, course load, location, program, and reciprocity agreements. Part-time tuition: $819 per credit hour. Part-time tuition and fees vary according to class time, course load, location, and reciprocity agreements. *Required fees:* $45 per credit hour part-time. *College room only:* $6006. Room and board charges vary according to board plan, housing facility, and location. *Payment plans:* installment, deferred payment. *Waivers:* senior citizens and employees or children of employees.

Financial Aid Of all full-time matriculated undergraduates who enrolled in 2009, 1,546 applied for aid, 1,406 were judged to have need, 146 had their need fully met. 95 Federal Work-Study jobs (averaging $1200). In 2009, 288 non-need-based awards were made. *Average percent of need met:* 58%. *Average financial aid package:* $14,188. *Average need-based loan:* $4084. *Average need-based gift aid:* $10,312. *Average non-need-based aid:* $10,608. *Average indebtedness upon graduation:* $21,000.

Applying *Options:* electronic application, early decision, deferred entrance. *Application fee:* $35. *Required:* high school transcript, minimum 2.25 GPA. *Required for some:* essay or personal statement, 2 letters of recommendation. *Recommended:* interview. *Application deadlines:* 8/1 (freshmen), 8/15 (transfers). *Notification:* continuous (freshmen), continuous (transfers).

Freshman Application Contact Danielle Blanchard, Assistant Director of Admission, Belmont Abbey College, 100 Belmont-Mt. Holly Road, Belmont, NC 28012-1802. *Phone:* 704-461-6668. *Toll-free phone:* 888-BAC-0110. *E-mail:* danielleblanchard@bac.edu. *Web site:* http://www.belmontabbeycollege.edu/.

Bennett College for Women
Greensboro, North Carolina

- **Independent United Methodist** 4-year, founded 1873
- **Urban** 55-acre campus
- **Endowment** $8.8 million
- **Women only**
- **Moderately difficult** entrance level

Faculty *Student/faculty ratio:* 11:1.

Academics *Calendar:* semesters. *Degree:* bachelor's.

Student Life *Campus security:* 24-hour patrols, late-night transport/escort service, controlled dormitory access.

Standardized Tests *Required for some:* SAT or ACT (for admission). *Recommended:* SAT or ACT (for admission).

Costs (2010–11) *One-time required fee:* $125. *Comprehensive fee:* $22,850 includes full-time tuition ($13,788), mandatory fees ($2056), and room and board ($7006). Part-time tuition: $575 per credit hour. *Required fees:* $849 per term part-time. *College room only:* $3488. Room and board charges vary according to housing facility.

Financial Aid *Of all full-time matriculated undergraduates who enrolled in 2005,* 526 applied for aid, 492 were judged to have need, 24 had their need fully met. 82 Federal Work-Study jobs (averaging $1800). *In 2005,* 46 non-need-based awards were made. *Average percent of need met:* 45. *Average financial aid package:* $9393. *Average need-based loan:* $3043. *Average need-based gift aid:* $7196. *Average non-need-based aid:* $16,857. *Average indebtedness upon graduation:* $15,531. *Financial aid deadline:* 3/15.

Applying *Options:* electronic application, deferred entrance. *Application fee:* $30. *Required:* essay or personal statement, high school transcript, minimum 2 GPA, 2 letters of recommendation. *Required for some:* interview.

Freshman Application Contact Ms. Jocelyn Biggs, Director of Admissions, Bennett College for Women, 900 East Washington Street, Campus Box H, Greensboro, NC 27401. *Phone:* 336-517-2167. *E-mail:* jbiggs@bennett.edu. *Web site:* http://www.bennett.edu/.

Brevard College
Brevard, North Carolina

- **Independent United Methodist** 4-year, founded 1853
- **Small-town** 120-acre campus
- **Endowment** $19.6 million
- **Coed** 638 undergraduate students, 97% full-time, 42% women, 58% men
- **Minimally difficult** entrance level, 53% of applicants were admitted

Undergraduates 619 full-time, 19 part-time. Students come from 34 states and territories; 10 other countries; 48% are from out of state; 11% Black or African American, non-Hispanic/Latino; 0.9% Hispanic/Latino; 0.3% Asian, non-Hispanic/Latino; 1% American Indian or Alaska Native, non-Hispanic/Latino; 5% Race/ethnicity unknown; 3% international; 7% transferred in; 76% live on campus. *Retention:* 57% of full-time freshmen returned.

Freshmen *Admission:* 1,342 applied, 706 admitted, 200 enrolled. *Average high school GPA:* 3.04. *Test scores:* SAT critical reading scores over 500: 37%; SAT math scores over 500: 44%; ACT scores over 18: 85%; SAT critical reading scores over 600: 11%; SAT math scores over 600: 12%; ACT scores over 24: 14%; SAT critical reading scores over 700: 3%; SAT math scores over 700: 1%.

Faculty *Total:* 91, 60% full-time, 57% with terminal degrees. *Student/faculty ratio:* 11:1.

Academics *Calendar:* semesters. *Degree:* bachelor's. *Special study options:* academic remediation for entering students, advanced placement credit, double majors, honors programs, independent study, internships, part-time degree program, services for LD students, student-designed majors, study abroad.

Computers on Campus 100 computers/terminals are available on campus for general student use. Students can access the following: campus intranet, computer help desk, free student e-mail accounts, online (class) grades, online (class) schedules. Campuswide network is available. 100% of college-owned or -operated housing units are wired for high-speed Internet access. Wireless service is available via learning centers, libraries, student centers.

Student Life *Housing:* on-campus residence required through senior year. *Options:* coed, men-only, women-only, disabled students. Campus housing is university owned. Freshman campus housing is guaranteed. *Activities and organizations:* drama/theater group, student-run newspaper, choral group, fine arts organizations, Omicron Delta Kappa, Fellowship of Christian Athletes, BC Greens, Acting Club. *Campus security:* 24-hour emergency response devices and patrols. *Student services:* health clinic, personal/psychological counseling, women's center.

Athletics Member NCAA. All Division II. *Intercollegiate sports:* baseball M(s), basketball M(s)/W(s), cheerleading W(s), cross-country running M(s)/W(s), football M(s), golf M(s)/W(s), soccer M(s)/W(s), softball W(s), tennis M(s)/W(s), track and field M(s)/W(s), volleyball W(s). *Intramural sports:* badminton M/W, basketball M/W, bowling M/W, fencing M(c)/W(c), football M/W, soccer M/W, softball M/W, tennis M/W, track and field M/W, ultimate Frisbee M/W, volleyball M/W, weight lifting M/W.

Standardized Tests *Required:* SAT or ACT (for admission).

Costs (2010–11) *Comprehensive fee:* $30,025 includes full-time tuition ($22,100), mandatory fees ($75), and room and board ($7850). Full-time tuition and fees vary according to course load. Part-time tuition: $815 per credit hour. Part-time tuition and fees vary according to course load. *Room and board:* Room and board charges vary according to board plan and housing facility. *Payment plan:* installment. *Waivers:* senior citizens and employees or children of employees.

Financial Aid Of all full-time matriculated undergraduates who enrolled in 2008, 512 applied for aid, 460 were judged to have need, 128 had their need fully met. 51 Federal Work-Study jobs (averaging $897). In 2008, 127 non-need-based awards were made. *Average percent of need met:* 83%. *Average financial aid package:* $20,500. *Average need-based loan:* $4260. *Average need-based gift aid:* $14,200. *Average non-need-based aid:* $2600. *Average indebtedness upon graduation:* $20,770.

Applying *Options:* electronic application, deferred entrance. *Application fee:* $30. *Required:* essay or personal statement, high school transcript, minimum 2 GPA. *Required for some:* interview, students in music require auditions, music tests; students in art require portfolio. *Application deadlines:* rolling (freshmen), rolling (out-of-state freshmen), rolling (transfers). *Notification:* continuous (freshmen), continuous (out-of-state freshmen), continuous (transfers).

Freshman Application Contact Ms. Karen Atkins, Associate Director of Admissions, Brevard College, One Brevard College Drive, Brevard, NC 28712. *Phone:* 828-884-8378. *Toll-free phone:* 800-527-9090. *Fax:* 828-884-3790. *E-mail:* admissions@brevard.edu. *Web site:* http://www.brevard.edu/.

Cabarrus College of Health Sciences
Concord, North Carolina

Freshman Application Contact Mr. Mark Ellison, Director of Admissions, Cabarrus College of Health Sciences, 401 Medical Park Drive, Concord, NC 28025-2077. *Phone:* 704-403-1616. *Fax:* 704-403-2077. *E-mail:* mellison@cabarruscollege.edu. *Web site:* http://www.cabarruscollege.edu/.

Campbell University
Buies Creek, North Carolina

Freshman Application Contact Ms. Peggy Mason, Director of Admissions, Campbell University, PO Box 546, 450 Leslie Campbell Avenue, Buies Creek, NC 27506. *Phone:* 910-893-1290. *Toll-free phone:* 800-334-4111. *Fax:* 910-893-1288. *E-mail:* adm@mailcenter.campbell.edu. *Web site:* http://www.campbell.edu/.

Carolina Christian College
Winston-Salem, North Carolina

- **Independent nondenominational** 4-year, founded 1949
- **Small-town** 2-acre campus
- **Endowment** $250,000
- **Coed** 47 undergraduate students, 81% full-time, 62% women, 38% men
- **Noncompetitive** entrance level, 100% of applicants were admitted

Undergraduates 38 full-time, 9 part-time. Students come from 1 other state; 1% are from out of state; 94% Black or African American, non-Hispanic/Latino; 4% Hispanic/Latino; 11% transferred in. *Retention:* 90% of full-time freshmen returned.

Freshmen *Admission:* 15 applied, 15 admitted, 15 enrolled. *Average high school GPA:* 3.2.

Faculty *Total:* 9, 11% full-time, 33% with terminal degrees. *Student/faculty ratio:* 40:1.

Academics *Calendar:* semesters. *Degrees:* associate and bachelor's. *Special study options:* accelerated degree program, adult/continuing education programs, external degree program, part-time degree program.

Computers on Campus 8 computers/terminals and 8 ports are available on campus for general student use. Wireless service is available via entire campus.

Student Life *Housing:* college housing not available. *Campus security:* 24-hour emergency response devices. *Student services:* personal/psychological counseling.

Costs (2011–12) *Tuition:* $7000 full-time, $875 per course part-time. *Required fees:* $200 full-time. *Payment plan:* installment.

Applying *Options:* electronic application. *Application fee:* $50. *Required:* essay or personal statement, high school transcript, 2 letters of recommendation, interview. *Application deadlines:* rolling (freshmen), rolling (out-of-state freshmen), rolling (transfers). *Notification:* continuous (freshmen), continuous (out-of-state freshmen), continuous (transfers).

Freshman Application Contact Carolina Christian College, 4209 Indiana Avenue, PO Box 777, Winston-Salem, NC 27102-0777. *Phone:* 336-744-0900 Ext. 106. *Web site:* http://www.carolina.edu/.

Catawba College

Salisbury, North Carolina

- **Independent** comprehensive, founded 1851, affiliated with United Church of Christ
- **Small-town** 210-acre campus with easy access to Charlotte
- **Endowment** $28.8 million
- **Coed**
- **Moderately difficult** entrance level

Faculty *Student/faculty ratio:* 16:1.

Academics *Calendar:* semesters. *Degrees:* bachelor's and master's.

Student Life *Campus security:* 24-hour emergency response devices and patrols, late-night transport/escort service, controlled dormitory access.

Athletics Member NCAA. All Division II.

Standardized Tests *Required:* SAT or ACT (for admission).

Costs (2010–11) *Comprehensive fee:* $33,860 includes full-time tuition ($25,160) and room and board ($8700). Part-time tuition: $655 per credit hour.

Financial Aid *Of all full-time matriculated undergraduates who enrolled in 2009,* 1,074 applied for aid, 940 were judged to have need, 213 had their need fully met. 199 Federal Work-Study jobs (averaging $1757), 268 state and other part-time jobs (averaging $1703). *In 2009,* 112 non-need-based awards were made. *Average percent of need met:* 70. *Average financial aid package:* $18,422. *Average need-based loan:* $4026. *Average need-based gift aid:* $5861. *Average non-need-based aid:* $5405. *Average indebtedness upon graduation:* $25,506.

Applying *Options:* electronic application, early admission, deferred entrance. *Application fee:* $25. *Required:* essay or personal statement, high school transcript, minimum 2 GPA, 2 letters of recommendation. *Recommended:* interview.

Freshman Application Contact Catawba College, 2300 West Innes Street, Salisbury, NC 28144-2488. *Phone:* 704-637-4414. *Toll-free phone:* 800-CATAWBA. *Web site:* http://www.catawba.edu/.

Chowan University

Murfreesboro, North Carolina

- **Independent Baptist** 4-year, founded 1848
- **Rural** 300-acre campus with easy access to Norfolk
- **Coed**
- **Minimally difficult** entrance level

Faculty *Student/faculty ratio:* 16:1.

Academics *Calendar:* semesters. *Degrees:* associate and bachelor's.

Student Life *Campus security:* 24-hour emergency response devices and patrols, late-night transport/escort service, controlled dormitory access.

Athletics Member NCAA, NCCAA. All NCAA Division II.

Standardized Tests *Required:* SAT or ACT (for admission).

Costs (2010–11) *One-time required fee:* $145. *Comprehensive fee:* $27,160 includes full-time tuition ($19,750) and room and board ($7410). *College room only:* $3560. Room and board charges vary according to board plan. *Payment plans:* installment, deferred payment.

Financial Aid *Of all full-time matriculated undergraduates who enrolled in 2009,* 1,172 applied for aid, 1,117 were judged to have need, 135 had their need fully met. 287 Federal Work-Study jobs (averaging $1252). 165 state and other part-time jobs (averaging $1162). *In 2009,* 50 non-need-based awards were made. *Average percent of need met:* 76. *Average financial aid package:* $16,365. *Average need-based loan:* $3226. *Average need-based gift aid:* $13,396. *Average non-need-based aid:* $6201. *Average indebtedness upon graduation:* $29,180.

Applying *Options:* electronic application. *Application fee:* $20. *Required:* high school transcript. *Required for some:* essay or personal statement, interview. *Recommended:* minimum 2 GPA, 2 letters of recommendation.

Freshman Application Contact Chowan University, One University Place, Murfreesboro, NC 27855. *Phone:* 252-398-6298. *Toll-free phone:* 888-4-Chowan. *Web site:* http://www.chowan.edu/.

Davidson College

Davidson, North Carolina

- **Independent Presbyterian** 4-year, founded 1837
- **Small-town** 665-acre campus with easy access to Charlotte
- **Endowment** $427.8 million
- **Coed** 1,742 undergraduate students, 100% full-time, 50% women, 50% men
- **Very difficult** entrance level, 29% of applicants were admitted

Undergraduates 1,742 full-time. Students come from 46 states and territories; 36 other countries; 74% are from out of state; 6% Black or African American, non-Hispanic/Latino; 5% Hispanic/Latino; 5% Asian, non-Hispanic/Latino; 0.1% Native Hawaiian or other Pacific Islander, non-Hispanic/Latino; 0.5% American Indian or Alaska Native, non-Hispanic/Latino; 0.6% Two or more races, non-Hispanic/Latino; 6% Race/ethnicity unknown; 4% international; 0.3% transferred in; 91% live on campus. *Retention:* 96% of full-time freshmen returned.

Freshmen *Admission:* 4,088 applied, 1,205 admitted, 499 enrolled. *Average high school GPA:* 4. *Test scores:* SAT critical reading scores over 500: 97%; SAT math scores over 500: 98%; SAT writing scores over 500: 99%; ACT scores over 18: 101%; SAT critical reading scores over 600: 83%; SAT math scores over 600: 89%; SAT writing scores over 600: 84%; ACT scores over 24: 98%; SAT critical reading scores over 700: 34%; SAT math scores over 700: 36%; SAT writing scores over 700: 33%; ACT scores over 30: 60%.

Faculty *Total:* 174, 96% full-time, 94% with terminal degrees. *Student/faculty ratio:* 10:1.

Academics *Calendar:* semesters. *Degree:* bachelor's. *Special study options:* advanced placement credit, double majors, honors programs, independent study, off-campus study, services for LD students, student-designed majors, study abroad. *ROTC:* Army (b), Air Force (c). *Unusual degree programs:* 3-2 engineering with Columbia University, Washington University in St. Louis.

Computers on Campus 142 computers/terminals are available on campus for general student use. Students can access the following: campus intranet, computer help desk, free student e-mail accounts, online (class) grades, online (class) registration, online (class) schedules. Campuswide network is available. 100% of college-owned or -operated housing units are wired for high-speed Internet access. Wireless service is available via entire campus.

Student Life *Housing:* on-campus residence required through senior year. *Options:* coed, men-only, women-only, cooperative. Campus housing is university owned. Freshman campus housing is guaranteed. *Activities and organizations:* drama/theater group, student-run newspaper, radio station, choral group, Inter-Varsity Christian Fellowship, Dean Rusk Program Student Advisory Council, music organizations, Community Service Council, Student Government Association, national fraternities, national sororities. *Campus security:* 24-hour emergency response devices and patrols, late-night transport/escort service, controlled dormitory access. *Student services:* health clinic, personal/psychological counseling, women's center.

Athletics Member NCAA. All Division I except football (Division I-AA). *Intercollegiate sports:* baseball M(s), basketball M(s)/W(s), crew M(c)/W(c), cross-country running M(s)/W(s), fencing M(c)/W(c), field hockey W(s), golf M(s), lacrosse W(s), rugby M(c), sailing M(c)/W(c), soccer M(s)/W(s), swimming and diving M(s)/W(s), tennis M(s)/W(s), track and field M(s)/W(s), ultimate Frisbee M(c)/W(c), volleyball W(s), weight lifting M(c)/W(c), wrestling M(s). *Intramural sports:* basketball M/W, equestrian sports W(c), field hockey M(c)/W(c), football M/W, lacrosse M(c)/W(c), soccer M(c)/W(c), softball M/W, swimming and diving M(c)/W(c), tennis M(c)/W(c), volleyball M/W(c), water polo M(c).

Standardized Tests *Required:* SAT or ACT (for admission). *Recommended:* SAT and SAT Subject Tests or ACT (for admission).

Costs (2011–12) *Comprehensive fee:* $49,723 includes full-time tuition ($38,481), mandatory fees ($385), and room and board ($10,857). *College room only:* $5733. Room and board charges vary according to board plan. *Waivers:* employees or children of employees.

Financial Aid Of all full-time matriculated undergraduates who enrolled in 2008, 851 applied for aid, 739 were judged to have need, 739 had their need fully met. 244 Federal Work-Study jobs (averaging $1425). 116 state and other part-time jobs (averaging $1473). In 2008, 184 non-need-based awards were made. *Average percent of need met:* 100%. *Average financial aid package:* $27,634. *Average need-based loan:* $3121. *Average need-based gift aid:* $24,873. *Average non-need-based aid:* $18,503. *Average indebtedness upon graduation:* $23,233. *Financial aid deadline:* 2/15.

Applying *Options:* electronic application, early admission, early decision, deferred entrance. *Application fee:* $50. *Required:* essay or personal statement, high school transcript, 3 letters of recommendation. *Recommended:* interview. *Application deadlines:* 1/2 (freshmen), 3/15 (transfers). *Early decision deadline:* 11/15. *Notification:* 4/1 (freshmen), 5/15 (transfers), 12/15 (early decision).

Freshman Application Contact Mr. Christopher J. Gruber, Vice President and Dean of Admission and Financial Aid, Davidson College, Box 7156, Davidson, NC 28035-7156. *Phone:* 704-894-2230. *Toll-free phone:* 800-768-0380. *Fax:* 704-894-2016. *E-mail:* admission@davidson.edu. *Web site:* http://www.davidson.edu/.

DeVry University

Charlotte, North Carolina

- **Proprietary** comprehensive, part of DeVry University
- **Coed**
- **Minimally difficult** entrance level

Faculty *Student/faculty ratio:* 64:1.

Academics *Calendar:* semesters. *Degrees:* associate, bachelor's, and master's.

Costs (2010–11) *Tuition:* $14,766 full-time, $580 per credit hour part-time. Full-time tuition and fees vary according to course load. Part-time tuition and fees vary according to course load. *Required fees:* $60 full-time, $30 per term part-time. *Payment plans:* installment, deferred payment.

Financial Aid *Of all full-time matriculated undergraduates who enrolled in 2007,* 34 applied for aid, 33 were judged to have need, 1 had their need fully met. *In 2007,* 2 non-need-based awards were made. *Average percent of need met:* 41. *Average financial aid package:* $12,613. *Average need-based loan:* $9286. *Average need-based gift aid:* $8335. *Average non-need-based aid:* $7635.

Applying *Options:* electronic application, deferred entrance. *Application fee:* $50. *Required:* high school transcript, interview.

Freshman Application Contact DeVry University, 2015 Ayrsley Town Boulevard, Suite 109, Charlotte, NC 28273-4068. *Web site:* http://www.devry.edu/.

Duke University
Durham, North Carolina

- **Independent** university, founded 1838, affiliated with United Methodist Church
- **Suburban** 8500-acre campus
- **Endowment** $4.4 billion
- **Coed**
- **Most difficult** entrance level

Faculty *Student/faculty ratio:* 8:1.

Academics *Calendar:* semesters. *Degrees:* bachelor's, master's, doctoral-professional, doctoral-research/scholarship, post-master's, and postbachelor's certificates.

Student Life *Campus security:* 24-hour emergency response devices and patrols, late-night transport/escort service, controlled dormitory access.

Athletics Member NCAA. All Division I except football (Division I-A).

Standardized Tests *Required:* SAT and SAT Subject Tests or ACT (for admission).

Costs (2010–11) *Comprehensive fee:* $51,865 includes full-time tuition ($38,985), mandatory fees ($1258), and room and board ($11,622). Part-time tuition: $4872 per course. Part-time tuition and fees vary according to course load. *College room only:* $6502. Room and board charges vary according to board plan and housing facility. *Payment plans:* tuition prepayment, installment, deferred payment.

Financial Aid *Of all full-time matriculated undergraduates who enrolled in 2009,* 3,233 applied for aid, 2,998 were judged to have need, 2,998 had their need fully met. 1,650 Federal Work-Study jobs (averaging $1884). 581 state and other part-time jobs (averaging $1665). *In 2009,* 485 non-need-based awards were made. *Average percent of need met:* 100. *Average financial aid package:* $39,186. *Average need-based loan:* $2585. *Average need-based gift aid:* $35,578. *Average non-need-based aid:* $21,158. *Average indebtedness upon graduation:* $21,884. *Financial aid deadline:* 3/1.

Applying *Options:* electronic application, early admission, early decision, deferred entrance. *Application fee:* $75. *Required:* essay or personal statement, high school transcript. *Required for some:* audition tape for dance, drama, or music; slides of work for art. *Recommended:* interview.

Freshman Application Contact Mr. Christoph Guttentag, Director of Admissions, Duke University, Durham, NC 27708-0586. *Phone:* 919-684-3214. *E-mail:* askduke@admiss.duke.edu. *Web site:* http://www.duke.edu/.

See page 1262 for the College Close-Up.

East Carolina University
Greenville, North Carolina

- **State-supported** university, founded 1907, part of University of North Carolina System
- **Urban** 1377-acre campus
- **Coed**
- **Moderately difficult** entrance level

Faculty *Student/faculty ratio:* 18:1.

Academics *Calendar:* semesters. *Degrees:* certificates, bachelor's, master's, doctoral-professional, doctoral-research/scholarship, post-master's, and postbachelor's certificates.

Student Life *Campus security:* 24-hour emergency response devices and patrols, student patrols, late-night transport/escort service, controlled dormitory access, Operation ID, Staff and Faculty Eyes, Campus Community Watch program.

Athletics Member NCAA. All Division I except football (Division I-A).

Standardized Tests *Required:* SAT or ACT (for admission).

Costs (2010–11) *Tuition:* state resident $2881 full-time; nonresident $14,955 full-time. Part-time tuition and fees vary according to course load. *Required fees:* $1916 full-time. *Room and board:* $7700; room only: $4450. Room and board charges vary according to board plan and housing facility. *Payment plans:* installment, deferred payment.

Financial Aid *Of all full-time matriculated undergraduates who enrolled in 2009,* 12,940 applied for aid, 10,340 were judged to have need, 1,139 had their need fully met. 400 Federal Work-Study jobs (averaging $2800). 1,600 state and other part-time jobs (averaging $2000). *In 2009,* 468 non-need-based awards were made. *Average percent of need met:* 72. *Average financial aid package:* $9557. *Average need-based loan:* $4126. *Average need-based gift aid:* $6634. *Average non-need-based aid:* $1844. *Average indebtedness upon graduation:* $17,243.

Applying *Options:* electronic application, early admission, deferred entrance. *Application fee:* $60. *Required:* high school transcript, minimum 2 GPA.

Freshman Application Contact East Carolina University, Undergraduate Admission, Whichard Building 106, Greenville, NC 27858-4353. *Phone:* 252-328-6769. *Web site:* http://www.ecu.edu/.

ECPI College of Technology
Greensboro, North Carolina

Admissions Office Contact ECPI College of Technology, 7802 Airport Center Drive, Greensboro, NC 27409. *Toll-free phone:* 866-708-6170. *Web site:* http://www.ecpi.edu/.

ECPI College of Technology
Raleigh, North Carolina

Freshman Application Contact Ms. Susan Wells, Campus President, ECPI College of Technology, 4101 Doie Cope Road, Raleigh, NC 27613. *Phone:* 919-571-0057. *Toll-free phone:* 800-986-1200. *Fax:* 919-571-0780. *E-mail:* swells@ecpi.edu. *Web site:* http://www.ecpi.edu/.

Elizabeth City State University
Elizabeth City, North Carolina

- **State-supported** comprehensive, founded 1891, part of University of North Carolina System
- **Small-town** 125-acre campus with easy access to Norfolk
- **Coed** 3,240 undergraduate students, 90% full-time, 60% women, 40% men
- **Moderately difficult** entrance level, 71% of applicants were admitted

Undergraduates 2,910 full-time, 330 part-time. Students come from 5 other countries; 12% are from out of state; 6% transferred in; 53% live on campus. *Retention:* 74% of full-time freshmen returned.

Freshmen *Admission:* 2,367 applied, 1,681 admitted, 523 enrolled. *Average high school GPA:* 2.67. *Test scores:* SAT critical reading scores over 500: 11%; SAT math scores over 500: 12%; SAT writing scores over 500: 7%; ACT scores over 18: 25%; SAT critical reading scores over 600: 1%; SAT math scores over 600: 1%; SAT writing scores over 600: 1%.

Faculty *Total:* 241, 63% full-time, 54% with terminal degrees. *Student/faculty ratio:* 18:1.

Academics *Calendar:* semesters. *Degrees:* bachelor's and master's. *Special study options:* academic remediation for entering students, adult/continuing education programs, advanced placement credit, cooperative education, distance learning, double majors, honors programs, independent study, internships, off-campus study, part-time degree program, services for LD students, study abroad, summer session for credit. *ROTC:* Army (b).

Computers on Campus 1,035 computers/terminals and 1,200 ports are available on campus for general student use. Students can access the following: campus intranet, computer help desk, free student e-mail accounts, online (class) registration, online (class) schedules. Campuswide network is available. 100% of college-owned or -operated housing units are wired for high-speed Internet access. Wireless service is available via entire campus.

Student Life *Housing options:* coed, men-only, women-only. Campus housing is university owned and leased by the school. Freshman campus housing is guaranteed. *Activities and organizations:* drama/theater group, student-run newspaper, choral group, marching band, Vans (Vikings Assisting New Students), Student Activities Committee, Vike Nu' Fashion Troupe, Pep Squad, Essence of Praise, national fraternities, national sororities. *Campus security:* 24-hour emergency response devices and patrols. *Student services:* health clinic, personal/psychological counseling.

Athletics Member NCAA. All Division II. *Intercollegiate sports:* baseball M(s), basketball M(s)/W(s), bowling W(s), cheerleading W, cross-country running M/W, football M(s), golf M(s), softball W(s), tennis W(s), volleyball W(s).

Standardized Tests *Required:* SAT or ACT (for admission). *Recommended:* SAT (for admission).

Costs (2010–11) *Tuition:* state resident $2204 full-time; nonresident $11,841 full-time. *Room and board:* $5639; room only: $3267.

Applying *Options:* electronic application, deferred entrance. *Application fee:* $30. *Required:* high school transcript, minimum 2 GPA. *Application dead-*

lines: 5/8 (freshmen), 5/8 (transfers). *Notification:* continuous (freshmen), continuous (transfers).
Freshman Application Contact Elizabeth City State University, 1704 Weeksville Road, Elizabeth City, NC 27909-7806. *Toll-free phone:* 800-347-3278. *Web site:* http://www.ecsu.edu/.

Elon University
Elon, North Carolina

- **Independent** comprehensive, founded 1889, affiliated with United Church of Christ
- **Suburban** 580-acre campus with easy access to Raleigh
- **Endowment** $103.4 million
- **Coed** 5,032 undergraduate students, 97% full-time, 59% women, 41% men
- **Moderately difficult** entrance level, 49% of applicants were admitted

Undergraduates 4,893 full-time, 139 part-time. Students come from 48 states and territories; 49 other countries; 72% are from out of state; 6% Black or African American, non-Hispanic/Latino; 3% Hispanic/Latino; 1% Asian, non-Hispanic/Latino; 0.2% American Indian or Alaska Native, non-Hispanic/Latino; 1% Two or more races, non-Hispanic/Latino; 6% Race/ethnicity unknown; 2% international; 1% transferred in; 59% live on campus. *Retention:* 90% of full-time freshmen returned.
Freshmen *Admission:* 9,771 applied, 4,740 admitted, 1,362 enrolled. *Average high school GPA:* 3.94. *Test scores:* SAT critical reading scores over 500: 94%; SAT math scores over 500: 94%; SAT writing scores over 500: 94%; ACT scores over 18: 99%; SAT critical reading scores over 600: 57%; SAT math scores over 600: 60%; SAT writing scores over 600: 61%; ACT scores over 24: 83%; SAT critical reading scores over 700: 9%; SAT math scores over 700: 11%; SAT writing scores over 700: 13%; ACT scores over 30: 18%.
Faculty *Total:* 501, 71% full-time, 78% with terminal degrees. *Student/faculty ratio:* 13:1.
Academics *Calendar:* semesters 3-week winter term. *Degrees:* bachelor's, master's, and doctoral-professional. *Special study options:* accelerated degree program, advanced placement credit, double majors, English as a second language, honors programs, independent study, internships, off-campus study, part-time degree program, services for LD students, student-designed majors, study abroad, summer session for credit. *ROTC:* Army (b), Air Force (c). *Unusual degree programs:* 3-2 engineering with North Carolina State University, North Carolina Agricultural and Technical State University, Virginia Polytechnic Institute and State University, Washington University, Columbia University, University of South Carolina, Georgia Tech, Notre Dame.
Computers on Campus 1,200 computers/terminals and 12,000 ports are available on campus for general student use. Students can access the following: computer help desk, free student e-mail accounts, online (class) grades, online (class) registration, online (class) schedules. Campuswide network is available. 100% of college-owned or -operated housing units are wired for high-speed Internet access. Wireless service is available via entire campus.
Student Life *Housing:* on-campus residence required through sophomore year. *Options:* coed, men-only, women-only. Campus housing is university owned and leased by the school. Freshman campus housing is guaranteed. *Activities and organizations:* drama/theater group, student-run newspaper, radio and television station, choral group, marching band, Elon volunteers, student media, intramural athletics, religious life, Habitat for Humanity, national fraternities, national sororities. *Campus security:* 24-hour emergency response devices and patrols, late-night transport/escort service, controlled dormitory access. *Student services:* health clinic, personal/psychological counseling, women's center.
Athletics Member NCAA. All Division I except football (Division I-AA). *Intercollegiate sports:* baseball M(s), basketball M(s)/W(s), cheerleading M/W, cross-country running M(s)/W(s), equestrian sports M(c)/W(c), field hockey W(c), golf M(s)/W(s), lacrosse M(c)/W(c), rugby M(c)/W(c), skiing (downhill) M(c)/W(c), soccer M(s)/W(s), softball W(s), swimming and diving M(c)/W(c), tennis M(s)/W(s), track and field W(s), ultimate Frisbee M(c)/W(c), volleyball W(s). *Intramural sports:* basketball M/W, bowling M/W, football M/W, golf M/W, racquetball M/W, soccer M/W, softball M/W, table tennis M/W, tennis M/W, volleyball M/W.
Standardized Tests *Required:* SAT or ACT (for admission).
Costs (2011–12) *Comprehensive fee:* $36,971 includes full-time tuition ($27,534), mandatory fees ($347), and room and board ($9090). Part-time tuition and fees vary according to course load. *College room only:* $4440. Room and board charges vary according to board plan and housing facility. *Payment plan:* installment. *Waivers:* employees or children of employees.
Financial Aid Of all full-time matriculated undergraduates who enrolled in 2009, 2,392 applied for aid, 1,786 were judged to have need. 1,204 Federal Work-Study jobs (averaging $2344). In 2009, 993 non-need-based awards were made. *Average percent of need met:* 71%. *Average financial aid package:* $17,388. *Average need-based loan:* $5087. *Average need-based gift aid:* $10,846. *Average non-need-based aid:* $5565. *Average indebtedness upon graduation:* $27,163.

Applying *Options:* electronic application, early admission, early decision, early action, deferred entrance. *Application fee:* $50. *Required:* essay or personal statement, high school transcript, minimum 2.7 GPA. *Required for some:* interview. *Application deadlines:* 1/10 (freshmen), rolling (transfers), 11/10 (early action). *Early decision deadline:* 11/1. *Notification:* 3/15 (freshmen), continuous (transfers), 12/1 (early decision), 12/19 (early action).
Freshman Application Contact Ms. Melinda Wood, Associate Director of Admissions and Director of Applications, Elon University, 100 Campus Box, Elon, NC 27244. *Phone:* 336-278-3566. *Toll-free phone:* 800-334-8448. *Fax:* 336-278-7699. *E-mail:* admissions@elon.edu. *Web site:* http://www.elon.edu/.

Fayetteville State University
Fayetteville, North Carolina

- **State-supported** comprehensive, founded 1867, part of University of North Carolina System
- **Urban** 156-acre campus with easy access to Raleigh
- **Endowment** $12.1 million
- **Coed** 5,103 undergraduate students, 76% full-time, 67% women, 33% men
- **Minimally difficult** entrance level, 61% of applicants were admitted

Undergraduates 3,884 full-time, 1,219 part-time. Students come from 29 states and territories; 6 other countries; 4% are from out of state; 72% Black or African American, non-Hispanic/Latino; 4% Hispanic/Latino; 1% Asian, non-Hispanic/Latino; 0.1% Native Hawaiian or other Pacific Islander, non-Hispanic/Latino; 1% American Indian or Alaska Native, non-Hispanic/Latino; 0.3% Two or more races, non-Hispanic/Latino; 6% Race/ethnicity unknown; 0.3% international; 12% transferred in; 26% live on campus. *Retention:* 69% of full-time freshmen returned.
Freshmen *Admission:* 2,596 applied, 1,584 admitted, 547 enrolled. *Average high school GPA:* 2.88.
Faculty *Total:* 336, 83% full-time, 75% with terminal degrees. *Student/faculty ratio:* 16:1.
Academics *Calendar:* semesters. *Degrees:* bachelor's, master's, and doctoral-research/scholarship. *Special study options:* academic remediation for entering students, accelerated degree program, adult/continuing education programs, advanced placement credit, cooperative education, distance learning, double majors, honors programs, independent study, internships, part-time degree program, services for LD students, study abroad, summer session for credit. *ROTC:* Army (c), Air Force (b). *Unusual degree programs:* 3-2 engineering with North Carolina State University.
Computers on Campus 538 computers/terminals and 1,800 ports are available on campus for general student use. Students can access the following: campus intranet, computer help desk, free student e-mail accounts, online (class) grades, online (class) registration, online (class) schedules. Campuswide network is available. 100% of college-owned or -operated housing units are wired for high-speed Internet access. Wireless service is available via classrooms, computer centers, computer labs, learning centers, libraries, student centers.
Student Life *Housing options:* coed, men-only, women-only, disabled students. Campus housing is university owned. Freshman applicants given priority for college housing. *Activities and organizations:* drama/theater group, student-run newspaper, choral group, marching band, Student Government Association, Student Activities Council, Pan-Hellenic Council, Residence Hall Association, Illusions and Black Millennium Modeling Clubs, national fraternities, national sororities. *Campus security:* 24-hour emergency response devices and patrols, late-night transport/escort service, controlled dormitory access. *Student services:* health clinic, personal/psychological counseling.
Athletics Member NCAA. All Division II. *Intercollegiate sports:* basketball M(s), bowling W(s), cheerleading M/W, cross-country running M/W, football M(s)/W(s), golf M(s), softball W(s), tennis W(s), volleyball W(s). *Intramural sports:* basketball M/W, football M/W, soccer M/W, softball M/W, volleyball M/W.
Standardized Tests *Required:* SAT or ACT (for admission).
Costs (2010–11) *Tuition:* state resident $2129 full-time; nonresident $12,593 full-time. Full-time tuition and fees vary according to course level, course load, degree level, location, and program. Part-time tuition and fees vary according to course level, course load, degree level, location, and program. *Required fees:* $1627 full-time. *Room and board:* $5812; room only: $3071. Room and board charges vary according to board plan and housing facility. *Payment plan:* installment. *Waivers:* senior citizens and employees or children of employees.
Financial Aid Of all full-time matriculated undergraduates who enrolled in 2009, 3,901 applied for aid, 3,581 were judged to have need, 199 had their need fully met. *Average indebtedness upon graduation:* $20,185. *Financial aid deadline:* 3/1.
Applying *Options:* electronic application, early admission, early decision, early action, deferred entrance. *Application fee:* $35. *Required:* high school transcript, minimum 2 GPA. *Recommended:* essay or personal statement.

Guilford College
Greensboro, North Carolina

- **Independent** 4-year, founded 1837, affiliated with Society of Friends
- **Suburban** 340-acre campus with easy access to Piedmont Triad
- **Endowment** $59.3 million
- **Coed** 2,828 undergraduate students, 84% full-time, 61% women, 39% men
- **Moderately difficult** entrance level, 53% of applicants were admitted

Undergraduates 2,376 full-time, 452 part-time. Students come from 43 states and territories; 13 other countries; 31% are from out of state; 26% Black or African American, non-Hispanic/Latino; 4% Hispanic/Latino; 2% Asian, non-Hispanic/Latino; 0.4% American Indian or Alaska Native, non-Hispanic/Latino; 3% Two or more races, non-Hispanic/Latino; 0.8% Race/ethnicity unknown; 0.8% international; 2% transferred in; 70% live on campus. *Retention:* 77% of full-time freshmen returned.

Freshmen *Admission:* 4,245 applied, 2,254 admitted, 384 enrolled. *Average high school GPA:* 3.15. *Test scores:* SAT critical reading scores over 500: 64%; SAT math scores over 500: 68%; SAT writing scores over 500: 62%; ACT scores over 18: 93%; SAT critical reading scores over 600: 31%; SAT math scores over 600: 29%; SAT writing scores over 600: 24%; ACT scores over 24: 51%; SAT critical reading scores over 700: 8%; SAT math scores over 700: 4%; SAT writing scores over 700: 3%; ACT scores over 30: 12%.

Faculty *Total:* 220, 55% full-time, 66% with terminal degrees. *Student/faculty ratio:* 17:1.

Academics *Calendar:* semesters. *Degree:* certificates and bachelor's. *Special study options:* academic remediation for entering students, accelerated degree program, adult/continuing education programs, advanced placement credit, cooperative education, double majors, English as a second language, honors programs, independent study, internships, off-campus study, part-time degree program, services for LD students, student-designed majors, study abroad, summer session for credit. *ROTC:* Army (c), Navy (c), Air Force (c). *Unusual degree programs:* 3-2 environmental studies, physician assistant.

Computers on Campus 275 computers/terminals are available on campus for general student use. Students can access the following: computer help desk, free student e-mail accounts, online (class) grades, online (class) registration, online (class) schedules, network storage. Campuswide network is available. 100% of college-owned or -operated housing units are wired for high-speed Internet access. Wireless service is available via libraries, student centers.

Student Life *Housing:* on-campus residence required through junior year. *Options:* coed, men-only, women-only, cooperative, disabled students. Campus housing is university owned. Freshman campus housing is guaranteed. *Activities and organizations:* drama/theater group, student-run newspaper, radio station, choral group, student government, student radio station, student newspaper, Project Community, African-American Cultural Society. *Campus security:* 24-hour emergency response devices and patrols, student patrols, late-night transport/escort service, controlled dormitory access. *Student services:* health clinic, personal/psychological counseling, women's center.

Athletics Member NCAA. All Division III. *Intercollegiate sports:* baseball M, basketball M/W, cross-country running M/W, football M, golf M, lacrosse M/W, rugby M/W, soccer M/W, softball W, swimming and diving W, tennis M/W, volleyball W. *Intramural sports:* archery M(c)/W(c), badminton M(c)/W(c), basketball M(c), bowling M(c)/W(c), cheerleading W(c), football M(c), rugby M(c)/W(c), soccer M(c)/W(c), softball W(c), table tennis M(c)/W(c), tennis M(c)/W(c), ultimate Frisbee M(c)/W(c), volleyball M(c)/W(c), water polo M(c)/W(c).

Standardized Tests *Recommended:* SAT or ACT (for admission).

Costs (2010–11) *Comprehensive fee:* $36,750 includes full-time tuition ($28,470), mandatory fees ($330), and room and board ($7950). Part-time tuition: $885 per credit hour. Part-time tuition and fees vary according to course load. *Room and board:* Room and board charges vary according to board plan and housing facility. *Payment plan:* installment. *Waivers:* employees or children of employees.

Financial Aid Of all full-time matriculated undergraduates who enrolled in 2009, 1,994 applied for aid, 1,598 were judged to have need, 293 had their need fully met. 213 Federal Work-Study jobs (averaging $1993). 121 state and other part-time jobs (averaging $1588). In 2009, 139 non-need-based awards were made. *Average percent of need met:* 91%. *Average financial aid package:* $21,918. *Average need-based loan:* $5126. *Average need-based gift aid:* $7857. *Average non-need-based aid:* $7307. *Average indebtedness upon graduation:* $24,580.

Applying *Options:* electronic application, early admission, early action, deferred entrance. *Application fee:* $25. *Required:* essay or personal statement, high school transcript, minimum 2 GPA. *Recommended:* minimum 3 GPA, 2 letters of recommendation, interview. *Application deadlines:* 2/15 (freshmen), 4/1 (transfers), 1/15 (early action). *Notification:* 4/1 (freshmen), continuous until 5/1 (transfers), 2/15 (early action).

Freshman Application Contact Tania Johnson-Rachkoskie, Associate Director of Admissions, Guilford College, 5800 West Friendly Avenue,

Greensboro, NC 27410. *Phone:* 336-316-2100. *Toll-free phone:* 800-992-7759. *Fax:* 336-316-2954. *E-mail:* admission@guilford.edu. *Web site:* http://www.guilford.edu/.

See page 1320 for the College Close-Up.

Heritage Bible College
Dunn, North Carolina

- **Independent Pentecostal Free Will Baptist** 4-year, founded 1971
- **Small-town** 82-acre campus with easy access to Raleigh-Durham
- **Endowment** $53,446
- **Coed**
- **Minimally difficult** entrance level

Faculty *Student/faculty ratio:* 20:1.
Academics *Calendar:* semesters. *Degrees:* associate and bachelor's.
Student Life *Campus security:* controlled dormitory access.
Costs (2010–11) *Comprehensive fee:* $12,060 includes full-time tuition ($7950), mandatory fees ($660), and room and board ($3450). Part-time tuition: $265 per credit hour. *Required fees:* $30 per credit hour part-time. *College room only:* $2400. Room and board charges vary according to board plan and housing facility. *Payment plans:* installment, deferred payment.
Financial Aid *Of all full-time matriculated undergraduates who enrolled in 2006,* 114 applied for aid, 85 were judged to have need, 85 had their need fully met. 3 Federal Work-Study jobs (averaging $300). *In 2006,* 10 non-need-based awards were made. *Average percent of need met:* 90. *Average financial aid package:* $4250. *Average need-based loan:* $3500. *Average need-based gift aid:* $250. *Average non-need-based aid:* $300. *Average indebtedness upon graduation:* $14,554. *Financial aid deadline:* 7/1.
Applying *Application fee:* $25. *Required:* essay or personal statement, high school transcript, medical history required for all, immunization record required for some. *Required for some:* interview.
Freshman Application Contact Mrs. Traci Newton, Director of Recruitment and Marketing, Heritage Bible College, PO Box 1628, Dunn, NC 28335-1628. *Phone:* 910-892-3178 Ext. 239. *Toll-free phone:* 800-297-6351 Ext. 230. *Fax:* 910-891-1660. *E-mail:* tnewton@heritagebiblecollege.edu. *Web site:* http://www.heritagebiblecollege.edu/.

High Point University
High Point, North Carolina

- **Independent United Methodist** comprehensive, founded 1924
- **Suburban** 200-acre campus with easy access to Charlotte
- **Endowment** $30.6 million
- **Coed**
- **Moderately difficult** entrance level

Faculty *Student/faculty ratio:* 16:1.
Academics *Calendar:* semesters. *Degrees:* bachelor's, master's, and post-bachelor's certificates.
Student Life *Campus security:* 24-hour emergency response devices and patrols, student patrols, late-night transport/escort service, controlled dormitory access.
Athletics Member NCAA. All Division I.
Standardized Tests *Required:* SAT or ACT (for admission). *Recommended:* SAT Subject Tests (for admission).
Costs (2010–11) *Comprehensive fee:* $35,900. Full-time tuition and fees vary according to class time, course load, and reciprocity agreements. Part-time tuition: $700 per credit hour. Part-time tuition and fees vary according to class time, course load, and reciprocity agreements. *Room and board:* Room and board charges vary according to board plan, housing facility, and location.
Financial Aid *Of all full-time matriculated undergraduates who enrolled in 2009,* 2,919 applied for aid, 2,070 were judged to have need, 1,180 had their need fully met. 633 Federal Work-Study jobs (averaging $1463). *In 2009,* 651 non-need-based awards were made. *Average percent of need met:* 56. *Average financial aid package:* $10,995. *Average need-based loan:* $5082. *Average need-based gift aid:* $2884. *Average non-need-based aid:* $2117. *Average indebtedness upon graduation:* $9437.
Applying *Options:* electronic application, early decision, early action, deferred entrance. *Application fee:* $40. *Required:* high school transcript, minimum 2 GPA, 2 letters of recommendation. *Recommended:* essay or personal statement, minimum 3 GPA, interview.
Freshman Application Contact Ms. Beth McCarthy, Director of Admissions, High Point University, University Station, Montlieu Avenue, High Point, NC 27262-3598. *Phone:* 336-841-9148. *Toll-free phone:* 800-345-6993. *Fax:* 336-888-6382. *E-mail:* jmcilrat@highpoint.edu. *Web site:* http://www.highpoint.edu/.

See page 1326 for the College Close-Up.

ITT Technical Institute

Charlotte, North Carolina

- **Proprietary** 4-year, part of ITT Educational Services, Inc.
- **Coed**
- **Minimally difficult** entrance level

Academics *Calendar:* quarters. *Degrees:* associate and bachelor's.
Freshman Application Contact Director of Recruitment, ITT Technical Institute, 10926 David Taylor Drive, Suite 100, Charlotte, NC 28262. *Phone:* 704-548-2300. *Toll-free phone:* 877-243-7685. *Web site:* http://www.itt-tech.edu/.

ITT Technical Institute

Charlotte, North Carolina

- **Proprietary** primarily 2-year
- **Coed**
- **Minimally difficult** entrance level

Academics *Degrees:* associate and bachelor's.
Student Life *Housing:* college housing not available.
Freshman Application Contact Director of Recruitment, ITT Technical Institute, 4135 Southstream Boulevard, Suite 200, Charlotte, NC 28217. *Phone:* 704-423-3100. *Toll-free phone:* 800-488-0173. *Web site:* http://www.itt-tech.edu/.

ITT Technical Institute

High Point, North Carolina

- **Proprietary** primarily 2-year, founded 2007, part of ITT Educational Services, Inc.
- **Coed**
- **Minimally difficult** entrance level

Academics *Calendar:* quarters. *Degrees:* associate and bachelor's.
Student Life *Housing:* college housing not available.
Freshman Application Contact Director of Recruitment, ITT Technical Institute, 4050 Piedmont Parkway, Suite 110, High Point, NC 27265. *Phone:* 336-819-5900. *Toll-free phone:* 877-536-5231. *Web site:* http://www.itt-tech.edu/.

ITT Technical Institute

Morrisville, North Carolina

- **Proprietary** primarily 2-year, part of ITT Educational Services, Inc.
- **Coed**
- **Minimally difficult** entrance level

Academics *Degrees:* associate and bachelor's.
Student Life *Housing:* college housing not available.
Freshman Application Contact Director of Recruitment, ITT Technical Institute, 5520 Dillard Drive, Suite 100, Morrisville, NC 27560. *Phone:* 919-233-2520. *Toll-free phone:* 877-203-5533. *Web site:* http://www.itt-tech.edu/.

Johnson & Wales University - Charlotte Campus

Charlotte, North Carolina

- **Independent** 4-year, founded 2004
- **Coed** 2,587 undergraduate students, 98% full-time, 59% women, 41% men
- **Moderately difficult** entrance level, 60% of applicants were admitted

Undergraduates 2,536 full-time, 51 part-time. 66% are from out of state; 20% Black or African American, non-Hispanic/Latino; 4% Hispanic/Latino; 1% Asian, non-Hispanic/Latino; 0.3% American Indian or Alaska Native, non-Hispanic/Latino; 0.1% Two or more races, non-Hispanic/Latino; 44% Race/ethnicity unknown; 2% international; 9% transferred in; 48% live on campus. *Retention:* 75% of full-time freshmen returned.
Freshmen *Admission:* 7,207 applied, 4,331 admitted, 732 enrolled. *Average high school GPA:* 3.1.
Faculty *Total:* 110, 80% full-time. *Student/faculty ratio:* 27:1.
Academics *Calendar:* quarters. *Degrees:* associate and bachelor's. *Special study options:* accelerated degree program, advanced placement credit, cooperative education, English as a second language, honors programs, independent study, internships, part-time degree program, services for LD students, study abroad.
Computers on Campus Students can access the following: computer help desk, free student e-mail accounts, online (class) grades, online (class) registration, online (class) schedules. Campuswide network is available.

Student Life *Housing:* on-campus residence required for freshman year. *Options:* coed. Campus housing is university owned. Freshman applicants given priority for college housing. *Activities and organizations:* student-run newspaper. *Campus security:* 24-hour emergency response devices and patrols, late-night transport/escort service, controlled dormitory access. *Student services:* health clinic, personal/psychological counseling.
Standardized Tests *Required for some:* SAT or ACT (for admission).
Costs (2011–12) *Comprehensive fee:* $35,721 includes full-time tuition ($23,955), mandatory fees ($1452), and room and board ($10,314). *Room and board:* Room and board charges vary according to board plan, housing facility, and location. *Payment plan:* installment. *Waivers:* employees or children of employees.
Financial Aid Of all full-time matriculated undergraduates who enrolled in 2009, 2,154 applied for aid, 1,951 were judged to have need, 275 had their need fully met. In 2009, 316 non-need-based awards were made. *Average percent of need met:* 71%. *Average financial aid package:* $17,625. *Average need-based loan:* $5205. *Average need-based gift aid:* $7894. *Average non-need-based aid:* $5275.
Applying *Options:* electronic application, early admission, deferred entrance. *Required:* high school transcript. *Required for some:* interview. *Recommended:* minimum 2 GPA. *Application deadlines:* rolling (freshmen), rolling (transfers). *Notification:* continuous (freshmen), continuous (transfers).
Freshman Application Contact Joseph Campos, Director of Admissions, Johnson & Wales University - Charlotte Campus, 801 West Trade Street, Charlotte, NC 28202. *Phone:* 980-598-1100. *Toll-free phone:* 866-598-2427. *Fax:* 980-598-1111. *E-mail:* clt@admissions.jwu.edu. *Web site:* http://www.jwu.edu/charlotte/.

Johnson C. Smith University

Charlotte, North Carolina

- **Independent** 4-year, founded 1867
- **Urban** 100-acre campus with easy access to Atlanta
- **Endowment** $45.2 million
- **Coed** 1,331 undergraduate students, 98% full-time, 59% women, 41% men
- **Moderately difficult** entrance level, 24% of applicants were admitted

Undergraduates 1,298 full-time, 33 part-time. Students come from 32 states and territories; 2 other countries; 64% are from out of state; 95% Black or African American, non-Hispanic/Latino; 0.4% Hispanic/Latino; 0.2% American Indian or Alaska Native, non-Hispanic/Latino; 0.3% Two or more races, non-Hispanic/Latino; 2% Race/ethnicity unknown; 2% international; 4% transferred in; 60% live on campus. *Retention:* 70% of full-time freshmen returned.
Freshmen *Admission:* 4,114 applied, 1,002 admitted, 223 enrolled. *Average high school GPA:* 2.98. *Test scores:* SAT critical reading scores over 500: 12%; SAT math scores over 500: 15%; ACT scores over 18: 44%; SAT critical reading scores over 600: 1%; SAT math scores over 600: 1%; ACT scores over 24: 5%.
Faculty *Total:* 130, 76% full-time, 65% with terminal degrees. *Student/faculty ratio:* 12:1.
Academics *Calendar:* semesters. *Degree:* bachelor's. *Special study options:* adult/continuing education programs, advanced placement credit, cooperative education, double majors, honors programs, independent study, internships, off-campus study, part-time degree program, services for LD students, study abroad, summer session for credit. *ROTC:* Army (b), Air Force (c).
Computers on Campus 335 computers/terminals are available on campus for general student use. Students can access the following: campus intranet, computer help desk, free student e-mail accounts, online (class) grades, online (class) registration, online (class) schedules. Campuswide network is available. 100% of college-owned or -operated housing units are wired for high-speed Internet access. Wireless service is available via entire campus.
Student Life *Housing:* on-campus residence required for freshman year. *Options:* coed, men-only, women-only. Campus housing is university owned. Freshman campus housing is guaranteed. *Activities and organizations:* drama/theater group, student-run newspaper, choral group, marching band, Student Government Association, Golden Bull Activities Committee, Black Ink Monks Poetry Society, National Pan-Hellenic Council, Student Ambassadors, national fraternities, national sororities. *Campus security:* 24-hour emergency response devices and patrols, late-night transport/escort service, controlled dormitory access. *Student services:* health clinic, personal/psychological counseling.
Athletics Member NCAA. All Division II. *Intercollegiate sports:* basketball M(s)/W(s), bowling W(s), cheerleading W(c), cross-country running M(s)/W(s), football M(s), golf M(s), softball W(s), tennis M(s)/W(s), track and field M(s)/W(s), volleyball W(s). *Intramural sports:* basketball M/W, football M, table tennis M/W.
Standardized Tests *Required:* SAT or ACT (for admission).
Costs (2010–11) *Comprehensive fee:* $22,981 includes full-time tuition ($14,029), mandatory fees ($2513), and room and board ($6439). Full-time tuition and fees vary according to course load. Part-time tuition: $379 per

credit hour. Part-time tuition and fees vary according to course load. *Required fees:* $346 per term part-time. *College room only:* $3706. Room and board charges vary according to board plan and housing facility. *Payment plan:* installment. *Waivers:* children of alumni and employees or children of employees.

Financial Aid Of all full-time matriculated undergraduates who enrolled in 2009, 1,228 applied for aid, 1,170 were judged to have need, 50 had their need fully met. In 2009, 34 non-need-based awards were made. *Average percent of need met:* 52%. *Average financial aid package:* $13,562. *Average need-based loan:* $4968. *Average need-based gift aid:* $9219. *Average non-need-based aid:* $18,311. *Average indebtedness upon graduation:* $29,218.

Applying *Options:* electronic application, early admission, early action, deferred entrance. *Application fee:* $25. *Required:* essay or personal statement, high school transcript. *Required for some:* 2 letters of recommendation. *Application deadlines:* 3/15 (freshmen), 5/30 (transfers), 12/1 (early action). *Notification:* continuous (freshmen), continuous (transfers).

Freshman Application Contact Mr. Dwight Sanchez, Interim Senior Associate Director of Admissions, Johnson C. Smith University, 100 Beatties Ford Road, Charlotte, NC 28216. *Phone:* 704-378-3500. *Toll-free phone:* 800-782-7303. *Fax:* 704-378-1242. *E-mail:* dsanchez@jcsu.edu. *Web site:* http://www.jcsu.edu/.

Laurel University

High Point, North Carolina

- **Independent interdenominational** comprehensive, founded 1932
- **Urban** 24-acre campus
- **Coed**
- **Minimally difficult** entrance level

Faculty *Student/faculty ratio:* 7:1.

Academics *Calendar:* semesters. *Degrees:* certificates, associate, and bachelor's.

Standardized Tests *Required for some:* College Board ACCUPLACER Test for English.

Costs (2010–11) *Tuition:* $10,000 full-time, $375 per credit hour part-time. Full-time tuition and fees vary according to course load and program. Part-time tuition and fees vary according to course load and program. *Required fees:* $730 full-time, $365 per term part-time. *Room only:* $2344. Room and board charges vary according to housing facility.

Financial Aid Of all full-time matriculated undergraduates who enrolled in 2008, 5 Federal Work-Study jobs (averaging $2500). 2 state and other part-time jobs (averaging $4500).

Applying *Options:* electronic application, early admission, deferred entrance. *Application fee:* $35. *Required:* high school transcript, 2 letters of recommendation, interview. *Recommended:* minimum 2 GPA.

Freshman Application Contact Jeremy Reese, Admissions Officer, Laurel University, 2314 North Centennial Street, High Point, NC 27265-3197. *Phone:* 336-889-2262 Ext. 127. *Fax:* 336-889-2261. *E-mail:* admissions@johnwesley.edu. *Web site:* http://www.laureluniversity.edu/.

Lees-McRae College

Banner Elk, North Carolina

- **Independent** 4-year, founded 1900, affiliated with Presbyterian Church (U.S.A.)
- **Rural** 400-acre campus
- **Coed**
- **Minimally difficult** entrance level

Faculty *Student/faculty ratio:* 16:1.

Academics *Calendar:* semesters. *Degree:* bachelor's.

Student Life *Campus security:* 24-hour patrols.

Athletics Member NCAA. All Division II.

Standardized Tests *Required:* SAT or ACT (for admission).

Costs (2010–11) *Comprehensive fee:* $29,025 includes full-time tuition ($21,625) and room and board ($7400). Part-time tuition: $600 per credit hour.

Financial Aid Of all full-time matriculated undergraduates who enrolled in 2009, 741 applied for aid, 647 were judged to have need, 26 had their need fully met. In 2009, 51 non-need-based awards were made. *Average percent of need met:* 74. *Average financial aid package:* $12,600. *Average need-based loan:* $5000. *Average need-based gift aid:* $9700. *Average non-need-based aid:* $5600.

Applying *Options:* electronic application. *Required:* high school transcript, minimum 2 GPA. *Required for some:* interview. *Recommended:* essay or personal statement.

Freshman Application Contact Mr. Bill Sliwa, Lees-McRae College, PO Box 128, Banner Elk, NC 28604-0128. *Phone:* 828-898-8723. *Toll-free phone:* 800-280-4562. *Fax:* 828-898-8707. *E-mail:* admissions@lmc.edu. *Web site:* http://www.lmc.edu/.

Lenoir-Rhyne University

Hickory, North Carolina

Director of Admissions Karen Feezor, Lenoir-Rhyne University, 625 7th Avenue NE, Hickory, NC 28601. *Phone:* 828-328-7300. *Toll-free phone:* 800-277-5721. *Fax:* 828-328-7378. *E-mail:* admission@lr.edu. *Web site:* http://www.lr.edu/.

Livingstone College

Salisbury, North Carolina

Freshman Application Contact Livingstone College, 701 West Monroe Street, Salifbury, NC 28144. *Phone:* 704-216-6001. *Toll-free phone:* 800-835-3435. *Fax:* 704-216-6215. *E-mail:* admissions@livingstone.edu. *Web site:* http://www.livingstone.edu/.

Mars Hill College

Mars Hill, North Carolina

- **Independent Baptist** 4-year, founded 1856
- **Small-town** 194-acre campus
- **Endowment** $37.5 million
- **Coed** 1,175 undergraduate students, 93% full-time, 51% women, 49% men
- **Moderately difficult** entrance level, 59% of applicants were admitted

Undergraduates 1,096 full-time, 79 part-time. Students come from 35 states and territories; 18 other countries; 30% are from out of state; 15% Black or African American, non-Hispanic/Latino; 3% Hispanic/Latino; 1% Asian, non-Hispanic/Latino; 0.3% Native Hawaiian or other Pacific Islander, non-Hispanic/Latino; 0.8% American Indian or Alaska Native, non-Hispanic/Latino; 3% Race/ethnicity unknown; 10% transferred in; 64% live on campus. *Retention:* 54% of full-time freshmen returned.

Freshmen *Admission:* 2,432 applied, 1,440 admitted, 274 enrolled. *Average high school GPA:* 3.17. *Test scores:* SAT critical reading scores over 500: 39%; SAT math scores over 500: 50%; ACT scores over 18: 80%; SAT critical reading scores over 600: 7%; SAT math scores over 600: 12%; ACT scores over 24: 20%; SAT critical reading scores over 700: 1%; SAT math scores over 700: 1%; ACT scores over 30: 2%.

Faculty *Total:* 147, 48% full-time. *Student/faculty ratio:* 12:1.

Academics *Calendar:* semesters. *Degree:* bachelor's. *Special study options:* academic remediation for entering students, accelerated degree program, adult/continuing education programs, advanced placement credit, cooperative education, double majors, English as a second language, honors programs, independent study, internships, part-time degree program, services for LD students, student-designed majors, study abroad, summer session for credit.

Computers on Campus 188 computers/terminals are available on campus for general student use. Students can access the following: campus intranet, computer help desk, free student e-mail accounts, online (class) grades, online (class) registration, online (class) schedules. Campuswide network is available. 80% of college-owned or -operated housing units are wired for high-speed Internet access. Wireless service is available via entire campus.

Student Life *Housing:* on-campus residence required through sophomore year. *Options:* men-only, women-only. Campus housing is university owned. Freshman campus housing is guaranteed. *Activities and organizations:* drama/theater group, student-run newspaper, choral group, marching band, Student Government Association, Fellowship of Christian Athletes, Christian Student Movement, Fraternity/Sorority, Athletic Trainers Association, national fraternities, national sororities. *Campus security:* 24-hour emergency response devices and patrols, late-night transport/escort service, controlled dormitory access. *Student services:* health clinic, personal/psychological counseling.

Athletics Member NCAA. All Division II. *Intercollegiate sports:* baseball M(s), basketball M(s)/W(s), cheerleading M(s)/W(s), cross-country running M(s)/W(s), football M(s), golf M(s)/W(s), lacrosse M(s), soccer M(s)/W(s), softball W(s), swimming and diving M(s)/W(s), tennis M(s)/W(s), track and field M(s)/W(s), volleyball W(s). *Intramural sports:* basketball M/W, football M/W, rock climbing M/W, skiing (downhill) M(c)/W(c), soccer M/W, track and field M(c)/W(c), ultimate Frisbee M/W, volleyball M/W, water polo M/W, weight lifting M/W.

Standardized Tests *Required:* SAT or ACT (for admission).

Costs (2010–11) *Comprehensive fee:* $29,629 includes full-time tuition ($19,907), mandatory fees ($2090), and room and board ($7632). Part-time tuition: $730 per credit hour. *Required fees:* $90 per credit hour part-time. *Room and board:* Room and board charges vary according to board plan and housing facility. *Payment plan:* installment. *Waivers:* employees or children of employees.

Financial Aid Of all full-time matriculated undergraduates who enrolled in 2008, 984 applied for aid, 856 were judged to have need, 235 had their need fully met. 200 Federal Work-Study jobs (averaging $1077). In 2008, 80 non-need-based awards were made. *Average percent of need met:* 79%. *Average* financial aid package: $15,620. *Average need-based loan:* $3437. *Average need-based gift aid:* $12,449. *Average non-need-based aid:* $6751. *Average indebtedness upon graduation:* $16,025.

Applying *Options:* electronic application, early admission, deferred entrance. *Application fee:* $25. *Required:* high school transcript, minimum 2 GPA. *Required for some:* interview. *Recommended:* essay or personal statement, minimum 3 GPA. *Application deadlines:* rolling (freshmen), rolling (transfers).

Freshman Application Contact Ed Hoffmeyer, Dean of Admissions and Financial Aid, Mars Hill College, PO Box 370, Mars Hill, NC 28754. *Phone:* 828-689-1201. *Toll-free phone:* 866-MHC-4-YOU. *Fax:* 828-689-1473. *E-mail:* ehoffmeyer@mhc.edu. *Web site:* http://www.mhc.edu/.

Meredith College
Raleigh, North Carolina

- **Independent** comprehensive, founded 1891
- **Urban** 225-acre campus
- **Endowment** $82.4 million
- **Undergraduate: women only; graduate: coed**
- **Moderately difficult** entrance level

Faculty *Student/faculty ratio:* 10:1.

Academics *Calendar:* semesters. *Degrees:* bachelor's, master's, and post-bachelor's certificates.

Student Life *Campus security:* 24-hour emergency response devices and patrols, late-night transport/escort service, controlled dormitory access, self-defense instruction.

Athletics Member NCAA. All Division III.

Standardized Tests *Required:* SAT or ACT (for admission). *Required for some:* SAT Subject Tests (for admission).

Costs (2010–11) *Comprehensive fee:* $33,700 includes full-time tuition ($26,150), mandatory fees ($50), and room and board ($7500). Full-time tuition and fees vary according to course load. Part-time tuition: $650 per credit hour. Part-time tuition and fees vary according to course load. *College room only:* $3750.

Financial Aid *Of all full-time matriculated undergraduates who enrolled in 2009,* 1,434 applied for aid, 1,245 were judged to have need, 209 had their need fully met. *In 2009,* 141 non-need-based awards were made. *Average percent of need met:* 78. *Average financial aid package:* $18,638. *Average need-based loan:* $4250. *Average need-based gift aid:* $14,917. *Average non-need-based aid:* $6790. *Average indebtedness upon graduation:* $32,350.

Applying *Options:* electronic application, early admission, early decision, deferred entrance. *Application fee:* $40. *Required:* high school transcript, minimum 2 GPA, 2 letters of recommendation. *Required for some:* essay or personal statement, interview.

Freshman Application Contact Ms. Megan Greer, Associate Director of Admissions, Meredith College, 3800 Hillsborough Street, Raleigh, NC 27807-5298. *Phone:* 919-760-8581. *Toll-free phone:* 800-MEREDITH. *Fax:* 919-760-2348. *E-mail:* admissions@meredith.edu. *Web site:* http://www.meredith.edu/.

See page 1422 for the College Close-Up.

Methodist University
Fayetteville, North Carolina

- **Independent United Methodist** comprehensive, founded 1956
- **Suburban** 600-acre campus with easy access to Raleigh-Durham
- **Endowment** $15.6 million
- **Coed**
- **Moderately difficult** entrance level

Faculty *Student/faculty ratio:* 12:1.

Academics *Calendar:* semesters. *Degrees:* associate, bachelor's, and master's.

Student Life *Campus security:* 24-hour emergency response devices and patrols, student patrols, late-night transport/escort service, controlled dormitory access, regular patrol by county sheriff department.

Athletics Member NCAA. All Division III.

Standardized Tests *Required:* SAT or ACT (for admission).

Costs (2010–11) *Comprehensive fee:* $33,120 includes full-time tuition ($23,780), mandatory fees ($440), and room and board ($8900). Full-time tuition and fees vary according to class time. Part-time tuition: $735 per semester hour. Part-time tuition and fees vary according to class time and course load. *Room and board:* Room and board charges vary according to housing facility.

Financial Aid *Of all full-time matriculated undergraduates who enrolled in 2008,* 1,727 applied for aid, 1,613 were judged to have need, 636 had their need fully met. 819 Federal Work-Study jobs (averaging $313). 117 state and other part-time jobs (averaging $1612). *In 2008,* 67 non-need-based awards were made. *Average percent of need met:* 82. *Average financial aid package:*

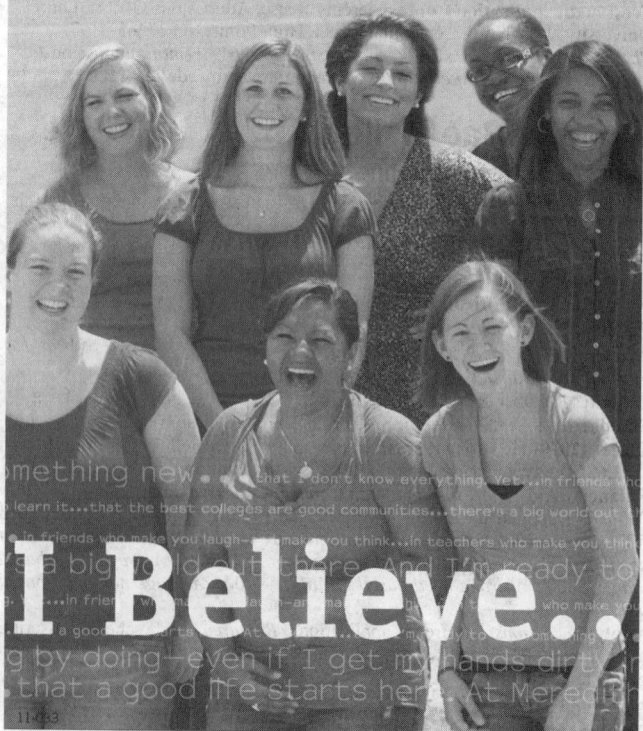

$23,733. Average need-based loan: $16,249. Average need-based gift aid: $9163. Average non-need-based aid: $5669. Average indebtedness upon graduation: $30,786.

Applying *Options:* deferred entrance. *Application fee:* $25. *Required:* high school transcript. *Required for some:* essay or personal statement, interview. *Recommended:* interview.

Freshman Application Contact Mr. Jamie Legg, Director of Admissions, Methodist University, 5400 Ramset Street, Fayetteville, NC 28311-1496. *Phone:* 910-630-7027. *Toll-free phone:* 800-488-7110 Ext. 7027. *Fax:* 910-630-7285. *E-mail:* admissions@methodist.edu. *Web site:* http://www.methodist.edu/.

Mid-Atlantic Christian University

Elizabeth City, North Carolina

- **Independent Christian** 4-year, founded 1948
- **Small-town** 19-acre campus with easy access to Norfolk
- **Endowment** $2.3 million
- **Coed** 179 undergraduate students, 75% full-time, 41% women, 59% men
- **Minimally difficult** entrance level, 39% of applicants were admitted

Undergraduates 135 full-time, 44 part-time. Students come from 10 states and territories; 1 other country; 39% are from out of state; 21% Black or African American, non-Hispanic/Latino; 3% Hispanic/Latino; 0.6% Asian, non-Hispanic/Latino; 12% transferred in; 60% live on campus. *Retention:* 64% of full-time freshmen returned.

Freshmen *Admission:* 132 applied, 52 admitted, 25 enrolled. *Average high school GPA:* 2.83. *Test scores:* SAT math scores over 500: 44%; SAT writing scores over 500: 51%; ACT scores over 18: 50%; SAT math scores over 600: 6%; SAT writing scores over 600: 13%; ACT scores over 24: 25%.

Faculty *Total:* 36, 14% full-time, 36% with terminal degrees. *Student/faculty ratio:* 12:1.

Academics *Calendar:* semesters. *Degrees:* certificates, associate, bachelor's, and postbachelor's certificates. *Special study options:* academic remediation for entering students, advanced placement credit, distance learning, double majors, internships, part-time degree program. *ROTC:* Army (c).

Computers on Campus 24 computers/terminals are available on campus for general student use. Students can access the following: free student e-mail accounts. Campuswide network is available. 100% of college-owned or -operated housing units are wired for high-speed Internet access. Wireless service is available via entire campus.

Student Life *Housing:* on-campus residence required through senior year. *Options:* men-only, women-only. Campus housing is university owned. Freshman campus housing is guaranteed. *Activities and organizations:* choral group, Student Advisory Council, Counseling Club, Drama Club, choral group. *Campus security:* 24-hour emergency response devices, controlled dormitory access. *Student services:* personal/psychological counseling.

Athletics *Intercollegiate sports:* basketball M/W, volleyball W. *Intramural sports:* basketball M/W, golf M/W, soccer M/W, softball M/W, table tennis M/W, tennis M/W, volleyball M/W.

Standardized Tests *Required:* SAT or ACT (for admission).

Costs (2011–12) *Comprehensive fee:* $18,800 includes full-time tuition ($11,200), mandatory fees ($400), and room and board ($7200). Part-time tuition: $350 per credit hour. *Required fees:* $21 per contact hour part-time. *College room only:* $3800. Room and board charges vary according to housing facility. *Payment plan:* deferred payment. *Waivers:* children of alumni, senior citizens, and employees or children of employees.

Financial Aid Of all full-time matriculated undergraduates who enrolled in 2008, 142 applied for aid, 129 were judged to have need, 7 had their need fully met. 19 Federal Work-Study jobs (averaging $699). In 2008, 10 non-need-based awards were made. *Average percent of need met:* 58%. *Average financial aid package:* $8832. *Average need-based loan:* $7795. *Average need-based gift aid:* $4954. *Average non-need-based aid:* $2550. *Average indebtedness upon graduation:* $32,413.

Applying *Options:* electronic application, early admission, deferred entrance. *Application fee:* $50. *Required:* essay or personal statement, high school transcript, minimum 2 GPA, 1 letter of recommendation, reference from church. *Required for some:* interview. *Application deadlines:* 8/1 (freshmen), 8/1 (transfers). *Notification:* continuous (freshmen), continuous (transfers).

Freshman Application Contact Mrs. Julie A. Fields, Mid-Atlantic Christian University, 715 North Poindexter Street, Elizabeth City, NC 27909-4054. *Phone:* 252-334-2028. *Toll-free phone:* 800-RBC-8980. *Fax:* 252-334-2064. *E-mail:* julie.fields@macuniversity.edu. *Web site:* http://www.macuniversity.edu/.

Montreat College

Montreat, North Carolina

- **Independent** comprehensive, founded 1916, affiliated with Presbyterian Church (U.S.A.)
- **Small-town** 112-acre campus
- **Endowment** $9.4 million
- **Coed** 850 undergraduate students, 94% full-time, 58% women, 42% men
- **Moderately difficult** entrance level, 50% of applicants were admitted

Undergraduates 799 full-time, 51 part-time. Students come from 31 states and territories; 12 other countries; 22% are from out of state; 24% Black or African American, non-Hispanic/Latino; 3% Hispanic/Latino; 1% Asian, non-Hispanic/Latino; 1% American Indian or Alaska Native, non-Hispanic/Latino; 1% Two or more races, non-Hispanic/Latino; 15% Race/ethnicity unknown; 1% international; 7% transferred in; 74% live on campus. *Retention:* 79% of full-time freshmen returned.

Freshmen *Admission:* 602 applied, 298 admitted, 111 enrolled. *Average high school GPA:* 3.15. *Test scores:* SAT critical reading scores over 500: 48%; SAT math scores over 500: 40%; ACT scores over 18: 83%; SAT critical reading scores over 600: 13%; SAT math scores over 600: 9%; ACT scores over 24: 23%; SAT critical reading scores over 700: 1%; ACT scores over 30: 6%.

Faculty *Total:* 147, 43% full-time, 44% with terminal degrees. *Student/faculty ratio:* 10:1.

Academics *Calendar:* semesters. *Degrees:* certificates, associate, bachelor's, and master's. *Special study options:* accelerated degree program, adult/continuing education programs, advanced placement credit, cooperative education, double majors, independent study, internships, off-campus study, part-time degree program, services for LD students, study abroad.

Computers on Campus 40 computers/terminals and 346 ports are available on campus for general student use. Students can access the following: campus intranet, computer help desk, free student e-mail accounts, online (class) grades, online (class) schedules. Campuswide network is available. 100% of college-owned or -operated housing units are wired for high-speed Internet access. Wireless service is available via entire campus.

Student Life *Housing:* on-campus residence required through sophomore year. *Options:* men-only, women-only. Campus housing is university owned. Freshman campus housing is guaranteed. *Activities and organizations:* drama/theater group, student-run newspaper, choral group, Fellowship of Christian Athletes, SEEDS (Student environmental stewardship organization), Phi Beta Lambda Business Club, Computer Club, Martial Arts Club. *Campus security:* 24-hour emergency response devices and patrols, controlled dormitory access. *Student services:* health clinic, personal/psychological counseling.

Athletics Member NAIA. *Intercollegiate sports:* baseball M(s), basketball M(s)/W(s), cross-country running M(s)/W(s), golf M(s), soccer M(s)/W(s), softball W(s), tennis M(s)/W(s), track and field M(s)/W(s), volleyball W(s). *Intramural sports:* basketball M/W, football M, softball M/W, table tennis M/W, tennis M/W, ultimate Frisbee M/W, volleyball M/W.

Standardized Tests *Required:* SAT or ACT (for admission).

Costs (2011–12) *Comprehensive fee:* $30,510 includes full-time tuition ($22,684), mandatory fees ($480), and room and board ($7346). Full-time tuition and fees vary according to course load, program, and reciprocity agreements. Part-time tuition: $600 per credit. Part-time tuition and fees vary according to course load, program, and reciprocity agreements. *Room and board:* Room and board charges vary according to board plan. *Payment plan:* installment. *Waivers:* employees or children of employees.

Financial Aid Of all full-time matriculated undergraduates who enrolled in 2009, 880 applied for aid, 790 were judged to have need, 148 had their need fully met. 85 Federal Work-Study jobs (averaging $1800). 50 state and other part-time jobs (averaging $1800). In 2009, 64 non-need-based awards were made. *Average percent of need met:* 66%. *Average financial aid package:* $12,337. *Average need-based loan:* $4183. *Average need-based gift aid:* $8571. *Average non-need-based aid:* $8132. *Average indebtedness upon graduation:* $19,295.

Applying *Options:* early admission, deferred entrance. *Application fee:* $30. *Required:* essay or personal statement, high school transcript, minimum 2.75 GPA. *Required for some:* 1 letter of recommendation, interview. *Application deadlines:* 8/15 (freshmen), 8/15 (out-of-state freshmen), rolling (transfers). *Notification:* continuous (freshmen), continuous (out-of-state freshmen), continuous (transfers).

Freshman Application Contact Mr. Joey Higgins, Director of Admissions, Montreat College, PO Box 1267, Montreat, NC 28757. *Phone:* 828-669-8012 Ext. 3782. *Toll-free phone:* 800-622-6968. *Fax:* 828-669-0120. *E-mail:* admissions@montreat.edu. *Web site:* http://www.montreat.edu/.

Mount Olive College

Mount Olive, North Carolina

- **Independent Free Will Baptist** 4-year, founded 1951
- **Small-town** 123-acre campus with easy access to Raleigh
- **Coed** 3,855 undergraduate students, 77% full-time, 67% women, 33% men
- **Minimally difficult** entrance level, 50% of applicants were admitted

Undergraduates 2,955 full-time, 900 part-time. Students come from 11 other countries; 5% are from out of state; 11% live on campus. *Retention:* 60% of full-time freshmen returned.

Freshmen *Admission:* 1,838 applied, 916 admitted, 369 enrolled. *Average high school GPA:* 2.85. *Test scores:* SAT critical reading scores over 500: 21%; SAT math scores over 500: 29%; ACT scores over 18: 70%; SAT critical reading scores over 600: 3%; SAT math scores over 600: 4%; ACT scores over 24: 9%.

Faculty *Total:* 183, 44% full-time, 62% with terminal degrees. *Student/faculty ratio:* 26:1.

Academics *Calendar:* semester or continuous accelerated programs. *Degrees:* associate and bachelor's. *Special study options:* accelerated degree program, adult/continuing education programs, advanced placement credit, cooperative education, double majors, external degree program, freshman honors college, honors programs, independent study, internships, off-campus study, part-time degree program, summer session for credit. *ROTC:* Air Force (c).

Computers on Campus Students can access the following: Web site. Campus-wide network is available. Wireless service is available via classrooms, computer centers, computer labs, dorm rooms, learning centers, libraries, student centers.

Student Life *Housing:* on-campus residence required for freshman year. *Options:* men-only, women-only. Campus housing is university owned. *Activities and organizations:* choral group, Student Government Association, Phi Beta Lambda, commuters organization, Christian Student Fellowship, English Society. *Campus security:* overnight security patrols; weekend patrols. *Student services:* health clinic, personal/psychological counseling.

Athletics Member NCAA. All Division II. *Intercollegiate sports:* baseball M(s), basketball M(s)/W(s), cheerleading W, cross-country running M(s)/W(s), golf M(s)/W(s), soccer M(s)/W(s), softball W(s), tennis M(s)/W(s), volleyball M(s)/W(s). *Intramural sports:* basketball M/W, football M/W, racquetball M/W, soccer M/W, softball W, table tennis M/W, tennis M/W, volleyball M/W.

Standardized Tests *Required for some:* SAT or ACT required for those under 21.

Costs (2010–11) *Comprehensive fee:* $21,700 includes full-time tuition ($15,500) and room and board ($6200). Part-time tuition: $380 per credit hour. *College room only:* $2400. Room and board charges vary according to board plan.

Financial Aid Of all full-time matriculated undergraduates who enrolled in 2008, 2,947 applied for aid, 2,492 were judged to have need, 371 had their need fully met. 160 Federal Work-Study jobs (averaging $1169). In 2008, 12 non-need-based awards were made. *Average percent of need met:* 65%. *Average financial aid package:* $8887. *Average need-based loan:* $3710. *Average need-based gift aid:* $5815. *Average non-need-based aid:* $2099. *Average indebtedness upon graduation:* $16,117.

Applying *Options:* electronic application, deferred entrance. *Application fee:* $20. *Required:* high school transcript. *Recommended:* 2 letters of recommendation, interview. *Application deadlines:* 8/18 (freshmen), rolling (transfers). *Notification:* continuous (freshmen).

Freshman Application Contact Mount Olive College, 634 Henderson Street, Mount Olive, NC 28365. *Phone:* 919-658-2502 Ext. 3009. *Toll-free phone:* 800-653-0854. *Web site:* http://www.moc.edu/.

New Life Theological Seminary

Charlotte, North Carolina

- **Independent religious** comprehensive, founded 1996
- **Urban** 3-acre campus
- **Coed**
- 100% of applicants were admitted

Faculty *Student/faculty ratio:* 6:1.

Academics *Calendar:* quarters. *Degrees:* certificates, associate, bachelor's, and master's.

Student Life *Campus security:* 24-hour emergency response devices.

Costs (2010–11) *Tuition:* $6800 full-time, $295 per credit hour part-time. *Required fees:* $220 full-time, $110 per term part-time.

Financial Aid *Of all full-time matriculated undergraduates who enrolled in 2008,* 56 applied for aid, 56 were judged to have need, 34 had their need fully met. 2 Federal Work-Study jobs (averaging $2358). *In 2008,* 1 non-need-based awards were made. *Average percent of need met:* 61. *Average financial aid package:* $8623. *Average need-based loan:* $3500. *Average need-based*

gift aid: $5135. *Average non-need-based aid:* $672. *Average indebtedness upon graduation:* $36,498.

Applying *Application fee:* $40. *Required:* essay or personal statement, high school transcript, 2 letters of recommendation, certification of Church membership and involvement.

Freshman Application Contact New Life Theological Seminary, PO Box 790106, Charlotte, NC 28206-7901. *Phone:* 704-334-6882 Ext. 08. *Web site:* http://www.nlts.org/.

North Carolina Agricultural and Technical State University

Greensboro, North Carolina

- **State-supported** university, founded 1891, part of University of North Carolina System
- **Suburban** 200-acre campus with easy access to Charlotte
- **Coed** 9,151 undergraduate students, 90% full-time, 53% women, 47% men
- **Moderately difficult** entrance level, 61% of applicants were admitted

Undergraduates 8,205 full-time, 946 part-time. 89% Black or African American, non-Hispanic/Latino; 2% Hispanic/Latino; 0.8% Asian, non-Hispanic/Latino; 0.4% American Indian or Alaska Native, non-Hispanic/Latino; 2% Race/ethnicity unknown; 1% international; 5% transferred in; 41% live on campus. *Retention:* 72% of full-time freshmen returned.

Freshmen *Admission:* 6,216 applied, 3,814 admitted, 2,053 enrolled. *Average high school GPA:* 3.04. *Test scores:* SAT critical reading scores over 500: 16%; SAT math scores over 500: 22%; SAT writing scores over 500: 7%; ACT scores over 18: 62%; SAT critical reading scores over 600: 2%; SAT math scores over 600: 3%; SAT writing scores over 600: 1%; ACT scores over 24: 9%; ACT scores over 30: 1%.

Faculty *Total:* 570, 91% full-time, 75% with terminal degrees. *Student/faculty ratio:* 18:1.

Academics *Calendar:* semesters. *Degrees:* bachelor's, master's, and doctoral-research/scholarship. *Special study options:* academic remediation for entering students, accelerated degree program, adult/continuing education programs, advanced placement credit, cooperative education, distance learning, double majors, honors programs, internships, part-time degree program, services for LD students, study abroad, summer session for credit. *ROTC:* Army (b), Air Force (b).

Computers on Campus Students can access the following: computer help desk, free student e-mail accounts, online (class) grades, online (class) registration, online (class) schedules. Campuswide network is available.

Student Life *Housing options:* coed, men-only, women-only. Campus housing is university owned and is provided by a third party. Freshman applicants given priority for college housing. *Activities and organizations:* drama/theater group, student-run newspaper, radio and television station, choral group, marching band, student government, national fraternities, national sororities. *Campus security:* 24-hour emergency response devices and patrols, late-night transport/escort service, controlled dormitory access. *Student services:* health clinic, personal/psychological counseling.

Athletics Member NCAA. All Division I except football (Division I-AA). *Intercollegiate sports:* baseball M(s), basketball M(s)/W(s), bowling W(s), cross-country running M(s)/W(s), softball W(s), swimming and diving W(s), tennis W(s), track and field M(s)/W(s), volleyball W(s). *Intramural sports:* baseball M, basketball M/W, football M, volleyball M/W.

Standardized Tests *Required:* SAT and SAT Subject Tests or ACT (for admission).

Costs (2010–11) *One-time required fee:* $140. *Tuition:* state resident $2621 full-time; nonresident $12,063 full-time. Full-time tuition and fees vary according to course load and student level. Part-time tuition and fees vary according to course load and student level. *Required fees:* $1795 full-time. *Room and board:* $6029; room only: $3429. Room and board charges vary according to board plan and housing facility. *Waivers:* senior citizens and employees or children of employees.

Financial Aid Of all full-time matriculated undergraduates who enrolled in 2009, 6,919 applied for aid, 6,919 were judged to have need, 1,305 had their need fully met. In 2009, 294 non-need-based awards were made. *Average percent of need met:* 84%. *Average financial aid package:* $12,838. *Average need-based loan:* $3915. *Average need-based gift aid:* $5247. *Average non-need-based aid:* $4733. *Average indebtedness upon graduation:* $21,644.

Applying *Options:* early admission, deferred entrance. *Application fee:* $45. *Required:* high school transcript, minimum 2 GPA. *Application deadlines:* rolling (freshmen), rolling (out-of-state freshmen), rolling (transfers). *Notification:* continuous (freshmen), continuous (out-of-state freshmen), continuous (transfers).

Freshman Application Contact Ms. Keyana Scales, Director of Admissions, North Carolina Agricultural and Technical State University, North Carolina Agricultural & Technical State University (Webb Hall), 1601 East Market Street, Greensboro, NC 27411. *Phone:* 336-334-7946. *Toll-free phone:* 800-

443-8964. *Fax:* 336-334-7478. *E-mail:* uadmit@ncat.edu. *Web site:* http://www.ncat.edu/.

North Carolina Central University

Durham, North Carolina

- **State-supported** comprehensive, founded 1910, part of University of North Carolina System
- **Urban** 115-acre campus
- **Endowment** $18.4 million
- **Coed**
- **Minimally difficult** entrance level

Faculty *Student/faculty ratio:* 15:1.

Academics *Calendar:* semesters. *Degrees:* bachelor's, master's, and doctoral-professional.

Student Life *Campus security:* 24-hour emergency response devices and patrols, student patrols, late-night transport/escort service, controlled dormitory access.

Athletics Member NCAA, NAIA. All NCAA Division II except baseball (Division I), men's and women's basketball (Division I), men's and women's bowling (Division I), men's and women's cross-country running (Division I), football (Division I), men's and women's golf (Division I), softball (Division I), men's and women's tennis (Division I), men's and women's track and field (Division I), volleyball (Division I).

Standardized Tests *Required:* SAT or ACT (for admission).

Costs (2010–11) *Tuition:* state resident $2812 full-time; nonresident $13,385 full-time. Part-time tuition and fees vary according to course load. *Required fees:* $2468 full-time. *Room and board:* $9509; room only: $6875. Room and board charges vary according to board plan, housing facility, and location.

Financial Aid *Of all full-time matriculated undergraduates who enrolled in 2005,* 3,974 applied for aid, 3,962 were judged to have need, 2,414 had their need fully met. *In 2005,* 69 non-need-based awards were made. *Average percent of need met:* 74. *Average financial aid package:* $8196. *Average need-based loan:* $3205. *Average need-based gift aid:* $1818. *Average non-need-based aid:* $3748. *Average indebtedness upon graduation:* $15,000.

Applying *Options:* electronic application, deferred entrance. *Application fee:* $40. *Required:* high school transcript, minimum 2.3 GPA, University of North Carolina System minimum course requirements. *Required for some:* essay or personal statement, interview.

Freshman Application Contact Mr. Anthony Brooks, Undergraduate Director of Admissions, North Carolina Central University, 1801 Fayetteville Street, McDougald House, Durham, NC 27707. *Phone:* 919-530-6298. *Toll-free phone:* 877-667-7533. *Fax:* 919-530-7625. *E-mail:* admissions@nccu.edu. *Web site:* http://www.nccu.edu/.

North Carolina State University

Raleigh, North Carolina

- **State-supported** university, founded 1887, part of University of North Carolina System
- **Urban** 2110-acre campus
- **Endowment** $503.1 million
- **Coed** 25,246 undergraduate students, 88% full-time, 44% women, 56% men
- **Very difficult** entrance level, 54% of applicants were admitted

Undergraduates 22,134 full-time, 3,112 part-time. Students come from 53 states and territories; 68 other countries; 7% are from out of state; 8% Black or African American, non-Hispanic/Latino; 3% Hispanic/Latino; 5% Asian, non-Hispanic/Latino; 0.1% Native Hawaiian or other Pacific Islander, non-Hispanic/Latino; 0.5% American Indian or Alaska Native, non-Hispanic/Latino; 1% Two or more races, non-Hispanic/Latino; 3% Race/ethnicity unknown; 2% international; 5% transferred in; 32% live on campus. *Retention:* 90% of full-time freshmen returned.

Freshman *Admission:* 19,503 applied, 10,519 admitted, 4,705 enrolled. *Average high school GPA:* 3.6. *Test scores:* SAT critical reading scores over 500: 87%; SAT math scores over 500: 95%; SAT writing scores over 500: 80%; ACT scores over 18: 99%; SAT critical reading scores over 600: 37%; SAT math scores over 600: 59%; SAT writing scores over 600: 31%; ACT scores over 24: 71%; SAT critical reading scores over 700: 6%; SAT math scores over 700: 12%; SAT writing scores over 700: 4%; ACT scores over 30: 14%.

Faculty *Total:* 1,918, 91% full-time, 85% with terminal degrees. *Student/faculty ratio:* 18:1.

Academics *Calendar:* semesters. *Degrees:* certificates, associate, bachelor's, master's, doctoral-professional, doctoral-research/scholarship, post-master's, and postbachelor's certificates. *Special study options:* academic remediation for entering students, accelerated degree program, adult/continuing education programs, advanced placement credit, cooperative education, distance learn-

ing, double majors, English as a second language, honors programs, independent study, internships, off-campus study, part-time degree program, services for LD students, student-designed majors, study abroad, summer session for credit. *ROTC:* Army (b), Navy (b), Air Force (b).

Computers on Campus 2,825 computers/terminals are available on campus for general student use. Students can access the following: campus intranet, computer help desk, free student e-mail accounts, online (class) grades, online (class) registration, online (class) schedules, course materials, online homework submission, online testing/quizzes, financial aid/cashier's office account balances, wiki space, blogging service, Web space, online storage space, on-site OS and virus removal, online/hybrid courses. Campuswide network is available. 100% of college-owned or -operated housing units are wired for high-speed Internet access. Wireless service is available via classrooms, computer centers, computer labs, dorm rooms, learning centers, libraries, student centers.

Student Life *Housing options:* coed, men-only, women-only, disabled students. Campus housing is university owned. Freshman applicants given priority for college housing. *Activities and organizations:* drama/theater group, student-run newspaper, radio and television station, choral group, marching band, Student Wolfpack Club, Inter-Fraternity Council, Panhellenic Association, Campus Crusade for Christ, Mechanical and Aerospace Engineering Graduate Student Association, national fraternities, national sororities. *Campus security:* 24-hour emergency response devices and patrols, student patrols, late-night transport/escort service, controlled dormitory access. *Student services:* health clinic, personal/psychological counseling, women's center, legal services.

Athletics Member NCAA. All Division I except football (Division I-A). *Intercollegiate sports:* badminton M(c)/W(c), baseball M(s), basketball M(s)/W(s), bowling M(c)/W(c), cheerleading M(s)/W(s), crew M(c)/W(c), cross-country running M(s)/W(s), equestrian sports M(c)/W(c), fencing M/W, field hockey M(c)/W(c), golf M(s)/W(s), gymnastics W(s), ice hockey M(c)/W(c), lacrosse M(c)/W(c), racquetball M(c)/W(c), riflery M(s)/W(s), rugby M(c)/W(c), sailing M(c)/W(c), skiing (downhill) M(c)/W(c), soccer M(s)/W(s), softball W(s), swimming and diving M(s)/W(s), table tennis M(c)/W(c), tennis M(s)/W(s), track and field M(s)/W(s), ultimate Frisbee M(c)/W(c), volleyball M(c)/W(s), water polo M(c)/W(c), wrestling M(s). *Intramural sports:* badminton M/W, baseball M, basketball M/W, bowling M/W, cheerleading W(c), crew M/W, cross-country running M/W, equestrian sports M/W, fencing M/W, field hockey W, football M/W, golf M/W, gymnastics W, ice hockey M, lacrosse M/W, racquetball M/W, rugby M/W, sailing M/W, skiing (downhill) M/W, soccer M/W, softball M/W, swimming and diving M/W, table tennis M/W, tennis M/W, track and field M/W, volleyball M/W, water polo M/W, wrestling M.

Standardized Tests *Required:* SAT or ACT (for admission). *Recommended:* SAT Subject Tests (for admission).

Costs (2010–11) *Tuition:* state resident $4853 full-time; nonresident $17,388 full-time. Full-time tuition and fees vary according to degree level and program. Part-time tuition and fees vary according to course load, degree level, and program. *Required fees:* $1676 full-time. *Room and board:* $8154; room only: $4976. Room and board charges vary according to board plan and housing facility. *Payment plan:* installment. *Waivers:* senior citizens and employees or children of employees.

Financial Aid Of all full-time matriculated undergraduates who enrolled in 2009, 14,308 applied for aid, 10,830 were judged to have need, 4,042 had their need fully met. 699 Federal Work-Study jobs (averaging $1000). 274 state and other part-time jobs (averaging $6599). In 2009, 746 non-need-based awards were made. *Average percent of need met:* 86%. *Average financial aid package:* $11,879. *Average need-based loan:* $3208. *Average need-based gift aid:* $9658. *Average non-need-based aid:* $5869. *Average indebtedness upon graduation:* $19,988.

Applying *Options:* electronic application, early action, deferred entrance. *Application fee:* $70. *Required:* high school transcript. *Required for some:* interview. *Recommended:* essay or personal statement. *Application deadlines:* 2/1 (freshmen), 4/1 (transfers), 11/1 (early action). *Notification:* continuous (freshmen), continuous (transfers), 1/15 (early action).

Freshman Application Contact Mr. Thomas Griffin, Director of Undergraduate Admissions, North Carolina State University, Box 7103, Raleigh, NC 27695. *Phone:* 919-515-2434. *Fax:* 919-515-5039. *E-mail:* undergrad_admissions@ncsu.edu. *Web site:* http://www.ncsu.edu/.

North Carolina Wesleyan College

Rocky Mount, North Carolina

Freshman Application Contact Ms. Cecelia Summers, Associate Director of Admissions, North Carolina Wesleyan College, 3400 North Wesleyan Boulevard, Rocky Mount, NC 27804. *Phone:* 252-985-5200. *Toll-free phone:* 800-488-6292. *Fax:* 252-985-5295. *E-mail:* adm@ncwc.edu. *Web site:* http://www.ncwc.edu/.

Peace College
Raleigh, North Carolina

- **Independent** 4-year, founded 1857, affiliated with Presbyterian Church (U.S.A.)
- **Urban** 19-acre campus
- **Endowment** $32.2 million
- **Women only**
- **Moderately difficult** entrance level

Faculty *Student/faculty ratio:* 14:1.

Academics *Calendar:* semesters. *Degrees:* certificates, diplomas, bachelor's, and postbachelor's certificates.

Student Life *Campus security:* 24-hour emergency response devices and patrols, late-night transport/escort service, controlled dormitory access.

Athletics Member NCAA. All Division III.

Standardized Tests *Required:* SAT or ACT (for admission). *Recommended:* SAT and SAT Subject Tests or ACT (for admission), SAT Subject Tests (for admission).

Costs (2010–11) *Comprehensive fee:* $33,720 includes full-time tuition ($25,058) and room and board ($8662). Full-time tuition and fees vary according to course load. Part-time tuition and fees vary according to course load. *Room and board:* Room and board charges vary according to board plan and housing facility.

Financial Aid *Of all full-time matriculated undergraduates who enrolled in 2009,* 601 applied for aid, 532 were judged to have need, 57 had their need fully met. 222 Federal Work-Study jobs (averaging $1840). 17 state and other part-time jobs (averaging $1307). *In 2009,* 120 non-need-based awards were made. *Average percent of need met:* 72. *Average financial aid package:* $19,858. *Average need-based loan:* $3978. *Average need-based gift aid:* $15,690. *Average non-need-based aid:* $7830. *Average indebtedness upon graduation:* $22,428.

Applying *Options:* electronic application. *Application fee:* $25. *Required:* high school transcript, minimum 2 GPA, Dean's Evaluation (transfers). *Recommended:* essay or personal statement, 2 letters of recommendation, interview.

Freshman Application Contact Mr. Matt Green, Dean of Enrollment, Peace College, 15 East Peace Street. *Phone:* 919-509-2000 Ext. 2016. *Toll-free phone:* 800-PEACE-47. *Fax:* 919-508-2326. *E-mail:* mtgreen@peace.edu. *Web site:* http://www.peace.edu/.

Pfeiffer University
Misenheimer, North Carolina

Freshman Application Contact Ms. Diane Martin, Associate Director of Admissions, Pfeiffer University, PO Box 960, Highway 52 North, Misenheimer, NC 28109. *Phone:* 704-463-3052. *Toll-free phone:* 800-338-2060. *Fax:* 704-463-1363. *E-mail:* admiss@pfeiffer.edu. *Web site:* http://www.pfeiffer.edu/.

Piedmont Baptist College and Graduate School
Winston-Salem, North Carolina

- **Independent Baptist** comprehensive, founded 1947
- **Urban** 12-acre campus
- **Coed**
- **Noncompetitive** entrance level

Academics *Calendar:* semesters. *Degrees:* associate, bachelor's, master's, and doctoral-research/scholarship.

Student Life *Campus security:* student patrols, late-night transport/escort service, controlled dormitory access, security guards on duty during evening hours.

Athletics Member NCCAA.

Standardized Tests *Required:* ACT (for admission).

Costs (2010–11) *Comprehensive fee:* $16,980 includes full-time tuition ($10,380), mandatory fees ($840), and room and board ($5760). Full-time tuition and fees vary according to course load, degree level, location, and program. Part-time tuition: $450 per credit hour. Part-time tuition and fees vary according to course load, degree level, location, and program. *Required fees:* $220 per term part-time.

Financial Aid *Financial aid deadline:* 8/31.

Applying *Options:* electronic application, early admission, early action, deferred entrance. *Application fee:* $50. *Required:* essay or personal statement, high school transcript, 2 letters of recommendation, medical history, proof of immunization. *Recommended:* minimum 2 GPA, interview.

Freshman Application Contact Piedmont Baptist College and Graduate School, 420 South Broad Street, Winston-Salem, NC 27101-5197. *Phone:*

336-725-8344 Ext. 2322. *Toll-free phone:* 800-937-5097. *Web site:* http://www.pbc.edu/.

Queens University of Charlotte
Charlotte, North Carolina

- **Independent Presbyterian** comprehensive, founded 1857
- **Suburban** 30-acre campus
- **Endowment** $52.7 million
- **Coed**
- **Moderately difficult** entrance level

Faculty *Student/faculty ratio:* 12:1.

Academics *Calendar:* semesters. *Degrees:* associate, bachelor's, master's, and postbachelor's certificates.

Student Life *Campus security:* 24-hour emergency response devices and patrols, late-night transport/escort service, controlled dormitory access.

Athletics Member NCAA. All Division II.

Standardized Tests *Required:* SAT or ACT (for admission).

Costs (2010–11) *Comprehensive fee:* $32,360 includes full-time tuition ($23,752) and room and board ($8608). Part-time tuition: $395 per credit hour. *Room and board:* Room and board charges vary according to board plan.

Financial Aid *Of all full-time matriculated undergraduates who enrolled in 2002,* 510 applied for aid, 382 were judged to have need, 110 had their need fully met. 134 Federal Work-Study jobs (averaging $879). 4 state and other part-time jobs (averaging $999). *In 2002,* 266 non-need-based awards were made. *Average percent of need met:* 74. *Average financial aid package:* $10,198. *Average need-based loan:* $2962. *Average need-based gift aid:* $7790. *Average non-need-based aid:* $7426. *Average indebtedness upon graduation:* $15,874.

Applying *Options:* electronic application, deferred entrance. *Application fee:* $40. *Required:* high school transcript, minimum 2.5 GPA. *Required for some:* essay or personal statement. *Recommended:* interview.

Freshman Application Contact Queens University of Charlotte, 1900 Selwyn Avenue, Harris Welcome Center, Charlotte, NC 28274. *Phone:* 704-337-2212. *Toll-free phone:* 800-849-0202. *Fax:* 704-337-2403. *E-mail:* admissions@queens.edu. *Web site:* http://www.queens.edu/.

St. Andrews Presbyterian College
Laurinburg, North Carolina

- **Independent Presbyterian** 4-year, founded 1958
- **Small-town** 600-acre campus
- **Endowment** $14.1 million
- **Coed** 441 undergraduate students, 94% full-time, 59% women, 41% men
- **Moderately difficult** entrance level, 69% of applicants were admitted

Undergraduates 416 full-time, 25 part-time. Students come from 33 states and territories; 8 other countries; 54% are from out of state; 14% Black or African American, non-Hispanic/Latino; 2% Hispanic/Latino; 2% Asian, non-Hispanic/Latino; 1% American Indian or Alaska Native, non-Hispanic/Latino; 0.7% Race/ethnicity unknown; 3% international; 7% transferred in; 94% live on campus.

Freshmen *Admission:* 582 applied, 404 admitted, 97 enrolled. *Average high school GPA:* 2.99. *Test scores:* SAT critical reading scores over 500: 42%; SAT math scores over 500: 43%; SAT critical reading scores over 600: 10%; SAT math scores over 600: 7%; SAT critical reading scores over 700: 1%.

Faculty *Total:* 64, 47% full-time, 50% with terminal degrees. *Student/faculty ratio:* 10:1.

Academics *Calendar:* semesters. *Degree:* certificates and bachelor's. *Special study options:* accelerated degree program, adult/continuing education programs, advanced placement credit, double majors, honors programs, independent study, internships, part-time degree program, services for LD students, student-designed majors, study abroad, summer session for credit. *Unusual degree programs:* 3-2 engineering with North Carolina State University; accounting with University of Georgia.

Computers on Campus 100 computers/terminals are available on campus for general student use. Students can access the following: campus intranet, computer help desk, free student e-mail accounts. Campuswide network is available. Wireless service is available via classrooms, libraries, student centers.

Student Life *Housing:* on-campus residence required through senior year. *Options:* coed, men-only, women-only. Campus housing is university owned. *Activities and organizations:* drama/theater group, student-run newspaper, choral group, Riding Council, Student Activities Union, Writer's Forum, Christian Student Union, Lion's Club. *Campus security:* 24-hour emergency response devices and patrols, late-night transport/escort service. *Student services:* health clinic, personal/psychological counseling.

Athletics Member NCAA. All Division II. *Intercollegiate sports:* baseball M(s), basketball M(s)/W(s), cross-country running M(s)/W(s), equestrian sports M(s)/W(s), golf M(s)/W(s), lacrosse M(s)/W(s), soccer M(s)/W(s), soft-

ball W(s), wrestling M. *Intramural sports:* basketball M/W, football M/W, rugby M(c)/W(c), softball M/W, table tennis M/W, volleyball M/W.
Standardized Tests *Required:* SAT or ACT (for admission).
Costs (2010–11) *Comprehensive fee:* $30,552 includes full-time tuition ($21,614) and room and board ($8938). Full-time tuition and fees vary according to course load and location. Part-time tuition: $450 per credit hour. Part-time tuition and fees vary according to location. *Room and board:* Room and board charges vary according to housing facility. *Payment plan:* installment. *Waivers:* adult students, senior citizens, and employees or children of employees.
Financial Aid *Of all full-time matriculated undergraduates who enrolled in 2009,* 435 applied for aid, 347 were judged to have need, 75 had their need fully met. 196 Federal Work-Study jobs (averaging $1800). 19 state and other part-time jobs (averaging $1800). *In 2009,* 77 non-need-based awards were made. *Average percent of need met:* 75%. *Average financial aid package:* $18,461. *Average need-based loan:* $4374. *Average need-based gift aid:* $14,177. *Average non-need-based aid:* $5270. *Average indebtedness upon graduation:* $22,599.
Applying *Options:* electronic application, early decision, deferred entrance. *Application fee:* $30. *Required:* high school transcript. *Required for some:* essay or personal statement, interview. *Recommended:* minimum 2 GPA. *Application deadlines:* rolling (freshmen), rolling (transfers). *Notification:* continuous (freshmen), continuous (transfers).
Freshman Application Contact Kristen Simmons, Director of Admissions, St. Andrews Presbyterian College, 1700 Dogwood Mile, Laurinburg, NC 28352. *Phone:* 910-277-5555. *Toll-free phone:* 800-763-0198. *Fax:* 910-277-5087. *E-mail:* admission@sapc.edu. *Web site:* http://www.sapc.edu/.

Saint Augustine's College
Raleigh, North Carolina

- **Independent Episcopal** 4-year, founded 1867
- **Urban** 105-acre campus
- **Endowment** $13.4 million
- **Coed**
- **Moderately difficult** entrance level

Faculty *Student/faculty ratio:* 16:1.
Academics *Calendar:* semesters. *Degree:* bachelor's.
Student Life *Campus security:* 24-hour emergency response devices and patrols, RAVE - Emergency Notification System.
Athletics Member NCAA. All Division II.
Standardized Tests *Required:* SAT or ACT (for admission).
Costs (2010–11) *Comprehensive fee:* $24,286 includes full-time tuition ($12,364), mandatory fees ($4796), and room and board ($7126). Full-time tuition and fees vary according to course load and program. Part-time tuition: $515 per semester hour. Part-time tuition and fees vary according to course load and program. *Required fees:* $200 per credit hour part-time. *College room only:* $2948. Room and board charges vary according to housing facility. *Payment plans:* installment, deferred payment.
Financial Aid *Of all full-time matriculated undergraduates who enrolled in 2009,* 1,222 applied for aid, 1,147 were judged to have need, 24 had their need fully met. 411 Federal Work-Study jobs (averaging $2500). 4 state and other part-time jobs (averaging $2500). *In 2009,* 11 non-need-based awards were made. *Average percent of need met:* 100. *Average financial aid package:* $2209. *Average need-based loan:* $2148. *Average need-based gift aid:* $1965. *Average non-need-based aid:* $2231. *Average indebtedness upon graduation:* $12,614.
Applying *Options:* electronic application, deferred entrance. *Application fee:* $25. *Required:* high school transcript, minimum 2 GPA, 2 letters of recommendation, medical history, social security card, background check. *Required for some:* essay or personal statement, interview. *Recommended:* minimum 2.5 GPA.
Freshman Application Contact Mr. Jorge E. Sousa, Director of Admissions, Saint Augustine's College, 1315 Oakwood Avenue, Raleigh, NC 27610-2298. *Phone:* 919-516-4012. *Toll-free phone:* 800-948-1126. *Fax:* 919-516-5805. *E-mail:* jesousa@st-aug.edu. *Web site:* http://www.st-aug.edu/.

Salem College
Winston-Salem, North Carolina

- **Independent religious** comprehensive, founded 1772
- **Urban** 67-acre campus with easy access to Charlotte
- **Coed, primarily women**
- **Moderately difficult** entrance level

Faculty *Student/faculty ratio:* 11:1.
Academics *Calendar:* 4-1-4. *Degrees:* bachelor's and master's (only students age 23 or over are eligible to enroll part-time).
Student Life *Campus security:* 24-hour emergency response devices and patrols, late-night transport/escort service, controlled dormitory access.

Athletics Member NCAA. All Division III.
Standardized Tests *Required:* SAT or ACT (for admission).
Costs (2010–11) *Comprehensive fee:* $33,485 includes full-time tuition ($21,610), mandatory fees ($355), and room and board ($11,520). Full-time tuition and fees vary according to degree level and program. Part-time tuition: $1074 per course. Part-time tuition and fees vary according to course load, degree level, and program. *Required fees:* $70 per term part-time.
Financial Aid *Of all full-time matriculated undergraduates who enrolled in 2008,* 476 applied for aid, 438 were judged to have need, 438 had their need fully met. 98 Federal Work-Study jobs (averaging $1009). *In 2008,* 38 non-need-based awards were made. *Average percent of need met:* 100. *Average financial aid package:* $18,755. *Average need-based loan:* $4406. *Average need-based gift aid:* $8440. *Average non-need-based aid:* $13,316. *Average indebtedness upon graduation:* $19,000.
Applying *Options:* electronic application, early admission, deferred entrance. *Application fee:* $30. *Required:* essay or personal statement, high school transcript, 2 letters of recommendation. *Recommended:* interview.
Freshman Application Contact Dean Katherine Knapp Watts, Dean of Admissions and Financial Aid, Salem College, Single Sisters House, 601 South Church Street, Winston-Salem, NC 27101. *Phone:* 336-721-2621. *Toll-free phone:* 800-327-2536. *Fax:* 336-917-5572. *E-mail:* admissions@salem.edu. *Web site:* http://www.salem.edu/.

Shaw University
Raleigh, North Carolina

- **Independent Baptist** comprehensive, founded 1865
- **Urban** 30-acre campus
- **Coed**
- **Minimally difficult** entrance level

Faculty *Student/faculty ratio:* 16:1.
Academics *Calendar:* semesters. *Degrees:* associate, bachelor's, master's, and doctoral-professional.
Student Life *Campus security:* 24-hour emergency response devices and patrols, late-night transport/escort service, 24-hour electronic surveillance cameras.
Athletics Member NCAA. All Division II.
Standardized Tests *Required:* SAT or ACT (for admission).
Costs (2010–11) *Comprehensive fee:* $20,140 includes full-time tuition ($9840), mandatory fees ($2740), and room and board ($7560). Part-time tuition: $410 per semester hour. *College room only:* $3570. *Payment plans:* installment, deferred payment.
Financial Aid *Of all full-time matriculated undergraduates who enrolled in 2005,* 2,197 applied for aid, 2,068 were judged to have need, 201 had their need fully met. 347 Federal Work-Study jobs (averaging $1120). *In 2005,* 117 non-need-based awards were made. *Average percent of need met:* 63. *Average financial aid package:* $8992. *Average need-based loan:* $3394. *Average need-based gift aid:* $5898. *Average non-need-based aid:* $9333. *Average indebtedness upon graduation:* $15,982. *Financial aid deadline:* 6/1.
Applying *Options:* electronic application, early admission, deferred entrance. *Application fee:* $25. *Required:* essay or personal statement, high school transcript, minimum 2 GPA.
Freshman Application Contact Ms. Sandy Clifton, Interim Director of Admissions and Recruitment, Shaw University, 118 East South Street, Raleigh, NC 27601-2399. *Phone:* 919-546-8275. *Toll-free phone:* 800-214-6683. *Fax:* 919-546-8271. *E-mail:* sclifton@shawu.edu. *Web site:* http://www.shawu.edu/.

South College–Asheville
Asheville, North Carolina

Freshman Application Contact Director of Admissions, South College–Asheville, 1567 Patton Avenue, Asheville, NC 28806. *Phone:* 828-277-5521. *Fax:* 828-277-6151. *Web site:* http://www.southcollegenc.edu.

Southeastern Baptist Theological Seminary
Wake Forest, North Carolina

- **Independent Southern Baptist** comprehensive, founded 1950
- **Small-town** 450-acre campus with easy access to Raleigh
- **Coed** 529 undergraduate students, 44% full-time, 42% women, 58% men
- **Minimally difficult** entrance level, 97% of applicants were admitted

Undergraduates 233 full-time, 296 part-time. Students come from 32 states and territories; 3 other countries; 15% are from out of state.
Freshmen *Admission:* 182 applied, 176 admitted, 69 enrolled.
Faculty *Total:* 85, 74% full-time, 80% with terminal degrees. *Student/faculty ratio:* 17:1.

Academics *Calendar:* semesters. *Degrees:* certificates, associate, bachelor's, and master's. *Special study options:* academic remediation for entering students, adult/continuing education programs, distance learning, double majors, independent study, internships, off-campus study, part-time degree program, summer session for credit.

Computers on Campus 7 computers/terminals are available on campus for general student use. Students can access the following: campus intranet, free student e-mail accounts, online (class) grades, online (class) registration, online (class) schedules. Campuswide network is available. Wireless service is available via classrooms, libraries, student centers.

Student Life *Housing options:* men-only, women-only. Campus housing is university owned and leased by the school. *Activities and organizations:* drama/theater group, choral group. *Campus security:* 24-hour emergency response devices and patrols, late-night transport/escort service. *Student services:* health clinic, personal/psychological counseling, women's center.

Athletics *Intramural sports:* basketball M/W, football M, golf M, racquetball M, table tennis M, tennis M, volleyball M, weight lifting M.

Standardized Tests *Required:* SAT or ACT (for admission).

Costs (2010–11) *Tuition:* $229 per credit hour part-time. Full-time tuition and fees vary according to degree level, location, and program. Part-time tuition and fees vary according to degree level, location, and program. *Required fees:* $165 per term part-time. *Room only:* Room and board charges vary according to housing facility. *Payment plan:* installment.

Applying *Application fee:* $25. *Required:* essay or personal statement, high school transcript. *Required for some:* interview. *Application deadlines:* 7/20 (freshmen), 7/20 (transfers). *Notification:* continuous until 8/20 (freshmen), continuous until 8/20 (transfers).

Freshman Application Contact Ms. Penny Keathley, Admissions Counselor, Southeastern Baptist Theological Seminary, PO Box 1889, Wake Forest, NC 27588-1889. *Phone:* 800-284-6317. *Toll-free phone:* 800-284-6317. *Web site:* http://www.sebts.edu/.

Strayer University - Greensboro Campus

Greensboro, North Carolina

- **Proprietary** comprehensive
- **Coed**

Academics *Degrees:* associate, bachelor's, master's, and postbachelor's certificates.

Costs (2010–11) *Tuition:* $13,635 full-time, $1590 per course part-time.

Freshman Application Contact Strayer University - Greensboro Campus, 4900 Koger Boulevard, Suite 400, Greensboro, NC 27407. *Web site:* http://www.strayer.edu/greensboro.

Strayer University - Huntersville Campus

Huntersville, North Carolina

- **Proprietary** comprehensive
- **Coed**

Academics *Degrees:* associate, bachelor's, master's, and postbachelor's certificates.

Costs (2010–11) *Tuition:* $13,635 full-time, $1590 per course part-time.

Freshman Application Contact Strayer University - Huntersville Campus, 13620 Reese Boulevard, Suite 130, Huntersville, NC 28078. *Web site:* http://www.strayer.edu/huntersville/.

Strayer University - North Charlotte Campus

Charlotte, North Carolina

- **Proprietary** comprehensive
- **Coed**

Academics *Degrees:* associate, bachelor's, master's, and postbachelor's certificates.

Costs (2010–11) *Tuition:* $13,635 full-time, $1590 per course part-time.

Freshman Application Contact Strayer University - North Charlotte Campus, 8335 IBM Drive, Suite 150, Charlotte, NC 28262. *Web site:* http://www.strayer.edu/north_charlotte.

Strayer University - North Raleigh Campus

Raleigh, North Carolina

- **Proprietary** comprehensive
- **Coed**

Academics *Degrees:* associate, bachelor's, master's, and postbachelor's certificates.

Costs (2010–11) *Tuition:* $13,635 full-time, $1590 per course part-time.

Freshman Application Contact Strayer University - North Raleigh Campus, 3200 Spring Forest Road, Suite 214, Raleigh, NC 27616. *Web site:* http://www.strayer.edu/north_raleigh.

Strayer University - RTP Campus

Morrisville, North Carolina

- **Proprietary** comprehensive
- **Coed**

Academics *Degrees:* associate, bachelor's, master's, and postbachelor's certificates.

Costs (2010–11) *Tuition:* $13,635 full-time, $1590 per course part-time.

Freshman Application Contact Strayer University - RTP Campus, 4 Copley Parkway, Morrisville, NC 27560. *Web site:* http://www.strayer.edu/rtp_campus/.

Strayer University - South Charlotte Campus

Charlotte, North Carolina

- **Proprietary** comprehensive
- **Coed**

Academics *Degrees:* associate, bachelor's, master's, and postbachelor's certificates.

Costs (2010–11) *Tuition:* $13,635 full-time, $1590 per course part-time.

Freshman Application Contact Strayer University - South Charlotte Campus, 9101 Kings Parade Boulevard, Suite 200, Charlotte, NC 28273. *Web site:* http://www.strayer.edu/south_charlotte.

Strayer University - South Raleigh Campus

Raleigh, North Carolina

- **Proprietary** comprehensive
- **Coed**

Academics *Degrees:* associate, bachelor's, master's, and postbachelor's certificates.

Costs (2010–11) *Tuition:* $13,635 full-time, $1590 per course part-time.

Freshman Application Contact Strayer University - South Raleigh Campus, 3421 Olympia Drive, Raleigh, NC 27603. *Web site:* http://www.strayer.edu/south_raleigh.

The University of North Carolina at Asheville

Asheville, North Carolina

- **State-supported** comprehensive, founded 1927, part of University of North Carolina System
- **Suburban** 265-acre campus
- **Endowment** $23.9 million
- **Coed** 3,916 undergraduate students, 83% full-time, 56% women, 44% men
- **Moderately difficult** entrance level, 77% of applicants were admitted

Undergraduates 3,238 full-time, 678 part-time. Students come from 39 states and territories; 20 other countries; 12% are from out of state; 9% transferred in; 33% live on campus. *Retention:* 82% of full-time freshmen returned.

Freshmen *Admission:* 2,362 applied, 1,824 admitted, 595 enrolled. *Average high school GPA:* 3.91. *Test scores:* SAT critical reading scores over 500: 88%; SAT math scores over 500: 88%; SAT writing scores over 500: 83%; ACT scores over 18: 95%; SAT critical reading scores over 600: 50%; SAT math scores over 600: 40%; SAT writing scores over 600: 38%; ACT scores over 24: 57%; SAT critical reading scores over 700: 12%; SAT math scores over 700: 4%; SAT writing scores over 700: 6%; ACT scores over 30: 8%.

Faculty *Total:* 309, 70% full-time, 71% with terminal degrees. *Student/faculty ratio:* 14:1.

Academics *Calendar:* semesters. *Degrees:* bachelor's, master's, and post-bachelor's certificates. *Special study options:* academic remediation for entering students, adult/continuing education programs, advanced placement credit, distance learning, double majors, honors programs, independent study, internships, off-campus study, part-time degree program, services for LD students, student-designed majors, study abroad, summer session for credit. *Unusual degree programs:* 3-2 chemistry and textile chemistry with North Carolina State University.

Computers on Campus 360 computers/terminals are available on campus for general student use. Students can access the following: computer help desk, free student e-mail accounts, online (class) grades, online (class) registration, online (class) schedules. Campuswide network is available. 100% of college-owned or -operated housing units are wired for high-speed Internet access. Wireless service is available via classrooms, libraries, student centers.

Student Life *Housing:* on-campus residence required for freshman year. *Options:* coed, men-only, women-only, disabled students. Campus housing is university owned and leased by the school. Freshman campus housing is guaranteed. *Activities and organizations:* drama/theater group, student-run newspaper, radio station, choral group, Student Government Association, Underdog Productions, Residence Hall Association, African-American Association, International Student Association, national fraternities, national sororities. *Campus security:* 24-hour emergency response devices and patrols, late-night transport/escort service, dorm entrances secured at night. *Student services:* health clinic, personal/psychological counseling, women's center.

Athletics Member NCAA. All Division I. *Intercollegiate sports:* baseball M(s), basketball M(s)/W(s), cheerleading M/W, cross-country running M(s)/W(s), soccer M(s)/W(s), tennis M(s)/W(s), track and field M(s)/W(s), volleyball W(s). *Intramural sports:* badminton M/W, basketball M/W, equestrian sports M(c)/W(c), football M/W, racquetball M/W, soccer M(c)/W, tennis M/W, ultimate Frisbee M(c)/W(c), volleyball M(c)/W(c).

Standardized Tests *Required:* SAT or ACT (for admission).

Costs (2010–11) *Tuition:* state resident $2626 full-time; nonresident $15,398 full-time. Full-time tuition and fees vary according to course load. Part-time tuition and fees vary according to course load. *Required fees:* $2146 full-time. *Room and board:* $7040; room only: $3990. Room and board charges vary according to housing facility. *Payment plan:* installment. *Waivers:* employees or children of employees.

Financial Aid Of all full-time matriculated undergraduates who enrolled in 2009, 2,264 applied for aid, 1,640 were judged to have need, 858 had their need fully met. 43 Federal Work-Study jobs (averaging $2654). In 2009, 160 non-need-based awards were made. *Average percent of need met:* 87%. *Average financial aid package:* $11,450. *Average need-based loan:* $4195. *Average need-based gift aid:* $6470. *Average non-need-based aid:* $3260. *Average indebtedness upon graduation:* $15,443.

Applying *Options:* electronic application, early action, deferred entrance. *Application fee:* $50. *Required:* essay or personal statement, high school transcript, 1 letter of recommendation, minimum course requirement. *Required for some:* interview. *Application deadlines:* 2/15 (freshmen), 4/15 (transfers), 11/15 (early action). *Notification:* 3/15 (freshmen), continuous (transfers), 12/15 (early action).

Freshman Application Contact Ms. Leigh McBride, Associate Director of Admissions, The University of North Carolina at Asheville, University Dining Hall, CPO # 1320, Asheville, NC 28804-8510. *Phone:* 828-251-6481. *Toll-free phone:* 800-531-9842. *Fax:* 828-251-6482. *E-mail:* admissions@unca.edu. *Web site:* http://www.unca.edu/.

The University of North Carolina at Chapel Hill

Chapel Hill, North Carolina

- **State-supported** university, founded 1789, part of University of North Carolina System
- **Suburban** 729-acre campus with easy access to Raleigh-Durham
- **Endowment** $2.0 billion
- **Coed** 18,579 undergraduate students, 94% full-time, 59% women, 41% men
- **Very difficult** entrance level, 32% of applicants were admitted

Undergraduates 17,513 full-time, 1,066 part-time. Students come from 51 states and territories; 63 other countries; 18% are from out of state; 9% Black or African American, non-Hispanic/Latino; 11% Hispanic/Latino; 6% Asian, non-Hispanic/Latino; 0.9% Native Hawaiian or other Pacific Islander, non-Hispanic/Latino; 0.6% American Indian or Alaska Native, non-Hispanic/

Latino; 2% Two or more races, non-Hispanic/Latino; 3% Race/ethnicity unknown; 2% international; 5% transferred in; 46% live on campus. *Retention:* 97% of full-time freshmen returned.

Freshmen *Admission:* 23,272 applied, 7,557 admitted, 3,960 enrolled. *Average high school GPA:* 4.47. *Test scores:* SAT critical reading scores over 500: 97%; SAT math scores over 500: 98%; SAT writing scores over 500: 96%; ACT scores over 18: 100%; SAT critical reading scores over 600: 74%; SAT math scores over 600: 83%; SAT writing scores over 600: 71%; ACT scores over 24: 93%; SAT critical reading scores over 700: 25%; SAT math scores over 700: 31%; SAT writing scores over 700: 24%; ACT scores over 30: 46%.

Faculty *Total:* 1,788, 93% full-time, 89% with terminal degrees. *Student/faculty ratio:* 14:1.

Academics *Calendar:* semesters. *Degrees:* certificates, bachelor's, master's, doctoral-professional, doctoral-research/scholarship, post-master's, and post-bachelor's certificates. *Special study options:* advanced placement credit, distance learning, double majors, English as a second language, honors programs, independent study, internships, off-campus study, part-time degree program, services for LD students, student-designed majors, study abroad, summer session for credit. *ROTC:* Army (b), Navy (b), Air Force (b).

Computers on Campus 740 computers/terminals and 9,999 ports are available on campus for general student use. Students can access the following: computer help desk, free student e-mail accounts, online (class) grades, online (class) registration, online (class) schedules. Campuswide network is available. 100% of college-owned or -operated housing units are wired for high-speed Internet access. Wireless service is available via entire campus.

Student Life *Housing:* on-campus residence required for freshman year. *Options:* coed, men-only, women-only, disabled students. Campus housing is university owned. Freshman campus housing is guaranteed. *Activities and organizations:* drama/theater group, student-run newspaper, radio and television station, choral group, marching band, Campus Y, Panhellenic Council, Campus Crusade for Christ (Cornerstone), Black Student Movement, Out-of-State Students Association, national fraternities, national sororities. *Campus security:* 24-hour emergency response devices and patrols, student patrols, late-night transport/escort service, controlled dormitory access, crime prevention programs (e.g., classes and workshops addressing acquaintance rape, workplace violence, alcohol abuse, self-defense). *Student services:* health clinic, personal/psychological counseling, women's center, legal services.

Athletics Member NCAA. All Division I except football (Division I-A). *Intercollegiate sports:* baseball M(s), basketball M(s)/W(s), crew W(s), cross-country running M(s)/W(s), fencing M/W, field hockey W(s), golf M(s)/W(s), gymnastics W(s), lacrosse M(s)/W(s), racquetball M(c)/W(c), soccer M(s)/W(s), softball W(s), swimming and diving M(s)/W(s), tennis M(s)/W(s), track and field M(s)/W(s), ultimate Frisbee M(c)/W(c), volleyball M(c)/W(s), water polo M(c)/W(c), wrestling M(s). *Intramural sports:* badminton M/W, baseball M(c), basketball M/W, cheerleading W(c), crew M(c), cross-country running M(c)/W(c), equestrian sports W(c), field hockey M(c)/W(c), football M(c), golf M(c)/W(c), gymnastics M(c)/W(c), ice hockey M(c), lacrosse M(c)/W(c), racquetball M/W, rugby M(c)/W(c), sailing M(c)/W(c), soccer M(c)/W(c), softball M/W, swimming and diving M(c)/W(c), table tennis M/W, tennis M(c)/W(c), track and field M(c)/W(c), ultimate Frisbee M/W, volleyball M/W, water polo M/W, wrestling M(c).

Standardized Tests *Required:* SAT or ACT (for admission).

Costs (2010–11) *Tuition:* state resident $4816 full-time; nonresident $23,430 full-time. Full-time tuition and fees vary according to program. Part-time tuition and fees vary according to course load and program. *Required fees:* $1850 full-time. *Room and board:* $9036; room only: $5408. Room and board charges vary according to board plan, housing facility, and location. *Payment plans:* installment, deferred payment. *Waivers:* employees or children of employees.

Financial Aid Of all full-time matriculated undergraduates who enrolled in 2008, 11,595 applied for aid, 6,276 were judged to have need, 6,064 had their need fully met. 1,645 Federal Work-Study jobs (averaging $1844). In 2008, 2621 non-need-based awards were made. *Average percent of need met:* 100%. *Average financial aid package:* $13,509. *Average need-based loan:* $4154. *Average need-based gift aid:* $11,080. *Average non-need-based aid:* $5117.

Applying *Options:* electronic application, early action, deferred entrance. *Application fee:* $70. *Required:* essay or personal statement, high school transcript, 1 letter of recommendation, counselor's statement. *Application deadlines:* 1/15 (freshmen), 3/1 (transfers), 11/2 (early action). *Notification:* 3/20 (freshmen), 4/15 (transfers), 1/30 (early action).

Freshman Application Contact The University of North Carolina at Chapel Hill, Chapel Hill, NC 27599. *Phone:* 919-966-3621. *Web site:* http://www.unc.edu/.

The University of North Carolina at Charlotte

Charlotte, North Carolina

- **State-supported** university, founded 1946, part of University of North Carolina System
- **Suburban** 1000-acre campus
- **Endowment** $126.4 million
- **Coed** 19,755 undergraduate students, 85% full-time, 51% women, 49% men
- **Moderately difficult** entrance level, 71% of applicants were admitted

Undergraduates 16,854 full-time, 2,901 part-time. Students come from 49 states and territories; 107 other countries; 8% are from out of state; 17% Black or African American, non-Hispanic/Latino; 5% Hispanic/Latino; 5% Asian, non-Hispanic/Latino; 0.1% Native Hawaiian or other Pacific Islander, non-Hispanic/Latino; 0.6% American Indian or Alaska Native, non-Hispanic/Latino; 1% Two or more races, non-Hispanic/Latino; 4% Race/ethnicity unknown; 3% international; 12% transferred in; 25% live on campus. *Retention:* 78% of full-time freshmen returned.

Freshmen *Admission:* 11,239 applied, 8,034 admitted, 2,985 enrolled. *Average high school GPA:* 3.65. *Test scores:* SAT critical reading scores over 500: 65%; SAT math scores over 500: 76%; SAT writing scores over 500: 56%; ACT scores over 18: 96%; SAT critical reading scores over 600: 16%; SAT math scores over 600: 24%; SAT writing scores over 600: 11%; ACT scores over 24: 35%; SAT critical reading scores over 700: 2%; SAT math scores over 700: 2%; SAT writing scores over 700: 1%; ACT scores over 30: 4%.

Faculty *Total:* 1,376, 71% full-time, 69% with terminal degrees. *Student/faculty ratio:* 19:1.

Academics *Calendar:* semesters. *Degrees:* bachelor's, master's, doctoral-research/scholarship, post-master's, and postbachelor's certificates. *Special study options:* accelerated degree program, adult/continuing education programs, advanced placement credit, cooperative education, distance learning, double majors, English as a second language, freshman honors college, honors programs, independent study, internships, off-campus study, part-time degree program, services for LD students, study abroad, summer session for credit. *ROTC:* Army (b), Air Force (b).

Computers on Campus 3,500 computers/terminals are available on campus for general student use. Students can access the following: computer help desk, free student e-mail accounts, online (class) grades, online (class) registration, online (class) schedules. Campuswide network is available. 100% of college-owned or -operated housing units are wired for high-speed Internet access. Wireless service is available via classrooms, computer centers, computer labs, learning centers, libraries, student centers.

Student Life *Housing options:* coed, men-only, women-only, disabled students. Campus housing is university owned. *Activities and organizations:* drama/theater group, student-run newspaper, radio and television station, choral group, Student Government Association, Student Alumni Ambassadors, Black Student Union, 49er Social and Ballroom Dance, Feminist Student Union, national fraternities, national sororities. *Campus security:* 24-hour emergency response devices and patrols, late-night transport/escort service, controlled dormitory access. *Student services:* health clinic, personal/psychological counseling.

Athletics Member NCAA. All Division I. *Intercollegiate sports:* baseball M(s), basketball M(s)/W(s), cheerleading M/W, cross-country running M(s)/W(s), golf M(s)/W(s), soccer M(s)/W(s), softball W(s), tennis M(s)/W(s), track and field M(s)/W(s), volleyball W(s). *Intramural sports:* archery M(c)/W(c), badminton M(c)/W(c), baseball M(c)/W(c), basketball M/W, bowling M(c)/W(c), fencing M(c)/W(c), football M/W, golf M/W, ice hockey M(c)/W(c), lacrosse M(c)/W(c), racquetball M(c)/W(c), rock climbing M/W, rugby M(c)/W(c), soccer M(c)/W(c), softball M(c)/W(c), swimming and diving M(c)/W(c), table tennis M/W, tennis M(c)/W(c), track and field M/W, ultimate Frisbee M(c)/W(c), volleyball M(c)/W(c), water polo M/W, wrestling M(c)/W(c).

Standardized Tests *Required:* SAT or ACT (for admission).

Costs (2010–11) *Tuition:* state resident $3044 full-time; nonresident $14,091 full-time. Full-time tuition and fees vary according to course load. Part-time tuition and fees vary according to course load. *Required fees:* $2094 full-time. *Room and board:* $7260; room only: $3830. Room and board charges vary according to board plan and housing facility. *Payment plan:* installment. *Waivers:* employees or children of employees.

Financial Aid Of all full-time matriculated undergraduates who enrolled in 2009, 11,270 applied for aid, 8,627 were judged to have need, 1,989 had their need fully met. 534 Federal Work-Study jobs (averaging $1670). 1,993 state and other part-time jobs (averaging $2071). In 2009, 225 non-need-based awards were made. *Average percent of need met:* 74%. *Average financial aid package:* $8642. *Average need-based loan:* $3724. *Average need-based gift aid:* $6096. *Average non-need-based aid:* $2427. *Average indebtedness upon graduation:* $17,964.

Applying *Options:* electronic application, early admission, early action. *Application fee:* $50. *Required:* high school transcript, minimum 2 GPA, med-

ical history, no criminal record. *Required for some:* interview. *Application deadlines:* 7/1 (freshmen), 7/1 (out-of-state freshmen), 7/1 (transfers), 10/15 (early action). *Notification:* continuous (freshmen), continuous (out-of-state freshmen), continuous (transfers), 12/15 (early action).

Freshman Application Contact Tina McEntire, Director of Admissions, The University of North Carolina at Charlotte, 9201 University City Boulevard, 1st Floor, Cato Hall, Charlotte, NC 28223-0001. *Phone:* 704-687-2213. *Fax:* 704-687-6483. *E-mail:* unccadm@uncc.edu. *Web site:* http://www.uncc.edu/.

The University of North Carolina at Greensboro

Greensboro, North Carolina

- **State-supported** university, founded 1891, part of University of North Carolina System
- **Urban** 357-acre campus
- **Endowment** $171.8 million
- **Coed** 14,714 undergraduate students, 89% full-time, 66% women, 34% men
- **Moderately difficult** entrance level, 58% of applicants were admitted

Undergraduates 13,057 full-time, 1,657 part-time. Students come from 51 states and territories; 75 other countries; 7% are from out of state; 23% Black or African American, non-Hispanic/Latino; 4% Hispanic/Latino; 3% Asian, non-Hispanic/Latino; 0.1% Native Hawaiian or other Pacific Islander, non-Hispanic/Latino; 0.4% American Indian or Alaska Native, non-Hispanic/Latino; 3% Two or more races, non-Hispanic/Latino; 0.5% Race/ethnicity unknown; 1% international; 11% transferred in; 29% live on campus. *Retention:* 77% of full-time freshmen returned.

Freshmen *Admission:* 11,574 applied, 6,679 admitted, 2,518 enrolled. *Average high school GPA:* 3.59. *Test scores:* SAT critical reading scores over 500: 54%; SAT math scores over 500: 58%; SAT writing scores over 500: 46%; SAT critical reading scores over 600: 14%; SAT math scores over 600: 14%; SAT writing scores over 600: 11%; SAT critical reading scores over 700: 2%; SAT math scores over 700: 1%; SAT writing scores over 700: 1%.

Faculty *Total:* 1,185, 71% full-time, 63% with terminal degrees. *Student/faculty ratio:* 17:1.

Academics *Calendar:* semesters. *Degrees:* bachelor's, master's, doctoral-research/scholarship, post-master's, and postbachelor's certificates. *Special study options:* academic remediation for entering students, accelerated degree program, adult/continuing education programs, advanced placement credit, distance learning, double majors, freshman honors college, honors programs, independent study, internships, off-campus study, part-time degree program, services for LD students, study abroad, summer session for credit. *ROTC:* Army (c), Air Force (c). *Unusual degree programs:* 3-2 business administration with North Carolina State University, University of North Carolina at Charlotte.

Computers on Campus 400 computers/terminals are available on campus for general student use. Students can access the following: computer help desk, free student e-mail accounts, online (class) grades, online (class) registration, online (class) schedules. Campuswide network is available. 100% of college-owned or -operated housing units are wired for high-speed Internet access. Wireless service is available via classrooms, computer centers, computer labs, dorm rooms, learning centers, libraries, student centers.

Student Life *Housing options:* coed, women-only. Campus housing is university owned. Freshman applicants given priority for college housing. *Activities and organizations:* drama/theater group, student-run newspaper, radio station, choral group, marching band, Campus Activities Board, religious organizations, Neo-Black Society, International Students Association, national fraternities, national sororities. *Campus security:* 24-hour emergency response devices and patrols, student patrols, late-night transport/escort service, controlled dormitory access. *Student services:* health clinic, personal/psychological counseling, women's center.

Athletics Member NCAA. All Division I. *Intercollegiate sports:* baseball M(s), basketball M(s)/W(s), cross-country running M(s)/W(s), golf M(s)/W(s), soccer M(s)/W(s), softball W(s), tennis M(s)/W(s), volleyball W(s), wrestling M(s). *Intramural sports:* basketball M(c)/W(c), cross-country running M(c)/W(c), equestrian sports M(c)/W(c), football W(c), lacrosse M(c), rugby M(c)/W(c), soccer W(c), swimming and diving M(c)/W(c), tennis M(c)/W(c), ultimate Frisbee M(c)/W(c), volleyball W(c).

Standardized Tests *Required:* SAT or ACT (for admission).

Costs (2011–12) *Tuition:* state resident $2790 full-time, $349 per course part-time; nonresident $14,551 full-time, $1819 per course part-time. Part-time tuition and fees vary according to course load. *Required fees:* $1730 full-time, $185 per course part-time. *Room only:* $3855. Room and board charges vary according to board plan and housing facility. *Payment plan:* installment. *Waivers:* employees or children of employees.

Financial Aid Of all full-time matriculated undergraduates who enrolled in 2009, 10,298 applied for aid, 9,980 were judged to have need, 2,252 had their need fully met. 278 Federal Work-Study jobs (averaging $1935). In 2009, 362 non-need-based awards were made. *Average percent of need met:* 58%. *Average financial aid package:* $9838. *Average need-based loan:* $4080. *Average need-based gift aid:* $6041. *Average non-need-based aid:* $2571. *Average indebtedness upon graduation:* $23,772.

Applying *Options:* electronic application, early admission, early action, deferred entrance. *Application fee:* $45. *Required:* high school transcript, minimum 2 GPA. *Application deadlines:* 3/1 (freshmen), 8/1 (transfers). *Notification:* continuous (freshmen), continuous (transfers).

Freshman Application Contact The University of North Carolina at Greensboro, Armfield-Preyer Admissions and Visitor Center, 1400 Spring Garden Street, Greensboro, NC 27412. *Phone:* 336-334-5243. *Fax:* 336-334-4180. *E-mail:* admissions@uncg.edu. *Web site:* http://www.uncg.edu/.

The University of North Carolina at Pembroke

Pembroke, North Carolina

- **State-supported** comprehensive, founded 1887, part of University of North Carolina System
- **Rural** 161-acre campus
- **Endowment** $11.8 million
- **Coed** 6,166 undergraduate students, 79% full-time, 62% women, 38% men
- **Moderately difficult** entrance level, 75% of applicants were admitted

Undergraduates 4,892 full-time, 1,274 part-time. Students come from 32 states and territories; 18 other countries; 3% are from out of state; 32% Black or African American, non-Hispanic/Latino; 4% Hispanic/Latino; 2% Asian, non-Hispanic/Latino; 0.1% Native Hawaiian or other Pacific Islander, non-Hispanic/Latino; 16% American Indian or Alaska Native, non-Hispanic/Latino; 2% Two or more races, non-Hispanic/Latino; 3% Race/ethnicity unknown; 1% international; 10% transferred in; 26% live on campus. *Retention:* 73% of full-time freshmen returned.

Freshmen *Admission:* 2,811 applied, 2,099 admitted, 1,057 enrolled. *Average high school GPA:* 3.12. *Test scores:* SAT critical reading scores over 500: 23%; SAT math scores over 500: 29%; SAT writing scores over 500: 17%; ACT scores over 18: 54%; SAT critical reading scores over 600: 4%; SAT math scores over 600: 4%; SAT writing scores over 600: 2%; ACT scores over 24: 7%; ACT scores over 30: 1%.

Faculty *Total:* 418, 79% full-time, 66% with terminal degrees. *Student/faculty ratio:* 16:1.

Academics *Calendar:* semesters. *Degrees:* bachelor's and master's. *Special study options:* academic remediation for entering students, accelerated degree program, adult/continuing education programs, advanced placement credit, cooperative education, distance learning, double majors, English as a second language, honors programs, independent study, internships, off-campus study, part-time degree program, services for LD students, study abroad, summer session for credit. *ROTC:* Army (b), Air Force (b).

Computers on Campus 875 computers/terminals are available on campus for general student use. Students can access the following: campus intranet, computer help desk, free student e-mail accounts, online (class) grades, online (class) registration, online (class) schedules, wireless network, online library, commuter/off campus connection to network, discounted computer software/hardware. Campuswide network is available. 100% of college-owned or -operated housing units are wired for high-speed Internet access. Wireless service is available via classrooms, computer centers, computer labs, dorm rooms, learning centers, libraries, student centers.

Student Life *Housing options:* coed, men-only, women-only. Campus housing is university owned and is provided by a third party. Freshman applicants given priority for college housing. *Activities and organizations:* drama/theater group, student-run newspaper, television station, choral group, marching band, NAACP, African Student Organization, English Club, International Student Organization, Voices of Serenity and Disabled Student Organization, national fraternities, national sororities. *Campus security:* 24-hour emergency response devices and patrols, late-night transport/escort service, controlled dormitory access. *Student services:* health clinic, personal/psychological counseling.

Athletics Member NCAA. All Division II. *Intercollegiate sports:* baseball M(s), basketball M(s)/W(s), cheerleading M/W, cross-country running M(s)/W(s), football M(s), golf M(s)/W(s), soccer M(s)/W(s), softball W(s), tennis W(s), track and field M(s)/W(s), volleyball W(s), wrestling M(s). *Intramural sports:* basketball M/W, bowling M/W, football M, golf M, racquetball M/W, soccer M, softball M/W, volleyball M/W, wrestling M.

Standardized Tests *Required:* SAT or ACT (for admission).

Costs (2010–11) *Tuition:* state resident $2423 full-time; nonresident $11,630 full-time. Full-time tuition and fees vary according to course load and location. Part-time tuition and fees vary according to course load and location. *Required fees:* $1717 full-time. *Room and board:* $5990; room only: $5040. Room and

board charges vary according to board plan and housing facility. *Payment plan:* installment. *Waivers:* employees or children of employees.

Financial Aid Of all full-time matriculated undergraduates who enrolled in 2009, 4,255 applied for aid, 3,757 were judged to have need, 917 had their need fully met. 143 Federal Work-Study jobs (averaging $1089). In 2009, 7 non-need-based awards were made. *Average percent of need met:* 80%. *Average financial aid package:* $10,246. *Average need-based loan:* $3648. *Average need-based gift aid:* $6210. *Average non-need-based aid:* $525.

Applying *Options:* electronic application, deferred entrance. *Application fee:* $40. *Required:* high school transcript. *Required for some:* 1 letter of recommendation, interview. *Recommended:* essay or personal statement, minimum 2 GPA. *Application deadlines:* rolling (freshmen), rolling (transfers). *Notification:* continuous (freshmen), continuous (transfers).

Freshman Application Contact Ms. Jennifer McNeil, Associate Director of Admissions, The University of North Carolina at Pembroke, PO Box 1510, Pembroke, NC 28372-1510. *Phone:* 910-521-6507. *Toll-free phone:* 800-949-UNCP. *Fax:* 910-521-6497. *E-mail:* jennifer.mcneill@uncp.edu. *Web site:* http://www.uncp.edu/.

University of North Carolina School of the Arts

Winston-Salem, North Carolina

- **State-supported** comprehensive, founded 1963, part of University of North Carolina System
- **Urban** 57-acre campus
- **Endowment** $16.8 million
- **Coed** 740 undergraduate students, 98% full-time, 39% women, 61% men
- **Very difficult** entrance level, 45% of applicants were admitted

Undergraduates 722 full-time, 18 part-time. Students come from 38 states and territories; 21 other countries; 54% are from out of state; 7% transferred in; 55% live on campus. *Retention:* 77% of full-time freshmen returned.

Freshmen *Admission:* 676 applied, 305 admitted, 161 enrolled. *Average high school GPA:* 3.3. *Test scores:* SAT critical reading scores over 500: 56%; SAT math scores over 500: 46%; SAT writing scores over 500: 50%; ACT scores over 18: 28%; SAT critical reading scores over 600: 32%; SAT math scores over 600: 18%; SAT writing scores over 600: 21%; ACT scores over 24: 16%; SAT critical reading scores over 700: 5%; SAT math scores over 700: 3%; SAT writing scores over 700: 4%; ACT scores over 30: 3%.

Faculty *Total:* 170, 77% full-time, 56% with terminal degrees. *Student/faculty ratio:* 7:1.

Academics *Calendar:* trimesters. *Degrees:* diplomas, bachelor's, master's, and post-master's certificates. *Special study options:* academic remediation for entering students, advanced placement credit, English as a second language, independent study, internships, services for LD students, summer session for credit.

Computers on Campus 60 computers/terminals are available on campus for general student use. Students can access the following: computer help desk, free student e-mail accounts, online (class) grades. Campuswide network is available. Wireless service is available via entire campus.

Student Life *Housing:* on-campus residence required through sophomore year. *Options:* coed. Campus housing is university owned. Freshman campus housing is guaranteed. *Activities and organizations:* drama/theater group, student-run newspaper, choral group, Pride (gay/lesbian organization), Appreciation of Black Artists. *Campus security:* 24-hour emergency response devices and patrols, controlled dormitory access. *Student services:* health clinic, personal/psychological counseling.

Standardized Tests *Required:* SAT or ACT (for admission).

Costs (2011–12) *Tuition:* state resident $180 per credit part-time; nonresident $695 per credit part-time. Full-time tuition and fees vary according to program. Part-time tuition and fees vary according to course load. *Room and board:* Room and board charges vary according to board plan and housing facility. *Payment plan:* installment. *Waivers:* senior citizens.

Financial Aid Of all full-time matriculated undergraduates who enrolled in 2008, 519 applied for aid, 405 were judged to have need, 67 had their need fully met. 108 Federal Work-Study jobs (averaging $460). In 2008, 108 non-need-based awards were made. *Average percent of need met:* 89%. *Average financial aid package:* $15,093. *Average need-based loan:* $4167. *Average need-based gift aid:* $7404. *Average non-need-based aid:* $3960. *Average indebtedness upon graduation:* $22,173.

Applying *Options:* electronic application. *Application fee:* $60. *Required:* high school transcript, 2 letters of recommendation, audition. *Required for some:* essay or personal statement, interview. *Application deadlines:* 3/1 (freshmen), rolling (transfers). *Notification:* continuous (freshmen), continuous (transfers).

Freshman Application Contact University of North Carolina School of the Arts, 1533 South Main Street, PO Box 12189, Winston-Salem, NC 27127-2188. *Phone:* 336-770-3290. *Web site:* http://www.uncsa.edu/.

The University of North Carolina Wilmington

Wilmington, North Carolina

- **State-supported** comprehensive, founded 1947, part of University of North Carolina System
- **Urban** 656-acre campus
- **Endowment** $47.9 million
- **Coed** 11,770 undergraduate students, 91% full-time, 60% women, 40% men
- **Moderately difficult** entrance level, 57% of applicants were admitted

Undergraduates 10,660 full-time, 1,110 part-time. Students come from 47 states and territories; 62 other countries; 14% are from out of state; 11% transferred in; 36% live on campus. *Retention:* 86% of full-time freshmen returned.

Freshmen *Admission:* 9,759 applied, 5,517 admitted, 1,992 enrolled. *Average high school GPA:* 3.8. *Test scores:* SAT critical reading scores over 500: 94%; SAT math scores over 500: 96%; SAT writing scores over 500: 84%; ACT scores over 18: 99%; SAT critical reading scores over 600: 38%; SAT math scores over 600: 46%; SAT writing scores over 600: 28%; ACT scores over 24: 61%; SAT critical reading scores over 700: 3%; SAT math scores over 700: 4%; SAT writing scores over 700: 2%; ACT scores over 30: 5%.

Faculty *Total:* 899, 65% full-time, 66% with terminal degrees. *Student/faculty ratio:* 17:1.

Academics *Calendar:* semesters. *Degrees:* bachelor's, master's, doctoral-research/scholarship, post-master's, and postbachelor's certificates. *Special study options:* academic remediation for entering students, accelerated degree program, advanced placement credit, cooperative education, distance learning, double majors, English as a second language, honors programs, independent study, internships, off-campus study, services for LD students, study abroad, summer session for credit.

Computers on Campus 1,111 computers/terminals and 3,481 ports are available on campus for general student use. Students can access the following: campus intranet, computer help desk, free student e-mail accounts, online (class) grades, online (class) registration, online (class) schedules. Campus-wide network is available. 100% of college-owned or -operated housing units are wired for high-speed Internet access. Wireless service is available via entire campus.

Student Life *Housing options:* coed, women-only, disabled students. Campus housing is university owned and is provided by a third party. Freshman applicants given priority for college housing. *Activities and organizations:* drama/theater group, student-run newspaper, radio and television station, choral group, Student Government Association, Association of Campus Entertainment, Residence Hall Association, national fraternities, national sororities. *Campus security:* 24-hour emergency response devices and patrols, late-night transport/escort service, controlled dormitory access. *Student services:* health clinic, personal/psychological counseling, women's center, legal services.

Athletics Member NCAA. All Division I. *Intercollegiate sports:* baseball M(s), basketball M(s)/W(s), cheerleading M/W(s), cross-country running M(s)/W(s), golf M(s)/W(s), soccer M(s)/W(s), softball W(s), swimming and diving M(s)/W(s), tennis M(s)/W(s), track and field M(s)/W(s), volleyball W(s). *Intramural sports:* baseball M(c), basketball W, crew M(c)/W(c), field hockey W(c), golf M/W, gymnastics W(c), ice hockey M, lacrosse M(c)/W(c), sailing M(c)/W(c), soccer M/W, softball M/W, swimming and diving M(c)/W(c), tennis M(c)/W(c), ultimate Frisbee M(c)/W(c), volleyball M/W.

Standardized Tests *Required:* SAT or ACT (for admission).

Costs (2010–11) *Tuition:* state resident $3029 full-time; nonresident $14,128 full-time. Full-time tuition and fees vary according to course load. Part-time tuition and fees vary according to course load. *Required fees:* $2387 full-time. *Room and board:* $7608; room only: $4458. Room and board charges vary according to board plan and housing facility. *Payment plan:* installment. *Waivers:* employees or children of employees.

Financial Aid Of all full-time matriculated undergraduates who enrolled in 2008, 6,690 applied for aid, 4,593 were judged to have need, 1,844 had their need fully met. 243 Federal Work-Study jobs (averaging $1481). In 2008, 342 non-need-based awards were made. *Average percent of need met:* 83%. *Average financial aid package:* $9078. *Average need-based loan:* $3547. *Average need-based gift aid:* $6030. *Average non-need-based aid:* $2272. *Average indebtedness upon graduation:* $16,115.

Applying *Options:* electronic application, early admission, early action, deferred entrance. *Application fee:* $60. *Required:* essay or personal statement, high school transcript. *Application deadlines:* 2/1 (freshmen), 3/1 (transfers), 11/1 (early action). *Notification:* 4/1 (freshmen), continuous (transfers), 1/20 (early action).

Freshman Application Contact Dr. Terrence M. Curran, Associate Provost, The University of North Carolina Wilmington, 601 South College Road, Wilmington, NC 28403-3297. *Phone:* 910-962-3876. *Toll-free phone:* 800-228-5571. *Fax:* 910-962-3922. *E-mail:* admissions@uncw.edu. *Web site:* http://www.uncw.edu/.

See page 1720 for the College Close-Up.

University of Phoenix–Charlotte Campus

Charlotte, North Carolina

Freshman Application Contact Ms. Audra McQuarie, Registrar/Executive Director, University of Phoenix–Charlotte Campus, 4035 South Riverpoint Parkway, Mail Stop CF-L101, Phoenix, AZ 85040. *Phone:* 480-557-6151. *Toll-free phone:* 800-776-4867 (in-state); 800-228-7240 (out-of-state). *Fax:* 480-643-3068. *E-mail:* audra.mcquarie@phoenix.edu. *Web site:* http://www.phoenix.edu/.

University of Phoenix–Raleigh Campus

Raleigh, North Carolina

Freshman Application Contact Ms. Audra McQuarie, Registrar/Executive Director, University of Phoenix–Raleigh Campus, 4035 South Riverpoint Parkway, Mail Stop CF-L101, Phoenix, AZ 85040. *Phone:* 480-557-6151. *Toll-free phone:* 800-776-4867 (in-state); 800-228-7240 (out-of-state). *Fax:* 480-643-3068. *E-mail:* audra.mcquarie@phoenix.edu. *Web site:* http://www.phoenix.edu/.

Wake Forest University

Winston-Salem, North Carolina

- **Independent** university, founded 1834
- **Suburban** 340-acre campus
- **Coed** 4,657 undergraduate students, 99% full-time, 52% women, 48% men
- **Very difficult** entrance level, 40% of applicants were admitted

Undergraduates 4,591 full-time, 66 part-time. 75% are from out of state; 7% Black or African American, non-Hispanic/Latino; 4% Hispanic/Latino; 5% Asian, non-Hispanic/Latino; 0.3% American Indian or Alaska Native, non-Hispanic/Latino; 0.8% Two or more races, non-Hispanic/Latino; 0.5% Race/ethnicity unknown; 2% international; 1% transferred in; 70% live on campus. *Retention:* 94% of full-time freshmen returned.
Freshmen *Admission:* 10,566 applied, 4,256 admitted, 1,219 enrolled. *Test scores:* SAT critical reading scores over 500: 95%; SAT math scores over 500: 98%; ACT scores over 18: 100%; SAT critical reading scores over 600: 78%; SAT math scores over 600: 83%; ACT scores over 24: 94%; SAT critical reading scores over 700: 20%; SAT math scores over 700: 32%; ACT scores over 30: 49%.
Faculty *Total:* 654, 77% full-time. *Student/faculty ratio:* 11:1.
Academics *Calendar:* semesters. *Degrees:* bachelor's, master's, doctoral-professional, and doctoral-research/scholarship. *Special study options:* advanced placement credit, double majors, honors programs, independent study, internships, off-campus study, part-time degree program, services for LD students, study abroad, summer session for credit. *ROTC:* Army (b).
Computers on Campus Students can access the following: campus intranet, computer help desk, free student e-mail accounts, online (class) grades, online (class) registration, online (class) schedules, financial information online, drop-add, transcript requests. Campuswide network is available. Wireless service is available via entire campus.
Student Life *Housing:* on-campus residence required through sophomore year. *Options:* coed. Campus housing is university owned. Freshman campus housing is guaranteed. *Activities and organizations:* drama/theater group, student-run newspaper, radio and television station, choral group, marching band, national fraternities, national sororities. *Campus security:* 24-hour emergency response devices and patrols, late-night transport/escort service, controlled dormitory access. *Student services:* health clinic, personal/psychological counseling.
Athletics Member NCAA. All Division I except football (Division I-A). *Intercollegiate sports:* baseball M(s), basketball M(s)/W(s), cross-country running M(s)/W(s), field hockey W(s), golf M(s)/W(s), soccer M(s)/W(s), tennis M(s)/W(s), track and field M(s)/W(s), volleyball W(s). *Intramural sports:* baseball M(c), basketball M/W, bowling M/W, cheerleading M(c)/W(c), crew M(c)/W(c), cross-country running M(c)/W(c), equestrian sports M(c)/W(c), fencing M(c)/W(c), field hockey W(c), football M, golf M(c)/W(c), ice hockey M(c)/W(c), lacrosse M(c)/W(c), racquetball M/W, rugby M(c), skiing (cross-country) M(c)/W(c), skiing (downhill) M(c)/W(c), soccer M(c)/W(c), softball

M/W(c), swimming and diving M/W, table tennis M/W, tennis M/W, ultimate Frisbee M/W, volleyball M/W, wrestling M(c).
Costs (2011–12) *Comprehensive fee:* $52,986 includes full-time tuition ($41,100), mandatory fees ($476), and room and board ($11,410). Part-time tuition: $1704 per semester hour. *College room only:* $7550.
Financial Aid Of all full-time matriculated undergraduates who enrolled in 2009, 2,042 applied for aid, 1,808 were judged to have need, 1,162 had their need fully met. In 2009, 482 non-need-based awards were made. *Average percent of need met:* 99%. *Average financial aid package:* $33,872. *Average need-based loan:* $11,670. *Average need-based gift aid:* $27,995. *Average non-need-based aid:* $15,023. *Average indebtedness upon graduation:* $32,237. *Financial aid deadline:* 3/1.
Applying *Options:* electronic application, early admission, early decision, early action. *Application fee:* $50. *Required:* essay or personal statement, high school transcript, 1 letter of recommendation. *Recommended:* interview. *Application deadlines:* 1/1 (freshmen), 11/15 (early action). *Early decision deadline:* 1/1. *Notification:* 4/1 (freshmen), rolling (early decision), 1/15 (early action).
Freshman Application Contact Wake Forest University, PO Box 7373 Reynolda Station, Winston-Salem, NC 27109. *Phone:* 336-758-5201. *Web site:* http://www.wfu.edu/.

Warren Wilson College

Swannanoa, North Carolina

Freshman Application Contact Mr. Richard Blomgren, Dean of Admission, Warren Wilson College, PO Box 9000, Asheville, NC 28815-9000. *Phone:* 828-771-2073. *Toll-free phone:* 800-934-3536. *Fax:* 828-298-1440. *E-mail:* admit@warren-wilson.edu. *Web site:* http://www.warren-wilson.edu/.

Western Carolina University

Cullowhee, North Carolina

- **State-supported** comprehensive, founded 1889, part of University of North Carolina System
- **Rural** 682-acre campus
- **Endowment** $33.9 million
- **Coed** 7,503 undergraduate students, 84% full-time, 53% women, 47% men
- **Moderately difficult** entrance level, 39% of applicants were admitted

Undergraduates 6,301 full-time, 1,202 part-time. Students come from 41 states and territories; 24 other countries; 7% are from out of state; 11% transferred in; 50% live on campus. *Retention:* 74% of full-time freshmen returned.
Freshmen *Admission:* 14,979 applied, 5,813 admitted, 1,440 enrolled. *Average high school GPA:* 3.51. *Test scores:* SAT critical reading scores over 500: 58%; SAT math scores over 500: 67%; SAT writing scores over 500: 42%; ACT scores over 18: 90%; SAT critical reading scores over 600: 14%; SAT math scores over 600: 16%; SAT writing scores over 600: 8%; ACT scores over 24: 26%; SAT critical reading scores over 700: 2%; SAT math scores over 700: 1%; SAT writing scores over 700: 1%; ACT scores over 30: 3%.
Faculty *Total:* 676, 69% full-time, 67% with terminal degrees. *Student/faculty ratio:* 15:1.
Academics *Calendar:* semesters. *Degrees:* bachelor's, master's, doctoral-research/scholarship, post-master's, and postbachelor's certificates. *Special study options:* advanced placement credit, cooperative education, distance learning, double majors, English as a second language, honors programs, independent study, internships, part-time degree program, services for LD students, student-designed majors, study abroad, summer session for credit.
Computers on Campus 103 computers/terminals and 6,590 ports are available on campus for general student use. Students can access the following: campus intranet, computer help desk, free student e-mail accounts, online (class) grades, online (class) registration, online (class) schedules, student Web pages, online music services. Campuswide network is available. 100% of college-owned or -operated housing units are wired for high-speed Internet access. Wireless service is available via classrooms, computer centers, computer labs, learning centers, libraries, student centers.
Student Life *Housing:* on-campus residence required for freshman year. *Options:* coed, men-only, women-only, disabled students. Campus housing is university owned, leased by the school and is provided by a third party. Freshman campus housing is guaranteed. *Activities and organizations:* drama/theater group, student-run newspaper, radio and television station, choral group, marching band, WCU Leadership Institute, Physical Therapy Club, UNITY, WCU Gaming Club, WCU Climbing Team, national fraternities, national sororities. *Campus security:* 24-hour emergency response devices and patrols, controlled dormitory access. *Student services:* health clinic, personal/psychological counseling, women's center.
Athletics Member NCAA. All Division I except football (Division I-AA). *Intercollegiate sports:* baseball M(s), basketball M(s)/W(s), cross-country running M(s)/W(s), equestrian sports M(c)/W(c), fencing M(c)/W(c), golf M(s)/

W(s), rock climbing M(c)/W(c), rugby M(c), soccer W(s), softball W(s), swimming and diving M(c)/W(c), tennis M(c)/W(s), track and field M(s)/W(s), ultimate Frisbee M(c)/W(c), volleyball W(s), wrestling M(c). *Intramural sports:* badminton M/W, basketball M/W, bowling M/W, cross-country running M/W, racquetball M/W, soccer M/W, softball M/W, swimming and diving M/W, table tennis M/W, tennis M/W, ultimate Frisbee M/W, volleyball M/W, water polo M/W, weight lifting M/W, wrestling M/W.

Standardized Tests *Required:* SAT or ACT (for admission). *Recommended:* SAT (for admission).

Costs (2011–12) *Tuition:* state resident $2998 full-time; nonresident $12,595 full-time. Full-time tuition and fees vary according to degree level. Part-time tuition and fees vary according to course load and degree level. *Required fees:* $2369 full-time. *Room and board:* $6980. Room and board charges vary according to board plan and housing facility. *Payment plan:* installment. *Waivers:* employees or children of employees.

Financial Aid Of all full-time matriculated undergraduates who enrolled in 2009, 5,077 applied for aid, 4,117 were judged to have need, 1,152 had their need fully met. In 2009, 236 non-need-based awards were made. *Average percent of need met:* 77%. *Average financial aid package:* $9322. *Average need-based loan:* $3586. *Average need-based gift aid:* $6736. *Average non-need-based aid:* $2051.

Applying *Options:* electronic application, early admission, early action. *Application fee:* $45. *Required:* high school transcript. *Application deadlines:* 3/1 (freshmen), 6/1 (transfers), 11/15 (early action). *Notification:* continuous (freshmen), continuous (transfers), 12/15 (early action).

Freshman Application Contact Mr. Chris Parrish, Senior Assistant Director of Admissions, Western Carolina University, 102 Cordelia Camp Building, Cullowhee, NC 28723. *Phone:* 828-227-7317. *Toll-free phone:* 877-WCU4YOU. *E-mail:* admiss@email.wcu.edu. *Web site:* http://www.wcu.edu/.

Wingate University

Wingate, North Carolina

- **Independent Baptist** comprehensive, founded 1896
- **Small-town** 330-acre campus with easy access to Charlotte
- **Coed** 1,622 undergraduate students, 97% full-time, 54% women, 46% men
- **Moderately difficult** entrance level, 88% of applicants were admitted

Undergraduates 1,574 full-time, 48 part-time. 19% are from out of state; 11% Black or African American, non-Hispanic/Latino; 3% Hispanic/Latino; 3% Asian, non-Hispanic/Latino; 0.9% American Indian or Alaska Native, non-Hispanic/Latino; 0.6% Two or more races, non-Hispanic/Latino; 15% Race/ethnicity unknown; 4% international; 3% transferred in; 84% live on campus. *Retention:* 74% of full-time freshmen returned.

Freshmen *Admission:* 3,512 applied, 3,079 admitted, 607 enrolled. *Average high school GPA:* 3.29. *Test scores:* SAT critical reading scores over 500: 51%; SAT math scores over 500: 56%; ACT scores over 18: 83%; SAT critical reading scores over 600: 16%; SAT math scores over 600: 18%; ACT scores over 24: 39%; SAT critical reading scores over 700: 1%; SAT math scores over 700: 2%; ACT scores over 30: 7%.

Faculty *Total:* 226, 53% full-time, 65% with terminal degrees. *Student/faculty ratio:* 14:1.

Academics *Calendar:* semesters. *Degrees:* bachelor's, master's, doctoral-professional, and doctoral-research/scholarship. *Special study options:* advanced placement credit, double majors, honors programs, independent study, internships, off-campus study, part-time degree program, services for LD students, study abroad, summer session for credit. *ROTC:* Army (c), Air Force (c).

Computers on Campus Students can access the following: online (class) registration. Campuswide network is available. 100% of college-owned or -operated housing units are wired for high-speed Internet access.

Student Life *Housing:* on-campus residence required through senior year. *Options:* men-only, women-only. Campus housing is university owned. Freshman campus housing is guaranteed. *Activities and organizations:* drama/theater group, student-run newspaper, television station, choral group, marching band, national fraternities, national sororities. *Campus security:* 24-hour emergency response devices and patrols, late-night transport/escort service, controlled dormitory access. *Student services:* health clinic, personal/psychological counseling.

Athletics Member NCAA. All Division II. *Intercollegiate sports:* baseball M(s), basketball M(s)/W(s), cross-country running M(s)/W, football M(s), golf M(s)/W(s), lacrosse M(s), soccer M(s)/W, softball W(s), swimming and diving M(s)/W(s), tennis M(s)/W(s), volleyball W(s). *Intramural sports:* basketball M/W, bowling M/W, cross-country running M, football M/W, golf M/W, racquetball M/W, swimming and diving M/W, table tennis M/W, tennis M/W, track and field M/W, volleyball M/W, water polo M/W, weight lifting M/W.

Standardized Tests *Required:* SAT or ACT (for admission).

Costs (2011–12) *Comprehensive fee:* $30,950 includes full-time tuition ($20,980), mandatory fees ($1200), and room and board ($8770). Part-time tuition: $700 per semester hour. Part-time tuition and fees vary according to course load. *Room and board:* Room and board charges vary according to board plan. *Payment plan:* installment. *Waivers:* employees or children of employees.

Financial Aid Of all full-time matriculated undergraduates who enrolled in 2008, 1,131 applied for aid, 933 were judged to have need, 287 had their need fully met. In 2008, 189 non-need-based awards were made. *Average percent of need met:* 85%. *Average financial aid package:* $17,769. *Average need-based loan:* $4165. *Average need-based gift aid:* $6952. *Average non-need-based aid:* $7313. *Average indebtedness upon graduation:* $23,279.

Applying *Options:* electronic application, early admission, deferred entrance. *Application fee:* $30. *Required:* high school transcript, minimum 2 GPA. *Recommended:* minimum 3 GPA, interview. *Application deadlines:* rolling (freshmen), rolling (transfers). *Notification:* continuous (freshmen), continuous (transfers).

Freshman Application Contact Ms. Lindsay Kreis, Director of Student Recruitment, Wingate University, PO Box 159, Wingate, NC 28174. *Phone:* 704-233-8000. *Toll-free phone:* 800-755-5550. *Fax:* 704-233-8110. *E-mail:* admit@wingate.edu. *Web site:* http://www.wingate.edu/.

Winston-Salem State University

Winston-Salem, North Carolina

- **State-supported** comprehensive, founded 1892, part of University of North Carolina System
- **Urban** 94-acre campus
- **Endowment** $19.5 million
- **Coed**
- **Minimally difficult** entrance level

Faculty *Student/faculty ratio:* 19:1.

Academics *Calendar:* semesters. *Degrees:* certificates, bachelor's, master's, and postbachelor's certificates.

Student Life *Campus security:* 24-hour emergency response devices and patrols.

Athletics Member NCAA. All Division I.

Standardized Tests *Required:* SAT or ACT (for admission).

Costs (2010–11) *Tuition:* state resident $2274 full-time; nonresident $11,420 full-time. Full-time tuition and fees vary according to location. Part-time tuition and fees vary according to course load and location. *Required fees:* $1814 full-time. *Room and board:* $7106; room only: $4626. Room and board charges vary according to board plan and housing facility.

Financial Aid *Of all full-time matriculated undergraduates who enrolled in 2006,* 4,644 applied for aid, 4,095 were judged to have need, 354 had their need fully met. 258 Federal Work-Study jobs (averaging $1361). 26 state and other part-time jobs (averaging $2755). *In 2006,* 54 non-need-based awards were made. *Average percent of need met:* 71. *Average financial aid package:* $5602. *Average need-based loan:* $2926. *Average need-based gift aid:* $2350. *Average non-need-based aid:* $4414. *Average indebtedness upon graduation:* $10,200. *Financial aid deadline:* 4/1.

Applying *Options:* deferred entrance. *Application fee:* $40. *Required:* high school transcript. *Recommended:* 1 letter of recommendation.

Freshman Application Contact Ms. Tomikia LeGrande, Assistant Vice Chancellor for Enrollment Services, Winston-Salem State University, 601 Martin Luther King, Jr. Drive, Thompson Center, Winston-Salem, NC 27110. *Phone:* 336-750-2070. *Toll-free phone:* 800-257-4052. *Fax:* 336-750-2079. *E-mail:* Legrandet@wssu.edu. *Web site:* http://www.wssu.edu/.

NORTH DAKOTA

Bismarck State College

Bismarck, North Dakota

Freshman Application Contact Greg Sturm, Dean of Admissions and Enrollment Services, Bismarck State College, PO Box 5587, Bismarck, ND 58506-5587. *Phone:* 701-224-5426. *Toll-free phone:* 800-445-5073. *Fax:* 701-224-5643. *E-mail:* gregory.sturm@bsc.nodak.edu. *Web site:* http://www.bismarckstate.edu/.

Dickinson State University

Dickinson, North Dakota

- **State-supported** 4-year, founded 1918, part of North Dakota University System
- **Small-town** 132-acre campus
- **Endowment** $9.9 million
- **Coed** 2,668 undergraduate students, 63% full-time, 61% women, 39% men
- **Minimally difficult** entrance level, 97% of applicants were admitted

Undergraduates 1,684 full-time, 984 part-time. Students come from 27 states and territories; 27 other countries; 23% are from out of state; 9% transferred in; 30% live on campus. *Retention:* 57% of full-time freshmen returned.
Freshmen *Admission:* 693 applied, 669 admitted, 369 enrolled. *Average high school GPA:* 3.18. *Test scores:* SAT critical reading scores over 500: 46%; SAT math scores over 500: 50%; SAT writing scores over 500: 32%; ACT scores over 18: 78%; SAT critical reading scores over 600: 9%; SAT math scores over 600: 12%; SAT writing scores over 600: 6%; ACT scores over 24: 21%; SAT critical reading scores over 700: 3%; SAT math scores over 700: 5%; ACT scores over 30: 1%.
Faculty *Total:* 233, 40% full-time, 32% with terminal degrees. *Student/faculty ratio:* 17:1.
Academics *Calendar:* semesters. *Degrees:* certificates, associate, and bachelor's. *Special study options:* academic remediation for entering students, accelerated degree program, adult/continuing education programs, advanced placement credit, cooperative education, distance learning, double majors, external degree program, honors programs, independent study, internships, off-campus study, part-time degree program, services for LD students, student-designed majors, study abroad, summer session for credit.
Computers on Campus 216 computers/terminals are available on campus for general student use. Students can access the following: campus intranet, computer help desk, free student e-mail accounts, online (class) grades, online (class) registration, online (class) schedules. Campuswide network is available. 100% of college-owned or -operated housing units are wired for high-speed Internet access. Wireless service is available via entire campus.
Student Life *Housing:* on-campus residence required through sophomore year. *Options:* coed, men-only, women-only, disabled students. Campus housing is university owned. Freshman campus housing is guaranteed. *Activities and organizations:* drama/theater group, student-run newspaper, choral group, marching band, Rodeo Club, Blue Hawk Brigade, chorale, Business Club, Navigators. *Campus security:* 24-hour emergency response devices and patrols, late-night transport/escort service. *Student services:* health clinic.
Athletics Member NAIA. *Intercollegiate sports:* badminton M/W, baseball M(s), basketball M(s)/W(s), cheerleading M/W, cross-country running M(s)/W(s), football M(s), golf M(s)/W(s), softball W(s), track and field M(s)/W(s), volleyball W(s), wrestling M(s). *Intramural sports:* badminton M/W, basketball M/W, football M/W, soccer M/W, softball W, squash M/W, table tennis M/W, tennis M/W, volleyball M/W, water polo M/W.
Standardized Tests *Required:* SAT or ACT (for admission).
Costs (2010–11) *Tuition:* state resident $5248 full-time; nonresident $12,195 full-time. *Required fees:* $1089 full-time. *Room and board:* $4262; room only: $1610. Room and board charges vary according to board plan. *Payment plan:* installment. *Waivers:* minority students, children of alumni, adult students, senior citizens, and employees or children of employees.
Financial Aid Of all full-time matriculated undergraduates who enrolled in 2009, 1,147 applied for aid, 901 were judged to have need, 872 had their need fully met. In 2009, 502 non-need-based awards were made. *Average percent of need met:* 35%. *Average financial aid package:* $7577. *Average need-based loan:* $3799. *Average need-based gift aid:* $4020. *Average non-need-based aid:* $1491. *Average indebtedness upon graduation:* $18,837.
Applying *Options:* electronic application, early admission, deferred entrance. *Application fee:* $35. *Required:* high school transcript, medical history, proof of measles-rubella shot. *Application deadlines:* rolling (freshmen), rolling (transfers). *Notification:* continuous (freshmen), continuous (transfers).
Freshman Application Contact Mr. Norman Coley, Director of Enrollment Services, Dickinson State University, Campus Box 169, Dickinson, ND 58601. *Phone:* 701-483-2175. *Toll-free phone:* 800-279-4295. *Fax:* 701-483-2409. *E-mail:* dsu.hawks@dsu.nodak.edu. *Web site:* http://www.dickinsonstate.edu.

Jamestown College

Jamestown, North Dakota

- **Independent Presbyterian** comprehensive, founded 1883
- **Small-town** 110-acre campus
- **Endowment** $23.6 million
- **Coed** 967 undergraduate students, 91% full-time, 54% women, 46% men
- **Minimally difficult** entrance level, 64% of applicants were admitted

Undergraduates 876 full-time, 91 part-time. Students come from 31 states and territories; 13 other countries; 48% are from out of state; 2% Black or African American, non-Hispanic/Latino; 3% Hispanic/Latino; 0.7% Asian, non-Hispanic/Latino; 0.7% Native Hawaiian or other Pacific Islander, non-Hispanic/Latino; 0.8% American Indian or Alaska Native, non-Hispanic/Latino; 5% international; 6% transferred in; 60% live on campus. *Retention:* 67% of full-time freshmen returned.
Freshmen *Admission:* 752 applied, 478 admitted, 208 enrolled. *Average high school GPA:* 3.41. *Test scores:* SAT critical reading scores over 500: 36%; SAT math scores over 500: 50%; ACT scores over 18: 93%; SAT critical reading scores over 600: 9%; SAT math scores over 600: 14%; ACT scores over 24: 42%; SAT math scores over 700: 5%; ACT scores over 30: 5%.
Faculty *Total:* 85, 68% full-time, 41% with terminal degrees. *Student/faculty ratio:* 14:1.
Academics *Calendar:* semesters. *Degrees:* bachelor's and master's. *Special study options:* advanced placement credit, cooperative education, distance learning, double majors, English as a second language, honors programs, independent study, internships, off-campus study, part-time degree program, services for LD students, student-designed majors, study abroad, summer session for credit. *Unusual degree programs:* 3-2 engineering with North Dakota State University, University of North Dakota, South Dakota State University, Washington University in St. Louis.
Computers on Campus 300 computers/terminals and 300 ports are available on campus for general student use. Students can access the following: campus intranet, computer help desk, free student e-mail accounts, online (class) grades, online (class) registration, online (class) schedules. Campuswide network is available. 100% of college-owned or -operated housing units are wired for high-speed Internet access. Wireless service is available via entire campus.
Student Life *Housing:* on-campus residence required through sophomore year. *Options:* coed. Campus housing is university owned. Freshman campus housing is guaranteed. *Activities and organizations:* drama/theater group, student-run newspaper, television station, choral group, Jimmie Ambassadors, Student Activities Committee, Nursing Students' Association, Building 28-Habitat for Humanity, Student Senate. *Campus security:* late-night transport/escort service, controlled dormitory access. *Student services:* personal/psychological counseling.
Athletics Member NAIA. *Intercollegiate sports:* baseball M(s), basketball M(s)/W(s), cross-country running M(s)/W(s), football M(s), golf M(s)/W(s), soccer M(s)/W(s), softball W(s), track and field M(s)/W(s), volleyball W(s), wrestling M(s)/W(s). *Intramural sports:* basketball M/W, football M/W, soccer M(c)/W(c), volleyball M/W.
Standardized Tests *Required:* SAT or ACT (for admission).
Costs (2011–12) *Comprehensive fee:* $22,970 includes full-time tuition ($16,850), mandatory fees ($420), and room and board ($5700). Part-time tuition and fees vary according to course load. *College room only:* $2530. Room and board charges vary according to board plan. *Payment plan:* installment. *Waivers:* employees or children of employees.
Financial Aid Of all full-time matriculated undergraduates who enrolled in 2009, 921 applied for aid, 642 were judged to have need, 132 had their need fully met. 230 Federal Work-Study jobs (averaging $1035). 59 state and other part-time jobs (averaging $901). In 2009, 252 non-need-based awards were made. *Average percent of need met:* 76%. *Average financial aid package:* $12,532. *Average need-based loan:* $4277. *Average need-based gift aid:* $8993. *Average non-need-based aid:* $5070. *Average indebtedness upon graduation:* $25,899.
Applying *Options:* electronic application, deferred entrance. *Application fee:* $35. *Required:* high school transcript, 1 letter of recommendation. *Recommended:* minimum 2.5 GPA. *Application deadlines:* rolling (freshmen), rolling (out-of-state freshmen), rolling (transfers).
Freshman Application Contact Jamestown College, 6000 College Lane, Jamestown, ND 58405. *Phone:* 701-252-3467 Ext. 5512. *Toll-free phone:* 800-336-2554. *Web site:* http://www.jc.edu/.

Mayville State University

Mayville, North Dakota

- **State-supported** 4-year, founded 1889, part of North Dakota University System
- **Rural** 60-acre campus
- **Coed** 982 undergraduate students, 56% full-time, 56% women, 44% men
- **Noncompetitive** entrance level, 55% of applicants were admitted

Undergraduates 552 full-time, 430 part-time. Students come from 41 states and territories; 3 other countries; 36% are from out of state; 6% Black or African American, non-Hispanic/Latino; 3% Hispanic/Latino; 2% Asian, non-Hispanic/Latino; 0.5% Native Hawaiian or other Pacific Islander, non-Hispanic/Latino; 3% American Indian or Alaska Native, non-Hispanic/Latino; 1% Two or more races, non-Hispanic/Latino; 3% international; 10% transferred in; 22% live on campus. *Retention:* 51% of full-time freshmen returned.
Freshmen *Admission:* 288 applied, 158 admitted, 133 enrolled. *Average high school GPA:* 2.84. *Test scores:* ACT scores over 18: 68%; ACT scores over 24: 16%; ACT scores over 30: 1%.

PROFILES

Faculty *Total:* 76, 49% full-time, 22% with terminal degrees. *Student/faculty ratio:* 14:1.

Academics *Calendar:* semesters. *Degrees:* associate and bachelor's. *Special study options:* academic remediation for entering students, accelerated degree program, adult/continuing education programs, advanced placement credit, cooperative education, distance learning, double majors, internships, off-campus study, part-time degree program, services for LD students, student-designed majors, summer session for credit. *ROTC:* Army (c), Air Force (c).

Computers on Campus Students can access the following: campus intranet, computer help desk, free student e-mail accounts, online (class) grades, online (class) registration, online (class) schedules. Campuswide network is available. 100% of college-owned or -operated housing units are wired for high-speed Internet access. Wireless service is available via entire campus.

Student Life *Housing:* on-campus residence required through sophomore year. *Options:* coed, men-only, women-only. Campus housing is university owned and is provided by a third party. Freshman campus housing is guaranteed. *Activities and organizations:* drama/theater group, student-run newspaper, radio station, choral group, Student Activities Council, Student Education Association, Health and Physical Education Club, Campus Crusade, Student Ambassadors. *Campus security:* controlled dormitory access. *Student services:* health clinic, personal/psychological counseling.

Athletics Member NAIA. *Intercollegiate sports:* baseball M(s), basketball M(s)/W(s), football M(s), softball W(s), volleyball W(s). *Intramural sports:* basketball M/W, bowling M/W, football M/W, golf M/W, ice hockey M, racquetball M/W, soccer M/W, softball M/W, table tennis M/W, tennis M/W, track and field M/W, volleyball M/W.

Standardized Tests *Required:* SAT or ACT (for admission).

Costs (2010–11) *One-time required fee:* $35. *Tuition:* state resident $4268 full-time, $178 per credit hour part-time; nonresident $6403 full-time, $267 per credit hour part-time. Full-time tuition and fees vary according to course load and reciprocity agreements. Part-time tuition and fees vary according to course load and reciprocity agreements. *Required fees:* $1669 full-time, $70 per credit hour part-time. *Room and board:* $4454; room only: $1676. Room and board charges vary according to board plan and housing facility. *Payment plan:* installment. *Waivers:* minority students, senior citizens, and employees or children of employees.

Financial Aid Of all full-time matriculated undergraduates who enrolled in 2009, 463 applied for aid, 364 were judged to have need, 358 had their need fully met. 56 Federal Work-Study jobs (averaging $1200). In 2009, 223 non-need-based awards were made. *Average percent of need met:* 59%. *Average financial aid package:* $8648. *Average need-based loan:* $4067. *Average need-based gift aid:* $4494. *Average non-need-based aid:* $742. *Average indebtedness upon graduation:* $19,986.

Applying *Options:* electronic application, deferred entrance. *Application fee:* $35. *Required:* high school transcript, minimum 2 GPA. *Recommended:* interview. *Application deadlines:* rolling (freshmen), rolling (out-of-state freshmen), rolling (transfers). *Notification:* continuous until 1/1 (freshmen), continuous (out-of-state freshmen), continuous until 1/1 (transfers).

Freshman Application Contact Jim Morowski, Director of Freshmen Enrollment Services, Mayville State University, 330 3rd Street, NE, Mayville, ND 58257-1299. *Phone:* 701-788-4842. *Toll-free phone:* 800-437-4104. *Fax:* 701-788-4748. *E-mail:* james.morowski@mayvillestate.edu. *Web site:* http://www.mayvillestate.edu/.

Medcenter One College of Nursing
Bismarck, North Dakota

- **Independent** upper-level, founded 1988, administratively affiliated with Medcenter One Health Systems
- **Small-town** 15-acre campus
- **Endowment** $791,956
- **Coed, primarily women** 91 undergraduate students, 99% full-time, 91% women, 9% men
- **Moderately difficult** entrance level, 54% of applicants were admitted

Undergraduates 90 full-time, 1 part-time. Students come from 3 states and territories; 4 other countries; 3% are from out of state; 4% Black or African American, non-Hispanic/Latino; 1% Hispanic/Latino; 1% Asian, non-Hispanic/Latino; 3% Two or more races, non-Hispanic/Latino; 53% transferred in.

Freshmen *Admission:* 100 applied, 54 admitted.

Faculty *Total:* 13, 77% full-time, 8% with terminal degrees. *Student/faculty ratio:* 8:1.

Academics *Calendar:* semesters. *Degree:* bachelor's. *Special study options:* independent study, internships.

Computers on Campus 25 computers/terminals are available on campus for general student use. Students can access the following: campus intranet, free student e-mail accounts. Campuswide network is available. Wireless service is available via entire campus.

Student Life *Housing:* college housing not available. *Activities and organizations:* Student Body Organization, Student Nurses Association. *Campus secu-*

rity: late-night transport/escort service. *Student services:* personal/psychological counseling.

Costs (2011–12) *One-time required fee:* $315. *Tuition:* $10,012 full-time, $417 per credit part-time. Part-time tuition and fees vary according to course load. *Required fees:* $839 full-time, $35 per credit part-time.

Financial Aid Of all full-time matriculated undergraduates who enrolled in 2008, 88 applied for aid, 69 were judged to have need, 51 had their need fully met. 5 Federal Work-Study jobs (averaging $1200). In 2008, 3 non-need-based awards were made. *Average percent of need met:* 98%. *Average financial aid package:* $13,210. *Average need-based loan:* $4253. *Average need-based gift aid:* $3521. *Average non-need-based aid:* $600.

Applying *Options:* early admission. *Application fee:* $40. *Application deadline:* 11/1 (transfers). *Notification:* continuous (transfers).

Application Contact Ms. Mary Smith, Director of Student Services, Medcenter One College of Nursing, 512 North 7th Street, Bismarck, ND 58501-4494. *Phone:* 701-323-6271. *Fax:* 701-323-6289. *E-mail:* msmith@mohs.org. *Web site:* http://www.medcenterone.com/collegeofnursing/index.asp.

Minot State University
Minot, North Dakota

- **State-supported** comprehensive, founded 1913, part of North Dakota University System
- **Small-town** 103-acre campus
- **Endowment** $2.4 million
- **Coed** 3,551 undergraduate students, 69% full-time, 61% women, 39% men
- **Moderately difficult** entrance level, 74% of applicants were admitted

Undergraduates 2,446 full-time, 1,105 part-time. Students come from 55 states and territories; 22 other countries; 27% are from out of state; 4% Black or African American, non-Hispanic/Latino; 2% Hispanic/Latino; 1% Asian, non-Hispanic/Latino; 4% American Indian or Alaska Native, non-Hispanic/Latino; 0.5% Two or more races, non-Hispanic/Latino; 3% Race/ethnicity unknown; 9% international; 9% transferred in; 16% live on campus. *Retention:* 71% of full-time freshmen returned.

Freshmen *Admission:* 837 applied, 618 admitted, 483 enrolled. *Average high school GPA:* 2.03. *Test scores:* ACT scores over 18: 91%; ACT scores over 24: 33%; ACT scores over 30: 3%.

Faculty *Total:* 189, 87% full-time, 56% with terminal degrees. *Student/faculty ratio:* 14:1.

Academics *Calendar:* semesters. *Degrees:* certificates, associate, bachelor's, master's, post-master's, and postbachelor's certificates. *Special study options:* academic remediation for entering students, accelerated degree program, adult/continuing education programs, advanced placement credit, cooperative education, distance learning, double majors, English as a second language, honors programs, independent study, internships, part-time degree program, services for LD students, student-designed majors, study abroad, summer session for credit. *Unusual degree programs:* business administration; nursing.

Computers on Campus 500 computers/terminals are available on campus for general student use. Students can access the following: campus intranet, computer help desk, free student e-mail accounts, online (class) grades, online (class) registration, online (class) schedules. Campuswide network is available. Wireless service is available via entire campus.

Student Life *Housing:* on-campus residence required for freshman year. *Options:* coed, men-only, women-only. Campus housing is university owned. Freshman campus housing is guaranteed. *Activities and organizations:* drama/theater group, student-run newspaper, radio and television station, choral group, Student ND Education Association, Minot State Club of Physical Education, Inter-Varsity Christian Fellowship, Residence Hall Association, National Student Speech and Hearing Association, national sororities. *Campus security:* controlled dormitory access, patrols by trained security personnel. *Student services:* health clinic, personal/psychological counseling, women's center.

Athletics Member NCAA, NAIA, NCCAA. All NCAA Division II. *Intercollegiate sports:* baseball M(s), basketball M(s)/W(s), cheerleading W, cross-country running M(s)/W(s), football M(s), golf M/W, ice hockey M(c), soccer W, softball M(s)/W(s), track and field M(s)/W(s), volleyball W(s), wrestling M. *Intramural sports:* basketball M/W, racquetball M/W, softball M/W, volleyball M/W.

Standardized Tests *Required:* SAT or ACT (for admission).

Costs (2011–12) *Tuition:* state resident $4477 full-time, $235 per credit hour part-time; nonresident $4477 full-time, $235 per credit hour part-time. Full-time tuition and fees vary according to class time, course load, degree level, location, and program. Part-time tuition and fees vary according to class time, degree level, location, and program. *Required fees:* $1161 full-time, $49 per credit hour part-time, $49 per credit hour part-time. *Room and board:* $4530; room only: $3000. Room and board charges vary according to board plan and housing facility. *Payment plan:* installment. *Waivers:* minority students, children of alumni, senior citizens, and employees or children of employees.

Financial Aid Of all full-time matriculated undergraduates who enrolled in 2009, 1,710 applied for aid, 1,321 were judged to have need, 1,292 had their need fully met. 102 Federal Work-Study jobs (averaging $2524). In 2009, 654 non-need-based awards were made. *Average percent of need met:* 54%. *Average financial aid package:* $7526. *Average need-based loan:* $3823. *Average need-based gift aid:* $4409. *Average non-need-based aid:* $966. *Average indebtedness upon graduation:* $20,272.

Applying *Options:* electronic application, deferred entrance. *Application fee:* $35. *Required:* high school transcript. *Required for some:* minimum 2.75 GPA. *Application deadlines:* rolling (freshmen), rolling (out-of-state freshmen), rolling (transfers). *Notification:* continuous (freshmen), continuous (out-of-state freshmen), continuous (transfers).

Freshman Application Contact Mr. Kevin Harmon, Dean of Enrollment Services, Minot State University, 500 University Avenue West, Minot, ND 58707-0002. *Phone:* 701-858-3126. *Toll-free phone:* 800-777-0750 Ext. 3350. *Fax:* 701-858-3825. *E-mail:* askmsu@minotstateu.edu. *Web site:* http://www.minotstateu.edu/.

North Dakota State University

Fargo, North Dakota

- **State-supported** university, founded 1890, part of North Dakota University System
- **Urban** 2100-acre campus
- **Endowment** $368,262
- **Coed** 11,977 undergraduate students, 90% full-time, 44% women, 56% men
- **Moderately difficult** entrance level, 77% of applicants were admitted

Undergraduates 10,818 full-time, 1,159 part-time. Students come from 46 states and territories; 68 other countries; 50% are from out of state; 2% Black or African American, non-Hispanic/Latino; 0.9% Hispanic/Latino; 1% Asian, non-Hispanic/Latino; 1% American Indian or Alaska Native, non-Hispanic/Latino; 0.7% Two or more races, non-Hispanic/Latino; 1% Race/ethnicity unknown; 5% international; 7% transferred in; 35% live on campus. *Retention:* 78% of full-time freshmen returned.

Freshmen *Admission:* 5,720 applied, 4,400 admitted, 2,400 enrolled. *Average high school GPA:* 3.37. *Test scores:* SAT critical reading scores over 500: 65%; SAT math scores over 500: 73%; ACT scores over 18: 96%; SAT critical reading scores over 600: 28%; SAT math scores over 600: 31%; ACT scores over 24: 50%; SAT critical reading scores over 700: 4%; SAT math scores over 700: 10%; ACT scores over 30: 8%.

Faculty *Total:* 796, 80% full-time, 71% with terminal degrees. *Student/faculty ratio:* 18:1.

Academics *Calendar:* semesters. *Degrees:* certificates, bachelor's, master's, doctoral-professional, doctoral-research/scholarship, post-master's, and post-bachelor's certificates. *Special study options:* academic remediation for entering students, advanced placement credit, cooperative education, distance learning, double majors, English as a second language, honors programs, independent study, internships, off-campus study, part-time degree program, services for LD students, student-designed majors, study abroad, summer session for credit. *ROTC:* Army (b), Air Force (b).

Computers on Campus 500 computers/terminals are available on campus for general student use. Students can access the following: computer help desk, free student e-mail accounts, online (class) grades, online (class) registration, online (class) schedules. Campuswide network is available. Wireless service is available via classrooms, computer centers, computer labs, libraries, student centers.

Student Life *Housing:* on-campus residence required for freshman year. *Options:* coed, men-only, women-only, disabled students. Campus housing is university owned. Freshman campus housing is guaranteed. *Activities and organizations:* drama/theater group, student-run newspaper, radio station, choral group, marching band, Saddle and Sirloin, Students Today, Leaders Forever, International Student Association, Chi Alpha Christian Organization, fraternities/sororities, national fraternities, national sororities. *Campus security:* 24-hour emergency response devices and patrols, student patrols, late-night transport/escort service, controlled dormitory access. *Student services:* health clinic, personal/psychological counseling.

Athletics Member NCAA. All Division I. *Intercollegiate sports:* archery M(c)/W(c), baseball M(s), basketball M(s)/W(s), bowling M(c)/W(c), cheerleading M(c)/W(c), cross-country running M(s)/W(s), football M(s), golf M/W(s), ice hockey M(c), lacrosse M(c), riflery M(c)/W(c), rugby M(c)/W(c), soccer M(c)/W(s), softball W(s), track and field M(s)/W(s), volleyball M(c)/W(s), wrestling M(s). *Intramural sports:* basketball M/W, football M/W, softball M/W, volleyball M/W, wrestling M.

Standardized Tests *Required:* SAT or ACT (for admission).

Costs (2010–11) *One-time required fee:* $70. *Tuition:* state resident $5639 full-time, $235 per credit hour part-time; nonresident $15,055 full-time, $627 per credit hour part-time. Full-time tuition and fees vary according to reciprocity agreements and student level. Part-time tuition and fees vary according to course load, reciprocity agreements, and student level. *Required fees:* $1022 full-time, $43 per credit hour part-time. *Room and board:* $6890; room only: $3040. Room and board charges vary according to board plan and housing facility. *Payment plan:* installment. *Waivers:* minority students, children of alumni, senior citizens, and employees or children of employees.

Financial Aid Of all full-time matriculated undergraduates who enrolled in 2007, 7,109 applied for aid, 4,917 were judged to have need, 980 had their need fully met. In 2007, 1763 non-need-based awards were made. *Average percent of need met:* 3%. *Average financial aid package:* $7030. *Average need-based loan:* $4378. *Average need-based gift aid:* $3419. *Average non-need-based aid:* $1533.

Applying *Options:* electronic application. *Application fee:* $35. *Required:* high school transcript, minimum 2.5 GPA. *Application deadlines:* 8/15 (freshmen), 8/15 (transfers). *Notification:* continuous (freshmen), continuous (transfers).

Freshman Application Contact Jobey Lichtblau, Director of Admission, North Dakota State University, PO Box 5454, Fargo, ND 58105-5454. *Phone:* 701-231-8643. *Toll-free phone:* 800-488-NDSU. *Fax:* 701-231-8802. *E-mail:* ndsu.admission@ndsu.edu. *Web site:* http://www.ndsu.edu/.

Rasmussen College Fargo

Fargo, North Dakota

Freshman Application Contact Ms. Elizabeth Largent, Director, Rasmussen College Fargo, 4012 19th Avenue, SW, Fargo, ND 58103. *Phone:* 701-277-3889. *Toll-free phone:* 800-817-0009. *Fax:* 701-277-5604. *Web site:* http://www.rasmussen.edu/.

Trinity Bible College

Ellendale, North Dakota

Director of Admissions Rev. Steve Tvedt, Vice President of College Relations, Trinity Bible College, 50 South 6th Avenue, Ellendale, ND 58436-7150. *Phone:* 701-349-3621 Ext. 2045. *Toll-free phone:* 888-TBC-2DAY. *Web site:* http://www.trinitybiblecollege.edu/.

University of Mary

Bismarck, North Dakota

- **Independent Roman Catholic** comprehensive, founded 1959
- **Rural** 107-acre campus
- **Endowment** $23.4 million
- **Coed**
- **Minimally difficult** entrance level

Faculty *Student/faculty ratio:* 15:1.

Academics *Calendar:* 4-4-1. *Degrees:* associate, bachelor's, master's, and doctoral-professional.

Student Life *Campus security:* 24-hour emergency response devices and patrols, late-night transport/escort service, controlled dormitory access, video cameras on campus.

Athletics Member NCAA. All Division II.

Standardized Tests *Required:* SAT or ACT (for admission).

Costs (2010–11) *Comprehensive fee:* $18,306 includes full-time tuition ($12,800), mandatory fees ($326), and room and board ($5180). Full-time tuition and fees vary according to course load, degree level, and program. Part-time tuition: $400 per credit hour. Part-time tuition and fees vary according to course load, degree level, and program. *College room only:* $2380. Room and board charges vary according to board plan and housing facility.

Financial Aid *Of all full-time matriculated undergraduates who enrolled in 2009,* 169 Federal Work-Study jobs (averaging $1447). 59 state and other part-time jobs (averaging $2015). *Average indebtedness upon graduation:* $25,287.

Applying *Options:* electronic application, early admission, deferred entrance. *Application fee:* $25. *Required:* high school transcript, 2.0 College Prep GPA. *Required for some:* essay or personal statement, interview. *Recommended:* minimum 2.5 GPA, 2 letters of recommendation.

Freshman Application Contact Pam Helm, University of Mary, 7500 University Drive, Bismarck, ND 58504-9652. *Phone:* 701-355-8390. *Toll-free phone:* 800-288-6279. *Fax:* 701-255-7687. *E-mail:* phelm@umary.edu. *Web site:* http://www.umary.edu/.

University of North Dakota
Grand Forks, North Dakota

- **State-supported** university, founded 1883, part of North Dakota University System
- **Urban** 550-acre campus
- **Endowment** $11.2 million
- **Coed** 11,139 undergraduate students, 83% full-time, 45% women, 55% men
- **Minimally difficult** entrance level, 70% of applicants were admitted

Undergraduates 9,232 full-time, 1,907 part-time. Students come from 57 states and territories; 35 other countries; 48% are from out of state; 1% Black or African American, non-Hispanic/Latino; 2% Hispanic/Latino; 1% Asian, non-Hispanic/Latino; 0.1% Native Hawaiian or other Pacific Islander, non-Hispanic/Latino; 2% American Indian or Alaska Native, non-Hispanic/Latino; 0.7% Two or more races, non-Hispanic/Latino; 4% Race/ethnicity unknown; 6% international; 8% transferred in; 34% live on campus. *Retention:* 79% of full-time freshmen returned.

Freshmen *Admission:* 4,796 applied, 3,357 admitted, 2,096 enrolled. *Average high school GPA:* 3.38. *Test scores:* ACT scores over 18: 96%; ACT scores over 24: 46%; ACT scores over 30: 6%.

Faculty *Total:* 680, 91% full-time, 73% with terminal degrees. *Student/faculty ratio:* 19:1.

Academics *Calendar:* semesters. *Degrees:* certificates, diplomas, bachelor's, master's, doctoral-professional, doctoral-research/scholarship, post-master's, and postbachelor's certificates. *Special study options:* accelerated degree program, adult/continuing education programs, advanced placement credit, cooperative education, distance learning, double majors, English as a second language, honors programs, independent study, internships, off-campus study, part-time degree program, services for LD students, student-designed majors, study abroad, summer session for credit. *ROTC:* Army (b), Air Force (b). *Unusual degree programs:* 3-2 engineering; applied economics, counseling, chemistry, public administration.

Computers on Campus 1,500 computers/terminals and 400 ports are available on campus for general student use. Students can access the following: campus intranet, computer help desk, free student e-mail accounts, online (class) grades, online (class) registration, online (class) schedules. Campus-wide network is available. 100% of college-owned or -operated housing units are wired for high-speed Internet access. Wireless service is available via classrooms, computer centers, computer labs, dorm rooms, learning centers, libraries, student centers.

Student Life *Housing options:* coed, men-only, women-only, disabled students. Campus housing is university owned and leased by the school. *Activities and organizations:* drama/theater group, student-run newspaper, radio and television station, choral group, marching band, student government, Greek Life, Association of Residence Halls, University of North Dakota Indian Association, Sioux Crew-student athletic boosters, national fraternities, national sororities. *Campus security:* 24-hour emergency response devices and patrols, student patrols, late-night transport/escort service, controlled dormitory access, emergency telephones. *Student services:* health clinic, personal/psychological counseling, women's center, legal services.

Athletics Member NCAA. All Division I. *Intercollegiate sports:* baseball M(s), basketball M(s)/W(s), cross-country running M(s)/W(s), football M(s), golf M(s)/W(s), ice hockey M(s)/W(s), soccer W(s), softball W(s), swimming and diving M(s)/W(s), tennis W(s), track and field M(s)/W(s), volleyball W(s). *Intramural sports:* badminton M/W, basketball M/W, football M, golf M/W, ice hockey M/W, racquetball M/W, soccer W, softball W, tennis W, ultimate Frisbee M/W, volleyball M/W.

Standardized Tests *Required:* SAT or ACT (for admission). *Recommended:* ACT (for admission).

Costs (2010–11) *Tuition:* state resident $5652 full-time, $236 per credit hour part-time; nonresident $15,091 full-time, $629 per credit hour part-time. Full-time tuition and fees vary according to degree level, program, and reciprocity agreements. Part-time tuition and fees vary according to course load, degree level, program, and reciprocity agreements. *Required fees:* $1282 full-time. *Room and board:* $5950; room only: $2350. Room and board charges vary according to board plan and housing facility. *Payment plan:* deferred payment. *Waivers:* minority students, adult students, senior citizens, and employees or children of employees.

Financial Aid Of all full-time matriculated undergraduates who enrolled in 2009, 6,900 applied for aid, 6,900 were judged to have need, 1,906 had their need fully met. 1,972 Federal Work-Study jobs. In 2009, 2539 non-need-based awards were made. *Average percent of need met:* 39%. *Average financial aid package:* $5723. *Average need-based loan:* $4130. *Average need-based gift aid:* $2892. *Average non-need-based aid:* $1469. *Average indebtedness upon graduation:* $22,137.

Applying *Options:* electronic application, deferred entrance. *Application fee:* $35. *Required:* high school transcript. *Recommended:* minimum 2.5 GPA. *Application deadline:* rolling (transfers). *Notification:* continuous (transfers).

Freshman Application Contact Deborah Melby, Director of Admissions, University of North Dakota, Stop 8357, 205 Twamley Hall, 264 Centennial Drive, Grand Forks, ND 58202. *Phone:* 701-777-3821. *Toll-free phone:* 800-CALLUND. *Fax:* 701-777-2721. *E-mail:* enrollmentservices@mail.und.nodak.edu. *Web site:* http://www.und.nodak.edu/.

Valley City State University
Valley City, North Dakota

- **State-supported** comprehensive, founded 1890, part of North Dakota University System
- **Small-town** 55-acre campus
- **Endowment** $4.1 million
- **Coed**
- **Noncompetitive** entrance level

Faculty *Student/faculty ratio:* 12:1.

Academics *Calendar:* semesters. *Degrees:* bachelor's and master's.

Student Life *Campus security:* controlled dormitory access, security cameras throughout campus.

Athletics Member NAIA.

Standardized Tests *Required for some:* SAT or ACT (for admission).

Costs (2010–11) *Tuition:* state resident $4433 full-time, $148 per semester hour part-time; nonresident $11,835 full-time, $395 per semester hour part-time. Full-time tuition and fees vary according to course load, location, program, and reciprocity agreements. Part-time tuition and fees vary according to course load, location, program, and reciprocity agreements. *Required fees:* $1642 full-time, $68 per semester hour part-time. *Room and board:* $4528; room only: $1812. Room and board charges vary according to board plan and housing facility.

Financial Aid Of all full-time matriculated undergraduates who enrolled in 2009, 565 applied for aid, 426 were judged to have need, 424 had their need fully met. 46 Federal Work-Study jobs (averaging $1673). In 2009, 329 non-need-based awards were made. *Average percent of need met:* 66. *Average financial aid package:* $8615. *Average need-based loan:* $4064. *Average need-based gift aid:* $4835. *Average non-need-based aid:* $1759. *Average indebtedness upon graduation:* $22,428.

Applying *Options:* electronic application, early admission, deferred entrance. *Application fee:* $35. *Required:* high school transcript. *Required for some:* minimum 0 GPA.

Freshman Application Contact Ms. Alison Kasowski, Admission Counselor, Valley City State University, 101 College Street, SW, Valley City, ND 58072. *Phone:* 701-845-7204. *Toll-free phone:* 800-532-8641 Ext. 37101. *Fax:* 701-845-7299. *E-mail:* alison.kasowski@vcsu.edu. *Web site:* http://www.vcsu.edu/.

OHIO

Akron Institute of Herzing University
Akron, Ohio

Admissions Office Contact Akron Institute of Herzing University, 1600 South Arlington Street, Suite 100, Akron, OH 44306. *Toll-free phone:* 800-311-0512. *Web site:* http://www.akroninstitute.com/.

Allegheny Wesleyan College
Salem, Ohio

Director of Admissions Admissions Office, Allegheny Wesleyan College, 2161 Woodsdale Road, Salem, OH 44460. *Phone:* 330-337-6403. *Toll-free phone:* 800-292-3153. *E-mail:* college@awc.edu. *Web site:* http://www.awc.edu/.

Antioch University Midwest
Yellow Springs, Ohio

- **Independent** upper-level, founded 1988, part of Antioch University
- **Small-town** 100-acre campus with easy access to Dayton
- **Coed** 159 undergraduate students, 39% full-time, 74% women, 26% men
- **Noncompetitive** entrance level

Undergraduates 62 full-time, 97 part-time. Students come from 1 other state; 16% Black or African American, non-Hispanic/Latino; 0.6% Hispanic/Latino; 0.6% American Indian or Alaska Native, non-Hispanic/Latino; 12% Race/ethnicity unknown; 12% transferred in.

Faculty *Total:* 52, 38% full-time. *Student/faculty ratio:* 12:1.

Academics *Calendar:* quarters. *Degrees:* certificates, bachelor's, master's, post-master's, and postbachelor's certificates. *Special study options:* accelerated degree program, adult/continuing education programs, advanced placement credit, cooperative education, distance learning, double majors, independent study, internships, part-time degree program, summer session for credit.

Computers on Campus 32 computers/terminals are available on campus for general student use. Students can access the following: campus intranet, computer help desk, free student e-mail accounts, online (class) grades, online (class) registration, online (class) schedules, online bill pay, and online view of financial aid award letter. Campuswide network is available. Wireless service is available via entire campus.

Student Life *Housing:* college housing not available. *Campus security:* 24-hour emergency response devices and patrols. *Student services:* personal/psychological counseling.

Costs (2010–11) *Tuition:* $20,480 full-time, $320 per credit hour part-time. *Required fees:* $600 full-time, $150 per term part-time. *Waivers:* employees or children of employees.

Financial Aid Of all full-time matriculated undergraduates who enrolled in 2009, 52 applied for aid, 51 were judged to have need. 9 Federal Work-Study jobs (averaging $2450). *Average percent of need met:* 30%. *Average financial aid package:* $3263. *Average need-based loan:* $5667. *Average need-based gift aid:* $2300. *Average indebtedness upon graduation:* $23,000.

Applying *Options:* electronic application, deferred entrance. *Application fee:* $45. *Application deadline:* rolling (transfers).

Application Contact Antioch University Midwest, 900 Dayton Street, Yellow Springs, OH 45387-1609. *Phone:* 937-769-1823. *Web site:* http://midwest.antioch.edu/.

Art Academy of Cincinnati
Cincinnati, Ohio

Freshman Application Contact Mr. John J. Wadell, Director of Admissions, Art Academy of Cincinnati, 1212 Jackson Street, Cincinnati, OH 45202-7106. *Phone:* 513-562-8744. *Toll-free phone:* 800-323-5692. *Fax:* 513-562-8778. *E-mail:* admissions@artacademy.edu. *Web site:* http://www.artacademy.edu/.

The Art Institute of Ohio–Cincinnati
Cincinnati, Ohio

- **Proprietary** primarily 2-year, part of Education Management Corporation
- **Urban** campus
- **Coed**

Academics *Calendar:* continuous. *Degrees:* diplomas, associate, and bachelor's.

Costs (2010–11) *Tuition:* Tuition cost varies by program. Prospective students should contact the school for current tuition costs. Other charges include a starting kit for all first-quarter students. Kits vary in price, depending on the program of study.

Freshman Application Contact The Art Institute of Ohio–Cincinnati, 8845 Governors Hill Drive, Cincinnati, OH 45249-3317. *Phone:* 513-833-2400. *Toll-free phone:* 866-613-5184. *Web site:* http://www.artinstitutes.edu/cincinnati/.

See page 1052 for the College Close-Up.

Ashland University
Ashland, Ohio

- **Independent** comprehensive, founded 1878, affiliated with Brethren Church
- **Small-town** 135-acre campus with easy access to Cleveland
- **Endowment** $39.4 million
- **Coed** 3,146 undergraduate students, 83% full-time, 54% women, 46% men
- **Moderately difficult** entrance level, 77% of applicants were admitted

Undergraduates 2,622 full-time, 524 part-time. Students come from 31 states and territories; 19 other countries; 10% are from out of state; 3% transferred in; 72% live on campus. *Retention:* 69% of full-time freshmen returned.

Freshmen *Admission:* 3,530 applied, 2,722 admitted, 675 enrolled. *Average high school GPA:* 3.37. *Test scores:* SAT critical reading scores over 500: 59%; SAT math scores over 500: 58%; ACT scores over 18: 96%; SAT critical reading scores over 600: 18%; SAT math scores over 600: 22%; ACT scores over 24: 40%; SAT critical reading scores over 700: 1%; SAT math scores over 700: 2%; ACT scores over 30: 4%.

Faculty *Total:* 591, 46% full-time, 56% with terminal degrees. *Student/faculty ratio:* 13:1.

Academics *Calendar:* semesters. *Degrees:* certificates, diplomas, associate, bachelor's, master's, doctoral-professional, and doctoral-research/scholarship. *Special study options:* academic remediation for entering students, adult/

continuing education programs, advanced placement credit, double majors, English as a second language, honors programs, independent study, internships, off-campus study, part-time degree program, services for LD students, student-designed majors, study abroad, summer session for credit.

Computers on Campus 760 computers/terminals are available on campus for general student use. Students can access the following: campus intranet, computer help desk, free student e-mail accounts, online (class) grades, online (class) registration, online (class) schedules. Campuswide network is available. 100% of college-owned or -operated housing units are wired for high-speed Internet access. Wireless service is available via classrooms, computer centers, computer labs, learning centers, libraries, student centers.

Student Life *Housing:* on-campus residence required through junior year. *Options:* coed, men-only, women-only, disabled students. Campus housing is university owned. Freshman campus housing is guaranteed. *Activities and organizations:* drama/theater group, student-run newspaper, radio and television station, choral group, marching band, Campus Activity Board, Fellowship of Christian Athletes, Hope Fellowship, intramurals, Community Care, national fraternities, national sororities. *Campus security:* 24-hour emergency response devices and patrols, student patrols, late-night transport/escort service, controlled dormitory access. *Student services:* health clinic, personal/psychological counseling, women's center.

Athletics Member NCAA. All Division II. *Intercollegiate sports:* baseball M(s), basketball M(s)/W(s), cross-country running M(s)/W(s), football M(s), golf M(s)/W(s), soccer M(s)/W(s), softball M/W(s), swimming and diving M(s)/W(s), tennis W, track and field M(s)/W(s), volleyball W(s), wrestling M(s). *Intramural sports:* badminton M/W, baseball M(c), basketball M/W, bowling M/W, cross-country running M/W, field hockey M/W, football M, golf M/W, lacrosse M(c), racquetball M/W, rugby M(c)/W(c), skiing (downhill) M(c)/W(c), soccer M/W, softball M(c)/W(c), swimming and diving M/W, table tennis M/W, tennis M/W, track and field M/W, ultimate Frisbee M/W, volleyball M(c)/W(c), weight lifting M(c)/W(c), wrestling M.

Standardized Tests *Required:* SAT or ACT (for admission).

Costs (2011–12) *Comprehensive fee:* $37,932 includes full-time tuition ($27,654), mandatory fees ($926), and room and board ($9352). Full-time tuition and fees vary according to degree level, location, and reciprocity agreements. Part-time tuition: $848 per semester hour. Part-time tuition and fees vary according to course load, degree level, location, and program. *Required fees:* $18 per semester hour part-time. *College room only:* $5022. Room and board charges vary according to board plan and housing facility. *Payment plan:* installment. *Waivers:* children of alumni, senior citizens, and employees or children of employees.

Financial Aid Of all full-time matriculated undergraduates who enrolled in 2009, 2,136 applied for aid, 1,769 were judged to have need. 1,249 Federal Work-Study jobs (averaging $2396). In 2009, 221 non-need-based awards were made. *Average percent of need met:* 90%. *Average financial aid package:* $23,254. *Average need-based loan:* $4717. *Average need-based gift aid:* $15,366. *Average non-need-based aid:* $8168. *Average indebtedness upon graduation:* $36,545.

Applying *Options:* electronic application, deferred entrance. *Required:* high school transcript, minimum 2.5 GPA. *Required for some:* interview. *Recommended:* interview. *Application deadlines:* rolling (freshmen), rolling (out-of-state freshmen), rolling (transfers). *Notification:* continuous (freshmen), continuous (transfers).

Freshman Application Contact Mr. Thomas Mansperger, Director of Admission, Ashland University, 401 College Avenue, Ashland, OH 44805. *Phone:* 419-289-5052. *Toll-free phone:* 800-882-1548. *Fax:* 419-289-5999. *E-mail:* enrollme@ashland.edu. *Web site:* http://www.exploreashland.com/.

Baldwin-Wallace College
Berea, Ohio

- **Independent Methodist** comprehensive, founded 1845
- **Suburban** 100-acre campus with easy access to Cleveland
- **Endowment** $103.9 million
- **Coed** 3,670 undergraduate students, 86% full-time, 57% women, 43% men
- **Moderately difficult** entrance level, 65% of applicants were admitted

Undergraduates 3,160 full-time, 510 part-time. Students come from 39 states and territories; 14 other countries; 13% are from out of state; 7% Black or African American, non-Hispanic/Latino; 3% Hispanic/Latino; 0.8% Asian, non-Hispanic/Latino; 0.1% American Indian or Alaska Native, non-Hispanic/Latino; 3% Two or more races, non-Hispanic/Latino; 0.8% Race/ethnicity unknown; 1% international; 4% transferred in; 60% live on campus. *Retention:* 82% of full-time freshmen returned.

Freshmen *Admission:* 3,553 applied, 2,303 admitted, 709 enrolled. *Average high school GPA:* 3.55. *Test scores:* SAT critical reading scores over 500: 74%; SAT math scores over 500: 71%; ACT scores over 18: 93%; SAT critical reading scores over 600: 31%; SAT math scores over 600: 33%; ACT scores over 24: 53%; SAT critical reading scores over 700: 4%; SAT math scores over 700: 8%; ACT scores over 30: 9%.

Faculty *Total:* 415, 40% full-time, 42% with terminal degrees. *Student/faculty ratio:* 15:1.

Academics *Calendar:* semesters. *Degrees:* certificates, bachelor's, and master's. *Special study options:* academic remediation for entering students, accelerated degree program, adult/continuing education programs, advanced placement credit, distance learning, double majors, English as a second language, honors programs, independent study, internships, off-campus study, part-time degree program, services for LD students, student-designed majors, study abroad, summer session for credit. *ROTC:* Army (c), Air Force (c). *Unusual degree programs:* 3-2 engineering with Case Western Reserve University and Columbia University; social work with Case Western Reserve University; 3/2 MBA Programs in Accounting, Computer Information Systems, Computer Science, and Human Resources.

Computers on Campus 565 computers/terminals and 100 ports are available on campus for general student use. Students can access the following: campus intranet, computer help desk, free student e-mail accounts, online (class) grades, online (class) registration, online (class) schedules. Campuswide network is available. 100% of college-owned or -operated housing units are wired for high-speed Internet access. Wireless service is available via entire campus.

Student Life *Housing:* on-campus residence required through sophomore year. *Options:* coed, disabled students. Campus housing is university owned. Freshman campus housing is guaranteed. *Activities and organizations:* drama/theater group, student-run newspaper, radio and television station, choral group, marching band, campus entertainment productions, Student Senate, Dance Marathon, Campus Crusade, Black Student Alliance, national fraternities, national sororities. *Campus security:* 24-hour emergency response devices and patrols, student patrols, late-night transport/escort service, controlled dormitory access. *Student services:* health clinic, personal/psychological counseling, women's center.

Athletics Member NCAA. All Division III. *Intercollegiate sports:* baseball M, basketball M/W, cross-country running M/W, football M, golf M/W, soccer M/W, softball W, swimming and diving M/W, tennis M/W, track and field M/

W, volleyball W, wrestling M. *Intramural sports:* archery M(c)/W(c), badminton M/W, basketball M/W, cheerleading W(c), crew M(c)/W(c), fencing M(c)/W(c), football M/W, golf M/W, gymnastics W(c), lacrosse M(c)/W(c), racquetball M/W, skiing (cross-country) M(c)/W(c), skiing (downhill) M(c)/W(c), soccer M/W, softball M/W, table tennis M(c)/W(c), tennis M/W, volleyball M/W, water polo M(c)/W(c), wrestling M.

Standardized Tests *Required for some:* SAT or ACT (for admission).

Costs (2010–11) *Comprehensive fee:* $33,560 includes full-time tuition ($25,260) and room and board ($8300). Full-time tuition and fees vary according to class time and course load. Part-time tuition: $785 per semester hour. Part-time tuition and fees vary according to class time and course load. *College room only:* $4056. *Payment plans:* installment, deferred payment. *Waivers:* children of alumni and employees or children of employees.

Financial Aid Of all full-time matriculated undergraduates who enrolled in 2009, 2,702 applied for aid, 2,431 were judged to have need, 872 had their need fully met. 909 Federal Work-Study jobs (averaging $710). 411 state and other part-time jobs (averaging $506). In 2009, 462 non-need-based awards were made. *Average percent of need met:* 86%. *Average financial aid package:* $20,739. *Average need-based loan:* $4564. *Average need-based gift aid:* $15,052. *Average non-need-based aid:* $8923. *Average indebtedness upon graduation:* $30,096. *Financial aid deadline:* 9/1.

Applying *Options:* electronic application, deferred entrance. *Application fee:* $25. *Required:* essay or personal statement, high school transcript, 1 letter of recommendation. *Recommended:* minimum 3.2 GPA, interview. *Application deadlines:* 3/1 (freshmen), 8/1 (transfers). *Notification:* continuous (freshmen), continuous (transfers).

Freshman Application Contact Patricia Skrha, Director of Undergraduate Admission, Baldwin-Wallace College, Bonds Administration Building, 275 Eastland Road, Berea, OH 44017. *Phone:* 440-826-2222. *Toll-free phone:* 877-BWAPPLY. *Fax:* 440-826-3830. *E-mail:* admission@bw.edu. *Web site:* http://www.bw.edu/.

See page 1100 for the College Close-Up.

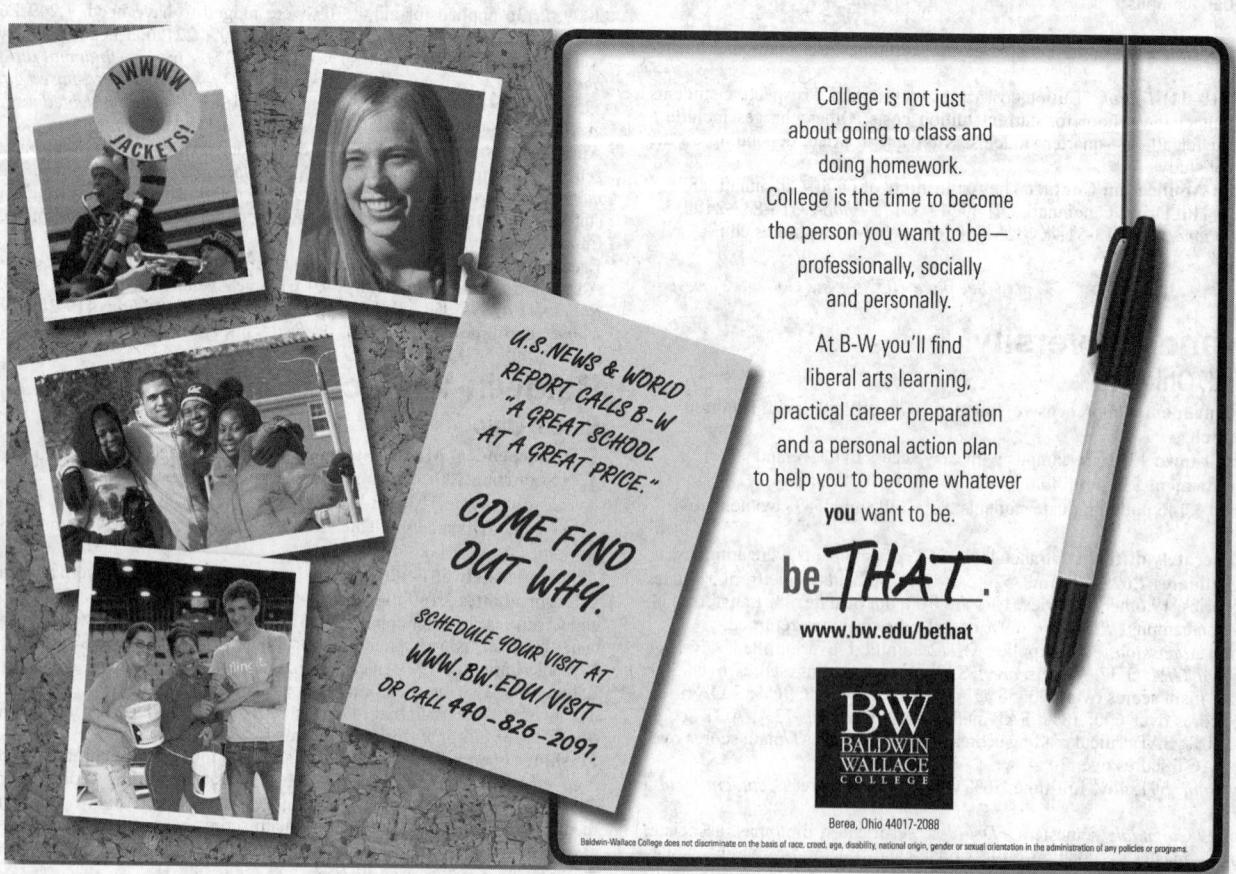

Bluffton University

Bluffton, Ohio

- **Independent Mennonite** comprehensive, founded 1899
- **Small-town** 65-acre campus with easy access to Toledo
- **Endowment** $16.1 million
- **Coed** 1,009 undergraduate students, 86% full-time, 53% women, 47% men
- **Moderately difficult** entrance level, 61% of applicants were admitted

Undergraduates 864 full-time, 145 part-time. Students come from 22 states and territories; 8 other countries; 15% are from out of state; 4% transferred in; 75% live on campus. *Retention:* 60% of full-time freshmen returned.

Freshmen *Admission:* 1,794 applied, 1,097 admitted, 219 enrolled. *Average high school GPA:* 3.2. *Test scores:* SAT critical reading scores over 500: 59%; SAT math scores over 500: 66%; ACT scores over 18: 79%; SAT critical reading scores over 600: 31%; SAT math scores over 600: 24%; ACT scores over 24: 29%; SAT critical reading scores over 700: 7%; SAT math scores over 700: 7%; ACT scores over 30: 5%.

Faculty *Total:* 104, 61% full-time, 49% with terminal degrees. *Student/faculty ratio:* 13:1.

Academics *Calendar:* semesters. *Degrees:* bachelor's and master's. *Special study options:* academic remediation for entering students, accelerated degree program, adult/continuing education programs, advanced placement credit, distance learning, double majors, external degree program, honors programs, independent study, internships, off-campus study, part-time degree program, services for LD students, student-designed majors, study abroad, summer session for credit.

Computers on Campus 170 computers/terminals and 1,300 ports are available on campus for general student use. Students can access the following: campus intranet, computer help desk, free student e-mail accounts, online (class) grades, online (class) registration, online (class) schedules. Campus-wide network is available. 100% of college-owned or -operated housing units are wired for high-speed Internet access. Wireless service is available via classrooms, computer centers, computer labs, dorm rooms, libraries, student centers.

Student Life *Housing:* on-campus residence required through senior year. *Options:* coed, men-only, women-only. Campus housing is university owned. Freshman campus housing is guaranteed. *Activities and organizations:* drama/theater group, student-run newspaper, radio station, choral groups, Brothers and Sisters in Christ, Campus Government, Student Union Board, music groups/chorale, chapel service. *Campus security:* 24-hour emergency response devices, late-night transport/escort service, controlled dormitory access, night security guards. *Student services:* health clinic, personal/psychological counseling.

Athletics Member NCAA. All Division III. *Intercollegiate sports:* baseball M, basketball M/W, cheerleading W, cross-country running M/W, football M, soccer M/W, softball W, track and field M/W, volleyball W. *Intramural sports:* basketball M/W, bowling M/W, football M/W, softball M/W, ultimate Frisbee M, volleyball M/W.

Standardized Tests *Required:* SAT or ACT (for admission).

Costs (2011–12) *Comprehensive fee:* $34,911 includes full-time tuition ($25,704), mandatory fees ($450), and room and board ($8757). Full-time tuition and fees vary according to course load. Part-time tuition: $1071 per credit hour. Part-time tuition and fees vary according to course load. *Required fees:* $113 per term part-time. *College room only:* $4302. Room and board charges vary according to board plan and housing facility. *Payment plan:* installment. *Waivers:* employees or children of employees.

Financial Aid Of all full-time matriculated undergraduates who enrolled in 2009, 726 applied for aid, 696 were judged to have need, 332 had their need fully met. 590 Federal Work-Study jobs (averaging $2297). 178 state and other part-time jobs (averaging $2470). In 2009, 73 non-need-based awards were made. *Average percent of need met:* 91%. *Average financial aid package:* $23,924. *Average need-based loan:* $4971. *Average need-based gift aid:* $16,937. *Average non-need-based aid:* $10,997. *Average indebtedness upon graduation:* $31,457. *Financial aid deadline:* 10/1.

Applying *Options:* electronic application, deferred entrance. *Application fee:* $20. *Required:* high school transcript, minimum 2.3 GPA, 1 letter of recommendation, rank in upper 50% of high school class or 19 on ACT. *Required for some:* essay or personal statement. *Recommended:* interview. *Application deadlines:* 8/15 (freshmen), rolling (transfers). *Notification:* continuous (freshmen), continuous (transfers).

Freshman Application Contact Mr. Chris Jebsen, Director of Admissions, Bluffton University, 1 University Drive, Bluffton, OH 45817. *Phone:* 419-358-3254. *Toll-free phone:* 800-488-3257. *Fax:* 419-358-3081. *E-mail:* admissions@bluffton.edu. *Web site:* http://www.bluffton.edu/.

Bowling Green State University

Bowling Green, Ohio

- **State-supported** university, founded 1910
- **Small-town** 1338-acre campus with easy access to Toledo
- **Endowment** $118.5 million
- **Coed** 14,807 undergraduate students, 92% full-time, 54% women, 46% men
- **Moderately difficult** entrance level, 80% of applicants were admitted

Undergraduates 13,687 full-time, 1,120 part-time. Students come from 53 states and territories; 39 other countries; 11% are from out of state; 11% Black or African American, non-Hispanic/Latino; 3% Hispanic/Latino; 0.9% Asian, non-Hispanic/Latino; 0.1% Native Hawaiian or other Pacific Islander, non-Hispanic/Latino; 0.6% American Indian or Alaska Native, non-Hispanic/Latino; 0.6% Two or more races, non-Hispanic/Latino; 3% Race/ethnicity unknown; 2% international; 5% transferred in; 43% live on campus. *Retention:* 77% of full-time freshmen returned.

Freshmen *Admission:* 13,996 applied, 11,211 admitted, 3,900 enrolled. *Average high school GPA:* 3.2. *Test scores:* SAT critical reading scores over 500: 56%; SAT math scores over 500: 60%; SAT writing scores over 500: 45%; ACT scores over 18: 90%; SAT critical reading scores over 600: 16%; SAT math scores over 600: 18%; SAT writing scores over 600: 9%; ACT scores over 24: 33%; SAT critical reading scores over 700: 2%; SAT math scores over 700: 1%; SAT writing scores over 700: 1%; ACT scores over 30: 4%.

Faculty *Total:* 919, 87% full-time. *Student/faculty ratio:* 19:1.

Academics *Calendar:* semesters. *Degrees:* certificates, bachelor's, master's, doctoral-research/scholarship, and post-master's certificates. *Special study options:* academic remediation for entering students, accelerated degree program, adult/continuing education programs, advanced placement credit, cooperative education, distance learning, double majors, English as a second language, honors programs, independent study, internships, off-campus study, part-time degree program, services for LD students, student-designed majors, study abroad, summer session for credit. *ROTC:* Army (b), Air Force (b).

Computers on Campus 958 computers/terminals and 500 ports are available on campus for general student use. Students can access the following: computer help desk, free student e-mail accounts, online (class) grades, online (class) registration, online (class) schedules, wireless networking, ePortfolio, MyFiles, Bursar billing information and payment, online mid-term grade reporting, view and change personal information, order official and unofficial transcripts, check meal plan balance, apply for graduation. Campuswide network is available. 100% of college-owned or -operated housing units are wired for high-speed Internet access. Wireless service is available via classrooms, computer centers, computer labs, dorm rooms, learning centers, libraries, student centers.

Student Life *Housing:* on-campus residence required through sophomore year. *Options:* coed, disabled students. Campus housing is university owned. Freshman campus housing is guaranteed. *Activities and organizations:* drama/theater group, student-run newspaper, radio station, choral group, marching band, Dance Marathon, University Activities Organization, BG Undead, Men's Rugby, Black Student Union, national fraternities, national sororities. *Campus security:* 24-hour emergency response devices and patrols, student patrols, late-night transport/escort service, controlled dormitory access. *Student services:* health clinic, personal/psychological counseling, women's center, legal services.

Athletics Member NCAA. All Division I. *Intercollegiate sports:* baseball M(s), basketball M(s)/W(s), cross-country running M(s)/W(s), football M(s), golf M(s)/W(s), gymnastics W(s), ice hockey M(s), soccer M(s)/W(s), softball W(s), swimming and diving W(s), tennis W(s), track and field W(s), volleyball W(s). *Intramural sports:* badminton M/W, baseball M, basketball M/W, bowling M(c)/W(c), football M/W, golf M/W, gymnastics M(c)/W(c), ice hockey M(c), lacrosse M(c), racquetball M/W, rugby M(c)/W(c), sailing M(c)/W(c), skiing (downhill) M(c)/W(c), soccer M/W, softball W, swimming and diving M(c)/W(c), tennis M(c)/W, track and field M(c)/W, ultimate Frisbee M/W, volleyball M(c)/W, water polo M/W, wrestling M(c)/W(c).

Standardized Tests *Required:* SAT or ACT (for admission).

Costs (2010–11) *Tuition:* state resident $8322 full-time, $347 per credit hour part-time; nonresident $15,630 full-time, $652 per credit hour part-time. Full-time tuition and fees vary according to course load and location. Part-time tuition and fees vary according to course load and location. *Required fees:* $1382 full-time, $57 per credit hour part-time. *Room and board:* $7800. Room and board charges vary according to board plan and housing facility. *Payment plan:* installment. *Waivers:* senior citizens and employees or children of employees.

Financial Aid Of all full-time matriculated undergraduates who enrolled in 2009, 11,557 applied for aid, 10,280 were judged to have need, 939 had their need fully met. 322 Federal Work-Study jobs (averaging $997). In 2009, 1960 non-need-based awards were made. *Average percent of need met:* 81%. *Average financial aid package:* $15,306. *Average need-based loan:* $7503. *Average need-based gift aid:* $6369. *Average non-need-based aid:* $3943. *Average indebtedness upon graduation:* $31,515.

Applying *Options:* electronic application, deferred entrance. *Application fee:* $40. *Required:* high school transcript, minimum 2.5 GPA. *Required for some:* interview. *Application deadlines:* 7/15 (freshmen), 7/15 (out-of-state freshmen), 7/15 (transfers). *Notification:* continuous (freshmen), continuous (out-of-state freshmen), continuous (transfers).

Freshman Application Contact Mr. Gary Swegan, Assistant Vice President/Director of Admissions, Bowling Green State University, 110 McFall, Bowling Green, OH 43403. *Phone:* 419-372-BGSU. *Fax:* 419-372-6955. *E-mail:* choosebgsu@bgsu.edu. *Web site:* http://www.bgsu.edu/.

See page 1132 for the College Close-Up.

Bowling Green State University-Firelands College

Huron, Ohio

- **State-supported** primarily 2-year, founded 1968, part of Bowling Green State University System
- **Rural** 216-acre campus with easy access to Cleveland and Toledo
- **Endowment** $2.0 million
- **Coed**
- **Noncompetitive** entrance level

Faculty *Student/faculty ratio:* 18:1.

Academics *Calendar:* semesters. *Degrees:* certificates, associate, and bachelor's (also offers some upper-level and graduate courses).

Student Life *Campus security:* 24-hour emergency response devices, late-night transport/escort service, patrols by trained security personnel.

Costs (2010–11) *Tuition:* state resident $4308 full-time, $2154 per year part-time; nonresident $11,616 full-time, $5814 per year part-time. Full-time tuition and fees vary according to course load and location. Part-time tuition and fees vary according to course load and location. *Required fees:* $220 full-time, $118 per year part-time. *Payment plans:* tuition prepayment, installment.

Applying *Options:* electronic application, early admission, deferred entrance. *Application fee:* $40. *Required:* high school transcript.

Freshman Application Contact Debralee Divers, Director of Admissions and Financial Aid, Bowling Green State University-Firelands College, One University Drive, Huron, OH 44839-9791. *Phone:* 419-433-5560. *Toll-free phone:* 800-322-4787. *Fax:* 419-372-0604. *E-mail:* divers@bgsu.edu. *Web site:* http://www.firelands.bgsu.edu/.

Bryant & Stratton College

Cleveland, Ohio

- **Proprietary** 4-year, founded 1929, part of Bryant and Stratton College, Inc.
- **Urban** campus
- **Coed**
- **Minimally difficult** entrance level

Faculty *Student/faculty ratio:* 10:1.

Academics *Calendar:* semesters. *Degrees:* associate and bachelor's.

Student Life *Campus security:* controlled dormitory access.

Standardized Tests *Required:* TABE (for admission). *Recommended:* SAT or ACT (for admission).

Financial Aid *Of all full-time matriculated undergraduates who enrolled in 2001,* 110 applied for aid, 108 were judged to have need, 90 had their need fully met. 8 Federal Work-Study jobs (averaging $3000). *Average percent of need met:* 89. *Average financial aid package:* $6200. *Average need-based loan:* $3065. *Average need-based gift aid:* $1500. *Average indebtedness upon graduation:* $12,000.

Applying *Options:* deferred entrance. *Required:* high school transcript, interview, entrance evaluation and placement evaluation.

Freshman Application Contact Bryant & Stratton College, Cleveland, OH 44114-3203. *Phone:* 216-771-1700. *Fax:* 216-771-7787. *Web site:* http://www.bryantstratton.edu/.

Bryant & Stratton College

Eastlake, Ohio

- **Proprietary** primarily 2-year, founded 1987, part of Bryant and Stratton College, Inc.
- **Suburban** campus with easy access to Cleveland
- **Coed**
- **Minimally difficult** entrance level

Faculty *Student/faculty ratio:* 12:1.

PROFILES

Academics *Calendar:* semesters. *Degrees:* associate and bachelor's.
Student Life *Campus security:* 24-hour emergency response devices, late-night transport/escort service.
Standardized Tests *Required:* CPAt (for admission). *Recommended:* SAT or ACT (for admission).
Financial Aid *Of all full-time matriculated undergraduates who enrolled in 2009,* 12 Federal Work-Study jobs (averaging $2800).
Applying *Options:* deferred entrance. *Application fee:* $35. *Required:* high school transcript, interview, entrance evaluation and placement evaluation. *Required for some:* essay or personal statement. *Recommended:* minimum 2 GPA.
Freshman Application Contact Ms. Melanie Pettit, Director of Admissions, Bryant & Stratton College, 35350 Curtis Boulevard, Eastlake, OH 44095. *Phone:* 440-510-1112. *Web site:* http://www.bryantstratton.edu/.

Bryant & Stratton College
Parma, Ohio

- **Proprietary** primarily 2-year, founded 1981, part of Bryant and Stratton College, Inc.
- **Suburban** 4-acre campus with easy access to Cleveland
- **Coed**
- **Minimally difficult** entrance level

Faculty *Student/faculty ratio:* 12:1.
Academics *Calendar:* semesters. *Degrees:* associate and bachelor's.
Student Life *Campus security:* 24-hour emergency response devices.
Standardized Tests *Required:* CPAt (for admission). *Recommended:* SAT or ACT (for admission).
Applying *Options:* deferred entrance. *Required:* high school transcript, interview, entrance evaluation and placement evaluation.
Freshman Application Contact Bryant & Stratton College, 12955 Snow Road, Parma, OH 44130-1013. *Phone:* 216-265-3151. *Toll-free phone:* 800-327-3151. *Web site:* http://www.bryantstratton.edu/.

Capital University
Columbus, Ohio

- **Independent** comprehensive, founded 1830, affiliated with Evangelical Lutheran Church in America
- **Suburban** 48-acre campus with easy access to Columbus
- **Endowment** $53.0 million
- **Coed** 2,754 undergraduate students, 89% full-time, 59% women, 41% men
- **Moderately difficult** entrance level, 75% of applicants were admitted

Undergraduates 2,451 full-time, 303 part-time. Students come from 32 states and territories; 18 other countries; 8% are from out of state; 9% Black or African American, non-Hispanic/Latino; 2% Hispanic/Latino; 1% Asian, non-Hispanic/Latino; 0.3% American Indian or Alaska Native, non-Hispanic/Latino; 1% Two or more races, non-Hispanic/Latino; 3% Race/ethnicity unknown; 1% international; 3% transferred in; 51% live on campus. *Retention:* 76% of full-time freshmen returned.
Freshmen *Admission:* 3,673 applied, 2,753 admitted, 720 enrolled. *Average high school GPA:* 3.45. *Test scores:* SAT critical reading scores over 500: 74%; SAT math scores over 500: 74%; SAT writing scores over 500: 65%; ACT scores over 18: 98%; SAT critical reading scores over 600: 29%; SAT math scores over 600: 29%; SAT writing scores over 600: 20%; ACT scores over 24: 53%; SAT critical reading scores over 700: 4%; SAT math scores over 700: 3%; SAT writing scores over 700: 1%; ACT scores over 30: 7%.
Faculty *Total:* 388, 52% full-time, 51% with terminal degrees. *Student/faculty ratio:* 12:1.
Academics *Calendar:* semesters. *Degrees:* bachelor's, master's, and doctoral-professional. *Special study options:* accelerated degree program, adult/continuing education programs, advanced placement credit, cooperative education, double majors, English as a second language, external degree program, freshman honors college, honors programs, independent study, internships, off-campus study, part-time degree program, services for LD students, student-designed majors, study abroad, summer session for credit. *ROTC:* Army (b), Air Force (c). *Unusual degree programs:* 3-2 engineering with Washington University in St. Louis, Case Western Reserve University; occupational therapy with Washington University in St. Louis, University of Indianapolis.
Computers on Campus 397 computers/terminals and 1,350 ports are available on campus for general student use. Students can access the following: campus intranet, computer help desk, free student e-mail accounts, online (class) grades, online (class) registration, online (class) schedules. Campus-wide network is available. 100% of college-owned or -operated housing units are wired for high-speed Internet access. Wireless service is available via entire campus.
Student Life *Housing:* on-campus residence required through sophomore year. *Options:* coed, disabled students. Campus housing is university owned. Fresh-

man campus housing is guaranteed. *Activities and organizations:* drama/theater group, student-run newspaper, radio and television station, choral group, Campus Crusade for Christ, student government, University Programming, College Republicans, American Marketing Association, national fraternities, national sororities. *Campus security:* 24-hour emergency response devices and patrols, late-night transport/escort service, controlled dormitory access. *Student services:* health clinic, personal/psychological counseling.
Athletics Member NCAA. All Division III. *Intercollegiate sports:* baseball M, basketball M/W, cross-country running M/W, football M, golf M/W, soccer M/W, softball W, tennis M/W, track and field M/W, volleyball W. *Intramural sports:* basketball M/W, bowling M/W, cheerleading M(c)/W(c), football M/W, lacrosse M(c)/W(c), skiing (downhill) M(c)/W(c), softball M/W, swimming and diving M(c)/W(c), volleyball M/W.
Standardized Tests *Required:* SAT or ACT (for admission).
Costs (2010–11) *Comprehensive fee:* $37,174 includes full-time tuition ($29,310) and room and board ($7864). Full-time tuition and fees vary according to course load. Part-time tuition: $977 per credit hour. Part-time tuition and fees vary according to course load. *Room and board:* Room and board charges vary according to board plan and housing facility. *Payment plan:* installment. *Waivers:* senior citizens and employees or children of employees.
Financial Aid Of all full-time matriculated undergraduates who enrolled in 2009, 2,083 applied for aid, 1,940 were judged to have need, 544 had their need fully met. In 2009, 294 non-need-based awards were made. *Average percent of need met:* 26%. *Average financial aid package:* $22,556. *Average need-based loan:* $3646. *Average need-based gift aid:* $17,075. *Average non-need-based aid:* $12,748.
Applying *Options:* electronic application, deferred entrance. *Application fee:* $25. *Required:* high school transcript, minimum 2.6 GPA. *Required for some:* 1 letter of recommendation, audition for Conservatory of Music. *Recommended:* interview. *Application deadlines:* 5/1 (freshmen), rolling (transfers). *Notification:* 9/30 (freshmen), continuous (transfers).
Freshman Application Contact Ms. Amanda Steiner, Director of Admission, Capital University, 1 College and Main, Columbus, OH 43209. *Phone:* 614-236-6574. *Toll-free phone:* 800-289-6289. *Fax:* 614-236-6926. *E-mail:* asteiner@capital.edu. *Web site:* http://www.capital.edu/.

See page 1188 for the College Close-Up.

Case Western Reserve University
Cleveland, Ohio

- **Independent** university, founded 1826
- **Urban** 155-acre campus
- **Endowment** $1.5 billion
- **Coed** 4,227 undergraduate students, 97% full-time, 43% women, 57% men
- **Very difficult** entrance level, 67% of applicants were admitted

Undergraduates 4,085 full-time, 142 part-time. Students come from 52 states and territories; 26 other countries; 51% are from out of state; 5% Black or African American, non-Hispanic/Latino; 3% Hispanic/Latino; 16% Asian, non-Hispanic/Latino; 0.1% Native Hawaiian or other Pacific Islander, non-Hispanic/Latino; 0.2% American Indian or Alaska Native, non-Hispanic/Latino; 1% Two or more races, non-Hispanic/Latino; 13% Race/ethnicity unknown; 6% international; 1% transferred in; 78% live on campus. *Retention:* 92% of full-time freshmen returned.
Freshmen *Admission:* 9,472 applied, 6,318 admitted, 1,021 enrolled. *Test scores:* SAT critical reading scores over 500: 97%; SAT math scores over 500: 99%; SAT writing scores over 500: 97%; ACT scores over 18: 100%; SAT critical reading scores over 600: 77%; SAT math scores over 600: 91%; SAT writing scores over 600: 72%; ACT scores over 24: 98%; SAT critical reading scores over 700: 29%; SAT math scores over 700: 51%; SAT writing scores over 700: 26%; ACT scores over 30: 59%.
Faculty *Total:* 932, 80% full-time, 86% with terminal degrees. *Student/faculty ratio:* 9:1.
Academics *Calendar:* semesters. *Degrees:* bachelor's, master's, doctoral-professional, doctoral-research/scholarship, and postbachelor's certificates. *Special study options:* accelerated degree program, adult/continuing education programs, advanced placement credit, cooperative education, double majors, English as a second language, honors programs, independent study, internships, off-campus study, part-time degree program, services for LD students, student-designed majors, study abroad, summer session for credit. *ROTC:* Army (c), Air Force (c). *Unusual degree programs:* 3-2 engineering.
Computers on Campus 265 computers/terminals and 1,000 ports are available on campus for general student use. Students can access the following: campus intranet, computer help desk, free student e-mail accounts, online (class) grades, online (class) registration, online (class) schedules, software library, online reference databases, electronic books and journals. Campuswide network is available. 100% of college-owned or -operated housing units are wired for high-speed Internet access. Wireless service is available via entire campus.

Student Life *Housing:* on-campus residence required through sophomore year. *Options:* coed. Campus housing is university owned. Freshman campus housing is guaranteed. *Activities and organizations:* drama/theater group, student-run newspaper, radio station, choral group, marching band, student government, radio station, Habitat for Humanity and service organizations, International Student Groups, Musical Theater/Dance Groups, national fraternities, national sororities. *Campus security:* 24-hour emergency response devices and patrols, student patrols, late-night transport/escort service, controlled dormitory access, crime prevention programs. *Student services:* health clinic, personal/psychological counseling, women's center, legal services.

Athletics Member NCAA. All Division III. *Intercollegiate sports:* archery M(c)/W(c), baseball M, basketball M/W, cheerleading M(c)/W(c), crew M(c)/W(c), cross-country running M/W, fencing M(c)/W(c), football M, ice hockey M(c)/W(c), soccer M/W, softball W, swimming and diving M/W, tennis M/W, track and field M/W, ultimate Frisbee M(c)/W(c), volleyball M(c)/W, wrestling M. *Intramural sports:* badminton M/W, basketball M/W, bowling M/W, cross-country running M/W, football M/W, golf M/W, racquetball M/W, soccer M/W, softball M/W, squash M/W, swimming and diving M/W, table tennis M/W, tennis M/W, track and field M/W, ultimate Frisbee M/W, volleyball M/W, water polo M/W, weight lifting M/W, wrestling M.

Standardized Tests *Required:* SAT or ACT (for admission).

Costs (2010–11) *One-time required fee:* $380. *Comprehensive fee:* $49,048 includes full-time tuition ($37,300), mandatory fees ($348), and room and board ($11,400). Part-time tuition: $1554 per credit hour. Part-time tuition and fees vary according to course load. *College room only:* $6550. Room and board charges vary according to board plan, housing facility, and student level. *Payment plan:* installment. *Waivers:* employees or children of employees.

Financial Aid Of all full-time matriculated undergraduates who enrolled in 2009, 2,889 applied for aid, 2,620 were judged to have need, 2,261 had their need fully met. 1,871 Federal Work-Study jobs (averaging $3058). In 2009, 799 non-need-based awards were made. *Average percent of need met:* 83%. *Average financial aid package:* $33,130. *Average need-based loan:* $7430. *Average need-based gift aid:* $23,585. *Average non-need-based aid:* $19,476. *Average indebtedness upon graduation:* $39,236.

Applying *Options:* electronic application, early admission, early action, deferred entrance. *Required:* essay or personal statement, high school transcript, 1 letter of recommendation. *Recommended:* interview. *Application deadlines:* 1/15 (freshmen), 5/15 (transfers), 11/1 (early action). *Notification:* 4/1 (freshmen), continuous until 7/1 (transfers), 12/15 (early action).
Freshman Application Contact Mr. Robert McCullough, Director of Undergraduate Admission, Case Western Reserve University, 10900 Euclid Avenue, Cleveland, OH 44106. *Phone:* 216-368-4450. *Fax:* 216-368-5111. *E-mail:* admission@case.edu. *Web site:* http://www.case.edu/.

See page 1204 for the College Close-Up.

Cedarville University
Cedarville, Ohio

- **Independent Baptist** comprehensive, founded 1887
- **Rural** 400-acre campus with easy access to Columbus and Dayton
- **Endowment** $13.1 million
- **Coed** 3,147 undergraduate students, 94% full-time, 54% women, 46% men
- **Moderately difficult** entrance level, 75% of applicants were admitted

Undergraduates 2,963 full-time, 184 part-time. Students come from 50 states and territories; 22 other countries; 65% are from out of state; 2% Black or African American, non-Hispanic/Latino; 2% Hispanic/Latino; 1% Asian, non-Hispanic/Latino; 0.1% Native Hawaiian or other Pacific Islander, non-Hispanic/Latino; 0.3% American Indian or Alaska Native, non-Hispanic/Latino; 0.2% Two or more races, non-Hispanic/Latino; 3% Race/ethnicity unknown; 1% international; 3% transferred in; 100% live on campus. *Retention:* 86% of full-time freshmen returned.

Freshmen *Admission:* 2,991 applied, 2,241 admitted, 859 enrolled. *Average high school GPA:* 3.64. *Test scores:* SAT critical reading scores over 500: 88%; SAT math scores over 500: 85%; SAT writing scores over 500: 83%; ACT scores over 18: 99%; SAT critical reading scores over 600: 50%; SAT math scores over 600: 44%; SAT writing scores over 600: 41%; ACT scores over 24: 75%; SAT critical reading scores over 700: 13%; SAT math scores over 700: 10%; SAT writing scores over 700: 9%; ACT scores over 30: 16%.
Faculty *Total:* 207, 95% full-time, 66% with terminal degrees. *Student/faculty ratio:* 15:1.

Academics *Calendar:* semesters. *Degrees:* certificates, bachelor's, and master's. *Special study options:* academic remediation for entering students, accelerated degree program, adult/continuing education programs, advanced

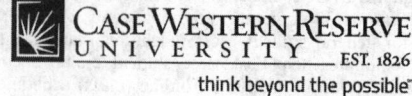

placement credit, distance learning, double majors, honors programs, independent study, internships, off-campus study, part-time degree program, services for LD students, study abroad, summer session for credit. *ROTC:* Army (c), Air Force (c).

Computers on Campus 2,600 computers/terminals are available on campus for general student use. Students can access the following: campus intranet, computer help desk, free student e-mail accounts, online (class) grades, online (class) registration, online (class) schedules, over 150 software packages. Campuswide network is available. Wireless service is available via entire campus.

Student Life *Housing:* on-campus residence required through senior year. *Options:* men-only, women-only, disabled students. Campus housing is university owned. Freshman campus housing is guaranteed. *Activities and organizations:* drama/theater group, student-run newspaper, radio station, choral group, Student Government Association, College Republicans, ASME (American Society of Mechanical Engineers), Chi Theta Pi, MENC. *Campus security:* 24-hour emergency response devices and patrols, student patrols, late-night transport/escort service, controlled dormitory access. *Student services:* health clinic, personal/psychological counseling.

Athletics Member NAIA, NCCAA. *Intercollegiate sports:* baseball M(s), basketball M(s)/W(s), cross-country running M(s)/W(s), golf M(s), soccer M(s)/W(s), softball W(s), tennis M(s)/W(s), track and field M(s)/W(s), volleyball W(s). *Intramural sports:* badminton M/W, basketball M/W, bowling M/W, cross-country running M/W, football M/W, golf M/W, racquetball M/W, rock climbing M/W, skiing (downhill) M/W, soccer M/W, softball M/W, table tennis M/W, tennis M/W, ultimate Frisbee M/W, volleyball M/W.

Standardized Tests *Required:* SAT or ACT (for admission). *Recommended:* SAT and SAT Subject Tests or ACT (for admission).

Costs (2011–12) *One-time required fee:* $130. *Comprehensive fee:* $28,586 includes full-time tuition ($23,500) and room and board ($5086). Part-time tuition: $870 per credit. Part-time tuition and fees vary according to course load. *College room only:* $2820. Room and board charges vary according to board plan. *Payment plan:* installment. *Waivers:* senior citizens and employees or children of employees.

Financial Aid Of all full-time matriculated undergraduates who enrolled in 2009, 2,184 applied for aid, 1,874 were judged to have need, 369 had their need fully met. 272 Federal Work-Study jobs (averaging $1192). 1,461 state and other part-time jobs (averaging $1150). In 2009, 590 non-need-based awards were made. *Average percent of need met:* 42%. *Average financial aid package:* $14,544. *Average need-based loan:* $6312. *Average need-based gift aid:* $4426. *Average non-need-based aid:* $14,213. *Average indebtedness upon graduation:* $29,177.

Applying *Options:* electronic application, early admission, deferred entrance. *Application fee:* $30. *Required:* essay or personal statement, high school transcript, minimum 3 GPA, 2 letters of recommendation, clear testimony of faith in Jesus Christ and evidence of consistent Christian lifestyle. *Required for some:* interview. *Application deadlines:* rolling (freshmen), rolling (transfers). *Notification:* continuous (freshmen), continuous (transfers).

Freshman Application Contact Mr. Mark Weinstein, Director of Admissions, Cedarville University, 251 North Main Street, Cedarville, OH 45314-0601. *Phone:* 937-766-7700. *Toll-free phone:* 800-CEDARVILLE. *Fax:* 937-766-7575. *E-mail:* admiss@cedarville.edu. *Web site:* http://www.cedarville.edu/.

Central State University
Wilberforce, Ohio

- **State-supported** comprehensive, founded 1887, part of Ohio Board of Regents
- **Rural** 60-acre campus with easy access to Dayton
- **Coed** 2,244 undergraduate students, 91% full-time, 49% women, 51% men
- **Minimally difficult** entrance level, 22% of applicants were admitted

Undergraduates 2,040 full-time, 204 part-time. Students come from 32 states and territories; 5 other countries; 49% are from out of state; 95% Black or African American, non-Hispanic/Latino; 0.7% Hispanic/Latino; 0.1% Asian, non-Hispanic/Latino; 0.1% American Indian or Alaska Native, non-Hispanic/Latino; 2% Race/ethnicity unknown; 0.1% international; 8% transferred in; 57% live on campus. *Retention:* 46% of full-time freshmen returned.

Freshmen *Admission:* 8,637 applied, 1,934 admitted, 507 enrolled. *Average high school GPA:* 2.4. *Test scores:* SAT critical reading scores over 500: 8%; SAT math scores over 500: 6%; ACT scores over 18: 26%; SAT critical reading scores over 600: 1%; ACT scores over 24: 2%.

Faculty *Total:* 189, 59% full-time, 45% with terminal degrees. *Student/faculty ratio:* 14:1.

Academics *Calendar:* semesters. *Degrees:* bachelor's and master's. *Special study options:* adult/continuing education programs, cooperative education, double majors, honors programs, independent study, internships, off-campus study, part-time degree program, services for LD students, study abroad, summer session for credit. *ROTC:* Army (b).

Computers on Campus 555 computers/terminals and 160 ports are available on campus for general student use. Students can access the following: campus intranet, free student e-mail accounts, online (class) grades, online (class) registration, online (class) schedules. Campuswide network is available. 100% of college-owned or -operated housing units are wired for high-speed Internet access. Wireless service is available via classrooms, computer centers, computer labs, dorm rooms, learning centers, libraries, student centers.

Student Life *Housing:* on-campus residence required for freshman year. *Options:* coed, men-only, women-only. Campus housing is university owned and leased by the school. Freshman campus housing is guaranteed. *Activities and organizations:* drama/theater group, student-run newspaper, radio and television station, choral group, marching band, Student Ambassadors, student government, Make it Happen (Inter-Faith), Daughters of Nia Anaya (Social Group), Evolutions (Modeling Troupe), national fraternities, national sororities. *Campus security:* 24-hour emergency response devices and patrols, controlled dormitory access. *Student services:* health clinic, personal/psychological counseling.

Athletics Member NCAA. All Division II. *Intercollegiate sports:* basketball M(s)/W(s), cheerleading M(s)/W(s), cross-country running M(s)/W(s), golf M(s)/W(s), tennis M(s)/W(s), track and field M(s)/W(s), volleyball W(s). *Intramural sports:* basketball M/W, bowling M/W, softball M/W, tennis M/W.

Standardized Tests *Required:* SAT or ACT (for admission). *Recommended:* ACT (for admission).

Costs (2010–11) *Tuition:* state resident $5480 full-time, $226 per credit hour part-time; nonresident $12,220 full-time, $529 per credit hour part-time. Full-time tuition and fees vary according to course load. Part-time tuition and fees vary according to course load. *Room and board:* $8198; room only: $4406. Room and board charges vary according to board plan. *Payment plans:* installment, deferred payment. *Waivers:* senior citizens and employees or children of employees.

Financial Aid Of all full-time matriculated undergraduates who enrolled in 2008, 1,899 applied for aid, 1,799 were judged to have need. 408 Federal Work-Study jobs (averaging $1720). In 2008, 33 non-need-based awards were made. *Average non-need-based aid:* $5125.

Applying *Options:* electronic application. *Application fee:* $20. *Required:* high school transcript. *Required for some:* essay or personal statement, minimum 2 GPA, 2 letters of recommendation, 2.5 high school GPA for nonresidents. *Recommended:* interview. *Application deadlines:* 6/15 (freshmen), 6/15 (transfers). *Notification:* continuous (freshmen), continuous (transfers).

Freshman Application Contact Ms. Robin Rucker, Director, Admissions, Central State University, PO Box 1004, 1400 Blush Row Road, Wilberforce, OH 45384. *Phone:* 937-376-6580. *Toll-free phone:* 800-388-CSU1. *Fax:* 937-376-6648. *E-mail:* admissions@centralstate.edu. *Web site:* http://www.centralstate.edu/.

Chancellor University
Cleveland, Ohio

Director of Admissions Vice President for Enrollment Management, Chancellor University, 3921 Chester Avenue, Cleveland, OH 44114-4624. *Phone:* 216-523-3806 Ext. 805. *Toll-free phone:* 877-366-9377. *E-mail:* admissions@myers.edu. *Web site:* http://www.chancelloru.edu/.

Cincinnati Christian University
Cincinnati, Ohio

- **Independent** comprehensive, founded 1924, affiliated with Church of Christ
- **Urban** 40-acre campus with easy access to Cincinnati
- **Coed** 760 undergraduate students, 66% full-time, 43% women, 57% men
- **Minimally difficult** entrance level, 98% of applicants were admitted

Undergraduates 498 full-time, 262 part-time. 33% are from out of state; 13% Black or African American, non-Hispanic/Latino; 1% Hispanic/Latino; 0.1% Asian, non-Hispanic/Latino; 0.1% American Indian or Alaska Native, non-Hispanic/Latino; 14% Race/ethnicity unknown; 1% international; 9% transferred in; 36% live on campus. *Retention:* 57% of full-time freshmen returned.

Freshmen *Admission:* 222 applied, 218 admitted, 152 enrolled. *Average high school GPA:* 2.91. *Test scores:* SAT critical reading scores over 500: 47%; SAT math scores over 500: 53%; SAT writing scores over 500: 50%; ACT scores over 18: 77%; SAT critical reading scores over 600: 13%; SAT math scores over 600: 16%; SAT writing scores over 600: 11%; ACT scores over 24: 28%; SAT critical reading scores over 700: 3%; SAT math scores over 700: 3%; SAT writing scores over 700: 3%; ACT scores over 30: 3%.

Faculty *Total:* 93, 35% full-time, 47% with terminal degrees. *Student/faculty ratio:* 12:1.

Academics *Calendar:* semesters. *Degrees:* associate, bachelor's, master's, and doctoral-professional. *Special study options:* academic remediation for entering students, adult/continuing education programs, advanced placement credit, cooperative education, distance learning, double majors, honors programs, independent study, internships, off-campus study, part-time degree program, services for LD students, summer session for credit.

Computers on Campus Students can access the following: campus intranet, computer help desk, free student e-mail accounts, online (class) grades, online (class) registration, online (class) schedules. Campuswide network is available. Wireless service is available via classrooms, computer labs, libraries, student centers.

Student Life *Housing:* on-campus residence required through junior year. *Options:* men-only, women-only. Campus housing is university owned. Freshman campus housing is guaranteed. *Activities and organizations:* drama/theater group, choral group. *Campus security:* 24-hour emergency response devices and patrols, student patrols, late-night transport/escort service, controlled dormitory access. *Student services:* health clinic, personal/psychological counseling.

Athletics Member NAIA. *Intercollegiate sports:* baseball M, basketball M(s)/W, cross-country running M/W, golf M, soccer M(s)/W, volleyball W. *Intramural sports:* soccer M/W, volleyball M/W.

Standardized Tests *Required:* SAT or ACT (for admission).

Costs (2010–11) *Comprehensive fee:* $20,490 includes full-time tuition ($13,280), mandatory fees ($500), and room and board ($6710). Full-time tuition and fees vary according to course load and student level. Part-time tuition: $425 per credit hour. Part-time tuition and fees vary according to course load and student level. *College room only:* $3210. Room and board charges vary according to board plan, housing facility, and student level. *Payment plan:* installment. *Waivers:* employees or children of employees.

Financial Aid Of all full-time matriculated undergraduates who enrolled in 2008, 478 applied for aid, 452 were judged to have need. In 2008, 44 non-need-based awards were made. *Average percent of need met:* 48%. *Average financial aid package:* $8830. *Average need-based loan:* $4492. *Average need-based gift aid:* $5000. *Average non-need-based aid:* $3390.

Applying *Options:* electronic application, early admission, deferred entrance. *Application fee:* $40. *Required:* essay or personal statement, high school transcript, 1 letter of recommendation. *Recommended:* minimum 2 GPA, interview. *Application deadlines:* 7/1 (freshmen), 7/1 (transfers). *Notification:* continuous (freshmen), continuous (transfers).

Freshman Application Contact Cincinnati Christian University, 2700 Glenway Avenue, PO Box 04320, Cincinnati, OH 45204-3200. *Toll-free phone:* 800-949-4228. *Web site:* http://www.ccuniversity.edu/.

Cincinnati College of Mortuary Science

Cincinnati, Ohio

- **Independent** 4-year, founded 1882
- **Urban** 10-acre campus
- **Coed** 165 undergraduate students, 100% full-time, 52% women, 48% men

Undergraduates 165 full-time. Students come from 13 states and territories; 14% Black or African American, non-Hispanic/Latino; 2% Hispanic/Latino; 94% transferred in. *Retention:* 95% of full-time freshmen returned.

Freshmen *Admission:* 10 enrolled.

Faculty *Total:* 7, 71% full-time. *Student/faculty ratio:* 33:1.

Academics *Calendar:* quarters. *Degrees:* associate and bachelor's. *Special study options:* adult/continuing education programs, summer session for credit.

Computers on Campus 16 computers/terminals are available on campus for general student use.

Student Life *Housing:* college housing not available.

Athletics *Intramural sports:* basketball M/W, bowling M/W, football M/W, softball M/W.

Standardized Tests *Required:* SAT or ACT (for admission).

Costs (2010–11) *Tuition:* $20,250 full-time. Full-time tuition and fees vary according to course load, degree level, and program. Part-time tuition and fees vary according to degree level. No tuition increase for student's term of enrollment.

Applying *Options:* deferred entrance. *Application fee:* $40. *Required:* high school transcript, minimum 2 GPA. *Application deadlines:* rolling (freshmen), rolling (transfers). *Notification:* continuous (freshmen), continuous (transfers).

Freshman Application Contact Cincinnati College of Mortuary Science, 645 West North Bend Road, Cincinnati, OH 45224-1462. *Phone:* 513-761-2020. *Fax:* 513-761-3333. *Web site:* http://www.ccms.edu/.

The Cleveland Institute of Art

Cleveland, Ohio

- **Independent** 4-year, founded 1882
- **Urban** 488-acre campus
- **Endowment** $23.5 million
- **Coed** 534 undergraduate students, 97% full-time, 55% women, 45% men
- **Moderately difficult** entrance level, 82% of applicants were admitted

Undergraduates 516 full-time, 18 part-time. Students come from 32 states and territories; 9 other countries; 32% are from out of state; 7% Black or African American, non-Hispanic/Latino; 3% Hispanic/Latino; 0.8% Asian, non-Hispanic/Latino; 4% Native Hawaiian or other Pacific Islander, non-Hispanic/Latino; 0.2% American Indian or Alaska Native, non-Hispanic/Latino; 2% Two or more races, non-Hispanic/Latino; 3% international; 7% transferred in; 21% live on campus. *Retention:* 88% of full-time freshmen returned.

Freshmen *Admission:* 593 applied, 486 admitted, 153 enrolled. *Average high school GPA:* 3.19. *Test scores:* SAT critical reading scores over 500: 64%; SAT math scores over 500: 55%; ACT scores over 18: 83%; SAT critical reading scores over 600: 33%; SAT math scores over 600: 14%; ACT scores over 24: 36%; SAT critical reading scores over 700: 2%; ACT scores over 30: 11%.

Faculty *Total:* 100, 48% full-time, 65% with terminal degrees. *Student/faculty ratio:* 8:1.

Academics *Calendar:* semesters. *Degree:* bachelor's. *Special study options:* academic remediation for entering students, advanced placement credit, double majors, honors programs, independent study, internships, off-campus study, part-time degree program, services for LD students, study abroad. *ROTC:* Army (c), Navy (c), Air Force (c).

Computers on Campus 80 computers/terminals are available on campus for general student use. Students can access the following: campus intranet, free student e-mail accounts, online (class) grades, online (class) registration, online (class) schedules. Campuswide network is available. 100% of college-owned or -operated housing units are wired for high-speed Internet access. Wireless service is available via classrooms, computer labs, learning centers, libraries, student centers.

Student Life *Housing:* on-campus residence required for freshman year. *Options:* coed. Campus housing is leased by the school. Freshman applicants given priority for college housing. *Activities and organizations:* Campus Activities Board, Student Independent Exhibition, Artists for Christ, Student Leadership Council, Community Service Club. *Campus security:* 24-hour emergency response devices and patrols, late-night transport/escort service, controlled dormitory access. *Student services:* health clinic, personal/psychological counseling, women's center, legal services.

Athletics *Intramural sports:* basketball M/W, cross-country running M/W, football M/W, golf M/W, ice hockey M/W, racquetball M/W, soccer M/W, softball M/W, swimming and diving M/W, tennis M/W, track and field M/W, ultimate Frisbee M/W, volleyball M/W.

Standardized Tests *Required:* SAT or ACT (for admission).

Costs (2011–12) *Comprehensive fee:* $45,248 includes full-time tuition ($31,760), mandatory fees ($2122), and room and board ($11,366). Full-time tuition and fees vary according to program, reciprocity agreements, and student level. Part-time tuition: $1325 per credit hour. Part-time tuition and fees vary according to course load, program, reciprocity agreements, and student level. *Required fees:* $142 per credit hour part-time, $105 per term part-time. *College room only:* $6516. Room and board charges vary according to board plan. *Payment plan:* installment. *Waivers:* employees or children of employees.

Financial Aid Of all full-time matriculated undergraduates who enrolled in 2009, 486 applied for aid, 459 were judged to have need, 39 had their need fully met. 358 Federal Work-Study jobs (averaging $2222). In 2009, 60 non-need-based awards were made. *Average percent of need met:* 57%. *Average financial aid package:* $21,225. *Average need-based loan:* $4818. *Average need-based gift aid:* $15,205. *Average non-need-based aid:* $9654. *Average indebtedness upon graduation:* $61,270.

Applying *Options:* electronic application, early action, deferred entrance. *Application fee:* $30. *Required:* essay or personal statement, high school transcript, minimum 2 GPA, 1 letter of recommendation, portfolio. *Recommended:* interview. *Application deadlines:* 3/1 (freshmen), 5/1 (transfers). *Notification:* continuous (freshmen), continuous (transfers).

Freshman Application Contact Office of Admissions, The Cleveland Institute of Art, 11141 East Boulevard, Cleveland, OH 44106-1700. *Phone:* 216-421-7418. *Toll-free phone:* 800-223-4700. *Fax:* 216-754-3634. *E-mail:* admissions@cia.edu. *Web site:* http://www.cia.edu/.

Cleveland Institute of Music

Cleveland, Ohio

Freshman Application Contact Mr. William Fay, Director of Admission, Cleveland Institute of Music, 11021 East Boulevard, Cleveland, OH 44106-

1776. *Phone:* 216-795-3107. *Fax:* 216-791-1530. *E-mail:* william.fay@case.edu. *Web site:* http://www.cim.edu/.

See page 1224 for the College Close-Up.

Cleveland State University
Cleveland, Ohio

- **State-supported** university, founded 1964, part of University System of Ohio
- **Urban** 82-acre campus
- **Endowment** $43.7 million
- **Coed** 11,481 undergraduate students, 71% full-time, 54% women, 46% men
- **Moderately difficult** entrance level, 64% of applicants were admitted

Undergraduates 8,115 full-time, 3,366 part-time. Students come from 29 states and territories; 66 other countries; 3% are from out of state; 22% Black or African American, non-Hispanic/Latino; 4% Hispanic/Latino; 2% Asian, non-Hispanic/Latino; 0.3% American Indian or Alaska Native, non-Hispanic/Latino; 0.6% Two or more races, non-Hispanic/Latino; 7% Race/ethnicity unknown; 3% international; 14% transferred in; 7% live on campus. *Retention:* 66% of full-time freshmen returned.
Freshmen *Admission:* 4,637 applied, 2,946 admitted, 1,220 enrolled. *Average high school GPA:* 3.14. *Test scores:* SAT critical reading scores over 500: 48%; SAT math scores over 500: 52%; ACT scores over 18: 81%; SAT critical reading scores over 600: 13%; SAT math scores over 600: 18%; ACT scores over 24: 27%; SAT critical reading scores over 700: 2%; SAT math scores over 700: 2%; ACT scores over 30: 3%.
Faculty *Total:* 1,069, 50% full-time, 51% with terminal degrees. *Student/faculty ratio:* 17:1.
Academics *Calendar:* semesters. *Degrees:* bachelor's, master's, doctoral-professional, doctoral-research/scholarship, post-master's, and postbachelor's certificates. *Special study options:* academic remediation for entering students, accelerated degree program, adult/continuing education programs, advanced placement credit, cooperative education, distance learning, double majors, English as a second language, freshman honors college, honors programs, independent study, internships, off-campus study, part-time degree program, services for LD students, student-designed majors, study abroad, summer session for credit. *ROTC:* Army (c), Air Force (c).
Computers on Campus 800 computers/terminals are available on campus for general student use. Students can access the following: campus intranet, computer help desk, free student e-mail accounts, online (class) grades, online (class) registration, online (class) schedules, each general purpose computer lab has a scanner and printer, and students are allowed free black and white printing up to 2,000 pages per semester. Campuswide network is available. 100% of college-owned or -operated housing units are wired for high-speed Internet access. Wireless service is available via entire campus.
Student Life *Housing options:* coed, disabled students. Campus housing is university owned. Freshman campus housing is guaranteed. *Activities and organizations:* drama/theater group, student-run newspaper, radio station, choral group, Friends of India, Psi Chi, C-SALAD (Cleveland State Animal Liberation and Defense), STAT (Students and Alumni Tomorrow), Math Club, national fraternities, national sororities. *Campus security:* 24-hour emergency response devices and patrols, student patrols, late-night transport/escort service, controlled dormitory access, Campus Watch, CSU Alert Notification System, Community Emergency and Response Team (CERT). *Student services:* health clinic, personal/psychological counseling, women's center.
Athletics Member NCAA. All Division I. *Intercollegiate sports:* baseball M(s), basketball M(s)/W(s), cheerleading M/W(c), cross-country running W(s), fencing M(s)/W(s), golf M(s)/W, soccer M(s)/W, softball W(s), swimming and diving M(s)/W(s), tennis M/W(s), track and field W(s), volleyball W(s), wrestling M(s). *Intramural sports:* badminton M/W, basketball M/W, bowling M/W, crew M(c)/W(c), cross-country running M/W, fencing M/W, field hockey M/W, football M, golf M/W, ice hockey M(c), racquetball M/W, sailing M/W, soccer M/W, softball M/W, squash M/W, swimming and diving M/W, table tennis M/W, tennis M/W, track and field M/W, volleyball M/W, water polo M(c)/W(c), weight lifting M(c)/W(c), wrestling M.
Standardized Tests *Required:* SAT or ACT (for admission).
Costs (2011–12) *Tuition:* state resident $8466 full-time, $353 per credit hour part-time; nonresident $11,387 full-time, $474 per credit hour part-time. Full-time tuition and fees vary according to course load, degree level, and program. Part-time tuition and fees vary according to course load, degree level, and program. *Room and board:* $10,285; room only: $6985. Room and board charges vary according to board plan and housing facility. *Payment plan:* installment. *Waivers:* senior citizens and employees or children of employees.
Financial Aid Of all full-time matriculated undergraduates who enrolled in 2009, 7,186 applied for aid, 6,697 were judged to have need, 370 had their need fully met. 703 Federal Work-Study jobs (averaging $3437). In 2009, 315 non-need-based awards were made. *Average percent of need met:* 48%. *Average financial aid package:* $8950. *Average need-based loan:* $4262. *Average

need-based gift aid:* $6188. *Average non-need-based aid:* $4786. *Average indebtedness upon graduation:* $19,537.
Applying *Options:* electronic application, early action, deferred entrance. *Application fee:* $30. *Required:* high school transcript, minimum 2 GPA, minimum ACT score of 16 or SAT of 750. *Application deadlines:* rolling (freshmen), 7/15 (transfers), 5/1 (early action). *Notification:* continuous (freshmen), continuous (transfers).
Freshman Application Contact Undergraduate Admissions Office, Cleveland State University, 2121 Euclid Avenue, RW 204, Cleveland, OH 44115. *Phone:* 216-687-2100. *Toll-free phone:* 888-CSU-OHIO. *E-mail:* admissions@csuohio.edu. *Web site:* http://www.csuohio.edu/.

College of Mount St. Joseph
Cincinnati, Ohio

- **Independent Roman Catholic** comprehensive, founded 1920
- **Suburban** 92-acre campus
- **Endowment** $21.0 million
- **Coed** 2,055 undergraduate students, 68% full-time, 64% women, 36% men
- **Moderately difficult** entrance level, 65% of applicants were admitted

Undergraduates 1,392 full-time, 663 part-time. Students come from 18 states and territories; 4 other countries; 18% are from out of state; 10% Black or African American, non-Hispanic/Latino; 1% Hispanic/Latino; 0.4% Asian, non-Hispanic/Latino; 0.1% Native Hawaiian or other Pacific Islander, non-Hispanic/Latino; 0.3% American Indian or Alaska Native, non-Hispanic/Latino; 4% Two or more races, non-Hispanic/Latino; 0.3% Race/ethnicity unknown; 0.2% international; 13% transferred in; 25% live on campus. *Retention:* 71% of full-time freshmen returned.
Freshmen *Admission:* 1,610 applied, 1,047 admitted, 391 enrolled. *Average high school GPA:* 3.22. *Test scores:* SAT critical reading scores over 500: 41%; SAT math scores over 500: 48%; ACT scores over 18: 90%; SAT critical reading scores over 600: 5%; SAT math scores over 600: 9%; ACT scores over 24: 24%; SAT math scores over 700: 1%; ACT scores over 30: 1%.
Faculty *Total:* 254, 47% full-time, 84% with terminal degrees. *Student/faculty ratio:* 12:1.
Academics *Calendar:* semesters. *Degrees:* certificates, associate, bachelor's, master's, doctoral-professional, and postbachelor's certificates. *Special study options:* academic remediation for entering students, accelerated degree program, advanced placement credit, cooperative education, distance learning, double majors, honors programs, independent study, internships, off-campus study, part-time degree program, services for LD students, study abroad, summer session for credit. *ROTC:* Army (c), Air Force (c).
Computers on Campus 140 computers/terminals are available on campus for general student use. Students can access the following: computer help desk, free student e-mail accounts, online (class) grades, online (class) registration, online (class) schedules, computer-aided instruction. Campuswide network is available. 100% of college-owned or -operated housing units are wired for high-speed Internet access. Wireless service is available via entire campus.
Student Life *Housing:* on-campus residence required through sophomore year. *Options:* coed, disabled students. Campus housing is university owned. Freshman applicants given priority for college housing. *Activities and organizations:* drama/theater group, student-run newspaper, choral group, Student Government Association, Black Student Union, Campus Ministry Leadership Team, Campus Activities Board, Campus Ambassadors. *Campus security:* 24-hour emergency response devices and patrols, late-night transport/escort service. *Student services:* health clinic, personal/psychological counseling.
Athletics Member NCAA. All Division III. *Intercollegiate sports:* baseball M, basketball M/W, cheerleading W, cross-country running M/W, football M, golf M/W, lacrosse M/W, soccer M/W, softball W, tennis M/W, track and field M/W, volleyball M/W, wrestling M. *Intramural sports:* basketball M/W, football M/W, racquetball M/W, soccer M/W, softball M/W, tennis M/W, volleyball M/W.
Standardized Tests *Required:* SAT or ACT (for admission).
Costs (2010–11) *One-time required fee:* $150. *Comprehensive fee:* $30,942 includes full-time tuition ($22,750), mandatory fees ($800), and room and board ($7392). Full-time tuition and fees vary according to course load and reciprocity agreements. Part-time tuition: $475 per credit hour. Part-time tuition and fees vary according to course load and reciprocity agreements. *Required fees:* $400 per year part-time. *College room only:* $3646. Room and board charges vary according to board plan and housing facility. *Payment plans:* installment, deferred payment. *Waivers:* senior citizens and employees or children of employees.
Financial Aid Of all full-time matriculated undergraduates who enrolled in 2009, 1,241 applied for aid, 1,136 were judged to have need, 191 had their need fully met. 240 Federal Work-Study jobs (averaging $1472). 131 state and other part-time jobs (averaging $1431). In 2009, 183 non-need-based awards were made. *Average percent of need met:* 73%. *Average financial aid package:* $16,827. *Average need-based loan:* $4507. *Average need-based gift aid:*

$12,764. *Average non-need-based aid:* $10,429. *Average indebtedness upon graduation:* $35,569.

Applying *Options:* electronic application, deferred entrance. *Application fee:* $25. *Required:* high school transcript. *Required for some:* essay or personal statement, 2 letters of recommendation, interview. *Recommended:* minimum 2 GPA. *Application deadlines:* 8/15 (freshmen), 8/1 (transfers). *Notification:* continuous (freshmen), continuous (transfers).

Freshman Application Contact Peggy Minnich, Director of Admission, College of Mount St. Joseph, 5701 Delhi Road, Cincinnati, OH 45233-1670. *Phone:* 513-244-4531. *Toll-free phone:* 800-654-9314. *Fax:* 513-244-4629. *E-mail:* admissions@mail.msj.edu. *Web site:* http://www.msj.edu/.

See page 1228 for the College Close-Up.

The College of Wooster
Wooster, Ohio

- **Independent** 4-year, founded 1866, affiliated with Presbyterian Church (U.S.A.)
- **Small-town** 240-acre campus with easy access to Cleveland
- **Endowment** $223.8 million
- **Coed** 2,003 undergraduate students, 97% full-time, 54% women, 46% men
- **Moderately difficult** entrance level, 67% of applicants were admitted

Undergraduates 1,949 full-time, 54 part-time. Students come from 45 states and territories; 33 other countries; 61% are from out of state; 7% Black or African American, non-Hispanic/Latino; 3% Hispanic/Latino; 3% Asian, non-Hispanic/Latino; 0.1% Native Hawaiian or other Pacific Islander, non-Hispanic/Latino; 0.8% American Indian or Alaska Native, non-Hispanic/Latino; 10% Race/ethnicity unknown; 6% international; 0.4% transferred in; 96% live on campus. *Retention:* 89% of full-time freshmen returned.

Freshmen *Admission:* 4,635 applied, 3,122 admitted, 622 enrolled. *Average high school GPA:* 3.64. *Test scores:* SAT critical reading scores over 500: 91%; SAT math scores over 500: 90%; SAT writing scores over 500: 89%; ACT scores over 18: 99%; SAT critical reading scores over 600: 57%; SAT math scores over 600: 57%; SAT writing scores over 600: 48%; ACT scores over 24: 81%; SAT critical reading scores over 700: 17%; SAT math scores over 700: 15%; SAT writing scores over 700: 7%; ACT scores over 30: 25%.

Faculty *Total:* 174, 79% full-time, 80% with terminal degrees. *Student/faculty ratio:* 12:1.

Academics *Calendar:* semesters. *Degree:* bachelor's. *Special study options:* advanced placement credit, cooperative education, double majors, independent study, internships, off-campus study, services for LD students, student-designed majors, study abroad. *Unusual degree programs:* 3-2 engineering with Case Western Reserve University, Washington University in St. Louis, University of Michigan; forestry with Duke University; nursing with Case Western Reserve University; social work with Case Western Reserve University; dentistry with Case Western Reserve University, architecture with Washington University in St. Louis.

Computers on Campus 500 computers/terminals and 3,000 ports are available on campus for general student use. Students can access the following: campus intranet, computer help desk, free student e-mail accounts, online (class) grades, online (class) registration, online (class) schedules, learning management system, campus blogging site. Campuswide network is available. 100% of college-owned or -operated housing units are wired for high-speed Internet access. Wireless service is available via classrooms, computer centers, computer labs, dorm rooms, learning centers, libraries, student centers.

Student Life *Housing:* on-campus residence required through senior year. *Options:* coed, women-only. Campus housing is university owned. Freshman campus housing is guaranteed. *Activities and organizations:* drama/theater group, student-run newspaper, radio station, choral group, marching band, Volunteer Network, International Student Association, Inter-Greek Council, Wooster Activities Crew, Women's Athletic and Recreation Association. *Campus security:* 24-hour emergency response devices and patrols, student patrols, late-night transport/escort service, controlled dormitory access. *Student services:* health clinic, personal/psychological counseling, women's center.

Athletics Member NCAA. All Division III. *Intercollegiate sports:* badminton M(c)/W(c), baseball M, basketball M/W, cheerleading W(c), cross-country running M/W, equestrian sports W(c), field hockey W, football M, golf M/W, lacrosse M/W, rugby M(c)/W(c), soccer M/W, softball W, swimming and diving M/W, tennis M/W, track and field M/W, ultimate Frisbee M(c)/W(c), volleyball M(c)/W. *Intramural sports:* badminton M/W, basketball M/W, bowling M/W, football M, golf M/W, soccer M/W, softball M/W, table tennis M/W, tennis M/W, track and field M/W, ultimate Frisbee M/W, volleyball M/W.

Standardized Tests *Required:* SAT or ACT (for admission).

Costs (2011–12) *Comprehensive fee:* $47,600 includes full-time tuition ($38,000), mandatory fees ($290), and room and board ($9310). Full-time tuition and fees vary according to course load. Part-time tuition and fees vary according to course load. *College room only:* $4275. Room and board charges vary according to board plan and housing facility. *Payment plan:* installment. *Waivers:* employees or children of employees.

Financial Aid Of all full-time matriculated undergraduates who enrolled in 2009, 1,368 applied for aid, 1,156 were judged to have need, 620 had their need fully met. 727 Federal Work-Study jobs (averaging $1366). 67 state and other part-time jobs (averaging $1954). In 2009, 744 non-need-based awards were made. *Average percent of need met:* 86%. *Average financial aid package:* $29,025. *Average need-based loan:* $3700. *Average need-based gift aid:* $23,088. *Average non-need-based aid:* $18,000. *Average indebtedness upon graduation:* $25,252. *Financial aid deadline:* 9/1.

Applying *Options:* electronic application, early admission, early decision, early action, deferred entrance. *Application fee:* $40. *Required:* essay or personal statement, high school transcript, 2 letters of recommendation. *Recommended:* interview. *Application deadlines:* 2/15 (freshmen), 6/1 (transfers), 12/15 (early action). *Early decision deadline:* 11/15. *Notification:* 3/15 (freshmen), continuous (transfers), 12/15 (early decision), 1/15 (early action).

Freshman Application Contact Mr. Cezar Mesquita, Director of Admissions, The College of Wooster, 1189 Beall Avenue, Wooster, OH 44691-2363. *Phone:* 330-263-2270. *Toll-free phone:* 800-877-9905. *Fax:* 330-263-2621. *E-mail:* admissions@wooster.edu. *Web site:* http://www.wooster.edu/.

See page 1238 for the College Close-Up.

Columbus College of Art & Design
Columbus, Ohio

- **Independent** comprehensive, founded 1879
- **Urban** 10-acre campus
- **Endowment** $6.2 million
- **Coed** 1,447 undergraduate students, 90% full-time, 61% women, 39% men
- **Moderately difficult** entrance level, 74% of applicants were admitted

Undergraduates 1,297 full-time, 150 part-time. Students come from 40 states and territories; 23 other countries; 16% are from out of state; 7% Black or African American, non-Hispanic/Latino; 4% Hispanic/Latino; 4% Asian, non-Hispanic/Latino; 0.1% Native Hawaiian or other Pacific Islander, non-Hispanic/Latino; 0.1% American Indian or Alaska Native, non-Hispanic/Latino; 4% Two or more races, non-Hispanic/Latino; 2% Race/ethnicity unknown; 4% international; 6% transferred in; 35% live on campus. *Retention:* 83% of full-time freshmen returned.

Freshmen *Admission:* 725 applied, 536 admitted, 174 enrolled. *Average high school GPA:* 3.12. *Test scores:* SAT critical reading scores over 500: 49%; SAT math scores over 500: 46%; SAT writing scores over 500: 42%; ACT scores over 18: 83%; SAT critical reading scores over 600: 21%; SAT math scores over 600: 11%; SAT writing scores over 600: 11%; ACT scores over 24: 32%; SAT critical reading scores over 700: 3%; SAT writing scores over 700: 2%; ACT scores over 30: 3%.

Faculty *Total:* 201, 36% full-time, 43% with terminal degrees. *Student/faculty ratio:* 12:1.

Academics *Calendar:* semesters. *Degrees:* bachelor's and master's. *Special study options:* academic remediation for entering students, advanced placement credit, distance learning, double majors, English as a second language, honors programs, independent study, internships, off-campus study, part-time degree program, services for LD students, study abroad, summer session for credit.

Computers on Campus 485 computers/terminals are available on campus for general student use. Students can access the following: campus intranet, computer help desk, free student e-mail accounts, online (class) grades, online (class) registration, online (class) schedules, online library. Campuswide network is available. 100% of college-owned or -operated housing units are wired for high-speed Internet access. Wireless service is available via classrooms, computer centers, computer labs, dorm rooms, learning centers, libraries, student centers.

Student Life *Housing:* on-campus residence required for freshman year. *Options:* coed, disabled students. Campus housing is university owned. Freshman campus housing is guaranteed. *Activities and organizations:* Student Government Association, Gay Straight Student Alliance, Sanctuary, Black Student Leadership Association, Student Programming Board. *Campus security:* 24-hour emergency response devices and patrols, late-night transport/escort service, controlled dormitory access. *Student services:* personal/psychological counseling.

Athletics *Intramural sports:* basketball M/W, soccer M/W, ultimate Frisbee M/W.

Standardized Tests *Required:* SAT or ACT (for admission).

Costs (2010–11) *Comprehensive fee:* $35,234 includes full-time tuition ($24,864), mandatory fees ($960), and room and board ($9410). Full-time tuition and fees vary according to course load. Part-time tuition: $1036 per credit hour. Part-time tuition and fees vary according to course load. *Required fees:* $180 per term part-time. *Room and board:* Room and board charges vary according to housing facility and student level. *Payment plans:* installment, deferred payment. *Waivers:* employees or children of employees.

Financial Aid Of all full-time matriculated undergraduates who enrolled in 2009, 1,217 applied for aid, 1,110 were judged to have need, 122 had their need fully met. 157 Federal Work-Study jobs (averaging $3150). 340 state and other part-time jobs (averaging $3075). In 2009, 181 non-need-based awards were made. *Average percent of need met:* 60%. *Average financial aid package:* $17,684. *Average need-based loan:* $5395. *Average need-based gift aid:* $12,565. *Average non-need-based aid:* $8908. *Average indebtedness upon graduation:* $37,355.

Applying *Options:* electronic application, deferred entrance. *Application fee:* $30. *Required:* essay or personal statement, high school transcript, minimum 2 GPA, 1 letter of recommendation, portfolio. *Recommended:* interview. *Application deadlines:* rolling (freshmen), rolling (transfers). *Notification:* continuous (freshmen), continuous (transfers).

Freshman Application Contact Columbus College of Art & Design, 60 Cleveland Avenue, Columbus, OH 43215-1758. *Phone:* 614-224-9101. *Toll-free phone:* 877-997-2223. *Fax:* 614-232-8344. *E-mail:* admissions@ccad.edu. *Web site:* http://www.ccad.edu/.

Defiance College
Defiance, Ohio

- **Independent** comprehensive, founded 1850, affiliated with United Church of Christ
- **Small-town** 150-acre campus with easy access to Toledo
- **Endowment** $12.3 million
- **Coed** 983 undergraduate students, 78% full-time, 51% women, 49% men
- **Moderately difficult** entrance level, 67% of applicants were admitted

Undergraduates 766 full-time, 217 part-time. Students come from 21 states and territories; 4 other countries; 22% are from out of state; 4% transferred in; 44% live on campus. *Retention:* 63% of full-time freshmen returned.

Freshmen *Admission:* 1,692 applied, 1,137 admitted, 267 enrolled. *Average high school GPA:* 3.08. *Test scores:* SAT critical reading scores over 500: 40%; SAT math scores over 500: 45%; SAT writing scores over 500: 31%; ACT scores over 18: 85%; SAT critical reading scores over 600: 9%; SAT math scores over 600: 6%; ACT scores over 24: 21%; SAT critical reading scores over 700: 3%; ACT scores over 30: 2%.

Faculty *Total:* 99, 43% full-time, 37% with terminal degrees. *Student/faculty ratio:* 12:1.

Academics *Calendar:* semesters. *Degrees:* associate, bachelor's, and master's. *Special study options:* academic remediation for entering students, adult/continuing education programs, advanced placement credit, cooperative education, distance learning, double majors, honors programs, independent study, internships, off-campus study, part-time degree program, services for LD students, student-designed majors, summer session for credit.

Computers on Campus 200 computers/terminals are available on campus for general student use. Students can access the following: campus intranet, computer help desk, free student e-mail accounts, online (class) grades, online (class) schedules. Campuswide network is available. 100% of college-owned or -operated housing units are wired for high-speed Internet access. Wireless service is available via entire campus.

Student Life *Housing:* on-campus residence required through junior year. *Options:* coed. Campus housing is university owned. Freshman campus housing is guaranteed. *Activities and organizations:* drama/theater group, student-run newspaper, choral group, Campus Activities Board, Criminal Justice Society, Student Senate, Black Action Student Association, DC Players, national sororities. *Campus security:* late-night transport/escort service, controlled dormitory access. *Student services:* health clinic, personal/psychological counseling.

Athletics Member NCAA. All Division III. *Intercollegiate sports:* baseball M, basketball M/W, cross-country running M/W, football M, golf M/W,

lacrosse M, soccer M/W, softball W, swimming and diving M/W, tennis M/W, track and field M/W, volleyball W. *Intramural sports:* baseball M, basketball M/W, cheerleading M/W, field hockey M/W, football M/W, racquetball M/W, soccer M/W, softball M/W, volleyball M/W, weight lifting M.

Standardized Tests *Required:* SAT or ACT (for admission).

Costs (2011–12) *One-time required fee:* $75. *Comprehensive fee:* $34,340 includes full-time tuition ($25,300), mandatory fees ($590), and room and board ($8450). Full-time tuition and fees vary according to program. Part-time tuition and fees vary according to course load. *College room only:* $4680. Room and board charges vary according to board plan and housing facility. *Payment plan:* installment. *Waivers:* senior citizens and employees or children of employees.

Financial Aid Of all full-time matriculated undergraduates who enrolled in 2009, 729 applied for aid, 700 were judged to have need, 92 had their need fully met. 465 Federal Work-Study jobs (averaging $1915). 63 state and other part-time jobs (averaging $1243). In 2009, 51 non-need-based awards were made. *Average percent of need met:* 75%. *Average financial aid package:* $18,433. *Average need-based loan:* $4544. *Average need-based gift aid:* $6007. *Average non-need-based aid:* $9308. *Average indebtedness upon graduation:* $25,388.

Applying *Options:* electronic application, deferred entrance. *Application fee:* $25. *Required:* high school transcript, minimum 2.25 GPA. *Required for some:* essay or personal statement, interview. *Recommended:* interview. *Application deadlines:* 8/15 (freshmen), 8/15 (transfers). *Notification:* continuous (freshmen), continuous (transfers).

Freshman Application Contact Mr. Brad Harsha, Director of Admissions, Defiance College, 701 North Clinton Street, Defiance, OH 43512. *Phone:* 419-783-2365. *Toll-free phone:* 800-520-4632 Ext. 2359. *Fax:* 419-783-2468. *E-mail:* bharsha@defiance.edu. *Web site:* http://www.defiance.edu/.

Denison University
Granville, Ohio

- **Independent** 4-year, founded 1831
- **Small-town** 800-acre campus with easy access to Columbus
- **Endowment** $585.0 million
- **Coed** 2,275 undergraduate students, 99% full-time, 56% women, 44% men
- **Very difficult** entrance level, 49% of applicants were admitted

Undergraduates 2,257 full-time, 18 part-time. Students come from 51 states and territories; 36 other countries; 73% are from out of state; 7% Black or African American, non-Hispanic/Latino; 4% Hispanic/Latino; 3% Asian, non-Hispanic/Latino; 0.2% American Indian or Alaska Native, non-Hispanic/Latino; 4% Two or more races, non-Hispanic/Latino; 0.3% Race/ethnicity unknown; 6% international; 0.9% transferred in; 98% live on campus. *Retention:* 89% of full-time freshmen returned.

Freshmen *Admission:* 4,723 applied, 2,326 admitted, 623 enrolled. *Average high school GPA:* 3.5. *Test scores:* SAT critical reading scores over 500: 98%; SAT math scores over 500: 99%; ACT scores over 18: 100%; SAT critical reading scores over 600: 76%; SAT math scores over 600: 69%; ACT scores over 24: 97%; SAT critical reading scores over 700: 25%; SAT math scores over 700: 20%; ACT scores over 30: 48%.

Faculty *Total:* 223, 92% full-time, 95% with terminal degrees. *Student/faculty ratio:* 10:1.

Academics *Calendar:* semesters plus optional May term. *Degree:* bachelor's. *Special study options:* advanced placement credit, double majors, honors programs, independent study, internships, off-campus study, part-time degree program, services for LD students, student-designed majors, study abroad. *ROTC:* Army (c). *Unusual degree programs:* 3-2 engineering with Case Western Reserve University, Columbia University, Rensselaer Polytechnic Institute, Washington University in St. Louis; forestry with Duke University; natural resources with University of Michigan; occupational therapy with Washington University in St. Louis; environmental management, dentistry with Case Western Reserve University; medical technology with Rochester General Hospital.

Computers on Campus Students can access the following: campus intranet, computer help desk, free student e-mail accounts, online (class) grades, online (class) registration, online (class) schedules. Campuswide network is available. Wireless service is available via entire campus.

Student Life *Housing:* on-campus residence required through senior year. *Options:* coed, men-only, women-only, cooperative. Campus housing is university owned. Freshman campus housing is guaranteed. *Activities and organizations:* drama/theater group, student-run newspaper, radio and television station, choral group, Community Association, Black Student Union, International Student Association, Student Activities Committee, national fraternities, national sororities. *Campus security:* 24-hour emergency response devices and patrols, student patrols, late-night transport/escort service, controlled dormitory access, security lighting, escort service. *Student services:* health clinic, personal/psychological counseling, women's center.

Athletics Member NCAA. All Division III. *Intercollegiate sports:* baseball M, basketball M/W, crew M(c), cross-country running M/W, equestrian sports

M(c)/W(c), field hockey W, football M, golf M, ice hockey M(c), lacrosse M/W, riflery M(c)/W(c), rugby M(c)/W(c), sailing M(c)/W(c), skiing (downhill) M(c)/W(c), soccer M/W, softball W, squash M(c)/W(c), swimming and diving M/W, tennis M/W, track and field M/W, volleyball W. *Intramural sports:* badminton M(c)/W(c), basketball M/W, cheerleading M/W, crew W(c), fencing M(c)/W(c), football M/W, lacrosse M(c), racquetball M/W, soccer M/W, softball M/W, squash M/W, table tennis M/W, tennis M/W, ultimate Frisbee M/W, volleyball M(c)/W, water polo M/W, weight lifting M/W.

Standardized Tests *Required for some:* SAT or ACT (for admission).

Costs (2011–12) *Comprehensive fee:* $50,170 includes full-time tuition ($39,330), mandatory fees ($880), and room and board ($9960). Part-time tuition: $1229 per semester hour. Part-time tuition and fees vary according to course load. *Required fees:* $440 per term part-time. *College room only:* $5480. Room and board charges vary according to board plan and housing facility. *Payment plan:* installment. *Waivers:* employees or children of employees.

Financial Aid Of all full-time matriculated undergraduates who enrolled in 2009, 1,306 applied for aid, 1,108 were judged to have need, 396 had their need fully met. In 2009, 1010 non-need-based awards were made. *Average percent of need met:* 97%. *Average financial aid package:* $33,286. *Average need-based loan:* $4631. *Average need-based gift aid:* $27,112. *Average non-need-based aid:* $15,552.

Applying *Options:* early admission, early decision, deferred entrance. *Application fee:* $40. *Required:* essay or personal statement, high school transcript, 2 letters of recommendation. *Recommended:* interview. *Application deadlines:* 1/15 (freshmen), 6/1 (transfers). *Early decision deadline:* 11/15 (for plan 1), 1/15 (for plan 2). *Notification:* 4/1 (freshmen), continuous (transfers), 1/1 (early decision).

Freshman Application Contact Mr. Perry Robinson, Director of Admissions, Denison University, Granville, OH 43023. *Phone:* 740-587-6276. *Toll-free phone:* 800-DENISON. *E-mail:* admissions@denison.edu. *Web site:* http://www.denison.edu/.

See page 1252 for the College Close-Up.

DeVry University
Columbus, Ohio

- **Proprietary** comprehensive, founded 1952, part of DeVry University
- **Urban** 21-acre campus
- **Coed** 3,409 undergraduate students, 43% full-time, 44% women, 56% men
- **Minimally difficult** entrance level

Undergraduates 1,452 full-time, 1,957 part-time. 17% are from out of state; 19% Black or African American, non-Hispanic/Latino; 2% Hispanic/Latino; 1% Asian, non-Hispanic/Latino; 0.4% American Indian or Alaska Native, non-Hispanic/Latino; 0.9% Two or more races, non-Hispanic/Latino; 27% Race/ethnicity unknown; 0.1% international; 24% transferred in.

Freshmen *Admission:* 635 enrolled.

Faculty *Total:* 100, 42% full-time. *Student/faculty ratio:* 37:1.

Academics *Calendar:* semesters. *Degrees:* associate, bachelor's, and master's. *Special study options:* academic remediation for entering students, accelerated degree program, adult/continuing education programs, advanced placement credit, distance learning, part-time degree program, services for LD students, summer session for credit.

Computers on Campus Students can access the following: online (class) registration. Campuswide network is available.

Student Life *Housing:* college housing not available. *Campus security:* late-night transport/escort service, security at evening activities.

Costs (2010–11) *Tuition:* $14,766 full-time, $580 per credit hour part-time. Full-time tuition and fees vary according to course load. Part-time tuition and fees vary according to course load. *Required fees:* $60 full-time, $30 per term part-time. *Payment plans:* installment, deferred payment. *Waivers:* employees or children of employees.

Financial Aid Of all full-time matriculated undergraduates who enrolled in 2007, 853 applied for aid, 826 were judged to have need, 35 had their need fully met. In 2007, 53 non-need-based awards were made. *Average percent of need met:* 46%. *Average financial aid package:* $14,130. *Average need-based loan:* $7868. *Average need-based gift aid:* $7762. *Average non-need-based aid:* $13,228. *Average indebtedness upon graduation:* $40,467.

Applying *Options:* electronic application, deferred entrance. *Application fee:* $50. *Required:* high school transcript, interview. *Application deadlines:* rolling (freshmen), rolling (transfers). *Notification:* continuous (freshmen), continuous (transfers).

Freshman Application Contact DeVry University, 1350 Alum Creek Drive, Columbus, OH 43209-2705. *Phone:* 614-253-7291. *Web site:* http://www.devry.edu/.

DeVry University
Columbus, Ohio

Admissions Office Contact DeVry University, 8800 Lyra Drive, Columbus, OH 43240. *Web site:* http://www.devry.edu/.

Franciscan University of Steubenville
Steubenville, Ohio

- **Independent Roman Catholic** comprehensive, founded 1946
- **Suburban** 242-acre campus with easy access to Pittsburgh
- **Endowment** $27.9 million
- **Coed**
- **Moderately difficult** entrance level

Faculty *Student/faculty ratio:* 15:1.

Academics *Calendar:* semesters. *Degrees:* associate, bachelor's, and master's.

Student Life *Campus security:* 24-hour emergency response devices and patrols, student patrols, late-night transport/escort service.

Athletics Member NCAA. All Division III.

Standardized Tests *Required:* SAT or ACT (for admission).

Costs (2010–11) *One-time required fee:* $150. *Comprehensive fee:* $27,220 includes full-time tuition ($19,900), mandatory fees ($420), and room and board ($6900). Part-time tuition: $665 per credit hour. Part-time tuition and fees vary according to class time and course load. *Required fees:* $15 per credit hour part-time. *Room and board:* Room and board charges vary according to board plan.

Financial Aid Of all full-time matriculated undergraduates who enrolled in 2009, 1,577 applied for aid, 1,324 were judged to have need, 183 had their need fully met. In 2009, 232 non-need-based awards were made. *Average percent of need met:* 60. *Average financial aid package:* $12,549. *Average need-based loan:* $4311. *Average need-based gift aid:* $8177. *Average non-need-based aid:* $4094. *Average indebtedness upon graduation:* $30,180.

Applying *Options:* electronic application, deferred entrance. *Application fee:* $20. *Required:* essay or personal statement, high school transcript, minimum 2.4 GPA. *Required for some:* 3 letters of recommendation. *Recommended:* interview.

Freshman Application Contact Mrs. Margaret Weber, Director of Admissions, Franciscan University of Steubenville, 1235 University Boulevard, Steubenville, OH 43952-1763. *Phone:* 740-283-6226. *Toll-free phone:* 800-783-6220. *Fax:* 740-284-5456. *E-mail:* admissions@franciscan.edu. *Web site:* http://www.franciscan.edu/.

Franklin University
Columbus, Ohio

- **Independent** comprehensive, founded 1902
- **Urban** 14-acre campus
- **Coed** 7,065 undergraduate students, 38% full-time, 59% women, 41% men
- **Noncompetitive** entrance level

Undergraduates 2,708 full-time, 4,357 part-time. Students come from 50 states and territories; 96 other countries; 25% are from out of state; 25% Black or African American, non-Hispanic/Latino; 2% Hispanic/Latino; 2% Asian, non-Hispanic/Latino; 0.7% American Indian or Alaska Native, non-Hispanic/Latino; 3% Race/ethnicity unknown; 2% international; 21% transferred in. *Retention:* 30% of full-time freshmen returned.

Freshmen *Admission:* 219 enrolled.

Faculty *Total:* 713, 8% full-time. *Student/faculty ratio:* 18:1.

Academics *Calendar:* trimesters. *Degrees:* associate, bachelor's, master's, and post-master's certificates. *Special study options:* academic remediation for entering students, accelerated degree program, adult/continuing education programs, advanced placement credit, cooperative education, distance learning, double majors, English as a second language, independent study, internships, off-campus study, part-time degree program, services for LD students, student-designed majors, study abroad, summer session for credit. *ROTC:* Army (c), Air Force (c).

Computers on Campus Students can access the following: online (class) registration. Campuswide network is available.

Student Life *Housing:* college housing not available. *Campus security:* 24-hour patrols, security personnel during operating hours.

Costs (2010–11) *Tuition:* $11,880 full-time, $330 per credit hour part-time. Full-time tuition and fees vary according to program. Part-time tuition and fees vary according to program. *Payment plans:* installment, deferred payment. *Waivers:* employees or children of employees.

Financial Aid Of all full-time matriculated undergraduates who enrolled in 2003, 1,135 applied for aid, 1,071 were judged to have need. 29 Federal Work-Study jobs (averaging $7702). In 2003, 108 non-need-based awards were made. *Average need-based loan:* $5091. *Average need-based gift aid:* $4436. *Average non-need-based aid:* $2211.

Applying *Options:* electronic application, deferred entrance. *Required for some:* high school transcript. *Application deadlines:* rolling (freshmen), rolling (transfers). *Notification:* continuous (transfers).

Freshman Application Contact Franklin University, 201 South Grant Avenue, Columbus, OH 43215-5399. *Toll-free phone:* 877-341-6300. *Web site:* http://www.franklin.edu/.

God's Bible School and College
Cincinnati, Ohio

Freshman Application Contact Steve Buckland, Director of Financial Aid and Admissions, God's Bible School and College, 1810 Young Street, Cincinnati, OH 45202-6838. *Phone:* 513-721-7944 Ext. 1161. *Toll-free phone:* 800-486-4637. *Fax:* 513-763-6649. *E-mail:* sbuckland@gbs.edu. *Web site:* http://www.gbs.edu/.

Heidelberg University
Tiffin, Ohio

- **Independent** comprehensive, founded 1850, affiliated with United Church of Christ
- **Small-town** 115-acre campus with easy access to Cleveland, Columbus, Detroit
- **Endowment** $32.1 million
- **Coed**
- **Moderately difficult** entrance level

Faculty *Student/faculty ratio:* 13:1.

Academics *Calendar:* semesters. *Degrees:* bachelor's and master's.

Student Life *Campus security:* 24-hour emergency response devices and patrols, student patrols, late-night transport/escort service, controlled dormitory access.

Athletics Member NCAA. All Division III.

Standardized Tests *Required:* SAT or ACT (for admission).

Costs (2010–11) *Comprehensive fee:* $31,416 includes full-time tuition ($22,242), mandatory fees ($538), and room and board ($8636). Full-time tuition and fees vary according to course load, degree level, and location. Part-time tuition: $612 per credit hour. Part-time tuition and fees vary according to course load, degree level, and location. *Required fees:* $269 per term part-time. *College room only:* $4088. Room and board charges vary according to housing facility and location.

Financial Aid *Of all full-time matriculated undergraduates who enrolled in 2009,* 1,086 applied for aid, 1,004 were judged to have need, 143 had their need fully met. 649 Federal Work-Study jobs (averaging $1870). 96 state and other part-time jobs (averaging $1575). *In 2009,* 131 non-need-based awards were made. *Average percent of need met:* 77. *Average financial aid package:* $19,020. *Average need-based loan:* $4694. *Average need-based gift aid:* $13,650. *Average non-need-based aid:* $9200. *Average indebtedness upon graduation:* $35,885.

Applying *Options:* electronic application, deferred entrance. *Application fee:* $25. *Required:* high school transcript, minimum 2.5 GPA. *Recommended:* essay or personal statement, interview.

Freshman Application Contact Ms. Lindsay Sooy, Director of Admission, Heidelberg University, 310 East Market Street, Tiffin, OH 44883. *Phone:* 419-448-2330. *Toll-free phone:* 800-434-3352. *Fax:* 419-448-2334. *E-mail:* adminfo@heidelberg.edu. *Web site:* http://www.heidelberg.edu/.

Herzing University
Toledo, Ohio

Admissions Office Contact Herzing University, 5212 Hill Avenue, Toledo, OH 43615. *Web site:* http://www.herzing.edu/toledo.

Hiram College
Hiram, Ohio

- **Independent** comprehensive, founded 1850, affiliated with Christian Church (Disciples of Christ)
- **Rural** 110-acre campus with easy access to Cleveland
- **Endowment** $62.7 million
- **Coed**
- **Moderately difficult** entrance level

Faculty *Student/faculty ratio:* 13:1.

Academics *Calendar:* semesters. *Degrees:* bachelor's and master's.

Student Life *Campus security:* 24-hour emergency response devices and patrols, late-night transport/escort service, controlled dormitory access.

Athletics Member NCAA. All Division III.

Standardized Tests *Required:* SAT or ACT (for admission).

Costs (2010–11) *Comprehensive fee:* $36,595 includes full-time tuition ($26,435), mandatory fees ($700), and room and board ($9460). Full-time tuition and fees vary according to student level. No tuition increase for student's term of enrollment. *College room only:* $4620. Room and board charges vary according to housing facility.

Financial Aid *Of all full-time matriculated undergraduates who enrolled in 2002,* 790 applied for aid, 736 were judged to have need, 699 had their need fully met. 587 Federal Work-Study jobs (averaging $1600). 18 state and other part-time jobs (averaging $1580). *In 2002,* 114 non-need-based awards were made. *Average percent of need met:* 95. *Average financial aid package:* $21,218. *Average need-based loan:* $6960. *Average need-based gift aid:* $8163. *Average non-need-based aid:* $8635. *Average indebtedness upon graduation:* $17,125.

Applying *Options:* electronic application, early admission, deferred entrance. *Required:* essay or personal statement, high school transcript. *Required for some:* interview. *Recommended:* 3 letters of recommendation, interview.

Freshman Application Contact Mr. Sherman C. Dean II, Director of Admission, Hiram College, PO Box 96, Hiram, OH 44234. *Phone:* 330-569-5169. *Toll-free phone:* 800-362-5280. *Fax:* 330-569-5944. *E-mail:* admission@hiram.edu. *Web site:* http://www.hiram.edu/.

ITT Technical Institute
Akron, Ohio

- **Proprietary** primarily 2-year
- **Coed**
- **Minimally difficult** entrance level

Academics *Degrees:* associate and bachelor's.

Freshman Application Contact ITT Technical Institute, 3428 West Market Street, Akron, OH 44333. *Phone:* 330-865-8600. *Toll-free phone:* 877-818-0154. *Web site:* http://www.itt-tech.edu/.

ITT Technical Institute
Dayton, Ohio

- **Proprietary** primarily 2-year, founded 1935, part of ITT Educational Services, Inc.
- **Suburban** campus
- **Coed**
- **Minimally difficult** entrance level

Academics *Calendar:* quarters. *Degrees:* associate and bachelor's.

Student Life *Housing:* college housing not available.

Freshman Application Contact Director of Recruitment, ITT Technical Institute, 3325 Stop 8 Road, Dayton, OH 45414. *Phone:* 937-264-7700. *Toll-free phone:* 800-568-3241. *Web site:* http://www.itt-tech.edu/.

ITT Technical Institute
Hilliard, Ohio

- **Proprietary** primarily 2-year, founded 2003, part of ITT Educational Services, Inc.
- **Coed**
- **Minimally difficult** entrance level

Academics *Calendar:* quarters. *Degrees:* associate and bachelor's.

Freshman Application Contact Director of Recruitment, ITT Technical Institute, 3781 Park Mill Run Drive, Hilliard, OH 43026. *Phone:* 614-771-4888. *Toll-free phone:* 888-483-4888. *Web site:* http://www.itt-tech.edu/.

ITT Technical Institute
Maumee, Ohio

- **Proprietary** primarily 2-year
- **Coed**

Academics *Degrees:* associate and bachelor's.

Student Life *Housing:* college housing not available.

Freshman Application Contact Director of Recruitment, ITT Technical Institute, 1656 Henthorne Drive, Suite B, Maumee, OH 43537. *Phone:* 419-861-6500. *Toll-free phone:* 877-205-4639. *Web site:* http://www.itt-tech.edu/.

ITT Technical Institute
Norwood, Ohio

- **Proprietary** primarily 2-year, founded 1995, part of ITT Educational Services, Inc.
- **Coed**
- **Minimally difficult** entrance level

Academics *Calendar:* quarters. *Degrees:* associate and bachelor's.

Student Life *Housing:* college housing not available.
Freshman Application Contact Director of Recruitment, ITT Technical Institute, 4750 Wesley Avenue, Norwood, OH 45212. *Phone:* 513-531-8300. *Toll-free phone:* 800-314-8324. *Web site:* http://www.itt-tech.edu/.

ITT Technical Institute
Strongsville, Ohio
- **Proprietary** primarily 2-year, founded 1994, part of ITT Educational Services, Inc.
- **Coed**
- **Minimally difficult** entrance level

Academics *Calendar:* quarters. *Degrees:* associate and bachelor's.
Student Life *Housing:* college housing not available.
Freshman Application Contact Director of Recruitment, ITT Technical Institute, 14955 Sprague Road, Strongsville, OH 44136. *Phone:* 440-234-9091. *Toll-free phone:* 800-331-1488. *Web site:* http://www.itt-tech.edu/.

ITT Technical Institute
Warrensville Heights, Ohio
- **Proprietary** primarily 2-year, founded 2005
- **Coed**
- **Minimally difficult** entrance level

Academics *Calendar:* quarters. *Degrees:* associate and bachelor's.
Student Life *Housing:* college housing not available.
Freshman Application Contact Director of Recruitment, ITT Technical Institute, 4700 Richmond Road, Warrensville Heights, OH 44128. *Phone:* 216-896-6500. *Toll-free phone:* 800-741-3494. *Web site:* http://www.itt-tech.edu/.

ITT Technical Institute
Youngstown, Ohio
- **Proprietary** primarily 2-year, founded 1967, part of ITT Educational Services, Inc.
- **Suburban** campus
- **Coed**
- **Minimally difficult** entrance level

Academics *Calendar:* quarters. *Degrees:* associate and bachelor's.
Student Life *Housing:* college housing not available.
Financial Aid Of all full-time matriculated undergraduates who enrolled in 2009, 5 Federal Work-Study jobs (averaging $3979).
Freshman Application Contact Director of Recruitment, ITT Technical Institute, 1030 North Meridian Road, Youngstown, OH 44509-4098. *Phone:* 330-270-1600. *Toll-free phone:* 800-832-5001. *Web site:* http://www.itt-tech.edu/.

John Carroll University
University Heights, Ohio
- **Independent Roman Catholic (Jesuit)** comprehensive, founded 1886
- **Suburban** 60-acre campus with easy access to Cleveland
- **Endowment** $147.1 million
- **Coed** 2,968 undergraduate students, 97% full-time, 51% women, 49% men
- **Moderately difficult** entrance level, 81% of applicants were admitted

Undergraduates 2,869 full-time, 99 part-time. Students come from 35 states and territories; 8 other countries; 29% are from out of state; 5% Black or African American, non-Hispanic/Latino; 4% Hispanic/Latino; 2% Asian, non-Hispanic/Latino; 0.2% American Indian or Alaska Native, non-Hispanic/Latino; 2% Two or more races, non-Hispanic/Latino; 4% Race/ethnicity unknown; 4% transferred in; 65% live on campus. *Retention:* 86% of full-time freshmen returned.
Freshmen *Admission:* 3,216 applied, 2,613 admitted, 703 enrolled. *Average high school GPA:* 3.38. *Test scores:* SAT critical reading scores over 500: 72%; SAT math scores over 500: 73%; SAT writing scores over 500: 72%; ACT scores over 18: 99%; SAT critical reading scores over 600: 21%; SAT math scores over 600: 28%; SAT writing scores over 600: 21%; ACT scores over 24: 54%; SAT critical reading scores over 700: 3%; SAT math scores over 700: 3%; SAT writing scores over 700: 2%; ACT scores over 30: 8%.
Faculty *Total:* 370, 54% full-time, 68% with terminal degrees. *Student/faculty ratio:* 13:1.
Academics *Calendar:* semesters. *Degrees:* bachelor's, master's, and post-master's certificates. *Special study options:* advanced placement credit, cooperative education, double majors, honors programs, independent study, internships, off-campus study, part-time degree program, services for LD students, student-designed majors, study abroad, summer session for credit. *ROTC:*

Army (b). *Unusual degree programs:* 3-2 engineering with Case Western Reserve University; nursing with Joint BA/BSN degree program with Ursuline College.
Computers on Campus 210 computers/terminals are available on campus for general student use. Students can access the following: campus intranet, computer help desk, free student e-mail accounts, online (class) grades, online (class) registration, online (class) schedules, online financial aid and billing; online course sites; online housing selection. Campuswide network is available. 100% of college-owned or -operated housing units are wired for high-speed Internet access. Wireless service is available via entire campus.
Student Life *Housing:* on-campus residence required through sophomore year. *Options:* coed, men-only, women-only, cooperative. Campus housing is university owned. Freshman campus housing is guaranteed. *Activities and organizations:* drama/theater group, student-run newspaper, radio and television station, choral group, Community Outreach/Volunteer Service Organization, Student Union, Carroll News, Pep Band, University Concert Choir, national fraternities, national sororities. *Campus security:* 24-hour emergency response devices and patrols, late-night transport/escort service, Distinctive Student EMS program fully staffed. *Student services:* health clinic, personal/psychological counseling, women's center.
Athletics Member NCAA. All Division III. *Intercollegiate sports:* baseball M, basketball M/W, cheerleading W(c), crew M(c)/W(c), cross-country running M/W, field hockey W(c), football M, golf M/W, ice hockey M(c), lacrosse M(c)/W(c), rugby M(c)/W(c), sailing M(c)/W(c), skiing (cross-country) M(c)/W(c), skiing (downhill) M(c)/W(c), soccer M/W, softball W, swimming and diving M/W, tennis M/W, track and field M/W, ultimate Frisbee M(c), volleyball M(c)/W, wrestling M. *Intramural sports:* basketball M/W, football M/W, golf M/W, racquetball M/W, rock climbing M/W, soccer M/W, softball M/W, swimming and diving M/W, table tennis M/W, tennis M/W, ultimate Frisbee M/W, volleyball M/W, water polo M/W.
Standardized Tests *Required:* SAT or ACT (for admission).
Costs (2011–12) *One-time required fee:* $325. *Comprehensive fee:* $40,860 includes full-time tuition ($30,660), mandatory fees ($1050), and room and board ($9150). Part-time tuition: $935 per credit hour. Part-time tuition and fees vary according to course load. *College room only:* $4850. Room and board charges vary according to board plan and housing facility. *Payment plans:* installment, deferred payment. *Waivers:* senior citizens and employees or children of employees.
Financial Aid Of all full-time matriculated undergraduates who enrolled in 2009, 2,486 applied for aid, 2,227 were judged to have need, 407 had their need fully met. 524 Federal Work-Study jobs (averaging $2200). In 2009, 539 non-need-based awards were made. *Average percent of need met:* 81%. *Average financial aid package:* $24,519. *Average need-based loan:* $4016. *Average need-based gift aid:* $19,440. *Average non-need-based aid:* $10,152. *Average indebtedness upon graduation:* $28,830. *Financial aid deadline:* 3/15.
Applying *Options:* electronic application, deferred entrance. *Required:* essay or personal statement, high school transcript, 1 letter of recommendation. *Required for some:* interview. *Application deadlines:* 2/1 (freshmen), 8/1 (transfers). *Notification:* continuous (freshmen).
Freshman Application Contact Mr. Steven P. Vitatoe, Executive Director of Enrollment, John Carroll University, 20700 North Park Boulevard, University Heights, OH 44118. *Phone:* 216-397-4294. *Fax:* 216-397-4981. *E-mail:* svitatoe@jcu.edu. *Web site:* http://www.jcu.edu/.

See page 1352 for the College Close-Up.

Kent State University
Kent, Ohio
- **State-supported** university, founded 1910, part of Kent State University System
- **Suburban** 1347-acre campus with easy access to Cleveland
- **Endowment** $76.7 million
- **Coed** 21,178 undergraduate students, 88% full-time, 58% women, 42% men
- **Moderately difficult** entrance level, 89% of applicants were admitted

Undergraduates 18,538 full-time, 2,640 part-time. Students come from 43 states and territories; 57 other countries; 10% are from out of state; 9% Black or African American, non-Hispanic/Latino; 2% Hispanic/Latino; 1% Asian, non-Hispanic/Latino; 0.4% American Indian or Alaska Native, non-Hispanic/Latino; 0.7% Two or more races, non-Hispanic/Latino; 4% Race/ethnicity unknown; 3% international; 6% transferred in; 34% live on campus. *Retention:* 79% of full-time freshmen returned.
Freshmen *Admission:* 12,325 applied, 10,926 admitted, 3,980 enrolled. *Average high school GPA:* 3.19. *Test scores:* SAT critical reading scores over 500: 58%; SAT math scores over 500: 59%; SAT writing scores over 500: 51%; ACT scores over 18: 93%; SAT critical reading scores over 600: 17%; SAT math scores over 600: 20%; SAT writing scores over 600: 13%; ACT scores

over 24: 35%; SAT critical reading scores over 700: 3%; SAT math scores over 700: 3%; SAT writing scores over 700: 3%; ACT scores over 30: 4%.

Faculty *Total:* 1,569, 56% full-time. *Student/faculty ratio:* 20:1.

Academics *Calendar:* semesters. *Degrees:* certificates, associate, bachelor's, master's, doctoral-other, doctoral-research/scholarship, post-master's, and postbachelor's certificates. *Special study options:* academic remediation for entering students, accelerated degree program, adult/continuing education programs, advanced placement credit, cooperative education, distance learning, double majors, English as a second language, external degree program, freshman honors college, honors programs, independent study, internships, off-campus study, part-time degree program, services for LD students, student-designed majors, study abroad, summer session for credit. *ROTC:* Army (b), Air Force (b).

Computers on Campus 1,700 computers/terminals and 1,200 ports are available on campus for general student use. Students can access the following: computer help desk, free student e-mail accounts, online (class) grades, online (class) registration, online (class) schedules. Campuswide network is available. 100% of college-owned or -operated housing units are wired for high-speed Internet access. Wireless service is available via entire campus.

Student Life *Housing:* on-campus residence required through sophomore year. *Options:* coed, men-only, women-only, disabled students. Campus housing is university owned. Freshman campus housing is guaranteed. *Activities and organizations:* drama/theater group, student-run newspaper, radio and television station, choral group, marching band, Kent Interhall Council, Black United Students, All Campus Programming Board, Delta Sigma Pi, Late Night Christian Fellowship, national fraternities, national sororities. *Campus security:* 24-hour emergency response devices and patrols, student patrols, late-night transport/escort service, controlled dormitory access, campus police and fire department, electronic locks on computer labs, studios and laboratory research areas. *Student services:* health clinic, personal/psychological counseling, women's center, legal services.

Athletics Member NCAA. All Division I. *Intercollegiate sports:* baseball M(s), basketball M(s)/W(s), cross-country running M(s)/W(s), field hockey W(s), football M(s), golf M(s)/W(s), gymnastics W(s), soccer W(s), softball W(s), track and field M(s)/W(s), volleyball W(s), wrestling M(s). *Intramural sports:* badminton M(c)/W(c), baseball M(c), basketball M/W, bowling M(c)/W(c), equestrian sports M(c)/W(c), fencing M(c)/W(c), field hockey W(c), football M/W, golf M(c)/W(c), gymnastics M(c)/W(c), ice hockey M(c), lacrosse M(c), racquetball M(c)/W(c), rugby M(c)/W(c), sailing M(c)/W(c), skiing (downhill) M(c)/W(c), soccer M(c)/W(c), softball M/W, swimming and diving M(c)/W(c), table tennis M/W, tennis M/W, ultimate Frisbee M/W, volleyball M(c)/W(c), water polo M/W, wrestling M.

Standardized Tests *Required:* SAT or ACT (for admission).

Costs (2010–11) *Tuition:* state resident $9030 full-time, $411 per credit hour part-time; nonresident $16,990 full-time, $773 per credit hour part-time. Full-time tuition and fees vary according to course load, program, and reciprocity agreements. Part-time tuition and fees vary according to course load, program, and reciprocity agreements. *Room and board:* $8376; room only: $5176. Room and board charges vary according to board plan and housing facility. *Payment plans:* installment, deferred payment. *Waivers:* senior citizens and employees or children of employees.

Financial Aid Of all full-time matriculated undergraduates who enrolled in 2009, 13,886 applied for aid, 12,120 were judged to have need, 4,593 had their need fully met. In 2009, 1877 non-need-based awards were made. *Average percent of need met:* 53%. *Average financial aid package:* $9250. *Average need-based loan:* $4083. *Average need-based gift aid:* $5886. *Average non-need-based aid:* $4230. *Average indebtedness upon graduation:* $28,186.

Applying *Options:* electronic application, early admission. *Application fee:* $40. *Required:* high school transcript, minimum 2.5 GPA. *Application deadlines:* rolling (freshmen), rolling (transfers). *Notification:* continuous (transfers).

Freshman Application Contact Mr. Christopher Buttenschon, Assistant Director of Admissions, Kent State University, 161 Michael Schwartz Center, Kent, OH 44242-0001. *Phone:* 330-672-2444. *Toll-free phone:* 800-988-KENT. *Fax:* 330-672-2499. *E-mail:* admissions@kent.edu. *Web site:* http://www.kent.edu/.

See page 1364 for the College Close-Up.

Kent State University at Ashtabula

Ashtabula, Ohio

- **State-supported** primarily 2-year, founded 1958, part of Kent State University System
- **Small-town** 120-acre campus with easy access to Cleveland
- **Coed** 2,486 undergraduate students, 55% full-time, 65% women, 35% men
- **Noncompetitive** entrance level, 98% of applicants were admitted

Undergraduates 1,360 full-time, 1,126 part-time. Students come from 5 states and territories; 2% are from out of state; 7% Black or African American, non-

Hispanic/Latino; 3% Hispanic/Latino; 0.5% Asian, non-Hispanic/Latino; 0.6% American Indian or Alaska Native, non-Hispanic/Latino; 1% Two or more races, non-Hispanic/Latino; 3% Race/ethnicity unknown; 9% transferred in. *Retention:* 59% of full-time freshmen returned.

Freshmen *Admission:* 613 applied, 601 admitted, 456 enrolled. *Average high school GPA:* 2.73. *Test scores:* ACT scores over 18: 71%; ACT scores over 24: 18%.

Faculty *Total:* 119, 45% full-time. *Student/faculty ratio:* 20:1.

Academics *Calendar:* semesters. *Degrees:* certificates, associate, and bachelor's (also offers some upper-level and graduate courses). *Special study options:* academic remediation for entering students, advanced placement credit, distance learning, double majors, English as a second language, freshman honors college, honors programs, internships, part-time degree program, services for LD students, student-designed majors, study abroad, summer session for credit. *ROTC:* Army (c), Air Force (c).

Computers on Campus 25 computers/terminals are available on campus for general student use. Students can access the following: computer help desk, free student e-mail accounts, online (class) grades, online (class) registration, online (class) schedules.

Student Life *Housing:* college housing not available. *Activities and organizations:* drama/theater group, student-run newspaper, student government, student veterans association, Student Nurses Association, Student Occupational Therapy Association (SOTA), Media Club. *Campus security:* 24-hour emergency response devices.

Standardized Tests *Required for some:* SAT or ACT (for admission). *Recommended:* SAT or ACT (for admission).

Costs (2010–11) *Tuition:* state resident $5110 full-time, $233 per credit hour part-time; nonresident $13,070 full-time, $595 per credit hour part-time. Full-time tuition and fees vary according to course level and course load. Part-time tuition and fees vary according to course level and course load. *Payment plans:* installment, deferred payment. *Waivers:* senior citizens and employees or children of employees.

Financial Aid Of all full-time matriculated undergraduates who enrolled in 2009, 1,037 applied for aid, 990 were judged to have need, 261 had their need fully met. In 2009, 3 non-need-based awards were made. *Average percent of need met:* 49%. *Average financial aid package:* $8074. *Average need-based loan:* $3587. *Average need-based gift aid:* $5295. *Average non-need-based aid:* $833.

Applying *Options:* early admission, deferred entrance. *Application fee:* $30. *Required:* high school transcript. *Application deadlines:* 8/1 (freshmen), 7/15 (out-of-state freshmen), 7/15 (transfers). *Notification:* continuous until 8/1 (freshmen), continuous until 7/15 (out-of-state freshmen), continuous until 7/15 (transfers).

Freshman Application Contact Kent State University at Ashtabula, 3300 Lake Road West, Ashtabula, OH 44004-2299. *Phone:* 440-964-4217. *Web site:* http://www.ashtabula.kent.edu/.

Kent State University at East Liverpool

East Liverpool, Ohio

- **State-supported** primarily 2-year, founded 1967, part of Kent State University System
- **Small-town** 4-acre campus with easy access to Pittsburgh
- **Coed** 1,371 undergraduate students, 57% full-time, 69% women, 31% men
- **Noncompetitive** entrance level, 99% of applicants were admitted

Undergraduates 785 full-time, 586 part-time. Students come from 7 states and territories; 5% are from out of state; 4% Black or African American, non-Hispanic/Latino; 0.9% Hispanic/Latino; 0.4% Asian, non-Hispanic/Latino; 0.1% Native Hawaiian or other Pacific Islander, non-Hispanic/Latino; 0.1% American Indian or Alaska Native, non-Hispanic/Latino; 0.9% Two or more races, non-Hispanic/Latino; 2% Race/ethnicity unknown; 6% transferred in. *Retention:* 63% of full-time freshmen returned.

Freshmen *Admission:* 229 applied, 226 admitted, 158 enrolled. *Average high school GPA:* 2.75. *Test scores:* ACT scores over 18: 71%; ACT scores over 24: 17%.

Faculty *Total:* 76, 37% full-time. *Student/faculty ratio:* 17:1.

Academics *Calendar:* semesters. *Degrees:* certificates, associate, and bachelor's (also offers some upper-level and graduate courses). *Special study options:* academic remediation for entering students, accelerated degree program, adult/continuing education programs, advanced placement credit, distance learning, double majors, English as a second language, freshman honors college, honors programs, internships, part-time degree program, services for LD students, student-designed majors, study abroad, summer session for credit. *ROTC:* Army (c), Air Force (c).

Computers on Campus 72 computers/terminals are available on campus for general student use. Campuswide network is available.

Student Life *Housing:* college housing not available. *Activities and organizations:* student-run newspaper, Student Senate, Student Nurses Association, Alpha Beta Gamma, Occupational Therapist Assistant Club, Physical Therapist Assistant Club. *Campus security:* student patrols, late-night transport/escort service.

Standardized Tests *Required for some:* SAT or ACT (for admission). *Recommended:* SAT or ACT (for admission).

Costs (2010–11) *Tuition:* state resident $5110 full-time, $233 per credit hour part-time; nonresident $13,070 full-time, $595 per credit hour part-time. Full-time tuition and fees vary according to course level and course load. Part-time tuition and fees vary according to course level and course load. *Payment plans:* installment, deferred payment. *Waivers:* senior citizens and employees or children of employees.

Financial Aid Of all full-time matriculated undergraduates who enrolled in 2009, 476 applied for aid, 459 were judged to have need, 94 had their need fully met. In 2009, 2 non-need-based awards were made. *Average percent of need met:* 47%. *Average financial aid package:* $8079. *Average need-based loan:* $3501. *Average need-based gift aid:* $5194. *Average non-need-based aid:* $1000.

Applying *Options:* early admission, deferred entrance. *Application fee:* $30. *Required:* high school transcript. *Application deadlines:* rolling (freshmen), rolling (transfers). *Notification:* continuous until 9/1 (freshmen), continuous until 9/1 (transfers).

Freshman Application Contact Melissa Ace, Director of Enrollment Management and Student Services, Kent State University at East Liverpool, 400 East 4th Street, East Liverpool, OH 43920-3497. *Phone:* 330-382—7462. *E-mail:* mpeter22@kent.edu. *Web site:* http://www.eliv.kent.edu/.

Kent State University at Geauga
Burton, Ohio

- **State-supported** founded 1964, part of Kent State University System
- **Rural** 87-acre campus with easy access to Cleveland
- **Coed** 2,190 undergraduate students, 58% full-time, 65% women, 35% men
- **Noncompetitive** entrance level

Undergraduates 1,272 full-time, 918 part-time. Students come from 10 states and territories; 7 other countries; 1% are from out of state; 9% Black or African American, non-Hispanic/Latino; 1% Hispanic/Latino; 2% Asian, non-Hispanic/Latino; 0.4% American Indian or Alaska Native, non-Hispanic/Latino; 0.7% Two or more races, non-Hispanic/Latino; 3% Race/ethnicity unknown; 0.3% international; 5% transferred in. *Retention:* 72% of full-time freshmen returned.

Freshmen *Admission:* 232 enrolled. *Average high school GPA:* 2.49. *Test scores:* SAT critical reading scores over 500: 35%; SAT math scores over 500: 31%; SAT writing scores over 500: 20%; SAT critical reading scores over 600: 8%; SAT math scores over 600: 8%; SAT writing scores over 600: 5%.

Faculty *Total:* 116, 26% full-time. *Student/faculty ratio:* 18:1.

Academics *Calendar:* semesters. *Degrees:* certificates, associate, and bachelor's. *Special study options:* academic remediation for entering students, advanced placement credit, distance learning, double majors, English as a second language, freshman honors college, honors programs, independent study, internships, part-time degree program, services for LD students, student-designed majors, study abroad, summer session for credit. *ROTC:* Army (c), Air Force (c).

Computers on Campus 270 computers/terminals and 110 ports are available on campus for general student use. Students can access the following: campus intranet, computer help desk, free student e-mail accounts, online (class) grades, online (class) registration, online (class) schedules. Campuswide network is available. Wireless service is available via entire campus.

Student Life *Housing:* college housing not available. *Activities and organizations:* Student Ambassadors, Campus Crusade for Christ, Gaia Society. *Campus security:* 24-hour emergency response devices.

Standardized Tests *Required for some:* SAT or ACT (for admission). *Recommended:* SAT or ACT (for admission).

Costs (2010–11) *Tuition:* state resident $5110 full-time, $233 per credit hour part-time; nonresident $13,070 full-time, $595 per credit hour part-time. Full-time tuition and fees vary according to course level and course load. Part-time tuition and fees vary according to course level and course load. *Payment plans:* installment, deferred payment. *Waivers:* senior citizens and employees or children of employees.

Financial Aid Of all full-time matriculated undergraduates who enrolled in 2009, 487 applied for aid, 447 were judged to have need, 138 had their need fully met. In 2009, 3 non-need-based awards were made. *Average percent of need met:* 48%. *Average financial aid package:* $7450. *Average need-based loan:* $3744. *Average need-based gift aid:* $4581. *Average non-need-based aid:* $398.

Applying *Options:* electronic application, deferred entrance. *Application fee:* $30. *Required:* high school transcript. *Application deadlines:* rolling (fresh-

men), rolling (transfers). *Notification:* continuous (freshmen), continuous (transfers).

Freshman Application Contact Thomas Hoiles, Kent State University at Geauga, 14111 Claridon-Troy Road, Burton, OH 44021. *Phone:* 440-834-4187. *Fax:* 440-834-8846. *E-mail:* thoiles@kent.edu. *Web site:* http://www.geauga.kent.edu/.

Kent State University at Salem
Salem, Ohio

- **State-supported** primarily 2-year, founded 1966, part of Kent State University System
- **Rural** 98-acre campus
- **Coed** 1,960 undergraduate students, 69% full-time, 69% women, 31% men
- **Noncompetitive** entrance level, 97% of applicants were admitted

Undergraduates 1,361 full-time, 599 part-time. Students come from 2 states and territories; 7 other countries; 2% are from out of state; 3% Black or African American, non-Hispanic/Latino; 1% Hispanic/Latino; 0.4% Asian, non-Hispanic/Latino; 0.7% American Indian or Alaska Native, non-Hispanic/Latino; 0.5% Two or more races, non-Hispanic/Latino; 2% Race/ethnicity unknown; 0.1% international; 8% transferred in. *Retention:* 57% of full-time freshmen returned.

Freshman *Admission:* 412 applied, 398 admitted, 261 enrolled. *Average high school GPA:* 2.79. *Test scores:* SAT writing scores over 500: 100%; ACT scores over 18: 69%; ACT scores over 24: 17%; ACT scores over 30: 1%.

Faculty *Total:* 123, 36% full-time. *Student/faculty ratio:* 18:1.

Academics *Calendar:* semesters. *Degrees:* associate and bachelor's (also offers some upper-level and graduate courses). *Special study options:* academic remediation for entering students, adult/continuing education programs, advanced placement credit, distance learning, double majors, freshman honors college, honors programs, internships, part-time degree program, services for LD students, study abroad, summer session for credit. *ROTC:* Army (c), Air Force (c).

Computers on Campus Students can access the following: computer help desk, free student e-mail accounts, online (class) grades, online (class) registration, online (class) schedules. Campuswide network is available.

Student Life *Housing:* college housing not available. *Activities and organizations:* Honors Club, Human Services Technology Club, Radiologic Technology Club, Student Government Organization, Students for Professional Nursing. *Campus security:* 24-hour emergency response devices, late-night transport/escort service. *Student services:* women's center.

Athletics *Intramural sports:* basketball M/W, skiing (downhill) M/W, table tennis M/W, tennis M/W, volleyball M/W.

Standardized Tests *Required for some:* SAT or ACT (for admission). *Recommended:* SAT or ACT (for admission).

Costs (2010–11) *Tuition:* state resident $5110 full-time, $233 per credit hour part-time; nonresident $13,070 full-time, $595 per credit hour part-time. Full-time tuition and fees vary according to course level and course load. Part-time tuition and fees vary according to course level and course load. *Payment plans:* installment, deferred payment. *Waivers:* senior citizens and employees or children of employees.

Financial Aid Of all full-time matriculated undergraduates who enrolled in 2009, 943 applied for aid, 894 were judged to have need, 225 had their need fully met. In 2009, 9 non-need-based awards were made. *Average percent of need met:* 49%. *Average financial aid package:* $7981. *Average need-based loan:* $3643. *Average need-based gift aid:* $5125. *Average non-need-based aid:* $581.

Applying *Options:* electronic application, early admission, deferred entrance. *Application fee:* $30. *Required:* high school transcript. *Required for some:* essay or personal statement. *Application deadlines:* rolling (freshmen), rolling (transfers).

Freshman Application Contact Mrs. Judy Heisler, Admissions Secretary, Kent State University at Salem, 2491 State Route 45 South, Salem, OH 44460-9412. *Phone:* 330-332-0361 Ext. 74201. *E-mail:* ask-us@salem.kent.edu. *Web site:* http://www.salem.kent.edu/.

Kent State University at Stark
Canton, Ohio

- **State-supported** comprehensive, founded 1967, part of Kent State University System
- **Suburban** 200-acre campus with easy access to Cleveland
- **Coed** 4,740 undergraduate students, 66% full-time, 60% women, 40% men
- **Noncompetitive** entrance level, 95% of applicants were admitted

Undergraduates 3,133 full-time, 1,607 part-time. Students come from 13 states and territories; 4 other countries; 1% are from out of state; 7% Black or African American, non-Hispanic/Latino; 2% Hispanic/Latino; 1% Asian, non-

Hispanic/Latino; 0.5% American Indian or Alaska Native, non-Hispanic/Latino; 0.7% Two or more races, non-Hispanic/Latino; 3% Race/ethnicity unknown; 0.2% international; 10% transferred in. *Retention:* 65% of full-time freshmen returned.

Freshmen *Admission:* 1,077 applied, 1,018 admitted, 714 enrolled. *Average high school GPA:* 2.71. *Test scores:* SAT critical reading scores over 500: 38%; SAT math scores over 500: 42%; SAT writing scores over 500: 21%; ACT scores over 18: 70%; SAT critical reading scores over 600: 4%; SAT math scores over 600: 4%; ACT scores over 24: 15%; ACT scores over 30: 1%.

Faculty *Total:* 243, 44% full-time. *Student/faculty ratio:* 22:1.

Academics *Calendar:* semesters. *Degrees:* certificates, associate, bachelor's, and master's (also offers some graduate courses). *Special study options:* academic remediation for entering students, accelerated degree program, adult/continuing education programs, advanced placement credit, distance learning, double majors, English as a second language, freshman honors college, honors programs, independent study, internships, off-campus study, part-time degree program, services for LD students, student-designed majors, study abroad, summer session for credit. *ROTC:* Army (c), Air Force (c).

Computers on Campus 575 computers/terminals are available on campus for general student use. Students can access the following: campus intranet, computer help desk, free student e-mail accounts, online (class) grades, online (class) registration, online (class) schedules. Campuswide network is available. Wireless service is available via entire campus.

Student Life *Housing:* college housing not available. *Activities and organizations:* drama/theater group, choral group, Club Sunaarashi (Japanese Animation, Magic the Gathering, and Dungeons and Dragons), Rooted in Faith-Bible Club (non-denominational), Kent State Stark Education Association (KSSEA), SCRUBS (nursing organization), Ohio Collegiate Music Education Association (OCMEA). *Campus security:* 24-hour emergency response devices, late-night transport/escort service. *Student services:* personal/psychological counseling.

Standardized Tests *Required for some:* SAT or ACT (for admission). *Recommended:* SAT or ACT (for admission).

Costs (2010–11) *Tuition:* state resident $5110 full-time, $233 per credit hour part-time; nonresident $13,070 full-time, $595 per credit hour part-time. Full-time tuition and fees vary according to course level and course load. Part-time tuition and fees vary according to course level and course load. *Payment plans:* installment, deferred payment. *Waivers:* senior citizens and employees or children of employees.

Financial Aid Of all full-time matriculated undergraduates who enrolled in 2009, 2,313 applied for aid, 2,092 were judged to have need, 646 had their need fully met. In 2009, 41 non-need-based awards were made. *Average percent of need met:* 52%. *Average financial aid package:* $7489. *Average need-based loan:* $3576. *Average need-based gift aid:* $4836. *Average non-need-based aid:* $2159.

Applying *Options:* electronic application, early admission, deferred entrance. *Application fee:* $30. *Required:* high school transcript. *Application deadlines:* rolling (freshmen), rolling (transfers).

Freshman Application Contact Ms. Deborah Ann Speck, Director of Admissions, Kent State University at Stark, 6000 Frank Avenue, NW, Canton, OH 44720-7599. *Phone:* 330-499-9600 Ext. 53259. *E-mail:* admit@stark.kent.edu. *Web site:* http://www.stark.kent.edu/.

Kent State University at Trumbull
Warren, Ohio

- **State-supported** primarily 2-year, founded 1954, part of Kent State University System
- **Suburban** 200-acre campus with easy access to Cleveland
- **Coed** 3,109 undergraduate students, 63% full-time, 63% women, 37% men
- **Noncompetitive** entrance level, 99% of applicants were admitted

Undergraduates 1,950 full-time, 1,164 part-time. Students come from 5 states and territories; 5 other countries; 1% are from out of state; 14% Black or African American, non-Hispanic/Latino; 2% Hispanic/Latino; 0.8% Asian, non-Hispanic/Latino; 0.1% Native Hawaiian or other Pacific Islander, non-Hispanic/Latino; 0.3% American Indian or Alaska Native, non-Hispanic/Latino; 0.8% Two or more races, non-Hispanic/Latino; 3% Race/ethnicity unknown; 0.1% international; 7% transferred in; 1% live on campus. *Retention:* 64% of full-time freshmen returned.

Freshmen *Admission:* 561 applied, 553 admitted, 455 enrolled. *Average high school GPA:* 2.56. *Test scores:* SAT math scores over 500: 100%; ACT scores over 18: 68%; SAT math scores over 600: 100%; ACT scores over 24: 12%.

Faculty *Total:* 127, 45% full-time. *Student/faculty ratio:* 24:1.

Academics *Calendar:* semesters. *Degrees:* certificates, associate, and bachelor's (also offers some upper-level and graduate courses). *Special study options:* academic remediation for entering students, adult/continuing education programs, advanced placement credit, cooperative education, distance learning, double majors, English as a second language, freshman honors col-

lege, honors programs, independent study, internships, part-time degree program, services for LD students, student-designed majors, study abroad, summer session for credit. *ROTC:* Army (c), Air Force (c).

Computers on Campus 300 computers/terminals are available on campus for general student use. Students can access the following: computer help desk, free student e-mail accounts, online (class) grades, online (class) registration, online (class) schedules. Campuswide network is available. Wireless service is available via entire campus.

Student Life *Housing:* college housing not available. *Activities and organizations:* drama/theater group, National Student Nurses Association, Spot On Improv Group, Amnesty International, Campus Crusade for Christ. *Campus security:* 24-hour emergency response devices, late-night transport/escort service, patrols by trained security personnel during open hours. *Student services:* personal/psychological counseling.

Standardized Tests *Required for some:* SAT or ACT (for admission). *Recommended:* SAT or ACT (for admission).

Costs (2010–11) *Tuition:* state resident $5110 full-time, $233 per credit hour part-time; nonresident $13,070 full-time, $595 per credit hour part-time. Full-time tuition and fees vary according to course level, course load, and location. Part-time tuition and fees vary according to course level, course load, and location. *Payment plans:* installment, deferred payment. *Waivers:* senior citizens and employees or children of employees.

Financial Aid Of all full-time matriculated undergraduates who enrolled in 2009, 1,294 applied for aid, 1,235 were judged to have need, 313 had their need fully met. In 2009, 4 non-need-based awards were made. *Average percent of need met:* 48%. *Average financial aid package:* $8015. *Average need-based loan:* $3575. *Average need-based gift aid:* $5087. *Average non-need-based aid:* $1995.

Applying *Options:* deferred entrance. *Application fee:* $30. *Required:* high school transcript. *Application deadlines:* rolling (freshmen), rolling (transfers). *Notification:* continuous until 8/30 (freshmen), continuous until 8/30 (transfers).

Freshman Application Contact Kent State University at Trumbull, Warren, OH 44483. *Phone:* 330-675-8935. *Web site:* http://www.trumbull.kent.edu/.

Kent State University at Tuscarawas
New Philadelphia, Ohio

- **State-supported** primarily 2-year, founded 1962, part of Kent State University System
- **Small-town** 172-acre campus with easy access to Cleveland
- **Coed** 2,778 undergraduate students, 60% full-time, 58% women, 42% men
- **Noncompetitive** entrance level, 96% of applicants were admitted

Undergraduates 1,663 full-time, 1,115 part-time. Students come from 4 states and territories; 3 other countries; 1% are from out of state; 2% Black or African American, non-Hispanic/Latino; 1% Hispanic/Latino; 0.5% Asian, non-Hispanic/Latino; 0.1% American Indian or Alaska Native, non-Hispanic/Latino; 0.7% Two or more races, non-Hispanic/Latino; 3% Race/ethnicity unknown; 0.1% international; 7% transferred in. *Retention:* 66% of full-time freshmen returned.

Freshmen *Admission:* 672 applied, 647 admitted, 515 enrolled. *Average high school GPA:* 2.74. *Test scores:* SAT critical reading scores over 500: 100%; SAT math scores over 500: 80%; SAT writing scores over 500: 60%; ACT scores over 18: 76%; SAT critical reading scores over 600: 20%; SAT math scores over 600: 20%; SAT writing scores over 600: 20%; ACT scores over 24: 17%; ACT scores over 30: 1%.

Faculty *Total:* 135, 37% full-time. *Student/faculty ratio:* 23:1.

Academics *Calendar:* semesters. *Degrees:* certificates, associate, and bachelor's (also offers some upper-level and graduate courses). *Special study options:* academic remediation for entering students, accelerated degree program, adult/continuing education programs, advanced placement credit, distance learning, double majors, freshman honors college, honors programs, independent study, internships, part-time degree program, services for LD students, student-designed majors, summer session for credit. *ROTC:* Army (c), Air Force (c).

Computers on Campus 194 computers/terminals are available on campus for general student use. Students can access the following: computer help desk, free student e-mail accounts, online (class) grades, online (class) registration, online (class) schedules. Campuswide network is available.

Student Life *Housing:* college housing not available. *Activities and organizations:* choral group, Society of Mechanical Engineers, IEEE, Imagineers, Criminal Justice Club, Salt and Light.

Athletics *Intramural sports:* basketball M/W, volleyball M/W.

Standardized Tests *Required for some:* SAT or ACT (for admission). *Recommended:* SAT or ACT (for admission).

Costs (2010–11) *Tuition:* state resident $5110 full-time, $233 per credit hour part-time; nonresident $13,070 full-time, $595 per credit hour part-time. Full-time tuition and fees vary according to course level and course load. Part-time tuition and fees vary according to course level and course load. *Payment*

plans: installment, deferred payment. *Waivers:* senior citizens and employees or children of employees.
Financial Aid Of all full-time matriculated undergraduates who enrolled in 2009, 1,257 applied for aid, 1,197 were judged to have need, 177 had their need fully met. In 2009, 15 non-need-based awards were made. *Average percent of need met:* 49%. *Average financial aid package:* $7855. *Average need-based loan:* $3483. *Average need-based gift aid:* $5030. *Average non-need-based aid:* $1125.
Applying *Options:* electronic application, early admission, deferred entrance. *Application fee:* $30. *Required:* high school transcript. *Application deadlines:* 9/1 (freshmen), 9/1 (transfers). *Notification:* continuous (freshmen), continuous (transfers).
Freshman Application Contact Mrs. Laurie R. Donley, Director of Enrollment Management and Student Services, Kent State University at Tuscarawas, 330 University Drive Northeast, New Philadelphia, OH 44663-9403. *Phone:* 330-339-3391 Ext. 47425. *Fax:* 330-339-3321. *E-mail:* ldonley@kent.edu. *Web site:* http://www.tusc.kent.edu/.

Kenyon College
Gambier, Ohio

- **Independent** 4-year, founded 1824
- **Rural** 1200-acre campus with easy access to Columbus
- **Endowment** $158.8 million
- **Coed** 1,632 undergraduate students, 99% full-time, 54% women, 46% men
- **Very difficult** entrance level, 39% of applicants were admitted

Undergraduates 1,619 full-time, 13 part-time. Students come from 50 states and territories; 57 other countries; 84% are from out of state; 4% Black or African American, non-Hispanic/Latino; 4% Hispanic/Latino; 6% Asian, non-Hispanic/Latino; 0.7% American Indian or Alaska Native, non-Hispanic/Latino; 3% Race/ethnicity unknown; 4% international; 0.3% transferred in; 98% live on campus. *Retention:* 92% of full-time freshmen returned.
Freshmen *Admission:* 4,066 applied, 1,598 admitted, 483 enrolled. *Average high school GPA:* 3.84. *Test scores:* SAT critical reading scores over 500: 99%; SAT math scores over 500: 99%; SAT writing scores over 500: 99%; ACT scores over 18: 100%; SAT critical reading scores over 600: 89%; SAT math scores over 600: 80%; SAT writing scores over 600: 84%; ACT scores over 24: 96%; SAT critical reading scores over 700: 46%; SAT math scores over 700: 23%; SAT writing scores over 700: 40%; ACT scores over 30: 61%.
Faculty *Total:* 199, 79% full-time, 91% with terminal degrees. *Student/faculty ratio:* 10:1.
Academics *Calendar:* semesters. *Degree:* bachelor's. *Special study options:* accelerated degree program, advanced placement credit, double majors, honors programs, independent study, off-campus study, services for LD students, student-designed majors, study abroad. *Unusual degree programs:* 3-2 engineering with Washington University in St. Louis, Case Western Reserve University, Rensselaer Polytechnic Institute; environmental science with Duke University, education with The Bank Street College of Education.
Computers on Campus Students can access the following: campus intranet, computer help desk, free student e-mail accounts, online (class) grades, online (class) schedules, commercial databases. Campuswide network is available. 99% of college-owned or -operated housing units are wired for high-speed Internet access. Wireless service is available via entire campus.
Student Life *Housing:* on-campus residence required through senior year. *Options:* coed, women-only, disabled students. Campus housing is university owned. Freshman campus housing is guaranteed. *Activities and organizations:* drama/theater group, student-run newspaper, radio station, choral group, Student Theater Organization, student radio station, musical groups, intramural sports and clubs, national fraternities, national sororities. *Campus security:* 24-hour emergency response devices and patrols, student patrols, late-night transport/escort service, controlled dormitory access. *Student services:* health clinic, personal/psychological counseling, women's center.
Athletics Member NCAA. All Division III. *Intercollegiate sports:* baseball M, basketball M/W, cross-country running M/W, field hockey W, football M, golf M, lacrosse M/W, soccer M/W, softball W, swimming and diving M/W, tennis M/W, track and field M/W, volleyball W. *Intramural sports:* archery M(c)/W(c), baseball M(c), basketball M/W, crew M(c)/W(c), equestrian sports M(c)/W(c), fencing M(c)/W(c), football M/W, lacrosse M(c), racquetball M/W, rugby M(c)/W(c), sailing M(c)/W(c), soccer M/W, squash M(c)/W(c), tennis M/W, ultimate Frisbee M(c)/W(c), volleyball M/W.
Standardized Tests *Required:* SAT or ACT (for admission).
Costs (2011–12) *Comprehensive fee:* $52,650 includes full-time tuition ($41,090), mandatory fees ($1540), and room and board ($10,020). *Payment plan:* installment. *Waivers:* employees or children of employees.
Financial Aid Of all full-time matriculated undergraduates who enrolled in 2009, 899 applied for aid, 772 were judged to have need, 367 had their need fully met. 244 Federal Work-Study jobs (averaging $1262). 162 state and other part-time jobs (averaging $1303). In 2009, 164 non-need-based awards were made. *Average percent of need met:* 98%. *Average financial aid package:*

$33,150. *Average need-based loan:* $4384. *Average need-based gift aid:* $30,415. *Average non-need-based aid:* $11,007. *Average indebtedness upon graduation:* $20,492.
Applying *Options:* electronic application, early admission, early decision, deferred entrance. *Application fee:* $50. *Required:* essay or personal statement, high school transcript, counselor recommendation. *Recommended:* minimum 3.5 GPA, 2 letters of recommendation, interview. *Application deadlines:* 1/15 (freshmen), 4/15 (transfers). *Early decision deadline:* 11/15 (for plan 1), 1/15 (for plan 2). *Notification:* 4/1 (freshmen), 5/15 (transfers), 12/15 (early decision plan 1), 2/1 (early decision plan 2).
Freshman Application Contact Ms. Jennifer Delahunty, Dean of Admissions, Kenyon College, Ransom Hall, Gambier, OH 43022. *Phone:* 740-427-5776. *Toll-free phone:* 800-848-2468. *Fax:* 740-427-5770. *E-mail:* admissions@kenyon.edu. *Web site:* http://www.kenyon.edu/.

Kettering College of Medical Arts
Kettering, Ohio

Freshman Application Contact Mrs. Becky McDonald, Director of Enrollment Services, Kettering College of Medical Arts, 3737 Southern Boulevard, Kettering, OH 45429-1299. *Phone:* 937-395-8628. *Toll-free phone:* 800-433-5262. *Fax:* 937-296-4238. *Web site:* http://www.kcma.edu/.

Lake Erie College
Painesville, Ohio

- **Independent** comprehensive, founded 1856
- **Small-town** 57-acre campus with easy access to Cleveland
- **Endowment** $31.1 million
- **Coed**
- **Moderately difficult** entrance level

Faculty *Student/faculty ratio:* 15:1.
Academics *Calendar:* semesters. *Degrees:* bachelor's, master's, and post-bachelor's certificates.
Student Life *Campus security:* 24-hour emergency response devices and patrols, late-night transport/escort service.
Athletics Member NCAA. All Division II.
Standardized Tests *Required:* SAT or ACT (for admission).
Costs (2010–11) *Comprehensive fee:* $33,866 includes full-time tuition ($24,308), mandatory fees ($1366), and room and board ($8192). Full-time tuition and fees vary according to course load and program. Part-time tuition: $665 per credit hour. Part-time tuition and fees vary according to course load and program. *Required fees:* $51 per credit hour part-time. *College room only:* $4057. Room and board charges vary according to board plan.
Financial Aid Of all full-time matriculated undergraduates who enrolled in 2009, 804 applied for aid, 764 were judged to have need, 98 had their need fully met. In 2009, 63 non-need-based awards were made. *Average percent of need met:* 69. *Average financial aid package:* $19,991. *Average need-based loan:* $4238. *Average need-based gift aid:* $16,203. *Average non-need-based aid:* $10,714.
Applying *Options:* electronic application, deferred entrance. *Application fee:* $30. *Required:* essay or personal statement, high school transcript, minimum 2.5 GPA. *Recommended:* interview.
Freshman Application Contact Mr. Eric Felver, Dean of Admissions and Financial Aid, Lake Erie College, 391 West Washington Street, Painesville, OH 44077-3389. *Phone:* 440-375-7050. *Toll-free phone:* 800-916-0904. *Fax:* 440-375-7005. *E-mail:* admissions@lec.edu. *Web site:* http://www.lec.edu/.

Laura and Alvin Siegal College of Judaic Studies
Beachwood, Ohio

- **Independent** comprehensive, founded 1963
- **Suburban** 2-acre campus with easy access to Cleveland
- **Coed**
- **Noncompetitive** entrance level

Academics *Calendar:* semesters. *Degrees:* bachelor's, master's, and post-bachelor's certificates.
Student Life *Campus security:* 24-hour emergency response devices, 24-hour ID check at all doors.
Costs (2010–11) *Tuition:* $13,608 full-time, $567 per credit hour part-time. *Required fees:* $230 full-time, $75 per term part-time.
Financial Aid Of all full-time matriculated undergraduates who enrolled in 2005, 1 applied for aid, 1 were judged to have need. *Average percent of need met:* 40. *Average financial aid package:* $1000. *Average need-based gift aid:* $1000.

Applying *Options:* deferred entrance. *Application fee:* $50. *Required:* essay or personal statement, high school transcript, 2 letters of recommendation, interview, personal interview.

Freshman Application Contact Ms. Ruth Kronick, Director of Student Services, Laura and Alvin Siegal College of Judaic Studies, 26500 Shaker Boulevard, Beachwood, OH 44122. *Phone:* 216-464-4050 Ext. 101. *Toll-free phone:* 888-336-2257. *Fax:* 216-464-5827. *E-mail:* admissions@siegalcollege.edu. *Web site:* http://www.siegalcollege.edu/.

Lourdes College

Sylvania, Ohio

- **Independent Roman Catholic** comprehensive, founded 1958
- **Suburban** 113-acre campus with easy access to Toledo
- **Endowment** $6.3 million
- **Coed** 2,223 undergraduate students, 53% full-time, 78% women, 22% men
- **Minimally difficult** entrance level, 77% of applicants were admitted

Undergraduates 1,169 full-time, 1,054 part-time. Students come from 11 states and territories; 9% are from out of state; 17% transferred in; 5% live on campus. *Retention:* 59% of full-time freshmen returned.

Freshmen *Admission:* 648 applied, 499 admitted, 178 enrolled. *Average high school GPA:* 2.77.

Faculty *Total:* 257, 35% full-time, 30% with terminal degrees. *Student/faculty ratio:* 11:1.

Academics *Calendar:* semesters. *Degrees:* certificates, associate, bachelor's, master's, and postbachelor's certificates. *Special study options:* academic remediation for entering students, adult/continuing education programs, advanced placement credit, distance learning, double majors, independent study, internships, part-time degree program, services for LD students, student-designed majors, study abroad, summer session for credit. *ROTC:* Army (c), Air Force (c).

Computers on Campus 181 computers/terminals are available on campus for general student use. Students can access the following: computer help desk, free student e-mail accounts, online (class) grades, online (class) registration, online (class) schedules, Sakai/eLearning, LiveText ePortfolio system, RRS news feeds, Facebook, Twitter, online polls. Campuswide network is available. 100% of college-owned or -operated housing units are wired for high-speed Internet access. Wireless service is available via entire campus.

Student Life *Housing:* on-campus residence required through junior year. *Options:* coed. Campus housing is university owned. Freshman applicants given priority for college housing. *Activities and organizations:* drama/theater group, choral group, Student Government Association, Drama Society, Student Nurses Association, Orbis Ars, Pre-Art Therapy Association. *Campus security:* 24-hour emergency response devices and patrols, late-night transport/escort service, controlled dormitory access. *Student services:* personal/psychological counseling.

Athletics Member NAIA. *Intercollegiate sports:* baseball M(s), basketball M(s)/W(s), golf M(s)/W(s), volleyball W(s). *Intramural sports:* basketball M/W, volleyball M/W.

Costs (2010–11) *Comprehensive fee:* $23,670 includes full-time tuition ($13,980), mandatory fees ($1890), and room and board ($7800). Full-time tuition and fees vary according to course load and location. Part-time tuition: $466 per credit hour. Part-time tuition and fees vary according to course load and location. *Required fees:* $63 per credit hour part-time. *College room only:* $4000. Room and board charges vary according to board plan and housing facility. *Payment plans:* installment, deferred payment. *Waivers:* senior citizens and employees or children of employees.

Financial Aid Of all full-time matriculated undergraduates who enrolled in 2009, 1,083 applied for aid, 971 were judged to have need. 102 Federal Work-Study jobs (averaging $2206). 100 state and other part-time jobs (averaging $1000). In 2009, 1 non-need-based awards were made. *Average financial aid package:* $8785. *Average need-based loan:* $3940. *Average need-based gift aid:* $6208. *Average non-need-based aid:* $1392.

Applying *Options:* electronic application, early admission, deferred entrance. *Application fee:* $25. *Required:* high school transcript. *Application deadlines:* rolling (freshmen), rolling (out-of-state freshmen), rolling (transfers). *Notification:* continuous (freshmen), continuous (out-of-state freshmen), continuous (transfers).

Freshman Application Contact Ms. Amy Mergen, Director of Admissions, Lourdes College, 6832 Convent Boulevard, Sylvania, OH 43560. *Phone:* 419-885-5291. *Toll-free phone:* 800-878-3210 Ext. 1299. *Fax:* 419-824-3916. *E-mail:* AdmissionsLCAdmits@lourdes.edu. *Web site:* http://www.lourdes.edu/.

Malone University

Canton, Ohio

- **Independent** comprehensive, founded 1892, affiliated with Evangelical Friends Church–Eastern Region
- **Suburban** 96-acre campus with easy access to Cleveland
- **Endowment** $16.1 million
- **Coed** 2,084 undergraduate students, 87% full-time, 59% women, 41% men
- **Moderately difficult** entrance level, 76% of applicants were admitted

Undergraduates 1,807 full-time, 277 part-time. Students come from 32 states and territories; 18 other countries; 13% are from out of state; 7% Black or African American, non-Hispanic/Latino; 1% Hispanic/Latino; 0.7% Asian, non-Hispanic/Latino; 0.3% American Indian or Alaska Native, non-Hispanic/Latino; 0.3% Two or more races, non-Hispanic/Latino; 1% Race/ethnicity unknown; 1% international; 5% transferred in; 53% live on campus. *Retention:* 71% of full-time freshmen returned.

Freshmen *Admission:* 1,455 applied, 1,112 admitted, 376 enrolled. *Average high school GPA:* 3.3. *Test scores:* SAT critical reading scores over 500: 65%; SAT math scores over 500: 69%; ACT scores over 18: 98%; SAT critical reading scores over 600: 28%; SAT math scores over 600: 31%; ACT scores over 24: 47%; SAT critical reading scores over 700: 1%; SAT math scores over 700: 1%; ACT scores over 30: 5%.

Faculty *Total:* 220, 49% full-time, 41% with terminal degrees. *Student/faculty ratio:* 14:1.

Academics *Calendar:* semesters. *Degrees:* bachelor's, master's, and postbachelor's certificates. *Special study options:* academic remediation for entering students, accelerated degree program, adult/continuing education programs, advanced placement credit, distance learning, double majors, honors programs, independent study, internships, off-campus study, part-time degree program, services for LD students, student-designed majors, study abroad, summer session for credit. *ROTC:* Army (c), Air Force (c).

Computers on Campus 225 computers/terminals and 250 ports are available on campus for general student use. Students can access the following: campus intranet, computer help desk, free student e-mail accounts, online (class) grades, online (class) registration, online (class) schedules, online advising, online financial aid information, and online credit card payments. Campuswide network is available. 100% of college-owned or -operated housing units are wired for high-speed Internet access. Wireless service is available via entire campus.

Student Life *Housing:* on-campus residence required through junior year. *Options:* men-only, women-only, disabled students. Campus housing is university owned. Freshman applicants given priority for college housing. *Activities and organizations:* drama/theater group, student-run newspaper, radio and television station, choral group, marching band, Celebration Worship Services, Student Activities Council, Student Senate, be: Justice, intramural athletics. *Campus security:* 24-hour emergency response devices and patrols, late-night transport/escort service, controlled dormitory access. *Student services:* health clinic, personal/psychological counseling.

Athletics Member NAIA, NCCAA. *Intercollegiate sports:* baseball M(s), basketball M(s)/W(s), cheerleading M/W, cross-country running M(s)/W(s), football M(s), golf M(s)/W(s), soccer M(s)/W(s), softball W(s), swimming and diving M(s)/W(s), tennis M(s)/W(s), track and field M(s)/W(s), volleyball W(s). *Intramural sports:* basketball M/W, bowling M/W, football M/W, lacrosse M(c)/W(c), skiing (cross-country) M/W, soccer M/W, softball M/W, table tennis M/W, ultimate Frisbee M(c)/W(c), volleyball M/W, weight lifting M/W.

Standardized Tests *Required:* SAT or ACT (for admission).

Costs (2011–12) *Comprehensive fee:* $31,508 includes full-time tuition ($22,832), mandatory fees ($588), and room and board ($8088). Part-time tuition: $425 per credit hour. Part-time tuition and fees vary according to course load. *Required fees:* $147 per term part-time. *College room only:* $4221. Room and board charges vary according to board plan. *Payment plan:* installment. *Waivers:* senior citizens and employees or children of employees.

Financial Aid Of all full-time matriculated undergraduates who enrolled in 2009, 1,513 applied for aid, 1,430 were judged to have need, 171 had their need fully met. 404 Federal Work-Study jobs (averaging $2185). 79 state and other part-time jobs (averaging $2518). In 2009, 195 non-need-based awards were made. *Average percent of need met:* 72%. *Average financial aid package:* $17,932. *Average need-based loan:* $4779. *Average need-based gift aid:* $13,659. *Average non-need-based aid:* $8068. *Average indebtedness upon graduation:* $32,306. *Financial aid deadline:* 7/31.

Applying *Options:* electronic application, early admission, deferred entrance. *Application fee:* $20. *Required:* high school transcript, minimum 2 GPA. *Required for some:* essay or personal statement. *Recommended:* interview. *Application deadlines:* 7/1 (freshmen), 7/1 (out-of-state freshmen), 7/1 (transfers). *Notification:* continuous (freshmen), continuous (out-of-state freshmen), continuous (transfers).

Freshman Application Contact Mr. David L. Kleffman, Director of Admissions, Malone University, 2600 Cleveland Avenue NW, Canton, OH

44709-3897. *Phone:* 330-471-8145. *Toll-free phone:* 800-521-1146. *Fax:* 330-471-8149. *E-mail:* admissions@malone.edu. *Web site:* http://www3.malone.edu/.

Marietta College

Marietta, Ohio

- **Independent** comprehensive, founded 1835
- **Small-town** 90-acre campus
- **Endowment** $55.7 million
- **Coed** 1,463 undergraduate students, 95% full-time, 49% women, 51% men
- **Moderately difficult** entrance level, 70% of applicants were admitted

Undergraduates 1,393 full-time, 70 part-time. Students come from 34 states and territories; 17 other countries; 32% are from out of state; 5% Black or African American, non-Hispanic/Latino; 1% Hispanic/Latino; 0.9% Asian, non-Hispanic/Latino; 0.5% American Indian or Alaska Native, non-Hispanic/Latino; 0.9% Two or more races, non-Hispanic/Latino; 8% Race/ethnicity unknown; 11% international; 2% transferred in; 81% live on campus. *Retention:* 78% of full-time freshmen returned.

Freshmen *Admission:* 3,523 applied, 2,451 admitted, 385 enrolled. *Average high school GPA:* 3.45. *Test scores:* SAT critical reading scores over 500: 71%; SAT math scores over 500: 78%; SAT writing scores over 500: 68%; ACT scores over 18: 98%; SAT critical reading scores over 600: 37%; SAT math scores over 600: 34%; SAT writing scores over 600: 29%; ACT scores over 24: 51%; SAT critical reading scores over 700: 7%; SAT math scores over 700: 4%; SAT writing scores over 700: 6%; ACT scores over 30: 7%.

Faculty *Total:* 147, 73% full-time, 84% with terminal degrees. *Student/faculty ratio:* 12:1.

Academics *Calendar:* semesters. *Degrees:* certificates, associate, bachelor's, and master's. *Special study options:* academic remediation for entering students, accelerated degree program, adult/continuing education programs, advanced placement credit, double majors, English as a second language, honors programs, independent study, internships, off-campus study, part-time degree program, services for LD students, student-designed majors, study abroad, summer session for credit. *Unusual degree programs:* 3-2 engineering with University of Pennsylvania, Columbia University, Case Western Reserve University, Washington University in St. Louis.

Computers on Campus 400 computers/terminals are available on campus for general student use. Students can access the following: campus intranet, computer help desk, free student e-mail accounts, online (class) grades, online (class) schedules. Campuswide network is available. 100% of college-owned or -operated housing units are wired for high-speed Internet access. Wireless service is available via classrooms, computer centers, computer labs, dorm rooms, learning centers, libraries, student centers.

Student Life *Housing:* on-campus residence required through senior year. *Options:* coed, men-only, women-only, disabled students. Campus housing is university owned, leased by the school and is provided by a third party. Freshman campus housing is guaranteed. *Activities and organizations:* drama/theater group, student-run newspaper, radio and television station, choral group, Student Programming Board, student government, Society of Petroleum Engineers, Inter-Varsity Christian Fellowship, Arts and Humanities Council, national fraternities, national sororities. *Campus security:* 24-hour emergency response devices and patrols, student patrols, late-night transport/escort service, controlled dormitory access. *Student services:* health clinic, personal/psychological counseling.

Athletics Member NCAA. All Division III. *Intercollegiate sports:* baseball M, basketball M/W, cheerleading W(c), crew M/W, cross-country running M/W, football M, lacrosse M(c), soccer M/W, softball W, tennis M/W, track and field M/W, volleyball W, wrestling M(c)/W(c). *Intramural sports:* badminton M/W, basketball M/W, bowling M/W, cross-country running M/W, football M/W, golf M/W, racquetball M/W, rock climbing M/W, soccer M/W, softball M/W, swimming and diving M/W, tennis M/W, ultimate Frisbee M/W, volleyball M/W, weight lifting M.

Standardized Tests *Required:* SAT or ACT (for admission). *Recommended:* SAT Subject Tests (for admission).

Costs (2010–11) *One-time required fee:* $280. *Comprehensive fee:* $36,780 includes full-time tuition ($27,640), mandatory fees ($700), and room and board ($8440). Full-time tuition and fees vary according to course load and degree level. Part-time tuition: $875 per credit hour. Part-time tuition and fees vary according to course load and degree level. *College room only:* $4580. Room and board charges vary according to board plan and housing facility. *Payment plan:* installment. *Waivers:* employees or children of employees.

Financial Aid Of all full-time matriculated undergraduates who enrolled in 2008, 1,299 applied for aid, 1,060 were judged to have need, 412 had their

need fully met. 897 Federal Work-Study jobs (averaging $1961). In 2008, 239 non-need-based awards were made. *Average percent of need met:* 89%. *Average financial aid package:* $24,212. *Average need-based loan:* $4611. *Average need-based gift aid:* $14,172. *Average non-need-based aid:* $8959. *Average indebtedness upon graduation:* $34,152.

Applying *Options:* electronic application, early admission, deferred entrance. *Application fee:* $25. *Required:* essay or personal statement, high school transcript, minimum 2 GPA, 1 letter of recommendation. *Recommended:* minimum 3 GPA, interview. *Application deadlines:* 5/1 (freshmen), rolling (transfers). *Notification:* continuous until 5/1 (freshmen), continuous (transfers).

Freshman Application Contact Mr. Jason Turley, Director of Admission, Marietta College, 215 Fifth Street, Marietta, OH 45750. *Phone:* 740-376-4600. *Toll-free phone:* 800-331-7896. *Fax:* 740-376-8888. *E-mail:* admit@marietta.edu. *Web site:* http://www.marietta.edu/.

Mercy College of Northwest Ohio

Toledo, Ohio

- **Independent** 4-year, founded 1993, affiliated with Roman Catholic Church, administratively affiliated with Mercy Health Partners
- **Urban** campus with easy access to Detroit
- **Endowment** $8.0 million
- **Coed, primarily women** 356,138 undergraduate students, 100% women
- **Moderately difficult** entrance level, 91% of applicants were admitted

Undergraduates 566 full-time, 355,572 part-time. Students come from 4 states and territories; 22% are from out of state; 8% Black or African American, non-Hispanic/Latino; 3% Hispanic/Latino; 0.5% Asian, non-Hispanic/Latino; 0.5% American Indian or Alaska Native, non-Hispanic/Latino; 2% Two or more races, non-Hispanic/Latino; 0.9% Race/ethnicity unknown; 0.1% transferred in; 5% live on campus. *Retention:* 90% of full-time freshmen returned.

Freshmen *Admission:* 164 applied, 149 admitted, 59 enrolled.

Faculty *Total:* 144, 42% full-time, 18% with terminal degrees. *Student/faculty ratio:* 12:1.

Academics *Calendar:* semesters. *Degrees:* certificates, associate, and bachelor's. *Special study options:* academic remediation for entering students, advanced placement credit, distance learning, double majors, independent study, internships, part-time degree program, services for LD students, summer session for credit.

Computers on Campus 40 computers/terminals and 40 ports are available on campus for general student use. Students can access the following: free student e-mail accounts, online (class) grades, online (class) registration, online (class) schedules, billing and payment, degree audit, and transcripts. Campuswide network is available. Wireless service is available via entire campus.

Student Life *Housing options:* coed. Campus housing is leased by the school. *Activities and organizations:* Student Senate, intramural sports, Student Nurses Association, Phi Theta Kappa. *Campus security:* 24-hour patrols, late-night transport/escort service, controlled dormitory access. *Student services:* personal/psychological counseling.

Standardized Tests *Required for some:* SAT or ACT (for admission). *Recommended:* SAT or ACT (for admission).

Costs (2010–11) *Tuition:* $9920 full-time, $342 per credit hour part-time. Full-time tuition and fees vary according to course load. Part-time tuition and fees vary according to course load. *Required fees:* $704 full-time, $22 per credit hour part-time. *Room only:* Room and board charges vary according to housing facility. *Payment plans:* installment, deferred payment. *Waivers:* employees or children of employees.

Financial Aid Of all full-time matriculated undergraduates who enrolled in 2008, 485 applied for aid, 443 were judged to have need, 17 had their need fully met. 29 Federal Work-Study jobs (averaging $1567). In 2008, 10 non-need-based awards were made. *Average percent of need met:* 37%. *Average financial aid package:* $7764. *Average need-based loan:* $4448. *Average need-based gift aid:* $5661. *Average non-need-based aid:* $1986. *Average indebtedness upon graduation:* $25,560.

Applying *Options:* electronic application. *Application fee:* $25. *Required:* high school transcript, minimum 2.3 GPA. *Application deadlines:* rolling (freshmen), rolling (transfers). *Notification:* continuous (freshmen), continuous (transfers).

Freshman Application Contact Admissions Counselor, Mercy College of Northwest Ohio, 2221 Madison Avenue, Toledo, OH 43604. *Phone:* 419-251-1313. *Toll-free phone:* 888-80-Mercy. *Fax:* 419-251-1462. *E-mail:* admissions@mercycollege.edu. *Web site:* http://www.mercycollege.edu/.

Miami University

Oxford, Ohio

- **State-related** university, founded 1809, part of Miami University System
- **Small-town** 2000-acre campus with easy access to Cincinnati
- **Endowment** $146.4 million
- **Coed** 14,872 undergraduate students, 98% full-time, 53% women, 47% men
- **Moderately difficult** entrance level, 79% of applicants were admitted

Undergraduates 14,605 full-time, 267 part-time. Students come from 51 states and territories; 47 other countries; 29% are from out of state; 4% Black or African American, non-Hispanic/Latino; 2% Hispanic/Latino; 3% Asian, non-Hispanic/Latino; 0.1% Native Hawaiian or other Pacific Islander, non-Hispanic/Latino; 0.5% American Indian or Alaska Native, non-Hispanic/Latino; 0.8% Two or more races, non-Hispanic/Latino; 2% Race/ethnicity unknown; 3% international; 2% transferred in; 49% live on campus. *Retention:* 89% of full-time freshmen returned.

Freshmen *Admission:* 16,960 applied, 13,358 admitted, 3,595 enrolled. *Average high school GPA:* 3.62. *Test scores:* SAT critical reading scores over 500: 84%; SAT math scores over 500: 92%; ACT scores over 18: 100%; SAT critical reading scores over 600: 37%; SAT math scores over 600: 55%; ACT scores over 24: 78%; SAT critical reading scores over 700: 7%; SAT math scores over 700: 10%; ACT scores over 30: 17%.

Faculty *Total:* 1,095, 77% full-time, 73% with terminal degrees. *Student/faculty ratio:* 17:1.

Academics *Calendar:* semesters. *Degrees:* certificates, associate, bachelor's, master's, doctoral-research/scholarship, and post-master's certificates. *Special study options:* adult/continuing education programs, advanced placement credit, cooperative education, double majors, English as a second language, honors programs, independent study, internships, off-campus study, services for LD students, student-designed majors, study abroad, summer session for credit. *ROTC:* Army (c), Navy (b), Air Force (b). *Unusual degree programs:* 3-2 engineering with Case Western Reserve University, Columbia University; forestry with Duke University.

Computers on Campus 400 computers/terminals and 11,200 ports are available on campus for general student use. Students can access the following: campus intranet, computer help desk, free student e-mail accounts, online (class) grades, online (class) registration, online (class) schedules. Campus-wide network is available. 100% of college-owned or -operated housing units are wired for high-speed Internet access. Wireless service is available via entire campus.

Student Life *Housing:* on-campus residence required through sophomore year. *Options:* coed, men-only, women-only, disabled students. Campus housing is university owned. Freshman campus housing is guaranteed. *Activities and organizations:* drama/theater group, student-run newspaper, radio and television station, choral group, marching band, Associated Student Government, Campus Crusade for Christ, College Democrats/College Republicans, Fraternities and Sororities, Red Alert, national fraternities, national sororities. *Campus security:* 24-hour emergency response devices and patrols, student patrols, late-night transport/escort service, controlled dormitory access. *Student services:* health clinic, personal/psychological counseling, women's center.

Athletics Member NCAA. All Division I except football (Division I-A). *Intercollegiate sports:* baseball M(s)/W(c), basketball M(s)/W(s), cross-country running M(s)/W(s), equestrian sports M(c)/W(c), fencing M(c)/W(c), field hockey M(c)/W(s), golf M(s), gymnastics M(c)/W(c), ice hockey M(s)/W(c), lacrosse M(c)/W(c), rugby M(c)/W(c), sailing M(c)/W(c), soccer M(c)/W(s), softball M(c)/W(s), swimming and diving M(s)/W(s), tennis M(c)/W(s), track and field M(s)/W(s), ultimate Frisbee M(c)/W(c), volleyball M(c)/W(s), water polo M(c)/W(c), weight lifting M(c)/W(c), wrestling M(c)/W(c). *Intramural sports:* badminton M(c)/W(c), baseball M/W, basketball M/W, golf M(c)/W(c), ice hockey M/W, racquetball M/W, soccer M/W, softball M/W, ultimate Frisbee M/W, volleyball M/W.

Standardized Tests *Required:* SAT or ACT (for admission).

Costs (2010–11) *Tuition:* state resident $12,198 full-time; nonresident $26,988 full-time. Full-time tuition and fees vary according to location and program. Part-time tuition and fees vary according to location and program. *Required fees:* $588 full-time. *Room and board:* $9786; room only: $4952. Room and board charges vary according to board plan and housing facility. *Payment plan:* installment. *Waivers:* employees or children of employees.

Financial Aid Of all full-time matriculated undergraduates who enrolled in 2009, 8,849 applied for aid, 6,622 were judged to have need, 806 had their need fully met. 1,081 Federal Work-Study jobs (averaging $2264). In 2009, 2225 non-need-based awards were made. *Average percent of need met:* 56%. *Average financial aid package:* $10,940. *Average need-based loan:* $4852. *Average need-based gift aid:* $6083. *Average non-need-based aid:* $4855. *Average indebtedness upon graduation:* $27,315.

Applying *Options:* electronic application, early decision, early action, deferred entrance. *Application fee:* $50. *Required:* essay or personal statement, high school transcript, 1 letter of recommendation. *Application deadlines:* 2/1 (freshmen), 5/1 (transfers), 12/1 (early action). *Early decision deadline:* 11/1.

Notification: 3/15 (freshmen), continuous (transfers), 12/15 (early decision), 2/1 (early action).

Freshman Application Contact Office of Admissions, Miami University, 301 South Campus Avenue, Oxford, OH 45056. *Phone:* 513-529-2531. *Fax:* 513-529-1550. *E-mail:* admission@muohio.edu. *Web site:* http://www.muohio.edu/.

Miami University Hamilton

Hamilton, Ohio

- **State-supported** comprehensive, founded 1968, part of Miami University System
- **Suburban** 78-acre campus with easy access to Cincinnati
- **Coed**
- **Noncompetitive** entrance level

Faculty *Student/faculty ratio:* 21:1.

Academics *Calendar:* semesters plus summer sessions. *Degrees:* certificates, associate, bachelor's, and master's (degrees awarded by Miami University main campus).

Student Life *Campus security:* 24-hour emergency response devices and patrols, late-night transport/escort service.

Costs (2010–11) *Tuition:* state resident $4230 full-time; nonresident $16,230 full-time. *Required fees:* $402 full-time.

Applying *Options:* electronic application. *Application fee:* $35. *Required:* high school transcript.

Freshman Application Contact Mr. Archie Nelson, Director of Admission and Financial Aid, Miami University Hamilton, 1601 Peck Boulevard, Hamilton, OH 45011-3399. *Phone:* 513-785-3111. *Fax:* 513-785-1807. *E-mail:* nelsona3@muohio.edu. *Web site:* http://www.ham.muohio.edu/.

Miami University–Middletown Campus

Middletown, Ohio

Freshman Application Contact Diane Cantonwine, Assistant Director of Admission and Financial Aid, Miami University–Middletown Campus, 4200 East University Boulevard, Middletown, OH 45042-3497. *Phone:* 513-727-3346. *Toll-free phone:* 866-426-4643. *Fax:* 513-727-3223. *E-mail:* cantondm@muohio.edu. *Web site:* http://www.mid.muohio.edu/.

Mount Carmel College of Nursing

Columbus, Ohio

- **Independent** comprehensive, founded 1903, administratively affiliated with Mount Carmel Health System
- **Urban** campus with easy access to Columbus
- **Endowment** $700,623
- **Coed, primarily women** 746 undergraduate students, 78% full-time, 91% women, 9% men
- **Moderately difficult** entrance level, 91% of applicants were admitted

Undergraduates 581 full-time, 165 part-time. Students come from 6 states and territories; 1% are from out of state; 6% Black or African American, non-Hispanic/Latino; 1% Hispanic/Latino; 2% Asian, non-Hispanic/Latino; 0.1% Native Hawaiian or other Pacific Islander, non-Hispanic/Latino; 0.4% American Indian or Alaska Native, non-Hispanic/Latino; 0.8% Two or more races, non-Hispanic/Latino; 3% Race/ethnicity unknown; 13% transferred in; 10% live on campus. *Retention:* 82% of full-time freshmen returned.

Freshmen *Admission:* 145 applied, 132 admitted, 85 enrolled. *Average high school GPA:* 3.54. *Test scores:* ACT scores over 18: 99%; ACT scores over 24: 38%.

Faculty *Total:* 76, 57% full-time, 20% with terminal degrees. *Student/faculty ratio:* 12:1.

Academics *Calendar:* semesters. *Degrees:* bachelor's, master's, and post-master's certificates. *Special study options:* accelerated degree program, adult/continuing education programs, distance learning, honors programs, summer session for credit. *ROTC:* Army (c), Navy (c), Air Force (c).

Computers on Campus 70 computers/terminals are available on campus for general student use. Students can access the following: campus intranet, computer help desk, free student e-mail accounts, online (class) grades, online (class) registration, online (class) schedules. Campuswide network is available. Wireless service is available via entire campus.

Student Life *Housing:* on-campus residence required through sophomore year. *Options:* coed. Campus housing is provided by a third party. Freshman applicants given priority for college housing. *Activities and organizations:* Student Nurses Association, Campus Ministry, Sigma Theta Tau, student government. *Campus security:* 24-hour emergency response devices and patrols, late-night transport/escort service, controlled dormitory access. *Student services:* health clinic, personal/psychological counseling.

Athletics *Intramural sports:* basketball W(c), softball W(c), volleyball M(c)/W(c).

Standardized Tests *Required for some:* SAT or ACT (for admission).

Costs (2010–11) *One-time required fee:* $225. *Tuition:* $15,332 full-time, $323 per semester hour part-time. Full-time tuition and fees vary according to course level, course load, and student level. Part-time tuition and fees vary according to course level, course load, and student level. *Required fees:* $312 full-time, $312 per year part-time. *Room only:* $4500. *Payment plan:* installment. *Waivers:* employees or children of employees.

Financial Aid Of all full-time matriculated undergraduates who enrolled in 2009, 521 applied for aid, 521 were judged to have need. In 2009, 5 non-need-based awards were made. *Average percent of need met:* 60%. *Average financial aid package:* $13,500. *Average need-based loan:* $4427. *Average need-based gift aid:* $1700. *Average non-need-based aid:* $2200. *Average indebtedness upon graduation:* $8675.

Applying *Application fee:* $30. *Required:* essay or personal statement, high school transcript, activities/interests resume. *Required for some:* interview. *Recommended:* minimum 3 GPA. *Application deadlines:* 4/1 (freshmen), 4/1 (out-of-state freshmen), 4/1 (transfers). *Notification:* continuous (freshmen), continuous (out-of-state freshmen), continuous (transfers).

Freshman Application Contact Kim Campbell, Direct, Admissions and Recruitment, Mount Carmel College of Nursing, 127 South Davis Avenue, Columbus, OH 43222-1504. *Phone:* 614-234-1085. *Fax:* 614-234-5427. *E-mail:* kcampbell@mccn.edu. *Web site:* http://www.mccn.edu/.

Mount Vernon Nazarene University
Mount Vernon, Ohio

- **Independent Nazarene** comprehensive, founded 1964
- **Small-town** 401-acre campus with easy access to Columbus
- **Endowment** $12.2 million
- **Coed** 1,923 undergraduate students, 90% full-time, 63% women, 37% men
- **Moderately difficult** entrance level, 75% of applicants were admitted

Undergraduates 1,738 full-time, 185 part-time. Students come from 27 states and territories; 6 other countries; 9% are from out of state; 5% Black or African American, non-Hispanic/Latino; 2% Hispanic/Latino; 0.7% Asian, non-Hispanic/Latino; 0.1% Native Hawaiian or other Pacific Islander, non-Hispanic/Latino; 0.2% American Indian or Alaska Native, non-Hispanic/Latino; 0.8% Two or more races, non-Hispanic/Latino; 4% Race/ethnicity unknown; 0.4% international; 3% transferred in; 75% live on campus. *Retention:* 74% of full-time freshmen returned.

Freshmen *Admission:* 983 applied, 736 admitted, 390 enrolled. *Average high school GPA:* 3.31. *Test scores:* SAT critical reading scores over 500: 65%; SAT math scores over 500: 61%; ACT scores over 18: 92%; SAT critical reading scores over 600: 26%; SAT math scores over 600: 24%; ACT scores over 24: 40%; SAT critical reading scores over 700: 6%; ACT scores over 30: 4%.

Faculty *Total:* 246, 43% full-time, 35% with terminal degrees. *Student/faculty ratio:* 14:1.

Academics *Calendar:* 4-1-4. *Degrees:* associate, bachelor's, and master's. *Special study options:* academic remediation for entering students, adult/continuing education programs, advanced placement credit, distance learning, double majors, honors programs, independent study, internships, off-campus study, part-time degree program, services for LD students, study abroad, summer session for credit. *Unusual degree programs:* 3-2 engineering with Olivet Nazarene University; pre-occupational therapy/physician assistant with Chatham University.

Computers on Campus 232 computers/terminals and 1,200 ports are available on campus for general student use. Students can access the following: campus intranet, computer help desk, free student e-mail accounts, online (class) grades, online (class) schedules. Campuswide network is available. 100% of college-owned or -operated housing units are wired for high-speed Internet access. Wireless service is available via classrooms, computer centers, computer labs, learning centers, libraries, student centers.

Student Life *Housing:* on-campus residence required through senior year. *Options:* men-only, women-only, disabled students. Campus housing is university owned. Freshman campus housing is guaranteed. *Activities and organizations:* drama/theater group, student-run newspaper, radio station, choral group, campus ministry groups, Student Government Association, Student Education Association, Drama Club, music department ensembles. *Campus security:* 24-hour emergency response devices and patrols, late-night transport/escort service, controlled dormitory access. *Student services:* health clinic, personal/psychological counseling.

Athletics Member NAIA, NCCAA. *Intercollegiate sports:* baseball M(s), basketball M(s)/W(s), cross-country running M(s)/W(s), golf M(s), soccer M(s)/W(s), softball W(s), volleyball W(s). *Intramural sports:* basketball M/W, bowling M/W, cheerleading M/W, football M/W, soccer M/W, softball M/W, table tennis M/W, ultimate Frisbee M/W, volleyball M/W.

Standardized Tests *Required:* SAT or ACT (for admission).

Costs (2011–12) *Comprehensive fee:* $28,710 includes full-time tuition ($22,280) and room and board ($6430). Full-time tuition and fees vary according to course load, program, and reciprocity agreements. Part-time tuition: $787 per credit hour. Part-time tuition and fees vary according to course load, program, and reciprocity agreements. *Required fees:* $21 per credit hour part-time. *College room only:* $3590. *Payment plan:* installment. *Waivers:* senior citizens and employees or children of employees.

Financial Aid Of all full-time matriculated undergraduates who enrolled in 2009, 1,356 applied for aid, 1,208 were judged to have need, 160 had their need fully met. 200 Federal Work-Study jobs (averaging $1500). 415 state and other part-time jobs (averaging $1600). In 2009, 100 non-need-based awards were made. *Average percent of need met:* 70%. *Average financial aid package:* $15,619. *Average need-based loan:* $3984. *Average need-based gift aid:* $9344. *Average non-need-based aid:* $4102. *Average indebtedness upon graduation:* $29,761.

Applying *Options:* electronic application, deferred entrance. *Application fee:* $25. *Required:* essay or personal statement, high school transcript, minimum 2.5 GPA, 2 letters of recommendation. *Application deadline:* 7/15 (freshmen). *Notification:* 9/1 (freshmen), continuous (transfers).

Freshman Application Contact James Smith, Director of Admissions and Student Recruitment, Mount Vernon Nazarene University, 800 Martinsburg Road, Mount Vernon, OH 43050. *Phone:* 740-392-6868 Ext. 4516. *Toll-free phone:* 866-462-6868. *Fax:* 740-393-0511. *E-mail:* admissions@mvnu.edu. *Web site:* http://www.mvnu.edu/.

Muskingum University
New Concord, Ohio

Freshman Application Contact Mrs. Beth DaLonzo, Director of Admission, Muskingum University, 163 Stormont Street, New Concord, OH 43762. *Phone:* 740-826-8137. *Toll-free phone:* 800-752-6082. *Fax:* 740-826-8100. *E-mail:* adminfo@muskingum.edu. *Web site:* http://www.muskingum.edu/.

See page 1458 for the College Close-Up.

Notre Dame College
South Euclid, Ohio

Freshman Application Contact Mr. David Armstrong, Dean of Admissions, Notre Dame College, 4545 College Road, South Euclid, OH 44121-4293. *Phone:* 216-373-5214. *Toll-free phone:* 800-632-1680. *Fax:* 216-381-3802. *E-mail:* admissinos@ndc.edu. *Web site:* http://www.notredamecollege.edu/.

See page 664 for Display. See page 1482 for the College Close-Up.

Oberlin College
Oberlin, Ohio

- **Independent** comprehensive, founded 1833
- **Small-town** 440-acre campus with easy access to Cleveland
- **Endowment** $603.4 million
- **Coed** 2,948 undergraduate students, 98% full-time, 55% women, 45% men
- **Very difficult** entrance level, 31% of applicants were admitted

Undergraduates 2,901 full-time, 47 part-time. Students come from 51 states and territories; 44 other countries; 91% are from out of state; 6% Black or African American, non-Hispanic/Latino; 6% Hispanic/Latino; 4% Asian, non-Hispanic/Latino; 0.2% American Indian or Alaska Native, non-Hispanic/Latino; 5% Two or more races, non-Hispanic/Latino; 0.4% Race/ethnicity unknown; 6% international; 0.9% transferred in; 89% live on campus. *Retention:* 94% of full-time freshmen returned.

Freshmen *Admission:* 7,222 applied, 2,207 admitted, 782 enrolled. *Average high school GPA:* 3.6. *Test scores:* SAT critical reading scores over 500: 100%; SAT math scores over 500: 99%; SAT writing scores over 500: 99%; ACT scores over 18: 100%; SAT critical reading scores over 600: 91%; SAT math scores over 600: 87%; SAT writing scores over 600: 90%; ACT scores over 24: 95%; SAT critical reading scores over 700: 53%; SAT math scores over 700: 35%; SAT writing scores over 700: 47%; ACT scores over 30: 62%.

Faculty *Total:* 285, 96% with terminal degrees. *Student/faculty ratio:* 9:1.

Academics *Calendar:* 4-1-4. *Degrees:* diplomas, bachelor's, master's, and postbachelor's certificates. *Special study options:* advanced placement credit, double majors, English as a second language, honors programs, independent study, internships, off-campus study, part-time degree program, services for LD students, student-designed majors, study abroad. *Unusual degree programs:* 3-2 engineering with Washington University in St. Louis, Case Western Reserve University, California Institute of Technology, Columbia University.

Computers on Campus 340 computers/terminals are available on campus for general student use. Students can access the following: campus intranet, computer help desk, free student e-mail accounts, online (class) grades, online (class) registration, online (class) schedules. Campuswide network is available.

100% of college-owned or -operated housing units are wired for high-speed Internet access. Wireless service is available via entire campus. **Student Life** *Housing:* on-campus residence required through junior year. *Options:* coed, women-only, cooperative, disabled students. Campus housing is university owned. Freshman campus housing is guaranteed. *Activities and organizations:* drama/theater group, student-run newspaper, radio station, choral group, marching band, Experimental College, Community Outreach, Student Government, Students Cooperative Association, student radio station. *Campus security:* 24-hour emergency response devices and patrols, student patrols, late-night transport/escort service, controlled dormitory access, crime prevention programs. *Student services:* health clinic, personal/psychological counseling, women's center.

Athletics Member NCAA. All Division III. *Intercollegiate sports:* baseball M, basketball M/W, cheerleading W(c), cross-country running M/W, equestrian sports M(c)/W(c), fencing M(c)/W(c), field hockey W, football M, golf M/W, ice hockey M(c)/W(c), lacrosse M/W, rugby M(c)/W(c), soccer M/W, softball W(c), swimming and diving M/W, tennis M/W, track and field M/W, ultimate Frisbee M(c)/W(c), volleyball M(c)/W, water polo M(c)/W(c). *Intramural sports:* baseball M, basketball M/W, bowling M/W, cross-country running M/W, football M, golf M/W, racquetball M/W, rock climbing M/W, soccer M/W, softball M/W, squash M/W, table tennis M/W, tennis M/W, track and field M/W, volleyball M/W, water polo M/W, weight lifting M/W.

Standardized Tests *Required:* SAT or ACT (for admission). *Recommended:* SAT Subject Tests (for admission).

Costs (2010–11) *Comprehensive fee:* $52,587 includes full-time tuition ($41,234), mandatory fees ($343), and room and board ($11,010). Part-time tuition: $1710 per credit hour. *College room only:* $5720. Room and board charges vary according to board plan and housing facility. *Payment plan:* installment. *Waivers:* employees or children of employees.

Financial Aid Of all full-time matriculated undergraduates who enrolled in 2009, 1,797 applied for aid, 1,570 were judged to have need, 1,570 had their need fully met. In 2009, 730 non-need-based awards were made. *Average percent of need met:* 100%. *Average financial aid package:* $32,508. *Average need-based loan:* $4776. *Average need-based gift aid:* $26,734. *Average non-need-based aid:* $11,812. *Average indebtedness upon graduation:* $18,604. *Financial aid deadline:* 2/1.

Applying *Options:* electronic application, early admission, early decision, deferred entrance. *Application fee:* $35. *Required:* essay or personal statement, high school transcript, 2 letters of recommendation. *Required for some:* interview, audition for applicants to the Conservatory of Music. *Application deadlines:* 1/15 (freshmen), 3/15 (transfers). *Early decision deadline:* 11/15 (for plan 1), 1/2 (for plan 2). *Notification:* 4/1 (freshmen), 5/15 (transfers), 12/15 (early decision plan 1), 2/1 (early decision plan 2).

Freshman Application Contact Ms. Debra Chermonte, Dean of Admissions and Financial Aid, Oberlin College, Admissions Office, Carnegie Building, Oberlin, OH 44074-1090. *Phone:* 440-775-8411. *Toll-free phone:* 800-622-OBIE. *Fax:* 440-775-6905. *E-mail:* college.admissions@oberlin.edu. *Web site:* http://www.oberlin.edu/.

See page 1484 for the College Close-Up.

Ohio Christian University
Circleville, Ohio

Director of Admissions Mike Egenreider, Associate Vice President for Enrollment, Ohio Christian University, 1476 Lancaster Pike, PO Box 458, Circleville, OH 43113-9487. *Phone:* 740-477-7741. *Toll-free phone:* 800-701-0222. *E-mail:* enroll@ohiochristian.edu. *Web site:* http://www.ohiochristian.edu/.

Ohio Dominican University
Columbus, Ohio

• **Independent Roman Catholic** comprehensive, founded 1911
• **Urban** 71-acre campus
• **Endowment** $15.1 million
• **Coed**
• **Moderately difficult** entrance level

Faculty *Student/faculty ratio:* 14:1.

Academics *Calendar:* semesters. *Degrees:* certificates, associate, bachelor's, and master's.

Student Life *Campus security:* 24-hour emergency response devices and patrols, late-night transport/escort service, controlled dormitory access.

Athletics Member NAIA.

Standardized Tests *Required:* SAT or ACT (for admission).

Costs (2010–11) *Comprehensive fee:* $33,602 includes full-time tuition ($24,780), mandatory fees ($500), and room and board ($8322). Part-time tuition: $501 per credit hour. *Required fees:* $135 per term part-time. *Room and board:* Room and board charges vary according to board plan and housing facility.

Financial Aid *Of all full-time matriculated undergraduates who enrolled in 2009,* 200 Federal Work-Study jobs (averaging $2000). *Average percent of need met:* 92. *Average financial aid package:* $12,467. *Average indebtedness upon graduation:* $13,500.
Applying *Options:* electronic application, deferred entrance. *Application fee:* $25. *Required:* high school transcript, minimum 2 GPA, interview. *Required for some:* essay or personal statement.
Freshman Application Contact Ms. Nicole A. Evans, Director of Admissions, Ohio Dominican University, 1216 Sunbury Road, Columbus, OH 43219. *Phone:* 614-251-4500. *Toll-free phone:* 800-854-2670. *Fax:* 614-251-0156. *E-mail:* admissions@ohiodominican.edu. *Web site:* http://www.ohiodominican.edu/.

Ohio Northern University
Ada, Ohio

- **Independent** comprehensive, founded 1871, affiliated with United Methodist Church
- **Small-town** 300-acre campus
- **Endowment** $172.7 million
- **Coed**
- **Moderately difficult** entrance level

Faculty *Student/faculty ratio:* 12:1.
Academics *Calendar:* quarters. *Degrees:* bachelor's, doctoral-professional, and postbachelor's certificates.
Student Life *Campus security:* 24-hour emergency response devices and patrols, late-night transport/escort service, controlled dormitory access.
Athletics Member NCAA. All Division III.
Standardized Tests *Required:* SAT or ACT (for admission).
Costs (2010–11) *Comprehensive fee:* $42,171 includes full-time tuition ($32,859), mandatory fees ($240), and room and board ($9072). Full-time tuition and fees vary according to course load, degree level, program, and student level. Part-time tuition: $913 per quarter hour. Part-time tuition and fees vary according to course load, degree level, program, and student level. *Required fees:* $30 per term part-time. *College room only:* $4725. Room and board charges vary according to board plan and housing facility.
Financial Aid *Of all full-time matriculated undergraduates who enrolled in 2009,* 2,199 applied for aid, 1,821 were judged to have need, 252 had their

need fully met. 1,354 Federal Work-Study jobs (averaging $1487). 169 state and other part-time jobs (averaging $2050). *In 2009,* 342 non-need-based awards were made. *Average percent of need met:* 76. *Average financial aid package:* $26,304. *Average need-based loan:* $4605. *Average need-based gift aid:* $21,219. *Average non-need-based aid:* $17,001. *Average indebtedness upon graduation:* $48,886.
Applying *Options:* electronic application, deferred entrance. *Application fee:* $30. *Required:* essay or personal statement, high school transcript, 1 letter of recommendation. *Recommended:* minimum 2.5 GPA, 2 letters of recommendation, interview.
Freshman Application Contact Ms. Deborah Miller, Director of Admission, Ohio Northern University, 525 South Main Street, Ada, OH 45810-1599. *Phone:* 419-772-2260 Ext. 2464. *Toll-free phone:* 888-408-4ONU. *Fax:* 419-772-2821. *E-mail:* admissions-ug@onu.cdu. *Web site:* http://www.onu.edu/.

See page 1486 for the College Close-Up.

The Ohio State University
Columbus, Ohio

- **State-supported** university, founded 1870, part of Ohio State University System
- **Urban** 3469-acre campus with easy access to Columbus
- **Endowment** $1.9 billion
- **Coed** 42,082 undergraduate students, 92% full-time, 47% women, 53% men
- **Very difficult** entrance level, 68% of applicants were admitted

Undergraduates 38,523 full-time, 3,559 part-time. Students come from 56 states and territories; 63 other countries; 11% are from out of state; 6% Black or African American, non-Hispanic/Latino; 3% Hispanic/Latino; 5% Asian, non-Hispanic/Latino; 0.3% American Indian or Alaska Native, non-Hispanic/Latino; 0.6% Two or more races, non-Hispanic/Latino; 2% Race/ethnicity unknown; 5% international; 5% transferred in; 25% live on campus. *Retention:* 93% of full-time freshmen returned.
Freshmen *Admission:* 24,302 applied, 16,531 admitted, 6,672 enrolled. *Test scores:* SAT critical reading scores over 500: 85%; SAT math scores over 500: 96%; SAT writing scores over 500: 88%; ACT scores over 18: 100%; SAT critical reading scores over 600: 51%; SAT math scores over 600: 75%; SAT writ-

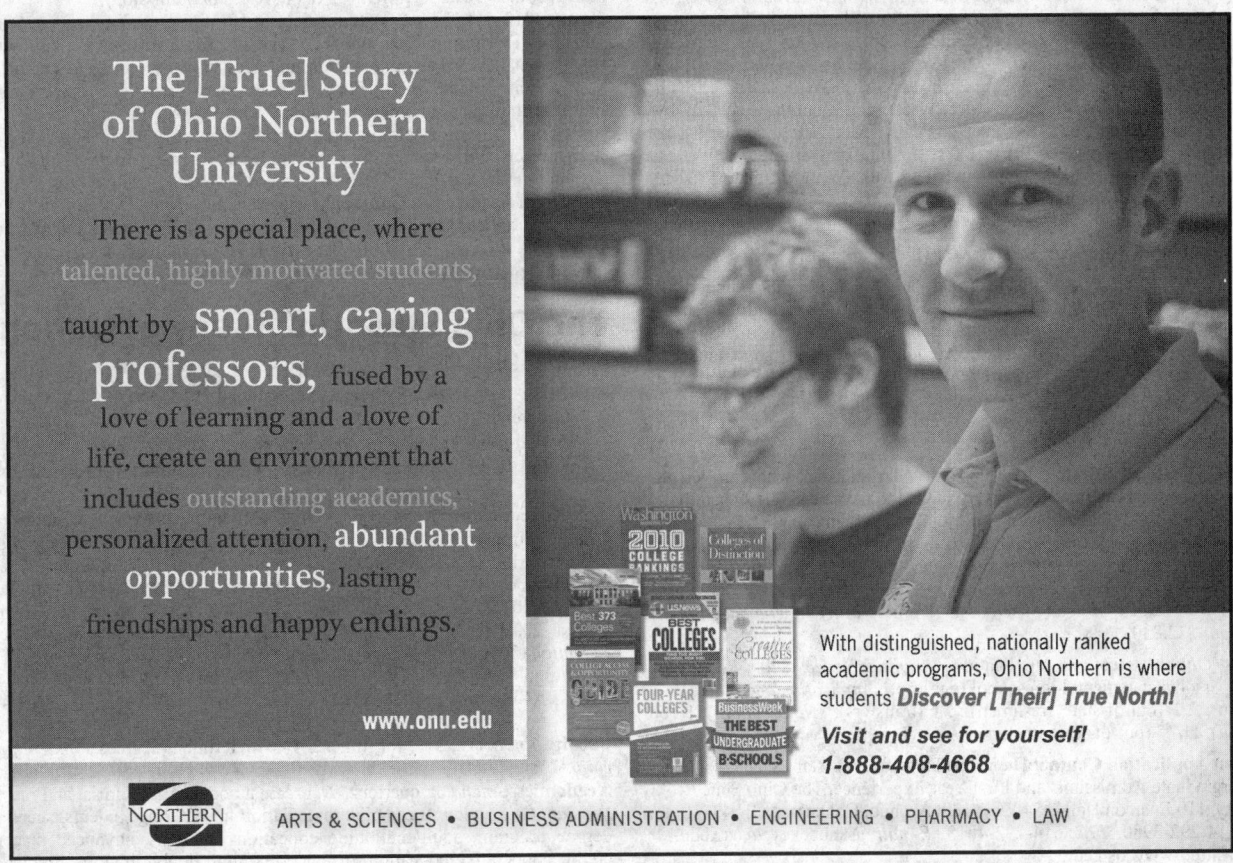

The [True] Story of Ohio Northern University

There is a special place, where talented, highly motivated students, taught by **smart, caring professors,** fused by a love of learning and a love of life, create an environment that includes outstanding academics, personalized attention, **abundant opportunities,** lasting friendships and happy endings.

www.onu.edu

With distinguished, nationally ranked academic programs, Ohio Northern is where students *Discover [Their] True North!*

Visit and see for yourself!
1-888-408-4668

NORTHERN   ARTS & SCIENCES • BUSINESS ADMINISTRATION • ENGINEERING • PHARMACY • LAW ing scores over 600: 46%; ACT scores over 24: 91%; SAT critical reading scores over 700: 12%; SAT math scores over 700: 28%; SAT writing scores over 700: 9%; ACT scores over 30: 31%.

Faculty *Total:* 4,632, 73% full-time, 72% with terminal degrees. *Student/faculty ratio:* 19:1.

Academics *Calendar:* quarters. *Degrees:* certificates, associate, bachelor's, master's, doctoral-professional, doctoral-research/scholarship, post-master's, and postbachelor's certificates. *Special study options:* academic remediation for entering students, accelerated degree program, adult/continuing education programs, advanced placement credit, cooperative education, distance learning, double majors, English as a second language, freshman honors college, honors programs, independent study, internships, off-campus study, part-time degree program, services for LD students, student-designed majors, study abroad, summer session for credit. *ROTC:* Army (b), Navy (b), Air Force (b). *Unusual degree programs:* 3-2 business administration.

Computers on Campus 675 computers/terminals are available on campus for general student use. Students can access the following: campus intranet, computer help desk, free student e-mail accounts, online (class) grades, online (class) registration, online (class) schedules, students can apply for admission, register, check grades, pay fees and obtain library resources, including books, online. Campuswide network is available. 100% of college-owned or -operated housing units are wired for high-speed Internet access. Wireless service is available via entire campus.

Student Life *Housing:* on-campus residence required for freshman year. *Options:* coed, women-only, cooperative, disabled students. Campus housing is university owned. Freshman campus housing is guaranteed. *Activities and organizations:* drama/theater group, student-run newspaper, radio and television station, choral group, marching band, African Student Union, Bisexual, Gay and Lesbian Alliance, Campus Crusade for Christ, University Wide Council of Hispanic Organizations, Asian-American Association, national fraternities, national sororities. *Campus security:* 24-hour emergency response devices and patrols, student patrols, late-night transport/escort service, controlled dormitory access, dorm entrances locked after 9 pm, lighted pathways and sidewalks, self-defense education. *Student services:* health clinic, personal/psychological counseling, women's center, legal services.

Athletics Member NCAA. All Division I except football (Division I-A). *Intercollegiate sports:* baseball M(s), basketball M(s)/W(s), cheerleading M/W, cross-country running M(s)/W(s), fencing M(s)/W(s), field hockey W(s), golf M(s)/W(s), gymnastics M(s)/W(s), ice hockey M(s)/W(s), lacrosse M(s)/W(s), riflery M/W, soccer M(s)/W(s), softball W(s), swimming and diving M(s)/W(s), tennis M(s)/W(s), track and field M(s)/W(s), volleyball M(s)/W(s), wrestling M(s). *Intramural sports:* badminton M(c)/W(c), baseball M(c), basketball M/W, bowling M(c)/W(c), crew M(c)/W, cross-country running M/W, equestrian sports M(c)/W(c), fencing M(c)/W(c), field hockey W, football M/W, golf M/W, gymnastics M(c)/W(c), ice hockey M(c)/W(c), lacrosse M(c)/W(c), racquetball M(c)/W(c), riflery M(c)/W(c), rock climbing M/W, rugby M(c)/W(c), sailing M(c)/W(c), skiing (downhill) M(c)/W(c), soccer M(c)/W(c), softball W(c), squash M(c)/W(c), swimming and diving M(c)/W(c), table tennis M/W, tennis M/W, track and field M(c)/W(c), ultimate Frisbee M(c)/W(c), volleyball M(c)/W(c), water polo M(c)/W(c), weight lifting M(c), wrestling M/W.

Standardized Tests *Required:* SAT or ACT (for admission).

Costs (2011–12) *Tuition:* state resident $250 per quarter hour part-time; nonresident $644 per quarter hour part-time. Full-time tuition and fees vary according to course load, location, program, and reciprocity agreements. Part-time tuition and fees vary according to course load, location, program, and reciprocity agreements. *Room and board:* $9180; room only: $6585. Room and board charges vary according to board plan, housing facility, and location. *Payment plan:* installment. *Waivers:* senior citizens and employees or children of employees.

Financial Aid Of all full-time matriculated undergraduates who enrolled in 2009, 26,410 applied for aid, 21,612 were judged to have need, 3,109 had their need fully met. 2,187 Federal Work-Study jobs (averaging $2034). 206 state and other part-time jobs (averaging $2432). In 2009, 6856 non-need-based awards were made. *Average percent of need met:* 57%. *Average financial aid package:* $10,575. *Average need-based loan:* $4696. *Average need-based gift aid:* $7789. *Average non-need-based aid:* $4704. *Average indebtedness upon graduation:* $22,830.

Applying *Options:* electronic application. *Application fee:* $40. *Required:* essay or personal statement, high school transcript. *Application deadlines:* 2/1 (freshmen), 2/1 (out-of-state freshmen), 6/1 (transfers). *Notification:* 11/15 (freshmen), 11/15 (out-of-state freshmen).

Freshman Application Contact Dr. Mabel Freeman, Assistant Vice President for Undergraduate Admissions and First Year Experience, The Ohio State University, 110 Enarson Hall, 154 West 12th Avenue, Columbus, OH 43210. *Phone:* 614-292-3980. *Fax:* 614-292-4818. *E-mail:* askabuckeye@osu.edu. *Web site:* http://www.osu.edu/.

The Ohio State University at Lima
Lima, Ohio

- **State-supported** comprehensive, founded 1960, part of Ohio State University System
- **Suburban** 565-acre campus
- **Coed** 1,430 undergraduate students, 85% full-time, 52% women, 48% men
- **Noncompetitive** entrance level, 99% of applicants were admitted

Undergraduates 1,219 full-time, 211 part-time. Students come from 6 states and territories; 5% Black or African American, non-Hispanic/Latino; 2% Hispanic/Latino; 0.8% Asian, non-Hispanic/Latino; 0.3% American Indian or Alaska Native, non-Hispanic/Latino; 0.7% Two or more races, non-Hispanic/Latino; 1% Race/ethnicity unknown; 8% transferred in. *Retention:* 63% of full-time freshmen returned.

Freshmen *Admission:* 1,141 applied, 1,129 admitted, 488 enrolled. *Test scores:* SAT critical reading scores over 500: 44%; SAT math scores over 500: 60%; SAT writing scores over 500: 40%; ACT scores over 18: 90%; SAT critical reading scores over 600: 16%; SAT math scores over 600: 16%; SAT writing scores over 600: 8%; ACT scores over 24: 31%; SAT critical reading scores over 700: 4%; SAT math scores over 700: 4%; ACT scores over 30: 1%.

Faculty *Total:* 86, 47% full-time. *Student/faculty ratio:* 23:1.

Academics *Calendar:* quarters. *Degrees:* associate, bachelor's, and master's. *Special study options:* academic remediation for entering students, accelerated degree program, adult/continuing education programs, advanced placement credit, cooperative education, distance learning, double majors, English as a second language, freshman honors college, honors programs, independent study, internships, off-campus study, part-time degree program, services for LD students, student-designed majors, study abroad, summer session for credit. *ROTC:* Army (c), Navy (c), Air Force (c).

Computers on Campus 150 computers/terminals are available on campus for general student use. Students can access the following: campus intranet, computer help desk, free student e-mail accounts, online (class) grades, online (class) registration, online (class) schedules. Campuswide network is available. Wireless service is available via entire campus.

Student Life *Housing:* college housing not available. *Activities and organizations:* choral group. *Campus security:* 24-hour emergency response devices and patrols, student patrols, late-night transport/escort service, lighted pathways/sidewalks. *Student services:* personal/psychological counseling.

Athletics *Intramural sports:* baseball M(c), basketball M(c)/W(c), football M/W, golf M(c)/W(c), soccer M/W, volleyball M(c)/W(c).

Standardized Tests *Required:* SAT or ACT (for admission).

Costs (2010–11) *Tuition:* state resident $6102 full-time; nonresident $20,286 full-time. Full-time tuition and fees vary according to course load, location, and student level. Part-time tuition and fees vary according to course load, location, and student level. *Payment plan:* installment. *Waivers:* senior citizens and employees or children of employees.

Applying *Options:* electronic application. *Application fee:* $40. *Required:* essay or personal statement, high school transcript. *Application deadline:* 7/1 (freshmen). *Notification:* 11/15 (freshmen).

Freshman Application Contact Ms. Garlene Smithson, Director of Admissions, The Ohio State University at Lima, 4240 Campus Drive, Lima, OH 45804. *Phone:* 419-995-8434. *Fax:* 419-995-8483. *E-mail:* admissions@lima.ohio-state.edu. *Web site:* http://lima.osu.edu/.

The Ohio State University at Marion
Marion, Ohio

- **State-supported** comprehensive, founded 1958, part of Ohio State University System
- **Small-town** 188-acre campus with easy access to Columbus
- **Coed** 1,749 undergraduate students, 85% full-time, 54% women, 46% men
- **Noncompetitive** entrance level, 97% of applicants were admitted

Undergraduates 1,492 full-time, 257 part-time. Students come from 4 states and territories; 10% Black or African American, non-Hispanic/Latino; 2% Hispanic/Latino; 4% Asian, non-Hispanic/Latino; 0.5% American Indian or Alaska Native, non-Hispanic/Latino; 0.4% Two or more races, non-Hispanic/Latino; 2% Race/ethnicity unknown; 0.1% international; 4% transferred in. *Retention:* 70% of full-time freshmen returned.

Freshmen *Admission:* 1,039 applied, 1,007 admitted, 597 enrolled. *Test scores:* ACT scores over 18: 85%; ACT scores over 24: 34%; ACT scores over 30: 2%.

Faculty *Total:* 118, 31% full-time, 31% with terminal degrees. *Student/faculty ratio:* 25:1.

Academics *Calendar:* quarters. *Degrees:* associate, bachelor's, and master's. *Special study options:* academic remediation for entering students, accelerated degree program, adult/continuing education programs, advanced placement credit, cooperative education, distance learning, double majors, English as a second language, freshman honors college, honors programs, independent study, internships, off-campus study, part-time degree program, services for LD students, student-designed majors, study abroad, summer session for credit. *ROTC:* Army (c), Navy (c), Air Force (c).

Computers on Campus 163 computers/terminals are available on campus for general student use. Students can access the following: campus intranet, computer help desk, free student e-mail accounts, online (class) grades, online (class) registration, online (class) schedules. Campuswide network is available. Wireless service is available via classrooms, libraries.

Student Life *Activities and organizations:* choral group. *Campus security:* 24-hour emergency response devices. *Student services:* personal/psychological counseling.

Athletics Member USCAA. *Intercollegiate sports:* basketball M, golf M, volleyball W. *Intramural sports:* cheerleading M(c)/W(c), rugby M(c)/W(c), skiing (downhill) M(c)/W(c), soccer M(c)/W(c), softball M(c)/W(c), table tennis M/W.

Standardized Tests *Required:* SAT or ACT (for admission).

Costs (2010–11) *Tuition:* state resident $6102 full-time; nonresident $20,286 full-time. Full-time tuition and fees vary according to course load and student level. Part-time tuition and fees vary according to course load and student level. *Payment plan:* installment. *Waivers:* senior citizens and employees or children of employees.

Applying *Options:* electronic application. *Application fee:* $40. *Required:* essay or personal statement, high school transcript. *Application deadlines:* 7/1 (freshmen), 7/1 (out-of-state freshmen), 7/1 (transfers). *Notification:* 11/15 (freshmen), 11/15 (out-of-state freshmen).

Freshman Application Contact Mr. Matthew Moreau, Admissions and Financial Aid Coordinator, The Ohio State University at Marion, 1465 Mount Vernon Avenue, Marion, OH 43302. *Phone:* 740-725-6337. *Fax:* 740-386-2439. *E-mail:* moreau.1@osu.edu. *Web site:* http://osumarion.osu.edu/.

The Ohio State University–Mansfield Campus
Mansfield, Ohio

- **State-supported** comprehensive, founded 1958, part of Ohio State University System
- **Small-town** 640-acre campus with easy access to Columbus and Cleveland
- **Coed** 1,341 undergraduate students, 86% full-time, 56% women, 44% men
- **Noncompetitive** entrance level, 98% of applicants were admitted

Undergraduates 1,147 full-time, 194 part-time. Students come from 5 states and territories; 6% Black or African American, non-Hispanic/Latino; 2% Hispanic/Latino; 1% Asian, non-Hispanic/Latino; 0.5% American Indian or Alaska Native, non-Hispanic/Latino; 0.2% Two or more races, non-Hispanic/Latino; 2% Race/ethnicity unknown; 6% transferred in; 15% live on campus. *Retention:* 67% of full-time freshmen returned.

Freshmen *Admission:* 1,526 applied, 1,500 admitted, 522 enrolled. *Test scores:* SAT critical reading scores over 500: 67%; SAT math scores over 500: 69%; SAT writing scores over 500: 59%; ACT scores over 18: 94%; SAT critical reading scores over 600: 8%; SAT math scores over 600: 10%; SAT writing scores over 600: 13%; ACT scores over 24: 41%; SAT math scores over 700: 2%; ACT scores over 30: 2%.

Faculty *Total:* 91, 48% full-time, 47% with terminal degrees. *Student/faculty ratio:* 20:1.

Academics *Calendar:* quarters. *Degrees:* associate, bachelor's, and master's. *Special study options:* academic remediation for entering students, accelerated degree program, adult/continuing education programs, advanced placement credit, cooperative education, distance learning, double majors, English as a second language, freshman honors college, honors programs, independent study, internships, off-campus study, part-time degree program, services for LD students, student-designed majors, study abroad, summer session for credit. *ROTC:* Army (c), Navy (c), Air Force (c).

Computers on Campus 260 computers/terminals are available on campus for general student use. Students can access the following: campus intranet, computer help desk, free student e-mail accounts, online (class) grades, online (class) registration, online (class) schedules. Campuswide network is available. 100% of college-owned or -operated housing units are wired for high-speed Internet access. Wireless service is available via computer centers, libraries, student centers.

Student Life *Housing options:* coed, disabled students. Campus housing is university owned. *Activities and organizations:* drama/theater group, choral group. *Campus security:* 24-hour emergency response devices and patrols, late-night transport/escort service. *Student services:* personal/psychological counseling.

Athletics *Intramural sports:* baseball M(c), basketball M(c)/W(c), bowling M/W, cheerleading M(c)/W(c), football M/W, golf M/W, soccer M(c), softball M/W, table tennis M/W, tennis M/W, volleyball M/W(c).

Standardized Tests *Required:* SAT or ACT (for admission).

Costs (2010–11) *Tuition:* state resident $6102 full-time; nonresident $20,286 full-time. Full-time tuition and fees vary according to course load, location, and student level. Part-time tuition and fees vary according to course load, location, and student level. *Room only:* $5205. Room and board charges vary according to housing facility. *Payment plan:* installment. *Waivers:* senior citizens and employees or children of employees.

Applying *Options:* electronic application. *Application fee:* $40. *Required:* essay or personal statement, high school transcript. *Application deadlines:* 7/1 (freshmen), 7/1 (out-of-state freshmen). *Notification:* 11/15 (freshmen), 11/15 (out-of-state freshmen).

Freshman Application Contact Mr. Henry D. Thomas, Coordinator of Admissions and Financial Aid, The Ohio State University–Mansfield Campus, 1760 University Drive, Mansfield, OH 44906. *Phone:* 419-755-4225. *Fax:* 419-755-4241. *E-mail:* admissions@mansfield.ohio-state.edu. *Web site:* http://www.mansfield.osu.edu/.

The Ohio State University–Newark Campus
Newark, Ohio

- **State-supported** comprehensive, founded 1957, part of Ohio State University System
- **Small-town** 106-acre campus with easy access to Columbus
- **Coed** 2,467 undergraduate students, 86% full-time, 49% women, 51% men
- **Noncompetitive** entrance level, 98% of applicants were admitted

Undergraduates 2,126 full-time, 341 part-time. Students come from 12 states and territories; 1% are from out of state; 12% Black or African American, non-Hispanic/Latino; 2% Hispanic/Latino; 3% Asian, non-Hispanic/Latino; 0.4% American Indian or Alaska Native, non-Hispanic/Latino; 0.7% Two or more races, non-Hispanic/Latino; 2% Race/ethnicity unknown; 4% transferred in; 7% live on campus. *Retention:* 61% of full-time freshmen returned.

Freshmen *Admission:* 2,676 applied, 2,624 admitted, 1,132 enrolled. *Test scores:* SAT critical reading scores over 500: 50%; SAT math scores over 500: 53%; SAT writing scores over 500: 34%; ACT scores over 18: 85%; SAT critical reading scores over 600: 7%; SAT math scores over 600: 13%; SAT writing scores over 600: 5%; ACT scores over 24: 29%; SAT math scores over 700: 1%; ACT scores over 30: 1%.

Faculty *Total:* 137, 39% full-time, 39% with terminal degrees. *Student/faculty ratio:* 27:1.

Academics *Calendar:* quarters. *Degrees:* associate, bachelor's, and master's. *Special study options:* academic remediation for entering students, accelerated degree program, adult/continuing education programs, advanced placement credit, cooperative education, distance learning, double majors, English as a second language, freshman honors college, honors programs, independent study, internships, off-campus study, part-time degree program, services for LD students, student-designed majors, study abroad, summer session for credit. *ROTC:* Army (b), Navy (c), Air Force (c).

Computers on Campus 1,100 computers/terminals are available on campus for general student use. Students can access the following: campus intranet, computer help desk, free student e-mail accounts, online (class) grades, online (class) registration, online (class) schedules. Campuswide network is available. 100% of college-owned or -operated housing units are wired for high-speed Internet access. Wireless service is available via entire campus.

Student Life *Housing options:* coed. Campus housing is university owned. *Activities and organizations:* choral group. *Campus security:* 24-hour emergency response devices and patrols, late-night transport/escort service, self-defense education. *Student services:* personal/psychological counseling.

Athletics *Intramural sports:* baseball M(c), basketball M(c)/W(c), football M(c)/W(c), golf M(c)/W(c), soccer M(c)/W(c), softball W(c), volleyball M(c)/W(c), weight lifting M(c)/W(c).

Standardized Tests *Required:* SAT or ACT (for admission).

Costs (2010–11) *Tuition:* state resident $6102 full-time; nonresident $20,286 full-time. Full-time tuition and fees vary according to course load and student level. Part-time tuition and fees vary according to course load and student level. *Room and board:* $7185; room only: $6075. Room and board charges vary according to housing facility. *Payment plan:* installment. *Waivers:* employees or children of employees.

Applying *Options:* electronic application. *Application fee:* $40. *Required:* essay or personal statement, high school transcript. *Application deadlines:* 7/1 (freshmen), 7/1 (out-of-state freshmen). *Notification:* 11/15 (freshmen), 11/15 (out-of-state freshmen).

Freshman Application Contact Ms. Ann Donahue, Director of Enrollment, The Ohio State University–Newark Campus, 1179 University Drive, Newark, OH 43055. *Phone:* 740-366-9333. *Fax:* 740-364-9645. *E-mail:* barclay.3@osu.edu. *Web site:* http://www.newark.osu.edu/.

Ohio University

Athens, Ohio

- **State-supported** university, founded 1804, part of Ohio Board of Regents, University System of Ohio
- **Small-town** 1762-acre campus
- **Endowment** $277.2 million
- **Coed** 20,994 undergraduate students, 82% full-time, 57% women, 43% men
- **Moderately difficult** entrance level, 85% of applicants were admitted

Undergraduates 17,117 full-time, 3,877 part-time. Students come from 46 states and territories; 43 other countries; 9% are from out of state; 5% Black or African American, non-Hispanic/Latino; 2% Hispanic/Latino; 0.8% Asian, non-Hispanic/Latino; 0.1% Native Hawaiian or other Pacific Islander, non-Hispanic/Latino; 0.3% American Indian or Alaska Native, non-Hispanic/Latino; 2% Two or more races, non-Hispanic/Latino; 1% Race/ethnicity unknown; 4% international; 2% transferred in; 40% live on campus. *Retention:* 81% of full-time freshmen returned.

Freshmen *Admission:* 13,366 applied, 11,372 admitted, 3,983 enrolled. *Average high school GPA:* 3.38. *Test scores:* SAT critical reading scores over 500: 72%; SAT math scores over 500: 74%; SAT writing scores over 500: 67%; ACT scores over 18: 99%; SAT critical reading scores over 600: 31%; SAT math scores over 600: 32%; SAT writing scores over 600: 23%; ACT scores over 24: 50%; SAT critical reading scores over 700: 6%; SAT math scores over 700: 5%; SAT writing scores over 700: 3%; ACT scores over 30: 9%.

Faculty *Total:* 1,181, 76% full-time, 79% with terminal degrees. *Student/faculty ratio:* 19:1.

Academics *Calendar:* quarters. *Degrees:* associate, bachelor's, master's, doctoral-professional, and doctoral-research/scholarship. *Special study options:* academic remediation for entering students, accelerated degree program, adult/continuing education programs, advanced placement credit, cooperative education, distance learning, double majors, English as a second language, external degree program, honors programs, independent study, internships, off-campus study, part-time degree program, services for LD students, student-designed majors, study abroad, summer session for credit. *ROTC:* Army (b), Air Force (b).

Computers on Campus 1,000 computers/terminals and 22,000 ports are available on campus for general student use. Students can access the following: computer help desk, free student e-mail accounts, online (class) grades, online (class) registration, online (class) schedules. Campuswide network is available. 100% of college-owned or -operated housing units are wired for high-speed Internet access. Wireless service is available via entire campus.

Student Life *Housing:* on-campus residence required through sophomore year. *Options:* coed, women-only, disabled students. Campus housing is university owned. Freshman campus housing is guaranteed. *Activities and organizations:* drama/theater group, student-run newspaper, radio and television station, choral group, marching band, Alpha Phi Omega, Golden Key Honor Society, International Student Union, Kappa Delta Pi, Campus Crusade for Christ, national fraternities, national sororities. *Campus security:* 24-hour emergency response devices and patrols, student patrols, late-night transport/escort service, Electronic dormitory access is being phased in gradually as part of renovations. *Student services:* health clinic, personal/psychological counseling, women's center, legal services.

Athletics Member NCAA. All Division I except football (Division I-A). *Intercollegiate sports:* baseball M(s), basketball M(s)/W(s), cheerleading M/W, cross-country running M(s)/W(s), field hockey W(s), golf M(s)/W(s), ice hockey M(c), soccer W(s), softball W(s), swimming and diving W(s), track and field W(s), volleyball W(s), wrestling M(s). *Intramural sports:* badminton M/W, baseball M(c), basketball M/W, crew M(c)/W(c), equestrian sports M(c)/W(c), fencing M(c)/W(c), field hockey M(c)/W(c), golf M/W, gymnastics M(c)/W(c), lacrosse M(c)/W(c), racquetball M/W, rugby M(c)/W(c), soccer M(c)/W(c), softball M/W, tennis M(c)/W(c), ultimate Frisbee M(c)/W(c), volleyball M(c)/W(c), water polo M(c)/W, wrestling M(c)/W(c).

Standardized Tests *Required:* SAT or ACT (for admission).

Costs (2010–11) *Tuition:* state resident $9603 full-time, $304 per quarter hour part-time; nonresident $18,567 full-time, $599 per quarter hour part-time. Full-time tuition and fees vary according to degree level, location, and program. Part-time tuition and fees vary according to course load, degree level, location, and program. *Room and board:* $9621; room only: $5325. Room and board charges vary according to board plan. *Payment plan:* installment. *Waivers:* senior citizens and employees or children of employees.

Financial Aid Of all full-time matriculated undergraduates who enrolled in 2009, 12,651 applied for aid, 9,117 were judged to have need, 1,393 had their need fully met. In 2009, 2123 non-need-based awards were made. *Average percent of need met:* 58%. *Average financial aid package:* $8484. *Average need-based loan:* $4287. *Average need-based gift aid:* $7145. *Average non-need-based aid:* $3656. *Average indebtedness upon graduation:* $22,095.

Applying *Options:* electronic application, early admission, deferred entrance. *Application fee:* $45. *Required:* high school transcript. *Required for some:* essay or personal statement, interview, auditions required for music and dance. *Recommended:* 2 letters of recommendation. *Application deadlines:* 2/1 (freshmen), 2/1 (out-of-state freshmen), 6/15 (transfers). *Notification:* continuous (freshmen), continuous (out-of-state freshmen), continuous (transfers).

Freshman Application Contact Undergraduate Admissions, Ohio University, Athens, OH 45701-2979. *Phone:* 740-593-4100. *Fax:* 740-593-0560. *E-mail:* admissions@ohio.edu. *Web site:* http://www.ohio.edu/.

Ohio University–Chillicothe

Chillicothe, Ohio

- **State-supported** comprehensive, founded 1946, part of Ohio Board of Regents
- **Small-town** 124-acre campus with easy access to Columbus
- **Coed** 2,558 undergraduate students
- **Noncompetitive** entrance level

Academics *Calendar:* quarters. *Degrees:* associate, bachelor's, and master's (offers first 2 years of most bachelor's degree programs available at the main campus in Athens; also offers several bachelor's degree programs that can be completed at this campus and several programs exclusive to this campus; also offers some graduate programs). *Special study options:* academic remediation for entering students, adult/continuing education programs, advanced placement credit, distance learning, external degree program, internships, part-time degree program, services for LD students, study abroad, summer session for credit.

Computers on Campus Students can access the following: online (class) registration. Campuswide network is available.

Student Life *Housing:* college housing not available. *Activities and organizations:* drama/theater group. *Campus security:* 24-hour emergency response devices, patrols by city police. *Student services:* personal/psychological counseling.

Athletics *Intramural sports:* baseball M(c), basketball M(c)/W(c), golf M(c), softball W(c), tennis M(c)/W(c), volleyball M(c)/W(c).

Standardized Tests *Required:* COMPASS (for admission).

Costs (2010–11) *Tuition:* state resident $3010 full-time; nonresident $5892 full-time. Full-time tuition and fees vary according to student level. Part-time tuition and fees vary according to student level. *Required fees:* $50 full-time.

Financial Aid Of all full-time matriculated undergraduates who enrolled in 2009, 1,450 applied for aid, 1,303 were judged to have need, 78 had their need fully met. In 2009, 28 non-need-based awards were made. *Average percent of need met:* 55%. *Average financial aid package:* $7751. *Average need-based loan:* $3794. *Average need-based gift aid:* $7730. *Average non-need-based aid:* $4362. *Average indebtedness upon graduation:* $22,095.

Applying *Options:* early admission, deferred entrance. *Required:* high school transcript. *Application deadlines:* 9/1 (freshmen), 9/1 (transfers). *Notification:* continuous (freshmen), continuous (transfers).

Freshman Application Contact Thomas Eveland, Manager, Recruitment and Admissions, Ohio University–Chillicothe, 101 University Drive, Chillicothe, OH 45601. *Phone:* 740-774-7241. *Toll-free phone:* 877-462-6824. *Fax:* 740-774-7214. *E-mail:* evelandt@ohio.edu. *Web site:* http://www.chillicothe.ohiou.edu/.

Ohio University–Eastern

St. Clairsville, Ohio

Director of Admissions N. Kip Howard, Assistant Vice President for Enrollment Services/Director of Admissions, Ohio University–Eastern, 45425 National Road, St. Clairsville, OH 43950-9724. *Phone:* 740-593-4120. *Toll-free phone:* 800-648-3331. *E-mail:* howardn@ohio.edu. *Web site:* http://www.eastern.ohiou.edu/.

Ohio University–Lancaster

Lancaster, Ohio

Director of Admissions Pat Fox, Enrollment Manager, Ohio University–Lancaster, 1570 Granville Pike, Lancaster, OH 43130-1097. *Phone:* 740-654-6711 Ext. 215. *Toll-free phone:* 888-446-4468 Ext. 215. *E-mail:* fox@ohio.edu. *Web site:* http://www.ohiou.edu/lancaster/.

Ohio University–Southern Campus

Ironton, Ohio

Director of Admissions Linda Harlow, Admission, Registration and Records Coordinator, Ohio University–Southern Campus, 1804 Liberty Avenue, Ironton, OH 45638-2214. *Phone:* 740-533-4584. *Toll-free phone:* 800-626-0513. *E-mail:* harlow@ohio.edu. *Web site:* http://www.ohiou.edu/.

Ohio University–Zanesville

Zanesville, Ohio

- **State-supported** comprehensive, founded 1946, administratively affiliated with Ohio University
- **Rural** 179-acre campus with easy access to Columbus
- **Coed** 1,983 undergraduate students, 59% full-time, 68% women, 32% men
- **Noncompetitive** entrance level, 84% of applicants were admitted

Undergraduates 1,166 full-time, 817 part-time. Students come from 2 states and territories; 1 other country; 1% are from out of state. *Retention:* 62% of full-time freshmen returned.
Freshmen *Admission:* 597 applied, 504 admitted, 330 enrolled. *Test scores:* ACT scores over 18: 74%; ACT scores over 24: 21%.
Faculty *Total:* 130, 24% full-time, 25% with terminal degrees. *Student/faculty ratio:* 23:1.
Academics *Calendar:* quarters. *Degrees:* associate and bachelor's (offers first 2 years of most bachelor's degree programs available at the main campus in Athens; also offers several bachelor's degree programs that can be completed at this campus; also offers some graduate courses). *Special study options:* academic remediation for entering students, adult/continuing education programs, advanced placement credit, distance learning, double majors, external degree program, independent study, off-campus study, part-time degree program, services for LD students, student-designed majors, summer session for credit.
Computers on Campus 200 computers/terminals are available on campus for general student use. Students can access the following: computer help desk, free student e-mail accounts, online (class) grades, online (class) registration, online (class) schedules. Campuswide network is available.
Student Life *Activities and organizations:* drama/theater group, student-run newspaper, radio station, Student Senate, Student Nurses Association, Drama Club, Green Bobcats, International Club. *Campus security:* night security. *Student services:* personal/psychological counseling.
Athletics *Intercollegiate sports:* baseball M, basketball M/W, golf M/W, softball W, tennis M/W, ultimate Frisbee M(s)/W(s), volleyball M(s)/W(s). *Intramural sports:* basketball M/W, bowling M/W, football M, golf M/W, skiing (downhill) M/W, soccer M/W, softball M/W, table tennis M/W, tennis M/W, ultimate Frisbee M/W, volleyball M/W.
Standardized Tests *Required for some:* SAT or ACT (for admission).
Costs (2011–12) *Tuition:* state resident $4662 full-time; nonresident $8985 full-time. Full-time tuition and fees vary according to student level. Part-time tuition and fees vary according to student level. *Payment plan:* installment. *Waivers:* senior citizens and employees or children of employees.
Financial Aid Of all full-time matriculated undergraduates who enrolled in 2009, 1,124 applied for aid, 959 were judged to have need, 90 had their need fully met. In 2009, 62 non-need-based awards were made. *Average percent of need met:* 59%. *Average financial aid package:* $7147. *Average need-based loan:* $3867. *Average need-based gift aid:* $7009. *Average non-need-based aid:* $2268. *Average indebtedness upon graduation:* $22,095.
Applying *Options:* electronic application. *Application fee:* $20. *Required:* high school transcript. *Application deadlines:* rolling (freshmen), rolling (transfers).
Freshman Application Contact Mrs. Karen Ragsdale, Student Services Secretary, Ohio University–Zanesville, Office of Student Services, 1425 Newark Road, Zanesville, OH 43701. *Phone:* 740-588-1440. *Fax:* 740-588-1444. *E-mail:* ouzservices@ohio.edu. *Web site:* http://www.zanesville.ohiou.edu/.

Ohio Wesleyan University

Delaware, Ohio

- **Independent United Methodist** 4-year, founded 1842
- **Small-town** 200-acre campus with easy access to Columbus
- **Coed** 1,919 undergraduate students, 99% full-time, 55% women, 45% men
- **Very difficult** entrance level, 69% of applicants were admitted

Undergraduates 1,899 full-time, 20 part-time. 48% are from out of state; 5% Black or African American, non-Hispanic/Latino; 2% Hispanic/Latino; 2% Asian, non-Hispanic/Latino; 0.6% American Indian or Alaska Native, non-Hispanic/Latino; 1% Two or more races, non-Hispanic/Latino; 2% Race/ethnicity unknown; 9% international; 1% transferred in; 89% live on campus. *Retention:* 87% of full-time freshmen returned.
Freshmen *Admission:* 4,139 applied, 2,873 admitted, 557 enrolled. *Average high school GPA:* 3.46. *Test scores:* SAT critical reading scores over 500: 81%; SAT math scores over 500: 80%; ACT scores over 18: 99%; SAT critical reading scores over 600: 43%; SAT math scores over 600: 46%; ACT scores over 24: 66%; SAT critical reading scores over 700: 12%; SAT math scores over 700: 11%; ACT scores over 30: 20%.
Faculty *Total:* 223, 61% full-time. *Student/faculty ratio:* 11:1.

Academics *Calendar:* semesters. *Degree:* bachelor's. *Special study options:* advanced placement credit, double majors, freshman honors college, honors programs, independent study, internships, off-campus study, part-time degree program, services for LD students, student-designed majors, study abroad, summer session for credit. *Unusual degree programs:* 3-2 engineering with Rensselaer Polytechnic Institute, California Institute of Technology, Case Western Reserve University, New York State College of Ceramics at Alfred University, Polytechnic Institute of New York, Washington University in St. Louis; medical technology, optometry, physical therapy.
Computers on Campus Campuswide network is available.
Student Life *Housing:* on-campus residence required through senior year. *Options:* coed, women-only. Campus housing is university owned. Freshman campus housing is guaranteed. *Activities and organizations:* drama/theater group, student-run newspaper, radio station, choral group, national fraternities, national sororities. *Campus security:* 24-hour emergency response devices and patrols, late-night transport/escort service, controlled dormitory access. *Student services:* health clinic, personal/psychological counseling, women's center.
Athletics Member NCAA. All Division III. *Intercollegiate sports:* baseball M, basketball M/W, cross-country running M/W, equestrian sports M(c)/W(c), field hockey W, football M, golf M, ice hockey M(c)/W(c), lacrosse M/W, rugby M(c)/W(c), sailing M(c)/W(c), soccer M/W, softball W, swimming and diving M/W, tennis M/W, track and field M/W, ultimate Frisbee M(c)/W(c), volleyball M(c)/W. *Intramural sports:* badminton M/W, basketball M/W, football M/W, golf M/W, lacrosse M/W, racquetball M/W, skiing (cross-country) M/W, skiing (downhill) M/W, soccer M/W, softball M/W, squash M/W, swimming and diving M/W, tennis M/W, track and field M/W, volleyball M/W, water polo M/W.
Standardized Tests *Required:* SAT or ACT (for admission).
Costs (2010–11) *Comprehensive fee:* $46,090 includes full-time tuition ($35,910), mandatory fees ($480), and room and board ($9700). Part-time tuition: $3920 per course. *College room only:* $4806. Room and board charges vary according to board plan. *Payment plan:* installment. *Waivers:* children of alumni and employees or children of employees.
Financial Aid Of all full-time matriculated undergraduates who enrolled in 2009, 1,310 applied for aid, 1,133 were judged to have need, 277 had their need fully met. 764 Federal Work-Study jobs (averaging $1717). 464 state and other part-time jobs (averaging $1965). In 2009, 667 non-need-based awards were made. *Average percent of need met:* 83%. *Average financial aid package:* $28,650. *Average need-based loan:* $5048. *Average need-based gift aid:* $28,217. *Average non-need-based aid:* $18,128. *Average indebtedness upon graduation:* $30,920. *Financial aid deadline:* 5/1.
Applying *Options:* electronic application, early admission, early action, deferred entrance. *Application fee:* $35. *Required:* essay or personal statement, high school transcript, minimum 2.5 GPA, 1 letter of recommendation. *Recommended:* 2 letters of recommendation, interview. *Application deadlines:* 3/1 (freshmen), rolling (transfers), 12/15 (early action). *Notification:* 3/1 (freshmen), continuous (transfers), 1/15 (early action).
Freshman Application Contact Ms. Carol DelPropost, Assistant Vice President of Admission and Financial Aid, Ohio Wesleyan University, 61 South Sandusky Street, Delaware, OH 43015. *Phone:* 740-368-3059. *Toll-free phone:* 800-922-8953. *Fax:* 740-368-3314. *E-mail:* cjdelpro@owu.edu. *Web site:* http://www.owu.edu/.

See page 670 for Display. See page 1488 for the College Close-Up.

Otterbein University

Westerville, Ohio

Freshman Application Contact Dr. Cass Johnson, Director of Admissions, Otterbein University, One Otterbein College, Westerville, OH 43081-9924. *Phone:* 614-823-1500. *Toll-free phone:* 800-488-8144. *Fax:* 614-823-1200. *E-mail:* uotterb@otterbein.edu. *Web site:* http://www.otterbein.edu/.

Pontifical College Josephinum

Columbus, Ohio

- **Independent Roman Catholic** comprehensive, founded 1888
- **Suburban** 100-acre campus
- **Endowment** $41.8 million
- **Men only**
- **Minimally difficult** entrance level

Faculty *Student/faculty ratio:* 7:1.
Academics *Calendar:* semesters. *Degrees:* bachelor's, master's, doctoral-professional, and postbachelor's certificates.
Student Life *Campus security:* 24-hour emergency response devices, controlled dormitory access.
Standardized Tests *Required:* SAT or ACT (for admission).

WHERE IN THE WORLD IS OHIO WESLEYAN?

EVERYWHERE.

On six continents and in more than 30 countries from Borneo to Brazil to Bangladesh, Ohio Wesleyan students are encountering the critical issues that will define their world.

As part of our unique travel-learning programs, they're turning classroom theory into practical solutions to real problems.

Ohio Wesleyan is located in Delaware, Ohio, but the world is our classroom.

This is one of many things that make us ...

THE OPPOSITE OF ORDINARY.

Ohio Wesleyan University

CONSIDER OWU.
www.owu.edu

Costs (2010–11) *Comprehensive fee:* $26,085 includes full-time tuition ($17,202), mandatory fees ($737), and room and board ($8146). *Part-time tuition:* $670 per credit hour. *College room only:* $4073.

Financial Aid *Of all full-time matriculated undergraduates who enrolled in 2007,* 63 applied for aid, 42 were judged to have need, 13 had their need fully met. 6 Federal Work-Study jobs (averaging $640). *In 2007,* 7 non-need-based awards were made. *Average percent of need met:* 74. *Average financial aid package:* $13,730. *Average need-based loan:* $4698. *Average need-based gift aid:* $1272. *Average non-need-based aid:* $2000. *Average indebtedness upon graduation:* $12,417.

Applying *Application fee:* $25. *Required:* essay or personal statement, high school transcript, 3 letters of recommendation, interview.

Freshman Application Contact Mrs. Arminda Crawford, Secretary for Admissions, Pontifical College Josephinum, 7825 North High Street, Columbus, OH 43235. *Phone:* 614-985-2241. *Toll-free phone:* 888-252-5812. *Fax:* 614-885-2307. *E-mail:* acrawford@pcj.edu. *Web site:* http://www.pcj.edu/.

Rabbinical College of Telshe
Wickliffe, Ohio

Freshman Application Contact Admissions Office, Rabbinical College of Telshe, 28400 Euclid Avenue, Wickliffe, OH 44092-2523. *Phone:* 440-943-5300.

Shawnee State University
Portsmouth, Ohio

- **State-supported** comprehensive, founded 1986
- **Small-town** 52-acre campus
- **Endowment** $10.8 million
- **Coed** 4,460 undergraduate students, 86% full-time, 58% women, 42% men
- **Noncompetitive** entrance level, 87% of applicants were admitted

Undergraduates 3,818 full-time, 642 part-time. Students come from 22 states and territories; 15 other countries; 8% are from out of state; 5% Black or African American, non-Hispanic/Latino; 0.5% Hispanic/Latino; 0.4% Asian, non-Hispanic/Latino; 0.1% Native Hawaiian or other Pacific Islander, non-Hispanic/Latino; 0.7% American Indian or Alaska Native, non-Hispanic/Latino; 0.7% Two or more races, non-Hispanic/Latino; 8% Race/ethnicity unknown; 0.7% international; 6% transferred in; 23% live on campus. *Retention:* 53% of full-time freshmen returned.

Freshmen *Admission:* 3,985 applied, 3,462 admitted, 1,171 enrolled. *Test scores:* ACT scores over 18: 71%; ACT scores over 24: 20%; ACT scores over 30: 2%.

Faculty *Total:* 327, 47% full-time. *Student/faculty ratio:* 19:1.

Academics *Calendar:* semesters. *Degrees:* certificates, associate, bachelor's, and master's. *Special study options:* academic remediation for entering students, accelerated degree program, adult/continuing education programs, advanced placement credit, distance learning, double majors, English as a second language, honors programs, independent study, internships, off-campus study, part-time degree program, services for LD students, student-designed majors, study abroad, summer session for credit.

Computers on Campus 620 computers/terminals are available on campus for general student use. Students can access the following: campus intranet, computer help desk, free student e-mail accounts, online (class) grades, online (class) registration, online (class) schedules, financial aid, student billing, courses, student service portal. Campuswide network is available. 100% of college-owned or -operated housing units are wired for high-speed Internet access. Wireless service is available via entire campus.

Student Life *Housing:* on-campus residence required for freshman year. *Options:* coed. Campus housing is university owned and leased by the school. Freshman applicants given priority for college housing. *Activities and organizations:* drama/theater group, student-run newspaper, choral group, campus ministry, Health Executives and Administrators Learning Society, Student Programming Board, Student Government Association, national fraternities. *Campus security:* 24-hour emergency response devices and patrols. *Student services:* health clinic, personal/psychological counseling, women's center.

Athletics Member NAIA. *Intercollegiate sports:* baseball M(s), basketball M(s)/W(s), cross-country running M(s)/W(s), golf M(s), soccer M(s)/W(s), softball W, tennis W(s), volleyball W(s). *Intramural sports:* basketball M/W, bowling M/W, golf M/W, racquetball M/W, softball M, swimming and diving M/W, table tennis M/W, tennis M/W, volleyball M/W.

Standardized Tests *Required for some:* ACT (for admission). *Recommended:* ACT (for admission).

Costs (2010–11) *Tuition:* state resident $5538 full-time, $231 per credit hour part-time; nonresident $10,182 full-time, $424 per credit hour part-time. Full-time tuition and fees vary according to course load, reciprocity agreements, and student level. Part-time tuition and fees vary according to course load, reciprocity agreements, and student level. *Required fees:* $1008 full-time, $42 per credit hour part-time. *Room and board:* $8416; room only: $5134. Room and board charges vary according to board plan and housing facility. *Payment plan:* installment. *Waivers:* senior citizens and employees or children of employees.

Applying *Options:* electronic application, deferred entrance. *Required:* high school transcript. *Required for some:* interview. *Application deadlines:* rolling (freshmen), rolling (out-of-state freshmen), rolling (transfers). *Notification:* continuous (freshmen), continuous (out-of-state freshmen), continuous (transfers).

Freshman Application Contact Shawnee State University, 940 Second Street, Portsmouth, OH 45662-4344. *Phone:* 740-351-3610 Ext. 610. *Toll-free phone:* 800-959-2SSU. *Web site:* http://www.shawnee.edu/.

Strayer University - Akron Campus
Akron, Ohio

- **Proprietary** comprehensive
- **Coed**

Academics *Degrees:* certificates, diplomas, associate, bachelor's, master's, and postbachelor's certificates.

Costs (2010–11) *Tuition:* $13,635 full-time, $1590 per course part-time.

Freshman Application Contact Strayer University - Akron Campus, 51 Park West Boulevard, Akron, OH 44320. *Web site:* http://strayer.edu/akron.

Strayer University - Cincinnati Campus
Cincinnati, Ohio

- **Proprietary** comprehensive
- **Coed**

Academics *Degrees:* certificates, diplomas, associate, bachelor's, master's, and postbachelor's certificates.

Freshman Application Contact Strayer University - Cincinnati Campus, 2135 Dana Avenue, Suite 300, Cincinnati, OH 45207. *Web site:* http://www.strayer.edu/cincinnati.

Strayer University - Columbus Campus
Columbus, Ohio

- **Proprietary** comprehensive
- **Coed**

Academics *Degrees:* certificates, diplomas, associate, bachelor's, master's, and postbachelor's certificates.

Costs (2010–11) *Tuition:* $13,635 full-time, $1590 per course part-time.

Freshman Application Contact Strayer University - Columbus Campus, 8425 Pulsar Place, Suite 400, Columbus, OH 43240. *Web site:* http://www.strayer.edu/columbus/.

Strayer University - Fairborn Campus
Fairborn, Ohio

- **Proprietary** comprehensive
- **Coed**

Academics *Degrees:* certificates, diplomas, associate, bachelor's, master's, and postbachelor's certificates.

Freshman Application Contact Strayer University - Fairborn Campus, 2600 Paramount Place, Suite 300, Fairborn, OH 45324. *Web site:* http://www.strayer.edu/fairborn.

Strayer University - Fairview Park Campus
Fairview Park, Ohio

- **Proprietary** comprehensive
- **Coed**

Academics *Degrees:* certificates, diplomas, associate, bachelor's, master's, and postbachelor's certificates.

Costs (2010–11) *Tuition:* $13,635 full-time, $1590 per course part-time.

Freshman Application Contact Strayer University - Fairview Park Campus, 22730 Fairview Center Drive, Suite 150, Fairview Park, OH 44126-3616. *Web site:* http://strayer.edu/fairview_park.

Strayer University - Mason Campus

Mason, Ohio

- **Proprietary** comprehensive
- **Coed**

Academics *Degrees:* certificates, diplomas, associate, bachelor's, master's, and postbachelor's certificates.
Costs (2010–11) *Tuition:* $13,635 full-time, $1590 per course part-time.
Freshman Application Contact Strayer University - Mason Campus, 4605 Duke Drive, Suite 700, Mason, OH 45040. *Web site:* http://www.strayer.edu/mason/.

Temple Baptist College

Cincinnati, Ohio

Admissions Office Contact Temple Baptist College, 11965 Kenn Road, Cincinnati, OH 45240. *Web site:* http://www.templebaptistcollege.com/.

Tiffin University

Tiffin, Ohio

- **Independent** comprehensive, founded 1888
- **Small-town** 110-acre campus with easy access to Toledo
- **Endowment** $5.0 million
- **Coed** 3,815 undergraduate students, 59% full-time, 59% women, 41% men
- **Moderately difficult** entrance level, 31% of applicants were admitted

Undergraduates 2,240 full-time, 1,582 part-time. Students come from 50 states and territories; 40 other countries; 29% are from out of state; 25% Black or African American, non-Hispanic/Latino; 4% Hispanic/Latino; 0.4% Asian, non-Hispanic/Latino; 0.1% Native Hawaiian or other Pacific Islander, non-Hispanic/Latino; 0.6% American Indian or Alaska Native, non-Hispanic/Latino; 20% Race/ethnicity unknown; 2% international; 9% transferred in; 22% live on campus. *Retention:* 62% of full-time freshmen returned.
Freshmen *Admission:* 6,630 applied, 2,078 admitted, 1,232 enrolled. *Average high school GPA:* 3.02. *Test scores:* SAT critical reading scores over 500: 39%; SAT math scores over 500: 39%; ACT scores over 18: 85%; SAT critical reading scores over 600: 13%; SAT math scores over 600: 6%; ACT scores over 24: 19%; ACT scores over 30: 1%.
Faculty *Total:* 403, 18% full-time, 33% with terminal degrees. *Student/faculty ratio:* 19:1.
Academics *Calendar:* semesters. *Degrees:* certificates, associate, bachelor's, master's, post-master's, and postbachelor's certificates. *Special study options:* academic remediation for entering students, accelerated degree program, adult/continuing education programs, advanced placement credit, distance learning, double majors, English as a second language, external degree program, freshman honors college, honors programs, independent study, internships, off-campus study, services for LD students, study abroad, summer session for credit. *ROTC:* Army (c), Air Force (c).
Computers on Campus 195 computers/terminals are available on campus for general student use. Students can access the following: campus intranet, computer help desk, free student e-mail accounts, online (class) grades, online (class) registration, online (class) schedules. Campuswide network is available. 100% of college-owned or -operated housing units are wired for high-speed Internet access. Wireless service is available via classrooms, computer centers, computer labs, dorm rooms, learning centers, libraries, student centers.
Student Life *Housing:* on-campus residence required through sophomore year. *Options:* coed, men-only, women-only, disabled students. Campus housing is university owned and leased by the school. Freshman campus housing is guaranteed. *Activities and organizations:* drama/theater group, student-run newspaper, choral group, marching band, Student Government Association, H2O, International Student Association, Global Affairs Organization, Circle K, national fraternities, national sororities. *Campus security:* 24-hour emergency response devices, student patrols, late-night transport/escort service. *Student services:* health clinic, personal/psychological counseling, women's center.
Athletics Member NCAA. All Division II. *Intercollegiate sports:* baseball M(s), basketball M(s)/W(s), cheerleading M(s)/W(s), cross-country running M(s)/W(s), equestrian sports M(s)/W(s), football M(s), golf M(s)/W(s), lacrosse M(s), soccer M(s)/W(s), softball W(s), tennis M(s)/W(s), track and field M(s)/W(s), volleyball W(s), wrestling M(s). *Intramural sports:* basketball M/W, bowling M/W, equestrian sports M(c)/W(c), football M, rugby M(c), soccer M/W, softball M/W, table tennis M/W, tennis M/W, ultimate Frisbee M/W, volleyball M/W, weight lifting M/W.
Standardized Tests *Required for some:* SAT or ACT (for admission).
Costs (2011–12) *Comprehensive fee:* $27,874 includes full-time tuition ($19,124) and room and board ($8750). Full-time tuition and fees vary according to course load, degree level, and location. Part-time tuition: $637 per credit hour. Part-time tuition and fees vary according to course load, degree level, and location. *College room only:* $4520. Room and board charges vary according

to board plan and housing facility. *Payment plan:* installment. *Waivers:* senior citizens and employees or children of employees.
Financial Aid Of all full-time matriculated undergraduates who enrolled in 2009, 1,965 applied for aid, 1,879 were judged to have need, 151 had their need fully met. 175 Federal Work-Study jobs (averaging $2416). *Average percent of need met:* 56%. *Average financial aid package:* $13,833. *Average need-based loan:* $4466. *Average need-based gift aid:* $19,087. *Average indebtedness upon graduation:* $29,130.
Applying *Options:* electronic application. *Application fee:* $20. *Required:* high school transcript. *Required for some:* essay or personal statement, interview. *Recommended:* minimum 3 GPA. *Application deadline:* rolling (freshmen). *Notification:* continuous (transfers).
Freshman Application Contact Mr. Jeremy Marinis, Director of Undergraduate Admissions, Tiffin University, 155 Miami Street, Tiffin, OH 44883. *Phone:* 419-448-3301. *Toll-free phone:* 800-968-6446. *Fax:* 419-443-5006. *E-mail:* marinisjj@tiffin.edu. *Web site:* http://www.tiffin.edu/.

Tri-State Bible College

South Point, Ohio

- **Independent nondenominational** 4-year, founded 1970
- **Suburban** 4-acre campus
- **Coed**

Academics *Calendar:* semesters. *Degrees:* associate and bachelor's.
Costs (2010–11) *One-time required fee:* $25. *Tuition:* $6000 full-time, $200 per semester hour part-time. *Required fees:* $298 full-time.
Applying *Application fee:* $25.
Freshman Application Contact Tri-State Bible College, 506 Margaret Street, PO Box 445, South Point, OH 45680-8402. *Phone:* 740-377-2520. *Web site:* http://www.tsbc.edu/.

Union Institute & University

Cincinnati, Ohio

- **Independent** university, founded 1969
- **Urban** 5-acre campus with easy access to Cincinnati
- **Endowment** $696,114
- **Coed** 968 undergraduate students, 68% full-time, 57% women, 43% men
- **Noncompetitive** entrance level

Undergraduates 661 full-time, 307 part-time. Students come from 41 states and territories; 2 other countries; 8% are from out of state; 29% Black or African American, non-Hispanic/Latino; 14% Hispanic/Latino; 1% Asian, non-Hispanic/Latino; 0.1% Native Hawaiian or other Pacific Islander, non-Hispanic/Latino; 1% American Indian or Alaska Native, non-Hispanic/Latino; 10% Race/ethnicity unknown; 30% transferred in. *Retention:* 79% of full-time freshmen returned.
Freshmen *Admission:* 19 enrolled.
Faculty *Total:* 294, 12% full-time, 51% with terminal degrees. *Student/faculty ratio:* 15:1.
Academics *Calendar:* trimesters some programs offer split (8wk) sessions. *Degrees:* bachelor's, master's, doctoral-research/scholarship, post-master's, and postbachelor's certificates. *Special study options:* accelerated degree program, adult/continuing education programs, advanced placement credit, distance learning, double majors, external degree program, independent study, internships, off-campus study, part-time degree program, services for LD students, summer session for credit.
Computers on Campus 65 computers/terminals are available on campus for general student use. Students can access the following: computer help desk, free student e-mail accounts, online (class) grades, online (class) registration, online (class) schedules, CampusWeb-online access to basic information and grades. Campuswide network is available. Wireless service is available via classrooms, computer labs, libraries.
Student Life *Campus security:* 24-hour emergency response devices, late-night transport/escort service, security personnel on site during business and class hours.
Costs (2010–11) *Tuition:* $11,016 full-time, $459 per semester hour part-time. *Required fees:* $116 full-time, $29 per term part-time. *Payment plan:* installment. *Waivers:* employees or children of employees.
Financial Aid Of all full-time matriculated undergraduates who enrolled in 2000, 587 applied for aid, 507 were judged to have need, 75 had their need fully met. 14 Federal Work-Study jobs (averaging $4500). *Average percent of need met:* 70%. *Average financial aid package:* $8000. *Average need-based loan:* $8000. *Average indebtedness upon graduation:* $26,250.
Applying *Options:* electronic application, deferred entrance. *Required:* essay or personal statement, recommendation from program faculty. *Required for some:* high school transcript, 1 letter of recommendation. *Recommended:* interview. *Application deadlines:* rolling (freshmen), rolling (out-of-state freshmen), rolling (transfers). *Notification:* continuous (freshmen), continuous (out-of-state freshmen), continuous (transfers).

Freshman Application Contact Union Institute & University, 440 East McMillan Street, Cincinnati, OH 45206-1925. *Phone:* 513-487-1173. *Toll-free phone:* 800-486-3116. *Web site:* http://www.myunion.edu/.

The University of Akron
Akron, Ohio

- **State-supported** university, founded 1870
- **Urban** 223-acre campus with easy access to Cleveland
- **Endowment** $156.0 million
- **Coed** 22,429 undergraduate students, 79% full-time, 49% women, 51% men
- **Moderately difficult** entrance level, 73% of applicants were admitted

Undergraduates 17,756 full-time, 4,673 part-time. Students come from 37 states and territories; 52 other countries; 3% are from out of state; 16% Black or African American, non-Hispanic/Latino; 2% Hispanic/Latino; 2% Asian, non-Hispanic/Latino; 0.1% Native Hawaiian or other Pacific Islander, non-Hispanic/Latino; 0.2% American Indian or Alaska Native, non-Hispanic/Latino; 1% Two or more races, non-Hispanic/Latino; 3% Race/ethnicity unknown; 1% international; 4% transferred in; 16% live on campus. *Retention:* 71% of full-time freshmen returned.

Freshmen *Admission:* 14,609 applied, 10,601 admitted, 4,648 enrolled. *Average high school GPA:* 2.98. *Test scores:* SAT critical reading scores over 500: 49%; SAT math scores over 500: 54%; ACT scores over 18: 76%; SAT critical reading scores over 600: 17%; SAT math scores over 600: 24%; ACT scores over 24: 28%; SAT critical reading scores over 700: 2%; SAT math scores over 700: 4%; ACT scores over 30: 4%.

Faculty *Total:* 1,731, 45% full-time, 53% with terminal degrees. *Student/faculty ratio:* 20:1.

Academics *Calendar:* semesters. *Degrees:* certificates, associate, bachelor's, master's, doctoral-professional, doctoral-research/scholarship, post-master's, and postbachelor's certificates. *Special study options:* academic remediation for entering students, accelerated degree program, adult/continuing education programs, advanced placement credit, cooperative education, distance learning, double majors, English as a second language, external degree program, freshman honors college, honors programs, independent study, internships, part-time degree program, services for LD students, student-designed majors, study abroad, summer session for credit. *ROTC:* Army (b), Air Force (c). *Unusual degree programs:* 3-2 accounting, BSMD (NEOUCOM), mathematics.

Computers on Campus 3,100 computers/terminals and 16,000 ports are available on campus for general student use. Students can access the following: campus intranet, computer help desk, free student e-mail accounts, online (class) grades, online (class) registration, online (class) schedules, library laptops for student checkout. Campuswide network is available. 100% of college-owned or -operated housing units are wired for high-speed Internet access. Wireless service is available via entire campus.

Student Life *Housing:* on-campus residence required for freshman year. *Options:* coed, men-only, women-only. Campus housing is university owned. Freshman applicants given priority for college housing. *Activities and organizations:* drama/theater group, student-run newspaper, radio and television station, choral group, marching band, Associated Student Government, Residence Hall Program Board, American Society of Mechanical Engineers, national fraternities, national sororities. *Campus security:* 24-hour emergency response devices and patrols, student patrols, late-night transport/escort service, controlled dormitory access. *Student services:* health clinic, personal/psychological counseling, women's center, legal services.

Athletics Member NCAA. All Division I except football (Division I-A). *Intercollegiate sports:* baseball M(s), basketball M(s)/W(s), cheerleading M/W, cross-country running M(s)/W(s), golf M(s)/W(s), riflery M/W(s), soccer M(s)/W(s), softball W(s), swimming and diving M/W, tennis W(s), track and field M(s)/W(s), volleyball W(s). *Intramural sports:* badminton M/W, basketball M/W, bowling M/W, cross-country running M/W, golf M/W, racquetball M/W, skiing (cross-country) M/W, skiing (downhill) M/W, soccer M/W, softball M/W, swimming and diving M/W, table tennis M/W, track and field M/W, volleyball W, wrestling M.

Standardized Tests *Required:* SAT or ACT (for admission).

Costs (2010–11) *Tuition:* state resident $7733 full-time, $322 per credit hour part-time; nonresident $15,389 full-time, $641 per credit hour part-time. Full-time tuition and fees vary according to course load, degree level, and location. Part-time tuition and fees vary according to course load, degree level, and location. *Required fees:* $1514 full-time, $49 per credit hour part-time. *Room and board:* $9160; room only: $5830. Room and board charges vary according to board plan and housing facility. *Payment plan:* installment. *Waivers:* senior citizens and employees or children of employees.

Financial Aid Of all full-time matriculated undergraduates who enrolled in 2009, 15,286 applied for aid, 13,853 were judged to have need, 2,744 had their need fully met. 637 Federal Work-Study jobs, 2,814 state and other part-time jobs. In 2009, 612 non-need-based awards were made. *Average percent of need met:* 61%. *Average financial aid package:* $7563. *Average need-based*

loan: $3919. *Average need-based gift aid:* $5021. *Average non-need-based aid:* $4118. *Average indebtedness upon graduation:* $28,421.

Applying *Options:* electronic application, early action, deferred entrance. *Application fee:* $40. *Required:* high school transcript. *Required for some:* essay or personal statement, 3 letters of recommendation, interview. *Application deadlines:* 8/11 (freshmen), rolling (transfers), 11/1 (early action). *Notification:* 9/15 (freshmen), continuous (transfers).

Freshman Application Contact The University of Akron, 302 Buchtel Common, Akron, OH 44325. *Phone:* 330-972-7100. *Toll-free phone:* 800-655-4884. *Web site:* http://www.uakron.edu/.

University of Cincinnati
Cincinnati, Ohio

- **State-supported** university, founded 1819, part of University System of Ohio
- **Urban** 137-acre campus with easy access to Cincinnati
- **Endowment** $1.1 billion
- **Coed** 22,449 undergraduate students, 83% full-time, 51% women, 49% men
- **Moderately difficult** entrance level, 62% of applicants were admitted

Undergraduates 18,704 full-time, 3,745 part-time. Students come from 53 states and territories; 87 other countries; 10% are from out of state; 9% Black or African American, non-Hispanic/Latino; 2% Hispanic/Latino; 3% Asian, non-Hispanic/Latino; 0.2% American Indian or Alaska Native, non-Hispanic/Latino; 0.6% Two or more races, non-Hispanic/Latino; 5% Race/ethnicity unknown; 2% international; 5% transferred in; 20% live on campus. *Retention:* 85% of full-time freshmen returned.

Freshmen *Admission:* 16,972 applied, 10,459 admitted, 3,758 enrolled. *Average high school GPA:* 3.44. *Test scores:* SAT critical reading scores over 500: 76%; SAT math scores over 500: 81%; SAT writing scores over 500: 70%; ACT scores over 18: 99%; SAT critical reading scores over 600: 34%; SAT math scores over 600: 43%; SAT writing scores over 600: 29%; ACT scores over 24: 62%; SAT critical reading scores over 700: 7%; SAT math scores over 700: 9%; SAT writing scores over 700: 5%; ACT scores over 30: 12%.

Faculty *Total:* 1,224, 97% full-time, 74% with terminal degrees. *Student/faculty ratio:* 17:1.

Academics *Calendar:* quarters. *Degrees:* certificates, associate, bachelor's, master's, doctoral-professional, doctoral-research/scholarship, post-master's, and postbachelor's certificates. *Special study options:* academic remediation for entering students, accelerated degree program, adult/continuing education programs, advanced placement credit, cooperative education, distance learning, double majors, English as a second language, honors programs, independent study, internships, off-campus study, part-time degree program, services for LD students, study abroad, summer session for credit. *ROTC:* Army (b), Air Force (b).

Computers on Campus Students can access the following: campus intranet, computer help desk, free student e-mail accounts, online (class) grades, online (class) registration, online (class) schedules. Campuswide network is available. 100% of college-owned or -operated housing units are wired for high-speed Internet access. Wireless service is available via entire campus.

Student Life *Housing:* on-campus residence required for freshman year. *Options:* coed, men-only, women-only, disabled students. Campus housing is university owned, leased by the school and is provided by a third party. Freshman campus housing is guaranteed. *Activities and organizations:* drama/theater group, student-run newspaper, radio station, choral group, marching band, Navigators, Criminal Justice Society, Serve Beyond Cincinnati, United Black Student Association, Engineering Tribunal, national fraternities, national sororities. *Campus security:* 24-hour emergency response devices and patrols, late-night transport/escort service, controlled dormitory access. *Student services:* health clinic, personal/psychological counseling, women's center.

Athletics Member NCAA. All Division I except football (Division I-A). *Intercollegiate sports:* baseball M(s), basketball M(s)/W(s), cheerleading M/W, cross-country running M(s)/W(s), golf M(s)/W(s), lacrosse W(s), soccer M(s)/W(s), swimming and diving M(s)/W(s), tennis W(s), track and field M(s)/W(s), volleyball W(s). *Intramural sports:* badminton M(c)/W(c), baseball M(c)/W(c), basketball M/W, bowling M(c)/W(c), crew M/W, fencing M(c)/W(c), football M(c)/W(c), golf M(c)/W(c), gymnastics W, ice hockey M(c), lacrosse M(c)/W(c), racquetball M/W, riflery M(c)/W(c), rugby M, soccer M/W, softball M/W, squash M/W, swimming and diving M/W, table tennis M(c)/W(c), tennis M(c)/W(c), track and field M(c)/W(c), ultimate Frisbee M(c)/W(c), volleyball M/W, water polo M(c)/W(c), weight lifting M, wrestling M(c)/W(c).

Standardized Tests *Required:* SAT or ACT (for admission).

Costs (2010–11) *Tuition:* state resident $8493 full-time, $236 per credit hour part-time; nonresident $23,016 full-time, $639 per credit hour part-time. Full-time tuition and fees vary according to course load, degree level, location, program, and reciprocity agreements. Part-time tuition and fees vary according to course load, degree level, location, program, and reciprocity agreements. *Required fees:* $1575 full-time, $44 per credit hour part-time. *Room and* *board:* $9702; room only: $5799. Room and board charges vary according to board plan and housing facility. *Payment plan:* installment. *Waivers:* employees or children of employees.

Financial Aid Of all full-time matriculated undergraduates who enrolled in 2009, 13,033 applied for aid, 10,458 were judged to have need, 481 had their need fully met. In 2009, 3090 non-need-based awards were made. *Average percent of need met:* 63%. *Average financial aid package:* $7843. *Average need-based loan:* $4223. *Average need-based gift aid:* $5883. *Average non-need-based aid:* $4755. *Average indebtedness upon graduation:* $25,878.

Applying *Options:* electronic application, deferred entrance. *Application fee:* $50. *Required:* essay or personal statement, high school transcript, minimum 2.7 GPA. *Required for some:* 2 letters of recommendation, audition. *Application deadlines:* 7/1 (freshmen), rolling (transfers). *Notification:* continuous (freshmen), continuous (transfers).

Freshman Application Contact Dr. Thomas Canepa EdD, Associate Vice President, Admissions, University of Cincinnati, Office of Admissions, PO Box210091, Cincinnati, OH 45221-0091. *Phone:* 513-556-1100. *Fax:* 513-556-1105. *E-mail:* admissions@uc.edu. *Web site:* http://www.uc.edu/.

University of Dayton
Dayton, Ohio

- **Independent Roman Catholic** university, founded 1850
- **Suburban** 373-acre campus with easy access to Cincinnati
- **Endowment** $346.6 million
- **Coed** 7,750 undergraduate students, 93% full-time, 49% women, 51% men
- **Moderately difficult** entrance level, 77% of applicants were admitted

Undergraduates 7,175 full-time, 575 part-time. Students come from 50 states and territories; 50 other countries; 40% are from out of state; 4% Black or African American, non-Hispanic/Latino; 3% Hispanic/Latino; 0.7% Asian, non-Hispanic/Latino; 0.1% Native Hawaiian or other Pacific Islander, non-Hispanic/Latino; 0.3% American Indian or Alaska Native, non-Hispanic/Latino; 0.8% Two or more races, non-Hispanic/Latino; 5% Race/ethnicity unknown; 3% international; 2% transferred in; 75% live on campus. *Retention:* 89% of full-time freshmen returned.

Freshmen *Admission:* 11,567 applied, 8,931 admitted, 2,036 enrolled. *Average high school GPA:* 3.51. *Test scores:* SAT critical reading scores over 500: 80%; SAT math scores over 500: 85%; SAT writing scores over 500: 76%; ACT scores over 18: 100%; SAT critical reading scores over 600: 33%; SAT math scores over 600: 41%; SAT writing scores over 600: 29%; ACT scores over 24: 77%; SAT critical reading scores over 700: 4%; SAT math scores over 700: 6%; SAT writing scores over 700: 4%; ACT scores over 30: 16%.

Faculty *Total:* 955, 51% full-time. *Student/faculty ratio:* 15:1.

Academics *Calendar:* semesters plus 2 6-week summer terms. *Degrees:* bachelor's, master's, doctoral-professional, doctoral-research/scholarship, post-master's, and postbachelor's certificates. *Special study options:* academic remediation for entering students, accelerated degree program, adult/continuing education programs, advanced placement credit, cooperative education, distance learning, double majors, English as a second language, honors programs, independent study, internships, off-campus study, part-time degree program, services for LD students, student-designed majors, study abroad, summer session for credit. *ROTC:* Army (b), Air Force (c). *Unusual degree programs:* 3-2 business administration; engineering.

Computers on Campus Students can access the following: campus intranet, computer help desk, free student e-mail accounts, online (class) grades, online (class) registration, online (class) schedules, applications, admission/enrollment status, virtual orientation, online digital resources, online courses, assistive technology, learning management system, multimedia labs, payment, cyber cafes, centrally-licensed, downloadable software and training. Campuswide network is available. 100% of college-owned or -operated housing units are wired for high-speed Internet access. Wireless service is available via entire campus.

Student Life *Housing:* on-campus residence required through sophomore year. *Options:* coed, men-only, women-only, disabled students. Campus housing is university owned. Freshman campus housing is guaranteed. *Activities and organizations:* drama/theater group, student-run newspaper, radio and television station, choral group, marching band, Student Government Association, marching band, Red Scare (basketball student cheering section), Campus Connection, Habitat for Humanity, national fraternities, national sororities. *Campus security:* 24-hour emergency response devices and patrols, student patrols, late-night transport/escort service, controlled dormitory access. *Student services:* health clinic, personal/psychological counseling, women's center.

Athletics Member NCAA. All Division I except football (Division I-AA). *Intercollegiate sports:* baseball M(s), basketball M(s)/W(s), cheerleading M/W, crew W, cross-country running M(s)/W(s), golf M(s)/W, soccer M(s)/W(s), softball W(s), tennis M(s)/W(s), track and field W(s), volleyball W(s). *Intramural sports:* badminton M/W, baseball M(c), basketball M/W, bowling M(c)/W(c), crew M(c), fencing M(c)/W(c), field hockey W(c), football M/W, golf M/W, gymnastics M(c)/W(c), ice hockey M(c), lacrosse M(c)/W(c), racquet-

ball M/W, rugby M(c)/W(c), soccer M(c)/W(c), softball M/W, tennis M/W, track and field M(c), ultimate Frisbee M(c)/W(c), volleyball M(c)/W(c), water polo M(c)/W(c), wrestling M(c)/W(c).

Standardized Tests *Required:* SAT or ACT (for admission).

Costs (2010–11) *Comprehensive fee:* $39,330 includes full-time tuition ($28,700), mandatory fees ($1230), and room and board ($9400). Full-time tuition and fees vary according to program. Part-time tuition: $957 per credit hour. Part-time tuition and fees vary according to course load and program. *Required fees:* $25 per term part-time. *College room only:* $5940. Room and board charges vary according to board plan and housing facility. *Payment plans:* installment, deferred payment. *Waivers:* senior citizens and employees or children of employees.

Financial Aid Of all full-time matriculated undergraduates who enrolled in 2009, 5,040 applied for aid, 4,034 were judged to have need, 1,464 had their need fully met. 1,235 Federal Work-Study jobs (averaging $2234), 4,251 state and other part-time jobs (averaging $2516). In 2009, 2968 non-need-based awards were made. *Average percent of need met:* 83%. *Average financial aid package:* $24,360. *Average need-based loan:* $5010. *Average need-based gift aid:* $12,490. *Average non-need-based aid:* $9961. *Average indebtedness upon graduation:* $35,421.

Applying *Options:* electronic application, early action, deferred entrance. *Required:* essay or personal statement, high school transcript, 1 letter of recommendation. *Required for some:* audition required for music, music therapy, music education programs. *Recommended:* interview. *Application deadlines:* 6/15 (transfers), 12/15 (early action). *Notification:* continuous (transfers), 1/15 (early action).

Freshman Application Contact Mr. Robert Durkle, Assistant Vice President and Dean of Admission, University of Dayton, 300 College Park, Dayton, OH 45469-1300. *Phone:* 937-229-4411. *Toll-free phone:* 800-837-7433. *Fax:* 937-229-4729. *E-mail:* admission@udayton.edu. *Web site:* http://www.udayton.edu/.

The University of Findlay
Findlay, Ohio

- **Independent** comprehensive, founded 1882, affiliated with Church of God
- **Urban** 390-acre campus with easy access to Toledo
- **Endowment** $22.4 million
- **Coed** 4,241 undergraduate students, 64% full-time, 62% women, 38% men
- **Moderately difficult** entrance level, 67% of applicants were admitted

Undergraduates 2,732 full-time, 1,509 part-time. Students come from 45 states and territories; 34 other countries; 19% are from out of state; 3% Black or African American, non-Hispanic/Latino; 2% Hispanic/Latino; 1% Asian, non-Hispanic/Latino; 0.3% American Indian or Alaska Native, non-Hispanic/Latino; 1% Two or more races, non-Hispanic/Latino; 20% Race/ethnicity unknown; 6% international; 2% transferred in; 40% live on campus. *Retention:* 73% of full-time freshmen returned.

Freshmen *Admission:* 2,887 applied, 1,945 admitted, 676 enrolled. *Average high school GPA:* 3.4. *Test scores:* SAT critical reading scores over 500: 68%; SAT math scores over 500: 66%; SAT writing scores over 500: 66%; ACT scores over 18: 93%; SAT critical reading scores over 600: 23%; SAT math scores over 600: 22%; SAT writing scores over 600: 20%; ACT scores over 24: 42%; SAT critical reading scores over 700: 4%; SAT math scores over 700: 2%; SAT writing scores over 700: 2%; ACT scores over 30: 8%.

Faculty *Total:* 305, 65% full-time, 49% with terminal degrees. *Student/faculty ratio:* 15:1.

Academics *Calendar:* semesters. *Degrees:* certificates, associate, bachelor's, master's, and doctoral-professional. *Special study options:* academic remediation for entering students, accelerated degree program, adult/continuing education programs, advanced placement credit, cooperative education, distance learning, double majors, English as a second language, honors programs, independent study, internships, off-campus study, part-time degree program, services for LD students, student-designed majors, study abroad, summer session for credit. *ROTC:* Army (c), Air Force (c). *Unusual degree programs:* 3-2 nursing with Mount Carmel College of Nursing.

Computers on Campus 274 computers/terminals are available on campus for general student use. Students can access the following: campus intranet, computer help desk, free student e-mail accounts, online (class) grades, online (class) registration, online (class) schedules. Campuswide network is available. 100% of college-owned or -operated housing units are wired for high-speed Internet access. Wireless service is available via entire campus.

Student Life *Housing:* on-campus residence required through junior year. *Options:* coed, men-only, women-only, disabled students. Campus housing is university owned. Freshman campus housing is guaranteed. *Activities and organizations:* drama/theater group, student-run newspaper, radio and television station, choral group, marching band, Campus Program Board, Pre-Vet Club, Horse Club, Circle K, International Club, national fraternities, national sororities. *Campus security:* 24-hour emergency response devices and patrols,

late-night transport/escort service. *Student services:* health clinic, personal/psychological counseling, women's center.
Athletics Member NCAA. All Division II. *Intercollegiate sports:* baseball M(s), basketball M(s)/W(s), cheerleading M/W, cross-country running M(s)/W(s), equestrian sports W, football M(s), golf M(s)/W(s), soccer M(s)/W(s), softball W(s), swimming and diving M(s)/W(s), tennis M(s)/W(s), track and field M(s)/W(s), volleyball W(s), water polo M(c)/W(c), wrestling M(s). *Intramural sports:* basketball M/W, bowling M/W, golf M/W, lacrosse M(c), soccer M/W, softball M/W, tennis M/W, volleyball M/W, water polo M/W.
Standardized Tests *Required:* SAT or ACT (for admission).
Costs (2010–11) *Comprehensive fee:* $35,608 includes full-time tuition ($26,016), mandatory fees ($782), and room and board ($8810). Full-time tuition and fees vary according to course load and program. Part-time tuition: $577 per semester hour. Part-time tuition and fees vary according to course load and program. *Required fees:* $682 per term part-time. *College room only:* $4396. *Payment plan:* installment. *Waivers:* children of alumni, senior citizens, and employees or children of employees.
Financial Aid Of all full-time matriculated undergraduates who enrolled in 2009, 2,064 applied for aid, 1,899 were judged to have need, 33 had their need fully met. 410 Federal Work-Study jobs (averaging $840). 300 state and other part-time jobs (averaging $840). In 2009, 254 non-need-based awards were made. *Average percent of need met:* 57%. *Average financial aid package:* $21,467. *Average need-based loan:* $5055. *Average need-based gift aid:* $2840. *Average non-need-based aid:* $11,250. *Average indebtedness upon graduation:* $32,822.
Applying *Options:* electronic application, deferred entrance. *Required:* essay or personal statement, high school transcript, minimum 2.3 GPA. *Required for some:* interview. *Application deadlines:* rolling (freshmen), rolling (transfers). *Notification:* continuous (freshmen), continuous (transfers).
Freshman Application Contact Mr. Donna Gruber, Director of Undergraduate Admissions, The University of Findlay, 1000 North Main Street, Findlay, OH 45840-3653. *Phone:* 419-434-4540. *Toll-free phone:* 800-548-0932. *Fax:* 419-434-4898. *E-mail:* admissions@findlay.edu. *Web site:* http://www.findlay.edu/.

See page 1692 for the College Close-Up.

University of Mount Union
Alliance, Ohio

- **Independent United Methodist** comprehensive, founded 1846
- **Suburban** 122-acre campus with easy access to Cleveland
- **Endowment** $115.1 million
- **Coed** 2,209 undergraduate students, 98% full-time, 48% women, 52% men
- **Moderately difficult** entrance level, 73% of applicants were admitted

Undergraduates 2,166 full-time, 43 part-time. Students come from 27 states and territories; 19 other countries; 12% are from out of state; 5% Black or African American, non-Hispanic/Latino; 1% Hispanic/Latino; 0.9% Asian, non-Hispanic/Latino; 0.1% American Indian or Alaska Native, non-Hispanic/Latino; 3% Two or more races, non-Hispanic/Latino; 3% Race/ethnicity unknown; 2% international; 2% transferred in; 75% live on campus. *Retention:* 74% of full-time freshmen returned.
Freshmen *Admission:* 2,705 applied, 1,964 admitted, 630 enrolled. *Average high school GPA:* 3.23. *Test scores:* SAT critical reading scores over 500: 45%; SAT math scores over 500: 63%; ACT scores over 18: 93%; SAT critical reading scores over 600: 11%; SAT math scores over 600: 15%; ACT scores over 24: 38%; SAT critical reading scores over 700: 1%; SAT math scores over 700: 1%; ACT scores over 30: 4%.
Faculty *Total:* 233, 52% full-time, 50% with terminal degrees. *Student/faculty ratio:* 14:1.
Academics *Calendar:* semesters. *Degrees:* bachelor's and master's. *Special study options:* accelerated degree program, adult/continuing education programs, advanced placement credit, cooperative education, double majors, English as a second language, honors programs, independent study, internships, off-campus study, part-time degree program, services for LD students, student-designed majors, study abroad, summer session for credit. *ROTC:* Army (c), Air Force (c).
Computers on Campus 265 computers/terminals are available on campus for general student use. Students can access the following: campus intranet, computer help desk, free student e-mail accounts, online (class) grades, online (class) registration, online (class) schedules. Campuswide network is available. 100% of college-owned or -operated housing units are wired for high-speed Internet access. Wireless service is available via entire campus.
Student Life *Housing:* on-campus residence required through sophomore year. *Options:* coed, men-only, women-only, disabled students. Campus housing is university owned and is provided by a third party. Freshman campus housing is guaranteed. *Activities and organizations:* drama/theater group, student-run newspaper, radio and television station, choral group, marching band, Association of Women Students, Student Senate, Black Student Union, Student Activi-

ties Council, Association of International Students, national fraternities, national sororities. *Campus security:* 24-hour emergency response devices and patrols, late-night transport/escort service, controlled dormitory access, 24-hour locked residence hall entrances, outside phones. *Student services:* health clinic, personal/psychological counseling.
Athletics Member NCAA. All Division III. *Intercollegiate sports:* baseball M, basketball M/W, cheerleading W, cross-country running M/W, football M, golf M/W, soccer M/W, softball W, swimming and diving M/W, tennis M/W, track and field M/W, volleyball W, wrestling M. *Intramural sports:* archery M/W, badminton M/W, basketball M/W, bowling M/W, football M, golf M/W, gymnastics M/W, racquetball M/W, soccer M/W, softball M/W, swimming and diving M/W, tennis M/W, track and field M/W, volleyball M/W, weight lifting M/W.
Standardized Tests *Required:* SAT or ACT (for admission).
Costs (2010–11) *Comprehensive fee:* $32,580 includes full-time tuition ($24,500), mandatory fees ($300), and room and board ($7780). Full-time tuition and fees vary according to course load. Part-time tuition: $1030 per credit hour. *Room and board:* Room and board charges vary according to board plan and housing facility. *Payment plans:* tuition prepayment, installment. *Waivers:* children of alumni, senior citizens, and employees or children of employees.
Financial Aid Of all full-time matriculated undergraduates who enrolled in 2009, 1,916 applied for aid, 1,742 were judged to have need, 172 had their need fully met. 741 Federal Work-Study jobs (averaging $699). 314 state and other part-time jobs (averaging $1505). In 2009, 365 non-need-based awards were made. *Average percent of need met:* 77%. *Average financial aid package:* $19,081. *Average need-based loan:* $5173. *Average need-based gift aid:* $13,650. *Average non-need-based aid:* $7307. *Average indebtedness upon graduation:* $25,804.
Applying *Options:* electronic application, early admission, deferred entrance. *Required:* essay or personal statement, high school transcript, minimum 2 GPA, 1 letter of recommendation. *Recommended:* interview. *Application deadlines:* rolling (freshmen), rolling (transfers). *Notification:* continuous (freshmen), continuous (transfers).
Freshman Application Contact Ms. Grace Chalker, Director of Admissions, University of Mount Union, 1972 Clark Avenue, Alliance, OH 44601. *Phone:* 330-823-2587. *Toll-free phone:* 800-334-6682 (in-state); 800-992-6682 (out-of-state). *Fax:* 330-823-5097. *E-mail:* admission@mountunion.edu. *Web site:* http://www.mountunion.edu/.

University of Northwestern Ohio
Lima, Ohio

Freshman Application Contact Mr. Dan Klopp, Vice President for Enrollment Management, University of Northwestern Ohio, 1441 North Cable Road, Lima, OH 45805-1498. *Phone:* 419-227-3141. *Fax:* 419-229-6926. *E-mail:* klopp_d@unoh.edu. *Web site:* http://www.unoh.edu/.

University of Phoenix–Cincinnati Campus
West Chester, Ohio

Freshman Application Contact Ms. Audra McQuarie, Registrar/Executive Director, University of Phoenix–Cincinnati Campus, 4035 South Riverpoint Parkway, Mail Stop CF-L101, Phoenix, AZ 85040. *Phone:* 480-557-6151. *Toll-free phone:* 800-776-4867 (in-state); 800-228-7240 (out-of-state). *Fax:* 480-643-3068. *E-mail:* audra.mcquarie@phoenix.edu. *Web site:* http://www.phoenix.edu/.

University of Phoenix–Cleveland Campus
Independence, Ohio

Freshman Application Contact Ms. Audra McQuarie, Registrar/Executive Director, University of Phoenix–Cleveland Campus, 4035 South Riverpoint Parkway, Mail Stop CF-L101, Phoenix, AZ 85040. *Phone:* 480-557-6151. *Toll-free phone:* 800-776-4867 (in-state); 800-228-7240 (out-of-state). *Fax:* 480-643-3068. *E-mail:* audra.mcquarie@phoenix.edu. *Web site:* http://www.phoenix.edu/.

University of Phoenix–Columbus Ohio Campus
Columbus, Ohio

Freshman Application Contact Ms. Audra McQuarie, Registrar/Executive Director, University of Phoenix–Columbus Ohio Campus, 4035 South Riverpoint Parkway, Mall Stop CF-L101, Phoenix, AZ 85040. *Phone:* 480-

557-6151. *Toll-free phone:* 800-776-4867 (in-state); 800-228-7240 (out-of-state). *Fax:* 480-643-3068. *E-mail:* audra.mcquarie@phoenix.edu. *Web site:* http://www.phoenix.edu/.

University of Rio Grande

Rio Grande, Ohio

- **Independent** comprehensive, founded 1876
- **Rural** 170-acre campus
- **Endowment** $18.1 million
- **Coed** 2,169 undergraduate students, 77% full-time, 59% women, 41% men
- **Noncompetitive** entrance level, 67% of applicants were admitted

Undergraduates 1,674 full-time, 495 part-time. Students come from 7 states and territories; 7 other countries; 2% are from out of state; 6% transferred in; 20% live on campus. *Retention:* 59% of full-time freshmen returned.

Freshmen *Admission:* 3,310 applied, 2,229 admitted, 311 enrolled. *Average high school GPA:* 3.06. *Test scores:* ACT scores over 18: 71%; ACT scores over 24: 11%; ACT scores over 30: 1%.

Faculty *Total:* 150, 60% full-time, 27% with terminal degrees. *Student/faculty ratio:* 15:1.

Academics *Calendar:* semesters. *Degrees:* certificates, associate, bachelor's, and master's. *Special study options:* academic remediation for entering students, accelerated degree program, adult/continuing education programs, advanced placement credit, cooperative education, distance learning, double majors, English as a second language, freshman honors college, honors programs, independent study, internships, part-time degree program, services for LD students, student-designed majors, study abroad, summer session for credit. *ROTC:* Army (c).

Computers on Campus 300 computers/terminals are available on campus for general student use. Students can access the following: computer help desk, free student e-mail accounts, online (class) grades, online (class) registration, online (class) schedules. Campuswide network is available. Wireless service is available via dorm rooms, libraries, student centers.

Student Life *Housing options:* coed, men-only, women-only. Campus housing is university owned. *Activities and organizations:* drama/theater group, student-run newspaper, radio and television station, choral group, student government, Honoraries, Bible studies, Students in Free Enterprise (SIFE), national fraternities. *Campus security:* 24-hour emergency response devices and patrols, late-night transport/escort service, controlled dormitory access. *Student services:* health clinic, personal/psychological counseling.

Athletics Member NAIA. *Intercollegiate sports:* archery M, baseball M(s), basketball M(s)/W(s), cross-country running M(s)/W(s), soccer M(s)/W, softball W(s), track and field M(s)/W(s), volleyball W(s). *Intramural sports:* basketball M/W, football M, golf M, gymnastics W, racquetball M/W, soccer M/W, table tennis M/W, tennis M/W, volleyball M/W.

Standardized Tests *Recommended:* ACT (for admission).

Costs (2010–11) *Comprehensive fee:* $26,636 includes full-time tuition ($18,808) and room and board ($7828). Full-time tuition and fees vary according to course level, course load, degree level, program, reciprocity agreements, and student level. Part-time tuition: $788 per credit hour. Part-time tuition and fees vary according to course level, course load, degree level, program, reciprocity agreements, and student level. *Room and board:* Room and board charges vary according to board plan, housing facility, and student level. *Payment plan:* installment. *Waivers:* senior citizens and employees or children of employees.

Financial Aid Of all full-time matriculated undergraduates who enrolled in 2008, 1,146 applied for aid, 1,138 were judged to have need, 856 had their need fully met. *Average percent of need met:* 91%. *Average financial aid package:* $12,420. *Average need-based gift aid:* $4836. *Average indebtedness upon graduation:* $18,689.

Applying *Options:* electronic application. *Application fee:* $25. *Required:* high school transcript, medical history. *Application deadlines:* rolling (freshmen), rolling (transfers). *Notification:* continuous (freshmen), continuous (transfers).

Freshman Application Contact Ms. Alicia Martin, Director of Admissions, University of Rio Grande, PO Box 500, Rio Grande, OH 45674. *Phone:* 740-245-7208. *Toll-free phone:* 800-282-7201. *Fax:* 740-245-7260. *E-mail:* admissions@rio.edu. *Web site:* http://www.rio.edu/.

The University of Toledo

Toledo, Ohio

- **State-supported** university, founded 1872
- **Suburban** 813-acre campus with easy access to Detroit
- **Endowment** $162.0 million
- **Coed** 18,130 undergraduate students, 82% full-time, 50% women, 50% men
- **Noncompetitive** entrance level, 90% of applicants were admitted

Undergraduates 14,883 full-time, 3,247 part-time. Students come from 41 states and territories; 90 other countries; 12% are from out of state; 15% Black or African American, non-Hispanic/Latino; 3% Hispanic/Latino; 2% Asian, non-Hispanic/Latino; 0.1% Native Hawaiian or other Pacific Islander, non-Hispanic/Latino; 0.2% American Indian or Alaska Native, non-Hispanic/Latino; 2% Two or more races, non-Hispanic/Latino; 8% Race/ethnicity unknown; 3% international; 6% transferred in; 21% live on campus. *Retention:* 65% of full-time freshmen returned.

Freshmen *Admission:* 12,128 applied, 10,959 admitted, 3,939 enrolled. *Average high school GPA:* 3.15. *Test scores:* ACT scores over 18: 82%; ACT scores over 24: 35%; ACT scores over 30: 4%.

Faculty *Total:* 1,138, 66% full-time. *Student/faculty ratio:* 19:1.

Academics *Calendar:* semesters. *Degrees:* certificates, associate, bachelor's, master's, doctoral-professional, doctoral-research/scholarship, post-master's, and postbachelor's certificates. *Special study options:* academic remediation for entering students, adult/continuing education programs, advanced placement credit, cooperative education, distance learning, double majors, English as a second language, honors programs, independent study, internships, off-campus study, part-time degree program, services for LD students, student-designed majors, study abroad, summer session for credit. *ROTC:* Army (b), Air Force (c).

Computers on Campus 5,000 computers/terminals and 7,450 ports are available on campus for general student use. Students can access the following: campus intranet, computer help desk, free student e-mail accounts, online (class) grades, online (class) registration, online (class) schedules, online transcripts, student account. Campuswide network is available. 100% of college-owned or -operated housing units are wired for high-speed Internet access. Wireless service is available via classrooms, libraries, student centers.

Student Life *Housing:* on-campus residence required for freshman year. *Options:* coed, disabled students. Campus housing is university owned. *Activities and organizations:* drama/theater group, student-run newspaper, radio station, choral group, marching band, student government, University YMCA, Newman Club, International Student Association, Campus Activities and Programming, national fraternities, national sororities. *Campus security:* 24-hour emergency response devices and patrols, student patrols, late-night transport/escort service, controlled dormitory access, bicycle patrols by security staff, crime prevention officer. *Student services:* health clinic, personal/psychological counseling, women's center, legal services.

Athletics Member NCAA. All Division I except football (Division I-A). *Intercollegiate sports:* baseball M(s), basketball M(s)/W(s), cross-country running M(s)/W(s), golf M(s)/W(s), soccer W(s), softball W(s), swimming and diving W(s), tennis M(s)/W(s), track and field W(s), volleyball W(s). *Intramural sports:* badminton M/W, basketball M/W, bowling M/W, cheerleading W, crew M(c)/W(c), fencing M(c)/W(c), football M/W, golf M/W, lacrosse M/W, racquetball M/W, sailing M(c)/W(c), skiing (cross-country) M(c)/W(c), skiing (downhill) M(c)/W(c), soccer M(c)/W(c), softball M/W, swimming and diving M/W, table tennis M/W, tennis M/W, track and field M/W, volleyball M/W, water polo M/W, weight lifting M/W, wrestling M.

Standardized Tests *Required:* SAT or ACT (for admission).

Costs (2011–12) *Tuition:* state resident $7301 full-time, $304 per semester hour part-time; nonresident $16,241 full-time, $684 per semester hour part-time. Full-time tuition and fees vary according to course load, program, and reciprocity agreements. Part-time tuition and fees vary according to course load, program, and reciprocity agreements. *Required fees:* $1190 full-time, $50 per semester hour part-time. *Room and board:* $9708; room only: $6478. Room and board charges vary according to board plan and housing facility. *Payment plan:* installment. *Waivers:* children of alumni and employees or children of employees.

Financial Aid Of all full-time matriculated undergraduates who enrolled in 2009, 12,343 applied for aid, 10,636 were judged to have need, 1,273 had their need fully met. 429 Federal Work-Study jobs (averaging $2146). In 2009, 2670 non-need-based awards were made. *Average percent of need met:* 58%. *Average financial aid package:* $10,372. *Average need-based loan:* $4087. *Average need-based gift aid:* $7654. *Average non-need-based aid:* $5118. *Average indebtedness upon graduation:* $27,378.

Applying *Options:* electronic application, deferred entrance. *Application fee:* $40. *Required:* high school transcript. *Required for some:* minimum 2 GPA, CORE high school curriculum. *Application deadlines:* rolling (freshmen), rolling (transfers). *Notification:* continuous (freshmen), continuous (transfers).

Freshman Application Contact Catherine Kwapick, Director of Undergraduate Admissions, The University of Toledo, 2801 West Bancroft,

Toledo, OH 43606-3390. *Phone:* 419-530-5704. *Toll-free phone:* 800-5TOLEDO. *Fax:* 419-530-1202. *E-mail:* cathi.kwapich@utoledo.edu. *Web site:* http://www.utoledo.edu/.

Urbana University
Urbana, Ohio

Freshman Application Contact Ms. Paula Brown, Director of Admissions, Urbana University, 579 College Way, Urbana, OH 43078. *Phone:* 937-484-1356. *Toll-free phone:* 800-7-URBANA. *Fax:* 937-652-6871. *E-mail:* admiss@urbana.edu. *Web site:* http://www.urbana.edu/.

Ursuline College
Pepper Pike, Ohio

- **Independent Roman Catholic** comprehensive, founded 1871
- **Suburban** 112-acre campus with easy access to Cleveland
- **Endowment** $27.5 million
- **Coed, primarily women** 1,022 undergraduate students, 64% full-time, 91% women, 9% men
- **Minimally difficult** entrance level, 90% of applicants were admitted

Undergraduates 655 full-time, 367 part-time. Students come from 12 states and territories; 14 other countries; 2% are from out of state; 27% Black or African American, non-Hispanic/Latino; 2% Hispanic/Latino; 1% Asian, non-Hispanic/Latino; 0.4% American Indian or Alaska Native, non-Hispanic/Latino; 2% Two or more races, non-Hispanic/Latino; 0.2% Race/ethnicity unknown; 0.7% international; 15% transferred in; 17% live on campus. *Retention:* 62% of full-time freshmen returned.

Freshmen *Admission:* 172 applied, 154 admitted, 83 enrolled. *Average high school GPA:* 3.09. *Test scores:* SAT critical reading scores over 500: 32%; SAT math scores over 500: 26%; SAT writing scores over 500: 26%; ACT scores over 18: 84%; SAT critical reading scores over 600: 11%; SAT math scores over 600: 5%; SAT writing scores over 600: 5%; ACT scores over 24: 18%.

Faculty *Total:* 224, 31% full-time, 35% with terminal degrees. *Student/faculty ratio:* 8:1.

Academics *Calendar:* semesters. *Degrees:* certificates, bachelor's, master's, doctoral-professional, post-master's, and postbachelor's certificates (applications from men are also accepted). *Special study options:* academic remediation for entering students, accelerated degree program, adult/continuing education programs, advanced placement credit, cooperative education, distance learning, double majors, independent study, internships, off-campus study, part-time degree program, services for LD students, summer session for credit. *ROTC:* Army (c). *Unusual degree programs:* 3-2 pharmacy with University of Toledo.

Computers on Campus 72 computers/terminals are available on campus for general student use. Students can access the following: campus intranet, computer help desk, free student e-mail accounts, online (class) grades, online (class) registration, online (class) schedules. Campuswide network is available. 100% of college-owned or -operated housing units are wired for high-speed Internet access. Wireless service is available via classrooms, computer centers, computer labs, libraries.

Student Life *Housing options:* coed, women-only. Campus housing is university owned. *Activities and organizations:* drama/theater group, choral group, Student Government Association, Student Nurses of Ursuline College, Fashion Focus, Students United for Black Awareness, Drama Club. *Campus security:* 24-hour emergency response devices and patrols, late-night transport/escort service, controlled dormitory access. *Student services:* personal/psychological counseling.

Athletics *Intercollegiate sports:* basketball W(s), bowling W(s), cross-country running W(s), golf W(s), soccer W(s), softball W(s), swimming and diving W(s), tennis W(s), track and field W(s), volleyball W(s).

Standardized Tests *Required:* SAT or ACT (for admission).

Costs (2010–11) *Comprehensive fee:* $31,910 includes full-time tuition ($23,700), mandatory fees ($240), and room and board ($7970). Full-time tuition and fees vary according to location. Part-time tuition: $790 per credit hour. Part-time tuition and fees vary according to location. *Required fees:* $80 per term part-time. *College room only:* $4072. Room and board charges vary according to board plan and housing facility. *Payment plan:* installment. *Waivers:* employees or children of employees.

Financial Aid Of all full-time matriculated undergraduates who enrolled in 2008, 739 applied for aid, 698 were judged to have need, 85 had their need fully met. 300 Federal Work-Study jobs (averaging $300,000). In 2008, 40 non-need-based awards were made. *Average percent of need met:* 63%. *Average financial aid package:* $14,643. *Average need-based loan:* $5364. *Average need-based gift aid:* $10,447. *Average non-need-based aid:* $5036. *Average indebtedness upon graduation:* $25,242.

Applying *Options:* electronic application, deferred entrance. *Application fee:* $25. *Required:* essay or personal statement, high school transcript. *Required*

for some: essay or personal statement, 1 letter of recommendation. *Recommended:* minimum 2 GPA, interview. *Application deadlines:* 2/1 (freshmen), 2/1 (out-of-state freshmen), rolling (transfers). *Notification:* continuous (freshmen), continuous (out-of-state freshmen), continuous (transfers).

Freshman Application Contact Ursuline College, 2550 Lander Road, Pepper Pike, OH 44124-4398. *Phone:* 440-449-4203. *Toll-free phone:* 888-URSULINE. *Web site:* http://www.ursuline.edu/.

Walsh University
North Canton, Ohio

- **Independent Roman Catholic** comprehensive, founded 1958
- **Small-town** 134-acre campus with easy access to Cleveland
- **Endowment** $8.9 million
- **Coed** 2,290 undergraduate students, 80% full-time, 62% women, 38% men
- **Moderately difficult** entrance level, 80% of applicants were admitted

Undergraduates 1,843 full-time, 447 part-time. Students come from 19 states and territories; 18 other countries; 3% are from out of state; 5% Black or African American, non-Hispanic/Latino; 1% Hispanic/Latino; 0.5% Asian, non-Hispanic/Latino; 0.1% Native Hawaiian or other Pacific Islander, non-Hispanic/Latino; 0.3% American Indian or Alaska Native, non-Hispanic/Latino; 2% Two or more races, non-Hispanic/Latino; 7% Race/ethnicity unknown; 0.9% international; 8% transferred in; 54% live on campus. *Retention:* 76% of full-time freshmen returned.

Freshmen *Admission:* 1,508 applied, 1,209 admitted, 447 enrolled. *Average high school GPA:* 3.31. *Test scores:* SAT critical reading scores over 500: 58%; SAT math scores over 500: 67%; ACT scores over 18: 93%; SAT critical reading scores over 600: 17%; SAT math scores over 600: 15%; ACT scores over 24: 30%; SAT critical reading scores over 700: 1%; ACT scores over 30: 3%.

Faculty *Total:* 314, 36% full-time, 36% with terminal degrees. *Student/faculty ratio:* 12:1.

Academics *Calendar:* semesters. *Degrees:* associate, bachelor's, master's, and doctoral-professional. *Special study options:* academic remediation for entering students, accelerated degree program, adult/continuing education programs, advanced placement credit, distance learning, double majors, English as a second language, honors programs, independent study, internships, off-campus study, part-time degree program, services for LD students, study abroad, summer session for credit. *Unusual degree programs:* 3-2 behavioral science/counseling; biology/physical therapy, theology.

Computers on Campus 335 computers/terminals and 1,000 ports are available on campus for general student use. Students can access the following: computer help desk, free student e-mail accounts, online (class) grades, online (class) registration, online (class) schedules. Campuswide network is available. 100% of college-owned or -operated housing units are wired for high-speed Internet access. Wireless service is available via classrooms, computer labs, dorm rooms, learning centers, libraries, student centers.

Student Life *Housing:* on-campus residence required through senior year. *Options:* men-only, women-only, disabled students. Campus housing is university owned. Freshman campus housing is guaranteed. *Activities and organizations:* drama/theater group, student-run newspaper, radio station, choral group, student government, University Programming Board, Business and Communication Club, Behavioral Science Club, Education Club. *Campus security:* 24-hour emergency response devices and patrols, late-night transport/escort service, controlled dormitory access. *Student services:* health clinic, personal/psychological counseling.

Athletics Member NAIA. *Intercollegiate sports:* baseball M(s), basketball M(s)/W(s), cheerleading W, cross-country running M(s)/W(s), football M(s), golf M(s)/W(s), soccer M(s)/W(s), softball W(s), tennis M(s)/W(s), track and field M(s)/W(s), volleyball W(s). *Intramural sports:* basketball M/W, bowling M/W, football M, golf M/W, lacrosse M(c), skiing (downhill) M(c)/W(c), soccer M/W, table tennis M/W, tennis M/W, ultimate Frisbee M(c)/W(c), volleyball M/W.

Standardized Tests *Required:* SAT or ACT (for admission).

Costs (2010–11) *One-time required fee:* $215. *Comprehensive fee:* $30,640 includes full-time tuition ($21,380), mandatory fees ($900), and room and board ($8360). Full-time tuition and fees vary according to location. Part-time tuition: $710 per semester hour. Part-time tuition and fees vary according to course load and location. *Required fees:* $30 per semester hour part-time. *College room only:* $4420. Room and board charges vary according to board plan and housing facility. *Payment plan:* installment. *Waivers:* children of alumni, senior citizens, and employees or children of employees.

Financial Aid Of all full-time matriculated undergraduates who enrolled in 2009, 1,726 applied for aid, 1,661 were judged to have need, 798 had their need fully met. In 2009, 180 non-need-based awards were made. *Average percent of need met:* 71%. *Average financial aid package:* $18,133. *Average need-based loan:* $4850. *Average need-based gift aid:* $6844. *Average non-need-based aid:* $9372. *Average indebtedness upon graduation:* $24,753.

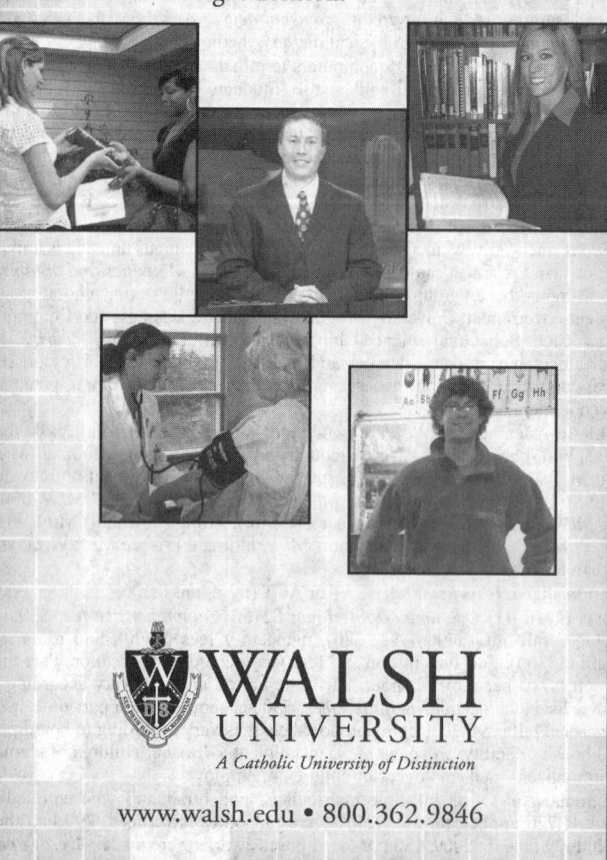
Applying *Options:* electronic application, early admission, deferred entrance. *Application fee:* $25. *Required:* high school transcript, minimum 2.4 GPA. *Required for some:* essay or personal statement, minimum 3 GPA, 2 letters of recommendation. *Recommended:* interview. *Application deadlines:* rolling (freshmen), rolling (transfers). *Notification:* continuous (freshmen), continuous (transfers).

Freshman Application Contact Mr. Brett Freshour, Vice President for Enrollment Management, Walsh University, 2020 East Maple, North Canton, OH 44720. *Phone:* 330-490-7171. *Toll-free phone:* 800-362-9846 (in-state); 800-362-8846 (out-of-state). *Fax:* 330-490-7165. *E-mail:* admissions@walsh.edu. *Web site:* http://www.walsh.edu/.

See page 1764 for the College Close-Up.

Wilberforce University
Wilberforce, Ohio

- **Independent** comprehensive, founded 1856, affiliated with African Methodist Episcopal Church
- **Rural** 125-acre campus with easy access to Dayton
- **Coed**
- **Minimally difficult** entrance level

Academics *Calendar:* semesters. *Degrees:* bachelor's and master's.
Student Life *Campus security:* 24-hour emergency response devices and patrols, controlled dormitory access.
Athletics Member NAIA.
Standardized Tests *Required:* SAT or ACT (for admission).
Financial Aid *Financial aid deadline:* 6/1.
Applying *Options:* electronic application, early admission, early decision, deferred entrance. *Application fee:* $25. *Required:* essay or personal statement, high school transcript, minimum 2 GPA, 2 letters of recommendation. *Recommended:* interview.
Freshman Application Contact Wilberforce University, 1055 North Bickett Road, Wilberforce, OH 45384. *Phone:* 937-708-5789. *Toll-free phone:* 800-367-8568. *Web site:* http://www.wilberforce.edu/.

Wilmington College
Wilmington, Ohio

- **Independent Friends** comprehensive, founded 1870
- **Small-town** 1465-acre campus with easy access to Cincinnati and Columbus
- **Coed** 1,364 undergraduate students, 82% full-time, 58% women, 42% men
- **Moderately difficult** entrance level, 88% of applicants were admitted

Undergraduates 1,121 full-time, 243 part-time. 5% are from out of state; 10% Black or African American, non-Hispanic/Latino; 0.7% Hispanic/Latino; 0.4% Asian, non-Hispanic/Latino; 0.5% American Indian or Alaska Native, non-Hispanic/Latino; 2% Two or more races, non-Hispanic/Latino; 14% Race/ethnicity unknown; 1% international; 7% transferred in; 75% live on campus. *Retention:* 70% of full-time freshmen returned.
Freshmen *Admission:* 1,352 applied, 1,195 admitted, 285 enrolled. *Average high school GPA:* 3.2. *Test scores:* SAT critical reading scores over 500: 38%; SAT math scores over 500: 40%; ACT scores over 18: 84%; SAT critical reading scores over 600: 19%; SAT math scores over 600: 12%; ACT scores over 24: 27%; SAT critical reading scores over 700: 2%; SAT math scores over 700: 2%; ACT scores over 30: 2%.
Faculty *Total:* 117, 57% full-time. *Student/faculty ratio:* 14:1.
Academics *Calendar:* semesters. *Degrees:* bachelor's and master's. *Special study options:* academic remediation for entering students, adult/continuing education programs, advanced placement credit, double majors, honors programs, independent study, internships, off-campus study, part-time degree program, services for LD students, student-designed majors, study abroad, summer session for credit.
Computers on Campus Students can access the following: online (class) registration, OhioLink. Campuswide network is available.
Student Life *Housing:* on-campus residence required through senior year. *Options:* coed, women-only. Campus housing is university owned. *Activities and organizations:* drama/theater group, student-run newspaper, choral group, national fraternities. *Campus security:* 24-hour emergency response devices and patrols, late-night transport/escort service, controlled dormitory access. *Student services:* health clinic, personal/psychological counseling.
Athletics Member NCAA. All Division III. *Intercollegiate sports:* baseball M, basketball M/W, cross-country running M/W, football M, golf M/W, soccer M/W, softball W, swimming and diving M/W, tennis M/W, track and field M/W, volleyball W, wrestling M. *Intramural sports:* basketball M/W, football M, racquetball M/W, soccer M/W, softball M/W, squash M/W, swimming and diving M/W, table tennis M/W, volleyball M/W.
Standardized Tests *Required:* SAT or ACT (for admission).

Costs (2011–12) *Comprehensive fee:* $34,234 includes full-time tuition ($25,214), mandatory fees ($500), and room and board ($8520). Part-time tuition and fees vary according to course load. *Room and board:* Room and board charges vary according to board plan and housing facility. *Payment plan:* installment. *Waivers:* employees or children of employees.

Financial Aid Of all full-time matriculated undergraduates who enrolled in 2008, 1,096 applied for aid, 1,021 were judged to have need, 306 had their need fully met. In 2008, 138 non-need-based awards were made. *Average percent of need met:* 81%. *Average financial aid package:* $21,500. *Average need-based loan:* $6000. *Average need-based gift aid:* $14,300. *Average non-need-based aid:* $7300.

Applying *Options:* deferred entrance. *Required:* high school transcript. *Recommended:* minimum 2.5 GPA, 1 letter of recommendation, interview. *Application deadlines:* 8/1 (freshmen), rolling (transfers). *Notification:* continuous (freshmen), continuous (transfers).

Freshman Application Contact Ms. Tina Garland, Director of Admission and Financial Aid, Wilmington College, 1870 Quaker Way, Wilmington, OH 45177. *Phone:* 937-382-6661 Ext. 426. *Toll-free phone:* 800-341-9318. *Fax:* 937-383-8542. *E-mail:* admissions@wilmington.edu. *Web site:* http://www.wilmington.edu/.

Wittenberg University
Springfield, Ohio

- **Independent** comprehensive, founded 1845, affiliated with Evangelical Lutheran Church
- **Suburban** 71-acre campus with easy access to Columbus and Dayton
- **Endowment** $88.5 million
- **Coed** 1,894 undergraduate students, 94% full-time, 56% women, 44% men
- **Moderately difficult** entrance level, 73% of applicants were admitted

Undergraduates 1,775 full-time, 119 part-time. Students come from 42 states and territories; 23 other countries; 27% are from out of state; 1% transferred in; 83% live on campus. *Retention:* 78% of full-time freshmen returned.

Freshmen *Admission:* 3,120 applied, 2,272 admitted, 500 enrolled. *Average high school GPA:* 3.44. *Test scores:* SAT critical reading scores over 500: 80%; SAT math scores over 500: 79%; ACT scores over 18: 97%; SAT critical reading scores over 600: 37%; SAT math scores over 600: 35%; ACT scores over 24: 66%; SAT critical reading scores over 700: 7%; SAT math scores over 700: 5%; ACT scores over 30: 16%.

Faculty *Total:* 200, 70% full-time, 75% with terminal degrees. *Student/faculty ratio:* 11:1.

Academics *Calendar:* semesters. *Degrees:* bachelor's and master's. *Special study options:* academic remediation for entering students, adult/continuing education programs, advanced placement credit, cooperative education, double majors, English as a second language, freshman honors college, honors programs, independent study, internships, off-campus study, part-time degree program, student-designed majors, study abroad, summer session for credit. *ROTC:* Army (c), Air Force (c). *Unusual degree programs:* 3-2 engineering with Georgia Institute of Technology, Washington University in St. Louis, Case Western Reserve University; forestry with Duke University; nursing with Case Western Reserve University, Johns Hopkins University; occupational therapy with Washington University in St. Louis.

Computers on Campus 500 computers/terminals and 1,200 ports are available on campus for general student use. Students can access the following: computer help desk, free student e-mail accounts, online (class) grades, online (class) registration, online (class) schedules. Campuswide network is available. Wireless service is available via entire campus.

Student Life *Housing:* on-campus residence required through sophomore year. *Options:* coed, women-only. Campus housing is university owned, leased by the school and is provided by a third party. Freshman campus housing is guaranteed. *Activities and organizations:* drama/theater group, student-run newspaper, radio station, choral group, Student Senate, Union Board, choirs, Weaver Chapel Association, national fraternities, national sororities. *Campus security:* 24-hour emergency response devices and patrols, student patrols, late-night transport/escort service, controlled dormitory access, crime prevention programs. *Student services:* health clinic, personal/psychological counseling, women's center.

Athletics Member NCAA. All Division III. *Intercollegiate sports:* baseball M, basketball M/W, crew M(c)/W(c), cross-country running M/W, field hockey W, football M, golf M/W, lacrosse M/W, rugby M(c)/W(c), soccer M/W, softball W, swimming and diving M/W, tennis M/W, track and field M/W, volleyball M(c)/W. *Intramural sports:* basketball M/W, football M, golf M/W, sailing M/W, soccer M/W, softball M/W, swimming and diving M/W, tennis M/W, track and field M/W, volleyball M/W.

Standardized Tests *Recommended:* submission of test scores are optional.

Costs (2011–12) *Comprehensive fee:* $45,728 includes full-time tuition ($35,884), mandatory fees ($550), and room and board ($9294). Part-time tuition: $1196 per credit. Part-time tuition and fees vary according to course load. *Required fees:* $1196 per credit part-time. *College room only:* $4826.

Room and board charges vary according to board plan and housing facility. *Payment plan:* installment. *Waivers:* minority students, children of alumni, adult students, senior citizens, and employees or children of employees.

Financial Aid Of all full-time matriculated undergraduates who enrolled in 2009, 1,546 applied for aid, 1,357 were judged to have need, 369 had their need fully met. 570 Federal Work-Study jobs (averaging $2612). 560 state and other part-time jobs (averaging $2316). In 2009, 433 non-need-based awards were made. *Average percent of need met:* 83%. *Average financial aid package:* $28,460. *Average need-based loan:* $4187. *Average need-based gift aid:* $22,549. *Average non-need-based aid:* $15,163. *Average indebtedness upon graduation:* $29,506.

Applying *Options:* electronic application, early admission, early decision, early action, deferred entrance. *Application fee:* $40. *Required:* essay or personal statement, high school transcript, interview. *Application deadlines:* rolling (transfers), 12/1 (early action). *Early decision deadline:* 11/15. *Notification:* continuous (freshmen), continuous (transfers), 12/15 (early decision), 1/1 (early action).

Freshman Application Contact Ms. Karen Hunt, Director of Admission, Wittenberg University, PO Box 720, Springfield, OH 45501-0720. *Phone:* 877-206-0332 Ext. 6377. *Toll-free phone:* 800-677-7558 Ext. 6314. *Fax:* 937-327-6379. *E-mail:* admission@wittenberg.edu. *Web site:* http://www.wittenberg.edu/.

Wright State University
Dayton, Ohio

- **State-supported** university, founded 1964, part of University System of Ohio
- **Suburban** 557-acre campus with easy access to Cincinnati
- **Endowment** $63.9 million
- **Coed** 14,366 undergraduate students, 83% full-time, 54% women, 46% men
- **Minimally difficult** entrance level, 84% of applicants were admitted

Undergraduates 11,955 full-time, 2,411 part-time. Students come from 46 states and territories; 50 other countries; 4% are from out of state; 16% Black or African American, non-Hispanic/Latino; 2% Hispanic/Latino; 2% Asian, non-Hispanic/Latino; 0.1% Native Hawaiian or other Pacific Islander, non-Hispanic/Latino; 0.3% American Indian or Alaska Native, non-Hispanic/Latino; 3% Two or more races, non-Hispanic/Latino; 1% Race/ethnicity unknown; 2% international; 8% transferred in; 21% live on campus. *Retention:* 71% of full-time freshmen returned.

Freshmen *Admission:* 6,798 applied, 5,742 admitted, 2,753 enrolled. *Average high school GPA:* 3.05. *Test scores:* SAT critical reading scores over 500: 54%; SAT math scores over 500: 53%; SAT writing scores over 500: 46%; ACT scores over 18: 79%; SAT critical reading scores over 600: 16%; SAT math scores over 600: 17%; SAT writing scores over 600: 11%; ACT scores over 24: 27%; SAT critical reading scores over 700: 3%; SAT math scores over 700: 3%; SAT writing scores over 700: 1%; ACT scores over 30: 3%.

Faculty *Total:* 656, 99% full-time. *Student/faculty ratio:* 23:1.

Academics *Calendar:* quarters. *Degrees:* certificates, associate, bachelor's, master's, doctoral-professional, and post-master's certificates. *Special study options:* academic remediation for entering students, adult/continuing education programs, advanced placement credit, cooperative education, distance learning, double majors, English as a second language, freshman honors college, honors programs, independent study, internships, off-campus study, part-time degree program, services for LD students, student-designed majors, study abroad, summer session for credit. *ROTC:* Army (b), Air Force (b).

Computers on Campus 450 computers/terminals are available on campus for general student use. Students can access the following: campus intranet, computer help desk, free student e-mail accounts, online (class) grades, online (class) registration, online (class) schedules. Campuswide network is available. Wireless service is available via entire campus.

Student Life *Housing options:* coed, disabled students. Campus housing is university owned and leased by the school. *Activities and organizations:* drama/theater group, student-run newspaper, radio and television station, choral group, student government, National Association for the Advancement of Colored People, Interfraternity Council, Panhellenic Council, Golden Key International Honor Society, national fraternities, national sororities. *Campus security:* 24-hour emergency response devices and patrols, student patrols, late-night transport/escort service, controlled dormitory access. *Student services:* health clinic, personal/psychological counseling, women's center, legal services.

Athletics Member NCAA. All Division I. *Intercollegiate sports:* baseball M(s), basketball M(s)/W(s), cross-country running M(s)/W(s), golf M(s), soccer M(s)/W(s), softball W(s), swimming and diving M(s)/W(s), tennis M(s)/W(s), track and field W(s), volleyball W(s). *Intramural sports:* baseball M, basketball M/W, cheerleading M/W, cross-country running M/W, football M/W, golf M/W, racquetball M(c)/W(c), rugby M(c)/W(c), skiing (downhill) M(c)/W(c), soccer M/W, softball M/W, squash M/W, table tennis M(c)/W(c), tennis M/W, volleyball M(c)/W.

Standardized Tests *Required:* SAT or ACT (for admission).
Costs (2010–11) *Tuition:* state resident $7797 full-time, $235 per credit hour part-time; nonresident $15,105 full-time, $459 per credit hour part-time. *Room and board:* $8125.
Financial Aid Of all full-time matriculated undergraduates who enrolled in 2009, 9,752 applied for aid, 8,712 were judged to have need, 668 had their need fully met. 2,284 Federal Work-Study jobs (averaging $1965). In 2009, 842 non-need-based awards were made. *Average percent of need met:* 52%. *Average financial aid package:* $9403. *Average need-based loan:* $4110. *Average need-based gift aid:* $6171. *Average non-need-based aid:* $4057. *Average indebtedness upon graduation:* $26,542.
Applying *Options:* electronic application, early admission, deferred entrance. *Application fee:* $30. *Required:* high school transcript. *Recommended:* minimum 2 GPA. *Application deadlines:* rolling (freshmen), rolling (transfers). *Notification:* continuous (freshmen), continuous (out-of-state freshmen), continuous (transfers).
Freshman Application Contact Ms. Cathy Davis, Director of Undergraduate Admissions, Wright State University, 3640 Colonel Glenn Highway, Dayton, OH 45435. *Phone:* 937-775-5700. *Toll-free phone:* 800-247-1770. *Fax:* 937-775-5795. *E-mail:* admissions@wright.edu. *Web site:* http://www.wright.edu/.

Xavier University
Cincinnati, Ohio

- **Independent Roman Catholic** comprehensive, founded 1831
- **Urban** 148-acre campus
- **Endowment** $101.0 million
- **Coed** 4,368 undergraduate students, 88% full-time, 53% women, 47% men
- **Moderately difficult** entrance level, 69% of applicants were admitted

Undergraduates 3,843 full-time, 525 part-time. Students come from 46 states and territories; 36 other countries; 40% are from out of state; 11% Black or African American, non-Hispanic/Latino; 4% Hispanic/Latino; 2% Asian, non-Hispanic/Latino; 0.3% American Indian or Alaska Native, non-Hispanic/Latino; 0.6% Two or more races, non-Hispanic/Latino; 2% Race/ethnicity unknown; 1% international; 3% transferred in; 45% live on campus. *Retention:* 85% of full-time freshmen returned.
Freshmen *Admission:* 9,353 applied, 6,473 admitted, 1,045 enrolled. *Average high school GPA:* 3.54. *Test scores:* SAT critical reading scores over 500: 76%; SAT math scores over 500: 79%; SAT writing scores over 500: 74%; ACT scores over 18: 99%; SAT critical reading scores over 600: 34%; SAT math scores over 600: 35%; SAT writing scores over 600: 29%; ACT scores over 24: 62%; SAT critical reading scores over 700: 5%; SAT math scores over 700: 6%; SAT writing scores over 700: 5%; ACT scores over 30: 15%.
Faculty *Total:* 677, 49% full-time, 49% with terminal degrees. *Student/faculty ratio:* 12:1.
Academics *Calendar:* semesters. *Degrees:* certificates, associate, bachelor's, master's, and doctoral-professional. *Special study options:* academic remediation for entering students, adult/continuing education programs, advanced placement credit, cooperative education, double majors, English as a second language, honors programs, independent study, internships, off-campus study, part-time degree program, services for LD students, study abroad, summer session for credit. *ROTC:* Army (b), Air Force (c). *Unusual degree programs:* 3-2 forestry with Duke University; environmental management, accounting.
Computers on Campus 320 computers/terminals and 8,000 ports are available on campus for general student use. Students can access the following: computer help desk, free student e-mail accounts, online (class) grades, online (class) registration, online (class) schedules. Campuswide network is available. 100% of college-owned or -operated housing units are wired for high-speed Internet access. Wireless service is available via entire campus.
Student Life *Housing:* on-campus residence required through sophomore year. *Options:* coed, disabled students. Campus housing is university owned. Freshman campus housing is guaranteed. *Activities and organizations:* drama/theater group, student-run newspaper, television station, choral group, Student Government Association, Black Student Association, X-treme Fans, Alternative Spring Break, Club Sports. *Campus security:* 24-hour emergency response devices and patrols, late-night transport/escort service, controlled dormitory access, campus-wide shuttle service. *Student services:* health clinic, personal/psychological counseling, women's center.
Athletics Member NCAA. All Division I. *Intercollegiate sports:* baseball M(s), basketball M(s)/W(s), cheerleading M(c)/W(c), crew M(c)/W(c), cross-country running M(s)/W(s), equestrian sports M(c)/W(c), fencing M(c)/W(c), field hockey M(c)/W(c), football M(c), golf M(s)/W(s), gymnastics M(c)/W(c), ice hockey M(c)/W(c), lacrosse M(c)/W(c), racquetball M(c)/W(c), rugby M(c)/W(c), soccer M(s)/W(s), softball M(c)/W(c), swimming and diving M(s)/W(s), tennis M(s)/W(s), track and field M(s)/W(s), ultimate Frisbee M(c)/W(c), volleyball M(c)/W(c), water polo M(c)/W(c). *Intramural sports:* baseball M(c), basketball M/W, bowling M/W, cross-country running M(c)/

W(c), football M/W, golf M(c), racquetball M/W, soccer M(c)/W(c), softball W, swimming and diving M(c)/W(c), tennis M/W, volleyball M/W.
Standardized Tests *Required:* SAT or ACT (for admission).
Costs (2010–11) *One-time required fee:* $190. *Comprehensive fee:* $39,870 includes full-time tuition ($29,300), mandatory fees ($670), and room and board ($9900). Full-time tuition and fees vary according to course load and program. Part-time tuition: $575 per credit hour. Part-time tuition and fees vary according to course load, location, and program. *College room only:* $5500. Room and board charges vary according to board plan and housing facility. *Payment plans:* installment, deferred payment. *Waivers:* senior citizens and employees or children of employees.
Financial Aid Of all full-time matriculated undergraduates who enrolled in 2009, 2,767 applied for aid, 2,323 were judged to have need, 351 had their need fully met. 516 Federal Work-Study jobs (averaging $2200). 18 state and other part-time jobs (averaging $1940). In 2009, 1199 non-need-based awards were made. *Average percent of need met:* 69%. *Average financial aid package:* $18,435. *Average need-based loan:* $4456. *Average need-based gift aid:* $13,747. *Average non-need-based aid:* $11,130. *Average indebtedness upon graduation:* $25,881.
Applying *Options:* electronic application, deferred entrance. *Application fee:* $35. *Required:* essay or personal statement, high school transcript, 1 letter of recommendation. *Required for some:* minimum 3 GPA, interview. *Application deadlines:* 2/1 (freshmen), rolling (transfers). *Notification:* 10/15 (freshmen), continuous (transfers).
Freshman Application Contact Xavier University, 3800 Victory Parkway, Cincinnati, OH 45207-5311. *Phone:* 513-745-2941. *Toll-free phone:* 800-344-4698. *E-mail:* xuadmit@xavier.edu. *Web site:* http://www.xu.edu/.

Youngstown State University
Youngstown, Ohio

- **State-supported** comprehensive, founded 1908
- **Urban** 200-acre campus with easy access to Cleveland and Pittsburgh
- **Endowment** $153.5 million
- **Coed** 13,890 undergraduate students, 78% full-time, 53% women, 47% men
- **Noncompetitive** entrance level, 87% of applicants were admitted

Undergraduates 10,820 full-time, 3,070 part-time. Students come from 31 states and territories; 55 other countries; 9% are from out of state; 18% Black or African American, non-Hispanic/Latino; 2% Hispanic/Latino; 1% Asian, non-Hispanic/Latino; 0.4% American Indian or Alaska Native, non-Hispanic/Latino; 0.1% Two or more races, non-Hispanic/Latino; 6% Race/ethnicity unknown; 0.6% international; 5% transferred in; 10% live on campus. *Retention:* 69% of full-time freshmen returned.
Freshmen *Admission:* 5,582 applied, 4,849 admitted, 2,890 enrolled. *Average high school GPA:* 2.8. *Test scores:* SAT critical reading scores over 500: 34%; SAT math scores over 500: 38%; SAT writing scores over 500: 28%; ACT scores over 18: 67%; SAT critical reading scores over 600: 8%; SAT math scores over 600: 12%; SAT writing scores over 600: 8%; ACT scores over 24: 21%; SAT critical reading scores over 700: 2%; SAT math scores over 700: 1%; SAT writing scores over 700: 1%; ACT scores over 30: 3%.
Faculty *Total:* 1,032, 44% full-time, 46% with terminal degrees. *Student/faculty ratio:* 19:1.
Academics *Calendar:* semesters. *Degrees:* certificates, diplomas, associate, bachelor's, master's, doctoral-professional, doctoral-research/scholarship, and postbachelor's certificates. *Special study options:* academic remediation for entering students, accelerated degree program, advanced placement credit, cooperative education, distance learning, double majors, English as a second language, honors programs, independent study, internships, off-campus study, part-time degree program, services for LD students, student-designed majors, study abroad, summer session for credit. *ROTC:* Army (b), Air Force (c). *Unusual degree programs:* 3-2 BS/MS Program in Chemistry; BS/MD Program.
Computers on Campus 170 computers/terminals are available on campus for general student use. Students can access the following: campus intranet, computer help desk, free student e-mail accounts, online (class) grades, online (class) registration, online (class) schedules. Campuswide network is available. 100% of college-owned or -operated housing units are wired for high-speed Internet access. Wireless service is available via entire campus.
Student Life *Housing options:* coed, women-only. Campus housing is university owned and is provided by a third party. *Activities and organizations:* drama/theater group, student-run newspaper, choral group, marching band, student government, Omicron Delta Kappa, Golden Key Society, Fraternities/Sororities (IFC, NPHC and Panhelenic Council, history club, national fraternities, national sororities. *Campus security:* 24-hour emergency response devices and patrols, student patrols, late-night transport/escort service, controlled dormitory access, residence hall patrols. *Student services:* health clinic, personal/psychological counseling, women's center.
Athletics Member NCAA. All Division I except football (Division I-AA). *Intercollegiate sports:* baseball M(s), basketball M(s)/W(s), cross-country run-

ning M(s)/W(s), golf M(s)/W(s), soccer W(s), softball W(s), swimming and diving W(s), tennis M(s)/W(s), track and field M(s)/W(s), volleyball W(s). *Intramural sports:* badminton M/W, basketball M/W, football M/W, racquetball M/W, soccer M/W, softball M/W, table tennis M/W, tennis M/W, ultimate Frisbee M/W, volleyball M/W, weight lifting M/W.

Standardized Tests *Required:* SAT or ACT (for admission).

Costs (2010–11) *Tuition:* state resident $6970 full-time, $290 per credit part-time; nonresident $12,643 full-time, $527 per credit part-time. Full-time tuition and fees vary according to course load. Part-time tuition and fees vary according to course load. *Required fees:* $229 full-time, $10 per credit part-time. *Room and board:* $7600. Room and board charges vary according to board plan and housing facility. *Payment plan:* installment. *Waivers:* senior citizens and employees or children of employees.

Financial Aid Of all full-time matriculated undergraduates who enrolled in 2008, 10,858 applied for aid, 9,695 were judged to have need, 495 had their need fully met. In 2008, 769 non-need-based awards were made. *Average percent of need met:* 29%. *Average financial aid package:* $8216. *Average need-based loan:* $3734. *Average need-based gift aid:* $5429. *Average non-need-based aid:* $2588.

Applying *Options:* electronic application, early admission, deferred entrance. *Application fee:* $30. *Required:* high school transcript. *Required for some:* interview. *Application deadlines:* 8/1 (freshmen), 8/1 (transfers). *Notification:* continuous (freshmen), continuous (transfers).

Freshman Application Contact Ms. Sue Davis, Director of Undergraduate Admissions, Youngstown State University, One University Plaza, Youngstown, OH 44555-0001. *Phone:* 330-941-2000. *Toll-free phone:* 877-468-6978. *Fax:* 330-941-3674. *E-mail:* enroll@ysu.edu. *Web site:* http://www.ysu.edu/.

OKLAHOMA

Bacone College

Muskogee, Oklahoma

Freshman Application Contact Bacone College, 2299 Old Bacone Road, Muskogee, OK 74403-1597. *Phone:* 918-781-7342. *Toll-free phone:* 888-682-5514 Ext. 7340. *Web site:* http://www.bacone.edu/.

Brown Mackie College–Tulsa

Tulsa, Oklahoma

- **Proprietary** primarily 2-year
- **Coed**

Academics *Degrees:* diplomas, associate, and bachelor's.

Costs (2010–11) *Tuition:* Tuition varies by program. Students should contact Brown Mackie College for tuition information.

Freshman Application Contact Brown Mackie College–Tulsa, 4608 South Garnett, Suite 110, Tulsa, OK 74146. *Phone:* 918-628-3700. *Toll-free phone:* 888-794-8411. *Web site:* http://www.brownmackie.edu/tulsa/.

Cameron University

Lawton, Oklahoma

- **State-supported** comprehensive, founded 1908, part of Oklahoma State Regents for Higher Education
- **Small-town** 160-acre campus
- **Endowment** $14.2 million
- **Coed** 5,883 undergraduate students, 67% full-time, 59% women, 41% men
- **Noncompetitive** entrance level, 100% of applicants were admitted

Undergraduates 3,920 full-time, 1,963 part-time. Students come from 36 states and territories; 39 other countries; 4% are from out of state; 9% Black or African American, non-Hispanic/Latino; 4% Hispanic/Latino; 2% Asian, non-Hispanic/Latino; 5% American Indian or Alaska Native, non-Hispanic/Latino; 45% Race/ethnicity unknown; 5% international; 6% transferred in; 9% live on campus. *Retention:* 54% of full-time freshmen returned.

Freshman *Admission:* 1,482 applied, 1,479 admitted, 1,058 enrolled. *Average high school GPA:* 3.13. *Test scores:* ACT scores over 18: 66%; ACT scores over 24: 18%; ACT scores over 30: 1%.

Faculty *Total:* 327, 56% full-time, 45% with terminal degrees. *Student/faculty ratio:* 21:1.

Academics *Calendar:* semesters. *Degrees:* associate, bachelor's, master's, and postbachelor's certificates. *Special study options:* academic remediation

for entering students, accelerated degree program, adult/continuing education programs, advanced placement credit, distance learning, double majors, honors programs, independent study, internships, off-campus study, part-time degree program, services for LD students, student-designed majors, summer session for credit. *ROTC:* Army (b).

Computers on Campus 334 computers/terminals are available on campus for general student use. Students can access the following: computer help desk, free student e-mail accounts, online (class) grades, online (class) schedules, online courses, student information system, library. Campuswide network is available. 100% of college-owned or -operated housing units are wired for high-speed Internet access. Wireless service is available via classrooms, computer centers, computer labs, dorm rooms, learning centers, libraries, student centers.

Student Life *Housing options:* coed, men-only, women-only. Campus housing is university owned. *Activities and organizations:* drama/theater group, student-run newspaper, television station, choral group, Student Government Association, Programming Activities Council, Student Housing Association, International Club, Greek Life, national fraternities, national sororities. *Campus security:* 24-hour emergency response devices and patrols, late-night transport/escort service, controlled dormitory access. *Student services:* health clinic, personal/psychological counseling.

Athletics Member NCAA. All Division II. *Intercollegiate sports:* baseball M(s), basketball M(s)/W(s), cross-country running M(s), golf M(s)/W(s), softball W(s), tennis M(s)/W(s), volleyball W(s). *Intramural sports:* archery M/W, badminton M/W, basketball M/W, bowling M/W, golf M/W, racquetball M/W, soccer M/W, swimming and diving M/W, table tennis M/W, tennis M/W, volleyball M/W.

Standardized Tests *Required:* SAT or ACT (for admission).

Costs (2010–11) *Tuition:* state resident $2963 full-time, $99 per credit hour part-time; nonresident $9180 full-time, $306 per credit hour part-time. Full-time tuition and fees vary according to course load, location, and program. Part-time tuition and fees vary according to course load, location, and program. *Required fees:* $1373 full-time, $46 per credit hour part-time. *Room and board:* $3668. Room and board charges vary according to board plan and housing facility. *Payment plan:* installment. *Waivers:* employees or children of employees.

Financial Aid Of all full-time matriculated undergraduates who enrolled in 2008, 2,532 applied for aid, 2,173 were judged to have need, 1,859 had their need fully met. In 2008, 1606 non-need-based awards were made. *Average percent of need met:* 89%. *Average financial aid package:* $12,100. *Average need-based loan:* $5000. *Average need-based gift aid:* $3500. *Average non-need-based aid:* $500. *Average indebtedness upon graduation:* $7000.

Applying *Options:* electronic application, deferred entrance. *Application fee:* $15. *Required for some:* high school transcript, minimum 2.7 GPA, Rank in top 50 percentile of high school graduating class. *Application deadlines:* rolling (freshmen), rolling (out-of-state freshmen), rolling (transfers). *Notification:* continuous (freshmen), continuous (out-of-state freshmen), continuous (transfers).

Freshman Application Contact Mr. Nate Todd, Coordinator of Prospective Student Services, Cameron University, Admissions, 2800 West Gore Boulevard, Lawton, OK 73505-6377. *Phone:* 580-581-5496. *Toll-free phone:* 888-454-7600. *Fax:* 580-581-5514. *E-mail:* admissions@cameron.edu. *Web site:* http://www.cameron.edu/.

DeVry University

Oklahoma City, Oklahoma

- **Proprietary** comprehensive
- **Coed**

Faculty *Student/faculty ratio:* 27:1.

Academics *Degrees:* associate, bachelor's, and master's.

Costs (2010–11) *Tuition:* $14,766 full-time, $580 per credit hour part-time. Full-time tuition and fees vary according to course load. Part-time tuition and fees vary according to course load. *Required fees:* $60 full-time, $30 per term part-time. *Payment plans:* installment, deferred payment.

Financial Aid *Of all full-time matriculated undergraduates who enrolled in 2007,* 16 applied for aid, 15 were judged to have need. *In 2007,* 1 non-need-based awards were made. *Average percent of need met:* 39. *Average financial aid package:* $10,842. *Average need-based loan:* $4877. *Average need-based gift aid:* $10,483. *Average non-need-based aid:* $14,400.

Applying *Options:* electronic application, deferred entrance. *Application fee:* $50.

Freshman Application Contact DeVry University, Lakepointe Towers, 4013 Northwest Expressway Street, Suite 100, Oklahoma City, OK 73116. *Web site:* http://www.devry.edu/.

East Central University
Ada, Oklahoma

- **State-supported** comprehensive, founded 1909, part of Oklahoma State Regents for Higher Education
- **Small-town** 140-acre campus with easy access to Oklahoma City
- **Endowment** $20.7 million
- **Coed** 3,956 undergraduate students, 81% full-time, 58% women, 42% men
- **Minimally difficult** entrance level, 92% of applicants were admitted

Undergraduates 3,218 full-time, 738 part-time. Students come from 31 states and territories; 36 other countries; 2% are from out of state; 5% Black or African American, non-Hispanic/Latino; 4% Hispanic/Latino; 0.3% Asian, non-Hispanic/Latino; 0.2% Native Hawaiian or other Pacific Islander, non-Hispanic/Latino; 19% American Indian or Alaska Native, non-Hispanic/Latino; 5% Two or more races, non-Hispanic/Latino; 2% Race/ethnicity unknown; 4% international; 11% transferred in; 46% live on campus. *Retention:* 68% of full-time freshmen returned.

Freshmen *Admission:* 972 applied, 897 admitted, 639 enrolled. *Average high school GPA:* 3.31. *Test scores:* SAT critical reading scores over 500: 32%; SAT math scores over 500: 44%; ACT scores over 18: 79%; SAT critical reading scores over 600: 10%; SAT math scores over 600: 13%; ACT scores over 24: 21%; SAT critical reading scores over 700: 1%; SAT math scores over 700: 1%; ACT scores over 30: 2%.

Faculty *Total:* 279, 60% full-time, 45% with terminal degrees. *Student/faculty ratio:* 18:1.

Academics *Calendar:* semesters. *Degrees:* bachelor's and master's. *Special study options:* academic remediation for entering students, adult/continuing education programs, advanced placement credit, distance learning, double majors, honors programs, independent study, internships, off-campus study, part-time degree program, services for LD students, study abroad, summer session for credit.

Computers on Campus 750 computers/terminals are available on campus for general student use. Students can access the following: campus intranet, computer help desk, free student e-mail accounts, online (class) grades, online (class) registration, online (class) schedules. Campuswide network is available. Wireless service is available via entire campus.

Student Life *Housing:* on-campus residence required for freshman year. *Options:* coed, women-only, disabled students. Campus housing is university owned. *Activities and organizations:* drama/theater group, student-run newspaper, choral group, marching band, BACCHUS, Fellowship of Christian Athletes, Human Resources, national fraternities, national sororities. *Campus security:* 24-hour emergency response devices and patrols, student patrols, late-night transport/escort service, agreements with all local, state, federal, and tribal police departments for added crime and violation prevention. *Student services:* health clinic, personal/psychological counseling.

Athletics Member NCAA, NAIA. All NCAA Division II. *Intercollegiate sports:* baseball M(s), basketball M(s)/W(s), cheerleading M/W, cross-country running M(s)/W(s), football M(s), golf M(s)/W, soccer W(s), softball W(s), tennis M(s)/W(s), track and field M/W, volleyball W(s). *Intramural sports:* basketball M/W, football M/W, racquetball M/W, soccer M/W, softball M/W, tennis M/W, volleyball M/W.

Standardized Tests *Required:* SAT or ACT (for admission). *Recommended:* ACT (for admission).

Costs (2010–11) *Tuition:* state resident $3223 full-time, $107 per semester hour part-time; nonresident $9539 full-time, $318 per semester hour part-time. No tuition increase for student's term of enrollment. *Required fees:* $1259 full-time, $39 per semester hour part-time, $48 per term part-time. *Room and board:* $4480; room only: $1762. Room and board charges vary according to board plan and housing facility. *Waivers:* senior citizens and employees or children of employees.

Financial Aid Of all full-time matriculated undergraduates who enrolled in 2006, 2,396 applied for aid, 2,085 were judged to have need, 756 had their need fully met. 175 Federal Work-Study jobs (averaging $2349). 232 state and other part-time jobs (averaging $572). In 2006, 542 non-need-based awards were made. *Average percent of need met:* 70%. *Average financial aid package:* $7597. *Average need-based loan:* $3835. *Average need-based gift aid:* $3420. *Average non-need-based aid:* $1567. *Average indebtedness upon graduation:* $19,190.

Applying *Options:* electronic application, early admission. *Application fee:* $20. *Required:* high school transcript. *Required for some:* minimum 2.7 GPA, rank in upper 50% of high school class. *Notification:* continuous (freshmen), continuous (transfers).

Freshman Application Contact Ms. Pam Denny, Freshman Admissions Officer, East Central University, PMBJ8, 1100 East 14th Street, Ada, OK 74820-6999. *Phone:* 580-310-5233 Ext. 233. *Fax:* 580-310-5432. *E-mail:* pdenny@ecok.edu. *Web site:* http://www.ecok.edu/.

Hillsdale Free Will Baptist College
Moore, Oklahoma

- **Independent Free Will Baptist** comprehensive, founded 1959
- **Suburban** 41-acre campus with easy access to Oklahoma City
- **Coed** 215 undergraduate students, 92% full-time, 38% women, 62% men
- **Noncompetitive** entrance level

Undergraduates 197 full-time, 18 part-time. 14% Black or African American, non-Hispanic/Latino; 4% Hispanic/Latino; 0.9% American Indian or Alaska Native, non-Hispanic/Latino; 6% Race/ethnicity unknown; 1% international. *Retention:* 52% of full-time freshmen returned.

Freshmen *Admission:* 52 enrolled. *Test scores:* ACT scores over 18: 71%; ACT scores over 24: 26%; ACT scores over 30: 4%.

Academics *Calendar:* semesters. *Degrees:* associate, bachelor's, and master's. *Special study options:* academic remediation for entering students, accelerated degree program, adult/continuing education programs, advanced placement credit, English as a second language, independent study, internships, part-time degree program, summer session for credit.

Computers on Campus 22 computers/terminals are available on campus for general student use. Students can access the following: campus intranet, free student e-mail accounts. Campuswide network is available.

Student Life *Housing:* on-campus residence required through sophomore year. *Options:* men-only, women-only. Campus housing is university owned. *Activities and organizations:* drama/theater group, choral group. *Campus security:* 24-hour emergency response devices, controlled dormitory access. *Student services:* personal/psychological counseling.

Athletics Member NCCAA. *Intercollegiate sports:* baseball M, basketball M/W, soccer M, softball W, volleyball W. *Intramural sports:* basketball M/W, volleyball M/W.

Standardized Tests *Required:* SAT or ACT (for admission).

Costs (2010–11) *One-time required fee:* $150. *Comprehensive fee:* $15,520 includes full-time tuition ($8400), mandatory fees ($1620), and room and board ($5500). Full-time tuition and fees vary according to course load. Part-time tuition: $350 per credit hour. Part-time tuition and fees vary according to course load. *Required fees:* $26 per credit hour part-time, $220 per term part-time. *College room only:* $2300. Room and board charges vary according to board plan and housing facility. *Payment plan:* installment. *Waivers:* children of alumni, senior citizens, and employees or children of employees.

Financial Aid Of all full-time matriculated undergraduates who enrolled in 2008, 172 applied for aid, 143 were judged to have need, 19 had their need fully met. 48 Federal Work-Study jobs (averaging $994). In 2008, 70 non-need-based awards were made. *Average percent of need met:* 49%. *Average financial aid package:* $9253. *Average need-based loan:* $3017. *Average need-based gift aid:* $3821. *Average non-need-based aid:* $3113. *Average indebtedness upon graduation:* $23,822.

Applying *Options:* electronic application, early admission, deferred entrance. *Application fee:* $20. *Required:* high school transcript. *Required for some:* interview. *Recommended:* minimum 2 GPA.

Freshman Application Contact Hillsdale Free Will Baptist College, PO Box 7208, Moore, OK 73160. *Phone:* 405-912-9007. *Fax:* 405-912-9050. *E-mail:* recruitment@hc.edu. *Web site:* http://www.hc.edu/.

ITT Technical Institute
Oklahoma City, Oklahoma

- **Proprietary** 4-year, founded 2006, part of ITT Educational Services, Inc.
- **Coed**
- **Minimally difficult** entrance level

Academics *Calendar:* quarters. *Degrees:* associate and bachelor's.
Student Life *Housing:* college housing not available.
Freshman Application Contact Director of Recruitment, ITT Technical Institute, 50 Penn Place Office Tower, 1900 Northwest Expressway, Suite 305R, Oklahoma City, OK 73118. *Phone:* 405-810-4100. *Toll-free phone:* 800-518-1612. *Web site:* http://www.itt-tech.edu/.

ITT Technical Institute
Tulsa, Oklahoma

- **Proprietary** primarily 2-year, founded 2005
- **Coed**
- **Minimally difficult** entrance level

Academics *Calendar:* quarters. *Degrees:* associate and bachelor's.
Student Life *Housing:* college housing not available.
Freshman Application Contact Director of Recruitment, ITT Technical Institute, 8421 East 61st Street, Suite U, Tulsa, OK 74133. *Phone:* 918-615-3900. *Toll-free phone:* 800-514-6535. *Web site:* http://www.itt-tech.edu/.

Langston University

Langston, Oklahoma

Freshman Application Contact Maurice Osborne, Assistant Director of Admission, Langston University, PO Box 667, Langston, OK 73050. *Phone:* 405-466-2984. *Web site:* http://www.lunet.edu/.

Mid-America Christian University

Oklahoma City, Oklahoma

Freshman Application Contact Mid-America Christian University, 3500 Southwest 119th Street, Oklahoma City, OK 73170-4504. *Phone:* 405-392-3180. *Web site:* http://www.macu.edu/.

Northeastern State University

Tahlequah, Oklahoma

- **State-supported** comprehensive, founded 1846, part of Regional University System of Oklahoma
- **Small-town** 160-acre campus with easy access to Tulsa
- **Endowment** $88,986
- **Coed** 8,372 undergraduate students, 73% full-time, 60% women, 40% men
- **Moderately difficult** entrance level, 74% of applicants were admitted

Undergraduates 6,100 full-time, 2,272 part-time. Students come from 25 states and territories; 54 other countries; 4% are from out of state; 6% Black or African American, non-Hispanic/Latino; 2% Hispanic/Latino; 2% Asian, non-Hispanic/Latino; 30% American Indian or Alaska Native, non-Hispanic/Latino; 0.1% Race/ethnicity unknown; 2% international; 13% transferred in; 19% live on campus. *Retention:* 64% of full-time freshmen returned.

Freshmen *Admission:* 2,807 applied, 2,091 admitted, 1,223 enrolled. *Average high school GPA:* 3.19. *Test scores:* ACT scores over 18: 76%; ACT scores over 24: 18%; ACT scores over 30: 1%.

Faculty *Total:* 535, 60% full-time, 51% with terminal degrees. *Student/faculty ratio:* 21:1.

Academics *Calendar:* semesters. *Degrees:* bachelor's, master's, doctoral-professional, post-master's, and postbachelor's certificates. *Special study options:* academic remediation for entering students, adult/continuing education programs, advanced placement credit, cooperative education, distance learning, double majors, honors programs, independent study, internships, part-time degree program, services for LD students, student-designed majors, summer session for credit. *ROTC:* Army (b).

Computers on Campus 1,172 computers/terminals and 1,200 ports are available on campus for general student use. Students can access the following: campus intranet, computer help desk, free student e-mail accounts, online (class) grades, online (class) schedules. Campuswide network is available. 100% of college-owned or -operated housing units are wired for high-speed Internet access. Wireless service is available via computer centers, computer labs, libraries, student centers.

Student Life *Housing:* on-campus residence required for freshman year. *Options:* coed, women-only, disabled students. Campus housing is university owned. Freshman applicants given priority for college housing. *Activities and organizations:* drama/theater group, student-run newspaper, television station, choral group, marching band, national fraternities, national sororities. *Campus security:* 24-hour emergency response devices and patrols, late-night transport/escort service, controlled dormitory access. *Student services:* health clinic, personal/psychological counseling.

Athletics Member NCAA. All Division II. *Intercollegiate sports:* baseball M(s), basketball M(s)/W(s), football M(s), golf M(s)/W(s), rock climbing M(c)/W(c), soccer M(s)/W(s), softball W(s), tennis W(s). *Intramural sports:* basketball M/W, bowling M/W, football M/W, golf M/W, racquetball M/W, soccer M/W, softball M/W, swimming and diving M/W, tennis M/W, volleyball M/W.

Standardized Tests *Required:* ACT (for admission).

Costs (2010–11) *Tuition:* state resident $3338 full-time, $111 per credit hour part-time; nonresident $9675 full-time, $323 per credit hour part-time. Full-time tuition and fees vary according to course load and program. Part-time tuition and fees vary according to course load and program. *Required fees:* $1047 full-time, $35 per credit hour part-time. *Room and board:* $5020. Room and board charges vary according to board plan and housing facility. *Waivers:* senior citizens and employees or children of employees.

Financial Aid Of all full-time matriculated undergraduates who enrolled in 2009, 5,058 applied for aid, 3,362 were judged to have need, 2,197 had their need fully met. 266 Federal Work-Study jobs (averaging $1733). 569 state and other part-time jobs (averaging $3393). In 2009, 401 non-need-based awards were made. *Average percent of need met:* 78%. *Average financial aid package:* $8860. *Average need-based loan:* $3884. *Average need-based gift aid:* $5244. *Average non-need-based aid:* $4160. *Average indebtedness upon graduation:* $23,155.

Applying *Options:* deferred entrance. *Application fee:* $25. *Required:* high school transcript, minimum 2.7 GPA, upper 50% of class or minimum ACT composite of 20. *Required for some:* interview. *Application deadlines:* 8/1 (freshmen), 8/1 (transfers). *Notification:* continuous (freshmen), continuous (transfers).

Freshman Application Contact Ms. Dawn Cain, Director of Admissions, Northeastern State University, 600 N Grand Ave, Tahlequah, OK 74464. *Phone:* 918-444-2211. *Toll-free phone:* 800-722-9614. *Fax:* 918-458-2342. *E-mail:* cain@nsuok.edu. *Web site:* http://www.nsuok.edu/.

Northwestern Oklahoma State University

Alva, Oklahoma

- **State-supported** comprehensive, founded 1897, part of Oklahoma State Regents for Higher Education
- **Small-town** 70-acre campus
- **Endowment** $15.6 million
- **Coed** 2,114 undergraduate students, 77% full-time, 55% women, 45% men
- **Moderately difficult** entrance level, 100% of applicants were admitted

Undergraduates 1,633 full-time, 481 part-time. Students come from 42 states and territories; 22 other countries; 21% are from out of state; 5% Black or African American, non-Hispanic/Latino; 5% Hispanic/Latino; 0.3% Asian, non-Hispanic/Latino; 0.1% Native Hawaiian or other Pacific Islander, non-Hispanic/Latino; 6% American Indian or Alaska Native, non-Hispanic/Latino; 6% Race/ethnicity unknown; 2% international; 13% transferred in; 30% live on campus. *Retention:* 63% of full-time freshmen returned.

Freshmen *Admission:* 851 applied, 851 admitted, 428 enrolled. *Average high school GPA:* 3.24. *Test scores:* ACT scores over 18: 69%; ACT scores over 24: 20%; ACT scores over 30: 2%.

Faculty *Total:* 160, 49% full-time, 32% with terminal degrees. *Student/faculty ratio:* 17:1.

Academics *Calendar:* semesters. *Degrees:* bachelor's, master's, post-master's, and postbachelor's certificates. *Special study options:* academic remediation for entering students, adult/continuing education programs, advanced placement credit, cooperative education, distance learning, honors programs, independent study, internships, off-campus study, part-time degree program, services for LD students, study abroad, summer session for credit.

Computers on Campus 260 computers/terminals are available on campus for general student use. Students can access the following: campus intranet, computer help desk, free student e-mail accounts, online (class) grades, online (class) registration, online (class) schedules. Campuswide network is available. 100% of college-owned or -operated housing units are wired for high-speed Internet access. Wireless service is available via classrooms, computer centers, computer labs, learning centers, libraries, student centers.

Student Life *Housing:* on-campus residence required for freshman year. *Options:* men-only, women-only. Campus housing is university owned. Freshman campus housing is guaranteed. *Activities and organizations:* drama/theater group, student-run newspaper, radio and television station, choral group, marching band, Student Government Association, Aggie Club, Phi Beta Lambda, Baptist Student Union. *Campus security:* 24-hour emergency response devices and patrols, late-night transport/escort service. *Student services:* personal/psychological counseling.

Athletics Member NAIA. *Intercollegiate sports:* baseball M(s), basketball M(s)/W(s), cheerleading M(s)/W(s), cross-country running M(s)/W(s), football M(s), golf M(s)/W(s), soccer W(s), softball W(s). *Intramural sports:* basketball M/W, football M, racquetball M/W, softball M/W, ultimate Frisbee M/W, volleyball M/W.

Standardized Tests *Required:* SAT or ACT (for admission).

Costs (2010–11) *Tuition:* state resident $3713 full-time; nonresident $9518 full-time. Full-time tuition and fees vary according to course load, location, and program. Part-time tuition and fees vary according to course load, location, and program. *Required fees:* $623 full-time. *Room and board:* $3640; room only: $1300. Room and board charges vary according to board plan. *Payment plan:* installment. *Waivers:* senior citizens and employees or children of employees.

Financial Aid Of all full-time matriculated undergraduates who enrolled in 2009, 1,012 applied for aid, 844 were judged to have need. 146 Federal Work-Study jobs (averaging $1086). 225 state and other part-time jobs (averaging $1408). *Average indebtedness upon graduation:* $14,281.

Applying *Options:* electronic application, early admission. *Application fee:* $15. *Required:* high school transcript. *Required for some:* essay or personal statement, minimum 2.7 GPA, 3 letters of recommendation. *Application deadlines:* rolling (freshmen), rolling (transfers). *Notification:* continuous (freshmen), continuous (transfers).

Freshman Application Contact Mr. Matt Adair, Director of Recruitment, Northwestern Oklahoma State University, 709 Oklahoma Boulevard, Alva,

OK 73717-2799. *Phone:* 580-327-8545. *Fax:* 580-327-8699. *E-mail:* wmadair@nwosu.edu. *Web site:* http://www.nwosu.edu/.

Oklahoma Baptist University
Shawnee, Oklahoma

- **Independent Southern Baptist** comprehensive, founded 1910
- **Small-town** 125-acre campus with easy access to Oklahoma City
- **Coed**
- **Moderately difficult** entrance level

Faculty *Student/faculty ratio:* 11:1.
Academics *Calendar:* 4-1-4. *Degrees:* associate, bachelor's, and master's.
Student Life *Campus security:* 24-hour emergency response devices and patrols, late-night transport/escort service, controlled dormitory access.
Athletics Member NAIA.
Standardized Tests *Required:* SAT or ACT (for admission).
Costs (2010–11) *One-time required fee:* $50. *Comprehensive fee:* $24,300 includes full-time tuition ($17,220), mandatory fees ($1450), and room and board ($5630). Full-time tuition and fees vary according to course load. Part-time tuition: $560 per credit hour. Part-time tuition and fees vary according to course load. *Room and board:* Room and board charges vary according to housing facility.
Financial Aid *Of all full-time matriculated undergraduates who enrolled in 2009,* 1,130 applied for aid, 998 were judged to have need, 146 had their need fully met. 144 Federal Work-Study jobs (averaging $1212). *In 2009,* 250 non-need-based awards were made. *Average percent of need met:* 70. *Average financial aid package:* $13,131. *Average need-based loan:* $4882. *Average need-based gift aid:* $5477. *Average non-need-based aid:* $2704. *Average indebtedness upon graduation:* $21,554.
Applying *Options:* early admission, deferred entrance. *Required:* high school transcript, minimum 2.5 GPA. *Required for some:* essay or personal statement, interview.
Freshman Application Contact Oklahoma Baptist University, 500 West University, Shawnee, OK 74804. *Phone:* 405-878-2033. *Toll-free phone:* 800-654-3285. *Web site:* http://www.okbu.edu/.

Oklahoma Christian University
Oklahoma City, Oklahoma

- **Independent** comprehensive, founded 1950, affiliated with Church of Christ
- **Suburban** 200-acre campus
- **Endowment** $61.9 million
- **Coed** 1,899 undergraduate students, 97% full-time, 49% women, 51% men
- **Noncompetitive** entrance level, 55% of applicants were admitted

Undergraduates 1,835 full-time, 64 part-time. Students come from 44 states and territories; 35 other countries; 57% are from out of state; 5% Black or African American, non-Hispanic/Latino; 3% Hispanic/Latino; 2% Asian, non-Hispanic/Latino; 0.3% Native Hawaiian or other Pacific Islander, non-Hispanic/Latino; 5% American Indian or Alaska Native, non-Hispanic/Latino; 6% Race/ethnicity unknown; 8% international; 5% transferred in; 79% live on campus. *Retention:* 72% of full-time freshmen returned.
Freshmen *Admission:* 1,829 applied, 1,012 admitted, 511 enrolled. *Average high school GPA:* 3.4. *Test scores:* SAT critical reading scores over 500: 66%; SAT math scores over 500: 67%; ACT scores over 18: 90%; SAT critical reading scores over 600: 31%; SAT math scores over 600: 33%; ACT scores over 24: 55%; SAT critical reading scores over 700: 8%; SAT math scores over 700: 6%; ACT scores over 30: 12%.
Faculty *Total:* 192, 57% full-time, 54% with terminal degrees. *Student/faculty ratio:* 13:1.
Academics *Calendar:* semesters. *Degrees:* bachelor's and master's. *Special study options:* academic remediation for entering students, accelerated degree program, advanced placement credit, distance learning, double majors, English as a second language, honors programs, independent study, internships, off-campus study, services for LD students, study abroad, summer session for credit. *ROTC:* Army (c), Air Force (c).
Computers on Campus 101 computers/terminals and 450 ports are available on campus for general student use. Students can access the following: campus intranet, computer help desk, free student e-mail accounts, online (class) grades, online (class) registration, online (class) schedules. Campuswide network is available. 100% of college-owned or -operated housing units are wired for high-speed Internet access. Wireless service is available via entire campus.
Student Life *Housing:* on-campus residence required through senior year. *Options:* men-only, women-only, disabled students. Campus housing is university owned. Freshman campus housing is guaranteed. *Activities and organizations:* drama/theater group, student-run newspaper, radio and television station, choral group, Outreach, Wishing Well Project, Acting on Aids, Young Republicans, College Democrats. *Campus security:* 24-hour emergency response devices and patrols, late-night transport/escort service, controlled dormitory access. *Student services:* health clinic, personal/psychological counseling.
Athletics Member NAIA. *Intercollegiate sports:* baseball M(s), basketball M(s)/W(s), cross-country running M(s)/W(s), golf M(s), soccer M(s)/W(s), softball W(s), tennis M(s)/W(s), track and field M(s)/W(s). *Intramural sports:* baseball M/W, basketball M/W, bowling M/W, cheerleading M/W, cross-country running M/W, football M/W, golf M/W, soccer M/W, softball M/W, swimming and diving M/W, table tennis M/W, tennis M/W, track and field M/W, volleyball M/W.
Standardized Tests *Required:* SAT or ACT (for admission).
Costs (2011–12) *Comprehensive fee:* $24,356 includes full-time tuition ($16,600), mandatory fees ($1856), and room and board ($5900). Full-time tuition and fees vary according to course load. Part-time tuition and fees vary according to course load. *College room only:* $3000. Room and board charges vary according to board plan and housing facility. *Payment plan:* installment. *Waivers:* employees or children of employees.
Financial Aid Of all full-time matriculated undergraduates who enrolled in 2008, 1,906 applied for aid, 1,272 were judged to have need, 265 had their need fully met. 589 Federal Work-Study jobs (averaging $1557). In 2008, 423 non-need-based awards were made. *Average percent of need met:* 55%. *Average financial aid package:* $15,613. *Average need-based loan:* $3877. *Average need-based gift aid:* $2506. *Average non-need-based aid:* $3941. *Average indebtedness upon graduation:* $22,333. *Financial aid deadline:* 8/31.
Applying *Options:* electronic application, early admission, deferred entrance. *Application fee:* $25. *Required:* high school transcript, 1 letter of recommendation. *Application deadlines:* rolling (freshmen), rolling (transfers). *Notification:* continuous (freshmen), continuous (transfers).
Freshman Application Contact Ms. Risa Forrester, Vice President for Enrollment Management, Oklahoma Christian University, Box 11000, Oklahoma City, OK 73136-1100. *Phone:* 405-425-5050. *Toll-free phone:* 800-877-5010. *Fax:* 405-425-5208. *E-mail:* info@oc.edu. *Web site:* http://www.oc.edu/.

Oklahoma City University
Oklahoma City, Oklahoma

- **Independent United Methodist** comprehensive, founded 1904
- **Urban** 75-acre campus with easy access to Oklahoma City
- **Endowment** $71.6 million
- **Coed** 2,314 undergraduate students, 82% full-time, 61% women, 39% men
- **Moderately difficult** entrance level, 76% of applicants were admitted

Undergraduates 1,899 full-time, 415 part-time. Students come from 45 states and territories; 42 other countries; 42% are from out of state; 8% Black or African American, non-Hispanic/Latino; 7% Hispanic/Latino; 2% Asian, non-Hispanic/Latino; 0.1% Native Hawaiian or other Pacific Islander, non-Hispanic/Latino; 4% American Indian or Alaska Native, non-Hispanic/Latino; 3% Two or more races, non-Hispanic/Latino; 2% Race/ethnicity unknown; 17% international; 9% transferred in; 69% live on campus. *Retention:* 77% of full-time freshmen returned.
Freshmen *Admission:* 1,253 applied, 952 admitted, 425 enrolled. *Average high school GPA:* 3.5. *Test scores:* SAT critical reading scores over 500: 80%; SAT math scores over 500: 82%; ACT scores over 18: 98%; SAT critical reading scores over 600: 34%; SAT math scores over 600: 40%; ACT scores over 24: 68%; SAT critical reading scores over 700: 8%; SAT math scores over 700: 3%; ACT scores over 30: 11%.
Faculty *Total:* 352, 57% full-time, 72% with terminal degrees. *Student/faculty ratio:* 11:1.
Academics *Calendar:* semesters. *Degrees:* bachelor's, master's, doctoral-professional, and doctoral-research/scholarship. *Special study options:* academic remediation for entering students, accelerated degree program, adult/continuing education programs, advanced placement credit, cooperative education, double majors, English as a second language, external degree program, honors programs, independent study, internships, off-campus study, part-time degree program, services for LD students, student-designed majors, study abroad, summer session for credit. *ROTC:* Army (c), Air Force (c). *Unusual degree programs:* 3-2 Oklahoma City University School of Law.
Computers on Campus 369 computers/terminals are available on campus for general student use. Students can access the following: campus intranet, computer help desk, free student e-mail accounts, online (class) grades, online (class) registration, online (class) schedules. Campuswide network is available. 100% of college-owned or -operated housing units are wired for high-speed Internet access. Wireless service is available via entire campus.
Student Life *Housing options:* men-only, women-only. Campus housing is university owned. Freshman applicants given priority for college housing. *Activities and organizations:* drama/theater group, student-run newspaper, television station, choral group, Delta Alpha Chi, Student Nursing Association, Fellowship of Christian Athletes, Multicultural Student Association, Chinese Student Association, national fraternities, national sororities. *Campus secu-*

rity: 24-hour emergency response devices and patrols, student patrols, late-night transport/escort service, controlled dormitory access, Operation ID; Emergency Electronic Network. *Student services:* health clinic, personal/psychological counseling.

Athletics Member NAIA. *Intercollegiate sports:* baseball M(s), basketball M(s)/W(s), cheerleading M(s)/W(s), crew M(s)/W(s), golf M(s)/W(s), sailing M(s)(c)/W(s)(c), soccer M(s)/W(s), softball W(s), track and field M(s)/W(s), volleyball W(s), wrestling M(s)/W(s). *Intramural sports:* basketball M/W, fencing M/W, football M, golf M/W, softball M/W, table tennis M/W, volleyball M/W.

Standardized Tests *Required:* SAT or ACT (for admission).

Costs (2011–12) *Comprehensive fee:* $33,260 includes full-time tuition ($23,360), mandatory fees ($2400), and room and board ($7500). Full-time tuition and fees vary according to program. Part-time tuition: $798 per credit hour. Part-time tuition and fees vary according to program. *Room and board:* Room and board charges vary according to board plan and housing facility. *Payment plans:* installment, deferred payment. *Waivers:* employees or children of employees.

Financial Aid Of all full-time matriculated undergraduates who enrolled in 2009, 1,425 applied for aid, 1,312 were judged to have need, 726 had their need fully met. 363 Federal Work-Study jobs (averaging $1362). 270 state and other part-time jobs (averaging $1692). In 2009, 349 non-need-based awards were made. *Average percent of need met:* 56%. *Average financial aid package:* $17,823. *Average need-based loan:* $5128. *Average need-based gift aid:* $14,465. *Average non-need-based aid:* $14,174. *Average indebtedness upon graduation:* $37,023.

Applying *Options:* electronic application, deferred entrance. *Application fee:* $50. *Required:* essay or personal statement, high school transcript, minimum 3 GPA, 2 letters of recommendation. *Required for some:* interview, audition for music and dance programs. *Recommended:* interview. *Application deadlines:* 8/21 (freshmen), rolling (out-of-state freshmen), rolling (transfers). *Notification:* continuous (freshmen), continuous (out-of-state freshmen), continuous (transfers).

Freshman Application Contact Ms. Michelle Lockhart, Senior Director, Admissions, Oklahoma City University, 2501 North Blackwelder, Oklahoma City, OK 73106. *Phone:* 405-208-5340. *Toll-free phone:* 800-633-7242. *Fax:* 405-208-5916. *E-mail:* mlockhart@okcu.edu. *Web site:* http://www.okcu.edu/.

Oklahoma Panhandle State University
Goodwell, Oklahoma

- **State-supported** 4-year, founded 1909, part of Oklahoma State Regents for Higher Education
- **Rural** 40-acre campus
- **Coed** 1,387 undergraduate students, 80% full-time, 50% women, 50% men
- **Noncompetitive** entrance level, 100% of applicants were admitted

Undergraduates 1,116 full-time, 271 part-time. Students come from 25 states and territories; 15 other countries; 50% are from out of state; 6% Black or African American, non-Hispanic/Latino; 18% Hispanic/Latino; 0.2% Asian, non-Hispanic/Latino; 4% American Indian or Alaska Native, non-Hispanic/Latino; 2% Two or more races, non-Hispanic/Latino; 3% Race/ethnicity unknown; 3% international; 12% transferred in. *Retention:* 53% of full-time freshmen returned.

Freshmen *Admission:* 316 applied, 316 admitted, 286 enrolled. *Test scores:* SAT critical reading scores over 500: 23%; SAT math scores over 500: 32%; ACT scores over 18: 58%; SAT critical reading scores over 600: 5%; SAT math scores over 600: 14%; ACT scores over 24: 13%; ACT scores over 30: 1%.

Faculty *Total:* 91, 71% full-time, 24% with terminal degrees. *Student/faculty ratio:* 16:1.

Academics *Calendar:* semesters. *Degrees:* associate and bachelor's. *Special study options:* academic remediation for entering students, advanced placement credit, distance learning, double majors, English as a second language, services for LD students, summer session for credit.

Computers on Campus Students can access the following: free student e-mail accounts, online (class) registration, online (class) schedules. Campuswide network is available. 85% of college-owned or -operated housing units are wired for high-speed Internet access. Wireless service is available via entire campus.

Student Life *Housing:* on-campus residence required for freshman year. *Options:* coed, men-only, women-only. Campus housing is university owned. Freshman campus housing is guaranteed. *Activities and organizations:* drama/theater group, student-run newspaper, radio station, choral group, marching band. *Campus security:* safety bars over door latches. *Student services:* health clinic, personal/psychological counseling.

Athletics Member NCAA. All Division II. *Intercollegiate sports:* baseball M(s), basketball M(s)/W(s), cheerleading W(s)(c), cross-country running M(s)/W(s), equestrian sports W(s)(c), football M(s), golf M(s)/W(s), soccer

M(c)/W(c), softball W(s), volleyball W(s). *Intramural sports:* basketball M/W, football M/W, golf M/W, softball M/W, table tennis M/W, volleyball M/W.

Standardized Tests *Recommended:* SAT or ACT (for admission).

Costs (2010–11) *Tuition:* state resident $2850 full-time, $95 per credit hour part-time; nonresident $8409 full-time, $280 per credit hour part-time. Full-time tuition and fees vary according to course level, program, and student level. Part-time tuition and fees vary according to course level, program, and student level. No tuition increase for student's term of enrollment. *Required fees:* $2494 full-time. *Room and board:* $3652; room only: $900. Room and board charges vary according to board plan and housing facility. *Payment plan:* installment. *Waivers:* senior citizens and employees or children of employees.

Financial Aid Of all full-time matriculated undergraduates who enrolled in 2008, 20 Federal Work-Study jobs (averaging $1747). 158 state and other part-time jobs (averaging $1311). *Average financial aid package:* $7890. *Average need-based gift aid:* $3337.

Applying *Options:* electronic application. *Required:* high school transcript. *Application deadlines:* rolling (freshmen), rolling (transfers).

Freshman Application Contact Mr. Bobby Jenkins, Registrar and Director of Admissions, Oklahoma Panhandle State University, PO Box 430, 323 Eagle Boulevard, Goodwell, OK 73939-0430. *Phone:* 580-349-1376. *Toll-free phone:* 800-664-6778. *Fax:* 580-349-1371. *E-mail:* opsu@opsu.edu. *Web site:* http://www.opsu.edu/.

Oklahoma State University
Stillwater, Oklahoma

- **State-supported** university, founded 1890, part of Oklahoma State University
- **Small-town** 840-acre campus with easy access to Oklahoma City and Tulsa
- **Endowment** $402.5 million
- **Coed** 18,197 undergraduate students, 87% full-time, 49% women, 51% men
- **Moderately difficult** entrance level, 81% of applicants were admitted

Undergraduates 15,776 full-time, 2,421 part-time. Students come from 51 states and territories; 88 other countries; 19% are from out of state; 5% Black or African American, non-Hispanic/Latino; 3% Hispanic/Latino; 2% Asian, non-Hispanic/Latino; 10% American Indian or Alaska Native, non-Hispanic/Latino; 3% international; 9% transferred in; 44% live on campus. *Retention:* 78% of full-time freshmen returned.

Freshmen *Admission:* 8,696 applied, 7,079 admitted, 3,554 enrolled. *Average high school GPA:* 3.52. *Test scores:* SAT critical reading scores over 500: 73%; SAT math scores over 500: 81%; ACT scores over 18: 98%; SAT critical reading scores over 600: 28%; SAT math scores over 600: 43%; ACT scores over 24: 65%; SAT critical reading scores over 700: 5%; SAT math scores over 700: 7%; ACT scores over 30: 15%.

Faculty *Total:* 1,285, 78% full-time, 77% with terminal degrees. *Student/faculty ratio:* 19:1.

Academics *Calendar:* semesters. *Degrees:* bachelor's, master's, doctoral-professional, doctoral-research/scholarship, post-master's, and postbachelor's certificates. *Special study options:* academic remediation for entering students, accelerated degree program, advanced placement credit, distance learning, double majors, English as a second language, freshman honors college, honors programs, independent study, internships, off-campus study, part-time degree program, services for LD students, student-designed majors, study abroad, summer session for credit. *ROTC:* Army (b), Air Force (b).

Computers on Campus Students can access the following: campus intranet, computer help desk, free student e-mail accounts, online (class) grades, online (class) registration, online (class) schedules. Campuswide network is available. Wireless service is available via classrooms, computer centers, computer labs, libraries, student centers.

Student Life *Housing:* on-campus residence required for freshman year. *Options:* coed, men-only, women-only, disabled students. Campus housing is university owned. Freshman campus housing is guaranteed. *Activities and organizations:* drama/theater group, student-run newspaper, radio and television station, choral group, marching band, national fraternities, national sororities. *Campus security:* 24-hour emergency response devices and patrols, student patrols, controlled dormitory access. *Student services:* health clinic, personal/psychological counseling, women's center.

Athletics Member NCAA. All Division I. *Intercollegiate sports:* baseball M(s), basketball M(s)/W(s), cross-country running M(s)/W(s), equestrian sports W(s), football M(s), golf M(s)/W(s), soccer W(s), softball W(s), tennis M(s)/W(s), track and field M(s)/W(s), wrestling M(s).

Standardized Tests *Required:* SAT or ACT (for admission).

Costs (2010–11) *One-time required fee:* $95. *Tuition:* state resident $4103 full-time, $137 per credit hour part-time; nonresident $14,925 full-time, $498 per credit hour part-time. Full-time tuition and fees vary according to program and student level. Part-time tuition and fees vary according to program and student level. *Required fees:* $2676 full-time, $89 per credit hour part-time.

Room and board: $6680; room only: $3600. Room and board charges vary according to board plan and housing facility. *Payment plan:* installment. *Waivers:* children of alumni.

Financial Aid Of all full-time matriculated undergraduates who enrolled in 2008, 9,891 applied for aid, 7,737 were judged to have need, 1,185 had their need fully met. 486 Federal Work-Study jobs (averaging $2117). 3,374 state and other part-time jobs (averaging $2416). In 2008, 3448 non-need-based awards were made. *Average percent of need met:* 72%. *Average financial aid package:* $11,277. *Average need-based loan:* $4258. *Average need-based gift aid:* $6271. *Average non-need-based aid:* $4352. *Average indebtedness upon graduation:* $19,934.

Applying *Options:* electronic application, deferred entrance. *Application fee:* $40. *Required:* high school transcript, minimum 3 GPA, class rank. *Required for some:* essay or personal statement, interview. *Application deadlines:* rolling (freshmen), rolling (out-of-state freshmen), rolling (transfers). *Notification:* continuous (freshmen), continuous (out-of-state freshmen), continuous (transfers).

Freshman Application Contact Oklahoma State University, Stillwater, OK 74078. *Phone:* 405-744-3087. *Toll-free phone:* 800-233-5019 Ext. 1 (in-state); 800-852-1255 (out-of-state). *Web site:* http://www.okstate.edu/.

Oklahoma State University, Oklahoma City

Oklahoma City, Oklahoma

- **State-supported** primarily 2-year, founded 1961, part of Oklahoma State University
- **Urban** 110-acre campus
- **Coed** 7,647 undergraduate students
- **Noncompetitive** entrance level, 100% of applicants were admitted

Undergraduates Students come from 9 states and territories; 8 other countries; 1% are from out of state. *Retention:* 36% of full-time freshmen returned.

Freshmen *Admission:* 1,082 applied, 1,082 admitted.

Faculty *Total:* 381, 22% full-time. *Student/faculty ratio:* 20:1.

Academics *Calendar:* semesters. *Degrees:* certificates, associate, and bachelor's. *Special study options:* academic remediation for entering students, advanced placement credit, cooperative education, distance learning, double majors, honors programs, independent study, part-time degree program, services for LD students, study abroad, summer session for credit.

Computers on Campus 600 computers/terminals are available on campus for general student use. Campuswide network is available.

Student Life *Housing:* college housing not available. *Activities and organizations:* Phi Theta Kappa, Deaf/Hearing Social Club, American Criminal Justice Association, Horticulture Club, Vet-Tech Club. *Campus security:* 24-hour patrols, late-night transport/escort service.

Costs (2010–11) *Tuition:* state resident $2889 full-time, $100 per credit hour part-time; nonresident $7749 full-time, $269 per credit hour part-time. Full-time tuition and fees vary according to course level, degree level, and program. Part-time tuition and fees vary according to course level, degree level, and program. No tuition increase for student's term of enrollment. *Required fees:* $30 full-time, $11 per credit hour part-time. *Payment plan:* installment. *Waivers:* senior citizens and employees or children of employees.

Applying *Options:* electronic application, early admission. *Required:* high school transcript. *Application deadlines:* rolling (freshmen), rolling (transfers). *Notification:* continuous (freshmen), continuous (transfers).

Freshman Application Contact Kyle Williams, Director, Enrollment Management, Oklahoma State University, Oklahoma City, 900 North Portland, AD202, Oklahoma City, OK 73107. *Phone:* 405-945-9152. *E-mail:* wilkylw@osuokc.edu. *Web site:* http://www.osuokc.edu/.

Oklahoma Wesleyan University

Bartlesville, Oklahoma

- **Independent** comprehensive, founded 1909, affiliated with Wesleyan Church
- **Small-town** 127-acre campus with easy access to Tulsa
- **Endowment** $2.8 million
- **Coed** 1,035 undergraduate students, 59% full-time, 59% women, 41% men
- **Minimally difficult** entrance level, 65% of applicants were admitted

Undergraduates 607 full-time, 428 part-time. Students come from 40 states and territories; 6 other countries; 38% are from out of state; 8% Black or African American, non-Hispanic/Latino; 4% Hispanic/Latino; 0.7% Asian, non-Hispanic/Latino; 0.1% Native Hawaiian or other Pacific Islander, non-Hispanic/Latino; 9% American Indian or Alaska Native, non-Hispanic/Latino; 2% Two or more races, non-Hispanic/Latino; 2% Race/ethnicity unknown; 3%

international; 16% transferred in; 28% live on campus. *Retention:* 62% of full-time freshmen returned.

Freshmen *Admission:* 1,894 applied, 1,226 admitted, 173 enrolled. *Average high school GPA:* 3.25. *Test scores:* SAT critical reading scores over 500: 44%; SAT math scores over 500: 33%; SAT writing scores over 500: 32%; ACT scores over 18: 81%; SAT critical reading scores over 600: 15%; SAT math scores over 600: 12%; SAT writing scores over 600: 17%; ACT scores over 24: 36%; SAT critical reading scores over 700: 2%; ACT scores over 30: 6%.

Faculty *Total:* 69, 43% full-time, 25% with terminal degrees. *Student/faculty ratio:* 19:1.

Academics *Calendar:* semesters. *Degrees:* certificates, diplomas, associate, bachelor's, and master's. *Special study options:* academic remediation for entering students, accelerated degree program, adult/continuing education programs, advanced placement credit, cooperative education, distance learning, double majors, external degree program, independent study, internships, off-campus study, part-time degree program, services for LD students, student-designed majors, study abroad, summer session for credit.

Computers on Campus 30 computers/terminals and 120 ports are available on campus for general student use. Students can access the following: campus intranet, computer help desk, free student e-mail accounts, online (class) grades, online (class) registration, online (class) schedules. Campuswide network is available. 100% of college-owned or -operated housing units are wired for high-speed Internet access. Wireless service is available via entire campus.

Student Life *Housing:* on-campus residence required through junior year. *Options:* men-only, women-only. Campus housing is university owned. Freshman campus housing is guaranteed. *Activities and organizations:* drama/theater group, student-run newspaper, choral group, Operation Saturation (Community Service Opportunities), Fellowship of Christian Athletes, Missions Support Groups, intramurals, Student Government groups. *Campus security:* 24-hour emergency response devices, student patrols. *Student services:* health clinic, personal/psychological counseling.

Athletics Member NAIA, NCCAA. *Intercollegiate sports:* baseball M(s), basketball M(s)/W(s), cross-country running M(s)/W(s), golf M(s), soccer M(s)/W(s), softball W(s), tennis M(s)/W(s), track and field M(s)/W(s), volleyball W(s). *Intramural sports:* basketball M/W, cheerleading W, football M/W, softball M/W, volleyball M/W.

Standardized Tests *Required:* SAT or ACT (for admission).

Costs (2011–12) *Comprehensive fee:* $27,034 includes full-time tuition ($19,060), mandatory fees ($1100), and room and board ($6874). Full-time tuition and fees vary according to course load. Part-time tuition: $755 per credit hour. *Required fees:* $55 per credit hour part-time, $60 per term part-time. *College room only:* $3634. Room and board charges vary according to board plan and housing facility. *Payment plans:* installment, deferred payment. *Waivers:* senior citizens and employees or children of employees.

Financial Aid Of all full-time matriculated undergraduates who enrolled in 2009, 674 applied for aid, 570 were judged to have need, 77 had their need fully met. 207 Federal Work-Study jobs (averaging $1085). 16 state and other part-time jobs (averaging $1585). In 2009, 55 non-need-based awards were made. *Average percent of need met:* 63%. *Average financial aid package:* $11,271. *Average need-based loan:* $4079. *Average need-based gift aid:* $8203. *Average non-need-based aid:* $5404. *Average indebtedness upon graduation:* $20,852.

Applying *Options:* electronic application. *Application fee:* $25. *Required:* high school transcript, ACT score 18 or higher. *Recommended:* minimum 2 GPA. *Application deadlines:* rolling (freshmen), rolling (out-of-state freshmen), rolling (transfers).

Freshman Application Contact Jennifer Weaver, Enrollment Counselor, Oklahoma Wesleyan University, 2201 Silver Lake Drive, Bartlesville, OK 74006. *Phone:* 866-222-8226. *Toll-free phone:* 866-222-8226. *Fax:* 918-335-6229. *E-mail:* admissions@okwu.edu. *Web site:* http://www.okwu.edu/.

Oral Roberts University

Tulsa, Oklahoma

- **Independent interdenominational** comprehensive, founded 1963
- **Urban** 263-acre campus
- **Coed**
- **Moderately difficult** entrance level

Faculty *Student/faculty ratio:* 12:1.

Academics *Calendar:* semesters. *Degrees:* bachelor's, master's, and doctoral-research/scholarship.

Student Life *Campus security:* 24-hour emergency response devices and patrols, late-night transport/escort service.

Athletics Member NCAA. All Division I.

Standardized Tests *Required:* SAT or ACT (for admission).

Costs (2010–11) *Comprehensive fee:* $28,348 includes full-time tuition ($19,382), mandatory fees ($662), and room and board ($8304). Full-time tuition and fees vary according to degree level. Part-time tuition: $810 per credit hour. Part-time tuition and fees vary according to degree level. *College* *room only:* $4254. Room and board charges vary according to board plan and housing facility.

Financial Aid *Of all full-time matriculated undergraduates who enrolled in 2008,* 1,978 applied for aid, 1,738 were judged to have need, 643 had their need fully met. *In 2008,* 501 non-need-based awards were made. *Average percent of need met:* 86. *Average financial aid package:* $18,229. *Average need-based loan:* $10,159. *Average need-based gift aid:* $9304. *Average non-need-based aid:* $7151. *Average indebtedness upon graduation:* $34,555.

Applying *Options:* early action, deferred entrance. *Application fee:* $35. *Required:* essay or personal statement, high school transcript, minimum 2 GPA, 1 letter of recommendation, proof of immunization. *Required for some:* interview. *Recommended:* interview.

Freshman Application Contact Director of Admissions, Oral Roberts University, 7777 South Lewis Avenue, Tulsa, OK 74171. *Phone:* 918-495-6529. *Toll-free phone:* 800-678-8876. *Fax:* 918-495-6222495-6222. *E-mail:* admissions@oru.edu. *Web site:* http://www.oru.edu/.

Rogers State University
Claremore, Oklahoma

- **State-supported** 4-year, founded 1909, part of Oklahoma State Regents for Higher Education
- **Small-town** 40-acre campus with easy access to Tulsa
- **Endowment** $6.4 million
- **Coed** 4,386 undergraduate students, 61% full-time, 63% women, 37% men
- **Noncompetitive** entrance level, 50% of applicants were admitted

Undergraduates 2,685 full-time, 1,701 part-time. Students come from 33 states and territories; 23 other countries; 4% are from out of state; 3% Black or African American, non-Hispanic/Latino; 3% Hispanic/Latino; 1% Asian, non-Hispanic/Latino; 0.1% Native Hawaiian or other Pacific Islander, non-Hispanic/Latino; 14% American Indian or Alaska Native, non-Hispanic/Latino; 17% Two or more races, non-Hispanic/Latino; 0.8% international; 8% transferred in; 6% live on campus. *Retention:* 54% of full-time freshmen returned.

Freshmen *Admission:* 2,098 applied, 1,057 admitted, 838 enrolled. *Average high school GPA:* 2.75. *Test scores:* ACT scores over 18: 75%; ACT scores over 24: 17%; ACT scores over 30: 1%.

Faculty *Total:* 260, 40% full-time, 35% with terminal degrees. *Student/faculty ratio:* 21:1.

Academics *Calendar:* semesters. *Degrees:* associate and bachelor's. *Special study options:* academic remediation for entering students, adult/continuing education programs, advanced placement credit, cooperative education, distance learning, double majors, honors programs, independent study, internships, off-campus study, part-time degree program, services for LD students, study abroad, summer session for credit.

Computers on Campus 254 computers/terminals are available on campus for general student use. Students can access the following: computer help desk, free student e-mail accounts, online (class) grades, online (class) registration, online (class) schedules, software to support courses. Campuswide network is available. 100% of college-owned or -operated housing units are wired for high-speed Internet access. Wireless service is available via classrooms, computer labs, learning centers, libraries, student centers.

Student Life *Housing options:* coed. Campus housing is university owned. *Activities and organizations:* drama/theater group, student-run newspaper, radio station, choral group, Student Veterans Association, EMSSA, Campus Crusade for Christ, Community Counseling Student Association, Student Nursing Association, national fraternities, national sororities. *Campus security:* 24-hour emergency response devices and patrols, student patrols, late-night transport/escort service. *Student services:* health clinic, personal/psychological counseling.

Athletics Member NAIA. *Intercollegiate sports:* baseball M(s), basketball M(s)/W(s), cheerleading M(s)/W(s), cross-country running M(s)/W(s), golf M(s)/W(s), soccer M(s)/W(s), softball W(s). *Intramural sports:* basketball M/W, soccer M/W, softball M/W, table tennis M/W, volleyball M/W.

Standardized Tests *Required:* SAT or ACT (for admission). *Required for some:* ACT COMPASS. *Recommended:* ACT (for admission).

Costs (2011–12) *Tuition:* state resident $2879 full-time, $96 per credit hour part-time; nonresident $8636 full-time, $288 per credit hour part-time. Full-time tuition and fees vary according to course level, course load, location, program, and student level. Part-time tuition and fees vary according to course level, course load, location, program, and student level. *Required fees:* $1634 full-time, $53 per credit hour part-time, $15 per credit hour part-time. *Room only:* $5990. Room and board charges vary according to board plan and housing facility. *Payment plan:* installment. *Waivers:* senior citizens and employees or children of employees.

Financial Aid *Of all full-time matriculated undergraduates who enrolled in 2009,* 1,171 applied for aid, 1,545 were judged to have need, 126 had their need fully met. 60 Federal Work-Study jobs (averaging $1914). 284 state and other part-time jobs (averaging $2549). *In 2009,* 38 non-need-based awards were made. *Average percent of need met:* 45%. *Average financial aid pack-*

age: $7956. *Average need-based loan:* $3799. *Average need-based gift aid:* $4875. *Average non-need-based aid:* $3391. *Average indebtedness upon graduation:* $15,962.

Applying *Options:* electronic application. *Required:* high school transcript, ACT or SAT scores. *Required for some:* minimum 2.7 GPA. *Application deadlines:* rolling (freshmen), rolling (out-of-state freshmen), rolling (transfers).

Freshman Application Contact Ms. Julie Rampey, Director of Admissions, Rogers State University, 1701 West Will Rogers Boulevard, Claremore, OK 74017. *Phone:* 918-343-7546. *Toll-free phone:* 800-256-7511. *Fax:* 918-343-7595. *E-mail:* info@rsu.edu. *Web site:* http://www.rsu.edu/.

St. Gregory's University
Shawnee, Oklahoma

Freshman Application Contact Director of Admissions, St. Gregory's University, 1900 West MacArthur Drive, Shawnee, OK 74804. *Phone:* 405-878-5447. *Toll-free phone:* 888-STGREGS. *Fax:* 405-878-5198. *E-mail:* admissions@stgregorys.edu. *Web site:* http://www.stgregorys.edu/.

Southeastern Oklahoma State University
Durant, Oklahoma

- **State-supported** comprehensive, founded 1909, part of Oklahoma State Regents for Higher Education
- **Small-town** 177-acre campus
- **Endowment** $9.7 million
- **Coed** 3,768 undergraduate students, 79% full-time, 56% women, 44% men
- **Moderately difficult** entrance level, 83% of applicants were admitted

Undergraduates 2,967 full-time, 801 part-time. Students come from 35 states and territories; 31 other countries; 24% are from out of state; 6% Black or African American, non-Hispanic/Latino; 3% Hispanic/Latino; 0.9% Asian, non-Hispanic/Latino; 0.3% Native Hawaiian or other Pacific Islander, non-Hispanic/Latino; 30% American Indian or Alaska Native, non-Hispanic/Latino; 2% international; 11% transferred in; 18% live on campus. *Retention:* 59% of full-time freshmen returned.

Freshmen *Admission:* 1,176 applied, 980 admitted, 672 enrolled. *Average high school GPA:* 3.29. *Test scores:* ACT scores over 18: 79%; ACT scores over 24: 21%; ACT scores over 30: 2%.

Faculty *Total:* 261, 56% full-time, 50% with terminal degrees. *Student/faculty ratio:* 18:1.

Academics *Calendar:* semesters. *Degrees:* bachelor's, master's, and post-master's certificates. *Special study options:* academic remediation for entering students, accelerated degree program, adult/continuing education programs, advanced placement credit, distance learning, double majors, honors programs, independent study, internships, off-campus study, part-time degree program, services for LD students, summer session for credit.

Computers on Campus 598 computers/terminals and 598 ports are available on campus for general student use. Students can access the following: campus intranet, computer help desk, free student e-mail accounts, online (class) grades, online (class) registration, online (class) schedules, campus Blackboard classes. Campuswide network is available. 100% of college-owned or -operated housing units are wired for high-speed Internet access. Wireless service is available via classrooms, computer labs, dorm rooms, learning centers, libraries, student centers.

Student Life *Housing:* on-campus residence required for freshman year. *Options:* coed, men-only, women-only, disabled students. Campus housing is university owned. Freshman campus housing is guaranteed. *Activities and organizations:* drama/theater group, student-run newspaper, radio station, choral group, marching band, Baptist Collegiate Ministries, Fellowship of Christian Athletes, Wesley Foundation, Resident Hall Association, national fraternities, national sororities. *Campus security:* 24-hour patrols, late-night transport/escort service. *Student services:* health clinic, personal/psychological counseling.

Athletics Member NCAA. All Division II. *Intercollegiate sports:* baseball M(s), basketball M(s)/W(s), cross-country running W(s), football M(s), golf M(s), softball W(s), tennis M(s)/W(s), volleyball W(s). *Intramural sports:* basketball M/W, football M.

Standardized Tests *Required:* SAT or ACT (for admission).

Costs (2010–11) *Tuition:* state resident $3875 full-time, $129 per credit hour part-time; nonresident $10,602 full-time, $353 per credit hour part-time. Full-time tuition and fees vary according to course level. Part-time tuition and fees vary according to course level and course load. *Required fees:* $677 full-time, $23 per credit hour part-time. *Room and board:* $4520; room only: $1980. Room and board charges vary according to board plan and housing facility. *Waivers:* minority students, children of alumni, senior citizens, and employees or children of employees.

Financial Aid Of all full-time matriculated undergraduates who enrolled in 2008, 2,056 applied for aid, 1,771 were judged to have need, 307 had their need fully met. 642 Federal Work-Study jobs (averaging $1571). 874 state and other part-time jobs (averaging $2032). In 2008, 12 non-need-based awards were made. *Average percent of need met: 24%. Average financial aid package:* $10,425. *Average need-based loan:* $1709. *Average need-based gift aid:* $1547. *Average non-need-based aid:* $1641. *Average indebtedness upon graduation:* $13,828.

Applying *Application fee:* $20. *Required:* high school transcript. *Required for some:* interview. *Application deadlines:* rolling (freshmen), rolling (transfers). *Notification:* continuous (freshmen), continuous (transfers).

Freshman Application Contact Southeastern Oklahoma State University, 1405 North 4th Avenue, Durant, OK 74701-0609. *Phone:* 580-745-2060. *Toll-free phone:* 800-435-1327. *Web site:* http://www.se.edu/.

Southern Nazarene University

Bethany, Oklahoma

- **Independent Nazarene** comprehensive, founded 1899
- **Suburban** 40-acre campus with easy access to Oklahoma City
- **Endowment** $19.9 million
- **Coed** 1,608 undergraduate students, 96% full-time, 51% women, 49% men
- **Noncompetitive** entrance level, 100% of applicants were admitted

Undergraduates 1,549 full-time, 59 part-time. Students come from 33 states and territories; 33 other countries; 23% are from out of state; 12% Black or African American, non-Hispanic/Latino; 5% Hispanic/Latino; 3% Asian, non-Hispanic/Latino; 5% American Indian or Alaska Native, non-Hispanic/Latino; 0.5% Race/ethnicity unknown; 1% international; 6% transferred in; 71% live on campus. *Retention:* 64% of full-time freshmen returned.

Freshmen *Admission:* 1,105 applied, 1,105 admitted, 279 enrolled. *Average high school GPA:* 3.3. *Test scores:* ACT scores over 18: 81%; ACT scores over 24: 34%; ACT scores over 30: 3%.

Faculty *Total:* 189, 37% full-time, 56% with terminal degrees. *Student/faculty ratio:* 18:1.

Academics *Calendar:* semesters. *Degrees:* associate, bachelor's, and master's. *Special study options:* academic remediation for entering students, accelerated degree program, adult/continuing education programs, advanced placement credit, distance learning, double majors, English as a second language, external degree program, honors programs, independent study, internships, off-campus study, part-time degree program, services for LD students, student-designed majors, study abroad, summer session for credit. *ROTC:* Army (c), Air Force (c).

Computers on Campus 120 computers/terminals are available on campus for general student use. Students can access the following: campus intranet, computer help desk, free student e-mail accounts, online (class) grades, online (class) schedules. Campuswide network is available. 100% of college-owned or -operated housing units are wired for high-speed Internet access. Wireless service is available via entire campus.

Student Life *Housing:* on-campus residence required through senior year. *Options:* men-only, women-only. Campus housing is university owned. Freshman campus housing is guaranteed. *Activities and organizations:* drama/theater group, student-run newspaper, choral group, Business Gaming Team, Campus Social Life Committee, intramural sports societies, Choral Society, Inter-Club. *Campus security:* 24-hour emergency response devices, student patrols, late-night transport/escort service, controlled dormitory access. *Student services:* health clinic, personal/psychological counseling.

Athletics Member NAIA. *Intercollegiate sports:* baseball M(s), basketball M(s)/W(s), cheerleading M(s)/W(s), cross-country running M(s)/W(s), equestrian sports M/W, football M(s), golf M(s)/W(s), soccer M(s)/W(s), softball W(s), tennis M(s)/W(s), track and field M(s)/W(s), volleyball W(s). *Intramural sports:* basketball M/W, football M/W, golf M/W, racquetball M/W, soccer M/W, softball M/W, swimming and diving M/W, table tennis M/W, tennis M/W, volleyball M/W, weight lifting M/W.

Standardized Tests *Required:* SAT or ACT (for admission). *Recommended:* ACT (for admission).

Costs (2011–12) *Comprehensive fee:* $27,394 includes full-time tuition ($19,170), mandatory fees ($624), and room and board ($7600). Part-time tuition: $639 per credit. Part-time tuition and fees vary according to course load. *Room and board:* Room and board charges vary according to board plan and housing facility. *Payment plans:* tuition prepayment, installment, deferred payment. *Waivers:* employees or children of employees.

Financial Aid Of all full-time matriculated undergraduates who enrolled in 2009, 1,485 applied for aid, 1,366 were judged to have need. 104 Federal

Work-Study jobs (averaging $2125). 115 state and other part-time jobs (averaging $3000).

Applying *Options:* electronic application, deferred entrance. *Application fee:* $35. *Required:* high school transcript, minimum 2 GPA, 2 letters of recommendation, interview. *Application deadlines:* 8/15 (freshmen), 8/15 (transfers). *Notification:* continuous (freshmen), continuous (transfers).

Freshman Application Contact Mr. Todd Brant, Director of Recruitment, Southern Nazarene University, 6729 Northwest 39th Expressway, Bethany, OK 73008. *Phone:* 405-491-6324. *Toll-free phone:* 800-648-9899. *Fax:* 405-491-6320. *E-mail:* admiss@snu.edu. *Web site:* http://www.snu.edu/.

Southwestern Christian University

Bethany, Oklahoma

Freshman Application Contact Southwestern Christian University, PO Box 340, Bethany, OK 73008-0340. *Phone:* 405-789-7661. *Web site:* http://www.swcu.edu/.

Southwestern Oklahoma State University

Weatherford, Oklahoma

- **State-supported** comprehensive, founded 1901, part of Southwestern Oklahoma State University
- **Small-town** 73-acre campus with easy access to Oklahoma City
- **Coed**
- **Minimally difficult** entrance level

Faculty *Student/faculty ratio:* 20:1.

Academics *Calendar:* semesters. *Degrees:* associate, bachelor's, master's, and doctoral-professional.

Student Life *Campus security:* late-night transport/escort service, controlled dormitory access, 20-hour campus emergency security.

Athletics Member NCAA. All Division II.

Standardized Tests *Required:* SAT or ACT (for admission).

Costs (2010–11) *Tuition:* state resident $3405 full-time, $114 per credit hour part-time; nonresident $9120 full-time, $304 per credit hour part-time. Full-time tuition and fees vary according to program. Part-time tuition and fees vary according to program. *Required fees:* $930 full-time, $31 per credit hour part-time. *Room and board:* $4100; room only: $1660. Room and board charges vary according to board plan.

Financial Aid Of all full-time matriculated undergraduates who enrolled in 2009, 2,758 applied for aid, 2,244 were judged to have need, 929 had their need fully met. In 2009, 1182 non-need-based awards were made. *Average percent of need met:* 89. *Average financial aid package:* $4890. *Average need-based loan:* $1677. *Average need-based gift aid:* $1463. *Average non-need-based aid:* $491. *Financial aid deadline:* 3/1.

Applying *Options:* deferred entrance. *Application fee:* $15. *Required:* high school transcript, minimum 2 GPA.

Freshman Application Contact Ms. Connie Phillips, Admission Counselor, Southwestern Oklahoma State University, 100 Campus Drive, Weatherford, OK 73096-3098. *Phone:* 580-774-3009. *Fax:* 580-774-3795. *E-mail:* ropers@swosu.edu. *Web site:* http://www.swosu.edu/.

Spartan College of Aeronautics and Technology

Tulsa, Oklahoma

- **Proprietary** primarily 2-year, founded 1928
- **Urban** 26-acre campus
- **Men only**
- **Noncompetitive** entrance level

Faculty *Student/faculty ratio:* 14:1.

Academics *Calendar:* calendar terms. *Degrees:* certificates, diplomas, associate, and bachelor's.

Financial Aid Of all full-time matriculated undergraduates who enrolled in 2009, 23 Federal Work-Study jobs (averaging $4341).

Applying *Application fee:* $100. *Required:* high school transcript. *Recommended:* interview.

Freshman Application Contact Mr. Mark Fowler, Vice President of Student Records and Finance, Spartan College of Aeronautics and Technology, 8820 East Pine Street, PO Box 582833, Tulsa, OK 74158-2833. *Phone:* 918-836-6886. *Toll-free phone:* 800-331-1204 (in-state); 800-331-124 (out-of-state). *Web site:* http://www.spartan.edu/.

University of Central Oklahoma

Edmond, Oklahoma

- **State-supported** comprehensive, founded 1890, part of Oklahoma State Regents for Higher Education
- **Suburban** 200-acre campus with easy access to Oklahoma City
- **Endowment** $8.6 million
- **Coed**
- **Minimally difficult** entrance level

Faculty *Student/faculty ratio:* 19:1.

Academics *Calendar:* semesters. *Degrees:* certificates, associate, bachelor's, and master's.

Student Life *Campus security:* 24-hour emergency response devices and patrols, late-night transport/escort service.

Athletics Member NCAA. All Division II.

Standardized Tests *Required:* SAT or ACT (for admission). *Required for some:* SAT and SAT Subject Tests or ACT (for admission). *Recommended:* SAT (for admission), ACT (for admission).

Costs (2010–11) *Tuition:* state resident $3914 full-time, $130 per credit hour part-time; nonresident $10,700 full-time, $357 per credit hour part-time. Full-time tuition and fees vary according to course load, degree level, and program. Part-time tuition and fees vary according to course load, degree level, and program. No tuition increase for student's term of enrollment. *Required fees:* $542 full-time, $18 per credit hour part-time. *Room and board:* $8005; room only: $4869. Room and board charges vary according to board plan and housing facility. *Payment plans:* installment, deferred payment.

Financial Aid *Of all full-time matriculated undergraduates who enrolled in 2008, 5,777 applied for aid, 4,770 were judged to have need, 412 had their need fully met. In 2008,* 4864 non-need-based awards were made. *Average percent of need met:* 67. *Average financial aid package:* $7249. *Average need-based loan:* $4339. *Average need-based gift aid:* $7378. *Average non-need-based aid:* $5549.

Applying *Options:* electronic application, deferred entrance. *Application fee:* $25. *Required:* high school transcript, minimum 2.7 GPA, rank in upper 50% of high school class.

Freshman Application Contact Ms. Linda Lofton, Director, Admissions and Records Processing, University of Central Oklahoma, Office of Enrollment Services, 100 North University Drive, Box 151, Edmond, OK 73034-5209. *Phone:* 405-974-2338 Ext. 2338. *Toll-free phone:* 800-254-4215. *Fax:* 405-341-4964. *E-mail:* admituco@uco.edu. *Web site:* http://www.uco.edu/.

University of Oklahoma

Norman, Oklahoma

- **State-supported** university, founded 1890
- **Suburban** 3754-acre campus with easy access to Oklahoma City
- **Endowment** $680.5 million
- **Coed** 19,781 undergraduate students, 87% full-time, 50% women, 50% men
- **Moderately difficult** entrance level, 85% of applicants were admitted

Undergraduates 17,168 full-time, 2,613 part-time. Students come from 54 states and territories; 101 other countries; 30% are from out of state; 5% Black or African American, non-Hispanic/Latino; 4% Hispanic/Latino; 6% Asian, non-Hispanic/Latino; 0.1% Native Hawaiian or other Pacific Islander, non-Hispanic/Latino; 6% American Indian or Alaska Native, non-Hispanic/Latino; 2% Two or more races, non-Hispanic/Latino; 9% Race/ethnicity unknown; 3% international; 7% transferred in; 35% live on campus. *Retention:* 83% of full-time freshmen returned.

Freshmen *Admission:* 9,996 applied, 8,498 admitted, 3,724 enrolled. *Average high school GPA:* 3.6. *Test scores:* SAT critical reading scores over 500: 80%; SAT math scores over 500: 85%; ACT scores over 18: 99%; SAT critical reading scores over 600: 40%; SAT math scores over 600: 50%; ACT scores over 24: 72%; SAT critical reading scores over 700: 14%; SAT math scores over 700: 14%; ACT scores over 30: 21%.

Faculty *Total:* 1,376, 82% full-time, 78% with terminal degrees. *Student/faculty ratio:* 19:1.

Academics *Calendar:* semesters. *Degrees:* bachelor's, master's, doctoral-professional, doctoral-research/scholarship, and postbachelor's certificates. *Special study options:* academic remediation for entering students, accelerated degree program, adult/continuing education programs, advanced placement credit, cooperative education, distance learning, double majors, English as a second language, external degree program, freshman honors college, honors programs, independent study, internships, off-campus study, part-time degree program, services for LD students, student-designed majors, study abroad, summer session for credit. *ROTC:* Army (b), Navy (b), Air Force (b). *Unusual degree programs:* 3-2 business administration; engineering; English; mathematics/biostatistics, computer science.

Computers on Campus 3,600 computers/terminals and 2,200 ports are available on campus for general student use. Students can access the following: campus intranet, computer help desk, free student e-mail accounts, online (class) grades, online (class) registration, online (class) schedules. Campus-wide network is available. 100% of college-owned or -operated housing units are wired for high-speed Internet access. Wireless service is available via classrooms, computer centers, computer labs, dorm rooms, learning centers, libraries, student centers.

Student Life *Housing:* on-campus residence required for freshman year. *Options:* coed, men-only, women-only, disabled students. Campus housing is university owned. Freshman campus housing is guaranteed. *Activities and organizations:* drama/theater group, student-run newspaper, radio and television station, choral group, marching band, Campus Activities Council, University of Oklahoma Student Association, OU Cousins, Fraternities/Sororities, The Big Event, national fraternities, national sororities. *Campus security:* 24-hour emergency response devices and patrols, student patrols, late-night transport/escort service, controlled dormitory access, crime prevention programs, police bicycle patrols, self-defense classes. *Student services:* health clinic, personal/psychological counseling, women's center, legal services.

Athletics Member NCAA. All Division I except football (Division I-A). *Intercollegiate sports:* baseball M(s), basketball M(s)/W(s), crew W(s), cross-country running M(s)/W(s), golf M(s)/W(s), gymnastics M(s)/W(s), soccer W(s), softball W(s), tennis M(s)/W(s), track and field M(s)/W(s), volleyball W(s), wrestling M(s). *Intramural sports:* badminton M/W, basketball M/W, crew M(c)/W(c), equestrian sports M(c)/W(c), golf M/W, ice hockey M(c), lacrosse M(c)/W(c), racquetball M/W, rugby M(c)/W(c), sailing M(c)/W(c), soccer M/W, softball M/W, table tennis M/W, ultimate Frisbee M(c)/W(c), volleyball M/W.

Standardized Tests *Required:* SAT or ACT (for admission).

Costs (2010–11) *Tuition:* state resident $2942 full-time, $123 per credit hour part-time; nonresident $11,287 full-time, $470 per credit hour part-time. Full-time tuition and fees vary according to course load, degree level, location, program, and reciprocity agreements. Part-time tuition and fees vary according to course load, degree level, location, program, and reciprocity agreements. No tuition increase for student's term of enrollment. *Required fees:* $2535 full-time, $95 per credit hour part-time, $127 per term part-time. *Room and board:* $7826; room only: $4284. Room and board charges vary according to board plan and housing facility. *Payment plan:* installment. *Waivers:* children of alumni, senior citizens, and employees or children of employees.

Financial Aid Of all full-time matriculated undergraduates who enrolled in 2008, 10,046 applied for aid, 7,305 were judged to have need, 6,385 had their need fully met. 633 Federal Work-Study jobs (averaging $3232). In 2008, 2147 non-need-based awards were made. *Average percent of need met:* 90%. *Average financial aid package:* $12,055. *Average need-based loan:* $4082. *Average need-based gift aid:* $6011. *Average non-need-based aid:* $2129. *Average indebtedness upon graduation:* $21,517.

Applying *Options:* electronic application. *Application fee:* $40. *Required:* high school transcript, 15 specified curricular units. *Application deadlines:* 4/1 (freshmen), 4/1 (out-of-state freshmen), 4/1 (transfers). *Notification:* continuous (freshmen), continuous (out-of-state freshmen), continuous (transfers).

Freshman Application Contact Mr. Craig Hayes, Executive Director of Recruitment Services, University of Oklahoma, 550 Parrington Oval, L-1, Norman, OK 73019-3032. *Phone:* 405-325-2151. *Toll-free phone:* 800-234-6868. *Fax:* 405-325-7478. *E-mail:* ou-pss@ou.edu. *Web site:* http://www.ou.edu/.

University of Oklahoma Health Sciences Center

Oklahoma City, Oklahoma

- **State-supported** upper-level, founded 1890, part of University of Oklahoma
- **Urban** 200-acre campus with easy access to Oklahoma City
- **Endowment** $974.5 million
- **Coed** 1,121 undergraduate students, 95% full-time, 86% women, 14% men

Undergraduates 1,068 full-time, 53 part-time. Students come from 47 states and territories; 42 other countries; 23% are from out of state; 3% Black or African American, non-Hispanic/Latino; 4% Hispanic/Latino; 7% Asian, non-Hispanic/Latino; 0.2% Native Hawaiian or other Pacific Islander, non-Hispanic/Latino; 5% American Indian or Alaska Native, non-Hispanic/Latino; 2% Two or more races, non-Hispanic/Latino; 2% Race/ethnicity unknown; 0.5% international; 33% transferred in.

Faculty *Total:* 456, 72% full-time, 72% with terminal degrees. *Student/faculty ratio:* 7:1.

Academics *Calendar:* semesters. *Degrees:* bachelor's, master's, doctoral-professional, doctoral-research/scholarship, post-master's, and postbachelor's certificates. *Special study options:* advanced placement credit, distance learning, honors programs, internships, part-time degree program, summer session for credit. *ROTC:* Army (c), Air Force (c).

Computers on Campus 140 computers/terminals are available on campus for general student use. Students can access the following: campus intranet, computer help desk, free student e-mail accounts, online (class) grades, online (class) registration, online (class) schedules, online bursar bill and payment. Campuswide network is available. 100% of college-owned or -operated housing units are wired for high-speed Internet access. Wireless service is available via classrooms, computer centers, computer labs, learning centers, libraries, student centers.

Student Life *Housing:* college housing not available. *Activities and organizations:* student-run newspaper, Student Government Association, Public Health Student Association, Student National Medical Association, Graduate Student Council, Student Medical Association. *Campus security:* 24-hour emergency response devices and patrols, late-night transport/escort service. *Student services:* health clinic, personal/psychological counseling, women's center.

Costs (2010–11) *Tuition:* state resident $3678 full-time, $123 per credit hour part-time; nonresident $14,109 full-time, $470 per credit hour part-time. Full-time tuition and fees vary according to course load, degree level, program, and student level. Part-time tuition and fees vary according to course load, degree level, program, and student level. *Required fees:* $2080 full-time, $53 per credit hour part-time, $238 per term part-time. *Payment plan:* installment. *Waivers:* employees or children of employees.

Applying *Options:* electronic application, deferred entrance. *Application deadline:* rolling (transfers). *Notification:* continuous (transfers).

Application Contact University of Oklahoma Health Sciences Center, PO Box 26901, Oklahoma City, OK 73190. *Phone:* 405-271-2359 Ext. 48916. *Web site:* http://www.ouhsc.edu/.

University of Phoenix–Oklahoma City Campus

Oklahoma City, Oklahoma

Freshman Application Contact Ms. Audra McQuarie, Registrar/Executive Director, University of Phoenix–Oklahoma City Campus, 4035 South Riverpoint Parkway, Mail Stop CF-L101, Phoenix, AZ 85040-1958. *Phone:* 480-557-3303. *Toll-free phone:* 800-776-4867 (in-state); 800-228-7240 (out-of-state). *Fax:* 480-643-1020. *E-mail:* audra.mcquarie@phoenix.edu. *Web site:* http://www.phoenix.edu/.

University of Phoenix–Tulsa Campus

Tulsa, Oklahoma

Freshman Application Contact Ms. Evelyn Gaskin, Registrar/Executive Director, University of Phoenix–Tulsa Campus, 4615 East Elwood Street, Mail Stop AA-K101, Phoenix, AZ 85040-1958. *Phone:* 480-557-3303. *Toll-free phone:* 800-776-4867 (in-state); 800-228-7240 (out-of-state). *Fax:* 480-643-1020. *E-mail:* evelyn.gaskin@phoenix.edu. *Web site:* http://www.phoenix.edu/.

University of Science and Arts of Oklahoma

Chickasha, Oklahoma

- **State-supported** 4-year, founded 1908, part of Oklahoma State Regents for Higher Education
- **Small-town** 75-acre campus with easy access to Oklahoma City
- **Endowment** $6.9 million
- **Coed** 1,050 undergraduate students, 86% full-time, 63% women, 37% men
- **Moderately difficult** entrance level, 56% of applicants were admitted

Undergraduates 907 full-time, 143 part-time. Students come from 17 states and territories; 15 other countries; 7% are from out of state; 4% Black or African American, non-Hispanic/Latino; 4% Hispanic/Latino; 1% Asian, non-Hispanic/Latino; 13% American Indian or Alaska Native, non-Hispanic/Latino; 5% international; 11% transferred in; 48% live on campus. *Retention:* 66% of full-time freshmen returned.

Freshmen *Admission:* 559 applied, 311 admitted, 223 enrolled. *Average high school GPA:* 3.42. *Test scores:* ACT scores over 18: 88%; ACT scores over 24: 43%; ACT scores over 30: 9%.

Faculty *Total:* 91, 62% full-time, 56% with terminal degrees. *Student/faculty ratio:* 14:1.

Academics *Calendar:* trimesters. *Degree:* bachelor's. *Special study options:* academic remediation for entering students, accelerated degree program, advanced placement credit, double majors, independent study, internships, off-campus study, part-time degree program, services for LD students, student-designed majors, summer session for credit.

Computers on Campus 150 computers/terminals are available on campus for general student use. Students can access the following: computer help desk, free student e-mail accounts, online (class) schedules, personal Web space. Campuswide network is available. 100% of college-owned or -operated housing units are wired for high-speed Internet access. Wireless service is available via entire campus.

Student Life *Housing:* on-campus residence required for freshman year. *Options:* coed. Campus housing is university owned and is provided by a third party. Freshman campus housing is guaranteed. *Activities and organizations:* drama/theater group, student-run newspaper, television station, choral group, Student Activities Council, Volunteer Action Council, Baptist Student Union, Intertribal Heritage Club, Psychology Club, national fraternities. *Campus security:* 24-hour emergency response devices and patrols, controlled dormitory access. *Student services:* health clinic, personal/psychological counseling.

Athletics Member NAIA. *Intercollegiate sports:* baseball M(s), basketball M(s)/W(s), cheerleading M(s)/W(s), soccer M(s)/W(s), softball W(s). *Intramural sports:* basketball M/W, football M/W, golf M/W, softball M/W, volleyball M/W.

Standardized Tests *Required:* SAT or ACT (for admission).

Costs (2010–11) *Tuition:* state resident $3510 full-time, $117 per credit hour part-time; nonresident $9960 full-time, $332 per credit hour part-time. No tuition increase for student's term of enrollment. *Required fees:* $1170 full-time, $39 per credit hour part-time. *Room and board:* $4990; room only: $2600. Room and board charges vary according to board plan and housing facility. *Payment plan:* installment. *Waivers:* senior citizens and employees or children of employees.

Financial Aid Of all full-time matriculated undergraduates who enrolled in 2009, 698 applied for aid, 599 were judged to have need, 82 had their need fully met. 136 Federal Work-Study jobs (averaging $1765). In 2009, 112 non-need-based awards were made. *Average percent of need met:* 66%. *Average financial aid package:* $8989. *Average need-based loan:* $2905. *Average need-based gift aid:* $7098. *Average non-need-based aid:* $2302. *Average indebtedness upon graduation:* $15,339.

Applying *Options:* electronic application, deferred entrance. *Application fee:* $25. *Required for some:* high school transcript, minimum 3 GPA, graduation in top 25% of high school class. *Recommended:* graduation in top 25% of high school class. *Application deadlines:* 9/1 (freshmen), 9/1 (out-of-state freshmen), 9/1 (transfers). *Notification:* continuous until 2/10 (freshmen), continuous until 2/10 (out-of-state freshmen), continuous (transfers).

Freshman Application Contact Ms. Kellee Johnson, Director of Admissions, University of Science and Arts of Oklahoma, 1727 West Alabama, Chickasha, OK 73018-5322. *Phone:* 405-574-1357. *Toll-free phone:* 800-933-8726 Ext. 1212. *Fax:* 405-574-1220. *E-mail:* usao-admissions@usao.edu. *Web site:* http://www.usao.edu/.

University of Tulsa

Tulsa, Oklahoma

- **Independent** university, founded 1894, affiliated with Presbyterian Church (U.S.A.)
- **Urban** 209-acre campus
- **Endowment** $691.9 million
- **Coed** 3,105 undergraduate students, 95% full-time, 45% women, 55% men
- **Very difficult** entrance level, 39% of applicants were admitted

Undergraduates 2,963 full-time, 142 part-time. Students come from 42 states and territories; 55 other countries; 42% are from out of state; 5% Black or African American, non-Hispanic/Latino; 4% Hispanic/Latino; 3% Asian, non-Hispanic/Latino; 4% American Indian or Alaska Native, non-Hispanic/Latino; 2% Two or more races, non-Hispanic/Latino; 4% Race/ethnicity unknown; 16% international; 5% transferred in; 70% live on campus. *Retention:* 88% of full-time freshmen returned.

Freshmen *Admission:* 5,737 applied, 2,244 admitted, 671 enrolled. *Average high school GPA:* 3.84. *Test scores:* SAT critical reading scores over 500: 90%; SAT math scores over 500: 93%; ACT scores over 18: 100%; SAT critical reading scores over 600: 63%; SAT math scores over 600: 68%; ACT scores over 24: 87%; SAT critical reading scores over 700: 30%; SAT math scores over 700: 29%; ACT scores over 30: 46%.

Faculty *Total:* 395, 79% full-time, 96% with terminal degrees. *Student/faculty ratio:* 11:1.

Academics *Calendar:* semesters. *Degrees:* bachelor's, master's, doctoral-professional, doctoral-research/scholarship, and postbachelor's certificates. *Special study options:* accelerated degree program, adult/continuing education programs, advanced placement credit, double majors, English as a second language, honors programs, independent study, internships, part-time degree program, services for LD students, student-designed majors, study abroad, summer session for credit. *ROTC:* Air Force (c). *Unusual degree programs:* 3-2 business administration.

Computers on Campus 900 computers/terminals are available on campus for general student use. Students can access the following: campus intranet, computer help desk, free student e-mail accounts, online (class) grades, online (class) registration, online (class) schedules. Campuswide network is available.

100% of college-owned or -operated housing units are wired for high-speed Internet access. Wireless service is available via entire campus.

Student Life *Housing:* on-campus residence required through sophomore year. *Options:* coed, men-only, women-only, disabled students. Campus housing is university owned. Freshman campus housing is guaranteed. *Activities and organizations:* drama/theater group, student-run newspaper, radio and television station, choral group, marching band, Student Association, Residence Hall Association, Pre-Professional organizations, Intramural sports, Greek life, national fraternities, national sororities. *Campus security:* 24-hour emergency response devices and patrols, late-night transport/escort service, controlled dormitory access. *Student services:* health clinic, personal/psychological counseling, women's center.

Athletics Member NCAA. All Division I except football (Division I-A). *Intercollegiate sports:* basketball M(s)/W(s), crew W(s), cross-country running M(s)/W(s), golf M(s)/W(s), soccer M(s)/W(s), softball W(s), tennis M(s)/W(s), track and field M(s)/W(s), volleyball W(s). *Intramural sports:* badminton M/W, basketball M/W, bowling M/W, crew M(c), cross-country running M/W, fencing M(c)/W(c), football M/W, golf M/W, racquetball M/W, rugby M(c), soccer M/W, softball M/W, squash M/W, swimming and diving M/W, table tennis M/W, tennis M/W, track and field M/W, volleyball M/W, water polo M/W, weight lifting M/W.

Standardized Tests *Required:* SAT or ACT (for admission).

Costs (2010–11) *One-time required fee:* $425. *Comprehensive fee:* $37,328 includes full-time tuition ($28,060), mandatory fees ($250), and room and board ($9018). Full-time tuition and fees vary according to course load. Part-time tuition: $1007 per credit. Part-time tuition and fees vary according to course load. *College room only:* $5010. Room and board charges vary according to board plan and housing facility. *Payment plans:* tuition prepayment, installment. *Waivers:* employees or children of employees.

Financial Aid Of all full-time matriculated undergraduates who enrolled in 2008, 2,559 applied for aid, 1,225 were judged to have need, 586 had their need fully met. 604 Federal Work-Study jobs (averaging $2964). 3 state and other part-time jobs (averaging $1269). In 2008, 1070 non-need-based awards were made. *Average percent of need met:* 85%. *Average financial aid package:* $26,961. *Average need-based loan:* $4211. *Average need-based gift aid:* $5996. *Average non-need-based aid:* $13,567. *Average indebtedness upon graduation:* $35,816.

Applying *Options:* electronic application, early admission, early action, deferred entrance. *Application fee:* $35. *Required:* essay or personal statement, high school transcript, 1 letter of recommendation, interview. *Recommended:* minimum 3 GPA. *Application deadlines:* rolling (freshmen), rolling (out-of-state freshmen), rolling (transfers), 11/1 (early action). *Notification:* continuous (freshmen), continuous (out-of-state freshmen), continuous (transfers), 11/22 (early action).

Freshman Application Contact Mr. Earl Johnson, Dean of Admission, University of Tulsa, 800 South Tucker Drive, Tulsa, OK 74104. *Phone:* 918-631-2307. *Toll-free phone:* 800-331-3050. *Fax:* 918-631-5003. *E-mail:* admission@utulsa.edu. *Web site:* http://www.utulsa.edu/.

See page 1750 for the College Close-Up.

OREGON

The Art Institute of Portland
Portland, Oregon

- **Proprietary** 4-year, founded 1963, part of Education Management Corporation
- **Urban** campus
- **Coed**

Academics *Calendar:* quarters. *Degrees:* diplomas, associate, and bachelor's.

Costs (2010–11) *Tuition:* Tuition cost varies by program. Prospective students should contact the school for current tuition costs. Other charges include a starting kit for all first-quarter students. Kits vary in price, depending on the program of study.

Freshman Application Contact The Art Institute of Portland, 1122 NW Davis Street, Portland, OR 97209. *Phone:* 503-228-6528. *Toll-free phone:* 888-228-6528. *Web site:* http://www.artinstitutes.edu/portland/.

See page 1060 for the College Close-Up.

Birthingway College of Midwifery
Portland, Oregon

Director of Admissions Director of Admission, Birthingway College of Midwifery, 12113 SE Foster Road, Portland, OR 97299. *Phone:* 503-760-3131. *E-mail:* info@birthingway.edu. *Web site:* http://www.birthingway.edu/.

Concordia University
Portland, Oregon

Freshman Application Contact Ms. Bobi Swan, Dean of Admission, Concordia University, 2811 Northeast Holman, Portland, OR 97211-6099. *Phone:* 503-493-6526. *Toll-free phone:* 800-321-9371. *Fax:* 503-280-8531. *E-mail:* admissions@cu-portland.edu. *Web site:* http://www.cu-portland.edu/.

Corban University
Salem, Oregon

- **Independent religious** comprehensive, founded 1935
- **Suburban** 145-acre campus with easy access to Portland
- **Endowment** $1.6 million
- **Coed** 923 undergraduate students, 86% full-time, 61% women, 39% men
- **Moderately difficult** entrance level, 39% of applicants were admitted

Undergraduates 792 full-time, 131 part-time. Students come from 20 states and territories; 4 other countries; 39% are from out of state; 2% Black or African American, non-Hispanic/Latino; 4% Hispanic/Latino; 4% Asian, non-Hispanic/Latino; 1% American Indian or Alaska Native, non-Hispanic/Latino; 3% Two or more races, non-Hispanic/Latino; 5% Race/ethnicity unknown; 0.9% international; 6% transferred in; 51% live on campus. *Retention:* 78% of full-time freshmen returned.

Freshmen *Admission:* 1,998 applied, 777 admitted, 213 enrolled. *Average high school GPA:* 3.54. *Test scores:* SAT critical reading scores over 500: 70%; SAT math scores over 500: 59%; SAT writing scores over 500: 54%; ACT scores over 18: 95%; SAT critical reading scores over 600: 23%; SAT math scores over 600: 22%; SAT writing scores over 600: 22%; ACT scores over 24: 42%; SAT critical reading scores over 700: 4%; SAT math scores over 700: 2%; SAT writing scores over 700: 3%; ACT scores over 30: 3%.

Faculty *Total:* 101, 45% full-time, 32% with terminal degrees. *Student/faculty ratio:* 13:1.

Academics *Calendar:* semesters. *Degrees:* certificates, associate, bachelor's, master's, and postbachelor's certificates. *Special study options:* accelerated degree program, adult/continuing education programs, advanced placement credit, cooperative education, distance learning, double majors, freshman honors college, honors programs, independent study, internships, off-campus study, services for LD students, student-designed majors, study abroad, summer session for credit. *ROTC:* Army (c), Air Force (c).

Computers on Campus 64 computers/terminals are available on campus for general student use. Students can access the following: computer help desk, free student e-mail accounts, online (class) grades, online (class) schedules. Campuswide network is available. 100% of college-owned or -operated housing units are wired for high-speed Internet access. Wireless service is available via computer centers, computer labs, dorm rooms, learning centers, libraries, student centers.

Student Life *Housing:* on-campus residence required through sophomore year. *Options:* men-only, women-only, disabled students. Campus housing is university owned. Freshman campus housing is guaranteed. *Activities and organizations:* drama/theater group, student-run newspaper, choral group, Student Fellowship Groups, Poetry Club, Worship Teams, Drama Club, Westrek Hiking Club. *Campus security:* 24-hour emergency response devices and patrols, student patrols, late-night transport/escort service. *Student services:* health clinic, personal/psychological counseling.

Athletics Member NAIA, NCCAA. *Intercollegiate sports:* baseball M(s), basketball M(s)/W(s), cross-country running M(s)/W(s), golf M(s)/W(s), soccer M(s)/W(s), softball W(s), track and field M(s)/W(s), volleyball W(s). *Intramural sports:* basketball M/W, football M, soccer M/W, softball W, volleyball M/W.

Standardized Tests *Required:* SAT or ACT (for admission).

Costs (2011–12) *One-time required fee:* $100. *Comprehensive fee:* $33,425 includes full-time tuition ($24,975), mandatory fees ($470), and room and board ($7980). Full-time tuition and fees vary according to program and reciprocity agreements. Part-time tuition: $1041 per credit hour. Part-time tuition and fees vary according to course load, program, and reciprocity agreements. *Room and board:* Room and board charges vary according to board plan. *Payment plan:* installment. *Waivers:* senior citizens and employees or children of employees.

Financial Aid Of all full-time matriculated undergraduates who enrolled in 2009, 679 applied for aid, 610 were judged to have need, 73 had their need fully met. 100 Federal Work-Study jobs (averaging $697). In 2009, 114 non-need-based awards were made. *Average percent of need met:* 64%. *Average financial aid package:* $18,182. *Average need-based loan:* $4420. *Average need-based gift aid:* $14,827. *Average non-need-based aid:* $6389. *Average indebtedness upon graduation:* $27,071.

Applying *Options:* electronic application. *Application fee:* $35. *Required:* essay or personal statement, high school transcript, minimum 2.7 GPA, 3 letters of recommendation. *Application deadlines:* 8/1 (freshmen), 8/1 (transfers). *Notification:* continuous (freshmen).

Freshman Application Contact Ms. Heidi Stowman, Director of Admissions, Corban University, 5000 Deer Park Drive, SE, Salem, OR 97301-9392. *Phone:* 503-375-7115. *Toll-free phone:* 800-845-3005. *Fax:* 503-585-4316. *E-mail:* admissions@corban.edu. *Web site:* http://www.corban.edu/.

DeVry University
Portland, Oregon

- **Proprietary** comprehensive, part of DeVry University
- **Coed**
- **Minimally difficult** entrance level

Faculty *Student/faculty ratio:* 11:1.

Academics *Calendar:* semesters. *Degrees:* associate, bachelor's, and master's.

Costs (2010–11) *Tuition:* $14,766 full-time, $580 per credit hour part-time. Full-time tuition and fees vary according to course load. Part-time tuition and fees vary according to course load. *Required fees:* $60 full-time, $30 per term part-time. *Payment plans:* installment, deferred payment.

Financial Aid *Of all full-time matriculated undergraduates who enrolled in 2007,* 17 applied for aid, 17 were judged to have need. *Average percent of need met:* 29. *Average financial aid package:* $9247. *Average need-based loan:* $6636. *Average need-based gift aid:* $4932.

Applying *Options:* electronic application, deferred entrance. *Application fee:* $50. *Required:* high school transcript, interview.

Freshman Application Contact DeVry University, 9755 Southwest Barnes Road, Suite 150, Portland, OR 97225-6651. *Web site:* http://www.devry.edu/.

Eastern Oregon University
La Grande, Oregon

- **State-supported** comprehensive, founded 1929, part of Oregon University System
- **Rural** 121-acre campus
- **Coed** 3,721 undergraduate students, 62% full-time, 61% women, 39% men
- **Moderately difficult** entrance level, 74% of applicants were admitted

Undergraduates 2,309 full-time, 1,412 part-time. Students come from 51 states and territories; 24 other countries; 28% are from out of state; 13% transferred in; 14% live on campus. *Retention:* 67% of full-time freshmen returned. **Freshmen** *Admission:* 1,061 applied, 786 admitted, 461 enrolled. *Average high school GPA:* 3.22. *Test scores:* SAT critical reading scores over 500: 40%; SAT math scores over 500: 47%; SAT writing scores over 500: 26%; ACT scores over 18: 79%; SAT critical reading scores over 600: 10%; SAT math scores over 600: 9%; SAT writing scores over 600: 4%; ACT scores over 24: 17%; SAT critical reading scores over 700: 2%; SAT math scores over 700: 1%; ACT scores over 30: 4%.

Faculty *Total:* 144, 80% full-time, 70% with terminal degrees. *Student/faculty ratio:* 22:1.

Academics *Calendar:* quarters. *Degrees:* certificates, associate, bachelor's, and master's. *Special study options:* adult/continuing education programs, advanced placement credit, cooperative education, distance learning, double majors, external degree program, honors programs, independent study, internships, off-campus study, part-time degree program, services for LD students, student-designed majors, study abroad, summer session for credit. *ROTC:* Army (b). *Unusual degree programs:* 3-2 nursing with Oregon Health Sciences University; agriculture with Oregon State University.

Computers on Campus Students can access the following: free student e-mail accounts, online (class) grades, online (class) registration, online (class) schedules. Campuswide network is available. Wireless service is available via entire campus.

Student Life *Housing:* on-campus residence required for freshman year. *Options:* coed. Campus housing is university owned. *Activities and organizations:* drama/theater group, student-run newspaper, radio station, choral group, Outdoor Club, Island Magic, student radio station, intramurals, student government. *Campus security:* 24-hour emergency response devices and patrols, late-night transport/escort service, controlled dormitory access. *Student services:* health clinic, personal/psychological counseling, women's center.

Athletics Member NCAA, NAIA. All NCAA Division III. *Intercollegiate sports:* basketball M/W, cross-country running M/W, football M, skiing (cross-country) M(c)/W(c), skiing (downhill) M(c)/W(c), soccer W, track and field M/W, volleyball W. *Intramural sports:* basketball M/W, football M, racquetball M/W, soccer W, softball M/W, volleyball W.

Standardized Tests *Required:* SAT or ACT (for admission).

Costs (2010–11) *Tuition:* state resident $5244 full-time, $118 per credit hour part-time; nonresident $5244 full-time, $118 per credit hour part-time. Full-time tuition and fees vary according to course load. Part-time tuition and fees vary according to course load. *Required fees:* $1395 full-time. *Room and board:* $8000; room only: $4335. Room and board charges vary according to

board plan and housing facility. *Payment plan:* installment. *Waivers:* senior citizens and employees or children of employees.

Financial Aid Of all full-time matriculated undergraduates who enrolled in 2009, 1,988 applied for aid, 1,795 were judged to have need, 700 had their need fully met. In 2009, 25 non-need-based awards were made. *Average percent of need met:* 50%. *Average financial aid package:* $9242. *Average need-based loan:* $3693. *Average need-based gift aid:* $5308. *Average non-need-based aid:* $1204.

Applying *Options:* electronic application, early admission, early action, deferred entrance. *Application fee:* $50. *Required:* high school transcript, minimum 3 GPA. *Required for some:* essay or personal statement, 2 letters of recommendation. *Application deadlines:* 9/1 (freshmen), rolling (transfers), 12/1 (early action). *Notification:* continuous (freshmen), 1/15 (early action).

Freshman Application Contact Tyler Dubsky, Assistant Director of Admissions, Eastern Oregon University, Eastern Oregon University, La Grande, OR. *Phone:* 541-962-3085. *Toll-free phone:* 800-452-8639 (in-state); 800-452-3393 (out-of-state). *Fax:* 541-962-3418. *E-mail:* admissions@eou.edu. *Web site:* http://www.eou.edu/.

George Fox University
Newberg, Oregon

- **Independent Friends** university, founded 1891
- **Small-town** 108-acre campus with easy access to Portland
- **Endowment** $16.7 million
- **Coed** 2,132 undergraduate students, 85% full-time, 57% women, 43% men
- **Moderately difficult** entrance level, 69% of applicants were admitted

Undergraduates 1,810 full-time, 322 part-time. Students come from 31 states and territories; 28 other countries; 30% are from out of state; 2% Black or African American, non-Hispanic/Latino; 7% Hispanic/Latino; 4% Asian, non-Hispanic/Latino; 0.5% Native Hawaiian or other Pacific Islander, non-Hispanic/Latino; 2% American Indian or Alaska Native, non-Hispanic/Latino; 2% Two or more races, non-Hispanic/Latino; 6% Race/ethnicity unknown; 6% international; 7% transferred in; 65% live on campus. *Retention:* 84% of full-time freshmen returned.

Freshmen *Admission:* 2,363 applied, 1,641 admitted, 491 enrolled. *Average high school GPA:* 3.58. *Test scores:* SAT critical reading scores over 500: 74%; SAT math scores over 500: 73%; SAT writing scores over 500: 69%; ACT scores over 18: 89%; SAT critical reading scores over 600: 38%; SAT math scores over 600: 36%; SAT writing scores over 600: 26%; ACT scores over 24: 52%; SAT critical reading scores over 700: 7%; SAT math scores over 700: 6%; SAT writing scores over 700: 4%; ACT scores over 30: 12%.

Faculty *Total:* 382, 44% full-time, 47% with terminal degrees. *Student/faculty ratio:* 13:1.

Academics *Calendar:* semesters. *Degrees:* bachelor's, master's, doctoral-professional, post-master's, and postbachelor's certificates. *Special study options:* academic remediation for entering students, accelerated degree program, adult/continuing education programs, advanced placement credit, distance learning, double majors, English as a second language, honors programs, independent study, internships, off-campus study, part-time degree program, services for LD students, student-designed majors, study abroad, summer session for credit. *ROTC:* Air Force (c). *Unusual degree programs:* 3-2 engineering.

Computers on Campus 130 computers/terminals are available on campus for general student use. Students can access the following: campus intranet, computer help desk, free student e-mail accounts, online (class) grades, online (class) registration, online (class) schedules, online acceptance of financial aid. Campuswide network is available. 100% of college-owned or -operated housing units are wired for high-speed Internet access. Wireless service is available via classrooms, computer centers, computer labs, dorm rooms, learning centers, libraries, student centers.

Student Life *Housing:* on-campus residence required through junior year. *Options:* men-only, women-only, disabled students. Campus housing is university owned. Freshman campus housing is guaranteed. *Activities and organizations:* drama/theater group, student-run newspaper, radio station, choral group, student government, Christian Ministries, Orientation Committee, Outdoor Club and Bruin Ambassadors. *Campus security:* 24-hour emergency response devices and patrols, student patrols, late-night transport/escort service, controlled dormitory access, parking lot cameras, and video surveillance of key buildings. *Student services:* health clinic, personal/psychological counseling.

Athletics Member NCAA. All Division III. *Intercollegiate sports:* baseball M, basketball M/W, cross-country running M/W, golf M/W, soccer M/W, softball W, tennis M/W, track and field M/W, volleyball W. *Intramural sports:* badminton M/W, basketball M/W, football M/W, golf M/W, racquetball M/W, rock climbing M/W, soccer M/W, table tennis M/W, tennis M/W, volleyball M/W.

Standardized Tests *Required:* SAT or ACT (for admission).

Costs (2010–11) *Comprehensive fee:* $36,600 includes full-time tuition ($27,640), mandatory fees ($330), and room and board ($8630). Part-time tuition: $840 per semester hour. Part-time tuition and fees vary according to

course load. *College room only:* $4880. Room and board charges vary according to board plan. *Payment plan:* installment. *Waivers:* senior citizens and employees or children of employees.
Financial Aid Of all full-time matriculated undergraduates who enrolled in 2009, 1,552 applied for aid, 1,413 were judged to have need, 534 had their need fully met. In 2009, 103 non-need-based awards were made. *Average percent of need met:* 87%. *Average financial aid package:* $25,387. *Average need-based loan:* $3602. *Average need-based gift aid:* $15,040. *Average non-need-based aid:* $7016. *Average indebtedness upon graduation:* $18,428.
Applying *Options:* electronic application, early action, deferred entrance. *Application fee:* $40. *Required:* essay or personal statement, high school transcript, 2 letters of recommendation. *Required for some:* interview. *Recommended:* minimum 2.6 GPA, interview. *Application deadlines:* rolling (freshmen), 6/1 (transfers), 12/1 (early action). *Notification:* continuous until 10/1 (freshmen), continuous (transfers), 12/15 (early action).
Freshman Application Contact Mr. Ryan Dougherty, Director of Undergraduate Admissions, George Fox University, 414 North Meridian Street, Newberg, OR 97132. *Phone:* 503-554-2240. *Toll-free phone:* 800-765-4369. *Fax:* 503-554-3110. *E-mail:* admissions@georgefox.edu. *Web site:* http://www.georgefox.edu/.

Gutenberg College
Eugene, Oregon

Freshman Application Contact Mr. Terry Stollar, Director of Admissions and Development, Gutenberg College, 1883 University Street, Eugene, OR 97403. *Phone:* 541-736-9071. *Fax:* 541-683-6997. *E-mail:* tstollar@gutenberg.edu. *Web site:* http://www.gutenberg.edu/.

ITT Technical Institute
Portland, Oregon

- **Proprietary** primarily 2-year, founded 1971, part of ITT Educational Services, Inc.
- **Urban** campus
- **Coed**
- **Minimally difficult** entrance level

Academics *Calendar:* quarters. *Degrees:* associate and bachelor's.
Student Life *Housing:* college housing not available.
Financial Aid Of all full-time matriculated undergraduates who enrolled in 2009, 15 Federal Work-Study jobs (averaging $5000).
Freshman Application Contact Director of Recruitment, ITT Technical Institute, 9500 Northeast Cascades Parkway, Portland, OR 97220. *Phone:* 503-255-6500. *Toll-free phone:* 800-234-5488. *Web site:* http://www.itt-tech.edu/.

Lewis & Clark College
Portland, Oregon

- **Independent** comprehensive, founded 1867
- **Suburban** 137-acre campus with easy access to Portland
- **Coed** 1,999 undergraduate students, 99% full-time, 60% women, 40% men
- **Very difficult** entrance level, 68% of applicants were admitted

Undergraduates 1,978 full-time, 21 part-time. 83% are from out of state; 2% Black or African American, non-Hispanic/Latino; 6% Hispanic/Latino; 6% Asian, non-Hispanic/Latino; 0.1% Native Hawaiian or other Pacific Islander, non-Hispanic/Latino; 1% American Indian or Alaska Native, non-Hispanic/Latino; 1% Two or more races, non-Hispanic/Latino; 20% Race/ethnicity unknown; 6% international; 4% transferred in; 65% live on campus. *Retention:* 83% of full-time freshmen returned.
Freshmen *Admission:* 5,281 applied, 3,598 admitted, 493 enrolled. *Average high school GPA:* 3.69. *Test scores:* SAT critical reading scores over 500: 98%; SAT math scores over 500: 98%; SAT writing scores over 500: 97%; ACT scores over 18: 100%; SAT critical reading scores over 600: 79%; SAT math scores over 600: 70%; SAT writing scores over 600: 68%; ACT scores

over 24: 96%; SAT critical reading scores over 700: 28%; SAT math scores over 700: 17%; SAT writing scores over 700: 16%; ACT scores over 30: 32%.
Faculty *Total:* 360, 64% full-time, 83% with terminal degrees. *Student/faculty ratio:* 12:1.

Academics *Calendar:* semesters. *Degrees:* bachelor's, master's, doctoral-professional, doctoral-research/scholarship, and post-master's certificates. *Special study options:* accelerated degree program, advanced placement credit, double majors, English as a second language, honors programs, independent study, internships, off-campus study, services for LD students, student-designed majors, study abroad, summer session for credit. *Unusual degree programs:* 3-2 engineering with Columbia University, Washington University in St. Louis, University of Southern California, Oregon Health Sciences University.

Computers on Campus Students can access the following: campus intranet, computer help desk, free student e-mail accounts, online (class) grades, online (class) registration, online (class) schedules. Campuswide network is available. 100% of college-owned or -operated housing units are wired for high-speed Internet access. Wireless service is available via classrooms, computer centers, computer labs, dorm rooms, learning centers, libraries, student centers.

Student Life *Housing:* on-campus residence required through sophomore year. *Options:* coed, women-only. Campus housing is university owned. Freshman campus housing is guaranteed. *Activities and organizations:* drama/theater group, student-run newspaper, radio and television station, choral group. *Campus security:* 24-hour emergency response devices and patrols, student patrols, late-night transport/escort service, controlled dormitory access. *Student services:* health clinic, personal/psychological counseling, women's center.

Athletics Member NCAA. All Division III. *Intercollegiate sports:* baseball M, basketball M/W, crew M/W, cross-country running M/W, football M, golf M/W, lacrosse M(c)/W(c), soccer M(c)/W, softball W, swimming and diving M/W, tennis M/W, track and field M/W, volleyball W. *Intramural sports:* badminton M/W, basketball M/W, cross-country running M/W, fencing M(c)/W(c), football M/W, rock climbing M(c)/W(c), rugby M(c)/W(c), sailing M(c)/W(c), skiing (cross-country) M/W, skiing (downhill) M/W, soccer W(c), softball M/W, swimming and diving M/W, table tennis M/W, tennis M/W, ultimate Frisbee M(c)/W(c), volleyball M/W, water polo M/W.

Standardized Tests *Required:* SAT or ACT, or academic portfolio. Students may apply via Portfolio Path where test scores are optional (for admission). *Required for some:* SAT or ACT (for admission).

Costs (2010–11) *Comprehensive fee:* $46,280 includes full-time tuition ($36,394), mandatory fees ($238), and room and board ($9648). Part-time tuition: $1832 per credit hour. *College room only:* $5058. Room and board charges vary according to board plan and housing facility. *Payment plan:* installment. *Waivers:* employees or children of employees.

Financial Aid Of all full-time matriculated undergraduates who enrolled in 2009, 1,323 applied for aid, 1,100 were judged to have need, 295 had their need fully met. In 2009, 308 non-need-based awards were made. *Average percent of need met:* 82%. *Average financial aid package:* $27,829. *Average need-based loan:* $20,995. *Average non-need-based aid:* $9523. *Average indebtedness upon graduation:* $22,148.

Applying *Options:* electronic application, early action, deferred entrance. *Application fee:* $50. *Required:* essay or personal statement, high school transcript, minimum 2 GPA, "portfolio path" applicants submit samples of writing. *Required for some:* 4 letters of recommendation. *Recommended:* minimum 3 GPA, interview.

Freshman Application Contact Ms. Jim Sumner, Interim Dean of Admissions, Lewis & Clark College, 0615 SW Palatine Hill Road, Portland, OR 97219. *Phone:* 503-768-7040. *Toll-free phone:* 800-444-4111. *Fax:* 503-768-7055. *E-mail:* admissions@lclark.edu. *Web site:* http://www.lclark.edu/.

See page 1380 for the College Close-Up.

Linfield College
McMinnville, Oregon

- **Independent American Baptist Churches in the USA** 4-year, founded 1849
- **Small-town** 193-acre campus with easy access to Portland
- **Endowment** $67.0 million
- **Coed** 1,729 undergraduate students, 98% full-time, 59% women, 41% men
- **Moderately difficult** entrance level, 77% of applicants were admitted

Undergraduates 1,694 full-time, 35 part-time. Students come from 19 states and territories; 22 other countries; 55% are from out of state; 2% Black or African American, non-Hispanic/Latino; 6% Hispanic/Latino; 8% Asian, non-Hispanic/Latino; 0.1% Native Hawaiian or other Pacific Islander, non-Hispanic/Latino; 2% American Indian or Alaska Native, non-Hispanic/Latino; 3% Two

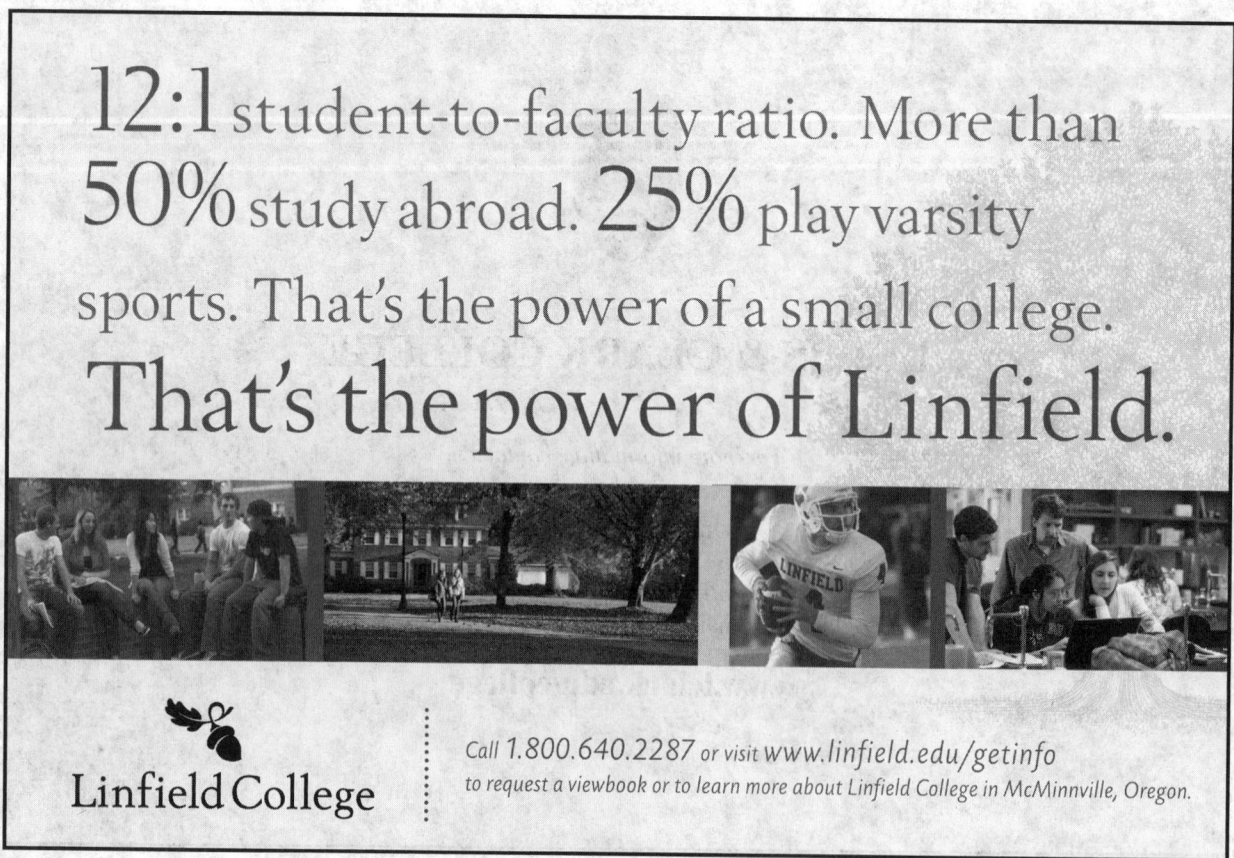

12:1 student-to-faculty ratio. More than 50% study abroad. 25% play varsity sports. That's the power of a small college. That's the power of Linfield.

Linfield College

Call 1.800.640.2287 *or visit* www.linfield.edu/getinfo
to request a viewbook or to learn more about Linfield College in McMinnville, Oregon.

or more races, non-Hispanic/Latino; 7% Race/ethnicity unknown; 4% international; 4% transferred in; 74% live on campus. *Retention:* 80% of full-time freshmen returned.

Freshmen *Admission:* 2,179 applied, 1,681 admitted, 529 enrolled. *Average high school GPA:* 3.56. *Test scores:* SAT critical reading scores over 500: 70%; SAT math scores over 500: 77%; SAT writing scores over 500: 67%; ACT scores over 18: 94%; SAT critical reading scores over 600: 27%; SAT math scores over 600: 27%; SAT writing scores over 600: 21%; ACT scores over 24: 48%; SAT critical reading scores over 700: 4%; SAT math scores over 700: 3%; SAT writing scores over 700: 1%; ACT scores over 30: 8%.

Faculty *Total:* 201, 55% full-time, 66% with terminal degrees. *Student/faculty ratio:* 12:1.

Academics *Calendar:* 4-1-4. *Degrees:* bachelor's and postbachelor's certificates. *Special study options:* accelerated degree program, adult/continuing education programs, advanced placement credit, distance learning, double majors, English as a second language, external degree program, independent study, internships, off-campus study, part-time degree program, services for LD students, student-designed majors, study abroad, summer session for credit. *ROTC:* Air Force (c). *Unusual degree programs:* 3-2 engineering with Washington State University, Oregon State University, University of Southern California.

Computers on Campus 250 computers/terminals are available on campus for general student use. Students can access the following: computer help desk, free student e-mail accounts, online (class) grades, online (class) registration, online (class) schedules. Campuswide network is available. 95% of college-owned or -operated housing units are wired for high-speed Internet access. Wireless service is available via classrooms, computer centers, computer labs, dorm rooms, learning centers, libraries, student centers.

Student Life *Housing:* on-campus residence required through junior year. *Options:* coed, men-only, women-only, disabled students. Campus housing is university owned. Freshman campus housing is guaranteed. *Activities and organizations:* drama/theater group, student-run newspaper, radio station, choral group, Fellowship of Christian Athletes, Linfield Ultimate Players Association, Hawaiian Club, International Club, Outdoor Club, national fraternities, national sororities. *Campus security:* 24-hour emergency response devices and patrols, late-night transport/escort service, controlled dormitory access. *Student services:* health clinic, personal/psychological counseling.

Athletics Member NCAA. All Division III. *Intercollegiate sports:* baseball M, basketball M/W, cross-country running M/W, football M, golf M/W, lacrosse W, soccer M/W, softball W, swimming and diving M/W, tennis M/W, track and field M/W, volleyball W. *Intramural sports:* basketball M/W, bowling M/W, soccer M/W, softball M/W, volleyball M/W.

Standardized Tests *Required:* SAT or ACT (for admission).

Costs (2010–11) *Comprehensive fee:* $39,254 includes full-time tuition ($30,300), mandatory fees ($304), and room and board ($8650). Full-time tuition and fees vary according to location. Part-time tuition: $945 per semester hour. Part-time tuition and fees vary according to course load and location. *College room only:* $4700. Room and board charges vary according to board plan, housing facility, and location. *Payment plan:* installment. *Waivers:* senior citizens and employees or children of employees.

Financial Aid Of all full-time matriculated undergraduates who enrolled in 2009, 1,210 applied for aid, 1,210 were judged to have need, 401 had their need fully met. 759 Federal Work-Study jobs (averaging $2201). 588 state and other part-time jobs (averaging $2273). In 2009, 331 non-need-based awards were made. *Average percent of need met:* 85%. *Average financial aid package:* $21,401. *Average need-based loan:* $4479. *Average need-based gift aid:* $11,736. *Average non-need-based aid:* $12,981. *Average indebtedness upon graduation:* $31,135.

Applying *Options:* electronic application, early action, deferred entrance. *Required:* essay or personal statement, high school transcript, 1 letter of recommendation. *Recommended:* interview. *Application deadlines:* 2/15 (freshmen), 4/15 (transfers), 11/15 (early action). *Notification:* 4/1 (freshmen), 5/15 (transfers), 1/15 (early action).

Freshman Application Contact Ms. Lisa Knodle-Bragiel, Director of Admission, Linfield College, 900 SE Baker Street, McMinnville, OR 97128. *Phone:* 503-883-2213. *Toll-free phone:* 800-640-2287. *Fax:* 503-883-2472. *E-mail:* admission@linfield.edu. *Web site:* http://www.linfield.edu/.

See page 1390 for the College Close-Up.

Marylhurst University
Marylhurst, Oregon

- **Independent Roman Catholic** comprehensive, founded 1893
- **Suburban** 73-acre campus with easy access to Portland
- **Endowment** $12.4 million
- **Coed, primarily women** 932 undergraduate students, 26% full-time, 71% women, 29% men
- **Noncompetitive** entrance level, 71% of applicants were admitted

Undergraduates 239 full-time, 693 part-time. Students come from 24 states and territories; 8 other countries; 8% are from out of state; 5% Black or African American, non-Hispanic/Latino; 5% Hispanic/Latino; 3% Asian, non-Hispanic/Latino; 0.5% Native Hawaiian or other Pacific Islander, non-Hispanic/Latino; 0.5% American Indian or Alaska Native, non-Hispanic/Latino; 3% Two or more races, non-Hispanic/Latino; 9% Race/ethnicity unknown; 2% international; 19% transferred in. *Retention:* 64% of full-time freshmen returned.

Freshmen *Admission:* 42 applied, 30 admitted, 18 enrolled.

Faculty *Total:* 260, 22% full-time, 35% with terminal degrees. *Student/faculty ratio:* 7:1.

Academics *Calendar:* quarters. *Degrees:* bachelor's, master's, post-master's, and postbachelor's certificates. *Special study options:* accelerated degree program, adult/continuing education programs, advanced placement credit, distance learning, double majors, English as a second language, independent study, internships, off-campus study, part-time degree program, services for LD students, student-designed majors, study abroad, summer session for credit.

Computers on Campus 50 computers/terminals are available on campus for general student use. Students can access the following: campus intranet, computer help desk, online (class) grades, online (class) registration, online (class) schedules. Campuswide network is available. Wireless service is available via entire campus.

Student Life *Housing:* college housing not available. *Activities and organizations:* student-run newspaper, choral group, Marylhurst's Writer's Club, Marylhurst Gerontology Association, Solutions: Marylhurst Mediation Resource, Marylhurst S.A.F.E. Community: Sexual Acceptance for Everyone, LABY: Labyrinth Alliance Balances You. *Campus security:* security is available during campus hours. *Student services:* personal/psychological counseling.

Costs (2010–11) *Tuition:* $17,730 full-time, $394 per credit part-time. Full-time tuition and fees vary according to course load and program. Part-time tuition and fees vary according to course load and program. *Payment plan:* installment. *Waivers:* senior citizens and employees or children of employees.

Financial Aid Of all full-time matriculated undergraduates who enrolled in 2009, 339 applied for aid, 312 were judged to have need, 8 had their need fully met. 41 Federal Work-Study jobs (averaging $3955). In 2009, 30 non-need-based awards were made. *Average percent of need met:* 48%. *Average financial aid package:* $10,399. *Average need-based loan:* $4510. *Average need-based gift aid:* $7613. *Average non-need-based aid:* $1713. *Average indebtedness upon graduation:* $10,278.

Applying *Options:* electronic application, deferred entrance. *Application fee:* $40. *Required:* essay or personal statement, high school transcript. *Required for some:* interview. *Recommended:* minimum 2.5 GPA. *Application deadlines:* rolling (freshmen), rolling (transfers). *Notification:* continuous (freshmen), continuous (transfers).

Freshman Application Contact Chris Sweet, Director of Admissions, Marylhurst University, 17600 Pacific Highway, PO Box 261, Marylhurst, OR 97036-0261. *Phone:* 503-636-8141. *Toll-free phone:* 800-634-9982. *Fax:* 503-635-6585. *E-mail:* admissions@marylhurst.edu. *Web site:* http://www.marylhurst.edu/.

Mount Angel Seminary
Saint Benedict, Oregon

Director of Admissions Registrar/Admissions Officer, Mount Angel Seminary, Saint Benedict, OR 97373. *Phone:* 503-845-3951 Ext. 14. *E-mail:* seminary@mountangelabbey.org. *Web site:* http://www.mountangelabbey.org/seminary/.

Multnomah University
Portland, Oregon

- **Independent interdenominational** comprehensive, founded 1936
- **Urban** 22-acre campus
- **Endowment** $6.4 million
- **Coed** 602 undergraduate students, 81% full-time, 43% women, 57% men
- **Moderately difficult** entrance level, 87% of applicants were admitted

Undergraduates 488 full-time, 114 part-time. Students come from 28 states and territories; 5 other countries; 50% are from out of state; 2% Black or African American, non-Hispanic/Latino; 4% Hispanic/Latino; 3% Asian, non-Hispanic/Latino; 0.3% Native Hawaiian or other Pacific Islander, non-Hispanic/Latino; 0.8% American Indian or Alaska Native, non-Hispanic/Latino; 1% Two or more races, non-Hispanic/Latino; 7% Race/ethnicity unknown; 0.7% international; 13% transferred in; 57% live on campus. *Retention:* 77% of full-time freshmen returned.

Freshmen *Admission:* 159 applied, 139 admitted, 78 enrolled. *Average high school GPA:* 3.1. *Test scores:* SAT critical reading scores over 500: 68%; SAT math scores over 500: 48%; SAT writing scores over 500: 60%; ACT scores over 18: 74%; SAT critical reading scores over 600: 33%; SAT math scores over 600: 14%; SAT writing scores over 600: 21%; ACT scores over 24: 42%; SAT critical reading scores over 700: 3%; SAT writing scores over 700: 2%; ACT scores over 30: 5%.

Faculty *Total:* 91, 37% full-time, 69% with terminal degrees. *Student/faculty ratio:* 14:1.

Academics *Calendar:* semesters. *Degrees:* bachelor's, master's, doctoral-professional, and postbachelor's certificates. *Special study options:* academic remediation for entering students, adult/continuing education programs, advanced placement credit, double majors, internships, part-time degree program, services for LD students, summer session for credit.

Computers on Campus 44 computers/terminals are available on campus for general student use. Students can access the following: campus intranet, computer help desk, free student e-mail accounts, online (class) grades, online (class) registration, online (class) schedules. Campuswide network is available. 80% of college-owned or -operated housing units are wired for high-speed Internet access. Wireless service is available via entire campus.

Student Life *Housing:* on-campus residence required through junior year. *Options:* men-only, women-only. Campus housing is university owned. Freshman campus housing is guaranteed. *Activities and organizations:* drama/theater group, choral group, Acting for Life, Prayer for the Persecuted, Community Response Team, MU Snow Club, Student World Outreach Team. *Campus security:* 24-hour emergency response devices and patrols, late-night transport/escort service, controlled dormitory access. *Student services:* health clinic, personal/psychological counseling.

Athletics Member NCCAA. *Intercollegiate sports:* basketball M, volleyball W. *Intramural sports:* basketball M/W, soccer M/W, ultimate Frisbee M/W, volleyball M/W.

Standardized Tests *Required:* SAT or ACT (for admission).

Costs (2010–11) *Comprehensive fee:* $20,770 includes full-time tuition ($14,280), mandatory fees ($150), and room and board ($6340). Full-time tuition and fees vary according to course load and location. Part-time tuition: $510 per credit hour. Part-time tuition and fees vary according to course load and location. *Required fees:* $30 per term part-time. *Room and board:* Room and board charges vary according to board plan and housing facility. *Payment plan:* installment. *Waivers:* employees or children of employees.

Financial Aid Of all full-time matriculated undergraduates who enrolled in 2009, 503 applied for aid, 441 were judged to have need, 11 had their need fully met. 75 Federal Work-Study jobs (averaging $1500). In 2009, 36 non-need-based awards were made. *Average percent of need met:* 50%. *Average financial aid package:* $9211. *Average need-based loan:* $4094. *Average need-based gift aid:* $5846. *Average non-need-based aid:* $1848. *Average indebtedness upon graduation:* $21,020.

Applying *Options:* deferred entrance. *Application fee:* $40. *Required:* essay or personal statement, high school transcript, minimum 2.5 GPA, 2 letters of recommendation. *Application deadlines:* 7/15 (freshmen), 7/15 (transfers). *Notification:* continuous (freshmen), continuous (transfers).

Freshman Application Contact Ms. Lisa Hezmalhalch, Admissions Assistant, Multnomah University, 8435 Northeast Glisan Street, Portland, OR 97220-5898. *Phone:* 503-255-5166. *Toll-free phone:* 800-275-4672. *Fax:* 503-254-1268. *E-mail:* admiss@multnomah.edu. *Web site:* http://www.multnomah.edu/.

New Hope Christian College
Eugene, Oregon

- **Independent** 4-year, founded 1925, affiliated with Open Bible Standard Churches
- **Suburban** 40-acre campus
- **Coed** 120 undergraduate students, 93% full-time, 42% women, 58% men
- **Minimally difficult** entrance level, 97% of applicants were admitted

Undergraduates 111 full-time, 9 part-time. 47% are from out of state; 23% transferred in; 40% live on campus. *Retention:* 51% of full-time freshmen returned.

Freshmen *Admission:* 61 applied, 59 admitted, 56 enrolled. *Average high school GPA:* 3.2.

Academics *Calendar:* semesters. *Degree:* certificates and bachelor's. *Special study options:* academic remediation for entering students, advanced placement credit, distance learning, double majors, independent study, internships, part-time degree program, summer session for credit.

Computers on Campus Students can access the following: campus intranet, free student e-mail accounts, online (class) grades. Campuswide network is available. Wireless service is available via dorm rooms, student centers.

Student Life *Housing:* on-campus residence required through junior year. *Options:* men-only, women-only. Campus housing is university owned. Freshman campus housing is guaranteed. *Activities and organizations:* drama/theater group, student-run newspaper, choral group. *Campus security:* 24-hour emergency response devices, student patrols, controlled dormitory access. *Student services:* personal/psychological counseling.

Athletics *Intercollegiate sports:* basketball M, soccer M/W, volleyball M/W. *Intramural sports:* basketball M/W, soccer M/W, ultimate Frisbee M/W, volleyball M/W.

Costs (2011–12) *Comprehensive fee:* $19,450 includes full-time tuition ($12,000), mandatory fees ($1190), and room and board ($6260). Part-time tuition: $500 per credit hour. Part-time tuition and fees vary according to class time and course load. *College room only:* $2500. Room and board charges vary according to housing facility. *Payment plan:* tuition prepayment. *Waivers:* senior citizens and employees or children of employees.

Financial Aid Of all full-time matriculated undergraduates who enrolled in 2006, 140 applied for aid, 140 were judged to have need, 1 had their need fully met. 6 Federal Work-Study jobs (averaging $2123). 23 state and other part-time jobs (averaging $2175). In 2006, 1 non-need-based awards were made. *Average percent of need met:* 42%. *Average financial aid package:* $8900. *Average need-based loan:* $3850. *Average need-based gift aid:* $3500. *Average non-need-based aid:* $100. *Average indebtedness upon graduation:* $10,550. *Financial aid deadline:* 9/1.

Applying *Options:* electronic application, deferred entrance. *Application fee:* $35. *Required:* essay or personal statement, high school transcript, minimum 2 GPA, 2 letters of recommendation. *Application deadlines:* 8/1 (freshmen), rolling (transfers). *Notification:* continuous (freshmen), continuous (transfers).

Freshman Application Contact Sarah Slater, Director of Admissions, New Hope Christian College, 2155 Bailey Hill Road, Eugene, OR 97405. *Phone:* 541-485-1780 Ext. 3115. *Toll-free phone:* 800-322-2638. *Fax:* 541-343-5801. *E-mail:* sarahslater@newhope.edu. *Web site:* http://www.newhope.edu/.

Northwest Christian University
Eugene, Oregon

- **Independent Christian** comprehensive, founded 1895
- **Urban** 8-acre campus with easy access to Portland
- **Endowment** $10.8 million
- **Coed** 479 undergraduate students, 81% full-time, 62% women, 38% men
- **Moderately difficult** entrance level, 93% of applicants were admitted

Undergraduates 386 full-time, 93 part-time. Students come from 14 states and territories; 19% are from out of state; 11% transferred in. *Retention:* 69% of full-time freshmen returned.

Freshmen *Admission:* 587 applied, 548 admitted, 75 enrolled. *Average high school GPA:* 3.37. *Test scores:* SAT critical reading scores over 500: 43%; SAT math scores over 500: 48%; SAT writing scores over 500: 34%; ACT scores over 18: 76%; SAT critical reading scores over 600: 11%; SAT math scores over 600: 8%; SAT writing scores over 600: 2%; ACT scores over 24: 24%.

Faculty *Total:* 28, 93% full-time, 68% with terminal degrees. *Student/faculty ratio:* 18:1.

Academics *Calendar:* quarters. *Degrees:* certificates, associate, bachelor's, master's, and postbachelor's certificates. *Special study options:* academic remediation for entering students, accelerated degree program, adult/continuing education programs, advanced placement credit, distance learning, double majors, independent study, internships, off-campus study, part-time degree program, services for LD students, student-designed majors, study abroad, summer session for credit.

Computers on Campus 60 computers/terminals are available on campus for general student use. Students can access the following: campus intranet, computer help desk, free student e-mail accounts, online (class) grades, online (class) schedules. Campuswide network is available. 100% of college-owned or -operated housing units are wired for high-speed Internet access. Wireless service is available via entire campus.

Student Life *Housing:* on-campus residence required for freshman year. *Options:* coed, men-only, women-only. Campus housing is university owned. Freshman campus housing is guaranteed. *Activities and organizations:* drama/theater group, student-run newspaper, choral group, Community Life Groups, Circle K, Believers Building Bonds through Boardgames, Parable. *Campus security:* 24-hour emergency response devices and patrols, late-night transport/escort service, controlled dormitory access, late-night patrols by trained security personnel. *Student services:* personal/psychological counseling.

Athletics Member NAIA. *Intercollegiate sports:* basketball M(s)/W(s), cross-country running M(s)/W(s), golf M(s)/W(s), soccer M(s)/W(s), softball W(s), track and field M(s)/W(s), volleyball W(s). *Intramural sports:* badminton M/W, basketball M/W, football M, skiing (downhill) M/W, ultimate Frisbee M/W, volleyball M/W.

Standardized Tests *Required:* SAT or ACT (for admission).
Costs (2011–12) *Comprehensive fee:* $31,000 includes full-time tuition ($23,600) and room and board ($7400). Full-time tuition and fees vary according to course load. Part-time tuition: $787 per credit. Part-time tuition and fees vary according to course load. *Room and board:* Room and board charges vary according to board plan and housing facility. *Payment plans:* installment, deferred payment. *Waivers:* employees or children of employees.
Financial Aid Of all full-time matriculated undergraduates who enrolled in 2009, 305 applied for aid, 284 were judged to have need, 48 had their need fully met. 70 Federal Work-Study jobs (averaging $945). 66 state and other part-time jobs (averaging $900). In 2009, 24 non-need-based awards were made. *Average percent of need met:* 75%. *Average financial aid package:* $19,742. *Average need-based loan:* $4921. *Average need-based gift aid:* $14,974. *Average non-need-based aid:* $6729. *Average indebtedness upon graduation:* $22,818.
Applying *Options:* electronic application, deferred entrance. *Required:* essay or personal statement, high school transcript, minimum 2.5 GPA. *Application deadlines:* rolling (freshmen), rolling (out-of-state freshmen), rolling (transfers). *Notification:* continuous (freshmen), continuous (out-of-state freshmen), continuous (transfers).
Freshman Application Contact Jennifer Samples, Director of Admissions, Northwest Christian University, 828 East 11th Avenue, Eugene, OR 97401-3745. *Phone:* 541-684-7201. *Toll-free phone:* 877-463-6622. *Fax:* 541-684-7317. *E-mail:* admissions@nwcu.edu. *Web site:* http://www.northwestchristian.edu/.

Oregon College of Art & Craft

Portland, Oregon

- **Independent** 4-year, founded 1907
- **Urban** 10-acre campus with easy access to Portland
- **Endowment** $12.6 million
- **Coed**
- **Minimally difficult** entrance level

Faculty *Student/faculty ratio:* 9:1.
Academics *Calendar:* semesters. *Degrees:* certificates, bachelor's, and post-bachelor's certificates.
Student Life *Campus security:* 24-hour emergency response devices, late-night transport/escort service.
Standardized Tests *Recommended:* SAT (for admission), ACT (for admission).
Costs (2010–11) *Comprehensive fee:* $28,070 includes full-time tuition ($20,938), mandatory fees ($922), and room and board ($6210). Part-time tuition: $914 per credit hour. *College room only:* $4185. Room and board charges vary according to board plan and housing facility.
Financial Aid *Of all full-time matriculated undergraduates who enrolled in 2008,* 84 applied for aid, 80 were judged to have need. 85 Federal Work-Study jobs (averaging $500). 86 state and other part-time jobs (averaging $1000). *In 2008,* 3 non-need-based awards were made. *Average percent of need met:* 38. *Average financial aid package:* $21,995. *Average need-based loan:* $4640. *Average need-based gift aid:* $9429. *Average non-need-based aid:* $3667. *Average indebtedness upon graduation:* $37,000.
Applying *Options:* electronic application, deferred entrance. *Application fee:* $35. *Required:* essay or personal statement, high school transcript, minimum 2.5 GPA, 2 letters of recommendation, portfolio. *Required for some:* interview.
Freshman Application Contact Ms. Devon Simpson, Assistant Director of Admissions, Oregon College of Art & Craft, 8245 Southwest Barnes Road, Portland, OR 97225-6349. *Phone:* 503-297-5544 Ext. 141. *Toll-free phone:* 800-390-0632 Ext. 129. *Fax:* 503-297-9651. *E-mail:* admissions@ocac.edu. *Web site:* http://www.ocac.edu/.

Oregon Health & Science University

Portland, Oregon

- **State-related** upper-level, founded 1974
- **Urban** 116-acre campus
- **Endowment** $257.9 million
- **Coed**

Academics *Calendar:* quarters. *Degrees:* certificates, bachelor's, master's, doctoral-professional, doctoral-research/scholarship, post-master's, and post-bachelor's certificates.
Student Life *Campus security:* 24-hour emergency response devices and patrols.
Costs (2010–11) *Tuition:* state resident $13,005 full-time, $289 per credit part-time; nonresident $24,615 full-time, $547 per credit part-time. Full-time tuition and fees vary according to course level, degree level, location, program, reciprocity agreements, and student level. Part-time tuition and fees vary according to course level, course load, degree level, location, program, reci-

procity agreements, and student level. *Required fees:* $5991 full-time. *Room and board:* Room and board charges vary according to housing facility and location.
Financial Aid *Of all full-time matriculated undergraduates who enrolled in 2009,* 300 applied for aid, 285 were judged to have need, 21 had their need fully met. 12 Federal Work-Study jobs (averaging $1275). *In 2009,* 2 non-need-based awards were made. *Average percent of need met:* 37. *Average financial aid package:* $11,215. *Average need-based loan:* $4326. *Average need-based gift aid:* $7961. *Average non-need-based aid:* $700.
Applying *Application fee:* $125.
Application Contact Jennifer Anderson, Director of Admissions, Oregon Health & Science University, 3181 Southwest Sam Jackson Park Road, Mail Code: 337A/SNADM, Portland, OR 97201-3098. *Phone:* 503-494-0647. *Fax:* 503-494-4350. *E-mail:* andersje@ohsu.edu. *Web site:* http://www.ohsu.edu/.

Oregon Institute of Technology

Klamath Falls, Oregon

- **State-supported** comprehensive, founded 1947, part of Oregon University System
- **Small-town** 173-acre campus
- **Coed**
- **Moderately difficult** entrance level

Faculty *Student/faculty ratio:* 20:1.
Academics *Calendar:* quarters. *Degrees:* certificates, associate, bachelor's, master's, and postbachelor's certificates.
Student Life *Campus security:* 24-hour emergency response devices and patrols, late-night transport/escort service.
Athletics Member NAIA.
Standardized Tests *Required:* SAT or ACT (for admission).
Costs (2010–11) *One-time required fee:* $150. *Tuition:* state resident $5850 full-time, $130 per credit part-time; nonresident $18,990 full-time, $130 per credit part-time. Full-time tuition and fees vary according to course level, course load, degree level, location, program, and reciprocity agreements. Part-time tuition and fees vary according to course level, course load, degree level, location, program, and reciprocity agreements. *Required fees:* $1410 full-time. *Room and board:* $8145. Room and board charges vary according to board plan and housing facility.
Financial Aid *Of all full-time matriculated undergraduates who enrolled in 2008,* 1,796 applied for aid, 1,665 were judged to have need, 396 had their need fully met. *In 2008,* 2 non-need-based awards were made. *Average percent of need met:* 19. *Average financial aid package:* $5554. *Average need-based loan:* $3988. *Average need-based gift aid:* $5361. *Average non-need-based aid:* $6617. *Average indebtedness upon graduation:* $27,266.
Applying *Options:* electronic application, deferred entrance. *Application fee:* $50. *Required:* high school transcript, minimum 3 GPA.
Freshman Application Contact Oregon Institute of Technology, 3201 Campus Drive, Klamath Falls, OR 97601-8801. *Phone:* 541-885-1151. *Toll-free phone:* 800-422-2017 (in-state); 800-343-6653 (out-of-state). *Web site:* http://www.oit.edu/.

Oregon State University

Corvallis, Oregon

- **State-supported** university, founded 1868, part of Oregon University System
- **Small-town** 422-acre campus
- **Endowment** $372.3 million
- **Coed** 19,559 undergraduate students, 84% full-time, 47% women, 53% men
- **Moderately difficult** entrance level, 81% of applicants were admitted

Undergraduates 16,383 full-time, 3,176 part-time. Students come from 50 states and territories; 91 other countries; 17% are from out of state; 1% Black or African American, non-Hispanic/Latino; 6% Hispanic/Latino; 8% Asian, non-Hispanic/Latino; 0.8% Native Hawaiian or other Pacific Islander, non-Hispanic/Latino; 1% American Indian or Alaska Native, non-Hispanic/Latino; 2% Two or more races, non-Hispanic/Latino; 8% Race/ethnicity unknown; 3% international; 7% transferred in; 21% live on campus. *Retention:* 83% of full-time freshmen returned.
Freshmen *Admission:* 11,428 applied, 9,269 admitted, 3,602 enrolled. *Average high school GPA:* 3.51. *Test scores:* SAT critical reading scores over 500: 63%; SAT math scores over 500: 73%; SAT writing scores over 500: 56%; ACT scores over 18: 92%; SAT critical reading scores over 600: 22%; SAT math scores over 600: 30%; SAT writing scores over 600: 16%; ACT scores over 24: 50%; SAT critical reading scores over 700: 3%; SAT math scores over 700: 5%; SAT writing scores over 700: 2%; ACT scores over 30: 8%.
Faculty *Total:* 980, 77% full-time, 71% with terminal degrees. *Student/faculty ratio:* 25:1.

Academics *Calendar:* quarters. *Degrees:* certificates, bachelor's, master's, doctoral-professional, doctoral-research/scholarship, post-master's, and post-bachelor's certificates. *Special study options:* academic remediation for entering students, accelerated degree program, advanced placement credit, cooperative education, distance learning, double majors, English as a second language, external degree program, freshman honors college, honors programs, independent study, internships, off-campus study, part-time degree program, services for LD students, student-designed majors, study abroad, summer session for credit. *ROTC:* Army (b), Navy (b), Air Force (b).

Computers on Campus 1,658 computers/terminals and 150 ports are available on campus for general student use. Students can access the following: campus intranet, computer help desk, free student e-mail accounts, online (class) grades, online (class) registration, online (class) schedules. Campus-wide network is available. 95% of college-owned or -operated housing units are wired for high-speed Internet access. Wireless service is available via entire campus.

Student Life *Housing options:* coed, cooperative, disabled students. Campus housing is university owned. Freshman applicants given priority for college housing. *Activities and organizations:* drama/theater group, student-run newspaper, radio and television station, choral group, marching band, Associated Students of OSU, International Students of OSU, Graduate Students Organization, Campus Crusade, MECHA, national fraternities, national sororities. *Campus security:* 24-hour emergency response devices and patrols, student patrols, late-night transport/escort service, controlled dormitory access, crime prevention office. *Student services:* health clinic, personal/psychological counseling, women's center, legal services.

Athletics Member NCAA. All Division I except football (Division I-A). *Intercollegiate sports:* baseball M(s), basketball M(s)/W(s), crew M/W, golf M(s)/W(s), gymnastics W(s), soccer M(s)/W(s), softball W(s), swimming and diving W(s), volleyball W(s), wrestling M(s). *Intramural sports:* archery M/W, badminton M/W, basketball M/W, bowling M/W, crew M/W, cross-country running M/W, equestrian sports M(c)/W(c), fencing M(c)/W(c), football M, golf M/W, lacrosse M(c)/W(c), racquetball M/W, riflery M(c)/W(c), rugby M(c)/W(c), sailing M(c)/W(c), skiing (cross-country) M(c)/W(c), skiing (downhill) M(c)/W(c), soccer M/W, softball M/W, squash M(c), swimming and diving M/W, table tennis M(c)/W(c), tennis M/W, track and field M/W, ultimate Frisbee M/W, volleyball M/W, water polo M/W, wrestling M.

Standardized Tests *Required:* SAT or ACT (for admission). *Required for some:* SAT Subject Tests (for admission).

Costs (2010–11) *Tuition:* state resident $5760 full-time, $160 per credit hour part-time; nonresident $19,080 full-time, $530 per credit hour part-time. Full-time tuition and fees vary according to course load. Full-time tuition and fees vary according to course load. *Required fees:* $1355 full-time. *Room and board:* Room and board charges vary according to board plan and housing facility. *Payment plan:* deferred payment. *Waivers:* employees or children of employees.

Financial Aid Of all full-time matriculated undergraduates who enrolled in 2009, 11,516 applied for aid, 9,197 were judged to have need, 1,161 had their need fully met. In 2009, 32 non-need-based awards were made. *Average percent of need met:* 56%. *Average financial aid package:* $9849. *Average need-based loan:* $4023. *Average need-based gift aid:* $3494. *Average non-need-based aid:* $4054.

Applying *Options:* electronic application, early action, deferred entrance. *Application fee:* $50. *Required:* essay or personal statement, high school transcript, minimum 3 GPA. *Application deadlines:* 9/1 (freshmen), 5/1 (transfers), 11/1 (early action). *Notification:* continuous (freshmen), continuous (transfers).

Freshman Application Contact Oregon State University, Corvallis, OR 97331. *Phone:* 541-737-4411. *Toll-free phone:* 800-291-4192. *Web site:* http://www.oregonstate.edu/.

See page 1492 for the College Close-Up.

Oregon State University–Cascades
Bend, Oregon

- **State-supported** comprehensive, founded 2001, part of Oregon University System
- **Small-town** 193-acre campus
- **Coed**

Faculty *Student/faculty ratio:* 15:1.

Academics *Calendar:* quarters. *Degrees:* bachelor's and master's.

Costs (2010–11) *Tuition:* state resident $5580 full-time, $155 per credit hour part-time; nonresident $19,080 full-time, $530 per credit hour part-time. Full-time tuition and fees vary according to program. Part-time tuition and fees vary according to program. *Required fees:* $540 full-time.

Oregon State UNIVERSITY **OSU**

For more information, contact:

Admissions Department
104 Kerr Administration Building
Corvallis, Oregon 97331
800-291-4192
E-mail: osuadmit@oregonstate.edu

Web site: http://oregonstate.edu

Applying *Application fee:* $50.
Freshman Application Contact Admissions Department, Oregon State University–Cascades, 2600 Northwest College Way, Bend, OR 97701. *Phone:* 541-322-3150. *E-mail:* cascadeadmit@osucascades.edu. *Web site:* http://www.osucascades.edu/.

Pacific Northwest College of Art

Portland, Oregon

- **Independent** comprehensive, founded 1909
- **Urban** 2-acre campus with easy access to Portland
- **Endowment** $13.7 million
- **Coed** 582 undergraduate students, 92% full-time, 64% women, 36% men
- **Minimally difficult** entrance level, 51% of applicants were admitted

Undergraduates 536 full-time, 46 part-time. 1% Black or African American, non-Hispanic/Latino; 3% Hispanic/Latino; 4% Asian, non-Hispanic/Latino; 0.5% Native Hawaiian or other Pacific Islander, non-Hispanic/Latino; 2% American Indian or Alaska Native, non-Hispanic/Latino; 9% Two or more races, non-Hispanic/Latino; 0.5% Race/ethnicity unknown; 0.3% international; 16% live on campus. *Retention:* 70% of full-time freshmen returned.
Freshmen *Admission:* 425 applied, 215 admitted, 93 enrolled. *Average high school GPA:* 3.12.
Faculty *Total:* 101, 26% full-time, 87% with terminal degrees. *Student/faculty ratio:* 9:1.
Academics *Calendar:* semesters. *Degrees:* bachelor's and master's. *Special study options:* advanced placement credit, cooperative education, independent study, internships, off-campus study, part-time degree program, services for LD students, student-designed majors, study abroad, summer session for credit.
Computers on Campus 300 computers/terminals are available on campus for general student use. Students can access the following: campus intranet, computer help desk, free student e-mail accounts, online (class) grades, online (class) registration, online (class) schedules. Campuswide network is available. Wireless service is available via entire campus.
Student Life *Housing options:* Campus housing is leased by the school. Freshman applicants given priority for college housing. *Campus security:* 24-hour emergency response devices, late-night transport/escort service, entrance security guards during open hours. *Student services:* personal/psychological counseling.
Costs (2011–12) *Comprehensive fee:* $37,932 includes full-time tuition ($28,440), mandatory fees ($1092), and room and board ($8400). Part-time tuition: $1185 per credit. *Required fees:* $42 per credit part-time. *Payment plans:* installment, deferred payment. *Waivers:* employees or children of employees.
Financial Aid Of all full-time matriculated undergraduates who enrolled in 2006, 264 applied for aid, 238 were judged to have need, 13 had their need fully met. 33 Federal Work-Study jobs (averaging $1200). 33 state and other part-time jobs (averaging $1200). In 2006, 10 non-need-based awards were made. *Average percent of need met:* 54%. *Average financial aid package:* $11,845. *Average need-based loan:* $4040. *Average need-based gift aid:* $4699. *Average non-need-based aid:* $2442. *Average indebtedness upon graduation:* $22,155.
Applying *Options:* electronic application, deferred entrance. *Required:* essay or personal statement, high school transcript, portfolio of artwork. *Recommended:* minimum 2 GPA, interview. *Application deadlines:* rolling (freshmen), rolling (out-of-state freshmen), rolling (transfers). *Notification:* continuous (freshmen), continuous (out-of-state freshmen), continuous (transfers).
Freshman Application Contact Pacific Northwest College of Art, 1241 NW Johnson Street, Portland, OR 97209. *Phone:* 503-821-8926. *Web site:* http://www.pnca.edu/.

Pacific University

Forest Grove, Oregon

- **Independent** comprehensive, founded 1849
- **Small-town** 60-acre campus with easy access to Portland
- **Endowment** $44.5 million
- **Coed** 1,640 undergraduate students, 96% full-time, 60% women, 40% men
- **Moderately difficult** entrance level, 75% of applicants were admitted

Undergraduates 1,573 full-time, 67 part-time. Students come from 36 states and territories; 48% are from out of state; 1% Black or African American, non-Hispanic/Latino; 7% Hispanic/Latino; 16% Asian, non-Hispanic/Latino; 3% Native Hawaiian or other Pacific Islander, non-Hispanic/Latino; 0.9% Ameri-

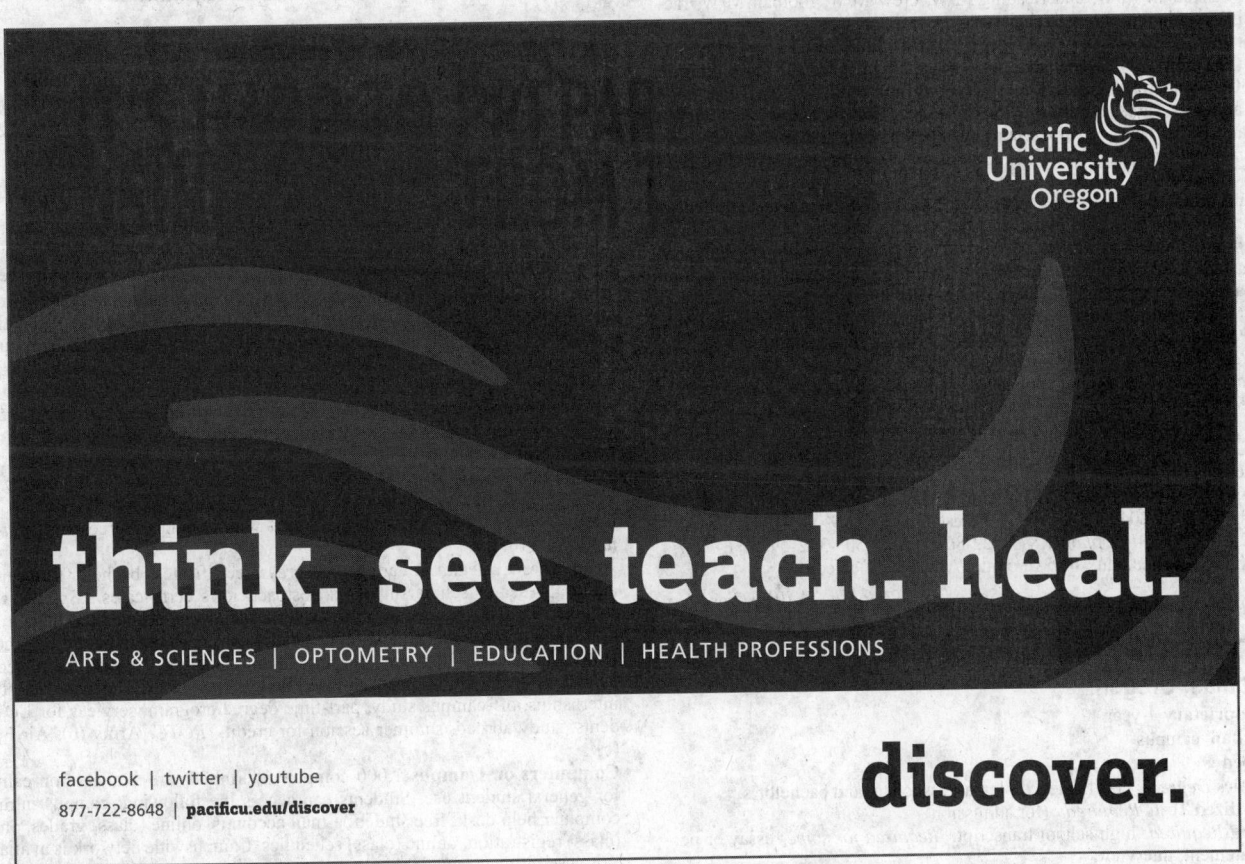

can Indian or Alaska Native, non-Hispanic/Latino; 2% Two or more races, non-Hispanic/Latino; 9% Race/ethnicity unknown; 3% international; 6% transferred in; 63% live on campus. *Retention:* 81% of full-time freshmen returned.

Freshmen *Admission:* 2,465 applied, 1,841 admitted, 475 enrolled. *Average high school GPA:* 3.58. *Test scores:* SAT critical reading scores over 500: 71%; SAT math scores over 500: 77%; ACT scores over 18: 92%; SAT critical reading scores over 600: 22%; SAT math scores over 600: 28%; ACT scores over 24: 51%; SAT critical reading scores over 700: 5%; SAT math scores over 700: 4%; ACT scores over 30: 6%.

Faculty *Total:* 385, 56% full-time, 52% with terminal degrees. *Student/faculty ratio:* 11:1.

Academics *Calendar:* semesters. *Degrees:* bachelor's, master's, doctoral-professional, post-master's, and postbachelor's certificates. *Special study options:* advanced placement credit, cooperative education, double majors, English as a second language, independent study, internships, off-campus study, services for LD students, study abroad, summer session for credit. *ROTC:* Army (c), Air Force (c). *Unusual degree programs:* 3-2 engineering with Washington State University, Washington University in St. Louis, Oregon Graduate Institute of Science and Technology, Oregon State University; medical technology, computer science, environmental science with Oregon Graduate Institute of Science and Technology.

Computers on Campus 315 computers/terminals and 5,900 ports are available on campus for general student use. Students can access the following: campus intranet, computer help desk, free student e-mail accounts, online (class) grades, online (class) schedules, Web space, printing, student and academic information, WebCT, computer peripherals. Campuswide network is available. 100% of college-owned or -operated housing units are wired for high-speed Internet access. Wireless service is available via entire campus.

Student Life *Housing:* on-campus residence required through sophomore year. *Options:* coed, disabled students. Campus housing is university owned. Freshman campus housing is guaranteed. *Activities and organizations:* drama/theater group, student-run newspaper, radio station, choral group, Pacific Outback activities, Hawaiian Club, Pacific Christian Fellowship (PCF), Business and Economics Club, Exercise Science Club. *Campus security:* 24-hour emergency response devices and patrols, late-night transport/escort service, controlled dormitory access. *Student services:* health clinic, personal/psychological counseling, women's center.

Athletics Member NCAA, NAIA. All NCAA Division III. *Intercollegiate sports:* baseball M, basketball M/W, cross-country running M/W, football M, golf M/W, lacrosse W, soccer M/W, softball W, swimming and diving M/W, tennis M/W, track and field M/W, volleyball W, wrestling M/W. *Intramural sports:* basketball M/W, cheerleading M/W, crew M/W, football M/W, racquetball W, softball M/W, volleyball M/W.

Standardized Tests *Required:* SAT or ACT (for admission).

Costs (2011–12) *Comprehensive fee:* $42,820 includes full-time tuition ($32,850), mandatory fees ($762), and room and board ($9208). Part-time tuition and fees vary according to course load. *College room only:* $4644. Room and board charges vary according to board plan and housing facility. *Payment plans:* installment, deferred payment. *Waivers:* employees or children of employees.

Financial Aid Of all full-time matriculated undergraduates who enrolled in 2009, 1,243 applied for aid, 1,113 were judged to have need, 263 had their need fully met. 753 Federal Work-Study jobs (averaging $1951). 140 state and other part-time jobs (averaging $993). In 2009, 257 non-need-based awards were made. *Average percent of need met:* 83%. *Average financial aid package:* $26,485. *Average need-based loan:* $4448. *Average need-based gift aid:* $14,309. *Average non-need-based aid:* $10,908. *Average indebtedness upon graduation:* $27,770.

Applying *Options:* electronic application, deferred entrance. *Application fee:* $40. *Required:* essay or personal statement, high school transcript, minimum 3 GPA, 1 letter of recommendation. *Recommended:* interview. *Application deadlines:* 8/15 (freshmen), rolling (transfers). *Notification:* continuous (freshmen), continuous (transfers).

Freshman Application Contact Ms. Karen Dunston, Executive Director, Pacific University, 2043 College Way, Forest Grove, OR 97116-1797. *Phone:* 503-352-2218. *Toll-free phone:* 877-722-8648. *Fax:* 503-352-2975. *E-mail:* admissions@pacificu.edu. *Web site:* http://www.pacificu.edu/.

See page 1496 for the College Close-Up.

Pioneer Pacific College
Clackamas, Oregon

- **Proprietary** 4-year
- **Urban** campus
- **Coed**

Academics *Degrees:* certificates, diplomas, associate, and bachelor's.

Standardized Tests *Required:* (for admission).

Applying *Required:* high school transcript. *Required for some:* essay or personal statement, interview.

Freshman Application Contact Admissions Office, Pioneer Pacific College, 8800 SE Sunnyside Road, Clackamas, OR 97015. *Phone:* 503-654-8000. *Toll-free phone:* 866-772-4636. *E-mail:* inquiries@pioneerpacific.edu. *Web site:* http://www.pioneerpacific.edu/.

Pioneer Pacific College
Wilsonville, Oregon

- **Proprietary** 4-year, founded 1981
- **Suburban** campus with easy access to Portland
- **Coed**
- **Noncompetitive** entrance level

Faculty *Student/faculty ratio:* 15:1.

Academics *Calendar:* continuous. *Degrees:* certificates, diplomas, associate, and bachelor's.

Standardized Tests *Required:* CPAt (for admission).

Applying *Required:* high school transcript, interview. *Required for some:* essay or personal statement.

Freshman Application Contact Ms. Kristin Lynn, Director of Admissions, Pioneer Pacific College, 27501 Southwest Parkway Avenue, Wilsonville, OR 97070. *Phone:* 866-772-4636. *Toll-free phone:* 866-PPC-INFO. *Fax:* 503-682-1514. *E-mail:* inquiries@pioneerpacific.edu. *Web site:* http://www.pioneerpacific.edu/.

Pioneer Pacific College–Eugene/Springfield Branch
Springfield, Oregon

- **Proprietary** 4-year
- **Urban** campus
- **Coed**

Academics *Degrees:* certificates, diplomas, associate, and bachelor's.

Standardized Tests *Required:* (for admission).

Applying *Required:* high school transcript. *Required for some:* essay or personal statement, interview.

Freshman Application Contact Admissions Office, Pioneer Pacific College–Eugene/Springfield Branch, 3800 Sports Way, Springfield, OR 97477. *Phone:* 541-684-4644. *Toll-free phone:* 866-772-4636. *E-mail:* inquiries@pioneerpacific.edu. *Web site:* http://www.pioneerpacific.edu/.

Portland State University
Portland, Oregon

- **State-supported** university, founded 1946, part of Oregon University System
- **Urban** 49-acre campus
- **Endowment** $50.0 million
- **Coed** 21,816 undergraduate students, 65% full-time, 53% women, 47% men
- **Moderately difficult** entrance level, 71% of applicants were admitted

Undergraduates 14,288 full-time, 7,528 part-time. Students come from 53 states and territories; 78 other countries; 12% are from out of state; 13% transferred in; 12% live on campus. *Retention:* 70% of full-time freshmen returned.

Freshmen *Admission:* 4,924 applied, 3,501 admitted, 1,495 enrolled. *Average high school GPA:* 3.34. *Test scores:* SAT critical reading scores over 500: 61%; SAT math scores over 500: 21%; SAT writing scores over 500: 50%; ACT scores over 18: 83%; SAT critical reading scores over 600: 22%; SAT math scores over 600: 17%; SAT writing scores over 600: 14%; ACT scores over 24: 36%; SAT critical reading scores over 700: 3%; SAT math scores over 700: 1%; SAT writing scores over 700: 1%; ACT scores over 30: 4%.

Faculty *Total:* 1,564, 57% full-time, 48% with terminal degrees. *Student/faculty ratio:* 18:1.

Academics *Calendar:* quarters. *Degrees:* certificates, bachelor's, master's, doctoral-research/scholarship, and postbachelor's certificates. *Special study options:* academic remediation for entering students, accelerated degree program, adult/continuing education programs, advanced placement credit, cooperative education, distance learning, double majors, English as a second language, freshman honors college, honors programs, independent study, internships, off-campus study, part-time degree program, services for LD students, study abroad, summer session for credit. *ROTC:* Army (b), Air Force (c).

Computers on Campus 1,000 computers/terminals are available on campus for general student use. Students can access the following: campus intranet, computer help desk, free student e-mail accounts, online (class) grades, online (class) registration, online (class) schedules. Campuswide network is available. Wireless service is available via entire campus.

Student Life *Housing options:* coed, disabled students. Campus housing is university owned. Freshman campus housing is guaranteed. *Activities and organizations:* drama/theater group, student-run newspaper, radio station, choral group, national fraternities, national sororities. *Campus security:* 24-hour emergency response devices and patrols, late-night transport/escort service, controlled dormitory access. *Student services:* health clinic, personal/psychological counseling, women's center, legal services.

Athletics Member NCAA. All Division I except football (Division I-AA). *Intercollegiate sports:* basketball M/W, cross-country running M/W, golf W, soccer W, softball W, tennis M/W, track and field M/W, volleyball W.

Standardized Tests *Required:* SAT or ACT (for admission).

Costs (2011–12) *One-time required fee:* $285. *Tuition:* state resident $5648 full-time, $126 per credit hour part-time; nonresident $20,160 full-time, $448 per credit hour part-time. Full-time tuition and fees vary according to program and reciprocity agreements. Part-time tuition and fees vary according to course level. *Required fees:* $1482 full-time, $18 per credit hour part-time, $96 per term part-time. *Room and board:* $10,065; room only: $7098. Room and board charges vary according to board plan and housing facility. *Payment plan:* installment. *Waivers:* minority students, senior citizens, and employees or children of employees.

Financial Aid Of all full-time matriculated undergraduates who enrolled in 2009, 9,885 applied for aid, 8,737 were judged to have need, 539 had their need fully met. 1,421 Federal Work-Study jobs (averaging $2876). In 2009, 76 non-need-based awards were made. *Average percent of need met:* 80%. *Average financial aid package:* $12,986. *Average need-based loan:* $4505. *Average need-based gift aid:* $5447. *Average non-need-based aid:* $1176. *Average indebtedness upon graduation:* $26,287.

Applying *Options:* electronic application, early admission, deferred entrance. *Application fee:* $50. *Required:* high school transcript, minimum 3 GPA. *Application deadlines:* rolling (freshmen), rolling (out-of-state freshmen), rolling (transfers). *Notification:* continuous (freshmen), continuous (out-of-state freshmen), continuous (transfers).

Freshman Application Contact Melissa Trifiletti, Director of New Student Programs, Portland State University, PO Box 751, Portland, OR 97207. *Phone:* 503-725-5504. *Toll-free phone:* 800-547-8887. *Fax:* 503-725-5525. *E-mail:* mtrifi@pdx.edu. *Web site:* http://www.pdx.edu/.

Reed College
Portland, Oregon

- **Independent** comprehensive, founded 1908
- **Urban** 116-acre campus
- **Endowment** $373.7 million
- **Coed** 1,447 undergraduate students, 97% full-time, 56% women, 44% men
- **Most difficult** entrance level, 43% of applicants were admitted

Undergraduates 1,408 full-time, 39 part-time. Students come from 50 states and territories; 46 other countries; 87% are from out of state; 2% Black or African American, non-Hispanic/Latino; 4% Hispanic/Latino; 6% Asian, non-Hispanic/Latino; 0.1% Native Hawaiian or other Pacific Islander, non-Hispanic/Latino; 0.5% American Indian or Alaska Native, non-Hispanic/Latino; 9% Two or more races, non-Hispanic/Latino; 17% Race/ethnicity unknown; 5% international; 2% transferred in; 67% live on campus. *Retention:* 90% of full-time freshmen returned.

Freshmen *Admission:* 3,075 applied, 1,311 admitted, 373 enrolled. *Average high school GPA:* 3.9. *Test scores:* SAT critical reading scores over 500: 100%; SAT math scores over 500: 99%; SAT writing scores over 500: 100%; ACT scores over 18: 100%; SAT critical reading scores over 600: 98%; SAT math scores over 600: 91%; SAT writing scores over 600: 98%; ACT scores over 24: 99%; SAT critical reading scores over 700: 61%; SAT math scores over 700: 35%; SAT writing scores over 700: 46%; ACT scores over 30: 76%.

Faculty *Total:* 139, 94% full-time, 92% with terminal degrees. *Student/faculty ratio:* 10:1.

Academics *Calendar:* semesters. *Degrees:* bachelor's and master's. *Special study options:* academic remediation for entering students, advanced placement credit, cooperative education, double majors, independent study, internships, off-campus study, part-time degree program, services for LD students, study abroad. *Unusual degree programs:* 3-2 engineering with California Institute of Technology, Rensselaer Polytechnic Institute, Columbia University School of Engineering and Applied Sciences; forestry with Nicholas School of the Environment of Duke University; Computer Science at University of Washington; Visual Arts at Pacific Northwest College of Art.

Computers on Campus 434 computers/terminals are available on campus for general student use. Students can access the following: campus intranet, computer help desk, free student e-mail accounts, online (class) registration, online

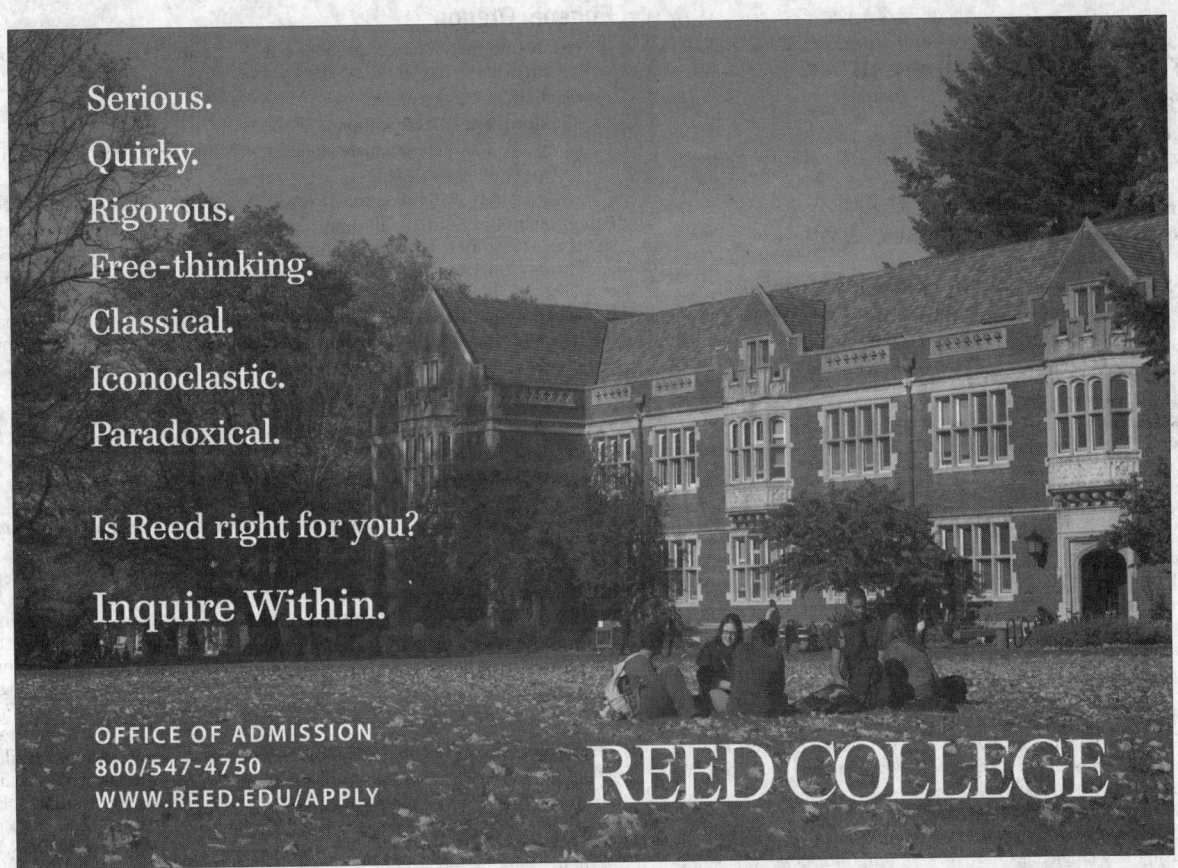

Serious.

Quirky.

Rigorous.

Free-thinking.

Classical.

Iconoclastic.

Paradoxical.

Is Reed right for you?

Inquire Within.

OFFICE OF ADMISSION
800/547-4750
WWW.REED.EDU/APPLY

REED COLLEGE

(class) schedules. Campuswide network is available. 100% of college-owned or -operated housing units are wired for high-speed Internet access. Wireless service is available via entire campus.

Student Life *Housing:* on-campus residence required for freshman year. *Options:* coed, women-only, cooperative, disabled students. Campus housing is university owned. Freshman campus housing is guaranteed. *Activities and organizations:* drama/theater group, student-run newspaper, radio station, choral group, GreenBoard, Movie Board, Reed Outing Club, Bike Co-op, Cookies For All. *Campus security:* 24-hour emergency response devices and patrols, student patrols, late-night transport/escort service, controlled dormitory access, 24-hour emergency dispatch. *Student services:* health clinic, personal/psychological counseling, women's center.

Athletics *Intercollegiate sports:* basketball M(c), fencing M(c)/W(c), rugby M(c)/W(c), soccer M(c)/W(c), squash M(c)/W(c). *Intramural sports:* basketball M/W, rugby M/W, soccer M/W, softball M/W, squash M/W, tennis M/W, ultimate Frisbee M/W.

Standardized Tests *Required:* SAT or ACT (for admission). *Recommended:* SAT Subject Tests (for admission).

Costs (2010–11) *Comprehensive fee:* $51,850 includes full-time tuition ($40,940), mandatory fees ($260), and room and board ($10,650). Part-time tuition: $1750 per semester hour. Part-time tuition and fees vary according to course load. *College room only:* $5550. Room and board charges according to board plan and housing facility. *Payment plan:* installment. *Waivers:* employees or children of employees.

Financial Aid Of all full-time matriculated undergraduates who enrolled in 2009, 841 applied for aid, 733 were judged to have need, 718 had their need fully met. 275 Federal Work-Study jobs (averaging $1388). 303 state and other part-time jobs (averaging $1304). *Average percent of need met:* 100%. *Average financial aid package:* $33,090. *Average need-based loan:* $4234. *Average need-based gift aid:* $30,710. *Average indebtedness upon graduation:* $20,750. *Financial aid deadline:* 2/1.

Applying *Options:* electronic application, early admission, early decision, deferred entrance. *Application fee:* $50. *Required:* essay or personal statement, high school transcript, 2 letters of recommendation. *Recommended:* interview. *Application deadlines:* 1/15 (freshmen), 3/1 (transfers). *Early decision deadline:* 11/15 (for plan 1), 12/20 (for plan 2). *Notification:* 4/1 (freshmen), 5/15 (transfers), 12/15 (early decision plan 1), 2/1 (early decision plan 2).

Freshman Application Contact Mr. Keith Todd, Dean of Admission, Reed College, 3203 Southeast Woodstock Boulevard, Portland, OR 97202-8199. *Phone:* 503-777-7511. *Toll-free phone:* 800-547-4750. *Fax:* 503-777-7553. *E-mail:* admission@reed.edu. *Web site:* http://www.reed.edu/.

See page 1524 for the College Close-Up.

Southern Oregon University
Ashland, Oregon

- **State-supported** comprehensive, founded 1926, part of Oregon University System
- **Small-town** 175-acre campus
- **Endowment** $13.0 million
- **Coed** 5,696 undergraduate students, 66% full-time, 59% women, 41% men
- **Moderately difficult** entrance level, 93% of applicants were admitted

Undergraduates 3,760 full-time, 1,936 part-time. Students come from 45 states and territories; 33 other countries; 30% are from out of state; 13% transferred in; 24% live on campus. *Retention:* 70% of full-time freshmen returned.

Freshmen *Admission:* 1,442 applied, 1,335 admitted, 715 enrolled. *Average high school GPA:* 3.2. *Test scores:* SAT critical reading scores over 500: 58%; SAT math scores over 500: 51%; ACT scores over 18: 88%; SAT critical reading scores over 600: 21%; SAT math scores over 600: 12%; ACT scores over 24: 44%; SAT critical reading scores over 700: 2%; SAT math scores over 700: 1%; ACT scores over 30: 5%.

Faculty *Total:* 290, 62% full-time. *Student/faculty ratio:* 21:1.

Academics *Calendar:* quarters. *Degrees:* bachelor's, master's, post-master's, and postbachelor's certificates. *Special study options:* academic remediation for entering students, accelerated degree program, adult/continuing education programs, advanced placement credit, cooperative education, distance learning, double majors, English as a second language, freshman honors college, honors programs, independent study, internships, off-campus study, part-time degree program, services for LD students, student-designed majors, study abroad, summer session for credit. *ROTC:* Army (b). *Unusual degree programs:* 3-2 engineering with Oregon State University.

Computers on Campus 750 computers/terminals are available on campus for general student use. Students can access the following: online (class) registration. Campuswide network is available.

Student Life *Housing:* on-campus residence required for freshman year. *Options:* coed, disabled students. Campus housing is university owned. Freshman campus housing is guaranteed. *Activities and organizations:* drama/the-

ater group, student-run newspaper, radio and television station, choral group, Native American Student Union, International Student Association, Impact (religious club), Ho'opa'a Hawaii Club, Omicron Delta Kappa. *Campus security:* 24-hour emergency response devices and patrols, student patrols, late-night transport/escort service. *Student services:* health clinic, personal/psychological counseling, women's center, legal services.

Athletics Member NAIA. *Intercollegiate sports:* basketball M(s)/W(s), cross-country running M(s)/W(s), football M(s), skiing (downhill) M/W, soccer W(s), softball W(s), tennis W(s), track and field M(s)/W(s), volleyball W(s), wrestling M(s). *Intramural sports:* basketball M/W, bowling M/W, cheerleading M/W, crew M/W, football M/W, golf M/W, racquetball M/W, rugby M/W, sailing M/W, skiing (cross-country) M/W, soccer M/W, softball M/W, swimming and diving M/W, table tennis M/W, tennis M/W, track and field M/W, ultimate Frisbee M/W, volleyball M/W, water polo M/W.

Standardized Tests *Required:* SAT or ACT (for admission). *Required for some:* SAT Subject Tests (for admission).

Costs (2010–11) *Tuition:* state resident $6729 full-time; nonresident $20,283 full-time. Full-time tuition and fees vary according to course load, location, and reciprocity agreements. Part-time tuition and fees vary according to course load, location, and reciprocity agreements. *Room and board:* $8508. Room and board charges vary according to board plan and housing facility. *Payment plan:* deferred payment. *Waivers:* senior citizens and employees or children of employees.

Financial Aid Of all full-time matriculated undergraduates who enrolled in 2008, 3,272 applied for aid, 2,860 were judged to have need, 273 had their need fully met. 316 Federal Work-Study jobs (averaging $1047). In 2008, 297 non-need-based awards were made. *Average percent of need met:* 60%. *Average financial aid package:* $10,226. *Average need-based loan:* $4003. *Average need-based gift aid:* $7816. *Average non-need-based aid:* $8905. *Average indebtedness upon graduation:* $24,132.

Applying *Options:* electronic application, early admission, deferred entrance. *Application fee:* $50. *Required:* high school transcript, minimum 2.75 GPA. *Required for some:* essay or personal statement. *Application deadlines:* rolling (freshmen), rolling (transfers). *Notification:* continuous (freshmen), continuous (transfers).

Freshman Application Contact Mr. Mark Bottorff, Director of Admissions, Southern Oregon University, 1250 Siskiyou Boulevard, Ashland, OR 97520. *Phone:* 541-552-6411. *Toll-free phone:* 800-482-7672. *Fax:* 541-552-6614. *E-mail:* admissions@sou.edu. *Web site:* http://www.sou.edu/.

University of Oregon
Eugene, Oregon

- **State-supported** university, founded 1872, part of Oregon University System
- **Urban** 295-acre campus
- **Endowment** $409.5 million
- **Coed** 19,528 undergraduate students, 91% full-time, 50% women, 50% men
- **Moderately difficult** entrance level, 79% of applicants were admitted

Undergraduates 17,820 full-time, 1,708 part-time. Students come from 51 states and territories; 86 other countries; 35% are from out of state; 2% Black or African American, non-Hispanic/Latino; 5% Hispanic/Latino; 5% Asian, non-Hispanic/Latino; 0.8% Native Hawaiian or other Pacific Islander, non-Hispanic/Latino; 0.9% American Indian or Alaska Native, non-Hispanic/Latino; 4% Two or more races, non-Hispanic/Latino; 3% Race/ethnicity unknown; 7% international; 8% transferred in; 19% live on campus. *Retention:* 86% of full-time freshmen returned.

Freshmen *Admission:* 18,515 applied, 14,588 admitted, 3,978 enrolled. *Average high school GPA:* 3.52. *Test scores:* SAT critical reading scores over 500: 75%; SAT math scores over 500: 75%; SAT critical reading scores over 600: 29%; SAT math scores over 600: 31%; SAT critical reading scores over 700: 5%; SAT math scores over 700: 4%.

Faculty *Total:* 1,386, 69% full-time, 92% with terminal degrees. *Student/faculty ratio:* 20:1.

Academics *Calendar:* quarters. *Degrees:* bachelor's, master's, doctoral-professional, doctoral-research/scholarship, and postbachelor's certificates. *Special study options:* adult/continuing education programs, advanced placement credit, cooperative education, distance learning, double majors, English as a second language, honors programs, independent study, internships, off-campus study, part-time degree program, services for LD students, student-designed majors, study abroad, summer session for credit. *ROTC:* Army (b), Air Force (c). *Unusual degree programs:* 3-2 engineering with Oregon State University.

Computers on Campus 833 computers/terminals and 500 ports are available on campus for general student use. Students can access the following: campus intranet, computer help desk, free student e-mail accounts, online (class) grades, online (class) registration, online (class) schedules. Campuswide network is available. 100% of college-owned or -operated housing units are wired for high-speed Internet access. Wireless service is available via entire campus.

Student Life *Housing options:* coed, cooperative. Campus housing is university owned. Freshman applicants given priority for college housing. *Activities and organizations:* drama/theater group, student-run newspaper, radio station, choral group, marching band, Political and Environmental Action, cultural organizations, major-specific organizations, community service organizations, Club Sports, national fraternities, national sororities. *Campus security:* 24-hour emergency response devices and patrols, late-night transport/escort service, controlled dormitory access. *Student services:* health clinic, personal/psychological counseling, women's center, legal services.

Athletics Member NCAA. All Division I except football (Division I-A). *Intercollegiate sports:* baseball M(s), basketball M(s)/W(s), cross-country running M(s)/W(s), golf M(s)/W(s), lacrosse W(s), soccer W(s), softball W(s), tennis M(s)/W(s), track and field M(s)/W(s), volleyball W(s). *Intramural sports:* archery M(c)/W(c), badminton M/W, baseball M(c), basketball M/W, bowling M(c)/W(c), crew M(c)/W(c), cross-country running M/W, equestrian sports M(c)/W(c), fencing M(c)/W(c), football M/W, golf M/W, ice hockey M(c)/W(c), lacrosse M(c)/W(c), racquetball M/W, rugby M(c)/W(c), sailing M(c)/W(c), skiing (downhill) M(c)/W(c), soccer M(c)/W(c), softball W(c), squash M(c)/W(c), swimming and diving M/W, table tennis M(c)/W(c), tennis M/W, track and field M(c)/W(c), ultimate Frisbee M(c)/W(c), volleyball M(c)/W(c), water polo M(c)/W(c).

Standardized Tests *Required:* SAT or ACT (for admission). *Required for some:* SAT and SAT Subject Tests or ACT (for admission).

Costs (2010–11) *One-time required fee:* $300. *Tuition:* state resident $6930 full-time, $154 per credit hour part-time; nonresident $24,570 full-time, $546 per credit hour part-time. Full-time tuition and fees vary according to course load. Part-time tuition and fees vary according to course load. *Required fees:* $1260 full-time. *Room and board:* $9429. Room and board charges vary according to board plan and housing facility. *Payment plan:* installment. *Waivers:* employees or children of employees.

Financial Aid Of all full-time matriculated undergraduates who enrolled in 2009, 10,654 applied for aid, 8,187 were judged to have need, 845 had their need fully met. 2,926 Federal Work-Study jobs (averaging $1478). 60 state and other part-time jobs (averaging $2600). In 2009, 846 non-need-based awards were made. *Average percent of need met:* 53%. *Average financial aid package:* $9343. *Average need-based loan:* $4663. *Average need-based gift aid:* $5573. *Average non-need-based aid:* $2679. *Average indebtedness upon graduation:* $20,928.

Applying *Options:* electronic application, early action. *Application fee:* $50. *Required:* essay or personal statement, high school transcript, 14 college preparatory units required, 16 recommended. *Required for some:* 2 letters of recommendation. *Recommended:* minimum 3 GPA. *Application deadlines:* 1/15 (freshmen), 5/15 (transfers), 11/1 (early action). *Notification:* 4/1 (freshmen), 12/15 (early action).

Freshman Application Contact University of Oregon, Eugene, OR 97403. *Phone:* 541-346-3201. *Toll-free phone:* 800-232-3825. *Web site:* http://www.uoregon.edu/.

See page 1722 for the College Close-Up.

University of Phoenix–Oregon Campus
Tigard, Oregon

Freshman Application Contact Ms. Audra McQuarie, Registrar/Executive Director, University of Phoenix–Oregon Campus, 4035 South Riverpoint Parkway, Mail Stop CF-L101, Phoenix, AZ 85040. *Phone:* 480-557-6151. *Toll-free phone:* 800-776-4867 (in-state); 800-228-7240 (out-of-state). *Fax:* 480-643-3068. *E-mail:* audra.mcquarie@phoenix.edu. *Web site:* http://www.phoenix.edu/.

University of Portland
Portland, Oregon

- **Independent Roman Catholic** comprehensive, founded 1901
- **Urban** 125-acre campus
- **Endowment** $80.0 million
- **Coed** 3,321 undergraduate students, 97% full-time, 60% women, 40% men
- **Moderately difficult** entrance level, 65% of applicants were admitted

Undergraduates 3,212 full-time, 109 part-time. Students come from 39 states and territories; 19 other countries; 62% are from out of state; 1% Black or African American, non-Hispanic/Latino; 8% Hispanic/Latino; 10% Asian, non-Hispanic/Latino; 1% Native Hawaiian or other Pacific Islander, non-Hispanic/Latino; 0.4% American Indian or Alaska Native, non-Hispanic/Latino; 5%

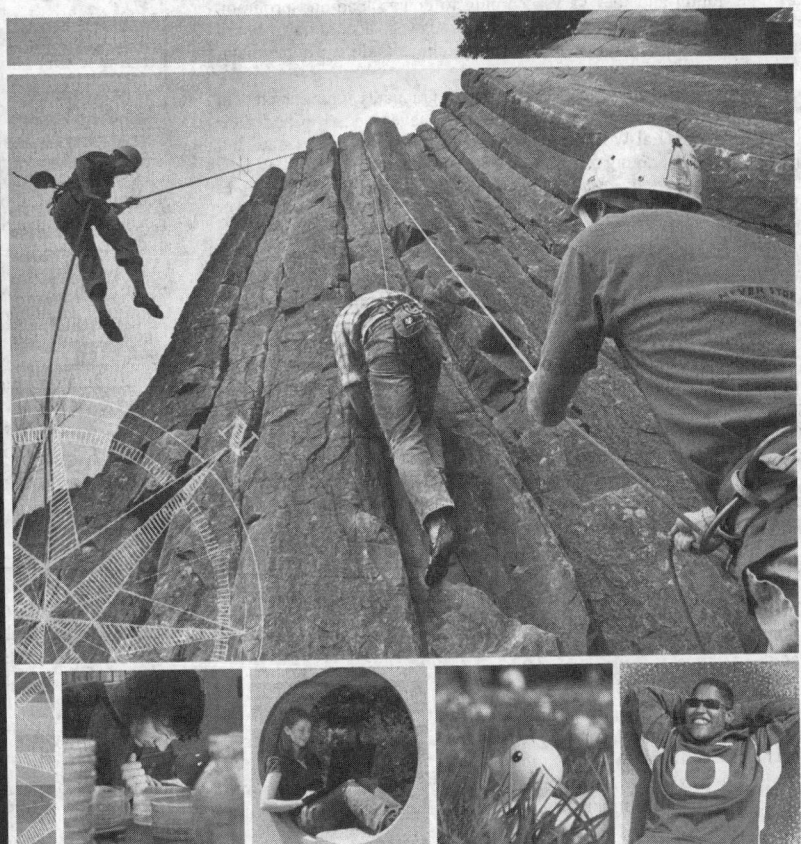

Two or more races, non-Hispanic/Latino; 7% Race/ethnicity unknown; 3% international; 3% transferred in; 57% live on campus. *Retention:* 89% of full-time freshmen returned.

Freshmen *Admission:* 8,156 applied, 5,300 admitted, 888 enrolled. *Average high school GPA:* 3.67. *Test scores:* SAT critical reading scores over 500: 91%; SAT math scores over 500: 91%; SAT critical reading scores over 600: 47%; SAT math scores over 600: 53%; SAT critical reading scores over 700: 12%; SAT math scores over 700: 10%.

Faculty *Total:* 321, 64% full-time, 61% with terminal degrees. *Student/faculty ratio:* 13:1.

Academics *Calendar:* semesters. *Degrees:* bachelor's, master's, doctoral-professional, and post-master's certificates. *Special study options:* adult/continuing education programs, advanced placement credit, double majors, honors programs, independent study, internships, off-campus study, part-time degree program, services for LD students, study abroad, summer session for credit. *ROTC:* Army (b), Air Force (b).

Computers on Campus 575 computers/terminals and 1,950 ports are available on campus for general student use. Students can access the following: campus intranet, computer help desk, free student e-mail accounts, online (class) grades, online (class) registration, online (class) schedules. Campuswide network is available. 100% of college-owned or -operated housing units are wired for high-speed Internet access. Wireless service is available via entire campus.

Student Life *Housing:* on-campus residence required for freshman year. *Options:* coed, men-only, women-only. Campus housing is university owned. Freshman campus housing is guaranteed. *Activities and organizations:* drama/theater group, student-run newspaper, radio station, choral group, English Society, International Club, Hawaiian Club, rugby club, Social Science Club. *Campus security:* 24-hour emergency response devices and patrols, student patrols, late-night transport/escort service, controlled dormitory access. *Student services:* health clinic, personal/psychological counseling.

Athletics Member NCAA. All Division I. *Intercollegiate sports:* baseball M(s), basketball M(s)/W(s), cross-country running M(s)/W(s), rugby M(c), soccer M(s)/W(s), tennis M(s)/W(s), track and field M(s)/W(s), volleyball W(s). *Intramural sports:* basketball M/W, crew M/W, cross-country running M/W, football M/W, rugby M, skiing (cross-country) M/W, skiing (downhill) M/W, soccer M(c)/W, softball M/W, swimming and diving M/W, tennis M/W, track and field M/W, volleyball M/W, water polo M/W, weight lifting M/W.

Standardized Tests *Required:* SAT or ACT (for admission).

Costs (2010–11) *Comprehensive fee:* $43,298 includes full-time tuition ($32,190), mandatory fees ($1348), and room and board ($9760). Full-time tuition and fees vary according to program. Part-time tuition: $1010 per credit hour. Part-time tuition and fees vary according to course load and program. *College room only:* $5290. Room and board charges vary according to board plan and housing facility. *Payment plans:* installment, deferred payment. *Waivers:* employees or children of employees.

Financial Aid Of all full-time matriculated undergraduates who enrolled in 2009, 2,427 applied for aid, 2,123 were judged to have need, 166 had their need fully met. 481 Federal Work-Study jobs (averaging $1337). 970 state and other part-time jobs (averaging $1742). In 2009, 784 non-need-based awards were made. *Average percent of need met:* 81%. *Average financial aid package:* $21,698. *Average need-based loan:* $4615. *Average need-based gift aid:* $18,359. *Average non-need-based aid:* $12,119. *Average indebtedness upon graduation:* $26,831.

Applying *Options:* electronic application, deferred entrance. *Application fee:* $50. *Required:* essay or personal statement, high school transcript, 1 letter of recommendation. *Application deadlines:* 6/1 (freshmen), 6/1 (transfers). *Notification:* continuous (freshmen), continuous (transfers).

Freshman Application Contact Mr. Jason McDonald, Dean of Admissions, University of Portland, 5000 North Willamette Boulevard, Portland, OR 97203-5798. *Phone:* 503-943-7147. *Toll-free phone:* 888-627-5601. *Fax:* 503-943-7315. *E-mail:* admissions@up.edu. *Web site:* http://www.up.edu/.

Warner Pacific College
Portland, Oregon

- **Independent** comprehensive, founded 1937, affiliated with Church of God
- **Urban** 15-acre campus with easy access to Portland
- **Endowment** $6.6 million
- **Coed**
- **Moderately difficult** entrance level

Faculty *Student/faculty ratio:* 22:1.

Academics *Calendar:* semesters. *Degrees:* associate, bachelor's, master's, and postbachelor's certificates.

Student Life *Campus security:* 24-hour emergency response devices and patrols, student patrols, late-night transport/escort service, controlled dormitory access.

Athletics Member NAIA, NCCAA.

Standardized Tests *Required:* SAT or ACT (for admission). *Recommended:* SAT Subject Tests (for admission).

Costs (2010–11) *Comprehensive fee:* $24,584 includes full-time tuition ($16,974), mandatory fees ($630), and room and board ($6980). Full-time tuition and fees vary according to course load, degree level, location, reciprocity agreements, and student level. Part-time tuition: $775 per credit. Part-time tuition and fees vary according to course load, degree level, location, and reciprocity agreements. *Required fees:* $315 per term part-time. *College room only:* $2800. Room and board charges vary according to board plan and housing facility.

Financial Aid Of all full-time matriculated undergraduates who enrolled in 2009, 439 applied for aid, 406 were judged to have need, 38 had their need fully met. 343 Federal Work-Study jobs (averaging $1502). In 2009, 28 non-need-based awards were made. *Average percent of need met:* 64. *Average financial aid package:* $15,003. *Average need-based loan:* $4267. *Average need-based gift aid:* $5714. *Average non-need-based aid:* $1807. *Average indebtedness upon graduation:* $30,559.

Applying *Options:* electronic application. *Application fee:* $50. *Required:* essay or personal statement, high school transcript, minimum 2.5 GPA. *Required for some:* 1 letter of recommendation, interview. *Recommended:* minimum 3 GPA, interview.

Freshman Application Contact Mrs. Shannon Mackey, Executive Director of Enrollment Management, Warner Pacific College, 2219 Southeast 68th Avenue, Portland, OR 97215. *Phone:* 503-517-1020. *Toll-free phone:* 800-804-1510. *Fax:* 503-517-1540. *E-mail:* admiss@warnerpacific.edu. *Web site:* http://www.warnerpacific.edu/.

Western Oregon University
Monmouth, Oregon

- **State-supported** comprehensive, founded 1856, part of Oregon University System
- **Rural** 157-acre campus with easy access to Portland
- **Coed** 5,318 undergraduate students, 86% full-time, 58% women, 42% men
- **Moderately difficult** entrance level, 89% of applicants were admitted

Undergraduates 4,580 full-time, 738 part-time. Students come from 33 states and territories; 22 other countries; 17% are from out of state; 3% Black or African American, non-Hispanic/Latino; 11% Hispanic/Latino; 2% Asian, non-Hispanic/Latino; 1% Native Hawaiian or other Pacific Islander, non-Hispanic/Latino; 2% American Indian or Alaska Native, non-Hispanic/Latino; 3% Two or more races, non-Hispanic/Latino; 1% Race/ethnicity unknown; 5% international; 11% transferred in. *Retention:* 72% of full-time freshmen returned.

Freshmen *Admission:* 2,578 applied, 2,293 admitted, 1,082 enrolled. *Average high school GPA:* 3.2.

Faculty *Total:* 452, 51% full-time, 41% with terminal degrees. *Student/faculty ratio:* 18:1.

Academics *Calendar:* quarters. *Degrees:* bachelor's, master's, and postbachelor's certificates. *Special study options:* academic remediation for entering students, advanced placement credit, distance learning, double majors, English as a second language, freshman honors college, honors programs, independent study, internships, off-campus study, part-time degree program, services for LD students, student-designed majors, study abroad, summer session for credit. *ROTC:* Army (b), Navy (c).

Computers on Campus 411 computers/terminals are available on campus for general student use. Students can access the following: computer help desk, free student e-mail accounts, online (class) grades, online (class) registration, online (class) schedules. Campuswide network is available. Wireless service is available via entire campus.

Student Life *Housing:* on-campus residence required for freshman year. *Options:* coed, disabled students. Campus housing is university owned. Freshman applicants given priority for college housing. *Activities and organizations:* drama/theater group, student-run newspaper, television station, choral group, Model United Nations, Multicultural Student Union, Oregon Student Association, Alternative Spring Break (community service), M.E.Ch.A. *Campus security:* 24-hour emergency response devices and patrols, student patrols, late-night transport/escort service, controlled dormitory access. *Student services:* health clinic, personal/psychological counseling, women's center.

Athletics Member NCAA. All Division II. *Intercollegiate sports:* baseball M(s), basketball M(s)/W(s), cross-country running M(s)/W(s), football M(s), soccer W(s), softball W(s), track and field M(s)/W(s), volleyball W(s). *Intramural sports:* badminton M/W, basketball M/W, bowling M/W, cross-country running M(c)/W(c), football M/W, golf M/W, lacrosse M(c), racquetball M(c)/W(c), riflery M/W, rugby M(c)/W(c), skiing (downhill) M/W, soccer M(c)/W(c), softball M/W, swimming and diving M(c)/W(c), table tennis M/W, tennis M/W, track and field M/W, volleyball M(c)/W(c), water polo M(c)/W(c), weight lifting M/W, wrestling M.

Costs (2011–12) *Tuition:* state resident $6855 full-time; nonresident $18,951 full-time. Full-time tuition and fees vary according to course level, course load, degree level, reciprocity agreements, and student level. Part-time tuition and fees vary according to course level, course load, degree level, reciprocity agreements, and student level. No tuition increase for student's term of enrollment. *Required fees:* $1200 full-time. *Room and board:* $8439. Room and board charges vary according to board plan and housing facility. *Payment plan:* deferred payment. *Waivers:* employees or children of employees.

Financial Aid Of all full-time matriculated undergraduates who enrolled in 2009, 3,743 applied for aid, 3,234 were judged to have need, 354 had their need fully met. 706 Federal Work-Study jobs (averaging $1074). In 2009, 151 non-need-based awards were made. *Average percent of need met:* 59%. *Average financial aid package:* $8601. *Average need-based loan:* $4146. *Average need-based gift aid:* $5948. *Average non-need-based aid:* $2333. *Average indebtedness upon graduation:* $24,131.

Applying *Options:* electronic application, deferred entrance. *Application fee:* $50. *Required:* high school transcript, minimum 2.75 GPA, general college preparatory program completion. *Application deadlines:* rolling (freshmen), rolling (transfers). *Notification:* continuous (freshmen), continuous (transfers).

Freshman Application Contact Mr. Rob Findtner, Assistant Director of Admissions, Western Oregon University, 345 North Monmouth Avenue, Monmouth, OR 97361. *Phone:* 503-838-8211. *Toll-free phone:* 877-877-1593. *Fax:* 503-838-8067. *E-mail:* wolfgram@wou.edu. *Web site:* http://www.wou.edu/.

Willamette University
Salem, Oregon

- **Independent United Methodist** comprehensive, founded 1842
- **Urban** 72-acre campus with easy access to Portland
- **Coed** 1,940 undergraduate students, 94% full-time, 56% women, 44% men
- **Very difficult** entrance level, 42% of applicants were admitted

Undergraduates 1,830 full-time, 110 part-time. 70% are from out of state; 2% Black or African American, non-Hispanic/Latino; 6% Hispanic/Latino; 7% Asian, non-Hispanic/Latino; 1% Native Hawaiian or other Pacific Islander, non-Hispanic/Latino; 0.9% American Indian or Alaska Native, non-Hispanic/Latino; 3% Two or more races, non-Hispanic/Latino; 15% Race/ethnicity unknown; 0.9% international; 2% transferred in; 70% live on campus. *Retention:* 90% of full-time freshmen returned.

Freshmen *Admission:* 7,785 applied, 3,306 admitted, 427 enrolled. *Average high school GPA:* 3.7. *Test scores:* SAT critical reading scores over 500: 98%; SAT math scores over 500: 98%; SAT writing scores over 500: 97%; ACT scores over 18: 100%; SAT critical reading scores over 600: 72%; SAT math scores over 600: 70%; SAT writing scores over 600: 67%; ACT scores over 24: 96%; SAT critical reading scores over 700: 20%; SAT math scores over 700: 13%; SAT writing scores over 700: 13%; ACT scores over 30: 35%.

Faculty *Total:* 298, 77% full-time, 86% with terminal degrees. *Student/faculty ratio:* 10:1.

Academics *Calendar:* semesters. *Degrees:* bachelor's, master's, and doctoral-professional. *Special study options:* accelerated degree program, advanced placement credit, double majors, independent study, internships, off-campus study, part-time degree program, services for LD students, student-designed majors, study abroad. *ROTC:* Army (c), Air Force (c). *Unusual degree programs:* 3-2 engineering with University of Southern California, Washington University in St. Louis, Columbia University; forestry with Duke University.

Computers on Campus Students can access the following: online (class) registration. Campuswide network is available. 100% of college-owned or -operated housing units are wired for high-speed Internet access.

Student Life *Housing:* on-campus residence required through sophomore year. *Options:* coed. Campus housing is university owned. Freshman campus housing is guaranteed. *Activities and organizations:* drama/theater group, student-run newspaper, radio station, choral group, national fraternities, national sororities. *Campus security:* 24-hour emergency response devices and patrols, student patrols, late-night transport/escort service, controlled dormitory access. *Student services:* health clinic, personal/psychological counseling, women's center.

Athletics Member NCAA. All Division III. *Intercollegiate sports:* baseball M, basketball M/W, crew M/W, cross-country running M/W, football M, golf M/W, lacrosse M(c), soccer M/W, softball W, swimming and diving M/W, tennis M/W, track and field M/W, volleyball W. *Intramural sports:* badminton M/W, basketball M/W, bowling M/W, cross-country running M/W, football M/W, golf M/W, racquetball M/W, skiing (cross-country) M(c)/W(c), skiing (downhill) M(c)/W(c), soccer M/W, softball M/W, table tennis M/W, tennis M/W, ultimate Frisbee M/W, volleyball M/W, water polo M/W, weight lifting M/W.

Standardized Tests *Required:* SAT or ACT (for admission).

Costs (2010–11) *Comprehensive fee:* $46,261 includes full-time tuition ($37,150), mandatory fees ($211), and room and board ($8900). Full-time tuition and fees vary according to course load. Part-time tuition: $4644 per course. Part-time tuition and fees vary according to course load. *Room and board:* Room and board charges vary according to board plan and housing

facility. *Payment plans:* tuition prepayment, installment. *Waivers:* employees or children of employees.

Financial Aid Of all full-time matriculated undergraduates who enrolled in 2009, 1,329 applied for aid, 1,173 were judged to have need, 469 had their need fully met. In 2009, 524 non-need-based awards were made. *Average percent of need met:* 88%. *Average financial aid package:* $31,308. *Average need-based loan:* $4242. *Average need-based gift aid:* $25,061. *Average non-need-based aid:* $12,488. *Average indebtedness upon graduation:* $23,248.

Applying *Options:* electronic application, early action, deferred entrance. *Application fee:* $50. *Required:* essay or personal statement, high school transcript, minimum 2 GPA, 1 letter of recommendation. *Required for some:* interview. *Recommended:* interview. *Application deadlines:* 2/1 (freshmen), 2/1 (transfers), 12/1 (early action). *Notification:* continuous until 4/1 (freshmen), 4/1 (transfers), 1/15 (early action).

Freshman Application Contact Susan Rauch, Vice President for Admission and Financial Aid, Willamette University, 900 State Street, Salem, OR 97301. *Phone:* 877-542-2787. *Toll-free phone:* 877-542-2787. *Fax:* 503-375-5363. *E-mail:* libarts@willamette.edu. *Web site:* http://www.willamette.edu/.

PENNSYLVANIA

Albright College
Reading, Pennsylvania

- **Independent** comprehensive, founded 1856, affiliated with United Methodist Church
- **Suburban** 118-acre campus with easy access to Philadelphia
- **Endowment** $43.0 million
- **Coed** 2,334 undergraduate students, 99% full-time, 58% women, 42% men
- **Moderately difficult** entrance level, 48% of applicants were admitted

Undergraduates 2,303 full-time, 31 part-time. Students come from 22 states and territories; 14 other countries; 35% are from out of state; 2% transferred in; 67% live on campus. *Retention:* 75% of full-time freshmen returned.

Freshmen *Admission:* 6,347 applied, 3,038 admitted, 485 enrolled. *Average high school GPA:* 3.35. *Test scores:* SAT critical reading scores over 500: 63%; SAT math scores over 500: 67%; SAT critical reading scores over 600: 16%; SAT math scores over 600: 20%; SAT critical reading scores over 700: 3%; SAT math scores over 700: 3%.

Faculty *Total:* 168, 71% full-time, 69% with terminal degrees. *Student/faculty ratio:* 13:1.

Academics *Calendar:* 4-1-4. *Degrees:* certificates, bachelor's, and master's. *Special study options:* accelerated degree program, advanced placement credit, double majors, English as a second language, honors programs, independent study, internships, part-time degree program, services for LD students, student-designed majors, study abroad, summer session for credit. *ROTC:* Army (c). *Unusual degree programs:* 3-2 forestry with Duke University; Environmental Studies - Duke University.

Computers on Campus 550 computers/terminals are available on campus for general student use. Students can access the following: campus intranet, computer help desk, free student e-mail accounts, online (class) grades, online (class) registration, online (class) schedules, online financial statements, housing choices, course management systems. Campuswide network is available. 100% of college-owned or -operated housing units are wired for high-speed Internet access. Wireless service is available via classrooms, computer centers, computer labs, learning centers, libraries, student centers.

Student Life *Housing:* on-campus residence required through sophomore year. *Options:* coed, men-only, women-only. Campus housing is university owned. Freshman campus housing is guaranteed. *Activities and organizations:* drama/theater group, student-run newspaper, radio station, choral group, Albright College Activities Council, Student Government Association, yearbook, newspaper, radio station, national fraternities, national sororities. *Campus security:* 24-hour emergency response devices and patrols, student patrols, late-night transport/escort service, controlled dormitory access, E2 campus test messaging, Rape Aggression Defense Training. *Student services:* health clinic, personal/psychological counseling, women's center.

Athletics Member NCAA. All Division III. *Intercollegiate sports:* badminton W(c), baseball M, basketball M/W, cheerleading M/W, cross-country running M/W, field hockey W, football M, golf M/W, lacrosse M/W, rugby M(c)/W(c), soccer M/W, softball W, swimming and diving M/W, tennis M/W, track and field M/W, volleyball W. *Intramural sports:* badminton W, basketball M/W, football M, racquetball M/W, soccer M/W, softball M/W, volleyball M/W.

Standardized Tests *Required:* students applying tests optional, must complete an on-campus admission interview (for admission). *Recommended:* SAT (for admission), ACT (for admission), SAT or ACT (for admission).

Costs (2010–11) *Comprehensive fee:* $41,598 includes full-time tuition ($31,940), mandatory fees ($800), and room and board ($8858). Full-time tuition and fees vary according to course load. Part-time tuition: $3993 per course. Part-time tuition and fees vary according to course load. *College room only:* $4919. Room and board charges vary according to board plan and housing facility. *Payment plan:* installment. *Waivers:* children of alumni, adult students, senior citizens, and employees or children of employees.

Applying *Options:* electronic application, early admission, deferred entrance. *Application fee:* $25. *Required:* essay or personal statement, high school transcript, 1 letter of recommendation, secondary school report (guidance department). *Recommended:* interview. *Application deadlines:* rolling (freshmen), rolling (transfers). *Notification:* continuous (freshmen), continuous (transfers).
Freshman Application Contact Mr. Gregory Eichhorn, Vice President for Enrollment Management, Albright College, PO Box 15234, 13th and Bern Streets, Reading, PA 19612-5234. *Phone:* 610-921-7260. *Toll-free phone:* 800-252-1856. *Fax:* 610-921-7294. *E-mail:* admission@albright.edu. *Web site:* http://www.albright.edu/.

Allegheny College
Meadville, Pennsylvania

- **Independent** 4-year, founded 1815
- **Suburban** 565-acre campus
- **Endowment** $134.6 million
- **Coed** 2,153 undergraduate students, 98% full-time, 55% women, 45% men
- **Very difficult** entrance level, 59% of applicants were admitted

Undergraduates 2,115 full-time, 38 part-time. Students come from 45 states and territories; 33 other countries; 45% are from out of state; 4% Black or African American, non-Hispanic/Latino; 4% Hispanic/Latino; 3% Asian, non-Hispanic/Latino; 0.1% American Indian or Alaska Native, non-Hispanic/Latino; 1% Two or more races, non-Hispanic/Latino; 0.3% Race/ethnicity unknown; 1% international; 1% transferred in; 85% live on campus. *Retention:* 86% of full-time freshmen returned.
Freshmen *Admission:* 4,341 applied, 2,550 admitted, 599 enrolled. *Average high school GPA:* 3.75. *Test scores:* SAT critical reading scores over 500: 91%; SAT math scores over 500: 91%; SAT writing scores over 500: 85%; ACT scores over 18: 100%; SAT critical reading scores over 600: 59%; SAT math scores over 600: 57%; SAT writing scores over 600: 45%; ACT scores over 24: 83%; SAT critical reading scores over 700: 15%; SAT math scores over 700: 11%; SAT writing scores over 700: 9%; ACT scores over 30: 20%.
Faculty *Total:* 197, 80% full-time, 82% with terminal degrees. *Student/faculty ratio:* 12:1.
Academics *Calendar:* semesters. *Degree:* bachelor's. *Special study options:* advanced placement credit, double majors, English as a second language, independent study, internships, off-campus study, services for LD students, student-designed majors, study abroad. *Unusual degree programs:* 3-2 engineering with Columbia University, Case Western Reserve University, Duke University, Washington University, University of Pittsburgh; nursing with Case Western Reserve University; arts management, public policy and management, health care policy and management and information systems management at Carnegie Mellon University; physician assistant, physical therapy and occupational therapy at Chatham; osteopathic medicine at PCOM and LECOM.
Computers on Campus 180 computers/terminals and 200 ports are available on campus for general student use. Students can access the following: campus intranet, computer help desk, free student e-mail accounts, online (class) grades, online (class) registration, online (class) schedules, online room selection, placement testing, course catalog, class lists, book buy, repair service, transcript review and ordering, billing, payroll time cards, internet kiosks, dataports for laptops, campus organizations, financial aid. Campuswide network is available. 100% of college-owned or -operated housing units are wired for high-speed Internet access. Wireless service is available via entire campus.
Student Life *Housing:* on-campus residence required through junior year. *Options:* coed, men-only, women-only, disabled students. Campus housing is university owned. Freshman campus housing is guaranteed. *Activities and organizations:* drama/theater group, student-run newspaper, radio and television station, choral group, student government, Gators Activity Programming, Alpha Phi Omega (service fraternity), Outing Club, Greek life, national fraternities, national sororities. *Campus security:* 24-hour emergency response devices and patrols, late-night transport/escort service, controlled dormitory access, local police patrol, emergency alert system, self defense education. *Student services:* health clinic, personal/psychological counseling.
Athletics Member NCAA. All Division III. *Intercollegiate sports:* baseball M, basketball M/W, cheerleading M(c)/W(c), cross-country running M/W, equestrian sports M(c)/W(c), fencing M(c)/W(c), football M, golf M/W, ice hockey M(c), lacrosse W, rugby M(c)/W(c), soccer M/W, softball W, swimming and diving M/W, tennis M/W, track and field M/W, ultimate Frisbee M(c)/W(c), volleyball M(c)/W. *Intramural sports:* basketball M/W, soccer M/W, volleyball M/W.
Standardized Tests *Required:* SAT or ACT (for admission).

Costs (2011–12) *Comprehensive fee:* $45,350 includes full-time tuition ($35,850), mandatory fees ($340), and room and board ($9160). Part-time tuition: $1494 per credit hour. Part-time tuition and fees vary according to course load. *Required fees:* $170 per term part-time. *College room only:* $4820. Room and board charges vary according to board plan and housing facility. *Payment plans:* tuition prepayment, installment. *Waivers:* employees or children of employees.
Financial Aid Of all full-time matriculated undergraduates who enrolled in 2009, 1,668 applied for aid, 1,487 were judged to have need, 507 had their need fully met. 1,222 Federal Work-Study jobs (averaging $2075). 95 state and other part-time jobs (averaging $4415). In 2009, 564 non-need-based awards were made. *Average percent of need met:* 89%. *Average financial aid package:* $28,033. *Average need-based loan:* $4789. *Average need-based gift aid:* $21,202. *Average non-need-based aid:* $12,460.
Applying *Options:* electronic application, early admission, early decision, deferred entrance. *Application fee:* $35. *Required:* essay or personal statement, high school transcript, 2 letters of recommendation, college preparatory program, standardized test scores. *Recommended:* interview. *Application deadlines:* 2/15 (freshmen), 7/1 (transfers). *Early decision deadline:* 11/15. *Notification:* 4/1 (freshmen), 8/1 (transfers), 12/15 (early decision).
Freshman Application Contact Ms. Jennifer Winge, Director of Admissions, Allegheny College, 520 North Main Street, Box 5, Meadville, PA 16335. *Phone:* 814-332-4351. *Toll-free phone:* 800-521-5293. *Fax:* 814-337-0431. *E-mail:* admissions@allegheny.edu. *Web site:* http://www.allegheny.edu/.

Alvernia University
Reading, Pennsylvania

- **Independent Roman Catholic** comprehensive, founded 1958
- **Suburban** 121-acre campus with easy access to Philadelphia
- **Endowment** $14.3 million
- **Coed** 2,110 undergraduate students, 78% full-time, 69% women, 31% men
- **Moderately difficult** entrance level, 81% of applicants were admitted

Undergraduates 1,654 full-time, 456 part-time. Students come from 20 states and territories; 5 other countries; 20% are from out of state; 10% Black or African American, non-Hispanic/Latino; 7% Hispanic/Latino; 1% Asian, non-Hispanic/Latino; 0.2% American Indian or Alaska Native, non-Hispanic/Latino; 1% Two or more races, non-Hispanic/Latino; 3% Race/ethnicity unknown; 0.2% international; 5% transferred in; 56% live on campus. *Retention:* 72% of full-time freshmen returned.
Freshmen *Admission:* 1,571 applied, 1,279 admitted, 388 enrolled. *Average high school GPA:* 3.13. *Test scores:* SAT critical reading scores over 500: 60%; SAT math scores over 500: 55%; SAT writing scores over 500: 60%; ACT scores over 18: 70%; SAT critical reading scores over 600: 10%; SAT math scores over 600: 11%; SAT writing scores over 600: 14%; ACT scores over 24: 7%; SAT critical reading scores over 700: 1%; ACT scores over 30: 1%.
Faculty *Total:* 308, 29% full-time, 34% with terminal degrees. *Student/faculty ratio:* 14:1.
Academics *Calendar:* semesters. *Degrees:* associate, bachelor's, master's, and doctoral-research/scholarship. *Special study options:* academic remediation for entering students, accelerated degree program, adult/continuing education programs, advanced placement credit, distance learning, double majors, English as a second language, honors programs, independent study, internships, off-campus study, part-time degree program, services for LD students, student-designed majors, study abroad, summer session for credit. *ROTC:* Army (c). *Unusual degree programs:* 3-2 occupational therapy.
Computers on Campus 360 computers/terminals and 1,020 ports are available on campus for general student use. Students can access the following: computer help desk, free student e-mail accounts, online (class) grades, online (class) registration, online (class) schedules. Campuswide network is available. 100% of college-owned or -operated housing units are wired for high-speed Internet access. Wireless service is available via classrooms, computer centers, computer labs, dorm rooms, learning centers, libraries, student centers.
Student Life *Housing:* on-campus residence required for freshman year. *Options:* coed, disabled students. Campus housing is university owned. Freshman campus housing is guaranteed. *Activities and organizations:* drama/theater group, student-run newspaper, choral group, Student Government Association, Student Nurses Association of Alvernia College (ASNA), Criminal Justice Association (CJA), Sports Management Association (SMA), Science Association. *Campus security:* 24-hour patrols, late-night transport/escort service, controlled dormitory access. *Student services:* health clinic, personal/psychological counseling.
Athletics Member NCAA. All Division III. *Intercollegiate sports:* baseball M, basketball M/W, cross-country running M/W, field hockey W, golf M, ice hockey M(c), lacrosse M/W, soccer M/W, softball W, tennis M/W, track and field M/W, volleyball W. *Intramural sports:* basketball M/W, cheerleading W(c), soccer M/W.
Standardized Tests *Required:* SAT or ACT (for admission).

Costs (2011–12) *Comprehensive fee:* $36,117 includes full-time tuition ($26,100), mandatory fees ($530), and room and board ($9487). Full-time tuition and fees vary according to class time and reciprocity agreements. Part-time tuition: $720 per credit hour. Part-time tuition and fees vary according to class time and course load. *College room only:* $4657. Room and board charges vary according to board plan and housing facility. *Payment plan:* installment. *Waivers:* senior citizens and employees or children of employees.
Financial Aid Of all full-time matriculated undergraduates who enrolled in 2008, 1,636 applied for aid, 1,536 were judged to have need, 143 had their need fully met. 205 Federal Work-Study jobs (averaging $1076). 17 state and other part-time jobs (averaging $1541). In 2008, 128 non-need-based awards were made. *Average percent of need met:* 63%. *Average financial aid package:* $15,576. *Average need-based loan:* $5699. *Average need-based gift aid:* $10,668. *Average non-need-based aid:* $5875. *Average indebtedness upon graduation:* $27,327.
Applying *Options:* electronic application, deferred entrance. *Application fee:* $25. *Required:* essay or personal statement, high school transcript. *Required for some:* 2 letters of recommendation, interview. *Recommended:* minimum 2 GPA, 1 letter of recommendation. *Application deadlines:* rolling (freshmen), rolling (transfers). *Notification:* continuous (freshmen).
Freshman Application Contact Mr. Jeff Dittman, Vice President for Enrollment Management, Alvernia University, 400 Saint Bernardine Street, Reading, PA 19607-1799. *Phone:* 610-796-8269. *Toll-free phone:* 888-ALVERNIA. *Fax:* 610-796-2873. *E-mail:* admissions@alvernia.edu. *Web site:* http://www.alvernia.edu/.

See page 990 for the College Close-Up.

Arcadia University
Glenside, Pennsylvania

- **Independent** comprehensive, founded 1853, affiliated with Presbyterian Church (U.S.A.)
- **Suburban** 71-acre campus with easy access to Philadelphia
- **Endowment** $40.2 million
- **Coed** 2,228 undergraduate students, 89% full-time, 72% women, 28% men
- **Moderately difficult** entrance level, 65% of applicants were admitted

Undergraduates 1,993 full-time, 235 part-time. Students come from 30 states and territories; 13 other countries; 39% are from out of state; 9% Black or African American, non-Hispanic/Latino; 5% Hispanic/Latino; 4% Asian, non-Hispanic/Latino; 0.3% American Indian or Alaska Native, non-Hispanic/Latino; 2% Two or more races, non-Hispanic/Latino; 5% Race/ethnicity unknown; 1% international; 6% transferred in; 55% live on campus. *Retention:* 76% of full-time freshmen returned.
Freshmen *Admission:* 5,938 applied, 3,844 admitted, 554 enrolled. *Average high school GPA:* 3.62. *Test scores:* SAT critical reading scores over 500: 82%; SAT math scores over 500: 76%; SAT writing scores over 500: 76%; ACT scores over 18: 98%; SAT critical reading scores over 600: 33%; SAT math scores over 600: 30%; SAT writing scores over 600: 31%; ACT scores over 24: 62%; SAT critical reading scores over 700: 5%; SAT math scores over 700: 2%; SAT writing scores over 700: 4%; ACT scores over 30: 10%.
Faculty *Total:* 467, 27% full-time. *Student/faculty ratio:* 13:1.
Academics *Calendar:* semesters. *Degrees:* bachelor's, master's, doctoral-professional, doctoral-research/scholarship, and postbachelor's certificates. *Special study options:* advanced placement credit, cooperative education, distance learning, double majors, English as a second language, honors programs, independent study, internships, off-campus study, part-time degree program, services for LD students, student-designed majors, study abroad, summer session for credit.
Computers on Campus 120 computers/terminals and 620 ports are available on campus for general student use. Students can access the following: campus intranet, computer help desk, free student e-mail accounts, online (class) grades, online (class) registration, online (class) schedules. Campuswide network is available.
Student Life *Housing options:* coed, women-only. Campus housing is university owned and leased by the school. Freshman campus housing is guaranteed. *Activities and organizations:* drama/theater group, student-run newspaper, radio station, choral group, Student Program Board, Residence Hall Council, student government, Arcadia Christian Fellowship, Student Alumni Association. *Campus security:* 24-hour emergency response devices and patrols, student patrols, late-night transport/escort service, controlled dormitory access. *Student services:* health clinic, personal/psychological counseling.
Athletics Member NCAA. All Division III. *Intercollegiate sports:* baseball M, basketball M/W, equestrian sports M/W, field hockey W, golf M/W, lacrosse W, soccer M/W, softball W, swimming and diving M/W, tennis M/W, volleyball W. *Intramural sports:* basketball M/W, cheerleading W(c), equestrian sports M/W, field hockey W, rock climbing M/W, soccer M/W, swimming and diving M, tennis M/W, volleyball M/W, weight lifting M/W.

Standardized Tests *Required:* SAT or ACT (for admission).
Costs (2011–12) *Comprehensive fee:* $45,790 includes full-time tuition ($33,490), mandatory fees ($660), and room and board ($11,640). Full-time tuition and fees vary according to course load, degree level, and program. *Room and board:* Room and board charges vary according to board plan. *Payment plans:* installment, deferred payment. *Waivers:* children of alumni and employees or children of employees.
Financial Aid Of all full-time matriculated undergraduates who enrolled in 2009, 1,868 applied for aid, 1,744 were judged to have need, 257 had their need fully met. 1,185 Federal Work-Study jobs (averaging $1626). 176 state and other part-time jobs (averaging $1575). In 2009, 268 non-need-based awards were made. *Average percent of need met:* 63%. *Average financial aid package:* $22,693. *Average need-based loan:* $4137. *Average need-based gift aid:* $18,407. *Average non-need-based aid:* $14,100. *Average indebtedness upon graduation:* $33,765.
Applying *Options:* electronic application, deferred entrance. *Application fee:* $30. *Required:* essay or personal statement, high school transcript, 2 letters of recommendation. *Required for some:* portfolio, audition. *Recommended:* minimum 3 GPA, interview. *Application deadlines:* 3/1 (freshmen), 6/15 (transfers). *Notification:* continuous until 9/1 (freshmen), continuous until 9/1 (transfers).
Freshman Application Contact Mr. Mark Laprezioza, Assistant Vice President of Enrollment Management, Arcadia University, 450 South Easton Road, Glenside, PA 19038. *Phone:* 215-572-2910. *Toll-free phone:* 877-ARCADIA. *Fax:* 215-572-4049. *E-mail:* admiss@arcadia.edu. *Web site:* http://www.arcadia.edu/.

See page 1000 for the College Close-Up.

The Art Institute of Philadelphia
Philadelphia, Pennsylvania

- **Proprietary** 4-year, founded 1966, part of Education Management Corporation
- **Urban** campus
- **Coed**

Academics *Calendar:* quarters. *Degrees:* diplomas, associate, and bachelor's.
Costs (2010–11) *Tuition:* Tuition cost varies by program. Prospective students should contact the school for current tuition costs. Other charges include a starting kit for all first-quarter students. Kits vary in price, depending on the program of study.
Freshman Application Contact The Art Institute of Philadelphia, 1622 Chestnut Street, Philadelphia, PA 19103. *Phone:* 215-567-7080. *Toll-free phone:* 800-275-2474. *Web site:* http://www.artinstitutes.edu/philadelphia/.

See page 1054 for the College Close-Up.

The Art Institute of Pittsburgh
Pittsburgh, Pennsylvania

- **Proprietary** 4-year, founded 1921, part of Education Management Corporation
- **Urban** campus
- **Coed**

Academics *Calendar:* quarters. *Degrees:* diplomas, associate, and bachelor's.
Costs (2010–11) *Tuition:* Tuition cost varies by program. Prospective students should contact the school for current tuition costs. Other charges include a starting kit for all first-quarter students. Kits vary in price, depending on the program of study.
Freshman Application Contact The Art Institute of Pittsburgh, 420 Boulevard of the Allies, Pittsburgh, PA 15219. *Phone:* 412-263-6600. *Toll-free phone:* 800-275-2470. *Web site:* http://www.artinstitutes.edu/pittsburgh/.

See page 1058 for the College Close-Up.

The Art Institute of York– Pennsylvania
York, Pennsylvania

- **Proprietary** primarily 2-year, founded 1952, part of Education Management Corporation
- **Suburban** campus
- **Coed**

Academics *Calendar:* quarters. *Degrees:* associate and bachelor's.
Costs (2010–11) *Tuition:* Tuition cost varies by program. Prospective students should contact the school for current tuition costs. Other charges include a starting kit for all first-quarter students. Kits vary in price, depending on the program of study.

Freshman Application Contact The Art Institute of York–Pennsylvania, 1409 Williams Road, York, PA 17402-9012. *Phone:* 717-755-2300. *Toll-free phone:* 800-864-7725. *Web site:* http://www.artinstitutes.edu/york/.

See page 1084 for the College Close-Up.

Baptist Bible College of Pennsylvania
Clarks Summit, Pennsylvania

- **Independent Baptist** comprehensive, founded 1932
- **Suburban** 124-acre campus
- **Endowment** $2.1 million
- **Coed** 595 undergraduate students, 86% full-time, 57% women, 43% men
- **Minimally difficult** entrance level, 84% of applicants were admitted

Undergraduates 512 full-time, 83 part-time. Students come from 32 states and territories; 6 other countries; 55% are from out of state; 12% transferred in; 91% live on campus. *Retention:* 77% of full-time freshmen returned.

Freshmen *Admission:* 425 applied, 356 admitted, 129 enrolled. *Average high school GPA:* 3.31. *Test scores:* SAT critical reading scores over 500: 63%; SAT math scores over 500: 44%; ACT scores over 18: 85%; SAT critical reading scores over 600: 24%; SAT math scores over 600: 14%; ACT scores over 24: 35%; SAT critical reading scores over 700: 8%; SAT math scores over 700: 1%; ACT scores over 30: 3%.

Faculty *Total:* 67, 66% full-time, 51% with terminal degrees. *Student/faculty ratio:* 12:1.

Academics *Calendar:* semesters. *Degrees:* certificates, associate, bachelor's, master's, doctoral-professional, and doctoral-research/scholarship. *Special study options:* academic remediation for entering students, adult/continuing education programs, advanced placement credit, distance learning, double majors, external degree program, independent study, internships, part-time degree program, student-designed majors, summer session for credit. *ROTC:* Army (c), Navy (c), Air Force (c).

Computers on Campus 25 computers/terminals are available on campus for general student use. Students can access the following: campus intranet, computer help desk, free student e-mail accounts, online (class) grades, online (class) registration, online (class) schedules. Campuswide network is available. 100% of college-owned or -operated housing units are wired for high-speed Internet access. Wireless service is available via classrooms, computer centers, computer labs, learning centers, libraries, student centers.

Student Life *Housing:* on-campus residence required through senior year. *Options:* men-only, women-only. Campus housing is university owned. Freshman campus housing is guaranteed. *Activities and organizations:* drama/theater group, choral group. *Campus security:* 24-hour patrols, student patrols, controlled dormitory access. *Student services:* health clinic, personal/psychological counseling.

Athletics Member NCAA, NCCAA. All NCAA Division III. *Intercollegiate sports:* baseball M, basketball M/W, cheerleading W, cross-country running M/W, golf M, soccer M/W, softball W, tennis W, track and field M/W, volleyball W. *Intramural sports:* basketball M, golf M, soccer M/W, softball M, volleyball W.

Standardized Tests *Required:* SAT or ACT (for admission).

Costs (2011–12) *Comprehensive fee:* $24,890 includes full-time tuition ($17,040), mandatory fees ($1200), and room and board ($6650). Part-time tuition: $598 per credit. Part-time tuition and fees vary according to course load. *Required fees:* $40 per credit part-time. *College room only:* $2400. Room and board charges vary according to board plan. *Payment plan:* installment. *Waivers:* employees or children of employees.

Financial Aid Of all full-time matriculated undergraduates who enrolled in 2007, 648 applied for aid, 569 were judged to have need, 81 had their need fully met. 10 state and other part-time jobs (averaging $2226). In 2007, 79 non-need-based awards were made. *Average percent of need met:* 68%. *Average financial aid package:* $10,987. *Average need-based loan:* $3967. *Average need-based gift aid:* $6918. *Average non-need-based aid:* $7112. *Average indebtedness upon graduation:* $17,990.

Applying *Options:* electronic application, early admission, deferred entrance. *Application fee:* $40. *Required:* essay or personal statement, high school transcript, 3 letters of recommendation, Christian testimony. *Required for some:* interview. *Application deadlines:* 8/15 (freshmen), rolling (transfers). *Notification:* continuous (freshmen).

Freshman Application Contact Mr. David Tassell, Admissions Counselor, Baptist Bible College of Pennsylvania, 538 Venard Road, Clarks Summit, PA 18411-1297. *Phone:* 800-451-7664. *Toll-free phone:* 800-451-7664. *Fax:* 570-585-9271. *E-mail:* admissions@bbc.edu. *Web site:* http://www.bbc.edu/.

Bloomsburg University of Pennsylvania
Bloomsburg, Pennsylvania

- **State-supported** comprehensive, founded 1839, part of Pennsylvania State System of Higher Education
- **Rural** 282-acre campus
- **Endowment** $16.3 million
- **Coed** 9,136 undergraduate students, 94% full-time, 57% women, 43% men
- **Moderately difficult** entrance level, 64% of applicants were admitted

Undergraduates 8,600 full-time, 536 part-time. Students come from 23 states and territories; 28 other countries; 11% are from out of state; 7% Black or African American, non-Hispanic/Latino; 4% Hispanic/Latino; 1% Asian, non-Hispanic/Latino; 0.1% American Indian or Alaska Native, non-Hispanic/Latino; 0.6% Two or more races, non-Hispanic/Latino; 6% Race/ethnicity unknown; 0.9% international; 5% transferred in; 48% live on campus. *Retention:* 81% of full-time freshmen returned.

Freshmen *Admission:* 11,866 applied, 7,648 admitted, 2,140 enrolled. *Average high school GPA:* 3.19. *Test scores:* SAT critical reading scores over 500: 47%; SAT math scores over 500: 59%; SAT critical reading scores over 600: 7%; SAT math scores over 600: 12%; SAT critical reading scores over 700: 1%; SAT math scores over 700: 1%.

Faculty *Total:* 487, 82% full-time, 70% with terminal degrees. *Student/faculty ratio:* 22:1.

Academics *Calendar:* semesters. *Degrees:* bachelor's, master's, doctoral-professional, post-master's, and postbachelor's certificates. *Special study options:* academic remediation for entering students, advanced placement credit, cooperative education, distance learning, double majors, English as a second language, freshman honors college, honors programs, independent study, internships, off-campus study, part-time degree program, services for LD students, study abroad, summer session for credit. *ROTC:* Army (b), Air Force (c). *Unusual degree programs:* 3-2 engineering with Pennsylvania State University, Wilkes University; B.S. Computer Forensics 2+2+2 Columbia Montour Vocational Technical School/Northumberland County Career & Technology Center/North Schuylkill School District/SUNTechnical Institute/Bloomsburg Area School District and Luzerne County Community College and Bloomsburg University.

Computers on Campus 1,557 computers/terminals are available on campus for general student use. Students can access the following: computer help desk, free student e-mail accounts, online (class) grades, online (class) registration, online (class) schedules. Campuswide network is available. 100% of college-owned or -operated housing units are wired for high-speed Internet access. Wireless service is available via entire campus.

Student Life *Housing:* on-campus residence required for freshman year. *Options:* coed. Campus housing is university owned and leased by the school. Freshman campus housing is guaranteed. *Activities and organizations:* drama/theater group, student-run newspaper, radio and television station, choral group, marching band, Living and Learning Communities, national fraternities, national sororities. *Campus security:* 24-hour emergency response devices and patrols, late-night transport/escort service, controlled dormitory access, monitored surveillance cameras. *Student services:* health clinic, personal/psychological counseling, women's center, legal services.

Athletics Member NCAA. All Division II except wrestling (Division I). *Intercollegiate sports:* baseball M(s), basketball M(s)/W(s), cross-country running M(s)/W(s), field hockey W(s), football M(s), lacrosse W(s), soccer M(s)/W(s), softball W(s), swimming and diving M(s)/W(s), tennis M(s)/W(s), track and field M(s)/W(s), wrestling M(s). *Intramural sports:* baseball M(c), basketball M/W, bowling M(c)/W(c), cheerleading M(c)/W(c), cross-country running M(c)/W(c), equestrian sports M(c)/W(c), field hockey W, football M, ice hockey M(c), lacrosse M(c), racquetball M/W, rugby M(c)/W(c), skiing (downhill) M(c)/W(c), soccer M(c)/W(c), softball M/W, table tennis M(c)/W(c), tennis M(c)/W(c), ultimate Frisbee M(c)/W(c), volleyball M(c)/W(c), water polo M(c)/W(c), weight lifting M(c).

Standardized Tests *Required:* SAT or ACT (for admission).

Costs (2010–11) *Tuition:* state resident $5804 full-time, $242 per credit part-time; nonresident $14,510 full-time, $605 per credit part-time. Full-time tuition and fees vary according to course load. Part-time tuition and fees vary according to course load. *Required fees:* $1652 full-time, $46 per credit part-time, $123 per term part-time. *Room and board:* $6890; room only: $4232. Room and board charges vary according to board plan and housing facility. *Payment plan:* installment. *Waivers:* minority students, senior citizens, and employees or children of employees.

Financial Aid Of all full-time matriculated undergraduates who enrolled in 2009, 7,419 applied for aid, 7,048 were judged to have need, 6,085 had their need fully met. 1,063 Federal Work-Study jobs (averaging $3732). 942 state and other part-time jobs (averaging $4111). In 2009, 145 non-need-based awards were made. *Average percent of need met:* 71%. *Average financial aid package:* $12,317. *Average need-based loan:* $4192. *Average need-based gift*

aid: $5655. *Average non-need-based aid:* $1941. *Average indebtedness upon graduation:* $23,882.

Applying *Options:* electronic application, early admission, early action, deferred entrance. *Application fee:* $35. *Required:* high school transcript. *Application deadlines:* rolling (freshmen), rolling (out-of-state freshmen), rolling (transfers), 10/31 (early action). *Notification:* continuous until 10/1 (freshmen), continuous (out-of-state freshmen), continuous (transfers).

Freshman Application Contact Mr. Christopher Keller, Director of Admissions, Bloomsburg University of Pennsylvania, 104 Student Services Center, Bloomsburg, PA 17815-1905. *Phone:* 570-389-4316. *Fax:* 570-389-4741. *E-mail:* buadmiss@bloomu.edu. *Web site:* http://www.bloomu.edu/.

Bryn Athyn College of the New Church

Bryn Athyn, Pennsylvania

- **Independent Christian** comprehensive, founded 1876, affiliated with Church of the New Jerusalem, part of The Academy of the New Church
- **Suburban** 130-acre campus with easy access to Philadelphia
- **Endowment** $227.2 million
- **Coed** 214 undergraduate students, 95% full-time, 54% women, 46% men
- **Minimally difficult** entrance level, 64% of applicants were admitted

Undergraduates 203 full-time, 11 part-time. Students come from 14 states and territories; 16 other countries; 14% are from out of state; 8% Black or African American, non-Hispanic/Latino; 3% Hispanic/Latino; 3% Asian, non-Hispanic/Latino; 0.5% American Indian or Alaska Native, non-Hispanic/Latino; 1% Two or more races, non-Hispanic/Latino; 19% international; 1% transferred in; 77% live on campus. *Retention:* 63% of full-time freshmen returned.

Freshmen *Admission:* 652 applied, 417 admitted, 72 enrolled. *Average high school GPA:* 3.3. *Test scores:* SAT critical reading scores over 500: 68%; SAT math scores over 500: 62%; SAT writing scores over 500: 56%; ACT scores over 18: 87%; SAT critical reading scores over 600: 32%; SAT math scores over 600: 25%; SAT writing scores over 600: 22%; ACT scores over 24: 25%; SAT critical reading scores over 700: 5%; SAT math scores over 700: 3%; SAT writing scores over 700: 5%.

Faculty *Total:* 53, 38% full-time, 38% with terminal degrees. *Student/faculty ratio:* 6:1.

Academics *Calendar:* trimesters. *Degrees:* associate, bachelor's, master's, and doctoral-professional. *Special study options:* academic remediation for entering students, accelerated degree program, advanced placement credit, cooperative education, English as a second language, independent study, internships, part-time degree program, services for LD students, student-designed majors, study abroad. *ROTC:* Army (c), Air Force (c).

Computers on Campus 59 computers/terminals are available on campus for general student use. Students can access the following: computer help desk, free student e-mail accounts. Campuswide network is available. 100% of college-owned or -operated housing units are wired for high-speed Internet access. Wireless service is available via entire campus.

Student Life *Housing:* on-campus residence required for freshman year. *Options:* men-only, women-only. Campus housing is university owned. Freshman campus housing is guaranteed. *Activities and organizations:* drama/theater group, student-run newspaper, choral group, C.A.R.E. (Community Service), Business Club, International Student Organization, Peer Advisory Council, Outing Club. *Campus security:* 24-hour emergency response devices, controlled dormitory access, 18-hour patrols by trained personnel. *Student services:* health clinic, personal/psychological counseling.

Athletics *Intercollegiate sports:* badminton M(c)/W(c), ice hockey M(c), lacrosse M(c), soccer M, volleyball W.

Standardized Tests *Required:* SAT or ACT (for admission).

Costs (2011–12) *Comprehensive fee:* $26,332 includes full-time tuition ($15,540), mandatory fees ($2352), and room and board ($8440). Part-time tuition: $507 per credit. *Required fees:* $70 per credit hour part-time. *College room only:* $3801. Room and board charges vary according to housing facility. *Payment plan:* installment. *Waivers:* senior citizens.

Financial Aid Of all full-time matriculated undergraduates who enrolled in 2008, 92 applied for aid, 66 were judged to have need, 30 had their need fully met. In 2008, 22 non-need-based awards were made. *Average percent of need met:* 95%. *Average financial aid package:* $9987. *Average need-based loan:* $3329. *Average need-based gift aid:* $8358. *Average non-need-based aid:* $2232. *Average indebtedness upon graduation:* $8299. *Financial aid deadline:* 7/1.

Applying *Options:* electronic application, deferred entrance. *Required:* essay or personal statement, high school transcript, minimum 2 GPA, 1 letter of recommendation, interest in the writings of Emanuel Swedenborg. *Required for some:* interview. *Application deadlines:* 7/1 (freshmen), 7/1 (transfers). *Notification:* continuous (freshmen), continuous (transfers).

Freshman Application Contact Admissions Office, Bryn Athyn College of the New Church, 2945 College Drive, Box 462, Bryn Athyn, PA 19009. *Phone:* 267-502-6000. *Fax:* 267-502-2593. *E-mail:* admissions@ brynathyn.edu. *Web site:* http://www.brynathyn.edu/.

Bryn Mawr College

Bryn Mawr, Pennsylvania

- **Independent** university, founded 1885
- **Suburban** 135-acre campus with easy access to Philadelphia
- **Endowment** $573.7 million
- **Undergraduate: women only; graduate: coed** 1,293 undergraduate students, 99% full-time, 100% women
- **Most difficult** entrance level, 48% of applicants were admitted

Undergraduates 1,283 full-time, 10 part-time. Students come from 47 states and territories; 62 other countries; 88% are from out of state; 6% Black or African American, non-Hispanic/Latino; 9% Hispanic/Latino; 12% Asian, non-Hispanic/Latino; 0.2% Native Hawaiian or other Pacific Islander, non-Hispanic/Latino; 4% Two or more races, non-Hispanic/Latino; 17% Race/ethnicity unknown; 12% international; 0.4% transferred in; 95% live on campus. *Retention:* 93% of full-time freshmen returned.

Freshmen *Admission:* 2,271 applied, 1,101 admitted, 369 enrolled. *Test scores:* SAT critical reading scores over 500: 97%; SAT math scores over 500: 96%; SAT writing scores over 500: 98%; ACT scores over 18: 100%; SAT critical reading scores over 600: 72%; SAT math scores over 600: 69%; SAT writing scores over 600: 79%; ACT scores over 24: 92%; SAT critical reading scores over 700: 32%; SAT math scores over 700: 25%; SAT writing scores over 700: 28%; ACT scores over 30: 33%.

Faculty *Total:* 211, 74% full-time, 93% with terminal degrees. *Student/faculty ratio:* 8:1.

Academics *Calendar:* semesters. *Degrees:* bachelor's, master's, doctoral-research/scholarship, and postbachelor's certificates. *Special study options:* academic remediation for entering students, accelerated degree program, advanced placement credit, double majors, independent study, internships, off-campus study, services for LD students, student-designed majors, study abroad, summer session for credit. *ROTC:* Air Force (c).

Computers on Campus 200 computers/terminals and 1,500 ports are available on campus for general student use. Students can access the following: online (class) registration. Campuswide network is available.

Student Life *Housing:* on-campus residence required for freshman year. *Options:* coed, women-only, cooperative. Campus housing is university owned. Freshman campus housing is guaranteed. *Activities and organizations:* drama/theater group, student-run newspaper, choral group, musical and theater groups, community service, Student Government Association, International Students Association, cultural groups. *Campus security:* 24-hour emergency response devices and patrols, late-night transport/escort service, controlled dormitory access, shuttle bus service, awareness programs, bicycle registration, security Web site. *Student services:* health clinic, personal/psychological counseling, women's center.

Athletics Member NCAA. All Division III. *Intercollegiate sports:* badminton W, basketball W, crew W, cross-country running W, field hockey W, lacrosse W, soccer W, swimming and diving W, tennis W, track and field W, volleyball W.

Standardized Tests *Required:* SAT and SAT Subject Tests or ACT (for admission).

Costs (2010–11) *Comprehensive fee:* $51,780 includes full-time tuition ($38,420), mandatory fees ($940), and room and board ($12,420). Part-time tuition: $4800 per course. *College room only:* $7100. *Payment plans:* tuition prepayment, installment.

Financial Aid Of all full-time matriculated undergraduates who enrolled in 2009, 823 applied for aid, 758 were judged to have need, 757 had their need fully met. 567 Federal Work-Study jobs (averaging $1958). 135 state and other part-time jobs (averaging $2039). In 2009, 25 non-need-based awards were made. *Average percent of need met:* 100%. *Average financial aid package:* $36,789. *Average need-based loan:* $4546. *Average need-based gift aid:* $31,543. *Average non-need-based aid:* $15,851. *Average indebtedness upon graduation:* $23,509. *Financial aid deadline:* 3/1.

Applying *Options:* electronic application, early admission, early decision, deferred entrance. *Application fee:* $50. *Required:* essay or personal statement, high school transcript, 3 letters of recommendation. *Recommended:* interview. *Application deadlines:* 1/15 (freshmen), 3/15 (transfers). *Early decision deadline:* 11/15 (for plan 1), 1/1 (for plan 2). *Notification:* 4/1 (freshmen), 6/1 (transfers), 12/15 (early decision plan 1), 2/1 (early decision plan 2).

Freshman Application Contact Ms. Laurie Koehler, Dean of Admissions, Bryn Mawr College, 101 North Merion Avenue, Bryn Mawr, PA 19010. *Phone:* 610-526-5152. *Toll-free phone:* 800-BMC-1885. *Fax:* 610-526-7471. *E-mail:* admissions@brynmawr.edu. *Web site:* http://www.brynmawr.edu/.

See page 710 for Display. See page 1168 for the College Close-Up.

Bucknell University

Lewisburg, Pennsylvania

- **Independent** comprehensive, founded 1846
- **Small-town** 446-acre campus
- **Endowment** $491.5 million
- **Coed** 3,508 undergraduate students, 99% full-time, 51% women, 49% men
- **Most difficult** entrance level, 31% of applicants were admitted

Undergraduates 3,488 full-time, 20 part-time. Students come from 48 states and territories; 54 other countries; 76% are from out of state; 3% Black or African American, non-Hispanic/Latino; 4% Hispanic/Latino; 3% Asian, non-Hispanic/Latino; 0.1% American Indian or Alaska Native, non-Hispanic/Latino; 2% Two or more races, non-Hispanic/Latino; 3% Race/ethnicity unknown; 4% international; 1% transferred in; 88% live on campus. *Retention:* 94% of full-time freshmen returned.

Freshmen *Admission:* 7,178 applied, 2,253 admitted, 929 enrolled. *Average high school GPA:* 3.5. *Test scores:* SAT critical reading scores over 500: 97%; SAT math scores over 500: 99%; SAT writing scores over 500: 93%; ACT scores over 18: 100%; SAT critical reading scores over 600: 75%; SAT math scores over 600: 88%; SAT writing scores over 600: 70%; ACT scores over 24: 95%; SAT critical reading scores over 700: 17%; SAT math scores over 700: 37%; SAT writing scores over 700: 20%; ACT scores over 30: 42%.

Faculty *Total:* 374, 95% full-time, 94% with terminal degrees. *Student/faculty ratio:* 10:1.

Academics *Calendar:* semesters. *Degrees:* bachelor's and master's. *Special study options:* advanced placement credit, double majors, honors programs, independent study, internships, off-campus study, part-time degree program, services for LD students, student-designed majors, study abroad, summer session for credit. *ROTC:* Army (b). *Unusual degree programs:* 3-2 engineering; biology, chemistry.

Computers on Campus 970 computers/terminals are available on campus for general student use. Students can access the following: campus intranet, computer help desk, free student e-mail accounts, online (class) grades, online (class) registration, online (class) schedules. Campuswide network is available. 100% of college-owned or -operated housing units are wired for high-speed Internet access. Wireless service is available via entire campus.

Student Life *Housing:* on-campus residence required through senior year. *Options:* coed, men-only, women-only, cooperative, disabled students. Campus housing is university owned. Freshman campus housing is guaranteed. *Activities and organizations:* drama/theater group, student-run newspaper, radio station, choral group, Alpha Phi Omega, Outing Club, Activities and Campus Events, Catholic Campus Ministries, CALVIN and HOBBES, national fraternities, national sororities. *Campus security:* 24-hour emergency response devices and patrols, student patrols, late-night transport/escort service, controlled dormitory access, well-lit pathways, self-defense education, safety/security orientation. *Student services:* health clinic, personal/psychological counseling, women's center.

Athletics Member NCAA. All Division I except football (Division I-AA). *Intercollegiate sports:* baseball M, basketball M(s)/W(s), cheerleading M(c)/W(c), crew M(c)/W, cross-country running M/W(s), equestrian sports M(c)/W(c), field hockey W, golf M/W, ice hockey M(c), lacrosse M(s)/W(s), rock climbing M(c)/W(c), rugby M(c)/W(c), skiing (downhill) M(c)/W(c), soccer M(s)/W(s), softball W, squash M(c)/W(c), swimming and diving M(s)/W(s), tennis M/W, track and field M/W, ultimate Frisbee M(c)/W(c), volleyball M(c)/W, water polo M/W, weight lifting M(c)/W(c), wrestling M(s). *Intramural sports:* badminton M/W, basketball M/W, bowling M/W, cross-country running M/W, golf M/W, racquetball M/W, soccer M/W, softball M/W, squash M/W, table tennis M/W, tennis M/W, ultimate Frisbee M/W, volleyball M/W, weight lifting M, wrestling M.

Standardized Tests *Required:* SAT or ACT (for admission).

Costs (2011–12) *Comprehensive fee:* $54,240 includes full-time tuition ($43,628), mandatory fees ($238), and room and board ($10,374). *College room only:* $6048. Room and board charges vary according to board plan and housing facility. *Payment plans:* tuition prepayment, installment. *Waivers:* employees or children of employees.

Financial Aid Of all full-time matriculated undergraduates who enrolled in 2009, 1,857 applied for aid, 1,592 were judged to have need, 1,507 had their need fully met. 700 Federal Work-Study jobs (averaging $1500). 50 state and other part-time jobs (averaging $1500). In 2009, 145 non-need-based awards were made. *Average percent of need met:* 95%. *Average financial aid package:* $25,600. *Average need-based loan:* $5400. *Average need-based gift aid:* $22,300. *Average non-need-based aid:* $11,641. *Average indebtedness upon graduation:* $18,900. *Financial aid deadline:* 1/15.

Applying *Options:* electronic application, early decision, deferred entrance. *Application fee:* $60. *Required:* essay or personal statement, high school transcript, 1 letter of recommendation. *Application deadlines:* 1/15 (freshmen), 3/15 (transfers). *Early decision deadline:* 11/15 (for plan 1), 1/15 (for plan 2). *Notification:* 4/1 (freshmen), 5/1 (transfers), 12/15 (early decision plan 1), 2/15 (early decision plan 2).
Freshman Application Contact Dean Robert Springall, Dean of Admissions, Bucknell University, Lewisburg, PA 17837. *Phone:* 570-577-1101. *Fax:* 570-577-3538. *E-mail:* admissions@bucknell.edu. *Web site:* http://www.bucknell.edu/.

See page 1170 for the College Close-Up.

Cabrini College
Radnor, Pennsylvania

- **Independent Roman Catholic** comprehensive, founded 1957
- **Suburban** 112-acre campus with easy access to Philadelphia
- **Coed** 1,415 undergraduate students, 93% full-time, 63% women, 37% men
- **Moderately difficult** entrance level, 70% of applicants were admitted

Undergraduates 1,309 full-time, 106 part-time. Students come from 21 states and territories; 19 other countries; 38% are from out of state; 5% Black or African American, non-Hispanic/Latino; 5% Hispanic/Latino; 2% Asian, non-Hispanic/Latino; 0.6% Native Hawaiian or other Pacific Islander, non-Hispanic/Latino; 0.1% American Indian or Alaska Native, non-Hispanic/Latino; 1% Two or more races, non-Hispanic/Latino; 6% Race/ethnicity unknown; 0.3% international; 5% transferred in; 55% live on campus. *Retention:* 68% of full-time freshmen returned.
Freshmen *Admission:* 2,501 applied, 1,761 admitted, 339 enrolled. *Average high school GPA:* 3. *Test scores:* SAT critical reading scores over 500: 31%; SAT math scores over 500: 32%; SAT critical reading scores over 600: 6%; SAT math scores over 600: 6%.
Faculty *Total:* 327, 22% full-time, 35% with terminal degrees. *Student/faculty ratio:* 14:1.
Academics *Calendar:* semesters. *Degrees:* bachelor's, master's, and post-bachelor's certificates. *Special study options:* academic remediation for entering students, adult/continuing education programs, advanced placement credit, cooperative education, double majors, honors programs, independent study, internships, off-campus study, part-time degree program, services for LD students, student-designed majors, study abroad, summer session for credit. *ROTC:* Army (c), Air Force (c). *Unusual degree programs:* 3-2 physical therapy, occupational therapy with Thomas Jefferson University.
Computers on Campus 469 computers/terminals and 1,050 ports are available on campus for general student use. Students can access the following: campus intranet, computer help desk, free student e-mail accounts, online (class) grades, online (class) registration, online (class) schedules, account balances and other services. Campuswide network is available. 100% of college-owned or -operated housing units are wired for high-speed Internet access. Wireless service is available via entire campus.
Student Life *Housing options:* coed, women-only, disabled students. Campus housing is university owned and leased by the school. Freshman applicants given priority for college housing. *Activities and organizations:* drama/theater group, student-run newspaper, radio station, choral group, Student Government Association, Campus Activities and Programming Board, Colleges Against Cancer/Relay for Life, Psychology Club, Habitat for Humanity. *Campus security:* 24-hour emergency response devices and patrols, student patrols, late-night transport/escort service, controlled dormitory access, resident assistants and directors on nightly duty. *Student services:* health clinic, personal/psychological counseling.
Athletics Member NCAA. All Division III. *Intercollegiate sports:* basketball M/W, cross-country running M/W, field hockey W, golf M, lacrosse M/W, soccer M/W, softball W, swimming and diving M/W, tennis M/W, volleyball W. *Intramural sports:* basketball M/W, cheerleading M(c)/W(c), football M/W, soccer M/W, squash M/W, ultimate Frisbee M/W, volleyball M/W.
Standardized Tests *Required:* SAT or ACT (for admission).
Costs (2010–11) *Comprehensive fee:* $43,484 includes full-time tuition ($31,174), mandatory fees ($910), and room and board ($11,400). Part-time tuition: $475 per credit hour. Part-time tuition and fees vary according to course load. *Required fees:* $45 per term part-time. *Room and board:* Room and board charges vary according to board plan and housing facility. *Payment plan:* installment. *Waivers:* children of alumni, senior citizens, and employees or children of employees.
Financial Aid Of all full-time matriculated undergraduates who enrolled in 2009, 1,078 applied for aid, 999 were judged to have need, 119 had their need fully met. 166 Federal Work-Study jobs (averaging $1047). In 2009, 267 non-need-based awards were made. *Average percent of need met:* 66%. *Average financial aid package:* $22,385. *Average need-based loan:* $4467. *Average need-based gift aid:* $9106. *Average non-need-based aid:* $11,494. *Average indebtedness upon graduation:* $30,637.

Applying *Options:* electronic application, deferred entrance. *Application fee:* $35. *Required:* high school transcript, minimum 2 GPA. *Recommended:* essay or personal statement, minimum 3 GPA, 3 letters of recommendation, interview. *Application deadlines:* rolling (freshmen), rolling (transfers).
Freshman Application Contact Mr. Eugene Soltys, Director of Admissions, Cabrini College, 610 King of Prussia Road, Radnor, PA 19087-3698. *Phone:* 610-902-8293. *Toll-free phone:* 800-848-1003. *Fax:* 610-902-8508. *E-mail:* admit@cabrini.edu. *Web site:* http://www.cabrini.edu/.

California University of Pennsylvania
California, Pennsylvania

Freshman Application Contact Mr. William Edmonds, Dean of Enrollment Management and Academic Services, California University of Pennsylvania, 250 University Avenue, California, PA 15419. *Phone:* 724-938-4404. *Toll-free phone:* 888-412-0479. *Fax:* 724-938-4564. *Web site:* http://www.cup.edu/.

See page 712 for Display. See page 1182 for the College Close-Up.

Carlow University
Pittsburgh, Pennsylvania

- **Independent Roman Catholic** comprehensive, founded 1929
- **Urban** 14-acre campus with easy access to Pittsburgh
- **Endowment** $11.9 million
- **Coed, primarily women** 1,929 undergraduate students, 55% full-time, 84% women, 16% men
- **Moderately difficult** entrance level, 62% of applicants were admitted

Undergraduates 1,066 full-time, 863 part-time. Students come from 13 states and territories; 3 other countries; 3% are from out of state; 17% Black or African American, non-Hispanic/Latino; 1% Hispanic/Latino; 1% Asian, non-Hispanic/Latino; 0.1% Native Hawaiian or other Pacific Islander, non-Hispanic/Latino; 0.6% American Indian or Alaska Native, non-Hispanic/Latino; 0.6% Two or more races, non-Hispanic/Latino; 20% Race/ethnicity unknown; 0.2% international; 13% transferred in; 25% live on campus. *Retention:* 65% of full-time freshmen returned.
Freshmen *Admission:* 1,136 applied, 707 admitted, 193 enrolled. *Average high school GPA:* 3.31. *Test scores:* SAT critical reading scores over 500: 44%; SAT math scores over 500: 48%; SAT writing scores over 500: 41%; ACT scores over 18: 84%; SAT critical reading scores over 600: 10%; SAT math scores over 600: 9%; SAT writing scores over 600: 9%; ACT scores over 24: 22%; SAT critical reading scores over 700: 1%; SAT math scores over 700: 1%; SAT writing scores over 700: 2%; ACT scores over 30: 2%.
Faculty *Total:* 306, 32% full-time, 44% with terminal degrees. *Student/faculty ratio:* 10:1.
Academics *Calendar:* semesters. *Degrees:* bachelor's, master's, doctoral-professional, post-master's, and postbachelor's certificates. *Special study options:* academic remediation for entering students, accelerated degree program, adult/continuing education programs, advanced placement credit, cooperative education, distance learning, double majors, honors programs, independent study, internships, off-campus study, part-time degree program, services for LD students, student-designed majors, study abroad, summer session for credit. *ROTC:* Army (c), Navy (c), Air Force (c). *Unusual degree programs:* 3-2 engineering with Carnegie Mellon University (Math/Engineering, Chemistry/Chemical Engineering, Biology/Environmental Engineering); Duquesne University (Biology/Environmental Science & Management).
Computers on Campus 162 computers/terminals are available on campus for general student use. Students can access the following: campus intranet, computer help desk, free student e-mail accounts, online (class) grades, online (class) registration, online (class) schedules. Campuswide network is available. 100% of college-owned or -operated housing units are wired for high-speed Internet access. Wireless service is available via entire campus.
Student Life *Housing options:* men-only, women-only. Campus housing is university owned. *Activities and organizations:* drama/theater group, student-run newspaper, choral group, Commuter Student Association, Resident Student Association, Student Athletic Association, Blessed (gospel choir), Student Government Association. *Campus security:* 24-hour emergency response devices and patrols, late-night transport/escort service, controlled dormitory access. *Student services:* health clinic, personal/psychological counseling.
Athletics Member NAIA. *Intercollegiate sports:* basketball W(s), crew W(c), soccer W(s), softball W(s), tennis W(s), volleyball W(s).
Standardized Tests *Required:* SAT or ACT (for admission).
Costs (2010–11) *Comprehensive fee:* $31,500 includes full-time tuition ($22,400), mandatory fees ($200), and room and board ($8900). Full-time tuition and fees vary according to course load, degree level, program, and reciprocity agreements. Part-time tuition: $710 per credit hour. Part-time tuition and fees vary according to course load, degree level, program, and reciprocity agreements. *College room only:* $4450. Room and board charges vary accord-

ing to board plan. *Payment plans:* installment, deferred payment. *Waivers:* children of alumni and employees or children of employees.

Financial Aid Of all full-time matriculated undergraduates who enrolled in 2003, 431 Federal Work-Study jobs (averaging $776).

Applying *Options:* electronic application, early admission, early action, deferred entrance. *Application fee:* $20. *Required:* high school transcript. *Recommended:* essay or personal statement, minimum 2.5 GPA, interview. *Application deadlines:* rolling (freshmen), rolling (transfers), 9/30 (early action). *Notification:* continuous (freshmen), continuous (transfers), 10/30 (early action).

Freshman Application Contact Ms. Susan Winstel, Director of Admissions, Carlow University, 3333 Fifth Avenue, Pittsburgh, PA 15213. *Phone:* 412-578-6059. *Toll-free phone:* 800-333-CARLOW. *Fax:* 412-578-6668. *E-mail:* admissions@carlow.edu. *Web site:* http://www.carlow.edu/.

See page 713 for Display. See page 1194 for the College Close-Up.

Carnegie Mellon University

Pittsburgh, Pennsylvania

- **Independent** university, founded 1900
- **Urban** 144-acre campus
- **Endowment** $815.0 million
- **Coed** 6,108 undergraduate students, 97% full-time, 42% women, 58% men
- **Most difficult** entrance level, 33% of applicants were admitted

Undergraduates 5,911 full-time, 197 part-time. Students come from 52 states and territories; 74 other countries; 67% are from out of state; 5% Black or African American, non-Hispanic/Latino; 4% Hispanic/Latino; 22% Asian, non-Hispanic/Latino; 0.0% Native Hawaiian or other Pacific Islander, non-Hispanic/Latino; 0.2% American Indian or Alaska Native, non-Hispanic/Latino; 5% Two or more races, non-Hispanic/Latino; 7% Race/ethnicity unknown; 16% international; 0.8% transferred in; 64% live on campus. *Retention:* 96% of full-time freshmen returned.

Freshmen *Admission:* 15,496 applied, 5,164 admitted, 1,486 enrolled. *Average high school GPA:* 3.64. *Test scores:* SAT critical reading scores over 500: 100%; SAT math scores over 500: 99%; SAT writing scores over 500: 99%; ACT scores over 18: 100%; SAT critical reading scores over 600: 85%; SAT

math scores over 600: 94%; SAT writing scores over 600: 88%; ACT scores over 24: 97%; SAT critical reading scores over 700: 37%; SAT math scores over 700: 68%; SAT writing scores over 700: 42%; ACT scores over 30: 69%.

Faculty *Total:* 972, 92% full-time, 98% with terminal degrees. *Student/faculty ratio:* 12:1.

Academics *Calendar:* semesters. *Degrees:* bachelor's, master's, doctoral-research/scholarship, and post-master's certificates. *Special study options:* advanced placement credit, cooperative education, distance learning, double majors, independent study, internships, off-campus study, part-time degree program, services for LD students, student-designed majors, study abroad, summer session for credit. *ROTC:* Army (b), Navy (b), Air Force (b). *Unusual degree programs:* 3-2 business administration; engineering; public management and policy.

Computers on Campus 458 computers/terminals are available on campus for general student use. Students can access the following: campus intranet, computer help desk, free student e-mail accounts, online (class) grades, online (class) registration, online (class) schedules. Campuswide network is available. 100% of college-owned or -operated housing units are wired for high-speed Internet access. Wireless service is available via entire campus.

Student Life *Housing:* on-campus residence required for freshman year. *Options:* coed, men-only, women-only, disabled students. Campus housing is university owned and leased by the school. Freshman campus housing is guaranteed. *Activities and organizations:* drama/theater group, student-run newspaper, radio and television station, choral group, marching band, Student Senate, Alpha Phi Omega, Tartan Club, Spirit Club, Greek Community, national fraternities, national sororities. *Campus security:* 24-hour emergency response devices and patrols, late-night transport/escort service, controlled dormitory access. *Student services:* health clinic, personal/psychological counseling, women's center, legal services.

Athletics Member NCAA. All Division III. *Intercollegiate sports:* badminton W(c), baseball M(c), basketball M/W, cheerleading M/W, crew M(c)/W(c), cross-country running M/W, fencing M(c)/W(c), football M, golf M, ice hockey M(c)/W(c), lacrosse M(c)/W(c), racquetball M(c)/W(c), rugby M(c)/W(c), soccer M/W, softball W(c), squash M(c)/W(c), swimming and diving M/W, tennis M/W, track and field M/W, ultimate Frisbee M(c)/W(c), volleyball M(c)/W, water polo M(c)/W(c). *Intramural sports:* badminton M/W, basketball M/W, bowling M/W, cross-country running M/W, fencing M/W, football M/W, golf M/W, racquetball M/W, soccer M/W, softball M/W, squash M/W,

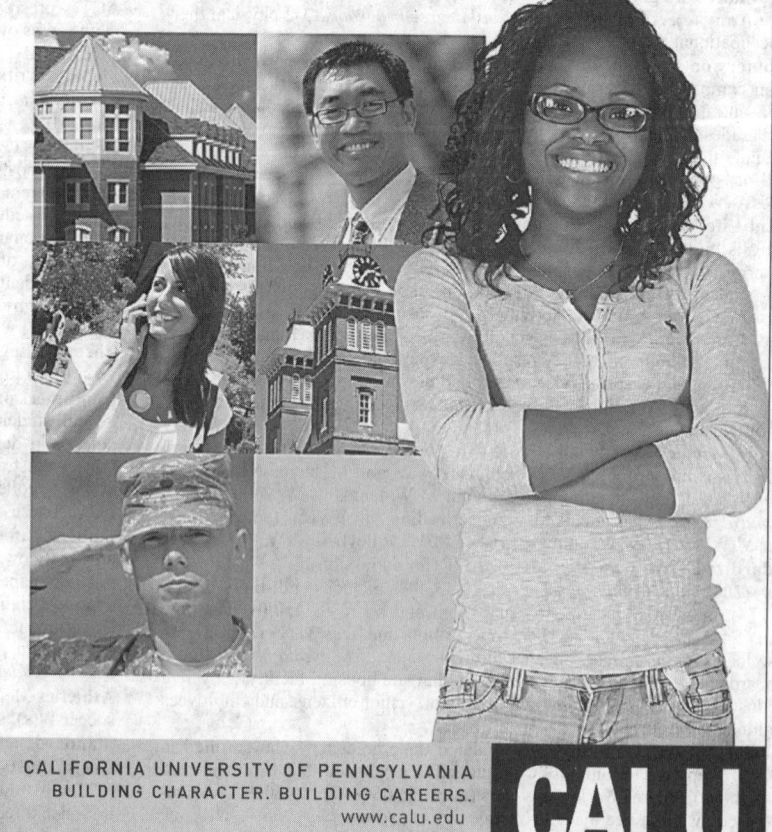

swimming and diving M/W, table tennis M/W, tennis M/W, track and field M/W, ultimate Frisbee M/W, volleyball M/W, water polo M/W.

Standardized Tests *Required:* SAT or ACT (for admission), SAT Subject Tests (for admission).

Costs (2010–11) *One-time required fee:* $192. *Comprehensive fee:* $52,690 includes full-time tuition ($41,500), mandatory fees ($440), and room and board ($10,750). Full-time tuition and fees vary according to student level. Part-time tuition and fees vary according to student level. *College room only:* $6300. Room and board charges vary according to board plan and housing facility. *Payment plan:* installment. *Waivers:* employees or children of employees.

Financial Aid Of all full-time matriculated undergraduates who enrolled in 2009, 3,433 applied for aid, 2,911 were judged to have need, 880 had their need fully met. 2,047 Federal Work-Study jobs (averaging $2600). 7 state and other part-time jobs (averaging $3174). In 2009, 442 non-need-based awards were made. *Average percent of need met:* 80%. *Average financial aid package:* $28,013. *Average need-based loan:* $4661. *Average need-based gift aid:* $22,789. *Average non-need-based aid:* $12,083. *Average indebtedness upon graduation:* $29,456. *Financial aid deadline:* 5/1.

Applying *Options:* electronic application, early admission, early decision, deferred entrance. *Application fee:* $70. *Required:* essay or personal statement, high school transcript, 2 letters of recommendation. *Required for some:* audition/portfolio required for certain majors/BFA. *Recommended:* interview. *Application deadlines:* 1/1 (freshmen), 3/1 (transfers). *Early decision deadline:* 11/1 (for plan 1), 12/1 (for plan 2). *Notification:* 4/15 (freshmen), 6/30 (transfers), 12/15 (early decision plan 1), 1/15 (early decision plan 2).

Freshman Application Contact Mr. Michael Steidel, Director of Admissions, Carnegie Mellon University, 5000 Forbes Avenue, Pittsburgh, PA 15213. *Phone:* 412-268-2082. *Fax:* 412-268-7838. *E-mail:* undergraduate-admissions@andrew.cmu.edu. *Web site:* http://www.cmu.edu/.

See page 714 for Display. See page 1196 for the College Close-Up.

Cedar Crest College

Allentown, Pennsylvania

- **Independent** comprehensive, founded 1867, affiliated with United Church of Christ
- **Suburban** 84-acre campus with easy access to Philadelphia
- **Endowment** $16.1 million
- **Coed, primarily women** 1,472 undergraduate students, 56% full-time, 95% women, 5% men
- **Moderately difficult** entrance level, 42% of applicants were admitted

Undergraduates 818 full-time, 654 part-time. Students come from 28 states and territories; 17% are from out of state; 9% Black or African American, non-Hispanic/Latino; 9% Hispanic/Latino; 3% Asian, non-Hispanic/Latino; 0.1% Native Hawaiian or other Pacific Islander, non-Hispanic/Latino; 1% American Indian or Alaska Native, non-Hispanic/Latino; 1% Two or more races, non-Hispanic/Latino; 2% Race/ethnicity unknown; 0.4% international; 4% transferred in; 61% live on campus. *Retention:* 71% of full-time freshmen returned.

Freshmen *Admission:* 825 applied, 345 admitted, 91 enrolled. *Average high school GPA:* 3.02. *Test scores:* SAT math scores over 500: 63%; SAT writing scores over 500: 61%; ACT scores over 18: 100%; SAT math scores over 600: 13%; SAT writing scores over 600: 11%; ACT scores over 24: 53%; SAT writing scores over 700: 2%; ACT scores over 30: 2%.

Faculty *Total:* 177, 49% full-time, 43% with terminal degrees. *Student/faculty ratio:* 10:1.

Academics *Calendar:* semesters. *Degrees:* bachelor's, master's, post-master's, and postbachelor's certificates. *Special study options:* academic remediation for entering students, advanced placement credit, double majors, honors programs, independent study, internships, off-campus study, part-time degree program, services for LD students, student-designed majors, summer session for credit. *ROTC:* Army (c).

Computers on Campus 207 computers/terminals and 587 ports are available on campus for general student use. Students can access the following: computer help desk, free student e-mail accounts, online (class) grades, online (class) registration, online (class) schedules. Campuswide network is available. 100% of college-owned or -operated housing units are wired for high-speed

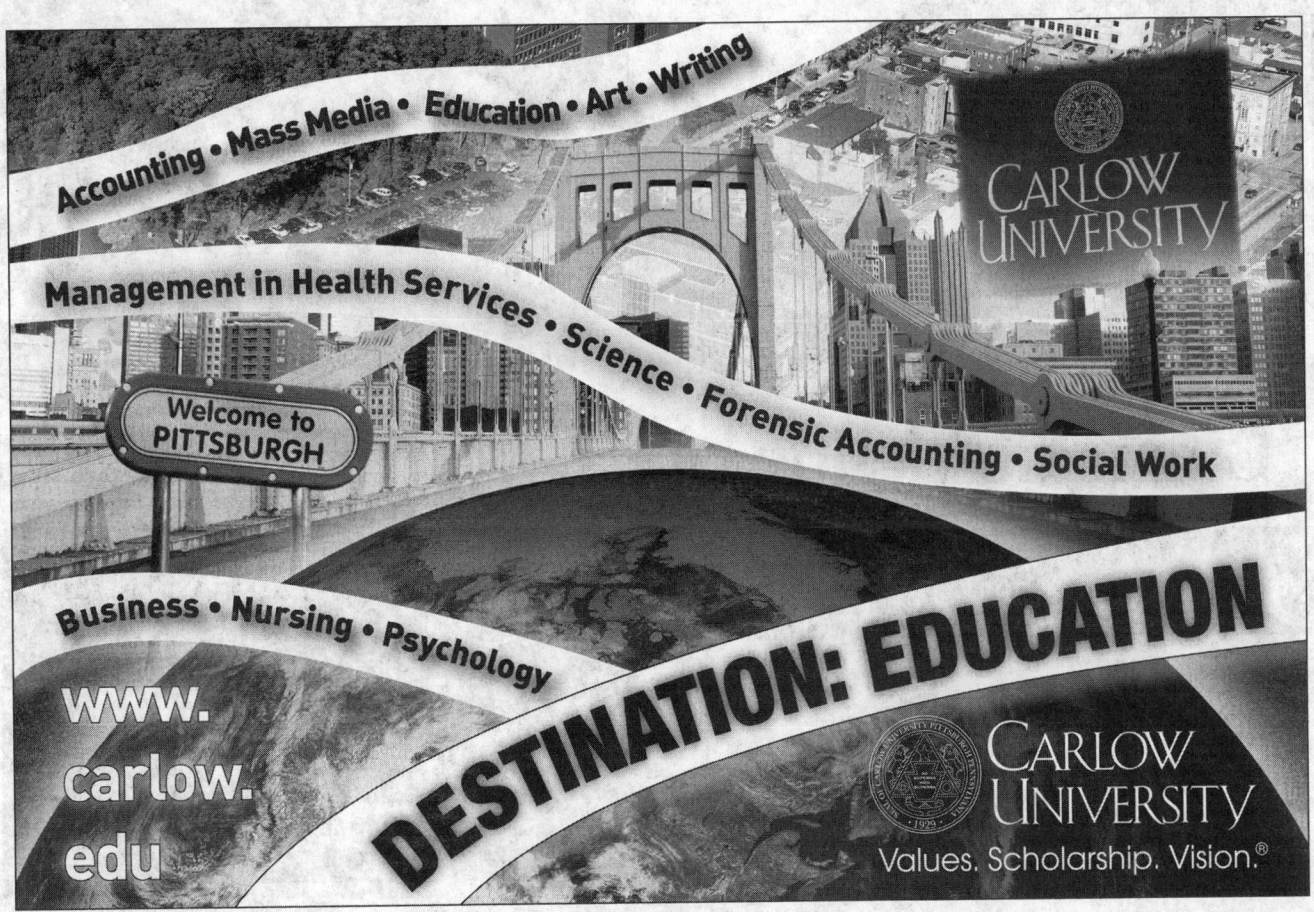

PROFILES

Choose your program Change the world

Carnegie Mellon University is looking for innovative minds like you.

Our seven schools and colleges offer focused disciplines in the fine arts, business, liberal arts, technology and the sciences. Throughout your college career you can work across disciplines, side-by-side with world-renowned faculty, with the opportunity to participate in research initiatives—even if you aren't a science major. Our graduating students are marketable upon graduation, as they gain real-world experience while attending Carnegie Mellon.

We believe in giving our students experiences beyond the classroom as well. They are involved in more than 225 clubs and organizations on campus and in the community.

Whether our students are studying or playing, to quote our founder, Andrew Carnegie, "Our hearts are in the work."

Carnegie Mellon

FROM ARTS TO TECHNOLOGY.
CREATING INNOVATION WITH IMPACT.

www.cmu.edu/admission
www.cmu.edu/admission/social

What will *you* do with a degree from Cedar Crest College?

Psychologist   Editor   Historian

Actor   Social worker   Anthropologist

Doctor   Writer   Dancer

Nutritionist   Conservation biologist

Chemist   Biologist

Accountant   Lawyer

Veterinarian

Marketing professional

Nurse   Neuroscientist

Poet   Mathematician

Therapist   Artist   Educator

Forensic scientist   Art therapist

 CEDAR CREST COLLEGE
1867

www.cedarcrest.edu
800-360-1222

free application

Internet access. Wireless service is available via classrooms, computer labs, dorm rooms, libraries, student centers.

Student Life *Housing:* on-campus residence required through sophomore year. *Options:* women-only, disabled students. Campus housing is university owned. Freshman campus housing is guaranteed. *Activities and organizations:* drama/ theater group, student-run newspaper, radio station, choral group, Alpha Phi Omega, Forensic Science Student Organization, Crestiad Student Newspaper, Student Activities Board, Student Government Association. *Campus security:* 24-hour emergency response devices and patrols, late-night transport/escort service, controlled dormitory access, crime prevention programs. *Student services:* health clinic, personal/psychological counseling.

Athletics Member NCAA. All Division III. *Intercollegiate sports:* basketball W, cross-country running W, equestrian sports W(c), field hockey W, lacrosse W, soccer W, softball W, tennis W, track and field W(c), volleyball W. *Intramural sports:* badminton W, basketball W, soccer W, softball W, tennis W, volleyball W.

Standardized Tests *Required:* SAT or ACT (for admission).

Costs (2010–11) *Comprehensive fee:* $38,507 includes full-time tuition ($28,567), mandatory fees ($400), and room and board ($9540). Full-time tuition and fees vary according to class time, course load, and program. Part-time tuition: $795 per credit hour. Part-time tuition and fees vary according to class time, course load, and program. *Required fees:* $75 per term part-time. *College room only:* $5010. Room and board charges vary according to board plan and housing facility. *Payment plans:* installment, deferred payment. *Waivers:* children of alumni and employees or children of employees.

Financial Aid Of all full-time matriculated undergraduates who enrolled in 2009, 659 applied for aid, 614 were judged to have need, 72 had their need fully met. 104 Federal Work-Study jobs (averaging $1500). In 2009, 65 non-need-based awards were made. *Average percent of need met:* 76%. *Average financial aid package:* $22,826. *Average need-based loan:* $4675. *Average need-based gift aid:* $18,215. *Average non-need-based aid:* $8719. *Average indebtedness upon graduation:* $32,225. *Financial aid deadline:* 5/1.

Applying *Options:* electronic application, early admission, deferred entrance. *Required:* essay or personal statement, high school transcript. *Required for some:* 2 letters of recommendation. *Recommended:* minimum 2 GPA, interview. *Application deadlines:* rolling (freshmen), rolling (transfers). *Notification:* continuous (freshmen), continuous (transfers).

Freshman Application Contact Andrea Stewart, Associate Director of Admissions, Cedar Crest College, 100 College Drive, Allentown, PA 18104. *Phone:* 610-606-4666. *Toll-free phone:* 800-360-1222. *E-mail:* astewart@cedarcrest.edu. *Web site:* http://www.cedarcrest.edu/.

See page 714 for Display. See page 1208 for the College Close-Up.

Central Pennsylvania College

Summerdale, Pennsylvania

- **Proprietary** 4-year, founded 1881
- **Small-town** 35-acre campus with easy access to Harrisburg
- **Coed** 1,482 undergraduate students, 55% full-time, 62% women, 38% men
- **Minimally difficult** entrance level, 48% of applicants were admitted

Undergraduates 822 full-time, 660 part-time. Students come from 15 states and territories; 1 other country; 7% are from out of state; 24% Black or African American, non-Hispanic/Latino; 3% Hispanic/Latino; 1% Asian, non-Hispanic/Latino; 0.1% Native Hawaiian or other Pacific Islander, non-Hispanic/Latino; 0.7% American Indian or Alaska Native, non-Hispanic/Latino; 7% Race/ethnicity unknown; 0.1% international; 19% live on campus. *Retention:* 52% of full-time freshmen returned.

Freshmen *Admission:* 2,285 applied, 1,093 admitted, 210 enrolled.

Faculty *Total:* 127, 19% full-time. *Student/faculty ratio:* 18:1.

Academics *Calendar:* quarters. *Degrees:* certificates, associate, and bachelor's. *Special study options:* academic remediation for entering students, adult/continuing education programs, advanced placement credit, distance learning, double majors, honors programs, independent study, internships, part-time degree program, study abroad, summer session for credit.

Computers on Campus 100 computers/terminals are available on campus for general student use. Students can access the following: campus intranet, computer help desk, free student e-mail accounts, online (class) grades, online (class) registration, online (class) schedules. Campuswide network is available. 100% of college-owned or -operated housing units are wired for high-speed Internet access. Wireless service is available via entire campus.

Student Life *Housing options:* men-only, women-only. Campus housing is university owned. Freshman applicants given priority for college housing. *Activities and organizations:* student-run newspaper, choral group, International Travel Club, Student Government Association, Toastmasters, Student Ambassadors. *Campus security:* 24-hour emergency response devices and patrols, late-night transport/escort service. *Student services:* personal/psychological counseling.

Athletics Member USCAA. *Intercollegiate sports:* basketball M/W, bowling M/W, golf M/W. *Intramural sports:* basketball M/W, football M, tennis M/W, volleyball M/W.

Standardized Tests *Recommended:* SAT or ACT (for admission).

Costs (2011–12) *Comprehensive fee:* $21,561 includes full-time tuition ($14,256), mandatory fees ($735), and room and board ($6570). Full-time tuition and fees vary according to course load and program. Part-time tuition: $396 per contact hour. Part-time tuition and fees vary according to course load and program. *Required fees:* $240 per term part-time. *College room only:* $4920. Room and board charges vary according to board plan and housing facility. *Payment plans:* installment, deferred payment. *Waivers:* employees or children of employees.

Financial Aid Of all full-time matriculated undergraduates who enrolled in 2006, 50 Federal Work-Study jobs (averaging $1500). *Financial aid deadline:* 5/1.

Applying *Options:* electronic application. *Required:* essay or personal statement, high school transcript, minimum 2 GPA, interview. *Required for some:* some majors have special requirements. *Application deadlines:* rolling (freshmen), rolling (out-of-state freshmen), rolling (transfers). *Notification:* continuous (freshmen), continuous (out-of-state freshmen), continuous (transfers).

Freshman Application Contact Ms. Stacy Scott, Director of Admissions, Central Pennsylvania College, College Hill and Valley Roads, Mechanicsburg, PA 17093. *Phone:* 717-728-2531. *Toll-free phone:* 800-759-2727 Ext. 2201. *Fax:* 717-728-2505. *E-mail:* stacyscott@centralpenn.edu. *Web site:* http://www.centralpenn.edu/.

Chatham University

Pittsburgh, Pennsylvania

- **Independent** university, founded 1869
- **Urban** 427-acre campus
- **Endowment** $48.7 million
- **Undergraduate: women only; graduate: coed** 1,044 undergraduate students, 65% full-time, 93% women, 7% men
- **Moderately difficult** entrance level, 62% of applicants were admitted

Undergraduates 680 full-time, 364 part-time. Students come from 28 states and territories; 20 other countries; 22% are from out of state; 14% Black or African American, non-Hispanic/Latino; 2% Hispanic/Latino; 2% Asian, non-Hispanic/Latino; 0.3% American Indian or Alaska Native, non-Hispanic/Latino; 2% Two or more races, non-Hispanic/Latino; 9% Race/ethnicity unknown; 8% international; 7% transferred in; 52% live on campus. *Retention:* 73% of full-time freshmen returned.

Freshmen *Admission:* 786 applied, 488 admitted, 151 enrolled. *Average high school GPA:* 3.42. *Test scores:* SAT critical reading scores over 500: 65%; SAT math scores over 500: 57%; ACT scores over 18: 89%; SAT critical reading scores over 600: 31%; SAT math scores over 600: 22%; ACT scores over 24: 44%; SAT critical reading scores over 700: 8%; SAT math scores over 700: 2%; ACT scores over 30: 19%.

Faculty *Total:* 273, 33% full-time. *Student/faculty ratio:* 10:1.

Academics *Calendar:* 4-4-1. *Degrees:* bachelor's, master's, doctoral-professional, post-master's, and postbachelor's certificates. *Special study options:* accelerated degree program, adult/continuing education programs, advanced placement credit, cooperative education, distance learning, double majors, English as a second language, honors programs, independent study, internships, off-campus study, part-time degree program, services for LD students, student-designed majors, study abroad, summer session for credit. *ROTC:* Army (c), Navy (c), Air Force (c). *Unusual degree programs:* 3-2 business administration; engineering with Carnegie Mellon University, Pennsylvania State University, University of Pittsburgh; arts management with Carnegie Mellon, biology, counseling psychology, film/digital technology, leadership/organizational transformation, occupational therapy, physician assistant studies, business, teaching, writing and creative writing, architecture (landscape and interior), global/public policy.

Computers on Campus 250 computers/terminals are available on campus for general student use. Students can access the following: campus intranet, computer help desk, free student e-mail accounts, online (class) grades, online (class) registration, online (class) schedules. Campuswide network is available. Wireless service is available via classrooms, computer centers, computer labs, learning centers, libraries.

Student Life *Housing:* on-campus residence required through sophomore year. *Options:* women-only. Campus housing is university owned. Freshman campus housing is guaranteed. *Activities and organizations:* drama/theater group, student-run newspaper, choral group, Chatham Student Government, choir, Chatham Feminist Collective, Students of Community Service, Activities Board. *Campus security:* 24-hour emergency response devices and patrols, late-night transport/escort service, controlled dormitory access, self-defense education, well-lighted pathways and sidewalks. *Student services:* health clinic, personal/psychological counseling.

Athletics Member NCAA. All Division III. *Intercollegiate sports:* basketball W, crew W(c), cross-country running W, ice hockey W, soccer W, softball W, swimming and diving W, tennis W, volleyball W, water polo W. *Intramural sports:* badminton W, basketball W, cross-country running W, football W, golf W, rock climbing W, skiing (downhill) W, softball W, squash W, swimming and diving W, volleyball W, water polo W, weight lifting W.

Costs (2010–11) *Comprehensive fee:* $38,061 includes full-time tuition ($28,088), mandatory fees ($1100), and room and board ($8873). Full-time tuition and fees vary according to degree level and student level. Part-time tuition: $681 per credit. Part-time tuition and fees vary according to course load. *College room only:* $4454. Room and board charges vary according to board plan and housing facility. *Payment plan:* installment. *Waivers:* employees or children of employees.

Financial Aid Of all full-time matriculated undergraduates who enrolled in 2009, 552 applied for aid, 517 were judged to have need, 80 had their need fully met. In 2009, 25 non-need-based awards were made. *Average percent of need met:* 66%. *Average financial aid package:* $15,515. *Average need-based loan:* $9265. *Average need-based gift aid:* $8645. *Average non-need-based aid:* $13,107.

Applying *Options:* electronic application, early admission, deferred entrance. *Application fee:* $35. *Required:* essay or personal statement, high school transcript, minimum 2 GPA, 1 letter of recommendation. *Recommended:* interview. *Application deadlines:* 8/1 (freshmen), rolling (transfers). *Notification:* continuous (transfers).

Freshman Application Contact Ms. Lisa D. Meyers, Director of Admissions, Chatham University, Woodland Road, Pittsburgh, PA 15232. *Phone:* 412-365-1672. *Toll-free phone:* 800-837-1290. *Fax:* 412-365-1609. *E-mail:* lmeyers@chatham.edu. *Web site:* http://www.chatham.edu/.

See page 1212 for the College Close-Up.

Chestnut Hill College
Philadelphia, Pennsylvania

- **Independent Roman Catholic** comprehensive, founded 1924
- **Suburban** 75-acre campus with easy access to Philadelphia
- **Endowment** $5.0 million
- **Coed** 1,574 undergraduate students, 78% full-time, 71% women, 29% men
- **Moderately difficult** entrance level, 68% of applicants were admitted

Undergraduates 1,235 full-time, 339 part-time. Students come from 25 states and territories; 11 other countries; 20% are from out of state; 35% Black or African American, non-Hispanic/Latino; 5% Hispanic/Latino; 2% Asian, non-Hispanic/Latino; 0.3% Native Hawaiian or other Pacific Islander, non-Hispanic/Latino; 0.1% American Indian or Alaska Native, non-Hispanic/Latino; 1% Two or more races, non-Hispanic/Latino; 11% Race/ethnicity unknown; 3% international; 4% transferred in; 31% live on campus. *Retention:* 67% of full-time freshmen returned.

Freshmen *Admission:* 2,566 applied, 1,736 admitted, 221 enrolled. *Average high school GPA:* 3.11. *Test scores:* SAT critical reading scores over 500: 49%; SAT math scores over 500: 43%; SAT writing scores over 500: 44%; ACT scores over 18: 91%; SAT critical reading scores over 600: 11%; SAT math scores over 600: 8%; SAT writing scores over 600: 9%; ACT scores over 24: 27%; SAT math scores over 700: 1%.

Faculty *Total:* 339, 24% full-time, 40% with terminal degrees. *Student/faculty ratio:* 11:1.

Academics *Calendar:* semesters. *Degrees:* certificates, associate, bachelor's, master's, doctoral-professional, post-master's, and postbachelor's certificates (profile includes figures from both traditional and accelerated (part-time) programs). *Special study options:* academic remediation for entering students, adult/continuing education programs, advanced placement credit, cooperative education, distance learning, double majors, English as a second language, honors programs, independent study, internships, off-campus study, part-time degree program, student-designed majors, study abroad, summer session for credit. *Unusual degree programs:* 3-2 Doctor of Podiatric Medicine with Temple University, medical technology with Thomas Jefferson University, physician assistant with Arcadia University, special education, instructional technology, human services administration, counseling psychology.

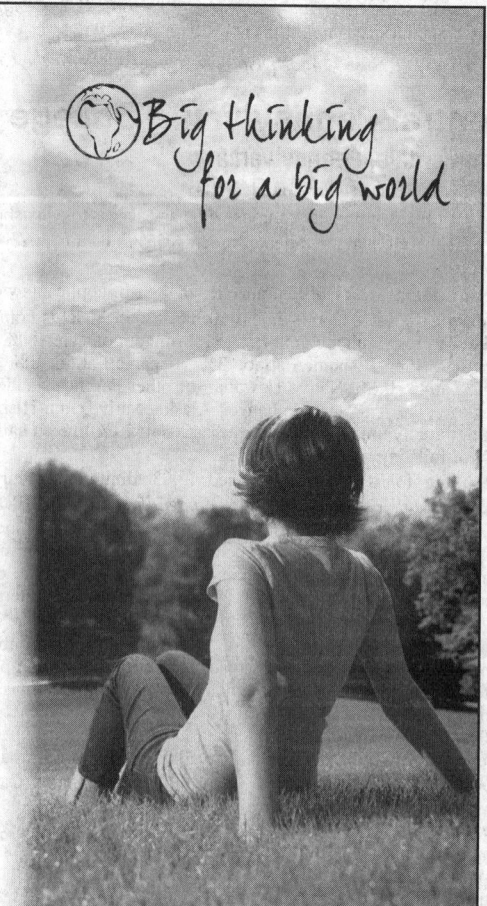

Computers on Campus 60 computers/terminals and 150 ports are available on campus for general student use. Students can access the following: campus intranet, computer help desk, free student e-mail accounts, online (class) grades, online (class) registration, online (class) schedules. Campuswide network is available. 90% of college-owned or -operated housing units are wired for high-speed Internet access. Wireless service is available via dorm rooms.

Student Life *Housing options:* coed. Campus housing is university owned. Freshman campus housing is guaranteed. *Activities and organizations:* drama/ theater group, student-run newspaper, television station, choral group, student government, Hispanics in Action, African American Awareness Society, Campus Ministry Community Service Group, Mosaic of Cultures Club. *Campus security:* 24-hour emergency response devices and patrols, late-night transport/ escort service, controlled dormitory access. *Student services:* health clinic, personal/psychological counseling.

Athletics Member NCAA. All Division II. *Intercollegiate sports:* baseball M(s), basketball M(s)/W(s), cross-country running M(s)/W(s), golf M(s), lacrosse M(s)/W(s), soccer M(s)/W(s), softball W(s), tennis M(s)/W(s), volleyball W(s).

Standardized Tests *Required:* SAT or ACT (for admission).

Costs (2010–11) *Comprehensive fee:* $37,265 includes full-time tuition ($28,100), mandatory fees ($100), and room and board ($9065). Part-time tuition: $600 per credit hour. *Required fees:* $50 per term part-time. *Room and board:* Room and board charges vary according to housing facility. *Payment plans:* installment, deferred payment. *Waivers:* senior citizens and employees or children of employees.

Financial Aid Of all full-time matriculated undergraduates who enrolled in 2009, 778 applied for aid, 705 were judged to have need, 119 had their need fully met. In 2009, 7 non-need-based awards were made. *Average percent of need met:* 73%. *Average financial aid package:* $21,066. *Average need-based loan:* $4680. *Average need-based gift aid:* $16,548. *Average non-need-based aid:* $3307.

Applying *Options:* electronic application, deferred entrance. *Application fee:* $35. *Required:* high school transcript. *Required for some:* interview. *Recommended:* essay or personal statement, minimum 2 GPA. *Application deadlines:* rolling (freshmen), rolling (out-of-state freshmen), rolling (transfers). *Notification:* continuous (freshmen), continuous (out-of-state freshmen), continuous (transfers).

Freshman Application Contact Ms. Leslie Harms, Chestnut Hill College, 9601 Germantown Avenue, Philadelphia, PA 19118-2693. *Phone:* 215-248-7001. *Toll-free phone:* 800-248-0052. *Fax:* 215-248-7082. *E-mail:* harmsl@ chc.edu. *Web site:* http://www.chc.edu/.

Cheyney University of Pennsylvania
Cheyney, Pennsylvania

- **State-supported** comprehensive, founded 1837, part of Pennsylvania State System of Higher Education
- **Suburban** 275-acre campus with easy access to Philadelphia
- **Coed**
- **Minimally difficult** entrance level

Faculty *Student/faculty ratio:* 15:1.

Academics *Calendar:* semesters. *Degrees:* associate, bachelor's, master's, and postbachelor's certificates.

Student Life *Campus security:* 24-hour emergency response devices and patrols.

Athletics Member NCAA. All Division II.

Standardized Tests *Required:* SAT (for admission), ACT (for admission), SAT and SAT Subject Tests or ACT (for admission).

Costs (2010–11) *One-time required fee:* $125. *Tuition:* state resident $5804 full-time, $242 per credit part-time; nonresident $14,510 full-time, $605 per credit part-time. Full-time tuition and fees vary according to course load. Part-time tuition and fees vary according to course load. *Required fees:* $1914 full-time, $479 per term part-time. *Room and board:* $8486; room only: $4770. Room and board charges vary according to board plan.

Financial Aid *Of all full-time matriculated undergraduates who enrolled in 2003,* 1,030 applied for aid, 1,005 were judged to have need, 451 had their need fully met. 215 Federal Work-Study jobs (averaging $1300). 133 state and other part-time jobs (averaging $600). *Average percent of need met:* 87. *Average financial aid package:* $11,789. *Average need-based loan:* $3700. *Average need-based gift aid:* $1975. *Average non-need-based aid:* $10,000. *Average indebtedness upon graduation:* $21,000.

Applying *Options:* electronic application, deferred entrance. *Application fee:* $20. *Required:* essay or personal statement, high school transcript. *Required for some:* 3 letters of recommendation. *Recommended:* interview.

The nation's *first...*

- *Responsive to the needs of the region,*
- *Building Centers of Excellence to prepare you for solid careers,*
- *Producing recognized leaders since 1837*

Dr. Michelle R. Howard-Vital, President

CHEYNEY UNIVERSITY OF PENNSYLVANIA 1837

Cheyney University of Pennsylvania

Visit us online at www.cheyney.edu or call 610-399-2000.

Freshman Application Contact Cheyney University of Pennsylvania, 1837 University Circle, PO Box 200, Cheyney, PA 19319. *Phone:* 610-399-2275. *Toll-free phone:* 800-CHEYNEY. *Web site:* http://www.cheyney.edu/.

See page 1214 for the College Close-Up.

Clarion University of Pennsylvania
Clarion, Pennsylvania

- **State-supported** comprehensive, founded 1867, part of Pennsylvania State System of Higher Education
- **Rural** 100-acre campus
- **Endowment** $17.6 million
- **Coed** 6,271 undergraduate students, 84% full-time, 62% women, 38% men
- **Minimally difficult** entrance level, 68% of applicants were admitted

Undergraduates 5,268 full-time, 1,003 part-time. Students come from 27 states and territories; 28 other countries; 5% are from out of state; 6% Black or African American, non-Hispanic/Latino; 0.9% Hispanic/Latino; 1% Asian, non-Hispanic/Latino; 0.4% American Indian or Alaska Native, non-Hispanic/Latino; 5% Race/ethnicity unknown; 7% transferred in; 33% live on campus. *Retention:* 71% of full-time freshmen returned.

Freshmen *Admission:* 4,777 applied, 3,271 admitted, 1,373 enrolled. *Average high school GPA:* 3.2. *Test scores:* SAT critical reading scores over 500: 34%; SAT math scores over 500: 38%; SAT critical reading scores over 600: 7%; SAT math scores over 600: 9%.

Faculty *Total:* 366, 71% full-time. *Student/faculty ratio:* 21:1.

Academics *Calendar:* semesters. *Degrees:* associate, bachelor's, master's, and post-master's certificates. *Special study options:* academic remediation for entering students, accelerated degree program, adult/continuing education programs, advanced placement credit, cooperative education, distance learning, double majors, honors programs, independent study, internships, off-campus study, part-time degree program, services for LD students, study abroad, summer session for credit. *ROTC:* Army (c). *Unusual degree programs:* 3-2 engineering with University of Pittsburgh, Case Western Reserve University.

Computers on Campus 400 computers/terminals are available on campus for general student use. Students can access the following: online (class) registration. Campuswide network is available. 100% of college-owned or -operated housing units are wired for high-speed Internet access. Wireless service is available via entire campus.

Student Life *Housing:* on-campus residence required for freshman year. *Options:* coed, men-only, women-only. Campus housing is university owned. Freshman campus housing is guaranteed. *Activities and organizations:* drama/theater group, student-run newspaper, radio and television station, choral group, marching band, national fraternities, national sororities. *Campus security:* 24-hour emergency response devices and patrols, student patrols, controlled dormitory access. *Student services:* health clinic, personal/psychological counseling, women's center.

Athletics Member NCAA. All Division II except wrestling (Division I). *Intercollegiate sports:* baseball M(s), basketball M(s)/W(s), cross-country running W(s), football M(s), golf M(s), softball W(s), swimming and diving M(s)/W(s), tennis W(s), track and field W(s), volleyball W(s), wrestling M(s). *Intramural sports:* badminton M/W, basketball M/W, bowling M/W, cross-country running W, football M, golf M/W, racquetball M/W, soccer M/W, swimming and diving M/W, tennis M/W, track and field W, volleyball M(c)/W, weight lifting M/W, wrestling M.

Standardized Tests *Required:* SAT or ACT (for admission).

Costs (2011–12) *One-time required fee:* $30. *Tuition:* state resident $6066 full-time, $252 per credit hour part-time; nonresident $12,130 full-time, $505 per credit hour part-time. Full-time tuition and fees vary according to course load. Part-time tuition and fees vary according to course load. *Required fees:* $2098 full-time, $57 per credit part-time. *Room and board:* $7000; room only: $4725. Room and board charges vary according to board plan, housing facility, and location. *Payment plan:* installment. *Waivers:* senior citizens and employees or children of employees.

Financial Aid Of all full-time matriculated undergraduates who enrolled in 2009, 4,610 applied for aid, 3,937 were judged to have need, 514 had their need fully met. In 2009, 260 non-need-based awards were made. *Average percent of need met:* 74%. *Average financial aid package:* $8384. *Average need-based loan:* $3937. *Average need-based gift aid:* $6010. *Average non-need-based aid:* $3029. *Financial aid deadline:* 4/15.

Applying *Options:* deferred entrance. *Application fee:* $30. *Required:* high school transcript. *Required for some:* essay or personal statement, interview. *Recommended:* essay or personal statement, interview. *Application deadlines:* rolling (freshmen), rolling (transfers).

Freshman Application Contact Clarion University of Pennsylvania, 890 Wood Street, Clarion, PA 16214. *Phone:* 814-393-2306. *Toll-free phone:* 800-672-7171. *Web site:* http://www.clarion.edu/.

Curtis Institute of Music
Philadelphia, Pennsylvania

Director of Admissions Mr. Christopher Hodges, Admissions Officer, Curtis Institute of Music, 1726 Locust Street, Philadelphia, PA 19103-6107. *Phone:* 215-893-5262. *E-mail:* chris.hodges@curtis.edu. *Web site:* http://www.curtis.edu/.

Delaware Valley College
Doylestown, Pennsylvania

- **Independent** comprehensive, founded 1896
- **Suburban** 600-acre campus with easy access to Philadelphia
- **Coed**
- **Moderately difficult** entrance level

Faculty *Student/faculty ratio:* 15:1.

Academics *Calendar:* semesters. *Degrees:* certificates, associate, bachelor's, and master's.

Student Life *Campus security:* 24-hour patrols, late-night transport/escort service, controlled dormitory access.

Athletics Member NCAA. All Division III.

Standardized Tests *Required:* SAT or ACT (for admission).

Costs (2010–11) *Comprehensive fee:* $39,610 includes full-time tuition ($27,234), mandatory fees ($2050), and room and board ($10,326). Part-time tuition: $750 per credit. *College room only:* $4682.

Financial Aid Of all full-time matriculated undergraduates who enrolled in 2009, 1,434 applied for aid, 1,306 were judged to have need, 149 had their need fully met. In 2009, 327 non-need-based awards were made. *Average percent of need met:* 68. *Average financial aid package:* $19,249. *Average need-based loan:* $4371. *Average need-based gift aid:* $14,435. *Average non-need-based aid:* $10,096. *Average indebtedness upon graduation:* $26,350. *Financial aid deadline:* 4/1.

Applying *Options:* electronic application, deferred entrance. *Application fee:* $50. *Required:* high school transcript, 1 letter of recommendation. *Required for some:* minimum 3 GPA. *Recommended:* minimum 2.75 GPA, interview.

Freshman Application Contact Mr. Stephen Zenko, Director of Admissions, Delaware Valley College, 700 East Butler Avenue, Doylestown, PA 18901-2697. *Phone:* 215-489-2211. *Toll-free phone:* 800-2DELVAL. *Fax:* 215-230-2968. *E-mail:* admitme@devalcol.edu. *Web site:* http://www.delval.edu/.

See page 1250 for the College Close-Up.

DeSales University
Center Valley, Pennsylvania

- **Independent Roman Catholic** comprehensive, founded 1964
- **Suburban** 480-acre campus with easy access to Philadelphia
- **Endowment** $38.9 million
- **Coed** 2,366 undergraduate students, 75% full-time, 60% women, 40% men
- **Moderately difficult** entrance level, 74% of applicants were admitted

Undergraduates 1,765 full-time, 601 part-time. Students come from 5 other countries; 74% are from out of state; 3% Black or African American, non-Hispanic/Latino; 5% Hispanic/Latino; 2% Asian, non-Hispanic/Latino; 0.5% American Indian or Alaska Native, non-Hispanic/Latino; 20% Race/ethnicity unknown; 4% transferred in; 58% live on campus. *Retention:* 83% of full-time freshmen returned.

Freshmen *Admission:* 2,158 applied, 1,591 admitted, 427 enrolled. *Test scores:* SAT critical reading scores over 500: 67%; SAT math scores over 500: 72%; ACT scores over 18: 92%; SAT critical reading scores over 600: 23%; SAT math scores over 600: 24%; ACT scores over 24: 35%; SAT critical reading scores over 700: 5%; SAT math scores over 700: 2%; ACT scores over 30: 4%.

Faculty *Total:* 293, 36% full-time. *Student/faculty ratio:* 14:1.

Academics *Calendar:* semesters. *Degrees:* bachelor's, master's, post-master's, and postbachelor's certificates. *Special study options:* academic remediation for entering students, accelerated degree program, advanced placement credit, cooperative education, distance learning, double majors, external degree program, freshman honors college, honors programs, independent study, internships, part-time degree program, services for LD students, study abroad, summer session for credit. *ROTC:* Army (c).

Computers on Campus 200 computers/terminals and 1 port are available on campus for general student use. Students can access the following: computer help desk, free student e-mail accounts, online (class) grades, online (class) registration, online (class) schedules. Campuswide network is available. 100% of college-owned or -operated housing units are wired for high-speed Internet access. Wireless service is available via classrooms, computer centers, computer labs, learning centers, libraries, student centers.

Student Life *Housing options:* men-only, women-only. Campus housing is university owned. Freshman campus housing is guaranteed. *Activities and* *organizations:* drama/theater group, student-run newspaper, radio and television station, choral group, Student Government Association, Student Night Life, Best Buddies, College vs. Cancer, National Security Club. *Campus security:* 24-hour emergency response devices and patrols, late-night transport/escort service, controlled dormitory access. *Student services:* health clinic, personal/psychological counseling.

Athletics Member NCAA. All Division III. *Intercollegiate sports:* baseball M, basketball M/W, cross-country running M/W, golf M, lacrosse M/W, soccer M/W, softball W, track and field M/W, volleyball W.

Standardized Tests *Required:* SAT or ACT (for admission).

Costs (2011–12) *Comprehensive fee:* $38,140 includes full-time tuition ($27,000), mandatory fees ($1000), and room and board ($10,140). Full-time tuition and fees vary according to class time. Part-time tuition: $1125 per credit hour. Part-time tuition and fees vary according to class time. *Room and board:* Room and board charges vary according to board plan. *Payment plan:* installment. *Waivers:* senior citizens and employees or children of employees.

Financial Aid Of all full-time matriculated undergraduates who enrolled in 2009, 1,542 applied for aid, 1,370 were judged to have need, 242 had their need fully met. 103 Federal Work-Study jobs (averaging $2426). 91 state and other part-time jobs (averaging $2501). In 2009, 307 non-need-based awards were made. *Average percent of need met:* 61%. *Average financial aid package:* $19,432. *Average need-based loan:* $4617. *Average need-based gift aid:* $14,648. *Average non-need-based aid:* $9224. *Average indebtedness upon graduation:* $33,835. *Financial aid deadline:* 5/1.

Applying *Options:* electronic application, early admission, deferred entrance. *Application fee:* $30. *Required:* high school transcript, 2 letters of recommendation. *Recommended:* essay or personal statement, interview. *Application deadlines:* 8/1 (freshmen), 8/1 (transfers). *Notification:* continuous (freshmen), continuous (transfers).

Freshman Application Contact Mr. Derrick Wetzel, Director of Admissions, DeSales University, 2755 Station Avenue, Center Valley, PA 18034-9568. *Phone:* 610-282-1100. *Toll-free phone:* 877-4DESALES. *E-mail:* admiss@ desales.edu. *Web site:* http://www.desales.edu/.

See page 1256 for the College Close-Up.

DeVry University
Fort Washington, Pennsylvania

- **Proprietary** comprehensive, founded 2002, part of DeVry University
- **Coed** 1,077 undergraduate students, 43% full-time, 31% women, 69% men
- **Minimally difficult** entrance level

Undergraduates 467 full-time, 610 part-time. 11% are from out of state; 28% Black or African American, non-Hispanic/Latino; 8% Hispanic/Latino; 4% Asian, non-Hispanic/Latino; 0.3% Native Hawaiian or other Pacific Islander, non-Hispanic/Latino; 0.4% American Indian or Alaska Native, non-Hispanic/Latino; 0.8% Two or more races, non-Hispanic/Latino; 21% Race/ethnicity unknown; 0.4% international; 23% transferred in.

Freshmen *Admission:* 223 enrolled.

Faculty *Total:* 133, 20% full-time. *Student/faculty ratio:* 12:1.

Academics *Calendar:* semesters. *Degrees:* associate, bachelor's, and master's. *Special study options:* academic remediation for entering students, accelerated degree program, adult/continuing education programs, advanced placement credit, distance learning, part-time degree program, services for LD students, summer session for credit.

Computers on Campus Students can access the following: online (class) registration. Campuswide network is available.

Student Life *Housing:* college housing not available.

Costs (2010–11) *Tuition:* $14,766 full-time, $580 per credit hour part-time. Full-time tuition and fees vary according to course load. Part-time tuition and fees vary according to course load. *Required fees:* $60 full-time, $30 per term part-time. *Payment plans:* installment, deferred payment. *Waivers:* employees or children of employees.

Financial Aid Of all full-time matriculated undergraduates who enrolled in 2007, 254 applied for aid, 244 were judged to have need, 2 had their need fully met. In 2007, 23 non-need-based awards were made. *Average percent of need met:* 34%. *Average financial aid package:* $12,114. *Average need-based loan:* $6836. *Average need-based gift aid:* $6835. *Average non-need-based aid:* $13,057. *Average indebtedness upon graduation:* $15,638.

Applying *Options:* electronic application, deferred entrance. *Application fee:* $50. *Required:* high school transcript, interview. *Application deadlines:* rolling (freshmen), rolling (transfers). *Notification:* continuous (freshmen), continuous (transfers).

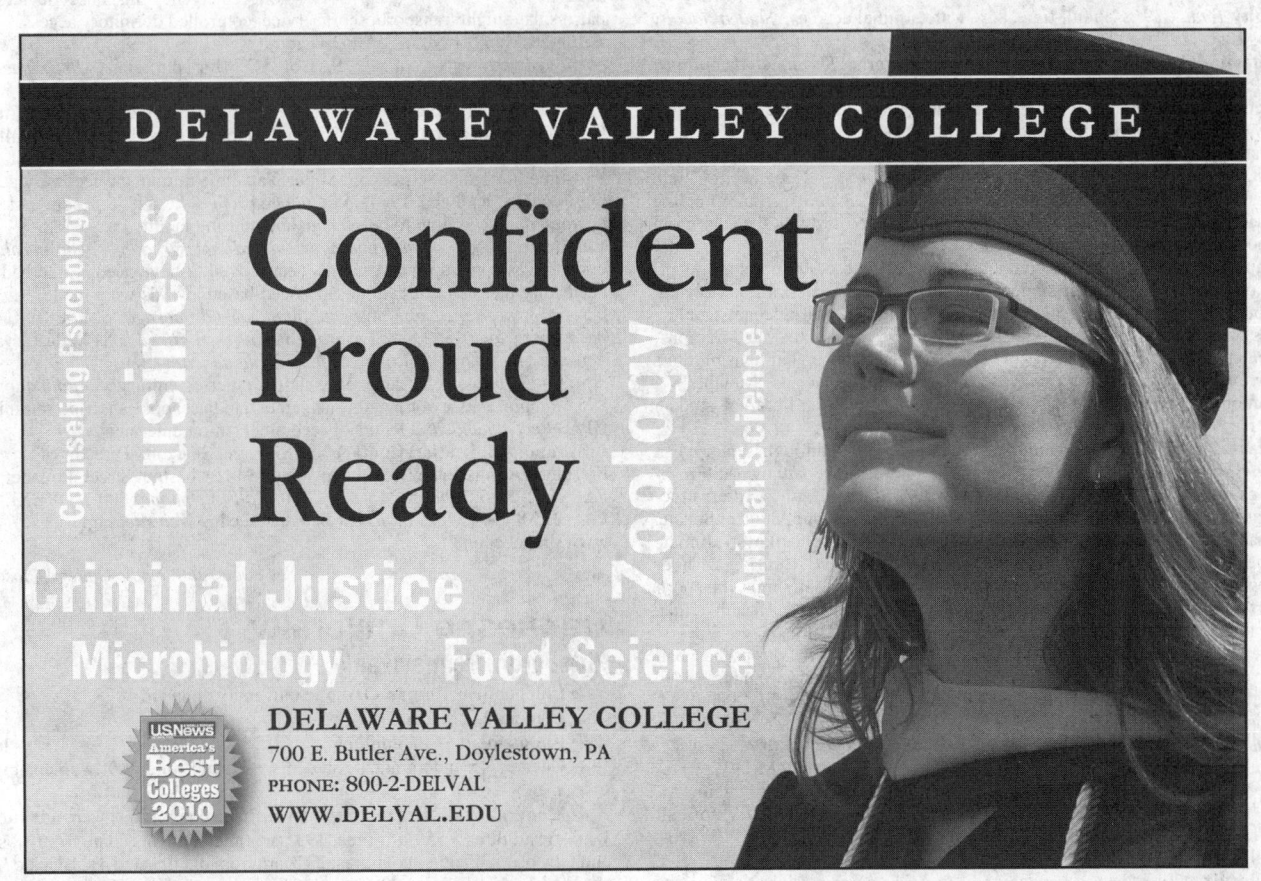

Freshman Application Contact DeVry University, 1140 Virginia Drive, Fort Washington, PA 19034. *Phone:* 215-591-5700. *Web site:* http://www.devry.edu/.

DeVry University
King of Prussia, Pennsylvania

Admissions Office Contact DeVry University, 150 Allendale Road, Builldlng 3, Suite 3201, King of Prussia, PA 19406-2926. *Web site:* http://www.devry.edu/.

DeVry University
Pittsburgh, Pennsylvania

Admissions Office Contact DeVry University, FreeMarkets Center, 210 Sixth Avenue, Suite 200, Pittsburgh, PA 15222-2606. *Toll-free phone:* 866-77DEVRY. *Web site:* http://www.devry.edu/.

Dickinson College
Carlisle, Pennsylvania

- **Independent** 4-year, founded 1773
- **Suburban** 120-acre campus with easy access to Harrisburg
- **Endowment** $278.0 million
- **Coed** 2,414 undergraduate students, 98% full-time, 55% women, 45% men
- **Very difficult** entrance level, 48% of applicants were admitted

Undergraduates 2,373 full-time, 41 part-time. Students come from 40 states and territories; 43 other countries; 76% are from out of state; 4% Black or African American, non-Hispanic/Latino; 5% Hispanic/Latino; 4% Asian, non-Hispanic/Latino; 0.3% American Indian or Alaska Native, non-Hispanic/Latino; 0.7% Two or more races, non-Hispanic/Latino; 2% Race/ethnicity unknown; 7% international; 1% transferred in; 94% live on campus. *Retention:* 90% of full-time freshmen returned.
Freshmen *Admission:* 5,033 applied, 2,405 admitted, 658 enrolled. *Test scores:* SAT critical reading scores over 500: 96%; SAT math scores over 500: 98%; ACT scores over 18: 100%; SAT critical reading scores over 600: 77%; SAT math scores over 600: 77%; ACT scores over 24: 99%; SAT critical reading scores over 700: 21%; SAT math scores over 700: 21%; ACT scores over 30: 37%.
Faculty *Total:* 239, 84% full-time, 85% with terminal degrees. *Student/faculty ratio:* 10:1.
Academics *Calendar:* semesters. *Degree:* bachelor's. *Special study options:* accelerated degree program, adult/continuing education programs, advanced placement credit, double majors, English as a second language, independent study, internships, off-campus study, part-time degree program, services for LD students, student-designed majors, study abroad, summer session for credit. *ROTC:* Army (b). *Unusual degree programs:* 3-2 engineering with Case Western Reserve University; Rensselaer Polytechnic Institute; nursing with Johns Hopkins University School of Nursing; pre-law with the Dickinson School of Law of the Pennsylvania State University.
Computers on Campus 702 computers/terminals and 5,000 ports are available on campus for general student use. Students can access the following: campus intranet, computer help desk, free student e-mail accounts, online (class) grades, online (class) registration, online (class) schedules. Campuswide network is available. 100% of college-owned or -operated housing units are wired for high-speed Internet access. Wireless service is available via classrooms, computer centers, computer labs, dorm rooms, libraries, student centers.
Student Life *Housing:* on-campus residence required through senior year. *Options:* coed, disabled students. Campus housing is university owned. Freshman campus housing is guaranteed. *Activities and organizations:* drama/theater group, student-run newspaper, radio station, choral group, Student Senate, Alpha Phi Omega, Multi-Organization Board, Hillel, Jive Turkeys (ultimate Frisbee), national fraternities, national sororities. *Campus security:* 24-hour emergency response devices and patrols, student patrols, late-night transport/escort service, controlled dormitory access. *Student services:* health clinic, personal/psychological counseling, women's center.
Athletics Member NCAA. All Division III. *Intercollegiate sports:* baseball M, basketball M/W, cheerleading M(c)/W(c), cross-country running M/W, equestrian sports M(c)/W(c), fencing M(c)/W(c), field hockey W, football M, golf M/W, ice hockey M(c), lacrosse M/W, skiing (downhill) M(c)/W(c), soccer M/W, softball W, squash M(c)/W(c), swimming and diving M/W, tennis M/W, track and field M/W, ultimate Frisbee M(c)/W(c), volleyball M(c)/W, wrestling M(c). *Intramural sports:* badminton M/W, basketball M, bowling M, field hockey W, football M, golf M/W, racquetball M/W, soccer M/W, softball M/W, squash M/W, table tennis M/W, tennis M/W, ultimate Frisbee M/W, volleyball M.
Standardized Tests *Recommended:* SAT or ACT (for admission).

Costs (2010–11) *One-time required fee:* $25. *Comprehensive fee:* $51,950 includes full-time tuition ($41,170), mandatory fees ($350), and room and board ($10,430). Part-time tuition: $5145 per course. *Required fees:* $44 per course part-time. *College room only:* $5380. Room and board charges vary according to board plan and housing facility. *Payment plan:* installment. *Waivers:* senior citizens and employees or children of employees.
Financial Aid Of all full-time matriculated undergraduates who enrolled in 2009, 1,430 applied for aid, 1,294 were judged to have need, 947 had their need fully met. 934 Federal Work-Study jobs (averaging $2231). 195 state and other part-time jobs (averaging $3386). In 2009, 225 non-need-based awards were made. *Average percent of need met:* 96%. *Average financial aid package:* $34,687. *Average need-based loan:* $5055. *Average need-based gift aid:* $28,994. *Average non-need-based aid:* $11,160. *Average indebtedness upon graduation:* $22,451. *Financial aid deadline:* 2/1.
Applying *Options:* electronic application, early decision, early action, deferred entrance. *Application fee:* $65. *Required:* essay or personal statement, high school transcript, 2 letters of recommendation. *Recommended:* minimum 3 GPA, interview. *Application deadlines:* 2/1 (freshmen), 2/1 (out-of-state freshmen), 4/1 (transfers), 12/1 (early action). *Early decision deadline:* 11/15 (for plan 1), 1/15 (for plan 2). *Notification:* 3/20 (freshmen), 3/20 (out-of-state freshmen), continuous until 5/1 (transfers), 12/15 (early decision plan 1), 2/15 (early decision plan 2), 2/1 (early action).
Freshman Application Contact Stephanie Balmer, Vice President for Enrollment and Communications/Dean of Admissions, Dickinson College, PO Box 1773, Admissions Office, Carlisle, PA 17013-2896. *Phone:* 717-245-1231. *Toll-free phone:* 800-644-1773. *Fax:* 717-245-1442. *E-mail:* admit@dickinson.edu. *Web site:* http://www.dickinson.edu/.

Drexel University
Philadelphia, Pennsylvania

- **Independent** university, founded 1891
- **Urban** 96-acre campus with easy access to Philadelphia
- **Endowment** $416.4 million
- **Coed**
- **Moderately difficult** entrance level

Faculty *Student/faculty ratio:* 9:1.
Academics *Calendar:* quarters. *Degrees:* certificates, associate, bachelor's, master's, doctoral-other, doctoral-professional, doctoral-research/scholarship, post-master's, and postbachelor's certificates.
Student Life *Campus security:* 24-hour emergency response devices and patrols, late-night transport/escort service, controlled dormitory access.
Athletics Member NCAA. All Division I.
Standardized Tests *Required:* SAT or ACT (for admission). *Recommended:* SAT (for admission).
Costs (2010–11) *Comprehensive fee:* $46,130 includes full-time tuition ($30,900), mandatory fees ($2105), and room and board ($13,125). Full-time tuition and fees vary according to course load, program, and student level. Part-time tuition: $850 per credit hour. Part-time tuition and fees vary according to course load and program. *College room only:* $7875. Room and board charges vary according to board plan and housing facility.
Financial Aid *Of all full-time matriculated undergraduates who enrolled in 2008,* 5,878 applied for aid, 5,833 were judged to have need, 1,826 had their need fully met. *In 2008,* 2086 non-need-based awards were made. *Average percent of need met:* 56. *Average financial aid package:* $21,488. *Average need-based loan:* $12,875. *Average need-based gift aid:* $13,204. *Average non-need-based aid:* $11,641. *Financial aid deadline:* 3/1.
Applying *Options:* electronic application, deferred entrance. *Application fee:* $75. *Required:* essay or personal statement, high school transcript, minimum 2 GPA. *Recommended:* 2 letters of recommendation, interview.
Freshman Application Contact Ms. Margaret Sparzani, Director of Freshman Admissions, Drexel University, 3141 Chestnut Street, Philadelphia, PA 19104-2875. *Phone:* 215-895-2400. *Toll-free phone:* 800-2-DREXEL. *Fax:* 215-895-5939. *E-mail:* enroll@drexel.edu. *Web site:* http://www.drexel.edu/.

See page 1260 for the College Close-Up.

Duquesne University
Pittsburgh, Pennsylvania

- **Independent Roman Catholic** university, founded 1878
- **Urban** 49-acre campus
- **Endowment** $140.8 million
- **Coed** 5,745 undergraduate students, 97% full-time, 56% women, 44% men
- **Moderately difficult** entrance level, 77% of applicants were admitted

Undergraduates 5,550 full-time, 195 part-time. Students come from 48 states and territories; 45 other countries; 23% are from out of state; 4% Black or African American, non-Hispanic/Latino; 2% Hispanic/Latino; 2% Asian, non-His-

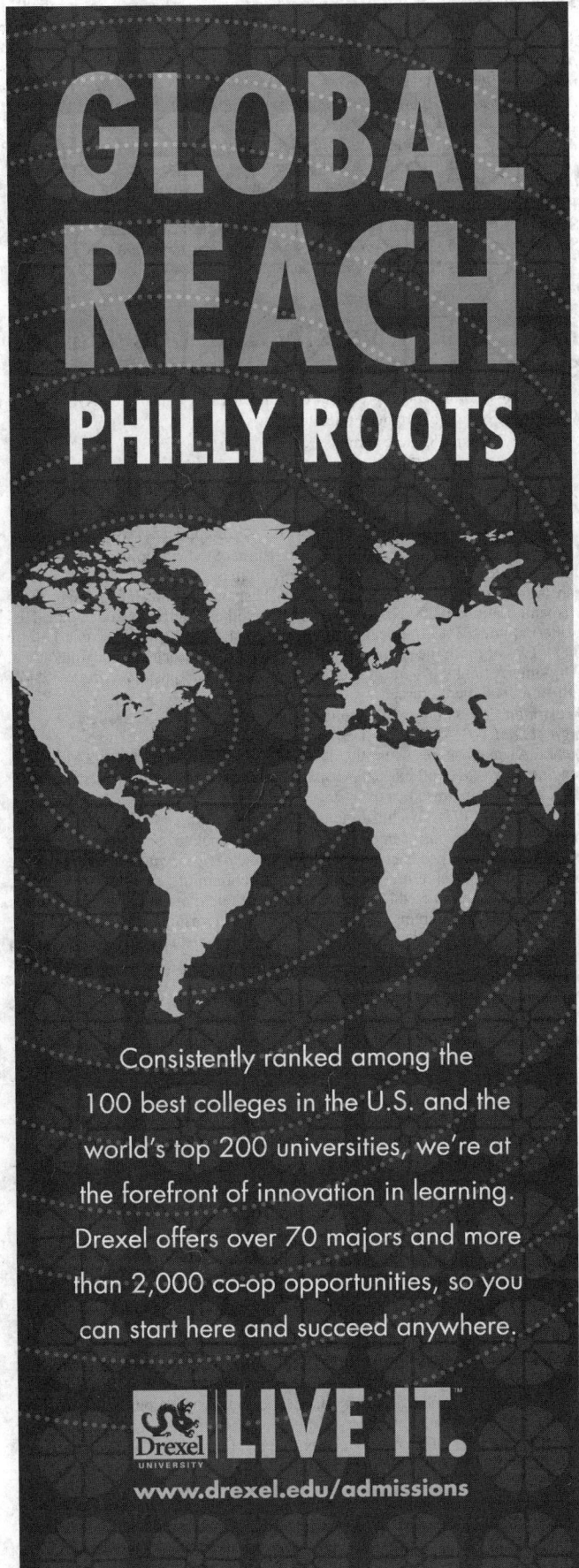

GLOBAL REACH

PHILLY ROOTS

Consistently ranked among the 100 best colleges in the U.S. and the world's top 200 universities, we're at the forefront of innovation in learning. Drexel offers over 70 majors and more than 2,000 co-op opportunities, so you can start here and succeed anywhere.

Drexel UNIVERSITY **LIVE IT.**

www.drexel.edu/admissions

panic/Latino; 0.3% American Indian or Alaska Native, non-Hispanic/Latino; 0.7% Two or more races, non-Hispanic/Latino; 4% Race/ethnicity unknown; 2% international; 3% transferred in; 57% live on campus. *Retention:* 84% of full-time freshmen returned.

Freshmen *Admission:* 6,502 applied, 4,989 admitted, 1,416 enrolled. *Average high school GPA:* 3.63. *Test scores:* SAT critical reading scores over 500: 83%; SAT math scores over 500: 86%; SAT writing scores over 500: 77%; ACT scores over 18: 98%; SAT critical reading scores over 600: 28%; SAT math scores over 600: 34%; SAT writing scores over 600: 27%; ACT scores over 24: 61%; SAT critical reading scores over 700: 4%; SAT math scores over 700: 4%; SAT writing scores over 700: 3%; ACT scores over 30: 6%.

Faculty *Total:* 992, 48% full-time. *Student/faculty ratio:* 14:1.

Academics *Calendar:* semesters. *Degrees:* bachelor's, master's, doctoral-other, doctoral-professional, doctoral-research/scholarship, post-master's, and postbachelor's certificates. *Special study options:* academic remediation for entering students, accelerated degree program, adult/continuing education programs, advanced placement credit, distance learning, double majors, English as a second language, external degree program, freshman honors college, honors programs, independent study, internships, off-campus study, part-time degree program, services for LD students, student-designed majors, study abroad, summer session for credit. *ROTC:* Army (b), Navy (c), Air Force (c). *Unusual degree programs:* 3-2 engineering with Case Western Reserve University, University of Pittsburgh.

Computers on Campus 850 computers/terminals are available on campus for general student use. Students can access the following: campus intranet, computer help desk, free student e-mail accounts, online (class) grades, online (class) registration, online (class) schedules. Campuswide network is available. 100% of college-owned or -operated housing units are wired for high-speed Internet access. Wireless service is available via classrooms, computer centers, computer labs, learning centers, libraries, student centers.

Student Life *Housing:* on-campus residence required through sophomore year. *Options:* coed, men-only, women-only, disabled students. Campus housing is university owned. Freshman campus housing is guaranteed. *Activities and organizations:* drama/theater group, student-run newspaper, radio and television station, choral group, marching band, Duquesne University Volunteers (DUV), Red and Blue Crew, Student Government Association, Duquesne Program Council, Residence Hall Association, national fraternities, national sororities. *Campus security:* 24-hour emergency response devices and patrols, late-night transport/escort service, controlled dormitory access, campus cameras monitor exterior 24 hours/day; card access for academic buildings; 8 Code Blue Emergency service stations. *Student services:* health clinic, personal/psychological counseling.

Athletics Member NCAA. All Division I except football (Division I-AA). *Intercollegiate sports:* basketball M(s)/W(s), cheerleading M(c)/W(c), crew M(c)/W(s), cross-country running M(s)/W(s), ice hockey M(c), lacrosse W(s), soccer M(s)/W(s), swimming and diving W(s), tennis M(s)/W(s), track and field M(s)/W(s), volleyball W(s). *Intramural sports:* basketball M/W, equestrian sports W(c), football M/W, racquetball M/W, rugby M(c), skiing (downhill) M(c)/W(c), soccer M/W, swimming and diving M/W, table tennis M(c)/W(c), tennis W, volleyball M(c)/W.

Standardized Tests *Required:* SAT or ACT (for admission).

Costs (2010–11) *Comprehensive fee:* $36,978 includes full-time tuition ($25,336), mandatory fees ($2166), and room and board ($9476). Full-time tuition and fees vary according to program. Part-time tuition: $826 per credit. Part-time tuition and fees vary according to program. *Required fees:* $84 per credit part-time. *College room only:* $5168. Room and board charges vary according to board plan and housing facility. *Payment plans:* installment, deferred payment. *Waivers:* senior citizens and employees or children of employees.

Financial Aid Of all full-time matriculated undergraduates who enrolled in 2008, 4,612 applied for aid, 3,881 were judged to have need, 979 had their need fully met. 2,939 Federal Work-Study jobs (averaging $3057). In 2008, 1360 non-need-based awards were made. *Average percent of need met:* 79%. *Average financial aid package:* $21,312. *Average need-based loan:* $4402. *Average need-based gift aid:* $13,231. *Average non-need-based aid:* $7800. *Financial aid deadline:* 5/1.

Applying *Options:* electronic application, early admission, early decision, early action, deferred entrance. *Application fee:* $50. *Required:* essay or personal statement, high school transcript, 1 letter of recommendation. *Required for some:* audition for School of Music applicants. *Recommended:* minimum 3 GPA, interview. *Application deadlines:* 7/1 (freshmen), 7/1 (transfers), 12/1 (early action). *Early decision deadline:* 11/1. *Notification:* continuous until 10/1 (freshmen), 12/15 (early decision), 1/15 (early action).

Freshman Application Contact Mr. Paul-James Cukanna, Associate Provost/Associate Academic Vice President for Enrollment Management/Director of Admissions, Duquesne University, 1st Floor Administration Building, 600 Forbes Avenue, Pittsburgh, PA 15282-0201. *Phone:* 412-396-5002. *Toll-free phone:* 800-456-0590. *Fax:* 412-396-6223. *E-mail:* admissions@duq.edu. *Web site:* http://www.duq.edu/.

Eastern University

St. Davids, Pennsylvania

Freshman Application Contact Mr. Michael Dziedziak, Director of Undergraduate Admissions, Eastern University, 1300 Eagle Road, St. Davids, PA 19087-3696. *Phone:* 610-341-1376. *Toll-free phone:* 800-452-0996. *Fax:* 610-341-1723. *E-mail:* ugadm@eastern.edu. *Web site:* http://www.eastern.edu/.

See page 1268 for the College Close-Up.

East Stroudsburg University of Pennsylvania

East Stroudsburg, Pennsylvania

- **State-supported** comprehensive, founded 1893, part of Pennsylvania State System of Higher Education
- **Small-town** 213-acre campus
- **Endowment** $15.1 million
- **Coed** 6,372 undergraduate students, 91% full-time, 55% women, 45% men
- **Moderately difficult** entrance level, 63% of applicants were admitted

Undergraduates 5,802 full-time, 570 part-time. Students come from 27 states and territories; 27 other countries; 26% are from out of state; 7% Black or African American, non-Hispanic/Latino; 7% Hispanic/Latino; 1% Asian, non-Hispanic/Latino; 0.1% Native Hawaiian or other Pacific Islander, non-Hispanic/Latino; 0.2% American Indian or Alaska Native, non-Hispanic/Latino; 0.5% Two or more races, non-Hispanic/Latino; 8% Race/ethnicity unknown; 0.8% international; 9% transferred in; 42% live on campus. *Retention:* 78% of full-time freshmen returned.

Freshmen *Admission:* 7,258 applied, 4,560 admitted, 1,163 enrolled. *Test scores:* SAT critical reading scores over 500: 42%; SAT math scores over 500: 52%; SAT writing scores over 500: 39%; SAT critical reading scores over 600: 6%; SAT math scores over 600: 9%; SAT writing scores over 600: 5%.

Faculty *Total:* 390, 85% full-time, 67% with terminal degrees. *Student/faculty ratio:* 17:1.

Academics *Calendar:* semesters. *Degrees:* associate, bachelor's, and master's. *Special study options:* academic remediation for entering students, accelerated degree program, adult/continuing education programs, advanced placement credit, distance learning, double majors, honors programs, independent study, internships, off-campus study, part-time degree program, services for LD students, student-designed majors, study abroad, summer session for credit. *ROTC:* Army (b), Air Force (c). *Unusual degree programs:* 3-2 engineering with Pennsylvania State University-University Park Campus, University of Pittsburgh.

Computers on Campus 500 computers/terminals are available on campus for general student use. Students can access the following: campus intranet, computer help desk, free student e-mail accounts, online (class) grades, online (class) registration, online (class) schedules, online classes. Campuswide network is available. 100% of college-owned or -operated housing units are wired for high-speed Internet access. Wireless service is available via classrooms, dorm rooms, libraries, student centers.

Student Life *Housing:* on-campus residence required for freshman year. *Options:* coed. Campus housing is university owned and is provided by a third party. Freshman campus housing is guaranteed. *Activities and organizations:* drama/theater group, student-run newspaper, radio station, choral group, marching band, Student Senate, Stage II, Council for Exceptional Children, United Campus Ministry/ESU Christian Fellowship, University Band/Vocal Performing Choirs, national fraternities, national sororities. *Campus security:* 24-hour emergency response devices and patrols, late-night transport/escort service, controlled dormitory access. *Student services:* health clinic, personal/psychological counseling, women's center.

Athletics Member NCAA. All Division II. *Intercollegiate sports:* baseball M(s), basketball M(s)/W(s), cross-country running M(s)/W(s), field hockey W(s), football M(s), golf W(s), lacrosse W(s), soccer M(s)/W(s), softball W(s), swimming and diving W(s), tennis M(s)/W(s), track and field M(s)/W(s), volleyball W(s), wrestling M(s). *Intramural sports:* badminton M/W, basketball M/W, equestrian sports M/W, golf M/W, ice hockey M/W, lacrosse M, racquetball M/W, rugby M/W, soccer M/W, softball W, tennis M/W, track and field M/W, ultimate Frisbee M/W, volleyball M/W, water polo M/W.

Standardized Tests *Required:* SAT or ACT (for admission).

Costs (2011–12) *Tuition:* state resident $5804 full-time, $242 per credit part-time; nonresident $14,510 full-time, $605 per credit part-time. Full-time tuition and fees vary according to course load. Part-time tuition and fees vary according to course load. *Required fees:* $1974 full-time, $68 per credit part-time. *Room and board:* $6658; room only: $4426. Room and board charges vary according to board plan and housing facility. *Payment plan:* installment. *Waivers:* senior citizens and employees or children of employees.

Financial Aid Of all full-time matriculated undergraduates who enrolled in 2008, 4,144 applied for aid, 3,013 were judged to have need, 1,773 had their need fully met. In 2008, 1047 non-need-based awards were made. *Average percent of need met:* 83%. *Average financial aid package:* $5933. *Average need-based loan:* $4106. *Average need-based gift aid:* $4312. *Average non-need-based aid:* $10,063. *Average indebtedness upon graduation:* $25,887. *Financial aid deadline:* 3/1.

Applying *Options:* electronic application. *Application fee:* $35. *Required for some:* high school transcript. *Application deadlines:* 4/1 (freshmen), 5/1 (transfers). *Notification:* 5/1 (freshmen), continuous (transfers).

Freshman Application Contact Mr. Jeff Jones, Director of Admissions, East Stroudsburg University of Pennsylvania, 200 Prospect Street, East Stroudsburg, PA 18301. *Phone:* 570-422-3542. *Toll-free phone:* 877-230-5547. *Fax:* 570-422-3933. *E-mail:* undergrads@po-box.esu.edu. *Web site:* http://www4.esu.edu/.

Edinboro University of Pennsylvania

Edinboro, Pennsylvania

- **State-supported** comprehensive, founded 1857, part of Pennsylvania State System of Higher Education
- **Small-town** 585-acre campus
- **Endowment** $4.7 million
- **Coed** 6,697 undergraduate students, 90% full-time, 58% women, 42% men
- **Moderately difficult** entrance level, 71% of applicants were admitted

Undergraduates 6,019 full-time, 678 part-time. Students come from 40 states and territories; 22 other countries; 11% are from out of state; 8% Black or African American, non-Hispanic/Latino; 2% Hispanic/Latino; 0.8% Asian, non-Hispanic/Latino; 0.2% Native Hawaiian or other Pacific Islander, non-Hispanic/Latino; 0.3% American Indian or Alaska Native, non-Hispanic/Latino; 0.8% Two or more races, non-Hispanic/Latino; 0.4% Race/ethnicity unknown; 0.8% international; 6% transferred in; 31% live on campus. *Retention:* 72% of full-time freshmen returned.

Freshmen *Admission:* 6,101 applied, 4,333 admitted, 1,575 enrolled. *Average high school GPA:* 3.21. *Test scores:* SAT critical reading scores over 500: 39%; SAT math scores over 500: 39%; ACT scores over 18: 69%; SAT critical reading scores over 600: 8%; SAT math scores over 600: 8%; ACT scores over 24: 18%; SAT math scores over 700: 1%.

Faculty *Total:* 407, 84% full-time. *Student/faculty ratio:* 18:1.

Academics *Calendar:* semesters. *Degrees:* associate, bachelor's, master's, post-master's, and postbachelor's certificates. *Special study options:* academic remediation for entering students, adult/continuing education programs, advanced placement credit, distance learning, double majors, freshman honors college, honors programs, independent study, internships, off-campus study, part-time degree program, services for LD students, student-designed majors, study abroad, summer session for credit. *ROTC:* Army (b). *Unusual degree programs:* 3-2 engineering with Pennsylvania State University-University Park Campus, University of Pittsburgh, Case Western Reserve University, Pennsylvania State University at Erie, The Behrend College; pre-pharmacy (2+3 at Lake Erie College of Osteopathic Medicine and School of Pharmacy), MA Counseling (3-2 program for Criminal Justice Majors).

Computers on Campus 998 computers/terminals and 2,000 ports are available on campus for general student use. Students can access the following: campus intranet, computer help desk, free student e-mail accounts, online (class) grades, online (class) registration, online (class) schedules, software. Campuswide network is available. 100% of college-owned or -operated housing units are wired for high-speed Internet access. Wireless service is available via classrooms, computer centers, computer labs, dorm rooms, learning centers, libraries, student centers.

Student Life *Housing:* on-campus residence required for freshman year. *Options:* coed, disabled students. Campus housing is university owned and is provided by a third party. Freshman campus housing is guaranteed. *Activities and organizations:* drama/theater group, student-run newspaper, radio and television station, choral group, marching band, Student Government Association, AFRICA, Gamma Sigma Sigma, Health and Physical Education Majors Club, national fraternities, national sororities. *Campus security:* 24-hour emergency response devices and patrols, controlled dormitory access, self-defense education. *Student services:* health clinic, personal/psychological counseling, women's center, legal services.

Athletics Member NCAA. All Division II except wrestling (Division I). *Intercollegiate sports:* basketball M(s)/W(s), cross-country running M(s)/W(s), football M(s), ice hockey M(c), lacrosse W(s), soccer W(s), softball W(s), swimming and diving M(s)/W(s), tennis M/W, track and field M(s)/W(s), volleyball W(s), wrestling M(s). *Intramural sports:* badminton M(c)/W(c), basketball M(c)/W(c), cheerleading W, equestrian sports M(c)/W(c), fencing M(c)/W(c), football M(c)/W(c), golf M(c)/W(c), ice hockey M(c)/W(c), racquetball M(c)/W(c), rock climbing M(c)/W(c), skiing (downhill) M(c)/W(c), soccer M(c)/W(c), softball M(c)/W(c), table tennis M(c)/W(c), tennis M(c)/

W(c), track and field M(c)/W(c), ultimate Frisbee M(c)/W(c), volleyball M(c)/W(c), weight lifting M(c)/W(c), wrestling M.

Standardized Tests *Required for some:* SAT or ACT (for admission).

Costs (2010–11) *Tuition:* state resident $5814 full-time, $242 per credit hour part-time; nonresident $8706 full-time, $363 per credit hour part-time. Part-time tuition and fees vary according to course load. *Required fees:* $1926 full-time, $77 per credit hour part-time, $68 per term part-time. *Room and board:* $7820; room only: $4980. Room and board charges vary according to board plan. *Payment plan:* installment. *Waivers:* minority students, senior citizens, and employees or children of employees.

Financial Aid Of all full-time matriculated undergraduates who enrolled in 2008, 4,952 applied for aid, 4,179 were judged to have need, 331 had their need fully met. 442 Federal Work-Study jobs (averaging $1474). 689 state and other part-time jobs (averaging $1515). In 2008, 333 non-need-based awards were made. *Average percent of need met:* 63%. *Average financial aid package:* $7473. *Average need-based loan:* $3622. *Average need-based gift aid:* $3080. *Average non-need-based aid:* $2100. *Average indebtedness upon graduation:* $28,392.

Applying *Options:* electronic application, deferred entrance. *Application fee:* $30. *Required:* high school transcript. *Required for some:* essay or personal statement, 1 letter of recommendation, interview, music auditions. *Recommended:* minimum 2.5 GPA. *Application deadline:* rolling (transfers). *Notification:* continuous (freshmen), continuous (transfers).

Freshman Application Contact Ms. Kimberly Fabrizio, Interim Director of Undergraduate Admissions, Edinboro University of Pennsylvania, Academy Hall, Edinboro, PA 16444. *Phone:* 814-732-2761. *Toll-free phone:* 888-846-2676 (in-state); 800-626-2203 (out-of-state). *Fax:* 814-732-2420. *E-mail:* eup_admissions@edinboro.edu. *Web site:* http://www.edinboro.edu/.

Elizabethtown College
Elizabethtown, Pennsylvania

- **Independent** comprehensive, founded 1899, affiliated with Church of the Brethren
- **Small-town** 201-acre campus with easy access to Baltimore and Philadelphia
- **Endowment** $48.2 million
- **Coed** 2,432 undergraduate students, 79% full-time, 64% women, 36% men
- **Moderately difficult** entrance level, 75% of applicants were admitted

Undergraduates 1,914 full-time, 518 part-time. Students come from 30 states and territories; 20 other countries; 29% are from out of state; 4% Black or African American, non-Hispanic/Latino; 3% Hispanic/Latino; 2% Asian, non-Hispanic/Latino; 0.1% Native Hawaiian or other Pacific Islander, non-Hispanic/Latino; 0.4% American Indian or Alaska Native, non-Hispanic/Latino; 0.3% Two or more races, non-Hispanic/Latino; 2% international; 1% transferred in; 69% live on campus. *Retention:* 88% of full-time freshmen returned.

Freshmen *Admission:* 3,329 applied, 2,481 admitted, 491 enrolled. *Test scores:* SAT critical reading scores over 500: 74%; SAT math scores over 500: 77%; SAT writing scores over 500: 70%; ACT scores over 18: 87%; SAT critical reading scores over 600: 27%; SAT math scores over 600: 32%; SAT writing scores over 600: 24%; ACT scores over 24: 44%; SAT critical reading scores over 700: 4%; SAT math scores over 700: 5%; SAT writing scores over 700: 2%; ACT scores over 30: 7%.

Faculty *Total:* 282, 46% full-time, 50% with terminal degrees. *Student/faculty ratio:* 11:1.

Academics *Calendar:* semesters. *Degrees:* certificates, associate, bachelor's, master's, and postbachelor's certificates. *Special study options:* academic remediation for entering students, adult/continuing education programs, advanced placement credit, distance learning, double majors, English as a second language, external degree program, honors programs, independent study, internships, off-campus study, part-time degree program, services for LD students, study abroad, summer session for credit. *Unusual degree programs:* 3-2 engineering with Pennsylvania State University - University Park Campus; forestry with Duke University; allied health programs with Thomas Jefferson University, Widener University, University of Maryland at Baltimore.

Computers on Campus 200 computers/terminals and 200 ports are available on campus for general student use. Students can access the following: campus intranet, computer help desk, free student e-mail accounts, online (class) grades, online (class) registration, online (class) schedules, file space, personal web page, financial aid, student billing. Campuswide network is available. 100% of college-owned or -operated housing units are wired for high-speed Internet access. Wireless service is available via classrooms, computer labs, learning centers, libraries, student centers.

Student Life *Housing:* on-campus residence required through senior year. *Options:* coed, women-only, disabled students. Campus housing is university owned and leased by the school. Freshman campus housing is guaranteed. *Activities and organizations:* drama/theater group, student-run newspaper, radio and television station, choral group, Students in Free Enterprise (SIFE), Emotion Dance Club, Student Senate, acapella groups, religious groups. *Cam-*

pus security: 24-hour emergency response devices and patrols, student patrols, late-night transport/escort service, controlled dormitory access, self-defense workshops, crime prevention program. *Student services:* health clinic, personal/psychological counseling.

Athletics Member NCAA. All Division III. *Intercollegiate sports:* baseball M, basketball M/W, cheerleading M(c)/W(c), cross-country running M/W, field hockey W, golf M, lacrosse M/W, soccer M/W, softball W, swimming and diving M/W, tennis M/W, track and field M/W, volleyball M(c)/W, wrestling M. *Intramural sports:* badminton M/W, basketball M/W, racquetball M/W, soccer M/W, softball M/W, tennis M/W, volleyball M/W, water polo M/W.

Standardized Tests *Required:* SAT or ACT (for admission).

Costs (2011–12) *Comprehensive fee:* $43,630 includes full-time tuition ($34,830) and room and board ($8800). Full-time tuition and fees vary according to course load. Part-time tuition: $845 per credit hour. Part-time tuition and fees vary according to class time and course load. *College room only:* $4400. Room and board charges vary according to board plan and housing facility. *Payment plan:* installment. *Waivers:* employees or children of employees.

Financial Aid Of all full-time matriculated undergraduates who enrolled in 2009, 1,568 applied for aid, 1,412 were judged to have need, 244 had their need fully met. 968 Federal Work-Study jobs (averaging $1351). In 2009, 392 non-need-based awards were made. *Average percent of need met:* 80%. *Average financial aid package:* $23,281. *Average need-based loan:* $4547. *Average need-based gift aid:* $18,578. *Average non-need-based aid:* $13,405.

Applying *Options:* electronic application, deferred entrance. *Application fee:* $30. *Required:* essay or personal statement, high school transcript, minimum 2 GPA, 2 letters of recommendation. *Required for some:* interview. *Recommended:* minimum 3 GPA, interview. *Application deadlines:* 3/1 (freshmen), 8/1 (transfers). *Notification:* continuous (freshmen), continuous (transfers).

Freshman Application Contact Ms. Debra Murray, Director of Admissions, Elizabethtown College, One Alpha Drive, Elizabethtown, PA 17022. *Phone:* 717-361-1400. *Fax:* 717-361-1365. *E-mail:* admissions@etown.edu. *Web site:* http://www.etown.edu/.

Franklin & Marshall College
Lancaster, Pennsylvania

- **Independent** 4-year, founded 1787
- **Suburban** 180-acre campus with easy access to Philadelphia
- **Coed** 2,179 undergraduate students, 98% full-time, 52% women, 48% men
- **Very difficult** entrance level, 45% of applicants were admitted

Undergraduates 2,132 full-time, 47 part-time. Students come from 43 states and territories; 44 other countries; 70% are from out of state; 3% Black or African American, non-Hispanic/Latino; 5% Hispanic/Latino; 3% Asian, non-Hispanic/Latino; 0.1% American Indian or Alaska Native, non-Hispanic/Latino; 2% Two or more races, non-Hispanic/Latino; 2% Race/ethnicity unknown; 9% international; 0.5% transferred in; 99% live on campus. *Retention:* 92% of full-time freshmen returned.

Freshmen *Admission:* 4,934 applied, 2,204 admitted, 629 enrolled. *Average high school GPA:* 3.52. *Test scores:* SAT critical reading scores over 500: 99%; SAT math scores over 500: 100%; ACT scores over 18: 100%; SAT critical reading scores over 600: 73%; SAT math scores over 600: 91%; ACT scores over 24: 100%; SAT critical reading scores over 700: 18%; SAT math scores over 700: 30%; ACT scores over 30: 44%.

Faculty *Total:* 265, 80% full-time, 90% with terminal degrees. *Student/faculty ratio:* 10:1.

Academics *Calendar:* semesters. *Degree:* bachelor's. *Special study options:* accelerated degree program, advanced placement credit, double majors, independent study, internships, off-campus study, services for LD students, student-designed majors, study abroad, summer session for credit. *Unusual degree programs:* 3-2 engineering with Rensselaer Polytechnic Institute, Washington University in St. Louis, Columbia University, Case Western Reserve University, Penn State University College of Engineering; forestry with Duke University; environmental studies with Duke University.

Computers on Campus 125 computers/terminals are available on campus for general student use. Students can access the following: campus intranet, computer help desk, free student e-mail accounts, online (class) grades, online (class) registration, online (class) schedules, online degree audit, unofficial transcripts, course material. Campuswide network is available. 100% of college-owned or -operated housing units are wired for high-speed Internet access. Wireless service is available via entire campus.

Student Life *Housing:* on-campus residence required through senior year. *Options:* coed, disabled students. Campus housing is university owned and is provided by a third party. Freshman campus housing is guaranteed. *Activities and organizations:* drama/theater group, student-run newspaper, radio station, choral group, Intervarsity, Hillel, Mi Gente Latina, Cia Bella, F&M Players, national fraternities, national sororities. *Campus security:* 24-hour emergency response devices and patrols, late-night transport/escort service, controlled dormitory access, residence hall security, campus security connected to city police and fire company. *Student services:* health clinic, personal/psychological counseling, women's center.

Athletics Member NCAA. All Division III except wrestling (Division I). *Intercollegiate sports:* baseball M, basketball M/W, crew M(c)/W, cross-country running M/W, equestrian sports W(c), field hockey W, football M, golf M/W, ice hockey M(c), lacrosse M/W, rugby M(c)/W(c), soccer M/W, softball W, squash M/W, swimming and diving M/W, tennis M/W, track and field M/W, ultimate Frisbee M(c)/W(c), volleyball M(c)/W, wrestling M. *Intramural sports:* basketball M/W, football M, soccer M/W, softball M/W, squash M/W, tennis M/W, volleyball M/W, wrestling M.

Costs (2010–11) *One-time required fee:* $200. *Comprehensive fee:* $52,070 includes full-time tuition ($41,090), mandatory fees ($60), and room and board ($10,920). *Part-time tuition:* $5136 per course. *College room only:* $6940. Room and board charges vary according to board plan and housing facility. *Payment plans:* installment, deferred payment. *Waivers:* employees or children of employees.

Financial Aid Of all full-time matriculated undergraduates who enrolled in 2009, 1,300 applied for aid, 1,065 were judged to have need, 746 had their need fully met. In 2009, 238 non-need-based awards were made. *Average percent of need met:* 95%. *Average financial aid package:* $32,018. *Average need-based loan:* $4339. *Average need-based gift aid:* $27,913. *Average non-need-based aid:* $11,291. *Average indebtedness upon graduation:* $28,451. *Financial aid deadline:* 2/15.

Applying *Options:* electronic application, early admission, early decision, deferred entrance. *Application fee:* $60. *Required:* essay or personal statement, high school transcript, 2 letters of recommendation, Common Application Supplement. *Required for some:* interview. *Application deadlines:* 2/1 (freshmen), 2/1 (out-of-state freshmen), 5/15 (transfers). *Early decision deadline:* 11/15 (for plan 1), 1/15 (for plan 2). *Notification:* 4/1 (freshmen), 4/1 (out-of-state freshmen), 12/15 (early decision plan 1), 2/15 (early decision plan 2).

Freshman Application Contact Julie Kerich, Interim Director of Admissions, Franklin & Marshall College, PO Box 3003, Lancaster, PA 17604-3003. *Phone:* 717-358-47433. *Fax:* 717-291-4389. *E-mail:* julie.kerich@fandm.edu. *Web site:* http://www.fandm.edu/.

Gannon University
Erie, Pennsylvania

- **Independent Roman Catholic** university, founded 1925
- **Urban** 13-acre campus with easy access to Cleveland, Buffalo, Pittsburgh
- **Endowment** $32.6 million
- **Coed** 2,992 undergraduate students, 82% full-time, 58% women, 42% men
- **Moderately difficult** entrance level, 80% of applicants were admitted

Undergraduates 2,468 full-time, 524 part-time. Students come from 36 states and territories; 22 other countries; 24% are from out of state; 6% Black or African American, non-Hispanic/Latino; 2% Hispanic/Latino; 1% Asian, non-Hispanic/Latino; 0.4% American Indian or Alaska Native, non-Hispanic/Latino; 4% Race/ethnicity unknown; 3% international; 4% transferred in; 46% live on campus. *Retention:* 79% of full-time freshmen returned.

Freshmen *Admission:* 3,089 applied, 2,483 admitted, 633 enrolled. *Average high school GPA:* 3.47. *Test scores:* SAT critical reading scores over 500: 59%; SAT math scores over 500: 63%; ACT scores over 18: 83%; SAT critical reading scores over 600: 16%; SAT math scores over 600: 25%; ACT scores over 24: 43%; SAT critical reading scores over 700: 2%; SAT math scores over 700: 2%; ACT scores over 30: 7%.

Faculty *Total:* 346, 57% full-time, 45% with terminal degrees. *Student/faculty ratio:* 14:1.

Academics *Calendar:* semesters plus 2 summer sessions. *Degrees:* certificates, associate, bachelor's, master's, doctoral-professional, doctoral-research/scholarship, post-master's, and postbachelor's certificates. *Special study options:* academic remediation for entering students, accelerated degree program, adult/continuing education programs, advanced placement credit, cooperative education, distance learning, double majors, English as a second language, honors programs, independent study, internships, off-campus study, part-time degree program, services for LD students, study abroad, summer session for credit. *ROTC:* Army (b). *Unusual degree programs:* 3-2 business administration; engineering with University of Pittsburgh; Occupational Therapy, Physician Assistant.

Computers on Campus 380 computers/terminals and 1,425 ports are available on campus for general student use. Students can access the following: campus intranet, computer help desk, free student e-mail accounts, online (class) grades, online (class) registration, online (class) schedules. Campuswide network is available. 100% of college-owned or -operated housing units are wired for high-speed Internet access. Wireless service is available via entire campus.

Student Life *Housing:* on-campus residence required through sophomore year. *Options:* coed, disabled students. Campus housing is university owned and leased by the school. Freshman campus housing is guaranteed. *Activities and organizations:* drama/theater group, student-run newspaper, radio station, choral group, Environmental Science Club, Habitat at Gannon, Social Concerns Club, Ski Club, PATCHES (Promoting Awareness Towards a Community of Healthy Educated Students), national fraternities, national sororities. *Campus security:* 24-hour emergency response devices and patrols, student patrols, late-night transport/escort service, controlled dormitory access, security cameras. *Student services:* health clinic, personal/psychological counseling.

Athletics Member NCAA. All Division II. *Intercollegiate sports:* baseball M(s), basketball M(s)/W(s), cheerleading M/W, cross-country running M(s)/W(s), football M(s), golf M(s)/W(s), lacrosse W(s), soccer M(s)/W(s), softball W(s), swimming and diving M(s)/W(s), volleyball W(s), water polo M(s)/W(s), wrestling M(s). *Intramural sports:* badminton M/W, basketball M/W, football M/W, racquetball M/W, soccer M/W, ultimate Frisbee M/W, volleyball M(c)/W, water polo M, weight lifting M, wrestling M.

Standardized Tests *Required:* SAT or ACT (for admission).

Costs (2010–11) *Comprehensive fee:* $34,302 includes full-time tuition ($24,040), mandatory fees ($542), and room and board ($9720). Full-time tuition and fees vary according to class time, course load, and program. Part-time tuition: $745 per credit hour. Part-time tuition and fees vary according to class time, course load, and program. *Required fees:* $18 per credit hour part-time. *College room only:* $5050. Room and board charges vary according to board plan and housing facility. *Payment plans:* installment, deferred payment. *Waivers:* senior citizens and employees or children of employees.

Financial Aid Of all full-time matriculated undergraduates who enrolled in 2009, 2,275 applied for aid, 2,129 were judged to have need, 475 had their need fully met. 598 Federal Work-Study jobs (averaging $2300). 149 state and other part-time jobs (averaging $2300). In 2009, 334 non-need-based awards were made. *Average percent of need met:* 76%. *Average financial aid package:* $20,647. *Average need-based loan:* $4251. *Average need-based gift aid:* $16,035. *Average non-need-based aid:* $9623. *Average indebtedness upon graduation:* $34,830.

Applying *Options:* electronic application, early admission, deferred entrance. *Application fee:* $25. *Required:* high school transcript, minimum 2 GPA. *Required for some:* minimum 3 GPA, 3 letters of recommendation, interview. *Recommended:* essay or personal statement, counselor's recommendation. *Application deadlines:* rolling (freshmen), rolling (transfers).

Freshman Application Contact Office of Admissions, Gannon University, 109 University Square, Erie, PA 16541. *Phone:* 814-871-7240. *Toll-free phone:* 800-GANNONU. *Fax:* 814-871-5803. *E-mail:* admissions@gannon.edu. *Web site:* http://www.gannon.edu/.

See page 1304 for the College Close-Up.

Geneva College
Beaver Falls, Pennsylvania

- **Independent** comprehensive, founded 1848, affiliated with Reformed Presbyterian Church of North America
- **Small-town** 55-acre campus with easy access to Pittsburgh
- **Endowment** $28.2 million
- **Coed** 1,445 undergraduate students, 98% full-time, 48% women, 52% men
- **Moderately difficult** entrance level, 80% of applicants were admitted

Undergraduates 1,415 full-time, 30 part-time. Students come from 37 states and territories; 8 other countries; 29% are from out of state; 4% Black or African American, non-Hispanic/Latino; 1% Hispanic/Latino; 1% Asian, non-Hispanic/Latino; 0.1% American Indian or Alaska Native, non-Hispanic/Latino; 1% Two or more races, non-Hispanic/Latino; 5% transferred in; 71% live on campus. *Retention:* 76% of full-time freshmen returned.

Freshmen *Admission:* 1,378 applied, 1,098 admitted, 412 enrolled. *Average high school GPA:* 3.47. *Test scores:* SAT critical reading scores over 500: 66%; SAT math scores over 500: 63%; ACT scores over 18: 93%; SAT critical reading scores over 600: 27%; SAT math scores over 600: 26%; ACT scores over 24: 39%; SAT critical reading scores over 700: 8%; SAT math scores over 700: 4%; ACT scores over 30: 7%.

Faculty *Total:* 171, 44% full-time. *Student/faculty ratio:* 13:1.

Academics *Calendar:* semesters. *Degrees:* associate, bachelor's, and master's (also offers non-traditional programs in Philadelphia and western Pennsylvania with significant enrollment not reflected in profile). *Special study options:* academic remediation for entering freshmen, accelerated degree program, adult/continuing education programs, advanced placement credit, cooperative education, double majors, English as a second language, honors programs, independent study, internships, off-campus study, part-time degree program,

services for LD students, student-designed majors, study abroad, summer session for credit. *ROTC:* Army (c). *Unusual degree programs:* 3-2 nursing with Roberts Wesleyan College; Master's of Divinity = with Reformed Presbyterian Theological Seminary.

Computers on Campus 150 computers/terminals and 400 ports are available on campus for general student use. Students can access the following: campus intranet, computer help desk, free student e-mail accounts, online (class) grades, online (class) registration, online (class) schedules. Campuswide network is available. 50% of college-owned or -operated housing units are wired for high-speed Internet access. Wireless service is available via entire campus.

Student Life *Housing:* on-campus residence required through senior year. *Options:* men-only, women-only. Campus housing is university owned. Freshman campus housing is guaranteed. *Activities and organizations:* drama/theater group, student-run newspaper, radio station, choral group, marching band, marching band, Genevans Choir, ministry groups, International Student Organization, discipleship. *Campus security:* 24-hour emergency response devices and patrols, late-night transport/escort service, controlled dormitory access. *Student services:* health clinic, personal/psychological counseling.

Athletics Member NCAA, NCCAA. All NCAA Division III. *Intercollegiate sports:* baseball M, basketball M/W, cross-country running M/W, football M, soccer M/W, softball W, tennis W, track and field M/W, volleyball M(c)/W. *Intramural sports:* basketball M/W, football M, ice hockey M(c), racquetball M/W, rugby M(c)/W(c), skiing (downhill) M(c)/W(c), soccer M/W, softball M/W, volleyball M/W.

Standardized Tests *Required:* SAT or ACT (for admission).

Costs (2010–11) *Comprehensive fee:* $30,236 includes full-time tuition ($22,236) and room and board ($8000). Full-time tuition and fees vary according to course load. Part-time tuition: $745 per credit. Part-time tuition and fees vary according to course load. *Room and board:* Room and board charges vary according to board plan. *Payment plan:* installment. *Waivers:* minority students and employees or children of employees.

Financial Aid Of all full-time matriculated undergraduates who enrolled in 2009, 1,367 applied for aid, 1,258 were judged to have need, 213 had their need fully met. 250 Federal Work-Study jobs (averaging $2000). In 2009, 200 non-need-based awards were made. *Average percent of need met:* 78%. *Average financial aid package:* $18,433. *Average need-based loan:* $4192. *Average need-based gift aid:* $14,096. *Average non-need-based aid:* $8179. *Average indebtedness upon graduation:* $24,000.

Applying *Options:* electronic application, early admission, early action, deferred entrance. *Application fee:* $40. *Required:* essay or personal statement, high school transcript, minimum 2 GPA. *Required for some:* interview. *Recommended:* minimum 3 GPA, 2 letters of recommendation, interview. *Application deadlines:* rolling (freshmen), rolling (transfers). *Notification:* continuous (freshmen), continuous (transfers).

Freshman Application Contact Mr. David Layton, Associate Vice President for Enrollment, Geneva College, 3200 College Avenue, Beaver Falls, PA 15010-3599. *Phone:* 724-847-6500. *Toll-free phone:* 800-847-8255. *E-mail:* admissions@geneva.edu. *Web site:* http://www.geneva.edu/.

Gettysburg College
Gettysburg, Pennsylvania

- **Independent** 4-year, founded 1832, affiliated with Evangelical Lutheran Church in America
- **Small-town** 200-acre campus with easy access to Baltimore and Washington, D.C.
- **Endowment** $215.2 million
- **Coed** 2,484 undergraduate students, 99% full-time, 53% women, 47% men
- **Most difficult** entrance level, 40% of applicants were admitted

Undergraduates 2,462 full-time, 22 part-time. Students come from 45 states and territories; 38 other countries; 75% are from out of state; 4% Black or African American, non-Hispanic/Latino; 4% Hispanic/Latino; 2% Asian, non-Hispanic/Latino; 0.1% American Indian or Alaska Native, non-Hispanic/Latino; 7% Race/ethnicity unknown; 2% international; 0.8% transferred in; 94% live on campus. *Retention:* 90% of full-time freshmen returned.

Freshmen *Admission:* 5,392 applied, 2,173 admitted, 731 enrolled. *Test scores:* SAT critical reading scores over 500: 100%; SAT math scores over 500: 100%; SAT critical reading scores over 600: 84%; SAT math scores over 600: 80%; SAT critical reading scores over 700: 19%; SAT math scores over 700: 13%.

Faculty *Total:* 291, 74% full-time, 77% with terminal degrees. *Student/faculty ratio:* 10:1.

Academics *Calendar:* semesters. *Degree:* bachelor's. *Special study options:* adult/continuing education programs, advanced placement credit, double majors, independent study, internships, off-campus study, student-designed majors, study abroad. *ROTC:* Army (c). *Unusual degree programs:* 3-2 engineering with Rensselaer Polytechnic Institute, Washington University, Columbia University; forestry with Duke University; nursing with Johns Hopkins University.

Computers on Campus Students can access the following: campus intranet, computer help desk, free student e-mail accounts, online (class) grades, online (class) registration, online (class) schedules. Campuswide network is available. 100% of college-owned or -operated housing units are wired for high-speed Internet access. Wireless service is available via entire campus.

Student Life *Housing:* on-campus residence required through senior year. *Options:* coed, men-only, women-only. Campus housing is university owned. Freshman campus housing is guaranteed. *Activities and organizations:* drama/theater group, student-run newspaper, radio and television station, choral group, marching band, community service, music, athletics, student government, national fraternities, national sororities. *Campus security:* 24-hour emergency response devices and patrols, late-night transport/escort service, controlled dormitory access. *Student services:* health clinic, personal/psychological counseling, women's center.

Athletics Member NCAA. All Division III. *Intercollegiate sports:* baseball M, basketball M/W, cheerleading M/W, cross-country running M/W, equestrian sports M(c)/W(c), field hockey W, football M, golf M/W, ice hockey M(c), lacrosse M/W, rugby M(c)/W(c), soccer M/W, softball W, swimming and diving M/W, tennis M/W, track and field M/W, ultimate Frisbee M(c)/W(c), volleyball W, water polo M(c)/W(c), wrestling M. *Intramural sports:* basketball M/W, cross-country running M/W, fencing M(c)/W(c), field hockey W, football M/W, golf M/W, lacrosse M/W, skiing (cross-country) M/W, skiing (downhill) M/W, soccer M/W, softball M/W, swimming and diving M/W, table tennis M/W, tennis M/W, track and field M/W, volleyball M/W, water polo M/W, wrestling M.

Standardized Tests *Required:* SAT or ACT (for admission). *Recommended:* SAT Subject Tests (for admission).

Costs (2010–11) *Comprehensive fee:* $50,880 includes full-time tuition ($41,070) and room and board ($9810). Full-time tuition and fees vary according to program. Part-time tuition and fees vary according to program. *College room only:* $5260. Room and board charges vary according to board plan and housing facility. *Payment plans:* tuition prepayment, installment. *Waivers:* employees or children of employees.

Financial Aid Of all full-time matriculated undergraduates who enrolled in 2009, 1,791 applied for aid, 1,485 were judged to have need, 1,425 had their need fully met. 740 Federal Work-Study jobs (averaging $919). 650 state and other part-time jobs (averaging $1250). In 2009, 359 non-need-based awards were made. *Average percent of need met:* 100%. *Average financial aid pack-age:* $32,938. *Average need-based loan:* $7139. *Average need-based gift aid:* $25,548. *Average non-need-based aid:* $11,498. *Average indebtedness upon graduation:* $24,981. *Financial aid deadline:* 2/15.

Applying *Options:* electronic application, early admission, early decision, deferred entrance. *Application fee:* $55. *Required:* essay or personal statement, high school transcript, 2 letters of recommendation. *Recommended:* minimum 3 GPA, interview, extracurricular activities. *Application deadlines:* 2/1 (freshmen), 11/1 (transfers). *Early decision deadline:* 11/15 (for plan 1), 1/15 (for plan 2). *Notification:* 4/1 (freshmen), continuous (transfers), 12/15 (early decision plan 1), 2/15 (early decision plan 2).

Freshman Application Contact Ms. Gail Sweezey, Director of Admissions, Gettysburg College, 300 North Washington Street, Gettysburg, PA 17325. *Phone:* 717-337-6100. *Toll-free phone:* 800-431-0803. *Fax:* 717-337-6145. *E-mail:* admiss@gettysburg.edu. *Web site:* http://www.gettysburg.edu/.

Gratz College

Melrose Park, Pennsylvania

Freshman Application Contact Admissions, Gratz College, 7605 Old York Road, Melrose Park, PA 19027. *Phone:* 215-635-7300. *Toll-free phone:* 800-475-4635. *Fax:* 215-635-1046. *E-mail:* admissions@gratz.edu. *Web site:* http://www.gratzcollege.edu/.

Grove City College

Grove City, Pennsylvania

- **Independent Presbyterian** 4-year, founded 1876
- **Small-town** 150-acre campus with easy access to Pittsburgh
- **Coed** 2,499 undergraduate students, 99% full-time, 50% women, 50% men
- **Very difficult** entrance level, 74% of applicants were admitted

Undergraduates 2,474 full-time, 25 part-time. Students come from 45 states and territories; 9 other countries; 53% are from out of state; 0.7% Black or African American, non-Hispanic/Latino; 2% Hispanic/Latino; 2% Asian, non-Hispanic/Latino; 0.1% American Indian or Alaska Native, non-Hispanic/Latino; 0.9% Two or more races, non-Hispanic/Latino; 0.6% international; 1%

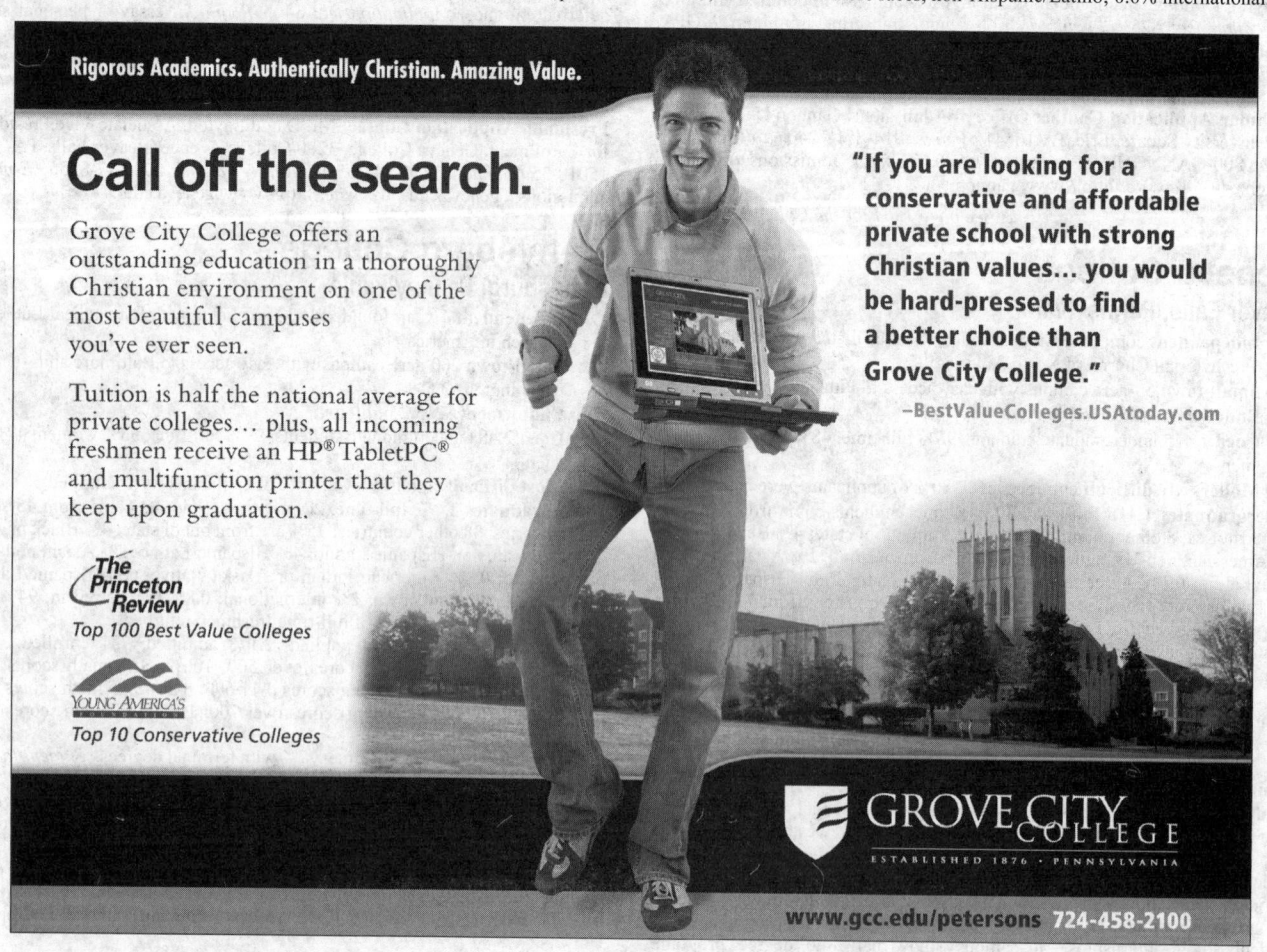

Rigorous Academics. Authentically Christian. Amazing Value.

Call off the search.

Grove City College offers an outstanding education in a thoroughly Christian environment on one of the most beautiful campuses you've ever seen.

Tuition is half the national average for private colleges... plus, all incoming freshmen receive an HP® TabletPC® and multifunction printer that they keep upon graduation.

The Princeton Review
Top 100 Best Value Colleges

YOUNG AMERICA'S
Top 10 Conservative Colleges

"If you are looking for a conservative and affordable private school with strong Christian values... you would be hard-pressed to find a better choice than Grove City College."

—BestValueColleges.USAtoday.com

GROVE CITY COLLEGE
ESTABLISHED 1876 · PENNSYLVANIA

www.gcc.edu/petersons   724-458-2100

transferred in; 94% live on campus. *Retention:* 91% of full-time freshmen returned.

Freshmen *Admission:* 1,660 applied, 1,222 admitted, 650 enrolled. *Average high school GPA:* 3.71. *Test scores:* SAT critical reading scores over 500: 97%; SAT math scores over 500: 98%; ACT scores over 18: 100%; SAT critical reading scores over 600: 68%; SAT math scores over 600: 65%; ACT scores over 24: 86%; SAT critical reading scores over 700: 21%; SAT math scores over 700: 14%; ACT scores over 30: 31%.

Faculty *Total:* 209, 61% full-time, 66% with terminal degrees. *Student/faculty ratio:* 16:1.

Academics *Calendar:* semesters. *Degree:* bachelor's. *Special study options:* advanced placement credit, double majors, independent study, internships, student-designed majors, study abroad. *ROTC:* Army (c).

Computers on Campus 50 computers/terminals are available on campus for general student use. Students can access the following: campus intranet, computer help desk, free student e-mail accounts, online (class) grades, online (class) registration, online (class) schedules. Campuswide network is available. 100% of college-owned or -operated housing units are wired for high-speed Internet access. Wireless service is available via classrooms, learning centers, student centers.

Student Life *Housing:* on-campus residence required through senior year. *Options:* men-only, women-only. Campus housing is university owned. Freshman campus housing is guaranteed. *Activities and organizations:* drama/theater group, student-run newspaper, radio and television station, choral group, marching band, Salt Company, Warriors for Christ, Orientation Board, Orchesis, Touring Choir. *Campus security:* 24-hour emergency response devices and patrols, student patrols, late-night transport/escort service, controlled dormitory access, security cameras located around campus and in parking lots. *Student services:* health clinic, personal/psychological counseling.

Athletics Member NCAA. All Division III. *Intercollegiate sports:* baseball M, basketball M/W, cheerleading W, cross-country running M/W, football M, golf M/W, soccer M/W, softball W, swimming and diving M/W, tennis M/W, track and field M/W, volleyball W, water polo W. *Intramural sports:* badminton M/W, basketball M/W, bowling M/W, football M, golf M/W, racquetball M/W, soccer W, softball M/W, table tennis M/W, tennis M/W, ultimate Frisbee M/W, volleyball M/W, weight lifting M.

Standardized Tests *Required:* SAT or ACT (for admission).

Costs (2010–11) *Comprehensive fee:* $20,220 includes full-time tuition ($13,088) and room and board ($7132). Full-time tuition and fees vary according to course load. Part-time tuition: $410 per credit hour. *Room and board:* Room and board charges vary according to housing facility. *Payment plan:* installment. *Waivers:* employees or children of employees.

Financial Aid Of all full-time matriculated undergraduates who enrolled in 2009, 1,235 applied for aid, 1,006 were judged to have need, 82 had their need fully met. In 2009, 266 non-need-based awards were made. *Average percent of need met:* 49%. *Average financial aid package:* $5820. *Average need-based gift aid:* $5820. *Average non-need-based aid:* $2298. *Average indebtedness upon graduation:* $25,773. *Financial aid deadline:* 4/15.

Applying *Options:* electronic application, early admission, early decision, deferred entrance. *Application fee:* $50. *Required:* essay or personal statement, high school transcript, 2 letters of recommendation. *Recommended:* interview. *Application deadlines:* 2/1 (freshmen), 8/15 (transfers). *Early decision deadline:* 11/15. *Notification:* 3/15 (freshmen), continuous (transfers), 12/15 (early decision).

Freshman Application Contact Mr. Jeffrey Mincey, Director of Admissions, Grove City College, 100 Campus Drive, Grove City, PA 16127-2104. *Phone:* 724-458-2100. *Fax:* 724-458-3395. *E-mail:* admissions@gcc.edu. *Web site:* http://www.gcc.edu/.

See page 1318 for the College Close-Up.

Gwynedd-Mercy College

Gwynedd Valley, Pennsylvania

- **Independent Roman Catholic** comprehensive, founded 1948
- **Suburban** 170-acre campus with easy access to Philadelphia
- **Endowment** $7.4 million
- **Coed**
- **Moderately difficult** entrance level

Faculty *Student/faculty ratio:* 13:1.

Academics *Calendar:* semesters. *Degrees:* certificates, associate, bachelor's, master's, post-master's, and postbachelor's certificates.

Student Life *Campus security:* 24-hour emergency response devices and patrols, late-night transport/escort service.

Athletics Member NCAA. All Division III.

Standardized Tests *Required:* SAT or ACT (for admission).

Costs (2010–11) *Comprehensive fee:* $35,420 includes full-time tuition ($25,160), mandatory fees ($500), and room and board ($9760). Full-time tuition and fees vary according to program. Part-time tuition: $515 per credit hour. Part-time tuition and fees vary according to program. *Required fees:* $10

per credit part-time. *Room and board:* Room and board charges vary according to board plan and housing facility.

Financial Aid Of all full-time matriculated undergraduates who enrolled in 2009, 1,308 applied for aid, 1,164 were judged to have need, 128 had their need fully met. 194 Federal Work-Study jobs (averaging $928). *In 2009,* 175 non-need-based awards were made. *Average percent of need met:* 71. *Average financial aid package:* $17,616. *Average need-based loan:* $4050. *Average need-based gift aid:* $14,042. *Average non-need-based aid:* $8925. *Average indebtedness upon graduation:* $34,520.

Applying *Options:* electronic application, deferred entrance. *Application fee:* $25. *Required:* high school transcript. *Required for some:* essay or personal statement, interview.

Freshman Application Contact Ms. Michelle Diehl, Director of Admissions, Gwynedd-Mercy College, 1325 Sumneytown Pike, Gwynedd Valley, PA 19437-0901. *Phone:* 215-646-7300. *Toll-free phone:* 800-DIAL-GMC. *Fax:* 215-641-5556. *E-mail:* admissions@gmc.edu. *Web site:* http://www.gmc.edu/ .

See page 1322 for the College Close-Up.

Harrisburg University of Science and Technology

Harrisburg, Pennsylvania

- **Independent** comprehensive, founded 2005
- **Urban** campus
- **Coed** 318 undergraduate students, 52% full-time, 52% women, 48% men
- **Minimally difficult** entrance level, 55% of applicants were admitted

Undergraduates 165 full-time, 153 part-time. Students come from 5 states and territories; 1 other country; 5% are from out of state; 7% transferred in. *Retention:* 60% of full-time freshmen returned.

Freshmen *Admission:* 163 applied, 89 admitted, 69 enrolled. *Average high school GPA:* 2.79.

Faculty *Total:* 27, 37% full-time, 44% with terminal degrees. *Student/faculty ratio:* 5:1.

Academics *Calendar:* semesters. *Degrees:* certificates, bachelor's, master's, and postbachelor's certificates. *Special study options:* academic remediation for entering students, adult/continuing education programs, advanced placement credit, double majors, independent study, internships, part-time degree program, services for LD students, student-designed majors, summer session for credit.

Computers on Campus 10 computers/terminals and 80 ports are available on campus for general student use. Students can access the following: campus intranet, computer help desk, free student e-mail accounts. Campuswide network is available. Wireless service is available via entire campus.

Student Life *Housing:* college housing not available. *Campus security:* 24-hour emergency response devices and patrols, trained security personnel during all university operating hours. *Student services:* personal/psychological counseling.

Standardized Tests *Recommended:* SAT or ACT (for admission).

Costs (2010–11) *Tuition:* $19,500 full-time, $850 per semester hour part-time. Part-time tuition and fees vary according to course load. *Payment plans:* installment, deferred payment.

Financial Aid Of all full-time matriculated undergraduates who enrolled in 2009, 10 Federal Work-Study jobs (averaging $1000). *Average percent of need met:* 49%. *Average financial aid package:* $13,708. *Average need-based gift aid:* $9894. *Average non-need-based aid:* $2812. *Average indebtedness upon graduation:* $21,500.

Applying *Options:* electronic application. *Required:* high school transcript. *Recommended:* essay or personal statement, interview. *Application deadline:* rolling (freshmen). *Notification:* continuous (freshmen).

Freshman Application Contact Harrisburg University of Science and Technology, 326 Market Street, Harrisburg, PA 17101. *Phone:* 717-901-5158. *Toll-free phone:* 866-HBG-UNIV. *Web site:* http://www.HarrisburgU.edu/.

Haverford College

Haverford, Pennsylvania

- **Independent** 4-year, founded 1833
- **Suburban** 200-acre campus with easy access to Philadelphia
- **Endowment** $355.5 million
- **Coed** 1,177 undergraduate students, 100% full-time, 53% women, 47% men
- **Most difficult** entrance level, 26% of applicants were admitted

Undergraduates 1,177 full-time. Students come from 45 states and territories; 33 other countries; 86% are from out of state; 7% Black or African American, non-Hispanic/Latino; 8% Hispanic/Latino; 8% Asian, non-Hispanic/Latino; 0.2% American Indian or Alaska Native, non-Hispanic/Latino; 5% Two or more races, non-Hispanic/Latino; 3% international; 0.4% transferred in; 99% live on campus. *Retention:* 96% of full-time freshmen returned.

Freshmen *Admission:* 3,312 applied, 860 admitted, 325 enrolled. *Test scores:* SAT critical reading scores over 500: 99%; SAT math scores over 500: 100%; SAT writing scores over 500: 100%; SAT critical reading scores over 600: 93%; SAT math scores over 600: 91%; SAT writing scores over 600: 91%; SAT critical reading scores over 700: 54%; SAT math scores over 700: 48%; SAT writing scores over 700: 54%.

Faculty *Total:* 139, 86% full-time, 91% with terminal degrees. *Student/faculty ratio:* 8:1.

Academics *Calendar:* semesters. *Degree:* bachelor's. *Special study options:* advanced placement credit, double majors, independent study, internships, off-campus study, services for LD students, student-designed majors, study abroad. *Unusual degree programs:* 3-2 engineering with California Institute of Technology.

Computers on Campus 300 computers/terminals and 1,600 ports are available on campus for general student use. Students can access the following: campus intranet, computer help desk, free student e-mail accounts, online (class) grades, online (class) registration, online (class) schedules. Campus-wide network is available. 100% of college-owned or -operated housing units are wired for high-speed Internet access. Wireless service is available via classrooms, computer centers, computer labs, dorm rooms, learning centers, libraries, student centers.

Student Life *Housing:* on-campus residence required for freshman year. *Options:* coed, disabled students. Campus housing is university owned. Freshman campus housing is guaranteed. *Activities and organizations:* drama/theater group, student-run newspaper, radio station, choral group, Volunteer Programs, student government, choral groups, Multicultural Groups, Orientation Team/Residential Life Leaders. *Campus security:* 24-hour emergency response devices and patrols, late-night transport/escort service, controlled dormitory access. *Student services:* health clinic, personal/psychological counseling, women's center.

Athletics Member NCAA. All Division III. *Intercollegiate sports:* badminton W(c), baseball M, basketball M/W, crew M(c)/W(c), cross-country running M/W, fencing M/W, field hockey W, golf M(c)/W(c), lacrosse M/W, rugby M(c), soccer M/W, softball W, squash M/W, tennis M/W, track and field M/W, ultimate Frisbee M(c)/W(c), volleyball M(c)/W, wrestling M(c). *Intramural sports:* basketball M/W, ice hockey M(c)/W(c), sailing M(c)/W(c), soccer M/W, softball M/W, tennis M/W, volleyball W.

Standardized Tests *Required:* SAT and SAT Subject Tests or ACT (for admission).

Costs (2010–11) *One-time required fee:* $200. *Comprehensive fee:* $52,970 includes full-time tuition ($40,260), mandatory fees ($364), and room and board ($12,346). *College room only:* $7026. *Payment plans:* tuition prepayment, installment. *Waivers:* employees or children of employees.

Financial Aid Of all full-time matriculated undergraduates who enrolled in 2009, 674 applied for aid, 616 were judged to have need, 616 had their need fully met. *Average percent of need met:* 100%. *Average financial aid package:* $37,509. *Average need-based loan:* $1274. *Average need-based gift aid:* $35,416. *Average indebtedness upon graduation:* $16,238. *Financial aid deadline:* 2/1.

Applying *Options:* electronic application, early admission, early decision, deferred entrance. *Application fee:* $60. *Required:* essay or personal statement, 2 letters of recommendation. *Required for some:* high school transcript. *Recommended:* interview. *Application deadlines:* 1/15 (freshmen), 3/31 (transfers). *Early decision deadline:* 11/15. *Notification:* 4/15 (freshmen), 6/1 (transfers), 12/15 (early decision).

Freshman Application Contact Mr. Jess Lord, Dean of Admissions and Financial Aid, Haverford College, 370 Lancaster Avenue, Haverford, PA 19041-1392. *Phone:* 610-896-1350. *Fax:* 610-896-1338. *E-mail:* admitme@haverford.edu. *Web site:* http://www.haverford.edu/.

Holy Family University
Philadelphia, Pennsylvania

- **Independent Roman Catholic** comprehensive, founded 1954
- **Suburban** 47-acre campus with easy access to Philadelphia
- **Endowment** $9.5 million
- **Coed** 2,176 undergraduate students, 73% full-time, 73% women, 27% men
- **Moderately difficult** entrance level, 72% of applicants were admitted

Undergraduates 1,597 full-time, 579 part-time. Students come from 18 states and territories; 9 other countries; 16% are from out of state; 6% Black or African American, non-Hispanic/Latino; 5% Hispanic/Latino; 5% Asian, non-Hispanic/Latino; 0.1% Native Hawaiian or other Pacific Islander, non-Hispanic/

Latino; 0.4% American Indian or Alaska Native, non-Hispanic/Latino; 16% Race/ethnicity unknown; 0.6% international; 10% transferred in; 18% live on campus. *Retention:* 75% of full-time freshmen returned.

Freshmen *Admission:* 1,284 applied, 924 admitted, 335 enrolled. *Average high school GPA:* 3.09. *Test scores:* SAT critical reading scores over 500: 39%; SAT math scores over 500: 33%; ACT scores over 18: 86%; SAT critical reading scores over 600: 6%; SAT math scores over 600: 6%.

Faculty *Total:* 259, 35% full-time, 53% with terminal degrees. *Student/faculty ratio:* 12:1.

Academics *Calendar:* semesters. *Degrees:* certificates, associate, bachelor's, master's, doctoral-professional, post-master's, and postbachelor's certificates. *Special study options:* academic remediation for entering students, accelerated degree program, adult/continuing education programs, advanced placement credit, cooperative education, double majors, English as a second language, freshman honors college, honors programs, independent study, internships, part-time degree program, services for LD students, study abroad, summer session for credit.

Computers on Campus 900 computers/terminals and 1,000 ports are available on campus for general student use. Students can access the following: campus intranet, computer help desk, free student e-mail accounts, online (class) grades, online (class) registration, online (class) schedules. Campuswide network is available. 100% of college-owned or -operated housing units are wired for high-speed Internet access. Wireless service is available via entire campus.

Student Life *Housing options:* coed, cooperative, disabled students. Campus housing is university owned. Freshman applicants given priority for college housing. *Activities and organizations:* drama/theater group, student-run newspaper, television station, choral group, Students at Your Service (S.A.Y.S.), student government, Campus Ministry Team, Habitat for Humanity, Tri-lite. *Campus security:* 24-hour emergency response devices and patrols, late-night transport/escort service, controlled dormitory access, video surveillance. *Student services:* health clinic, personal/psychological counseling.

Athletics Member NCAA. All Division II. *Intercollegiate sports:* basketball M(s)/W(s), cheerleading W, cross-country running M(s)/W(s), golf M(s), lacrosse W(s), soccer M(s)/W(s), softball W(s), tennis W(s), track and field M(s)/W(s), volleyball W(s). *Intramural sports:* basketball M/W, football M, racquetball M/W, rugby M, table tennis M/W, ultimate Frisbee M/W, volleyball M/W.

Standardized Tests *Required:* SAT or ACT (for admission).

Costs (2011–12) *Comprehensive fee:* $36,300 includes full-time tuition ($23,900), mandatory fees ($650), and room and board ($11,750). Full-time tuition and fees vary according to course load and program. Part-time tuition: $515 per credit. Part-time tuition and fees vary according to course load and program. *Required fees:* $60 per term part-time. *College room only:* $6500. Room and board charges vary according to board plan and housing facility. *Payment plans:* installment, deferred payment. *Waivers:* senior citizens and employees or children of employees.

Financial Aid Of all full-time matriculated undergraduates who enrolled in 2009, 1,447 applied for aid, 1,284 were judged to have need, 216 had their need fully met. 324 Federal Work-Study jobs (averaging $1518). In 2009, 124 non-need-based awards were made. *Average percent of need met:* 71%. *Average financial aid package:* $16,005. *Average need-based loan:* $4351. *Average need-based gift aid:* $11,705. *Average non-need-based aid:* $8093. *Average indebtedness upon graduation:* $31,855.

Applying *Options:* electronic application, deferred entrance. *Application fee:* $25. *Required:* essay or personal statement, high school transcript, minimum 2 GPA, 2 letters of recommendation. *Recommended:* interview. *Application deadlines:* rolling (freshmen), rolling (out-of-state freshmen), rolling (transfers). *Notification:* continuous (freshmen), continuous (out-of-state freshmen), continuous (transfers).

Freshman Application Contact Ms. Lauren Campbell, Director of Admissions, Holy Family University, 9801 Frankford Avenue, Philadelphia, PA 19114-2009. *Phone:* 215-637-3050. *Toll-free phone:* 800-637-1191. *Fax:* 215-281-1022. *E-mail:* admissions@holyfamily.edu. *Web site:* http://www.holyfamily.edu/.

See page 1334 for the College Close-Up.

Immaculata University
Immaculata, Pennsylvania

- **Independent Roman Catholic** comprehensive, founded 1920
- **Suburban** 400-acre campus with easy access to Philadelphia
- **Coed, primarily women** 3,223 undergraduate students, 38% full-time, 76% women, 24% men
- **Moderately difficult** entrance level, 78% of applicants were admitted

Undergraduates 1,239 full-time, 1,984 part-time. 25% are from out of state; 15% Black or African American, non-Hispanic/Latino; 3% Hispanic/Latino; 3% Asian, non-Hispanic/Latino; 0.2% Native Hawaiian or other Pacific Islander, non-Hispanic/Latino; 0.4% American Indian or Alaska Native, non-

Hispanic/Latino; 1% Two or more races, non-Hispanic/Latino; 2% Race/ethnicity unknown; 0.8% international; 3% transferred in; 18% live on campus. *Retention:* 84% of full-time freshmen returned.

Freshmen *Admission:* 1,534 applied, 1,195 admitted, 278 enrolled. *Average high school GPA:* 3.06. *Test scores:* SAT critical reading scores over 500: 32%; SAT math scores over 500: 28%; SAT writing scores over 500: 31%; ACT scores over 18: 70%; SAT critical reading scores over 600: 10%; SAT math scores over 600: 7%; SAT writing scores over 600: 10%; ACT scores over 24: 10%; SAT critical reading scores over 700: 2%; SAT writing scores over 700: 1%; ACT scores over 30: 7%.

Faculty *Total:* 423, 24% full-time. *Student/faculty ratio:* 10:1.

Academics *Calendar:* semesters. *Degrees:* certificates, associate, bachelor's, master's, and doctoral-research/scholarship. *Special study options:* academic remediation for entering students, accelerated degree program, advanced placement credit, distance learning, double majors, honors programs, independent study, internships, off-campus study, services for LD students, study abroad, summer session for credit. *ROTC:* Army (c).

Computers on Campus Campuswide network is available.

Student Life *Housing options:* coed, men-only, women-only, disabled students. Campus housing is university owned. Freshman campus housing is guaranteed. *Activities and organizations:* drama/theater group, student-run newspaper, choral group. *Campus security:* 24-hour emergency response devices and patrols, late-night transport/escort service, controlled dormitory access. *Student services:* health clinic, personal/psychological counseling.

Athletics Member NCAA. All Division III. *Intercollegiate sports:* basketball W, cross-country running W, field hockey W, lacrosse W, soccer W, softball W, tennis W, volleyball W. *Intramural sports:* archery W, badminton W, cheerleading W(c), equestrian sports W(c), fencing W, swimming and diving W.

Standardized Tests *Required:* SAT or ACT (for admission).

Costs (2010–11) *Comprehensive fee:* $39,330 includes full-time tuition ($27,870) and room and board ($11,460). Full-time tuition and fees vary according to student level. Part-time tuition: $440 per credit hour. No tuition increase for student's term of enrollment. *College room only:* $6160. Room and board charges vary according to board plan and housing facility. *Payment plan:* installment. *Waivers:* senior citizens and employees or children of employees.

Financial Aid Of all full-time matriculated undergraduates who enrolled in 2007, 810 applied for aid, 697 were judged to have need, 201 had their need fully met. *Average percent of need met:* 24%. *Average financial aid package:* $15,657. *Average need-based loan:* $4132. *Average need-based gift aid:* $5516. *Average non-need-based aid:* $6508.

Applying *Options:* electronic application. *Application fee:* $35. *Required:* high school transcript, minimum 2 GPA. *Required for some:* essay or personal statement. *Recommended:* minimum 3 GPA, interview. *Application deadlines:* rolling (freshmen), rolling (transfers). *Notification:* continuous (freshmen), continuous (transfers).

Freshman Application Contact Director of Admissions, Immaculata University, PO Box 642, Immaculata, PA 19345-0702. *Phone:* 610-647-4400 Ext. 3046. *Toll-free phone:* 877-428-6329. *Fax:* 610-640-0836. *E-mail:* admiss@immaculata.edu. *Web site:* http://www.immaculata.edu/.

See page 730 for Display. See page 1346 for the College Close-Up.

Indiana University of Pennsylvania
Indiana, Pennsylvania

- **State-supported** university, founded 1875, part of Pennsylvania State System of Higher Education
- **Small-town** 374-acre campus with easy access to Pittsburgh
- **Endowment** $34.4 million
- **Coed** 12,827 undergraduate students, 93% full-time, 56% women, 44% men
- **Moderately difficult** entrance level, 60% of applicants were admitted

Undergraduates 11,932 full-time, 895 part-time. Students come from 38 states and territories; 51 other countries; 6% are from out of state; 11% Black or African American, non-Hispanic/Latino; 2% Hispanic/Latino; 1% Asian, non-Hispanic/Latino; 0.2% American Indian or Alaska Native, non-Hispanic/Latino; 0.6% Two or more races, non-Hispanic/Latino; 4% Race/ethnicity unknown; 1% international; 5% transferred in. *Retention:* 75% of full-time freshmen returned.

Freshmen *Admission:* 12,114 applied, 7,294 admitted, 2,995 enrolled. *Test scores:* SAT critical reading scores over 500: 44%; SAT math scores over 500: 50%; SAT writing scores over 500: 36%; SAT critical reading scores over 600: 8%; SAT math scores over 600: 10%; SAT writing scores over 600: 6%; SAT critical reading scores over 700: 1%; SAT math scores over 700: 1%; SAT writing scores over 700: 1%.

Faculty *Total:* 701, 89% full-time. *Student/faculty ratio:* 18:1.

Academics *Calendar:* semesters. *Degrees:* certificates, associate, bachelor's, master's, doctoral-research/scholarship, post-master's, and postbachelor's certificates. *Special study options:* academic remediation for entering students, accelerated degree program, adult/continuing education programs, advanced placement credit, cooperative education, distance learning, double majors, English as a second language, freshman honors college, honors programs, independent study, internships, off-campus study, part-time degree program, services for LD students, study abroad, summer session for credit. *ROTC:* Army (b). *Unusual degree programs:* 3-2 engineering with Drexel University, University of Pittsburgh; forestry with Duke University; chiropractic with Logan College of Chiropractic, New York Chiropractic College, Parker College of Straight Chiropractic; dentistry with Temple University School of Dentistry; optometry with Pennsylvania College of Optometry.

Computers on Campus 1,200 computers/terminals and 8,000 ports are available on campus for general student use. Students can access the following: computer help desk, free student e-mail accounts, online (class) registration, online (class) schedules. Campuswide network is available. 100% of college-owned or -operated housing units are wired for high-speed Internet access. Wireless service is available via entire campus.

Student Life *Housing:* on-campus residence required for freshman year. *Options:* coed, women-only, disabled students. Campus housing is university owned and is provided by a third party. Freshman campus housing is guaranteed. *Activities and organizations:* drama/theater group, student-run newspaper, radio and television station, choral group, marching band, Student Government Association, Panhellenic Association, Interfraternity Council, NAACP, Alpha Phi Omega, national fraternities, national sororities. *Campus security:* 24-hour emergency response devices and patrols, late-night transport/escort service, controlled dormitory access. *Student services:* health clinic, personal/psychological counseling, women's center, legal services.

Athletics Member NCAA. All Division II. *Intercollegiate sports:* baseball M(s), basketball M(s)/W(s), cross-country running M(s)/W(s), field hockey W(s), football M(s), golf M(s), lacrosse W(s), soccer W(s), softball W(s), swimming and diving M(s)/W(s), tennis W(s), track and field M(s)/W(s), volleyball W(s). *Intramural sports:* basketball M/W, bowling M/W, cheerleading M(c)/W(c), equestrian sports M(c)/W(c), fencing M(c), football M/W, golf M/W, gymnastics M(c)/W(c), ice hockey W(c), lacrosse M(c), racquetball M/W, riflery M(c)/W(c), rugby M(c)/W(c), sailing M(c)/W(c), skiing (downhill) M(c)/W(c), soccer M(c)/W(c), softball M/W, swimming and diving M(c)/W(c), tennis M(c)/W(c), track and field M(c)/W(c), ultimate Frisbee M(c)/W(c), volleyball M(c)/W.

Standardized Tests *Required:* SAT or ACT (for admission).

Costs (2010–11) *Tuition:* state resident $5804 full-time, $242 per credit hour part-time; nonresident $14,510 full-time, $605 per credit hour part-time. Full-time tuition and fees vary according to course load and reciprocity agreements. Part-time tuition and fees vary according to course load and reciprocity agreements. *Required fees:* $1767 full-time, $24 per credit hour part-time, $262 per term part-time. *Room and board:* $9300; room only: $6840. Room and board charges vary according to board plan, housing facility, and location. *Payment plans:* installment, deferred payment. *Waivers:* senior citizens and employees or children of employees.

Financial Aid Of all full-time matriculated undergraduates who enrolled in 2008, 9,293 applied for aid, 7,380 were judged to have need, 725 had their need fully met. 1,158 Federal Work-Study jobs (averaging $1827). 1,767 state and other part-time jobs (averaging $2550). In 2008, 383 non-need-based awards were made. *Average percent of need met:* 70%. *Average financial aid package:* $8991. *Average need-based loan:* $4093. *Average need-based gift aid:* $5035. *Average non-need-based aid:* $2705. *Average indebtedness upon graduation:* $25,224. *Financial aid deadline:* 4/15.

Applying *Options:* electronic application, early admission, deferred entrance. *Application fee:* $40. *Required:* high school transcript. *Recommended:* essay or personal statement, 2 letters of recommendation. *Application deadlines:* rolling (freshmen), rolling (transfers). *Notification:* 9/1 (freshmen), continuous (transfers).

Freshman Application Contact Office of Admissions, Indiana University of Pennsylvania, 1011 South Drive, Sutton Hall 214, Indiana, PA 15705. *Phone:* 724-357-2230. *Toll-free phone:* 800-442-6830. *Fax:* 724-357-6281. *E-mail:* admissions-inquiry@iup.edu. *Web site:* http://www.iup.edu/.

Juniata College

Huntingdon, Pennsylvania

- **Independent** 4-year, founded 1876, affiliated with Church of the Brethren
- **Small-town** 110-acre campus
- **Endowment** $64.1 million
- **Coed** 1,593 undergraduate students, 96% full-time, 56% women, 44% men
- **Moderately difficult** entrance level, 72% of applicants were admitted

Undergraduates 1,527 full-time, 66 part-time. Students come from 38 states and territories; 38 other countries; 30% are from out of state; 2% Black or African American, non-Hispanic/Latino; 2% Hispanic/Latino; 2% Asian, non-Hispanic/Latino; 0.1% American Indian or Alaska Native, non-Hispanic/Latino; 1% Two or more races, non-Hispanic/Latino; 3% Race/ethnicity unknown; 8% international; 1% transferred in; 80% live on campus. *Retention:* 84% of full-time freshmen returned.

Freshmen *Admission:* 2,198 applied, 1,592 admitted, 421 enrolled. *Average high school GPA:* 3.75. *Test scores:* SAT critical reading scores over 500: 86%; SAT math scores over 500: 90%; SAT critical reading scores over 600: 48%; SAT math scores over 600: 49%; SAT critical reading scores over 700: 12%; SAT math scores over 700: 10%.

Faculty *Total:* 150, 68% full-time, 72% with terminal degrees. *Student/faculty ratio:* 13:1.

Academics *Calendar:* semesters. *Degree:* bachelor's. *Special study options:* accelerated degree program, advanced placement credit, double majors, English as a second language, freshman honors college, honors programs, independent study, internships, off-campus study, part-time degree program, services for LD students, student-designed majors, study abroad, summer session for credit. *Unusual degree programs:* 3-2 engineering with Columbia University, Penn State University, Washington University-St. Louis, Clarkson University; nursing with Case Western University, Johns Hopkins University.

Computers on Campus 340 computers/terminals and 500 ports are available on campus for general student use. Students can access the following: computer help desk, free student e-mail accounts, online (class) grades, online (class) registration, online (class) schedules. Campuswide network is available. 100% of college-owned or -operated housing units are wired for high-speed Internet access. Wireless service is available via classrooms, computer centers, computer labs, dorm rooms, learning centers, libraries, student centers.

Student Life *Housing:* on-campus residence required through senior year. *Options:* coed, women-only. Campus housing is university owned. Freshman campus housing is guaranteed. *Activities and organizations:* drama/theater group, student-run newspaper, radio and television station, choral group, student government, Juniata Activities Board (JAB), Colleges Against Cancer, habitat for Humanity, Model UN. *Campus security:* 24-hour emergency response devices and patrols, student patrols, late-night transport/escort service, controlled dormitory access, fire safety training, adopt-an-officer program, security web site, weather/terror alerts, travel forecast, crime statistics. *Student services:* health clinic, personal/psychological counseling, women's center.

Athletics Member NCAA. All Division III. *Intercollegiate sports:* baseball M, basketball M/W, cross-country running M/W, equestrian sports M(c)/W(c), field hockey W, football M, golf M(c)/W(c), lacrosse M(c), rugby M(c)/W(c), soccer M/W, softball W, swimming and diving W, tennis M/W, track and field M/W, ultimate Frisbee M(c)/W(c), volleyball M/W. *Intramural sports:* basketball M/W, cheerleading W(c), field hockey M(c)/W(c), lacrosse W(c), racquetball M(c)/W(c), skiing (downhill) M(c)/W(c), soccer M/W, volleyball M(c)/W(c).

Standardized Tests *Recommended:* SAT or ACT (for admission).

Costs (2011–12) *Comprehensive fee:* $43,420 includes full-time tuition ($33,370), mandatory fees ($720), and room and board ($9330). Part-time tuition: $1385 per credit hour. *College room only:* $4920. Room and board charges vary according to board plan. *Payment plan:* installment. *Waivers:* adult students, senior citizens, and employees or children of employees.

Financial Aid Of all full-time matriculated undergraduates who enrolled in 2009, 1,199 applied for aid, 1,076 were judged to have need, 233 had their need fully met. 352 Federal Work-Study jobs (averaging $644). 365 state and other part-time jobs (averaging $1022). In 2009, 402 non-need-based awards were made. *Average percent of need met:* 82%. *Average financial aid package:* $24,962. *Average need-based loan:* $4745. *Average need-based gift aid:* $19,811. *Average non-need-based aid:* $14,471. *Average indebtedness upon graduation:* $23,637. *Financial aid deadline:* 3/1.

Applying *Options:* electronic application, early admission, early decision, early action, deferred entrance. *Application fee:* $30. *Required:* essay or personal statement, high school transcript, minimum 3 GPA, 1 letter of recommendation. *Recommended:* interview. *Application deadlines:* 3/15 (freshmen), 6/15 (transfers), 1/1 (early action). *Early decision deadline:* 12/1. *Notification:* continuous (freshmen), continuous (transfers), 12/31 (early decision), 1/30 (early action).

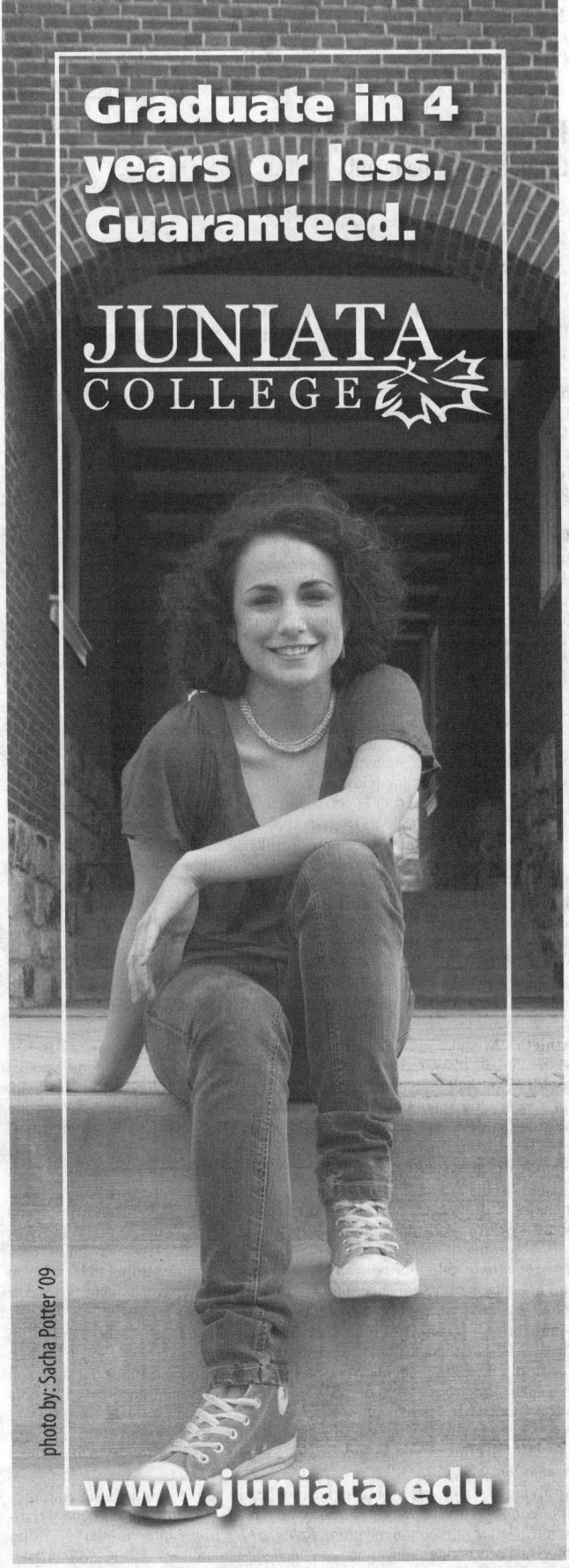

Graduate in 4 years or less. Guaranteed.

JUNIATA COLLEGE

photo by: Sacha Potter '09

www.juniata.edu

Freshman Application Contact Terri Bollman-Dalansky, Director of Admissions, Juniata College, 1700 Moore Street, Huntingdon, PA 16652-2119. *Phone:* 814-641-3424. *Toll-free phone:* 877-JUNIATA. *Fax:* 814-641-3100. *E-mail:* admissions@juniata.edu. *Web site:* http://www.juniata.edu/.

See page 1360 for the College Close-Up.

Keystone College
La Plume, Pennsylvania

- **Independent** 4-year, founded 1868
- **Small-town** 270-acre campus
- **Endowment** $6.6 million
- **Coed** 1,707 undergraduate students, 79% full-time, 60% women, 40% men
- **Minimally difficult** entrance level, 94% of applicants were admitted

Undergraduates 1,354 full-time, 353 part-time. Students come from 14 states and territories; 9 other countries; 11% are from out of state; 4% Black or African American, non-Hispanic/Latino; 2% Hispanic/Latino; 1% Asian, non-Hispanic/Latino; 0.2% Native Hawaiian or other Pacific Islander, non-Hispanic/Latino; 0.2% American Indian or Alaska Native, non-Hispanic/Latino; 0.7% Two or more races, non-Hispanic/Latino; 20% Race/ethnicity unknown; 0.5% international; 9% transferred in; 17% live on campus. *Retention:* 65% of full-time freshmen returned.
Freshman *Admission:* 1,138 applied, 1,068 admitted, 357 enrolled. *Test scores:* ACT scores over 18: 55%; ACT scores over 24: 10%.
Faculty *Total:* 265, 26% full-time, 22% with terminal degrees. *Student/faculty ratio:* 11:1.
Academics *Calendar:* semesters. *Degrees:* certificates, associate, bachelor's, and postbachelor's certificates. *Special study options:* academic remediation for entering students, adult/continuing education programs, advanced placement credit, cooperative education, distance learning, double majors, English as a second language, honors programs, independent study, internships, part-time degree program, services for LD students, study abroad, summer session for credit. *ROTC:* Army (c), Air Force (c).
Computers on Campus 100 computers/terminals are available on campus for general student use. Students can access the following: campus intranet, computer help desk, free student e-mail accounts, online (class) grades, online (class) registration, online (class) schedules. Campuswide network is available. 100% of college-owned or -operated housing units are wired for high-speed Internet access. Wireless service is available via entire campus.
Student Life *Housing:* on-campus residence required for freshman year. *Options:* coed, women-only, disabled students. Campus housing is university owned. Freshman campus housing is guaranteed. *Activities and organizations:* drama/theater group, student-run newspaper, radio station, choral group, Art Society, Inter-Hall Council, O.P.E.N. (Opposing Prejudice Ending Negativity), S.M.A.R.T. (Sports Management and Recreation Team), Keystone College Mofyah Step Team. *Campus security:* 24-hour emergency response devices and patrols, student patrols, late-night transport/escort service, controlled dormitory access. *Student services:* health clinic, personal/psychological counseling, women's center.
Athletics Member NCAA. All Division III. *Intercollegiate sports:* baseball M, basketball M/W, cross-country running M/W, field hockey W, golf M, soccer M/W, softball W, tennis M/W, track and field M/W, volleyball W. *Intramural sports:* basketball M/W, cheerleading M(c)/W(c), football M/W, skiing (downhill) M/W, soccer M/W, softball M/W, table tennis M/W, tennis M/W, wrestling M(c).
Standardized Tests *Required:* SAT or ACT (for admission).
Costs (2011–12) *One-time required fee:* $300. *Comprehensive fee:* $28,820 includes full-time tuition ($18,770), mandatory fees ($850), and room and board ($9200). *Part-time tuition:* $400 per credit. Part-time tuition and fees vary according to course load. *Required fees:* $200 per term part-time. *College room only:* $4650. Room and board charges vary according to board plan and housing facility. *Payment plans:* installment, deferred payment. *Waivers:* senior citizens and employees or children of employees.
Financial Aid Of all full-time matriculated undergraduates who enrolled in 2008, 1,123 applied for aid, 1,033 were judged to have need, 352 had their need fully met. 202 Federal Work-Study jobs (averaging $1450). 50 state and other part-time jobs (averaging $1450). In 2008, 39 non-need-based awards were made. *Average percent of need met:* 77%. *Average financial aid package:* $22,554. *Average need-based loan:* $6500. *Average need-based gift aid:* $20,719. *Average non-need-based aid:* $11,868. *Average indebtedness upon graduation:* $24,750.
Applying *Options:* electronic application, early admission, deferred entrance. *Application fee:* $30. *Required:* essay or personal statement, high school transcript, 1 letter of recommendation. *Required for some:* interview, art portfolio for visual arts and art education. *Recommended:* interview. *Application deadlines:* 7/15 (freshmen), 8/1 (transfers). *Notification:* continuous (freshmen), continuous (transfers).

Freshman Application Contact Jessica Lopez, Senior Administrative Assistant, Keystone College, One College Green, PO Box 50, La Plume, PA 18440-1099. *Phone:* 570-945-8111. *Toll-free phone:* 877-4COLLEGE Ext. 1. *Fax:* 570-945-7916. *E-mail:* admissions@keystone.edu. *Web site:* http://www.keystone.edu/.

See page 1368 for the College Close-Up.

King's College
Wilkes-Barre, Pennsylvania

- **Independent Roman Catholic** comprehensive, founded 1946
- **Urban** 48-acre campus
- **Endowment** $48.4 million
- **Coed** 2,356 undergraduate students, 85% full-time, 50% women, 50% men
- **Moderately difficult** entrance level, 74% of applicants were admitted

Undergraduates 1,999 full-time, 357 part-time. Students come from 20 states and territories; 6 other countries; 28% are from out of state; 3% Black or African American, non-Hispanic/Latino; 5% Hispanic/Latino; 1% Asian, non-Hispanic/Latino; 0.2% American Indian or Alaska Native, non-Hispanic/Latino; 0.3% Two or more races, non-Hispanic/Latino; 9% Race/ethnicity unknown; 0.3% international; 3% transferred in; 53% live on campus. *Retention:* 79% of full-time freshmen returned.
Freshmen *Admission:* 2,420 applied, 1,796 admitted, 528 enrolled. *Average high school GPA:* 3.3. *Test scores:* SAT critical reading scores over 500: 56%; SAT math scores over 500: 61%; SAT writing scores over 500: 56%; SAT critical reading scores over 600: 13%; SAT math scores over 600: 14%; SAT writing scores over 600: 12%; SAT math scores over 700: 2%.
Faculty *Total:* 230, 57% full-time, 58% with terminal degrees. *Student/faculty ratio:* 13:1.
Academics *Calendar:* semesters. *Degrees:* certificates, associate, bachelor's, master's, and postbachelor's certificates. *Special study options:* accelerated degree program, adult/continuing education programs, advanced placement credit, distance learning, double majors, English as a second language, honors programs, independent study, internships, off-campus study, part-time degree program, services for LD students, student-designed majors, study abroad, summer session for credit. *ROTC:* Army (b), Air Force (c).
Computers on Campus 470 computers/terminals are available on campus for general student use. Students can access the following: computer help desk, free student e-mail accounts, online (class) grades, online (class) registration, online (class) schedules. Campuswide network is available. 100% of college-owned or -operated housing units are wired for high-speed Internet access. Wireless service is available via classrooms, computer labs, libraries, student centers.
Student Life *Housing:* on-campus residence required through sophomore year. *Options:* coed, men-only, women-only, cooperative, disabled students. Campus housing is university owned. Freshman campus housing is guaranteed. *Activities and organizations:* drama/theater group, student-run newspaper, radio station, choral group, Association of Campus Events, Student Government Association, Accounting Association, International/Multicultural Club, Biology Club. *Campus security:* 24-hour emergency response devices and patrols, student patrols, late-night transport/escort service, bicycle patrols. *Student services:* health clinic, personal/psychological counseling, women's center.
Athletics Member NCAA. All Division III. *Intercollegiate sports:* baseball M, basketball M/W, cheerleading M/W, cross-country running M/W, field hockey W, football M, golf M, lacrosse M/W, soccer M/W, softball W, swimming and diving M/W, tennis M/W, volleyball W, wrestling M. *Intramural sports:* basketball M/W, ice hockey M(c), soccer M/W, track and field M(c)/W(c).
Standardized Tests *Recommended:* SAT or ACT (for admission).
Costs (2010–11) *Comprehensive fee:* $36,712 includes full-time tuition ($26,644) and room and board ($10,068). *Part-time tuition:* $495 per credit hour. *College room only:* $4808. Room and board charges vary according to board plan. *Payment plans:* installment, deferred payment. *Waivers:* senior citizens and employees or children of employees.
Financial Aid Of all full-time matriculated undergraduates who enrolled in 2009, 1,812 applied for aid, 1,668 were judged to have need, 260 had their need fully met. 290 Federal Work-Study jobs (averaging $1178). 333 state and other part-time jobs (averaging $1099). In 2009, 294 non-need-based awards were made. *Average percent of need met:* 72%. *Average financial aid package:* $19,426. *Average need-based loan:* $4796. *Average need-based gift aid:* $14,831. *Average non-need-based aid:* $11,719. *Average indebtedness upon graduation:* $31,113.
Applying *Options:* electronic application, deferred entrance. *Application fee:* $30. *Required:* essay or personal statement, high school transcript. *Recommended:* interview. *Application deadlines:* rolling (freshmen), rolling (out-of-state freshmen), rolling (transfers). *Notification:* continuous (freshmen), continuous (out-of-state freshmen), continuous (transfers).

Freshman Application Contact Mr. James Anderson, Director of Admission, King's College, 133 North River Street, Wilkes-Barre, PA 18711-0801. *Phone:* 570-208-5858. *Toll-free phone:* 888-KINGSPA. *Fax:* 570-208-5971. *E-mail:* admissions@kings.edu. *Web site:* http://www.kings.edu/.

See page 1370 for the College Close-Up.

Kutztown University of Pennsylvania

Kutztown, Pennsylvania

- **State-supported** comprehensive, founded 1866, part of Pennsylvania State System of Higher Education
- **Rural** 289-acre campus with easy access to Philadelphia
- **Endowment** $14.3 million
- **Coed** 9,728 undergraduate students, 91% full-time, 58% women, 42% men
- **Moderately difficult** entrance level, 63% of applicants were admitted

Undergraduates 8,848 full-time, 880 part-time. Students come from 23 states and territories; 50 other countries; 10% are from out of state; 6% Black or African American, non-Hispanic/Latino; 5% Hispanic/Latino; 1% Asian, non-Hispanic/Latino; 0.3% American Indian or Alaska Native, non-Hispanic/Latino; 0.5% Two or more races, non-Hispanic/Latino; 2% Race/ethnicity unknown; 0.8% international; 8% transferred in; 47% live on campus. *Retention:* 77% of full-time freshmen returned.

Freshmen *Admission:* 10,142 applied, 6,429 admitted, 2,013 enrolled. *Average high school GPA:* 3.03. *Test scores:* SAT critical reading scores over 500: 41%; SAT math scores over 500: 43%; SAT writing scores over 500: 35%; ACT scores over 18: 80%; SAT critical reading scores over 600: 8%; SAT math scores over 600: 8%; SAT writing scores over 600: 5%; ACT scores over 24: 16%; SAT critical reading scores over 700: 1%; SAT math scores over 700: 1%; ACT scores over 30: 1%.

Faculty *Total:* 476, 90% full-time, 77% with terminal degrees. *Student/faculty ratio:* 20:1.

Academics *Calendar:* semesters. *Degrees:* bachelor's, master's, and post-bachelor's certificates. *Special study options:* academic remediation for entering students, accelerated degree program, adult/continuing education programs, advanced placement credit, distance learning, double majors, honors programs, independent study, internships, off-campus study, part-time degree program, services for LD students, student-designed majors, study abroad, summer session for credit. *ROTC:* Army (c). *Unusual degree programs:* 3-2 engineering with Pennsylvania State University–University Park Campus.

Computers on Campus 1,075 computers/terminals and 100 ports are available on campus for general student use. Students can access the following: computer help desk, free student e-mail accounts, online (class) grades, online (class) registration, online (class) schedules. Campuswide network is available. 100% of college-owned or -operated housing units are wired for high-speed Internet access. Wireless service is available via classrooms, learning centers, libraries, student centers.

Student Life *Housing options:* coed, women-only, cooperative. Campus housing is university owned and leased by the school. Freshman campus housing is guaranteed. *Activities and organizations:* drama/theater group, student-run newspaper, radio and television station, choral group, marching band, Student Government Board, Student Pennsylvania State Education Association, National Art Education Association, Residence Hall Association, Association of Campus Events, national fraternities, national sororities. *Campus security:* 24-hour emergency response devices and patrols, student patrols, late-night transport/escort service, secondary door electronic alarm system in residence halls, 24-hour student desk personnel at main entrance of residence halls. *Student services:* health clinic, personal/psychological counseling, women's center.

Athletics Member NCAA. All Division II. *Intercollegiate sports:* baseball M(s), basketball M(s)/W(s), bowling W(s), cheerleading W(c), cross-country running M(s)/W(s), equestrian sports M(c)/W(c), field hockey W(s), football M(s), golf W(s), ice hockey M(c), lacrosse M(c)/W(s), rugby M(c)/W(c), skiing (downhill) M(c)/W(c), soccer M(c)/W(s), softball W(s), swimming and diving W(s), tennis M(s)/W(s), track and field M(s)/W(s), ultimate Frisbee M(c)/W(c), volleyball M(c)/W(s), wrestling M(s). *Intramural sports:* basketball M/W, fencing M/W, football M/W, lacrosse W(c), racquetball M/W, rock climbing M/W, skiing (downhill) M/W, soccer M/W, softball M/W, swimming and diving M/W, table tennis M/W, tennis M/W, volleyball M/W.

Standardized Tests *Required:* SAT or ACT (for admission). *Required for some:* SAT Subject Tests (for admission).

Costs (2010–11) *Tuition:* state resident $5804 full-time, $242 per credit hour part-time; nonresident $14,510 full-time, $605 per credit hour part-time. Part-time tuition and fees vary according to course load. *Required fees:* $1928 full-time, $99 per credit hour part-time, $68 per term part-time. *Room and board:* $8094; room only: $5024. Room and board charges vary according to board plan and housing facility. *Payment plans:* installment, deferred payment. *Waivers:* senior citizens and employees or children of employees.

Financial Aid Of all full-time matriculated undergraduates who enrolled in 2008, 7,724 applied for aid, 5,796 were judged to have need, 2,457 had their need fully met. 311 Federal Work-Study jobs (averaging $1065). In 2008, 298 non-need-based awards were made. *Average percent of need met:* 55%. *Average financial aid package:* $7739. *Average need-based loan:* $4068. *Average need-based gift aid:* $5290. *Average non-need-based aid:* $1843. *Average indebtedness upon graduation:* $22,670.

Applying *Options:* electronic application, early admission, deferred entrance. *Application fee:* $35. *Required:* high school transcript, minimum 2 GPA. *Required for some:* audition for music; portfolio and/or art test for arts. *Application deadlines:* rolling (freshmen), rolling (transfers). *Notification:* continuous (freshmen), continuous (transfers).

Freshman Application Contact Kutztown University of Pennsylvania, 15200 Kutztown Road, Kutztown, PA 19530-0730. *Phone:* 610-683-4060. *Toll-free phone:* 877-628-1915. *Web site:* http://www.kutztown.edu/.

Lafayette College

Easton, Pennsylvania

- **Independent** 4-year, founded 1826, affiliated with Presbyterian Church (U.S.A.)
- **Suburban** 340-acre campus with easy access to New York City and Philadelphia
- **Endowment** $567.9 million
- **Coed** 2,414 undergraduate students, 98% full-time, 47% women, 53% men
- **Most difficult** entrance level, 42% of applicants were admitted

Undergraduates 2,362 full-time, 52 part-time. Students come from 40 states and territories; 46 other countries; 77% are from out of state; 5% Black or African American, non-Hispanic/Latino; 5% Hispanic/Latino; 4% Asian, non-Hispanic/Latino; 0.1% Native Hawaiian or other Pacific Islander, non-Hispanic/Latino; 2% Two or more races, non-Hispanic/Latino; 6% international; 0.4% transferred in; 94% live on campus. *Retention:* 94% of full-time freshmen returned.

Freshmen *Admission:* 5,822 applied, 2,430 admitted, 648 enrolled. *Average high school GPA:* 3.41. *Test scores:* SAT critical reading scores over 500: 96%; SAT math scores over 500: 98%; SAT writing scores over 500: 97%; ACT scores over 18: 100%; SAT critical reading scores over 600: 62%; SAT math scores over 600: 81%; SAT writing scores over 600: 69%; ACT scores over 24: 94%; SAT critical reading scores over 700: 16%; SAT math scores over 700: 25%; SAT writing scores over 700: 18%; ACT scores over 30: 30%.

Faculty *Total:* 259, 82% full-time, 90% with terminal degrees. *Student/faculty ratio:* 10:1.

Academics *Calendar:* semesters plus interim January program. *Degree:* bachelor's. *Special study options:* academic remediation for entering students, accelerated degree program, advanced placement credit, honors programs, internships, off-campus study, part-time degree program, services for LD students, student-designed majors, study abroad, summer session for credit. *ROTC:* Army (c).

Computers on Campus 600 computers/terminals and 600 ports are available on campus for general student use. Students can access the following: online (class) registration. Campuswide network is available.

Student Life *Housing:* on-campus residence required through senior year. *Options:* coed. Campus housing is university owned. Freshman campus housing is guaranteed. *Activities and organizations:* drama/theater group, student-run newspaper, radio station, choral group, Association of Biscer Collegians, International Student Association, Activities Forum, national fraternities, national sororities. *Campus security:* 24-hour emergency response devices and patrols, student patrols, late-night transport/escort service, controlled dormitory access. *Student services:* health clinic, personal/psychological counseling, women's center.

Athletics Member NCAA. All Division I except football (Division I-AA). *Intercollegiate sports:* baseball M, basketball M/W, crew M(c)/W(c), cross-country running M/W, equestrian sports M(c)/W(c), fencing M/W, field hockey W, golf M, ice hockey M(c), lacrosse M/W, rugby M(c)/W(c), skiing (downhill) M(c)/W(c), soccer M/W, softball W, squash M(c), swimming and diving M/W, tennis M/W, track and field M/W, volleyball W, weight lifting M(c)/W(c), wrestling M(c). *Intramural sports:* badminton M/W, baseball M, basketball M/W, bowling M/W, cross-country running M/W, fencing M/W, field hockey W, football M, golf M/W, lacrosse M/W, racquetball M/W, sailing M(c)/W(c), skiing (cross-country) M(c)/W(c), soccer M/W, softball M/W, squash M/W, swimming and diving M/W, table tennis M/W, tennis M/W, track and field M/W, volleyball M/W, weight lifting M/W, wrestling M.

Standardized Tests *Required:* SAT or ACT (for admission). *Recommended:* SAT Subject Tests (for admission).

Costs (2010–11) *One-time required fee:* $700. *Comprehensive fee:* $51,074 includes full-time tuition ($38,810), mandatory fees ($305), and room and board ($11,959). Part-time tuition: $1735 per course. *College room only:*

$7265. Room and board charges vary according to board plan. *Payment plans:* tuition prepayment, installment.

Financial Aid Of all full-time matriculated undergraduates who enrolled in 2009, 1,409 applied for aid, 1,050 were judged to have need, 923 had their need fully met. In 2009, 160 non-need-based awards were made. *Average percent of need met:* 99%. *Average financial aid package:* $35,451. *Average need-based loan:* $4316. *Average need-based gift aid:* $30. *Average non-need-based aid:* $17,613. *Average indebtedness upon graduation:* $20,687. *Financial aid deadline:* 3/1.

Applying *Options:* electronic application, early admission, early decision, deferred entrance. *Application fee:* $65. *Required:* essay or personal statement, high school transcript, 1 letter of recommendation. *Recommended:* interview. *Application deadlines:* 1/1 (freshmen), 5/1 (transfers). *Early decision deadline:* 12/1. *Notification:* 4/1 (freshmen), continuous (transfers), 3/1 (early decision).

Freshman Application Contact Ms. Carol Rowlands, Director of Admissions, Lafayette College, Easton, PA 18042-1798. *Phone:* 610-330-5100. *Fax:* 610-330-5355. *E-mail:* rowlandc@lafayette.edu. *Web site:* http://www.lafayette.edu/.

See page 1372 for the College Close-Up.

Lancaster Bible College & Graduate School

Lancaster, Pennsylvania

Freshman Application Contact Mrs. Joanne M. Roper, Associate Vice President for Admissions, Lancaster Bible College & Graduate School, PO Box 83403, Lancaster, PA 17608. *Phone:* 717-560-8271. *Toll-free phone:* 866-LBC4YOU. *Fax:* 717-560-8213. *E-mail:* admissions@lbc.edu. *Web site:* http://www.lbc.edu/.

La Roche College

Pittsburgh, Pennsylvania

- **Independent** comprehensive, founded 1963, affiliated with Roman Catholic Church
- **Suburban** 43-acre campus
- **Endowment** $3.7 million
- **Coed** 1,292 undergraduate students, 81% full-time, 60% women, 40% men
- **Minimally difficult** entrance level, 57% of applicants were admitted

Undergraduates 1,046 full-time, 246 part-time. Students come from 19 states and territories; 38 other countries; 6% are from out of state; 7% Black or African American, non-Hispanic/Latino; 1% Hispanic/Latino; 0.5% Asian, non-Hispanic/Latino; 0.1% American Indian or Alaska Native, non-Hispanic/Latino; 0.7% Two or more races, non-Hispanic/Latino; 17% Race/ethnicity unknown; 11% international; 15% transferred in; 35% live on campus. *Retention:* 69% of full-time freshmen returned.

Freshmen *Admission:* 1,341 applied, 759 admitted, 273 enrolled. *Average high school GPA:* 3.08. *Test scores:* SAT critical reading scores over 500: 34%; SAT math scores over 500: 31%; SAT writing scores over 500: 29%; ACT scores over 18: 62%; SAT critical reading scores over 600: 5%; SAT math scores over 600: 6%; SAT writing scores over 600: 7%; ACT scores over 24: 18%; SAT math scores over 700: 1%.

Faculty *Total:* 171, 36% full-time, 35% with terminal degrees. *Student/faculty ratio:* 12:1.

Academics *Calendar:* semesters plus summer term. *Degrees:* certificates, associate, bachelor's, master's, and postbachelor's certificates. *Special study options:* academic remediation for entering students, accelerated degree program, adult/continuing education programs, advanced placement credit, distance learning, double majors, English as a second language, honors programs, independent study, internships, part-time degree program, services for LD students, student-designed majors, study abroad, summer session for credit. *ROTC:* Army (c), Air Force (c). *Unusual degree programs:* 3-2 engineering with University of Pittsburgh; physical therapy, physician's assistant, speech language pathologist, athletic trainer, occupational therapy with Duquesne University.

Computers on Campus 186 computers/terminals are available on campus for general student use. Students can access the following: campus intranet, computer help desk, free student e-mail accounts, online (class) grades, online (class) registration, online (class) schedules. Campuswide network is available. 100% of college-owned or -operated housing units are wired for high-speed Internet access. Wireless service is available via classrooms, computer labs, learning centers, libraries, student centers.

Student Life *Housing options:* coed. Campus housing is university owned. Freshman campus housing is guaranteed. *Activities and organizations:* drama/theater group, student-run newspaper, radio station, choral group, American Society of Interior Design, student government, Visions (environmental club),

Helping Hands, Project Achievement. *Campus security:* 24-hour emergency response devices and patrols, student patrols, late-night transport/escort service, controlled dormitory access. *Student services:* health clinic, personal/psychological counseling.

Athletics Member NCAA. All Division III. *Intercollegiate sports:* baseball M, basketball M/W, cross-country running M/W, golf M, lacrosse M, soccer M/W, softball W, tennis W, volleyball W. *Intramural sports:* basketball M/W, weight lifting M/W.

Standardized Tests *Required:* SAT or ACT (for admission).

Costs (2010–11) *Comprehensive fee:* $31,392 includes full-time tuition ($21,776), mandatory fees ($700), and room and board ($8916). Full-time tuition and fees vary according to program. Part-time tuition: $550 per credit hour. Part-time tuition and fees vary according to program. *College room only:* $5644. Room and board charges vary according to board plan. *Payment plan:* installment. *Waivers:* senior citizens and employees or children of employees.

Financial Aid Of all full-time matriculated undergraduates who enrolled in 2009, 811 applied for aid, 753 were judged to have need, 269 had their need fully met. 149 Federal Work-Study jobs (averaging $2000). In 2009, 58 non-need-based awards were made. *Average percent of need met:* 95%. *Average financial aid package:* $23,616. *Average need-based loan:* $4238. *Average need-based gift aid:* $2443. *Average non-need-based aid:* $13,496. *Average indebtedness upon graduation:* $18,719.

Applying *Options:* electronic application, early admission, deferred entrance. *Application fee:* $50. *Required:* high school transcript, minimum 2 GPA, 2 letters of recommendation. *Recommended:* essay or personal statement, minimum 3 GPA, interview. *Application deadlines:* rolling (freshmen), rolling (transfers). *Notification:* 9/15 (freshmen).

Freshman Application Contact Mr. David McFarland, Director of Admissions, La Roche College, 9000 Babcock Boulevard, Pittsburgh, PA 15237. *Phone:* 412-536-1275. *Toll-free phone:* 800-838-4LRC. *Fax:* 412-536-1048. *E-mail:* admissions@laroche.edu. *Web site:* http://www.laroche.edu/.

La Salle University

Philadelphia, Pennsylvania

- **Independent Roman Catholic** comprehensive, founded 1863
- **Urban** 130-acre campus
- **Endowment** $56.9 million
- **Coed** 4,487 undergraduate students, 74% full-time, 65% women, 35% men
- **Moderately difficult** entrance level, 65% of applicants were admitted

Undergraduates 3,311 full-time, 1,176 part-time. Students come from 37 states and territories; 14 other countries; 39% are from out of state; 18% Black or African American, non-Hispanic/Latino; 10% Hispanic/Latino; 4% Asian, non-Hispanic/Latino; 0.1% Native Hawaiian or other Pacific Islander, non-Hispanic/Latino; 0.3% American Indian or Alaska Native, non-Hispanic/Latino; 12% Race/ethnicity unknown; 0.9% international; 3% transferred in; 61% live on campus. *Retention:* 77% of full-time freshmen returned.

Freshmen *Admission:* 5,839 applied, 3,824 admitted, 986 enrolled. *Average high school GPA:* 3.35. *Test scores:* SAT critical reading scores over 500: 52%; SAT math scores over 500: 53%; ACT scores over 18: 79%; SAT critical reading scores over 600: 12%; SAT math scores over 600: 14%; ACT scores over 24: 24%; SAT critical reading scores over 700: 2%; SAT math scores over 700: 2%; ACT scores over 30: 2%.

Faculty *Total:* 419, 55% full-time. *Student/faculty ratio:* 13:1.

Academics *Calendar:* semesters. *Degrees:* associate, bachelor's, master's, doctoral-research/scholarship, post-master's, and postbachelor's certificates. *Special study options:* academic remediation for entering students, accelerated degree program, adult/continuing education programs, advanced placement credit, cooperative education, double majors, freshman honors college, honors programs, independent study, internships, off-campus study, part-time degree program, services for LD students, student-designed majors, study abroad, summer session for credit. *ROTC:* Army (c), Air Force (c). *Unusual degree programs:* 3-2 occupational therapy with Thomas Jefferson University, speech pathology.

Computers on Campus 1,100 computers/terminals are available on campus for general student use. Students can access the following: campus intranet, computer help desk, free student e-mail accounts, online (class) grades, online (class) registration, online (class) schedules, Blackboard Course Management System. Campuswide network is available. 100% of college-owned or -operated housing units are wired for high-speed Internet access. Wireless service is available via classrooms, computer centers, computer labs, dorm rooms, learning centers, libraries, student centers.

Student Life *Housing options:* coed, men-only, women-only, disabled students. Campus housing is university owned and leased by the school. Freshman campus housing is guaranteed. *Activities and organizations:* drama/theater group, student-run newspaper, radio and television station, choral group, Student Government Association, Community service organization, La Salle Entertainment Organization, The Explorer (yearbook), The Masque (the-

ater group), national fraternities, national sororities. *Campus security:* 24-hour emergency response devices and patrols, student patrols, late-night transport/escort service, controlled dormitory access. *Student services:* health clinic, personal/psychological counseling, women's center.

Athletics Member NCAA. All Division I. *Intercollegiate sports:* baseball M(s), basketball M(s)/W(s), crew M(s)/W(s), cross-country running M(s)/W(s), field hockey W(s), golf M(s)/W(s), lacrosse W(s), soccer M(s)/W(s), softball W(s), swimming and diving M(s)/W(s), tennis M(s)/W(s), track and field M(s)/W(s), volleyball W(s). *Intramural sports:* baseball M(c), basketball M/W, crew M/W, field hockey W, football M/W, golf M/W, ice hockey M(c), lacrosse M(c)/W(c), rugby M(c)/W(c), soccer M(c)/W(c), softball W, swimming and diving M/W, tennis M(c)/W(c), track and field M/W, ultimate Frisbee M(c)/W(c), volleyball M/W, water polo M(c)/W(c).

Standardized Tests *Required:* SAT or ACT (for admission).

Costs (2011–12) *One-time required fee:* $150. *Comprehensive fee:* $46,820 includes full-time tuition ($34,840), mandatory fees ($300), and room and board ($11,680). Full-time tuition and fees vary according to course load and program. Part-time tuition: $475 per credit hour. Part-time tuition and fees vary according to course load and program. *Required fees:* $125 per term part-time. *College room only:* $6150. Room and board charges vary according to board plan and housing facility. *Payment plans:* installment, deferred payment. *Waivers:* employees or children of employees.

Financial Aid Of all full-time matriculated undergraduates who enrolled in 2009, 2,841 applied for aid, 2,555 were judged to have need, 577 had their need fully met. In 2009, 601 non-need-based awards were made. *Average percent of need met:* 82%. *Average financial aid package:* $17,373. *Average need-based loan:* $4663. *Average need-based gift aid:* $13,462. *Average non-need-based aid:* $9373. *Average indebtedness upon graduation:* $24,345.

Applying *Options:* electronic application, early admission, early decision, early action, deferred entrance. *Application fee:* $35. *Required:* essay or personal statement, high school transcript, 1 letter of recommendation. *Recommended:* interview. *Application deadlines:* 8/15 (transfers), 11/15 (early action). *Notification:* continuous (freshmen), continuous (transfers), 12/15 (early action).

Freshman Application Contact Mr. James Plunkett, Executive Director of Undergraduate Admission, La Salle University, 1900 West Olney Avenue, Philadelphia, PA 19141-1199. *Phone:* 215-951-1500. *Toll-free phone:* 800-328-1910. *Fax:* 215-951-1656. *E-mail:* admiss@lasalle.edu. *Web site:* http://www.lasalle.edu/.

Lebanon Valley College

Annville, Pennsylvania

- **Independent United Methodist** comprehensive, founded 1866
- **Small-town** 340-acre campus
- **Endowment** $46.6 million
- **Coed** 1,776 undergraduate students, 91% full-time, 57% women, 43% men
- **Moderately difficult** entrance level, 70% of applicants were admitted

Undergraduates 1,611 full-time, 165 part-time. Students come from 19 states and territories; 2 other countries; 20% are from out of state; 2% Black or African American, non-Hispanic/Latino; 3% Hispanic/Latino; 1% Asian, non-Hispanic/Latino; 0.2% Native Hawaiian or other Pacific Islander, non-Hispanic/Latino; 0.2% American Indian or Alaska Native, non-Hispanic/Latino; 0.8% Two or more races, non-Hispanic/Latino; 4% Race/ethnicity unknown; 0.1% international; 2% transferred in; 76% live on campus. *Retention:* 83% of full-time freshmen returned.

Freshmen *Admission:* 2,633 applied, 1,833 admitted, 460 enrolled. *Test scores:* SAT critical reading scores over 500: 66%; SAT math scores over 500: 76%; SAT writing scores over 500: 64%; ACT scores over 18: 93%; SAT critical reading scores over 600: 23%; SAT math scores over 600: 35%; SAT writing scores over 600: 20%; ACT scores over 24: 57%; SAT critical reading scores over 700: 3%; SAT math scores over 700: 6%; SAT writing scores over 700: 2%; ACT scores over 30: 13%.

Faculty *Total:* 212, 48% full-time, 56% with terminal degrees. *Student/faculty ratio:* 13:1.

Academics *Calendar:* semesters. *Degrees:* certificates, associate, bachelor's, master's, doctoral-professional, and postbachelor's certificates. *Special study options:* academic remediation for entering students, adult/continuing education programs, advanced placement credit, double majors, independent study, internships, off-campus study, part-time degree program, services for LD students, student-designed majors, study abroad, summer session for credit. *ROTC:* Army (c). *Unusual degree programs:* 3-2 engineering with Case Western Reserve University, The Pennsylvania State University.

Computers on Campus 186 computers/terminals are available on campus for general student use. Students can access the following: campus intranet, computer help desk, free student e-mail accounts, online (class) grades, online (class) registration, online (class) schedules. Campuswide network is available. 100% of college-owned or -operated housing units are wired for high-speed

Internet access. Wireless service is available via classrooms, computer centers, computer labs, dorm rooms, learning centers, libraries, student centers.

Student Life *Housing:* on-campus residence required through senior year. *Options:* coed, women-only, disabled students. Campus housing is university owned. Freshman campus housing is guaranteed. *Activities and organizations:* drama/theater group, student-run newspaper, radio station, choral group, marching band, LVC PSEA, Corner Stone, College Against Cancer, Wig and Buckle Theater Group, Habitat for Humanity, national fraternities, national sororities. *Campus security:* 24-hour emergency response devices and patrols, late-night transport/escort service, controlled dormitory access, residence hall entrances locked 24 hours a day. *Student services:* health clinic, personal/psychological counseling, women's center.

Athletics Member NCAA. All Division III. *Intercollegiate sports:* baseball M, basketball M/W, cross-country running M/W, field hockey W, football M, golf M, ice hockey M(c), lacrosse M/W, soccer M/W, softball W, swimming and diving M/W, tennis M/W, track and field M/W, volleyball W. *Intramural sports:* basketball M/W, football M/W, racquetball M/W, rugby W(c), softball M/W, volleyball M(c).

Costs (2011–12) *Comprehensive fee:* $42,000 includes full-time tuition ($32,490), mandatory fees ($710), and room and board ($8800). Part-time tuition and fees vary according to class time and degree level. *College room only:* $4300. Room and board charges vary according to board plan and housing facility. *Payment plans:* tuition prepayment, installment. *Waivers:* senior citizens and employees or children of employees.

Financial Aid Of all full-time matriculated undergraduates who enrolled in 2009, 1,456 applied for aid, 1,347 were judged to have need, 276 had their need fully met. 977 Federal Work-Study jobs (averaging $1507). In 2009, 221 non-need-based awards were made. *Average percent of need met:* 80%. *Average financial aid package:* $22,755. *Average need-based loan:* $4332. *Average need-based gift aid:* $19,787. *Average non-need-based aid:* $12,532. *Average indebtedness upon graduation:* $32,428.

Applying *Options:* electronic application. *Application fee:* $30. *Required:* high school transcript. *Required for some:* essay or personal statement, audition for music majors. *Recommended:* 2 letters of recommendation, interview. *Application deadlines:* rolling (freshmen), rolling (transfers). *Notification:* continuous (freshmen), continuous (transfers).

Freshman Application Contact Ms. Erin Sanno, Associate Director of Admission, Lebanon Valley College, 101 North College Avenue, Annville, PA

17003. *Phone:* 717-867-6181. *Toll-free phone:* 866-LVC-4ADM. *Fax:* 717-867-6026. *E-mail:* admission@lvc.edu. *Web site:* http://www.lvc.edu/.

See page 1376 for the College Close-Up.

Lehigh University
Bethlehem, Pennsylvania

- **Independent** university, founded 1865
- **Suburban** 1600-acre campus with easy access to Philadelphia
- **Endowment** $940.4 million
- **Coed** 4,781 undergraduate students, 99% full-time, 41% women, 59% men
- **Most difficult** entrance level, 38% of applicants were admitted

Undergraduates 4,723 full-time, 58 part-time. Students come from 55 states and territories; 50 other countries; 77% are from out of state; 4% Black or African American, non-Hispanic/Latino; 7% Hispanic/Latino; 6% Asian, non-Hispanic/Latino; 0.1% Native Hawaiian or other Pacific Islander, non-Hispanic/Latino; 2% Two or more races, non-Hispanic/Latino; 6% Race/ethnicity unknown; 5% international; 1% transferred in; 69% live on campus. *Retention:* 93% of full-time freshmen returned.

Freshmen *Admission:* 10,328 applied, 3,913 admitted, 1,212 enrolled. *Test scores:* SAT critical reading scores over 500: 95%; SAT math scores over 500: 98%; ACT scores over 18: 100%; SAT critical reading scores over 600: 67%; SAT math scores over 600: 88%; ACT scores over 24: 96%; SAT critical reading scores over 700: 14%; SAT math scores over 700: 39%; ACT scores over 30: 44%.

Faculty *Total:* 666, 71% full-time, 68% with terminal degrees. *Student/faculty ratio:* 10:1.

Academics *Calendar:* semesters. *Degrees:* bachelor's, master's, doctoral-research/scholarship, post-master's, and postbachelor's certificates. *Special study options:* accelerated degree program, advanced placement credit, cooperative education, distance learning, double majors, English as a second language, external degree program, honors programs, independent study, internships, off-campus study, services for LD students, study abroad, summer session for credit. *ROTC:* Army (b). *Unusual degree programs:* 3-2 engineering; education.

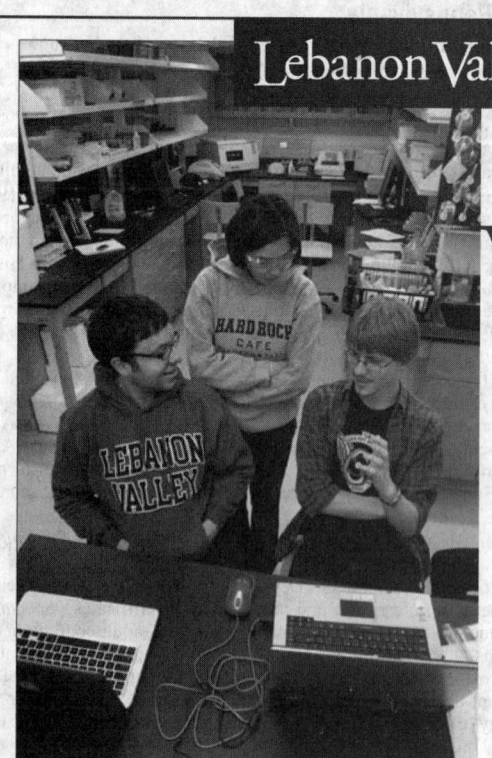

Computers on Campus 638 computers/terminals are available on campus for general student use. Students can access the following: campus intranet, computer help desk, free student e-mail accounts, online (class) grades, online (class) registration, online (class) schedules. Campuswide network is available. 100% of college-owned or -operated housing units are wired for high-speed Internet access. Wireless service is available via classrooms, computer centers, computer labs, dorm rooms, learning centers, libraries, student centers.
Student Life *Housing:* on-campus residence required through sophomore year. *Options:* coed, disabled students. Campus housing is university owned. Freshman campus housing is guaranteed. *Activities and organizations:* drama/theater group, student-run newspaper, radio station, choral group, marching band, WLVR Radio Station, Association of Student Alumni, University Productions, Accounting Club, Business Careers in Entertainment Club, national fraternities, national sororities. *Campus security:* 24-hour emergency response devices and patrols, student patrols, late-night transport/escort service, controlled dormitory access. *Student services:* health clinic, personal/psychological counseling, women's center.
Athletics Member NCAA. All Division I except football (Division I-AA). *Intercollegiate sports:* baseball M, basketball M(s)/W(s), cheerleading M(c)/W(c), crew M(c)/W(s), cross-country running M(s)/W(s), equestrian sports M(c)/W(c), fencing M(c)/W(c), field hockey W(s), golf M(s)/W(s), ice hockey M(c), lacrosse M(s)/W(s), rugby M(c)/W(c), skiing (downhill) M(c)/W(c), soccer M(s)/W(s), softball W(s), swimming and diving M(s)/W(s), tennis M(s)/W(s), track and field M(s)/W(s), volleyball M(c)/W(s), wrestling M(s). *Intramural sports:* badminton M(c)/W(c), baseball M(c), basketball M/W, cross-country running M(c)/W(c), field hockey W(c), football M/W, golf M(c)/W(c), gymnastics M(c)/W(c), ice hockey M(c), lacrosse M(c)/W(c), racquetball M(c)/W(c), rock climbing M/W, skiing (cross-country) M(c)/W(c), soccer M(c)/W(c), softball M/W, squash M(c)/W(c), swimming and diving M(c)/W(c), table tennis M(c)/W(c), tennis M(c)/W(c), ultimate Frisbee M(c)/W(c), volleyball M/W, water polo M(c)/W(c), wrestling M(c).
Standardized Tests *Required:* SAT or ACT (for admission).
Costs (2010–11) *Comprehensive fee:* $50,300 includes full-time tuition ($39,480), mandatory fees ($300), and room and board ($10,520). Part-time tuition: $1650 per credit hour. *College room only:* $6060. Room and board charges vary according to board plan and housing facility. *Payment plans:* tuition prepayment, installment. *Waivers:* employees or children of employees.
Financial Aid Of all full-time matriculated undergraduates who enrolled in 2009, 2,765 applied for aid, 2,129 were judged to have need, 1,894 had their need fully met. 1,222 Federal Work-Study jobs (averaging $1816). 98 state and other part-time jobs (averaging $1996). In 2009, 301 non-need-based awards were made. *Average percent of need met:* 97%. *Average financial aid package:* $30,528. *Average need-based loan:* $4426. *Average need-based gift aid:* $29,498. *Average non-need-based aid:* $10,232. *Average indebtedness upon graduation:* $31,922. *Financial aid deadline:* 2/15.
Applying *Options:* electronic application, early admission, early decision, deferred entrance. *Application fee:* $70. *Required:* essay or personal statement, high school transcript, 2 letters of recommendation. *Application deadlines:* 1/1 (freshmen), 4/1 (transfers). *Early decision deadline:* 11/15 (for plan 1), 1/15 (for plan 2). *Notification:* 4/1 (freshmen), 5/1 (transfers), 12/15 (early decision plan 1), 2/15 (early decision plan 2).
Freshman Application Contact J. Bruce Gardiner, Director of Admissions, Lehigh University, 27 Memorial Drive West, Bethlehem, PA 18015. *Phone:* 610-758-3100. *Fax:* 610-758-4361. *E-mail:* admissions@lehigh.edu. *Web site:* http://www.lehigh.edu/.

Lincoln University
Lincoln University, Pennsylvania

- **State-related** comprehensive, founded 1854
- **Rural** 422-acre campus with easy access to Philadelphia
- **Endowment** $19.5 million
- **Coed**
- **Moderately difficult** entrance level

Faculty *Student/faculty ratio:* 19:1.
Academics *Calendar:* semesters. *Degrees:* bachelor's and master's.
Student Life *Campus security:* 24-hour emergency response devices and patrols, late-night transport/escort service.
Athletics Member NCAA. All Division II.
Standardized Tests *Required:* SAT or ACT (for admission).
Costs (2010–11) *Tuition:* state resident $6038 full-time, $254 per credit hour part-time; nonresident $10,276 full-time, $431 per credit hour part-time. Full-time tuition and fees vary according to student level. Part-time tuition and fees vary according to course load. *Required fees:* $2434 full-time, $108 per credit hour part-time. *Room and board:* $8004; room only: $4346. Room and board charges vary according to board plan and housing facility. *Payment plans:* installment, deferred payment.
Financial Aid *Of all full-time matriculated undergraduates who enrolled in 2009,* 1,913 applied for aid, 1,797 were judged to have need, 51 had their need

fully met. 146 Federal Work-Study jobs (averaging $1294). *In 2009,* 31 non-need-based awards were made. *Average percent of need met:* 49. *Average financial aid package:* $9060. *Average need-based loan:* $3740. *Average need-based gift aid:* $5122. *Average non-need-based aid:* $3740. *Average indebtedness upon graduation:* $30,818. *Financial aid deadline:* 5/1.
Applying *Options:* electronic application, early admission, deferred entrance. *Application fee:* $20. *Required:* essay or personal statement, high school transcript, minimum 2 GPA, 2 letters of recommendation. *Recommended:* interview.
Freshman Application Contact Ms. Germel Eaton-Clarke, Interim Director of Admissions, Lincoln University, PO Box 179, Lincoln University, PA 19352. *Phone:* 484-365-7218. *Toll-free phone:* 800-790-0191. *Fax:* 484-365-8109. *E-mail:* admiss@lincoln.edu. *Web site:* http://www.lincoln.edu/.

Lock Haven University of Pennsylvania
Lock Haven, Pennsylvania

- **State-supported** comprehensive, founded 1870, part of Pennsylvania State System of Higher Education
- **Rural** 165-acre campus
- **Endowment** $5.5 million
- **Coed** 5,114 undergraduate students, 93% full-time, 56% women, 44% men
- **Moderately difficult** entrance level, 72% of applicants were admitted

Undergraduates 4,766 full-time, 348 part-time. Students come from 26 states and territories; 32 other countries; 10% are from out of state; 7% Black or African American, non-Hispanic/Latino; 2% Hispanic/Latino; 0.7% Asian, non-Hispanic/Latino; 0.2% American Indian or Alaska Native, non-Hispanic/Latino; 0.5% Two or more races, non-Hispanic/Latino; 0.5% Race/ethnicity unknown; 0.7% international; 5% transferred in; 36% live on campus. *Retention:* 69% of full-time freshmen returned.
Freshmen *Admission:* 5,039 applied, 3,603 admitted, 1,195 enrolled. *Average high school GPA:* 3.25. *Test scores:* SAT critical reading scores over 500: 34%; SAT math scores over 500: 41%; SAT writing scores over 500: 28%; ACT scores over 18: 58%; SAT critical reading scores over 600: 5%; SAT math scores over 600: 7%; SAT writing scores over 600: 3%; ACT scores over 24: 8%.
Faculty *Total:* 253, 93% full-time, 70% with terminal degrees. *Student/faculty ratio:* 21:1.
Academics *Calendar:* semesters. *Degrees:* associate, bachelor's, and master's. *Special study options:* academic remediation for entering students, adult/continuing education programs, advanced placement credit, cooperative education, distance learning, double majors, English as a second language, freshman honors college, honors programs, independent study, internships, off-campus study, part-time degree program, services for LD students, student-designed majors, study abroad, summer session for credit. *ROTC:* Army (b). *Unusual degree programs:* 3-2 engineering with Pennsylvania State University-University Park Campus; nursing with Clarion University of Pennsylvania.
Computers on Campus 290 computers/terminals are available on campus for general student use. Students can access the following: online (class) registration. Campuswide network is available.
Student Life *Housing:* on-campus residence required for freshman year. *Options:* coed. Campus housing is university owned and is provided by a third party. Freshman applicants given priority for college housing. *Activities and organizations:* drama/theater group, student-run newspaper, radio and television station, choral group, marching band, student government, Residence Hall Association, national fraternities, national sororities. *Campus security:* 24-hour emergency response devices and patrols, late-night transport/escort service, controlled dormitory access. *Student services:* health clinic, personal/psychological counseling, women's center.
Athletics Member NCAA. All Division II except field hockey (Division I), wrestling (Division I). *Intercollegiate sports:* baseball M(s), basketball M(s)/W(s), cross-country running M(s)/W(s), field hockey W(s), football M(s), lacrosse W(s), soccer M(s)/W(s), softball W(s), swimming and diving W(s), track and field M(s)/W(s), volleyball W(s), wrestling M(s). *Intramural sports:* badminton M/W, basketball M/W, cross-country running M/W, fencing M/W, field hockey W, football M, golf M/W, ice hockey M, lacrosse M/W, racquetball M/W, rugby M/W, skiing (cross-country) M/W, skiing (downhill) M/W, soccer M/W, softball M/W, swimming and diving M/W, tennis M/W, track and field M/W, ultimate Frisbee M/W, volleyball M/W, water polo M, weight lifting M/W, wrestling M.
Standardized Tests *Required:* SAT or ACT (for admission).
Costs (2011–12) *Tuition:* state resident $5804 full-time, $242 per credit hour part-time; nonresident $12,510 full-time, $521 per credit hour part-time. Full-time tuition and fees vary according to course load and location. Part-time tuition and fees vary according to course load and location. *Required fees:* $1736 full-time, $46 per credit hour part-time, $135 per term part-time. *Room*

and board: $6695; room only: $3872. Room and board charges vary according to board plan and housing facility. *Payment plan:* installment. *Waivers:* minority students, senior citizens, and employees or children of employees.

Financial Aid Of all full-time matriculated undergraduates who enrolled in 2009, 4,428 applied for aid, 3,410 were judged to have need, 1,875 had their need fully met. 250 Federal Work-Study jobs (averaging $1350). 750 state and other part-time jobs (averaging $1616). In 2009, 80 non-need-based awards were made. *Average percent of need met:* 75%. *Average financial aid package:* $8256. *Average need-based loan:* $4094. *Average need-based gift aid:* $6843. *Average non-need-based aid:* $996. *Average indebtedness upon graduation:* $22,883. *Financial aid deadline:* 3/15.

Applying *Options:* electronic application, deferred entrance. *Application fee:* $25. *Required:* high school transcript. *Required for some:* essay or personal statement. *Recommended:* interview. *Application deadlines:* rolling (freshmen), rolling (transfers). *Notification:* continuous (freshmen), continuous (transfers).

Freshman Application Contact Mr. Steven Lee, Director of Admissions, Lock Haven University of Pennsylvania, Office of Admission, Akeley Hall, Lock Haven, PA 17745. *Phone:* 570-484-2027. *Toll-free phone:* 800-332-8900 (in-state); 800-233-8978 (out-of-state). *Fax:* 570-484-2201. *E-mail:* admissions@lhup.edu. *Web site:* http://www.lhup.edu/.

Lycoming College
Williamsport, Pennsylvania

- **Independent United Methodist** 4-year, founded 1812
- **Small-town** 35-acre campus
- **Endowment** $127.0 million
- **Coed** 1,321 undergraduate students, 98% full-time, 56% women, 44% men
- **Moderately difficult** entrance level, 64% of applicants were admitted

Undergraduates 1,298 full-time, 23 part-time. Students come from 29 states and territories; 10 other countries; 34% are from out of state; 3% Black or African American, non-Hispanic/Latino; 3% Hispanic/Latino; 0.5% Asian, non-Hispanic/Latino; 0.2% Native Hawaiian or other Pacific Islander, non-Hispanic/Latino; 0.3% American Indian or Alaska Native, non-Hispanic/Latino; 2% Two or more races, non-Hispanic/Latino; 6% Race/ethnicity unknown; 2% international; 2% transferred in; 84% live on campus. *Retention:* 77% of full-time freshmen returned.

Freshmen *Admission:* 2,078 applied, 1,334 admitted, 341 enrolled. *Test scores:* SAT critical reading scores over 500: 65%; SAT math scores over 500: 65%; SAT writing scores over 500: 59%; ACT scores over 18: 94%; SAT critical reading scores over 600: 20%; SAT math scores over 600: 20%; SAT writing scores over 600: 17%; ACT scores over 24: 52%; SAT critical reading scores over 700: 5%; SAT math scores over 700: 2%; SAT writing scores over 700: 2%; ACT scores over 30: 4%.

Faculty *Total:* 124, 69% full-time, 66% with terminal degrees. *Student/faculty ratio:* 13:1.

Academics *Calendar:* semesters. *Degree:* bachelor's. *Special study options:* accelerated degree program, advanced placement credit, double majors, honors programs, independent study, internships, off-campus study, part-time degree program, services for LD students, student-designed majors, study abroad, summer session for credit. *ROTC:* Army (c). *Unusual degree programs:* 3-2 forestry with Duke University; environmental management with Duke University.

Computers on Campus 140 computers/terminals are available on campus for general student use. Students can access the following: campus intranet, computer help desk, free student e-mail accounts, online (class) grades, online (class) registration, online (class) schedules. Campuswide network is available. 100% of college-owned or -operated housing units are wired for high-speed Internet access. Wireless service is available via entire campus.

Student Life *Housing:* on-campus residence required through senior year. *Options:* coed, women-only. Campus housing is university owned. Freshman campus housing is guaranteed. *Activities and organizations:* drama/theater group, student-run newspaper, radio station, choral group, Campus Activities Board, Lycoming Dance Club, Habitat for Humanity, Circle K, United Campus Ministry, national fraternities, national sororities. *Campus security:* 24-hour emergency response devices and patrols, student patrols, late-night transport/escort service, controlled dormitory access. *Student services:* health clinic, personal/psychological counseling.

Athletics Member NCAA. All Division III. *Intercollegiate sports:* badminton M(c)/W(c), basketball M/W, cheerleading M(c)/W(c), crew M(c)/W(c), cross-country running M/W, equestrian sports M(c)/W(c), fencing M(c)/W(c), football M, golf M/W, lacrosse M/W, rugby M(c), soccer M/W, softball W, swimming and diving M/W, tennis M/W, ultimate Frisbee M(c)/W(c), volleyball W, water polo M(c)/W(c), wrestling M. *Intramural sports:* basketball M/W, football M/W, soccer M/W, softball M/W, table tennis M/W, volleyball M/W.

Standardized Tests *Recommended:* SAT or ACT (for admission).

Costs (2011–12) *Comprehensive fee:* $39,342 includes full-time tuition ($30,240), mandatory fees ($560), and room and board ($8542). Part-time

---

tuition: $945 per credit hour. Part-time tuition and fees vary according to course load. *Room and board:* Room and board charges vary according to board plan and housing facility. *Payment plan:* installment. *Waivers:* employees or children of employees.

Financial Aid Of all full-time matriculated undergraduates who enrolled in 2009, 1,220 applied for aid, 1,137 were judged to have need, 172 had their need fully met. 364 Federal Work-Study jobs (averaging $1102). In 2009, 166 non-need-based awards were made. *Average percent of need met:* 78%. *Average financial aid package:* $23,264. *Average need-based loan:* $4760. *Average need-based gift aid:* $18,340. *Average non-need-based aid:* $10,852. *Average indebtedness upon graduation:* $29,478.

Applying *Options:* electronic application, deferred entrance. *Application fee:* $35. *Required:* essay or personal statement, high school transcript, 2 letters of recommendation. *Recommended:* minimum 2.3 GPA, interview. *Application deadlines:* 5/1 (freshmen), rolling (transfers). *Notification:* continuous (freshmen), continuous (transfers).

Freshman Application Contact Mr. James Spencer, Vice President of Admissions and Financial Aid, Lycoming College, 700 College Place, Williamsport, PA 17701. *Phone:* 570-321-4026. *Toll-free phone:* 800-345-3920 Ext. 4026. *Fax:* 570-321-4317. *E-mail:* admissions@lycoming.edu. *Web site:* http://www.lycoming.edu/.

Mansfield University of Pennsylvania
Mansfield, Pennsylvania

- **State-supported** comprehensive, founded 1857, part of Pennsylvania State System of Higher Education
- **Small-town** 174-acre campus
- **Endowment** $9.2 million
- **Coed** 2,945 undergraduate students, 93% full-time, 58% women, 42% men
- **Moderately difficult** entrance level, 73% of applicants were admitted

Undergraduates 2,753 full-time, 192 part-time. Students come from 35 states and territories; 20 other countries; 20% are from out of state; 7% Black or African American, non-Hispanic/Latino; 2% Hispanic/Latino; 1% Asian, non-Hispanic/Latino; 1% American Indian or Alaska Native, non-Hispanic/Latino; 9% Race/ethnicity unknown; 1% international; 9% transferred in; 50% live on campus. *Retention:* 69% of full-time freshmen returned.

Freshmen *Admission:* 2,711 applied, 1,977 admitted, 640 enrolled. *Average high school GPA:* 3.25. *Test scores:* SAT critical reading scores over 500: 40%; SAT math scores over 500: 43%; SAT writing scores over 500: 33%; SAT critical reading scores over 600: 9%; SAT math scores over 600: 11%; SAT writing scores over 600: 6%; SAT critical reading scores over 700: 1%; SAT math scores over 700: 1%.

Faculty *Total:* 212, 70% full-time. *Student/faculty ratio:* 17:1.

Academics *Calendar:* semesters. *Degrees:* associate, bachelor's, master's, and post-master's certificates. *Special study options:* academic remediation for entering students, accelerated degree program, adult/continuing education programs, advanced placement credit, distance learning, double majors, freshman honors college, honors programs, independent study, internships, off-campus study, part-time degree program, services for LD students, student-designed majors, study abroad, summer session for credit. *ROTC:* Army (c). *Unusual degree programs:* 3-2 engineering.

Computers on Campus 661 computers/terminals and 4,600 ports are available on campus for general student use. Students can access the following: campus intranet, computer help desk, free student e-mail accounts, online (class) grades, online (class) registration, online (class) schedules. Campuswide network is available. 100% of college-owned or -operated housing units are wired for high-speed Internet access. Wireless service is available via classrooms, computer centers, computer labs, dorm rooms, learning centers, libraries, student centers.

Student Life *Housing:* on-campus residence required through sophomore year. *Options:* coed. Campus housing is university owned. Freshman campus housing is guaranteed. *Activities and organizations:* drama/theater group, student-run newspaper, radio and television station, choral group, marching band, Mansfield International Student Organization, P.R. Society, PSEA, Ski Club, Activities Council, national fraternities, national sororities. *Campus security:* 24-hour emergency response devices and patrols, student patrols, late-night transport/escort service, controlled dormitory access. *Student services:* health clinic, personal/psychological counseling, women's center.

Athletics Member NCAA. All Division II. *Intercollegiate sports:* baseball M(s), basketball M(s)/W(s), cross-country running M(s)/W(s), field hockey W(s), football M(c), soccer W(s), softball W(s), swimming and diving W, track and field M(s)/W(s). *Intramural sports:* badminton M/W, basketball M/W, bowling M/W, cheerleading W, cross-country running M/W, equestrian sports M/W, football M/W, golf M/W, racquetball M/W, skiing (cross-country) M/W, skiing (downhill) M/W, soccer M/W, softball M/W, swimming and diving M/W, tennis M/W, track and field M/W, volleyball M/W, water polo M/W, weight lifting M/W.

Standardized Tests *Required:* SAT or ACT (for admission).

Costs (2010–11) *Tuition:* state resident $5804 full-time, $242 per credit hour part-time; nonresident $9578 full-time, $399 per credit hour part-time. Part-time tuition and fees vary according to course load. *Required fees:* $2254 full-time, $884 per year part-time. *Room and board:* $7070; room only: $4370. Room and board charges vary according to board plan. *Payment plans:* installment, deferred payment. *Waivers:* senior citizens and employees or children of employees.

Financial Aid Of all full-time matriculated undergraduates who enrolled in 2008, 2,210 were judged to have need, 727 had their need fully met. In 2008, 7 non-need-based awards were made. *Average percent of need met:* 81%. *Average financial aid package:* $2694. *Average need-based loan:* $3309. *Average need-based gift aid:* $2404. *Average non-need-based aid:* $594. *Average indebtedness upon graduation:* $28,937.

Applying *Options:* electronic application, early admission, deferred entrance. *Application fee:* $25. *Required:* high school transcript. *Required for some:* interview. *Recommended:* essay or personal statement, minimum 2.5 GPA. *Application deadlines:* rolling (freshmen), rolling (transfers). *Notification:* continuous (freshmen), continuous (transfers).

Freshman Application Contact Mr. Brian Barden, Director of Admissions, Mansfield University of Pennsylvania, Academy Street, Mansfield, PA 16933. *Phone:* 570-662-4813. *Toll-free phone:* 800-577-6826. *E-mail:* admissions@ mnsfld.edu. *Web site:* http://www.mansfield.edu/.

Marywood University

Scranton, Pennsylvania

- **Independent Roman Catholic** comprehensive, founded 1915
- **Suburban** 115-acre campus
- **Endowment** $41.5 million
- **Coed** 2,267 undergraduate students, 93% full-time, 70% women, 30% men
- **Moderately difficult** entrance level, 71% of applicants were admitted

Undergraduates 2,106 full-time, 161 part-time. 27% are from out of state; 1% Black or African American, non-Hispanic/Latino; 3% Hispanic/Latino; 2% Asian, non-Hispanic/Latino; 0.1% American Indian or Alaska Native, non-Hispanic/Latino; 0.1% Two or more races, non-Hispanic/Latino; 6% Race/ethnicity unknown; 0.7% international; 6% transferred in; 56% live on campus. *Retention:* 81% of full-time freshmen returned.

Freshmen *Admission:* 2,062 applied, 1,455 admitted, 458 enrolled. *Average high school GPA:* 3.21. *Test scores:* SAT critical reading scores over 500: 66%; SAT math scores over 500: 64%; SAT writing scores over 500: 64%; ACT scores over 18: 97%; SAT critical reading scores over 600: 14%; SAT math scores over 600: 16%; SAT writing scores over 600: 15%; ACT scores over 24: 29%; SAT critical reading scores over 700: 1%; SAT math scores over 700: 1%; SAT writing scores over 700: 4%; ACT scores over 30: 4%.

Faculty *Total:* 398, 38% full-time. *Student/faculty ratio:* 13:1.

Academics *Calendar:* semesters. *Degrees:* bachelor's, master's, doctoral-professional, doctoral-research/scholarship, post-master's, and postbachelor's certificates. *Special study options:* adult/continuing education programs, advanced placement credit, double majors, English as a second language, honors programs, independent study, internships, off-campus study, part-time degree program, services for LD students, student-designed majors, study abroad, summer session for credit. *ROTC:* Army (c), Air Force (c). *Unusual degree programs:* 3-2 physician assistant, communication sciences disorders, criminal justice, biotechnology, health services administration.

Computers on Campus 460 computers/terminals are available on campus for general student use. Students can access the following: computer help desk, free student e-mail accounts, online (class) registration, online (class) schedules. Campuswide network is available. 100% of college-owned or -operated housing units are wired for high-speed Internet access. Wireless service is available via entire campus.

Student Life *Housing:* on-campus residence required through sophomore year. *Options:* coed, men-only, women-only, disabled students. Campus housing is university owned. Freshman campus housing is guaranteed. *Activities and organizations:* drama/theater group, student-run newspaper, radio and television station, choral group. *Campus security:* 24-hour emergency response devices and patrols, late-night transport/escort service, controlled dormitory access, apartments with deadbolts, self-defense education, lighted pathways, seminars on safety. *Student services:* health clinic, personal/psychological counseling.

Athletics Member NCAA. All Division III. *Intercollegiate sports:* baseball M, basketball M/W, cheerleading M(c)/W(c), cross-country running M/W, field hockey W, golf M/W, lacrosse M/W, skiing (cross-country) M(c)/W(c), soccer M/W, softball W, swimming and diving M/W, tennis M/W, track and field M(c)/W(c), volleyball W. *Intramural sports:* badminton M/W, basketball M/W, cross-country running M(c)/W(c), golf M(c)/W, racquetball M/W, soccer M(c)/W(c), softball M/W, table tennis M/W, tennis M/W, volleyball M/W, water polo M/W.

Standardized Tests *Required:* SAT or ACT (for admission).

Costs (2010–11) *Comprehensive fee:* $39,322 includes full-time tuition ($26,000), mandatory fees ($1150), and room and board ($12,172). Full-time tuition and fees vary according to course load. Part-time tuition: $590 per credit. Part-time tuition and fees vary according to course load. *Required fees:* $100 per term part-time. *College room only:* $6922. Room and board charges vary according to board plan and housing facility. *Payment plans:* installment, deferred payment. *Waivers:* senior citizens and employees or children of employees.

Financial Aid Of all full-time matriculated undergraduates who enrolled in 2009, 1,939 applied for aid, 1,807 were judged to have need, 416 had their need fully met. In 2009, 135 non-need-based awards were made. *Average percent of need met:* 79%. *Average financial aid package:* $22,829. *Average need-based loan:* $5283. *Average need-based gift aid:* $16,968. *Average non-need-based aid:* $11,376. *Average indebtedness upon graduation:* $27,736.

Applying *Options:* electronic application, early admission, deferred entrance. *Application fee:* $35. *Required:* high school transcript, 1 letter of recommendation. *Required for some:* essay or personal statement, interview, art majors require portfolio, music majors require audition. *Recommended:* essay or personal statement, interview. *Application deadlines:* rolling (freshmen), rolling (transfers). *Notification:* continuous (freshmen), continuous (transfers).

Freshman Application Contact Mr. Christian DiGregorio, Director of University Admissions, Marywood University, 2300 Adams Avenue, Scranton, PA 18509. *Phone:* 570-348-6234. *Toll-free phone:* 866-279-9663. *Fax:* 570-961-4763. *E-mail:* yourfuture@marywood.edu. *Web site:* http://www.marywood.edu/.

See page 1416 for the College Close-Up.

Mercyhurst College

Erie, Pennsylvania

- **Independent Roman Catholic** comprehensive, founded 1926
- **Suburban** 88-acre campus with easy access to Buffalo
- **Endowment** $26.9 million
- **Coed**
- **Moderately difficult** entrance level

Faculty *Student/faculty ratio:* 16:1.

Academics *Calendar:* 4-3-3. *Degrees:* certificates, associate, bachelor's, master's, and postbachelor's certificates.

Student Life *Campus security:* 24-hour emergency response devices and patrols, campus-wide camera system.

Athletics Member NCAA. All Division II except men's and women's ice hockey (Division I).

Standardized Tests *Required:* SAT or ACT (for admission). *Recommended:* SAT Subject Tests (for admission).

Costs (2010–11) *Comprehensive fee:* $35,541 includes full-time tuition ($24,648), mandatory fees ($1698), and room and board ($9195). Full-time tuition and fees vary according to program. Part-time tuition: $822 per credit hour. Part-time tuition and fees vary according to class time, course load, degree level, and location. *College room only:* $4542. Room and board charges vary according to board plan and housing facility.

Financial Aid *Of all full-time matriculated undergraduates who enrolled in 2009,* 2,230 applied for aid, 1,865 were judged to have need, 579 had their need fully met. 345 Federal Work-Study jobs (averaging $1208). 853 state and other part-time jobs (averaging $1239). *In 2009,* 570 non-need-based awards were made. *Average percent of need met:* 62. *Average financial aid package:* $19,803. *Average need-based loan:* $5913. *Average need-based gift aid:* $10,956. *Average non-need-based aid:* $10,475. *Average indebtedness upon graduation:* $22,630. *Financial aid deadline:* 5/1.

Applying *Options:* electronic application, deferred entrance. *Application fee:* $30. *Required:* essay or personal statement, high school transcript. *Required for some:* 1 letter of recommendation. *Recommended:* interview.

Freshman Application Contact Christopher Coons, Director of Undergraduate Admissions, Mercyhurst College, 501 East 38th Street, Erie, PA 16546-0001. *Phone:* 814-824-2202. *Toll-free phone:* 800-825-1926 Ext. 2202. *Fax:* 814-824-2071. *E-mail:* ccoons@mercyhurst.edu. *Web site:* http://www.mercyhurst.edu/.

Mercyhurst North East

North East, Pennsylvania

Director of Admissions Travis Lindahl, Director of Admissions, Mercyhurst North East, 16 West Division Street, North East, PA 16428. *Phone:* 814-725-6217. *Toll-free phone:* 866-846-6042. *Fax:* 814-725-6251. *E-mail:* neadmiss@mercyhurst.edu. *Web site:* http://northeast.mercyhurst.edu/.

www.facebook.com/find.colleges 739

Messiah College
Grantham, Pennsylvania

- **Independent interdenominational** comprehensive, founded 1909
- **Small-town** 485-acre campus
- **Endowment** $111.6 million
- **Coed** 2,808 undergraduate students, 98% full-time, 62% women, 38% men
- **Moderately difficult** entrance level, 68% of applicants were admitted

Undergraduates 2,739 full-time, 69 part-time. Students come from 35 states and territories; 29 other countries; 41% are from out of state; 4% transferred in; 87% live on campus. *Retention:* 85% of full-time freshmen returned.

Freshmen *Admission:* 3,066 applied, 2,071 admitted, 721 enrolled. *Average high school GPA:* 3.7. *Test scores:* SAT critical reading scores over 500: 81%; SAT math scores over 500: 82%; SAT writing scores over 500: 79%; ACT scores over 18: 98%; SAT critical reading scores over 600: 38%; SAT math scores over 600: 41%; SAT writing scores over 600: 36%; ACT scores over 24: 68%; SAT critical reading scores over 700: 9%; SAT math scores over 700: 6%; SAT writing scores over 700: 6%; ACT scores over 30: 21%.

Faculty *Total:* 281, 62% full-time. *Student/faculty ratio:* 13:1.

Academics *Calendar:* semesters. *Degrees:* bachelor's, master's, and post-master's certificates. *Special study options:* accelerated degree program, adult/continuing education programs, advanced placement credit, cooperative education, distance learning, double majors, English as a second language, freshman honors college, honors programs, independent study, internships, off-campus study, part-time degree program, services for LD students, student-designed majors, study abroad, summer session for credit. *Unusual degree programs:* 3-2 Biopsychology (B.S.)/EMOT in Occupational Therapy: Thomas Jefferson University; Health and Exercise Science (B.A.)/EMOT in Occupational Therapy: Thomas Jefferson University.

Computers on Campus 571 computers/terminals are available on campus for general student use. Students can access the following: campus intranet, computer help desk, free student e-mail accounts, online (class) grades, online (class) registration, online (class) schedules, access to software. Campuswide network is available. 100% of college-owned or -operated housing units are wired for high-speed Internet access. Wireless service is available via entire campus.

Student Life *Housing:* on-campus residence required through senior year. *Options:* coed, men-only, women-only, disabled students. Campus housing is university owned. Freshman campus housing is guaranteed. *Activities and organizations:* drama/theater group, student-run newspaper, radio station, choral group, Outreach teams, student government, choral groups and ensembles, Small Group Program, Outdoors Club. *Campus security:* 24-hour emergency response devices and patrols, student patrols, late-night transport/escort service, controlled dormitory access, bicycle patrols, security lighting, self-defense classes, prevention/awareness programs. *Student services:* health clinic, personal/psychological counseling.

Athletics Member NCAA. All Division III. *Intercollegiate sports:* baseball M, basketball M/W, cross-country running M/W, field hockey W, golf M, lacrosse M/W, soccer M/W, softball W, swimming and diving M/W, tennis M/W, track and field M/W, volleyball W, wrestling M. *Intramural sports:* basketball M/W, football M/W, ice hockey M(c), racquetball M/W, soccer M/W, softball M/W, ultimate Frisbee M/W, volleyball M/W.

Standardized Tests *Required for some:* SAT or ACT (for admission). *Recommended:* SAT or ACT (for admission).

Costs (2011–12) *Comprehensive fee:* $36,776 includes full-time tuition ($27,536), mandatory fees ($820), and room and board ($8420). Part-time tuition: $1147 per credit. *College room only:* $4460. Room and board charges vary according to board plan, housing facility, and location. *Payment plan:* installment. *Waivers:* minority students, children of alumni, adult students, senior citizens, and employees or children of employees.

Financial Aid Of all full-time matriculated undergraduates who enrolled in 2009, 2,206 applied for aid, 1,964 were judged to have need, 355 had their need fully met. 874 Federal Work-Study jobs (averaging $2085). 707 state and other part-time jobs (averaging $2060). In 2009, 699 non-need-based awards were made. *Average percent of need met:* 69%. *Average financial aid package:* $18,977. *Average need-based loan:* $4549. *Average need-based gift aid:* $13,502. *Average non-need-based aid:* $10,174. *Average indebtedness upon graduation:* $34,132.

Applying *Options:* electronic application, deferred entrance. *Application fee:* $30. *Required:* essay or personal statement, high school transcript, 1 letter of recommendation. *Recommended:* interview. *Application deadlines:* rolling (freshmen), rolling (transfers). *Notification:* continuous (freshmen), continuous (transfers).

Freshman Application Contact Mr. John Chopka, Vice President for Enrollment Management, Messiah College, PO Box 3005, One College Avenue, Grantham, PA 17027. *Phone:* 717-691-6000. *Toll-free phone:* 800-233-4220. *Fax:* 717-791-2307. *E-mail:* admiss@messiah.edu. *Web site:* http://www.messiah.edu/.

See page 1424 for the College Close-Up.

Millersville University of Pennsylvania
Millersville, Pennsylvania

- **State-supported** comprehensive, founded 1855, part of Pennsylvania State System of Higher Education
- **Small-town** 250-acre campus
- **Endowment** $2.0 million
- **Coed** 7,604 undergraduate students, 91% full-time, 56% women, 44% men
- **Moderately difficult** entrance level, 58% of applicants were admitted

Undergraduates 6,908 full-time, 696 part-time. Students come from 14 states and territories; 47 other countries; 4% are from out of state; 7% Black or African American, non-Hispanic/Latino; 5% Hispanic/Latino; 1% Asian, non-Hispanic/Latino; 0.1% Native Hawaiian or other Pacific Islander, non-Hispanic/Latino; 0.2% American Indian or Alaska Native, non-Hispanic/Latino; 1% Two or more races, non-Hispanic/Latino; 1% Race/ethnicity unknown; 0.3% international; 9% transferred in; 32% live on campus. *Retention:* 81% of full-time freshmen returned.

Freshmen *Admission:* 7,292 applied, 4,210 admitted, 1,322 enrolled. *Test scores:* SAT critical reading scores over 500: 63%; SAT math scores over 500: 69%; SAT writing scores over 500: 58%; ACT scores over 18: 86%; SAT critical reading scores over 600: 13%; SAT math scores over 600: 18%; SAT writing scores over 600: 12%; ACT scores over 24: 30%; SAT critical reading scores over 700: 1%; SAT math scores over 700: 1%; SAT writing scores over 700: 1%; ACT scores over 30: 4%.

Faculty *Total:* 431, 69% full-time, 77% with terminal degrees. *Student/faculty ratio:* 23:1.

Academics *Calendar:* 4-1-4. *Degrees:* associate, bachelor's, master's, post-master's, and postbachelor's certificates. *Special study options:* academic remediation for entering students, accelerated degree program, adult/continuing education programs, advanced placement credit, cooperative education, distance learning, double majors, honors programs, independent study, internships, off-campus study, part-time degree program, services for LD students, study abroad, summer session for credit. *ROTC:* Army (b). *Unusual degree programs:* 3-2 engineering with Pennsylvania State University and University of Southern California.

Computers on Campus 712 computers/terminals are available on campus for general student use. Students can access the following: computer help desk, free student e-mail accounts, online (class) grades, online (class) registration, online (class) schedules. Campuswide network is available. 100% of college-owned or -operated housing units are wired for high-speed Internet access. Wireless service is available via entire campus.

Student Life *Housing:* on-campus residence required through sophomore year. *Options:* coed. Campus housing is university owned. Freshman campus housing is guaranteed. *Activities and organizations:* drama/theater group, student-run newspaper, radio and television station, choral group, marching band, John Newman Association, University Christian Fellowship, marching band, University Activities Board (UAB), Student Senate, national fraternities, national sororities. *Campus security:* 24-hour emergency response devices and patrols, student patrols, late-night transport/escort service, controlled dormitory access, crime awareness programs, self-defense education, shuttle buses, lighted pathways / sidewalks. *Student services:* health clinic, personal/psychological counseling, women's center.

Athletics Member NCAA. All Division II except wrestling (Division I). *Intercollegiate sports:* baseball M(s), basketball M(s)/W(s), cheerleading W, cross-country running M(s)/W(s), field hockey W(s), football M(s), golf M(s), lacrosse W(s), soccer M(s)/W(s), softball W(s), swimming and diving W(s), tennis M(s)/W(s), track and field M(s)/W(s), volleyball W(s), wrestling M(s). *Intramural sports:* badminton M/W, basketball M/W, bowling M(c)/W(c), fencing M(c)/W(c), golf M/W, ice hockey M(c), lacrosse M(c), racquetball M/W, rock climbing M/W, rugby M(c)/W(c), soccer M/W, softball M/W, tennis M/W, ultimate Frisbee M/W, volleyball M(c)/W, water polo M(c)/W(c).

Standardized Tests *Required:* SAT or ACT (for admission).

Costs (2010–11) *Tuition:* state resident $5804 full-time, $242 per credit part-time; nonresident $14,510 full-time, $605 per credit part-time. Full-time tuition and fees vary according to degree level. Part-time tuition and fees vary according to course load and degree level. *Required fees:* $1896 full-time, $69 per credit part-time, $68 per term part-time. *Room and board:* $8298; room only: $4872. Room and board charges vary according to board plan and housing facility. *Payment plan:* installment. *Waivers:* senior citizens and employees or children of employees.

Financial Aid Of all full-time matriculated undergraduates who enrolled in 2008, 5,303 applied for aid, 3,942 were judged to have need, 479 had their need fully met. 283 Federal Work-Study jobs (averaging $1314). 1,722 state and other part-time jobs (averaging $1459). In 2008, 154 non-need-based awards were made. *Average percent of need met:* 77%. *Average financial aid package:* $8050. *Average need-based loan:* $4046. *Average need-based gift aid:* $5463. *Average non-need-based aid:* $2702. *Average indebtedness upon graduation:* $25,876.

Applying *Options:* electronic application, early admission, deferred entrance. *Application fee:* $50. *Required:* high school transcript, minimum 2 GPA. *Required for some:* essay or personal statement, interview. *Recommended:* essay or personal statement. *Application deadlines:* rolling (freshmen), rolling (out-of-state freshmen), rolling (transfers). *Notification:* continuous (freshmen), continuous (out-of-state freshmen), continuous (transfers).

Freshman Application Contact Dr. Jose Aviles, Director of Admissions, Millersville University of Pennsylvania, PO Box 1002, Millersville, PA 17551-0302. *Phone:* 717-872-3371. *Toll-free phone:* 800-MU-ADMIT. *Fax:* 717-871-2147. *E-mail:* admissions@millersville.edu. *Web site:* http://www.millersville.edu/.

See page 1432 for the College Close-Up.

Misericordia University

Dallas, Pennsylvania

- **Independent Roman Catholic** comprehensive, founded 1924
- **Small-town** 100-acre campus
- **Endowment** $19.7 million
- **Coed, primarily women** 2,409 undergraduate students, 71% full-time, 71% women, 29% men
- **Moderately difficult** entrance level, 67% of applicants were admitted

Undergraduates 1,699 full-time, 710 part-time. Students come from 22 states and territories; 17% are from out of state; 1% Black or African American, non-Hispanic/Latino; 2% Hispanic/Latino; 0.9% Asian, non-Hispanic/Latino; 0.1% American Indian or Alaska Native, non-Hispanic/Latino; 0.7% Two or more races, non-Hispanic/Latino; 5% transferred in; 37% live on campus. *Retention:* 81% of full-time freshmen returned.

Freshmen *Admission:* 1,551 applied, 1,032 admitted, 375 enrolled. *Average high school GPA:* 3.3. *Test scores:* SAT critical reading scores over 500: 63%; SAT math scores over 500: 70%; ACT scores over 18: 98%; SAT critical reading scores over 600: 16%; SAT math scores over 600: 15%; ACT scores over 24: 42%; SAT critical reading scores over 700: 1%; SAT math scores over 700: 1%; ACT scores over 30: 2%.

Faculty *Total:* 292, 36% full-time, 37% with terminal degrees. *Student/faculty ratio:* 12:1.

Academics *Calendar:* semesters. *Degrees:* bachelor's, master's, doctoral-professional, post-master's, and postbachelor's certificates. *Special study options:* academic remediation for entering students, accelerated degree program, adult/continuing education programs, advanced placement credit, cooperative education, distance learning, double majors, external degree program, honors programs, independent study, internships, off-campus study, part-time degree program, services for LD students, student-designed majors, study abroad, summer session for credit. *ROTC:* Army (c), Air Force (c). *Unusual degree programs:* 3-2 occupational therapy, physical therapy, speech-language pathology.

Computers on Campus 100 computers/terminals and 1,000 ports are available on campus for general student use. Students can access the following: campus intranet, computer help desk, free student e-mail accounts, online (class) grades, online (class) registration, online (class) schedules, student leadership transcript. Campuswide network is available. 100% of college-owned or -operated housing units are wired for high-speed Internet access. Wireless service is available via entire campus.

Student Life *Housing options:* coed. Campus housing is university owned. Freshman applicants given priority for college housing. *Activities and organizations:* drama/theater group, student-run newspaper, radio station, choral group, Circle K, SOAR - Student Outdoor Adventure and Recreation, BACCHUS, Peer Advocates, Commuter Council. *Campus security:* 24-hour emergency response devices and patrols, late-night transport/escort service. *Student services:* health clinic, personal/psychological counseling, women's center.

Athletics Member NCAA. All Division III. *Intercollegiate sports:* baseball M, basketball M/W, cheerleading W, cross-country running M/W, field hockey W, football M, golf M, lacrosse M/W, soccer M/W, softball W, swimming and diving M/W, tennis M/W, track and field M/W, volleyball W. *Intramural sports:* basketball M/W, cross-country running M/W, football M/W, racquetball M/W, soccer M/W, softball M/W, tennis M/W, ultimate Frisbee M/W, volleyball M/W.

Standardized Tests *Required:* SAT or ACT (for admission).

Costs (2010–11) *Comprehensive fee:* $35,400 includes full-time tuition ($23,750), mandatory fees ($1240), and room and board ($10,410). Part-time tuition: $450 per credit. Part-time tuition and fees vary according to class time, degree level, and location. *College room only:* $6040. Room and board charges vary according to board plan and housing facility. *Payment plans:* installment, deferred payment. *Waivers:* employees or children of employees.

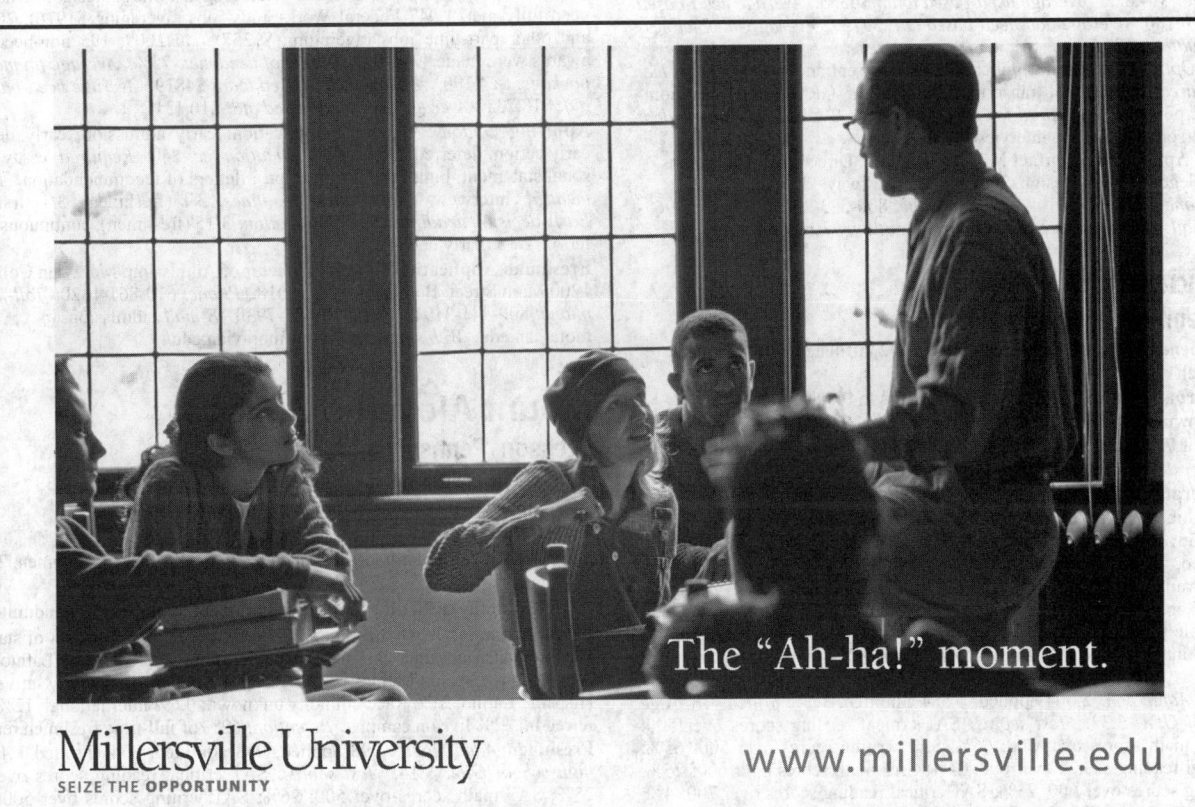

Financial Aid Of all full-time matriculated undergraduates who enrolled in 2009, 1,579 applied for aid, 1,428 were judged to have need, 196 had their need fully met. In 2009, 145 non-need-based awards were made. *Average percent of need met:* 73%. *Average financial aid package:* $18,120. *Average need-based loan:* $8345. *Average need-based gift aid:* $12,564. *Average non-need-based aid:* $7284. *Average indebtedness upon graduation:* $36,742.

Applying *Options:* electronic application, early admission, deferred entrance. *Application fee:* $25. *Required:* high school transcript. *Required for some:* essay or personal statement, minimum 2 GPA, 2 letters of recommendation. *Recommended:* interview. *Application deadlines:* rolling (freshmen), rolling (transfers). *Notification:* continuous (freshmen), continuous (transfers).

Freshman Application Contact Mr. Glenn Bozinski, Director of Admissions, Misericordia University, 301 Lake Street, Dallas, PA 18612-1098. *Phone:* 570-675-6264. *Toll-free phone:* 866-262-6363. *Fax:* 570-674-6232. *E-mail:* admiss@misericordia.edu. *Web site:* http://www.misericordia.edu/.

See page 1440 for the College Close-Up.

Moore College of Art & Design
Philadelphia, Pennsylvania

- **Independent** comprehensive, founded 1848
- **Urban** 3-acre campus
- **Endowment** $8.1 million
- **Women only**
- **Moderately difficult** entrance level

Faculty *Student/faculty ratio:* 9:1.

Academics *Calendar:* semesters. *Degrees:* certificates, bachelor's, master's, and postbachelor's certificates.

Student Life *Campus security:* 24-hour patrols, late-night transport/escort service.

Standardized Tests *Required for some:* SAT or ACT (for admission).

Costs (2010–11) *Comprehensive fee:* $41,778 includes full-time tuition ($29,266), mandatory fees ($1144), and room and board ($11,368). Part-time tuition: $1221 per credit. Part-time tuition and fees vary according to course load and program. *Required fees:* $251 per term part-time. *College room only:* $6844. Room and board charges vary according to board plan and housing facility.

Financial Aid *Of all full-time matriculated undergraduates who enrolled in 2006,* 383 applied for aid, 357 were judged to have need, 9 had their need fully met. 87 Federal Work-Study jobs (averaging $1500). In 2006, 93 non-need-based awards were made. *Average percent of need met:* 45. *Average financial aid package:* $14,823. *Average need-based loan:* $4355. *Average need-based gift aid:* $10,180. *Average non-need-based aid:* $9729. *Average indebtedness upon graduation:* $36,778.

Applying *Options:* electronic application, deferred entrance. *Application fee:* $40. *Required:* high school transcript, minimum 2.5 GPA, 1 letter of recommendation, portfolio. *Required for some:* minimum 3 GPA. *Recommended:* essay or personal statement, interview.

Freshman Application Contact Ms. Heesung Lee, Director of Admissions, Moore College of Art & Design, 20th and The Parkway, Philadelphia, PA 19103. *Phone:* 215-965-4014. *Toll-free phone:* 800-523-2025. *Fax:* 215-965-8544. *E-mail:* enroll@moore.edu. *Web site:* http://www.moore.edu/.

Moravian College
Bethlehem, Pennsylvania

- **Independent** comprehensive, founded 1742, affiliated with Moravian Church
- **Suburban** 60-acre campus with easy access to Philadelphia
- **Endowment** $74.1 million
- **Coed** 1,773 undergraduate students, 88% full-time, 60% women, 40% men
- **Moderately difficult** entrance level, 79% of applicants were admitted

Undergraduates 1,559 full-time, 214 part-time. Students come from 14 other countries; 36% are from out of state; 3% Black or African American, non-Hispanic/Latino; 7% Hispanic/Latino; 2% Asian, non-Hispanic/Latino; 0.1% Native Hawaiian or other Pacific Islander, non-Hispanic/Latino; 0.1% American Indian or Alaska Native, non-Hispanic/Latino; 2% Two or more races, non-Hispanic/Latino; 0.8% Race/ethnicity unknown; 1% international; 5% transferred in; 76% live on campus. *Retention:* 80% of full-time freshmen returned.

Freshmen *Admission:* 2,004 applied, 1,584 admitted, 373 enrolled. *Average high school GPA:* 3.33. *Test scores:* SAT critical reading scores over 500: 66%; SAT math scores over 500: 66%; SAT writing scores over 500: 65%; SAT critical reading scores over 600: 24%; SAT math scores over 600: 25%; SAT writing scores over 600: 23%; SAT critical reading scores over 700: 4%; SAT math scores over 700: 4%; SAT writing scores over 700: 1%.

Faculty *Total:* 202, 57% full-time, 65% with terminal degrees. *Student/faculty ratio:* 11:1.

Academics *Calendar:* semesters. *Degrees:* bachelor's, master's, and post-bachelor's certificates. *Special study options:* adult/continuing education programs, advanced placement credit, double majors, honors programs, independent study, internships, off-campus study, part-time degree program, services for LD students, student-designed majors, study abroad, summer session for credit. *ROTC:* Army (c). *Unusual degree programs:* 3-2 engineering with Washington University in St. Louis; Lehigh University; forestry with Duke University; occupational therapy with Thomas Jefferson University, Dental School, Temple University.

Computers on Campus 180 computers/terminals are available on campus for general student use. Students can access the following: campus intranet, computer help desk, free student e-mail accounts, online (class) grades, online (class) schedules. Campuswide network is available. 100% of college-owned or -operated housing units are wired for high-speed Internet access. Wireless service is available via classrooms, computer centers, computer labs, learning centers, libraries, student centers.

Student Life *Housing:* on-campus residence required through junior year. *Options:* coed, men-only, women-only. Campus housing is university owned. Freshman campus housing is guaranteed. *Activities and organizations:* drama/theater group, student-run newspaper, radio station, choral group, marching band, Student Alumni Association, United Student Government, Moravian College Choir, Twenty-six Points (student ambassador group), Multicultural Club, national fraternities, national sororities. *Campus security:* 24-hour emergency response devices and patrols, late-night transport/escort service, controlled dormitory access. *Student services:* health clinic, personal/psychological counseling.

Athletics Member NCAA. All Division III. *Intercollegiate sports:* baseball M, basketball M/W, cheerleading W(c), cross-country running M/W, equestrian sports M(c)/W(c), field hockey W, football M, golf M/W(c), ice hockey M(c)/W(c), soccer M/W, softball W, tennis M/W, track and field M/W, volleyball W. *Intramural sports:* badminton M/W, basketball M/W, football M/W, racquetball M/W, rugby M/W, skiing (downhill) M(c)/W(c), soccer M/W, softball M/W, table tennis M/W, tennis M/W, volleyball M/W.

Standardized Tests *Required:* SAT or ACT (for admission).

Costs (2010–11) *Comprehensive fee:* $41,341 includes full-time tuition ($31,662), mandatory fees ($515), and room and board ($9164). Part-time tuition: $880 per credit hour. Part-time tuition and fees vary according to class time. *College room only:* $5149. Room and board charges vary according to board plan and housing facility. *Payment plan:* installment. *Waivers:* employees or children of employees.

Financial Aid Of all full-time matriculated undergraduates who enrolled in 2009, 1,337 applied for aid, 1,222 were judged to have need, 184 had their need fully met. 1,047 Federal Work-Study jobs (averaging $1916). 268 state and other part-time jobs (averaging $1257). In 2009, 195 non-need-based awards were made. *Average percent of need met:* 75%. *Average financial aid package:* $24,190. *Average need-based loan:* $4819. *Average need-based gift aid:* $18,231. *Average non-need-based aid:* $10,131.

Applying *Options:* electronic application, early admission, early decision, early action, deferred entrance. *Application fee:* $40. *Required:* essay or personal statement, high school transcript, 3 letters of recommendation. *Recommended:* interview. *Application deadlines:* 3/1 (freshmen), 3/1 (transfers). *Early decision deadline:* 2/1. *Notification:* 3/15 (freshmen), continuous (transfers), 12/15 (early decision).

Freshman Application Contact Director of Admission, Moravian College, 1200 Main Street, Bethlehem, PA 18018. *Phone:* 610-861-1320. *Toll-free phone:* 800-441-3191. *Fax:* 610-625-7930. *E-mail:* admissions@moravian.edu. *Web site:* http://www.moravian.edu/.

Mount Aloysius College
Cresson, Pennsylvania

- **Independent Roman Catholic** comprehensive, founded 1939
- **Small-town** 193-acre campus
- **Endowment** $15.3 million
- **Coed** 1,573 undergraduate students, 79% full-time, 71% women, 29% men
- **Minimally difficult** entrance level, 72% of applicants were admitted

Undergraduates 1,241 full-time, 332 part-time. 5% are from out of state; 3% Black or African American, non-Hispanic/Latino; 1% Hispanic/Latino; 0.4% Asian, non-Hispanic/Latino; 0.2% American Indian or Alaska Native, non-Hispanic/Latino; 21% Race/ethnicity unknown; 0.6% international; 12% transferred in; 32% live on campus. *Retention:* 62% of full-time freshmen returned.

Freshmen *Admission:* 1,298 applied, 938 admitted, 364 enrolled. *Average high school GPA:* 3.14. *Test scores:* SAT critical reading scores over 500: 25%; SAT math scores over 500: 26%; SAT writing scores over 500: 18%; ACT scores over 18: 56%; SAT critical reading scores over 600: 2%; SAT math scores over 600: 2%; SAT writing scores over 600: 1%; ACT scores over 24: 10%; ACT scores over 30: 1%.

Faculty *Total:* 171, 40% full-time, 21% with terminal degrees. *Student/faculty ratio:* 14:1.

Academics *Calendar:* semesters. *Degrees:* certificates, associate, bachelor's, and master's. *Special study options:* academic remediation for entering students, accelerated degree program, advanced placement credit, distance learning, double majors, external degree program, honors programs, independent study, internships, part-time degree program, student-designed majors, study abroad, summer session for credit.

Computers on Campus Students can access the following: campus intranet, computer help desk, free student e-mail accounts, online (class) grades, online (class) registration, online (class) schedules. Campuswide network is available. 100% of college-owned or -operated housing units are wired for high-speed Internet access. Wireless service is available via entire campus.

Student Life *Housing:* on-campus residence required for freshman year. *Options:* coed. Campus housing is university owned. Freshman campus housing is guaranteed. *Activities and organizations:* drama/theater group, student-run newspaper, choral group. *Campus security:* 24-hour emergency response devices and patrols, student patrols, late-night transport/escort service, controlled dormitory access. *Student services:* health clinic, personal/psychological counseling, women's center.

Athletics Member NCAA. All Division III. *Intercollegiate sports:* baseball M, basketball M/W, cross-country running M/W, golf M/W, soccer M/W, softball W, volleyball W. *Intramural sports:* baseball M, basketball M/W, cheerleading M(c)/W(c), football M/W, skiing (cross-country) M/W, skiing (downhill) M/W, soccer M/W, softball M/W, table tennis M/W, tennis M/W, ultimate Frisbee M/W, volleyball M/W, weight lifting M/W.

Standardized Tests *Required:* SAT or ACT (for admission).

Costs (2010–11) *Comprehensive fee:* $25,660 includes full-time tuition ($17,240), mandatory fees ($760), and room and board ($7660). Full-time tuition and fees vary according to program. Part-time tuition: $520 per credit. Part-time tuition and fees vary according to program. *Required fees:* $200 per term part-time. *College room only:* $3940. Room and board charges vary according to board plan. *Payment plan:* installment. *Waivers:* employees or children of employees.

Financial Aid Of all full-time matriculated undergraduates who enrolled in 2009, 1,206 applied for aid, 1,185 were judged to have need. 220 Federal Work-Study jobs (averaging $1000). In 2009, 21 non-need-based awards were made. *Average percent of need met:* 35%. *Average financial aid package:* $12,668. *Average need-based loan:* $4179. *Average need-based gift aid:* $4830. *Average non-need-based aid:* $3600. *Average indebtedness upon graduation:* $32,312.

Applying *Options:* electronic application, early admission, deferred entrance. *Application fee:* $30. *Required:* high school transcript. *Required for some:* essay or personal statement, interview. *Recommended:* interview. *Application deadlines:* rolling (freshmen), rolling (transfers). *Notification:* continuous (freshmen), continuous (transfers).

Freshman Application Contact Mr. Frank C. Crouse Jr., Vice President for Enrollment Management/Dean of Admissions, Mount Aloysius College, 7373 Admiral Peary Highway, Cresson, PA 16630-1999. *Phone:* 814-886-6383. *Toll-free phone:* 888-823-2220. *Fax:* 814-886-6441. *E-mail:* admissions@mtaloy.edu. *Web site:* http://www.mtaloy.edu/.

See page 1452 for the College Close-Up.

Muhlenberg College
Allentown, Pennsylvania

- **Independent** 4-year, founded 1848, affiliated with Lutheran Church
- **Suburban** 75-acre campus with easy access to Philadelphia
- **Endowment** $126.5 million
- **Coed** 2,515 undergraduate students, 94% full-time, 57% women, 43% men
- **Very difficult** entrance level, 49% of applicants were admitted

Undergraduates 2,370 full-time, 145 part-time. Students come from 34 states and territories; 7 other countries; 70% are from out of state; 0.5% transferred in; 92% live on campus. *Retention:* 93% of full-time freshmen returned.

Freshmen *Admission:* 4,505 applied, 2,195 admitted, 603 enrolled. *Average high school GPA:* 3.3. *Test scores:* SAT critical reading scores over 500: 93%; SAT math scores over 500: 95%; SAT writing scores over 500: 95%; ACT scores over 18: 100%; SAT critical reading scores over 600: 60%; SAT math scores over 600: 64%; SAT writing scores over 600: 60%; ACT scores over 24: 86%; SAT critical reading scores over 700: 15%; SAT math scores over 700: 11%; SAT writing scores over 700: 15%; ACT scores over 30: 25%.

Faculty *Total:* 257, 65% full-time, 66% with terminal degrees. *Student/faculty ratio:* 12:1.

THE HORIZON IS JUST YOUR STARTING LINE

Mount Aloysius College

ON-CAMPUS · OPPORTUNITIES · ONLINE

888-823-2220 · mtaloy.edu

Academics *Calendar:* semesters. *Degrees:* certificates, associate, and bachelor's. *Special study options:* accelerated degree program, adult/continuing education programs, advanced placement credit, double majors, honors programs, independent study, internships, off-campus study, part-time degree program, services for LD students, student-designed majors, study abroad, summer session for credit. *ROTC:* Army (c). *Unusual degree programs:* 3-2 engineering with Columbia University; forestry with Duke University.

Computers on Campus 490 computers/terminals and 100 ports are available on campus for general student use. Students can access the following: campus intranet, computer help desk, free student e-mail accounts, online (class) grades, online (class) registration, online (class) schedules. Campuswide network is available. 100% of college-owned or -operated housing units are wired for high-speed Internet access. Wireless service is available via classrooms, dorm rooms, libraries, student centers.

Student Life *Housing:* on-campus residence required for freshman year. *Options:* coed, women-only, disabled students. Campus housing is university owned and leased by the school. Freshman campus housing is guaranteed. *Activities and organizations:* drama/theater group, student-run newspaper, radio and television station, choral group, Theater Association, Environmental Action Team, Jefferson School Partnership, Select Choir, Habitat for Humanity, national fraternities, national sororities. *Campus security:* 24-hour emergency response devices and patrols, late-night transport/escort service, controlled dormitory access. *Student services:* health clinic, personal/psychological counseling.

Athletics Member NCAA. All Division III. *Intercollegiate sports:* baseball M, basketball M/W, cheerleading M/W, cross-country running M/W, field hockey W, football M, golf M/W, lacrosse M/W, soccer M/W, softball W, tennis M/W, track and field M/W, volleyball W, wrestling M. *Intramural sports:* basketball M/W, cross-country running M/W, football M/W, ice hockey M, racquetball M/W, rugby M/W, soccer M/W, softball M, swimming and diving M/W, tennis M/W, ultimate Frisbee M, volleyball M/W.

Standardized Tests *Required for some:* SAT or ACT (for admission).

Costs (2010–11) *Comprehensive fee:* $47,115 includes full-time tuition ($38,110), mandatory fees ($270), and room and board ($8735). Part-time tuition and fees vary according to program. *College room only:* $5035. Room and board charges vary according to board plan, housing facility, and location. *Payment plan:* installment. *Waivers:* employees or children of employees.

Financial Aid Of all full-time matriculated undergraduates who enrolled in 2008, 1,318 applied for aid, 1,038 were judged to have need, 943 had their need fully met. In 2008, 594 non-need-based awards were made. *Average percent of need met:* 92%. *Average financial aid package:* $22,294. *Average need-based loan:* $4238. *Average need-based gift aid:* $19,598. *Average non-need-based aid:* $12,312. *Average indebtedness upon graduation:* $18,542. *Financial aid deadline:* 2/15.

Applying *Options:* electronic application, early admission, early decision, deferred entrance. *Application fee:* $50. *Required:* essay or personal statement, high school transcript, 2 letters of recommendation. *Required for some:* interview, graded paper. *Recommended:* interview. *Application deadlines:* 2/15 (freshmen), 6/15 (transfers). *Early decision deadline:* 2/1. *Notification:* 3/15 (freshmen), continuous until 7/1 (transfers).

Freshman Application Contact Mr. Christopher Hooker-Haring, Director of Undergraduate Admissions, Muhlenberg College, 2400 Chew Street, Allentown, PA 18104. *Phone:* 484-664-3245. *Fax:* 484-664-3234. *E-mail:* adm@muhlenberg.edu. *Web site:* http://www.muhlenberg.edu/.

See page 1456 for the College Close-Up.

Neumann University
Aston, Pennsylvania

- **Independent Roman Catholic** comprehensive, founded 1965
- **Suburban** 50-acre campus with easy access to Philadelphia
- **Endowment** $18.9 million
- **Coed** 2,524 undergraduate students, 81% full-time, 66% women, 34% men
- **Moderately difficult** entrance level, 93% of applicants were admitted

Undergraduates 2,043 full-time, 481 part-time. Students come from 18 states and territories; 14 other countries; 30% are from out of state; 4% transferred in; 40% live on campus. *Retention:* 73% of full-time freshmen returned.

Freshmen *Admission:* 2,478 applied, 2,295 admitted, 552 enrolled. *Average high school GPA:* 3.25. *Test scores:* SAT critical reading scores over 500: 22%; SAT math scores over 500: 23%; SAT critical reading scores over 600: 3%; SAT math scores over 600: 2%; SAT critical reading scores over 700: 1%.

Faculty *Total:* 315, 30% full-time, 47% with terminal degrees. *Student/faculty ratio:* 14:1.

MUHLENBERG COLLEGE

Excellence in the liberal arts and pre-professional studies.

For more information, contact:

Christopher Hooker-Haring
Dean of Admission & Financial Aid
Office of Admission
2400 Chew Street
Allentown, Pennsylvania 18104
Phone: 484-664-3200
E-mail: admission@muhlenberg.edu

Web site: www.muhlenberg.edu

Academics *Calendar:* semesters. *Degrees:* certificates, associate, bachelor's, master's, doctoral-other, doctoral-professional, post-master's, and postbachelor's certificates. *Special study options:* academic remediation for entering students, accelerated degree program, adult/continuing education programs, advanced placement credit, cooperative education, distance learning, double majors, freshman honors college, honors programs, independent study, internships, off-campus study, part-time degree program, services for LD students, student-designed majors, study abroad, summer session for credit. *ROTC:* Army (c).

Computers on Campus 500 computers/terminals are available on campus for general student use. Students can access the following: campus intranet, computer help desk, free student e-mail accounts, online (class) grades, online (class) registration, online (class) schedules. Campuswide network is available. 100% of college-owned or -operated housing units are wired for high-speed Internet access. Wireless service is available via computer centers, libraries.

Student Life *Housing options:* coed. Campus housing is university owned and leased by the school. Freshman applicants given priority for college housing. *Activities and organizations:* drama/theater group, student-run newspaper, radio station, choral group, Professional Education Society, Student Nurses Association, theater ensemble, Environmental Club, community chorus. *Campus security:* 24-hour emergency response devices and patrols, late-night transport/escort service, controlled dormitory access. *Student services:* health clinic, personal/psychological counseling.

Athletics Member NCAA. All Division III. *Intercollegiate sports:* baseball M, basketball M/W, cross-country running M/W, field hockey W, golf M, ice hockey M/W, lacrosse M/W, soccer M/W, softball W, tennis M/W, track and field M/W, volleyball W. *Intramural sports:* basketball M/W, lacrosse M, softball W, tennis M/W, volleyball M/W.

Standardized Tests *Required:* SAT or ACT (for admission).

Costs (2010–11) *Comprehensive fee:* $32,418 includes full-time tuition ($21,456), mandatory fees ($800), and room and board ($10,162). Part-time tuition: $490 per credit hour. *Required fees:* $30 per semester hour part-time. *College room only:* $5976. Room and board charges vary according to board plan. *Payment plan:* installment. *Waivers:* employees or children of employees.

Financial Aid Of all full-time matriculated undergraduates who enrolled in 2009, 1,820 applied for aid, 1,820 were judged to have need, 1,100 had their need fully met. 180 Federal Work-Study jobs (averaging $1400). *Average per-*cent of need met: 65%. *Average financial aid package:* $19,000. *Average need-based loan:* $5000. *Average need-based gift aid:* $11,000. *Average indebtedness upon graduation:* $30,000.

Applying *Application fee:* $35. *Required:* high school transcript, minimum 2 GPA. *Recommended:* interview. *Application deadlines:* 4/1 (freshmen), rolling (transfers). *Notification:* continuous (freshmen), continuous (transfers).

Freshman Application Contact Mr. Dennis J. Murphy, Vice President for Enrollment Management, Neumann University, One Neumann Drive, Aston, PA 19014-1298. *Phone:* 610-361-2448. *Toll-free phone:* 800-963-8626. *Fax:* 610-558-5652. *E-mail:* neumann@neumann.edu. *Web site:* http://www.neumann.edu/.

See page 1462 for the College Close-Up.

Peirce College
Philadelphia, Pennsylvania

- **Independent** 4-year, founded 1865
- **Urban** 1-acre campus
- **Endowment** $13.5 million
- **Coed, primarily women** 2,139 undergraduate students, 36% full-time, 71% women, 29% men
- **Noncompetitive** entrance level

Undergraduates 762 full-time, 1,377 part-time. Students come from 29 states and territories; 28 other countries; 14% are from out of state; 61% Black or African American, non-Hispanic/Latino; 6% Hispanic/Latino; 2% Asian, non-Hispanic/Latino; 0.2% Native Hawaiian or other Pacific Islander, non-Hispanic/Latino; 0.5% American Indian or Alaska Native, non-Hispanic/Latino; 0.6% Two or more races, non-Hispanic/Latino; 2% Race/ethnicity unknown; 1% international. *Retention:* 100% of full-time freshmen returned.

Freshmen *Admission:* 115 enrolled.

Faculty *Total:* 155, 21% full-time, 33% with terminal degrees. *Student/faculty ratio:* 17:1.

Academics *Calendar:* semesters. *Degrees:* certificates, associate, and bachelor's. *Special study options:* accelerated degree program, adult/continuing education programs, advanced placement credit, cooperative education, distance learning, internships, part-time degree program, services for LD students, summer session for credit.

Computers on Campus 43 computers/terminals are available on campus for general student use. Students can access the following: campus intranet, computer help desk, free student e-mail accounts, online (class) grades, online (class) registration, online (class) schedules. Campuswide network is available. Wireless service is available via entire campus.

Student Life *Housing:* college housing not available. *Campus security:* 24-hour emergency response devices and patrols, late-night transport/escort service, 24-hour security cameras.

Costs (2011–12) *Tuition:* $14,850 full-time, $495 per credit part-time. Full-time tuition and fees vary according to course load. Part-time tuition and fees vary according to course load. *Required fees:* $1050 full-time. *Payment plan:* installment. *Waivers:* children of alumni and employees or children of employees.

Financial Aid Of all full-time matriculated undergraduates who enrolled in 2008, 615 applied for aid, 554 were judged to have need, 15 had their need fully met. 32 Federal Work-Study jobs (averaging $3600). In 2008, 38 non-need-based awards were made. *Average percent of need met:* 56%. *Average financial aid package:* $10,628. *Average need-based loan:* $4944. *Average need-based gift aid:* $6323. *Average non-need-based aid:* $2221. *Average indebtedness upon graduation:* $18,721.

Applying *Options:* electronic application. *Application fee:* $50. *Required:* high school transcript. *Application deadlines:* rolling (freshmen), rolling (out-of-state freshmen), rolling (transfers). *Notification:* continuous (freshmen), continuous (out-of-state freshmen), continuous (transfers).

Freshman Application Contact Mr. Paul Ballentine, Supervisor, Admissions, Peirce College, 1420 Pine Street, Philadelphia, PA 19102. *Phone:* 215-670-9214. *Toll-free phone:* 888-467-3472. *Fax:* 215-670-9366. *E-mail:* info@peirce.edu. *Web site:* http://www.peirce.edu/.

Penn State Abington

Abington, Pennsylvania

- **State-related** 4-year, founded 1950, part of Pennsylvania State University
- **Small-town** 45-acre campus with easy access to Philadelphia
- **Coed** 3,423 undergraduate students, 82% full-time, 49% women, 51% men
- **Very difficult** entrance level

Undergraduates 2,792 full-time, 631 part-time. 6% are from out of state; 13% Black or African American, non-Hispanic/Latino; 8% Hispanic/Latino; 15% Asian, non-Hispanic/Latino; 0.1% Native Hawaiian or other Pacific Islander, non-Hispanic/Latino; 0.2% American Indian or Alaska Native, non-Hispanic/Latino; 2% Two or more races, non-Hispanic/Latino; 4% Race/ethnicity unknown; 1% international; 4% transferred in. *Retention:* 76% of full-time freshmen returned.

Freshmen *Admission:* 2,111 applied, 833 enrolled. *Average high school GPA:* 3.02. *Test scores:* SAT critical reading scores over 500: 32%; SAT math scores over 500: 43%; SAT writing scores over 500: 29%; SAT critical reading scores over 600: 5%; SAT math scores over 600: 14%; SAT writing scores over 600: 6%; SAT critical reading scores over 700: 1%; SAT math scores over 700: 2%; SAT writing scores over 700: 1%.

Faculty *Total:* 245, 44% full-time, 45% with terminal degrees. *Student/faculty ratio:* 20:1.

Academics *Calendar:* semesters. *Degrees:* associate and bachelor's (enrollment figures include students enrolled at The Graduate School at Penn State who are taking courses at this location). *Special study options:* academic remediation for entering students, accelerated degree program, adult/continuing education programs, advanced placement credit, cooperative education, distance learning, double majors, English as a second language, external degree program, freshman honors college, honors programs, independent study, internships, off-campus study, part-time degree program, services for LD students, student-designed majors, study abroad, summer session for credit. *ROTC:* Army (b), Air Force (c). *Unusual degree programs:* 3-2 biotechnology, cytotechnology, medical technology, occupational therapy with Thomas Jefferson University, Jefferson College of Health Professions; clinical health psychology with Philadelphia College of Osteopathic Medicine.

Computers on Campus Students can access the following: campus intranet, computer help desk, free student e-mail accounts, online (class) grades, online (class) registration, online (class) schedules. Campuswide network is available.

Student Life *Housing:* college housing not available. *Activities and organizations:* drama/theater group, student-run newspaper, choral group. *Campus security:* 24-hour emergency response devices and patrols. *Student services:* health clinic, personal/psychological counseling.

Athletics *Intercollegiate sports:* baseball M, basketball M/W, golf M, soccer M/W, softball W, tennis M/W, volleyball W. *Intramural sports:* basketball M/W, cross-country running M/W, football M, soccer M/W, softball M, tennis M/W, volleyball M/W.

Standardized Tests *Required:* SAT or ACT (for admission).

Costs (2010–11) *Tuition:* state resident $11,892 full-time, $481 per credit part-time; nonresident $18,148 full-time, $756 per credit part-time. Full-time tuition and fees vary according to course level, degree level, location, program, and student level. Part-time tuition and fees vary according to course level, course load, degree level, location, program, and student level. *Required fees:* $838 full-time. *Payment plans:* installment, deferred payment. *Waivers:* senior citizens and employees or children of employees.

Financial Aid Of all full-time matriculated undergraduates who enrolled in 2008, 2,217 applied for aid, 1,803 were judged to have need, 68 had their need fully met. In 2008, 85 non-need-based awards were made. *Average percent of need met:* 58%. *Average financial aid package:* $9852. *Average need-based loan:* $3937. *Average need-based gift aid:* $6978. *Average non-need-based aid:* $1795. *Average indebtedness upon graduation:* $31,135.

Applying *Options:* electronic application, early admission, deferred entrance. *Application fee:* $50. *Required:* high school transcript. *Required for some:* interview. *Recommended:* essay or personal statement. *Application deadlines:* rolling (freshmen), rolling (transfers). *Notification:* continuous (freshmen), continuous (transfers).

Freshman Application Contact Admissions Office, Penn State Abington, 1600 Woodland Road, Abington, PA 19001. *Phone:* 215-881-7600. *Fax:* 215-881-7655. *E-mail:* abingtonadmissions@psu.edu. *Web site:* http://www.abington.psu.edu/.

Penn State Altoona

Altoona, Pennsylvania

- **State-related** 4-year, founded 1939, part of Pennsylvania State University
- **Suburban** 150-acre campus
- **Coed** 4,128 undergraduate students, 94% full-time, 47% women, 53% men
- **Very difficult** entrance level

Undergraduates 3,888 full-time, 240 part-time. 15% are from out of state; 6% Black or African American, non-Hispanic/Latino; 4% Hispanic/Latino; 2% Asian, non-Hispanic/Latino; 0.1% Native Hawaiian or other Pacific Islander, non-Hispanic/Latino; 0.1% American Indian or Alaska Native, non-Hispanic/Latino; 2% Two or more races, non-Hispanic/Latino; 2% Race/ethnicity unknown; 1% international; 2% transferred in; 22% live on campus. *Retention:* 86% of full-time freshmen returned.

Freshmen *Admission:* 2,437 applied, 1,441 enrolled. *Average high school GPA:* 3.04. *Test scores:* SAT critical reading scores over 500: 45%; SAT math scores over 500: 56%; SAT writing scores over 500: 42%; SAT critical reading scores over 600: 7%; SAT math scores over 600: 14%; SAT writing scores over 600: 6%; SAT math scores over 700: 1%.

Faculty *Total:* 327, 56% full-time, 50% with terminal degrees. *Student/faculty ratio:* 17:1.

Academics *Calendar:* semesters. *Degrees:* certificates, associate, and bachelor's (enrollment figures include students enrolled at The Graduate School at Penn State who are taking courses at this location). *Special study options:* academic remediation for entering students, accelerated degree program, adult/continuing education programs, advanced placement credit, cooperative education, distance learning, double majors, English as a second language, freshman honors college, honors programs, independent study, internships, off-campus study, part-time degree program, services for LD students, student-designed majors, study abroad, summer session for credit. *ROTC:* Army (c), Air Force (c).

Computers on Campus Students can access the following: campus intranet, computer help desk, free student e-mail accounts, online (class) grades, online (class) registration, online (class) schedules. Campuswide network is available.

Student Life *Housing options:* coed, disabled students. Campus housing is university owned. *Activities and organizations:* drama/theater group, student-run newspaper, choral group, national fraternities, national sororities. *Campus security:* 24-hour emergency response devices and patrols, late-night transport/escort service. *Student services:* health clinic, personal/psychological counseling.

Athletics Member NCAA. All Division III. *Intercollegiate sports:* baseball M, basketball M/W, cross-country running M/W, golf M/W, soccer M/W, softball W, swimming and diving M/W, tennis M/W. *Intramural sports:* badminton M/W, baseball M/W, basketball M/W, football M/W, golf M/W, racquetball M/W, soccer M/W, softball M/W, table tennis M/W, tennis M/W, track and field M/W, volleyball M/W, weight lifting M/W.

Standardized Tests *Required:* SAT or ACT (for admission).

Costs (2010–11) *Tuition:* state resident $12,412 full-time, $517 per credit part-time; nonresident $18,990 full-time, $791 per credit part-time. Full-time tuition and fees vary according to course level, degree level, location, program, and student level. Part-time tuition and fees vary according to course level, course load, degree level, location, program, and student level. *Required fees:* $838 full-time. *Room and board:* $8370; room only: $4540. Room and board charges vary according to board plan, housing facility, and location. *Payment plans:* installment, deferred payment. *Waivers:* employees or children of employees.

Financial Aid Of all full-time matriculated undergraduates who enrolled in 2008, 3,238 applied for aid, 2,698 were judged to have need, 126 had their need fully met. In 2008, 120 non-need-based awards were made. *Average percent of need met:* 55%. *Average financial aid package:* $9298. *Average need-based loan:* $4083. *Average need-based gift aid:* $6126. *Average non-need-based aid:* $1473. *Average indebtedness upon graduation:* $31,135.

Applying *Options:* electronic application, early admission, deferred entrance. *Application fee:* $50. *Required:* high school transcript. *Required for some:* interview. *Recommended:* essay or personal statement. *Application deadlines:* rolling (freshmen), rolling (transfers). *Notification:* continuous (freshmen), continuous (transfers).

Freshman Application Contact Admissions Office, Penn State Altoona, 3000 Ivyside Park, Altoona, PA 16601-3760. *Phone:* 814-949-5466. *Toll-free phone:* 800-848-9843. *Fax:* 814-949-5564. *E-mail:* aaadmit@psu.edu. *Web site:* http://www.aa.psu.edu/.

Penn State Beaver

Monaca, Pennsylvania

- **State-related** primarily 2-year, founded 1964, part of Pennsylvania State University
- **Small-town** 91-acre campus with easy access to Pittsburgh
- **Coed** 906 undergraduate students, 76% full-time, 48% women, 52% men
- **Moderately difficult** entrance level

Undergraduates 690 full-time, 216 part-time. 7% are from out of state; 9% Black or African American, non-Hispanic/Latino; 2% Hispanic/Latino; 2% Asian, non-Hispanic/Latino; 0.1% American Indian or Alaska Native, non-Hispanic/Latino; 2% Two or more races, non-Hispanic/Latino; 2% Race/ethnicity unknown; 0.3% international; 5% transferred in; 20% live on campus. *Retention:* 67% of full-time freshmen returned.

Freshmen *Admission:* 454 applied, 271 enrolled. *Average high school GPA:* 2.92. *Test scores:* SAT critical reading scores over 500: 38%; SAT math scores over 500: 49%; SAT writing scores over 500: 30%; SAT critical reading scores over 600: 4%; SAT math scores over 600: 12%; SAT writing scores over 600: 4%.

Faculty *Total:* 64, 52% full-time, 41% with terminal degrees. *Student/faculty ratio:* 18:1.

Academics *Calendar:* semesters. *Degrees:* associate, bachelor's, and master's. *Special study options:* academic remediation for entering students, adult/continuing education programs, advanced placement credit, distance learning, double majors, English as a second language, honors programs, independent study, internships, services for LD students, study abroad, summer session for credit.

Computers on Campus Students can access the following: online (class) registration. Campuswide network is available.

Student Life *Housing options:* coed. Campus housing is university owned. Freshman campus housing is guaranteed. *Activities and organizations:* drama/theater group, student-run newspaper, radio station. *Campus security:* 24-hour patrols, controlled dormitory access. *Student services:* health clinic, personal/psychological counseling.

Athletics Member NJCAA. *Intercollegiate sports:* baseball M, basketball M, softball M/W, volleyball W. *Intramural sports:* basketball M/W, cheerleading M(c)/W(c), cross-country running M/W, football M, golf M/W, soccer M/W, softball M/W, table tennis M/W.

Standardized Tests *Required:* SAT or ACT (for admission).

Costs (2010–11) *Tuition:* state resident $11,892 full-time, $481 per credit part-time; nonresident $18,148 full-time, $756 per credit part-time. Full-time tuition and fees vary according to course level, degree level, location, program, and student level. Part-time tuition and fees vary according to course level, course load, degree level, location, program, and student level. *Required fees:* $838 full-time. *Room and board:* $8370; room only: $4540. Room and board charges vary according to board plan, housing facility, and location. *Payment plans:* installment, deferred payment. *Waivers:* employees or children of employees.

Financial Aid Of all full-time matriculated undergraduates who enrolled in 2008, 573 applied for aid, 473 were judged to have need, 32 had their need fully met. In 2008, 48 non-need-based awards were made. *Average percent of need met:* 61%. *Average financial aid package:* $10,069. *Average need-based loan:* $3936. *Average need-based gift aid:* $6603. *Average non-need-based aid:* $2040. *Average indebtedness upon graduation:* $31,135.

Applying *Options:* electronic application, early admission, deferred entrance. *Application fee:* $50. *Required:* high school transcript. *Required for some:* interview. *Recommended:* essay or personal statement. *Application deadlines:* rolling (freshmen), rolling (transfers). *Notification:* continuous (freshmen), continuous (transfers).

Freshman Application Contact Admissions Office, Penn State Beaver, 100 University Drive, Monaca, PA 15061. *Phone:* 724-773-3800. *Fax:* 724-773-3658. *E-mail:* br-admissions@psu.edu. *Web site:* http://www.br.psu.edu/.

Penn State Berks

Reading, Pennsylvania

- **State-related** 4-year, founded 1924, part of Pennsylvania State University
- **Suburban** 258-acre campus with easy access to Philadelphia
- **Coed** 2,701 undergraduate students, 89% full-time, 43% women, 57% men
- **Very difficult** entrance level

Undergraduates 2,398 full-time, 303 part-time. 8% are from out of state; 7% Black or African American, non-Hispanic/Latino; 7% Hispanic/Latino; 4% Asian, non-Hispanic/Latino; 0.2% American Indian or Alaska Native, non-Hispanic/Latino; 2% Two or more races, non-Hispanic/Latino; 2% Race/ethnicity unknown; 1% international; 4% transferred in; 30% live on campus. *Retention:* 83% of full-time freshmen returned.

Freshmen *Admission:* 1,789 applied, 894 enrolled. *Average high school GPA:* 2.9. *Test scores:* SAT critical reading scores over 500: 37%; SAT math scores over 500: 52%; SAT writing scores over 500: 36%; SAT critical reading scores over 600: 6%; SAT math scores over 600: 14%; SAT writing scores over 600: 6%; SAT critical reading scores over 700: 1%; SAT math scores over 700: 1%.

Faculty *Total:* 211, 55% full-time, 45% with terminal degrees. *Student/faculty ratio:* 17:1.

Academics *Calendar:* semesters. *Degrees:* associate and bachelor's (enrollment figures include students enrolled at The Graduate School at Penn State who are taking courses at this location). *Special study options:* academic remediation for entering students, accelerated degree program, adult/continuing education programs, advanced placement credit, cooperative education, distance learning, English as a second language, freshman honors college, honors programs, independent study, internships, off-campus study, part-time degree program, services for LD students, study abroad, summer session for credit. *ROTC:* Army (c).

Computers on Campus Students can access the following: campus intranet, computer help desk, free student e-mail accounts, online (class) grades, online (class) registration, online (class) schedules. Campuswide network is available.

Student Life *Housing options:* coed, disabled students. Campus housing is university owned. *Activities and organizations:* drama/theater group, student-run newspaper, radio and television station, choral group. *Campus security:* 24-hour emergency response devices and patrols, late-night transport/escort service, controlled dormitory access. *Student services:* health clinic, personal/psychological counseling.

Athletics Member NJCAA. *Intercollegiate sports:* baseball M, basketball M/W, cheerleading M/W, cross-country running M/W, golf M, soccer M/W, softball W, tennis M/W, volleyball W. *Intramural sports:* badminton M/W, basketball M/W, football M/W, golf M/W, table tennis M/W, volleyball M/W.

Standardized Tests *Required:* SAT or ACT (for admission).

Costs (2010–11) *Tuition:* state resident $12,412 full-time, $517 per credit part-time; nonresident $18,990 full-time, $791 per credit part-time. Full-time tuition and fees vary according to course level, degree level, location, program, and student level. Part-time tuition and fees vary according to course level, course load, degree level, location, program, and student level. *Required fees:* $838 full-time. *Room and board:* $9160; room only: $5330. Room and board charges vary according to board plan, housing facility, and location. *Payment plans:* installment, deferred payment. *Waivers:* employees or children of employees.

Financial Aid Of all full-time matriculated undergraduates who enrolled in 2008, 1,915 applied for aid, 1,513 were judged to have need, 54 had their need fully met. In 2008, 40 non-need-based awards were made. *Average percent of need met:* 55%. *Average financial aid package:* $9088. *Average need-based loan:* $4113. *Average need-based gift aid:* $6344. *Average non-need-based aid:* $1513. *Average indebtedness upon graduation:* $31,135.

Applying *Options:* electronic application, early admission, deferred entrance. *Application fee:* $50. *Required:* high school transcript. *Required for some:* interview. *Recommended:* essay or personal statement. *Application deadlines:* rolling (freshmen), rolling (transfers). *Notification:* continuous (freshmen), continuous (transfers).

Freshman Application Contact Admissions Office, Penn State Berks, Tulpehocken Road, PO Box 7009, Reading, PA 19610-6009. *Phone:* 610-396-6060. *Fax:* 610-396-6077. *E-mail:* admissionsbk@psu.edu. *Web site:* http://www.bk.psu.edu/.

Penn State Brandywine
Media, Pennsylvania

- **State-related** primarily 2-year, founded 1966, part of Pennsylvania State University
- **Small-town** 87-acre campus with easy access to Philadelphia
- **Coed** 1,613 undergraduate students, 85% full-time, 42% women, 58% men
- **Moderately difficult** entrance level

Undergraduates 1,376 full-time, 237 part-time. 5% are from out of state; 12% Black or African American, non-Hispanic/Latino; 4% Hispanic/Latino; 6% Asian, non-Hispanic/Latino; 2% Two or more races, non-Hispanic/Latino; 3% Race/ethnicity unknown; 0.3% international; 3% transferred in. *Retention:* 73% of full-time freshmen returned.

Freshmen *Admission:* 761 applied, 390 enrolled. *Average high school GPA:* 2.91. *Test scores:* SAT critical reading scores over 500: 36%; SAT math scores over 500: 50%; SAT writing scores over 500: 5%; SAT critical reading scores over 600: 6%; SAT math scores over 600: 14%; SAT writing scores over 600: 5%; SAT critical reading scores over 700: 1%; SAT math scores over 700: 2%.

Faculty *Total:* 129, 47% full-time, 43% with terminal degrees. *Student/faculty ratio:* 17:1.

Academics *Calendar:* semesters. *Degrees:* certificates, associate, and bachelor's. *Special study options:* academic remediation for entering students, adult/continuing education programs, advanced placement credit, distance learning, double majors, English as a second language, honors programs, independent study, internships, services for LD students, study abroad, summer session for credit. *ROTC:* Army (c), Air Force (c).

Computers on Campus Students can access the following: online (class) registration. Campuswide network is available.

Student Life *Housing:* college housing not available. *Activities and organizations:* student-run newspaper, choral group. *Campus security:* late-night transport/escort service, part-time trained security personnel. *Student services:* health clinic, personal/psychological counseling, women's center.

Athletics Member NJCAA. *Intercollegiate sports:* baseball M, basketball M/W, soccer M/W, tennis M/W, volleyball W. *Intramural sports:* basketball M/W, cheerleading M(c)/W(c), golf M/W, ice hockey M(c)/W(c), lacrosse M/W, soccer M/W, softball W(c), tennis M/W, volleyball M(c)/W.

Standardized Tests *Required:* SAT or ACT (for admission).

Costs (2010–11) *Tuition:* state resident $11,892 full-time, $481 per credit part-time; nonresident $18,148 full-time, $756 per credit part-time. Full-time tuition and fees vary according to course level, degree level, location, program, and student level. Part-time tuition and fees vary according to course level, course load, degree level, location, program, and student level. *Required fees:* $838 full-time. *Payment plans:* installment, deferred payment. *Waivers:* employees or children of employees.

Financial Aid Of all full-time matriculated undergraduates who enrolled in 2008, 1,003 applied for aid, 750 were judged to have need, 33 had their need fully met. In 2008, 116 non-need-based awards were made. *Average percent of need met:* 58%. *Average financial aid package:* $9078. *Average need-based loan:* $3921. *Average need-based gift aid:* $6280. *Average non-need-based aid:* $2367. *Average indebtedness upon graduation:* $31,135.

Applying *Options:* electronic application, early admission, deferred entrance. *Application fee:* $50. *Required:* high school transcript. *Required for some:* interview. *Recommended:* essay or personal statement. *Application deadlines:* rolling (freshmen), rolling (transfers). *Notification:* continuous (freshmen), continuous (transfers).

Freshman Application Contact Admissions Office, Penn State Brandywine, 25 Yearsley Mill Road, Media, PA 19063-5596. *Phone:* 610-892-1200. *Fax:* 610-892-1320. *E-mail:* bwadmissions@psu.edu. *Web site:* http://www.brandywine.psu.edu/.

Penn State DuBois
DuBois, Pennsylvania

- **State-related** primarily 2-year, founded 1935, part of Pennsylvania State University
- **Small-town** 20-acre campus
- **Coed** 919 undergraduate students, 78% full-time, 52% women, 48% men
- **Moderately difficult** entrance level

Undergraduates 721 full-time, 198 part-time. 2% are from out of state; 0.9% Black or African American, non-Hispanic/Latino; 2% Hispanic/Latino; 0.3% Asian, non-Hispanic/Latino; 0.9% Two or more races, non-Hispanic/Latino; 1% Race/ethnicity unknown; 0.3% international; 3% transferred in. *Retention:* 73% of full-time freshmen returned.

Freshmen *Admission:* 313 applied, 207 enrolled. *Average high school GPA:* 2.9. *Test scores:* SAT critical reading scores over 500: 25%; SAT math scores over 500: 32%; SAT writing scores over 500: 24%; SAT critical reading scores over 600: 4%; SAT math scores over 600: 8%; SAT writing scores over 600: 2%.

Faculty *Total:* 87, 53% full-time, 43% with terminal degrees. *Student/faculty ratio:* 13:1.

Academics *Calendar:* semesters. *Degrees:* associate, bachelor's, and master's. *Special study options:* academic remediation for entering students, accelerated degree program, adult/continuing education programs, advanced placement credit, distance learning, double majors, honors programs, independent study, internships, services for LD students, student-designed majors, study abroad, summer session for credit.

Computers on Campus Students can access the following: online (class) registration. Campuswide network is available.

Student Life *Housing:* college housing not available. *Activities and organizations:* drama/theater group, student-run newspaper, choral group. *Student services:* health clinic, personal/psychological counseling, women's center.

Athletics Member NJCAA. *Intercollegiate sports:* basketball M, cross-country running M/W, golf M/W, volleyball W. *Intramural sports:* basketball M/W, football M, soccer M/W, table tennis M/W, volleyball M/W.

Standardized Tests *Required:* SAT or ACT (for admission).

Costs (2010–11) *Tuition:* state resident $11,892 full-time, $481 per credit part-time; nonresident $18,148 full-time, $756 per credit part-time. Full-time tuition and fees vary according to course level, degree level, location, program, and student level. Part-time tuition and fees vary according to course level, course load, degree level, location, program, and student level. *Required fees:* $704 full-time. *Payment plans:* installment, deferred payment. *Waivers:* employees or children of employees.

Financial Aid Of all full-time matriculated undergraduates who enrolled in 2008, 642 applied for aid, 586 were judged to have need, 29 had their need fully met. In 2008, 4 non-need-based awards were made. *Average percent of need met:* 61%. *Average financial aid package:* $10,851. *Average need-based loan:* $3821. *Average need-based gift aid:* $6569. *Average non-need-based aid:* $2000. *Average indebtedness upon graduation:* $31,135.

Applying *Options:* electronic application, early admission, deferred entrance. *Application fee:* $50. *Required:* high school transcript. *Required for some:* interview. *Recommended:* essay or personal statement. *Application deadlines:* rolling (freshmen), rolling (transfers). *Notification:* continuous (freshmen), continuous (transfers).

Freshman Application Contact Admissions Office, Penn State DuBois, College Place, DuBois, PA 15801-3199. *Phone:* 814-375-4720. *Toll-free phone:* 800-346-7627. *Fax:* 814-375-4784. *E-mail:* duboisinfo@psi.edu. *Web site:* http://www.ds.psu.edu/.

Penn State Erie, The Behrend College
Erie, Pennsylvania

- **State-related** comprehensive, founded 1948, part of Pennsylvania State University
- **Suburban** 725-acre campus
- **Coed** 4,252 undergraduate students, 92% full-time, 36% women, 64% men
- **Very difficult** entrance level

Undergraduates 3,929 full-time, 323 part-time. 8% are from out of state; 3% Black or African American, non-Hispanic/Latino; 3% Hispanic/Latino; 2% Asian, non-Hispanic/Latino; 0.1% Native Hawaiian or other Pacific Islander, non-Hispanic/Latino; 0.1% American Indian or Alaska Native, non-Hispanic/Latino; 2% Two or more races, non-Hispanic/Latino; 2% Race/ethnicity unknown; 2% international; 2% transferred in; 39% live on campus. *Retention:* 84% of full-time freshmen returned.

Freshmen *Admission:* 1,876 applied, 1,032 enrolled. *Average high school GPA:* 3.15. *Test scores:* SAT critical reading scores over 500: 57%; SAT math scores over 500: 69%; SAT writing scores over 500: 50%; SAT critical reading scores over 600: 14%; SAT math scores over 600: 25%; SAT writing scores over 600: 9%; SAT critical reading scores over 700: 2%; SAT math scores over 700: 2%; SAT writing scores over 700: 1%.

Faculty *Total:* 282, 81% full-time, 53% with terminal degrees. *Student/faculty ratio:* 17:1.

Academics *Calendar:* semesters. *Degrees:* certificates, associate, bachelor's, and master's. *Special study options:* academic remediation for entering students, accelerated degree program, adult/continuing education programs, advanced placement credit, cooperative education, distance learning, double majors, freshman honors college, honors programs, independent study, internships, off-campus study, part-time degree program, services for LD students, study abroad, summer session for credit. *ROTC:* Army (b).

Computers on Campus Students can access the following: campus intranet, computer help desk, free student e-mail accounts, online (class) grades, online (class) registration, online (class) schedules. Campuswide network is available.

Student Life *Housing options:* coed, men-only, women-only, disabled students. Campus housing is university owned. *Activities and organizations:* drama/theater group, student-run newspaper, radio station, choral group, national fraternities, national sororities. *Campus security:* 24-hour emergency response devices and patrols, student patrols, late-night transport/escort service, controlled dormitory access. *Student services:* health clinic, personal/psychological counseling.

Athletics Member NCAA. All Division III. *Intercollegiate sports:* baseball M, basketball M/W, cheerleading M/W, cross-country running M/W, golf M/W, ice hockey M(c), lacrosse M(c), skiing (downhill) M(c)/W(c), soccer M/W, softball W, swimming and diving M/W, tennis M/W, track and field M/W, volleyball M(c)/W, water polo M/W. *Intramural sports:* badminton M/W, basketball M/W, bowling M/W, cross-country running M/W, football M/W, golf M/W, skiing (downhill) M/W, soccer M/W, softball M/W, swimming and diving M/W, table tennis M/W, tennis M/W, volleyball M/W.

Standardized Tests *Required:* SAT or ACT (for admission).

Costs (2010–11) *Tuition:* state resident $12,412 full-time, $517 per credit part-time; nonresident $18,990 full-time, $791 per credit part-time. Full-time tuition and fees vary according to course level, degree level, location, program, and student level. Part-time tuition and fees vary according to course level, course load, degree level, location, program, and student level. *Required fees:* $838 full-time. *Room and board:* $8370; room only: $4540. Room and board charges vary according to board plan, housing facility, and location. *Payment plans:* installment, deferred payment. *Waivers:* employees or children of employees.

Financial Aid Of all full-time matriculated undergraduates who enrolled in 2008, 3,418 applied for aid, 2,917 were judged to have need, 122 had their need fully met. In 2008, 65 non-need-based awards were made. *Average percent of need met:* 58%. *Average financial aid package:* $9651. *Average need-based loan:* $4454. *Average need-based gift aid:* $6176. *Average non-need-based aid:* $3967. *Average indebtedness upon graduation:* $31,135.

Applying *Options:* electronic application, early admission, deferred entrance. *Application fee:* $50. *Required:* high school transcript. *Required for some:* interview. *Recommended:* essay or personal statement. *Application deadlines:* rolling (freshmen), rolling (transfers). *Notification:* continuous (freshmen), continuous (transfers).

Freshman Application Contact Admissions Office, Penn State Erie, The Behrend College, 4701 College Drive, Erie, PA 16563-0001. *Phone:* 814-898-6100. *Toll-free phone:* 866-374-3378. *Fax:* 814-898-6044. *E-mail:* behrend.admissions@psu.edu. *Web site:* http://www.pserie.psu.edu/.

See page 1500 for the College Close-Up.

Penn State Fayette, The Eberly Campus

Uniontown, Pennsylvania

- **State-related** primarily 2-year, founded 1934, part of Pennsylvania State University
- **Small-town** 92-acre campus
- **Coed** 1,037 undergraduate students, 77% full-time, 59% women, 41% men
- **Moderately difficult** entrance level

Undergraduates 802 full-time, 235 part-time. 3% are from out of state; 5% Black or African American, non-Hispanic/Latino; 1% Hispanic/Latino; 0.5% Asian, non-Hispanic/Latino; 0.2% American Indian or Alaska Native, non-Hispanic/Latino; 0.9% Two or more races, non-Hispanic/Latino; 3% Race/ethnicity unknown; 0.9% international; 5% transferred in. *Retention:* 77% of full-time freshmen returned.

Freshmen *Admission:* 458 applied, 248 enrolled. *Average high school GPA:* 3.04. *Test scores:* SAT critical reading scores over 500: 28%; SAT math scores over 500: 37%; SAT writing scores over 500: 22%; SAT critical reading scores over 600: 6%; SAT math scores over 600: 8%; SAT writing scores over 600: 5%; SAT critical reading scores over 700: 1%; SAT math scores over 700: 1%; SAT writing scores over 700: 1%.

Faculty *Total:* 92, 61% full-time, 38% with terminal degrees. *Student/faculty ratio:* 13:1.

Academics *Calendar:* semesters. *Degrees:* associate and bachelor's. *Special study options:* academic remediation for entering students, accelerated degree program, adult/continuing education programs, advanced placement credit, distance learning, double majors, honors programs, independent study, internships, services for LD students, student-designed majors, study abroad, summer session for credit.

Computers on Campus Students can access the following: online (class) registration. Campuswide network is available.

Student Life *Housing:* college housing not available. *Activities and organizations:* drama/theater group. *Campus security:* student patrols, 8-hour patrols by trained security personnel. *Student services:* health clinic, personal/psychological counseling.

Athletics Member NJCAA. *Intercollegiate sports:* baseball M, basketball M, softball W, volleyball W. *Intramural sports:* badminton M/W, basketball M/W, cheerleading M(c)/W(c), equestrian sports M(c)/W(c), football M/W, golf M(c)/W(c), softball M/W, tennis M/W, volleyball M/W, weight lifting M/W.

Standardized Tests *Required:* SAT or ACT (for admission).

Costs (2010–11) *Tuition:* state resident $11,892 full-time, $481 per credit part-time; nonresident $18,148 full-time, $756 per credit part-time. Full-time tuition and fees vary according to course level, degree level, location, program, and student level. Part-time tuition and fees vary according to course level, course load, degree level, location, program, and student level. *Required fees:* $724 full-time. *Payment plans:* installment, deferred payment. *Waivers:* employees or children of employees.

Financial Aid Of all full-time matriculated undergraduates who enrolled in 2008, 677 applied for aid, 615 were judged to have need, 36 had their need fully met. In 2008, 23 non-need-based awards were made. *Average percent of need met:* 60%. *Average financial aid package:* $10,051. *Average need-based loan:* $3893. *Average need-based gift aid:* $6339. *Average non-need-based aid:* $2304. *Average indebtedness upon graduation:* $31,135.

Applying *Options:* electronic application, early admission, deferred entrance. *Application fee:* $50. *Required:* high school transcript. *Required for some:* interview. *Recommended:* essay or personal statement. *Application deadlines:* rolling (freshmen), rolling (transfers). *Notification:* continuous (freshmen), continuous (transfers).

Freshman Application Contact Admissions Office, Penn State Fayette, The Eberly Campus, 1 University Drive, PO Box 519, Uniontown, PA 15401-0519. *Phone:* 724-430-4130. *Toll-free phone:* 877-568-4130. *Fax:* 724-430-4175. *E-mail:* feadm@psu.edu. *Web site:* http://www.fe.psu.edu/.

Penn State Greater Allegheny
McKeesport, Pennsylvania

- **State-related** primarily 2-year, founded 1947, part of Pennsylvania State University
- **Small-town** 40-acre campus with easy access to Pittsburgh
- **Coed** 768 undergraduate students, 86% full-time, 45% women, 55% men
- **Moderately difficult** entrance level

Undergraduates 657 full-time, 111 part-time. 9% are from out of state; 28% Black or African American, non-Hispanic/Latino; 2% Hispanic/Latino; 3% Asian, non-Hispanic/Latino; 0.1% Native Hawaiian or other Pacific Islander, non-Hispanic/Latino; 0.1% American Indian or Alaska Native, non-Hispanic/Latino; 3% Two or more races, non-Hispanic/Latino; 2% Race/ethnicity unknown; 2% international; 3% transferred in; 27% live on campus. *Retention:* 69% of full-time freshmen returned.

Freshmen *Admission:* 569 applied, 279 enrolled. *Average high school GPA:* 2.8. *Test scores:* SAT critical reading scores over 500: 24%; SAT math scores over 500: 30%; SAT writing scores over 500: 21%; SAT critical reading scores over 600: 5%; SAT math scores over 600: 6%; SAT writing scores over 600: 4%; SAT math scores over 700: 1%.

Faculty *Total:* 63, 57% full-time, 49% with terminal degrees. *Student/faculty ratio:* 15:1.

Academics *Calendar:* semesters. *Degrees:* certificates, associate, bachelor's, and master's. *Special study options:* academic remediation for entering students, adult/continuing education programs, advanced placement credit, distance learning, double majors, English as a second language, honors programs, independent study, internships, services for LD students, student-designed majors, study abroad, summer session for credit.

Computers on Campus Students can access the following: online (class) registration. Campuswide network is available.

Student Life *Housing options:* coed, disabled students. Campus housing is university owned. Freshman campus housing is guaranteed. *Activities and organizations:* drama/theater group, student-run newspaper, radio and television station, choral group. *Campus security:* 24-hour patrols, controlled dormitory access. *Student services:* health clinic, personal/psychological counseling, women's center.

Athletics Member NJCAA. *Intercollegiate sports:* baseball M, basketball M, softball W, volleyball W. *Intramural sports:* basketball M/W, cheerleading M(c)/W(c), football M/W, ice hockey M(c), racquetball M/W, skiing (cross-country) M(c)/W(c), skiing (downhill) M(c)/W(c), soccer M(c)/W(c), softball M/W, tennis M/W, volleyball M/W.

Standardized Tests *Required:* SAT or ACT (for admission).

Costs (2010–11) *Tuition:* state resident $11,892 full-time, $481 per credit part-time; nonresident $18,148 full-time, $756 per credit part-time. Full-time tuition and fees vary according to course level, degree level, location, program, and student level. Part-time tuition and fees vary according to course level, course load, degree level, location, program, and student level. *Required fees:* $838 full-time. *Room and board:* $8370; room only: $4540. Room and board charges vary according to board plan, housing facility, and location. *Payment plans:* installment, deferred payment. *Waivers:* employees or children of employees.

Financial Aid Of all full-time matriculated undergraduates who enrolled in 2008, 544 applied for aid, 481 were judged to have need, 10 had their need fully met. In 2008, 27 non-need-based awards were made. *Average percent of need met:* 62%. *Average financial aid package:* $11,087. *Average need-based loan:* $3817. *Average need-based gift aid:* $7344. *Average non-need-based aid:* $3515. *Average indebtedness upon graduation:* $31,135.

Applying *Options:* electronic application, early admission, deferred entrance. *Application fee:* $50. *Required:* high school transcript. *Required for some:* interview. *Recommended:* essay or personal statement. *Application deadlines:* rolling (freshmen), rolling (transfers). *Notification:* continuous (freshmen), continuous (transfers).

Freshman Application Contact Admissions Office, Penn State Greater Allegheny, 4000 University Drive, McKeesport, PA 15132-7698. *Phone:* 412-675-9010. *Fax:* 412-675-9046. *E-mail:* psuga@psu.edu. *Web site:* http://www.ga.psu.edu/.

Penn State Harrisburg
Middletown, Pennsylvania

- **State-related** comprehensive, founded 1966, part of Pennsylvania State University
- **Small-town** 218-acre campus
- **Coed** 2,963 undergraduate students, 84% full-time, 45% women, 55% men
- **Very difficult** entrance level

Undergraduates 2,482 full-time, 481 part-time. 13% are from out of state; 9% Black or African American, non-Hispanic/Latino; 5% Hispanic/Latino; 6% Asian, non-Hispanic/Latino; 0.1% Native Hawaiian or other Pacific Islander, non-Hispanic/Latino; 0.2% American Indian or Alaska Native, non-Hispanic/Latino; 2% Two or more races, non-Hispanic/Latino; 4% Race/ethnicity unknown; 3% international; 9% transferred in; 14% live on campus. *Retention:* 85% of full-time freshmen returned.

Freshmen *Admission:* 1,046 applied, 534 enrolled. *Average high school GPA:* 3.04. *Test scores:* SAT critical reading scores over 500: 45%; SAT math scores over 500: 57%; SAT writing scores over 500: 42%; SAT critical reading scores over 600: 8%; SAT math scores over 600: 23%; SAT writing scores over 600: 6%; SAT math scores over 700: 4%; SAT writing scores over 700: 1%.

Faculty *Total:* 313, 65% full-time, 66% with terminal degrees. *Student/faculty ratio:* 13:1.

Academics *Calendar:* semesters. *Degrees:* certificates, associate, bachelor's, master's, and doctoral-research/scholarship. *Special study options:* academic remediation for entering students, adult/continuing education programs, advanced placement credit, cooperative education, distance learning, double majors, freshman honors college, honors programs, independent study, internships, off-campus study, part-time degree program, services for LD students, student-designed majors, study abroad, summer session for credit. *ROTC:* Army (c).

Computers on Campus Students can access the following: campus intranet, computer help desk, free student e-mail accounts, online (class) grades, online (class) registration, online (class) schedules. Campuswide network is available.

Student Life *Housing options:* disabled students. Campus housing is university owned. *Activities and organizations:* drama/theater group, student-run newspaper, radio station, choral group. *Campus security:* 24-hour emergency response devices and patrols, student patrols, late-night transport/escort service, controlled dormitory access. *Student services:* health clinic, personal/psychological counseling.

Athletics *Intercollegiate sports:* baseball M, basketball M/W, cross-country running M/W, golf M/W, soccer M/W, softball W, tennis M/W, volleyball W. *Intramural sports:* badminton M/W, basketball M/W, racquetball M/W, tennis M/W.

Standardized Tests *Required:* SAT or ACT (for admission).

Costs (2010–11) *Tuition:* state resident $12,412 full-time, $517 per credit part-time; nonresident $18,990 full-time, $791 per credit part-time. Full-time tuition and fees vary according to course level, degree level, location, program, and student level. Part-time tuition and fees vary according to course level, course load, degree level, location, program, and student level. *Required fees:* $828 full-time. *Room and board:* $9580; room only: $5750. Room and board charges vary according to board plan, housing facility, and location. *Payment plans:* installment, deferred payment. *Waivers:* employees or children of employees.

Financial Aid Of all full-time matriculated undergraduates who enrolled in 2008, 1,743 applied for aid, 1,429 were judged to have need, 93 had their need fully met. In 2008, 32 non-need-based awards were made. *Average percent of need met:* 56%. *Average financial aid package:* $9974. *Average need-based loan:* $4565. *Average need-based gift aid:* $6524. *Average non-need-based aid:* $1272. *Average indebtedness upon graduation:* $31,135.

Applying *Options:* electronic application, early admission, deferred entrance. *Application fee:* $50. *Required:* high school transcript. *Required for some:* interview. *Recommended:* essay or personal statement. *Application deadlines:*

rolling (freshmen), rolling (transfers). *Notification:* continuous (freshmen), continuous (transfers).

Freshman Application Contact Admissions Office, Penn State Harrisburg, 777 West Harrisburg Pike, Middletown, PA 17057-4898. *Phone:* 717-948-6250. *Toll-free phone:* 800-222-2056. *Fax:* 717-948-6325. *E-mail:* hbgadmit@psu.edu. *Web site:* http://www.hbg.psu.edu/.

Penn State Hazleton

Hazleton, Pennsylvania

- **State-related** primarily 2-year, founded 1934, part of Pennsylvania State University
- **Small-town** 98-acre campus
- **Coed** 1,245 undergraduate students, 96% full-time, 43% women, 57% men
- **Moderately difficult** entrance level

Undergraduates 1,191 full-time, 54 part-time. 28% are from out of state; 3% transferred in; 38% live on campus. *Retention:* 79% of full-time freshmen returned.

Freshmen *Admission:* 1,514 applied, 564 enrolled. *Average high school GPA:* 2.81. *Test scores:* SAT critical reading scores over 500: 34%; SAT math scores over 500: 38%; SAT writing scores over 500: 29%; SAT critical reading scores over 600: 4%; SAT math scores over 600: 11%; SAT writing scores over 600: 5%; SAT math scores over 700: 1%.

Faculty *Total:* 85, 64% full-time, 45% with terminal degrees. *Student/faculty ratio:* 19:1.

Academics *Calendar:* semesters. *Degrees:* associate, bachelor's, and master's. *Special study options:* academic remediation for entering students, accelerated degree program, adult/continuing education programs, advanced placement credit, distance learning, double majors, English as a second language, honors programs, independent study, internships, services for LD students, student-designed majors, study abroad, summer session for credit. *ROTC:* Army (b), Air Force (c).

Computers on Campus Students can access the following: online (class) registration. Campuswide network is available.

Student Life *Housing options:* coed. Campus housing is university owned. Freshman campus housing is guaranteed. *Activities and organizations:* drama/theater group, student-run newspaper, radio station, choral group. *Campus security:* 24-hour patrols, late-night transport/escort service, controlled dormitory access. *Student services:* health clinic, personal/psychological counseling, women's center, legal services.

Athletics Member NJCAA. *Intercollegiate sports:* baseball M, basketball M/W, cheerleading M/W, soccer M, softball W(s), tennis M/W, volleyball M/W. *Intramural sports:* basketball M/W, skiing (downhill) M(c)/W(c), soccer M/W, volleyball M/W.

Standardized Tests *Required:* SAT or ACT (for admission).

Costs (2010–11) *Tuition:* state resident $11,892 full-time, $481 per credit part-time; nonresident $18,148 full-time, $756 per credit part-time. Full-time tuition and fees vary according to course level, degree level, location, program, and student level. Part-time tuition and fees vary according to course level, course load, degree level, location, program, and student level. *Required fees:* $786 full-time. *Room and board:* $8370; room only: $4540. Room and board charges vary according to board plan, housing facility, and location. *Payment plans:* installment, deferred payment. *Waivers:* employees or children of employees.

Financial Aid Of all full-time matriculated undergraduates who enrolled in 2008, 1,031 applied for aid, 886 were judged to have need, 30 had their need fully met. In 2008, 93 non-need-based awards were made. *Average percent of need met:* 55%. *Average financial aid package:* $9388. *Average need-based loan:* $3692. *Average need-based gift aid:* $6639. *Average non-need-based aid:* $2689. *Average indebtedness upon graduation:* $31,135.

Applying *Options:* electronic application, early admission, deferred entrance. *Application fee:* $50. *Required:* high school transcript. *Required for some:* interview. *Recommended:* essay or personal statement. *Application deadlines:* rolling (freshmen), rolling (transfers). *Notification:* continuous (freshmen), continuous (transfers).

Freshman Application Contact Admissions Office, Penn State Hazleton, Hazleton, PA 18202-1291. *Phone:* 570-450-3142. *Toll-free phone:* 800-279-8495. *Fax:* 570-450-3182. *E-mail:* admissions-hn@psu.edu. *Web site:* http://www.hn.psu.edu/.

Penn State Lehigh Valley

Fogelsville, Pennsylvania

- **State-related** primarily 2-year, founded 1912, part of Pennsylvania State University
- **Small-town** 42-acre campus
- **Coed** 914 undergraduate students, 77% full-time, 46% women, 54% men
- **Moderately difficult** entrance level

Undergraduates 707 full-time, 207 part-time. 4% are from out of state; 3% Black or African American, non-Hispanic/Latino; 13% Hispanic/Latino; 7% Asian, non-Hispanic/Latino; 0.1% Native Hawaiian or other Pacific Islander, non-Hispanic/Latino; 0.4% American Indian or Alaska Native, non-Hispanic/Latino; 2% Two or more races, non-Hispanic/Latino; 3% Race/ethnicity unknown; 0.1% international; 7% transferred in. *Retention:* 72% of full-time freshmen returned.

Freshmen *Admission:* 483 applied, 279 enrolled. *Average high school GPA:* 2.89. *Test scores:* SAT critical reading scores over 500: 45%; SAT math scores over 500: 54%; SAT writing scores over 500: 37%; SAT critical reading scores over 600: 14%; SAT math scores over 600: 19%; SAT writing scores over 600: 6%; SAT critical reading scores over 700: 2%; SAT math scores over 700: 2%.

Faculty *Total:* 92, 36% full-time, 39% with terminal degrees. *Student/faculty ratio:* 15:1.

Academics *Calendar:* semesters. *Degrees:* associate and bachelor's (enrollment figures include students enrolled at The Graduate School at Penn State who are taking courses at this location). *Special study options:* academic remediation for entering students, accelerated degree program, adult/continuing education programs, advanced placement credit, cooperative education, distance learning, honors programs, independent study, internships, services for LD students, study abroad, summer session for credit. *ROTC:* Army (c).

Computers on Campus Students can access the following: online (class) registration. Campuswide network is available.

Student Life *Housing:* college housing not available. *Activities and organizations:* drama/theater group, student-run newspaper.

Athletics Member NJCAA. *Intercollegiate sports:* baseball M, basketball M/W, bowling M(c)/W(c), cheerleading M/W, cross-country running M/W, football M(c), golf M(c)/W(c), ice hockey M(c)/W(c), skiing (downhill) M(c)/W(c), soccer M(c)/W, tennis M/W, volleyball M(c)/W. *Intramural sports:* badminton M/W, basketball M/W, football M/W, golf M/W, soccer M/W, volleyball M/W.

Standardized Tests *Required:* SAT or ACT (for admission).

Costs (2010–11) *Tuition:* state resident $11,892 full-time, $481 per credit part-time; nonresident $18,148 full-time, $756 per credit part-time. Full-time tuition and fees vary according to course level, degree level, location, program, and student level. Part-time tuition and fees vary according to course level, course load, degree level, location, program, and student level. *Required fees:* $828 full-time. *Payment plans:* installment, deferred payment. *Waivers:* employees or children of employees.

Financial Aid Of all full-time matriculated undergraduates who enrolled in 2008, 478 applied for aid, 382 were judged to have need, 13 had their need fully met. In 2008, 40 non-need-based awards were made. *Average percent of need met:* 58%. *Average financial aid package:* $9147. *Average need-based loan:* $3877. *Average need-based gift aid:* $6720. *Average non-need-based aid:* $2129. *Average indebtedness upon graduation:* $31,135.

Applying *Options:* electronic application, early admission, deferred entrance. *Application fee:* $50. *Required:* high school transcript. *Application deadlines:* rolling (freshmen), rolling (transfers). *Notification:* continuous (freshmen), continuous (transfers).

Freshman Application Contact Admissions Office, Penn State Lehigh Valley, 2809 Saucon Valley Road, Fogelsville, PA 18051-9999. *Phone:* 610-285-5000. *Fax:* 610-285-5220. *E-mail:* admissions-lv@psu.edu. *Web site:* http://www.lv.psu.edu/.

Penn State Mont Alto

Mont Alto, Pennsylvania

- **State-related** primarily 2-year, founded 1929, part of Pennsylvania State University
- **Small-town** 64-acre campus
- **Coed** 1,252 undergraduate students, 76% full-time, 58% women, 42% men
- **Moderately difficult** entrance level

Undergraduates 957 full-time, 295 part-time. 17% are from out of state; 12% Black or African American, non-Hispanic/Latino; 4% Hispanic/Latino; 1% Asian, non-Hispanic/Latino; 0.1% Native Hawaiian or other Pacific Islander, non-Hispanic/Latino; 0.3% American Indian or Alaska Native, non-Hispanic/Latino; 2% Two or more races, non-Hispanic/Latino; 2% Race/ethnicity unknown; 0.4% international; 6% transferred in; 34% live on campus. *Retention:* 79% of full-time freshmen returned.

Freshmen *Admission:* 595 applied, 417 enrolled. *Average high school GPA:* 2.9. *Test scores:* SAT critical reading scores over 500: 37%; SAT math scores over 500: 41%; SAT writing scores over 500: 29%; SAT critical reading scores over 600: 7%; SAT math scores over 600: 9%; SAT writing scores over 600: 3%; SAT critical reading scores over 700: 1%; SAT math scores over 700: 1%; SAT writing scores over 700: 1%.

Faculty *Total:* 121, 48% full-time, 35% with terminal degrees. *Student/faculty ratio:* 13:1.

Academics *Calendar:* semesters. *Degrees:* associate and bachelor's. *Special study options:* academic remediation for entering students, accelerated degree program, adult/continuing education programs, advanced placement credit, distance learning, double majors, honors programs, independent study, internships, services for LD students, study abroad, summer session for credit. *ROTC:* Army (c).

Computers on Campus Students can access the following: online (class) registration. Campuswide network is available.

Student Life *Housing options:* coed, disabled students. Campus housing is university owned. Freshman campus housing is guaranteed. *Activities and organizations:* drama/theater group, student-run newspaper. *Campus security:* 24-hour patrols, controlled dormitory access. *Student services:* health clinic, women's center.

Athletics Member NJCAA. *Intercollegiate sports:* basketball M/W, cheerleading M/W, cross-country running M/W, golf M/W, soccer M/W, softball W, tennis M/W, volleyball W. *Intramural sports:* badminton M/W, basketball M/W, cheerleading M(c)/W(c), racquetball M/W, soccer M/W, softball W, volleyball M/W.

Standardized Tests *Required:* SAT or ACT (for admission).

Costs (2010–11) *Tuition:* state resident $11,892 full-time, $481 per credit part-time; nonresident $18,148 full-time, $756 per credit part-time. Full-time tuition and fees vary according to course level, degree level, location, program, and student level. Part-time tuition and fees vary according to course level, course load, degree level, location, program, and student level. *Required fees:* $838 full-time. *Room and board:* $8370; room only: $4540. Room and board charges vary according to board plan, housing facility, and location. *Payment plans:* installment, deferred payment. *Waivers:* employees or children of employees.

Financial Aid Of all full-time matriculated undergraduates who enrolled in 2008, 774 applied for aid, 651 were judged to have need, 34 had their need fully met. In 2008, 47 non-need-based awards were made. *Average percent of need met:* 58%. *Average financial aid package:* $9783. *Average need-based loan:* $3768. *Average need-based gift aid:* $6075. *Average non-need-based aid:* $3204. *Average indebtedness upon graduation:* $31,135.

Applying *Options:* electronic application, early admission, deferred entrance. *Application fee:* $50. *Required:* high school transcript. *Required for some:* interview. *Recommended:* essay or personal statement. *Application deadlines:* rolling (freshmen), rolling (transfers). *Notification:* continuous (freshmen), continuous (transfers).

Freshman Application Contact Admissions Office, Penn State Mont Alto, 1 Campus Drive, Mont Alto, PA 17237-9703. *Phone:* 717-749-6130. *Toll-free phone:* 800-392-6173. *Fax:* 717-749-6132. *E-mail:* psuma@psu.edu. *Web site:* http://www.ma.psu.edu/.

Penn State New Kensington
New Kensington, Pennsylvania

- **State-related** primarily 2-year, founded 1958, part of Pennsylvania State University
- **Small-town** 71-acre campus with easy access to Pittsburgh
- **Coed** 870 undergraduate students, 76% full-time, 40% women, 60% men
- **Moderately difficult** entrance level

Undergraduates 657 full-time, 213 part-time. 17% are from out of state; 4% Black or African American, non-Hispanic/Latino; 1% Hispanic/Latino; 0.3% Asian, non-Hispanic/Latino; 0.1% American Indian or Alaska Native, non-Hispanic/Latino; 2% Two or more races, non-Hispanic/Latino; 2% Race/ethnicity unknown; 0.1% international; 5% transferred in; 29% live on campus. *Retention:* 75% of full-time freshmen returned.

Freshmen *Admission:* 552 applied, 226 enrolled. *Average high school GPA:* 2.68. *Test scores:* SAT critical reading scores over 500: 22%; SAT math scores over 500: 27%; SAT writing scores over 500: 18%; SAT critical reading scores over 600: 6%; SAT math scores over 600: 5%; SAT writing scores over 600: 4%; SAT critical reading scores over 700: 1%; SAT math scores over 700: 1%.

Faculty *Total:* 77, 57% full-time, 49% with terminal degrees. *Student/faculty ratio:* 17:1.

Academics *Calendar:* semesters. *Degrees:* associate, bachelor's, and master's. *Special study options:* academic remediation for entering students, adult/continuing education programs, advanced placement credit, distance learning, double majors, honors programs, independent study, internships, services for LD students, study abroad, summer session for credit.

Computers on Campus Students can access the following: online (class) registration. Campuswide network is available.

Student Life *Housing options:* disabled students. *Activities and organizations:* drama/theater group, student-run newspaper, choral group. *Campus security:* part-time trained security personnel. *Student services:* health clinic, women's center.

Athletics Member NJCAA. *Intercollegiate sports:* baseball M, basketball M/W, cheerleading M/W, golf M/W, softball W, volleyball W. *Intramural sports:* badminton M/W, basketball M/W, bowling M/W, cheerleading M(c)/W(c), football M/W, ice hockey M(c)/W(c), racquetball M/W, skiing (downhill) M(c)/W(c), soccer M/W, softball W, volleyball M/W.

Standardized Tests *Required:* SAT or ACT (for admission).

Costs (2010–11) *Tuition:* state resident $11,892 full-time, $481 per credit part-time; nonresident $18,148 full-time, $756 per credit part-time. Full-time tuition and fees vary according to course level, degree level, location, program, and student level. Part-time tuition and fees vary according to course level, course load, degree level, location, program, and student level. *Required fees:* $786 full-time. *Payment plans:* installment, deferred payment. *Waivers:* employees or children of employees.

Financial Aid Of all full-time matriculated undergraduates who enrolled in 2008, 776 applied for aid, 720 were judged to have need, 30 had their need fully met. In 2008, 15 non-need-based awards were made. *Average percent of need met:* 58%. *Average financial aid package:* $10,943. *Average need-based loan:* $3996. *Average need-based gift aid:* $7125. *Average non-need-based aid:* $2132. *Average indebtedness upon graduation:* $31,135.

Applying *Options:* electronic application, early admission, deferred entrance. *Application fee:* $50. *Required:* high school transcript. *Required for some:* interview. *Recommended:* essay or personal statement. *Application deadlines:* rolling (freshmen), rolling (transfers). *Notification:* continuous (freshmen), continuous (transfers).

Freshman Application Contact Admissions Office, Penn State New Kensington, 3550 Seventh Street Road, New Kensington, PA 15068. *Phone:* 724-334-5466. *Toll-free phone:* 888-968-7297. *Fax:* 724-334-6111. *E-mail:* nkadmissions@psu.edu. *Web site:* http://www.nk.psu.edu/.

Penn State Schuylkill
Schuylkill Haven, Pennsylvania

- **State-related** primarily 2-year, founded 1934, part of Pennsylvania State University
- **Small-town** 42-acre campus
- **Coed** 1,034 undergraduate students, 85% full-time, 55% women, 45% men
- **Moderately difficult** entrance level

Undergraduates 876 full-time, 158 part-time. 17% are from out of state; 29% Black or African American, non-Hispanic/Latino; 6% Hispanic/Latino; 3% Asian, non-Hispanic/Latino; 0.2% American Indian or Alaska Native, non-Hispanic/Latino; 2% Two or more races, non-Hispanic/Latino; 3% Race/ethnicity unknown; 0.5% international; 4% transferred in; 29% live on campus. *Retention:* 74% of full-time freshmen returned.

Freshmen *Admission:* 552 applied, 388 enrolled. *Average high school GPA:* 2.68. *Test scores:* SAT critical reading scores over 500: 20%; SAT math scores over 500: 21%; SAT writing scores over 500: 18%; SAT critical reading scores over 600: 4%; SAT math scores over 600: 3%; SAT writing scores over 600: 2%; SAT critical reading scores over 700: 1%.

Faculty *Total:* 77, 57% full-time, 49% with terminal degrees. *Student/faculty ratio:* 17:1.

Academics *Calendar:* semesters. *Degrees:* certificates, associate, and bachelor's (bachelor's degree programs completed at the Harrisburg campus). *Special study options:* academic remediation for entering students, accelerated degree program, adult/continuing education programs, advanced placement credit, cooperative education, distance learning, double majors, honors programs, independent study, internships, services for LD students, student-designed majors, study abroad, summer session for credit.

Computers on Campus Students can access the following: online (class) registration. Campuswide network is available.

Student Life *Housing options:* disabled students. Campus housing is provided by a third party. Freshman campus housing is guaranteed. *Activities and organizations:* drama/theater group, student-run newspaper, choral group. *Campus security:* 24-hour patrols, controlled dormitory access.

Athletics Member NJCAA. *Intercollegiate sports:* basketball M, cross-country running M/W, golf M, soccer M, softball W, volleyball W. *Intramural sports:* basketball M/W, football M, soccer M/W, softball M/W, table tennis M/W, volleyball M/W.

Standardized Tests *Required:* SAT or ACT (for admission).

Costs (2010–11) *Tuition:* state resident $11,892 full-time, $481 per credit part-time; nonresident $18,148 full-time, $756 per credit part-time. Full-time tuition and fees vary according to course level, degree level, location, program, and student level. Part-time tuition and fees vary according to course level, course load, degree level, location, program, and student level. *Required fees:* $734 full-time. *Payment plans:* installment, deferred payment. *Waivers:* employees or children of employees.

Financial Aid Of all full-time matriculated undergraduates who enrolled in 2008, 776 applied for aid, 720 were judged to have need, 30 had their need fully met. In 2008, 15 non-need-based awards were made. *Average percent of need met:* 58%. *Average financial aid package:* $10,943. *Average need-based loan:* $3996. *Average need-based gift aid:* $7125. *Average non-need-based aid:* $2132. *Average indebtedness upon graduation:* $31,135.

Applying *Options:* electronic application, early admission, deferred entrance. *Application fee:* $50. *Required:* high school transcript. *Application deadlines:* rolling (freshmen), rolling (transfers). *Notification:* continuous (freshmen), continuous (transfers).

Freshman Application Contact Admissions Office, Penn State Schuylkill, 200 University Drive, Schuylkill Haven, PA 17972-2208. *Phone:* 570-385-6252. *Fax:* 570-385-6272. *E-mail:* sl-admissions@psu.edu. *Web site:* http://www.sl.psu.edu/.

Penn State Shenango

Sharon, Pennsylvania

- **State-related** primarily 2-year, founded 1965, part of Pennsylvania State University
- **Small-town** 14-acre campus
- **Coed** 714 undergraduate students, 63% full-time, 63% women, 37% men
- **Moderately difficult** entrance level

Undergraduates 450 full-time, 264 part-time. 17% are from out of state; 8% Black or African American, non-Hispanic/Latino; 2% Hispanic/Latino; 0.7% Asian, non-Hispanic/Latino; 0.2% American Indian or Alaska Native, non-Hispanic/Latino; 0.8% Two or more races, non-Hispanic/Latino; 3% Race/ethnicity unknown; 0.2% international; 5% transferred in. *Retention:* 58% of full-time freshmen returned.

Freshmen *Admission:* 217 applied, 108 enrolled. *Average high school GPA:* 2.83. *Test scores:* SAT critical reading scores over 500: 22%; SAT math scores over 500: 25%; SAT writing scores over 500: 10%; SAT critical reading scores over 600: 1%; SAT math scores over 600: 4%; SAT math scores over 700: 3%.

Faculty *Total:* 71, 42% full-time, 34% with terminal degrees. *Student/faculty ratio:* 12:1.

Academics *Calendar:* semesters. *Degrees:* certificates, associate, and bachelor's. *Special study options:* academic remediation for entering students, accelerated degree program, adult/continuing education programs, advanced placement credit, distance learning, double majors, honors programs, independent study, internships, services for LD students, student-designed majors, study abroad, summer session for credit.

Computers on Campus Students can access the following: online (class) registration. Campuswide network is available.

Student Life *Housing:* college housing not available. *Activities and organizations:* choral group. *Campus security:* part-time trained security personnel. *Student services:* health clinic, women's center.

Athletics *Intramural sports:* basketball M(c)/W, bowling M/W, football M(c), golf M/W, softball M/W, tennis M/W, volleyball M/W.

Standardized Tests *Required:* SAT or ACT (for admission).

Costs (2010–11) *Tuition:* state resident $11,892 full-time, $481 per credit part-time; nonresident $18,148 full-time, $756 per credit part-time. Full-time tuition and fees vary according to course level, degree level, location, program, and student level. Part-time tuition and fees vary according to course level, course load, degree level, location, program, and student level. *Required fees:* $630 full-time. *Payment plans:* installment, deferred payment. *Waivers:* employees or children of employees.

Financial Aid Of all full-time matriculated undergraduates who enrolled in 2008, 438 applied for aid, 410 were judged to have need, 18 had their need fully met. In 2008, 10 non-need-based awards were made. *Average percent of need met:* 56%. *Average financial aid package:* $10,771. *Average need-based loan:* $3779. *Average need-based gift aid:* $6548. *Average non-need-based aid:* $2569. *Average indebtedness upon graduation:* $31,135.

Applying *Options:* electronic application, early admission, deferred entrance. *Application fee:* $50. *Required:* high school transcript. *Required for some:* interview. *Recommended:* essay or personal statement. *Application deadlines:* rolling (freshmen), rolling (transfers). *Notification:* continuous (freshmen), continuous (transfers).

Freshman Application Contact Admissions Office, Penn State Shenango, 147 Shenango Avenue, Sharon, PA 16146-1537. *Phone:* 724-983-2803. *Fax:* 724-983-2820. *E-mail:* psushenango@psu.edu. *Web site:* http://www.shenango.psu.edu/.

Penn State University Park

State College, Pennsylvania

- **State-related** university, founded 1855, part of Pennsylvania State University
- **Small-town** 8556-acre campus with easy access to Harrisburg
- **Endowment** $1.4 billion
- **Coed** 38,594 undergraduate students, 97% full-time, 45% women, 55% men
- **Very difficult** entrance level, 55% of applicants were admitted

Undergraduates 37,347 full-time, 1,247 part-time. Students come from 57 states and territories; 119 other countries; 27% are from out of state; 4% Black or African American, non-Hispanic/Latino; 5% Hispanic/Latino; 5% Asian, non-Hispanic/Latino; 0.1% American Indian or Alaska Native, non-Hispanic/Latino; 2% Two or more races, non-Hispanic/Latino; 3% Race/ethnicity unknown; 5% international; 1% transferred in; 37% live on campus. *Retention:* 93% of full-time freshmen returned.

Freshmen *Admission:* 41,545 applied, 22,761 admitted, 7,262 enrolled. *Average high school GPA:* 3.53. *Test scores:* SAT critical reading scores over 500: 85%; SAT math scores over 500: 92%; SAT writing scores over 500: 88%; SAT critical reading scores over 600: 38%; SAT math scores over 600: 62%; SAT writing scores over 600: 45%; SAT critical reading scores over 700: 5%; SAT math scores over 700: 15%; SAT writing scores over 700: 7%.

Faculty *Total:* 2,888, 85% full-time, 71% with terminal degrees. *Student/faculty ratio:* 17:1.

Academics *Calendar:* semesters. *Degrees:* certificates, associate, bachelor's, master's, doctoral-professional, doctoral-research/scholarship, post-master's, and postbachelor's certificates. *Special study options:* academic remediation for entering students, accelerated degree program, adult/continuing education programs, advanced placement credit, cooperative education, distance learning, double majors, English as a second language, external degree program, freshman honors college, honors programs, independent study, internships, off-campus study, part-time degree program, services for LD students, student-designed majors, study abroad, summer session for credit. *ROTC:* Army (b), Navy (b), Air Force (b). *Unusual degree programs:* 3-2 engineering with Please see: http://www.cheme.psu.edu/Ugrad/prospective/3_2.htm; 3-2 Cooperative Program in GeoScience.

Computers on Campus 6,150 computers/terminals and 23,225 ports are available on campus for general student use. Students can access the following: campus intranet, computer help desk, free student e-mail accounts, online (class) grades, online (class) registration, online (class) schedules. Campuswide network is available. 50% of college-owned or -operated housing units are wired for high-speed Internet access. Wireless service is available via classrooms, computer centers, computer labs, dorm rooms, learning centers, libraries, student centers.

Student Life *Housing:* on-campus residence required for freshman year. *Options:* coed, men-only, women-only, disabled students. Campus housing is university owned. Freshman campus housing is guaranteed. *Activities and organizations:* drama/theater group, student-run newspaper, radio and television station, choral group, marching band, national fraternities, national sororities. *Campus security:* 24-hour emergency response devices and patrols, student patrols, late-night transport/escort service, controlled dormitory access. *Student services:* health clinic, personal/psychological counseling, women's center.

Athletics Member USCAA and NCAA. All Division I except football (Division I-A). *Intercollegiate sports:* archery M(c)/W(c), badminton M(c)/W(c), baseball M(s), basketball M(s)/W(s), bowling M(c), cheerleading M/W, cross-country running M(s)/W(s), equestrian sports M(c)/W(c), fencing M(s)/W(s), field hockey W(s), golf M(s)/W(s), gymnastics M(s)/W(s), ice hockey M(c)/W(c), lacrosse M(s)/W(s), rugby M(c)/W(c), skiing (downhill) M(c)/W(c), soccer M(s)/W(s), softball W, swimming and diving M(s)/W(s), table tennis M(c), tennis M(s)/W(s), track and field M(s)/W(s), volleyball M(s)/W(s), water polo M(c)/W(c), weight lifting M(c)/W(c), wrestling M(s). *Intramural sports:* badminton M/W, basketball M/W, bowling M/W, crew M(c)/W(c), cross-country running M/W, fencing M(c)/W(c), field hockey W, football M, golf M/W, gymnastics M(c)/W(c), lacrosse M(c)/W(c), racquetball M/W, riflery M(c)/W(c), sailing M(c)/W(c), soccer M/W, softball M/W, squash M/W, tennis M/W, track and field M/W, ultimate Frisbee M(c)/W(c), volleyball M/W, wrestling M.

Standardized Tests *Required:* SAT or ACT (for admission).

Costs (2010–11) *Tuition:* state resident $14,412 full-time, $601 per credit part-time; nonresident $26,276 full-time, $1095 per credit part-time. Full-time tuition and fees vary according to course level, degree level, location, program, and student level. Part-time tuition and fees vary according to course level, course load, degree level, location, program, and student level. *Required fees:* $838 full-time. *Room and board:* $8370; room only: $4540. Room and board charges vary according to board plan, housing facility, and location. *Payment plans:* installment, deferred payment. *Waivers:* employees or children of employees.

Financial Aid Of all full-time matriculated undergraduates who enrolled in 2009, 25,071 applied for aid, 19,537 were judged to have need, 1,481 had their need fully met. In 2009, 2673 non-need-based awards were made. *Average percent of need met:* 58%. *Average financial aid package:* $10,124. *Average need-based loan:* $4676. *Average need-based gift aid:* $6607. *Average non-need-based aid:* $3178. *Average indebtedness upon graduation:* $31,135.

Applying *Options:* electronic application, early admission, deferred entrance. *Application fee:* $50. *Required:* high school transcript. *Required for some:* interview. *Recommended:* essay or personal statement. *Application deadlines:* rolling (freshmen), rolling (transfers). *Notification:* continuous (freshmen), continuous (transfers).

Freshman Application Contact Anne L. Rohrbach, Director for Undergraduate Admissions, Penn State University Park, 201 Shields Building, Box 3000, University Park, PA 16804-3000. *Phone:* 814-865-4700. *Fax:* 814-863-7590. *E-mail:* admissions@psu.edu. *Web site:* http://www.psu.edu/.

Penn State Wilkes-Barre

Lehman, Pennsylvania

- **State-related** primarily 2-year, founded 1916, part of Pennsylvania State University
- **Rural** 156-acre campus
- **Coed** 719 undergraduate students, 85% full-time, 30% women, 70% men
- **Moderately difficult** entrance level

Undergraduates 609 full-time, 110 part-time. 5% are from out of state; 4% Black or African American, non-Hispanic/Latino; 3% Hispanic/Latino; 2% Asian, non-Hispanic/Latino; 0.2% American Indian or Alaska Native, non-Hispanic/Latino; 1% Two or more races, non-Hispanic/Latino; 1% Race/ethnicity unknown; 0.2% international; 3% transferred in. *Retention:* 80% of full-time freshmen returned.

Freshmen *Admission:* 333 applied, 208 enrolled. *Average high school GPA:* 2.91. *Test scores:* SAT critical reading scores over 500: 40%; SAT math scores over 500: 39%; SAT writing scores over 500: 29%; SAT critical reading scores over 600: 6%; SAT math scores over 600: 12%; SAT writing scores over 600: 3%; SAT critical reading scores over 700: 1%; SAT math scores over 700: 1%.

Faculty *Total:* 63, 57% full-time, 44% with terminal degrees. *Student/faculty ratio:* 15:1.

Academics *Calendar:* semesters. *Degrees:* certificates, associate, and bachelor's (enrollment figures include students enrolled at The Graduate School at Penn State who are taking courses at this location). *Special study options:* academic remediation for entering students, accelerated degree program, adult/continuing education programs, advanced placement credit, distance learning, double majors, honors programs, independent study, internships, services for LD students, student-designed majors, study abroad, summer session for credit. *ROTC:* Army (c), Air Force (c).

Computers on Campus Students can access the following: online (class) registration. Campuswide network is available.

Student Life *Housing:* college housing not available. *Activities and organizations:* student-run newspaper, radio station. *Campus security:* part-time trained security personnel. *Student services:* health clinic, personal/psychological counseling.

Athletics Member NJCAA. *Intercollegiate sports:* baseball M, basketball M, cross-country running M/W, golf M/W, soccer M/W, volleyball W. *Intramural sports:* basketball M/W, bowling M(c)/W(c), cheerleading M(c)/W(c), football M, racquetball M/W, softball M/W, volleyball M(c)/W.

Standardized Tests *Required:* SAT or ACT (for admission).

Costs (2010–11) *Tuition:* state resident $11,892 full-time, $481 per credit part-time; nonresident $18,148 full-time, $756 per credit part-time. Full-time tuition and fees vary according to course level, degree level, location, program, and student level. Part-time tuition and fees vary according to course level, course load, degree level, location, program, and student level. *Required fees:* $724 full-time. *Payment plans:* installment, deferred payment. *Waivers:* employees or children of employees.

Financial Aid Of all full-time matriculated undergraduates who enrolled in 2008, 495 applied for aid, 408 were judged to have need, 16 had their need fully met. In 2008, 40 non-need-based awards were made. *Average percent of need met:* 59%. *Average financial aid package:* $9495. *Average need-based loan:* $3920. *Average need-based gift aid:* $6367. *Average non-need-based aid:* $2415. *Average indebtedness upon graduation:* $31,135.

Applying *Options:* electronic application, early admission, deferred entrance. *Application fee:* $50. *Required:* high school transcript. *Required for some:* interview. *Recommended:* essay or personal statement. *Application deadlines:* rolling (freshmen), rolling (transfers). *Notification:* continuous (freshmen), continuous (transfers).

Freshman Application Contact Admissions Office, Penn State Wilkes-Barre, PO PSU, Lehman, PA 18627-0217. *Phone:* 570-675-9238. *Toll-free phone:* 800-966-6613. *Fax:* 570-675-9113. *E-mail:* wbadmissions@psu.edu. *Web site:* http://www.wb.psu.edu/.

Penn State Worthington Scranton

Dunmore, Pennsylvania

- **State-related** primarily 2-year, founded 1923, part of Pennsylvania State University
- **Small-town** 43-acre campus
- **Coed** 1,386 undergraduate students, 79% full-time, 52% women, 48% men
- **Moderately difficult** entrance level

Undergraduates 1,096 full-time, 290 part-time. 2% are from out of state; 2% Black or African American, non-Hispanic/Latino; 4% Hispanic/Latino; 3% Asian, non-Hispanic/Latino; 0.1% American Indian or Alaska Native, non-Hispanic/Latino; 2% Two or more races, non-Hispanic/Latino; 3% Race/ethnicity unknown; 0.2% international; 5% transferred in. *Retention:* 69% of full-time freshmen returned.

Freshmen *Admission:* 587 applied, 362 enrolled. *Average high school GPA:* 2.83. *Test scores:* SAT critical reading scores over 500: 33%; SAT math scores over 500: 38%; SAT writing scores over 500: 28%; SAT critical reading scores over 600: 5%; SAT math scores over 600: 12%; SAT writing scores over 600: 5%; SAT critical reading scores over 700: 1%; SAT writing scores over 700: 1%.

Faculty *Total:* 103, 54% full-time, 39% with terminal degrees. *Student/faculty ratio:* 17:1.

Academics *Calendar:* semesters. *Degrees:* certificates, associate, and bachelor's. *Special study options:* academic remediation for entering students, accelerated degree program, adult/continuing education programs, advanced placement credit, cooperative education, distance learning, double majors, honors programs, independent study, internships, services for LD students, study abroad, summer session for credit. *ROTC:* Army (c), Air Force (c).

Computers on Campus Students can access the following: online (class) registration. Campuswide network is available.

Student Life *Housing:* college housing not available. *Activities and organizations:* drama/theater group, student-run newspaper, choral group. *Campus security:* part-time trained security personnel. *Student services:* health clinic, personal/psychological counseling, women's center.

Athletics Member NJCAA. *Intercollegiate sports:* baseball M, basketball M/W, cheerleading M/W, cross-country running M/W, soccer M, softball W, volleyball W. *Intramural sports:* basketball M/W, bowling M(c)/W(c), skiing (downhill) M(c)/W(c), soccer M/W, softball M/W, volleyball M/W(c), weight lifting M(c)/W(c).

Standardized Tests *Required:* SAT or ACT (for admission).

Costs (2010–11) *Tuition:* state resident $11,892 full-time, $481 per credit part-time; nonresident $18,148 full-time, $756 per credit part-time. Full-time tuition and fees vary according to course level, degree level, location, program, and student level. Part-time tuition and fees vary according to course level, course load, degree level, location, program, and student level. *Required fees:* $704 full-time. *Payment plans:* installment, deferred payment. *Waivers:* employees or children of employees.

Financial Aid Of all full-time matriculated undergraduates who enrolled in 2008, 904 applied for aid, 760 were judged to have need, 26 had their need fully met. In 2008, 54 non-need-based awards were made. *Average percent of need met:* 59%. *Average financial aid package:* $9067. *Average need-based loan:* $3888. *Average need-based gift aid:* $6009. *Average non-need-based aid:* $2838. *Average indebtedness upon graduation:* $31,135.

Applying *Options:* electronic application, early admission, deferred entrance. *Application fee:* $50. *Required:* high school transcript. *Required for some:* interview. *Recommended:* essay or personal statement. *Application deadlines:* rolling (freshmen), rolling (transfers). *Notification:* continuous (freshmen), continuous (transfers).

Freshman Application Contact Admissions Office, Penn State Worthington Scranton, 120 Ridge View Drive, Dunmore, PA 18512-1699. *Phone:* 570-963-2500. *Fax:* 570-963-2524. *E-mail:* wsadmissions@psu.edu. *Web site:* http://www.sn.psu.edu/.

Penn State York

York, Pennsylvania

- **State-related** primarily 2-year, founded 1926, part of Pennsylvania State University
- **Suburban** 53-acre campus
- **Coed** 1,393 undergraduate students, 68% full-time, 43% women, 57% men
- **Moderately difficult** entrance level

Undergraduates 948 full-time, 445 part-time. 7% are from out of state; 7% Black or African American, non-Hispanic/Latino; 6% Hispanic/Latino; 5% Asian, non-Hispanic/Latino; 0.1% Native Hawaiian or other Pacific Islander, non-Hispanic/Latino; 0.2% American Indian or Alaska Native, non-Hispanic/Latino; 2% Two or more races, non-Hispanic/Latino; 2% Race/ethnicity unknown; 4% international; 4% transferred in. *Retention:* 76% of full-time freshmen returned.

Freshmen *Admission:* 678 applied, 325 enrolled. *Average high school GPA:* 2.85. *Test scores:* SAT critical reading scores over 500: 38%; SAT math scores over 500: 53%; SAT writing scores over 500: 32%; SAT critical reading scores over 600: 9%; SAT math scores over 600: 17%; SAT writing scores over 600: 6%; SAT math scores over 700: 2%.

Faculty *Total:* 112, 53% full-time, 42% with terminal degrees. *Student/faculty ratio:* 15:1.

Academics *Calendar:* semesters. *Degrees:* certificates, associate, bachelor's, and master's (also offers up to 2 years of most bachelor's degree programs offered at University Park campus). *Special study options:* academic remediation for entering students, accelerated degree program, adult/continuing education programs, advanced placement credit, distance learning, double majors, English as a second language, honors programs, independent study, internships, services for LD students, student-designed majors, study abroad, summer session for credit.

Computers on Campus Students can access the following: online (class) registration. Campuswide network is available.

Student Life *Housing:* college housing not available. *Activities and organizations:* drama/theater group, student-run newspaper. *Campus security:* part-time trained security personnel. *Student services:* health clinic, personal/psychological counseling, women's center.

Athletics Member NJCAA.

Standardized Tests *Required:* SAT or ACT (for admission).

Costs (2010–11) *Tuition:* state resident $11,892 full-time, $481 per credit part-time; nonresident $18,148 full-time, $756 per credit part-time. Full-time tuition and fees vary according to course level, degree level, location, program, and student level. Part-time tuition and fees vary according to course level, course load, degree level, location, program, and student level. *Required fees:* $704 full-time. *Payment plans:* installment, deferred payment. *Waivers:* employees or children of employees.

Financial Aid Of all full-time matriculated undergraduates who enrolled in 2008, 758 applied for aid, 597 were judged to have need, 33 had their need fully met. In 2008, 59 non-need-based awards were made. *Average percent of need met:* 58%. *Average financial aid package:* $9160. *Average need-based loan:* $3819. *Average need-based gift aid:* $5905. *Average non-need-based aid:* $2670. *Average indebtedness upon graduation:* $31,135.

Applying *Options:* electronic application, early admission, deferred entrance. *Application fee:* $50. *Required:* high school transcript. *Required for some:* interview. *Recommended:* essay or personal statement. *Application deadlines:* rolling (freshmen), rolling (transfers). *Notification:* continuous (freshmen), continuous (transfers).

Freshman Application Contact Admissions Office, Penn State York, 1031 Edgecomb Avenue, York, PA 17403-3398. *Phone:* 717-771-4040. *Toll-free phone:* 800-778-6227. *Fax:* 717-771-4005. *E-mail:* ykadmissions@psu.edu. *Web site:* http://www.yk.psu.edu/.

Pennsylvania College of Art & Design
Lancaster, Pennsylvania

- **Independent** 4-year, founded 1982
- **Urban** campus with easy access to Philadelphia and Baltimore
- **Endowment** $835,049
- **Coed** 282 undergraduate students, 95% full-time, 63% women, 37% men
- **Moderately difficult** entrance level, 48% of applicants were admitted

Undergraduates 267 full-time, 15 part-time. Students come from 7 states and territories; 22% are from out of state; 4% Black or African American, non-Hispanic/Latino; 4% Hispanic/Latino; 3% Asian, non-Hispanic/Latino; 0.7% American Indian or Alaska Native, non-Hispanic/Latino; 3% Two or more races, non-Hispanic/Latino; 6% Race/ethnicity unknown; 9% transferred in. *Retention:* 75% of full-time freshmen returned.

Freshmen *Admission:* 350 applied, 168 admitted, 89 enrolled. *Average high school GPA:* 3.02.

Faculty *Total:* 53, 28% full-time. *Student/faculty ratio:* 10:1.

Academics *Calendar:* semesters. *Degree:* certificates and bachelor's. *Special study options:* advanced placement credit, internships, part-time degree program.

Computers on Campus 74 computers/terminals are available on campus for general student use. Students can access the following: campus intranet, computer help desk, free student e-mail accounts, online (class) grades, online (class) schedules. Campuswide network is available. Wireless service is available via entire campus.

Student Life *Housing:* college housing not available. *Activities and organizations:* Student Council, Anime Club. *Campus security:* late-night transport/escort service, trained evening/weekend security personnel.

Standardized Tests *Recommended:* SAT (for admission), ACT (for admission).

Costs (2010–11) *Tuition:* $17,200 full-time, $717 per credit part-time. Part-time tuition and fees vary according to course load. *Required fees:* $980 full-

time, $717 per credit part-time. *Payment plan:* installment. *Waivers:* employees or children of employees.

Applying *Options:* electronic application, deferred entrance. *Application fee:* $40. *Required:* essay or personal statement, high school transcript, minimum 2.5 GPA, interview, portfolio. *Required for some:* 2 letters of recommendation. *Application deadlines:* rolling (freshmen), rolling (transfers). *Notification:* continuous (transfers).

Freshman Application Contact Director of Admissions Marketing and Recruitment, Pennsylvania College of Art & Design, 204 North Prince Street, PO Box 59, Lancaster, PA 17608. *Phone:* 717-396-7833. *Fax:* 717-396-1339. *E-mail:* admissions@pcad.edu. *Web site:* http://www.pcad.edu/.

Pennsylvania College of Technology
Williamsport, Pennsylvania

- **State-related** 4-year, founded 1965, administratively affiliated with Pennsylvania State University
- **Small-town** 997-acre campus
- **Endowment** $5.4 million
- **Coed** 6,290 undergraduate students, 85% full-time, 36% women, 64% men
- **Noncompetitive** entrance level, 92% of applicants were admitted

Undergraduates 5,347 full-time, 943 part-time. Students come from 34 states and territories; 14 other countries; 11% are from out of state; 4% Black or African American, non-Hispanic/Latino; 2% Hispanic/Latino; 0.7% Asian, non-Hispanic/Latino; 0.1% Native Hawaiian or other Pacific Islander, non-Hispanic/Latino; 0.3% American Indian or Alaska Native, non-Hispanic/Latino; 1% Two or more races, non-Hispanic/Latino; 0.4% international; 10% transferred in; 27% live on campus. *Retention:* 64% of full-time freshmen returned.

Freshmen *Admission:* 3,642 applied, 3,347 admitted, 1,380 enrolled.

Faculty *Total:* 489, 61% full-time. *Student/faculty ratio:* 18:1.

Academics *Calendar:* semesters. *Degrees:* certificates, associate, and bachelor's. *Special study options:* academic remediation for entering students, advanced placement credit, cooperative education, distance learning, English as a second language, independent study, internships, off-campus study, part-time degree program, services for LD students, student-designed majors, study abroad, summer session for credit. *ROTC:* Army (c).

Computers on Campus 2,400 computers/terminals are available on campus for general student use. Students can access the following: campus intranet, computer help desk, free student e-mail accounts, online (class) grades, online (class) registration, online (class) schedules. Campuswide network is available. 100% of college-owned or -operated housing units are wired for high-speed Internet access. Wireless service is available via entire campus.

Student Life *Housing options:* coed, disabled students. Campus housing is university owned. *Activities and organizations:* student-run radio station, Student Government Association, Residence Hall Association, Wildcats Event Board, Association of Computing Machinery, Campus Crusade for Christ, national fraternities, national sororities. *Campus security:* 24-hour emergency response devices and patrols, late-night transport/escort service, controlled dormitory access. *Student services:* health clinic, personal/psychological counseling.

Athletics Member USCAA. *Intercollegiate sports:* archery M/W, baseball M, basketball M/W, bowling M/W, cross-country running M/W, golf M/W, soccer M/W, softball W, tennis M/W, volleyball M/W, wrestling M. *Intramural sports:* archery M/W, badminton M/W, basketball M/W, bowling M/W, football M/W, golf M/W, lacrosse M/W, racquetball M/W, soccer M/W, softball M/W, table tennis M/W, tennis M/W, ultimate Frisbee M/W, volleyball M/W, weight lifting M/W.

Standardized Tests *Required for some:* SAT (for admission).

Costs (2010–11) *Tuition:* state resident $11,040 full-time, $368 per credit hour part-time; nonresident $14,340 full-time, $478 per credit hour part-time. Full-time tuition and fees vary according to course load and program. Part-time tuition and fees vary according to course load and program. *Required fees:* $2040 full-time, $68 per credit part-time. *Room and board:* $9500; room only: $5500. Room and board charges vary according to board plan and housing facility. *Payment plan:* deferred payment. *Waivers:* employees or children of employees.

Financial Aid Of all full-time matriculated undergraduates who enrolled in 2008, 6,763 applied for aid, 5,296 were judged to have need. 191 Federal Work-Study jobs (averaging $1658). 374 state and other part-time jobs (averaging $1580). *Average percent of need met:* 78%. *Average financial aid package:* $14,006. *Average need-based gift aid:* $3243.

Applying *Options:* electronic application, early admission, deferred entrance. *Application fee:* $50. *Required:* high school transcript. *Application deadlines:* 7/1 (freshmen), rolling (transfers).

Freshman Application Contact Mr. Dennis L. Correll, Associate Dean for Admissions/Financial Aid, Pennsylvania College of Technology, One College Avenue, DIF #119, Williamsport, PA 17701. *Phone:* 570-327-4761 Ext. 7337. *Toll-free phone:* 800-367-9222. *Fax:* 570-321-5551. *E-mail:* dcorrell@pct.edu. *Web site:* http://www.pct.edu/.

Philadelphia Biblical University

Langhorne, Pennsylvania

- **Independent nondenominational** comprehensive, founded 1913
- **Suburban** 105-acre campus with easy access to Philadelphia
- **Endowment** $7.8 million
- **Coed** 1,005 undergraduate students, 91% full-time, 53% women, 47% men
- **Moderately difficult** entrance level, 73% of applicants were admitted

Undergraduates 919 full-time, 86 part-time. Students come from 36 states and territories; 18 other countries; 42% are from out of state; 15% Black or African American, non-Hispanic/Latino; 4% Hispanic/Latino; 4% Asian, non-Hispanic/Latino; 0.5% American Indian or Alaska Native, non-Hispanic/Latino; 1% Two or more races, non-Hispanic/Latino; 1% Race/ethnicity unknown; 2% international; 10% transferred in; 62% live on campus. *Retention:* 75% of full-time freshmen returned.

Freshmen *Admission:* 611 applied, 445 admitted, 164 enrolled. *Average high school GPA:* 3.37. *Test scores:* SAT critical reading scores over 500: 71%; SAT math scores over 500: 63%; ACT scores over 18: 96%; SAT critical reading scores over 600: 23%; SAT math scores over 600: 21%; ACT scores over 24: 50%; SAT critical reading scores over 700: 2%; SAT math scores over 700: 1%.

Faculty *Total:* 121, 41% full-time, 39% with terminal degrees. *Student/faculty ratio:* 14:1.

Academics *Calendar:* semesters. *Degrees:* certificates, bachelor's, master's, and postbachelor's certificates. *Special study options:* academic remediation for entering students, accelerated degree program, adult/continuing education programs, advanced placement credit, double majors, honors programs, internships, off-campus study, part-time degree program, services for LD students, study abroad, summer session for credit. *ROTC:* Air Force (c).

Computers on Campus 79 computers/terminals are available on campus for general student use. Students can access the following: campus intranet, computer help desk, free student e-mail accounts, online (class) grades, online (class) registration, online (class) schedules. Campuswide network is available. 100% of college-owned or -operated housing units are wired for high-speed Internet access. Wireless service is available via classrooms, computer labs, dorm rooms, learning centers, libraries.

Student Life *Housing:* on-campus residence required through senior year. *Options:* men-only, women-only, disabled students. Campus housing is university owned and leased by the school. Freshman campus housing is guaranteed. *Activities and organizations:* drama/theater group, student-run newspaper, choral group, Student Senate, Chi Beta Sigma (Social Work Club), Students in Free Enterprise, Student Missionary Fellowship, Culture & Arts Association. *Campus security:* 24-hour emergency response devices and patrols, student patrols, late-night transport/escort service, controlled dormitory access. *Student services:* health clinic, personal/psychological counseling.

Athletics Member NCAA, NCCAA. All NCAA Division III. *Intercollegiate sports:* baseball M, basketball M/W, cross-country running M/W, golf M, soccer M/W, softball W, tennis W, volleyball M/W. *Intramural sports:* basketball M/W, soccer M/W, tennis M/W, ultimate Frisbee M/W, volleyball M/W.

Standardized Tests *Required:* SAT or ACT (for admission).

Costs (2011–12) *Comprehensive fee:* $29,163 includes full-time tuition ($20,688), mandatory fees ($200), and room and board ($8275). Full-time tuition and fees vary according to course load and location. Part-time tuition: $613 per credit. Part-time tuition and fees vary according to course load and location. *College room only:* $4400. Room and board charges vary according to board plan, housing facility, and location. *Payment plan:* installment. *Waivers:* employees or children of employees.

Financial Aid Of all full-time matriculated undergraduates who enrolled in 2009, 988 applied for aid, 838 were judged to have need, 96 had their need fully met. 92 Federal Work-Study jobs (averaging $989). In 2009, 60 non-need-based awards were made. *Average percent of need met:* 66%. *Average financial aid package:* $14,502. *Average need-based loan:* $5062. *Average need-based gift aid:* $10,340. *Average non-need-based aid:* $6646. *Average indebtedness upon graduation:* $25,971.

Applying *Options:* electronic application, early admission, deferred entrance. *Application fee:* $25. *Required:* essay or personal statement, high school transcript, minimum 2 GPA. *Required for some:* interview. *Recommended:* interview. *Application deadlines:* rolling (freshmen), rolling (transfers). *Notification:* continuous (freshmen), continuous (transfers).

Freshman Application Contact Mr. Jamie Gleason, Director of Undergraduate Admissions, Philadelphia Biblical University, 200 Manor Avenue, Langhorne, PA 19047. *Phone:* 215-702-4250. *Toll-free phone:* 800-366-0049. *Fax:* 215-702-4248. *E-mail:* admissions@pbu.edu. *Web site:* http://www.pbu.edu/.

Philadelphia University

Philadelphia, Pennsylvania

- **Independent** comprehensive, founded 1884
- **Suburban** 100-acre campus
- **Coed** 2,999 undergraduate students, 93% full-time, 66% women, 34% men
- **Moderately difficult** entrance level, 73% of applicants were admitted

Undergraduates 2,802 full-time, 197 part-time. 52% are from out of state; 10% Black or African American, non-Hispanic/Latino; 6% Hispanic/Latino; 4% Asian, non-Hispanic/Latino; 0.2% Native Hawaiian or other Pacific Islander, non-Hispanic/Latino; 0.2% American Indian or Alaska Native, non-Hispanic/Latino; 2% Two or more races, non-Hispanic/Latino; 8% Race/ethnicity unknown; 2% international; 4% transferred in; 48% live on campus. *Retention:* 79% of full-time freshmen returned.

Freshmen *Admission:* 4,138 applied, 3,039 admitted, 703 enrolled. *Average high school GPA:* 3.43. *Test scores:* SAT critical reading scores over 500: 67%; SAT math scores over 500: 72%; SAT writing scores over 500: 61%; SAT critical reading scores over 600: 14%; SAT math scores over 600: 23%; SAT writing scores over 600: 13%; SAT critical reading scores over 700: 1%; SAT math scores over 700: 2%; SAT writing scores over 700: 1%.

Faculty *Total:* 482, 23% full-time, 17% with terminal degrees. *Student/faculty ratio:* 14:1.

Academics *Calendar:* semesters. *Degrees:* certificates, associate, bachelor's, master's, doctoral-research/scholarship, post-master's, and postbachelor's certificates. *Special study options:* academic remediation for entering students, accelerated degree program, adult/continuing education programs, advanced placement credit, distance learning, double majors, freshman honors college, honors programs, independent study, internships, off-campus study, part-time degree program, services for LD students, study abroad, summer session for credit.

Computers on Campus Students can access the following: online (class) registration. Campuswide network is available.

Student Life *Housing options:* coed, women-only, disabled students. Campus housing is university owned and leased by the school. Freshman campus housing is guaranteed. *Activities and organizations:* drama/theater group, student-run newspaper, choral group, national fraternities, national sororities. *Campus security:* 24-hour emergency response devices and patrols, late-night transport/escort service, controlled dormitory access. *Student services:* health clinic, personal/psychological counseling.

Athletics Member NCAA. All Division II except soccer (Division I). *Intercollegiate sports:* baseball M(s), basketball M(s)/W(s), field hockey W(s), golf M(s), lacrosse W(s), soccer M(s)/W(s), softball W(s), tennis M(s)/W(s), volleyball W(s). *Intramural sports:* basketball M/W, cross-country running M/W, football M, skiing (downhill) M(c)/W(c), soccer M/W, softball M/W, swimming and diving M/W, table tennis M/W, tennis M/W, volleyball M/W, weight lifting M/W.

Standardized Tests *Required:* SAT or ACT (for admission).

Costs (2010–11) *Comprehensive fee:* $38,392 includes full-time tuition ($28,800), mandatory fees ($90), and room and board ($9502). Full-time tuition and fees vary according to degree level and program. Part-time tuition: $510 per credit hour. Part-time tuition and fees vary according to class time, course load, degree level, and program. *College room only:* $4698. Room and board charges vary according to board plan and housing facility. *Payment plans:* installment, deferred payment. *Waivers:* employees or children of employees.

Financial Aid Of all full-time matriculated undergraduates who enrolled in 2009, 2,216 applied for aid, 1,946 were judged to have need, 175 had their need fully met. In 2009, 729 non-need-based awards were made. *Average percent of need met:* 72%. *Average financial aid package:* $21,048. *Average need-based loan:* $5277. *Average need-based gift aid:* $13,751. *Average non-need-based aid:* $5137. *Average indebtedness upon graduation:* $32,037. *Financial aid deadline:* 4/15.

Applying *Options:* electronic application, deferred entrance. *Application fee:* $40. *Required:* high school transcript. *Recommended:* essay or personal statement, 2 letters of recommendation, interview. *Application deadlines:* rolling (freshmen), rolling (transfers). *Notification:* continuous (freshmen).

Freshman Application Contact Ms. Christine Greb, Director of Admissions, Philadelphia University, School House Lane and Henry Avenue, Philadelphia, PA 19144-5497. *Phone:* 215-951-2800. *Fax:* 215-951-2907. *E-mail:* admissions@philau.edu. *Web site:* http://www.philau.edu/.

See page 1502 for the College Close-Up.

Point Park University

Pittsburgh, Pennsylvania

- **Independent** comprehensive, founded 1960
- **Urban** campus
- **Endowment** $21.9 million
- **Coed** 3,493 undergraduate students, 76% full-time, 61% women, 39% men
- **Moderately difficult** entrance level, 74% of applicants were admitted

Undergraduates 2,666 full-time, 827 part-time. Students come from 43 states and territories; 21 other countries; 18% are from out of state; 18% Black or African American, non-Hispanic/Latino; 3% Hispanic/Latino; 0.8% Asian, non-Hispanic/Latino; 0.2% Native Hawaiian or other Pacific Islander, non-Hispanic/Latino; 0.4% American Indian or Alaska Native, non-Hispanic/Latino; 3% Two or more races, non-Hispanic/Latino; 1% Race/ethnicity unknown; 0.9% international; 14% transferred in; 25% live on campus. *Retention:* 77% of full-time freshmen returned.

Freshmen *Admission:* 2,971 applied, 2,204 admitted, 538 enrolled. *Average high school GPA:* 3.23. *Test scores:* SAT critical reading scores over 500: 61%; SAT math scores over 500: 50%; SAT writing scores over 500: 58%; ACT scores over 18: 91%; SAT critical reading scores over 600: 20%; SAT math scores over 600: 12%; SAT writing scores over 600: 15%; ACT scores over 24: 36%; SAT critical reading scores over 700: 3%; SAT math scores over 700: 1%; SAT writing scores over 700: 2%; ACT scores over 30: 4%.

Faculty *Total:* 451, 28% full-time. *Student/faculty ratio:* 14:1.

Academics *Calendar:* semesters. *Degrees:* certificates, associate, bachelor's, master's, and postbachelor's certificates. *Special study options:* academic remediation for entering students, accelerated degree program, adult/continuing education programs, advanced placement credit, cooperative education, distance learning, double majors, English as a second language, honors programs, independent study, internships, off-campus study, part-time degree program, services for LD students, student-designed majors, study abroad, summer session for credit. *ROTC:* Army (c), Air Force (c).

Computers on Campus 247 computers/terminals and 112 ports are available on campus for general student use. Students can access the following: campus intranet, computer help desk, free student e-mail accounts, online (class) grades, online (class) registration, online (class) schedules. Campuswide network is available. 100% of college-owned or -operated housing units are wired for high-speed Internet access. Wireless service is available via classrooms, computer labs, libraries, student centers.

Student Life *Housing options:* coed, women-only, disabled students. Campus housing is university owned and leased by the school. Freshman campus housing is guaranteed. *Activities and organizations:* drama/theater group, student-run newspaper, radio and television station, choral group, Black Student Union, student radio station, Dance Club, The Body Christian Fellowship, College Students in Broadcasting. *Campus security:* 24-hour emergency response devices and patrols, late-night transport/escort service, controlled dormitory access, 24-hour security desk, video security. *Student services:* health clinic, personal/psychological counseling.

Athletics Member NAIA. *Intercollegiate sports:* baseball M(s), basketball M(s)/W(s), cross-country running M(s)/W(s), golf M(s)/W(s), soccer M(s)/W(s), softball W(s), volleyball W(s). *Intramural sports:* basketball M, bowling M/W, football M, golf M, tennis M/W, volleyball M/W, weight lifting M/W.

Standardized Tests *Required:* SAT or ACT (for admission).

Costs (2010–11) *Comprehensive fee:* $31,980 includes full-time tuition ($21,700), mandatory fees ($800), and room and board ($9480). Full-time tuition and fees vary according to program. Part-time tuition: $602 per credit. Part-time tuition and fees vary according to program. *Required fees:* $30 per credit part-time. *College room only:* $4520. Room and board charges vary according to board plan and housing facility. *Payment plans:* installment, deferred payment. *Waivers:* employees or children of employees.

Financial Aid Of all full-time matriculated undergraduates who enrolled in 2009, 2,737 applied for aid, 2,489 were judged to have need, 262 had their need fully met. 295 Federal Work-Study jobs (averaging $2260). 293 state and other part-time jobs (averaging $3008). In 2009, 208 non-need-based awards were made. *Average percent of need met:* 63%. *Average financial aid package:* $16,546. *Average need-based loan:* $5015. *Average need-based gift aid:* $10,862. *Average non-need-based aid:* $6788. *Average indebtedness upon graduation:* $26,687. *Financial aid deadline:* 3/15.

Applying *Options:* electronic application, early admission, deferred entrance. *Application fee:* $40. *Required:* high school transcript. *Required for some:* 2 letters of recommendation, interview, audition. *Recommended:* essay or personal statement, minimum 2.5 GPA. *Application deadlines:* rolling (freshmen), rolling (transfers). *Notification:* continuous (freshmen), continuous (transfers).

Freshman Application Contact Point Park University, 201 Wood Street, Pittsburgh, PA 15222-1984. *Phone:* 412-392-3430. *Toll-free phone:* 800-321-0129. *Web site:* http://www.pointpark.edu/.

The Restaurant School at Walnut Hill College

Philadelphia, Pennsylvania

- **Proprietary** primarily 2-year, founded 1974
- **Urban** 2-acre campus
- **Coed** 423 undergraduate students, 100% full-time, 47% women, 53% men
- **97%** of applicants were admitted

Undergraduates 423 full-time. Students come from 2 other countries; 33% are from out of state; 17% Black or African American, non-Hispanic/Latino; 5% Hispanic/Latino; 2% Asian, non-Hispanic/Latino; 0.5% Two or more races, non-Hispanic/Latino; 30% Race/ethnicity unknown; 9% transferred in. *Retention:* 64% of full-time freshmen returned.

Freshmen *Admission:* 174 applied, 168 admitted, 212 enrolled.

Faculty *Total:* 19, 95% full-time. *Student/faculty ratio:* 22:1.

Academics *Calendar:* quarters. *Degrees:* associate and bachelor's. *Special study options:* internships, part-time degree program.

Computers on Campus 56 computers/terminals are available on campus for general student use. Students can access the following: campus intranet, computer help desk, free student e-mail accounts, online (class) grades, online (class) schedules. Campuswide network is available. 100% of college-owned or -operated housing units are wired for high-speed Internet access. Wireless service is available via entire campus.

Student Life *Housing options:* coed. Campus housing is leased by the school. *Activities and organizations:* Wine Club, Book Club, Coffee & Tea Club, Craft Club, Flair Bartending. *Campus security:* 24-hour emergency response devices and patrols, student patrols, controlled dormitory access.

Standardized Tests *Recommended:* SAT or ACT (for admission).

Costs (2011–12) *One-time required fee:* $200. *Tuition:* $17,850 full-time. *Required fees:* $3300 full-time. *Room only:* $4500. Room and board charges vary according to housing facility. *Payment plans:* installment, deferred payment.

Applying *Options:* electronic application, early admission, early decision, deferred entrance. *Application fee:* $50. *Required:* essay or personal statement, high school transcript, 2 letters of recommendation, interview. *Required for some:* entrance exam. *Recommended:* minimum 2 GPA. *Application deadline:* rolling (freshmen).

Freshman Application Contact Miss Toni Morelli, Director of Admissions, The Restaurant School at Walnut Hill College, 4207 Walnut Street, Philadelphia, PA 19104-3518. *Phone:* 267-295-2353. *Toll-free phone:* 877-925-6884 Ext. 3011. *Fax:* 215-222-4219. *E-mail:* tmorelli@walnuthillcollege.edu. *Web site:* http://www.walnuthillcollege.edu/.

Robert Morris University

Moon Township, Pennsylvania

- **Independent** university, founded 1921
- **Suburban** 230-acre campus with easy access to Pittsburgh
- **Endowment** $19.5 million
- **Coed** 3,803 undergraduate students, 88% full-time, 44% women, 56% men
- **Minimally difficult** entrance level, 89% of applicants were admitted

Undergraduates 3,334 full-time, 469 part-time. Students come from 38 states and territories; 38 other countries; 15% are from out of state; 8% Black or African American, non-Hispanic/Latino; 1% Hispanic/Latino; 1% Asian, non-Hispanic/Latino; 0.2% American Indian or Alaska Native, non-Hispanic/Latino; 0.2% Two or more races, non-Hispanic/Latino; 13% Race/ethnicity unknown; 3% international; 8% transferred in; 40% live on campus. *Retention:* 73% of full-time freshmen returned.

Freshmen *Admission:* 5,125 applied, 4,538 admitted, 900 enrolled. *Average high school GPA:* 3.32. *Test scores:* SAT critical reading scores over 500: 50%; SAT math scores over 500: 58%; SAT writing scores over 500: 46%; ACT scores over 18: 91%; SAT critical reading scores over 600: 10%; SAT math scores over 600: 22%; SAT writing scores over 600: 9%; ACT scores over 24: 41%; SAT critical reading scores over 700: 1%; SAT math scores over 700: 3%; ACT scores over 30: 3%.

Faculty *Total:* 411, 46% full-time, 56% with terminal degrees. *Student/faculty ratio:* 15:1.

Academics *Calendar:* semesters. *Degrees:* certificates, bachelor's, master's, doctoral-professional, and postbachelor's certificates. *Special study options:*

academic remediation for entering students, accelerated degree program, adult/continuing education programs, advanced placement credit, cooperative education, distance learning, honors programs, independent study, internships, off-campus study, part-time degree program, services for LD students, study abroad, summer session for credit. *ROTC:* Army (b), Air Force (c).

Computers on Campus 300 computers/terminals are available on campus for general student use. Students can access the following: campus intranet, computer help desk, free student e-mail accounts, online (class) grades, online (class) registration, online (class) schedules, online payment. Campuswide network is available. 100% of college-owned or -operated housing units are wired for high-speed Internet access. Wireless service is available via classrooms, computer centers, computer labs, learning centers, libraries, student centers.

Student Life *Housing:* on-campus residence required for freshman year. *Options:* coed, men-only, women-only, disabled students. Campus housing is university owned. Freshman applicants given priority for college housing. *Activities and organizations:* drama/theater group, student-run newspaper, radio and television station, choral group, marching band, Student Government Association, Residence Hall Association, R-MOVE, National Society of Collegiate Scholars, Black Student Union, national fraternities, national sororities. *Campus security:* 24-hour emergency response devices and patrols, late-night transport/escort service, controlled dormitory access. *Student services:* health clinic, personal/psychological counseling.

Athletics Member NCAA. All Division I. *Intercollegiate sports:* baseball M(c), basketball M(s)/W(s), cheerleading M(c)/W(c), crew W(s), field hockey W(s), football M(s), golf M(s)/W(s), ice hockey M(s)/W(s), lacrosse M(s)/W(s), soccer M(s)/W(s), softball W(s), tennis M(s)/W(s), track and field M(s)/W(s), volleyball W(s). *Intramural sports:* basketball M/W, bowling M(c)/W(c), football M, ice hockey M(c), rugby M(c), softball M/W, volleyball M(c)/W.

Standardized Tests *Required:* SAT or ACT (for admission).

Costs (2010–11) *Comprehensive fee:* $32,210 includes full-time tuition ($20,940), mandatory fees ($610), and room and board ($10,660). Full-time tuition and fees vary according to degree level and program. Part-time tuition: $695 per credit hour. Part-time tuition and fees vary according to course load, degree level, and program. *Required fees:* $30 per credit hour part-time. *College room only:* $5110. Room and board charges vary according to board plan and housing facility. *Payment plans:* installment, deferred payment. *Waivers:* employees or children of employees.

Financial Aid Of all full-time matriculated undergraduates who enrolled in 2009, 2,903 applied for aid, 2,660 were judged to have need, 335 had their need fully met. In 2009, 503 non-need-based awards were made. *Average percent of need met:* 69%. *Average financial aid package:* $17,227. *Average need-based loan:* $5482. *Average need-based gift aid:* $11,155. *Average non-need-based aid:* $8990. *Average indebtedness upon graduation:* $37,523.

Applying *Options:* electronic application, deferred entrance. *Application fee:* $30. *Required:* high school transcript, minimum 2.5 GPA. *Required for some:* interview. *Recommended:* minimum 3 GPA, interview. *Application deadlines:* 7/1 (freshmen), 7/1 (transfers). *Notification:* continuous until 9/1 (freshmen), continuous (transfers).

Freshman Application Contact Enrollment Services Department, Robert Morris University, 6001 University Boulevard, Moon Township, PA 15108-1189. *Phone:* 412-397-5200. *Toll-free phone:* 800-762-0097. *Fax:* 412-397-2425. *E-mail:* admissionsoffice@rmu.edu. *Web site:* http://www.rmu.edu/.

See page 1538 for the College Close-Up.

Rosemont College

Rosemont, Pennsylvania

- **Independent Roman Catholic** comprehensive, founded 1921
- **Suburban** 56-acre campus with easy access to Philadelphia
- **Endowment** $12.2 million
- **Coed** 501 undergraduate students, 81% full-time, 77% women, 23% men
- **Moderately difficult** entrance level, 51% of applicants were admitted

Undergraduates 408 full-time, 93 part-time. Students come from 10 states and territories; 5 other countries; 20% are from out of state; 45% Black or African American, non-Hispanic/Latino; 7% Hispanic/Latino; 5% Asian, non-Hispanic/Latino; 9% Race/ethnicity unknown; 1% international; 5% transferred in; 70% live on campus. *Retention:* 66% of full-time freshmen returned.

Freshmen *Admission:* 1,090 applied, 561 admitted, 101 enrolled. *Average high school GPA:* 3.4. *Test scores:* SAT critical reading scores over 500: 48%; SAT math scores over 500: 50%; SAT writing scores over 500: 42%; ACT scores over 18: 83%; SAT critical reading scores over 600: 15%; SAT math scores over 600: 9%; SAT writing scores over 600: 10%; ACT scores over 24: 24%; SAT critical reading scores over 700: 2%; SAT math scores over 700: 4%; SAT writing scores over 700: 4%; ACT scores over 30: 6%.

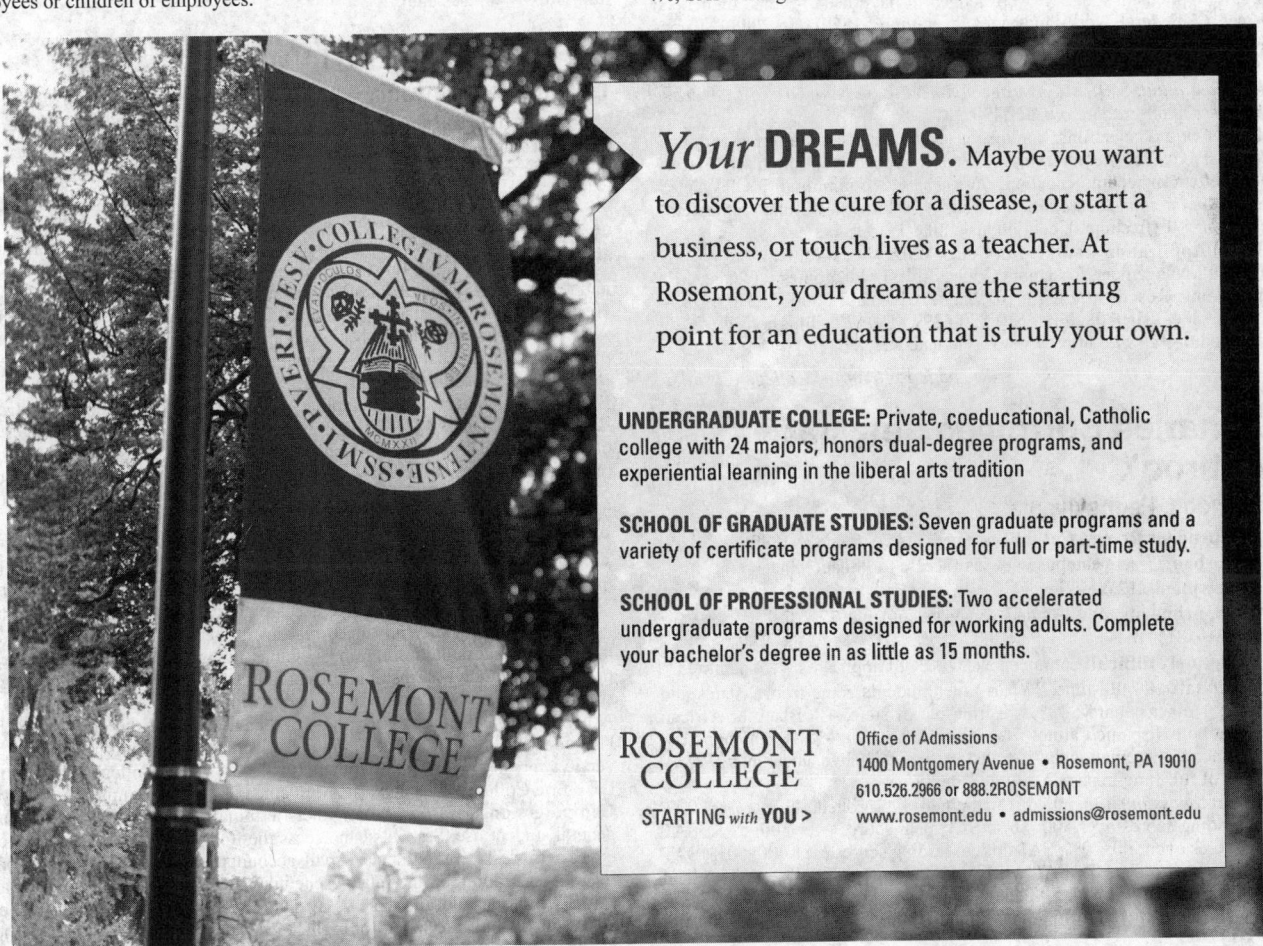

Faculty *Total:* 136, 21% full-time, 86% with terminal degrees. *Student/faculty ratio:* 8:1.

Academics *Calendar:* semesters. *Degrees:* bachelor's, master's, and post-bachelor's certificates. *Special study options:* academic remediation for entering students, accelerated degree program, adult/continuing education programs, advanced placement credit, double majors, English as a second language, honors programs, independent study, internships, off-campus study, part-time degree program, services for LD students, student-designed majors, study abroad, summer session for credit. *ROTC:* Army (c). *Unusual degree programs:* 3-2 nursing with Villanova University, Drexel University; counseling psychology, dentistry, art therapy, physical therapy, creative arts in therapy, nursing with Drexel University.

Computers on Campus 100 computers/terminals and 250 ports are available on campus for general student use. Students can access the following: campus intranet, computer help desk, free student e-mail accounts, online (class) grades, online (class) registration, online (class) schedules. Campuswide network is available. 100% of college-owned or -operated housing units are wired for high-speed Internet access. Wireless service is available via classrooms, computer centers, computer labs, dorm rooms, learning centers, libraries, student centers.

Student Life *Housing:* on-campus residence required through junior year. *Options:* coed, women-only. Campus housing is university owned. Freshman campus housing is guaranteed. *Activities and organizations:* drama/theater group, student-run newspaper, choral group, student government, Triad, Jest and Gesture, Best Buddies, Political Science Club. *Campus security:* 24-hour emergency response devices and patrols, late-night transport/escort service, controlled dormitory access. *Student services:* health clinic, personal/psychological counseling, women's center, legal services.

Athletics Member NCAA. All Division III. *Intercollegiate sports:* basketball M/W, cross-country running M/W, field hockey W, golf M, lacrosse M/W, soccer M/W, softball W, tennis M/W, volleyball W.

Standardized Tests *Required:* SAT or ACT (for admission).

Costs (2011–12) *Comprehensive fee:* $40,490 includes full-time tuition ($28,100), mandatory fees ($950), and room and board ($11,440). Part-time tuition: $1070 per credit hour. *Room and board:* Room and board charges vary according to board plan and housing facility. *Payment plan:* installment. *Waivers:* senior citizens and employees or children of employees.

Financial Aid Of all full-time matriculated undergraduates who enrolled in 2008, 407 applied for aid, 393 were judged to have need, 42 had their need fully met. 65 Federal Work-Study jobs (averaging $1550). In 2008, 27 non-need-based awards were made. *Average percent of need met:* 71%. *Average financial aid package:* $22,845. *Average need-based loan:* $3330. *Average need-based gift aid:* $19,781. *Average non-need-based aid:* $10,657. *Average indebtedness upon graduation:* $21,490.

Applying *Options:* electronic application, early admission, deferred entrance. *Application fee:* $35. *Required:* essay or personal statement, high school transcript, 2 letters of recommendation. *Recommended:* minimum 3 GPA, interview. *Application deadlines:* rolling (freshmen), rolling (transfers). *Notification:* 8/1 (freshmen), continuous until 8/1 (transfers).

Freshman Application Contact Mr. Chuck Walz, Vice President for Enrollment Management, Rosemont College, 1400 Montgomery Avenue, Main Building, Rosemont, PA 19010. *Phone:* 610-527-0200 Ext. 2905. *Toll-free phone:* 800-331-0708. *Fax:* 610-520-4399. *E-mail:* admissions@rosemont.edu. *Web site:* http://www.rosemont.edu/.

See page 1546 for the College Close-Up.

St. Charles Borromeo Seminary, Overbrook

Wynnewood, Pennsylvania

- **Independent Roman Catholic** comprehensive, founded 1832
- **Suburban** 77-acre campus with easy access to Philadelphia
- **Endowment** $12.0 million
- **Coed, primarily men** 134 undergraduate students, 72% full-time, 19% women, 81% men
- **Moderately difficult** entrance level, 100% of applicants were admitted

Undergraduates 97 full-time, 37 part-time. Students come from 9 states and territories; 1 other country; 13% are from out of state; 4% Black or African American, non-Hispanic/Latino; 7% Hispanic/Latino; 4% Asian, non-Hispanic/Latino; 1% international; 7% transferred in; 94% live on campus. *Retention:* 77% of full-time freshmen returned.

Freshmen *Admission:* 13 applied, 13 admitted, 17 enrolled. *Test scores:* SAT critical reading scores over 500: 86%; SAT math scores over 500: 57%; SAT writing scores over 500: 79%; SAT critical reading scores over 600: 50%; SAT math scores over 600: 7%; SAT writing scores over 600: 29%; SAT critical reading scores over 700: 7%; SAT math scores over 700: 7%.

Faculty *Total:* 30, 47% full-time, 47% with terminal degrees. *Student/faculty ratio:* 8:1.

Academics *Calendar:* semesters. *Degrees:* certificates, bachelor's, master's, doctoral-professional, and postbachelor's certificates (also offers coed part-time programs). *Special study options:* academic remediation for entering students, accelerated degree program, adult/continuing education programs, advanced placement credit, English as a second language, independent study, summer session for credit.

Computers on Campus 60 computers/terminals are available on campus for general student use. Students can access the following: campus intranet. Campuswide network is available. Wireless service is available via classrooms, computer centers, computer labs, libraries.

Student Life *Housing:* on-campus residence required through senior year. *Options:* men-only. Campus housing is university owned. Freshman campus housing is guaranteed. *Activities and organizations:* drama/theater group, student-run newspaper, choral group, Seminarians for Life, Student Council. *Campus security:* 24-hour emergency response devices and patrols. *Student services:* health clinic, personal/psychological counseling.

Athletics *Intramural sports:* basketball M, football M, soccer M, volleyball M.

Standardized Tests *Recommended:* SAT or ACT (for admission).

Costs (2010–11) *Comprehensive fee:* $29,700 includes full-time tuition ($17,088), mandatory fees ($1140), and room and board ($11,472). Part-time tuition: $831 per course. *Room and board:* Room and board charges vary according to board plan. *Payment plan:* installment. *Waivers:* employees or children of employees.

Financial Aid Of all full-time matriculated undergraduates who enrolled in 2009, 54 applied for aid, 45 were judged to have need, 25 had their need fully met. In 2009, 25 non-need-based awards were made. *Average percent of need met:* 80%. *Average financial aid package:* $19,000. *Average need-based loan:* $5000. *Average need-based gift aid:* $5600. *Average non-need-based aid:* $20,790. *Average indebtedness upon graduation:* $19,000.

Applying *Options:* deferred entrance. *Required:* essay or personal statement, high school transcript, minimum 2 GPA, 3 letters of recommendation, interview, sponsorship by diocese or religious community. *Application deadlines:* 7/15 (freshmen), 7/15 (transfers). *Notification:* continuous (freshmen), continuous (transfers).

Freshman Application Contact Rev. Joseph W. Bongard, Vice Rector, St. Charles Borromeo Seminary, Overbrook, 100 East Wynnewood Road, Wynnewood, PA 19096. *Phone:* 610-785-6271. *Fax:* 610-617-9267. *Web site:* http://www.scs.edu/.

Saint Francis University

Loretto, Pennsylvania

- **Independent Roman Catholic** comprehensive, founded 1847
- **Rural** 600-acre campus
- **Endowment** $26.6 million
- **Coed** 1,832 undergraduate students, 87% full-time, 59% women, 41% men
- **Moderately difficult** entrance level, 72% of applicants were admitted

Undergraduates 1,594 full-time, 238 part-time. Students come from 33 states and territories; 23% are from out of state; 5% Black or African American, non-Hispanic/Latino; 1% Hispanic/Latino; 0.7% Asian, non-Hispanic/Latino; 0.1% American Indian or Alaska Native, non-Hispanic/Latino; 4% Race/ethnicity unknown; 3% international; 3% transferred in; 93% live on campus. *Retention:* 83% of full-time freshmen returned.

Freshmen *Admission:* 1,575 applied, 1,132 admitted, 450 enrolled. *Average high school GPA:* 3.47. *Test scores:* SAT critical reading scores over 500: 66%; SAT math scores over 500: 68%; ACT scores over 18: 92%; SAT critical reading scores over 600: 17%; SAT math scores over 600: 24%; ACT scores over 24: 60%; SAT critical reading scores over 700: 1%; SAT math scores over 700: 3%; ACT scores over 30: 5%.

Faculty *Total:* 190, 59% full-time. *Student/faculty ratio:* 14:1.

Academics *Calendar:* semesters. *Degrees:* certificates, associate, bachelor's, master's, and doctoral-research/scholarship. *Special study options:* academic remediation for entering students, accelerated degree program, adult/continuing education programs, advanced placement credit, distance learning, double majors, external degree program, freshman honors college, honors programs, independent study, internships, off-campus study, part-time degree program, student-designed majors, study abroad, summer session for credit. *ROTC:* Army (b). *Unusual degree programs:* 3-2 engineering with Pennsylvania State University - University Park Campus, University of Pittsburgh, Clarkson University; forestry with Duke University; Pennsylvania College of Optometry, Lake Erie College of Osteopathic Medicine (LECOM), Temple University.

Computers on Campus 75 computers/terminals are available on campus for general student use. Students can access the following: campus intranet, computer help desk, free student e-mail accounts, online (class) grades, online (class) registration, online (class) schedules, wireless access throughout all of campus. Campuswide network is available. 95% of college-owned or -operated housing units are wired for high-speed Internet access. Wireless service is available via entire campus.

Student Life *Housing:* on-campus residence required through junior year. *Options:* men-only, women-only. Campus housing is university owned and leased by the school. Freshman campus housing is guaranteed. *Activities and organizations:* drama/theater group, student-run newspaper, radio station, choral group, marching band, Student Activities Organization, Club Baseball, Student Government Association, Best Buddies, Ultimate Frisbee Club, national fraternities, national sororities. *Campus security:* 24-hour emergency response devices and patrols, late-night transport/escort service, controlled dormitory access. *Student services:* health clinic, personal/psychological counseling.

Athletics Member NCAA. All Division I. *Intercollegiate sports:* basketball M(s)/W(s), bowling W, cross-country running M(s)/W(s), field hockey W(s), football M, golf M(s)/W(s), lacrosse W, soccer M(s)/W(s), softball W(s), swimming and diving M(s)/W(s), tennis M(s)/W(s), track and field M(s)/W(s), volleyball M(s)/W(s). *Intramural sports:* baseball M(c), basketball M/W, cheerleading M/W, cross-country running M/W, football M, golf M/W, lacrosse W, racquetball M/W, skiing (cross-country) M/W, skiing (downhill) M/W, soccer M/W, softball W, swimming and diving M/W, table tennis M/W, tennis M/W, track and field M/W, ultimate Frisbee M/W, volleyball M/W.

Standardized Tests *Required:* SAT or ACT (for admission).

Costs (2010–11) *Comprehensive fee:* $35,600 includes full-time tuition ($25,484), mandatory fees ($1050), and room and board ($9066). Full-time tuition and fees vary according to course load, degree level, and program. Part-time tuition: $796 per credit hour. Part-time tuition and fees vary according to class time, degree level, and program. *Required fees:* $376 per credit hour part-time. *College room only:* $4510. Room and board charges vary according to board plan and housing facility. *Waivers:* employees or children of employees.

Financial Aid Of all full-time matriculated undergraduates who enrolled in 2009, 1,457 applied for aid, 1,287 were judged to have need, 223 had their need fully met. 257 Federal Work-Study jobs (averaging $1000). 474 state and other part-time jobs (averaging $1000). In 2009, 223 non-need-based awards were made. *Average percent of need met:* 69%. *Average financial aid package:* $17,896. *Average need-based loan:* $4317. *Average need-based gift aid:* $15,543. *Average non-need-based aid:* $14,125. *Average indebtedness upon graduation:* $10,632.

Applying *Options:* electronic application, deferred entrance. *Application fee:* $30. *Required:* essay or personal statement, high school transcript, 1 letter of recommendation. *Required for some:* interview. *Recommended:* interview.

Application deadlines: rolling (freshmen), rolling (out-of-state freshmen), rolling (transfers). *Notification:* continuous (transfers).

Freshman Application Contact Robert Beener, Dean for Enrollment Management, Saint Francis University, PO Box 600, 117 Evergreen Drive, Loretto, PA 15940-0600. *Phone:* 814-472-3100. *Toll-free phone:* 800-342-5732. *E-mail:* rbeener@francis.edu. *Web site:* http://www.francis.edu/.

See page 1558 for the College Close-Up.

Saint Joseph's University
Philadelphia, Pennsylvania

- **Independent Roman Catholic (Jesuit)** comprehensive, founded 1851
- **Suburban** 103-acre campus
- **Endowment** $145.1 million
- **Coed** 5,471 undergraduate students, 84% full-time, 53% women, 47% men
- **Moderately difficult** entrance level, 80% of applicants were admitted

Undergraduates 4,619 full-time, 852 part-time. Students come from 43 states and territories; 32 other countries; 54% are from out of state; 7% Black or African American, non-Hispanic/Latino; 4% Hispanic/Latino; 2% Asian, non-Hispanic/Latino; 0.1% Native Hawaiian or other Pacific Islander, non-Hispanic/Latino; 0.2% American Indian or Alaska Native, non-Hispanic/Latino; 1% Two or more races, non-Hispanic/Latino; 2% Race/ethnicity unknown; 1% international; 1% transferred in; 59% live on campus. *Retention:* 89% of full-time freshmen returned.

Freshmen *Admission:* 6,974 applied, 5,606 admitted, 1,214 enrolled. *Average high school GPA:* 3.43. *Test scores:* SAT critical reading scores over 500: 81%; SAT math scores over 500: 85%; ACT scores over 18: 97%; SAT critical reading scores over 600: 28%; SAT math scores over 600: 35%; ACT scores over 24: 56%; SAT critical reading scores over 700: 3%; SAT math scores over 700: 4%; ACT scores over 30: 6%.

Faculty *Total:* 726, 40% full-time. *Student/faculty ratio:* 14:1.

Academics *Calendar:* semesters. *Degrees:* certificates, associate, bachelor's, master's, doctoral-research/scholarship, post-master's, and postbachelor's certificates. *Special study options:* accelerated degree program, adult/continuing education programs, advanced placement credit, cooperative education, distance learning, double majors, English as a second language, honors programs, independent study, internships, off-campus study, part-time degree program, services for LD students, student-designed majors, study abroad, summer session for credit. *ROTC:* Army (c), Navy (c), Air Force (b).

Computers on Campus 720 computers/terminals are available on campus for general student use. Students can access the following: campus intranet, computer help desk, free student e-mail accounts, online (class) grades, online (class) registration, online (class) schedules. Campuswide network is available. 100% of college-owned or -operated housing units are wired for high-speed Internet access. Wireless service is available via entire campus.

Student Life *Housing:* on-campus residence required through sophomore year. *Options:* coed, men-only, women-only, disabled students. Campus housing is university owned, leased by the school and is provided by a third party. Freshman campus housing is guaranteed. *Activities and organizations:* drama/theater group, student-run newspaper, radio station, choral group, Student Union Board, Hand-in-Hand, Collegiate Challenge, Appalachian Experience, Weekly Service, national fraternities, national sororities. *Campus security:* 24-hour emergency response devices and patrols, late-night transport/escort service, controlled dormitory access, 24-hour shuttle/escort service, bicycle patrols. *Student services:* health clinic, personal/psychological counseling.

Athletics Member NCAA. All Division I. *Intercollegiate sports:* baseball M(s), basketball M(s)/W(s), cheerleading M(c)/W(c), crew M(s)/W(s), cross-country running M(s)/W(s), field hockey W(s), golf M(s), lacrosse M(s)/W(s), soccer M(s)/W(s), softball W(s), tennis M(s)/W(s), track and field M(s)/W(s). *Intramural sports:* baseball M(c), basketball M(c)/W(c), field hockey W(c), football M/W, golf M(c)/W(c), ice hockey M(c), lacrosse M(c)/W(c), racquetball M/W, rugby M(c)/W(c), soccer M(c)/W(c), softball M/W, swimming and diving M(c)/W(c), tennis M(c)/W(c), ultimate Frisbee M(c)/W(c), volleyball M(c)/W(c).

Standardized Tests *Required:* SAT or ACT (for admission).

Costs (2010–11) *One-time required fee:* $225. *Comprehensive fee:* $47,155 includes full-time tuition ($35,080), mandatory fees ($150), and room and board ($11,925). Full-time tuition and fees vary according to course load. Part-time tuition: $466 per credit. *College room only:* $7500. Room and board charges vary according to board plan and housing facility. *Payment plans:* installment, deferred payment. *Waivers:* employees or children of employees.

Financial Aid Of all full-time matriculated undergraduates who enrolled in 2009, 2,971 applied for aid, 2,483 were judged to have need, 558 had their need fully met. In 2009, 1736 non-need-based awards were made. *Average percent of need met:* 75%. *Average financial aid package:* $19,762. *Average need-based loan:* $4400. *Average need-based gift aid:* $15,719. *Average non-need-based aid:* $10,500. *Average indebtedness upon graduation:* $45,530.

Applying *Options:* electronic application, early action, deferred entrance. *Application fee:* $60. *Required:* essay or personal statement, high school transcript. *Application deadlines:* 2/1 (freshmen), 3/1 (transfers), 11/15 (early action). *Notification:* 3/15 (freshmen), continuous (transfers), 12/25 (early action).

Freshman Application Contact Office of Admissions, Saint Joseph's University, 5600 City Avenue, Philadelphia, PA 19131-1395. *Phone:* 610-660-1300. *Toll-free phone:* 888-BEAHAWK. *Fax:* 610-660-1314. *E-mail:* admit@sju.edu. *Web site:* http://www.sju.edu/.

See page 1568 for the College Close-Up.

Saint Vincent College
Latrobe, Pennsylvania

- **Independent Roman Catholic** comprehensive, founded 1846
- **Suburban** 200-acre campus with easy access to Pittsburgh
- **Endowment** $68.8 million
- **Coed**
- **Moderately difficult** entrance level

Faculty *Student/faculty ratio:* 13:1.

Academics *Calendar:* semesters. *Degrees:* certificates, bachelor's, master's, and postbachelor's certificates.

Student Life *Campus security:* 24-hour emergency response devices and patrols, late-night transport/escort service, controlled dormitory access, limited access to residence halls on weekends.

Athletics Member NCAA. All Division III.

Standardized Tests *Required:* SAT or ACT (for admission).

Costs (2010–11) *Comprehensive fee:* $36,238 includes full-time tuition ($26,350), mandatory fees ($840), and room and board ($9048). Part-time tuition: $824 per credit. *College room only:* $4896. Room and board charges vary according to board plan and housing facility.

Financial Aid *Of all full-time matriculated undergraduates who enrolled in 2009,* 1,492 applied for aid, 1,282 were judged to have need, 315 had their need fully met. *In 2009,* 386 non-need-based awards were made. *Average percent of need met:* 81. *Average financial aid package:* $21,705. *Average need-based loan:* $4662. *Average need-based gift aid:* $16,506. *Average non-need-based aid:* $12,349. *Financial aid deadline:* 5/1.

Applying *Options:* electronic application, early admission, deferred entrance. *Application fee:* $25. *Required:* essay or personal statement, high school transcript, minimum 2.5 GPA. *Required for some:* interview. *Recommended:* minimum 3.2 GPA, 3 letters of recommendation, interview.

Freshman Application Contact Mr. David Collins, Assistant Vice President of Admission and Financial Aid, Saint Vincent College, 300 Fraser Purchase Road, Latrobe, PA 15650-2690. *Phone:* 800-782-5549. *Toll-free phone:* 800-782-5549. *Fax:* 724-532-5069. *E-mail:* admission@stvincent.edu. *Web site:* http://www.stvincent.edu/.

Seton Hill University
Greensburg, Pennsylvania

- **Independent Roman Catholic** comprehensive, founded 1883
- **Small-town** 200-acre campus with easy access to Pittsburgh
- **Endowment** $24.4 million
- **Coed** 1,810 undergraduate students, 84% full-time, 62% women, 38% men
- **Moderately difficult** entrance level, 66% of applicants were admitted

Undergraduates 1,527 full-time, 283 part-time. Students come from 31 states and territories; 15 other countries; 23% are from out of state; 6% transferred in; 55% live on campus. *Retention:* 74% of full-time freshmen returned.

Freshmen *Admission:* 2,039 applied, 1,344 admitted, 372 enrolled. *Average high school GPA:* 3.34.

Faculty *Total:* 194, 45% full-time, 54% with terminal degrees. *Student/faculty ratio:* 15:1.

Academics *Calendar:* semesters. *Degrees:* certificates, bachelor's, master's, post-master's, and postbachelor's certificates. *Special study options:* academic remediation for entering students, adult/continuing education programs, advanced placement credit, distance learning, double majors, English as a second language, honors programs, independent study, internships, part-time degree program, services for LD students, student-designed majors, study abroad, summer session for credit. *ROTC:* Army (b). *Unusual degree programs:* 3-2 engineering with University of Pittsburgh, Pennsylvania State University - University Park Campus, Georgia Institute of Technology; physician assistant with Seton Hill University, BS/DO and BS/DPharm with Lake Erie College of Osteopathic Medicine.

Computers on Campus 450 computers/terminals and 750 ports are available on campus for general student use. Students can access the following: campus intranet, computer help desk, free student e-mail accounts, online (class) grades, online (class) registration, online (class) schedules. Campuswide network is available. 100% of college-owned or -operated housing units are wired for high-speed Internet access. Wireless service is available via entire campus.

Student Life *Housing:* on-campus residence required for freshman year. *Options:* coed, men-only, women-only, disabled students. Campus housing is university owned. Freshman campus housing is guaranteed. *Activities and organizations:* drama/theater group, student-run newspaper, choral group, marching band, Student body activities council, SHU-A-thon, Chemistry Club, Biology Club, SITA - Students in the Arts. *Campus security:* 24-hour emergency response devices and patrols, late-night transport/escort service, controlled dormitory access. *Student services:* health clinic, personal/psychological counseling.

Athletics Member NCAA. All Division II. *Intercollegiate sports:* baseball M(s), basketball M(s)/W(s), cross-country running M(s)/W(s), equestrian sports W(s), field hockey W(s), football M(s), golf W(s), lacrosse M(s)/W(s), soccer M(s)/W(s), softball W(s), tennis W(s), track and field M(s)/W(s), volleyball W(s), wrestling M(s).

Standardized Tests *Recommended:* SAT or ACT (for admission).

Costs (2010–11) *Comprehensive fee:* $36,358 includes full-time tuition ($26,848), mandatory fees ($700), and room and board ($8810). Full-time tuition and fees vary according to course load and program. Part-time tuition: $720 per credit. Part-time tuition and fees vary according to course load and program. *Required fees:* $25 per credit part-time, $40 per term part-time. *Room and board:* Room and board charges vary according to board plan and housing facility. *Payment plan:* installment. *Waivers:* employees or children of employees.

Financial Aid Of all full-time matriculated undergraduates who enrolled in 2009, 1,473 applied for aid, 1,277 were judged to have need, 211 had their need fully met. 543 Federal Work-Study jobs (averaging $1594), 131 state and other part-time jobs (averaging $1536). In 2009, 147 non-need-based awards were made. *Average percent of need met:* 74%. *Average financial aid package:* $21,753. *Average need-based loan:* $5253. *Average need-based gift aid:* $16,995. *Average non-need-based aid:* $11,482. *Average indebtedness upon graduation:* $30,997.

Applying *Options:* electronic application, deferred entrance. *Application fee:* $35. *Required:* essay or personal statement, high school transcript, 1 letter of recommendation, portfolio for art, audition for music and theatre. *Recommended:* interview. *Application deadlines:* rolling (freshmen), rolling (out-of-state freshmen), rolling (transfers). *Notification:* continuous (freshmen), continuous (out-of-state freshmen), continuous (transfers).

See page 1600 for the College Close-Up.

Shippensburg University of Pennsylvania

Shippensburg, Pennsylvania

- **State-supported** comprehensive, founded 1871, part of Pennsylvania State System of Higher Education
- **Rural** 200-acre campus
- **Endowment** $27.4 million
- **Coed** 7,143 undergraduate students, 96% full-time, 52% women, 48% men
- **Moderately difficult** entrance level, 69% of applicants were admitted

Undergraduates 6,836 full-time, 307 part-time. Students come from 20 states and territories; 11 other countries; 6% are from out of state; 6% Black or African American, non-Hispanic/Latino; 2% Hispanic/Latino; 1% Asian, non-Hispanic/Latino; 0.1% Native Hawaiian or other Pacific Islander, non-Hispanic/Latino; 0.2% American Indian or Alaska Native, non-Hispanic/Latino; 0.9% Two or more races, non-Hispanic/Latino; 5% Race/ethnicity unknown; 0.2% international; 6% transferred in; 37% live on campus. *Retention:* 74% of full-time freshmen returned.

Freshmen *Admission:* 6,949 applied, 4,770 admitted, 1,712 enrolled. *Average high school GPA:* 3.21. *Test scores:* SAT critical reading scores over 500: 48%; SAT math scores over 500: 53%; ACT scores over 18: 76%; SAT critical reading scores over 600: 10%; SAT math scores over 600: 12%; ACT scores over 24: 17%; SAT critical reading scores over 700: 1%; SAT math scores over 700: 1%; ACT scores over 30: 1%.

Faculty *Total:* 420, 80% full-time, 78% with terminal degrees. *Student/faculty ratio:* 20:1.

Academics *Calendar:* semesters. *Degrees:* certificates, bachelor's, master's, post-master's, and postbachelor's certificates. *Special study options:* academic remediation for entering students, accelerated degree program, advanced placement credit, cooperative education, distance learning, double majors, honors programs, independent study, internships, off-campus study, part-time degree program, services for LD students, study abroad, summer session for credit. *ROTC:* Army (b). *Unusual degree programs:* 3-2 engineering with Pennsylvania State University - University Park and Harrisburg Campus, University of Maryland College Park.

Computers on Campus 1,100 computers/terminals are available on campus for general student use. Students can access the following: campus intranet, computer help desk, free student e-mail accounts, online (class) grades, online (class) registration, online (class) schedules, personal Web pages. Campuswide network is available. 100% of college-owned or -operated housing units are wired for high-speed Internet access. Wireless service is available via classrooms, computer centers, computer labs, learning centers, libraries, student centers.

Student Life *Housing:* on-campus residence required for freshman year. *Options:* coed. Campus housing is university owned and leased by the school. Freshman campus housing is guaranteed. *Activities and organizations:* drama/theater group, student-run newspaper, radio and television station, choral group, marching band, national fraternities, national sororities. *Campus security:* 24-hour emergency response devices and patrols, late-night transport/escort service, controlled dormitory access, surveillance cameras in certain parking lots and buildings, foot, vehicular and bicycle patrols by security officers. *Student services:* health clinic, personal/psychological counseling, women's center.

Athletics Member NCAA. All Division II. *Intercollegiate sports:* baseball M(s), basketball M(s)/W(s), cross-country running M(s)/W(s), field hockey W(s), football M(s), lacrosse W(s), soccer M(s)/W(s), softball W(s), swimming and diving M(s)/W(s), tennis W(s), track and field M(s)/W(s), volleyball W(s), wrestling M(s). *Intramural sports:* basketball M/W, bowling M(c)/W(c), lacrosse M(c), racquetball W, rugby M(c)/W(c), soccer M/W, softball M/W, tennis M(c)/W(c), ultimate Frisbee M/W, volleyball M/W.

Standardized Tests *Required:* SAT or ACT (for admission).

Costs (2010–11) *Tuition:* state resident $5804 full-time, $242 per credit hour part-time; nonresident $14,510 full-time, $605 per credit hour part-time. *Required fees:* $2252 full-time, $255 per course part-time, $68 per term part-time. *Room and board:* $7400; room only: $3870. Room and board charges vary according to board plan and housing facility. *Payment plan:* installment. *Waivers:* senior citizens and employees or children of employees.

Financial Aid Of all full-time matriculated undergraduates who enrolled in 2009, 5,549 applied for aid, 4,329 were judged to have need, 293 had their need fully met. 97 Federal Work-Study jobs (averaging $801). 491 state and other part-time jobs (averaging $1192). In 2009, 489 non-need-based awards were made. *Average percent of need met: 62%. Average financial aid package: $7902. Average need-based loan: $4009. Average need-based gift aid: $5668. Average non-need-based aid: $4334. Average indebtedness upon graduation:* $24,165.

Applying *Options:* electronic application, early admission, early action, deferred entrance. *Application fee:* $30. *Required:* high school transcript. *Required for some:* interview. *Recommended:* essay or personal statement, class rank, letters of recommendation optional. *Application deadlines:* rolling (freshmen), rolling (transfers). *Notification:* continuous (freshmen), continuous (transfers).

Freshman Application Contact Dr. Thomas Speakman, Dean of Enrollment Services, Shippensburg University of Pennsylvania, 1871 Old Main Drive, Shippensburg, PA 17257-2299. *Phone:* 717-477-1231. *Toll-free phone:* 800-822-8028. *Fax:* 717-477-4016. *E-mail:* admiss@ship.edu. *Web site:* http://www.ship.edu/.

See page 1602 for the College Close-Up.

Slippery Rock University of Pennsylvania

Slippery Rock, Pennsylvania

- **State-supported** comprehensive, founded 1889, part of Pennsylvania State System of Higher Education
- **Rural** 650-acre campus with easy access to Pittsburgh
- **Endowment** $14.7 million
- **Coed** 8,026 undergraduate students, 93% full-time, 57% women, 43% men
- **Moderately difficult** entrance level, 67% of applicants were admitted

Undergraduates 7,437 full-time, 589 part-time. Students come from 32 states and territories; 38 other countries; 9% are from out of state; 5% Black or African American, non-Hispanic/Latino; 1% Hispanic/Latino; 0.6% Asian, non-Hispanic/Latino; 0.1% American Indian or Alaska Native, non-Hispanic/Latino; 0.8% Two or more races, non-Hispanic/Latino; 6% Race/ethnicity unknown; 0.9% international; 8% transferred in; 36% live on campus. *Retention:* 81% of full-time freshmen returned.

Freshmen *Admission:* 5,932 applied, 4,002 admitted, 1,575 enrolled. *Average high school GPA:* 3.39. *Test scores:* SAT critical reading scores over 500: 51%; SAT math scores over 500: 61%; SAT writing scores over 500: 46%; ACT scores over 18: 91%; SAT critical reading scores over 600: 8%; SAT math scores over 600: 12%; SAT writing scores over 600: 8%; ACT scores over 24: 30%; SAT critical reading scores over 700: 1%; ACT scores over 30: 2%.

Faculty *Total:* 405, 86% full-time, 80% with terminal degrees. *Student/faculty ratio:* 20:1.

Academics *Calendar:* semesters. *Degrees:* certificates, bachelor's, master's, doctoral-professional, and postbachelor's certificates. *Special study options:* academic remediation for entering students, adult/continuing education programs, advanced placement credit, distance learning, double majors, honors programs, independent study, internships, off-campus study, part-time degree program, services for LD students, student-designed majors, study abroad, summer session for credit. *ROTC:* Army (b). *Unusual degree programs:* 3-2 engineering with Pennsylvania State University, University Park Campus; Youngstown State University; accelerated pre-med and pre-pharmacy options with the Lake Erie College of Osteopathic Medicine (LECOM); pre-chiropractic option with Logan College of Chiropractic.

Computers on Campus 1,323 computers/terminals and 75 ports are available on campus for general student use. Students can access the following: computer help desk, free student e-mail accounts, online (class) grades, online (class) registration, online (class) schedules. Campuswide network is available. 100% of college-owned or -operated housing units are wired for high-speed Internet access. Wireless service is available via classrooms, computer labs, dorm rooms, libraries, student centers.

Student Life *Housing:* on-campus residence required for freshman year. *Options:* coed, disabled students. Campus housing is university owned. Freshman campus housing is guaranteed. *Activities and organizations:* drama/theater group, student-run newspaper, radio and television station, choral group, marching band, Panhellenic Council, Council for Exceptional Children, Hunting and Fishing Club, Building Bridges, Campus Crusade for Christ, national fraternities, national sororities. *Campus security:* 24-hour emergency response devices and patrols, late-night transport/escort service, controlled dormitory

access. *Student services:* health clinic, personal/psychological counseling, women's center, legal services.

Athletics Member NCAA. All Division II. *Intercollegiate sports:* baseball M(s), basketball M(s)/W(s), cheerleading M/W, cross-country running M(s)/W(s), equestrian sports M(c)/W(c), field hockey W(s), football M(s), golf M(c)/W(c), gymnastics W(c), ice hockey M(c)/W(c), lacrosse M(c)/W(s), racquetball M(c)/W(c), rugby M(c)/W(c), skiing (downhill) M(c)/W(c), soccer M(s)/W(s), softball W(s), swimming and diving M(c)/W(c), tennis M(c)/W(s), track and field M(s)/W(s), ultimate Frisbee M(c)/W(c), volleyball M(c)/W(s), water polo M(c), wrestling M(c)/W(c). *Intramural sports:* badminton M/W, basketball M/W, bowling M/W, football M/W, lacrosse W(c), racquetball M/W, soccer M/W, softball M/W, tennis M/W(c), volleyball M/W, water polo M/W.

Standardized Tests *Required:* SAT or ACT (for admission).

Costs (2010–11) *Tuition:* state resident $5804 full-time, $242 per credit hour part-time; nonresident $8706 full-time, $484 per credit hour part-time. Full-time tuition and fees vary according to course load and degree level. Part-time tuition and fees vary according to course load and degree level. *Required fees:* $1862 full-time, $93 per credit hour part-time, $68 per term part-time. *Room and board:* $8884; room only: $5964. Room and board charges vary according to board plan and housing facility. *Payment plan:* installment. *Waivers:* minority students, senior citizens, and employees or children of employees.

Financial Aid Of all full-time matriculated undergraduates who enrolled in 2009, 6,773 applied for aid, 5,274 were judged to have need, 1,803 had their need fully met. In 2009, 189 non-need-based awards were made. *Average percent of need met: 63%. Average financial aid package: $8169. Average need-based loan: $4137. Average need-based gift aid: $5285. Average non-need-based aid:* $1483. *Average indebtedness upon graduation:* $26,452.

Applying *Options:* electronic application, deferred entrance. *Application fee:* $30. *Required:* high school transcript, minimum 2 GPA. *Notification:* 6/15 (freshmen), continuous (transfers).

Freshman Application Contact Slippery Rock University of Pennsylvania, 1 Morrow Way, Slippery Rock, PA 16057-1383. *Phone:* 724-738-2015. *Toll-free phone:* 800-SRU-9111. *Web site:* http://www.sru.edu/.

Strayer University - Allentown Campus

Center Valley, Pennsylvania

- **Proprietary** comprehensive
- **Coed**

Academics *Degrees:* certificates, diplomas, associate, bachelor's, master's, and postbachelor's certificates.

Costs (2010–11) *Tuition:* $13,635 full-time, $1590 per course part-time.

Freshman Application Contact Strayer University - Allentown Campus, 3800 Sierra Circle, Suite 300, Center Valley, PA 18034. *Web site:* http://www.strayer.edu/allentown/.

Strayer University - Center City Campus

Philadelphia, Pennsylvania

- **Proprietary** comprehensive
- **Coed**

Academics *Degrees:* certificates, diplomas, associate, bachelor's, master's, and postbachelor's certificates.

Costs (2010–11) *Tuition:* $13,635 full-time, $1590 per course part-time.

Freshman Application Contact Strayer University - Center City Campus, 1601 Cherry Street, Suite 100, Philadelphia, PA 19102. *Web site:* http://www.strayer.edu/center_city.

Strayer University - Cranberry Woods Campus

Cranberry Township, Pennsylvania

- **Proprietary** comprehensive
- **Coed**

Academics *Degrees:* certificates, diplomas, associate, bachelor's, master's, and postbachelor's certificates.

Costs (2010–11) *Tuition:* $13,635 full-time, $1590 per course part-time.

Freshman Application Contact Strayer University - Cranberry Woods Campus, Regional Learning Alliance, 850 Cranberry Woods Drive, Suite 2241, Cranberry Township, PA 16066. *Web site:* http://www.strayer.edu/cranberry_woods.

Strayer University - Delaware County Campus

Springfield, Pennsylvania

- **Proprietary** comprehensive
- **Coed**

Academics *Degrees:* certificates, diplomas, associate, bachelor's, master's, and postbachelor's certificates.
Costs (2010–11) *Tuition:* $13,635 full-time, $1590 per course part-time.
Freshman Application Contact Strayer University - Delaware County Campus, 760 West Sproul Road, Suite 200, Springfield, PA 19064-1215. *Web site:* http://www.strayer.edu/delaware_county.

Strayer University - King of Prussia Campus

King of Prussia, Pennsylvania

- **Proprietary** comprehensive
- **Coed**

Academics *Degrees:* certificates, diplomas, associate, bachelor's, master's, and postbachelor's certificates.
Costs (2010–11) *Tuition:* $13,635 full-time, $1590 per course part-time.
Freshman Application Contact Strayer University - King of Prussia Campus, 234 Mall Boulevard, Suite G-50, King of Prussia, PA 19406. *Web site:* http://www.strayer.edu/king_of_prussia.

Strayer University - Lower Bucks County Campus

Trevose, Pennsylvania

- **Proprietary** comprehensive
- **Coed**

Academics *Degrees:* certificates, diplomas, associate, bachelor's, master's, and postbachelor's certificates.
Costs (2010–11) *Tuition:* $13,635 full-time, $1590 per course part-time.
Freshman Application Contact Strayer University - Lower Bucks County Campus, 3600 Horizon Boulevard, Suite 100, Trevose, PA 19053. *Web site:* http://www.strayer.edu/lower_bucks_county/.

Strayer University - Penn Center West Campus

Pittsburgh, Pennsylvania

- **Proprietary** comprehensive
- **Coed**

Academics *Degrees:* certificates, diplomas, associate, bachelor's, master's, and postbachelor's certificates.
Costs (2010–11) *Tuition:* $13,635 full-time, $1590 per course part-time.
Freshman Application Contact Strayer University - Penn Center West Campus, One Penn Center West, Suite 320, Pittsburgh, PA 15276. *Web site:* http://www.strayer.edu/penn_center_west/.

Susquehanna University

Selinsgrove, Pennsylvania

- **Independent** 4-year, founded 1858, affiliated with Evangelical Lutheran Church in America
- **Small-town** 306-acre campus with easy access to Harrisburg
- **Endowment** $93.0 million
- **Coed** 2,305 undergraduate students, 97% full-time, 55% women, 45% men
- **Moderately difficult** entrance level, 70% of applicants were admitted

Undergraduates 2,230 full-time, 75 part-time. Students come from 36 states and territories; 17 other countries; 45% are from out of state; 3% Black or African American, non-Hispanic/Latino; 4% Hispanic/Latino; 1% Asian, non-Hispanic/Latino; 0.1% American Indian or Alaska Native, non-Hispanic/Latino; 0.9% Two or more races, non-Hispanic/Latino; 0.7% international; 1% transferred in; 76% live on campus. *Retention:* 83% of full-time freshmen returned.
Freshmen *Admission:* 3,186 applied, 2,243 admitted, 642 enrolled. *Average high school GPA:* 3.39. *Test scores:* SAT critical reading scores over 500: 77%; SAT math scores over 500: 83%; SAT writing scores over 500: 77%; ACT scores over 18: 100%; SAT critical reading scores over 600: 30%; SAT math scores over 600: 32%; SAT writing scores over 600: 27%; ACT scores over 24: 52%; SAT critical reading scores over 700: 6%; SAT math scores over 700: 3%; SAT writing scores over 700: 4%; ACT scores over 30: 5%.
Faculty *Total:* 244, 57% full-time, 68% with terminal degrees. *Student/faculty ratio:* 13:1.
Academics *Calendar:* semesters. *Degrees:* bachelor's (also offers evening associate degree program limited to local adult students). *Special study options:* accelerated degree program, advanced placement credit, distance learning, double majors, honors programs, independent study, internships, off-campus study, part-time degree program, services for LD students, student-designed majors, study abroad, summer session for credit. *ROTC:* Army (c). *Unusual degree programs:* forestry with Duke University.
Computers on Campus 300 computers/terminals and 60 ports are available on campus for general student use. Students can access the following: campus intranet, computer help desk, free student e-mail accounts, online (class) grades, online (class) registration, online (class) schedules, class listings and assignments, online voting booth. Campuswide network is available. 100% of college-owned or -operated housing units are wired for high-speed Internet access. Wireless service is available via classrooms, computer centers, computer labs, dorm rooms, learning centers, libraries, student centers.
Student Life *Housing:* on-campus residence required through junior year. *Options:* coed. Campus housing is university owned. Freshman campus housing is guaranteed. *Activities and organizations:* drama/theater group, student-run newspaper, radio and television station, choral group, Student Government Association, community service organizations, music performance groups, theater performance groups, intramurals and outdoor recreation, national fraternities, national sororities. *Campus security:* 24-hour emergency response devices and patrols, late-night transport/escort service, controlled dormitory access. *Student services:* health clinic, personal/psychological counseling.
Athletics Member NCAA. All Division III. *Intercollegiate sports:* baseball M, basketball M/W, cheerleading M(c)/W(c), crew M(c)/W(c), cross-country running M/W, equestrian sports M(c)/W(c), field hockey W, football M, golf M/W, lacrosse M/W, rugby M(c)/W(c), soccer M/W, softball W, swimming and diving M/W, tennis M/W, track and field M/W, volleyball M(c)/W. *Intramural sports:* basketball M/W, racquetball M/W, soccer M/W, softball M/W, tennis M/W, volleyball M/W.
Standardized Tests *Recommended:* SAT or ACT (for admission).
Costs (2010–11) *Comprehensive fee:* $41,650 includes full-time tuition ($32,450), mandatory fees ($400), and room and board ($8800). Part-time tuition: $1065 per semester hour. *College room only:* $4600. Room and board charges vary according to board plan and housing facility. *Payment plans:* tuition prepayment, installment. *Waivers:* employees or children of employees.
Financial Aid Of all full-time matriculated undergraduates who enrolled in 2009, 1,712 applied for aid, 1,496 were judged to have need, 248 had their need fully met. 1,124 Federal Work-Study jobs (averaging $2044). 84 state and other part-time jobs (averaging $4425). In 2009, 537 non-need-based awards were made. *Average percent of need met:* 79%. *Average financial aid package:* $23,880. *Average need-based loan:* $4390. *Average need-based gift aid:* $19,015. *Average non-need-based aid:* $10,081. *Average indebtedness upon graduation:* $20,915.
Applying *Options:* electronic application, early admission, early decision, deferred entrance. *Application fee:* $35. *Required:* essay or personal statement, high school transcript, minimum 2.5 GPA, 1 letter of recommendation. *Required for some:* writing portfolio, auditions for music programs. *Recommended:* minimum 3 GPA, interview. *Application deadlines:* 3/1 (freshmen), 7/1 (transfers). *Early decision deadline:* 11/15. *Notification:* continuous until 1/15 (freshmen), 8/1 (transfers), 12/1 (early decision).
Freshman Application Contact Mr. Chris Markle, Director of Admissions, Susquehanna University, 514 University Avenue, Selinsgrove, PA 17870. *Phone:* 570-372-4260. *Toll-free phone:* 800-326-9672. *Fax:* 570-372-2722. *E-mail:* suadmiss@susqu.edu. *Web site:* http://www.susqu.edu/.

See page 1654 for the College Close-Up.

Swarthmore College

Swarthmore, Pennsylvania

- **Independent** 4-year, founded 1864
- **Suburban** 425-acre campus with easy access to Philadelphia
- **Coed** 1,524 undergraduate students, 99% full-time, 51% women, 49% men
- **Most difficult** entrance level, 16% of applicants were admitted

Undergraduates 1,510 full-time, 14 part-time. Students come from 54 states and territories; 43 other countries; 88% are from out of state; 6% Black or African American, non-Hispanic/Latino; 12% Hispanic/Latino; 14% Asian, non-Hispanic/Latino; 0.4% American Indian or Alaska Native, non-Hispanic/Latino; 6% Two or more races, non-Hispanic/Latino; 9% Race/ethnicity unknown; 7% international; 0.7% transferred in; 94% live on campus. *Retention:* 94% of full-time freshmen returned.

Freshmen *Admission:* 6,041 applied, 974 admitted, 388 enrolled. *Test scores:* SAT critical reading scores over 500: 100%; SAT math scores over 500: 100%; SAT writing scores over 500: 100%; ACT scores over 18: 100%; SAT critical reading scores over 600: 97%; SAT math scores over 600: 94%; SAT writing scores over 600: 95%; ACT scores over 24: 100%; SAT critical reading scores over 700: 65%; SAT math scores over 700: 61%; SAT writing scores over 700: 69%; ACT scores over 30: 74%.

Faculty *Total:* 212, 81% full-time, 92% with terminal degrees. *Student/faculty ratio:* 8:1.

Academics *Calendar:* semesters. *Degree:* bachelor's. *Special study options:* accelerated degree program, advanced placement credit, double majors, honors programs, independent study, internships, off-campus study, services for LD students, student-designed majors, study abroad. *ROTC:* Army (c), Navy (c), Air Force (c).

Computers on Campus 313 computers/terminals and 3,300 ports are available on campus for general student use. Students can access the following: campus intranet, computer help desk, free student e-mail accounts, online (class) grades, online (class) registration, online (class) schedules. Campuswide network is available. 100% of college-owned or -operated housing units are wired for high-speed Internet access. Wireless service is available via entire campus.

Student Life *Housing:* on-campus residence required for freshman year. *Options:* coed, men-only, women-only. Campus housing is university owned. Freshman campus housing is guaranteed. *Activities and organizations:* drama/theater group, student-run newspaper, radio station, choral group, community service and activist groups, club sports and intramurals, social/cultural clubs, music/acappella groups, political and debate clubs, national fraternities. *Campus security:* 24-hour emergency response devices and patrols, late-night transport/escort service. *Student services:* health clinic, personal/psychological counseling, women's center.

Athletics Member NCAA. All Division III. *Intercollegiate sports:* badminton M(c)/W, baseball M, basketball M/W, cross-country running M/W, fencing M(c)/W(c), field hockey W, golf M, ice hockey M(c)/W(c), lacrosse M/W, rugby M(c)/W(c), soccer M/W, softball W, squash M(c)/W(c), swimming and diving M/W, tennis M/W, track and field M/W, ultimate Frisbee M(c)/W(c), volleyball M(c)/W, water polo M(c)/W(c). *Intramural sports:* basketball M/W, football M/W, soccer M/W, softball M/W, table tennis M/W, tennis M/W, volleyball M/W.

Standardized Tests *Required:* SAT and SAT Subject Tests or ACT (for admission).

Costs (2010–11) *Comprehensive fee:* $51,500 includes full-time tuition ($39,260), mandatory fees ($340), and room and board ($11,900). *College room only:* $6100. Room and board charges vary according to board plan. *Payment plan:* installment. *Waivers:* employees or children of employees.

Financial Aid Of all full-time matriculated undergraduates who enrolled in 2009, 856 applied for aid, 756 were judged to have need, 756 had their need fully met. 705 Federal Work-Study jobs (averaging $1651). In 2009, 10 non-need-based awards were made. *Average percent of need met:* 100%. *Average financial aid package:* $36,571. *Average need-based gift aid:* $35,033. *Average non-need-based aid:* $39,260. *Average indebtedness upon graduation:* $18,739. *Financial aid deadline:* 2/15.

Applying *Options:* electronic application, early admission, early decision, deferred entrance. *Application fee:* $60. *Required:* essay or personal statement, high school transcript, 3 letters of recommendation. *Recommended:* interview. *Application deadlines:* 1/2 (freshmen), 4/1 (transfers). *Early decision deadline:* 11/15 (for plan 1), 1/2 (for plan 2). *Notification:* 4/1 (freshmen), 5/30 (transfers), 12/15 (early decision plan 1), 2/15 (early decision plan 2).

Freshman Application Contact Mr. James L. Bock, Dean of Admissions and Financial Aid, Swarthmore College, 500 College Avenue, Swarthmore, PA 19081. *Phone:* 610-328-8300. *Toll-free phone:* 800-667-3110. *Fax:* 610-328-8580. *E-mail:* admissions@swarthmore.edu. *Web site:* http://www.swarthmore.edu/.

Talmudical Yeshiva of Philadelphia

Philadelphia, Pennsylvania

Freshman Application Contact Rabbi Shmuel Kamenetsky, Co-Dean, Talmudical Yeshiva of Philadelphia, 6063 Drexel Road, Philadelphia, PA 19131-1296. *Phone:* 215-473-1212.

Temple University

Philadelphia, Pennsylvania

- **State-related** university, founded 1884
- **Urban** 115-acre campus with easy access to Philadelphia
- **Coed** 27,623 undergraduate students, 89% full-time, 52% women, 48% men
- **Moderately difficult** entrance level, 65% of applicants were admitted

Undergraduates 24,644 full-time, 2,979 part-time. Students come from 46 states and territories; 100 other countries; 19% are from out of state; 15% Black or African American, non-Hispanic/Latino; 4% Hispanic/Latino; 10% Asian, non-Hispanic/Latino; 0.4% American Indian or Alaska Native, non-Hispanic/Latino; 0.7% Two or more races, non-Hispanic/Latino; 8% Race/ethnicity unknown; 2% international; 10% transferred in; 18% live on campus. *Retention:* 88% of full-time freshmen returned.

Freshmen *Admission:* 17,051 applied, 11,022 admitted, 4,329 enrolled. *Average high school GPA:* 3.39. *Test scores:* SAT critical reading scores over 500: 77%; SAT math scores over 500: 82%; SAT writing scores over 500: 75%; ACT scores over 18: 93%; SAT critical reading scores over 600: 27%; SAT math scores over 600: 31%; SAT writing scores over 600: 25%; ACT scores over 24: 45%; SAT critical reading scores over 700: 4%; SAT math scores over 700: 4%; SAT writing scores over 700: 3%; ACT scores over 30: 5%.

Faculty *Total:* 2,936, 49% full-time. *Student/faculty ratio:* 16:1.

Academics *Calendar:* semesters. *Degrees:* certificates, diplomas, associate, bachelor's, master's, doctoral-professional, doctoral-research/scholarship, post-master's, and postbachelor's certificates. *Special study options:* academic remediation for entering students, adult/continuing education programs, advanced placement credit, cooperative education, distance learning, double majors, English as a second language, external degree program, honors programs, independent study, internships, off-campus study, part-time degree program, services for LD students, student-designed majors, study abroad, summer session for credit. *ROTC:* Army (b), Navy (c), Air Force (c). *Unusual degree programs:* 3-2 physical therapy, pharmacy, chemistry, physics.

Computers on Campus 3,670 computers/terminals are available on campus for general student use. Students can access the following: computer help desk, free student e-mail accounts, online (class) grades, online (class) registration, online (class) schedules, student accounts, Web hosting. Campuswide network is available. 100% of college-owned or -operated housing units are wired for high-speed Internet access. Wireless service is available via entire campus.

Student Life *Housing options:* coed. Campus housing is university owned, leased by the school and is provided by a third party. Freshman campus housing is guaranteed. *Activities and organizations:* drama/theater group, student-run newspaper, radio station, choral group, marching band, American Society of Mechanical Engineers, Anthropology Association, Cherry Crusade, Habitat for Humanity, Student Peace Alliance, national fraternities, national sororities. *Campus security:* 24-hour emergency response devices and patrols, late-night transport/escort service, controlled dormitory access. *Student services:* health clinic, personal/psychological counseling, legal services.

Athletics Member NCAA. All Division I except football (Division I-A). *Intercollegiate sports:* baseball M(s), basketball M(s)/W(s), cheerleading M(s)/W(s), crew M(s)/W(s), cross-country running M(s)/W(s), fencing W(s), field hockey W(s), golf M(s), gymnastics M(s)/W(s), lacrosse W(s), soccer M(s)/W(s), softball M/W(s), tennis M(s)/W(s), track and field M(s)/W(s), volleyball W(s). *Intramural sports:* badminton M(c)/W(c), basketball M/W, bowling M(c)/W(c), equestrian sports M(c)/W(c), fencing M(c)/W(c), gymnastics M(c)/W(c), ice hockey M(c), lacrosse M(c)/W(c), racquetball M(c)/W(c), rugby M(c)/W(c), soccer M/W, softball W, tennis M/W, ultimate Frisbee M(c)/W(c), volleyball M/W.

Standardized Tests *Required:* SAT or ACT (for admission).

Costs (2010–11) *Tuition:* state resident $11,834 full-time, $457 per credit hour part-time; nonresident $21,662 full-time, $771 per credit hour part-time. Full-time tuition and fees vary according to course load, program, and reciprocity agreements. Part-time tuition and fees vary according to course load, program, and reciprocity agreements. *Required fees:* $590 full-time, $213 per semester part-time. *Room and board:* $9550; room only: $6370. Room and board charges vary according to board plan and housing facility. *Payment plan:* installment. *Waivers:* employees or children of employees.

Financial Aid Of all full-time matriculated undergraduates who enrolled in 2008, 21,583 applied for aid, 17,042 were judged to have need, 5,139 had their need fully met. 1,288 Federal Work-Study jobs. In 2008, 2864 non-need-based awards were made. *Average percent of need met:* 85%. *Average financial aid package:* $15,362. *Average need-based loan:* $4137. *Average need-based gift aid:* $5753. *Average non-need-based aid:* $8759. *Average indebtedness upon graduation:* $31,123.

Applying *Options:* electronic application, early admission, deferred entrance. *Application fee:* $50. *Required:* essay or personal statement, high school transcript. *Recommended:* minimum 3 GPA. *Application deadlines:* 3/1 (freshmen), 6/1 (transfers). *Notification:* continuous (freshmen), continuous (transfers).

Freshman Application Contact Temple University, 1801 North Broad Street, Philadelphia, PA 19122-6096. *Phone:* 215-204-7200. *Toll-free phone:* 888-340-2222. *Web site:* http://www.temple.edu/.

See page 1660 for the College Close-Up.

Thiel College
Greenville, Pennsylvania

- **Independent** 4-year, founded 1866, affiliated with Evangelical Lutheran Church in America
- **Rural** 135-acre campus with easy access to Cleveland and Pittsburgh
- **Endowment** $20.9 million
- **Coed** 1,096 undergraduate students, 95% full-time, 46% women, 54% men
- **Moderately difficult** entrance level, 68% of applicants were admitted

Undergraduates 1,038 full-time, 58 part-time. Students come from 23 states and territories; 8 other countries; 35% are from out of state; 6% Black or African American, non-Hispanic/Latino; 1% Hispanic/Latino; 0.5% Asian, non-Hispanic/Latino; 0.2% American Indian or Alaska Native, non-Hispanic/Latino; 1% Two or more races, non-Hispanic/Latino; 21% Race/ethnicity unknown; 6% international; 4% transferred in; 84% live on campus. *Retention:* 67% of full-time freshmen returned.
Freshmen *Admission:* 1,856 applied, 1,255 admitted, 357 enrolled. *Average high school GPA:* 3.02. *Test scores:* SAT critical reading scores over 500: 29%; SAT math scores over 500: 38%; ACT scores over 18: 80%; SAT critical reading scores over 600: 5%; SAT math scores over 600: 8%; ACT scores over 24: 26%; SAT math scores over 700: 1%; ACT scores over 30: 1%.
Faculty *Total:* 114, 56% full-time, 45% with terminal degrees. *Student/faculty ratio:* 13:1.
Academics *Calendar:* semesters. *Degrees:* associate and bachelor's. *Special study options:* academic remediation for entering students, adult/continuing education programs, advanced placement credit, cooperative education, distance learning, double majors, honors programs, independent study, internships, off-campus study, part-time degree program, services for LD students, study abroad, summer session for credit. *Unusual degree programs:* 3-2 engineering with Case Western Reserve University, Point Park College, University of Pittsburgh; forestry with Duke University; physician assistant with Chatham University.
Computers on Campus 130 computers/terminals and 1,705 ports are available on campus for general student use. Students can access the following: campus intranet, computer help desk, free student e-mail accounts, online (class) grades, online (class) registration, online (class) schedules. Campuswide network is available. 100% of college-owned or -operated housing units are wired for high-speed Internet access. Wireless service is available via classrooms, computer centers, computer labs, learning centers, libraries, student centers.
Student Life *Housing:* on-campus residence required through senior year. *Options:* coed. Campus housing is university owned and leased by the school. Freshman campus housing is guaranteed. *Activities and organizations:* drama/theater group, student-run newspaper, radio and television station, choral group, marching band, Thiel Players Theatre Group, student government, Thiel Choir, Ski Club, Thiel Christian Fellowship, national fraternities, national sororities. *Campus security:* 24-hour emergency response devices and patrols, late-night transport/escort service, controlled dormitory access. *Student services:* health clinic, personal/psychological counseling, women's center.
Athletics Member NCAA. All Division III. *Intercollegiate sports:* baseball M, basketball M/W, cheerleading M/W, cross-country running M/W, football M, golf M/W, lacrosse M/W, soccer M/W, softball W, tennis M/W, track and field M/W, volleyball M/W, wrestling M. *Intramural sports:* badminton M/W, basketball M/W, riflery M/W, skiing (downhill) M/W, softball M/W, volleyball M/W.
Standardized Tests *Required:* SAT or ACT (for admission).
Costs (2011–12) *One-time required fee:* $300. *Comprehensive fee:* $34,508 includes full-time tuition ($23,076), mandatory fees ($1780), and room and board ($9652). Part-time tuition: $770 per credit. Part-time tuition and fees vary according to course load. *Required fees:* $73 per credit part-time. *College room only:* $4826. Room and board charges vary according to board plan and housing facility. *Payment plan:* installment. *Waivers:* senior citizens and employees or children of employees.
Financial Aid Of all full-time matriculated undergraduates who enrolled in 2009, 1,001 applied for aid, 964 were judged to have need, 76 had their need fully met. 62 Federal Work-Study jobs, 277 state and other part-time jobs. In 2009, 112 non-need-based awards were made. *Average percent of need met:* 67%. *Average financial aid package:* $19,220. *Average need-based loan:* $4244. *Average need-based gift aid:* $15,076. *Average non-need-based aid:* $8565. *Average indebtedness upon graduation:* $34,606.
Applying *Options:* electronic application, deferred entrance. *Application fee:* $35. *Required:* essay or personal statement, high school transcript, minimum 2 GPA, 1 letter of recommendation. *Required for some:* interview. *Application deadlines:* rolling (freshmen), rolling (out-of-state freshmen), rolling (transfers). *Notification:* continuous (freshmen), continuous (out-of-state freshmen), continuous (transfers).
Freshman Application Contact Ms. Amy Becker, Chief Admissions Officer, Thiel College, 75 College Avenue, Greenville, PA 16125. *Phone:* 724-589-2182. *Toll-free phone:* 800-248-4435. *Fax:* 724-589-2013. *E-mail:* admissions@thiel.edu. *Web site:* http://www.thiel.edu/.

Thomas Jefferson University
Philadelphia, Pennsylvania

Freshman Application Contact Ms. Karen Jacobs, Director of Admissions, Thomas Jefferson University, Edison Building, 130 South Ninth Street, Philadelphia, PA 19107. *Phone:* 215-503-8890. *Toll-free phone:* 877-533-3247. *Fax:* 215-503-7241. *E-mail:* chpadmissions@mail.tju.edu. *Web site:* http://www.jefferson.edu/.

University of Pennsylvania
Philadelphia, Pennsylvania

- **Independent** university, founded 1740
- **Urban** 279-acre campus
- **Endowment** $5.7 billion
- **Coed** 9,865 undergraduate students, 97% full-time, 51% women, 49% men
- **Most difficult** entrance level, 14% of applicants were admitted

Undergraduates 9,590 full-time, 275 part-time. Students come from 54 states and territories; 126 other countries; 83% are from out of state; 7% Black or African American, non-Hispanic/Latino; 7% Hispanic/Latino; 19% Asian, non-Hispanic/Latino; 0.1% Native Hawaiian or other Pacific Islander, non-Hispanic/Latino; 0.5% American Indian or Alaska Native, non-Hispanic/Latino; 1% Two or more races, non-Hispanic/Latino; 9% Race/ethnicity unknown; 11% international; 3% transferred in; 62% live on campus. *Retention:* 99% of full-time freshmen returned.
Freshmen *Admission:* 26,941 applied, 3,841 admitted, 2,370 enrolled. *Average high school GPA:* 3.89. *Test scores:* SAT critical reading scores over 500: 100%; SAT math scores over 500: 100%; SAT writing scores over 500: 100%; ACT scores over 18: 100%; SAT critical reading scores over 600: 93%; SAT math scores over 600: 97%; SAT writing scores over 600: 95%; ACT scores over 24: 99%; SAT critical reading scores over 700: 57%; SAT math scores over 700: 71%; SAT writing scores over 700: 67%; ACT scores over 30: 78%.
Faculty *Total:* 2,161, 64% full-time, 100% with terminal degrees. *Student/faculty ratio:* 6:1.
Academics *Calendar:* semesters plus 2 5-week summer sessions. *Degrees:* certificates, associate, bachelor's, master's, doctoral-other, doctoral-professional, doctoral-research/scholarship, post-master's, and postbachelor's certificates (also offers evening program with significant enrollment not reflected in profile). *Special study options:* academic remediation for entering students, accelerated degree program, adult/continuing education programs, advanced placement credit, cooperative education, distance learning, double majors, English as a second language, honors programs, independent study, internships, off-campus study, part-time degree program, services for LD students, student-designed majors, study abroad, summer session for credit. *ROTC:* Army (c), Navy (b), Air Force (c).
Computers on Campus Students can access the following: campus intranet, computer help desk, free student e-mail accounts, online (class) grades, online (class) registration, online (class) schedules, billing information, financial aid application, status, academic records, student services. Campuswide network is available. 100% of college-owned or -operated housing units are wired for high-speed Internet access. Wireless service is available via entire campus.
Student Life *Housing options:* coed, disabled students. Campus housing is university owned. Freshman campus housing is guaranteed. *Activities and organizations:* drama/theater group, student-run newspaper, radio and television station, choral group, marching band, Kite and Key Society, Social Planning and Events Committee, Hillel at Penn, Sports Club Council, Interfraternity Council, national fraternities, national sororities. *Campus security:* 24-hour emergency response devices and patrols, late-night transport/escort service, controlled dormitory access. *Student services:* health clinic, personal/psychological counseling, women's center, legal services.
Athletics Member NCAA. All Division I except football (Division I-AA). *Intercollegiate sports:* baseball M, basketball M/W, crew M/W, cross-country running M/W, fencing M/W, field hockey W, golf M/W, gymnastics W, lacrosse M/W, soccer M/W, softball W, squash M/W, swimming and diving M/W, tennis M/W, track and field M/W, volleyball W, wrestling M. *Intramural sports:* badminton M(c)/W(c), baseball M(c)/W(c), basketball M(c)/W(c), cheerleading M/W, equestrian sports M(c)/W(c), field hockey M(c)/W(c), golf M(c)/W(c), gymnastics M(c)/W(c), ice hockey M(c)/W(c), lacrosse M/W, rugby M(c)/W(c), sailing M(c)/W(c), skiing (downhill) M(c)/W(c), soccer M/

Pennsylvania

W, softball M/W, squash M/W, swimming and diving M/W, table tennis M/W, tennis M/W, ultimate Frisbee M(c)/W(c), volleyball M/W, water polo M(c)/W(c).

Standardized Tests *Required:* SAT and SAT Subject Tests or ACT (for admission).

Costs (2011–12) *Comprehensive fee:* $53,976 includes full-time tuition ($37,620), mandatory fees ($4478), and room and board ($11,878). Part-time tuition and fees vary according to course load. *College room only:* $7592. Room and board charges vary according to board plan and housing facility. *Payment plans:* tuition prepayment, installment. *Waivers:* employees or children of employees.

Financial Aid Of all full-time matriculated undergraduates who enrolled in 2008, 4,815 applied for aid, 4,346 were judged to have need, 4,346 had their need fully met. 3,355 Federal Work-Study jobs (averaging $2871). 645 state and other part-time jobs (averaging $2071). *Average percent of need met:* 100%. *Average financial aid package:* $35,580. *Average need-based loan:* $393. *Average need-based gift aid:* $32,443. *Average indebtedness upon graduation:* $17,013.

Applying *Options:* electronic application, early admission, early decision, deferred entrance. *Application fee:* $75. *Required:* essay or personal statement, high school transcript, 2 letters of recommendation. *Application deadlines:* 1/1 (freshmen), 3/15 (transfers). *Early decision deadline:* 11/1. *Notification:* 4/1 (freshmen), 5/15 (transfers), 12/15 (early decision).

Freshman Application Contact University of Pennsylvania, 1 College Hall, Levy Park, Philadelphia, PA 19104. *Phone:* 215-898-7507. *E-mail:* info@admissions.ugao.upenn.edu. *Web site:* http://www.upenn.edu/.

University of Phoenix–Philadelphia Campus
Wayne, Pennsylvania

Freshman Application Contact Ms. Audra McQuarie, Registrar/Executive Director, University of Phoenix–Philadelphia Campus, 4035 South Riverpoint Parkway, Mail Stop CF-L101, Phoenix, AZ 85040. *Phone:* 480-557-6151. *Toll-free phone:* 800-776-4867 (in-state); 800-228-7240 (out-of-state). *Fax:* 480-643-3068. *E-mail:* audra.mcquarie@phoenix.edu. *Web site:* http://www.phoenix.edu/.

University of Phoenix–Pittsburgh Campus
Pittsburgh, Pennsylvania

Freshman Application Contact Ms. Audra McQuarie, Registrar/Executive Director, University of Phoenix–Pittsburgh Campus, 4035 South Riverpoint Parkway, Mail Stop CF-L101, Phoenix, AZ 85040. *Phone:* 480-557-6151. *Toll-free phone:* 800-776-4867 (in-state); 800-228-7240 (out-of-state). *Fax:* 480-643-3068. *E-mail:* audra.mcquarie@phoenix.edu. *Web site:* http://www.phoenix.edu/.

University of Pittsburgh
Pittsburgh, Pennsylvania

- **State-related** university, founded 1787, part of Commonwealth System of Higher Education
- **Urban** 132-acre campus with easy access to Pittsburgh
- **Endowment** $2.0 billion
- **Coed** 18,371 undergraduate students, 93% full-time, 51% women, 49% men
- **Moderately difficult** entrance level, 58% of applicants were admitted

Undergraduates 17,083 full-time, 1,288 part-time. Students come from 53 states and territories; 48 other countries; 22% are from out of state; 7% Black or African American, non-Hispanic/Latino; 2% Hispanic/Latino; 5% Asian, non-Hispanic/Latino; 0.1% Native Hawaiian or other Pacific Islander, non-Hispanic/Latino; 1% Two or more races, non-Hispanic/Latino; 4% Race/ethnicity unknown; 2% international; 5% transferred in; 45% live on campus. *Retention:* 92% of full-time freshmen returned.

Freshmen *Admission:* 22,616 applied, 13,066 admitted, 3,710 enrolled. *Average high school GPA:* 3.91. *Test scores:* SAT critical reading scores over 500: 98%; SAT math scores over 500: 99%; SAT writing scores over 500: 95%; ACT scores over 18: 99%; SAT critical reading scores over 600: 63%; SAT math scores over 600: 77%; SAT writing scores over 600: 56%; ACT scores over 24: 91%; SAT critical reading scores over 700: 21%; SAT math scores over 700: 24%; SAT writing scores over 700: 12%; ACT scores over 30: 32%.

Faculty *Total:* 2,265, 72% full-time. *Student/faculty ratio:* 15:1.

Academics *Calendar:* semesters plus summer term. *Degrees:* certificates, bachelor's, master's, doctoral-professional, doctoral-research/scholarship, post-master's, and postbachelor's certificates. *Special study options:* academic

remediation for entering students, accelerated degree program, adult/continuing education programs, advanced placement credit, cooperative education, distance learning, double majors, English as a second language, external degree program, freshman honors college, honors programs, independent study, internships, off-campus study, part-time degree program, services for LD students, student-designed majors, study abroad, summer session for credit. *ROTC:* Army (b), Navy (c), Air Force (b). *Unusual degree programs:* 3-2 engineering; statistics.

Computers on Campus 2,000 computers/terminals and 2,000 ports are available on campus for general student use. Students can access the following: campus intranet, computer help desk, free student e-mail accounts, online (class) grades, online (class) registration, online (class) schedules, online class listings, online tuition payment. Campuswide network is available. 100% of college-owned or -operated housing units are wired for high-speed Internet access. Wireless service is available via entire campus.

Student Life *Housing options:* coed, women-only, disabled students. Campus housing is university owned. Freshman campus housing is guaranteed. *Activities and organizations:* drama/theater group, student-run newspaper, radio and television station, choral group, marching band, Resident Student Association, Black Action Society, Engineering Student Council, Interfraternity Council, Panhellenic Association, national fraternities, national sororities. *Campus security:* 24-hour emergency response devices and patrols, late-night transport/escort service, controlled dormitory access, on-call van transportation. *Student services:* health clinic, personal/psychological counseling.

Athletics Member NCAA. All Division I except football (Division I-A). *Intercollegiate sports:* baseball M(s), basketball M(s)/W(s), cross-country running M(s)/W(s), gymnastics W(s), soccer M(s)/W(s), softball W(s), swimming and diving M(s)/W(s), tennis W(s), track and field M(s)/W(s), volleyball W(s), wrestling M(s). *Intramural sports:* badminton M/W, basketball M/W, equestrian sports M(c)/W(c), football M, ice hockey M(c)/W(c), racquetball M/W, rugby M(c)/W(c), soccer M/W, softball W(c), squash M/W, tennis W, ultimate Frisbee M/W, volleyball M/W, water polo M(c)/W(c), wrestling M.

Standardized Tests *Required:* SAT or ACT (for admission).

Costs (2010–11) *Tuition:* state resident $14,076 full-time, $586 per credit part-time; nonresident $23,732 full-time, $988 per credit part-time. Full-time tuition and fees vary according to program. Part-time tuition and fees vary according to program. *Required fees:* $860 full-time, $860 per term part-time. *Room and board:* $9230; room only: $5500. Room and board charges vary according to board plan and housing facility. *Payment plans:* installment, deferred payment. *Waivers:* employees or children of employees.

Financial Aid Of all full-time matriculated undergraduates who enrolled in 2009, 12,176 applied for aid, 9,729 were judged to have need, 3,401 had their need fully met. 1,308 Federal Work-Study jobs (averaging $2452). In 2009, 1220 non-need-based awards were made. *Average percent of need met:* 76%. *Average financial aid package:* $10,140. *Average need-based loan:* $4930. *Average need-based gift aid:* $8281. *Average non-need-based aid:* $15,076. *Average indebtedness upon graduation:* $26,612.

Applying *Options:* electronic application, early admission. *Application fee:* $45. *Required:* high school transcript. *Recommended:* essay or personal statement, interview. *Application deadlines:* rolling (freshmen), rolling (transfers). *Notification:* continuous (freshmen), continuous (transfers).

Freshman Application Contact Dr. Betsy A. Porter, Director of Office of Admissions and Financial Aid, University of Pittsburgh, 4227 Fifth Avenue, First Floor, Alumni Hall, Pittsburgh, PA 15260. *Phone:* 412-624-7488. *Fax:* 412-648-8815. *E-mail:* oafa@pitt.edu. *Web site:* http://www.pitt.edu/.

University of Pittsburgh at Bradford
Bradford, Pennsylvania

- **State-related** 4-year, founded 1963, part of University of Pittsburgh System
- **Small-town** 317-acre campus with easy access to Buffalo
- **Endowment** $15.3 million
- **Coed** 1,627 undergraduate students, 88% full-time, 53% women, 47% men
- **Minimally difficult** entrance level, 44% of applicants were admitted

Undergraduates 1,436 full-time, 191 part-time. Students come from 20 states and territories; 10 other countries; 16% are from out of state; 7% Black or African American, non-Hispanic/Latino; 2% Hispanic/Latino; 2% Asian, non-Hispanic/Latino; 0.2% Native Hawaiian or other Pacific Islander, non-Hispanic/Latino; 0.7% American Indian or Alaska Native, non-Hispanic/Latino; 4% Race/ethnicity unknown; 1% international; 7% transferred in; 55% live on campus. *Retention:* 68% of full-time freshmen returned.

Freshmen *Admission:* 926 applied, 406 admitted, 350 enrolled. *Average high school GPA:* 3.18. *Test scores:* SAT critical reading scores over 500: 47%; SAT math scores over 500: 54%; SAT writing scores over 500: 44%; ACT scores over 18: 81%; SAT critical reading scores over 600: 10%; SAT math scores over 600: 16%; SAT writing scores over 600: 7%; ACT scores over 24: 31%; SAT critical reading scores over 700: 1%; SAT math scores over 700: 2%; ACT scores over 30: 2%.

Faculty *Total:* 154, 47% full-time, 39% with terminal degrees. *Student/faculty ratio:* 18:1.

Academics *Calendar:* semesters. *Degrees:* associate and bachelor's. *Special study options:* academic remediation for entering students, accelerated degree program, adult/continuing education programs, advanced placement credit, distance learning, double majors, independent study, internships, off-campus study, part-time degree program, services for LD students, study abroad, summer session for credit. *ROTC:* Army (c).

Computers on Campus 120 computers/terminals and 1,056 ports are available on campus for general student use. Students can access the following: computer help desk, free student e-mail accounts, online (class) grades, online (class) registration, online (class) schedules, online bills. Campuswide network is available. 100% of college-owned or -operated housing units are wired for high-speed Internet access. Wireless service is available via entire campus.

Student Life *Housing:* on-campus residence required for freshman year. *Options:* coed, disabled students. Campus housing is university owned. Freshman campus housing is guaranteed. *Activities and organizations:* drama/theater group, student-run newspaper, radio station, choral group, Student Government Association, Student Activities Board, The Source (student newspaper), Alpha Phi Omega, WDRQ (student radio station). *Campus security:* 24-hour emergency response devices and patrols, late-night transport/escort service, controlled dormitory access. *Student services:* health clinic, personal/psychological counseling.

Athletics Member NCAA. All Division III. *Intercollegiate sports:* baseball M, basketball M/W, cross-country running M/W, golf M/W, soccer M/W, softball W, swimming and diving M/W, tennis M/W, volleyball W. *Intramural sports:* basketball M/W, bowling M/W, cheerleading W(c), football M/W, golf M/W, ice hockey M/W, rock climbing M/W, rugby M(c)/W(c), skiing (cross-country) M/W, skiing (downhill) M/W, soccer M/W, softball M/W, swimming and diving M/W, table tennis M/W, ultimate Frisbee M/W, volleyball M/W, water polo M/W.

Standardized Tests *Required:* SAT or ACT (for admission).

Costs (2010–11) *One-time required fee:* $90. *Tuition:* state resident $11,286 full-time, $470 per credit hour part-time; nonresident $21,086 full-time, $878 per credit hour part-time. Full-time tuition and fees vary according to course load and program. Part-time tuition and fees vary according to course load and program. *Required fees:* $760 full-time, $130 per term part-time. *Room and board:* $7650; room only: $4680. Room and board charges vary according to board plan and housing facility. *Payment plan:* installment. *Waivers:* employees or children of employees.

Financial Aid Of all full-time matriculated undergraduates who enrolled in 2008, 1,449 applied for aid, 1,318 were judged to have need, 778 had their need fully met. 199 Federal Work-Study jobs (averaging $1740). 1 state and other part-time job (averaging $1740). In 2008, 267 non-need-based awards were made. *Average percent of need met:* 90%. *Average financial aid package:* $12,625. *Average need-based loan:* $4432. *Average need-based gift aid:* $5524. *Average non-need-based aid:* $5587. *Average indebtedness upon graduation:* $21,695.

Applying *Options:* electronic application, deferred entrance. *Application fee:* $45. *Required:* high school transcript, minimum 2 GPA. *Required for some:* minimum 3 GPA. *Recommended:* essay or personal statement, 2 letters of recommendation, interview. *Application deadlines:* rolling (freshmen), rolling (out-of-state freshmen), rolling (transfers). *Notification:* continuous (freshmen), continuous (out-of-state freshmen), continuous (transfers).

Freshman Application Contact Ms. Vicky Pingie, Associate Director of Admissions, University of Pittsburgh at Bradford, 300 Campus Drive, Bradford, PA 16701. *Phone:* 814-362-7552. *Toll-free phone:* 800-872-1787. *Fax:* 814-362-5150. *E-mail:* monti@pitt.edu. *Web site:* http://www.upb.pitt.edu/.

See page 1724 for the College Close-Up.

University of Pittsburgh at Greensburg

Greensburg, Pennsylvania

- **State-related** 4-year, founded 1963, part of University of Pittsburgh System
- **Small-town** 219-acre campus with easy access to Pittsburgh
- **Coed** 1,803 undergraduate students, 93% full-time, 50% women, 50% men
- **Moderately difficult** entrance level, 85% of applicants were admitted

Undergraduates 1,673 full-time, 130 part-time. Students come from 13 states and territories; 4 other countries; 2% are from out of state; 5% Black or African American, non-Hispanic/Latino; 2% Hispanic/Latino; 2% Asian, non-Hispanic/Latino; 0.2% American Indian or Alaska Native, non-Hispanic/Latino; 1% Two or more races, non-Hispanic/Latino; 10% Race/ethnicity unknown; 0.3% international; 8% transferred in; 35% live on campus. *Retention:* 78% of full-time freshmen returned.

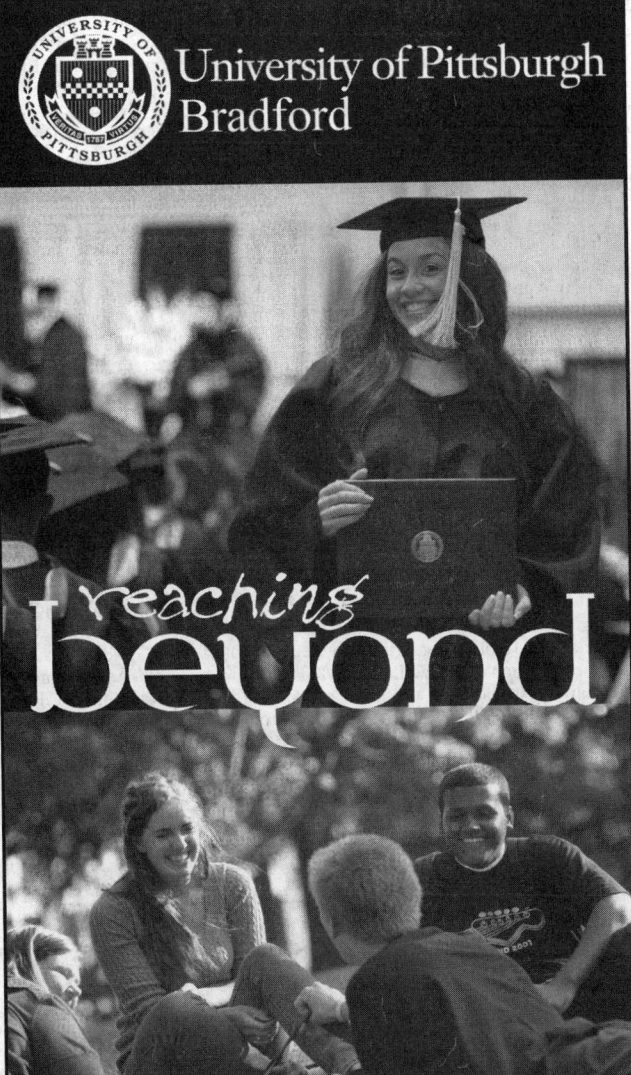

Freshmen *Admission:* 1,249 applied, 1,057 admitted, 412 enrolled. *Average high school GPA:* 3.39. *Test scores:* SAT critical reading scores over 500: 51%; SAT math scores over 500: 64%; SAT writing scores over 500: 48%; ACT scores over 18: 81%; SAT critical reading scores over 600: 8%; SAT math scores over 600: 13%; SAT writing scores over 600: 6%; ACT scores over 24: 16%; SAT math scores over 700: 1%.

Faculty *Total:* 133, 55% full-time. *Student/faculty ratio:* 18:1.

Academics *Calendar:* semesters. *Degree:* certificates and bachelor's. *Special study options:* academic remediation for entering students, accelerated degree program, adult/continuing education programs, advanced placement credit, distance learning, double majors, independent study, internships, off-campus study, part-time degree program, services for LD students, student-designed majors, study abroad, summer session for credit. *ROTC:* Army (c), Air Force (c).

Computers on Campus 400 computers/terminals are available on campus for general student use. Students can access the following: campus intranet, computer help desk, free student e-mail accounts, online (class) grades, online (class) registration, online (class) schedules. Campuswide network is available. 100% of college-owned or -operated housing units are wired for high-speed Internet access. Wireless service is available via classrooms, computer centers, computer labs, learning centers, libraries, student centers.

Student Life *Housing options:* coed. Campus housing is university owned. *Activities and organizations:* drama/theater group, student-run newspaper, radio station, choral group, Student Government Association, Circle K, Freshmen Honor Society-Phi Eta Sigma, Senior Honor Society-Phi Kappa Phi, Student Activities Board. *Campus security:* 24-hour emergency response devices and patrols, late-night transport/escort service, controlled dormitory access. *Student services:* health clinic, personal/psychological counseling.

Athletics Member NCAA. All Division III. *Intercollegiate sports:* baseball M, basketball M/W, cross-country running M/W, golf M/W, soccer M/W, softball W, tennis M, volleyball W. *Intramural sports:* baseball M, basketball M/W, bowling M/W, football M/W, golf M/W, racquetball M/W, skiing (cross-country) M/W, skiing (downhill) M/W, soccer M/W, softball M/W, table tennis M/W, tennis M/W, volleyball M/W, weight lifting M/W.

Standardized Tests *Required:* SAT or ACT (for admission).

Costs (2010–11) *Tuition:* state resident $11,286 full-time, $470 per credit hour part-time; nonresident $21,086 full-time, $878 per credit hour part-time. *Required fees:* $890 full-time. *Room and board:* $8110. Room and board

charges vary according to board plan and housing facility. *Payment plan:* installment. *Waivers:* senior citizens and employees or children of employees.

Financial Aid Of all full-time matriculated undergraduates who enrolled in 2008, 1,468 applied for aid, 1,271 were judged to have need, 107 had their need fully met. In 2008, 44 non-need-based awards were made. *Average percent of need met:* 79%. *Average financial aid package:* $12,647. *Average need-based loan:* $4391. *Average need-based gift aid:* $6219. *Average non-need-based aid:* $3242. *Average indebtedness upon graduation:* $26,163.

Applying *Options:* electronic application, early admission, deferred entrance. *Application fee:* $45. *Required:* high school transcript, minimum 2.5 GPA. *Recommended:* essay or personal statement, interview. *Application deadlines:* 8/1 (freshmen), 8/1 (transfers). *Notification:* continuous (freshmen), continuous (transfers).

Freshman Application Contact Ms. Heather Kabala, Director of Admissions, University of Pittsburgh at Greensburg, 150 Finoli Drive, Greensburg, PA 15601. *Phone:* 724-836-9880. *Fax:* 724-836-7471. *E-mail:* upgadmit@pitt.edu. *Web site:* http://www.greensburg.pitt.edu/.

University of Pittsburgh at Johnstown
Johnstown, Pennsylvania

- **State-related** 4-year, founded 1927, part of University of Pittsburgh System
- **Suburban** 650-acre campus with easy access to Pittsburgh
- **Coed** 2,982 undergraduate students, 96% full-time, 46% women, 54% men
- **Moderately difficult** entrance level, 88% of applicants were admitted

Undergraduates 2,864 full-time, 118 part-time. Students come from 14 states and territories; 12 other countries; 2% are from out of state; 3% Black or African American, non-Hispanic/Latino; 1% Hispanic/Latino; 1% Asian, non-Hispanic/Latino; 0.8% Two or more races, non-Hispanic/Latino; 2% Race/ethnicity unknown; 0.8% international; 3% transferred in; 59% live on campus. *Retention:* 74% of full-time freshmen returned.

Freshmen *Admission:* 1,667 applied, 1,473 admitted, 752 enrolled. *Average high school GPA:* 3.36. *Test scores:* SAT critical reading scores over 500: 51%; SAT math scores over 500: 61%; SAT writing scores over 500: 40%; ACT scores over 18: 82%; SAT critical reading scores over 600: 10%; SAT math scores over 600: 15%; SAT writing scores over 600: 7%; ACT scores

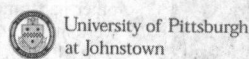
University of Pittsburgh at Johnstown

UNIVERSITY OF PITTSBURGH AT JOHNSTOWN

Founded in 1927, the University of Pittsburgh at Johnstown is the first and largest regional campus of the University of Pittsburgh. A vital knowledge center and a foremost contributor to the region's educational, social, cultural, and economic development, Pitt-Johnstown provides a high-quality educational experience that is purposefully designed to prepare students for the real world of the 21st century. Pitt-Johnstown's record of excellence is reflected, in part, by the accomplishments of students, faculty, and staff; the record of achievements of more than 19,000 alumni; the satisfaction of area employers; and the commendations of many external organizations. Pitt-Johnstown offers a high-quality educational experience in a supportive living-learning environment, which is grounded in the liberal arts and sciences, is current, and is responsive to both our students' personal and professional needs and to our communities' needs. Our campus is located on 655 picturesque acres in the Laurel Highlands of Pennsylvania, 70 miles east of Pittsburgh.

For more information, contact:

BJ Sarneso
Office of Admissions
450 Schoolhouse Road
Johnstown, Pennsylvania 15904
800-765-4875 (toll-free)
E-mail: upjadmit@pitt.edu

Web site: http://upj.pitt.edu

over 24: 22%; SAT critical reading scores over 700: 1%; SAT math scores over 700: 2%; ACT scores over 30: 3%.

Faculty *Total:* 171, 78% full-time, 62% with terminal degrees. *Student/faculty ratio:* 20:1.

Academics *Calendar:* semesters. *Degrees:* certificates, associate, and bachelor's. *Special study options:* accelerated degree program, adult/continuing education programs, advanced placement credit, cooperative education, distance learning, double majors, independent study, internships, off-campus study, part-time degree program, services for LD students, student-designed majors, study abroad, summer session for credit.

Computers on Campus 222 computers/terminals and 100 ports are available on campus for general student use. Students can access the following: computer help desk, free student e-mail accounts, online (class) grades, online (class) registration, online (class) schedules. Campuswide network is available. 100% of college-owned or -operated housing units are wired for high-speed Internet access. Wireless service is available via entire campus.

Student Life *Housing options:* coed, disabled students. Campus housing is university owned. Freshman campus housing is guaranteed. *Activities and organizations:* drama/theater group, student-run newspaper, radio and television station, choral group, Dance Ensemble, Student Senate, Programming Board, academic clubs, national fraternities, national sororities. *Campus security:* 24-hour emergency response devices and patrols, late-night transport/escort service, controlled dormitory access. *Student services:* health clinic, personal/psychological counseling.

Athletics Member NCAA. All Division II. *Intercollegiate sports:* baseball M, basketball M(s)/W(s), cheerleading W, cross-country running W, golf M/W, soccer M/W, track and field W, volleyball W, wrestling M(s). *Intramural sports:* archery M(c)/W(c), basketball M/W, football M/W, ice hockey M(c), lacrosse M(c), rock climbing M(c)/W(c), rugby M(c)/W(c), sailing M(c)/W(c), skiing (downhill) M(c)/W(c), soccer M/W, softball M/W, ultimate Frisbee M(c)/W(c), volleyball M/W, water polo M/W.

Standardized Tests *Required:* SAT or ACT (for admission).

Costs (2010–11) *Tuition:* state resident $11,286 full-time, $470 per credit part-time; nonresident $21,086 full-time, $878 per credit part-time. Full-time tuition and fees vary according to program. Part-time tuition and fees vary according to program. *Required fees:* $792 full-time, $87 per term part-time. *Room and board:* $7826; room only: $4970. Room and board charges vary according to board plan and housing facility. *Payment plan:* installment. *Waivers:* employees or children of employees.

Financial Aid Of all full-time matriculated undergraduates who enrolled in 2008, 2,591 applied for aid, 2,147 were judged to have need, 297 had their need fully met. 142 Federal Work-Study jobs (averaging $1797). 318 state and other part-time jobs (averaging $2742). In 2008, 42 non-need-based awards were made. *Average percent of need met:* 53%. *Average financial aid package:* $10,441. *Average need-based loan:* $4322. *Average need-based gift aid:* $5411. *Average non-need-based aid:* $3063. *Average indebtedness upon graduation:* $21,220.

Applying *Options:* electronic application, early admission, deferred entrance. *Application fee:* $45. *Required:* high school transcript, minimum 2 GPA. *Required for some:* interview. *Recommended:* essay or personal statement, 3 letters of recommendation. *Application deadlines:* rolling (freshmen), rolling (out-of-state freshmen), rolling (transfers). *Notification:* continuous (freshmen), continuous (out-of-state freshmen), continuous (transfers).

Freshman Application Contact Office of Admissions, University of Pittsburgh at Johnstown, 157 Blackington Hall, Johnstown, PA 15904. *Phone:* 814-269-7050. *Toll-free phone:* 800-765-4875. *E-mail:* upjadmit@pitt.edu. *Web site:* http://www.upj.pitt.edu/.

See page 1726 for the College Close-Up.

University of Pittsburgh at Titusville

Titusville, Pennsylvania

- **State-related** primarily 2-year, founded 1963, part of University of Pittsburgh System
- **Small-town** 10-acre campus
- **Endowment** $850,000
- **Coed** 514 undergraduate students, 86% full-time, 63% women, 37% men
- **Minimally difficult** entrance level

Undergraduates 442 full-time, 72 part-time. Students come from 15 states and territories; 8% are from out of state; 19% Black or African American, non-Hispanic/Latino; 2% Hispanic/Latino; 2% Asian, non-Hispanic/Latino; 0.2% American Indian or Alaska Native, non-Hispanic/Latino; 3% Two or more races, non-Hispanic/Latino; 3% Race/ethnicity unknown; 8% transferred in; 55% live on campus.

Freshmen *Admission:* 183 enrolled. *Average high school GPA:* 3.02. *Test scores:* SAT critical reading scores over 500: 21%; SAT math scores over 500: 27%; SAT writing scores over 500: 23%; ACT scores over 18: 67%; SAT critical reading scores over 600: 4%; SAT math scores over 600: 4%; SAT writing

scores over 600: 4%; ACT scores over 24: 10%; SAT math scores over 700: 1%; ACT scores over 30: 3%.

Academics *Calendar:* semesters. *Degrees:* certificates, associate, and bachelor's. *Special study options:* academic remediation for entering students, advanced placement credit, distance learning, internships, part-time degree program, study abroad, summer session for credit.

Computers on Campus 62 computers/terminals are available on campus for general student use. Students can access the following: campus intranet, computer help desk, free student e-mail accounts, online (class) grades, online (class) registration, online (class) schedules. Campuswide network is available. 100% of college-owned or -operated housing units are wired for high-speed Internet access. Wireless service is available via entire campus.

Student Life *Housing:* on-campus residence required through sophomore year. *Options:* coed, disabled students. Campus housing is university owned. Freshman campus housing is guaranteed. *Activities and organizations:* drama/theater group, Phi Theta Kappa, Weight Club, SAB, Students in Free Enterprise (SIFE), Diversity Club. *Campus security:* 24-hour emergency response devices and patrols, controlled dormitory access. *Student services:* health clinic, personal/psychological counseling.

Athletics Member NJCAA. *Intercollegiate sports:* basketball M(s)/W(s). *Intramural sports:* badminton M/W, basketball M/W, bowling M/W, football M/W, golf M/W, racquetball M/W, softball M/W, table tennis M/W, tennis M/W, volleyball M/W, weight lifting M/W.

Standardized Tests *Required:* SAT or ACT (for admission). *Recommended:* SAT (for admission).

Costs (2010–11) *Tuition:* state resident $9942 full-time, $414 per credit part-time; nonresident $18,778 full-time, $782 per credit part-time. Full-time tuition and fees vary according to program. Part-time tuition and fees vary according to program. *Required fees:* $780 full-time, $128 per term part-time. *Room and board:* $8556. Room and board charges vary according to board plan. *Payment plan:* installment.

Financial Aid Of all full-time matriculated undergraduates who enrolled in 2009, 445 applied for aid, 426 were judged to have need, 15 had their need fully met. *Average percent of need met:* 84%. *Average financial aid package:* $17,138. *Average need-based loan:* $7905. *Average need-based gift aid:* $8156.

Applying *Options:* electronic application, early admission, deferred entrance. *Application fee:* $45. *Required:* high school transcript, minimum 2 GPA. *Required for some:* essay or personal statement, 1 letter of recommendation. *Recommended:* interview. *Application deadlines:* rolling (freshmen), rolling (transfers). *Notification:* continuous (freshmen).

Freshman Application Contact Mr. John R. Mumford, Executive Director of Enrollment Management, University of Pittsburgh at Titusville, PO Box 287, Titusville, PA 16354. *Phone:* 814-827-4409. *Toll-free phone:* 888-878-0462. *Fax:* 814-827-4519. *E-mail:* uptadm@pitt.edu. *Web site:* http://www.upt.pitt.edu/.

The University of Scranton

Scranton, Pennsylvania

- **Independent Roman Catholic (Jesuit)** comprehensive, founded 1888
- **Urban** 50-acre campus
- **Endowment** $108.5 million
- **Coed** 4,100 undergraduate students, 95% full-time, 56% women, 44% men
- **Moderately difficult** entrance level, 74% of applicants were admitted

Undergraduates 3,880 full-time, 220 part-time. Students come from 18 states and territories; 12 other countries; 54% are from out of state; 1% Black or African American, non-Hispanic/Latino; 5% Hispanic/Latino; 1% Asian, non-Hispanic/Latino; 0.7% Native Hawaiian or other Pacific Islander, non-Hispanic/Latino; 0.3% American Indian or Alaska Native, non-Hispanic/Latino; 0.6% Two or more races, non-Hispanic/Latino; 6% Race/ethnicity unknown; 2% international; 2% transferred in; 54% live on campus. *Retention:* 89% of full-time freshmen returned.

Freshmen *Admission:* 7,810 applied, 5,809 admitted, 953 enrolled. *Average high school GPA:* 3.33. *Test scores:* SAT critical reading scores over 500: 80%; SAT math scores over 500: 84%; ACT scores over 18: 100%; SAT critical reading scores over 600: 26%; SAT math scores over 600: 34%; ACT scores over 24: 52%; SAT critical reading scores over 700: 3%; SAT math scores over 700: 3%; ACT scores over 30: 4%.

Faculty *Total:* 518, 52% full-time, 48% with terminal degrees. *Student/faculty ratio:* 12:1.

Academics *Calendar:* 4-1-4. *Degrees:* certificates, associate, bachelor's, master's, doctoral-professional, post-master's, and postbachelor's certificates. *Special study options:* academic remediation for entering students, accelerated degree program, adult/continuing education programs, advanced placement credit, distance learning, double majors, honors programs, independent study, internships, off-campus study, part-time degree program, services for LD students, student-designed majors, study abroad, summer session for credit. *ROTC:* Army (b), Air Force (c).

Computers on Campus 945 computers/terminals are available on campus for general student use. Students can access the following: computer help desk, free student e-mail accounts, online (class) grades, online (class) registration, online (class) schedules. Campuswide network is available. 100% of college-owned or -operated housing units are wired for high-speed Internet access. Wireless service is available via classrooms, computer centers, computer labs, dorm rooms, learning centers, libraries, student centers.
Student Life *Housing:* on-campus residence required through sophomore year. *Options:* coed, men-only, women-only, disabled students. Campus housing is university owned. Freshman campus housing is guaranteed. *Activities and organizations:* drama/theater group, student-run newspaper, radio and television station, choral group, Service-Oriented Students Club, United Colors, retreat program, Biology/Pre-Medicine Club, Pre-Law Society. *Campus security:* 24-hour emergency response devices and patrols, student patrols, late-night transport/escort service, controlled dormitory access. *Student services:* health clinic, personal/psychological counseling, women's center.
Athletics Member NCAA. All Division III. *Intercollegiate sports:* baseball M, basketball M/W, bowling M(c)/W(c), crew M(c)/W(c), cross-country running M/W, equestrian sports M(c)/W(c), field hockey W, golf M, ice hockey M(c), lacrosse M/W(c), rugby M(c)/W(c), skiing (downhill) M(c)/W(c), soccer M/W, softball M/W, swimming and diving M/W, tennis M/W, track and field M(c)/W(c), volleyball M(c)/W, wrestling M. *Intramural sports:* badminton M/W, baseball M, basketball M/W, bowling M/W, cross-country running M/W, football M, golf M/W, racquetball M/W, soccer M/W, softball M/W, swimming and diving M/W, table tennis M/W, tennis M/W, ultimate Frisbee M/W, volleyball M/W, weight lifting M/W, wrestling M.
Standardized Tests *Required for some:* SAT or ACT (for admission).
Costs (2011–12) *Comprehensive fee:* $48,474 includes full-time tuition ($35,692), mandatory fees ($350), and room and board ($12,432). Part-time tuition: $917 per credit. *College room only:* $7282. Room and board charges vary according to board plan and housing facility. *Payment plan:* installment. *Waivers:* senior citizens and employees or children of employees.
Financial Aid Of all full-time matriculated undergraduates who enrolled in 2009, 3,161 applied for aid, 2,718 were judged to have need, 288 had their need fully met. 805 Federal Work-Study jobs (averaging $1800). 620 state and other part-time jobs (averaging $1800). In 2009, 631 non-need-based awards were made. *Average percent of need met:* 74%. *Average financial aid package:* $22,585. *Average need-based loan:* $4590. *Average need-based gift aid:* $16,794. *Average non-need-based aid:* $9932. *Average indebtedness upon graduation:* $30,920.
Applying *Options:* electronic application, early admission, early action, deferred entrance. *Required:* essay or personal statement, high school transcript. *Required for some:* interview. *Application deadlines:* 3/1 (freshmen), rolling (transfers), 11/15 (early action). *Notification:* continuous until 1/15 (freshmen), continuous (transfers), 12/15 (early action).
Freshman Application Contact Mr. Joseph Roback, Associate Vice President, Undergraduate Admissions and Enrollment, The University of Scranton, 800 Linden Street, The Estate Room 208, Scranton, PA 18510-4501. *Phone:* 570-941-7540. *Toll-free phone:* 888-SCRANTON. *Fax:* 570-941-5928. *E-mail:* admissions@scranton.edu. *Web site:* http://www.scranton.edu/.

The University of the Arts

Philadelphia, Pennsylvania

- **Independent** comprehensive, founded 1870
- **Urban** 18-acre campus
- **Coed** 2,099 undergraduate students, 98% full-time, 57% women, 43% men
- **Moderately difficult** entrance level, 67% of applicants were admitted

Undergraduates 2,053 full-time, 46 part-time. Students come from 39 states and territories; 22 other countries; 65% are from out of state; 5% transferred in; 35% live on campus. *Retention:* 81% of full-time freshmen returned.
Freshmen *Admission:* 1,855 applied, 1,236 admitted, 505 enrolled. *Average high school GPA:* 2.8. *Test scores:* SAT critical reading scores over 500: 61%; SAT math scores over 500: 48%; SAT writing scores over 500: 60%; ACT scores over 18: 88%; SAT critical reading scores over 600: 23%; SAT math scores over 600: 13%; SAT writing scores over 600: 20%; ACT scores over 24: 39%; SAT critical reading scores over 700: 2%; SAT math scores over 700: 1%; SAT writing scores over 700: 3%; ACT scores over 30: 6%.
Faculty *Total:* 476, 25% full-time. *Student/faculty ratio:* 10:1.
Academics *Calendar:* semesters. *Degrees:* certificates, diplomas, bachelor's, master's, and postbachelor's certificates. *Special study options:* academic remediation for entering students, advanced placement credit, double majors, English as a second language, independent study, internships, off-campus study, part-time degree program, services for LD students, study abroad.
Computers on Campus 400 computers/terminals are available on campus for general student use. Students can access the following: campus intranet, computer help desk, free student e-mail accounts, online (class) grades, online (class) registration, online (class) schedules. Campuswide network is available.

100% of college-owned or -operated housing units are wired for high-speed Internet access. Wireless service is available via entire campus.
Student Life *Housing options:* coed. Campus housing is university owned and leased by the school. Freshman applicants given priority for college housing. *Activities and organizations:* drama/theater group, student-run radio station, choral group, Ladies of Service, Peer Support/Peer Education, Gallery One, Student Council, Cataclysmic (create fashion shows). *Campus security:* 24-hour emergency response devices and patrols, late-night transport/escort service, crime prevention workshops and seminars. *Student services:* health clinic, personal/psychological counseling.
Athletics *Intramural sports:* fencing M/W.
Standardized Tests *Required for some:* SAT or ACT (for admission).
Costs (2011–12) *Comprehensive fee:* $45,800 includes full-time tuition ($33,500) and room and board ($12,300). *College room only:* $8100. Room and board charges vary according to housing facility. *Payment plan:* installment. *Waivers:* children of alumni and employees or children of employees.
Financial Aid In 2002, 561 non-need-based awards were made. *Average percent of need met:* 65%. *Average financial aid package:* $16,500. *Average indebtedness upon graduation:* $17,000.
Applying *Options:* electronic application, early admission, deferred entrance. *Application fee:* $60. *Required:* essay or personal statement, high school transcript, 1 letter of recommendation, portfolio or audition. *Required for some:* interview. *Recommended:* minimum 2 GPA, interview. *Application deadlines:* rolling (freshmen), rolling (transfers). *Notification:* continuous (freshmen), continuous (transfers).
Freshman Application Contact Ms. Susan Gandy, Dean of Admission, The University of the Arts, 320 South Broad Street, Philadelphia, PA 19102-4944. *Phone:* 215-717-6049. *Toll-free phone:* 800-616-ARTS. *Fax:* 215-717-6045. *E-mail:* admissions@uarts.edu. *Web site:* http://www.uarts.edu/.

See page 1742 for the College Close-Up.

University of the Sciences in Philadelphia

Philadelphia, Pennsylvania

- **Independent** university, founded 1821
- **Urban** 35-acre campus
- **Endowment** $135.2 million
- **Coed** 2,526 undergraduate students, 98% full-time, 61% women, 39% men
- **Moderately difficult** entrance level, 64% of applicants were admitted

Undergraduates 2,479 full-time, 47 part-time. Students come from 30 states and territories; 11 other countries; 54% are from out of state; 4% Black or African American, non-Hispanic/Latino; 2% Hispanic/Latino; 38% Asian, non-Hispanic/Latino; 0.1% Native Hawaiian or other Pacific Islander, non-Hispanic/Latino; 0.2% American Indian or Alaska Native, non-Hispanic/Latino; 6% Race/ethnicity unknown; 2% international; 2% transferred in; 30% live on campus. *Retention:* 85% of full-time freshmen returned.
Freshmen *Admission:* 4,494 applied, 2,892 admitted, 467 enrolled. *Average high school GPA:* 3.6. *Test scores:* SAT critical reading scores over 500: 90%; SAT math scores over 500: 96%; SAT writing scores over 500: 88%; ACT scores over 18: 100%; SAT critical reading scores over 600: 31%; SAT math scores over 600: 66%; SAT writing scores over 600: 40%; ACT scores over 24: 73%; SAT critical reading scores over 700: 4%; SAT math scores over 700: 15%; SAT writing scores over 700: 5%; ACT scores over 30: 8%.
Faculty *Total:* 267, 60% full-time. *Student/faculty ratio:* 12:1.
Academics *Calendar:* semesters. *Degrees:* bachelor's, master's, doctoral-professional, doctoral-research/scholarship, and postbachelor's certificates. *Special study options:* academic remediation for entering students, adult/continuing education programs, advanced placement credit, cooperative education, distance learning, double majors, English as a second language, honors programs, internships, off-campus study, part-time degree program, services for LD students, study abroad, summer session for credit. *ROTC:* Army (c), Air Force (c). *Unusual degree programs:* 3-2 occupational therapy, pharmacy, physical therapy.
Computers on Campus 165 computers/terminals are available on campus for general student use. Students can access the following: campus intranet, computer help desk, free student e-mail accounts, online (class) grades, online (class) registration, online (class) schedules. Campuswide network is available. 100% of college-owned or -operated housing units are wired for high-speed Internet access. Wireless service is available via classrooms, computer centers, computer labs, dorm rooms, learning centers, libraries, student centers.
Student Life *Housing:* on-campus residence required through sophomore year. *Options:* coed. Campus housing is university owned and leased by the school. Freshman campus housing is guaranteed. *Activities and organizations:* drama/theater group, student-run newspaper, choral group, student government, Bharat, Academy of Students of Pharmacy, Student Physical Therapy Association, Asian Student Association, national fraternities, national sororities. *Campus security:* 24-hour emergency response devices and patrols, late-night

transport/escort service, controlled dormitory access. *Student services:* health clinic, personal/psychological counseling.

Athletics Member NCAA, NAIA. All NCAA Division II. *Intercollegiate sports:* baseball M(s), basketball M(s)/W(s), cross-country running M/W, golf M/W, riflery M/W, softball W(s), tennis M/W, volleyball W(s). *Intramural sports:* archery M/W, basketball M/W, bowling M/W, riflery M/W, softball M/W, table tennis M/W, volleyball M/W.

Standardized Tests *Required:* SAT or ACT (for admission). *Recommended:* SAT (for admission).

Costs (2010–11) *Comprehensive fee:* $42,828 includes full-time tuition ($29,290), mandatory fees ($1504), and room and board ($12,034). Full-time tuition and fees vary according to program. Part-time tuition: $1220 per credit hour. Part-time tuition and fees vary according to course load and program. *Room and board:* Room and board charges vary according to board plan. *Payment plans:* tuition prepayment, installment. *Waivers:* employees or children of employees.

Financial Aid Of all full-time matriculated undergraduates who enrolled in 2008, 1,778 applied for aid, 1,684 were judged to have need, 632 had their need fully met. In 2008, 96 non-need-based awards were made. *Average percent of need met:* 98%. *Average financial aid package:* $8554. *Average need-based loan:* $6047. *Average need-based gift aid:* $7361. *Average non-need-based aid:* $7984. *Average indebtedness upon graduation:* $34,019.

Applying *Options:* electronic application, deferred entrance. *Application fee:* $45. *Required:* high school transcript. *Recommended:* minimum 3 GPA. *Application deadline:* rolling (freshmen). *Notification:* continuous (freshmen), continuous (transfers).

Freshman Application Contact Ms. Dianna Collins, Executive Director of Admission and Enrollment Services, University of the Sciences in Philadelphia, 600 South 43rd Street, Philadelphia, PA 19104-4495. *Phone:* 215-596-8815. *Toll-free phone:* 888-996-8747. *Fax:* 215-596-8821. *E-mail:* admit@usp.edu. *Web site:* http://www.usciences.edu/.

See page 1746 for the College Close-Up.

Ursinus College

Collegeville, Pennsylvania

- **Independent** 4-year, founded 1869
- **Suburban** 168-acre campus with easy access to Philadelphia
- **Endowment** $91.7 million
- **Coed**
- **Very difficult** entrance level

Faculty *Student/faculty ratio:* 12:1.

Academics *Calendar:* semesters. *Degree:* bachelor's.

Student Life *Campus security:* 24-hour emergency response devices and patrols, late-night transport/escort service, student EMT Corps for first aid/emergency first response.

Athletics Member NCAA. All Division III.

Standardized Tests *Required for some:* SAT or ACT (for admission).

Costs (2010–11) *Comprehensive fee:* $49,870 includes full-time tuition ($39,950), mandatory fees ($170), and room and board ($9750). Part-time tuition: $1249 per credit hour. *Required fees:* $170 per year part-time. *College room only:* $4875.

Financial Aid Of all full-time matriculated undergraduates who enrolled in 2009, 1,440 applied for aid, 1,210 were judged to have need, 263 had their need fully met. 743 Federal Work-Study jobs (averaging $1822). In 2009, 407 non-need-based awards were made. *Average percent of need met:* 80. *Average financial aid package:* $27,194. *Average need-based loan:* $4306. *Average need-based gift aid:* $22,868. *Average non-need-based aid:* $13,512. *Average indebtedness upon graduation:* $25,875. *Financial aid deadline:* 2/15.

Applying *Options:* electronic application, early admission, early decision, early action, deferred entrance. *Required:* essay or personal statement, high school transcript, graded paper. *Recommended:* 2 letters of recommendation, interview.

Freshman Application Contact Mr. Richard Floyd, Dean of Admission, Ursinus College, PO Box 1000, Main Street, Collegeville, PA 19426. *Phone:* 610-409-3200. *Fax:* 610-409-3197. *E-mail:* admissions@ursinus.edu. *Web site:* http://www.ursinus.edu/.

PROFILES

Valley Forge Christian College

Phoenixville, Pennsylvania

- **Independent Assemblies of God** comprehensive, founded 1938
- **Small-town** 106-acre campus with easy access to Philadelphia
- **Endowment** $1.2 million
- **Coed**
- **Minimally difficult** entrance level

Faculty *Student/faculty ratio:* 19:1.

Academics *Calendar:* semesters. *Degrees:* certificates, associate, bachelor's, and master's.

Student Life *Campus security:* 24-hour emergency response devices and patrols, student patrols, late-night transport/escort service, controlled dormitory access, 16-hour patrols by trained security personnel.

Athletics Member NCCAA.

Standardized Tests *Required:* SAT or ACT (for admission).

Costs (2010–11) *One-time required fee:* $75. *Comprehensive fee:* $23,806 includes full-time tuition ($14,600), mandatory fees ($1650), and room and board ($7556). Full-time tuition and fees vary according to course load, location, and program. Part-time tuition: $564 per credit. Part-time tuition and fees vary according to course load, location, and program. *Required fees:* $250 per term part-time. *College room only:* $3860. Room and board charges vary according to board plan and housing facility.

Financial Aid *Of all full-time matriculated undergraduates who enrolled in 2009,* 769 applied for aid, 714 were judged to have need, 52 had their need fully met. 26 Federal Work-Study jobs (averaging $2059). *In 2009,* 74 non-need-based awards were made. *Average percent of need met:* 49. *Average financial aid package:* $10,406. *Average need-based loan:* $4001. *Average need-based gift aid:* $7060. *Average non-need-based aid:* $4634. *Average indebtedness upon graduation:* $32,581.

Applying *Options:* electronic application, early admission, deferred entrance. *Application fee:* $25. *Required:* essay or personal statement, high school transcript, 1 letter of recommendation. *Required for some:* interview.

Freshman Application Contact Rev. William Chenco, Director of Admissions, Valley Forge Christian College, 1401 Charlestown Road, Phoenixville, PA 19460. *Phone:* 610-935-0450 Ext. 1430. *Toll-free phone:* 800-432-8322. *Fax:* 610-917-2069. *E-mail:* admissions@vfcc.edu. *Web site:* http://www.vfcc.edu/.

Villanova University

Villanova, Pennsylvania

- **Independent Roman Catholic** comprehensive, founded 1842
- **Suburban** 254-acre campus with easy access to Philadelphia
- **Endowment** $297.7 million
- **Coed** 7,146 undergraduate students, 92% full-time, 51% women, 49% men
- **Very difficult** entrance level, 45% of applicants were admitted

Undergraduates 6,590 full-time, 556 part-time. Students come from 50 states and territories; 54 other countries; 76% are from out of state; 5% Black or African American, non-Hispanic/Latino; 7% Hispanic/Latino; 6% Asian, non-Hispanic/Latino; 0.1% Native Hawaiian or other Pacific Islander, non-Hispanic/Latino; 0.1% American Indian or Alaska Native, non-Hispanic/Latino; 1% Two or more races, non-Hispanic/Latino; 1% Race/ethnicity unknown; 3% international; 2% transferred in; 70% live on campus. *Retention:* 95% of full-time freshmen returned.

Freshmen *Admission:* 14,361 applied, 6,483 admitted, 1,651 enrolled. *Average high school GPA:* 3.82. *Test scores:* SAT critical reading scores over 500: 96%; SAT math scores over 500: 97%; ACT scores over 18: 100%; SAT critical reading scores over 600: 73%; SAT math scores over 600: 85%; ACT scores over 24: 95%; SAT critical reading scores over 700: 16%; SAT math scores over 700: 30%; ACT scores over 30: 53%.

Faculty *Total:* 934, 62% full-time, 70% with terminal degrees. *Student/faculty ratio:* 11:1.

Academics *Calendar:* semesters. *Degrees:* bachelor's, master's, doctoral-professional, doctoral-research/scholarship, post-master's, and postbachelor's certificates. *Special study options:* accelerated degree program, adult/continuing education programs, advanced placement credit, cooperative education, distance learning, double majors, English as a second language, honors programs, independent study, internships, off-campus study, part-time degree program, services for LD students, study abroad, summer session for credit. *ROTC:* Army (c), Navy (b), Air Force (c). *Unusual degree programs:* 3-2 engineering with Civil Engineering, Chemical Engineering, Computer Engineering, Electrical Engineering, and Mechanical Engineering; Arts/Liberal Studies; Classical Studies; Communication; Criminal Justice; Political Science; Psychology; Spanish; Religious Studies; Computer Science; Biology; Chemistry; Mathematics; Mathematics/Applied Statistics; Human Resources Development; Business Information Systems/Software Engineering.

Computers on Campus 6,609 computers/terminals and 20,000 ports are available on campus for general student use. Students can access the following: campus intranet, computer help desk, free student e-mail accounts, online (class) grades, online (class) registration, online (class) schedules, learning management system with anti-plagiarism software, testing software, online faculty hours, videoconferencing; electronic portfolios; data vaulting/backup service; emergency notification system; Citrix-based library of advanced software. Campuswide network is available. 100% of college-owned or -operated housing units are wired for high-speed Internet access. Wireless service is available via classrooms, computer centers, computer labs, dorm rooms, learning centers, libraries, student centers.

Student Life *Housing options:* coed, men-only, women-only, disabled students. Campus housing is university owned. Freshman campus housing is guaranteed. *Activities and organizations:* drama/theater group, student-run newspaper, radio and television station, choral group, marching band, Blue Key Society, New Student Orientation Counselor Program, Special Olympics, Campus Activities Team, Student Government Association, national fraternities, national sororities. *Campus security:* 24-hour emergency response devices and patrols, late-night transport/escort service, controlled dormitory access, Nova Alert - email, text messaging re: emergency situations. *Student services:* health clinic, personal/psychological counseling.

Athletics Member NCAA. All Division I except football (Division I-AA). *Intercollegiate sports:* baseball M(s), basketball M(s)/W(s), cheerleading M/W, crew M(c)/W, cross-country running M(s)/W(s), equestrian sports W(c), field hockey W(s), golf M, ice hockey M(c)/W(c), lacrosse M(s)/W(s), sailing M(c)/W(c), skiing (downhill) M(c)/W(c), soccer M(s)/W(s), softball W(s), swimming and diving M/W(s), tennis M/W, track and field M(s)/W(s), volleyball M(c)/W(s), water polo M(c)/W. *Intramural sports:* badminton M(c)/W(c), baseball M(c), basketball M(c)/W(c), crew M(c), equestrian sports W(c), field hockey W(c), football M/W, golf M(c)/W(c), ice hockey M(c)/W(c), lacrosse M(c)/W(c), rugby M(c), sailing M(c)/W(c), skiing (downhill) M(c)/W(c), soccer M(c)/W(c), softball M/W, swimming and diving M(c)/W(c), tennis M(c)/W(c), ultimate Frisbee M(c)/W(c), volleyball M(c)/W(c), water polo M(c).

Standardized Tests *Required:* SAT or ACT (for admission).

Costs (2010–11) *Comprehensive fee:* $50,305 includes full-time tuition ($39,085), mandatory fees ($580), and room and board ($10,640). Part-time tuition: $1595 per course. *Required fees:* $30 per year part-time. *College room only:* $5640. Room and board charges vary according to board plan and housing facility. *Payment plan:* installment. *Waivers:* senior citizens and employees or children of employees.

Financial Aid Of all full-time matriculated undergraduates who enrolled in 2009, 3,916 applied for aid, 3,198 were judged to have need, 505 had their need fully met. 2,568 Federal Work-Study jobs (averaging $2666). 48 state and other part-time jobs (averaging $2855). In 2009, 404 non-need-based awards were made. *Average percent of need met:* 79%. *Average financial aid package:* $28,445. *Average need-based loan:* $4431. *Average need-based gift aid:* $23,525. *Average non-need-based aid:* $10,361. *Average indebtedness upon graduation:* $37,267. *Financial aid deadline:* 2/7.

Applying *Options:* electronic application, early action, deferred entrance. *Application fee:* $75. *Required:* essay or personal statement, high school transcript, 1 letter of recommendation. *Application deadlines:* 1/7 (freshmen), 1/7 (out-of-state freshmen), 6/1 (transfers), 11/1 (early action). *Notification:* 4/1 (freshmen), 4/1 (out-of-state freshmen), continuous (transfers), 12/20 (early action).

Freshman Application Contact Mr. Michael Gaynor, Director of University Admission, Villanova University, 800 Lancaster Avenue, Villanova, PA 19085-1672. *Phone:* 610-519-4000. *Fax:* 610-519-6450. *E-mail:* gotovu@villanova.edu. *Web site:* http://www.villanova.edu/.

See page 1760 for the College Close-Up.

Washington & Jefferson College

Washington, Pennsylvania

- **Independent** 4-year, founded 1781
- **Small-town** 60-acre campus with easy access to Pittsburgh
- **Endowment** $83.7 million
- **Coed** 1,460 undergraduate students, 99% full-time, 50% women, 50% men
- **Very difficult** entrance level, 39% of applicants were admitted

Undergraduates 1,443 full-time, 17 part-time. Students come from 38 states and territories; 11 other countries; 26% are from out of state; 3% Black or African American, non-Hispanic/Latino; 2% Hispanic/Latino; 1% Asian, non-Hispanic/Latino; 0.1% Native Hawaiian or other Pacific Islander, non-Hispanic/Latino; 0.3% American Indian or Alaska Native, non-Hispanic/Latino; 1% Two or more races, non-Hispanic/Latino; 9% Race/ethnicity unknown; 2% international; 0.6% transferred in; 90% live on campus. *Retention:* 83% of full-time freshmen returned.

Freshmen *Admission:* 6,820 applied, 2,652 admitted, 395 enrolled. *Average high school GPA:* 3.35. *Test scores:* SAT critical reading scores over 500: 89%; SAT math scores over 500: 92%; ACT scores over 18: 100%; SAT critical reading scores over 600: 33%; SAT math scores over 600: 45%; ACT scores over 24: 69%; SAT critical reading scores over 700: 3%; SAT math scores over 700: 4%; ACT scores over 30: 10%.

Faculty *Total:* 168, 67% full-time, 75% with terminal degrees. *Student/faculty ratio:* 11:1.

Academics *Calendar:* 4-1-4. *Degree:* bachelor's. *Special study options:* academic remediation for entering students, accelerated degree program, advanced placement credit, double majors, honors programs, independent study, internships, off-campus study, part-time degree program, services for LD students, student-designed majors, study abroad, summer session for credit. *ROTC:* Army (c), Air Force (c). *Unusual degree programs:* 3-2 engineering with Columbia University in New York City; Case Western Reserve University in Ohio, Washington University in St. Louis; 3-4 podiatry with PA and Ohio Colleges of Podiatry and 3-4 optometry with PA College of Optometry, integrated pre-health enrichment program, pre-physical therapy program, pre-occupational therapy programs, and physician program, 3-3 Law with Duquesne University Law and University of Pittsburgh.

Computers on Campus 450 computers/terminals and 2,000 ports are available on campus for general student use. Students can access the following: campus intranet, computer help desk, free student e-mail accounts, online (class) grades, online (class) registration, online (class) schedules. Campuswide network is available. 100% of college-owned or -operated housing units are wired for high-speed Internet access. Wireless service is available via entire campus.

Student Life *Housing:* on-campus residence required through senior year. *Options:* coed, men-only, women-only, disabled students. Campus housing is university owned and leased by the school. Freshman campus housing is guaranteed. *Activities and organizations:* drama/theater group, student-run newspaper, radio station, choral group, Student Government Association, Student Activities Board, Black Student Union, Pre-Legal Society, W&J American Mock Trial Association, national fraternities, national sororities. *Campus security:* 24-hour emergency response devices and patrols, late-night transport/escort service, controlled dormitory access, security cameras throughout campus, card access to buildings. *Student services:* health clinic, personal/psychological counseling, women's center.

Athletics Member NCAA. All Division III. *Intercollegiate sports:* baseball M, basketball M/W, cross-country running M/W, field hockey W, football M, golf M/W, lacrosse M/W, soccer M/W, softball W, swimming and diving M/W, tennis M/W, track and field M/W, volleyball W, water polo M/W, wrestling M. *Intramural sports:* basketball M/W, bowling M/W, cross-country running M/W, equestrian sports M(c)/W(c), ice hockey M(c), racquetball M/W, rugby M(c)/W(c), soccer M/W, table tennis M/W, tennis M/W, ultimate Frisbee M(c)/W(c), volleyball M/W.

Costs (2010–11) *Comprehensive fee:* $43,890 includes full-time tuition ($34,150), mandatory fees ($460), and room and board ($9280). Full-time tuition and fees vary according to reciprocity agreements. Part-time tuition: $856 per credit hour. Part-time tuition and fees vary according to course load. *College room only:* $5520. Room and board charges vary according to board plan and housing facility. *Payment plans:* installment, deferred payment. *Waivers:* employees or children of employees.

Financial Aid Of all full-time matriculated undergraduates who enrolled in 2009, 1,215 applied for aid, 1,095 were judged to have need, 175 had their need fully met. 613 Federal Work-Study jobs (averaging $1617). 270 state and other part-time jobs (averaging $888). In 2009, 286 non-need-based awards were made. *Average percent of need met:* 74%. *Average financial aid package:* $24,185. *Average need-based loan:* $4607. *Average need-based gift aid:* $10,070. *Average non-need-based aid:* $11,924. *Average indebtedness upon graduation:* $30,000.

Applying *Options:* electronic application, early admission, early decision, early action, deferred entrance. *Application fee:* $25. *Required:* essay or personal statement, high school transcript, 1 letter of recommendation. *Required for some:* interview. *Recommended:* interview. *Application deadlines:* 3/1 (freshmen), rolling (transfers), 1/15 (early action). *Early decision deadline:* 12/1. *Notification:* 3/15 (freshmen), 12/15 (early decision), 2/15 (early action).

Freshman Application Contact Mr. Alton E. Newell, Vice President for Enrollment, Washington & Jefferson College, 60 South Lincoln Street, Washington, PA 15301. *Phone:* 724-223-6025. *Toll-free phone:* 888-WANDJAY. *Fax:* 724-223-6534. *E-mail:* admission@washjeff.edu. *Web site:* http://www.washjeff.edu/.

Waynesburg University

Waynesburg, Pennsylvania

- **Independent** comprehensive, founded 1849, affiliated with Presbyterian Church (U.S.A.)
- **Small-town** 30-acre campus with easy access to Pittsburgh
- **Coed** 1,801 undergraduate students, 92% full-time, 63% women, 37% men
- **Moderately difficult** entrance level, 65% of applicants were admitted

Undergraduates 1,660 full-time, 141 part-time. Students come from 27 states and territories; 5 other countries; 14% are from out of state; 3% Black or African American, non-Hispanic/Latino; 1% Hispanic/Latino; 0.3% Asian, non-Hispanic/Latino; 0.2% American Indian or Alaska Native, non-Hispanic/Latino; 0.2% Two or more races, non-Hispanic/Latino; 1% Race/ethnicity unknown; 0.4% international; 3% transferred in; 56% live on campus. *Retention:* 78% of full-time freshmen returned.

Freshmen *Admission:* 2,162 applied, 1,409 admitted, 402 enrolled. *Average high school GPA:* 3.46.

Faculty *Total:* 301, 25% full-time, 32% with terminal degrees. *Student/faculty ratio:* 14:1.

Academics *Calendar:* semesters. *Degrees:* associate, bachelor's, master's, and doctoral-professional. *Special study options:* academic remediation for entering students, accelerated degree program, adult/continuing education programs, advanced placement credit, distance learning, double majors, honors programs, independent study, internships, part-time degree program, services for LD students, study abroad. *ROTC:* Army (c). *Unusual degree programs:* 3-2 engineering with Washington University in St. Louis, Pennsylvania State University - University Park Campus.

Computers on Campus 150 computers/terminals are available on campus for general student use. Students can access the following: campus intranet, computer help desk, free student e-mail accounts, online (class) grades, online (class) registration, online (class) schedules. Campuswide network is available. 100% of college-owned or -operated housing units are wired for high-speed Internet access. Wireless service is available via classrooms, computer labs, libraries.

Student Life *Housing:* on-campus residence required through junior year. *Options:* men-only, women-only. Campus housing is university owned. Freshman campus housing is guaranteed. *Activities and organizations:* drama/theater group, student-run newspaper, radio and television station, choral group, marching band, Student Senate, Student Activities Board, Student Nurses Association, Christian Fellowship. *Campus security:* 24-hour emergency response devices and patrols, late-night transport/escort service, controlled dormitory access. *Student services:* health clinic, personal/psychological counseling.

Athletics Member NCAA. All Division III. *Intercollegiate sports:* baseball M, basketball M/W, cross-country running M/W, football M, golf M/W, lacrosse W, soccer M/W, softball W, tennis M/W, track and field M/W, volleyball W, wrestling M. *Intramural sports:* basketball M/W, bowling M/W, racquetball M/W, softball M/W, table tennis M/W, volleyball M/W.

Standardized Tests *Required:* SAT or ACT (for admission).

Costs (2010–11) *Comprehensive fee:* $25,990 includes full-time tuition ($18,050), mandatory fees ($360), and room and board ($7580). Full-time tuition and fees vary according to class time. Part-time tuition: $760 per credit hour. Part-time tuition and fees vary according to class time, course load, and location. *College room only:* $3850. Room and board charges vary according to board plan. *Payment plan:* installment. *Waivers:* employees or children of employees.

Financial Aid Of all full-time matriculated undergraduates who enrolled in 2009, 408 applied for aid, 378 were judged to have need, 73 had their need fully met. 225 Federal Work-Study jobs (averaging $1000). In 2009, 22 non-need-based awards were made. *Average percent of need met:* 79%. *Average financial aid package:* $15,171. *Average need-based loan:* $3546. *Average need-based gift aid:* $11,695. *Average non-need-based aid:* $7157. *Average indebtedness upon graduation:* $25,000.

Applying *Options:* electronic application, early admission. *Application fee:* $20. *Required:* high school transcript, minimum 2.75 GPA. *Required for some:* essay or personal statement, 2 letters of recommendation. *Recommended:* minimum 3 GPA, interview. *Application deadlines:* rolling (freshmen), rolling (transfers). *Notification:* continuous (freshmen), continuous (transfers).

Freshman Application Contact Ms. Robin L. King, Dean of Admissions, Waynesburg University, 51 West College Street, Waynesburg, PA 15370. *Phone:* 724-852-3333. *Toll-free phone:* 800-225-7393. *Fax:* 724-627-8124. *E-mail:* admissions@waynesburg.edu. *Web site:* http://www.waynesburg.edu/.

West Chester University of Pennsylvania

West Chester, Pennsylvania

- **State-supported** comprehensive, founded 1871, part of Pennsylvania State System of Higher Education
- **Suburban** 405-acre campus with easy access to Philadelphia
- **Endowment** $14.0 million
- **Coed** 12,232 undergraduate students, 91% full-time, 59% women, 41% men
- **Moderately difficult** entrance level, 41% of applicants were admitted

Undergraduates 11,139 full-time, 1,093 part-time. Students come from 25 states and territories; 52 other countries; 12% are from out of state; 9% Black or African American, non-Hispanic/Latino; 4% Hispanic/Latino; 2% Asian, non-Hispanic/Latino; 0.4% American Indian or Alaska Native, non-Hispanic/Latino; 0.0% Two or more races, non-Hispanic/Latino; 0.4% Race/ethnicity unknown; 0.3% international; 10% transferred in; 37% live on campus. *Retention:* 85% of full-time freshmen returned.

Freshmen *Admission:* 15,124 applied, 6,269 admitted, 2,067 enrolled. *Average high school GPA:* 3.48. *Test scores:* SAT critical reading scores over 500: 79%; SAT math scores over 500: 74%; SAT writing scores over 500: 69%; SAT critical reading scores over 600: 24%; SAT math scores over 600: 17%; SAT writing scores over 600: 17%; SAT critical reading scores over 700: 2%; SAT math scores over 700: 1%; SAT writing scores over 700: 1%.

Faculty *Total:* 827, 66% full-time, 66% with terminal degrees. *Student/faculty ratio:* 18:1.

Academics *Calendar:* semesters. *Degrees:* bachelor's, master's, post-master's, and postbachelor's certificates. *Special study options:* academic remediation for entering students, adult/continuing education programs, advanced placement credit, cooperative education, distance learning, double majors, honors programs, independent study, internships, off-campus study, part-time degree program, services for LD students, student-designed majors, study abroad, summer session for credit. *ROTC:* Army (c), Air Force (c). *Unusual degree programs:* 3-2 engineering with Pennsylvania State University, Philadelphia University.

Computers on Campus 1,700 computers/terminals are available on campus for general student use. Students can access the following: campus intranet, computer help desk, free student e-mail accounts, online (class) grades, online (class) registration, online (class) schedules. Campuswide network is available. 100% of college-owned or -operated housing units are wired for high-speed Internet access. Wireless service is available via classrooms, computer centers, computer labs, learning centers, libraries, student centers.

Student Life *Housing options:* coed, disabled students. Campus housing is university owned and is provided by a third party. Freshman applicants given priority for college housing. *Activities and organizations:* drama/theater group, student-run newspaper, radio and television station, choral group, marching band, Off Campus and Commuter Association, Residence Hall Association, Student Government Association, Sports Club Council, national fraternities, national sororities. *Campus security:* 24-hour emergency response devices and patrols, late-night transport/escort service, controlled dormitory access. *Student services:* health clinic, personal/psychological counseling, women's center, legal services.

Athletics Member NCAA. All Division II except field hockey (Division I). *Intercollegiate sports:* baseball M(s), basketball M(s)/W(s), bowling M(c)/W(c), cheerleading W, cross-country running M(s)/W(s), equestrian sports M(c)/W(c), fencing M(c)/W(c), field hockey W(s), football M(s), golf M(s)/W(s), gymnastics W(s), ice hockey M(c)/W(c), lacrosse M(c)/W(s), rugby M(c)/W(s), skiing (downhill) M(c)/W(c), soccer M(s)/W(s), softball W(s), swimming and diving M(s)/W(s), tennis M(s)/W(s), track and field M(s)/W(s), volleyball M(c)/W(s), water polo W(c), wrestling M(c). *Intramural sports:* basketball M/W, field hockey M/W, soccer M/W, softball M/W, tennis M/W, volleyball M/W.

Standardized Tests *Required:* SAT or ACT (for admission).

Costs (2010–11) *Tuition:* state resident $5804 full-time, $242 per credit part-time; nonresident $14,510 full-time, $605 per credit part-time. Full-time tuition and fees vary according to course load. Part-time tuition and fees vary according to course load. *Required fees:* $1876 full-time, $62 per unit part-time. *Room and board:* $7188; room only: $4810. Room and board charges vary according to board plan and housing facility. *Payment plan:* installment. *Waivers:* senior citizens and employees or children of employees.

Financial Aid Of all full-time matriculated undergraduates who enrolled in 2008, 8,007 applied for aid, 5,667 were judged to have need, 1,994 had their need fully met. In 2008, 214 non-need-based awards were made. *Average percent of need met:* 53%. *Average financial aid package:* $7559. *Average need-*

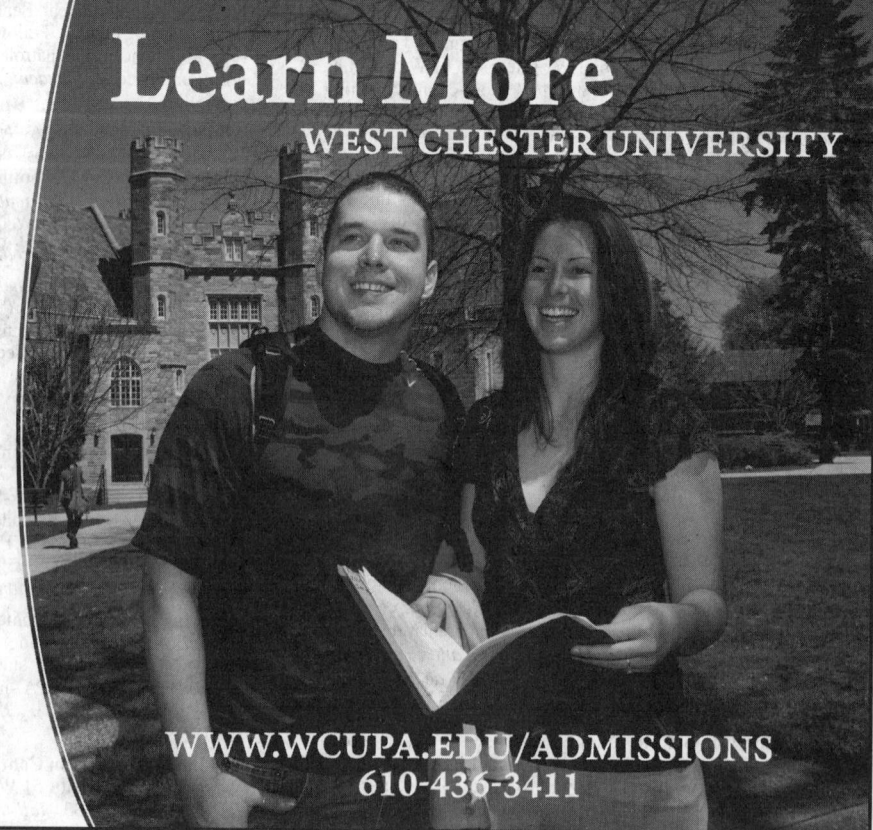

based loan: $4282. *Average need-based gift aid:* $5402. *Average non-need-based aid:* $3466. *Average indebtedness upon graduation:* $25,159.

Applying *Options:* electronic application, early admission, deferred entrance. *Application fee:* $35. *Required:* essay or personal statement, high school transcript. *Required for some:* interview. *Recommended:* minimum 3 GPA. *Application deadlines:* rolling (freshmen), rolling (transfers). *Notification:* continuous (freshmen), continuous (transfers).

Freshman Application Contact West Chester University of Pennsylvania, University Avenue and High Street, West Chester, PA 19383. *Phone:* 610-436-3414. *Toll-free phone:* 877-315-2165. *Web site:* http://www.wcupa.edu/.

See page 1776 for the College Close-Up.

Westminster College
New Wilmington, Pennsylvania

Freshman Application Contact Bradley Tokar, Director of Admissions, Westminster College, 319 South Market Street, New Wilmington, PA 16172-0001. *Phone:* 724-946-7100. *Toll-free phone:* 800-942-8033. *Fax:* 724-946-7171. *E-mail:* tokarbp@westminster.edu. *Web site:* http://www.westminster.edu/.

Widener University
Chester, Pennsylvania

- **Independent** comprehensive, founded 1821
- **Suburban** 110-acre campus with easy access to Philadelphia
- **Endowment** $61.3 million
- **Coed** 3,365 undergraduate students, 80% full-time, 56% women, 44% men
- **Moderately difficult** entrance level, 70% of applicants were admitted

Undergraduates 2,707 full-time, 658 part-time. Students come from 22 states and territories; 17 other countries; 37% are from out of state; 16% Black or African American, non-Hispanic/Latino; 3% Hispanic/Latino; 3% Asian, non-Hispanic/Latino; 0.2% Native Hawaiian or other Pacific Islander, non-Hispanic/Latino; 0.3% American Indian or Alaska Native, non-Hispanic/Latino; 2% Two or more races, non-Hispanic/Latino; 2% Race/ethnicity unknown; 2% international; 5% transferred in; 48% live on campus. *Retention:* 73% of full-time freshmen returned.

Freshmen *Admission:* 4,739 applied, 3,322 admitted, 735 enrolled. *Average high school GPA:* 3.32. *Test scores:* SAT critical reading scores over 500: 49%; SAT math scores over 500: 57%; SAT critical reading scores over 600: 10%; SAT math scores over 600: 18%; SAT critical reading scores over 700: 1%; SAT math scores over 700: 2%.

Faculty *Total:* 665, 48% full-time, 65% with terminal degrees. *Student/faculty ratio:* 12:1.

Academics *Calendar:* semesters. *Degrees:* associate, bachelor's, master's, doctoral-professional, and doctoral-research/scholarship. *Special study options:* academic remediation for entering students, accelerated degree program, adult/continuing education programs, advanced placement credit, cooperative education, distance learning, double majors, English as a second language, honors programs, independent study, internships, off-campus study, part-time degree program, services for LD students, student-designed majors, study abroad, summer session for credit. *ROTC:* Army (b), Navy (c), Air Force (c). *Unusual degree programs:* 3-2 business administration; engineering; social work; physical therapy, education.

Computers on Campus 345 computers/terminals are available on campus for general student use. Students can access the following: campus intranet, computer help desk, free student e-mail accounts, online (class) grades, online (class) registration, online (class) schedules. Campuswide network is available. 100% of college-owned or -operated housing units are wired for high-speed Internet access. Wireless service is available via classrooms, computer centers, computer labs, dorm rooms, learning centers, libraries, student centers.

Student Life *Housing:* on-campus residence required through sophomore year. *Options:* coed, men-only, women-only, cooperative, disabled students. Campus housing is university owned. Freshman campus housing is guaranteed. *Activities and organizations:* drama/theater group, student-run newspaper, radio and television group, WDNR Radio, Black Student Union, volunteer services, rugby club, Theatre Widener, national fraternities, national sororities. *Campus security:* 24-hour emergency response devices and patrols, late-night transport/escort service, controlled dormitory access, blue light emergency phones located throughout campus. *Student services:* health clinic, personal/psychological counseling.

Athletics Member NCAA. All Division III. *Intercollegiate sports:* baseball M, basketball M/W, cheerleading W, cross-country running M/W, field hockey W, football M, golf M, lacrosse M/W, soccer M/W, softball W, swimming and diving M/W, tennis M/W, track and field M/W, volleyball W. *Intramural sports:* crew M, ice hockey M(c), rock climbing M(c)/W(c), skiing (downhill) M(c)/W(c), soccer M, volleyball M(c), water polo M(c)/W(c).

Standardized Tests *Required:* SAT or ACT (for admission).

Costs (2010–11) *Comprehensive fee:* $44,990 includes full-time tuition ($32,750), mandatory fees ($520), and room and board ($11,720). Full-time tuition and fees vary according to class time, course load, and program. Part-time tuition: $1090 per credit hour. *College room only:* $6052. Room and board charges vary according to board plan and housing facility. *Payment plan:* installment. *Waivers:* senior citizens and employees or children of employees.

Financial Aid Of all full-time matriculated undergraduates who enrolled in 2009, 2,537 applied for aid, 2,189 were judged to have need, 300 had their need fully met. 1,646 Federal Work-Study jobs (averaging $1400). 468 state and other part-time jobs (averaging $1200). In 2009, 330 non-need-based awards were made. *Average percent of need met:* 73%. *Average financial aid package:* $24,475. *Average need-based loan:* $4971. *Average need-based gift aid:* $8492. *Average non-need-based aid:* $12,145. *Average indebtedness upon graduation:* $40,386.

Applying *Options:* electronic application, deferred entrance. *Application fee:* $35. *Required:* essay or personal statement, high school transcript. *Required for some:* minimum 2.85 GPA. *Recommended:* interview. *Application deadlines:* rolling (freshmen), rolling (transfers). *Notification:* continuous (freshmen), continuous (transfers).

Freshman Application Contact Office of Admissions, Widener University, One University Place, Chester, PA 19013. *Phone:* 610-499-4126. *Toll-free phone:* 888-WIDENER. *Fax:* 610-499-4676. *E-mail:* admissions.office@widener.edu. *Web site:* http://www.widener.edu/.

Wilkes University
Wilkes-Barre, Pennsylvania

- **Independent** comprehensive, founded 1933
- **Urban** 25-acre campus
- **Endowment** $32.7 million
- **Coed** 2,184 undergraduate students, 90% full-time, 49% women, 51% men
- **Moderately difficult** entrance level, 75% of applicants were admitted

Undergraduates 1,968 full-time, 216 part-time. Students come from 19 states and territories; 12 other countries; 20% are from out of state; 3% Black or African American, non-Hispanic/Latino; 3% Hispanic/Latino; 2% Asian, non-Hispanic/Latino; 0.1% American Indian or Alaska Native, non-Hispanic/Latino; 1% Two or more races, non-Hispanic/Latino; 9% Race/ethnicity unknown; 3% international; 6% transferred in; 39% live on campus. *Retention:* 79% of full-time freshmen returned.

Freshmen *Admission:* 2,485 applied, 1,875 admitted, 502 enrolled. *Test scores:* SAT critical reading scores over 500: 61%; SAT math scores over 500: 70%; SAT writing scores over 500: 58%; SAT critical reading scores over 600: 15%; SAT math scores over 600: 27%; SAT writing scores over 600: 14%; SAT critical reading scores over 700: 1%; SAT math scores over 700: 3%; SAT writing scores over 700: 1%.

Faculty *Total:* 465, 34% full-time. *Student/faculty ratio:* 14:1.

Academics *Calendar:* semesters. *Degrees:* bachelor's, master's, doctoral-professional, and doctoral-research/scholarship. *Special study options:* academic remediation for entering students, accelerated degree program, adult/continuing education programs, advanced placement credit, cooperative education, distance learning, double majors, English as a second language, external degree program, honors programs, independent study, internships, off-campus study, part-time degree program, services for LD students, student-designed majors, study abroad, summer session for credit. *ROTC:* Army (c), Air Force (b).

Computers on Campus 739 computers/terminals are available on campus for general student use. Students can access the following: campus intranet, computer help desk, free student e-mail accounts, online (class) grades, online (class) registration, online (class) schedules. Campuswide network is available. Wireless service is available via libraries, student centers.

Student Life *Housing:* on-campus residence required through sophomore year. *Options:* coed, men-only, women-only. Campus housing is university owned. Freshman campus housing is guaranteed. *Activities and organizations:* drama/theater group, student-run newspaper, radio and television station, choral group. *Campus security:* 24-hour emergency response devices and patrols, late-night transport/escort service, controlled dormitory access. *Student services:* health clinic, personal/psychological counseling.

Athletics Member NCAA. All Division III. *Intercollegiate sports:* baseball M, basketball M/W, cross-country running M/W, field hockey W, football M, golf M, lacrosse M/W, soccer M/W, softball W, tennis M/W, volleyball W, wrestling M. *Intramural sports:* basketball M/W, football M, racquetball M/W, volleyball M/W, weight lifting M/W.

Standardized Tests *Required:* SAT or ACT (for admission).

Costs (2010–11) *Comprehensive fee:* $38,648 includes full-time tuition ($25,802), mandatory fees ($1376), and room and board ($11,470). Part-time tuition: $715 per credit hour. *College room only:* $6880. Room and board charges vary according to board plan and housing facility. *Payment plans:* installment, deferred payment. *Waivers:* employees or children of employees.

Financial Aid Of all full-time matriculated undergraduates who enrolled in 2009, 1,738 applied for aid, 1,611 were judged to have need, 192 had their need fully met. In 2009, 229 non-need-based awards were made. *Average percent of need met:* 71%. *Average financial aid package:* $19,886. *Average need-based loan:* $4392. *Average need-based gift aid:* $15,415. *Average non-need-based aid:* $10,070. *Average indebtedness upon graduation:* $35,244.

Applying *Options:* electronic application, early admission, deferred entrance. *Application fee:* $40. *Required:* high school transcript. *Required for some:* 2 letters of recommendation. *Recommended:* interview. *Application deadlines:* rolling (freshmen), rolling (transfers). *Notification:* 8/30 (freshmen), continuous until 8/30 (transfers).

Freshman Application Contact Ms. Melanie Mickelson, Vice President of Enrollment Services, Wilkes University, 84 West South Street, Wilkes-Barre, PA 18766. *Phone:* 570-408-4400. *Toll-free phone:* 800-945-5378 Ext. 4400. *Fax:* 570-408-4904. *E-mail:* admissions@wilkes.edu. *Web site:* http://www.wilkes.edu/.

See page 1792 for the College Close-Up.

Wilson College
Chambersburg, Pennsylvania

- **Independent** comprehensive, founded 1869, affiliated with Presbyterian Church (U.S.A.)
- **Small-town** 300-acre campus
- **Endowment** $50.3 million
- **Coed, primarily women**
- **Moderately difficult** entrance level

Faculty *Student/faculty ratio:* 10:1.

Academics *Calendar:* 4-1-4. *Degrees:* associate, bachelor's, and master's.

Student Life *Campus security:* 24-hour emergency response devices and patrols, late-night transport/escort service, controlled dormitory access.

Athletics Member NCAA. All Division III.

Standardized Tests *Required for some:* SAT or ACT (for admission), SAT/ACT optional for HS GPA of 3.0 and specified college prep curriculum from regionally accredited schools.

Costs (2010–11) *Comprehensive fee:* $37,650 includes full-time tuition ($27,640), mandatory fees ($580), and room and board ($9430). Part-time tuition: $2765 per course. Part-time tuition and fees vary according to course load. *Required fees:* $45 per course part-time, $50 per term part-time. *College room only:* $4910. Room and board charges vary according to board plan.

Financial Aid Of all full-time matriculated undergraduates who enrolled in 2009, 317 applied for aid, 290 were judged to have need, 53 had their need fully met. 42 Federal Work-Study jobs (averaging $2000). 115 state and other part-time jobs (averaging $2000). In 2009, 49 non-need-based awards were made. *Average percent of need met:* 78. *Average financial aid package:* $22,148. *Average need-based loan:* $4344. *Average need-based gift aid:* $18,314. *Average non-need-based aid:* $12,357. *Average indebtedness upon graduation:* $33,673.

Applying *Options:* electronic application, early admission, deferred entrance. *Application fee:* $35. *Required:* essay or personal statement, high school transcript, 1 letter of recommendation. *Recommended:* minimum 2.7 GPA, interview.

Freshman Application Contact Deborah Arthur, Admissions Administrator, Wilson College, 1015 Philadelphia Avenue, Chambersburg, PA 17201. *Phone:* 717-262-2002. *Toll-free phone:* 800-421-8402. *Fax:* 717-262-2546. *E-mail:* admissions@wilson.edu. *Web site:* http://www.wilson.edu/.

Yeshiva Beth Moshe
Scranton, Pennsylvania

Director of Admissions Dean, Yeshiva Beth Moshe, 930 Hickory Street, PO Box 1141, Scranton, PA 18505-2124. *Phone:* 717-346-1747.

York College of Pennsylvania
York, Pennsylvania

- **Independent** comprehensive, founded 1787
- **Suburban** 190-acre campus with easy access to Baltimore
- **Endowment** $54.5 million
- **Coed** 5,346 undergraduate students, 87% full-time, 56% women, 44% men
- **Moderately difficult** entrance level, 77% of applicants were admitted

Undergraduates 4,669 full-time, 677 part-time. Students come from 33 states and territories; 7 other countries; 39% are from out of state; 4% Black or African American, non-Hispanic/Latino; 3% Hispanic/Latino; 1% Asian, non-Hispanic/Latino; 0.1% Native Hawaiian or other Pacific Islander, non-Hispanic/Latino; 0.3% American Indian or Alaska Native, non-Hispanic/Latino; 0.3% Two or more races, non-Hispanic/Latino; 4% Race/ethnicity unknown; 0.4%

international; 5% transferred in; 44% live on campus. *Retention:* 76% of full-time freshmen returned.

Freshmen *Admission:* 10,412 applied, 7,973 admitted, 1,238 enrolled. *Average high school GPA:* 3.49. *Test scores:* SAT critical reading scores over 500: 79%; SAT math scores over 500: 72%; ACT scores over 18: 94%; SAT critical reading scores over 600: 24%; SAT math scores over 600: 16%; ACT scores over 24: 30%; SAT critical reading scores over 700: 2%; SAT math scores over 700: 1%; ACT scores over 30: 3%.

Faculty *Total:* 540, 31% full-time, 39% with terminal degrees. *Student/faculty ratio:* 17:1.

Academics *Calendar:* semesters. *Degrees:* associate, bachelor's, master's, and doctoral-professional. *Special study options:* academic remediation for entering students, advanced placement credit, cooperative education, double majors, independent study, internships, part-time degree program, services for LD students, student-designed majors, study abroad, summer session for credit. *ROTC:* Army (c). *Unusual degree programs:* 3-2 business administration.

Computers on Campus 893 computers/terminals are available on campus for general student use. Students can access the following: campus intranet, computer help desk, free student e-mail accounts, online (class) grades, online (class) registration, online (class) schedules. Campuswide network is available. 100% of college-owned or -operated housing units are wired for high-speed Internet access. Wireless service is available via classrooms, computer centers, computer labs, dorm rooms, learning centers, libraries, student centers.

Student Life *Housing:* on-campus residence required through junior year. *Options:* coed, men-only, women-only, disabled students. Campus housing is university owned. Freshman campus housing is guaranteed. *Activities and organizations:* drama/theater group, student-run newspaper, radio station, choral group, Campus Activities Board, Ski and Outdoor Club, Intervarsity Christian Fellowship, Students in Free Enterprise (SIFE), Rugby, national fraternities, national sororities. *Campus security:* 24-hour emergency response devices and patrols, late-night transport/escort service. *Student services:* health clinic, personal/psychological counseling.

Athletics Member NCAA. All Division III. *Intercollegiate sports:* baseball M, basketball M/W, cheerleading W, cross-country running M/W, field hockey W, golf M, lacrosse M/W, soccer M/W, softball W, swimming and diving M/W, tennis M/W, track and field M/W, volleyball M(c)/W, wrestling M. *Intramural sports:* badminton M/W, basketball M/W, football M, lacrosse M(c)/W(c), rugby M(c)/W(c), soccer M/W, softball M/W, table tennis M, volleyball M/W.

Standardized Tests *Required:* SAT or ACT (for admission).

Costs (2011–12) *Comprehensive fee:* $24,800 includes full-time tuition ($14,320), mandatory fees ($1560), and room and board ($8920). Full-time tuition and fees vary according to program. Part-time tuition: $445 per credit. *Required fees:* $340 per term part-time. *College room only:* $4990. Room and board charges vary according to housing facility. *Payment plans:* tuition prepayment, installment. *Waivers:* employees or children of employees.

Financial Aid Of all full-time matriculated undergraduates who enrolled in 2009, 3,839 applied for aid, 3,021 were judged to have need, 679 had their need fully met. 293 Federal Work-Study jobs (averaging $1962). 18 state and other part-time jobs (averaging $1688). In 2009, 688 non-need-based awards were made. *Average percent of need met:* 66%. *Average financial aid package:* $11,189. *Average need-based loan:* $6287. *Average need-based gift aid:* $5189. *Average non-need-based aid:* $3618. *Average indebtedness upon graduation:* $28,851.

Applying *Options:* electronic application, deferred entrance. *Application fee:* $30. *Required:* essay or personal statement, high school transcript, minimum 2 GPA. *Required for some:* interview. *Recommended:* 1 letter of recommendation. *Application deadlines:* 8/15 (freshmen), 8/15 (out-of-state freshmen), rolling (transfers). *Notification:* continuous (freshmen), continuous (out-of-state freshmen), continuous (transfers).

Freshman Application Contact York College of Pennsylvania, York, PA 17405-7199. *Phone:* 717-849-1600. *Toll-free phone:* 800-455-8018. *Web site:* http://www.ycp.edu/.

RHODE ISLAND

Brown University
Providence, Rhode Island

- **Independent** university, founded 1764
- **Urban** 140-acre campus with easy access to Boston
- **Coed** 6,318 undergraduate students, 96% full-time, 53% women, 47% men
- **Most difficult** entrance level, 9% of applicants were admitted

Undergraduates 6,092 full-time, 226 part-time. 95% are from out of state; 6% Black or African American, non-Hispanic/Latino; 9% Hispanic/Latino; 15% Asian, non-Hispanic/Latino; 0.1% Native Hawaiian or other Pacific Islander, non-Hispanic/Latino; 0.4% American Indian or Alaska Native, non-Hispanic/Latino; 3% Two or more races, non-Hispanic/Latino; 11% Race/ethnicity unknown; 10% international; 2% transferred in; 79% live on campus. *Retention:* 98% of full-time freshmen returned.

Freshmen *Admission:* 30,135 applied, 2,815 admitted, 1,499 enrolled. *Test scores:* SAT critical reading scores over 500: 100%; SAT math scores over 500: 100%; SAT writing scores over 500: 100%; ACT scores over 18: 100%; SAT critical reading scores over 600: 90%; SAT math scores over 600: 95%; SAT writing scores over 600: 93%; ACT scores over 24: 99%; SAT critical reading scores over 700: 60%; SAT math scores over 700: 65%; SAT writing scores over 700: 65%; ACT scores over 30: 70%.

Faculty *Total:* 977, 81% full-time, 88% with terminal degrees. *Student/faculty ratio:* 9:1.

Academics *Calendar:* semesters. *Degrees:* bachelor's, master's, doctoral-professional, and doctoral-research/scholarship. *Special study options:* adult/continuing education programs, advanced placement credit, double majors, honors programs, independent study, internships, off-campus study, part-time degree program, services for LD students, student-designed majors, study abroad, summer session for credit. *ROTC:* Army (c).

Computers on Campus Students can access the following: campus intranet, computer help desk, free student e-mail accounts, online (class) grades, online (class) registration, online (class) schedules. Campuswide network is available. Wireless service is available via entire campus.

Student Life *Housing:* on-campus residence required through junior year. *Options:* coed, cooperative, disabled students. Campus housing is university owned. Freshman campus housing is guaranteed. *Activities and organizations:* drama/theater group, student-run newspaper, radio and television station, choral group, marching band, national fraternities, national sororities. *Campus security:* 24-hour emergency response devices and patrols, late-night transport/escort service, controlled dormitory access. *Student services:* health clinic, personal/psychological counseling, women's center.

Athletics Member NCAA. All Division I except football (Division I-AA). *Intercollegiate sports:* baseball M, basketball M/W, crew M/W, cross-country running M/W, equestrian sports W, fencing M/W, field hockey W, golf M/W, gymnastics W, ice hockey M/W, lacrosse M/W, rugby M(c)/W(c), sailing M(c)/W(c), skiing (downhill) M(c)/W, soccer M/W, softball W, squash M/W, swimming and diving M/W, tennis M/W, track and field M/W, volleyball M(c)/W, water polo M/W, wrestling M. *Intramural sports:* badminton M(c)/W(c), basketball M/W, cheerleading M/W, fencing M/W, field hockey W, football M, ice hockey M/W, lacrosse M/W, racquetball M(c)/W(c), rugby M/W, skiing (downhill) M/W, soccer M/W, softball M/W, squash M/W, swimming and diving M/W, table tennis M(c)/W(c), tennis M/W, ultimate Frisbee M(c)/W(c), volleyball M/W, water polo M/W.

Standardized Tests *Required:* SAT and SAT Subject Tests or ACT (for admission).

Costs (2011–12) *Comprehensive fee:* $53,136 includes full-time tuition ($41,328), mandatory fees ($902), and room and board ($10,906). *College room only:* $6748. Room and board charges vary according to board plan. *Payment plan:* installment. *Waivers:* employees or children of employees.

Financial Aid Of all full-time matriculated undergraduates who enrolled in 2009, 2,970 applied for aid, 2,772 were judged to have need, 2,772 had their need fully met. 1,479 Federal Work-Study jobs (averaging $2280). 316 state and other part-time jobs (averaging $2339). In 2009, 5 non-need-based awards were made. *Average percent of need met:* 100%. *Average financial aid package:* $36,815. *Average need-based loan:* $5320. *Average need-based gift aid:* $33,861. *Average non-need-based aid:* $11,600. *Average indebtedness upon graduation:* $22,468. *Financial aid deadline:* 2/1.

Applying *Options:* electronic application, early decision, deferred entrance. *Required:* essay or personal statement, high school transcript, 2 letters of recommendation, Common application; Brown University supplement. *Application deadlines:* 1/1 (freshmen), 3/1 (transfers). *Early decision deadline:* 11/1. *Notification:* 4/1 (freshmen), 5/15 (transfers), 12/15 (early decision).

Freshman Application Contact Mr. James Miller, Dean of Admission, Brown University, Box 1876, Providence, RI 02912. *Phone:* 401-863-2378. *Fax:* 401-863-9300. *E-mail:* admission_undergraduate@brown.edu. *Web site:* http://www.brown.edu/.

Bryant University
Smithfield, Rhode Island

- **Independent** comprehensive, founded 1863
- **Suburban** 420-acre campus with easy access to Boston and Providence
- **Coed** 3,365 undergraduate students, 96% full-time, 42% women, 58% men
- **Moderately difficult** entrance level, 69% of applicants were admitted

Undergraduates 3,225 full-time, 140 part-time. Students come from 30 states and territories; 60 other countries; 85% are from out of state; 4% Black or African American, non-Hispanic/Latino; 4% Hispanic/Latino; 3% Asian, non-Hispanic/Latino; 0.3% American Indian or Alaska Native, non-Hispanic/Latino;

3% Race/ethnicity unknown; 6% international; 3% transferred in; 82% live on campus. *Retention:* 87% of full-time freshmen returned.

Freshmen *Admission:* 5,050 applied, 3,492 admitted, 833 enrolled. *Test scores:* SAT critical reading scores over 500: 79%; SAT math scores over 500: 93%; SAT writing scores over 500: 80%; ACT scores over 18: 99%; SAT critical reading scores over 600: 21%; SAT math scores over 600: 44%; SAT writing scores over 600: 24%; ACT scores over 24: 60%; SAT critical reading scores over 700: 1%; SAT math scores over 700: 4%; SAT writing scores over 700: 2%; ACT scores over 30: 6%.

Faculty *Total:* 288, 56% full-time, 53% with terminal degrees. *Student/faculty ratio:* 16:1.

Academics *Calendar:* semesters. *Degrees:* bachelor's and master's. *Special study options:* adult/continuing education programs, advanced placement credit, double majors, English as a second language, honors programs, independent study, internships, part-time degree program, services for LD students, study abroad, summer session for credit. *ROTC:* Army (b).

Computers on Campus 478 computers/terminals and 9,000 ports are available on campus for general student use. Students can access the following: campus intranet, computer help desk, free student e-mail accounts, online (class) grades, online (class) registration, online (class) schedules, e-mail, online library, wireless network, student Web hosts. Campuswide network is available. 100% of college-owned or -operated housing units are wired for high-speed Internet access. Wireless service is available via entire campus.

Student Life *Housing options:* coed, women-only, disabled students. Campus housing is university owned. Freshman campus housing is guaranteed. *Activities and organizations:* drama/theater group, student-run newspaper, radio and television station, choral group, Bryant Outdoor Activities Club, Student Programming Board, Rhythm and Pride Dance Team, WJMF Radio, Bryant Players (drama club), national fraternities, national sororities. *Campus security:* 24-hour emergency response devices and patrols, late-night transport/escort service, controlled dormitory access, prevention/awareness programs; pamphlets/posters/films; monitored one point access to campus; bicycle patrols; video cameras. *Student services:* health clinic, personal/psychological counseling, women's center.

Athletics Member NCAA. All Division I except football (Division I-AA). *Intercollegiate sports:* badminton M(c)/W(c), baseball M(s), basketball M(s)/W(s), bowling M(c)/W(c), cheerleading M(c)/W(c), cross-country running M(s)/W(s), field hockey W(s), golf M(s), ice hockey M(c), lacrosse M(s)/W(s), racquetball M(c)/W(c), rugby M(c)/W(c), soccer M(s)/W(s), softball W(s), squash M(c)/W(c), swimming and diving M(s)/W(s), table tennis M(c)/W(c), tennis M(s)/W(s), track and field M(s)/W(s), ultimate Frisbee M(c)/W(c), volleyball M(c)/W(s), wrestling M(c). *Intramural sports:* basketball M/W, field hockey W, football M, soccer M/W, softball M/W, volleyball M/W.

Standardized Tests *Required:* SAT or ACT (for admission).

Costs (2011–12) *Comprehensive fee:* $47,453 includes full-time tuition ($34,288), mandatory fees ($336), and room and board ($12,829). Part-time tuition: $1998 per course. Part-time tuition and fees vary according to course load. *College room only:* $7530. Room and board charges vary according to board plan and housing facility. *Payment plan:* installment. *Waivers:* employees or children of employees.

Financial Aid Of all full-time matriculated undergraduates who enrolled in 2009, 2,465 applied for aid, 2,203 were judged to have need, 1,102 had their need fully met. In 2009, 397 non-need-based awards were made. *Average percent of need met:* 51%. *Average financial aid package:* $21,206. *Average need-based loan:* $4899. *Average need-based gift aid:* $11,553. *Average non-need-based aid:* $13,225. *Average indebtedness upon graduation:* $39,490.

Applying *Options:* electronic application, early decision, early action, deferred entrance. *Application fee:* $50. *Required:* essay or personal statement, high school transcript, 1 letter of recommendation, senior year first-quarter grades; SAT Reasoning Test or ACT results. *Recommended:* minimum 3.3 GPA, interview. *Application deadlines:* 2/1 (freshmen), 2/1 (out-of-state freshmen), rolling (transfers), 12/1 (early action). *Early decision deadline:* 11/15 (for plan 1), 1/14 (for plan 2). *Notification:* 3/20 (freshmen), 3/20 (out-of-state freshmen), continuous (transfers), 12/15 (early decision plan 1), 2/14 (early decision plan 2), 1/20 (early action).

Freshman Application Contact Ms. Michelle Beauregard, Director of Admission, Bryant University, 1150 Douglas Pike, Smithfield, RI 02917. *Phone:* 401-232-6100. *Toll-free phone:* 800-622-7001. *Fax:* 401-232-6741. *E-mail:* admission@bryant.edu. *Web site:* http://www.bryant.edu/.

Johnson & Wales University
Providence, Rhode Island

- **Independent** comprehensive, founded 1914
- **Urban** 47-acre campus with easy access to Boston
- **Coed** 9,703 undergraduate students, 91% full-time, 56% women, 44% men
- **Moderately difficult** entrance level, 70% of applicants were admitted

Undergraduates 8,843 full-time, 860 part-time. 81% are from out of state; 7% Black or African American, non-Hispanic/Latino; 7% Hispanic/Latino; 2%

Asian, non-Hispanic/Latino; 0.3% American Indian or Alaska Native, non-Hispanic/Latino; 0.5% Two or more races, non-Hispanic/Latino; 30% Race/ethnicity unknown; 9% international; 7% transferred in; 42% live on campus. *Retention:* 75% of full-time freshmen returned.

Freshmen *Admission:* 13,850 applied, 9,694 admitted, 2,259 enrolled. *Average high school GPA:* 3.1.

Faculty *Total:* 519, 57% full-time. *Student/faculty ratio:* 27:1.

Academics *Calendar:* quarters. *Degrees:* certificates, associate, bachelor's, master's, doctoral-other, and post-master's certificates (branch locations in Charlotte, NC; Denver, CO; North Miami, FL). *Special study options:* academic remediation for entering students, accelerated degree program, adult/continuing education programs, advanced placement credit, cooperative education, English as a second language, freshman honors college, honors programs, independent study, internships, part-time degree program, services for LD students, study abroad, summer session for credit. *ROTC:* Army (b).

Computers on Campus Students can access the following: computer help desk, free student e-mail accounts, online (class) grades, online (class) registration, online (class) schedules. Campuswide network is available.

Student Life *Housing:* on-campus residence required for freshman year. *Options:* coed. Campus housing is university owned. Freshman campus housing is guaranteed. *Activities and organizations:* student-run newspaper, national fraternities, national sororities. *Campus security:* 24-hour emergency response devices and patrols, student patrols, late-night transport/escort service. *Student services:* health clinic, personal/psychological counseling, women's center.

Athletics Member NCAA. All Division III. *Intercollegiate sports:* baseball M(c), basketball M/W, cross-country running M/W, equestrian sports M(c)/W(c), golf M/W, ice hockey M(c), sailing M/W, soccer M/W, softball W, tennis M/W, volleyball M/W, wrestling M. *Intramural sports:* badminton M/W, basketball M/W, bowling M(c)/W(c), cheerleading M/W, football M/W, skiing (downhill) M(c)/W(c), soccer M/W, softball M/W, table tennis M/W, tennis M(c)/W(c), volleyball M/W.

Standardized Tests *Required for some:* SAT or ACT (for admission).

Costs (2010–11) *One-time required fee:* $288. *Tuition:* $23,034 full-time. *Required fees:* $1107 full-time. *Room only:* Room and board charges vary according to board plan, housing facility, and location. *Payment plan:* installment. *Waivers:* employees or children of employees.

Financial Aid Of all full-time matriculated undergraduates who enrolled in 2009, 6,745 applied for aid, 5,959 were judged to have need, 687 had their need fully met. In 2009, 1444 non-need-based awards were made. *Average percent of need met:* 68%. *Average financial aid package:* $15,772. *Average need-based loan:* $5297. *Average need-based gift aid:* $7226. *Average non-need-based aid:* $4618.

Applying *Options:* electronic application, early admission, deferred entrance. *Required:* high school transcript. *Required for some:* essay or personal statement, minimum 2.75 GPA, interview. *Recommended:* minimum 2 GPA. *Application deadlines:* rolling (freshmen), rolling (transfers). *Notification:* continuous (freshmen), continuous (transfers).

Freshman Application Contact Amy Podbelski, Dean of Undergraduate Admissions, Johnson & Wales University, 8 Abbott Park Place, Providence, RI 02903-3703. *Phone:* 401-598-2310. *Toll-free phone:* 800-598-1000 (in-state); 800-342-5598 (out-of-state). *Fax:* 401-598-2948. *E-mail:* pvd@admissions.jwu.edu. *Web site:* http://www.jwu.edu/.

See page 1358 for the College Close-Up.

Mater Ecclesiae College
Greenville, Rhode Island

Freshman Application Contact Admissions, Mater Ecclesiae College, 60 Austin Avenue, Greenville, RI 02828. *Phone:* 401-949-2820. *E-mail:* info@mecollege.org. *Web site:* http://www.materecclesiae.net/.

New England Institute of Technology
Warwick, Rhode Island

- **Independent** primarily 2-year, founded 1940
- **Suburban** 10-acre campus with easy access to Boston
- **Coed** 3,258 undergraduate students, 87% full-time, 23% women, 77% men
- **Noncompetitive** entrance level

Undergraduates 2,829 full-time, 429 part-time. Students come from 10 states and territories; 22 other countries; 7% Black or African American, non-Hispanic/Latino; 7% Hispanic/Latino; 2% Asian, non-Hispanic/Latino; 0.6%

American Indian or Alaska Native, non-Hispanic/Latino; 0.5% Two or more races, non-Hispanic/Latino; 13% Race/ethnicity unknown; 3% international.

Freshmen *Admission:* 596 enrolled.

Faculty *Total:* 310, 36% full-time, 10% with terminal degrees.

Academics *Calendar:* quarters. *Degrees:* associate, bachelor's, and master's. *Special study options:* academic remediation for entering students, adult/continuing education programs, advanced placement credit, distance learning, English as a second language, internships, part-time degree program, services for LD students, summer session for credit.

Computers on Campus 325 computers/terminals are available on campus for general student use. Students can access the following: free student e-mail accounts, online (class) registration. Campuswide network is available. Wireless service is available via entire campus.

Student Life *Housing:* college housing not available. *Campus security:* security personnel during open hours. *Student services:* personal/psychological counseling.

Costs (2011–12) *Tuition:* $18,825 full-time, $430 per credit hour part-time. Full-time tuition and fees vary according to degree level and program. Part-time tuition and fees vary according to degree level and program. No tuition increase for student's term of enrollment. *Required fees:* $890 full-time. *Payment plans:* tuition prepayment, installment. *Waivers:* employees or children of employees.

Financial Aid Of all full-time matriculated undergraduates who enrolled in 2009, 250 Federal Work-Study jobs (averaging $2290).

Applying *Options:* early admission, deferred entrance. *Application fee:* $25. *Required:* high school transcript, interview. *Application deadlines:* rolling (freshmen), rolling (transfers).

Freshman Application Contact Mr. Mark Blondin, Director of Admissions, New England Institute of Technology, 2500 Post Road, Warwick, RI 02886-2244. *Phone:* 401-739-5000. *Fax:* 401-738-5122. *E-mail:* neit@ids.net. *Web site:* http://www.neit.edu/.

Providence College
Providence, Rhode Island

- **Independent Roman Catholic** comprehensive, founded 1917
- **Suburban** 105-acre campus with easy access to Boston
- **Endowment** $137.7 million
- **Coed** 3,898 undergraduate students, 100% full-time, 57% women, 43% men
- **Very difficult** entrance level, 67% of applicants were admitted

Undergraduates 3,885 full-time, 13 part-time. Students come from 39 states and territories; 18 other countries; 92% are from out of state; 3% Black or African American, non-Hispanic/Latino; 4% Hispanic/Latino; 2% Asian, non-Hispanic/Latino; 0.1% Native Hawaiian or other Pacific Islander, non-Hispanic/Latino; 0.1% American Indian or Alaska Native, non-Hispanic/Latino; 2% Two or more races, non-Hispanic/Latino; 12% Race/ethnicity unknown; 1% international; 2% transferred in; 80% live on campus. *Retention:* 91% of full-time freshmen returned.

Freshmen *Admission:* 8,398 applied, 5,640 admitted, 1,103 enrolled. *Average high school GPA:* 3.37. *Test scores:* SAT critical reading scores over 500: 84%; SAT math scores over 500: 86%; SAT writing scores over 500: 87%; ACT scores over 18: 98%; SAT critical reading scores over 600: 36%; SAT math scores over 600: 45%; SAT writing scores over 600: 47%; ACT scores over 24: 70%; SAT critical reading scores over 700: 6%; SAT math scores over 700: 5%; SAT writing scores over 700: 8%; ACT scores over 30: 14%.

Faculty *Total:* 387, 76% full-time, 84% with terminal degrees. *Student/faculty ratio:* 12:1.

Academics *Calendar:* semesters. *Degrees:* certificates, associate, bachelor's, and master's. *Special study options:* adult/continuing education programs, advanced placement credit, cooperative education, double majors, honors programs, independent study, internships, part-time degree program, services for LD students, student-designed majors, study abroad, summer session for credit. *ROTC:* Army (b). *Unusual degree programs:* 3-2 engineering with Columbia University, Washington University in St. Louis.

Computers on Campus 350 computers/terminals and 5,000 ports are available on campus for general student use. Students can access the following: campus intranet, computer help desk, free student e-mail accounts, online (class) grades, online (class) registration, online (class) schedules. Campuswide network is available. 100% of college-owned or -operated housing units are wired for high-speed Internet access. Wireless service is available via classrooms, computer centers, computer labs, learning centers, libraries, student centers.

Student Life *Housing:* on-campus residence required through sophomore year. *Options:* coed, men-only, women-only, disabled students. Campus housing is university owned. Freshman campus housing is guaranteed. *Activities and organizations:* drama/theater group, student-run newspaper, radio and television station, choral group, Student Congress, Campus Ministry, Board of Multicultural Students Affairs, Future Friar Executives, Urban Action. *Campus security:* 24-hour emergency response devices and patrols, student patrols,

late-night transport/escort service, controlled dormitory access. *Student services:* health clinic, personal/psychological counseling.

Athletics Member NCAA. All Division I. *Intercollegiate sports:* basketball M(s)/W(s), cheerleading W, cross-country running M(s)/W(s), field hockey W(s), golf M(c)/W(c), ice hockey M(s)/W(s), lacrosse M(s), racquetball M(c)/W(c), rugby M(c)/W(c), sailing M(c)/W(c), soccer M(s)/W(s), softball W(s), swimming and diving M(s)/W(s), tennis W(s), track and field M(s)/W(s), volleyball M(c)/W(s). *Intramural sports:* basketball M/W, field hockey W, football M/W, ice hockey M/W, lacrosse M/W, racquetball M/W, soccer M/W, softball M/W, tennis M/W, ultimate Frisbee M/W, volleyball M/W.

Costs (2011–12) *Comprehensive fee:* $51,125 includes full-time tuition ($38,610), mandatory fees ($825), and room and board ($11,690). Full-time tuition and fees vary according to degree level and student level. Part-time tuition: $1287 per credit hour. Part-time tuition and fees vary according to degree level. *College room only:* $6790. Room and board charges vary according to board plan and housing facility. *Payment plan:* installment. *Waivers:* senior citizens and employees or children of employees.

Financial Aid Of all full-time matriculated undergraduates who enrolled in 2009, 2,740 applied for aid, 2,242 were judged to have need, 902 had their need fully met. 700 Federal Work-Study jobs (averaging $1800). 700 state and other part-time jobs (averaging $1800). In 2009, 286 non-need-based awards were made. *Average percent of need met:* 83%. *Average financial aid package:* $24,085. *Average need-based loan:* $4946. *Average need-based gift aid:* $18,866. *Average non-need-based aid:* $26,763. *Average indebtedness upon graduation:* $32,850. *Financial aid deadline:* 2/1.

Applying *Options:* electronic application, early admission, early action, deferred entrance. *Application fee:* $55. *Required:* essay or personal statement, high school transcript, 2 letters of recommendation. *Application deadlines:* 1/15 (freshmen), 4/1 (transfers), 11/1 (early action). *Notification:* 4/1 (freshmen), 5/30 (transfers), 1/1 (early action).

Freshman Application Contact Providence College, 1 Cunningham Square, Providence, RI 02918. *Phone:* 401-865-2535. *Toll-free phone:* 800-721-6444. *Web site:* http://www.providence.edu/.

See page 1512 for the College Close-Up.

Rhode Island College
Providence, Rhode Island

- **State-supported** comprehensive, founded 1854
- **Suburban** 180-acre campus with easy access to Boston
- **Endowment** $15.0 million
- **Coed** 7,778 undergraduate students, 75% full-time, 66% women, 34% men
- **Moderately difficult** entrance level, 75% of applicants were admitted

Undergraduates 5,797 full-time, 1,981 part-time. Students come from 23 states and territories; 2 other countries; 15% are from out of state; 6% Black or African American, non-Hispanic/Latino; 9% Hispanic/Latino; 2% Asian, non-Hispanic/Latino; 0.1% Native Hawaiian or other Pacific Islander, non-Hispanic/Latino; 0.4% American Indian or Alaska Native, non-Hispanic/Latino; 1% Two or more races, non-Hispanic/Latino; 14% Race/ethnicity unknown; 0.2% international; 9% transferred in; 16% live on campus. *Retention:* 76% of full-time freshmen returned.

Freshmen *Admission:* 3,955 applied, 2,976 admitted, 1,127 enrolled. *Test scores:* SAT critical reading scores over 500: 37%; SAT math scores over 500: 38%; SAT writing scores over 500: 36%; ACT scores over 18: 50%; SAT critical reading scores over 600: 7%; SAT math scores over 600: 7%; SAT writing scores over 600: 5%; ACT scores over 24: 8%; SAT critical reading scores over 700: 1%; ACT scores over 30: 2%.

Faculty *Total:* 760, 42% full-time. *Student/faculty ratio:* 15:1.

Academics *Calendar:* semesters. *Degrees:* certificates, bachelor's, master's, doctoral-research/scholarship, post-master's, and postbachelor's certificates. *Special study options:* academic remediation for entering students, adult/continuing education programs, advanced placement credit, double majors, English as a second language, honors programs, independent study, internships, off-campus study, part-time degree program, services for LD students, student-designed majors, study abroad, summer session for credit. *ROTC:* Army (c). *Unusual degree programs:* 3-2 public administration with University of Rhode Island.

Computers on Campus 267 computers/terminals and 24 ports are available on campus for general student use. Students can access the following: campus intranet, computer help desk, free student e-mail accounts, online (class) grades, online (class) registration, online (class) schedules. Campuswide network is available. 100% of college-owned or -operated housing units are wired for high-speed Internet access. Wireless service is available via classrooms, computer centers, computer labs, dorm rooms, learning centers, libraries, student centers.

Student Life *Housing options:* coed, women-only, disabled students. Campus housing is university owned. Freshman applicants given priority for college housing. *Activities and organizations:* drama/theater group, student-run newspaper, radio and television station, choral group, student government, newspaper (The Anchor), campus radio station (WXIN), Programming Board, Resident Student Association. *Campus security:* 24-hour emergency response devices and patrols, late-night transport/escort service, controlled dormitory access. *Student services:* health clinic, personal/psychological counseling, women's center.

Athletics Member NCAA. All Division III. *Intercollegiate sports:* baseball M, basketball M/W, cross-country running M/W, golf M, gymnastics W, lacrosse W, soccer M/W, softball W, tennis M/W, track and field M/W, volleyball W, wrestling M. *Intramural sports:* badminton M/W, basketball M/W, football M, golf M/W, gymnastics W, sailing M/W, soccer M/W, softball M/W, swimming and diving M/W, tennis M/W, volleyball M/W, water polo M/W.

Standardized Tests *Required:* SAT or ACT (for admission).

Costs (2010–11) *Tuition:* state resident $5988 full-time, $250 per credit part-time; nonresident $15,880 full-time, $604 per credit part-time. Part-time tuition and fees vary according to course load. *Required fees:* $998 full-time, $28 per credit part-time, $72 per term part-time. *Room and board:* $9256; room only: $5266. Room and board charges vary according to housing facility. *Payment plan:* installment. *Waivers:* employees or children of employees.

Financial Aid Of all full-time matriculated undergraduates who enrolled in 2009, 4,417 applied for aid, 3,370 were judged to have need, 1,035 had their need fully met. In 2009, 138 non-need-based awards were made. *Average percent of need met:* 75%. *Average financial aid package:* $8365. *Average need-based loan:* $3759. *Average need-based gift aid:* $5360. *Average non-need-based aid:* $1819. *Average indebtedness upon graduation:* $18,352.

Applying *Options:* electronic application, early admission. *Application fee:* $50. *Required:* essay or personal statement, high school transcript, 1 letter of recommendation, one letter from guidance counselor. *Required for some:* interview. *Recommended:* minimum 3 GPA. *Application deadlines:* 3/15 (freshmen), 3/15 (out-of-state freshmen), 6/1 (transfers). *Notification:* continuous (freshmen), continuous (out-of-state freshmen), continuous (transfers).

Freshman Application Contact Deborah Johnson, Interim Director of Admissions, Rhode Island College, 600 Mount Pleasant Avenue, Providence, RI 02908-1927. *Phone:* 401-456-8234. *Toll-free phone:* 800-669-5760. *Fax:* 401-456-8817. *E-mail:* admissions@ric.edu. *Web site:* http://www.ric.edu/.

Rhode Island School of Design
Providence, Rhode Island

Freshman Application Contact Mr. Edward Newhall, Director of Admissions, Rhode Island School of Design, 2 College Street, Providence, RI 02905-2791. *Phone:* 401-454-6307. *Toll-free phone:* 800-364-7473. *Fax:* 401-454-6309. *E-mail:* admissions@risd.edu. *Web site:* http://www.risd.edu/.

Roger Williams University
Bristol, Rhode Island

Freshman Application Contact Mr. Didier Bouvet, Dean of Undergraduate Admission, Roger Williams University, 1 Old Ferry Road, Bristol, RI 02809. *Phone:* 401-254-3500. *Toll-free phone:* 800-458-7144. *Fax:* 401-254-3557. *E-mail:* admit@rwu.edu. *Web site:* http://www.rwu.edu/.

See page 1544 for the College Close-Up.

Salve Regina University
Newport, Rhode Island

- **Independent Roman Catholic** comprehensive, founded 1934
- **Suburban** 75-acre campus with easy access to Boston and Providence
- **Endowment** $36.1 million
- **Coed** 2,022 undergraduate students, 95% full-time, 69% women, 31% men
- **Moderately difficult** entrance level, 70% of applicants were admitted

Undergraduates 1,931 full-time, 91 part-time. Students come from 36 states and territories; 20 other countries; 73% are from out of state; 1% Black or African American, non-Hispanic/Latino; 3% Hispanic/Latino; 2% Asian, non-Hispanic/Latino; 0.5% American Indian or Alaska Native, non-Hispanic/Latino; 0.5% Two or more races, non-Hispanic/Latino; 17% Race/ethnicity unknown; 0.3% international; 2% transferred in; 63% live on campus. *Retention:* 84% of full-time freshmen returned.

Freshmen *Admission:* 4,922 applied, 3,425 admitted, 600 enrolled. *Average high school GPA:* 3.38.

Faculty *Total:* 265, 42% full-time, 67% with terminal degrees. *Student/faculty ratio:* 14:1.

Academics *Calendar:* semesters. *Degrees:* certificates, associate, bachelor's, master's, doctoral-research/scholarship, post-master's, and postbachelor's certificates. *Special study options:* accelerated degree program, adult/continuing education programs, advanced placement credit, distance learning, double majors, English as a second language, honors programs, independent study, internships, off-campus study, part-time degree program, services for LD students, study abroad, summer session for credit. *ROTC:* Army (c). *Unusual degree programs:* 3-2 business administration; administration of justice, holistic counseling, international relations, management, rehabilitation counseling.

Computers on Campus 163 computers/terminals are available on campus for general student use. Students can access the following: campus intranet, computer help desk, free student e-mail accounts, online (class) grades, online (class) registration, online (class) schedules. Campuswide network is available. 90% of college-owned or -operated housing units are wired for high-speed Internet access. Wireless service is available via classrooms, computer centers, computer labs, learning centers, libraries, student centers.

Student Life *Housing:* on-campus residence required through sophomore year. *Options:* coed, men-only, women-only, disabled students. Campus housing is university owned and leased by the school. Freshman campus housing is guaranteed. *Activities and organizations:* drama/theater group, student-run newspaper, radio station, choral group, Orpheus Musical Society, Student Government Association, Student Outdoor Adventures, Student Nurse Organization, Stagefright Theatre Company. *Campus security:* 24-hour emergency response devices and patrols, late-night transport/escort service, controlled dormitory access. *Student services:* health clinic, personal/psychological counseling.

Athletics Member NCAA. All Division III. *Intercollegiate sports:* baseball M, basketball M/W, cross-country running M/W, equestrian sports M(c)/W(c), field hockey W, football M, ice hockey M/W, lacrosse M/W, rugby M(c), sailing M/W, soccer M/W, softball W, tennis M/W, track and field W, volleyball W. *Intramural sports:* baseball M, basketball M/W, cheerleading W, field hockey W, football M/W, soccer M/W, softball M/W, tennis M/W, track and field W, volleyball M/W, weight lifting M/W.

Standardized Tests *Required for some:* SAT or ACT (for admission).

Costs (2010–11) *Comprehensive fee:* $42,750 includes full-time tuition ($31,250), mandatory fees ($200), and room and board ($11,300). Part-time tuition: $1042 per credit hour. Part-time tuition and fees vary according to course load. *Required fees:* $40 per term part-time. *Room and board:* Room and board charges vary according to board plan and housing facility. *Payment plan:* installment. *Waivers:* employees or children of employees.

Financial Aid Of all full-time matriculated undergraduates who enrolled in 2009, 1,604 applied for aid, 1,437 were judged to have need, 105 had their need fully met. 532 Federal Work-Study jobs (averaging $801). 160 state and other part-time jobs (averaging $1312). In 2009, 233 non-need-based awards were made. *Average percent of need met:* 68%. *Average financial aid package:* $22,199. *Average need-based loan:* $4542. *Average need-based gift aid:* $17,596. *Average non-need-based aid:* $8240. *Average indebtedness upon graduation:* $35,737.

Applying *Options:* electronic application, early action, deferred entrance. *Application fee:* $50. *Required:* essay or personal statement, high school transcript, 2 letters of recommendation. *Recommended:* minimum 2.7 GPA. *Application deadlines:* 2/1 (freshmen), rolling (transfers), 11/1 (early action). *Notification:* 4/1 (freshmen), continuous (transfers), 12/25 (early action).

Freshman Application Contact Ms. Colleen Emerson, Dean of Undergraduate Admissions, Salve Regina University, 100 Ochre Point Avenue, Newport, RI 02840-4192. *Phone:* 401-341-2908. *Toll-free phone:* 888-GO SALVE. *Fax:* 401-848-2823. *E-mail:* sruadmis@salve.edu. *Web site:* http://www.salve.edu/.

University of Rhode Island
Kingston, Rhode Island

- **State-supported** university, founded 1892, part of Rhode Island Board of Governors for Higher Education
- **Small-town** 1200-acre campus
- **Endowment** $84.9 million
- **Coed** 13,093 undergraduate students, 88% full-time, 55% women, 45% men
- **Moderately difficult** entrance level, 78% of applicants were admitted

Undergraduates 11,556 full-time, 1,537 part-time. Students come from 42 states and territories; 57 other countries; 38% are from out of state; 5% Black or African American, non-Hispanic/Latino; 6% Hispanic/Latino; 3% Asian, non-Hispanic/Latino; 0.1% Native Hawaiian or other Pacific Islander, non-Hispanic/Latino; 0.3% American Indian or Alaska Native, non-Hispanic/Latino; 0.6% Two or more races, non-Hispanic/Latino; 12% Race/ethnicity unknown; 0.3% international; 5% transferred in; 45% live on campus. *Retention:* 80% of full-time freshmen returned.

Freshmen *Admission:* 19,564 applied, 15,205 admitted, 2,767 enrolled. *Average high school GPA:* 3.12. *Test scores:* SAT critical reading scores over 500: 61%; SAT math scores over 500: 66%; SAT writing scores over 500: 62%; ACT scores over 18: 96%; SAT critical reading scores over 600: 15%; SAT math scores over 600: 20%; SAT writing scores over 600: 15%; ACT scores over 24: 41%; SAT critical reading scores over 700: 1%; SAT math scores over 700: 1%; SAT writing scores over 700: 1%; ACT scores over 30: 4%.

Faculty *Total:* 1,229, 54% full-time. *Student/faculty ratio:* 16:1.

Academics *Calendar:* semesters. *Degrees:* bachelor's, master's, doctoral-professional, doctoral-research/scholarship, and postbachelor's certificates. *Special study options:* academic remediation for entering students, adult/continuing education programs, advanced placement credit, distance learning, double majors, honors programs, independent study, internships, off-campus study, part-time degree program, services for LD students, study abroad, summer session for credit. *ROTC:* Army (b). *Unusual degree programs:* 3-2 engineering; nursing; accounting, pharmacy, chemistry, education, psychology.

Computers on Campus 488 computers/terminals are available on campus for general student use. Students can access the following: campus intranet, computer help desk, free student e-mail accounts, online (class) grades, online (class) registration, online (class) schedules. Campuswide network is available. 100% of college-owned or -operated housing units are wired for high-speed Internet access. Wireless service is available via entire campus.

Student Life *Housing options:* coed, cooperative, disabled students. Campus housing is university owned and leased by the school. Freshman campus housing is guaranteed. *Activities and organizations:* drama/theater group, student-run newspaper, radio and television station, choral group, marching band, Student Entertainment Committee, Student radio station, Intramural sport clubs, Student Alumni Association, student newspaper, national fraternities, national sororities. *Campus security:* 24-hour emergency response devices and patrols, student patrols, late-night transport/escort service, controlled dormitory access. *Student services:* health clinic, personal/psychological counseling, women's center.

Athletics Member NCAA. All Division I. *Intercollegiate sports:* baseball M(s), basketball M(s)/W(s), crew W(s), cross-country running M(s)/W(s), football M(s), golf M(s), soccer M(s)/W(s), softball W(s), swimming and diving W(s), tennis W(s), track and field M(s)/W(s), volleyball W(s). *Intramural sports:* crew M(c), equestrian sports M(c)/W(c), field hockey W(c), football M, gymnastics W(c), ice hockey M(c)/W(c), lacrosse M(c)/W(c), rugby M(c)/W(c), sailing M(c)/W(c), skiing (downhill) M(c)/W(c), soccer M/W, swimming and diving M(c), ultimate Frisbee M(c)/W(c), volleyball M(c), wrestling M(c).

Standardized Tests *Required:* SAT or ACT (for admission).

Costs (2010–11) *Tuition:* state resident $9014 full-time, $376 per credit part-time; nonresident $25,720 full-time, $1072 per credit part-time. Full-time tuition and fees vary according to course load, location, and reciprocity agreements. Part-time tuition and fees vary according to course load, location, and

reciprocity agreements. *Required fees:* $34 per credit part-time, $58 per term part-time. *Room and board:* $10,854; room only: $6994. Room and board charges vary according to board plan and housing facility. *Payment plan:* installment. *Waivers:* minority students, senior citizens, and employees or children of employees.

Financial Aid Of all full-time matriculated undergraduates who enrolled in 2009, 10,466 applied for aid, 8,833 were judged to have need, 6,048 had their need fully met. In 2009, 404 non-need-based awards were made. *Average percent of need met:* 57%. *Average financial aid package:* $12,794. *Average need-based loan:* $5499. *Average need-based gift aid:* $7540. *Average non-need-based aid:* $5057. *Average indebtedness upon graduation:* $23,000.

Applying *Options:* electronic application, early admission, early action, deferred entrance. *Application fee:* $65. *Required:* essay or personal statement, high school transcript, 1 letter of recommendation, minimum of 18 units of college preparatory work. *Application deadlines:* 2/1 (freshmen), 6/1 (transfers), 12/1 (early action). *Notification:* 3/31 (freshmen), continuous (transfers), 1/31 (early action).

Freshman Application Contact Ms. Joanne Lynch, Assistant Dean of Admissions, University of Rhode Island, Undergraduate Admission Office, Newman Hall, 14 Upper College Road, Kingston, RI 02881. *Phone:* 401-874-7110. *Fax:* 401-874-5523. *E-mail:* lynch@uri.edu. *Web site:* http://www.uri.edu/.

See page 1732 for the College Close-Up.

SOUTH CAROLINA

Allen University
Columbia, South Carolina

- **Independent African Methodist Episcopal** 4-year, founded 1870
- **Suburban** campus
- **Coed**
- **Minimally difficult** entrance level

Academics *Calendar:* semesters. *Degree:* bachelor's.

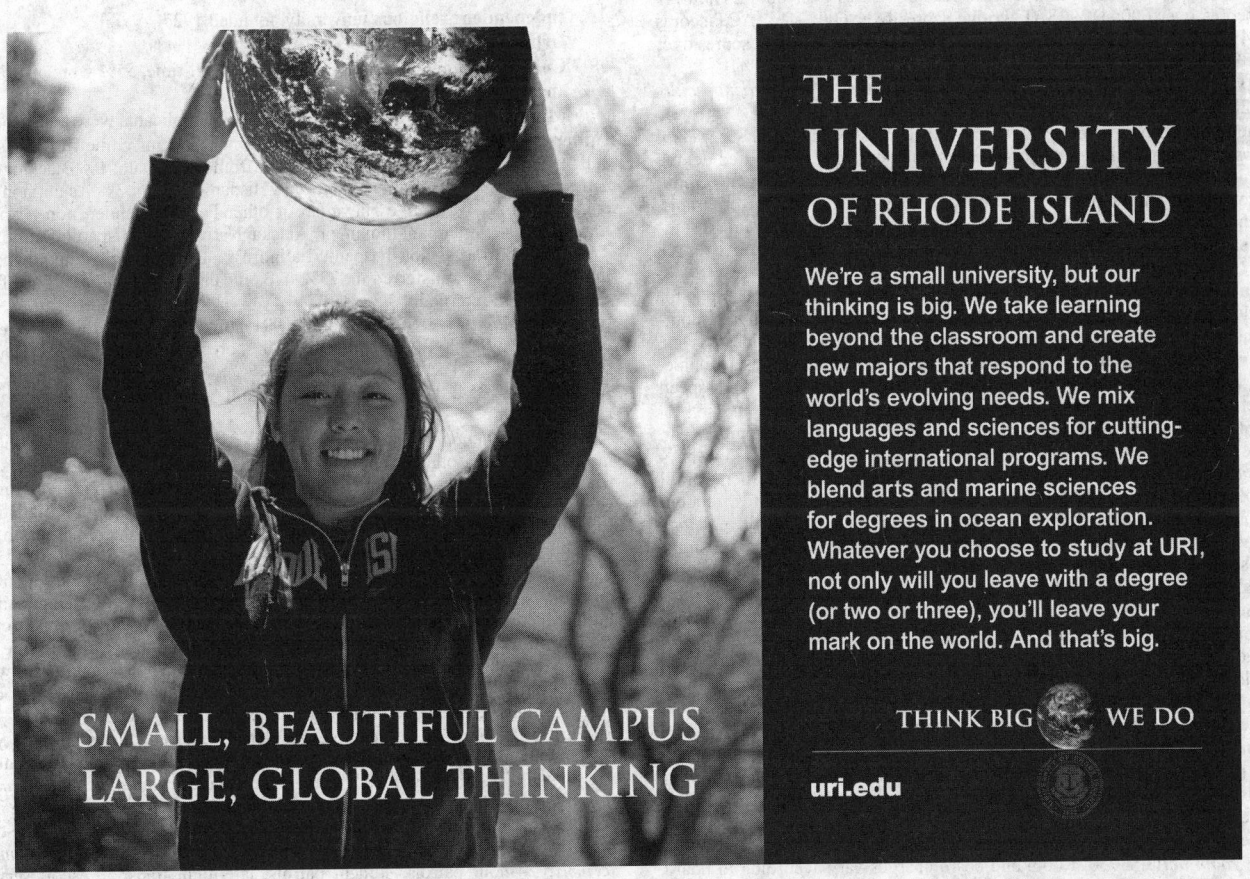

SMALL, BEAUTIFUL CAMPUS
LARGE, GLOBAL THINKING

THE
UNIVERSITY
OF RHODE ISLAND

We're a small university, but our thinking is big. We take learning beyond the classroom and create new majors that respond to the world's evolving needs. We mix languages and sciences for cutting-edge international programs. We blend arts and marine sciences for degrees in ocean exploration. Whatever you choose to study at URI, not only will you leave with a degree (or two or three), you'll leave your mark on the world. And that's big.

THINK BIG   WE DO

uri.edu

Student Life *Campus security:* 24-hour emergency response devices and patrols, controlled dormitory access.

Athletics Member NAIA.

Standardized Tests *Recommended:* SAT or ACT (for admission).

Costs (2010–11) *Comprehensive fee:* $16,124 includes full-time tuition ($10,884) and room and board ($5240). Part-time tuition: $450 per credit hour.

Financial Aid *Of all full-time matriculated undergraduates who enrolled in 2003,* 552 applied for aid, 442 were judged to have need, 54 had their need fully met. 160 Federal Work-Study jobs (averaging $1000). *In 2003,* 3 non-need-based awards were made. *Average percent of need met:* 74. *Average financial aid package:* $8081. *Average need-based loan:* $4833. *Average need-based gift aid:* $2213. *Average non-need-based aid:* $3609. *Average indebtedness upon graduation:* $13,037.

Applying *Options:* electronic application. *Application fee:* $20. *Required:* essay or personal statement, high school transcript, 2 letters of recommendation.

Freshman Application Contact Terri Parker, Director of Admission, Allen University, 1530 Harden Street, Columbia, SC 29204. *Phone:* 803-376-5733. *Toll-free phone:* 877-625-5368. *E-mail:* tparker@allenuniversity.edu. *Web site:* http://www.allenuniversity.edu/.

Anderson University
Anderson, South Carolina

- **Independent Baptist** comprehensive, founded 1911
- **Suburban** 271-acre campus with easy access to Greenville
- **Endowment** $22.6 million
- **Coed** 2,334 undergraduate students, 81% full-time, 68% women, 32% men
- **Minimally difficult** entrance level, 68% of applicants were admitted

Undergraduates 1,883 full-time, 451 part-time. Students come from 28 states and territories; 24 other countries; 15% are from out of state; 12% Black or African American, non-Hispanic/Latino; 2% Hispanic/Latino; 0.9% Asian, non-Hispanic/Latino; 0.9% Native Hawaiian or other Pacific Islander, non-Hispanic/Latino; 0.2% American Indian or Alaska Native, non-Hispanic/Latino; 1% Race/ethnicity unknown; 2% international; 4% transferred in; 55% live on campus. *Retention:* 70% of full-time freshmen returned.

Freshmen *Admission:* 1,926 applied, 1,319 admitted, 515 enrolled. *Average high school GPA:* 3.28. *Test scores:* SAT critical reading scores over 500: 61%; SAT math scores over 500: 62%; SAT writing scores over 500: 55%; ACT scores over 18: 90%; SAT critical reading scores over 600: 23%; SAT math scores over 600: 18%; SAT writing scores over 600: 15%; ACT scores over 24: 37%; SAT critical reading scores over 700: 3%; SAT math scores over 700: 1%; SAT writing scores over 700: 1%; ACT scores over 30: 3%.

Faculty *Total:* 254, 31% full-time, 39% with terminal degrees. *Student/faculty ratio:* 20:1.

Academics *Calendar:* semesters. *Degrees:* bachelor's and master's. *Special study options:* academic remediation for entering students, accelerated degree program, adult/continuing education programs, advanced placement credit, cooperative education, distance learning, double majors, honors programs, independent study, internships, part-time degree program, services for LD students, study abroad, summer session for credit. *ROTC:* Army (c), Air Force (c).

Computers on Campus 192 computers/terminals are available on campus for general student use. Students can access the following: campus intranet, computer help desk, free student e-mail accounts, online (class) grades, online (class) registration, online (class) schedules. Campuswide network is available. 100% of college-owned or -operated housing units are wired for high-speed Internet access. Wireless service is available via entire campus.

Student Life *Housing:* on-campus residence required through sophomore year. *Options:* men-only, women-only. Campus housing is university owned. *Activities and organizations:* drama/theater group, student-run newspaper, choral group, Baptist Campus Ministries, Fellowship of Christian Athletes, Student Government Association, Gamma Beta Phi, Student Alumni Council. *Campus security:* 24-hour emergency response devices and patrols, late-night transport/escort service, controlled dormitory access. *Student services:* health clinic, personal/psychological counseling.

Athletics Member NCAA. All Division II. *Intercollegiate sports:* baseball M(s), basketball M(s)/W(s), cheerleading W(s), cross-country running M(s)/W(s), golf M(s)/W(s), soccer M(s)/W(s), softball W(s), tennis M(s)/W(s), track and field M(s)/W(s), volleyball W(s), wrestling M(s). *Intramural sports:* basketball M/W, football M/W, racquetball M/W, softball M/W, table tennis M/W, ultimate Frisbee M/W, volleyball M/W, weight lifting M.

Standardized Tests *Required:* SAT or ACT (for admission).

Costs (2011–12) *Comprehensive fee:* $30,395 includes full-time tuition ($20,910), mandatory fees ($1660), and room and board ($7825). Full-time tuition and fees vary according to course load and program. Part-time tuition: $480 per credit hour. Part-time tuition and fees vary according to program. *College room only:* $3950. Room and board charges vary according to board plan and housing facility. *Payment plan:* installment. *Waivers:* employees or children of employees.

Financial Aid *Financial aid deadline:* 7/30.

Applying *Options:* electronic application, deferred entrance. *Application fee:* $25. *Required:* high school transcript. *Required for some:* essay or personal statement, 2 letters of recommendation, interview. *Recommended:* minimum 2.5 GPA. *Application deadline:* 7/1 (freshmen). *Notification:* continuous (freshmen), continuous (transfers).

Freshman Application Contact Mrs. Pam Bryant-Ross, Anderson University, 316 Boulevard, Anderson, SC 29621-4035. *Phone:* 864-231-2030. *Toll-free phone:* 800-542-3594. *Web site:* http://www.andersonuniversity.edu/.

The Art Institute of Charleston
Charleston, South Carolina

- **Proprietary** 4-year, founded 2007, part of Education Management Corporation
- **Urban** campus
- **Coed**

Academics *Calendar:* quarters. *Degrees:* certificates, associate, and bachelor's.

Costs (2010–11) *Tuition:* Tuition cost varies by program. Prospective students should contact the school for current tuition costs. Other charges include a starting kit for all first-quarter students. Kits vary in price, depending on the program of study.

Freshman Application Contact The Art Institute of Charleston, 24 North Market Street, Charleston, SC 29401. *Phone:* 843-727-3500. *Toll-free phone:* 866-211-0107. *Web site:* http://www.artinstitutes.edu/charleston/.

See page 1028 for the College Close-Up.

Benedict College
Columbia, South Carolina

Freshman Application Contact Benedict College, 1600 Harden Street, Columbia, SC 29204. *Phone:* 803-705-4491. *Toll-free phone:* 800-868-6598. *Web site:* http://www.benedict.edu/.

Bob Jones University
Greenville, South Carolina

- **Independent religious** university, founded 1927
- **Urban** 225-acre campus
- **Coed** 3,317 undergraduate students, 98% full-time, 55% women, 45% men
- **Minimally difficult** entrance level, 75% of applicants were admitted

Undergraduates 3,235 full-time, 82 part-time. Students come from 57 states and territories; 47 other countries; 69% are from out of state; 1% Black or African American, non-Hispanic/Latino; 2% Hispanic/Latino; 3% Asian, non-Hispanic/Latino; 0.4% Native Hawaiian or other Pacific Islander, non-Hispanic/Latino; 0.2% American Indian or Alaska Native, non-Hispanic/Latino; 3% Two or more races, non-Hispanic/Latino; 3% Race/ethnicity unknown; 4% international; 4% transferred in; 73% live on campus. *Retention:* 75% of full-time freshmen returned.

Freshmen *Admission:* 1,329 applied, 991 admitted, 642 enrolled. *Average high school GPA:* 3.42. *Test scores:* ACT scores over 18: 100%; ACT scores over 24: 46%; ACT scores over 30: 7%.

Faculty *Total:* 354, 65% full-time, 31% with terminal degrees. *Student/faculty ratio:* 13:1.

Academics *Calendar:* semesters. *Degrees:* certificates, associate, bachelor's, master's, doctoral-other, doctoral-research/scholarship, and post-master's certificates. *Special study options:* accelerated degree program, adult/continuing education programs, advanced placement credit, distance learning, English as a second language, internships, off-campus study, part-time degree program, services for LD students, summer session for credit.

Computers on Campus 450 computers/terminals and 500 ports are available on campus for general student use. Students can access the following: campus intranet, computer help desk, free student e-mail accounts, online (class) grades, online (class) registration, online (class) schedules. Campuswide network is available. 100% of college-owned or -operated housing units are wired for high-speed Internet access. Wireless service is available via classrooms, computer labs, dorm rooms, learning centers, libraries, student centers.

Student Life *Housing:* on-campus residence required through senior year. *Options:* men-only, women-only, disabled students. Campus housing is university owned. Freshman campus housing is guaranteed. *Activities and organizations:* drama/theater group, student-run newspaper, radio and television station, choral group, Community Relations Council, Extension Ministries, Societies, Mission Prayer Band, University Business Association. *Campus security:* 24-hour patrols, student patrols, late-night transport/escort service, controlled dormitory access, 24/7 emergency dispatcher. *Student services:* health clinic, personal/psychological counseling.

Athletics *Intramural sports:* badminton M/W, basketball M/W, cheerleading W, racquetball M, soccer M/W, softball M/W, table tennis M/W, tennis M/W, volleyball M/W, water polo W.

Standardized Tests *Required:* ACT (for admission).

Costs (2011–12) *One-time required fee:* $610. *Comprehensive fee:* $17,220 includes full-time tuition ($12,120) and room and board ($5100). Part-time tuition: $576 per unit. *Payment plan:* installment. *Waivers:* senior citizens and employees or children of employees.

Financial Aid Of all full-time matriculated undergraduates who enrolled in 2009, 2,425 applied for aid, 2,267 were judged to have need, 61 had their need fully met. *Average financial aid package:* $9400. *Average need-based loan:* $3930. *Average need-based gift aid:* $7000. *Average indebtedness upon graduation:* $28,000.

Applying *Options:* electronic application. *Required:* essay or personal statement, high school transcript, 3 letters of recommendation. *Application deadlines:* 8/1 (freshmen), 8/1 (transfers).

Freshman Application Contact Mr. Gary Deedrick, Director of Admissions, Bob Jones University, 1700 Wade Hampton Boulevard, Greenville, SC 29614. *Phone:* 864-242-5100. *Toll-free phone:* 800-BJANDME. *Fax:* 800-232-9258. *E-mail:* admission@bju.edu. *Web site:* http://www.bju.edu/.

Brown Mackie College–Greenville

Greenville, South Carolina

- **Proprietary** primarily 2-year
- **Coed**

Academics *Degrees:* certificates, associate, and bachelor's.

Costs (2010–11) *Tuition:* Tuition varies by program. Students should contact Brown Mackie College for tuition information.

Freshman Application Contact Brown Mackie College–Greenville, Two Liberty Square, 75 Beattie Place, Suite 100, Greenville, SC 29601. *Phone:* 864-239-5300. *Toll-free phone:* 877-479-8465. *Web site:* http://www.brownmackie.edu/greenville/.

See page 1144 for the College Close-Up.

Charleston Southern University

Charleston, South Carolina

Freshman Application Contact Mr. Jim Rhoden, Director of Enrollment Management, Charleston Southern University, Charleston, SC 29423-8087. *Phone:* 843-863-7050. *Toll-free phone:* 800-947-7474. *E-mail:* enroll@csuniv.edu. *Web site:* http://www.charlestonsouthern.edu/.

The Citadel, The Military College of South Carolina

Charleston, South Carolina

- **State-supported** comprehensive, founded 1842
- **Suburban** 300-acre campus
- **Endowment** $48.1 million
- **Coed, primarily men** 2,455 undergraduate students, 94% full-time, 9% women, 91% men
- **Moderately difficult** entrance level, 57% of applicants were admitted

Undergraduates 2,299 full-time, 156 part-time. Students come from 45 states and territories; 12 other countries; 48% are from out of state; 3% transferred in; 100% live on campus. *Retention:* 80% of full-time freshmen returned.

Freshmen *Admission:* 2,426 applied, 1,384 admitted, 626 enrolled. *Average high school GPA:* 3.38. *Test scores:* SAT critical reading scores over 500: 65%; SAT math scores over 500: 75%; ACT scores over 18: 95%; SAT critical reading scores over 600: 22%; SAT math scores over 600: 24%; ACT scores over 24: 24%; SAT critical reading scores over 700: 3%; SAT math scores over 700: 3%; ACT scores over 30: 1%.

Faculty *Total:* 240, 71% full-time, 80% with terminal degrees. *Student/faculty ratio:* 14:1.

Academics *Calendar:* semesters. *Degrees:* bachelor's, master's, and post-master's certificates. *Special study options:* advanced placement credit, cooperative education, distance learning, double majors, English as a second language, honors programs, independent study, internships, off-campus study, services for LD students, study abroad, summer session for credit. *ROTC:* Army (b), Navy (b), Air Force (b).

Computers on Campus 350 computers/terminals are available on campus for general student use. Students can access the following: campus intranet, computer help desk, free student e-mail accounts, online (class) grades, online (class) registration, online (class) schedules. Campuswide network is available. Wireless service is available via classrooms, dorm rooms, libraries, student centers.

Student Life *Housing:* on-campus residence required through senior year. *Options:* coed. Campus housing is university owned. Freshman campus housing is guaranteed. *Activities and organizations:* student-run newspaper, choral group, marching band, The Republican Society, Semper Fi Society, HESS Majors, Rod & Gun Club, Cordell Airborne Rangers. *Campus security:* 24-hour patrols. *Student services:* health clinic, personal/psychological counseling.

Athletics Member NCAA. All Division I except football (Division I-AA). *Intercollegiate sports:* baseball M(s), basketball M(s), cross-country running M(s)/W(s), golf W(s), ice hockey M(c), lacrosse M(c), riflery M(s)/W(s), rugby M(c)/W(c), skiing (downhill) M(c)/W(c), soccer M(c), tennis M(s), track and field M(s)/W(s), volleyball W(s), wrestling M(s). *Intramural sports:* badminton M/W, basketball M/W, football M, golf M/W, racquetball M/W, soccer M/W, softball M/W, swimming and diving M/W, table tennis M/W, tennis M/W, track and field M/W, ultimate Frisbee M/W, volleyball M/W, weight lifting M/W, wrestling M/W.

Standardized Tests *Required:* SAT or ACT (for admission).

Costs (2010–11) *Tuition:* state resident $9871 full-time, $365 per credit part-time; nonresident $24,800 full-time, $640 per credit part-time. *Required fees:* $1149 full-time. *Room and board:* $5889. *Waivers:* senior citizens and employees or children of employees.

Financial Aid Of all full-time matriculated undergraduates who enrolled in 2009, 1,581 applied for aid, 1,189 were judged to have need, 360 had their need fully met. 34 Federal Work-Study jobs (averaging $1250). In 2009, 216 non-need-based awards were made. *Average percent of need met:* 71%. *Average financial aid package:* $14,910. *Average need-based loan:* $4361. *Average need-based gift aid:* $10,908. *Average non-need-based aid:* $9626. *Average indebtedness upon graduation:* $25,817.

Applying *Options:* electronic application. *Application fee:* $40. *Required:* high school transcript. *Recommended:* interview. *Application deadlines:* rolling (freshmen), rolling (transfers). *Notification:* continuous (freshmen), continuous (transfers).

Freshman Application Contact Lt. Col. John W. Powell Jr., Director of Admissions, The Citadel, The Military College of South Carolina, 171 Moultrie Street, Charleston, SC 29409. *Phone:* 843-953-5230. *Toll-free phone:* 800-868-1842. *Fax:* 843-953-7036. *E-mail:* john.powell@citadel.edu. *Web site:* http://www.citadel.edu/.

Claflin University

Orangeburg, South Carolina

- **Independent United Methodist** comprehensive, founded 1869
- **Small-town** 46-acre campus with easy access to Columbia
- **Endowment** $16.8 million
- **Coed** 1,831 undergraduate students, 96% full-time, 65% women, 35% men
- **Minimally difficult** entrance level, 35% of applicants were admitted

Undergraduates 1,755 full-time, 76 part-time. Students come from 28 states and territories; 13 other countries; 20% are from out of state; 93% Black or African American, non-Hispanic/Latino; 2% Hispanic/Latino; 0.2% Asian, non-Hispanic/Latino; 1% American Indian or Alaska Native, non-Hispanic/Latino; 0.3% Two or more races, non-Hispanic/Latino; 0.1% Race/ethnicity unknown; 2% international; 3% transferred in. *Retention:* 70% of full-time freshmen returned.

Freshmen *Admission:* 4,204 applied, 1,453 admitted, 423 enrolled. *Average high school GPA:* 3. *Test scores:* SAT critical reading scores over 500: 29%; SAT math scores over 500: 26%; SAT critical reading scores over 600: 6%; SAT math scores over 600: 6%.

Faculty *Total:* 158, 73% full-time, 65% with terminal degrees. *Student/faculty ratio:* 14:1.

Academics *Calendar:* semesters. *Degrees:* bachelor's and master's. *Special study options:* academic remediation for entering students, adult/continuing education programs, advanced placement credit, cooperative education, freshman honors college, honors programs, independent study, internships, off-campus study, part-time degree program, summer session for credit. *ROTC:* Army (c). *Unusual degree programs:* 3-2 engineering with Clemson University, South Carolina State University.

Computers on Campus 530 computers/terminals are available on campus for general student use. Students can access the following: computer help desk, free student e-mail accounts, online (class) grades, online (class) registration, online (class) schedules. Campuswide network is available. 100% of college-owned or -operated housing units are wired for high-speed Internet access. Wireless service is available via classrooms, computer centers, computer labs, learning centers, libraries, student centers.

Student Life *Housing options:* men-only, women-only. Campus housing is university owned. *Activities and organizations:* drama/theater group, student-run newspaper, radio and television station, choral group, national fraternities, national sororities. *Campus security:* 24-hour emergency response devices and patrols, student patrols, controlled dormitory access. *Student services:* health clinic, personal/psychological counseling.

Athletics Member NCAA. All Division II. *Intercollegiate sports:* baseball M(s)/W(s), basketball M(s)/W(s), cross-country running M(s)/W(s), softball W(s), track and field M(s)/W(s), volleyball W(s).

Standardized Tests *Required:* SAT or ACT (for admission). *Recommended:* SAT Subject Tests (for admission).

Costs (2010–11) *Comprehensive fee:* $20,250 includes full-time tuition ($11,044), mandatory fees ($2128), and room and board ($7078). Full-time tuition and fees vary according to class time. Part-time tuition: $338 per credit hour. Part-time tuition and fees vary according to class time. *Required fees:* $54 per credit hour part-time. *College room only:* $3156. Room and board charges vary according to housing facility. *Payment plans:* installment, deferred payment. *Waivers:* employees or children of employees.

Financial Aid Of all full-time matriculated undergraduates who enrolled in 2006, 1,517 applied for aid, 1,475 were judged to have need, 144 had their need fully met. In 2006, 300 non-need-based awards were made. *Average percent of need met:* 56%. *Average financial aid package:* $10,917. *Average need-based loan:* $3734. *Average need-based gift aid:* $8220. *Average non-need-based aid:* $17,712. *Average indebtedness upon graduation:* $19,993.

Applying *Options:* electronic application, deferred entrance. *Application fee:* $21. *Required:* essay or personal statement, high school transcript, minimum 2 GPA. *Application deadlines:* rolling (freshmen), rolling (transfers). *Notification:* continuous (freshmen), continuous (transfers).

Freshman Application Contact Claflin University, 400 Magnolia Street, Orangeburg, SC 29115. *Phone:* 803-5355340. *Toll-free phone:* 800-922-1276. *Web site:* http://www.claflin.edu/.

Clemson University

Clemson, South Carolina

- **State-supported** university, founded 1889
- **Small-town** 1400-acre campus
- **Endowment** $301.2 million
- **Coed** 14,713 undergraduate students, 94% full-time, 46% women, 54% men
- **Moderately difficult** entrance level, 63% of applicants were admitted

Undergraduates 13,780 full-time, 933 part-time. Students come from 53 states and territories; 84 other countries; 29% are from out of state; 7% transferred in; 37% live on campus. *Retention:* 92% of full-time freshmen returned.

Freshmen *Admission:* 16,282 applied, 10,224 admitted, 2,923 enrolled. *Average high school GPA:* 3.89. *Test scores:* SAT critical reading scores over 500: 92%; SAT math scores over 500: 96%; ACT scores over 18: 99%; SAT critical reading scores over 600: 51%; SAT math scores over 600: 71%; ACT scores over 24: 86%; SAT critical reading scores over 700: 9%; SAT math scores over 700: 17%; ACT scores over 30: 27%.

Faculty *Total:* 1,277, 87% full-time. *Student/faculty ratio:* 14:1.

Academics *Calendar:* semesters. *Degrees:* bachelor's, master's, doctoral-research/scholarship, and post-master's certificates. *Special study options:* academic remediation for entering students, advanced placement credit, cooperative education, distance learning, double majors, honors programs, independent study, internships, part-time degree program, services for LD students, study abroad, summer session for credit. *ROTC:* Army (b), Air Force (b).

Computers on Campus 1,250 computers/terminals are available on campus for general student use. Students can access the following: online (class) registration. Campuswide network is available. 100% of college-owned or -operated housing units are wired for high-speed Internet access. Wireless service is available via entire campus.

Student Life *Housing:* on-campus residence required for freshman year. *Options:* coed, men-only, women-only. Campus housing is university owned. Freshman campus housing is guaranteed. *Activities and organizations:* drama/theater group, student-run newspaper, radio and television station, choral group, marching band, student government, Fellowship of Christian Athletes, Tiger Band, national fraternities, national sororities. *Campus security:* 24-hour emergency response devices and patrols, late-night transport/escort service, controlled dormitory access. *Student services:* health clinic, personal/psychological counseling, legal services.

Athletics Member NCAA. All Division I except football (Division I-A). *Intercollegiate sports:* baseball M, basketball M(s)/W(s), bowling M(c)/W(c), cheerleading M/W, crew M(c)/W(s), cross-country running M(s)/W(s), equestrian sports M(c)/W(c), fencing M(c)/W(c), field hockey M(c)/W(c), golf M(s), ice hockey M(c)/W(c), lacrosse M(c)/W(c), riflery M(c)/W(c), rugby M(c)/W(c), sailing M(c)/W(c), soccer M(s)/W(s), softball W(c), swimming and diving M(s)/W(s), tennis M(s)/W(s), track and field M(s)/W(s), ultimate Frisbee M(c)/W(c), volleyball M(c)/W(s), weight lifting M(c)/W(c), wrestling M(c). *Intramural sports:* basketball M/W, golf M/W, racquetball M/W, soccer M/W, softball M/W, swimming and diving M(c)/W(c), table tennis M/W, tennis M(c)/W(c), volleyball M/W, water polo M/W.

Standardized Tests *Required:* SAT or ACT (for admission).

Costs (2010–11) *One-time required fee:* $1300. *Tuition:* state resident $12,346 full-time, $499 per credit hour part-time; nonresident $27,858 full-time, $1171

per credit hour part-time. Full-time tuition and fees vary according to course load, location, and program. Part-time tuition and fees vary according to program. *Required fees:* $9 per credit hour part-time, $4 per term part-time. *Room and board:* Room and board charges vary according to board plan, housing facility, and location. *Payment plan:* installment. *Waivers:* senior citizens. **Financial Aid** Of all full-time matriculated undergraduates who enrolled in 2009, 8,608 applied for aid, 6,722 were judged to have need, 1,407 had their need fully met. 589 Federal Work-Study jobs (averaging $2346). 3,700 state and other part-time jobs (averaging $2100). In 2009, 2617 non-need-based awards were made. *Average percent of need met:* 57%. *Average financial aid package:* $11,253. *Average need-based loan:* $4285. *Average need-based gift aid:* $4778. *Average non-need-based aid:* $2360. *Average indebtedness upon graduation:* $18,463.
Applying *Options:* electronic application. *Application fee:* $50. *Required:* high school transcript. *Recommended:* essay or personal statement. *Application deadlines:* 5/1 (freshmen), 7/1 (transfers). *Notification:* continuous (freshmen), continuous (transfers).
Freshman Application Contact Ms. Audrey R. Bodell, Associate Director of Admissions, Clemson University, PO Box 345124, 105 Sikes Hall, Clemson, SC 29634. *Phone:* 864-656-2287. *Fax:* 864-656-2464. *E-mail:* cuadmissions@clemson.edu. *Web site:* http://www.clemson.edu/.

See page 1222 for the College Close-Up.

Coastal Carolina University
Conway, South Carolina

- **State-supported** comprehensive, founded 1954
- **Suburban** 631-acre campus
- **Endowment** $28.0 million
- **Coed** 8,203 undergraduate students, 92% full-time, 53% women, 47% men
- **Moderately difficult** entrance level, 74% of applicants were admitted

Undergraduates 7,539 full-time, 664 part-time. Students come from 47 states and territories; 43 other countries; 48% are from out of state; 18% Black or African American, non-Hispanic/Latino; 3% Hispanic/Latino; 0.8% Asian, non-Hispanic/Latino; 0.1% Native Hawaiian or other Pacific Islander, non-Hispanic/Latino; 0.3% American Indian or Alaska Native, non-Hispanic/Latino; 2% Two or more races, non-Hispanic/Latino; 0.3% Race/ethnicity unknown; 1% international; 10% transferred in; 40% live on campus. *Retention:* 65% of full-time freshmen returned.
Freshmen *Admission:* 9,639 applied, 7,170 admitted, 2,006 enrolled. *Average high school GPA:* 3.34. *Test scores:* SAT critical reading scores over 500: 44%; SAT math scores over 500: 57%; ACT scores over 18: 86%; SAT critical reading scores over 600: 8%; SAT math scores over 600: 13%; ACT scores over 24: 12%; SAT critical reading scores over 700: 1%; SAT math scores over 700: 1%.
Faculty *Total:* 613, 56% full-time, 54% with terminal degrees. *Student/faculty ratio:* 17:1.
Academics *Calendar:* semesters. *Degrees:* bachelor's, master's, and post-bachelor's certificates. *Special study options:* accelerated degree program, adult/continuing education programs, advanced placement credit, cooperative education, distance learning, double majors, honors programs, independent study, internships, part-time degree program, services for LD students, student-designed majors, study abroad, summer session for credit. *ROTC:* Army (b).
Computers on Campus 700 computers/terminals are available on campus for general student use. Students can access the following: computer help desk, free student e-mail accounts, online (class) grades, online (class) registration, online (class) schedules. Campuswide network is available. Wireless service is available via classrooms, computer centers, computer labs, dorm rooms, learning centers, libraries, student centers.
Student Life *Housing:* on-campus residence required through sophomore year. *Options:* coed, disabled students. Campus housing is university owned. Freshman applicants given priority for college housing. *Activities and organizations:* drama/theater group, student-run newspaper, radio station, choral group, marching band, Student Government Association, Campus Activities Board, STAR (Students Taking Active Responsibility), Refuge, Leadership Challenge, national fraternities, national sororities. *Campus security:* 24-hour emergency response devices and patrols, late-night transport/escort service. *Student services:* health clinic, personal/psychological counseling, women's center.
Athletics Member NCAA. All Division I. *Intercollegiate sports:* baseball M(s), basketball M(s)/W(s), cheerleading M(c)/W(c), cross-country running M(s)/W(s), equestrian sports M(c)/W(c), football M(s), golf M(s)/W(s), lacrosse M(c)/W(c), rugby M(c)/W(c), soccer M(s)/W(s), softball W(s), swimming and diving M(c)/W(c), tennis M(s)/W(s), track and field M(s)/W(s), volleyball M(c)/W(c), wrestling M(c). *Intramural sports:* badminton M/W, basketball M/W, football M/W, golf M/W, soccer M/W, softball M/W, table tennis M/W, volleyball M/W, water polo M/W.
Standardized Tests *Required:* SAT or ACT (for admission).

Costs (2010–11) *Tuition:* state resident $9310 full-time, $382 per credit hour part-time; nonresident $20,190 full-time, $830 per credit hour part-time. Full-time tuition and fees vary according to course load and degree level. Part-time tuition and fees vary according to course load and degree level. *Required fees:* $80 full-time. *Room and board:* $7350; room only: $4750. Room and board charges vary according to board plan and housing facility. *Payment plan:* installment. *Waivers:* senior citizens and employees or children of employees.
Financial Aid Of all full-time matriculated undergraduates who enrolled in 2008, 5,816 applied for aid, 4,679 were judged to have need, 485 had their need fully met. 103 Federal Work-Study jobs (averaging $939). 985 state and other part-time jobs (averaging $2220). In 2008, 1172 non-need-based awards were made. *Average percent of need met:* 48%. *Average financial aid package:* $8886. *Average need-based loan:* $8051. *Average need-based gift aid:* $5309. *Average non-need-based aid:* $11,090. *Average indebtedness upon graduation:* $31,907.
Applying *Options:* electronic application, deferred entrance. *Application fee:* $45. *Required:* high school transcript, minimum 2 GPA. *Recommended:* essay or personal statement, 1 letter of recommendation, interview. *Application deadlines:* 8/15 (freshmen), 8/15 (transfers). *Notification:* 9/15 (freshmen), continuous until 8/15 (transfers).
Freshman Application Contact Coastal Carolina University, PO Box 261954, Conway, SC 29528-6054. *Phone:* 843-349-2037. *Toll-free phone:* 800-277-7000. *Web site:* http://www.coastal.edu/.

Coker College
Hartsville, South Carolina

- **Independent** 4-year, founded 1908
- **Small-town** 30-acre campus with easy access to Charlotte
- **Coed** 678 undergraduate students, 97% full-time, 63% women, 37% men
- **Moderately difficult** entrance level, 52% of applicants were admitted

Undergraduates 656 full-time, 22 part-time. Students come from 26 states and territories; 10 other countries; 19% are from out of state; 27% Black or African American, non-Hispanic/Latino; 2% Hispanic/Latino; 0.1% Asian, non-Hispanic/Latino; 0.1% Native Hawaiian or other Pacific Islander, non-Hispanic/Latino; 0.7% American Indian or Alaska Native, non-Hispanic/Latino; 0.3% Race/ethnicity unknown; 3% international; 8% transferred in; 72% live on campus. *Retention:* 71% of full-time freshmen returned.
Freshmen *Admission:* 1,148 applied, 592 admitted, 189 enrolled. *Average high school GPA:* 3.37. *Test scores:* SAT critical reading scores over 500: 49%; SAT math scores over 500: 50%; ACT scores over 18: 82%; SAT critical reading scores over 600: 14%; SAT math scores over 600: 13%; ACT scores over 24: 18%; SAT critical reading scores over 700: 1%.
Faculty *Total:* 58. *Student/faculty ratio:* 12:1.
Academics *Calendar:* semesters. *Degrees:* bachelor's (also offers evening program with significant enrollment not reflected in profile). *Special study options:* adult/continuing education programs, distance learning, double majors, honors programs, independent study, internships, part-time degree program, student-designed majors, study abroad, summer session for credit.
Computers on Campus Students can access the following: campus intranet, free student e-mail accounts, online (class) grades, online (class) registration, online (class) schedules. Campuswide network is available. Wireless service is available via entire campus.
Student Life *Housing:* on-campus residence required through junior year. *Options:* coed. Campus housing is university owned. Freshman campus housing is guaranteed. *Activities and organizations:* drama/theater group, choral group, Student Government Association. *Campus security:* 24-hour patrols, late-night transport/escort service, controlled dormitory access.
Athletics Member NCAA. All Division II. *Intercollegiate sports:* baseball M(s), basketball M(s)/W(s), cross-country running M(s)/W(s), golf M(s), soccer M(s)/W(s), softball W(s), tennis M(s)/W(s), volleyball W(s). *Intramural sports:* basketball M/W, football M/W, table tennis M/W, track and field M/W, volleyball M/W, weight lifting M/W.
Standardized Tests *Required:* SAT or ACT (for admission).
Costs (2010–11) *Comprehensive fee:* $27,408 includes full-time tuition ($20,328), mandatory fees ($490), and room and board ($6590). Part-time tuition: $847 per semester hour. *College room only:* $3220. *Waivers:* employees or children of employees.
Financial Aid Of all full-time matriculated undergraduates who enrolled in 2009, 605 applied for aid, 564 were judged to have need, 165 had their need fully met. 98 Federal Work-Study jobs (averaging $974). In 2009, 50 non-need-based awards were made. *Average percent of need met:* 85%. *Average financial aid package:* $20,486. *Average need-based loan:* $4527. *Average need-based gift aid:* $7456. *Average non-need-based aid:* $7196. *Average indebtedness upon graduation:* $25,593. *Financial aid deadline:* 6/1.
Applying *Options:* electronic application, deferred entrance. *Application fee:* $15. *Application deadlines:* 8/1 (freshmen), rolling (transfers). *Notification:* 9/1 (freshmen).
Freshman Application Contact Director of Admissions, Coker College, 300 East College Avenue, Hartsville, SC 29550. *Phone:* 843-383-8050. *Toll-free*

phone: 800-950-1908. *Fax:* 843-383-8056. *E-mail:* admissions@coker.edu. *Web site:* http://www.coker.edu/.

College of Charleston
Charleston, South Carolina

- **State-supported** comprehensive, founded 1770
- **Urban** 52-acre campus
- **Endowment** $45.6 million
- **Coed** 10,121 undergraduate students, 93% full-time, 62% women, 38% men
- **Moderately difficult** entrance level, 70% of applicants were admitted

Undergraduates 9,397 full-time, 724 part-time. Students come from 50 states and territories; 62 other countries; 36% are from out of state; 6% Black or African American, non-Hispanic/Latino; 3% Hispanic/Latino; 2% Asian, non-Hispanic/Latino; 0.3% Native Hawaiian or other Pacific Islander, non-Hispanic/Latino; 0.4% American Indian or Alaska Native, non-Hispanic/Latino; 2% Two or more races, non-Hispanic/Latino; 2% Race/ethnicity unknown; 1% international; 8% transferred in; 32% live on campus. *Retention:* 82% of full-time freshmen returned.

Freshmen *Admission:* 11,280 applied, 7,896 admitted, 2,010 enrolled. *Average high school GPA:* 3.87. *Test scores:* SAT critical reading scores over 500: 98%; SAT math scores over 500: 98%; ACT scores over 18: 100%; SAT critical reading scores over 600: 55%; SAT math scores over 600: 55%; ACT scores over 24: 71%; SAT critical reading scores over 700: 7%; SAT math scores over 700: 6%; ACT scores over 30: 6%.

Faculty *Total:* 909, 58% full-time, 65% with terminal degrees. *Student/faculty ratio:* 16:1.

Academics *Calendar:* semesters. *Degrees:* bachelor's, master's, post-master's, and postbachelor's certificates (also offers graduate degree programs through University of Charleston, South Carolina). *Special study options:* accelerated degree program, adult/continuing education programs, advanced placement credit, cooperative education, distance learning, double majors, English as a second language, honors programs, independent study, internships, off-campus study, part-time degree program, services for LD students, study abroad, summer session for credit. *ROTC:* Air Force (c).

Computers on Campus 578 computers/terminals are available on campus for general student use. Students can access the following: computer help desk, free student e-mail accounts, online (class) registration, online (class) schedules. Campuswide network is available. 100% of college-owned or -operated housing units are wired for high-speed Internet access. Wireless service is available via entire campus.

Student Life *Housing options:* coed, men-only, women-only, disabled students. Campus housing is university owned. Freshman campus housing is guaranteed. *Activities and organizations:* drama/theater group, student-run newspaper, radio station, choral group, Student Government Association, Cougar Productions, intramural basketball, Black Student Union, national fraternities, national sororities. *Campus security:* 24-hour emergency response devices and patrols, student patrols, late-night transport/escort service, controlled dormitory access. *Student services:* health clinic, personal/psychological counseling, women's center, legal services.

Athletics Member NCAA. All Division I. *Intercollegiate sports:* baseball M(s), basketball M(s)/W(s), cross-country running M(s)/W(s), equestrian sports W, golf M(s)/W(s), sailing M/W, soccer M(s)/W(s), softball M/W(s), swimming and diving M(s)/W(s), tennis M(s)/W(s), track and field W(s), volleyball W(s). *Intramural sports:* badminton M/W, basketball M/W, crew M(c)/W(c), golf M(c)/W(c), gymnastics M(c)/W(c), ice hockey M(c), lacrosse M(c), racquetball M/W, rugby M(c)/W(c), soccer M/W, softball W, squash M(c)/W(c), swimming and diving M(c)/W(c), table tennis M/W, tennis M/W, ultimate Frisbee M/W, volleyball M/W, weight lifting M/W.

Standardized Tests *Required:* SAT or ACT (for admission).

Costs (2010–11) *Tuition:* state resident $10,314 full-time, $430 per semester hour part-time; nonresident $23,172 full-time, $965 per semester hour part-time. Full-time tuition and fees vary according to degree level. Part-time tuition and fees vary according to course load and degree level. *Room and board:* $9843; room only: $6743. Room and board charges vary according to board plan and housing facility. *Payment plan:* installment. *Waivers:* senior citizens.

Financial Aid Of all full-time matriculated undergraduates who enrolled in 2008, 5,407 applied for aid, 4,072 were judged to have need, 1,070 had their need fully met. In 2008, 1078 non-need-based awards were made. *Average percent of need met:* 63%. *Average financial aid package:* $12,882. *Average need-based loan:* $4008. *Average need-based gift aid:* $3173. *Average non-need-based aid:* $11,423. *Average indebtedness upon graduation:* $19,875.

Applying *Options:* electronic application, early action, deferred entrance. *Application fee:* $50. *Required:* essay or personal statement, high school transcript. *Application deadlines:* 4/1 (freshmen), 5/1 (transfers), 11/1 (early action). *Notification:* 5/15 (freshmen), 6/1 (transfers), 12/15 (early action).

Freshman Application Contact Ms. Suzette Stille, Director of Undergraduate Admissions, College of Charleston, 66 George Street, Charleston, SC 29424-0001. *Phone:* 843-953-5670. *Toll-free phone:* 843-953-5670. *Fax:* 843-953-6322. *E-mail:* admissions@cofc.edu. *Web site:* http://www.cofc.edu/.

Columbia College
Columbia, South Carolina

- **Independent United Methodist** comprehensive, founded 1854
- **Suburban** 33-acre campus
- **Endowment** $19.0 million
- **Undergraduate: women only; graduate: coed** 1,164 undergraduate students, 79% full-time, 98% women, 2% men
- **Moderately difficult** entrance level, 76% of applicants were admitted

Undergraduates 925 full-time, 239 part-time. Students come from 23 states and territories; 11 other countries; 10% are from out of state; 40% Black or African American, non-Hispanic/Latino; 2% Hispanic/Latino; 1% Asian, non-Hispanic/Latino; 0.4% American Indian or Alaska Native, non-Hispanic/Latino; 7% Race/ethnicity unknown; 1% international; 10% transferred in; 44% live on campus. *Retention:* 63% of full-time freshmen returned.

Freshmen *Admission:* 1,141 applied, 871 admitted, 214 enrolled. *Average high school GPA:* 3.5. *Test scores:* SAT critical reading scores over 500: 58%; SAT math scores over 500: 51%; SAT writing scores over 500: 47%; ACT scores over 18: 86%; SAT critical reading scores over 600: 20%; SAT math scores over 600: 19%; SAT writing scores over 600: 19%; ACT scores over 24: 32%; SAT critical reading scores over 700: 5%; SAT math scores over 700: 1%; SAT writing scores over 700: 3%; ACT scores over 30: 8%.

Faculty *Total:* 147, 49% full-time, 59% with terminal degrees. *Student/faculty ratio:* 12:1.

Academics *Calendar:* semesters. *Degrees:* bachelor's, master's, and doctoral-professional. *Special study options:* academic remediation for entering students, adult/continuing education programs, advanced placement credit, distance learning, double majors, honors programs, independent study, internships, off-campus study, part-time degree program, student-designed majors, study abroad, summer session for credit. *ROTC:* Army (c), Navy (c), Air Force (c).

Computers on Campus 150 computers/terminals are available on campus for general student use. Students can access the following: campus intranet, computer help desk, free student e-mail accounts, online (class) grades, online (class) registration, online (class) schedules. Campuswide network is available. 100% of college-owned or -operated housing units are wired for high-speed Internet access. Wireless service is available via student centers.

Student Life *Housing:* on-campus residence required through sophomore year. *Options:* women-only. Campus housing is university owned. Freshman campus housing is guaranteed. *Activities and organizations:* drama/theater group, student-run newspaper, choral group, Student Government Association, African-American Student Association, Columbia College Activities Board, Heavenly Creations Gospel Choir, Student Christian Association. *Campus security:* 24-hour emergency response devices and patrols, late-night transport/escort service, controlled dormitory access. *Student services:* health clinic, personal/psychological counseling, women's center.

Athletics Member NAIA. *Intercollegiate sports:* basketball W(s), soccer W(s), softball W(s), tennis W(s), volleyball W(s).

Standardized Tests *Required:* SAT or ACT (for admission).

Costs (2011–12) *Comprehensive fee:* $31,688 includes full-time tuition ($24,600), mandatory fees ($450), and room and board ($6638). Full-time tuition and fees vary according to class time. Part-time tuition: $660 per semester hour. Part-time tuition and fees vary according to course load. *Room and board:* Room and board charges vary according to board plan and housing facility. *Payment plan:* installment. *Waivers:* employees or children of employees.

Financial Aid Of all full-time matriculated undergraduates who enrolled in 2005, 794 applied for aid, 698 were judged to have need, 310 had their need fully met. 200 Federal Work-Study jobs (averaging $1000). In 2005, 152 non-need-based awards were made. *Average percent of need met:* 70%. *Average financial aid package:* $20,052. *Average need-based loan:* $3810. *Average need-based gift aid:* $8495. *Average non-need-based aid:* $7775. *Average indebtedness upon graduation:* $25,333.

Applying *Options:* electronic application. *Application fee:* $25. *Required:* high school transcript, minimum 2 GPA, 1 letter of recommendation. *Required for some:* interview. *Recommended:* essay or personal statement. *Application deadlines:* 8/1 (freshmen), 8/1 (transfers).

Freshman Application Contact Ms. Julie King, Director of Admissions, Columbia College, 1301 Columbia College Drive, Columbia, SC 29203. *Phone:* 803-786-3765. *Toll-free phone:* 800-277-1301. *Fax:* 803-786-3674. *E-mail:* admissions@colacoll.edu. *Web site:* http://www.columbiacollegesc.edu/.

Columbia International University
Columbia, South Carolina

- **Independent nondenominational** university, founded 1923
- **Suburban** 450-acre campus
- **Endowment** $3.8 million
- **Coed**
- **Minimally difficult** entrance level

Faculty *Student/faculty ratio:* 20:1.

Academics *Calendar:* semesters. *Degrees:* certificates, associate, bachelor's, master's, doctoral-other, and postbachelor's certificates.

Student Life *Campus security:* 24-hour emergency response devices and patrols, late-night transport/escort service.

Standardized Tests *Required:* SAT or ACT (for admission).

Costs (2010–11) *Comprehensive fee:* $23,805 includes full-time tuition ($16,850), mandatory fees ($545), and room and board ($6410). Full-time tuition and fees vary according to course load. Part-time tuition: $695 per credit. Part-time tuition and fees vary according to course load. *Required fees:* $273 per term part-time. *Room and board:* Room and board charges vary according to board plan.

Financial Aid *Of all full-time matriculated undergraduates who enrolled in 2008,* 318 applied for aid, 292 were judged to have need, 1 had their need fully met. 68 Federal Work-Study jobs (averaging $2500). *In 2008,* 93 non-need-based awards were made. *Average percent of need met:* 47. *Average financial aid package:* $6150. *Average need-based loan:* $4200. *Average non-need-based aid:* $4000. *Average indebtedness upon graduation:* $16,500.

Applying *Options:* electronic application, deferred entrance. *Application fee:* $45. *Required:* essay or personal statement, minimum 2 GPA, 4 letters of recommendation. *Required for some:* high school transcript, interview.

Freshman Application Contact Columbia International University, PO Box 3122, Columbia, SC 29230-3122. *Phone:* 803-807-5024. *Toll-free phone:* 800-777-2227 Ext. 3024. *Fax:* 803-786-4041. *E-mail:* yesciu@ciu.edu. *Web site:* http://www.ciu.edu/.

Converse College
Spartanburg, South Carolina

- **Independent** comprehensive, founded 1889
- **Urban** 70-acre campus
- **Endowment** $71.4 million
- **Undergraduate: women only; graduate: coed**
- **Moderately difficult** entrance level

Faculty *Student/faculty ratio:* 9:1.

Academics *Calendar:* 4-2-4. *Degrees:* bachelor's, master's, and post-master's certificates.

Student Life *Campus security:* 24-hour emergency response devices and patrols, late-night transport/escort service, controlled dormitory access.

Athletics Member NCAA. All Division II.

Standardized Tests *Required:* SAT or ACT (for admission).

Costs (2010–11) *One-time required fee:* $100. *Comprehensive fee:* $34,170 includes full-time tuition ($26,138) and room and board ($8032). Full-time tuition and fees vary according to program and reciprocity agreements. Part-time tuition: $825 per credit hour. Part-time tuition and fees vary according to program. *Room and board:* Room and board charges vary according to housing facility.

Financial Aid *Of all full-time matriculated undergraduates who enrolled in 2009,* 570 applied for aid, 538 were judged to have need, 127 had their need fully met. 107 Federal Work-Study jobs (averaging $1595). 60 state and other part-time jobs (averaging $1000). *In 2009,* 80 non-need-based awards were made. *Average percent of need met:* 78. *Average financial aid package:* $22,546. *Average need-based loan:* $4717. *Average need-based gift aid:* $18,918. *Average non-need-based aid:* $13,341. *Average indebtedness upon graduation:* $24,187.

Applying *Options:* electronic application, early admission, deferred entrance. *Required:* high school transcript, 1 letter of recommendation. *Recommended:* essay or personal statement, minimum 3 GPA, interview.

Freshman Application Contact Ms. April Lewis, Director of Admissions, Converse College, 580 East Main Street, Spartanburg, SC 29302. *Phone:* 864-596-9040 Ext. 9746. *Toll-free phone:* 800-766-1125. *Fax:* 864-596-9225. *E-mail:* admissions@converse.edu. *Web site:* http://www.converse.edu/.

ECPI College of Technology
Charleston, South Carolina

Admissions Office Contact ECPI College of Technology, 7410 Northside Drive, Suite 100, Charleston, SC 29420. *Toll-free phone:* 866-708-6166. *Web site:* http://www.ecpi.edu/.

ECPI College of Technology
Columbia, South Carolina

Admissions Office Contact ECPI College of Technology, 250 Berryhill Road, #300, Columbia, SC 29210. *Toll-free phone:* 866-708-6168 (in-state); 866-708-6768 (out-of-state). *Web site:* http://www.ecpi.edu/.

ECPI College of Technology
Greenville, South Carolina

Admissions Office Contact ECPI College of Technology, 1001 Keys Drive, #100, Greenville, SC 29615. *Toll-free phone:* 866-708-6171. *Web site:* http://www.ecpi.edu/.

Erskine College
Due West, South Carolina

- **Independent** comprehensive, founded 1839, affiliated with Associate Reformed Presbyterian Church, administratively affiliated with Erskine Theological Seminary
- **Rural** 90-acre campus
- **Endowment** $43.6 million
- **Coed** 553 undergraduate students, 98% full-time, 53% women, 47% men
- **Moderately difficult** entrance level, 75% of applicants were admitted

Undergraduates 541 full-time, 12 part-time. Students come from 19 states and territories; 8 other countries; 24% are from out of state; 8% Black or African American, non-Hispanic/Latino; 1% Hispanic/Latino; 1% Asian, non-Hispanic/Latino; 0.7% Two or more races, non-Hispanic/Latino; 16% Race/ethnicity unknown; 4% international; 3% transferred in; 89% live on campus. *Retention:* 77% of full-time freshmen returned.

Freshmen *Admission:* 500 applied, 373 admitted, 144 enrolled. *Test scores:* SAT critical reading scores over 500: 60%; SAT math scores over 500: 63%; ACT scores over 18: 95%; SAT critical reading scores over 600: 24%; SAT math scores over 600: 28%; ACT scores over 24: 45%; SAT critical reading scores over 700: 5%; SAT math scores over 700: 5%; ACT scores over 30: 8%.

Faculty *Total:* 70, 59% full-time, 59% with terminal degrees. *Student/faculty ratio:* 11:1.

Academics *Calendar:* 4-1-4. *Degrees:* certificates, bachelor's, master's, and doctoral-research/scholarship. *Special study options:* advanced placement credit, double majors, independent study, internships, off-campus study, part-time degree program, study abroad, summer session for credit. *Unusual degree programs:* 3-2 engineering with Clemson University, University of Tennessee, Knoxville; allied health programs with Medical University of South Carolina.

Computers on Campus Students can access the following: free student e-mail accounts. Campuswide network is available. Wireless service is available via classrooms, dorm rooms, libraries, student centers.

Student Life *Housing:* on-campus residence required through senior year. *Options:* men-only, women-only. Campus housing is university owned. Freshman campus housing is guaranteed. *Activities and organizations:* drama/theater group, student-run newspaper, radio station, choral group, literary societies, religious organizations, Student Government Organization, publications, honor societies. *Campus security:* 24-hour patrols, late-night transport/escort service, controlled dormitory access. *Student services:* health clinic, personal/psychological counseling.

Athletics Member NCAA. All Division II. *Intercollegiate sports:* baseball M(s), basketball M(s)/W(s), cross-country running M(s)/W(s), equestrian sports W(c), golf M(s)/W(s), lacrosse W(s), soccer M(s)/W(s), softball W(s), tennis M(s)/W(s), volleyball W(s). *Intramural sports:* basketball M/W, football M/W, soccer M/W, softball M/W, tennis M/W, volleyball M/W.

Standardized Tests *Required:* SAT or ACT (for admission).

Costs (2010–11) *Comprehensive fee:* $35,250 includes full-time tuition ($24,750), mandatory fees ($1725), and room and board ($8775). Part-time tuition: $917 per semester hour. *Payment plan:* installment. *Waivers:* children of alumni and employees or children of employees.

Financial Aid Of all full-time matriculated undergraduates who enrolled in 2008, 498 applied for aid, 400 were judged to have need, 156 had their need fully met. In 2008, 121 non-need-based awards were made. *Average percent of need met:* 86%. *Average financial aid package:* $21,093. *Average need-based loan:* $4750. *Average need-based gift aid:* $16,222. *Average non-need-based aid:* $10,725. *Average indebtedness upon graduation:* $24,450.

Applying *Options:* electronic application, early admission, early action, deferred entrance. *Application fee:* $25. *Required:* essay or personal statement, high school transcript, 1 letter of recommendation. *Recommended:* interview. *Application deadlines:* rolling (freshmen), rolling (transfers), 11/1 (early action). *Notification:* continuous (freshmen), continuous (transfers), 11/15 (early action).

Freshman Application Contact Erskine College, 2 Washington Street, PO Box 338, Due West, SC 29639. *Phone:* 864-379-8838. *Toll-free phone:* 800-241-8721. *Web site:* http://www.erskine.edu/.

Francis Marion University

Florence, South Carolina

- **State-supported** comprehensive, founded 1970
- **Rural** 400-acre campus
- **Endowment** $22.4 million
- **Coed** 3,771 undergraduate students, 90% full-time, 67% women, 33% men
- **Moderately difficult** entrance level, 60% of applicants were admitted

Undergraduates 3,410 full-time, 361 part-time. Students come from 33 states and territories; 15 other countries; 4% are from out of state; 46% Black or African American, non-Hispanic/Latino; 1% Hispanic/Latino; 1% Asian, non-Hispanic/Latino; 0.1% Native Hawaiian or other Pacific Islander, non-Hispanic/Latino; 0.5% American Indian or Alaska Native, non-Hispanic/Latino; 0.1% Two or more races, non-Hispanic/Latino; 3% Race/ethnicity unknown; 1% international; 8% transferred in; 39% live on campus. *Retention:* 68% of full-time freshmen returned.

Freshmen *Admission:* 3,596 applied, 2,142 admitted, 738 enrolled. *Average high school GPA:* 3.55. *Test scores:* SAT critical reading scores over 500: 42%; SAT math scores over 500: 45%; SAT writing scores over 500: 31%; ACT scores over 18: 81%; SAT critical reading scores over 600: 11%; SAT math scores over 600: 11%; SAT writing scores over 600: 5%; ACT scores over 24: 20%; SAT critical reading scores over 700: 1%; SAT math scores over 700: 1%; ACT scores over 30: 2%.

Faculty *Total:* 293, 69% full-time, 66% with terminal degrees. *Student/faculty ratio:* 15:1.

Academics *Calendar:* semesters. *Degrees:* bachelor's, master's, and postmaster's certificates. *Special study options:* accelerated degree program, adult/continuing education programs, advanced placement credit, distance learning, double majors, honors programs, independent study, internships, off-campus study, part-time degree program, services for LD students, study abroad, summer session for credit. *Unusual degree programs:* 3-2 engineering with Clemson University; forestry with Clemson University.

Computers on Campus 590 computers/terminals are available on campus for general student use. Students can access the following: computer help desk, online (class) registration, Blackboard. Campuswide network is available. 100% of college-owned or -operated housing units are wired for high-speed Internet access. Wireless service is available via classrooms, computer labs, dorm rooms, libraries.

Student Life *Housing options:* men-only, women-only, disabled students. Campus housing is provided by a third party. Freshman applicants given priority for college housing. *Activities and organizations:* drama/theater group, student-run newspaper, choral group, Baptist Collegiate Ministries, University Programming Board, National Pan-Hellenic Association, Student Alumni Association, Student Government Association, national fraternities, national sororities. *Campus security:* 24-hour emergency response devices and patrols, late-night transport/escort service, controlled dormitory access. *Student services:* health clinic, personal/psychological counseling.

Athletics Member NCAA. All Division II except golf (Division I), soccer (Division I). *Intercollegiate sports:* baseball M(s), basketball M(s)/W(s), cross-country running M(s)/W(s), golf M(s), soccer M(s)/W(s), softball W(s), tennis M(s)/W(s), track and field M/W, volleyball W(s). *Intramural sports:* basketball M/W, bowling M/W, cheerleading M(c)/W(c), football M/W, golf M/W, racquetball M/W, soccer M/W, softball M/W, table tennis M/W, tennis M/W, track and field M/W, ultimate Frisbee M/W, volleyball M/W.

Standardized Tests *Required:* SAT or ACT (for admission).

Costs (2010–11) *Tuition:* state resident $8145 full-time, $407 per credit hour part-time; nonresident $16,290 full-time, $815 per credit hour part-time. Part-time tuition and fees vary according to course load. *Required fees:* $335 full-time, $12 per credit hour part-time, $30 per term part-time. *Room and board:* $6380; room only: $3600. Room and board charges vary according to board plan and housing facility. *Payment plan:* installment. *Waivers:* senior citizens and employees or children of employees.

Financial Aid Of all full-time matriculated undergraduates who enrolled in 2009, 2,960 applied for aid, 2,723 were judged to have need. In 2009, 24 non-need-based awards were made. *Average non-need-based aid:* $2367. *Average indebtedness upon graduation:* $26,453.

Applying *Options:* electronic application, early admission, deferred entrance. *Application fee:* $30. *Required:* high school transcript, minimum 2 GPA. *Application deadlines:* rolling (freshmen), rolling (transfers). *Notification:* continuous (freshmen).

Freshman Application Contact Mrs. Perry Wilson, Director of Admissions, Francis Marion University, PO Box 100547, Florence, SC 29502-0547. *Phone:* 843-661-1231. *Toll-free phone:* 800-368-7551. *Fax:* 843-661-4635. *E-mail:* admission@fmarion.edu. *Web site:* http://www.fmarion.edu/.

Furman University

Greenville, South Carolina

- **Independent** comprehensive, founded 1826
- **Suburban** 800-acre campus
- **Endowment** $498.3 million
- **Coed** 2,761 undergraduate students, 94% full-time, 58% women, 42% men
- **Very difficult** entrance level, 70% of applicants were admitted

Undergraduates 2,586 full-time, 175 part-time. Students come from 46 states and territories; 47 other countries; 68% are from out of state; 6% Black or African American, non-Hispanic/Latino; 3% Hispanic/Latino; 2% Asian, non-Hispanic/Latino; 0.1% American Indian or Alaska Native, non-Hispanic/Latino; 1% Two or more races, non-Hispanic/Latino; 4% Race/ethnicity unknown; 1% international; 0.8% transferred in; 96% live on campus. *Retention:* 90% of full-time freshmen returned.

Freshmen *Admission:* 4,611 applied, 3,206 admitted, 688 enrolled. *Average high school GPA:* 3.8. *Test scores:* SAT critical reading scores over 500: 97%; SAT math scores over 500: 98%; SAT writing scores over 500: 94%; ACT scores over 18: 100%; SAT critical reading scores over 600: 70%; SAT math scores over 600: 69%; SAT writing scores over 600: 69%; ACT scores over 24: 93%; SAT critical reading scores over 700: 21%; SAT math scores over 700: 20%; SAT writing scores over 700: 21%; ACT scores over 30: 38%.

Faculty *Total:* 267, 88% full-time, 89% with terminal degrees. *Student/faculty ratio:* 11:1.

Academics *Calendar:* 3-2-3. *Degrees:* bachelor's, master's, and postbachelor's certificates. *Special study options:* accelerated degree program, adult/continuing education programs, advanced placement credit, double majors, independent study, internships, part-time degree program, services for LD students, student-designed majors, study abroad, summer session for credit. *ROTC:* Army (b). *Unusual degree programs:* 3-2 engineering with Georgia Institute of Technology, Clemson University, Auburn University, North Carolina State University, Washington University in St. Louis; forestry with Duke University.

Computers on Campus 425 computers/terminals and 3,500 ports are available on campus for general student use. Students can access the following: campus intranet, computer help desk, free student e-mail accounts, online (class) grades, online (class) registration, online (class) schedules. Campuswide network is available. 100% of college-owned or -operated housing units are wired for high-speed Internet access. Wireless service is available via entire campus.

Student Life *Housing:* on-campus residence required through senior year. *Options:* coed, men-only, women-only. Campus housing is university owned. Freshman campus housing is guaranteed. *Activities and organizations:* drama/theater group, student-run newspaper, radio and television station, choral group, marching band, Collegiate Educational Service Corps, Fellowship of Christian Athletes, Baptist Student Union, Student Activities Board, Furman Singers, national fraternities, national sororities. *Campus security:* 24-hour emergency response devices and patrols, student patrols, late-night transport/escort service, controlled dormitory access. *Student services:* health clinic, personal/psychological counseling, women's center.

Athletics Member NCAA. All Division I except football (Division I-AA). *Intercollegiate sports:* baseball M(s), basketball M(s)/W(s), cheerleading M/W, crew M(c)/W(c), cross-country running M(s)/W(s), equestrian sports W(c), fencing M(c)/W(c), golf M(s)/W(s), ice hockey M(c), lacrosse M(c)/W(c), rugby M(c)/W(c), soccer M(s)/W(s), softball W(s), swimming and diving M(c)/W(c), tennis M(s)/W(s), track and field M(s)/W(s), ultimate Frisbee M(c)/W(c), volleyball W(s), weight lifting M(c)/W(c), wrestling M(c). *Intramural sports:* basketball M/W, bowling M/W, cross-country running M/W, football M/W, golf M/W, racquetball M/W, soccer M/W, softball M/W, swimming and diving M/W, tennis M/W, track and field M/W, volleyball M/W.

Standardized Tests *Recommended:* SAT or ACT (for admission).

Costs (2010–11) *Comprehensive fee:* $47,660 includes full-time tuition ($37,728), mandatory fees ($360), and room and board ($9572). Part-time tuition: $1179 per credit. Part-time tuition and fees vary according to course load. *College room only:* $5198. Room and board charges vary according to board plan and housing facility. *Payment plan:* installment. *Waivers:* employees or children of employees.

Financial Aid Of all full-time matriculated undergraduates who enrolled in 2009, 1,487 applied for aid, 1,243 were judged to have need, 448 had their need fully met. 680 Federal Work-Study jobs (averaging $1446). In 2009, 801 non-need-based awards were made. *Average percent of need met:* 81%. *Average financial aid package:* $29,184. *Average need-based loan:* $4600. *Average need-based gift aid:* $23,124. *Average non-need-based aid:* $18,924. *Average indebtedness upon graduation:* $26,202. *Financial aid deadline:* 1/15.

Applying *Options:* electronic application, early admission, early decision. *Required:* essay or personal statement, high school transcript. *Required for some:* interview. *Application deadlines:* 1/15 (freshmen), 6/1 (transfers).

Early decision deadline: 11/15. *Notification:* 3/15 (freshmen), 6/15 (transfers), 12/15 (early decision).
Freshman Application Contact Mr. Brad Pochard, Director of Admissions, Furman University, 3300 Poinsett Highway, Greenville, SC 29613. *Phone:* 864-294-2034. *Fax:* 864-294-2018. *E-mail:* admissions@furman.edu. *Web site:* http://www.furman.edu/.

ITT Technical Institute
Columbia, South Carolina

- **Proprietary** primarily 2-year, part of ITT Educational Services, Inc.
- **Coed**

Academics *Degrees:* associate and bachelor's.
Student Life *Housing:* college housing not available.
Freshman Application Contact Director of Recruitment, ITT Technical Institute, 1628 Browning Road, Suite 180, Columbia, SC 29210. *Phone:* 803-216-6000. *Toll-free phone:* 800-242-5158. *Web site:* http://www.itt-tech.edu/.

ITT Technical Institute
Greenville, South Carolina

- **Proprietary** primarily 2-year, founded 1992, part of ITT Educational Services, Inc.
- **Coed**
- **Minimally difficult** entrance level

Academics *Calendar:* quarters. *Degrees:* associate and bachelor's.
Student Life *Housing:* college housing not available.
Financial Aid Of all full-time matriculated undergraduates who enrolled in 2009, 3 Federal Work-Study jobs.
Freshman Application Contact Director of Recruitment, ITT Technical Institute, 6 Independence Pointe, Greenville, SC 29615. *Phone:* 864-288-0777. *Toll-free phone:* 800-932-4488. *Web site:* http://www.itt-tech.edu/.

Lander University
Greenwood, South Carolina

Freshman Application Contact Dr. Bettie R. Horne, Director of Admissions, Lander University, Greenwood, SC 29649. *Phone:* 864-388-8307. *Toll-free phone:* 888-452-6337. *Fax:* 864-388-8125. *E-mail:* admissions@lander.edu. *Web site:* http://www.lander.edu/.

Limestone College
Gaffney, South Carolina

- **Independent** 4-year, founded 1845
- **Suburban** 117-acre campus with easy access to Charlotte
- **Endowment** $10.4 million
- **Coed** 859 undergraduate students, 98% full-time, 42% women, 58% men
- **Minimally difficult** entrance level, 59% of applicants were admitted

Undergraduates 842 full-time, 17 part-time. Students come from 26 states and territories; 17 other countries; 41% are from out of state; 20% Black or African American, non-Hispanic/Latino; 3% Hispanic/Latino; 0.6% Asian, non-Hispanic/Latino; 0.7% American Indian or Alaska Native, non-Hispanic/Latino; 2% Race/ethnicity unknown; 7% international; 10% transferred in; 51% live on campus. *Retention:* 65% of full-time freshmen returned.
Freshmen *Admission:* 1,328 applied, 777 admitted, 244 enrolled. *Average high school GPA:* 3.06. *Test scores:* SAT critical reading scores over 500: 37%; SAT math scores over 500: 44%; ACT scores over 18: 69%; SAT critical reading scores over 600: 7%; SAT math scores over 600: 8%; ACT scores over 24: 18%; SAT critical reading scores over 700: 1%.
Faculty *Total:* 80, 76% full-time, 70% with terminal degrees. *Student/faculty ratio:* 13:1.
Academics *Calendar:* semesters. *Degrees:* associate and bachelor's. *Special study options:* academic remediation for entering students, accelerated degree program, adult/continuing education programs, advanced placement credit, distance learning, double majors, honors programs, independent study, internships, part-time degree program, services for LD students, student-designed majors, summer session for credit. *ROTC:* Army (b).
Computers on Campus 98 computers/terminals are available on campus for general student use. Students can access the following: computer help desk, free student e-mail accounts, online (class) grades, online registration for Internet classes only. Campuswide network is available. 100% of college-owned or -operated housing units are wired for high-speed Internet access. Wireless service is available via classrooms, learning centers, libraries, student centers.
Student Life *Housing:* on-campus residence required through junior year. *Options:* men-only, women-only. Campus housing is university owned and leased by the school. Freshman applicants given priority for college housing. *Activities and organizations:* drama/theater group, choral group, Fellowship of

Christian Athletes, Student Government Association, Student Alumni Leadership Council, Students in Free Enterprise (SIFE), Limestone Activities Board. *Campus security:* 24-hour patrols, late-night transport/escort service, controlled dormitory access. *Student services:* health clinic, personal/psychological counseling.
Athletics Member NCAA. All Division II. *Intercollegiate sports:* baseball M(s), basketball M(s)/W(s), cross-country running M(s)/W(s), field hockey W(s), golf M(s)/W(s), lacrosse M(s)/W(s), soccer M(s)/W(s), softball W(s), swimming and diving M(s)/W(s), tennis M(s)/W(s), track and field M(s)/W(s), volleyball M(s)/W(s), wrestling M(s). *Intramural sports:* baseball M, bowling M/W, cheerleading M/W, softball M/W, table tennis M/W, volleyball M/W.
Standardized Tests *Required:* SAT or ACT (for admission).
Costs (2011–12) *Comprehensive fee:* $27,500 includes full-time tuition ($20,000) and room and board ($7500). Full-time tuition and fees vary according to class time, course load, and location. Part-time tuition: $835 per semester hour. Part-time tuition and fees vary according to class time, course load, and location. *College room only:* $3750. Room and board charges vary according to housing facility. *Payment plan:* installment. *Waivers:* employees or children of employees.
Financial Aid Of all full-time matriculated undergraduates who enrolled in 2008, 735 applied for aid, 660 were judged to have need, 100 had their need fully met. 172 Federal Work-Study jobs (averaging $1322). 66 state and other part-time jobs (averaging $824). In 2008, 165 non-need-based awards were made. *Average percent of need met:* 60%. *Average financial aid package:* $13,805. *Average need-based loan:* $3553. *Average need-based gift aid:* $10,565. *Average non-need-based aid:* $5200. *Average indebtedness upon graduation:* $28,939.
Applying *Options:* electronic application. *Application fee:* $25. *Required:* high school transcript, minimum 2 GPA. *Recommended:* 2 letters of recommendation, interview. *Application deadlines:* rolling (freshmen), rolling (out-of-state freshmen), rolling (transfers). *Notification:* continuous (freshmen), continuous (out-of-state freshmen), continuous (transfers).
Freshman Application Contact Ms. Sharon Chery, Admissions Office Manager, Limestone College, 1115 College Drive, Gaffney, SC 29340-3799. *Phone:* 864-488-4554. *Toll-free phone:* 800-795-7151 Ext. 554. *Fax:* 864-487-8706. *E-mail:* cphenicie@limestone.edu. *Web site:* http://www.limestone.edu/.

See page 1386 for the College Close-Up.

Medical University of South Carolina
Charleston, South Carolina

- **State-supported** upper-level, founded 1824
- **Urban** 80-acre campus
- **Endowment** $181.6 million
- **Coed** 237 undergraduate students, 86% full-time, 80% women, 20% men
- **Very difficult** entrance level

Undergraduates 203 full-time, 34 part-time. Students come from 23 states and territories; 10% are from out of state; 7% Black or African American, non-Hispanic/Latino; 4% Hispanic/Latino; 5% Asian, non-Hispanic/Latino; 0.9% American Indian or Alaska Native, non-Hispanic/Latino; 11% Race/ethnicity unknown.
Faculty *Total:* 227, 56% full-time, 78% with terminal degrees. *Student/faculty ratio:* 8:1.
Academics *Calendar:* semesters. *Degrees:* bachelor's, master's, doctoral-professional, doctoral-research/scholarship, post-master's, and postbachelor's certificates. *Special study options:* accelerated degree program, distance learning, internships, off-campus study, services for LD students. *ROTC:* Air Force (c).
Computers on Campus 200 computers/terminals are available on campus for general student use. Students can access the following: campus intranet, computer help desk, free student e-mail accounts, online (class) grades, online (class) registration, online (class) schedules. Campuswide network is available. Wireless service is available via entire campus.
Student Life *Housing:* college housing not available. *Activities and organizations:* choral group, MUSC Student Government Association, Multicultural Group Advisory Board, Public Health Interest Group, International Association, Crisis Ministries. *Campus security:* 24-hour emergency response devices and patrols, late-night transport/escort service. *Student services:* health clinic, personal/psychological counseling, legal services.
Athletics *Intramural sports:* basketball M/W, softball M/W, volleyball M/W.
Standardized Tests *Required for some:* SAT or ACT (for admission).
Costs (2010–11) *One-time required fee:* $485. *Tuition:* state resident $13,924 full-time, $630 per semester hour part-time; nonresident $22,266 full-time, $1030 per semester hour part-time. Full-time tuition and fees vary according to program. Part-time tuition and fees vary according to course load and program. *Required fees:* $1110 full-time, $938 per term part-time. *Payment plan:* installment. *Waivers:* minority students, adult students, senior citizens, and employees or children of employees.

Financial Aid Of all full-time matriculated undergraduates who enrolled in 2008, 210 applied for aid, 188 were judged to have need, 25 had their need fully met. In 2008, 1 non-need-based awards were made. *Average percent of need met:* 53%. *Average financial aid package:* $14,637. *Average need-based loan:* $10,158. *Average need-based gift aid:* $3471. *Average non-need-based aid:* $2500.

Applying *Options:* electronic application, deferred entrance. *Application fee:* $95.

Application Contact Lyla E. Hudson, Director of Admissions, Medical University of South Carolina, 41 Bee Street MSC203, Charleston, SC 29425-2030. *Phone:* 843-792-7408. *E-mail:* hudsonly@musc.edu. *Web site:* http://www.musc.edu/.

Morris College

Sumter, South Carolina

- **Independent** 4-year, founded 1908, affiliated with Baptist Educational and Missionary Convention of South Carolina
- **Small-town** 34-acre campus
- **Endowment** $11.3 million
- **Coed** 1,048 undergraduate students, 99% full-time, 56% women, 44% men
- **Noncompetitive** entrance level, 92% of applicants were admitted

Undergraduates 1,034 full-time, 14 part-time. Students come from 22 states and territories; 1 other country; 17% are from out of state; 99% Black or African American, non-Hispanic/Latino; 0.2% Hispanic/Latino; 0.2% Two or more races, non-Hispanic/Latino; 5% transferred in; 77% live on campus. *Retention:* 63% of full-time freshmen returned.

Freshmen *Admission:* 2,053 applied, 1,888 admitted, 321 enrolled. *Average high school GPA:* 2.45.

Faculty *Total:* 65, 74% full-time, 55% with terminal degrees. *Student/faculty ratio:* 19:1.

Academics *Calendar:* semesters. *Degree:* bachelor's. *Special study options:* academic remediation for entering students, accelerated degree program, adult/continuing education programs, advanced placement credit, cooperative education, double majors, honors programs, internships, summer session for credit. *ROTC:* Army (b). *Unusual degree programs:* 3-2 engineering with North Carolina Agricultural and Technical State University.

Computers on Campus 252 computers/terminals and 688 ports are available on campus for general student use. Students can access the following: campus intranet, free student e-mail accounts, online (class) grades, online (class) registration, online (class) schedules. Campuswide network is available. 100% of college-owned or -operated housing units are wired for high-speed Internet access. Wireless service is available via entire campus.

Student Life *Housing options:* men-only, women-only. Campus housing is university owned. Freshman applicants given priority for college housing. *Activities and organizations:* drama/theater group, student-run newspaper, radio station, choral group, Student Government Association, New Emphasis on Nontraditional Students, Block M Club, Pre Alumni Council, Baptist Student Union, national fraternities, national sororities. *Campus security:* 24-hour patrols, controlled dormitory access, cameras in select locations. *Student services:* health clinic, personal/psychological counseling.

Athletics Member NAIA. *Intercollegiate sports:* baseball M(s), basketball M(s)/W(s), cheerleading M(s)/W(s), cross-country running M(s)/W(s), golf M(s), softball W(s), tennis M(s)/W(s), track and field M(s)/W(s), volleyball W(s). *Intramural sports:* basketball M/W, football M/W, softball M/W, table tennis M/W, tennis M/W, volleyball M/W.

Costs (2010–11) *Comprehensive fee:* $14,787 includes full-time tuition ($10,015), mandatory fees ($275), and room and board ($4497). Part-time tuition: $417 per credit hour. *Required fees:* $63 per term part-time. *Payment plan:* installment.

Financial Aid Of all full-time matriculated undergraduates who enrolled in 2009, 887 applied for aid, 859 were judged to have need, 10 had their need fully met. 300 Federal Work-Study jobs (averaging $818). *Average percent of need met:* 85%. *Average financial aid package:* $12,100. *Average need-based loan:* $3900. *Average need-based gift aid:* $7400. *Average indebtedness upon graduation:* $17,125.

Applying *Options:* deferred entrance. *Application fee:* $20. *Required:* high school transcript, minimum 2 GPA, medical examination. *Required for some:* interview. *Application deadlines:* rolling (freshmen), rolling (out-of-state freshmen), rolling (transfers). *Notification:* continuous (freshmen), continuous (out-of-state freshmen), continuous (transfers).

Freshman Application Contact Ms. Deborah C. Calhoun, Director of Admissions and Records, Morris College, 100 West College Street, Sumter, SC 29150-3599. *Phone:* 803-934-3225. *Toll-free phone:* 866-853-1345. *Fax:* 803-773-8241. *E-mail:* dcalhoun@morris.edu. *Web site:* http://www.morris.edu/.

Newberry College

Newberry, South Carolina

- **Independent Evangelical Lutheran** 4-year, founded 1856
- **Small-town** 90-acre campus
- **Endowment** $20.8 million
- **Coed** 1,155 undergraduate students, 97% full-time, 45% women, 55% men
- **Moderately difficult** entrance level, 61% of applicants were admitted

Undergraduates 1,117 full-time, 38 part-time. Students come from 30 states and territories; 14 other countries; 16% are from out of state; 24% Black or African American, non-Hispanic/Latino; 3% Hispanic/Latino; 0.9% Asian, non-Hispanic/Latino; 0.3% American Indian or Alaska Native, non-Hispanic/Latino; 3% Two or more races, non-Hispanic/Latino; 0.6% Race/ethnicity unknown; 2% international; 68% live on campus. *Retention:* 61% of full-time freshmen returned.

Freshmen *Admission:* 1,206 applied, 736 admitted, 288 enrolled. *Average high school GPA:* 3.45. *Test scores:* SAT math scores over 500: 57%; SAT math scores over 600: 16%; SAT math scores over 700: 1%.

Faculty *Total:* 80, 73% full-time, 64% with terminal degrees. *Student/faculty ratio:* 17:1.

Academics *Calendar:* semesters. *Degree:* bachelor's. *Special study options:* academic remediation for entering students, accelerated degree program, adult/continuing education programs, advanced placement credit, cooperative education, distance learning, double majors, honors programs, independent study, internships, off-campus study, part-time degree program, services for LD students, student-designed majors, study abroad, summer session for credit. *ROTC:* Army (b). *Unusual degree programs:* 3-2 forestry with Duke University; law with Charleston School of Law, medical technology with Palmetto Baptist Medical Center.

Computers on Campus 20 computers/terminals are available on campus for general student use. Students can access the following: campus intranet, computer help desk, free student e-mail accounts, online (class) grades, online (class) registration, online (class) schedules. Campuswide network is available. 100% of college-owned or -operated housing units are wired for high-speed Internet access. Wireless service is available via entire campus.

Student Life *Housing:* on-campus residence required through senior year. *Options:* coed, men-only, women-only. Campus housing is university owned. Freshman applicants given priority for college housing. *Activities and organizations:* drama/theater group, student-run newspaper, radio and television station, choral group, marching band, Future Educators Association, Multi Cultural Student Association, American Chemistry Society, Blue key Honor Club, Baptist Collegiate Ministry, national fraternities, national sororities. *Campus security:* 24-hour emergency response devices and patrols, controlled dormitory access. *Student services:* health clinic, personal/psychological counseling.

Athletics Member NCAA. All Division II. *Intercollegiate sports:* baseball M(s), basketball M(s)/W(s), cheerleading W(s), cross-country running M(s)/W(s), football M(s), golf M(s)/W(s), soccer M(s)/W(s), softball W(s), tennis M(s)/W(s), volleyball W(s), wrestling M(s). *Intramural sports:* basketball M/W, football M.

Standardized Tests *Required:* SAT or ACT (for admission).

Costs (2010–11) *Comprehensive fee:* $32,143 includes full-time tuition ($21,500), mandatory fees ($2493), and room and board ($8150). Full-time tuition and fees vary according to class time, course load, and student level. Part-time tuition: $525 per credit hour. Part-time tuition and fees vary according to class time, course load, and student level. *Required fees:* $100 per term part-time. *College room only:* $4000. Room and board charges vary according to housing facility. *Payment plan:* installment. *Waivers:* employees or children of employees.

Financial Aid Of all full-time matriculated undergraduates who enrolled in 2009, 977 applied for aid, 895 were judged to have need, 219 had their need fully met. In 2009, 147 non-need-based awards were made. *Average percent of need met:* 76%. *Average financial aid package:* $20,440. *Average need-based loan:* $4474. *Average need-based gift aid:* $16,969. *Average non-need-based aid:* $11,552. *Average indebtedness upon graduation:* $30,693.

Applying *Options:* electronic application, deferred entrance. *Application fee:* $30. *Required:* high school transcript, minimum 2 GPA. *Required for some:* essay or personal statement. *Recommended:* 1 letter of recommendation, interview. *Application deadlines:* rolling (freshmen), rolling (transfers). *Notification:* continuous (freshmen), continuous (transfers).

Freshman Application Contact Mrs. Julie Nelson, Director of Admissions, Newberry College, 2100 College Street, Holland Hall, Newberry, SC 29108. *Phone:* 803-321-5131. *Toll-free phone:* 800-845-4955 Ext. 5127. *Fax:* 803-321-5138. *E-mail:* julie.nelson@newberry.edu. *Web site:* http://www.newberry.edu/.

North Greenville University

Tigerville, South Carolina

- **Independent Southern Baptist** comprehensive, founded 1892
- **Rural** 330-acre campus with easy access to Greenville
- **Endowment** $14.0 million
- **Coed** 2,152 undergraduate students, 89% full-time, 51% women, 49% men
- **Minimally difficult** entrance level, 59% of applicants were admitted

Undergraduates 1,926 full-time, 226 part-time. Students come from 34 states and territories; 15 other countries; 14% are from out of state; 7% Black or African American, non-Hispanic/Latino; 1% Hispanic/Latino; 0.3% Asian, non-Hispanic/Latino; 18% Race/ethnicity unknown; 0.7% international; 7% transferred in; 70% live on campus. *Retention:* 71% of full-time freshmen returned.

Freshmen *Admission:* 1,479 applied, 877 admitted, 482 enrolled. *Average high school GPA:* 3.6. *Test scores:* SAT critical reading scores over 500: 86%; SAT math scores over 500: 79%; SAT writing scores over 500: 84%; ACT scores over 18: 82%; SAT critical reading scores over 600: 39%; SAT math scores over 600: 33%; SAT writing scores over 600: 35%; ACT scores over 24: 32%; SAT critical reading scores over 700: 9%; SAT math scores over 700: 8%; SAT writing scores over 700: 9%; ACT scores over 30: 12%.

Faculty *Total:* 190, 66% full-time, 51% with terminal degrees. *Student/faculty ratio:* 14:1.

Academics *Calendar:* semesters. *Degrees:* bachelor's and master's. *Special study options:* academic remediation for entering students, accelerated degree program, advanced placement credit, cooperative education, distance learning, double majors, English as a second language, freshman honors college, honors programs, independent study, internships, part-time degree program, services for LD students, student-designed majors, study abroad, summer session for credit. *ROTC:* Army (c).

Computers on Campus 95 computers/terminals and 6 ports are available on campus for general student use. Students can access the following: campus intranet, computer help desk, free student e-mail accounts, online (class) grades, online (class) registration, online (class) schedules. Campuswide network is available. 100% of college-owned or -operated housing units are wired for high-speed Internet access. Wireless service is available via libraries, student centers.

Student Life *Housing:* on-campus residence required through sophomore year. *Options:* men-only, women-only. Campus housing is university owned. Freshman campus housing is guaranteed. *Activities and organizations:* drama/theater group, student-run newspaper, radio station, choral group, marching band, Baptist Student Union, Fellowship of Christians in Service, Fellowship of Christian Athletes, Black Student Fellowship, Education Club. *Campus security:* 24-hour emergency response devices and patrols, late-night transport/escort service, controlled dormitory access. *Student services:* health clinic, personal/psychological counseling.

Athletics Member NCAA, NCCAA. All NCAA Division II. *Intercollegiate sports:* baseball M(s), basketball M(s)/W(s), cheerleading M(s)/W(s), cross-country running M(s)/W(s), football M(s), golf M(s)/W(s), soccer M(s)/W(s), softball W(s), tennis M(s)/W(s), track and field M(s)/W(s), volleyball W(s). *Intramural sports:* basketball M/W, bowling M/W, football M, golf M/W, softball M/W, table tennis M/W, tennis M/W, ultimate Frisbee M/W, volleyball W, weight lifting M/W.

Standardized Tests *Required:* SAT or ACT (for admission). *Required for some:* CPT. *Recommended:* CPT.

Costs (2010–11) *Comprehensive fee:* $20,330 includes full-time tuition ($12,820) and room and board ($7510). Full-time tuition and fees vary according to course load. Part-time tuition: $220 per credit hour. *College room only:* $3470. Room and board charges vary according to housing facility. *Payment plan:* installment. *Waivers:* employees or children of employees.

Financial Aid Of all full-time matriculated undergraduates who enrolled in 2009, 1,800 applied for aid, 1,782 were judged to have need, 1,603 had their need fully met. *Average percent of need met:* 96%. *Average indebtedness upon graduation:* $18,200.

Applying *Options:* electronic application, early admission, deferred entrance. *Application fee:* $25. *Required:* high school transcript. *Required for some:* interview. *Recommended:* minimum 2 GPA. *Application deadlines:* 8/18 (freshmen), 8/21 (transfers). *Notification:* continuous (freshmen), continuous (transfers).

Freshman Application Contact North Greenville University, PO Box 1892, Tigerville, SC 29688-1892. *Phone:* 864-977-7052. *Toll-free phone:* 800-468-6642 Ext. 7001. *Web site:* http://www.ngu.edu/.

Presbyterian College

Clinton, South Carolina

- **Independent** comprehensive, founded 1880, affiliated with Presbyterian Church (U.S.A.)
- **Small-town** 240-acre campus with easy access to Greenville and Spartanburg
- **Endowment** $71.7 million
- **Coed** 1,188 undergraduate students, 97% full-time, 52% women, 48% men
- **Very difficult** entrance level, 68% of applicants were admitted

Undergraduates 1,154 full-time, 34 part-time. Students come from 34 states and territories; 6 other countries; 65% are from out of state; 9% Black or African American, non-Hispanic/Latino; 2% Hispanic/Latino; 0.6% Asian, non-Hispanic/Latino; 0.1% Native Hawaiian or other Pacific Islander, non-Hispanic/Latino; 0.3% American Indian or Alaska Native, non-Hispanic/Latino; 2% Two or more races, non-Hispanic/Latino; 0.3% Race/ethnicity unknown; 1% international; 2% transferred in; 98% live on campus. *Retention:* 84% of full-time freshmen returned.

Freshmen *Admission:* 1,499 applied, 1,012 admitted, 304 enrolled. *Average high school GPA:* 3.46. *Test scores:* SAT critical reading scores over 500: 72%; SAT math scores over 500: 79%; ACT scores over 18: 92%; SAT critical reading scores over 600: 23%; SAT math scores over 600: 37%; ACT scores over 24: 45%; SAT critical reading scores over 700: 3%; SAT math scores over 700: 4%; ACT scores over 30: 4%.

Faculty *Total:* 130, 77% full-time, 78% with terminal degrees. *Student/faculty ratio:* 12:1.

Academics *Calendar:* semesters. *Degrees:* bachelor's and doctoral-professional. *Special study options:* advanced placement credit, double majors, honors programs, independent study, internships, off-campus study, services for LD students, study abroad, summer session for credit. *ROTC:* Army (b). *Unusual degree programs:* 3-2 engineering with Auburn University, Clemson University, Vanderbilt University, University of South Carolina.

Computers on Campus 100 computers/terminals and 275 ports are available on campus for general student use. Students can access the following: campus intranet, free student e-mail accounts, online (class) grades, online (class) registration, online (class) schedules. Campuswide network is available. 100% of college-owned or -operated housing units are wired for high-speed Internet access. Wireless service is available via entire campus.

Student Life *Housing:* on-campus residence required through senior year. *Options:* coed, men-only, women-only, disabled students. Campus housing is university owned. Freshman campus housing is guaranteed. *Activities and organizations:* drama/theater group, student-run newspaper, radio station, choral group, Student Volunteer Services, intramural sports, Student Union Board, Fellowship of Christian Athletes, Student Government Association, national fraternities, national sororities. *Campus security:* 24-hour emergency response devices and patrols, late-night transport/escort service, controlled dormitory access. *Student services:* health clinic, personal/psychological counseling.

Athletics Member NCAA. All Division I. *Intercollegiate sports:* baseball M(s), basketball M(s)/W(s), cheerleading M(s)/W(s), cross-country running M(s)/W(s), football M(s), golf M(s)/W(s), lacrosse M(s)/W(s), soccer M(s)/W(s), softball W(s), tennis M(s)/W(s), volleyball W(s). *Intramural sports:* basketball M/W, football M/W, golf M/W, rock climbing M/W, skiing (cross-country) M/W, soccer M/W, softball M/W, table tennis M/W, tennis M/W, ultimate Frisbee M/W, volleyball M/W.

Standardized Tests *Required:* SAT or ACT (for admission).

Costs (2010–11) *Comprehensive fee:* $38,850 includes full-time tuition ($27,580), mandatory fees ($2600), and room and board ($8670). Full-time tuition and fees vary according to program and reciprocity agreements. Part-time tuition: $1150 per credit hour. Part-time tuition and fees vary according to course load and program. *Required fees:* $25 per credit hour part-time, $23 per term part-time. *Room and board:* Room and board charges vary according to board plan and housing facility. *Payment plan:* installment. *Waivers:* senior citizens and employees or children of employees.

Financial Aid Of all full-time matriculated undergraduates who enrolled in 2009, 886 applied for aid, 805 were judged to have need, 364 had their need fully met. In 2009, 280 non-need-based awards were made. *Average percent of need met:* 86%. *Average financial aid package:* $30,827. *Average need-based loan:* $4169. *Average need-based gift aid:* $28,564. *Average non-need-based aid:* $13,003. *Average indebtedness upon graduation:* $24,067. *Financial aid deadline:* 6/30.

Applying *Options:* electronic application, early admission, early decision, early action, deferred entrance. *Application fee:* $40. *Required:* essay or personal statement, high school transcript, 1 letter of recommendation. *Recommended:* interview. *Application deadlines:* 2/1 (freshmen), 2/1 (out-of-state freshmen), 7/1 (transfers), 11/15 (early action). *Early decision deadline:* 11/1. *Notification:* 3/15 (freshmen), 3/15 (out-of-state freshmen), 7/15 (transfers), 12/1 (early decision), 12/15 (early action).

Freshman Application Contact Mr. Brian J. Fortman, Dean of Admissions, Presbyterian College, 503 South Broad Street, Clinton, SC 29325. *Phone:*

864-833-8258. *Toll-free phone:* 800-476-7272. *Fax:* 864-833-8481. *E-mail:* bjfortman@presby.edu. *Web site:* http://www.presby.edu/.

See page 1510 for the College Close-Up.

South Carolina State University

Orangeburg, South Carolina

- **State-supported** comprehensive, founded 1896, part of South Carolina Commission on Higher Education
- **Small-town** 160-acre campus
- **Endowment** $914,098
- **Coed**
- **Minimally difficult** entrance level

Faculty *Student/faculty ratio:* 16:1.

Academics *Calendar:* semesters. *Degrees:* bachelor's, master's, doctoral-research/scholarship, post-master's, and postbachelor's certificates.

Student Life *Campus security:* 24-hour emergency response devices and patrols, late-night transport/escort service, controlled dormitory access.

Athletics Member NCAA. All Division I except football (Division I-AA).

Standardized Tests *Required:* SAT or ACT (for admission). *Recommended:* SAT Subject Tests (for admission).

Costs (2010–11) *Tuition:* state resident $8898 full-time, $371 per credit hour part-time; nonresident $17,470 full-time, $728 per credit hour part-time. *Room and board:* $9238; room only: $6300. Room and board charges vary according to housing facility. *Payment plans:* installment, deferred payment.

Financial Aid *Of all full-time matriculated undergraduates who enrolled in 2007,* 343 Federal Work-Study jobs (averaging $1048). 360 state and other part-time jobs (averaging $2050). *Average indebtedness upon graduation:* $26,678.

Applying *Options:* electronic application, deferred entrance. *Application fee:* $25. *Required:* high school transcript, minimum 2 GPA.

Freshman Application Contact Mr. Antonio Boyle, Assistant Vice President of Enrollment Management, South Carolina State University, 300 College Street Northeast, Orangeburg, SC 29117-0001. *Phone:* 803-536-7186. *Toll-free phone:* 800-260-5956. *Fax:* 803-536-8990. *E-mail:* admissions@scsu.edu. *Web site:* http://www.scsu.edu/.

Southern Methodist College

Orangeburg, South Carolina

Freshman Application Contact Ms. Juanta Webb, Recruitment Officer, Southern Methodist College, PO Box 1027, Orangeburg, SC 29116-7827. *Phone:* 803-268-1322. *Toll-free phone:* 800-360-1503. *Fax:* 803-534-7827. *E-mail:* jwebb@smcollege.edu. *Web site:* http://www.smcollege.edu/.

Southern Wesleyan University

Central, South Carolina

- **Independent** comprehensive, founded 1906, affiliated with Wesleyan Church
- **Small-town** 350-acre campus
- **Endowment** $3.5 million
- **Coed** 1,456 undergraduate students, 99% full-time, 60% women, 40% men
- **Minimally difficult** entrance level, 94% of applicants were admitted

Undergraduates 1,440 full-time, 16 part-time. Students come from 25 states and territories; 9 other countries; 16% are from out of state; 27% Black or African American, non-Hispanic/Latino; 2% Hispanic/Latino; 0.4% Asian, non-Hispanic/Latino; 0.6% American Indian or Alaska Native, non-Hispanic/Latino; 8% Race/ethnicity unknown; 0.8% international; 6% transferred in; 55% live on campus. *Retention:* 70% of full-time freshmen returned.

Freshmen *Admission:* 575 applied, 540 admitted, 157 enrolled. *Average high school GPA:* 3.5. *Test scores:* SAT critical reading scores over 500: 40%; SAT math scores over 500: 50%; SAT writing scores over 500: 35%; ACT scores over 18: 78%; SAT critical reading scores over 600: 13%; SAT math scores over 600: 9%; SAT writing scores over 600: 8%; ACT scores over 24: 13%; SAT critical reading scores over 700: 3%; SAT math scores over 700: 1%; SAT writing scores over 700: 1%.

Faculty *Total:* 193, 30% full-time, 48% with terminal degrees. *Student/faculty ratio:* 18:1.

Academics *Calendar:* semesters. *Degrees:* associate, bachelor's, and master's. *Special study options:* academic remediation for entering students, accelerated degree program, adult/continuing education programs, advanced placement credit, distance learning, double majors, English as a second language, honors programs, independent study, internships, off-campus study,

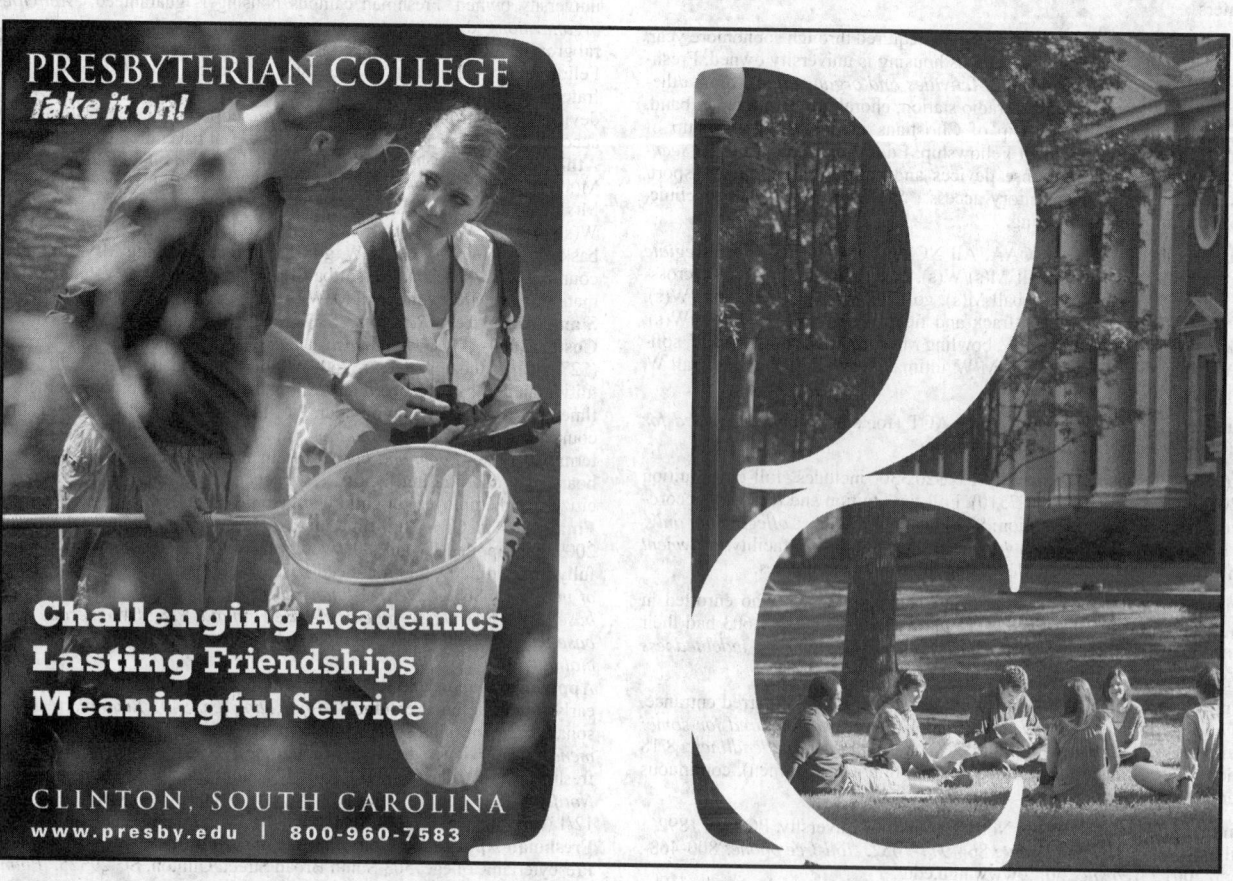
PROFILES

part-time degree program, services for LD students, student-designed majors, study abroad, summer session for credit. *ROTC:* Army (c), Air Force (c).

Computers on Campus 95 computers/terminals are available on campus for general student use. Students can access the following: campus intranet, computer help desk, free student e-mail accounts, online (class) grades, online (class) registration, online (class) schedules. Campuswide network is available. 100% of college-owned or -operated housing units are wired for high-speed Internet access. Wireless service is available via entire campus.

Student Life *Housing:* on-campus residence required through senior year. *Options:* coed, women-only, disabled students. Campus housing is university owned. Freshman campus housing is guaranteed. *Activities and organizations:* drama/theater group, choral group, Student Government Association, Student Missions Focus, Ministry Teams, Music Club, Ignite student athlete fellowship group. *Campus security:* 24-hour emergency response devices, late night security patrols until 2:00 am, restricted access to campus after midnight. *Student services:* health clinic, personal/psychological counseling.

Athletics Member NAIA, NCCAA. *Intercollegiate sports:* baseball M(s), basketball M(s)/W(s), cheerleading M/W, cross-country running M(s)/W(s), golf M(s), soccer M(s)/W(s), softball W(s), volleyball W(s). *Intramural sports:* basketball M/W, football M/W, softball M/W, table tennis M/W, tennis M/W, ultimate Frisbee M/W, volleyball M/W.

Standardized Tests *Required:* SAT or ACT (for admission).

Costs (2011–12) *Comprehensive fee:* $28,100 includes full-time tuition ($19,950), mandatory fees ($600), and room and board ($7550). Full-time tuition and fees vary according to class time, course load, degree level, location, and program. Part-time tuition: $825 per credit. Part-time tuition and fees vary according to class time, course load, degree level, location, and program. *College room only:* $2750. Room and board charges vary according to board plan and housing facility. *Payment plan:* installment. *Waivers:* senior citizens and employees or children of employees.

Financial Aid Of all full-time matriculated undergraduates who enrolled in 2006, 437 applied for aid, 387 were judged to have need, 128 had their need fully met. 158 Federal Work-Study jobs (averaging $1150). 73 state and other part-time jobs (averaging $1150). In 2006, 90 non-need-based awards were made. *Average percent of need met:* 78%. *Average financial aid package:* $14,094. *Average need-based loan:* $4844. *Average need-based gift aid:* $9962. *Average non-need-based aid:* $9196. *Average indebtedness upon graduation:* $25,971.

Applying *Options:* electronic application, deferred entrance. *Application fee:* $25. *Required:* high school transcript, minimum 2.3 GPA. *Required for some:* interview. *Application deadlines:* 8/1 (freshmen), 8/1 (transfers). *Notification:* continuous (freshmen), continuous (transfers).

Freshman Application Contact Mrs. Beth Roe, Director of First Year Experience, Southern Wesleyan University, PO Box 1020, 907 Wesleyan Drive, Central, SC 29630-1020. *Phone:* 864-644-5149. *Toll-free phone:* 800-289-1292 Ext. 5550. *Fax:* 864-644-5901. *E-mail:* broe@swu.edu. *Web site:* http://www.swu.edu/.

South University

Columbia, South Carolina

- **Proprietary** comprehensive, founded 1935, part of Education Management Corporation
- **Coed**

Academics *Calendar:* quarters. *Degrees:* certificates, associate, bachelor's, and master's.

Costs (2010–11) *Tuition:* Information about tuition and fees can be obtained by contacting the South University Admissions Office.

Freshman Application Contact South University, 9 Science Court, Columbia, SC 29203. *Phone:* 803-799-9082. *Toll-free phone:* 866-629-3031. *Web site:* http://www.southuniversity.edu/columbia/.

See page 1630 for the College Close-Up.

Strayer University - Charleston Campus

North Charleston, South Carolina

- **Proprietary** comprehensive
- **Coed**

Academics *Degrees:* certificates, associate, bachelor's, master's, and post-bachelor's certificates.

Costs (2010–11) *Tuition:* $13,635 full-time, $1590 per course part-time.

Freshman Application Contact Strayer University - Charleston Campus, 5010 Wetland Crossing, North Charleston, SC 29418. *Web site:* http://www.strayer.edu/charleston/.

Strayer University - Columbia Campus

Columbia, South Carolina

- **Proprietary** comprehensive
- **Coed**

Academics *Degrees:* certificates, associate, bachelor's, master's, and post-bachelor's certificates.

Costs (2010–11) *Tuition:* $13,635 full-time, $1590 per course part-time.

Freshman Application Contact Strayer University - Columbia Campus, 200 Center Point Circle, Suite 300, Columbia, SC 29210. *Web site:* http://www.strayer.edu/columbia.

Strayer University - Greenville Campus

Greenville, South Carolina

- **Proprietary** comprehensive
- **Coed**

Academics *Degrees:* certificates, associate, bachelor's, master's, and post-bachelor's certificates.

Costs (2010–11) *Tuition:* $13,635 full-time, $1590 per course part-time.

Freshman Application Contact Strayer University - Greenville Campus, 555 North Pleasantburg Drive, Suite 300, Greenville, SC 29607. *Web site:* http://www.strayer.edu/greenville.

University of South Carolina

Columbia, South Carolina

- **State-supported** university, founded 1801, part of University of South Carolina System
- **Urban** 315-acre campus
- **Endowment** $414.0 million
- **Coed** 21,383 undergraduate students, 93% full-time, 54% women, 46% men
- **Moderately difficult** entrance level, 70% of applicants were admitted

Undergraduates 19,823 full-time, 1,560 part-time. Students come from 54 states and territories; 112 other countries; 28% are from out of state; 11% Black or African American, non-Hispanic/Latino; 3% Hispanic/Latino; 3% Asian, non-Hispanic/Latino; 0.1% Native Hawaiian or other Pacific Islander, non-Hispanic/Latino; 0.3% American Indian or Alaska Native, non-Hispanic/Latino; 3% Two or more races, non-Hispanic/Latino; 0.5% Race/ethnicity unknown; 1% international; 8% transferred in; 36% live on campus. *Retention:* 86% of full-time freshmen returned.

Freshmen *Admission:* 18,485 applied, 12,914 admitted, 4,468 enrolled. *Average high school GPA:* 3.89. *Test scores:* SAT critical reading scores over 500: 90%; SAT math scores over 500: 95%; ACT scores over 18: 100%; SAT critical reading scores over 600: 42%; SAT math scores over 600: 54%; ACT scores over 24: 78%; SAT critical reading scores over 700: 7%; SAT math scores over 700: 9%; ACT scores over 30: 17%.

Faculty *Total:* 1,869, 71% full-time, 72% with terminal degrees. *Student/faculty ratio:* 19:1.

Academics *Calendar:* semesters. *Degrees:* bachelor's, master's, doctoral-professional, doctoral-research/scholarship, post-master's, and postbachelor's certificates. *Special study options:* accelerated degree program, adult/continuing education programs, advanced placement credit, cooperative education, distance learning, double majors, English as a second language, freshman honors college, honors programs, independent study, internships, part-time degree program, services for LD students, student-designed majors, study abroad, summer session for credit. *ROTC:* Army (b), Navy (b), Air Force (b).

Computers on Campus 2,800 computers/terminals are available on campus for general student use. Students can access the following: computer help desk, free student e-mail accounts, online (class) grades, online (class) registration, online (class) schedules. Campuswide network is available. 100% of college-owned or -operated housing units are wired for high-speed Internet access. Wireless service is available via entire campus.

Student Life *Housing:* on-campus residence required for freshman year. *Options:* coed, men-only, women-only, disabled students. Campus housing is university owned. Freshman campus housing is guaranteed. *Activities and organizations:* drama/theater group, student-run newspaper, radio station, choral group, marching band, Residence Hall Association, Alpha Lampda Delta, Student Bar Association, Student Nurses Association, Social Work Student Association, national fraternities, national sororities. *Campus security:* 24-hour emergency response devices and patrols, student patrols, late-night transport/escort service, controlled dormitory access. *Student services:* health clinic, personal/psychological counseling.

Athletics Member NCAA. All Division I except football (Division I-A). *Intercollegiate sports:* baseball M(s), basketball M(s)/W(s), cross-country running W(s), equestrian sports W(s), golf M(s)/W(s), soccer M(s)/W(s), softball W(s), swimming and diving M(s)/W(s), tennis M(s)/W(s), track and field M(s)/W(s), volleyball W(s). *Intramural sports:* badminton M(c)/W(c), baseball M(c), basketball M/W, bowling M/W, equestrian sports M(c)/W(c), fencing M(c)/W(c), field hockey W(c), football M/W, golf M/W, ice hockey M(c), lacrosse M(c)/W(c), racquetball M/W, rock climbing M(c)/W(c), rugby M(c)/W(c), sailing M(c)/W(c), soccer M/W, softball M/W, swimming and diving M/W, table tennis M/W, tennis M/W, ultimate Frisbee M/W, volleyball M/W, water polo M(c)/W(c), weight lifting M/W, wrestling M(c).
Standardized Tests *Required:* SAT or ACT (for admission).
Costs (2011–12) *Tuition:* state resident $9386 full-time, $400 per credit hour part-time; nonresident $24,962 full-time, $1050 per credit hour part-time. Full-time tuition and fees vary according to program and reciprocity agreements. Part-time tuition and fees vary according to course load. *Required fees:* $400 full-time, $17 per credit hour part-time. *Room and board:* $7764; room only: $4965. Room and board charges vary according to board plan, housing facility, and location. *Payment plan:* deferred payment. *Waivers:* senior citizens and employees or children of employees.
Financial Aid Of all full-time matriculated undergraduates who enrolled in 2008, 12,213 applied for aid, 9,007 were judged to have need, 2,021 had their need fully met. 657 Federal Work-Study jobs (averaging $2115). 2,732 state and other part-time jobs (averaging $1739). In 2008, 6563 non-need-based awards were made. *Average percent of need met:* 74%. *Average financial aid package:* $12,570. *Average need-based loan:* $3962. *Average need-based gift aid:* $5027. *Average non-need-based aid:* $6260. *Average indebtedness upon graduation:* $21,811.
Applying *Options:* electronic application, early action. *Application fee:* $50. *Required:* high school transcript, minimum 2 GPA. *Application deadlines:* 12/1 (freshmen), 6/1 (transfers), 10/15 (early action). *Notification:* continuous (transfers), 12/20 (early action).
Freshman Application Contact Dr. Mary Wagner, Senior Associate Director, Undergraduate Admissions, University of South Carolina, Columbia, SC 29208. *Phone:* 803-777-7700. *Toll-free phone:* 800-868-5872. *Fax:* 803-777-0101. *E-mail:* admissions-ugrad@sc.edu. *Web site:* http://www.sc.edu/.

University of South Carolina Aiken
Aiken, South Carolina

- **State-supported** comprehensive, founded 1961, part of University of South Carolina System
- **Suburban** 453-acre campus with easy access to Columbia
- **Endowment** $17.7 million
- **Coed** 3,184 undergraduate students, 80% full-time, 67% women, 33% men
- **Moderately difficult** entrance level, 39% of applicants were admitted

Undergraduates 2,532 full-time, 652 part-time. Students come from 33 states and territories; 20 other countries; 9% are from out of state; 28% Black or African American, non-Hispanic/Latino; 4% Hispanic/Latino; 0.7% Asian, non-Hispanic/Latino; 0.2% Native Hawaiian or other Pacific Islander, non-Hispanic/Latino; 0.4% American Indian or Alaska Native, non-Hispanic/Latino; 3% Two or more races, non-Hispanic/Latino; 1% Race/ethnicity unknown; 1% international; 8% transferred in; 29% live on campus. *Retention:* 73% of full-time freshmen returned.
Freshmen *Admission:* 2,721 applied, 1,069 admitted, 630 enrolled. *Average high school GPA:* 3.55. *Test scores:* SAT critical reading scores over 500: 47%; SAT math scores over 500: 50%; SAT writing scores over 500: 36%; ACT scores over 18: 86%; SAT critical reading scores over 600: 14%; SAT math scores over 600: 14%; SAT writing scores over 600: 6%; ACT scores over 24: 25%; SAT critical reading scores over 700: 1%; SAT math scores over 700: 1%; ACT scores over 30: 1%.
Faculty *Total:* 229, 66% full-time, 57% with terminal degrees. *Student/faculty ratio:* 16:1.
Academics *Calendar:* semesters. *Degrees:* bachelor's and master's. *Special study options:* adult/continuing education programs, advanced placement credit, cooperative education, distance learning, double majors, English as a second language, honors programs, independent study, internships, off-campus study, part-time degree program, services for LD students, student-designed majors, study abroad, summer session for credit.
Computers on Campus 546 computers/terminals and 796 ports are available on campus for general student use. Students can access the following: computer help desk, free student e-mail accounts, online (class) grades, online (class) registration, online (class) schedules. Campuswide network is available. 100% of college-owned or -operated housing units are wired for high-speed Internet access. Wireless service is available via entire campus.
Student Life *Housing options:* coed, disabled students. Campus housing is university owned. Freshman applicants given priority for college housing. *Activities and organizations:* drama/theater group, student-run newspaper, choral group, student government, Pacesetters, Student Alumni Ambassadors,

African-American Student Alliance, Pacer Union Board, national fraternities, national sororities. *Campus security:* 24-hour emergency response devices and patrols, late-night transport/escort service, controlled dormitory access. *Student services:* health clinic, personal/psychological counseling.
Athletics Member NCAA. All Division II. *Intercollegiate sports:* baseball M(s), basketball M(s)/W(s), cross-country running W(s), golf M(s), soccer M(s)/W(s), softball W(s), tennis M(s)/W(s), volleyball W(s). *Intramural sports:* basketball M/W, cheerleading M(c)/W(c), equestrian sports M(c)/W(c), soccer M/W, ultimate Frisbee M/W, volleyball M/W.
Standardized Tests *Required:* SAT or ACT (for admission).
Costs (2010–11) *Tuition:* state resident $8134 full-time, $353 per credit hour part-time; nonresident $16,302 full-time, $706 per credit hour part-time. Full-time tuition and fees vary according to reciprocity agreements. Part-time tuition and fees vary according to course load and reciprocity agreements. *Required fees:* $290 full-time, $9 per credit hour part-time, $25 per term part-time. *Room and board:* $6450. Room and board charges vary according to board plan and housing facility. *Payment plan:* deferred payment. *Waivers:* senior citizens and employees or children of employees.
Financial Aid Of all full-time matriculated undergraduates who enrolled in 2008, 2,172 applied for aid, 1,401 were judged to have need, 267 had their need fully met. In 2008, 522 non-need-based awards were made. *Average percent of need met:* 69%. *Average financial aid package:* $9108. *Average need-based loan:* $4254. *Average need-based gift aid:* $6552. *Average non-need-based aid:* $5686.
Applying *Options:* electronic application, early admission, deferred entrance. *Application fee:* $45. *Required:* high school transcript. *Application deadlines:* 8/1 (freshmen), 8/1 (out-of-state freshmen), 8/1 (transfers). *Notification:* continuous (freshmen), continuous (out-of-state freshmen), continuous (transfers).
Freshman Application Contact Mr. Andrew Hendrix, Director of Admissions, University of South Carolina Aiken, 471 University Parkway, Aiken, SC 29801-6309. *Phone:* 803-641-3366. *Toll-free phone:* 888-WOW-USCA. *Fax:* 803-641-3727. *E-mail:* admit@usca.edu. *Web site:* http://www.usca.edu/.

University of South Carolina Beaufort
Bluffton, South Carolina

- **State-supported** 4-year, founded 1959, part of University of South Carolina System
- **Small-town** 200-acre campus
- **Coed** 1,754 undergraduate students, 76% full-time, 61% women, 39% men
- **Minimally difficult** entrance level, 75% of applicants were admitted

Undergraduates 1,340 full-time, 414 part-time. Students come from 38 states and territories; 12 other countries; 19% are from out of state; 17% Black or African American, non-Hispanic/Latino; 6% Hispanic/Latino; 1% Asian, non-Hispanic/Latino; 0.2% Native Hawaiian or other Pacific Islander, non-Hispanic/Latino; 0.3% American Indian or Alaska Native, non-Hispanic/Latino; 3% Two or more races, non-Hispanic/Latino; 1% Race/ethnicity unknown; 0.5% international; 18% live on campus.
Freshmen *Admission:* 1,366 applied, 1,020 admitted.
Faculty *Total:* 141, 42% full-time. *Student/faculty ratio:* 17:1.
Academics *Calendar:* semesters. *Degrees:* certificates, associate, and bachelor's. *Special study options:* adult/continuing education programs, advanced placement credit, distance learning, double majors, independent study, internships, off-campus study, part-time degree program, services for LD students, study abroad, summer session for credit.
Computers on Campus Students can access the following: free student e-mail accounts, online (class) grades, online (class) registration, online (class) schedules. Campuswide network is available. 100% of college-owned or -operated housing units are wired for high-speed Internet access. Wireless service is available via entire campus.
Student Life *Housing:* on-campus residence required for freshman year. *Options:* Campus housing is university owned and leased by the school. *Activities and organizations:* drama/theater group, student-run newspaper, Student Government Association, Gamma Beta Phi, Black Student Organization, Business Club, Environmental Awareness Club. *Campus security:* 24-hour emergency response devices, evening security service. *Student services:* personal/psychological counseling.
Athletics Member NAIA. *Intercollegiate sports:* baseball M(s), cross-country running M(s)/W(s), golf M(s)/W(s), softball W, track and field M(s)/W(s).
Standardized Tests *Required:* SAT or ACT (for admission).
Costs (2010–11) *Tuition:* state resident $7604 full-time, $317 per credit hour part-time; nonresident $16,186 full-time, $676 per credit hour part-time. Full-time tuition and fees vary according to reciprocity agreements. Part-time tuition and fees vary according to reciprocity agreements. *Required fees:* $416 full-time, $14 per credit hour part-time. *Room and board:* $6380; room only: $4600. Room and board charges vary according to board plan and housing facility. *Payment plan:* deferred payment. *Waivers:* senior citizens and employees or children of employees.

Financial Aid Of all full-time matriculated undergraduates who enrolled in 2008, 30 Federal Work-Study jobs (averaging $2800).
Applying *Options:* electronic application, deferred entrance. *Application fee:* $40. *Required:* high school transcript. *Recommended:* minimum 2 GPA. *Application deadlines:* rolling (freshmen), rolling (transfers). *Notification:* continuous (freshmen).
Freshman Application Contact Ms. Monica Williams, University of South Carolina Beaufort, 1 University Boulevard, Bluffton, SC 29909. *Phone:* 843-208-8112. *Fax:* 843-208-8015. *E-mail:* mrwilli5@uscb.edu. *Web site:* http://www.uscb.edu/.

University of South Carolina Upstate
Spartanburg, South Carolina

- **State-supported** comprehensive, founded 1967, part of University of South Carolina System
- **Urban** 300-acre campus with easy access to Charlotte
- **Endowment** $3.3 million
- **Coed** 5,439 undergraduate students, 78% full-time, 64% women, 36% men
- **Moderately difficult** entrance level, 80% of applicants were admitted

Undergraduates 4,267 full-time, 1,172 part-time. Students come from 34 states and territories; 30 other countries; 4% are from out of state; 27% Black or African American, non-Hispanic/Latino; 4% Hispanic/Latino; 2% Asian, non-Hispanic/Latino; 0.1% Native Hawaiian or other Pacific Islander, non-Hispanic/Latino; 0.2% American Indian or Alaska Native, non-Hispanic/Latino; 3% Two or more races, non-Hispanic/Latino; 2% Race/ethnicity unknown; 1% international; 14% transferred in; 17% live on campus. *Retention:* 69% of full-time freshmen returned.
Freshmen *Admission:* 2,885 applied, 2,297 admitted, 891 enrolled. *Average high school GPA:* 3.64. *Test scores:* SAT critical reading scores over 500: 38%; SAT math scores over 500: 47%; SAT writing scores over 500: 29%; ACT scores over 18: 85%; SAT critical reading scores over 600: 8%; SAT math scores over 600: 9%; SAT writing scores over 600: 5%; ACT scores over 24: 15%; SAT critical reading scores over 700: 1%; SAT math scores over 700: 1%; ACT scores over 30: 1%.
Faculty *Total:* 406, 51% full-time, 65% with terminal degrees. *Student/faculty ratio:* 17:1.
Academics *Calendar:* semesters. *Degrees:* bachelor's, master's, and post-bachelor's certificates. *Special study options:* academic remediation for entering students, accelerated degree program, adult/continuing education programs, advanced placement credit, cooperative education, distance learning, double majors, English as a second language, honors programs, independent study, internships, off-campus study, part-time degree program, services for LD students, student-designed majors, study abroad, summer session for credit. *ROTC:* Army (c).
Computers on Campus 400 computers/terminals are available on campus for general student use. Students can access the following: computer help desk, free student e-mail accounts, online (class) grades, online (class) registration. Campuswide network is available. Wireless service is available via classrooms, computer centers, computer labs, dorm rooms, libraries, student centers.
Student Life *Housing options:* coed, disabled students. Campus housing is university owned. Freshman applicants given priority for college housing. *Activities and organizations:* drama/theater group, student-run newspaper, choral group, African-American Association, Campus Activity Board, Student Nurses Association, Student Government Association, Impact, national fraternities, national sororities. *Campus security:* 24-hour emergency response devices and patrols, late-night transport/escort service, campus security cameras. *Student services:* health clinic, personal/psychological counseling, women's center.
Athletics Member NCAA. All Division I. *Intercollegiate sports:* baseball M(s), basketball M(s)/W(s), cheerleading M(s)/W(s), cross-country running M(s)/W(s), golf M(s)/W(s), soccer M(s)/W(s), softball W(s), tennis M(s)/W(s), track and field M(s)/W(s), volleyball W(s). *Intramural sports:* badminton M/W, baseball M, basketball M/W, bowling M/W, football M/W, golf M/W, racquetball M/W, soccer M/W, softball M/W, table tennis M/W, tennis M/W, track and field M/W, volleyball M/W.
Standardized Tests *Required:* SAT or ACT (for admission).
Costs (2010–11) *Tuition:* state resident $8792 full-time, $375 per semester hour part-time; nonresident $17,864 full-time, $759 per semester hour part-time. Full-time tuition and fees vary according to course load and program. Part-time tuition and fees vary according to course load and program. *Required fees:* $500 full-time. *Room and board:* $6400; room only: $4300. Room and board charges vary according to board plan and housing facility. *Payment plan:* deferred payment. *Waivers:* senior citizens.
Financial Aid Of all full-time matriculated undergraduates who enrolled in 2008, 3,328 applied for aid, 2,782 were judged to have need, 408 had their need fully met. 97 Federal Work-Study jobs (averaging $1730). 439 state and other part-time jobs (averaging $1244). In 2008, 94 non-need-based awards

were made. *Average percent of need met:* 53%. *Average financial aid package:* $8944. *Average need-based loan:* $4011. *Average need-based gift aid:* $4214. *Average non-need-based aid:* $2048. *Average indebtedness upon graduation:* $18,762.
Applying *Options:* electronic application, deferred entrance. *Application fee:* $40. *Required:* high school transcript, minimum 2 GPA, college preparatory courses. *Notification:* continuous (freshmen), continuous (transfers).
Freshman Application Contact Ms. Donette Stewart, Assistant Vice Chancellor for Enrollment Services, University of South Carolina Upstate, 800 University Way, Spartanburg, SC 29303. *Phone:* 864-503-5280. *Toll-free phone:* 800-277-8727. *Fax:* 864-503-5727. *E-mail:* dstewart@uscupstate.edu. *Web site:* http://www.uscupstate.edu/.

Voorhees College
Denmark, South Carolina

- **Independent Episcopal** 4-year, founded 1897
- **Rural** 350-acre campus
- **Endowment** $5.0 million
- **Coed**
- **Moderately difficult** entrance level

Faculty *Student/faculty ratio:* 16:1.
Academics *Calendar:* semesters. *Degree:* bachelor's.
Student Life *Campus security:* 24-hour emergency response devices and patrols, student patrols, late-night transport/escort service.
Athletics Member NAIA.
Standardized Tests *Recommended:* SAT or ACT (for admission).
Costs (2010–11) *Comprehensive fee:* $18,126 includes full-time tuition ($10,180), mandatory fees ($600), and room and board ($7346). *College room only:* $3676. Room and board charges vary according to housing facility.
Financial Aid Of all full-time matriculated undergraduates who enrolled in 2004, 813 applied for aid, 791 were judged to have need, 61 had their need fully met. 223 Federal Work-Study jobs (averaging $2000). In 2004, 65 non-need-based awards were made. *Average percent of need met:* 51. *Average financial aid package:* $7449. *Average need-based loan:* $2840. *Average need-based gift aid:* $4805. *Average non-need-based aid:* $9582. *Average indebtedness upon graduation:* $13,383.
Applying *Options:* electronic application, deferred entrance. *Application fee:* $25. *Required:* high school transcript, minimum 2 GPA, secondary school GPA. *Required for some:* interview.
Freshman Application Contact Dr. Willie Jefferson, Dean of Enrollment Management, Voorhees College, PO Box 678, Denmark, SC 29042. *Phone:* 803-703-1049. *Toll-free phone:* 866-685-9904. *E-mail:* williej@voorhees.edu. *Web site:* http://www.voorhees.edu/.

Winthrop University
Rock Hill, South Carolina

- **State-supported** comprehensive, founded 1886, part of South Carolina Commission on Higher Education
- **Suburban** 445-acre campus with easy access to Charlotte
- **Endowment** $27.4 million
- **Coed** 4,933 undergraduate students, 88% full-time, 68% women, 32% men
- **Moderately difficult** entrance level, 69% of applicants were admitted

Undergraduates 4,352 full-time, 581 part-time. 12% are from out of state; 27% Black or African American, non-Hispanic/Latino; 2% Hispanic/Latino; 2% Asian, non-Hispanic/Latino; 0.5% American Indian or Alaska Native, non-Hispanic/Latino; 2% Race/ethnicity unknown; 3% international; 7% transferred in; 44% live on campus. *Retention:* 69% of full-time freshmen returned.
Freshmen *Admission:* 4,030 applied, 2,792 admitted, 961 enrolled. *Average high school GPA:* 3.68. *Test scores:* SAT critical reading scores over 500: 62%; SAT math scores over 500: 64%; ACT scores over 18: 95%; SAT critical reading scores over 600: 19%; SAT math scores over 600: 17%; ACT scores over 24: 35%; SAT critical reading scores over 700: 4%; SAT math scores over 700: 2%; ACT scores over 30: 6%.
Faculty *Total:* 569, 50% full-time, 58% with terminal degrees. *Student/faculty ratio:* 15:1.
Academics *Calendar:* semesters. *Degrees:* bachelor's, master's, post-master's, and postbachelor's certificates. *Special study options:* adult/continuing education programs, advanced placement credit, cooperative education, distance learning, double majors, honors programs, independent study, internships, off-campus study, part-time degree program, services for LD students, study abroad, summer session for credit. *ROTC:* Army (c).
Computers on Campus 620 computers/terminals are available on campus for general student use. Students can access the following: campus intranet, computer help desk, free student e-mail accounts, online (class) grades, online (class) registration, online (class) schedules, vast majority of university ser-

vices are available online. Campuswide network is available. 100% of college-owned or -operated housing units are wired for high-speed Internet access. Wireless service is available via entire campus.

Student Life *Housing:* on-campus residence required for freshman year. *Options:* coed, men-only, women-only, disabled students. Campus housing is university owned. Freshman campus housing is guaranteed. *Activities and organizations:* drama/theater group, student-run newspaper, radio station, choral group, Ebonites, Campus Ministries, Student Government Association, Dinkins Student Union, national fraternities, national sororities. *Campus security:* 24-hour emergency response devices and patrols, late-night transport/escort service, controlled dormitory access. *Student services:* health clinic, personal/psychological counseling.

Athletics Member NCAA. All Division I. *Intercollegiate sports:* baseball M(s), basketball M(s)/W(s), cheerleading M(c)/W(c), cross-country running M(s)/W(s), fencing M(c)/W(c), golf M(s)/W(s), lacrosse M(c)/W(c), rugby M(c), soccer M(s), softball W(s), tennis M(s)/W(s), track and field M(s)/W(s), volleyball W(s). *Intramural sports:* badminton M/W, basketball M/W, cross-country running M/W, equestrian sports M(c)/W(c), football M/W, golf M/W, racquetball M/W, soccer M/W, softball M/W, swimming and diving M/W, table tennis M/W, tennis M/W, ultimate Frisbee M/W, volleyball M/W, water polo M/W, weight lifting M/W.

Standardized Tests *Required:* SAT or ACT (for admission).

Costs (2010–11) *Tuition:* state resident $12,176 full-time, $508 per credit hour part-time; nonresident $22,892 full-time, $954 per credit hour part-time. Full-time tuition and fees vary according to reciprocity agreements and student level. Part-time tuition and fees vary according to student level. *Room and board:* $6922; room only: $4452. Room and board charges vary according to board plan and housing facility. *Payment plan:* installment. *Waivers:* senior citizens and employees or children of employees.

Financial Aid Of all full-time matriculated undergraduates who enrolled in 2009, 3,597 applied for aid, 3,041 were judged to have need, 511 had their need fully met. 273 Federal Work-Study jobs (averaging $916). In 2009, 335 non-need-based awards were made. *Average percent of need met:* 59%. *Average financial aid package:* $10,109. *Average need-based loan:* $4281. *Average need-based gift aid:* $7768. *Average non-need-based aid:* $4539. *Average indebtedness upon graduation:* $24,463.

Applying *Options:* electronic application, deferred entrance. *Application fee:* $40. *Required:* high school transcript, minimum 3 GPA. *Required for some:* essay or personal statement. *Application deadline:* 5/1 (freshmen). *Notification:* continuous (freshmen), continuous (transfers).

Freshman Application Contact Winthrop University, 701 Oakland Avenue, Rock Hill, SC 29733. *Phone:* 803-323-2191. *Toll-free phone:* 800-763-0230. *Web site:* http://www.winthrop.edu/.

Wofford College
Spartanburg, South Carolina

- **Independent** 4-year, founded 1854, affiliated with United Methodist Church
- **Urban** 170-acre campus with easy access to Charlotte
- **Endowment** $138.2 million
- **Coed** 1,506 undergraduate students, 98% full-time, 48% women, 52% men
- **Very difficult** entrance level, 62% of applicants were admitted

Undergraduates 1,472 full-time, 34 part-time. Students come from 35 states and territories; 16 other countries; 40% are from out of state; 7% Black or African American, non-Hispanic/Latino; 2% Hispanic/Latino; 3% Asian, non-Hispanic/Latino; 0.1% Native Hawaiian or other Pacific Islander, non-Hispanic/Latino; 0.3% American Indian or Alaska Native, non-Hispanic/Latino; 2% Two or more races, non-Hispanic/Latino; 3% Race/ethnicity unknown; 0.9% international; 1% transferred in; 94% live on campus. *Retention:* 90% of full-time freshmen returned.

Freshmen *Admission:* 2,595 applied, 1,607 admitted, 431 enrolled. *Average high school GPA:* 3.56. *Test scores:* SAT critical reading scores over 500: 93%; SAT math scores over 500: 96%; SAT writing scores over 500: 88%; ACT scores over 18: 99%; SAT critical reading scores over 600: 62%; SAT math scores over 600: 73%; SAT writing scores over 600: 55%; ACT scores over 24: 66%; SAT critical reading scores over 700: 16%; SAT math scores over 700: 20%; SAT writing scores over 700: 11%; ACT scores over 30: 16%.

Faculty *Total:* 159, 75% full-time, 85% with terminal degrees. *Student/faculty ratio:* 11:1.

Academics *Calendar:* 4-1-4. *Degree:* bachelor's. *Special study options:* accelerated degree program, advanced placement credit, double majors, independent study, internships, off-campus study, part-time degree program, student-designed majors, study abroad, summer session for credit. *ROTC:* Army (b).

Computers on Campus 106 computers/terminals are available on campus for general student use. Students can access the following: campus intranet, computer help desk, free student e-mail accounts, online (class) grades, online (class) registration, online (class) schedules. Campuswide network is available.

100% of college-owned or -operated housing units are wired for high-speed Internet access. Wireless service is available via classrooms, computer centers, computer labs, libraries, student centers.

Student Life *Housing:* on-campus residence required through senior year. *Options:* coed. Campus housing is university owned. Freshman applicants given priority for college housing. *Activities and organizations:* drama/theater group, student-run newspaper, choral group, Ultimate Frisbee Club, W.A.C. (Wofford Activities Council), Psychology Kingdom, Beta Beta Beta (Biology), Twin Towers (Service), national fraternities, national sororities. *Campus security:* 24-hour emergency response devices and patrols, late-night transport/escort service, controlled dormitory access. *Student services:* health clinic, personal/psychological counseling.

Athletics Member NCAA. All Division I except football (Division I-AA). *Intercollegiate sports:* baseball M(s), basketball M(s)/W(s), cheerleading W, cross-country running M(s)/W(s), golf M(s)/W(s), riflery M/W, soccer M(s)/W(s), tennis M(s)/W(s), track and field M(s)/W(s), volleyball W(s). *Intramural sports:* basketball M/W, bowling M/W, football M/W, lacrosse M(c)/W(c), racquetball M/W, soccer M/W, softball M/W, tennis M/W, ultimate Frisbee M/W, volleyball M/W, weight lifting M/W.

Standardized Tests *Required:* SAT or ACT (for admission).

Costs (2010–11) *Comprehensive fee:* $40,580 includes full-time tuition ($31,710) and room and board ($8870). Part-time tuition: $1255 per credit hour. *Payment plan:* installment. *Waivers:* employees or children of employees.

Financial Aid Of all full-time matriculated undergraduates who enrolled in 2009, 1,019 applied for aid, 870 were judged to have need, 414 had their need fully met. In 2009, 371 non-need-based awards were made. *Average percent of need met:* 85%. *Average financial aid package:* $29,792. *Average need-based loan:* $4224. *Average need-based gift aid:* $26,674. *Average non-need-based aid:* $13,857. *Average indebtedness upon graduation:* $23,103.

Applying *Options:* electronic application, early admission, early decision, deferred entrance. *Application fee:* $35. *Required:* essay or personal statement, high school transcript. *Recommended:* 2 letters of recommendation, interview. *Application deadlines:* 2/1 (freshmen), rolling (transfers). *Early decision deadline:* 11/15. *Notification:* 3/15 (freshmen), continuous (transfers), 12/5 (early decision).

Freshman Application Contact Mr. S. Wells Shepard, Director of Admission, Wofford College, 429 North Church Street, Spartanburg, SC 29303-3663. *Phone:* 864-597-4130. *Fax:* 864-597-4147. *E-mail:* admission@wofford.edu. *Web site:* http://www.wofford.edu/.

SOUTH DAKOTA

Augustana College
Sioux Falls, South Dakota

- **Independent** comprehensive, founded 1860, affiliated with Evangelical Lutheran Church in America
- **Urban** 100-acre campus
- **Endowment** $49.9 million
- **Coed** 1,794 undergraduate students, 94% full-time, 63% women, 37% men
- **Moderately difficult** entrance level, 83% of applicants were admitted

Undergraduates 1,694 full-time, 100 part-time. Students come from 32 states and territories; 23 other countries; 51% are from out of state; 1% Black or African American, non-Hispanic/Latino; 0.7% Hispanic/Latino; 0.8% Asian, non-Hispanic/Latino; 0.1% Native Hawaiian or other Pacific Islander, non-Hispanic/Latino; 0.4% American Indian or Alaska Native, non-Hispanic/Latino; 1% Two or more races, non-Hispanic/Latino; 0.1% Race/ethnicity unknown; 4% international; 4% transferred in; 73% live on campus. *Retention:* 86% of full-time freshmen returned.

Freshmen *Admission:* 1,231 applied, 1,021 admitted, 419 enrolled. *Average high school GPA:* 3.6. *Test scores:* ACT scores over 18: 100%; ACT scores over 24: 68%; ACT scores over 30: 11%.

Faculty *Total:* 171, 74% full-time, 64% with terminal degrees. *Student/faculty ratio:* 12:1.

Academics *Calendar:* 4-1-4. *Degrees:* bachelor's and master's. *Special study options:* academic remediation for entering students, accelerated degree program, advanced placement credit, cooperative education, double majors, freshman honors college, honors programs, independent study, internships, off-campus study, part-time degree program, services for LD students, student-designed majors, study abroad, summer session for credit. *ROTC:* Army (c), Air Force (c). *Unusual degree programs:* 3-2 engineering with Washington University in St. Louis and University of Minnesota; Medical Laboratory Scientist programs with Sanford Heath in Sioux Falls and St. Luke in Sioux City.

Computers on Campus 270 computers/terminals and 1,400 ports are available on campus for general student use. Students can access the following:

campus intranet, computer help desk, free student e-mail accounts, online (class) grades, online (class) registration, online (class) schedules. Campus-wide network is available. 100% of college-owned or -operated housing units are wired for high-speed Internet access. Wireless service is available via learning centers, libraries, student centers.

Student Life *Housing:* on-campus residence required through junior year. *Options:* coed, disabled students. Campus housing is university owned. Freshman campus housing is guaranteed. *Activities and organizations:* drama/theater group, student-run newspaper, choral group, Augieholics (student athletics support organization), Intramurals, Union Board of Governors (student union), Augie Green, Campus Ministries. *Campus security:* 24-hour emergency response devices and patrols, late-night transport/escort service, controlled dormitory access. *Student services:* health clinic, personal/psychological counseling.

Athletics Member NCAA. All Division II. *Intercollegiate sports:* baseball M(s), basketball M(s)/W(s), cheerleading W, cross-country running M(s)/W(s), football M(s), golf M/W(s), rugby W(c), soccer M(c)/W(s), softball W(s), tennis M(s)/W(s), track and field M(s)/W(s), volleyball W(s), wrestling M(s). *Intramural sports:* basketball M/W, bowling M/W, cross-country running M/W, football M, golf M/W, racquetball M/W, rock climbing M/W, skiing (cross-country) M/W, soccer M/W, softball M/W, swimming and diving M/W, table tennis M/W, tennis M/W, ultimate Frisbee M/W, volleyball M/W, weight lifting M/W.

Standardized Tests *Required:* SAT or ACT (for admission), minimum ACT score of 20 (for admission).

Costs (2010–11) *Comprehensive fee:* $31,364 includes full-time tuition ($24,790), mandatory fees ($314), and room and board ($6260). Full-time tuition and fees vary according to course load and degree level. Part-time tuition: $375 per credit hour. Part-time tuition and fees vary according to course load and degree level. *College room only:* $3048. Room and board charges vary according to board plan and housing facility. *Payment plan:* installment. *Waivers:* employees or children of employees.

Financial Aid Of all full-time matriculated undergraduates who enrolled in 2009, 1,362 applied for aid, 1,174 were judged to have need, 263 had their need fully met. 349 Federal Work-Study jobs (averaging $1643). 187 state and other part-time jobs (averaging $1159). In 2009, 500 non-need-based awards were made. *Average percent of need met:* 88%. *Average financial aid package:* $20,828. *Average need-based loan:* $5440. *Average need-based gift aid:* $15,916. *Average non-need-based aid:* $10,754. *Average indebtedness upon graduation:* $31,520.

Applying *Options:* electronic application, deferred entrance. *Required:* essay or personal statement, high school transcript, minimum 2.7 GPA, 1 letter of recommendation. *Recommended:* interview. *Application deadlines:* 8/1 (freshmen), rolling (transfers). *Notification:* continuous (freshmen).

Freshman Application Contact Ms. Nancy Davidson, Vice President for Enrollment, Augustana College, 2001 South Summit Avenue, Sioux Falls, SD 57197. *Phone:* 605-274-5516. *Toll-free phone:* 800-727-2844 Ext. 5516 (in-state); 800-727-2844 (out-of-state). *Fax:* 605-274-5518. *E-mail:* admission@augie.edu. *Web site:* http://www.augie.edu/.

Black Hills State University
Spearfish, South Dakota

- **State-supported** comprehensive, founded 1883, part of South Dakota State University System
- **Small-town** 123-acre campus
- **Endowment** $7.5 million
- **Coed**
- **Minimally difficult** entrance level

Faculty *Student/faculty ratio:* 19:1.

Academics *Calendar:* semesters. *Degrees:* associate, bachelor's, master's, post-master's, and postbachelor's certificates.

Student Life *Campus security:* 24-hour patrols, late-night transport/escort service, controlled dormitory access.

Athletics Member NAIA.

Standardized Tests *Required:* SAT or ACT (for admission).

Costs (2010–11) *Tuition:* state resident $3194 full-time, $100 per credit hour part-time; nonresident $4790 full-time, $150 per credit hour part-time. Full-time tuition and fees vary according to course load and reciprocity agreements. Part-time tuition and fees vary according to course load and reciprocity agreements. *Required fees:* $3757 full-time, $117 per credit hour part-time. *Room and board:* $5729; room only: $2738. Room and board charges vary according to board plan and housing facility. *Payment plans:* installment, deferred payment.

Financial Aid *Of all full-time matriculated undergraduates who enrolled in 2008,* 242 Federal Work-Study jobs (averaging $1596). 369 state and other part-time jobs (averaging $1723). *Average indebtedness upon graduation:* $21,069.

Applying *Options:* electronic application. *Application fee:* $20. *Required:* high school transcript, minimum 2.0 high school GPA in core curriculum.

Freshman Application Contact Black Hills State University, 1200 University Station, USB 9502, Spearfish, SD 57799-9502. *Phone:* 605-642-6343. *Toll-free phone:* 800-255-2478. *Fax:* 605-642-6254. *E-mail:* admissions@bhsu.edu. *Web site:* http://www.bhsu.edu/.

Colorado Technical University Sioux Falls
Sioux Falls, South Dakota

Freshman Application Contact Colorado Technical University Sioux Falls, 3901 West 59th Street, Sioux Falls, SD 57108. *Phone:* 605-361-0200. *Web site:* http://www.ctu-siouxfalls.com/.

Dakota State University
Madison, South Dakota

- **State-supported** comprehensive, founded 1881, part of South Dakota Board of Regents
- **Rural** 56-acre campus with easy access to Sioux Falls
- **Endowment** $5.7 million
- **Coed** 2,753 undergraduate students, 43% full-time, 53% women, 47% men
- **Minimally difficult** entrance level, 90% of applicants were admitted

Undergraduates 1,190 full-time, 1,563 part-time. Students come from 41 states and territories; 9 other countries; 21% are from out of state; 2% Black or African American, non-Hispanic/Latino; 2% Hispanic/Latino; 1% Asian, non-Hispanic/Latino; 0.4% Native Hawaiian or other Pacific Islander, non-Hispanic/Latino; 0.9% American Indian or Alaska Native, non-Hispanic/Latino; 2% Two or more races, non-Hispanic/Latino; 1% Race/ethnicity unknown; 3% international; 7% transferred in; 39% live on campus. *Retention:* 64% of full-time freshmen returned.

Freshmen *Admission:* 729 applied, 654 admitted, 348 enrolled. *Average high school GPA:* 3.1. *Test scores:* SAT math scores over 500: 58%; ACT scores over 18: 87%; SAT math scores over 600: 11%; ACT scores over 24: 35%; SAT math scores over 700: 5%; ACT scores over 30: 3%.

Faculty *Total:* 127, 76% full-time, 60% with terminal degrees. *Student/faculty ratio:* 17:1.

Academics *Calendar:* semesters. *Degrees:* certificates, associate, bachelor's, master's, and doctoral-research/scholarship. *Special study options:* academic remediation for entering students, adult/continuing education programs, advanced placement credit, cooperative education, distance learning, double majors, English as a second language, honors programs, independent study, internships, off-campus study, part-time degree program, services for LD students, summer session for credit. *ROTC:* Air Force (c).

Computers on Campus 165 computers/terminals and 356 ports are available on campus for general student use. Students can access the following: computer help desk, free student e-mail accounts, online (class) grades, online (class) registration, online (class) schedules, wireless computing initiative requires full-time students to have a tablet computer. Campuswide network is available. 100% of college-owned or -operated housing units are wired for high-speed Internet access. Wireless service is available via entire campus.

Student Life *Housing:* on-campus residence required through sophomore year. *Options:* coed, men-only, women-only. Campus housing is university owned and leased by the school. Freshman campus housing is guaranteed. *Activities and organizations:* drama/theater group, student-run newspaper, radio station, choral group, Gaming Club, Students in Free Enterprise, Phi Beta Lambda Business Club, Student Senate, Student Activities Board. *Campus security:* late-night transport/escort service, controlled dormitory access, night watchman. *Student services:* health clinic, personal/psychological counseling.

Athletics Member NAIA. *Intercollegiate sports:* baseball M(s), basketball M(s)/W(s), cheerleading M/W, cross-country running M(s)/W(s), football M(s), softball W(s), track and field M(s)/W(s), volleyball W(s). *Intramural sports:* basketball M/W, softball M/W, volleyball M/W.

Standardized Tests *Required:* SAT or ACT (for admission).

Costs (2010–11) *Tuition:* state resident $2994 full-time, $100 per credit hour part-time; nonresident $4491 full-time, $150 per credit hour part-time. Full-time tuition and fees vary according to location and reciprocity agreements. Part-time tuition and fees vary according to location and reciprocity agreements. *Required fees:* $4177 full-time, $115 per credit hour part-time. *Room and board:* $5004; room only: $2676. Room and board charges vary according to board plan and housing facility. *Payment plans:* installment, deferred payment. *Waivers:* senior citizens and employees or children of employees.

Financial Aid Of all full-time matriculated undergraduates who enrolled in 2008, 985 applied for aid, 772 were judged to have need, 123 had their need fully met. 110 Federal Work-Study jobs (averaging $2382). 18 state and other part-time jobs (averaging $5749). In 2008, 107 non-need-based awards were made. *Average percent of need met:* 84%. *Average financial aid package:* $7897. *Average need-based loan:* $3868. *Average need-based gift aid:* $4756.

Average non-need-based aid: $3454. *Average indebtedness upon graduation:* $21,811.

Applying *Options:* electronic application, deferred entrance. *Application fee:* $20. *Required:* high school transcript, minimum 2.7 GPA, rank in upper two-thirds of high school class. *Application deadlines:* rolling (freshmen), rolling (out-of-state freshmen), rolling (transfers). *Notification:* continuous (freshmen), continuous (out-of-state freshmen), continuous (transfers).

Freshman Application Contact Ms. Dana Hoff, Admissions Secretary, Dakota State University, 820 North Washington, Madison, SD 57042-1799. *Phone:* 605-256-5139. *Toll-free phone:* 888-DSU-9988. *Fax:* 605-256-5020. *E-mail:* yourfuture@dsu.edu. *Web site:* http://www.dsu.edu/.

Dakota Wesleyan University
Mitchell, South Dakota

- **Independent United Methodist** comprehensive, founded 1885
- **Small-town** 50-acre campus
- **Endowment** $20.0 million
- **Coed** 744 undergraduate students, 89% full-time, 58% women, 42% men
- **Moderately difficult** entrance level, 79% of applicants were admitted

Undergraduates 659 full-time, 85 part-time. Students come from 29 states and territories; 22% are from out of state; 6% Black or African American, non-Hispanic/Latino; 2% Hispanic/Latino; 0.7% Asian, non-Hispanic/Latino; 2% American Indian or Alaska Native, non-Hispanic/Latino; 2% Two or more races, non-Hispanic/Latino; 0.8% international; 17% transferred in; 45% live on campus. *Retention:* 57% of full-time freshmen returned.

Freshmen *Admission:* 507 applied, 398 admitted, 172 enrolled. *Average high school GPA:* 3.08. *Test scores:* SAT critical reading scores over 500: 46%; SAT writing scores over 500: 16%; ACT scores over 18: 91%; SAT critical reading scores over 600: 23%; SAT writing scores over 600: 8%; ACT scores over 24: 24%.

Faculty *Total:* 71, 72% full-time, 69% with terminal degrees. *Student/faculty ratio:* 12:1.

Academics *Calendar:* semesters. *Degrees:* associate, bachelor's, and master's. *Special study options:* academic remediation for entering students, advanced placement credit, cooperative education, distance learning, double majors, honors programs, independent study, internships, off-campus study, part-time degree program, services for LD students, student-designed majors, study abroad, summer session for credit. *ROTC:* Army (b).

Computers on Campus 100 computers/terminals are available on campus for general student use. Students can access the following: computer help desk, free student e-mail accounts, online (class) grades, online (class) registration, portal, course management system. Campuswide network is available. 100% of college-owned or -operated housing units are wired for high-speed Internet access. Wireless service is available via entire campus.

Student Life *Housing:* on-campus residence required through sophomore year. *Options:* coed, men-only, women-only. Campus housing is university owned and leased by the school. Freshman campus housing is guaranteed. *Activities and organizations:* drama/theater group, student-run newspaper, choral group, Future Teachers Organization, Student Nurses Association, Multi-Culture Club, Human Services Club, Student Ministry Council. *Campus security:* 24-hour emergency response devices, student patrols, late-night transport/escort service, controlled dormitory access, campus patrol from 2am to 6am by special request only. *Student services:* health clinic, personal/psychological counseling.

Athletics Member NAIA. *Intercollegiate sports:* baseball M(s), basketball M(s)/W(s), cheerleading M(s)/W(s), cross-country running M(s)/W(s), football M(s), golf M(s)/W(s), softball W(s), track and field M(s)/W(s), volleyball W(s), wrestling M(s). *Intramural sports:* basketball M/W, softball M/W, volleyball M/W, weight lifting M/W.

Standardized Tests *Required:* SAT or ACT (for admission).

Costs (2010–11) *Comprehensive fee:* $25,780 includes full-time tuition ($19,850) and room and board ($5930). Part-time tuition: $430 per credit hour. *College room only:* $2400. Room and board charges vary according to board plan and housing facility. *Waivers:* senior citizens.

Financial Aid Of all full-time matriculated undergraduates who enrolled in 2009, 613 applied for aid, 572 were judged to have need, 107 had their need fully met. 100 Federal Work-Study jobs (averaging $1400). 3 state and other part-time jobs (averaging $1200). In 2009, 87 non-need-based awards were made. *Average percent of need met:* 70%. *Average financial aid package:* $17,000. *Average need-based loan:* $4400. *Average need-based gift aid:* $12,700. *Average non-need-based aid:* $8100. *Average indebtedness upon graduation:* $32,400.

Applying *Options:* electronic application. *Application fee:* $25. *Required:* high school transcript. *Recommended:* minimum 2 GPA. *Application deadlines:* 8/27 (freshmen), 8/27 (transfers). *Notification:* continuous (freshmen), continuous (transfers).

Freshman Application Contact Mrs. Melissa Herr-Valburg, Director of Admissions, Dakota Wesleyan University, 1200 West University Avenue, Mitchell, SD 57301-4398. *Phone:* 605-995-2600 Ext. 2652. *Toll-free phone:*

800-333-8506. *Fax:* 605-995-2699. *E-mail:* admissions@dwu.edu. *Web site:* http://www.dwu.edu/.

Globe University
Sioux Falls, South Dakota

Director of Admissions Jason Crandall, Director of Admissions, Globe University, 5101 South Broadband Lane, Sioux Falls, SD 57108-2208. *Phone:* 605-977-0705. *Toll-free phone:* 866-437-0705. *Fax:* 605-977-0784. *E-mail:* jcrandall@globeuniversity.edu. *Web site:* http://www.globeuniversity.edu/.

Mount Marty College
Yankton, South Dakota

- **Independent Roman Catholic** comprehensive, founded 1936
- **Small-town** 80-acre campus
- **Endowment** $12.1 million
- **Coed** 1,137 undergraduate students, 55% full-time, 61% women, 39% men
- **Minimally difficult** entrance level, 65% of applicants were admitted

Undergraduates 628 full-time, 509 part-time. Students come from 12 states and territories; 28% are from out of state; 6% transferred in; 60% live on campus. *Retention:* 70% of full-time freshmen returned.

Freshmen *Admission:* 362 applied, 235 admitted, 137 enrolled. *Average high school GPA:* 3.32. *Test scores:* SAT critical reading scores over 500: 60%; SAT math scores over 500: 20%; SAT writing scores over 500: 60%; ACT scores over 18: 93%; SAT critical reading scores over 600: 20%; ACT scores over 24: 30%; ACT scores over 30: 2%.

Faculty *Total:* 61, 70% full-time, 46% with terminal degrees. *Student/faculty ratio:* 13:1.

Academics *Calendar:* semesters. *Degrees:* certificates, associate, bachelor's, and master's. *Special study options:* academic remediation for entering students, accelerated degree program, adult/continuing education programs, advanced placement credit, cooperative education, distance learning, double majors, honors programs, independent study, internships, off-campus study, part-time degree program, services for LD students, student-designed majors, summer session for credit. *ROTC:* Army (c).

Computers on Campus 25 computers/terminals are available on campus for general student use. Students can access the following: campus intranet, computer help desk, free student e-mail accounts, online (class) grades, online (class) registration, online (class) schedules. Campuswide network is available. 100% of college-owned or -operated housing units are wired for high-speed Internet access. Wireless service is available via entire campus.

Student Life *Housing:* on-campus residence required through senior year. *Options:* men-only, women-only. Campus housing is university owned. Freshman campus housing is guaranteed. *Activities and organizations:* drama/theater group, student-run newspaper, choral group, Campus Ministry, Student Government Association, Nursing Club, Education Club, Theater Club. *Campus security:* 24-hour emergency response devices and patrols, controlled dormitory access. *Student services:* health clinic, personal/psychological counseling.

Athletics Member NAIA. *Intercollegiate sports:* archery M(c)/W(c), baseball M(s), basketball M(s)/W(s), cross-country running M(s)/W(s), golf M(s)/W(s), soccer M(s)/W(s), softball W(s), track and field M(s)/W(s), volleyball W(s). *Intramural sports:* archery M/W, basketball M/W, soccer M/W, softball W, volleyball M/W.

Standardized Tests *Required:* SAT or ACT (for admission).

Costs (2010–11) *Comprehensive fee:* $25,568 includes full-time tuition ($18,102), mandatory fees ($1830), and room and board ($5636). Full-time tuition and fees vary according to location. Part-time tuition: $211 per credit hour. Part-time tuition and fees vary according to course load and location. *Required fees:* $25 per credit hour part-time. *Room and board:* Room and board charges vary according to board plan. *Payment plan:* installment. *Waivers:* employees or children of employees.

Financial Aid Of all full-time matriculated undergraduates who enrolled in 2009, 587 applied for aid, 541 were judged to have need, 237 had their need fully met. 206 Federal Work-Study jobs (averaging $1500). 49 state and other part-time jobs (averaging $1500). In 2009, 36 non-need-based awards were made. *Average percent of need met:* 98%. *Average financial aid package:* $21,311. *Average need-based loan:* $5551. *Average need-based gift aid:* $7502. *Average non-need-based aid:* $6646. *Average indebtedness upon graduation:* $34,983.

Applying *Options:* electronic application, early admission, deferred entrance. *Application fee:* $35. *Required:* high school transcript, minimum 2 GPA. *Recommended:* interview. *Application deadlines:* rolling (freshmen), rolling (transfers). *Notification:* continuous (freshmen), continuous (transfers).

Freshman Application Contact Paula Tacke, Vice President for Enrollment Management, Mount Marty College, 1105 West 8th Street, Yankton, SD

57078. *Phone:* 605-668-1545. *Toll-free phone:* 800-658-4552. *E-mail:* paula.tacke@mtmc.edu. *Web site:* http://www.mtmc.edu/.

National American University
Rapid City, South Dakota

Freshman Application Contact Ms. Angela Beck, Director of Enrollment Management, National American University, 321 Kansas City Street, Rapid City, SD 57701. *Phone:* 605-394-4902. *Toll-free phone:* 800-843-8892. *Fax:* 605-394-4871. *E-mail:* abeck@national.edu. *Web site:* http://www.national.edu/Locations/RapidCity/.

National American University–Sioux Falls Branch
Sioux Falls, South Dakota

Freshman Application Contact Ms. Lisa Houtsma, Director of Admissions, National American University–Sioux Falls Branch, 2801 South Kiwanis Avenue, Suite 100, Sioux Falls, SD 57105-4293. *Phone:* 605-336-4600. *Toll-free phone:* 800-388-5430. *Fax:* 605-336-4605. *E-mail:* lhoutsma@national.edu. *Web site:* http://www.national.edu/.

Northern State University
Aberdeen, South Dakota

- **State-supported** comprehensive, founded 1901, part of South Dakota Board of Regents
- **Small-town** 72-acre campus
- **Endowment** $17.9 million
- **Coed** 2,686 undergraduate students, 61% full-time, 59% women, 41% men
- **Minimally difficult** entrance level, 93% of applicants were admitted

Undergraduates 1,640 full-time, 1,046 part-time. Students come from 44 states and territories; 16 other countries; 28% are from out of state; 6% transferred in; 60% live on campus. *Retention:* 69% of full-time freshmen returned.
Freshmen *Admission:* 1,051 applied, 976 admitted, 410 enrolled. *Average high school GPA:* 3.05. *Test scores:* SAT critical reading scores over 500: 38%; SAT math scores over 500: 46%; ACT scores over 18: 83%; SAT critical reading scores over 600: 8%; SAT math scores over 600: 15%; ACT scores over 24: 28%; SAT critical reading scores over 700: 4%; ACT scores over 30: 1%.
Faculty *Total:* 95, 100% full-time, 81% with terminal degrees. *Student/faculty ratio:* 18:1.
Academics *Calendar:* semesters. *Degrees:* certificates, bachelor's, master's, and postbachelor's certificates. *Special study options:* academic remediation for entering students, accelerated degree program, adult/continuing education programs, advanced placement credit, cooperative education, distance learning, double majors, English as a second language, freshman honors college, honors programs, independent study, internships, off-campus study, part-time degree program, services for LD students, student-designed majors, study abroad, summer session for credit.
Computers on Campus 135 computers/terminals are available on campus for general student use. Students can access the following: campus intranet, computer help desk, free student e-mail accounts, online (class) grades, online (class) registration, online (class) schedules. Campuswide network is available. 100% of college-owned or -operated housing units are wired for high-speed Internet access. Wireless service is available via entire campus.
Student Life *Housing:* on-campus residence required through sophomore year. *Options:* coed. Campus housing is university owned. *Activities and organizations:* drama/theater group, student-run newspaper, television station, choral group, marching band, Student Ambassadors, Choices, honor society, Native American Student Association, International Student Association. *Campus security:* 24-hour emergency response devices, controlled dormitory access, evening patrols. *Student services:* health clinic, personal/psychological counseling, women's center, legal services.
Athletics Member NCAA. All Division II. *Intercollegiate sports:* baseball M(s), basketball M(s)/W(s), cheerleading W(s), cross-country running M(s)/W(s), football M(s), golf M(s)/W(s), soccer W(s), softball W(s), swimming and diving W(s), tennis W(s), track and field W(s), volleyball W(s), wrestling M(s). *Intramural sports:* basketball M/W, football M/W, rugby M(c), soccer M(c), softball M/W, volleyball M/W.
Standardized Tests *Required:* SAT or ACT (for admission).
Costs (2011–12) *Tuition:* state resident $2994 full-time; nonresident $4491 full-time. Full-time tuition and fees vary according to course level, course load, and reciprocity agreements. Part-time tuition and fees vary according to course level, course load, and reciprocity agreements. *Required fees:* $3357 full-time.

Room and board: $5068; room only: $2611. Room and board charges vary according to board plan. *Payment plan:* installment.
Financial Aid Of all full-time matriculated undergraduates who enrolled in 2009, 1,263 applied for aid, 998 were judged to have need, 194 had their need fully met. 300 Federal Work-Study jobs (averaging $2000). 367 state and other part-time jobs (averaging $1328). In 2009, 117 non-need-based awards were made. *Average percent of need met:* 73%. *Average financial aid package:* $7607. *Average need-based loan:* $4882. *Average need-based gift aid:* $4004. *Average non-need-based aid:* $1580.
Applying *Options:* electronic application, early admission, deferred entrance. *Application fee:* $20. *Required:* high school transcript, minimum 2.6 GPA. *Notification:* continuous (freshmen), continuous (transfers).
Freshman Application Contact Mr. Allan Vogel, Director of Admissions, Northern State University, 1200 South Jay Street, Aberdeen, SD 57401. *Phone:* 605-626-2544. *Toll-free phone:* 800-678-5330. *Fax:* 605-626-2587. *E-mail:* admission2@northern.edu. *Web site:* http://www.northern.edu/.

Oglala Lakota College
Kyle, South Dakota

Director of Admissions Director of Admissions, Oglala Lakota College, 490 Piya Wiconi Road, Kyle, SD 57752-0490. *Phone:* 605-455-2321 Ext. 236. *E-mail:* lmeseteth@olc.edu. *Web site:* http://www.olc.edu/.

Presentation College
Aberdeen, South Dakota

- **Independent Roman Catholic** 4-year, founded 1951
- **Small-town** 100-acre campus
- **Endowment** $7.3 million
- **Coed, primarily women** 718 undergraduate students, 59% full-time, 80% women, 20% men
- **Noncompetitive** entrance level

Undergraduates 422 full-time, 296 part-time. Students come from 19 states and territories; 45% are from out of state; 3% Black or African American, non-Hispanic/Latino; 2% Hispanic/Latino; 0.7% Asian, non-Hispanic/Latino; 0.2% Native Hawaiian or other Pacific Islander, non-Hispanic/Latino; 5% American Indian or Alaska Native, non-Hispanic/Latino; 0.3% Two or more races, non-Hispanic/Latino; 11% Race/ethnicity unknown; 18% transferred in; 26% live on campus. *Retention:* 62% of full-time freshmen returned.
Freshmen *Admission:* 147 applied, 61 enrolled. *Average high school GPA:* 3. *Test scores:* ACT scores over 18: 69%; ACT scores over 24: 12%; ACT scores over 30: 2%.
Faculty *Total:* 69, 58% full-time, 22% with terminal degrees. *Student/faculty ratio:* 11:1.
Academics *Calendar:* semesters. *Degrees:* certificates, associate, and bachelor's. *Special study options:* academic remediation for entering students, accelerated degree program, adult/continuing education programs, advanced placement credit, cooperative education, distance learning, double majors, external degree program, internships, part-time degree program, summer session for credit.
Computers on Campus 60 computers/terminals and 150 ports are available on campus for general student use. Students can access the following: computer help desk, free student e-mail accounts, online (class) grades, online (class) schedules, wireless network has 100% coverage for students. Campuswide network is available. 100% of college-owned or -operated housing units are wired for high-speed Internet access. Wireless service is available via entire campus.
Student Life *Housing:* on-campus residence required through sophomore year. *Options:* men-only, women-only, disabled students. Campus housing is university owned. Freshman campus housing is guaranteed. *Activities and organizations:* drama/theater group, student-run newspaper, choral group, Wellness/athletics, National Student Nursing Association, Social Work Organization, Rad Tech Organization, Student Ambassadors. *Campus security:* 24-hour emergency response devices, late-night transport/escort service, controlled dormitory access. *Student services:* health clinic, personal/psychological counseling.
Athletics Member NCAA. All Division III. *Intercollegiate sports:* baseball M, basketball M/W, cross-country running M/W, golf M/W, soccer M/W, softball W, volleyball W.
Standardized Tests *Required:* SAT or ACT (for admission).
Costs (2010–11) *Comprehensive fee:* $20,460 includes full-time tuition ($14,960) and room and board ($5500). Full-time tuition and fees vary according to course load, location, and program. Part-time tuition: $550 per credit. Part-time tuition and fees vary according to course load, location, and program. *College room only:* $4100. Room and board charges vary according to board plan. *Payment plan:* installment. *Waivers:* senior citizens and employees or children of employees.

Financial Aid Of all full-time matriculated undergraduates who enrolled in 2007, 494 applied for aid, 471 were judged to have need, 66 had their need fully met. 56 Federal Work-Study jobs (averaging $1874). 39 state and other part-time jobs (averaging $1950). In 2007, 23 non-need-based awards were made. *Average percent of need met:* 43%. *Average financial aid package:* $8737. *Average need-based loan:* $3741. *Average need-based gift aid:* $3769. *Average non-need-based aid:* $2814. *Average indebtedness upon graduation:* $27,430.

Applying *Options:* electronic application. *Application fee:* $25. *Required:* high school transcript. *Required for some:* 2 letters of recommendation, GED, if applicable; college transcripts. *Recommended:* minimum 2 GPA. *Application deadlines:* rolling (freshmen), rolling (transfers). *Notification:* continuous (freshmen), continuous (transfers).

Freshman Application Contact Ms. Jo Ellen Lindner, Vice President for Enrollment, Presentation College, 1500 North Main Street, Aberdeen, SD 57401. *Phone:* 605-229-8492. *Toll-free phone:* 800-437-6060. *Fax:* 605-229-8425. *E-mail:* admit@presentation.edu. *Web site:* http://www.presentation.edu/.

Sinte Gleska University
Mission, South Dakota

Director of Admissions Mr. Jack Herman, Registrar and Director of Admissions, Sinte Gleska University, 101 Antelope Lake Circle, PO Box 105, Mission, SD 57555. *Phone:* 605-856-8100 Ext. 8479. *Web site:* http://www.sintegleska.edu/.

South Dakota School of Mines and Technology
Rapid City, South Dakota

- **State-supported** university, founded 1885, part of South Dakota State Board of Regents University System
- **Suburban** 120-acre campus
- **Endowment** $32.7 million
- **Coed** 2,050 undergraduate students, 78% full-time, 29% women, 71% men
- **Moderately difficult** entrance level, 89% of applicants were admitted

Undergraduates 1,608 full-time, 442 part-time. Students come from 40 states and territories; 38 other countries; 45% are from out of state; 5% transferred in; 33% live on campus. *Retention:* 78% of full-time freshmen returned.

Freshmen *Admission:* 993 applied, 886 admitted, 437 enrolled. *Average high school GPA:* 3.47. *Test scores:* SAT critical reading scores over 500: 77%; SAT math scores over 500: 94%; ACT scores over 18: 100%; SAT critical reading scores over 600: 38%; SAT math scores over 600: 54%; ACT scores over 24: 72%; SAT critical reading scores over 700: 13%; SAT math scores over 700: 8%; ACT scores over 30: 15%.

Faculty *Total:* 152, 88% full-time, 79% with terminal degrees. *Student/faculty ratio:* 14:1.

Academics *Calendar:* semesters. *Degrees:* associate, bachelor's, master's, and doctoral-research/scholarship. *Special study options:* academic remediation for entering students, adult/continuing education programs, advanced placement credit, cooperative education, distance learning, English as a second language, independent study, internships, off-campus study, part-time degree program, services for LD students, study abroad, summer session for credit. *ROTC:* Army (b).

Computers on Campus 105 computers/terminals and 662 ports are available on campus for general student use. Students can access the following: campus intranet, computer help desk, free student e-mail accounts, online (class) grades, online (class) registration, online (class) schedules, laptop rental, our whole campus has wireless connections. Campuswide network is available. 100% of college-owned or -operated housing units are wired for high-speed Internet access. Wireless service is available via entire campus.

Student Life *Housing:* on-campus residence required through sophomore year. *Options:* coed, men-only, women-only, disabled students. Campus housing is university owned and leased by the school. Freshman campus housing is guaranteed. *Activities and organizations:* drama/theater group, student-run newspaper, radio station, choral group, ASCE (American Society of Civil Engineers), ASME (American Society of Mechanical Engineers), Drill and Crucible Club, Tau Beta Pi, Formula SAE (Mini Indy race car team), national fraternities, national sororities. *Campus security:* 24-hour emergency response devices and patrols, student patrols, late-night transport/escort service, controlled dormitory access. *Student services:* health clinic, personal/psychological counseling.

Athletics Member NAIA. *Intercollegiate sports:* basketball M(s)/W(s), cross-country running M(s)/W(s), football M(s), golf M(s)/W(s), track and field M(s)/W(s), volleyball W(s). *Intramural sports:* basketball M/W, cheerleading M(c)/W(c), football M/W, racquetball M/W, riflery M(c)/W(c), rock climbing

M(c)/W(c), skiing (downhill) M(c)/W(c), soccer M(c)/W(c), tennis M(c)/W(c), volleyball M/W, weight lifting M/W.

Standardized Tests *Required:* SAT or ACT (for admission). *Required for some:* SAT or ACT (for admission). *Recommended:* SAT or ACT (for admission).

Costs (2010–11) *Tuition:* state resident $3000 full-time, $100 per credit hour part-time; nonresident $4490 full-time, $150 per credit hour part-time. Full-time tuition and fees vary according to course load, location, program, and reciprocity agreements. Part-time tuition and fees vary according to course load, location, program, and reciprocity agreements. *Required fees:* $4130 full-time. *Room and board:* $5610; room only: $3000. Room and board charges vary according to board plan and housing facility. *Payment plan:* installment. *Waivers:* senior citizens and employees or children of employees.

Financial Aid Of all full-time matriculated undergraduates who enrolled in 2009, 1,417 applied for aid, 939 were judged to have need, 355 had their need fully met. 118 Federal Work-Study jobs (averaging $1857). In 2009, 296 non-need-based awards were made. *Average percent of need met:* 78%. *Average financial aid package:* $12,199. *Average need-based loan:* $3993. *Average need-based gift aid:* $4014. *Average non-need-based aid:* $2538. *Average indebtedness upon graduation:* $16,045.

Applying *Options:* electronic application. *Application fee:* $20. *Required:* high school transcript. *Recommended:* minimum 2.75 GPA. *Application deadlines:* rolling (freshmen), rolling (out-of-state freshmen), rolling (transfers). *Notification:* continuous (freshmen), continuous (out-of-state freshmen), continuous (transfers).

Freshman Application Contact Genene Sigler, Applications Processor, South Dakota School of Mines and Technology, 501 East Saint Joseph Street, Rapid City, SD 57701-3995. *Phone:* 605-394-2414 Ext. 5209. *Toll-free phone:* 800-544-8162 Ext. 2414. *Fax:* 605-394-1979. *E-mail:* admissions@sdsmt.edu. *Web site:* http://www.sdsmt.edu/.

South Dakota State University
Brookings, South Dakota

- **State-supported** university, founded 1881, part of South Dakota Board of Regents
- **Small-town** 272-acre campus
- **Endowment** $54.5 million
- **Coed** 11,062 undergraduate students, 79% full-time, 52% women, 48% men
- **Minimally difficult** entrance level, 91% of applicants were admitted

Undergraduates 8,743 full-time, 2,319 part-time. Students come from 50 states and territories; 66 other countries; 30% are from out of state; 7% transferred in; 41% live on campus. *Retention:* 77% of full-time freshmen returned.

Freshmen *Admission:* 4,604 applied, 4,205 admitted, 2,247 enrolled. *Average high school GPA:* 3.27. *Test scores:* ACT scores over 18: 94%; ACT scores over 24: 44%; ACT scores over 30: 5%.

Faculty *Total:* 695, 69% full-time, 54% with terminal degrees. *Student/faculty ratio:* 17:1.

Academics *Calendar:* semesters. *Degrees:* certificates, associate, bachelor's, master's, doctoral-professional, doctoral-research/scholarship, post-master's, and postbachelor's certificates. *Special study options:* academic remediation for entering students, accelerated degree program, adult/continuing education programs, advanced placement credit, cooperative education, distance learning, double majors, English as a second language, freshman honors college, honors programs, independent study, internships, off-campus study, part-time degree program, services for LD students, study abroad, summer session for credit. *ROTC:* Army (b), Air Force (b). *Unusual degree programs:* 3-2 economics.

Computers on Campus 437 computers/terminals and 938 ports are available on campus for general student use. Students can access the following: computer help desk, free student e-mail accounts, online (class) grades, online (class) registration. Campuswide network is available. 100% of college-owned or -operated housing units are wired for high-speed Internet access. Wireless service is available via classrooms, dorm rooms, libraries, student centers.

Student Life *Housing:* on-campus residence required through sophomore year. *Options:* coed, disabled students. Campus housing is university owned. Freshman campus housing is guaranteed. *Activities and organizations:* drama/theater group, student-run newspaper, radio station, choral group, marching band, Student Association, University Programming Council, Block and Bridle Club, national fraternities, national sororities. *Campus security:* 24-hour emergency response devices and patrols, student patrols, late-night transport/escort service, controlled dormitory access. *Student services:* health clinic, personal/psychological counseling, women's center, legal services.

Athletics Member NCAA. All Division I. *Intercollegiate sports:* baseball M(s), basketball M(s)/W(s), bowling M(c)/W(c), cheerleading M(c)/W(c), cross-country running M(s)/W(s), equestrian sports W, football M(s), golf M(s)/W(s), ice hockey M(c)/W(c), rugby M(c)/W(c), soccer M(c)/W(c), softball W(s), swimming and diving M(s)/W(s), tennis M(s)/W(s), track and field

M(s)/W(s), volleyball W(s), wrestling M(s). *Intramural sports:* badminton M/W, basketball M/W, football M/W, golf M/W, racquetball M/W, soccer W, softball M/W, swimming and diving M/W, table tennis M/W, track and field M/W, volleyball M/W, wrestling M.
Standardized Tests *Required:* SAT or ACT (for admission).
Costs (2010–11) *Tuition:* state resident $2994 full-time, $100 per credit hour part-time; nonresident $4491 full-time, $150 per credit hour part-time. Full-time tuition and fees vary according to course level, course load, location, program, and reciprocity agreements. Part-time tuition and fees vary according to course level, course load, location, program, and reciprocity agreements. *Required fees:* $3450 full-time. *Room and board:* $5899; room only: $2540. Room and board charges vary according to board plan and housing facility. *Payment plans:* installment, deferred payment. *Waivers:* children of alumni, senior citizens, and employees or children of employees.
Financial Aid Of all full-time matriculated undergraduates who enrolled in 2009, 7,471 applied for aid, 6,518 were judged to have need, 5,031 had their need fully met. 462 Federal Work-Study jobs (averaging $1520). 1,651 state and other part-time jobs (averaging $1730). In 2009, 1802 non-need-based awards were made. *Average percent of need met:* 87%. *Average financial aid package:* $9711. *Average need-based loan:* $4963. *Average need-based gift aid:* $4858. *Average non-need-based aid:* $1482. *Average indebtedness upon graduation:* $20,733.
Applying *Options:* electronic application, deferred entrance. *Application fee:* $20. *Required:* high school transcript, minimum 2.6 GPA. *Application deadlines:* rolling (freshmen), rolling (transfers). *Notification:* continuous (freshmen), continuous (transfers).
Freshman Application Contact Ms. Michelle Kuebler, Assistant Director of Admissions, South Dakota State University, PO Box 2201, Brookings, SD 57007. *Phone:* 605-688-4121. *Toll-free phone:* 800-952-3541. *Fax:* 605-688-6891. *E-mail:* sdsu.admissions@sdstate.edu. *Web site:* http://www.sdstate.edu/.

University of Sioux Falls

Sioux Falls, South Dakota

- **Independent American Baptist Churches in the USA** comprehensive, founded 1883
- **Suburban** 24-acre campus
- **Endowment** $17.2 million
- **Coed** 1,243 undergraduate students, 81% full-time, 53% women, 47% men
- **Moderately difficult** entrance level, 97% of applicants were admitted

Undergraduates 1,011 full-time, 232 part-time. Students come from 30 states and territories; 5 other countries; 32% are from out of state; 7% transferred in; 47% live on campus. *Retention:* 68% of full-time freshmen returned.
Freshmen *Admission:* 645 applied, 624 admitted, 292 enrolled. *Average high school GPA:* 3.3. *Test scores:* SAT critical reading scores over 500: 56%; SAT math scores over 500: 45%; ACT scores over 18: 92%; SAT critical reading scores over 600: 22%; SAT math scores over 600: 11%; ACT scores over 24: 41%; SAT critical reading scores over 700: 22%; SAT math scores over 700: 11%; ACT scores over 30: 5%.
Faculty *Total:* 140, 43% full-time. *Student/faculty ratio:* 15:1.
Academics *Calendar:* 4-1-4. *Degrees:* associate, bachelor's, master's, and post-master's certificates. *Special study options:* academic remediation for entering students, accelerated degree program, adult/continuing education programs, advanced placement credit, distance learning, double majors, honors programs, independent study, internships, off-campus study, part-time degree program, services for LD students, student-designed majors, study abroad, summer session for credit. *ROTC:* Air Force (b). *Unusual degree programs:* 3-2 engineering with South Dakota State University, Washington University in St. Louis; theology and philosophy with North American Baptist Seminary.
Computers on Campus 150 computers/terminals are available on campus for general student use. Students can access the following: campus intranet, computer help desk, free student e-mail accounts, online (class) grades, online (class) registration, online (class) schedules. Campuswide network is available. 100% of college-owned or -operated housing units are wired for high-speed Internet access. Wireless service is available via entire campus.
Student Life *Housing:* on-campus residence required through sophomore year. *Options:* coed, men-only, women-only. Campus housing is university owned and leased by the school. Freshman applicants given priority for college housing. *Activities and organizations:* drama/theater group, student-run newspaper, radio and television station, choral group, Fellowship of Christian Athletes, Campus Ministry Outreach, Student Senate, Association of Cougar Education Students (ACES), 1980's Music Video Remake Club. *Campus security:* 24-hour emergency response devices and patrols, student patrols, late-night transport/escort service, controlled dormitory access. *Student services:* personal/psychological counseling.
Athletics Member NAIA. *Intercollegiate sports:* baseball M(s), basketball M(s)/W(s), cheerleading M(s)/W(s), cross-country running M(s)/W(s), football M(s), golf M(s)/W(s), soccer M(s)/W(s), softball W(s), tennis M(s)/W(s),

track and field M(s)/W(s), volleyball W(s), wrestling M(s). *Intramural sports:* basketball M/W, football M/W, ice hockey M/W, table tennis M/W, ultimate Frisbee M/W, volleyball M/W.
Standardized Tests *Required:* SAT or ACT (for admission).
Costs (2011–12) *Comprehensive fee:* $29,420 includes full-time tuition ($22,090), mandatory fees ($760), and room and board ($6570). Full-time tuition and fees vary according to course load, degree level, and program. Part-time tuition: $300 per semester hour. Part-time tuition and fees vary according to course load, degree level, and program. *Required fees:* $150 per year part-time. *College room only:* $3070. Room and board charges vary according to board plan, housing facility, and student level. *Payment plan:* installment. *Waivers:* employees or children of employees.
Financial Aid Of all full-time matriculated undergraduates who enrolled in 2004, 130 Federal Work-Study jobs (averaging $1200).
Applying *Options:* electronic application. *Application fee:* $25. *Required:* high school transcript. *Required for some:* 2 letters of recommendation, interview. *Recommended:* essay or personal statement, minimum 2.8 GPA. *Application deadlines:* rolling (freshmen), rolling (transfers). *Notification:* continuous (freshmen), continuous (transfers).
Freshman Application Contact Mrs. Laura Glanville, Operations Manager, University of Sioux Falls, 1101 West 22nd Street, Sioux Falls, SD 57105. *Phone:* 605-331-6600 Ext. 6700. *Toll-free phone:* 800-888-1047. *Fax:* 605-331-6615. *E-mail:* admissions@usiouxfalls.edu. *Web site:* http://www.usiouxfalls.edu/.

The University of South Dakota

Vermillion, South Dakota

- **State-supported** university, founded 1862, part of South Dakota Board of Regents
- **Small-town** 275-acre campus
- **Endowment** $125.5 million
- **Coed** 7,220 undergraduate students, 61% full-time, 63% women, 37% men
- **Moderately difficult** entrance level, 85% of applicants were admitted

Undergraduates 4,422 full-time, 2,798 part-time. Students come from 46 states and territories; 14 other countries; 29% are from out of state; 11% transferred in; 26% live on campus. *Retention:* 76% of full-time freshmen returned.
Freshmen *Admission:* 3,452 applied, 2,927 admitted, 1,175 enrolled. *Average high school GPA:* 3.25. *Test scores:* SAT critical reading scores over 500: 60%; SAT math scores over 500: 65%; ACT scores over 18: 93%; SAT critical reading scores over 600: 33%; SAT math scores over 600: 35%; ACT scores over 24: 42%; SAT critical reading scores over 700: 4%; SAT math scores over 700: 5%; ACT scores over 30: 5%.
Faculty *Total:* 504, 73% full-time, 55% with terminal degrees. *Student/faculty ratio:* 17:1.
Academics *Calendar:* semesters. *Degrees:* certificates, associate, bachelor's, master's, doctoral-professional, doctoral-research/scholarship, post-master's, and postbachelor's certificates. *Special study options:* academic remediation for entering students, accelerated degree program, adult/continuing education programs, advanced placement credit, cooperative education, distance learning, double majors, English as a second language, external degree program, honors programs, independent study, internships, off-campus study, part-time degree program, services for LD students, student-designed majors, study abroad, summer session for credit. *ROTC:* Army (b). *Unusual degree programs:* 3-2 business administration; social work; accounting, political science, public administration.
Computers on Campus 917 computers/terminals are available on campus for general student use. Students can access the following: campus intranet, computer help desk, free student e-mail accounts, online (class) registration. Campuswide network is available. Wireless service is available via computer centers, computer labs, learning centers, libraries, student centers.
Student Life *Housing:* on-campus residence required through sophomore year. *Options:* coed, men-only, women-only, disabled students. Campus housing is university owned. Freshman campus housing is guaranteed. *Activities and organizations:* drama/theater group, student-run newspaper, radio station, choral group, marching band, Program Council, Residence Hall Association, Student Ambassadors, Delta Sigma Pi, national fraternities, national sororities. *Campus security:* 24-hour emergency response devices and patrols, student patrols, late-night transport/escort service, controlled dormitory access. *Student services:* health clinic, personal/psychological counseling, legal services.
Athletics Member NCAA. All Division I. *Intercollegiate sports:* basketball M(s)/W(s), cross-country running M(s)/W(s), football M(s), golf M(s)/W(s), soccer W(s), softball W(s), swimming and diving M(s)/W(s), tennis W(s), track and field M(s)/W(s), volleyball W(s). *Intramural sports:* baseball M(c), basketball M/W, crew M(c)/W(c), fencing M(c)/W(c), football M, ice hockey M(c), lacrosse M(c)/W(c), rock climbing M(c), rugby M(c)/W(c), soccer M(c)/W(c), softball W(c), tennis W.
Standardized Tests *Required:* SAT or ACT (for admission).

Costs (2010–11) *Tuition:* state resident $2994 full-time, $100 per credit hour part-time; nonresident $4491 full-time, $150 per credit hour part-time. Full-time tuition and fees vary according to course load. Part-time tuition and fees vary according to course load. *Required fees:* $3768 full-time, $126 per credit hour part-time. *Room and board:* $6123; room only: $3003. Room and board charges vary according to board plan and housing facility. *Payment plan:* deferred payment. *Waivers:* children of alumni, senior citizens, and employees or children of employees.

Financial Aid Of all full-time matriculated undergraduates who enrolled in 2008, 4,153 applied for aid, 3,170 were judged to have need, 1,997 had their need fully met. In 2008, 887 non-need-based awards were made. *Average percent of need met:* 80%. *Average financial aid package:* $7005. *Average need-based loan:* $4354. *Average need-based gift aid:* $4697. *Average non-need-based aid:* $3792. *Average indebtedness upon graduation:* $22,954.

Applying *Options:* electronic application, early admission, deferred entrance. *Application fee:* $20. *Required:* high school transcript. *Recommended:* minimum 2 GPA. *Application deadlines:* rolling (freshmen), rolling (transfers). *Notification:* continuous (freshmen), continuous (transfers).

Freshman Application Contact Mr. Scott Pohlson, Director of Enrollment Services, The University of South Dakota, 414 East Clark Street, Vermillion, SD 57069-2390. *Phone:* 605-677-5434. *Toll-free phone:* 877-269-6837. *Fax:* 605-677-6753. *E-mail:* admiss@usd.edu. *Web site:* http://www.usd.edu/.

TENNESSEE

American Baptist College of American Baptist Theological Seminary

Nashville, Tennessee

- **Independent Baptist** 4-year, founded 1924
- **Urban** 52-acre campus
- **Endowment** $875,540
- **Coed**
- **Noncompetitive** entrance level

Faculty *Student/faculty ratio:* 14:1.

Academics *Calendar:* semesters. *Degrees:* certificates, associate, and bachelor's.

Student Life *Campus security:* student patrols, security patrols from 10 pm to 7 am.

Costs (2010–11) *Tuition:* $5760 full-time, $240 per credit hour part-time. *Required fees:* $400 full-time, $200 per term part-time. *Room only:* $2000. Room and board charges vary according to board plan and housing facility.

Financial Aid *Of all full-time matriculated undergraduates who enrolled in 2009,* 60 applied for aid, 60 were judged to have need. 1 Federal Work-Study job (averaging $6741). *Average percent of need met:* 75. *Average financial aid package:* $2675. *Average need-based gift aid:* $1161. *Financial aid deadline:* 7/23.

Applying *Options:* deferred entrance. *Application fee:* $20. *Required:* essay or personal statement, high school transcript, minimum 2 GPA, 3 letters of recommendation, interview.

Freshman Application Contact Ms. Marcella Lockhart, Director of Enrollment Management, American Baptist College of American Baptist Theological Seminary, 1800 Baptist World Center Drive, Nashville, TN 37207. *Phone:* 615-687-6896. *Fax:* 615-226-7855. *E-mail:* mlockhart@abcnash.edu. *Web site:* http://www.abcnash.edu/.

Aquinas College

Nashville, Tennessee

- **Independent Roman Catholic** 4-year, founded 1961, administratively affiliated with The Dominican Sisters of the Saint Cecilia Congregation
- **Urban** 92-acre campus
- **Coed** 721 undergraduate students, 35% full-time, 85% women, 15% men
- **Minimally difficult** entrance level, 65% of applicants were admitted

Undergraduates 255 full-time, 466 part-time. 13% Black or African American, non-Hispanic/Latino; 2% Hispanic/Latino; 2% Asian, non-Hispanic/Latino; 1% Native Hawaiian or other Pacific Islander, non-Hispanic/Latino; 0.1% American Indian or Alaska Native, non-Hispanic/Latino; 0.4% Two or more races, non-Hispanic/Latino; 6% Race/ethnicity unknown; 18% transferred in. *Retention:* 80% of full-time freshmen returned.

Freshmen *Admission:* 82 applied, 53 admitted, 36 enrolled. *Average high school GPA:* 3.22.

Faculty *Total:* 91, 37% full-time, 31% with terminal degrees. *Student/faculty ratio:* 8:1.

Academics *Calendar:* semesters. *Degrees:* associate, bachelor's, and post-bachelor's certificates. *Special study options:* academic remediation for entering students, accelerated degree program, advanced placement credit, cooperative education, independent study, internships, part-time degree program, summer session for credit.

Computers on Campus Students can access the following: computer help desk, free student e-mail accounts, online (class) grades, online (class) schedules. Campuswide network is available.

Student Life *Housing:* college housing not available. *Activities and organizations:* student-run newspaper. *Campus security:* 24-hour emergency response devices, patrols by security after class hours.

Standardized Tests *Required for some:* SAT or ACT (for admission).

Costs (2010–11) *Tuition:* $17,730 full-time, $591 per credit hour part-time. Full-time tuition and fees vary according to course load and program. Part-time tuition and fees vary according to course load and program. *Required fees:* $600 full-time, $300 per term part-time. *Payment plan:* installment. *Waivers:* employees or children of employees.

Applying *Options:* electronic application, deferred entrance. *Application fee:* $25. *Required:* high school transcript, minimum 2.2 GPA. *Required for some:* essay or personal statement. *Application deadlines:* rolling (freshmen), rolling (transfers). *Notification:* continuous (freshmen), continuous (transfers).

Freshman Application Contact Ms. Connie Hansom, Director of Admission, Aquinas College, 4210 Harding Road, Nashville, TN 37205-2005. *Phone:* 615-297-7545 Ext. 411. *Toll-free phone:* 800-649-9956. *Fax:* 615-279-3893. *E-mail:* hansomc@aquinascollege.edu. *Web site:* http://www.aquinascollege.edu/.

Argosy University, Nashville

Nashville, Tennessee

- **Proprietary** university, founded 2001
- **Coed**

Academics *Calendar:* semesters. *Degrees:* bachelor's, master's, and doctoral-professional.

Costs (2010–11) *Tuition:* Tuition varies by program. Students should contact Argosy University for tuition information.

Freshman Application Contact Argosy University, Nashville, 100 Centerview Drive, Suite 225, Nashville, TN 37214. *Phone:* 615-525-2800. *Toll-free phone:* 866-833-6598. *Web site:* http://www.argosy.edu/nashville/.

See page 1002 for the College Close-Up.

The Art Institute of Tennessee–Nashville

Nashville, Tennessee

- **Proprietary** 4-year, founded 2006, part of Education Management Corporation
- **Urban** campus
- **Coed**

Academics *Degrees:* diplomas, associate, and bachelor's.

Costs (2010–11) *Tuition:* Tuition cost varies by program. Prospective students should contact the school for current tuition costs. Other charges include a starting kit for all first-quarter students. Kits vary in price, depending on the program of study.

Freshman Application Contact The Art Institute of Tennessee–Nashville, 100 Centerview Drive, Suite 250, Nashville, TN 37214. *Phone:* 615-874-1067. *Toll-free phone:* 866-747-5770. *Web site:* http://www.artinstitutes.edu/nashville/.

See page 1072 for the College Close-Up.

Austin Peay State University

Clarksville, Tennessee

- **State-supported** comprehensive, founded 1927, part of Tennessee Board of Regents
- **Suburban** 200-acre campus with easy access to Nashville
- **Endowment** $5.7 million
- **Coed** 9,835 undergraduate students, 74% full-time, 61% women, 39% men
- **Moderately difficult** entrance level, 88% of applicants were admitted

Undergraduates 7,317 full-time, 2,518 part-time. Students come from 37 states and territories; 21 other countries; 9% are from out of state; 19% Black or African American, non-Hispanic/Latino; 6% Hispanic/Latino; 2% Asian, non-Hispanic/Latino; 0.5% Native Hawaiian or other Pacific Islander, non-Hispanic/Latino; 0.6% American Indian or Alaska Native, non-Hispanic/Latino; 4% Two or more races, non-Hispanic/Latino; 2% Race/ethnicity

unknown; 0.5% international; 9% transferred in; 14% live on campus. *Retention:* 70% of full-time freshmen returned.

Freshmen *Admission:* 3,464 applied, 3,034 admitted, 1,718 enrolled. *Average high school GPA:* 3.12. *Test scores:* SAT critical reading scores over 500: 43%; SAT math scores over 500: 36%; ACT scores over 18: 88%; SAT critical reading scores over 600: 12%; SAT math scores over 600: 13%; ACT scores over 24: 25%; SAT critical reading scores over 700: 4%; ACT scores over 30: 3%.

Faculty *Total:* 592, 55% full-time. *Student/faculty ratio:* 21:1.

Academics *Calendar:* semesters. *Degrees:* certificates, associate, bachelor's, master's, post-master's, and postbachelor's certificates. *Special study options:* academic remediation for entering students, accelerated degree program, adult/continuing education programs, advanced placement credit, cooperative education, distance learning, double majors, English as a second language, honors programs, independent study, internships, part-time degree program, services for LD students, study abroad, summer session for credit. *ROTC:* Army (b), Air Force (c).

Computers on Campus 790 computers/terminals are available on campus for general student use. Students can access the following: campus intranet, computer help desk, free student e-mail accounts, online (class) grades, online (class) registration, online (class) schedules. Campuswide network is available. Wireless service is available via entire campus.

Student Life *Housing:* on-campus residence required for freshman year. *Options:* coed, men-only, women-only, disabled students. Campus housing is university owned. Freshman campus housing is guaranteed. *Activities and organizations:* drama/theater group, student-run newspaper, radio and television station, choral group, marching band, national fraternities, national sororities. *Campus security:* 24-hour emergency response devices and patrols, late-night transport/escort service, controlled dormitory access. *Student services:* health clinic, personal/psychological counseling.

Athletics Member NCAA. All Division I except football (Division I-AA). *Intercollegiate sports:* baseball M(s), basketball M(s)/W(s), cheerleading M(s)/W(s), cross-country running M(s)/W(s), golf M(s)/W(s), soccer W(s), softball W(s), tennis M(s)/W(s), track and field W(s), volleyball W(s). *Intramural sports:* badminton M/W, basketball M/W, football M/W, golf M/W, ice hockey M/W, racquetball M/W, soccer M/W, softball M/W, ultimate Frisbee M/W, volleyball M/W, wrestling M.

Standardized Tests *Required for some:* SAT or ACT (for admission).

Costs (2010–11) *Tuition:* state resident $4824 full-time, $201 per credit hour part-time; nonresident $17,352 full-time, $723 per credit hour part-time. Full-time tuition and fees vary according to location and program. Part-time tuition and fees vary according to location and program. *Required fees:* $1224 full-time, $61 per credit hour part-time. *Room and board:* $6450; room only: $3960. Room and board charges vary according to board plan and housing facility. *Payment plan:* installment. *Waivers:* senior citizens and employees or children of employees.

Financial Aid Of all full-time matriculated undergraduates who enrolled in 2008, 6,216 applied for aid, 5,268 were judged to have need. 177 Federal Work-Study jobs (averaging $1946). 409 state and other part-time jobs (averaging $1580). In 2008, 633 non-need-based awards were made. *Average financial aid package:* $8902. *Average need-based loan:* $3811. *Average need-based gift aid:* $5158. *Average non-need-based aid:* $4315. *Average indebtedness upon graduation:* $19,149.

Applying *Options:* electronic application, early admission, deferred entrance. *Application fee:* $15. *Required:* high school transcript. *Required for some:* minimum 2.75 GPA. *Application deadlines:* 7/23 (freshmen), rolling (transfers). *Notification:* continuous (freshmen), continuous (transfers).

Freshman Application Contact Mr. Ryan Forsythe, Director of Admissions, Austin Peay State University, 601 College Street, Clarksville, TN 37044. *Phone:* 931-221-7661. *Toll-free phone:* 800-844-2778. *Fax:* 931-221-6168. *E-mail:* admissions@apsu.edu. *Web site:* http://www.apsu.edu/.

Baptist College of Health Sciences
Memphis, Tennessee

- **Independent Southern Baptist** 4-year, founded 1994, administratively affiliated with Baptist Memorial Health Care
- **Urban** campus
- **Coed, primarily women** 1,021 undergraduate students
- **Moderately difficult** entrance level

Undergraduates Students come from 10 states and territories; 31% are from out of state; 35% Black or African American, non-Hispanic/Latino; 1% Hispanic/Latino; 2% Asian, non-Hispanic/Latino; 0.1% American Indian or Alaska Native, non-Hispanic/Latino; 5% Race/ethnicity unknown; 10% live on campus. *Retention:* 84% of full-time freshmen returned.

Faculty *Total:* 106, 57% full-time. *Student/faculty ratio:* 14:1.

Academics *Calendar:* trimesters. *Degree:* bachelor's. *Special study options:* accelerated degree program, advanced placement credit, distance learning, part-time degree program, services for LD students, summer session for credit.

Computers on Campus 64 computers/terminals and 64 ports are available on campus for general student use. Students can access the following: campus intranet, computer help desk, free student e-mail accounts, online (class) grades, online (class) registration, online (class) schedules. Campuswide network is available. 100% of college-owned or -operated housing units are wired for high-speed Internet access. Wireless service is available via entire campus.

Student Life *Housing options:* coed. Campus housing is university owned. *Activities and organizations:* Student Government Association, Student Nursing Association, Allied Health Organization. *Campus security:* 24-hour emergency response devices, late-night transport/escort service, controlled dormitory access, 16 to 20-hour trained security personnel. *Student services:* health clinic, personal/psychological counseling.

Standardized Tests *Required:* ACT (for admission), Health Occupations Basic Entrance Test (for admission).

Costs (2010–11) *Tuition:* $9420 full-time, $314 per credit hour part-time. *Required fees:* $850 full-time, $25 per credit hour part-time, $50 per term part-time. *Room only:* $900. Room and board charges vary according to housing facility.

Applying *Options:* electronic application, early admission. *Application fee:* $25. *Required:* high school transcript, minimum 2.75 GPA, 3 letters of recommendation, immunizations, health physical. *Required for some:* essay or personal statement, interview. *Application deadlines:* 5/1 (freshmen), 5/1 (transfers).

Freshman Application Contact Baptist College of Health Sciences, 1003 Monroe Avenue, Memphis, TN 38104. *Phone:* 901-572-2441. *Toll-free phone:* 866-575-2247. *Web site:* http://www.bchs.edu/.

Belhaven University
Memphis, Tennessee

Director of Admissions Don Jones, Director of Admission, Belhaven University, 5100 Poplar Avenue, Suite 200, Memphis, TN 38137. *Phone:* 901-888-3343. *Fax:* 901-888-0771. *E-mail:* memphisadmission@belhaven.edu. *Web site:* http://memphis.belhaven.edu/.

Belmont University
Nashville, Tennessee

- **Independent Christian** comprehensive, founded 1951
- **Urban** 66-acre campus
- **Endowment** $73.4 million
- **Coed** 4,603 undergraduate students, 93% full-time, 57% women, 43% men
- **Moderately difficult** entrance level, 81% of applicants were admitted

Undergraduates 4,274 full-time, 329 part-time. Students come from 49 states and territories; 27 other countries; 57% are from out of state; 4% Black or African American, non-Hispanic/Latino; 3% Hispanic/Latino; 3% Asian, non-Hispanic/Latino; 0.2% Native Hawaiian or other Pacific Islander, non-Hispanic/Latino; 1% American Indian or Alaska Native, non-Hispanic/Latino; 0.1% Two or more races, non-Hispanic/Latino; 0.7% Race/ethnicity unknown; 1% international; 9% transferred in; 45% live on campus. *Retention:* 82% of full-time freshmen returned.

Freshmen *Admission:* 3,322 applied, 2,704 admitted, 1,019 enrolled. *Average high school GPA:* 3.53. *Test scores:* SAT critical reading scores over 500: 90%; SAT math scores over 500: 89%; ACT scores over 18: 100%; SAT critical reading scores over 600: 46%; SAT math scores over 600: 45%; ACT scores over 24: 75%; SAT critical reading scores over 700: 11%; SAT math scores over 700: 7%; ACT scores over 30: 20%.

Faculty *Total:* 648, 44% full-time, 51% with terminal degrees. *Student/faculty ratio:* 13:1.

Academics *Calendar:* semesters. *Degrees:* bachelor's, master's, doctoral-other, doctoral-professional, and post-master's certificates. *Special study options:* accelerated degree program, adult/continuing education programs, advanced placement credit, cooperative education, distance learning, double majors, English as a second language, honors programs, independent study, internships, off-campus study, part-time degree program, student-designed majors, study abroad, summer session for credit. *ROTC:* Army (c), Navy (c), Air Force (c). *Unusual degree programs:* 3-2 engineering with Auburn University, Georgia Institute of Technology, University of Tennessee.

Computers on Campus 500 computers/terminals are available on campus for general student use. Students can access the following: campus intranet, free student e-mail accounts, online (class) grades, online (class) registration, online (class) schedules, individual student information via BANNER Web. Campuswide network is available. 100% of college-owned or -operated housing units are wired for high-speed Internet access. Wireless service is available via entire campus.

Student Life *Housing:* on-campus residence required through sophomore year. *Options:* men-only, women-only. Campus housing is university owned. Freshman applicants given priority for college housing. *Activities and organiza-*

tions: drama/theater group, student-run newspaper, radio and television station, choral group, marching band, Service Corp, Alpha Sigma Tau, Phi Mu, Phi Kappa Tau, MOB, national fraternities, national sororities. *Campus security:* 24-hour emergency response devices and patrols, late-night transport/ escort service, controlled dormitory access, bicycle patrol. *Student services:* health clinic, personal/psychological counseling, women's center.

Athletics Member NCAA. All Division I. *Intercollegiate sports:* baseball M(s), basketball M(s)/W(s), cross-country running M(s)/W(s), golf M(s)/W(s), soccer M(s)/W(s), softball W(s), tennis M(s)/W(s), track and field M(s)/W(s), volleyball W(s). *Intramural sports:* basketball M/W, bowling M/W, football M, golf M, ice hockey M/W, racquetball M/W, table tennis M/W, tennis M/W, volleyball M/W.

Standardized Tests *Required:* SAT or ACT (for admission).

Costs (2010–11) *Comprehensive fee:* $35,360 includes full-time tuition ($22,530), mandatory fees ($1150), and room and board ($11,680). Full-time tuition and fees vary according to class time and course load. Part-time tuition: $865 per credit hour. Part-time tuition and fees vary according to course load. *Required fees:* $410 per term part-time. *College room only:* $7650. Room and board charges vary according to board plan, housing facility, and location. *Payment plans:* installment, deferred payment. *Waivers:* senior citizens and employees or children of employees.

Financial Aid Of all full-time matriculated undergraduates who enrolled in 2009, 4,001 applied for aid, 2,599 were judged to have need, 648 had their need fully met. 534 Federal Work-Study jobs (averaging $6297). In 2009, 522 non-need-based awards were made. *Average percent of need met:* 79%. *Average financial aid package:* $12,214. *Average need-based loan:* $4434. *Average need-based gift aid:* $6896. *Average non-need-based aid:* $6851. *Average indebtedness upon graduation:* $29,058.

Applying *Options:* electronic application, early admission, deferred entrance. *Application fee:* $50. *Required:* essay or personal statement, high school transcript, minimum 3 GPA, 2 letters of recommendation, resume of activities. *Required for some:* interview. *Application deadlines:* 8/1 (freshmen), 8/1 (transfers). *Notification:* continuous (freshmen), continuous (transfers).

Freshman Application Contact Mr. David Mee, Dean of Enrollment Services, Belmont University, 1900 Belmont Boulevard, Nashville, TN 37212-3757. *Phone:* 615-460-6785. *Toll-free phone:* 800-56E-NROL. *Fax:* 615-460-5434. *E-mail:* buadmission@belmont.edu. *Web site:* http://www.belmont.edu/.

See page 1116 for the College Close-Up.

Bethel University
McKenzie, Tennessee

- **Independent Cumberland Presbyterian** comprehensive, founded 1842
- **Small-town** 100-acre campus
- **Endowment** $8.1 million
- **Coed** 2,550 undergraduate students, 99% full-time, 59% women, 41% men
- **Minimally difficult** entrance level, 54% of applicants were admitted

Undergraduates 2,515 full-time, 35 part-time. Students come from 25 states and territories; 19 other countries; 9% are from out of state; 2% transferred in; 29% live on campus. *Retention:* 64% of full-time freshmen returned.

Freshmen *Admission:* 1,057 applied, 566 admitted, 353 enrolled. *Average high school GPA:* 3.05.

Faculty *Total:* 291, 33% full-time. *Student/faculty ratio:* 19:1.

Academics *Calendar:* semesters. *Degrees:* bachelor's and master's. *Special study options:* academic remediation for entering students, accelerated degree program, adult/continuing education programs, advanced placement credit, cooperative education, distance learning, double majors, honors programs, independent study, internships, off-campus study, part-time degree program, services for LD students, student-designed majors, summer session for credit. *Unusual degree programs:* 3-2 engineering with Tennessee Technological University; pharmacy with University of Tennessee, Memphis.

Computers on Campus 12 computers/terminals and 30 ports are available on campus for general student use. Students can access the following: campus intranet, computer help desk, free student e-mail accounts, online (class) grades, online (class) registration, online (class) schedules. Campuswide network is available. 100% of college-owned or -operated housing units are wired for high-speed Internet access. Wireless service is available via classrooms, computer labs, dorm rooms, libraries, student centers.

Student Life *Housing:* on-campus residence required through junior year. *Options:* coed, men-only, women-only, disabled students. Campus housing is university owned and leased by the school. Freshman applicants given priority for college housing. *Activities and organizations:* drama/theater group, choral group, marching band, Campus Crusade for Christ, STEA (Education), Student Government Association, Students in Free Enterprise (SIFE), Arete. *Campus security:* night patrols by trained security personnel. *Student services:* personal/psychological counseling.

Athletics Member NAIA. *Intercollegiate sports:* baseball M(s), basketball M(s)/W(s), bowling M(s)/W(s), cheerleading M(s)/W(s), cross-country running M(s)/W(s), football M(s), golf M(s)/W(s), riflery M(s)/W(s), soccer M(s)/W(s), softball M(s), tennis M(s)/W(s), track and field M(s)/W(s), volleyball W(s). *Intramural sports:* basketball M/W, football M/W, soccer M/W, softball M/W, table tennis M/W, tennis M/W, volleyball M/W.

Standardized Tests *Recommended:* SAT or ACT (for admission).

Costs (2011–12) *Comprehensive fee:* $21,334 includes full-time tuition ($12,902), mandatory fees ($650), and room and board ($7782). Full-time tuition and fees vary according to program. Part-time tuition: $398 per credit hour. Part-time tuition and fees vary according to course load and program. *Payment plan:* installment. *Waivers:* employees or children of employees.

Applying *Options:* electronic application, early admission, deferred entrance. *Application fee:* $30. *Required:* high school transcript, minimum 2 GPA. *Required for some:* essay or personal statement, interview. *Application deadlines:* rolling (freshmen), rolling (transfers). *Notification:* continuous (freshmen), continuous (transfers).

Freshman Application Contact Tina Hodges, Enrollment Director of Admissions and Financial Aid, Bethel University, 325 Cherry Avenue, McKenzie, TN 38201. *Phone:* 731-352-4030. *Fax:* 731-352-4069. *E-mail:* hodgest@bethelu.edu. *Web site:* http://www.bethel-college.edu/.

Bryan College
Dayton, Tennessee

- **Independent interdenominational** comprehensive, founded 1930
- **Small-town** 100-acre campus
- **Coed** 1,222 undergraduate students, 84% full-time, 53% women, 47% men
- **Moderately difficult** entrance level, 53% of applicants were admitted

Undergraduates 1,029 full-time, 193 part-time. 50% are from out of state; 5% Black or African American, non-Hispanic/Latino; 2% Hispanic/Latino; 0.6% Asian, non-Hispanic/Latino; 0.2% American Indian or Alaska Native, non-Hispanic/Latino; 3% Race/ethnicity unknown; 1% international; 3% transferred in; 82% live on campus.

Freshmen *Admission:* 897 applied, 477 admitted, 239 enrolled. *Average high school GPA:* 3.59. *Test scores:* SAT critical reading scores over 500: 82%; SAT math scores over 500: 67%; SAT writing scores over 500: 72%; ACT scores over 18: 92%; SAT critical reading scores over 600: 41%; SAT math scores over 600: 33%; SAT writing scores over 600: 32%; ACT scores over 24: 50%; SAT critical reading scores over 700: 7%; SAT writing scores over 700: 3%; ACT scores over 30: 6%.

Faculty *Total:* 66, 65% full-time, 80% with terminal degrees. *Student/faculty ratio:* 23:1.

Academics *Calendar:* semesters. *Degrees:* certificates, diplomas, associate, bachelor's, and master's. *Special study options:* academic remediation for entering students, adult/continuing education programs, advanced placement credit, distance learning, double majors, honors programs, independent study, internships, part-time degree program, study abroad, summer session for credit. *Unusual degree programs:* 3-2 nursing with Vanderbilt University.

Computers on Campus Students can access the following: campus intranet, computer help desk, free student e-mail accounts, online (class) grades, online (class) schedules. Campuswide network is available.

Student Life *Housing:* on-campus residence required through senior year. *Options:* men-only, women-only. Campus housing is university owned. Freshman campus housing is guaranteed. *Activities and organizations:* drama/theater group, student-run newspaper, choral group. *Campus security:* student patrols, late-night transport/escort service, controlled dormitory access, police patrols. *Student services:* health clinic, personal/psychological counseling.

Athletics Member NAIA, NCCAA. *Intercollegiate sports:* baseball M(s), basketball M(s)/W(s), cross-country running M(s)/W(s), soccer M(s)/W(s), track and field M/W, volleyball W(s). *Intramural sports:* basketball M/W, football M/W, golf M, soccer M/W, softball M/W, table tennis M/W, tennis M/W, volleyball M/W.

Standardized Tests *Required:* SAT or ACT (for admission).

Costs (2011–12) *Comprehensive fee:* $24,194 includes full-time tuition ($18,620), mandatory fees ($120), and room and board ($5454). Full-time tuition and fees vary according to course load. Part-time tuition: $775 per credit. Part-time tuition and fees vary according to course load. *Room and board:* Room and board charges vary according to board plan and housing facility. *Payment plan:* installment. *Waivers:* employees or children of employees.

Financial Aid Of all full-time matriculated undergraduates who enrolled in 2009, 832 applied for aid, 734 were judged to have need, 371 had their need fully met. In 2009, 102 non-need-based awards were made. *Average percent of need met:* 76%. *Average financial aid package:* $14,768. *Average need-based loan:* $3678. *Average need-based gift aid:* $8587. *Average non-need-based aid:* $4703. *Average indebtedness upon graduation:* $14,976.

Applying *Options:* electronic application, early action, deferred entrance. *Application fee:* $35. *Required:* essay or personal statement, high school transcript, minimum 2 GPA, 3 letters of recommendation. *Required for some:* interview. *Application deadlines:* rolling (freshmen), rolling (transfers), 5/1 (early action). *Notification:* continuous (freshmen), rolling (early action). **Freshman Application Contact** Michael Sapienza, Vice President for Enrollment Management, Bryan College, PO Box 7000, Dayton, TN 37321-7000. *Phone:* 423-775-2041. *Toll-free phone:* 800-277-9522. *Fax:* 423-775-7199. *E-mail:* admissions@bryan.edu. *Web site:* http://www.bryan.edu/.

Carson-Newman College

Jefferson City, Tennessee

- **Independent Southern Baptist** comprehensive, founded 1851
- **Small-town** 90-acre campus with easy access to Knoxville
- **Endowment** $41.7 million
- **Coed** 1,763 undergraduate students, 96% full-time, 55% women, 45% men
- **Moderately difficult** entrance level, 69% of applicants were admitted

Undergraduates 1,698 full-time, 65 part-time. Students come from 31 states and territories; 23 other countries; 31% are from out of state; 9% Black or African American, non-Hispanic/Latino; 2% Hispanic/Latino; 0.3% Asian, non-Hispanic/Latino; 0.3% American Indian or Alaska Native, non-Hispanic/Latino; 2% Two or more races, non-Hispanic/Latino; 1% Race/ethnicity unknown; 4% international; 8% transferred in; 51% live on campus. *Retention:* 68% of full-time freshmen returned.

Freshmen *Admission:* 3,174 applied, 2,187 admitted, 428 enrolled. *Average high school GPA:* 3.4. *Test scores:* ACT scores over 18: 94%; ACT scores over 24: 42%; ACT scores over 30: 7%.

Faculty *Total:* 204, 60% full-time, 47% with terminal degrees. *Student/faculty ratio:* 12:1.

Academics *Calendar:* semesters. *Degrees:* associate, bachelor's, and master's. *Special study options:* academic remediation for entering students, accelerated degree program, adult/continuing education programs, advanced placement credit, English as a second language, honors programs, internships, off-campus study, part-time degree program, services for LD students, student-designed majors, study abroad, summer session for credit. *ROTC:* Army (b), Air Force (c). *Unusual degree programs:* 3-2 engineering with Georgia Institute of Technology, University of Tennessee, Tennessee Technological University; pharmacy with Campbell University, Mercer University, University of Georgia.

Computers on Campus 200 computers/terminals are available on campus for general student use. Campuswide network is available.

Student Life *Housing:* on-campus residence required through junior year. *Options:* men-only, women-only. Freshman campus housing is guaranteed. *Activities and organizations:* drama/theater group, student-run newspaper, choral group, marching band, Baptist Student Union, Fellowship of Christian Athletes, Student Government Association, Student Ambassadors Association, Columbians, national fraternities, national sororities. *Campus security:* 24-hour emergency response devices and patrols, late-night transport/escort service, controlled dormitory access. *Student services:* health clinic, personal/psychological counseling.

Athletics Member NCAA. All Division II. *Intercollegiate sports:* baseball M(s), basketball M(s)/W(s), cross-country running M(s)/W(s), football M(s), golf M(s), soccer M(s)/W(s), softball W(s), tennis M(s)/W(s), track and field M(s)/W(s), volleyball W(s), wrestling M(s). *Intramural sports:* badminton M/W, baseball M/W, basketball M/W, football M/W, golf M/W, racquetball M/W, skiing (downhill) M/W, soccer M/W, softball M/W, table tennis M/W, tennis M/W, volleyball M/W.

Standardized Tests *Required:* SAT or ACT (for admission).

Costs (2011–12) *Comprehensive fee:* $28,024 includes full-time tuition ($20,786), mandatory fees ($992), and room and board ($6246). Full-time tuition and fees vary according to class time and course load. Part-time tuition: $818 per semester hour. *Room and board:* Room and board charges vary according to board plan, gender, and housing facility. *Payment plans:* installment, deferred payment. *Waivers:* senior citizens and employees or children of employees.

Financial Aid Of all full-time matriculated undergraduates who enrolled in 2009, 1,556 applied for aid, 1,366 were judged to have need, 287 had their need fully met. 119 Federal Work-Study jobs (averaging $1596). 14 state and other part-time jobs (averaging $814). In 2009, 247 non-need-based awards were made. *Average percent of need met:* 70%. *Average financial aid package:* $16,621. *Average need-based loan:* $3693. *Average need-based gift aid:* $12,279. *Average non-need-based aid:* $7864. *Average indebtedness upon graduation:* $20,528.

Applying *Options:* electronic application, deferred entrance. *Application fee:* $25. *Required:* high school transcript, minimum 2.25 GPA, medical history.

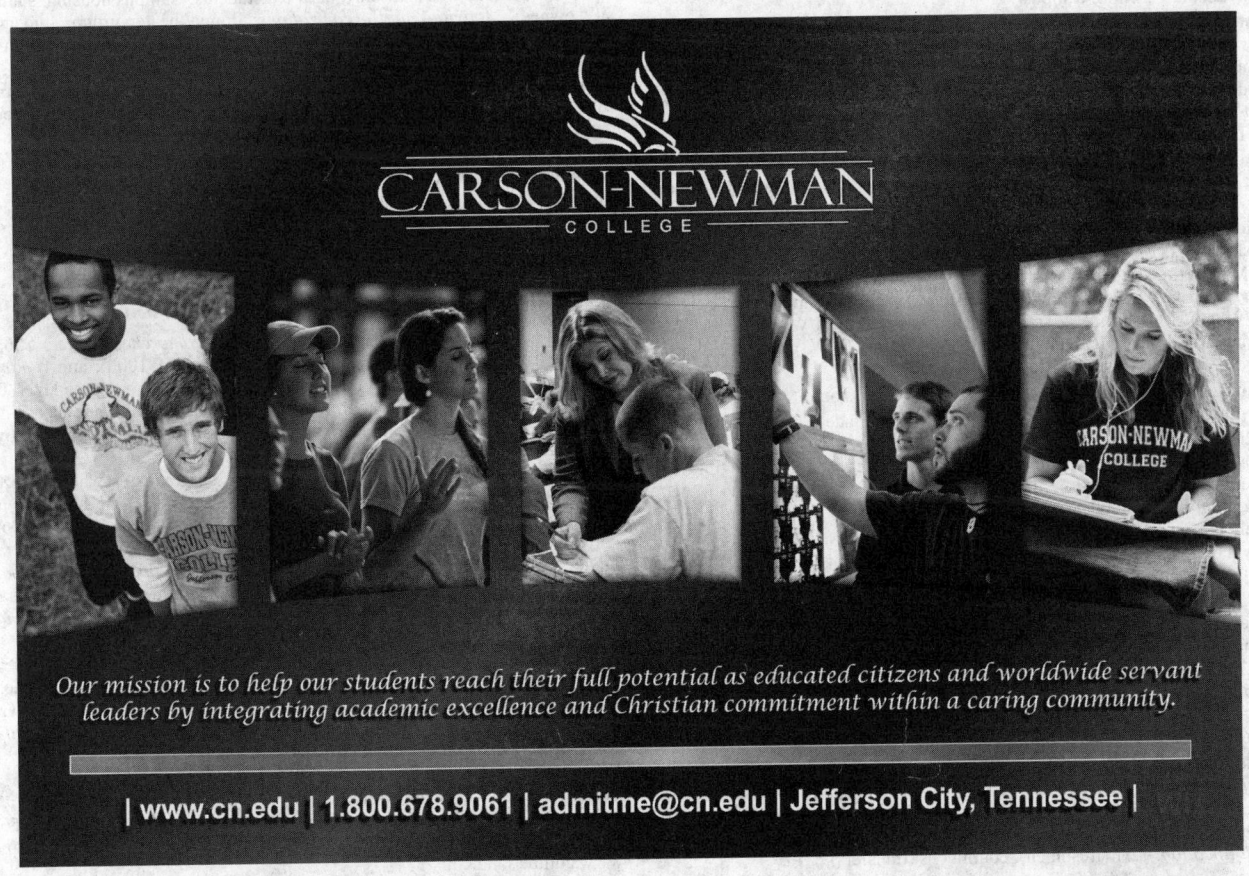

Required for some: essay or personal statement, interview. *Recommended:* interview. *Application deadlines:* 8/1 (freshmen), 8/1 (transfers). *Notification:* continuous (freshmen), continuous (transfers).

Freshman Application Contact Melanie Redding, Director of Admissions, Carson-Newman College, 1646 Russell Avenue, PO Box 557, Jefferson City, TN 37760. *Phone:* 865-471-3223. *Toll-free phone:* 800-678-9061. *Fax:* 865-471-3502. *E-mail:* cnadmiss@cn.edu. *Web site:* http://www.cn.edu/.

See page 1202 for the College Close-Up.

Christian Brothers University
Memphis, Tennessee

- **Independent Roman Catholic** comprehensive, founded 1871
- **Urban** 75-acre campus
- **Endowment** $24.8 million
- **Coed** 1,351 undergraduate students, 88% full-time, 54% women, 46% men
- **Moderately difficult** entrance level, 48% of applicants were admitted

Undergraduates 1,195 full-time, 156 part-time. Students come from 22 states and territories; 22 other countries; 21% are from out of state; 5% transferred in; 40% live on campus. *Retention:* 74% of full-time freshmen returned.

Freshmen *Admission:* 1,853 applied, 889 admitted, 289 enrolled. *Average high school GPA:* 3.66. *Test scores:* ACT scores over 18: 100%; ACT scores over 24: 54%; ACT scores over 30: 10%.

Faculty *Total:* 167, 60% full-time, 67% with terminal degrees. *Student/faculty ratio:* 13:1.

Academics *Calendar:* semesters. *Degrees:* bachelor's, master's, and post-bachelor's certificates. *Special study options:* accelerated degree program, adult/continuing education programs, advanced placement credit, distance learning, double majors, honors programs, independent study, internships, off-campus study, part-time degree program, services for LD students, study abroad, summer session for credit. *ROTC:* Army (c), Navy (c), Air Force (c). *Unusual degree programs:* 3-2 engineering.

Computers on Campus 310 computers/terminals are available on campus for general student use. Students can access the following: campus intranet, computer help desk, free student e-mail accounts, online (class) grades, online (class) registration, online (class) schedules, online class listings, course assignments. Campuswide network is available. 100% of college-owned or -operated housing units are wired for high-speed Internet access. Wireless service is available via entire campus.

Student Life *Housing:* on-campus residence required through sophomore year. *Options:* men-only, women-only. Campus housing is university owned. Freshman applicants given priority for college housing. *Activities and organizations:* drama/theater group, student-run radio station, choral group, Black Student Association, BACCHUS Alcohol Awareness Group, Intercultural Club, The Chosen Generation, Lasallian Collegians, national fraternities, national sororities. *Campus security:* 24-hour emergency response devices and patrols, student patrols, late-night transport/escort service, controlled dormitory access. *Student services:* health clinic, personal/psychological counseling.

Athletics Member NCAA. All Division II. *Intercollegiate sports:* baseball M(s), basketball M(s)/W(s), cross-country running M(s)/W(s), golf M(s)/W(s), soccer M(s)/W(s), softball W(s), tennis M(s)/W(s), volleyball W(s). *Intramural sports:* basketball M/W, bowling M/W, cross-country running M/W, football M/W, golf M, lacrosse M, racquetball M/W, soccer M/W, softball M/W, swimming and diving M/W, table tennis M/W, tennis M/W, ultimate Frisbee M/W, volleyball M/W, weight lifting M.

Standardized Tests *Required:* SAT or ACT (for admission).

Costs (2010–11) *Comprehensive fee:* $31,280 includes full-time tuition ($24,320), mandatory fees ($550), and room and board ($6410). Full-time tuition and fees vary according to class time and course load. Part-time tuition: $870 per credit hour. Part-time tuition and fees vary according to class time. *College room only:* $3000. Room and board charges vary according to board plan and housing facility. *Payment plans:* installment, deferred payment. *Waivers:* children of alumni and employees or children of employees.

Financial Aid Of all full-time matriculated undergraduates who enrolled in 2009, 1,080 applied for aid, 920 were judged to have need, 217 had their need fully met. 157 Federal Work-Study jobs (averaging $988). 186 state and other part-time jobs (averaging $978). In 2009, 198 non-need-based awards were made. *Average percent of need met:* 81%. *Average financial aid package:* $20,985. *Average need-based loan:* $4413. *Average need-based gift aid:* $6590. *Average non-need-based aid:* $9265. *Average indebtedness upon graduation:* $29,207.

Applying *Options:* electronic application, early admission, deferred entrance. *Application fee:* $25. *Required:* essay or personal statement, high school transcript, minimum 2 GPA. *Required for some:* 2 letters of recommendation. *Recommended:* interview. *Application deadlines:* 8/1 (freshmen), 8/23 (transfers). *Notification:* 12/1 (freshmen), continuous (transfers).

Freshman Application Contact Dr. Anne Kenworthy, Dean of Admissions, Christian Brothers University, 650 East Parkway South, Memphis, TN 38104. *Phone:* 901-321-3205. *Toll-free phone:* 800-288-7576. *Fax:* 901-321-3202. *E-mail:* admissions@cbu.edu. *Web site:* http://www.cbu.edu/.

Cumberland University
Lebanon, Tennessee

- **Independent** comprehensive, founded 1842
- **Small-town** 44-acre campus with easy access to Nashville
- **Endowment** $8.4 million
- **Coed** 1,120 undergraduate students, 86% full-time, 56% women, 44% men
- **Moderately difficult** entrance level, 56% of applicants were admitted

Undergraduates 965 full-time, 155 part-time. Students come from 26 states and territories; 19 other countries; 10% are from out of state; 11% Black or African American, non-Hispanic/Latino; 3% Hispanic/Latino; 1% Asian, non-Hispanic/Latino; 0.4% American Indian or Alaska Native, non-Hispanic/Latino; 6% Race/ethnicity unknown; 3% international; 17% transferred in; 30% live on campus. *Retention:* 68% of full-time freshmen returned.

Freshmen *Admission:* 592 applied, 334 admitted, 164 enrolled. *Average high school GPA:* 3.4. *Test scores:* SAT critical reading scores over 500: 45%; SAT math scores over 500: 75%; SAT writing scores over 500: 35%; ACT scores over 18: 95%; SAT critical reading scores over 600: 5%; SAT math scores over 600: 25%; ACT scores over 24: 33%; ACT scores over 30: 1%.

Faculty *Total:* 122, 39% full-time, 39% with terminal degrees. *Student/faculty ratio:* 15:1.

Academics *Calendar:* semesters. *Degrees:* associate, bachelor's, and master's. *Special study options:* academic remediation for entering students, accelerated degree program, adult/continuing education programs, advanced placement credit, cooperative education, double majors, freshman honors college, honors programs, internships, part-time degree program, services for LD students, summer session for credit. *ROTC:* Army (b).

Computers on Campus 150 computers/terminals are available on campus for general student use. Students can access the following: campus intranet, computer help desk, free student e-mail accounts, online (class) grades, online (class) schedules. Campuswide network is available. 100% of college-owned or -operated housing units are wired for high-speed Internet access. Wireless service is available via entire campus.

Student Life *Housing:* on-campus residence required for freshman year. *Options:* men-only, women-only, disabled students. Campus housing is university owned. *Activities and organizations:* drama/theater group, student-run newspaper, radio station, choral group, marching band, African-American Student Association, Baptist Collegiate Ministry, Law and Government Club, Student Government Association, Student Nurses' Association, national fraternities, national sororities. *Campus security:* 24-hour emergency response devices and patrols, late-night transport/escort service. *Student services:* personal/psychological counseling.

Athletics Member NAIA. *Intercollegiate sports:* baseball M(s), basketball M(s)/W(s), bowling M(s)/W(s), cheerleading M(s)/W(s), football M(s), golf M(s)/W(s), soccer M(s)/W(s), softball W(s), tennis M(s)/W(s), volleyball W(s), wrestling M(s). *Intramural sports:* basketball M/W, bowling M/W, softball W, table tennis M/W, volleyball M/W.

Standardized Tests *Required:* SAT or ACT (for admission). *Recommended:* SAT (for admission).

Costs (2011–12) *One-time required fee:* $100. *Comprehensive fee:* $26,800 includes full-time tuition ($18,200), mandatory fees ($1000), and room and board ($7600). Full-time tuition and fees vary according to degree level. Part-time tuition: $758 per credit hour. Part-time tuition and fees vary according to course load and degree level. *Payment plan:* installment. *Waivers:* employees or children of employees.

Financial Aid Of all full-time matriculated undergraduates who enrolled in 2007, 837 applied for aid, 713 were judged to have need, 135 had their need fully met. 120 Federal Work-Study jobs (averaging $750). 16 state and other part-time jobs (averaging $750). In 2007, 125 non-need-based awards were made. *Average percent of need met:* 54%. *Average financial aid package:* $12,176. *Average need-based loan:* $4073. *Average need-based gift aid:* $5669. *Average non-need-based aid:* $8069. *Average indebtedness upon graduation:* $21,562.

Applying *Options:* electronic application, deferred entrance. *Application fee:* $25. *Required:* high school transcript. *Required for some:* 3 letters of recommendation. *Recommended:* essay or personal statement, minimum 2.5 GPA. *Application deadlines:* rolling (freshmen), rolling (transfers). *Notification:* continuous (freshmen), continuous (transfers).

Freshman Application Contact Ms. Beatrice LaChance, Director of Enrollment Services, Cumberland University, One Cumberland Square, Lebanon, TN 37087. *Phone:* 615-547-1244. *Toll-free phone:* 800-467-0562. *Fax:* 615-444-2569. *E-mail:* admissions@cumberland.edu. *Web site:* http://www.cumberland.edu/.

Daymar Institute

Clarksville, Tennessee

- **Proprietary** 4-year, founded 1987
- **Small-town** campus
- **Coed**
- **Noncompetitive** entrance level

Faculty *Student/faculty ratio:* 7:1.

Academics *Calendar:* quarters. *Degrees:* certificates, diplomas, associate, and bachelor's.

Costs (2010–11) *Tuition:* $10,440 full-time, $290 per quarter hour part-time. Full-time tuition and fees vary according to course level, course load, location, and program. Part-time tuition and fees vary according to course level, course load, location, and program.

Financial Aid *Of all full-time matriculated undergraduates who enrolled in 2009,* 20 Federal Work-Study jobs (averaging $1000).

Applying *Required:* high school transcript, interview.

Freshman Application Contact Daymar Institute, 1860 Wilma Rudolph Boulevard, Clarksville, TN 37040. *Phone:* 931-552-7600 Ext. 204. *Web site:* http://www.daymarinstitute.edu/.

DeVry University

Memphis, Tennessee

- **Proprietary** comprehensive, founded 2007
- **Coed**

Academics *Degrees:* associate, bachelor's, and master's.

Costs (2010–11) *Tuition:* $14,766 full-time, $580 per credit hour part-time. Full-time tuition and fees vary according to course load. Part-time tuition and fees vary according to course load. *Required fees:* $60 full-time, $30 per term part-time. *Payment plans:* installment, deferred payment.

Financial Aid *Of all full-time matriculated undergraduates who enrolled in 2007,* 6 applied for aid, 6 were judged to have need, 1 had their need fully met. *Average percent of need met:* 42. *Average financial aid package:* $11,341. *Average need-based loan:* $7566. *Average need-based gift aid:* $4530.

Applying *Options:* deferred entrance. *Application fee:* $50.

Freshman Application Contact DeVry University, 6401 Poplar Avenue, Suite 600, Memphis, TN 38119. *Toll-free phone:* 888-563-3879. *Web site:* http://www.devry.edu/.

DeVry University

Nashville, Tennessee

Admissions Office Contact DeVry University, 3343 Perimeter Hill Drive, Suite 200, Nashville, TN 37211-4147. *Web site:* http://www.devry.edu/.

East Tennessee State University

Johnson City, Tennessee

- **State-supported** university, founded 1911, part of State University and Community College System of Tennessee; Tennessee Board of Regents
- **Small-town** 366-acre campus
- **Endowment** $79.2 million
- **Coed** 12,175 undergraduate students, 85% full-time, 57% women, 43% men
- **Moderately difficult** entrance level, 82% of applicants were admitted

Undergraduates 10,296 full-time, 1,879 part-time. Students come from 44 states and territories; 45 other countries; 12% are from out of state; 5% Black or African American, non-Hispanic/Latino; 2% Hispanic/Latino; 1% Asian, non-Hispanic/Latino; 0.1% Native Hawaiian or other Pacific Islander, non-Hispanic/Latino; 0.4% American Indian or Alaska Native, non-Hispanic/Latino; 2% Two or more races, non-Hispanic/Latino; 0.3% Race/ethnicity unknown; 1% international; 9% transferred in; 20% live on campus. *Retention:* 72% of full-time freshmen returned.

Freshmen *Admission:* 5,245 applied, 4,295 admitted, 2,099 enrolled. *Average high school GPA:* 3.26. *Test scores:* SAT critical reading scores over 500: 46%; SAT math scores over 500: 50%; SAT writing scores over 500: 43%; ACT scores over 18: 88%; SAT critical reading scores over 600: 14%; SAT math scores over 600: 17%; SAT writing scores over 600: 13%; ACT scores over 24: 34%; SAT critical reading scores over 700: 2%; SAT math scores over 700: 2%; SAT writing scores over 700: 1%; ACT scores over 30: 5%.

Faculty *Total:* 841, 63% full-time, 52% with terminal degrees. *Student/faculty ratio:* 19:1.

Academics *Calendar:* semesters. *Degrees:* bachelor's, master's, doctoral-professional, doctoral-research/scholarship, post-master's, and postbachelor's certificates. *Special study options:* adult/continuing education programs, advanced placement credit, cooperative education, distance learning, double majors, English as a second language, external degree program, freshman hon-

ors college, honors programs, independent study, internships, off-campus study, part-time degree program, services for LD students, student-designed majors, study abroad, summer session for credit. *ROTC:* Army (b).

Computers on Campus 1,400 computers/terminals are available on campus for general student use. Students can access the following: computer help desk, free student e-mail accounts, online (class) grades, online (class) registration, online (class) schedules. Campuswide network is available. Wireless service is available via entire campus.

Student Life *Housing options:* coed, men-only, women-only, disabled students. Campus housing is university owned. *Activities and organizations:* drama/theater group, student-run newspaper, radio and television station, choral group, honor societies, Volunteer ETSU, religious groups, residence hall councils, national fraternities, national sororities. *Campus security:* 24-hour emergency response devices and patrols, student patrols, late-night transport/escort service, controlled dormitory access. *Student services:* health clinic, personal/psychological counseling, women's center.

Athletics Member NCAA. All Division I. *Intercollegiate sports:* baseball M(s), basketball M(s)/W(s), cross-country running M(s)/W(s), golf M(s)/W(s), soccer M(s)/W(s), softball W(s), tennis M(s)/W(s), track and field M(s)/W(s), volleyball W(s). *Intramural sports:* basketball M/W, cross-country running M/W, football M/W, golf M/W, racquetball M/W, softball M/W, tennis M/W, volleyball W, weight lifting M.

Standardized Tests *Required:* SAT or ACT (for admission).

Costs (2010–11) *Tuition:* state resident $4824 full-time, $201 per credit hour part-time; nonresident $17,352 full-time, $723 per credit hour part-time. Full-time tuition and fees vary according to course load and program. Part-time tuition and fees vary according to course load and program. *Required fees:* $999 full-time, $64 per credit hour part-time. *Room and board:* $5783; room only: $2930. Room and board charges vary according to board plan and housing facility. *Payment plans:* installment, deferred payment. *Waivers:* senior citizens and employees or children of employees.

Financial Aid Of all full-time matriculated undergraduates who enrolled in 2009, 8,339 applied for aid, 6,053 were judged to have need, 2,784 had their need fully met. 595 Federal Work-Study jobs (averaging $1117). In 2009, 1220 non-need-based awards were made. *Average percent of need met:* 81%. *Average financial aid package:* $5079. *Average need-based loan:* $3408. *Average need-based gift aid:* $3560. *Average non-need-based aid:* $3826. *Average indebtedness upon graduation:* $20,984.

Applying *Options:* electronic application, early admission. *Application fee:* $15. *Required:* high school transcript, minimum 2.3 GPA, 2.3 high school GPA or 19 ACT. *Application deadlines:* rolling (freshmen), rolling (out-of-state freshmen), rolling (transfers). *Notification:* continuous (freshmen), continuous (out-of-state freshmen), continuous (transfers).

Freshman Application Contact Mr. Mike Pitts, Director of Admissions, East Tennessee State University, PO Box 70731, Johnson City, TN 37614-0734. *Phone:* 423-439-4213. *Toll-free phone:* 800-462-3878. *Fax:* 423-439-4630. *E-mail:* go2etsu@etsu.edu. *Web site:* http://www.etsu.edu/.

Fisk University

Nashville, Tennessee

- **Independent** comprehensive, founded 1866, affiliated with United Church of Christ
- **Urban** 40-acre campus
- **Endowment** $12.1 million
- **Coed**
- **Moderately difficult** entrance level

Faculty *Student/faculty ratio:* 9:1.

Academics *Calendar:* semesters. *Degrees:* bachelor's, master's, and post-bachelor's certificates.

Student Life *Campus security:* 24-hour patrols, late-night transport/escort service.

Athletics Member NAIA.

Standardized Tests *Required:* SAT or ACT (for admission).

Costs (2010–11) *Comprehensive fee:* $26,944 includes full-time tuition ($16,848), mandatory fees ($1510), and room and board ($8586). Full-time tuition and fees vary according to course load. Part-time tuition: $702 per credit hour. Part-time tuition and fees vary according to course load. *College room only:* $4976. Room and board charges vary according to board plan.

Financial Aid *Of all full-time matriculated undergraduates who enrolled in 2009,* 541 applied for aid, 541 were judged to have need, 147 had their need fully met. 181 Federal Work-Study jobs (averaging $1573). *Average percent of need met:* 71. *Average financial aid package:* $14,957. *Average need-based loan:* $4387. *Average need-based gift aid:* $12,028. *Average indebtedness upon graduation:* $27,345. *Financial aid deadline:* 6/1.

Applying *Options:* electronic application. *Application fee:* $50. *Required:* essay or personal statement, high school transcript, minimum 2.5 GPA, 2 letters of recommendation.

Freshman Application Contact Fisk University, 1000 17th Avenue North, Nashville, TN 37208-3051. *Phone:* 615-329-8665. *Toll-free phone:* 800-443-

FISK. *Fax:* 615-329-8774. *E-mail:* admit@fisk.edu. *Web site:* http://www.fisk.edu/.

Fountainhead College of Technology

Knoxville, Tennessee

Freshman Application Contact Director of Administration, Fountainhead College of Technology, 3203 Tazewell Pike, Knoxville, TN 37918-2530. *Phone:* 865-688-9422. *Toll-free phone:* 888-218-7335. *Fax:* 865-688-2419. *Web site:* http://www.fountainheadcollege.edu/.

Freed-Hardeman University

Henderson, Tennessee

- **Independent** comprehensive, founded 1869, affiliated with Church of Christ
- **Small-town** 96-acre campus
- **Coed** 1,490 undergraduate students, 95% full-time, 54% women, 46% men
- 100% of applicants were admitted

Undergraduates 1,409 full-time, 81 part-time. Students come from 31 states and territories; 21 other countries; 45% are from out of state; 6% Black or African American, non-Hispanic/Latino; 0.5% Hispanic/Latino; 0.2% Asian, non-Hispanic/Latino; 0.5% American Indian or Alaska Native, non-Hispanic/Latino; 0.1% Two or more races, non-Hispanic/Latino; 1% Race/ethnicity unknown; 2% international; 5% transferred in. *Retention:* 75% of full-time freshmen returned.

Freshmen *Admission:* 1,441 applied, 1,439 admitted, 373 enrolled. *Average high school GPA:* 3.5. *Test scores:* SAT critical reading scores over 500: 65%; SAT math scores over 500: 56%; ACT scores over 18: 91%; SAT critical reading scores over 600: 28%; SAT math scores over 600: 16%; ACT scores over 24: 44%; SAT critical reading scores over 700: 5%; SAT math scores over 700: 3%; ACT scores over 30: 8%.

Faculty *Total:* 145, 68% full-time, 61% with terminal degrees. *Student/faculty ratio:* 15:1.

Academics *Calendar:* semesters. *Degrees:* associate, bachelor's, master's, doctoral-professional, post-master's, and postbachelor's certificates. *Special study options:* academic remediation for entering students, accelerated degree program, advanced placement credit, cooperative education, distance learning, double majors, honors programs, independent study, internships, off-campus study, part-time degree program, services for LD students, student-designed majors, summer session for credit.

Computers on Campus 250 computers/terminals are available on campus for general student use. Students can access the following: online (class) registration. Campuswide network is available. Wireless service is available via entire campus.

Student Life *Housing:* on-campus residence required through senior year. *Options:* men-only, women-only. Campus housing is university owned. Freshman campus housing is guaranteed. *Activities and organizations:* drama/theater group, student-run newspaper, radio and television station, choral group, Student Alumni Association, University Program Council, University Student Ambassadors, Evangelism Forum. *Campus security:* 24-hour emergency response devices and patrols, late-night transport/escort service, controlled dormitory access. *Student services:* health clinic, personal/psychological counseling.

Athletics Member NAIA. *Intercollegiate sports:* baseball M(s), basketball M(s)/W(s), cheerleading W(s), cross-country running M(s)/W(s), soccer M(s)/W(s), softball W(s), volleyball W(s). *Intramural sports:* basketball M/W, football M/W, racquetball M/W, softball M/W, table tennis M/W, volleyball M/W.

Standardized Tests *Required:* SAT or ACT (for admission).

Costs (2010–11) *Comprehensive fee:* $23,138 includes full-time tuition ($12,840), mandatory fees ($3082), and room and board ($7216). Full-time tuition and fees vary according to course load and degree level. Part-time tuition: $428 per semester hour. Part-time tuition and fees vary according to course load and degree level. *College room only:* $3980. Room and board charges vary according to board plan and housing facility. *Payment plan:* installment. *Waivers:* senior citizens and employees or children of employees.

Financial Aid Of all full-time matriculated undergraduates who enrolled in 2009, 1,308 applied for aid, 1,112 were judged to have need, 248 had their need fully met. In 2009, 237 non-need-based awards were made. *Average percent of need met:* 66%. *Average financial aid package:* $13,942. *Average*

need-based loan: $4188. *Average need-based gift aid:* $10,139. *Average non-need-based aid:* $6191. *Average indebtedness upon graduation:* $33,659.

Applying *Options:* early admission, deferred entrance. *Required:* high school transcript, minimum 2.25 GPA. *Required for some:* interview. *Recommended:* essay or personal statement. *Application deadlines:* rolling (freshmen), rolling (transfers). *Notification:* continuous (freshmen), continuous until 9/1 (transfers).

Freshman Application Contact Mr. Joseph Askew, Interim Director of Admissions, Freed-Hardeman University, 158 East Main Street, Henderson, TN 38340-2399. *Phone:* 731-989-6651. *Toll-free phone:* 800-630-3480. *Fax:* 731-989-6047. *E-mail:* admissions@fhu.edu. *Web site:* http://www.fhu.edu/.

Free Will Baptist Bible College

Nashville, Tennessee

- **Independent Free Will Baptist** 4-year, founded 1942
- **Urban** 10-acre campus with easy access to Nashville
- **Endowment** $720,467
- **Coed** 282 undergraduate students, 68% full-time, 45% women, 55% men
- **Noncompetitive** entrance level, 95% of applicants were admitted

Undergraduates 192 full-time, 90 part-time. Students come from 23 states and territories; 5 other countries; 64% are from out of state; 8% Black or African American, non-Hispanic/Latino; 2% Hispanic/Latino; 0.8% international; 10% transferred in; 55% live on campus. *Retention:* 61% of full-time freshmen returned.

Freshmen *Admission:* 78 applied, 74 admitted, 49 enrolled. *Average high school GPA:* 3.01. *Test scores:* ACT scores over 18: 77%; ACT scores over 24: 35%; ACT scores over 30: 3%.

Faculty *Total:* 55, 38% full-time, 35% with terminal degrees. *Student/faculty ratio:* 10:1.

Academics *Calendar:* semesters. *Degrees:* associate and bachelor's. *Special study options:* academic remediation for entering students, advanced placement credit, distance learning, double majors, internships, part-time degree program, student-designed majors, summer session for credit. *ROTC:* Army (c), Air Force (c). *Unusual degree programs:* nursing.

Computers on Campus 41 computers/terminals are available on campus for general student use. Students can access the following: campus intranet, computer help desk, free student e-mail accounts, online (class) grades, online (class) schedules. Campuswide network is available. Wireless service is available via computer centers, computer labs, dorm rooms, libraries, student centers.

Student Life *Housing:* on-campus residence required through senior year. *Options:* men-only, women-only. Campus housing is university owned. Freshman campus housing is guaranteed. *Activities and organizations:* drama/theater group, choral group, GMF-Global Missions Fellowship, Four Women's Societies, Four Men's Societies. *Campus security:* 24-hour emergency response devices, student patrols, late-night transport/escort service, controlled dormitory access. *Student services:* personal/psychological counseling.

Athletics Member NCCAA. *Intercollegiate sports:* baseball M, basketball M/W, golf M/W, volleyball W. *Intramural sports:* basketball M/W, tennis M/W, volleyball M/W.

Standardized Tests *Required:* SAT or ACT (for admission).

Costs (2011–12) *Comprehensive fee:* $20,348 includes full-time tuition ($13,410), mandatory fees ($896), and room and board ($6042). Part-time tuition: $447 per credit. *Room and board:* Room and board charges vary according to board plan. *Payment plans:* installment, deferred payment. *Waivers:* employees or children of employees.

Financial Aid Of all full-time matriculated undergraduates who enrolled in 2008, 163 applied for aid, 163 were judged to have need. 6 Federal Work-Study jobs (averaging $3434). 84 state and other part-time jobs (averaging $1414). *Average percent of need met:* 70%. *Average financial aid package:* $11,469. *Average need-based loan:* $5617. *Average need-based gift aid:* $4438. *Average indebtedness upon graduation:* $18,487.

Applying *Options:* electronic application, early admission, deferred entrance. *Application fee:* $35. *Required:* essay or personal statement, high school transcript, 3 letters of recommendation, medical history. *Application deadlines:* rolling (freshmen), rolling (out-of-state freshmen), rolling (transfers). *Notification:* continuous (freshmen), continuous (out-of-state freshmen), continuous (transfers).

Freshman Application Contact Mr. Rusty Campbell, Director of Enrollment Services, Free Will Baptist Bible College, 3606 West End Avenue, Nashville, TN 37205. *Phone:* 615-844-5269. *Toll-free phone:* 800-763-9222. *Fax:* 615-269-6028. *E-mail:* rcampbell@fwbbc.edu. *Web site:* http://www.fwbbc.edu/.

PROFILES

Huntington College of Health Sciences

Knoxville, Tennessee

- **Proprietary** comprehensive, founded 1984
- **Suburban** campus
- **Coed** 400 undergraduate students, 100% full-time, 64% women, 36% men
- **Noncompetitive** entrance level, 100% of applicants were admitted

Undergraduates 400 full-time. Students come from 49 states and territories; 15 other countries; 98% are from out of state; 46% transferred in. *Retention:* 10% of full-time freshmen returned.

Freshmen *Admission:* 33 applied, 33 admitted, 25 enrolled.

Faculty *Total:* 20, 15% full-time, 35% with terminal degrees. *Student/faculty ratio:* 29:1.

Academics *Calendar:* continuous. *Degrees:* certificates, diplomas, associate, bachelor's, master's, and postbachelor's certificates (offers only external degree programs conducted through home study). *Special study options:* academic remediation for entering students, adult/continuing education programs, distance learning, external degree program, independent study, part-time degree program, student-designed majors, summer session for credit.

Costs (2010–11) *Tuition:* $165 per semester hour part-time. Full-time tuition and fees vary according to course load and program. Part-time tuition and fees vary according to course load and program. No tuition increase for student's term of enrollment. *Payment plans:* tuition prepayment, installment. *Waivers:* employees or children of employees.

Applying *Options:* electronic application, deferred entrance. *Application fee:* $200. *Required for some:* high school transcript, interview. *Recommended:* minimum 2 GPA. *Application deadlines:* rolling (freshmen), rolling (transfers). *Notification:* continuous (freshmen), continuous (transfers).

Freshman Application Contact Ms. Cheryl Freeman, Director/Registrar, Huntington College of Health Sciences, 1204 Kenesaw Avenue, Suite D, Knoxville, TN 37919. *Phone:* 800-290-4226. *Toll-free phone:* 800-290-4226. *Fax:* 865-524-8339. *E-mail:* cfreeman@hchs.edu. *Web site:* http://www.hchs.edu/.

ITT Technical Institute

Chattanooga, Tennessee

- **Proprietary** primarily 2-year, part of ITT Educational Services, Inc.
- **Coed**
- **Minimally difficult** entrance level

Academics *Degrees:* associate and bachelor's.

Student Life *Housing:* college housing not available.

Freshman Application Contact Director of Recruitment, ITT Technical Institute, 5600 Brainerd Road, Suite G-1, Chattanooga, TN 37411. *Phone:* 423-510-6800. *Toll-free phone:* 877-474-8312. *Web site:* http://www.itt-tech.edu/.

ITT Technical Institute

Cordova, Tennessee

- **Proprietary** primarily 2-year, founded 1994, part of ITT Educational Services, Inc.
- **Suburban** campus
- **Coed**
- **Minimally difficult** entrance level

Academics *Calendar:* quarters. *Degrees:* associate and bachelor's.

Student Life *Housing:* college housing not available.

Freshman Application Contact Director of Recruitment, ITT Technical Institute, 7260 Goodlett Farms Parkway, Cordova, TN 38016. *Phone:* 901-381-0200. *Toll-free phone:* 866-444-5141. *Web site:* http://www.itt-tech.edu/.

ITT Technical Institute

Johnson City, Tennessee

- **Proprietary** primarily 2-year
- **Coed**
- **Minimally difficult** entrance level

Academics *Degrees:* associate and bachelor's.

Freshman Application Contact Director of Recruitment, ITT Technical Institute, 4721 Lake Park Drive, Suite 100, Johnson City, TN 37615. *Phone:* 423-952-4400. *Toll-free phone:* 877-301-9691. *Web site:* http://www.itt-tech.edu/.

ITT Technical Institute

Knoxville, Tennessee

- **Proprietary** primarily 2-year, founded 1988, part of ITT Educational Services, Inc.
- **Suburban** campus
- **Coed**
- **Minimally difficult** entrance level

Academics *Calendar:* quarters. *Degrees:* associate and bachelor's.

Student Life *Housing:* college housing not available.

Freshman Application Contact Director of Recruitment, ITT Technical Institute, 10208 Technology Drive, Knoxville, TN 37932. *Phone:* 865-671-2800. *Toll-free phone:* 800-671-2801. *Web site:* http://www.itt-tech.edu/.

ITT Technical Institute

Nashville, Tennessee

- **Proprietary** primarily 2-year, founded 1984, part of ITT Educational Services, Inc.
- **Urban** campus
- **Coed**
- **Minimally difficult** entrance level

Academics *Calendar:* quarters. *Degrees:* associate and bachelor's.

Student Life *Housing:* college housing not available.

Freshman Application Contact Director of Recruitment, ITT Technical Institute, 2845 Elm Hill Pike, Nashville, TN 37214. *Phone:* 615-889-8700. *Toll-free phone:* 800-331-8386. *Web site:* http://www.itt-tech.edu/.

Johnson Bible College

Knoxville, Tennessee

- **Independent** comprehensive, founded 1893, affiliated with Christian Churches and Churches of Christ
- **Rural** 75-acre campus
- **Endowment** $99.9 million
- **Coed** 680 undergraduate students, 95% full-time, 47% women, 53% men
- **Moderately difficult** entrance level, 66% of applicants were admitted

Undergraduates 649 full-time, 31 part-time. Students come from 34 states and territories; 13 other countries; 72% are from out of state; 2% Black or African American, non-Hispanic/Latino; 3% Hispanic/Latino; 0.3% Asian, non-Hispanic/Latino; 0.1% Native Hawaiian or other Pacific Islander, non-Hispanic/Latino; 0.6% American Indian or Alaska Native, non-Hispanic/Latino; 2% Two or more races, non-Hispanic/Latino; 2% international; 17% transferred in; 85% live on campus. *Retention:* 69% of full-time freshmen returned.

Freshmen *Admission:* 466 applied, 308 admitted, 158 enrolled. *Average high school GPA:* 3.06. *Test scores:* SAT writing scores over 500: 58%; ACT scores over 18: 85%; SAT writing scores over 600: 13%; ACT scores over 24: 30%.

Faculty *Total:* 62, 55% full-time, 48% with terminal degrees. *Student/faculty ratio:* 14:1.

Academics *Calendar:* semesters. *Degrees:* certificates, associate, bachelor's, and master's. *Special study options:* academic remediation for entering students, accelerated degree program, adult/continuing education programs, advanced placement credit, cooperative education, distance learning, double majors, English as a second language, honors programs, independent study, internships, part-time degree program, services for LD students, study abroad, summer session for credit.

Computers on Campus Students can access the following: campus intranet, computer help desk, free student e-mail accounts, online (class) grades, online (class) registration, online (class) schedules. Campuswide network is available. 100% of college-owned or -operated housing units are wired for high-speed Internet access. Wireless service is available via classrooms.

Student Life *Housing:* on-campus residence required through senior year. *Options:* men-only, women-only. Campus housing is university owned. *Activities and organizations:* student-run radio station, choral group, Quest, Timothy Club, International Harvesters. *Campus security:* 24-hour emergency response devices, student patrols, controlled dormitory access. *Student services:* health clinic, personal/psychological counseling.

Athletics Member NCCAA. *Intercollegiate sports:* baseball M, basketball M/W, cheerleading M/W, cross-country running M/W, soccer M/W, volleyball W. *Intramural sports:* basketball M, tennis M/W, ultimate Frisbee M/W, volleyball M/W.

Standardized Tests *Required:* SAT or ACT (for admission). *Required for some:* ACT (for admission).

Costs (2010–11) *Comprehensive fee:* $14,200 includes full-time tuition ($8300), mandatory fees ($800), and room and board ($5100). Part-time tuition: $332 per credit hour. Part-time tuition and fees vary according to course load. *Required fees:* $35 per credit hour part-time. *College room only:* $2400. Room and board charges vary according to board plan and housing facility. *Payment plan:* installment. *Waivers:* employees or children of employees.

Financial Aid Of all full-time matriculated undergraduates who enrolled in 2009, 649 applied for aid, 543 were judged to have need, 51 had their need fully met. 64 Federal Work-Study jobs (averaging $1602). 335 state and other part-time jobs (averaging $1611). *Average percent of need met:* 63%. *Average financial aid package:* $11,642. *Average need-based loan:* $3414. *Average need-based gift aid:* $6471. *Average indebtedness upon graduation:* $18,494.

Applying *Options:* electronic application, deferred entrance. *Application fee:* $35. *Required:* essay or personal statement, high school transcript, 3 letters of recommendation. *Required for some:* interview. *Application deadlines:* 7/1 (freshmen), 7/1 (transfers). *Notification:* continuous (freshmen), continuous (transfers).

Freshman Application Contact Mr. Tim Wingfield, Director of Admissions, Johnson Bible College, 7900 Johnson Drive, Knoxville, TN 37998-1001. *Phone:* 865-251-2346. *Toll-free phone:* 800-827-2122. *Fax:* 865-251-2336. *E-mail:* twingfield@jbc.edu. *Web site:* http://www.jbc.edu/.

King College
Bristol, Tennessee

- **Independent** comprehensive, founded 1867, affiliated with Presbyterian Church (U.S.A.)
- **Suburban** 135-acre campus
- **Endowment** $24.0 million
- **Coed** 1,671 undergraduate students, 90% full-time, 64% women, 36% men
- **Moderately difficult** entrance level, 62% of applicants were admitted

Undergraduates 1,504 full-time, 167 part-time. Students come from 31 states and territories; 20 other countries; 36% are from out of state; 4% Black or African American, non-Hispanic/Latino; 2% Hispanic/Latino; 0.5% Asian, non-Hispanic/Latino; 0.1% American Indian or Alaska Native, non-Hispanic/Latino; 0.2% Two or more races, non-Hispanic/Latino; 16% Race/ethnicity unknown; 2% international; 9% transferred in; 27% live on campus. *Retention:* 68% of full-time freshmen returned.

Freshmen *Admission:* 898 applied, 553 admitted, 228 enrolled. *Average high school GPA:* 3.34. *Test scores:* SAT critical reading scores over 500: 37%; SAT math scores over 500: 56%; SAT writing scores over 500: 43%; ACT scores over 18: 92%; SAT critical reading scores over 600: 12%; SAT math scores over 600: 16%; SAT writing scores over 600: 9%; ACT scores over 24: 30%; SAT math scores over 700: 1%; SAT writing scores over 700: 1%; ACT scores over 30: 2%.

Faculty *Total:* 172, 50% full-time, 55% with terminal degrees. *Student/faculty ratio:* 15:1.

Academics *Calendar:* semesters. *Degrees:* bachelor's, master's, and post-master's certificates. *Special study options:* adult/continuing education programs, advanced placement credit, cooperative education, double majors, honors programs, independent study, internships, off-campus study, part-time degree program, services for LD students, student-designed majors, study abroad, summer session for credit. *ROTC:* Army (c). *Unusual degree programs:* 3-2 engineering with University of Tennessee, Vanderbilt University.

Computers on Campus 90 computers/terminals and 500 ports are available on campus for general student use. Students can access the following: campus intranet, computer help desk, free student e-mail accounts, online (class) grades, online (class) registration, online (class) schedules, student portal. Campuswide network is available. 100% of college-owned or -operated housing units are wired for high-speed Internet access. Wireless service is available via classrooms, computer centers, computer labs, learning centers, libraries, student centers.

Student Life *Housing:* on-campus residence required through junior year. *Options:* men-only, women-only, disabled students. Campus housing is university owned. Freshman campus housing is guaranteed. *Activities and organizations:* drama/theater group, student-run newspaper, choral group, Student Government Association, Campus Life Committee, World Christian Fellowship, Fellowship of Christian Athletes, Drama Club. *Campus security:* 24-hour patrols, late-night transport/escort service, controlled dormitory access. *Student services:* personal/psychological counseling.

Athletics Member NCAA. All Division II. *Intercollegiate sports:* baseball M(s), basketball M(s)/W(s), cheerleading M(s)/W(s), cross-country running M(s)/W(s), golf M(s)/W(s), soccer M(s)/W(s), softball W(s), swimming and diving M(s)/W(s), tennis M(s)/W(s), track and field M(s)/W(s), volleyball W(s), wrestling M(s)/W(s). *Intramural sports:* badminton M/W, basketball M/W, soccer M/W, softball M/W, table tennis M/W, tennis M/W, ultimate Frisbee M/W, volleyball M/W, weight lifting M.

Standardized Tests *Required:* SAT or ACT (for admission).

Costs (2010–11) *Comprehensive fee:* $30,698 includes full-time tuition ($21,620), mandatory fees ($1288), and room and board ($7790). Full-time tuition and fees vary according to course load and program. Part-time tuition: $600 per credit hour. Part-time tuition and fees vary according to course load and program. *Required fees:* $120 per credit hour part-time. *College room*

only: $3912. Room and board charges vary according to board plan. *Payment plan:* installment. *Waivers:* senior citizens and employees or children of employees.

Financial Aid Of all full-time matriculated undergraduates who enrolled in 2009, 768 applied for aid, 702 were judged to have need, 71 had their need fully met. In 2009, 44 non-need-based awards were made. *Average percent of need met:* 69%. *Average financial aid package:* $16,736. *Average need-based loan:* $4773. *Average need-based gift aid:* $14,125. *Average non-need-based aid:* $8610. *Average indebtedness upon graduation:* $15,757.

Applying *Options:* electronic application, early admission, deferred entrance. *Application fee:* $20. *Required:* high school transcript, minimum 2.4 GPA. *Required for some:* essay or personal statement. *Recommended:* interview. *Application deadlines:* rolling (freshmen), rolling (out-of-state freshmen), rolling (transfers). *Notification:* continuous (freshmen), continuous (out-of-state freshmen), continuous (transfers).

Freshman Application Contact Mr. Greg King, Director of Recruitment, King College, 1350 King College Road, Bristol, TN 37620. *Phone:* 423-652-4861. *Toll-free phone:* 800-362-0014. *Fax:* 423-652-4727. *E-mail:* admissions@king.edu. *Web site:* http://www.king.edu/.

Lambuth University
Jackson, Tennessee

Freshman Application Contact Ms. Karen Myers, Director of Financial Aid, Lambuth University, 705 Lambuth Boulevard, Jackson, TN 38301. *Phone:* 731-425-3332. *Toll-free phone:* 800-526-2884. *Fax:* 731-425-3496. *E-mail:* myers-k@lambuth.edu. *Web site:* http://www.lambuth.edu/.

Lane College
Jackson, Tennessee

- **Independent** 4-year, founded 1882, affiliated with Christian Methodist Episcopal Church
- **Suburban** 25-acre campus with easy access to Memphis
- **Endowment** $3.3 million
- **Coed** 2,222 undergraduate students, 99% full-time, 53% women, 47% men
- **Minimally difficult** entrance level, 37% of applicants were admitted

Undergraduates 2,210 full-time, 12 part-time. Students come from 33 states and territories; 3 other countries; 33% are from out of state; 100% Black or African American, non-Hispanic/Latino; 0.1% Hispanic/Latino; 0.1% international; 6% transferred in; 62% live on campus. *Retention:* 57% of full-time freshmen returned.

Freshmen *Admission:* 6,060 applied, 2,216 admitted, 696 enrolled. *Average high school GPA:* 2.8. *Test scores:* ACT scores over 18: 17%; ACT scores over 24: 1%.

Faculty *Total:* 104, 96% full-time, 79% with terminal degrees. *Student/faculty ratio:* 21:1.

Academics *Calendar:* semesters. *Degrees:* bachelor's and postbachelor's certificates. *Special study options:* academic remediation for entering students, accelerated degree program, adult/continuing education programs, advanced placement credit, cooperative education, honors programs, independent study, internships, part-time degree program, study abroad, summer session for credit.

Computers on Campus 258 computers/terminals and 258 ports are available on campus for general student use. Students can access the following: campus intranet, computer help desk, free student e-mail accounts, online admissions and advising. Campuswide network is available. 100% of college-owned or -operated housing units are wired for high-speed Internet access. Wireless service is available via classrooms, computer centers, computer labs, dorm rooms, learning centers, libraries, student centers.

Student Life *Housing:* on-campus residence required for freshman year. *Options:* men-only, women-only. Campus housing is university owned. Freshman applicants given priority for college housing. *Activities and organizations:* drama/theater group, choral group, marching band, Student Government Association, Pre-Law Club, Student Christian Association, Drama Club, Computer Science Club, national fraternities, national sororities. *Campus security:* 24-hour emergency response devices and patrols, surveillance cameras, lighted parking areas. *Student services:* health clinic, personal/psychological counseling.

Athletics Member NCAA. All Division II. *Intercollegiate sports:* baseball M(s), basketball M(s)/W(s), cheerleading W, cross-country running M/W, football M(s), softball W, tennis M/W, track and field M/W, volleyball W. *Intramural sports:* basketball M/W, swimming and diving M/W, table tennis M/W, track and field M/W, volleyball M/W.

Standardized Tests *Required:* SAT or ACT (for admission).

Costs (2011–12) *Comprehensive fee:* $14,020 includes full-time tuition ($7550), mandatory fees ($670), and room and board ($5800). Full-time tuition and fees vary according to course load. Part-time tuition: $315 per credit hour.

Part-time tuition and fees vary according to course load. *Required fees:* $670 per year part-time. *Payment plans:* installment, deferred payment. *Waivers:* adult students and employees or children of employees.

Financial Aid Of all full-time matriculated undergraduates who enrolled in 2009, 2,102 applied for aid, 2,008 were judged to have need, 898 had their need fully met. In 2009, 42 non-need-based awards were made. *Average percent of need met:* 43%. *Average financial aid package:* $3304. *Average need-based loan:* $1968. *Average need-based gift aid:* $1730. *Average non-need-based aid:* $2713. *Average indebtedness upon graduation:* $8769.

Applying *Options:* electronic application, deferred entrance. *Required:* high school transcript, 2 letters of recommendation. *Application deadlines:* rolling (freshmen), rolling (out-of-state freshmen), rolling (transfers). *Notification:* continuous (freshmen), continuous (transfers).

Freshman Application Contact Ms. Kelly Boyd, Director of Enrollment Management, Lane College, 545 Lane Avenue, Jackson, TN 38301. *Phone:* 731-426-7533. *Toll-free phone:* 800-960-7533. *Fax:* 731-426-7559. *E-mail:* kboyd@lanecollege.edu. *Web site:* http://www.lanecollege.edu/.

Lee University
Cleveland, Tennessee

- **Independent** comprehensive, founded 1918, affiliated with Church of God
- **Small-town** 120-acre campus with easy access to Chattanooga
- **Endowment** $8.5 million
- **Coed** 4,006 undergraduate students, 88% full-time, 58% women, 42% men
- **Minimally difficult** entrance level, 64% of applicants were admitted

Undergraduates 3,544 full-time, 462 part-time. Students come from 48 states and territories; 60 other countries; 55% are from out of state; 5% Black or African American, non-Hispanic/Latino; 3% Hispanic/Latino; 1% Asian, non-Hispanic/Latino; 0.2% Native Hawaiian or other Pacific Islander, non-Hispanic/Latino; 0.2% American Indian or Alaska Native, non-Hispanic/Latino; 0.8% Two or more races, non-Hispanic/Latino; 5% Race/ethnicity unknown; 5% international; 7% transferred in; 46% live on campus. *Retention:* 71% of full-time freshmen returned.

Freshmen *Admission:* 1,750 applied, 1,126 admitted, 853 enrolled. *Average high school GPA:* 3.44. *Test scores:* SAT critical reading scores over 500: 64%; SAT math scores over 500: 59%; ACT scores over 18: 90%; SAT critical reading scores over 600: 27%; SAT math scores over 600: 22%; ACT scores over 24: 56%; SAT critical reading scores over 700: 3%; SAT math scores over 700: 3%; ACT scores over 30: 12%.

Faculty *Total:* 344, 46% full-time, 46% with terminal degrees. *Student/faculty ratio:* 18:1.

Academics *Calendar:* semesters. *Degrees:* bachelor's, master's, and post-master's certificates. *Special study options:* academic remediation for entering students, adult/continuing education programs, advanced placement credit, cooperative education, distance learning, double majors, English as a second language, external degree program, honors programs, independent study, internships, services for LD students, study abroad, summer session for credit.

Computers on Campus 410 computers/terminals and 410 ports are available on campus for general student use. Students can access the following: campus intranet, computer help desk, free student e-mail accounts, online (class) grades, online (class) registration, online (class) schedules. Campuswide network is available. 95% of college-owned or -operated housing units are wired for high-speed Internet access. Wireless service is available via entire campus.

Student Life *Housing:* on-campus residence required through sophomore year. *Options:* men-only, women-only. Campus housing is university owned. Freshman campus housing is guaranteed. *Activities and organizations:* drama/theater group, student-run newspaper, choral group, Student Leadership Council, Pioneers for Christ, International Student Fellowship, Starlite Ministries, Back Yard Ministry. *Campus security:* 24-hour emergency response devices and patrols, late-night transport/escort service, controlled dormitory access. *Student services:* health clinic, personal/psychological counseling.

Athletics Member NAIA, NCCAA. *Intercollegiate sports:* baseball M(s), basketball M(s)/W(s), cheerleading M(c)/W(c), cross-country running M(s)/W(s), golf M(s), rugby M(c)/W(c), soccer M(s)/W(s), softball W(s), tennis M(s)/W(s), volleyball W(s). *Intramural sports:* badminton M/W, basketball M/W, bowling M/W, football M/W, racquetball M/W, soccer M/W, softball M/W, table tennis M/W, tennis M/W, ultimate Frisbee M/W, volleyball M/W, wrestling M.

Standardized Tests *Required:* SAT or ACT (for admission).

Costs (2011–12) *Comprehensive fee:* $18,690 includes full-time tuition ($12,120), mandatory fees ($560), and room and board ($6010). Full-time tuition and fees vary according to course load. Part-time tuition: $506 per credit hour. Part-time tuition and fees vary according to course load. *Required fees:* $506 per credit hour part-time. *College room only:* $2900. Room and board charges vary according to board plan and housing facility. *Payment plan:* deferred payment. *Waivers:* employees or children of employees.

Financial Aid Of all full-time matriculated undergraduates who enrolled in 2009, 2,927 applied for aid, 2,445 were judged to have need, 390 had their need fully met. 560 Federal Work-Study jobs (averaging $1235). In 2009, 130 non-need-based awards were made. *Average percent of need met:* 56%. *Average financial aid package:* $10,703. *Average need-based loan:* $4230. *Average need-based gift aid:* $8217. *Average non-need-based aid:* $7947. *Average indebtedness upon graduation:* $28,911.

Applying *Options:* electronic application, early admission, deferred entrance. *Application fee:* $25. *Required:* high school transcript, minimum 2 GPA, MMR immunization record. *Required for some:* 3 letters of recommendation. *Application deadlines:* 9/1 (freshmen), 9/1 (transfers). *Notification:* continuous (freshmen), continuous (transfers).

Freshman Application Contact Mr. Phillip Cook, Vice President for Enrollment, Lee University, PO Box 3450, Cleveland, TN 37320-3450. *Phone:* 423-614-8500. *Toll-free phone:* 800-533-9930. *Fax:* 423-614-8533. *E-mail:* admissions@leeuniversity.edu. *Web site:* http://www.leeuniversity.edu/.

LeMoyne-Owen College
Memphis, Tennessee

Freshman Application Contact LeMoyne-Owen College, 807 Walker Avenue, Memphis, TN 38126-6595. *Phone:* 901-435-1500. *Web site:* http://www.loc.edu/.

Lincoln Memorial University
Harrogate, Tennessee

- **Independent** comprehensive, founded 1897
- **Small-town** 1000-acre campus
- **Endowment** $25.8 million
- **Coed** 1,786 undergraduate students, 82% full-time, 70% women, 30% men
- **Moderately difficult** entrance level, 93% of applicants were admitted

Undergraduates 1,459 full-time, 327 part-time. Students come from 46 states and territories; 25 other countries; 33% are from out of state; 17% transferred in; 36% live on campus. *Retention:* 62% of full-time freshmen returned.

Freshmen *Admission:* 1,136 applied, 1,060 admitted, 355 enrolled. *Average high school GPA:* 3.47. *Test scores:* SAT critical reading scores over 500: 49%; SAT math scores over 500: 58%; ACT scores over 18: 93%; SAT critical reading scores over 600: 14%; SAT math scores over 600: 14%; ACT scores over 24: 43%; SAT critical reading scores over 700: 2%; ACT scores over 30: 5%.

Faculty *Total:* 253, 67% full-time, 57% with terminal degrees. *Student/faculty ratio:* 13:1.

Academics *Calendar:* semesters. *Degrees:* associate, bachelor's, master's, doctoral-professional, doctoral-research/scholarship, and post-master's certificates. *Special study options:* academic remediation for entering students, accelerated degree program, adult/continuing education programs, advanced placement credit, distance learning, double majors, English as a second language, honors programs, independent study, internships, part-time degree program, summer session for credit.

Computers on Campus Students can access the following: campus intranet, computer help desk, free student e-mail accounts, online (class) grades, online (class) registration, online (class) schedules. Campuswide network is available. 100% of college-owned or -operated housing units are wired for high-speed Internet access.

Student Life *Housing options:* coed, men-only, women-only, disabled students. Campus housing is university owned. *Activities and organizations:* drama/theater group, student-run radio and television station, choral group, Students in Free Enterprise (SIFE), Baptist Campus Ministries, Pre-Med Club, Fishing Club, Earth Club. *Campus security:* 24-hour emergency response devices and patrols. *Student services:* health clinic, personal/psychological counseling.

Athletics Member NCAA. All Division II. *Intercollegiate sports:* baseball M(s), basketball M(s)/W(s), cross-country running M(s)/W(s), golf M(s)/W(s), soccer M(s)/W(s), softball W(s), tennis M(s)/W(s), volleyball W(s). *Intramural sports:* basketball M/W, football M/W, soccer M/W, softball M/W, swimming and diving M/W, table tennis M/W, tennis M/W, ultimate Frisbee M/W, volleyball M/W.

Standardized Tests *Required:* SAT or ACT (for admission).

Costs (2010–11) *Comprehensive fee:* $21,980 includes full-time tuition ($16,200) and room and board ($5780). Part-time tuition: $675 per credit hour. Part-time tuition and fees vary according to course load. *Room and board:* Room and board charges vary according to board plan and housing facility. *Payment plan:* installment. *Waivers:* senior citizens and employees or children of employees.

Financial Aid Of all full-time matriculated undergraduates who enrolled in 2009, 1,185 applied for aid, 1,106 were judged to have need, 442 had their

need fully met. In 2009, 23 non-need-based awards were made. *Average percent of need met:* 72%. *Average financial aid package:* $16,166. *Average need-based loan:* $2625. *Average need-based gift aid:* $11,463. *Average non-need-based aid:* $1793. *Average indebtedness upon graduation:* $10,623.
Applying *Options:* electronic application. *Application fee:* $25. *Required:* high school transcript, minimum 2.3 GPA, immunization records, financial aid application. *Application deadlines:* rolling (freshmen), rolling (transfers). *Notification:* continuous (freshmen), continuous (transfers).
Freshman Application Contact Lincoln Memorial University, 6965 Cumberland Gap Parkway, Harrogate, TN 37752-1901. *Phone:* 423-869-6280. *Toll-free phone:* 800-325-0900. *Web site:* http://www.lmunet.edu/.

Lipscomb University
Nashville, Tennessee

- **Independent** comprehensive, founded 1891, affiliated with Church of Christ
- **Suburban** 65-acre campus
- **Endowment** $50.8 million
- **Coed** 2,644 undergraduate students, 92% full-time, 58% women, 42% men
- **Moderately difficult** entrance level, 60% of applicants were admitted

Undergraduates 2,425 full-time, 219 part-time. Students come from 43 states and territories; 19 other countries; 30% are from out of state; 7% Black or African American, non-Hispanic/Latino; 3% Hispanic/Latino; 3% Asian, non-Hispanic/Latino; 0.2% American Indian or Alaska Native, non-Hispanic/Latino; 3% Race/ethnicity unknown; 2% international; 5% transferred in; 54% live on campus. *Retention:* 73% of full-time freshmen returned.
Freshmen *Admission:* 2,694 applied, 1,627 admitted, 668 enrolled. *Average high school GPA:* 3.5. *Test scores:* SAT critical reading scores over 500: 79%; SAT math scores over 500: 77%; ACT scores over 18: 99%; SAT critical reading scores over 600: 32%; SAT math scores over 600: 35%; ACT scores over 24: 58%; SAT critical reading scores over 700: 4%; SAT math scores over 700: 4%; ACT scores over 30: 16%.
Faculty *Total:* 363, 39% full-time. *Student/faculty ratio:* 16:1.
Academics *Calendar:* semesters. *Degrees:* bachelor's, master's, doctoral-professional, and postbachelor's certificates. *Special study options:* academic remediation for entering students, accelerated degree program, adult/continuing education programs, advanced placement credit, distance learning, double majors, honors programs, independent study, internships, part-time degree program, services for LD students, study abroad, summer session for credit. *ROTC:* Army (c), Air Force (c). *Unusual degree programs:* 3-2 engineering with Vanderbilt University, Tennessee Technical University, University of Tennessee.
Computers on Campus 185 computers/terminals are available on campus for general student use. Students can access the following: computer help desk, free student e-mail accounts, online (class) grades, online (class) registration, online (class) schedules. Campuswide network is available. 100% of college-owned or -operated housing units are wired for high-speed Internet access. Wireless service is available via entire campus.
Student Life *Housing:* on-campus residence required through junior year. *Options:* men-only, women-only. Campus housing is university owned. Freshman applicants given priority for college housing. *Activities and organizations:* drama/theater group, student-run newspaper, radio and television station, choral group, Sigma Pi Beta, business fraternities, Multicultural Association, Alpha Phi Chi men's service club, Pi Kappa Sigma women's service club. *Campus security:* 24-hour emergency response devices and patrols, late-night transport/escort service, controlled dormitory access. *Student services:* health clinic, personal/psychological counseling.
Athletics Member NCAA. All Division I. *Intercollegiate sports:* baseball M(s), basketball M(s)/W(s), cross-country running M(s)/W(s), golf M(s)/W(s), soccer M(s)/W(s), softball W(s), tennis M(s)/W(s), volleyball W(s). *Intramural sports:* basketball M/W, football M/W, soccer M/W, softball M/W, table tennis M/W, volleyball M/W.
Standardized Tests *Required:* SAT or ACT (for admission).
Costs (2011–12) *Comprehensive fee:* $32,284 includes full-time tuition ($21,896), mandatory fees ($1598), and room and board ($8790). Full-time tuition and fees vary according to class time, course load, and degree level. Part-time tuition: $915 per hour. Part-time tuition and fees vary according to class time, course load, and degree level. *Required fees:* $50 per credit hour part-time. *College room only:* $4940. Room and board charges vary according to board plan and housing facility. *Payment plans:* installment, deferred payment. *Waivers:* employees or children of employees.
Financial Aid Of all full-time matriculated undergraduates who enrolled in 2009, 2,297 applied for aid, 1,616 were judged to have need, 414 had their need fully met. In 2009, 387 non-need-based awards were made. *Average percent of need met:* 62%. *Average financial aid package:* $18,174. *Average need-based loan:* $5366. *Average need-based gift aid:* $6804. *Average non-need-based aid:* $6992. *Average indebtedness upon graduation:* $21,034.

Applying *Options:* electronic application, early admission, deferred entrance. *Application fee:* $25. *Required:* high school transcript, minimum 2.25 GPA, 1 letter of recommendation, interview. *Recommended:* essay or personal statement. *Application deadlines:* rolling (freshmen), rolling (transfers). *Notification:* continuous (freshmen), continuous (transfers).
Freshman Application Contact Office of Admissions, Lipscomb University, One University Park Drive, Nashville, TN 37204-3951. *Phone:* 615-966-1776. *Toll-free phone:* 877-582-4766. *Fax:* 615-966-1804. *E-mail:* admissions@lipscomb.edu. *Web site:* http://www.lipscomb.edu/.

Martin Methodist College
Pulaski, Tennessee

Freshman Application Contact Lisa Smith, Director of Admissions, Martin Methodist College, 433 West Madison Street, Pulaski, TN 38478-2716. *Phone:* 931-363-9868. *Toll-free phone:* 800-467-1273. *Fax:* 931-363-9818. *E-mail:* admit@martinmethodist.edu. *Web site:* http://www.martinmethodist.edu/.

Maryville College
Maryville, Tennessee

- **Independent Presbyterian** 4-year, founded 1819
- **Suburban** 350-acre campus
- **Coed** 1,080 undergraduate students, 98% full-time, 53% women, 47% men
- **Moderately difficult** entrance level, 70% of applicants were admitted

Undergraduates 1,060 full-time, 20 part-time. Students come from 25 states and territories; 20 other countries; 21% are from out of state; 6% Black or African American, non-Hispanic/Latino; 2% Hispanic/Latino; 1% Asian, non-Hispanic/Latino; 0.5% American Indian or Alaska Native, non-Hispanic/Latino; 2% Two or more races, non-Hispanic/Latino; 0.4% Race/ethnicity unknown; 4% international; 4% transferred in; 75% live on campus. *Retention:* 72% of full-time freshmen returned.
Freshmen *Admission:* 1,322 applied, 920 admitted, 277 enrolled. *Average high school GPA:* 3.5. *Test scores:* SAT critical reading scores over 500: 55%; SAT math scores over 500: 59%; SAT writing scores over 500: 47%; ACT scores over 18: 97%; SAT critical reading scores over 600: 22%; SAT math scores over 600: 22%; SAT writing scores over 600: 15%; ACT scores over 24: 51%; SAT critical reading scores over 700: 1%; SAT math scores over 700: 1%; SAT writing scores over 700: 1%; ACT scores over 30: 11%.
Faculty *Total:* 121, 64% with terminal degrees. *Student/faculty ratio:* 11:1.
Academics *Calendar:* 4-1-4. *Degree:* bachelor's. *Special study options:* academic remediation for entering students, accelerated degree program, adult/continuing education programs, advanced placement credit, double majors, English as a second language, honors programs, independent study, internships, off-campus study, part-time degree program, services for LD students, student-designed majors, study abroad, summer session for credit. *Unusual degree programs:* 3-2 engineering with Vanderbilt University, Washington University in St. Louis, Auburn University, Tennessee Technological University; nursing with Vanderbilt University.
Computers on Campus 290 computers/terminals are available on campus for general student use. Students can access the following: campus intranet, computer help desk, free student e-mail accounts, online (class) registration. Campuswide network is available. 100% of college-owned or -operated housing units are wired for high-speed Internet access. Wireless service is available via entire campus.
Student Life *Housing:* on-campus residence required through senior year. *Options:* coed, men-only, women-only, disabled students. Campus housing is university owned. Freshman campus housing is guaranteed. *Activities and organizations:* drama/theater group, student-run newspaper, choral group, Voices of Praise, student government, Student Programming Board, Global Citizenship, Peer Mentors. *Campus security:* 24-hour emergency response devices and patrols, late-night transport/escort service, controlled dormitory access, Campus wide emergency alert system via cell phones, home phones, and email. *Student services:* health clinic, personal/psychological counseling.
Athletics Member NCAA. All Division III. *Intercollegiate sports:* baseball M, basketball M/W, cheerleading M/W, cross-country running M/W, equestrian sports M(c)/W(c), football M, golf M/W, soccer M/W, softball W, swimming and diving M/W, tennis M/W, ultimate Frisbee M(c)/W(c), volleyball W. *Intramural sports:* archery M/W, badminton M/W, basketball M/W, bowling M/W, football M/W, racquetball M/W, rugby M/W, skiing (downhill) M/W, soccer M/W, softball M/W, table tennis M/W, tennis M/W, track and field M/W, ultimate Frisbee M/W, volleyball M/W, water polo M/W.
Standardized Tests *Required:* SAT or ACT (for admission).
Costs (2011–12) *Comprehensive fee:* $39,158 includes full-time tuition ($29,230), mandatory fees ($694), and room and board ($9234). Full-time tuition and fees vary according to course load. Part-time tuition: $1218 per credit hour. Part-time tuition and fees vary according to course load. *College*

room only: $4584. Room and board charges vary according to board plan and housing facility. *Payment plan:* installment. *Waivers:* employees or children of employees.

Financial Aid Of all full-time matriculated undergraduates who enrolled in 2009, 1,060 applied for aid, 876 were judged to have need, 209 had their need fully met. 549 Federal Work-Study jobs (averaging $1753). 50 state and other part-time jobs (averaging $1632). In 2009, 164 non-need-based awards were made. *Average percent of need met:* 85%. *Average financial aid package:* $27,657. *Average need-based loan:* $4825. *Average need-based gift aid:* $32,153. *Average non-need-based aid:* $14,003. *Average indebtedness upon graduation:* $21,343.

Applying *Options:* electronic application, early admission, early decision, early action, deferred entrance. *Required:* essay or personal statement, high school transcript, minimum 2.5 GPA. *Required for some:* interview. *Recommended:* minimum 3 GPA. *Application deadlines:* 3/1 (freshmen), rolling (transfers), 10/1 (early action). *Early decision deadline:* 11/15. *Notification:* 4/1 (freshmen), 8/15 (transfers), 12/1 (early decision), 10/15 (early action).

Freshman Application Contact Ms. Linda L. Moore, Administrative Assistant of Admissions, Maryville College, 502 East Lamar Alexander Parkway, Maryville, TN 37804-5907. *Phone:* 865-981-8096. *Toll-free phone:* 800-597-2687. *Fax:* 865-981-8005. *E-mail:* admissions@maryvillecollege.edu. *Web site:* http://www.maryvillecollege.edu/.

Memphis College of Art
Memphis, Tennessee

- **Independent** comprehensive, founded 1936
- **Urban** 340-acre campus
- **Coed**
- **Moderately difficult** entrance level

Faculty *Student/faculty ratio:* 10:1.
Academics *Calendar:* semesters. *Degrees:* bachelor's and master's.
Student Life *Campus security:* 24-hour emergency response devices and patrols, late-night transport/escort service, controlled dormitory access.
Standardized Tests *Required:* SAT or ACT (for admission).
Costs (2010–11) *Comprehensive fee:* $31,950 includes full-time tuition ($23,300), mandatory fees ($650), and room and board ($8000). Part-time tuition: $1012 per course. Part-time tuition and fees vary according to course load. *Required fees:* $650 per year part-time. *College room only:* $6000. Room and board charges vary according to housing facility.
Financial Aid Of all full-time matriculated undergraduates who enrolled in 2009, 302 applied for aid, 277 were judged to have need, 64 had their need fully met. 340 Federal Work-Study jobs (averaging $500). In 2009, 40 non-need-based awards were made. *Average percent of need met:* 80. *Average financial aid package:* $10,862. *Average need-based loan:* $5500. *Average need-based gift aid:* $6252. *Average non-need-based aid:* $9000. *Average indebtedness upon graduation:* $34,360.
Applying *Options:* electronic application, deferred entrance. *Application fee:* $25. *Required:* high school transcript, minimum 2 GPA, portfolio. *Recommended:* essay or personal statement, interview.
Freshman Application Contact Memphis College of Art, Overton Park, 1930 Poplar Avenue, Memphis, TN 38104-2764. *Phone:* 901-272-5153. *Toll-free phone:* 800-727-1088. *Web site:* http://www.mca.edu/.

See page 1418 for the College Close-Up.

Middle Tennessee State University
Murfreesboro, Tennessee

- **State-supported** university, founded 1911, part of Tennessee Board of Regents
- **Urban** 500-acre campus with easy access to Nashville
- **Endowment** $53.2 million
- **Coed** 23,401 undergraduate students, 84% full-time, 52% women, 48% men
- **Moderately difficult** entrance level, 71% of applicants were admitted

Undergraduates 19,717 full-time, 3,684 part-time. 4% are from out of state; 17% Black or African American, non-Hispanic/Latino; 3% Hispanic/Latino; 3% Asian, non-Hispanic/Latino; 0.1% Native Hawaiian or other Pacific Islander, non-Hispanic/Latino; 0.3% American Indian or Alaska Native, non-Hispanic/Latino; 2% Two or more races, non-Hispanic/Latino; 2% Race/ethnicity unknown; 10% transferred in; 11% live on campus.
Freshmen *Admission:* 10,542 applied, 7,511 admitted, 3,777 enrolled. *Test scores:* SAT critical reading scores over 500: 64%; SAT math scores over 500: 65%; ACT scores over 18: 93%; SAT critical reading scores over 600: 27%; SAT math scores over 600: 25%; ACT scores over 24: 33%; SAT critical reading scores over 700: 4%; SAT math scores over 700: 3%; ACT scores over 30: 4%.
Faculty *Total:* 1,346, 70% full-time. *Student/faculty ratio:* 21:1.

Bachelor of Fine Arts

Animation	Graphic Design	Printmaking
Digital Cinema	Illustration	Sculpture
Digital Media	Painting	Sequential Narrative
Drawing	Photography	

Master of Fine Arts | Master of Arts in Art Education
Master of Arts in Teaching

1.800.727.1088
info@mca.edu | www.mca.edu

Memphis College *of* **Art**
1930 Poplar Avenue, Overton Park • Memphis, TN 38104

Academics *Calendar:* semesters. *Degrees:* bachelor's, master's, doctoral-research/scholarship, post-master's, and postbachelor's certificates. *Special study options:* academic remediation for entering students, adult/continuing education programs, advanced placement credit, distance learning, double majors, freshman honors college, honors programs, independent study, internships, off-campus study, part-time degree program, services for LD students, study abroad, summer session for credit. *ROTC:* Army (b), Air Force (c). *Unusual degree programs:* 3-2 engineering with University of Tennessee, Knoxville; Georgia Institute of Technology; Tennessee Technological University; The University of Memphis; Tennessee State University; Vanderbilt University.

Computers on Campus Students can access the following: online (class) registration. Campuswide network is available.

Student Life *Housing options:* coed, men-only, women-only. Campus housing is university owned. *Activities and organizations:* drama/theater group, student-run newspaper, radio and television station, choral group, marching band, national fraternities, national sororities. *Campus security:* 24-hour emergency response devices and patrols, student patrols, late-night transport/escort service, controlled dormitory access. *Student services:* health clinic, personal/psychological counseling, women's center, legal services.

Athletics Member NCAA. All Division I except football (Division I-A). *Intercollegiate sports:* baseball M(s), basketball M(s)/W(s), cheerleading M(s)/W(s), cross-country running M(s)/W(s), equestrian sports M/W, golf M(s), soccer W(s), softball W(s), tennis M(s)/W(s), track and field M(s)/W(s), volleyball W(s). *Intramural sports:* badminton M/W, basketball M/W, bowling M(c)/W(c), fencing M(c)/W(c), field hockey M(c)/W(c), football M, ice hockey M(c), lacrosse M(c)/W(c), racquetball M(c)/W(c), riflery M, rugby M(c)/W(c), soccer M(c)/W, softball M/W, swimming and diving M/W, tennis M/W, ultimate Frisbee M(c)/W(c), volleyball M(c)/W(c), wrestling M(c)/W(c).

Standardized Tests *Required:* SAT or ACT (for admission).

Costs (2010–11) *Tuition:* state resident $4824 full-time, $201 per credit hour part-time; nonresident $17,352 full-time, $723 per credit hour part-time. Full-time tuition and fees vary according to course load. Part-time tuition and fees vary according to course load. *Required fees:* $1474 full-time, $62 per credit hour part-time. *Room and board:* $7132; room only: $4232. Room and board charges vary according to board plan and housing facility.

Financial Aid Of all full-time matriculated undergraduates who enrolled in 2009, 16,524 applied for aid, 12,781 were judged to have need, 2,003 had their need fully met. 261 Federal Work-Study jobs (averaging $3480). In 2009, 652 non-need-based awards were made. *Average percent of need met:* 65%. *Average financial aid package:* $8949. *Average need-based loan:* $3936. *Average need-based gift aid:* $5262. *Average non-need-based aid:* $2766. *Average indebtedness upon graduation:* $14,822.

Applying *Options:* electronic application. *Application fee:* $25. *Required:* high school transcript, minimum 3 GPA. *Required for some:* essay or personal statement. *Notification:* continuous (freshmen).

Freshman Application Contact Ms. Lynn Palmer, Director of Admissions, Middle Tennessee State University, 1301 East Main Street, Murfreesboro, TN 37132. *Phone:* 615-898-2111. *Fax:* 615-898-5478. *E-mail:* admissions@mtsu.edu. *Web site:* http://www.mtsu.edu/.

Milligan College
Milligan College, Tennessee

- **Independent Christian** comprehensive, founded 1866
- **Suburban** 181-acre campus
- **Endowment** $12.7 million
- **Coed** 931 undergraduate students, 89% full-time, 59% women, 41% men
- **Moderately difficult** entrance level, 67% of applicants were admitted

Undergraduates 832 full-time, 99 part-time. Students come from 34 states and territories; 18 other countries; 35% are from out of state; 6% Black or African American, non-Hispanic/Latino; 3% Hispanic/Latino; 0.5% Asian, non-Hispanic/Latino; 0.2% American Indian or Alaska Native, non-Hispanic/Latino; 2% Two or more races, non-Hispanic/Latino; 0.6% Race/ethnicity unknown; 2% international; 9% transferred in; 74% live on campus. *Retention:* 81% of full-time freshmen returned.

Freshmen *Admission:* 655 applied, 439 admitted, 177 enrolled. *Average high school GPA:* 3.56. *Test scores:* SAT critical reading scores over 500: 74%; SAT math scores over 500: 58%; SAT writing scores over 500: 57%; ACT scores over 18: 97%; SAT critical reading scores over 600: 20%; SAT math scores over 600: 20%; SAT writing scores over 600: 9%; ACT scores over 24: 45%; SAT math scores over 700: 2%; ACT scores over 30: 3%.

Faculty *Total:* 115, 58% full-time, 58% with terminal degrees. *Student/faculty ratio:* 13:1.

Academics *Calendar:* semesters. *Degrees:* bachelor's and master's. *Special study options:* academic remediation for entering students, adult/continuing education programs, advanced placement credit, cooperative education, distance learning, double majors, independent study, internships, off-campus study, part-time degree program, study abroad, summer session for credit.

ROTC: Army (c). *Unusual degree programs:* 3-2 pharmacy with Gatton College of Pharmacy at East Tennessee State University.

Computers on Campus 97 computers/terminals are available on campus for general student use. Students can access the following: campus intranet, computer help desk, free student e-mail accounts, online (class) grades, online (class) registration, online (class) schedules. Campuswide network is available. 100% of college-owned or -operated housing units are wired for high-speed Internet access. Wireless service is available via classrooms, computer centers, computer labs, dorm rooms, libraries, student centers.

Student Life *Housing:* on-campus residence required through senior year. *Options:* men-only, women-only. Campus housing is university owned. Freshman campus housing is guaranteed. *Activities and organizations:* drama/theater group, student-run newspaper, radio station, choral group, Social Affairs Committee, Buffalo Ramblers, Concert Council, Volunteer Milligan, Students for Life. *Campus security:* 24-hour emergency response devices and patrols, late-night transport/escort service. *Student services:* health clinic, personal/psychological counseling.

Athletics Member NAIA. *Intercollegiate sports:* baseball M(s), basketball M(s)/W(s), cross-country running M(s)/W(s), golf M(s)/W(s), soccer M(s)/W(s), softball W(s), swimming and diving M(s)/W(s), tennis M(s)/W(s), volleyball W(s). *Intramural sports:* basketball M/W, cheerleading W, football M/W, softball M/W, swimming and diving M/W, table tennis M/W, tennis M/W, ultimate Frisbee M/W, volleyball M/W, weight lifting M/W.

Standardized Tests *Required:* SAT or ACT (for admission).

Costs (2011–12) *One-time required fee:* $75. *Comprehensive fee:* $30,910 includes full-time tuition ($24,360), mandatory fees ($900), and room and board ($5650). Full-time tuition and fees vary according to course load. Part-time tuition: $360 per credit hour. Part-time tuition and fees vary according to course load. *College room only:* $2650. Room and board charges vary according to housing facility. *Payment plan:* installment. *Waivers:* employees or children of employees.

Financial Aid Of all full-time matriculated undergraduates who enrolled in 2009, 766 applied for aid, 674 were judged to have need, 173 had their need fully met. 168 Federal Work-Study jobs (averaging $1200). 129 state and other part-time jobs (averaging $1607). In 2009, 111 non-need-based awards were made. *Average percent of need met:* 77%. *Average financial aid package:* $17,370. *Average need-based loan:* $4098. *Average need-based gift aid:* $14,415. *Average non-need-based aid:* $7209. *Average indebtedness upon graduation:* $22,360.

Applying *Options:* electronic application, deferred entrance. *Application fee:* $30. *Required:* essay or personal statement, high school transcript, minimum 2 GPA, 2 letters of recommendation. *Required for some:* interview. *Recommended:* minimum 3 GPA. *Application deadlines:* 8/1 (freshmen), rolling (transfers). *Notification:* continuous (freshmen), continuous (transfers).

Freshman Application Contact Ms. Tracy Brinn, Director of Enrollment Management, Milligan College, PO Box 210, Milligan College, TN 37682. *Phone:* 423-461-8730. *Toll-free phone:* 800-262-8337. *Fax:* 423-461-8982. *E-mail:* admissions@milligan.edu. *Web site:* http://www.milligan.edu/.

See page 1434 for the College Close-Up.

National College
Bristol, Tennessee

Freshman Application Contact National College, 1328 Highway 11 West, Bristol, TN 37620. *Phone:* 423-878-4440. *Web site:* http://www.national-college.edu/.

Nossi College of Art
Goodlettsville, Tennessee

- **Independent** primarily 2-year
- **Urban** 10-acre campus with easy access to Nashville
- **Coed** 660 undergraduate students, 100% full-time, 55% women, 45% men
- 63% of applicants were admitted

Undergraduates 660 full-time. Students come from 10 states and territories; 1 other country; 10% are from out of state; 16% Black or African American, non-Hispanic/Latino; 2% Hispanic/Latino; 0.8% Asian, non-Hispanic/Latino; 1% Race/ethnicity unknown. *Retention:* 75% of full-time freshmen returned.

Freshmen *Admission:* 210 applied, 133 admitted.

Faculty *Total:* 37, 16% full-time. *Student/faculty ratio:* 10:1.

Academics *Calendar:* semesters. *Degrees:* associate and bachelor's. *Special study options:* independent study, internships, services for LD students, summer session for credit.

Computers on Campus 125 computers/terminals and 200 ports are available on campus for general student use. Students can access the following: campus intranet, free student e-mail accounts. Wireless service is available via entire campus.

Student Life *Housing:* college housing not available. *Activities and organizations:* national fraternities. *Campus security:* Campus has a gated entrance and all doors are kept locked. Active students and staff have key cards which open doors.

Costs (2011–12) *Tuition:* $14,100 full-time, $4700 per term part-time. Full-time tuition and fees vary according to course load, degree level, and program. Part-time tuition and fees vary according to course load, degree level, and program. No tuition increase for student's term of enrollment. *Payment plan:* installment.

Applying *Options:* electronic application, early admission. *Application fee:* $100. *Required:* essay or personal statement, high school transcript, interview, A portfolio of work is required for those applying to the following programs: Associate or Bachelor of Graphic Art and Design and a Bachelor of Illustration.

Freshman Application Contact Ms. Mary Alexander, Admissions Director, Nossi College of Art, 590 Cheron Road, Madison, TN 37115. *Phone:* 615-514-2787 (ARTS). *Toll-free phone:* 877-860-1601. *Fax:* 615-514-2788. *E-mail:* admissions@nossi.edu. *Web site:* http://www.nossi.edu/.

O'More College of Design

Franklin, Tennessee

- **Independent** 4-year, founded 1970
- **Small-town** 6-acre campus with easy access to Nashville
- **Coed, primarily women** 202 undergraduate students, 90% full-time, 89% women, 11% men
- **Moderately difficult** entrance level, 89% of applicants were admitted

Undergraduates 182 full-time, 20 part-time. *Retention:* 82% of full-time freshmen returned.

Freshmen *Admission:* 53 applied, 47 admitted, 33 enrolled. *Average high school GPA:* 3.3. *Test scores:* ACT scores over 18: 100%; ACT scores over 24: 40%; ACT scores over 30: 3%.

Faculty *Total:* 40, 30% full-time, 20% with terminal degrees. *Student/faculty ratio:* 7:1.

Academics *Calendar:* semesters. *Degree:* bachelor's. *Special study options:* academic remediation for entering students, advanced placement credit, cooperative education, double majors, independent study, internships, off-campus study, part-time degree program, summer session for credit.

Computers on Campus 20 computers/terminals and 16 ports are available on campus for general student use. Students can access the following: free student e-mail accounts, library card catalog. Wireless service is available via entire campus.

Student Life *Housing:* college housing not available. *Activities and organizations:* American Society for Interior Design, Student Government Association, O'More Fashion Merchandising Association, Visual Communications Forum. *Campus security:* 24-hour emergency response devices, security provided until midnight.

Standardized Tests *Required:* SAT or ACT (for admission).

Costs (2011–12) *Tuition:* $23,170 full-time, $934 per credit part-time. *Required fees:* $75 per term part-time. *Room only:* Room and board charges vary according to board plan and housing facility. *Payment plan:* installment. *Waivers:* employees or children of employees.

Applying *Options:* electronic application, deferred entrance. *Application fee:* $50. *Required:* essay or personal statement, high school transcript, minimum 2.25 GPA. *Required for some:* interview, portfolio. *Application deadlines:* 8/1 (freshmen), 8/1 (out-of-state freshmen), 8/1 (transfers). *Notification:* continuous (freshmen), continuous (out-of-state freshmen), continuous (transfers).

Freshman Application Contact Mr. Chris Lee, Vice President of Enrollment, O'More College of Design, 423 South Margin Street, Franklin, TN 37064-2816. *Phone:* 615-794-4254 Ext. 232. *Fax:* 615-790-1662. *E-mail:* clee@omorecollege.edu. *Web site:* http://www.omorecollege.edu/.

Remington College–Memphis Campus

Memphis, Tennessee

Director of Admissions Randal Hayes, Director of Recruitment, Remington College–Memphis Campus, 2731 Nonconnah Boulevard, Memphis, TN 38132-2131. *Phone:* 901-345-1000. *Fax:* 901-396-8310. *E-mail:* randal.hayes@remingtoncollege.edu. *Web site:* http://www.remingtoncollege.edu/.

Rhodes College

Memphis, Tennessee

- **Independent** comprehensive, founded 1848
- **Suburban** 100-acre campus
- **Coed** 1,712 undergraduate students, 99% full-time, 58% women, 42% men
- **Very difficult** entrance level, 45% of applicants were admitted

Undergraduates 1,695 full-time, 17 part-time. 73% are from out of state; 7% Black or African American, non-Hispanic/Latino; 3% Hispanic/Latino; 5% Asian, non-Hispanic/Latino; 0.8% American Indian or Alaska Native, non-Hispanic/Latino; 1% Two or more races, non-Hispanic/Latino; 5% Race/ethnicity unknown; 3% international; 0.7% transferred in; 73% live on campus. *Retention:* 88% of full-time freshmen returned.

Freshmen *Admission:* 5,598 applied, 2,543 admitted, 502 enrolled. *Average high school GPA:* 3.78. *Test scores:* SAT critical reading scores over 500: 97%; SAT math scores over 500: 99%; ACT scores over 18: 100%; SAT critical reading scores over 600: 74%; SAT math scores over 600: 75%; ACT scores over 24: 97%; SAT critical reading scores over 700: 26%; SAT math scores over 700: 22%; ACT scores over 30: 38%.

Faculty *Total:* 196, 85% full-time, 88% with terminal degrees. *Student/faculty ratio:* 10:1.

Academics *Calendar:* semesters. *Degrees:* bachelor's and master's (master's degree in accounting only). *Special study options:* advanced placement credit, cooperative education, double majors, honors programs, independent study, internships, off-campus study, part-time degree program, services for LD students, student-designed majors, study abroad. *ROTC:* Army (c), Air Force (c). *Unusual degree programs:* 3-2 engineering with Washington University in St. Louis.

Computers on Campus Students can access the following: computer help desk, free student e-mail accounts, online (class) grades, online (class) registration, online (class) schedules. Campuswide network is available. Wireless service is available via entire campus.

Student Life *Housing:* on-campus residence required through sophomore year. *Options:* coed, men-only, women-only. Campus housing is university owned. Freshman campus housing is guaranteed. *Activities and organizations:* drama/theater group, student-run newspaper, radio and television station, choral group, national fraternities, national sororities. *Campus security:* 24-hour emergency response devices and patrols, student patrols, late-night transport/escort service, 24-hour monitored security cameras in parking areas, fenced campus with monitored access at night. *Student services:* health clinic, personal/psychological counseling, women's center.

Athletics Member NCAA. All Division III. *Intercollegiate sports:* baseball M, basketball M/W, cheerleading W(c), cross-country running M/W, field hockey W, football M, golf M/W, lacrosse M(c)/W(c), rugby M(c), soccer M/W, softball W, swimming and diving M/W, tennis M/W, track and field M/W, volleyball W. *Intramural sports:* basketball M/W, football M/W, racquetball M/W, soccer M/W, softball M/W, squash M, volleyball M/W.

Standardized Tests *Required:* SAT or ACT (for admission).

Costs (2011–12) *Comprehensive fee:* $43,060 includes full-time tuition ($34,270), mandatory fees ($310), and room and board ($8480). *Room and board:* Room and board charges vary according to board plan and housing facility. *Payment plan:* installment. *Waivers:* employees or children of employees.

Financial Aid Of all full-time matriculated undergraduates who enrolled in 2009, 1,051 applied for aid, 887 were judged to have need, 280 had their need fully met. In 2009, 155 non-need-based awards were made. *Average percent of need met:* 85%. *Average financial aid package:* $31,392. *Average need-based loan:* $5525. *Average need-based gift aid:* $22,182. *Average non-need-based aid:* $16,711. *Average indebtedness upon graduation:* $24,946. *Financial aid deadline:* 3/1.

Applying *Options:* electronic application, early admission, early decision, deferred entrance. *Application fee:* $45. *Required:* essay or personal statement, high school transcript, 2 letters of recommendation. *Recommended:* interview. *Application deadlines:* 1/15 (freshmen), 1/15 (transfers). *Early decision deadline:* 11/1 (for plan 1), 1/1 (for plan 2). *Notification:* 4/1 (freshmen), 4/1 (transfers), 12/1 (early decision plan 1), 2/1 (early decision plan 2).

Freshman Application Contact Rhodes College, 2000 North Parkway, Memphis, TN 38112-1690. *Phone:* 901-843-3700. *Toll-free phone:* 800-844-5969. *Web site:* http://www.rhodes.edu/.

Sewanee: The University of the South
Sewanee, Tennessee

- **Independent Episcopal** comprehensive, founded 1857
- **Small-town** 13,000-acre campus
- **Endowment** $272.5 million
- **Coed** 1,455 undergraduate students, 99% full-time, 53% women, 47% men
- **Very difficult** entrance level, 68% of applicants were admitted

Undergraduates 1,436 full-time, 19 part-time. Students come from 39 states and territories; 23 other countries; 77% are from out of state; 4% Black or African American, non-Hispanic/Latino; 3% Hispanic/Latino; 2% Asian, non-Hispanic/Latino; 0.4% American Indian or Alaska Native, non-Hispanic/Latino; 4% Two or more races, non-Hispanic/Latino; 0.6% Race/ethnicity unknown; 3% international; 1% transferred in; 96% live on campus. *Retention:* 90% of full-time freshmen returned.

Freshmen *Admission:* 2,481 applied, 1,688 admitted, 401 enrolled. *Average high school GPA:* 3.6. *Test scores:* SAT critical reading scores over 500: 93%; SAT math scores over 500: 96%; SAT writing scores over 500: 96%; ACT scores over 18: 100%; SAT critical reading scores over 600: 66%; SAT math scores over 600: 66%; SAT writing scores over 600: 61%; ACT scores over 24: 91%; SAT critical reading scores over 700: 22%; SAT math scores over 700: 13%; SAT writing scores over 700: 15%; ACT scores over 30: 33%.

Faculty *Total:* 172, 78% full-time, 88% with terminal degrees. *Student/faculty ratio:* 11:1.

Academics *Calendar:* semesters. *Degrees:* bachelor's, master's, doctoral-professional, post-master's, and postbachelor's certificates. *Special study options:* advanced placement credit, double majors, independent study, internships, services for LD students, student-designed majors, study abroad, summer session for credit. *Unusual degree programs:* 3-2 engineering with Washington University in St. Louis, Vanderbilt University, Rensselaer Polytechnic Institute, Columbia University; forestry with Duke University.

Computers on Campus 340 computers/terminals are available on campus for general student use. Students can access the following: campus intranet, computer help desk, free student e-mail accounts, online (class) grades, online (class) registration, online (class) schedules. Campuswide network is available. 100% of college-owned or -operated housing units are wired for high-speed Internet access. Wireless service is available via entire campus.

Student Life *Housing:* on-campus residence required through senior year. *Options:* coed, men-only, women-only, disabled students. Campus housing is university owned. Freshman campus housing is guaranteed. *Activities and organizations:* drama/theater group, student-run newspaper, radio station, choral group, Sewanee Outing Program, Community Service Council, Student Activities Programming Board, student radio station, BACCHUS (alcohol and drug education), national fraternities. *Campus security:* 24-hour emergency response devices and patrols, late-night transport/escort service, controlled dormitory access, security lighting. *Student services:* health clinic, personal/psychological counseling, women's center, legal services.

Athletics Member NCAA. All Division III. *Intercollegiate sports:* baseball M, basketball M/W, crew M(c)/W(c), cross-country running M/W, equestrian sports M(c)/W(c), fencing M(c)/W(c), field hockey W, football M, golf M/W, lacrosse M(c)/W(c), rugby M(c), soccer M/W, softball W(c), swimming and diving M/W, tennis M/W, track and field M/W, volleyball W. *Intramural sports:* basketball M/W, cross-country running M/W, football M, golf M/W, racquetball M/W, soccer M/W, softball M/W, swimming and diving M/W, table tennis M/W, tennis M/W, track and field M/W, volleyball M/W.

Standardized Tests *Required for some:* TEOFL for International Students. *Recommended:* SAT or ACT (for admission).

Costs (2011–12) *Comprehensive fee:* $41,518 includes full-time tuition ($32,020), mandatory fees ($272), and room and board ($9226). Part-time tuition: $1162 per credit hour. *College room only:* $4796. *Payment plans:* installment, deferred payment. *Waivers:* employees or children of employees.

Financial Aid Of all full-time matriculated undergraduates who enrolled in 2007, 749 applied for aid, 722 were judged to have need, 588 had their need fully met. 350 Federal Work-Study jobs (averaging $1444). 99 state and other part-time jobs (averaging $1423). In 2007, 339 non-need-based awards were made. *Average percent of need met:* 97%. *Average financial aid package:* $25,169. *Average need-based loan:* $4177. *Average need-based gift aid:* $20,536. *Average non-need-based aid:* $14,523. *Average indebtedness upon graduation:* $15,885.

Applying *Options:* electronic application, early admission, early decision, deferred entrance. *Application fee:* $45. *Required:* essay or personal statement, high school transcript, 2 letters of recommendation. *Recommended:* interview. *Application deadlines:* 2/1 (freshmen), 4/1 (transfers). *Early decision deadline:* 11/15 (for plan 1), 1/2 (for plan 2). *Notification:* 3/17 (freshmen), continuous (transfers), 12/17 (early decision plan 1), 2/8 (early decision plan 2).

Freshman Application Contact Ms. Lee Ann Afton, Dean of Admission and Financial Aid, Sewanee: The University of the South, 735 University Avenue, Sewanee, TN 37383-1000. *Phone:* 931-598-1238. *Toll-free phone:* 800-522-2234. *Fax:* 931-598-3248. *E-mail:* admiss@sewanee.edu. *Web site:* http://www.sewanee.edu/.

South College
Knoxville, Tennessee

Director of Admissions Mr. Walter Hosea, Director of Admissions, South College, 720 North Fifth Avenue, Knoxville, TN 37917. *Phone:* 865-524-3043 Ext. 1825. *E-mail:* whosea@southcollegetn.edu. *Web site:* http://www.southcollegetn.edu/.

Southern Adventist University
Collegedale, Tennessee

- **Independent Seventh-day Adventist** comprehensive, founded 1892
- **Small-town** 1000-acre campus with easy access to Chattanooga
- **Endowment** $21.1 million
- **Coed** 2,732 undergraduate students, 85% full-time, 55% women, 45% men
- **Moderately difficult** entrance level, 80% of applicants were admitted

Undergraduates 2,323 full-time, 409 part-time. Students come from 49 states and territories; 69% are from out of state; 12% Black or African American, non-Hispanic/Latino; 18% Hispanic/Latino; 5% Asian, non-Hispanic/Latino; 0.7% Native Hawaiian or other Pacific Islander, non-Hispanic/Latino; 0.4% American Indian or Alaska Native, non-Hispanic/Latino; 0.1% Two or more races, non-Hispanic/Latino; 4% international; 7% transferred in; 61% live on campus. *Retention:* 72% of full-time freshmen returned.

Freshmen *Admission:* 1,452 applied, 1,167 admitted, 628 enrolled. *Average high school GPA:* 3.36. *Test scores:* SAT critical reading scores over 500: 56%; SAT math scores over 500: 48%; ACT scores over 18: 89%; SAT critical reading scores over 600: 20%; SAT math scores over 600: 16%; ACT scores over 24: 37%; SAT critical reading scores over 700: 4%; SAT math scores over 700: 3%; ACT scores over 30: 6%.

Faculty *Total:* 269, 54% full-time, 53% with terminal degrees. *Student/faculty ratio:* 15:1.

Academics *Calendar:* semesters. *Degrees:* certificates, associate, bachelor's, master's, and post-master's certificates. *Special study options:* advanced placement credit, double majors, English as a second language, honors programs, independent study, internships, off-campus study, services for LD students, study abroad, summer session for credit.

Computers on Campus 200 computers/terminals are available on campus for general student use. Students can access the following: campus intranet, computer help desk, free student e-mail accounts, online (class) grades, online (class) registration, online (class) schedules. Campuswide network is available. 80% of college-owned or -operated housing units are wired for high-speed Internet access. Wireless service is available via entire campus.

Student Life *Housing:* on-campus residence required through junior year. *Options:* men-only, women-only. Campus housing is university owned. Freshman campus housing is guaranteed. *Activities and organizations:* drama/theater group, student-run newspaper, radio and television station, choral group, Student Association, Black Christian Union, Campus Ministries. *Campus security:* 24-hour patrols, late-night transport/escort service, controlled dormitory access. *Student services:* health clinic, personal/psychological counseling.

Athletics *Intramural sports:* basketball M/W, football M/W, soccer M/W, softball M/W, volleyball M/W.

Standardized Tests *Required:* SAT or ACT (for admission).

Costs (2011–12) *Comprehensive fee:* $24,110 includes full-time tuition ($17,534), mandatory fees ($790), and room and board ($5786). Part-time tuition: $740 per semester hour. Part-time tuition and fees vary according to course load. *College room only:* $3286. Room and board charges vary according to housing facility. *Payment plans:* tuition prepayment, installment, deferred payment. *Waivers:* senior citizens and employees or children of employees.

Financial Aid Of all full-time matriculated undergraduates who enrolled in 2009, 1,709 applied for aid, 1,217 were judged to have need, 1,062 had their need fully met. In 2009, 468 non-need-based awards were made. *Average percent of need met:* 85%. *Average financial aid package:* $20,692. *Average need-based loan:* $4800. *Average need-based gift aid:* $9713. *Average non-need-based aid:* $5427. *Average indebtedness upon graduation:* $27,121.

Applying *Options:* deferred entrance. *Application fee:* $25. *Required:* high school transcript, minimum 2.25 GPA. *Required for some:* essay or personal statement. *Application deadlines:* rolling (freshmen), rolling (transfers). *Notification:* continuous (freshmen), continuous (transfers).

Freshman Application Contact Mr. Marc Grundy, Associate Vice President, Marketing and Enrollment Services, Southern Adventist University, PO Box 370, Collegedale, TN 37315-0370. *Phone:* 423-236-2844. *Toll-free phone:* 800-768-8437. *Fax:* 423-236-1844. *E-mail:* admissions@southern.edu. *Web site:* http://www.southern.edu/.

Strayer University - Knoxville Campus

Knoxville, Tennessee

- **Proprietary** comprehensive
- **Coed**

Academics *Degrees:* certificates, diplomas, associate, bachelor's, master's, and postbachelor's certificates.

Costs (2010–11) *Tuition:* $13,635 full-time, $1590 per course part-time.

Freshman Application Contact Strayer University - Knoxville Campus, 10118 Parkside Drive, Suite 200, Knoxville, TN 37922. *Web site:* http://www.strayer.edu/knoxville/.

Strayer University - Nashville Campus

Nashville, Tennessee

- **Proprietary** comprehensive
- **Coed**

Academics *Degrees:* certificates, diplomas, associate, bachelor's, master's, and postbachelor's certificates.

Costs (2010–11) *Tuition:* $14,310 full-time, $1590 per course part-time.

Freshman Application Contact Strayer University - Nashville Campus, 1809 Dabbs Avenue, Nashville, TN 37210. *Web site:* http://www.strayer.edu/nashville.

Strayer University - Shelby Oaks Campus

Memphis, Tennessee

- **Proprietary** comprehensive
- **Coed**

Academics *Degrees:* certificates, diplomas, associate, bachelor's, master's, and postbachelor's certificates.

Costs (2010–11) *Tuition:* $14,310 full-time, $1590 per course part-time.

Freshman Application Contact Strayer University - Shelby Oaks Campus, 6211 Shelby Oaks Drive, Suite 100, Memphis, TN 38134. *Web site:* http://www.strayer.edu/shelby_oaks.

Strayer University - Thousand Oaks Campus

Memphis, Tennessee

- **Proprietary** comprehensive
- **Coed**

Academics *Degrees:* certificates, diplomas, associate, bachelor's, master's, and postbachelor's certificates.

Costs (2010–11) *Tuition:* $14,310 full-time, $1590 per course part-time.

Freshman Application Contact Strayer University - Thousand Oaks Campus, 2620 Thousand Oaks Boulevard, Suite 1100, Memphis, TN 38118. *Web site:* http://www.strayer.edu/thousand_oaks_campus.

Tennessee State University

Nashville, Tennessee

Freshman Application Contact Ms. Vernella Smith, Admissions Coordinator, Tennessee State University, 3500 John A Merritt Boulevard, Nashville, TN 37209-1561. *Phone:* 615-963-5104. *Fax:* 615-963-5108. *E-mail:* vsmith@tnstate.edu. *Web site:* http://www.tnstate.edu/.

Tennessee Technological University

Cookeville, Tennessee

- **State-supported** university, founded 1915, part of Tennessee Board of Regents
- **Small-town** 235-acre campus
- **Endowment** $50.0 million
- **Coed** 9,436 undergraduate students, 90% full-time, 47% women, 53% men
- **Moderately difficult** entrance level, 94% of applicants were admitted

Undergraduates 8,506 full-time, 930 part-time. Students come from 43 states and territories; 60 other countries; 4% are from out of state; 4% Black or African American, non-Hispanic/Latino; 2% Hispanic/Latino; 1% Asian, non-Hispanic/Latino; 0.1% Native Hawaiian or other Pacific Islander, non-Hispanic/Latino; 0.3% American Indian or Alaska Native, non-Hispanic/Latino; 2% Two or more races, non-Hispanic/Latino; 0.6% Race/ethnicity unknown; 3% international; 8% transferred in; 30% live on campus. *Retention:* 76% of full-time freshmen returned.

Freshmen *Admission:* 4,553 applied, 4,277 admitted, 1,909 enrolled. *Average high school GPA:* 3.4. *Test scores:* SAT critical reading scores over 500: 70%; SAT math scores over 500: 74%; ACT scores over 18: 95%; SAT critical reading scores over 600: 25%; SAT math scores over 600: 44%; ACT scores over 24: 39%; SAT critical reading scores over 700: 2%; SAT math scores over 700: 9%; ACT scores over 30: 7%.

Faculty *Total:* 640, 61% full-time, 56% with terminal degrees. *Student/faculty ratio:* 21:1.

Academics *Calendar:* semesters. *Degrees:* bachelor's, master's, doctoral-research/scholarship, post-master's, and postbachelor's certificates. *Special study options:* academic remediation for entering students, accelerated degree program, adult/continuing education programs, advanced placement credit, cooperative education, distance learning, double majors, English as a second language, honors programs, independent study, internships, off-campus study, part-time degree program, services for LD students, study abroad, summer session for credit. *ROTC:* Army (b), Air Force (c).

Computers on Campus 227 computers/terminals are available on campus for general student use. Students can access the following: campus intranet, computer help desk, free student e-mail accounts, online (class) grades, online (class) registration, online (class) schedules, 590 additional computers are available for student use in individual departmental labs. Campuswide network is available. 100% of college-owned or -operated housing units are wired for high-speed Internet access. Wireless service is available via entire campus.

Student Life *Housing:* on-campus residence required through sophomore year. *Options:* coed, men-only, women-only. Campus housing is university owned. Freshman campus housing is guaranteed. *Activities and organizations:* drama/theater group, student-run newspaper, radio station, choral group, marching band, Baptist Collegiate Center, Fellowship of Christian Athletes, University Christian Student Center, Residence Hall Association, national fraternities, national sororities. *Campus security:* 24-hour emergency response devices and patrols, late-night transport/escort service, student safety organization, lighted pathways. *Student services:* health clinic, personal/psychological counseling, women's center.

Athletics Member NCAA. All Division I except football (Division I-AA). *Intercollegiate sports:* baseball M(s), basketball M(s)/W(s), cheerleading M(s)/W(s), cross-country running M(s)/W(s), golf M(s)/W(s), soccer W(s), softball W(s), tennis M(s), track and field W(s), volleyball W(s). *Intramural sports:* basketball M/W, bowling M/W, fencing M(c)/W(c), football M/W, golf M/W, racquetball M/W, rugby M(c)/W(c), soccer M/W, softball M/W, tennis M/W, ultimate Frisbee M/W, volleyball M/W, wrestling M.

Standardized Tests *Required:* SAT or ACT (for admission). *Recommended:* ACT (for admission).

Costs (2010–11) *Tuition:* state resident $5828 full-time, $268 per credit hour part-time; nonresident $18,356 full-time, $790 per credit hour part-time. Full-time tuition and fees vary according to course load and program. Part-time tuition and fees vary according to course load and program. *Room and board:* $7158; room only: $3700. Room and board charges vary according to board plan and housing facility. *Payment plan:* installment. *Waivers:* employees or children of employees.

Financial Aid Of all full-time matriculated undergraduates who enrolled in 2009, 7,177 applied for aid, 5,746 were judged to have need, 1,515 had their need fully met. 515 Federal Work-Study jobs (averaging $754). In 2009, 639 non-need-based awards were made. *Average percent of need met:* 67%. *Average financial aid package:* $7217. *Average need-based loan:* $3916. *Average need-based gift aid:* $4211. *Average non-need-based aid:* $2537. *Average indebtedness upon graduation:* $9510.

Applying *Options:* electronic application, early admission, deferred entrance. *Application fee:* $25. *Required:* high school transcript, minimum 2.5 GPA. *Recommended:* interview. *Application deadlines:* 8/1 (freshmen), 8/1 (transfers). *Notification:* continuous (freshmen), continuous (transfers).

Freshman Application Contact Ms. Vanessa Palmer, Director of Admissions, Tennessee Technological University, PO Box 5006, Cookeville, TN 38505. *Phone:* 931-372-3888. *Toll-free phone:* 800-255-8881. *Fax:* 931-372-6250. *E-mail:* admissions@tntech.edu. *Web site:* http://www.tntech.edu/.

Tennessee Temple University

Chattanooga, Tennessee

Director of Admissions Eric Lovett, Director of Recruitment, Tennessee Temple University, 1815 Union Avenue, Chattanooga, TN 37404-3587. *Phone:* 423-493-4371. *Toll-free phone:* 800-553-4050. *E-mail:* eric.lovett@tntemple.edu. *Web site:* http://www.tntemple.edu/.

Tennessee Wesleyan College

Athens, Tennessee

- **Independent United Methodist** 4-year, founded 1857
- **Small-town** 40-acre campus with easy access to Knoxville and Chattanooga
- **Coed** 1,103 undergraduate students, 88% full-time, 66% women, 34% men
- **Minimally difficult** entrance level, 88% of applicants were admitted

Undergraduates 975 full-time, 128 part-time. 11% are from out of state; 4% Black or African American, non-Hispanic/Latino; 1% Hispanic/Latino; 1% Asian, non-Hispanic/Latino; 0.1% Native Hawaiian or other Pacific Islander, non-Hispanic/Latino; 0.3% American Indian or Alaska Native, non-Hispanic/Latino; 0.6% Two or more races, non-Hispanic/Latino; 4% Race/ethnicity unknown; 3% international; 15% transferred in; 30% live on campus. *Retention:* 68% of full-time freshmen returned.

Freshmen *Admission:* 410 applied, 361 admitted, 219 enrolled. *Average high school GPA:* 3.28. *Test scores:* SAT critical reading scores over 500: 29%; SAT math scores over 500: 26%; ACT scores over 18: 90%; SAT critical reading scores over 600: 7%; SAT math scores over 600: 15%; ACT scores over 24: 33%; ACT scores over 30: 3%.

Faculty *Total:* 89, 57% full-time, 54% with terminal degrees. *Student/faculty ratio:* 16:1.

Academics *Calendar:* semesters. *Degrees:* bachelor's (profile includes information for both the main and branch campuses). *Special study options:* academic remediation for entering students, accelerated degree program, adult/continuing education programs, advanced placement credit, double majors, honors programs, independent study, internships, off-campus study, part-time degree program, services for LD students, student-designed majors, study abroad, summer session for credit.

Computers on Campus Students can access the following: campus intranet, computer help desk, online (class) schedules. Campuswide network is available. Wireless service is available via classrooms, dorm rooms, libraries.

Student Life *Housing:* on-campus residence required through senior year. *Options:* men-only, women-only. Campus housing is university owned. Freshman campus housing is guaranteed. *Activities and organizations:* drama/theater group, student-run newspaper, choral group, national sororities. *Campus security:* 24-hour patrols, late-night transport/escort service, controlled dormitory access, night patrols by trained security personnel. *Student services:* health clinic, personal/psychological counseling.

Athletics Member NAIA. *Intercollegiate sports:* baseball M(s), basketball M(s)/W(s), cheerleading M(s)/W(s), cross-country running M(s)/W(s), golf M(s)/W(s), lacrosse M(s), soccer M(s)/W(s), softball W(s), tennis M(s)/W(s), volleyball W(s).

Standardized Tests *Required:* SAT or ACT (for admission).

Costs (2010–11) *Comprehensive fee:* $25,450 includes full-time tuition ($18,500), mandatory fees ($600), and room and board ($6350). Full-time tuition and fees vary according to location. Part-time tuition: $510 per credit hour. Part-time tuition and fees vary according to class time and location. *Required fees:* $10 per credit hour part-time. *Room and board:* Room and board charges vary according to housing facility. *Payment plans:* installment, deferred payment. *Waivers:* employees or children of employees.

Financial Aid Of all full-time matriculated undergraduates who enrolled in 2008, 871 applied for aid, 739 were judged to have need, 157 had their need fully met. In 2008, 87 non-need-based awards were made. *Average percent of need met:* 70%. *Average financial aid package:* $14,087. *Average need-based loan:* $3876. *Average need-based gift aid:* $11,682. *Average non-need-based aid:* $6221. *Average indebtedness upon graduation:* $16,304.

Applying *Options:* electronic application, deferred entrance. *Application fee:* $25. *Required:* high school transcript, minimum 2.25 GPA, 1 letter of recommendation. *Required for some:* interview. *Recommended:* essay or personal statement.

Freshman Application Contact Stan Harrison, Vice President of Enrollment Services and Director of Athletics, Tennessee Wesleyan College, 204 East College Street, Athens, TN 37303. *Phone:* 423-746-5287. *Toll-free phone:* 800-PICK-TWC. *Fax:* 423-745-9335. *E-mail:* admissions@twcnet.edu. *Web site:* http://www.twcnet.edu/.

Trevecca Nazarene University

Nashville, Tennessee

- **Independent Nazarene** comprehensive, founded 1901
- **Urban** 65-acre campus
- **Endowment** $16.1 million
- **Coed** 1,312 undergraduate students, 90% full-time, 57% women, 43% men
- **Moderately difficult** entrance level, 74% of applicants were admitted

Undergraduates 1,176 full-time, 136 part-time. Students come from 36 states and territories; 11 other countries; 33% are from out of state; 9% Black or Afri-

can American, non-Hispanic/Latino; 3% Hispanic/Latino; 0.8% Asian, non-Hispanic/Latino; 0.4% American Indian or Alaska Native, non-Hispanic/Latino; 0.6% Two or more races, non-Hispanic/Latino; 5% Race/ethnicity unknown; 1% international; 6% transferred in; 51% live on campus. *Retention:* 78% of full-time freshmen returned.

Freshmen *Admission:* 960 applied, 710 admitted, 235 enrolled. *Average high school GPA:* 3.22. *Test scores:* SAT critical reading scores over 500: 56%; SAT math scores over 500: 49%; ACT scores over 18: 83%; SAT critical reading scores over 600: 23%; SAT math scores over 600: 18%; ACT scores over 24: 33%; SAT critical reading scores over 700: 5%; SAT math scores over 700: 5%; ACT scores over 30: 4%.

Faculty *Total:* 229, 38% full-time, 60% with terminal degrees. *Student/faculty ratio:* 16:1.

Academics *Calendar:* semesters. *Degrees:* associate, bachelor's, master's, and doctoral-research/scholarship. *Special study options:* academic remediation for entering students, adult/continuing education programs, advanced placement credit, distance learning, double majors, internships, services for LD students, study abroad, summer session for credit. *ROTC:* Army (c).

Computers on Campus 200 computers/terminals and 1,460 ports are available on campus for general student use. Students can access the following: campus intranet, computer help desk, free student e-mail accounts, online (class) grades, online (class) schedules, traditional undergraduate registration on-line by advisors. Campuswide network is available. 100% of college-owned or -operated housing units are wired for high-speed Internet access. Wireless service is available via entire campus.

Student Life *Housing:* on-campus residence required through senior year. *Options:* men-only, women-only. Campus housing is university owned. *Activities and organizations:* drama/theater group, student-run newspaper, choral group, marching band. *Campus security:* 24-hour patrols, late-night transport/escort service. *Student services:* health clinic, personal/psychological counseling.

Athletics Member NAIA. *Intercollegiate sports:* baseball M(s), basketball M(s)/W(s), golf M(s)/W(s), soccer M(s)/W(s), softball W(s), track and field M(s)/W(s), volleyball W(s). *Intramural sports:* badminton M/W, basketball M/W, football M/W, golf M/W, racquetball M/W, softball M/W, table tennis M/W, track and field M/W, volleyball M/W.

Standardized Tests *Required:* SAT or ACT (for admission).

Costs (2010–11) *Comprehensive fee:* $26,252 includes full-time tuition ($18,318), mandatory fees ($200), and room and board ($7734). Full-time tuition and fees vary according to course load. Part-time tuition: $708 per credit hour. Part-time tuition and fees vary according to course load. *College room only:* $3582. Room and board charges vary according to board plan. *Payment plans:* tuition prepayment, installment. *Waivers:* senior citizens and employees or children of employees.

Financial Aid *Financial aid deadline:* 8/1.

Applying *Options:* electronic application, early admission, deferred entrance. *Application fee:* $25. *Required:* high school transcript, minimum 2.5 GPA, medical history and immunization records. *Application deadlines:* 8/1 (freshmen), rolling (transfers). *Notification:* continuous (freshmen), continuous (transfers).

Freshman Application Contact Mr. Michael Cantrell, Director of Undergraduate Admissions, Trevecca Nazarene University, 333 Murfreesboro Road, Nashville, TN 37210-2834. *Phone:* 615-248-1320. *Toll-free phone:* 888-210-4TNU. *Fax:* 615-248-7406. *E-mail:* admissions_und@trevecca.edu. *Web site:* http://www.trevecca.edu/.

Tusculum College

Greeneville, Tennessee

- **Independent Presbyterian** comprehensive, founded 1794
- **Small-town** 140-acre campus
- **Endowment** $15.3 million
- **Coed**
- **Moderately difficult** entrance level

Faculty *Student/faculty ratio:* 16:1.

Academics *Calendar:* semesters. *Degrees:* bachelor's and master's.

Student Life *Campus security:* 24-hour emergency response devices and patrols, student patrols, late-night transport/escort service, controlled dormitory access, trained security personnel on duty.

Athletics Member NCAA. All Division II.

Standardized Tests *Required:* SAT or ACT (for admission).

Costs (2010–11) *Comprehensive fee:* $27,920 includes full-time tuition ($19,920) and room and board ($8000). Full-time tuition and fees vary according to degree level and reciprocity agreements. Part-time tuition: $625 per semester hour. Part-time tuition and fees vary according to degree level and reciprocity agreements.

Financial Aid *Of all full-time matriculated undergraduates who enrolled in 2008,* 2,069 applied for aid, 1,470 were judged to have need. 264 Federal Work-Study jobs (averaging $2285). 16 state and other part-time jobs (averaging $2000). *In 2008,* 618 non-need-based awards were made. *Average finan-*

cial aid package: $17,651. *Average non-need-based aid:* $4088. *Average indebtedness upon graduation:* $8632.

Applying *Options:* electronic application, early admission, deferred entrance. *Required:* essay or personal statement, high school transcript, minimum 2 GPA. *Required for some:* 3 letters of recommendation. *Recommended:* interview.

Freshman Application Contact Ms. Melissa Ripley, Director of Operations, Tusculum College, PO Box 5047, Greeneville, TN 37743-9997. *Phone:* 423-636-7300 Ext. 5374. *Toll-free phone:* 800-729-0256. *Fax:* 423-798-1622. *E-mail:* admissions@tusculum.edu. *Web site:* http://www.tusculum.edu/.

Union University

Jackson, Tennessee

- **Independent Southern Baptist** comprehensive, founded 1823
- **Small-town** 360-acre campus with easy access to Memphis
- **Endowment** $27.5 million
- **Coed** 2,818 undergraduate students, 78% full-time, 60% women, 40% men
- **Moderately difficult** entrance level, 79% of applicants were admitted

Undergraduates 2,212 full-time, 606 part-time. Students come from 44 states and territories; 36 other countries; 29% are from out of state; 5% transferred in; 55% live on campus. *Retention:* 84% of full-time freshmen returned.

Freshmen *Admission:* 1,747 applied, 1,374 admitted, 508 enrolled. *Average high school GPA:* 3.65. *Test scores:* SAT critical reading scores over 500: 87%; SAT math scores over 500: 81%; ACT scores over 18: 98%; SAT critical reading scores over 600: 54%; SAT math scores over 600: 52%; ACT scores over 24: 63%; SAT critical reading scores over 700: 20%; SAT math scores over 700: 15%; ACT scores over 30: 19%.

Faculty *Total:* 237, 98% full-time, 73% with terminal degrees. *Student/faculty ratio:* 12:1.

Academics *Calendar:* 4-1-4. *Degrees:* certificates, diplomas, associate, bachelor's, master's, doctoral-other, doctoral-professional, doctoral-research/scholarship, and post-master's certificates. *Special study options:* academic remediation for entering students, accelerated degree program, adult/continuing education programs, advanced placement credit, cooperative education, distance learning, double majors, English as a second language, honors programs, independent study, internships, off-campus study, part-time degree pro-

gram, services for LD students, study abroad, summer session for credit. *ROTC:* Army (c).

Computers on Campus 236 computers/terminals are available on campus for general student use. Students can access the following: campus intranet, computer help desk, free student e-mail accounts, online (class) grades, online (class) registration, online (class) schedules. Campuswide network is available. 100% of college-owned or -operated housing units are wired for high-speed Internet access. Wireless service is available via entire campus.

Student Life *Housing:* on-campus residence required through junior year. *Options:* men-only, women-only, disabled students. Campus housing is university owned. Freshman applicants given priority for college housing. *Activities and organizations:* drama/theater group, student-run newspaper, choral group, Campus Ministries, Student Government Association, Student Activities Council, Students in Free Enterprise (SIFE), national fraternities, national sororities. *Campus security:* 24-hour emergency response devices and patrols, student patrols, late-night transport/escort service. *Student services:* health clinic, personal/psychological counseling.

Athletics Member NAIA, NCCAA. *Intercollegiate sports:* baseball M(s), basketball M(s)/W(s), cheerleading W(s), cross-country running M/W(s), golf M(s), soccer M(s)/W(s), softball W(s), track and field M/W, volleyball W(s). *Intramural sports:* basketball M/W, bowling M/W, cross-country running M/W, football M/W, golf M/W, racquetball M/W, soccer W, softball M/W, swimming and diving M/W, table tennis M/W, track and field M/W, ultimate Frisbee M/W, volleyball M/W.

Standardized Tests *Required:* SAT or ACT (for admission). *Recommended:* SAT Subject Tests (for admission).

Costs (2010–11) *Comprehensive fee:* $29,850 includes full-time tuition ($21,700), mandatory fees ($690), and room and board ($7460). Full-time tuition and fees vary according to course load. Part-time tuition: $735 per credit hour. *Required fees:* $220 per term part-time. *Room and board:* Room and board charges vary according to board plan and housing facility. *Payment plans:* installment, deferred payment. *Waivers:* children of alumni and employees or children of employees.

Financial Aid Of all full-time matriculated undergraduates who enrolled in 2009, 1,521 applied for aid, 1,279 were judged to have need, 323 had their need fully met. 141 Federal Work-Study jobs (averaging $1235). 373 state and other part-time jobs (averaging $1188). In 2009, 203 non-need-based awards were made. *Average percent of need met:* 69%. *Average financial aid pack-*

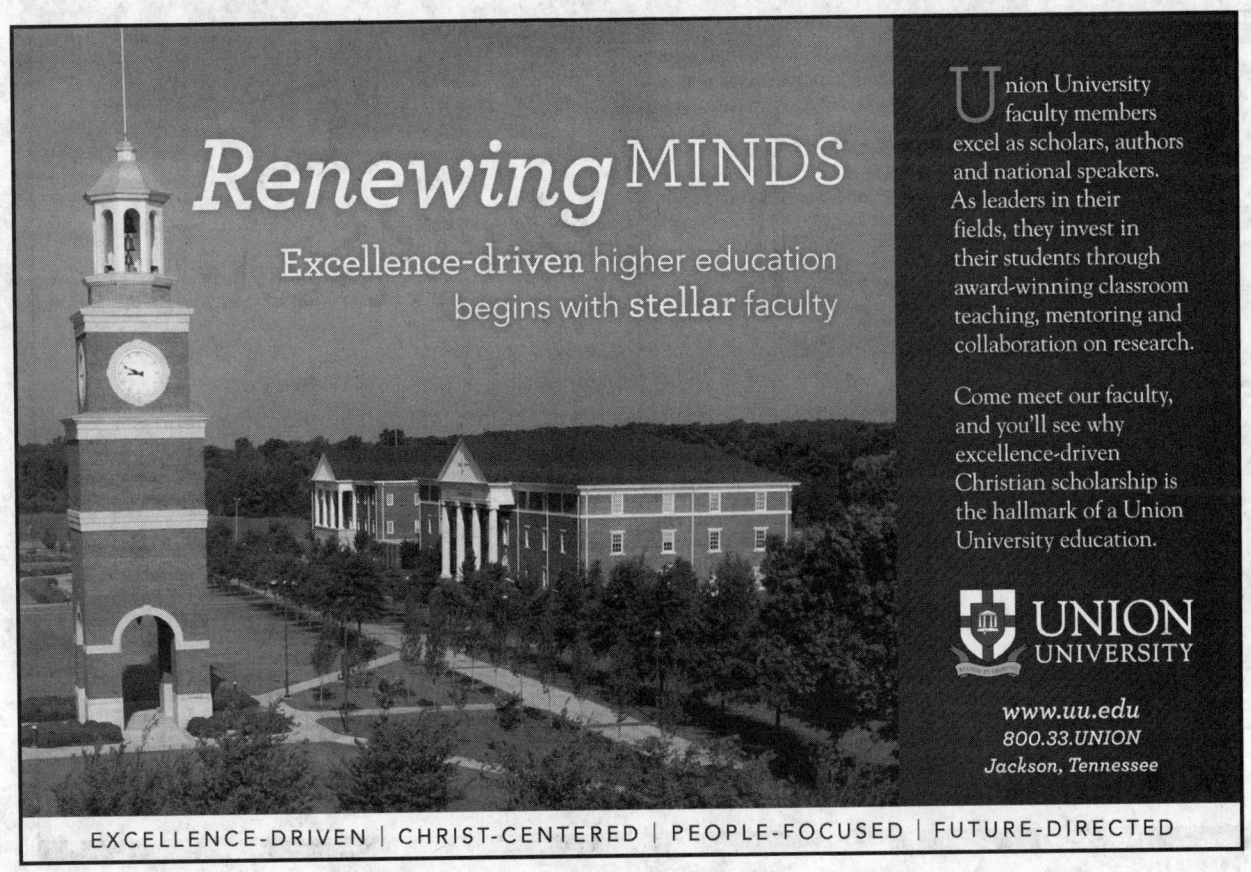

age: $19,643. *Average need-based loan:* $4453. *Average need-based gift aid:* $5479. *Average non-need-based aid:* $7432. *Average indebtedness upon graduation:* $24,253.

Applying *Options:* electronic application, early admission, early action, deferred entrance. *Application fee:* $35. *Required:* high school transcript, minimum 2.5 GPA. *Required for some:* 3 letters of recommendation. *Recommended:* essay or personal statement, interview. *Application deadlines:* rolling (freshmen), rolling (transfers), 12/1 (early action). *Notification:* 8/1 (freshmen), continuous until 8/15 (transfers), 12/15 (early action).

Freshman Application Contact Mr. Robbie Graves, Director of Enrollment Services, Union University, 1050 Union University Drive, Jackson, TN 38305-3697. *Phone:* 731-661-5590. *Toll-free phone:* 800-33-UNION. *Fax:* 731-661-5017. *E-mail:* rgraves@uu.edu. *Web site:* http://www.uu.edu/.

See page 1674 for the College Close-Up.

University of Memphis

Memphis, Tennessee

- **State-supported** university, founded 1912, part of Tennessee Board of Regents
- **Urban** 1160-acre campus
- **Coed** 17,510 undergraduate students, 74% full-time, 61% women, 39% men
- **Moderately difficult** entrance level, 67% of applicants were admitted

Undergraduates 12,879 full-time, 4,631 part-time. 10% are from out of state; 40% Black or African American, non-Hispanic/Latino; 2% Hispanic/Latino; 2% Asian, non-Hispanic/Latino; 0.2% American Indian or Alaska Native, non-Hispanic/Latino; 2% Two or more races, non-Hispanic/Latino; 4% Race/ethnicity unknown; 1% international; 9% transferred in; 18% live on campus. *Retention:* 78% of full-time freshmen returned.

Freshmen *Admission:* 6,583 applied, 4,381 admitted, 2,432 enrolled. *Average high school GPA:* 3.46. *Test scores:* ACT scores over 18: 82%; ACT scores over 24: 29%; ACT scores over 30: 3%.

Faculty *Total:* 1,377, 61% full-time, 62% with terminal degrees. *Student/faculty ratio:* 15:1.

Academics *Calendar:* semesters. *Degrees:* bachelor's, master's, doctoral-professional, doctoral-research/scholarship, post-master's, and postbachelor's certificates. *Special study options:* academic remediation for entering students, accelerated degree program, adult/continuing education programs, advanced placement credit, cooperative education, distance learning, double majors, English as a second language, external degree program, honors programs, independent study, internships, off-campus study, part-time degree program, services for LD students, student-designed majors, study abroad, summer session for credit. *ROTC:* Army (b), Navy (b), Air Force (b).

Computers on Campus 1,600 computers/terminals and 35 ports are available on campus for general student use. Students can access the following: campus intranet, computer help desk, free student e-mail accounts, online (class) grades, online (class) registration, online (class) schedules. Campuswide network is available. Wireless service is available via entire campus.

Student Life *Housing options:* coed, men-only, women-only, disabled students. Campus housing is university owned. *Activities and organizations:* drama/theater group, student-run newspaper, radio station, choral group, marching band, Blue Crew, Up 'til Dawn, Black Student Association, national fraternities, national sororities. *Campus security:* 24-hour emergency response devices and patrols, student patrols, late-night transport/escort service, controlled dormitory access. *Student services:* health clinic, personal/psychological counseling, women's center.

Athletics Member NCAA. All Division I except football (Division I-A). *Intercollegiate sports:* baseball M(s), basketball M(s)/W(s), cheerleading M(s)/W(s), cross-country running M(s)/W(s), golf M(s)/W(s), racquetball M(c)/W(c), riflery M(s)/W(s), soccer M(s)/W(s), softball W, swimming and diving M(c)/W(c), tennis M(s)/W(s), track and field M(s)/W(s), volleyball W(s). *Intramural sports:* basketball M/W, bowling M/W, golf M/W, racquetball M/W, soccer M/W, softball M/W, table tennis M/W, tennis M/W, track and field M/W, ultimate Frisbee M/W, volleyball M/W, water polo M/W.

Standardized Tests *Required:* SAT or ACT (for admission).

Costs (2010–11) *Tuition:* state resident $5778 full-time, $232 per credit hour part-time; nonresident $19,644 full-time, $789 per credit hour part-time. Full-time tuition and fees vary according to course load, degree level, program, and reciprocity agreements. Part-time tuition and fees vary according to course load, degree level, and program. *Required fees:* $1212 full-time, $79 per credit part-time. *Room and board:* $6190. Room and board charges vary according to board plan and housing facility. *Payment plan:* installment. *Waivers:* senior citizens and employees or children of employees.

Financial Aid Of all full-time matriculated undergraduates who enrolled in 2009, 11,774 applied for aid, 9,847 were judged to have need, 528 had their need fully met. 235 Federal Work-Study jobs (averaging $1714). In 2009, 1854 non-need-based awards were made. *Average percent of need met:* 68%. *Average financial aid package:* $8803. *Average need-based loan:* $3991. *Average need-based gift aid:* $5483. *Average non-need-based aid:* $7668. *Average indebtedness upon graduation:* $20,856.

Applying *Options:* electronic application, early admission. *Application fee:* $25. *Required:* high school transcript. *Required for some:* minimum 2 GPA, 2 letters of recommendation, interview. *Application deadlines:* 7/1 (freshmen), 7/1 (transfers). *Notification:* continuous (freshmen), continuous (transfers).

Freshman Application Contact University of Memphis, Memphis, TN 38152. *Phone:* 901-678-2111. *Toll-free phone:* 800-669-2678. *Web site:* http://www.memphis.edu/.

See page 1710 for the College Close-Up.

University of Phoenix–Nashville Campus
Nashville, Tennessee

Freshman Application Contact Ms. Audra McQuarie, Registrar/Executive Director, University of Phoenix–Nashville Campus, 4035 South Riverpoint Parkway, Mail Stop CF-L101, Phoenix, AZ 85040. *Phone:* 480-557-6151. *Toll-free phone:* 800-776-4867 (in-state); 800-228-7240 (out-of-state). *Fax:* 480-643-3068. *E-mail:* audra.mcquarie@phoenix.edu. *Web site:* http://www.phoenix.edu/.

The University of Tennessee
Knoxville, Tennessee

- **State-supported** university, founded 1794, part of University of Tennessee System
- **Urban** 560-acre campus
- **Endowment** $541.0 million
- **Coed** 21,393 undergraduate students, 94% full-time, 48% women, 52% men
- **Moderately difficult** entrance level, 74% of applicants were admitted

Undergraduates 20,199 full-time, 1,194 part-time. Students come from 46 other countries; 14% are from out of state; 7% Black or African American, non-Hispanic/Latino; 2% Hispanic/Latino; 3% Asian, non-Hispanic/Latino; 0.3% American Indian or Alaska Native, non-Hispanic/Latino; 2% Two or more races, non-Hispanic/Latino; 1% Race/ethnicity unknown; 1% international; 6% transferred in; 35% live on campus. *Retention:* 86% of full-time freshmen returned.

Freshmen *Admission:* 12,555 applied, 9,352 admitted, 4,214 enrolled. *Average high school GPA:* 3.76. *Test scores:* SAT critical reading scores over 500: 85%; SAT math scores over 500: 87%; ACT scores over 18: 100%; SAT critical reading scores over 600: 42%; SAT math scores over 600: 47%; ACT scores over 24: 80%; SAT critical reading scores over 700: 9%; SAT math scores over 700: 8%; ACT scores over 30: 21%.

Faculty *Total:* 1,911, 84% full-time, 76% with terminal degrees. *Student/faculty ratio:* 15:1.

Academics *Calendar:* semesters. *Degrees:* certificates, bachelor's, master's, doctoral-professional, doctoral-research/scholarship, post-master's, and post-bachelor's certificates. *Special study options:* accelerated degree program, advanced placement credit, cooperative education, distance learning, double majors, English as a second language, freshman honors college, honors programs, independent study, internships, off-campus study, part-time degree program, services for LD students, student-designed majors, study abroad, summer session for credit. *ROTC:* Army (b), Air Force (b).

Computers on Campus 600 computers/terminals are available on campus for general student use. Students can access the following: campus intranet, computer help desk, free student e-mail accounts, online (class) grades, online (class) registration, online (class) schedules, Blackboard Course Management System. Campuswide network is available. 100% of college-owned or -operated housing units are wired for high-speed Internet access. Wireless service is available via entire campus.

Student Life *Housing:* on-campus residence required for freshman year. *Options:* men-only, women-only, disabled students. Campus housing is university owned. Freshman campus housing is guaranteed. *Activities and organizations:* drama/theater group, student-run newspaper, radio and television station, choral group, marching band, Fraternities/Sororities, religious organizations, Central Program Council, Black Cultural Program, student government, national fraternities, national sororities. *Campus security:* 24-hour emergency response devices and patrols, late-night transport/escort service, controlled dormitory access, Security cameras on all building entrances; card entry into the living sections of residence hall buildings. *Student services:* health clinic, personal/psychological counseling, women's center.

Athletics Member NCAA. All Division I. *Intercollegiate sports:* baseball M(s)(c), basketball M(s)/W(s), crew M(c)/W(s)(c), equestrian sports M(c)/W(c), fencing M(c)/W(c), golf M(s)(c)/W(s)(c), gymnastics M(c)/W(c), ice hockey M(c)/W(c), lacrosse M(c)/W(c), rugby M(c)/W(c), sailing M(c)/W(c), skiing (downhill) M(c)/W(c), soccer W(s), softball W(s), swimming and diving M(s)(c)/W(s)(c), tennis M(s)(c)/W(s)(c), track and field M(s)/W(s), volleyball W(s), weight lifting M/W, wrestling M(c). *Intramural sports:* badminton M(c)/W(c), basketball M/W, bowling M/W, crew M(c)/W(c), cross-country running M/W, field hockey M(c)/W(c), football M, golf M/W, racquetball M(c)/W(c), soccer M(c)/W(c), softball M/W, swimming and diving M/W, table tennis M/W, tennis M(c)/W(c), ultimate Frisbee M(c)/W(c), volleyball M(c)/W(c), water polo M(c)/W(c).

Standardized Tests *Required:* SAT or ACT (for admission).

Costs (2010–11) *Tuition:* state resident $7382 full-time, $270 per hour part-time; nonresident $22,720 full-time, $897 per hour part-time. Full-time tuition and fees vary according to course level and program. Part-time tuition and fees vary according to course level and program. *Required fees:* $43 per hour part-time. *Room and board:* $7800. Room and board charges vary according to board plan and housing facility. *Payment plan:* installment. *Waivers:* senior citizens and employees or children of employees.

Financial Aid Of all full-time matriculated undergraduates who enrolled in 2009, 17,764 applied for aid, 11,417 were judged to have need, 2,371 had their need fully met. 402 Federal Work-Study jobs (averaging $2200). In 2009, 2160 non-need-based awards were made. *Average percent of need met:* 70%. *Average financial aid package:* $11,215. *Average need-based loan:* $4361. *Average need-based gift aid:* $3142. *Average non-need-based aid:* $2346. *Average indebtedness upon graduation:* $19,987.

Applying *Options:* electronic application, early admission. *Application fee:* $30. *Required:* high school transcript, minimum 2 GPA, specific high school units. *Recommended:* essay or personal statement. *Application deadlines:* 12/1 (freshmen), 7/1 (transfers). *Notification:* 3/15 (freshmen), continuous (transfers).

Freshman Application Contact Ms. Norma Harrington, Senior Associate Director, The University of Tennessee, 320 Student Services Building, 1331 Circle Park, Knoxville, TN 37996-0230. *Phone:* 865-974-2184. *Toll-free phone:* 800-221-8657. *Fax:* 865-974-4689. *E-mail:* admissions@utk.edu. *Web site:* http://www.utk.edu.

The University of Tennessee at Chattanooga
Chattanooga, Tennessee

- **State-supported** comprehensive, founded 1886, part of University of Tennessee System
- **Urban** 120-acre campus with easy access to Atlanta
- **Coed** 9,229 undergraduate students, 89% full-time, 55% women, 45% men
- **Moderately difficult** entrance level, 68% of applicants were admitted

Undergraduates 8,230 full-time, 999 part-time. 6% are from out of state; 12% Black or African American, non-Hispanic/Latino; 2% Hispanic/Latino; 2% Asian, non-Hispanic/Latino; 2% Two or more races, non-Hispanic/Latino; 14% Race/ethnicity unknown; 0.7% international; 8% transferred in. *Retention:* 68% of full-time freshmen returned.

Freshmen *Admission:* 6,661 applied, 4,512 admitted, 1,948 enrolled. *Average high school GPA:* 3.31. *Test scores:* SAT critical reading scores over 500: 65%; SAT math scores over 500: 65%; ACT scores over 18: 99%; SAT critical reading scores over 600: 29%; SAT math scores over 600: 19%; ACT scores over 24: 38%; SAT critical reading scores over 700: 6%; SAT math scores over 700: 3%; ACT scores over 30: 4%.

Faculty *Total:* 740, 58% full-time, 51% with terminal degrees. *Student/faculty ratio:* 18:1.

Academics *Calendar:* semesters. *Degrees:* certificates, bachelor's, master's, doctoral-professional, doctoral-research/scholarship, post-master's, and post-bachelor's certificates. *Special study options:* academic remediation for entering students, adult/continuing education programs, advanced placement credit, cooperative education, distance learning, double majors, English as a second language, honors programs, independent study, internships, off-campus study, part-time degree program, services for LD students, study abroad, summer session for credit. *ROTC:* Army (b). *Unusual degree programs:* 3-2 engineering.

Computers on Campus 965 computers/terminals are available on campus for general student use. Students can access the following: campus intranet, computer help desk, free student e-mail accounts, online (class) grades, online (class) registration, online (class) schedules, pay fees. Campuswide network is available. 100% of college-owned or -operated housing units are wired for high-speed Internet access. Wireless service is available via classrooms, computer labs, dorm rooms, libraries.

Student Life *Housing:* on-campus residence required for freshman year. *Options:* coed. Campus housing is university owned. Freshman applicants given priority for college housing. *Activities and organizations:* drama/theater group, student-run newspaper, radio station, choral group, marching band, Student Government Association, Black Student Association, Association for Campus Entertainment, International Student Association, Baptist Student Union, national fraternities, national sororities. *Campus security:* 24-hour emergency response devices and patrols, late-night transport/escort service, controlled dormitory access. *Student services:* health clinic, personal/psychological counseling.

Athletics Member NCAA. All Division I except football (Division I-AA). *Intercollegiate sports:* basketball M(s)/W(s), cross-country running M(s)/W(s), golf M(s)/W(s), soccer W(s), softball W(s), tennis M(s)/W(s), track and field M(s)/W(s), volleyball W(s), wrestling M(s). *Intramural sports:* badminton M/W, baseball M(c), basketball M/W, crew M(c)/W(c), cross-country running M/W, fencing M(c)/W(c), golf M/W, racquetball M/W, soccer M/W, swimming and diving M/W, tennis M/W, ultimate Frisbee M(c)/W(c), volleyball W, wrestling M.

Standardized Tests *Required:* SAT or ACT (for admission).

Costs (2011–12) *Tuition:* state resident $4912 full-time, $205 per credit hour part-time; nonresident $17,226 full-time, $718 per credit hour part-time. *Required fees:* $1150 full-time. *Room and board:* $8210; room only: $5300. Room and board charges vary according to board plan and housing facility. *Payment plan:* installment. *Waivers:* senior citizens and employees or children of employees.

Financial Aid Of all full-time matriculated undergraduates who enrolled in 2008, 7,018 applied for aid, 4,743 were judged to have need, 522 had their need fully met. 164 Federal Work-Study jobs (averaging $2213). 45 state and other part-time jobs (averaging $3633). In 2008, 1055 non-need-based awards were made. *Average percent of need met:* 66%. *Average financial aid package:* $6197. *Average need-based loan:* $3414. *Average need-based gift aid:* $5808. *Average non-need-based aid:* $3470. *Average indebtedness upon graduation:* $13,845.

Applying *Options:* electronic application, deferred entrance. *Application fee:* $30. *Required:* high school transcript. *Recommended:* essay or personal statement. *Application deadlines:* 8/1 (freshmen), 8/1 (out-of-state freshmen), 8/1 (transfers). *Notification:* continuous (freshmen), continuous (out-of-state freshmen), continuous (transfers).

Freshman Application Contact Mr. Yancy Freeman, Director, Admissions and Recruitment, The University of Tennessee at Chattanooga, 715 Oak Street, Dept. 5105, Guerry Hall, Chattanooga, TN 37403. *Phone:* 423-425-4662. *Toll-free phone:* 800-UTC-MOCS. *Fax:* 423-425-4157. *E-mail:* yancy-freeman@utc.edu. *Web site:* http://www.utc.edu/.

The University of Tennessee at Martin
Martin, Tennessee

- **State-supported** comprehensive, founded 1900, part of University of Tennessee System
- **Small-town** 250-acre campus
- **Endowment** $18.8 million
- **Coed** 7,947 undergraduate students, 77% full-time, 58% women, 42% men
- **Moderately difficult** entrance level, 75% of applicants were admitted

Undergraduates 6,103 full-time, 1,844 part-time. Students come from 38 states and territories; 21 other countries; 4% are from out of state; 17% Black or African American, non-Hispanic/Latino; 1% Hispanic/Latino; 0.5% Asian, non-Hispanic/Latino; 0.2% American Indian or Alaska Native, non-Hispanic/Latino; 0.5% Two or more races, non-Hispanic/Latino; 2% international; 8% transferred in; 27% live on campus. *Retention:* 71% of full-time freshmen returned.

Freshmen *Admission:* 3,402 applied, 2,551 admitted, 1,288 enrolled. *Average high school GPA:* 3.4. *Test scores:* ACT scores over 18: 95%; ACT scores over 24: 33%; ACT scores over 30: 2%.

Faculty *Total:* 532, 52% full-time, 45% with terminal degrees. *Student/faculty ratio:* 19:1.

Academics *Calendar:* semesters. *Degrees:* bachelor's and master's. *Special study options:* accelerated degree program, adult/continuing education programs, advanced placement credit, cooperative education, distance learning, double majors, English as a second language, honors programs, independent study, internships, off-campus study, part-time degree program, services for LD students, student-designed majors, study abroad, summer session for credit. *ROTC:* Army (b). *Unusual degree programs:* veterinary, medicine, dentistry, medicine, and pharmacy.

Computers on Campus 786 computers/terminals and 2,719 ports are available on campus for general student use. Students can access the following: campus intranet, computer help desk, free student e-mail accounts, online (class) grades, online (class) registration, online (class) schedules, online fee payments, degree progress, financial aid data, housing applications, transcripts. Campuswide network is available. 100% of college-owned or -operated housing units are wired for high-speed Internet access. Wireless service is available via entire campus.

Student Life *Housing:* on-campus residence required for freshman year. *Options:* men-only, women-only, disabled students. Campus housing is university owned. Freshman applicants given priority for college housing. *Activities and organizations:* drama/theater group, student-run newspaper, radio and television station, choral group, marching band, Student Government Association, Student Activities Council, Sigma Theta Tau, Gamma Beta Phi, Student Tennessee Education Association, national fraternities, national sororities. *Campus security:* 24-hour emergency response devices and patrols, student patrols, controlled dormitory access. *Student services:* health clinic, personal/psychological counseling, women's center.

Athletics Member NCAA. All Division I except football (Division I-AA). *Intercollegiate sports:* baseball M(s), basketball M(s)/W(s), cheerleading W(s), cross-country running M(s)/W(s), equestrian sports W(s), golf M(s), riflery M(s)/W(s), soccer W(s), softball W(s), tennis W(s), volleyball W(s). *Intramural sports:* basketball M/W, cross-country running M/W, football M/W, golf M/W, racquetball M/W, rugby M/W, soccer M/W, softball M/W, table tennis M/W, tennis M/W, volleyball M/W, water polo M/W.

Standardized Tests *Required:* SAT or ACT (for admission).

Costs (2010–11) *Tuition:* state resident $5132 full-time, $214 per credit hour part-time; nonresident $17,542 full-time, $732 per credit hour part-time. Part-time tuition and fees vary according to course load. *Required fees:* $1058 full-time, $45 per credit hour part-time. *Room and board:* $5104; room only: $2530. Room and board charges vary according to board plan and housing facility. *Payment plan:* deferred payment. *Waivers:* senior citizens and employees or children of employees.

Financial Aid Of all full-time matriculated undergraduates who enrolled in 2009, 5,814 applied for aid, 4,544 were judged to have need, 1,539 had their need fully met. 314 Federal Work-Study jobs (averaging $2500). In 2009, 983 non-need-based awards were made. *Average percent of need met:* 81%. *Average financial aid package:* $12,655. *Average need-based loan:* $4204. *Average need-based gift aid:* $6246. *Average non-need-based aid:* $5675. *Average indebtedness upon graduation:* $19,048.

Applying *Options:* electronic application, early admission, deferred entrance. *Application fee:* $30. *Required:* high school transcript, minimum 2.5 GPA. *Application deadlines:* rolling (freshmen), rolling (transfers). *Notification:* 8/1 (freshmen), continuous until 8/1 (transfers).

Freshman Application Contact Ms. Judy Rayburn, Director of Admissions, The University of Tennessee at Martin, 200 Hall-Moody Administration Building, Martin, TN 38238. *Phone:* 731-881-7032. *Toll-free phone:* 800-829-8861. *Fax:* 731-881-7029. *E-mail:* jrayburn@utm.edu. *Web site:* http://www.utm.edu/.

Vanderbilt University
Nashville, Tennessee

- **Independent** university, founded 1873
- **Urban** 330-acre campus
- **Endowment** $3.0 billion
- **Coed** 6,879 undergraduate students, 99% full-time, 51% women, 49% men
- **Very difficult** entrance level, 18% of applicants were admitted

Undergraduates 6,831 full-time, 48 part-time. Students come from 54 states and territories; 36 other countries; 84% are from out of state; 8% Black or African American, non-Hispanic/Latino; 7% Hispanic/Latino; 7% Asian, non-Hispanic/Latino; 0.3% American Indian or Alaska Native, non-Hispanic/Latino; 3% Two or more races, non-Hispanic/Latino; 5% Race/ethnicity unknown; 5% international; 3% transferred in; 85% live on campus. *Retention:* 97% of full-time freshmen returned.

Freshmen *Admission:* 21,811 applied, 3,914 admitted, 1,600 enrolled. *Average high school GPA:* 3.7. *Test scores:* SAT critical reading scores over 500: 98%; SAT math scores over 500: 99%; SAT writing scores over 500: 99%; ACT scores over 18: 100%; SAT critical reading scores over 600: 93%; SAT math scores over 600: 95%; SAT writing scores over 600: 93%; ACT scores over 24: 99%; SAT critical reading scores over 700: 62%; SAT math scores over 700: 73%; SAT writing scores over 700: 58%; ACT scores over 30: 84%.

Faculty *Total:* 1,108, 81% full-time. *Student/faculty ratio:* 8:1.

Academics *Calendar:* semesters. *Degrees:* bachelor's, master's, doctoral-professional, and doctoral-research/scholarship. *Special study options:* accelerated degree program, advanced placement credit, cooperative education, distance learning, double majors, English as a second language, honors programs, independent study, internships, off-campus study, services for LD students, student-designed majors, study abroad, summer session for credit. *ROTC:* Army (b), Navy (b), Air Force (c).

Computers on Campus 400 computers/terminals are available on campus for general student use. Students can access the following: campus intranet, computer help desk, free student e-mail accounts, online (class) grades, online (class) registration, online (class) schedules, productivity and educational software. Campuswide network is available. Wireless service is available via entire campus.

Student Life *Housing:* on-campus residence required for freshman year. *Options:* coed, men-only, women-only, disabled students. Campus housing is university owned. Freshman campus housing is guaranteed. *Activities and organizations:* drama/theater group, student-run newspaper, radio and television station, choral group, marching band, national fraternities, national sororities. *Campus security:* 24-hour emergency response devices and patrols, student patrols, late-night transport/escort service, controlled dormitory access. *Student services:* health clinic, personal/psychological counseling, women's center.

Athletics Member NCAA. All Division I except football (Division I-A). *Intercollegiate sports:* baseball M(s), basketball M(s)/W(s), bowling W(s), cross-country running M(s)/W(s), golf M(s)/W(s), lacrosse W(s), soccer W(s), swimming and diving W, tennis M(s)/W(s), track and field W(s). *Intramural sports:* badminton M(c)/W(c), baseball M(c), basketball M/W, bowling M(c)/W(c), crew M(c)/W(c), cross-country running M(c)/W(c), equestrian sports M(c)/W(c), fencing M(c)/W(c), field hockey M(c)/W(c), football M/W, golf M(c)/W(c), ice hockey M(c), lacrosse M(c)/W(c), racquetball M(c)/W(c), rugby M(c), sailing M(c)/W(c), soccer M(c)/W(c), softball M/W, squash M(c)/W(c), swimming and diving M(c)/W(c), table tennis M/W, tennis M(c)/W(c), track and field M(c), ultimate Frisbee M(c)/W(c), volleyball M(c)/W(c), water polo M(c)/W(c), weight lifting M/W, wrestling M(c).

Standardized Tests *Required:* SAT or ACT (for admission).

Costs (2010–11) *One-time required fee:* $642. *Comprehensive fee:* $52,988 includes full-time tuition ($38,952), mandatory fees ($978), and room and board ($13,058). Part-time tuition: $1623 per credit hour. *College room only:* $8528. Room and board charges vary according to board plan. *Payment plans:* tuition prepayment, installment. *Waivers:* employees or children of employees.

Financial Aid Of all full-time matriculated undergraduates who enrolled in 2009, 3,609 applied for aid, 3,232 were judged to have need, 3,227 had their need fully met. In 2009, 606 non-need-based awards were made. *Average percent of need met:* 100%. *Average financial aid package:* $41,835. *Average need-based loan:* $3292. *Average need-based gift aid:* $36,352. *Average non-need-based aid:* $22,182. *Average indebtedness upon graduation:* $18,605.

Applying *Options:* electronic application, early admission, early decision, deferred entrance. *Application fee:* $50. *Required:* essay or personal statement, high school transcript, 2 letters of recommendation. *Application deadlines:* 1/3 (freshmen), 3/1 (transfers). *Early decision deadline:* 11/1 (for plan 1), 1/3 (for plan 2). *Notification:* 4/1 (freshmen), 4/1 (transfers), 12/15 (early decision plan 1), 2/15 (early decision plan 2).

Freshman Application Contact John O. Gaines, Director of Admissions, Vanderbilt University, 2305 West End Avenue, Nashville, TN 37203. *Phone:* 615-936-2811. *Toll-free phone:* 800-288-0432. *Fax:* 615-343-8326. *E-mail:* admissions@vanderbilt.edu. *Web site:* http://www.vanderbilt.edu/.

Victory University
Memphis, Tennessee

- **Independent** comprehensive, founded 1941
- **Urban** 7-acre campus with easy access to Memphis
- **Coed** 694 undergraduate students, 65% full-time, 74% women, 26% men
- **Minimally difficult** entrance level, 29% of applicants were admitted

Undergraduates 449 full-time, 245 part-time. Students come from 13 states and territories; 4 other countries; 8% are from out of state; 80% Black or African American, non-Hispanic/Latino; 1% Hispanic/Latino; 0.3% Asian, non-Hispanic/Latino; 0.4% Native Hawaiian or other Pacific Islander, non-Hispanic/Latino; 0.1% Two or more races, non-Hispanic/Latino; 3% Race/ethnicity unknown; 0.6% international; 13% transferred in. *Retention:* 70% of full-time freshmen returned.

Freshmen *Admission:* 145 applied, 42 admitted, 33 enrolled. *Average high school GPA:* 2.8. *Test scores:* ACT scores over 18: 85%; ACT scores over 24: 5%.

Faculty *Total:* 63, 56% full-time, 57% with terminal degrees. *Student/faculty ratio:* 12:1.

Academics *Calendar:* semesters. *Degrees:* certificates, associate, bachelor's, master's, and postbachelor's certificates. *Special study options:* academic remediation for entering students, accelerated degree program, adult/continuing education programs, advanced placement credit, distance learning, double majors, honors programs, independent study, off-campus study, part-time degree program, services for LD students, student-designed majors, study abroad, summer session for credit.

Computers on Campus 31 computers/terminals are available on campus for general student use. Students can access the following: campus intranet, computer help desk, free student e-mail accounts, online (class) grades, online (class) registration, online (class) schedules. Campuswide network is available. Wireless service is available via entire campus.

Student Life *Housing:* college housing not available. *Activities and organizations:* drama/theater group, student-run newspaper, choral group. *Campus security:* 24-hour patrols.

Athletics Member NCCAA. *Intercollegiate sports:* basketball M(s).

Standardized Tests *Required for some:* SAT or ACT (for admission).

Costs (2010–11) *Tuition:* $10,050 full-time, $335 per credit hour part-time. Full-time tuition and fees vary according to course load and location. Part-time tuition and fees vary according to course load and location. No tuition increase for student's term of enrollment. *Required fees:* $570 full-time, $19 per credit hour part-time. *Payment plan:* installment. *Waivers:* senior citizens and employees or children of employees.

Financial Aid Of all full-time matriculated undergraduates who enrolled in 2008, 385 applied for aid, 358 were judged to have need, 29 had their need fully met. 50 Federal Work-Study jobs (averaging $2085). *Average percent of need met:* 76%. *Average financial aid package:* $9029. *Average need-based loan:* $4376. *Average need-based gift aid:* $6488. *Average indebtedness upon graduation:* $27,625.

Applying *Options:* electronic application, deferred entrance. *Application fee:* $25. *Required:* minimum 2 GPA. *Required for some:* essay or personal statement, high school transcript, 3 letters of recommendation, transfer students must have a 2.0 college GPA. *Recommended:* interview. *Application deadlines:* rolling (freshmen), rolling (transfers). *Notification:* continuous (freshmen), continuous (transfers).

Freshman Application Contact Ms. Shelley Dunn, Director of Admissions, Victory University, 255 North Highland, Memphis, TN 38111-1375. *Phone:* 901-320-9777. *Toll-free phone:* 800-960-9777. *Fax:* 901-320-9791. *E-mail:* admissions@victory.edu. *Web site:* http://www.victory.edu/.

Watkins College of Art, Design, & Film
Nashville, Tennessee

- **Independent** 4-year, founded 1885
- **Urban** 13-acre campus
- **Endowment** $1.3 million
- **Coed** 396 undergraduate students, 68% full-time, 52% women, 48% men
- **Moderately difficult** entrance level, 83% of applicants were admitted

Undergraduates 270 full-time, 126 part-time. Students come from 29 states and territories; 3 other countries; 30% are from out of state; 9% Black or African American, non-Hispanic/Latino; 2% Hispanic/Latino; 2% Asian, non-Hispanic/Latino; 0.3% Native Hawaiian or other Pacific Islander, non-Hispanic/Latino; 0.3% American Indian or Alaska Native, non-Hispanic/Latino; 3% Two or more races, non-Hispanic/Latino; 5% Race/ethnicity unknown; 1% international; 24% live on campus. *Retention:* 82% of full-time freshmen returned.

Freshmen *Admission:* 113 applied, 94 admitted. *Average high school GPA:* 3.01. *Test scores:* SAT critical reading scores over 500: 70%; ACT scores over 18: 93%; SAT critical reading scores over 600: 10%; ACT scores over 24: 32%; ACT scores over 30: 4%.

Faculty *Total:* 57, 35% full-time, 54% with terminal degrees. *Student/faculty ratio:* 7:1.

Academics *Calendar:* semesters. *Degree:* certificates and bachelor's. *Special study options:* advanced placement credit, cooperative education, independent study, internships, off-campus study, part-time degree program, services for LD students, study abroad, summer session for credit.

Computers on Campus 200 computers/terminals and 150 ports are available on campus for general student use. Students can access the following: campus intranet, computer help desk, free student e-mail accounts, online (class) registration, online (class) schedules. Campuswide network is available. 100% of college-owned or -operated housing units are wired for high-speed Internet access. Wireless service is available via entire campus.

Student Life *Housing:* on-campus residence required for freshman year. *Options:* men-only, women-only, disabled students. Campus housing is university owned. Freshman applicants given priority for college housing. *Activities and organizations:* Art Society, Film club, sports club, OWL (One Wise Life). *Campus security:* 24-hour emergency response devices and patrols, late-night transport/escort service, controlled dormitory access, monitored 24 hour camera security. *Student services:* health clinic, personal/psychological counseling.

Standardized Tests *Required:* SAT or ACT (for admission).

Costs (2011–12) *One-time required fee:* $50. *Tuition:* $18,900 full-time, $630 per credit part-time. *Required fees:* $1560 full-time, $52 per credit part-time. *Room only:* $6200. *Payment plan:* installment. *Waivers:* employees or children of employees.

Financial Aid Of all full-time matriculated undergraduates who enrolled in 2008, 174 applied for aid, 174 were judged to have need, 30 had their need fully met. 17 Federal Work-Study jobs (averaging $1300). 25 state and other part-time jobs (averaging $2000). In 2008, 30 non-need-based awards were made. *Average percent of need met:* 45%. *Average financial aid package:* $11,150. *Average need-based loan:* $4750. *Average need-based gift aid:* $4000. *Average non-need-based aid:* $4000. *Average indebtedness upon graduation:* $15,000.

Applying *Options:* electronic application, early admission, deferred entrance. *Application fee:* $50. *Required:* essay or personal statement, high school transcript, minimum 2.6 GPA, 1 letter of recommendation. *Required for some:*

high school transcript, artistic exercises, optional portfolio. *Application deadlines:* 7/15 (freshmen), 7/15 (transfers). *Notification:* 8/1 (freshmen), 8/1 (transfers).
Freshman Application Contact Ms. Linda E. Schwab, Director of Admissions, Watkins College of Art, Design, & Film, 2298 Rosa L. Parks Boulevard, Nashville, TN 37228. *Phone:* 615-383-4848 Ext. 7458. *Fax:* 615-383-4849. *E-mail:* admissions@watkins.edu. *Web site:* http://www.watkins.edu/.

Williamson Christian College

Franklin, Tennessee

Freshman Application Contact Ms. Mary Newby, Recruiter, Williamson Christian College, 200 Seaboard Lane, Franklin, TN 37067. *Phone:* 615-771-7821. *Fax:* 615-771-7810. *E-mail:* mary@williamsoncc.edu. *Web site:* http://www.williamsoncc.edu/.

TEXAS

Abilene Christian University

Abilene, Texas

- **Independent** comprehensive, founded 1906, affiliated with Church of Christ
- **Urban** 208-acre campus
- **Endowment** $266.1 million
- **Coed** 3,806 undergraduate students, 95% full-time, 54% women, 46% men
- **Moderately difficult** entrance level, 53% of applicants were admitted

Undergraduates 3,624 full-time, 182 part-time. Students come from 50 states and territories; 42 other countries; 15% are from out of state; 7% Black or African American, non-Hispanic/Latino; 8% Hispanic/Latino; 1% Asian, non-Hispanic/Latino; 0.1% Native Hawaiian or other Pacific Islander, non-Hispanic/Latino; 0.4% American Indian or Alaska Native, non-Hispanic/Latino; 2% Two or more races, non-Hispanic/Latino; 0.1% Race/ethnicity unknown; 4% international; 5% transferred in; 43% live on campus. *Retention:* 71% of full-time freshmen returned.
Freshmen *Admission:* 4,106 applied, 2,157 admitted, 980 enrolled. *Average high school GPA:* 3.69. *Test scores:* SAT critical reading scores over 500: 75%; SAT math scores over 500: 81%; ACT scores over 18: 98%; SAT critical reading scores over 600: 31%; SAT math scores over 600: 36%; ACT scores over 24: 62%; SAT critical reading scores over 700: 8%; SAT math scores over 700: 5%; ACT scores over 30: 16%.
Faculty *Total:* 368, 67% full-time, 63% with terminal degrees. *Student/faculty ratio:* 15:1.
Academics *Calendar:* semesters. *Degrees:* certificates, associate, bachelor's, master's, doctoral-other, post-master's, and postbachelor's certificates. *Special study options:* adult/continuing education programs, advanced placement credit, distance learning, double majors, English as a second language, honors programs, independent study, internships, off-campus study, part-time degree program, services for LD students, student-designed majors, study abroad, summer session for credit. *Unusual degree programs:* 3-2 engineering with The University of Texas at Arlington.
Computers on Campus 530 computers/terminals are available on campus for general student use. Students can access the following: campus intranet, computer help desk, free student e-mail accounts, online (class) grades, online (class) registration, online (class) schedules. Campuswide network is available. 100% of college-owned or -operated housing units are wired for high-speed Internet access. Wireless service is available via entire campus.
Student Life *Housing:* on-campus residence required through sophomore year. *Options:* men-only, women-only. Campus housing is university owned. Freshman campus housing is guaranteed. *Activities and organizations:* drama/theater group, student-run newspaper, radio and television station, choral group, marching band, Student Association, Graduate Students Association, Spring Break Campaigns, International Students Association, LYNAY. *Campus security:* 24-hour emergency response devices and patrols, student patrols, late-night transport/escort service, controlled dormitory access. *Student services:* health clinic, personal/psychological counseling.
Athletics Member NCAA. All Division II. *Intercollegiate sports:* baseball M(s), basketball M(s)/W(s), cross-country running M(s)/W(s), football M(s), golf M(s), soccer W(s), softball W(s), tennis M(s)/W(s), track and field M(s)/W(s), volleyball W(s). *Intramural sports:* basketball M/W, bowling M/W, football M/W, golf M/W, racquetball M/W, soccer M/W, softball M/W, tennis M/W, volleyball M/W, water polo M/W.
Standardized Tests *Required:* SAT or ACT (for admission).
Costs (2010–11) *Comprehensive fee:* $30,644 includes full-time tuition ($21,510), mandatory fees ($1250), and room and board ($7884). Full-time

tuition and fees vary according to course load. Part-time tuition: $717 per semester hour. Part-time tuition and fees vary according to course load. *Required fees:* $62 per semester hour part-time, $10 per term part-time. *College room only:* $3460. Room and board charges vary according to board plan and student level. *Payment plans:* tuition prepayment, installment. *Waivers:* employees or children of employees.
Financial Aid Of all full-time matriculated undergraduates who enrolled in 2009, 2,824 applied for aid, 2,371 were judged to have need, 513 had their need fully met. 244 Federal Work-Study jobs (averaging $1632). 14 state and other part-time jobs (averaging $5348). In 2009, 394 non-need-based awards were made. *Average percent of need met:* 66%. *Average financial aid package:* $15,102. *Average need-based loan:* $4358. *Average need-based gift aid:* $11,289. *Average non-need-based aid:* $7272. *Average indebtedness upon graduation:* $38,634.
Applying *Options:* electronic application, early admission. *Application fee:* $50. *Required:* essay or personal statement, high school transcript, ACT or SAT score. *Application deadlines:* 2/15 (freshmen), rolling (transfers). *Notification:* 3/15 (freshmen), continuous until 9/1 (transfers).
Freshman Application Contact Abilene Christian University, ACU Box 29000, Abilene, TX 79699-9000. *Phone:* 325-674-2650. *Fax:* 325-674-2130. *E-mail:* info@admissions.acu.edu. *Web site:* http://www.acu.edu/.

Amberton University

Garland, Texas

- **Independent nondenominational** upper-level, founded 1971
- **Suburban** 5-acre campus with easy access to Dallas-Fort Worth
- **Endowment** $10.0 million
- **Coed** 389 undergraduate students, 57% full-time, 60% women, 40% men
- **Minimally difficult** entrance level

Undergraduates 221 full-time, 168 part-time. Students come from 1 other state; 27% Black or African American, non-Hispanic/Latino; 6% Hispanic/Latino; 3% Asian, non-Hispanic/Latino; 9% Race/ethnicity unknown.
Faculty *Total:* 40, 38% full-time, 88% with terminal degrees. *Student/faculty ratio:* 25:1.
Academics *Calendar:* 4 10-week terms. *Degrees:* bachelor's and master's. *Special study options:* adult/continuing education programs, distance learning, external degree program, internships, part-time degree program, student-designed majors, summer session for credit.
Computers on Campus 30 computers/terminals are available on campus for general student use. Students can access the following: campus intranet, computer help desk, free student e-mail accounts, online (class) schedules.
Student Life *Housing:* college housing not available. *Campus security:* 24-hour emergency response devices and patrols.
Costs (2011–12) *Tuition:* $5600 full-time, $700 per course part-time. *Payment plan:* installment.
Applying *Options:* electronic application, deferred entrance. *Application deadline:* rolling (transfers). *Notification:* continuous (transfers).
Application Contact Dr. Don Hebbard, Academic Dean, Amberton University, 1700 Eastgate Drive, Garland, TX 75041-5595. *Phone:* 972-279-6511. *E-mail:* advisor@amberton.edu. *Web site:* http://www.amberton.edu/.

American InterContinental University Houston

Houston, Texas

Freshman Application Contact American InterContinental University Houston, 9999 Richmond Avenue, Houston, TX 77042. *Phone:* 877-564-6248. *Toll-free phone:* 888-607-9888. *Web site:* http://www.aiuniv.edu/.

Angelo State University

San Angelo, Texas

- **State-supported** comprehensive, founded 1928, part of Texas Tech University System
- **Urban** 268-acre campus
- **Endowment** $103.0 million
- **Coed** 6,155 undergraduate students, 84% full-time, 55% women, 45% men
- **Moderately difficult** entrance level, 95% of applicants were admitted

Undergraduates 5,194 full-time, 961 part-time. Students come from 42 states and territories; 19 other countries; 3% are from out of state; 9% Black or African American, non-Hispanic/Latino; 26% Hispanic/Latino; 1% Asian, non-Hispanic/Latino; 0.6% American Indian or Alaska Native, non-Hispanic/Latino; 0.6% Two or more races, non-Hispanic/Latino; 0.5% Race/ethnicity unknown; 0.8% international; 8% transferred in; 33% live on campus. *Retention:* 64% of full-time freshmen returned.

Freshmen *Admission:* 3,128 applied, 2,979 admitted, 1,475 enrolled. *Test scores:* SAT critical reading scores over 500: 35%; SAT math scores over 500: 45%; ACT scores over 18: 77%; SAT critical reading scores over 600: 8%; SAT math scores over 600: 12%; ACT scores over 24: 23%; ACT scores over 30: 2%.

Faculty *Total:* 346, 75% full-time, 60% with terminal degrees. *Student/faculty ratio:* 20:1.

Academics *Calendar:* semesters. *Degrees:* associate, bachelor's, master's, and doctoral-professional. *Special study options:* academic remediation for entering students, advanced placement credit, distance learning, double majors, English as a second language, honors programs, independent study, internships, part-time degree program, study abroad, summer session for credit. *ROTC:* Air Force (b). *Unusual degree programs:* 3-2 accounting.

Computers on Campus 610 computers/terminals and 3,600 ports are available on campus for general student use. Students can access the following: campus intranet, computer help desk, free student e-mail accounts, online (class) grades, online (class) registration, online (class) schedules, online courses, tuition payments, purchase books, purchase parking permits, university calendar, library card catalog and library resources. Discounted hardware and software programs for personally owned computers. Campuswide network is available. 100% of college-owned or -operated housing units are wired for high-speed Internet access. Wireless service is available via entire campus.

Student Life *Housing:* on-campus residence required through sophomore year. *Options:* coed, disabled students. Campus housing is university owned. *Activities and organizations:* drama/theater group, student-run newspaper, radio and television station, choral group, marching band, Block and Bridle Club, Baptist Student Union, Delta Sigma Pi, Air Force ROTC, Association of Mexican-American Students, national fraternities, national sororities. *Campus security:* 24-hour emergency response devices and patrols, student patrols, late-night transport/escort service, controlled dormitory access. *Student services:* health clinic, personal/psychological counseling.

Athletics Member NCAA. All Division II. *Intercollegiate sports:* baseball M(s), basketball M(s)/W(s), cross-country running M(s)/W(s), football M(s), golf W(s), soccer W(s), softball W(s), track and field M(s)/W(s), volleyball W(s). *Intramural sports:* badminton M/W, basketball M/W, bowling M/W, football M/W, golf M/W, racquetball M/W, soccer M/W, softball M/W, swimming and diving M/W, table tennis M/W, tennis M/W, ultimate Frisbee M/W, volleyball M/W, weight lifting M/W.

Standardized Tests *Required:* SAT or ACT (for admission).

Costs (2011–12) *Tuition:* state resident $4560 full-time, $152 per hour part-time; nonresident $13,860 full-time, $462 per hour part-time. *Required fees:* $2132 full-time, $39 per hour part-time, $572 per term part-time. *Room and board:* $6666; room only: $4066. Room and board charges vary according to board plan and housing facility. *Payment plan:* installment. *Waivers:* senior citizens and employees or children of employees.

Financial Aid Of all full-time matriculated undergraduates who enrolled in 2009, 2,616 applied for aid, 2,192 were judged to have need, 441 had their need fully met. In 2009, 203 non-need-based awards were made. *Average percent of need met:* 85%. *Average financial aid package:* $10,780. *Average need-based loan:* $3603. *Average need-based gift aid:* $2986. *Average non-need-based aid:* $2815. *Average indebtedness upon graduation:* $10,712.

Applying *Options:* electronic application, early admission, deferred entrance. *Application fee:* $30. *Required:* high school transcript, high school class rank. *Application deadlines:* rolling (freshmen), rolling (out-of-state freshmen), rolling (transfers). *Notification:* continuous (freshmen), continuous (out-of-state freshmen), continuous (transfers).

Freshman Application Contact Ms. Megan Wheeler, Coordinator of Recruiting, Angelo State University, 2601 West Avenue N, San Angelo, TX 76909. *Phone:* 325-942-2259 Ext. 233. *Toll-free phone:* 800-946-8627. *Fax:* 325-942-2128. *E-mail:* admissions@angelo.edu. *Web site:* http://www.angelo.edu/.

See page 996 for the College Close-Up.

Argosy University, Dallas
Farmers Branch, Texas

- **Proprietary** university, founded 2002, part of Education Management Corporation
- **Urban** campus
- **Coed**

Academics *Calendar:* semesters. *Degrees:* bachelor's, master's, and doctoral-professional.

Costs (2010–11) *Tuition:* Tuition varies by program. Students should contact Argosy University for tuition information.

Freshman Application Contact Argosy University, Dallas, 5001 Lyndon B. Johnson Freeway, Heritage Square, Farmers Branch, TX 75244. *Phone:* 214-890-9900. *Toll-free phone:* 866-954-9900. *Web site:* http://www.argosy.edu/dallas/.

See page 1002 for the College Close-Up.

Arlington Baptist College

Arlington, Texas

- **Independent Baptist** comprehensive, founded 1939
- **Urban** 32-acre campus with easy access to Dallas-Fort Worth
- **Endowment** $17,000
- **Coed** 211 undergraduate students, 89% full-time, 42% women, 58% men
- **Noncompetitive** entrance level, 100% of applicants were admitted

Undergraduates 187 full-time, 24 part-time. Students come from 14 states and territories; 4 other countries; 12% are from out of state; 16% Black or African American, non-Hispanic/Latino; 10% Hispanic/Latino; 1% Asian, non-Hispanic/Latino; 0.5% American Indian or Alaska Native, non-Hispanic/Latino; 3% international; 23% transferred in; 45% live on campus. *Retention:* 77% of full-time freshmen returned.

Freshmen *Admission:* 64 applied, 64 admitted, 51 enrolled. *Average high school GPA:* 3.04.

Faculty *Total:* 17, 53% full-time, 12% with terminal degrees. *Student/faculty ratio:* 6:1.

Academics *Calendar:* semesters. *Degrees:* certificates, diplomas, bachelor's, and master's. *Special study options:* academic remediation for entering students, advanced placement credit, distance learning, double majors, independent study, internships, part-time degree program, summer session for credit.

Computers on Campus 23 computers/terminals are available on campus for general student use. Campuswide network is available. Wireless service is available via computer labs, dorm rooms, libraries.

Student Life *Housing:* on-campus residence required through senior year. *Options:* men-only, women-only. Campus housing is university owned. Freshman campus housing is guaranteed. *Activities and organizations:* choral group, Student Missionary Association, 4-12 Group. *Campus security:* student patrols, controlled dormitory access, night security guards. *Student services:* personal/psychological counseling.

Athletics *Intercollegiate sports:* baseball M, basketball M, volleyball W.

Costs (2011–12) *Comprehensive fee:* $10,940 includes full-time tuition ($6000), mandatory fees ($740), and room and board ($4200). Full-time tuition and fees vary according to course load. Part-time tuition: $220 per credit. Part-time tuition and fees vary according to course load. *Payment plan:* installment. *Waivers:* employees or children of employees.

Financial Aid Of all full-time matriculated undergraduates who enrolled in 2006, 164 applied for aid, 118 were judged to have need, 93 had their need fully met. *Average financial aid package:* $6847. *Average indebtedness upon graduation:* $4838.

Applying *Options:* electronic application, early admission, deferred entrance. *Application fee:* $15. *Required:* essay or personal statement, high school transcript, 1 letter of recommendation, pastoral recommendation, medical examination. *Required for some:* interview. *Application deadlines:* rolling (freshmen), rolling (transfers). *Notification:* continuous (freshmen), continuous (transfers).

Freshman Application Contact Ms. Janie Taylor, Registrar/Admissions, Arlington Baptist College, 3001 West Division, Arlington, TX 76012-3425. *Phone:* 817-461-8741 Ext. 105. *Fax:* 817-274-1138. *E-mail:* jhall@abconline.org. *Web site:* http://www.abconline.edu/.

The Art Institute of Austin

Austin, Texas

- **Proprietary** 4-year, part of Education Management Corporation
- **Coed**

Academics *Degrees:* associate and bachelor's.

Costs (2010–11) *Tuition:* Tuition cost varies by program. Prospective students should contact the school for current tuition costs. Other charges include a starting kit for all first-quarter students. Kits vary in price, depending on the program of study.

Freshman Application Contact The Art Institute of Austin, 101 W. Louis Henna Boulevard, Suite 100, Austin, TX 78728. *Phone:* 512-691-1707. *Toll-free phone:* 866-583-7952. *Web site:* http://www.artinstitutes.edu/austin.

See page 1010 for the College Close-Up.

The Art Institute of Dallas

Dallas, Texas

- **Proprietary** 4-year, founded 1978, part of Education Management Corporation
- **Urban** 2-acre campus
- **Coed**

Academics *Calendar:* quarters. *Degrees:* certificates, associate, and bachelor's.

Costs (2010–11) *Tuition:* Tuition cost varies by program. Prospective students should contact the school for current tuition costs. Other charges include a starting kit for all first-quarter students. Kits vary in price, depending on the program of study.

Freshman Application Contact The Art Institute of Dallas, 8080 Park Lane, Suite 100, Dallas, TX 75231-5993. *Phone:* 214-692-8080. *Toll-free phone:* 800-275-4243. *Web site:* http://www.artinstitutes.edu/dallas/.

See page 1034 for the College Close-Up.

The Art Institute of Fort Worth

Fort Worth, Texas

- **Proprietary** 4-year
- **Coed**

Academics *Degrees:* associate and bachelor's.

Costs (2010–11) *Tuition:* Tuition cost varies by program. Prospective students should contact the school for current tuition costs. Other charges include a starting kit for all first-quarter students. Kits vary in price, depending on the program of study.

Freshman Application Contact The Art Institute of Fort Worth, 7000 Calmont Avenue, Suite 150, Fort Worth, TX 76116. *Phone:* 817-210-0808. *Toll-free phone:* 888-422-9686. *Web site:* http://www.artinstitutes.edu/fort-worth/.

See page 1038 for the College Close-Up.

The Art Institute of Houston

Houston, Texas

- **Proprietary** 4-year, founded 1978, part of Education Management Corporation
- **Urban** campus
- **Coed**

Academics *Calendar:* quarters. *Degrees:* diplomas, associate, and bachelor's.

Costs (2010–11) *Tuition:* Tuition cost varies by program. Prospective students should contact the school for current tuition costs. Other charges include a starting kit for all first-quarter students. Kits vary in price, depending on the program of study.

Freshman Application Contact The Art Institute of Houston, 1900 Yorktown Street, Houston, TX 77056. *Phone:* 713-623-2040. *Toll-free phone:* 800-275-4244. *Web site:* http://www.artinstitutes.edu/houston/.

See page 1040 for the College Close-Up.

The Art Institute of Houston - North

Houston, Texas

- **Proprietary** 4-year
- **Coed**

Costs (2010–11) *Tuition:* Tuition cost varies by program. Prospective students should contact the school for current tuition costs. Other charges include a starting kit for all first-quarter students. Kits vary in price, depending on the program of study.

Freshman Application Contact The Art Institute of Houston - North, 10740 North Gessner Drive, Suite 190, Houston, TX 77064. *Phone:* 281-671-3381. *Toll-free phone:* 866-830-4450. *Web site:* http://www.artinstitutes.edu/houston-north.

See page 1042 for the College Close-Up.

The Art Institute of San Antonio

San Antonio, Texas

- **Proprietary** 4-year
- **Coed**

Academics *Degrees:* associate and bachelor's.

Costs (2010–11) *Tuition:* Tuition cost varies by program. Prospective students should contact the school for current tuition costs. Other charges include a starting kit for all first-quarter students. Kits vary in price, depending on the program of study.

Freshman Application Contact The Art Institute of San Antonio, 1000 IH-10 West, Suite 200, San Antonio, TX 78230. *Phone:* 210-338-7320. *Toll-free phone:* 888-222-0040. *Web site:* http://www.artinstitutes.edu/san-antonio/.

See page 1066 for the College Close-Up.

Austin College
Sherman, Texas

- **Independent Presbyterian** comprehensive, founded 1849
- **Small-town** 60-acre campus with easy access to Dallas-Fort Worth
- **Endowment** $112.7 million
- **Coed** 1,293 undergraduate students, 100% full-time, 56% women, 44% men
- **Very difficult** entrance level, 83% of applicants were admitted

Undergraduates 1,287 full-time, 6 part-time. Students come from 33 states and territories; 16 other countries; 8% are from out of state; 4% Black or African American, non-Hispanic/Latino; 12% Hispanic/Latino; 14% Asian, non-Hispanic/Latino; 0.3% American Indian or Alaska Native, non-Hispanic/Latino; 4% Two or more races, non-Hispanic/Latino; 1% Race/ethnicity unknown; 2% international; 3% transferred in; 71% live on campus. *Retention:* 84% of full-time freshmen returned.

Freshmen *Admission:* 1,608 applied, 1,335 admitted, 319 enrolled. *Average high school GPA:* 3.68. *Test scores:* SAT critical reading scores over 500: 90%; SAT math scores over 500: 95%; SAT writing scores over 500: 84%; ACT scores over 18: 99%; SAT critical reading scores over 600: 59%; SAT math scores over 600: 67%; SAT writing scores over 600: 48%; ACT scores over 24: 67%; SAT critical reading scores over 700: 12%; SAT math scores over 700: 17%; SAT writing scores over 700: 12%; ACT scores over 30: 15%.

Faculty *Total:* 127, 73% full-time, 80% with terminal degrees. *Student/faculty ratio:* 13:1.

Academics *Calendar:* 4-1-4. *Degrees:* bachelor's and master's. *Special study options:* adult/continuing education programs, advanced placement credit, double majors, honors programs, independent study, internships, off-campus study, part-time degree program, student-designed majors, study abroad, summer session for credit. *Unusual degree programs:* 3-2 engineering with University of Texas at Dallas, Texas A&M University, Washington University in St. Louis, Columbia University.

Computers on Campus 160 computers/terminals are available on campus for general student use. Students can access the following: campus intranet, computer help desk, free student e-mail accounts, online (class) grades, online (class) registration, online (class) schedules. Campuswide network is available. 100% of college-owned or -operated housing units are wired for high-speed Internet access. Wireless service is available via entire campus.

Student Life *Housing:* on-campus residence required through junior year. *Options:* coed, men-only, women-only, disabled students. Campus housing is university owned. Freshman campus housing is guaranteed. *Activities and organizations:* drama/theater group, student-run newspaper, choral group, Fellowship of Christian Athletes, Campus Activity Board, Indian Cultural Association, Student Development Board, International Relations Club. *Campus security:* 24-hour emergency response devices and patrols, late-night transport/escort service, controlled dormitory access. *Student services:* health clinic, personal/psychological counseling.

Athletics Member NCAA. All Division III. *Intercollegiate sports:* baseball M, basketball M/W, cheerleading M/W, football M, soccer M/W, softball W, swimming and diving M/W, tennis M/W, volleyball W. *Intramural sports:* basketball M/W, football M/W, soccer M/W, softball W, swimming and diving M/W, table tennis M/W, tennis M/W, ultimate Frisbee M/W, volleyball W.

Standardized Tests *Required:* SAT or ACT (for admission).

Costs (2011–12) *One-time required fee:* $25. *Comprehensive fee:* $41,348 includes full-time tuition ($31,110), mandatory fees ($160), and room and board ($10,078). Full-time tuition and fees vary according to student level. Part-time tuition: $4424 per course. *Room and board:* Room and board charges vary according to board plan. *Payment plan:* installment. *Waivers:* employees or children of employees.

Financial Aid Of all full-time matriculated undergraduates who enrolled in 2009, 980 applied for aid, 816 were judged to have need, 773 had their need fully met. 297 Federal Work-Study jobs (averaging $1628). 217 state and other part-time jobs (averaging $1469). In 2009, 293 non-need-based awards were made. *Average percent of need met:* 95%. *Average financial aid package:* $26,331. *Average need-based loan:* $6200. *Average need-based gift aid:* $19,001. *Average non-need-based aid:* $12,949.

Applying *Options:* electronic application, early admission, deferred entrance. *Required:* essay or personal statement, high school transcript, 2 letters of recommendation. *Required for some:* interview. *Recommended:* minimum 3 GPA, interview. *Application deadlines:* 5/1 (freshmen), 5/1 (transfers).

Freshman Application Contact Ms. Nan Davis, Vice President for Institutional Enrollment, Austin College, 900 North Grand Avenue, Suite 6N, Sherman, TX 75090-4400. *Phone:* 903-813-3000. *Toll-free phone:* 800-442-5363. *Fax:* 903-813-3198. *E-mail:* admission@austincollege.edu. *Web site:* http://www.austincollege.edu/.

See page 1094 for the College Close-Up.

Austin Graduate School of Theology
Austin, Texas

- **Independent** upper-level, founded 1917, affiliated with Church of Christ
- **Urban** 2-acre campus with easy access to Austin
- **Endowment** $3.6 million
- **Coed**
- **Minimally difficult** entrance level

Academics *Calendar:* semesters. *Degrees:* bachelor's and master's.

Student Life *Campus security:* 24-hour emergency response devices.

Costs (2010–11) *Tuition:* $7080 full-time, $295 per semester hour part-time. Full-time tuition and fees vary according to course load. Part-time tuition and fees vary according to course load. *Required fees:* $150 full-time, $75 per term part-time.

Financial Aid Of all full-time matriculated undergraduates who enrolled in 2008, 5 Federal Work-Study jobs (averaging $860).

Application Contact Mrs. Celeste Scarbrough, Director of Admissions, Austin Graduate School of Theology, 7640 Guadalupe Street, Austin, TX 78752. *Phone:* 512-476-2772. *Toll-free phone:* 866-AUS-GRAD. *Fax:* 512-476-3919. *E-mail:* registrar@austingrad.edu. *Web site:* http://www.austingrad.edu/.

Baptist Missionary Association Theological Seminary
Jacksonville, Texas

Director of Admissions Dr. Philip Attebery, Dean and Registrar, Baptist Missionary Association Theological Seminary, 1530 East Pine Street, Jacksonville, TX 75766-5407. *Phone:* 903-586-2501 Ext. 229. *E-mail:* attebery@bmats.edu. *Web site:* http://www.bmats.edu/.

Baptist University of the Americas
San Antonio, Texas

Freshman Application Contact Baptist University of the Americas, 8019 South Pan Am Expressway, San Antonio, TX 78224-2701. *Phone:* 210-924-4338 Ext. 202. *Toll-free phone:* 800-721-1396. *Web site:* http://www.bua.edu/.

Baylor University
Waco, Texas

- **Independent Baptist** university, founded 1845
- **Urban** 508-acre campus with easy access to Dallas-Fort Worth
- **Endowment** $880.3 million
- **Coed**
- **Moderately difficult** entrance level

Faculty *Student/faculty ratio:* 15:1.

Academics *Calendar:* semesters. *Degrees:* certificates, bachelor's, master's, doctoral-professional, doctoral-research/scholarship, and post-master's certificates.

Student Life *Campus security:* 24-hour emergency response devices and patrols, late-night transport/escort service, controlled dormitory access, bicycle patrols.

Athletics Member NCAA. All Division I except football (Division I-A).

Standardized Tests *Required:* SAT or ACT (for admission), (for admission).

Costs (2010–11) *Comprehensive fee:* $38,085 includes full-time tuition ($26,996), mandatory fees ($2758), and room and board ($8331). Part-time tuition: $1124 per semester hour. *College room only:* $4494. Room and board charges vary according to board plan and housing facility.

Financial Aid Of all full-time matriculated undergraduates who enrolled in 2009, 8,053 applied for aid, 7,000 were judged to have need, 1,081 had their need fully met. 4,864 Federal Work-Study jobs (averaging $2827). In 2009, 3692 non-need-based awards were made. *Average percent of need met:* 66. *Average financial aid package:* $21,568. *Average need-based loan:* $4870. *Average need-based gift aid:* $16,079. *Average non-need-based aid:* $9913.

Applying *Options:* electronic application, early admission, early action. *Application fee:* $50. *Required:* high school transcript. *Required for some:* essay or personal statement, minimum 2.5 GPA, 2 letters of recommendation. *Recommended:* interview.

Freshman Application Contact Ms. Jessica King Gereghty, Director of Admissions, Baylor University, PO Box 97056, Waco, TX 76798. *Phone:* 254-710-3435. *Toll-free phone:* 800-BAYLORU. *Fax:* 254-710-3436. *E-mail:* admissions@baylor.edu. *Web site:* http://www.baylor.edu/.

Brazosport College
Lake Jackson, Texas

Freshman Application Contact Brazosport College, 500 College Drive, Lake Jackson, TX 77566-3199. *Phone:* 979-230-3020. *Web site:* http://www.brazosport.edu/.

Brown Mackie College–San Antonio
San Antonio, Texas

- **Proprietary** 4-year
- **Coed**

Academics *Degrees:* associate and bachelor's.
Director of Admissions Director of Admissions, Brown Mackie College–San Antonio, 4715 Fredericksburg Road, Suite 100, San Antonio, TX 78229. *Phone:* 210-428-2210. *Toll-free phone:* 877-460-1714. *Web site:* http://www.brownmackie.edu/san-antonio.

See page 1162 for the College Close-Up.

College of Biblical Studies–Houston
Houston, Texas

- **Independent nondenominational** comprehensive, founded 1979
- **Urban** 12-acre campus with easy access to Houston
- **Endowment** $1.4 million
- **Coed**
- **Noncompetitive** entrance level

Academics *Calendar:* trimesters. *Degrees:* certificates, associate, and bachelor's.
Student Life *Campus security:* 24-hour emergency response devices, late-night transport/escort service, hourly patrols by trained security guards and police.
Costs (2010–11) *Tuition:* $5616 full-time, $234 per credit hour part-time. *Required fees:* $240 full-time, $120 per term part-time.
Applying *Options:* electronic application. *Application fee:* $40. *Required:* essay or personal statement, high school transcript.
Freshman Application Contact Admissions, College of Biblical Studies–Houston, 7000 Regency Square Boulevard, Houston, TX 77036. *Phone:* 832-252-3377. *Fax:* 713-532-8150. *E-mail:* admissions@cbshouston.edu. *Web site:* http://www.cbshouston.edu/.

The College of Saint Thomas More
Fort Worth, Texas

Freshman Application Contact Dr. James A. Patrick, The College of Saint Thomas More, 3020 Lubbock Avenue, Fort Worth, TX 76109-2323. *Phone:* 817-928-8459. *Toll-free phone:* 800-583-6489. *Fax:* 817-924-3206. *E-mail:* more-info@cstm.edu. *Web site:* http://www.cstm.edu/.

Concordia University Texas
Austin, Texas

- **Independent** comprehensive, founded 1926, affiliated with Lutheran Church–Missouri Synod, part of Concordia University System
- **Urban** 20-acre campus with easy access to San Antonio
- **Coed**
- **Moderately difficult** entrance level

Faculty *Student/faculty ratio:* 10:1.
Academics *Calendar:* semesters. *Degrees:* certificates, associate, bachelor's, master's, and postbachelor's certificates.
Student Life *Campus security:* 24-hour emergency response devices, student patrols, late-night transport/escort service, controlled dormitory access.
Athletics Member NCAA. All Division III.
Standardized Tests *Required:* SAT or ACT (for admission).
Costs (2010–11) *Comprehensive fee:* $29,960 includes full-time tuition ($21,700), mandatory fees ($100), and room and board ($8160). Full-time tuition and fees vary according to course load, degree level, location, and program. Part-time tuition: $720 per hour. Part-time tuition and fees vary according to course load, degree level, location, and program. *College room only:* $4700. Room and board charges vary according to board plan.
Financial Aid *Of all full-time matriculated undergraduates who enrolled in 2008,* 210 applied for aid, 156 were judged to have need, 96 had their need fully met. 77 Federal Work-Study jobs (averaging $1326). 4 state and other part-time jobs (averaging $3164). *In 2008,* 42 non-need-based awards were made. *Average percent of need met:* 90. *Average financial aid package:* $17,507. *Average need-based loan:* $8900. *Average need-based gift aid:* $9126. *Average non-need-based aid:* $6936. *Average indebtedness upon graduation:* $22,095.

Applying *Options:* early admission, deferred entrance. *Application fee:* $25. *Required:* high school transcript, minimum 2.5 GPA. *Required for some:* essay or personal statement, interview.
Freshman Application Contact Kristi Kirk, Director of Enrollment Services, Concordia University Texas, 11400 Concordia University Drive, Austin, TX 78726. *Phone:* 512-486-2000 Ext. 1156. *Toll-free phone:* 800-865-4282. *Fax:* 512-459-8517. *E-mail:* ctxadmis@crf.cuis.edu. *Web site:* http://www.concordia.edu/.

The Criswell College
Dallas, Texas

Director of Admissions Admissions, The Criswell College, 4010 Gaston Avenue, Dallas, TX 75246-1537. *Phone:* 214-821-5433. *Toll-free phone:* 800-899-0012. *Fax:* 214-818-1310. *Web site:* http://www.criswell.edu/.

Dallas Baptist University
Dallas, Texas

- **Independent** comprehensive, founded 1965, affiliated with Baptist General Convention of Texas
- **Urban** 293-acre campus
- **Endowment** $28.9 million
- **Coed** 3,523 undergraduate students, 65% full-time, 59% women, 41% men
- **Moderately difficult** entrance level, 43% of applicants were admitted

Undergraduates 2,303 full-time, 1,220 part-time. Students come from 39 states and territories; 38 other countries; 6% are from out of state; 19% Black or African American, non-Hispanic/Latino; 9% Hispanic/Latino; 2% Asian, non-Hispanic/Latino; 0.3% Native Hawaiian or other Pacific Islander, non-Hispanic/Latino; 0.8% American Indian or Alaska Native, non-Hispanic/Latino; 8% international; 8% transferred in; 44% live on campus. *Retention:* 76% of full-time freshmen returned.
Freshmen *Admission:* 1,718 applied, 741 admitted, 376 enrolled. *Average high school GPA:* 3.47. *Test scores:* SAT critical reading scores over 500: 73%; SAT math scores over 500: 78%; ACT scores over 18: 99%; SAT critical reading scores over 600: 20%; SAT math scores over 600: 24%; ACT scores over 24: 35%; SAT critical reading scores over 700: 5%; SAT math scores over 700: 2%; ACT scores over 30: 2%.
Faculty *Total:* 532, 23% full-time, 44% with terminal degrees. *Student/faculty ratio:* 14:1.
Academics *Calendar:* 4-1-4. *Degrees:* certificates, associate, bachelor's, master's, doctoral-research/scholarship, post-master's, and postbachelor's certificates. *Special study options:* academic remediation for entering students, accelerated degree program, adult/continuing education programs, advanced placement credit, distance learning, double majors, English as a second language, honors programs, independent study, internships, off-campus study, part-time degree program, services for LD students, study abroad, summer session for credit. *ROTC:* Army (c), Air Force (c).
Computers on Campus 208 computers/terminals are available on campus for general student use. Students can access the following: computer help desk, free student e-mail accounts, online (class) grades, online (class) registration, online (class) schedules. Campuswide network is available. 100% of college-owned or -operated housing units are wired for high-speed Internet access. Wireless service is available via entire campus.
Student Life *Housing:* on-campus residence required through senior year. *Options:* men-only, women-only, disabled students. Campus housing is university owned and leased by the school. Freshman applicants given priority for college housing. *Activities and organizations:* drama/theater group, choral group, Student Activities Board, Baptist Student Ministry, Student Government Association, Student Education Association, International Student Organization. *Campus security:* 24-hour emergency response devices and patrols, late-night transport/escort service, controlled dormitory access. *Student services:* health clinic, personal/psychological counseling.
Athletics Member NCAA, NCCAA. All NCAA Division II. *Intercollegiate sports:* baseball M(s), basketball M(s), cheerleading W(c), cross-country running M/W(s), football W(s), golf M/W(s), ice hockey M(c), soccer W(s), tennis M/W(s), track and field M/W(s), volleyball W(s). *Intramural sports:* basketball M/W, cross-country running M/W, football M/W, golf M/W, soccer M/W, softball M/W, table tennis M/W, tennis M/W, ultimate Frisbee M/W, volleyball M/W.
Standardized Tests *Required:* SAT or ACT (for admission).
Costs (2010–11) *Comprehensive fee:* $24,558 includes full-time tuition ($18,690) and room and board ($5868). Part-time tuition: $623 per credit hour. *College room only:* $2326. Room and board charges vary according to board plan and housing facility. *Payment plans:* installment, deferred payment. *Waivers:* employees or children of employees.
Financial Aid Of all full-time matriculated undergraduates who enrolled in 2009, 2,017 applied for aid, 1,511 were judged to have need, 565 had their

need fully met. 130 Federal Work-Study jobs (averaging $2575). 56 state and other part-time jobs (averaging $663). In 2009, 369 non-need-based awards were made. *Average percent of need met:* 65%. *Average financial aid package:* $14,769. *Average need-based loan:* $4094. *Average need-based gift aid:* $3515. *Average non-need-based aid:* $7469. *Average indebtedness upon graduation:* $18,629.
Applying *Options:* electronic application, early admission, deferred entrance. *Application fee:* $25. *Required:* essay or personal statement, high school transcript, minimum 2.5 GPA, rank in upper 50% of high school class. *Recommended:* interview. *Application deadlines:* rolling (freshmen), rolling (transfers). *Notification:* continuous (freshmen), continuous (transfers).
Freshman Application Contact Mr. Jason Williams, Assistant Vice President for Enrollment Services, Dallas Baptist University, 3000 Mountain Creek Parkway, Dallas, TX 75211-9299. *Phone:* 214-333-5360. *Toll-free phone:* 800-460-1328. *Fax:* 214-333-5447. *E-mail:* admiss@dbu.edu. *Web site:* http://www.dbu.edu/.

Dallas Christian College

Dallas, Texas

Freshman Application Contact Ms. Kristi Boggs, Director of Admissions, Dallas Christian College, 2700 Christian Parkway, Dallas, TX 75234-7299. *Phone:* 972-241-3371 Ext. 161. *Fax:* 972-241-8021. *E-mail:* kboggs@dallas.edu. *Web site:* http://www.dallas.edu/.

DeVry University

Houston, Texas

- **Proprietary** comprehensive
- **Coed** 1,959 undergraduate students, 39% full-time, 49% women, 51% men
- **Minimally difficult** entrance level

Undergraduates 759 full-time, 1,200 part-time. 1% are from out of state; 28% Black or African American, non-Hispanic/Latino; 34% Hispanic/Latino; 3% Asian, non-Hispanic/Latino; 0.4% Native Hawaiian or other Pacific Islander, non-Hispanic/Latino; 0.1% American Indian or Alaska Native, non-Hispanic/Latino; 0.3% Two or more races, non-Hispanic/Latino; 20% Race/ethnicity unknown; 0.6% international; 25% transferred in.
Freshmen *Admission:* 382 enrolled.
Faculty *Total:* 183, 11% full-time. *Student/faculty ratio:* 18:1.
Academics *Calendar:* semesters. *Degrees:* associate, bachelor's, and master's. *Special study options:* academic remediation for entering students, accelerated degree program, advanced placement credit, distance learning, summer session for credit.
Costs (2010–11) *Tuition:* $14,766 full-time, $580 per credit hour part-time. Full-time tuition and fees vary according to course load. Part-time tuition and fees vary according to course load. *Required fees:* $60 full-time, $30 per term part-time. *Payment plans:* installment, deferred payment. *Waivers:* employees or children of employees.
Financial Aid Of all full-time matriculated undergraduates who enrolled in 2007, 306 applied for aid, 299 were judged to have need, 3 had their need fully met. In 2007, 20 non-need-based awards were made. *Average percent of need met:* 39%. *Average financial aid package:* $12,662. *Average need-based loan:* $7855. *Average need-based gift aid:* $5374. *Average non-need-based aid:* $14,939. *Average indebtedness upon graduation:* $30,068.
Applying *Options:* electronic application, deferred entrance. *Application fee:* $50. *Application deadlines:* rolling (freshmen), rolling (transfers). *Notification:* continuous (freshmen), continuous (transfers).
Freshman Application Contact DeVry University, 11125 Equity Drive, Houston, TX 77041. *Phone:* 713-973-3100. *Toll-free phone:* 866-703-3879. *Web site:* http://www.devry.edu/.

DeVry University

Irving, Texas

- **Proprietary** comprehensive, founded 1969, part of DeVry University
- **Suburban** 13-acre campus with easy access to Dallas
- **Coed** 1,898 undergraduate students, 42% full-time, 33% women, 67% men
- **Minimally difficult** entrance level

Undergraduates 806 full-time, 1,092 part-time. 3% are from out of state; 25% Black or African American, non-Hispanic/Latino; 22% Hispanic/Latino; 3% Asian, non-Hispanic/Latino; 0.2% Native Hawaiian or other Pacific Islander, non-Hispanic/Latino; 0.6% American Indian or Alaska Native, non-Hispanic/Latino; 0.6% Two or more races, non-Hispanic/Latino; 19% Race/ethnicity unknown; 0.2% international; 21% transferred in.
Freshmen *Admission:* 329 enrolled.
Faculty *Total:* 100, 44% full-time. *Student/faculty ratio:* 22:1.

Academics *Calendar:* semesters. *Degrees:* associate, bachelor's, and master's. *Special study options:* academic remediation for entering students, accelerated degree program, adult/continuing education programs, advanced placement credit, distance learning, part-time degree program, services for LD students, summer session for credit.
Computers on Campus Students can access the following: online (class) registration. Campuswide network is available.
Student Life *Housing:* college housing not available. *Campus security:* 24-hour emergency response devices, student patrols, late-night transport/escort service, lighted pathways/sidewalks.
Costs (2010–11) *Tuition:* $14,766 full-time, $580 per credit hour part-time. Full-time tuition and fees vary according to course load. Part-time tuition and fees vary according to course load. *Required fees:* $60 full-time, $30 per term part-time. *Payment plans:* installment, deferred payment. *Waivers:* employees or children of employees.
Financial Aid Of all full-time matriculated undergraduates who enrolled in 2007, 354 applied for aid, 343 were judged to have need, 9 had their need fully met. In 2007, 33 non-need-based awards were made. *Average percent of need met:* 40%. *Average financial aid package:* $12,581. *Average need-based loan:* $8675. *Average need-based gift aid:* $5995. *Average non-need-based aid:* $17,309. *Average indebtedness upon graduation:* $31,895.
Applying *Options:* electronic application, deferred entrance. *Application fee:* $50. *Required:* high school transcript, interview. *Application deadlines:* rolling (freshmen), rolling (transfers). *Notification:* continuous (freshmen), continuous (transfers).
Freshman Application Contact DeVry University, 4800 Regent Boulevard, Irving, TX 75063-2439. *Phone:* 972-929-6777. *Web site:* http://www.devry.edu/.

DeVry University

Richardson, Texas

Admissions Office Contact DeVry University, Richardson Center, 2201 North Central Expressway, Richardson, TX 75080. *Web site:* http://www.devry.edu/.

East Texas Baptist University

Marshall, Texas

- **Independent Baptist** 4-year, founded 1912
- **Small-town** 200-acre campus
- **Endowment** $51.1 million
- **Coed** 1,197 undergraduate students, 89% full-time, 50% women, 50% men
- **Moderately difficult** entrance level, 51% of applicants were admitted

Undergraduates 1,060 full-time, 137 part-time. Students come from 18 states and territories; 10 other countries; 10% are from out of state; 16% Black or African American, non-Hispanic/Latino; 9% Hispanic/Latino; 0.9% Asian, non-Hispanic/Latino; 1% American Indian or Alaska Native, non-Hispanic/Latino; 0.8% Two or more races, non-Hispanic/Latino; 0.4% Race/ethnicity unknown; 1% international; 9% transferred in; 82% live on campus. *Retention:* 64% of full-time freshmen returned.
Freshmen *Admission:* 1,078 applied, 547 admitted, 284 enrolled. *Average high school GPA:* 3.32. *Test scores:* SAT critical reading scores over 500: 38%; SAT math scores over 500: 48%; ACT scores over 18: 86%; SAT critical reading scores over 600: 7%; SAT math scores over 600: 8%; ACT scores over 24: 18%; SAT critical reading scores over 700: 1%; ACT scores over 30: 1%.
Faculty *Total:* 98, 65% full-time, 64% with terminal degrees. *Student/faculty ratio:* 15:1.
Academics *Calendar:* semesters 4-4-1. *Degree:* certificates and bachelor's. *Special study options:* accelerated degree program, adult/continuing education programs, advanced placement credit, distance learning, double majors, honors programs, independent study, internships, off-campus study, part-time degree program, services for LD students, student-designed majors, study abroad, summer session for credit.
Computers on Campus 200 computers/terminals and 720 ports are available on campus for general student use. Students can access the following: campus intranet, computer help desk, free student e-mail accounts, online (class) grades, online (class) registration, online (class) schedules. Campuswide network is available. 100% of college-owned or -operated housing units are wired for high-speed Internet access. Wireless service is available via entire campus.
Student Life *Housing:* on-campus residence required through senior year. *Options:* men-only, women-only. Campus housing is university owned. Freshman campus housing is guaranteed. *Activities and organizations:* drama/theater group, student-run newspaper, radio station, choral group, marching band, Baptist Student Ministry, Student Activities Board, Blue Crew, Student Government Association, Student Foundation. *Campus security:* 24-hour emergency response devices, controlled dormitory access. *Student services:* personal/psychological counseling.

Athletics Member NCAA. All Division III. *Intercollegiate sports:* baseball M, basketball M/W, cross-country running M/W, football M, soccer M/W, softball W, volleyball W. *Intramural sports:* basketball M/W, football M/W, racquetball M/W, soccer M/W, softball M/W, table tennis M/W, ultimate Frisbee M/W, volleyball M/W.

Standardized Tests *Required:* SAT or ACT (for admission).

Costs (2011–12) *Comprehensive fee:* $26,166 includes full-time tuition ($19,680), mandatory fees ($820), and room and board ($5666). Part-time tuition: $656 per credit hour. *College room only:* $2400. Room and board charges vary according to board plan and housing facility. *Payment plan:* installment. *Waivers:* employees or children of employees.

Financial Aid Of all full-time matriculated undergraduates who enrolled in 2008, 1,024 applied for aid, 894 were judged to have need, 183 had their need fully met. 87 Federal Work-Study jobs (averaging $1437). 217 state and other part-time jobs (averaging $1461). In 2008, 188 non-need-based awards were made. *Average percent of need met:* 48%. *Average financial aid package:* $14,472. *Average need-based loan:* $3703. *Average need-based gift aid:* $6273. *Average non-need-based aid:* $6700. *Average indebtedness upon graduation:* $25,284.

Applying *Options:* electronic application. *Application fee:* $25. *Required:* high school transcript. *Required for some:* interview. *Application deadlines:* 8/15 (freshmen), 8/15 (out-of-state freshmen), 8/15 (transfers). *Notification:* continuous (freshmen), continuous (out-of-state freshmen), continuous (transfers).

Freshman Application Contact East Texas Baptist University, 1209 North Grove, Marshall, TX 75670-1498. *Phone:* 903-923-2000. *Toll-free phone:* 800-804-ETBU. *Web site:* http://www.etbu.edu/.

Hallmark College of Technology
San Antonio, Texas

- **Proprietary** primarily 2-year, founded 1969, administratively affiliated with Hallmark College of Aeronautics
- **Suburban** 3-acre campus
- **Coed** 356 undergraduate students, 100% full-time, 55% women, 45% men
- **Moderately difficult** entrance level

Undergraduates 356 full-time. Students come from 1 other state; 15% Black or African American, non-Hispanic/Latino; 54% Hispanic/Latino; 0.6% Asian, non-Hispanic/Latino; 0.3% Native Hawaiian or other Pacific Islander, non-Hispanic/Latino; 4% Two or more races, non-Hispanic/Latino; 1% Race/ethnicity unknown.

Freshmen *Admission:* 356 enrolled.

Faculty *Total:* 43, 47% full-time, 7% with terminal degrees. *Student/faculty ratio:* 8:1.

Academics *Calendar:* continuous. *Degrees:* certificates, associate, and bachelor's. *Special study options:* accelerated degree program, internships.

Computers on Campus 227 computers/terminals and 227 ports are available on campus for general student use. Students can access the following: campus intranet, computer help desk, free student e-mail accounts. Campuswide network is available. Wireless service is available via classrooms, computer centers, computer labs, libraries.

Student Life *Housing:* college housing not available. *Activities and organizations:* Alpha Beta Kappa Honor Society. *Campus security:* 24-hour emergency response devices.

Standardized Tests *Required:* Wonderlic aptitude test (for admission).

Applying *Application fee:* $110. *Required:* high school transcript, interview, tour. *Required for some:* essay or personal statement. *Application deadlines:* rolling (freshmen), rolling (transfers). *Notification:* continuous (freshmen), continuous (transfers).

Freshman Application Contact Hallmark College of Technology, 10401 IH 10 West, San Antonio, TX 78230. *Phone:* 210-690-9000 Ext. 212. *Toll-free phone:* 800-880-6600. *Web site:* http://www.hallmarkcollege.edu/.

Hardin-Simmons University
Abilene, Texas

- **Independent Baptist** comprehensive, founded 1891
- **Urban** 120-acre campus
- **Endowment** $105.7 million
- **Coed** 1,877 undergraduate students, 91% full-time, 55% women, 45% men
- **Moderately difficult** entrance level, 35% of applicants were admitted

Undergraduates 1,715 full-time, 162 part-time. Students come from 25 states and territories; 17 other countries; 5% are from out of state; 6% Black or African American, non-Hispanic/Latino; 12% Hispanic/Latino; 1% Asian, non-Hispanic/Latino; 0.2% Native Hawaiian or other Pacific Islander, non-Hispanic/Latino; 0.9% American Indian or Alaska Native, non-Hispanic/Latino; 0.4% Two or more races, non-Hispanic/Latino; 4% Race/ethnicity unknown;

1% international; 8% transferred in; 47% live on campus. *Retention:* 67% of full-time freshmen returned.

Freshmen *Admission:* 1,963 applied, 682 admitted, 403 enrolled. *Average high school GPA:* 3.55. *Test scores:* SAT critical reading scores over 500: 54%; SAT math scores over 500: 67%; SAT writing scores over 500: 51%; ACT scores over 18: 92%; SAT critical reading scores over 600: 19%; SAT math scores over 600: 20%; SAT writing scores over 600: 14%; ACT scores over 24: 36%; SAT critical reading scores over 700: 1%; SAT math scores over 700: 3%; SAT writing scores over 700: 2%; ACT scores over 30: 5%.

Faculty *Total:* 203, 67% full-time, 66% with terminal degrees. *Student/faculty ratio:* 13:1.

Academics *Calendar:* semesters. *Degrees:* bachelor's, master's, doctoral-professional, doctoral-research/scholarship, post-master's, and postbachelor's certificates. *Special study options:* academic remediation for entering students, accelerated degree program, adult/continuing education programs, advanced placement credit, distance learning, double majors, honors programs, independent study, internships, off-campus study, part-time degree program, services for LD students, study abroad, summer session for credit.

Computers on Campus 230 computers/terminals and 1,000 ports are available on campus for general student use. Students can access the following: campus intranet, computer help desk, free student e-mail accounts, online (class) grades, online (class) schedules. Campuswide network is available. 100% of college-owned or -operated housing units are wired for high-speed Internet access. Wireless service is available via entire campus.

Student Life *Housing:* on-campus residence required through sophomore year. *Options:* men-only, women-only, disabled students. Campus housing is university owned. Freshman campus housing is guaranteed. *Activities and organizations:* drama/theater group, student-run newspaper, choral group, marching band, Baptist Student Ministry, Student Foundation, Student Congress, Fellowship of Christian Athletes, Unity Group. *Campus security:* 24-hour emergency response devices and patrols, late-night transport/escort service, controlled dormitory access. *Student services:* health clinic, personal/psychological counseling.

Athletics Member NCAA. All Division III. *Intercollegiate sports:* baseball M, basketball M/W, cheerleading M(c)/W(c), cross-country running M/W, football M, golf M/W, soccer M/W, softball W, tennis M/W, track and field M/W, volleyball W. *Intramural sports:* badminton M/W, basketball M/W, bowling M/W, football M/W, golf M/W, gymnastics M(c)/W(c), racquetball M/W, rock climbing M(c)/W(c), soccer M/W, softball M/W, table tennis M(c)/W(c), tennis M(c)/W(c), ultimate Frisbee M/W, volleyball M/W.

Standardized Tests *Required:* SAT or ACT (for admission).

Costs (2011–12) *Comprehensive fee:* $29,264 includes full-time tuition ($21,450), mandatory fees ($1010), and room and board ($6804). Full-time tuition and fees vary according to program. Part-time tuition: $715 per credit hour. Part-time tuition and fees vary according to course load and program. No tuition increase for student's term of enrollment. *Required fees:* $150 per term part-time. *College room only:* $3384. Room and board charges vary according to board plan and housing facility. *Payment plan:* installment. *Waivers:* employees or children of employees.

Financial Aid Of all full-time matriculated undergraduates who enrolled in 2009, 1,682 applied for aid, 1,274 were judged to have need, 244 had their need fully met. 119 Federal Work-Study jobs (averaging $1900). 221 state and other part-time jobs (averaging $1900). In 2009, 356 non-need-based awards were made. *Average percent of need met:* 68%. *Average financial aid package:* $23,956. *Average need-based loan:* $4203. *Average need-based gift aid:* $7520. *Average non-need-based aid:* $8214. *Average indebtedness upon graduation:* $37,383.

Applying *Options:* electronic application, deferred entrance. *Application fee:* $50. *Required:* high school transcript, minimum 2 GPA. *Recommended:* 3 letters of recommendation. *Application deadlines:* rolling (freshmen), rolling (transfers). *Notification:* continuous (freshmen), continuous (transfers).

Freshman Application Contact Ms. Brynn Reynolds, Visitor Coordinator, Hardin-Simmons University, Box 16050, Abilene, TX 79698-0001. *Phone:* 325-670-5890. *Toll-free phone:* 877-464-7889. *Fax:* 325-671-2115. *E-mail:* breynolds@hsutx.edu. *Web site:* http://www.hsutx.edu/.

Houston Baptist University
Houston, Texas

- **Independent Baptist** comprehensive, founded 1960
- **Urban** 100-acre campus
- **Endowment** $85.5 million
- **Coed**
- **Moderately difficult** entrance level

Faculty *Student/faculty ratio:* 15:1.

Academics *Calendar:* semesters. *Degrees:* bachelor's, master's, post-master's, and postbachelor's certificates.

Student Life *Campus security:* 24-hour emergency response devices and patrols, late-night transport/escort service.

Athletics Member NCAA. All Division I.

Standardized Tests *Required:* SAT or ACT (for admission).

Costs (2010–11) *Comprehensive fee:* $30,155 includes full-time tuition ($21,970), mandatory fees ($1210), and room and board ($6975). Part-time tuition: $750 per semester hour. Part-time tuition and fees vary according to course load. *Room and board:* Room and board charges vary according to board plan and housing facility.

Financial Aid *Of all full-time matriculated undergraduates who enrolled in 2009,* 1,496 applied for aid, 1,372 were judged to have need, 423 had their need fully met. 988 Federal Work-Study jobs. *In 2009,* 112 non-need-based awards were made. *Average percent of need met:* 88. *Average financial aid package:* $19,578. *Average need-based loan:* $3873. *Average need-based gift aid:* $6259. *Average non-need-based aid:* $4348. *Financial aid deadline:* 4/15.

Applying *Options:* electronic application, early admission. *Required:* high school transcript. *Required for some:* essay or personal statement, interview.

Freshman Application Contact Eduardo Borges, Director of Admissions, Houston Baptist University, 7502 Fondren Road, Houston, TX 77074-3298. *Phone:* 281-649-3299. *Toll-free phone:* 800-696-3210. *Fax:* 281-649-3217. *E-mail:* eborges@hbu.edu. *Web site:* http://www.hbu.edu/.

Howard Payne University

Brownwood, Texas

- **Independent** comprehensive, founded 1889, affiliated with Baptist General Convention of Texas
- **Small-town** 30-acre campus
- **Endowment** $37.6 million
- **Coed**
- **Moderately difficult** entrance level

Faculty *Student/faculty ratio:* 10:1.

Academics *Calendar:* semesters. *Degrees:* certificates, associate, bachelor's, and master's.

Student Life *Campus security:* 24-hour emergency response devices and patrols, late-night transport/escort service, controlled dormitory access, 12-hour patrols by trained security personnel.

Athletics Member NCAA. All Division III.

Standardized Tests *Required:* SAT or ACT (for admission). *Required for some:* ACCUPLACER.

Costs (2010–11) *Comprehensive fee:* $25,642 includes full-time tuition ($18,850), mandatory fees ($1100), and room and board ($5692). Full-time tuition and fees vary according to course load, location, and program. Part-time tuition: $575 per credit hour. Part-time tuition and fees vary according to location and program. *College room only:* $2400. Room and board charges vary according to board plan and housing facility.

Financial Aid *Of all full-time matriculated undergraduates who enrolled in 2009,* 823 applied for aid, 736 were judged to have need, 254 had their need fully met. 105 Federal Work-Study jobs (averaging $1217). 9 state and other part-time jobs (averaging $1333). *In 2009,* 169 non-need-based awards were made. *Average percent of need met:* 86. *Average financial aid package:* $15,273. *Average need-based loan:* $3927. *Average need-based gift aid:* $10,858. *Average non-need-based aid:* $6166. *Average indebtedness upon graduation:* $28,400.

Applying *Options:* electronic application. *Required:* high school transcript, minimum 3 GPA. *Recommended:* essay or personal statement, interview.

Freshman Application Contact Ms. Cheryl Mangrum, Associate Director of Admission, Howard Payne University, 1000 Fisk Street, Brownwood, TX 76801. *Phone:* 325-649-8027. *Toll-free phone:* 800-880-4478. *Fax:* 325-649-8901. *E-mail:* enroll@hputx.edu. *Web site:* http://www.hputx.edu/.

Huston-Tillotson University

Austin, Texas

- **Independent interdenominational** 4-year, founded 1875
- **Urban** 23-acre campus
- **Endowment** $8.0 million
- **Coed** 895 undergraduate students, 93% full-time, 51% women, 49% men
- **Moderately difficult** entrance level, 96% of applicants were admitted

Undergraduates 834 full-time, 61 part-time. Students come from 20 states and territories; 11 other countries; 4% are from out of state; 72% Black or African American, non-Hispanic/Latino; 19% Hispanic/Latino; 0.3% Two or more races, non-Hispanic/Latino; 3% international; 8% transferred in; 39% live on campus. *Retention:* 50% of full-time freshmen returned.

Freshmen *Admission:* 652 applied, 628 admitted, 270 enrolled. *Average high school GPA:* 2.79. *Test scores:* SAT critical reading scores over 500: 13%; SAT math scores over 500: 14%; ACT scores over 18: 41%; SAT critical reading scores over 600: 2%; SAT math scores over 600: 2%; ACT scores over 24: 6%; SAT critical reading scores over 700: 1%; ACT scores over 30: 1%.

Faculty *Total:* 86, 55% full-time, 44% with terminal degrees. *Student/faculty ratio:* 15:1.

Academics *Calendar:* semesters. *Degrees:* bachelor's and postbachelor's certificates. *Special study options:* academic remediation for entering students, advanced placement credit, cooperative education, distance learning, double majors, honors programs, independent study, internships, services for LD students, study abroad, summer session for credit. *ROTC:* Army (c). *Unusual degree programs:* 3-2 engineering with Prairie View A&M University.

Computers on Campus 400 computers/terminals are available on campus for general student use. Students can access the following: free student e-mail accounts, online (class) grades. Campuswide network is available. 100% of college-owned or -operated housing units are wired for high-speed Internet access. Wireless service is available via entire campus.

Student Life *Housing:* on-campus residence required for freshman year. *Options:* men-only, women-only. Campus housing is university owned. Freshman campus housing is guaranteed. *Activities and organizations:* drama/theater group, choral group, Student Government Association, Toastmasters, Pre-Alumni Council, national fraternities, national sororities. *Campus security:* 24-hour patrols. *Student services:* health clinic, personal/psychological counseling.

Athletics Member NAIA. *Intercollegiate sports:* baseball M, basketball M/W, cross-country running M, soccer M/W, softball W, track and field M/W, volleyball W.

Standardized Tests *Required:* SAT or ACT (for admission).

Costs (2010–11) *Comprehensive fee:* $19,376 includes full-time tuition ($10,396), mandatory fees ($2034), and room and board ($6946). Full-time tuition and fees vary according to course load. Part-time tuition: $347 per credit hour. Part-time tuition and fees vary according to course load. *Required fees:* $138 per credit hour part-time. *College room only:* $3020. Room and board charges vary according to housing facility. *Payment plan:* deferred payment. *Waivers:* employees or children of employees.

Financial Aid Of all full-time matriculated undergraduates who enrolled in 2009, 775 applied for aid, 768 were judged to have need, 158 had their need fully met. In 2009, 4 non-need-based awards were made. *Average percent of need met:* 78%. *Average financial aid package:* $14,885. *Average need-based loan:* $4875. *Average need-based gift aid:* $9772.

Applying *Options:* electronic application, deferred entrance. *Application fee:* $25. *Required:* high school transcript, minimum 2 GPA. *Required for some:* essay or personal statement, interview. *Application deadlines:* 7/1 (freshmen), 7/1 (transfers).

Freshman Application Contact Ms. Shakitha Stinson, Director of Admission, Huston-Tillotson University, 900 Chicon Street, Austin, TX 78702. *Phone:* 512-505-3029. *Fax:* 512-505-3192. *E-mail:* slstinson@htu.edu. *Web site:* http://www.htu.edu/.

ITT Technical Institute

Arlington, Texas

- **Proprietary** primarily 2-year, founded 1982, part of ITT Educational Services, Inc.
- **Suburban** campus
- **Coed**
- **Minimally difficult** entrance level

Academics *Calendar:* quarters. *Degrees:* associate and bachelor's.

Student Life *Housing:* college housing not available.

Freshman Application Contact Director of Recruitment, ITT Technical Institute, 551 Ryan Plaza Drive, Arlington, TX 76011. *Phone:* 817-794-5100. *Toll-free phone:* 888-288-4950. *Fax:* 817-275-8446. *Web site:* http://www.itt-tech.edu/.

ITT Technical Institute

Austin, Texas

- **Proprietary** primarily 2-year, founded 1985, part of ITT Educational Services, Inc.
- **Urban** campus
- **Coed**
- **Minimally difficult** entrance level

Academics *Calendar:* quarters. *Degrees:* associate and bachelor's.

Student Life *Housing:* college housing not available.

Financial Aid Of all full-time matriculated undergraduates who enrolled in 2009, 1 Federal Work-Study job.

Freshman Application Contact Director of Recruitment, ITT Technical Institute, 6330 Highway 290 East, Austin, TX 78723. *Phone:* 512-467-6800. *Toll-free phone:* 800-431-0677. *Fax:* 512-467-6677. *Web site:* http://www.itt-tech.edu/.

ITT Technical Institute

DeSoto, Texas

- **Proprietary** primarily 2-year
- **Coed**
- **Minimally difficult** entrance level

Academics *Degrees:* associate and bachelor's.

Freshman Application Contact Director of Recruitment, ITT Technical Institute, 921 West Belt Line Road, Suite 181, DeSoto, TX 75115. *Phone:* 972-274-8600. *Toll-free phone:* 877-854-5728. *Web site:* http://www.itt-tech.edu/.

ITT Technical Institute

Houston, Texas

- **Proprietary** primarily 2-year, founded 1985, part of ITT Educational Services, Inc.
- **Suburban** campus
- **Coed**
- **Minimally difficult** entrance level

Academics *Calendar:* quarters. *Degrees:* associate and bachelor's.

Student Life *Housing:* college housing not available.

Freshman Application Contact Director of Recruitment, ITT Technical Institute, 15651 North Freeway, Houston, TX 77090. *Phone:* 281-873-0512. *Toll-free phone:* 800-879-6486. *Web site:* http://www.itt-tech.edu/.

ITT Technical Institute

Houston, Texas

- **Proprietary** primarily 2-year, founded 1983, part of ITT Educational Services, Inc.
- **Urban** campus
- **Coed**
- **Minimally difficult** entrance level

Academics *Calendar:* quarters. *Degrees:* associate and bachelor's.

Student Life *Housing:* college housing not available.

Freshman Application Contact Director of Recruitment, ITT Technical Institute, 2950 South Gessner, Houston, TX 77063-3751. *Phone:* 713-952-2294. *Toll-free phone:* 800-235-4787. *Web site:* http://www.itt-tech.edu/.

ITT Technical Institute

Richardson, Texas

- **Proprietary** primarily 2-year, founded 1989, part of ITT Educational Services, Inc.
- **Suburban** campus
- **Coed**
- **Minimally difficult** entrance level

Academics *Calendar:* quarters. *Degrees:* associate and bachelor's.

Student Life *Housing:* college housing not available.

Financial Aid Of all full-time matriculated undergraduates who enrolled in 2009, 5 Federal Work-Study jobs (averaging $5000).

Director of Admissions Director of Recruitment, ITT Technical Institute, 2101 Waterview Parkway, Richardson, TX 75080. *Phone:* 972-690-9100. *Toll-free phone:* 888-488-5761. *Web site:* http://www.itt-tech.edu/.

ITT Technical Institute

San Antonio, Texas

- **Proprietary** primarily 2-year, founded 1988, part of ITT Educational Services, Inc.
- **Urban** campus
- **Coed**
- **Minimally difficult** entrance level

Academics *Calendar:* quarters. *Degrees:* associate and bachelor's.

Student Life *Housing:* college housing not available.

Freshman Application Contact Director of Recruitment, ITT Technical Institute, 5700 Northwest Parkway, San Antonio, TX 78249-3303. *Phone:* 210-694-4612. *Toll-free phone:* 800-880-0570. *Web site:* http://www.itt-tech.edu/.

ITT Technical Institute

Webster, Texas

- **Proprietary** primarily 2-year, founded 1995, part of ITT Educational Services, Inc.
- **Coed**
- **Minimally difficult** entrance level

Academics *Calendar:* quarters. *Degrees:* associate and bachelor's.

Student Life *Housing:* college housing not available.

Freshman Application Contact Director of Recruitment, ITT Technical Institute, 1001 Magnolia Avenue, Webster, TX 77598. *Phone:* 281-316-4700. *Toll-free phone:* 888-488-9347. *Web site:* http://www.itt-tech.edu/.

Jarvis Christian College

Hawkins, Texas

- **Independent** 4-year, founded 1912, affiliated with Christian Church (Disciples of Christ)
- **Rural** 465-acre campus
- **Endowment** $8.5 million
- **Coed** 521 undergraduate students, 98% full-time, 46% women, 54% men
- **Minimally difficult** entrance level, 84% of applicants were admitted

Undergraduates 508 full-time, 13 part-time. Students come from 18 states and territories; 3 other countries; 12% are from out of state; 93% Black or African American, non-Hispanic/Latino; 4% Hispanic/Latino; 0.6% international; 7% transferred in; 98% live on campus.

Freshmen *Admission:* 390 applied, 327 admitted, 91 enrolled. *Average high school GPA:* 2.6. *Test scores:* SAT writing scores over 500: 3%; ACT scores over 18: 14%; ACT scores over 24: 5%.

Faculty *Total:* 51, 67% full-time, 24% with terminal degrees. *Student/faculty ratio:* 10:1.

Academics *Calendar:* semesters. *Degree:* bachelor's. *Special study options:* academic remediation for entering students, advanced placement credit, cooperative education, distance learning, double majors, English as a second language, honors programs, independent study, internships, off-campus study, student-designed majors, summer session for credit. *Unusual degree programs:* 3-2 engineering with University of Texas at Arlington; nursing with University of Texas at Tyler; mass communication with University of North Texas.

Computers on Campus 100 computers/terminals and 500 ports are available on campus for general student use. Students can access the following: campus intranet, computer help desk, free student e-mail accounts, online (class) grades, online (class) registration, online (class) schedules. Campuswide network is available. 100% of college-owned or -operated housing units are wired for high-speed Internet access. Wireless service is available via classrooms, computer centers, computer labs, dorm rooms, learning centers, libraries, student centers.

Student Life *Housing options:* men-only, women-only, disabled students. Campus housing is university owned. *Activities and organizations:* choral group, Student Government Association, Students in Free Enterprise (SIFE), Student Ministers' Association, SNEA, national fraternities, national sororities. *Campus security:* 24-hour patrols, student patrols. *Student services:* health clinic, personal/psychological counseling.

Athletics Member NAIA. *Intercollegiate sports:* baseball M, basketball M/W, cheerleading W. *Intramural sports:* baseball M, basketball M/W, football M/W, golf M, soccer M, softball M/W, swimming and diving M/W, table tennis M/W, tennis M/W, volleyball M/W, water polo M/W, weight lifting M/W.

Standardized Tests *Recommended:* SAT or ACT (for admission).

Costs (2011–12) *Comprehensive fee:* $18,934 includes full-time tuition ($9892), mandatory fees ($1254), and room and board ($7788). Part-time tuition: $412 per semester hour. *Required fees:* $412 per semester hour part-time, $627 per term part-time. *College room only:* $4312. Room and board charges vary according to board plan and housing facility. *Payment plan:* installment.

Financial Aid Of all full-time matriculated undergraduates who enrolled in 2009, 535 applied for aid, 535 were judged to have need, 19 had their need fully met. 152 Federal Work-Study jobs (averaging $1475). 2 state and other part-time jobs (averaging $2745). *Average percent of need met:* 82%. *Average financial aid package:* $11,535. *Average need-based loan:* $3551. *Average need-based gift aid:* $9730. *Average indebtedness upon graduation:* $18,500.

Applying *Options:* electronic application. *Application fee:* $50. *Required:* high school transcript. *Recommended:* minimum 2 GPA. *Application deadlines:* 8/1 (freshmen), rolling (transfers). *Notification:* 8/15 (freshmen).

Freshman Application Contact Dr. Robert Harper, Admissions Counselor, Jarvis Christian College, PO Box 1470, Hawkins, TX 75765-9989. *Phone:* 903-769-5734. *Fax:* 903-769-4842. *E-mail:* rharper@jarvis.edu. *Web site:* http://www.jarvis.edu/.

Lamar University

Beaumont, Texas

- **State-supported** university, founded 1923, part of Texas State University System

- **Suburban** 200-acre campus with easy access to Houston

- **Coed** 9,463 undergraduate students, 73% full-time, 60% women, 40% men

- **Minimally difficult** entrance level, 47% of applicants were admitted

Undergraduates 6,905 full-time, 2,558 part-time. Students come from 66 other countries; 2% are from out of state; 32% Black or African American, non-Hispanic/Latino; 8% Hispanic/Latino; 3% Asian, non-Hispanic/Latino; 0.5% American Indian or Alaska Native, non-Hispanic/Latino; 3% Race/ethnicity unknown; 0.6% international; 10% transferred in. *Retention:* 65% of full-time freshmen returned.

Freshmen *Admission:* 6,139 applied, 2,899 admitted, 1,514 enrolled. *Test scores:* SAT critical reading scores over 500: 32%; SAT math scores over 500: 39%; SAT writing scores over 500: 28%; ACT scores over 18: 67%; SAT critical reading scores over 600: 8%; SAT math scores over 600: 10%; SAT writing scores over 600: 6%; ACT scores over 24: 12%; SAT critical reading scores over 700: 1%; SAT math scores over 700: 1%; SAT writing scores over 700: 1%; ACT scores over 30: 1%.

Faculty *Total:* 600, 74% full-time, 59% with terminal degrees. *Student/faculty ratio:* 23:1.

Academics *Calendar:* semesters. *Degrees:* associate, bachelor's, master's, and doctoral-other. *Special study options:* academic remediation for entering students, accelerated degree program, advanced placement credit, cooperative education, English as a second language, honors programs, internships, off-campus study, part-time degree program, services for LD students, student-designed majors, summer session for credit.

Computers on Campus 120 computers/terminals are available on campus for general student use. Campuswide network is available. Wireless service is available via entire campus.

Student Life *Housing options:* coed. *Activities and organizations:* drama/theater group, student-run newspaper, television station, choral group, national fraternities, national sororities. *Campus security:* 24-hour emergency response devices and patrols, student patrols, late-night transport/escort service. *Student services:* health clinic, personal/psychological counseling.

Athletics Member NCAA. All Division I except football (Division I-AA). *Intercollegiate sports:* baseball M(s), basketball M(s)/W(s), cheerleading M/W, cross-country running M(s)/W(s), golf M(s)/W(s), soccer W(s), tennis M(s)/W(s), track and field M(s)/W(s), volleyball W(s). *Intramural sports:* basketball M/W, cross-country running M/W, football M, golf M/W, gymnastics W, racquetball M/W, rugby M/W, sailing M/W, soccer M/W, swimming and diving M/W, table tennis M, tennis M/W, track and field M/W, volleyball M/W, weight lifting M/W.

Standardized Tests *Required:* SAT or ACT (for admission). *Required for some:* SAT Subject Tests (for admission).

Costs (2011–12) *Tuition:* state resident $4750 full-time, $158 per credit hour part-time; nonresident $14,040 full-time, $468 per credit hour part-time. Full-time tuition and fees vary according to course load. Part-time tuition and fees vary according to course load. *Required fees:* $2184 full-time. *Room and board:* $7010; room only: $4500. Room and board charges vary according to board plan. *Payment plan:* installment. *Waivers:* senior citizens and employees or children of employees.

Financial Aid Of all full-time matriculated undergraduates who enrolled in 2009, 4,827 applied for aid, 3,321 were judged to have need. 182 Federal Work-Study jobs (averaging $3159). 62 state and other part-time jobs (averaging $1228). *Average percent of need met:* 64%. *Average financial aid package:* $4618. *Average need-based loan:* $2107. *Average need-based gift aid:* $2134. *Average indebtedness upon graduation:* $8234.

Applying *Options:* electronic application, early admission. *Required:* high school transcript. *Required for some:* essay or personal statement. *Application deadlines:* 8/1 (freshmen), 8/1 (transfers). *Notification:* continuous (freshmen).

Freshman Application Contact Ms. Melissa Chesser, Director of Recruitment, Lamar University, PO Box 10009, Beaumont, TX 77710. *Phone:* 409-880-8888. *Fax:* 409-880-8463. *E-mail:* admissions@lamar.edu. *Web site:* http://www.lamar.edu/.

LeTourneau University

Longview, Texas

- **Independent nondenominational** comprehensive, founded 1946

- **Suburban** 162-acre campus

- **Coed** 2,844 undergraduate students, 96% full-time, 54% women, 46% men

- **Moderately difficult** entrance level, 54% of applicants were admitted

Undergraduates 2,733 full-time, 111 part-time. 51% are from out of state; 18% Black or African American, non-Hispanic/Latino; 8% Hispanic/Latino; 0.8% Asian, non-Hispanic/Latino; 0.3% American Indian or Alaska Native, non-Hispanic/Latino; 0.7% Two or more races, non-Hispanic/Latino; 3% Race/ethnicity unknown; 2% international; 4% transferred in; 75% live on campus. *Retention:* 78% of full-time freshmen returned.

Freshmen *Admission:* 1,976 applied, 1,061 admitted, 444 enrolled. *Average high school GPA:* 3.56. *Test scores:* SAT critical reading scores over 500: 74%; SAT math scores over 500: 87%; SAT writing scores over 500: 65%; ACT scores over 18: 97%; SAT critical reading scores over 600: 41%; SAT math scores over 600: 50%; SAT writing scores over 600: 31%; ACT scores over 24: 62%; SAT critical reading scores over 700: 13%; SAT math scores over 700: 12%; SAT writing scores over 700: 7%; ACT scores over 30: 19%.

Academics *Calendar:* semesters. *Degrees:* associate, bachelor's, and master's. *Special study options:* academic remediation for entering students, accelerated degree program, adult/continuing education programs, advanced placement credit, cooperative education, distance learning, double majors, honors programs, independent study, internships, off-campus study, part-time degree program, services for LD students, study abroad, summer session for credit.

Computers on Campus Students can access the following: campus intranet, computer help desk, free student e-mail accounts, online (class) grades, online (class) registration, online (class) schedules. Campuswide network is available. 100% of college-owned or -operated housing units are wired for high-speed Internet access. Wireless service is available via classrooms, computer centers, computer labs, dorm rooms, learning centers, libraries, student centers.

Student Life *Housing:* on-campus residence required through junior year. *Options:* men-only, women-only, disabled students. Campus housing is university owned. Freshman campus housing is guaranteed. *Activities and organizations:* drama/theater group, student-run newspaper, choral group. *Campus security:* 24-hour emergency response devices and patrols, late-night transport/escort service, controlled dormitory access, University police department. *Student services:* health clinic, personal/psychological counseling.

Athletics Member NCAA, NCCAA. All NCAA Division III. *Intercollegiate sports:* baseball M, basketball M/W, cross-country running M/W, golf M/W, soccer M/W, softball W, tennis M/W, volleyball W. *Intramural sports:* badminton M/W, basketball M/W, bowling M/W, cross-country running M/W, football M/W, golf M/W, racquetball M/W, soccer M/W, softball M/W, swimming and diving M/W, table tennis M/W, tennis M/W, volleyball M/W.

Standardized Tests *Required:* SAT or ACT (for admission).

Costs (2010–11) *Comprehensive fee:* $30,370 includes full-time tuition ($21,510), mandatory fees ($470), and room and board ($8390). Part-time tuition: $858 per credit hour. Part-time tuition and fees vary according to course load. *Room and board:* Room and board charges vary according to board plan. *Payment plan:* installment. *Waivers:* employees or children of employees.

Financial Aid Of all full-time matriculated undergraduates who enrolled in 2009, 1,266 applied for aid, 1,113 were judged to have need, 103 had their need fully met. In 2009, 177 non-need-based awards were made. *Average percent of need met:* 58%. *Average financial aid package:* $15,500. *Average need-based loan:* $4215. *Average need-based gift aid:* $11,558. *Average non-need-based aid:* $6697.

Applying *Options:* electronic application, deferred entrance. *Application fee:* $35. *Application deadlines:* rolling (freshmen), rolling (transfers). *Notification:* continuous (freshmen), continuous (transfers).

Freshman Application Contact Mr. James Townsend, Director of Admissions, LeTourneau University, PO Box 7001, Longview, TX 75607-7001. *Phone:* 903-233-3400. *Toll-free phone:* 800-759-8811. *Fax:* 903-233-3411. *E-mail:* admissions@letu.edu. *Web site:* http://www.letu.edu/.

Lubbock Christian University

Lubbock, Texas

- **Independent** comprehensive, founded 1957, affiliated with Church of Christ
- **Suburban** 120-acre campus
- **Endowment** $11.3 million
- **Coed** 1,629 undergraduate students, 84% full-time, 57% women, 43% men
- **Moderately difficult** entrance level, 60% of applicants were admitted

Undergraduates 1,364 full-time, 265 part-time. Students come from 36 states and territories; 18 other countries; 10% are from out of state; 7% Black or African American, non-Hispanic/Latino; 18% Hispanic/Latino; 0.4% Asian, non-Hispanic/Latino; 0.2% Native Hawaiian or other Pacific Islander, non-Hispanic/Latino; 0.6% American Indian or Alaska Native, non-Hispanic/Latino; 2% international; 15% transferred in; 34% live on campus. *Retention:* 61% of full-time freshmen returned.

Freshmen *Admission:* 1,542 applied, 925 admitted, 343 enrolled. *Average high school GPA:* 3.43. *Test scores:* SAT critical reading scores over 500: 38%; SAT math scores over 500: 46%; SAT writing scores over 500: 30%; ACT scores over 18: 85%; SAT critical reading scores over 600: 9%; SAT math scores over 600: 13%; SAT writing scores over 600: 7%; ACT scores over 24: 28%; SAT writing scores over 700: 1%; ACT scores over 30: 4%.

Faculty *Total:* 159, 49% full-time, 54% with terminal degrees. *Student/faculty ratio:* 15:1.

Academics *Calendar:* semesters. *Degrees:* associate, bachelor's, and master's. *Special study options:* academic remediation for entering students, adult/continuing education programs, advanced placement credit, distance learning, double majors, English as a second language, honors programs, internships, part-time degree program, services for LD students, student-designed majors, study abroad, summer session for credit. *ROTC:* Army (c), Air Force (c). *Unusual degree programs:* 3-2 engineering with Texas Tech University.

Computers on Campus 159 computers/terminals are available on campus for general student use. Students can access the following: campus intranet, computer help desk, free student e-mail accounts, online (class) grades, online (class) registration, online (class) schedules. Campuswide network is available. 100% of college-owned or -operated housing units are wired for high-speed Internet access. Wireless service is available via entire campus.

Student Life *Housing:* on-campus residence required through sophomore year. *Options:* men-only, women-only, disabled students. Campus housing is university owned. Freshman campus housing is guaranteed. *Activities and organizations:* drama/theater group, student-run newspaper, choral group. *Campus security:* 24-hour patrols. *Student services:* health clinic, personal/psychological counseling.

Athletics Member NAIA. *Intercollegiate sports:* baseball M(s), basketball M(s)/W(s), cheerleading M(s)/W(s), cross-country running M(s)/W(s), golf M(s)/W(s), soccer M(s)/W(s), softball W(s), track and field M/W, volleyball W(s). *Intramural sports:* badminton M/W, basketball M/W, bowling M/W, cross-country running M/W, football M/W, golf M/W, racquetball M/W, rock climbing M/W, soccer M/W, softball M/W, table tennis M/W, tennis M/W, track and field M/W, volleyball M/W.

Standardized Tests *Required:* SAT or ACT (for admission).

Costs (2010–11) *Comprehensive fee:* $22,548 includes full-time tuition ($14,900), mandatory fees ($1280), and room and board ($6368). Full-time tuition and fees vary according to degree level and program. Part-time tuition: $480 per semester hour. Part-time tuition and fees vary according to course load, degree level, and program. *Required fees:* $495 per term part-time. *Room and board:* Room and board charges vary according to board plan and housing facility. *Payment plan:* installment. *Waivers:* employees or children of employees.

Financial Aid Of all full-time matriculated undergraduates who enrolled in 2009, 1,149 applied for aid, 1,013 were judged to have need, 65 had their need fully met. 849 Federal Work-Study jobs (averaging $1763). 89 state and other part-time jobs (averaging $257). In 2009, 169 non-need-based awards were made. *Average percent of need met:* 65%. *Average financial aid package:* $13,401. *Average need-based loan:* $4211. *Average need-based gift aid:* $9021. *Average non-need-based aid:* $4220. *Average indebtedness upon graduation:* $26,440.

Applying *Options:* electronic application. *Application fee:* $25. *Required:* high school transcript. *Application deadlines:* 8/1 (freshmen), rolling (transfers). *Notification:* continuous (freshmen), continuous (transfers).

Freshman Application Contact Mr. Charles Webb, Director of Admissions, Lubbock Christian University, 5601 19th Street, Lubbock, TX 79407. *Phone:* 806-720-7156. *Toll-free phone:* 800-933-7601. *Fax:* 806-720-7162. *E-mail:* admissions@lcu.edu. *Web site:* http://www.lcu.edu/.

McMurry University

Abilene, Texas

- **Independent United Methodist** 4-year, founded 1923
- **Suburban** 43-acre campus with easy access to Fort Worth and Austin
- **Endowment** $54.4 million
- **Coed** 1,414 undergraduate students, 83% full-time, 48% women, 52% men
- **Moderately difficult** entrance level, 54% of applicants were admitted

Undergraduates 1,177 full-time, 237 part-time. Students come from 23 states and territories; 3 other countries; 4% are from out of state; 15% Black or African American, non-Hispanic/Latino; 19% Hispanic/Latino; 0.3% Asian, non-Hispanic/Latino; 0.1% Native Hawaiian or other Pacific Islander, non-Hispanic/Latino; 0.6% American Indian or Alaska Native, non-Hispanic/Latino; 3% Two or more races, non-Hispanic/Latino; 1% Race/ethnicity unknown; 0.4% international; 11% transferred in; 46% live on campus. *Retention:* 53% of full-time freshmen returned.

Freshmen *Admission:* 1,423 applied, 772 admitted, 280 enrolled. *Average high school GPA:* 3.39. *Test scores:* SAT critical reading scores over 500: 32%; SAT math scores over 500: 40%; ACT scores over 18: 79%; SAT critical reading scores over 600: 7%; SAT math scores over 600: 13%; ACT scores over 24: 22%; SAT critical reading scores over 700: 2%; SAT math scores over 700: 2%; ACT scores over 30: 2%.

Faculty *Total:* 143, 55% full-time, 51% with terminal degrees. *Student/faculty ratio:* 13:1.

Academics *Calendar:* semesters plus May term. *Degree:* bachelor's. *Special study options:* academic remediation for entering students, accelerated degree program, adult/continuing education programs, advanced placement credit, double majors, honors programs, independent study, internships, part-time degree program, services for LD students, student-designed majors, study abroad, summer session for credit. *Unusual degree programs:* 3-2 dentistry at University of Texas Health Science Center at San Antonio-San Antonio School of Dentistry.

Computers on Campus 130 computers/terminals and 705 ports are available on campus for general student use. Students can access the following: campus intranet, computer help desk, free student e-mail accounts, online (class) grades, online (class) registration, online (class) schedules, Moodle. Campuswide network is available. 100% of college-owned or -operated housing units are wired for high-speed Internet access. Wireless service is available via entire campus.

Student Life *Housing:* on-campus residence required through junior year. *Options:* coed, men-only, women-only. Campus housing is university owned and is provided by a third party. Freshman campus housing is guaranteed. *Activities and organizations:* drama/theater group, student-run newspaper, choral group, marching band, Alpha Phi Omega, Religious Life Council, McMurry Student Government, Campus Activity Board, Servant Leadership. *Campus security:* 24-hour emergency response devices and patrols, late-night transport/escort service, controlled dormitory access. *Student services:* health clinic, personal/psychological counseling.

Athletics Member NCAA. All Division III. *Intercollegiate sports:* baseball M, basketball M/W, cross-country running M/W, football M, golf M/W, soccer M/W, swimming and diving M/W, tennis M/W, track and field M/W, volleyball W. *Intramural sports:* basketball M/W, football M/W, golf M/W, racquetball M/W, soccer M/W, softball M/W, tennis M/W, ultimate Frisbee M/W, volleyball M/W.

Standardized Tests *Required:* SAT or ACT (for admission).

Costs (2010–11) *One-time required fee:* $150. *Comprehensive fee:* $27,656 includes full-time tuition ($19,820), mandatory fees ($860), and room and board ($6976). Full-time tuition and fees vary according to course load. Part-time tuition: $620 per semester hour. Part-time tuition and fees vary according to course load. *College room only:* $3360. Room and board charges vary according to board plan and housing facility. *Payment plan:* installment. *Waivers:* employees or children of employees.

Financial Aid Of all full-time matriculated undergraduates who enrolled in 2009, 1,088 applied for aid, 1,022 were judged to have need, 129 had their need fully met. 298 Federal Work-Study jobs (averaging $2129). 59 state and other part-time jobs (averaging $2424). In 2009, 67 non-need-based awards were made. *Average percent of need met:* 80%. *Average financial aid package:* $17,698. *Average need-based loan:* $4428. *Average need-based gift aid:* $9903. *Average non-need-based aid:* $5864. *Average indebtedness upon graduation:* $33,212.

Applying *Options:* electronic application, deferred entrance. *Application fee:* $25. *Required:* essay or personal statement, high school transcript, minimum 2 GPA. *Required for some:* 3 letters of recommendation, interview. *Application deadlines:* 8/15 (freshmen), 8/5 (out-of-state freshmen), 8/15 (transfers). *Notification:* continuous (freshmen), continuous (out-of-state freshmen), continuous (transfers).

Freshman Application Contact McMurry University, McMurry Station 278, Abilene, TX 79697. *Phone:* 325-793-4700. *Toll-free phone:* 800-477-0077.

Fax: 325-793-4701. *E-mail:* admissions@mcm.edu. *Web site:* http://www.mcm.edu/.

Midland College
Midland, Texas

- **State and locally supported** 4-year, founded 1969
- **Suburban** 163-acre campus
- **Coed**
- **Noncompetitive** entrance level

Faculty *Student/faculty ratio:* 18:1.
Academics *Calendar:* semesters. *Degrees:* certificates, associate, and bachelor's.
Student Life *Campus security:* 24-hour patrols.
Athletics Member NJCAA.
Costs (2010–11) *Tuition:* area resident $1890 full-time, $105 per credit hour part-time; state resident $2610 full-time, $129 per credit hour part-time; nonresident $3600 full-time, $162 per credit hour part-time. Full-time tuition and fees vary according to course load, program, and reciprocity agreements. Part-time tuition and fees vary according to course load. *Required fees:* $400 full-time. *Room and board:* $3900. *Payment plans:* installment, deferred payment.
Financial Aid *Of all full-time matriculated undergraduates who enrolled in 2008,* 75 Federal Work-Study jobs (averaging $2700). 5 state and other part-time jobs (averaging $2700).
Applying *Required:* high school transcript.
Freshman Application Contact Mr. Ryan Gibbs, Director of Admissions, Midland College, 3600 North Garfield, Midland, TX 79705-6399. *Phone:* 432-685-5502. *Fax:* 432-685-6401. *E-mail:* rgibbs@midland.edu. *Web site:* http://www.midland.edu/.

Midwestern State University
Wichita Falls, Texas

- **State-supported** comprehensive, founded 1922
- **Urban** 255-acre campus
- **Endowment** $14.9 million
- **Coed** 5,712 undergraduate students, 75% full-time, 57% women, 43% men
- **Moderately difficult** entrance level, 64% of applicants were admitted

Undergraduates 4,287 full-time, 1,425 part-time. Students come from 26 states and territories; 51 other countries; 8% are from out of state; 13% Black or African American, non-Hispanic/Latino; 9% Hispanic/Latino; 3% Asian, non-Hispanic/Latino; 0.2% Native Hawaiian or other Pacific Islander, non-Hispanic/Latino; 1% American Indian or Alaska Native, non-Hispanic/Latino; 1% Two or more races, non-Hispanic/Latino; 2% Race/ethnicity unknown; 7% international; 11% transferred in; 23% live on campus. *Retention:* 71% of full-time freshmen returned.
Freshmen *Admission:* 2,531 applied, 1,609 admitted, 756 enrolled. *Average high school GPA:* 3.45. *Test scores:* SAT critical reading scores over 500: 47%; SAT math scores over 500: 57%; SAT writing scores over 500: 38%; ACT scores over 18: 91%; SAT critical reading scores over 600: 9%; SAT math scores over 600: 14%; SAT writing scores over 600: 7%; ACT scores over 24: 24%; SAT critical reading scores over 700: 1%; SAT math scores over 700: 1%; ACT scores over 30: 1%.
Faculty *Total:* 332, 66% full-time, 59% with terminal degrees. *Student/faculty ratio:* 19:1.
Academics *Calendar:* semesters. *Degrees:* associate, bachelor's, master's, and postbachelor's certificates. *Special study options:* academic remediation for entering students, adult/continuing education programs, advanced placement credit, distance learning, double majors, English as a second language, honors programs, independent study, internships, part-time degree program, services for LD students, study abroad, summer session for credit. *ROTC:* Air Force (c). *Unusual degree programs:* 3-2 business administration.
Computers on Campus 405 computers/terminals are available on campus for general student use. Students can access the following: campus intranet, computer help desk, free student e-mail accounts, online (class) grades, online (class) registration, online (class) schedules. Campuswide network is available. 100% of college-owned or -operated housing units are wired for high-speed Internet access. Wireless service is available via entire campus.
Student Life *Housing:* on-campus residence required through sophomore year. *Options:* coed, men-only, women-only, disabled students. Campus housing is university owned. Freshman applicants given priority for college housing. *Activities and organizations:* drama/theater group, student-run newspaper, television station, choral group, marching band, Caribbean Students Organization, Baptist Student Ministry, Catholic Campus Ministry, African Students Organization, University Programming Board, national fraternities, national sororities. *Campus security:* 24-hour emergency response devices and patrols, controlled dormitory access. *Student services:* health clinic, personal/psychological counseling, legal services.

Athletics Member NCAA. All Division II. *Intercollegiate sports:* basketball M(s)/W(s), cheerleading M(s)(c)/W(s)(c), cross-country running W(s), fencing M(c)/W(c), football M(s), golf M(s)/W(s), soccer M(s)/W(s), softball W(s), tennis M(s)/W(s), volleyball W(s). *Intramural sports:* archery M/W, badminton M/W, basketball M/W, bowling M/W, football M/W, golf M/W, rugby M(c), soccer M/W, softball M/W, table tennis M/W, tennis M/W, ultimate Frisbee M/W, volleyball M/W, weight lifting M/W.
Standardized Tests *Required:* SAT or ACT (for admission).
Costs (2010–11) *Tuition:* state resident $1500 full-time, $50 per credit hour part-time; nonresident $2400 full-time, $80 per credit hour part-time. Full-time tuition and fees vary according to course load, location, and program. Part-time tuition and fees vary according to course load, location, and program. *Required fees:* $5220 full-time, $163 per credit hour part-time, $179 per term part-time. *Room and board:* $5940; room only: $3100. Room and board charges vary according to board plan and housing facility. *Payment plan:* installment. *Waivers:* senior citizens and employees or children of employees.
Financial Aid Of all full-time matriculated undergraduates who enrolled in 2009, 2,994 applied for aid, 2,353 were judged to have need, 425 had their need fully met. 59 Federal Work-Study jobs (averaging $4055). In 2009, 513 non-need-based awards were made. *Average percent of need met:* 69%. *Average financial aid package:* $8992. *Average need-based loan:* $6967. *Average need-based gift aid:* $6250. *Average non-need-based aid:* $1722. *Average indebtedness upon graduation:* $16,620.
Applying *Options:* electronic application, early action. *Application fee:* $25. *Required:* essay or personal statement, high school transcript. *Application deadlines:* 8/7 (freshmen), 8/7 (transfers). *Notification:* continuous (freshmen), continuous (transfers).
Freshman Application Contact Ms. Barbara Merkle, Director of Admissions, Midwestern State University, Wichita Falls, TX 76308. *Phone:* 940-397-4334. *Toll-free phone:* 800-842-1922. *Fax:* 940-397-4672. *E-mail:* admissions@mwsu.edu. *Web site:* http://www.mwsu.edu/.

Northwood University, Texas Campus
Cedar Hill, Texas

Freshman Application Contact Ms. Sylvia Correa, Director of Admissions, Northwood University, Texas Campus, 1114 West FM 1382, Cedar Hill, TX 75104. *Phone:* 972-293-5400. *Toll-free phone:* 800-927-9663. *Fax:* 972-291-3824. *E-mail:* txadmit@northwood.edu. *Web site:* http://www.northwood.edu/.

Our Lady of the Lake University of San Antonio
San Antonio, Texas

- **Independent Roman Catholic** comprehensive, founded 1895
- **Urban** 75-acre campus
- **Coed** 1,588 undergraduate students, 80% full-time, 74% women, 26% men
- **Moderately difficult** entrance level, 48% of applicants were admitted

Undergraduates 1,278 full-time, 310 part-time. 2% are from out of state; 8% Black or African American, non-Hispanic/Latino; 63% Hispanic/Latino; 0.7% Asian, non-Hispanic/Latino; 0.4% Native Hawaiian or other Pacific Islander, non-Hispanic/Latino; 1% American Indian or Alaska Native, non-Hispanic/Latino; 1% Two or more races, non-Hispanic/Latino; 8% Race/ethnicity unknown; 1% international; 12% transferred in. *Retention:* 60% of full-time freshmen returned.
Freshmen *Admission:* 2,129 applied, 1,024 admitted, 300 enrolled. *Average high school GPA:* 3.3. *Test scores:* SAT critical reading scores over 500: 26%; SAT math scores over 500: 39%; ACT scores over 18: 59%; SAT critical reading scores over 600: 6%; SAT math scores over 600: 8%; ACT scores over 24: 15%; SAT critical reading scores over 700: 2%; SAT math scores over 700: 1%; ACT scores over 30: 1%.
Faculty *Total:* 249, 41% full-time. *Student/faculty ratio:* 15:1.
Academics *Calendar:* semesters plus 2 summer sessions. *Degrees:* bachelor's, master's, doctoral-professional, doctoral-research/scholarship, post-master's, and postbachelor's certificates. *Special study options:* academic remediation for entering students, accelerated degree program, adult/continuing education programs, advanced placement credit, cooperative education, distance learning, double majors, honors programs, independent study, internships, off-campus study, part-time degree program, services for LD students, study abroad, summer session for credit. *ROTC:* Army (c), Air Force (c). *Unusual degree programs:* 3-2 engineering with Washington University in St. Louis.
Computers on Campus 230 computers/terminals are available on campus for general student use. Students can access the following: computer help desk, free student e-mail accounts, online (class) registration. Campuswide network is available. 100% of college-owned or -operated housing units are wired for high-speed Internet access. Wireless service is available via entire campus.

Student Life *Housing options:* coed, men-only, women-only. Campus housing is university owned. *Activities and organizations:* drama/theater group, student-run newspaper, television station, choral group, Student Government Association, Leadership Institute for Freshman Excellence, Health Occupations Student of America, Epsilon Sigma Alpha Service Sorority, University Programming Council. *Campus security:* 24-hour emergency response devices and patrols, late-night transport/escort service, controlled dormitory access. *Student services:* health clinic, personal/psychological counseling, women's center.

Athletics Member NAIA. *Intercollegiate sports:* baseball M, basketball M(s)/W(s), cross-country running M(s)/W(s), golf M(s), soccer M(s)/W(s), softball W(s), tennis M(s)/W(s), volleyball W(s). *Intramural sports:* cheerleading M/W, football M/W, volleyball M.

Standardized Tests *Required:* SAT or ACT (for admission).

Costs (2010–11) *Comprehensive fee:* $28,738 includes full-time tuition ($21,400), mandatory fees ($500), and room and board ($6838). Full-time tuition and fees vary according to degree level and location. Part-time tuition: $690 per credit hour. Part-time tuition and fees vary according to degree level and location. *Required fees:* $12 per credit hour part-time, $58 per term part-time. *College room only:* $3988. Room and board charges vary according to board plan. *Payment plans:* installment, deferred payment. *Waivers:* employees or children of employees.

Financial Aid Of all full-time matriculated undergraduates who enrolled in 2009, 1,169 applied for aid, 1,120 were judged to have need, 230 had their need fully met. In 2009, 4 non-need-based awards were made. *Average percent of need met:* 82%. *Average financial aid package:* $24,580. *Average need-based loan:* $4382. *Average need-based gift aid:* $16,288. *Average non-need-based aid:* $11,762. *Average indebtedness upon graduation:* $32,356.

Applying *Options:* electronic application, deferred entrance. *Application fee:* $25. *Required:* high school transcript. *Required for some:* interview. *Application deadlines:* rolling (freshmen), rolling (transfers). *Notification:* continuous (freshmen), continuous (transfers).

Freshman Application Contact Gilberto Becerra, Assistant Director of Undergraduate Admissions, Our Lady of the Lake University of San Antonio, 411 Southwest 24th Street, San Antonio, TX 78207-4689. *Phone:* 210-434-6711 Ext. 4129. *Toll-free phone:* 800-436-6558. *Fax:* 210-431-4036. *E-mail:* admission@lake.ollusa.edu. *Web site:* http://www.ollusa.edu/.

Paul Quinn College
Dallas, Texas

Director of Admissions Ms. Nena Taylor-Richey, Director of Admissions and Recruitment, Paul Quinn College, 3837 Simpson-Stuart Road, Dallas, TX 75241-4331. *Phone:* 214-302-3575. *Toll-free phone:* 800-237-2648. *Web site:* http://www.pqc.edu/.

Prairie View A&M University
Prairie View, Texas

- **State-supported** university, founded 1878, part of Texas A&M University System
- **Small-town** 1502-acre campus with easy access to Houston
- **Endowment** $51.8 million
- **Coed** 6,973 undergraduate students, 92% full-time, 58% women, 42% men
- **Moderately difficult** entrance level

Undergraduates 6,417 full-time, 556 part-time. Students come from 39 states and territories; 36 other countries; 7% are from out of state; 88% Black or African American, non-Hispanic/Latino; 5% Hispanic/Latino; 2% Asian, non-Hispanic/Latino; 0.2% American Indian or Alaska Native, non-Hispanic/Latino; 0.7% Race/ethnicity unknown; 1% international; 5% transferred in; 68% live on campus. *Retention:* 71% of full-time freshmen returned.

Freshmen *Admission:* 7,904 applied, 1,730 enrolled. *Average high school GPA:* 2.9. *Test scores:* SAT critical reading scores over 500: 11%; SAT math scores over 500: 15%; SAT writing scores over 500: 10%; ACT scores over 18: 38%; SAT critical reading scores over 600: 1%; SAT math scores over 600: 2%; ACT scores over 24: 4%.

Faculty *Total:* 501, 79% full-time, 62% with terminal degrees. *Student/faculty ratio:* 17:1.

Academics *Calendar:* semesters. *Degrees:* bachelor's, master's, and doctoral-professional. *Special study options:* academic remediation for entering students, accelerated degree program, advanced placement credit, cooperative education, distance learning, double majors, English as a second language, honors programs, independent study, internships, off-campus study, part-time degree program, services for LD students, study abroad, summer session for credit. *ROTC:* Army (b), Navy (b).

Computers on Campus 4,400 computers/terminals and 4,400 ports are available on campus for general student use. Students can access the following: campus intranet, computer help desk, free student e-mail accounts, online

(class) grades, online (class) registration, online (class) schedules. Campuswide network is available. 100% of college-owned or -operated housing units are wired for high-speed Internet access. Wireless service is available via entire campus.

Student Life *Housing:* on-campus residence required for freshman year. *Options:* coed, men-only, women-only. Campus housing is provided by a third party. Freshman campus housing is guaranteed. *Activities and organizations:* drama/theater group, student-run newspaper, radio station, choral group, marching band, National Society of Black Engineers, National Association of Black Accountants, National Organization of Black Chemists and Chemical Engineers, Toastmasters International, Baptist Student Movement, national fraternities, national sororities. *Campus security:* 24-hour emergency response devices and patrols, late-night transport/escort service, controlled dormitory access. *Student services:* health clinic, personal/psychological counseling.

Athletics Member NCAA, NAIA. All NCAA Division I except football (Division I-AA). *Intercollegiate sports:* baseball M(s), basketball M(s)/W(s), cross-country running M(s)/W(s), golf M(s)/W(s), soccer W(s), softball W(s), tennis M(s)/W(s), track and field M(s)/W(s), volleyball W(s). *Intramural sports:* baseball M, basketball M/W, bowling W, cross-country running M/W, golf M/W, soccer W, softball W, tennis M/W, track and field M/W, volleyball M/W.

Standardized Tests *Required:* SAT or ACT (for admission).

Costs (2011–12) *Tuition:* state resident $5076 full-time, $169 per credit hour part-time; nonresident $14,376 full-time, $479 per credit hour part-time. Full-time tuition and fees vary according to course load and program. Part-time tuition and fees vary according to course load and program. *Required fees:* $1779 full-time. *Room and board:* $7064; room only: $4752. Room and board charges vary according to board plan, housing facility, and student level. *Payment plan:* installment. *Waivers:* senior citizens.

Financial Aid Of all full-time matriculated undergraduates who enrolled in 2002, 4,622 applied for aid, 4,311 were judged to have need. 732 Federal Work-Study jobs (averaging $1934). 328 state and other part-time jobs (averaging $1146). In 2002, 271 non-need-based awards were made. *Average percent of need met:* 75%. *Average financial aid package:* $6920. *Average need-based loan:* $4000. *Average need-based gift aid:* $3300. *Average non-need-based aid:* $1400. *Average indebtedness upon graduation:* $11,000.

Applying *Options:* electronic application, deferred entrance. *Application fee:* $25. *Required:* high school transcript, minimum 2.5 GPA. *Application deadlines:* 6/1 (freshmen), 6/1 (transfers). *Notification:* continuous (freshmen), continuous (transfers).

Freshman Application Contact Ms. Mary Gooch, Director of Admissions, Prairie View A&M University, PO Box 519, MS #1009, Prairie View, TX 77446-0188. *Phone:* 936-261-1066. *E-mail:* megooch@pvamu.edu. *Web site:* http://www.pvamu.edu/.

Rice University
Houston, Texas

- **Independent** university, founded 1912
- **Urban** 300-acre campus with easy access to Houston
- **Endowment** $3.8 billion
- **Coed** 3,529 undergraduate students, 98% full-time, 48% women, 52% men
- **Most difficult** entrance level, 21% of applicants were admitted

Undergraduates 3,475 full-time, 54 part-time. Students come from 52 states and territories; 47 other countries; 44% are from out of state; 7% Black or African American, non-Hispanic/Latino; 11% Hispanic/Latino; 21% Asian, non-Hispanic/Latino; 0.4% American Indian or Alaska Native, non-Hispanic/Latino; 7% Race/ethnicity unknown; 10% international; 2% transferred in; 77% live on campus. *Retention:* 95% of full-time freshmen returned.

Freshmen *Admission:* 12,393 applied, 2,639 admitted, 949 enrolled. *Test scores:* SAT critical reading scores over 500: 98%; SAT math scores over 500: 99%; SAT writing scores over 500: 98%; ACT scores over 18: 100%; SAT critical reading scores over 600: 92%; SAT math scores over 600: 96%; SAT writing scores over 600: 92%; ACT scores over 24: 97%; SAT critical reading scores over 700: 55%; SAT math scores over 700: 72%; SAT writing scores over 700: 58%; ACT scores over 30: 82%.

Faculty *Total:* 752, 83% full-time, 93% with terminal degrees. *Student/faculty ratio:* 6:1.

Academics *Calendar:* semesters. *Degrees:* bachelor's, master's, and doctoral-research/scholarship. *Special study options:* accelerated degree program, advanced placement credit, double majors, English as a second language, honors programs, independent study, internships, off-campus study, services for LD students, student-designed majors, study abroad, summer session for credit. *ROTC:* Army (c), Navy (b), Air Force (c).

Computers on Campus 543 computers/terminals are available on campus for general student use. Students can access the following: campus intranet, computer help desk, free student e-mail accounts, online (class) grades, online (class) registration. Campuswide network is available. Wireless service is available via entire campus.

Student Life *Housing options:* coed. Campus housing is university owned. Freshman campus housing is guaranteed. *Activities and organizations:* drama/theater group, student-run newspaper, radio and television station, choral group, marching band, Drama Club, volunteer program, intramural sports, college government, Marching Owl Band. *Campus security:* 24-hour emergency response devices and patrols, late-night transport/escort service, controlled dormitory access. *Student services:* health clinic, personal/psychological counseling, women's center.

Athletics Member NCAA. All Division I except football (Division I-A). *Intercollegiate sports:* badminton M(c)/W(c), baseball M(s), basketball M(s)/W(s), cheerleading M(c)/W(c), crew M(c)/W(c), cross-country running M(s)/W(s), equestrian sports M(c)/W(c), fencing M(c)/W(c), field hockey W(c), golf M(s), lacrosse M(c)/W(c), riflery M(c)/W(c), rugby M(c)/W(c), sailing M(c)/W(c), soccer M(c)/W(s), softball W(s), swimming and diving W(s), tennis M(s)/W(s), track and field M(s)/W(s), ultimate Frisbee M(c)/W(c), volleyball M(c)/W(s), water polo M(c)/W(c). *Intramural sports:* badminton M/W, basketball M/W, cross-country running M/W, football M/W, racquetball M/W, soccer M/W, softball M/W, swimming and diving M/W, table tennis M/W, tennis M/W, track and field M/W, ultimate Frisbee M/W, volleyball M/W.

Standardized Tests *Required:* SAT and SAT Subject Tests or ACT (for admission).

Costs (2011–12) *Comprehensive fee:* $47,821 includes full-time tuition ($34,900), mandatory fees ($651), and room and board ($12,270). Full-time tuition and fees vary according to student level. Part-time tuition and fees vary according to course load. *College room only:* $8270. Room and board charges vary according to board plan. *Payment plan:* installment. *Waivers:* employees or children of employees.

Financial Aid Of all full-time matriculated undergraduates who enrolled in 2009, 2,343 applied for aid, 1,391 were judged to have need, 1,391 had their need fully met. In 2009, 701 non-need-based awards were made. *Average percent of need met:* 100%. *Average financial aid package:* $29,739. *Average need-based loan:* $1404. *Average need-based gift aid:* $27,671. *Average non-need-based aid:* $14,772. *Average indebtedness upon graduation:* $13,944.

Applying *Options:* electronic application, early decision, deferred entrance. *Application fee:* $70. *Required:* essay or personal statement, high school transcript, 2 letters of recommendation. *Required for some:* portfolio for architecture; audition for music. *Recommended:* interview. *Application deadlines:* 1/1 (freshmen), 3/15 (transfers). *Early decision deadline:* 11/1 (freshmen), 5/15 (transfers), 12/15 (early decision).

Freshman Application Contact Office of Admission, Rice University, Office of Admission, PO Box 1892, MS 17, Houston, TX 77251-1892. *Phone:* 713-348-RICE. *Toll-free phone:* 800-527-OWLS. *E-mail:* admi@rice.edu. *Web site:* http://www.rice.edu/.

Rio Grande Bible Institute

Edinburg, Texas

Director of Admissions David Loyola, Director of Admissions, Rio Grande Bible Institute, 4300 S US Hwy 281, Edinburg, TX 78539. *Phone:* 956-380-8100. *Fax:* 956-380-8256. *E-mail:* admisiones@riogrande.edu. *Web site:* http://www.riogrande.edu/.

St. Edward's University

Austin, Texas

- **Independent Roman Catholic** comprehensive, founded 1885
- **Urban** 160-acre campus
- **Endowment** $49.9 million
- **Coed** 4,476 undergraduate students, 79% full-time, 60% women, 40% men
- **Moderately difficult** entrance level, 63% of applicants were admitted

Undergraduates 3,526 full-time, 950 part-time. Students come from 44 states and territories; 35 other countries; 7% are from out of state; 4% Black or African American, non-Hispanic/Latino; 31% Hispanic/Latino; 2% Asian, non-Hispanic/Latino; 0.1% Native Hawaiian or other Pacific Islander, non-Hispanic/Latino; 0.8% American Indian or Alaska Native, non-Hispanic/Latino; 2% Two or more races, non-Hispanic/Latino; 3% Race/ethnicity unknown; 3% international; 5% transferred in; 38% live on campus. *Retention:* 83% of full-time freshmen returned.

Freshmen *Admission:* 3,759 applied, 2,362 admitted, 780 enrolled. *Test scores:* SAT critical reading scores over 500: 86%; SAT math scores over 500: 80%; SAT writing scores over 500: 77%; ACT scores over 18: 100%; SAT critical reading scores over 600: 36%; SAT math scores over 600: 29%; SAT writing scores over 600: 26%; ACT scores over 24: 58%; SAT critical reading scores over 700: 4%; SAT math scores over 700: 2%; SAT writing scores over 700: 3%; ACT scores over 30: 9%.

Faculty *Total:* 497, 40% full-time, 67% with terminal degrees. *Student/faculty ratio:* 15:1.

Academics *Calendar:* semesters. *Degrees:* bachelor's, master's, and post-bachelor's certificates. *Special study options:* academic remediation for entering students, adult/continuing education programs, advanced placement credit, double majors, honors programs, independent study, internships, part-time degree program, services for LD students, study abroad, summer session for credit. *ROTC:* Army (c), Air Force (c).

Computers on Campus 790 computers/terminals and 7,200 ports are available on campus for general student use. Students can access the following: computer help desk, free student e-mail accounts, online (class) grades, online (class) registration, online (class) schedules, online library, ability to change address and biographical data, look at transcripts, pull up statements of account, grades, online progress reports and degree audit, campus job postings, student timesheets, financial aid information. Campuswide network is available. 100% of college-owned or -operated housing units are wired for high-speed Internet access. Wireless service is available via classrooms, computer centers, computer labs, dorm rooms, learning centers, libraries, student centers.

Student Life *Housing:* on-campus residence required for freshman year. *Options:* coed, women-only, disabled students. Campus housing is university owned. Freshman campus housing is guaranteed. *Activities and organizations:* drama/theater group, student-run newspaper, choral group, Academy of Science, Student Government Association, Sigma Alpha Pi Leadership Society, Fellowship of Christian Athletes, Delta Sigma Pi Business Fraternity. *Campus security:* 24-hour emergency response devices and patrols, late-night transport/escort service, controlled dormitory access, self-defense education, informal discussions, pamphlets, posters, films, lighted pathways and sidewalks. *Student services:* health clinic, personal/psychological counseling.

Athletics Member NCAA. All Division II. *Intercollegiate sports:* baseball M(s), basketball M(s)/W(s), golf M(s)/W(s), soccer M(s)/W(s), softball W(s), tennis M(s)/W(s), volleyball W(s). *Intramural sports:* baseball M(c), basketball M/W, bowling M/W, crew M(c)/W(c), cross-country running M(c)/W(c), golf M/W, lacrosse M(c)/W(c), racquetball M/W, rugby M(c), soccer M(c)/W(c), swimming and diving M/W, tennis M/W, track and field M(c)/W(c), ultimate Frisbee M(c)/W(c), volleyball M/W.

Standardized Tests *Required:* SAT or ACT (for admission).

Costs (2011–12) *Comprehensive fee:* $38,484 includes full-time tuition ($28,300), mandatory fees ($400), and room and board ($9784). Full-time tuition and fees vary according to course load and degree level. Part-time tuition: $944 per credit hour. Part-time tuition and fees vary according to course load and degree level. *Required fees:* $50 per term part-time. *College room only:* $5784. Room and board charges vary according to board plan and housing facility. *Payment plans:* installment, deferred payment. *Waivers:* employees or children of employees.

Financial Aid Of all full-time matriculated undergraduates who enrolled in 2009, 2,865 applied for aid, 2,188 were judged to have need, 208 had their need fully met. 168 Federal Work-Study jobs (averaging $2088). 2 state and other part-time jobs (averaging $2501). In 2009, 202 non-need-based awards were made. *Average percent of need met:* 64%. *Average financial aid package:* $20,324. *Average need-based loan:* $4262. *Average need-based gift aid:* $12,252. *Average non-need-based aid:* $8312. *Average indebtedness upon graduation:* $32,515. *Financial aid deadline:* 5/1.

Applying *Options:* electronic application, deferred entrance. *Application fee:* $45. *Required:* essay or personal statement, high school transcript, 1 letter of recommendation. *Recommended:* interview. *Application deadlines:* 5/1 (freshmen), 5/1 (out-of-state freshmen), 7/1 (transfers). *Notification:* continuous (freshmen), continuous (out-of-state freshmen), continuous (transfers).

Freshman Application Contact Ms. Karen Gregg, Inquiry Coordinator, St. Edward's University, 3001 South Congress Avenue, Austin, TX 78704. *Phone:* 512-448-8580. *Toll-free phone:* 800-555-0164. *Fax:* 512-464-8877. *E-mail:* seu.admit@stedwards.edu. *Web site:* http://www.gotostedwards.com/.

St. Mary's University

San Antonio, Texas

- **Independent Roman Catholic** comprehensive, founded 1852
- **Urban** 135-acre campus
- **Endowment** $116.5 million
- **Coed**
- **Moderately difficult** entrance level

Faculty *Student/faculty ratio:* 13:1.

Academics *Calendar:* semesters. *Degrees:* bachelor's, master's, doctoral-professional, and doctoral-research/scholarship.

Student Life *Campus security:* 24-hour emergency response devices and patrols, late-night transport/escort service, controlled dormitory access.

Athletics Member NCAA. All Division II.

Standardized Tests *Required:* SAT or ACT (for admission).

Costs (2010–11) *Comprehensive fee:* $30,106 includes full-time tuition ($21,980), mandatory fees ($576), and room and board ($7550). Full-time tuition and fees vary according to course load. Part-time tuition: $660 per credit hour. Part-time tuition and fees vary according to course load. *Required fees:* $163 per term part-time. *College room only:* $4750. Room and board charges vary according to board plan and housing facility. *Payment plans:* tuition prepayment, installment.

Financial Aid *Of all full-time matriculated undergraduates who enrolled in 2009,* 1,747 applied for aid, 1,633 were judged to have need, 406 had their need fully met. *In 2009,* 509 non-need-based awards were made. *Average percent of need met:* 76. *Average financial aid package:* $20,138. *Average need-based loan:* $6124. *Average need-based gift aid:* $14,206. *Average non-need-based aid:* $7292. *Average indebtedness upon graduation:* $22,592.

Applying *Options:* electronic application, deferred entrance. *Application fee:* $30. *Required:* high school transcript. *Recommended:* essay or personal statement, minimum 2 GPA, interview.

Freshman Application Contact Mr. Chadd J. Bridwell, Director of Undergraduate Admission, St. Mary's University, One Camino Santa Maria, San Antonio, TX 78228. *Phone:* 210-436-3126. *Toll-free phone:* 800-FOR-STMU. *Fax:* 210-431-6742. *E-mail:* uadm@stmarytx.edu. *Web site:* http://www.stmarytx.edu/.

Sam Houston State University
Huntsville, Texas

- **State-supported** university, founded 1879, part of Texas State University System
- **Small-town** 1256-acre campus with easy access to Houston
- **Coed** 14,689 undergraduate students, 84% full-time, 57% women, 43% men
- **Moderately difficult** entrance level, 47% of applicants were admitted

Undergraduates 12,282 full-time, 2,407 part-time. Students come from 45 states and territories; 44 other countries; 1% are from out of state; 16% Black or African American, non-Hispanic/Latino; 16% Hispanic/Latino; 1% Asian, non-Hispanic/Latino; 0.5% American Indian or Alaska Native, non-Hispanic/Latino; 1% Two or more races, non-Hispanic/Latino; 0.2% Race/ethnicity unknown; 1% international; 14% transferred in; 22% live on campus. *Retention:* 71% of full-time freshmen returned.

Freshmen *Admission:* 11,464 applied, 5,418 admitted, 2,259 enrolled. *Test scores:* SAT critical reading scores over 500: 46%; SAT math scores over 500: 56%; ACT scores over 18: 85%; SAT critical reading scores over 600: 10%; SAT math scores over 600: 12%; ACT scores over 24: 21%; SAT critical reading scores over 700: 1%; SAT math scores over 700: 1%; ACT scores over 30: 1%.

Faculty *Total:* 843, 78% full-time, 55% with terminal degrees. *Student/faculty ratio:* 20:1.

Academics *Calendar:* semesters. *Degrees:* bachelor's, master's, and doctoral-other. *Special study options:* academic remediation for entering students, advanced placement credit, distance learning, double majors, English as a second language, external degree program, honors programs, independent study, internships, off-campus study, part-time degree program, services for LD students, summer session for credit. *ROTC:* Army (b).

Computers on Campus 607 computers/terminals are available on campus for general student use. Students can access the following: campus intranet, computer help desk, free student e-mail accounts, online (class) grades, online (class) registration, online (class) schedules. Campuswide network is available. Wireless service is available via entire campus.

Student Life *Housing:* on-campus residence required for freshman year. *Options:* coed, men-only, women-only, disabled students. Campus housing is university owned and is provided by a third party. Freshman campus housing is guaranteed. *Activities and organizations:* drama/theater group, student-run newspaper, radio and television station, choral group, marching band, Chi Alpha Christian Fellowship, Non-Traditional Student Organization, Sigma Alpha Pi Leadership Society, Baptist Student Ministry, Bearkats for Life, national fraternities, national sororities. *Campus security:* 24-hour emergency response devices and patrols, student patrols, late-night transport/escort service. *Student services:* health clinic, personal/psychological counseling, legal services.

Athletics Member NCAA. All Division I except football (Division I-AA). *Intercollegiate sports:* baseball M(s), basketball M(s)/W(s), bowling W(s), cross-country running M/W, golf M(s)/W(s), soccer W(s), softball W(s), tennis W(s), track and field M(s)/W(s), volleyball W(s). *Intramural sports:* basketball M/W, football M, lacrosse M, racquetball M/W, rugby M/W, soccer M/W, softball W, tennis M/W, volleyball M/W.

Standardized Tests *Required:* SAT or ACT (for admission).

Costs (2011–12) *Tuition:* state resident $4890 full-time, $163 per credit hour part-time; nonresident $14,190 full-time, $473 per credit hour part-time. Full-time tuition and fees vary according to course level, course load, degree level, location, program, and student level. Part-time tuition and fees vary according to course level, course load, degree level, location, program, and student level. *Required fees:* $2110 full-time. *Room and board:* $7022; room only: $3914. Room and board charges vary according to board plan and housing facility. *Payment plan:* installment. *Waivers:* employees or children of employees.

Financial Aid *Of all full-time matriculated undergraduates who enrolled in 2008,* 8,023 applied for aid, 3,703 were judged to have need, 4 had their need

fully met. 291 Federal Work-Study jobs (averaging $1563). 90 state and other part-time jobs (averaging $1206). In 2008, 708 non-need-based awards were made. *Average percent of need met:* 31%. *Average financial aid package:* $4340. *Average need-based loan:* $189. *Average need-based gift aid:* $906. *Average non-need-based aid:* $322. *Average indebtedness upon graduation:* $6196.

Applying *Options:* electronic application. *Application fee:* $40. *Required:* high school transcript, minimum 2 GPA. *Application deadlines:* 8/1 (freshmen), 8/1 (out-of-state freshmen), 8/1 (transfers). *Notification:* continuous (freshmen), continuous (transfers).

Freshman Application Contact Mr. Trevor B. Thorn, Director of Admissions and Recruitment, Sam Houston State University, PO Box 2418, Huntsville, TX 77341. *Phone:* 936-294-1828. *Toll-free phone:* 866-232-7528 Ext. 1828. *Fax:* 936-294-3758. *E-mail:* admissions@shsu.edu. *Web site:* http://www.shsu.edu/.

Schreiner University
Kerrville, Texas

- **Independent Presbyterian** comprehensive, founded 1923
- **Small-town** 175-acre campus with easy access to San Antonio and Austin
- **Endowment** $46.6 million
- **Coed** 1,043 undergraduate students, 96% full-time, 56% women, 44% men
- **Moderately difficult** entrance level, 60% of applicants were admitted

Undergraduates 1,002 full-time, 41 part-time. 4% are from out of state; 4% Black or African American, non-Hispanic/Latino; 24% Hispanic/Latino; 0.8% Asian, non-Hispanic/Latino; 0.2% American Indian or Alaska Native, non-Hispanic/Latino; 3% Two or more races, non-Hispanic/Latino; 0.5% international; 7% transferred in; 67% live on campus. *Retention:* 63% of full-time freshmen returned.

Freshmen *Admission:* 1,000 applied, 601 admitted, 253 enrolled. *Average high school GPA:* 3.55. *Test scores:* SAT critical reading scores over 500: 46%; SAT math scores over 500: 56%; SAT writing scores over 500: 41%; ACT scores over 18: 87%; SAT critical reading scores over 600: 14%; SAT math scores over 600: 13%; SAT writing scores over 600: 8%; ACT scores over 24: 28%; ACT scores over 30: 2%.

Faculty *Total:* 114, 56% full-time, 47% with terminal degrees. *Student/faculty ratio:* 13:1.

Academics *Calendar:* semesters. *Degrees:* certificates, associate, bachelor's, and master's. *Special study options:* academic remediation for entering students, accelerated degree program, advanced placement credit, cooperative education, double majors, honors programs, independent study, internships, part-time degree program, services for LD students, student-designed majors, study abroad, summer session for credit. *Unusual degree programs:* 3-2 engineering with University of Texas at Austin, Texas A&M University.

Computers on Campus 120 computers/terminals are available on campus for general student use. Students can access the following: computer help desk, free student e-mail accounts, online (class) grades, online (class) registration, online (class) schedules. Campuswide network is available. 100% of college-owned or -operated housing units are wired for high-speed Internet access. Wireless service is available via classrooms, computer centers, computer labs, dorm rooms, learning centers, libraries, student centers.

Student Life *Housing:* on-campus residence required through junior year. *Options:* coed, disabled students. Campus housing is university owned. Freshman campus housing is guaranteed. *Activities and organizations:* drama/theater group, student-run newspaper, choral group, Student Senate, Greek Life, Campus Ministry, honor societies, Hall Councils, national fraternities, national sororities. *Campus security:* 24-hour emergency response devices and patrols, late-night transport/escort service. *Student services:* health clinic, personal/psychological counseling.

Athletics Member NCAA. All Division III. *Intercollegiate sports:* baseball M, basketball M/W, cross-country running M/W, golf M/W, soccer M/W, softball W, tennis M/W, volleyball W. *Intramural sports:* cheerleading W.

Standardized Tests *Required:* SAT or ACT (for admission).

Costs (2011–12) *Comprehensive fee:* $30,030 includes full-time tuition ($19,754), mandatory fees ($600), and room and board ($9676). Part-time tuition: $843 per credit. *Required fees:* $115 per term part-time. *College room only:* $5410. Room and board charges vary according to board plan and housing facility. *Payment plan:* installment. *Waivers:* employees or children of employees.

Financial Aid Of all full-time matriculated undergraduates who enrolled in 2009, 708 applied for aid, 607 were judged to have need, 102 had their need fully met. In 2009, 183 non-need-based awards were made. *Average percent of need met:* 72%. *Average financial aid package:* $14,453. *Average need-based loan:* $3608. *Average need-based gift aid:* $11,211. *Average non-need-based aid:* $6612. *Average indebtedness upon graduation:* $27,986. *Financial aid deadline:* 8/1.

Applying *Options:* electronic application, deferred entrance. *Application fee:* $25. *Required:* essay or personal statement, high school transcript. *Recommended:* interview. *Application deadlines:* 5/1 (freshmen), 5/1 (transfers). *Notification:* continuous (freshmen), continuous (transfers).
Freshman Application Contact Ms. Sandy Speed, Dean of Admission and Financial Aid, Schreiner University, 2100 Memorial Boulevard, Kerrville, TX 78028. *Phone:* 830-792-7217. *Toll-free phone:* 800-343-4919. *E-mail:* admissions@schreiner.edu. *Web site:* http://www.schreiner.edu/.

Southern Methodist University

Dallas, Texas

- **Independent** university, founded 1911, affiliated with United Methodist Church
- **Suburban** 231-acre campus
- **Endowment** $1.1 billion
- **Coed** 6,192 undergraduate students, 96% full-time, 53% women, 47% men
- **Moderately difficult** entrance level, 59% of applicants were admitted

Undergraduates 5,939 full-time, 253 part-time. Students come from 51 states and territories; 77 other countries; 49% are from out of state; 5% Black or African American, non-Hispanic/Latino; 10% Hispanic/Latino; 6% Asian, non-Hispanic/Latino; 0.5% Native Hawaiian or other Pacific Islander, non-Hispanic/Latino; 0.6% American Indian or Alaska Native, non-Hispanic/Latino; 0.7% Two or more races, non-Hispanic/Latino; 1% Race/ethnicity unknown; 6% international; 4% transferred in; 33% live on campus. *Retention:* 89% of full-time freshmen returned.
Freshmen *Admission:* 8,239 applied, 4,899 admitted, 1,479 enrolled. *Average high school GPA:* 3.36. *Test scores:* SAT critical reading scores over 500: 94%; SAT math scores over 500: 95%; SAT writing scores over 500: 92%; ACT scores over 18: 99%; SAT critical reading scores over 600: 61%; SAT math scores over 600: 69%; SAT writing scores over 600: 58%; ACT scores over 24: 88%; SAT critical reading scores over 700: 14%; SAT math scores over 700: 18%; SAT writing scores over 700: 12%; ACT scores over 30: 34%.
Faculty *Total:* 1,040, 64% full-time, 72% with terminal degrees. *Student/faculty ratio:* 12:1.
Academics *Calendar:* semesters. *Degrees:* bachelor's, master's, doctoral-professional, doctoral-research/scholarship, and postbachelor's certificates. *Special study options:* academic remediation for entering students, accelerated degree program, adult/continuing education programs, advanced placement credit, cooperative education, distance learning, double majors, English as a second language, honors programs, independent study, internships, part-time degree program, services for LD students, student-designed majors, study abroad, summer session for credit. *ROTC:* Army (b), Air Force (c). *Unusual degree programs:* 3-2 engineering.
Computers on Campus 758 computers/terminals are available on campus for general student use. Students can access the following: campus intranet, computer help desk, free student e-mail accounts, online (class) grades, online (class) registration, online (class) schedules, online billing/payment processing. Campuswide network is available. Wireless service is available via classrooms, computer centers, computer labs, dorm rooms, learning centers, libraries, student centers.
Student Life *Housing:* on-campus residence required for freshman year. *Options:* coed, disabled students. Campus housing is university owned. Freshman campus housing is guaranteed. *Activities and organizations:* drama/theater group, student-run newspaper, radio and television station, choral group, marching band, Program Council, Student Senate, Student Foundation, Residence Hall Association, SPARC (Students Promoting Awareness, Responsibility, and Citizenship), national fraternities, national sororities. *Campus security:* 24-hour emergency response devices and patrols, late-night transport/escort service, controlled dormitory access. *Student services:* health clinic, personal/psychological counseling, women's center.
Athletics Member NCAA. All Division I except football (Division I-A). *Intercollegiate sports:* baseball M(c), basketball M(s)/W(s), cheerleading M(s)(c)/W(s)(c), crew W(s), cross-country running W(s), equestrian sports W(s), fencing M(c)/W(c), golf M(s)/W(s), ice hockey M(c), lacrosse M(c), rugby M(c)/W(c), soccer M(s)/W(s), swimming and diving M(s)/W(s), tennis M(s)/W(s), track and field W, volleyball W(s), wrestling M(c). *Intramural sports:* basketball M/W, bowling M/W, football M, golf M/W, racquetball M/W, rock climbing M(c)/W(c), soccer M/W, softball M/W, swimming and diving M/W, table tennis M(c)/W(c), tennis M/W, ultimate Frisbee M/W, volleyball M/W, water polo M/W, weight lifting M(c)/W(c).
Standardized Tests *Required:* SAT or ACT (for admission). *Required for some:* SAT Subject Tests (for admission).
Costs (2011–12) *Tuition:* $34,990 full-time. Full-time tuition and fees vary according to class time. Part-time tuition and fees vary according to class time and course load. *Required fees:* $4440 full-time. *Room only:* Room and board charges vary according to board plan and housing facility. *Payment plans:* tuition prepayment, installment. *Waivers:* employees or children of employees.

Financial Aid Of all full-time matriculated undergraduates who enrolled in 2009, 2,733 applied for aid, 2,344 were judged to have need, 827 had their need fully met. 1,540 Federal Work-Study jobs (averaging $3472). 11 state and other part-time jobs (averaging $3223). In 2009, 1943 non-need-based awards were made. *Average percent of need met:* 86%. *Average financial aid package:* $32,632. *Average need-based loan:* $3709. *Average need-based gift aid:* $18,433. *Average non-need-based aid:* $15,334. *Average indebtedness upon graduation:* $24,569.
Applying *Options:* electronic application, early admission, early action, deferred entrance. *Application fee:* $60. *Required:* high school transcript, minimum 2 GPA, 1 letter of recommendation, statement of good standing from prior institution(s). *Recommended:* essay or personal statement, minimum 2.7 GPA. *Application deadlines:* 1/15 (freshmen), 7/1 (transfers), 11/1 (early action). *Notification:* continuous (freshmen), continuous (transfers), 12/31 (early action).
Freshman Application Contact Dr. Stephanie Dupaul, Interim Dean of Undergraduate Admission and Executive Director of Enrollment Services, Southern Methodist University, PO Box 750181, Dallas, TX 75275-0181. *Phone:* 214-768-2058. *Toll-free phone:* 800-323-0672. *Fax:* 214-768-0103. *E-mail:* ugadmission@smu.edu. *Web site:* http://www.smu.edu/.

South Texas College

McAllen, Texas

Freshman Application Contact Mr. Matthew Hebbard, Director of Enrollment Services and Registrar, South Texas College, 3201 West Pecan, McAllen, TX 78501. *Phone:* 956-872-2147. *Toll-free phone:* 800-742-7822. *E-mail:* mshebbar@southtexascollege.edu. *Web site:* http://www.southtexascollege.edu/.

Southwestern Adventist University

Keene, Texas

- **Independent Seventh-day Adventist** comprehensive, founded 1894
- **Small-town** 150-acre campus with easy access to Dallas-Fort Worth
- **Endowment** $10.9 million
- **Coed** 785 undergraduate students, 86% full-time, 57% women, 43% men
- **Minimally difficult** entrance level, 56% of applicants were admitted

Undergraduates 674 full-time, 111 part-time. Students come from 36 states and territories; 32 other countries; 29% are from out of state; 14% Black or African American, non-Hispanic/Latino; 28% Hispanic/Latino; 4% Asian, non-Hispanic/Latino; 0.8% Native Hawaiian or other Pacific Islander, non-Hispanic/Latino; 0.4% American Indian or Alaska Native, non-Hispanic/Latino; 1% Two or more races, non-Hispanic/Latino; 0.6% Race/ethnicity unknown; 19% international; 40% live on campus. *Retention:* 62% of full-time freshmen returned.
Freshmen *Admission:* 663 applied, 370 admitted, 132 enrolled. *Test scores:* SAT critical reading scores over 500: 43%; SAT math scores over 500: 28%; ACT scores over 18: 79%; SAT critical reading scores over 600: 9%; SAT math scores over 600: 3%; ACT scores over 24: 18%; SAT critical reading scores over 700: 1%; ACT scores over 30: 2%.
Faculty *Total:* 78, 67% full-time, 44% with terminal degrees. *Student/faculty ratio:* 12:1.
Academics *Calendar:* semesters. *Degrees:* associate, bachelor's, and master's. *Special study options:* academic remediation for entering students, accelerated degree program, adult/continuing education programs, advanced placement credit, double majors, English as a second language, external degree program, honors programs, independent study, internships, off-campus study, part-time degree program, services for LD students, student-designed majors, study abroad, summer session for credit.
Computers on Campus 100 computers/terminals are available on campus for general student use. Students can access the following: campus intranet, computer help desk, free student e-mail accounts, online (class) grades, online (class) registration, online (class) schedules. Campuswide network is available. 100% of college-owned or -operated housing units are wired for high-speed Internet access. Wireless service is available via entire campus.
Student Life *Housing:* on-campus residence required through sophomore year. *Options:* men-only, women-only, cooperative. Campus housing is university owned. Freshman campus housing is guaranteed. *Activities and organizations:* drama/theater group, student-run newspaper, radio and television station, choral group, Student Association, Students in Free Enterprise (SIFE), Education/Psychology Club, Theology Club, Nursing Club. *Campus security:* 24-hour emergency response devices, student patrols. *Student services:* health clinic, personal/psychological counseling.
Athletics *Intramural sports:* basketball M(c)/W(c), football M/W, racquetball M/W, soccer M(c)/W(c), softball M/W, table tennis M/W, tennis M/W, volleyball M/W(c).
Standardized Tests *Required:* SAT or ACT (for admission).

Costs (2011–12) *Comprehensive fee:* $24,542 includes full-time tuition ($16,682), mandatory fees ($400), and room and board ($7460). Full-time tuition and fees vary according to course load and program. Part-time tuition and fees vary according to course load and program. *College room only:* $3319. Room and board charges vary according to board plan. *Payment plans:* installment, deferred payment. *Waivers:* employees or children of employees.
Applying *Options:* electronic application, deferred entrance. *Required:* high school transcript, minimum 2 GPA. *Required for some:* essay or personal statement, 1 letter of recommendation, interview. *Application deadlines:* 8/31 (freshmen), 8/31 (transfers). *Notification:* 9/1 (freshmen), 9/1 (transfers).
Freshman Application Contact Ms. Diem Dennis, Associate Director of Admissions and Records, Southwestern Adventist University, 100 West Hillcrest, Keene, TX 76059. *Phone:* 817-202-6252. *Toll-free phone:* 800-433-2240. *E-mail:* ddennis@swau.edu. *Web site:* http://www.swau.edu/.

Southwestern Assemblies of God University
Waxahachie, Texas

- **Independent** comprehensive, founded 1927, affiliated with Assemblies of God
- **Small-town** 70-acre campus with easy access to Dallas
- **Endowment** $3.1 million
- **Coed** 1,742 undergraduate students, 84% full-time, 49% women, 51% men
- **Noncompetitive** entrance level

Undergraduates 1,458 full-time, 284 part-time. Students come from 49 states and territories; 11 other countries; 40% are from out of state; 15% transferred in; 85% live on campus. *Retention:* 67% of full-time freshmen returned.
Freshmen *Admission:* 296 enrolled.
Faculty *Total:* 142, 49% full-time, 33% with terminal degrees. *Student/faculty ratio:* 16:1.
Academics *Calendar:* semesters. *Degrees:* associate, bachelor's, and master's. *Special study options:* academic remediation for entering students, adult/continuing education programs, advanced placement credit, distance learning, double majors, external degree program, independent study, internships, part-time degree program, services for LD students, summer session for credit. *ROTC:* Air Force (c).
Computers on Campus 96 computers/terminals and 1,000 ports are available on campus for general student use. Students can access the following: computer help desk, free student e-mail accounts, online (class) grades, online (class) registration, online (class) schedules. Campuswide network is available. 95% of college-owned or -operated housing units are wired for high-speed Internet access. Wireless service is available via entire campus.
Student Life *Housing:* on-campus residence required through senior year. *Options:* coed. Campus housing is university owned. Freshman campus housing is guaranteed. *Activities and organizations:* drama/theater group, student-run newspaper, choral group, Student Congress, Southwestern Missions Association, Street Hope, Gold Jackets, Women in Ministry. *Campus security:* 24-hour patrols, late-night transport/escort service, controlled dormitory access, 2 dorms electronic access; 4 dorms key access to rooms, camera surveillance, 24 hour dispatch monitored fire alarm systems (offsite). *Student services:* health clinic, personal/psychological counseling.
Athletics Member NAIA, NCCAA. *Intercollegiate sports:* baseball M(s), basketball M(s)/W(s), football M(s), soccer M(s)/W(s), volleyball W(s). *Intramural sports:* basketball M/W, soccer M(c)/W, softball M/W, table tennis M/W, tennis M/W, volleyball M/W.
Standardized Tests *Required:* SAT or ACT (for admission).
Costs (2011–12) *Comprehensive fee:* $22,156 includes full-time tuition ($14,850), mandatory fees ($880), and room and board ($6426). Part-time tuition: $495 per credit. *College room only:* $3390. Room and board charges vary according to housing facility. *Payment plan:* deferred payment. *Waivers:* employees or children of employees.
Financial Aid Of all full-time matriculated undergraduates who enrolled in 2000, 1,116 applied for aid, 1,002 were judged to have need, 110 had their need fully met. 178 Federal Work-Study jobs, 7 state and other part-time jobs (averaging $890). In 2000, 316 non-need-based awards were made. *Average percent of need met:* 64%. *Average financial aid package:* $6728. *Average need-based loan:* $3177. *Average need-based gift aid:* $3511. *Average indebtedness upon graduation:* $13,938. *Financial aid deadline:* 7/1.
Applying *Options:* early admission, deferred entrance. *Application fee:* $35. *Required:* essay or personal statement, high school transcript, minimum 2 GPA, 1 letter of recommendation, medical history, evidence of approved Christian character. *Application deadlines:* rolling (freshmen), rolling (transfers).
Freshman Application Contact Mr. Bryan Brooks, Assistant Dean of Admissions, Southwestern Assemblies of God University, 1200 Sycamore Street, Waxahachie, TX 75165. *Phone:* 972-825-4821. *Toll-free phone:* 888-937-7248. *Fax:* 972-923-8131. *E-mail:* bbrooks@sagu.edu. *Web site:* http://www.sagu.edu/.

Southwestern Christian College
Terrell, Texas

Freshman Application Contact Admissions Department, Southwestern Christian College, Box 10, 200 Bowser Street, Terrell, TX 75160. *Phone:* 214-524-3341. *Web site:* http://www.swcc.edu/.

Southwestern University
Georgetown, Texas

- **Independent Methodist** 4-year, founded 1840
- **Suburban** 700-acre campus with easy access to Austin
- **Endowment** $226.9 million
- **Coed**
- **Very difficult** entrance level

Faculty *Student/faculty ratio:* 10:1.
Academics *Calendar:* semesters. *Degree:* bachelor's.
Student Life *Campus security:* 24-hour emergency response devices and patrols, student patrols, late-night transport/escort service, controlled dormitory access.
Athletics Member NCAA. All Division III.
Standardized Tests *Required:* SAT (for admission). *Required for some:* SAT and SAT Subject Tests or ACT (for admission).
Costs (2010–11) *Comprehensive fee:* $41,400 includes full-time tuition ($31,630) and room and board ($9770). Part-time tuition: $1320 per semester hour. Part-time tuition and fees vary according to course load. *College room only:* $5100. Room and board charges vary according to board plan and housing facility.
Financial Aid *Of all full-time matriculated undergraduates who enrolled in 2009,* 936 applied for aid, 805 were judged to have need, 259 had their need fully met. 147 Federal Work-Study jobs (averaging $1865). 548 state and other part-time jobs (averaging $2123). *In 2009,* 444 non-need-based awards were made. *Average percent of need met:* 88. *Average financial aid package:* $27,424. *Average need-based loan:* $5346. *Average need-based gift aid:* $22,109. *Average non-need-based aid:* $13,480. *Average indebtedness upon graduation:* $29,548. *Financial aid deadline:* 3/1.
Applying *Options:* electronic application, early decision, early action, deferred entrance. *Application fee:* $40. *Required:* essay or personal statement, high school transcript, 1 letter of recommendation. *Required for some:* interview. *Recommended:* interview.
Freshman Application Contact Mr. Tom Oliver, Vice President for Enrollment Services, Southwestern University, 1001 East University Avenue, Georgetown, TX 78626. *Phone:* 512-863-1200. *Toll-free phone:* 800-252-3166. *Fax:* 512-863-9601. *E-mail:* admission@southwestern.edu. *Web site:* http://www.southwestern.edu/.

Stephen F. Austin State University
Nacogdoches, Texas

- **State-supported** comprehensive, founded 1923
- **Small-town** 400-acre campus
- **Coed** 11,269 undergraduate students, 85% full-time, 62% women, 38% men
- **Moderately difficult** entrance level, 65% of applicants were admitted

Undergraduates 9,555 full-time, 1,714 part-time. 2% are from out of state; 24% Black or African American, non-Hispanic/Latino; 10% Hispanic/Latino; 0.9% Asian, non-Hispanic/Latino; 0.6% American Indian or Alaska Native, non-Hispanic/Latino; 0.6% Two or more races, non-Hispanic/Latino; 3% Race/ethnicity unknown; 0.9% international; 9% transferred in; 44% live on campus. *Retention:* 64% of full-time freshmen returned.
Freshmen *Admission:* 9,190 applied, 5,993 admitted, 2,177 enrolled. *Test scores:* SAT critical reading scores over 500: 38%; SAT math scores over 500: 45%; SAT writing scores over 500: 33%; ACT scores over 18: 78%; SAT critical reading scores over 600: 8%; SAT math scores over 600: 11%; SAT writing scores over 600: 5%; ACT scores over 24: 21%; SAT critical reading scores over 700: 1%; ACT scores over 30: 1%.
Faculty *Student/faculty ratio:* 19:1.
Academics *Calendar:* semesters. *Degrees:* bachelor's, master's, and doctoral-research/scholarship. *Special study options:* academic remediation for entering students, accelerated degree program, adult/continuing education programs, advanced placement credit, distance learning, double majors, freshman honors college, honors programs, independent study, internships, off-campus study, part-time degree program, services for LD students, student-designed majors, study abroad, summer session for credit. *ROTC:* Army (b). *Unusual degree programs:* 3-2 professional accountancy.

Computers on Campus 1,000 computers/terminals are available on campus for general student use. Students can access the following: campus intranet, computer help desk, free student e-mail accounts, online (class) grades, online (class) registration, online (class) schedules. Campuswide network is available. 100% of college-owned or -operated housing units are wired for high-speed Internet access. Wireless service is available via classrooms, computer centers, computer labs, dorm rooms, libraries, student centers.

Student Life *Housing:* on-campus residence required through sophomore year. *Options:* coed, men-only, women-only, disabled students. Campus housing is university owned. Freshman campus housing is guaranteed. *Activities and organizations:* drama/theater group, student-run newspaper, radio and television station, choral group, marching band, Baptist Student Ministry, National Society of Collegiate Scholars, Residence Hall Association, Crosspoint (Christian fellowship), Biology Club, national fraternities, national sororities. *Campus security:* 24-hour emergency response devices and patrols, student patrols, late-night transport/escort service, controlled dormitory access. *Student services:* health clinic, personal/psychological counseling, legal services.

Athletics Member NCAA. All Division I except football (Division I-AA). *Intercollegiate sports:* baseball M(s), basketball M(s)/W(s), bowling W(s), cross-country running M(s)/W(s), equestrian sports W, golf M(s)/W(s), soccer W(s), softball W(s), tennis W(s), track and field M(s)/W(s), volleyball W(s). *Intramural sports:* badminton M/W, baseball M(c), basketball M/W, football M/W, golf M/W, lacrosse M(c)/W(c), racquetball M(c)/W(c), rock climbing M/W, soccer M/W, softball M/W, table tennis M/W, tennis M/W, ultimate Frisbee M/W, volleyball M/W.

Standardized Tests *Required:* SAT or ACT (for admission).

Costs (2010–11) *Tuition:* state resident $5096 full-time, $170 per credit hour part-time; nonresident $14,396 full-time, $480 per credit hour part-time. Full-time tuition and fees vary according to course load, degree level, and location. Part-time tuition and fees vary according to course load, degree level, and location. *Required fees:* $1902 full-time, $147 per credit hour part-time. *Room and board:* $7670. Room and board charges vary according to board plan and housing facility. *Payment plan:* installment. *Waivers:* senior citizens and employees or children of employees.

Financial Aid Of all full-time matriculated undergraduates who enrolled in 2008, 7,618 applied for aid, 6,318 were judged to have need, 3,722 had their need fully met. In 2008, 341 non-need-based awards were made. *Average percent of need met:* 89%. *Average financial aid package:* $9233. *Average need-based loan:* $4040. *Average need-based gift aid:* $5349. *Average non-need-based aid:* $2775. *Average indebtedness upon graduation:* $20,483.

Applying *Options:* electronic application. *Application fee:* $35. *Required:* high school transcript. *Application deadlines:* rolling (freshmen), rolling (out-of-state freshmen), rolling (transfers). *Notification:* continuous (freshmen), continuous (out-of-state freshmen), continuous (transfers).

Freshman Application Contact Ms. Beth Smith, Associate Director of Admissions, Stephen F. Austin State University, PO Box 13051, SFA Station, Nacogdoches, TX 75962. *Phone:* 936-468-2504. *Toll-free phone:* 800-731-2902. *Fax:* 936-468-3849. *E-mail:* admissions@sfasu.edu. *Web site:* http://www.sfasu.edu/.

See page 1646 for the College Close-Up.

Strayer University - Cedar Hill Campus
Cedar Hill, Texas
- **Proprietary** comprehensive
- **Coed**

Academics *Degrees:* certificates, diplomas, associate, bachelor's, master's, and postbachelor's certificates.

Freshman Application Contact Strayer University - Cedar Hill Campus, 610 Uptown Boulevard, Suite 3500, Cedar Hill, TX 75104. *Web site:* http://www.strayer.edu/cedarhill.

Strayer University - Irving Campus
Irving, Texas
- **Proprietary** comprehensive
- **Coed**

Academics *Degrees:* certificates, diplomas, associate, bachelor's, master's, and postbachelor's certificates.

Costs (2010–11) *Tuition:* $13,635 full-time, $1590 per course part-time.

Freshman Application Contact Strayer University - Irving Campus, 7701 Las Colinas Ridge, Suite 450, Irving, TX 75063. *Web site:* http://www.strayer.edu/irving.

Strayer University - Katy Campus
Houston, Texas
- **Proprietary** comprehensive
- **Coed**

Academics *Degrees:* certificates, diplomas, associate, bachelor's, master's, and postbachelor's certificates.

Freshman Application Contact Strayer University - Katy Campus, 14511 Old Katy Road, Suite 200, Houston, TX 77079. *Web site:* http://www.strayer.edu/katy.

Strayer University - North Austin Campus
Austin, Texas
- **Proprietary** comprehensive
- **Coed**

Academics *Degrees:* certificates, diplomas, associate, bachelor's, master's, and postbachelor's certificates.

Costs (2010–11) *Tuition:* $13,635 full-time, $1590 per course part-time.

Freshman Application Contact Strayer University - North Austin Campus, 8501 North Mopac Expressway, Suite 100, Austin, TX 78759. *Web site:* http://www.strayer.edu/north_austin.

Strayer University - Northwest Houston Campus
Houston, Texas
- **Proprietary** comprehensive
- **Coed**

Academics *Degrees:* certificates, diplomas, associate, bachelor's, master's, and postbachelor's certificates.

Costs (2010–11) *Tuition:* $13,635 full-time, $1590 per course part-time.

Freshman Application Contact Strayer University - Northwest Houston Campus, 10940 W. Sam Houston Parkway N., Suite 200, Houston, TX 77064. *Web site:* http://www.strayer.edu/northwest_houston.

Strayer University - Plano Campus
Plano, Texas
- **Proprietary** comprehensive
- **Coed**

Academics *Degrees:* certificates, diplomas, associate, bachelor's, master's, and postbachelor's certificates.

Costs (2010–11) *Tuition:* $13,635 full-time, $1590 per course part-time.

Freshman Application Contact Strayer University - Plano Campus, 2701 North Dallas Parkway, Suite 300, Plano, TX 75093. *Web site:* http://www.strayer.edu/plano.

Sul Ross State University
Alpine, Texas
- **State-supported** comprehensive, founded 1920, part of Texas State University System
- **Small-town** 640-acre campus
- **Coed** 2,237 undergraduate students, 64% full-time, 57% women, 43% men
- **Noncompetitive** entrance level, 98% of applicants were admitted

Undergraduates 1,436 full-time, 801 part-time. 2% are from out of state; 5% Black or African American, non-Hispanic/Latino; 64% Hispanic/Latino; 0.4% Asian, non-Hispanic/Latino; 0.1% Native Hawaiian or other Pacific Islander, non-Hispanic/Latino; 0.4% American Indian or Alaska Native, non-Hispanic/Latino; 1% Two or more races, non-Hispanic/Latino; 7% Race/ethnicity unknown; 0.5% international; 14% transferred in; 28% live on campus.

Freshmen *Admission:* 851 applied, 837 admitted, 323 enrolled. *Average high school GPA:* 3.09. *Test scores:* SAT critical reading scores over 500: 15%; SAT math scores over 500: 15%; SAT writing scores over 500: 21%; ACT scores over 18: 52%; SAT critical reading scores over 600: 2%; SAT math scores over 600: 3%; ACT scores over 24: 8%; ACT scores over 30: 1%.

Faculty *Total:* 174, 73% full-time. *Student/faculty ratio:* 14:1.

Academics *Calendar:* semesters. *Degrees:* certificates, diplomas, associate, bachelor's, master's, and postbachelor's certificates. *Special study options:* academic remediation for entering students, advanced placement credit, distance learning, honors programs, internships, part-time degree program, summer session for credit.

Computers on Campus Students can access the following: campus intranet, computer help desk, free student e-mail accounts, online (class) grades. Campuswide network is available.

Student Life *Housing:* on-campus residence required through sophomore year. *Options:* coed. Campus housing is university owned. Freshman campus housing is guaranteed. *Activities and organizations:* drama/theater group, student-run newspaper, radio station, choral group. *Campus security:* 24-hour patrols, late-night transport/escort service. *Student services:* health clinic, personal/psychological counseling.

Athletics Member NCAA. All Division III. *Intercollegiate sports:* baseball M, basketball M/W, cheerleading M/W, cross-country running W, football M, softball W, tennis M/W, track and field M/W, volleyball W. *Intramural sports:* basketball M/W, cheerleading M/W, equestrian sports M/W, football M/W, racquetball M/W, soccer M/W, softball M, tennis M/W, ultimate Frisbee M/W, volleyball M/W, water polo M/W, weight lifting M/W.

Standardized Tests *Required:* SAT or ACT (for admission).

Costs (2010–11) *Tuition:* state resident $2928 full-time; nonresident $9576 full-time. *Room and board:* $6370; room only: $3820. Room and board charges vary according to board plan and housing facility. *Payment plan:* installment. *Waivers:* senior citizens and employees or children of employees.

Financial Aid Of all full-time matriculated undergraduates who enrolled in 2008, 999 applied for aid, 730 were judged to have need. In 2008, 156 non-need-based awards were made. *Average percent of need met:* 12%. *Average financial aid package:* $11,857. *Average need-based loan:* $6482. *Average need-based gift aid:* $5046. *Average non-need-based aid:* $1424. *Financial aid deadline:* 4/1.

Applying *Options:* electronic application, deferred entrance. *Application fee:* $25. *Required:* high school transcript. *Recommended:* interview. *Application deadlines:* rolling (freshmen), rolling (transfers). *Notification:* continuous (freshmen), continuous (transfers).

Freshman Application Contact Sul Ross State University, PO Box C - 114, Alpine, TX 79832. *Phone:* 432-837-8050. *Toll-free phone:* 888-722-7778. *Web site:* http://www.sulross.edu/.

Tarleton State University
Stephenville, Texas

- **State-supported** comprehensive, founded 1899, part of Texas A&M University System
- **Small-town** 175-acre campus with easy access to Fort Worth
- **Endowment** $25.2 million
- **Coed** 7,902 undergraduate students, 79% full-time, 58% women, 42% men
- **Moderately difficult** entrance level, 88% of applicants were admitted

Undergraduates 6,277 full-time, 1,625 part-time. Students come from 45 states and territories; 22 other countries; 2% are from out of state; 6% Black or African American, non-Hispanic/Latino; 11% Hispanic/Latino; 0.5% Asian, non-Hispanic/Latino; 0.1% Native Hawaiian or other Pacific Islander, non-Hispanic/Latino; 0.8% American Indian or Alaska Native, non-Hispanic/Latino; 2% Two or more races, non-Hispanic/Latino; 0.2% Race/ethnicity unknown; 0.7% international; 15% transferred in; 23% live on campus. *Retention:* 68% of full-time freshmen returned.

Freshmen *Admission:* 3,270 applied, 2,867 admitted, 1,572 enrolled. *Test scores:* SAT critical reading scores over 500: 38%; SAT math scores over 500: 45%; SAT writing scores over 500: 30%; ACT scores over 18: 80%; SAT critical reading scores over 600: 7%; SAT math scores over 600: 9%; SAT writing scores over 600: 4%; ACT scores over 24: 21%; SAT critical reading scores over 700: 1%; SAT math scores over 700: 1%; ACT scores over 30: 1%.

Faculty *Total:* 535, 53% full-time. *Student/faculty ratio:* 20:1.

Academics *Calendar:* semesters. *Degrees:* associate, bachelor's, master's, and doctoral-research/scholarship. *Special study options:* academic remediation for entering students, accelerated degree program, adult/continuing education programs, advanced placement credit, cooperative education, distance learning, double majors, honors programs, independent study, internships, off-campus study, part-time degree program, services for LD students, study abroad, summer session for credit. *ROTC:* Army (b).

Computers on Campus 1,000 computers/terminals are available on campus for general student use. Students can access the following: campus intranet, computer help desk, free student e-mail accounts, online (class) grades, online (class) registration, online (class) schedules. Campuswide network is available. 100% of college-owned or -operated housing units are wired for high-speed Internet access. Wireless service is available via classrooms, computer centers, computer labs, learning centers, libraries, student centers.

Student Life *Housing:* on-campus residence required through sophomore year. *Options:* coed, men-only, women-only. Campus housing is university owned and leased by the school. Freshman campus housing is guaranteed. *Activities and organizations:* drama/theater group, student-run newspaper, radio station, choral group, marching band, Student Government Association, Student Programming Association, Kappa Delta Rho, Delta Zeta, Chi Alpha, national fraternities, national sororities. *Campus security:* 24-hour emergency response

devices and patrols, student patrols, late-night transport/escort service, controlled dormitory access. *Student services:* health clinic, personal/psychological counseling, legal services.

Athletics Member NCAA. All Division II. *Intercollegiate sports:* baseball M(s), basketball M(s)/W(s), cheerleading M(s)/W(s), cross-country running M(s)/W(s), football M(s), golf W(s), softball W(s), tennis W(s), track and field M(s)/W(s), volleyball W(s). *Intramural sports:* archery M/W, basketball M/W, football M/W, golf M/W, racquetball M/W, soccer M/W, softball M/W, table tennis M/W, tennis M/W, volleyball M/W.

Standardized Tests *Required:* SAT or ACT (for admission).

Costs (2010–11) *Tuition:* state resident $4319 full-time, $144 per credit hour part-time; nonresident $13,619 full-time, $454 per credit hour part-time. Full-time tuition and fees vary according to course load and degree level. Part-time tuition and fees vary according to course load and degree level. *Required fees:* $1880 full-time. *Room and board:* $6591; room only: $3381. Room and board charges vary according to board plan and housing facility. *Payment plan:* installment.

Financial Aid Of all full-time matriculated undergraduates who enrolled in 2009, 10,919 applied for aid, 9,230 were judged to have need, 1,922 had their need fully met. In 2009, 2055 non-need-based awards were made. *Average percent of need met:* 43%. *Average financial aid package:* $9988. *Average need-based loan:* $2344. *Average need-based gift aid:* $2722. *Average non-need-based aid:* $3193. *Average indebtedness upon graduation:* $14,879. *Financial aid deadline:* 11/1.

Applying *Options:* electronic application, early action. *Application fee:* $30. *Required:* high school transcript. *Application deadlines:* 8/1 (freshmen), 7/1 (transfers), 11/30 (early action).

Freshman Application Contact Ms. Cindy Hess, Director of Undergraduate Admissions, Tarleton State University, Box T-0030, Tarleton Station, Stephenville, TX 76402. *Phone:* 254-968-9123. *Toll-free phone:* 800-687-8236. *Fax:* 254-968-9951. *E-mail:* uadm@tarleton.edu. *Web site:* http://www.tarleton.edu/.

Texas A&M Health Science Center
College Station, Texas

- **State-supported** upper-level, founded 1999, part of Texas A&M University System Health Science Center
- **Urban** campus
- **Coed**

Academics *Calendar:* semesters. *Degrees:* bachelor's, master's, doctoral-professional, and post-master's certificates.

Student Life *Campus security:* 24-hour emergency response devices and patrols, late-night transport/escort service, electronically operated building access.

Applying *Application fee:* $35.

Application Contact Dr. Jack L. Long, Associate Dean for Student Services, Texas A&M Health Science Center, PO Box 660677, 3302 Gaston Avenue, Dallas, TX 75266-0677. *Phone:* 214-828-8232. *Fax:* 214-874-4567. *Web site:* http://www.tamhsc.edu/.

Texas A&M International University
Laredo, Texas

- **State-supported** comprehensive, founded 1969, part of Texas A&M University System
- **Urban** 300-acre campus
- **Endowment** $27.4 million
- **Coed** 5,823 undergraduate students, 63% full-time, 59% women, 41% men
- **Moderately difficult** entrance level, 52% of applicants were admitted

Undergraduates 3,676 full-time, 2,147 part-time. Students come from 23 states and territories; 16 other countries; 0.8% are from out of state; 0.7% Black or African American, non-Hispanic/Latino; 93% Hispanic/Latino; 0.6% Asian, non-Hispanic/Latino; 0.1% American Indian or Alaska Native, non-Hispanic/Latino; 0.1% Two or more races, non-Hispanic/Latino; 1% Race/ethnicity unknown; 2% international; 8% transferred in; 13% live on campus. *Retention:* 73% of full-time freshmen returned.

Freshmen *Admission:* 4,055 applied, 2,123 admitted, 866 enrolled. *Average high school GPA:* 3.6. *Test scores:* SAT critical reading scores over 500: 17%; SAT math scores over 500: 30%; SAT writing scores over 500: 18%; ACT scores over 18: 52%; SAT critical reading scores over 600: 3%; SAT math scores over 600: 5%; SAT writing scores over 600: 1%; ACT scores over 24: 8%; ACT scores over 30: 1%.

Faculty *Total:* 326, 56% full-time, 50% with terminal degrees. *Student/faculty ratio:* 21:1.

Academics *Calendar:* semesters. *Degrees:* bachelor's, master's, and doctoral-research/scholarship. *Special study options:* academic remediation for entering students, advanced placement credit, distance learning, double majors,

English as a second language, honors programs, independent study, internships, part-time degree program, services for LD students, study abroad, summer session for credit. *ROTC:* Army (b).

Computers on Campus 410 computers/terminals are available on campus for general student use. Students can access the following: campus intranet, computer help desk, free student e-mail accounts, online (class) grades, online (class) registration, online (class) schedules. Campuswide network is available. 100% of college-owned or -operated housing units are wired for high-speed Internet access. Wireless service is available via classrooms, computer centers, computer labs, learning centers, libraries, student centers.

Student Life *Housing options:* coed. Campus housing is provided by a third party. Freshman applicants given priority for college housing. *Activities and organizations:* drama/theater group, student-run newspaper, choral group, marching band, Fellowship of Christian Athletes (FCA), National Student Speech Language Hearing Association (NSSLHA), Association of International Students (AIS), Campus Activities Board (CAB), Student Government Association (SGA), national fraternities, national sororities. *Campus security:* 24-hour emergency response devices and patrols, late-night transport/escort service, controlled dormitory access. *Student services:* health clinic, personal/psychological counseling, women's center.

Athletics Member NCAA. All Division II. *Intercollegiate sports:* baseball M(s), basketball M(s)/W(s), cross-country running M(s)/W(s), golf M(s)/W(s), soccer M(s)/W(s), softball W(s), volleyball W(s). *Intramural sports:* badminton M/W, basketball M/W, soccer M/W, softball M/W, table tennis M/W, volleyball M/W, weight lifting M/W.

Standardized Tests *Required:* SAT or ACT (for admission).

Costs (2011–12) *Tuition:* state resident $4215 full-time; nonresident $13,515 full-time. Full-time tuition and fees vary according to course load. Part-time tuition and fees vary according to course load and reciprocity agreements. *Required fees:* $1938 full-time. *Room and board:* $6918; room only: $4842. Room and board charges vary according to board plan and housing facility. *Payment plan:* installment. *Waivers:* senior citizens.

Financial Aid Of all full-time matriculated undergraduates who enrolled in 2009, 3,514 applied for aid, 3,236 were judged to have need, 355 had their need fully met. 104 Federal Work-Study jobs (averaging $2361). 16 state and other part-time jobs (averaging $2361). In 2009, 157 non-need-based awards were made. *Average percent of need met:* 67%. *Average financial aid package:* $10,749. *Average need-based loan:* $4095. *Average need-based gift aid:* $6408. *Average non-need-based aid:* $3604. *Average indebtedness upon graduation:* $19,400. *Financial aid deadline:* 8/1.

Applying *Options:* electronic application, early admission, deferred entrance. *Required:* high school transcript. *Application deadlines:* 7/1 (freshmen), 7/1 (transfers). *Notification:* 7/15 (freshmen), 7/15 (transfers).

Freshman Application Contact Ms. Rosa Dickinson, Director of Admissions, Texas A&M International University, 5201 University Boulevard, Laredo, TX 78041-1900. *Phone:* 956-326-2200. *Toll-free phone:* 888-489-2648. *E-mail:* adms@tamiu.edu. *Web site:* http://www.tamiu.edu/.

Texas A&M University
College Station, Texas

- **State-supported** university, founded 1876, part of Texas A&M University System
- **Suburban** 5200-acre campus with easy access to Houston
- **Endowment** $5.7 billion
- **Coed** 39,150 undergraduate students, 92% full-time, 47% women, 53% men
- **Moderately difficult** entrance level, 69% of applicants were admitted

Undergraduates 35,889 full-time, 3,261 part-time. Students come from 52 states and territories; 128 other countries; 3% are from out of state; 3% Black or African American, non-Hispanic/Latino; 16% Hispanic/Latino; 5% Asian, non-Hispanic/Latino; 0.1% Native Hawaiian or other Pacific Islander, non-Hispanic/Latino; 0.4% American Indian or Alaska Native, non-Hispanic/Latino; 2% Two or more races, non-Hispanic/Latino; 0.1% Race/ethnicity unknown; 2% international; 4% transferred in; 25% live on campus. *Retention:* 91% of full-time freshmen returned.

Freshmen *Admission:* 23,407 applied, 16,130 admitted, 8,178 enrolled. *Test scores:* SAT critical reading scores over 500: 85%; SAT math scores over 500: 93%; SAT writing scores over 500: 79%; ACT scores over 18: 99%; SAT critical reading scores over 600: 48%; SAT math scores over 600: 66%; SAT writing scores over 600: 36%; ACT scores over 24: 81%; SAT critical reading scores over 700: 9%; SAT math scores over 700: 17%; SAT writing scores over 700: 5%; ACT scores over 30: 27%.

Faculty *Total:* 2,818, 82% full-time, 88% with terminal degrees. *Student/faculty ratio:* 19:1.

Academics *Calendar:* semesters. *Degrees:* bachelor's, master's, doctoral-professional, doctoral-research/scholarship, and postbachelor's certificates. *Special study options:* academic remediation for entering students, accelerated degree program, advanced placement credit, cooperative education, distance learning, double majors, English as a second language, honors programs, inde-

pendent study, internships, off-campus study, part-time degree program, services for LD students, study abroad, summer session for credit. *ROTC:* Army (b), Navy (b), Air Force (b).

Computers on Campus 1,840 computers/terminals and 5,000 ports are available on campus for general student use. Students can access the following: campus intranet, computer help desk, free student e-mail accounts, online (class) grades, online (class) registration, online (class) schedules. Campuswide network is available. 100% of college-owned or -operated housing units are wired for high-speed Internet access. Wireless service is available via classrooms, computer labs, learning centers, libraries, student centers.

Student Life *Housing options:* coed, men-only, women-only, disabled students. Campus housing is university owned. *Activities and organizations:* drama/theater group, student-run newspaper, radio and television station, choral group, marching band, Memorial Student Center, Corps of Cadets, Fish Camp, student government, national fraternities, national sororities. *Campus security:* 24-hour emergency response devices and patrols, late-night transport/escort service, controlled dormitory access, student escorts. *Student services:* health clinic, personal/psychological counseling, women's center, legal services.

Athletics Member NCAA. All Division I except football (Division I-A). *Intercollegiate sports:* archery W(s), baseball M(s), basketball M(s)/W(s), cross-country running M(s)/W(s), equestrian sports W(s), golf M(s)/W(s), soccer W(s), softball W(s), swimming and diving M(s)/W(s), tennis M(s)/W(s), track and field M(s)/W(s), volleyball W(s). *Intramural sports:* archery M/W, badminton M/W, basketball M/W, bowling M/W, cross-country running M/W, fencing M(c)/W(c), field hockey M(c)/W(c), football M/W, golf M/W, gymnastics M(c)/W(c), lacrosse M(c)/W(c), racquetball M(c)/W(c), riflery M/W, rugby M(c)/W(c), sailing M(c)/W(c), soccer M/W, softball M/W, squash M/W, swimming and diving M/W, table tennis M/W, tennis M/W, track and field M/W, ultimate Frisbee M(c)/W(c), volleyball M/W, water polo M/W, weight lifting M(c)/W(c), wrestling M(c).

Standardized Tests *Required:* SAT or ACT (for admission).

Costs (2010–11) *Tuition:* state resident $5297 full-time, $177 per credit hour part-time; nonresident $19,727 full-time, $658 per credit hour part-time. *Required fees:* $3090 full-time. *Room and board:* $8008. Room and board charges vary according to board plan, housing facility, and location. *Payment plan:* installment.

Financial Aid Of all full-time matriculated undergraduates who enrolled in 2009, 20,677 applied for aid, 14,739 were judged to have need, 6,618 had their need fully met. 693 Federal Work-Study jobs (averaging $2567). 109 state and other part-time jobs (averaging $2320). In 2009, 1925 non-need-based awards were made. *Average percent of need met:* 71%. *Average financial aid package:* $14,950. *Average need-based loan:* $6454. *Average need-based gift aid:* $9278. *Average non-need-based aid:* $3532. *Average indebtedness upon graduation:* $22,243.

Applying *Options:* electronic application. *Application fee:* $60. *Required:* essay or personal statement, high school transcript. *Application deadlines:* 1/15 (freshmen), 3/15 (transfers). *Notification:* continuous (freshmen), continuous (transfers).

Freshman Application Contact Mr. Scott McDonald, Director of Admissions, Texas A&M University, 217 John J. Koldus Building, College Station, TX 77843-1265. *Phone:* 979-845-3741. *Fax:* 979-845-8737. *E-mail:* admissions@tamu.edu. *Web site:* http://www.tamu.edu/.

Texas A&M University at Galveston
Galveston, Texas

- **State-supported** comprehensive, founded 1962, part of Texas A&M University System
- **Suburban** 122-acre campus with easy access to Houston
- **Endowment** $2.2 million
- **Coed**
- **Moderately difficult** entrance level

Faculty *Student/faculty ratio:* 12:1.

Academics *Calendar:* semesters. *Degrees:* bachelor's and master's.

Student Life *Campus security:* 24-hour emergency response devices and patrols.

Standardized Tests *Required:* SAT or ACT (for admission). *Recommended:* SAT Subject Tests (for admission).

Costs (2010–11) *One-time required fee:* $75. *Tuition:* state resident $5456 full-time, $182 per credit hour part-time; nonresident $14,756 full-time, $492 per credit hour part-time. Full-time tuition and fees vary according to course load and program. Part-time tuition and fees vary according to course load and program. *Required fees:* $1702 full-time, $846 per term part-time. *Room and board:* $6276; room only: $2750. Room and board charges vary according to board plan and housing facility.

Financial Aid *Of all full-time matriculated undergraduates who enrolled in 2007,* 804 applied for aid, 714 were judged to have need, 130 had their need fully met. 6 Federal Work-Study jobs (averaging $2383). 1 state and other part-time job (averaging $500). *In 2007,* 40 non-need-based awards were made.

Average percent of need met: 18. *Average financial aid package:* $11,234. *Average need-based loan:* $3452. *Average need-based gift aid:* $5016. *Average non-need-based aid:* $5267. *Average indebtedness upon graduation:* $16,800.

Applying *Options:* electronic application, early admission, deferred entrance. *Application fee:* $45. *Required:* essay or personal statement, high school transcript. *Required for some:* interview. *Recommended:* 2 letters of recommendation, community involvement.

Freshman Application Contact Ms. Sarah Trombley, Associate Director of Admissions and Records, Texas A&M University at Galveston, PO Box 1675, Galveston, TX 77553-1675. *Phone:* 409-740-4448. *Fax:* 409-740-4731. *E-mail:* seaaggie@tamug.edu. *Web site:* http://www.tamug.edu/.

Texas A&M University–Commerce
Commerce, Texas

- **State-supported** university, founded 1889, part of Texas A&M University System
- **Small-town** 1883-acre campus with easy access to Dallas-Fort Worth
- **Endowment** $12.6 million
- **Coed**
- **Moderately difficult** entrance level

Faculty *Student/faculty ratio:* 17:1.

Academics *Calendar:* semesters. *Degrees:* bachelor's, master's, and doctoral-research/scholarship.

Student Life *Campus security:* 24-hour emergency response devices and patrols, controlled dormitory access.

Athletics Member NCAA. All Division II.

Standardized Tests *Required:* SAT or ACT (for admission).

Costs (2010–11) *Tuition:* state resident $4490 full-time; nonresident $13,790 full-time. Full-time tuition and fees vary according to course load. Part-time tuition and fees vary according to course load. *Required fees:* $1508 full-time. *Room and board:* $7090. Room and board charges vary according to board plan and housing facility.

Financial Aid *Of all full-time matriculated undergraduates who enrolled in 2009,* 3,853 applied for aid, 3,398 were judged to have need, 1,047 had their need fully met. 117 Federal Work-Study jobs (averaging $4019). 39 state and other part-time jobs (averaging $2743). *In 2009,* 339 non-need-based awards were made. *Average percent of need met:* 64. *Average financial aid package:* $10,412. *Average need-based loan:* $4140. *Average need-based gift aid:* $7946. *Average non-need-based aid:* $2343. *Average indebtedness upon graduation:* $26,090.

Applying *Options:* electronic application, early admission. *Application fee:* $25. *Required:* high school transcript.

Freshman Application Contact Hope Young, Director of Admissions, Texas A&M University–Commerce, PO Box 3011, Commerce, TX 75429. *Phone:* 903-886-5103. *Toll-free phone:* 800-331-3878. *Fax:* 903-886-5888. *E-mail:* admissions@tamu-commerce.edu. *Web site:* http://www.tamu-commerce.edu/.

Texas A&M University–Corpus Christi
Corpus Christi, Texas

- **State-supported** university, founded 1947, part of Texas A&M University System
- **Suburban** 240-acre campus
- **Endowment** $5.2 million
- **Coed** 8,054 undergraduate students, 80% full-time, 59% women, 41% men
- **Moderately difficult** entrance level, 85% of applicants were admitted

Undergraduates 6,406 full-time, 1,648 part-time. Students come from 45 states and territories; 42 other countries; 3% are from out of state; 5% Black or African American, non-Hispanic/Latino; 41% Hispanic/Latino; 3% Asian, non-Hispanic/Latino; 0.5% American Indian or Alaska Native, non-Hispanic/Latino; 0.2% Two or more races, non-Hispanic/Latino; 1% Race/ethnicity unknown; 3% international; 11% transferred in; 16% live on campus. *Retention:* 65% of full-time freshmen returned.

Freshmen *Admission:* 5,094 applied, 4,312 admitted, 1,356 enrolled. *Average high school GPA:* 3.3. *Test scores:* SAT critical reading scores over 500: 39%; SAT math scores over 500: 45%; SAT writing scores over 500: 31%; ACT scores over 18: 72%; SAT critical reading scores over 600: 8%; SAT math scores over 600: 11%; SAT writing scores over 600: 4%; ACT scores over 24: 14%; ACT scores over 30: 1%.

Faculty *Total:* 579, 58% full-time, 81% with terminal degrees. *Student/faculty ratio:* 19:1.

Academics *Calendar:* semesters. *Degrees:* bachelor's, master's, and doctoral-research/scholarship. *Special study options:* academic remediation for entering students, advanced placement credit, cooperative education, distance learning, double majors, English as a second language, honors programs,

independent study, internships, off-campus study, part-time degree program, services for LD students, study abroad, summer session for credit. *ROTC:* Army (b). *Unusual degree programs:* engineering; nursing; accounting.

Computers on Campus 500 computers/terminals are available on campus for general student use. Students can access the following: campus intranet, computer help desk, free student e-mail accounts, online (class) grades, online (class) registration, online (class) schedules. Campuswide network is available. 100% of college-owned or -operated housing units are wired for high-speed Internet access. Wireless service is available via entire campus.

Student Life *Housing options:* coed, men-only, women-only. Campus housing is provided by a third party. *Activities and organizations:* drama/theater group, student-run newspaper, choral group, marching band, Student Accounting Society, Student Art Association, Islander Cultural Alliance, Graduate Student Association, Student Nurses Association, national fraternities, national sororities. *Campus security:* 24-hour emergency response devices and patrols, late-night transport/escort service, controlled dormitory access. *Student services:* health clinic, personal/psychological counseling, women's center.

Athletics Member NCAA. All Division I. *Intercollegiate sports:* baseball M(s), basketball M(s)/W(s), cross-country running M(s)/W(s), golf W(s), softball W(s), tennis M(s)/W(s), track and field M/W, volleyball W(s). *Intramural sports:* baseball M, basketball M/W, cross-country running M/W, golf W, racquetball M/W, softball W, tennis M/W, track and field M/W, volleyball W.

Standardized Tests *Required:* SAT or ACT (for admission).

Costs (2011–12) *Tuition:* state resident $4494 full-time, $157 per credit part-time; nonresident $13,794 full-time, $467 per credit part-time. Full-time tuition and fees vary according to course level, course load, and degree level. Part-time tuition and fees vary according to course level, course load, and degree level. *Required fees:* $2020 full-time, $120 per credit hour part-time. *Room and board:* $9528; room only: $6677. Room and board charges vary according to housing facility and location. *Payment plan:* installment. *Waivers:* senior citizens and employees or children of employees.

Financial Aid Of all full-time matriculated undergraduates who enrolled in 2009, 3,401 applied for aid, 2,812 were judged to have need, 308 had their need fully met. 132 Federal Work-Study jobs (averaging $3599). 124 state and other part-time jobs (averaging $3384). In 2009, 472 non-need-based awards were made. *Average percent of need met:* 65%. *Average financial aid package:* $9559. *Average need-based loan:* $4183. *Average need-based gift aid:* $6498. *Average non-need-based aid:* $1984. *Average indebtedness upon graduation:* $18,314.

Applying *Options:* electronic application. *Application fee:* $25. *Required:* high school transcript, minimum 2 GPA. *Application deadlines:* 7/1 (freshmen), 7/1 (out-of-state freshmen), 7/1 (transfers). *Notification:* continuous (freshmen), continuous (out-of-state freshmen), continuous (transfers).

Freshman Application Contact Mrs. Monica Martinez, Assistant Director of Admissions, Texas A&M University–Corpus Christi, SSC 107, 6300 Ocean Drive, Unit 5774, Corpus Christi, TX 78412-5774. *Phone:* 361-825-2624. *Toll-free phone:* 800-482-6822. *Fax:* 361-825-5887. *E-mail:* monica.martinez@tamucc.edu. *Web site:* http://www.tamucc.edu/.

Texas A&M University–Kingsville
Kingsville, Texas

- **State-supported** university, founded 1925, part of Texas A&M University System
- **Small-town** 255-acre campus
- **Endowment** $15.0 million
- **Coed** 5,269 undergraduate students, 84% full-time, 46% women, 54% men
- **Moderately difficult** entrance level, 98% of applicants were admitted

Undergraduates 4,444 full-time, 825 part-time. Students come from 32 states and territories; 24 other countries; 0.2% are from out of state; 7% Black or African American, non-Hispanic/Latino; 66% Hispanic/Latino; 1% Asian, non-Hispanic/Latino; 0.5% American Indian or Alaska Native, non-Hispanic/Latino; 2% Race/ethnicity unknown; 2% international; 8% transferred in. *Retention:* 59% of full-time freshmen returned.

Freshmen *Admission:* 3,863 applied, 3,791 admitted, 1,272 enrolled. *Average high school GPA:* 3.39. *Test scores:* SAT critical reading scores over 500: 18%; SAT math scores over 500: 30%; SAT writing scores over 500: 16%; ACT scores over 18: 55%; SAT math scores over 600: 6%; SAT writing scores over 600: 2%; ACT scores over 24: 8%; ACT scores over 30: 1%.

Faculty *Total:* 388, 78% full-time. *Student/faculty ratio:* 17:1.

Academics *Calendar:* semesters. *Degrees:* bachelor's, master's, doctoral-research/scholarship, and postbachelor's certificates. *Special study options:* academic remediation for entering students, advanced placement credit, cooperative education, distance learning, double majors, English as a second language, honors programs, internships, off-campus study, part-time degree program, services for LD students, study abroad, summer session for credit. *ROTC:* Army (b). *Unusual degree programs:* 3-2 business administration.

Computers on Campus Students can access the following: campus intranet, computer help desk, free student e-mail accounts, online (class) grades, online (class) registration, online (class) schedules, Blackboard. Campuswide network is available. Wireless service is available via classrooms, computer centers, computer labs, dorm rooms, learning centers, libraries.

Student Life *Housing:* on-campus residence required for freshman year. *Options:* coed, men-only, women-only. Campus housing is university owned. Freshman campus housing is guaranteed. *Activities and organizations:* drama/theater group, student-run newspaper, radio and television station, choral group, marching band, national fraternities, national sororities. *Campus security:* 24-hour emergency response devices and patrols, late-night transport/escort service, controlled dormitory access. *Student services:* health clinic, personal/psychological counseling, women's center.

Athletics Member NCAA, NAIA. All NCAA Division II. *Intercollegiate sports:* baseball M(s), basketball M(s)/W(s), cross-country running M(s)/W(s), equestrian sports M/W, football M(s), golf W(s), softball W(s), track and field M(s)/W(s), volleyball W(s). *Intramural sports:* badminton M/W, basketball M/W, bowling M/W, fencing M/W, football M/W, golf M/W, racquetball M/W, soccer M/W, swimming and diving M/W, tennis M/W, volleyball W, weight lifting M/W.

Standardized Tests *Required:* SAT or ACT (for admission).

Costs (2010–11) *Tuition:* state resident $6346 full-time; nonresident $15,646 full-time. Full-time tuition and fees vary according to course load and degree level. Part-time tuition and fees vary according to course load and degree level. *Room and board:* $5130. Room and board charges vary according to board plan and housing facility. *Payment plans:* tuition prepayment, installment, deferred payment. *Waivers:* senior citizens and employees or children of employees.

Financial Aid Of all full-time matriculated undergraduates who enrolled in 2005, 4,449 applied for aid, 4,214 were judged to have need, 2,899 had their need fully met. *Average financial aid package:* $6500. *Average need-based loan:* $3875. *Average need-based gift aid:* $6500. *Average indebtedness upon graduation:* $2867.

Applying *Options:* electronic application, early admission, deferred entrance. *Application fee:* $15. *Required:* high school transcript. *Required for some:* interview. *Recommended:* minimum 2 GPA. *Application deadlines:* rolling (freshmen), rolling (transfers). *Notification:* continuous (freshmen), continuous (transfers).

Freshman Application Contact Laura Knippers, Associate Director of Admissions and Enrollment Management, Texas A&M University–Kingsville,

MSC 116, 700 University Boulevard, Kingsville, TX 78363. *Phone:* 361-593-3907. *Toll-free phone:* 800-687-6000. *Fax:* 361-593-2991. *E-mail:* laura.knippers@tamuk.edu. *Web site:* http://www.tamuk.edu/.

Texas A&M University–San Antonio
San Antonio, Texas

Freshman Application Contact Jennifer Zamarripa, Director of Admissions and Registrar, Texas A&M University–San Antonio, 1450 Gillette Boulevard, San Antonio, TX 78224. *Phone:* 210-932-6201. *E-mail:* jennifer.zamarripa@tamusa.tamus.edu. *Web site:* http://www.tamuk.edu/sanantonio/.

Texas A&M University–Texarkana
Texarkana, Texas

Application Contact Mrs. Patricia Black, Director of Admissions and Registrar, Texas A&M University–Texarkana, PO Box 5518, Texarkana, TX 75505-5518. *Phone:* 903-223-3068. *Fax:* 903-223-3140. *E-mail:* admissions@tamut.edu. *Web site:* http://www.tamut.edu/.

Texas Christian University
Fort Worth, Texas

- **Independent** university, founded 1873, affiliated with Christian Church (Disciples of Christ)
- **Suburban** 272-acre campus with easy access to Dallas-Fort Worth
- **Endowment** $1.1 billion
- **Coed** 7,853 undergraduate students, 96% full-time, 59% women, 41% men
- **Moderately difficult** entrance level, 53% of applicants were admitted

Undergraduates 7,538 full-time, 315 part-time. Students come from 49 states and territories; 88 other countries; 25% are from out of state; 5% Black or African American, non-Hispanic/Latino; 10% Hispanic/Latino; 2% Asian, non-Hispanic/Latino; 0.2% Native Hawaiian or other Pacific Islander, non-Hispanic/Latino; 0.8% American Indian or Alaska Native, non-Hispanic/Latino; 0.5% Two or more races, non-Hispanic/Latino; 2% Race/ethnicity unknown;

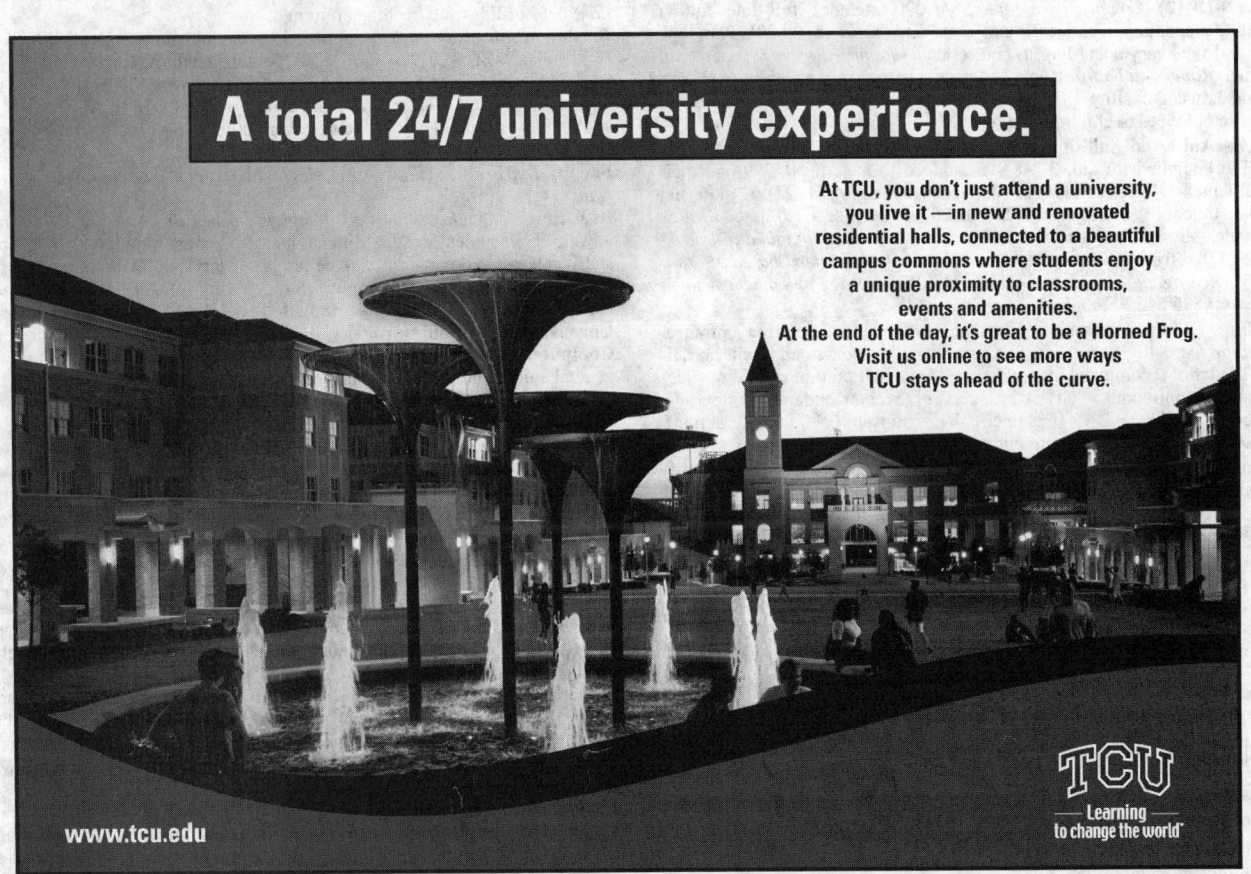

5% international; 6% transferred in; 50% live on campus. *Retention:* 86% of full-time freshmen returned.

Freshmen *Admission:* 14,085 applied, 7,428 admitted, 1,827 enrolled.

Faculty *Total:* 845, 63% full-time, 66% with terminal degrees. *Student/faculty ratio:* 13:1.

Academics *Calendar:* semesters. *Degrees:* certificates, diplomas, bachelor's, master's, doctoral-professional, doctoral-research/scholarship, post-master's, and postbachelor's certificates. *Special study options:* accelerated degree program, adult/continuing education programs, advanced placement credit, distance learning, double majors, English as a second language, freshman honors college, honors programs, independent study, internships, part-time degree program, services for LD students, study abroad, summer session for credit. *ROTC:* Army (b), Air Force (b). *Unusual degree programs:* The Four-One Option allows outstanding students to combine a bachelor's degree with the Master of Education (M.Ed.) in only five years.

Computers on Campus 1,200 computers/terminals and 10,000 ports are available on campus for general student use. Students can access the following: campus intranet, computer help desk, free student e-mail accounts, online (class) grades, online (class) registration, online (class) schedules. Campus-wide network is available. 100% of college-owned or -operated housing units are wired for high-speed Internet access. Wireless service is available via entire campus.

Student Life *Housing:* on-campus residence required through sophomore year. *Options:* coed, women-only. Campus housing is university owned. Freshman campus housing is guaranteed. *Activities and organizations:* drama/theater group, student-run newspaper, radio and television station, choral group, marching band, national fraternities, national sororities. *Campus security:* 24-hour emergency response devices and patrols, student patrols, late-night transport/escort service, controlled dormitory access, emergency call boxes, video camera surveillance in parking lots, self-defense educ., lighted sidewalks, emergency notification system. *Student services:* health clinic, personal/psychological counseling, women's center, legal services.

Athletics Member NCAA. All Division I. *Intercollegiate sports:* baseball M(s), basketball M(s)/W(s), cross-country running M(s)/W(s), equestrian sports W(s), football M(s), golf M(s)/W(s), riflery W(s), soccer W(s), swimming and diving M(s)/W(s), tennis M(s)/W(s), track and field M(s)/W(s), volleyball W(s). *Intramural sports:* baseball M(c), basketball M/W, bowling M/W, gymnastics M(c)/W(c), lacrosse M(c)/W(c), racquetball M/W, rugby M(c)/W(c), soccer M(c)/W(c), softball M/W, table tennis M/W, tennis M(c)/W(c), ultimate Frisbee M(c)/W(c), volleyball W(c), wrestling M(c)/W(c).

Standardized Tests *Required:* SAT or ACT (for admission).

Costs (2011–12) *Comprehensive fee:* $43,090 includes full-time tuition ($32,400), mandatory fees ($90), and room and board ($10,600). Part-time tuition and fees vary according to course load. *Required fees:* $90 per term part-time. *Room and board:* Room and board charges vary according to board plan and housing facility. *Payment plans:* tuition prepayment, installment. *Waivers:* employees or children of employees.

Financial Aid Of all full-time matriculated undergraduates who enrolled in 2009, 3,941 applied for aid, 3,248 were judged to have need, 799 had their need fully met. 1,420 Federal Work-Study jobs (averaging $1722). 32 state and other part-time jobs (averaging $1927). In 2009, 1763 non-need-based awards were made. *Average percent of need met:* 64%. *Average financial aid package:* $20,378. *Average need-based loan:* $4405. *Average need-based gift aid:* $17,417. *Average non-need-based aid:* $11,301. *Average indebtedness upon graduation:* $36,546. *Financial aid deadline:* 5/1.

Applying *Options:* electronic application, early action, deferred entrance. *Application fee:* $40. *Required:* essay or personal statement, high school transcript, 1 letter of recommendation. *Required for some:* minimum 2 GPA. *Recommended:* minimum 3 GPA, 2 letters of recommendation, interview. *Application deadlines:* 2/15 (freshmen), 4/15 (transfers), 11/1 (early action). *Notification:* 4/1 (freshmen), continuous (transfers), 1/1 (early action).

Freshman Application Contact Mr. Wes Waggoner, Director of Freshman Admissions, Texas Christian University, 2800 South University Drive, Fort Worth, TX 76129-0002. *Phone:* 817-257-7490. *Toll-free phone:* 800-828-3764. *Fax:* 817-257-7268. *E-mail:* frogmail@tcu.edu. *Web site:* http://www.tcu.edu/.

See page 1662 for the College Close-Up.

Texas College

Tyler, Texas

- **Independent** 4-year, founded 1894, affiliated with Christian Methodist Episcopal Church
- **Urban** 25-acre campus
- **Endowment** $1.3 million
- **Coed**
- **Noncompetitive** entrance level

Faculty *Student/faculty ratio:* 24:1.

Academics *Calendar:* semesters. *Degrees:* associate, bachelor's, and post-bachelor's certificates.

Student Life *Campus security:* 24-hour emergency response devices and patrols, late-night transport/escort service.

Athletics Member NAIA.

Standardized Tests *Required:* SAT or ACT (for admission).

Costs (2010–11) *One-time required fee:* $20. *Comprehensive fee:* $16,090 includes full-time tuition ($8000), mandatory fees ($1490), and room and board ($6600). Part-time tuition: $333 per credit hour. *Required fees:* $745 per term part-time. *College room only:* $3600.

Financial Aid Of all full-time matriculated undergraduates who enrolled in 2008, 837 applied for aid, 815 were judged to have need, 30 had their need fully met. 144 Federal Work-Study jobs (averaging $1528). 19 state and other part-time jobs (averaging $1057). In 2008, 31 non-need-based awards were made. *Average percent of need met:* 58. *Average financial aid package:* $9402. *Average need-based loan:* $3304. *Average need-based gift aid:* $6375. *Average non-need-based aid:* $3099. *Average indebtedness upon graduation:* $27,158.

Applying *Options:* electronic application, early admission. *Application fee:* $20. *Required:* high school transcript, minimum 2 GPA.

Freshman Application Contact Mr. John Roberts, Director of Admissions, Texas College, 2404 North Grand Avenue, Tyler, TX 75702. *Phone:* 903-593-8311 Ext. 2297. *Toll-free phone:* 800-306-6299. *Fax:* 903-596-0001. *E-mail:* jroberts@texascollege.edu. *Web site:* http://www.texascollege.edu/.

Texas Lutheran University

Seguin, Texas

- **Independent** 4-year, founded 1891, affiliated with Evangelical Lutheran Church
- **Suburban** 196-acre campus with easy access to San Antonio
- **Endowment** $67.5 million
- **Coed** 1,340 undergraduate students, 95% full-time, 52% women, 48% men
- **Moderately difficult** entrance level, 65% of applicants were admitted

Undergraduates 1,272 full-time, 68 part-time. Students come from 23 states and territories; 12 other countries; 4% are from out of state; 10% Black or African American, non-Hispanic/Latino; 23% Hispanic/Latino; 0.9% Asian, non-Hispanic/Latino; 0.2% American Indian or Alaska Native, non-Hispanic/Latino; 2% Two or more races, non-Hispanic/Latino; 3% Race/ethnicity unknown; 1% international; 6% transferred in; 60% live on campus. *Retention:* 67% of full-time freshmen returned.

Freshmen *Admission:* 1,625 applied, 1,050 admitted, 340 enrolled. *Average high school GPA:* 3.5. *Test scores:* SAT critical reading scores over 500: 43%; SAT math scores over 500: 60%; ACT scores over 18: 85%; SAT critical reading scores over 600: 12%; SAT math scores over 600: 18%; ACT scores over 24: 29%; SAT critical reading scores over 700: 2%; SAT math scores over 700: 1%; ACT scores over 30: 3%.

Faculty *Total:* 140, 51% full-time, 57% with terminal degrees. *Student/faculty ratio:* 14:1.

Academics *Calendar:* semesters. *Degree:* bachelor's. *Special study options:* advanced placement credit, double majors, honors programs, independent study, internships, part-time degree program, services for LD students, study abroad, summer session for credit. *ROTC:* Army (c), Air Force (c). *Unusual degree programs:* 3-2 engineering with Texas A&M University, Texas Tech University, Texas State University.

Computers on Campus 237 computers/terminals are available on campus for general student use. Students can access the following: campus intranet, computer help desk, free student e-mail accounts, online (class) grades, online (class) registration, online (class) schedules, free printing. Campuswide network is available. 100% of college-owned or -operated housing units are wired for high-speed Internet access. Wireless service is available via classrooms, computer centers, computer labs, learning centers, libraries, student centers.

Student Life *Housing:* on-campus residence required through senior year. *Options:* coed, men-only, women-only. Campus housing is university owned. Freshman campus housing is guaranteed. *Activities and organizations:* drama/theater group, student-run newspaper, choral group, Campus Ministry, Mexican American Student Association, Student Government Association. *Campus security:* 24-hour emergency response devices and patrols, late-night transport/escort service, controlled dormitory access. *Student services:* health clinic, personal/psychological counseling, women's center.

Athletics Member NCAA. All Division III. *Intercollegiate sports:* baseball M, basketball M/W, cross-country running W, football M, golf M/W, soccer M/W, softball W, tennis M/W, track and field W, volleyball W. *Intramural sports:* basketball M/W, bowling M/W, football M, racquetball M/W, softball M/W, tennis M/W, volleyball M/W.

Standardized Tests *Required:* SAT or ACT (for admission).

Costs (2010–11) *Comprehensive fee:* $29,630 includes full-time tuition ($22,760), mandatory fees ($130), and room and board ($6740). Full-time tuition and fees vary according to course load. Part-time tuition: $760 per

semester hour. Part-time tuition and fees vary according to course load. *Required fees:* $65 per term part-time. *College room only:* $3400. Room and board charges vary according to board plan, housing facility, and location. *Payment plan:* installment. *Waivers:* children of alumni and employees or children of employees.

Financial Aid Of all full-time matriculated undergraduates who enrolled in 2009, 1,081 applied for aid, 950 were judged to have need, 350 had their need fully met. 533 Federal Work-Study jobs (averaging $1812). 35 state and other part-time jobs (averaging $1662). In 2009, 261 non-need-based awards were made. *Average percent of need met:* 37%. *Average financial aid package:* $18,482. *Average need-based loan:* $4844. *Average need-based gift aid:* $13,472. *Average non-need-based aid:* $8785. *Average indebtedness upon graduation:* $29,200.

Applying *Options:* electronic application, deferred entrance. *Application fee:* $40. *Required:* essay or personal statement, high school transcript, 2 letters of recommendation. *Required for some:* minimum 2 GPA. *Recommended:* interview. *Application deadlines:* rolling (freshmen), rolling (transfers). *Notification:* 8/1 (freshmen), continuous until 8/1 (transfers).

Freshman Application Contact Mr. Norm Jones, Vice President for Enrollment Services, Texas Lutheran University, 1000 West Court Street, Seguin, TX 78155-5999. *Phone:* 830-372-8053. *Toll-free phone:* 800-771-8521. *Fax:* 830-372-8096. *E-mail:* njones@tlu.edu. *Web site:* http://www.tlu.edu/.

Texas Southern University

Houston, Texas

- **State-supported** university, founded 1947, part of Texas Higher Education Coordinating Board
- **Urban** 147-acre campus
- **Coed** 6,964 undergraduate students, 84% full-time, 57% women, 43% men
- **Noncompetitive** entrance level, 36% of applicants were admitted

Undergraduates 5,828 full-time, 1,136 part-time. Students come from 44 states and territories; 14% are from out of state; 89% Black or African American, non-Hispanic/Latino; 4% Hispanic/Latino; 2% Asian, non-Hispanic/Latino; 0.2% American Indian or Alaska Native, non-Hispanic/Latino; 3% international; 9% transferred in; 21% live on campus. *Retention:* 61% of full-time freshmen returned.

Freshmen *Admission:* 8,787 applied, 3,201 admitted, 1,188 enrolled. *Average high school GPA:* 2.7. *Test scores:* SAT critical reading scores over 500: 9%; SAT math scores over 500: 13%; SAT writing scores over 500: 9%; ACT scores over 18: 34%; SAT critical reading scores over 600: 1%; SAT math scores over 600: 2%; SAT writing scores over 600: 1%; ACT scores over 24: 3%.

Faculty *Total:* 585, 59% full-time. *Student/faculty ratio:* 20:1.

Academics *Calendar:* semesters. *Degrees:* bachelor's, master's, doctoral-professional, and doctoral-research/scholarship. *Special study options:* academic remediation for entering students, accelerated degree program, adult/continuing education programs, cooperative education, distance learning, English as a second language, honors programs, independent study, internships, off-campus study, part-time degree program, services for LD students, study abroad, summer session for credit. *ROTC:* Army (c), Navy (c).

Computers on Campus Students can access the following: computer help desk, free student e-mail accounts, online (class) grades, online (class) registration, online (class) schedules, Blackboard Learning and Community Portal System (E-education). Campuswide network is available. Wireless service is available via entire campus.

Student Life *Housing options:* coed, men-only, women-only. Campus housing is university owned, leased by the school and is provided by a third party. Freshman campus housing is guaranteed. *Activities and organizations:* drama/theater group, student-run newspaper, radio station, choral group, marching band, Debate Team, University Program Council, Student Government Association, band, national fraternities, national sororities. *Campus security:* 24-hour emergency response devices and patrols, student patrols, late-night transport/escort service. *Student services:* health clinic, personal/psychological counseling, legal services.

Athletics Member NCAA. All Division I except football (Division I-AA). *Intercollegiate sports:* baseball M(s), basketball M(s)/W(s), bowling W(s), cross-country running M(s)/W(s), golf M(s), soccer M/W(s), softball W(s), tennis M(s)/W(s), track and field M(s)/W(s), volleyball M/W(s). *Intramural sports:* softball M/W, swimming and diving M/W, tennis M/W, volleyball M/W.

Standardized Tests *Required:* SAT or ACT (for admission).

Costs (2010–11) *Tuition:* state resident $7462 full-time; nonresident $15,772 full-time. Full-time tuition and fees vary according to course level, course load, degree level, and program. Part-time tuition and fees vary according to course level, course load, degree level, and program. *Room and board:* $11,880. Room and board charges vary according to board plan and housing facility.

Payment plans: installment, deferred payment. *Waivers:* minority students and senior citizens.

Financial Aid Of all full-time matriculated undergraduates who enrolled in 2009, 6,477 applied for aid, 5,141 were judged to have need, 1,365 had their need fully met. 380 Federal Work-Study jobs (averaging $4000). 29 state and other part-time jobs (averaging $4000). *Average percent of need met:* 53%. *Average financial aid package:* $15,918. *Average need-based loan:* $6520. *Average need-based gift aid:* $12,353. *Average indebtedness upon graduation:* $7883.

Applying *Options:* electronic application. *Application fee:* $42. *Required:* high school transcript, minimum 2 GPA. *Application deadlines:* 8/15 (freshmen), 8/13 (transfers). *Notification:* 8/28 (freshmen), continuous until 8/28 (transfers).

Freshman Application Contact Enrollment Services Customer Service Center, Texas Southern University, 3100 Cleburne Street, Houston, TX 77004-4598. *Phone:* 713-313-7071. *Fax:* 713-313-7851. *E-mail:* eservices@em.tsu.edu. *Web site:* http://www.tsu.edu/.

Texas State University–San Marcos

San Marcos, Texas

- **State-supported** university, founded 1899, part of Texas State University System
- **Suburban** 423-acre campus with easy access to San Antonio and Austin
- **Endowment** $86.9 million
- **Coed** 27,448 undergraduate students, 81% full-time, 55% women, 45% men
- **Moderately difficult** entrance level, 76% of applicants were admitted

Undergraduates 22,331 full-time, 5,117 part-time. Students come from 44 states and territories; 44 other countries; 1% are from out of state; 6% Black or African American, non-Hispanic/Latino; 26% Hispanic/Latino; 2% Asian, non-Hispanic/Latino; 0.1% Native Hawaiian or other Pacific Islander, non-Hispanic/Latino; 0.6% American Indian or Alaska Native, non-Hispanic/Latino; 1% Two or more races, non-Hispanic/Latino; 1% Race/ethnicity unknown; 0.3% international; 13% transferred in; 20% live on campus. *Retention:* 79% of full-time freshmen returned.

Freshmen *Admission:* 13,311 applied, 10,054 admitted, 3,930 enrolled. *Test scores:* SAT critical reading scores over 500: 62%; SAT math scores over 500: 71%; SAT writing scores over 500: 53%; ACT scores over 18: 96%; SAT critical reading scores over 600: 17%; SAT math scores over 600: 21%; SAT writing scores over 600: 11%; ACT scores over 24: 41%; SAT critical reading scores over 700: 2%; SAT math scores over 700: 1%; SAT writing scores over 700: 1%; ACT scores over 30: 4%.

Faculty *Total:* 1,546, 70% full-time, 64% with terminal degrees. *Student/faculty ratio:* 19:1.

Academics *Calendar:* semesters. *Degrees:* bachelor's, master's, doctoral-professional, doctoral-research/scholarship, and postbachelor's certificates. *Special study options:* academic remediation for entering students, accelerated degree program, adult/continuing education programs, advanced placement credit, distance learning, double majors, English as a second language, honors programs, independent study, internships, off-campus study, part-time degree program, services for LD students, study abroad, summer session for credit. *ROTC:* Army (b), Air Force (b). *Unusual degree programs:* 3-2 engineering with University of Texas at Austin, Texas A&M University, Texas Tech University, University of Texas at San Antonio.

Computers on Campus 1,792 computers/terminals are available on campus for general student use. Students can access the following: computer help desk, free student e-mail accounts, online (class) grades, online (class) registration, online (class) schedules. Campuswide network is available. 100% of college-owned or -operated housing units are wired for high-speed Internet access. Wireless service is available via entire campus.

Student Life *Housing:* on-campus residence required through sophomore year. *Options:* coed, men-only, women-only. Campus housing is university owned. Freshman campus housing is guaranteed. *Activities and organizations:* drama/theater group, student-run newspaper, radio station, choral group, marching band, Non-traditional Students Association, Student Association for Campus Activities, Association Student Government, national fraternities, national sororities. *Campus security:* 24-hour emergency response devices and patrols, late-night transport/escort service, controlled dormitory access. *Student services:* health clinic, personal/psychological counseling, legal services.

Athletics Member NCAA. All Division I except football (Division I-AA). *Intercollegiate sports:* baseball M(s), basketball M(s)/W(s), cheerleading M/W, cross-country running M(s)/W(s), equestrian sports M(c)/W(c), fencing M(c)/W(c), golf M(s)/W(s), gymnastics M(c)/W(c), lacrosse M(c)/W(c), rugby M(c)/W(c), soccer M(c)/W(s), softball M(c)/W(s), tennis M(c)/W(s), track and field M(s)/W(s), ultimate Frisbee M(c)/W(c), volleyball W(s), water polo M(c)/W(c), weight lifting M(c)/W(c), wrestling M(c)/W(c). *Intramural sports:* basketball M/W, bowling M/W, cross-country running M/W, football M/W, golf M/W, racquetball M/W, soccer M/W, softball M/W, tennis M/W, ultimate Frisbee M, volleyball M/W.

Standardized Tests *Required:* SAT or ACT (for admission).

Costs (2010–11) *Tuition:* state resident $5730 full-time, $191 per credit hour part-time; nonresident $15,030 full-time, $501 per credit hour part-time. Full-time tuition and fees vary according to course load and degree level. Part-time tuition and fees vary according to course load and degree level. *Required fees:* $2108 full-time, $48 per credit hour part-time, $379 per term part-time. *Room and board:* $6810; room only: $4380. Room and board charges vary according to board plan and housing facility. *Payment plan:* installment. *Waivers:* employees or children of employees.

Financial Aid Of all full-time matriculated undergraduates who enrolled in 2009, 16,045 applied for aid, 12,910 were judged to have need, 1,218 had their need fully met. 675 Federal Work-Study jobs (averaging $2228). 120 state and other part-time jobs (averaging $2093). In 2009, 390 non-need-based awards were made. *Average percent of need met:* 65%. *Average financial aid package:* $14,112. *Average need-based loan:* $4278. *Average need-based gift aid:* $6518. *Average non-need-based aid:* $2239. *Average indebtedness upon graduation:* $21,667.

Applying *Options:* electronic application, early admission, deferred entrance. *Application fee:* $60. *Required:* essay or personal statement, high school transcript. *Application deadlines:* 5/1 (freshmen), 5/1 (out-of-state freshmen), 7/1 (transfers). *Notification:* continuous (freshmen), continuous (transfers).

Freshman Application Contact Texas State University–San Marcos, 601 University Drive, San Marcos, TX 78666. *Phone:* 512-245-2364 Ext. 2803. *Web site:* http://www.txstate.edu/.

Texas Tech University

Lubbock, Texas

- **State-supported** university, founded 1923, part of Texas Tech University System
- **Urban** 1839-acre campus
- **Endowment** $429.2 million
- **Coed** 25,462 undergraduate students, 90% full-time, 45% women, 55% men
- **Moderately difficult** entrance level, 72% of applicants were admitted

Undergraduates 22,959 full-time, 2,503 part-time. Students come from 51 states and territories; 111 other countries; 5% are from out of state; 5% Black or African American, non-Hispanic/Latino; 16% Hispanic/Latino; 3% Asian, non-Hispanic/Latino; 0.1% Native Hawaiian or other Pacific Islander, non-Hispanic/Latino; 0.6% American Indian or Alaska Native, non-Hispanic/Latino; 0.9% Two or more races, non-Hispanic/Latino; 2% Race/ethnicity unknown; 3% international; 10% transferred in; 26% live on campus. *Retention:* 82% of full-time freshmen returned.

Freshmen *Admission:* 16,349 applied, 11,720 admitted, 4,858 enrolled. *Test scores:* SAT critical reading scores over 500: 67%; SAT math scores over 500: 80%; SAT writing scores over 500: 59%; ACT scores over 18: 97%; SAT critical reading scores over 600: 20%; SAT math scores over 600: 31%; SAT writing scores over 600: 14%; ACT scores over 24: 47%; SAT critical reading scores over 700: 2%; SAT math scores over 700: 4%; SAT writing scores over 700: 1%; ACT scores over 30: 7%.

Faculty *Total:* 1,390, 85% full-time, 74% with terminal degrees. *Student/faculty ratio:* 23:1.

Academics *Calendar:* semesters. *Degrees:* bachelor's, master's, doctoral-professional, doctoral-research/scholarship, and postbachelor's certificates. *Special study options:* academic remediation for entering students, accelerated degree program, advanced placement credit, cooperative education, distance learning, double majors, English as a second language, external degree program, freshman honors college, honors programs, independent study, internships, off-campus study, part-time degree program, services for LD students, student-designed majors, study abroad, summer session for credit. *ROTC:* Army (b), Air Force (b). *Unusual degree programs:* 3-2 business administration; engineering; architecture, agriculture and applied economics, mathematics, computer science.

Computers on Campus 3,000 computers/terminals are available on campus for general student use. Students can access the following: computer help desk, free student e-mail accounts, online (class) grades, online (class) registration, online (class) schedules, online degree plans, accounts, transcripts, schedules. Campuswide network is available. 100% of college-owned or -operated housing units are wired for high-speed Internet access. Wireless service is available via entire campus.

Student Life *Housing:* on-campus residence required for freshman year. *Options:* coed, men-only, women-only, disabled students. Campus housing is university owned. Freshman campus housing is guaranteed. *Activities and organizations:* drama/theater group, student-run newspaper, choral group, marching band, Red Raider Club, Alpha Lambda Delta, Phi Eta Sigma, Paradigm, Campus Crusade for Christ, national fraternities, national sororities. *Campus security:* 24-hour emergency response devices and patrols, late-night transport/escort service, controlled dormitory access. *Student services:* health clinic, personal/psychological counseling, legal services.

Athletics Member NCAA. All Division I except football (Division I-A). *Intercollegiate sports:* baseball M(s), basketball M(s)/W(s), cross-country running M(s)/W(s), golf M(s)/W(s), soccer W(s), softball W(s), tennis M(s)/W(s), track and field M(s)/W(s), volleyball W(s). *Intramural sports:* badminton M/W, baseball M(c), basketball M(c), bowling M(c)/W, equestrian sports M(c)/W(c), fencing M(c)/W(c), football M/W, golf M/W, gymnastics M(c)/W(c), lacrosse M(c)/W(c), racquetball M/W, rock climbing M(c)/W(c), rugby M(c)/W(c), skiing (downhill) M(c)/W(c), soccer M(c)/W(c), softball M/W, swimming and diving M/W, table tennis M/W, tennis M(c)/W(c), ultimate Frisbee M(c)/W(c), volleyball M/W, water polo M(c)/W(c), weight lifting M/W, wrestling M(c)/W(c).

Standardized Tests *Required:* SAT or ACT (for admission).

Costs (2010–11) *Tuition:* state resident $5370 full-time, $179 per credit hour part-time; nonresident $14,670 full-time, $489 per credit hour part-time. Full-time tuition and fees vary according to course load, program, and reciprocity agreements. Part-time tuition and fees vary according to course load, program, and reciprocity agreements. *Required fees:* $2890 full-time, $36 per credit hour part-time, $905 per term part-time. *Room and board:* $7800; room only: $4100. Room and board charges vary according to board plan and housing facility. *Payment plan:* installment. *Waivers:* senior citizens and employees or children of employees.

Financial Aid Of all full-time matriculated undergraduates who enrolled in 2008, 13,607 applied for aid, 9,784 were judged to have need, 631 had their need fully met. In 2008, 2605 non-need-based awards were made. *Average percent of need met:* 53%. *Average financial aid package:* $9301. *Average need-based loan:* $4223. *Average need-based gift aid:* $7005. *Average non-need-based aid:* $3581.

Applying *Options:* electronic application, early admission. *Application fee:* $50. *Required:* high school transcript. *Recommended:* essay or personal statement. *Application deadlines:* 5/1 (freshmen), rolling (transfers). *Notification:* continuous (freshmen), continuous (transfers).

Freshman Application Contact Texas Tech University, Lubbock, TX 79409. *Phone:* 806-742-1480. *Web site:* http://www.ttu.edu/.

Texas Wesleyan University

Fort Worth, Texas

- **Independent United Methodist** comprehensive, founded 1890
- **Urban** 74-acre campus with easy access to Dallas-Fort Worth
- **Endowment** $47.2 million
- **Coed** 1,844 undergraduate students, 69% full-time, 63% women, 37% men
- **Moderately difficult** entrance level, 49% of applicants were admitted

Undergraduates 1,266 full-time, 578 part-time. Students come from 15 states and territories; 27 other countries; 7% are from out of state; 16% transferred in; 20% live on campus. *Retention:* 66% of full-time freshmen returned.

Freshmen *Admission:* 1,006 applied, 489 admitted, 215 enrolled. *Average high school GPA:* 3.3. *Test scores:* SAT critical reading scores over 500: 37%; SAT math scores over 500: 55%; SAT writing scores over 500: 47%; ACT scores over 18: 88%; SAT critical reading scores over 600: 5%; SAT math scores over 600: 8%; ACT scores over 24: 21%; SAT math scores over 700: 1%; SAT writing scores over 700: 1%; ACT scores over 30: 2%.

Faculty *Total:* 279, 60% full-time, 54% with terminal degrees. *Student/faculty ratio:* 14:1.

Academics *Calendar:* semesters. *Degrees:* bachelor's, master's, and doctoral-other. *Special study options:* accelerated degree program, advanced placement credit, distance learning, double majors, English as a second language, external degree program, independent study, internships, off-campus study, part-time degree program, services for LD students, study abroad, summer session for credit. *ROTC:* Army (c), Navy (c), Air Force (c).

Computers on Campus 77 computers/terminals are available on campus for general student use. Students can access the following: free student e-mail accounts, online (class) grades, online (class) registration, online (class) schedules. Campuswide network is available. Wireless service is available via computer labs, dorm rooms, libraries.

Student Life *Housing options:* coed, men-only, women-only. Campus housing is university owned. *Activities and organizations:* drama/theater group, student-run newspaper, choral group, national fraternities, national sororities. *Campus security:* 24-hour emergency response devices and patrols, student patrols, late-night transport/escort service, controlled dormitory access. *Student services:* health clinic, personal/psychological counseling.

Athletics Member NAIA. *Intercollegiate sports:* baseball M(s), basketball M(s)/W(s), cross-country running M(s)/W(s), golf M(s), soccer M(s)/W(s), softball W(s), table tennis M(s)/W(s), track and field M(s)/W(s), volleyball W(s). *Intramural sports:* basketball M/W, golf M/W, table tennis M/W.

Standardized Tests *Required:* SAT or ACT (for admission).

Costs (2010–11) *Comprehensive fee:* $25,620 includes full-time tuition ($16,985), mandatory fees ($1725), and room and board ($6910). Full-time tuition and fees vary according to degree level and program. Part-time tuition:

$575 per credit hour. Part-time tuition and fees vary according to degree level and program. *Required fees:* $65 per credit hour part-time. *College room only:* $4050. Room and board charges vary according to housing facility. *Payment plans:* installment, deferred payment. *Waivers:* employees or children of employees.
Financial Aid Of all full-time matriculated undergraduates who enrolled in 2004, 974 applied for aid, 799 were judged to have need. *Average percent of need met:* 74%.
Applying *Options:* electronic application, deferred entrance. *Application fee:* $25. *Required:* minimum 2 GPA. *Required for some:* essay or personal statement, high school transcript. *Application deadlines:* rolling (freshmen), rolling (transfers). *Notification:* continuous (freshmen), continuous (transfers).
Freshman Application Contact Texas Wesleyan University, 1201 Wesleyan Street, Fort Worth, TX 76105-1536. *Phone:* 817-531-4422. *Toll-free phone:* 800-580-8980. *Fax:* 817-531-7515. *E-mail:* admission@txwes.edu. *Web site:* http://www.txwes.edu/.

Texas Woman's University
Denton, Texas

- **State-supported** university, founded 1901
- **Suburban** 270-acre campus with easy access to Dallas-Fort Worth
- **Endowment** $9.2 million
- **Coed, primarily women** 8,483 undergraduate students, 69% full-time, 91% women, 9% men
- **Minimally difficult** entrance level, 91% of applicants were admitted

Undergraduates 5,811 full-time, 2,672 part-time. Students come from 47 states and territories; 61 other countries; 1% are from out of state; 20% Black or African American, non-Hispanic/Latino; 20% Hispanic/Latino; 8% Asian, non-Hispanic/Latino; 0.2% Native Hawaiian or other Pacific Islander, non-Hispanic/Latino; 0.8% American Indian or Alaska Native, non-Hispanic/Latino; 0.7% Two or more races, non-Hispanic/Latino; 0.6% Race/ethnicity unknown; 2% international; 14% transferred in; 20% live on campus. *Retention:* 64% of full-time freshmen returned.
Freshmen *Admission:* 3,182 applied, 2,895 admitted, 734 enrolled. *Average high school GPA:* 3.12. *Test scores:* SAT critical reading scores over 500: 30%; SAT math scores over 500: 35%; ACT scores over 18: 66%; SAT critical reading scores over 600: 5%; SAT math scores over 600: 5%; ACT scores over 24: 14%.
Faculty *Total:* 801, 59% full-time. *Student/faculty ratio:* 17:1.
Academics *Calendar:* semesters. *Degrees:* bachelor's, master's, doctoral-professional, doctoral-research/scholarship, post-master's, and postbachelor's certificates. *Special study options:* academic remediation for entering students, accelerated degree program, adult/continuing education programs, advanced placement credit, cooperative education, distance learning, double majors, honors programs, independent study, internships, off-campus study, part-time degree program, services for LD students, study abroad, summer session for credit. *ROTC:* Army (c), Air Force (c).
Computers on Campus 1,000 computers/terminals are available on campus for general student use. Students can access the following: campus intranet, computer help desk, free student e-mail accounts, online (class) grades, online (class) registration, online (class) schedules. Campuswide network is available. 100% of college-owned or -operated housing units are wired for high-speed Internet access. Wireless service is available via libraries, student centers.
Student Life *Housing:* on-campus residence required through sophomore year. *Options:* coed, women-only, disabled students. Campus housing is university owned. Freshman campus housing is guaranteed. *Activities and organizations:* drama/theater group, student-run newspaper, choral group, Helping Hands, Athenian Honor Society, Campus Activities Board, Nursing Student Organization, Graduate Library and Information Studies Association, national fraternities, national sororities. *Campus security:* 24-hour emergency response devices and patrols, late-night transport/escort service, controlled dormitory access. *Student services:* health clinic, personal/psychological counseling.
Athletics Member NCAA. All Division II. *Intercollegiate sports:* basketball W(s), gymnastics W(s), soccer W(s), softball W(s), volleyball W(s). *Intramural sports:* badminton M/W, basketball M(c)/W(c), football M/W, golf M(c)/W(c), soccer M(c)/W(c), softball M(c)/W(c), tennis M/W, track and field M(c)/W(c), volleyball M/W, weight lifting M(c)/W(c), wrestling M(c)/W(c).
Standardized Tests *Required for some:* SAT or ACT (for admission).
Costs (2011–12) *Tuition:* state resident $5040 full-time, $168 per credit hour part-time; nonresident $14,340 full-time, $478 per credit hour part-time. Full-time tuition and fees vary according to course load, program, and reciprocity agreements. Part-time tuition and fees vary according to course load, program, and reciprocity agreements. *Required fees:* $1920 full-time. *Room and board:* $6210; room only: $3410. Room and board charges vary according to board plan and housing facility. *Payment plan:* installment. *Waivers:* senior citizens.
Financial Aid Of all full-time matriculated undergraduates who enrolled in 2009, 4,198 applied for aid, 3,397 were judged to have need, 1,184 had their need fully met. 236 Federal Work-Study jobs (averaging $1598). 52 state and other part-time jobs (averaging $1341). In 2009, 566 non-need-based awards

were made. *Average percent of need met:* 88%. *Average financial aid package:* $7813. *Average need-based loan:* $3703. *Average need-based gift aid:* $7592. *Average non-need-based aid:* $3000. *Average indebtedness upon graduation:* $22,293.
Applying *Options:* electronic application, early admission, deferred entrance. *Application fee:* $50. *Required:* high school transcript, minimum 2 GPA. *Application deadlines:* 7/15 (freshmen), 7/15 (transfers). *Notification:* 8/15 (freshmen), continuous until 8/15 (transfers).
Freshman Application Contact Ms. Erma Nieto-Brecht, Director of Admissions, Texas Woman's University, 304 Administration Drive, Denton, TX 76201. *Phone:* 940-898-3188. *Toll-free phone:* 866-809-6130. *Fax:* 940-898-3081. *E-mail:* admissions@twu.edu. *Web site:* http://www.twu.edu/.

Trinity University
San Antonio, Texas

- **Independent** comprehensive, founded 1869, affiliated with Presbyterian Church
- **Urban** 113-acre campus
- **Endowment** $862.1 million
- **Coed** 2,417 undergraduate students, 98% full-time, 54% women, 46% men
- **Very difficult** entrance level, 63% of applicants were admitted

Undergraduates 2,372 full-time, 45 part-time. Students come from 50 states and territories; 70 other countries; 30% are from out of state; 3% Black or African American, non-Hispanic/Latino; 12% Hispanic/Latino; 7% Asian, non-Hispanic/Latino; 0.7% American Indian or Alaska Native, non-Hispanic/Latino; 2% Two or more races, non-Hispanic/Latino; 7% Race/ethnicity unknown; 7% international; 1% transferred in; 74% live on campus. *Retention:* 90% of full-time freshmen returned.
Freshmen *Admission:* 4,292 applied, 2,693 admitted, 587 enrolled. *Average high school GPA:* 3.52. *Test scores:* SAT critical reading scores over 500: 98%; SAT math scores over 500: 99%; ACT scores over 18: 100%; SAT critical reading scores over 600: 67%; SAT math scores over 600: 74%; ACT scores over 24: 94%; SAT critical reading scores over 700: 20%; SAT math scores over 700: 23%; ACT scores over 30: 42%.
Faculty *Total:* 306, 77% full-time, 83% with terminal degrees. *Student/faculty ratio:* 9:1.
Academics *Calendar:* semesters. *Degrees:* bachelor's and master's. *Special study options:* accelerated degree program, advanced placement credit, double majors, honors programs, independent study, internships, part-time degree program, services for LD students, study abroad, summer session for credit. *ROTC:* Air Force (c).
Computers on Campus 450 computers/terminals are available on campus for general student use. Students can access the following: campus intranet, computer help desk, free student e-mail accounts, online (class) grades, online (class) registration, online (class) schedules. Campuswide network is available. 100% of college-owned or -operated housing units are wired for high-speed Internet access. Wireless service is available via entire campus.
Student Life *Housing:* on-campus residence required through junior year. *Options:* coed. Campus housing is university owned. Freshman campus housing is guaranteed. *Activities and organizations:* drama/theater group, student-run newspaper, radio and television station, choral group, Voluntary Action Center, Alpha Phi Omega, Association of Student Representatives, Activities Council, Multicultural Network. *Campus security:* 24-hour emergency response devices and patrols, late-night transport/escort service, controlled dormitory access. *Student services:* health clinic, personal/psychological counseling.
Athletics Member NCAA. All Division III. *Intercollegiate sports:* baseball M, basketball M/W, cross-country running M/W, fencing M(c)/W(c), football M, golf M/W, lacrosse M(c)/W(c), riflery M(c)/W(c), soccer M/W, softball W, swimming and diving M/W, tennis M/W, track and field M/W, volleyball M(c)/W, water polo M(c)/W(c). *Intramural sports:* basketball M/W, cross-country running M/W, equestrian sports M(c)/W(c), football M, racquetball M/W, soccer M/W, softball M/W, swimming and diving M/W, table tennis M/W, tennis M/W, ultimate Frisbee M/W, volleyball M/W, wrestling M/W.
Standardized Tests *Required:* SAT or ACT (for admission).
Costs (2010–11) *Comprehensive fee:* $40,324 includes full-time tuition ($29,832), mandatory fees ($180), and room and board ($10,312). Full-time tuition and fees vary according to course load. Part-time tuition: $1243 per credit hour. Part-time tuition and fees vary according to course load. *College room only:* $6896. Room and board charges vary according to board plan. *Payment plan:* installment. *Waivers:* employees or children of employees.
Financial Aid Of all full-time matriculated undergraduates who enrolled in 2009, 1,245 applied for aid, 953 were judged to have need, 438 had their need fully met. In 2009, 1061 non-need-based awards were made. *Average percent of need met:* 90%. *Average financial aid package:* $23,645. *Average need-based loan:* $6658. *Average need-based gift aid:* $16,619. *Average non-need-based aid:* $12,112. *Financial aid deadline:* 4/1.

Applying *Options:* electronic application, early decision, early action, deferred entrance. *Application fee:* $50. *Required:* essay or personal statement, high school transcript, 2 letters of recommendation. *Recommended:* interview. *Application deadlines:* 2/1 (freshmen), 3/1 (transfers), 11/1 (early action). *Early decision deadline:* 11/1. *Notification:* 4/1 (freshmen), 4/1 (transfers), 12/1 (early decision), 12/15 (early action).
Freshman Application Contact Mr. Christopher Ellertson, Dean of Admissions and Financial Aid, Trinity University, One Trinity Place, San Antonio, TX 78212-7200. *Phone:* 210-999-7207. *Toll-free phone:* 800-TRINITY. *Fax:* 210-999-8164. *E-mail:* admissions@trinity.edu. *Web site:* http://www.trinity.edu/.

University of Dallas
Irving, Texas

- **Independent Roman Catholic** university, founded 1955
- **Suburban** 215-acre campus with easy access to Dallas-Fort Worth
- **Endowment** $43.7 million
- **Coed** 1,337 undergraduate students, 99% full-time, 51% women, 49% men
- **Moderately difficult** entrance level, 91% of applicants were admitted

Undergraduates 1,322 full-time, 15 part-time. Students come from 49 states and territories; 12 other countries; 55% are from out of state; 1% Black or African American, non-Hispanic/Latino; 16% Hispanic/Latino; 4% Asian, non-Hispanic/Latino; 0.1% Native Hawaiian or other Pacific Islander, non-Hispanic/Latino; 0.2% American Indian or Alaska Native, non-Hispanic/Latino; 2% Two or more races, non-Hispanic/Latino; 4% Race/ethnicity unknown; 2% international; 3% transferred in; 55% live on campus. *Retention:* 82% of full-time freshmen returned.
Freshmen *Admission:* 1,041 applied, 948 admitted, 376 enrolled. *Average high school GPA:* 3.75. *Test scores:* SAT critical reading scores over 500: 92%; SAT math scores over 500: 86%; SAT writing scores over 500: 88%; ACT scores over 18: 99%; SAT critical reading scores over 600: 62%; SAT math scores over 600: 47%; SAT writing scores over 600: 53%; ACT scores over 24: 71%; SAT critical reading scores over 700: 25%; SAT math scores over 700: 10%; SAT writing scores over 700: 16%; ACT scores over 30: 25%.
Faculty *Total:* 239, 56% full-time. *Student/faculty ratio:* 12:1.
Academics *Calendar:* semesters. *Degrees:* bachelor's, master's, doctoral-research/scholarship, post-master's, and postbachelor's certificates. *Special study options:* advanced placement credit, double majors, independent study, internships, off-campus study, part-time degree program, services for LD students, student-designed majors, study abroad, summer session for credit. *ROTC:* Army (c), Air Force (c). *Unusual degree programs:* 3-2 business administration; psychology, philosophy.
Computers on Campus 125 computers/terminals are available on campus for general student use. Students can access the following: campus intranet, computer help desk, free student e-mail accounts, online (class) grades, online (class) registration, online (class) schedules. Campuswide network is available. 100% of college-owned or -operated housing units are wired for high-speed Internet access. Wireless service is available via entire campus.
Student Life *Housing:* on-campus residence required through junior year. *Options:* men-only, women-only. Campus housing is university owned. Freshman campus housing is guaranteed. *Activities and organizations:* drama/theater group, student-run newspaper, choral group, SPUD (Programming Board), Residence Hall Association, student government, Best Buddies, Alpha Phi Omega. *Campus security:* 24-hour emergency response devices and patrols, late-night transport/escort service, controlled dormitory access. *Student services:* health clinic, personal/psychological counseling.
Athletics Member NCAA. All Division III. *Intercollegiate sports:* baseball M, basketball M/W, cross-country running M/W, golf M, lacrosse M/W, soccer M/W, softball W, track and field M/W, volleyball W. *Intramural sports:* basketball M, equestrian sports M(c)/W(c), football M/W, rugby M(c)/W(c), sailing M(c)/W(c), soccer M/W, softball M/W, tennis M(c)/W(c), ultimate Frisbee M(c)/W(c), volleyball M/W.
Standardized Tests *Required:* SAT or ACT (for admission).
Costs (2011–12) *Comprehensive fee:* $38,651 includes full-time tuition ($27,500), mandatory fees ($1825), and room and board ($9326). Part-time tuition: $1150 per credit. *Required fees:* $1825 per year part-time. *College room only:* $5300. Room and board charges vary according to board plan and housing facility. *Payment plan:* installment. *Waivers:* employees or children of employees.
Financial Aid Of all full-time matriculated undergraduates who enrolled in 2009, 900 applied for aid, 817 were judged to have need, 180 had their need fully met. 251 Federal Work-Study jobs (averaging $1422). 13 state and other part-time jobs (averaging $1262). In 2009, 434 non-need-based awards were made. *Average percent of need met:* 73%. *Average financial aid package:* $21,844. *Average need-based loan:* $5330. *Average need-based gift aid:* $17,215. *Average non-need-based aid:* $12,105. *Average indebtedness upon graduation:* $28,020.

Applying *Options:* electronic application, early action, deferred entrance. *Application fee:* $40. *Required:* essay or personal statement, high school transcript, 2 letters of recommendation. *Required for some:* interview. *Application deadlines:* 3/1 (freshmen), 3/1 (out-of-state freshmen), 8/1 (transfers), 12/1 (early action). *Notification:* continuous (freshmen), continuous (transfers), 1/15 (early action).
Freshman Application Contact Mr. Andrew Klein, Campus Visit Coordinator, University of Dallas, 1845 East Northgate Drive, Irving, TX 75062-4736. *Phone:* 800-628-6999. *Toll-free phone:* 800-628-6999. *Fax:* 972-721-5017. *E-mail:* ugadmis@udallas.edu. *Web site:* http://www.udallas.edu/.

University of Houston
Houston, Texas

- **State-supported** university, founded 1927, part of University of Houston System
- **Urban** 594-acre campus
- **Endowment** $442.3 million
- **Coed** 30,688 undergraduate students, 73% full-time, 50% women, 50% men
- **Moderately difficult** entrance level, 70% of applicants were admitted

Undergraduates 22,327 full-time, 8,361 part-time. Students come from 52 states and territories; 127 other countries; 1% are from out of state; 14% Black or African American, non-Hispanic/Latino; 26% Hispanic/Latino; 21% Asian, non-Hispanic/Latino; 0.3% Native Hawaiian or other Pacific Islander, non-Hispanic/Latino; 0.3% American Indian or Alaska Native, non-Hispanic/Latino; 2% Two or more races, non-Hispanic/Latino; 0.8% Race/ethnicity unknown; 4% international; 14% transferred in; 15% live on campus. *Retention:* 82% of full-time freshmen returned.
Freshmen *Admission:* 12,571 applied, 8,847 admitted, 3,637 enrolled. *Test scores:* SAT critical reading scores over 500: 64%; SAT math scores over 500: 80%; ACT scores over 18: 91%; SAT critical reading scores over 600: 20%; SAT math scores over 600: 34%; ACT scores over 24: 40%; SAT critical reading scores over 700: 2%; SAT math scores over 700: 5%; ACT scores over 30: 5%.
Faculty *Total:* 1,757, 73% full-time, 77% with terminal degrees. *Student/faculty ratio:* 23:1.
Academics *Calendar:* semesters. *Degrees:* bachelor's, master's, doctoral-professional, and doctoral-research/scholarship. *Special study options:* academic remediation for entering students, adult/continuing education programs, advanced placement credit, cooperative education, distance learning, double majors, English as a second language, freshman honors college, honors programs, independent study, internships, off-campus study, part-time degree program, services for LD students, study abroad, summer session for credit. *ROTC:* Army (b), Navy (c), Air Force (b). *Unusual degree programs:* 3-2 business administration.
Computers on Campus 1,476 computers/terminals and 25,000 ports are available on campus for general student use. Students can access the following: computer help desk, free student e-mail accounts, online (class) grades, online (class) registration, online (class) schedules. Campuswide network is available. 100% of college-owned or -operated housing units are wired for high-speed Internet access. Wireless service is available via classrooms, computer centers, computer labs, dorm rooms, learning centers, libraries, student centers.
Student Life *Housing options:* coed, disabled students. Campus housing is university owned. *Activities and organizations:* drama/theater group, student-run newspaper, television station, choral group, marching band, Student Government Association, Council of Ethnic Organizations, National Society of Collegiate Scholars, Optometric Student Association, Cougars for Kids, national fraternities, national sororities. *Campus security:* 24-hour emergency response devices and patrols, student patrols, late-night transport/escort service, controlled dormitory access, vehicle assistance. *Student services:* health clinic, personal/psychological counseling, women's center, legal services.
Athletics Member NCAA. All Division I except football (Division I-A). *Intercollegiate sports:* baseball M(s), basketball M(s)/W(s), cross-country running M(s)/W(s), football M(s)/W, golf M(s), soccer W(s), softball W(s), swimming and diving W(s), tennis W(s), track and field M(s)/W(s), volleyball W(s). *Intramural sports:* badminton M/W, basketball M/W, bowling M(c)/W, cross-country running M/W, fencing M(c)/W(c), football M, golf M/W, racquetball M/W, rock climbing M/W, rugby M(c), soccer M(c)/W(c), softball M/W, swimming and diving M/W, table tennis M/W, tennis M/W, ultimate Frisbee M(c), volleyball M/W(c), water polo M.
Standardized Tests *Required:* SAT or ACT (for admission).
Costs (2010–11) *Tuition:* state resident $6270 full-time, $209 per credit hour part-time; nonresident $15,570 full-time, $519 per credit hour part-time. Full-time tuition and fees vary according to course level, course load, and program. Part-time tuition and fees vary according to course level, course load, and program. *Required fees:* $2730 full-time. *Room and board:* $7300. Room and board charges vary according to board plan and housing facility. *Payment*

plans: installment, deferred payment. *Waivers:* employees or children of employees.

Financial Aid Of all full-time matriculated undergraduates who enrolled in 2009, 15,241 applied for aid, 13,609 were judged to have need, 3,440 had their need fully met. 504 Federal Work-Study jobs (averaging $2832). 67 state and other part-time jobs (averaging $2723). In 2009, 353 non-need-based awards were made. *Average percent of need met:* 76%. *Average financial aid package:* $12,365. *Average need-based loan:* $7224. *Average need-based gift aid:* $6896. *Average non-need-based aid:* $4162. *Average indebtedness upon graduation:* $14,922.

Applying *Options:* electronic application. *Application fee:* $50. *Required:* high school transcript. *Application deadlines:* 4/1 (freshmen), 6/1 (transfers). *Notification:* continuous (freshmen), continuous (transfers).

Freshman Application Contact Jeff Fuller, Director, Student Recruitment, University of Houston, Welcome Center, 4400 University Boulevard, Houston, TX 77204-2023. *Phone:* 713-743-1010. *Fax:* 713-743-9633. *E-mail:* jdfuller@central.uh.edu. *Web site:* http://www.uh.edu/.

See page 1700 for the College Close-Up.

University of Houston–Clear Lake
Houston, Texas

- **State-supported** upper-level, founded 1971, part of University of Houston System
- **Suburban** 487-acre campus
- **Endowment** $16.7 million
- **Coed** 4,592 undergraduate students, 46% full-time, 68% women, 32% men
- **Minimally difficult** entrance level

Undergraduates 2,101 full-time, 2,491 part-time. 1% are from out of state; 9% Black or African American, non-Hispanic/Latino; 28% Hispanic/Latino; 6% Asian, non-Hispanic/Latino; 0.2% Native Hawaiian or other Pacific Islander, non-Hispanic/Latino; 0.6% American Indian or Alaska Native, non-Hispanic/Latino; 0.8% Two or more races, non-Hispanic/Latino; 0.7% Race/ethnicity unknown; 2% international; 1% live on campus.

Faculty *Total:* 525, 44% full-time, 57% with terminal degrees. *Student/faculty ratio:* 12:1.

Academics *Calendar:* semesters. *Degrees:* certificates, bachelor's, master's, and doctoral-other. *Special study options:* accelerated degree program, advanced placement credit, cooperative education, distance learning, double majors, English as a second language, independent study, internships, off-campus study, part-time degree program, services for LD students, student-designed majors, study abroad, summer session for credit.

Computers on Campus 715 computers/terminals are available on campus for general student use. Students can access the following: campus intranet, computer help desk, free student e-mail accounts, online (class) grades, online (class) registration, online (class) schedules. Campuswide network is available. Wireless service is available via entire campus.

Student Life *Housing options:* coed. Campus housing is provided by a third party. *Activities and organizations:* student-run newspaper, Beta Alpha Psi, National Society of Leadership and Success, Applied Behavior Student Analysis Student Organization, Student Government Association, Accounting Association. *Campus security:* 24-hour emergency response devices and patrols, late-night transport/escort service. *Student services:* health clinic, personal/psychological counseling, women's center.

Costs (2011–12) *Tuition:* state resident $5036 full-time, $159 per credit hour part-time; nonresident $15,356 full-time, $503 per credit hour part-time. Full-time tuition and fees vary according to course load, location, and program. Part-time tuition and fees vary according to course load, location, and program. *Required fees:* $1152 full-time, $438 per term part-time. *Room only:* $10,340. Room and board charges vary according to housing facility. *Payment plans:* installment, deferred payment. *Waivers:* senior citizens.

Financial Aid Of all full-time matriculated undergraduates who enrolled in 2009, 1,677 applied for aid, 1,536 were judged to have need, 459 had their need fully met. 38 Federal Work-Study jobs (averaging $3207). 26 state and other part-time jobs (averaging $3222). In 2009, 56 non-need-based awards were made. *Average percent of need met:* 44%. *Average financial aid package:* $7218. *Average need-based loan:* $4460. *Average need-based gift aid:* $2972. *Average non-need-based aid:* $869. *Average indebtedness upon graduation:* $8061.

Applying *Options:* electronic application, early admission, deferred entrance. *Application fee:* $35. *Application deadline:* rolling (transfers). *Notification:* continuous (transfers).

Application Contact Ms. Rauchelle Jones, Executive Director of Admissions, University of Houston–Clear Lake, 2700 Bay Area Boulevard, Box 13,

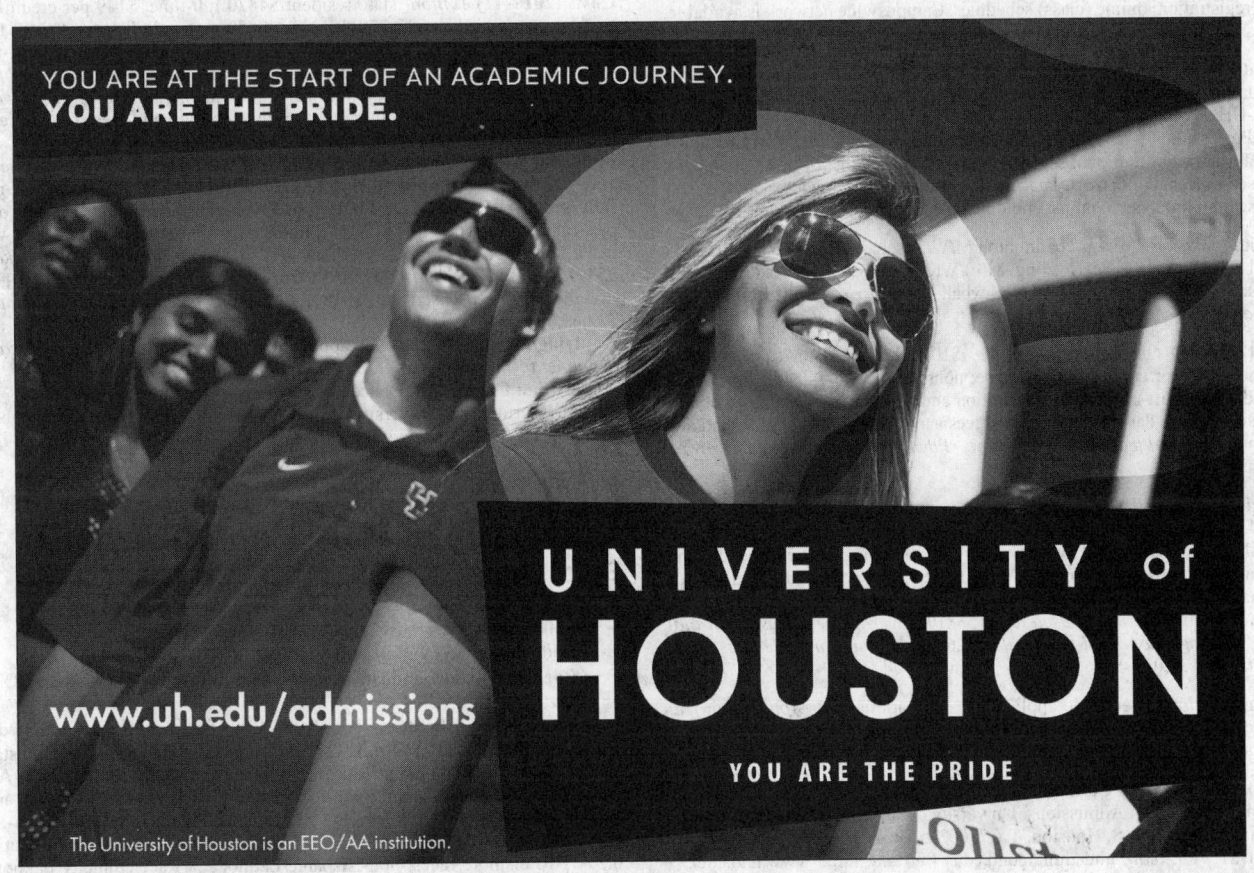

Houston, TX 77058-1098. *Phone:* 281-283-2518. *Fax:* 281-283-2530. *E-mail:* admissions@uhcl.edu. *Web site:* http://www.uhcl.edu/.

University of Houston–Downtown

Houston, Texas

- **State-supported** comprehensive, founded 1974, part of University of Houston System

- **Urban** 24-acre campus

- **Endowment** $19.5 million

- **Coed** 12,746 undergraduate students, 47% full-time, 62% women, 38% men

- **Noncompetitive** entrance level, 100% of applicants were admitted

Undergraduates 6,038 full-time, 6,708 part-time. Students come from 28 states and territories; 78 other countries; 1% are from out of state; 28% Black or African American, non-Hispanic/Latino; 37% Hispanic/Latino; 9% Asian, non-Hispanic/Latino; 0.1% Native Hawaiian or other Pacific Islander, non-Hispanic/Latino; 0.3% American Indian or Alaska Native, non-Hispanic/Latino; 1% Two or more races, non-Hispanic/Latino; 0.3% Race/ethnicity unknown; 5% international; 16% transferred in. *Retention:* 59% of full-time freshmen returned.

Freshmen *Admission:* 2,485 applied, 2,480 admitted, 1,114 enrolled.

Faculty *Total:* 626, 51% full-time, 59% with terminal degrees. *Student/faculty ratio:* 20:1.

Academics *Calendar:* semesters. *Degrees:* bachelor's and master's. *Special study options:* academic remediation for entering students, advanced placement credit, distance learning, double majors, English as a second language, honors programs, independent study, internships, off-campus study, part-time degree program, services for LD students, study abroad, summer session for credit. *ROTC:* Army (c), Air Force (c).

Computers on Campus 1,860 computers/terminals and 450 ports are available on campus for general student use. Students can access the following: computer help desk, free student e-mail accounts, online (class) grades, online (class) registration, online (class) schedules. Campuswide network is available. Wireless service is available via entire campus.

Student Life *Housing:* college housing not available. *Activities and organizations:* drama/theater group, student-run newspaper, American Marketing Association-UHD Chapter, Mathematical Association of America, Photography Club, Professional Accounting Society, Student Government Association, national fraternities, national sororities. *Campus security:* 24-hour emergency response devices and patrols, late-night transport/escort service. *Student services:* health clinic, personal/psychological counseling, legal services.

Athletics *Intramural sports:* badminton M/W, baseball M(c), basketball M(c)/W(c), bowling M/W, cheerleading M(c)/W(c), football M/W, soccer M(c)/W(c), softball M/W, tennis M/W, volleyball M(c)/W(c), weight lifting M(c)/W(c).

Costs (2010–11) *One-time required fee:* $10. *Tuition:* state resident $4440 full-time, $148 per credit hour part-time; nonresident $13,740 full-time, $458 per credit hour part-time. Full-time tuition and fees vary according to course load and program. Part-time tuition and fees vary according to course load and program. *Required fees:* $1052 full-time. *Payment plan:* installment. *Waivers:* senior citizens.

Financial Aid Of all full-time matriculated undergraduates who enrolled in 2009, 4,890 applied for aid, 4,890 were judged to have need, 194 had their need fully met. 169 Federal Work-Study jobs (averaging $3265). 26 state and other part-time jobs (averaging $2471). In 2009, 119 non-need-based awards were made. *Average percent of need met:* 49%. *Average financial aid package:* $8126. *Average need-based loan:* $3819. *Average need-based gift aid:* $5465. *Average non-need-based aid:* $2669. *Average indebtedness upon graduation:* $13,204.

Applying *Options:* electronic application, early admission. *Application fee:* $35. *Required:* high school transcript. *Application deadlines:* 6/1 (freshmen), 7/15 (transfers). *Notification:* continuous (freshmen), continuous (transfers).

Freshman Application Contact Ms. Patricia Santos, Assistant Director of Admissions-Freshman Admissions, University of Houston–Downtown, One Main Street, Suite 350-S, Houston, TX 77002. *Phone:* 713-221-8522. *Fax:* 713-221-8157. *E-mail:* uhdadmit@uhd.edu. *Web site:* http://www.uhd.edu/.

University of Houston–Victoria

Victoria, Texas

- **State-supported** upper-level, founded 1973, part of University of Houston System

- **Small-town** 20-acre campus

- **Endowment** $7.5 million

- **Coed** 2,289 undergraduate students, 47% full-time, 67% women, 33% men

- **Minimally difficult** entrance level, 41% of applicants were admitted

Undergraduates 1,071 full-time, 1,218 part-time. Students come from 7 states and territories; 25 other countries; 1% are from out of state; 13% Black or African American, non-Hispanic/Latino; 25% Hispanic/Latino; 7% Asian, non-Hispanic/Latino; 0.2% Native Hawaiian or other Pacific Islander, non-Hispanic/Latino; 0.2% American Indian or Alaska Native, non-Hispanic/Latino; 1% Two or more races, non-Hispanic/Latino; 1% Race/ethnicity unknown; 1% international; 22% transferred in; 15% live on campus.

Freshmen *Admission:* 1,273 applied, 520 admitted.

Faculty *Total:* 195, 59% full-time, 68% with terminal degrees. *Student/faculty ratio:* 17:1.

Academics *Calendar:* semesters. *Degrees:* bachelor's, master's, post-master's, and postbachelor's certificates. *Special study options:* accelerated degree program, adult/continuing education programs, distance learning, double majors, external degree program, honors programs, independent study, internships, off-campus study, part-time degree program, services for LD students, study abroad, summer session for credit. *ROTC:* Air Force (c).

Computers on Campus 200 computers/terminals are available on campus for general student use. Students can access the following: campus intranet, computer help desk, free student e-mail accounts, online (class) grades, online (class) registration, online (class) schedules. Campuswide network is available. 100% of college-owned or -operated housing units are wired for high-speed Internet access. Wireless service is available via entire campus.

Student Life *Housing options:* coed. Campus housing is university owned. Freshman applicants given priority for college housing. *Activities and organizations:* UHV Student Education Association, Mexican American Student Organization, Psi Chi, Gamma Beta Phi, Criminal Justice Society. *Campus security:* 24-hour emergency response devices and patrols, controlled dormitory access. *Student services:* personal/psychological counseling.

Athletics Member NAIA. *Intercollegiate sports:* baseball M, golf M/W, soccer M/W, softball W.

Standardized Tests *Required for some:* SAT or ACT (for admission).

Costs (2010–11) *Tuition:* state resident $4470 full-time, $149 per credit hour part-time; nonresident $13,770 full-time, $459 per credit hour part-time. Full-time tuition and fees vary according to course level and course load. Part-time tuition and fees vary according to course level and course load. *Required fees:* $1134 full-time, $54 per credit hour part-time. *Room and board:* $6550. *Payment plan:* installment. *Waivers:* senior citizens and employees or children of employees.

Financial Aid Of all full-time matriculated undergraduates who enrolled in 2007, 201 applied for aid, 168 were judged to have need, 32 had their need fully met. 17 Federal Work-Study jobs (averaging $2755). 7 state and other part-time jobs (averaging $1272). In 2007, 4 non-need-based awards were made. *Average percent of need met:* 41%. *Average financial aid package:* $5311. *Average need-based loan:* $3676. *Average need-based gift aid:* $1376. *Average non-need-based aid:* $818. *Average indebtedness upon graduation:* $17,695.

Applying *Options:* electronic application, deferred entrance. *Application deadline:* rolling (transfers). *Notification:* continuous (transfers).

Application Contact Dr. Denee Thomas, Senior Director of LEAD and Student Recruitment, University of Houston–Victoria, 3007 North Ben Wilson, Victoria, TX 77901. *Phone:* 877-970-4848 Ext. 4184. *Toll-free phone:* 877-970-4848 Ext. 110. *E-mail:* recruitment@uhv.edu. *Web site:* http://www.uhv.edu/.

University of Mary Hardin-Baylor

Belton, Texas

- **Independent Southern Baptist** comprehensive, founded 1845

- **Small-town** 100-acre campus with easy access to Austin

- **Endowment** $57.9 million

- **Coed** 2,653 undergraduate students, 90% full-time, 62% women, 38% men

- **Moderately difficult** entrance level, 37% of applicants were admitted

Undergraduates 2,381 full-time, 272 part-time. Students come from 26 states and territories; 43 other countries; 2% are from out of state; 13% Black or African American, non-Hispanic/Latino; 14% Hispanic/Latino; 2% Asian, non-Hispanic/Latino; 0.5% Native Hawaiian or other Pacific Islander, non-Hispanic/Latino; 0.6% American Indian or Alaska Native, non-Hispanic/Latino; 0.2% Two or more races, non-Hispanic/Latino; 2% Race/ethnicity unknown;

PROFILES

1% international; 12% transferred in; 48% live on campus. *Retention:* 60% of full-time freshmen returned.

Freshmen *Admission:* 8,323 applied, 3,114 admitted, 608 enrolled. *Test scores:* SAT critical reading scores over 500: 54%; SAT math scores over 500: 65%; SAT writing scores over 500: 44%; ACT scores over 18: 96%; SAT critical reading scores over 600: 16%; SAT math scores over 600: 20%; SAT writing scores over 600: 7%; ACT scores over 24: 42%; SAT critical reading scores over 700: 1%; SAT math scores over 700: 1%; SAT writing scores over 700: 1%; ACT scores over 30: 5%.

Faculty *Total:* 233, 59% full-time, 54% with terminal degrees. *Student/faculty ratio:* 14:1.

Academics *Calendar:* semesters. *Degrees:* bachelor's, master's, and doctoral-research/scholarship. *Special study options:* academic remediation for entering students, accelerated degree program, advanced placement credit, distance learning, double majors, English as a second language, honors programs, independent study, internships, part-time degree program, services for LD students, student-designed majors, study abroad, summer session for credit. *ROTC:* Army (b), Air Force (c). *Unusual degree programs:* 3-2 business administration.

Computers on Campus 275 computers/terminals are available on campus for general student use. Students can access the following: campus intranet, computer help desk, free student e-mail accounts, online (class) grades, online (class) registration, online (class) schedules. Campuswide network is available. Wireless service is available via entire campus.

Student Life *Housing:* on-campus residence required through sophomore year. *Options:* men-only, women-only, disabled students. Campus housing is university owned. Freshman applicants given priority for college housing. *Activities and organizations:* drama/theater group, student-run newspaper, choral group, marching band, Baptist Student Ministry, Student Government Association, Residence Hall Association, Campus Activities Board, Focus. *Campus security:* 24-hour emergency response devices and patrols, late-night transport/ escort service, controlled dormitory access, campus police force, lighted pathways and sidewalks. *Student services:* health clinic, personal/psychological counseling.

Athletics Member NCAA. All Division III. *Intercollegiate sports:* baseball M, basketball M/W, football M, golf M/W, soccer M/W, softball W, tennis M/ W, volleyball W. *Intramural sports:* basketball M/W, football M/W, golf M/ W, soccer M/W, softball M/W, table tennis M/W, tennis M/W, ultimate Frisbee M/W, volleyball M/W.

Standardized Tests *Required:* SAT or ACT (for admission).

Costs (2011–12) *Comprehensive fee:* $29,271 includes full-time tuition ($20,700), mandatory fees ($2350), and room and board ($6221). Full-time tuition and fees vary according to course load. Part-time tuition and fees vary according to course load. *Room and board:* Room and board charges vary according to board plan and housing facility. *Payment plan:* installment. *Waivers:* employees or children of employees.

Financial Aid Of all full-time matriculated undergraduates who enrolled in 2009, 2,195 applied for aid, 2,002 were judged to have need, 182 had their need fully met. 234 Federal Work-Study jobs (averaging $2390). 300 state and other part-time jobs (averaging $2324). In 2009, 304 non-need-based awards were made. *Average percent of need met:* 60%. *Average financial aid package:* $13,642. *Average need-based loan:* $4535. *Average need-based gift aid:* $9666. *Average non-need-based aid:* $5656. *Average indebtedness upon graduation:* $17,500.

Applying *Options:* electronic application, early admission, deferred entrance. *Application fee:* $35. *Required:* high school transcript. *Required for some:* essay or personal statement, interview. *Application deadlines:* rolling (freshmen), rolling (transfers). *Notification:* continuous (freshmen), continuous (transfers).

Freshman Application Contact Mr. Brent Burks, Director of Admissions, University of Mary Hardin-Baylor, UMHB Station Box 8004, 900 College Street, Belton, TX 76513-2599. *Phone:* 254-295-4520. *Toll-free phone:* 800-727-8642. *Fax:* 254-295-5049. *E-mail:* admission@umhb.edu. *Web site:* http://www.umhb.edu/.

University of North Texas

Denton, Texas

- **State-supported** university, founded 1890, part of University of North Texas System
- **Suburban** 875-acre campus with easy access to Dallas-Fort Worth
- **Endowment** $90.8 million
- **Coed** 28,283 undergraduate students, 79% full-time, 53% women, 47% men
- **Moderately difficult** entrance level, 65% of applicants were admitted

Undergraduates 22,467 full-time, 5,816 part-time. Students come from 52 states and territories; 139 other countries; 3% are from out of state; 13% Black or African American, non-Hispanic/Latino; 15% Hispanic/Latino; 6% Asian,

non-Hispanic/Latino; 1% American Indian or Alaska Native, non-Hispanic/ Latino; 1% Race/ethnicity unknown; 2% international; 14% transferred in; 16% live on campus. *Retention:* 78% of full-time freshmen returned.

Freshmen *Admission:* 13,737 applied, 8,969 admitted, 3,746 enrolled. *Test scores:* SAT critical reading scores over 500: 71%; SAT math scores over 500: 77%; ACT scores over 18: 98%; SAT critical reading scores over 600: 27%; SAT math scores over 600: 31%; ACT scores over 24: 48%; SAT critical reading scores over 700: 4%; SAT math scores over 700: 6%; ACT scores over 30: 7%.

Faculty *Total:* 1,456, 72% full-time, 64% with terminal degrees. *Student/faculty ratio:* 24:1.

Academics *Calendar:* semesters. *Degrees:* bachelor's, master's, doctoral-professional, doctoral-research/scholarship, and postbachelor's certificates. *Special study options:* academic remediation for entering students, accelerated degree program, adult/continuing education programs, advanced placement credit, cooperative education, distance learning, double majors, English as a second language, freshman honors college, honors programs, internships, off-campus study, part-time degree program, services for LD students, study abroad, summer session for credit. *ROTC:* Army (b), Air Force (b).

Computers on Campus 755 computers/terminals and 5,554 ports are available on campus for general student use. Students can access the following: campus intranet, computer help desk, free student e-mail accounts, online (class) grades, online (class) registration, online (class) schedules. Campuswide network is available. 100% of college-owned or -operated housing units are wired for high-speed Internet access. Wireless service is available via entire campus.

Student Life *Housing:* on-campus residence required for freshman year. *Options:* coed, women-only, disabled students. Campus housing is university owned. Freshman applicants given priority for college housing. *Activities and organizations:* drama/theater group, student-run newspaper, radio and television station, choral group, marching band, Student Government Association, Residence Hall Association, Panhellenic Association, Interfraternity Council, College Life, national fraternities, national sororities. *Campus security:* 24-hour emergency response devices and patrols, late-night transport/escort service, controlled dormitory access. *Student services:* health clinic, personal/ psychological counseling, women's center, legal services.

Athletics Member NCAA. All Division I except football (Division I-A). *Intercollegiate sports:* baseball M(c), basketball M(s)/W(s), bowling M(c)/ W(c), cross-country running M(s)/W(s), fencing M(c)/W(c), golf M(s)/W(s), ice hockey M(c), lacrosse M(c)/W(c), racquetball M(c)/W(c), rock climbing M(c), sailing M(c)/W(c), soccer M(c)/W(s), softball M(s)/W, swimming and diving M(c)/W(s), tennis M(c)/W, track and field M(s)/W(s), ultimate Frisbee M(c)/W(c), volleyball W(s). *Intramural sports:* basketball M/W, bowling M/ W, football M, golf M/W, racquetball M/W, soccer M/W, softball M/W, table tennis M/W, tennis M/W, volleyball M/W.

Standardized Tests *Required:* SAT or ACT (for admission).

Costs (2011–12) *Tuition:* state resident $5660 full-time, $189 per credit part-time; nonresident $14,960 full-time, $499 per credit part-time. *Required fees:* $2300 full-time, $153 per credit part-time. *Room and board:* $6716. Room and board charges vary according to board plan and housing facility. *Payment plan:* installment. *Waivers:* senior citizens and employees or children of employees.

Financial Aid Of all full-time matriculated undergraduates who enrolled in 2009, 15,995 applied for aid, 12,864 were judged to have need, 3,548 had their need fully met. In 2009, 2426 non-need-based awards were made. *Average percent of need met:* 70%. *Average financial aid package:* $11,125. *Average need-based loan:* $4397. *Average need-based gift aid:* $6684. *Average non-need-based aid:* $4912.

Applying *Options:* electronic application, early admission, deferred entrance. *Application fee:* $60. *Required:* high school transcript. *Required for some:* essay or personal statement, 3 letters of recommendation, interview. *Application deadlines:* 8/1 (freshmen), rolling (transfers). *Notification:* continuous (freshmen), continuous (transfers).

Freshman Application Contact Mr. Jasiel Perez, Associate Director of Admissions, University of North Texas, Denton, TX 76203. *Phone:* 940-369-7664. *Toll-free phone:* 800-868-8211. *E-mail:* jasiel.perez@unt.edu. *Web site:* http://www.unt.edu/.

University of Phoenix–Dallas Campus

Dallas, Texas

Freshman Application Contact Ms. Audra McQuarie, Registrar/Executive Director, University of Phoenix–Dallas Campus, 4035 South Riverpoint Parkway, Mail Stop CF-L101, Phoenix, AZ 85040. *Phone:* 480-557-6151. *Toll-free phone:* 800-776-4867 (in-state); 800-228-7240 (out-of-state). *Fax:* 480-643-3068. *E-mail:* audra.mcquarie@phoenix.edu. *Web site:* http:// www.phoenix.edu/.

University of Phoenix–Houston Campus

Houston, Texas

Freshman Application Contact Ms. Audra McQuarie, Registrar/Executive Director, University of Phoenix–Houston Campus, 4305 South Riverpoint Parkway, Mail Stop CF-L101, Phoenix, AZ 85040. *Phone:* 480-557-6151. *Toll-free phone:* 800-776-4867 (in-state); 800-228-7240 (out-of-state). *Fax:* 480-643-3068. *E-mail:* audra.mcquarie@phoenix.edu. *Web site:* http://www.phoenix.edu/.

University of St. Thomas

Houston, Texas

- **Independent Roman Catholic** comprehensive, founded 1947
- **Urban** 20-acre campus
- **Endowment** $46.1 million
- **Coed** 1,627 undergraduate students, 74% full-time, 61% women, 39% men
- **Moderately difficult** entrance level, 81% of applicants were admitted

Undergraduates 1,201 full-time, 426 part-time. Students come from 25 states and territories; 56 other countries; 3% are from out of state; 5% Black or African American, non-Hispanic/Latino; 37% Hispanic/Latino; 12% Asian, non-Hispanic/Latino; 0.1% Native Hawaiian or other Pacific Islander, non-Hispanic/Latino; 0.3% American Indian or Alaska Native, non-Hispanic/Latino; 2% Two or more races, non-Hispanic/Latino; 2% Race/ethnicity unknown; 6% international; 9% transferred in; 16% live on campus. *Retention:* 75% of full-time freshmen returned.
Freshmen *Admission:* 725 applied, 586 admitted, 194 enrolled. *Average high school GPA:* 3.46. *Test scores:* SAT critical reading scores over 500: 87%; SAT math scores over 500: 83%; SAT writing scores over 500: 80%; ACT scores over 18: 100%; SAT critical reading scores over 600: 43%; SAT math scores over 600: 38%; SAT writing scores over 600: 27%; ACT scores over 24: 75%; SAT critical reading scores over 700: 8%; SAT math scores over 700: 7%; SAT writing scores over 700: 5%; ACT scores over 30: 17%.
Faculty *Total:* 299, 46% full-time, 79% with terminal degrees. *Student/faculty ratio:* 11:1.
Academics *Calendar:* semesters. *Degrees:* diplomas, bachelor's, master's, and doctoral-research/scholarship. *Special study options:* accelerated degree program, adult/continuing education programs, advanced placement credit, distance learning, double majors, honors programs, independent study, internships, off-campus study, part-time degree program, services for LD students, student-designed majors, study abroad, summer session for credit. *ROTC:* Army (c), Air Force (c). *Unusual degree programs:* 3-2 business administration; engineering with University of Notre Dame, University of Houston, Texas A&M University.
Computers on Campus 287 computers/terminals and 400 ports are available on campus for general student use. Students can access the following: campus intranet, computer help desk, free student e-mail accounts, online (class) grades, online (class) registration, online (class) schedules. Campuswide network is available. 95% of college-owned or -operated housing units are wired for high-speed Internet access. Wireless service is available via entire campus.
Student Life *Housing options:* coed. Campus housing is university owned. Freshman applicants given priority for college housing. *Activities and organizations:* drama/theater group, student-run newspaper, choral group, Health Occupations Students of America (HOSA), Pre Health Professions Society, Student Activities Board (SAB), American Chemical Society, tennis. *Campus security:* 24-hour emergency response devices and patrols, late-night transport/escort service, controlled dormitory access. *Student services:* personal/psychological counseling.
Athletics Member NAIA. *Intercollegiate sports:* basketball M(s)(c), cheerleading M(c)/W(c), fencing M(c)/W(c), rugby M(c), soccer M(s)/W(c), tennis M(c)/W(c), ultimate Frisbee M(c)/W(c), volleyball W(s). *Intramural sports:* basketball M/W, bowling M/W, racquetball M/W, soccer M/W, table tennis M/W, tennis M/W, ultimate Frisbee M/W, volleyball M/W.
Standardized Tests *Required:* SAT or ACT (for admission).
Costs (2010–11) *Comprehensive fee:* $31,400 includes full-time tuition ($23,160), mandatory fees ($340), and room and board ($7900). Full-time tuition and fees vary according to course load. Part-time tuition: $772 per credit hour. Part-time tuition and fees vary according to course load. *College room only:* $4800. Room and board charges vary according to board plan and housing facility. *Payment plans:* installment, deferred payment. *Waivers:* senior citizens and employees or children of employees.
Financial Aid Of all full-time matriculated undergraduates who enrolled in 2009, 808 applied for aid, 731 were judged to have need, 79 had their need fully met. 42 Federal Work-Study jobs (averaging $3533). 3 state and other part-time jobs (averaging $3869). In 2009, 282 non-need-based awards were made. *Average percent of need met:* 62%. *Average financial aid package:* $15,983. *Average need-based loan:* $4965. *Average need-based gift aid:*

$12,300. *Average non-need-based aid:* $8816. *Average indebtedness upon graduation:* $29,245.
Applying *Options:* electronic application, early action, deferred entrance. *Application fee:* $25. *Required:* essay or personal statement, high school transcript, minimum 2.8 GPA, 1070 SAT (Critical Reading and Math) or 23 ACT. *Application deadlines:* 5/1 (freshmen), 5/1 (out-of-state freshmen), rolling (transfers), 11/1 (early action). *Notification:* continuous until 11/15 (freshmen), continuous until 11/15 (out-of-state freshmen), continuous (transfers), 12/15 (early action).
Freshman Application Contact Mr. Arthur Ortiz, University of St. Thomas, 3800 Montrose Boulevard, Houston, TX 77006-4696. *Phone:* 713-525-3848. *Toll-free phone:* 800-856-8565. *Fax:* 713-525-3558. *E-mail:* admissions@stthom.edu. *Web site:* http://www.stthom.edu/.

The University of Texas at Arlington

Arlington, Texas

- **State-supported** university, founded 1895, part of University of Texas System
- **Urban** 400-acre campus with easy access to Dallas-Fort Worth
- **Endowment** $63.6 million
- **Coed** 25,106 undergraduate students, 61% full-time, 55% women, 45% men
- **Moderately difficult** entrance level, 70% of applicants were admitted

Undergraduates 15,408 full-time, 9,698 part-time. Students come from 50 states and territories; 69 other countries; 2% are from out of state; 15% Black or African American, non-Hispanic/Latino; 19% Hispanic/Latino; 10% Asian, non-Hispanic/Latino; 0.2% Native Hawaiian or other Pacific Islander, non-Hispanic/Latino; 0.4% American Indian or Alaska Native, non-Hispanic/Latino; 2% Two or more races, non-Hispanic/Latino; 4% Race/ethnicity unknown; 5% international; 17% transferred in; 13% live on campus. *Retention:* 73% of full-time freshmen returned.
Freshmen *Admission:* 8,866 applied, 6,219 admitted, 2,536 enrolled. *Test scores:* SAT critical reading scores over 500: 60%; SAT math scores over 500: 76%; ACT scores over 18: 87%; SAT critical reading scores over 600: 20%; SAT math scores over 600: 32%; ACT scores over 24: 43%; SAT critical reading scores over 700: 2%; SAT math scores over 700: 4%; ACT scores over 30: 5%.
Faculty *Total:* 1,283, 67% full-time. *Student/faculty ratio:* 24:1.
Academics *Calendar:* semesters. *Degrees:* bachelor's, master's, doctoral-professional, doctoral-research/scholarship, post-master's, and postbachelor's certificates. *Special study options:* academic remediation for entering students, adult/continuing education programs, advanced placement credit, cooperative education, distance learning, double majors, English as a second language, freshman honors college, honors programs, independent study, internships, off-campus study, part-time degree program, services for LD students, student-designed majors, study abroad, summer session for credit. *ROTC:* Army (b), Air Force (c). *Unusual degree programs:* 3-2 business administration; psychology, health care administration.
Computers on Campus 600 computers/terminals and 6,000 ports are available on campus for general student use. Students can access the following: campus intranet, computer help desk, free student e-mail accounts, online (class) grades, online (class) registration, online (class) schedules. Campuswide network is available. 90% of college-owned or -operated housing units are wired for high-speed Internet access. Wireless service is available via classrooms, computer labs, learning centers, libraries, student centers.
Student Life *Housing options:* coed, men-only, women-only. Campus housing is university owned and leased by the school. *Activities and organizations:* drama/theater group, student-run newspaper, radio station, choral group, marching band, Student Alumni Association, Golden Key International Honor Society, National Society of Leadership & Success, National Society of Collegiate Scholars, University Catholic Community, national fraternities, national sororities. *Campus security:* 24-hour emergency response devices and patrols, late-night transport/escort service, controlled dormitory access, remote emergency telephones, bicycle patrols, crime prevention program, student shuttle service. *Student services:* health clinic, personal/psychological counseling, legal services.
Athletics Member NCAA. All Division I. *Intercollegiate sports:* baseball M(s), basketball M(s)/W(s), golf M, softball W(s), tennis M(s)/W(s), track and field M/W, volleyball W(s). *Intramural sports:* badminton M/W, basketball M/W, bowling M/W, golf M, racquetball M/W, soccer M/W, softball M/W, table tennis M/W, tennis M/W, volleyball M/W.
Standardized Tests *Required:* SAT or ACT (for admission).
Costs (2010–11) *Tuition:* state resident $8500 full-time; nonresident $17,800 full-time. Full-time tuition and fees vary according to course level, course load, and program. Part-time tuition and fees vary according to course level, course load, and program. *Room and board:* $6224; room only: $2932. Room and board charges vary according to board plan and housing facility. *Payment plan:* installment. *Waivers:* employees or children of employees.

Financial Aid Of all full-time matriculated undergraduates who enrolled in 2009, 11,453 applied for aid, 10,293 were judged to have need, 1,654 had their need fully met. 2,054 Federal Work-Study jobs (averaging $2984). 186 state and other part-time jobs (averaging $1395). In 2009, 222 non-need-based awards were made. *Average percent of need met:* 73%. *Average financial aid package:* $12,829. *Average need-based loan:* $4309. *Average need-based gift aid:* $6862. *Average non-need-based aid:* $5227. *Average indebtedness upon graduation:* $18,749.

Applying *Options:* electronic application, deferred entrance. *Application fee:* $35. *Required:* high school transcript, class rank. *Application deadlines:* 6/1 (freshmen), rolling (transfers). *Notification:* continuous (freshmen), continuous (transfers).

Freshman Application Contact Dr. Hans Gatterdam, Executive Director of Admissions and Records, The University of Texas at Arlington, UTA Box 19088, 701 South Nedderman Drive, Arlington, TX 76019-0088. *Phone:* 817-272-3275. *Fax:* 817-272-3435. *E-mail:* admissions@uta.edu. *Web site:* http://www.uta.edu/.

The University of Texas at Austin

Austin, Texas

- **State-supported** university, founded 1883, part of University of Texas System
- **Urban** 431-acre campus with easy access to San Antonio
- **Endowment** $2.6 billion
- **Coed** 38,420 undergraduate students, 93% full-time, 51% women, 49% men
- **Very difficult** entrance level, 47% of applicants were admitted

Undergraduates 35,558 full-time, 2,862 part-time. Students come from 50 states and territories; 96 other countries; 5% are from out of state; 5% Black or African American, non-Hispanic/Latino; 20% Hispanic/Latino; 18% Asian, non-Hispanic/Latino; 0.4% American Indian or Alaska Native, non-Hispanic/Latino; 1% Two or more races, non-Hispanic/Latino; 0.4% Race/ethnicity unknown; 5% international; 6% transferred in; 20% live on campus. *Retention:* 92% of full-time freshmen returned.

Freshmen *Admission:* 31,022 applied, 14,583 admitted, 7,275 enrolled. *Test scores:* SAT critical reading scores over 500: 85%; SAT math scores over 500: 93%; SAT writing scores over 500: 85%; ACT scores over 18: 98%; SAT critical reading scores over 600: 53%; SAT math scores over 600: 69%; SAT writing scores over 600: 52%; ACT scores over 24: 81%; SAT critical reading scores over 700: 15%; SAT math scores over 700: 27%; SAT writing scores over 700: 15%; ACT scores over 30: 36%.

Faculty *Total:* 2,976, 91% full-time, 88% with terminal degrees. *Student/faculty ratio:* 18:1.

Academics *Calendar:* semesters. *Degrees:* bachelor's, master's, doctoral-professional, and doctoral-research/scholarship. *Special study options:* academic remediation for entering students, accelerated degree program, advanced placement credit, cooperative education, distance learning, double majors, English as a second language, honors programs, independent study, internships, off-campus study, part-time degree program, services for LD students, student-designed majors, study abroad, summer session for credit. *ROTC:* Army (b), Navy (b), Air Force (b). *Unusual degree programs:* 3-2 business administration; engineering; Computer Science.

Computers on Campus 503 computers/terminals and 9,000 ports are available on campus for general student use. Students can access the following: computer help desk, free student e-mail accounts, online (class) grades, online (class) registration, online (class) schedules. Campuswide network is available. 100% of college-owned or -operated housing units are wired for high-speed Internet access. Wireless service is available via entire campus.

Student Life *Housing options:* coed, men-only, women-only. Campus housing is university owned. Freshman applicants given priority for college housing. *Activities and organizations:* drama/theater group, student-run newspaper, radio and television station, choral group, marching band, Alpha Phi Omega, Student Events Center, Texas Exes-Student Chapter, Longhorn Band Student Organization, Student Volunteer Board, national fraternities, national sororities. *Campus security:* 24-hour emergency response devices and patrols, late-night transport/escort service, controlled dormitory access. *Student services:* health clinic, personal/psychological counseling, women's center, legal services.

Athletics Member NCAA. All Division I except football (Division I-A). *Intercollegiate sports:* archery M(c)/W(c), badminton M(c)/W(c), baseball M(s)/W(c), basketball M(s)/W(s), crew M(c)/W(s), cross-country running M(s)/W(s), fencing M(c)/W(c), golf M(s)/W(s), gymnastics M(c)/W(c), ice hockey M(c)/W(c), lacrosse M(c)/W(c), racquetball M(c)/W(c), rugby M(c)/W(s), sailing M(c)/W(s), soccer M(c)/W(s), softball W(s), swimming and diving M(s)/W(s), table tennis M(c)/W(c), tennis M(s)/W(s), track and field M(s)/W(s), ultimate Frisbee M(c)/W(c), volleyball M(c)/W(s), water polo M(c)/W(c), weight lifting M(c)/W(c), wrestling M(c)/W(c). *Intramural sports:* basketball M/W, football M/W, golf M/W, racquetball M/W, soccer M/W, softball M/W, tennis M/W, track and field M/W, ultimate Frisbee M/W, volleyball M/W.

Standardized Tests *Required:* SAT or ACT (for admission). *Required for some:* SAT Subject Tests (for admission).

Costs (2011–12) *Tuition:* state resident $9794 full-time; nonresident $32,506 full-time. Full-time tuition and fees vary according to course load and program. Part-time tuition and fees vary according to course load and program. *Room and board:* Room and board charges vary according to housing facility. *Payment plan:* installment. *Waivers:* senior citizens and employees or children of employees.

Financial Aid Of all full-time matriculated undergraduates who enrolled in 2009, 21,253 applied for aid, 15,336 were judged to have need, 3,668 had their need fully met. In 2009, 1827 non-need-based awards were made. *Average percent of need met:* 75%. *Average financial aid package:* $12,388. *Average need-based loan:* $4204. *Average need-based gift aid:* $8822. *Average indebtedness upon graduation:* $22,102.

Applying *Options:* electronic application, deferred entrance. *Application fee:* $60. *Required:* essay or personal statement, high school transcript. *Application deadlines:* 12/1 (freshmen), 3/1 (transfers). *Notification:* continuous (freshmen), continuous (transfers).

Freshman Application Contact Dr. Kedra Ishop, Vice Provost and Director of Admissions, The University of Texas at Austin, Office of Admissions, Freshman Admissions Center, PO Box 8058, Austin, TX 78713-8058. *Phone:* 512-475-7387. *Fax:* 512-475-7478. *Web site:* http://www.utexas.edu/.

The University of Texas at Brownsville

Brownsville, Texas

- **State-supported** comprehensive, founded 1973, part of University of Texas System
- **Urban** 380-acre campus
- **Coed**
- **Noncompetitive** entrance level

Faculty *Student/faculty ratio:* 21:1.

Academics *Calendar:* semesters. *Degrees:* certificates, associate, bachelor's, master's, and doctoral-research/scholarship.

Student Life *Campus security:* 24-hour emergency response devices and patrols, late-night transport/escort service.

Athletics Member NAIA.

Costs (2010–11) *Tuition:* state resident $3395 full-time, $141 per credit hour part-time; nonresident $10,835 full-time, $451 per credit hour part-time. Full-time tuition and fees vary according to class time, course level, course load, location, and program. Part-time tuition and fees vary according to class time, course level, course load, location, and program. *Required fees:* $1371 full-time, $36 per credit hour part-time, $253 per term part-time. *Room and board:* $5782; room only: $2992. Room and board charges vary according to board plan.

Financial Aid *Of all full-time matriculated undergraduates who enrolled in 2009,* 4,609 applied for aid, 4,373 were judged to have need. 140 Federal Work-Study jobs (averaging $3508). 27 state and other part-time jobs (averaging $4141). *In 2009,* 119 non-need-based awards were made. *Average percent of need met:* 57. *Average financial aid package:* $8618. *Average need-based loan:* $3824. *Average need-based gift aid:* $6883. *Average non-need-based aid:* $2814.

Applying *Options:* electronic application, early admission. *Required:* high school transcript.

Freshman Application Contact Carlo Tamayo, New Student Relations Coordinator, The University of Texas at Brownsville, 80 Fort Brown, Brownsville, TX 78520-4991. *Phone:* 956-882-8860. *Toll-free phone:* 800-850-0160. *Fax:* 956-882-8959. *E-mail:* admissions@utb.edu. *Web site:* http://www.utb.edu/.

The University of Texas at Dallas

Richardson, Texas

- **State-supported** university, founded 1969, part of University of Texas System
- **Suburban** 500-acre campus with easy access to Dallas
- **Endowment** $220.0 million
- **Coed** 10,648 undergraduate students, 75% full-time, 44% women, 56% men
- **Very difficult** entrance level, 50% of applicants were admitted

Undergraduates 8,019 full-time, 2,629 part-time. Students come from 46 states and territories; 79 other countries; 3% are from out of state; 7% Black or African American, non-Hispanic/Latino; 14% Hispanic/Latino; 22% Asian, non-Hispanic/Latino; 0.5% American Indian or Alaska Native, non-Hispanic/Latino; 1% Two or more races, non-Hispanic/Latino; 3% Race/ethnicity

unknown; 4% international; 15% transferred in; 23% live on campus. *Retention:* 85% of full-time freshmen returned.

Freshmen *Admission:* 5,644 applied, 2,816 admitted, 1,377 enrolled. *Average high school GPA:* 3.78. *Test scores:* SAT critical reading scores over 500: 88%; SAT math scores over 500: 95%; SAT writing scores over 500: 84%; ACT scores over 18: 98%; SAT critical reading scores over 600: 55%; SAT math scores over 600: 73%; SAT writing scores over 600: 45%; ACT scores over 24: 84%; SAT critical reading scores over 700: 14%; SAT math scores over 700: 28%; SAT writing scores over 700: 10%; ACT scores over 30: 32%.

Faculty *Total:* 898, 68% full-time, 82% with terminal degrees. *Student/faculty ratio:* 19:1.

Academics *Calendar:* semesters. *Degrees:* bachelor's, master's, doctoral-professional, doctoral-research/scholarship, and postbachelor's certificates. *Special study options:* academic remediation for entering students, accelerated degree program, adult/continuing education programs, advanced placement credit, cooperative education, distance learning, double majors, freshman honors college, honors programs, independent study, internships, part-time degree program, services for LD students, student-designed majors, study abroad, summer session for credit. *ROTC:* Army (c), Air Force (c). *Unusual degree programs:* 3-2 engineering with Abilene Christian University, Austin College, Paul Quinn College, Texas Woman's University.

Computers on Campus 630 computers/terminals are available on campus for general student use. Students can access the following: computer help desk, free student e-mail accounts, online (class) grades, online (class) registration, online (class) schedules. Campuswide network is available. 100% of college-owned or -operated housing units are wired for high-speed Internet access. Wireless service is available via classrooms, computer centers, dorm rooms, libraries, student centers.

Student Life *Housing options:* coed. Campus housing is university owned and is provided by a third party. Freshman applicants given priority for college housing. *Activities and organizations:* drama/theater group, student-run newspaper, radio and television station, choral group, Student Government Association, Golden Key National Honor Society, Muslim Students Association, Indian Student Association, Friendship Association of Chinese Students and Scholars, national fraternities, national sororities. *Campus security:* 24-hour emergency response devices and patrols, student patrols, late-night transport/escort service, controlled dormitory access. *Student services:* health clinic, personal/psychological counseling, women's center, legal services.

Athletics Member NCAA. All Division III. *Intercollegiate sports:* baseball M, basketball M/W, cross-country running M/W, golf M/W, soccer M/W, softball W, tennis M/W, volleyball W. *Intramural sports:* badminton M(c)/W(c), basketball M/W, cheerleading M/W, cross-country running M(c)/W(c), field hockey M(c)/W(c), football M(c)/W(c), golf M/W, racquetball M(c)/W(c), rugby M(c)/W(c), soccer M(c)/W(c), softball M/W, squash M(c)/W(c), swimming and diving M(c)/W(c), table tennis M(c)/W(c), tennis M(c)/W(c), ultimate Frisbee M(c)/W(c), volleyball M/W, water polo M/W, weight lifting M(c), wrestling M(c).

Standardized Tests *Required:* SAT or ACT (for admission). *Required for some:* Texas Higher Education Assessment.

Costs (2010–11) *Tuition:* state resident $10,744 full-time, $358 per credit hour part-time; nonresident $25,866 full-time, $862 per credit hour part-time. Full-time tuition and fees vary according to course load and degree level. Part-time tuition and fees vary according to course load and degree level. No tuition increase for student's term of enrollment. *Room and board:* $8210. Room and board charges vary according to board plan and housing facility. *Payment plan:* installment. *Waivers:* senior citizens and employees or children of employees.

Financial Aid Of all full-time matriculated undergraduates who enrolled in 2008, 4,496 applied for aid, 3,684 were judged to have need, 845 had their need fully met. 254 Federal Work-Study jobs (averaging $4333). In 2008, 300 non-need-based awards were made. *Average percent of need met:* 67%. *Average financial aid package:* $10,378. *Average need-based loan:* $4285. *Average need-based gift aid:* $6664. *Average non-need-based aid:* $7455. *Average indebtedness upon graduation:* $17,384.

Applying *Options:* electronic application, deferred entrance. *Application fee:* $50. *Required:* essay or personal statement, high school transcript. *Required for some:* interview. *Recommended:* 3 letters of recommendation. *Application deadline:* 7/1 (freshmen). *Notification:* continuous (freshmen), continuous (transfers).

Freshman Application Contact Enrollment Services, The University of Texas at Dallas, 800 West Campbell Road, Mail Station ROC11, Richardson, TX 75083-0688. *Phone:* 972-883-2270. *Toll-free phone:* 800-889-2443. *Fax:* 972-883-2599. *E-mail:* interest@utdallas.edu. *Web site:* http://www.utdallas.edu/.

The University of Texas at El Paso
El Paso, Texas

- **State-supported** university, founded 1913
- **Urban** 360-acre campus
- **Coed**
- **Minimally difficult** entrance level

Faculty *Student/faculty ratio:* 20:1.
Academics *Calendar:* semesters. *Degrees:* bachelor's, master's, and doctoral-research/scholarship.
Student Life *Campus security:* 24-hour emergency response devices and patrols, late-night transport/escort service.
Athletics Member NCAA. All Division I except football (Division I-A).
Standardized Tests *Required for some:* SAT or ACT (for admission).
Costs (2010–11) *One-time required fee:* $166. *Tuition:* state resident $5063 full-time, $169 per credit hour part-time; nonresident $14,363 full-time, $479 per credit hour part-time. Full-time tuition and fees vary according to course load and degree level. Part-time tuition and fees vary according to course load and degree level. No tuition increase for student's term of enrollment. *Required fees:* $1472 full-time, $46 per credit hour part-time, $125 per term part-time. *Room and board:* Room and board charges vary according to housing facility.
Financial Aid Of all full-time matriculated undergraduates who enrolled in 2008, 8,696 applied for aid, 7,259 were judged to have need, 1,686 had their need fully met. In 2008, 741 non-need-based awards were made. *Average percent of need met:* 73. *Average financial aid package:* $14,508. *Average need-based loan:* $6671. *Average need-based gift aid:* $9294. *Average non-need-based aid:* $2501. *Average indebtedness upon graduation:* $18,773.
Applying *Options:* deferred entrance. *Required:* high school transcript.
Freshman Application Contact Director of Admissions, The University of Texas at El Paso, 500 West University Avenue, El Paso, TX 79968-0001. *Phone:* 915-747-5588. *Toll-free phone:* 877-746-4636. *Fax:* 915-747-8893. *E-mail:* futureminer@utep.edu. *Web site:* http://www.utep.edu/.

The University of Texas at San Antonio
San Antonio, Texas

- **State-supported** university, founded 1969, part of University of Texas System
- **Suburban** 600-acre campus
- **Coed** 25,794 undergraduate students, 80% full-time, 49% women, 51% men
- **Moderately difficult** entrance level, 83% of applicants were admitted

Undergraduates 20,622 full-time, 5,172 part-time. 2% are from out of state; 9% Black or African American, non-Hispanic/Latino; 46% Hispanic/Latino; 5% Asian, non-Hispanic/Latino; 0.2% Native Hawaiian or other Pacific Islander, non-Hispanic/Latino; 0.2% American Indian or Alaska Native, non-Hispanic/Latino; 2% Two or more races, non-Hispanic/Latino; 3% Race/ethnicity unknown; 2% international; 11% transferred in; 12% live on campus. *Retention:* 57% of full-time freshmen returned.
Freshmen *Admission:* 12,882 applied, 10,724 admitted, 4,936 enrolled. *Test scores:* SAT critical reading scores over 500: 51%; SAT math scores over 500: 65%; SAT writing scores over 500: 41%; ACT scores over 18: 88%; SAT critical reading scores over 600: 12%; SAT math scores over 600: 20%; SAT writing scores over 600: 9%; ACT scores over 24: 28%; SAT critical reading scores over 700: 2%; SAT math scores over 700: 2%; SAT writing scores over 700: 1%; ACT scores over 30: 2%.
Faculty *Total:* 1,250, 79% full-time, 69% with terminal degrees. *Student/faculty ratio:* 23:1.
Academics *Calendar:* semesters. *Degrees:* bachelor's, master's, doctoral-research/scholarship, and postbachelor's certificates. *Special study options:* academic remediation for entering students, adult/continuing education programs, advanced placement credit, cooperative education, distance learning, double majors, English as a second language, honors programs, independent study, internships, off-campus study, part-time degree program, services for LD students, study abroad, summer session for credit. *ROTC:* Army (b), Air Force (b).
Computers on Campus Students can access the following: computer help desk, free student e-mail accounts, online (class) grades, online (class) registration, online (class) schedules. Campuswide network is available. Wireless service is available via entire campus.
Student Life *Housing options:* coed, disabled students. Campus housing is university owned and is provided by a third party. *Activities and organizations:* drama/theater group, student-run newspaper, choral group, national fraternities, national sororities. *Campus security:* 24-hour emergency response devices and patrols, crime prevention program, PSA commercials on campus TV, educational programs for students, faculty, and staff; security surveys. *Student services:* health clinic, personal/psychological counseling.

Athletics Member NCAA. All Division I. *Intercollegiate sports:* baseball M(s), basketball M(s)/W(s), cross-country running M(s)/W(s), golf M(s), softball W(s), tennis M(s)/W(s), track and field M(s)/W(s), volleyball W(s). *Intramural sports:* badminton M/W, baseball M, basketball M/W, cross-country running M/W, football M/W, golf M, soccer M/W, softball M/W, table tennis M/W, tennis M/W, track and field M/W, volleyball M/W, weight lifting M/W.

Costs (2011–12) *Tuition:* state resident $5783 full-time, $193 per hour part-time; nonresident $15,683 full-time, $523 per hour part-time. Full-time tuition and fees vary according to course level, course load, and degree level. Part-time tuition and fees vary according to course level, course load, and degree level. *Required fees:* $2500 full-time. *Room and board:* $8696; room only: $5796. Room and board charges vary according to board plan and housing facility. *Payment plans:* installment, deferred payment. *Waivers:* employees or children of employees.

Financial Aid Of all full-time matriculated undergraduates who enrolled in 2008, 14,582 applied for aid, 12,197 were judged to have need, 1,722 had their need fully met. 712 Federal Work-Study jobs (averaging $2169). 89 state and other part-time jobs (averaging $2038). In 2008, 580 non-need-based awards were made. *Average percent of need met:* 53%. *Average financial aid package:* $9075. *Average need-based loan:* $4073. *Average need-based gift aid:* $5969. *Average non-need-based aid:* $1810. *Average indebtedness upon graduation:* $24,017.

Applying *Options:* electronic application. *Required:* high school transcript. *Application deadlines:* 6/1 (freshmen), 7/1 (transfers). *Notification:* continuous (transfers).

Freshman Application Contact Ms. Jennifer Ehlers, Director of Admissions, The University of Texas at San Antonio, One UTSA Circle, San Antonio, TX 78249-0617. *Phone:* 210-458-4536. *Toll-free phone:* 800-669-0919. *Fax:* 210-458-2001. *E-mail:* prospects@utsa.edu. *Web site:* http://www.utsa.edu/.

The University of Texas at Tyler

Tyler, Texas

- **State-supported** comprehensive, founded 1971, part of University of Texas System
- **Urban** 200-acre campus
- **Coed** 5,064 undergraduate students, 76% full-time, 58% women, 42% men
- **Moderately difficult** entrance level

Undergraduates 3,830 full-time, 1,234 part-time. 2% are from out of state; 9% Black or African American, non-Hispanic/Latino; 8% Hispanic/Latino; 2% Asian, non-Hispanic/Latino; 0.7% American Indian or Alaska Native, non-Hispanic/Latino; 0.6% Two or more races, non-Hispanic/Latino; 10% Race/ethnicity unknown; 1% international; 16% transferred in; 14% live on campus. *Retention:* 64% of full-time freshmen returned.

Freshmen *Admission:* 2,384 applied, 573 enrolled. *Average high school GPA:* 3.4. *Test scores:* SAT critical reading scores over 500: 63%; SAT math scores over 500: 76%; SAT writing scores over 500: 58%; ACT scores over 18: 98%; SAT critical reading scores over 600: 19%; SAT math scores over 600: 24%; SAT writing scores over 600: 13%; ACT scores over 24: 44%; SAT critical reading scores over 700: 2%; SAT math scores over 700: 3%; SAT writing scores over 700: 1%; ACT scores over 30: 2%.

Faculty *Total:* 383, 70% full-time, 60% with terminal degrees. *Student/faculty ratio:* 16:1.

Academics *Calendar:* semesters. *Degrees:* bachelor's, master's, doctoral-research/scholarship, and postbachelor's certificates. *Special study options:* adult/continuing education programs, advanced placement credit, cooperative education, distance learning, double majors, honors programs, independent study, internships, part-time degree program, services for LD students, student-designed majors, study abroad, summer session for credit.

Computers on Campus Students can access the following: computer help desk, free student e-mail accounts, online (class) grades, online (class) registration, online (class) schedules. Campuswide network is available. 100% of college-owned or -operated housing units are wired for high-speed Internet access. Wireless service is available via classrooms, computer centers, computer labs, learning centers, libraries, student centers.

Student Life *Housing:* on-campus residence required for freshman year. *Options:* coed. Campus housing is university owned and is provided by a third party. Freshman applicants given priority for college housing. *Activities and organizations:* student-run newspaper, choral group, national fraternities, national sororities. *Campus security:* 24-hour emergency response devices and patrols, late-night transport/escort service, controlled dormitory access. *Student services:* health clinic, personal/psychological counseling.

Athletics Member NCAA. All Division III. *Intercollegiate sports:* baseball M, basketball M/W, cheerleading M/W, cross-country running M/W, golf M/W, soccer M/W, tennis M/W, track and field M/W, volleyball W. *Intramural sports:* baseball M, basketball M/W, bowling M/W, football M/W, golf M/W, racquetball M/W, soccer M/W, softball M/W, swimming and diving M/W, table tennis M/W, tennis M/W, ultimate Frisbee M/W, volleyball W, wrestling M.

Standardized Tests *Required:* SAT or ACT (for admission).

Costs (2010–11) *Tuition:* state resident $4920 full-time, $50 per semester hour part-time; nonresident $14,220 full-time, $360 per semester hour part-time. Full-time tuition and fees vary according to course level, course load, and degree level. *Required fees:* $1402 full-time. *Room and board:* $8106; room only: $5090. Room and board charges vary according to board plan and housing facility. *Payment plan:* installment. *Waivers:* senior citizens and employees or children of employees.

Financial Aid Of all full-time matriculated undergraduates who enrolled in 2008, 2,488 applied for aid, 2,009 were judged to have need, 243 had their need fully met. 105 Federal Work-Study jobs (averaging $3408). 14 state and other part-time jobs (averaging $4444). In 2008, 357 non-need-based awards were made. *Average percent of need met:* 57%. *Average financial aid package:* $8496. *Average need-based loan:* $4077. *Average need-based gift aid:* $5899. *Average non-need-based aid:* $2451. *Average indebtedness upon graduation:* $18,041.

Applying *Options:* electronic application, deferred entrance. *Application fee:* $25. *Required:* high school transcript. *Application deadlines:* rolling (freshmen), rolling (transfers). *Notification:* continuous (freshmen), continuous (transfers).

Freshman Application Contact Ms. Sarah Bowdin, Director of Admissions, The University of Texas at Tyler, 3900 University Boulevard, Tyler, TX 75799-0001. *Phone:* 903-566-7057. *Toll-free phone:* 800-UTTYLER. *Fax:* 903-566-7068. *E-mail:* admissions@uttyler.edu. *Web site:* http://www.uttyler.edu/.

The University of Texas Health Science Center at Houston

Houston, Texas

- **State-supported** upper-level, founded 1972, part of University of Texas System
- **Urban** campus with easy access to Houston
- **Endowment** $113.5 million
- **Coed**
- **Moderately difficult** entrance level

Faculty *Student/faculty ratio:* 11:1.

Academics *Calendar:* semesters. *Degrees:* certificates, bachelor's, master's, doctoral-other, doctoral-professional, doctoral-research/scholarship, post-master's, and postbachelor's certificates.

Student Life *Campus security:* 24-hour emergency response devices and patrols, late-night transport/escort service, controlled access to all buildings.

Standardized Tests *Required:* HESI A2-Nursing Entrance Test for BSN programs (for admission).

Costs (2010–11) *Tuition:* state resident $149 per credit hour part-time; nonresident $623 per credit hour part-time. *Required fees:* $157 per credit hour part-time.

Financial Aid *Of all full-time matriculated undergraduates who enrolled in 2008,* 266 applied for aid, 241 were judged to have need, 30 had their need fully met. *In 2008,* 34 non-need-based awards were made. *Average percent of need met:* 45. *Average financial aid package:* $9508. *Average need-based loan:* $5158. *Average need-based gift aid:* $5195. *Average non-need-based aid:* $2176.

Applying *Options:* electronic application. *Application fee:* $30.

Application Contact Mr. Robert L. Jenkins, Registrar, The University of Texas Health Science Center at Houston, PO Box 20036, Houston, TX 77225-0036. *Phone:* 713-500-3361. *Fax:* 713-500-3356. *E-mail:* registrar@uth.tmc.edu. *Web site:* http://www.uthouston.edu/.

The University of Texas Health Science Center at San Antonio

San Antonio, Texas

Application Contact The University of Texas Health Science Center at San Antonio, 7703 Floyd Curl Drive, San Antonio, TX 78229-3900. *Phone:* 210-567-2659. *Web site:* http://www.uthscsa.edu/.

The University of Texas Medical Branch

Galveston, Texas

- **State-supported** comprehensive, founded 1891, part of University of Texas System
- **Small-town** 85-acre campus with easy access to Houston
- **Endowment** $368.5 million
- **Coed**
- **Very difficult** entrance level

Academics *Calendar:* semesters (early semester). *Degrees:* bachelor's, master's, doctoral-professional, doctoral-research/scholarship, and post-master's certificates.

Student Life *Campus security:* 24-hour emergency response devices and patrols, late-night transport/escort service.

Costs (2010–11) *Tuition:* state resident $4770 full-time, $159 per credit hour part-time; nonresident $14,070 full-time, $469 per credit hour part-time. Full-time tuition and fees vary according to course load, degree level, and program. Part-time tuition and fees vary according to course load, degree level, and program. *Required fees:* $970 full-time, $16 per credit hour part-time, $220 per term part-time. *Room and board:* Room and board charges vary according to housing facility.

Financial Aid *Of all full-time matriculated undergraduates who enrolled in 2008,* 491 applied for aid, 407 were judged to have need, 60 had their need fully met. 21 Federal Work-Study jobs (averaging $48,797). *In 2008,* 356 non-need-based awards were made. *Average percent of need met:* 83. *Average financial aid package:* $15,827. *Average need-based loan:* $5216. *Average need-based gift aid:* $5163. *Average non-need-based aid:* $9647.

Applying *Options:* electronic application. *Application fee:* $30.

Freshman Application Contact The University of Texas Medical Branch, 301 University Boulevard, Galveston, TX 77555. *Phone:* 409-772-1215. *Web site:* http://www.utmb.edu/.

The University of Texas of the Permian Basin

Odessa, Texas

- **State-supported** comprehensive, founded 1969, part of University of Texas System
- **Urban** 600-acre campus
- **Endowment** $16.8 million
- **Coed** 3,177 undergraduate students, 67% full-time, 60% women, 40% men
- **Moderately difficult** entrance level, 81% of applicants were admitted

Undergraduates 2,132 full-time, 1,045 part-time. Students come from 28 states and territories; 11 other countries; 3% are from out of state; 5% Black or African American, non-Hispanic/Latino; 42% Hispanic/Latino; 1% Asian, non-Hispanic/Latino; 0.1% Native Hawaiian or other Pacific Islander, non-Hispanic/Latino; 0.5% American Indian or Alaska Native, non-Hispanic/Latino; 2% Two or more races, non-Hispanic/Latino; 0.8% Race/ethnicity unknown; 0.4% international; 15% transferred in; 15% live on campus. *Retention:* 61% of full-time freshmen returned.

Freshmen *Admission:* 854 applied, 692 admitted, 337 enrolled. *Test scores:* SAT critical reading scores over 500: 44%; SAT math scores over 500: 56%; ACT scores over 18: 90%; SAT critical reading scores over 600: 13%; SAT math scores over 600: 21%; ACT scores over 24: 27%; SAT critical reading scores over 700: 1%; SAT math scores over 700: 2%; ACT scores over 30: 2%.

Faculty *Total:* 197, 66% full-time, 64% with terminal degrees. *Student/faculty ratio:* 19:1.

Academics *Calendar:* semesters. *Degrees:* bachelor's and master's. *Special study options:* academic remediation for entering students, advanced placement credit, distance learning, double majors, English as a second language, honors programs, independent study, internships, off-campus study, part-time degree program, services for LD students, study abroad, summer session for credit.

Computers on Campus 170 computers/terminals are available on campus for general student use. Students can access the following: campus intranet, computer help desk, free student e-mail accounts, online (class) grades, online (class) registration, online (class) schedules. Campuswide network is available. 100% of college-owned or -operated housing units are wired for high-speed Internet access. Wireless service is available via entire campus.

Student Life *Housing options:* coed. Campus housing is university owned. *Activities and organizations:* drama/theater group, student-run newspaper, choral group, Catholic Student Association (CSA), Baptist Student Ministries, Christians on Campus, Students in Free Enterprise (SIFE), Accounting Association, national fraternities. *Campus security:* 24-hour patrols, late-night transport/escort service. *Student services:* health clinic, personal/psychological counseling.

Athletics Member NCAA. All Division II. *Intercollegiate sports:* baseball M(s), basketball M(s)/W(s), cheerleading M(s)/W(s), cross-country running M(s)/W(s), soccer M(s)/W(s), softball W(s), swimming and diving M(s)/W(s), volleyball W(s). *Intramural sports:* basketball M/W, racquetball M/W, tennis M/W, ultimate Frisbee M(c)/W(c), volleyball M/W, water polo M/W.

Standardized Tests *Required:* SAT or ACT (for admission).

Costs (2010–11) *Tuition:* state resident $4380 full-time, $146 per credit hour part-time; nonresident $12,690 full-time, $423 per credit hour part-time. Full-time tuition and fees vary according to course load and location. Part-time tuition and fees vary according to course load and location. *Required fees:* $1219 full-time, $41 per credit hour part-time. *Room and board:* $6964; room only: $3880. Room and board charges vary according to board plan and housing facility. *Payment plan:* installment. *Waivers:* senior citizens and employees or children of employees.

Financial Aid Of all full-time matriculated undergraduates who enrolled in 2009, 1,364 applied for aid, 1,092 were judged to have need, 252 had their need fully met. 20 Federal Work-Study jobs (averaging $2474). 15 state and other part-time jobs (averaging $1382). In 2009, 256 non-need-based awards were made. *Average percent of need met:* 81%. *Average financial aid package:* $7384. *Average need-based loan:* $3540. *Average need-based gift aid:* $6842. *Average non-need-based aid:* $2460. *Average indebtedness upon graduation:* $18,507.

Applying *Options:* electronic application, deferred entrance. *Required:* high school transcript. *Application deadlines:* 7/15 (freshmen), rolling (transfers). *Notification:* continuous (freshmen), continuous (transfers).

Freshman Application Contact The University of Texas of the Permian Basin, 4901 East University Boulevard, Odessa, TX 79762-0001. *Phone:* 432-552-2605. *Toll-free phone:* 866-552-UTPB. *Web site:* http://www.utpb.edu/.

The University of Texas–Pan American

Edinburg, Texas

- **State-supported** comprehensive, founded 1927, part of University of Texas System
- **Small-town** 289-acre campus with easy access to McAllen-Edinburg-Mission MSA
- **Coed** 16,266 undergraduate students, 74% full-time, 56% women, 44% men
- **Noncompetitive** entrance level, 70% of applicants were admitted

Undergraduates 12,010 full-time, 4,256 part-time. 1% are from out of state; 0.5% Black or African American, non-Hispanic/Latino; 90% Hispanic/Latino; 0.6% Asian, non-Hispanic/Latino; 0.1% American Indian or Alaska Native, non-Hispanic/Latino; 0.3% Two or more races, non-Hispanic/Latino; 2% Race/ethnicity unknown; 2% international; 6% transferred in; 5% live on campus. *Retention:* 73% of full-time freshmen returned.

Freshmen *Admission:* 7,470 applied, 5,197 admitted, 2,925 enrolled. *Test scores:* SAT critical reading scores over 500: 35%; SAT math scores over 500: 43%; SAT writing scores over 500: 29%; ACT scores over 18: 68%; SAT critical reading scores over 600: 9%; SAT math scores over 600: 12%; SAT writing scores over 600: 6%; ACT scores over 24: 10%; SAT critical reading scores over 700: 2%; SAT math scores over 700: 1%; SAT writing scores over 700: 1%.

Faculty *Total:* 800, 83% full-time, 78% with terminal degrees. *Student/faculty ratio:* 21:1.

Academics *Calendar:* semesters. *Degrees:* bachelor's, master's, and doctoral-research/scholarship. *Special study options:* academic remediation for entering students, accelerated degree program, adult/continuing education programs, advanced placement credit, cooperative education, distance learning, double majors, English as a second language, honors programs, independent study, internships, part-time degree program, services for LD students, study abroad, summer session for credit. *ROTC:* Army (b). *Unusual degree programs:* accounting.

Computers on Campus Students can access the following: campus intranet, computer help desk, free student e-mail accounts, online (class) grades, online (class) registration, online (class) schedules. Campuswide network is available. Wireless service is available via entire campus.

Student Life *Housing options:* coed, men-only, women-only. Campus housing is university owned. *Activities and organizations:* drama/theater group, student-run newspaper, choral group, national fraternities, national sororities. *Campus security:* 24-hour emergency response devices and patrols, late-night transport/escort service. *Student services:* health clinic, personal/psychological counseling.

Athletics Member NCAA. All Division I. *Intercollegiate sports:* baseball M(s), basketball M(s)/W(s), cross-country running M(s)/W(s), golf M(s)/W(s), tennis M(s)/W(s), track and field M(s)/W(s), volleyball W(s). *Intramural sports:* badminton M/W, basketball M/W, bowling M/W, cheerleading M/W, football M/W, racquetball M/W, soccer M/W, softball M/W, tennis M/W, volleyball M/W.

Standardized Tests *Required:* SAT or ACT (for admission).

Costs (2010–11) *Tuition:* state resident $3528 full-time, $65 per credit hour part-time; nonresident $10,176 full-time, $342 per credit hour part-time. Full-time tuition and fees vary according to course load. Part-time tuition and fees vary according to course load. *Required fees:* $1032 full-time, $275 per credit hour part-time, $516 per term part-time. *Room and board:* $5298; room only: $3328. Room and board charges vary according to board plan and housing facility. *Payment plan:* installment. *Waivers:* senior citizens.

Financial Aid Of all full-time matriculated undergraduates who enrolled in 2008, 9,827 applied for aid, 9,451 were judged to have need, 620 had their need fully met. 837 Federal Work-Study jobs (averaging $2283). 219 state and other part-time jobs (averaging $1619). In 2008, 315 non-need-based awards were made. *Average percent of need met:* 71%. *Average financial aid package:* $10,252. *Average need-based loan:* $4429. *Average need-based gift aid:* $10,877. *Average non-need-based aid:* $3055. *Average indebtedness upon graduation:* $13,480.

Applying *Options:* electronic application. *Required:* high school transcript, minimum 2 GPA. *Required for some:* interview. *Application deadlines:* 8/11 (freshmen), 8/11 (transfers). *Notification:* continuous (freshmen), continuous (transfers).

Freshman Application Contact Dr. Magdalena Hinojosa, Dean of Admissions and Enrollment Services, The University of Texas–Pan American, Office of Admissions and Records, 1201 West University Drive, Edinburg, TX 78539. *Phone:* 956-665-2999. *Fax:* 956-665-2212. *E-mail:* admissions@utpa.edu. *Web site:* http://www.utpa.edu/.

The University of Texas Southwestern Medical Center at Dallas

Dallas, Texas

- **State-supported** upper-level, founded 1943, part of University of Texas System
- **Urban** 98-acre campus
- **Endowment** $1.4 billion
- **Coed** 65 undergraduate students, 94% full-time, 80% women, 20% men
- **Moderately difficult** entrance level, 36% of applicants were admitted

Undergraduates 61 full-time, 4 part-time. Students come from 4 states and territories; 4 other countries; 6% are from out of state; 22% Black or African American, non-Hispanic/Latino; 18% Hispanic/Latino; 8% Asian, non-Hispanic/Latino; 17% Race/ethnicity unknown; 3% international; 8% transferred in.

Freshmen *Admission:* 87 applied, 31 admitted.

Faculty *Total:* 2,038.

Academics *Calendar:* semesters. *Degrees:* bachelor's, master's, doctoral-professional, doctoral-research/scholarship, post-master's, and postbachelor's certificates. *Special study options:* advanced placement credit, distance learning, independent study, internships, off-campus study, services for LD students.

Computers on Campus 150 computers/terminals are available on campus for general student use. Students can access the following: campus intranet, free student e-mail accounts, online (class) grades, online (class) schedules. Campuswide network is available. Wireless service is available via classrooms, computer labs, libraries, student centers.

Student Life *Campus security:* 24-hour emergency response devices and patrols, late-night transport/escort service. *Student services:* health clinic, personal/psychological counseling.

Athletics *Intramural sports:* badminton M/W, basketball M/W, football M, golf M/W, racquetball M/W, soccer M/W, table tennis M/W, tennis M/W, volleyball M/W.

Costs (2010–11) *Tuition:* state resident $4500 full-time, $125 per credit hour part-time; nonresident $16,530 full-time, $435 per credit hour part-time. Full-time tuition and fees vary according to course load and program. Part-time tuition and fees vary according to course load and program. *Required fees:* $1220 full-time. *Room and board:* $11,353. *Payment plan:* installment.

Financial Aid Of all full-time matriculated undergraduates who enrolled in 2008, 89 applied for aid, 89 were judged to have need. 10 Federal Work-Study jobs (averaging $1933).

Applying *Options:* electronic application. *Application fee:* $10. *Application deadline:* rolling (transfers). *Notification:* continuous (transfers).

Application Contact The University of Texas Southwestern Medical Center at Dallas, 5323 Harry Hines Boulevard, Dallas, TX 75390. *Phone:* 214-648-5617. *Web site:* http://www.utsouthwestern.edu/.

University of the Incarnate Word

San Antonio, Texas

- **Independent Roman Catholic** comprehensive, founded 1881
- **Urban** 200-acre campus
- **Coed** 5,464 undergraduate students, 68% full-time, 64% women, 36% men
- **Moderately difficult** entrance level, 96% of applicants were admitted

Undergraduates 3,706 full-time, 1,758 part-time. Students come from 41 states and territories; 40 other countries; 5% are from out of state; 7% Black or African American, non-Hispanic/Latino; 57% Hispanic/Latino; 2% Asian, non-Hispanic/Latino; 0.1% Native Hawaiian or other Pacific Islander, non-Hispanic/Latino; 0.4% American Indian or Alaska Native, non-Hispanic/Latino; 0.2% Two or more races, non-Hispanic/Latino; 8% Race/ethnicity unknown; 3% international; 11% transferred in; 21% live on campus. *Retention:* 75% of full-time freshmen returned.

Freshmen *Admission:* 2,435 applied, 2,327 admitted, 885 enrolled. *Average high school GPA:* 3.48. *Test scores:* SAT critical reading scores over 500: 42%; SAT math scores over 500: 46%; SAT writing scores over 500: 37%; ACT scores over 18: 79%; SAT critical reading scores over 600: 8%; SAT math scores over 600: 11%; SAT writing scores over 600: 5%; ACT scores over 24: 23%; SAT critical reading scores over 700: 1%; SAT math scores over 700: 1%; ACT scores over 30: 2%.

Faculty *Total:* 524, 47% full-time.

Academics *Calendar:* semesters. *Degrees:* associate, bachelor's, master's, doctoral-professional, and doctoral-research/scholarship. *Special study options:* academic remediation for entering students, accelerated degree program, adult/continuing education programs, advanced placement credit, cooperative education, distance learning, double majors, English as a second language, freshman honors college, honors programs, independent study, internships, off-campus study, part-time degree program, services for LD students, student-designed majors, study abroad, summer session for credit. *ROTC:* Army (c), Air Force (c). *Unusual degree programs:* 3-2 business administration; communications and accounting.

Computers on Campus 180 computers/terminals are available on campus for general student use. Students can access the following: computer help desk, free student e-mail accounts, online (class) grades, online (class) registration, online (class) schedules. Campuswide network is available. 100% of college-owned or -operated housing units are wired for high-speed Internet access. Wireless service is available via entire campus.

Student Life *Housing options:* coed, men-only, women-only, disabled students. Campus housing is university owned. Freshman campus housing is guaranteed. *Activities and organizations:* drama/theater group, student-run newspaper, radio and television station, choral group, Society of Leadership and Success, Pre-Pharmacy Association, Alpha Sigma Alpha, Lambda Chi Alpha, Student Government Association House, national fraternities, national sororities. *Campus security:* 24-hour emergency response devices and patrols, late-night transport/escort service, controlled dormitory access. *Student services:* health clinic, personal/psychological counseling.

Athletics Member NCAA. All Division II. *Intercollegiate sports:* baseball M(s), basketball M(s)/W(s), cross-country running M(s)/W(s), football M(s), golf M(s)/W(s), soccer M(s)/W(s), softball W(s), swimming and diving M(s)/W(s), tennis M(s)/W(s), track and field M(s)/W(s), volleyball W(s). *Intramural sports:* basketball M/W, cheerleading M/W, football M/W, racquetball M/W, soccer M/W, softball M/W, tennis M/W, ultimate Frisbee M/W, volleyball M/W, water polo M/W.

Standardized Tests *Required:* SAT or ACT (for admission).

Costs (2011–12) *Comprehensive fee:* $32,448 includes full-time tuition ($21,900), mandatory fees ($890), and room and board ($9658). Full-time tuition and fees vary according to course load, degree level, location, program, and reciprocity agreements. Part-time tuition: $725 per hour. Part-time tuition and fees vary according to course load, degree level, location, program, and reciprocity agreements. *College room only:* $5760. Room and board charges vary according to board plan and housing facility. *Payment plan:* installment. *Waivers:* senior citizens and employees or children of employees.

Financial Aid Of all full-time matriculated undergraduates who enrolled in 2008, 2,820 applied for aid, 2,629 were judged to have need, 698 had their need fully met. In 2008, 170 non-need-based awards were made. *Average percent of need met:* 68%. *Average financial aid package:* $17,171. *Average need-based loan:* $4427. *Average need-based gift aid:* $11,344. *Average non-need-based aid:* $6698.

Applying *Options:* electronic application, deferred entrance. *Application fee:* $20. *Required:* high school transcript. *Required for some:* essay or personal statement, interview. *Recommended:* minimum 2 GPA, 1 letter of recommendation. *Application deadlines:* rolling (freshmen), rolling (transfers). *Notification:* continuous (freshmen), continuous (transfers).

Freshman Application Contact Ms. Heather M. Rodriguez, Director of Undergraduate Admissions, University of the Incarnate Word, 4301 Broadway Avenue, University of the Incarnate Word, San Antonio, TN 78209. *Phone:*

210-829-6005. *Toll-free phone:* 800-749-WORD. *Fax:* 210-829-3921. *E-mail:* hrodrig1@uiwtx.edu. *Web site:* http://www.uiw.edu/.

Wade College

Dallas, Texas

- **Proprietary** primarily 2-year, founded 1965
- **Urban** 175-acre campus
- **Coed, primarily women** 238 undergraduate students
- **Minimally difficult** entrance level

Undergraduates 5% are from out of state. *Retention:* 49% of full-time freshmen returned.

Faculty *Total:* 18, 50% full-time, 11% with terminal degrees. *Student/faculty ratio:* 15:1.

Academics *Calendar:* trimesters. *Degrees:* associate and bachelor's. *Special study options:* academic remediation for entering students, advanced placement credit, double majors, part-time degree program, summer session for credit.

Computers on Campus Students can access the following: campus intranet, free student e-mail accounts. Campuswide network is available. Wireless service is available via entire campus.

Student Life *Housing options:* coed, men-only, women-only. Campus housing is leased by the school and is provided by a third party. *Activities and organizations:* Merchandising Design Student Association. *Campus security:* 24-hour emergency response devices and patrols, late-night transport/escort service, controlled dormitory access.

Costs (2010–11) *One-time required fee:* $125. *Tuition:* $10,900 full-time, $1265 per course part-time. Full-time tuition and fees vary according to course load and degree level. Part-time tuition and fees vary according to course load and degree level. No tuition increase for student's term of enrollment. *Required fees:* $1050 full-time. *Room only:* $4400. *Payment plan:* installment.

Applying *Options:* electronic application. *Required:* high school transcript, interview. *Application deadlines:* rolling (freshmen), rolling (transfers).

Freshman Application Contact Wade College, INFOMart, 1950 Stemmons Freeway, Suite 4080, LB 562, Dallas, TX 75207. *Phone:* 214-637-3530. *Toll-free phone:* 800-624-4850. *Web site:* http://www.wadecollege.edu/.

Wayland Baptist University

Plainview, Texas

- **Independent Baptist** comprehensive, founded 1908
- **Small-town** 80-acre campus
- **Endowment** $58.4 million
- **Coed** 1,088 undergraduate students, 77% full-time, 50% women, 50% men
- **Minimally difficult** entrance level, 100% of applicants were admitted

Undergraduates 833 full-time, 255 part-time. Students come from 41 states and territories; 14 other countries; 16% are from out of state; 8% Black or African American, non-Hispanic/Latino; 29% Hispanic/Latino; 0.2% Asian, non-Hispanic/Latino; 0.1% Native Hawaiian or other Pacific Islander, non-Hispanic/Latino; 1% American Indian or Alaska Native, non-Hispanic/Latino; 2% Two or more races, non-Hispanic/Latino; 4% Race/ethnicity unknown; 3% international; 9% transferred in; 61% live on campus. *Retention:* 58% of full-time freshmen returned.

Freshmen *Admission:* 368 applied, 367 admitted, 247 enrolled. *Average high school GPA:* 3.22. *Test scores:* SAT critical reading scores over 500: 28%; SAT math scores over 500: 39%; SAT writing scores over 500: 21%; ACT scores over 18: 75%; SAT critical reading scores over 600: 10%; SAT math scores over 600: 8%; SAT writing scores over 600: 5%; ACT scores over 24: 17%; SAT critical reading scores over 700: 3%; SAT math scores over 700: 1%; SAT writing scores over 700: 1%; ACT scores over 30: 2%.

Faculty *Total:* 132, 70% full-time, 52% with terminal degrees. *Student/faculty ratio:* 8:1.

Academics *Calendar:* semesters. *Degrees:* associate, bachelor's, and master's (branch locations in Anchorage, AK; Amarillo, TX; Luke Air Force Base, AZ; Glorieta, NM; Aiea, HI; Lubbock, TX; San Antonio, TX; Wichita Falls, TX). *Special study options:* academic remediation for entering students, accelerated degree program, adult/continuing education programs, advanced placement credit, distance learning, double majors, external degree program, honors programs, part-time degree program, services for LD students, study abroad, summer session for credit. *ROTC:* Army (c), Air Force (c). *Unusual degree programs:* 3-2 engineering with Texas Tech University.

Computers on Campus 231 computers/terminals are available on campus for general student use. Students can access the following: computer help desk,

free student e-mail accounts, online (class) grades, online (class) registration, online (class) schedules. Campuswide network is available. 100% of college-owned or -operated housing units are wired for high-speed Internet access. Wireless service is available via classrooms, computer labs, dorm rooms, libraries, student centers.

Student Life *Housing:* on-campus residence required through junior year. *Options:* men-only, women-only. Campus housing is university owned. Freshman campus housing is guaranteed. *Activities and organizations:* drama/theater group, student-run newspaper, radio and television station, choral group, marching band, student government, national fraternities, national sororities. *Campus security:* 24-hour emergency response devices and patrols, security lighting, campus police department. *Student services:* health clinic, personal/psychological counseling.

Athletics Member NAIA. *Intercollegiate sports:* baseball M(s), basketball M(s)/W(s), cheerleading M(s)/W(s), cross-country running M(s)/W(s), golf M(s)/W(s), soccer M(s)/W(s), track and field M(s)/W(s), volleyball W(s), wrestling M(s)/W(s). *Intramural sports:* basketball M/W, football M/W, soccer M/W, softball M/W, table tennis M/W, volleyball M/W.

Standardized Tests *Required:* SAT or ACT (for admission).

Costs (2010–11) *Comprehensive fee:* $17,424 includes full-time tuition ($12,450), mandatory fees ($890), and room and board ($4084). Full-time tuition and fees vary according to course load and location. Part-time tuition: $415 per credit hour. Part-time tuition and fees vary according to course load and location. *Required fees:* $60 per term part-time. *College room only:* $1328. Room and board charges vary according to board plan and housing facility. *Payment plan:* installment. *Waivers:* employees or children of employees.

Financial Aid Of all full-time matriculated undergraduates who enrolled in 2009, 719 applied for aid, 626 were judged to have need, 94 had their need fully met. 169 Federal Work-Study jobs (averaging $1582). 318 state and other part-time jobs (averaging $1969). In 2009, 143 non-need-based awards were made. *Average percent of need met:* 70%. *Average financial aid package:* $12,015. *Average need-based loan:* $3517. *Average need-based gift aid:* $9120. *Average non-need-based aid:* $8128. *Average indebtedness upon graduation:* $26,959.

Applying *Options:* electronic application. *Application fee:* $35. *Required:* high school transcript. *Required for some:* interview. *Application deadlines:* 8/1 (freshmen), rolling (transfers). *Notification:* continuous (freshmen), continuous (transfers).

Freshman Application Contact Ms. Debbie Stennett, Director of Student Admissions, Wayland Baptist University, 1900 West 7th Street, CMB 712, Plainview, TX 79072. *Phone:* 806-291-3500. *Toll-free phone:* 800-588-1928. *Fax:* 806-291-1973. *E-mail:* admityou@wbu.edu. *Web site:* http://www.wbu.edu/.

West Texas A&M University

Canyon, Texas

Freshman Application Contact Mr. Shawn Thomas, Director of Admissions, West Texas A&M University, WT Box 60907, Canyon, TX 79016-0001. *Phone:* 806-651-2020. *Toll-free phone:* 800-99-WTAMU. *Fax:* 806-651-5285. *E-mail:* sthomas@mail.wtamu.edu. *Web site:* http://www.wtamu.edu/.

Westwood College–Dallas

Dallas, Texas

- **Proprietary** 4-year, founded 2002
- **Coed**

Academics *Calendar:* continuous. *Degrees:* diplomas, associate, and bachelor's.

Freshman Application Contact Westwood College–Dallas, 8390 LBJ Freeway, Executive Center 1, Suite 100, Dallas, TX 75243. *Phone:* 214-570-9100. *Toll-free phone:* 800-803-3140. *Web site:* http://www.westwood.edu/.

Westwood College–Fort Worth

Fort Worth, Texas

- **Proprietary** 4-year
- **Coed**

Academics *Calendar:* continuous. *Degrees:* diplomas, associate, and bachelor's.

Freshman Application Contact Westwood College–Fort Worth, 4232 North Freeway, Fort Worth, TX 76137. *Phone:* 817-547-9601. *Toll-free phone:* 866-533-9997. *Web site:* http://www.westwood.edu/.

Westwood College–Houston South Campus

Houston, Texas

- **Proprietary** primarily 2-year, founded 2003
- **Coed**

Academics *Calendar:* continuous. *Degrees:* diplomas, associate, and bachelor's.

Freshman Application Contact Westwood College–Houston South Campus, 7322 Southwest Freeway #110, Houston, TX 77074. *Phone:* 713-777-4779. *Toll-free phone:* 888-227-4260. *Web site:* http://www.westwood.edu/.

Wiley College

Marshall, Texas

Director of Admissions Ms. Alvena Jones, Interim Director of Admissions/Recruitment, Wiley College, 711 Wiley Avenue, Marshall, TX 75670-5199. *Phone:* 903-927-3222. *Toll-free phone:* 800-658-6889. *Fax:* 903-923-8878. *E-mail:* ajones@wileyc.edu. *Web site:* http://www.wileyc.edu/.

UTAH

Argosy University, Salt Lake City

Draper, Utah

- **Proprietary** university, founded 2008
- **Coed**

Costs (2010–11) *Tuition:* Tuition varies by program. Students should contact Argosy University for tuition information.

Freshman Application Contact Argosy University, Salt Lake City, 121 West Election Road, Suite 300, Draper, UT 84020. *Phone:* 801-601-5000. *Toll-free phone:* 888-639-4756. *Web site:* http://www.argosy.edu/saltlakecity/.

See page 1002 for the College Close-Up.

The Art Institute of Salt Lake City

Draper, Utah

- **Proprietary** 4-year, part of Education Management Corporation
- **Coed**

Academics *Degrees:* certificates, diplomas, associate, and bachelor's.

Costs (2010–11) *Tuition:* Tuition cost varies by program. Prospective students should contact the school for current tuition costs. Other charges include a starting kit for all first-quarter students. Kits vary in price, depending on the program of study.

Freshman Application Contact The Art Institute of Salt Lake City, 121 West Election Road, Suite 100, Draper, UT 84020-9492. *Phone:* 801-601-4700. *Toll-free phone:* 800-978-0096. *Web site:* http://www.artinstitutes.edu/SaltLakeCity/.

See page 1064 for the College Close-Up.

Brigham Young University

Provo, Utah

- **Independent** university, founded 1875, affiliated with The Church of Jesus Christ of Latter-day Saints, part of Church Education System (CES) of The Church of Jesus Christ of Latter-day Saints
- **Suburban** 557-acre campus with easy access to Salt Lake City
- **Coed** 30,409 undergraduate students, 92% full-time, 49% women, 51% men
- **Moderately difficult** entrance level, 64% of applicants were admitted

Undergraduates 27,852 full-time, 2,557 part-time. 67% are from out of state; 0.4% Black or African American, non-Hispanic/Latino; 5% Hispanic/Latino; 2% Asian, non-Hispanic/Latino; 0.6% Native Hawaiian or other Pacific Islander, non-Hispanic/Latino; 0.4% American Indian or Alaska Native, non-Hispanic/Latino; 3% Two or more races, non-Hispanic/Latino; 1% Race/ethnicity unknown; 5% international; 2% transferred in; 19% live on campus. *Retention:* 84% of full-time freshmen returned.

Freshmen *Admission:* 10,913 applied, 7,020 admitted, 5,234 enrolled. *Average high school GPA:* 3.77. *Test scores:* SAT critical reading scores over 500: 93%; SAT math scores over 500: 95%; ACT scores over 18: 100%; SAT critical reading scores over 600: 63%; SAT math scores over 600: 68%; ACT scores over 24: 91%; SAT critical reading scores over 700: 21%; SAT math scores over 700: 20%; ACT scores over 30: 34%.

Faculty *Total:* 1,728, 73% full-time, 76% with terminal degrees. *Student/faculty ratio:* 21:1.

Academics *Calendar:* semesters. *Degrees:* bachelor's, master's, doctoral-professional, and doctoral-research/scholarship. *Special study options:* academic remediation for entering students, accelerated degree program, adult/continuing education programs, advanced placement credit, cooperative education, distance learning, double majors, English as a second language, external degree program, freshman honors college, honors programs, independent study, internships, off-campus study, part-time degree program, services for LD students, study abroad, summer session for credit. *ROTC:* Army (b), Air Force (b).

Computers on Campus Students can access the following: campus intranet, computer help desk, online (class) grades, online (class) registration, online (class) schedules. Campuswide network is available.

Student Life *Housing options:* men-only, women-only, disabled students. Campus housing is university owned. *Activities and organizations:* drama/theater group, student-run newspaper, radio and television station, choral group, marching band. *Campus security:* 24-hour emergency response devices and patrols, late-night transport/escort service, controlled dormitory access. *Student services:* health clinic, personal/psychological counseling, women's center, legal services.

Athletics Member NCAA. All Division I except football (Division I-A). *Intercollegiate sports:* baseball M(s), basketball M(s)/W(s), cheerleading M(s)/W(s), cross-country running M(s)/W(s), golf M(s)/W(s), gymnastics W(s), lacrosse M(c), racquetball M/W, rugby M(c), soccer M(c)/W(s), softball W(s), swimming and diving M(s)/W(s), tennis M(s)/W(s), track and field M(s)/W(s), volleyball M(s)/W(s). *Intramural sports:* badminton W, basketball M/W, field hockey M, football M/W, golf M/W, racquetball M/W, soccer M/W, softball M/W, table tennis M/W, tennis M/W, ultimate Frisbee M/W, volleyball M/W, water polo M/W, wrestling M.

Standardized Tests *Required:* SAT or ACT (for admission).

Costs (2010–11) *Comprehensive fee:* $11,680 includes full-time tuition ($4560) and room and board ($7120). Part-time tuition: $234 per credit hour. Part-time tuition and fees vary according to course load. Latter Day Saints full-time student $4,560 per year, non-LDS full-time student $9,120. *Room and board:* Room and board charges vary according to board plan, housing facility, and location. *Waivers:* employees or children of employees.

Financial Aid Of all full-time matriculated undergraduates who enrolled in 2008, 15,850 applied for aid, 13,475 were judged to have need, 495 had their need fully met. In 2008, 7426 non-need-based awards were made. *Average percent of need met:* 40%. *Average financial aid package:* $7405. *Average need-based loan:* $4274. *Average need-based gift aid:* $5491. *Average non-need-based aid:* $3436. *Average indebtedness upon graduation:* $13,354.

Applying *Options:* electronic application, early admission, deferred entrance. *Application fee:* $35. *Required:* essay or personal statement, high school transcript, 1 letter of recommendation, interview. *Application deadlines:* 2/1 (freshmen), 3/1 (transfers). *Notification:* continuous (freshmen), continuous (transfers).

Freshman Application Contact Mr. Tom Gourley, Dean of Admissions and Records, Brigham Young University, A-153 Abraham Smoot Building, Provo, UT 84602. *Phone:* 801-422-2507. *Fax:* 801-422-0005. *E-mail:* admissions@byu.edu. *Web site:* http://www.byu.edu/.

Broadview University

West Jordan, Utah

Freshman Application Contact Ms. Karma Cooper, Director of Admissions, Broadview University, 1902 West 7800 South, West Jordan, UT 84088. *Phone:* 801-304-4224 Ext. 158. *Toll-free phone:* 866-304-4224. *Fax:* 801-304-4229. *E-mail:* kcooper@utahcollege.edu. *Web site:* http://www.broadviewuniversity.edu/.

Broadview University-Layton

Layton, Utah

Director of Admissions Jeremy Smithson, Director of Admissions, Broadview University-Layton, 869 West Hill Field Road, Layton, UT 84041. *Phone:* 801-666-6000. *Toll-free phone:* 866-253-7744. *Fax:* 801-660-6001. *Web site:* http://www.broadviewuniversity.edu/.

Broadview University-Orem

Orem, Utah

Director of Admissions Matthew Moon, Director of Admissions, Broadview University-Orem, 898 North 1200 West, Orem, UT 84057. *Phone:* 801-822-5800. *Toll-free phone:* 877-822-5838. *Fax:* 801-822-5801. *Web site:* http://www.broadviewuniversity.edu/.

Broadview University-Salt Lake City

Salt Lake City, Utah

Director of Admissions Jeannie Carr, Director of Admission, Broadview University-Salt Lake City, 240 East Morris Avenue, Salt Lake City, UT 84115. *Phone:* 801-300-4300. *Toll-free phone:* 877-801-8889. *Fax:* 801-300-4301. *Web site:* http://www.broadviewuniversity.edu/.

DeVry University

Sandy, Utah

- **Proprietary** comprehensive
- **Coed**

Faculty *Student/faculty ratio:* 13:1.

Academics *Degrees:* associate, bachelor's, and master's.

Costs (2010–11) *Tuition:* $14,766 full-time, $580 per credit hour part-time. Full-time tuition and fees vary according to course load. Part-time tuition and fees vary according to course load. *Required fees:* $60 full-time, $30 per term part-time. *Payment plans:* installment, deferred payment.

Financial Aid *Of all full-time matriculated undergraduates who enrolled in 2007,* 9 applied for aid, 8 were judged to have need, 1 had their need fully met. In 2007, 1 non-need-based awards were made. *Average percent of need met:* 34. *Average financial aid package:* $11,508. *Average need-based loan:* $9109. *Average need-based gift aid:* $4798. *Average non-need-based aid:* $6900.

Applying *Options:* electronic application, deferred entrance. *Application fee:* $50.

Freshman Application Contact DeVry University, 9350 South 150 E, Suite 420, Sandy, UT 84070. *Web site:* http://www.devry.edu/.

Dixie State College of Utah

St. George, Utah

- **State-supported** 4-year, founded 1911, part of Utah System of Higher Education
- **Small-town** 117-acre campus
- **Endowment** $8.8 million
- **Coed** 8,553 undergraduate students, 61% full-time, 52% women, 48% men
- **Noncompetitive** entrance level, 70% of applicants were admitted

Undergraduates 5,220 full-time, 3,333 part-time. 14% are from out of state; 7% transferred in; 3% live on campus. *Retention:* 63% of full-time freshmen returned.

Freshmen *Admission:* 4,171 applied, 2,927 admitted, 1,828 enrolled. *Average high school GPA:* 3.15. *Test scores:* SAT critical reading scores over 500: 36%; SAT math scores over 500: 32%; ACT scores over 18: 78%; SAT critical reading scores over 600: 6%; SAT math scores over 600: 10%; ACT scores over 24: 22%; SAT critical reading scores over 700: 1%; SAT math scores over 700: 3%; ACT scores over 30: 2%.

Faculty *Total:* 508, 29% full-time, 18% with terminal degrees. *Student/faculty ratio:* 24:1.

Academics *Calendar:* semesters. *Degrees:* certificates, diplomas, associate, and bachelor's. *Special study options:* academic remediation for entering students, accelerated degree program, adult/continuing education programs, advanced placement credit, cooperative education, distance learning, double majors, English as a second language, honors programs, independent study, internships, off-campus study, part-time degree program, services for LD students, student-designed majors, study abroad, summer session for credit. *ROTC:* Army (b).

Computers on Campus 400 computers/terminals and 350 ports are available on campus for general student use. Students can access the following: computer help desk, free student e-mail accounts, online (class) grades, online (class) registration, online (class) schedules. Campuswide network is available. 100% of college-owned or -operated housing units are wired for high-speed Internet access. Wireless service is available via entire campus.

Student Life *Housing options:* coed, men-only. Campus housing is university owned. *Activities and organizations:* drama/theater group, student-run newspaper, radio and television station, choral group, marching band, Dixie Spirit, Outdoor Club, Association of Women Students, intramurals. *Campus security:* 24-hour emergency response devices and patrols. *Student services:* health clinic, personal/psychological counseling.

Athletics Member NCAA. except baseball (Division II), men's and women's basketball (Division II), men's and women's cross-country running (Division II), football (Division II), golf (Division II), men's and women's soccer (Division II), softball (Division II), tennis (Division II), volleyball (Division II) *Intercollegiate sports:* baseball M(s), basketball M(s)/W(s), cross-country running M(s)/W(s), football M(s), golf M(s), soccer M(s)/W(s), softball W(s), tennis W(s), volleyball W(s). *Intramural sports:* basketball M/W, soccer M/W, table tennis M/W, tennis M/W.

Standardized Tests *Recommended:* SAT or ACT (for admission).

Costs (2010–11) *Tuition:* state resident $2940 full-time, $123 per credit hour part-time; nonresident $11,568 full-time, $482 per credit hour part-time. Full-time tuition and fees vary according to course load and program. Part-time tuition and fees vary according to course load and program. *Required fees:* $550 full-time. *Room and board:* $4100; room only: $1450. Room and board charges vary according to board plan and housing facility. *Payment plan:* installment. *Waivers:* children of alumni, senior citizens, and employees or children of employees.

Financial Aid Of all full-time matriculated undergraduates who enrolled in 2008, 3,221 applied for aid, 2,788 were judged to have need, 53 had their need fully met. In 2008, 919 non-need-based awards were made. *Average percent of need met:* 37%. *Average financial aid package:* $7614. *Average need-based loan:* $3826. *Average need-based gift aid:* $5917. *Average non-need-based aid:* $3241. *Average indebtedness upon graduation:* $15,564. *Financial aid deadline:* 5/1.

Applying *Options:* electronic application, deferred entrance. *Application fee:* $35. *Required:* high school transcript. *Application deadlines:* rolling (freshmen), rolling (out-of-state freshmen), rolling (transfers). *Notification:* continuous (freshmen), continuous (out-of-state freshmen), continuous (transfers).

Freshman Application Contact Dixie State College of Utah, 225 South 700 East, St. George, UT 84770-3876. *Phone:* 435-652-7698. *Toll-free phone:* 888-GO2DIXIE. *Web site:* http://www.dixie.edu/.

Independence University

Salt Lake City, Utah

Freshman Application Contact Ms. Deborah Hopkins, Enrollment Manager, Independence University, 5295 South Commerce Drive, Salt Lake City, UT 84107. *Toll-free phone:* 800-791-7353. *Web site:* http://www.independence.edu/.

ITT Technical Institute

Murray, Utah

- **Proprietary** primarily 2-year, founded 1984, part of ITT Educational Services, Inc.
- **Suburban** campus
- **Coed**
- **Minimally difficult** entrance level

Academics *Calendar:* quarters. *Degrees:* associate and bachelor's.

Student Life *Housing:* college housing not available.

Freshman Application Contact Director of Recruitment, ITT Technical Institute, 920 West Levoy Drive, Murray, UT 84123-2500. *Phone:* 801-263-3313. *Toll-free phone:* 800-365-2136. *Web site:* http://www.itt-tech.edu/.

Midwives College of Utah

Salt Lake City, Utah

- **Independent** comprehensive, founded 1980
- **Suburban** campus with easy access to Salt Lake City
- **Women only**
- **Noncompetitive** entrance level

Academics *Calendar:* semesters. *Degrees:* certificates, diplomas, associate, bachelor's, and master's.

Applying *Options:* electronic application. *Application fee:* $35. *Required:* essay or personal statement, high school transcript, interview.

Freshman Application Contact Kristi Ridd-Young, President, Midwives College of Utah, 1174 East 2700 South, Suite 2, Salt Lake City, UT 84106. *Phone:* 801-649-5230. *Toll-free phone:* 866-764-9068. *Fax:* 866-207-2024. *E-mail:* office@midwifery.edu. *Web site:* http://www.midwifery.edu/.

Neumont University

South Jordan, Utah

- **Proprietary** comprehensive, founded 2002
- **Suburban** campus with easy access to Salt Lake City
- **Coed, primarily men** 272 undergraduate students, 100% full-time, 8% women, 92% men
- **Moderately difficult** entrance level, 85% of applicants were admitted

Undergraduates 272 full-time. 50% live on campus. *Retention:* 70% of full-time freshmen returned.

Freshmen *Admission:* 487 applied, 415 admitted, 130 enrolled. *Test scores:* ACT scores over 18: 91%; ACT scores over 24: 51%; ACT scores over 30: 19%.

Faculty *Total:* 36, 31% full-time.

Academics *Calendar:* quarters. *Degrees:* bachelor's and master's. *Special study options:* accelerated degree program, services for LD students.

Computers on Campus Students can access the following: campus intranet, computer help desk, free student e-mail accounts, online (class) grades, online (class) registration, online (class) schedules. Campuswide network is available. Wireless service is available via entire campus.

Student Life *Housing options:* men-only, women-only, disabled students. Campus housing is leased by the school and is provided by a third party. Freshman campus housing is guaranteed. *Activities and organizations:* Unified Student Government, Neumont Chapter of the Society of Women Engineers, Robotics and Science Club, Rhythm-based Game Lovers Association, Athletic Club. *Student services:* health clinic, personal/psychological counseling.

Athletics *Intramural sports:* basketball M(c), soccer M(c), table tennis M(c)/W(c).

Standardized Tests *Required:* SAT or ACT (for admission).

Costs (2011–12) *Tuition:* $21,600 full-time. No tuition increase for student's term of enrollment. *Required fees:* $1500 full-time. *Room only:* $4044. *Payment plans:* tuition prepayment, installment. *Waivers:* employees or children of employees.

Applying *Options:* electronic application. *Application fee:* $35. *Required:* essay or personal statement, high school transcript. *Required for some:* interview. *Recommended:* 2 letters of recommendation. *Application deadlines:* rolling (freshmen), rolling (transfers).

Freshman Application Contact Karick Heaton, Enrollment Manager, Neumont University, 10701 South River Front Parkway, Suite 200, South Jordan, UT 84095. *Phone:* 801-302-2879. *Toll-free phone:* 866-622-3448. *Fax:* 801-302-2811. *E-mail:* karick.heaton@neumont.edu. *Web site:* http://www.neumont.edu/.

Southern Utah University
Cedar City, Utah

- **State-supported** comprehensive, founded 1897, part of Utah System of Higher Education
- **Small-town** 113-acre campus
- **Coed** 7,231 undergraduate students, 79% full-time, 58% women, 42% men
- **Moderately difficult** entrance level, 77% of applicants were admitted

Undergraduates 5,690 full-time, 1,541 part-time. 13% are from out of state; 2% Black or African American, non-Hispanic/Latino; 4% Hispanic/Latino; 0.8% Asian, non-Hispanic/Latino; 1% Native Hawaiian or other Pacific Islander, non-Hispanic/Latino; 2% American Indian or Alaska Native, non-Hispanic/Latino; 2% Race/ethnicity unknown; 3% international; 13% live on campus. *Retention:* 63% of full-time freshmen returned.

Freshmen *Admission:* 3,876 applied, 3,003 admitted, 1,319 enrolled. *Average high school GPA:* 3.49. *Test scores:* SAT critical reading scores over 500: 60%; SAT math scores over 500: 52%; ACT scores over 18: 90%; SAT critical reading scores over 600: 19%; SAT math scores over 600: 13%; ACT scores over 24: 41%; SAT critical reading scores over 700: 2%; SAT math scores over 700: 1%; ACT scores over 30: 5%.

Faculty *Total:* 328, 71% full-time, 64% with terminal degrees. *Student/faculty ratio:* 25:1.

Academics *Calendar:* semesters. *Degrees:* certificates, diplomas, associate, bachelor's, and master's. *Special study options:* academic remediation for entering students, adult/continuing education programs, advanced placement credit, cooperative education, distance learning, double majors, English as a second language, honors programs, independent study, internships, part-time degree program, services for LD students, summer session for credit. *ROTC:* Army (b).

Computers on Campus Campuswide network is available.

Student Life *Housing options:* coed, men-only, women-only, disabled students. *Activities and organizations:* drama/theater group, student-run newspaper, radio and television station, choral group, marching band, national fraternities, national sororities. *Campus security:* 24-hour emergency response devices, student patrols, late-night transport/escort service, controlled dormitory access. *Student services:* health clinic, personal/psychological counseling, women's center.

Athletics Member NCAA. All Division I except football (Division I-AA). *Intercollegiate sports:* baseball M(s), basketball M(s)/W(s), cross-country running M/W, golf M(s), gymnastics W(s), softball W(s), tennis W(s), track and field M(s)/W(s). *Intramural sports:* basketball M/W, football M, golf M/W, soccer M/W, tennis M/W, track and field M/W, volleyball M/W.

Standardized Tests *Required:* SAT or ACT (for admission).

Costs (2010–11) *Tuition:* state resident $4196 full-time, $200 per credit hour part-time; nonresident $13,846 full-time, $660 per credit hour part-time. Part-time tuition and fees vary according to course load. *Required fees:* $540 full-time, $270 per term part-time. *Room only:* $2086. Room and board charges vary according to board plan and housing facility. *Payment plan:* installment. *Waivers:* employees or children of employees.

Financial Aid Of all full-time matriculated undergraduates who enrolled in 2008, 4,069 applied for aid, 3,469 were judged to have need, 354 had their need fully met. In 2008, 2065 non-need-based awards were made. *Average*

percent of need met: 62%. *Average financial aid package:* $7659. *Average need-based loan:* $3868. *Average need-based gift aid:* $5874. *Average non-need-based aid:* $7489. *Average indebtedness upon graduation:* $11,170.

Applying *Options:* electronic application, early admission, early action, deferred entrance. *Application fee:* $40. *Required:* high school transcript, minimum 2 GPA. *Notification:* continuous (freshmen).

Freshman Application Contact Southern Utah University, 351 West University Boulevard, Cedar City, UT 84720-2498. *Phone:* 435-586-7740. *Web site:* http://www.suu.edu/.

Stevens-Henager College
West Haven, Utah

Freshman Application Contact Admissions Office, Stevens-Henager College, 1890 South 1350 West, West Haven, UT 84401. *Phone:* 801-394-7791. *Toll-free phone:* 800-622-2640. *Web site:* http://www.stevenshenager.edu/.

Strayer University - Salt Lake Campus
Sandy, Utah

- **Proprietary** comprehensive
- **Coed**

Academics *Degrees:* certificates, diplomas, associate, bachelor's, master's, and postbachelor's certificates.

Costs (2010–11) *Tuition:* $13,635 full-time, $1590 per course part-time.

Freshman Application Contact Strayer University - Salt Lake Campus, 9815 South Monroe Street, Suite 200, Sandy, UT 84070. *Web site:* http://www.strayer.edu/salt_lake/.

University of Phoenix–Utah Campus
Salt Lake City, Utah

Freshman Application Contact Ms. Evelyn Gaskin, Registrar/Executive Director, University of Phoenix–Utah Campus, 4615 East Elwood Street, Mail Stop AA-K101, Phoenix, AZ 85040-1958. *Phone:* 480-557-3303. *Toll-free phone:* 800-776-4867 (in-state); 800-228-7240 (out-of-state). *Fax:* 480-643-1020. *E-mail:* evelyn.gaskin@phoenix.edu. *Web site:* http://www.phoenix.edu/.

University of Utah
Salt Lake City, Utah

- **State-supported** university, founded 1850, part of Utah System of Higher Education
- **Urban** 1535-acre campus with easy access to Salt Lake City
- **Endowment** $474.0 million
- **Coed** 23,371 undergraduate students, 70% full-time, 45% women, 55% men
- **Moderately difficult** entrance level, 83% of applicants were admitted

Undergraduates 16,364 full-time, 7,007 part-time. Students come from 53 states and territories; 118 other countries; 16% are from out of state; 1% Black or African American, non-Hispanic/Latino; 6% Hispanic/Latino; 5% Asian, non-Hispanic/Latino; 0.6% Native Hawaiian or other Pacific Islander, non-Hispanic/Latino; 0.6% American Indian or Alaska Native, non-Hispanic/Latino; 2% Two or more races, non-Hispanic/Latino; 5% Race/ethnicity unknown; 4% international; 9% transferred in; 13% live on campus. *Retention:* 85% of full-time freshmen returned.

Freshmen *Admission:* 8,364 applied, 6,931 admitted, 3,110 enrolled. *Average high school GPA:* 3.52. *Test scores:* SAT critical reading scores over 500: 75%; SAT math scores over 500: 80%; SAT writing scores over 500: 73%; ACT scores over 18: 96%; SAT critical reading scores over 600: 38%; SAT math scores over 600: 41%; SAT writing scores over 600: 31%; ACT scores over 24: 54%; SAT critical reading scores over 700: 9%; SAT math scores over 700: 7%; SAT writing scores over 700: 5%; ACT scores over 30: 14%.

Faculty *Total:* 1,957, 68% full-time, 65% with terminal degrees. *Student/faculty ratio:* 15:1.

Academics *Calendar:* semesters. *Degrees:* bachelor's, master's, doctoral-professional, doctoral-research/scholarship, post-master's, and postbachelor's certificates. *Special study options:* academic remediation for entering students, accelerated degree program, advanced placement credit, cooperative education, distance learning, double majors, English as a second language, freshman honors college, honors programs, independent study, internships, off-campus study, part-time degree program, services for LD students, student-designed majors, study abroad, summer session for credit. *ROTC:* Army (b), Navy (b), Air Force (b). *Unusual degree programs:* 3-2 physical therapy, occupational therapy.

Computers on Campus 3,000 computers/terminals are available on campus for general student use. Students can access the following: campus intranet, computer help desk, free student e-mail accounts, online (class) grades, online (class) registration, online (class) schedules, online classes. Campuswide network is available. 100% of college-owned or -operated housing units are wired for high-speed Internet access. Wireless service is available via entire campus.

Student Life *Housing options:* coed, men-only, women-only, disabled students. Campus housing is university owned. *Activities and organizations:* drama/theater group, student-run newspaper, radio and television station, choral group, marching band, Latter-Day Saints Student Association, Bennion Center, Newman Center, Center for Ethnic Student Affairs, national fraternities, national sororities. *Campus security:* 24-hour emergency response devices and patrols, student patrols, late-night transport/escort service, controlled dormitory access. *Student services:* health clinic, personal/psychological counseling, women's center, legal services.

Athletics Member NCAA. All Division I. *Intercollegiate sports:* baseball M(s), basketball M(s)/W(s), cheerleading M(s)/W(s), cross-country running W(s), football M(s), golf M(s), gymnastics W(s), rugby M(c), skiing (cross-country) M(s)/W(s), skiing (downhill) M(s)/W(s), soccer W(s), softball W(s), swimming and diving M(s)/W(s), table tennis M(c)/W(c), tennis M(s)/W(s), track and field W(s), volleyball W(s), water polo M(c)/W(c). *Intramural sports:* badminton M/W, basketball M/W, bowling M/W, fencing M/W, field hockey M/W, football M, ice hockey M, lacrosse M, racquetball M/W, riflery M/W, rugby M/W, soccer M/W, softball M/W, squash M/W, tennis M/W, ultimate Frisbee M/W, volleyball M/W.

Standardized Tests *Required:* ACT (for admission), SAT or ACT (for admission).

Costs (2010–11) *Tuition:* state resident $5427 full-time, $152 per credit hour part-time; nonresident $18,994 full-time, $524 per credit hour part-time. Full-time tuition and fees vary according to course level, course load, degree level, program, and student level. Part-time tuition and fees vary according to course level, course load, degree level, program, and student level. *Required fees:* $847 full-time. *Room and board:* $6240; room only: $3096. Room and board charges vary according to board plan and housing facility. *Payment plans:* installment, deferred payment. *Waivers:* children of alumni, senior citizens, and employees or children of employees.

Financial Aid Of all full-time matriculated undergraduates who enrolled in 2008, 6,129 applied for aid, 5,302 were judged to have need, 655 had their need fully met. In 2008, 715 non-need-based awards were made. *Average percent of need met:* 58%. *Average financial aid package:* $9146. *Average need-based loan:* $4797. *Average need-based gift aid:* $4803. *Average non-need-based aid:* $4619. *Average indebtedness upon graduation:* $11,749.

Applying *Options:* electronic application, early admission. *Application fee:* $45. *Required:* high school transcript, minimum 2.6 GPA. *Required for some:* essay or personal statement. *Recommended:* minimum 3 GPA. *Application deadlines:* 4/1 (freshmen), 4/1 (out-of-state freshmen), 4/1 (transfers). *Notification:* continuous (freshmen), continuous (out-of-state freshmen), continuous (transfers).

Freshman Application Contact Mateo Remsburg, Director of High School Services, University of Utah, 200 Central Campus Drive, Room 280, Salt Lake City, UT 84112. *Phone:* 801-581-8761. *Toll-free phone:* 800-444-8638. *Fax:* 801-585-3257. *E-mail:* mremsburg@sa.utah.edu. *Web site:* http://www.utah.edu/.

Utah State University

Logan, Utah

- **State-supported** university, founded 1888, part of Utah System of Higher Education
- **Urban** 456-acre campus
- **Endowment** $172.4 million
- **Coed** 14,649 undergraduate students, 85% full-time, 49% women, 51% men
- **Moderately difficult** entrance level, 97% of applicants were admitted

Undergraduates 12,384 full-time, 2,265 part-time. Students come from 52 states and territories; 48 other countries; 21% are from out of state; 1% Black or African American, non-Hispanic/Latino; 3% Hispanic/Latino; 1% Asian, non-Hispanic/Latino; 0.4% Native Hawaiian or other Pacific Islander, non-Hispanic/Latino; 0.5% American Indian or Alaska Native, non-Hispanic/Latino; 0.8% Two or more races, non-Hispanic/Latino; 4% Race/ethnicity unknown; 3% international; 7% transferred in.

Freshmen *Admission:* 7,374 applied, 7,176 admitted, 3,113 enrolled. *Average high school GPA:* 3.54. *Test scores:* SAT critical reading scores over 500: 69%; SAT math scores over 500: 72%; ACT scores over 18: 96%; SAT critical reading scores over 600: 33%; SAT math scores over 600: 30%; ACT scores over 24: 52%; SAT critical reading scores over 700: 6%; SAT math scores over 700: 4%; ACT scores over 30: 11%.

Faculty *Total:* 879, 80% full-time. *Student/faculty ratio:* 19:1.

Academics *Calendar:* semesters. *Degrees:* certificates, associate, bachelor's, master's, doctoral-professional, doctoral-research/scholarship, post-master's,

and postbachelor's certificates. *Special study options:* academic remediation for entering students, accelerated degree program, adult/continuing education programs, advanced placement credit, cooperative education, distance learning, double majors, English as a second language, freshman honors college, honors programs, independent study, internships, off-campus study, part-time degree program, services for LD students, student-designed majors, study abroad, summer session for credit. *ROTC:* Army (b), Air Force (b).

Computers on Campus 1,000 computers/terminals are available on campus for general student use. Students can access the following: computer help desk, free student e-mail accounts, online (class) grades, online (class) registration, online (class) schedules. Campuswide network is available. 100% of college-owned or -operated housing units are wired for high-speed Internet access. Wireless service is available via classrooms, computer centers, computer labs, dorm rooms, learning centers, libraries, student centers.

Student Life *Housing options:* coed, men-only, women-only, disabled students. Campus housing is university owned. *Activities and organizations:* drama/theater group, student-run newspaper, radio station, choral group, marching band, Latter-Day Saints Student Association, multicultural clubs, volunteer groups, college councils, national fraternities, national sororities. *Campus security:* 24-hour emergency response devices and patrols, student patrols, late-night transport/escort service, video monitors in pedestrian tunnels. *Student services:* health clinic, personal/psychological counseling, women's center, legal services.

Athletics Member NCAA. All Division I except football (Division I-A). *Intercollegiate sports:* baseball M(c), basketball M(s)/W(s), cross-country running M(s)/W(s), equestrian sports M(c)/W(c), golf M(s), gymnastics W(s), ice hockey M(c), rugby M(c)/W(c), soccer M(c)/W(s), softball W(s), tennis M(s)/W(s), track and field M(s)/W(s), volleyball M(c)/W(s). *Intramural sports:* badminton M/W, basketball M/W, cross-country running M/W, fencing M(c)/W(c), football M/W, golf M/W, ice hockey W(c), lacrosse M(c), racquetball M(c)/W(c), skiing (cross-country) M(c)/W(c), skiing (downhill) M(c)/W(c), soccer M/W, softball M/W, squash M/W, swimming and diving M/W, table tennis M/W, tennis M/W, ultimate Frisbee M(c)/W(c), volleyball M/W, water polo M(c)/W(c).

Standardized Tests *Required:* SAT or ACT (for admission).

Costs (2010–11) *Tuition:* state resident $4346 full-time; nonresident $13,993 full-time. Full-time tuition and fees vary according to course load, program, reciprocity agreements, and student level. Part-time tuition and fees vary according to course load, program, reciprocity agreements, and student level. *Required fees:* $804 full-time. *Room and board:* $5070; room only: $1670. Room and board charges vary according to board plan and housing facility. *Payment plan:* deferred payment. *Waivers:* minority students, children of alumni, adult students, senior citizens, and employees or children of employees.

Financial Aid Of all full-time matriculated undergraduates who enrolled in 2009, 7,749 applied for aid, 6,799 were judged to have need, 792 had their need fully met. 244 Federal Work-Study jobs (averaging $3050). 126 state and other part-time jobs (averaging $3050). In 2009, 315 non-need-based awards were made. *Average percent of need met:* 62%. *Average financial aid package:* $8800. *Average need-based loan:* $4260. *Average need-based gift aid:* $4800. *Average non-need-based aid:* $2700. *Average indebtedness upon graduation:* $15,194.

Applying *Options:* electronic application, early admission, deferred entrance. *Application fee:* $40. *Required:* high school transcript. *Recommended:* minimum 2.75 GPA. *Application deadlines:* rolling (freshmen), rolling (transfers). *Notification:* continuous (freshmen), continuous (transfers).

Freshman Application Contact Ms. Jenn Putnam, Director, Admissions Office, Utah State University, 0160 Old Main Hill, Logan, UT 84322-0160. *Phone:* 435-797-1079. *Toll-free phone:* 800-488-8108. *Fax:* 435-797-3708. *E-mail:* admit@usu.edu. *Web site:* http://www.usu.edu/.

Utah Valley University

Orem, Utah

- **State-supported** comprehensive, founded 1941, affiliated with Advent Christian Church, part of Utah System of Higher Education
- **Suburban** 312-acre campus with easy access to Salt Lake City
- **Endowment** $11.0 million
- **Coed** 32,573 undergraduate students, 51% full-time, 43% women, 57% men
- **Noncompetitive** entrance level, 100% of applicants were admitted

Undergraduates 16,461 full-time, 16,112 part-time. Students come from 50 states and territories; 54 other countries; 14% are from out of state; 6% transferred in. *Retention:* 57% of full-time freshmen returned.

Freshmen *Admission:* 6,203 applied, 6,203 admitted, 4,895 enrolled. *Average high school GPA:* 3.26. *Test scores:* SAT critical reading scores over 500: 47%; SAT math scores over 500: 54%; SAT writing scores over 500: 46%; ACT scores over 18: 98%; SAT critical reading scores over 600: 13%; SAT math scores over 600: 18%; SAT writing scores over 600: 8%; ACT scores

over 24: 72%; SAT critical reading scores over 700: 2%; SAT math scores over 700: 2%; ACT scores over 30: 18%.

Faculty *Total:* 1,508, 34% full-time, 25% with terminal degrees. *Student/faculty ratio:* 26:1.

Academics *Calendar:* semesters. *Degrees:* certificates, diplomas, associate, bachelor's, and master's. *Special study options:* academic remediation for entering students, advanced placement credit, cooperative education, distance learning, double majors, English as a second language, honors programs, independent study, internships, off-campus study, part-time degree program, services for LD students, student-designed majors, study abroad, summer session for credit. *ROTC:* Army (b), Air Force (c).

Computers on Campus 1,000 computers/terminals are available on campus for general student use. Students can access the following: campus intranet, computer help desk, free student e-mail accounts, online (class) grades, online (class) registration, online (class) schedules. Campuswide network is available. Wireless service is available via entire campus.

Student Life *Housing:* college housing not available. *Activities and organizations:* drama/theater group, student-run newspaper, television station, choral group, LDSSA Orem Institute, Center for the Advancement of Leadership. *Campus security:* 24-hour patrols. *Student services:* health clinic, personal/psychological counseling, women's center, legal services.

Athletics Member NCAA. All Division I. *Intercollegiate sports:* baseball M(s), basketball M(s)/W(s), cross-country running M(s)/W(s), golf M(s)/W(s), soccer W(s), softball W(s), track and field M(s)/W(s), volleyball W(s), wrestling M(s). *Intramural sports:* basketball M/W, bowling M/W, football M/W, golf M/W, racquetball M/W, rock climbing M/W, soccer M/W, softball M/W, tennis M/W, ultimate Frisbee M/W, volleyball W.

Standardized Tests *Required:* SAT or ACT (for admission). *Recommended:* ACT (for admission).

Costs (2010–11) *Tuition:* state resident $3672 full-time, $154 per credit hour part-time; nonresident $12,246 full-time, $488 per credit hour part-time. Full-time tuition and fees vary according to course load. Part-time tuition and fees vary according to course load. *Required fees:* $616 full-time, $616 per year part-time. *Room and board:* $8904; room only: $6678. Room and board charges vary according to housing facility. *Payment plans:* installment, deferred payment. *Waivers:* employees or children of employees.

Financial Aid Of all full-time matriculated undergraduates who enrolled in 2009, 12,621 applied for aid, 11,149 were judged to have need, 261 had their need fully met. In 2009, 1108 non-need-based awards were made. *Average percent of need met:* 92%. *Average financial aid package:* $22,561. *Average need-based loan:* $11,189. *Average need-based gift aid:* $14,484. *Average non-need-based aid:* $4985. *Average indebtedness upon graduation:* $15,593. *Financial aid deadline:* 5/1.

Applying *Options:* electronic application, early admission, deferred entrance. *Application fee:* $35. *Recommended:* high school transcript. *Application deadlines:* 8/15 (freshmen), 8/15 (transfers). *Notification:* continuous (freshmen), continuous (transfers).

Freshman Application Contact Mrs. Liz Childs, Senior Director of Admissions, Utah Valley University, 800 West University Parkway, Orem, UT 84058-5999. *Phone:* 801-863-8460. *Fax:* 801-225-4677. *E-mail:* info@uvsc.edu. *Web site:* http://www.uvu.edu/.

Weber State University
Ogden, Utah

- **State-supported** comprehensive, founded 1889, part of Utah System of Higher Education
- **Urban** 526-acre campus with easy access to Salt Lake City
- **Endowment** $62.2 million
- **Coed** 23,401 undergraduate students, 43% full-time, 47% women, 53% men
- **Noncompetitive** entrance level, 100% of applicants were admitted

Undergraduates 9,985 full-time, 13,416 part-time. Students come from 52 states and territories; 49 other countries; 8% are from out of state; 5% transferred in; 4% live on campus. *Retention:* 73% of full-time freshmen returned.

Freshmen *Admission:* 8,152 applied, 8,152 admitted, 2,608 enrolled. *Average high school GPA:* 3.35. *Test scores:* ACT scores over 18: 81%; ACT scores over 24: 30%; ACT scores over 30: 2%.

Faculty *Total:* 837, 55% full-time, 40% with terminal degrees. *Student/faculty ratio:* 22:1.

Academics *Calendar:* semesters. *Degrees:* certificates, associate, bachelor's, master's, and postbachelor's certificates. *Special study options:* academic remediation for entering students, accelerated degree program, adult/continuing education programs, advanced placement credit, cooperative education, distance learning, double majors, English as a second language, external degree program, freshman honors college, honors programs, independent study, internships, off-campus study, part-time degree program, services for LD students, student-designed majors, study abroad, summer session for credit. *ROTC:* Army (b), Navy (b), Air Force (b).

Computers on Campus 600 computers/terminals are available on campus for general student use. Students can access the following: campus intranet, computer help desk, free student e-mail accounts, online (class) grades, online (class) registration, online (class) schedules. Campuswide network is available. 100% of college-owned or -operated housing units are wired for high-speed Internet access. Wireless service is available via entire campus.

Student Life *Housing options:* men-only, women-only, cooperative, disabled students. Campus housing is university owned and is provided by a third party. *Activities and organizations:* drama/theater group, student-run newspaper, radio and television station, choral group, marching band, LDSSA, Mountaineering Club, Rodeo Club, Beta Alpha Psi, Student Nurses Organization, national fraternities, national sororities. *Campus security:* 24-hour emergency response devices and patrols, student patrols, late-night transport/escort service, controlled dormitory access. *Student services:* health clinic, personal/psychological counseling, women's center, legal services.

Athletics Member NCAA. All Division I except football (Division I-AA). *Intercollegiate sports:* baseball M(c), basketball M(s)/W(s), bowling M(c)/W(c), cheerleading M(s)/W(s), cross-country running M(s)/W(s), fencing M(c)/W(c), golf M(s)/W(s), ice hockey M(c), lacrosse M(c)/W(c), racquetball M(c)/W(c), rugby M(c)/W(c), skiing (downhill) M(c)/W(c), soccer M(c)/W(s), softball W(s), swimming and diving M(c)/W(c), tennis M(s)/W(s), track and field M(s)/W(s), volleyball W(s), water polo M(c)/W(c). *Intramural sports:* baseball M/W, basketball M/W, bowling M/W, cross-country running M/W, football M/W, golf M/W, racquetball M/W, soccer M/W, softball M/W, tennis M/W, volleyball M/W.

Standardized Tests *Required for some:* ACCUPLACER. *Recommended:* SAT or ACT (for admission).

Costs (2011–12) *Tuition:* state resident $4088 full-time; nonresident $11,554 full-time. Full-time tuition and fees vary according to course load. Part-time tuition and fees vary according to course load. *Room and board:* $4000. Room and board charges vary according to housing facility. *Payment plan:* installment. *Waivers:* children of alumni and employees or children of employees.

Financial Aid Of all full-time matriculated undergraduates who enrolled in 2007, 4,981 applied for aid, 4,509 were judged to have need, 174 had their need fully met. In 2007, 1562 non-need-based awards were made. *Average percent of need met:* 50%. *Average financial aid package:* $5878. *Average need-based loan:* $4079. *Average need-based gift aid:* $3622. *Average non-need-based aid:* $2033.

Applying *Options:* electronic application, early admission, deferred entrance. *Application fee:* $30. *Required:* high school transcript. *Application deadlines:* 8/22 (freshmen), rolling (transfers). *Notification:* continuous (freshmen), continuous (transfers).

Freshman Application Contact Laura Albright, Student Recruitment, Weber State University, 1137 University Circle, Ogden, UT 84408-1137. *Phone:* 801-626-6050. *Toll-free phone:* 800-634-6568 (in-state); 800-848-7770 (out-of-state). *Fax:* 801-626-6744. *E-mail:* admissions@weber.edu. *Web site:* http://www.weber.edu/.

Western Governors University
Salt Lake City, Utah

Freshman Application Contact Western Governors University, 4001 South 700 East, Suite 700, Salt Lake City, UT 84107. *Phone:* 801-274-3280 Ext. 336. *Toll-free phone:* 877-435-7948. *Web site:* http://www.wgu.edu/.

Westminster College
Salt Lake City, Utah

- **Independent** comprehensive, founded 1875
- **Suburban** 27-acre campus
- **Endowment** $50.8 million
- **Coed** 2,343 undergraduate students, 94% full-time, 57% women, 43% men
- **Moderately difficult** entrance level, 78% of applicants were admitted

Undergraduates 2,193 full-time, 150 part-time. Students come from 40 states and territories; 29 other countries; 30% are from out of state; 1% Black or African American, non-Hispanic/Latino; 9% Hispanic/Latino; 3% Asian, non-Hispanic/Latino; 0.3% Native Hawaiian or other Pacific Islander, non-Hispanic/Latino; 0.6% American Indian or Alaska Native, non-Hispanic/Latino; 1% Two or more races, non-Hispanic/Latino; 7% Race/ethnicity unknown; 4% international; 9% transferred in; 27% live on campus. *Retention:* 79% of full-time freshmen returned.

Freshmen *Admission:* 1,963 applied, 1,526 admitted, 540 enrolled. *Average high school GPA:* 3.5. *Test scores:* SAT critical reading scores over 500: 76%; SAT math scores over 500: 80%; ACT scores over 18: 96%; SAT critical reading scores over 600: 34%; SAT math scores over 600: 36%; ACT scores over 24: 59%; SAT critical reading scores over 700: 6%; SAT math scores over 700: 5%; ACT scores over 30: 10%.

Faculty *Total:* 354, 40% full-time, 55% with terminal degrees. *Student/faculty ratio:* 11:1.

Academics *Calendar:* 4-4-1. *Degrees:* bachelor's, master's, and postbachelor's certificates. *Special study options:* academic remediation for entering students, accelerated degree program, advanced placement credit, cooperative education, distance learning, double majors, English as a second language, external degree program, freshman honors college, honors programs, independent study, internships, off-campus study, part-time degree program, services for LD students, student-designed majors, study abroad, summer session for credit. *ROTC:* Army (c), Navy (c), Air Force (c). *Unusual degree programs:* 3-2 engineering with University of Southern California, Washington University in St. Louis.

Computers on Campus 403 computers/terminals and 650 ports are available on campus for general student use. Students can access the following: campus intranet, computer help desk, free student e-mail accounts, online (class) grades, online (class) registration, online (class) schedules. Campuswide network is available. 100% of college-owned or -operated housing units are wired for high-speed Internet access. Wireless service is available via entire campus.

Student Life *Housing:* on-campus residence required for freshman year. *Options:* cooperative, disabled students. Campus housing is university owned. Freshman applicants given priority for college housing. *Activities and organizations:* drama/theater group, student-run newspaper, choral group, Associated Students of Westminster College (Student Government), Associated Residents of Westminster College (Residential Government), Westminster Ski and Snowboard Club (WSSC), Associated Commuters of Westminster College, Latter Day Saints Student Association (LDSSA). *Campus security:* 24-hour emergency response devices and patrols, student patrols, late-night transport/escort service, controlled dormitory access. *Student services:* health clinic, personal/psychological counseling.

Athletics Member NAIA. *Intercollegiate sports:* basketball M(s)/W(s), cross-country running M(s)/W(s), golf M(s)/W, lacrosse M/W, skiing (downhill) M/W, soccer M(s)/W(s), track and field M/W, volleyball W(s). *Intramural sports:* basketball M/W, soccer M/W, volleyball M/W.

Standardized Tests *Required:* SAT or ACT (for admission).

Costs (2011–12) *Comprehensive fee:* $34,766 includes full-time tuition ($26,712), mandatory fees ($470), and room and board ($7584). Full-time tuition and fees vary according to course load. Part-time tuition: $1113 per credit hour. Part-time tuition and fees vary according to course load. *Room and board:* Room and board charges vary according to board plan. *Payment plans:* installment, deferred payment. *Waivers:* employees or children of employees.

Financial Aid Of all full-time matriculated undergraduates who enrolled in 2009, 1,485 applied for aid, 1,336 were judged to have need, 396 had their need fully met. 352 Federal Work-Study jobs (averaging $2513). 227 state and other part-time jobs (averaging $2423). In 2009, 755 non-need-based awards were made. *Average percent of need met:* 76%. *Average financial aid package:* $19,342. *Average need-based loan:* $4787. *Average need-based gift aid:* $14,303. *Average non-need-based aid:* $10,996. *Average indebtedness upon graduation:* $20,002.

Applying *Options:* electronic application, deferred entrance. *Application fee:* $50. *Required:* essay or personal statement, high school transcript, minimum 2.5 GPA, 1 letter of recommendation. *Recommended:* interview. *Application deadlines:* rolling (freshmen), rolling (out-of-state freshmen), rolling (transfers). *Notification:* continuous (freshmen), continuous (out-of-state freshmen), continuous (transfers).

Freshman Application Contact Elizabeth Key, Director of Admissions, Westminster College, 1840 South 1300 East, Salt Lake City, UT 84105-3697. *Phone:* 801-832-2200. *Toll-free phone:* 800-748-4753. *Fax:* 801-832-3101. *E-mail:* admission@westminstercollege.edu. *Web site:* http://www.westminstercollege.edu/.

See page 1784 for the College Close-Up.

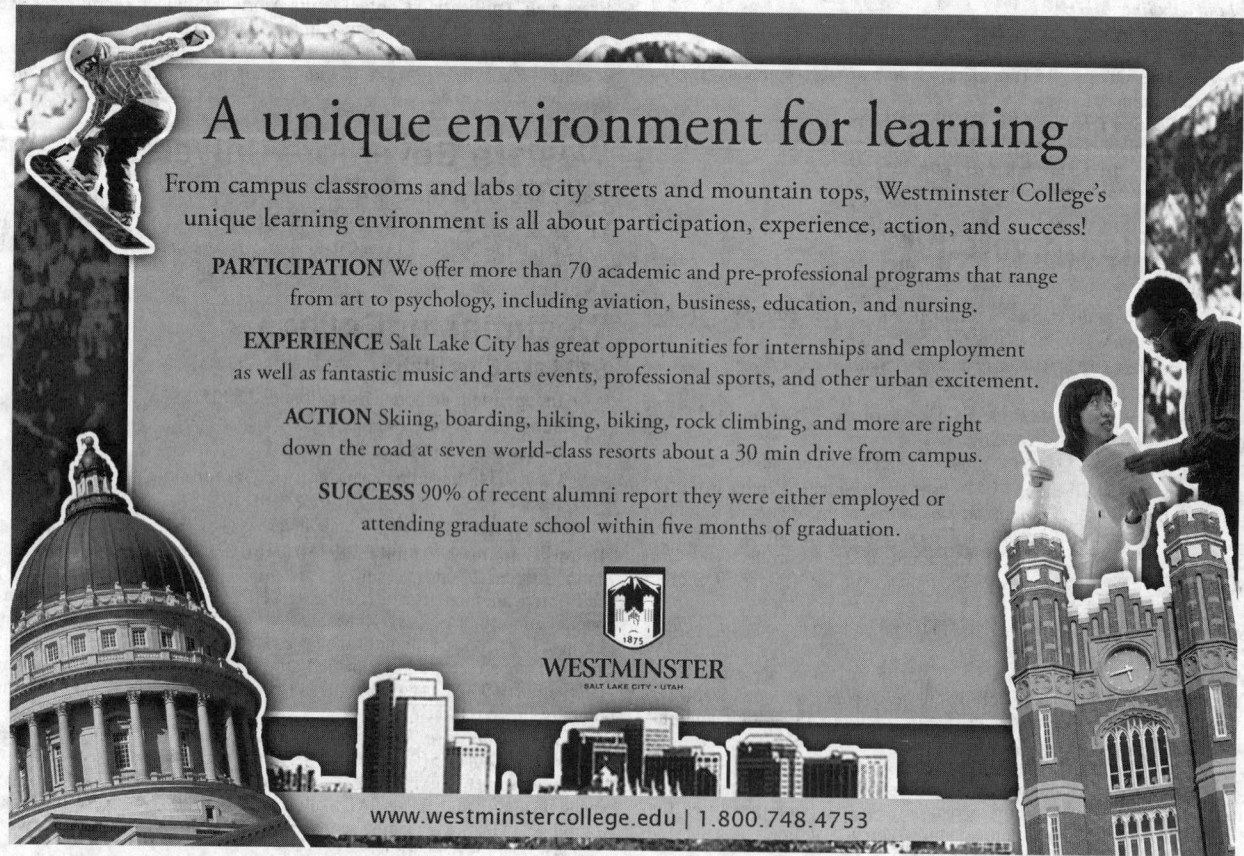

VERMONT

Bennington College

Bennington, Vermont

- **Independent** comprehensive, founded 1932
- **Small-town** 470-acre campus with easy access to Albany, NY
- **Endowment** $14.0 million
- **Coed** 668 undergraduate students, 99% full-time, 67% women, 33% men
- **Very difficult** entrance level, 65% of applicants were admitted

Undergraduates 664 full-time, 4 part-time. Students come from 25 states and territories; 15 other countries; 95% are from out of state; 2% Black or African American, non-Hispanic/Latino; 3% Hispanic/Latino; 2% Asian, non-Hispanic/Latino; 0.6% American Indian or Alaska Native, non-Hispanic/Latino; 0.1% Two or more races, non-Hispanic/Latino; 6% Race/ethnicity unknown; 7% international; 2% transferred in; 94% live on campus. *Retention:* 85% of full-time freshmen returned.

Freshmen *Admission:* 1,089 applied, 708 admitted, 169 enrolled. *Average high school GPA:* 3.41. *Test scores:* SAT critical reading scores over 500: 99%; SAT math scores over 500: 89%; SAT writing scores over 500: 99%; ACT scores over 18: 100%; SAT critical reading scores over 600: 89%; SAT math scores over 600: 45%; SAT writing scores over 600: 77%; ACT scores over 24: 93%; SAT critical reading scores over 700: 31%; SAT math scores over 700: 10%; SAT writing scores over 700: 27%; ACT scores over 30: 30%.

Faculty *Total:* 77, 81% full-time, 69% with terminal degrees. *Student/faculty ratio:* 10:1.

Academics *Calendar:* semesters plus winter work term in January and February. *Degrees:* bachelor's, master's, and postbachelor's certificates. *Special study options:* accelerated degree program, double majors, independent study, internships, part-time degree program, services for LD students, student-designed majors, study abroad. *Unusual degree programs:* 3-2 teaching.

Computers on Campus 100 computers/terminals and 25 ports are available on campus for general student use. Students can access the following: campus intranet, computer help desk, free student e-mail accounts, online (class) schedules. Campuswide network is available. 100% of college-owned or -operated housing units are wired for high-speed Internet access. Wireless service is available via entire campus.

Student Life *Housing:* on-campus residence required through senior year. *Options:* coed, cooperative. Campus housing is university owned. Freshman campus housing is guaranteed. *Activities and organizations:* drama/theater group, student-run newspaper, choral group, Program Activity Council, Community Outreach and Action, Bennington Free Press, Student Endowment for the Arts, SILO: Student Journal of Arts and Letters. *Campus security:* 24-hour emergency response devices and patrols, late-night transport/escort service, prevention/awareness program. *Student services:* health clinic, personal/psychological counseling.

Athletics *Intercollegiate sports:* basketball M(c)/W(c), soccer M(c)/W(c). *Intramural sports:* archery M/W, badminton M/W, basketball M/W, bowling M/W, cross-country running M/W, equestrian sports M/W, fencing M/W, golf M/W, skiing (cross-country) M/W, skiing (downhill) M/W, soccer M/W, softball M/W, swimming and diving M/W, table tennis M/W, tennis M/W, ultimate Frisbee M/W, volleyball M/W, weight lifting M/W.

Costs (2010–11) *Comprehensive fee:* $52,900 includes full-time tuition ($40,280), mandatory fees ($1070), and room and board ($11,550). Part-time tuition: $1340 per credit hour. *College room only:* $6190. *Payment plan:* installment. *Waivers:* employees or children of employees.

Financial Aid Of all full-time matriculated undergraduates who enrolled in 2009, 486 applied for aid, 421 were judged to have need, 34 had their need fully met. 367 Federal Work-Study jobs (averaging $2200). 36 state and other part-time jobs (averaging $2200). In 2009, 117 non-need-based awards were made. *Average percent of need met:* 82%. *Average financial aid package:* $34,170. *Average need-based loan:* $4098. *Average need-based gift aid:* $29,493. *Average non-need-based aid:* $19,633. *Average indebtedness upon graduation:* $26,224. *Financial aid deadline:* 2/15.

Applying *Options:* electronic application, early admission, early decision, early action, deferred entrance. *Application fee:* $60. *Required:* essay or personal statement, high school transcript, 2 letters of recommendation, graded analytic paper. *Recommended:* interview. *Application deadlines:* 1/3 (freshmen), 3/15 (transfers). *Early decision deadline:* 11/15 (for plan 1), 1/3 (for plan 2). *Notification:* 4/1 (freshmen), 5/1 (transfers), 12/15 (early decision plan 1), 2/15 (early decision plan 2).

Freshman Application Contact Mr. Ken Himmelman, Dean of Admissions and Financial Aid, Bennington College, One College Drive, Bennington, VT 05201-6003. *Phone:* 802-440-4312. *Toll-free phone:* 800-833-6845. *Fax:* 802-440-4320. *E-mail:* admissions@bennington.edu. *Web site:* http://www.bennington.edu/.

Burlington College

Burlington, Vermont

- **Independent** 4-year, founded 1972
- **Urban** 32-acre campus with easy access to Montreal
- **Endowment** $100,784
- **Coed** 192 undergraduate students, 75% full-time, 49% women, 51% men
- **Moderately difficult** entrance level, 88% of applicants were admitted

Undergraduates 144 full-time, 48 part-time. Students come from 22 states and territories; 5 other countries; 46% are from out of state; 0.5% Black or African American, non-Hispanic/Latino; 3% Hispanic/Latino; 0.5% Asian, non-Hispanic/Latino; 0.5% Native Hawaiian or other Pacific Islander, non-Hispanic/Latino; 1% American Indian or Alaska Native, non-Hispanic/Latino; 0.5% Two or more races, non-Hispanic/Latino; 10% Race/ethnicity unknown; 0.5% international; 15% transferred in; 18% live on campus. *Retention:* 76% of full-time freshmen returned.

Freshmen *Admission:* 146 applied, 128 admitted, 34 enrolled. *Average high school GPA:* 2.8. *Test scores:* SAT critical reading scores over 500: 50%; SAT math scores over 500: 40%; SAT writing scores over 500: 30%; ACT scores over 18: 50%; SAT critical reading scores over 600: 10%; SAT math scores over 600: 10%; SAT writing scores over 600: 10%; ACT scores over 24: 50%.

Faculty *Total:* 80, 6% full-time, 30% with terminal degrees. *Student/faculty ratio:* 5:1.

Academics *Calendar:* semesters. *Degrees:* certificates, associate, and bachelor's. *Special study options:* advanced placement credit, distance learning, double majors, external degree program, independent study, internships, off-campus study, part-time degree program, services for LD students, student-designed majors, study abroad, summer session for credit.

Computers on Campus 21 computers/terminals and 12 ports are available on campus for general student use. Students can access the following: campus intranet, computer help desk, free student e-mail accounts. Campuswide network is available. 100% of college-owned or -operated housing units are wired for high-speed Internet access. Wireless service is available via entire campus.

Student Life *Housing:* on-campus residence required for freshman year. *Options:* cooperative. Campus housing is university owned. Freshman campus housing is guaranteed. *Activities and organizations:* Student Association. *Campus security:* student patrols. *Student services:* legal services.

Costs (2010–11) *Tuition:* $21,340 full-time, $705 per credit hour part-time. Full-time tuition and fees vary according to course load, program, and reciprocity agreements. Part-time tuition and fees vary according to course load, program, and reciprocity agreements. Resident students should expect to spend $2,700 per year for meals as the college does not offer a dining service. *Required fees:* $125 full-time. *Room only:* $7100. Room and board charges vary according to housing facility. *Payment plan:* installment. *Waivers:* employees or children of employees.

Financial Aid Of all full-time matriculated undergraduates who enrolled in 2009, 115 applied for aid, 109 were judged to have need, 3 had their need fully met. In 2009, 3 non-need-based awards were made. *Average percent of need met:* 46%. *Average financial aid package:* $12,710. *Average need-based loan:* $5255. *Average need-based gift aid:* $8011. *Average non-need-based aid:* $1833. *Average indebtedness upon graduation:* $21,670.

Applying *Options:* electronic application, deferred entrance. *Application fee:* $50. *Required:* essay or personal statement, high school transcript, 2 letters of recommendation. *Recommended:* minimum 2 GPA, interview. *Application deadlines:* 8/15 (freshmen), 8/15 (out-of-state freshmen), 8/15 (transfers). *Notification:* continuous (freshmen), continuous (out-of-state freshmen), continuous (transfers).

Freshman Application Contact Ms. Gillian Homsted, Admissions Director, Burlington College, 95 North Avenue, Burlington, VT 05401-2998. *Phone:* 802-862-9616 Ext. 104. *Toll-free phone:* 800-862-9616. *Fax:* 802-660-4331. *E-mail:* admissions@burlington.edu. *Web site:* http://www.burlington.edu/.

See page 870 for Display. See page 1172 for the College Close-Up.

Castleton State College

Castleton, Vermont

- **State-supported** comprehensive, founded 1787, part of Vermont State Colleges System
- **Rural** 165-acre campus
- **Endowment** $4.9 million
- **Coed** 2,091 undergraduate students, 90% full-time, 53% women, 47% men
- **Moderately difficult** entrance level, 73% of applicants were admitted

Undergraduates 1,877 full-time, 214 part-time. Students come from 9 states and territories; 5 other countries; 36% are from out of state; 1% Black or African American, non-Hispanic/Latino; 2% Hispanic/Latino; 0.7% Asian, non-Hispanic/Latino; 0.8% American Indian or Alaska Native, non-Hispanic/Latino; 0.4% Two or more races, non-Hispanic/Latino; 6% Race/ethnicity unknown; 0.9% international; 8% transferred in; 57% live on campus. *Retention:* 71% of full-time freshmen returned.

Freshmen *Admission:* 2,262 applied, 1,650 admitted, 496 enrolled. *Average high school GPA:* 2.9. *Test scores:* SAT critical reading scores over 500: 38%; SAT math scores over 500: 42%; SAT writing scores over 500: 35%; ACT scores over 18: 87%; SAT critical reading scores over 600: 5%; SAT math scores over 600: 7%; SAT writing scores over 600: 4%; ACT scores over 24: 18%; SAT critical reading scores over 700: 1%.

Faculty *Total:* 220, 43% full-time, 57% with terminal degrees. *Student/faculty ratio:* 14:1.

Academics *Calendar:* semesters. *Degrees:* associate, bachelor's, master's, post-master's, and postbachelor's certificates. *Special study options:* academic remediation for entering students, advanced placement credit, cooperative education, double majors, honors programs, independent study, internships, off-campus study, part-time degree program, services for LD students, student-designed majors, study abroad, summer session for credit. *ROTC:* Army (c).

Computers on Campus 225 computers/terminals are available on campus for general student use. Students can access the following: campus intranet, computer help desk, free student e-mail accounts, online (class) grades. Campus-wide network is available. Wireless service is available via classrooms, dorm rooms, libraries.

Student Life *Housing:* on-campus residence required for freshman year. *Options:* coed. Campus housing is university owned. Freshman campus housing is guaranteed. *Activities and organizations:* drama/theater group, student-run newspaper, radio station, choral group, community service, Sustainability group, Women's issues organization, Outing Club, Skiing/Snowboarding. *Campus security:* 24-hour emergency response devices and patrols, student patrols, late-night transport/escort service, controlled dormitory access. *Student services:* health clinic, personal/psychological counseling.

Athletics Member NCAA. All Division III. *Intercollegiate sports:* baseball M, basketball M/W, cheerleading M(c)/W(c), cross-country running M/W, equestrian sports W(c), field hockey W, football M, golf M, ice hockey M/W, lacrosse M/W, rugby M(c)/W(c), skiing (downhill) M/W, soccer M/W, softball W, tennis M/W, volleyball W. *Intramural sports:* basketball M/W, racquetball M/W, rock climbing M/W, soccer M/W, softball M/W, table tennis M/W, tennis M/W, volleyball M/W, water polo M/W.

Standardized Tests *Required:* SAT or ACT (for admission).

Costs (2011–12) *One-time required fee:* $200. *Tuition:* state resident $8568 full-time, $357 per credit part-time; nonresident $20,112 full-time, $838 per credit part-time. Part-time tuition and fees vary according to course load. *Required fees:* $900 full-time. *Room and board:* $8446. Room and board charges vary according to board plan. *Payment plan:* installment. *Waivers:* senior citizens and employees or children of employees.

Financial Aid Of all full-time matriculated undergraduates who enrolled in 2006, 1,471 applied for aid, 1,174 were judged to have need, 371 had their need fully met. 360 Federal Work-Study jobs (averaging $1000). In 2006, 40 non-need-based awards were made. *Average percent of need met:* 72%. *Average financial aid package:* $9213. *Average need-based loan:* $3715. *Average need-based gift aid:* $4307. *Average non-need-based aid:* $3247. *Average indebtedness upon graduation:* $25,474.

Applying *Options:* electronic application, deferred entrance. *Application fee:* $40. *Required:* essay or personal statement, high school transcript, minimum 2.5 GPA, 2 letters of recommendation. *Recommended:* interview. *Application deadlines:* rolling (freshmen), rolling (transfers). *Notification:* continuous (freshmen), continuous (transfers).

Freshman Application Contact Mr. Maurice Ouimet, Admissions Director, Castleton State College, Castleton, VT 05735. *Phone:* 802-468-1213. *Toll-free phone:* 800-639-8521. *Fax:* 802-468-1476. *E-mail:* info@castleton.edu. *Web site:* http://www.castleton.edu/.

See page 871 for Display. See page 1206 for the College Close-Up.

Champlain College
Burlington, Vermont

- **Independent** comprehensive, founded 1878
- **Suburban** 21-acre campus with easy access to Montreal
- **Endowment** $7.6 million
- **Coed** 2,068 undergraduate students, 98% full-time, 39% women, 61% men
- **Moderately difficult** entrance level, 85% of applicants were admitted

Undergraduates 2,034 full-time, 34 part-time. Students come from 37 states and territories; 23 other countries; 77% are from out of state; 1% Black or African American, non-Hispanic/Latino; 2% Hispanic/Latino; 2% Asian, non-Hispanic/Latino; 0.3% American Indian or Alaska Native, non-Hispanic/Latino;

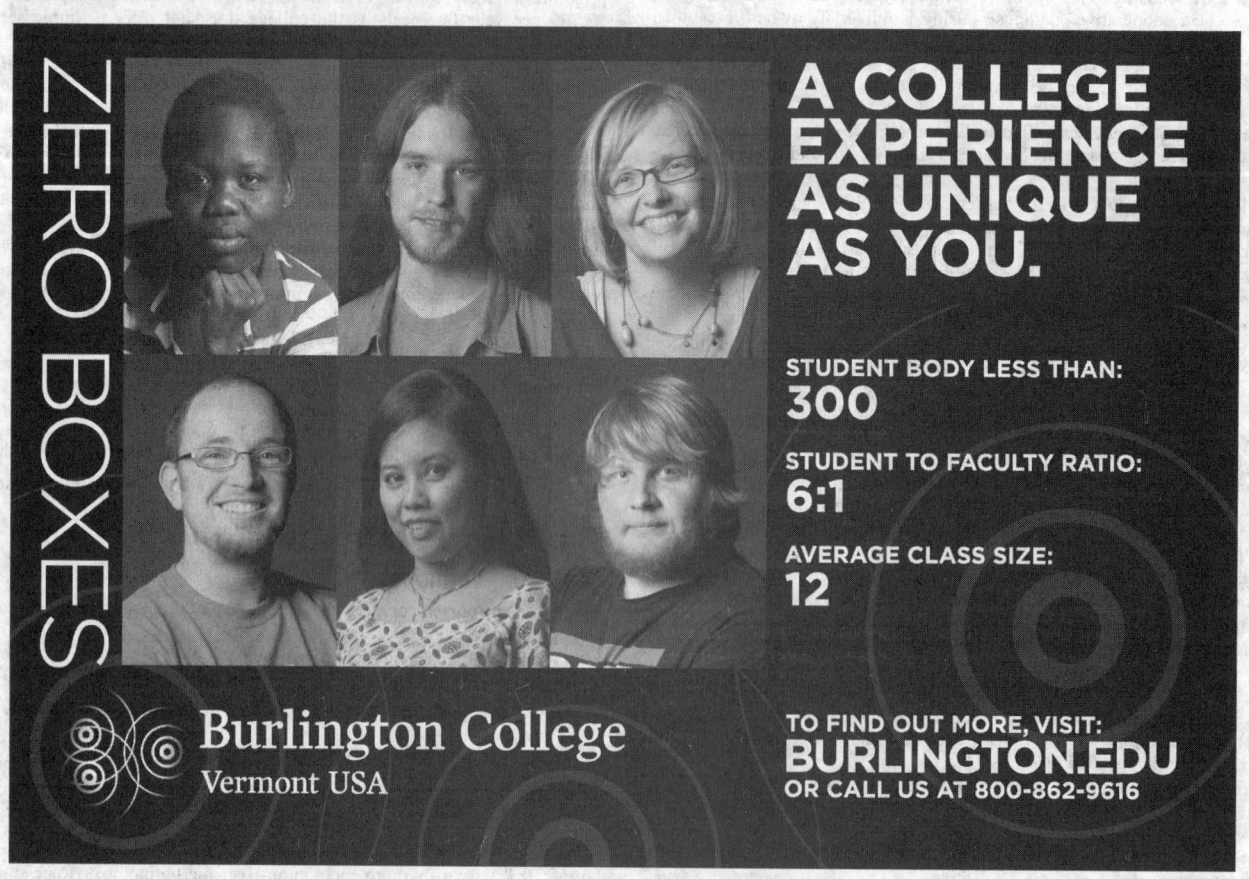

0.4% Two or more races, non-Hispanic/Latino; 24% Race/ethnicity unknown; 0.1% international; 3% transferred in; 41% live on campus. *Retention:* 76% of full-time freshmen returned.

Freshmen *Admission:* 3,077 applied, 2,604 admitted, 658 enrolled. *Test scores:* SAT critical reading scores over 500: 74%; SAT math scores over 500: 76%; ACT scores over 18: 100%; SAT critical reading scores over 600: 25%; SAT math scores over 600: 23%; ACT scores over 24: 47%; SAT critical reading scores over 700: 2%; SAT math scores over 700: 2%; ACT scores over 30: 8%.

Faculty *Total:* 324, 30% full-time, 35% with terminal degrees. *Student/faculty ratio:* 14:1.

Academics *Calendar:* semesters. *Degrees:* associate, bachelor's, and master's. *Special study options:* adult/continuing education programs, advanced placement credit, cooperative education, distance learning, double majors, independent study, internships, off-campus study, part-time degree program, services for LD students, study abroad, summer session for credit. *ROTC:* Army (c).

Computers on Campus 260 computers/terminals are available on campus for general student use. Students can access the following: campus intranet, computer help desk, free student e-mail accounts, online (class) registration, wireless laptops available. Campuswide network is available.

Student Life *Housing options:* coed. Campus housing is university owned and leased by the school. Freshman campus housing is guaranteed. *Activities and organizations:* drama/theater group, student-run newspaper, choral group, Diversity Champlain, International Club, community service organization, Champlain Players (theater group), Outing Club/Skiing Snowboarding Club. *Campus security:* 24-hour emergency response devices and patrols, late-night transport/escort service, controlled dormitory access. *Student services:* health clinic, personal/psychological counseling.

Athletics *Intramural sports:* basketball M/W, bowling M/W, cross-country running M/W, golf M/W, ice hockey M/W, lacrosse M, sailing M/W, skiing (cross-country) M/W, skiing (downhill) M/W, soccer M/W, ultimate Frisbee M/W, volleyball M/W.

Standardized Tests *Required:* SAT or ACT (for admission).

Costs (2011–12) *Comprehensive fee:* $40,920 includes full-time tuition ($28,350), mandatory fees ($50), and room and board ($12,520). Full-time tuition and fees vary according to course load. Part-time tuition: $1180 per credit. Part-time tuition and fees vary according to course load. *College room only:* $7620. Room and board charges vary according to housing facility. *Payment plan:* installment. *Waivers:* employees or children of employees.

Financial Aid Of all full-time matriculated undergraduates who enrolled in 2009, 1,590 applied for aid, 1,375 were judged to have need, 82 had their need fully met. 1,086 Federal Work-Study jobs (averaging $2484). In 2009, 206 non-need-based awards were made. *Average percent of need met:* 64%. *Average financial aid package:* $16,489. *Average need-based loan:* $6880. *Average need-based gift aid:* $9093. *Average non-need-based aid:* $3917. *Average indebtedness upon graduation:* $34,658.

Applying *Options:* electronic application, early decision. *Application fee:* $50. *Required:* essay or personal statement, high school transcript. *Recommended:* 1 letter of recommendation, interview. *Application deadlines:* 1/31 (freshmen), rolling (transfers). *Notification:* 3/25 (freshmen), continuous (transfers).

Freshman Application Contact Ian Mortimer, Director of Admissions, Champlain College, 163 South Willard Street, Burlington, VT 05401. *Phone:* 802-860-2727. *Toll-free phone:* 800-570-5858. *Fax:* 802-860-2767. *E-mail:* admission@champlain.edu. *Web site:* http://www.champlain.edu/.

College of St. Joseph
Rutland, Vermont

- **Independent Roman Catholic** comprehensive, founded 1950
- **Small-town** 117-acre campus
- **Endowment** $3.5 million
- **Coed** 247 undergraduate students, 67% full-time, 61% women, 39% men
- **Minimally difficult** entrance level, 70% of applicants were admitted

Undergraduates 165 full-time, 82 part-time. Students come from 16 states and territories; 24% are from out of state; 9% Black or African American, non-Hispanic/Latino; 0.9% Hispanic/Latino; 0.5% Asian, non-Hispanic/Latino; 0.5% Native Hawaiian or other Pacific Islander, non-Hispanic/Latino; 1% American Indian or Alaska Native, non-Hispanic/Latino; 15% transferred in; 35% live on campus. *Retention:* 48% of full-time freshmen returned.

Freshmen *Admission:* 149 applied, 104 admitted, 54 enrolled. *Average high school GPA:* 2.7. *Test scores:* SAT critical reading scores over 500: 19%; SAT math scores over 500: 16%; SAT writing scores over 500: 18%; ACT scores over 18: 60%; SAT critical reading scores over 600: 8%; SAT math scores over 600: 3%; SAT writing scores over 600: 8%; ACT scores over 24: 10%.

Faculty *Total:* 66, 23% full-time, 27% with terminal degrees. *Student/faculty ratio:* 9:1.

Academics *Calendar:* semesters. *Degrees:* associate, bachelor's, master's, and postbachelor's certificates. *Special study options:* academic remediation

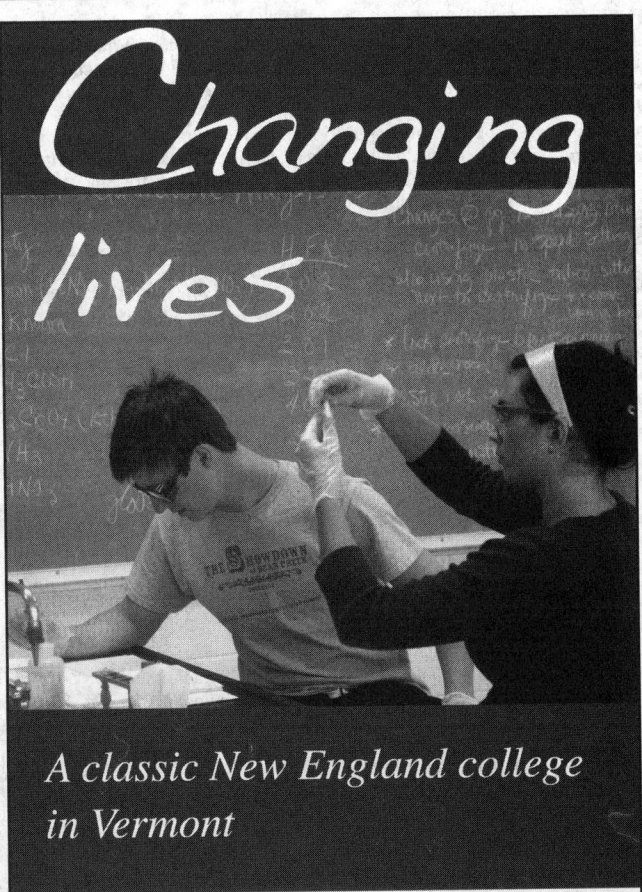

for entering students, accelerated degree program, adult/continuing education programs, advanced placement credit, double majors, independent study, internships, part-time degree program, services for LD students, summer session for credit.

Computers on Campus 33 computers/terminals are available on campus for general student use. Students can access the following: campus intranet, computer help desk, free student e-mail accounts. Campuswide network is available. 100% of college-owned or -operated housing units are wired for high-speed Internet access. Wireless service is available via libraries.

Student Life *Housing:* on-campus residence required through sophomore year. *Options:* men-only, women-only. Campus housing is university owned. Freshman campus housing is guaranteed. *Activities and organizations:* choral group, Humans vs. Zombies Club, Business Club, Human Services Club, Student Government Association, chorus. *Campus security:* 24-hour emergency response devices, trained security personnel from 8 pm to 6 am. *Student services:* personal/psychological counseling.

Athletics Member NAIA. *Intercollegiate sports:* basketball M/W, cross-country running M/W, soccer M/W.

Standardized Tests *Required:* SAT or ACT (for admission).

Costs (2011–12) *Comprehensive fee:* $28,665 includes full-time tuition ($18,990), mandatory fees ($475), and room and board ($9200). Full-time tuition and fees vary according to course load, degree level, and program. Part-time tuition: $260 per credit. Part-time tuition and fees vary according to course load, degree level, and program. No tuition increase for student's term of enrollment. *Room and board:* Room and board charges vary according to housing facility. *Payment plan:* installment. *Waivers:* senior citizens and employees or children of employees.

Financial Aid Of all full-time matriculated undergraduates who enrolled in 2008, 166 applied for aid, 158 were judged to have need, 13 had their need fully met. 32 Federal Work-Study jobs (averaging $886). 37 state and other part-time jobs (averaging $651). In 2008, 8 non-need-based awards were made. *Average percent of need met:* 87%. *Average financial aid package:* $19,062. *Average need-based loan:* $8905. *Average need-based gift aid:* $10,133. *Average non-need-based aid:* $2843. *Average indebtedness upon graduation:* $25,848.

Applying *Options:* electronic application, early admission, deferred entrance. *Application fee:* $25. *Required:* essay or personal statement, high school transcript, minimum 2 GPA, 2 letters of recommendation. *Recommended:* interview. *Application deadlines:* rolling (freshmen), rolling (out-of-state freshmen), rolling (transfers). *Notification:* continuous (freshmen), continuous (out-of-state freshmen), continuous (transfers).

Freshman Application Contact Mr. Alan Young, Dean of Admissions, College of St. Joseph, 71 Clement Road, Rutland, VT 05701-3899. *Phone:* 802-773-5900 Ext. 3227. *Toll-free phone:* 877-270-9998. *Fax:* 802-776-5258. *E-mail:* admissions@csj.edu. *Web site:* http://www.csj.edu/.

Goddard College

Plainfield, Vermont

- **Independent** comprehensive, founded 1938
- **Rural** 200-acre campus
- **Endowment** $932,377
- **Coed** 275 undergraduate students, 100% full-time, 63% women, 37% men
- **Moderately difficult** entrance level, 83% of applicants were admitted

Undergraduates 275 full-time. Students come from 40 states and territories; 3 other countries; 86% are from out of state; 30% transferred in. *Retention:* 67% of full-time freshmen returned.

Freshmen *Admission:* 12 applied, 10 admitted, 8 enrolled.

Faculty *Total:* 140, 5% full-time, 89% with terminal degrees.

Academics *Calendar:* semesters. *Degrees:* bachelor's and master's. *Special study options:* adult/continuing education programs, advanced placement credit, distance learning, double majors, external degree program, independent study, internships, off-campus study, services for LD students, student-designed majors.

Computers on Campus 55 computers/terminals are available on campus for general student use. Students can access the following: campus intranet, computer help desk, free student e-mail accounts, online (class) schedules, library services. Campuswide network is available. 80% of college-owned or -operated housing units are wired for high-speed Internet access. Wireless service is available via entire campus.

Student Life *Housing options:* coed, women-only, disabled students. Campus housing is university owned. *Activities and organizations:* student-run radio station. *Campus security:* 24-hour patrols, patrols by trained security personnel 9 pm to 6 am. *Student services:* personal/psychological counseling.

Costs (2010–11) *Comprehensive fee:* $14,174 includes full-time tuition ($12,854), mandatory fees ($168), and room and board ($1152). Full-time tuition and fees vary according to program. *Payment plan:* installment. *Waivers:* employees or children of employees.

Financial Aid Of all full-time matriculated undergraduates who enrolled in 2007, 252 applied for aid, 229 were judged to have need, 10 had their need fully met. *Average percent of need met:* 40%. *Average financial aid package:* $6356. *Average need-based loan:* $4133. *Average need-based gift aid:* $3809. *Average indebtedness upon graduation:* $21,639.

Applying *Options:* electronic application, deferred entrance. *Application fee:* $40. *Required:* essay or personal statement, high school transcript, 2 letters of recommendation, interview. *Application deadlines:* rolling (freshmen), rolling (out-of-state freshmen), rolling (transfers). *Notification:* continuous (freshmen), continuous (out-of-state freshmen), continuous (transfers).

Freshman Application Contact Erin Johnson, Admissions Counselor, Goddard College, 123 Pitkin Road, Plainfield, VT 05667-9432. *Phone:* 800-906-8312 Ext. 262. *Toll-free phone:* 800-906-8312. *Fax:* 802-454-1029. *E-mail:* admissions@goddard.edu. *Web site:* http://www.goddard.edu/.

Green Mountain College

Poultney, Vermont

- **Independent** comprehensive, founded 1834
- **Small-town** 155-acre campus
- **Endowment** $2.9 million
- **Coed**
- **Moderately difficult** entrance level

Faculty *Student/faculty ratio:* 14:1.

Academics *Calendar:* semesters. *Degrees:* bachelor's and master's.

Student Life *Campus security:* 24-hour emergency response devices and patrols, late-night transport/escort service.

Athletics Member NCAA. All Division III.

Standardized Tests *Recommended:* SAT or ACT (for admission).

Costs (2010–11) *One-time required fee:* $250. *Comprehensive fee:* $38,087 includes full-time tuition ($26,920), mandatory fees ($1025), and room and board ($10,142). Full-time tuition and fees vary according to course load, location, and program. Part-time tuition: $898 per credit hour. Part-time tuition and fees vary according to course load, location, and program. *College room only:* $6022. Room and board charges vary according to housing facility.

Financial Aid *Of all full-time matriculated undergraduates who enrolled in 2009,* 607 applied for aid, 554 were judged to have need, 68 had their need fully met. 213 Federal Work-Study jobs (averaging $1700). 104 state and other part-time jobs (averaging $1700). *In 2009,* 115 non-need-based awards were made. *Average percent of need met:* 65. *Average financial aid package:* $19,432. *Average need-based loan:* $4162. *Average need-based gift aid:* $15,462. *Average non-need-based aid:* $12,669. *Average indebtedness upon graduation:* $39,983.

Applying *Options:* electronic application, deferred entrance. *Application fee:* $30. *Required:* essay or personal statement, high school transcript, 1 letter of recommendation. *Required for some:* interview. *Recommended:* minimum 2.5 GPA, interview.

Freshman Application Contact Green Mountain College, One Brennan Circle, Poultney, VT 05764. *Phone:* 802-287-8207. *Toll-free phone:* 800-776-6675. *Web site:* http://www.greenmtn.edu/.

Johnson State College

Johnson, Vermont

- **State-supported** comprehensive, founded 1828, part of Vermont State Colleges System
- **Rural** 350-acre campus with easy access to Montreal
- **Coed** 1,701 undergraduate students, 69% full-time, 62% women, 38% men
- **Moderately difficult** entrance level, 81% of applicants were admitted

Undergraduates 1,175 full-time, 526 part-time. Students come from 18 states and territories; 20 other countries; 19% are from out of state; 2% Black or African American, non-Hispanic/Latino; 2% Hispanic/Latino; 1% Asian, non-Hispanic/Latino; 1% American Indian or Alaska Native, non-Hispanic/Latino; 7% Race/ethnicity unknown; 0.1% international; 9% transferred in; 60% live on campus. *Retention:* 65% of full-time freshmen returned.

Freshmen *Admission:* 928 applied, 752 admitted, 259 enrolled. *Average high school GPA:* 3.32. *Test scores:* SAT critical reading scores over 500: 45%; SAT math scores over 500: 36%; SAT critical reading scores over 600: 11%; SAT math scores over 600: 6%; SAT critical reading scores over 700: 1%.

Faculty *Total:* 143, 36% full-time, 55% with terminal degrees. *Student/faculty ratio:* 19:1.

Academics *Calendar:* semesters. *Degrees:* certificates, associate, bachelor's, master's, and post-master's certificates. *Special study options:* accelerated degree program, advanced placement credit, cooperative education, distance learning, double majors, English as a second language, external degree program, honors programs, independent study, internships, off-campus study, part-time degree program, services for LD students, study abroad, summer session for credit. *ROTC:* Army (c).

Computers on Campus 160 computers/terminals are available on campus for general student use. Students can access the following: campus intranet, computer help desk, free student e-mail accounts, online (class) grades, online (class) registration, online (class) schedules. Campuswide network is available. Wireless service is available via classrooms, libraries, student centers.

Student Life *Housing:* on-campus residence required through sophomore year. *Options:* coed. Campus housing is university owned. Freshman applicants given priority for college housing. *Activities and organizations:* drama/theater group, student-run newspaper, radio station, choral group, SERVE (Break Away), A Global partnership: Students for Children's Right, Ski/Snowboarding Club, Dance Club, Christian Fellowship Club. *Campus security:* 24-hour emergency response devices and patrols, student patrols, late-night transport/escort service, controlled dormitory access. *Student services:* health clinic, personal/psychological counseling, women's center.

Athletics Member NCAA. All Division III. *Intercollegiate sports:* basketball M/W, cross-country running M/W, golf M, lacrosse W, soccer M/W, softball W, tennis M/W, volleyball W. *Intramural sports:* badminton M/W, basketball M/W, cross-country running M/W, golf M(c)/W(c), ice hockey M(c)/W(c), lacrosse M(c)/W, racquetball M/W, rock climbing M(c)/W(c), soccer M/W, softball M/W, swimming and diving M(c)/W(c), table tennis M/W, tennis M/W, volleyball M/W, water polo M/W, weight lifting M/W.

Standardized Tests *Required:* SAT or ACT (for admission).

Costs (2011–12) *Tuition:* state resident $8568 full-time, $459 per credit hour part-time; nonresident $19,008 full-time, $990 per credit hour part-time. Full-time tuition and fees vary according to course load. Part-time tuition and fees vary according to course load. *Required fees:* $1104 full-time. *Room and board:* $8444; room only: $5029. Room and board charges vary according to board plan. *Payment plan:* installment. *Waivers:* employees or children of employees.

Financial Aid *Average percent of need met:* 80%. *Average financial aid package:* $7835. *Average indebtedness upon graduation:* $16,910.

Applying *Options:* electronic application, early action, deferred entrance. *Application fee:* $40. *Required:* essay or personal statement, high school transcript, minimum 2 GPA, 1 letter of recommendation. *Recommended:* minimum 2.5 GPA, interview. *Application deadlines:* rolling (freshmen), rolling (transfers). *Notification:* continuous (freshmen), continuous (transfers). **Freshman Application Contact** Bethany Harrington, Admissions Specialist, Johnson State College, 337 College Hill, Johnson, VT 05656. *Phone:* 802-635-1219. *Toll-free phone:* 800-635-2356. *Fax:* 802-635-1230. *E-mail:* jscadmissions@jsc.edu. *Web site:* http://www.jsc.edu/.

Lyndon State College

Lyndonville, Vermont

- **State-supported** comprehensive, founded 1911, part of Vermont State Colleges System
- **Rural** 175-acre campus
- **Endowment** $2.8 million
- **Coed** 1,323 undergraduate students, 92% full-time, 46% women, 54% men
- **Moderately difficult** entrance level, 93% of applicants were admitted

Undergraduates 1,213 full-time, 110 part-time. Students come from 19 states and territories; 11 other countries; 39% are from out of state; 2% Black or African American, non-Hispanic/Latino; 2% Hispanic/Latino; 1% Asian, non-Hispanic/Latino; 1% American Indian or Alaska Native, non-Hispanic/Latino; 3% Race/ethnicity unknown; 0.4% international; 6% transferred in; 51% live on campus. *Retention:* 59% of full-time freshmen returned.

Freshmen *Admission:* 1,021 applied, 952 admitted, 334 enrolled. *Average high school GPA:* 2.5. *Test scores:* SAT critical reading scores over 500: 34%; SAT math scores over 500: 29%; SAT critical reading scores over 600: 7%; SAT math scores over 600: 3%; SAT critical reading scores over 700: 1%.

Faculty *Total:* 160, 36% full-time, 58% with terminal degrees. *Student/faculty ratio:* 15:1.

Academics *Calendar:* semesters. *Degrees:* associate, bachelor's, and master's. *Special study options:* academic remediation for entering students, accelerated degree program, adult/continuing education programs, advanced placement credit, cooperative education, double majors, honors programs, independent study, internships, part-time degree program, services for LD students, student-designed majors, study abroad, summer session for credit. *ROTC:* Air Force (c).

Computers on Campus 125 computers/terminals are available on campus for general student use. Students can access the following: computer help desk, free student e-mail accounts, online (class) grades. Campuswide network is available.

Student Life *Housing:* on-campus residence required through sophomore year. *Options:* coed, women-only, disabled students. Campus housing is university owned and leased by the school. Freshman applicants given priority for college housing. *Activities and organizations:* drama/theater group, student-run newspaper, radio and television station, choral group, American Meteorological Society, ASSIST (A Society of Students in Service Together), Student Senate,

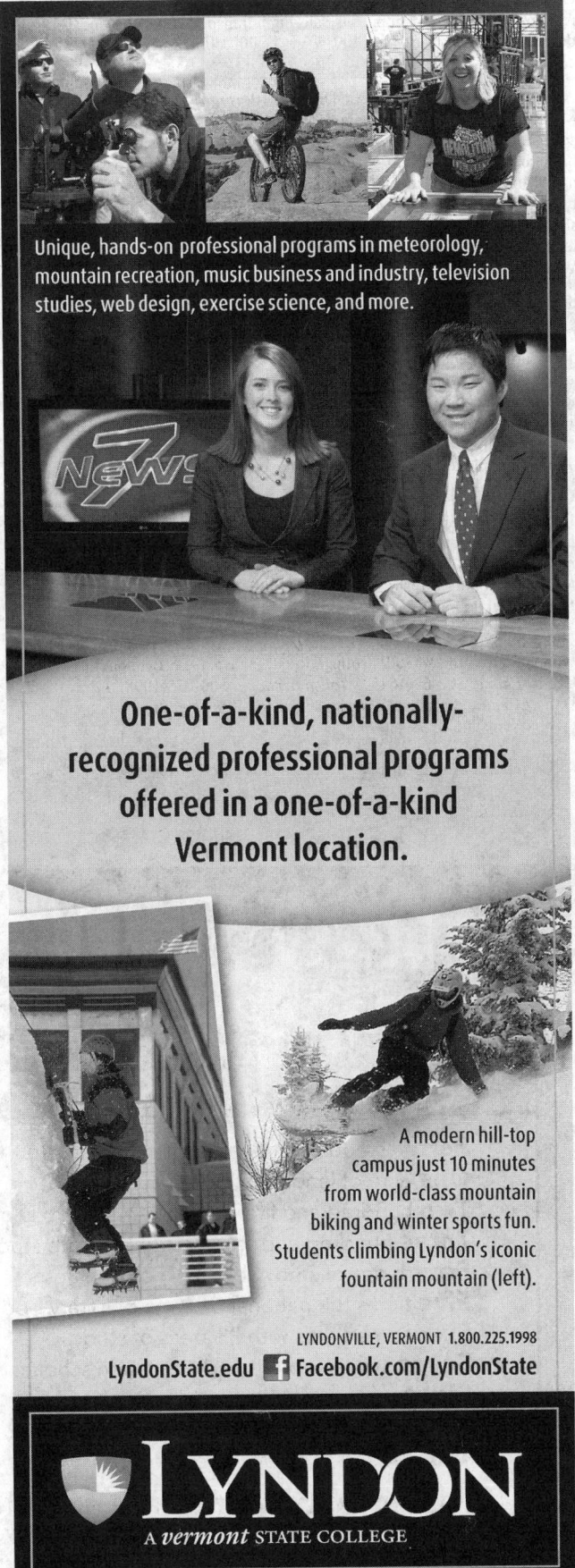

Unique, hands-on professional programs in meteorology, mountain recreation, music business and industry, television studies, web design, exercise science, and more.

One-of-a-kind, nationally-recognized professional programs offered in a one-of-a-kind Vermont location.

A modern hill-top campus just 10 minutes from world-class mountain biking and winter sports fun. Students climbing Lyndon's iconic fountain mountain (left).

LYNDONVILLE, VERMONT 1.800.225.1998

LyndonState.edu **f** Facebook.com/LyndonState

LYNDON
A *vermont* STATE COLLEGE

Campus Activities Board, Outing Club. *Campus security:* 24-hour emergency response devices, student patrols, late-night transport/escort service, controlled dormitory access. *Student services:* health clinic, personal/psychological counseling.

Athletics Member NCAA. All Division III. *Intercollegiate sports:* baseball M, basketball M/W, cross-country running M/W, lacrosse M, soccer M/W, softball W, tennis M/W, volleyball W. *Intramural sports:* badminton M/W, basketball M/W, bowling M(c)/W(c), cheerleading W(c), cross-country running M/W, field hockey M/W, football M/W, ice hockey M(c)/W(c), racquetball M/W, rock climbing M/W, rugby M(c)/W(c), skiing (cross-country) M/W, skiing (downhill) M(c)/W(c), softball M/W, swimming and diving M/W, table tennis M/W, tennis M/W, track and field M(c)/W(c), ultimate Frisbee M(c)/W(c), volleyball M/W, water polo M/W.

Standardized Tests *Required:* SAT or ACT (for admission).

Costs (2011–12) *Tuition:* state resident $8568 full-time, $357 per credit part-time; nonresident $18,456 full-time, $769 per credit part-time. Full-time tuition and fees vary according to course load. Part-time tuition and fees vary according to course load. *Required fees:* $1380 full-time, $75 per credit part-time. *Room and board:* $8444; room only: $5029. Room and board charges vary according to board plan and housing facility. *Payment plan:* installment. *Waivers:* employees or children of employees.

Applying *Options:* electronic application, early admission, deferred entrance. *Application fee:* $36. *Required:* high school transcript, minimum 2 GPA, 1 letter of recommendation. *Required for some:* essay or personal statement, minimum 3 GPA. *Recommended:* minimum 3 GPA, interview. *Application deadlines:* rolling (freshmen), rolling (transfers). *Notification:* continuous (freshmen), continuous (transfers).

Freshman Application Contact Ms. Cheri Goldrick, Admissions Assistant, Lyndon State College, 1001 College Road, PO Box 919, Lyndonville, VT 05851. *Phone:* 802-626-6451. *Toll-free phone:* 800-225-1998. *Fax:* 802-626-6335. *E-mail:* admissions@lyndonstate.edu. *Web site:* http://www.lyndonstate.edu/.

See page 1400 for the College Close-Up.

Marlboro College
Marlboro, Vermont

- **Independent** comprehensive, founded 1946
- **Rural** 350-acre campus
- **Endowment** $36.6 million
- **Coed** 281 undergraduate students, 99% full-time, 49% women, 51% men
- **Moderately difficult** entrance level, 76% of applicants were admitted

Undergraduates 277 full-time, 4 part-time. Students come from 4 other countries; 88% are from out of state; 1% Black or African American, non-Hispanic/Latino; 3% Hispanic/Latino; 2% Asian, non-Hispanic/Latino; 0.4% Native Hawaiian or other Pacific Islander, non-Hispanic/Latino; 0.4% American Indian or Alaska Native, non-Hispanic/Latino; 3% Two or more races, non-Hispanic/Latino; 23% Race/ethnicity unknown; 0.7% international; 6% transferred in; 80% live on campus. *Retention:* 80% of full-time freshmen returned.

Freshmen *Admission:* 318 applied, 243 admitted, 42 enrolled. *Average high school GPA:* 3.2. *Test scores:* SAT critical reading scores over 500: 96%; SAT math scores over 500: 77%; ACT scores over 18: 100%; SAT critical reading scores over 600: 72%; SAT math scores over 600: 43%; ACT scores over 24: 77%; SAT critical reading scores over 700: 21%; SAT math scores over 700: 6%; ACT scores over 30: 12%.

Faculty *Total:* 52, 81% full-time, 87% with terminal degrees. *Student/faculty ratio:* 6:1.

Academics *Calendar:* semesters. *Degrees:* bachelor's, master's, and doctoral-professional. *Special study options:* accelerated degree program, advanced placement credit, double majors, independent study, internships, off-campus study, part-time degree program, services for LD students, student-designed majors, study abroad.

Computers on Campus 47 computers/terminals are available on campus for general student use. Students can access the following: campus intranet, computer help desk, free student e-mail accounts, online (class) registration, online (class) schedules. Campuswide network is available. 85% of college-owned or -operated housing units are wired for high-speed Internet access. Wireless service is available via entire campus.

Student Life *Housing:* on-campus residence required for freshman year. *Options:* coed, women-only, cooperative. Campus housing is university owned. Freshman campus housing is guaranteed. *Activities and organizations:*

drama/theater group, student-run newspaper, radio station, choral group, outdoor program, theater, farm program, Gay/Lesbian/Bisexual Alliance, madrigal and a cappella groups. *Campus security:* 24-hour emergency response devices and patrols. *Student services:* health clinic, personal/psychological counseling, women's center.

Athletics *Intercollegiate sports:* soccer M/W. *Intramural sports:* basketball M/W, fencing M/W, rock climbing M/W, skiing (cross-country) M/W, skiing (downhill) M/W, soccer M/W, softball M/W, table tennis M/W, ultimate Frisbee M/W.

Costs (2011–12) *Comprehensive fee:* $46,200 includes full-time tuition ($35,250), mandatory fees ($1310), and room and board ($9640). Full-time tuition and fees vary according to degree level, location, and program. Part-time tuition: $1175 per credit. Part-time tuition and fees vary according to course load, degree level, location, and program. *College room only:* $5310. *Payment plan:* installment. *Waivers:* senior citizens and employees or children of employees.

Financial Aid Of all full-time matriculated undergraduates who enrolled in 2009, 207 applied for aid, 193 were judged to have need. 173 Federal Work-Study jobs (averaging $2050). In 2009, 34 non-need-based awards were made. *Average percent of need met:* 87%. *Average financial aid package:* $20,263. *Average need-based gift aid:* $18,598. *Average non-need-based aid:* $7971. *Average indebtedness upon graduation:* $22,456. *Financial aid deadline:* 3/1.

Applying *Options:* electronic application, early admission, early decision, early action, deferred entrance. *Application fee:* $50. *Required:* essay or personal statement, high school transcript, 2 letters of recommendation, expository essay. *Required for some:* interview. *Recommended:* interview. *Application deadlines:* 3/1 (freshmen), 4/1 (transfers), 2/1 (early action). *Early decision deadline:* 12/1. *Notification:* 5/1 (freshmen), 5/1 (transfers), 12/15 (early decision), 2/15 (early action).

Freshman Application Contact Mr. Mark Crowther, Associate Director of Admission, Marlboro College, PO Box A, South Road, Marlboro, VT 05344-0300. *Toll-free phone:* 800-343-0049. *Fax:* 800-451-7555. *E-mail:* admissions@marlboro.edu. *Web site:* http://www.marlboro.edu/.

See page 1412 for the College Close-Up.

Middlebury College
Middlebury, Vermont

- **Independent** comprehensive, founded 1800
- **Small-town** 350-acre campus
- **Endowment** $783.2 million
- **Coed** 2,532 undergraduate students, 99% full-time, 51% women, 49% men
- **Most difficult** entrance level, 17% of applicants were admitted

Undergraduates 2,505 full-time, 27 part-time. Students come from 52 states and territories; 71 other countries; 95% are from out of state; 2% Black or African American, non-Hispanic/Latino; 6% Hispanic/Latino; 6% Asian, non-Hispanic/Latino; 0.2% American Indian or Alaska Native, non-Hispanic/Latino; 4% Two or more races, non-Hispanic/Latino; 5% Race/ethnicity unknown; 10% international; 97% live on campus. *Retention:* 96% of full-time freshmen returned.

Freshmen *Admission:* 7,984 applied, 1,375 admitted, 577 enrolled. *Test scores:* SAT critical reading scores over 500: 99%; SAT math scores over 500: 99%; SAT writing scores over 500: 99%; ACT scores over 18: 100%; SAT critical reading scores over 600: 86%; SAT math scores over 600: 94%; SAT writing scores over 600: 90%; ACT scores over 24: 98%; SAT critical reading scores over 700: 47%; SAT math scores over 700: 48%; SAT writing scores over 700: 53%; ACT scores over 30: 78%.

Faculty *Total:* 310, 84% full-time, 93% with terminal degrees. *Student/faculty ratio:* 9:1.

Academics *Calendar:* 4-1-4. *Degrees:* bachelor's, master's, and doctoral-research/scholarship. *Special study options:* accelerated degree program, advanced placement credit, double majors, honors programs, independent study, internships, off-campus study, services for LD students, student-designed majors, study abroad, summer session for credit. *ROTC:* Army (c). *Unusual degree programs:* 3-2 business administration with University of Chicago; New York University; Rutgers, The State University of New Jersey, Graduate School of Management; University of Rochester; Columbia University; Boston University; Dartmouth College; engineering with Columbia University, Rensselaer Polytechnic Institute, University of Rochester; forestry with Duke University; nursing with Columbia University.

Computers on Campus 494 computers/terminals are available on campus for general student use. Students can access the following: computer help desk, free student e-mail accounts, online (class) registration, online (class) schedules, help-line, personal Web pages, file servers. Campuswide network is available. Wireless service is available via entire campus.

Student Life *Housing:* on-campus residence required through junior year. *Options:* coed, disabled students. Campus housing is university owned. Freshman campus housing is guaranteed. *Activities and organizations:* drama/the-

ater group, student-run newspaper, radio station, choral group, Volunteer Service Organization, International Students Organization, Mountain Club, Activities Board, WRMC radio. *Campus security:* 24-hour patrols, student patrols, late-night transport/escort service, controlled dormitory access. *Student services:* health clinic, personal/psychological counseling, women's center.

Athletics Member NCAA. All Division III except men's and women's skiing (downhill) (Division I). *Intercollegiate sports:* baseball M, basketball M/W, cross-country running M/W, field hockey W, football M, golf M/W, ice hockey M/W, lacrosse M/W, skiing (cross-country) M/W, skiing (downhill) M/W, soccer M/W, softball W, squash W, swimming and diving M/W, tennis M/W, track and field M/W, volleyball W. *Intramural sports:* badminton M/W, basketball M/W, crew M(c)/W(c), cross-country running M/W, equestrian sports M(c)/W(c), football M/W, golf M/W, ice hockey M/W, rock climbing M(c)/W(c), rugby M(c)/W(c), sailing M(c)/W(c), skiing (cross-country) M/W, skiing (downhill) M/W, soccer M/W, softball M/W, squash M(c)/W, swimming and diving M/W, table tennis M/W, tennis M/W, ultimate Frisbee M(c)/W(c), volleyball M/W, water polo M(c)/W(c).

Standardized Tests *Required:* three tests to include: a writing test, a quantitative test, and an area of the applicant's choice (for admission).

Costs (2010–11) *Comprehensive fee:* $52,500. *Payment plan:* tuition prepayment. *Waivers:* employees or children of employees.

Financial Aid Of all full-time matriculated undergraduates who enrolled in 2008, 1,421 applied for aid, 1,158 were judged to have need, 1,158 had their need fully met. *Average percent of need met:* 100%. *Average financial aid package:* $35,470. *Average need-based loan:* $2804. *Average need-based gift aid:* $32,236. *Average indebtedness upon graduation:* $21,520. *Financial aid deadline:* 2/1.

Applying *Options:* electronic application, early admission, early decision, deferred entrance. *Application fee:* $65. *Required:* essay or personal statement, high school transcript, 3 letters of recommendation. *Recommended:* interview. *Application deadlines:* 1/1 (freshmen), 3/1 (transfers). *Early decision deadline:* 11/1 (for plan 1), 12/15 (for plan 2). *Notification:* 4/1 (freshmen), 4/10 (transfers), 12/15 (early decision plan 1), 2/15 (early decision plan 2).

Freshman Application Contact Mr. Robert Clagett, Dean of Admissions, Middlebury College, Emma Willard House, Middlebury, VT 05753-6002. *Phone:* 802-443-3000. *Fax:* 802-443-2056. *E-mail:* admissions@middlebury.edu. *Web site:* http://www.middlebury.edu/.

New England Culinary Institute
Montpelier, Vermont

Freshman Application Contact Jan Knutsen, Vice President of Enrollment, New England Culinary Institute, 56 College Street, Montpelier, VT 05602-3115. *Toll-free phone:* 877-223-6324. *Fax:* 802-225-3280. *E-mail:* janknutsen@neci.edu. *Web site:* http://www.neci.edu/.

Norwich University
Northfield, Vermont

Director of Admissions Ms. Shelby Wallace, Director of Admissions, Norwich University, 158 Harmon Drive, Northfield, VT 05663. *Phone:* 802-485-2658. *Toll-free phone:* 800-468-6679. *E-mail:* nuadm@norwich.edu. *Web site:* http://www.norwich.edu/.

See page 1480 for the College Close-Up.

Saint Michael's College
Colchester, Vermont

- **Independent Roman Catholic** comprehensive, founded 1904
- **Suburban** 440-acre campus with easy access to Montreal
- **Endowment** $58.2 million
- **Coed** 1,899 undergraduate students, 98% full-time, 52% women, 48% men
- **Moderately difficult** entrance level, 82% of applicants were admitted

Undergraduates 1,854 full-time, 45 part-time. Students come from 39 states and territories; 17 other countries; 79% are from out of state; 1% Black or African American, non-Hispanic/Latino; 3% Hispanic/Latino; 1% Asian, non-Hispanic/Latino; 0.2% American Indian or Alaska Native, non-Hispanic/Latino; 0.6% Two or more races, non-Hispanic/Latino; 0.4% Race/ethnicity unknown; 2% international; 2% transferred in; 98% live on campus. *Retention:* 89% of full-time freshmen returned.

Freshmen *Admission:* 3,363 applied, 2,773 admitted, 548 enrolled. *Average high school GPA:* 3.5. *Test scores:* SAT critical reading scores over 500: 82%; SAT math scores over 500: 81%; SAT writing scores over 500: 82%; ACT scores over 18: 97%; SAT critical reading scores over 600: 38%; SAT math scores over 600: 37%; SAT writing scores over 600: 37%; ACT scores over 24:

67%; SAT critical reading scores over 700: 6%; SAT math scores over 700: 3%; SAT writing scores over 700: 3%; ACT scores over 30: 9%.

Faculty *Total:* 202, 73% full-time, 77% with terminal degrees. *Student/faculty ratio:* 12:1.

Academics *Calendar:* semesters. *Degrees:* bachelor's, master's, post-master's, and postbachelor's certificates. *Special study options:* advanced placement credit, distance learning, double majors, English as a second language, honors programs, independent study, internships, off-campus study, part-time degree program, services for LD students, student-designed majors, study abroad, summer session for credit. *ROTC:* Army (c), Air Force (c). *Unusual degree programs:* 3-2 business administration with Clarkson University; engineering with University of Vermont, and Clarkson University; Pre-pharmacy duel degree (B.S., D.Pharm.) with Albany College of Pharmacy and Health Sciences.

Computers on Campus 375 computers/terminals and 5,000 ports are available on campus for general student use. Students can access the following: computer help desk, free student e-mail accounts, online (class) grades, online (class) registration, online (class) schedules. Campuswide network is available. 100% of college-owned or -operated housing units are wired for high-speed Internet access. Wireless service is available via classrooms, computer centers, computer labs, dorm rooms, libraries, student centers.

Student Life *Housing:* on-campus residence required through senior year. *Options:* coed, men-only, women-only, disabled students. Campus housing is university owned. Freshman campus housing is guaranteed. *Activities and organizations:* drama/theater group, student-run newspaper, radio station, choral group, Student Association (governing board), Mobilization of Volunteer Efforts (MOVE), WWPV-FM (student run radio station), Wilderness Program, student newspaper/online publication (The Defender). *Campus security:* 24-hour emergency response devices and patrols, student patrols, late-night transport/escort service, controlled dormitory access, bicycle patrols; Fire and Rescue Squad serving the surrounding community with professionally trained student volunteers. *Student services:* health clinic, personal/psychological counseling, women's center.

Athletics Member NCAA. All Division II. *Intercollegiate sports:* baseball M, basketball M(s)/W(s), cheerleading M(c)/W(c), cross-country running M/W, field hockey W, golf M, ice hockey M/W, lacrosse M/W, rugby M(c)/W(c), skiing (cross-country) M/W, skiing (downhill) M/W, soccer M/W, softball W, swimming and diving M/W, tennis M/W, volleyball W. *Intramural sports:* basketball M/W, cross-country running M/W, ice hockey M/W, racquetball M/W, rock climbing M/W, skiing (cross-country) M/W, skiing (downhill) M/W, soccer M/W, softball M/W, squash M/W, swimming and diving M/W, table tennis M/W, tennis M/W, track and field M(c)/W(c), ultimate Frisbee M(c)/W(c), volleyball M/W.

Standardized Tests *Recommended:* SAT or ACT (for admission), scores are considered if submitted.

Costs (2011–12) *Comprehensive fee:* $45,270 includes full-time tuition ($35,940), mandatory fees ($300), and room and board ($9030). Part-time tuition: $1200 per credit. *Room and board:* Room and board charges vary according to housing facility. *Payment plan:* installment. *Waivers:* employees or children of employees.

Financial Aid Of all full-time matriculated undergraduates who enrolled in 2009, 1,344 applied for aid, 1,159 were judged to have need, 330 had their need fully met. In 2009, 519 non-need-based awards were made. *Average percent of need met:* 77%. *Average financial aid package:* $23,468. *Average need-based loan:* $5193. *Average need-based gift aid:* $16,639. *Average non-need-based aid:* $9960. *Average indebtedness upon graduation:* $29,410.

Applying *Options:* electronic application, early action, deferred entrance. *Application fee:* $50. *Required:* essay or personal statement, high school transcript. *Recommended:* minimum 3 GPA, 3 letters of recommendation, interview. *Application deadlines:* 2/1 (freshmen), 3/15 (transfers), 11/1 (early action). *Notification:* 4/1 (freshmen), 4/15 (transfers), 1/1 (early action).

Freshman Application Contact Ms. Jacqueline Murphy, Director of Admission, Saint Michael's College, One Winooski Park, Colchester, VT 05452. *Phone:* 802-654-3000. *Toll-free phone:* 800-762-8000. *Fax:* 802-654-2906. *E-mail:* admission@smcvt.edu. *Web site:* http://www.smcvt.edu/.

See page 1580 for the College Close-Up.

Southern Vermont College

Bennington, Vermont

- **Independent** 4-year, founded 1926
- **Small-town** 371-acre campus with easy access to Albany, NY
- **Endowment** $1.2 million
- **Coed** 491 undergraduate students, 90% full-time, 63% women, 37% men
- **Minimally difficult** entrance level, 99% of applicants were admitted

Undergraduates 441 full-time, 50 part-time. Students come from 15 states and territories; 3 other countries; 60% are from out of state; 8% Black or African American, non-Hispanic/Latino; 3% Hispanic/Latino; 2% Asian, non-Hispanic/Latino; 0.4% Native Hawaiian or other Pacific Islander, non-Hispanic/

Latino; 0.2% American Indian or Alaska Native, non-Hispanic/Latino; 7% Race/ethnicity unknown; 1% international; 14% transferred in; 50% live on campus. *Retention:* 56% of full-time freshmen returned.

Freshmen *Admission:* 402 applied, 398 admitted, 106 enrolled. *Average high school GPA:* 2.69. *Test scores:* SAT critical reading scores over 500: 22%; SAT math scores over 500: 25%; SAT writing scores over 500: 20%; SAT critical reading scores over 600: 3%; SAT math scores over 600: 1%; SAT writing scores over 600: 1%; SAT critical reading scores over 700: 1%.

Faculty *Total:* 72, 33% full-time, 24% with terminal degrees. *Student/faculty ratio:* 17:1.

Academics *Calendar:* semesters. *Degrees:* associate and bachelor's. *Special study options:* academic remediation for entering students, accelerated degree program, adult/continuing education programs, advanced placement credit, cooperative education, distance learning, double majors, external degree program, honors programs, independent study, internships, off-campus study, part-time degree program, services for LD students, student-designed majors, study abroad, summer session for credit.

Computers on Campus 60 computers/terminals are available on campus for general student use. Students can access the following: campus intranet, free student e-mail accounts. Campuswide network is available.

Student Life *Housing:* on-campus residence required through sophomore year. *Options:* coed. Campus housing is university owned. Freshman campus housing is guaranteed. *Activities and organizations:* drama/theater group, student-run newspaper, Student Government Association, The Student Activities Squad, Japanese Culture and Anime Club, Big Brothers Big Sisters, Moosecorps. *Campus security:* 24-hour patrols, late-night transport/escort service, controlled dormitory access. *Student services:* health clinic, personal/psychological counseling.

Athletics Member NCAA. All Division III. *Intercollegiate sports:* baseball M, basketball M/W, cross-country running M/W, rugby M/W, soccer M/W, softball W, track and field M/W, volleyball M/W. *Intramural sports:* baseball M/W, basketball M/W, cheerleading W(c), football M/W, golf M/W, rugby M(c)/W(c), skiing (cross-country) M(c)/W(c), skiing (downhill) M(c)/W(c), soccer M/W, softball M/W, volleyball M/W.

Standardized Tests *Required:* SAT or ACT (for admission).

Costs (2010–11) *Comprehensive fee:* $28,630 includes full-time tuition ($19,430) and room and board ($9200). Full-time tuition and fees vary according to program. Part-time tuition: $660 per credit hour. Part-time tuition and fees vary according to course load and program. *College room only:* $4600. Room and board charges vary according to board plan and housing facility. *Payment plan:* installment. *Waivers:* employees or children of employees.

Financial Aid Of all full-time matriculated undergraduates who enrolled in 2006, 287 applied for aid, 262 were judged to have need, 32 had their need fully met. 71 Federal Work-Study jobs (averaging $1200). In 2006, 18 non-need-based awards were made. *Average percent of need met:* 65%. *Average financial aid package:* $12,689. *Average need-based loan:* $4231. *Average need-based gift aid:* $9088. *Average non-need-based aid:* $3461. *Average indebtedness upon graduation:* $20,244.

Applying *Options:* electronic application, early admission, deferred entrance. *Application fee:* $30. *Required:* essay or personal statement, high school transcript, 2 letters of recommendation. *Required for some:* interview. *Recommended:* minimum 2 GPA, interview. *Application deadlines:* rolling (freshmen), rolling (transfers). *Notification:* continuous (freshmen), continuous (transfers).

Freshman Application Contact Southern Vermont College, 982 Mansion Drive, Bennington, VT 05201. *Phone:* 802-447-6304. *Toll-free phone:* 800-378-2782. *Fax:* 802-447-4695. *E-mail:* admis@svc.edu. *Web site:* http://www.svc.edu/.

Sterling College

Craftsbury Common, Vermont

- **Independent** 4-year, founded 1958
- **Rural** 430-acre campus
- **Endowment** $732,390
- **Coed** 99 undergraduate students, 95% full-time, 43% women, 57% men
- **Moderately difficult** entrance level, 75% of applicants were admitted

Undergraduates 94 full-time, 5 part-time. Students come from 24 states and territories; 1 other country; 76% are from out of state; 1% Native Hawaiian or other Pacific Islander, non-Hispanic/Latino; 2% Two or more races, non-Hispanic/Latino; 20% Race/ethnicity unknown; 1% international; 14% transferred in; 86% live on campus. *Retention:* 58% of full-time freshmen returned.

Freshmen *Admission:* 71 applied, 53 admitted, 17 enrolled.

Faculty *Total:* 26, 38% full-time, 31% with terminal degrees. *Student/faculty ratio:* 7:1.

Academics *Calendar:* semesters. *Degrees:* associate and bachelor's. *Special study options:* advanced placement credit, double majors, independent study, internships, off-campus study, services for LD students, student-designed majors, study abroad, summer session for credit.

Computers on Campus 18 computers/terminals are available on campus for general student use. Students can access the following: campus intranet, computer help desk, free student e-mail accounts. Campuswide network is available. 100% of college-owned or -operated housing units are wired for high-speed Internet access. Wireless service is available via entire campus.

Student Life *Housing options:* coed. Campus housing is university owned. Freshman campus housing is guaranteed. *Activities and organizations:* drama/theater group, choral group, Outing Club, Timbersports Team, Student Union, Art Club, Musical Groups. *Campus security:* 24-hour pager. *Student services:* health clinic, personal/psychological counseling.

Costs (2011–12) *Comprehensive fee:* $35,242 includes full-time tuition ($26,802), mandatory fees ($350), and room and board ($8090). Full-time tuition and fees vary according to course load. Part-time tuition: $848 per credit. Part-time tuition and fees vary according to course load. *College room only:* $3684. Room and board charges vary according to board plan. *Payment plan:* installment. *Waivers:* employees or children of employees.

Financial Aid Of all full-time matriculated undergraduates who enrolled in 2008, 86 applied for aid, 86 were judged to have need, 7 had their need fully met. 39 Federal Work-Study jobs (averaging $339). 108 state and other part-time jobs (averaging $1595). In 2008, 11 non-need-based awards were made. *Average percent of need met:* 80%. *Average financial aid package:* $20,771. *Average need-based loan:* $3944. *Average need-based gift aid:* $15,839. *Average non-need-based aid:* $6018. *Average indebtedness upon graduation:* $19,751.

Applying *Options:* electronic application, early admission, early action, deferred entrance. *Application fee:* $35. *Required:* essay or personal statement, high school transcript, 2 letters of recommendation. *Recommended:* minimum 2 GPA, interview. *Application deadlines:* rolling (freshmen), rolling (transfers), 12/15 (early action). *Notification:* continuous (freshmen), continuous (transfers), 1/15 (early action).

Freshman Application Contact Ms. Lynne A. Birdsall, Director of Admissions, Sterling College, PO Box 72, Craftsbury Common, VT 05827. *Phone:* 802-586-7711 Ext. 135. *Toll-free phone:* 800-648-3591 Ext. 100. *Fax:* 802-586-2596. *E-mail:* lbirdsall@sterlingcollege.edu. *Web site:* http://www.sterlingcollege.edu/.

University of Vermont

Burlington, Vermont

- **State-supported** university, founded 1791
- **Suburban** 459-acre campus
- **Endowment** $269.0 million
- **Coed** 11,605 undergraduate students, 89% full-time, 57% women, 43% men
- **Moderately difficult** entrance level, 71% of applicants were admitted

Undergraduates 10,317 full-time, 1,288 part-time. Students come from 49 states and territories; 30 other countries; 66% are from out of state; 4% transferred in; 51% live on campus. *Retention:* 87% of full-time freshmen returned.

Freshmen *Admission:* 22,317 applied, 15,772 admitted, 2,472 enrolled. *Test scores:* SAT critical reading scores over 500: 89%; SAT math scores over 500: 92%; SAT writing scores over 500: 89%; ACT scores over 18: 100%; SAT critical reading scores over 600: 47%; SAT math scores over 600: 52%; SAT writing scores over 600: 46%; ACT scores over 24: 81%; SAT critical reading scores over 700: 9%; SAT math scores over 700: 7%; SAT writing scores over 700: 7%; ACT scores over 30: 18%.

Faculty *Total:* 764, 80% full-time, 78% with terminal degrees. *Student/faculty ratio:* 17:1.

Academics *Calendar:* semesters. *Degrees:* bachelor's, master's, doctoral-professional, doctoral-research/scholarship, post-master's, and postbachelor's certificates. *Special study options:* adult/continuing education programs, advanced placement credit, cooperative education, distance learning, double majors, freshman honors college, honors programs, independent study, internships, off-campus study, part-time degree program, services for LD students, student-designed majors, study abroad, summer session for credit. *ROTC:* Army (b). *Unusual degree programs:* 3-2 computer science; physical therapy.

Computers on Campus 850 computers/terminals and 299 ports are available on campus for general student use. Students can access the following: campus intranet, computer help desk, free student e-mail accounts, online (class) grades, online (class) registration, online (class) schedules, Web pages, online course support. Campuswide network is available. 100% of college-owned or -operated housing units are wired for high-speed Internet access. Wireless service is available via classrooms, computer centers, computer labs, learning centers, libraries, student centers.

Student Life *Housing:* on-campus residence required through sophomore year. *Options:* coed. Campus housing is university owned. Freshman campus housing is guaranteed. *Activities and organizations:* drama/theater group, student-run newspaper, radio and television station, choral group, Volunteers in Action, Outing Club, Ski and Snowboard Club, national fraternities, national sororities. *Campus security:* 24-hour emergency response devices and patrols, late-night transport/escort service, controlled dormitory access. *Student services:*

health clinic, personal/psychological counseling, women's center, legal services.

Athletics Member NCAA. All Division I. *Intercollegiate sports:* basketball M(s)/W(s), cheerleading M(c)/W(c), crew M(c)/W(c), cross-country running M(s)/W(s), equestrian sports M(c)/W(c), fencing M(c)/W(c), field hockey W(s), gymnastics M(c)/W(c), ice hockey M(s)/W(s), lacrosse M(s)/W(s), rugby M(c)/W(c), sailing M(c)/W(c), skiing (cross-country) M(s)/W(s), skiing (downhill) M(s)/W(s), soccer M(s)/W(s), swimming and diving W(s), table tennis M(c)/W(c), track and field M(s)/W(s), ultimate Frisbee M(c)/W(c), volleyball M(c)/W(c), water polo M(c)/W(c). *Intramural sports:* basketball M/W, bowling M/W, football M/W, ice hockey M/W, lacrosse M/W, racquetball M/W, soccer M/W, softball M/W, tennis M/W, volleyball M/W, water polo M/W.

Standardized Tests *Required:* SAT or ACT (for admission).

Costs (2010–11) *Tuition:* state resident $12,180 full-time, $508 per credit hour part-time; nonresident $30,744 full-time, $1281 per credit hour part-time. Part-time tuition and fees vary according to course load. *Required fees:* $1856 full-time. *Room and board:* $9382; room only: $6196. Room and board charges vary according to board plan and housing facility. *Payment plans:* installment, deferred payment. *Waivers:* senior citizens and employees or children of employees.

Financial Aid Of all full-time matriculated undergraduates who enrolled in 2009, 7,084 applied for aid, 5,909 were judged to have need, 1,180 had their need fully met. 2,437 Federal Work-Study jobs (averaging $1462). In 2009, 1790 non-need-based awards were made. *Average percent of need met:* 71%. *Average financial aid package:* $18,364. *Average need-based loan:* $6413. *Average need-based gift aid:* $14,576. *Average non-need-based aid:* $2426. *Average indebtedness upon graduation:* $27,696.

Applying *Options:* electronic application, early action, deferred entrance. *Application fee:* $55. *Required:* essay or personal statement, high school transcript, 1 letter of recommendation. *Application deadlines:* 1/15 (freshmen), 4/15 (transfers), 11/1 (early action). *Notification:* 3/31 (freshmen), continuous (transfers), 12/15 (early action).

Freshman Application Contact Beth A. Wiser PhD, Director of Admissions, University of Vermont, Office of Admissions, 194 South Prospect Street, Burlington, VT 05401-3596. *Phone:* 802-656-3370. *Fax:* 802-656-8611. *E-mail:* admissions@uvm.edu. *Web site:* http://www.uvm.edu/.

Vermont Technical College

Randolph Center, Vermont

- **State-supported** 4-year, founded 1866, part of Vermont State Colleges System
- **Rural** 544-acre campus
- **Endowment** $4.6 million
- **Coed** 1,658 undergraduate students, 78% full-time, 43% women, 57% men
- **Moderately difficult** entrance level, 64% of applicants were admitted

Undergraduates 1,299 full-time, 359 part-time. Students come from 17 states and territories; 8 other countries; 15% are from out of state; 0.9% Black or African American, non-Hispanic/Latino; 0.8% Hispanic/Latino; 2% Asian, non-Hispanic/Latino; 0.6% American Indian or Alaska Native, non-Hispanic/Latino; 0.4% international; 19% transferred in; 35% live on campus. *Retention:* 70% of full-time freshmen returned.

Freshmen *Admission:* 880 applied, 559 admitted, 273 enrolled. *Average high school GPA:* 2.96. *Test scores:* SAT critical reading scores over 500: 41%; SAT math scores over 500: 43%; SAT writing scores over 500: 30%; ACT scores over 18: 65%; SAT critical reading scores over 600: 9%; SAT math scores over 600: 8%; SAT writing scores over 600: 7%; ACT scores over 24: 22%; SAT critical reading scores over 700: 1%; SAT math scores over 700: 1%.

Faculty *Total:* 183, 45% full-time, 16% with terminal degrees. *Student/faculty ratio:* 12:1.

Academics *Calendar:* semesters. *Degrees:* certificates, associate, and bachelor's. *Special study options:* academic remediation for entering students, accelerated degree program, advanced placement credit, cooperative education, distance learning, double majors, English as a second language, honors programs, independent study, internships, part-time degree program, services for LD students, summer session for credit. *ROTC:* Army (c).

Computers on Campus 480 computers/terminals and 600 ports are available on campus for general student use. Students can access the following: campus intranet, computer help desk, free student e-mail accounts, online (class) grades, online (class) registration, online (class) schedules, online (network) file storage, wireless network. Campuswide network is available. 98% of college-owned or -operated housing units are wired for high-speed Internet access. Wireless service is available via entire campus.

Student Life *Housing:* on-campus residence required through sophomore year. *Options:* coed. Campus housing is university owned. *Activities and organizations:* student-run radio and television station, choral group, Student Council (student government), Adventurer's Guild (board & video gaming), WVTC

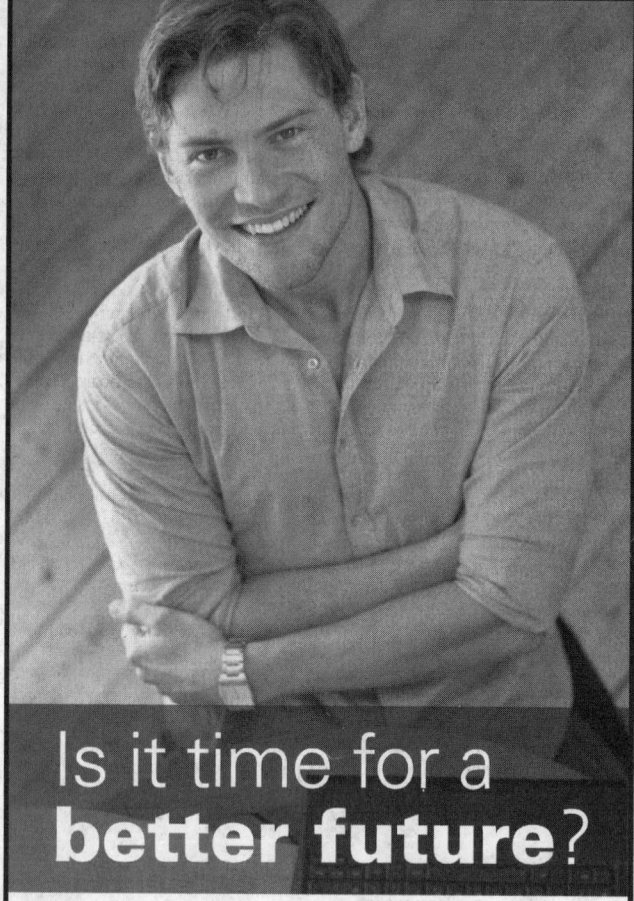

Is it time for a better future?

Then come make it happen at Vermont Tech.
Vermont Technical College offers more than 25 bachelor's and associate degree programs in today's most sought after fields, including business, computer technology, engineering technology, equine studies, fire science, architectural engineering technology, landscape design, diversified agriculture, dental hygiene, automotive and diesel technology, nursing, respiratory therapy and more.

Located in the heart of the Green Mountains, Vermont Tech offers a wide range of activities, including varsity and intramural sports, more than 20 clubs and organizations, plus a 450 acre campus just minutes from I-89 and close to some of Vermont's finest ski resorts.

To learn more about Vermont Tech, including our 95% job placement rate, call one of our Admissions Counselors or visit us online today.

VERMONT TECH Choose **Success.**

LEARN MORE: **800.442.8821** | vtc.edu

(student radio station), Outing Club, Veterinary Technology Club. *Campus security:* 24-hour emergency response devices and patrols, late-night transport/ escort service, controlled dormitory access. *Student services:* health clinic.

Athletics Member USCAA. *Intercollegiate sports:* baseball M, basketball M/ W, golf M/W, soccer M/W, softball W. *Intramural sports:* basketball M/W, bowling M(c)/W(c), cross-country running M/W, fencing M(c)/W(c), football M/W, golf M(c)/W(c), ice hockey M(c)/W(c), racquetball M/W, riflery M(c)/ W(c), rock climbing M(c)/W(c), rugby M(c), skiing (cross-country) M(c)/ W(c), skiing (downhill) M(c)/W(c), soccer M/W, softball M/W, swimming and diving M/W, table tennis M/W, tennis M/W, volleyball M/W, water polo M/W, weight lifting M(c)/W(c).

Standardized Tests *Required for some:* SAT or ACT (for admission).

Costs (2011–12) *Tuition:* state resident $10,656 full-time, $444 per credit part-time; nonresident $20,376 full-time, $849 per credit part-time. Full-time tuition and fees vary according to course load and program. Part-time tuition and fees vary according to program. *Required fees:* $899 full-time. *Room and board:* $8445. Room and board charges vary according to board plan. *Payment plan:* installment. *Waivers:* employees or children of employees.

Financial Aid Of all full-time matriculated undergraduates who enrolled in 2008, 1,046 applied for aid, 923 were judged to have need, 112 had their need fully met. 150 Federal Work-Study jobs (averaging $900). In 2008, 19 non-need-based awards were made. *Average percent of need met:* 60%. *Average financial aid package:* $8856. *Average need-based loan:* $39,476. *Average need-based gift aid:* $5620. *Average non-need-based aid:* $4146. *Average indebtedness upon graduation:* $24,000.

Applying *Options:* electronic application. *Application fee:* $40. *Required:* high school transcript. *Required for some:* essay or personal statement, 2 letters of recommendation, interview. *Recommended:* minimum 3 GPA, 2 letters of recommendation, interview. *Application deadlines:* rolling (freshmen), rolling (transfers). *Notification:* continuous (freshmen), continuous (transfers).

Freshman Application Contact Dwight A. Cross, Assistant Dean of Enrollment, Vermont Technical College, PO Box 500, Randolph Center, VT 05061. *Phone:* 802-728-1244. *Toll-free phone:* 800-442-VTC1. *Fax:* 802-728-1390. *E-mail:* admissions@vtc.edu. *Web site:* http://www.vtc.edu/.

See page 1758 for the College Close-Up.

VIRGINIA

Argosy University, Washington DC
Arlington, Virginia

- **Proprietary** university, founded 1994, part of Argosy Education Group
- **Urban** campus
- **Coed**

Academics *Calendar:* semesters. *Degrees:* bachelor's, master's, and doctoral-professional.

Costs (2010–11) *Tuition:* Tuition varies by program. Students should contact Argosy University for tuition information.

Freshman Application Contact Argosy University, Washington DC, 1550 Wilson Boulevard, Suite 600, Arlington, VA 22209. *Phone:* 703-526-5800. *Toll-free phone:* 866-703-2777. *Web site:* http://www.argosy.edu/ washingtondc/.

See page 1002 for the College Close-Up.

The Art Institute of Virginia Beach
Virginia Beach, Virginia

- **Proprietary** 4-year
- **Coed**

Academics *Degrees:* associate and bachelor's.

Costs (2010–11) *Tuition:* Tuition cost varies by program. Prospective students should contact the school for current tuition costs. Other charges include a starting kit for all first-quarter students. Kits vary in price, depending on the program of study.

Freshman Application Contact The Art Institute of Virginia Beach, Two Columbus Center, 4500 Main Street, Suite 100, Virginia Beach, VA 23462. *Phone:* 757-493-6700. *Toll-free phone:* 877-437-4428. *Web site:* http:// www.artinstitutes.edu/virginia-beach/.

See page 1076 for the College Close-Up.

The Art Institute of Washington
Arlington, Virginia
- **Proprietary** 4-year, founded 2000, part of Education Management Corporation
- **Urban** campus
- **Coed**

Academics *Calendar:* quarters. *Degrees:* diplomas, associate, and bachelor's.
Costs (2010–11) *Tuition:* Tuition cost varies by program. Prospective students should contact the school for current tuition costs. Other charges include a starting kit for all first-quarter students. Kits vary in price, depending on the program of study.
Freshman Application Contact The Art Institute of Washington, 1820 North Fort Meyer Drive, Arlington, VA 22209. *Phone:* 703-358-9550. *Toll-free phone:* 877-303-3771. *Web site:* http://www.artinstitutes.edu/arlington/.

See page 1078 for the College Close-Up.

The Art Institute of Washington–Northern Virginia
Sterling, Virginia
- **Proprietary** 4-year
- **Coed**

Academics *Degrees:* associate and bachelor's.
Costs (2010–11) *Tuition:* Tuition cost varies by program. Prospective students should contact the school for current tuition costs. Other charges include a starting kit for all first-quarter students. Kits vary in price, depending on the program of study.
Freshman Application Contact The Art Institute of Washington–Northern Virginia, The Corporate Office Park at Dulles Town Center, 21000 Atlantic Boulevard, Suite 100, Sterling, VA 20166. *Phone:* 571-449-4400. *Toll-free phone:* 888-627-5008. *Web site:* http://www.artinstitutes.edu/northern-virginia/.

See page 1080 for the College Close-Up.

Averett University
Danville, Virginia
- **Independent** comprehensive, founded 1859, affiliated with Baptist General Association of Virginia
- **Small-town** 19-acre campus with easy access to Greensboro and Raleigh
- **Endowment** $23.8 million
- **Coed** 857 undergraduate students, 94% full-time, 46% women, 54% men
- **Moderately difficult** entrance level, 86% of applicants were admitted

Undergraduates 807 full-time, 50 part-time. Students come from 30 states and territories; 15 other countries; 37% are from out of state; 26% Black or African American, non-Hispanic/Latino; 3% Hispanic/Latino; 0.6% Asian, non-Hispanic/Latino; 0.1% Native Hawaiian or other Pacific Islander, non-Hispanic/Latino; 0.5% American Indian or Alaska Native, non-Hispanic/Latino; 2% Two or more races, non-Hispanic/Latino; 0.5% Race/ethnicity unknown; 9% international; 9% transferred in; 56% live on campus. *Retention:* 57% of full-time freshmen returned.
Freshmen *Admission:* 1,237 applied, 1,065 admitted, 239 enrolled. *Average high school GPA:* 3.1. *Test scores:* SAT critical reading scores over 500: 31%; SAT math scores over 500: 32%; ACT scores over 18: 67%; SAT critical reading scores over 600: 5%; SAT math scores over 600: 7%; ACT scores over 24: 18%.
Faculty *Total:* 81, 67% full-time, 57% with terminal degrees. *Student/faculty ratio:* 13:1.
Academics *Calendar:* semesters. *Degrees:* associate, bachelor's, and master's. *Special study options:* academic remediation for entering students, accelerated degree program, advanced placement credit, cooperative education, distance learning, double majors, external degree program, honors programs, independent study, internships, off-campus study, part-time degree program, services for LD students, student-designed majors, study abroad, summer session for credit.
Computers on Campus 150 computers/terminals are available on campus for general student use. Students can access the following: computer help desk, free student e-mail accounts, online (class) grades, online (class) registration, online (class) schedules. Campuswide network is available. Wireless service is available via libraries, student centers.
Student Life *Housing:* on-campus residence required through junior year. *Options:* coed, men-only, women-only. Campus housing is university owned. *Activities and organizations:* drama/theater group, student-run newspaper, choral group, Student Government Association, Campus Activities Board, Christian Student Union, Averett Gospel Choir, Averett Anime Association, national fraternities, national sororities. *Campus security:* 24-hour emergency response devices and patrols, late-night transport/escort service, controlled dormitory access. *Student services:* personal/psychological counseling.
Athletics Member NCAA. All Division III. *Intercollegiate sports:* baseball M, basketball M/W, cross-country running M/W, equestrian sports M/W, football M, golf M, soccer M/W, softball W, tennis M/W, volleyball W. *Intramural sports:* basketball M/W, cheerleading M/W, football M/W, golf M/W, racquetball M/W, soccer M/W, softball M/W, table tennis M/W, tennis M/W, volleyball M/W.
Standardized Tests *Required:* SAT or ACT (for admission).
Costs (2010–11) *Comprehensive fee:* $31,230 includes full-time tuition ($21,956), mandatory fees ($1000), and room and board ($8274). Full-time tuition and fees vary according to course load, degree level, location, and program. Part-time tuition: $375 per credit hour. Part-time tuition and fees vary according to course load, degree level, location, and program. *College room only:* $5492. Room and board charges vary according to board plan and housing facility. *Payment plan:* installment. *Waivers:* senior citizens and employees or children of employees.
Financial Aid Of all full-time matriculated undergraduates who enrolled in 2008, 775 applied for aid, 705 were judged to have need, 145 had their need fully met. 164 Federal Work-Study jobs (averaging $938). In 2008, 176 non-need-based awards were made. *Average percent of need met:* 74%. *Average financial aid package:* $17,442. *Average need-based loan:* $4114. *Average need-based gift aid:* $13,971. *Average non-need-based aid:* $8525. *Average indebtedness upon graduation:* $39,110.
Applying *Options:* electronic application, deferred entrance. *Required:* high school transcript, minimum 2.2 GPA, college preparatory curriculum. *Recommended:* essay or personal statement, 1 letter of recommendation, interview. *Application deadlines:* 7/15 (freshmen), 8/15 (transfers). *Notification:* continuous (freshmen), continuous (transfers).
Freshman Application Contact Averett University, 420 West Main Street, Danville, VA 24541-3692. *Phone:* 434-791-5663. *Toll-free phone:* 800-AVERETT. *Web site:* http://www.averett.edu/.

Bluefield College
Bluefield, Virginia
- **Independent Southern Baptist** 4-year, founded 1922
- **Small-town** 85-acre campus
- **Endowment** $4.6 million
- **Coed** 692 undergraduate students, 83% full-time, 57% women, 43% men
- **Moderately difficult** entrance level, 47% of applicants were admitted

Undergraduates 577 full-time, 115 part-time. Students come from 23 states and territories; 10 other countries; 20% are from out of state; 21% Black or African American, non-Hispanic/Latino; 3% Hispanic/Latino; 2% Asian, non-Hispanic/Latino; 0.1% American Indian or Alaska Native, non-Hispanic/Latino; 8% Race/ethnicity unknown; 0.1% international; 21% transferred in; 39% live on campus. *Retention:* 59% of full-time freshmen returned.
Freshmen *Admission:* 747 applied, 350 admitted, 113 enrolled. *Average high school GPA:* 3.03. *Test scores:* SAT critical reading scores over 500: 36%; SAT math scores over 500: 32%; ACT scores over 18: 74%; SAT critical reading scores over 600: 8%; SAT math scores over 600: 8%; ACT scores over 24: 14%; SAT math scores over 700: 1%.
Faculty *Total:* 100, 38% full-time, 52% with terminal degrees. *Student/faculty ratio:* 11:1.
Academics *Calendar:* semesters. *Degree:* bachelor's. *Special study options:* academic remediation for entering students, accelerated degree program, adult/continuing education programs, advanced placement credit, cooperative education, distance learning, double majors, external degree program, honors programs, independent study, internships, part-time degree program, services for LD students, study abroad, summer session for credit.
Computers on Campus 105 computers/terminals and 150 ports are available on campus for general student use. Students can access the following: campus intranet, free student e-mail accounts, online (class) grades, online (class) registration, online (class) schedules. Campuswide network is available. 100% of college-owned or -operated housing units are wired for high-speed Internet access. Wireless service is available via libraries, student centers.
Student Life *Housing:* on-campus residence required through junior year. *Options:* coed, men-only, women-only, disabled students. Campus housing is university owned. Freshman campus housing is guaranteed. *Activities and organizations:* drama/theater group, student-run newspaper, choral group, Baptist Collegiate Ministries, Fellowship of Christian Athletes, Student Union Board, Student Government Association, Art Club. *Campus security:* controlled dormitory access, night security patrols. *Student services:* personal/psychological counseling.
Athletics Member NCAA, NAIA, NCCAA. All NCAA Division II. *Intercollegiate sports:* baseball M(s), basketball M(s)/W(s), cross-country running M(s)/W(s), football M(s)(c), golf M(s), soccer M(s)/W(s), softball W(s), tennis M(s)/W(s), volleyball W(s). *Intramural sports:* badminton M/W, baseball M, basketball M/W, bowling M/W, football M/W, softball M/W, table tennis M/W, tennis M/W, volleyball M/W.

Standardized Tests *Required:* SAT or ACT (for admission).

Costs (2010–11) *Comprehensive fee:* $26,150 includes full-time tuition ($17,990), mandatory fees ($810), and room and board ($7350). Full-time tuition and fees vary according to program. Part-time tuition: $750 per credit hour. Part-time tuition and fees vary according to program. *Required fees:* $300 per term part-time. *Room and board:* Room and board charges vary according to housing facility. *Payment plan:* installment. *Waivers:* senior citizens and employees or children of employees.

Financial Aid Of all full-time matriculated undergraduates who enrolled in 2009, 545 applied for aid, 495 were judged to have need, 67 had their need fully met. 65 Federal Work-Study jobs (averaging $1125). In 2009, 69 non-need-based awards were made. *Average percent of need met:* 62%. *Average financial aid package:* $14,035. *Average need-based loan:* $4960. *Average need-based gift aid:* $9827. *Average non-need-based aid:* $5345. *Average indebtedness upon graduation:* $18,661.

Applying *Options:* electronic application, deferred entrance. *Application fee:* $30. *Required:* high school transcript, minimum 2 GPA. *Required for some:* essay or personal statement, 2 letters of recommendation. *Application deadlines:* rolling (freshmen), rolling (transfers). *Notification:* continuous (freshmen), continuous (transfers).

Freshman Application Contact Mr. Mark Hipes, Bluefield College, 3000 College Drive, Bluefield, VA 24605-1799. *Phone:* 276-326-4340. *Toll-free phone:* 800-872-0175. *Fax:* 276-326-4395. *E-mail:* mhipes@bluefield.edu. *Web site:* http://www.bluefield.edu/.

Bridgewater College
Bridgewater, Virginia

- **Independent** 4-year, founded 1880, affiliated with Church of the Brethren
- **Small-town** 300-acre campus
- **Endowment** $57.2 million
- **Coed** 1,688 undergraduate students, 99% full-time, 58% women, 42% men
- **Moderately difficult** entrance level

Undergraduates 1,672 full-time, 16 part-time. Students come from 24 states and territories; 5 other countries; 19% are from out of state; 9% Black or African American, non-Hispanic/Latino; 2% Hispanic/Latino; 0.8% Asian, non-Hispanic/Latino; 0.1% Native Hawaiian or other Pacific Islander, non-Hispanic/Latino; 0.2% American Indian or Alaska Native, non-Hispanic/Latino; 2% Two or more races, non-Hispanic/Latino; 5% Race/ethnicity unknown; 0.3% international; 2% transferred in; 84% live on campus. *Retention:* 70% of full-time freshmen returned.

Freshmen *Admission:* 5,530 applied, 552 enrolled. *Average high school GPA:* 3.5. *Test scores:* SAT critical reading scores over 500: 59%; SAT math scores over 500: 63%; SAT writing scores over 500: 56%; ACT scores over 18: 86%; SAT critical reading scores over 600: 20%; SAT math scores over 600: 17%; SAT writing scores over 600: 14%; ACT scores over 24: 29%; SAT critical reading scores over 700: 2%; SAT math scores over 700: 1%; SAT writing scores over 700: 1%; ACT scores over 30: 1%.

Faculty *Total:* 143, 73% full-time, 68% with terminal degrees. *Student/faculty ratio:* 14:1.

Academics *Calendar:* 4-1-4. *Degree:* bachelor's. *Special study options:* adult/continuing education programs, advanced placement credit, double majors, honors programs, independent study, internships, off-campus study, part-time degree program, services for LD students, study abroad, summer session for credit. *Unusual degree programs:* 3-2 engineering with George Washington University; Virginia Tech; nursing with Vanderbilt University; physical therapy with Shenandoah University (3-4 program); veterinary science with Virginia Polytechnic Institute and State University (3-4 program).

Computers on Campus 197 computers/terminals are available on campus for general student use. Students can access the following: campus intranet, computer help desk, free student e-mail accounts, online (class) grades, online (class) registration, online (class) schedules, Moodle (course management system), campus bulletin board system. Campuswide network is available. 100% of college-owned or -operated housing units are wired for high-speed Internet access. Wireless service is available via entire campus.

Student Life *Housing:* on-campus residence required through senior year. *Options:* coed, men-only, women-only, disabled students. Campus housing is university owned. Freshman campus housing is guaranteed. *Activities and organizations:* drama/theater group, student-run newspaper, radio station, choral group, Equestrian Club, Student Ambassadors, Campus Crusade for Christ (CRU), Eagle Productions (program board), Civil War Club. *Campus security:* 24-hour emergency response devices and patrols, controlled dormitory access, emergency alert system. *Student services:* health clinic, personal/psychological counseling.

Athletics Member NCAA. All Division III. *Intercollegiate sports:* baseball M, basketball M/W, cheerleading M(c)/W(c), cross-country running M/W, equestrian sports M/W, field hockey W, football M, golf M, lacrosse M(c)/W, soccer M/W, softball W, swimming and diving W, tennis M/W, track and field

M/W, volleyball W. *Intramural sports:* badminton M/W, basketball M/W, bowling M/W, football M/W, golf M/W, racquetball M/W, soccer M/W, softball M/W, table tennis M/W, tennis M/W, ultimate Frisbee M/W, volleyball M/W.

Standardized Tests *Required:* SAT or ACT (for admission).

Costs (2010–11) *Comprehensive fee:* $35,850 includes full-time tuition ($25,500) and room and board ($10,350). Part-time tuition: $850 per credit hour. *Required fees:* $30 per term part-time. *College room only:* $5260. Room and board charges vary according to board plan and housing facility. *Payment plan:* installment. *Waivers:* senior citizens and employees or children of employees.

Financial Aid Of all full-time matriculated undergraduates who enrolled in 2009, 1,345 applied for aid, 1,190 were judged to have need, 171 had their need fully met. In 2009, 376 non-need-based awards were made. *Average percent of need met:* 79%. *Average financial aid package:* $21,596. *Average need-based loan:* $4923. *Average need-based gift aid:* $17,183. *Average non-need-based aid:* $9887. *Average indebtedness upon graduation:* $29,331.

Applying *Options:* electronic application, deferred entrance. *Application fee:* $30. *Required:* high school transcript, minimum 2.5 GPA, 1 letter of recommendation. *Required for some:* interview. *Recommended:* minimum 2.8 GPA, interview. *Application deadlines:* rolling (freshmen), rolling (transfers). *Notification:* continuous (freshmen), continuous (transfers).

Freshman Application Contact Bridgewater College, 402 East College Street, Bridgewater, VA 22812-1599. *Phone:* 540-828-5375. *Toll-free phone:* 800-759-8328. *Web site:* http://www.bridgewater.edu/.

Bryant & Stratton College - Richmond Campus
Richmond, Virginia

- **Proprietary** primarily 2-year, founded 1952, part of Bryant and Stratton Business Institute, Inc.
- **Suburban** campus
- **Coed**
- **Minimally difficult** entrance level

Faculty *Student/faculty ratio:* 10:1.

Academics *Calendar:* semesters. *Degrees:* associate and bachelor's.

Student Life *Campus security:* late-night transport/escort service.

Standardized Tests *Required:* TABE, CPAt (for admission). *Recommended:* SAT or ACT (for admission).

Applying *Options:* deferred entrance. *Required:* high school transcript, interview, entrance evaluation and placement evaluation.

Freshman Application Contact Mr. David K. Mayle, Director of Admissions, Bryant & Stratton College - Richmond Campus, 8141 Hull Street Road, Richmond, VA 23235-6411. *Phone:* 804-745-2444. *Fax:* 804-745-6884. *E-mail:* tlawson@bryanstratton.edu. *Web site:* http://www.bryantstratton.edu/.

Bryant & Stratton College - Virginia Beach
Virginia Beach, Virginia

- **Proprietary** primarily 2-year, founded 1952, part of Bryant and Stratton Business Institute, Inc.
- **Suburban** campus
- **Coed**
- **Minimally difficult** entrance level

Faculty *Student/faculty ratio:* 12:1.

Academics *Calendar:* semesters. *Degrees:* associate and bachelor's.

Student Life *Campus security:* 24-hour emergency response devices, late-night transport/escort service.

Standardized Tests *Required:* CPAt (for admission).

Financial Aid Of all full-time matriculated undergraduates who enrolled in 2009, 30 Federal Work-Study jobs (averaging $5000).

Applying *Options:* electronic application. *Application fee:* $35. *Required:* essay or personal statement, high school transcript, interview.

Freshman Application Contact Bryant & Stratton College - Virginia Beach, 301 Centre Pointe Drive, Virginia Beach, VA 23462-4417. *Phone:* 757-499-7900 Ext. 173. *Web site:* http://www.bryantstratton.edu/.

Centura College
Virginia Beach, Virginia

Freshman Application Contact Admissions Office, Centura College, 2697 Dean Drive, Suite 100, Virginia Beach, VA 23452. *Phone:* 757-340-2121. *Toll-free phone:* 877-575-5627. *Fax:* 757-340-9704. *Web site:* http://www.centuracollege.edu/.

Christendom College

Front Royal, Virginia

- **Independent Roman Catholic** comprehensive, founded 1977
- **Rural** 100-acre campus with easy access to Washington, D.C.
- **Endowment** $3.1 million
- **Coed** 409 undergraduate students, 100% full-time, 53% women, 47% men
- **Very difficult** entrance level, 82% of applicants were admitted

Undergraduates 407 full-time, 2 part-time. Students come from 45 states and territories; 7 other countries; 75% are from out of state; 2% transferred in; 95% live on campus. *Retention:* 93% of full-time freshmen returned.

Freshmen *Admission:* 302 applied, 247 admitted, 112 enrolled. *Average high school GPA:* 3.6. *Test scores:* SAT critical reading scores over 500: 95%; SAT math scores over 500: 77%; SAT writing scores over 500: 90%; SAT critical reading scores over 600: 64%; SAT math scores over 600: 34%; SAT writing scores over 600: 54%; SAT critical reading scores over 700: 24%; SAT math scores over 700: 5%; SAT writing scores over 700: 13%.

Faculty *Total:* 44, 48% full-time, 52% with terminal degrees. *Student/faculty ratio:* 13:1.

Academics *Calendar:* semesters. *Degrees:* associate, bachelor's, and master's. *Special study options:* academic remediation for entering students, accelerated degree program, advanced placement credit, cooperative education, double majors, independent study, internships, services for LD students, study abroad, summer session for credit.

Computers on Campus 60 computers/terminals are available on campus for general student use. Students can access the following: campus intranet, computer help desk, free student e-mail accounts. Wireless service is available via computer labs, libraries, student centers.

Student Life *Housing options:* men-only, women-only. Campus housing is university owned. Freshman campus housing is guaranteed. *Activities and organizations:* drama/theater group, student-run newspaper, choral group, drama, choir, Shield of Roses, Legion of Mary, debate team. *Campus security:* 24-hour emergency response devices, late-night transport/escort service, night patrols by trained security personnel. *Student services:* health clinic, personal/psychological counseling.

Athletics Member USCAA. *Intercollegiate sports:* baseball M, basketball M/W, soccer M/W, volleyball W. *Intramural sports:* basketball M/W, fencing M/W, football M/W, racquetball M/W, rugby M, soccer M/W, table tennis M/W, tennis M/W, volleyball M/W.

Standardized Tests *Required:* SAT or ACT (for admission).

Costs (2011–12) *Comprehensive fee:* $28,090 includes full-time tuition ($19,884), mandatory fees ($550), and room and board ($7656). *Payment plan:* installment. *Waivers:* employees or children of employees.

Financial Aid Of all full-time matriculated undergraduates who enrolled in 2009, 230 applied for aid, 213 were judged to have need, 213 had their need fully met. 145 state and other part-time jobs (averaging $1980). In 2009, 87 non-need-based awards were made. *Average percent of need met:* 90%. *Average financial aid package:* $13,440. *Average need-based loan:* $6360. *Average need-based gift aid:* $7325. *Average non-need-based aid:* $7700. *Average indebtedness upon graduation:* $26,614.

Applying *Options:* electronic application, early admission, early action. *Application fee:* $25. *Required:* essay or personal statement, high school transcript, 2 letters of recommendation. *Recommended:* minimum 3 GPA, interview. *Application deadlines:* 3/1 (freshmen), 3/1 (transfers), 12/1 (early action). *Notification:* 4/1 (freshmen), continuous until 4/1 (transfers), 12/15 (early action).

Freshman Application Contact Christendom College, 134 Christendom Drive, Front Royal, VA 22630-5103. *Phone:* 540-636-2900 Ext. 1290. *Toll-free phone:* 800-877-5456 Ext. 290. *Web site:* http://www.christendom.edu/.

Christopher Newport University

Newport News, Virginia

- **State-supported** comprehensive, founded 1960
- **Suburban** 260-acre campus with easy access to Williamsburg, Virginia Beach
- **Endowment** $12.5 million
- **Coed** 4,778 undergraduate students, 97% full-time, 57% women, 43% men
- 60% of applicants were admitted

Undergraduates 4,634 full-time, 144 part-time. Students come from 27 states and territories; 35 other countries; 7% are from out of state; 8% Black or African American, non-Hispanic/Latino; 4% Hispanic/Latino; 2% Asian, non-His-

panic/Latino; 0.4% Native Hawaiian or other Pacific Islander, non-Hispanic/Latino; 0.3% American Indian or Alaska Native, non-Hispanic/Latino; 4% Two or more races, non-Hispanic/Latino; 0.2% Race/ethnicity unknown; 0.5% international; 4% transferred in; 61% live on campus. *Retention:* 81% of full-time freshmen returned.

Freshmen *Admission:* 7,492 applied, 4,514 admitted, 1,150 enrolled. *Average high school GPA:* 3.64. *Test scores:* SAT critical reading scores over 500: 95%; SAT math scores over 500: 96%; ACT scores over 18: 96%; SAT critical reading scores over 600: 51%; SAT math scores over 600: 53%; ACT scores over 24: 58%; SAT critical reading scores over 700: 8%; SAT math scores over 700: 6%; ACT scores over 30: 6%.

Faculty *Total:* 350, 69% full-time, 67% with terminal degrees. *Student/faculty ratio:* 17:1.

Academics *Calendar:* semesters. *Degrees:* bachelor's and master's. *Special study options:* advanced placement credit, double majors, honors programs, independent study, internships, services for LD students, student-designed majors, study abroad, summer session for credit. *ROTC:* Army (b).

Computers on Campus 450 computers/terminals are available on campus for general student use. Students can access the following: campus intranet, computer help desk, free student e-mail accounts, online (class) grades, online (class) registration, online (class) schedules, online degree audit; 80% of campus is wireless. Campuswide network is available. 100% of college-owned or -operated housing units are wired for high-speed Internet access. Wireless service is available via classrooms, computer centers, computer labs, dorm rooms, learning centers, libraries, student centers.

Student Life *Housing:* on-campus residence required through junior year. *Options:* coed, disabled students. Campus housing is university owned and leased by the school. Freshman campus housing is guaranteed. *Activities and organizations:* drama/theater group, student-run newspaper, radio and television station, choral group, marching band, student government, Campus Activities Board, Multicultural Student Association, Intervarsity Christian Fellowship, Residence Hall Association, national fraternities, national sororities. *Campus security:* 24-hour emergency response devices and patrols, late-night transport/escort service, controlled dormitory access, Campus Police; Emergency Notification System; Crime Prevention Programs. *Student services:* health clinic, personal/psychological counseling.

Athletics Member NCAA. All Division III. *Intercollegiate sports:* baseball M, basketball M/W, cheerleading M/W, cross-country running M/W, field hockey W, football M, golf M, lacrosse M(c)/W(c), sailing M/W, soccer M/W, softball W, tennis M/W, track and field M/W, volleyball W. *Intramural sports:* badminton M/W, basketball M/W, equestrian sports M(c)/W(c), football M/W, ice hockey M(c), lacrosse M(c), rock climbing M(c)/W(c), rugby M(c), soccer M/W, softball M/W, swimming and diving M(c)/W(c), table tennis M(c)/W(c), tennis M/W, ultimate Frisbee M(c)/W(c), volleyball M(c)/W(c).

Standardized Tests *Required for some:* SAT or ACT (for admission).

Costs (2010–11) *Tuition:* state resident $9250 full-time, $385 per semester hour part-time; nonresident $17,992 full-time, $665 per semester hour part-time. Full-time tuition and fees vary according to course load. Part-time tuition and fees vary according to course load. *Required fees:* $3970 full-time, $165 per semester hour part-time. *Room and board:* $9540; room only: $6420. Room and board charges vary according to board plan and housing facility. *Payment plan:* installment. *Waivers:* senior citizens and employees or children of employees.

Financial Aid Of all full-time matriculated undergraduates who enrolled in 2009, 3,047 applied for aid, 2,160 were judged to have need, 339 had their need fully met. 117 Federal Work-Study jobs (averaging $833). 1,762 state and other part-time jobs (averaging $1177). In 2009, 482 non-need-based awards were made. *Average percent of need met:* 69%. *Average financial aid package:* $8099. *Average need-based loan:* $4033. *Average need-based gift aid:* $5087. *Average non-need-based aid:* $1772. *Average indebtedness upon graduation:* $21,572.

Applying *Options:* electronic application, early admission, early decision, early action, deferred entrance. *Application fee:* $50. *Required:* high school transcript, minimum 3 GPA. *Required for some:* essay or personal statement, 3 letters of recommendation, interview. *Application deadlines:* 2/1 (freshmen), 3/1 (transfers), 12/1 (early action). *Early decision deadline:* 11/15. *Notification:* continuous (freshmen), 5/21 (transfers), 12/15 (early decision), 1/15 (early action).

Freshman Application Contact Mr. Curtis Davidson, Senior Associate Director of Admissions, Christopher Newport University, 1 University Place, Newport News, VA 23606-2998. *Phone:* 757-594-7015. *Toll-free phone:* 800-333-4268. *Fax:* 757-594-7333. *E-mail:* admit@cnu.edu. *Web site:* http://www.cnu.edu/.

See page 1216 for the College Close-Up.

The College of William and Mary
Williamsburg, Virginia

- **State-supported** university, founded 1693
- **Small-town** 1200-acre campus with easy access to Richmond
- **Endowment** $539.5 million
- **Coed** 5,898 undergraduate students, 99% full-time, 55% women, 45% men
- **Most difficult** entrance level, 32% of applicants were admitted

Undergraduates 5,842 full-time, 56 part-time. Students come from 46 states and territories; 32 other countries; 32% are from out of state; 7% Black or African American, non-Hispanic/Latino; 8% Hispanic/Latino; 7% Asian, non-Hispanic/Latino; 0.1% Native Hawaiian or other Pacific Islander, non-Hispanic/Latino; 0.6% American Indian or Alaska Native, non-Hispanic/Latino; 2% Two or more races, non-Hispanic/Latino; 17% Race/ethnicity unknown; 3% international; 3% transferred in; 74% live on campus. *Retention:* 95% of full-time freshmen returned.

Freshmen *Admission:* 12,537 applied, 3,978 admitted, 1,398 enrolled. *Average high school GPA:* 4.05. *Test scores:* SAT critical reading scores over 500: 98%; SAT math scores over 500: 99%; SAT writing scores over 500: 98%; ACT scores over 18: 100%; SAT critical reading scores over 600: 86%; SAT math scores over 600: 86%; SAT writing scores over 600: 85%; ACT scores over 24: 95%; SAT critical reading scores over 700: 42%; SAT math scores over 700: 36%; SAT writing scores over 700: 35%; ACT scores over 30: 61%.

Academics *Calendar:* semesters. *Degrees:* bachelor's, master's, doctoral-professional, doctoral-research/scholarship, and post-master's certificates. *Special study options:* accelerated degree program, advanced placement credit, double majors, honors programs, independent study, internships, off-campus study, part-time degree program, services for LD students, student-designed majors, study abroad, summer session for credit. *ROTC:* Army (b). *Unusual degree programs:* 3-2 engineering with Columbia University, Rensselaer Polytechnic Institute, Washington University in St. Louis.

Computers on Campus 350 computers/terminals and 6,500 ports are available on campus for general student use. Students can access the following: campus intranet, computer help desk, free student e-mail accounts, online (class) grades, online (class) registration, online (class) schedules. Campuswide network is available. 100% of college-owned or -operated housing units are wired for high-speed Internet access. Wireless service is available via entire campus.

Student Life *Housing:* on-campus residence required for freshman year. *Options:* coed. Campus housing is university owned and leased by the school. Freshman campus housing is guaranteed. *Activities and organizations:* drama/theater group, student-run newspaper, radio and television station, choral group, Alma Mater Productions, College Partnership for Kids, Student Assembly, Flat Hat (student newspaper), Resident Hall Association, national fraternities, national sororities. *Campus security:* 24-hour emergency response devices and patrols, late-night transport/escort service, controlled dormitory access, Certified police officers, accredited police department, foot, bicycle, and patrols provided by marked and unmarked police vehicles. *Student services:* health clinic, personal/psychological counseling, legal services.

Athletics Member NCAA. All Division I except football (Division I-AA). *Intercollegiate sports:* baseball M(s), basketball M(s)/W(s), cross-country running M(s)/W(s), field hockey W(s), golf M(s)/W(s), gymnastics M(s)/W(s), lacrosse W(s), soccer M(s)/W(s), swimming and diving M/W, tennis M(s)/W(s), track and field M(s)/W(s), volleyball W(s). *Intramural sports:* badminton M(c)/W(c), baseball M(c), basketball M/W, bowling M/W, crew M(c)/W(c), cross-country running M(c)/W(c), equestrian sports M(c)/W(c), fencing M(c)/W(c), field hockey W(c), football M/W, golf M(c)/W(c), gymnastics M(c)/W(c), ice hockey M(c), lacrosse M(c)/W(c), racquetball M(c)/W(c), rock climbing M(c)/W(c), rugby M(c)/W(c), sailing M(c)/W(c), soccer M/W, softball M/W, squash M(c)/W(c), swimming and diving M(c)/W(c), table tennis M(c)/W(c), tennis M(c)/W(c), ultimate Frisbee M(c)/W(c), volleyball M/W, water polo M(c)/W(c), weight lifting M/W, wrestling M(c).

Standardized Tests *Required:* SAT or ACT (for admission). *Recommended:* SAT Subject Tests (for admission).

Costs (2010–11) *One-time required fee:* $157. *Tuition:* state resident $7523 full-time, $260 per credit hour part-time; nonresident $28,547 full-time, $920 per credit hour part-time. *Required fees:* $4665 full-time. *Room and board:* $8684; room only: $5232. Room and board charges vary according to board plan and housing facility. *Payment plan:* installment. *Waivers:* senior citizens.

Financial Aid Of all full-time matriculated undergraduates who enrolled in 2008, 3,005 applied for aid, 1,902 were judged to have need, 326 had their need fully met. 98 Federal Work-Study jobs (averaging $960). In 2008, 285 non-need-based awards were made. *Average percent of need met:* 79%. *Average financial aid package:* $15,606. *Average need-based loan:* $4467. *Average need-based gift aid:* $11,555. *Average non-need-based aid:* $5977. *Average indebtedness upon graduation:* $21,367.

Applying *Options:* electronic application, early admission, early decision, deferred entrance. *Application fee:* $60. *Required:* essay or personal statement, high school transcript, 1 letter of recommendation. *Recommended:* 2 letters of recommendation. *Application deadlines:* 1/1 (freshmen), 3/1 (transfers). *Early decision deadline:* 11/1. *Notification:* 4/1 (freshmen), 5/1 (transfers), 12/1 (early decision).

Freshman Application Contact Timothy Wolfe, Dean of Admissions, The College of William and Mary, PO Box 8795, Williamsburg, VA 23187-8795. *Phone:* 757-221-4223. *Fax:* 757-221-1242. *E-mail:* admission@wm.edu. *Web site:* http://www.wm.edu/.

Culinary Institute of Virginia
Norfolk, Virginia

- **Proprietary** 4-year, administratively affiliated with ECPI College of Technology
- **Urban** campus
- **Coed**
- **Minimally difficult** entrance level

Academics *Degrees:* certificates, diplomas, associate, and bachelor's.

Student Life *Campus security:* trained evening security personnel.

Financial Aid *Of all full-time matriculated undergraduates who enrolled in 2002,* 633 applied for aid, 569 were judged to have need, 491 had their need fully met. 206 Federal Work-Study jobs (averaging $2164). *In 2002,* 24 non-need-based awards were made. *Average percent of need met:* 67. *Average financial aid package:* $10,866. *Average need-based loan:* $5398. *Average need-based gift aid:* $4015. *Average non-need-based aid:* $3025. *Average indebtedness upon graduation:* $13,277.

Applying *Options:* electronic application. *Application fee:* $100. *Required:* interview.

Freshman Application Contact Director of Admissions, Culinary Institute of Virginia, 2428 Almeda Avenue, Suite 316, Norfolk, VA 23513. *Phone:* 757-858-2433. *Toll-free phone:* 866-619-CHEF. *E-mail:* hsadmissions@chefva.com. *Web site:* http://www.chefva.com/.

DeVry University
Arlington, Virginia

- **Proprietary** comprehensive, founded 2001, part of DeVry University
- **Coed** 749 undergraduate students, 46% full-time, 29% women, 71% men
- **Minimally difficult** entrance level

Undergraduates 347 full-time, 402 part-time. 60% are from out of state; 44% Black or African American, non-Hispanic/Latino; 11% Hispanic/Latino; 3% Asian, non-Hispanic/Latino; 0.5% Native Hawaiian or other Pacific Islander, non-Hispanic/Latino; 0.4% American Indian or Alaska Native, non-Hispanic/Latino; 0.8% Two or more races, non-Hispanic/Latino; 22% Race/ethnicity unknown; 1% international; 21% transferred in.

Freshmen *Admission:* 144 enrolled.

Faculty *Total:* 158, 9% full-time. *Student/faculty ratio:* 10:1.

Academics *Calendar:* semesters. *Degrees:* associate, bachelor's, and master's. *Special study options:* academic remediation for entering students, accelerated degree program, adult/continuing education programs, advanced placement credit, distance learning, part-time degree program, services for LD students, summer session for credit.

Computers on Campus Students can access the following: online (class) registration. Campuswide network is available.

Student Life *Housing:* college housing not available.

Costs (2010–11) *Tuition:* $14,766 full-time, $580 per credit hour part-time. Full-time tuition and fees vary according to course load. Part-time tuition and fees vary according to course load. *Required fees:* $60 full-time, $30 per term part-time. *Payment plans:* installment, deferred payment. *Waivers:* employees or children of employees.

Financial Aid Of all full-time matriculated undergraduates who enrolled in 2007, 175 applied for aid, 164 were judged to have need, 9 had their need fully met. In 2007, 21 non-need-based awards were made. *Average percent of need met:* 38%. *Average financial aid package:* $11,581. *Average need-based loan:* $7979. *Average need-based gift aid:* $5610. *Average non-need-based aid:* $18,172. *Average indebtedness upon graduation:* $12,479.

Applying *Options:* electronic application, deferred entrance. *Application fee:* $50. *Required:* high school transcript, interview. *Application deadlines:* rolling (freshmen), rolling (transfers). *Notification:* continuous (freshmen), continuous (transfers).

Freshman Application Contact DeVry University, 2450 Crystal Drive, Arlington, VA 22202. *Phone:* 703-414-4000. *Web site:* http://www.devry.edu/

DeVry University
Chesapeake, Virginia

Admissions Office Contact DeVry University, 1317 Executive Boulevard, Suite 100, Chesapeake, VA 23320-3671. *Web site:* http://www.devry.edu/.

DeVry University

Manassas, Virginia

Admissions Office Contact DeVry University, 10432 Balls Ford Road, Suite 130, Manassas, VA 20109-3173. *Web site:* http://www.devry.edu/.

Eastern Mennonite University

Harrisonburg, Virginia

- **Independent Mennonite** comprehensive, founded 1917
- **Small-town** 93-acre campus
- **Endowment** $14.9 million
- **Coed**
- **Moderately difficult** entrance level

Faculty *Student/faculty ratio:* 7:1.

Academics *Calendar:* semesters. *Degrees:* certificates, associate, bachelor's, master's, doctoral-professional, and postbachelor's certificates.

Student Life *Campus security:* 24-hour emergency response devices, controlled dormitory access, night watchman.

Athletics Member NCAA. All Division III.

Standardized Tests *Required:* SAT or ACT (for admission).

Costs (2010–11) *Comprehensive fee:* $33,100 includes full-time tuition ($25,060) and room and board ($8040). Part-time tuition: $1050 per credit hour. Part-time tuition and fees vary according to course load. *Room and board:* Room and board charges vary according to board plan, housing facility, and student level.

Financial Aid *Of all full-time matriculated undergraduates who enrolled in 2003,* 735 applied for aid, 652 were judged to have need, 246 had their need fully met. 326 Federal Work-Study jobs (averaging $1787). *In 2003,* 82 non-need-based awards were made. *Average percent of need met:* 87. *Average financial aid package:* $15,530. *Average need-based loan:* $5665. *Average need-based gift aid:* $5520. *Average non-need-based aid:* $7765. *Average indebtedness upon graduation:* $18,208.

Applying *Options:* electronic application, deferred entrance. *Application fee:* $25. *Required:* high school transcript, minimum 2.2 GPA, statement of commitment. *Required for some:* 2 letters of recommendation. *Recommended:* interview.

Freshman Application Contact Mrs. Stephanie C. Shafer, Director of Admissions, Eastern Mennonite University, 1200 Park Road, Harrisonburg, VA 22802-2462. *Phone:* 540-432-4118. *Toll-free phone:* 800-368-2665. *Fax:* 540-432-4444. *E-mail:* admiss@emu.edu. *Web site:* http://www.emu.edu/.

ECPI College of Technology

Glen Allen, Virginia

Freshman Application Contact Mr. Jacob Pope, Director, ECPI College of Technology, 4305 Cox Road, Glen Allen, VA 23060. *Phone:* 804-934-0100. *Toll-free phone:* 800-986-1200. *Fax:* 804-934-0054. *E-mail:* jpope@ecpi.edu. *Web site:* http://www.ecpi.edu/.

ECPI College of Technology

Manassas, Virginia

Admissions Office Contact ECPI College of Technology, 10021 Balls Ford Road, Manassas, VA 20109. *Toll-free phone:* 866-708-6172. *Web site:* http://www.ecpi.edu/.

ECPI College of Technology

Newport News, Virginia

Freshman Application Contact Ms. Cheryl Lokey, Provost, ECPI College of Technology, 1001 Omni Boulevard, #100, Newport News, VA 23606. *Phone:* 757-838-9191. *Toll-free phone:* 866-499-0335. *Fax:* 757-829-5351. *Web site:* http://www.ecpi.edu/.

ECPI College of Technology

Richmond, Virginia

Freshman Application Contact Director, ECPI College of Technology, 800 Moorefield Park Drive, Richmond, VA 23236. *Phone:* 804-330-5533. *Toll-free phone:* 800-986-1200. *Fax:* 804-330-5577. *E-mail:* agerard@ecpi.edu. *Web site:* http://www.ecpi.edu/.

ECPI College of Technology

Virginia Beach, Virginia

- **Proprietary** 4-year, founded 1966
- **Suburban** 8-acre campus
- **Coed** 13,717 undergraduate students, 100% full-time, 58% women, 42% men
- **Moderately difficult** entrance level, 80% of applicants were admitted

Undergraduates 13,717 full-time. Students come from 6 states and territories; 10% are from out of state; 41% Black or African American, non-Hispanic/Latino; 5% Hispanic/Latino; 3% Asian, non-Hispanic/Latino; 0.6% American Indian or Alaska Native, non-Hispanic/Latino; 0.7% Two or more races, non-Hispanic/Latino; 8% Race/ethnicity unknown. *Retention:* 73% of full-time freshmen returned.

Freshmen *Admission:* 1,328 applied, 1,063 admitted, 850 enrolled.

Faculty *Total:* 1,371, 41% full-time. *Student/faculty ratio:* 17:1.

Academics *Calendar:* continuous. *Degrees:* certificates, diplomas, associate, and bachelor's. *Special study options:* academic remediation for entering students, accelerated degree program, adult/continuing education programs, advanced placement credit, distance learning, double majors, freshman honors college, honors programs, independent study, internships, off-campus study, part-time degree program, study abroad, summer session for credit.

Computers on Campus 6,500 computers/terminals are available on campus for general student use. Students can access the following: campus intranet, computer help desk, free student e-mail accounts, online (class) grades, online (class) registration, online (class) schedules. Campuswide network is available. Wireless service is available via libraries.

Student Life *Housing options:* Campus housing is provided by a third party. *Activities and organizations:* Student Electronic Technicians Association (SETA), Institute of Electrical & Electronic Engineers (IEEE), Phi Theta Kappa Honor Society, Information Technology Exchange (ITE), Medical Student Association, national fraternities, national sororities. *Campus security:* building and parking lot security. *Student services:* personal/psychological counseling.

Standardized Tests *Required:* ACT (for admission). *Recommended:* SAT (for admission), SAT or ACT (for admission), SAT Subject Tests (for admission).

Financial Aid Of all full-time matriculated undergraduates who enrolled in 2009, 8,775 applied for aid.

Applying *Options:* electronic application, deferred entrance. *Application fee:* $45. *Required:* high school transcript, interview. *Notification:* continuous (freshmen), continuous (transfers).

Freshman Application Contact Mrs. Bernadette Rozman Bellas, Vice President, Accreditation and Regulatory Affairs, ECPI College of Technology, 5555 Greenwich Road, Suite 100, Virginia Beach, VA 23462. *Phone:* 757-671-7171. *Toll-free phone:* 866-499-0336. *Fax:* 757-671-8661. *E-mail:* rballance@ecpi.edu. *Web site:* http://www.ecpi.edu/.

Emory & Henry College

Emory, Virginia

- **Independent United Methodist** comprehensive, founded 1836
- **Rural** 331-acre campus
- **Endowment** $70.7 million
- **Coed** 908 undergraduate students, 96% full-time, 48% women, 52% men
- **Moderately difficult** entrance level, 70% of applicants were admitted

Undergraduates 871 full-time, 37 part-time. Students come from 24 states and territories; 6 other countries; 31% are from out of state; 9% Black or African American, non-Hispanic/Latino; 1% Hispanic/Latino; 0.6% Asian, non-Hispanic/Latino; 0.7% American Indian or Alaska Native, non-Hispanic/Latino; 7% Race/ethnicity unknown; 0.2% international; 73% live on campus. *Retention:* 71% of full-time freshmen returned.

Freshmen *Admission:* 1,308 applied, 920 admitted, 300 enrolled. *Average high school GPA:* 3.47.

Faculty *Total:* 127, 55% full-time, 61% with terminal degrees. *Student/faculty ratio:* 10:1.

Academics *Calendar:* semesters. *Degrees:* bachelor's and master's. *Special study options:* advanced placement credit, cooperative education, double majors, honors programs, independent study, internships, services for LD students, student-designed majors, study abroad, summer session for credit.

Computers on Campus 250 computers/terminals are available on campus for general student use. Students can access the following: computer help desk, free student e-mail accounts, online (class) grades, online (class) registration, online (class) schedules. Campuswide network is available. Wireless service is available via entire campus.

Student Life *Housing:* on-campus residence required for freshman year. *Options:* coed, men-only, women-only, disabled students. Campus housing is university owned. Freshman campus housing is guaranteed. *Activities and organizations:* drama/theater group, student-run newspaper, radio and television station, choral group, Alpha Phi Omega, intramural sports, Campus Christian Fellowship, Psychology Club, student radio station. *Campus security:* 24-hour emergency response devices and patrols, late-night transport/escort service, controlled dormitory access. *Student services:* health clinic, personal/psychological counseling.

Athletics Member NCAA. All Division III. *Intercollegiate sports:* baseball M, basketball M/W, cross-country running M/W, football M, golf M, soccer M/W, softball W, tennis M/W, volleyball W. *Intramural sports:* basketball M/W, cheerleading W(c), football M/W, golf M/W, racquetball M/W, skiing (cross-country) M(c)/W(c), skiing (downhill) M(c), soccer M/W, softball M/W, table tennis M/W, tennis M/W, ultimate Frisbee M/W, volleyball M/W, water polo M/W, weight lifting M/W.

Standardized Tests *Required:* SAT or ACT (for admission).

Costs (2010–11) *Comprehensive fee:* $34,570 includes full-time tuition ($26,000) and room and board ($8570). Full-time tuition and fees vary according to course load and degree level. Part-time tuition: $1040 per credit hour. Part-time tuition and fees vary according to course load and degree level. *College room only:* $4140. Room and board charges vary according to board plan. *Payment plan:* installment. *Waivers:* employees or children of employees.

Financial Aid Of all full-time matriculated undergraduates who enrolled in 2009, 774 applied for aid, 717 were judged to have need, 106 had their need fully met. 231 Federal Work-Study jobs (averaging $1071). In 2009, 149 non-need-based awards were made. *Average percent of need met:* 87%. *Average financial aid package:* $24,225. *Average need-based loan:* $4334. *Average need-based gift aid:* $20,940. *Average non-need-based aid:* $12,173. *Average indebtedness upon graduation:* $23,049.

Applying *Options:* electronic application, early action, deferred entrance. *Application fee:* $30. *Required:* high school transcript, 1 letter of recommendation. *Recommended:* essay or personal statement, interview. *Application deadlines:* rolling (freshmen), rolling (transfers), 12/1 (early action). *Notification:* continuous (freshmen), continuous (transfers), 1/1 (early action).

Freshman Application Contact Emory & Henry College, PO Box 947, Emory, VA 24327-0947. *Phone:* 276-944-6133. *Toll-free phone:* 800-848-5493. *Web site:* http://www.ehc.edu/.

See page 1278 for the College Close-Up.

Ferrum College
Ferrum, Virginia

- **Independent United Methodist** 4-year, founded 1913
- **Rural** 720-acre campus
- **Endowment** $35.8 million
- **Coed** 1,484 undergraduate students, 98% full-time, 47% women, 53% men
- **Minimally difficult** entrance level, 76% of applicants were admitted

Undergraduates 1,458 full-time, 26 part-time. Students come from 27 states and territories; 7 other countries; 15% are from out of state; 33% Black or African American, non-Hispanic/Latino; 3% Hispanic/Latino; 0.9% Asian, non-Hispanic/Latino; 0.3% Native Hawaiian or other Pacific Islander, non-Hispanic/Latino; 0.2% American Indian or Alaska Native, non-Hispanic/Latino; 3% Two or more races, non-Hispanic/Latino; 9% Race/ethnicity unknown; 0.7% international; 5% transferred in. *Retention:* 59% of full-time freshmen returned.

Freshmen *Admission:* 2,865 applied, 2,181 admitted, 565 enrolled. *Average high school GPA:* 2.8. *Test scores:* SAT critical reading scores over 500: 29%; SAT math scores over 500: 29%; ACT scores over 18: 9%; SAT critical reading scores over 600: 5%; SAT math scores over 600: 3%.

Faculty *Total:* 123, 59% full-time, 58% with terminal degrees. *Student/faculty ratio:* 17:1.

Academics *Calendar:* semesters. *Degree:* bachelor's. *Special study options:* academic remediation for entering students, adult/continuing education programs, advanced placement credit, double majors, honors programs, internships, services for LD students, student-designed majors, study abroad, summer session for credit. *Unusual degree programs:* 3-2 Sherman College of Straight Chiropractic.

Computers on Campus Students can access the following: campus intranet, computer help desk, free student e-mail accounts, online (class) grades, online (class) schedules. Campuswide network is available. Wireless service is available via entire campus.

Student Life *Housing:* on-campus residence required through senior year. *Options:* coed, women-only, disabled students. Campus housing is university owned. Freshman campus housing is guaranteed. *Activities and organizations:* drama/theater group, student-run newspaper, radio station, choral group, Student Government Association, Agriculture Club, BACCHUS, Panther Productions, African American Student Association, Students in Free Enterprise

(SIFE). *Campus security:* 24-hour emergency response devices and patrols, student patrols, late-night transport/escort service, controlled dormitory access. *Student services:* health clinic, personal/psychological counseling.

Athletics Member NCAA. All Division III. *Intercollegiate sports:* baseball M, basketball M/W, cheerleading M/W, cross-country running M/W, football M, golf M, lacrosse M/W, soccer M/W, softball W, swimming and diving W, tennis M/W, volleyball W. *Intramural sports:* basketball M/W, football M/W, racquetball M/W, softball M/W, tennis M/W.

Standardized Tests *Required:* SAT or ACT (for admission).

Costs (2010–11) *Comprehensive fee:* $33,025 includes full-time tuition ($24,900), mandatory fees ($45), and room and board ($8080). Full-time tuition and fees vary according to course load. Part-time tuition: $500 per credit hour. Part-time tuition and fees vary according to course load. *Room and board:* Room and board charges vary according to board plan and housing facility. *Payment plan:* installment. *Waivers:* employees or children of employees.

Financial Aid Of all full-time matriculated undergraduates who enrolled in 2009, 1,455 applied for aid, 1,346 were judged to have need. 834 Federal Work-Study jobs (averaging $2042). 83 state and other part-time jobs (averaging $1778). In 2009, 143 non-need-based awards were made. *Average percent of need met:* 64%. *Average financial aid package:* $19,984. *Average need-based loan:* $3824. *Average need-based gift aid:* $7438. *Average non-need-based aid:* $6899. *Average indebtedness upon graduation:* $30,460.

Applying *Options:* electronic application, early admission, deferred entrance. *Application fee:* $25. *Required:* high school transcript. *Required for some:* interview. *Recommended:* essay or personal statement, minimum 2 GPA, 2 letters of recommendation, interview. *Application deadline:* rolling (freshmen). *Notification:* continuous (freshmen).

Freshman Application Contact Ms. Gilda Q. Woods, Dean of Admissions, Ferrum College, Spilman-Daniel House, PO Box 1000, Ferrum, VA 24088-9001. *Phone:* 540-365-4290. *Toll-free phone:* 800-868-9797. *Fax:* 540-365-4266. *E-mail:* admissions@ferrum.edu. *Web site:* http://www.ferrum.edu/.

George Mason University
Fairfax, Virginia

- **State-supported** university, founded 1957
- **Suburban** 806-acre campus with easy access to Washington, D.C.
- **Endowment** $41.9 million
- **Coed**
- **Moderately difficult** entrance level

Faculty *Student/faculty ratio:* 16:1.

Academics *Calendar:* semesters. *Degrees:* bachelor's, master's, doctoral-professional, doctoral-research/scholarship, post-master's, and postbachelor's certificates.

Student Life *Campus security:* 24-hour emergency response devices and patrols, student patrols, late-night transport/escort service, controlled dormitory access.

Athletics Member NCAA. All Division I.

Standardized Tests *Required for some:* SAT or ACT (for admission). *Recommended:* SAT and SAT Subject Tests or ACT (for admission).

Costs (2010–11) *Tuition:* state resident $6320 full-time, $263 per credit hour part-time; nonresident $23,084 full-time, $962 per credit hour part-time. Full-time tuition and fees vary according to course load. Part-time tuition and fees vary according to course load. *Required fees:* $2364 full-time, $99 per credit hour part-time. *Room and board:* $8220; room only: $4720. Room and board charges vary according to board plan and housing facility. *Payment plans:* installment, deferred payment.

Financial Aid *Of all full-time matriculated undergraduates who enrolled in 2009,* 9,912 applied for aid, 7,689 were judged to have need, 649 had their need fully met. 275 Federal Work-Study jobs (averaging $1394). *In 2009,* 444 non-need-based awards were made. *Average percent of need met:* 67. *Average financial aid package:* $11,715. *Average need-based loan:* $4350. *Average need-based gift aid:* $6909. *Average non-need-based aid:* $5987. *Average indebtedness upon graduation:* $22,219.

Applying *Options:* electronic application, early admission, early action, deferred entrance. *Application fee:* $75. *Required:* essay or personal statement, high school transcript, minimum 2 GPA. *Required for some:* 3 letters of recommendation, score-optional students must submit 3 letters. *Recommended:* minimum 3 GPA.

Freshman Application Contact Mr. Eddie Tallent, Assistant Dean, Executive Director of Undergraduate Admissions, George Mason University, Fairfax, VA 22030-4444. *Phone:* 703-993-2398. *E-mail:* etallent@gmu.edu. *Web site:* http://www.gmu.edu/.

Hampden-Sydney College

Hampden-Sydney, Virginia

- **Independent** 4-year, founded 1776, affiliated with Presbyterian Church (U.S.A.)
- **Rural** 1340-acre campus with easy access to Richmond
- **Endowment** $118.3 million
- **Men only** 1,058 undergraduate students, 100% full-time
- **Moderately difficult** entrance level, 54% of applicants were admitted

Undergraduates 1,058 full-time. Students come from 28 states and territories; 17 other countries; 31% are from out of state; 6% Black or African American, non-Hispanic/Latino; 2% Hispanic/Latino; 0.7% Asian, non-Hispanic/Latino; 0.6% American Indian or Alaska Native, non-Hispanic/Latino; 1% Two or more races, non-Hispanic/Latino; 3% Race/ethnicity unknown; 2% international; 2% transferred in; 95% live on campus. *Retention:* 78% of full-time freshmen returned.

Freshmen *Admission:* 2,528 applied, 1,365 admitted, 315 enrolled. *Average high school GPA:* 3.4. *Test scores:* SAT critical reading scores over 500: 77%; SAT math scores over 500: 82%; SAT critical reading scores over 600: 29%; SAT math scores over 600: 34%; SAT critical reading scores over 700: 6%; SAT math scores over 700: 5%.

Faculty *Total:* 113, 87% full-time, 82% with terminal degrees. *Student/faculty ratio:* 10:1.

Academics *Calendar:* semesters. *Degree:* bachelor's. *Special study options:* academic remediation for entering students, advanced placement credit, double majors, honors programs, independent study, internships, off-campus study, study abroad, summer session for credit. *ROTC:* Army (c). *Unusual degree programs:* 3-2 engineering with University of Virginia.

Computers on Campus 200 computers/terminals are available on campus for general student use. Students can access the following: campus intranet, computer help desk, free student e-mail accounts, online (class) grades, online (class) registration, online (class) schedules. Campuswide network is available. 100% of college-owned or -operated housing units are wired for high-speed Internet access. Wireless service is available via classrooms, computer centers, computer labs, libraries, student centers.

Student Life *Housing:* on-campus residence required through senior year. *Options:* men-only. Campus housing is university owned. Freshman campus housing is guaranteed. *Activities and organizations:* drama/theater group, student-run newspaper, radio station, choral group, Republican Society, Pre-Health Society, Outsiders Club, Tiger Athletic Club, Pre-Law Society, national fraternities. *Campus security:* 24-hour emergency response devices and patrols. *Student services:* health clinic, personal/psychological counseling.

Athletics Member NCAA. All Division III. *Intercollegiate sports:* baseball M, basketball M, crew M(c), cross-country running M, fencing M(c), football M, golf M, lacrosse M, riflery M(c), rugby M(c), soccer M, tennis M, ultimate Frisbee M(c). *Intramural sports:* basketball M, football M, soccer M, softball M, volleyball M.

Standardized Tests *Required:* SAT or ACT (for admission). *Recommended:* SAT Subject Tests (for admission).

Costs (2010–11) *Comprehensive fee:* $42,490 includes full-time tuition ($30,994), mandatory fees ($1370), and room and board ($10,126). *Room and board:* Room and board charges vary according to board plan and housing facility. *Payment plan:* installment. *Waivers:* employees or children of employees.

Financial Aid Of all full-time matriculated undergraduates who enrolled in 2009, 695 applied for aid, 590 were judged to have need, 158 had their need fully met. 356 Federal Work-Study jobs (averaging $1699). In 2009, 435 non-need-based awards were made. *Average percent of need met:* 81%. *Average financial aid package:* $25,250. *Average need-based loan:* $4892. *Average need-based gift aid:* $20,089. *Average non-need-based aid:* $10,815. *Average indebtedness upon graduation:* $25,426.

Applying *Options:* electronic application, early admission, early decision, early action. *Application fee:* $30. *Required:* essay or personal statement, high school transcript, minimum 2 GPA, 2 letters of recommendation. *Recommended:* minimum 3 GPA, interview. *Application deadlines:* 3/1 (freshmen), 7/1 (transfers), 1/15 (early action). *Early decision deadline:* 11/15. *Notification:* 4/15 (freshmen), 7/31 (transfers), 12/15 (early decision), 2/15 (early action).

Freshman Application Contact Ms. Anita Garland, Dean of Admissions, Hampden-Sydney College, PO Box 667, Hampden-Sydney, VA 23943-0667. *Phone:* 434-223-6120. *Toll-free phone:* 800-755-0733. *Fax:* 434-223-6346. *E-mail:* hsapp@hsc.edu. *Web site:* http://www.hsc.edu/.

Hampton University

Hampton, Virginia

- **Independent** comprehensive, founded 1868
- **Urban** 210-acre campus with easy access to Norfolk
- **Endowment** $185.8 million
- **Coed**
- **Moderately difficult** entrance level

Faculty *Student/faculty ratio:* 13:1.

Academics *Calendar:* semesters. *Degrees:* certificates, associate, bachelor's, master's, doctoral-professional, doctoral-research/scholarship, and post-master's certificates.

Student Life *Campus security:* 24-hour emergency response devices and patrols, controlled dormitory access, emergency call boxes.

Athletics Member NCAA. All Division I.

Standardized Tests *Required:* SAT or ACT (for admission).

Costs (2010–11) *Comprehensive fee:* $26,122 includes full-time tuition ($16,238), mandatory fees ($1836), and room and board ($8048). Full-time tuition and fees vary according to course load, degree level, and program. Part-time tuition: $410 per credit hour. *College room only:* $4186. Room and board charges vary according to board plan and housing facility.

Financial Aid *Of all full-time matriculated undergraduates who enrolled in 2009,* 2,524 applied for aid, 2,230 were judged to have need, 1,053 had their need fully met. 127 Federal Work-Study jobs (averaging $1127). 18 state and other part-time jobs (averaging $1179). *In 2009,* 102 non-need-based awards were made. *Average percent of need met:* 51. *Average financial aid package:* $4563. *Average need-based loan:* $3450. *Average need-based gift aid:* $4035. *Average non-need-based aid:* $12,587. *Average indebtedness upon graduation:* $11,334. *Financial aid deadline:* 4/15.

Applying *Options:* electronic application, early admission, deferred entrance. *Application fee:* $35. *Required:* essay or personal statement, high school transcript, minimum 2.5 GPA, 3 letters of recommendation.

Freshman Application Contact Ms. Patra Johnson, Director, Freshman Studies, Hampton University, 200 Student Center, Hampton University, Hampton, VA 23668. *Phone:* 757-727-5901. *Toll-free phone:* 800-624-3328. *Fax:* 757-727-5095. *E-mail:* patra.johnson@hamptonu.edu. *Web site:* http://www.hamptonu.edu/.

Hollins University

Roanoke, Virginia

- **Independent** comprehensive, founded 1842
- **Suburban** 475-acre campus
- **Endowment** $128.7 million
- **Undergraduate: women only; graduate: coed** 775 undergraduate students, 96% full-time, 100% women
- **Moderately difficult** entrance level, 89% of applicants were admitted

Undergraduates 747 full-time, 28 part-time. Students come from 32 states and territories; 13 other countries; 43% are from out of state; 10% Black or African American, non-Hispanic/Latino; 4% Hispanic/Latino; 1% Asian, non-Hispanic/Latino; 0.1% Native Hawaiian or other Pacific Islander, non-Hispanic/Latino; 0.7% American Indian or Alaska Native, non-Hispanic/Latino; 3% Two or more races, non-Hispanic/Latino; 4% international; 3% transferred in; 78% live on campus. *Retention:* 74% of full-time freshmen returned.

Freshmen *Admission:* 687 applied, 611 admitted, 185 enrolled. *Average high school GPA:* 3.45. *Test scores:* SAT critical reading scores over 500: 76%; SAT math scores over 500: 63%; SAT writing scores over 500: 76%; ACT scores over 18: 94%; SAT critical reading scores over 600: 45%; SAT math scores over 600: 22%; SAT writing scores over 600: 36%; ACT scores over 24: 53%; SAT critical reading scores over 700: 12%; SAT math scores over 700: 4%; SAT writing scores over 700: 7%; ACT scores over 30: 11%.

Faculty *Total:* 99, 72% full-time, 88% with terminal degrees. *Student/faculty ratio:* 11:1.

Academics *Calendar:* 4-1-4. *Degrees:* bachelor's, master's, post-master's, and postbachelor's certificates. *Special study options:* accelerated degree program, adult/continuing education programs, advanced placement credit, double majors, independent study, internships, off-campus study, part-time degree program, services for LD students, student-designed majors, study abroad.

Computers on Campus 100 computers/terminals and 100 ports are available on campus for general student use. Students can access the following: campus intranet, computer help desk, free student e-mail accounts, online (class) grades, online (class) registration, online (class) schedules, applications software. Campuswide network is available. 100% of college-owned or -operated housing units are wired for high-speed Internet access. Wireless service is available via entire campus.

Student Life *Housing:* on-campus residence required through senior year. *Options:* women-only, disabled students. Campus housing is university owned. Freshman campus housing is guaranteed. *Activities and organizations:* drama/theater group, student-run newspaper, television station, choral group, Student

Government Association, SHARE (volunteer group), Religious Life Association, Student Athletic Association, campus political organizations. *Campus security:* 24-hour emergency response devices and patrols, late-night transport/escort service, controlled dormitory access, emergency call boxes. *Student services:* health clinic, personal/psychological counseling, women's center.

Athletics Member NCAA. All Division III. *Intercollegiate sports:* basketball W, cross-country running W(c), equestrian sports W, fencing W(c), golf W, lacrosse W, soccer W, softball W(c), swimming and diving W, tennis W, volleyball W.

Standardized Tests *Required:* SAT or ACT (for admission).

Costs (2010–11) *Comprehensive fee:* $39,685 includes full-time tuition ($28,910), mandatory fees ($575), and room and board ($10,200). Part-time tuition: $903 per credit hour. *Required fees:* $146 per term part-time. *College room only:* $6050. *Payment plans:* tuition prepayment, installment. *Waivers:* employees or children of employees.

Financial Aid Of all full-time matriculated undergraduates who enrolled in 2009, 662 applied for aid, 608 were judged to have need, 86 had their need fully met. 327 Federal Work-Study jobs (averaging $2347). 96 state and other part-time jobs (averaging $2421). In 2009, 121 non-need-based awards were made. *Average percent of need met:* 81%. *Average financial aid package:* $22,803. *Average need-based loan:* $5164. *Average need-based gift aid:* $17,890. *Average non-need-based aid:* $15,435. *Average indebtedness upon graduation:* $19,982. *Financial aid deadline:* 2/15.

Applying *Options:* electronic application, early admission, early decision, deferred entrance. *Application fee:* $40. *Required:* essay or personal statement, high school transcript, 2 letters of recommendation. *Recommended:* interview. *Application deadline:* rolling (freshmen). *Early decision deadline:* 12/1. *Notification:* continuous (freshmen), 12/15 (early decision).

Freshman Application Contact Ms. Nicole Johnson Williams, Associate Dean of Admissions, Hollins University, PO Box 9707, Roanoke, VA 24020-1707. *Phone:* 540-362-6401. *Toll-free phone:* 800-456-9595. *Fax:* 540-362-6218. *E-mail:* huadm@hollins.edu. *Web site:* http://www.hollins.edu/.

See page 1332 for the College Close-Up.

ITT Technical Institute
Chantilly, Virginia

- **Proprietary** primarily 2-year, founded 2002, part of ITT Educational Services, Inc.
- **Coed**
- **Minimally difficult** entrance level

Academics *Calendar:* quarters. *Degrees:* associate and bachelor's.
Student Life *Housing:* college housing not available.
Freshman Application Contact Director of Recruitment, ITT Technical Institute, 14420 Abermarle Point Place, Suite 100, Chantilly, VA 20151. *Phone:* 703-263-2541. *Toll-free phone:* 888-895-8324. *Web site:* http://www.itt-tech.edu/.

ITT Technical Institute
Norfolk, Virginia

- **Proprietary** primarily 2-year, founded 1988, part of ITT Educational Services, Inc.
- **Suburban** campus
- **Coed**
- **Minimally difficult** entrance level

Academics *Calendar:* quarters. *Degrees:* associate and bachelor's.
Student Life *Housing:* college housing not available.
Financial Aid Of all full-time matriculated undergraduates who enrolled in 2009, 3 Federal Work-Study jobs (averaging $5000).
Freshman Application Contact Director of Recruitment, ITT Technical Institute, 863 Glenrock Road, Suite 100, Norfolk, VA 23502-3701. *Phone:* 757-466-1260. *Toll-free phone:* 888-253-8324. *Web site:* http://www.itt-tech.edu/.

ITT Technical Institute
Richmond, Virginia

- **Proprietary** primarily 2-year, founded 1999, part of ITT Educational Services, Inc.
- **Coed**
- **Minimally difficult** entrance level

Academics *Calendar:* quarters. *Degrees:* associate and bachelor's.
Student Life *Housing:* college housing not available.
Freshman Application Contact Director of Recruitment, ITT Technical Institute, 300 Gateway Centre Parkway, Richmond, VA 23235. *Phone:* 804-330-4992. *Toll-free phone:* 888-330-4888. *Web site:* http://www.itt-tech.edu/.

ITT Technical Institute
Salem, Virginia

- **Proprietary** primarily 2-year
- **Coed**
- **Minimally difficult** entrance level

Academics *Degrees:* associate and bachelor's.
Freshman Application Contact Director of Recruitment, ITT Technical Institute, 2159 Apperson Drive, Salem, VA 24153. *Phone:* 540-989-2500. *Toll-free phone:* 877-208-6132. *Web site:* http://www.itt-tech.edu/.

ITT Technical Institute
Springfield, Virginia

- **Proprietary** primarily 2-year, founded 2002, part of ITT Educational Services, Inc.
- **Coed**
- **Minimally difficult** entrance level

Academics *Calendar:* quarters. *Degrees:* associate and bachelor's.
Student Life *Housing:* college housing not available.
Freshman Application Contact Director of Recruitment, ITT Technical Institute, 7300 Boston Boulevard, Springfield, VA 22153. *Phone:* 703-440-9535. *Toll-free phone:* 866-817-8324. *Web site:* http://www.itt-tech.edu/.

James Madison University
Harrisonburg, Virginia

- **State-supported** comprehensive, founded 1908
- **Small-town** 714-acre campus
- **Endowment** $48.8 million
- **Coed** 17,657 undergraduate students, 95% full-time, 60% women, 40% men
- **Very difficult** entrance level, 60% of applicants were admitted

Undergraduates 16,845 full-time, 812 part-time. Students come from 41 states and territories; 70 other countries; 28% are from out of state; 4% Black or African American, non-Hispanic/Latino; 3% Hispanic/Latino; 5% Asian, non-Hispanic/Latino; 0.4% Native Hawaiian or other Pacific Islander, non-Hispanic/Latino; 0.2% American Indian or Alaska Native, non-Hispanic/Latino; 0.9% Two or more races, non-Hispanic/Latino; 6% Race/ethnicity unknown; 1% international; 4% transferred in; 35% live on campus. *Retention:* 91% of full-time freshmen returned.

Freshmen *Admission:* 22,221 applied, 13,307 admitted, 4,001 enrolled. *Average high school GPA:* 3.84. *Test scores:* SAT critical reading scores over 500: 82%; ACT scores over 18: 98%; SAT critical reading scores over 600: 29%; ACT scores over 24: 65%; SAT critical reading scores over 700: 3%; ACT scores over 30: 6%.

Faculty *Total:* 1,350, 67% full-time, 60% with terminal degrees. *Student/faculty ratio:* 16:1.

Academics *Calendar:* semesters. *Degrees:* bachelor's, master's, doctoral-professional, doctoral-research/scholarship, and post-master's certificates (also offers specialist in education degree). *Special study options:* accelerated degree program, adult/continuing education programs, advanced placement credit, distance learning, double majors, English as a second language, freshman honors college, honors programs, independent study, internships, off-campus study, part-time degree program, services for LD students, student-designed majors, study abroad, summer session for credit. *ROTC:* Army (b), Air Force (c). *Unusual degree programs:* 3-2 forestry with Virginia Polytechnic Institute and State University.

Computers on Campus 600 computers/terminals and 7,000 ports are available on campus for general student use. Students can access the following: campus intranet, computer help desk, free student e-mail accounts, online (class) grades, online (class) registration, online (class) schedules. Campus-wide network is available. 100% of college-owned or -operated housing units are wired for high-speed Internet access. Wireless service is available via classrooms, dorm rooms, learning centers, libraries, student centers.

Student Life *Housing:* on-campus residence required for freshman year. *Options:* coed. Campus housing is university owned and leased by the school. Freshman campus housing is guaranteed. *Activities and organizations:* drama/theater group, student-run newspaper, radio station, choral group, marching band, national fraternities, national sororities. *Campus security:* 24-hour emergency response devices and patrols, student patrols, late-night transport/escort service, controlled dormitory access, lighted pathways. *Student services:* health clinic, personal/psychological counseling, women's center.

Athletics Member NCAA. All Division I except football (Division I-AA). *Intercollegiate sports:* baseball M(s), basketball M(s)/W(s), cheerleading M/W, cross-country running W(s), field hockey W(s), golf M(s)/W(s), lacrosse W(s), soccer M(s)/W(s), softball W(s), swimming and diving W(s), tennis M(s)/W(s), track and field W(s), volleyball W(s). *Intramural sports:* archery M(c)/W(c), baseball M(c), basketball M/W, bowling M/W, cheerleading W(c), crew M(c)/W(c), cross-country running M(c)/W(c), equestrian sports M(c)/W(c), fencing M(c)/W(c), field hockey W(c), football M/W, golf M/W, gymnastics M(c)/W(c), ice hockey M(c)/W(c), lacrosse M(c)/W(c), racquetball M/W, rugby M(c)/W(c), skiing (downhill) M(c)/W(c), soccer M/W, softball M/W, squash M(c)/W(c), swimming and diving M(c)/W(c), table tennis M/W, tennis M/W, track and field M(c)/W(c), ultimate Frisbee M(c)/W(c), volleyball M/W, water polo M(c)/W(c), wrestling M(c).

Standardized Tests *Required:* SAT or ACT (for admission).

Costs (2010–11) *Tuition:* state resident $4182 full-time, $139 per credit hour part-time; nonresident $16,946 full-time, $547 per credit hour part-time. Part-time tuition and fees vary according to course load. *Required fees:* $3678 full-time. *Room and board:* $8020; room only: $4028. Room and board charges vary according to board plan and housing facility. *Payment plan:* installment. *Waivers:* senior citizens and employees or children of employees.

Financial Aid Of all full-time matriculated undergraduates who enrolled in 2009, 15,833 applied for aid, 7,312 were judged to have need, 4,565 had their need fully met. 275 Federal Work-Study jobs (averaging $1998). 2,448 state and other part-time jobs (averaging $2206). In 2009, 122 non-need-based awards were made. *Average percent of need met:* 48%. *Average financial aid package:* $7967. *Average need-based loan:* $4224. *Average need-based gift aid:* $6680. *Average non-need-based aid:* $3120. *Average indebtedness upon graduation:* $20,417.

Applying *Options:* electronic application, early action, deferred entrance. *Application fee:* $50. *Required:* high school transcript. *Recommended:* minimum 3 GPA. *Application deadlines:* 1/15 (freshmen), 3/1 (transfers), 11/1 (early action). *Notification:* 4/1 (freshmen), 4/15 (transfers), 1/15 (early action).

Freshman Application Contact James Madison University, 800 South Main Street, Harrisonburg, VA 22807. *Phone:* 540-568-5681. *Web site:* http://www.jmu.edu/.

Jefferson College of Health Sciences
Roanoke, Virginia

- **Independent** comprehensive, founded 1982
- **Urban** 1-acre campus
- **Endowment** $1.6 million
- **Coed** 833 undergraduate students, 76% full-time, 83% women, 17% men
- **Moderately difficult** entrance level, 39% of applicants were admitted

Undergraduates 636 full-time, 197 part-time. Students come from 22 states and territories; 10 other countries; 4% are from out of state; 11% Black or African American, non-Hispanic/Latino; 1% Hispanic/Latino; 0.7% Asian, non-Hispanic/Latino; 0.1% Native Hawaiian or other Pacific Islander, non-Hispanic/Latino; 0.2% American Indian or Alaska Native, non-Hispanic/Latino; 1% Two or more races, non-Hispanic/Latino; 3% Race/ethnicity unknown; 0.1% international; 27% transferred in; 5% live on campus. *Retention:* 71% of full-time freshmen returned.

Freshmen *Admission:* 572 applied, 222 admitted, 67 enrolled. *Average high school GPA:* 3.19. *Test scores:* SAT critical reading scores over 500: 41%; SAT math scores over 500: 35%; SAT writing scores over 500: 33%; ACT scores over 18: 58%; SAT critical reading scores over 600: 3%; SAT math scores over 600: 2%; SAT writing scores over 600: 3%; ACT scores over 24: 5%; SAT critical reading scores over 700: 1%.

Faculty *Total:* 128, 54% full-time, 37% with terminal degrees. *Student/faculty ratio:* 10:1.

Academics *Calendar:* semesters. *Degrees:* certificates, associate, bachelor's, and master's. *Special study options:* accelerated degree program, adult/continuing education programs, advanced placement credit, cooperative education, distance learning, double majors, English as a second language, independent study, internships, off-campus study, part-time degree program, services for LD students, summer session for credit.

Computers on Campus 72 computers/terminals are available on campus for general student use. Students can access the following: free student e-mail accounts, online (class) grades, online (class) registration, online (class) schedules. Campuswide network is available. 100% of college-owned or -operated housing units are wired for high-speed Internet access. Wireless service is available via classrooms, computer labs, learning centers, libraries.

Student Life *Housing options:* coed. Campus housing is university owned. *Activities and organizations:* student-run newspaper, choral group, Jefferson Activities Group (JAG), Student Ambassadors, Hands of Healing, American Medical Students Association (AMSA), Student Nurses Association. *Campus security:* 24-hour emergency response devices and patrols, late-night transport/escort service, controlled dormitory access. *Student services:* personal/psychological counseling.

Athletics *Intercollegiate sports:* basketball M(c), cross-country running M(c)/W(c), softball M(c)/W(c), tennis M(c)/W(c), volleyball M(c)/W(c). *Intramural sports:* table tennis M(c)/W(c).

Standardized Tests *Required:* SAT or ACT (for admission). *Recommended:* SAT (for admission).

Costs (2010–11) *Tuition:* $18,810 full-time, $545 per credit hour part-time. *Room only:* $4700. *Payment plan:* installment. *Waivers:* employees or children of employees.

Financial Aid Of all full-time matriculated undergraduates who enrolled in 2009, 1,281 applied for aid, 1,108 were judged to have need, 52 had their need fully met. 91 Federal Work-Study jobs (averaging $1050). 106 state and other part-time jobs (averaging $1552). In 2009, 69 non-need-based awards were made. *Average percent of need met:* 45%. *Average financial aid package:* $11,255. *Average need-based loan:* $4252. *Average need-based gift aid:* $8482. *Average non-need-based aid:* $3148. *Average indebtedness upon graduation:* $17,327.

Applying *Options:* electronic application, deferred entrance. *Application fee:* $35. *Required:* high school transcript, minimum 2 GPA. *Required for some:* interview. *Application deadlines:* rolling (freshmen), rolling (transfers). *Notification:* continuous (freshmen), continuous (transfers).

Freshman Application Contact Jefferson College of Health Sciences, PO Box 13186, Roanoke, VA 24031-3186. *Phone:* 540-985-9083. *Toll-free phone:* 888-985-8483. *Web site:* http://www.jchs.edu/.

Liberty University
Lynchburg, Virginia

- **Independent nondenominational** comprehensive, founded 1971
- **Suburban** 6500-acre campus
- **Coed** 11,142 undergraduate students, 98% full-time, 53% women, 47% men
- **Minimally difficult** entrance level, 95% of applicants were admitted

Undergraduates 10,877 full-time, 265 part-time. Students come from 52 states and territories; 95 other countries; 55% are from out of state; 7% Black or African American, non-Hispanic/Latino; 3% Hispanic/Latino; 1% Asian, non-Hispanic/Latino; 0.2% Native Hawaiian or other Pacific Islander, non-Hispanic/Latino; 0.4% American Indian or Alaska Native, non-Hispanic/Latino; 0.1% Two or more races, non-Hispanic/Latino; 17% Race/ethnicity unknown; 7% international; 5% transferred in; 63% live on campus. *Retention:* 74% of full-time freshmen returned.

Freshmen *Admission:* 5,300 applied, 5,048 admitted, 2,657 enrolled. *Average high school GPA:* 3.34. *Test scores:* SAT critical reading scores over 500: 60%; SAT math scores over 500: 55%; SAT writing scores over 500: 52%; ACT scores over 18: 87%; SAT critical reading scores over 600: 20%; SAT math scores over 600: 18%; SAT writing scores over 600: 16%; ACT scores over 24: 38%; SAT critical reading scores over 700: 3%; SAT math scores over 700: 2%; SAT writing scores over 700: 2%; ACT scores over 30: 6%.

Faculty *Total:* 555, 70% full-time. *Student/faculty ratio:* 27:1.

Academics *Calendar:* semesters. *Degrees:* certificates, associate, bachelor's, master's, doctoral-professional, doctoral-research/scholarship, and post-master's certificates (also offers external degree program with significant enrollment not reflected in profile). *Special study options:* academic remediation for entering students, accelerated degree program, advanced placement credit, cooperative education, distance learning, double majors, English as a second language, external degree program, honors programs, independent study, internships, off-campus study, part-time degree program, services for LD students, student-designed majors, study abroad, summer session for credit. *ROTC:* Army (b), Air Force (c).

Computers on Campus 1,200 computers/terminals are available on campus for general student use. Students can access the following: computer help desk, free student e-mail accounts, online (class) grades, online (class) registration, online (class) schedules. Campuswide network is available. 100% of college-owned or -operated housing units are wired for high-speed Internet access. Wireless service is available via entire campus.

Student Life *Housing:* on-campus residence required through senior year. *Options:* men-only, women-only, disabled students. Campus housing is university owned and leased by the school. Freshman campus housing is guaranteed. *Activities and organizations:* drama/theater group, student-run newspaper, radio station, choral group, marching band, College Republicans, Campus Serve. *Campus security:* 24-hour patrols, late-night transport/escort service, 24-hour emergency dispatch. *Student services:* health clinic, personal/psychological counseling.

Athletics Member NCAA. All Division I except football (Division I-AA). *Intercollegiate sports:* baseball M(s), basketball M(s)/W(s), cheerleading M(s)/W(s), crew M(c)/W(c), cross-country running M(s)/W(s), equestrian sports W(c), field hockey W, golf M(s), ice hockey M(c)/W(c), lacrosse W(s), soccer M(s)/W(s), softball W(s), swimming and diving W(s), tennis M(s)/W(s), track and field M(s)/W(s), volleyball W(s), wrestling M(s). *Intramural sports:* basketball M/W, football M/W, soccer M/W, softball M/W, table tennis M/W, tennis M/W, ultimate Frisbee M/W, volleyball M/W.

Standardized Tests *Required:* SAT or ACT (for admission).

Costs (2011–12) *Comprehensive fee:* $25,834 includes full-time tuition ($17,806), mandatory fees ($1348), and room and board ($6680). Full-time tuition and fees vary according to course load. Part-time tuition: $594 per hour. Part-time tuition and fees vary according to course load. *Room and board:*

Room and board charges vary according to housing facility. *Payment plan:* installment. *Waivers:* employees or children of employees.

Financial Aid Of all full-time matriculated undergraduates who enrolled in 2009, 17,357 applied for aid, 15,306 were judged to have need, 1,011 had their need fully met. In 2009, 871 non-need-based awards were made. *Average percent of need met:* 42%. *Average financial aid package:* $8734. *Average need-based loan:* $2887. *Average need-based gift aid:* $6455. *Average non-need-based aid:* $6976. *Average indebtedness upon graduation:* $32,936. *Financial aid deadline:* 3/1.

Applying *Options:* electronic application, early admission, deferred entrance. *Application fee:* $40. *Required:* essay or personal statement, high school transcript, minimum 2 GPA, 800 SAT (Math and Verbal), 17 ACT. *Recommended:* minimum 2 GPA. *Application deadlines:* rolling (freshmen), rolling (out-of-state freshmen), rolling (transfers). *Notification:* continuous until 8/15 (freshmen), continuous (out-of-state freshmen), continuous (transfers).

Freshman Application Contact Mr. Terry Elam, Director of Admissions, Liberty University, 1971 University Boulevard, Lynchburg, VA 24502. *Phone:* 434-592-3966. *Toll-free phone:* 800-543-5317. *Fax:* 800-542-2311. *E-mail:* admissions@liberty.edu. *Web site:* http://www.liberty.edu/.

See page 1382 for the College Close-Up.

Longwood University

Farmville, Virginia

- **State-supported** comprehensive, founded 1839, part of The State Council of Higher Education for Virginia
- **Small-town** 160-acre campus with easy access to Richmond
- **Coed** 4,125 undergraduate students, 94% full-time, 66% women, 34% men
- **Moderately difficult** entrance level, 73% of applicants were admitted

Undergraduates 3,869 full-time, 256 part-time. Students come from 15 other countries; 4% are from out of state; 6% Black or African American, non-Hispanic/Latino; 3% Hispanic/Latino; 1% Asian, non-Hispanic/Latino; 0.2% Native Hawaiian or other Pacific Islander, non-Hispanic/Latino; 0.4% American Indian or Alaska Native, non-Hispanic/Latino; 2% Two or more races, non-Hispanic/Latino; 3% Race/ethnicity unknown; 0.7% international; 5%

transferred in; 74% live on campus. *Retention:* 79% of full-time freshmen returned.

Freshmen *Admission:* 4,402 applied, 3,207 admitted, 967 enrolled. *Average high school GPA:* 3.34. *Test scores:* SAT critical reading scores over 500: 65%; SAT math scores over 500: 62%; ACT scores over 18: 99%; SAT critical reading scores over 600: 13%; SAT math scores over 600: 11%; ACT scores over 24: 23%; SAT critical reading scores over 700: 1%.

Faculty *Total:* 274, 78% full-time, 53% with terminal degrees. *Student/faculty ratio:* 18:1.

Academics *Calendar:* semesters. *Degrees:* bachelor's, master's, post-master's, and postbachelor's certificates. *Special study options:* accelerated degree program, advanced placement credit, distance learning, double majors, honors programs, independent study, internships, off-campus study, part-time degree program, services for LD students, study abroad, summer session for credit. *ROTC:* Army (b). *Unusual degree programs:* 3-2 engineering with University of Virginia, Old Dominion University, University of Tennessee, Virginia Polytechnic Institute and University, Christopher Newport University.

Computers on Campus 265 computers/terminals and 650 ports are available on campus for general student use. Students can access the following: campus intranet, computer help desk, free student e-mail accounts, online (class) grades, online (class) registration, online (class) schedules. Campuswide network is available. 100% of college-owned or -operated housing units are wired for high-speed Internet access. Wireless service is available via classrooms, computer centers, computer labs, libraries, student centers.

Student Life *Housing:* on-campus residence required through sophomore year. *Options:* coed, women-only, disabled students. Campus housing is university owned. Freshman campus housing is guaranteed. *Activities and organizations:* drama/theater group, student-run newspaper, radio and television station, choral group, Student Government Association, Alpha Phi Omega, Inter-Varsity Christian Fellowship, Longwood Ambassadors, Wellness Advocates, national fraternities, national sororities. *Campus security:* 24-hour emergency response devices and patrols, late-night transport/escort service, controlled dormitory access, security lighting. *Student services:* health clinic, personal/psychological counseling.

Athletics Member NCAA. All Division I. *Intercollegiate sports:* baseball M(s), basketball M(s)/W(s), cross-country running M(s)/W(s), equestrian sports M(c)/W(c), field hockey W(s), golf M(s)/W(s), lacrosse W(s), rugby M(c)/W(c), soccer M(s)/W(s), softball W(s), swimming and diving M(c)/W(c),

tennis M(s)/W(s), track and field M(c)/W(c), volleyball M(c)/W(c), wrestling M(c). *Intramural sports:* badminton M/W, basketball W, bowling M/W, cheerleading M/W, football M/W, golf M/W, racquetball M/W, soccer M/W, softball M/W, table tennis M/W, tennis M/W, ultimate Frisbee M/W, volleyball M/W.

Standardized Tests *Required:* SAT or ACT (for admission).

Costs (2010–11) *Tuition:* state resident $5370 full-time, $179 per credit hour part-time; nonresident $15,600 full-time, $520 per credit hour part-time. Full-time tuition and fees vary according to course load. Part-time tuition and fees vary according to course load. *Required fees:* $4485 full-time. *Room and board:* $8114; room only: $5260. Room and board charges vary according to board plan, housing facility, and location. *Payment plan:* installment. *Waivers:* senior citizens.

Financial Aid Of all full-time matriculated undergraduates who enrolled in 2008, 2,776 applied for aid, 1,929 were judged to have need, 952 had their need fully met. 310 Federal Work-Study jobs (averaging $1298). 450 state and other part-time jobs (averaging $1217). In 2008, 223 non-need-based awards were made. *Average percent of need met:* 82%. *Average financial aid package:* $11,038. *Average need-based loan:* $6156. *Average need-based gift aid:* $5768. *Average non-need-based aid:* $3461. *Average indebtedness upon graduation:* $23,379.

Applying *Options:* electronic application, early admission, early action, deferred entrance. *Application fee:* $40. *Required:* essay or personal statement, high school transcript. *Required for some:* interview. *Application deadlines:* 3/1 (freshmen), 3/1 (out-of-state freshmen), 3/1 (transfers), 12/1 (early action). *Notification:* 6/1 (freshmen), 6/1 (out-of-state freshmen), continuous until 6/1 (transfers), 1/15 (early action).

Freshman Application Contact Mr. Robert J. Chonko, Dean of Admissions, Longwood University, 201 High Street, Farmville, VA 23909. *Phone:* 434-395-2060. *Toll-free phone:* 800-281-4677. *Fax:* 434-395-2332. *E-mail:* admissions@longwood.edu. *Web site:* http://www.longwood.edu/.

Lynchburg College

Lynchburg, Virginia

- **Independent** comprehensive, founded 1903, affiliated with Christian Church (Disciples of Christ)
- **Suburban** 214-acre campus
- **Endowment** $67.6 million
- **Coed** 2,197 undergraduate students, 96% full-time, 59% women, 41% men
- **Moderately difficult** entrance level, 67% of applicants were admitted

Undergraduates 2,102 full-time, 95 part-time. Students come from 36 states and territories; 5 other countries; 34% are from out of state; 9% Black or African American, non-Hispanic/Latino; 2% Hispanic/Latino; 1% Asian, non-Hispanic/Latino; 0.5% American Indian or Alaska Native, non-Hispanic/Latino; 0.4% Two or more races, non-Hispanic/Latino; 8% Race/ethnicity unknown; 0.4% international; 4% transferred in; 79% live on campus. *Retention:* 72% of full-time freshmen returned.

Freshmen *Admission:* 4,574 applied, 3,049 admitted, 571 enrolled. *Average high school GPA:* 3.14. *Test scores:* SAT critical reading scores over 500: 52%; SAT math scores over 500: 55%; SAT writing scores over 500: 47%; ACT scores over 18: 86%; SAT critical reading scores over 600: 12%; SAT math scores over 600: 14%; SAT writing scores over 600: 10%; ACT scores over 24: 27%; SAT critical reading scores over 700: 1%; SAT math scores over 700: 1%; SAT writing scores over 700: 1%; ACT scores over 30: 2%.

Faculty *Total:* 274, 62% full-time, 60% with terminal degrees. *Student/faculty ratio:* 12:1.

Academics *Calendar:* semesters. *Degrees:* bachelor's, master's, doctoral-professional, post-master's, and postbachelor's certificates. *Special study options:* accelerated degree program, adult/continuing education programs, advanced placement credit, double majors, honors programs, independent study, internships, off-campus study, part-time degree program, services for LD students, study abroad, summer session for credit. *Unusual degree programs:* 3-2 engineering with Old Dominion University, University of Virginia.

Computers on Campus 300 computers/terminals are available on campus for general student use. Students can access the following: campus intranet, computer help desk, free student e-mail accounts, online (class) grades, online (class) registration, online (class) schedules. Campuswide network is available. 100% of college-owned or -operated housing units are wired for high-speed Internet access. Wireless service is available via classrooms, learning centers, libraries, student centers.

Student Life *Housing:* on-campus residence required through junior year. *Options:* coed, disabled students. Campus housing is university owned. Freshman campus housing is guaranteed. *Activities and organizations:* drama/theater group, student-run newspaper, choral group, Student Government Association, Student Activities Board, Enrollment Student Ambassadors, Emergency Services, Greek Life, national fraternities, national sororities. *Campus security:* 24-hour emergency response devices and patrols, late-night

Lynchburg College
in Virginia

Where *Going Above and Beyond* is a way of life

Academics: Liberal arts curriculum: 38 majors, 45 minors, 14 pre-professional programs; **doctoral studies** in physical therapy, proposed program in educational leadership; **master's degrees** including M.A., M.B.A., M.Ed., M.S.N.

Athletics: Outstanding Division III sports. Unranked 2010 men's soccer team second in NCAA Division III championship; Coach Chris Yeager national coach of the year

National Recognition: *Colleges That Change Lives* by Loren Pope; *U. S. News & World Report;* The Princeton Review; John Templeton Foundation's Honor Roll of Character-Building Colleges

Student Body: 2,700 undergraduate and graduate students from 36 states and 14 foreign countries

Location: Central Virginia metropolitan area of 225,000

Beyond The Classroom: 470-acre Claytor Nature Study Center for environmental study; faculty/student research; study abroad; honors program; performing and visual arts, service learning, Bonner Leaders program

Financial Aid: 96% of LC students benefit from some type of financial assistance.

Information: www.lynchburg.edu or 800.426.8101, ext. 8300

transport/escort service, controlled dormitory access. *Student services:* health clinic, personal/psychological counseling.

Athletics Member NCAA. All Division III. *Intercollegiate sports:* baseball M, basketball M/W, cheerleading M/W, cross-country running M/W, equestrian sports M/W, field hockey W, golf M, lacrosse M/W, soccer M/W, softball W, tennis M/W, track and field M/W, volleyball W. *Intramural sports:* basketball M(c)/W(c), equestrian sports M(c)/W(c), field hockey W(c), golf M(c)/W(c), ice hockey M(c), lacrosse M(c)/W(c), rugby M/W, soccer M(c)/W(c), softball W(c), tennis M(c)/W(c), volleyball M/W, wrestling M(c).

Standardized Tests *Required:* SAT or ACT (for admission).

Costs (2011–12) *Comprehensive fee:* $39,015 includes full-time tuition ($29,860), mandatory fees ($945), and room and board ($8210). Part-time tuition: $415 per credit hour. Part-time tuition and fees vary according to course load. *Required fees:* $5 per credit hour part-time. *College room only:* $4190. Room and board charges vary according to board plan and housing facility. *Payment plans:* tuition prepayment, installment. *Waivers:* adult students, senior citizens, and employees or children of employees.

Financial Aid Of all full-time matriculated undergraduates who enrolled in 2009, 1,715 applied for aid, 1,464 were judged to have need, 317 had their need fully met. In 2009, 563 non-need-based awards were made. *Average percent of need met:* 78%. *Average financial aid package:* $20,193. *Average need-based loan:* $3526. *Average need-based gift aid:* $16,607. *Average non-need-based aid:* $9958. *Average indebtedness upon graduation:* $30,954.

Applying *Options:* electronic application, early admission, early decision, deferred entrance. *Application fee:* $30. *Required:* high school transcript. *Recommended:* essay or personal statement, 2 letters of recommendation, interview. *Application deadlines:* rolling (freshmen), rolling (transfers). *Early decision deadline:* 11/15. *Notification:* continuous (freshmen), continuous (transfers), 12/15 (early decision).

Freshman Application Contact Lynchburg College, 1501 Lakeside Drive, Lynchburg, VA 24501-3199. *Phone:* 434-544-8300. *Toll-free phone:* 800-426-8101. *Web site:* http://www.lynchburg.edu/.

See page 1398 for the College Close-Up.

Mary Baldwin College
Staunton, Virginia

- **Independent** comprehensive, founded 1842
- **Small-town** 54-acre campus
- **Endowment** $29.3 million
- **Coed, primarily women** 1,535 undergraduate students, 68% full-time, 93% women, 7% men
- **Moderately difficult** entrance level, 52% of applicants were admitted

Undergraduates 1,049 full-time, 486 part-time. Students come from 32 states and territories; 4 other countries; 34% are from out of state; 25% Black or African American, non-Hispanic/Latino; 5% Hispanic/Latino; 3% Asian, non-Hispanic/Latino; 0.1% Native Hawaiian or other Pacific Islander, non-Hispanic/Latino; 0.7% American Indian or Alaska Native, non-Hispanic/Latino; 1% Two or more races, non-Hispanic/Latino; 5% Race/ethnicity unknown; 1% international; 4% transferred in; 62% live on campus. *Retention:* 62% of full-time freshmen returned.

Freshmen *Admission:* 3,129 applied, 1,638 admitted, 272 enrolled. *Average high school GPA:* 3.27. *Test scores:* SAT critical reading scores over 500: 51%; SAT math scores over 500: 113%; SAT writing scores over 500: 45%; ACT scores over 18: 74%; SAT critical reading scores over 600: 17%; SAT math scores over 600: 82%; SAT writing scores over 600: 14%; ACT scores over 24: 24%; SAT critical reading scores over 700: 4%; SAT math scores over 700: 1%; SAT writing scores over 700: 3%; ACT scores over 30: 4%.

Faculty *Total:* 138, 58% full-time, 111% with terminal degrees. *Student/faculty ratio:* 11:1.

Academics *Calendar:* 4-1-4. *Degrees:* certificates, bachelor's, and master's. *Special study options:* academic remediation for entering students, accelerated degree program, adult/continuing education programs, advanced placement credit, double majors, English as a second language, external degree program, freshman honors college, honors programs, independent study, internships, off-campus study, part-time degree program, services for LD students, student-designed majors, study abroad. *ROTC:* Army (b), Navy (c), Air Force (c). *Unusual degree programs:* 3-2 engineering with University of Virginia; nursing with Vanderbilt University.

Computers on Campus 244 computers/terminals are available on campus for general student use. Students can access the following: computer help desk, free student e-mail accounts, online (class) grades, online (class) registration, online (class) schedules, we are 100% wireless. Campuswide network is available. 100% of college-owned or -operated housing units are wired for high-speed Internet access. Wireless service is available via entire campus.

Student Life *Housing:* on-campus residence required through senior year. *Options:* women-only. Campus housing is university owned. Freshman campus housing is guaranteed. *Activities and organizations:* drama/theater group, student-run newspaper, radio station, choral group, marching band, Interna-

tional Club council, Minority Clubs United, Student Senate, Baldwin Program Board, Resident Hall Association. *Campus security:* 24-hour emergency response devices and patrols, late-night transport/escort service, controlled dormitory access. *Student services:* health clinic, personal/psychological counseling.

Athletics Member NCAA. All Division III. *Intercollegiate sports:* basketball W, cross-country running W, soccer W, softball W, swimming and diving W(c), tennis W, volleyball W. *Intramural sports:* basketball W, fencing W(c), racquetball W, swimming and diving W, volleyball W.

Standardized Tests *Required:* SAT or ACT (for admission).

Costs (2010–11) *Comprehensive fee:* $32,975 includes full-time tuition ($25,340), mandatory fees ($215), and room and board ($7420). Full-time tuition and fees vary according to degree level. Part-time tuition and fees vary according to degree level. *College room only:* $4732. Room and board charges vary according to housing facility. *Payment plan:* installment. *Waivers:* employees or children of employees.

Financial Aid Of all full-time matriculated undergraduates who enrolled in 2009, 874 applied for aid, 801 were judged to have need, 113 had their need fully met. 382 Federal Work-Study jobs (averaging $1759). 90 state and other part-time jobs (averaging $1334). In 2009, 61 non-need-based awards were made. *Average percent of need met:* 77%. *Average financial aid package:* $19,749. *Average need-based loan:* $4885. *Average need-based gift aid:* $15,304. *Average non-need-based aid:* $10,768. *Average indebtedness upon graduation:* $25,665.

Applying *Options:* electronic application, early admission, early decision, deferred entrance. *Application fee:* $35. *Required:* high school transcript, minimum 2 GPA, 1 letter of recommendation. *Recommended:* interview. *Application deadlines:* rolling (freshmen), rolling (transfers). *Early decision deadline:* 11/15. *Notification:* continuous (freshmen), continuous (transfers), 12/1 (early decision).

Freshman Application Contact Ms. Roberta Palmer, Director of Admissions, Mary Baldwin College, Frederick and New Streets, Staunton, VA 24401. *Phone:* 540-887-7260. *Toll-free phone:* 800-468-2262. *Fax:* 540-887-7229. *E-mail:* rpalmer@mbc.edu. *Web site:* http://www.mbc.edu/.

Marymount University
Arlington, Virginia

- **Independent** comprehensive, founded 1950, affiliated with Roman Catholic Church
- **Suburban** 21-acre campus with easy access to Washington, D.C.
- **Endowment** $21.7 million
- **Coed** 2,289 undergraduate students, 88% full-time, 72% women, 28% men
- **Moderately difficult** entrance level, 83% of applicants were admitted

Undergraduates 2,022 full-time, 267 part-time. Students come from 38 states and territories; 59 other countries; 38% are from out of state; 16% Black or African American, non-Hispanic/Latino; 13% Hispanic/Latino; 7% Asian, non-Hispanic/Latino; 0.1% Native Hawaiian or other Pacific Islander, non-Hispanic/Latino; 0.3% American Indian or Alaska Native, non-Hispanic/Latino; 15% Race/ethnicity unknown; 10% international; 12% transferred in; 38% live on campus. *Retention:* 65% of full-time freshmen returned.

Freshmen *Admission:* 1,827 applied, 1,514 admitted, 420 enrolled. *Average high school GPA:* 3.13. *Test scores:* SAT critical reading scores over 500: 53%; SAT math scores over 500: 48%; SAT writing scores over 500: 46%; ACT scores over 18: 81%; SAT critical reading scores over 600: 13%; SAT math scores over 600: 10%; SAT writing scores over 600: 9%; ACT scores over 24: 23%; SAT critical reading scores over 700: 1%; SAT math scores over 700: 1%; SAT writing scores over 700: 1%; ACT scores over 30: 1%.

Faculty *Total:* 346, 42% full-time, 65% with terminal degrees. *Student/faculty ratio:* 14:1.

Academics *Calendar:* semesters plus 2 summer terms. *Degrees:* certificates, bachelor's, master's, doctoral-professional, post-master's, and postbachelor's certificates. *Special study options:* academic remediation for entering students, accelerated degree program, advanced placement credit, distance learning, double majors, English as a second language, honors programs, independent study, internships, off-campus study, part-time degree program, services for LD students, student-designed majors, study abroad, summer session for credit. *ROTC:* Army (c).

Computers on Campus 260 computers/terminals are available on campus for general student use. Students can access the following: computer help desk, free student e-mail accounts, online (class) grades, online (class) registration, online (class) schedules, online drive space. Campuswide network is available. 100% of college-owned or -operated housing units are wired for high-speed Internet access. Wireless service is available via classrooms, computer centers, dorm rooms, learning centers, libraries, student centers.

Student Life *Housing:* on-campus residence required through sophomore year. *Options:* coed, men-only, women-only. Campus housing is university owned and leased by the school. Freshman applicants given priority for college housing. *Activities and organizations:* drama/theater group, student-run newspaper, choral group, Interior Design Alliance, Student Nurses Association, Fashion Club, International Club, One 2 One (drama club). *Campus security:* 24-hour emergency response devices and patrols, late-night transport/escort service, controlled dormitory access. *Student services:* health clinic, personal/psychological counseling.

Athletics Member NCAA. All Division III. *Intercollegiate sports:* basketball M/W, cross-country running M/W, golf M, lacrosse M/W, soccer M/W, swimming and diving M/W, volleyball W. *Intramural sports:* basketball M/W, cheerleading W, football M/W, soccer M/W, volleyball M/W.

Standardized Tests *Required:* SAT or ACT (for admission).

Costs (2011–12) *Comprehensive fee:* \$34,554 includes full-time tuition (\$23,700), mandatory fees (\$274), and room and board (\$10,580). *Room and board:* Room and board charges vary according to housing facility. *Payment plan:* installment. *Waivers:* senior citizens and employees or children of employees.

Financial Aid Of all full-time matriculated undergraduates who enrolled in 2009, 1,361 applied for aid, 1,141 were judged to have need, 164 had their need fully met. 692 Federal Work-Study jobs (averaging \$1722). In 2009, 374 non-need-based awards were made. *Average percent of need met:* 67%. *Average financial aid package:* \$15,574. *Average need-based loan:* \$4337. *Average need-based gift aid:* \$6427. *Average non-need-based aid:* \$9553. *Average indebtedness upon graduation:* \$22,946.

Applying *Options:* electronic application, deferred entrance. *Application fee:* \$40. *Required:* high school transcript, minimum 2.5 GPA, 1 letter of recommendation. *Recommended:* essay or personal statement, interview. *Application deadlines:* rolling (freshmen), rolling (transfers). *Notification:* continuous (freshmen), continuous (transfers).

Freshman Application Contact Mr. Mike Canfield, Director of Undergraduate Admissions, Marymount University, 2807 North Glebe Road, Arlington, VA 22207-4299. *Phone:* 703-284-1500. *Toll-free phone:* 800-548-7638. *Fax:* 703-522-0349. *E-mail:* admissions@marymount.edu. *Web site:* http://www.marymount.edu/.

National College

Danville, Virginia

Freshman Application Contact Admissions Office, National College, 734 Main Street, Danville, VA 24541-1819. *Phone:* 434-793-6822. *Toll-free phone:* 800-664-1886. *Web site:* http://www.national-college.edu/.

National College

Harrisonburg, Virginia

Director of Admissions Jack Evey, Campus Director, National College, 51 B Burgess Road, Harrisonburg, VA 22801-9709. *Phone:* 540-432-0943. *Toll-free phone:* 800-664-1886. *Web site:* http://www.national-college.edu/.

National College

Lynchburg, Virginia

Freshman Application Contact Admissions Representative, National College, 104 Candlewood Court, Lynchburg, VA 24502-2653. *Phone:* 804-239-3500. *Toll-free phone:* 800-664-1886. *Web site:* http://www.national-college.edu/.

National College

Salem, Virginia

Freshman Application Contact Director of Admissions, National College, 1813 East Main Street, Salem, VA 24153. *Phone:* 540-986-1800. *Toll-free phone:* 800-664-1886. *Fax:* 540-444-4198. *Web site:* http://www.national-college.edu/.

Norfolk State University

Norfolk, Virginia

- **State-supported** comprehensive, founded 1935, part of State Council of Higher Education for Virginia
- **Urban** 134-acre campus
- **Coed**
- **Moderately difficult** entrance level

Faculty *Student/faculty ratio:* 18:1.

Academics *Calendar:* semesters. *Degrees:* associate, bachelor's, master's, and doctoral-research/scholarship.

Student Life *Campus security:* 24-hour emergency response devices and patrols, late-night transport/escort service.

Athletics Member NCAA. All Division I.

Standardized Tests *Required:* SAT or ACT (for admission).

Costs (2010–11) *Tuition:* state resident \$5694 full-time, \$275 per credit hour part-time; nonresident \$14,742 full-time, \$711 per credit hour part-time. Full-time tuition and fees vary according to course load. Part-time tuition and fees vary according to course load. *Required fees:* \$3468 full-time. *Room and board:* \$7719; room only: \$4857. Room and board charges vary according to board plan and housing facility.

Financial Aid *Of all full-time matriculated undergraduates who enrolled in 2008,* 5,073 applied for aid, 4,427 were judged to have need, 1,755 had their need fully met. *Average percent of need met:* 82. *Average financial aid package:* \$13,168. *Average need-based loan:* \$4140. *Average need-based gift aid:* \$6743. *Average indebtedness upon graduation:* \$19,371. *Financial aid deadline:* 5/31.

Applying *Options:* electronic application, deferred entrance. *Application fee:* \$35. *Required:* high school transcript, minimum 2.3 GPA.

Freshman Application Contact Mr. Kevin M. Holmes, Director of Recruitment and Admissions, Norfolk State University, 700 Park Avenue, Norfolk, VA 23504. *Phone:* 757-823-9222. *Fax:* 757-823-2078. *E-mail:* admissions@nsu.edu. *Web site:* http://www.nsu.edu/.

Old Dominion University

Norfolk, Virginia

- **State-supported** university, founded 1930
- **Urban** 188-acre campus with easy access to Virginia Beach
- **Endowment** \$144.3 million
- **Coed** 18,965 undergraduate students, 76% full-time, 54% women, 46% men
- **Moderately difficult** entrance level, 69% of applicants were admitted

Undergraduates 14,445 full-time, 4,520 part-time. Students come from 46 states and territories; 75 other countries; 7% are from out of state; 23% Black or African American, non-Hispanic/Latino; 5% Hispanic/Latino; 4% Asian, non-Hispanic/Latino; 0.7% Native Hawaiian or other Pacific Islander, non-Hispanic/Latino; 0.5% American Indian or Alaska Native, non-Hispanic/Latino; 3% Two or more races, non-Hispanic/Latino; 6% Race/ethnicity unknown; 2% international; 12% transferred in; 25% live on campus. *Retention:* 80% of full-time freshmen returned.

Freshmen *Admission:* 10,515 applied, 7,291 admitted, 2,663 enrolled. *Average high school GPA:* 3.26. *Test scores:* SAT critical reading scores over 500: 64%; SAT math scores over 500: 70%; SAT writing scores over 500: 54%; ACT scores over 18: 86%; SAT critical reading scores over 600: 15%; SAT math scores over 600: 19%; SAT writing scores over 600: 10%; ACT scores over 24: 24%; SAT critical reading scores over 700: 1%; SAT math scores over 700: 2%; SAT writing scores over 700: 1%; ACT scores over 30: 2%.

Faculty *Total:* 1,197, 58% full-time, 46% with terminal degrees. *Student/faculty ratio:* 21:1.

Academics *Calendar:* semesters. *Degrees:* bachelor's, master's, doctoral-professional, doctoral-research/scholarship, and post-master's certificates. *Special study options:* accelerated degree program, adult/continuing education programs, advanced placement credit, cooperative education, distance learning, double majors, English as a second language, freshman honors college, honors programs, independent study, internships, off-campus study, part-time degree program, services for LD students, student-designed majors, study abroad, summer session for credit. *ROTC:* Army (b), Navy (b). *Unusual degree programs:* 3-2 business administration; engineering; nursing; international studies, dental hygiene, communications/humanities, English, English/applied linguistics, history, interdisciplinary studies/humanities, computer science, women's studies/humanities, philosophy/humanities, health science/public health, environmental health/public health.

Computers on Campus 1,130 computers/terminals and 10,000 ports are available on campus for general student use. Students can access the following: campus intranet, computer help desk, free student e-mail accounts, online (class) grades, online (class) registration, online (class) schedules, online courses. Campuswide network is available. 100% of college-owned or -operated housing units are wired for high-speed Internet access. Wireless service is available via classrooms, computer centers, computer labs, dorm rooms, learning centers, libraries, student centers.

Student Life *Housing options:* coed, disabled students. Campus housing is university owned and leased by the school. Freshman applicants given priority for college housing. *Activities and organizations:* drama/theater group, student-run newspaper, radio and television station, choral group, marching band, Student Activities Council, F.O.R.E.I.G.N.E.R.S, Monarch Maniacs, Anime Club, Ebony Impact Gospel Choir, national fraternities, national sororities. *Campus security:* 24-hour emergency response devices and patrols, student patrols, late-night transport/escort service, controlled dormitory access. *Student services:* health clinic, personal/psychological counseling, women's center.

Athletics Member NCAA. All Division I. *Intercollegiate sports:* baseball M(s), basketball M(s)/W(s), crew M(c)/W(s), cross-country running M(c)/W(c), fencing M(c)/W(c), field hockey W(s), football M(s), golf M(s)/W(s), ice hockey M(c)/W(c), lacrosse M(c)/W(s), rock climbing M(c)/W(c), rugby

M(c), sailing M/W, soccer M(s)/W(s), softball W(c), swimming and diving M(s)/W(s), tennis M(s)/W(s), ultimate Frisbee M(c)/W(c), volleyball M(c)/W(c), wrestling M(s). *Intramural sports:* badminton M/W, basketball M/W, bowling M/W, cross-country running M/W, golf M/W, racquetball M/W, rock climbing M/W, sailing M/W, soccer M/W, softball M/W, table tennis M/W, tennis M/W, ultimate Frisbee M/W, volleyball M/W.

Standardized Tests *Required:* SAT or ACT (for admission).

Costs (2010–11) *Tuition:* state resident $7470 full-time, $249 per credit hour part-time; nonresident $20,910 full-time, $697 per credit hour part-time. Full-time tuition and fees vary according to course level and course load. Part-time tuition and fees vary according to course level and course load. *Required fees:* $238 full-time, $59 per term part-time. *Room and board:* $8322; room only: $4840. Room and board charges vary according to board plan and housing facility. *Payment plans:* installment, deferred payment. *Waivers:* senior citizens and employees or children of employees.

Financial Aid Of all full-time matriculated undergraduates who enrolled in 2009, 10,826 applied for aid, 8,255 were judged to have need, 3,315 had their need fully met. 174 Federal Work-Study jobs (averaging $1854). In 2009, 299 non-need-based awards were made. *Average percent of need met:* 72%. *Average financial aid package:* $8049. *Average need-based loan:* $4272. *Average need-based gift aid:* $4846. *Average non-need-based aid:* $3364. *Average indebtedness upon graduation:* $17,250. *Financial aid deadline:* 3/15.

Applying *Options:* electronic application, early admission, early action, deferred entrance. *Application fee:* $50. *Required:* high school transcript, minimum 2.7 GPA, test scores. *Required for some:* interview. *Recommended:* essay or personal statement, 1 letter of recommendation. *Application deadlines:* 2/1 (freshmen), 2/1 (out-of-state freshmen), 5/1 (transfers), 12/1 (early action). *Notification:* continuous (freshmen), continuous (out-of-state freshmen), continuous (transfers), 1/15 (early action).

Freshman Application Contact Ms. Shereen Williams, Customer Service Manager, Admissions Office, Old Dominion University, 108 Rollins Hall, 5215 Hampton Boulevard, Norfolk, VA 23529. *Phone:* 757-683-3648. *Toll-free phone:* 800-348-7926. *Fax:* 757-683-3255. *E-mail:* admit@odu.edu. *Web site:* http://www.odu.edu/.

Patrick Henry College
Purcellville, Virginia

- **Independent nondenominational** 4-year, founded 1999
- **Small-town** 106-acre campus with easy access to Washington, D.C.
- **Coed** 355 undergraduate students, 77% full-time, 50% women, 50% men
- **Very difficult** entrance level, 83% of applicants were admitted

Undergraduates 274 full-time, 81 part-time. Students come from 38 states and territories; 87% are from out of state; 81% live on campus. *Retention:* 88% of full-time freshmen returned.

Freshmen *Admission:* 132 applied, 110 admitted, 34 enrolled. *Average high school GPA:* 3.73. *Test scores:* SAT critical reading scores over 500: 100%; SAT math scores over 500: 90%; SAT writing scores over 500: 96%; ACT scores over 18: 100%; SAT critical reading scores over 600: 88%; SAT math scores over 600: 50%; SAT writing scores over 600: 79%; ACT scores over 24: 90%; SAT critical reading scores over 700: 48%; SAT math scores over 700: 10%; SAT writing scores over 700: 27%; ACT scores over 30: 45%.

Faculty *Total:* 50, 42% full-time, 68% with terminal degrees. *Student/faculty ratio:* 10:1.

Academics *Calendar:* semesters. *Degree:* bachelor's. *Special study options:* advanced placement credit, distance learning, independent study, internships, off-campus study, summer session for credit.

Computers on Campus 6 computers/terminals and 100 ports are available on campus for general student use. Students can access the following: campus intranet, computer help desk, free student e-mail accounts, online (class) grades, online (class) registration, online (class) schedules. Campuswide network is available. 100% of college-owned or -operated housing units are wired for high-speed Internet access. Wireless service is available via entire campus.

Student Life *Housing:* on-campus residence required through sophomore year. *Options:* men-only, women-only. Campus housing is university owned. Freshman applicants given priority for college housing. *Activities and organizations:* drama/theater group, student-run newspaper, choral group, Drama Club, Eden Troupe, student government, chorale, College Republicans, Debate/Moot Court. *Campus security:* 24-hour emergency response devices, student patrols, late-night transport/escort service, controlled dormitory access, after hours patrols by trained security personnel.

Athletics *Intercollegiate sports:* basketball M/W, soccer M/W. *Intramural sports:* baseball M, basketball M/W, fencing M(c)/W(c), football M(c), racquetball M(c)/W(c), rugby M(c), table tennis M(c)/W(c), tennis M/W, ultimate Frisbee M/W, volleyball M/W.

Standardized Tests *Required:* SAT or ACT (for admission).

Costs (2010–11) *Comprehensive fee:* $30,050 includes full-time tuition ($21,270), mandatory fees ($250), and room and board ($8530). Full-time tuition and fees vary according to course load and degree level. Part-time tuition: $400 per credit hour. Part-time tuition and fees vary according to

course level, course load, and degree level. *Room and board:* Room and board charges vary according to board plan. *Payment plan:* installment. *Waivers:* employees or children of employees.

Financial Aid Of all full-time matriculated undergraduates who enrolled in 2008, 129 applied for aid, 120 were judged to have need. In 2008, 190 non-need-based awards were made. *Average percent of need met:* 54%. *Average financial aid package:* $10,879. *Average need-based gift aid:* $8372. *Average non-need-based aid:* $5688. *Financial aid deadline:* 6/15.

Applying *Options:* electronic application, early action, deferred entrance. *Application fee:* $40. *Required:* essay or personal statement, high school transcript, 2 letters of recommendation, interview. *Application deadlines:* 6/15 (freshmen), 11/1 (early action). *Notification:* continuous (freshmen).

Freshman Application Contact Patrick Henry College, Ten Patrick Henry Circle, Purcellville, VA 20132. *Phone:* 540-338-1776. *Web site:* http://www.phc.edu/.

Potomac College
Herndon, Virginia

Freshman Application Contact Admissions Office, Potomac College, 1029 Herndon Parkway, Herndon, VA 20170. *Phone:* 703-709-5875. *Fax:* 703-709-8972. *E-mail:* admissions@potomac.edu. *Web site:* http://www.potomac.edu/.

Radford University
Radford, Virginia

- **State-supported** comprehensive, founded 1910
- **Small-town** 191-acre campus
- **Endowment** $34.7 million
- **Coed** 7,950 undergraduate students, 96% full-time, 57% women, 43% men
- **Moderately difficult** entrance level, 75% of applicants were admitted

Undergraduates 7,627 full-time, 323 part-time. Students come from 39 states and territories; 28 other countries; 6% are from out of state; 6% Black or African American, non-Hispanic/Latino; 3% Hispanic/Latino; 2% Asian, non-Hispanic/Latino; 0.2% Native Hawaiian or other Pacific Islander, non-Hispanic/Latino; 0.4% American Indian or Alaska Native, non-Hispanic/Latino; 0.8% Two or more races, non-Hispanic/Latino; 2% Race/ethnicity unknown; 0.7% international; 9% transferred in; 37% live on campus. *Retention:* 76% of full-time freshmen returned.

Freshmen *Admission:* 7,098 applied, 5,328 admitted, 1,837 enrolled. *Average high school GPA:* 3.22. *Test scores:* SAT critical reading scores over 500: 56%; SAT math scores over 500: 58%; SAT writing scores over 500: 46%; ACT scores over 18: 88%; SAT critical reading scores over 600: 11%; SAT math scores over 600: 11%; SAT writing scores over 600: 7%; ACT scores over 24: 9%; SAT critical reading scores over 700: 1%; SAT math scores over 700: 1%.

Faculty *Total:* 608, 65% full-time, 62% with terminal degrees. *Student/faculty ratio:* 18:1.

Academics *Calendar:* semesters. *Degrees:* certificates, bachelor's, master's, doctoral-other, post-master's, and postbachelor's certificates. *Special study options:* accelerated degree program, advanced placement credit, distance learning, double majors, honors programs, independent study, internships, off-campus study, part-time degree program, services for LD students, student-designed majors, study abroad, summer session for credit. *ROTC:* Army (b).

Computers on Campus 772 computers/terminals are available on campus for general student use. Students can access the following: campus intranet, computer help desk, free student e-mail accounts, online (class) grades, online (class) registration, online (class) schedules, online financial aid status and student accounts payable. Campuswide network is available. 100% of college-owned or -operated housing units are wired for high-speed Internet access. Wireless service is available via entire campus.

Student Life *Housing:* on-campus residence required through sophomore year. *Options:* coed, disabled students. Campus housing is university owned and leased by the school. Freshman campus housing is guaranteed. *Activities and organizations:* drama/theater group, student-run newspaper, radio and television station, choral group, Alpha Sigma Pi (Greek fraternity), Delta Zeta (Greek sorority), Environmental Club, Men's Rugby Club, Photography Club, national fraternities, national sororities. *Campus security:* 24-hour emergency response devices and patrols, late-night transport/escort service, controlled dormitory access. *Student services:* health clinic, personal/psychological counseling.

Athletics Member NCAA. All Division I. *Intercollegiate sports:* baseball M(s), basketball M(s)/W(s), cross-country running M(s)/W(s), field hockey W(s), golf M(s)/W(s), soccer M(s)/W(s), softball W(s), swimming and diving W(s), tennis M(s)/W(s), track and field M(s)/W(s), volleyball W(s). *Intramural sports:* baseball M(c), basketball M/W, bowling M/W, cheerleading M(c)/W(c), cross-country running M/W, equestrian sports M(c)/W(c), football M/W, golf M(c)/W(c), gymnastics M(c)/W(c), ice hockey M(c)/W(c), lacrosse M(c)/W(c), racquetball M/W, riflery M(c)/W(c), rock climbing M/W, rugby M(c), soccer M/W, softball M/W, table tennis M/W, tennis M/W, ultimate Frisbee M/W, volleyball M/W, weight lifting M/W, wrestling M(c)/W(c).

Standardized Tests *Required:* SAT or ACT (for admission).

Costs (2010–11) *Tuition:* state resident $5012 full-time, $209 per credit hour part-time; nonresident $15,336 full-time, $639 per credit hour part-time. *Required fees:* $3092 full-time, $137 per credit hour part-time. *Room and board:* $7302; room only: $3932. Room and board charges vary according to board plan and housing facility. *Payment plan:* installment. *Waivers:* senior citizens and employees or children of employees.

Financial Aid Of all full-time matriculated undergraduates who enrolled in 2009, 5,116 applied for aid, 3,797 were judged to have need, 1,283 had their need fully met. 340 Federal Work-Study jobs (averaging $2610). 472 state and other part-time jobs (averaging $2610). In 2009, 219 non-need-based awards were made. *Average percent of need met:* 85%. *Average financial aid package:* $9564. *Average need-based loan:* $3942. *Average need-based gift aid:* $7691. *Average non-need-based aid:* $3800. *Average indebtedness upon graduation:* $20,678.

Applying *Options:* electronic application, early admission, early action, deferred entrance. *Application fee:* $50. *Required:* high school transcript. *Application deadlines:* 2/1 (freshmen), 6/1 (transfers), 12/1 (early action). *Notification:* 4/1 (freshmen), continuous (transfers), 1/15 (early action).

Freshman Application Contact Mr. James A. Pennix, Dean of Admissions, Radford University, PO Box 6903, Radford, VA 24142. *Phone:* 540-831-5371. *Toll-free phone:* 800-890-4265. *Fax:* 540-831-5038. *E-mail:* admissions@radford.edu. *Web site:* http://www.radford.edu/.

Randolph College

Lynchburg, Virginia

- **Independent Methodist** comprehensive, founded 1891
- **Suburban** 100-acre campus
- **Endowment** $135.2 million
- **Coed** 517 undergraduate students, 97% full-time, 66% women, 34% men
- **Moderately difficult** entrance level, 90% of applicants were admitted

Undergraduates 499 full-time, 18 part-time. Students come from 35 states and territories; 30 other countries; 42% are from out of state; 10% Black or African American, non-Hispanic/Latino; 5% Hispanic/Latino; 2% Asian, non-Hispanic/Latino; 1% American Indian or Alaska Native, non-Hispanic/Latino; 2% Two or more races, non-Hispanic/Latino; 13% international; 5% transferred in; 90% live on campus. *Retention:* 79% of full-time freshmen returned.

Freshmen *Admission:* 734 applied, 663 admitted, 163 enrolled. *Average high school GPA:* 3.4. *Test scores:* SAT critical reading scores over 500: 74%; SAT math scores over 500: 72%; ACT scores over 18: 94%; SAT critical reading scores over 600: 21%; SAT math scores over 600: 30%; ACT scores over 24: 46%; SAT critical reading scores over 700: 3%; SAT math scores over 700: 8%; ACT scores over 30: 9%.

Faculty *Total:* 69. *Student/faculty ratio:* 7:1.

Academics *Calendar:* semesters. *Degrees:* bachelor's and master's. *Special study options:* accelerated degree program, adult/continuing education programs, advanced placement credit, double majors, honors programs, independent study, internships, off-campus study, part-time degree program, services for LD students, student-designed majors, study abroad. *Unusual degree programs:* 3-2 engineering with University of Virginia, Vanderbilt University, Washington University, Virginia Commonwealth University; nursing with Johns Hopkins University, Vanderbilt University.

Computers on Campus 154 computers/terminals and 10 ports are available on campus for general student use. Students can access the following: campus intranet, computer help desk, free student e-mail accounts, online (class) grades, online (class) registration, online (class) schedules. Campuswide network is available. 100% of college-owned or -operated housing units are wired for high-speed Internet access. Wireless service is available via entire campus.

Student Life *Housing:* on-campus residence required through senior year. *Options:* coed. Campus housing is university owned. Freshman campus housing is guaranteed. *Activities and organizations:* drama/theater group, student-run newspaper, radio station, choral group, Pan World Club, Macon Activities Council, Model United Nations, BIONIC (Believe It or Not, I Care volunteer organization), Black Students Alliance. *Campus security:* 24-hour emergency response devices and patrols, late-night transport/escort service. *Student services:* health clinic, personal/psychological counseling.

Athletics Member NCAA. All Division III. *Intercollegiate sports:* basketball M/W, cross-country running M/W, equestrian sports M/W, lacrosse M/W, soccer M/W, softball W, tennis M/W, volleyball W.

Standardized Tests *Required:* SAT or ACT (for admission).

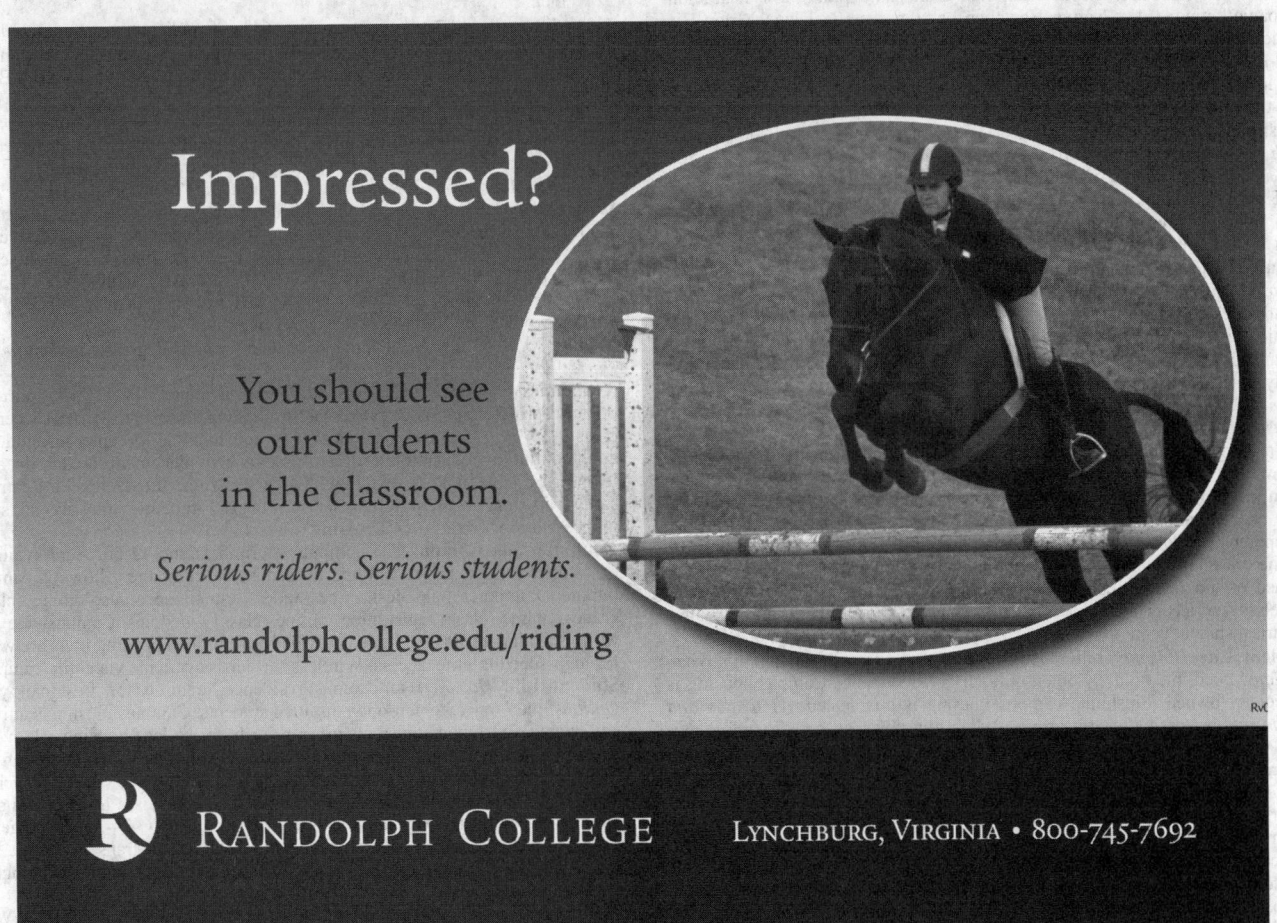

Costs (2010–11) *Comprehensive fee:* $39,249 includes full-time tuition ($28,744), mandatory fees ($510), and room and board ($9995). Part-time tuition: $1200 per credit hour. Part-time tuition and fees vary according to course load. *Required fees:* $103 per term part-time. *Payment plan:* installment. *Waivers:* adult students and employees or children of employees.

Financial Aid Of all full-time matriculated undergraduates who enrolled in 2009, 407 applied for aid, 369 were judged to have need, 73 had their need fully met. 180 Federal Work-Study jobs (averaging $1860). 119 state and other part-time jobs (averaging $1800). In 2009, 132 non-need-based awards were made. *Average percent of need met:* 75%. *Average financial aid package:* $24,013. *Average need-based loan:* $5370. *Average need-based gift aid:* $18,359. *Average non-need-based aid:* $16,268. *Average indebtedness upon graduation:* $22,000.

Applying *Options:* electronic application, early admission, early action, deferred entrance. *Application fee:* $50. *Required:* essay or personal statement, high school transcript, 2 letters of recommendation. *Recommended:* interview. *Application deadlines:* 4/1 (freshmen), 7/1 (transfers), 2/1 (early action). *Notification:* 4/15 (freshmen), continuous (transfers), 2/15 (early action).

Freshman Application Contact Ms. Margaret Blount, Director of Admissions, Randolph College, 2500 Rivermont Avenue, Lynchburg, VA 24503-1555. *Phone:* 434-947-8100. *Toll-free phone:* 800-745-7692. *Fax:* 434-947-8996. *E-mail:* admissions@randolphcollege.edu. *Web site:* http://www.randolphcollege.edu/.

See page 1522 for the College Close-Up.

Randolph-Macon College
Ashland, Virginia

- **Independent United Methodist** 4-year, founded 1830
- **Suburban** 120-acre campus with easy access to Richmond
- **Endowment** $105.2 million
- **Coed** 1,222 undergraduate students, 98% full-time, 53% women, 47% men
- **Moderately difficult** entrance level, 56% of applicants were admitted

Undergraduates 1,196 full-time, 26 part-time. Students come from 29 states and territories; 15 other countries; 32% are from out of state; 12% Black or African American, non-Hispanic/Latino; 3% Hispanic/Latino; 2% Asian, non-Hispanic/Latino; 0.1% Native Hawaiian or other Pacific Islander, non-Hispanic/Latino; 0.6% American Indian or Alaska Native, non-Hispanic/Latino; 2% Two or more races, non-Hispanic/Latino; 0.2% Race/ethnicity unknown; 3% international; 2% transferred in; 77% live on campus. *Retention:* 75% of full-time freshmen returned.

Freshmen *Admission:* 4,659 applied, 2,586 admitted, 343 enrolled. *Average high school GPA:* 3.39. *Test scores:* SAT critical reading scores over 500: 72%; SAT math scores over 500: 73%; SAT writing scores over 500: 58%; SAT critical reading scores over 600: 22%; SAT math scores over 600: 21%; SAT writing scores over 600: 17%; SAT critical reading scores over 700: 2%; SAT math scores over 700: 2%; SAT writing scores over 700: 1%.

Faculty *Total:* 147, 63% full-time, 69% with terminal degrees. *Student/faculty ratio:* 11:1.

Academics *Calendar:* 4-1-4. *Degree:* bachelor's. *Special study options:* academic remediation for entering students, accelerated degree program, advanced placement credit, double majors, honors programs, independent study, internships, off-campus study, part-time degree program, services for LD students, study abroad, summer session for credit. *ROTC:* Army (c). *Unusual degree programs:* 3-2 engineering with Columbia University, University of Virginia; forestry with Duke University; accounting with Virginia Commonwealth University.

Computers on Campus 356 computers/terminals and 1,500 ports are available on campus for general student use. Students can access the following: computer help desk, free student e-mail accounts, online (class) registration, online (class) schedules. Campuswide network is available. 100% of college-owned or -operated housing units are wired for high-speed Internet access. Wireless service is available via classrooms, computer labs, dorm rooms, libraries, student centers.

Student Life *Housing:* on-campus residence required through junior year. *Options:* coed, men-only, women-only, disabled students. Campus housing is university owned. Freshman campus housing is guaranteed. *Activities and organizations:* drama/theater group, student-run newspaper, radio and television station, choral group, Residence Hall Association, Campus Activities Board, Student Government Association, Drama Guild, Student Honors Association, national fraternities, national sororities. *Campus security:* 24-hour emergency response devices and patrols, late-night transport/escort service, controlled dormitory access. *Student services:* health clinic, personal/psychological counseling, women's center.

Athletics Member NCAA. All Division III. *Intercollegiate sports:* baseball M, basketball M/W, equestrian sports M(c)/W(c), field hockey W, football M, golf M, lacrosse M/W, soccer M/W, softball W, swimming and diving M/W,

tennis M/W, volleyball W. *Intramural sports:* basketball M/W, cheerleading M/W, cross-country running M/W, football M/W, lacrosse M/W, racquetball M/W, rugby M/W, soccer M/W, softball M/W, swimming and diving M, table tennis M/W, tennis M/W, ultimate Frisbee M/W, volleyball M/W.

Standardized Tests *Required:* SAT or ACT (for admission). *Recommended:* SAT Subject Tests (for admission).

Costs (2010–11) *One-time required fee:* $100. *Comprehensive fee:* $39,934 includes full-time tuition ($29,788), mandatory fees ($820), and room and board ($9326). Full-time tuition and fees vary according to reciprocity agreements. Part-time tuition: $3310 per course. *Required fees:* $840 per year part-time. *Room and board:* Room and board charges vary according to housing facility. *Payment plan:* installment. *Waivers:* employees or children of employees.

Financial Aid Of all full-time matriculated undergraduates who enrolled in 2009, 968 applied for aid, 842 were judged to have need, 193 had their need fully met. 235 Federal Work-Study jobs (averaging $2000). In 2009, 332 non-need-based awards were made. *Average percent of need met:* 79%. *Average financial aid package:* $23,140. *Average need-based loan:* $4560. *Average need-based gift aid:* $18,955. *Average non-need-based aid:* $12,029. *Average indebtedness upon graduation:* $31,603.

Applying *Options:* electronic application, early admission, early action, deferred entrance. *Application fee:* $30. *Required:* essay or personal statement, high school transcript, minimum 2 GPA, 1 letter of recommendation. *Recommended:* interview. *Application deadlines:* 3/1 (freshmen), 4/1 (transfers), 11/15 (early action). *Notification:* 4/1 (freshmen), 5/1 (transfers), 1/1 (early action).

Freshman Application Contact Anthony Ambrogi, Director of Admissions and Enrollment Research, Randolph-Macon College, PO Box 5005, Ashland, VA 23005-5505. *Phone:* 804-752-7305. *Toll-free phone:* 800-888-1762. *Fax:* 804-752-4707. *E-mail:* admissions@rmc.edu. *Web site:* http://www.rmc.edu/.

Regent University
Virginia Beach, Virginia

- **Independent religious** comprehensive, founded 1977
- **Suburban** 70-acre campus
- **Endowment** $188.0 million
- **Coed** 2,242 undergraduate students, 55% full-time, 63% women, 37% men
- **Minimally difficult** entrance level, 64% of applicants were admitted

Undergraduates 1,236 full-time, 1,006 part-time. Students come from 49 states and territories; 14 other countries; 54% are from out of state; 26% Black or African American, non-Hispanic/Latino; 7% Hispanic/Latino; 2% Asian, non-Hispanic/Latino; 0.7% American Indian or Alaska Native, non-Hispanic/Latino; 9% Race/ethnicity unknown; 0.4% international; 21% transferred in; 24% live on campus. *Retention:* 68% of full-time freshmen returned.

Freshmen *Admission:* 223 applied, 143 admitted, 174 enrolled. *Average high school GPA:* 3. *Test scores:* SAT critical reading scores over 500: 59%; SAT math scores over 500: 51%; SAT writing scores over 500: 54%; ACT scores over 18: 93%; SAT critical reading scores over 600: 29%; SAT math scores over 600: 21%; SAT writing scores over 600: 22%; ACT scores over 24: 57%; SAT critical reading scores over 700: 5%; SAT math scores over 700: 1%; SAT writing scores over 700: 6%; ACT scores over 30: 7%.

Faculty *Total:* 588, 32% full-time, 65% with terminal degrees. *Student/faculty ratio:* 17:1.

Academics *Calendar:* trimesters. *Degrees:* associate, bachelor's, master's, doctoral-professional, doctoral-research/scholarship, and post-master's certificates. *Special study options:* academic remediation for entering students, adult/continuing education programs, advanced placement credit, distance learning, double majors, external degree program, internships, off-campus study, part-time degree program, services for LD students, study abroad, summer session for credit. *ROTC:* Army (c).

Computers on Campus 123 computers/terminals and 32 ports are available on campus for general student use. Students can access the following: campus intranet, computer help desk, free student e-mail accounts, online (class) grades, online (class) registration, online (class) schedules. Campuswide network is available. 100% of college-owned or -operated housing units are wired for high-speed Internet access. Wireless service is available via entire campus.

Student Life *Housing:* on-campus residence required for freshman year. *Options:* men-only, women-only, disabled students. Campus housing is university owned. Freshman applicants given priority for college housing. *Activities and organizations:* drama/theater group, student-run newspaper, choral group, Regent Undergraduate Council, Students in Free Enterprise (SIFE), Psychology Club, Student Alumni Ambassadors, Jabez Praise Dance Ministry, national fraternities, national sororities. *Campus security:* 24-hour emergency response devices and patrols, student patrols, late-night transport/escort service, controlled dormitory access. *Student services:* personal/psychological counseling.

Athletics *Intramural sports:* basketball M/W, soccer M/W, volleyball M/W.

Standardized Tests *Required for some:* SAT or ACT (for admission).

Costs (2010–11) *Tuition:* $14,850 full-time, $495 per credit hour part-time. Full-time tuition and fees vary according to course level, course load, program, and student level. Part-time tuition and fees vary according to course level, course load, program, and student level. *Required fees:* $458 full-time, $495 per credit hour part-time. *Room only:* $5900. Room and board charges vary according to housing facility. *Payment plan:* installment. *Waivers:* employees or children of employees.

Applying *Options:* electronic application. *Application fee:* $50. *Required:* essay or personal statement. *Required for some:* high school transcript, minimum 3 GPA. *Application deadlines:* 8/1 (freshmen), 8/1 (transfers).

Freshman Application Contact Mr. Ken Baker, Director of Admissions, Regent University, 1000 Regent University Drive, SC 218, Virginia Beach, VA 23464. *Phone:* 757-352-4845. *Toll-free phone:* 800-373-5504. *Fax:* 757-352-4509. *E-mail:* kbaker@regent.edu. *Web site:* http://www.regent.edu/.

Roanoke College

Salem, Virginia

- **Independent** 4-year, founded 1842, affiliated with Evangelical Lutheran Church in America
- **Suburban** 80-acre campus
- **Endowment** $105.3 million
- **Coed** 2,104 undergraduate students, 95% full-time, 56% women, 44% men
- **Moderately difficult** entrance level, 66% of applicants were admitted

Undergraduates 2,004 full-time, 100 part-time. Students come from 41 states and territories; 22 other countries; 45% are from out of state; 4% Black or African American, non-Hispanic/Latino; 3% Hispanic/Latino; 1% Asian, non-Hispanic/Latino; 0.4% American Indian or Alaska Native, non-Hispanic/Latino; 0.8% Two or more races, non-Hispanic/Latino; 4% Race/ethnicity unknown; 2% international; 4% transferred in; 66% live on campus. *Retention:* 81% of full-time freshmen returned.

Freshmen *Admission:* 4,498 applied, 2,987 admitted, 565 enrolled. *Average high school GPA:* 3.39. *Test scores:* SAT critical reading scores over 500: 75%; SAT math scores over 500: 75%; SAT writing scores over 500: 70%; ACT scores over 18: 98%; SAT critical reading scores over 600: 23%; SAT math scores over 600: 20%; SAT writing scores over 600: 19%; ACT scores over 24: 43%; SAT critical reading scores over 700: 2%; SAT writing scores over 700: 2%; ACT scores over 30: 5%.

Faculty *Total:* 207, 79% full-time, 71% with terminal degrees. *Student/faculty ratio:* 12:1.

Academics *Calendar:* semesters. *Degree:* bachelor's. *Special study options:* accelerated degree program, adult/continuing education programs, advanced placement credit, double majors, English as a second language, honors programs, independent study, internships, off-campus study, part-time degree program, services for LD students, study abroad, summer session for credit. *Unusual degree programs:* 3-2 engineering with Virginia Polytechnic Institute and State University, University of Tennessee-Knoxville.

Computers on Campus 339 computers/terminals are available on campus for general student use. Students can access the following: campus intranet, computer help desk, free student e-mail accounts, online (class) grades, online (class) registration, online (class) schedules, discounts on computer hardware and software purchases, free Microsoft Office software. Campuswide network is available. 100% of college-owned or -operated housing units are wired for high-speed Internet access. Wireless service is available via entire campus.

Student Life *Housing:* on-campus residence required through senior year. *Options:* coed, women-only. Campus housing is university owned. Freshman campus housing is guaranteed. *Activities and organizations:* drama/theater group, student-run newspaper, radio station, choral group, Outdoor Adventures, Habitat for Humanity, Honors Association, Campus Activities Board, Inter-Varsity Christian Fellowship, national fraternities, national sororities. *Campus security:* 24-hour emergency response devices and patrols, late-night transport/escort service, controlled dormitory access. *Student services:* health clinic, personal/psychological counseling.

Athletics Member NCAA. All Division III. *Intercollegiate sports:* baseball M, basketball M/W, cross-country running M/W, field hockey W, golf M/W, lacrosse M/W, soccer M/W, softball W, tennis M/W, track and field M/W, volleyball W. *Intramural sports:* badminton M/W, basketball M/W, cheerleading M/W, equestrian sports W(c), field hockey W, football M/W, ice hockey M(c), lacrosse M, racquetball M/W, rugby M(c), soccer M(c)/W(c), softball M/W, table tennis M/W, tennis M/W, ultimate Frisbee M(c)/W(c), volleyball M/W, water polo M/W.

Standardized Tests *Required:* SAT or ACT (for admission).

Costs (2011–12) *One-time required fee:* $125. *Comprehensive fee:* $43,672 includes full-time tuition ($31,950), mandatory fees ($950), and room and board ($10,772). Part-time tuition: $1530 per course. Part-time tuition and fees vary according to course load. *College room only:* $5004. Room and board charges vary according to board plan and housing facility. *Payment plan:* installment. *Waivers:* senior citizens and employees or children of employees.

Financial Aid Of all full-time matriculated undergraduates who enrolled in 2009, 1,617 applied for aid, 1,412 were judged to have need, 323 had their need fully met. 1,016 Federal Work-Study jobs (averaging $1500). In 2009, 545 non-need-based awards were made. *Average percent of need met:* 79%. *Average financial aid package:* $24,218. *Average need-based loan:* $4644. *Average need-based gift aid:* $19,306. *Average non-need-based aid:* $11,717. *Average indebtedness upon graduation:* $27,984.

Applying *Options:* electronic application, early admission, early decision, early action, deferred entrance. *Application fee:* $30. *Required:* high school transcript. *Recommended:* essay or personal statement, 3 letters of recommendation, interview. *Application deadlines:* 3/15 (freshmen), 8/1 (transfers). *Early decision deadline:* 11/1. *Notification:* 4/1 (freshmen), 8/15 (transfers), 12/1 (early decision), 10/1 (early action).

Freshman Application Contact Admissions Office, Roanoke College, 221 College Lane, Salem, VA 24153. *Phone:* 540-375-2270. *Toll-free phone:* 800-388-2276. *Fax:* 540-375-2267. *E-mail:* admissions@roanoke.edu. *Web site:* http://www.roanoke.edu/.

Saint Paul's College

Lawrenceville, Virginia

- **Independent Episcopal** 4-year, founded 1888
- **Small-town** 75-acre campus with easy access to Richmond
- **Coed**
- **Minimally difficult** entrance level

Faculty *Student/faculty ratio:* 17:1.

Academics *Calendar:* semesters. *Degree:* bachelor's.

Student Life *Campus security:* 24-hour emergency response devices and patrols, late-night transport/escort service, alarms on doors.

Athletics Member NCAA. All Division II.

Standardized Tests *Required:* SAT or ACT (for admission).

Costs (2010–11) *Comprehensive fee:* $19,850 includes full-time tuition ($11,880), mandatory fees ($1330), and room and board ($6640). Part-time tuition: $495 per credit hour. *Required fees:* $29 per credit hour part-time. *College room only:* $3140. Room and board charges vary according to board plan. *Payment plans:* installment, deferred payment.

Financial Aid Of all full-time matriculated undergraduates who enrolled in 2009, 613 applied for aid, 598 were judged to have need, 66 had their need fully met. *Average percent of need met:* 57. *Average financial aid package:* $8147. *Average need-based loan:* $1337. *Average need-based gift aid:* $4508. *Average indebtedness upon graduation:* $21,917.

Applying *Options:* deferred entrance. *Application fee:* $20. *Required:* high school transcript, 1 letter of recommendation. *Recommended:* essay or personal statement, interview.

Freshman Application Contact Saint Paul's College, 115 College Drive, Lawrenceville, VA 23868-1202. *Phone:* 434-848-6493. *Toll-free phone:* 800-678-7071. *Web site:* http://www.saintpauls.edu/.

Shenandoah University

Winchester, Virginia

- **Independent United Methodist** comprehensive, founded 1875
- **Small-town** 100-acre campus with easy access to Baltimore and Washington, D.C.
- **Endowment** $47.2 million
- **Coed** 1,882 undergraduate students, 96% full-time, 59% women, 41% men
- **Moderately difficult** entrance level, 81% of applicants were admitted

Undergraduates 1,801 full-time, 81 part-time. Students come from 37 states and territories; 49 other countries; 33% are from out of state; 13% Black or African American, non-Hispanic/Latino; 2% Hispanic/Latino; 2% Asian, non-Hispanic/Latino; 0.3% Native Hawaiian or other Pacific Islander, non-Hispanic/Latino; 0.4% American Indian or Alaska Native, non-Hispanic/Latino; 0.9% Two or more races, non-Hispanic/Latino; 10% Race/ethnicity unknown; 3% international; 11% transferred in; 45% live on campus. *Retention:* 72% of full-time freshmen returned.

Freshmen *Admission:* 1,498 applied, 1,215 admitted, 408 enrolled. *Average high school GPA:* 3.34. *Test scores:* SAT critical reading scores over 500: 54%; SAT math scores over 500: 57%; SAT writing scores over 500: 52%; ACT scores over 18: 87%; SAT critical reading scores over 600: 16%; SAT math scores over 600: 16%; SAT writing scores over 600: 14%; ACT scores over 24: 29%; SAT critical reading scores over 700: 2%; SAT math scores over 700: 2%; SAT writing scores over 700: 1%; ACT scores over 30: 3%.

Faculty *Total:* 432, 50% full-time, 60% with terminal degrees. *Student/faculty ratio:* 9:1.

Academics *Calendar:* semesters. *Degrees:* certificates, diplomas, bachelor's, master's, doctoral-professional, doctoral-research/scholarship, post-master's, and postbachelor's certificates. *Special study options:* accelerated degree program, adult/continuing education programs, advanced placement credit, cooperative education, distance learning, double majors, English as a second language, independent study, internships, off-campus study, part-time degree program, services for LD students, student-designed majors, study abroad, summer session for credit. *Unusual degree programs:* 3-2 MS in Athletic Training program utilizes 3+2 model where student may apply as an undergraduate student who has completed the prerequisite courses without having earned an undergraduate degree. Applicant must have a minimum of 90 college credits (grade C or better) for the 52 required prereq credits.

Computers on Campus 142 computers/terminals and 50 ports are available on campus for general student use. Students can access the following: campus intranet, computer help desk, free student e-mail accounts, online (class) grades, online (class) registration, online (class) schedules, online student account information. Campuswide network is available. 100% of college-owned or -operated housing units are wired for high-speed Internet access. Wireless service is available via entire campus.

Student Life *Housing:* on-campus residence required through sophomore year. *Options:* coed, disabled students. Campus housing is university owned and is provided by a third party. Freshman campus housing is guaranteed. *Activities and organizations:* drama/theater group, student-run newspaper, television station, choral group, American Pharmacists Association Academy of Student Pharmacists, Alpha Lambda Delta, Kappa Psi Pharmaceutical Fraternity, Inc, Sigma Alpha Iota, Phi Delta Chi. *Campus security:* 24-hour emergency response devices and patrols, late-night transport/escort service, controlled dormitory access, side door alarms. *Student services:* health clinic, personal/psychological counseling.

Athletics Member NCAA. All Division III. *Intercollegiate sports:* baseball M, basketball M/W, cross-country running M/W, field hockey W, football M, golf M, lacrosse M/W, soccer M/W, softball W, tennis M/W, track and field M/W, volleyball W. *Intramural sports:* basketball M/W, cheerleading M/W, football M/W, soccer M/W, softball M/W, tennis M/W, ultimate Frisbee M/W, volleyball M/W.

Standardized Tests *Required:* SAT or ACT (for admission).

Costs (2010–11) *Comprehensive fee:* $33,950 includes full-time tuition ($24,780), mandatory fees ($300), and room and board ($8870). Full-time tuition and fees vary according to course load, location, and program. Part-time tuition: $723 per credit hour. Part-time tuition and fees vary according to course load, location, and program. *Room and board:* Room and board charges vary according to board plan and housing facility. *Payment plan:* installment. *Waivers:* employees or children of employees.

Financial Aid Of all full-time matriculated undergraduates who enrolled in 2009, 1,231 applied for aid, 1,151 were judged to have need, 71 had their need fully met. 732 Federal Work-Study jobs (averaging $1935). 384 state and other part-time jobs (averaging $1980). In 2009, 146 non-need-based awards were made. *Average percent of need met:* 71%. *Average financial aid package:* $19,000. *Average need-based loan:* $4500. *Average need-based gift aid:* $8000. *Average non-need-based aid:* $5000. *Average indebtedness upon graduation:* $27,000.

Applying *Options:* electronic application, deferred entrance. *Application fee:* $30. *Required:* high school transcript, 1 letter of recommendation. *Required for some:* essay or personal statement, interview, Audition and/or portfolio for Conservatory applicants. *Recommended:* minimum 2.4 GPA. *Application deadlines:* rolling (freshmen), rolling (transfers). *Notification:* continuous (freshmen), continuous (transfers).

Freshman Application Contact Mr. David Anthony, Dean of Admissions, Shenandoah University, 1460 University Drive, Winchester, VA 22601-5195. *Phone:* 540-665-4581. *Toll-free phone:* 800-432-2266. *Fax:* 540-665-4627. *E-mail:* admit@su.edu. *Web site:* http://www.su.edu/.

Skyline College
Roanoke, Virginia

- **Proprietary** 4-year, founded 1966
- **Suburban** 3-acre campus
- **Coed** 321 undergraduate students, 100% full-time, 59% women, 41% men
- **Moderately difficult** entrance level, 81% of applicants were admitted

Undergraduates 321 full-time. Students come from 4 states and territories; 2% are from out of state; 28% Black or African American, non-Hispanic/Latino; 2% Hispanic/Latino; 0.3% Two or more races, non-Hispanic/Latino. *Retention:* 54% of full-time freshmen returned.

Freshmen *Admission:* 52 applied, 42 admitted, 33 enrolled.

Faculty *Total:* 46, 46% full-time. *Student/faculty ratio:* 11:1.

Academics *Calendar:* semesters. *Degrees:* certificates, diplomas, associate, and bachelor's. *Special study options:* academic remediation for entering students, accelerated degree program, adult/continuing education programs, advanced placement credit, distance learning, double majors, honors programs, independent study, internships, off-campus study, part-time degree program, study abroad, summer session for credit.

Computers on Campus 120 computers/terminals are available on campus for general student use. Students can access the following: campus intranet, com-

puter help desk, free student e-mail accounts, online (class) grades, online (class) registration, online (class) schedules. Campuswide network is available.

Student Life *Housing:* college housing not available. *Activities and organizations:* National Vocational Technical Honor Society, Electronics Technician's Association, American Red Cross blood mobile drives. *Campus security:* building and parking lot security.

Standardized Tests *Required:* ACT (for admission). *Recommended:* SAT (for admission), SAT Subject Tests (for admission).

Financial Aid Of all full-time matriculated undergraduates who enrolled in 2008, 425 applied for aid, 410 were judged to have need.

Applying *Options:* electronic application, deferred entrance. *Application fee:* $45. *Required:* high school transcript, interview. *Application deadlines:* rolling (freshmen), rolling (transfers). *Notification:* continuous (freshmen), continuous (transfers).

Freshman Application Contact Dr. Walter Merchant, Campus Provost (Interim), Skyline College, 5234 Airport Road, Roanoke, VA 24012. *Phone:* 540-563-8080. *Toll-free phone:* 866-708-6178. *Fax:* 540-362-5400. *E-mail:* wmerchant@ecpi.edu. *Web site:* http://www.skyline.edu/.

Southern Virginia University
Buena Vista, Virginia

Freshman Application Contact Mr. Tony Caputo, Dean of Admissions, Southern Virginia University, One University Hill Drive, Buena Vista, VA 24416. *Phone:* 540-261-2756. *Toll-free phone:* 800-229-8420. *Fax:* 540-261-8559. *E-mail:* admissions@southernvirginia.edu. *Web site:* http://www.svu.edu/.

South University
Glen Allen, Virginia

- **Proprietary** comprehensive
- **Coed**

Academics *Degrees:* bachelor's and master's.

Costs (2010–11) *Tuition:* Information about tuition and fees can be obtained by contacting the South University Admissions Office.

Freshman Application Contact South University, 2151 Old Brick Road, Glen Allen, VA 23060. *Phone:* 804-727-6800. *Toll-free phone:* 888-422-5076. *Web site:* http://www.southuniversity.edu/richmond.

See page 1632 for the College Close-Up.

South University
Virginia Beach, Virginia

- **Proprietary** comprehensive
- **Coed**

Academics *Degrees:* associate, bachelor's, and master's.

Costs (2010–11) *Tuition:* Information about tuition and fees can be obtained by contacting the South University Admissions Office.

Freshman Application Contact South University, 301 Bendix Road, Suite 100, Virginia Beach, VA 23452. *Phone:* 757-493-6900. *Toll-free phone:* 877-206-1845. *Web site:* http://www.southuniversity.edu/virginia-beach.

See page 1634 for the College Close-Up.

Stratford University
Falls Church, Virginia

- **Proprietary** comprehensive, founded 1976
- **Suburban** campus with easy access to Washington, D.C.
- **Coed** 1,023 undergraduate students, 13% full-time, 73% women, 27% men
- **Minimally difficult** entrance level

Undergraduates 136 full-time, 887 part-time. 52% are from out of state. *Retention:* 52% of full-time freshmen returned.

Freshmen *Admission:* 350 enrolled.

Faculty *Total:* 72, 15% full-time, 36% with terminal degrees. *Student/faculty ratio:* 13:1.

Academics *Calendar:* quarters. *Degrees:* diplomas, associate, bachelor's, and master's. *Special study options:* accelerated degree program, advanced placement credit, cooperative education, distance learning, English as a second language, internships, part-time degree program, summer session for credit.

Computers on Campus 104 computers/terminals are available on campus for general student use. Students can access the following: campus intranet, computer help desk, free student e-mail accounts, online (class) registration, online (class) schedules. Campuswide network is available. Wireless service is available via entire campus.

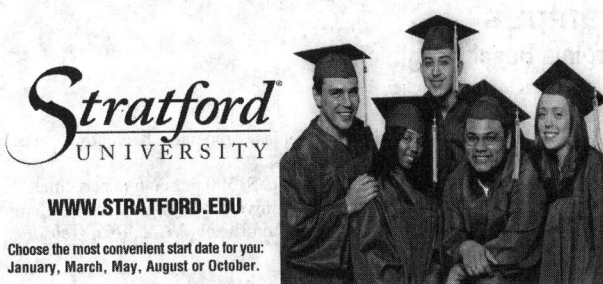

Student Life *Housing:* college housing not available. *Options:* Campus housing is provided by a third party. *Campus security:* 24-hour emergency response devices.

Costs (2011–12) *Comprehensive fee:* $22,330 includes full-time tuition ($14,985), mandatory fees ($345), and room and board ($7000). Full-time tuition and fees vary according to course load and program. Part-time tuition and fees vary according to course load and program. *Room and board:* Room and board charges vary according to housing facility. *Payment plans:* installment, deferred payment. *Waivers:* employees or children of employees.

Applying *Options:* electronic application, deferred entrance. *Application fee:* $50. *Required:* minimum 2 GPA, interview, proof of high school graduation or equivalent is required for all students. Personal statement, transcript, and letters of recommendation are only required for the Nursing program. *Required for some:* essay or personal statement, high school transcript, 2 letters of recommendation. *Application deadlines:* 8/5 (freshmen), 8/5 (transfers). *Notification:* continuous until 8/5 (freshmen), continuous until 8/5 (transfers).

Freshman Application Contact James W. Ray, Director of Admissions, Stratford University, 7777 Leesburg Pike, Falls Church, VA 22043. *Phone:* 703-821-8570. *Toll-free phone:* 800-444-0804. *Fax:* 703-734-5339. *E-mail:* jray@stratford.edu. *Web site:* http://www.stratford.edu/.

See page 1652 for the College Close-Up.

Stratford University
Woodbridge, Virginia

- **Proprietary** comprehensive
- **Coed**

Academics *Degrees:* certificates, diplomas, associate, bachelor's, and master's.

Costs (2010–11) *Tuition:* $370 per credit hour part-time.

Applying *Options:* electronic application. *Application fee:* $50.

Freshman Application Contact Director of Admissions, Stratford University, 14349 Gideon Drive, Woodbridge, VA 22192. *Phone:* 703-897-1982. *Toll-free phone:* 888-546-1250. *E-mail:* admissions@stratford.edu. *Web site:* http://www.stratford.edu/.

Strayer University - Alexandria Campus
Alexandria, Virginia

- **Proprietary** comprehensive
- **Coed**

Academics *Degrees:* certificates, diplomas, associate, bachelor's, master's, and postbachelor's certificates.

Costs (2010–11) *Tuition:* $13,635 full-time, $1590 per course part-time.

Freshman Application Contact Strayer University - Alexandria Campus, 2730 Eisenhower Avenue, Alexandria, VA 22314. *Web site:* http://www.strayer.edu/alexandria.

Strayer University - Arlington Campus
Arlington, Virginia

- **Proprietary** comprehensive
- **Coed**

Academics *Degrees:* certificates, diplomas, associate, bachelor's, master's, and postbachelor's certificates.

Costs (2010–11) *Tuition:* $13,635 full-time, $1590 per course part-time.

Freshman Application Contact Strayer University - Arlington Campus, 2121 15th Street North, Arlington, VA 22201. *Web site:* http://www.strayer.edu/arlington.

Strayer University - Chesapeake Campus
Chesapeake, Virginia

- **Proprietary** comprehensive
- **Coed**

Academics *Degrees:* certificates, diplomas, associate, bachelor's, master's, and postbachelor's certificates.

Costs (2010–11) *Tuition:* $13,635 full-time, $1590 per course part-time.

Freshman Application Contact Strayer University - Chesapeake Campus, 700 Independent Parkway, Suite 400, Chesapeake, VA 23320. *Web site:* http://www.strayer.edu/chesapeake/.

Strayer University - Chesterfield Campus

Midlothian, Virginia

- **Proprietary** comprehensive
- **Coed**

Academics *Degrees:* certificates, diplomas, associate, bachelor's, master's, and postbachelor's certificates.
Costs (2010–11) *Tuition:* $13,635 full-time, $1590 per course part-time.
Freshman Application Contact Strayer University - Chesterfield Campus, 2820 Waterford Lake Drive, Suite 100, Midlothian, VA 23112. *Web site:* http://www.strayer.edu/chesterfield/.

Strayer University - Fredericksburg Campus

Fredericksburg, Virginia

- **Proprietary** comprehensive
- **Coed**

Academics *Degrees:* certificates, diplomas, associate, bachelor's, master's, and postbachelor's certificates.
Costs (2010–11) *Tuition:* $13,635 full-time, $1590 per course part-time.
Freshman Application Contact Strayer University - Fredericksburg Campus, 150 Riverside Parkway, Suite 100, Fredericksburg, VA 22406. *Web site:* http://www.strayer.edu/fredericksburg.

Strayer University - Henrico Campus

Glen Allen, Virginia

- **Proprietary** comprehensive, founded 1892
- **Coed**

Academics *Degrees:* certificates, diplomas, associate, bachelor's, master's, and postbachelor's certificates.
Costs (2010–11) *Tuition:* $13,635 full-time, $1590 per course part-time.
Freshman Application Contact Strayer University - Henrico Campus, 11501 Nuckols Road, Glen Allen, VA 23059. *Web site:* http://www.strayer.edu/henrico.

Strayer University - Loudoun Campus

Ashburn, Virginia

- **Proprietary** comprehensive
- **Coed**

Academics *Degrees:* certificates, diplomas, associate, bachelor's, master's, and postbachelor's certificates.
Costs (2010–11) *Tuition:* $13,635 full-time, $1590 per course part-time.
Freshman Application Contact Strayer University - Loudoun Campus, 45150 Russell Branch Parkway, Suite 200, Ashburn, VA 20147. *Web site:* http://www.strayer.edu/loudoun.

Strayer University - Manassas Campus

Manassas, Virginia

- **Proprietary** comprehensive
- **Coed**

Academics *Degrees:* certificates, diplomas, associate, bachelor's, master's, and postbachelor's certificates.
Costs (2010–11) *Tuition:* $13,635 full-time, $1590 per course part-time.
Freshman Application Contact Strayer University - Manassas Campus, 9990 Battleview Parkway, Manassas, VA 20109. *Web site:* http://www.strayer.edu/manassas.

Strayer University - Newport News Campus

Newport News, Virginia

- **Proprietary** comprehensive
- **Coed**

Academics *Degrees:* certificates, diplomas, associate, bachelor's, master's, and postbachelor's certificates.
Costs (2010–11) *Tuition:* $13,635 full-time, $1590 per course part-time.
Freshman Application Contact Strayer University - Newport News Campus, 813 Diligence Drive, Suite 100, Newport News, VA 23606. *Web site:* http://www.strayer.edu/newport_news.

Strayer University - Virginia Beach Campus

Virginia Beach, Virginia

- **Proprietary** comprehensive
- **Coed**

Academics *Degrees:* certificates, diplomas, associate, bachelor's, master's, and postbachelor's certificates.
Costs (2010–11) *Tuition:* $13,635 full-time, $1590 per course part-time.
Freshman Application Contact Strayer University - Virginia Beach Campus, 249 Central Park Avenue, Suite 350, Virginia Beach, VA 23462. *Web site:* http://www.strayer.edu/virginia_beach.

Strayer University - Woodbridge Campus

Woodbridge, Virginia

- **Proprietary** comprehensive
- **Coed**

Academics *Degrees:* certificates, diplomas, associate, bachelor's, master's, and postbachelor's certificates.
Costs (2010–11) *Tuition:* $13,635 full-time, $1590 per course part-time.
Freshman Application Contact Strayer University - Woodbridge Campus, 13385 Minnieville Road, Woodbridge, VA 22192. *Web site:* http://www.strayer.edu/woodbridge.

Sweet Briar College

Sweet Briar, Virginia

- **Independent** comprehensive, founded 1901
- **Rural** 3250-acre campus
- **Endowment** $81.9 million
- **Women only** 747 undergraduate students, 97% full-time
- **Moderately difficult** entrance level, 84% of applicants were admitted

Undergraduates 723 full-time, 24 part-time. 91% live on campus. *Retention:* 76% of full-time freshmen returned.
Freshmen *Admission:* 606 applied, 507 admitted, 180 enrolled.
Faculty *Total:* 115, 73% full-time. *Student/faculty ratio:* 7:1.
Academics *Calendar:* semesters. *Degrees:* bachelor's and master's. *Special study options:* accelerated degree program, adult/continuing education programs, advanced placement credit, double majors, honors programs, independent study, internships, off-campus study, part-time degree program, services for LD students, student-designed majors, study abroad, summer session for credit. *Unusual degree programs:* 3-2 engineering with Virginia Polytechnic Institute and State University, University of Virginia, Columbia University, Washington University in St. Louis.
Computers on Campus 128 computers/terminals and 3,000 ports are available on campus for general student use. Students can access the following: campus intranet, computer help desk, free student e-mail accounts, online (class) grades, online (class) registration, online (class) schedules. Campus-wide network is available. 100% of college-owned or -operated housing units are wired for high-speed Internet access. Wireless service is available via entire campus.
Student Life *Housing:* on-campus residence required through senior year. *Options:* women-only. Campus housing is university owned. Freshman campus housing is guaranteed. *Activities and organizations:* drama/theater group, student-run newspaper, radio and television station, choral group, Student Government Association, Campus Events Organization, Interclub Council, PnP, Environmental Club. *Campus security:* 24-hour emergency response devices and patrols, late-night transport/escort service, controlled dormitory access, front gate security. *Student services:* health clinic, personal/psychological counseling.
Athletics Member NCAA. All Division III. *Intercollegiate sports:* equestrian sports W(c), fencing W(c), field hockey W, lacrosse W, soccer W, softball W(c), swimming and diving W, tennis W, volleyball W.
Standardized Tests *Required:* SAT or ACT (for admission).
Costs (2010–11) *Comprehensive fee:* $40,975 includes full-time tuition ($29,720), mandatory fees ($475), and room and board ($10,780). Full-time tuition and fees vary according to program. Part-time tuition: $760 per credit hour. Part-time tuition and fees vary according to program. *Room and board:* Room and board charges vary according to board plan. *Payment plan:* installment. *Waivers:* adult students, senior citizens, and employees or children of employees.
Financial Aid Of all full-time matriculated undergraduates who enrolled in 2008, 422 applied for aid, 408 were judged to have need, 354 had their need fully met. 99 Federal Work-Study jobs (averaging $945). 115 state and other part-time jobs (averaging $949). *Average percent of need met:* 70%. *Average*

financial aid package: $13,633. *Average need-based loan:* $4585. *Average need-based gift aid:* $11,479. *Average indebtedness upon graduation:* $20,118.

Applying *Options:* electronic application, early admission, deferred entrance. *Application fee:* $40. *Required:* essay or personal statement, high school transcript, 2 letters of recommendation. *Required for some:* portfolio with courses taken, list of texts covered, essay about homeschooling, campus visit, interview for homeschooled applicants. *Recommended:* interview. *Application deadlines:* 2/1 (freshmen), 5/1 (transfers). *Notification:* continuous (freshmen), 5/15 (transfers).

Freshman Application Contact Sweet Briar College, PO Box B, Sweet Briar, VA 24595. *Phone:* 434-381-6142. *Toll-free phone:* 800-381-6142. *E-mail:* admissions@sbc.edu. *Web site:* http://www.sbc.edu/.

See page 1656 for the College Close-Up.

University of Management and Technology
Arlington, Virginia

Freshman Application Contact Vice President, University of Management and Technology, Suite 700, 1901 North Fort Meyers Drive, Arlington, VA 22209. *Phone:* 703-516-0035. *Toll-free phone:* 800-924-4885. *Fax:* 703-516-0985. *E-mail:* admissions@umtweb.edu. *Web site:* http://www.umtweb.edu/.

University of Mary Washington
Fredericksburg, Virginia

- **State-supported** comprehensive, founded 1908
- **Small-town** 176-acre campus with easy access to Richmond and Washington, D.C.
- **Endowment** $35.7 million
- **Coed** 4,354 undergraduate students, 88% full-time, 64% women, 36% men
- **Very difficult** entrance level, 77% of applicants were admitted

Undergraduates 3,834 full-time, 520 part-time. Students come from 42 states and territories; 21 other countries; 20% are from out of state; 5% Black or African American, non-Hispanic/Latino; 4% Hispanic/Latino; 5% Asian, non-Hispanic/Latino; 0.3% American Indian or Alaska Native, non-Hispanic/Latino; 26% Race/ethnicity unknown; 0.8% international; 5% transferred in; 57% live on campus. *Retention:* 84% of full-time freshmen returned.

Freshmen *Admission:* 4,766 applied, 3,681 admitted, 960 enrolled. *Average high school GPA:* 3.58. *Test scores:* SAT critical reading scores over 500: 87%; SAT math scores over 500: 85%; SAT writing scores over 500: 85%; ACT scores over 18: 100%; SAT critical reading scores over 600: 46%; SAT math scores over 600: 34%; SAT writing scores over 600: 40%; ACT scores over 24: 82%; SAT critical reading scores over 700: 8%; SAT math scores over 700: 3%; SAT writing scores over 700: 6%; ACT scores over 30: 10%.

Faculty *Total:* 387, 62% full-time, 70% with terminal degrees. *Student/faculty ratio:* 15:1.

Academics *Calendar:* semesters. *Degrees:* certificates, bachelor's, master's, and postbachelor's certificates. *Special study options:* accelerated degree program, adult/continuing education programs, advanced placement credit, cooperative education, distance learning, double majors, independent study, internships, part-time degree program, services for LD students, student-designed majors, study abroad, summer session for credit. *ROTC:* Army (c). *Unusual degree programs:* computer science, elementary education.

Computers on Campus 306 computers/terminals are available on campus for general student use. Students can access the following: campus intranet, computer help desk, free student e-mail accounts, online (class) grades, online (class) registration, online (class) schedules, Library resources, foreign languages resources, course management system. Campuswide network is available. 100% of college-owned or -operated housing units are wired for high-speed Internet access. Wireless service is available via entire campus.

Student Life *Housing:* on-campus residence required through sophomore year. *Options:* coed, men-only, women-only, disabled students. Campus housing is university owned and leased by the school. Freshman campus housing is guaranteed. *Activities and organizations:* drama/theater group, student-run newspaper, radio station, choral group, Students Helping Honduras, Black Student Association, Giant Productions (campus entertainment group), PRISM, Cheap Seats Cinema. *Campus security:* 24-hour emergency response devices and patrols, student patrols, late-night transport/escort service, controlled dormitory access, self-defense and safety classes. *Student services:* health clinic, personal/psychological counseling.

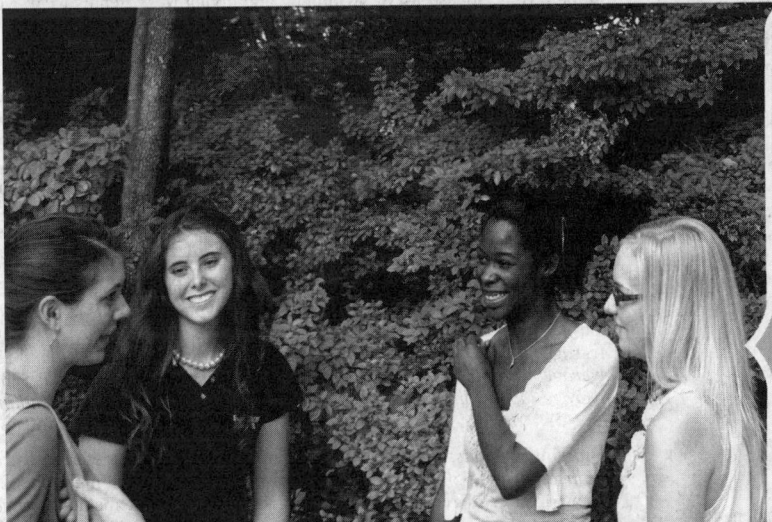

Athletics Member NCAA. All Division III. *Intercollegiate sports:* baseball M, basketball M/W, cheerleading M(c)/W(c), crew M/W, cross-country running M/W, equestrian sports M/W, field hockey W, lacrosse M/W, rugby M(c)/W(c), soccer M/W, softball W, swimming and diving M/W, tennis M/W, track and field M/W, volleyball M(c)/W. *Intramural sports:* badminton M/W, baseball M(c), basketball M/W, bowling M/W, cheerleading M(c)/W(c), fencing M(c)/W(c), football M/W, golf M/W, lacrosse M/W(c), soccer M/W, softball M/W, tennis M(c)/W(c), ultimate Frisbee M(c)/W(c), volleyball M/W, water polo M/W.

Standardized Tests *Required:* SAT or ACT (for admission). *Recommended:* SAT Subject Tests (for admission).

Costs (2011–12) *One-time required fee:* $75. *Tuition:* state resident $4460 full-time, $195 per credit hour part-time; nonresident $16,190 full-time, $740 per credit hour part-time. Part-time tuition and fees vary according to course load and location. *Required fees:* $4340 full-time, $110 per credit hour part-time, $30 per term part-time. *Room and board:* $8900; room only: $5350. Room and board charges vary according to board plan and housing facility. *Payment plan:* installment. *Waivers:* senior citizens.

Financial Aid Of all full-time matriculated undergraduates who enrolled in 2008, 2,150 applied for aid, 1,350 were judged to have need, 190 had their need fully met. 25 Federal Work-Study jobs (averaging $1760). 750 state and other part-time jobs (averaging $1820). In 2008, 330 non-need-based awards were made. *Average percent of need met:* 53%. *Average financial aid package:* $8200. *Average need-based loan:* $4100. *Average need-based gift aid:* $6500. *Average non-need-based aid:* $2400. *Average indebtedness upon graduation:* $16,000. *Financial aid deadline:* 5/15.

Applying *Options:* electronic application, deferred entrance. *Application fee:* $50. *Required:* essay or personal statement, high school transcript. *Application deadlines:* 2/1 (freshmen), 3/1 (transfers). *Notification:* 4/1 (freshmen), 5/15 (transfers).

Freshman Application Contact Ms. Kimberly Johnston, Dean of Admissions, University of Mary Washington, 1301 College Avenue, Fredericksburg, VA 22401-5358. *Phone:* 540-654-2000. *Toll-free phone:* 800-468-5614. *Fax:* 540-654-1857. *E-mail:* admit@umw.edu. *Web site:* http://www.umw.edu/.

University of Phoenix–Northern Virginia Campus

Reston, Virginia

Freshman Application Contact Ms. Audra McQuarie, Registrar/Executive Director, University of Phoenix–Northern Virginia Campus, 4035 South Riverpoint Parkway, Mail Stop CF-L101, Phoenix, AZ 85040. *Phone:* 480-557-6151. *Toll-free phone:* 800-776-4867 (in-state); 800-228-7240 (out-of-state). *Fax:* 480-643-3068. *E-mail:* audra.mcquarie@phoenix.edu. *Web site:* http://www.phoenix.edu/.

University of Phoenix–Richmond Campus

Richmond, Virginia

Freshman Application Contact Ms. Audra McQuarie, Registrar/Executive Director, University of Phoenix–Richmond Campus, 4035 South Riverpoint Parkway, Mail Stop CF-L101, Phoenix, AZ 85040. *Phone:* 480-557-6151. *Toll-free phone:* 800-776-4867 (in-state); 800-228-7240 (out-of-state). *Fax:* 480-643-3068. *E-mail:* audra.mcquarie@phoenix.edu. *Web site:* http://www.phoenix.edu/.

University of Richmond

Richmond, Virginia

- **Independent** comprehensive, founded 1830
- **Suburban** 350-acre campus
- **Endowment** $1.6 billion
- **Coed** 3,048 undergraduate students, 98% full-time, 54% women, 46% men
- **Very difficult** entrance level, 33% of applicants were admitted

Undergraduates 2,999 full-time, 49 part-time. Students come from 45 states and territories; 67 other countries; 79% are from out of state; 7% Black or African American, non-Hispanic/Latino; 5% Hispanic/Latino; 5% Asian, non-Hispanic/Latino; 0.3% American Indian or Alaska Native, non-Hispanic/Latino; 1% Two or more races, non-Hispanic/Latino; 12% Race/ethnicity unknown;

6% international; 2% transferred in; 91% live on campus. *Retention:* 93% of full-time freshmen returned.

Freshmen *Admission:* 8,661 applied, 2,857 admitted, 818 enrolled. *Test scores:* SAT critical reading scores over 500: 93%; SAT math scores over 500: 98%; SAT writing scores over 500: 96%; ACT scores over 18: 99%; SAT critical reading scores over 600: 70%; SAT math scores over 600: 79%; SAT writing scores over 600: 76%; ACT scores over 24: 93%; SAT critical reading scores over 700: 18%; SAT math scores over 700: 26%; SAT writing scores over 700: 22%; ACT scores over 30: 49%.

Faculty *Total:* 392, 78% full-time, 72% with terminal degrees. *Student/faculty ratio:* 9:1.

Academics *Calendar:* semesters. *Degrees:* bachelor's, master's, and doctoral-professional. *Special study options:* adult/continuing education programs, advanced placement credit, double majors, English as a second language, honors programs, independent study, internships, off-campus study, part-time degree program, services for LD students, student-designed majors, study abroad, summer session for credit. *ROTC:* Army (b). *Unusual degree programs:* 3-2 engineering with Columbia University School of Engineering & Applied Science; George Washington University School of Engineering & Applied Science; UVA School of Engineering; VCU School of Engineering; Virginia Polytechnic Institute College of Engineering.

Computers on Campus 1,079 computers/terminals and 3,300 ports are available on campus for general student use. Students can access the following: campus intranet, computer help desk, free student e-mail accounts, online (class) grades, online (class) registration, online (class) schedules. Campus-wide network is available. 100% of college-owned or -operated housing units are wired for high-speed Internet access. Wireless service is available via entire campus.

Student Life *Housing options:* coed, men-only, women-only. Campus housing is university owned. Freshman campus housing is guaranteed. *Activities and organizations:* drama/theater group, student-run newspaper, radio station, choral group, Amnesty International, Student Government Association, Volunteer Action Council, Multicultural Student Union, Campus Activities Board, national fraternities, national sororities. *Campus security:* 24-hour emergency response devices and patrols, late-night transport/escort service, controlled dormitory access, campus police. *Student services:* health clinic, personal/psychological counseling, women's center.

Athletics Member NCAA. All Division I except football (Division I-AA). *Intercollegiate sports:* badminton M(c)/W(c), baseball M(s), basketball M(s)/W(s), cheerleading W(c), crew M(c)/W(c), cross-country running M/W(s), equestrian sports M(c)/W(c), field hockey W(s), golf M(s)/W(s), gymnastics M(c)/W(c), ice hockey M(c), lacrosse M(c)/W(s), rugby M(c)/W(c), soccer M(s)/W(s), squash M(c)/W(c), swimming and diving M(c)/W(s), tennis M(s)/W(s), track and field M/W(s), ultimate Frisbee M(c)/W(c), volleyball M(c)/W(c), water polo M(c)/W(c). *Intramural sports:* baseball M(c), basketball M/W, field hockey W(c), football M, golf M/W, lacrosse W(c), soccer M(c)/W(c), softball M/W, squash M/W, swimming and diving M/W, tennis M/W, volleyball M/W.

Standardized Tests *Required:* SAT or ACT (for admission).

Costs (2011–12) *Comprehensive fee:* $52,420 includes full-time tuition ($43,170) and room and board ($9250). Full-time tuition and fees vary according to course load and student level. Part-time tuition: $7554 per unit. Part-time tuition and fees vary according to course load and student level. *College room only:* $4170. Room and board charges vary according to board plan and housing facility. *Payment plans:* installment, deferred payment. *Waivers:* employees or children of employees.

Financial Aid Of all full-time matriculated undergraduates who enrolled in 2009, 1,738 applied for aid, 1,500 were judged to have need, 1,409 had their need fully met. 393 Federal Work-Study jobs (averaging $1295). In 2009, 403 non-need-based awards were made. *Average percent of need met:* 100%. *Average financial aid package:* $38,676. *Average need-based loan:* $3112. *Average need-based gift aid:* $35,002. *Average non-need-based aid:* $23,209. *Average indebtedness upon graduation:* $23,070. *Financial aid deadline:* 2/15.

Applying *Options:* electronic application, early decision, deferred entrance. *Application fee:* $50. *Required:* essay or personal statement, high school transcript, 1 letter of recommendation, Signed character statement. *Application deadlines:* 1/15 (freshmen), 2/15 (transfers). *Early decision deadline:* 11/15 (for plan 1), 1/15 (for plan 2). *Notification:* 4/1 (freshmen), 4/15 (transfers), 12/15 (early decision plan 1), 2/15 (early decision plan 2).

Freshman Application Contact Mr. Gil Villanueva, Dean of Admission, University of Richmond, Brunet Memorial Hall, 28 Westhampton Way, University of Richmond, VA 23173. *Phone:* 804-289-8640. *Toll-free phone:* 800-700-1662. *Fax:* 804-287-6003. *E-mail:* admissions@richmond.edu. *Web site:* http://www.richmond.edu/.

University of Virginia

Charlottesville, Virginia

- **State-supported** university, founded 1819
- **Suburban** 1167-acre campus with easy access to Richmond
- **Endowment** $3.9 billion
- **Coed** 15,595 undergraduate students, 95% full-time, 55% women, 45% men
- **Very difficult** entrance level, 33% of applicants were admitted

Undergraduates 14,748 full-time, 847 part-time. Students come from 49 states and territories; 136 other countries; 26% are from out of state; 8% Black or African American, non-Hispanic/Latino; 5% Hispanic/Latino; 11% Asian, non-Hispanic/Latino; 0.2% Native Hawaiian or other Pacific Islander, non-Hispanic/Latino; 0.2% American Indian or Alaska Native, non-Hispanic/Latino; 2% Two or more races, non-Hispanic/Latino; 8% Race/ethnicity unknown; 6% international; 4% transferred in; 42% live on campus. *Retention:* 96% of full-time freshmen returned.

Freshmen *Admission:* 22,124 applied, 7,212 admitted, 3,243 enrolled. *Average high school GPA:* 4.17. *Test scores:* SAT critical reading scores over 500: 97%; SAT math scores over 500: 98%; SAT writing scores over 500: 97%; ACT scores over 18: 100%; SAT critical reading scores over 600: 78%; SAT math scores over 600: 85%; SAT writing scores over 600: 81%; ACT scores over 24: 96%; SAT critical reading scores over 700: 33%; SAT math scores over 700: 43%; SAT writing scores over 700: 35%; ACT scores over 30: 57%.

Faculty *Total:* 1,309, 95% full-time, 91% with terminal degrees. *Student/faculty ratio:* 16:1.

Academics *Calendar:* semesters. *Degrees:* bachelor's, master's, doctoral-professional, doctoral-research/scholarship, and post-master's certificates. *Special study options:* accelerated degree program, adult/continuing education programs, advanced placement credit, cooperative education, double majors, English as a second language, honors programs, independent study, internships, part-time degree program, services for LD students, student-designed majors, study abroad, summer session for credit. *ROTC:* Army (b), Navy (b), Air Force (b). *Unusual degree programs:* 3-2 joint BA in College of Arts and Sciences/MT in Education.

Computers on Campus 691 computers/terminals are available on campus for general student use. Students can access the following: campus intranet, computer help desk, free student e-mail accounts, online (class) grades, online (class) registration, online (class) schedules, online course management tool. Campuswide network is available. 100% of college-owned or -operated housing units are wired for high-speed Internet access. Wireless service is available via classrooms, computer centers, computer labs, dorm rooms, learning centers, libraries, student centers.

Student Life *Housing:* on-campus residence required for freshman year. *Options:* coed. Campus housing is university owned. Freshman campus housing is guaranteed. *Activities and organizations:* drama/theater group, student-run newspaper, radio and television station, choral group, marching band, Madison House, student government, university guides, University Union, The Cavalier Daily, national fraternities, national sororities. *Campus security:* 24-hour emergency response devices and patrols, late-night transport/escort service, controlled dormitory access. *Student services:* health clinic, personal/psychological counseling, women's center, legal services.

Athletics Member NCAA. All Division I except football (Division I-A). *Intercollegiate sports:* baseball M(s), basketball M(s)/W(s), crew W(s), cross-country running M(s)/W(s), field hockey W(s), golf M(s)/W(s), lacrosse M(s)/W(s), soccer M(s)/W(s), softball W(s), swimming and diving M(s)/W(s), tennis M(s)/W(s), track and field M(s)/W(s), volleyball W(s), wrestling M(s). *Intramural sports:* archery M(c)/W(c), badminton M(c)/W(c), baseball M(c), basketball M(c)/W(c), cheerleading M(c)/W(c), crew M(c)/W, cross-country running M(c)/W(c), equestrian sports M/W, fencing M(c)/W(c), field hockey W(c), football M, golf M(c)/W(c), gymnastics M(c)/W(c), ice hockey M(c)/W(c), lacrosse M(c)/W(c), racquetball M(c)/W(c), riflery M(c)/W(c), rugby M(c)/W(c), sailing M(c)/W(c), skiing (downhill) M(c)/W(c), soccer M(c)/W(c), softball M/W, squash M(c)/W(c), swimming and diving M(c)/W(c), table tennis M(c)/W(c), tennis M(c)/W(c), track and field M(c)/W(c), ultimate Frisbee M(c)/W(c), volleyball M(c)/W(c), water polo M(c)/W(c), weight lifting M(c)/W(c), wrestling M.

Standardized Tests *Required:* SAT or ACT (for admission). *Recommended:* SAT Subject Tests (for admission), Either SAT or ACT plus optional ACT writing test (ACT alone does not satisfy requirement). At least two SAT subject tests (student's choice) are recommended.

Costs (2010–11) *Tuition:* state resident $8356 full-time, $278 per credit hour part-time; nonresident $30,630 full-time, $1022 per credit hour part-time. *Required fees:* $2272 full-time, $2272 per year part-time. *Room and board:* $8652; room only: $4732. Room and board charges vary according to board

plan and housing facility. *Payment plan:* installment. *Waivers:* senior citizens and employees or children of employees.

Financial Aid Of all full-time matriculated undergraduates who enrolled in 2009, 7,886 applied for aid, 4,446 were judged to have need, 4,446 had their need fully met. In 2009, 1358 non-need-based awards were made. *Average percent of need met:* 100%. *Average financial aid package:* $21,215. *Average need-based loan:* $5509. *Average need-based gift aid:* $16,488. *Average non-need-based aid:* $10,332. *Average indebtedness upon graduation:* $19,384.

Applying *Options:* electronic application, deferred entrance. *Application fee:* $60. *Required:* essay or personal statement, high school transcript, 1 letter of recommendation. *Application deadlines:* 1/1 (freshmen), 3/1 (transfers). *Notification:* 4/1 (freshmen), 5/1 (transfers).

Freshman Application Contact Mr. Gregory W. Roberts, Dean of Admission, University of Virginia, PO Box 400160, Charlottesville, VA 22904-4727. *Phone:* 434-982-3200. *Fax:* 434-924-3587. *E-mail:* undergrad-admission@virginia.edu. *Web site:* http://www.virginia.edu/.

The University of Virginia's College at Wise

Wise, Virginia

- **State-supported** 4-year, founded 1954, part of University of Virginia
- **Small-town** 396-acre campus
- **Endowment** $34.2 million
- **Coed**
- **Moderately difficult** entrance level

Faculty *Student/faculty ratio:* 14:1.

Academics *Calendar:* semesters. *Degrees:* bachelor's and postbachelor's certificates.

Student Life *Campus security:* 24-hour emergency response devices and patrols, student patrols, late-night transport/escort service, self-defense, informal discussions, pamphlets/posters/films, and crime prevention office.

Athletics Member NAIA.

Standardized Tests *Required:* SAT or ACT (for admission).

Costs (2010–11) *Tuition:* state resident $3910 full-time, $167 per credit hour part-time; nonresident $16,500 full-time, $699 per credit hour part-time. Part-time tuition and fees vary according to course load. *Required fees:* $3284 full-time, $97 per credit hour part-time, $1067 per term part-time. *Room and board:* $8351; room only: $4394. Room and board charges vary according to board plan and housing facility. *Payment plans:* installment, deferred payment.

Financial Aid Of all full-time matriculated undergraduates who enrolled in 2009, 1,347 applied for aid, 1,130 were judged to have need, 826 had their need fully met. In 2009, 124 non-need-based awards were made. *Average percent of need met:* 74. *Average financial aid package:* $9212. *Average need-based loan:* $3168. *Average need-based gift aid:* $5474. *Average non-need-based aid:* $3456. *Average indebtedness upon graduation:* $12,120.

Applying *Options:* early admission, early action. *Application fee:* $25. *Required:* high school transcript, minimum 2.3 GPA. *Required for some:* interview. *Recommended:* 2 letters of recommendation.

Freshman Application Contact Mr. Russell D. Necessary, Vice Chancellor for Enrollment Management, The University of Virginia's College at Wise, 1 College Avenue, Wise, VA 24293. *Phone:* 276-328-0322. *Toll-free phone:* 888-282-9324. *Fax:* 276-328-0251. *E-mail:* admissions@uvawise.edu. *Web site:* http://www.uvawise.edu/.

Valley Forge Christian College Woodbridge Campus

Woodbridge, Virginia

- **Independent Assemblies of God** 4-year, administratively affiliated with Valley Forge Christian College
- **Suburban** campus with easy access to Washington, D.C.
- **Coed**
- **Minimally difficult** entrance level

Academics *Degree:* certificates and bachelor's.

Costs (2010–11) *Tuition:* $7980 full-time. *Required fees:* $350 full-time. *Payment plans:* tuition prepayment, installment.

Freshman Application Contact Admissions Office, Valley Forge Christian College Woodbridge Campus, 13909 Smoketown Road, Woodbridge, VA 22192. *Phone:* 703-580-4810. *Toll-free phone:* 800-432-8322. *Web site:* http://www.vfcc.edu/woodbridge/.

Virginia Commonwealth University

Richmond, Virginia

- **State-supported** university, founded 1838
- **Urban** 143-acre campus
- **Endowment** $280.7 million
- **Coed** 23,483 undergraduate students, 83% full-time, 57% women, 43% men
- 66% of applicants were admitted

Undergraduates 19,600 full-time, 3,883 part-time. Students come from 48 states and territories; 85 other countries; 7% are from out of state; 19% Black or African American, non-Hispanic/Latino; 6% Hispanic/Latino; 12% Asian, non-Hispanic/Latino; 0.2% Native Hawaiian or other Pacific Islander, non-Hispanic/Latino; 0.4% American Indian or Alaska Native, non-Hispanic/Latino; 3% Two or more races, non-Hispanic/Latino; 3% Race/ethnicity unknown; 3% international; 9% transferred in; 21% live on campus. *Retention:* 86% of full-time freshmen returned.

Freshmen *Admission:* 14,086 applied, 9,246 admitted, 3,615 enrolled. *Average high school GPA:* 3.48. *Test scores:* SAT critical reading scores over 500: 72%; SAT math scores over 500: 71%; SAT writing scores over 500: 66%; ACT scores over 18: 92%; SAT critical reading scores over 600: 28%; SAT math scores over 600: 26%; SAT writing scores over 600: 21%; ACT scores over 24: 42%; SAT critical reading scores over 700: 4%; SAT math scores over 700: 3%; SAT writing scores over 700: 3%; ACT scores over 30: 7%.

Faculty *Total:* 3,158, 63% full-time. *Student/faculty ratio:* 18:1.

Academics *Calendar:* semesters. *Degrees:* certificates, bachelor's, master's, doctoral-professional, doctoral-research/scholarship, post-master's, and post-bachelor's certificates. *Special study options:* academic remediation for entering students, accelerated degree program, adult/continuing education programs, advanced placement credit, cooperative education, distance learning, double majors, English as a second language, freshman honors college, honors programs, independent study, internships, off-campus study, part-time degree program, services for LD students, student-designed majors, study abroad, summer session for credit. *ROTC:* Army (c).

Computers on Campus 1,450 computers/terminals and 60,654 ports are available on campus for general student use. Students can access the following: campus intranet, computer help desk, free student e-mail accounts, online (class) grades, online (class) registration, online (class) schedules. Campuswide network is available. 100% of college-owned or -operated housing units are wired for high-speed Internet access. Wireless service is available via classrooms, computer centers, computer labs, dorm rooms, learning centers, libraries, student centers.

Student Life *Housing options:* coed. Campus housing is university owned. *Activities and organizations:* drama/theater group, student-run newspaper, radio and television station, choral group, national fraternities, national sororities. *Campus security:* 24-hour emergency response devices and patrols, student patrols, late-night transport/escort service, controlled dormitory access, security personnel in residence halls. *Student services:* health clinic, personal/psychological counseling, women's center.

Athletics Member NCAA. All Division I. *Intercollegiate sports:* baseball M(s), basketball M(s)/W(s), cross-country running M(s)/W(s), field hockey W(s), golf M(s), soccer M(s)/W(s), tennis M(s)/W(s), track and field M(s)/W(s), volleyball W(s). *Intramural sports:* badminton M/W, basketball M(c)/W(c), field hockey W(c), gymnastics W(c), ice hockey M(c), lacrosse M(c)/W(c), racquetball M/W, rugby M(c)/W(c), soccer M(c)/W(c), softball M/W, swimming and diving M(c)/W(c), table tennis M(c)/W(c), tennis M(c)/W(c), ultimate Frisbee M(c)/W(c), volleyball M/W, weight lifting M(c)/W(c), wrestling M(c).

Standardized Tests *Required:* SAT (for admission), SAT or ACT (for admission).

Costs (2010–11) *Tuition:* state resident $6853 full-time, $291 per credit hour part-time; nonresident $19,672 full-time, $821 per credit hour part-time. *Required fees:* $1864 full-time, $70 per credit hour part-time. *Room and board:* $8526; room only: $5186. Room and board charges vary according to board plan. *Payment plan:* installment. *Waivers:* senior citizens and employees or children of employees.

Financial Aid Of all full-time matriculated undergraduates who enrolled in 2008, 11,665 applied for aid, 9,680 were judged to have need, 1,033 had their need fully met. 661 Federal Work-Study jobs (averaging $1574). In 2008, 1426 non-need-based awards were made. *Average percent of need met:* 59%. *Average financial aid package:* $9259. *Average need-based loan:* $4325. *Average need-based gift aid:* $5841. *Average non-need-based aid:* $6385. *Average indebtedness upon graduation:* $25,151.

Applying *Options:* electronic application, early admission. *Application fee:* $40. *Required:* high school transcript. *Application deadline:* 1/15 (freshmen). *Notification:* 11/1 (freshmen).

Freshman Application Contact Ms. Sybil Halloran, Director of Undergraduate Admissions, Virginia Commonwealth University, 821 West Franklin Street, Box 842526, Richmond, VA 23284-2526. *Phone:* 804-828-6125. *Toll-free phone:* 800-841-3638. *Fax:* 804-828-1899. *E-mail:* schallor@vcu.edu. *Web site:* http://www.vcu.edu/.

Virginia Intermont College

Bristol, Virginia

- **Independent** 4-year, founded 1884, affiliated with Baptist Church
- **Small-town** 13-acre campus
- **Endowment** $4.0 million
- **Coed** 591 undergraduate students, 89% full-time, 70% women, 30% men
- **Minimally difficult** entrance level, 41% of applicants were admitted

Undergraduates 525 full-time, 66 part-time. Students come from 34 states and territories; 8 other countries; 42% are from out of state; 8% Black or African American, non-Hispanic/Latino; 1% Hispanic/Latino; 1% Asian, non-Hispanic/Latino; 0.7% American Indian or Alaska Native, non-Hispanic/Latino; 4% Race/ethnicity unknown; 2% international; 15% transferred in; 46% live on campus. *Retention:* 70% of full-time freshmen returned.

Freshmen *Admission:* 2,907 applied, 1,196 admitted, 129 enrolled. *Average high school GPA:* 3.11. *Test scores:* SAT critical reading scores over 500: 46%; SAT math scores over 500: 48%; SAT writing scores over 500: 36%; ACT scores over 18: 83%; SAT critical reading scores over 600: 9%; SAT math scores over 600: 8%; SAT writing scores over 600: 7%; ACT scores over 24: 28%; ACT scores over 30: 4%.

Faculty *Total:* 99, 42% full-time, 51% with terminal degrees. *Student/faculty ratio:* 13:1.

Academics *Calendar:* semesters. *Degrees:* associate and bachelor's. *Special study options:* academic remediation for entering students, accelerated degree program, adult/continuing education programs, advanced placement credit, double majors, English as a second language, honors programs, independent study, internships, off-campus study, part-time degree program, services for LD students, study abroad, summer session for credit.

Computers on Campus 80 computers/terminals are available on campus for general student use. Students can access the following: campus intranet, computer help desk, free student e-mail accounts, online (class) grades, online (class) registration, online (class) schedules. Campuswide network is available. 100% of college-owned or -operated housing units are wired for high-speed Internet access. Wireless service is available via libraries, student centers.

Student Life *Housing:* on-campus residence required through junior year. *Options:* coed, women-only. Campus housing is university owned and leased by the school. Freshman campus housing is guaranteed. *Activities and organizations:* drama/theater group, student-run newspaper, choral group, Poetry Club, Gay-Straight Alliance, Student Government Association, equestrian club, International Issues Club. *Campus security:* 24-hour patrols, late-night transport/escort service. *Student services:* health clinic, personal/psychological counseling.

Athletics Member NAIA. *Intercollegiate sports:* baseball M(s), basketball M(s)/W(s), cheerleading W(s), equestrian sports M(s)/W(s), golf M(s), soccer M(s), softball W(s), volleyball W(s). *Intramural sports:* basketball M/W, bowling M/W, football M/W, golf M/W, softball M/W, table tennis M/W, ultimate Frisbee M/W, volleyball M/W.

Standardized Tests *Required:* SAT or ACT (for admission).

Costs (2011–12) *Comprehensive fee:* $32,232 includes full-time tuition ($24,542) and room and board ($7690). Full-time tuition and fees vary according to class time, course load, program, and reciprocity agreements. Part-time tuition: $491 per credit hour. Part-time tuition and fees vary according to class time, course level, course load, program, and reciprocity agreements. *College room only:* $3760. Room and board charges vary according to board plan, housing facility, and location. *Payment plan:* installment. *Waivers:* senior citizens and employees or children of employees.

Financial Aid Of all full-time matriculated undergraduates who enrolled in 2009, 479 applied for aid, 445 were judged to have need, 21 had their need fully met. 98 Federal Work-Study jobs (averaging $1000). In 2009, 60 non-need-based awards were made. *Average percent of need met:* 60%. *Average financial aid package:* $15,499. *Average need-based loan:* $3853. *Average need-based gift aid:* $11,767. *Average non-need-based aid:* $8961. *Average indebtedness upon graduation:* $16,337.

Applying *Options:* electronic application, early admission, deferred entrance. *Application fee:* $25. *Required:* high school transcript, minimum 2.5 GPA. *Required for some:* essay or personal statement, 2 letters of recommendation, interview. *Application deadlines:* rolling (freshmen), rolling (out-of-state freshmen), rolling (transfers). *Notification:* continuous (freshmen), continuous (out-of-state freshmen), continuous (transfers).

Freshman Application Contact Ms. Robin Brooks, Director of Admissions, Virginia Intermont College, 1013 Moore Street, Campus Box D-460, Bristol, VA 24201. *Phone:* 276-466-7856. *Toll-free phone:* 800-451-1842. *Fax:* 276-466-7885. *E-mail:* viadmit@vic.edu. *Web site:* http://www.vic.edu/.

Virginia International University

Fairfax, Virginia

Freshman Application Contact Admissions Department, Virginia International University, 11200 Waples Mill Road, Fairfax, VA 22030. *Phone:* 703-591-7042 Ext. 313. *Toll-free phone:* 800-514 6848. *Fax:* 703-591-7048. *E-mail:* admissions@viu.edu. *Web site:* http://www.viu.edu/.

Virginia Military Institute

Lexington, Virginia

- **State-supported** 4-year, founded 1839
- **Small-town** 134-acre campus
- **Coed, primarily men** 1,569 undergraduate students, 100% full-time, 9% women, 91% men
- **Moderately difficult** entrance level, 56% of applicants were admitted

Undergraduates 1,569 full-time. 40% are from out of state; 5% Black or African American, non-Hispanic/Latino; 4% Hispanic/Latino; 5% Asian, non-Hispanic/Latino; 0.3% American Indian or Alaska Native, non-Hispanic/Latino; 0.4% Two or more races, non-Hispanic/Latino; 2% international; 2% transferred in; 100% live on campus. *Retention:* 83% of full-time freshmen returned.

Freshmen *Admission:* 1,598 applied, 889 admitted, 441 enrolled. *Average high school GPA:* 3.47. *Test scores:* SAT critical reading scores over 500: 82%; SAT math scores over 500: 89%; SAT writing scores over 500: 71%; ACT scores over 18: 96%; SAT critical reading scores over 600: 32%; SAT math scores over 600: 38%; SAT writing scores over 600: 21%; ACT scores over 24: 61%; SAT critical reading scores over 700: 4%; SAT math scores over 700: 4%; SAT writing scores over 700: 2%; ACT scores over 30: 6%.

Faculty *Total:* 180, 66% full-time, 78% with terminal degrees. *Student/faculty ratio:* 11:1.

Academics *Calendar:* semesters. *Degree:* bachelor's. *Special study options:* advanced placement credit, double majors, honors programs, independent study, internships, services for LD students, study abroad, summer session for credit. *ROTC:* Army (b), Navy (b), Air Force (b).

Computers on Campus 200 ports are available on campus for general student use. Students can access the following: computer help desk, free student e-mail accounts. Campuswide network is available. 100% of college-owned or -operated housing units are wired for high-speed Internet access.

Student Life *Housing:* on-campus residence required through senior year. *Options:* Campus housing is university owned. Freshman campus housing is guaranteed. *Activities and organizations:* drama/theater group, student-run newspaper, choral group, marching band, Newman Club, Officers Christian Fellowship, strength and fitness organizations, Promaji, Pre-Law Society. *Campus security:* 24-hour emergency response devices and patrols, student patrols. *Student services:* health clinic, personal/psychological counseling.

Athletics Member NCAA. All Division I. *Intercollegiate sports:* baseball M(s), basketball M(s), cross-country running M(s)/W(s), football M(s), golf M(s), lacrosse M(s), riflery M(s)/W(s), soccer M(s)/W, swimming and diving M(s)/W, track and field M(s)/W(s), water polo W, wrestling M(s).

Standardized Tests *Required:* SAT or ACT (for admission).

Costs (2010–11) *Tuition:* state resident $6024 full-time; nonresident $24,016 full-time. *Required fees:* $6304 full-time. *Room and board:* $7132. *Payment plan:* installment.

Financial Aid Of all full-time matriculated undergraduates who enrolled in 2008, 934 applied for aid, 704 were judged to have need, 351 had their need fully met. In 2008, 271 non-need-based awards were made. *Average percent of need met:* 90%. *Average financial aid package:* $19,333. *Average need-based loan:* $3706. *Average need-based gift aid:* $8847. *Average non-need-based aid:* $3659. *Average indebtedness upon graduation:* $18,063.

Applying *Options:* electronic application, early admission, early decision. *Application fee:* $40. *Required:* high school transcript. *Recommended:* essay or personal statement, 2 letters of recommendation, interview. *Application deadlines:* 2/1 (freshmen), 2/1 (transfers). *Early decision deadline:* 11/15. *Notification:* continuous (freshmen), continuous (transfers), 12/15 (early decision).

Freshman Application Contact Lt. Col. Tom Mortenson, Associate Director of Admissions, Virginia Military Institute, Admissions Office, Lexington, VA 24450. *Phone:* 540-464-7211. *Toll-free phone:* 800-767-4207. *Fax:* 540-464-7746. *E-mail:* admissions@vmi.edu. *Web site:* http://www.vmi.edu/.

See page 1762 for the College Close-Up.

Virginia Polytechnic Institute and State University

Blacksburg, Virginia

- **State-supported** university, founded 1872
- **Small-town** 2600-acre campus
- **Endowment** $502.4 million
- **Coed** 23,690 undergraduate students, 98% full-time, 42% women, 58% men
- **Moderately difficult** entrance level, 67% of applicants were admitted

Undergraduates 23,241 full-time, 449 part-time. Students come from 113 other countries; 4% Black or African American, non-Hispanic/Latino; 4% Hispanic/Latino; 8% Asian, non-Hispanic/Latino; 0.1% Native Hawaiian or other Pacific Islander, non-Hispanic/Latino; 0.2% American Indian or Alaska Native, non-Hispanic/Latino; 2% Two or more races, non-Hispanic/Latino; 5% Race/ethnicity unknown; 2% international; 4% transferred in; 39% live on campus. *Retention:* 92% of full-time freshmen returned.

Freshmen *Admission:* 19,981 applied, 13,389 admitted, 5,205 enrolled. *Average high school GPA:* 3.96. *Test scores:* SAT critical reading scores over 500: 75%; SAT math scores over 500: 83%; SAT writing scores over 500: 73%; SAT critical reading scores over 600: 32%; SAT math scores over 600: 43%; SAT writing scores over 600: 25%; SAT critical reading scores over 700: 5%; SAT math scores over 700: 8%; SAT writing scores over 700: 3%.

Faculty *Total:* 1,579, 83% full-time. *Student/faculty ratio:* 16:1.

Academics *Calendar:* semesters. *Degrees:* associate, bachelor's, master's, doctoral-professional, doctoral-research/scholarship, and post-master's certificates. *Special study options:* accelerated degree program, adult/continuing education programs, advanced placement credit, cooperative education, distance learning, double majors, English as a second language, honors programs, independent study, internships, part-time degree program, services for LD students, study abroad, summer session for credit. *ROTC:* Army (b), Navy (b), Air Force (b).

Computers on Campus 8,000 computers/terminals are available on campus for general student use. Students can access the following: campus intranet, computer help desk, free student e-mail accounts, online (class) grades, online (class) registration, online (class) schedules. Campuswide network is available. Wireless service is available via entire campus.

Student Life *Housing:* on-campus residence required for freshman year. *Options:* coed, men-only, women-only. Campus housing is university owned. Freshman campus housing is guaranteed. *Activities and organizations:* drama/theater group, student-run newspaper, radio and television station, choral group, marching band, Virginia Tech Union, Student Government Association, international student organizations, national fraternities, national sororities. *Campus security:* 24-hour emergency response devices and patrols, student patrols, late-night transport/escort service, controlled dormitory access. *Student services:* health clinic, personal/psychological counseling, women's center, legal services.

Athletics Member NCAA. All Division I except football (Division I-A). *Intercollegiate sports:* baseball M, basketball M, cross-country running M/W, golf M(s), lacrosse W(s), soccer M(s)/W(s), swimming and diving M(s)/W(s), tennis M(s)/W(s), track and field M(s)/W(s), ultimate Frisbee M/W, volleyball W. *Intramural sports:* baseball M(c), basketball M, bowling M/W, crew M(c)/W(c), cross-country running M/W, equestrian sports M(c)/W(c), fencing M(c)/W(c), field hockey M(c)/W(c), football M/W, golf M/W, gymnastics M(c)/W(c), ice hockey M/W, lacrosse M(c)/W(c), racquetball M/W, riflery M(c)/W(c), rugby M(c)/W(c), soccer M/W, softball M/W, swimming and diving M/W, table tennis M/W, tennis M/W, volleyball M/W, water polo M/W.

Standardized Tests *Required:* SAT or ACT (for admission). *Required for some:* SAT and SAT Subject Tests or ACT (for admission).

Costs (2010–11) *Tuition:* state resident $7309 full-time; nonresident $20,498 full-time. *Required fees:* $2149 full-time. *Room and board:* $6290. Room and board charges vary according to board plan. *Payment plan:* installment. *Waivers:* senior citizens and employees or children of employees.

Financial Aid Of all full-time matriculated undergraduates who enrolled in 2008, 13,931 applied for aid, 8,538 were judged to have need, 2,132 had their need fully met. In 2008, 2043 non-need-based awards were made. *Average percent of need met:* 71%. *Average financial aid package:* $10,909. *Average need-based loan:* $4104. *Average need-based gift aid:* $5579. *Average non-need-based aid:* $2667. *Average indebtedness upon graduation:* $22,070.

Applying *Options:* electronic application, early admission, early decision, deferred entrance. *Application fee:* $60. *Required:* high school transcript. *Recommended:* minimum 3 GPA. *Application deadlines:* 1/15 (freshmen), 2/15 (transfers). *Early decision deadline:* 11/1. *Notification:* 4/1 (freshmen), 5/1 (transfers), 12/15 (early decision).

Freshman Application Contact Virginia Polytechnic Institute and State University, Blacksburg, VA 24061. *Phone:* 540-231-6267. *Web site:* http://www.vt.edu/.

Virginia State University

Petersburg, Virginia

- **State-supported** comprehensive, founded 1882, part of State Council of Higher Education for Virginia
- **Suburban** 236-acre campus with easy access to Richmond
- **Endowment** $17.0 million
- **Coed** 5,075 undergraduate students, 93% full-time, 61% women, 39% men
- **Minimally difficult** entrance level, 51% of applicants were admitted

Undergraduates 4,732 full-time, 343 part-time. Students come from 39 states and territories; 32% are from out of state; 90% Black or African American, non-Hispanic/Latino; 1% Hispanic/Latino; 0.2% Asian, non-Hispanic/Latino; 0.2% American Indian or Alaska Native, non-Hispanic/Latino; 7% Race/ethnicity unknown; 6% transferred in; 63% live on campus.

Freshmen *Admission:* 8,567 applied, 4,406 admitted, 1,260 enrolled. *Average high school GPA:* 2.7. *Test scores:* SAT critical reading scores over 500: 13%; SAT math scores over 500: 14%; SAT writing scores over 500: 9%; ACT scores over 18: 45%; SAT critical reading scores over 600: 2%; SAT math scores over 600: 1%; SAT writing scores over 600: 1%; ACT scores over 24: 5%.

Faculty *Total:* 456, 58% full-time. *Student/faculty ratio:* 16:1.

Academics *Calendar:* semesters. *Degrees:* associate, bachelor's, master's, doctoral-research/scholarship, post-master's, and postbachelor's certificates. *Special study options:* adult/continuing education programs, advanced placement credit, cooperative education, double majors, honors programs, independent study, internships, off-campus study, part-time degree program, services for LD students, student-designed majors, study abroad, summer session for credit. *ROTC:* Army (b).

Computers on Campus 1,461 computers/terminals are available on campus for general student use. Students can access the following: computer help desk, free student e-mail accounts, online (class) grades, online (class) registration, online (class) schedules. Campuswide network is available.

Student Life *Housing:* on-campus residence required for freshman year. *Options:* coed, men-only, women-only. Campus housing is university owned. Freshman applicants given priority for college housing. *Activities and organizations:* drama/theater group, student-run newspaper, choral group, marching band, Betterment of Brothers/Sisters, The VSU Gospel Chorale, Alpha Kappa Alpha Sorority, Inc, Panic 2000, Hospitality Management Program Students Association, national fraternities, national sororities. *Campus security:* 24-hour emergency response devices and patrols, late-night transport/escort service, controlled dormitory access. *Student services:* health clinic, personal/psychological counseling.

Athletics Member NCAA. All Division II. *Intercollegiate sports:* baseball M(s), basketball M(s)/W(s), bowling W(s), cheerleading M/W, cross-country running M(s)/W(s), football M(s), golf M(s)/W(s), softball W(s), tennis M(s)/W(s), track and field M(s)/W(s), volleyball W(s). *Intramural sports:* basketball M/W, football M, tennis M/W, track and field M/W, volleyball W.

Standardized Tests *Required:* SAT or ACT (for admission).

Costs (2010–11) *Tuition:* state resident $3886 full-time, $226 per credit hour part-time; nonresident $12,452 full-time, $500 per credit hour part-time. Full-time tuition and fees vary according to course load, degree level, and program. Part-time tuition and fees vary according to course load, degree level, and program. *Required fees:* $2684 full-time, $10 per credit hour part-time. *Room and board:* $8152; room only: $4640. Room and board charges vary according to board plan and housing facility. *Payment plan:* installment. *Waivers:* senior citizens.

Financial Aid Of all full-time matriculated undergraduates who enrolled in 2009, 4,771 applied for aid, 4,568 were judged to have need, 685 had their need fully met. 400 Federal Work-Study jobs (averaging $2000). In 2009, 507 non-need-based awards were made. *Average percent of need met:* 65%. *Average financial aid package:* $10,200. *Average need-based loan:* $5500. *Average need-based gift aid:* $5500. *Average non-need-based aid:* $1000. *Average indebtedness upon graduation:* $28,250.

Applying *Options:* electronic application. *Application fee:* $25. *Required:* essay or personal statement, high school transcript, minimum 2.2 GPA, 2 letters of recommendation. *Application deadlines:* 5/1 (freshmen), 5/1 (transfers). *Notification:* continuous (freshmen), continuous (transfers).

Freshman Application Contact Mrs. Irene Logan, Director of Admissions, Virginia State University, Office of Admissions, Petersburg, VA 23806-2096. *Phone:* 804-524-5902. *Toll-free phone:* 800-871-7611. *Fax:* 804-524-5055. *E-mail:* ilogan@vsu.edu. *Web site:* http://www.vsu.edu/.

Virginia Union University

Richmond, Virginia

- **Independent Baptist** comprehensive, founded 1865
- **Urban** 72-acre campus
- **Coed**
- **Moderately difficult** entrance level

Faculty *Student/faculty ratio:* 15:1.

Academics *Calendar:* semesters. *Degrees:* bachelor's, master's, doctoral-professional, and doctoral-research/scholarship.

Student Life *Campus security:* 24-hour emergency response devices and patrols, controlled dormitory access.

Athletics Member NCAA. All Division II.

Standardized Tests *Required:* SAT or ACT (for admission).

Costs (2010–11) *Comprehensive fee:* $21,460 includes full-time tuition ($13,314), mandatory fees ($1316), and room and board ($6830). Full-time tuition and fees vary according to course level and course load. Part-time tuition: $422 per credit hour. Part-time tuition and fees vary according to course level and course load. *Required fees:* $40 per credit hour part-time. *College room only:* $3084. Room and board charges vary according to housing facility. *Payment plans:* installment, deferred payment.

Financial Aid *Of all full-time matriculated undergraduates who enrolled in 2009,* 1,163 applied for aid, 1,101 were judged to have need. *Average financial aid package:* $10,921. *Average need-based loan:* $3894. *Average need-based gift aid:* $5371.

Applying *Options:* electronic application, deferred entrance. *Application fee:* $25. *Required:* high school transcript, minimum 2.25 GPA. *Required for some:* interview. *Recommended:* essay or personal statement, minimum 2.5 GPA, 3 letters of recommendation.

Freshman Application Contact Mr. Gil Powell, Director of Admissions, Virginia Union University, 1500 North Lombardy Street, Richmond, VA 23220-1170. *Phone:* 804-257-5881. *Toll-free phone:* 800-368-3227. *Fax:* 804-329-8477. *E-mail:* gpowell@vuu.edu. *Web site:* http://www.vuu.edu/.

Virginia University of Lynchburg

Lynchburg, Virginia

- **Independent religious** comprehensive, founded 1886
- **Urban** campus
- **Coed**
- **Noncompetitive** entrance level

Faculty *Student/faculty ratio:* 9:1.

Academics *Calendar:* semesters. *Degrees:* certificates, associate, bachelor's, master's, and doctoral-other.

Student Life *Campus security:* 24-hour emergency response devices, Monitored camera security system with electronic backup saved.

Costs (2010–11) *Comprehensive fee:* $8900 includes full-time tuition ($5000), mandatory fees ($300), and room and board ($3600). Full-time tuition and fees vary according to location and program. Part-time tuition: $167 per credit hour. Part-time tuition and fees vary according to location and program.

Financial Aid *Of all full-time matriculated undergraduates who enrolled in 2009,* 9 Federal Work-Study jobs. *Average indebtedness upon graduation:* $9500.

Applying *Application fee:* $25. *Required:* high school transcript.

Freshman Application Contact Ms. Cheryl Glass, Director of Admissions, Virginia University of Lynchburg, 2058 Garfield Avenue, Lynchburg, VA 24501. *Phone:* 434-528-5276 Ext. 106. *Fax:* 434-528-4275. *E-mail:* cglass@vul.edu. *Web site:* http://www.vul.edu/.

Virginia Wesleyan College

Norfolk, Virginia

- **Independent United Methodist** 4-year, founded 1961
- **Urban** 300-acre campus with easy access to Norfolk and Virginia Beach
- **Endowment** $38.0 million
- **Coed** 1,279 undergraduate students, 87% full-time, 62% women, 38% men
- **Moderately difficult** entrance level, 75% of applicants were admitted

Undergraduates 1,111 full-time, 168 part-time. Students come from 31 states and territories; 7 other countries; 21% are from out of state; 22% Black or African American, non-Hispanic/Latino; 5% Hispanic/Latino; 1% Asian, non-Hispanic/Latino; 0.2% Native Hawaiian or other Pacific Islander, non-Hispanic/Latino; 1% Two or more races, non-Hispanic/Latino; 4% Race/ethnicity unknown; 0.2% international; 7% transferred in; 58% live on campus. *Retention:* 63% of full-time freshmen returned.

Freshmen *Admission:* 1,461 applied, 1,090 admitted, 295 enrolled. *Average high school GPA:* 3.1. *Test scores:* SAT critical reading scores over 500: 47%; SAT math scores over 500: 44%; SAT writing scores over 500: 42%; ACT scores over 18: 83%; SAT critical reading scores over 600: 12%; SAT math

scores over 600: 11%; SAT writing scores over 600: 11%; ACT scores over 24: 29%; SAT critical reading scores over 700: 3%; SAT math scores over 700: 1%; SAT writing scores over 700: 2%.
Faculty *Total:* 128, 67% full-time. *Student/faculty ratio:* 11:1.
Academics *Calendar:* 4-1-4. *Degree:* bachelor's. *Special study options:* academic remediation for entering students, adult/continuing education programs, advanced placement credit, double majors, freshman honors college, honors programs, independent study, internships, off-campus study, part-time degree program, services for LD students, student-designed majors, study abroad, summer session for credit. *ROTC:* Army (c).
Computers on Campus 118 computers/terminals are available on campus for general student use. Students can access the following: campus intranet, computer help desk, free student e-mail accounts, online (class) grades, online (class) registration, online (class) schedules. Campuswide network is available. 100% of college-owned or -operated housing units are wired for high-speed Internet access. Wireless service is available via classrooms, computer centers, computer labs, learning centers, libraries, student centers.
Student Life *Housing:* on-campus residence required through senior year. *Options:* coed, women-only, disabled students. Campus housing is university owned. Freshman campus housing is guaranteed. *Activities and organizations:* drama/theater group, student-run newspaper, radio station, choral group, Wesleyan Activities Council, Community service, Student Government Association, student newspaper, Black Student Union, national fraternities, national sororities. *Campus security:* 24-hour emergency response devices and patrols, late-night transport/escort service, controlled dormitory access, well-lit pathways. *Student services:* health clinic, personal/psychological counseling, women's center.
Athletics Member NCAA. All Division III. *Intercollegiate sports:* baseball M, basketball M/W, cheerleading W, cross-country running M/W, field hockey W, golf M, lacrosse M/W, soccer M/W, softball W, tennis M/W, track and field M/W, volleyball W. *Intramural sports:* basketball M/W, crew M(c)/W(c), fencing M(c)/W(c), field hockey W, football M/W, racquetball M/W, soccer M/W, softball M/W, table tennis M/W, ultimate Frisbee M/W, volleyball M/W.
Standardized Tests *Required for some:* SAT or ACT (for admission).
Costs (2011–12) *One-time required fee:* $250. *Comprehensive fee:* $37,668 includes full-time tuition ($29,180), mandatory fees ($500), and room and board ($7988). Full-time tuition and fees vary according to course load. Part-time tuition: $1216 per credit hour. Part-time tuition and fees vary according to course load. *Required fees:* $500 per year part-time. *Room and board:* Room and board charges vary according to board plan and housing facility. *Payment plans:* installment, deferred payment. *Waivers:* adult students, senior citizens, and employees or children of employees.
Financial Aid Of all full-time matriculated undergraduates who enrolled in 2008, 1,204 applied for aid, 943 were judged to have need, 90 had their need fully met. 195 Federal Work-Study jobs (averaging $1054). In 2008, 210 non-need-based awards were made. *Average percent of need met:* 70%. *Average financial aid package:* $19,757. *Average need-based loan:* $7584. *Average need-based gift aid:* $15,373. *Average non-need-based aid:* $8422. *Average indebtedness upon graduation:* $29,679.
Applying *Options:* electronic application. *Application fee:* $40. *Required:* essay or personal statement, high school transcript, minimum 2.5 GPA. *Required for some:* interview. *Application deadlines:* rolling (freshmen), rolling (transfers). *Notification:* continuous (freshmen), continuous (transfers).
Freshman Application Contact Mrs. Sara Gastler, Director of Admissions, Virginia Wesleyan College, 1584 Wesleyan Drive, Norfolk, VA 23502-5599. *Phone:* 757-455-3208. *Toll-free phone:* 800-737-8684. *Fax:* 757-461-5238. *E-mail:* admissions@vwc.edu. *Web site:* http://www.vwc.edu/.

Washington and Lee University
Lexington, Virginia

- **Independent** comprehensive, founded 1749
- **Small-town** 322-acre campus
- **Endowment** $533.4 million
- **Coed** 1,759 undergraduate students, 100% full-time, 50% women, 50% men
- **Most difficult** entrance level, 19% of applicants were admitted

Undergraduates 1,758 full-time, 1 part-time. Students come from 49 states and territories; 46 other countries; 85% are from out of state; 0.1% transferred in; 60% live on campus. *Retention:* 95% of full-time freshmen returned.
Freshmen *Admission:* 6,627 applied, 1,259 admitted, 471 enrolled. *Test scores:* SAT critical reading scores over 500: 100%; SAT math scores over 500: 100%; SAT writing scores over 500: 100%; ACT scores over 18: 100%; SAT critical reading scores over 600: 97%; SAT math scores over 600: 95%; SAT writing scores over 600: 91%; ACT scores over 24: 100%; SAT critical reading scores over 700: 45%; SAT math scores over 700: 46%; SAT writing scores over 700: 42%; ACT scores over 30: 60%.
Faculty *Total:* 282, 77% full-time, 91% with terminal degrees. *Student/faculty ratio:* 9:1.

Academics *Calendar:* 4-4-2. *Degrees:* bachelor's, master's, and doctoral-professional. *Special study options:* advanced placement credit, double majors, honors programs, independent study, internships, off-campus study, services for LD students, student-designed majors, study abroad. *ROTC:* Army (c).
Computers on Campus 320 computers/terminals and 1,500 ports are available on campus for general student use. Students can access the following: computer help desk, free student e-mail accounts, online (class) grades, online (class) registration, online (class) schedules. Campuswide network is available. 100% of college-owned or -operated housing units are wired for high-speed Internet access. Wireless service is available via entire campus.
Student Life *Housing:* on-campus residence required through sophomore year. *Options:* coed, men-only, women-only, disabled students. Campus housing is university owned. Freshman campus housing is guaranteed. *Activities and organizations:* drama/theater group, student-run newspaper, radio and television station, choral group, Outing Club, Student Activities Board, Nabors Service League, Mock Convention, College Republicans, national fraternities, national sororities. *Campus security:* 24-hour emergency response devices and patrols, late-night transport/escort service, controlled dormitory access, Emergency Alert System. *Student services:* health clinic, personal/psychological counseling, women's center.
Athletics Member NCAA. All Division III. *Intercollegiate sports:* baseball M, basketball M/W, cheerleading M(c)/W(c), cross-country running M/W, equestrian sports W, fencing M(c)/W(c), field hockey W, football M, golf M/W, ice hockey M(c)/W(c), lacrosse M/W, rugby M(c), skiing (cross-country) M(c)/W(c), soccer M/W, softball W(c), swimming and diving M/W, tennis M/W, track and field M/W, ultimate Frisbee M(c)/W(c), volleyball M(c)/W, wrestling M. *Intramural sports:* badminton M/W, baseball M(c), basketball M/W, equestrian sports W(c), football M/W, golf M/W, lacrosse M(c)/W(c), racquetball M/W, rock climbing M(c), skiing (downhill) M(c)/W(c), soccer M/W, softball M/W, squash M(c)/W(c), swimming and diving M/W, table tennis M/W, tennis M/W, track and field M/W, ultimate Frisbee M/W, volleyball M/W, wrestling M.
Standardized Tests *Required:* SAT or ACT (for admission), 2 unrelated SAT Subject Tests (for admission).
Costs (2010–11) *Comprehensive fee:* $50,630 includes full-time tuition ($39,500), mandatory fees ($887), and room and board ($10,243). Part-time tuition: $1411 per credit hour. *College room only:* $4993. Room and board charges vary according to board plan and housing facility. *Payment plan:* installment. *Waivers:* employees or children of employees.
Financial Aid Of all full-time matriculated undergraduates who enrolled in 2009, 748 applied for aid, 647 were judged to have need, 646 had their need fully met. 152 Federal Work-Study jobs (averaging $1790). 383 state and other part-time jobs (averaging $2018). In 2009, 162 non-need-based awards were made. *Average percent of need met:* 100%. *Average financial aid package:* $41,076. *Average need-based loan:* $1313. *Average need-based gift aid:* $34,315. *Average non-need-based aid:* $27,117. *Average indebtedness upon graduation:* $23,807. *Financial aid deadline:* 2/15.
Applying *Options:* electronic application, early decision, deferred entrance. *Application fee:* $50. *Required:* high school transcript, 3 letters of recommendation. *Recommended:* essay or personal statement, interview. *Application deadlines:* 1/15 (freshmen), 4/1 (transfers). *Early decision deadline:* 11/15 (for plan 1), 1/3 (for plan 2). *Notification:* 4/1 (freshmen), continuous (transfers), 12/21 (early decision plan 1), 2/1 (early decision plan 2).
Freshman Application Contact Mr. William M. Hartog, Dean of Admissions and Financial Aid, Washington and Lee University, 204 West Washington Street, Lexington, VA 24450-2116. *Phone:* 540-458-8710. *Fax:* 540-458-8062. *E-mail:* admissions@wlu.edu. *Web site:* http://www.wlu.edu/.

Westwood College–Annandale Campus
Annandale, Virginia

- **Proprietary** 4-year, part of Westwood Colleges, Inc.
- **Coed**

Academics *Degrees:* associate and bachelor's.
Freshman Application Contact Westwood College–Annandale Campus, 7619 Little River Turnpike, 5th Floor, Annandale, VA 22003. *Phone:* 703-642-3633. *Toll-free phone:* 877-268-5218. *Web site:* http://www.westwood.edu/.

Westwood College–Arlington Ballston Campus
Arlington, Virginia

- **Proprietary** 4-year, part of Westwood Colleges, Inc.
- **Coed**

Academics *Degrees:* associate and bachelor's.

Freshman Application Contact Westwood College–Arlington Ballston Campus, 4300 Wilson Boulevard, Suite 200, Arlington, VA 22203. *Phone:* 703-243-1662. *Toll-free phone:* 877-268-5218. *Web site:* http://www.westwood.edu/.

World College
Virginia Beach, Virginia

- **Proprietary** 4-year, founded 1992
- **Suburban** campus
- **Coed** 489 undergraduate students
- **Noncompetitive** entrance level

Undergraduates Students come from 50 states and territories; 25 other countries.

Faculty *Total:* 5, 60% full-time.

Academics *Calendar:* semesters. *Degrees:* bachelor's (offers only external degree programs). *Special study options:* accelerated degree program, adult/continuing education programs, distance learning, external degree program, independent study, part-time degree program.

Costs (2011–12) *Tuition:* $3770 full-time. No tuition increase for student's term of enrollment. *Payment plans:* tuition prepayment, installment.

Applying *Options:* electronic application, early admission. *Required:* high school transcript. *Application deadline:* rolling (freshmen). *Notification:* continuous (freshmen).

Freshman Application Contact Mrs. Audre Piratzky, Admissions Counselor, World College, 5193 Shore Drive, Suite 105, Virginia Beach, VA 23455. *Phone:* 757-464-4600. *Toll-free phone:* 800-696-7532. *Fax:* 757-464-3687. *E-mail:* instruct@cie-wc.edu. *Web site:* http://www.worldcollege.edu/.

WASHINGTON

Antioch University Seattle
Seattle, Washington

- **Independent** university, founded 1975, part of Antioch University
- **Urban** campus
- **Coed**
- **Noncompetitive** entrance level

Faculty *Student/faculty ratio:* 8:1.

Academics *Calendar:* quarters. *Degrees:* certificates, bachelor's, master's, and doctoral-research/scholarship.

Costs (2010–11) *Tuition:* $18,000 full-time, $500 per credit hour part-time. *Required fees:* $270 full-time, $500 per credit hour part-time.

Financial Aid *Of all full-time matriculated undergraduates who enrolled in 2006, 259 applied for aid, 150 had their need fully met. 18 Federal Work-Study jobs (averaging $6000). 2 state and other part-time jobs (averaging $5000). Average percent of need met: 75. Average financial aid package: $6701. Average need-based loan: $5500. Average need-based gift aid: $4000. Average indebtedness upon graduation: $15,999.*

Applying *Options:* electronic application, deferred entrance. *Application fee:* $75.

Freshman Application Contact Admissions Office, Antioch University Seattle, 2326 Sixth Avenue, Seattle, WA 98121-1814. *Phone:* 206-268-4202. *E-mail:* admissions@antiochseattle.edu. *Web site:* http://www.antiochsea.edu/.

Argosy University, Seattle
Seattle, Washington

- **Proprietary** university, founded 1995, part of Education Management Corporation
- **Urban** campus
- **Coed**

Academics *Calendar:* semesters. *Degrees:* bachelor's, master's, and doctoral-professional.

Costs (2010–11) *Tuition:* Tuition varies by program. Students should contact Argosy University for tuition information.

Freshman Application Contact Argosy University, Seattle, 2601-A Elliott Avenue, Seattle, WA 98121. *Phone:* 206-283-4500. *Toll-free phone:* 866-283-2777. *Web site:* http://www.argosy.edu/seattle/.

See page 1002 for the College Close-Up.

The Art Institute of Seattle
Seattle, Washington

- **Proprietary** primarily 2-year, founded 1982, part of Education Management Corporation
- **Urban** campus
- **Coed**

Academics *Calendar:* quarters. *Degrees:* diplomas, associate, and bachelor's.

Costs (2010–11) *Tuition:* Tuition cost varies by program. Prospective students should contact the school for current tuition costs. Other charges include a starting kit for all first-quarter students. Kits vary in price, depending on the program of study.

Freshman Application Contact The Art Institute of Seattle, 2323 Elliott Avenue, Seattle, WA 98121-1642. *Phone:* 206-448-6600. *Toll-free phone:* 800-275-2471. *Web site:* http://www.artinstitutes.edu/seattle/.

See page 1068 for the College Close-Up.

Bastyr University
Kenmore, Washington

- **Independent** upper-level, founded 1978
- **Suburban** 51-acre campus with easy access to Seattle
- **Coed** 253 undergraduate students, 72% full-time, 85% women, 15% men

Undergraduates 181 full-time, 72 part-time. Students come from 24 states and territories; 7 other countries; 22% are from out of state; 7% live on campus.

Faculty *Total:* 153, 35% full-time. *Student/faculty ratio:* 9:1.

Academics *Calendar:* quarters. *Degrees:* bachelor's, master's, doctoral-professional, post-master's, and postbachelor's certificates. *Special study options:* cooperative education, double majors, independent study, internships, part-time degree program, summer session for credit.

Computers on Campus 71 computers/terminals and 20 ports are available on campus for general student use. Students can access the following: campus intranet, computer help desk, free student e-mail accounts, online (class) grades, online (class) schedules. Campuswide network is available. 100% of college-owned or -operated housing units are wired for high-speed Internet access. Wireless service is available via entire campus.

Student Life *Housing options:* coed. Campus housing is university owned. *Activities and organizations:* Naturopaths Without Borders, Nature Club, Multicultural Student Association of Natural Medicine, Environmental Action Team, Venture Grant. *Campus security:* student patrols, late-night transport/escort service, controlled dormitory access. *Student services:* health clinic, personal/psychological counseling.

Athletics *Intramural sports:* basketball M, soccer M/W, ultimate Frisbee M/W, volleyball M/W.

Costs (2011–12) *Tuition:* $19,995 full-time, $528 per credit hour part-time. Full-time tuition and fees vary according to course load and program. Part-time tuition and fees vary according to course load and program. *Required fees:* $1020 full-time. *Room only:* Room and board charges vary according to housing facility. *Waivers:* employees or children of employees.

Financial Aid Of all full-time matriculated undergraduates who enrolled in 2008, 189 applied for aid, 178 were judged to have need. 40 Federal Work-Study jobs (averaging $3000). 31 state and other part-time jobs (averaging $3000). In 2008, 10 non-need-based awards were made. *Average percent of need met:* 50%. *Average financial aid package:* $17,600. *Average need-based loan:* $5500. *Average need-based gift aid:* $8750. *Average non-need-based aid:* $500. *Average indebtedness upon graduation:* $32,500.

Applying *Options:* electronic application, deferred entrance. *Application fee:* $60. *Application deadline:* 3/15 (transfers). *Notification:* continuous until 9/1 (transfers).

Application Contact Mr. Ted Olsen, Director of Admissions, Bastyr University, 14500 Juanita Drive NE, Kenmore, WA 98028-4966. *Phone:* 425-602-3101. *Fax:* 425-602-3090. *E-mail:* admissions@bastyr.edu. *Web site:* http://www.bastyr.edu/.

See page 1110 for the College Close-Up.

Bellevue College
Bellevue, Washington

Freshman Application Contact Morenika Jacobs, Associate Dean of Enrollment Services, Bellevue College, 3000 Landerholm Circle, SE, Bellevue, WA 98007-6484. *Phone:* 425-564-2205. *Fax:* 425-564-4065. *Web site:* http://www.bcc.ctc.edu/.

Central Washington University

Ellensburg, Washington

Freshman Application Contact Ms. Lisa Garcia-Hanson, Director of Admissions, Central Washington University, 400 East University Way, Ellensburg, WA 98926-7463. *Phone:* 509-963-1211. *Toll-free phone:* 866-298-4968. *Fax:* 509-963-3022. *E-mail:* cwuadmis@cwu.edu. *Web site:* http://www.cwu.edu/.

City University of Seattle

Bellevue, Washington

- **Independent** comprehensive, founded 1973
- **Suburban** campus with easy access to Seattle
- **Coed**
- **Noncompetitive** entrance level

Faculty *Student/faculty ratio:* 13:1.

Academics *Calendar:* quarters. *Degrees:* certificates, diplomas, associate, bachelor's, master's, and postbachelor's certificates.

Student Life *Campus security:* 24-hour emergency response devices.

Financial Aid *Of all full-time matriculated undergraduates who enrolled in 2003,* 824 applied for aid, 721 were judged to have need. 1 Federal Work-Study job (averaging $1300). *In 2003,* 18 non-need-based awards were made. *Average percent of need met:* 15. *Average financial aid package:* $4943. *Average need-based loan:* $4353. *Average need-based gift aid:* $2344. *Average non-need-based aid:* $3738. *Average indebtedness upon graduation:* $16,369.

Applying *Options:* electronic application, deferred entrance. *Application fee:* $50. *Recommended:* high school transcript.

Freshman Application Contact Student Services Center, City University of Seattle, 11900 NE First Street, Bellvue, WA 98005. *Phone:* 888-422-4898. *Toll-free phone:* 888-42-CITYU. *Fax:* 425-709-5361. *E-mail:* info@cityu.edu. *Web site:* http://www.cityu.edu/.

Cornish College of the Arts

Seattle, Washington

- **Independent** 4-year, founded 1914
- **Urban** 4-acre campus
- **Endowment** $6.6 million
- **Coed**
- **Moderately difficult** entrance level

Faculty *Student/faculty ratio:* 8:1.

Academics *Calendar:* semesters. *Degree:* bachelor's.

Student Life *Campus security:* 24-hour emergency response devices and patrols, late-night transport/escort service.

Standardized Tests *Recommended:* SAT or ACT (for admission).

Costs (2010–11) *Comprehensive fee:* $37,537 includes full-time tuition ($28,750), mandatory fees ($487), and room and board ($8300). Part-time tuition: $1200 per credit. *College room only:* $5900. Room and board charges vary according to board plan.

Financial Aid *Of all full-time matriculated undergraduates who enrolled in 2008,* 578 applied for aid, 490 were judged to have need, 47 had their need fully met. *In 2008,* 123 non-need-based awards were made. *Average percent of need met:* 56. *Average financial aid package:* $15,185. *Average need-based loan:* $4719. *Average need-based gift aid:* $8788. *Average non-need-based aid:* $5157. *Average indebtedness upon graduation:* $36,026.

Applying *Options:* electronic application, deferred entrance. *Application fee:* $35. *Required:* essay or personal statement, high school transcript, minimum 2.5 GPA, portfolio or audition. *Required for some:* 2 letters of recommendation. *Recommended:* 2 letters of recommendation, interview.

Freshman Application Contact Ms. Sharron Starling, Director of Admissions, Cornish College of the Arts, 1000 Lenora Street, Seattle, WA 98121. *Phone:* 206-726-5017. *Toll-free phone:* 800-726-ARTS. *Fax:* 206-720-1011. *E-mail:* admissions@cornish.edu. *Web site:* http://www.cornish.edu/.

DeVry University

Bellevue, Washington

Admissions Office Contact DeVry University, 600 108th Avenue NE, Suite 230, Bellevue, WA 98004-5110. *Web site:* http://www.devry.edu/.

DeVry University

Federal Way, Washington

- **Proprietary** comprehensive, founded 2001, part of DeVry University
- **Suburban** 12-acre campus
- **Coed** 836 undergraduate students, 57% full-time, 30% women, 70% men
- **Minimally difficult** entrance level

Undergraduates 479 full-time, 357 part-time. 5% are from out of state; 11% Black or African American, non-Hispanic/Latino; 8% Hispanic/Latino; 5% Asian, non-Hispanic/Latino; 1% Native Hawaiian or other Pacific Islander, non-Hispanic/Latino; 1% American Indian or Alaska Native, non-Hispanic/Latino; 1% Two or more races, non-Hispanic/Latino; 26% Race/ethnicity unknown; 0.2% international; 28% transferred in.

Freshmen *Admission:* 135 enrolled.

Faculty *Total:* 86, 22% full-time. *Student/faculty ratio:* 16:1.

Academics *Calendar:* semesters. *Degrees:* associate, bachelor's, and master's. *Special study options:* academic remediation for entering students, accelerated degree program, adult/continuing education programs, advanced placement credit, distance learning, part-time degree program, services for LD students, summer session for credit.

Computers on Campus Students can access the following: online (class) registration. Campuswide network is available.

Student Life *Housing:* college housing not available. *Campus security:* 24-hour emergency response devices and patrols, lighted pathways, emergency response team.

Costs (2010–11) *Tuition:* $14,766 full-time, $580 per credit hour part-time. Full-time tuition and fees vary according to course load. Part-time tuition and fees vary according to course load. *Required fees:* $60 full-time, $30 per term part-time. *Payment plans:* installment, deferred payment. *Waivers:* employees or children of employees.

Financial Aid Of all full-time matriculated undergraduates who enrolled in 2007, 259 applied for aid, 250 were judged to have need, 8 had their need fully met. In 2007, 15 non-need-based awards were made. *Average percent of need met:* 34%. *Average financial aid package:* $10,833. *Average need-based loan:* $6622. *Average need-based gift aid:* $5975. *Average non-need-based aid:* $20,202. *Average indebtedness upon graduation:* $50,600.

Applying *Options:* electronic application, deferred entrance. *Application fee:* $50. *Required:* high school transcript, interview. *Application deadlines:* rolling (freshmen), rolling (transfers). *Notification:* continuous (freshmen), continuous (transfers).

Freshman Application Contact DeVry University, 3600 South 344th Way, Federal Way, WA 98001. *Phone:* 253-943-2800. *Web site:* http://www.devry.edu/.

DigiPen Institute of Technology

Redmond, Washington

- **Proprietary** comprehensive, founded 1988
- **Suburban** 2-acre campus with easy access to Seattle
- **Coed** 867 undergraduate students
- **Minimally difficult** entrance level, 37% of applicants were admitted

Undergraduates Students come from 32 other countries; 0.5% Black or African American, non-Hispanic/Latino; 6% Hispanic/Latino; 7% Asian, non-Hispanic/Latino; 0.1% Native Hawaiian or other Pacific Islander, non-Hispanic/Latino; 0.2% American Indian or Alaska Native, non-Hispanic/Latino; 5% Two or more races, non-Hispanic/Latino; 14% Race/ethnicity unknown; 10% international. *Retention:* 76% of full-time freshmen returned.

Freshmen *Admission:* 351 applied, 131 admitted.

Faculty *Total:* 75, 64% full-time. *Student/faculty ratio:* 12:1.

Academics *Calendar:* semesters. *Degrees:* bachelor's and master's. *Special study options:* academic remediation for entering students, advanced placement credit, independent study, internships, services for LD students, summer session for credit.

Computers on Campus 650 computers/terminals are available on campus for general student use. Students can access the following: campus intranet, computer help desk, free student e-mail accounts, online (class) grades, online (class) registration, online (class) schedules. Campuswide network is available. Wireless service is available via entire campus.

Student Life *Housing:* college housing not available. *Options:* Campus housing is provided by a third party. *Activities and organizations:* Game Testing Club, Guilty Gear Club, Student Association, Audio Freaks, Japanese Club. *Campus security:* late-night transport/escort service, controlled dormitory access, on-site security during campus hours. *Student services:* personal/psychological counseling.

Standardized Tests *Required for some:* SAT or ACT (for admission).

Costs (2011–12) *One-time required fee:* $150. *Tuition:* $25,000 full-time, $618 per semester hour part-time. Full-time tuition and fees vary according to course load and program. Part-time tuition and fees vary according to course load and program. *Required fees:* $160 full-time, $80 per term part-time.

Room only: Room and board charges vary according to housing facility. *Payment plan:* installment. *Waivers:* employees or children of employees.

Applying *Options:* electronic application, deferred entrance. *Application fee:* $35. *Required:* essay or personal statement, high school transcript, minimum 2.5 GPA. *Required for some:* art portfolio for BFA in Digital Art and Animation applicants; specific essay requirements for Game Design applicants. *Recommended:* 2 letters of recommendation. *Application deadlines:* rolling (freshmen), rolling (out-of-state freshmen), rolling (transfers). *Notification:* continuous (freshmen), continuous (out-of-state freshmen), continuous (transfers).

Freshman Application Contact Ms. Angela Kugler, Admissions Director, DigiPen Institute of Technology, 9931 Willows Road NE, Redmond, WA 98052. *Phone:* 425-895-4438. *Fax:* 425-558-0378. *E-mail:* admissions@ digipen.edu. *Web site:* http://www.digipen.edu/.

Eastern Washington University
Cheney, Washington

- **State-supported** comprehensive, founded 1882
- **Small-town** 335-acre campus with easy access to Spokane
- **Endowment** $17.9 million
- **Coed** 10,218 undergraduate students, 88% full-time, 55% women, 45% men
- **Moderately difficult** entrance level, 82% of applicants were admitted

Undergraduates 9,033 full-time, 1,185 part-time. 6% are from out of state; 4% Black or African American, non-Hispanic/Latino; 9% Hispanic/Latino; 4% Asian, non-Hispanic/Latino; 0.4% Native Hawaiian or other Pacific Islander, non-Hispanic/Latino; 2% American Indian or Alaska Native, non-Hispanic/Latino; 3% Two or more races, non-Hispanic/Latino; 11% Race/ethnicity unknown; 2% international; 12% transferred in; 16% live on campus. *Retention:* 73% of full-time freshmen returned.

Freshmen *Admission:* 3,949 applied, 3,233 admitted, 1,545 enrolled. *Average high school GPA:* 3.17. *Test scores:* SAT critical reading scores over 500: 42%; SAT math scores over 500: 44%; SAT writing scores over 500: 35%; ACT scores over 18: 77%; SAT critical reading scores over 600: 11%; SAT math scores over 600: 10%; SAT writing scores over 600: 6%; ACT scores over 24: 24%; SAT critical reading scores over 700: 1%; SAT math scores over 700: 1%; ACT scores over 30: 1%.

Faculty *Total:* 628, 66% full-time, 63% with terminal degrees. *Student/faculty ratio:* 22:1.

Academics *Calendar:* quarters. *Degrees:* certificates, bachelor's, master's, doctoral-other, and post-master's certificates. *Special study options:* academic remediation for entering students, advanced placement credit, distance learning, double majors, English as a second language, honors programs, independent study, internships, off-campus study, part-time degree program, services for LD students, student-designed majors, study abroad, summer session for credit. *ROTC:* Army (b).

Computers on Campus 812 computers/terminals and 250 ports are available on campus for general student use. Students can access the following: computer help desk, free student e-mail accounts, online (class) grades, online (class) registration, online (class) schedules, 15 gb network disk storage per student; discounted Microsoft and Adobe software; laptops, still and video cameras, projectors for checkout; print credit; black white laser, color laser, and color photo options, large format print service. Campuswide network is available. 100% of college-owned or -operated housing units are wired for high-speed Internet access. Wireless service is available via classrooms, computer centers, computer labs, dorm rooms, learning centers, libraries, student centers.

Student Life *Housing options:* coed, disabled students. Campus housing is university owned. *Activities and organizations:* drama/theater group, student-run newspaper, radio station, choral group, marching band, Campus Crusade for Christ, Hockey Club, M.E. Ch.A. Chicano Community, Black Student Union, EWU Gamers Club, national fraternities, national sororities. *Campus security:* 24-hour emergency response devices and patrols, student patrols, late-night transport/escort service, controlled dormitory access, emergency call boxes. *Student services:* health clinic, personal/psychological counseling, women's center.

Athletics Member NCAA. All Division I except football (Division I-AA). *Intercollegiate sports:* archery M(c)/W(c), baseball M(c), basketball M(s)/W(s), cheerleading W(c), cross-country running M(s)/W(s), equestrian sports M(c)/W(c), fencing M(c)/W(c), golf W(s), ice hockey M(c)/W(c), rugby M(c)/W(c), soccer M(c)/W(s), softball W(c), tennis M(s)/W(s), track and field M(s)/W(s), volleyball W(s). *Intramural sports:* baseball M/W, basketball M/W, bowling M/W, cross-country running M/W, football M, golf W, racquetball M/W, soccer M/W, softball M/W, tennis M/W, track and field M/W, ultimate Frisbee M(c)/W(c), volleyball M/W, wrestling M(c)/W(c).

Standardized Tests *Required:* SAT or ACT (for admission).

Costs (2011–12) *Tuition:* state resident $6063 full-time, $202 per credit part-time; nonresident $14,781 full-time, $493 per credit part-time. Full-time tuition and fees vary according to course load and program. Part-time tuition

and fees vary according to course load and program. *Required fees:* $541 full-time, $541 per year part-time. *Room and board:* $7470; room only: $3960. Room and board charges vary according to board plan and housing facility. *Payment plan:* installment.

Financial Aid Of all full-time matriculated undergraduates who enrolled in 2008, 6,490 applied for aid, 5,227 were judged to have need, 1,443 had their need fully met. 230 Federal Work-Study jobs (averaging $2322). 335 state and other part-time jobs (averaging $2683). In 2008, 465 non-need-based awards were made. *Average percent of need met:* 71%. *Average financial aid package:* $11,827. *Average need-based loan:* $2958. *Average need-based gift aid:* $7281. *Average non-need-based aid:* $2945. *Average indebtedness upon graduation:* $20,114.

Applying *Options:* electronic application, deferred entrance. *Application fee:* $50. *Required:* high school transcript, minimum 2 GPA. *Required for some:* essay or personal statement. *Recommended:* minimum 3 GPA. *Application deadlines:* 5/15 (freshmen), 7/1 (transfers). *Notification:* continuous (freshmen), continuous (transfers).

Freshman Application Contact Ms. Shannon Carr, Director of Admissions, Eastern Washington University, Eastern Washington University, 101 Sutton Hall, Cheney, WA 99004-2447. *Phone:* 509-359-6582. *Fax:* 509-359-6692. *E-mail:* admissions@mail.ewu.edu. *Web site:* http://www.ewu.edu/.

The Evergreen State College
Olympia, Washington

- **State-supported** comprehensive, founded 1967, part of Washington State Public Baccalaureate Institution
- **Rural** 1000-acre campus with easy access to Seattle
- **Endowment** $2.3 million
- **Coed** 4,489 undergraduate students, 90% full-time, 54% women, 46% men
- **Moderately difficult** entrance level, 94% of applicants were admitted

Undergraduates 4,046 full-time, 443 part-time. Students come from 49 states and territories; 15 other countries; 27% are from out of state; 4% Black or African American, non-Hispanic/Latino; 5% Hispanic/Latino; 3% Asian, non-Hispanic/Latino; 0.4% Native Hawaiian or other Pacific Islander, non-Hispanic/Latino; 3% American Indian or Alaska Native, non-Hispanic/Latino; 4% Two or more races, non-Hispanic/Latino; 10% Race/ethnicity unknown; 0.4% international; 18% transferred in; 21% live on campus. *Retention:* 73% of full-time freshmen returned.

Freshmen *Admission:* 1,965 applied, 1,854 admitted, 624 enrolled. *Average high school GPA:* 3.08. *Test scores:* SAT critical reading scores over 500: 83%; SAT math scores over 500: 60%; SAT writing scores over 500: 71%; ACT scores over 18: 93%; SAT critical reading scores over 600: 46%; SAT math scores over 600: 22%; SAT writing scores over 600: 25%; ACT scores over 24: 56%; SAT critical reading scores over 700: 11%; SAT math scores over 700: 1%; SAT writing scores over 700: 3%; ACT scores over 30: 12%.

Faculty *Total:* 247, 68% full-time, 75% with terminal degrees. *Student/faculty ratio:* 23:1.

Academics *Calendar:* quarters. *Degrees:* bachelor's and master's. *Special study options:* accelerated degree program, advanced placement credit, double majors, independent study, internships, off-campus study, part-time degree program, services for LD students, student-designed majors, study abroad, summer session for credit.

Computers on Campus 408 computers/terminals are available on campus for general student use. Students can access the following: campus intranet, computer help desk, free student e-mail accounts, online (class) grades, online (class) registration, online (class) schedules, online payment and student accounts history, online housing application. Campuswide network is available. 100% of college-owned or -operated housing units are wired for high-speed Internet access. Wireless service is available via entire campus.

Student Life *Housing options:* coed, disabled students. Campus housing is university owned. Freshman campus housing is guaranteed. *Activities and organizations:* drama/theater group, student-run newspaper, radio and television station, choral group, Common Bread, Giant Robot Appreciation Society (GRAS)/Anime Club, Gaming Guild, Black Student Union, Folk Dance Alliance. *Campus security:* 24-hour emergency response devices and patrols, student patrols, late-night transport/escort service, controlled dormitory access. *Student services:* health clinic, personal/psychological counseling, women's center.

Athletics Member NAIA. *Intercollegiate sports:* basketball M(s)/W(s), crew M(c)/W(c), cross-country running M(s)/W(s), soccer M(s)/W(s), track and field M(s)/W(s), volleyball W(s). *Intramural sports:* basketball M/W, wrestling M(c)/W(c).

Standardized Tests *Required:* SAT or ACT (for admission).

Costs (2010–11) *Tuition:* state resident $6108 full-time, $204 per credit hour part-time; nonresident $17,235 full-time, $575 per credit hour part-time. Full-time tuition and fees vary according to course load and location. Part-time tuition and fees vary according to course load and location. *Required fees:* $571 full-time, $8 per credit hour part-time, $69 per term part-time. *Room and* *board:* $8460; room only: $5730. Room and board charges vary according to board plan, housing facility, location, and student level. *Payment plan:* installment. *Waivers:* senior citizens and employees or children of employees.

Financial Aid Of all full-time matriculated undergraduates who enrolled in 2009, 2,936 applied for aid, 2,589 were judged to have need, 444 had their need fully met. 125 Federal Work-Study jobs (averaging $3357). 263 state and other part-time jobs (averaging $3300). In 2009, 302 non-need-based awards were made. *Average percent of need met:* 67%. *Average financial aid package:* $11,459. *Average need-based loan:* $4298. *Average need-based gift aid:* $8596. *Average non-need-based aid:* $2460. *Average indebtedness upon graduation:* $16,700.

Applying *Options:* electronic application, deferred entrance. *Application fee:* $50. *Required:* high school transcript, minimum 2 GPA. *Required for some:* essay or personal statement. *Recommended:* essay or personal statement. *Application deadlines:* 3/1 (freshmen), 3/1 (transfers). *Notification:* continuous until 11/1 (freshmen), continuous until 11/1 (transfers).

Freshman Application Contact The Evergreen State College, 2700 Evergreen Parkway, NW, Olympia, WA 98505. *Phone:* 360-867-6170. *Web site:* http://www.evergreen.edu/.

Gonzaga University

Spokane, Washington

- **Independent Roman Catholic** comprehensive, founded 1887
- **Urban** 130-acre campus
- **Coed**
- **Moderately difficult** entrance level

Faculty *Student/faculty ratio:* 10:1.

Academics *Calendar:* semesters. *Degrees:* bachelor's, master's, doctoral-professional, doctoral-research/scholarship, and post-master's certificates.

Student Life *Campus security:* 24-hour emergency response devices and patrols, late-night transport/escort service, controlled dormitory access.

Athletics Member NCAA. All Division I.

Standardized Tests *Required:* SAT or ACT (for admission).

Costs (2010–11) *Comprehensive fee:* $39,225 includes full-time tuition ($30,440), mandatory fees ($485), and room and board ($8300). Full-time tuition and fees vary according to course load, location, program, reciprocity agreements, and student level. Part-time tuition and fees vary according to course load, location, program, reciprocity agreements, and student level. *Required fees:* $850 per credit hour part-time. *College room only:* $4240. Room and board charges vary according to board plan and housing facility. *Payment plans:* installment, deferred payment.

Financial Aid *Of all full-time matriculated undergraduates who enrolled in 2009,* 3,364 applied for aid, 2,646 were judged to have need, 532 had their need fully met. 443 Federal Work-Study jobs (averaging $2935). 412 state and other part-time jobs (averaging $4308). *In 2009,* 1704 non-need-based awards were made. *Average percent of need met:* 71. *Average financial aid package:* $20,412. *Average need-based loan:* $5225. *Average need-based gift aid:* $17,477. *Average non-need-based aid:* $10,673. *Average indebtedness upon graduation:* $27,136.

Applying *Options:* electronic application, early action, deferred entrance. *Application fee:* $50. *Required:* essay or personal statement, high school transcript, minimum 3 GPA, 1 letter of recommendation. *Recommended:* interview.

Freshman Application Contact Ms. Julie McCulloh, Dean of Admission, Gonzaga University, 502 East Boone Avenue, Spokane, WA 99258-0102. *Phone:* 509-313-6591. *Toll-free phone:* 800-322-2584 Ext. 6572. *Fax:* 509-313-5780. *E-mail:* admissions@gonzaga.edu. *Web site:* http://www.gonzaga.edu/.

See page 1310 for the College Close-Up.

Heritage University

Toppenish, Washington

Freshman Application Contact Miguel Puente, Director of Admissions and Recruitment, Heritage University, 3240 Fort Road, Toppenish, WA 98948-9599. *Phone:* 509-865-8508. *Toll-free phone:* 888-272-6190. *Fax:* 509-865-4469. *E-mail:* admissions@heritage.edu. *Web site:* http://www.heritage.edu/.

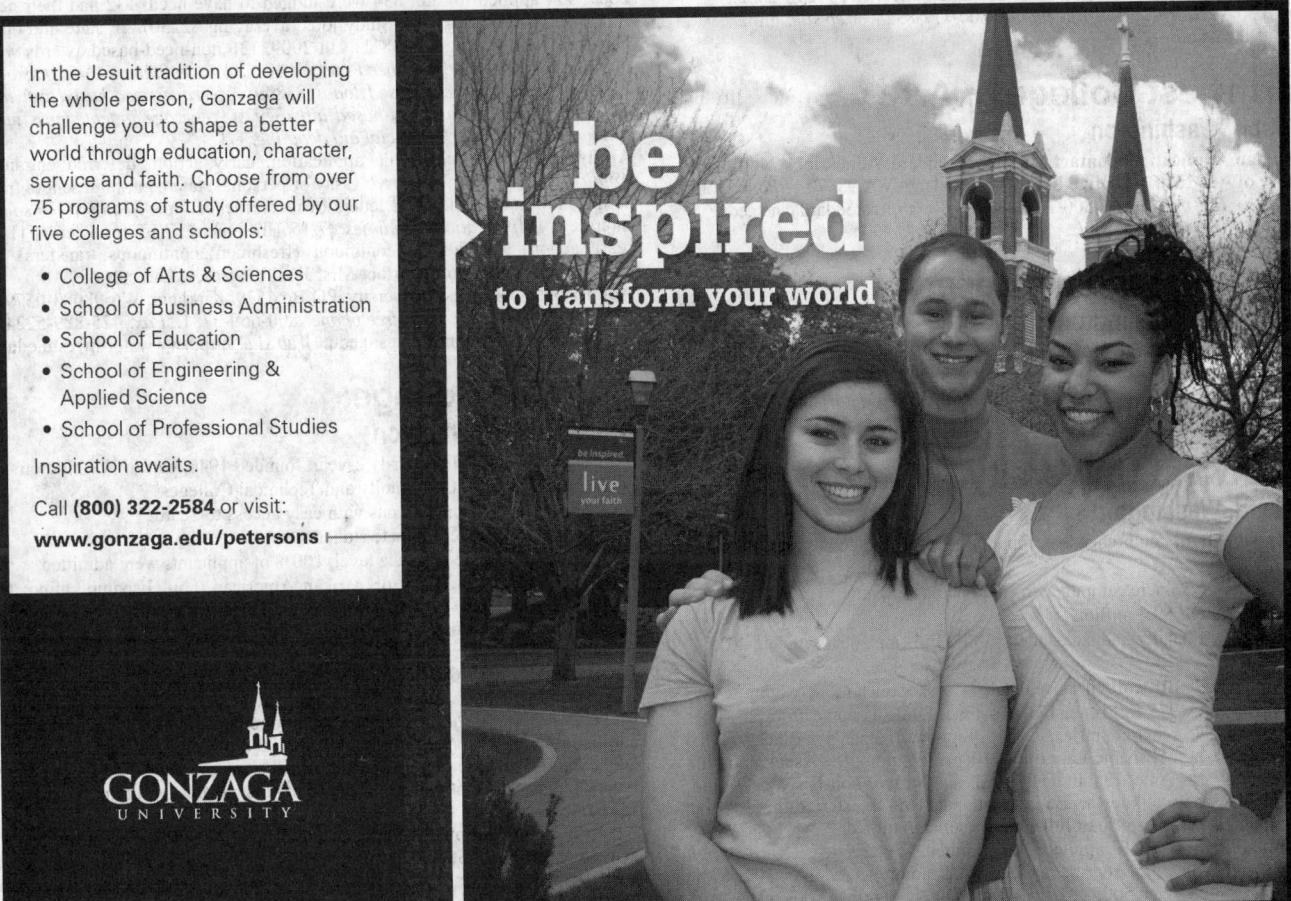

ITT Technical Institute
Everett, Washington

- **Proprietary** primarily 2-year, part of ITT Educational Services, Inc.
- **Coed**
- **Minimally difficult** entrance level

Academics *Degrees:* associate and bachelor's.
Freshman Application Contact Director of Recruitment, ITT Technical Institute, 1615 75th Street SW, Everett, WA 98203. *Phone:* 425-583-0200. *Toll-free phone:* 800-272-3791. *Web site:* http://www.itt-tech.edu/.

ITT Technical Institute
Seattle, Washington

- **Proprietary** primarily 2-year, founded 1932, part of ITT Educational Services, Inc.
- **Urban** campus
- **Coed**
- **Minimally difficult** entrance level

Academics *Calendar:* quarters. *Degrees:* associate and bachelor's.
Student Life *Housing:* college housing not available.
Freshman Application Contact Director of Recruitment, ITT Technical Institute, 12720 Gateway Drive, Suite 100, Seattle, WA 98168-3333. *Phone:* 206-244-3300. *Toll-free phone:* 800-422-2029. *Web site:* http://www.itt-tech.edu/.

ITT Technical Institute
Spokane Valley, Washington

- **Proprietary** primarily 2-year, founded 1985, part of ITT Educational Services, Inc.
- **Suburban** campus
- **Coed**
- **Minimally difficult** entrance level

Academics *Calendar:* quarters. *Degrees:* associate and bachelor's.
Student Life *Housing:* college housing not available.
Freshman Application Contact Director of Recruitment, ITT Technical Institute, 13518 East Indiana Avenue, Spokane Valley, WA 99212-2682. *Phone:* 509-926-2900. *Toll-free phone:* 800-777-8324. *Web site:* http://www.itt-tech.edu/.

Northwest College of Art
Poulsbo, Washington

Freshman Application Contact Mr. Mark Stoddard, Admissions, Northwest College of Art, 16301 Creative Drive, NE, Poulsbo, WA 98370. *Phone:* 360-779-9993. *Toll-free phone:* 800-769-ARTS. *E-mail:* mstoddard@nca.edu. *Web site:* http://www.nca.edu/.

Northwest Indian College
Bellingham, Washington

Freshman Application Contact Office of Admissions, Northwest Indian College, 2522 Kwina Road, Bellingham, WA 98226. *Phone:* 360-676-2772. *Toll-free phone:* 866-676-2772. *Fax:* 360-392-4333. *E-mail:* admissions@nwic.edu. *Web site:* http://www.nwic.edu/.

Northwest University
Kirkland, Washington

- **Independent** comprehensive, founded 1934, affiliated with Assemblies of God
- **Suburban** 56-acre campus with easy access to Seattle
- **Endowment** $9.3 million
- **Coed** 1,148 undergraduate students, 85% full-time, 60% women, 40% men
- **Moderately difficult** entrance level, 74% of applicants were admitted

Undergraduates 975 full-time, 173 part-time. Students come from 24 states and territories; 15 other countries; 8% are from out of state; 5% Black or African American, non-Hispanic/Latino; 6% Hispanic/Latino; 6% Asian, non-Hispanic/Latino; 2% American Indian or Alaska Native, non-Hispanic/Latino; 12% Race/ethnicity unknown; 2% international; 16% transferred in; 55% live on campus. *Retention:* 69% of full-time freshmen returned.
Freshmen *Admission:* 471 applied, 349 admitted, 159 enrolled. *Average high school GPA:* 3.34. *Test scores:* SAT critical reading scores over 500: 63%; SAT math scores over 500: 48%; SAT writing scores over 500: 52%; ACT scores over 18: 74%; SAT critical reading scores over 600: 20%; SAT math scores over 600: 14%; SAT writing scores over 600: 19%; ACT scores over 24: 29%; SAT critical reading scores over 700: 3%; SAT writing scores over 700: 2%.
Faculty *Total:* 108, 50% full-time, 36% with terminal degrees. *Student/faculty ratio:* 17:1.
Academics *Calendar:* semesters. *Degrees:* certificates, diplomas, associate, bachelor's, master's, and doctoral-professional. *Special study options:* academic remediation for entering students, accelerated degree program, adult/continuing education programs, advanced placement credit, cooperative education, double majors, English as a second language, independent study, internships, part-time degree program, study abroad, summer session for credit. *ROTC:* Army (c), Air Force (c).
Computers on Campus 134 computers/terminals are available on campus for general student use. Students can access the following: campus intranet, computer help desk, free student e-mail accounts, online (class) grades, online (class) registration, online (class) schedules, online classes. Campuswide network is available. 100% of college-owned or -operated housing units are wired for high-speed Internet access. Wireless service is available via entire campus.
Student Life *Housing:* on-campus residence required through sophomore year. *Options:* men-only, women-only. Campus housing is university owned. Freshman campus housing is guaranteed. *Activities and organizations:* drama/theater group, student-run newspaper, radio station, choral group, Student Ministries, Pursuit (worship service), Northwest University Business Club, Environmental Stewardship Club. *Campus security:* 24-hour emergency response devices and patrols, late-night transport/escort service, controlled dormitory access. *Student services:* health clinic, personal/psychological counseling.
Athletics Member NAIA. *Intercollegiate sports:* basketball M(s)/W(s), cross-country running M(s)/W(s), soccer M(s)/W(s), track and field M(s)/W(s), volleyball W(s).
Standardized Tests *Required:* SAT or ACT (for admission).
Costs (2011–12) *One-time required fee:* $40. *Comprehensive fee:* $30,284 includes full-time tuition ($23,030), mandatory fees ($370), and room and board ($6884). Full-time tuition and fees vary according to class time, location, and program. Part-time tuition: $960 per credit hour. Part-time tuition and fees vary according to course load and location. *Room and board:* Room and board charges vary according to board plan, housing facility, and location. *Payment plan:* installment. *Waivers:* employees or children of employees.
Financial Aid Of all full-time matriculated undergraduates who enrolled in 2009, 934 applied for aid, 834 were judged to have need, 132 had their need fully met. 70 Federal Work-Study jobs (averaging $2230). 26 state and other part-time jobs (averaging $3811). In 2009, 136 non-need-based awards were made. *Average percent of need met:* 70%. *Average financial aid package:* $15,696. *Average need-based loan:* $3899. *Average need-based gift aid:* $11,690. *Average non-need-based aid:* $7920. *Average indebtedness upon graduation:* $29,160. *Financial aid deadline:* 8/1.
Applying *Options:* electronic application, early action, deferred entrance. *Application fee:* $30. *Required:* essay or personal statement, high school transcript, minimum 2.3 GPA, 2 letters of recommendation. *Required for some:* interview. *Application deadlines:* 7/15 (freshmen), 7/15 (transfers), 11/15 (early action). *Notification:* continuous (freshmen), continuous (transfers).
Freshman Application Contact Mrs. Jessica Velasco, Director of Admissions, Northwest University, PO Box 579, Kirkland, WA 98083-0579. *Phone:* 425-889-5212. *Toll-free phone:* 800-669-3781. *Fax:* 425-889-5224. *E-mail:* admissions@northwestu.edu. *Web site:* http://www.northwestu.edu/.

Olympic College
Bremerton, Washington

- **State-supported** primarily 2-year, founded 1946, part of Washington State Board for Community and Technical Colleges
- **Suburban** 33-acre campus with easy access to Seattle
- **Coed** 8,533 undergraduate students
- **Noncompetitive** entrance level, 100% of applicants were admitted

Undergraduates 4% Black or African American, non-Hispanic/Latino; 6% Hispanic/Latino; 8% Asian, non-Hispanic/Latino; 2% American Indian or Alaska Native, non-Hispanic/Latino; 0.6% international.
Freshmen *Admission:* 805 applied, 805 admitted.
Faculty *Total:* 459, 26% full-time. *Student/faculty ratio:* 28:1.
Academics *Calendar:* quarters. *Degrees:* certificates, diplomas, associate, and bachelor's. *Special study options:* academic remediation for entering students, adult/continuing education programs, advanced placement credit, cooperative education, distance learning, English as a second language, honors programs, independent study, off-campus study, part-time degree program, services for LD students, summer session for credit.
Computers on Campus 650 computers/terminals are available on campus for general student use. Students can access the following: campus intranet, computer help desk, free student e-mail accounts, online (class) grades, online (class) registration, online (class) schedules. Campuswide network is available. Wireless service is available via entire campus.

Student Life *Housing:* college housing not available. *Activities and organizations:* drama/theater group, student-run newspaper, choral group, Phi Theta Kappa, International Student Club, Oceans (Nursing), ASOC, ASAD. *Campus security:* 24-hour emergency response devices and patrols, student patrols, late-night transport/escort service. *Student services:* personal/psychological counseling, women's center.

Athletics *Intercollegiate sports:* baseball M(s), basketball M(s)/W(s), cross-country running M/W, golf M/W, soccer M(s)/W(s), softball W(s), volleyball W(s). *Intramural sports:* basketball M/W, table tennis M/W, volleyball M/W, weight lifting M/W.

Costs (2010–11) *Tuition:* state resident $3135 full-time, $87 per quarter hour part-time; nonresident $3536 full-time, $100 per quarter hour part-time. Full-time tuition and fees vary according to course level, course load, and degree level. Part-time tuition and fees vary according to course level, course load, and degree level. *Required fees:* $240 full-time, $5 per credit hour part-time, $65 per term part-time. *Payment plan:* installment. *Waivers:* senior citizens.

Financial Aid Of all full-time matriculated undergraduates who enrolled in 2009, 105 Federal Work-Study jobs (averaging $2380). 31 state and other part-time jobs (averaging $2880).

Applying *Options:* electronic application, early admission, deferred entrance. *Required for some:* high school transcript. *Application deadlines:* rolling (freshmen), rolling (transfers). *Notification:* continuous (freshmen), continuous (transfers).

Freshman Application Contact Ms. Jennifer Fyllingness, Director of Admissions and Outreach, Olympic College, 1600 Chester Avenue, Bremerton, WA 98337-1699. *Phone:* 360-475-7128. *Toll-free phone:* 800-259-6718. *Fax:* 360-475-7202. *E-mail:* jfyllingness@olympic.edu. *Web site:* http://www.olympic.edu/.

Pacific Lutheran University
Tacoma, Washington

- **Independent** comprehensive, founded 1890, affiliated with Evangelical Lutheran Church in America
- **Suburban** 126-acre campus with easy access to Seattle
- **Endowment** $69.2 million
- **Coed** 3,267 undergraduate students, 95% full-time, 63% women, 37% men
- **Moderately difficult** entrance level, 78% of applicants were admitted

Undergraduates 3,103 full-time, 164 part-time. Students come from 50 states and territories; 186 other countries; 24% are from out of state; 3% Black or African American, non-Hispanic/Latino; 5% Hispanic/Latino; 5% Asian, non-Hispanic/Latino; 0.8% Native Hawaiian or other Pacific Islander, non-Hispanic/Latino; 0.6% American Indian or Alaska Native, non-Hispanic/Latino; 6% Two or more races, non-Hispanic/Latino; 2% Race/ethnicity unknown; 5% international; 6% transferred in; 49% live on campus. *Retention:* 82% of full-time freshmen returned.

Freshmen *Admission:* 2,837 applied, 2,199 admitted, 689 enrolled. *Average high school GPA:* 3.65. *Test scores:* SAT critical reading scores over 500: 76%; SAT math scores over 500: 76%; SAT writing scores over 500: 72%; ACT scores over 18: 94%; SAT critical reading scores over 600: 37%; SAT math scores over 600: 35%; SAT writing scores over 600: 30%; ACT scores over 24: 65%; SAT critical reading scores over 700: 7%; SAT math scores over 700: 7%; SAT writing scores over 700: 5%; ACT scores over 30: 18%.

Faculty *Total:* 310, 68% full-time, 70% with terminal degrees. *Student/faculty ratio:* 14:1.

Academics *Calendar:* 4-1-4. *Degrees:* bachelor's, master's, and postbachelor's certificates. *Special study options:* advanced placement credit, cooperative education, double majors, English as a second language, independent study, internships, part-time degree program, services for LD students, student-designed majors, study abroad, summer session for credit. *ROTC:* Army (b). *Unusual degree programs:* 3-2 engineering with Columbia University in New York and Washington University in Missouri.

Computers on Campus 435 computers/terminals and 1,200 ports are available on campus for general student use. Students can access the following: campus intranet, computer help desk, free student e-mail accounts, online (class) grades, online (class) registration, online (class) schedules. Campus-wide network is available. 100% of college-owned or -operated housing units are wired for high-speed Internet access. Wireless service is available via entire campus.

Student Life *Housing:* on-campus residence required through sophomore year. *Options:* coed, women-only. Campus housing is university owned. Freshman campus housing is guaranteed. *Activities and organizations:* drama/theater group, student-run newspaper, radio and television station, choral group, Ignite, Circle K, Adult Students Club, Residence Hall Government, Inter-Varsity Fellowship. *Campus security:* 24-hour emergency response devices and patrols, student patrols, late-night transport/escort service. *Student services:* health clinic, personal/psychological counseling, women's center.

Athletics Member NCAA. All Division III. *Intercollegiate sports:* baseball M, basketball M/W, cheerleading M/W, crew M/W, cross-country running M/W, football M, golf M/W, lacrosse M(c)/W(c), soccer M/W, softball W, swimming and diving M/W, tennis M/W, track and field M/W, ultimate Frisbee M(c)/W(c), volleyball M(c)/W(c). *Intramural sports:* badminton M/W, basketball M/W, cross-country running M/W, football M/W, racquetball M/W, soccer M/W, softball W, squash M/W, volleyball M/W.

Standardized Tests *Required:* SAT or ACT (for admission).

Costs (2011–12) *Comprehensive fee:* $40,200 includes full-time tuition ($30,950) and room and board ($9250). *Room and board:* Room and board charges vary according to board plan and housing facility. *Payment plan:* installment. *Waivers:* children of alumni and employees or children of employees.

Financial Aid Of all full-time matriculated undergraduates who enrolled in 2009, 2,528 applied for aid, 2,229 were judged to have need, 673 had their need fully met. 576 Federal Work-Study jobs (averaging $2266). 1,156 state and other part-time jobs (averaging $3178). In 2009, 740 non-need-based awards were made. *Average percent of need met:* 87%. *Average financial aid package:* $28,473. *Average need-based loan:* $8631. *Average need-based gift aid:* $16,843. *Average non-need-based aid:* $12,374. *Average indebtedness upon graduation:* $28,640.

Applying *Options:* electronic application, early admission, deferred entrance. *Application fee:* $40. *Required:* essay or personal statement, high school transcript, 1 letter of recommendation. *Required for some:* interview. *Recommended:* minimum 2.5 GPA. *Application deadlines:* rolling (freshmen), rolling (transfers). *Notification:* continuous (freshmen), continuous (transfers).

Freshman Application Contact Jennifer Olsen Krengel, Director of Admission, Pacific Lutheran University, Tacoma, WA 98447. *Phone:* 253-535-7151. *Toll-free phone:* 800-274-6758. *Fax:* 253-536-5136. *E-mail:* admission@plu.edu. *Web site:* http://www.plu.edu/.

Peninsula College
Port Angeles, Washington

Freshman Application Contact Ms. Pauline Marvin, Peninsula College, 1502 East Lauridsen Boulevard, Port Angeles, WA 98362. *Phone:* 360-417-6596. *Fax:* 360-457-8100. *E-mail:* admissions@pcadmin.ctc.edu. *Web site:* http://www.pc.ctc.edu/.

Pima Medical Institute
Seattle, Washington

- **Proprietary** primarily 2-year, founded 1989, part of Vocational Training Institutes, Inc.
- **Urban** campus
- **Coed** 357 undergraduate students
- **Minimally difficult** entrance level

Academics *Calendar:* modular. *Degrees:* certificates, associate, and bachelor's. *Special study options:* distance learning.

Student Life *Housing:* college housing not available.

Standardized Tests *Required:* Wonderlic aptitude test (for admission).

Applying *Required:* interview. *Required for some:* high school transcript.

Freshman Application Contact Admissions Office, Pima Medical Institute, 9709 Third Avenue NE, Suite 400, Seattle, WA 98115. *Phone:* 206-322-6100. *Toll-free phone:* 888-898-9048. *Web site:* http://www.pmi.edu/.

Saint Martin's University
Lacey, Washington

- **Independent Roman Catholic** comprehensive, founded 1895
- **Suburban** 380-acre campus with easy access to Tacoma
- **Endowment** $16.1 million
- **Coed** 1,465 undergraduate students, 77% full-time, 50% women, 50% men
- **Moderately difficult** entrance level, 80% of applicants were admitted

Undergraduates 1,134 full-time, 331 part-time. Students come from 36 states and territories; 21 other countries; 23% are from out of state; 18% transferred in; 30% live on campus. *Retention:* 73% of full-time freshmen returned.

Freshmen *Admission:* 808 applied, 644 admitted, 236 enrolled. *Average high school GPA:* 3.26. *Test scores:* SAT critical reading scores over 500: 50%; SAT math scores over 500: 57%; SAT writing scores over 500: 46%; ACT scores over 18: 81%; SAT critical reading scores over 600: 18%; SAT math scores over 600: 21%; SAT writing scores over 600: 9%; ACT scores over 24: 29%; SAT critical reading scores over 700: 1%; SAT math scores over 700: 3%; SAT writing scores over 700: 1%; ACT scores over 30: 1%.

Faculty *Total:* 204, 39% full-time, 43% with terminal degrees. *Student/faculty ratio:* 12:1.

Academics *Calendar:* semesters. *Degrees:* bachelor's, master's, post-master's, and postbachelor's certificates. *Special study options:* academic remediation for entering students, accelerated degree program, adult/continuing education programs, advanced placement credit, cooperative education, distance learning, double majors, English as a second language, independent study, internships, off-campus study, part-time degree program, services for LD students, study abroad, summer session for credit. *ROTC:* Army (c), Air Force (c).

Computers on Campus 80 computers/terminals and 130 ports are available on campus for general student use. Students can access the following: campus intranet, computer help desk, free student e-mail accounts, online (class) grades, online (class) registration, online (class) schedules. Campuswide network is available. 100% of college-owned or -operated housing units are wired for high-speed Internet access. Wireless service is available via entire campus.

Student Life *Housing:* on-campus residence required through sophomore year. *Options:* coed. Campus housing is university owned and leased by the school. Freshman campus housing is guaranteed. *Activities and organizations:* drama/theater group, student-run newspaper, choral group, International Club, Minorities in Action, Hui O Hawaii, American Society of Civil Engineers, Chemistry. *Campus security:* 24-hour emergency response devices and patrols, late-night transport/escort service, controlled dormitory access. *Student services:* health clinic, personal/psychological counseling.

Athletics Member NCAA. All Division II. *Intercollegiate sports:* baseball M(s), basketball M(s)/W(s), cross-country running M(s)/W(s), golf M(s)/W(s), soccer M/W(s), softball W(s), track and field M(s)/W(s), volleyball W(s). *Intramural sports:* basketball M/W, bowling M/W, golf M/W, soccer M/W, softball M/W, table tennis M/W, tennis M/W, ultimate Frisbee M/W, volleyball M/W.

Standardized Tests *Required:* SAT or ACT (for admission).

Costs (2011–12) *Comprehensive fee:* $36,581 includes full-time tuition ($27,300), mandatory fees ($321), and room and board ($8960). Full-time tuition and fees vary according to degree level and location. Part-time tuition: $910 per credit hour. Part-time tuition and fees vary according to course load, degree level, and location. *College room only:* $4460. Room and board charges vary according to board plan. *Payment plan:* installment. *Waivers:* children of alumni and employees or children of employees.

Financial Aid Of all full-time matriculated undergraduates who enrolled in 2008, 975 applied for aid, 892 were judged to have need, 212 had their need fully met. 192 Federal Work-Study jobs (averaging $1996). 193 state and other part-time jobs (averaging $4058). In 2008, 124 non-need-based awards were made. *Average percent of need met:* 77%. *Average financial aid package:* $18,977. *Average need-based loan:* $4380. *Average need-based gift aid:* $14,385. *Average non-need-based aid:* $6988. *Average indebtedness upon graduation:* $22,966.

Applying *Options:* electronic application. *Application fee:* $35. *Required:* high school transcript, minimum 2.5 GPA, 1 letter of recommendation. *Required for some:* interview. *Recommended:* essay or personal statement. *Application deadline:* 8/1 (transfers). *Notification:* 8/15 (freshmen), continuous until 8/15 (transfers).

Freshman Application Contact Kellen Willis, Assistant Director of Admissions, Saint Martin's University, 5300 Pacific Avenue SE, Lacey, WA 98503-7500. *Phone:* 360-438-4596. *Toll-free phone:* 800-368-8803. *Fax:* 360-412-6189. *E-mail:* admissions@stmartin.edu. *Web site:* http://www.stmartin.edu/.

Seattle Pacific University
Seattle, Washington

- **Independent Free Methodist** comprehensive, founded 1891
- **Urban** 35-acre campus
- **Endowment** $42.4 million
- **Coed** 3,139 undergraduate students, 96% full-time, 67% women, 33% men
- **Moderately difficult** entrance level, 77% of applicants were admitted

Undergraduates 3,020 full-time, 119 part-time. Students come from 41 states and territories; 26 other countries; 38% are from out of state; 3% Black or African American, non-Hispanic/Latino; 5% Hispanic/Latino; 8% Asian, non-Hispanic/Latino; 0.1% Native Hawaiian or other Pacific Islander, non-Hispanic/Latino; 0.5% American Indian or Alaska Native, non-Hispanic/Latino; 7% Two or more races, non-Hispanic/Latino; 3% Race/ethnicity unknown; 1% international; 8% transferred in; 51% live on campus. *Retention:* 88% of full-time freshmen returned.

Freshmen *Admission:* 3,261 applied, 2,519 admitted, 726 enrolled. *Average high school GPA:* 3.6. *Test scores:* SAT critical reading scores over 500: 84%; SAT math scores over 500: 82%; SAT writing scores over 500: 81%; ACT scores over 18: 99%; SAT critical reading scores over 600: 41%; SAT math scores over 600: 39%; SAT writing scores over 600: 37%; ACT scores over 24: 67%; SAT critical reading scores over 700: 8%; SAT math scores over 700: 5%; SAT writing scores over 700: 7%; ACT scores over 30: 14%.

Faculty *Total:* 355, 55% full-time, 52% with terminal degrees. *Student/faculty ratio:* 15:1.

Academics *Calendar:* quarters. *Degrees:* bachelor's, master's, doctoral-research/scholarship, and post-master's certificates. *Special study options:* academic remediation for entering students, adult/continuing education pro-

grams, advanced placement credit, distance learning, double majors, external degree program, honors programs, independent study, internships, off-campus study, part-time degree program, services for LD students, student-designed majors, study abroad, summer session for credit. *ROTC:* Army (c), Navy (c), Air Force (c).

Computers on Campus 150 computers/terminals are available on campus for general student use. Students can access the following: campus intranet, computer help desk, free student e-mail accounts, online (class) grades, online (class) registration, online (class) schedules. Campuswide network is available. Wireless service is available via entire campus.

Student Life *Housing:* on-campus residence required through sophomore year. *Options:* coed, disabled students. Campus housing is university owned. Freshman campus housing is guaranteed. *Activities and organizations:* drama/theater group, student-run newspaper, radio station, choral group, Centurions, Falconettes, forensics organization, Amnesty International, University Players. *Campus security:* 24-hour emergency response devices and patrols, student patrols, late-night transport/escort service, closed-circuit TV monitors. *Student services:* health clinic, personal/psychological counseling.

Athletics Member NCAA. All Division II. *Intercollegiate sports:* basketball M(s)/W(s), crew M/W(s), cross-country running M(s)/W(s), gymnastics W(s), soccer M(s)/W(s), track and field M(s)/W(s), volleyball W(s). *Intramural sports:* archery M/W, basketball M/W, bowling M/W, cross-country running M/W, football M/W, soccer M/W(c), softball M/W, tennis M/W, volleyball M(c)/W(c), weight lifting M/W.

Standardized Tests *Required:* SAT or ACT (for admission).

Costs (2011–12) *Comprehensive fee:* $39,420 includes full-time tuition ($29,976), mandatory fees ($363), and room and board ($9081). Part-time tuition and fees vary according to course load. *College room only:* $4944. Room and board charges vary according to board plan and housing facility. *Payment plans:* installment, deferred payment. *Waivers:* senior citizens and employees or children of employees.

Financial Aid Of all full-time matriculated undergraduates who enrolled in 2009, 2,294 applied for aid, 1,990 were judged to have need, 140 had their need fully met. 373 Federal Work-Study jobs, 309 state and other part-time jobs. In 2009, 645 non-need-based awards were made. *Average percent of need met:* 82%. *Average financial aid package:* $26,479. *Average need-based loan:* $5251. *Average need-based gift aid:* $21,498. *Average non-need-based aid:* $14,897. *Average indebtedness upon graduation:* $30,073.

Applying *Options:* electronic application, early admission, early action. *Application fee:* $50. *Required:* essay or personal statement, high school transcript, minimum 2.5 GPA, 2 letters of recommendation. *Recommended:* interview. *Application deadlines:* 2/1 (freshmen), 8/1 (transfers), 11/15 (early action). *Notification:* 3/1 (freshmen), continuous (transfers), 1/5 (early action).

Freshman Application Contact Mr. Jobe Korb-Nice, Director of Admissions, Seattle Pacific University, 3307 3rd Avenue, West, Seattle, WA 98119-1997. *Phone:* 206-281-2021. *Toll-free phone:* 800-366-3344. *Fax:* 206-281-2669. *E-mail:* admissions@spu.edu. *Web site:* http://www.spu.edu/.

See page 1594 for the College Close-Up.

Seattle University

Seattle, Washington

- **Independent Roman Catholic** comprehensive, founded 1891
- **Urban** 50-acre campus
- **Endowment** $184.7 million
- **Coed**
- **Moderately difficult** entrance level

Faculty *Student/faculty ratio:* 13:1.

Academics *Calendar:* quarters. *Degrees:* bachelor's, master's, doctoral-professional, doctoral-research/scholarship, post-master's, and postbachelor's certificates.

Student Life *Campus security:* 24-hour emergency response devices and patrols, late-night transport/escort service, controlled dormitory access, bicycle patrols.

Athletics Member NCAA, NAIA. All NCAA Division I.

Standardized Tests *Required:* SAT or ACT (for admission).

Costs (2010–11) *Comprehensive fee:* $40,140 includes full-time tuition ($30,825) and room and board ($9315). Full-time tuition and fees vary according to course load. Part-time tuition: $685 per credit hour. Part-time tuition and fees vary according to course load. *College room only:* $5805. Room and board charges vary according to board plan.

Financial Aid *Of all full-time matriculated undergraduates who enrolled in 2009,* 3,316 applied for aid, 2,596 were judged to have need, 574 had their need fully met. *In 2009,* 9 non-need-based awards were made. *Average percent of need met:* 77. *Average financial aid package:* $28,428. *Average need-based loan:* $4766. *Average need-based gift aid:* $16,432. *Average non-need-based loan:* $5402. *Average indebtedness upon graduation:* $26,665.

Applying *Options:* electronic application, early action, deferred entrance. *Application fee:* $50. *Required:* essay or personal statement, high school transcript, minimum 2.5 GPA, 2 letters of recommendation.

Freshman Application Contact Melore Nielsen, Acting Dean of Admissions, Seattle University, 901 12th Avenue, PO Box 222000, Seattle, WA 98122-1090. *Phone:* 206-296-2000. *Toll-free phone:* 800-542-0833 (in-state); 800-426-7123 (out-of-state). *Fax:* 206-296-5656. *E-mail:* admissions@seattleu.edu. *Web site:* http://www.seattleu.edu/.

See page 1596 for the College Close-Up.

Trinity Lutheran College

Issaquah, Washington

- **Independent Lutheran** 4-year, founded 1944
- **Urban** 1-acre campus with easy access to Seattle
- **Coed** 150 undergraduate students
- **Minimally difficult** entrance level, 51% of applicants were admitted

Undergraduates Students come from 13 states and territories; 6 other countries; 10% are from out of state.

Freshmen *Admission:* 113 applied, 58 admitted. *Average high school GPA:* 3.1.

Faculty *Total:* 28, 46% full-time.

Academics *Calendar:* quarters. *Degrees:* certificates, associate, bachelor's, and postbachelor's certificates. *Special study options:* academic remediation for entering students, advanced placement credit, double majors, English as a second language, independent study, internships, off-campus study, part-time degree program, services for LD students, study abroad.

Computers on Campus 15 computers/terminals are available on campus for general student use. Students can access the following: free student e-mail accounts, online (class) grades, online (class) registration, online (class) schedules. Campuswide network is available.

Student Life *Housing options:* coed, men-only, women-only. Campus housing is university owned. Freshman campus housing is guaranteed. *Activities and organizations:* drama/theater group, choral group, Environmental Commission, student government, Worship Commission, Global Concerns, Activities Commission. *Campus security:* 24-hour emergency response devices, student patrols, controlled dormitory access. *Student services:* health clinic, personal/psychological counseling.

Athletics *Intramural sports:* basketball M/W, softball M/W, tennis M/W, volleyball M/W.

Standardized Tests *Required:* SAT or ACT (for admission).

Costs (2010–11) *Comprehensive fee:* $27,103 includes full-time tuition ($19,870), mandatory fees ($500), and room and board ($6733). Part-time tuition: $830 per credit hour. Part-time tuition and fees vary according to course load and program. *Required fees:* $830 per credit hour part-time, $150 per term part-time. *Room and board:* Room and board charges vary according to board plan and housing facility. *Payment plan:* installment. *Waivers:* children of alumni, senior citizens, and employees or children of employees.

Financial Aid Of all full-time matriculated undergraduates who enrolled in 2007, 45 Federal Work-Study jobs (averaging $744).

Applying *Options:* electronic application, early admission, deferred entrance. *Application fee:* $30. *Required:* essay or personal statement, high school transcript, minimum 2 GPA, 1 letter of recommendation. *Required for some:* interview. *Application deadlines:* 9/15 (freshmen), 9/15 (transfers).

Freshman Application Contact Mr. Chad Larson, Admissions Counselor, Trinity Lutheran College, 2802 Wetmore AVE, Everett, WA 98201. *Phone:* 425-249-4741. *Toll-free phone:* 800-843-5659. *Fax:* 425-249-4801. *E-mail:* chad.larson@tlc.edu. *Web site:* http://www.tlc.edu/.

University of Phoenix–Eastern Washington Campus

Spokane Valley, Washington

Freshman Application Contact Ms. Audra McQuarie, Registrar/Executive Director, University of Phoenix–Eastern Washington Campus, 4035 South Riverpoint Parkway, Mail Stop CF-L101, Phoenix, AZ 85040. *Phone:* 480-557-6151. *Toll-free phone:* 800-697-8223 (in-state); 800-228-7240 (out-of-state). *Fax:* 480-643-3068. *E-mail:* audra.mcquarie@phoenix.edu. *Web site:* http://www.phoenix.edu/.

University of Phoenix–Washington Campus

Seattle, Washington

Freshman Application Contact Ms. Evelyn Gaskin, Registrar/Executive Director, University of Phoenix–Washington Campus, 4615 East Elwood Street, Mail Stop AA-K101, Phoenix, AZ 85040-1958. *Phone:* 480-557-3303.

Toll-free phone: 800-776-4867 (in-state); 800-228-7240 (out-of-state). *Fax:* 480-643-1020. *E-mail:* evelyn.gaskin@phoenix.edu. *Web site:* http://www.phoenix.edu/.

University of Puget Sound

Tacoma, Washington

- **Independent** comprehensive, founded 1888
- **Suburban** 97-acre campus with easy access to Seattle
- **Endowment** $195.5 million
- **Coed** 2,582 undergraduate students, 99% full-time, 59% women, 41% men
- **Very difficult** entrance level, 52% of applicants were admitted

Undergraduates 2,549 full-time, 33 part-time. Students come from 51 states and territories; 11 other countries; 76% are from out of state; 2% Black or African American, non-Hispanic/Latino; 5% Hispanic/Latino; 9% Asian, non-Hispanic/Latino; 0.5% Native Hawaiian or other Pacific Islander, non-Hispanic/Latino; 1% American Indian or Alaska Native, non-Hispanic/Latino; 2% Two or more races, non-Hispanic/Latino; 7% Race/ethnicity unknown; 0.5% international; 3% transferred in; 58% live on campus. *Retention:* 86% of full-time freshmen returned.

Freshmen *Admission:* 6,586 applied, 3,448 admitted, 625 enrolled. *Average high school GPA:* 3.52. *Test scores:* SAT critical reading scores over 500: 95%; SAT math scores over 500: 93%; SAT writing scores over 500: 93%; ACT scores over 18: 99%; SAT critical reading scores over 600: 66%; SAT math scores over 600: 56%; SAT writing scores over 600: 58%; ACT scores over 24: 87%; SAT critical reading scores over 700: 17%; SAT math scores over 700: 9%; SAT writing scores over 700: 14%; ACT scores over 30: 27%.

Faculty *Total:* 285, 80% full-time, 78% with terminal degrees. *Student/faculty ratio:* 12:1.

Academics *Calendar:* semesters. *Degrees:* bachelor's, master's, doctoral-professional, and post-master's certificates. *Special study options:* advanced placement credit, cooperative education, double majors, honors programs, independent study, internships, part-time degree program, student-designed majors, study abroad, summer session for credit. *ROTC:* Army (c). *Unusual degree programs:* 3-2 engineering with Washington University in St. Louis, Columbia University, Duke University, and University of Southern California.

Computers on Campus 320 computers/terminals and 6,500 ports are available on campus for general student use. Students can access the following: campus intranet, computer help desk, free student e-mail accounts, online (class) grades, online (class) registration, online (class) schedules, financial aid, admission, student employment. Campuswide network is available. 100% of college-owned or -operated housing units are wired for high-speed Internet access. Wireless service is available via entire campus.

Student Life *Housing:* on-campus residence required for freshman year. *Options:* coed, women-only, disabled students. Campus housing is university owned. Freshman campus housing is guaranteed. *Activities and organizations:* drama/theater group, student-run newspaper, radio station, choral group, Puget Sound Outdoors, Repertory Dance Group, Hui-O-Hawaii, Student Theatre Productions, Relay for Life, national fraternities, national sororities. *Campus security:* 24-hour emergency response devices and patrols, student patrols, late-night transport/escort service, controlled dormitory access, 24-hour locked residence hall entrances. *Student services:* health clinic, personal/psychological counseling, legal services.

Athletics Member NCAA. All Division III. *Intercollegiate sports:* baseball M, basketball M/W, cheerleading M/W, crew M/W, cross-country running M/W, fencing M(c)/W(c), football M, golf M/W, ice hockey M(c)/W(c), lacrosse M(c)/W, rugby M(c), sailing M(c)/W(c), skiing (downhill) M(c)/W(c), soccer M/W, softball W, swimming and diving M/W, tennis M/W, track and field M/W, volleyball W. *Intramural sports:* basketball M/W, football M/W, racquetball M/W, soccer M/W, softball M/W, tennis M/W, ultimate Frisbee M/W, volleyball M/W, water polo M(c)/W(c).

Standardized Tests *Required:* SAT or ACT (for admission).

Costs (2011–12) *Comprehensive fee:* $48,740 includes full-time tuition ($38,510), mandatory fees ($210), and room and board ($10,020). Full-time tuition and fees vary according to course load. Part-time tuition and fees vary according to course load. *College room only:* $5550. Room and board charges vary according to board plan and housing facility. *Payment plans:* installment, deferred payment. *Waivers:* employees or children of employees.

Financial Aid Of all full-time matriculated undergraduates who enrolled in 2009, 1,801 applied for aid, 1,645 were judged to have need, 306 had their need fully met. 544 Federal Work-Study jobs (averaging $2835). 788 state and other part-time jobs (averaging $2770). In 2009, 593 non-need-based awards were made. *Average percent of need met:* 80%. *Average financial aid package:* $28,813. *Average need-based loan:* $5257. *Average need-based gift aid:*

$23,776. *Average non-need-based aid:* $10,055. *Average indebtedness upon graduation:* $28,660.

Applying *Options:* electronic application, early admission, early decision, deferred entrance. *Application fee:* $50. *Required:* essay or personal statement, high school transcript, school report, application supplement, 2 recommendations. *Recommended:* minimum 3 GPA, interview. *Application deadlines:* 1/15 (freshmen), 7/1 (transfers). *Early decision deadline:* 11/1 (for plan 1), 1/2 (for plan 2). *Notification:* 4/1 (freshmen), continuous (transfers), 12/15 (early decision plan 1), 2/15 (early decision plan 2).

Freshman Application Contact Dr. George Mills, Vice President for Enrollment, University of Puget Sound, 1500 North Warner Street, Tacoma, WA 98416. *Phone:* 253-879-3211. *Toll-free phone:* 800-396-7191. *Fax:* 253-879-3993. *E-mail:* admission@ups.edu. *Web site:* http://www.pugetsound.edu.

See page 1728 for the College Close-Up.

University of Washington
Seattle, Washington

- **State-supported** university, founded 1861
- **Urban** 703-acre campus
- **Endowment** $1.6 billion
- **Coed** 29,302 undergraduate students, 91% full-time, 52% women, 48% men
- **Moderately difficult** entrance level, 57% of applicants were admitted

Undergraduates 26,600 full-time, 2,702 part-time. Students come from 52 states and territories; 105 other countries; 12% are from out of state; 3% Black or African American, non-Hispanic/Latino; 6% Hispanic/Latino; 26% Asian, non-Hispanic/Latino; 0.7% Native Hawaiian or other Pacific Islander, non-Hispanic/Latino; 1% American Indian or Alaska Native, non-Hispanic/Latino; 8% Race/ethnicity unknown; 7% international; 6% transferred in; 25% live on campus. *Retention:* 93% of full-time freshmen returned.

Freshmen *Admission:* 22,843 applied, 12,965 admitted, 5,497 enrolled. *Test scores:* SAT critical reading scores over 500: 83%; SAT math scores over 500: 93%; SAT writing scores over 500: 83%; ACT scores over 18: 97%; SAT critical reading scores over 600: 48%; SAT math scores over 600: 67%; SAT writing scores over 600: 43%; ACT scores over 24: 79%; SAT critical reading scores over 700: 12%; SAT math scores over 700: 22%; SAT writing scores over 700: 9%; ACT scores over 30: 26%.

Faculty *Total:* 3,752, 81% full-time.

Academics *Calendar:* quarters. *Degrees:* bachelor's, master's, doctoral-professional, doctoral-research/scholarship, and post-master's certificates. *Special study options:* academic remediation for entering students, adult/continuing education programs, advanced placement credit, cooperative education, distance learning, double majors, English as a second language, honors programs, independent study, internships, part-time degree program, services for LD students, student-designed majors, study abroad, summer session for credit. *ROTC:* Army (b), Navy (b), Air Force (b).

Computers on Campus 2,000 computers/terminals are available on campus for general student use. Students can access the following: computer help desk, free student e-mail accounts, online (class) grades, online (class) registration, online (class) schedules. Campuswide network is available. 100% of college-owned or -operated housing units are wired for high-speed Internet access. Wireless service is available via entire campus.

Student Life *Housing options:* coed, disabled students. Campus housing is university owned, leased by the school and is provided by a third party. *Activities and organizations:* drama/theater group, student-run newspaper, radio and television station, choral group, marching band, national fraternities, national sororities. *Campus security:* 24-hour emergency response devices and patrols, late-night transport/escort service, controlled dormitory access. *Student services:* health clinic, personal/psychological counseling, women's center, legal services.

Athletics Member NCAA. All Division I except football (Division I-A). *Intercollegiate sports:* baseball M(s), basketball M(s)/W(s), cheerleading M/W, crew M(s)/W(s), cross-country running M(s)/W(s), golf M(s)/W(s), gymnastics W(s), soccer M(s)/W(s), softball W(s), tennis M(s)/W(s), track and field M(s)/W(s), volleyball W(s). *Intramural sports:* archery M(c)/W(c), badminton M/W, basketball M/W, bowling M/W, crew M(c)/W(c), fencing M(c)/W(c), field hockey M(c)/W(c), football M/W, golf M/W, gymnastics M(c)/W(c), ice hockey M(c), lacrosse M(c)/W(c), racquetball M(c)/W(c), rock climbing M/W, rugby M(c)/W(c), sailing M(c)/W(c), skiing (cross-country) M(c)/W(c), skiing (downhill) M(c)/W(c), soccer M(c)/W(c), squash M(c)/W(c), table tennis M/W, tennis M/W, track and field M/W, ultimate Frisbee M(c)/W(c), volleyball M/W, water polo M(c)/W(c).

Standardized Tests *Required:* SAT or ACT (for admission).

Costs (2011–12) *Tuition:* state resident $8701 full-time; nonresident $25,329 full-time. Full-time tuition and fees vary according to course load. Part-time tuition and fees vary according to course load. *Required fees:* $272 full-time. *Room and board:* $8169. Room and board charges vary according to board

plan and housing facility. *Waivers:* senior citizens and employees or children of employees.

Financial Aid Of all full-time matriculated undergraduates who enrolled in 2008, 13,572 applied for aid, 9,824 were judged to have need, 3,250 had their need fully met. 478 Federal Work-Study jobs (averaging $2800). 327 state and other part-time jobs (averaging $3160). In 2008, 706 non-need-based awards were made. *Average percent of need met:* 79%. *Average financial aid package:* $11,560. *Average need-based loan:* $2860. *Average need-based gift aid:* $8720. *Average non-need-based aid:* $4430. *Average indebtedness upon graduation:* $16,800.

Applying *Options:* electronic application, early admission. *Application fee:* $60. *Required:* essay or personal statement, minimum 2 GPA. *Required for some:* high school transcript. *Application deadlines:* 12/1 (freshmen), 2/15 (transfers).

Freshman Application Contact Emily Leggio, Senior Associate Director of Admissions, University of Washington, Seattle, WA 98195. *Phone:* 206-543-9686. *Fax:* 206-685-3655. *Web site:* http://www.washington.edu/.

University of Washington, Bothell
Bothell, Washington

- **State-supported** comprehensive, founded 1990, part of University of Washington
- **Suburban** 128-acre campus with easy access to Seattle
- **Endowment** $2.6 million
- **Coed** 2,747 undergraduate students, 77% full-time, 53% women, 47% men
- **Moderately difficult** entrance level, 72% of applicants were admitted

Undergraduates 2,122 full-time, 625 part-time. Students come from 16 states and territories; 19 other countries; 1% are from out of state; 4% Black or African American, non-Hispanic/Latino; 6% Hispanic/Latino; 26% Asian, non-Hispanic/Latino; 0.6% Native Hawaiian or other Pacific Islander, non-Hispanic/Latino; 1% American Indian or Alaska Native, non-Hispanic/Latino; 7% Race/ethnicity unknown; 3% international; 17% transferred in; 3% live on campus. *Retention:* 83% of full-time freshmen returned.

Freshmen *Admission:* 1,733 applied, 1,244 admitted, 401 enrolled. *Average high school GPA:* 3.28. *Test scores:* SAT critical reading scores over 500: 49%; SAT math scores over 500: 64%; SAT writing scores over 500: 43%; ACT scores over 18: 82%; SAT critical reading scores over 600: 13%; SAT math scores over 600: 21%; SAT writing scores over 600: 9%; ACT scores over 24: 33%; SAT critical reading scores over 700: 2%; SAT math scores over 700: 3%; SAT writing scores over 700: 1%; ACT scores over 30: 4%.

Faculty *Total:* 162, 73% full-time, 75% with terminal degrees. *Student/faculty ratio:* 20:1.

Academics *Degrees:* bachelor's and master's. *Special study options:* adult/continuing education programs, advanced placement credit, cooperative education, double majors, honors programs, independent study, internships, off-campus study, part-time degree program, services for LD students, student-designed majors, study abroad, summer session for credit. *ROTC:* Army (c), Air Force (c).

Computers on Campus 350 computers/terminals and 1,000 ports are available on campus for general student use. Students can access the following: computer help desk, free student e-mail accounts, online (class) grades, online (class) registration, online (class) schedules, online course management system. Campuswide network is available. 100% of college-owned or -operated housing units are wired for high-speed Internet access. Wireless service is available via entire campus.

Student Life *Housing options:* coed. Campus housing is leased by the school. Freshman applicants given priority for college housing. *Activities and organizations:* student-run newspaper, Dodge Ball, Beta Alpha Psi, Collegiate DECA, Campus Events Board, basketball. *Campus security:* 24-hour emergency response devices and patrols, late-night transport/escort service. *Student services:* personal/psychological counseling.

Athletics *Intramural sports:* basketball M(c)/W(c), cheerleading M(c)/W(c), golf M(c)/W(c), soccer M(c)/W(c), softball M(c)/W(c), table tennis M(c)/W(c), ultimate Frisbee M(c)/W(c), volleyball M(c)/W(c).

Standardized Tests *Required:* SAT or ACT (for admission).

Costs (2010–11) *Tuition:* state resident $8124 full-time; nonresident $24,750 full-time. Full-time tuition and fees vary according to course load. Part-time tuition and fees vary according to course load. *Required fees:* $495 full-time. *Room and board:* $6075. Room and board charges vary according to housing facility. *Payment plan:* installment. *Waivers:* employees or children of employees.

Applying *Options:* electronic application, early admission, deferred entrance. *Application fee:* $60. *Required:* essay or personal statement, high school transcript, minimum 2 GPA. *Application deadlines:* 1/15 (freshmen), 4/1 (transfers). *Notification:* continuous (freshmen).

Freshman Application Contact Lindsey Wille, Associate Director of Admissions, University of Washington, Bothell, 18115 Campus Way NE, Box

358500, Bothell, WA 98011-8246. *Phone:* 425-352-5000. *Fax:* 425-352-5455. *E-mail:* freshmen@uwb.edu. *Web site:* http://www.uwb.edu/.

University of Washington, Tacoma
Tacoma, Washington

- **State-supported** comprehensive, founded 1990, part of University of Washington
- **Urban** 46-acre campus with easy access to Seattle
- **Endowment** $22.6 million
- **Coed**
- **Minimally difficult** entrance level

Faculty *Student/faculty ratio:* 16:1.

Academics *Calendar:* quarters. *Degrees:* bachelor's, master's, post-master's, and postbachelor's certificates.

Student Life *Campus security:* 24-hour emergency response devices and patrols, late-night transport/escort service, key card access to buildings after hours.

Standardized Tests *Required:* SAT or ACT (for admission).

Costs (2010–11) *Tuition:* state resident $8122 full-time, $290 per credit part-time; nonresident $24,750 full-time, $844 per credit part-time. Full-time tuition and fees vary according to course load. Part-time tuition and fees vary according to course load. *Required fees:* $567 full-time. *Room only:* $8949. Room and board charges vary according to housing facility.

Financial Aid *Of all full-time matriculated undergraduates who enrolled in 2009,* 1,486 applied for aid, 1,268 were judged to have need, 321 had their need fully met. *In 2009,* 27 non-need-based awards were made. *Average percent of need met:* 77. *Average financial aid package:* $13,800. *Average need-based loan:* $6900. *Average need-based gift aid:* $11,200. *Average non-need-based aid:* $6300. *Average indebtedness upon graduation:* $17,900.

Applying *Options:* electronic application, early decision, deferred entrance. *Application fee:* $60. *Required:* essay or personal statement, minimum 2 GPA. *Required for some:* high school transcript.

Freshman Application Contact Ms. Fiona Johnson, Admissions Advising and Outreach, University of Washington, Tacoma, 1900 Commerce Street, Tacoma, WA 98402-3100. *Phone:* 253-692-4742. *Toll-free phone:* 800-736-7750. *Fax:* 253-692-4788. *E-mail:* fionaj@u.washington.edu. *Web site:* http://www.tacoma.washington.edu/.

Walla Walla University
College Place, Washington

- **Independent Seventh-day Adventist** comprehensive, founded 1892
- **Small-town** 77-acre campus
- **Coed** 1,549 undergraduate students, 93% full-time, 50% women, 50% men
- **Moderately difficult** entrance level, 89% of applicants were admitted

Undergraduates 1,447 full-time, 102 part-time. 59% are from out of state; 8% transferred in; 63% live on campus. *Retention:* 78% of full-time freshmen returned.

Freshmen *Admission:* 626 applied, 557 admitted, 299 enrolled.

Faculty *Total:* 207, 54% full-time, 51% with terminal degrees. *Student/faculty ratio:* 12:1.

Academics *Calendar:* quarters. *Degrees:* diplomas, associate, bachelor's, and master's. *Special study options:* academic remediation for entering students, advanced placement credit, cooperative education, distance learning, double majors, freshman honors college, honors programs, independent study, internships, off-campus study, part-time degree program, services for LD students, study abroad, summer session for credit.

Computers on Campus Students can access the following: campus intranet, computer help desk, free student e-mail accounts, online (class) grades, online (class) registration, online (class) schedules, online forum, online classifieds, online student directory. Campuswide network is available. 100% of college-owned or -operated housing units are wired for high-speed Internet access. Wireless service is available via entire campus.

Student Life *Housing:* on-campus residence required through junior year. *Options:* men-only, women-only, disabled students. Campus housing is university owned and leased by the school. Freshman campus housing is guaranteed. *Activities and organizations:* drama/theater group, student-run newspaper, radio and television station, choral group. *Campus security:* 24-hour emergency response devices and patrols, student patrols, late-night transport/escort service, controlled dormitory access. *Student services:* health clinic, personal/psychological counseling.

Athletics Member NAIA. *Intercollegiate sports:* basketball M/W, golf M, ice hockey M, soccer M, softball W, volleyball M/W. *Intramural sports:* basketball M/W, football M/W, gymnastics M/W, ice hockey M, racquetball M/W, softball M/W, table tennis M/W, tennis M/W, volleyball M/W.

Standardized Tests *Required:* SAT or ACT (for admission). *Recommended:* ACT (for admission).

Costs (2010–11) *Comprehensive fee:* $28,785 includes full-time tuition ($23,229), mandatory fees ($225), and room and board ($5331). Full-time tuition and fees vary according to course load and degree level. Part-time tuition and fees vary according to degree level. *Room and board:* Room and board charges vary according to housing facility and location. *Payment plans:* installment, deferred payment.

Financial Aid Of all full-time matriculated undergraduates who enrolled in 2007, 1,330 applied for aid, 1,027 were judged to have need, 208 had their need fully met. 653 Federal Work-Study jobs (averaging $2680). 71 state and other part-time jobs (averaging $3111). In 2007, 243 non-need-based awards were made. *Average percent of need met:* 88%. *Average financial aid package:* $20,564. *Average need-based loan:* $6509. *Average need-based gift aid:* $7619. *Average non-need-based aid:* $3843. *Average indebtedness upon graduation:* $28,287.

Applying *Options:* electronic application, early decision, deferred entrance. *Application fee:* $40. *Required:* high school transcript, minimum 2.5 GPA. *Application deadlines:* rolling (freshmen), rolling (transfers). *Notification:* continuous (freshmen), continuous (transfers).

Freshman Application Contact Walla Walla University, 204 South College Avenue, College Place, WA 99324-1198. *Phone:* 509-527-2327. *Toll-free phone:* 800-541-8900. *Web site:* http://www.wallawalla.edu/.

Washington State University
Pullman, Washington

- **State-supported** university, founded 1890
- **Small-town** 620-acre campus
- **Endowment** $638.4 million
- **Coed** 21,816 undergraduate students, 86% full-time, 52% women, 48% men
- **Moderately difficult** entrance level, 69% of applicants were admitted

Undergraduates 18,806 full-time, 3,010 part-time. Students come from 49 states and territories; 58 other countries; 8% are from out of state; 2% Black or African American, non-Hispanic/Latino; 7% Hispanic/Latino; 6% Asian, non-Hispanic/Latino; 0.4% Native Hawaiian or other Pacific Islander, non-Hispanic/Latino; 1% American Indian or Alaska Native, non-Hispanic/Latino; 3% Two or more races, non-Hispanic/Latino; 5% Race/ethnicity unknown; 4% international; 12% transferred in; 33% live on campus. *Retention:* 82% of full-time freshmen returned.

Freshmen *Admission:* 12,427 applied, 8,634 admitted, 3,288 enrolled. *Average high school GPA:* 3.44. *Test scores:* SAT critical reading scores over 500: 68%; SAT math scores over 500: 78%; SAT writing scores over 500: 62%; ACT scores over 18: 95%; SAT critical reading scores over 600: 21%; SAT math scores over 600: 31%; SAT writing scores over 600: 15%; ACT scores over 24: 50%; SAT critical reading scores over 700: 3%; SAT math scores over 700: 3%; SAT writing scores over 700: 1%; ACT scores over 30: 5%.

Faculty *Total:* 1,640, 73% full-time, 78% with terminal degrees. *Student/faculty ratio:* 15:1.

Academics *Calendar:* semesters. *Degrees:* certificates, bachelor's, master's, doctoral-professional, doctoral-research/scholarship, post-master's, and post-bachelor's certificates. *Special study options:* accelerated degree program, adult/continuing education programs, advanced placement credit, cooperative education, distance learning, double majors, English as a second language, external degree program, honors programs, independent study, internships, off-campus study, part-time degree program, services for LD students, student-designed majors, study abroad, summer session for credit. *ROTC:* Army (b), Navy (c), Air Force (b).

Computers on Campus 2,500 computers/terminals and 2,500 ports are available on campus for general student use. Students can access the following: campus intranet, computer help desk, free student e-mail accounts, online (class) grades, online (class) registration, online (class) schedules. Campuswide network is available. 100% of college-owned or -operated housing units are wired for high-speed Internet access. Wireless service is available via classrooms, computer centers, computer labs, dorm rooms, learning centers, libraries, student centers.

Student Life *Housing:* on-campus residence required for freshman year. *Options:* coed, men-only, women-only, disabled students. Campus housing is university owned. Freshman campus housing is guaranteed. *Activities and organizations:* drama/theater group, student-run newspaper, radio and television station, choral group, marching band, Panhellenic Association - Sororities, Interfraternity Council - Fraternities, Student Entertainment Board, International Students Council, ChiLaStAl (Chicana/o Latina/o Student Alliance, national fraternities, national sororities. *Campus security:* 24-hour emergency response devices and patrols, student patrols, late-night transport/escort service, controlled dormitory access. *Student services:* health clinic, personal/psychological counseling, women's center, legal services.

Athletics Member NCAA. All Division I except football (Division I-A). *Intercollegiate sports:* baseball M(s), basketball M(s)/W(s), bowling M(c)/W(c), cheerleading M/W, crew M(c)/W(s), cross-country running M(s)/W(s), fencing M/W(c), golf M(s)/W(s), ice hockey M(c), lacrosse M(c)/W(c), rugby

M(c)/W(c), sailing M(c)/W(c), skiing (cross-country) M(c)/W(c), skiing (downhill) M(c)/W(c), soccer M(c)/W(s), softball W(c), swimming and diving W(s), tennis M(c)/W(s), track and field M(s)/W(s), ultimate Frisbee M(c)/W(c), volleyball M(c)/W(s), water polo M(c)/W(c). *Intramural sports:* badminton M/W, basketball M/W, football M/W, golf M/W, racquetball M/W, rock climbing M/W, soccer M/W, softball M/W, table tennis M/W, tennis M/W, ultimate Frisbee M/W, volleyball M/W.

Standardized Tests *Required:* SAT or ACT (for admission).

Costs (2010–11) *Tuition:* state resident $8080 full-time, $430 per credit hour part-time; nonresident $19,122 full-time, $934 per credit hour part-time. Full-time tuition and fees vary according to location and reciprocity agreements. Part-time tuition and fees vary according to course load, location, and reciprocity agreements. *Required fees:* $1409 full-time. *Room and board:* $9644; room only: $5536. Room and board charges vary according to board plan, housing facility, and location. *Waivers:* senior citizens and employees or children of employees.

Financial Aid Of all full-time matriculated undergraduates who enrolled in 2008, 12,877 applied for aid, 9,965 were judged to have need, 2,574 had their need fully met. 296 Federal Work-Study jobs (averaging $2500). 834 state and other part-time jobs (averaging $2500). In 2008, 2397 non-need-based awards were made. *Average percent of need met:* 76%. *Average financial aid package:* $12,441. *Average need-based loan:* $4415. *Average need-based gift aid:* $8428. *Average non-need-based aid:* $3566.

Applying *Options:* electronic application. *Application fee:* $50. *Required:* high school transcript, minimum 2 GPA. *Recommended:* essay or personal statement. *Application deadlines:* 1/31 (freshmen), 1/31 (out-of-state freshmen), 1/31 (transfers). *Notification:* continuous until 11/1 (freshmen), continuous until 11/1 (out-of-state freshmen), continuous until 11/1 (transfers).

Freshman Application Contact Ms. Wendy Peterson, Director of Admissions, Washington State University, PO Box 641067, Pullman, WA 99164-1067. *Phone:* 888-468-6978. *Toll-free phone:* 888-468-6978. *Fax:* 509-335-4902. *E-mail:* admissions@wsu.edu. *Web site:* http://www.wsu.edu/.

Washington State University Vancouver
Vancouver, Washington

Admissions Office Contact Washington State University Vancouver, 14204 Northeast Salmon Creek Avenue, Vancouver, WA 98686. *Web site:* http://www.vancouver.wsu.edu/.

Western Washington University
Bellingham, Washington

- **State-supported** comprehensive, founded 1893
- **Small-town** 223-acre campus with easy access to Seattle and Vancouver
- **Endowment** $33.4 million
- **Coed**
- **Moderately difficult** entrance level

Faculty *Student/faculty ratio:* 19:1.
Academics *Calendar:* quarters. *Degrees:* certificates, bachelor's, master's, post-master's, and postbachelor's certificates.
Student Life *Campus security:* 24-hour emergency response devices and patrols, student patrols, late-night transport/escort service, controlled dormitory access.
Athletics Member NCAA. All Division II.
Standardized Tests *Required:* SAT or ACT (for admission).
Costs (2010–11) *Tuition:* state resident $6081 full-time, $203 per credit hour part-time; nonresident $16,428 full-time, $548 per credit hour part-time. Full-time tuition and fees vary according to course load and location. Part-time tuition and fees vary according to course load and location. *Required fees:* $777 full-time, $26 per credit hour part-time. *Room and board:* $8749. Room and board charges vary according to board plan and housing facility.
Financial Aid *Of all full-time matriculated undergraduates who enrolled in 2009,* 8,280 applied for aid, 5,869 were judged to have need, 1,220 had their need fully met. 266 Federal Work-Study jobs (averaging $32). 541 state and other part-time jobs (averaging $3290). *In 2009,* 237 non-need-based awards were made. *Average percent of need met:* 84. *Average financial aid package:* $11,730. *Average need-based loan:* $4415. *Average need-based gift aid:*

$8037. *Average non-need-based aid:* $1710. *Average indebtedness upon graduation:* $17,652.

Applying *Options:* electronic application, deferred entrance. *Application fee:* $50. *Required:* high school transcript. *Recommended:* essay or personal statement.

Freshman Application Contact Ms. Karen Copetas, Director of Admissions, Western Washington University, 516 High Street, Bellingham, WA 98225-9009. *Phone:* 360-650-3440. *Fax:* 360-650-7369. *E-mail:* admit@wwu.edu. *Web site:* http://www.wwu.edu/.

See page 1782 for the College Close-Up.

Whitman College
Walla Walla, Washington

- **Independent** 4-year, founded 1859
- **Small-town** 117-acre campus
- **Endowment** $334.8 million
- **Coed** 1,555 undergraduate students, 98% full-time, 58% women, 42% men
- **Very difficult** entrance level, 47% of applicants were admitted

Undergraduates 1,529 full-time, 26 part-time. Students come from 43 states and territories; 29 other countries; 62% are from out of state; 1% Black or African American, non-Hispanic/Latino; 6% Hispanic/Latino; 7% Asian, non-Hispanic/Latino; 0.5% Native Hawaiian or other Pacific Islander, non-Hispanic/Latino; 0.8% American Indian or Alaska Native, non-Hispanic/Latino; 4% Two or more races, non-Hispanic/Latino; 9% Race/ethnicity unknown; 3% international; 1% transferred in; 62% live on campus. *Retention:* 92% of full-time freshmen returned.

Freshmen *Admission:* 3,164 applied, 1,493 admitted, 415 enrolled. *Average high school GPA:* 3.8. *Test scores:* SAT critical reading scores over 500: 97%; SAT math scores over 500: 97%; SAT writing scores over 500: 98%; ACT scores over 18: 100%; SAT critical reading scores over 600: 79%; SAT math scores over 600: 80%; SAT writing scores over 600: 83%; ACT scores over 24: 93%; SAT critical reading scores over 700: 33%; SAT math scores over 700: 31%; SAT writing scores over 700: 29%; ACT scores over 30: 38%.

Faculty *Total:* 196, 68% full-time, 83% with terminal degrees. *Student/faculty ratio:* 10:1.

Academics *Calendar:* semesters. *Degree:* bachelor's. *Special study options:* accelerated degree program, advanced placement credit, cooperative education, double majors, honors programs, independent study, off-campus study, services for LD students, student-designed majors, study abroad. *Unusual degree programs:* 3-2 engineering with California Institute of Technology, Columbia University, Duke University, University of Washington, Washington University in St. Louis; forestry with Duke University; international studies with Monterey Institute of International Studies; oceanography with University of Washington; teacher education with Bank Street College of Education; law with Columbia University.

Computers on Campus 397 computers/terminals are available on campus for general student use. Students can access the following: computer help desk, free student e-mail accounts, online (class) grades, online (class) registration, online (class) schedules, course registration information. Campuswide network is available. 100% of college-owned or -operated housing units are wired for high-speed Internet access. Wireless service is available via classrooms, computer centers, computer labs, dorm rooms, learning centers, libraries, student centers.

Student Life *Housing:* on-campus residence required through sophomore year. *Options:* coed, women-only. Campus housing is university owned. Freshman campus housing is guaranteed. *Activities and organizations:* drama/theater group, student-run newspaper, radio station, choral group, Associated Students, Outdoor Program, Center for Community Service, national fraternities, national sororities. *Campus security:* 24-hour emergency response devices and patrols, student patrols, late-night transport/escort service, controlled dormitory access. *Student services:* health clinic, personal/psychological counseling, women's center.

Athletics Member NCAA. All Division III. *Intercollegiate sports:* baseball M, basketball M/W, cross-country running M/W, fencing M(c)/W(c), golf M/W, ice hockey M(c), lacrosse M(c)/W(c), rugby M(c)/W(c), skiing (cross-country) M(c)/W(c), skiing (downhill) M(c)/W(c), soccer M/W, softball W(c), swimming and diving M/W, tennis M/W, track and field M(c)/W(c), ultimate Frisbee M(c)/W(c), volleyball M(c)/W. *Intramural sports:* basketball M/W, bowling M/W, football M/W, soccer M/W, softball M/W, tennis M/W, ultimate Frisbee M/W, volleyball M/W.

Standardized Tests *Required:* SAT or ACT (for admission).

Costs (2011–12) *Comprehensive fee:* $50,656 includes full-time tuition ($40,180), mandatory fees ($316), and room and board ($10,160). Part-time tuition: $1674 per credit. *College room only:* $4700. Room and board charges vary according to board plan and housing facility. *Payment plan:* deferred payment. *Waivers:* employees or children of employees.

Financial Aid Of all full-time matriculated undergraduates who enrolled in 2008, 915 applied for aid, 767 were judged to have need, 532 had their need fully met. 525 Federal Work-Study jobs (averaging $1883). 200 state and other part-time jobs (averaging $1019). In 2008, 405 non-need-based awards were made. *Average percent of need met:* 92%. *Average financial aid package:* $32,208. *Average need-based loan:* $4435. *Average need-based gift aid:* $26,526. *Average non-need-based aid:* $8790. *Average indebtedness upon graduation:* $14,285. *Financial aid deadline:* 2/1.

Applying *Options:* electronic application, early decision, deferred entrance. *Application fee:* $50. *Required:* essay or personal statement, high school transcript, 1 letter of recommendation. *Recommended:* interview. *Application deadlines:* 1/15 (freshmen), 3/1 (transfers). *Early decision deadline:* 11/15. *Notification:* 4/1 (freshmen), 4/15 (transfers), 12/21 (early decision).

Freshman Application Contact Mr. Tony Cabasco, Dean of Admission and Financial Aid, Whitman College, 515 Boyer Avenue, Walla Walla, WA 99362-2083. *Phone:* 509-527-5176. *Toll-free phone:* 877-462-9448. *Fax:* 509-527-4967. *E-mail:* admission@whitman.edu. *Web site:* http://www.whitman.edu/.

See page 1790 for the College Close-Up.

Whitworth University

Spokane, Washington

Freshman Application Contact Ms. Marianne Hansen, Director of Admission, Whitworth University, 300 West, Hawthorne Road, Spokane, WA 99251. *Phone:* 509-777-4348. *Toll-free phone:* 800-533-4668. *Fax:* 509-777-3758. *E-mail:* admission@whitworth.edu. *Web site:* http://www.whitworth.edu/.

WEST VIRGINIA

Alderson-Broaddus College

Philippi, West Virginia

- **Independent** comprehensive, founded 1871, affiliated with American Baptist Churches in the U.S.A.
- **Rural** 170-acre campus
- **Endowment** $16.0 million
- **Coed** 566 undergraduate students, 95% full-time, 64% women, 36% men
- **Moderately difficult** entrance level, 71% of applicants were admitted

Undergraduates 535 full-time, 31 part-time. Students come from 28 states and territories; 6 other countries; 20% are from out of state; 3% Black or African American, non-Hispanic/Latino; 2% Hispanic/Latino; 1% Asian, non-Hispanic/Latino; 0.5% American Indian or Alaska Native, non-Hispanic/Latino; 0.5% Two or more races, non-Hispanic/Latino; 2% international; 4% transferred in; 63% live on campus. *Retention:* 65% of full-time freshmen returned.

Freshmen *Admission:* 791 applied, 560 admitted, 132 enrolled. *Average high school GPA:* 3.3. *Test scores:* SAT critical reading scores over 500: 44%; SAT math scores over 500: 43%; SAT writing scores over 500: 35%; ACT scores over 18: 93%; SAT critical reading scores over 600: 14%; SAT math scores over 600: 16%; SAT writing scores over 600: 5%; ACT scores over 24: 32%; ACT scores over 30: 1%.

Faculty *Total:* 85, 67% full-time, 40% with terminal degrees. *Student/faculty ratio:* 9:1.

Academics *Calendar:* semesters. *Degrees:* certificates, associate, bachelor's, and master's. *Special study options:* advanced placement credit, double majors, honors programs, independent study, internships, part-time degree program, services for LD students, study abroad, summer session for credit.

Computers on Campus 100 computers/terminals and 750 ports are available on campus for general student use. Students can access the following: campus intranet, computer help desk, free student e-mail accounts, online (class) grades, online (class) schedules, course materials, student record information. Campuswide network is available. 100% of college-owned or -operated housing units are wired for high-speed Internet access. Wireless service is available via entire campus.

Student Life *Housing:* on-campus residence required through senior year. *Options:* coed, women-only, disabled students. Campus housing is university owned. Freshman campus housing is guaranteed. *Activities and organizations:* drama/theater group, student-run newspaper, radio and television station, choral group, AAPA/Hu C. Myers Society, Alpha Beta Nu, Student Athletic Advisory Committee, Sigma Alpha Iota, Kappa Xi Omega. *Campus security:* 24-hour patrols, controlled dormitory access, emergency notification system, lighted pathways and sidewalks. *Student services:* health clinic, personal/psychological counseling.

Athletics Member NCAA. All Division II. *Intercollegiate sports:* baseball M(s), basketball M(s)/W(s), cross-country running M(s)/W(s), soccer M(s)/W(s), softball W(s), track and field M(s)/W(s), volleyball W(s). *Intramural sports:* basketball M/W, bowling M/W, football M/W, golf M/W, gymnastics M/W, racquetball M/W, soccer M/W, softball W, tennis M/W, ultimate Frisbee M/W, volleyball M/W.

Standardized Tests *Required:* SAT and SAT Subject Tests or ACT (for admission).

Costs (2010–11) *Comprehensive fee:* $29,426 includes full-time tuition ($21,994), mandatory fees ($210), and room and board ($7222). Full-time tuition and fees vary according to program and student level. Part-time tuition: $733 per credit hour. Part-time tuition and fees vary according to program and student level. *Required fees:* $53 per term part-time. *College room only:* $3556. Room and board charges vary according to housing facility. *Payment plan:* installment. *Waivers:* employees or children of employees.

Financial Aid Of all full-time matriculated undergraduates who enrolled in 2009, 520 applied for aid, 495 were judged to have need, 131 had their need fully met. 189 Federal Work-Study jobs (averaging $1390). 90 state and other part-time jobs (averaging $2198). In 2009, 33 non-need-based awards were made. *Average percent of need met:* 81%. *Average financial aid package:* $21,596. *Average need-based loan:* $4838. *Average need-based gift aid:* $17,655. *Average non-need-based aid:* $8942. *Average indebtedness upon graduation:* $31,751.

Applying *Options:* electronic application, deferred entrance. *Application fee:* $25. *Required:* high school transcript, minimum 2 GPA. *Required for some:* 3 letters of recommendation, interview. *Application deadlines:* rolling (freshmen), rolling (transfers). *Notification:* 8/31 (freshmen), continuous until 8/31 (transfers).

Freshman Application Contact Ms. Kimberly N. Klaus, Director of Admissions, Alderson-Broaddus College, 101 College Hill Drive, Campus Box 2003, Philippi, WV 26416. *Phone:* 304-457-1700. *Toll-free phone:* 800-263-1549. *Fax:* 304-457-6239. *E-mail:* admissions@ab.edu. *Web site:* http://www.ab.edu/.

American Public University System

Charles Town, West Virginia

- **Proprietary** comprehensive, founded 1991, administratively affiliated with American Military University/American Public University
- **Rural** campus with easy access to Washington, D.C.
- **Coed** 29,746 undergraduate students, 11% full-time, 33% women, 67% men
- **Noncompetitive** entrance level, 100% of applicants were admitted

Undergraduates 3,273 full-time, 26,473 part-time. Students come from 55 states and territories; 43 other countries; 15% transferred in.

Freshmen *Admission:* 3,261 applied, 3,261 admitted, 3,261 enrolled.

Faculty *Total:* 1,461, 17% full-time. *Student/faculty ratio:* 24:1.

Academics *Calendar:* courses start on the first Monday of each month. *Degrees:* certificates, associate, bachelor's, master's, and postbachelor's certificates (profile includes American Public University, American Military University and American Community College). *Special study options:* adult/continuing education programs, distance learning, external degree program, independent study, part-time degree program.

Computers on Campus Students can access the following: free student e-mail accounts, online (class) grades, online (class) registration, online (class) schedules.

Student Life *Housing:* college housing not available.

Costs (2011–12) *Tuition:* $6000 full-time, $250 per credit hour part-time. *Payment plan:* installment. *Waivers:* employees or children of employees.

Applying *Options:* electronic application, deferred entrance. *Required:* high school transcript, Complete no-fee orientation. *Application deadlines:* rolling (freshmen), rolling (transfers).

Freshman Application Contact Ms. Terry Grant, Associate Vice President, Enrollment Management, American Public University System, 111 West Congress Street, Charles Town, WV 25414. *Phone:* 877-468-6268. *Fax:* 304-724-3788. *E-mail:* info@apus.edu. *Web site:* http://www.apus.edu/.

Appalachian Bible College

Bradley, West Virginia

- **Independent nondenominational** comprehensive, founded 1950
- **Small-town** 110-acre campus
- **Endowment** $316,677
- **Coed** 258 undergraduate students, 81% full-time, 47% women, 53% men
- **Noncompetitive** entrance level, 62% of applicants were admitted

Undergraduates 209 full-time, 49 part-time. Students come from 36 states and territories; 10 other countries; 10% transferred in; 95% live on campus. *Retention:* 71% of full-time freshmen returned.

Freshmen *Admission:* 117 applied, 73 admitted, 58 enrolled. *Test scores:* SAT critical reading scores over 500: 63%; SAT math scores over 500: 46%; ACT scores over 18: 86%; SAT critical reading scores over 600: 25%; SAT math scores over 600: 21%; ACT scores over 24: 40%; SAT critical reading scores over 700: 8%; ACT scores over 30: 2%.

Faculty *Total:* 18, 61% full-time, 28% with terminal degrees. *Student/faculty ratio:* 17:1.

Academics *Calendar:* semesters. *Degrees:* certificates, diplomas, associate, bachelor's, master's, and postbachelor's certificates. *Special study options:* academic remediation for entering students, adult/continuing education programs, advanced placement credit, distance learning, double majors, honors programs, independent study, internships, part-time degree program, student-designed majors, summer session for credit.

Computers on Campus 30 computers/terminals are available on campus for general student use. Students can access the following: campus intranet, computer help desk, free student e-mail accounts. Campuswide network is available. 100% of college-owned or -operated housing units are wired for high-speed Internet access. Wireless service is available via computer labs, libraries, student centers.

Student Life *Housing:* on-campus residence required through senior year. *Options:* men-only, women-only. Campus housing is university owned. Freshman campus housing is guaranteed. *Activities and organizations:* drama/theater group, choral group. *Campus security:* 24-hour emergency response devices, patrols by trained security personnel. *Student services:* health clinic, personal/psychological counseling.

Athletics Member NCCAA. *Intercollegiate sports:* basketball M/W, soccer M, volleyball W.

Standardized Tests *Required:* SAT or ACT (for admission).

Costs (2010–11) *Comprehensive fee:* $16,724 includes full-time tuition ($9384), mandatory fees ($1550), and room and board ($5790). Full-time tuition and fees vary according to program. Part-time tuition and fees vary according to program. *Required fees:* $391 per credit hour part-time. *Room and board:* Room and board charges vary according to housing facility. *Payment plans:* tuition prepayment, installment. *Waivers:* children of alumni, adult students, senior citizens, and employees or children of employees.

Financial Aid Of all full-time matriculated undergraduates who enrolled in 2009, 352 applied for aid, 321 were judged to have need, 13 had their need fully met. 44 Federal Work-Study jobs (averaging $461). In 2009, 30 non-need-based awards were made. *Average percent of need met:* 38%. *Average financial aid package:* $7293. *Average need-based loan:* $3359. *Average need-based gift aid:* $5799. *Average non-need-based aid:* $1919. *Financial aid deadline:* 6/15.

Applying *Options:* electronic application, early admission. *Application fee:* $20. *Required:* essay or personal statement, high school transcript, 3 letters of recommendation, interview. *Required for some:* interview. *Recommended:* minimum 2.5 GPA. *Application deadlines:* rolling (freshmen), rolling (transfers).

Freshman Application Contact Miss Rachel Delevan, Admissions Assistant, Appalachian Bible College, PO Box ABC, Bradley, WV 25818. *Phone:* 304-877-6428 Ext. 3213. *Toll-free phone:* 800-678-9ABC Ext. 3213. *Fax:* 304-877-5082. *E-mail:* admissions2@abc.edu. *Web site:* http://www.abc.edu/.

Bethany College

Bethany, West Virginia

- **Independent** comprehensive, founded 1840, affiliated with Christian Church (Disciples of Christ)
- **Rural** 1300-acre campus with easy access to Pittsburgh
- **Coed** 887 undergraduate students, 99% full-time, 45% women, 55% men
- **Moderately difficult** entrance level

Undergraduates 878 full-time, 9 part-time. Students come from 29 states and territories; 4 other countries; 78% are from out of state; 11% Black or African American, non-Hispanic/Latino; 2% Hispanic/Latino; 0.6% Asian, non-Hispanic/Latino; 0.2% American Indian or Alaska Native, non-Hispanic/Latino; 0.8% Two or more races, non-Hispanic/Latino; 9% Race/ethnicity unknown; 0.7% international; 4% transferred in; 90% live on campus. *Retention:* 63% of full-time freshmen returned.

Freshmen *Admission:* 1,378 applied, 272 enrolled. *Average high school GPA:* 2.9. *Test scores:* SAT critical reading scores over 500: 30%; SAT math scores over 500: 30%; SAT writing scores over 500: 24%; ACT scores over 18: 61%; SAT critical reading scores over 600: 6%; SAT math scores over 600: 4%; SAT writing scores over 600: 5%; ACT scores over 24: 26%; ACT scores over 30: 2%.

Faculty *Total:* 80, 64% full-time, 59% with terminal degrees. *Student/faculty ratio:* 15:1.

Academics *Calendar:* 4-1-4. *Degrees:* bachelor's and master's. *Special study options:* academic remediation for entering students, advanced placement credit, distance learning, double majors, independent study, internships, off-campus study, part-time degree program, services for LD students, student-designed majors, study abroad. *Unusual degree programs:* 3-2 engineering with Columbia University, Case Western Reserve University; Duquesne University.

Computers on Campus 150 computers/terminals are available on campus for general student use. Students can access the following: computer help desk, free student e-mail accounts, online (class) grades, online (class) registration, online (class) schedules. Campuswide network is available. 100% of college-owned or -operated housing units are wired for high-speed Internet access. Wireless service is available via classrooms, computer centers, computer labs, learning centers, libraries, student centers.

Student Life *Housing:* on-campus residence required through senior year. *Options:* coed, men-only, women-only, disabled students. Campus housing is university owned. Freshman campus housing is guaranteed. *Activities and organizations:* drama/theater group, student-run newspaper, radio and television station, choral group, Student Board of Governors, Outdoor Club, Model United Nations, Public Relations Society, International Student Association, national fraternities, national sororities. *Campus security:* 24-hour emergency response devices and patrols, late-night transport/escort service, controlled dormitory access. *Student services:* health clinic, personal/psychological counseling.

Athletics Member NCAA. All Division III. *Intercollegiate sports:* baseball M, basketball M/W, cross-country running M/W, football M, golf M/W, lacrosse M, soccer M/W, softball W, swimming and diving M/W, tennis M/W, track and field M/W, volleyball W.

Standardized Tests *Required:* SAT or ACT (for admission).

Costs (2010–11) *Comprehensive fee:* $31,896 includes full-time tuition ($21,696), mandatory fees ($900), and room and board ($9300). Part-time tuition: $650 per credit hour. *Room and board:* Room and board charges vary according to housing facility. *Payment plan:* installment. *Waivers:* children of alumni and employees or children of employees.

Financial Aid Of all full-time matriculated undergraduates who enrolled in 2009, 777 applied for aid, 699 were judged to have need. In 2009, 60 non-need-based awards were made. *Average percent of need met:* 49%. *Average need-based loan:* $7258. *Average need-based gift aid:* $9824. *Average non-need-based aid:* $7189.

Applying *Options:* electronic application, deferred entrance. *Required:* essay or personal statement, high school transcript, minimum 2 GPA, 1 letter of recommendation, documentation of student involvement. *Required for some:* interview. *Recommended:* interview. *Application deadlines:* rolling (freshmen), rolling (out-of-state freshmen), rolling (transfers). *Notification:* 8/15 (freshmen), 8/15 (out-of-state freshmen), continuous until 8/15 (transfers).

Freshman Application Contact Mother R.J. Zitzelsberger, Director of Admission, Bethany College, Office of Admission, Bethany, WV 26032. *Phone:* 304-829-7611. *Toll-free phone:* 800-922-7611. *Fax:* 304-829-7142. *E-mail:* admission@bethanywv.edu. *Web site:* http://www.bethanywv.edu/.

Bluefield State College

Bluefield, West Virginia

- **State-supported** 4-year, founded 1895, part of West Virginia Higher Education Policy Commission
- **Small-town** 45-acre campus
- **Coed** 2,063 undergraduate students, 77% full-time, 63% women, 37% men
- **Noncompetitive** entrance level, 69% of applicants were admitted

Undergraduates 1,586 full-time, 477 part-time. 12% are from out of state; 12% Black or African American, non-Hispanic/Latino; 0.8% Hispanic/Latino; 0.2% Asian, non-Hispanic/Latino; 0.2% Native Hawaiian or other Pacific Islander, non-Hispanic/Latino; 0.2% American Indian or Alaska Native, non-Hispanic/Latino; 0.2% Two or more races, non-Hispanic/Latino; 4% Race/ethnicity unknown; 11% transferred in. *Retention:* 61% of full-time freshmen returned.

Freshmen *Admission:* 558 applied, 383 admitted, 301 enrolled. *Average high school GPA:* 3.44. *Test scores:* SAT critical reading scores over 500: 45%; SAT math scores over 500: 43%; ACT scores over 18: 70%; SAT critical reading scores over 600: 2%; SAT math scores over 600: 10%; ACT scores over 24: 11%.

Faculty *Total:* 147, 53% full-time, 34% with terminal degrees. *Student/faculty ratio:* 17:1.

Academics *Calendar:* semesters. *Degrees:* associate and bachelor's. *Special study options:* academic remediation for entering students, adult/continuing education programs, advanced placement credit, distance learning, double majors, honors programs, independent study, internships, part-time degree program, summer session for credit.

Computers on Campus Students can access the following: computer help desk, free student e-mail accounts, online (class) grades, online (class) registration. Campuswide network is available. Wireless service is available via entire campus.

Student Life *Housing:* college housing not available. *Activities and organizations:* drama/theater group, student-run newspaper, radio station, choral group, national fraternities, national sororities. *Campus security:* 24-hour emergency response devices and patrols, student patrols. *Student services:* health clinic, personal/psychological counseling.

Athletics Member NCAA. All Division II. *Intercollegiate sports:* baseball M(s), basketball M(s)/W(s), cheerleading W, cross-country running M(s)/W(s), golf M(s), softball W(s), tennis M(s)/W(s). *Intramural sports:* badminton M/W, basketball M/W, football M, soccer M, swimming and diving M/W, table tennis M/W, volleyball M/W, water polo M/W.

Standardized Tests *Required:* SAT or ACT (for admission).

Costs (2010–11) *Tuition:* state resident $4596 full-time, $192 per credit hour part-time; nonresident $9288 full-time, $387 per credit hour part-time. *Payment plan:* installment. *Waivers:* adult students and senior citizens.

Financial Aid Of all full-time matriculated undergraduates who enrolled in 2009, 1,310 applied for aid, 1,120 were judged to have need, 440 had their need fully met. 42 Federal Work-Study jobs (averaging $2750). 110 state and other part-time jobs (averaging $3100). In 2009, 400 non-need-based awards were made. *Average percent of need met:* 70%. *Average financial aid package:* $6800. *Average need-based loan:* $3600. *Average need-based gift aid:* $3500. *Average non-need-based aid:* $1500. *Average indebtedness upon graduation:* $22,000.

Applying *Options:* electronic application, early admission, deferred entrance. *Required:* high school transcript, minimum 2 GPA. *Application deadlines:* rolling (freshmen), rolling (transfers). *Notification:* continuous (freshmen), continuous (transfers).

Freshman Application Contact Bluefield State College, 219 Rock Street, Bluefield, WV 24701-2198. *Phone:* 304-327-4067. *Toll-free phone:* 800-344-8892 Ext. 4065 (in-state); 800-654-7798 Ext. 4065 (out-of-state). *Web site:* http://www.bluefieldstate.edu/.

Concord University
Athens, West Virginia

- **State-supported** comprehensive, founded 1872, part of State College System of West Virginia
- **Rural** 100-acre campus
- **Endowment** $21.4 million
- **Coed** 2,857 undergraduate students, 83% full-time, 57% women, 43% men
- **Minimally difficult** entrance level, 61% of applicants were admitted

Undergraduates 2,373 full-time, 484 part-time. Students come from 27 states and territories; 23 other countries; 22% are from out of state; 6% Black or African American, non-Hispanic/Latino; 0.8% Hispanic/Latino; 2% Asian, non-Hispanic/Latino; 0.3% American Indian or Alaska Native, non-Hispanic/Latino; 6% transferred in; 38% live on campus. *Retention:* 65% of full-time freshmen returned.

Freshmen *Admission:* 2,290 applied, 1,388 admitted, 575 enrolled. *Average high school GPA:* 3.21. *Test scores:* SAT critical reading scores over 500: 43%; SAT math scores over 500: 36%; ACT scores over 18: 79%; SAT critical reading scores over 600: 6%; SAT math scores over 600: 5%; ACT scores over 24: 28%; ACT scores over 30: 2%.

Faculty *Total:* 207, 58% full-time, 43% with terminal degrees. *Student/faculty ratio:* 17:1.

Academics *Calendar:* semesters. *Degrees:* associate, bachelor's, and master's. *Special study options:* academic remediation for entering students, accelerated degree program, advanced placement credit, cooperative education, distance learning, double majors, English as a second language, external degree program, honors programs, independent study, internships, off-campus study, part-time degree program, services for LD students, student-designed majors, study abroad, summer session for credit.

Computers on Campus 250 computers/terminals are available on campus for general student use. Students can access the following: campus intranet, computer help desk, free student e-mail accounts, online (class) grades, online (class) registration, online (class) schedules. Campuswide network is available. 100% of college-owned or -operated housing units are wired for high-speed Internet access. Wireless service is available via classrooms, computer centers, computer labs, libraries, student centers.

Student Life *Housing:* on-campus residence required through senior year. *Options:* coed, men-only, women-only. Campus housing is university owned. Freshman campus housing is guaranteed. *Activities and organizations:* drama/theater group, student-run newspaper, radio and television station, choral group, marching band, Service Groups, student government, student-run publications, Intramurals, Student Activities Committee, national fraternities, national sororities. *Campus security:* 24-hour emergency response devices and patrols, student patrols, late-night transport/escort service, controlled dormitory access. *Student services:* health clinic, personal/psychological counseling.

Athletics Member NCAA. All Division II. *Intercollegiate sports:* baseball M(s), basketball M(s)/W(s), cheerleading M/W, cross-country running M(s)/W(s), football M(s), golf M(s), soccer W(s), tennis M(s)/W(s), track and field M(s)/W(s), volleyball W(s). *Intramural sports:* basketball M/W, bowling M/W, football M, golf M/W, lacrosse M, racquetball M/W, soccer M/W, tennis M/W, volleyball M/W, water polo M/W, weight lifting M/W, wrestling M.

Standardized Tests *Required:* SAT or ACT (for admission).

Costs (2011–12) *Tuition:* state resident $4974 full-time, $207 per credit part-time; nonresident $11,050 full-time, $460 per credit part-time. Full-time tuition and fees vary according to course load. Part-time tuition and fees vary according to course load. *Room and board:* $6962; room only: $3546. *Payment plan:* installment. *Waivers:* adult students, senior citizens, and employees or children of employees.

Financial Aid Of all full-time matriculated undergraduates who enrolled in 2009, 2,092 applied for aid, 1,702 were judged to have need, 533 had their need fully met. 248 Federal Work-Study jobs (averaging $1205). 385 state and other part-time jobs (averaging $1191). In 2009, 175 non-need-based awards were made. *Average percent of need met:* 93%. *Average financial aid package:* $11,726. *Average need-based loan:* $6642. *Average need-based gift aid:* $5292. *Average non-need-based aid:* $2760. *Average indebtedness upon graduation:* $14,700.

Applying *Options:* electronic application, early admission, early decision. *Required:* high school transcript, minimum 2 GPA. *Required for some:* essay or personal statement, interview. *Recommended:* interview. *Application deadlines:* rolling (freshmen), 1/15 (out-of-state freshmen), rolling (transfers). *Notification:* continuous (freshmen), continuous (transfers).

Freshman Application Contact Mr. Kent Gamble, Director of Enrollment, Concord University, 1000 Vermillion Street, Athens, WV 24712. *Phone:* 304-384-5316. *Toll-free phone:* 888-384-5249. *Fax:* 304-384-9044. *E-mail:* admissions@concord.edu. *Web site:* http://www.concord.edu/.

Davis & Elkins College
Elkins, West Virginia

Freshman Application Contact Ms. Rene Heckel, Director of Enrollment Management, Davis & Elkins College, 100 Campus Drive, Elkins, WV 26241. *Phone:* 304-637-1974. *Toll-free phone:* 800-624-3157 Ext. 1230. *Fax:* 304-637-1800. *E-mail:* admiss@davisandelkins.edu. *Web site:* http://www.davisandelkins.edu/.

Fairmont State University
Fairmont, West Virginia

- **State-supported** comprehensive, founded 1865, part of State College System of West Virginia
- **Small-town** 120-acre campus
- **Endowment** $14.8 million
- **Coed** 4,362 undergraduate students, 87% full-time, 56% women, 44% men
- **Minimally difficult** entrance level, 57% of applicants were admitted

Undergraduates 3,786 full-time, 576 part-time. Students come from 23 states and territories; 20 other countries; 5% are from out of state; 4% Black or African American, non-Hispanic/Latino; 1% Hispanic/Latino; 0.3% Asian, non-Hispanic/Latino; 0.1% Native Hawaiian or other Pacific Islander, non-Hispanic/Latino; 0.3% American Indian or Alaska Native, non-Hispanic/Latino; 2% Two or more races, non-Hispanic/Latino; 0.9% Race/ethnicity unknown; 2% international; 11% transferred in; 18% live on campus. *Retention:* 67% of full-time freshmen returned.

Freshmen *Admission:* 3,354 applied, 1,906 admitted, 776 enrolled. *Average high school GPA:* 3.12. *Test scores:* SAT critical reading scores over 500: 31%; SAT math scores over 500: 35%; ACT scores over 18: 80%; SAT critical reading scores over 600: 2%; SAT math scores over 600: 2%; ACT scores over 24: 21%; ACT scores over 30: 1%.

Faculty *Total:* 334, 49% full-time, 51% with terminal degrees. *Student/faculty ratio:* 18:1.

Academics *Calendar:* semesters. *Degrees:* certificates, associate, bachelor's, and master's. *Special study options:* academic remediation for entering students, accelerated degree program, adult/continuing education programs, advanced placement credit, cooperative education, distance learning, double majors, English as a second language, honors programs, independent study, internships, off-campus study, part-time degree program, services for LD students, study abroad, summer session for credit. *ROTC:* Army (b), Air Force (c).

Computers on Campus 1,350 computers/terminals are available on campus for general student use. Students can access the following: campus intranet, computer help desk, free student e-mail accounts, online (class) grades, online (class) registration, online (class) schedules. Campuswide network is available. Wireless service is available via entire campus.

Student Life *Housing:* on-campus residence required through sophomore year. *Options:* coed, men-only, women-only. Campus housing is university owned. Freshman campus housing is guaranteed. *Activities and organizations:* drama/theater group, student-run newspaper, choral group, marching band, Alpha Phi Omega, Circle K, Society for Non-traditional Students, Criminal Justice Club, Honors Association, national fraternities, national sororities. *Campus security:* 24-hour emergency response devices and patrols, student patrols, controlled dormitory access. *Student services:* health clinic, personal/psychological counseling, legal services.

Athletics Member NCAA. All Division II. *Intercollegiate sports:* baseball M, basketball M(s)/W(s), cross-country running M/W, football M(s), golf M(s)/W, softball W, swimming and diving M(s)/W(s), tennis M(s)/W(s), volleyball W. *Intramural sports:* archery M/W, basketball M/W, bowling M/W, cross-country running M/W, football M, golf M/W, swimming and diving M/W, table tennis M/W, tennis M/W, volleyball M/W, wrestling M.

Standardized Tests *Required:* SAT or ACT (for admission).

Costs (2010–11) *Tuition:* state resident $5172 full-time, $216 per credit hour part-time; nonresident $10,904 full-time, $454 per credit hour part-time. Full-time tuition and fees vary according to degree level and location. Part-time tuition and fees vary according to course load, degree level, and location. *Room and board:* $7236; room only: $3388. Room and board charges vary according to board plan and housing facility. *Payment plan:* installment. *Waivers:* employees or children of employees.

Financial Aid Of all full-time matriculated undergraduates who enrolled in 2008, 2,896 applied for aid, 2,359 were judged to have need, 326 had their need fully met. In 2008, 394 non-need-based awards were made. *Average financial aid package:* $7654. *Average need-based loan:* $3635. *Average need-based gift aid:* $11,064. *Average non-need-based aid:* $1109.

Applying *Options:* electronic application. *Required:* high school transcript. *Recommended:* minimum 2 GPA. *Application deadlines:* rolling (freshmen), rolling (transfers). *Notification:* continuous (freshmen), continuous (transfers).

Freshman Application Contact Mrs. Lori Schoonmaker, Director of Admissions and Recruiting (Interim Associate), Fairmont State University, 1201 Locust Avenue, Fairmont, WV 26554. *Phone:* 304-367-4892. *Toll-free phone:* 800-641-5678. *Fax:* 304-367-4938. *E-mail:* admit@fairmontstate.edu. *Web site:* http://www.fairmontstate.edu/.

Glenville State College

Glenville, West Virginia

- **State-supported** 4-year, founded 1872, part of West Virginia Higher Education Policy Commission
- **Rural** 331-acre campus
- **Endowment** $10.8 million
- **Coed**
- **Noncompetitive** entrance level

Faculty *Student/faculty ratio:* 18:1.

Academics *Calendar:* semesters. *Degrees:* associate and bachelor's.

Student Life *Campus security:* 24-hour emergency response devices and patrols, student patrols, late-night transport/escort service, controlled dormitory access.

Athletics Member NCAA. All Division II.

Standardized Tests *Required:* SAT or ACT (for admission).

Costs (2010–11) *Tuition:* state resident $4888 full-time, $204 per credit hour part-time; nonresident $12,000 full-time, $500 per credit hour part-time. Full-time tuition and fees vary according to course load. *Required fees:* $204 per credit hour part-time. *Room and board:* $7350; room only: $4000. Room and board charges vary according to board plan and housing facility.

Financial Aid Of all full-time matriculated undergraduates who enrolled in 2009, 1,114 applied for aid, 1,027 were judged to have need, 228 had their need fully met. 94 Federal Work-Study jobs (averaging $1500). 255 state and other part-time jobs (averaging $2200). In 2009, 49 non-need-based awards were made. *Average percent of need met:* 73. *Average financial aid package:* $11,686. *Average need-based loan:* $3727. *Average need-based gift aid:* $5299. *Average non-need-based aid:* $2077. *Average indebtedness upon graduation:* $25,145.

Applying *Options:* electronic application, deferred entrance. *Application fee:* $10. *Required:* high school transcript, minimum 3 GPA, college preparatory program. *Required for some:* interview.

Freshman Application Contact Mr. Tommy Oldaker, Admission Counselor, Glenville State College, 200 High Street, Glenville, WV 26351-1200. *Phone:*

304-462-4128 Ext. 6133. *Toll-free phone:* 800-924-2010. *Fax:* 304-462-8619. *E-mail:* tommy.oldaker@glenville.edu. *Web site:* http://www.glenville.edu/.

Marshall University

Huntington, West Virginia

- **State-supported** university, founded 1837, part of University System of West Virginia
- **Urban** 70-acre campus
- **Coed** 10,018 undergraduate students, 85% full-time, 56% women, 44% men
- **Moderately difficult** entrance level, 84% of applicants were admitted

Undergraduates 8,529 full-time, 1,489 part-time. Students come from 44 states and territories; 34 other countries; 24% are from out of state; 6% Black or African American, non-Hispanic/Latino; 1% Hispanic/Latino; 0.9% Asian, non-Hispanic/Latino; 0.4% American Indian or Alaska Native, non-Hispanic/Latino; 0.2% Two or more races, non-Hispanic/Latino; 3% Race/ethnicity unknown; 1% international; 8% transferred in; 17% live on campus. *Retention:* 70% of full-time freshmen returned.

Freshmen *Admission:* 2,768 applied, 2,324 admitted, 1,951 enrolled. *Average high school GPA:* 3.33. *Test scores:* SAT critical reading scores over 500: 49%; SAT math scores over 500: 45%; ACT scores over 18: 90%; SAT critical reading scores over 600: 8%; SAT math scores over 600: 11%; ACT scores over 24: 34%; SAT critical reading scores over 700: 1%; SAT math scores over 700: 1%; ACT scores over 30: 4%.

Faculty *Total:* 740, 66% full-time, 55% with terminal degrees. *Student/faculty ratio:* 20:1.

Academics *Calendar:* semesters. *Degrees:* associate, bachelor's, master's, doctoral-professional, doctoral-research/scholarship, post-master's, and post-bachelor's certificates. *Special study options:* academic remediation for entering students, accelerated degree program, adult/continuing education programs, advanced placement credit, cooperative education, distance learning, double majors, English as a second language, honors programs, independent study, internships, off-campus study, part-time degree program, services for LD students, study abroad, summer session for credit. *ROTC:* Army (b). *Unusual degree programs:* 3-2 forestry with Duke University.

Computers on Campus 1,461 computers/terminals and 2,900 ports are available on campus for general student use. Students can access the following: campus intranet, computer help desk, free student e-mail accounts, online (class) grades, online (class) registration, online (class) schedules, Virtual Computer Lab - MU Remote and Web Conferencing. Campuswide network is available. 100% of college-owned or -operated housing units are wired for high-speed Internet access. Wireless service is available via classrooms, computer centers, computer labs, dorm rooms, learning centers, libraries, student centers.

Student Life *Housing:* on-campus residence required through sophomore year. *Options:* coed, men-only, women-only, disabled students. Campus housing is university owned. Freshman campus housing is guaranteed. *Activities and organizations:* drama/theater group, student-run newspaper, radio and television station, choral group, marching band, Campus Crusade for Christ, Gamma Beta Phi, The International Students' Organization, Newman Association, Phi Alpha Theta, national fraternities, national sororities. *Campus security:* 24-hour emergency response devices and patrols, student patrols, late-night transport/escort service, controlled dormitory access. *Student services:* health clinic, personal/psychological counseling, women's center, legal services.

Athletics Member NCAA. All Division I except football (Division I-A). *Intercollegiate sports:* baseball M(s), basketball M(s)/W(s), cross-country running M(s)/W(s), golf M(s)/W(s), lacrosse M(c), rugby M(c)/W(c), soccer M(s)/W(s), softball W(s), swimming and diving W(s), tennis W(s), track and field M(s)/W(s), volleyball W(s). *Intramural sports:* basketball M/W, bowling M/W, football M/W, golf M/W, racquetball M/W, soccer M/W, softball M/W, swimming and diving M/W, tennis M/W, track and field M/W, volleyball M/W.

Standardized Tests *Required:* SAT or ACT (for admission).

Costs (2010–11) *Tuition:* state resident $4319 full-time, $180 per credit hour part-time; nonresident $11,930 full-time, $497 per credit hour part-time. Full-time tuition and fees vary according to degree level, location, program, and reciprocity agreements. Part-time tuition and fees vary according to course load, degree level, location, program, and reciprocity agreements. *Required fees:* $966 full-time, $41 per credit hour part-time. *Room and board:* $7858; room only: $4652. Room and board charges vary according to board plan and housing facility. *Payment plan:* installment. *Waivers:* senior citizens and employees or children of employees.

Financial Aid Of all full-time matriculated undergraduates who enrolled in 2009, 6,416 applied for aid, 5,173 were judged to have need, 1,739 had their need fully met. 189 Federal Work-Study jobs (averaging $1807). In 2009, 1238 non-need-based awards were made. *Average percent of need met:* 55%. *Average financial aid package:* $9628. *Average need-based loan:* $7066. *Average need-based gift aid:* $5933. *Average non-need-based aid:* $5643. *Average indebtedness upon graduation:* $21,156.

Applying *Options:* electronic application, deferred entrance. *Application fee:* $30. *Required for some:* high school transcript. *Application deadlines:* rolling (freshmen), rolling (transfers). *Notification:* continuous (freshmen), continuous (transfers).

Freshman Application Contact Dr. Tammy Johnson, Director of Admissions, Marshall University, 1 John Marshall Drive, Huntington, WV 25755. *Phone:* 800-642-3499. *Toll-free phone:* 800-642-3499. *Fax:* 304-696-3135. *E-mail:* admissions@marshall.edu. *Web site:* http://www.marshall.edu/.

Mountain State University

Beckley, West Virginia

- **Independent** comprehensive, founded 1933
- **Small-town** 35-acre campus
- **Endowment** $9.1 million
- **Coed** 4,890 undergraduate students, 67% full-time, 67% women, 33% men
- **Noncompetitive** entrance level, 100% of applicants were admitted

Undergraduates 3,267 full-time, 1,623 part-time. Students come from 50 states and territories; 46 other countries; 31% are from out of state; 16% Black or African American, non-Hispanic/Latino; 3% Hispanic/Latino; 0.9% Asian, non-Hispanic/Latino; 0.2% Native Hawaiian or other Pacific Islander, non-Hispanic/Latino; 0.6% American Indian or Alaska Native, non-Hispanic/Latino; 0.1% Two or more races, non-Hispanic/Latino; 12% Race/ethnicity unknown; 5% international; 16% transferred in; 37% live on campus. *Retention:* 24% of full-time freshmen returned.

Freshmen *Admission:* 1,633 applied, 1,633 admitted, 531 enrolled. *Average high school GPA:* 2.98. *Test scores:* ACT scores over 18: 53%; ACT scores over 24: 12%.

Faculty *Total:* 419, 25% full-time, 25% with terminal degrees. *Student/faculty ratio:* 13:1.

Academics *Calendar:* semesters. *Degrees:* certificates, associate, bachelor's, master's, doctoral-other, post-master's, and postbachelor's certificates. *Special study options:* academic remediation for entering students, accelerated degree program, adult/continuing education programs, advanced placement credit, cooperative education, distance learning, double majors, English as a second language, external degree program, independent study, internships, part-time degree program, student-designed majors, summer session for credit.

Computers on Campus 230 computers/terminals are available on campus for general student use. Students can access the following: campus intranet, computer help desk, free student e-mail accounts, online (class) grades, online (class) registration, online (class) schedules. Campuswide network is available. 100% of college-owned or -operated housing units are wired for high-speed Internet access. Wireless service is available via entire campus.

Student Life *Housing:* on-campus residence required through sophomore year. *Options:* coed. Campus housing is university owned. *Activities and organizations:* drama/theater group, student-run newspaper, choral group, FIA-Forensics Investigation Association, SNA-Student Nursing Association, Students in Free Enterprise (SIFE), Cougar Culinarians, Student Government Association, national fraternities, national sororities. *Campus security:* 24-hour emergency response devices and patrols, late-night transport/escort service, controlled dormitory access.

Athletics Member NAIA. *Intercollegiate sports:* basketball M(s), cheerleading M/W(s), cross-country running M(s)/W(s), soccer M(s)/W(s), track and field M(s)/W(s), volleyball W(s). *Intramural sports:* basketball M, soccer M/W, volleyball W.

Standardized Tests *Required for some:* SAT (for admission), ACT (for admission), SAT or ACT (for admission). *Recommended:* SAT Subject Tests (for admission).

Costs (2011–12) *Comprehensive fee:* $16,545 includes full-time tuition ($7680) and room and board ($8865). Full-time tuition and fees vary according to course load, degree level, location, and program. Part-time tuition: $245 per credit hour. Part-time tuition and fees vary according to course load, degree level, location, and program. *College room only:* $5625. Room and board charges vary according to board plan and housing facility. *Payment plan:* installment. *Waivers:* senior citizens and employees or children of employees.

Financial Aid Of all full-time matriculated undergraduates who enrolled in 2009, 2,052 applied for aid, 1,877 were judged to have need, 1,877 had their need fully met. 100 Federal Work-Study jobs (averaging $1819). In 2009, 15 non-need-based awards were made. *Average percent of need met:* 48%. *Average financial aid package:* $7033. *Average need-based loan:* $4592. *Average need-based gift aid:* $4211. *Average non-need-based aid:* $4214. *Average indebtedness upon graduation:* $33,218.

Applying *Options:* electronic application, early admission, deferred entrance. *Application fee:* $25. *Required:* high school transcript. *Required for some:* essay or personal statement, interview. *Application deadlines:* rolling (freshmen), rolling (transfers).

Freshman Application Contact Ms. Tammy Kyle, Mountain State University, 408 South Kanawha Street, Beckley, WV 25801. *Phone:* 304-929-1563. *Toll-free phone:* 800-766-6067 Ext. 1433. *Fax:* 304-253-5072. *E-mail:* gomsu@mountainstate.edu. *Web site:* http://www.mountainstate.edu/.

Ohio Valley University

Vienna, West Virginia

- **Independent** comprehensive, founded 1960, affiliated with Church of Christ
- **Small-town** 299-acre campus
- **Coed** 443 undergraduate students, 85% full-time, 50% women, 50% men
- **Minimally difficult** entrance level, 56% of applicants were admitted

Undergraduates 377 full-time, 66 part-time. Students come from 28 states and territories; 10 other countries; 58% are from out of state; 4% Black or African American, non-Hispanic/Latino; 3% Hispanic/Latino; 1% Two or more races, non-Hispanic/Latino; 5% Race/ethnicity unknown; 5% international; 9% transferred in; 40% live on campus. *Retention:* 63% of full-time freshmen returned.

Freshmen *Admission:* 722 applied, 407 admitted, 107 enrolled. *Test scores:* SAT critical reading scores over 500: 42%; SAT math scores over 500: 42%; SAT writing scores over 500: 39%; ACT scores over 18: 90%; SAT critical reading scores over 600: 17%; SAT math scores over 600: 4%; ACT scores over 24: 21%; ACT scores over 30: 3%.

Faculty *Total:* 75, 29% full-time, 40% with terminal degrees. *Student/faculty ratio:* 9:1.

Academics *Calendar:* semesters. *Degrees:* certificates, associate, bachelor's, master's, and postbachelor's certificates. *Special study options:* academic remediation for entering students, adult/continuing education programs, advanced placement credit, double majors, English as a second language, external degree program, honors programs, independent study, internships, part-time degree program, services for LD students, study abroad, summer session for credit.

Computers on Campus 30 computers/terminals and 30 ports are available on campus for general student use. Students can access the following: campus intranet, computer help desk, free student e-mail accounts, online (class) grades, online (class) registration, online (class) schedules. Campuswide network is available. 100% of college-owned or -operated housing units are wired for high-speed Internet access. Wireless service is available via entire campus.

Student Life *Housing:* on-campus residence required through sophomore year. *Options:* men-only, women-only. Campus housing is university owned. Freshman campus housing is guaranteed. *Activities and organizations:* drama/theater group, student-run newspaper, choral group, Alpha Chi Honor Society, SNEA, Ambassadors for Christ, Timothy Club. *Campus security:* 24-hour emergency response devices and patrols, controlled dormitory access.

Athletics Member NCAA. All Division II. *Intercollegiate sports:* baseball M(s), basketball M(s)/W(s), cross-country running M(s)/W(s), golf M(s)/W(s), lacrosse M(s), soccer M(s)/W(s), softball W(s), volleyball W(s), wrestling M(s). *Intramural sports:* basketball M/W, bowling M/W, football M/W, golf M/W, soccer M/W, softball M/W, volleyball M/W.

Standardized Tests *Required:* SAT or ACT (for admission).

Costs (2011–12) *One-time required fee:* $60. *Comprehensive fee:* $20,496 includes full-time tuition ($12,538), mandatory fees ($1512), and room and board ($6446). Full-time tuition and fees vary according to course load and location. Part-time tuition: $525 per credit. Part-time tuition and fees vary according to course load and location. *Required fees:* $63 per credit hour part-time. *College room only:* $3269. Room and board charges vary according to board plan and housing facility. *Payment plan:* installment. *Waivers:* employees or children of employees.

Financial Aid Of all full-time matriculated undergraduates who enrolled in 2009, 373 applied for aid, 338 were judged to have need, 64 had their need fully met. 119 Federal Work-Study jobs (averaging $984). 8 state and other part-time jobs (averaging $1510). In 2009, 47 non-need-based awards were made. *Average percent of need met:* 69%. *Average financial aid package:* $13,188. *Average need-based loan:* $3947. *Average need-based gift aid:* $9922. *Average non-need-based aid:* $6171. *Average indebtedness upon graduation:* $21,735.

Applying *Options:* electronic application, early admission, deferred entrance. *Application fee:* $20. *Required:* high school transcript. *Required for some:* essay or personal statement, interview. *Application deadlines:* 8/15 (freshmen), rolling (transfers). *Notification:* continuous (freshmen), continuous (transfers).

Freshman Application Contact Mrs. Valerie Wright, Admissions Office Manager, Ohio Valley University, 1 Campus View Drive, Vienna, WV 26105. *Phone:* 304-865-6200. *Toll-free phone:* 877-446-8668 Ext. 6200. *Fax:* 304-865-6001. *E-mail:* admissions@ovu.edu. *Web site:* http://www.ovu.edu/.

Potomac State College of West Virginia University

Keyser, West Virginia

- **State-supported** primarily 2-year, founded 1901, part of West Virginia Higher Education Policy Commission
- **Small-town** 18-acre campus
- **Coed** 1,836 undergraduate students, 77% full-time, 51% women, 49% men
- **Noncompetitive** entrance level

Undergraduates 1,415 full-time, 421 part-time. Students come from 18 states and territories; 3 other countries; 29% are from out of state; 14% Black or African American, non-Hispanic/Latino; 3% Hispanic/Latino; 0.7% Asian, non-Hispanic/Latino; 0.2% Native Hawaiian or other Pacific Islander, non-Hispanic/Latino; 1% American Indian or Alaska Native, non-Hispanic/Latino; 0.3% Two or more races, non-Hispanic/Latino; 2% Race/ethnicity unknown; 0.3% international; 4% transferred in. *Retention:* 50% of full-time freshmen returned.

Freshmen *Admission:* 1,006 admitted, 710 enrolled. *Average high school GPA:* 2.78. *Test scores:* SAT critical reading scores over 500: 17%; SAT math scores over 500: 15%; ACT scores over 18: 63%; SAT critical reading scores over 600: 3%; SAT math scores over 600: 2%; ACT scores over 24: 16%; ACT scores over 30: 1%.

Faculty *Total:* 100, 41% full-time, 15% with terminal degrees. *Student/faculty ratio:* 25:1.

Academics *Calendar:* semesters. *Degrees:* certificates, associate, and bachelor's. *Special study options:* academic remediation for entering students, adult/continuing education programs, advanced placement credit, distance learning, double majors, honors programs, independent study, internships, part-time degree program, services for LD students, study abroad, summer session for credit.

Computers on Campus Students can access the following: campus intranet, computer help desk, free student e-mail accounts, online (class) grades, online (class) registration, online (class) schedules. Campuswide network is available. 100% of college-owned or -operated housing units are wired for high-speed Internet access. Wireless service is available via classrooms, computer labs, libraries, student centers.

Student Life *Housing:* on-campus residence required for freshman year. *Options:* coed. Campus housing is university owned. Freshman applicants given priority for college housing. *Activities and organizations:* drama/theater group, student-run newspaper, choral group, Community Chorus, Circle K, Agriculture and Forestry Club, Business Club. *Campus security:* 24-hour patrols, late-night transport/escort service, controlled dormitory access. *Student services:* health clinic, personal/psychological counseling.

Athletics Member NJCAA. *Intercollegiate sports:* baseball M(s), basketball M(s)/W(s), golf M(s)/W(s), soccer M/W, softball W(s), volleyball W(s). *Intramural sports:* basketball M/W, football M/W, volleyball M/W.

Standardized Tests *Required for some:* SAT or ACT (for admission).

Costs (2010–11) *Tuition:* state resident $2280 full-time, $95 per credit hour part-time; nonresident $8140 full-time, $340 per credit hour part-time. Part-time tuition and fees vary according to course load. *Required fees:* $606 full-time, $26 per credit hour part-time.

Financial Aid Of all full-time matriculated undergraduates who enrolled in 2009, 70 Federal Work-Study jobs (averaging $1300).

Applying *Options:* electronic application, early admission. *Required:* high school transcript. *Application deadlines:* rolling (freshmen), rolling (transfers).

Freshman Application Contact Ms. Beth Little, Director of Enrollment Services, Potomac State College of West Virginia University, 75 Arnold Street, Keyser, WV 26726. *Phone:* 304-788-6820. *Toll-free phone:* 800-262-7332 Ext. 6820. *Fax:* 304-788-6939. *E-mail:* go2psc@mail.wvu.edu. *Web site:* http://www.potomacstatecollege.edu/.

Salem International University

Salem, West Virginia

Freshman Application Contact Ms. Gina Cossey, Vice President, Recruiting and Admissions, Salem International University, PO Box 500, Salem, WV 26426-0500. *Phone:* 304-326-1359. *Toll-free phone:* 800-283-4562. *Fax:* 304-326-1592. *E-mail:* admissions@salemiu.edu. *Web site:* http://www.salemu.edu/.

Shepherd University

Shepherdstown, West Virginia

- **State-supported** comprehensive, founded 1871, part of West Virginia Higher Education Policy Commission
- **Small-town** 320-acre campus with easy access to Washington, D.C.
- **Endowment** $24.8 million
- **Coed** 4,080 undergraduate students, 82% full-time, 57% women, 43% men
- **Moderately difficult** entrance level, 88% of applicants were admitted

Undergraduates 3,363 full-time, 717 part-time. Students come from 49 states and territories; 9 other countries; 40% are from out of state; 9% transferred in; 34% live on campus. *Retention:* 70% of full-time freshmen returned.

Freshmen *Admission:* 2,024 applied, 1,776 admitted, 769 enrolled. *Average high school GPA:* 3.23. *Test scores:* SAT critical reading scores over 500: 54%; SAT math scores over 500: 50%; ACT scores over 18: 95%; SAT critical reading scores over 600: 12%; SAT math scores over 600: 11%; ACT scores over 24: 34%; SAT critical reading scores over 700: 1%; SAT math scores over 700: 1%; ACT scores over 30: 2%.

Faculty *Total:* 343, 36% full-time, 49% with terminal degrees. *Student/faculty ratio:* 19:1.

Academics *Calendar:* semesters. *Degrees:* bachelor's and master's. *Special study options:* academic remediation for entering students, accelerated degree program, adult/continuing education programs, advanced placement credit, cooperative education, distance learning, double majors, honors programs, independent study, internships, part-time degree program, services for LD students, study abroad, summer session for credit. *ROTC:* Air Force (c).

Computers on Campus 350 computers/terminals and 150 ports are available on campus for general student use. Students can access the following: campus intranet, computer help desk, free student e-mail accounts, online (class) grades, online (class) registration, online (class) schedules, personal Web pages. Campuswide network is available. 100% of college-owned or -operated housing units are wired for high-speed Internet access. Wireless service is available via classrooms, computer labs, libraries, student centers.

Student Life *Housing:* on-campus residence required through senior year. *Options:* coed. Campus housing is university owned. Freshman applicants given priority for college housing. *Activities and organizations:* drama/theater group, student-run newspaper, radio station, choral group, marching band, Student Government Association, Sigma Sigma Sigma, Delta Zeta, Relay for Life, marching band, national fraternities, national sororities. *Campus security:* 24-hour emergency response devices and patrols, late-night transport/escort service, controlled dormitory access, student security in academic buildings. *Student services:* health clinic, personal/psychological counseling.

Athletics Member NCAA. All Division II. *Intercollegiate sports:* baseball M(s), basketball M(s)/W(s), football M(s), golf M(s), lacrosse W(s), soccer M(s)/W(s), softball W(s), tennis M(s)/W(s), volleyball W(s). *Intramural sports:* basketball M/W, bowling M/W, football M/W, racquetball M/W, soccer M/W, softball M/W, swimming and diving M/W, table tennis M/W, tennis M/W, ultimate Frisbee M/W, volleyball M/W, water polo M/W, weight lifting M/W, wrestling M/W.

Standardized Tests *Required:* SAT or ACT (for admission).

Costs (2010–11) *Tuition:* state resident $5234 full-time, $214 per credit hour part-time; nonresident $14,046 full-time, $581 per credit hour part-time. Full-time tuition and fees vary according to program and reciprocity agreements. Part-time tuition and fees vary according to program. *Room and board:* $7720. Room and board charges vary according to board plan and housing facility. *Payment plan:* installment. *Waivers:* minority students, senior citizens, and employees or children of employees.

Financial Aid Of all full-time matriculated undergraduates who enrolled in 2009, 3,051 applied for aid, 2,013 were judged to have need, 542 had their need fully met. 142 Federal Work-Study jobs (averaging $1532). 484 state and other part-time jobs (averaging $2324). In 2009, 717 non-need-based awards were made. *Average percent of need met:* 80%. *Average financial aid package:* $11,294. *Average need-based loan:* $3973. *Average need-based gift aid:* $5129. *Average non-need-based aid:* $9351. *Average indebtedness upon graduation:* $20,429.

Applying *Options:* electronic application, early admission, early action, deferred entrance. *Application fee:* $45. *Required:* high school transcript, minimum 2 GPA. *Recommended:* essay or personal statement, minimum 3 GPA, 3 letters of recommendation. *Application deadlines:* rolling (freshmen), rolling (out-of-state freshmen), rolling (transfers), 11/15 (early action). *Notification:* continuous until 8/15 (freshmen), continuous until 8/15 (out-of-state freshmen), continuous until 8/15 (transfers), 12/15 (early action).

Freshman Application Contact Mr. Randall Friend, Director of Admissions, Shepherd University, PO Box 5000, Shepherdstown, WV 25443-5000. *Phone:* 304-876-5212. *Toll-free phone:* 800-344-5231. *Fax:* 304-876-5165. *E-mail:* admissions@shepherd.edu. *Web site:* http://www.shepherd.edu/.

Strayer University - Teays Valley Campus
Scott Depot, West Virginia
- **Proprietary** comprehensive
- **Coed**

Academics *Degrees:* certificates, diplomas, associate, bachelor's, master's, and postbachelor's certificates.
Costs (2010–11) *Tuition:* $13,635 full-time, $1590 per course part-time.
Freshman Application Contact Strayer University - Teays Valley Campus, 100 Corporate Center Drive, Scott Depot, WV 25560. *Web site:* http://www.strayer.edu/teays_valley.

University of Charleston
Charleston, West Virginia
- **Independent** comprehensive, founded 1888
- **Urban** 40-acre campus
- **Endowment** $28.1 million
- **Coed** 1,135 undergraduate students, 96% full-time, 60% women, 40% men
- **Moderately difficult** entrance level, 56% of applicants were admitted

Undergraduates 1,095 full-time, 40 part-time. Students come from 37 states and territories; 35 other countries; 37% are from out of state; 10% Black or African American, non-Hispanic/Latino; 0.7% Hispanic/Latino; 0.8% Asian, non-Hispanic/Latino; 0.4% American Indian or Alaska Native, non-Hispanic/Latino; 2% Two or more races, non-Hispanic/Latino; 19% Race/ethnicity unknown; 13% international; 10% transferred in; 59% live on campus. *Retention:* 70% of full-time freshmen returned.
Freshmen *Admission:* 1,780 applied, 1,002 admitted, 339 enrolled. *Average high school GPA:* 3.35. *Test scores:* SAT critical reading scores over 500: 36%; SAT math scores over 500: 51%; ACT scores over 18: 95%; SAT critical reading scores over 600: 7%; SAT math scores over 600: 12%; ACT scores over 24: 39%; SAT critical reading scores over 700: 1%; SAT math scores over 700: 2%; ACT scores over 30: 3%.
Faculty *Total:* 130, 61% full-time, 40% with terminal degrees. *Student/faculty ratio:* 16:1.
Academics *Calendar:* semesters. *Degrees:* associate, bachelor's, master's, and doctoral-professional. *Special study options:* academic remediation for entering students, accelerated degree program, adult/continuing education programs, advanced placement credit, distance learning, double majors, English as a second language, independent study, internships, part-time degree program, services for LD students, student-designed majors, study abroad, summer session for credit. *ROTC:* Army (b). *Unusual degree programs:* 3-2 business administration.
Computers on Campus 200 computers/terminals are available on campus for general student use. Students can access the following: campus intranet, computer help desk, free student e-mail accounts, online (class) grades, online (class) registration, online (class) schedules. Campuswide network is available. 100% of college-owned or -operated housing units are wired for high-speed Internet access. Wireless service is available via entire campus.
Student Life *Housing:* on-campus residence required through sophomore year. *Options:* coed, disabled students. Campus housing is university owned. Freshman campus housing is guaranteed. *Activities and organizations:* drama/theater group, student-run newspaper, choral group, Student Activities Board, American Society of Interior Designers, Student Government Association, Capitol Association of Nursing Students, International Student Organization, national fraternities. *Campus security:* 24-hour emergency response devices and patrols, student patrols, late-night transport/escort service, controlled dormitory access, radio connection to city police and ambulance. *Student services:* health clinic, personal/psychological counseling.
Athletics Member NCAA. All Division II. *Intercollegiate sports:* baseball M(s), basketball M(s)/W(s), cheerleading W(s), crew M(s)/W(s), cross-country running M(s)/W(s), football M(s), golf M(s), soccer M(s)/W(s), softball W(s), swimming and diving M(s)/W(s), tennis M(s)/W(s), track and field M(s)/W(s), volleyball W(s). *Intramural sports:* basketball M/W, bowling M/W, football M/W, tennis M/W, volleyball M/W, water polo M/W.
Standardized Tests *Required:* SAT or ACT (for admission).
Costs (2011–12) *Comprehensive fee:* $33,800 includes full-time tuition ($25,000) and room and board ($8800). Part-time tuition: $410 per credit hour. Part-time tuition and fees vary according to program. *College room only:* $4800. Room and board charges vary according to board plan and housing facility. *Payment plan:* installment. *Waivers:* children of alumni, senior citizens, and employees or children of employees.
Financial Aid Of all full-time matriculated undergraduates who enrolled in 2008, 995 applied for aid, 875 were judged to have need, 297 had their need fully met. *Average percent of need met:* 87%. *Average financial aid package:* $21,500. *Average need-based loan:* $8100. *Average need-based gift aid:* $7150. *Average indebtedness upon graduation:* $23,250.

Applying *Options:* electronic application, early admission, deferred entrance. *Application fee:* $25. *Required:* high school transcript, minimum 2.25 GPA. *Required for some:* interview. *Recommended:* essay or personal statement, 3 letters of recommendation. *Application deadlines:* rolling (freshmen), rolling (transfers). *Notification:* continuous (freshmen), continuous (transfers).
Freshman Application Contact Amanda Pritt, Dean of Admissions, University of Charleston, 2300 MacCorkle Avenue, SE, Charleston, WV 25304. *Phone:* 304-357-4750. *Toll-free phone:* 800-995-GOUC. *E-mail:* admissions@ucwv.edu. *Web site:* http://www.ucwv.edu/.

West Liberty University
West Liberty, West Virginia
- **State-supported** comprehensive, founded 1837, part of West Virginia Higher Education Policy Commission
- **Rural** campus with easy access to Pittsburgh, PA
- **Endowment** $9.1 million
- **Coed** 2,687 undergraduate students, 87% full-time, 57% women, 43% men
- **Minimally difficult** entrance level

Undergraduates 2,331 full-time, 356 part-time. Students come from 24 states and territories; 29 other countries; 30% are from out of state; 10% transferred in; 47% live on campus. *Retention:* 74% of full-time freshmen returned.
Freshmen *Admission:* 1,941 applied, 534 enrolled. *Average high school GPA:* 3.25. *Test scores:* SAT critical reading scores over 500: 40%; SAT math scores over 500: 49%; SAT writing scores over 500: 30%; ACT scores over 18: 75%; SAT critical reading scores over 600: 11%; SAT math scores over 600: 19%; SAT writing scores over 600: 6%; ACT scores over 24: 19%; SAT math scores over 700: 9%; ACT scores over 30: 1%.
Faculty *Total:* 197, 60% full-time, 32% with terminal degrees. *Student/faculty ratio:* 18:1.
Academics *Calendar:* semesters. *Degrees:* associate, bachelor's, and master's. *Special study options:* academic remediation for entering students, accelerated degree program, adult/continuing education programs, advanced placement credit, double majors, external degree program, honors programs, independent study, internships, off-campus study, part-time degree program, student-designed majors, summer session for credit. *ROTC:* Army (b).
Computers on Campus 400 computers/terminals are available on campus for general student use. Students can access the following: campus intranet, computer help desk, free student e-mail accounts, online (class) grades, online (class) registration, online (class) schedules. Campuswide network is available. 100% of college-owned or -operated housing units are wired for high-speed Internet access. Wireless service is available via classrooms, computer labs, dorm rooms, learning centers, libraries, student centers.
Student Life *Housing options:* coed, men-only, women-only, disabled students. Campus housing is university owned. *Activities and organizations:* drama/theater group, student-run newspaper, radio and television station, choral group, marching band, Delta Sigma Pi, student government, Drama Club, Students in Free Enterprise (SIFE), Chi Nu, national fraternities, national sororities. *Campus security:* 24-hour emergency response devices and patrols, controlled dormitory access. *Student services:* health clinic, personal/psychological counseling.
Athletics Member NCAA. All Division II. *Intercollegiate sports:* baseball M(s), basketball M(s)/W(s), cross-country running M(s)/W(s), football M(s), golf M(s)/W(s), softball W(s), tennis M(s)/W(s), track and field M(s)/W(s), volleyball W(s), wrestling M(s). *Intramural sports:* basketball M/W, golf M/W, racquetball M/W, softball M/W, table tennis M/W, tennis M/W, volleyball M/W.
Standardized Tests *Required:* SAT or ACT (for admission).
Costs (2010–11) *Tuition:* state resident $4880 full-time, $203 per credit hour part-time; nonresident $12,750 full-time, $531 per credit hour part-time. Full-time tuition and fees vary according to course load, degree level, and program. Part-time tuition and fees vary according to course load, degree level, and program. *Room and board:* $7310; room only: $4250. Room and board charges vary according to board plan and housing facility. *Payment plans:* installment, deferred payment. *Waivers:* senior citizens and employees or children of employees.
Financial Aid Of all full-time matriculated undergraduates who enrolled in 2008, 2,006 applied for aid, 1,679 were judged to have need, 782 had their need fully met. In 2008, 58 non-need-based awards were made. *Average percent of need met:* 68%. *Average financial aid package:* $8924. *Average need-based loan:* $4064. *Average need-based gift aid:* $6162. *Average non-need-based aid:* $1745. *Average indebtedness upon graduation:* $19,200.
Applying *Options:* electronic application. *Required:* high school transcript, minimum 2 GPA. *Recommended:* interview. *Application deadlines:* rolling (freshmen), rolling (transfers). *Notification:* continuous (freshmen), continuous (transfers).
Freshman Application Contact Ms. Stephanie North, Admissions Counselor, West Liberty University, PO Box 295, West Liberty, WV 26074. *Phone:* 304-

336-8078. *Toll-free phone:* 800-732-6204 Ext. 8076. *Fax:* 304-336-8403. *E-mail:* wladmsn1@westliberty.edu. *Web site:* http://www.westliberty.edu/.

West Virginia State University
Institute, West Virginia

- **State-supported** comprehensive, founded 1891, part of State College System of West Virginia
- **Suburban** 98-acre campus
- **Coed**
- **Minimally difficult** entrance level

Faculty *Student/faculty ratio:* 19:1.
Academics *Calendar:* semesters. *Degrees:* bachelor's and master's.
Student Life *Campus security:* 24-hour emergency response devices and patrols, late-night transport/escort service.
Athletics Member NCAA. All Division II.
Standardized Tests *Required for some:* SAT or ACT (for admission). *Recommended:* SAT (for admission).
Financial Aid *Financial aid deadline:* 6/15.
Applying *Options:* electronic application, early admission. *Required:* high school transcript.
Freshman Application Contact Mr. Christopher D. Jackson, Interim Director of Recruiting, West Virginia State University, Campus Box 197, PO Box 1000, Ferrell Hall, Room 106, Institute, WV 25112-1000. *Phone:* 304-766-3033. *Toll-free phone:* 800-987-2112. *Fax:* 304-766-5182. *E-mail:* jacksoc@wvstateu.edu. *Web site:* http://www.wvstateu.edu/.

West Virginia University
Morgantown, West Virginia

- **State-supported** university, founded 1867, part of West Virginia Higher Education Policy Commission
- **Small-town** 1400-acre campus with easy access to Pittsburgh
- **Endowment** $322.4 million
- **Coed** 22,303 undergraduate students, 93% full-time, 45% women, 55% men
- **Moderately difficult** entrance level, 86% of applicants were admitted

Undergraduates 20,809 full-time, 1,494 part-time. Students come from 52 states and territories; 67 other countries; 45% are from out of state; 3% Black or African American, non-Hispanic/Latino; 3% Hispanic/Latino; 1% Asian, non-Hispanic/Latino; 0.1% Native Hawaiian or other Pacific Islander, non-Hispanic/Latino; 0.3% American Indian or Alaska Native, non-Hispanic/Latino; 2% Two or more races, non-Hispanic/Latino; 0.7% Race/ethnicity unknown; 2% international; 4% transferred in; 24% live on campus. *Retention:* 80% of full-time freshmen returned.
Freshmen *Admission:* 14,905 applied, 12,838 admitted, 5,034 enrolled. *Average high school GPA:* 3.32. *Test scores:* SAT critical reading scores over 500: 56%; SAT math scores over 500: 68%; ACT scores over 18: 96%; SAT critical reading scores over 600: 13%; SAT math scores over 600: 20%; ACT scores over 24: 48%; SAT critical reading scores over 700: 2%; SAT math scores over 700: 2%; ACT scores over 30: 7%.
Faculty *Total:* 1,235, 76% full-time, 68% with terminal degrees. *Student/faculty ratio:* 23:1.
Academics *Calendar:* semesters. *Degrees:* bachelor's, master's, doctoral-professional, and doctoral-research/scholarship. *Special study options:* academic remediation for entering students, accelerated degree program, adult/continuing education programs, advanced placement credit, distance learning, double majors, English as a second language, external degree program, honors programs, independent study, internships, off-campus study, part-time degree program, services for LD students, student-designed majors, study abroad, summer session for credit. *ROTC:* Army (b), Air Force (b). *Unusual degree programs:* 3-2 education, business/foreign language, occupational therapy, physical therapy, social work.
Computers on Campus 2,500 computers/terminals are available on campus for general student use. Students can access the following: campus intranet, computer help desk, free student e-mail accounts, online (class) grades, online (class) registration, online (class) schedules. Campuswide network is available. 100% of college-owned or -operated housing units are wired for high-speed Internet access. Wireless service is available via classrooms, computer centers, dorm rooms, libraries, student centers.
Student Life *Housing:* on-campus residence required for freshman year. *Options:* coed, men-only, women-only, cooperative, disabled students. Campus housing is university owned and leased by the school. Freshman campus housing is guaranteed. *Activities and organizations:* drama/theater group, student-run newspaper, radio station, choral group, marching band, Residential Hall Association, Alpha Phi Omega, WVU Greek System, Mountaineer Maniacs, Campus Crusade for Christ, national fraternities, national sororities. *Campus security:* 24-hour emergency response devices and patrols, student patrols, late-night transport/escort service, controlled dormitory access, patrol officers

just for housing. *Student services:* health clinic, personal/psychological counseling, women's center, legal services.
Athletics Member NCAA. All Division I except football (Division I-A). *Intercollegiate sports:* baseball M(s), basketball M(s)/W(s), cheerleading M(s)/W(s), crew W(s), cross-country running W(s), gymnastics W(s), riflery M(s)/W(s), soccer M(s)/W(s), swimming and diving M(s)/W(s), tennis W(s), track and field W(s), volleyball W(s), wrestling M(s). *Intramural sports:* basketball M(c)/W(c), cheerleading M(c)/W(c), crew M(c)/W(c), equestrian sports M(c)/W(c), fencing M(c)/W(c), football M, golf M(c)/W(c), ice hockey M(c), lacrosse M(c)/W(c), riflery M/W, rock climbing M(c)/W(c), rugby M(c)/W(c), skiing (cross-country) M(c)/W(c), skiing (downhill) M(c)/W(c), soccer M/W, softball M(c)/W(c), swimming and diving M/W, tennis M(c)/W(c), track and field M(c)/W, ultimate Frisbee M(c)/W(c), volleyball M(c)/W, wrestling M(c).
Standardized Tests *Required:* SAT or ACT (for admission).
Costs (2010–11) *Tuition:* state resident $5406 full-time, $225 per credit hour part-time; nonresident $17,002 full-time, $708 per credit hour part-time. Full-time tuition and fees vary according to location, program, and reciprocity agreements. Part-time tuition and fees vary according to course load, location, program, and reciprocity agreements. *Room and board:* $8120. Room and board charges vary according to board plan, housing facility, and location. *Payment plan:* installment. *Waivers:* senior citizens and employees or children of employees.
Financial Aid Of all full-time matriculated undergraduates who enrolled in 2009, 16,197 applied for aid, 12,634 were judged to have need, 3,120 had their need fully met. In 2009, 3567 non-need-based awards were made. *Average percent of need met:* 75%. *Average financial aid package:* $7200. *Average need-based loan:* $4675. *Average need-based gift aid:* $5029. *Average non-need-based aid:* $2081. *Financial aid deadline:* 3/1.
Applying *Options:* early admission, deferred entrance. *Application fee:* $25. *Required:* high school transcript, minimum 2 GPA. *Required for some:* essay or personal statement, minimum 2.25 GPA. *Application deadlines:* 8/1 (freshmen), 8/1 (transfers). *Notification:* continuous (transfers).
Freshman Application Contact Ms. Kim Guynn, Assistant Director of Admissions, West Virginia University, PO Box 6009, Morgantown, WV 26506-6009. *Phone:* 304-293-2124. *Toll-free phone:* 800-344-9881. *Fax:* 304-293-3080. *Web site:* http://www.wvu.edu/.

West Virginia University at Parkersburg
Parkersburg, West Virginia

Freshman Application Contact Christine Post, Associate Dean of Enrollment Management, West Virginia University at Parkersburg, 300 Campus Drive, Parkersburg, WV 26104. *Phone:* 304-424-8223 Ext. 223. *Toll-free phone:* 800-WVA-WVUP. *Fax:* 304-424-8332. *E-mail:* christine.post@mail.wvu.edu. *Web site:* http://www.wvup.edu/.

West Virginia University Institute of Technology
Montgomery, West Virginia

- **State-supported** comprehensive, founded 1895, part of University System of West Virginia
- **Small-town** 200-acre campus with easy access to Charleston
- **Endowment** $1.9 million
- **Coed**
- **Minimally difficult** entrance level

Faculty *Student/faculty ratio:* 14:1.
Academics *Calendar:* semesters. *Degrees:* certificates, associate, bachelor's, and master's.
Student Life *Campus security:* 24-hour emergency response devices and patrols, late-night transport/escort service.
Athletics Member NAIA.
Standardized Tests *Required:* SAT or ACT (for admission). *Required for some:* TOEFL or IELTS.
Costs (2010–11) *Tuition:* state resident $4460 full-time, $215 per credit hour part-time; nonresident $12,560 full-time, $553 per credit hour part-time. Full-time tuition and fees vary according to program. Part-time tuition and fees vary according to course load and program. *Required fees:* $704 full-time. *Room and board:* $8130; room only: $4800. Room and board charges vary according to board plan and housing facility.
Financial Aid Of all full-time matriculated undergraduates who enrolled in 2009, 975 applied for aid, 825 were judged to have need, 271 had their need fully met. 79 Federal Work-Study jobs (averaging $1151). 127 state and other part-time jobs (averaging $1006). In 2009, 50 non-need-based awards were made. *Average percent of need met:* 34. *Average financial aid package:* $9374. *Average need-based loan:* $3612. *Average need-based gift aid:* $4779.

Average non-need-based aid: $5227. *Average indebtedness upon graduation:* $18,319.

Applying *Options:* electronic application, early admission. *Required:* high school transcript, minimum 2 GPA.

Freshman Application Contact West Virginia University Institute of Technology, 405 Fayette Pike, Montgomery, WV 25136. *Phone:* 304-981-6240. *Toll-free phone:* 888-554-8324. *Web site:* http://www.wvutech.edu/.

West Virginia Wesleyan College
Buckhannon, West Virginia

- **Independent** comprehensive, founded 1890, affiliated with United Methodist Church
- **Small-town** 80-acre campus
- **Endowment** $30.7 million
- **Coed**
- **Moderately difficult** entrance level

Faculty *Student/faculty ratio:* 13:1.

Academics *Calendar:* semesters. *Degrees:* bachelor's and master's.

Student Life *Campus security:* 24-hour emergency response devices and patrols, student patrols, late-night transport/escort service, controlled dormitory access.

Athletics Member NCAA. All Division II.

Standardized Tests *Required:* SAT or ACT (for admission). *Required for some:* SAT Subject Tests (for admission).

Costs (2010–11) *Comprehensive fee:* $31,120 includes full-time tuition ($23,130), mandatory fees ($850), and room and board ($7140). Full-time tuition and fees vary according to course load. Part-time tuition and fees vary according to course load. *Room and board:* Room and board charges vary according to board plan and housing facility.

Financial Aid *Of all full-time matriculated undergraduates who enrolled in 2009,* 1,302 applied for aid, 1,009 were judged to have need, 331 had their need fully met. *In 2009,* 262 non-need-based awards were made. *Average percent of need met:* 78. *Average financial aid package:* $23,785. *Average need-based loan:* $4189. *Average need-based gift aid:* $18,591. *Average non-need-based aid:* $12,053. *Average indebtedness upon graduation:* $21,502.

Applying *Options:* electronic application, deferred entrance. *Application fee:* $35. *Required:* high school transcript. *Recommended:* essay or personal statement, interview.

Freshman Application Contact John Waltz, Director of Admission, West Virginia Wesleyan College, 59 College Avenue, Buckhannon, WV 26201. *Phone:* 304-473-8510. *Toll-free phone:* 800-722-9933. *Fax:* 304-473-8108. *E-mail:* admission@wvwc.edu. *Web site:* http://www.wvwc.edu/.

Wheeling Jesuit University
Wheeling, West Virginia

- **Independent Roman Catholic (Jesuit)** comprehensive, founded 1954
- **Suburban** 65-acre campus with easy access to Pittsburgh
- **Endowment** $14.7 million
- **Coed** 1,062 undergraduate students, 84% full-time, 60% women, 40% men
- **Moderately difficult** entrance level, 72% of applicants were admitted

Undergraduates 892 full-time, 170 part-time. Students come from 27 states and territories; 13 other countries; 63% are from out of state; 4% Black or African American, non-Hispanic/Latino; 1% Hispanic/Latino; 1% Asian, non-Hispanic/Latino; 0.1% American Indian or Alaska Native, non-Hispanic/Latino; 54% Race/ethnicity unknown; 4% international; 2% transferred in; 78% live on campus. *Retention:* 85% of full-time freshmen returned.

Freshmen *Admission:* 1,285 applied, 920 admitted, 259 enrolled. *Average high school GPA:* 3.5. *Test scores:* SAT critical reading scores over 500: 58%; SAT math scores over 500: 65%; ACT scores over 18: 96%; SAT critical reading scores over 600: 15%; SAT math scores over 600: 15%; ACT scores over 24: 44%; SAT critical reading scores over 700: 1%; SAT math scores over 700: 2%; ACT scores over 30: 3%.

Faculty *Total:* 138, 56% full-time, 53% with terminal degrees. *Student/faculty ratio:* 12:1.

Academics *Calendar:* semesters. *Degrees:* bachelor's, master's, doctoral-professional, and postbachelor's certificates. *Special study options:* academic remediation for entering students, accelerated degree program, adult/continuing education programs, advanced placement credit, distance learning, double majors, English as a second language, external degree program, honors programs, independent study, internships, off-campus study, part-time degree program, services for LD students, student-designed majors, study abroad, summer session for credit. *Unusual degree programs:* 3-2 engineering with Case Western Reserve University.

Computers on Campus 245 computers/terminals are available on campus for general student use. Students can access the following: campus intranet, computer help desk, free student e-mail accounts, online (class) grades, online (class) registration, online (class) schedules. Campuswide network is available. 100% of college-owned or -operated housing units are wired for high-speed Internet access. Wireless service is available via entire campus.

Student Life *Housing:* on-campus residence required for freshman year. *Options:* coed, men-only, women-only, cooperative, disabled students. Campus housing is university owned. Freshman campus housing is guaranteed. *Activities and organizations:* drama/theater group, student-run newspaper, television station, choral group, Campus Activity Board (CAB), Theater Guild, Student Senate, International Student Club, Campus Ministry. *Campus security:* 24-hour emergency response devices and patrols, student patrols, late-night transport/escort service, controlled dormitory access. *Student services:* health clinic, personal/psychological counseling, women's center.

Athletics Member NCAA. All Division II. *Intercollegiate sports:* baseball M(s), basketball M(s)/W(s), cheerleading M(c)/W(c), cross-country running M(s)/W(s), golf M(s)/W(s), lacrosse M(s)/W(s), rugby M(c)/W(c), soccer M(s)/W(s), softball W(s), swimming and diving M(s)/W(s), track and field M(s)/W(s), volleyball W(s). *Intramural sports:* basketball M/W, cross-country running M/W, football M, racquetball M/W, soccer M/W, softball M/W, tennis M/W, ultimate Frisbee M/W, volleyball M/W.

Standardized Tests *Required:* SAT or ACT (for admission).

Costs (2011–12) *Comprehensive fee:* $33,884 includes full-time tuition ($23,950), mandatory fees ($1060), and room and board ($8874). Full-time tuition and fees vary according to program. Part-time tuition: $655 per hour. Part-time tuition and fees vary according to program. *College room only:* $3906. Room and board charges vary according to board plan and housing facility. *Payment plan:* installment. *Waivers:* employees or children of employees.

Financial Aid Of all full-time matriculated undergraduates who enrolled in 2009, 809 applied for aid, 707 were judged to have need, 220 had their need fully met. 151 Federal Work-Study jobs (averaging $2200). 157 state and other part-time jobs (averaging $2200). In 2009, 88 non-need-based awards were made. *Average percent of need met:* 84%. *Average financial aid package:* $22,153. *Average need-based loan:* $4850. *Average need-based gift aid:* $6399. *Average non-need-based aid:* $11,853. *Average indebtedness upon graduation:* $32,927.

Applying *Options:* electronic application, deferred entrance. *Application fee:* $25. *Required:* high school transcript. *Required for some:* interview. *Recommended:* essay or personal statement, minimum 2.5 GPA, 2 letters of recommendation, interview. *Application deadlines:* rolling (freshmen), rolling (transfers). *Notification:* continuous (freshmen), continuous (transfers).

Freshman Application Contact Ms. Beth Loy, Director of Admissions, Wheeling Jesuit University, 316 Washington Avenue, Wheeling, WV 26003. *Phone:* 304-243-2425. *Toll-free phone:* 800-624-6992 Ext. 2359. *Fax:* 304-243-2397. *E-mail:* bloy@wju.edu. *Web site:* http://www.wju.edu/.

WISCONSIN

Alverno College
Milwaukee, Wisconsin

- **Independent Roman Catholic** comprehensive, founded 1887
- **Urban** 46-acre campus
- **Endowment** $17.4 million
- **Undergraduate: women only; graduate: coed** 2,324 undergraduate students, 72% full-time, 100% women
- **Moderately difficult** entrance level, 78% of applicants were admitted

Undergraduates 1,665 full-time, 659 part-time. Students come from 12 states and territories; 14 other countries; 3% are from out of state; 18% Black or African American, non-Hispanic/Latino; 15% Hispanic/Latino; 5% Asian, non-Hispanic/Latino; 0.1% Native Hawaiian or other Pacific Islander, non-Hispanic/Latino; 1% American Indian or Alaska Native, non-Hispanic/Latino; 2% Two or more races, non-Hispanic/Latino; 0.6% international; 10% transferred in; 9% live on campus. *Retention:* 69% of full-time freshmen returned.

Freshmen *Admission:* 647 applied, 507 admitted, 264 enrolled. *Average high school GPA:* 2.8. *Test scores:* ACT scores over 18: 63%; ACT scores over 24: 10%.

Faculty *Total:* 262, 46% full-time, 76% with terminal degrees. *Student/faculty ratio:* 12:1.

Academics *Calendar:* semesters. *Degrees:* associate, bachelor's, master's, post-master's, and postbachelor's certificates (also offers weekend program with significant enrollment not reflected in profile). *Special study options:* academic remediation for entering students, adult/continuing education programs, advanced placement credit, double majors, independent study, internships, part-time degree program, services for LD students, student-designed majors, study abroad, summer session for credit. *ROTC:* Army (c), Air Force (c).

Computers on Campus 604 computers/terminals are available on campus for general student use. Students can access the following: campus intranet, free student e-mail accounts, online (class) registration, online (class) schedules. Campuswide network is available. 100% of college-owned or -operated housing units are wired for high-speed Internet access. Wireless service is available via classrooms, computer centers, computer labs, dorm rooms, libraries.

Student Life *Housing options:* women-only. Campus housing is university owned. Freshman campus housing is guaranteed. *Activities and organizations:* drama/theater group, student-run newspaper, radio station, choral group, Student Nurses Association, Association for Women in Communication, Women of Asian Ethnicity, Circle K, Gay-Straight Alliance. *Campus security:* 24-hour emergency response devices and patrols, late-night transport/escort service, controlled dormitory access, well-lit parking lots and pathways, emergency first-aid and CPR, crisis intervention team and plan in place. *Student services:* health clinic, personal/psychological counseling.

Athletics Member NCAA. All Division III. *Intercollegiate sports:* basketball W, cross-country running W, soccer W, softball W, tennis W, volleyball W.

Standardized Tests *Required:* SAT or ACT (for admission).

Costs (2011–12) *Comprehensive fee:* $28,029 includes full-time tuition ($20,538), mandatory fees ($525), and room and board ($6966). Full-time tuition and fees vary according to program. Part-time tuition and fees vary according to program. *Room and board:* Room and board charges vary according to board plan and housing facility. *Payment plans:* installment, deferred payment. *Waivers:* employees or children of employees.

Financial Aid Of all full-time matriculated undergraduates who enrolled in 2009, 1,548 applied for aid, 1,440 were judged to have need. 183 Federal Work-Study jobs (averaging $2324). In 2009, 166 non-need-based awards were made. *Average financial aid package:* $15,269. *Average need-based loan:* $4058. *Average need-based gift aid:* $11,209. *Average non-need-based aid:* $6159. *Average indebtedness upon graduation:* $33,220.

Applying *Options:* electronic application, deferred entrance. *Application fee:* $20. *Required:* essay or personal statement, high school transcript, 2.0 on any college work. *Recommended:* minimum 2 GPA, interview. *Application deadlines:* rolling (freshmen), rolling (transfers). *Notification:* continuous (freshmen), continuous (transfers).

Freshman Application Contact Ms. Holly Baer, Assistant Director for High School Admissions, Alverno College, 3400 South 43 Street, PO Box 343922, Milwaukee, WI 53234-3922. *Phone:* 414-382-6103. *Toll-free phone:* 800-933-3401. *Fax:* 414-382-6055. *E-mail:* admissions@alverno.edu. *Web site:* http://www.alverno.edu/.

The Art Institute of Wisconsin
Milwaukee, Wisconsin

Director of Admissions Director of Admissions, The Art Institute of Wisconsin, 320 East Buffalo Street, Suite 600, Milwaukee, WI 53202. *Phone:* 414-978-5000. *Toll-free phone:* 877-285-4234. *Fax:* 414-978-5182. *Web site:* http://www.artinstitutes.edu/milwaukee.

See page 1082 for the College Close-Up.

Bellin College
Green Bay, Wisconsin

Freshman Application Contact Dr. Penny Croghan, Admissions Director, Bellin College, 3201 Eaton Road, Green Bay, WI 54305. *Phone:* 920-433-5803. *Toll-free phone:* 800-236-8707. *Fax:* 920-433-7416. *E-mail:* admissio@bcon.edu. *Web site:* http://www.bellincollege.edu/.

Beloit College
Beloit, Wisconsin

- **Independent** 4-year, founded 1846
- **Small-town** 65-acre campus with easy access to Chicago and Milwaukee
- **Coed** 1,397 undergraduate students, 95% full-time, 57% women, 43% men
- **Very difficult** entrance level, 72% of applicants were admitted

Undergraduates 1,324 full-time, 73 part-time. 77% are from out of state; 3% Black or African American, non-Hispanic/Latino; 7% Hispanic/Latino; 2% Asian, non-Hispanic/Latino; 0.4% American Indian or Alaska Native, non-Hispanic/Latino; 4% Two or more races, non-Hispanic/Latino; 2% Race/ethnicity unknown; 9% international; 2% transferred in; 94% live on campus. *Retention:* 88% of full-time freshmen returned.

Freshmen *Admission:* 2,003 applied, 1,439 admitted, 333 enrolled. *Average high school GPA:* 3.42. *Test scores:* SAT critical reading scores over 500: 90%; SAT math scores over 500: 89%; ACT scores over 18: 100%; SAT criti-

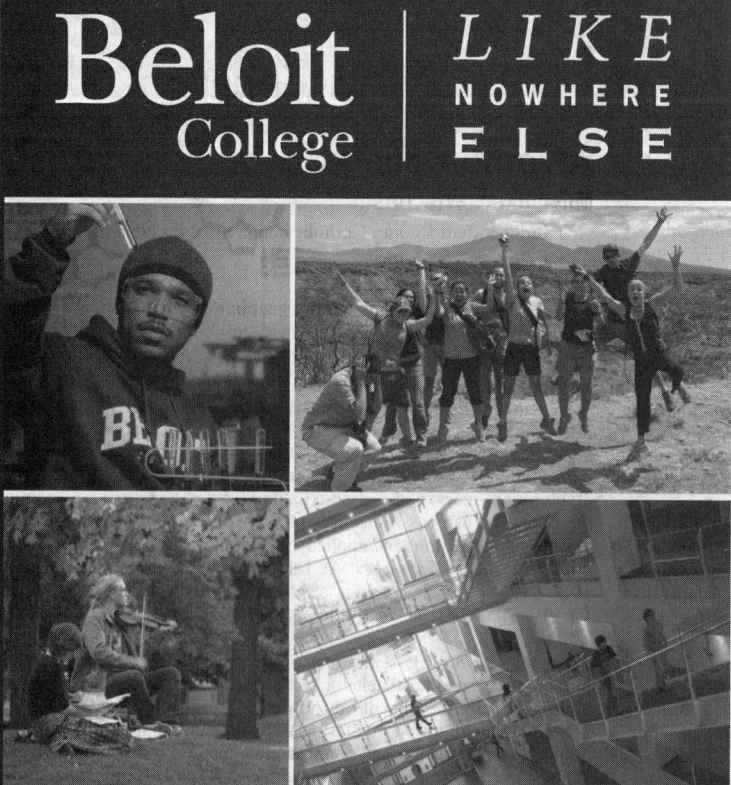

cal reading scores over 600: 69%; SAT math scores over 600: 60%; ACT scores over 24: 82%; SAT critical reading scores over 700: 28%; SAT math scores over 700: 19%; ACT scores over 30: 32%.

Faculty *Total:* 138, 93% full-time, 91% with terminal degrees. *Student/faculty ratio:* 10:1.

Academics *Calendar:* semesters. *Degree:* bachelor's. *Special study options:* adult/continuing education programs, advanced placement credit, double majors, English as a second language, independent study, internships, off-campus study, services for LD students, student-designed majors, study abroad, summer session for credit. *Unusual degree programs:* 3-2 engineering with University of Illinois at Urbana-Champaign, University of Michigan, Rensselaer Polytechnic Institute, Georgia Institute of Technology; forestry with Duke University; nursing with Rush University; medical technology with Rush University.

Computers on Campus Students can access the following: campus intranet, computer help desk, free student e-mail accounts, online (class) grades, online (class) schedules. Campuswide network is available. 100% of college-owned or -operated housing units are wired for high-speed Internet access. Wireless service is available via classrooms, computer centers, computer labs, dorm rooms, libraries, student centers.

Student Life *Housing:* on-campus residence required through junior year. *Options:* coed, women-only, cooperative. Campus housing is university owned. Freshman campus housing is guaranteed. *Activities and organizations:* drama/theater group, student-run newspaper, radio and television station, choral group, national fraternities, national sororities. *Campus security:* 24-hour emergency response devices and patrols, late-night transport/escort service, controlled dormitory access. *Student services:* health clinic, personal/psychological counseling, women's center.

Athletics Member NCAA. All Division III. *Intercollegiate sports:* baseball M, basketball M/W, crew M(c)/W(c), cross-country running M/W, fencing M(c)/W(c), football M, golf M, ice hockey M(c)/W(c), lacrosse M(c)/W(c), soccer M/W, softball W, swimming and diving M/W, tennis M/W, track and field M/W, volleyball W. *Intramural sports:* badminton M/W, basketball M/W, bowling M/W, football M, racquetball M/W, sailing M/W, soccer M/W, tennis M/W, ultimate Frisbee M/W, volleyball M/W, water polo M/W.

Standardized Tests *Required:* SAT or ACT (for admission).

Costs (2010–11) *Comprehensive fee:* $42,202 includes full-time tuition ($34,808), mandatory fees ($230), and room and board ($7164). Part-time tuition: $4351 per course. *College room only:* $3512. Room and board charges vary according to board plan. *Payment plan:* installment. *Waivers:* employees or children of employees.

Financial Aid Of all full-time matriculated undergraduates who enrolled in 2009, 1,004 applied for aid, 868 were judged to have need, 572 had their need fully met. 629 Federal Work-Study jobs (averaging $1741). 419 state and other part-time jobs (averaging $1253). In 2009, 331 non-need-based awards were made. *Average percent of need met:* 96%. *Average financial aid package:* $32,229. *Average need-based loan:* $7236. *Average need-based gift aid:* $22,612. *Average non-need-based aid:* $14,169. *Average indebtedness upon graduation:* $19,930.

Applying *Options:* electronic application, early admission, early action, deferred entrance. *Application fee:* $35. *Required:* essay or personal statement, high school transcript, 1 letter of recommendation. *Required for some:* interview. *Recommended:* interview. *Application deadlines:* 1/15 (freshmen), rolling (transfers), 12/1 (early action). *Notification:* 4/1 (freshmen), continuous (transfers), 1/1 (early action).

Freshman Application Contact Mr. James S. Zielinski, Director of Admissions, Beloit College, 700 College Street, Beloit, WI 53511-5596. *Phone:* 608-363-2500. *Toll-free phone:* 800-9-BELOIT. *Fax:* 608-363-2075. *E-mail:* admiss@beloit.edu. *Web site:* http://www.beloit.edu/.

See page 1118 for the College Close-Up.

Bryant & Stratton College
Milwaukee, Wisconsin

- **Proprietary** primarily 2-year, founded 1863, part of Bryant and Stratton College, Inc.
- **Urban** campus
- **Coed** 828 undergraduate students, 56% full-time, 84% women, 16% men
- **Minimally difficult** entrance level, 89% of applicants were admitted

Undergraduates 460 full-time, 368 part-time. Students come from 1 other state; 33% transferred in. *Retention:* 70% of full-time freshmen returned.

Freshmen *Admission:* 433 applied, 387 admitted, 385 enrolled.

Faculty *Total:* 102, 19% full-time. *Student/faculty ratio:* 13:1.

Academics *Calendar:* semesters. *Degrees:* associate and bachelor's. *Special study options:* academic remediation for entering students, adult/continuing education programs, advanced placement credit, cooperative education, distance learning, double majors, independent study, internships, part-time degree program, summer session for credit.

Computers on Campus 130 computers/terminals are available on campus for general student use. Campuswide network is available.

Student Life *Housing:* college housing not available. *Activities and organizations:* student-run newspaper, Phi Beta Lambda, Association of Information Technology Professionals, Allied Health Association, Institute of Management Accountants, Student Advisory Board. *Campus security:* 24-hour emergency response devices and patrols.

Standardized Tests *Required:* CPAt; ACCUPLACER (for admission). *Recommended:* SAT or ACT (for admission).

Applying *Options:* electronic application. *Required:* high school transcript, interview, entrance and placement evaluations. *Application deadlines:* rolling (freshmen), rolling (transfers). *Notification:* continuous (freshmen), continuous (transfers).

Freshman Application Contact Mr. Dan Basile, Director of Admissions, Bryant & Stratton College, 310 West Wisconsin Avenue, Suite 500 East, Milwaukee, WI 53203-2214. *Phone:* 414-276-5200. *Web site:* http://www.bryantstratton.edu/.

Bryant & Stratton College - Wauwatosa Campus
Wauwatosa, Wisconsin

- **Proprietary** 4-year
- **Suburban** campus with easy access to Milwaukee
- **Coed** 1,264 undergraduate students, 74% full-time, 86% women, 14% men

Undergraduates 930 full-time, 334 part-time. Students come from 2 states and territories. *Retention:* 88% of full-time freshmen returned.

Faculty *Student/faculty ratio:* 10:1.

Academics *Calendar:* semesters. *Degrees:* associate and bachelor's. *Special study options:* academic remediation for entering students, adult/continuing education programs, advanced placement credit, cooperative education, distance learning, double majors, independent study, internships, part-time degree program, services for LD students.

Computers on Campus 125 computers/terminals are available on campus for general student use. Students can access the following: campus intranet, computer help desk, free student e-mail accounts, online (class) grades, online (class) registration, online (class) schedules. Campuswide network is available.

Student Life *Housing:* college housing not available.

Standardized Tests *Required:* TABE, CPAt (for admission). *Recommended:* SAT or ACT (for admission).

Applying *Options:* electronic application. *Required:* high school transcript, interview, entrance and placement evaluation. *Application deadlines:* rolling (freshmen), rolling (transfers). *Notification:* continuous (freshmen), continuous (transfers).

Freshman Application Contact Bryant & Stratton College - Wauwatosa Campus, 10950 W. Potter Road, Wauwatosa, WI 53226. *Phone:* 414-302-7000 Ext. 502. *Web site:* http://www.bryantstratton.edu/.

Cardinal Stritch University
Milwaukee, Wisconsin

Freshman Application Contact Ms. Kristine Bueno, Associate Director of Admissions, Cardinal Stritch University, 6801 North Yates Road, Milwaukee, WI 53217-3985. *Phone:* 414-410-4040. *Toll-free phone:* 800-347-8822 Ext. 4040. *Fax:* 414-410-4058. *E-mail:* admityou@stritch.edu. *Web site:* http://www.stritch.edu/.

Carroll University
Waukesha, Wisconsin

- **Independent Presbyterian** comprehensive, founded 1846
- **Suburban** 52-acre campus with easy access to Milwaukee
- **Endowment** $32.7 million
- **Coed** 3,139 undergraduate students, 85% full-time, 66% women, 34% men
- **Moderately difficult** entrance level, 79% of applicants were admitted

Undergraduates 2,675 full-time, 464 part-time. Students come from 25 states and territories; 25 other countries; 23% are from out of state; 6% transferred in; 52% live on campus. *Retention:* 75% of full-time freshmen returned.

Freshmen *Admission:* 2,512 applied, 1,996 admitted, 760 enrolled. *Average high school GPA:* 3.3. *Test scores:* ACT scores over 18: 97%; ACT scores over 24: 51%; ACT scores over 30: 6%.

Faculty *Total:* 330, 38% full-time, 35% with terminal degrees. *Student/faculty ratio:* 15:1.

Academics *Calendar:* semesters. *Degrees:* bachelor's, master's, and doctoral-professional. *Special study options:* academic remediation for entering students, adult/continuing education programs, advanced placement credit, distance learning, double majors, English as a second language, honors programs, independent study, internships, part-time degree program, services for LD students, student-designed majors, study abroad, summer session for credit. *ROTC:* Army (c), Air Force (c). *Unusual degree programs:* 3-2 engineering with University of Wisconsin-Platteville, University of Wisconsin-Milwaukee; Pharmacy - Rosalind Franklin University of Medicine and Science.

Computers on Campus 400 computers/terminals and 100 ports are available on campus for general student use. Students can access the following: campus intranet, computer help desk, free student e-mail accounts, online (class) grades, online (class) registration, online (class) schedules. Campuswide network is available. 100% of college-owned or -operated housing units are wired for high-speed Internet access. Wireless service is available via classrooms, computer centers, computer labs, libraries, student centers.

Student Life *Housing:* on-campus residence required through sophomore year. *Options:* coed, women-only, disabled students. Campus housing is university owned. Freshman campus housing is guaranteed. *Activities and organizations:* drama/theater group, student-run newspaper, radio station, choral group, College Activities Board, Student Senate, Black Student Union, Intervarsity Christian Fellowship, Latin American Student Organization, national sororities. *Campus security:* 24-hour emergency response devices and patrols, student patrols, late-night transport/escort service, controlled dormitory access. *Student services:* health clinic, personal/psychological counseling.

Athletics Member NCAA. All Division III. *Intercollegiate sports:* baseball M, basketball M/W, cross-country running M/W, football M, golf M/W, soccer M/W, swimming and diving M/W, tennis M/W, track and field M/W, volleyball W. *Intramural sports:* basketball M/W, bowling M/W, cheerleading M/W, football M/W, soccer M/W, tennis M/W, ultimate Frisbee M/W, volleyball M/W.

Standardized Tests *Required:* SAT or ACT (for admission). *Recommended:* ACT (for admission).

Costs (2011–12) *Comprehensive fee:* $32,984 includes full-time tuition ($24,749), mandatory fees ($499), and room and board ($7736). Full-time tuition and fees vary according to program. Part-time tuition: $310 per credit. Part-time tuition and fees vary according to course load and program. *College room only:* $4222. Room and board charges vary according to board plan and housing facility. *Payment plan:* installment. *Waivers:* employees or children of employees.

Financial Aid Of all full-time matriculated undergraduates who enrolled in 2009, 2,399 applied for aid, 2,136 were judged to have need, 838 had their need fully met. 897 Federal Work-Study jobs (averaging $2187). 782 state and other part-time jobs (averaging $2082). In 2009, 520 non-need-based awards were made. *Average percent of need met:* 100%. *Average financial aid package:* $19,499. *Average need-based loan:* $4549. *Average need-based gift aid:* $13,117. *Average non-need-based aid:* $10,437. *Average indebtedness upon graduation:* $28,777.

Applying *Options:* electronic application, deferred entrance. *Required:* high school transcript, minimum 2 GPA, 1 letter of recommendation. *Required for some:* essay or personal statement. *Recommended:* interview. *Application deadlines:* rolling (freshmen), rolling (transfers). *Notification:* 8/20 (freshmen), continuous until 8/20 (transfers).

Freshman Application Contact Mr. James Wiseman, Vice President of Enrollment, Carroll University, 100 North East Avenue, Waukesha, WI 53186-5593. *Phone:* 262-524-7221. *Toll-free phone:* 800-CARROLL. *Fax:* 262-524-7139. *E-mail:* info@carrollu.edu. *Web site:* http://www.carrollu.edu/.

See page 1200 for the College Close-Up.

Carthage College

Kenosha, Wisconsin

Freshman Application Contact Carthage College, 2001 Alford Park Drive, Kenosha, WI 53140. *Phone:* 262-551-6000. *Toll-free phone:* 800-351-4058. *Web site:* http://www.carthage.edu/.

Columbia College of Nursing

Milwaukee, Wisconsin

- **Independent** 4-year, founded 1901
- **Urban** 1-acre campus with easy access to Milwaukee
- **Endowment** $700,000
- **Coed, primarily women** 169 undergraduate students, 91% full-time, 96% women, 4% men
- **Moderately difficult** entrance level

Undergraduates 154 full-time, 15 part-time. Students come from 3 states and territories; 4% are from out of state; 8% Black or African American, non-Hispanic/Latino; 4% Hispanic/Latino; 2% Asian, non-Hispanic/Latino; 0.6% American Indian or Alaska Native, non-Hispanic/Latino; 8% Race/ethnicity unknown; 14% transferred in. *Retention:* 88% of full-time freshmen returned.

Freshmen *Average high school GPA:* 2.9. *Test scores:* ACT scores over 18: 100%; ACT scores over 24: 38%; ACT scores over 30: 2%.

Faculty *Total:* 21, 86% full-time, 24% with terminal degrees. *Student/faculty ratio:* 9:1.

Academics *Calendar:* semesters. *Degrees:* bachelor's (nursing degree is awarded in conjunction with Mount Mary College). *Special study options:* academic remediation for entering students, advanced placement credit, cooperative education, double majors, honors programs, independent study, off-campus study, part-time degree program, study abroad, summer session for credit.

Computers on Campus 46 computers/terminals are available on campus for general student use. Students can access the following: campus intranet, computer help desk, free student e-mail accounts, online (class) grades, online (class) registration, online (class) schedules. Campuswide network is available. Wireless service is available via entire campus.

Student Life *Housing:* college housing not available. *Activities and organizations:* Student Senate, Student Nurses Association. *Campus security:* 24-hour emergency response devices and patrols, student patrols, late-night transport/escort service, Security card entrances to academic areas. *Student services:* health clinic, personal/psychological counseling.

Standardized Tests *Required:* SAT or ACT (for admission).

Costs (2011–12) *Tuition:* $22,318 full-time, $668 per credit part-time. Part-time tuition and fees vary according to program. *Required fees:* $1200 full-time, $55 per credit part-time. *Payment plan:* installment. *Waivers:* employees or children of employees.

Financial Aid Of all full-time matriculated undergraduates who enrolled in 2000, 1,782 applied for aid, 1,336 were judged to have need, 1,336 had their need fully met. In 2000, 426 non-need-based awards were made. *Average percent of need met:* 100%. *Average financial aid package:* $13,219. *Average need-based loan:* $3186. *Average need-based gift aid:* $9050. *Average non-need-based aid:* $7051. *Average indebtedness upon graduation:* $16,000.

Applying *Options:* electronic application. *Application fee:* $25. *Required:* high school transcript, minimum 2.8 GPA, minimum 2.8 GPA in college level natural and social sciences. *Required for some:* essay or personal statement, interview. *Recommended:* essay or personal statement, 1 letter of recommendation. *Application deadline:* 3/1 (transfers). *Notification:* 4/15 (transfers).

Freshman Application Contact Columbia College of Nursing, 4425 N. Port Washington Road, Milwaukee, WI 53212. *Phone:* 414-326-2336. *Toll-free phone:* 800-321-6265. *Web site:* http://www.ccon.edu/.

Concordia University Wisconsin

Mequon, Wisconsin

- **Independent** comprehensive, founded 1881, affiliated with Lutheran Church–Missouri Synod, part of Concordia University System
- **Suburban** 192-acre campus with easy access to Milwaukee
- **Coed** 4,344 undergraduate students, 57% full-time, 65% women, 35% men
- **Moderately difficult** entrance level, 64% of applicants were admitted

Undergraduates 2,478 full-time, 1,866 part-time. 20% are from out of state; 17% Black or African American, non-Hispanic/Latino; 2% Hispanic/Latino; 1% Asian, non-Hispanic/Latino; 1% American Indian or Alaska Native, non-Hispanic/Latino; 0.3% Two or more races, non-Hispanic/Latino; 14% Race/ethnicity unknown; 0.8% international; 3% transferred in; 63% live on campus. *Retention:* 80% of full-time freshmen returned.

Freshmen *Admission:* 2,386 applied, 1,524 admitted, 538 enrolled. *Average high school GPA:* 3.36. *Test scores:* ACT scores over 18: 95%; ACT scores over 24: 41%; ACT scores over 30: 6%.

Faculty *Total:* 277, 46% full-time, 42% with terminal degrees. *Student/faculty ratio:* 12:1.

Academics *Calendar:* 4-1-4. *Degrees:* certificates, associate, bachelor's, master's, doctoral-professional, doctoral-research/scholarship, and postbachelor's certificates. *Special study options:* academic remediation for entering students, accelerated degree program, adult/continuing education programs, advanced placement credit, distance learning, double majors, English as a second language, independent study, internships, off-campus study, part-time degree program, services for LD students, student-designed majors, study abroad, summer session for credit.

Computers on Campus 225 computers/terminals are available on campus for general student use. Students can access the following: computer help desk, free student e-mail accounts. Campuswide network is available.

Student Life *Housing options:* men-only, women-only. Campus housing is university owned. Freshman applicants given priority for college housing. *Activities and organizations:* drama/theater group, student-run newspaper, radio station, choral group. *Campus security:* 24-hour patrols, student patrols, late-night transport/escort service, controlled dormitory access. *Student services:* health clinic, personal/psychological counseling.

Athletics Member NCAA. All Division III. *Intercollegiate sports:* baseball M, basketball M/W, cross-country running M/W, football M, golf M/W, ice hockey M/W, soccer M/W, softball W, tennis M/W, track and field M/W, volleyball W, wrestling M. *Intramural sports:* basketball M/W, softball M/W, volleyball M/W.

Standardized Tests *Required:* ACT (for admission).

Costs (2010–11) *Comprehensive fee:* $30,460 includes full-time tuition ($21,940), mandatory fees ($210), and room and board ($8310). Full-time tuition and fees vary according to program. Part-time tuition: $915 per credit hour. Part-time tuition and fees vary according to program. No tuition increase for student's term of enrollment. *Room and board:* Room and board charges vary according to board plan. *Payment plans:* installment, deferred payment. *Waivers:* employees or children of employees.

Financial Aid Of all full-time matriculated undergraduates who enrolled in 2009, 2,023 applied for aid, 1,814 were judged to have need, 579 had their need fully met. 250 Federal Work-Study jobs (averaging $1621). In 2009, 276 non-need-based awards were made. *Average percent of need met:* 81%. *Average financial aid package:* $20,585. *Average need-based loan:* $5944. *Average need-based gift aid:* $12,024. *Average non-need-based aid:* $8772. *Average indebtedness upon graduation:* $28,247.

Applying *Application fee:* $35. *Required:* high school transcript, minimum 2 GPA. *Required for some:* essay or personal statement, minimum 3 GPA, 3 letters of recommendation. *Recommended:* interview. *Application deadlines:* 8/15 (freshmen), rolling (transfers). *Notification:* continuous (freshmen), continuous (transfers).

Freshman Application Contact Ms. Julie Schroeder, Concordia University Wisconsin, Admissions Office, 12800 North Lake Drive, Mequon, WI 53097. *Phone:* 262-243-4305 Ext. 4305. *Toll-free phone:* 888-628-9472. *E-mail:* admission@cuw.edu. *Web site:* http://www.cuw.edu/.

DeVry University
Milwaukee, Wisconsin

- **Proprietary** comprehensive, part of DeVry University
- **Coed**
- **Minimally difficult** entrance level

Faculty *Student/faculty ratio:* 9:1.

Academics *Calendar:* semesters. *Degrees:* associate, bachelor's, and master's.

Costs (2010–11) *Tuition:* $14,766 full-time, $580 per credit hour part-time. Full-time tuition and fees vary according to course load. Part-time tuition and fees vary according to course load. *Required fees:* $60 full-time, $30 per term part-time. *Payment plans:* installment, deferred payment.

Financial Aid *Of all full-time matriculated undergraduates who enrolled in 2007,* 12 applied for aid, 12 were judged to have need. *Average percent of need met:* 35. *Average financial aid package:* $11,858. *Average need-based loan:* $7870. *Average need-based gift aid:* $5981.

Applying *Options:* electronic application, deferred entrance. *Application fee:* $50. *Required:* high school transcript, interview.

Freshman Application Contact DeVry University, 411 East Wisconsin Avenue, Suite 300, Milwaukee, WI 53202. *Web site:* http://www.devry.edu/.

DeVry University
Waukesha, Wisconsin

Admissions Office Contact DeVry University, N14 W23833 Stone Ridge Drive, Suite 450, Waukesha, WI 53188-1157. *Web site:* http://www.devry.edu/.

Edgewood College
Madison, Wisconsin

- **Independent Roman Catholic** comprehensive, founded 1927
- **Urban** 55-acre campus
- **Endowment** $16.6 million
- **Coed, primarily women** 1,941 undergraduate students, 80% full-time, 71% women, 29% men
- **Moderately difficult** entrance level, 76% of applicants were admitted

Undergraduates 1,560 full-time, 381 part-time. Students come from 22 states and territories; 24 other countries; 7% are from out of state; 3% Black or African American, non-Hispanic/Latino; 4% Hispanic/Latino; 2% Asian, non-Hispanic/Latino; 0.1% Native Hawaiian or other Pacific Islander, non-Hispanic/Latino; 0.5% American Indian or Alaska Native, non-Hispanic/Latino; 2% Two or more races, non-Hispanic/Latino; 2% Race/ethnicity unknown; 2% international; 11% transferred in; 29% live on campus. *Retention:* 78% of full-time freshmen returned.

Freshmen *Admission:* 1,321 applied, 1,001 admitted, 326 enrolled. *Average high school GPA:* 3.3. *Test scores:* ACT scores over 18: 94%; ACT scores over 24: 35%; ACT scores over 30: 3%.

Faculty *Total:* 332, 33% full-time, 56% with terminal degrees. *Student/faculty ratio:* 11:1.

Academics *Calendar:* semesters. *Degrees:* associate, bachelor's, master's, and doctoral-research/scholarship. *Special study options:* academic remediation for entering students, accelerated degree program, adult/continuing education programs, advanced placement credit, cooperative education, double majors, honors programs, independent study, internships, part-time degree program, services for LD students, student-designed majors, study abroad, summer session for credit. *ROTC:* Army (c). *Unusual degree programs:* 3-2 business administration with Accountancy.

Computers on Campus 100 computers/terminals and 200 ports are available on campus for general student use. Students can access the following: campus intranet, computer help desk, free student e-mail accounts, online (class) grades, online (class) registration, online (class) schedules. Campuswide network is available. 100% of college-owned or -operated housing units are wired for high-speed Internet access. Wireless service is available via entire campus.

Student Life *Housing:* on-campus residence required through sophomore year. *Options:* coed, women-only, disabled students. Campus housing is university owned. Freshman applicants given priority for college housing. *Activities and organizations:* drama/theater group, student-run newspaper, choral group, Circle K, Student Government Association, Association for Latino/a Students (ALaS), The Wood's Edge, Student Education Association. *Campus security:* 24-hour emergency response devices and patrols, student patrols, late-night transport/escort service, controlled dormitory access. *Student services:* health clinic, personal/psychological counseling.

Athletics Member NCAA. All Division III. *Intercollegiate sports:* baseball M, basketball M/W, cheerleading W, cross-country running M/W, golf M/W, soccer M/W, softball W, tennis M/W, track and field M/W, volleyball W. *Intramural sports:* basketball M/W, bowling M/W, football M/W, soccer M/W, volleyball M/W.

Standardized Tests *Required:* SAT or ACT (for admission).

Costs (2010–11) *Comprehensive fee:* $29,372 includes full-time tuition ($21,988) and room and board ($7384). Full-time tuition and fees vary according to degree level. Part-time tuition: $692 per credit. Part-time tuition and fees vary according to course load and degree level. *College room only:* $3750. Room and board charges vary according to housing facility. *Payment plan:* installment. *Waivers:* employees or children of employees.

Financial Aid Of all full-time matriculated undergraduates who enrolled in 2008, 1,321 applied for aid, 1,272 were judged to have need, 154 had their need fully met. In 2008, 237 non-need-based awards were made. *Average percent of need met:* 71%. *Average financial aid package:* $15,719. *Average need-based loan:* $5106. *Average need-based gift aid:* $10,446. *Average non-need-based aid:* $3922. *Average indebtedness upon graduation:* $29,745.

Applying *Options:* electronic application, deferred entrance. *Application fee:* $25. *Required:* high school transcript, minimum 2.5 GPA. *Required for some:* essay or personal statement, interview. *Application deadlines:* 8/14 (freshmen), 8/14 (transfers). *Notification:* continuous (freshmen), continuous (transfers).

Freshman Application Contact Ms. Christine Benedict, Director of Undergraduate Admissions, Edgewood College, 1000 Edgewood College Drive, Madison, WI 53711-1997. *Phone:* 608-663-2294. *Toll-free phone:* 800-444-4861 Ext. 2294. *Fax:* 608-663-2214. *E-mail:* admissions@edgewood.edu. *Web site:* http://www.edgewood.edu/.

Herzing University
Brookfield, Wisconsin

Admissions Office Contact Herzing University, 555 South Executive Drive, Brookfield, WI 53005. *Web site:* http://www.herzing.edu/brookfield.

Herzing University
Kenosha, Wisconsin

Admissions Office Contact Herzing University, 4006 Washington Road, Kenosha, WI 53144. *Web site:* http://www.herzing.edu/kenosha.

Herzing University
Madison, Wisconsin

- **Proprietary** 4-year, founded 1948, part of Herzing Institutes, Inc.
- **Suburban** campus with easy access to Madison and Milwaukee
- **Coed, primarily men** 857 undergraduate students

Faculty *Total:* 48, 58% full-time, 10% with terminal degrees.

Academics *Calendar:* semesters. *Degrees:* diplomas, associate, and bachelor's. *Special study options:* academic remediation for entering students, accelerated degree program, adult/continuing education programs, advanced placement credit, cooperative education, distance learning, honors programs, independent study, internships, part-time degree program, services for LD students, study abroad.

Computers on Campus 363 computers/terminals are available on campus for general student use. Campuswide network is available.

Student Life *Housing:* college housing not available. *Campus security:* 24-hour emergency response devices. *Student services:* personal/psychological counseling.

Costs (2011–12) *Tuition:* $16,920 full-time, $9660 per year part-time.

Financial Aid *Financial aid deadline:* 6/30.

Applying *Required:* high school transcript, interview. *Application deadline:* rolling (freshmen).

Freshman Application Contact Mr. Matthew Schneider, Admissions Director, Herzing University, 5218 East Terrace Drive, Madison, WI 53718. *Phone:* 608-663-0806. *Toll-free phone:* 800-582-1227. *Fax:* 608-249-8593. *E-mail:* info@msn.herzing.edu. *Web site:* http://www.herzing.edu/madison/.

Herzing University Online

Milwaukee, Wisconsin

Admissions Office Contact Herzing University Online, 525 North 6th Street, Milwaukee, WI 53203. *Web site:* http://www.herzingonline.edu/.

ITT Technical Institute

Green Bay, Wisconsin

- **Proprietary** primarily 2-year, founded 2000, part of ITT Educational Services, Inc.
- **Coed**
- **Minimally difficult** entrance level

Academics *Calendar:* quarters. *Degrees:* associate and bachelor's.

Student Life *Housing:* college housing not available.

Freshman Application Contact Director of Recruitment, ITT Technical Institute, 470 Security Boulevard, Green Bay, WI 54313. *Phone:* 920-662-9000. *Toll-free phone:* 888-884-3626. *Fax:* 920-662-9384. *Web site:* http://www.itt-tech.edu/.

ITT Technical Institute

Greenfield, Wisconsin

- **Proprietary** primarily 2-year, founded 1968, part of ITT Educational Services, Inc.
- **Suburban** campus
- **Coed**
- **Minimally difficult** entrance level

Academics *Calendar:* quarters. *Degrees:* associate and bachelor's.

Student Life *Housing:* college housing not available.

Freshman Application Contact Director of Recruitment, ITT Technical Institute, 6300 West Layton Avenue, Greenfield, WI 53220-4612. *Phone:* 414-282-9494. *Web site:* http://www.itt-tech.edu/.

ITT Technical Institute

Madison, Wisconsin

- **Proprietary** primarily 2-year, part of ITT Educational Services, Inc.
- **Coed**
- **Minimally difficult** entrance level

Academics *Degrees:* associate and bachelor's.

Freshman Application Contact Director of Recruitment, ITT Technical Institute, 2450 Rimrock Road, Suite 100, Madison, WI 53713. *Phone:* 608-288-6301. *Toll-free phone:* 877-628-5960. *Web site:* http://www.itt-tech.edu/.

Lakeland College

Sheboygan, Wisconsin

- **Independent** comprehensive, founded 1862, affiliated with United Church of Christ
- **Rural** 240-acre campus with easy access to Milwaukee
- **Endowment** $9.3 million
- **Coed**
- **Minimally difficult** entrance level

Faculty *Student/faculty ratio:* 17:1.

Academics *Calendar:* 4-4-1. *Degrees:* bachelor's and master's.

Student Life *Campus security:* 24-hour emergency response devices, student patrols, late-night transport/escort service, controlled dormitory access.

Athletics Member NCAA. All Division III.

Standardized Tests *Required:* SAT or ACT (for admission).

Costs (2010–11) *Comprehensive fee:* $26,656 includes full-time tuition ($19,640) and room and board ($7016). Full-time tuition and fees vary according to degree level. Part-time tuition: $657 per credit. Part-time tuition and fees vary according to class time, course load, degree level, and location. No tuition increase for student's term of enrollment. *Room and board:* Room and board

charges vary according to board plan and housing facility. *Payment plans:* tuition prepayment, installment, deferred payment.

Financial Aid *Of all full-time matriculated undergraduates who enrolled in 2009,* 1,372 applied for aid, 1,232 were judged to have need, 114 had their need fully met. 262 Federal Work-Study jobs (averaging $2500). 150 state and other part-time jobs (averaging $2500). *In 2009,* 189 non-need-based awards were made. *Average percent of need met:* 65. *Average financial aid package:* $11,992. *Average need-based loan:* $4441. *Average need-based gift aid:* $8840. *Average non-need-based aid:* $8075. *Financial aid deadline:* 7/1.

Applying *Options:* electronic application, deferred entrance. *Required:* essay or personal statement, high school transcript, minimum 2 GPA. *Required for some:* interview.

Freshman Application Contact Mr. Nick Spaeth, Director of Admissions, Lakeland College, PO Box 359, Nash Visitors Center, Sheboygan, WI 53082-0359. *Phone:* 920-565-1007. *Toll-free phone:* 800-242-3347. *Fax:* 920-565-1215. *E-mail:* admissions@lakeland.edu. *Web site:* http://www.lakeland.edu/.

Lawrence University

Appleton, Wisconsin

- **Independent** 4-year, founded 1847
- **Small-town** 84-acre campus
- **Endowment** $180.3 million
- **Coed** 1,566 undergraduate students, 97% full-time, 54% women, 46% men
- **Very difficult** entrance level, 66% of applicants were admitted

Undergraduates 1,515 full-time, 51 part-time. Students come from 47 states and territories; 38 other countries; 66% are from out of state; 3% Black or African American, non-Hispanic/Latino; 4% Hispanic/Latino; 3% Asian, non-Hispanic/Latino; 0.2% Native Hawaiian or other Pacific Islander, non-Hispanic/Latino; 0.5% American Indian or Alaska Native, non-Hispanic/Latino; 3% Two or more races, non-Hispanic/Latino; 1% Race/ethnicity unknown; 9% international; 1% transferred in; 99% live on campus. *Retention:* 88% of full-time freshmen returned.

Freshmen *Admission:* 2,625 applied, 1,739 admitted, 452 enrolled. *Average high school GPA:* 3.66. *Test scores:* SAT critical reading scores over 500: 90%; SAT math scores over 500: 96%; SAT writing scores over 500: 92%; ACT scores over 18: 100%; SAT critical reading scores over 600: 71%; SAT math scores over 600: 74%; SAT writing scores over 600: 66%; ACT scores over 24: 94%; SAT critical reading scores over 700: 30%; SAT math scores over 700: 26%; SAT writing scores over 700: 22%; ACT scores over 30: 48%.

Faculty *Total:* 193, 81% full-time, 79% with terminal degrees. *Student/faculty ratio:* 9:1.

Academics *Calendar:* trimesters. *Degree:* bachelor's. *Special study options:* advanced placement credit, double majors, independent study, internships, off-campus study, services for LD students, student-designed majors, study abroad. *Unusual degree programs:* 3-2 engineering with Rensselaer Polytechnic Institute, Washington University in St. Louis, Columbia University; forestry with Duke University; occupational therapy with Washington University.

Computers on Campus 354 computers/terminals and 1,055 ports are available on campus for general student use. Students can access the following: campus intranet, computer help desk, free student e-mail accounts, online (class) grades, online (class) registration, online (class) schedules, online transcripts, financial aid, financial account information. Campuswide network is available. 100% of college-owned or -operated housing units are wired for high-speed Internet access. Wireless service is available via classrooms, computer centers, computer labs, dorm rooms, learning centers, libraries, student centers.

Student Life *Housing:* on-campus residence required through senior year. *Options:* coed, men-only, women-only, cooperative, disabled students. Campus housing is university owned. Freshman campus housing is guaranteed. *Activities and organizations:* drama/theater group, student-run newspaper, radio station, choral group, Lawrence Swing Dancers, Lawrence International, Outdoor Recreation Club, Lawrence Christian Fellowship, Greenfire, national fraternities, national sororities. *Campus security:* 24-hour emergency response devices and patrols, student patrols, late-night transport/escort service, controlled dormitory access, evening patrols by trained security personnel. *Student services:* health clinic, personal/psychological counseling.

Athletics Member NCAA. All Division III. *Intercollegiate sports:* baseball M, basketball M/W, crew M(c)/W(c), cross-country running M/W, fencing M/W, football M, golf M, ice hockey M/W(c), soccer M/W, softball W, swimming and diving M/W, tennis M/W, track and field M/W, ultimate Frisbee M(c)/W(c), volleyball M(c)/W. *Intramural sports:* badminton M/W, basketball M/W, bowling M/W, cheerleading W, cross-country running M/W, equestrian sports M/W, fencing M/W, golf M/W, racquetball M/W, squash M/W, swimming and diving M/W, table tennis M/W, tennis M/W, track and field M/W, volleyball M/W, water polo M/W, weight lifting M/W.

Costs (2011–12) *Comprehensive fee:* $46,371 includes full-time tuition ($38,205), mandatory fees ($276), and room and board ($7890). *Room and board:* Room and board charges vary according to board plan. *Payment plans:*

tuition prepayment, installment. *Waivers:* employees or children of employees.

Financial Aid Of all full-time matriculated undergraduates who enrolled in 2009, 1,072 applied for aid, 879 were judged to have need, 408 had their need fully met. 654 Federal Work-Study jobs (averaging $2345). 321 state and other part-time jobs (averaging $2230). In 2009, 513 non-need-based awards were made. *Average percent of need met:* 90%. *Average financial aid package:* $27,473. *Average need-based loan:* $4331. *Average need-based gift aid:* $21,032. *Average non-need-based aid:* $14,587. *Average indebtedness upon graduation:* $30,224.

Applying *Options:* electronic application, early admission, early decision, early action, deferred entrance. *Application fee:* $40. *Required:* essay or personal statement, high school transcript, 2 letters of recommendation, audition for music program. *Recommended:* minimum 3 GPA, interview. *Application deadlines:* 1/15 (freshmen), 5/1 (transfers), 12/1 (early action). *Early decision deadline:* 11/15. *Notification:* 4/1 (freshmen), 6/1 (transfers), 12/1 (early decision), 1/15 (early action).

Freshman Application Contact Mr. Steven T. Syverson, Vice President for Enrollment Management, Lawrence University, 711 East Boldt Way, Appleton, WI 54912. *Phone:* 920-832-6500. *Toll-free phone:* 800-227-0982. *Fax:* 920-832-6782. *E-mail:* excel@lawrence.edu. *Web site:* http://www.lawrence.edu/.

Maranatha Baptist Bible College

Watertown, Wisconsin

- **Independent Baptist** comprehensive, founded 1968
- **Small-town** 60-acre campus with easy access to Milwaukee
- **Endowment** $218,513
- **Coed** 879 undergraduate students, 87% full-time, 56% women, 44% men
- **Noncompetitive** entrance level, 50% of applicants were admitted

Undergraduates 765 full-time, 114 part-time. Students come from 43 states and territories; 10 other countries; 70% are from out of state; 1% Black or African American, non-Hispanic/Latino; 1% Hispanic/Latino; 1% Asian, non-Hispanic/Latino; 1% Two or more races, non-Hispanic/Latino; 0.3% Race/ethnicity unknown; 5% transferred in; 69% live on campus. *Retention:* 81% of full-time freshmen returned.

Freshmen *Admission:* 435 applied, 219 admitted, 207 enrolled. *Test scores:* SAT critical reading scores over 500: 62%; SAT math scores over 500: 47%; ACT scores over 18: 92%; SAT critical reading scores over 600: 22%; SAT math scores over 600: 4%; ACT scores over 24: 44%; SAT critical reading scores over 700: 4%; SAT math scores over 700: 4%; ACT scores over 30: 6%.

Faculty *Total:* 81, 54% full-time, 23% with terminal degrees. *Student/faculty ratio:* 14:1.

Academics *Calendar:* semesters. *Degrees:* certificates, associate, bachelor's, and master's. *Special study options:* academic remediation for entering students, accelerated degree program, distance learning, double majors, independent study, internships, off-campus study, part-time degree program, summer session for credit. *ROTC:* Army (b), Air Force (c).

Computers on Campus 120 computers/terminals are available on campus for general student use. Students can access the following: campus intranet, computer help desk, free student e-mail accounts, online (class) grades, online (class) registration, online (class) schedules. Campuswide network is available. 100% of college-owned or -operated housing units are wired for high-speed Internet access. Wireless service is available via classrooms, computer centers, computer labs, dorm rooms, libraries, student centers.

Student Life *Housing:* on-campus residence required through senior year. *Options:* men-only, women-only. Campus housing is university owned. Freshman campus housing is guaranteed. *Activities and organizations:* drama/theater group, choral group. *Campus security:* student patrols, late-night transport/escort service, controlled dormitory access. *Student services:* health clinic, personal/psychological counseling.

Athletics Member NCAA, NCCAA. All NCAA Division III. *Intercollegiate sports:* baseball M, basketball M/W, cross-country running M/W, football M, soccer M/W, softball W, volleyball W, wrestling M. *Intramural sports:* basketball M/W.

Standardized Tests *Required:* SAT or ACT (for admission).

Costs (2010–11) *Comprehensive fee:* $17,840 includes full-time tuition ($10,500), mandatory fees ($1050), and room and board ($6290). Full-time tuition and fees vary according to course load. Part-time tuition: $437 per credit hour. Part-time tuition and fees vary according to course load. *Payment plan:* installment. *Waivers:* employees or children of employees.

Financial Aid Of all full-time matriculated undergraduates who enrolled in 2008, 662 applied for aid, 602 were judged to have need, 33 had their need fully met. In 2008, 28 non-need-based awards were made. *Average percent of need met:* 53%. *Average financial aid package:* $8279. *Average need-based loan:* $4358. *Average need-based gift aid:* $4299. *Average non-need-based aid:* $1481. *Average indebtedness upon graduation:* $19,191.

Applying *Options:* electronic application. *Application fee:* $50. *Required:* essay or personal statement, high school transcript, 4 letters of recommenda-

tion. *Application deadlines:* rolling (freshmen), rolling (transfers). *Notification:* continuous (freshmen), continuous (transfers).

Freshman Application Contact Dr. James Harrison, Director of Admissions, Maranatha Baptist Bible College, 745 West Main Street, Watertown, WI 53094. *Phone:* 920-206-2327. *Toll-free phone:* 800-622-2947. *Fax:* 920-261-9109. *E-mail:* admissions@mbbc.edu. *Web site:* http://www.mbbc.edu/.

Marian University

Fond du Lac, Wisconsin

- **Independent Roman Catholic** comprehensive, founded 1936
- **Small-town** 104-acre campus with easy access to Milwaukee
- **Endowment** $7.1 million
- **Coed** 1,999 undergraduate students, 77% full-time, 73% women, 27% men
- **Moderately difficult** entrance level, 81% of applicants were admitted

Undergraduates 1,548 full-time, 451 part-time. Students come from 18 states and territories; 8 other countries; 5% are from out of state; 6% Black or African American, non-Hispanic/Latino; 4% Hispanic/Latino; 2% Asian, non-Hispanic/Latino; 0.2% Native Hawaiian or other Pacific Islander, non-Hispanic/Latino; 0.9% American Indian or Alaska Native, non-Hispanic/Latino; 0.4% Two or more races, non-Hispanic/Latino; 1% Race/ethnicity unknown; 1% international; 12% transferred in; 32% live on campus. *Retention:* 67% of full-time freshmen returned.

Freshmen *Admission:* 977 applied, 787 admitted, 310 enrolled. *Average high school GPA:* 3. *Test scores:* ACT scores over 18: 72%; ACT scores over 24: 15%; ACT scores over 30: 1%.

Faculty *Total:* 309, 27% full-time, 25% with terminal degrees. *Student/faculty ratio:* 12:1.

Academics *Calendar:* semesters. *Degrees:* certificates, bachelor's, master's, and doctoral-research/scholarship. *Special study options:* academic remediation for entering students, accelerated degree program, advanced placement credit, cooperative education, distance learning, double majors, English as a second language, honors programs, independent study, internships, part-time degree program, services for LD students, student-designed majors, study abroad, summer session for credit. *ROTC:* Army (b).

Computers on Campus 450 computers/terminals are available on campus for general student use. Students can access the following: campus intranet, computer help desk, free student e-mail accounts, online (class) grades, online (class) registration, online (class) schedules. Campuswide network is available. 100% of college-owned or -operated housing units are wired for high-speed Internet access. Wireless service is available via entire campus.

Student Life *Housing:* on-campus residence required through sophomore year. *Options:* coed, disabled students. Campus housing is university owned. Freshman campus housing is guaranteed. *Activities and organizations:* student-run newspaper, choral group, Student Senate, Student Nurses Association, Student Education Association, Science and Math Association, African American Student Union, national fraternities, national sororities. *Campus security:* 24-hour emergency response devices and patrols, student patrols, late-night transport/escort service, controlled dormitory access. *Student services:* health clinic, personal/psychological counseling.

Athletics Member NCAA. All Division III. *Intercollegiate sports:* baseball M, basketball M/W, cross-country running M/W, golf M/W, ice hockey M/W, soccer M/W, softball W, tennis M/W, volleyball W. *Intramural sports:* basketball M/W, bowling M/W, football M, skiing (downhill) M/W, tennis M/W, volleyball M/W.

Standardized Tests *Required:* SAT or ACT (for admission).

Costs (2010–11) *One-time required fee:* $100. *Comprehensive fee:* $27,190 includes full-time tuition ($21,140), mandatory fees ($350), and room and board ($5700). Full-time tuition and fees vary according to course load, degree level, and program. Part-time tuition: $330 per credit hour. Part-time tuition and fees vary according to course load, degree level, and program. *College room only:* $3950. Room and board charges vary according to board plan and housing facility. *Payment plan:* installment. *Waivers:* senior citizens and employees or children of employees.

Financial Aid Of all full-time matriculated undergraduates who enrolled in 2008, 1,320 applied for aid, 1,182 were judged to have need, 451 had their need fully met. 193 Federal Work-Study jobs (averaging $679). 449 state and other part-time jobs (averaging $1341). In 2008, 137 non-need-based awards were made. *Average percent of need met:* 90%. *Average financial aid package:* $19,444. *Average need-based loan:* $7089. *Average need-based gift aid:* $11,769. *Average non-need-based aid:* $4503. *Average indebtedness upon graduation:* $22,125.

Applying *Options:* electronic application, deferred entrance. *Application fee:* $20. *Required:* high school transcript. *Required for some:* interview. *Recommended:* minimum 2 GPA, interview. *Application deadlines:* rolling (freshmen), rolling (transfers). *Notification:* 8/15 (freshmen), continuous until 8/15 (transfers).

Freshman Application Contact Shannon LaLuzerne, Senior Director of Admissions, Marian University, 45 South National Avenue, Fond du Lac, WI

54935-4699. *Phone:* 800-262-7426. *Toll-free phone:* 800-2-MARIAN Ext. 7652. *Fax:* 920-923-8755. *E-mail:* admit@marianuniversity.edu. *Web site:* http://www.marianuniversity.edu/.

Marquette University
Milwaukee, Wisconsin

- **Independent Roman Catholic (Jesuit)** university, founded 1881
- **Urban** 93-acre campus with easy access to Milwaukee
- **Endowment** $326.0 million
- **Coed** 8,113 undergraduate students, 95% full-time, 52% women, 48% men
- **Moderately difficult** entrance level, 62% of applicants were admitted

Undergraduates 7,715 full-time, 398 part-time. Students come from 51 states and territories; 47 other countries; 59% are from out of state; 5% Black or African American, non-Hispanic/Latino; 7% Hispanic/Latino; 4% Asian, non-Hispanic/Latino; 0.3% Native Hawaiian or other Pacific Islander, non-Hispanic/Latino; 0.3% American Indian or Alaska Native, non-Hispanic/Latino; 2% Two or more races, non-Hispanic/Latino; 0.3% Race/ethnicity unknown; 2% international; 2% transferred in; 55% live on campus. *Retention:* 88% of full-time freshmen returned.

Freshmen *Admission:* 19,930 applied, 12,398 admitted, 1,938 enrolled. *Test scores:* SAT critical reading scores over 500: 89%; SAT math scores over 500: 90%; SAT writing scores over 500: 88%; ACT scores over 18: 100%; SAT critical reading scores over 600: 45%; SAT math scores over 600: 54%; SAT writing scores over 600: 46%; ACT scores over 24: 83%; SAT critical reading scores over 700: 7%; SAT math scores over 700: 9%; SAT writing scores over 700: 7%; ACT scores over 30: 25%.

Faculty *Total:* 1,118, 56% full-time, 71% with terminal degrees. *Student/faculty ratio:* 15:1.

Academics *Calendar:* semesters. *Degrees:* bachelor's, master's, doctoral-professional, doctoral-research/scholarship, post-master's, and postbachelor's certificates. *Special study options:* accelerated degree program, adult/continuing education programs, advanced placement credit, cooperative education, distance learning, double majors, English as a second language, honors programs, independent study, internships, off-campus study, part-time degree program, services for LD students, student-designed majors, study abroad, summer session for credit. *ROTC:* Army (b), Navy (b), Air Force (b).

Computers on Campus 1,500 computers/terminals and 500 ports are available on campus for general student use. Students can access the following: campus intranet, computer help desk, free student e-mail accounts, online (class) grades, online (class) registration, online (class) schedules, AV Software, MATLAB. Campuswide network is available. 100% of college-owned or -operated housing units are wired for high-speed Internet access. Wireless service is available via classrooms, computer centers, computer labs, dorm rooms, learning centers, libraries, student centers.

Student Life *Housing:* on-campus residence required through sophomore year. *Options:* coed, men-only, women-only, disabled students. Campus housing is university owned. Freshman campus housing is guaranteed. *Activities and organizations:* drama/theater group, student-run newspaper, radio and television station, choral group, student government, club sports, community service organizations, band/jazz/orchestra, Residence Hall Association, national fraternities, national sororities. *Campus security:* 24-hour emergency response devices and patrols, student patrols, late-night transport/escort service, 24-hour desk attendants in residence halls. *Student services:* health clinic, personal/psychological counseling.

Athletics Member NCAA. All Division I. *Intercollegiate sports:* baseball M(c), basketball M(s)/W(s), cheerleading M/W, crew M(c)/W(c), cross-country running M(s)/W(s), football M(c)/W(c), golf M(s), ice hockey M(c), lacrosse M(c)/W(c), rugby M(c)/W(c), sailing M(c)/W(c), skiing (downhill) M(c)/W(c), soccer M(s)/W(s), softball W(c), swimming and diving M(c)/W(c), tennis M(s)/W(s), track and field M(s)/W(s), ultimate Frisbee M(c)/W(c), volleyball M(c)/W(s). *Intramural sports:* badminton M/W, basketball M/W, fencing M(c)/W(c), football M, racquetball M/W, soccer M/W, softball M/W, tennis M/W, track and field M/W, ultimate Frisbee M/W, volleyball M/W, water polo M/W, weight lifting M/W.

Standardized Tests *Required:* SAT or ACT (for admission).

Costs (2011–12) *Comprehensive fee:* $42,192 includes full-time tuition ($31,400), mandatory fees ($422), and room and board ($10,370). Full-time tuition and fees vary according to course load and program. Part-time tuition: $915 per credit. Part-time tuition and fees vary according to program. *Room and board:* Room and board charges vary according to board plan and housing facility. *Payment plan:* installment. *Waivers:* adult students, senior citizens, and employees or children of employees.

Financial Aid Of all full-time matriculated undergraduates who enrolled in 2009, 5,672 applied for aid, 4,764 were judged to have need, 1,231 had their need fully met. In 2009, 2115 non-need-based awards were made. *Average percent of need met:* 76%. *Average financial aid package:* $21,936. *Average need-based loan:* $5434. *Average need-based gift aid:* $15,219. *Average non-need-based aid:* $8480. *Average indebtedness upon graduation:* $32,824.

Applying *Options:* electronic application, deferred entrance. *Required:* essay or personal statement, high school transcript, minimum 2.5 GPA, 1 letter of recommendation. *Recommended:* minimum 3.4 GPA. *Application deadline:* 12/1 (freshmen). *Notification:* 1/31 (freshmen).

Freshman Application Contact Mr. Robert Blust, Dean of Undergraduate Admissions, Marquette University, PO Box 1881, Milwaukee, WI 53201-1881. *Phone:* 414-288-7004. *Toll-free phone:* 800-222-6544. *Fax:* 414-288-3764. *E-mail:* admissions@marquette.edu. *Web site:* http://www.marquette.edu/.

Milwaukee Institute of Art and Design
Milwaukee, Wisconsin

Freshman Application Contact Stacey Steinberg, Director of Admissions, Milwaukee Institute of Art and Design, 273 East Erie Street, Milwaukee, WI 53202. *Phone:* 414-847-3200. *Toll-free phone:* 888-749-MIAD. *Fax:* 414-291-8077. *E-mail:* admissions@miad.edu. *Web site:* http://www.miad.edu/.

Milwaukee School of Engineering
Milwaukee, Wisconsin

- **Independent** comprehensive, founded 1903
- **Urban** 15-acre campus
- **Endowment** $37.5 million
- **Coed, primarily men** 2,393 undergraduate students, 91% full-time, 20% women, 80% men
- **Moderately difficult** entrance level, 71% of applicants were admitted

Undergraduates 2,180 full-time, 213 part-time. Students come from 36 states and territories; 22 other countries; 29% are from out of state; 3% Black or African American, non-Hispanic/Latino; 4% Hispanic/Latino; 3% Asian, non-Hispanic/Latino; 0.1% Native Hawaiian or other Pacific Islander, non-Hispanic/Latino; 0.4% American Indian or Alaska Native, non-Hispanic/Latino; 2% Two or more races, non-Hispanic/Latino; 2% Race/ethnicity unknown; 3% international; 6% transferred in; 35% live on campus. *Retention:* 79% of full-time freshmen returned.

Freshmen *Admission:* 2,037 applied, 1,442 admitted, 493 enrolled. *Average high school GPA:* 3.61. *Test scores:* SAT critical reading scores over 500: 84%; SAT math scores over 500: 100%; ACT scores over 18: 100%; SAT critical reading scores over 600: 37%; SAT math scores over 600: 67%; ACT scores over 24: 81%; SAT critical reading scores over 700: 10%; SAT math scores over 700: 10%; ACT scores over 30: 24%.

Faculty *Total:* 253, 51% full-time, 51% with terminal degrees. *Student/faculty ratio:* 14:1.

Academics *Calendar:* quarters. *Degrees:* bachelor's and master's. *Special study options:* academic remediation for entering students, adult/continuing education programs, advanced placement credit, distance learning, double majors, English as a second language, independent study, internships, part-time degree program, services for LD students, study abroad, summer session for credit. *ROTC:* Army (c), Navy (c), Air Force (c).

Computers on Campus 125 computers/terminals and 2,000 ports are available on campus for general student use. Students can access the following: campus intranet, computer help desk, free student e-mail accounts, online (class) grades, online (class) registration, online (class) schedules. Campuswide network is available. 100% of college-owned or -operated housing units are wired for high-speed Internet access. Wireless service is available via entire campus.

Student Life *Housing:* on-campus residence required through sophomore year. *Options:* coed, disabled students. Campus housing is university owned. Freshman campus housing is guaranteed. *Activities and organizations:* drama/theater group, student-run radio station, choral group, Architectural Engineering and Construction Management Societies, Student Athletic Advisory Committee, MAGE, Student Government Association, Student Union Board, national fraternities, national sororities. *Campus security:* 24-hour emergency response devices and patrols, late-night transport/escort service, controlled dormitory access. *Student services:* health clinic, personal/psychological counseling, women's center.

Athletics Member NCAA. All Division III. *Intercollegiate sports:* baseball M, basketball M/W, cheerleading M/W, crew M, cross-country running M/W, golf M/W, ice hockey M, lacrosse M, soccer M/W, softball W, tennis M/W, track and field M/W, volleyball M/W, wrestling M. *Intramural sports:* basketball M/W, bowling M(c)/W(c), fencing M(c)/W(c), football M/W, gymnastics M(c)/W(c), rugby M(c), soccer M/W, softball M/W, ultimate Frisbee M(c), volleyball M/W, weight lifting M(c)/W(c).

Standardized Tests *Required:* SAT or ACT (for admission).

Costs (2011–12) *Comprehensive fee:* $38,784 includes full-time tuition ($30,990) and room and board ($7794). Part-time tuition: $538 per quarter hour. Part-time tuition and fees vary according to course load. *College room only:* $4974. Room and board charges vary according to board plan and housing facility. *Payment plan:* installment. *Waivers:* employees or children of employees.

Financial Aid Of all full-time matriculated undergraduates who enrolled in 2008, 2,113 applied for aid, 1,936 were judged to have need, 286 had their need fully met. 284 Federal Work-Study jobs (averaging $1429). In 2008, 346 non-need-based awards were made. *Average percent of need met:* 68%. *Average financial aid package:* $19,411. *Average need-based loan:* $3547. *Average need-based gift aid:* $16,192. *Average non-need-based aid:* $10,136. *Average indebtedness upon graduation:* $35,236.

Applying *Options:* electronic application, deferred entrance. *Application fee:* $25. *Required:* high school transcript, minimum 2.5 GPA. *Required for some:* essay or personal statement, interview. *Application deadlines:* rolling (freshmen), rolling (transfers). *Notification:* continuous (freshmen), continuous (transfers).

Freshman Application Contact Dana-Marie Grennier, Director of Admissions, Milwaukee School of Engineering, 1025 North Broadway, Milwaukee, WI 53202-3109. *Phone:* 414-277-6761. *Toll-free phone:* 800-332-6763. *Fax:* 414-277-7475. *E-mail:* grennier@msoe.edu. *Web site:* http://www.msoe.edu/.

See page 1438 for the College Close-Up.

Mount Mary College
Milwaukee, Wisconsin

- **Independent Roman Catholic** comprehensive, founded 1913
- **Urban** 80-acre campus
- **Endowment** $9.0 million
- **Undergraduate: women only; graduate: coed**
- **Moderately difficult** entrance level

Faculty *Student/faculty ratio:* 13:1.

Academics *Calendar:* semesters. *Degrees:* bachelor's, master's, post-master's, and postbachelor's certificates.

Student Life *Campus security:* 24-hour patrols, late-night transport/escort service, controlled dormitory access.

Athletics Member NCAA. All Division III.

Standardized Tests *Required:* SAT or ACT (for admission).

Costs (2010–11) *Comprehensive fee:* $29,616 includes full-time tuition ($21,668), mandatory fees ($450), and room and board ($7498). Full-time

tuition and fees vary according to degree level and program. Part-time tuition: $648 per credit hour. Part-time tuition and fees vary according to course load, degree level, and program. *Required fees:* $120 per term part-time. *Room and board:* Room and board charges vary according to board plan.

Financial Aid *Of all full-time matriculated undergraduates who enrolled in 2009,* 1,018 applied for aid, 960 were judged to have need, 75 had their need fully met. 157 Federal Work-Study jobs (averaging $1373). 43 state and other part-time jobs (averaging $1247). *In 2009,* 122 non-need-based awards were made. *Average percent of need met:* 68. *Average financial aid package:* $16,408. *Average need-based loan:* $4576. *Average need-based gift aid:* $11,587. *Average non-need-based aid:* $5148. *Average indebtedness upon graduation:* $24,614.

Applying *Options:* electronic application, deferred entrance. *Application fee:* $25. *Required:* high school transcript, minimum 2.5 GPA. *Required for some:* essay or personal statement, 2 letters of recommendation. *Recommended:* interview.

Freshman Application Contact Mary Ellen Strieter, Admission Counselor Assistant/Receptionist, Mount Mary College, 2900 North Menomonee River Parkway, Milwaukee, WI 53222. *Phone:* 414-258-4810 Ext. 219. *Fax:* 414-256-0180. *E-mail:* admiss@mtmary.edu. *Web site:* http://www.mtmary.edu/.

See page 1454 for the College Close-Up.

Northland College
Ashland, Wisconsin

- **Independent** 4-year, founded 1892, affiliated with United Church of Christ
- **Small-town** 130-acre campus
- **Endowment** $15.9 million
- **Coed** 557 undergraduate students, 96% full-time, 53% women, 47% men
- **Moderately difficult** entrance level, 76% of applicants were admitted

Undergraduates 532 full-time, 25 part-time. Students come from 34 states and territories; 5 other countries; 58% are from out of state; 0.4% Black or African American, non-Hispanic/Latino; 1% Hispanic/Latino; 0.9% Asian, non-Hispanic/Latino; 0.2% Native Hawaiian or other Pacific Islander, non-Hispanic/Latino; 3% American Indian or Alaska Native, non-Hispanic/Latino; 1% Two or more races, non-Hispanic/Latino; 6% Race/ethnicity unknown; 3%

international; 8% transferred in; 67% live on campus. *Retention:* 75% of full-time freshmen returned.

Freshmen *Admission:* 602 applied, 458 admitted, 129 enrolled. *Average high school GPA:* 3.1. *Test scores:* SAT critical reading scores over 500: 58%; SAT math scores over 500: 52%; ACT scores over 18: 92%; SAT critical reading scores over 600: 19%; SAT math scores over 600: 19%; ACT scores over 24: 45%; ACT scores over 30: 7%.

Faculty *Total:* 59, 68% full-time, 73% with terminal degrees. *Student/faculty ratio:* 12:1.

Academics *Calendar:* 4-4-1. *Degree:* bachelor's. *Special study options:* advanced placement credit, cooperative education, distance learning, double majors, honors programs, independent study, internships, off-campus study, part-time degree program, services for LD students, student-designed majors, study abroad, summer session for credit. *Unusual degree programs:* 3-2 engineering with Michigan Technological University, Washington University in St. Louis.

Computers on Campus 125 computers/terminals are available on campus for general student use. Students can access the following: campus intranet, computer help desk, free student e-mail accounts, online (class) grades, online (class) registration, online (class) schedules. Campuswide network is available. 100% of college-owned or -operated housing units are wired for high-speed Internet access. Wireless service is available via classrooms, computer centers, computer labs, learning centers, libraries, student centers.

Student Life *Housing:* on-campus residence required through sophomore year. *Options:* coed, women-only, cooperative. Campus housing is university owned. Freshman campus housing is guaranteed. *Activities and organizations:* drama/theater group, student-run newspaper, radio station, choral group, Northland Volunteer Program, Northland College Student Association, Native American Student Association, Environmental Council, N Club. *Campus security:* 24-hour emergency response devices and patrols, late-night transport/escort service, controlled dormitory access. *Student services:* health clinic, personal/psychological counseling.

Athletics Member NCAA. All Division III. *Intercollegiate sports:* baseball M, basketball M/W, cross-country running M/W, ice hockey M, soccer M/W, softball W, volleyball W. *Intramural sports:* basketball M/W, football M/W, ice hockey M(c)/W(c), skiing (cross-country) M(c)/W(c), soccer M/W, softball M/W, table tennis M/W, ultimate Frisbee M/W, volleyball M/W.

Standardized Tests *Required:* SAT or ACT (for admission).

Costs (2011–12) *Comprehensive fee:* $33,776 includes full-time tuition ($25,725), mandatory fees ($841), and room and board ($7210). Full-time tuition and fees vary according to course load. Part-time tuition: $475 per credit hour. Part-time tuition and fees vary according to course load. *College room only:* $2990. Room and board charges vary according to board plan and housing facility. *Payment plan:* installment. *Waivers:* employees or children of employees.

Financial Aid Of all full-time matriculated undergraduates who enrolled in 2009, 548 applied for aid.

Applying *Options:* electronic application, deferred entrance. *Required:* high school transcript. *Recommended:* minimum 2 GPA. *Application deadlines:* rolling (freshmen), rolling (transfers). *Notification:* continuous (freshmen), continuous (transfers).

Freshman Application Contact Northland College, 1411 Ellis Avenue, Ashland, WI 54806-3925. *Phone:* 715-682-1257. *Toll-free phone:* 800-753-1840 (in-state); 800-753-1040 (out-of-state). *Web site:* http://www.northland.edu/.

Ripon College
Ripon, Wisconsin

- **Independent** 4-year, founded 1851
- **Small-town** 250-acre campus with easy access to Milwaukee
- **Endowment** $50.4 million
- **Coed** 1,065 undergraduate students, 99% full-time, 52% women, 48% men
- **Moderately difficult** entrance level, 78% of applicants were admitted

Undergraduates 1,054 full-time, 11 part-time. Students come from 31 states and territories; 18 other countries; 26% are from out of state; 2% Black or African American, non-Hispanic/Latino; 4% Hispanic/Latino; 1% Asian, non-Hispanic/Latino; 0.7% American Indian or Alaska Native, non-Hispanic/Latino; 1% Two or more races, non-Hispanic/Latino; 0.4% Race/ethnicity unknown; 3% international; 2% transferred in; 90% live on campus. *Retention:* 85% of full-time freshmen returned.

Freshmen *Admission:* 1,160 applied, 899 admitted, 289 enrolled. *Average high school GPA:* 3.38. *Test scores:* SAT critical reading scores over 500: 47%; SAT math scores over 500: 64%; ACT scores over 18: 94%; SAT critical reading scores over 600: 12%; SAT math scores over 600: 26%; ACT scores

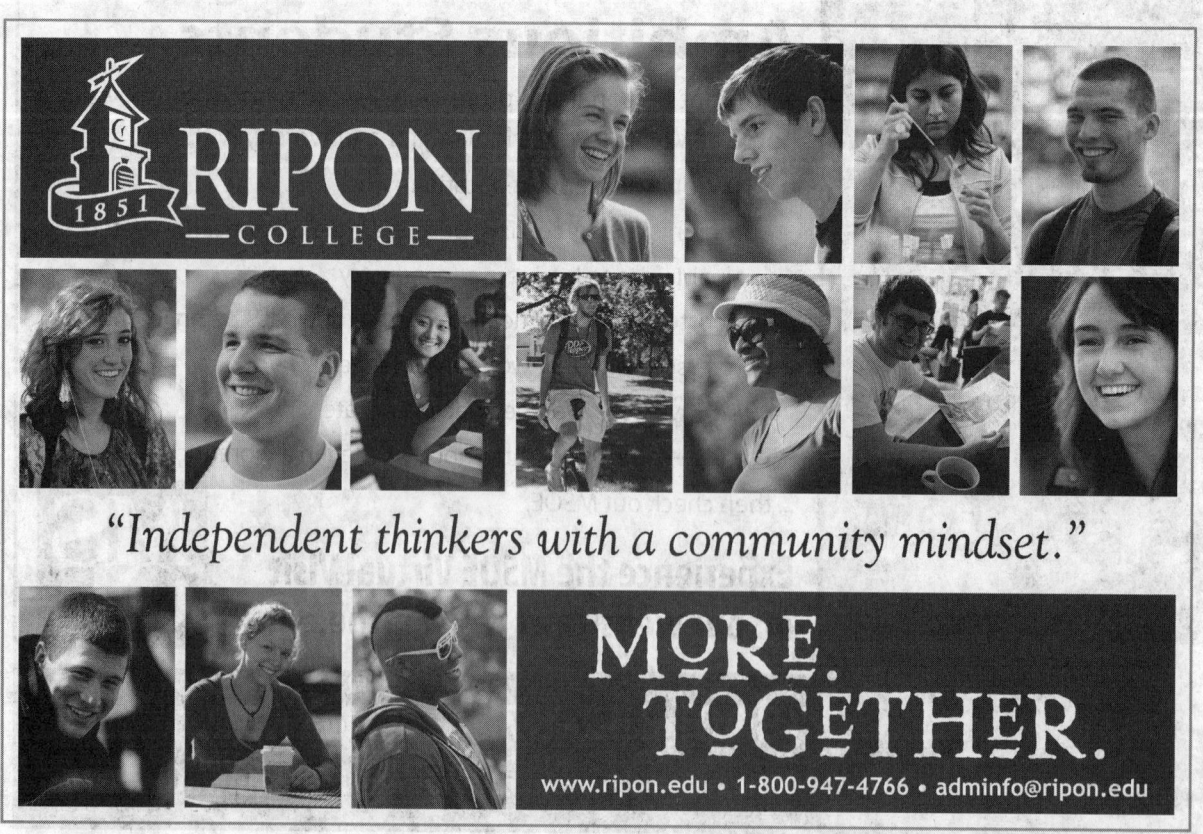

over 24: 49%; SAT critical reading scores over 700: 3%; SAT math scores over 700: 3%; ACT scores over 30: 10%.

Faculty *Total:* 98, 65% full-time, 76% with terminal degrees. *Student/faculty ratio:* 15:1.

Academics *Calendar:* semesters. *Degree:* bachelor's. *Special study options:* accelerated degree program, advanced placement credit, double majors, internships, off-campus study, part-time degree program, services for LD students, student-designed majors, study abroad. *ROTC:* Army (b). *Unusual degree programs:* 3-2 engineering with Rensselaer Polytechnic Institute, Washington University in St. Louis, University of Wisconsin-Madison; forestry with Duke University; nursing with Rush University; environmental studies with Duke University.

Computers on Campus 150 computers/terminals are available on campus for general student use. Students can access the following: campus intranet, computer help desk, free student e-mail accounts. Campuswide network is available. 100% of college-owned or -operated housing units are wired for high-speed Internet access. Wireless service is available via classrooms, libraries, student centers.

Student Life *Housing:* on-campus residence required through senior year. *Options:* coed, men-only, women-only. Campus housing is university owned. Freshman campus housing is guaranteed. *Activities and organizations:* drama/theater group, student-run newspaper, radio station, choral group, Environmental Group, Student Senate, Community Service Coalition, SMAC (Student Media and Activities Committee), national fraternities, national sororities. *Campus security:* 24-hour emergency response devices and patrols, student patrols, late-night transport/escort service, controlled dormitory access. *Student services:* health clinic, personal/psychological counseling.

Athletics Member NCAA. All Division III. *Intercollegiate sports:* baseball M, basketball M/W, cheerleading M(c)/W, cross-country running M/W, football M, golf M/W, rugby M(c)/W(c), soccer M/W, softball W, swimming and diving M/W, tennis M/W, track and field M/W, volleyball W. *Intramural sports:* basketball M/W, bowling M/W, equestrian sports M(c)/W(c), fencing M/W, football M/W, golf M/W, lacrosse M/W, racquetball M/W, soccer M/W, softball M/W, table tennis M/W, tennis M/W, ultimate Frisbee M/W, volleyball M/W.

Standardized Tests *Required:* SAT or ACT (for admission).

Costs (2011–12) *Comprehensive fee:* $36,959 includes full-time tuition ($28,414), mandatory fees ($275), and room and board ($8270). *College room*

only: $4390. *Payment plan:* installment. *Waivers:* employees or children of employees.

Financial Aid Of all full-time matriculated undergraduates who enrolled in 2009, 943 applied for aid, 862 were judged to have need, 270 had their need fully met. 454 Federal Work-Study jobs (averaging $1531). 569 state and other part-time jobs (averaging $1449). In 2009, 168 non-need-based awards were made. *Average percent of need met:* 89%. *Average financial aid package:* $22,365. *Average need-based loan:* $4378. *Average need-based gift aid:* $17,850. *Average non-need-based aid:* $10,587. *Average indebtedness upon graduation:* $26,073.

Applying *Options:* electronic application, deferred entrance. *Application fee:* $30. *Required:* essay or personal statement, high school transcript, minimum 2 GPA, 1 letter of recommendation. *Required for some:* interview. *Recommended:* interview. *Application deadlines:* rolling (freshmen), rolling (transfers). *Notification:* continuous (freshmen), continuous (transfers).

Freshman Application Contact Office of Admission, Ripon College, 300 Seward Street, PO Box 248, Ripon, WI 54971. *Phone:* 920-748-8337. *Toll-free phone:* 800-947-4766. *Fax:* 920-748-8335. *E-mail:* adminfo@ripon.edu. *Web site:* http://www.ripon.edu/.

See page 1532 for the College Close-Up.

St. Norbert College

De Pere, Wisconsin

- **Independent Roman Catholic** comprehensive, founded 1898
- **Suburban** 93-acre campus
- **Endowment** $59.6 million
- **Coed** 2,172 undergraduate students, 97% full-time, 59% women, 41% men
- **Moderately difficult** entrance level, 81% of applicants were admitted

Undergraduates 2,112 full-time, 60 part-time. Students come from 29 states and territories; 37 other countries; 31% are from out of state; 0.7% Black or African American, non-Hispanic/Latino; 2% Hispanic/Latino; 1% Asian, non-Hispanic/Latino; 0.6% American Indian or Alaska Native, non-Hispanic/Latino; 2% Two or more races, non-Hispanic/Latino; 5% international; 3% transferred in; 77% live on campus. *Retention:* 84% of full-time freshmen returned.

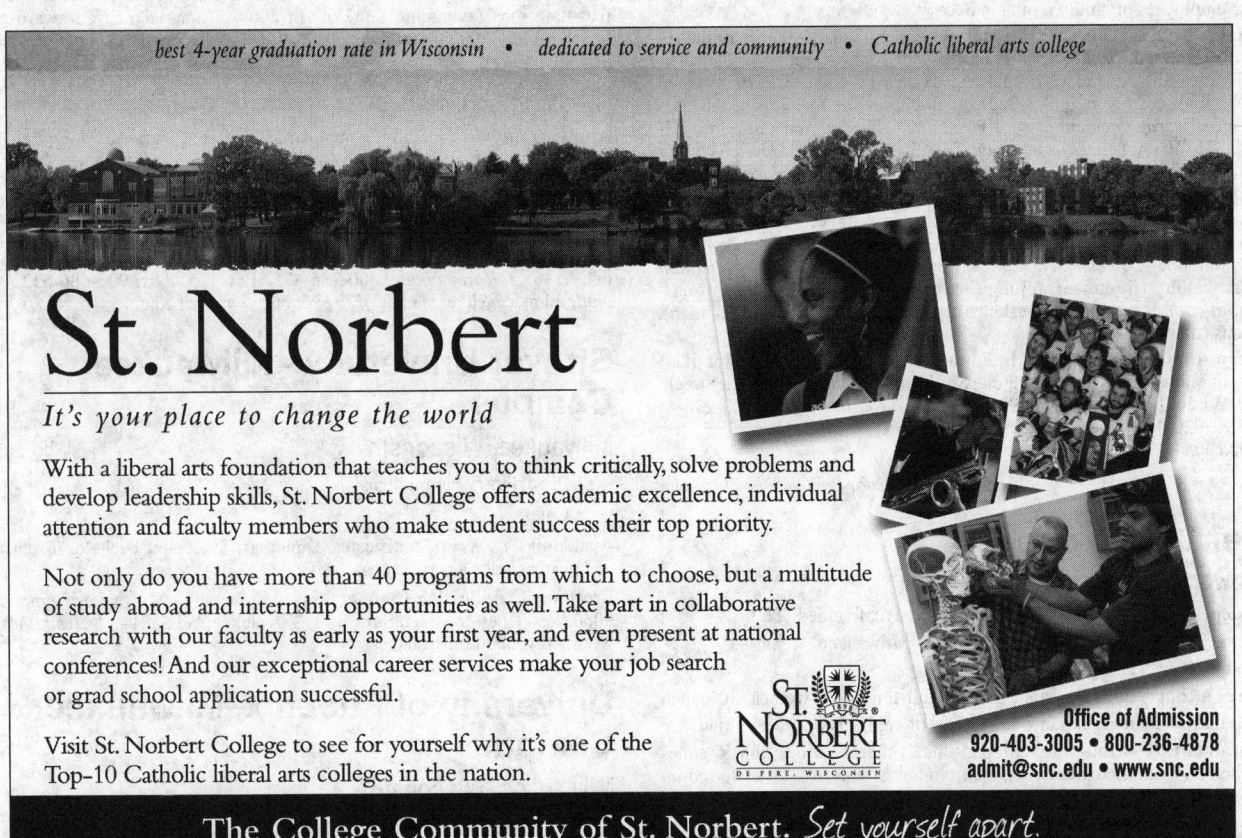

Freshmen *Admission:* 2,160 applied, 1,750 admitted, 604 enrolled. *Average high school GPA:* 3.47. *Test scores:* ACT scores over 18: 100%; ACT scores over 24: 63%; ACT scores over 30: 8%.

Faculty *Total:* 196, 69% full-time, 69% with terminal degrees. *Student/faculty ratio:* 15:1.

Academics *Calendar:* semesters. *Degrees:* bachelor's and master's. *Special study options:* academic remediation for entering students, advanced placement credit, distance learning, double majors, English as a second language, honors programs, independent study, internships, off-campus study, part-time degree program, services for LD students, student-designed majors, study abroad, summer session for credit. *ROTC:* Army (b).

Computers on Campus 247 computers/terminals are available on campus for general student use. Students can access the following: campus intranet, computer help desk, free student e-mail accounts, online (class) grades, online (class) registration, online (class) schedules. Campuswide network is available. 100% of college-owned or -operated housing units are wired for high-speed Internet access. Wireless service is available via classrooms, computer centers, computer labs, dorm rooms, learning centers, libraries, student centers.

Student Life *Housing:* on-campus residence required through senior year. *Options:* coed, women-only, disabled students. Campus housing is university owned. Freshman campus housing is guaranteed. *Activities and organizations:* drama/theater group, student-run newspaper, radio and television station, choral group, Student Education Association, SNC Radio, Circle K, Pre-Health Sciences, Spanish Club, national fraternities, national sororities. *Campus security:* 24-hour emergency response devices and patrols, student patrols, late-night transport/escort service, controlled dormitory access, crime prevention programs. *Student services:* health clinic, personal/psychological counseling, women's center.

Athletics Member NCAA. All Division III. *Intercollegiate sports:* baseball M, basketball M/W, cross-country running M/W, football M, golf M/W, ice hockey M/W, soccer M/W, softball W, tennis M/W, track and field M/W, volleyball W. *Intramural sports:* badminton M/W, basketball M/W, cheerleading M(c)/W(c), crew M(c)/W(c), football M/W, lacrosse M, racquetball M/W, skiing (downhill) M(c)/W(c), softball M/W, volleyball M/W.

Standardized Tests *Required:* SAT or ACT (for admission).

Costs (2010–11) *Comprehensive fee:* $35,392 includes full-time tuition ($27,583), mandatory fees ($460), and room and board ($7349). Full-time tuition and fees vary according to course load. Part-time tuition: $862 per credit. Part-time tuition and fees vary according to course load. *College room only:* $3854. Room and board charges vary according to board plan, housing facility, and student level. *Payment plans:* installment, deferred payment. *Waivers:* employees or children of employees.

Financial Aid Of all full-time matriculated undergraduates who enrolled in 2008, 1,617 applied for aid, 1,373 were judged to have need, 542 had their need fully met. 331 Federal Work-Study jobs (averaging $1223). 670 state and other part-time jobs (averaging $1225). In 2008, 580 non-need-based awards were made. *Average percent of need met:* 87%. *Average financial aid package:* $20,341. *Average need-based loan:* $4613. *Average need-based gift aid:* $15,113. *Average non-need-based aid:* $8957. *Average indebtedness upon graduation:* $29,836.

Applying *Options:* electronic application, deferred entrance. *Application fee:* $25. *Required:* high school transcript, 1 letter of recommendation. *Required for some:* interview. *Recommended:* essay or personal statement. *Application deadlines:* rolling (freshmen), rolling (out-of-state freshmen), rolling (transfers). *Notification:* continuous (freshmen), continuous (out-of-state freshmen), continuous (transfers).

Freshman Application Contact Mr. Edward Lamm, Executive Director of Enrollment Management and Marketing, St. Norbert College, 100 Grant Street, De Pere, WI 54115-2099. *Phone:* 920-403-3005. *Toll-free phone:* 800-236-4878. *Fax:* 920-403-4072. *E-mail:* admit@snc.edu. *Web site:* http://www.snc.edu/.

See page 1582 for the College Close-Up.

Silver Lake College

Manitowoc, Wisconsin

- **Independent Roman Catholic** comprehensive, founded 1869
- **Rural** 30-acre campus with easy access to Milwaukee
- **Endowment** $5.2 million
- **Coed** 482 undergraduate students, 40% full-time, 70% women, 30% men
- **Minimally difficult** entrance level, 72% of applicants were admitted

Undergraduates 194 full-time, 288 part-time. Students come from 6 states and territories; 4 other countries; 4% are from out of state; 14% transferred in; 18% live on campus. *Retention:* 63% of full-time freshmen returned.

Freshmen *Admission:* 116 applied, 84 admitted, 41 enrolled. *Average high school GPA:* 2.98. *Test scores:* ACT scores over 18: 68%; ACT scores over 24: 17%; ACT scores over 30: 2%.

Faculty *Total:* 109, 32% full-time, 29% with terminal degrees. *Student/faculty ratio:* 7:1.

Academics *Calendar:* semesters. *Degrees:* certificates, associate, bachelor's, master's, and postbachelor's certificates. *Special study options:* academic remediation for entering students, accelerated degree program, adult/continuing education programs, advanced placement credit, distance learning, double majors, independent study, internships, part-time degree program, services for LD students, student-designed majors, summer session for credit.

Computers on Campus 88 computers/terminals are available on campus for general student use. Students can access the following: free student e-mail accounts, online (class) grades, online (class) registration, online (class) schedules. Campuswide network is available. 100% of college-owned or -operated housing units are wired for high-speed Internet access. Wireless service is available via classrooms, computer centers, computer labs, dorm rooms, learning centers, libraries, student centers.

Student Life *Housing:* on-campus residence required through junior year. *Options:* coed, men-only, women-only, disabled students. Campus housing is university owned. Freshman campus housing is guaranteed. *Activities and organizations:* choral group, Campus Ministry projects, Education-related clubs, Student Forum (Student government), Optimist Club, Tri Beta (Biology). *Campus security:* 24-hour emergency response devices, student patrols, late-night transport/escort service, controlled dormitory access. *Student services:* health clinic, personal/psychological counseling.

Athletics Member USCAA. *Intercollegiate sports:* basketball M(s)/W(s), cross-country running M(s)/W(s), golf M(s)/W(s). *Intramural sports:* bowling M/W, football M/W, soccer M(c)/W(c), table tennis M/W, ultimate Frisbee M/W, volleyball M/W.

Standardized Tests *Required:* SAT or ACT (for admission).

Costs (2011–12) *Comprehensive fee:* $30,320 includes full-time tuition ($21,580), mandatory fees ($240), and room and board ($8500). Full-time tuition and fees vary according to degree level, location, program, and reciprocity agreements. Part-time tuition: $720 per credit. Part-time tuition and fees vary according to course load, degree level, location, and program. *Required fees:* $65 per term part-time. *College room only:* $4900. Room and board charges vary according to board plan and housing facility. *Payment plans:* installment, deferred payment. *Waivers:* senior citizens and employees or children of employees.

Financial Aid Of all full-time matriculated undergraduates who enrolled in 2009, 151 applied for aid, 145 were judged to have need, 17 had their need fully met. 88 Federal Work-Study jobs (averaging $1989). 3 state and other part-time jobs (averaging $2475). In 2009, 7 non-need-based awards were made. *Average percent of need met:* 67%. *Average financial aid package:* $17,932. *Average need-based loan:* $4576. *Average need-based gift aid:* $9602. *Average non-need-based aid:* $9713. *Average indebtedness upon graduation:* $19,386.

Applying *Options:* electronic application, deferred entrance. *Required:* high school transcript, minimum 2 GPA. *Required for some:* interview. *Application deadlines:* 8/1 (freshmen), 8/1 (transfers). *Notification:* continuous (freshmen), continuous (transfers).

Freshman Application Contact Dan Connolly, Admissions Counselor, Silver Lake College, 2406 South Alverno Road, Manitowoc, WI 54220. *Phone:* 920-686-6186. *Toll-free phone:* 800-236-4752 Ext. 175. *Fax:* 920-686-6322. *E-mail:* admslc@silver.sl.edu. *Web site:* http://www.sl.edu/.

Strayer University - Milwaukee Campus

Milwaukee, Wisconsin

- **Proprietary** comprehensive
- **Coed**

Academics *Degrees:* certificates, diplomas, associate, bachelor's, master's, and postbachelor's certificates.

Freshman Application Contact Strayer University - Milwaukee Campus, 9000 West Chester Street, Suite 300, Milwaukee, WI 53214. *Web site:* http://www.strayer.edu/milwaukee.

University of Phoenix–Milwaukee Campus

Milwaukee, Wisconsin

Admissions Office Contact University of Phoenix–Milwaukee Campus, 20075 Watertower Boulevard, Milwaukee, WI 53045. *Toll-free phone:* 866-766-0766. *Web site:* http://www.phoenix.edu/.

University of Wisconsin–Eau Claire
Eau Claire, Wisconsin

- **State-supported** comprehensive, founded 1916, part of University of Wisconsin System
- **Small-town** 333-acre campus with easy access to Minneapolis-St. Paul
- **Endowment** $26.8 million
- **Coed** 10,784 undergraduate students, 91% full-time, 59% women, 41% men
- **Moderately difficult** entrance level, 71% of applicants were admitted

Undergraduates 9,851 full-time, 933 part-time. Students come from 22 states and territories; 41 other countries; 21% are from out of state; 0.6% Black or African American, non-Hispanic/Latino; 2% Hispanic/Latino; 3% Asian, non-Hispanic/Latino; 0.5% American Indian or Alaska Native, non-Hispanic/Latino; 0.8% Two or more races, non-Hispanic/Latino; 1% Race/ethnicity unknown; 2% international; 6% transferred in; 39% live on campus. *Retention:* 82% of full-time freshmen returned.

Freshmen *Admission:* 7,108 applied, 5,047 admitted, 2,070 enrolled. *Test scores:* SAT critical reading scores over 500: 68%; SAT math scores over 500: 88%; ACT scores over 18: 99%; SAT critical reading scores over 600: 44%; SAT math scores over 600: 53%; ACT scores over 24: 60%; SAT critical reading scores over 700: 9%; SAT math scores over 700: 12%; ACT scores over 30: 6%.

Faculty *Total:* 529, 80% full-time, 69% with terminal degrees. *Student/faculty ratio:* 22:1.

Academics *Calendar:* semesters. *Degrees:* certificates, associate, bachelor's, master's, doctoral-professional, post-master's, and postbachelor's certificates. *Special study options:* academic remediation for entering students, accelerated degree program, adult/continuing education programs, advanced placement credit, cooperative education, distance learning, double majors, English as a second language, external degree program, honors programs, independent study, internships, off-campus study, part-time degree program, services for LD students, student-designed majors, study abroad, summer session for credit. *ROTC:* Army (b).

Computers on Campus 900 computers/terminals are available on campus for general student use. Students can access the following: campus intranet, computer help desk, free student e-mail accounts, online (class) grades, online (class) registration, online (class) schedules, course management system, library reference staff online chat, ability to check where there are open seats in the general access computer labs, laptop check out pool. Campuswide network is available. 100% of college-owned or -operated housing units are wired for high-speed Internet access. Wireless service is available via classrooms, computer centers, computer labs, learning centers, libraries, student centers.

Student Life *Housing:* on-campus residence required through sophomore year. *Options:* coed, men-only, women-only. Campus housing is university owned. Freshman campus housing is guaranteed. *Activities and organizations:* drama/theater group, student-run newspaper, radio and television station, choral group, marching band, American Marketing Association, Beta Upsilon Sigma, Blue Gold Marching Band, Singing Statesmen, Navigators, national fraternities, national sororities. *Campus security:* 24-hour emergency response devices and patrols, student patrols, late-night transport/escort service, controlled dormitory access. *Student services:* health clinic, personal/psychological counseling, women's center, legal services.

Athletics Member NCAA. All Division III. *Intercollegiate sports:* basketball M/W, cross-country running M/W, football M, golf M/W, gymnastics W, ice hockey M/W, soccer W, softball W, swimming and diving M/W, tennis M/W, track and field M/W, volleyball W, wrestling M. *Intramural sports:* baseball M(c), basketball M/W, bowling M(c)/W(c), cheerleading M(c)/W(c), equestrian sports M(c)/W(c), football M/W, ice hockey M, lacrosse M(c)/W(c), racquetball M/W, rock climbing M(c)/W(c), rugby M(c)/W(c), skiing (cross-country) M(c)/W(c), skiing (downhill) M(c)/W(c), soccer M/W, softball M/W, table tennis M(c)/W(c), tennis M/W, ultimate Frisbee M/W, volleyball M/W.

Standardized Tests *Required:* SAT or ACT (for admission).

Costs (2010–11) *Tuition:* state resident $6122 full-time, $255 per credit part-time; nonresident $13,695 full-time, $571 per credit part-time. Full-time tuition and fees vary according to reciprocity agreements. Part-time tuition and fees vary according to reciprocity agreements. *Required fees:* $1242 full-time, $52 per credit part-time, $2 per term part-time. *Room and board:* $5830; room only: $2920. Room and board charges vary according to board plan and housing facility. *Payment plan:* installment. *Waivers:* minority students.

Financial Aid Of all full-time matriculated undergraduates who enrolled in 2008, 7,054 applied for aid, 4,704 were judged to have need, 2,860 had their need fully met. 2,510 Federal Work-Study jobs (averaging $1711). 1,737 state and other part-time jobs (averaging $1553). In 2008, 817 non-need-based awards were made. *Average percent of need met:* 91%. *Average financial aid package:* $8506. *Average need-based loan:* $4595. *Average need-based gift aid:* $5288. *Average non-need-based aid:* $1768. *Average indebtedness upon graduation:* $21,185.

Applying *Options:* electronic application, early admission. *Application fee:* $44. *Required:* high school transcript. *Recommended:* essay or personal state-

ment. *Application deadlines:* rolling (freshmen), 7/1 (transfers). *Notification:* continuous (freshmen), continuous (transfers).

Freshman Application Contact Ms. Kristina Anderson, Executive Director of Enrollment Management and Director of Admissions, University of Wisconsin–Eau Claire, PO Box 4004, Eau Claire, WI 54702-4004. *Phone:* 715-836-5415. *Fax:* 715-836-2409. *E-mail:* admissions@uwec.edu. *Web site:* http://www.uwec.edu/.

University of Wisconsin–Green Bay
Green Bay, Wisconsin

- **State-supported** comprehensive, founded 1968, part of University of Wisconsin System
- **Suburban** 700-acre campus with easy access to Milwaukee
- **Endowment** $16.8 million
- **Coed** 6,389 undergraduate students, 75% full-time, 63% women, 37% men
- **Moderately difficult** entrance level, 66% of applicants were admitted

Undergraduates 4,815 full-time, 1,574 part-time. Students come from 38 states and territories; 30 other countries; 6% are from out of state; 0.9% Black or African American, non-Hispanic/Latino; 2% Hispanic/Latino; 3% Asian, non-Hispanic/Latino; 0.1% Native Hawaiian or other Pacific Islander, non-Hispanic/Latino; 2% American Indian or Alaska Native, non-Hispanic/Latino; 1% Two or more races, non-Hispanic/Latino; 1% Race/ethnicity unknown; 1% international; 12% transferred in; 32% live on campus. *Retention:* 73% of full-time freshmen returned.

Freshmen *Admission:* 3,211 applied, 2,130 admitted, 906 enrolled. *Average high school GPA:* 3.32. *Test scores:* SAT critical reading scores over 500: 64%; SAT math scores over 500: 77%; SAT writing scores over 500: 66%; ACT scores over 18: 97%; SAT critical reading scores over 600: 19%; SAT math scores over 600: 41%; SAT writing scores over 600: 14%; ACT scores over 24: 39%; SAT critical reading scores over 700: 5%; SAT math scores over 700: 9%; ACT scores over 30: 4%.

Faculty *Total:* 356, 56% full-time, 55% with terminal degrees. *Student/faculty ratio:* 22:1.

Academics *Calendar:* semesters. *Degrees:* associate, bachelor's, master's, and postbachelor's certificates. *Special study options:* academic remediation for entering students, adult/continuing education programs, advanced placement credit, distance learning, double majors, external degree program, independent study, internships, off-campus study, part-time degree program, services for LD students, student-designed majors, study abroad, summer session for credit. *ROTC:* Army (c). *Unusual degree programs:* 3-2 engineering with University of Wisconsin-Milwaukee.

Computers on Campus 550 computers/terminals are available on campus for general student use. Students can access the following: computer help desk, free student e-mail accounts, online (class) grades, online (class) registration, online (class) schedules, online degree progress, online financial records and bill paying. Campuswide network is available. 100% of college-owned or -operated housing units are wired for high-speed Internet access. Wireless service is available via entire campus.

Student Life *Housing options:* coed. Campus housing is university owned and is provided by a third party. Freshman applicants given priority for college housing. *Activities and organizations:* drama/theater group, student-run newspaper, radio station, choral group, Good Times, Psychology and Human Development Club, Student Ambassadors, Residence Hall Apartment Association, Student Government Association. *Campus security:* 24-hour emergency response devices and patrols, late-night transport/escort service, controlled dormitory access. *Student services:* health clinic, personal/psychological counseling.

Athletics Member NCAA. All Division I. *Intercollegiate sports:* basketball M(s)/W(s), cross-country running M(s)/W(s), golf M(s)/W(s), skiing (cross-country) M(s)/W(s), soccer M(s)/W(s), softball W(s), swimming and diving M(s)/W(s), tennis M(s)/W(s), volleyball W(s). *Intramural sports:* basketball M/W, bowling M/W, cheerleading M/W, football M/W, golf M/W, racquetball M/W, sailing M/W, skiing (cross-country) M/W, soccer M/W, softball M/W, swimming and diving M/W, tennis M/W, ultimate Frisbee M/W, volleyball M/W, weight lifting M/W.

Standardized Tests *Required:* SAT or ACT (for admission).

Costs (2010–11) *One-time required fee:* $200. *Tuition:* state resident $5659 full-time, $236 per credit hour part-time; nonresident $13,232 full-time, $551 per credit hour part-time. Full-time tuition and fees vary according to course load and reciprocity agreements. Part-time tuition and fees vary according to reciprocity agreements. *Required fees:* $1314 full-time, $52 per credit hour part-time. *Room and board:* $7290; room only: $4320. Room and board charges vary according to board plan and housing facility. *Payment plan:* installment. *Waivers:* senior citizens.

Financial Aid Of all full-time matriculated undergraduates who enrolled in 2009, 3,950 applied for aid, 3,237 were judged to have need, 1,427 had their need fully met. 250 Federal Work-Study jobs (averaging $2000). In 2009, 47 non-need-based awards were made. *Average percent of need met:* 84%. *Average financial aid package: $10,711. *Average need-based loan:* $5163. *Average need-based gift aid:* $6251. *Average non-need-based aid:* $1721. *Average indebtedness upon graduation:* $22,399.

Applying *Options:* electronic application, deferred entrance. *Application fee:* $44. *Required:* essay or personal statement, high school transcript. *Required for some:* interview. *Application deadlines:* rolling (freshmen), rolling (out-of-state freshmen), rolling (transfers). *Notification:* continuous (freshmen), continuous (out-of-state freshmen), continuous (transfers).

Freshman Application Contact Ms. Pam Harvey-Jacobs, Director of Admissions, University of Wisconsin–Green Bay, 2420 Nicolet Drive, Green Bay, WI 54311-7001. *Phone:* 920-465-2111. *Toll-free phone:* 888-367-8942. *Fax:* 920-465-5754. *E-mail:* uwgb@uwgb.edu. *Web site:* http://www.uwgb.edu/.

University of Wisconsin–La Crosse
La Crosse, Wisconsin

- **State-supported** comprehensive, founded 1909, part of University of Wisconsin System
- **Suburban** 121-acre campus
- **Endowment** $13.8 million
- **Coed** 8,958 undergraduate students, 94% full-time, 57% women, 43% men
- **Moderately difficult** entrance level, 78% of applicants were admitted

Undergraduates 8,460 full-time, 498 part-time. Students come from 28 states and territories; 34 other countries; 15% are from out of state; 1% Black or African American, non-Hispanic/Latino; 2% Hispanic/Latino; 3% Asian, non-Hispanic/Latino; 0.1% Native Hawaiian or other Pacific Islander, non-Hispanic/Latino; 0.4% American Indian or Alaska Native, non-Hispanic/Latino; 1% Two or more races, non-Hispanic/Latino; 1% Race/ethnicity unknown; 3% international; 6% transferred in; 34% live on campus. *Retention:* 86% of full-time freshmen returned.

Freshmen *Admission:* 6,004 applied, 4,658 admitted, 1,837 enrolled. *Test scores:* ACT scores over 18: 99%; ACT scores over 24: 66%; ACT scores over 30: 6%.

Faculty *Total:* 546, 76% full-time, 52% with terminal degrees. *Student/faculty ratio:* 20:1.

Academics *Calendar:* semesters. *Degrees:* certificates, associate, bachelor's, master's, doctoral-other, and postbachelor's certificates. *Special study options:* academic remediation for entering students, adult/continuing education programs, advanced placement credit, cooperative education, distance learning, double majors, English as a second language, independent study, internships, off-campus study, part-time degree program, services for LD students, study abroad, summer session for credit. *ROTC:* Army (b). *Unusual degree programs:* 3-2 engineering with University of Wisconsin-Madison, University of Wisconsin-Milwaukee, University of Wisconsin- Platteville, University of Minnesota; physical therapy and physics, physical therapy and biology, occupational therapy and psychology.

Computers on Campus 575 computers/terminals and 125 ports are available on campus for general student use. Students can access the following: campus intranet, computer help desk, free student e-mail accounts, online (class) grades, online (class) registration, online (class) schedules. Campuswide network is available. 100% of college-owned or -operated housing units are wired for high-speed Internet access. Wireless service is available via classrooms, computer centers, computer labs, dorm rooms, learning centers, libraries, student centers.

Student Life *Housing:* on-campus residence required for freshman year. *Options:* coed, disabled students. Campus housing is university owned. Freshman applicants given priority for college housing. *Activities and organizations:* drama/theater group, student-run newspaper, radio and television station, choral group, marching band, Sports and Activities Club, Residential Hall Council, religious/spiritual organizations, Human Diversity Organizations, departmental/professional, national fraternities, national sororities. *Campus security:* 24-hour emergency response devices and patrols, late-night transport/escort service, controlled dormitory access. *Student services:* health clinic, personal/psychological counseling, women's center, legal services.

Athletics Member NCAA. All Division III. *Intercollegiate sports:* baseball M, basketball M/W, cross-country running M/W, football M, gymnastics W, soccer W, softball W, swimming and diving M/W, tennis M/W, track and field M/W, volleyball W, weight lifting M/W, wrestling M. *Intramural sports:* badminton M/W, basketball M/W, cheerleading M/W, equestrian sports W(c), football M/W, golf M/W, ice hockey W(c), lacrosse M(c)/W(c), racquetball M/W, rugby M(c)/W(c), skiing (downhill) M(c)/W(c), soccer M(c)/W, softball M/W, table tennis M/W, tennis M/W, ultimate Frisbee M/W, volleyball M(c)/W(c).

Standardized Tests *Required:* SAT or ACT (for admission).

Costs (2010–11) *Tuition:* state resident $6809 full-time, $284 per credit hour part-time; nonresident $14,382 full-time, $599 per credit hour part-time. Full-time tuition and fees vary according to program and reciprocity agreements. Part-time tuition and fees vary according to course load, program, and reci-

procity agreements. *Required fees:* $1102 full-time. *Room and board:* $5630; room only: $3240. Room and board charges vary according to board plan and housing facility. *Payment plan:* installment. *Waivers:* minority students.

Financial Aid Of all full-time matriculated undergraduates who enrolled in 2008, 5,492 applied for aid, 3,720 were judged to have need, 787 had their need fully met. In 2008, 311 non-need-based awards were made. *Average percent of need met:* 73%. *Average financial aid package:* $6891. *Average need-based loan:* $3995. *Average need-based gift aid:* $5335. *Average non-need-based aid:* $1070. *Average indebtedness upon graduation:* $21,420.

Applying *Options:* electronic application. *Application fee:* $44. *Required:* essay or personal statement, high school transcript. *Required for some:* interview. *Application deadlines:* rolling (freshmen), rolling (out-of-state freshmen), rolling (transfers). *Notification:* continuous (freshmen), continuous (out-of-state freshmen), continuous (transfers).

Freshman Application Contact Ms. Kathryn Kiefer, Director of Admissions, University of Wisconsin–La Crosse, 1725 State Street, La Crosse, WI 54601. *Phone:* 608-785-8939. *Fax:* 608-785-8940. *E-mail:* admissions@uwlax.edu. *Web site:* http://www.uwlax.edu/.

University of Wisconsin–Madison
Madison, Wisconsin

- **State-supported** university, founded 1848, part of University of Wisconsin System
- **Urban** 1050-acre campus with easy access to Milwaukee
- **Endowment** $1.6 billion
- **Coed** 30,555 undergraduate students, 92% full-time, 52% women, 48% men
- **Very difficult** entrance level, 57% of applicants were admitted

Undergraduates 28,021 full-time, 2,534 part-time. Students come from 52 states and territories; 92 other countries; 32% are from out of state; 2% Black or African American, non-Hispanic/Latino; 4% Hispanic/Latino; 5% Asian, non-Hispanic/Latino; 0.1% Native Hawaiian or other Pacific Islander, non-Hispanic/Latino; 0.4% American Indian or Alaska Native, non-Hispanic/Latino; 1% Two or more races, non-Hispanic/Latino; 3% Race/ethnicity unknown; 6% international; 4% transferred in; 25% live on campus. *Retention:* 95% of full-time freshmen returned.

Freshmen *Admission:* 25,522 applied, 14,423 admitted, 5,927 enrolled. *Average high school GPA:* 3.69. *Test scores:* SAT critical reading scores over 500: 87%; SAT math scores over 500: 98%; SAT writing scores over 500: 96%; ACT scores over 18: 100%; SAT critical reading scores over 600: 53%; SAT math scores over 600: 84%; SAT writing scores over 600: 70%; ACT scores over 24: 94%; SAT critical reading scores over 700: 15%; SAT math scores over 700: 45%; SAT writing scores over 700: 17%; ACT scores over 30: 35%.

Faculty *Total:* 2,864, 84% full-time, 87% with terminal degrees. *Student/faculty ratio:* 17:1.

Academics *Calendar:* semesters. *Degrees:* bachelor's, master's, doctoral-professional, doctoral-research/scholarship, and post-master's certificates. *Special study options:* accelerated degree program, adult/continuing education programs, advanced placement credit, cooperative education, distance learning, double majors, English as a second language, honors programs, independent study, internships, part-time degree program, services for LD students, student-designed majors, study abroad, summer session for credit. *ROTC:* Army (b), Navy (b), Air Force (b).

Computers on Campus 1,000 computers/terminals are available on campus for general student use. Students can access the following: computer help desk, free student e-mail accounts, online (class) grades, online (class) registration, online (class) schedules. Campuswide network is available. 100% of college-owned or -operated housing units are wired for high-speed Internet access. Wireless service is available via entire campus.

Student Life *Housing options:* coed, men-only, women-only, cooperative. Campus housing is university owned. Freshman applicants given priority for college housing. *Activities and organizations:* drama/theater group, student-run newspaper, radio station, choral group, marching band, national fraternities, national sororities. *Campus security:* 24-hour emergency response devices and patrols, late-night transport/escort service, controlled dormitory access. *Student services:* health clinic, personal/psychological counseling, women's center.

Athletics Member NCAA. All Division I except football (Division I-A). *Intercollegiate sports:* basketball M(s)/W(s), cheerleading M/W, crew M/W, cross-country running M(s)/W(s), golf M(s)/W(s), ice hockey M(s)/W(s), sailing M(c)/W(c), soccer M(s)/W(s), softball W(s), swimming and diving M(s)/W(s), tennis M(s)/W(s), track and field M(s)/W(s), ultimate Frisbee M(c)/W(c), volleyball W(s), water polo M(c)/W(c), wrestling M(s).

Standardized Tests *Required:* SAT or ACT (for admission).

Costs (2010–11) *Tuition:* state resident $7933 full-time, $376 per credit hour part-time; nonresident $23,183 full-time, $1012 per credit hour part-time. Full-time tuition and fees vary according to program and reciprocity agreements. Part-time tuition and fees vary according to course load, program, and reciprocity agreements. *Required fees:* $1054 full-time, $46 per credit hour part-time. *Room and board:* $7690. Room and board charges vary according to board plan and housing facility.

Financial Aid Of all full-time matriculated undergraduates who enrolled in 2009, 15,444 applied for aid, 11,468 were judged to have need, 2,403 had their need fully met. In 2009, 2168 non-need-based awards were made. *Average percent of need met:* 66%. *Average financial aid package:* $11,268. *Average need-based loan:* $4862. *Average need-based gift aid:* $6222. *Average non-need-based aid:* $3214. *Average indebtedness upon graduation:* $22,872.

Applying *Options:* electronic application, deferred entrance. *Application fee:* $44. *Required:* essay or personal statement, high school transcript. *Recommended:* 2 letters of recommendation. *Application deadlines:* 2/1 (freshmen), 2/1 (transfers). *Notification:* continuous (freshmen), continuous (transfers).

Freshman Application Contact Office of Admissions and Recruitment, University of Wisconsin–Madison, 702 West Johnson Street, Suite 101, Madison, WI 53706-1481. *Phone:* 608-262-3961. *Fax:* 608-262-7706. *E-mail:* onwisconsin@admissions.wisc.edu. *Web site:* http://www.wisc.edu/.

University of Wisconsin–Milwaukee

Milwaukee, Wisconsin

- **State-supported** university, founded 1956, part of University of Wisconsin System
- **Urban** 90-acre campus
- **Coed**
- **Moderately difficult** entrance level

Faculty *Student/faculty ratio:* 21:1.

Academics *Calendar:* semesters. *Degrees:* certificates, bachelor's, master's, doctoral-professional, doctoral-research/scholarship, post-master's, and post-bachelor's certificates.

Student Life *Campus security:* 24-hour emergency response devices, late-night transport/escort service.

Athletics Member NCAA. All Division I.

Standardized Tests *Required:* SAT or ACT (for admission), ACT for state residents (for admission).

Costs (2010–11) *Tuition:* state resident $8151 full-time, $340 per credit hour part-time; nonresident $17,880 full-time, $745 per credit hour part-time. Full-time tuition and fees vary according to location, program, and reciprocity agreements. Part-time tuition and fees vary according to course load, location, program, and reciprocity agreements. *Required fees:* $924 full-time. *Room only:* $4310. Room and board charges vary according to board plan and housing facility.

Financial Aid Of all full-time matriculated undergraduates who enrolled in 2008, 16,237 applied for aid, 13,398 were judged to have need, 3,368 had their need fully met. In 2008, 101 non-need-based awards were made. *Average percent of need met:* 57. *Average financial aid package:* $7311. *Average need-based loan:* $4499. *Average need-based gift aid:* $5996. *Average non-need-based aid:* $2606. *Average indebtedness upon graduation:* $15,772.

Applying *Options:* electronic application, deferred entrance. *Application fee:* $44. *Required:* high school transcript. *Recommended:* essay or personal statement.

Freshman Application Contact Ms. Jan Ford, Director, Recruitment and Outreach, University of Wisconsin–Milwaukee, PO Box 413, Milwaukee, WI 53201-0413. *Phone:* 414-229-4397. *Fax:* 414-229-6940. *E-mail:* uwmlook@uwm.edu. *Web site:* http://www.uwm.edu/.

University of Wisconsin–Oshkosh

Oshkosh, Wisconsin

- **State-supported** comprehensive, founded 1871, part of University of Wisconsin System
- **Suburban** 192-acre campus with easy access to Milwaukee
- **Coed**
- **Moderately difficult** entrance level

Faculty *Student/faculty ratio:* 21:1.

Academics *Calendar:* semesters. *Degrees:* certificates, associate, bachelor's, master's, and postbachelor's certificates.

Student Life *Campus security:* 24-hour emergency response devices and patrols, student patrols, late-night transport/escort service, controlled dormitory access.

Athletics Member NCAA. All Division III.

Standardized Tests *Required:* SAT or ACT (for admission), ACT required for state residents (for admission).

Costs (2010–11) *Tuition:* state resident $6682 full-time; nonresident $14,670 full-time. *Room and board:* $6922.

Financial Aid Of all full-time matriculated undergraduates who enrolled in 2008, 6,020 applied for aid, 4,093 were judged to have need, 686 had their need fully met. In 2008, 1500 non-need-based awards were made. *Average percent of need met:* 35. *Average financial aid package:* $4500. *Average*

need-based loan: $4000. *Average need-based gift aid:* $1000. *Average non-need-based aid:* $800. *Average indebtedness upon graduation:* $19,000.

Applying *Options:* electronic application, deferred entrance. *Application fee:* $35. *Required:* high school transcript. *Recommended:* essay or personal statement.

Freshman Application Contact Mr. Richard Hillman, Associate Director of Admissions, University of Wisconsin–Oshkosh, 800 Algoma Boulevard, Oshkosh, WI 54901. *Phone:* 920-424-0202. *E-mail:* oshadmuw@uwosh.edu. *Web site:* http://www.uwosh.edu/.

University of Wisconsin–Parkside

Kenosha, Wisconsin

- **State-supported** comprehensive, founded 1968, part of University of Wisconsin System
- **Suburban** 700-acre campus with easy access to Chicago and Milwaukee
- **Endowment** $2.0 million
- **Coed** 5,015 undergraduate students, 72% full-time, 53% women, 47% men
- **Moderately difficult** entrance level, 65% of applicants were admitted

Undergraduates 3,632 full-time, 1,383 part-time. Students come from 27 states and territories; 15 other countries; 11% are from out of state; 11% Black or African American, non-Hispanic/Latino; 10% Hispanic/Latino; 3% Asian, non-Hispanic/Latino; 0.2% Native Hawaiian or other Pacific Islander, non-Hispanic/Latino; 0.3% American Indian or Alaska Native, non-Hispanic/Latino; 2% Two or more races, non-Hispanic/Latino; 1% Race/ethnicity unknown; 1% international; 7% transferred in; 18% live on campus. *Retention:* 65% of full-time freshmen returned.

Freshmen *Admission:* 2,267 applied, 1,468 admitted, 805 enrolled. *Test scores:* ACT scores over 18: 85%; ACT scores over 24: 20%; ACT scores over 30: 1%.

Faculty *Total:* 300, 60% full-time. *Student/faculty ratio:* 19:1.

Academics *Calendar:* semesters. *Degrees:* certificates, bachelor's, and master's. *Special study options:* academic remediation for entering students, accelerated degree program, advanced placement credit, distance learning, double majors, external degree program, honors programs, independent study, internships, off-campus study, part-time degree program, services for LD students, study abroad, summer session for credit. *ROTC:* Army (c). *Unusual degree programs:* 3-2 molecular biology.

Computers on Campus 84 computers/terminals are available on campus for general student use. Students can access the following: campus intranet, computer help desk, free student e-mail accounts, online (class) grades, online (class) registration, online (class) schedules. Campuswide network is available. 100% of college-owned or -operated housing units are wired for high-speed Internet access. Wireless service is available via entire campus.

Student Life *Housing:* on-campus residence required through sophomore year. *Options:* coed, disabled students. Campus housing is university owned. *Activities and organizations:* drama/theater group, student-run newspaper, radio station, choral group, Black Student Union, Parkside Asian Organization, Parkside Activities Board, Latinos Unidos, Men's Rugby Club, national fraternities, national sororities. *Campus security:* 24-hour emergency response devices and patrols, late-night transport/escort service, controlled dormitory access. *Student services:* health clinic, personal/psychological counseling, women's center.

Athletics Member NCAA. All Division II. *Intercollegiate sports:* baseball M(s), basketball M(s)/W(s), cross-country running M(s)/W(s), golf M(s), soccer M(s)/W(s), softball W(s), track and field M(s)/W(s), volleyball W(s), wrestling M(s). *Intramural sports:* basketball M/W, cheerleading M(c)/W(c), football M(c), racquetball M/W, rugby M(c)/W(c), soccer M/W, softball M/W, table tennis M/W, tennis M/W, volleyball M/W.

Standardized Tests *Required for some:* SAT or ACT (for admission).

Costs (2011–12) *Tuition:* state resident $5659 full-time, $236 per credit hour part-time; nonresident $13,232 full-time, $551 per credit hour part-time. Full-time tuition and fees vary according to course load and reciprocity agreements. Part-time tuition and fees vary according to course load. *Required fees:* $964 full-time, $40 per credit hour part-time. *Room and board:* $6828; room only: $4108. Room and board charges vary according to board plan and housing facility. *Payment plan:* installment. *Waivers:* senior citizens.

Financial Aid Of all full-time matriculated undergraduates who enrolled in 2008, 2,843 applied for aid, 2,297 were judged to have need, 804 had their need fully met. *Average percent of need met:* 68%. *Average financial aid package:* $8487. *Average need-based gift aid:* $6315. *Average indebtedness upon graduation:* $18,254.

Applying *Options:* electronic application. *Application fee:* $44. *Required:* high school transcript, minimum of 17 high school units distribution. *Application deadlines:* 8/1 (freshmen), 7/15 (transfers). *Notification:* continuous (freshmen), continuous (transfers).

Freshman Application Contact Mrs. DeAnn Possehl, Interim Director, Enrollment Management, University of Wisconsin–Parkside, PO Box 2000,

900 Wood Road, Kenosha, WI 53141-2000. *Phone:* 262-595-2454. *E-mail:* possehl@uwp.edu. *Web site:* http://www.uwp.edu/.

University of Wisconsin–Platteville
Platteville, Wisconsin

- **State-supported** comprehensive, founded 1866, part of University of Wisconsin System
- **Small-town** 820-acre campus
- **Endowment** $2.1 million
- **Coed** 7,159 undergraduate students, 91% full-time, 35% women, 65% men
- **Minimally difficult** entrance level, 81% of applicants were admitted

Undergraduates 6,497 full-time, 662 part-time. Students come from 19 states and territories; 17 other countries; 21% are from out of state; 2% Black or African American, non-Hispanic/Latino; 1% Hispanic/Latino; 1% Asian, non-Hispanic/Latino; 0.1% Native Hawaiian or other Pacific Islander, non-Hispanic/Latino; 0.7% American Indian or Alaska Native, non-Hispanic/Latino; 1% Race/ethnicity unknown; 0.9% international; 5% transferred in; 40% live on campus. *Retention:* 76% of full-time freshmen returned.
Freshmen *Admission:* 3,660 applied, 2,973 admitted, 1,515 enrolled. *Test scores:* ACT scores over 18: 94%; ACT scores over 24: 40%; ACT scores over 30: 4%.
Faculty *Student/faculty ratio:* 20:1.
Academics *Calendar:* semesters. *Degrees:* associate, bachelor's, master's, and postbachelor's certificates. *Special study options:* academic remediation for entering students, adult/continuing education programs, advanced placement credit, cooperative education, distance learning, double majors, external degree program, independent study, internships, off-campus study, part-time degree program, services for LD students, student-designed majors, study abroad, summer session for credit. *ROTC:* Army (c).
Computers on Campus 1,200 computers/terminals and 1,000 ports are available on campus for general student use. Students can access the following: campus intranet, computer help desk, free student e-mail accounts, online (class) grades, online (class) registration, online (class) schedules. Campus-wide network is available. 100% of college-owned or -operated housing units are wired for high-speed Internet access. Wireless service is available via classrooms, libraries, student centers.
Student Life *Housing:* on-campus residence required for freshman year. *Options:* coed, men-only, women-only, disabled students. Campus housing is university owned. Freshman campus housing is guaranteed. *Activities and organizations:* drama/theater group, student-run newspaper, radio and television station, choral group, marching band, Intervarsity Christian Fellowship, Student Senate, Greek Life, Paintball Club, CPR, national fraternities, national sororities. *Campus security:* 24-hour emergency response devices and patrols, student patrols, late-night transport/escort service. *Student services:* health clinic, personal/psychological counseling, women's center.
Athletics Member NCAA. All Division III. *Intercollegiate sports:* baseball M, basketball M/W, bowling M(c)/W(c), cheerleading M/W, cross-country running M/W, football M, golf W, ice hockey M(c)/W(c), lacrosse M(c)/W(c), rugby M(c)/W(c), soccer M/W, softball W, track and field M/W, ultimate Frisbee M(c)/W(c), volleyball M(c)/W, wrestling M. *Intramural sports:* badminton M/W, basketball M/W, bowling M/W, cheerleading M(c)/W(c), football M/W, racquetball M/W, soccer M/W, softball M/W, tennis M/W, ultimate Frisbee M/W, volleyball M/W, water polo M/W.
Standardized Tests *Required:* SAT or ACT (for admission). *Recommended:* ACT (for admission).
Costs (2010–11) *Tuition:* state resident $5466 full-time; nonresident $13,039 full-time. Full-time tuition and fees vary according to course load, degree level, and reciprocity agreements. Part-time tuition and fees vary according to course load, degree level, and reciprocity agreements. *Required fees:* $990 full-time. *Room and board:* $5628; room only: $3100. Room and board charges vary according to board plan, housing facility, and location. *Payment plan:* installment. *Waivers:* senior citizens.
Financial Aid Of all full-time matriculated undergraduates who enrolled in 2002, 3,289 applied for aid, 2,468 were judged to have need. 382 Federal Work-Study jobs (averaging $1392). In 2002, 652 non-need-based awards were made. *Average financial aid package:* $6161. *Average need-based loan:* $3499. *Average need-based gift aid:* $3599. *Average non-need-based aid:* $1427. *Average indebtedness upon graduation:* $15,785.
Applying *Options:* electronic application, deferred entrance. *Application fee:* $44. *Required:* high school transcript. *Recommended:* essay or personal statement. *Application deadlines:* rolling (freshmen), rolling (out-of-state freshmen), rolling (transfers). *Notification:* continuous (transfers).
Freshman Application Contact Mrs. Angela Udelhofen, Director of Admissions and Enrollment Management, University of Wisconsin–Platteville, 1 University Plaza, 120 Brigham Hall, Platteville, WI 53818-3099. *Phone:* 608-342-1125. *Toll-free phone:* 800-362-5515. *Fax:* 608-342-1122. *E-mail:* admit@uwplatt.edu. *Web site:* http://www.uwplatt.edu/.

University of Wisconsin–River Falls
River Falls, Wisconsin

- **State-supported** comprehensive, founded 1874, part of University of Wisconsin System
- **Suburban** 225-acre campus with easy access to Minneapolis-St. Paul
- **Coed** 6,373 undergraduate students, 92% full-time, 59% women, 41% men
- **Moderately difficult** entrance level, 76% of applicants were admitted

Undergraduates 5,833 full-time, 540 part-time. 50% are from out of state; 1% Black or African American, non-Hispanic/Latino; 0.7% Hispanic/Latino; 2% Asian, non-Hispanic/Latino; 0.1% Native Hawaiian or other Pacific Islander, non-Hispanic/Latino; 0.3% American Indian or Alaska Native, non-Hispanic/Latino; 2% Two or more races, non-Hispanic/Latino; 1% Race/ethnicity unknown; 0.9% international; 7% transferred in; 39% live on campus. *Retention:* 75% of full-time freshmen returned.
Freshmen *Admission:* 3,358 applied, 2,566 admitted, 1,775 enrolled. *Test scores:* SAT critical reading scores over 500: 48%; SAT math scores over 500: 52%; SAT writing scores over 500: 48%; ACT scores over 18: 93%; SAT critical reading scores over 600: 9%; SAT math scores over 600: 22%; SAT writing scores over 600: 13%; ACT scores over 24: 33%; SAT math scores over 700: 4%; SAT writing scores over 700: 4%; ACT scores over 30: 2%.
Faculty *Total:* 372, 74% full-time. *Student/faculty ratio:* 23:1.
Academics *Calendar:* semesters. *Degrees:* certificates, bachelor's, master's, post-master's, and postbachelor's certificates. *Special study options:* academic remediation for entering students, adult/continuing education programs, advanced placement credit, distance learning, double majors, English as a second language, external degree program, honors programs, independent study, internships, off-campus study, part-time degree program, services for LD students, study abroad, summer session for credit. *ROTC:* Army (b). *Unusual degree programs:* 3-2 engineering with University of Wisconsin-Madison and University of Minnesota-Twin Cities.
Computers on Campus Students can access the following: computer help desk, free student e-mail accounts, online (class) grades, online (class) registration, online (class) schedules. Campuswide network is available. Wireless service is available via classrooms, computer centers, computer labs, dorm rooms, learning centers, libraries, student centers.
Student Life *Housing:* on-campus residence required through sophomore year. *Options:* coed, women-only, disabled students. Campus housing is university owned. Freshman campus housing is guaranteed. *Activities and organizations:* drama/theater group, student-run newspaper, radio and television station, choral group, Falcon Programs, Badminton Club, Dairy Club, Agricultural Education Society, Intervarsity Christian Fellowship, national fraternities, national sororities. *Campus security:* 24-hour emergency response devices and patrols, student patrols, late-night transport/escort service, controlled dormitory access. *Student services:* health clinic, personal/psychological counseling.
Athletics Member NCAA. All Division III. *Intercollegiate sports:* badminton M(c)/W(c), baseball M(c), basketball M/W, cheerleading M(c), cross-country running M/W, equestrian sports M(c)/W(c), football M(c)/W, golf M(c)/W, ice hockey M/W, lacrosse M(c)/W(c), racquetball M(c)/W(c), rugby M(c)/W(c), soccer M(c)/W, softball W, swimming and diving M/W, tennis W, track and field M/W, ultimate Frisbee M(c)/W(c), volleyball M(c)/W(c), weight lifting M(c)/W(c). *Intramural sports:* badminton M/W, basketball M/W, bowling M/W, football M, golf M/W, racquetball M/W, soccer M/W, softball M/W, tennis M/W, volleyball M/W.
Standardized Tests *Required:* SAT or ACT (for admission). *Recommended:* ACT (for admission).
Costs (2010–11) *Tuition:* state resident $5730 full-time, $239 per credit part-time; nonresident $13,303 full-time, $556 per credit part-time. Full-time tuition and fees vary according to course load, degree level, and reciprocity agreements. Part-time tuition and fees vary according to course load, degree level, and reciprocity agreements. *Required fees:* $1163 full-time, $239 per credit part-time. *Room and board:* $5730; room only: $3400. Room and board charges vary according to board plan and housing facility. *Payment plan:* installment. *Waivers:* children of alumni.
Financial Aid Of all full-time matriculated undergraduates who enrolled in 2008, 5,068 applied for aid, 4,806 were judged to have need. *Average percent of need met:* 84%. *Average financial aid package:* $2810. *Average need-based gift aid:* $2062. *Average indebtedness upon graduation:* $8000.
Applying *Options:* electronic application, deferred entrance. *Application fee:* $44. *Required:* essay or personal statement, high school transcript. *Recommended:* rank in upper 40% of high school class. *Application deadlines:* rolling (freshmen), rolling (transfers). *Notification:* continuous (freshmen), continuous (transfers).
Freshman Application Contact University of Wisconsin–River Falls, 410 South Third Street, River Falls, WI 54022. *Phone:* 715-425-3500. *Web site:* http://www.uwrf.edu/.

University of Wisconsin–Stevens Point

Stevens Point, Wisconsin

- **State-supported** comprehensive, founded 1894, part of University of Wisconsin System
- **Small-town** 400-acre campus
- **Endowment** $13.9 million
- **Coed** 9,054 undergraduate students, 96% full-time, 52% women, 48% men
- **Moderately difficult** entrance level, 72% of applicants were admitted

Undergraduates 8,687 full-time, 367 part-time. Students come from 34 states and territories; 29 other countries; 8% are from out of state; 1% Black or African American, non-Hispanic/Latino; 2% Hispanic/Latino; 2% Asian, non-Hispanic/Latino; 0.5% American Indian or Alaska Native, non-Hispanic/Latino; 1% Two or more races, non-Hispanic/Latino; 1% Race/ethnicity unknown; 2% international; 7% transferred in; 36% live on campus. *Retention:* 82% of full-time freshmen returned.

Freshmen *Admission:* 5,072 applied, 3,655 admitted, 1,652 enrolled. *Average high school GPA:* 3.43. *Test scores:* ACT scores over 18: 98%; ACT scores over 24: 44%; ACT scores over 30: 5%.

Faculty *Total:* 469, 87% full-time, 77% with terminal degrees. *Student/faculty ratio:* 21:1.

Academics *Calendar:* semesters. *Degrees:* associate, bachelor's, master's, and doctoral-other. *Special study options:* academic remediation for entering students, accelerated degree program, advanced placement credit, cooperative education, distance learning, double majors, English as a second language, honors programs, independent study, internships, off-campus study, part-time degree program, services for LD students, student-designed majors, study abroad, summer session for credit. *ROTC:* Army (b).

Computers on Campus 1,233 computers/terminals and 3,963 ports are available on campus for general student use. Students can access the following: computer help desk, free student e-mail accounts, online (class) grades, online (class) registration, online (class) schedules. Campuswide network is available. 100% of college-owned or -operated housing units are wired for high-speed Internet access. Wireless service is available via entire campus.

Student Life *Housing:* on-campus residence required through sophomore year. *Options:* coed, men-only, women-only. Campus housing is university owned. Freshman campus housing is guaranteed. *Activities and organizations:* drama/theater group, student-run newspaper, radio and television station, choral group, The Wildlife Society, Student Impact, WWSP 90-FM radio station, Gender and Sexuality Alliance, Student Wisconsin Education Association, national fraternities, national sororities. *Campus security:* 24-hour emergency response devices and patrols, student patrols, late-night transport/escort service, controlled dormitory access. *Student services:* health clinic, personal/psychological counseling.

Athletics Member NCAA. All Division III. *Intercollegiate sports:* baseball M, basketball M/W, cross-country running M/W, football M, golf W, ice hockey M/W, soccer W, softball W, swimming and diving M/W, tennis W, track and field M/W, volleyball W, wrestling M. *Intramural sports:* archery M(c)/W(c), badminton M/W, basketball M/W, football M, golf M/W, ice hockey M/W, lacrosse M(c), racquetball M/W, rugby M(c)/W(c), skiing (downhill) M(c)/W(c), soccer M/W, softball M/W, table tennis M/W, tennis M/W, ultimate Frisbee M/W, volleyball M/W.

Standardized Tests *Required:* SAT or ACT (for admission).

Costs (2011–12) *Tuition:* state resident $5659 full-time, $236 per credit hour part-time; nonresident $13,232 full-time, $551 per credit hour part-time. Full-time tuition and fees vary according to course load, program, and reciprocity agreements. Part-time tuition and fees vary according to course load, program, and reciprocity agreements. *Required fees:* $1190 full-time, $340 per credit hour part-time. *Room and board:* $5760; room only: $3438. Room and board charges vary according to board plan and housing facility. *Payment plan:* installment. *Waivers:* children of alumni.

Financial Aid Of all full-time matriculated undergraduates who enrolled in 2008, 6,691 applied for aid, 4,914 were judged to have need, 3,430 had their need fully met. 963 Federal Work-Study jobs (averaging $1424). 2,497 state and other part-time jobs (averaging $1887). In 2008, 550 non-need-based awards were made. *Average percent of need met:* 72%. *Average financial aid package:* $8109. *Average need-based loan:* $4721. *Average need-based gift aid:* $6590. *Average non-need-based aid:* $2031. *Average indebtedness upon graduation:* $22,370. *Financial aid deadline:* 5/1.

Applying *Options:* electronic application, deferred entrance. *Application fee:* $44. *Required:* high school transcript, SAT or ACT. *Recommended:* essay or personal statement, 3 letters of recommendation. *Application deadlines:* rolling (freshmen), rolling (transfers). *Notification:* continuous (freshmen), continuous (transfers).

Freshman Application Contact Ms. Catherine Glennon, Director of Admissions, University of Wisconsin–Stevens Point, 102 Student Services Center, University of Wisconsin-Stevens Point, Stevens Point, WI 54481. *Phone:* 715-346-2441. *Fax:* 715-346-3296. *E-mail:* cglennon@uwsp.edu. *Web site:* http://www.uwsp.edu/.

University of Wisconsin–Stout

Menomonie, Wisconsin

- **State-supported** comprehensive, founded 1891, part of University of Wisconsin System
- **Small-town** 120-acre campus with easy access to Minneapolis-St. Paul
- **Coed** 8,303 undergraduate students, 84% full-time, 48% women, 52% men
- **Moderately difficult** entrance level, 80% of applicants were admitted

Undergraduates 7,006 full-time, 1,297 part-time. 30% are from out of state; 8% transferred in; 40% live on campus. *Retention:* 74% of full-time freshmen returned.

Freshmen *Admission:* 3,631 applied, 2,892 admitted, 1,601 enrolled. *Average high school GPA:* 3.2. *Test scores:* ACT scores over 18: 92%; ACT scores over 24: 28%; ACT scores over 30: 2%.

Faculty *Total:* 453, 77% full-time, 69% with terminal degrees. *Student/faculty ratio:* 20:1.

Academics *Calendar:* 4-1-4. *Degrees:* certificates, bachelor's, master's, post-master's, and postbachelor's certificates. *Special study options:* accelerated degree program, adult/continuing education programs, cooperative education, distance learning, double majors, external degree program, honors programs, independent study, internships, off-campus study, part-time degree program, services for LD students, study abroad, summer session for credit. *ROTC:* Army (b), Air Force (c).

Computers on Campus 590 computers/terminals are available on campus for general student use. Students can access the following: computer help desk, free student e-mail accounts, online (class) grades, online (class) registration, online (class) schedules, all undergraduates receive a laptop computer and have unlimited access to Internet. Campuswide network is available. 100% of college-owned or -operated housing units are wired for high-speed Internet access. Wireless service is available via entire campus.

Student Life *Housing:* on-campus residence required through sophomore year. *Options:* coed, disabled students. Campus housing is university owned. Freshman campus housing is guaranteed. *Activities and organizations:* drama/theater group, student-run newspaper, radio and television station, choral group, marching band, national fraternities, national sororities. *Campus security:* 24-hour emergency response devices and patrols, student patrols, controlled dormitory access. *Student services:* health clinic, personal/psychological counseling, legal services.

Athletics Member NCAA. All Division III. *Intercollegiate sports:* baseball M, basketball M/W, cross-country running M/W, football M, gymnastics W, ice hockey M/W(c), soccer M(c)/W, softball W, tennis W, track and field M/W, volleyball M(c)/W. *Intramural sports:* baseball M, basketball M/W, bowling M(c)/W(c), football M/W, golf M/W, ice hockey M/W, racquetball M/W, rugby M(c)/W(c), skiing (cross-country) M(c)/W(c), skiing (downhill) M(c)/W(c), softball M/W, ultimate Frisbee M/W, volleyball M/W.

Standardized Tests *Required:* SAT or ACT (for admission).

Costs (2011–12) *Tuition:* state resident $6302 full-time, $210 per credit hour part-time; nonresident $14,048 full-time, $468 per credit hour part-time. Full-time tuition and fees vary according to degree level and reciprocity agreements. Part-time tuition and fees vary according to degree level and reciprocity agreements. *Required fees:* $1797 full-time. *Room and board:* $5560; room only: $3300. Room and board charges vary according to board plan and housing facility. *Payment plan:* installment.

Financial Aid Of all full-time matriculated undergraduates who enrolled in 2009, 5,512 applied for aid, 4,170 were judged to have need, 1,994 had their need fully met. 1,234 Federal Work-Study jobs (averaging $1771). In 2009, 63 non-need-based awards were made. *Average percent of need met:* 87%. *Average financial aid package:* $9715. *Average need-based loan:* $4399. *Average need-based gift aid:* $2656. *Average non-need-based aid:* $1630. *Average indebtedness upon graduation:* $25,855.

Applying *Options:* electronic application. *Application fee:* $44. *Required:* high school transcript. *Required for some:* minimum 2.75 GPA. *Recommended:* minimum 2.5 GPA. *Application deadlines:* rolling (freshmen), rolling (out-of-state freshmen), rolling (transfers). *Notification:* continuous (freshmen), continuous (out-of-state freshmen), continuous (transfers).

Freshman Application Contact Dr. Pamela Holsinger-Fuchs, Executive Director of Enrollment Services, University of Wisconsin-Stout, Admissions, Bowman Hall, Menomonie, WI 54751. *Phone:* 715-232-2639. *Toll-free phone:* 800-HI-STOUT. *Fax:* 715-232-1667. *E-mail:* admissions@uwstout.edu. *Web site:* http://www.uwstout.edu/.

University of Wisconsin–Superior
Superior, Wisconsin

- **State-supported** comprehensive, founded 1893, part of University of Wisconsin System
- **Suburban** 230-acre campus
- **Endowment** $7.3 million
- **Coed** 2,631 undergraduate students, 81% full-time, 57% women, 43% men
- **Moderately difficult** entrance level, 75% of applicants were admitted

Undergraduates 2,127 full-time, 504 part-time. Students come from 24 states and territories; 31 other countries; 44% are from out of state; 1% Black or African American, non-Hispanic/Latino; 1% Hispanic/Latino; 1% Asian, non-Hispanic/Latino; 0.1% Native Hawaiian or other Pacific Islander, non-Hispanic/Latino; 3% American Indian or Alaska Native, non-Hispanic/Latino; 2% Two or more races, non-Hispanic/Latino; 1% Race/ethnicity unknown; 7% international; 13% transferred in; 40% live on campus. *Retention:* 69% of full-time freshmen returned.

Freshmen *Admission:* 980 applied, 739 admitted, 380 enrolled. *Test scores:* ACT scores over 18: 90%; ACT scores over 24: 29%; ACT scores over 30: 2%.

Faculty *Total:* 175, 73% full-time, 62% with terminal degrees. *Student/faculty ratio:* 17:1.

Academics *Calendar:* semesters. *Degrees:* certificates, associate, bachelor's, master's, and post-master's certificates. *Special study options:* academic remediation for entering students, accelerated degree program, adult/continuing education programs, advanced placement credit, cooperative education, distance learning, double majors, English as a second language, external degree program, freshman honors college, independent study, internships, off-campus study, part-time degree program, services for LD students, student-designed majors, study abroad, summer session for credit. *ROTC:* Air Force (c). *Unusual degree programs:* 3-2 engineering with Michigan Technological University, University of Wisconsin-Madison; forestry with Michigan Technological University.

Computers on Campus 343 computers/terminals are available on campus for general student use. Students can access the following: campus intranet, computer help desk, free student e-mail accounts, online (class) grades, online (class) registration, online (class) schedules. Campuswide network is available. 100% of college-owned or -operated housing units are wired for high-speed Internet access. Wireless service is available via entire campus.

Student Life *Housing:* on-campus residence required through sophomore year. *Options:* coed, women-only, disabled students. Campus housing is university owned. Freshman campus housing is guaranteed. *Activities and organizations:* drama/theater group, student-run newspaper, radio station, choral group, Student Senate, Student Activities Board, Residence Hall Association, Inter-Varsity Christian Fellowship, World Student Association. *Campus security:* 24-hour emergency response devices and patrols, student patrols, late-night transport/escort service, controlled dormitory access. *Student services:* health clinic, personal/psychological counseling, women's center.

Athletics Member NCAA. All Division III. *Intercollegiate sports:* baseball M, basketball M/W, cheerleading M/W, cross-country running M/W, golf W, ice hockey M/W, soccer M/W, softball W, track and field M/W, volleyball W. *Intramural sports:* badminton M/W, baseball M/W, basketball M/W, bowling M/W, cross-country running M/W, football M/W, golf M/W, ice hockey M, racquetball M/W, riflery M/W, rock climbing M/W, rugby M, skiing (cross-country) M/W, skiing (downhill) M/W, soccer M/W, softball M/W, table tennis M/W, tennis M/W, volleyball M/W.

Standardized Tests *Required:* SAT or ACT (for admission).

Costs (2010–11) *Tuition:* state resident $5865 full-time, $424 per semester hour part-time; nonresident $13,438 full-time, $740 per semester hour part-time. Full-time tuition and fees vary according to course load, program, and reciprocity agreements. Part-time tuition and fees vary according to course load, program, and reciprocity agreements. *Required fees:* $1304 full-time. *Room and board:* $5730; room only: $3050. Room and board charges vary according to board plan, housing facility, and student level. *Payment plan:* installment.

Financial Aid Of all full-time matriculated undergraduates who enrolled in 2009, 1,450 applied for aid, 1,204 were judged to have need, 284 had their need fully met. In 2009, 46 non-need-based awards were made. *Average need-based loan:* $3811. *Average need-based gift aid:* $5452. *Average non-need-based aid:* $1769. *Average indebtedness upon graduation:* $22,516.

Applying *Options:* electronic application, early admission, deferred entrance. *Application fee:* $44. *Required:* high school transcript. *Required for some:* essay or personal statement. *Recommended:* interview. *Application deadlines:* rolling (freshmen), rolling (transfers). *Notification:* continuous (freshmen), continuous (out-of-state freshmen), continuous (transfers).

Freshman Application Contact Ms. Tonya Roth, Director of Admission, University of Wisconsin–Superior, Belknap and Catlin, PO Box 2000, Superior, WI 54880-4500. *Phone:* 715-394-8217. *Fax:* 715-394-8407. *E-mail:* admissions@uwsuper.edu. *Web site:* http://www.uwsuper.edu/.

University of Wisconsin–Whitewater
Whitewater, Wisconsin

- **State-supported** comprehensive, founded 1868, part of University of Wisconsin System
- **Small-town** 385-acre campus with easy access to Milwaukee
- **Endowment** $13.0 million
- **Coed** 10,144 undergraduate students, 93% full-time, 49% women, 51% men
- **Moderately difficult** entrance level, 71% of applicants were admitted

Undergraduates 9,456 full-time, 688 part-time. Students come from 32 states and territories; 37 other countries; 9% are from out of state; 5% Black or African American, non-Hispanic/Latino; 3% Hispanic/Latino; 1% Asian, non-Hispanic/Latino; 0.1% Native Hawaiian or other Pacific Islander, non-Hispanic/Latino; 0.3% American Indian or Alaska Native, non-Hispanic/Latino; 0.9% Two or more races, non-Hispanic/Latino; 0.6% Race/ethnicity unknown; 1% international; 7% transferred in. *Retention:* 79% of full-time freshmen returned.

Freshmen *Admission:* 6,309 applied, 4,477 admitted, 2,044 enrolled. *Average high school GPA:* 3.2. *Test scores:* SAT critical reading scores over 500: 49%; SAT math scores over 500: 49%; ACT scores over 18: 91%; SAT critical reading scores over 600: 12%; SAT math scores over 600: 22%; ACT scores over 24: 33%; SAT critical reading scores over 700: 2%; SAT math scores over 700: 2%; ACT scores over 30: 2%.

Faculty *Total:* 529, 77% full-time, 73% with terminal degrees. *Student/faculty ratio:* 23:1.

Academics *Calendar:* semesters. *Degrees:* associate, bachelor's, and master's. *Special study options:* academic remediation for entering students, accelerated degree program, adult/continuing education programs, advanced placement credit, cooperative education, distance learning, double majors, English as a second language, external degree program, honors programs, independent study, internships, part-time degree program, services for LD students, student-designed majors, study abroad, summer session for credit. *ROTC:* Army (b), Air Force (b).

Computers on Campus Students can access the following: campus intranet, computer help desk, free student e-mail accounts, online (class) grades, online (class) registration, online (class) schedules. Campuswide network is available. 100% of college-owned or -operated housing units are wired for high-speed Internet access. Wireless service is available via entire campus.

Student Life *Housing:* on-campus residence required through sophomore year. *Options:* coed, women-only. Campus housing is university owned. Freshman campus housing is guaranteed. *Activities and organizations:* drama/theater group, student-run newspaper, radio and television station, choral group, marching band, Finance Association, American Marketing Association, Black Student Union, Golden Key Honor Society, Wisconsin Education Association, national fraternities, national sororities. *Campus security:* 24-hour emergency response devices, late-night transport/escort service, controlled dormitory access. *Student services:* health clinic, personal/psychological counseling, women's center, legal services.

Athletics Member NCAA. All Division III. *Intercollegiate sports:* baseball M, basketball M/W, bowling M(c)/W, cheerleading M(c)/W(c), cross-country running M/W, football M, golf W, gymnastics W, ice hockey M(c)/W(c), lacrosse M(c), rugby M(c)/W(c), soccer M/W, softball W, swimming and diving M/W, tennis M/W, track and field M/W, volleyball M(c)/W, weight lifting M(c), wrestling M. *Intramural sports:* basketball M/W, bowling M/W, football M/W, golf M/W, racquetball M/W, rock climbing M(c)/W(c), skiing (downhill) M(c)/W(c), soccer M, softball M/W, table tennis M/W, tennis M/W, ultimate Frisbee M(c)/W(c), volleyball M/W, water polo M/W.

Standardized Tests *Required for some:* ACT (for admission). *Recommended:* SAT or ACT (for admission).

Costs (2011–12) *Tuition:* state resident $5857 full-time, $195 per credit part-time; nonresident $13,430 full-time, $448 per credit part-time. Full-time tuition and fees vary according to degree level and reciprocity agreements. *Required fees:* $979 full-time. *Room and board:* $5402; room only: $3232. Room and board charges vary according to board plan. *Payment plan:* installment. *Waivers:* children of alumni and senior citizens.

Financial Aid Of all full-time matriculated undergraduates who enrolled in 2009, 7,074 applied for aid, 4,924 were judged to have need, 2,989 had their need fully met. 505 Federal Work-Study jobs (averaging $1261). 1,723 state and other part-time jobs (averaging $2031). In 2009, 396 non-need-based awards were made. *Average percent of need met:* 73%. *Average financial aid package:* $7957. *Average need-based loan:* $3984. *Average need-based gift aid:* $5220. *Average non-need-based aid:* $1424. *Average indebtedness upon graduation:* $20,715.

Applying *Options:* electronic application, deferred entrance. *Application fee:* $44. *Required:* high school transcript. *Application deadlines:* rolling (freshmen), rolling (transfers). *Notification:* 9/15 (freshmen), continuous (transfers).

Freshman Application Contact Mrs. Jodi Hare, Interim Director of Admissions, University of Wisconsin–Whitewater, 800 West Main Street,

Whitewater, WI 53190-1790. *Phone:* 262-472-1440 Ext. 1512. *Fax:* 262-472-1515. *E-mail:* uwwadmit@uww.edu. *Web site:* http://www.uww.edu/.

Viterbo University
La Crosse, Wisconsin

- **Independent Roman Catholic** comprehensive, founded 1890
- **Suburban** 72-acre campus
- **Endowment** $23.9 million
- **Coed** 2,207 undergraduate students, 74% full-time, 70% women, 30% men
- **Moderately difficult** entrance level, 87% of applicants were admitted

Undergraduates 1,633 full-time, 574 part-time. Students come from 29 states and territories; 12 other countries; 22% are from out of state; 15% transferred in; 28% live on campus. *Retention:* 66% of full-time freshmen returned.

Freshmen *Admission:* 1,463 applied, 1,272 admitted, 417 enrolled. *Average high school GPA:* 3.35. *Test scores:* ACT scores over 18: 95%; ACT scores over 24: 37%; ACT scores over 30: 5%.

Faculty *Total:* 283, 40% full-time, 33% with terminal degrees. *Student/faculty ratio:* 12:1.

Academics *Calendar:* semesters. *Degrees:* associate, bachelor's, master's, post-master's, and postbachelor's certificates. *Special study options:* academic remediation for entering students, accelerated degree program, adult/continuing education programs, advanced placement credit, distance learning, double majors, honors programs, independent study, internships, off-campus study, part-time degree program, services for LD students, student-designed majors, study abroad, summer session for credit. *ROTC:* Army (c). *Unusual degree programs:* 3-2 business administration.

Computers on Campus 314 computers/terminals and 570 ports are available on campus for general student use. Students can access the following: campus intranet, computer help desk, free student e-mail accounts, online (class) grades, online (class) registration, online (class) schedules, Blackboard courses. Campuswide network is available. 100% of college-owned or -operated housing units are wired for high-speed Internet access. Wireless service is available via entire campus.

Student Life *Housing:* on-campus residence required through sophomore year. *Options:* coed, men-only, women-only. Campus housing is university owned. Freshman campus housing is guaranteed. *Activities and organizations:* drama/theater group, student-run newspaper, choral group, Viterbo Student Nurses Association, Campus Ministry (volunteer services and service trips), Global Rhythms, Student Government Association, Residence Hall Council. *Campus security:* 24-hour emergency response devices, late-night transport/escort service, controlled dormitory access, security officers on campus 5:00 pm to 7:00 am, lighted pathways, emergency evacuation plan, self-defense education programs. *Student services:* health clinic, personal/psychological counseling.

Athletics Member NAIA. *Intercollegiate sports:* baseball M(s), basketball M(s)/W(s), bowling M(s)/W(s), cross-country running M(s)/W(s), golf M(s)/W(s), soccer M(s)/W(s), softball W(s), volleyball W(s). *Intramural sports:* badminton M/W, basketball M/W, bowling M/W, cross-country running M/W, golf M/W, racquetball M/W, rugby M/W, skiing (cross-country) M/W, skiing (downhill) M/W, soccer M/W, softball M/W, swimming and diving M/W, table tennis M/W, tennis M/W, ultimate Frisbee M/W, volleyball M/W.

Standardized Tests *Required:* ACT (for admission).

Costs (2010–11) *Comprehensive fee:* $27,820 includes full-time tuition ($20,360), mandatory fees ($490), and room and board ($6970). Part-time tuition: $600 per credit. *Required fees:* $15 per credit part-time, $45 per term part-time. *College room only:* $3120. Room and board charges vary according to board plan and housing facility. *Waivers:* employees or children of employees.

Financial Aid Of all full-time matriculated undergraduates who enrolled in 2003, 1,311 applied for aid, 1,208 were judged to have need, 309 had their need fully met. 387 Federal Work-Study jobs (averaging $1680). 19 state and other part-time jobs (averaging $1615). In 2003, 223 non-need-based awards were made. *Average percent of need met:* 71%. *Average financial aid package:* $13,534. *Average need-based loan:* $4317. *Average need-based gift aid:* $8859. *Average non-need-based aid:* $5629. *Average indebtedness upon graduation:* $16,619.

Applying *Options:* electronic application, deferred entrance. *Application fee:* $25. *Required:* high school transcript, minimum 2 GPA. *Required for some:* essay or personal statement, interview, audition for theater and music, portfolio for art. *Application deadlines:* rolling (freshmen), rolling (out-of-state freshmen), rolling (transfers). *Notification:* 8/15 (freshmen), continuous until 8/15 (out-of-state freshmen), continuous until 8/15 (transfers).

Freshman Application Contact Mr. Wayne Wojciechowski, Assistant Academic Vice President, Viterbo University, 900 Viterbo Drive, LaCrosse, WI 54601. *Phone:* 608-796-3085. *Toll-free phone:* 800-VITERBO Ext. 3010. *Fax:* 608-796-3020. *E-mail:* admission@viterbo.edu. *Web site:* http://www.viterbo.edu/.

Wisconsin Lutheran College
Milwaukee, Wisconsin

Freshman Application Contact Ms. Meghan Wieselmann, Admissions Office Manager, Wisconsin Lutheran College, 8800 West Bluemound Road, Milwaukee, WI 53226-9942. *Phone:* 414-443-8718. *Toll-free phone:* 888-WIS LUTH. *Fax:* 414-443-8547. *E-mail:* meg.wieselmann@wlc.edu. *Web site:* http://www.wlc.edu/.

WYOMING

University of Wyoming
Laramie, Wyoming

- **State-supported** university, founded 1886
- **Small-town** 785-acre campus
- **Endowment** $249.4 million
- **Coed** 10,079 undergraduate students, 83% full-time, 52% women, 48% men
- **Moderately difficult** entrance level, 95% of applicants were admitted

Undergraduates 8,360 full-time, 1,719 part-time. Students come from 53 states and territories; 72 other countries; 29% are from out of state; 1% Black or African American, non-Hispanic/Latino; 5% Hispanic/Latino; 1% Asian, non-Hispanic/Latino; 0.2% Native Hawaiian or other Pacific Islander, non-Hispanic/Latino; 0.9% American Indian or Alaska Native, non-Hispanic/Latino; 2% Two or more races, non-Hispanic/Latino; 6% Race/ethnicity unknown; 3% international; 11% transferred in; 20% live on campus. *Retention:* 73% of full-time freshmen returned.

Freshmen *Admission:* 3,713 applied, 3,542 admitted, 1,472 enrolled. *Average high school GPA:* 3.43. *Test scores:* SAT critical reading scores over 500: 72%; SAT math scores over 500: 73%; ACT scores over 18: 97%; SAT critical reading scores over 600: 28%; SAT math scores over 600: 28%; ACT scores over 24: 56%; SAT critical reading scores over 700: 4%; SAT math scores over 700: 1%; ACT scores over 30: 10%.

Faculty *Total:* 800, 93% full-time, 80% with terminal degrees. *Student/faculty ratio:* 14:1.

Academics *Calendar:* semesters. *Degrees:* certificates, bachelor's, master's, doctoral-professional, doctoral-research/scholarship, post-master's, and post-bachelor's certificates. *Special study options:* accelerated degree program, advanced placement credit, distance learning, double majors, external degree program, honors programs, independent study, internships, off-campus study, part-time degree program, services for LD students, student-designed majors, study abroad, summer session for credit. *ROTC:* Army (b), Air Force (b).

Computers on Campus 1,443 computers/terminals are available on campus for general student use. Students can access the following: campus intranet, computer help desk, free student e-mail accounts, online (class) grades, online (class) registration, online (class) schedules. Campuswide network is available. 100% of college-owned or -operated housing units are wired for high-speed Internet access. Wireless service is available via classrooms, computer centers, computer labs, learning centers, libraries, student centers.

Student Life *Housing:* on-campus residence required for freshman year. *Options:* coed, men-only, women-only, disabled students. Campus housing is university owned. Freshman campus housing is guaranteed. *Activities and organizations:* drama/theater group, student-run newspaper, radio and television station, choral group, marching band, national fraternities, national sororities. *Campus security:* 24-hour emergency response devices and patrols, student patrols, late-night transport/escort service, controlled dormitory access, 24-hour front desk coverage at campus housing and at campus police. *Student services:* health clinic, personal/psychological counseling, women's center, legal services.

Athletics Member NCAA. All Division I except football (Division I-A). *Intercollegiate sports:* badminton M(c)/W(c), baseball M(c), basketball M(s)/W(s), cheerleading M(s)/W(s), cross-country running M(s)/W(s), equestrian sports M(c)/W(c), fencing M(c)/W(c), golf M(s)/W(s), ice hockey M(c)/W(c), lacrosse M(c)/W(c), racquetball M(c)/W(c), riflery M(c)/W(c), rugby M(c)/W(c), skiing (cross-country) M(c)/W(c), soccer M(c)/W(s), softball W(c), swimming and diving M(s)/W(s), tennis W(s), track and field M(s)/W(s), ultimate Frisbee M(c)/W(c), volleyball W(s), wrestling M(s). *Intramural sports:* badminton M/W, basketball M/W, bowling M/W, football M/W, golf M/W, racquetball M/W, rock climbing M/W, soccer M/W, softball M/W, swimming and diving M/W, table tennis M/W, tennis M/W, track and field M/W, ultimate Frisbee M/W, volleyball M/W, water polo M/W, wrestling M.

Standardized Tests *Required:* SAT or ACT (for admission).

Costs (2010–11) *One-time required fee:* $40. *Tuition:* state resident $2970 full-time, $99 per credit hour part-time; nonresident $11,280 full-time, $376 per credit hour part-time. Full-time tuition and fees vary according to course load, location, and reciprocity agreements. Part-time tuition and fees vary according to course load, location, and reciprocity agreements. *Required fees:* $957 full-time, $239 per term part-time. *Room and board:* $8360; room only: $3612. Room and board charges vary according to board plan and housing facility. *Payment plan:* installment. *Waivers:* children of alumni, senior citizens, and employees or children of employees.

Financial Aid Of all full-time matriculated undergraduates who enrolled in 2009, 5,295 applied for aid, 3,856 were judged to have need, 747 had their need fully met. 289 Federal Work-Study jobs (averaging $1422). In 2009, 3047 non-need-based awards were made. *Average percent of need met:* 42%. *Average financial aid package:* $8690. *Average need-based loan:* $2388. *Average need-based gift aid:* $3154. *Average non-need-based aid:* $5057. *Average indebtedness upon graduation:* $20,571.

Applying *Options:* electronic application, deferred entrance. *Application fee:* $40. *Required:* high school transcript, minimum 2.75 GPA, pre-college curriculum, SAT or ACT score. *Required for some:* minimum 3 GPA. *Application deadlines:* 8/10 (freshmen), 8/10 (out-of-state freshmen), 8/10 (transfers). *Notification:* continuous (freshmen), continuous (out-of-state freshmen), continuous (transfers).

Freshman Application Contact Mary Aguayo, Assistant Director of Admissions, University of Wyoming, 1000 East University Avenue, Department 3435, Laramie, WY 82071. *Phone:* 307-766-4075. *Toll-free phone:* 800-342-5996. *Fax:* 307-766-4042. *E-mail:* why-wyo@uwyo.edu. *Web site:* http://www.uwyo.edu/.

See page 1754 for the College Close-Up.

GUAM

Pacific Islands University
Mangilao, Guam

Freshman Application Contact Ethel Laco, Admissions Office, Pacific Islands University, PO Box 22619, Guam Main Facility, GU 96921-2619. *Phone:* 671-734-1812. *Fax:* 671-734-1813. *E-mail:* guamcampus@pibc.edu. *Web site:* http://www.piu.edu/.

University of Guam
Mangilao, Guam

- **Territory-supported** comprehensive, founded 1952
- **Suburban** 100-acre campus
- **Endowment** $7.9 million
- **Coed**
- **Noncompetitive** entrance level

Faculty *Student/faculty ratio:* 14:1.

Academics *Calendar:* semesters. *Degrees:* certificates, associate, bachelor's, master's, and postbachelor's certificates.

Student Life *Campus security:* 24-hour emergency response devices and patrols, late-night transport/escort service.

Costs (2011–12) *Tuition:* territory resident $5320 full-time, $190 per credit hour part-time; nonresident $15,820 full-time, $565 per credit hour part-time. Part-time tuition and fees vary according to course load and degree level. *Required fees:* $498 full-time, $249 per term part-time. *Room only:* $9559. Room and board charges vary according to housing facility.

Applying *Options:* electronic application, early admission, deferred entrance. *Application fee:* $49. *Required:* high school transcript.

Freshman Application Contact Ms. Angelica Anthonio, Admissions Supervisor, University of Guam, Admissions and Records Office, UOG Station, Mangilao, GU 96923. *Phone:* 671-735-2201. *Fax:* 671-735-2203. *E-mail:* admitme@uguam.uog.edu. *Web site:* http://www.uog.edu/.

NORTHERN MARIANA ISLANDS

Northern Marianas College
Saipan, Northern Mariana Islands

Freshman Application Contact Ms. Leilani M. Basa-Alam, Admission Specialist, Northern Marianas College, PO Box 501250, Saipan, MP 96950-1250. *Phone:* 670-234-3690 Ext. 1539. *Fax:* 670-235-4967. *E-mail:* leilanib@nmcnet.edu. *Web site:* http://www.nmcnet.edu/.

PUERTO RICO

American University of Puerto Rico
Bayamón, Puerto Rico

Freshman Application Contact Ms. Margarita Cruz Santiago, Director of Admissions, American University of Puerto Rico, PO Box 2037, Bayamón, PR 00960-2037. *Phone:* 787-740-6410. *Fax:* 787-785-7377. *Web site:* http://www.aupr.edu/.

Atlantic College
Guaynabo, Puerto Rico

Director of Admissions Ms. Zaida Perez, Admission's Officer, Atlantic College, PO Box 3918, Guaynabo, PR 00970. *Phone:* 787-720-1022 Ext. 13. *E-mail:* admisiones@atlanticcollege.edu. *Web site:* http://www.atlanticcollege.edu/.

Bayamón Central University
Bayamón, Puerto Rico

Director of Admissions Sra. Christine M. Hernandez, Director of Admissions, Bayamón Central University, PO Box 1725, Bayamón, PR 00960-1725. *Phone:* 787-786-3030 Ext. 2102. *Web site:* http://www.ucb.edu.pr/.

Caribbean University
Bayamón, Puerto Rico

Director of Admissions Mr. Hector Gracia, Director of Admissions, Caribbean University, Box 493, Bayamón, PR 00960-0493. *Phone:* 787-780-0070 Ext. 226. *Web site:* http://www.caribbean.edu/.

Carlos Albizu University
San Juan, Puerto Rico

- **Independent** university, founded 1966
- **Urban** campus
- **Endowment** $732,270
- **Coed, primarily women**
- **Noncompetitive** entrance level

Faculty *Student/faculty ratio:* 33:1.

Academics *Calendar:* semesters. *Degrees:* bachelor's, master's, and doctoral-other.

Student Life *Campus security:* 24-hour emergency response devices, late-night transport/escort service, security cameras.

Standardized Tests *Required:* CEEB or SAT (for admission).

Costs (2010–11) *Tuition:* $5940 full-time, $165 per credit part-time. *Required fees:* $999 full-time, $333 per term part-time.

Financial Aid *Of all full-time matriculated undergraduates who enrolled in 2009,* 55 applied for aid, 55 were judged to have need. 6 Federal Work-Study jobs (averaging $1118). *Average percent of need met:* 30. *Average financial aid package:* $6548. *Average need-based loan:* $5450. *Average need-based gift aid:* $3789.

Applying *Options:* early admission, deferred entrance. *Application fee:* $75. *Required:* minimum 2 GPA, 3 letters of recommendation. *Required for some:* health certificate, Good Conduct Crete, official university transcript.

Freshman Application Contact Carlos Albizu University, 151 Tanca Street, San Juan, PR 00901. *Phone:* 787-725-6500 Ext. 1521. *Web site:* http://www.albizu.edu/.

Colegio Pentecostal Mizpa
Río Piedras, Puerto Rico

Director of Admissions Omar Alicea, Recruitment, Colegio Pentecostal Mizpa, Bo Caimito Road 199, Apartado 20966, Río Piedras, PR 00928-0966. *Phone:* 787-720-4476. *Fax:* 787-720-2012. *Web site:* http://www.colmizpa.edu/.

Colegio Universitario de San Juan
San Juan, Puerto Rico

Freshman Application Contact Colegio Universitario de San Juan, Jose R. Oliver Street, Hato Rey, PR 00918. *Phone:* 787-250-7111 Ext. 2227. *Web site:* http://www.cunisanjuan.edu/.

Columbia Centro Universitario

Yauco, Puerto Rico

- **Proprietary** 4-year, founded 1976, administratively affiliated with Columbia Centro Universitario, Recinto Caguas
- **Urban** campus
- **Coed** 559 undergraduate students, 55% full-time, 75% women, 25% men
- 54% of applicants were admitted

Undergraduates 308 full-time, 251 part-time.

Freshmen *Admission:* 419 applied, 228 admitted. *Average high school GPA:* 2.

Faculty *Total:* 58, 17% full-time, 14% with terminal degrees. *Student/faculty ratio:* 9:1.

Academics *Calendar:* trimesters. *Degrees:* certificates, associate, and bachelor's. *Special study options:* cooperative education, honors programs.

Computers on Campus 83 computers/terminals are available on campus for general student use. Students can access the following: computer help desk. Wireless service is available via entire campus.

Student Life *Activities and organizations:* Nursing Group, Librarian Group. *Campus security:* late-night transport/escort service. *Student services:* personal/psychological counseling.

Costs (2011–12) *Tuition:* $9435 full-time. Full-time tuition and fees vary according to program. Part-time tuition and fees vary according to program. *Required fees:* $100 full-time. *Payment plan:* installment. *Waivers:* employees or children of employees.

Applying *Options:* electronic application. *Application fee:* $50. *Required:* high school transcript. *Required for some:* interview. *Application deadline:* rolling (freshmen). *Notification:* continuous (freshmen).

Freshman Application Contact Mrs. Rosario Padilla, Admissions, Columbia Centro Universitario, Calle Betances #3, Box 3062, Yauco, PR 00698. *Phone:* 787-856-0845 Ext. 11. *Fax:* 787-267-2335. *E-mail:* rpadilla@columbiaco.edu. *Web site:* http://www.columbiaco.edu/.

Columbia College

Caguas, Puerto Rico

- **Proprietary** comprehensive, founded 1966
- **Rural** 6-acre campus with easy access to San Juan
- **Coed** 1,258 undergraduate students, 56% full-time, 70% women, 30% men
- **Noncompetitive** entrance level

Undergraduates 699 full-time, 559 part-time. *Retention:* 43% of full-time freshmen returned.

Freshmen *Admission:* 404 applied, 226 enrolled. *Average high school GPA:* 2.

Faculty *Total:* 93, 15% full-time. *Student/faculty ratio:* 21:1.

Academics *Calendar:* semesters. *Degrees:* certificates, associate, bachelor's, and master's. *Special study options:* accelerated degree program, independent study, part-time degree program.

Computers on Campus 68 computers/terminals are available on campus for general student use. Students can access the following: campus intranet, free student e-mail accounts.

Student Life *Housing:* college housing not available. *Campus security:* 24-hour patrols. *Student services:* personal/psychological counseling.

Costs (2011–12) *Tuition:* $9435 full-time. Full-time tuition and fees vary according to program. Part-time tuition and fees vary according to program. *Payment plan:* installment. *Waivers:* employees or children of employees.

Financial Aid *Of all full-time matriculated undergraduates who enrolled in 2008, 974 applied for aid, 818 were judged to have need. 61 Federal Work-Study jobs (averaging $982). Average percent of need met:* 11%. *Average financial aid package:* $4035.

Applying *Options:* electronic application. *Application fee:* $50. *Required:* high school transcript. *Required for some:* essay or personal statement, minimum 2 GPA, 3 letters of recommendation, interview. *Application deadline:* rolling (freshmen). *Notification:* continuous (freshmen).

Freshman Application Contact Mrs. Xiomara Sanchez, Admission Coordinator, Columbia College, PO Box 8517, Caguas, PR 00726. *Phone:* 787-743-4041 Ext. 239. *Toll-free phone:* 800-981-4877 Ext. 239. *Fax:* 787-744-7031. *E-mail:* xsanchez@columbianco.edu. *Web site:* http://www.columbiaco.edu/.

Conservatorio de Musica

San Juan, Puerto Rico

Director of Admissions Eutimia Santiago, Admissions Director, Conservatorio de Musica, 951 Ave Ponce de Len, Esquina F. D. Roosevelt, San Juan, PR 00907. *Phone:* 787-751-0160 Ext. 275. *Fax:* 787-766-1216. *E-mail:* esantiago@cmpr.gobierno.pr. *Web site:* http://www.cmpr.edu/.

Conservatory of Music of Puerto Rico

San Juan, Puerto Rico

Freshman Application Contact Conservatory of Music of Puerto Rico, 350 Rafael Lamar St at FDR Ave, San Juan, PR 00918. *Phone:* 787-751-0160 Ext. 275. *Web site:* http://www.cmpr.edu/.

EDP College of Puerto Rico, Inc.

Hato Rey, Puerto Rico

- **Proprietary** comprehensive, founded 1968
- **Urban** 1-acre campus
- **Coed**
- **Minimally difficult** entrance level

Faculty *Student/faculty ratio:* 19:1.

Academics *Calendar:* semesters. *Degrees:* associate, bachelor's, master's, and postbachelor's certificates.

Student Life *Campus security:* security and emergency telephones in working hours.

Standardized Tests *Required:* CEEB Placement Test, Institution Admission Exam (for admission).

Costs (2010–11) *Tuition:* $5400 full-time, $156 per credit part-time. Full-time tuition and fees vary according to course load and program. Part-time tuition and fees vary according to course load and program. *Required fees:* $720 full-time, $156 per credit part-time, $360 per term part-time.

Applying *Options:* deferred entrance. *Application fee:* $15. *Required:* high school transcript, minimum 1.6 GPA, placement test or College Board exam, vaccination certificate, copy of social security number. *Required for some:* minimum 2.5 GPA, interview, placement test or College Board exam, vaccination certificate, copy of social security number.

Freshman Application Contact Ms. Leila M. Andino, Student Affairs Dean, EDP College of Puerto Rico, Inc., Avenue Ponce de Leon, #560, Hato Rey, PR 00918. *Phone:* 787-765-3560 Ext. 262. *Fax:* 787-777-0024. *E-mail:* landino@edpcollege.edu. *Web site:* http://www.edpcollege.edu/.

EDP College of Puerto Rico– San Sebastian

San Sebastian, Puerto Rico

- **Proprietary** 4-year, founded 1976
- **Rural** campus
- **Coed**
- **Minimally difficult** entrance level

Academics *Calendar:* semesters. *Degrees:* associate and bachelor's.

Standardized Tests *Required:* College Board or institutional entrance test (for admission).

Costs (2010–11) *Tuition:* $5400 full-time, $156 per credit hour part-time. Full-time tuition and fees vary according to course load and program. Part-time tuition and fees vary according to course load and program. *Required fees:* $720 full-time, $156 per credit hour part-time, $360 per term part-time.

Financial Aid *Of all full-time matriculated undergraduates who enrolled in 2008, 1,348 applied for aid, 1,337 were judged to have need. 81 Federal Work-Study jobs (averaging $2500). Average percent of need met:* 77. *Average financial aid package:* $6000. *Average need-based loan:* $2500. *Average need-based gift aid:* $250. *Average indebtedness upon graduation:* $2500.

Applying *Application fee:* $15. *Required:* high school transcript, minimum 2 GPA. *Required for some:* interview.

Freshman Application Contact EDP College of Puerto Rico–San Sebastian, Avenue Betances #49, San Sebastian, PR 00685. *Phone:* 787-896-2252 Ext. 300. *Web site:* http://www.edpcollege.edu/.

Escuela de Artes Plasticas de Puerto Rico

San Juan, Puerto Rico

- **Commonwealth-supported** 4-year, founded 1966, administratively affiliated with Instituto de Cultura de Puerto Rico
- **Urban** campus
- **Endowment** $905,165
- **Coed** 522 undergraduate students, 63% full-time, 57% women, 43% men
- **Moderately difficult** entrance level, 71% of applicants were admitted

Undergraduates 327 full-time, 195 part-time. Students come from 1 other state; 100% Hispanic/Latino; 0.2% Asian, non-Hispanic/Latino; 6% transferred in. *Retention:* 75% of full-time freshmen returned.

Freshmen *Admission:* 125 applied, 89 admitted, 79 enrolled. *Average high school GPA:* 3.12.

Faculty *Total:* 66, 27% full-time, 53% with terminal degrees. *Student/faculty ratio:* 12:1.

Academics *Calendar:* 3 semesters each calendar year; participant in Year Round Pell. *Degree:* bachelor's. *Special study options:* accelerated degree program, adult/continuing education programs, advanced placement credit, internships, off-campus study, part-time degree program, services for LD students.

Computers on Campus 120 computers/terminals and 120 ports are available on campus for general student use. Students can access the following: computer help desk, library online catalog, wireless access. Wireless service is available via entire campus.

Student Life *Housing:* college housing not available. *Activities and organizations:* student government, literary magazine. *Campus security:* 24-hour emergency response devices and patrols, security cameras and institutional police of privacy. *Student services:* personal/psychological counseling.

Standardized Tests *Recommended:* SAT (for admission).

Costs (2010–11) *Tuition:* commonwealth resident $4404 full-time, $90 per credit part-time; nonresident $7644 full-time, $180 per credit part-time. Full-time tuition and fees vary according to course load and program. Part-time tuition and fees vary according to course load and program. *Required fees:* $375 full-time. *Payment plan:* deferred payment. *Waivers:* employees or children of employees.

Financial Aid Of all full-time matriculated undergraduates who enrolled in 2007, 276 applied for aid, 276 were judged to have need. 10 Federal Work-Study jobs (averaging $1850). *Average percent of need met:* 82%. *Financial aid deadline:* 5/25.

Applying *Application fee:* $25. *Required:* essay or personal statement, high school transcript, minimum 2 GPA, interview, The applicants must approve an evaluation regarding artistic skills through a portfolio or seminar and complete the security seminar. *Application deadlines:* 10/6 (freshmen), 10/6 (out-of-state freshmen), 10/6 (transfers). *Notification:* 10/30 (freshmen), 10/30 (out-of-state freshmen), 10/30 (transfers).

Freshman Application Contact Mrs. Ivelisse Torres, Acting as Promotion and Recruitment Officer, Escuela de Artes Plasticas de Puerto Rico, PO Box 902112, San Juan, PR 00902-1112. *Phone:* 787-725-8120 Ext. 337. *Fax:* 787-721-3798. *E-mail:* itorres@eap.edu. *Web site:* http://www.eap.edu/.

Inter American University of Puerto Rico, Aguadilla Campus

Aguadilla, Puerto Rico

- **Independent** comprehensive, founded 1957, part of Inter American University of Puerto Rico
- **Small-town** 50-acre campus
- **Endowment** $757,235
- **Coed**
- **Moderately difficult** entrance level

Faculty *Student/faculty ratio:* 29:1.

Academics *Calendar:* semesters. *Degrees:* certificates, associate, bachelor's, and master's.

Student Life *Campus security:* 24-hour emergency response devices and patrols.

Standardized Tests *Required:* PAA (for admission). *Required for some:* SAT or ACT (for admission).

Costs (2010–11) *Tuition:* $5017 full-time. *Required fees:* $478 full-time. *Payment plans:* installment, deferred payment.

Applying *Options:* electronic application. *Required:* high school transcript, minimum 2 GPA.

Freshman Application Contact Mrs. Doris Perez, Admissions Director, Inter American University of Puerto Rico, Aguadilla Campus, PO Box 20,000, Road 459 Intersection 463, Aguadilla, PR 00605. *Phone:* 787-891-0925 Ext. 2101. *Fax:* 787-882-3020. *Web site:* http://www.aguadilla.inter.edu/.

Inter American University of Puerto Rico, Arecibo Campus

Arecibo, Puerto Rico

- **Independent** comprehensive, founded 1957, part of Inter American University of Puerto Rico
- **Urban** 20-acre campus with easy access to San Juan
- **Coed**
- **Moderately difficult** entrance level

Faculty *Student/faculty ratio:* 24:1.

Academics *Calendar:* semesters. *Degrees:* certificates, associate, bachelor's, and master's.

Student Life *Campus security:* 24-hour emergency response devices and patrols.

Standardized Tests *Required:* PAA, CEEB (for admission).

Costs (2010–11) *Comprehensive fee:* $13,857 includes full-time tuition ($4080), mandatory fees ($516), and room and board ($9261). Full-time tuition and fees vary according to course load. Part-time tuition: $170 per credit hour. Part-time tuition and fees vary according to course load. *College room only:* $4761.

Financial Aid *Of all full-time matriculated undergraduates who enrolled in 2008,* 2,486 applied for aid, 2,474 were judged to have need, 2 had their need fully met. 238 Federal Work-Study jobs (averaging $1600). *Average percent of need met:* 8. *Average financial aid package:* $1439. *Average need-based loan:* $2332. *Average need-based gift aid:* $292.

Applying *Options:* electronic application, early admission, deferred entrance. *Required:* high school transcript, minimum 2 GPA. *Required for some:* interview. *Recommended:* minimum 3 GPA.

Freshman Application Contact Ms. Provi Montalvo, Admission Director, Inter American University of Puerto Rico, Arecibo Campus, PO Box 4050, Arecibo, PR 00614-4050. *Phone:* 787-878-5475. *Fax:* 787-880-1624. *E-mail:* pmontalvo@arecibo.inter.edu. *Web site:* http://www.arecibo.inter.edu/.

Inter American University of Puerto Rico, Barranquitas Campus

Barranquitas, Puerto Rico

Freshman Application Contact Mrs. Aramilda Cartagena, Dean of Students, Inter American University of Puerto Rico, Barranquitas Campus, PO Box 517, Barranquitas, PR 00794. *Phone:* 787-857-3600 Ext. 2009. *Fax:* 787-857-2125. *E-mail:* acartagena@br.inter.edu. *Web site:* http://www.br.inter.edu/.

Inter American University of Puerto Rico, Bayamón Campus

Bayamón, Puerto Rico

- **Independent** comprehensive, founded 1912, part of Inter American University of Puerto Rico
- **Urban** 51-acre campus with easy access to San Juan
- **Endowment** $121.9 million
- **Coed** 4,992 undergraduate students, 86% full-time, 45% women, 55% men
- **42%** of applicants were admitted

Undergraduates 4,296 full-time, 696 part-time. Students come from 1 other state; 4 other countries; 100% Hispanic/Latino; 4% transferred in. *Retention:* 73% of full-time freshmen returned.

Freshmen *Admission:* 3,250 applied, 1,376 admitted, 1,265 enrolled. *Average high school GPA:* 3.

Faculty *Total:* 321, 34% full-time, 20% with terminal degrees. *Student/faculty ratio:* 23:1.

Academics *Calendar:* semesters. *Degrees:* certificates, associate, bachelor's, and master's. *Special study options:* accelerated degree program, adult/continuing education programs, advanced placement credit, cooperative education, distance learning, external degree program, honors programs, independent study, internships, part-time degree program, services for LD students, summer session for credit. *ROTC:* Army (c).

Computers on Campus 610 computers/terminals are available on campus for general student use. Students can access the following: computer help desk, free student e-mail accounts, online (class) grades, online (class) registration. Campuswide network is available.

Student Life *Housing options:* Campus housing is university owned. *Activities and organizations:* student-run newspaper, choral group, Asociacion de Estudiantes de Administracion de Empresas, Estudiantes Unidos por la Ciencia, Asociacion Estudiantes de Aviacion, Consejo de Estudiante, Asociacion Estudiantes de Ingenieria. *Campus security:* 24-hour patrols. *Student services:* health clinic, personal/psychological counseling.

Athletics *Intercollegiate sports:* baseball M(s), basketball M(s)/W(s), cross-country running M(s)/W(s), softball M(s)/W(s), swimming and diving M(s)/W(s), table tennis M(s)/W(s), track and field M(s)/W(s), volleyball M(s)/W(s), weight lifting M(s). *Intramural sports:* basketball M/W, cross-country running M/W, softball M/W, swimming and diving M/W, table tennis M/W, tennis M/W, track and field M/W, volleyball M/W, weight lifting M.

Standardized Tests *Required:* CEEB (for admission). *Required for some:* SAT (for admission).

Costs (2011–12) *Tuition:* $5100 full-time, $258 per semester hour part-time. Full-time tuition and fees vary according to course load and program. Part-time tuition and fees vary according to course load and program. *Required fees:* $516 full-time. *Payment plan:* deferred payment.

Financial Aid Of all full-time matriculated undergraduates who enrolled in 2009, 2,985 applied for aid, 2,955 were judged to have need, 4 had their need fully met. *Average percent of need met:* 8%. *Average financial aid package:* $983. *Average need-based loan:* $1580. *Average need-based gift aid:* $387.

Applying *Options:* electronic application. *Required:* high school transcript, minimum 2 GPA, 2.5 GPA for engineering programs. *Application deadline:* 7/30 (freshmen). *Notification:* continuous (freshmen), continuous (transfers).
Freshman Application Contact Inter American University of Puerto Rico, Bayamón Campus, 500 Road 830, Bayamón, PR 00957. *Phone:* 787-279-1912 Ext. 2017. *Web site:* http://www.bc.inter.edu/.

Inter American University of Puerto Rico, Fajardo Campus

Fajardo, Puerto Rico

- **Independent** comprehensive, founded 1965, part of Inter American University of Puerto Rico
- **Small-town** 11-acre campus with easy access to San Juan
- **Coed**
- **Moderately difficult** entrance level

Faculty *Student/faculty ratio:* 11:1.
Academics *Calendar:* semesters. *Degrees:* associate, bachelor's, and master's.
Student Life *Campus security:* 24-hour patrols.
Standardized Tests *Required:* College Board (for admission).
Costs (2010–11) *Tuition:* $170 per credit part-time. Full-time tuition and fees vary according to degree level. Part-time tuition and fees vary according to degree level. *Payment plans:* installment, deferred payment.
Applying *Options:* electronic application, early admission, deferred entrance. *Required:* high school transcript. *Required for some:* interview.
Freshman Application Contact Ms. Jackeline Melèndez, Administrative Assistant II, Inter American University of Puerto Rico, Fajardo Campus, Call Box 70003, Fajardo, PR 00738-7003. *Phone:* 787-863-2390 Ext. 2210. *Fax:* 787-860-3470. *E-mail:* jackeline.melendez@fajardo.inter.edu. *Web site:* http://www.fajardo.inter.edu/.

Inter American University of Puerto Rico, Guayama Campus

Guayama, Puerto Rico

- **Independent** comprehensive, founded 1958, part of Inter American University of Puerto Rico
- **Small-town** 50-acre campus
- **Endowment** $782,124
- **Coed** 2,285 undergraduate students, 83% full-time, 66% women, 34% men
- **Moderately difficult** entrance level, 62% of applicants were admitted

Undergraduates 1,902 full-time, 383 part-time. 100% Hispanic/Latino. *Retention:* 61% of full-time freshmen returned.
Freshmen *Admission:* 575 applied, 356 admitted, 332 enrolled.
Faculty *Total:* 203, 22% full-time, 16% with terminal degrees. *Student/faculty ratio:* 23:1.
Academics *Calendar:* semesters. *Degrees:* certificates, associate, bachelor's, and master's. *Special study options:* academic remediation for entering students, adult/continuing education programs, distance learning, English as a second language, external degree program, honors programs, independent study, off-campus study, part-time degree program, summer session for credit. *ROTC:* Army (c).
Computers on Campus 288 computers/terminals are available on campus for general student use. Students can access the following: campus intranet, computer help desk, free student e-mail accounts, online (class) grades, online (class) registration, online (class) schedules. Campuswide network is available. Wireless service is available via entire campus.
Student Life *Housing:* college housing not available. *Activities and organizations:* drama/theater group, Criminal Justice, Honor's Program, Human Resources, Natural Sciences, Health Sciences. *Campus security:* 24-hour emergency response devices. *Student services:* health clinic.
Athletics *Intercollegiate sports:* baseball M, basketball M(s)/W(s), cross-country running M(s)/W(s), swimming and diving M. *Intramural sports:* baseball M, basketball M/W, cross-country running M/W, soccer M, softball M/W, swimming and diving M, table tennis W, tennis W, track and field M/W.
Standardized Tests *Required:* SAT (for admission), PAA (for admission).
Costs (2011–12) *Tuition:* $4080 full-time. *Required fees:* $478 full-time. *Payment plan:* deferred payment. *Waivers:* employees or children of employees.
Financial Aid Of all full-time matriculated undergraduates who enrolled in 2009, 1,607 applied for aid, 1,604 were judged to have need. *Average percent of need met:* 16%. *Average financial aid package:* $2821. *Average need-based loan:* $3281. *Average need-based gift aid:* $528.
Applying *Options:* electronic application. *Required:* high school transcript, minimum 2 GPA. *Required for some:* essay or personal statement, interview. *Application deadlines:* 8/1 (freshmen), 8/1 (transfers).

Freshman Application Contact Inter American University of Puerto Rico, Guayama Campus, Call Box 10004, Guayama, PR 00785. *Phone:* 787-864-2222 Ext. 220. *Toll-free phone:* 787-864-2222 Ext. 2243. *Web site:* http://www.guayama.inter.edu/.

Inter American University of Puerto Rico, Metropolitan Campus

San Juan, Puerto Rico

- **Independent** comprehensive, founded 1960, part of Inter American University of Puerto Rico
- **Urban** campus
- **Endowment** $7.5 million
- **Coed** 6,961 undergraduate students, 81% full-time, 54% women, 46% men
- **Moderately difficult** entrance level, 27% of applicants were admitted

Undergraduates 5,652 full-time, 1,309 part-time.
Freshmen *Admission:* 4,379 applied, 1,202 admitted, 972 enrolled. *Average high school GPA:* 3.07.
Faculty *Total:* 599, 36% full-time, 43% with terminal degrees.
Academics *Calendar:* semesters. *Degrees:* certificates, associate, bachelor's, master's, doctoral-research/scholarship, and postbachelor's certificates. *Special study options:* accelerated degree program, adult/continuing education programs, cooperative education, distance learning, English as a second language, external degree program, honors programs, independent study, internships, part-time degree program, services for LD students, study abroad, summer session for credit. *ROTC:* Army (c), Navy (c), Air Force (c).
Computers on Campus 625 computers/terminals are available on campus for general student use. Students can access the following: campus intranet, computer help desk, free student e-mail accounts, online (class) grades, online (class) registration, online (class) schedules. Campuswide network is available. Wireless service is available via classrooms, computer centers, computer labs, learning centers, libraries, student centers.
Student Life *Housing:* college housing not available. *Activities and organizations:* drama/theater group, student-run newspaper, choral group, Intercultural Student Association, Club Rotaract, Biological Science, Abriendo Camino, Alpha Phi Omega. *Campus security:* 24-hour emergency response devices and patrols, video security system. *Student services:* health clinic, personal/psychological counseling.
Athletics *Intercollegiate sports:* baseball M, basketball M, soccer M, table tennis M/W, tennis M/W, volleyball W.
Standardized Tests *Required:* CEEB (for admission). *Required for some:* SAT (for admission).
Costs (2010–11) *Tuition:* $4590 full-time, $170 per credit part-time. *Required fees:* $516 full-time, $516 per year part-time. *Payment plan:* deferred payment. *Waivers:* employees or children of employees.
Financial Aid Of all full-time matriculated undergraduates who enrolled in 1999, 4,328 applied for aid, 3,935 were judged to have need, 29 had their need fully met. *Average percent of need met:* 11%. *Average financial aid package:* $2144. *Average need-based loan:* $1149. *Average need-based gift aid:* $1617. *Financial aid deadline:* 4/30.
Applying *Options:* electronic application. *Required:* high school transcript. *Application deadlines:* 5/15 (freshmen), 5/15 (out-of-state freshmen), 5/15 (transfers).
Freshman Application Contact Ms. Ida G. Betancourt, Official Admission, Inter American University of Puerto Rico, Metropolitan Campus, PO Box 191293, San Juan, PR 00919-1293. *Phone:* 787-250-1912 Ext. 2188. *Fax:* 787-250-1025. *E-mail:* jbetancourt@metro.inter.edu. *Web site:* http://metro.inter.edu/.

Inter American University of Puerto Rico, Ponce Campus

Mercedita, Puerto Rico

- **Independent** comprehensive, founded 1962, part of Inter American University of Puerto Rico
- **Urban** 50-acre campus with easy access to San Juan
- **Coed** 6,038 undergraduate students, 83% full-time, 61% women, 39% men
- **Moderately difficult** entrance level

Undergraduates 5,025 full-time, 1,013 part-time. Students come from 1 other state; 4% transferred in. *Retention:* 72% of full-time freshmen returned.
Freshmen *Admission:* 3,018 applied, 1,103 enrolled.
Faculty *Total:* 347, 29% full-time, 19% with terminal degrees. *Student/faculty ratio:* 31:1.
Academics *Calendar:* semesters. *Degrees:* associate, bachelor's, and master's. *Special study options:* academic remediation for entering students, adult/

continuing education programs, cooperative education, distance learning, English as a second language, honors programs, independent study, internships, off-campus study, part-time degree program, services for LD students, study abroad, summer session for credit.

Computers on Campus 700 computers/terminals are available on campus for general student use. Students can access the following: online (class) registration. Campuswide network is available.

Student Life *Housing:* college housing not available. *Activities and organizations:* drama/theater group, choral group, marching band, IKARUS Drama Association, American Marketing Association, ABACUS, ECOS, Cheer-Leaders. *Campus security:* 24-hour patrols. *Student services:* health clinic, personal/psychological counseling.

Athletics *Intercollegiate sports:* baseball M(s)/W, cross-country running M/W, softball M(s)/W, table tennis M/W, track and field M(s)/W(s), volleyball M/W, weight lifting M(s)/W. *Intramural sports:* basketball M/W, table tennis M/W, weight lifting M.

Standardized Tests *Required:* CEEB (for admission). *Required for some:* SAT (for admission).

Costs (2010–11) *Tuition:* $4080 full-time, $170 per credit part-time. Full-time tuition and fees vary according to course load and program. Part-time tuition and fees vary according to course load and program. *Required fees:* $516 full-time, $422 per year part-time. *Payment plan:* deferred payment.

Financial Aid Of all full-time matriculated undergraduates who enrolled in 2008, 3,209 applied for aid, 3,194 were judged to have need, 1 had their need fully met. *Average percent of need met:* 10%. *Average financial aid package:* $1702. *Average need-based loan:* $2248. *Average need-based gift aid:* $537.

Applying *Options:* deferred admission. *Required:* high school transcript, minimum 2 GPA. *Application deadlines:* 5/15 (freshmen), 5/15 (transfers).

Freshman Application Contact Mr. Franco Diaz, Admissions Officer, Inter American University of Puerto Rico, Ponce Campus, 104 Turpo Industrial Park, Road #1, Mercedita, PR 00715-1602. *Phone:* 787-284-1912 Ext. 2025. *Fax:* 787-841-0103. *E-mail:* fidiaz@ponce.inter.edu. *Web site:* http://www.ponce.inter.edu/.

Inter American University of Puerto Rico, San Germán Campus

San Germán, Puerto Rico

- **Independent** university, founded 1912, part of Inter American University of Puerto Rico
- **Small-town** 260-acre campus with easy access to Ponce, Aguadilla, Mayaguez
- **Endowment** $22.0 million
- **Coed** 8,820 undergraduate students, 93% full-time, 27% women, 73% men
- **Moderately difficult** entrance level, 80% of applicants were admitted

Undergraduates 8,222 full-time, 598 part-time. Students come from 10 states and territories; 1% are from out of state; 2% transferred in; 10% live on campus. *Retention:* 72% of full-time freshmen returned.

Freshmen *Admission:* 1,675 applied, 1,345 admitted, 935 enrolled. *Average high school GPA:* 2.9.

Faculty *Total:* 308, 42% full-time, 31% with terminal degrees. *Student/faculty ratio:* 23:1.

Academics *Calendar:* semesters. *Degrees:* certificates, associate, bachelor's, master's, doctoral-research/scholarship, and postbachelor's certificates. *Special study options:* academic remediation for entering students, accelerated degree program, adult/continuing education programs, advanced placement credit, cooperative education, distance learning, double majors, English as a second language, external degree program, honors programs, independent study, internships, off-campus study, part-time degree program, services for LD students, summer session for credit. *ROTC:* Army (c), Navy (c), Air Force (c).

Computers on Campus 1,200 computers/terminals are available on campus for general student use. Students can access the following: free student e-mail accounts, online (class) grades, online (class) registration, online (class) schedules. Campuswide network is available. Wireless service is available via computer centers, computer labs, dorm rooms, learning centers, libraries, student centers.

Student Life *Housing options:* men-only, women-only. Campus housing is university owned. *Activities and organizations:* drama/theater group, student-run newspaper, choral group, Asociacion de Pre-Medica-Caduceus, Honors Program, Asociacion De Estudiantes De Psicologia (AEPSI), Asociacion de Estudiantes Inter Tecnicos (AEITEC), national fraternities, national sororities. *Campus security:* 24-hour emergency response devices and patrols. *Student services:* personal/psychological counseling.

Athletics *Intercollegiate sports:* baseball M(s), basketball M(s)/W(s), cross-country running M(s)/W(s), soccer M(s), softball M/W, swimming and diving M/W, table tennis M(s)/W(s), tennis M(s)/W(s), track and field M(s)/W(s), volleyball M(s)/W(s), weight lifting M(s). *Intramural sports:* badminton M/

W, basketball M/W, cross-country running M/W, softball M/W, table tennis M/W, tennis M/W, track and field M/W, volleyball M/W.

Standardized Tests *Required:* CEEB (for admission). *Required for some:* SAT or ACT (for admission).

Costs (2011–12) *Comprehensive fee:* $8116 includes full-time tuition ($5100), mandatory fees ($516), and room and board ($2500). Part-time tuition: $170 per credit. *Required fees:* $170 per credit part-time, $258 per term part-time. *College room only:* $1000. Room and board charges vary according to board plan and housing facility. *Payment plan:* installment. *Waivers:* employees or children of employees.

Financial Aid Of all full-time matriculated undergraduates who enrolled in 2008, 2,797 applied for aid, 2,755 were judged to have need, 4 had their need fully met. *Average percent of need met:* 12%. *Average financial aid package:* $2009. *Average need-based loan:* $3080. *Average need-based gift aid:* $642.

Applying *Options:* electronic application, early admission. *Required:* high school transcript, medical history, vaccination. *Required for some:* 1 letter of recommendation, interview. *Recommended:* essay or personal statement, minimum 2 GPA. *Application deadlines:* 5/15 (freshmen), 5/15 (transfers). *Notification:* continuous (freshmen), continuous (transfers).

Freshman Application Contact Prof. Mildred Camacho, Director of Admissions, Inter American University of Puerto Rico, San Germán Campus, PO Box 5100, San Germán, PR 00683-5008. *Phone:* 787-264-1912 Ext. 7283. *Fax:* 787-892-7020. *E-mail:* milcama@sg.inter.edu. *Web site:* http://www.sg.inter.edu/.

National University College

Bayamón, Puerto Rico

Freshman Application Contact Admissions, National University College, PO Box 2036, National College Plaza Building, Bayamón, PR 00960. *Phone:* 787-780-5134. *Toll-free phone:* 800-780-5134. *Fax:* 787-779-4909. *E-mail:* infobayamon@nuc.edu. *Web site:* http://www.nuc.edu/.

Polytechnic University of Puerto Rico

Hato Rey, Puerto Rico

- **Independent** comprehensive, founded 1966
- **Urban** 10-acre campus with easy access to San Juan
- **Endowment** $10.8 million
- **Coed, primarily men** 4,894 undergraduate students, 53% full-time, 22% women, 78% men
- **Minimally difficult** entrance level, 94% of applicants were admitted

Undergraduates 2,607 full-time, 2,287 part-time. Students come from 2 states and territories; 12 other countries. *Retention:* 74% of full-time freshmen returned.

Freshmen *Admission:* 773 applied, 727 admitted, 559 enrolled. *Average high school GPA:* 2.45.

Faculty *Total:* 279, 62% full-time, 30% with terminal degrees. *Student/faculty ratio:* 20:1.

Academics *Calendar:* trimesters. *Degrees:* bachelor's and master's. *Special study options:* academic remediation for entering students, distance learning, English as a second language, independent study, part-time degree program, student-designed majors, summer session for credit. *ROTC:* Army (c).

Computers on Campus 375 computers/terminals are available on campus for general student use. Students can access the following: free student e-mail accounts. Campuswide network is available. Wireless service is available via entire campus.

Student Life *Activities and organizations:* choral group, Society of Women Engineers, American Civil Engineering - Student Chapter, Society of Hispanic Professional Engineers, Society of Automotive Engineers, Capitulo Estudiantil Ingenieros Electricos. *Campus security:* 24-hour patrols. *Student services:* personal/psychological counseling.

Athletics *Intercollegiate sports:* basketball M(s), cross-country running M(s)/W(s), table tennis M(s)/W(s), tennis M(s)/W(s), track and field M(s)/W(s), volleyball M(s)/W(s), wrestling M(s). *Intramural sports:* basketball M.

Costs (2010–11) *Comprehensive fee:* $18,967 includes full-time tuition ($6588), mandatory fees ($675), and room and board ($11,704). Full-time tuition and fees vary according to course load, degree level, and program. Part-time tuition: $180 per credit hour. Part-time tuition and fees vary according to course load, degree level, and program. *Payment plan:* deferred payment. *Waivers:* employees or children of employees.

Financial Aid Of all full-time matriculated undergraduates who enrolled in 2008, 2,749 applied for aid, 2,679 were judged to have need, 25 had their need fully met. 121 Federal Work-Study jobs (averaging $1733). *Average percent of need met:* 63%. *Average financial aid package:* $5350. *Average need-based loan:* $4550. *Average need-based gift aid:* $4454. *Financial aid deadline:* 5/15.

Applying *Options:* early admission, deferred entrance. *Application fee:* $30. *Required:* high school transcript. *Application deadline:* 8/15 (freshmen).

Freshman Application Contact Ms. Teresa Cardona, Director of Admissions, Polytechnic University of Puerto Rico, PO Box 192017, San Juan, PR 00919-2017. *Phone:* 787-754-8000 Ext. 240. *Fax:* 787-764-8712. *E-mail:* tcardona@pupr.edu. *Web site:* http://www.pupr.edu/.

Pontifical Catholic University of Puerto Rico

Ponce, Puerto Rico

- **Independent Roman Catholic** university, founded 1948
- **Urban** 120-acre campus with easy access to San Juan
- **Coed**
- **Moderately difficult** entrance level

Faculty *Student/faculty ratio:* 23:1.

Academics *Calendar:* semesters. *Degrees:* associate, bachelor's, master's, doctoral-professional, doctoral-research/scholarship, and postbachelor's certificates (branch locations in Arecibo, Guayana, Mayagüez).

Student Life *Campus security:* 24-hour emergency response devices and patrols.

Athletics Member NAIA.

Standardized Tests *Required:* College Entrance Examination Board (CEEB) Aptitude Test for Admission, Achievement Test for placement (for admission). *Required for some:* SAT (for admission).

Costs (2010–11) *Tuition:* $4950 full-time, $165 per credit part-time. Full-time tuition and fees vary according to location. Part-time tuition and fees vary according to location. *Required fees:* $518 full-time. *Room only:* $1300.

Financial Aid *Of all full-time matriculated undergraduates who enrolled in 2009,* 6,953 applied for aid, 6,149 were judged to have need, 262 had their need fully met. 780 Federal Work-Study jobs (averaging $1329). 105 state and other part-time jobs (averaging $239). *Average percent of need met:* 61. *Average financial aid package:* $7118. *Average need-based loan:* $3563. *Average need-based gift aid:* $5533. *Average indebtedness upon graduation:* $12,707. *Financial aid deadline:* 5/15.

Applying *Options:* early admission, deferred entrance. *Application fee:* $15. *Required:* high school transcript, minimum 2.5 GPA. *Required for some:* essay or personal statement, minimum 3 GPA, 1 letter of recommendation, interview.

Freshman Application Contact Sra. Ana O. Bonilla, Director of Admissions, Pontifical Catholic University of Puerto Rico, 2250 Avenida Las Americas Avenue, Suite 584, Ponce, PR 00717-9777. *Phone:* 787-841-2000 Ext. 1004. *Toll-free phone:* 800-981-5040. *Fax:* 787-840-4295. *E-mail:* admissions@email.pucpr.edu. *Web site:* http://www.pucpr.edu/.

Universidad Adventista de las Antillas

Mayagüez, Puerto Rico

- **Independent Seventh-day Adventist** comprehensive, founded 1957
- **Rural** 284-acre campus
- **Endowment** $134,104
- **Coed**
- **Minimally difficult** entrance level

Faculty *Student/faculty ratio:* 17:1.

Academics *Calendar:* semesters. *Degrees:* associate, bachelor's, and master's.

Student Life *Campus security:* 24-hour emergency response devices and patrols, student patrols, controlled dormitory access.

Standardized Tests *Recommended:* SAT or ACT (for admission), CEEB.

Costs (2010–11) *Comprehensive fee:* $8570 includes full-time tuition ($4650), mandatory fees ($1020), and room and board ($2900). Part-time tuition: $158 per credit hour. *College room only:* $1100. Room and board charges vary according to board plan.

Financial Aid *Of all full-time matriculated undergraduates who enrolled in 2009,* 955 applied for aid, 955 were judged to have need. *Average percent of need met:* 70. *Average need-based loan:* $3250. *Average need-based gift aid:* $6472. *Average indebtedness upon graduation:* $4400.

Applying *Options:* electronic application, early admission. *Application fee:* $20. *Required:* high school transcript, minimum 2 GPA. *Required for some:* essay or personal statement, interview.

Freshman Application Contact Ms. Evelyn del Valle, Director of Admissions, Universidad Adventista de las Antillas, Oficina de Admisiones, PO Box 118, Mayaguez, PR 00681-0118. *Phone:* 787-834-9595 Ext. 2208. *Fax:* 787-834-9597. *E-mail:* admissions@uaa.edu. *Web site:* http://www.uaa.edu/.

Universidad Central del Caribe

Bayamón, Puerto Rico

Director of Admissions Admissions Department, Universidad Central del Caribe, PO Box 60-327, Bayamón, PR 00960-6032. *Phone:* 787-740-1611. *Toll-free phone:* 809-616-1616. *Web site:* http://www.uccaribe.edu/.

Universidad del Este

Carolina, Puerto Rico

Freshman Application Contact Universidad del Este, PO Box 2010, Carolina, PR 00984. *Phone:* 787-257-7373 Ext. 3401. *Web site:* http://www.suagm.edu/une/.

Universidad del Turabo

Gurabo, Puerto Rico

Director of Admissions Carmen Rivera, Director of Admissions and Financial Aid, Universidad del Turabo, PO Box 3030, Gurabo, PR 00778-3030. *Phone:* 787-743-7979 Ext. 4352. *E-mail:* ut_crivera@suagm.edu. *Web site:* http://www.suagm.edu/ut/.

Universidad Metropolitana

San Juan, Puerto Rico

Freshman Application Contact Mr. Julio Rodriguez Soiza, Director of Admissions, Universidad Metropolitana, Box 21150, San Juan, PR 00928-1150. *Phone:* 787-766-1717 Ext. 6587. *Toll-free phone:* 800-747-8362. *Fax:* 787-751-0992. *E-mail:* um_frivera@suagm1.suagm.edu. *Web site:* http://www.suagm.edu/umet/.

Universidad Teologica del Caribe

St. Just, Puerto Rico

- **Independent Pentecostal** 4-year, founded 1956
- **Suburban** 4-acre campus with easy access to San Juan
- **Endowment** $1.0 million
- **Coed** 261 undergraduate students, 41% full-time, 41% women, 59% men
- 94% of applicants were admitted

Undergraduates 106 full-time, 155 part-time. Students come from 1 other state; 3 other countries; 1% are from out of state; 100% Hispanic/Latino; 12% transferred in. *Retention:* 53% of full-time freshmen returned.

Freshmen *Admission:* 48 applied, 45 admitted, 60 enrolled.

Faculty *Total:* 26, 23% full-time, 23% with terminal degrees. *Student/faculty ratio:* 10:1.

Academics *Calendar:* semesters. *Degree:* certificates, diplomas, and bachelor's. *Special study options:* honors programs, independent study, internships, off-campus study, part-time degree program, services for LD students, summer session for credit.

Computers on Campus 3 computers/terminals and 3 ports are available on campus for general student use. Students can access the following: online (class) schedules. Wireless service is available via classrooms, computer labs, libraries, student centers.

Student Life *Housing options:* coed. Campus housing is university owned. *Activities and organizations:* Asociacion Pioneros por Cristo, Asociacion Misionera, Asociacion Ministerial, FESI. *Student services:* personal/psychological counseling.

Costs (2011–12) *One-time required fee:* $13. *Comprehensive fee:* $6280 includes full-time tuition ($3500), mandatory fees ($380), and room and board ($2400). Part-time tuition: $18 per credit. *Required fees:* $130 per credit part-time, $2720 per term part-time. *College room only:* $1200. Room and board charges vary according to board plan. *Payment plan:* deferred payment.

Financial Aid Of all full-time matriculated undergraduates who enrolled in 2009, 83 applied for aid, 83 were judged to have need. *Financial aid deadline:* 6/30.

Applying *Options:* electronic application, early admission. *Application fee:* $25. *Required:* interview, medical certificate. *Required for some:* high school transcript.

Freshman Application Contact Ms. Isabel Mojica, Admissions Officer, Universidad Teologica del Caribe, PO Box 901, Saint Just, PR 00978-901. *Phone:* 787-761-0640 Ext. 246. *Fax:* 787-748-9220. *E-mail:* reclutamiento.utc@gmail.com. *Web site:* http://www.utcpr.edu/.

University of Phoenix–Puerto Rico Campus

Guaynabo, Puerto Rico

Freshman Application Contact Ms. Audra McQuarie, Registrar/Executive Director, University of Phoenix–Puerto Rico Campus, 4035 South Riverpoint Parkway, Mail Stop CF-L101, Phoenix, AZ 85040. *Phone:* 480-557-6151. *Toll-free phone:* 800-776-4867 (in-state); 800-228-7240 (out-of-state). *Fax:* 480-643-3068. *E-mail:* audra.mcquarie@phoenix.edu. *Web site:* http://www.phoenix.edu/.

University of Puerto Rico, Aguadilla University College

Aguadilla, Puerto Rico

Director of Admissions Ms. Melba Serrano Lugo, Admissions Officer, University of Puerto Rico, Aguadilla University College, PO Box 6150, Aguadilla, PR 00604. *Phone:* 787-890-2681 Ext. 280. *Web site:* http://www.uprag.edu/.

University of Puerto Rico at Arecibo

Arecibo, Puerto Rico

Freshman Application Contact University of Puerto Rico at Arecibo, PO Box 4010, Arecibo, PR 00613. *Phone:* 787-878-2830 Ext. 4101. *Web site:* http://www.upra.edu/.

University of Puerto Rico at Bayamón

Bayamón, Puerto Rico

- **Commonwealth-supported** 4-year, founded 1971, part of University of Puerto Rico System
- **Urban** 78-acre campus with easy access to San Juan
- **Coed**
- **Very difficult** entrance level

Faculty *Student/faculty ratio:* 20:1.
Academics *Calendar:* semesters. *Degrees:* associate and bachelor's.
Student Life *Campus security:* 24-hour patrols.
Athletics Member NCAA.
Standardized Tests *Required:* College Board (for admission).
Costs (2010–11) *Tuition:* commonwealth resident $1734 full-time, $51 per credit part-time; nonresident $4039 full-time. Full-time tuition and fees vary according to class time, course load, degree level, and program. Part-time tuition and fees vary according to class time, course load, degree level, and program. No tuition increase for student's term of enrollment. *Required fees:* $342 full-time, $144 per term part-time. *Room and board:* Room and board charges vary according to housing facility.
Applying *Options:* electronic application. *Application fee:* $15. *Required:* high school transcript.
Freshman Application Contact Ms. Carmen I. Montes, Admissions Director, University of Puerto Rico at Bayamón, OPEI Office, Street 174 #170 Minillas Industrial Park, Bayamon, PR 00959. *Phone:* 787-993-8952. *Fax:* 787-993-8929. *E-mail:* cmontes@upr.edu. *Web site:* http://www.uprb.edu/.

University of Puerto Rico at Carolina

Carolina, Puerto Rico

Director of Admissions Ms. Celia Mendez, Admissions Officer, University of Puerto Rico at Carolina, PO Box 4800, Carolina, PR 00984-4800. *Phone:* 787-757-1485. *Web site:* http://uprc.edu/.

University of Puerto Rico at Humacao

Humacao, Puerto Rico

- **Commonwealth-supported** 4-year, founded 1962, part of University of Puerto Rico System
- **Suburban** 62-acre campus with easy access to San Juan
- **Coed** 4,314 undergraduate students, 91% full-time, 66% women, 34% men
- **Moderately difficult** entrance level, 41% of applicants were admitted

Undergraduates 3,945 full-time, 369 part-time. 100% Race/ethnicity unknown; 0.4% transferred in. *Retention:* 82% of full-time freshmen returned.
Freshmen *Admission:* 2,410 applied, 998 admitted, 841 enrolled. *Average high school GPA:* 3.64.

Faculty *Total:* 291, 87% full-time, 44% with terminal degrees. *Student/faculty ratio:* 16:1.
Academics *Calendar:* semesters. *Degrees:* associate and bachelor's. *Special study options:* academic remediation for entering students, advanced placement credit, English as a second language, honors programs, internships, part-time degree program, services for LD students, summer session for credit.
Computers on Campus Students can access the following: free student e-mail accounts, online (class) grades, online (class) registration, online (class) schedules. Campuswide network is available. Wireless service is available via libraries, student centers.
Student Life *Housing:* college housing not available. *Activities and organizations:* drama/theater group, student-run radio station, choral group, marching band, Recreational Organization, Accounting Students Association, Management Students Association, Microbiology Students Association, Human Resources Students Association, national fraternities, national sororities. *Campus security:* 24-hour patrols, 24-hour gate security. *Student services:* personal/psychological counseling, women's center.
Athletics *Intercollegiate sports:* baseball M(s), basketball M(s)/W(s), cheerleading M(s)/W(s), cross-country running M(s)/W(s), softball W(s), swimming and diving M(s)/W(s), table tennis M(s)/W(s), tennis W(s), track and field M(s)/W(s), volleyball M(s)/W(s), weight lifting M(s)/W(s), wrestling M(s). *Intramural sports:* softball W, volleyball M/W.
Standardized Tests *Required:* Pruebas de Admision y Evaluacion Universitaria (PEAU) (for admission). *Required for some:* SAT or ACT (for admission), SAT Subject Tests (for admission).
Costs (2010–11) *Tuition:* commonwealth resident $1734 full-time, $51 per credit hour part-time. Full-time tuition and fees vary according to class time, course load, and student level. Part-time tuition and fees vary according to class time, course load, and student level. No tuition increase for student's term of enrollment. *Required fees:* $1142 full-time. *Room and board:* $8280; room only: $3000. *Payment plan:* deferred payment. *Waivers:* employees or children of employees.
Financial Aid Of all full-time matriculated undergraduates who enrolled in 2001, 3,515 applied for aid, 2,883 were judged to have need, 7 had their need fully met. 278 Federal Work-Study jobs (averaging $1318). *Average percent of need met:* 50%. *Average financial aid package:* $3929. *Average need-based loan:* $3295. *Average need-based gift aid:* $3664. *Average indebtedness upon graduation:* $2749. *Financial aid deadline:* 6/30.
Applying *Options:* deferred entrance. *Application fee:* $20. *Required:* high school transcript. *Required for some:* interview. *Application deadlines:* 1/31 (freshmen), 3/9 (transfers). *Notification:* 4/15 (freshmen), continuous until 6/30 (transfers).
Freshman Application Contact Mrs. Elizabeth Gerena, Acting Director of Admissions, University of Puerto Rico at Humacao, HUC Station 100, Road 908, Humacao, PR 00791. *Phone:* 787-850-9301. *Fax:* 787-850-9428. *E-mail:* elizabeth.gerena@upr.edu. *Web site:* http://www.uprh.edu/.

University of Puerto Rico at Ponce

Ponce, Puerto Rico

Freshman Application Contact University of Puerto Rico at Ponce, PO Box 7186, Ponce, PR 00732-7186. *Phone:* 787-844-8181 Ext. 2533. *Web site:* http://upr-ponce.upr.edu/.

University of Puerto Rico at Utuado

Utuado, Puerto Rico

- **Commonwealth-supported** 4-year, founded 1979, part of University of Puerto Rico System
- **Small-town** 180-acre campus with easy access to San Juan
- **Coed**
- **Moderately difficult** entrance level

Faculty *Student/faculty ratio:* 18:1.
Academics *Calendar:* semesters. *Degrees:* associate and bachelor's.
Student Life *Campus security:* 24-hour emergency response devices and patrols.
Standardized Tests *Required:* SAT Subject Tests (for admission), CEEB required (for admission).
Financial Aid *Of all full-time matriculated undergraduates who enrolled in 2006,* 143 Federal Work-Study jobs. *Financial aid deadline:* 6/15.
Applying *Options:* electronic application, early admission, deferred entrance. *Application fee:* $20.
Freshman Application Contact Mrs. Maria Robles Serrano, Admissions Officer, University of Puerto Rico at Utuado, PO Box 2500, Utuado, PR 00641-2500. *Phone:* 787-894-2828 Ext. 2240. *Web site:* http://www.uprutuado.edu/.

University of Puerto Rico, Cayey University College

Cayey, Puerto Rico

- **Commonwealth-supported** 4-year, founded 1967, part of University of Puerto Rico System
- **Urban** 177-acre campus with easy access to San Juan
- **Coed**
- **Moderately difficult** entrance level

Faculty *Student/faculty ratio:* 21:1.

Academics *Calendar:* semesters. *Degrees:* associate and bachelor's.

Student Life *Campus security:* 24-hour emergency response devices and patrols, late-night transport/escort service.

Standardized Tests *Required:* CEEB (for admission). *Required for some:* SAT (for admission).

Costs (2010–11) *Tuition:* commonwealth resident $1350 full-time; nonresident $3740 full-time. Full-time tuition and fees vary according to class time and student level. Part-time tuition and fees vary according to class time and student level. *Required fees:* $498 full-time. *Room and board:* $8180. Room and board charges vary according to housing facility.

Financial Aid *Of all full-time matriculated undergraduates who enrolled in 2000,* 2,866 applied for aid, 2,819 were judged to have need. 281 Federal Work-Study jobs. *Average financial aid package:* $4200. *Average need-based loan:* $3000. *Average need-based gift aid:* $3300.

Applying *Options:* early admission, early decision. *Application fee:* $20. *Required:* high school transcript.

Freshman Application Contact University of Puerto Rico, Cayey University College, 205 Avenue Antonio R. Barcelo, Cayey, PR 00736. *Phone:* 787-738-2161 Ext. 2233. *Web site:* http://www.cayey.upr.edu/.

University of Puerto Rico, Mayagüez Campus

Mayagüez, Puerto Rico

Freshman Application Contact Ms. Sheila Marty-Rodriquez, Director, Admissions Office, University of Puerto Rico, Mayagüez Campus, PO Box 9000, Mayagüez, PR 00681-9000. *Phone:* 787-265-5465. *Fax:* 787-265-5465. *E-mail:* smarty@uprm.edu. *Web site:* http://www.uprm.edu/.

University of Puerto Rico, Medical Sciences Campus

San Juan, Puerto Rico

Freshman Application Contact University of Puerto Rico, Medical Sciences Campus, PO Box 365067, San Juan, PR 00936-5067. *Phone:* 787-758-2525 Ext. 5214. *Web site:* http://www.rcm.upr.edu/.

University of Puerto Rico, Río Piedras

San Juan, Puerto Rico

- **Commonwealth-supported** university, founded 1903, part of University of Puerto Rico System
- **Urban** 281-acre campus
- **Coed**
- **Very difficult** entrance level

Faculty *Student/faculty ratio:* 16:1.

Academics *Calendar:* semesters. *Degrees:* bachelor's, master's, doctoral-professional, doctoral-research/scholarship, post-master's, and postbachelor's certificates.

Student Life *Campus security:* 24-hour emergency response devices, late-night transport/escort service.

Athletics Member NCAA, NAIA. All NCAA Division II.

Standardized Tests *Required:* SAT (for admission), Aptitude Test in mathematics and verbal reasoning and the Academic Achievement Test in English, mathematics and Spanish offered by the College Entrance Examination Board (CEEB) (for admission).

Costs (2010–11) *Tuition:* commonwealth resident $1224 full-time, $51 per credit part-time; nonresident $4056 full-time, $169 per credit part-time. Full-time tuition and fees vary according to degree level and reciprocity agreements. Part-time tuition and fees vary according to degree level and reciprocity agreements. *Required fees:* $144 full-time, $72 per credit part-time. *Room and board:* $8280.

Financial Aid *Financial aid deadline:* 4/25.

Applying *Options:* electronic application. *Application fee:* $20. *Required:* high school transcript. *Required for some:* interview.

Freshman Application Contact University of Puerto Rico, Río Piedras, PO Box 23300, San Juan, PR 00931-3300. *Phone:* 787-764-0000 Ext. 85700. *Web site:* http://www.uprrp.edu/.

University of the Sacred Heart

San Juan, Puerto Rico

Director of Admissions Mr. Luis Heviquez, Director of Admissions, University of the Sacred Heart, PO Box 12383, San Juan, PR 00914-0383. *Phone:* 787-728-1515 Ext. 3237. *Web site:* http://www.sagrado.edu/.

VIRGIN ISLANDS

University of the Virgin Islands

Saint Thomas, Virgin Islands

- **Territory-supported** comprehensive, founded 1962
- **Small-town** 518-acre campus
- **Endowment** $26.4 million
- **Coed** 2,520 undergraduate students, 64% full-time, 72% women, 28% men
- **Minimally difficult** entrance level, 52% of applicants were admitted

Undergraduates 1,601 full-time, 919 part-time. Students come from 28 states and territories; 16 other countries; 2% are from out of state; 76% Black or African American, non-Hispanic/Latino; 7% Hispanic/Latino; 0.1% Asian, non-Hispanic/Latino; 6% Race/ethnicity unknown; 7% international; 4% transferred in; 14% live on campus. *Retention:* 72% of full-time freshmen returned.

Freshmen Admission: 1,718 applied, 889 admitted, 483 enrolled. *Average high school GPA:* 2.73. *Test scores:* SAT critical reading scores over 500: 15%; SAT math scores over 500: 11%; SAT writing scores over 500: 13%; ACT scores over 18: 40%; SAT critical reading scores over 600: 1%; SAT math scores over 600: 1%.

Faculty *Total:* 241, 48% full-time, 48% with terminal degrees. *Student/faculty ratio:* 17:1.

Academics *Calendar:* semesters. *Degrees:* associate, bachelor's, master's, and post-master's certificates. *Special study options:* academic remediation for entering students, adult/continuing education programs, advanced placement credit, distance learning, double majors, external degree program, honors programs, independent study, internships, off-campus study, part-time degree program, services for LD students, summer session for credit. *ROTC:* Army (b). *Unusual degree programs:* 3-2 engineering with Columbia University, University of Florida, University of South Carolina.

Computers on Campus 500 computers/terminals are available on campus for general student use. Students can access the following: campus intranet, computer help desk, free student e-mail accounts, online (class) grades, online (class) registration, online (class) schedules. Campuswide network is available. 100% of college-owned or -operated housing units are wired for high-speed Internet access. Wireless service is available via entire campus.

Student Life *Housing options:* men-only, women-only. Campus housing is university owned. *Activities and organizations:* drama/theater group, student-run newspaper, choral group, The Squad, Predators, Golden Key Honor Society, National Student Exchange Club, St. Kitts and Nevis, national sororities. *Campus security:* 24-hour patrols. *Student services:* health clinic, personal/psychological counseling.

Athletics Member NCAA. *Intercollegiate sports:* basketball M/W, cheerleading W, cross-country running M/W, swimming and diving M/W, table tennis M/W, track and field M/W, volleyball M. *Intramural sports:* basketball M/W, sailing M/W, table tennis M/W, tennis M/W, volleyball M/W.

Standardized Tests *Required:* SAT or ACT (for admission).

Costs (2011–12) *Tuition:* territory resident $3990 full-time; nonresident $11,970 full-time. Full-time tuition and fees vary according to reciprocity agreements. Part-time tuition and fees vary according to course load and reciprocity agreements. *Required fees:* $604 full-time. *Room and board:* $9386; room only: $3606. Room and board charges vary according to board plan and housing facility. *Payment plan:* deferred payment. *Waivers:* senior citizens and employees or children of employees.

Financial Aid Of all full-time matriculated undergraduates who enrolled in 2007, 1,202 applied for aid, 1,118 were judged to have need, 10 had their need fully met. 39 Federal Work-Study jobs (averaging $2130). 28 state and other part-time jobs (averaging $1900). In 2007, 5 non-need-based awards were made. *Average financial aid package:* $4450. *Average need-based loan:* $3240. *Average need-based gift aid:* $3440. *Average non-need-based aid:* $8500. *Average indebtedness upon graduation:* $9480.

Applying *Options:* electronic application, early admission, deferred entrance. *Application fee:* $25. *Recommended:* high school transcript, minimum 2 GPA. *Application deadlines:* 4/30 (freshmen), 4/30 (transfers). *Notification:* continuous (freshmen), 6/15 (transfers).

Freshman Application Contact Dr. Xuri Maurice Allen, Director of Admissions/Recruitment, University of the Virgin Islands, University of the Virgin Islands, #2 John Brewers Bay, St. Thomas, VI 00802. *Phone:* 340-693- 1224. *Fax:* 340-693-1167. *E-mail:* xallen@uvi.edu. *Web site:* http://www.uvi.edu/.

CANADA

CANADA

Acadia University
Wolfville, Nova Scotia, Canada

- **Province-supported** comprehensive, founded 1838
- **Small-town** 250-acre campus
- **Coed** 3,005 undergraduate students, 96% full-time, 56% women, 44% men
- **Moderately difficult** entrance level, 31% of applicants were admitted

Undergraduates 2,881 full-time, 124 part-time. Students come from 25 provinces and territories; 54 other countries; 41% are from out of state; 6% transferred in; 50% live on campus. *Retention:* 79% of full-time freshmen returned.
Freshmen *Admission:* 3,055 applied, 960 admitted, 760 enrolled.
Faculty *Total:* 331, 73% full-time. *Student/faculty ratio:* 10:1.
Academics *Calendar:* Canadian standard year. *Degrees:* bachelor's and master's. *Special study options:* academic remediation for entering students, advanced placement credit, cooperative education, distance learning, double majors, English as a second language, honors programs, internships, off-campus study, part-time degree program, study abroad, summer session for credit.
Computers on Campus 7,000 ports are available on campus for general student use. Students can access the following: campus intranet, computer help desk, free student e-mail accounts, online (class) grades, online (class) registration, online (class) schedules. Campuswide network is available. 100% of college-owned or -operated housing units are wired for high-speed Internet access. Wireless service is available via learning centers, libraries, student centers.
Student Life *Housing options:* coed, women-only. Campus housing is university owned. Freshman campus housing is guaranteed. *Activities and organizations:* drama/theater group, student-run newspaper, radio station, choral group, Dance Acadia, Power Cheerleading, Water Watch Canada, LINC, Biology. *Campus security:* 24-hour emergency response devices and patrols, student patrols, late-night transport/escort service, controlled dormitory access, Video surveillance, emergency response, emergency notification, emergency management planning. *Student services:* health clinic, personal/psychological counseling, women's center, legal services.
Athletics Member CIS. *Intercollegiate sports:* basketball M(s)/W(s), cross-country running W, football M(s), ice hockey M(s), rugby W(s), soccer M(s)/W(s), swimming and diving M(s)/W(s), track and field W, volleyball W.
Costs (2010–11) *Tuition:* province resident $7221 full-time; International tuition $13,410 full-time. Full-time tuition and fees vary according to course level, course load, degree level, and program. Part-time tuition and fees vary according to course level, course load, degree level, and program. *Required fees:* $247 full-time. *Room and board:* $8195; room only: $4610. Room and board charges vary according to board plan and housing facility. *Payment plan:* installment. *Waivers:* senior citizens and employees or children of employees.
Applying *Options:* electronic application, deferred entrance. *Application fee:* $25 Canadian dollars. *Required:* high school transcript, minimum 2.5 GPA. *Required for some:* essay or personal statement, 1 letter of recommendation, interview. *Application deadlines:* 7/1 (freshmen), 7/1 (out-of-state freshmen), 7/1 (transfers). *Notification:* continuous (freshmen), continuous (out-of-state freshmen), continuous (transfers).
Freshman Application Contact Ms. Anne Scott, Manager of Admissions, Acadia University, Wolfville, NS B4P 2R6, Canada. *Phone:* 902-585-1016. *Fax:* 902-585-1092. *E-mail:* admissions@acadiau.ca. *Web site:* http://www.acadiau.ca/.

Alberta Bible College
Calgary, Alberta, Canada

Director of Admissions Brad Olorenshaw, Recruitment Officer, Alberta Bible College, 635 Northmount Drive, NW, Calgary, AB T2K 3J6, Canada. *Phone:* 403-282-2994 Ext. 225. *Toll-free phone:* 877-542-9492. *E-mail:* admissions@abccampus.ca. *Web site:* http://www.abccampus.ca/.

Alberta College of Art & Design
Calgary, Alberta, Canada

- **Province-supported** 4-year, founded 1926
- **Urban** 1-acre campus
- **Endowment** $4.4 million
- **Coed** 1,195 undergraduate students, 90% full-time, 71% women, 29% men
- **Moderately difficult** entrance level, 46% of applicants were admitted

Undergraduates 1,080 full-time, 115 part-time. Students come from 10 provinces and territories; 14 other countries; 12% are from out of state; 96% Race/ethnicity unknown; 4% international; 6% transferred in; 9% live on campus. *Retention:* 78% of full-time freshmen returned.
Freshmen *Admission:* 659 applied, 300 admitted, 300 enrolled.
Faculty *Total:* 111, 36% full-time. *Student/faculty ratio:* 18:1.
Academics *Calendar:* semesters. *Degree:* bachelor's. *Special study options:* academic remediation for entering students, adult/continuing education programs, advanced placement credit, independent study, internships, part-time degree program, services for LD students, study abroad, summer session for credit.
Computers on Campus 80 computers/terminals are available on campus for general student use. Students can access the following: campus intranet, computer help desk, free student e-mail accounts, online (class) grades, online (class) registration, online (class) schedules. Campuswide network is available. 100% of college-owned or -operated housing units are wired for high-speed Internet access. Wireless service is available via entire campus.
Student Life *Housing options:* coed, disabled students. Campus housing is provided by a third party. *Activities and organizations:* student-run newspaper, The Rendez-Vous Collective, Team NCECA, Full Print Friday Society, 2DD Drink + Draw, Feminist Book Club. *Campus security:* 24-hour emergency response devices and patrols, late-night transport/escort service, controlled dormitory access. *Student services:* health clinic, personal/psychological counseling.
Athletics *Intercollegiate sports:* baseball W, basketball M/W, cross-country running M/W, ice hockey M/W, soccer M/W, volleyball M/W. *Intramural sports:* basketball M/W, bowling M/W, ice hockey M/W, soccer M/W, softball M/W, volleyball M/W.
Costs (2011–12) *Tuition:* province resident $4371 Canadian dollars full-time, $146 Canadian dollars per credit part-time; nonresident $468 Canadian dollars per credit part-time; International tuition $14,044 Canadian dollars full-time. Full-time tuition and fees vary according to course load, program, and student level. Part-time tuition and fees vary according to course load, program, and student level. *Required fees:* $819 Canadian dollars full-time, $202 Canadian dollars per term part-time. *Room only:* $5640 Canadian dollars. Room and board charges vary according to housing facility. *Waivers:* senior citizens.
Applying *Options:* electronic application, early admission, early decision. *Application fee:* $85 Canadian dollars. *Required:* essay or personal statement, high school transcript, minimum 2 GPA, portfolio of artwork. *Application deadlines:* 4/1 (freshmen), 4/1 (out-of-state freshmen), 3/1 (transfers). *Early decision deadline:* 2/1. *Notification:* 5/15 (freshmen), 5/15 (out-of-state freshmen), 4/15 (transfers), 3/15 (early decision).
Freshman Application Contact Ms. Jill Flaman, Admissions Officer, Alberta College of Art & Design, 1407-14 Avenue NW, Calgary, AB T2N 4R3, Canada. *Phone:* 403-284-7678. *Toll-free phone:* 800-251-8290. *Fax:* 403-284-7644. *E-mail:* admissions@acad.ca. *Web site:* http://www.acad.ca/.

Ambrose University College
Calgary, Alberta, Canada

Director of Admissions Admissions Officer, Ambrose University College, 630, 833 4th Avenue, SW, Calgary, AB T2P 3T5, Canada. *Toll-free phone:* 800-461-1222. *E-mail:* enrolment@ambrose.edu. *Web site:* http://www.ambrose.edu/.

Athabasca University

Athabasca, Alberta, Canada

- **Province-supported** comprehensive, founded 1970
- **Small-town** 480-acre campus
- **Endowment** $1.2 million
- **Coed** 34,367 undergraduate students, 68% women, 32% men
- **Noncompetitive** entrance level

Undergraduates 34,367 part-time. Students come from 33 provinces and territories; 87 other countries; 47% are from out of state.

Faculty *Total:* 166.

Academics *Calendar:* continuous. *Degrees:* certificates, diplomas, bachelor's, master's, doctoral-other, post-master's, and postbachelor's certificates (offers only external degree programs). *Special study options:* academic remediation for entering students, accelerated degree program, adult/continuing education programs, advanced placement credit, distance learning, English as a second language, external degree program, off-campus study, part-time degree program, services for LD students, student-designed majors, study abroad, summer session for credit.

Computers on Campus 28 computers/terminals are available on campus for general student use. Students can access the following: online (class) registration. Campuswide network is available.

Student Life *Housing:* college housing not available. *Activities and organizations:* student-run newspaper. *Campus security:* 24-hour emergency response devices.

Costs (2010–11) *Tuition:* province resident $646 per course part-time; nonresident $751 per course part-time. Full-time tuition and fees vary according to degree level. Part-time tuition and fees vary according to degree level. *Waivers:* employees or children of employees.

Applying *Options:* electronic application. *Application fee:* $60 Canadian dollars. *Application deadlines:* rolling (freshmen), rolling (transfers). *Notification:* continuous (freshmen), continuous (transfers).

Freshman Application Contact Information Centre, Athabasca University, 1 University Drive, Athabasca, AB T9S 3A3, Canada. *Phone:* 800-788-9041. *Toll-free phone:* 800-788-9041. *Fax:* 780-675-6437. *E-mail:* reginfo@ cs.athabascau.ca. *Web site:* http://www.athabascau.ca/.

Bethany Bible College

Sussex, New Brunswick, Canada

- **Independent** 4-year, founded 1945, affiliated with Wesleyan Church
- **Small-town** 57-acre campus
- **Endowment** $249,921
- **Coed** 215 undergraduate students, 95% full-time, 45% women, 55% men
- **Moderately difficult** entrance level, 56% of applicants were admitted

Undergraduates 204 full-time, 11 part-time. Students come from 7 provinces and territories; 4 other countries; 69% are from out of state; 2% transferred in; 70% live on campus. *Retention:* 73% of full-time freshmen returned.

Freshmen *Admission:* 201 applied, 113 admitted, 48 enrolled. *Average high school GPA:* 2.96. *Test scores:* SAT critical reading scores over 500: 58%; SAT math scores over 500: 86%; SAT writing scores over 500: 58%; ACT scores over 18: 86%; SAT critical reading scores over 600: 29%; SAT math scores over 600: 29%; SAT writing scores over 600: 29%; ACT scores over 24: 43%; ACT scores over 30: 29%.

Faculty *Total:* 26, 42% full-time, 31% with terminal degrees. *Student/faculty ratio:* 14:1.

Academics *Calendar:* semesters. *Degrees:* associate and bachelor's. *Special study options:* advanced placement credit, double majors, internships, part-time degree program, summer session for credit.

Computers on Campus 20 computers/terminals are available on campus for general student use. Students can access the following: campus intranet, free student e-mail accounts, online (class) grades, online (class) schedules. 100% of college-owned or -operated housing units are wired for high-speed Internet access. Wireless service is available via entire campus.

Student Life *Housing:* on-campus residence required through junior year. *Options:* men-only, women-only. Campus housing is university owned. Freshman campus housing is guaranteed. *Activities and organizations:* drama/theater group, choral group, Ministerial Association, Athletic Association, Student Mission Fellowship, Social Committee, Drama Club. *Campus security:* controlled dormitory access. *Student services:* personal/psychological counseling.

Athletics *Intercollegiate sports:* basketball M/W, ice hockey M, soccer M/W, softball M/W, volleyball W. *Intramural sports:* basketball M/W, table tennis M/W, volleyball M/W.

Standardized Tests *Required for some:* SAT or ACT (for admission).

Costs (2010–11) *Comprehensive fee:* $13,650 includes full-time tuition ($8550) and room and board ($5100). Part-time tuition: $285 per credit hour. *College room only:* $2150. Room and board charges vary according to board plan and housing facility. *Payment plan:* installment. *Waivers:* senior citizens and employees or children of employees.

Financial Aid *Financial aid deadline:* 7/15.

Applying *Options:* electronic application, early admission. *Application fee:* $20 Canadian dollars. *Required:* high school transcript, 2 letters of recommendation. *Recommended:* interview. *Application deadlines:* rolling (freshmen), rolling (transfers).

Freshman Application Contact Mrs. Shelley Vail, Associate Director of Admissions and Financial Aid, Bethany Bible College, Bethany Bible College, PO Box 5125, Sussex, NB E4E 5L2. *Phone:* 506-432-4422. *Toll-free phone:* 888-432-4422. *Fax:* 506-432-4442. *E-mail:* vails@bbc.ca. *Web site:* http://www.bbc.ca.

Bishop's University

Sherbrooke, Quebec, Canada

- **Province-supported** comprehensive, founded 1843, part of Association of Universities and Colleges of Canada (AUCC)
- **Small-town** 500-acre campus
- **Endowment** $32.5 million
- **Coed**
- **Moderately difficult** entrance level

Faculty *Student/faculty ratio:* 16:1.

Academics *Calendar:* semesters most students study from September to late April. Spring semester is May-June. *Degrees:* certificates, bachelor's, and master's.

Student Life *Campus security:* 24-hour emergency response devices and patrols, student patrols, late-night transport/escort service, controlled dormitory access.

Athletics Member CIS.

Standardized Tests *Required:* SAT or ACT (for admission).

Costs (2010–11) *Tuition:* province resident $2000 Canadian dollars full-time; nonresident $5500 Canadian dollars full-time; International tuition $13,500 Canadian dollars full-time. Full-time tuition and fees vary according to course load, program, reciprocity agreements, and student level. Part-time tuition and fees vary according to course load, program, and student level. *Required fees:* $1090 Canadian dollars full-time. *Room and board:* $6900 Canadian dollars. Room and board charges vary according to board plan and housing facility.

Applying *Options:* electronic application, early admission, early decision, early action, deferred entrance. *Application fee:* $60 Canadian dollars. *Required:* high school transcript, minimum 3 GPA, birth certificate, copy of student visa. *Required for some:* essay or personal statement. *Recommended:* essay or personal statement.

Freshman Application Contact Mrs. Jacqueline Belleau, Coordinator of Student Recruitment, Bishop's University, 2600 College Street, Sherbrooke, QC J1M 0C8, Canada. *Phone:* 819-822-9600 Ext. 2691. *Toll-free phone:* 877-822-8200. *Fax:* 819-822-9661. *E-mail:* recruitment@ubishops.ca. *Web site:* http://www.ubishops.ca/.

Booth University College

Winnipeg, Manitoba, Canada

Director of Admissions Chantel Burt, Director of Admission, Booth University College, 447 Webb Place, Winnipeg, MB R3B 2P2, Canada. *Phone:* 204-924-4867. *Toll-free phone:* 800-781-6044. *E-mail:* cburt@ boothcollege.ca. *Web site:* http://www.boothcollege.ca/.

Brandon University

Brandon, Manitoba, Canada

Freshman Application Contact Murray Kerr, Director of Admissions, Brandon University, 270 18th Street, Brandon, MB R7A 6A9, Canada. *Phone:* 204-727-7352. *Toll-free phone:* 800-644-7644. *Fax:* 204-728-3221. *E-mail:* kerr@brandonu.ca. *Web site:* http://www.brandonu.ca/.

Briercrest College

Caronport, Saskatchewan, Canada

Freshman Application Contact Mr. Mike Benallick, Director of Admissions, Briercrest College, 510 College Drive, Caronport, SK S0H 0S0, Canada. *Phone:* 306-756-3200. *Toll-free phone:* 800-667-5199. *E-mail:* info@ briercrest.ca. *Web site:* http://www.briercrest.ca/.

British Columbia Institute of Technology

Burnaby, British Columbia, Canada

Freshman Application Contact Ms. Anna Dosen, Supervisor of Admissions, British Columbia Institute of Technology, 3700 Willingdon Avenue, Burnaby, BC V5G 3H2, Canada. *Phone:* 604-432-8496. *Fax:* 604-431-6917. *Web site:* http://www.bcit.ca/.

Brock University

St. Catharines, Ontario, Canada

- **Province-supported** university, founded 1964
- **Urban** 540-acre campus with easy access to Toronto, ON and Buffalo, NY
- **Coed** 16,341 undergraduate students, 100% full-time, 58% women, 42% men

Undergraduates 16,341 full-time. Students come from 70 other countries; 14% live on campus. *Retention:* 86% of full-time freshmen returned.

Freshmen *Admission:* 19,885 applied. *Average high school GPA:* 3.

Faculty *Total:* 578, 100% full-time. *Student/faculty ratio:* 30:1.

Academics *Calendar:* Canadian standard year. *Degrees:* certificates, bachelor's, master's, and doctoral-research/scholarship. *Special study options:* academic remediation for entering students, accelerated degree program, adult/continuing education programs, advanced placement credit, cooperative education, double majors, English as a second language, honors programs, internships, part-time degree program, services for LD students, student-designed majors, study abroad, summer session for credit.

Computers on Campus 429 computers/terminals are available on campus for general student use. Students can access the following: computer help desk, free student e-mail accounts, online (class) grades, online (class) registration, online (class) schedules. Campuswide network is available. 100% of college-owned or -operated housing units are wired for high-speed Internet access. Wireless service is available via classrooms, computer centers, computer labs, learning centers, libraries, student centers.

Student Life *Housing options:* coed, disabled students. Campus housing is university owned and leased by the school. Freshman campus housing is guaranteed. *Activities and organizations:* drama/theater group, student-run newspaper, radio and television station, choral group, International Students Association, Brock University Student Association, Business Administration Association, Brock Christian Fellowship, Ace Brock. *Campus security:* 24-hour emergency response devices and patrols, student patrols, late-night transport/escort service, controlled dormitory access. *Student services:* health clinic, personal/psychological counseling, women's center.

Athletics Member CIS. *Intercollegiate sports:* baseball M, basketball M(s)/W(s), cheerleading M/W, crew M(s)/W(s), cross-country running M/W, fencing M/W, field hockey W(c), ice hockey M(s)/W(s), lacrosse M, rugby M/W, soccer M(s)/W(s), swimming and diving M/W, volleyball W, wrestling M(s)/W(s). *Intramural sports:* badminton M/W, basketball M/W, football M/W, ice hockey M/W, skiing (downhill) M/W, soccer M/W, softball M/W, swimming and diving M/W, ultimate Frisbee M/W, volleyball M/W, water polo M/W.

Standardized Tests *Required:* SAT or ACT (for admission).

Costs (2010–11) *Tuition:* province resident $5478 full-time, $1096 per credit part-time; International tuition $14,160 full-time. Full-time tuition and fees vary according to course load, program, and student level. Part-time tuition and fees vary according to course load, program, and student level. *Room and board:* $8455; room only: $4705. Room and board charges vary according to board plan and housing facility. *Payment plan:* installment. *Waivers:* senior citizens and employees or children of employees.

Applying *Options:* electronic application. *Required:* high school transcript. *Required for some:* essay or personal statement, interview, audition for Dramatic Arts and Music programs, profile questionnaire for Concurrent Education programs. *Recommended:* minimum 3 GPA.

Freshman Application Contact Mrs. Lynn Thompson-Dovi, International Admissions Officer, Brock University, 500 Glenridge Avenue, L2S 3A1, Canada. *Phone:* 905-688-5550 Ext. 3431. *Fax:* 905-688-5488. *E-mail:* admissns@brocku.ca. *Web site:* http://www.brocku.ca/.

Canadian Mennonite University

Winnipeg, Manitoba, Canada

Freshman Application Contact Mr. Abe Bergen, Director of Enrollment Services, Canadian Mennonite University, 500 Shaftesbury Boulevard, Winnipeg, MB R3P 2N2, Canada. *Phone:* 204-487-3300 Ext. 652. *Toll-free phone:* 877-231-4570. *Fax:* 204-487-3858. *E-mail:* cu@cmu.ca. *Web site:* http://www.cmu.ca/.

Cape Breton University

Sydney, Nova Scotia, Canada

- **Province-supported** comprehensive, founded 1974
- **Urban** campus
- **Endowment** $12.3 million
- **Coed**
- **Moderately difficult** entrance level

Faculty *Student/faculty ratio:* 15:1.

Academics *Calendar:* semesters. *Degrees:* certificates, diplomas, bachelor's, master's, and postbachelor's certificates.

Student Life *Campus security:* 24-hour emergency response devices and patrols, student patrols, late-night transport/escort service, controlled dormitory access.

Athletics Member CIS.

Costs (2010–11) *One-time required fee:* $126. *Tuition:* province resident $4638 full-time; nonresident $5660 full-time; International tuition $11,320 full-time. *Room and board:* $6560; room only: $3360. Room and board charges vary according to board plan and housing facility.

Applying *Options:* electronic application, early admission, deferred entrance. *Application fee:* $35 Canadian dollars. *Required:* high school transcript. *Required for some:* essay or personal statement, 3 letters of recommendation, interview.

Freshman Application Contact Cape Breton University, Box 5300, 1250 Grand Lake Road, Sydney, NS B1P 6L2, Canada. *Phone:* 902-563-1117. *Toll-free phone:* 888-959-9995. *Web site:* http://www.cbu.ca/.

Carleton University

Ottawa, Ontario, Canada

Freshman Application Contact Ms. Jean Mullan, Director, Undergraduate Recruitment Office, Carleton University, 1125 Colonel By Drive, Ottawa, ON K1S 5B6, Canada. *Phone:* 613-520-3663. *Toll-free phone:* 888-354-4414. *E-mail:* liaison@admissions.carleton.ca. *Web site:* http://www.carleton.ca/.

Centennial College

Scarborough, Ontario, Canada

Freshman Application Contact Enrolment Services, Centennial College, PO Box 631, Station 'A', Scarborough, ON M1K 5E9, Canada. *Phone:* 416-289-5325. *Toll-free phone:* 800-268-4419. *E-mail:* success@centennialcollege.ca. *Web site:* http://www.centennialcollege.ca/.

Collège Dominicain de Philosophie et de Théologie

Ottawa, Ontario, Canada

- **Independent Roman Catholic** university, founded 1909, administratively affiliated with Institut de Pastorale
- **Urban** campus
- **Endowment** $7.9 million
- **Coed**
- **Noncompetitive** entrance level

Faculty *Student/faculty ratio:* 3:1.

Academics *Calendar:* semesters. *Degrees:* certificates, bachelor's, master's, and doctoral-research/scholarship.

Student Life *Campus security:* late-night transport/escort service, controlled dormitory access.

Costs (2010–11) *Comprehensive fee:* $10,350 Canadian dollars includes full-time tuition ($3430 Canadian dollars), mandatory fees ($120 Canadian dollars), and room and board ($6800 Canadian dollars). Full-time tuition and fees vary according to degree level. Part-time tuition: $150 Canadian dollars per credit. Part-time tuition and fees vary according to course load and degree level. International tuition: $7000 Canadian dollars full-time. *Required fees:* $85 Canadian dollars per year part-time.

Financial Aid *Of all full-time matriculated undergraduates who enrolled in 2009,* 24 applied for aid, 24 were judged to have need. *Average financial aid package:* $1000. *Average need-based gift aid:* $915. *Financial aid deadline:* 10/15.

Applying *Options:* deferred entrance. *Application fee:* $35 Canadian dollars. *Required:* high school transcript. *Required for some:* essay or personal statement, interview.

Freshman Application Contact Fr. Herve Tremblay OP, Registrar, Collège Dominicain de Philosophie et de Théologie, 96 Empress Avenue, Ottawa, ON K1R 7G3, Canada. *Phone:* 613-233-5696 Ext. 308. *Fax:* 613-233-6064. *E-mail:* registraire@collegedominicain.ca. *Web site:* http://www.collegedominicain.ca/.

Collège universitaire de Saint-Boniface
Saint-Boniface, Manitoba, Canada

Admissions Office Contact Collège universitaire de Saint-Boniface, 200 avenue de la Cathèdrale, Saint-Boniface, MB R2H 0H7, Canada. *Web site:* http://www.ustboniface.mb.ca/.

Columbia Bible College
Abbotsford, British Columbia, Canada

- **Independent Mennonite Brethren** 4-year, founded 1936
- **Urban** 9-acre campus with easy access to Vancouver
- **Endowment** $556,224
- **Coed** 468 undergraduate students
- **Noncompetitive** entrance level, 78% of applicants were admitted

Undergraduates Students come from 12 provinces and territories; 6 other countries; 26% are from out of state. *Retention:* 25% of full-time freshmen returned.

Freshmen *Admission:* 258 applied, 201 admitted.

Faculty *Total:* 45, 31% full-time, 13% with terminal degrees. *Student/faculty ratio:* 20:1.

Academics *Calendar:* semesters. *Degree:* certificates, diplomas, and bachelor's. *Special study options:* academic remediation for entering students, advanced placement credit, distance learning, independent study, internships, off-campus study, part-time degree program, services for LD students, study abroad.

Computers on Campus 30 computers/terminals are available on campus for general student use. Students can access the following: campus intranet, online (class) grades, online (class) schedules. Campuswide network is available. 85% of college-owned or -operated housing units are wired for high-speed Internet access. Wireless service is available via classrooms, computer labs, dorm rooms, libraries, student centers.

Student Life *Housing:* on-campus residence required through sophomore year. *Options:* men-only, women-only. Campus housing is university owned and leased by the school. Freshman applicants given priority for college housing. *Activities and organizations:* choral group. *Campus security:* late-night transport/escort service, controlled dormitory access, night watchman 11 pm to 6 am. *Student services:* personal/psychological counseling.

Athletics *Intercollegiate sports:* basketball M/W, golf M/W, ice hockey M, soccer M/W, volleyball M/W.

Costs (2011–12) *Comprehensive fee:* $14,180 Canadian dollars includes full-time tuition ($8970 Canadian dollars) and room and board ($5210 Canadian dollars). Full-time tuition and fees vary according to course load. Part-time tuition: $299 Canadian dollars per credit. Part-time tuition and fees vary according to course load. *Room and board:* Room and board charges vary according to board plan. *Payment plans:* installment, deferred payment. *Waivers:* senior citizens and employees or children of employees.

Financial Aid *Financial aid deadline:* 5/15.

Applying *Options:* electronic application, early admission, early decision, deferred entrance. *Application fee:* $50. *Required:* essay or personal statement, high school transcript, minimum 2 GPA, 3 letters of recommendation, must be Christian. *Required for some:* interview. *Application deadlines:* 8/15 (freshmen), 8/15 (out-of-state freshmen), 8/15 (transfers). *Early decision deadline:* 5/15. *Notification:* continuous (freshmen), continuous (out-of-state freshmen), continuous (transfers).

Freshman Application Contact Candice Green, Director of Admissions, Columbia Bible College, 2940 Clearbrook Road, Abbotsford, BC V2T 2Z8, Canada. *Phone:* 604-853-3358 Ext. 309. *Toll-free phone:* 800-283-0881. *Fax:* 604-853-3063. *E-mail:* candice.green@columbiabc.edu. *Web site:* http://www.columbiabc.edu/.

Concordia University
Montréal, Quebec, Canada

- **Province-supported** university, founded 1974, part of Quebec University Network
- **Urban** 52-acre campus with easy access to Montreal
- **Endowment** $77.5 million
- **Coed** 29,435 undergraduate students, 66% full-time, 52% women, 48% men
- **Moderately difficult** entrance level, 67% of applicants were admitted

Undergraduates 19,351 full-time, 10,084 part-time. Students come from 13 provinces and territories; 148 other countries; 10% are from out of state; 2% live on campus. *Retention:* 87% of full-time freshmen returned.

Freshmen *Admission:* 14,920 applied, 9,969 admitted, 5,437 enrolled.

Faculty *Total:* 1,616, 59% full-time. *Student/faculty ratio:* 19:1.

Academics *Calendar:* semesters. *Degrees:* certificates, diplomas, bachelor's, master's, doctoral-research/scholarship, and postbachelor's certificates. *Special study options:* academic remediation for entering students, accelerated degree program, adult/continuing education programs, advanced placement credit, cooperative education, distance learning, double majors, English as a second language, honors programs, independent study, internships, off-campus study, part-time degree program, services for LD students, student-designed majors, study abroad, summer session for credit.

Computers on Campus 350 computers/terminals and 3,000 ports are available on campus for general student use. Students can access the following: campus intranet, computer help desk, free student e-mail accounts, online (class) grades, online (class) registration, online (class) schedules, specialized software applications. Campuswide network is available. 67% of college-owned or -operated housing units are wired for high-speed Internet access. Wireless service is available via classrooms, computer centers, computer labs, learning centers, libraries, student centers.

Student Life *Housing options:* coed, men-only, women-only, disabled students. Campus housing is university owned. Freshman applicants given priority for college housing. *Activities and organizations:* drama/theater group, student-run newspaper, radio and television station, choral group, undergraduate student union, departmental clubs, religious clubs, ethnic clubs, social action groups, national fraternities, national sororities. *Campus security:* 24-hour emergency response devices and patrols, student patrols, late-night transport/escort service, controlled dormitory access. *Student services:* health clinic, personal/psychological counseling, women's center.

Athletics Member CIS. *Intercollegiate sports:* baseball M, basketball M(s)/W(s), cross-country running M(c)/W(c), football M(s), golf M(c)/W(c), ice hockey M(s)/W(s), rugby M(s)/W(s), skiing (downhill) M(c)/W(c), soccer M(s)/W(s), wrestling M(s)/W(s). *Intramural sports:* basketball M/W, cross-country running M/W, ice hockey M/W, soccer M/W, ultimate Frisbee M/W, volleyball M/W.

Costs (2010–11) *Tuition:* province resident $2068 full-time, $69 per credit part-time; nonresident $5668 full-time, $189 per credit part-time; International tuition $16,159 full-time. Full-time tuition and fees vary according to course load. Part-time tuition and fees vary according to course load. *Required fees:* $1388 full-time, $38 per credit part-time, $305 per year part-time. *Room and board:* $6769. Room and board charges vary according to board plan and housing facility. *Payment plan:* installment. *Waivers:* senior citizens and employees or children of employees.

Financial Aid Of all full-time matriculated undergraduates who enrolled in 2009, 349 state and other part-time jobs (averaging $1286). *Financial aid deadline:* 3/31.

Applying *Options:* electronic application, deferred entrance. *Application fee:* $90 Canadian dollars. *Required:* high school transcript, minimum 2.5 GPA. *Required for some:* essay or personal statement, minimum 2.9 GPA, 2 letters of recommendation, interview, Portfolio/auditions required for all Performing and Visual Arts. Communications and Journalism require interview/essay/portfolio. *Application deadlines:* 3/1 (freshmen), 3/1 (out-of-state freshmen), 3/1 (transfers). *Notification:* continuous (freshmen), continuous (transfers).

Freshman Application Contact Ms. Assunta Fargnoli, Assistant Registrar, Concordia University, 1455 de Maisonneuve Boulevard West, Building LB-719-2, Montreal, QC H3G 1M8, Canada. *Phone:* 514-848-2424 Ext. 2628. *Fax:* 514-848-2621. *E-mail:* fargnoli@alcor.concordia.ca. *Web site:* http://www.concordia.ca/.

Concordia University College of Alberta
Edmonton, Alberta, Canada

- **Independent Lutheran** comprehensive, founded 1921
- **Urban** 15-acre campus
- **Coed**
- **Moderately difficult** entrance level

Faculty *Student/faculty ratio:* 18:1.

Academics *Calendar:* semesters. *Degrees:* certificates, diplomas, bachelor's, master's, and postbachelor's certificates.

Student Life *Campus security:* 24-hour patrols, late-night transport/escort service.

Athletics Member CIS.

Costs (2010–11) *Tuition:* $7950 Canadian dollars full-time, $265 Canadian dollars per credit hour part-time. Full-time tuition and fees vary according to class time, course load, degree level, program, and student level. Part-time tuition and fees vary according to class time, course load, degree level, program, and student level. *Required fees:* $598 Canadian dollars full-time, $33 Canadian dollars per credit hour part-time. *Room only:* Room and board charges vary according to board plan and housing facility.

Applying *Options:* electronic application, early admission. *Required:* high school transcript, minimum 2 GPA. *Required for some:* essay or personal statement, 2 letters of recommendation, interview.

Freshman Application Contact Student and Enrollment Services, Concordia University College of Alberta, 7128 Ada Boulevard, Edmonton, AB T5B 4E4, Canada. *Phone:* 780-479-9220. *Toll-free phone:* 866-479-5200. *Fax:* 780-378-8460. *E-mail:* admits@concordia.ab.ca. *Web site:* http://www.concordia.ab.ca/.

Crandall University

Moncton, New Brunswick, Canada

- **Independent Baptist** 4-year, founded 1949, administratively affiliated with The Council of Christian Colleges and Universities
- **Urban** 220-acre campus
- **Coed** 719 undergraduate students, 90% full-time, 66% women, 34% men
- **Minimally difficult** entrance level, 89% of applicants were admitted

Undergraduates 648 full-time, 71 part-time. Students come from 11 provinces and territories; 3 other countries; 15% are from out of state; 4% transferred in; 22% live on campus. *Retention:* 71% of full-time freshmen returned.

Freshmen *Admission:* 207 applied, 185 admitted, 99 enrolled. *Average high school GPA:* 2.67.

Faculty *Total:* 60. *Student/faculty ratio:* 17:1.

Academics *Calendar:* semesters. *Degrees:* certificates, bachelor's, post-master's, and postbachelor's certificates. *Special study options:* accelerated degree program, adult/continuing education programs, advanced placement credit, cooperative education, double majors, English as a second language, honors programs, internships, off-campus study, part-time degree program, summer session for credit.

Computers on Campus Students can access the following: campus intranet, computer help desk, free student e-mail accounts, online (class) schedules. Campuswide network is available. 100% of college-owned or -operated housing units are wired for high-speed Internet access. Wireless service is available via entire campus.

Student Life *Housing options:* men-only, women-only, disabled students. Campus housing is university owned. *Activities and organizations:* drama/theater group, student-run newspaper, choral group, Student Association, Business Society, intramurals, debate team, International Student Association. *Campus security:* 24-hour emergency response devices, student patrols, controlled dormitory access.

Athletics *Intercollegiate sports:* baseball M, basketball M/W, cross-country running M/W, soccer M/W. *Intramural sports:* badminton M/W, basketball M/W, football M/W, golf M/W, ice hockey M, skiing (downhill) M/W, soccer M/W, softball M/W, table tennis M/W, volleyball M/W, weight lifting M/W.

Costs (2010–11) *Comprehensive fee:* $13,570 includes full-time tuition ($7075), mandatory fees ($765), and room and board ($5730). Part-time tuition: $740 per course. *College room only:* $2430. Room and board charges vary according to board plan and housing facility. *Waivers:* employees or children of employees.

Financial Aid *Financial aid deadline:* 5/15.

Applying *Options:* electronic application, early admission, early decision, deferred entrance. *Application fee:* $35 Canadian dollars. *Required:* high school transcript, minimum 2.67 GPA, 3 letters of recommendation. *Required for some:* essay or personal statement, interview. *Application deadlines:* rolling (freshmen), rolling (transfers). *Early decision deadline:* 11/30. *Notification:* 9/15 (freshmen), continuous until 9/15 (transfers), 12/31 (early decision).

Freshman Application Contact Mrs. Laura Lutes, Administrative Officer, Admissions and Recruitment, Crandall University, Box 6004, Moncton, NB E1C 9L7, Canada. *Phone:* 506-858-8970 Ext. 6433. *Toll-free phone:* 888-YOU-N-ABU. *Fax:* 506-858-9694. *E-mail:* Laura.lutes@crandallu.ca. *Web site:* http://www.crandallu.ca/.

Dalhousie University

Halifax, Nova Scotia, Canada

Freshman Application Contact Mairead Barry, Associate Registrar and Director of Admissions, Dalhousie University, Office of the Registrar, Halifax, NS B3H 4H6, Canada. *Phone:* 902-494-2148. *Fax:* 902-494-1630. *E-mail:* admissions@dal.ca. *Web site:* http://www.dal.ca/.

École Polytechnique de Montréal

Montréal, Quebec, Canada

Admissions Office Contact École Polytechnique de Montréal, CP 6079, Succursale Centre-Ville, Montréal, QC H3C 3A7, Canada. *Web site:* http://www.polymtl.ca/.

Emily Carr University of Art + Design

Vancouver, British Columbia, Canada

- **Province-supported** comprehensive, founded 1925
- **Urban** campus
- **Coed** 1,558 undergraduate students
- **Moderately difficult** entrance level

Undergraduates *Retention:* 87% of full-time freshmen returned.

Faculty *Total:* 220, 25% full-time. *Student/faculty ratio:* 18:1.

Academics *Degrees:* bachelor's and master's. *Special study options:* advanced placement credit, cooperative education, part-time degree program, services for LD students, study abroad.

Computers on Campus Students can access the following: campus intranet, computer help desk, free student e-mail accounts, online (class) registration, online (class) schedules. Campuswide network is available. Wireless service is available via entire campus.

Student Life *Housing:* college housing not available. *Activities and organizations:* student-run newspaper. *Campus security:* 24-hour emergency response devices and patrols. *Student services:* personal/psychological counseling.

Costs (2011–12) *Tuition:* province resident $3600 full-time, $120 per credit part-time; International tuition $11,845 full-time. *Required fees:* $295 full-time, $8 per credit part-time. *Payment plan:* installment. *Waivers:* employees or children of employees.

Applying *Options:* electronic application, deferred entrance. *Required:* essay or personal statement, high school transcript, 2 letters of recommendation, portfolio + questionnaire. *Application deadlines:* 1/15 (freshmen), 1/15 (transfers). *Notification:* 3/1 (freshmen), 3/1 (transfers).

Freshman Application Contact Admissions, Emily Carr University of Art + Design, 1399 Johnston Street, Vancouver, BC V6H 3R9, Canada. *Phone:* 604-844-3800. *Toll-free phone:* 800-832-7788. *Fax:* 604-844-3801. *E-mail:* admissions@ecuad.ca. *Web site:* http://www.ecuad.ca/.

Emmanuel Bible College

Kitchener, Ontario, Canada

- **Independent** 4-year, founded 1940, affiliated with Missionary Church
- **Urban** 12-acre campus with easy access to Toronto
- **Coed**
- **Moderately difficult** entrance level

Academics *Calendar:* semesters. *Degree:* bachelor's.

Costs (2010–11) *Comprehensive fee:* $13,925 includes full-time tuition ($8896), mandatory fees ($35), and room and board ($4994). Part-time tuition: $278 per credit hour. *Required fees:* $35 per degree program part-time. *College room only:* $3174. Room and board charges vary according to student level.

Financial Aid *Financial aid deadline:* 7/1.

Applying *Options:* deferred entrance. *Application fee:* $100. *Required:* essay or personal statement, high school transcript, 3 letters of recommendation, interview, Christian testimony.

Freshman Application Contact Emmanuel Bible College, 100 Fergus Avenue, Kitchener, ON N2A 2H2, Canada. *Phone:* 519-894-8900 Ext. 224. *Web site:* http://www.ebcollege.on.ca/.

Eston College

Eston, Saskatchewan, Canada

Freshman Application Contact Admissions, Eston College, 730 1st Street E., Box 579, Eston, SK S0L 1A0, Canada. *Phone:* 306-962-3621. *Toll-free phone:* 888-440-3424. *Fax:* 306-962-3810. *E-mail:* admissions@estoncollege.ca. *Web site:* http://www.estoncollege.ca/.

HEC Montreal

Montréal, Quebec, Canada

- **Province-supported** comprehensive, founded 1910, part of Universite de Montreal
- **Urban** 9-acre campus
- **Coed** 9,372 undergraduate students, 49% full-time, 50% women, 50% men
- **Moderately difficult** entrance level, 60% of applicants were admitted

Undergraduates 4,554 full-time, 4,818 part-time. Students come from 4 provinces and territories; 32 other countries; 0.3% are from out of state. *Retention:* 89% of full-time freshmen returned.

Freshmen *Admission:* 2,614 applied, 1,577 admitted, 910 enrolled.

Faculty *Total:* 629, 44% full-time, 37% with terminal degrees. *Student/faculty ratio:* 21:1.

Academics *Calendar:* trimesters. *Degrees:* certificates, bachelor's, master's, doctoral-research/scholarship, and postbachelor's certificates. *Special study* *options:* academic remediation for entering students, adult/continuing education programs, English as a second language, honors programs, independent study, off-campus study, student-designed majors, study abroad, summer session for credit.

Computers on Campus 250 computers/terminals and 10,000 ports are available on campus for general student use. Students can access the following: campus intranet, computer help desk, free student e-mail accounts, online (class) grades, online (class) registration, online (class) schedules, corporate calendar and web site for all the resources available for classes. Wireless service is available via entire campus.

Student Life *Housing options:* Campus housing is provided by a third party. *Activities and organizations:* student-run newspaper, radio station, choral group, AEMBA (MBA Students' Association), AEMD (MSc and PhD Students' Association), AEDES (Post-Bachelor's Certificate Students' Association), AEHEC (BBA Students' Association), AEPC (Certificate Students' Association). *Campus security:* 24-hour emergency response devices and patrols. *Student services:* health clinic, personal/psychological counseling.

Costs (2010–11) *Tuition:* province resident $2068 full-time, $69 per credit part-time; nonresident $5668 full-time, $189 per credit part-time; International tuition $16,160 full-time. Full-time tuition and fees vary according to program. Part-time tuition and fees vary according to program. *Required fees:* $1006 full-time, $29 per credit part-time, $70 per term part-time. *Room only:* $3530. Room and board charges vary according to board plan and housing facility. *Waivers:* employees or children of employees.

Financial Aid Of all full-time matriculated undergraduates who enrolled in 2008, 2,400 applied for aid, 2,150 were judged to have need. *Average financial aid package:* $6000. *Average need-based loan:* $3200. *Average need-based gift aid:* $5100.

Applying *Options:* electronic application, deferred entrance. *Application fee:* $78 Canadian dollars. *Required:* high school transcript. *Required for some:* cote de rendement collegial. *Application deadlines:* 3/1 (freshmen), 2/15 (out-of-state freshmen). *Notification:* 3/30 (freshmen), 4/30 (out-of-state freshmen).

Freshman Application Contact Mrs. Yolaine Martineau, Head Admissions Officer, HEC Montreal, 3000 Chemin de la Cote-Sainte-Catherine, Montreal, QC H3T 2A7, Canada. *Phone:* 514-340-6151. *Fax:* 514-340-5640. *E-mail:* admission.info@hec.ca. *Web site:* http://www.hec.ca/.

Heritage Baptist College and Heritage Theological Seminary

Cambridge, Ontario, Canada

- **Independent Baptist** comprehensive, founded 1993
- **Urban** 7-acre campus with easy access to Toronto
- **Endowment** $1.1 million
- **Coed**
- **Noncompetitive** entrance level

Faculty *Student/faculty ratio:* 11:1.

Academics *Calendar:* Canadian standard year. *Degrees:* certificates, diplomas, associate, bachelor's, and master's.

Student Life *Campus security:* controlled dormitory access.

Costs (2010–11) *One-time required fee:* $50. *Comprehensive fee:* $13,220 includes full-time tuition ($8800), mandatory fees ($100), and room and board ($4320). Part-time tuition: $275 per credit hour. *College room only:* $3420. *Payment plans:* installment, deferred payment.

Financial Aid *Of all full-time matriculated undergraduates who enrolled in 2009,* 12 state and other part-time jobs.

Applying *Options:* deferred entrance. *Application fee:* $50 Canadian dollars. *Required:* essay or personal statement, high school transcript. *Required for some:* audition.

Freshman Application Contact Mr. Mark Walther, Assistant Dean of Students, Heritage Baptist College and Heritage Theological Seminary, New York, NY 10023-6588. *Phone:* 519-651-2869 Ext. 251. *Fax:* 519-651-2870. *E-mail:* mwalther@heritagecollege.net. *Web site:* http://www.heritage-theo.edu/.

Horizon College & Seminary

Saskatoon, Saskatchewan, Canada

- **Independent** 4-year, founded 1930, affiliated with Pentecostal Assemblies of Canada, administratively affiliated with University of Saskatchewan
- **Urban** 5-acre campus
- **Coed**
- **Noncompetitive** entrance level

Faculty *Student/faculty ratio:* 11:1.

Academics *Calendar:* semesters. *Degree:* certificates, diplomas, and bachelor's.

Student Life *Campus security:* 24-hour emergency response devices, late-night transport/escort service, controlled dormitory access.

Costs (2010–11) *Comprehensive fee:* $11,735 Canadian dollars includes full-time tuition ($5920 Canadian dollars), mandatory fees ($815 Canadian dollars), and room and board ($5000 Canadian dollars). Full-time tuition and fees vary according to course load and program. Part-time tuition: $185 Canadian dollars per credit hour. Part-time tuition and fees vary according to course load and program. *Required fees:* $370 Canadian dollars per year part-time.

Applying *Options:* electronic application, deferred entrance. *Application fee:* $50 Canadian dollars. *Required:* essay or personal statement, high school transcript, 3 letters of recommendation. *Required for some:* interview.

Freshman Application Contact Mrs. Shannon Olson, Assistant Registrar, Horizon College & Seminary, 1303 Jackson Avenue, Saskatoon, SK S7H 2M9, Canada. *Phone:* 306-374-6655. *Toll-free phone:* 877-374.6655. *Fax:* 306-373-6968. *E-mail:* admissions@horizon.edu. *Web site:* http://www.horizon.edu/.

The King's University College

Edmonton, Alberta, Canada

- **Independent interdenominational** 4-year, founded 1979
- **Suburban** 20-acre campus
- **Endowment** $2.0 million
- **Coed** 591 undergraduate students, 93% full-time, 58% women, 42% men
- **Moderately difficult** entrance level, 90% of applicants were admitted

Undergraduates 551 full-time, 40 part-time. Students come from 7 provinces and territories; 12 other countries; 15% are from out of state; 15% transferred in; 33% live on campus. *Retention:* 72% of full-time freshmen returned.

Freshmen *Admission:* 299 applied, 268 admitted, 134 enrolled. *Average high school GPA:* 3.3.

Faculty *Total:* 115, 39% full-time, 57% with terminal degrees. *Student/faculty ratio:* 9:1.

Academics *Calendar:* Canadian standard year. *Degrees:* certificates, diplomas, bachelor's, and postbachelor's certificates. *Special study options:* adult/continuing education programs, advanced placement credit, double majors, English as a second language, independent study, internships, off-campus study, part-time degree program, services for LD students, study abroad, summer session for credit. *Unusual degree programs:* 3-2 elementary education, secondary education.

Computers on Campus 48 computers/terminals are available on campus for general student use. Students can access the following: campus intranet, computer help desk, free student e-mail accounts, online (class) grades, online (class) registration, online (class) schedules. Campuswide network is available. 100% of college-owned or -operated housing units are wired for high-speed Internet access. Wireless service is available via entire campus.

Student Life *Housing options:* coed, women-only. Campus housing is university owned. Freshman applicants given priority for college housing. *Activities and organizations:* drama/theater group, student-run newspaper, choral group, Micah Action and Awareness, The King's Players (drama club), Chamber and Concert Choirs, King's Science Society, The King's Commerce Association. *Campus security:* 24-hour emergency response devices, student patrols, controlled dormitory access. *Student services:* personal/psychological counseling.

Athletics *Intercollegiate sports:* basketball M(s)/W(s), soccer M(s)/W(s), volleyball M(s)/W(s). *Intramural sports:* basketball M/W, ice hockey M, soccer M/W, ultimate Frisbee M/W, volleyball M/W.

Costs (2011–12) *Comprehensive fee:* $15,586 includes full-time tuition ($9331), mandatory fees ($525), and room and board ($5730). Full-time tuition and fees vary according to course load. Part-time tuition: $301 per credit. Part-time tuition and fees vary according to course load. *Required fees:* $113 per term part-time. *College room only:* $3100. Room and board charges vary according to board plan and housing facility. *Waivers:* employees or children of employees.

Financial Aid Of all full-time matriculated undergraduates who enrolled in 2007, 215 applied for aid, 146 were judged to have need. 70 state and other part-time jobs. In 2007, 283 non-need-based awards were made. *Financial aid deadline:* 3/31.

Applying *Options:* electronic application. *Application fee:* $65 Canadian dollars. *Required:* high school transcript, minimum 2 GPA, 1 letter of recommendation. *Required for some:* essay or personal statement, interview. *Application deadlines:* rolling (freshmen), rolling (transfers). *Notification:* 8/15 (freshmen), 8/15 (transfers).

Freshman Application Contact Mr. Glenn Keeler, Registrar/Director of Admissions, The King's University College, 9125-50 Street, Edmonton, AB T6B 2H3, Canada. *Phone:* 780-465-3500 Ext. 8035. *Toll-free phone:* 800-661-8582. *Fax:* 780-465-3534. *E-mail:* admissions@kingsu.ca. *Web site:* http://www.kingsu.ca/.

Kwantlen Polytechnic University

Surrey, British Columbia, Canada

- **Province-supported** 4-year, founded 1981
- **Suburban** campus with easy access to Vancouver
- **Endowment** $6.7 million
- **Coed**
- 41% of applicants were admitted

Faculty *Student/faculty ratio:* 35:1.

Academics *Calendar:* semesters. *Degrees:* certificates, diplomas, associate, bachelor's, and postbachelor's certificates (profile includes information from Langley, Richmond, Newton and Surrey campuses).

Student Life *Campus security:* 24-hour emergency response devices and patrols, late-night transport/escort service.

Costs (2010–11) *Tuition:* province resident $3634 Canadian dollars full-time, $121 Canadian dollars per credit part-time; International tuition $13,500 Canadian dollars full-time. Full-time tuition and fees vary according to course load and program. Part-time tuition and fees vary according to course load and program. *Required fees:* $636 Canadian dollars full-time, $15 Canadian dollars per credit part-time, $8 Canadian dollars per term part-time.

Financial Aid *Of all full-time matriculated undergraduates who enrolled in 2009,* 4 applied for aid, 4 were judged to have need. *Average percent of need met:* 17. *Average financial aid package:* $3625. *Average need-based loan:* $3625.

Applying *Options:* electronic application, early admission, early decision, early action. *Application fee:* $40 Canadian dollars. *Required for some:* essay or personal statement, minimum 2 GPA, interview, portfolio, external testing, some certifications. *Recommended:* high school transcript.

Freshman Application Contact Admissions, Kwantlen Polytechnic University, 12666 - 72nd Avenue, Surrey, BC V3W 2M8, Canada. *Phone:* 604-599-2000. *Fax:* 604-599-2086. *E-mail:* admission@kwantlen.ca. *Web site:* http://www.kwantlen.ca/.

Lakehead University

Thunder Bay, Ontario, Canada

- **Province-supported** comprehensive, founded 1965
- **Suburban** 345-acre campus
- **Endowment** $33.9 million
- **Coed** 7,998 undergraduate students, 80% full-time, 59% women, 41% men
- **Moderately difficult** entrance level, 78% of applicants were admitted

Undergraduates 6,426 full-time, 1,572 part-time. Students come from 12 provinces and territories; 28 other countries; 20% live on campus. *Retention:* 88% of full-time freshmen returned.

Freshmen *Admission:* 8,294 applied, 6,482 admitted, 1,870 enrolled. *Average high school GPA:* 3.

Faculty *Total:* 315.

Academics *Calendar:* Canadian standard year. *Degrees:* certificates, diplomas, bachelor's, master's, doctoral-other, doctoral-professional, doctoral-research/scholarship, and postbachelor's certificates. *Special study options:* accelerated degree program, advanced placement credit, cooperative education, distance learning, double majors, external degree program, honors programs, independent study, internships, off-campus study, part-time degree program, services for LD students, study abroad, summer session for credit. *Unusual degree programs:* 3-2 social work; Concurrent Education.

Computers on Campus 594 computers/terminals and 3,000 ports are available on campus for general student use. Students can access the following: campus intranet, computer help desk, free student e-mail accounts, online (class) grades, online (class) registration, online (class) schedules. Campus-wide network is available. 100% of college-owned or -operated housing units are wired for high-speed Internet access. Wireless service is available via learning centers, libraries, student centers.

Student Life *Housing options:* coed, disabled students. Campus housing is university owned. Freshman campus housing is guaranteed. *Activities and organizations:* student-run newspaper, radio station, choral group, Outdoor Recreation Students Association, Engineering Students Society, Business Association, Educational Students Association, Native Students Association. *Campus security:* 24-hour emergency response devices and patrols, student patrols, late-night transport/escort service, controlled dormitory access. *Student services:* health clinic, personal/psychological counseling, women's center.

Athletics Member CIS. *Intercollegiate sports:* basketball M/W, cross-country running M/W, golf M(c), ice hockey M, skiing (cross-country) M/W, soccer M(c)/W(c), track and field M/W, volleyball M/W, wrestling M/W. *Intramural sports:* badminton M/W, basketball M/W, cross-country running M(c)/W(c), ice hockey M/W, lacrosse M(c), rugby M(c)/W(c), skiing (cross-country) M/

W, soccer M/W, ultimate Frisbee M/W, volleyball M(c)/W(c), wrestling M(c)/W(c).

Standardized Tests *Required:* SAT or ACT (for admission).

Costs (2010–11) *Tuition:* nonresident $5100 full-time; International tuition $13,600 full-time. Full-time tuition and fees vary according to course level, degree level, location, program, and student level. Part-time tuition and fees vary according to course level, course load, degree level, location, program, and student level. tuition rates vary depending upon program and year level. *Required fees:* $881 full-time. *Room and board:* $7565; room only: $5785. Room and board charges vary according to board plan, housing facility, and location. *Payment plan:* installment. *Waivers:* senior citizens and employees or children of employees.

Financial Aid *Financial aid deadline:* 6/30.

Applying *Options:* electronic application, early admission, deferred entrance. *Application fee:* $120 Canadian dollars. *Required:* portfolio for visual arts program, audition for music program. *Required for some:* essay or personal statement, high school transcript. *Recommended:* minimum 3 GPA. *Application deadlines:* 9/21 (freshmen), 9/21 (transfers). *Notification:* continuous (transfers).

Freshman Application Contact Mrs. Andrea Huillery, Manager of Undergraduate Admissions, Lakehead University, 955 Oliver Road, Thunder Bay, ON P7B 5E1, Canada. *Phone:* 807-343-8153. *Toll-free phone:* 800-465-3959. *Fax:* 807-766-7209. *E-mail:* admissions@lakeheadu.ca. *Web site:* http://www.lakeheadu.ca/.

Laurentian University

Sudbury, Ontario, Canada

- **Province-supported** comprehensive, founded 1960
- **Suburban** 700-acre campus
- **Coed** 8,478 undergraduate students

Undergraduates Students come from 46 other countries.

Academics *Calendar:* Canadian standard year. *Degrees:* certificates, diplomas, bachelor's, master's, doctoral-research/scholarship, and postbachelor's certificates. *Special study options:* academic remediation for entering students, accelerated degree program, adult/continuing education programs, cooperative education, distance learning, English as a second language, external degree program, honors programs, internships, off-campus study, part-time degree program, services for LD students, study abroad, summer session for credit.

Computers on Campus 450 computers/terminals are available on campus for general student use. Students can access the following: computer help desk, free student e-mail accounts, online (class) grades, online (class) registration, online (class) schedules. Campuswide network is available. 100% of college-owned or -operated housing units are wired for high-speed Internet access. Wireless service is available via entire campus.

Student Life *Housing options:* coed. Campus housing is university owned. *Activities and organizations:* drama/theater group, student-run newspaper, radio station, Students General Association, Association des Étudiantes/Étudiants francophones, Association of Mature and Part-time Students, Graduate Students Association. *Campus security:* 24-hour emergency response devices and patrols, late-night transport/escort service, controlled dormitory access. *Student services:* health clinic, personal/psychological counseling, women's center.

Athletics Member CIS. *Intercollegiate sports:* basketball M/W, cross-country running W, skiing (downhill) M, soccer M, swimming and diving M/W, track and field W, volleyball M. *Intramural sports:* badminton M/W, basketball M/W, golf M, lacrosse M(c)/W(c), rock climbing M(c)/W(c), skiing (downhill) M(c)/W(c), soccer M/W, swimming and diving M(c)/W(c), volleyball M/W, water polo M/W.

Costs (2010–11) *Tuition:* province resident $5114 full-time, $1023 per course part-time; International tuition $13,700 full-time. Full-time tuition and fees vary according to program. Part-time tuition and fees vary according to course load. *Required fees:* $616 full-time, $37 per term part-time. *Room only:* $3825. Room and board charges vary according to housing facility. *Payment plan:* installment. *Waivers:* senior citizens and employees or children of employees.

Financial Aid Of all full-time matriculated undergraduates who enrolled in 2009, 241 state and other part-time jobs (averaging $1563).

Applying *Options:* electronic application, early admission. *Application fee:* $40 Canadian dollars. *Required:* high school transcript. *Required for some:* essay or personal statement, 2 letters of recommendation, interview. *Application deadlines:* 4/1 (freshmen), rolling (transfers).

Freshman Application Contact Laurentian University, Ramsey Lake Road, P3E 2C6, Canada. *Phone:* 705-675-1151. *Fax:* 705-675-4891. *E-mail:* admissions@laurentian.ca. *Web site:* http://www.laurentian.ca/.

Master's College and Seminary
Toronto, Ontario, Canada

- **Independent Pentecostal** 4-year, founded 1939
- **Suburban** campus with easy access to Toronto
- **Endowment** $331,500
- **Coed** 238 undergraduate students
- **Noncompetitive** entrance level, 89% of applicants were admitted

Undergraduates Students come from 4 provinces and territories; 2 other countries; 5% are from out of state; 65% live on campus. *Retention:* 78% of full-time freshmen returned.
Freshman *Admission:* 70 applied, 62 admitted.
Faculty *Total:* 33, 12% full-time, 24% with terminal degrees. *Student/faculty ratio:* 8:1.
Academics *Calendar:* semesters. *Degree:* certificates, diplomas, and bachelor's. *Special study options:* academic remediation for entering students, accelerated degree program, distance learning, independent study, internships, off-campus study, part-time degree program, services for LD students, summer session for credit.
Computers on Campus 6 computers/terminals are available on campus for general student use. Students can access the following: free student e-mail accounts, online (class) registration, online (class) schedules. Campuswide network is available. Wireless service is available via entire campus.
Student Life *Housing:* on-campus residence required for freshman year. *Options:* men-only, women-only. Campus housing is leased by the school. Freshman campus housing is guaranteed. *Campus security:* 24-hour emergency response devices, student patrols, controlled dormitory access.
Athletics *Intercollegiate sports:* volleyball W.
Costs (2010–11) *Comprehensive fee:* $11,762 includes full-time tuition ($5600), mandatory fees ($962), and room and board ($5200). Full-time tuition and fees vary according to course load and program. Part-time tuition: $175 per credit hour. Part-time tuition and fees vary according to course load and program. *Required fees:* $18 per credit hour part-time. *Payment plans:* installment, deferred payment. *Waivers:* adult students, senior citizens, and employees or children of employees.
Applying *Options:* deferred entrance. *Application fee:* $75 Canadian dollars. *Required:* essay or personal statement, high school transcript, 3 letters of recommendation, Christian commitment. *Required for some:* interview. *Recommended:* minimum 2 GPA. *Application deadlines:* 8/31 (freshmen), 8/31 (transfers).
Freshman Application Contact Ms. Flora Anthony, Admissions, Master's College and Seminary, 780 Argyle Street, Peterborough, ON K9H 5T2, Canada. *Phone:* 800-295-6368. *Toll-free phone:* 800-295-6368 Ext. 243. *Fax:* 705-749-0417. *E-mail:* flora.anthony@mcs.edu. *Web site:* http://www.mcs.edu/.

McGill University
Montréal, Quebec, Canada

Freshman Application Contact Enrollment Services, McGill University, 845 Sherbrooke Street West, James Administration Building, Room 205, Montreal, QC H3A 2T5, Canada. *Phone:* 514-398-3910. *Fax:* 514-398-4193. *E-mail:* admissions@mcgill.ca. *Web site:* http://www.mcgill.ca/.

McMaster University
Hamilton, Ontario, Canada

Freshman Application Contact Olivia Demerling, Admissions Officer, McMaster University, 1280 Main Street West, Hamilton, ON L8S 4M2, Canada. *Phone:* 905-525-4600. *Fax:* 905-527-1105. *E-mail:* admitmac@mcmaster.ca. *Web site:* http://www.mcmaster.ca/.

Memorial University of Newfoundland
St. John's, Newfoundland and Labrador, Canada

- **Province-supported** university, founded 1925, administratively affiliated with Marine Institute, Sir Wilfred Grenfell College, WRSON, CNS
- **Urban** 250-acre campus
- **Endowment** $60.0 million
- **Coed**
- **Moderately difficult** entrance level

Faculty *Student/faculty ratio:* 12:1.
Academics *Calendar:* trimesters. *Degrees:* certificates, diplomas, bachelor's, master's, doctoral-other, and postbachelor's certificates.
Student Life *Campus security:* 24-hour emergency response devices and patrols, student patrols, late-night transport/escort service.

Athletics Member CIS.
Costs (2010–11) *Tuition:* province resident $2550 full-time, $85 per credit hour part-time; International tuition $8800 full-time. Full-time tuition and fees vary according to course load and program. Part-time tuition and fees vary according to course load and program. *Required fees:* $494 full-time, $29 per term part-time. *Room and board:* $6204; room only: $2174. Room and board charges vary according to board plan, housing facility, and location.
Applying *Options:* electronic application, early admission, early decision, deferred entrance. *Application fee:* $40 Canadian dollars. *Required:* high school transcript. *Required for some:* essay or personal statement, 2 letters of recommendation, interview, audition, portfolio.
Freshman Application Contact Ms. Marian Abbott, Admissions Office, Memorial University of Newfoundland, Elizabeth Avenue, St. John's, NL A1C 5S7, Canada. *Phone:* 709-737-3705. *E-mail:* sturecru@morgan.ucs.mun.ca. *Web site:* http://www.mun.ca/.

Mount Allison University
Sackville, New Brunswick, Canada

- **Province-supported** comprehensive, founded 1839
- **Small-town** 50-acre campus
- **Endowment** $65.0 million
- **Coed** 2,611 undergraduate students, 96% full-time, 60% women, 40% men
- **Moderately difficult** entrance level, 74% of applicants were admitted

Undergraduates 2,505 full-time, 106 part-time. Students come from 19 provinces and territories; 42 other countries; 59% are from out of state; 2% transferred in; 50% live on campus. *Retention:* 79% of full-time freshmen returned.
Freshmen *Admission:* 2,110 applied, 1,551 admitted, 771 enrolled. *Average high school GPA:* 3.25.
Faculty *Total:* 187, 71% full-time, 88% with terminal degrees. *Student/faculty ratio:* 16:1.
Academics *Calendar:* Canadian standard year. *Degrees:* certificates, bachelor's, and master's. *Special study options:* academic remediation for entering students, adult/continuing education programs, advanced placement credit, distance learning, double majors, honors programs, independent study, internships, off-campus study, part-time degree program, services for LD students, student-designed majors, study abroad, summer session for credit.
Computers on Campus 100 computers/terminals and 240 ports are available on campus for general student use. Students can access the following: computer help desk, free student e-mail accounts, online (class) grades, online (class) registration, online (class) schedules, online student account/Websis. Campuswide network is available. 100% of college-owned or -operated housing units are wired for high-speed Internet access. Wireless service is available via entire campus.
Student Life *Housing options:* coed, women-only, cooperative. Campus housing is university owned. Freshman campus housing is guaranteed. *Activities and organizations:* drama/theater group, student-run newspaper, radio station, choral group, Commerce Society, Windsor Theatre, President's Leadership Development Certificate, Leadership Mount Allison, Garnet and Gold Society. *Campus security:* 24-hour emergency response devices, late-night transport/escort service. *Student services:* health clinic, personal/psychological counseling.
Athletics Member CIS. *Intercollegiate sports:* basketball M/W, football M, ice hockey W, rugby M/W, soccer M/W, swimming and diving M/W. *Intramural sports:* badminton M/W, baseball M/W, basketball M/W, football M/W, golf M/W, ice hockey M/W, rugby M/W, skiing (cross-country) M/W, skiing (downhill) M/W, soccer M/W, softball M/W, tennis M/W, ultimate Frisbee M/W, volleyball M/W, weight lifting M/W.
Costs (2011–12) *Tuition:* province resident $6720 full-time, $672 per course part-time; nonresident $1411 per course part-time; International tuition $14,110 full-time. Full-time tuition and fees vary according to course load. Part-time tuition and fees vary according to course load. *Required fees:* $289 full-time, $38 per term part-time. *Room and board:* $7389; room only: $3873. Room and board charges vary according to board plan and housing facility. *Payment plans:* installment, deferred payment. *Waivers:* senior citizens and employees or children of employees.
Applying *Options:* electronic application, deferred entrance. *Application fee:* $50 Canadian dollars. *Required:* high school transcript, minimum 2.5 GPA. *Required for some:* essay or personal statement, interview. *Recommended:* 2 letters of recommendation. *Application deadlines:* rolling (freshmen), rolling (transfers). *Notification:* continuous (freshmen), continuous (transfers).
Freshman Application Contact Mr. Joceylyn Ollerhead, Manager of Admissions, Mount Allison University, 65 York Street, Sackville, NB E4L 1E4, Canada. *Phone:* 506-364-3294. *Fax:* 506-364-2272. *E-mail:* admissions@mta.ca. *Web site:* http://www.mta.ca/.

Mount Royal University

Calgary, Alberta, Canada

Freshman Application Contact Admissions Office, Mount Royal University, 4825 Mount Royal Gate SW, Calgary, AB T3E 6K6, Canada. *Phone:* 403-440-5000. *Toll-free phone:* 877-440-5001. *Web site:* http://www.mtroyal.ca/.

Mount Saint Vincent University

Halifax, Nova Scotia, Canada

Freshman Application Contact Ms. Heidi Tattrie, Assistant Registrar/Admissions, Mount Saint Vincent University, 166 Bedford Highway, Halifax, NS B3M2J6, Canada. *Phone:* 902-457-6117. *Fax:* 902-457-6498. *E-mail:* admissions@msvu.ca. *Web site:* http://www.msvu.ca/.

Ner Israel Yeshiva College of Toronto

Thornhill, Ontario, Canada

Director of Admissions Rabbi Y. Kravetz, Director of Admissions, Ner Israel Yeshiva College of Toronto, 8950 Bathurst Street, Thornhill, ON L4J 8A7, Canada. *Phone:* 905-731-1224.

Nipissing University

North Bay, Ontario, Canada

- **Province-supported** comprehensive, founded 1992, part of Ontario Ministry of Training, Colleges and Universities
- **Urban** 290-hectare campus
- **Coed**
- **Moderately difficult** entrance level

Academics *Calendar:* semesters. *Degrees:* bachelor's, master's, doctoral-professional, and postbachelor's certificates.

Student Life *Campus security:* 24-hour emergency response devices and patrols, student patrols, late-night transport/escort service, controlled dormitory access.

Athletics Member CIS.

Standardized Tests *Required:* SAT and SAT Subject Tests or ACT (for admission).

Applying *Options:* electronic application, early admission, early decision. *Required:* high school transcript. *Required for some:* essay or personal statement.

Freshman Application Contact Ms. Lori-Ann Beckford, Assistant Registrar, Liaison, Nipissing University, 100 College Drive, Box 5002, North Bay, ON P1B 8L7, Canada. *Phone:* 705-474-3461 Ext. 4518. *Fax:* 705-474-1947. *E-mail:* liaison@nipissingu.ca. *Web site:* http://www.nipissingu.ca/.

Nova Scotia Agricultural College

Truro, Nova Scotia, Canada

- **Province-supported** comprehensive, founded 1905, administratively affiliated with Dalhousie University
- **Small-town** 408-acre campus with easy access to Halifax
- **Coed**
- **Minimally difficult** entrance level

Faculty *Student/faculty ratio:* 12:1.

Academics *Calendar:* semesters. *Degrees:* diplomas, bachelor's, and master's.

Student Life *Campus security:* 24-hour patrols, student patrols.

Costs (2010–11) *Tuition:* province resident $5500 full-time, $550 per course part-time; nonresident $1100 per course part-time; International tuition $11,000 full-time. Full-time tuition and fees vary according to course load, degree level, program, and reciprocity agreements. Part-time tuition and fees vary according to course load, degree level, program, and reciprocity agreements. *Required fees:* $550 full-time, $60 per course part-time. *Room and board:* $7360. Room and board charges vary according to board plan and housing facility.

Applying *Options:* electronic application. *Application fee:* $25 Canadian dollars. *Required:* high school transcript, minimum 2.5 GPA. *Required for some:* essay or personal statement, 1 letter of recommendation, interview.

Freshman Application Contact Ms. Elizabeth Johnson, Admissions Officer, Nova Scotia Agricultural College, PO Box 550, Truro, NS B2N 5E3, Canada. *Phone:* 902-893-8212. *Toll-free phone:* 888-700-6722. *Fax:* 902-895-5529. *E-mail:* recruit@nsac.ca. *Web site:* http://nsac.ca/.

NSCAD University

Halifax, Nova Scotia, Canada

Freshman Application Contact Mr. Terry Bailey, Director of Admissions and Enrollment Services, NSCAD University, 5163 Duke Street, Halifax, NS B3J 3J6, Canada. *Phone:* 902-494-8129. *Fax:* 902-425-2987. *E-mail:* admissions@nscad.ca. *Web site:* http://www.nscad.ca/.

Okanagan College

Kelowna, British Columbia, Canada

Freshman Application Contact Mr. Paul Campo, Okanagan College, 1000 KLO Road, Kelowna, BC V1Y 4X8, Canada. *Phone:* 250-762-5445 Ext. 4332. *E-mail:* pgcampo@okanagan.bc.ca. *Web site:* http://www.okanagan.bc.ca/.

Prairie Bible Institute

Three Hills, Alberta, Canada

Director of Admissions Mr. Kevin Kirk, Vice President, Marketing and Enrollment Management, Prairie Bible Institute, 330 Sixth Avenue North, PO Box 4000, Three Hills, AB T0M 2N0, Canada. *Phone:* 403-443-5511 Ext. 3007. *Toll-free phone:* 800-661-2425. *E-mail:* admissions@prairie.edu. *Web site:* http://www.prairie.edu/.

Providence College and Theological Seminary

Otterburne, Manitoba, Canada

Freshman Application Contact Mr. Adrian Enns, Director of College Enrollment, Providence College and Theological Seminary, 10 College Crescent, Otterburne, MB R0A 1G0, Canada. *Phone:* 204-433-7488. *Toll-free phone:* 800-668-7768. *Fax:* 204-433-7158. *E-mail:* info@prov.ca. *Web site:* http://www.prov.ca/.

Queen's University at Kingston

Kingston, Ontario, Canada

- **Province-supported** university, founded 1841
- **Urban** 160-acre campus
- **Endowment** $601.9 million
- **Coed**
- **Most difficult** entrance level

Faculty *Student/faculty ratio:* 15:1.

Academics *Calendar:* Canadian standard year. *Degrees:* certificates, bachelor's, master's, and doctoral-research/scholarship.

Student Life *Campus security:* 24-hour emergency response devices and patrols, student patrols, late-night transport/escort service, controlled dormitory access.

Athletics Member CIS.

Standardized Tests *Required:* SAT or ACT (for admission).

Costs (2010–11) *Tuition:* province resident $5461 Canadian dollars full-time, $1066 Canadian dollars per course part-time; nonresident $3766 Canadian dollars per course part-time; International tuition $18,730 Canadian dollars full-time. Full-time tuition and fees vary according to course load, degree level, and program. Part-time tuition and fees vary according to course load, degree level, and program. *Required fees:* $1035 Canadian dollars full-time, $20 Canadian dollars per credit part-time. *Room and board:* $10,265 Canadian dollars; room only: $5737 Canadian dollars. Room and board charges vary according to board plan and location. *Payment plans:* installment, deferred payment.

Financial Aid *Of all full-time matriculated undergraduates who enrolled in 2008,* 361 state and other part-time jobs (averaging $1068). *Average financial aid package:* $8861.

Applying *Options:* deferred entrance. *Application fee:* $180 Canadian dollars. *Required:* essay or personal statement, high school transcript, minimum 2.7 GPA. *Required for some:* 1 letter of recommendation.

Freshman Application Contact Ms. Wendy Smith, Admission Coordinator, Queen's University at Kingston, Undergraduate Admissions, Gordon Hall, 74 Union Street, Kingston, ON K7L 3N6, Canada. *Phone:* 613-533-2218. *Fax:* 613-533-6810. *E-mail:* admission@queensu.ca. *Web site:* http://www.queensu.ca/.

Redeemer University College
Ancaster, Ontario, Canada
- **Independent interdenominational** 4-year, founded 1980
- **Small-town** 86-acre campus with easy access to Toronto
- **Endowment** $3.1 million
- **Coed**
- **Moderately difficult** entrance level

Faculty *Student/faculty ratio:* 13:1.
Academics *Calendar:* semesters. *Degree:* certificates and bachelor's.
Student Life *Campus security:* 24-hour emergency response devices, student patrols, late-night transport/escort service, controlled dormitory access, path lighting.
Standardized Tests *Required for some:* SAT or ACT (for admission).
Costs (2010–11) *Comprehensive fee:* $19,617 Canadian dollars includes full-time tuition ($13,212 Canadian dollars), mandatory fees ($479 Canadian dollars), and room and board ($5926 Canadian dollars). Full-time tuition and fees vary according to course load and program. Part-time tuition: $1326 Canadian dollars per course. Part-time tuition and fees vary according to course load and program. *Required fees:* $35 Canadian dollars per course part-time. *Room and board:* Room and board charges vary according to board plan and housing facility.
Applying *Options:* electronic application, deferred entrance. *Application fee:* $40 Canadian dollars. *Required:* essay or personal statement, high school transcript, minimum 2 GPA, 2 letters of recommendation, personal reference. *Required for some:* interview.
Freshman Application Contact Recruitment, Redeemer University College, 777 Garner Road East, Ancaster, ON L9K 1J4, Canada. *Phone:* 905-648-2139 Ext. 4280. *Toll-free phone:* 800-263-6467 Ext. 4280. *Fax:* 905-648-9545. *E-mail:* recruitment@redeemer.ca. *Web site:* http://www.redeemer.ca/.

Rocky Mountain College
Calgary, Alberta, Canada
Freshman Application Contact Rocky Mountain College, 4039 Brentwood Road, NW, Calgary, AB T2L 1L1, Canada. *Phone:* 403-284-5100. *Toll-free phone:* 877-YOUnRMC. *Web site:* http://www.rockymountaincollege.ca/.

Royal Military College of Canada
Kingston, Ontario, Canada
- **Federally supported** comprehensive, founded 1876, part of Council of Ontario Universities
- **Urban** 90-acre campus
- **Coed**
- **Most difficult** entrance level

Academics *Calendar:* Canadian standard year. *Degrees:* certificates, diplomas, bachelor's, master's, and doctoral-other.
Student Life *Campus security:* 24-hour emergency response devices and patrols, controlled dormitory access.
Athletics Member CIS.
Costs (2010–11) *Tuition:* province resident $3390 Canadian dollars full-time, $1695 Canadian dollars per term part-time; International tuition $16,000 Canadian dollars full-time. Full-time tuition and fees vary according to program. Part-time tuition and fees vary according to program. *Room and board:* Room and board charges vary according to housing facility and student level.
Applying *Options:* electronic application, early decision. *Required:* high school transcript, interview, medical, aptitude and physical fitness testing.
Freshman Application Contact Royal Military College of Canada, PO Box 17000, Station Forces, Kingston, ON K7K 7B4, Canada. *Phone:* 613-541-6000 Ext. 6579. *Web site:* http://www.rmc.ca/.

Royal Roads University
Victoria, British Columbia, Canada
- **Province-supported** upper-level, founded 1996
- **Suburban** 565-acre campus
- **Coed**
- **Moderately difficult** entrance level

Academics *Calendar:* continuous. *Degrees:* certificates, diplomas, bachelor's, master's, and doctoral-research/scholarship.
Student Life *Campus security:* 24-hour emergency response devices and patrols, late-night transport/escort service.
Costs (2010–11) *Tuition:* province resident $14,380 full-time; International tuition $28,760 full-time. No tuition increase for student's term of enrollment. *Payment plans:* tuition prepayment, installment.
Applying *Options:* electronic application. *Application fee:* $102 Canadian dollars.

Application Contact Royal Roads University, 2005 Sooke Road, Victoria, BC V9B 5Y2, Canada. *Phone:* 250-391-2511. *Toll-free phone:* 800-788-8028. *Web site:* http://www.royalroads.ca/.

Ryerson University
Toronto, Ontario, Canada
Freshman Application Contact Michelle Beaton, Manager of International Student Recruitment, Ryerson University, 350 Victoria Street, Toronto, ON M5B 2K3, Canada. *Phone:* 416-979-5080. *Fax:* 416-979-5067. *E-mail:* inquire@ryerson.ca. *Web site:* http://www.ryerson.ca/.

See page 1550 for the College Close-Up.

St. Francis Xavier University
Antigonish, Nova Scotia, Canada
- **Independent Roman Catholic** comprehensive, founded 1853
- **Small-town** 100-acre campus
- **Endowment** $67.4 million
- **Coed** 4,255 undergraduate students, 52% full-time, 62% women, 38% men
- **Moderately difficult** entrance level, 65% of applicants were admitted

Undergraduates 2,209 full-time, 2,046 part-time. Students come from 13 provinces and territories; 37 other countries; 43% are from out of state; 5% transferred in; 45% live on campus. *Retention:* 90% of full-time freshmen returned.
Freshmen *Admission:* 2,851 applied, 1,859 admitted, 890 enrolled. *Average high school GPA:* 83.3.
Faculty *Total:* 318, 79% full-time, 74% with terminal degrees. *Student/faculty ratio:* 12:1.
Academics *Calendar:* Canadian standard year. *Degrees:* certificates, diplomas, bachelor's, and master's. *Special study options:* academic remediation for entering students, accelerated degree program, adult/continuing education programs, advanced placement credit, cooperative education, distance learning, double majors, English as a second language, honors programs, independent study, internships, off-campus study, part-time degree program, services for LD students, student-designed majors, study abroad, summer session for credit.
Computers on Campus 500 computers/terminals and 500 ports are available on campus for general student use. Students can access the following: campus intranet, computer help desk, free student e-mail accounts, online (class) grades, online (class) registration, online (class) schedules, online financial account, personal network storage, personal Web publishing, WirelessSynch iPodsSmartphones. Campuswide network is available. 100% of college-owned or -operated housing units are wired for high-speed Internet access. Wireless service is available via entire campus.
Student Life *Housing options:* coed, men-only, women-only, disabled students. Campus housing is university owned. Freshman campus housing is guaranteed. *Activities and organizations:* drama/theater group, student-run newspaper, radio station, choral group, X-Project, Blue Crew, orientation committee, X-Debate, ACE (Advancing Canadian Entrepreneurship). *Campus security:* 24-hour emergency response devices and patrols, student patrols, late-night transport/escort service, controlled dormitory access. *Student services:* health clinic, personal/psychological counseling, women's center.
Athletics Member CIS. *Intercollegiate sports:* baseball M(c), basketball M(s)/W(s), cheerleading W(c), crew M(c)/W(c), cross-country running M(s)/W(s), equestrian sports W(c), field hockey W(c), football M(s), ice hockey M(s)/W(s), lacrosse M, rugby M(c)/W(s), soccer M/W(s), track and field M/W, volleyball W(s). *Intramural sports:* badminton M/W, basketball M/W, football M/W, golf M/W, ice hockey M/W, racquetball M/W, soccer M/W, softball M/W, squash M/W, swimming and diving M/W, table tennis M/W, track and field M/W, ultimate Frisbee M/W, volleyball M/W, water polo M/W.
Standardized Tests *Required for some:* SAT or ACT (for admission). *Recommended:* SAT or ACT (for admission), SAT Subject Tests (for admission).
Costs (2011–12) *Tuition:* province resident $5108 Canadian dollars full-time, $182 Canadian dollars per credit part-time; nonresident $6130 Canadian dollars full-time, $216 Canadian dollars per credit part-time; International tuition $12,782 Canadian dollars full-time. Full-time tuition and fees vary according to degree level and program. Part-time tuition and fees vary according to course load, degree level, and program. *Required fees:* $621 Canadian dollars full-time, $16 Canadian dollars per credit part-time. *Room and board:* $9005 Canadian dollars; room only: $4825 Canadian dollars. Room and board charges vary according to board plan and housing facility. *Payment plan:* installment. *Waivers:* senior citizens and employees or children of employees.
Applying *Options:* electronic application, early admission, early decision, deferred entrance. *Application fee:* $40 Canadian dollars. *Required:* essay or personal statement, high school transcript, 2 letters of recommendation. *Application deadlines:* rolling (freshmen), rolling (transfers). *Early decision dead-*

line: 1/31. *Notification:* continuous until 8/15 (freshmen), continuous until 8/15 (transfers).

Freshman Application Contact Ms. Sarah Murray, Admissions Officer, St. Francis Xavier University, PO Box 5000, Antigonish, NS B2G 2W5, Canada. *Phone:* 902-867-2219. *Toll-free phone:* 877-867-7839 (in-state); 877-867-STFX (out-of-state). *Fax:* 902-867-2329. *E-mail:* mbarry@stfx.ca. *Web site:* http://www.stfx.ca/.

Saint Mary's University
Halifax, Nova Scotia, Canada

Director of Admissions Mr. Greg Ferguson, Director of Admissions, Saint Mary's University, Halifax, NS B3H 3C3, Canada. *Phone:* 902-420-5415. *Fax:* 902-496-8100. *E-mail:* greg.ferguson@smu.ca. *Web site:* http://www.smu.ca/.

Saint Paul University
Ottawa, Ontario, Canada

Director of Admissions Admission and Recruitment Office, Saint Paul University, 223 Main Street, Ottawa, ON K1S 1C4, Canada. *Phone:* 613-236-1393 Ext. 8990. *Toll-free phone:* 800-637-6859. *Fax:* 613-782-3014. *E-mail:* admission@ustpaul.ca. *Web site:* http://www.ustpaul.ca/.

St. Thomas University
Fredericton, New Brunswick, Canada

- **Independent Roman Catholic** 4-year, founded 1910
- **Small-town** 16-acre campus
- **Endowment** $27.6 million
- **Coed** 2,435 undergraduate students, 92% full-time, 67% women, 33% men
- **Moderately difficult** entrance level, 77% of applicants were admitted

Undergraduates 2,241 full-time, 194 part-time. Students come from 12 provinces and territories; 31 other countries; 22% are from out of state; 97% Race/ethnicity unknown; 3% international; 5% transferred in; 33% live on campus. *Retention:* 73% of full-time freshmen returned.
Freshmen *Admission:* 1,334 applied, 1,028 admitted, 709 enrolled. *Average high school GPA:* 3.3.
Faculty *Total:* 199, 54% full-time, 66% with terminal degrees. *Student/faculty ratio:* 19:1.
Academics *Calendar:* semesters. *Degrees:* certificates, bachelor's, and post-bachelor's certificates. *Special study options:* academic remediation for entering students, accelerated degree program, advanced placement credit, double majors, English as a second language, honors programs, independent study, internships, off-campus study, part-time degree program, services for LD students, student-designed majors, study abroad, summer session for credit.
Computers on Campus 130 computers/terminals are available on campus for general student use. Students can access the following: computer help desk, free student e-mail accounts, online (class) grades, online (class) registration, online (class) schedules, Moodle. Campuswide network is available. 100% of college-owned or -operated housing units are wired for high-speed Internet access. Wireless service is available via entire campus.
Student Life *Housing options:* coed, women-only, disabled students. Campus housing is university owned. Freshman campus housing is guaranteed. *Activities and organizations:* drama/theater group, student-run newspaper, radio station, choral group, Theatre St. Thomas, St. Thomas Student Union, Criminology Society, Model UN, International Students' Association. *Campus security:* 24-hour emergency response devices and patrols, student patrols, late-night transport/escort service, controlled dormitory access. *Student services:* health clinic, personal/psychological counseling, women's center.
Athletics Member CIS. *Intercollegiate sports:* basketball M/W, cross-country running M/W, golf M/W, ice hockey M(s)/W(s), soccer M/W, volleyball M/W. *Intramural sports:* badminton M/W, basketball M/W, cross-country running M/W, fencing M/W, football M, ice hockey M/W, rock climbing M/W, soccer M/W, softball M/W, squash M/W, swimming and diving M/W, table tennis M/W, track and field M/W, ultimate Frisbee M/W, volleyball M/W, water polo M/W.
Standardized Tests *Recommended:* SAT (for admission).
Costs (2010–11) *Comprehensive fee:* $12,376 Canadian dollars includes full-time tuition ($4570 Canadian dollars), mandatory fees ($306 Canadian dollars), and room and board ($7500 Canadian dollars). Full-time tuition and fees vary according to course load, degree level, and program. Part-time tuition: $510 Canadian dollars per course. Part-time tuition and fees vary according to course load. International tuition: $12,480 Canadian dollars full-time. *Required fees:* $31 Canadian dollars per course part-time. *Room and board:* Room and board charges vary according to board plan, housing facility, and location. *Payment plans:* installment, deferred payment. *Waivers:* senior citizens and employees or children of employees.

Financial Aid *Financial aid deadline:* 3/1.
Applying *Options:* electronic application, early action. *Application fee:* $35 Canadian dollars. *Required:* high school transcript, minimum 3 GPA. *Required for some:* essay or personal statement, interview. *Application deadlines:* 8/31 (freshmen), 8/31 (transfers), 12/7 (early action). *Notification:* continuous (freshmen), continuous (transfers).
Freshman Application Contact Ms. Kathryn Monti, Director of Admissions, St. Thomas University, Admissions and Welcome Building, Fredericton, NB E3B 5G3, Canada. *Phone:* 506-452-0532. *Fax:* 506-452-0617. *E-mail:* admissions@stu.ca. *Web site:* http://www.stu.ca/.

Simon Fraser University
Burnaby, British Columbia, Canada

- **Province-supported** university, founded 1965
- **Suburban** campus with easy access to Vancouver
- **Endowment** $176.9 million
- **Coed** 23,985 undergraduate students, 51% full-time, 55% women, 45% men
- **Moderately difficult** entrance level, 77% of applicants were admitted

Undergraduates 12,186 full-time, 11,799 part-time. Students come from 11 provinces and territories; 84 other countries; 8% are from out of state; 5% transferred in; 9% live on campus. *Retention:* 87% of full-time freshmen returned.
Freshmen *Admission:* 10,200 applied, 7,843 admitted, 3,194 enrolled. *Average high school GPA:* 3.35.
Faculty *Total:* 939, 98% full-time, 89% with terminal degrees. *Student/faculty ratio:* 24:1.
Academics *Calendar:* trimesters. *Degrees:* certificates, diplomas, bachelor's, master's, doctoral-research/scholarship, post-master's, and postbachelor's certificates. *Special study options:* academic remediation for entering students, adult/continuing education programs, advanced placement credit, cooperative education, distance learning, double majors, English as a second language, honors programs, independent study, internships, off-campus study, part-time degree program, services for LD students, study abroad, summer session for credit.
Computers on Campus 900 computers/terminals are available on campus for general student use. Students can access the following: free student e-mail accounts, online (class) grades, online (class) registration, online (class) schedules. Campuswide network is available. 100% of college-owned or -operated housing units are wired for high-speed Internet access. Wireless service is available via entire campus.
Student Life *Housing options:* coed, women-only, disabled students. Campus housing is university owned. Freshman applicants given priority for college housing. *Activities and organizations:* drama/theater group, student-run newspaper, radio station, The Peak Newspaper, orientation leaders, Crisis line, Women's Centre, Simon Fraser Public Interest Research Group. *Campus security:* 24-hour emergency response devices and patrols, student patrols, late-night transport/escort service, controlled dormitory access, safe-walk stations, 24-hour safe study area. *Student services:* health clinic, personal/psychological counseling, women's center.
Athletics Member NCAA. All Division II. *Intercollegiate sports:* basketball M(s)/W(s), cross-country running M(s)/W(s), field hockey W, football M(s), golf M(s), gymnastics M, soccer M(s)/W(s), softball W(s), swimming and diving M(s)/W(s), track and field M(s)/W(s), volleyball W(s), wrestling M(s)/W(s). *Intramural sports:* archery M(c)/W(c), badminton M(c)/W(c), basketball M/W, cheerleading M(c)/W(c), crew M(c)/W(c), fencing M(c)/W(c), field hockey W(c), football M/W, golf W(c), gymnastics W(c), ice hockey W(c), lacrosse M(c), rugby M(c)/W(c), soccer M/W, softball M/W, squash M(c)/W(c), table tennis M(c)/W(c), tennis M/W, ultimate Frisbee M(c)/W(c), volleyball M(c)/W(c), water polo M(c)/W(c).
Standardized Tests *Required for some:* SAT or ACT (for admission).
Costs (2010–11) *Tuition:* province resident $4815 full-time, $161 per credit hour part-time; nonresident $527 per credit hour part-time; International tuition $15,816 full-time. Full-time tuition and fees vary according to course level and program. *Required fees:* $547 full-time, $274 per term part-time. *Room and board:* $7630; room only: $4930. Room and board charges vary according to board plan and housing facility. *Waivers:* employees or children of employees.
Financial Aid Of all full-time matriculated undergraduates who enrolled in 2008, 420 state and other part-time jobs (averaging $1131). *Financial aid deadline:* 11/15.
Applying *Options:* electronic application, early admission, deferred entrance. *Application fee:* $100 Canadian dollars. *Required:* high school transcript, minimum 3 GPA. *Required for some:* essay or personal statement, interview. *Application deadlines:* 4/30 (freshmen), rolling (transfers). *Notification:* continuous until 6/30 (freshmen), continuous (transfers).
Freshman Application Contact Ms. Louise Legris, Director of Admissions, Simon Fraser University, 8888 University Drive, Burnaby, BC V5A 1S6,

Canada. *Phone:* 778-782-3498. *Fax:* 778-782-4969. *E-mail:* undergraduate-admissions@sfu.ca. *Web site:* http://www.sfu.ca/.

Southern Alberta Institute of Technology
Calgary, Alberta, Canada
- **Province-supported** primarily 2-year, founded 1916
- **Urban** 96-acre campus
- **Coed** 7,672 undergraduate students, 91% full-time, 42% women, 58% men

Undergraduates 6,954 full-time, 718 part-time.
Faculty *Total:* 962.
Academics *Calendar:* trimesters. *Degree:* certificates, diplomas, and bachelor's. *Special study options:* cooperative education, distance learning, independent study, internships, off-campus study, services for LD students.
Computers on Campus Students can access the following: campus intranet, computer help desk, free student e-mail accounts, online (class) grades, online (class) registration, online (class) schedules. Campuswide network is available. 100% of college-owned or -operated housing units are wired for high-speed Internet access. Wireless service is available via classrooms, computer centers, computer labs, dorm rooms, learning centers, libraries, student centers.
Student Life *Housing options:* coed, disabled students. Campus housing is university owned. *Activities and organizations:* drama/theater group, student-run newspaper, radio and television station, SAIT Petroleum Society, Business Student's Association, Global Passport, Environmental Technology Students Organization, Civil Engineering Technology Concrete Toboggan. *Campus security:* 24-hour emergency response devices and patrols, late-night transport/escort service. *Student services:* health clinic, personal/psychological counseling.
Athletics *Intercollegiate sports:* basketball M(s)/W(s), cross-country running M/W, ice hockey M(s)/W(s), soccer M(s)/W(s), volleyball M(s)/W(s). *Intramural sports:* basketball M/W, football M/W, ice hockey M/W, soccer M/W, softball M/W, volleyball M/W.
Applying *Options:* electronic application, early admission, early decision. *Application fee:* $50 Canadian dollars. *Required:* high school transcript. *Required for some:* essay or personal statement, interview. *Application deadlines:* rolling (freshmen), rolling (out-of-state freshmen), rolling (transfers). *Early decision deadline:* rolling.
Freshman Application Contact Southern Alberta Institute of Technology, 1301 16th Avenue NW, Calgary, AB T2M 0L4, Canada. *Phone:* 403-284-8857. *Toll-free phone:* 877-284-SAIT. *Web site:* http://www.sait.ca/.

Steinbach Bible College
Steinbach, Manitoba, Canada
- **Independent Mennonite** 4-year, founded 1936
- **Urban** 16-acre campus with easy access to Winnipeg
- **Coed**
- **Minimally difficult** entrance level

Faculty *Student/faculty ratio:* 18:1.
Academics *Calendar:* semesters. *Degree:* certificates, diplomas, and bachelor's.
Costs (2010–11) *Comprehensive fee:* $10,697 Canadian dollars includes full-time tuition ($6080 Canadian dollars), mandatory fees ($297 Canadian dollars), and room and board ($4320 Canadian dollars). Part-time tuition: $190 Canadian dollars per credit hour. *Required fees:* $60 Canadian dollars per year part-time.
Applying *Options:* electronic application. *Application fee:* $50 Canadian dollars.
Freshman Application Contact Mrs. Kaylene Buhler, Admissions Counselor, Steinbach Bible College, 50 PTH 12 North, Steinbach, MB R5G 1T4, Canada. *Phone:* 204-326-6451 Ext. 232. *Toll-free phone:* 800-230-8478. *Fax:* 204-326-6908. *E-mail:* info@sbcollege.ca. *Web site:* http://www.sbcollege.ca/.

Summit Pacific College
Abbotsford, British Columbia, Canada
Director of Admissions Ms. Melody Deeley, Admissions and Registration, Summit Pacific College, Box 1700, Abbotsford, BC V2S 7E7, Canada. *Phone:* 604-851-7225. *Toll-free phone:* 800-976-8388. *E-mail:* registrar@summitpacific.ca. *Web site:* http://www.summitpacific.ca/.

Télé-université
Québec, Quebec, Canada
Freshman Application Contact Ms. Louise Bertrand, Registraire, Télé-université, 455, rue de l'Église, C.P. 4800, succ. Terminus, Québec, QC G1K

9H5, Canada. *Phone:* 418-657-2262 Ext. 5307. *Toll-free phone:* 888-843-4333. *Web site:* http://www.teluq.uquebec.ca/.

Thompson Rivers University
Kamloops, British Columbia, Canada
- **Province-supported** comprehensive, founded 1970, part of Ministry of Advanced Education, Province of British Columbia
- **Small-town** 100-acre campus
- **Endowment** $7.3 million
- **Coed**
- **50%** of applicants were admitted

Faculty *Student/faculty ratio:* 12:1.
Academics *Calendar:* semesters. *Degrees:* certificates, diplomas, associate, bachelor's, master's, and postbachelor's certificates.
Student Life *Campus security:* 24-hour emergency response devices and patrols, student patrols, late-night transport/escort service, controlled dormitory access.
Athletics Member CIS.
Costs (2010–11) *Tuition:* province resident $3610 Canadian dollars full-time; $120 Canadian dollars per credit hour part-time; International tuition $13,800 Canadian dollars full-time. Full-time tuition and fees vary according to course load and program. Part-time tuition and fees vary according to course load and program. *Required fees:* $850 Canadian dollars full-time, $23 Canadian dollars per credit hour part-time, $69 Canadian dollars per course part-time. *Room only:* $3900 Canadian dollars. Room and board charges vary according to housing facility.
Financial Aid *Of all full-time matriculated undergraduates who enrolled in 2009,* 85 state and other part-time jobs (averaging $2400). *Financial aid deadline:* 3/1.
Applying *Options:* electronic application. *Application fee:* $25 Canadian dollars. *Required:* high school transcript. *Required for some:* essay or personal statement, interview.
Freshman Application Contact Mr. Josh Keller, Director, Student Recruitment and Liaison, Thompson Rivers University, PO Box 3010, 900 McGill Road, Kamloops, BC V2C 5N3, Canada. *Phone:* 250-828-5008. *Fax:* 250-828-5159. *E-mail:* jkeller@tru.ca. *Web site:* http://www.tru.ca/.

Trent University
Peterborough, Ontario, Canada
- **Province-supported** university, founded 1963
- **Suburban** 1400-acre campus with easy access to Toronto
- **Coed** 7,417 undergraduate students, 83% full-time, 65% women, 35% men
- **Moderately difficult** entrance level, 90% of applicants were admitted

Undergraduates 6,187 full-time, 1,230 part-time. Students come from 13 provinces and territories; 91 other countries; 2% are from out of state; 9% transferred in; 17% live on campus. *Retention:* 83% of full-time freshmen returned.
Freshmen *Admission:* 6,722 applied, 6,036 admitted, 1,618 enrolled.
Faculty *Total:* 524, 62% full-time. *Student/faculty ratio:* 18:1.
Academics *Calendar:* Canadian standard year. *Degrees:* diplomas, bachelor's, master's, and doctoral-research/scholarship. *Special study options:* academic remediation for entering students, accelerated degree program, advanced placement credit, cooperative education, distance learning, double majors, English as a second language, honors programs, independent study, internships, off-campus study, part-time degree program, services for LD students, student-designed majors, study abroad, summer session for credit.
Computers on Campus Students can access the following: campus intranet, computer help desk, free student e-mail accounts, online (class) grades, online (class) registration, online (class) schedules, online tuition payment. Campuswide network is available. 100% of college-owned or -operated housing units are wired for high-speed Internet access. Wireless service is available via entire campus.
Student Life *Housing options:* coed, women-only. Campus housing is university owned. Freshman applicants given priority for college housing. *Activities and organizations:* drama/theater group, student-run newspaper, radio station, choral group, Trent Radio, Trent International Program, Trent Central Student Association, Arthur (student newspaper), Excalibur (yearbook). *Campus security:* 24-hour emergency response devices and patrols, student patrols, late-night transport/escort service. *Student services:* health clinic, personal/psychological counseling, women's center.
Athletics Member CIS. *Intercollegiate sports:* crew M/W, cross-country running M/W, fencing M/W, lacrosse M, rugby M/W, soccer M/W, swimming and diving M/W, volleyball M/W. *Intramural sports:* badminton M/W, baseball M/W, basketball M/W, cross-country running M/W, football M/W, ice hockey M/W, soccer M/W, softball M/W, squash M/W, swimming and diving M/W,

tennis M/W, track and field M/W, ultimate Frisbee M/W, volleyball M/W, water polo M/W.

Costs (2010–11) *Tuition:* province resident $5214 Canadian dollars full-time, $1043 Canadian dollars per course part-time; International tuition $14,497 Canadian dollars full-time. Full-time tuition and fees vary according to location and student level. Part-time tuition and fees vary according to course load and student level. *Required fees:* $1331 Canadian dollars full-time, $112 Canadian dollars per course part-time. *Room and board:* $8625 Canadian dollars. Room and board charges vary according to board plan, housing facility, and location. *Payment plans:* installment, deferred payment. *Waivers:* employees or children of employees.

Applying *Options:* electronic application, deferred entrance. *Application fee:* $120 Canadian dollars. *Required:* high school transcript, minimum 2.8 GPA. *Required for some:* essay or personal statement, interview. *Application deadlines:* 6/1 (freshmen), 6/1 (transfers). *Notification:* continuous (freshmen), continuous (transfers).

Freshman Application Contact Lois Fleming, Admissions Officer, Trent University, 1600 West Bank Drive, Peterborough, ON K9J 7B8, Canada. *Phone:* 705-748-1215. *Fax:* 705-748-1629. *E-mail:* leaders@trentu.ca. *Web site:* http://www.trentu.ca/.

Trinity Western University
Langley, British Columbia, Canada

Director of Admissions Director of Admissions, Trinity Western University, 7600 Glover Road, Langley, BC V2Y 1Y1, Canada. *Phone:* 604-888-7511 Ext. 3005. *Toll-free phone:* 888-468-6898. *E-mail:* admissions@twu.ca. *Web site:* http://www.twu.ca/.

Tyndale University College & Seminary
Toronto, Ontario, Canada

Freshman Application Contact Tricia McKenley, Admissions Office Coordinator, Tyndale University College & Seminary, 25 Ballyconnor Court, Toronto, ON M2M 4B3, Canada. *Phone:* 416-218-6757 Ext. 6738. *Toll-free phone:* 800-663-6052. *E-mail:* admissions@tydale.ca. *Web site:* http://www.tyndale.ca/.

Université de Moncton
Moncton, New Brunswick, Canada

Freshman Application Contact Miss Nicole Savois, Chief Admission Officer, Université de Moncton, Moncton, NB E1A 3E9, Canada. *Phone:* 506-858-4115. *Toll-free phone:* 800-363-8336. *E-mail:* gallanrm@umoncton.ca. *Web site:* http://www.umoncton.ca/.

Université de Montréal
Montréal, Quebec, Canada

Freshman Application Contact Mr. Pierre Chenard, Registrar, Université de Montréal, CP 6128, Succursale Centre-ville, Montréal, QC H3C 3J7, Canada. *Phone:* 514-343-2214. *Fax:* 514-343-2097. *E-mail:* pierre.chenard@umontreal.ca. *Web site:* http://www.umontreal.ca/.

Université de Sherbrooke
Sherbrooke, Quebec, Canada

- **Independent** university, founded 1954
- **Urban** 800-acre campus with easy access to Montreal
- **Coed** 15,364 undergraduate students, 67% full-time, 54% women, 46% men
- **Moderately difficult** entrance level, 61% of applicants were admitted

Undergraduates 10,347 full-time, 5,017 part-time. Students come from 3 provinces and territories; 53 other countries; 3% are from out of state; 5% transferred in.

Freshmen *Admission:* 17,960 applied, 11,027 admitted, 3,523 enrolled.

Faculty *Total:* 1,331, 66% full-time.

Academics *Calendar:* Canadian standard year. *Degrees:* certificates, diplomas, bachelor's, master's, doctoral-professional, and doctoral-research/scholarship. *Special study options:* accelerated degree program, adult/continuing education programs, cooperative education, English as a second language, internships, off-campus study, part-time degree program, services for LD students, student-designed majors, study abroad, summer session for credit.

Computers on Campus 300 computers/terminals are available on campus for general student use. Students can access the following: computer help desk, free student e-mail accounts, online (class) registration, online (class) schedules. Campuswide network is available. Wireless service is available via classrooms, computer centers, computer labs, learning centers, libraries.

Student Life *Housing options:* coed. Campus housing is university owned. *Activities and organizations:* drama/theater group, student-run newspaper, radio station. *Campus security:* 24-hour emergency response devices and patrols. *Student services:* health clinic, personal/psychological counseling, legal services.

Athletics Member CIS. *Intercollegiate sports:* badminton M/W, cheerleading M/W, golf M/W, rugby M/W. *Intramural sports:* badminton M/W, basketball M/W, field hockey M/W, ice hockey M, racquetball M/W, soccer M/W, squash M/W, track and field M/W, ultimate Frisbee M/W, volleyball M/W, water polo M/W.

Financial Aid *Financial aid deadline:* 3/31.

Applying *Options:* electronic application, early admission. *Application fee:* $70 Canadian dollars. *Required:* high school transcript. *Required for some:* interview. *Application deadline:* 3/1 (freshmen). *Notification:* continuous until 5/15 (freshmen).

Freshman Application Contact Ms. Lisa Bedard or Valerie Bergeron, Admissions Officers, Université de Sherbrooke, 2500, Boulevard de l'Universite, Sherbrooke, QC J1K 2R1, Canada. *Phone:* 819-821-7687. *Toll-free phone:* 800-267-UDES. *Web site:* http://www.usherbrooke.ca/.

Université du Québec à Chicoutimi
Chicoutimi, Quebec, Canada

Freshman Application Contact Mr. Claudio Zoccastello, Admissions Officer, Université du Québec à Chicoutimi, 555, boulevard de L'Université, Chicoutimi, QC G7H 2B1, Canada. *Phone:* 418-545-5005. *E-mail:* czoccast@uqac.uquebec.ca. *Web site:* http://www.uqac.ca/.

Université du Québec à Montréal
Montréal, Quebec, Canada

Freshman Application Contact Ms. Lucille Boisselle-Roy, Admissions Officer, Université du Québec à Montréal, CP 8888, Succursale Centreville, Montréal, QC H2L 4S8, Canada. *Phone:* 514-987-3132. *E-mail:* admission@uqam.ca. *Web site:* http://www.uqam.ca/.

Université du Québec à Rimouski
Rimouski, Quebec, Canada

Freshman Application Contact Ms. Marie Saint-Laurent, Admissions Officer, Université du Québec à Rimouski, 300 Allee des Ursulines, CP3300, Rimouski QC G5L 3A1, Canada. *Phone:* 418-724-1433. *E-mail:* philippe_horth@uqar.uquebec.ca. *Web site:* http://www.uqar.ca/.

Université du Québec à Trois-Rivières
Trois-Rivières, Quebec, Canada

Freshman Application Contact Ms. Jean Bois, Admissions Officer, Université du Québec à Trois-Rivières, 3351 blvd des Forges, Case post 500, Trois-Rivières, QC G9A 5H7, Canada. *Phone:* 819-376-5011. *Toll-free phone:* 800-365-0922. *Fax:* 819-376-5232. *E-mail:* registraire@uqtr.ca. *Web site:* http://www.uqtr.ca/.

Université du Québec, École de technologie supérieure
Montréal, Quebec, Canada

Director of Admissions Mme. Francine Gamache, Registraire, Université du Québec, École de technologie supérieure, 1100, rue Notre Dame Ouest, Montréal, QC H3C 1K3, Canada. *Phone:* 514-396-8885. *E-mail:* admission@ets.mtl.ca. *Web site:* http://www.etsmtl.ca/.

Université du Québec en Abitibi-Témiscamingue
Rouyn-Noranda, Quebec, Canada

Freshman Application Contact Mrs. Monique Fay, Admissions Officer, Université du Québec en Abitibi-Témiscamingue, 445 boulevard de l'Université, Rouyn-Noranda, QC J9X 5E4, Canada. *Phone:* 819-762-0971. *E-mail:* micheline.chevalier@uqat.uquebec.ca. *Web site:* http://www.uqat.ca/.

Université du Québec en Outaouais
Gatineau, Quebec, Canada

- **Province-supported** university, founded 1981, part of Universite du Quebec
- **Small-town** campus with easy access to Ottawa
- **Coed** 4,781 undergraduate students
- **Noncompetitive** entrance level

Undergraduates Students come from 34 other countries.

Academics *Calendar:* trimesters. *Degrees:* certificates, bachelor's, master's, doctoral-professional, doctoral-research/scholarship, and postbachelor's certificates. *Special study options:* accelerated degree program, adult/continuing education programs, cooperative education, independent study, internships, off-campus study, part-time degree program, services for LD students, study abroad, summer session for credit.

Computers on Campus 500 computers/terminals are available on campus for general student use. Students can access the following: computer help desk, free student e-mail accounts, online (class) registration, online (class) schedules, pay tuition fees online. Campuswide network is available. Wireless service is available via entire campus.

Student Life *Housing options:* coed. Campus housing is university owned. *Activities and organizations:* student-run newspaper, radio station, AGE (Association Generale des Etudiants), AIESEC (Association Internationale des Etudiants en Sciences Economiques et Commerciales, AEME (Association for Events Management Education), REMAA (Regroupement des Etudiants du Monde de l'Administration des Affaires. *Campus security:* 24-hour emergency response devices and patrols. *Student services:* personal/psychological counseling.

Athletics *Intercollegiate sports:* cheerleading M/W, golf M/W, soccer M/W, swimming and diving M/W, volleyball W. *Intramural sports:* badminton M/W, basketball M/W, ice hockey M, rock climbing M/W, soccer M/W, swimming and diving M/W, table tennis M/W, volleyball M/W, water polo M/W, weight lifting M/W.

Costs (2011–12) *Tuition:* province resident $2755 full-time; nonresident $6445 full-time; International tuition $15,113 full-time. Full-time tuition and fees vary according to class time, course load, degree level, program, and reciprocity agreements. Part-time tuition and fees vary according to class time, course load, degree level, and program. *Room only:* $5400. Room and board charges vary according to housing facility. *Payment plan:* installment.

Applying *Options:* electronic application. *Application fee:* $60 Canadian dollars. *Required:* high school transcript, Birth certificate. *Required for some:* essay or personal statement, 3 letters of recommendation, interview.

Freshman Application Contact Registrar Office, Université du Québec en Outaouais, CP 1250, Succursale Hull, 101 St-Jean-Bosco, 101 rue Saint-Jean-Bosco, Gatineau, QC J8X 3X7, Canada. *Phone:* 819-595-3900. *Toll-free phone:* 800-567-1283 Ext. 1840. *Fax:* 819-773-1835. *E-mail:* registraire@uqo.ca. *Web site:* http://www.uqo.ca/.

Université Laval
Québec, Quebec, Canada

Freshman Application Contact Promotion and Recruitment Division, Université Laval, Quebec, QC G1K 7P4, Canada. *Phone:* 418-656-2764. *Toll-free phone:* 877-785-2825. *Fax:* 418-656-5216. *E-mail:* info@dap.ulaval.ca. *Web site:* http://www.ulaval.ca/.

Université Sainte-Anne
Church Point, Nova Scotia, Canada

Freshman Application Contact Mrs. Blanche Thériault, Admissions Officer, Université Sainte-Anne, Church Point, NS B0W 1M0, Canada. *Phone:* 902-769-2114 Ext. 116. *E-mail:* admission@ustanne.ednet.ns.ca. *Web site:* http://www.usainteanne.ca/.

University of Alberta
Edmonton, Alberta, Canada

- **Province-supported** university, founded 1906
- **Urban** 154-acre campus
- **Endowment** $602.4 million
- **Coed**
- **Moderately difficult** entrance level

Faculty *Student/faculty ratio:* 21:1.

Academics *Calendar:* Canadian standard year. *Degrees:* bachelor's, master's, and doctoral-research/scholarship.

Student Life *Campus security:* 24-hour emergency response devices and patrols, student patrols, late-night transport/escort service, controlled dormitory access.

Athletics Member CIS.

Standardized Tests *Recommended:* SAT (for admission), ACT (for admission), SAT or ACT (for admission), SAT and SAT Subject Tests or ACT (for admission), SAT Subject Tests (for admission).

Applying *Options:* electronic application, deferred entrance. *Required:* high school transcript. *Required for some:* essay or personal statement, interview, portfolios/ auditions required for some programs. *Recommended:* minimum 2 GPA.

Freshman Application Contact Ms. Patricia Dalton, Associate Registrar/Director of Enrollment Management, University of Alberta, 105 Administration Building, Edmonton, AB T6G 2M7, Canada. *Phone:* 780-492-3113. *Fax:* 780-492-4380. *E-mail:* registrar@ualberta.ca. *Web site:* http://www.ualberta.ca/.

The University of British Columbia
Vancouver, British Columbia, Canada

- **Province-supported** university, founded 1915
- **Urban** 1000-acre campus with easy access to Vancouver
- **Endowment** $969.6 million
- **Coed** 31,788 undergraduate students, 69% full-time, 55% women, 45% men
- **Very difficult** entrance level, 24% of applicants were admitted

Undergraduates 21,870 full-time, 9,918 part-time. Students come from 40 provinces and territories; 144 other countries; 5% transferred in; 25% live on campus. *Retention:* 90% of full-time freshmen returned.

Freshmen *Admission:* 32,037 applied, 7,739 admitted, 5,116 enrolled.

Faculty *Total:* 2,735, 98% full-time. *Student/faculty ratio:* 15:1.

Academics *Calendar:* Canadian standard year. *Degrees:* certificates, diplomas, bachelor's, master's, doctoral-professional, doctoral-research/scholarship, and postbachelor's certificates. *Special study options:* academic remediation for entering students, adult/continuing education programs, advanced placement credit, cooperative education, distance learning, double majors, English as a second language, freshman honors college, honors programs, internships, off-campus study, part-time degree program, services for LD students, study abroad, summer session for credit.

Computers on Campus 1,500 computers/terminals are available on campus for general student use. Students can access the following: free student e-mail accounts, online (class) grades, online (class) registration, online (class) schedules. Campuswide network is available. Wireless service is available via entire campus.

Student Life *Housing options:* coed, men-only, women-only, disabled students. Campus housing is university owned. Freshman applicants given priority for college housing. *Activities and organizations:* drama/theater group, student-run newspaper, radio station, choral group, Ski and Board Club, Dance Club, AIESEC (international leadership organization), UBC Film Society, Varsity Outdoors Club, national fraternities, national sororities. *Campus security:* 24-hour emergency response devices and patrols, student patrols, late-night transport/escort service, 24-hour desk attendants in residence halls. *Student services:* health clinic, personal/psychological counseling, women's center, legal services.

Athletics Member NAIA, CIS. *Intercollegiate sports:* baseball M(s), basketball M(s)/W(s), cheerleading M(c)/W(c), crew M(s)/W(s), cross-country running M(s)/W(s), equestrian sports M/W, fencing M(c)/W(c), field hockey M(s)/W(s), football M(s), golf M(s)/W(s), ice hockey M(s)/W(s), rock climbing M(s)/W(s), rugby M/W, skiing (downhill) M/W, soccer M(s)/W(s), swimming and diving M(s)/W(s), track and field M(s)/W(s), volleyball M(s)/W(s). *Intramural sports:* badminton M/W, basketball M/W, cross-country running M/W, football M/W, gymnastics M/W, ice hockey M/W, racquetball M/W, rugby M/W, sailing M/W, skiing (cross-country) M/W, skiing (downhill) M/W, soccer M/W, softball M/W, squash M/W, swimming and diving M/W, table tennis M/W, tennis M/W, ultimate Frisbee M/W, volleyball M/W, water polo M/W, weight lifting M/W, wrestling M/W.

Standardized Tests *Required for some:* SAT or ACT plus Writing required of applicants following US curriculum.

Costs (2010–11) *Tuition:* province resident $4518 full-time, $151 per credit part-time; nonresident $704 per credit part-time; International tuition $21,118 full-time. Full-time tuition and fees vary according to course load, program, and student level. Part-time tuition and fees vary according to course load, program, and student level. *Required fees:* $605 full-time. *Room and board:* $8390. Room and board charges vary according to board plan, housing facility, and location. *Waivers:* senior citizens.

Financial Aid Of all full-time matriculated undergraduates who enrolled in 2008, 12,299 were judged to have need. 1,992 state and other part-time jobs (averaging $1561). In 2008, 6848 non-need-based awards were made. *Average financial aid package:* $10,938. *Average need-based loan:* $9066. *Average need-based gift aid:* $3219. *Average non-need-based aid:* $2495. *Financial aid deadline:* 9/15.

Applying *Options:* electronic application, deferred entrance. *Application fee:* $100 Canadian dollars. *Required:* high school transcript, minimum 2.6 GPA, English Language Admission Standard. *Required for some:* essay or personal statement. *Application deadlines:* 2/28 (freshmen), 2/28 (out-of-state freshmen), 2/28 (transfers). *Notification:* continuous (freshmen), continuous (out-of-state freshmen), continuous (transfers).

Freshman Application Contact Acting Associate Director, Undergraduate Admissions, The University of British Columbia, 1874 East Mall, V6T 1Z1, Canada. *Phone:* 604-822-8999. *Toll-free phone:* 877-292-1422. *Fax:* 604-822-9888. *Web site:* http://www.ubc.ca/.

The University of British Columbia–Okanagan

Kelowna, British Columbia, Canada

- **Province-supported** university, founded 2005
- **Urban** 260-acre campus with easy access to Kelowna
- **Endowment** $969.6 million
- **Coed** 6,362 undergraduate students, 77% full-time, 56% women, 44% men
- **Moderately difficult** entrance level, 31% of applicants were admitted

Undergraduates 4,893 full-time, 1,469 part-time. Students come from 19 provinces and territories; 74 other countries; 40% live on campus. *Retention:* 76% of full-time freshmen returned.

Freshmen *Admission:* 5,428 applied, 1,657 admitted, 1,570 enrolled.

Faculty *Total:* 315. *Student/faculty ratio:* 15:1.

Academics *Degrees:* certificates, diplomas, bachelor's, master's, doctoral-research/scholarship, and postbachelor's certificates. *Special study options:* academic remediation for entering students, advanced placement credit, cooperative education, distance learning, double majors, English as a second language, freshman honors college, honors programs, internships, off-campus study, part-time degree program, services for LD students, student-designed majors, study abroad, summer session for credit.

Computers on Campus Students can access the following: campus intranet, computer help desk, free student e-mail accounts, online (class) grades, online (class) registration, online (class) schedules. Campuswide network is available. 100% of college-owned or -operated housing units are wired for high-speed Internet access. Wireless service is available via entire campus.

Student Life *Housing options:* coed, men-only, women-only. Campus housing is university owned. Freshman applicants given priority for college housing. *Activities and organizations:* drama/theater group, student-run newspaper, radio station, choral group, Save the World, Student Leadership, UBCSUO Mountain Riders Ski and Snowboard Club, Model United Nations, UBCSUO Asian Students' Association. *Campus security:* 24-hour emergency response devices and patrols, controlled dormitory access, 24-hour desk attendants in residence halls. *Student services:* health clinic, personal/psychological counseling, women's center, legal services.

Athletics Member CIS. *Intercollegiate sports:* basketball M(s)/W(s), soccer M(s)/W(s), volleyball M(s)/W(s). *Intramural sports:* basketball M/W, cross-country running M/W, field hockey M/W, golf M/W, gymnastics M/W, ice hockey M/W, soccer M/W, tennis M/W, volleyball M/W.

Standardized Tests *Required for some:* SAT or ACT (for admission).

Costs (2010–11) *Tuition:* province resident $4518 full-time, $151 per credit part-time; nonresident $704 per credit part-time; International tuition $21,118 full-time. Full-time tuition and fees vary according to course load, program, and student level. Part-time tuition and fees vary according to course load, program, and student level. *Required fees:* $735 full-time. *Room and board:* $7785. Room and board charges vary according to board plan, housing facility, and location. *Waivers:* senior citizens.

Applying *Options:* electronic application, deferred entrance. *Application fee:* $100 Canadian dollars. *Required:* high school transcript, minimum 2.6 GPA. *Required for some:* essay or personal statement. *Application deadlines:* 2/28 (freshmen), 2/28 (out-of-state freshmen), 2/28 (transfers). *Notification:* continuous (freshmen), continuous (transfers).

Freshman Application Contact International Student Recruitment, The University of British Columbia–Okanagan, UC222 University Centre, 3333 University Way, Kelowna, BC V1V 1V7, Canada. *Phone:* 604-822-3014. *Fax:* 604-822-3599. *Web site:* http://www.ubc.ca/okanagan/welcome.html.

University of Calgary

Calgary, Alberta, Canada

Freshman Application Contact Kim Vandam, Associate Director of Admissions, University of Calgary, 2500 University Drive NW, Calgary, AB T2N 1N4, Canada. *Phone:* 403-220-3825. *E-mail:* vandam@ucalgary.ca. *Web site:* http://www.ucalgary.ca/.

University of Guelph

Guelph, Ontario, Canada

- **Province-supported** university, founded 1964
- **Urban** 1017-acre campus with easy access to Toronto
- **Coed** 16,878 undergraduate students
- **Moderately difficult** entrance level, 73% of applicants were admitted

Undergraduates Students come from 100 other countries; 24% live on campus. *Retention:* 91% of full-time freshmen returned.

Freshmen *Admission:* 21,327 applied, 15,516 admitted. *Average high school GPA:* 3.5.

Faculty *Total:* 869. *Student/faculty ratio:* 22:1.

Academics *Calendar:* trimesters. *Degrees:* certificates, diplomas, bachelor's, master's, doctoral-professional, and doctoral-research/scholarship. *Special study options:* academic remediation for entering students, accelerated degree program, advanced placement credit, cooperative education, distance learning, double majors, English as a second language, freshman honors college, honors programs, independent study, internships, off-campus study, part-time degree program, services for LD students, student-designed majors, study abroad, summer session for credit.

Computers on Campus 1,500 computers/terminals and 16,000 ports are available on campus for general student use. Students can access the following: campus intranet, computer help desk, free student e-mail accounts, online (class) registration. Campuswide network is available. 100% of college-owned or -operated housing units are wired for high-speed Internet access. Wireless service is available via entire campus.

Student Life *Housing options:* coed, men-only, women-only, cooperative, disabled students. Campus housing is university owned and is provided by a third party. Freshman campus housing is guaranteed. *Activities and organizations:* drama/theater group, student-run newspaper, radio station, choral group, Guelph Gryphon Athletics, Habitat for Humanity, Curtain Call Productions, West Indian Students Association, OXFAM-Guelph Chapter. *Campus security:* 24-hour emergency response devices and patrols, student patrols, late-night transport/escort service, controlled dormitory access, video camera surveillance in parking lots, alarms in women's locker room. *Student services:* health clinic, personal/psychological counseling, women's center, legal services.

Athletics Member CIS. *Intercollegiate sports:* baseball M, basketball M/W, crew M/W, cross-country running M/W, field hockey W, football M, golf M/W, ice hockey M/W, lacrosse M/W, rugby M/W, skiing (cross-country) M/W, soccer M/W, swimming and diving M/W, track and field M/W, volleyball M/W, wrestling M/W. *Intramural sports:* archery M(c)/W(c), badminton M/W, basketball M/W, cheerleading M(c)/W(c), fencing M(c)/W(c), football M/W, ice hockey M/W, lacrosse M(c)/W(c), rock climbing M(c)/W(c), soccer M/W, softball M/W, squash M(c)/W(c), tennis M/W, ultimate Frisbee M/W, volleyball M/W, water polo M(c)/W(c).

Standardized Tests *Required:* SAT or ACT (for admission).

Costs (2010–11) *Tuition:* province resident $5212 full-time, $1042 per credit part-time; International tuition $16,922 full-time. Full-time tuition and fees vary according to course level and program. Part-time tuition and fees vary according to course level, course load, and program. No tuition increase for student's term of enrollment. tuition varies by major. Contact institution for tuition information. *Required fees:* $1210 full-time, $40 per credit part-time, $390 per term part-time. *Room and board:* $9552; room only: $5002. Room and board charges vary according to board plan and housing facility. *Payment plan:* installment. *Waivers:* senior citizens and employees or children of employees.

Applying *Options:* electronic application, early admission. *Application fee:* $125 Canadian dollars. *Required:* high school transcript, minimum 3 GPA. *Required for some:* essay or personal statement. *Application deadlines:* 3/1 (freshmen), 5/1 (transfers). *Notification:* 5/25 (freshmen), continuous until 8/1 (transfers).

Freshman Application Contact Ms. Janette Hogan, Assistant Registrar, Admissions, University of Guelph, L-3 University Centre, Guelph, ON N1G 2W1, Canada. *Phone:* 519-824-4120 Ext. 58529. *Fax:* 519-766-9481. *E-mail:* jhogan@registrar.uoguelph.ca. *Web site:* http://www.uoguelph.ca/.

See page 1696 for the College Close-Up.

University of King's College

Halifax, Nova Scotia, Canada

- **Province-supported** 4-year, founded 1789, administratively affiliated with Dalhousie University
- **Urban** 4-acre campus
- **Endowment** $28,540
- **Coed**
- **Moderately difficult** entrance level

Faculty *Student/faculty ratio:* 21:1.

Academics *Calendar:* Canadian standard year. *Degree:* bachelor's.

Student Life *Campus security:* student patrols, late-night transport/escort service, controlled dormitory access.

Standardized Tests *Required for some:* SAT (for admission).

Costs (2010–11) *Tuition:* province resident $7232 Canadian dollars full-time, $201 Canadian dollars per credit hour part-time; nonresident $7232 Canadian dollars full-time; International tuition $14,492 Canadian dollars full-time. Full-time tuition and fees vary according to course load and program. Part-time tuition and fees vary according to course load and program. *Room and board:* $8741 Canadian dollars; room only: $5565 Canadian dollars. Room and board charges vary according to board plan and housing facility.

Applying *Options:* electronic application, early admission, early decision, deferred entrance. *Application fee:* $45 Canadian dollars. *Required:* high school transcript, minimum 3 GPA. *Required for some:* essay or personal statement, writing sample.

Freshman Application Contact Ms. Jill MacBeath, Admissions and Recruitment Coordinator, University of King's College, Registrar's Office, Halifax, NS B3H 3A1, Canada. *Phone:* 902-422-1271. *Fax:* 902-425-8183. *E-mail:* admissions@ukings.ns.ca. *Web site:* http://www.ukings.ca/.

University of Lethbridge

Lethbridge, Alberta, Canada

- **Province-supported** university, founded 1967
- **Urban** 576-acre campus
- **Endowment** $29.5 million
- **Coed** 7,850 undergraduate students, 88% full-time, 57% women, 43% men
- **Moderately difficult** entrance level, 55% of applicants were admitted

Undergraduates 6,946 full-time, 904 part-time. Students come from 13 provinces and territories; 59 other countries; 12% are from out of state; 10% live on campus. *Retention:* 74% of full-time freshmen returned.

Freshmen *Admission:* 2,525 applied, 1,394 admitted.

Faculty *Total:* 668, 90% full-time, 61% with terminal degrees. *Student/faculty ratio:* 12:1.

Academics *Calendar:* semesters. *Degrees:* certificates, diplomas, bachelor's, master's, doctoral-research/scholarship, post-master's, and postbachelor's certificates. *Special study options:* academic remediation for entering students, accelerated degree program, cooperative education, distance learning, double

majors, English as a second language, independent study, internships, off-campus study, part-time degree program, services for LD students, student-designed majors, study abroad, summer session for credit. *Unusual degree programs:* 3-2 education.

Computers on Campus 761 computers/terminals are available on campus for general student use. Students can access the following: computer help desk, free student e-mail accounts, online (class) grades, online (class) registration, online (class) schedules. Campuswide network is available. 100% of college-owned or -operated housing units are wired for high-speed Internet access. Wireless service is available via entire campus.

Student Life *Housing options:* coed. Campus housing is university owned. *Activities and organizations:* drama/theater group, student-run newspaper, radio station, choral group, Management Students Society, Inter-Varsity Christian Fellowship, Organization of Residence Students, Geography Club, Education Undergraduate Society. *Campus security:* 24-hour emergency response devices and patrols, student patrols, late-night transport/escort service, controlled dormitory access, video camera monitored entrances, hallways. *Student services:* health clinic, personal/psychological counseling, women's center.

Athletics Member CIS. *Intercollegiate sports:* cross-country running M(s)/W(s), ice hockey M(s)/W(s), soccer M(s)/W(s), swimming and diving M(s)/W(s), track and field M(s)/W(s), volleyball W. *Intramural sports:* archery M, fencing M(c)/W(c), football M/W, golf M/W, gymnastics M/W, ice hockey M/W, racquetball M/W, rugby M(c)/W(c), skiing (cross-country) M/W, skiing (downhill) M/W, soccer M/W, softball M/W, squash M/W, tennis M(c)/W(c), volleyball M/W, water polo M/W, weight lifting M/W.

Costs (2011–12) *Tuition:* province resident $4855 Canadian dollars full-time, $486 Canadian dollars per course part-time; nonresident $4855 Canadian dollars full-time, $486 Canadian dollars per course part-time; International tuition $10,990 Canadian dollars full-time. Full-time tuition and fees vary according to course load. Part-time tuition and fees vary according to course load. *Required fees:* $676 Canadian dollars full-time, $113 Canadian dollars per course part-time. *Room and board:* $7830 Canadian dollars; room only: $4664 Canadian dollars. Room and board charges vary according to board plan and housing facility. *Waivers:* employees or children of employees.

Applying *Options:* electronic application, deferred entrance. *Application fee:* $75 Canadian dollars. *Required:* high school transcript, minimum 2 GPA. *Required for some:* minimum 3 GPA, interview. *Application deadlines:* 6/1

UNIVERSITY OF GUELPH

For more information, contact:

Leanne Stillman
International Admissions, Admission Services
50 Stone Road East
Guelph, ON N1G 2W1
E-mail: www.uoguelph.ca

Web site: http://www.uoguelph.ca/

(freshmen), 6/1 (transfers). *Notification:* continuous (freshmen), continuous (transfers).

Freshman Application Contact Ms. Alice Miller, Assistant Registrar, University of Lethbridge, 4401 University Drive, Lethbridge, AB T1K 3M4, Canada. *Phone:* 403-320-5700. *Fax:* 403-329-5159. *E-mail:* inquiries@ uleth.ca. *Web site:* http://www.uleth.ca/.

University of Manitoba
Winnipeg, Manitoba, Canada

- **Province-supported** university, founded 1877
- **Suburban** 685-acre campus
- **Coed** 23,929 undergraduate students, 82% full-time, 56% women, 44% men
- **Moderately difficult** entrance level

Undergraduates 19,522 full-time, 4,407 part-time.
Faculty *Total:* 2,385.
Academics *Calendar:* 8-month academic year plus 6-week summer session. *Degrees:* certificates, diplomas, bachelor's, master's, doctoral-other, doctoral-professional, doctoral-research/scholarship, post-master's, and postbachelor's certificates. *Special study options:* academic remediation for entering students, accelerated degree program, adult/continuing education programs, advanced placement credit, cooperative education, distance learning, double majors, English as a second language, external degree program, honors programs, independent study, internships, off-campus study, part-time degree program, services for LD students, student-designed majors, study abroad, summer session for credit.
Computers on Campus Students can access the following: computer help desk, free student e-mail accounts, online (class) grades, online (class) registration, online (class) schedules. Campuswide network is available.
Student Life *Housing options:* coed. Campus housing is university owned. *Activities and organizations:* drama/theater group, student-run newspaper, radio station, choral group, national fraternities, national sororities. *Campus security:* 24-hour emergency response devices, student patrols, late-night transport/escort service. *Student services:* health clinic, personal/psychological counseling, women's center.
Athletics Member CIS. *Intercollegiate sports:* basketball M/W, cross-country running M/W, field hockey M/W, football M/W, gymnastics M/W, ice hockey M/W, swimming and diving M/W, track and field M/W, volleyball M/W. *Intramural sports:* basketball M/W, cross-country running M/W, fencing M/W, field hockey M/W, football M/W, golf M/W, gymnastics M/W, ice hockey M/W, lacrosse M/W, skiing (cross-country) M/W, skiing (downhill) M/W, soccer M/W, squash M/W, swimming and diving M/W, tennis M/W, track and field M/W, volleyball M/W, wrestling M/W.
Financial Aid Of all full-time matriculated undergraduates who enrolled in 2009, 50 state and other part-time jobs (averaging $900).
Applying *Options:* electronic application, early admission. *Application fee:* $65 Canadian dollars. *Required:* high school transcript.
Freshman Application Contact Mr. Peter Dueck, Director of Enrollment Services, University of Manitoba, Winnipeg, MB R3T 2N2, Canada. *Phone:* 204-474-6382. *Web site:* http://www.umanitoba.ca/.

University of New Brunswick Fredericton
Fredericton, New Brunswick, Canada

- **Province-supported** university, founded 1785
- **Urban** 7100-acre campus
- **Endowment** $116.0 million
- **Coed** 9,191 undergraduate students, 87% full-time, 54% women, 46% men
- **Moderately difficult** entrance level, 79% of applicants were admitted

Undergraduates 7,957 full-time, 1,234 part-time. Students come from 13 provinces and territories; 71 other countries; 19% are from out of state; 20% live on campus. *Retention:* 72% of full-time freshmen returned.
Freshmen *Admission:* 3,695 applied, 2,907 admitted.
Faculty *Total:* 641, 89% full-time.
Academics *Calendar:* Canadian standard year. *Degrees:* bachelor's, master's, and doctoral-research/scholarship. *Special study options:* accelerated degree program, adult/continuing education programs, advanced placement credit, cooperative education, distance learning, double majors, English as a second language, external degree program, honors programs, independent study, internships, off-campus study, part-time degree program, services for LD students, student-designed majors, study abroad, summer session for credit.
Computers on Campus 1,400 computers/terminals are available on campus for general student use. Students can access the following: campus intranet, computer help desk, free student e-mail accounts, online (class) grades, online (class) registration, online (class) schedules. Campuswide network is available.

100% of college-owned or -operated housing units are wired for high-speed Internet access. Wireless service is available via classrooms, computer centers, computer labs, learning centers, libraries, student centers.
Student Life *Housing options:* coed, men-only, women-only, disabled students. Campus housing is university owned. Freshman campus housing is guaranteed. *Activities and organizations:* drama/theater group, student-run newspaper, radio station, choral group. *Campus security:* 24-hour emergency response devices and patrols, student patrols, late-night transport/escort service, controlled dormitory access. *Student services:* health clinic, personal/psychological counseling, women's center, legal services.
Athletics Member CIS. *Intercollegiate sports:* basketball M/W, cross-country running M/W, soccer M/W, swimming and diving M/W, volleyball W, wrestling M/W. *Intramural sports:* badminton M/W, baseball M/W, basketball M/W, cheerleading M/W, crew M/W, fencing M/W, field hockey W, ice hockey M/W, rock climbing M/W, rugby M/W, soccer M/W, swimming and diving M/W, volleyball M/W.
Standardized Tests *Required for some:* SAT (for admission).
Costs (2010–11) *Tuition:* province resident $5482 full-time, $548 per term part-time; International tuition $11,912 full-time. Full-time tuition and fees vary according to program. Part-time tuition and fees vary according to course load. *Required fees:* $698 full-time, $33 per term part-time. *Room and board:* $7864. Room and board charges vary according to board plan. *Payment plan:* installment. *Waivers:* employees or children of employees.
Financial Aid Of all full-time matriculated undergraduates who enrolled in 2007, 123 state and other part-time jobs (averaging $1264). *Financial aid deadline:* 5/15.
Applying *Options:* electronic application, early admission, deferred entrance. *Application fee:* $45 Canadian dollars. *Required:* high school transcript. *Required for some:* essay or personal statement, 1 letter of recommendation, interview. *Application deadlines:* 3/31 (freshmen), 3/31 (transfers). *Notification:* continuous until 8/31 (freshmen), continuous until 8/31 (transfers).
Freshman Application Contact University of New Brunswick Fredericton, PO Box 4400, Fredericton, NB E3B 5A3, Canada. *Phone:* 506-453-4865. *Web site:* http://www.unb.ca/.

University of New Brunswick Saint John
Saint John, New Brunswick, Canada

- **Province-supported** comprehensive, founded 1964
- **Urban** 250-acre campus
- **Coed**
- **Moderately difficult** entrance level

Undergraduates 5% live on campus.
Academics *Calendar:* Canadian standard year. *Degrees:* certificates, diplomas, bachelor's, master's, doctoral-other, and postbachelor's certificates. *Special study options:* academic remediation for entering students, accelerated degree program, adult/continuing education programs, advanced placement credit, cooperative education, distance learning, double majors, English as a second language, honors programs, independent study, internships, off-campus study, part-time degree program, services for LD students, student-designed majors, study abroad, summer session for credit.
Computers on Campus 100 computers/terminals are available on campus for general student use. Students can access the following: campus intranet, computer help desk, free student e-mail accounts, online (class) grades, online (class) registration, online (class) schedules. Campuswide network is available.
Student Life *Housing options:* coed. Campus housing is university owned. *Activities and organizations:* drama/theater group, student-run newspaper, radio station, choral group, Business Administration Society, OPTAMUS, International Student Association, Chinese Cultural Association, Muslim Student Association. *Campus security:* 24-hour emergency response devices and patrols, student patrols, late-night transport/escort service, controlled dormitory access. *Student services:* personal/psychological counseling, women's center.
Athletics *Intercollegiate sports:* badminton M/W, basketball M/W, crew M/W, cross-country running M/W, fencing M/W, ice hockey M/W, rugby M/W, soccer M/W, volleyball M/W. *Intramural sports:* badminton M/W, basketball M/W, fencing M/W, golf M/W, soccer M/W, table tennis M/W, tennis M/W, volleyball M/W.
Standardized Tests *Required:* SAT (for admission).
Costs (2010–11) *Tuition:* province resident $5482 full-time. Full-time tuition and fees vary according to program. *Required fees:* $699 full-time. *Room and board:* Room and board charges vary according to board plan and housing facility. *Payment plan:* installment.
Financial Aid Of all full-time matriculated undergraduates who enrolled in 2009, 140 state and other part-time jobs (averaging $500).
Applying *Options:* electronic application, early admission, deferred entrance. *Application fee:* $45 Canadian dollars. *Required:* high school transcript. *Application deadlines:* rolling (freshmen), 3/31 (out-of-state freshmen), rolling

(transfers). *Notification:* continuous until 8/31 (freshmen), continuous (out-of-state freshmen), continuous until 8/31 (transfers).
Freshman Application Contact University of New Brunswick Saint John, PO Box 5050, Saint John, NB E2L 4L5, Canada. *Web site:* http://www.unb.ca/.

University of Northern British Columbia

Prince George, British Columbia, Canada

Freshman Application Contact Mr. Grant Kerr, Assistant Registrar, Admissions, University of Northern British Columbia, Office of the Registrar, 3333 University Way, Prince George, BC V2N 4Z9, Canada. *Phone:* 250-960-6347. *Fax:* 250-960-6330. *E-mail:* registrar-info@unbc.ca. *Web site:* http://www.unbc.ca/.

University of Ottawa

Ottawa, Ontario, Canada

- **Province-supported** university, founded 1848, administratively affiliated with Saint-Paul University (Ottawa, Ontario)
- **Urban** 43-hectare campus with easy access to Ottawa-Gatineau
- **Endowment** $164.6 million
- **Coed** 33,917 undergraduate students, 83% full-time, 61% women, 39% men
- **Moderately difficult** entrance level, 61% of applicants were admitted

Undergraduates 28,005 full-time, 5,912 part-time. Students come from 13 provinces and territories; 152 other countries; 20% are from out of state; 9% live on campus. *Retention:* 86% of full-time freshmen returned.
Freshmen *Admission:* 34,980 applied, 21,370 admitted. *Average high school GPA:* 3.27.
Faculty *Total:* 2,123, 60% full-time. *Student/faculty ratio:* 23:1.
Academics *Calendar:* semesters. *Degrees:* certificates, diplomas, bachelor's, master's, doctoral-research/scholarship, and postbachelor's certificates. *Special study options:* academic remediation for entering students, advanced placement credit, cooperative education, distance learning, double majors, English as a second language, honors programs, internships, off-campus study, part-time degree program, services for LD students, study abroad, summer session for credit. *Unusual degree programs:* 3-2 law, education.
Computers on Campus 1,540 computers/terminals are available on campus for general student use. Students can access the following: computer help desk, free student e-mail accounts, online (class) grades, online (class) registration, online (class) schedules, wireless connection available on campus. Campus-wide network is available. 100% of college-owned or -operated housing units are wired for high-speed Internet access. Wireless service is available via entire campus.
Student Life *Housing options:* coed, disabled students. Campus housing is university owned. Freshman campus housing is guaranteed. *Activities and organizations:* drama/theater group, student-run newspaper, radio station, choral group, Student Federation of the University of Ottawa, Graduate Students Association, national fraternities, national sororities. *Campus security:* 24-hour emergency response devices and patrols, student patrols, late-night transport/escort service, controlled dormitory access. *Student services:* health clinic, personal/psychological counseling, women's center, legal services.
Athletics Member CIS. *Intercollegiate sports:* badminton M(c)/W(c), baseball M(c)/W(c), basketball M(s)/W(s), cheerleading M(c)/W(c), crew M(c)/W(c), cross-country running M(s)/W(s), equestrian sports M(c)/W(c), fencing M(c)/W(c), football M(s), golf M(c)/W(c), ice hockey M(s)/W(s), rugby W(s), soccer M(s)(c)/W(s), swimming and diving M(s)/W(s), track and field M(s)/W(s), ultimate Frisbee M(c)/W(c), volleyball M(c)/W(s), water polo M(c)/W(c). *Intramural sports:* basketball M/W, football M, ice hockey M/W, soccer M/W, ultimate Frisbee M/W, volleyball M/W.
Standardized Tests *Required for some:* SAT or ACT required for American citizens.
Costs (2010–11) *One-time required fee:* $290. *Tuition:* province resident $5187 full-time, $206 per credit part-time; nonresident $613 per credit part-time; International tuition $15,815 full-time. Full-time tuition and fees vary according to program and student level. Part-time tuition and fees vary according to program. *Required fees:* $629 full-time, $109 per term part-time. *Room and board:* $6416; room only: $4316. Room and board charges vary according to board plan and housing facility. *Waivers:* employees or children of employees.
Financial Aid Of all full-time matriculated undergraduates who enrolled in 2009, 1,313 state and other part-time jobs (averaging $3000). *Financial aid deadline:* 1/31.
Applying *Options:* electronic application, early admission, deferred entrance. *Application fee:* $165 Canadian dollars. *Required:* high school transcript, minimum 3 GPA. *Required for some:* interview. *Application deadline:* 6/1 (freshmen). *Notification:* continuous until 8/30 (freshmen).

Freshman Application Contact Ms. Emilie Bertrand, University of Ottawa, 550 Cumberland Street, PO Box 450, Station A, Ottawa, ON K1N 6N5, Canada. *Phone:* 613-562-5800 Ext. 1593. *Fax:* 613-562-5790. *E-mail:* cpharand@uottawa.ca. *Web site:* http://www.uottawa.ca/.

University of Phoenix–Vancouver Campus

Burnaby, British Columbia, Canada

Freshman Application Contact Ms. Audra McQuarie, Registrar/Executive Director, University of Phoenix–Vancouver Campus, 4035 South Riverpoint Parkway, Mail Stop CF-L101, Phoenix, AZ 85040. *Phone:* 480-557-6151. *Toll-free phone:* 800-776-4867 (in-state); 800-228-7240 (out-of-state). *Fax:* 480-643-3068. *E-mail:* audra.mcquarie@phoenix.edu. *Web site:* http://www.phoenix.edu/.

University of Prince Edward Island

Charlottetown, Prince Edward Island, Canada

Freshman Application Contact University of Prince Edward Island, 550 University Avenue, Charlottetown, PE C1A 4P3, Canada. *Phone:* 902-566-0634. *Web site:* http://www.upei.ca/.

University of Regina

Regina, Saskatchewan, Canada

- **Province-supported** university, founded 1974
- **Urban** 445-acre campus
- **Endowment** $26.6 million
- **Coed** 10,625 undergraduate students, 75% full-time, 61% women, 39% men
- **Minimally difficult** entrance level, 85% of applicants were admitted

Undergraduates 7,958 full-time, 2,667 part-time. Students come from 13 provinces and territories; 91 other countries; 5% are from out of state; 9% transferred in; 10% live on campus. *Retention:* 76% of full-time freshmen returned.
Freshmen *Admission:* 2,465 applied, 2,086 admitted, 1,298 enrolled. *Average high school GPA:* 3.5.
Faculty *Total:* 546, 100% full-time, 70% with terminal degrees. *Student/faculty ratio:* 17:1.
Academics *Calendar:* semesters. *Degrees:* certificates, diplomas, bachelor's, master's, doctoral-research/scholarship, and postbachelor's certificates. *Special study options:* academic remediation for entering students, adult/continuing education programs, advanced placement credit, cooperative education, distance learning, double majors, English as a second language, honors programs, independent study, internships, off-campus study, part-time degree program, services for LD students, student-designed majors, study abroad, summer session for credit.
Computers on Campus 193 computers/terminals and 1,200 ports are available on campus for general student use. Students can access the following: campus intranet, computer help desk, free student e-mail accounts, online (class) grades, online (class) registration, online (class) schedules. Campus-wide network is available. 100% of college-owned or -operated housing units are wired for high-speed Internet access. Wireless service is available via entire campus.
Student Life *Housing options:* disabled students. Campus housing is university owned. *Activities and organizations:* drama/theater group, student-run newspaper, television station, choral group, Business Administration Students' Society, Education Students' Society, Engineering Students Society, Chinese Students and Scholars Association, Luther Student Association. *Campus security:* 24-hour emergency response devices and patrols, late-night transport/escort service, controlled dormitory access, crime prevention assistance, CCTV, card access and some alarm monitoring. *Student services:* health clinic, personal/psychological counseling, women's center.
Athletics Member NAIA, CIS. *Intercollegiate sports:* basketball M(s)/W(s), cross-country running M(s)/W(s), football M(s), ice hockey M(s)/W(s), soccer W(s), swimming and diving M(s)/W(s), track and field M(s)/W(s), volleyball M(s)/W(s), wrestling M(s)/W(s). *Intramural sports:* badminton M/W, basketball M/W, cheerleading M(c)/W(c), football M, soccer M/W, softball M/W(c), tennis M/W, ultimate Frisbee M/W, volleyball M/W, water polo M/W.
Standardized Tests *Required for some:* SAT or ACT (for admission), SAT Subject Tests (for admission).
Costs (2011–12) *Tuition:* province resident $5059 Canadian dollars full-time, $147 Canadian dollars per credit hour part-time; nonresident $147 Canadian dollars per credit hour part-time; International tuition $13,879 Canadian dollars full-time. Full-time tuition and fees vary according to course load and program. Part-time tuition and fees vary according to course load and program. *Required fees:* $384 Canadian dollars full-time, $132 Canadian dollars per

term part-time. *Room and board:* $8088 Canadian dollars; room only: $5588 Canadian dollars. Room and board charges vary according to board plan and housing facility. *Waivers:* senior citizens and employees or children of employees.

Applying *Options:* electronic application, early admission, early action, deferred entrance. *Application fee:* $100 Canadian dollars. *Required:* high school transcript, minimum 2.3 GPA. *Required for some:* essay or personal statement, 1 letter of recommendation, interview, portfolio, audition. *Application deadlines:* 7/1 (freshmen), 7/1 (transfers), 3/15 (early action).

Freshman Application Contact University of Regina, 3737 Wascana Parkway, Regina, SK S4S 0A2, Canada. *Phone:* 306-585-4942. *Toll-free phone:* 800-664-4756. *Web site:* http://www.uregina.ca/.

University of Saskatchewan
Saskatoon, Saskatchewan, Canada

- **Province-supported** university, founded 1907
- **Urban** 1865-acre campus
- **Coed** 16,590 undergraduate students

Faculty *Total:* 1,119.

Academics *Calendar:* Canadian standard year. *Degrees:* certificates, diplomas, bachelor's, master's, doctoral-professional, doctoral-research/scholarship, and postbachelor's certificates. *Special study options:* accelerated degree program, advanced placement credit, cooperative education, distance learning, double majors, English as a second language, honors programs, independent study, internships, off-campus study, part-time degree program, services for LD students, study abroad, summer session for credit.

Computers on Campus Students can access the following: computer help desk, free student e-mail accounts, online (class) grades, online (class) registration, online (class) schedules, student portal. 100% of college-owned or -operated housing units are wired for high-speed Internet access. Wireless service is available via entire campus.

Student Life *Housing options:* coed. Campus housing is university owned. *Activities and organizations:* drama/theater group, student-run newspaper, choral group. *Campus security:* 24-hour emergency response devices and patrols, student patrols, late-night transport/escort service, controlled dormitory access. *Student services:* health clinic, personal/psychological counseling, women's center, legal services.

Athletics Member CIS. *Intercollegiate sports:* basketball M/W, cross-country running M/W, football M, ice hockey M/W, soccer M/W, track and field M/W, volleyball M/W, wrestling M/W(c). *Intramural sports:* badminton M/W, basketball M/W, football M/W, ice hockey M/W, soccer M/W, ultimate Frisbee M/W, volleyball M/W.

Standardized Tests *Recommended:* scores sometimes used for home-educated students.

Costs (2011–12) *Tuition:* province resident $178 Canadian dollars per credit part-time; nonresident $178 Canadian dollars per credit part-time. Full-time tuition and fees vary according to course load and program. Part-time tuition and fees vary according to course load and program. *Room and board:* Room and board charges vary according to board plan, housing facility, and location. *Payment plan:* installment. *Waivers:* senior citizens and employees or children of employees.

Financial Aid *Financial aid deadline:* 3/15.

Applying *Options:* electronic application, early admission. *Application fee:* $90 Canadian dollars. *Required:* high school transcript. *Required for some:* essay or personal statement, interview. *Application deadlines:* 5/1 (freshmen), 5/1 (transfers). *Notification:* continuous (freshmen), continuous (transfers).

Freshman Application Contact University of Saskatchewan, 105 Administration Place, Saskatoon, SK S7N 5A2, Canada. *Phone:* 306-966-5788. *Web site:* http://www.usask.ca/.

University of the Fraser Valley
Abbotsford, British Columbia, Canada

Freshman Application Contact Ms. Robin Smith, Admissions Coordinator, University of the Fraser Valley, 33844 King Road, Abbotsford, BC V2S 7M8, Canada. *Phone:* 604-504-7441 Ext. 4540. *Toll-free phone:* 808-504-7441. *Fax:* 604-853-0138. *E-mail:* reginfo@ucfv.ca. *Web site:* http://www.ufv.ca/.

University of Toronto
Toronto, Ontario, Canada

- **Province-supported** university, founded 1827
- **Urban** 714-hectare campus
- **Endowment** $1.3 billion
- **Coed**
- **Very difficult** entrance level

Faculty *Student/faculty ratio:* 24:1.

Academics *Calendar:* Canadian standard year. *Degrees:* certificates, diplomas, bachelor's, master's, and doctoral-research/scholarship.

Student Life *Campus security:* 24-hour emergency response devices and patrols, student patrols, late-night transport/escort service.

Athletics Member CIS.

Standardized Tests *Required:* SAT and SAT Subject Tests or ACT (for admission).

Costs (2010–11) *Tuition:* province resident $5216 Canadian dollars full-time; nonresident $5216 Canadian dollars full-time; International tuition $23,478 Canadian dollars full-time. Full-time tuition and fees vary according to course level, course load, and program. Part-time tuition and fees vary according to course load. *Required fees:* $1200 Canadian dollars full-time. *Room and board:* $12,000 Canadian dollars; room only: $7000 Canadian dollars. Room and board charges vary according to board plan, housing facility, and location.

Applying *Options:* deferred entrance. *Application fee:* $115 Canadian dollars. *Required:* high school transcript. *Required for some:* interview.

Freshman Application Contact University of Toronto, Toronto, ON M5S 1A1, Canada. *Phone:* 416-978-2190. *Fax:* 416-978-7022. *E-mail:* admissions.help@utoronto.ca. *Web site:* http://www.utoronto.ca/uoft.html.

University of Victoria
Victoria, British Columbia, Canada

Freshman Application Contact Mr. Bruno Rocca, Student Recruitment Director, University of Victoria, PO Box 1700, STN CSC, Victoria, BC V8W 2Y2, Canada. *Phone:* 250-721-8121 Ext. 8109. *Fax:* 250-721-6225. *E-mail:* admit@uvic.ca. *Web site:* http://www.uvic.ca/.

University of Waterloo
Waterloo, Ontario, Canada

- **Province-supported** university, founded 1957
- **Suburban** 1000-acre campus with easy access to Toronto
- **Coed** 23,276 undergraduate students, 96% full-time, 43% women, 57% men
- **Moderately difficult** entrance level, 50% of applicants were admitted

Undergraduates 22,330 full-time, 946 part-time. Students come from 115 other countries; 26% live on campus. *Retention:* 88% of full-time freshmen returned.

Freshmen *Admission:* 41,952 applied, 20,794 admitted.

Faculty *Total:* 1,888, 55% full-time.

Academics *Calendar:* trimesters. *Degrees:* certificates, diplomas, bachelor's, master's, doctoral-other, doctoral-professional, and postbachelor's certificates. *Special study options:* academic remediation for entering students, accelerated degree program, advanced placement credit, cooperative education, distance learning, double majors, English as a second language, honors programs, independent study, internships, off-campus study, part-time degree program, services for LD students, student-designed majors, study abroad, summer session for credit.

Computers on Campus 6,000 computers/terminals are available on campus for general student use. Students can access the following: computer help desk, free student e-mail accounts, online (class) grades, online (class) registration, online (class) schedules. Campuswide network is available. 100% of college-owned or -operated housing units are wired for high-speed Internet access. Wireless service is available via entire campus.

Student Life *Housing options:* coed, men-only, women-only. Campus housing is university owned. Freshman campus housing is guaranteed. *Activities and organizations:* drama/theater group, student-run newspaper, radio station, choral group, marching band, national fraternities, national sororities. *Campus security:* 24-hour emergency response devices and patrols, student patrols, late-night transport/escort service. *Student services:* health clinic, personal/psychological counseling, women's center, legal services.

Athletics Member CIS. *Intercollegiate sports:* badminton M/W, baseball M, basketball M/W, cheerleading M/W, cross-country running M/W, field hockey M, football M, golf M/W, ice hockey M/W, rugby M/W, skiing (cross-country) M/W, soccer M/W, squash M, swimming and diving M/W, tennis M/W, track and field M/W, volleyball M/W. *Intramural sports:* archery M(c)/W(c), badminton M(c)/W(c), baseball M/W, basketball M/W, crew M(c)/W(c), equestrian sports M(c)/W(c), fencing M(c)/W(c), golf M(c)/W(c), ice hockey M/W, racquetball M(c)/W(c), rock climbing M(c)/W(c), skiing (cross-country) M(c)/W(c), skiing (downhill) M(c)/W(c), soccer M(c)/W(c), squash M(c)/W(c), swimming and diving M(c)/W(c), table tennis M(c)/W(c), tennis M/W, ultimate Frisbee M(c)/W(c), volleyball M/W, water polo M(c)/W(c), weight lifting M(c)/W(c).

Standardized Tests *Required for some:* SAT or ACT (for admission), SAT Subject Tests (for admission).

Costs (2010–11) *Tuition:* province resident $5200 full-time; International tuition $18,100 full-time. Full-time tuition and fees vary according to course load, degree level, location, and program. Part-time tuition and fees vary according to course load, degree level, location, and program. tuition varies by major. Contact institution for tuition information. *Room and board:* $7800. Room and board charges vary according to board plan, housing facility, and location. *Payment plan:* installment. *Waivers:* minority students, children of alumni, adult students, senior citizens, and employees or children of employees.

Applying *Options:* electronic application, early admission, deferred entrance. *Application fee:* $110 Canadian dollars. *Required:* high school transcript. *Required for some:* essay or personal statement, minimum 3 GPA, interview. *Application deadline:* 3/31 (freshmen). *Notification:* 5/30 (freshmen), continuous (transfers).

Freshman Application Contact University of Waterloo, 200 University Avenue West, Waterloo, ON N2L 3G1, Canada. *Phone:* 519-888-4567 Ext. 32265. *Web site:* http://www.uwaterloo.ca/.

The University of Western Ontario
London, Ontario, Canada

- **Province-supported** university, founded 1878, administratively affiliated with Brescia University College, Huron University College, King's University College
- **Suburban** 496-hectare campus
- **Coed** 28,543 undergraduate students, 91% full-time, 56% women, 44% men
- **Very difficult** entrance level, 55% of applicants were admitted

Undergraduates 25,963 full-time, 2,580 part-time. Students come from 13 provinces and territories; 116 other countries; 6% are from out of state; 1% transferred in; 19% live on campus. *Retention:* 93% of full-time freshmen returned.

Freshmen *Admission:* 32,163 applied, 17,817 admitted, 4,905 enrolled. *Average high school GPA:* 3.9.

Faculty *Total:* 1,381, 100% full-time. *Student/faculty ratio:* 20:1.

Academics *Calendar:* Canadian standard year. *Degrees:* certificates, diplomas, bachelor's, master's, and doctoral-other. *Special study options:* academic remediation for entering students, accelerated degree program, adult/continuing education programs, advanced placement credit, cooperative education, distance learning, double majors, English as a second language, honors programs, independent study, internships, off-campus study, part-time degree program, services for LD students, student-designed majors, study abroad, summer session for credit.

Computers on Campus 414 computers/terminals are available on campus for general student use. Students can access the following: campus intranet, computer help desk, free student e-mail accounts, online (class) grades, online (class) registration, online (class) schedules. Campuswide network is available. 100% of college-owned or -operated housing units are wired for high-speed Internet access. Wireless service is available via classrooms, computer centers, computer labs, learning centers, libraries, student centers.

Student Life *Housing options:* coed, disabled students. Campus housing is university owned. Freshman campus housing is guaranteed. *Activities and organizations:* drama/theater group, student-run newspaper, radio and television station, choral group, marching band, Purple Spur Society, Pre-Medical Society, Western Investment Club, Western Snowboarding Federation (WSF), Canadian Asian International Students' Association, national fraternities, national sororities. *Campus security:* 24-hour emergency response devices and patrols, student patrols, late-night transport/escort service, controlled dormitory access, Campus Community Police, SERT: Student Emergency Response Team, Western Foot Patrol. *Student services:* health clinic, personal/psychological counseling, legal services.

Athletics Member CIS. *Intercollegiate sports:* badminton M(s)/W(s), baseball M(s), basketball M(s)/W(s), cheerleading M/W, crew M(s)/W(s), cross-country running M(s)/W(s), equestrian sports M(c)/W(c), fencing M(s)/W(s), field hockey W(s), football M(s), golf M(s)/W(s), ice hockey M(s)/W(s), lacrosse M(c)/W(c), rugby M(s)/W(s), soccer M(s)/W(s), softball W(c), squash M(s)/W(s), swimming and diving M(s)/W(s), tennis M(s)/W(s), track and field M(s)/W(s), volleyball M(s)/W(s), water polo M(s), wrestling M(s)/W(s). *Intramural sports:* badminton M/W, basketball M/W, equestrian sports M(c)/W(c), fencing M(c)/W(c), football M/W, ice hockey M/W, racquetball M/W, skiing (downhill) M(c)/W(c), soccer M/W, softball M/W, squash M(c)/W(c), swimming and diving M(c)/W(c), table tennis M(c)/W(c), tennis M/W, ultimate Frisbee M/W, volleyball M/W, water polo M/W.

Standardized Tests *Required:* SAT or ACT (for admission).

Costs (2010–11) *Tuition:* province resident $5159 Canadian dollars full-time; $1032 Canadian dollars per course part-time; nonresident $3106 Canadian dollars per course part-time; International tuition $15,530 Canadian dollars full-time. Full-time tuition and fees vary according to program and student level. Part-time tuition and fees vary according to course load, location, program, and student level. *Required fees:* $994 Canadian dollars full-time, $141 Canadian dollars per course part-time. *Room and board:* $8770 Canadian dollars; room only: $5425 Canadian dollars. Room and board charges vary according to board plan, housing facility, and location. *Payment plans:* installment,

deferred payment. *Waivers:* senior citizens and employees or children of employees.

Financial Aid Of all full-time matriculated undergraduates who enrolled in 2008, 1,419 state and other part-time jobs (averaging $1809).

Applying *Options:* electronic application, deferred entrance. *Application fee:* $125 Canadian dollars. *Required:* high school transcript, minimum 3.5 GPA. *Application deadlines:* 6/1 (freshmen), 5/15 (out-of-state freshmen), 6/1 (transfers). *Notification:* continuous (freshmen), continuous (out-of-state freshmen).

Freshman Application Contact Undergraduate Recruitment and Admissions, The University of Western Ontario, The University of Western Ontario, Western Student Services Building, Room 3140, London, ON N6A 3K7, Canada. *Phone:* 519-661-2100. *Fax:* 519-661-3710. *E-mail:* reg-admissions@uwo.ca. *Web site:* http://www.uwo.ca/.

University of Windsor
Windsor, Ontario, Canada

- **Province-supported** university, founded 1857
- **Urban** 125-acre campus with easy access to Detroit
- **Endowment** $56.0 million
- **Coed**
- **Moderately difficult** entrance level

Faculty *Student/faculty ratio:* 21:1.

Academics *Calendar:* semesters. *Degrees:* certificates, bachelor's, master's, doctoral-professional, doctoral-research/scholarship, and postbachelor's certificates.

Student Life *Campus security:* 24-hour emergency response devices and patrols, student patrols, late-night transport/escort service, controlled dormitory access.

Athletics Member NAIA, CIS.

Standardized Tests *Required for some:* SAT or ACT (for admission), SAT and SAT Subject Tests or ACT (for admission), SAT Subject Tests (for admission).

Costs (2010–11) *Tuition:* province resident $5910 Canadian dollars full-time; International tuition $16,396 Canadian dollars full-time. Full-time tuition and fees vary according to course load, degree level, location, and program. Part-time tuition and fees vary according to course load, degree level, location, and program. *Room and board:* $8206 Canadian dollars; room only: $4692 Canadian dollars. Room and board charges vary according to board plan and housing facility.

Financial Aid *Of all full-time matriculated undergraduates who enrolled in 2009,* 450 state and other part-time jobs (averaging $1166). *Financial aid deadline:* 6/15.

Applying *Options:* electronic application, early admission. *Application fee:* $60 Canadian dollars. *Required:* high school transcript, minimum 3 GPA. *Required for some:* essay or personal statement, minimum 3.3 GPA, 1 letter of recommendation, interview.

Freshman Application Contact Ms. Charlene Yates, Manager of Undergraduate Admissions, University of Windsor, Office of the Registrar, 401 Sunset Avenue, Windsor, ON N9B 3P4, Canada. *Phone:* 519-253-3000 Ext. 3315. *Toll-free phone:* 800-864-2860. *Fax:* 519-971-3653. *E-mail:* registr@uwindsor.ca. *Web site:* http://www.uwindsor.ca/.

See page 1752 for the College Close-Up.

The University of Winnipeg
Winnipeg, Manitoba, Canada

Director of Admissions Mr. Colin Russell, Registrar, The University of Winnipeg, 515 Portage Avenue, Winnipeg, MB R3B 2E9, Canada. *Phone:* 204-786-9776. *Fax:* 204-786-8656. *E-mail:* admissions@uwinnipeg.ca. *Web site:* http://www.uwinnipeg.ca/.

Vancouver Island University
Nanaimo, British Columbia, Canada

Freshman Application Contact Ms. Leslie Peterson, Admissions Manager, Vancouver Island University, 900 Fifth Street, Nanaimo, BC V9R 5S5, Canada. *Phone:* 250-740-6355. *Fax:* 250-740-6479. *Web site:* http://www.viu.ca/.

Vanguard College
Edmonton, Alberta, Canada

Director of Admissions Tim Bratton, Recruitment Director, Vanguard College, 11617 106 Avenue, NW, Edmonton, AB T5H 0S1, Canada. *Phone:* 780-452-0808 Ext. 231. *Toll-free phone:* 866-222-0808. *Fax:* 780-452-5803. *E-mail:* tbratton@vanguardcollege.com. *Web site:* http://www.vanguardcollege.com/.

Western Christian College

Regina, Saskatchewan, Canada

- **Independent** 4-year, founded 1957, affiliated with Church of Christ, administratively affiliated with Faulkner University
- **Urban** campus
- **Coed**

Academics *Calendar:* semesters. *Degree:* certificates and bachelor's.
Student Life *Housing:* college housing not available. *Activities and organizations:* drama/theater group, choral group.
Standardized Tests *Required for some:* SAT or ACT (for admission).
Costs (2011–12) *Tuition:* $235 per credit hour part-time. Full-time tuition and fees vary according to course load. Part-time tuition and fees vary according to course load. *Payment plan:* installment. *Waivers:* employees or children of employees.
Applying *Options:* electronic application. *Application fee:* $50 Canadian dollars. *Required:* essay or personal statement, high school transcript. *Required for some:* interview.
Freshman Application Contact Ms. Trish Thompson, Registrar, Western Christian College, 100-400 Fourth Avenue, Regina, SK S4T 0H8, Canada. *Phone:* 306-545-1515 Ext. 500. *Fax:* 306-352-2198. *E-mail:* registrar@westernchristian.ca. *Web site:* http://www.westernchristian.ca/.

Wilfrid Laurier University

Waterloo, Ontario, Canada

- **Province-supported** comprehensive, founded 1911
- **Urban** 40-acre campus with easy access to Toronto
- **Coed** 15,896 undergraduate students, 88% full-time, 58% women, 42% men
- **Minimally difficult** entrance level, 70% of applicants were admitted

Undergraduates 13,954 full-time, 1,942 part-time. Students come from 57 other countries; 25% live on campus. *Retention:* 89% of full-time freshmen returned.
Freshmen *Admission:* 24,597 applied, 17,219 admitted, 4,337 enrolled.
Faculty *Total:* 516. *Student/faculty ratio:* 25:1.
Academics *Calendar:* semesters Canadian standard year. *Degrees:* certificates, diplomas, bachelor's, master's, and doctoral-research/scholarship. *Special study options:* academic remediation for entering students, accelerated degree program, adult/continuing education programs, advanced placement credit, cooperative education, distance learning, double majors, English as a second language, honors programs, internships, off-campus study, part-time degree program, services for LD students, study abroad, summer session for credit. *Unusual degree programs:* 3-2 education.
Computers on Campus 383 computers/terminals are available on campus for general student use. Students can access the following: campus intranet, computer help desk, free student e-mail accounts, online (class) grades, online (class) registration, online (class) schedules. Campuswide network is available. 100% of college-owned or -operated housing units are wired for high-speed Internet access. Wireless service is available via entire campus.
Student Life *Housing options:* coed, men-only, women-only, disabled students. Campus housing is university owned. Freshman campus housing is guaranteed. *Activities and organizations:* drama/theater group, student-run newspaper, radio station, Habitat for Humanity of WLU, Laurier Musical Theatre, East Meets West, Laurier SOS, Laurier Ski and Snowboarding Club, national fraternities, national sororities. *Campus security:* 24-hour emergency response devices and patrols, student patrols, late-night transport/escort service, controlled dormitory access. *Student services:* health clinic, personal/psychological counseling, women's center, legal services.
Athletics Member CIS. *Intercollegiate sports:* baseball M, basketball M/W, cheerleading M/W, cross-country running M/W, football M, golf M, ice hockey M/W, lacrosse W, rugby M/W, soccer M/W, swimming and diving M/W, volleyball M/W. *Intramural sports:* badminton M/W, basketball M/W, football M/W, ice hockey M/W, lacrosse M(c), rock climbing M/W, skiing (cross-country) M(c)/W(c), skiing (downhill) M(c)/W(c), soccer M/W, softball M/W, squash M/W, swimming and diving M/W, tennis M/W, ultimate Frisbee M/W, volleyball M/W, water polo M/W, weight lifting W.
Standardized Tests *Required for some:* SAT or ACT (for admission).
Costs (2011–12) *Tuition:* province resident $5214 Canadian dollars full-time; International tuition $18,869 Canadian dollars full-time. Full-time tuition and fees vary according to course load, degree level, location, program, and student level. Part-time tuition and fees vary according to course load, degree level, location, program, and student level. *Required fees:* $964 Canadian dollars full-time. *Room and board:* $8047 Canadian dollars; room only: $4641 Canadian dollars. Room and board charges vary according to board plan, housing facility, and location. *Waivers:* senior citizens and employees or children of employees.
Financial Aid *Financial aid deadline:* 1/15.
Applying *Options:* electronic application, early admission, early decision, deferred entrance. *Application fee:* $120 Canadian dollars. *Required:* high school transcript. *Required for some:* essay or personal statement, interview, audition for music programs. *Application deadlines:* 5/1 (freshmen), 5/1 (out-of-state freshmen), 5/1 (transfers). *Notification:* continuous until 5/25 (freshmen), continuous (out-of-state freshmen), continuous (transfers).
Freshman Application Contact Wilfrid Laurier University, 75 University Avenue West, Waterloo, ON N2L 3C5, Canada. *Phone:* 519-884-0710 Ext. 6099. *Web site:* http://www.wlu.ca/.

York University

Toronto, Ontario, Canada

- **Province-supported** university, founded 1959
- **Urban** 457-acre campus
- **Endowment** $245.0 million
- **Coed**
- **Moderately difficult** entrance level

Faculty *Student/faculty ratio:* 19:1.
Academics *Calendar:* semesters. *Degrees:* certificates, diplomas, bachelor's, master's, doctoral-research/scholarship, post-master's, and postbachelor's certificates.
Student Life *Campus security:* 24-hour emergency response devices and patrols, student patrols, late-night transport/escort service, controlled dormitory access.
Athletics Member CIS.
Standardized Tests *Required:* SAT or ACT (for admission).
Costs (2010–11) *Tuition:* province resident $6003 Canadian dollars full-time; International tuition $16,403 Canadian dollars full-time. Full-time tuition and fees vary according to course load and program. Part-time tuition and fees vary according to course load and program. *Room and board:* $7956 Canadian dollars; room only: $4456 Canadian dollars. Room and board charges vary according to board plan and housing facility.
Financial Aid *Financial aid deadline:* 3/15.
Applying *Options:* electronic application, deferred entrance. *Application fee:* $210 Canadian dollars. *Required:* high school transcript, minimum 3 GPA, audition for fine arts, supplemental application for business. *Required for some:* essay or personal statement, interview.
Freshman Application Contact Ms. Amber Holliday, International Recruitment Officer, York University, N301 Bennett Centre for Student Services, 4700 Keele Street, Toronto, ON M3J 1P3, Canada. *Phone:* 416-736-2100 Ext. 60595. *Fax:* 416-736-5741. *E-mail:* aburkett@yorku.ca. *Web site:* http://www.yorku.ca/.

INTERNATIONAL

BULGARIA

American University in Bulgaria

Blagoevgrad, Bulgaria

- **Independent** comprehensive, founded 1991
- **Small-town** campus with easy access to Sofia
- **Endowment** $17.0 million
- **Coed** 1,040 undergraduate students, 100% full-time, 53% women, 48% men
- **Very difficult** entrance level, 65% of applicants were admitted

Undergraduates 1,040 full-time. Students come from 38 other countries; 96% live on campus. *Retention:* 97% of full-time freshmen returned.
Freshmen *Admission:* 636 applied, 413 admitted, 302 enrolled. *Average high school GPA:* 3.5. *Test scores:* SAT critical reading scores over 500: 60%; SAT math scores over 500: 100%; SAT critical reading scores over 600: 10%; SAT math scores over 600: 70%; SAT math scores over 700: 19%.
Faculty *Total:* 73, 70% full-time, 73% with terminal degrees. *Student/faculty ratio:* 18:1.
Academics *Calendar:* semesters. *Degrees:* bachelor's and master's. *Special study options:* advanced placement credit, double majors, honors programs, independent study, internships, services for LD students, study abroad.

Computers on Campus 289 computers/terminals are available on campus for general student use. Students can access the following: computer help desk, free student e-mail accounts, online (class) grades, online (class) registration, online (class) schedules. Campuswide network is available. Wireless service is available via entire campus.

Student Life *Housing:* on-campus residence required through senior year. *Options:* disabled students. Campus housing is university owned. Freshman campus housing is guaranteed. *Activities and organizations:* drama/theater group, student-run newspaper, radio station, choral group, Computer Science Student Union, Debate Club, Better Community Club, AUBG Broadway Performance Club, Business Club. *Campus security:* 24-hour patrols. *Student services:* health clinic, personal/psychological counseling.

Athletics *Intramural sports:* basketball M/W, cheerleading W(c), equestrian sports M(c)/W(c), football M(c), gymnastics W, soccer M(c), softball M/W, volleyball M/W.

Standardized Tests *Required:* SAT or ACT (for admission). *Required for some:* TOEFL, IELTS, or ESOL for students whose primary language is not English.

Costs (2011–12) *Comprehensive fee:* $11,520 includes full-time tuition ($9300), mandatory fees ($250), and room and board ($1970). Part-time tuition: $388 per credit hour. *College room only:* $1170. Room and board charges vary according to housing facility. *Waivers:* employees or children of employees.

Applying *Options:* electronic application, early admission, deferred entrance. *Application fee:* $25. *Required:* essay or personal statement, high school transcript, minimum 3 GPA, 3 letters of recommendation. *Application deadlines:* 6/1 (freshmen), 6/1 (transfers).

Freshman Application Contact American University in Bulgaria, Blagoevgrad 2700, Bulgaria. *Phone:* 359-73 888 235. *Web site:* http://www.aubg.bg/.

CAYMAN ISLANDS

International College of the Cayman Islands

Newlands, Cayman Islands

Freshman Application Contact International College of the Cayman Islands, PO Box 136, Savannah Post Office, Newlands, Grand Cayman, Cayman Islands. *Phone:* 345-325-6454. *Web site:* http://www.icci.edu.ky/.

EGYPT

The American University in Cairo

Cairo, Egypt

Freshman Application Contact Ms. Randa Kamel, Director of Enrollment Services, The American University in Cairo, The Office of Student Affairs, 420 Fifth Avenue, 3rd Floor, New York, NY 10018-2728. *Phone:* 212-797-5551. *E-mail:* randa_k@aucnyo.edu. *Web site:* http://www.aucegypt.edu/.

FRANCE

The American University of Paris

Paris, France

- **Independent** comprehensive, founded 1962
- **Urban** campus
- **Endowment** $680,752
- **Coed** 736 undergraduate students, 94% full-time, 69% women, 31% men
- **Moderately difficult** entrance level, 79% of applicants were admitted

Undergraduates 693 full-time, 43 part-time. Students come from 39 states and territories; 69 other countries; 6% transferred in. *Retention:* 71% of full-time freshmen returned.

Freshmen *Admission:* 497 applied, 394 admitted, 142 enrolled.

Faculty *Total:* 124, 54% full-time, 62% with terminal degrees. *Student/faculty ratio:* 13:1.

Academics *Calendar:* semesters. *Degrees:* bachelor's and master's. *Special study options:* advanced placement credit, cooperative education, double majors, English as a second language, honors programs, independent study, internships, off-campus study, part-time degree program, student-designed majors, study abroad, summer session for credit.

Computers on Campus 100 computers/terminals are available on campus for general student use. Students can access the following: campus intranet, computer help desk, free student e-mail accounts, online (class) grades, online (class) registration, online (class) schedules. Campuswide network is available. Wireless service is available via entire campus.

Student Life *Housing:* college housing not available. *Options:* Campus housing is provided by a third party. *Activities and organizations:* drama/theater group, student-run newspaper, radio and television station, choral group, AUP Student Media (ASM) - Print, Video, Audio, White Mask (Theatre), Student Senate, Student Government Association, Sports Association. *Campus security:* 24-hour emergency response devices. *Student services:* personal/psychological counseling.

Athletics *Intramural sports:* basketball M/W, equestrian sports M/W, football M, golf M/W, racquetball M/W, soccer M/W, squash M/W, tennis M/W, volleyball M/W.

Standardized Tests *Required for some:* SAT or ACT (for admission), TOEFL, TOEIC or IELTS for students whose primary language is not English.

Costs (2011–12) *Tuition:* 24,490 euros full-time. Full-time tuition and fees vary according to course load. Part-time tuition and fees vary according to course load. *Room only:* Room and board charges vary according to board plan and housing facility. *Payment plan:* installment. *Waivers:* children of alumni and employees or children of employees.

Financial Aid Of all full-time matriculated undergraduates who enrolled in 2008, 218 applied for aid, 218 were judged to have need. In 2008, 17 non-need-based awards were made. *Average percent of need met:* 42%. *Average financial aid package:* $13,900. *Average need-based loan:* $5100. *Average need-based gift aid:* $11,600. *Average non-need-based aid:* $1500.

Applying *Options:* electronic application, deferred entrance. *Application fee:* $65. *Required:* essay or personal statement, high school transcript, 2 letters of recommendation. *Recommended:* minimum 3 GPA, interview. *Application deadlines:* 3/15 (freshmen), 3/15 (transfers). *Notification:* continuous (freshmen), continuous (transfers).

Freshman Application Contact International Admissions Office, The American University of Paris, 6 rue du Colonel Combes, Paris 75007, France. *Phone:* -+33 1 40 62 07 20. *Fax:* +33 1 47 05 34 32. *E-mail:* admissions@aup.edu. *Web site:* http://www.aup.edu/.

Parsons Paris School of Art + Design

Paris, France

Freshman Application Contact Sara Krauskopf, Parsons Paris School of Art + Design, 14 rue Letellier, F-75015 Paris, France. *Phone:* -331 4577 40 17. *Fax:* 331 4577 44 12. *E-mail:* sara.krauskopf@parsons-paris.com. *Web site:* http://www.parsons-paris.com/.

Schiller International University

Paris, France

Freshman Application Contact Ms. Kamala Dontamsetti, Associate Director of Admissions, Schiller International University, 300 East Bay Drive, Largo, FL 33770. *Phone:* 727-736-5082 Ext. 234. *Fax:* 727-734-0347. *E-mail:* admissions@schiller.edu. *Web site:* http://www.schiller.edu/.

GERMANY

Schiller International University

Heidelberg, Germany

Freshman Application Contact Ms. Kamala Dontamsetti, Associate Director of Admissions, Schiller International University, 300 East Bay Drive, Largo, FL 33770. *Phone:* 727-736-5082 Ext. 234. *Fax:* 727-734-0359. *E-mail:* kamala_dontamsetti@schiller.edu. *Web site:* http://www.schiller.edu/.

GREECE

American College of Thessaloniki
Pylea, Greece

- **Independent** comprehensive, founded 1886, administratively affiliated with Anatolia College
- **Suburban** 40-acre campus with easy access to Thessaloniki
- **Endowment** $3.7 million
- **Coed** 433 undergraduate students, 78% full-time, 57% women, 43% men
- **Minimally difficult** entrance level, 93% of applicants were admitted

Undergraduates 336 full-time, 97 part-time. Students come from 24 other countries; 0.2% transferred in; 35% live on campus. *Retention:* 73% of full-time freshmen returned.

Freshmen *Admission:* 94 applied, 87 admitted, 60 enrolled. *Average high school GPA:* 3.

Faculty *Total:* 39, 38% full-time, 49% with terminal degrees. *Student/faculty ratio:* 16:1.

Academics *Calendar:* semesters. *Degrees:* certificates, bachelor's, and master's. *Special study options:* academic remediation for entering students, accelerated degree program, advanced placement credit, double majors, English as a second language, independent study, internships, part-time degree program, services for LD students, study abroad, summer session for credit.

Computers on Campus 180 computers/terminals and 20 ports are available on campus for general student use. Students can access the following: campus intranet, computer help desk, free student e-mail accounts, online (class) grades, online (class) schedules. Campuswide network is available. 100% of college-owned or -operated housing units are wired for high-speed Internet access. Wireless service is available via classrooms, computer centers, learning centers, libraries, student centers.

Student Life *Housing options:* coed. Campus housing is university owned and leased by the school. Freshman applicants given priority for college housing. *Activities and organizations:* student-run radio station, InterACT, Community Service, Field Trip Club, scuba diving club, Photography Club. *Campus security:* 24-hour patrols. *Student services:* personal/psychological counseling.

Athletics *Intercollegiate sports:* basketball M/W, soccer M/W, table tennis M/W, tennis M/W, volleyball M/W. *Intramural sports:* basketball M, sailing M/W, soccer M/W, table tennis M/W, tennis M/W, volleyball M/W.

Costs (2010–11) *Tuition:* 8250 euros full-time, 275 euros per credit hour part-time. Part-time tuition and fees vary according to course load. *Required fees:* 100 euros full-time, 50 euros per term part-time. *Room only:* 4800 euros. Room and board charges vary according to housing facility. *Waivers:* employees or children of employees.

Applying *Options:* electronic application, deferred entrance. *Application fee:* 95 euros. *Required:* high school transcript, proficiency in English. *Required for some:* essay or personal statement, interview. *Recommended:* minimum 2 GPA. *Application deadlines:* rolling (freshmen), rolling (transfers). *Notification:* continuous (freshmen), continuous (transfers).

Freshman Application Contact Mrs. Roula Lebetli, Director of Admissions, American College of Thessaloniki, PO Box 21021, Pylea, Thessaloniki 55510, Greece. *Phone:* -30 2310-398239. *Fax:* 30 2310-398389. *E-mail:* admissions@act.edu. *Web site:* http://www.act.edu/.

The American University of Athens
Athens, Greece

Director of Admissions Ms. Thalia Poulos, Director of Admissions, The American University of Athens, 4 Sohou Street and Kifissias Avenue, Neo Psychiko, GR-115 25 Athens, Greece. *Phone:* -30 210-725-9301. *E-mail:* admissions@aua.edu. *Web site:* http://www.aua.edu/.

DEREE - The American College of Greece
Athens, Greece

- **Independent** comprehensive, founded 1875
- **Suburban** 60-acre campus
- **Coed** 2,954 undergraduate students, 53% full-time, 51% women, 49% men
- **Moderately difficult** entrance level, 70% of applicants were admitted

Undergraduates 1,558 full-time, 1,396 part-time. Students come from 39 other countries; 1% live on campus. *Retention:* 80% of full-time freshmen returned.

Freshmen *Admission:* 959 applied, 667 admitted. *Average high school GPA:* 3.18. *Test scores:* SAT critical reading scores over 500: 61%; SAT math scores over 500: 63%; SAT critical reading scores over 600: 6%; SAT math scores over 600: 8%.

Faculty *Total:* 201, 71% full-time, 43% with terminal degrees. *Student/faculty ratio:* 11:1.

Academics *Calendar:* 4-1-4. *Degrees:* bachelor's, master's, and postbachelor's certificates. *Special study options:* academic remediation for entering students, accelerated degree program, adult/continuing education programs, advanced placement credit, double majors, English as a second language, freshman honors college, independent study, internships, part-time degree program, services for LD students, student-designed majors, study abroad, summer session for credit.

Computers on Campus 280 computers/terminals are available on campus for general student use. Students can access the following: computer help desk, free student e-mail accounts, online (class) grades, online (class) registration, online (class) schedules. 100% of college-owned or -operated housing units are wired for high-speed Internet access. Wireless service is available via computer labs, dorm rooms, libraries.

Student Life *Housing options:* coed. Campus housing is university owned. *Activities and organizations:* drama/theater group, student-run newspaper, choral group, Debate Club, MUN (Model United Nations), SAB (Students Activity Board), Environmental Club, DEREE College Ambassadors. *Campus security:* 24-hour emergency response devices and patrols. *Student services:* health clinic, personal/psychological counseling.

Athletics *Intercollegiate sports:* basketball M/W, soccer M, swimming and diving M/W, tennis M/W, volleyball M/W, water polo M. *Intramural sports:* basketball M/W, football M/W, rock climbing M/W, skiing (downhill) M/W, soccer M, softball M/W, swimming and diving M/W, table tennis M/W, tennis M/W, track and field M/W, volleyball M/W, water polo M.

Financial Aid *Financial aid deadline:* 9/1.

Applying *Options:* electronic application, deferred entrance. *Required:* essay or personal statement, high school transcript, minimum 2 GPA, 1 letter of recommendation, interview. *Application deadlines:* rolling (freshmen), rolling (transfers). *Notification:* 7/25 (freshmen), 7/25 (transfers).

Freshman Application Contact Ms. Nancy Parkes, DEREE - The American College of Greece, 6 Gravias Street, GR-153-42 Aghia Paraskevi, Athens, Greece. *Phone:* -30 210-600-9800 Ext. 1472. *E-mail:* dereeadm@hol.gr. *Web site:* http://www.acg.edu/.

IRELAND

Institute of Public Administration
Dublin, Ireland

Director of Admissions Dr. Denis O'Brien, Registrar, Institute of Public Administration, 57-61 Lansdowne Road, Dublin 4, Ireland. *Phone:* 353-1-240-3600. *Fax:* 353-1-668-9135. *E-mail:* undergrad@ipa.ie. *Web site:* http://www.ipa.ie/.

ITALY

The American University of Rome
Rome, Italy

Freshman Application Contact Ms. Mara Nisdeo, Director of Admissions, The American University of Rome, Via Pietro Roselli 4, Rome 00153, Italy. *Phone:* -39 06-58330919 Ext. 206. *Toll-free phone:* 888-791-8327. *E-mail:* admissions@aur.edu. *Web site:* http://www.aur.edu/.

John Cabot University
Rome, Italy

- **Independent** 4-year, founded 1972
- **Urban** campus with easy access to Rome
- **Coed**
- **Moderately difficult** entrance level

Faculty *Student/faculty ratio:* 18:1.

Academics *Calendar:* semesters. *Degrees:* associate and bachelor's.

Student Life *Campus security:* 24-hour emergency response devices.

Standardized Tests *Required for some:* SAT or ACT (for admission).

Applying *Options:* electronic application, early decision, deferred entrance. *Application fee:* $50. *Required:* essay or personal statement, high school transcript, 2 letters of recommendation. *Recommended:* minimum 2.7 GPA, interview.

Freshman Application Contact Ms. Jill Peacock, Director of Admissions, John Cabot University, Via della Lungara 233, Roma 00165, Italy. *Phone:* -39

06 681 9121. *Toll-free phone:* 866-227-0112. *Fax:* 39 06 589 7429. *E-mail:* admissions@johncabot.edu. *Web site:* http://www.johncabot.edu/.

See page 1350 for the College Close-Up.

KENYA

United States International University
Nairobi, Kenya

- **Independent** comprehensive, founded 1977, part of Alliant International University
- **Urban** 120-acre campus
- **Coed** 4,028 undergraduate students, 91% full-time, 54% women, 46% men
- **Moderately difficult** entrance level, 77% of applicants were admitted

Undergraduates 3,650 full-time, 378 part-time.

Freshmen *Admission:* 833 applied, 644 admitted, 427 enrolled. *Average high school GPA:* 2.79.

Faculty *Total:* 219, 39% full-time, 34% with terminal degrees. *Student/faculty ratio:* 30:1.

Academics *Calendar:* trimesters. *Degrees:* bachelor's and master's. *Special study options:* adult/continuing education programs, off-campus study, part-time degree program, summer session for credit.

Student Life *Housing options:* Campus housing is university owned and is provided by a third party. Freshman applicants given priority for college housing. *Campus security:* 24-hour patrols.

Standardized Tests *Required for some:* TOEFL for students whose high school language of instruction was not English.

Costs (2010–11) *Comprehensive fee:* 321,828 Kenyan shillings includes full-time tuition (162,888 Kenyan shillings), mandatory fees (13,900 Kenyan shillings), and room and board (145,040 Kenyan shillings). Full-time tuition and fees vary according to course load and program. Part-time tuition: 6787 Kenyan shillings per unit. Part-time tuition and fees vary according to course load and program. *College room only:* 52,920 Kenyan shillings. *Payment plan:* installment. *Waivers:* children of alumni and employees or children of employees.

Applying *Options:* deferred entrance. *Application fee:* 50 Kenyan shillings. *Required:* high school transcript, minimum 2.5 GPA. *Required for some:* interview. *Application deadlines:* rolling (freshmen), rolling (transfers). *Notification:* continuous (freshmen), continuous (transfers).

Freshman Application Contact United States International University, PO Box 14634, Thika Road Kasarani, Nairobi 00800, Kenya. *Phone:* 254-02-3606563. *Web site:* http://www.usiu.ac.ke/.

LEBANON

American University of Beirut
Beirut, Lebanon

- **Independent** university, founded 1866
- **Urban** 61-acre campus with easy access to Beirut
- **Endowment** $417.6 million
- **Coed** 6,424 undergraduate students, 96% full-time, 47% women, 53% men
- **36%** of applicants were admitted

Undergraduates 6,183 full-time, 241 part-time. Students come from 73 other countries; 0.7% transferred in; 15% live on campus. *Retention:* 92% of full-time freshmen returned.

Freshmen *Admission:* 4,258 applied, 1,516 admitted, 1,523 enrolled. *Average high school GPA:* 3. *Test scores:* SAT critical reading scores over 500: 49%; SAT math scores over 500: 97%; SAT writing scores over 500: 64%; SAT critical reading scores over 600: 9%; SAT math scores over 600: 77%; SAT writing scores over 600: 15%; SAT critical reading scores over 700: 1%; SAT math scores over 700: 27%; SAT writing scores over 700: 1%.

Faculty *Total:* 744, 62% full-time, 72% with terminal degrees. *Student/faculty ratio:* 13:1.

Academics *Calendar:* semesters. *Degrees:* certificates, diplomas, bachelor's, master's, doctoral-other, doctoral-professional, and doctoral-research/scholarship. *Special study options:* academic remediation for entering students, advanced placement credit, English as a second language, honors programs, independent study, internships, services for LD students, study abroad, summer session for credit.

Computers on Campus 1,851 computers/terminals and 1,500 ports are available on campus for general student use. Students can access the following: campus intranet, computer help desk, free student e-mail accounts, online (class) grades, online (class) registration, online (class) schedules. Campuswide network is available. 100% of college-owned or -operated housing units are wired for high-speed Internet access. Wireless service is available via entire campus.

Student Life *Housing:* on-campus residence required for freshman year. *Options:* men-only, women-only. Campus housing is university owned. Freshman campus housing is guaranteed. *Activities and organizations:* drama/theater group, student-run newspaper, choral group, Red Cross Club, Biology Society, Business Society, Music Club, Palestinian Cultural Club. *Campus security:* 24-hour emergency response devices and patrols, late-night transport/escort service, staff monitors entrance 24/7. *Student services:* health clinic, personal/psychological counseling, legal services.

Athletics *Intercollegiate sports:* basketball M/W, cross-country running M/W, rugby M, skiing (downhill) M/W, soccer M/W, squash M/W, swimming and diving M/W, table tennis M/W, tennis M/W, track and field M/W, volleyball M/W, water polo M. *Intramural sports:* basketball M/W, cross-country running M/W, racquetball M/W, soccer M/W, squash M/W, swimming and diving M/W, table tennis M/W, tennis M/W, volleyball M/W, weight lifting M/W.

Standardized Tests *Required:* SAT (for admission). *Required for some:* SAT Subject Tests (for admission).

Costs (2010–11) *Tuition:* $13,082 full-time, $545 per credit part-time. Full-time tuition and fees vary according to course load, degree level, and program. Part-time tuition and fees vary according to course load, degree level, and program. *Required fees:* $499 full-time. *Room only:* $2954. Room and board charges vary according to housing facility and location. *Payment plan:* deferred payment. *Waivers:* employees or children of employees.

Applying *Options:* electronic application, early admission, early action, deferred entrance. *Application fee:* $50. *Required:* high school transcript. *Required for some:* interview. *Recommended:* essay or personal statement. *Application deadlines:* 2/1 (freshmen), 4/30 (transfers), 11/30 (early action). *Notification:* 4/30 (freshmen), continuous until 6/30 (transfers), 1/31 (early action).

Freshman Application Contact Dr. Salim Kanaan, Director of Admissions Office, American University of Beirut, PO Box 11-0236, Riad El-Solh, 1107 2020, Lebanon. *Phone:* -961 1-374 374 Ext. 2592. *Fax:* 961 1-750 775. *E-mail:* admissions@aub.edu.lb. *Web site:* http://www.aub.edu.lb/.

Lebanese American University

Beirut, Lebanon

- **Private** comprehensive, founded 1835
- **Urban** 49-acre campus
- **Endowment** $249.5 million
- **Coed** 7,183 undergraduate students, 91% full-time, 47% women, 53% men
- **Moderately difficult** entrance level, 73% of applicants were admitted

Undergraduates 6,551 full-time, 632 part-time. Students come from 79 other countries; 21% are from out of state; 1% transferred in; 3% live on campus. *Retention:* 91% of full-time freshmen returned.

Freshmen *Admission:* 3,533 applied, 2,568 admitted, 1,553 enrolled. *Average high school GPA:* 2.84. *Test scores:* SAT critical reading scores over 500: 16%; SAT math scores over 500: 76%; SAT writing scores over 500: 28%; SAT critical reading scores over 600: 1%; SAT math scores over 600: 34%; SAT writing scores over 600: 3%; SAT math scores over 700: 4%.

Faculty *Total:* 608, 39% full-time, 43% with terminal degrees. *Student/faculty ratio:* 20:1.

Academics *Degrees:* certificates, diplomas, associate, bachelor's, master's, and doctoral-professional. *Special study options:* academic remediation for entering students, double majors, part-time degree program, services for LD students, study abroad, summer session for credit.

Computers on Campus 825 computers/terminals and 500 ports are available on campus for general student use. Students can access the following: campus intranet, computer help desk, free student e-mail accounts, online (class) grades, online (class) registration, online (class) schedules, online library book reservation. Campuswide network is available. 100% of college-owned or -operated housing units are wired for high-speed Internet access. Wireless service is available via entire campus.

Student Life *Housing options:* men-only, women-only, disabled students. Campus housing is university owned. Freshman applicants given priority for college housing. *Activities and organizations:* drama/theater group, student-run newspaper, choral group, Model United Nations, Social Work Club, Engineering and Pharmacy Students professional Clubs, UNESCO club, Lebanese Students Front Club. *Campus security:* 24-hour patrols, 24/7 security at Residence Halls. *Student services:* health clinic, personal/psychological counseling, women's center.

Athletics *Intercollegiate sports:* basketball M(s)/W(s), rugby M(s), soccer M(s)/W(s), swimming and diving M(s)/W(s), table tennis M(s)/W, tennis M/W(s), track and field M/W, volleyball M/W. *Intramural sports:* basketball M/W, skiing (downhill) M(c)/W(c), soccer M/W, swimming and diving M/W, table tennis M/W, tennis M/W, volleyball M/W.

Standardized Tests *Required:* SAT (for admission). *Required for some:* SAT Subject Tests (for admission).

Costs (2010–11) *Tuition:* Full-time tuition and fees vary according to course load and program. Part-time tuition and fees vary according to course load and program. Tuition and fees vary depending upon program. Please contact school directly for costs. *Room and board:* Room and board charges vary according to housing facility and location. *Payment plan:* deferred payment. *Waivers:* employees or children of employees.

Applying *Options:* electronic application, early admission, early action, deferred entrance. *Application fee:* $50. *Required:* high school transcript, Official High School Diploma, SAT I, Institutional English Test (English Entrance Exam EEE) or International TOFEL. *Application deadlines:* 7/31 (freshmen), 7/31 (out-of-state freshmen), 7/31 (transfers), 1/31 (early action). *Notification:* 4/1 (freshmen), 4/1 (out-of-state freshmen), 4/1 (transfers), 3/1 (early action).

Freshman Application Contact Lebanese American University, PO Box 13-5053, Beirut, Lebanon. *Phone:* -961 1 786456 Ext. 1162. *Web site:* http://www.lau.edu.lb/.

MEXICO

Alliant International University–México City

Mexico City, Mexico

- **Independent** comprehensive, founded 1970, part of Alliant International University
- **Urban** campus with easy access to Mexico City
- **Coed**
- **Moderately difficult** entrance level

Faculty *Student/faculty ratio:* 12:1.

Academics *Calendar:* semesters. *Degrees:* bachelor's and master's.

Standardized Tests *Recommended:* SAT or ACT (for admission).

Applying *Options:* electronic application, deferred entrance. *Application fee:* 500 Mexican pesos. *Required:* essay or personal statement, high school transcript, minimum 2 GPA, 1 letter of recommendation. *Required for some:* interview. *Recommended:* minimum 3 GPA.

Freshman Application Contact Alliant International University–México City, Hamburgo #115, Col. Juarez, Mexico D.F. 06600, Mexico. *Phone:* -52 5555257651. *E-mail:* mexicoadmissions@alliant.edu. *Web site:* http://www.alliant.edu/wps/wcm/connect/website/Home/Campuses/Mexico+City+Campus/.

Instituto Tecnológico y de Estudios Superiores de Monterrey, Campus Central de Veracruz

Córdoba, Mexico

Director of Admissions Ing. Luis Pablo Villareal, Registrar, Instituto Tecnológico y de Estudios Superiores de Monterrey, Campus Central de Veracruz, Avenida Eugenio Garza Sada 1, Apartado Postal 314, 94500 Córdoba, Veracruz, Mexico. *Phone:* -27-13-23-40 Ext. 123. *Web site:* http://www.ver.itesm.mx/.

Instituto Tecnológico y de Estudios Superiores de Monterrey, Campus Chiapas

Tuxtla Gutiérrez, Mexico

Director of Admissions Lic. Luis Enrique Cancino, Registrar, Instituto Tecnológico y de Estudios Superiores de Monterrey, Campus Chiapas, Carretera a Tapanatepec Km 149&746, Apartado Postal 312, 29000 Tuxtla Gutiérrez, Chiapas, Mexico. *Phone:* -96-15-1723. *Web site:* http://www.chs.itesm.mx/.

Instituto Tecnológico y de Estudios Superiores de Monterrey, Campus Chihuahua

Chihuahua, Mexico

Director of Admissions Ing. Juan Manuel Fernandez, Registrar, Instituto Tecnológico y de Estudios Superiores de Monterrey, Campus Chihuahua, Colegio Militar 4700, Colonia Nombre de Dios, Apartado Postal 728, 31300 Chihuahua, Chihuahua, Mexico. *Phone:* -14-17-48-58 Ext. 117. *Web site:* http://www.chi.itesm.mx/.

Instituto Tecnológico y de Estudios Superiores de Monterrey, Campus Ciudad de México

Ciudad de Mexico, Mexico

Freshman Application Contact Admissions Office, Instituto Tecnológico y de Estudios Superiores de Monterrey, Campus Ciudad de México, Calle del Puente #222 esquina con Periférico, 14380 Colonia Huipulco, Tlalpan, MDF, Mexico. *Phone:* -5-673-6488. *Web site:* http://www.ccm.itesm.mx/.

Instituto Tecnológico y de Estudios Superiores de Monterrey, Campus Ciudad Juárez

Ciudad Juárez, Mexico

Director of Admissions Lic. Alberto Trejo, Registrar, Instituto Tecnológico y de Estudios Superiores de Monterrey, Campus Ciudad Juárez, Boulevard Tomas Fernandez y Avenida A J Bermudez, Apartado Postal 3105-J, 32320 Ciudad Juárez, Chihuahua, Mexico. *Phone:* -16-17-88-07 Ext. 113. *Web site:* http://www.cdj.itesm.mx/.

Instituto Tecnológico y de Estudios Superiores de Monterrey, Campus Ciudad Obregón

Ciudad Obregón, Mexico

Director of Admissions Lic. Judith Almeida, Registrar, Instituto Tecnológico y de Estudios Superiores de Monterrey, Campus Ciudad Obregón, Dr Norman E Borlaug Km 14, Apartado Postal 662, 85000 Ciudad Obregón, Sonora, Mexico. *Phone:* -64-15-03-12. *Web site:* http://www.cob.itesm.mx/.

Instituto Tecnológico y de Estudios Superiores de Monterrey, Campus Colima

Colima, Mexico

Director of Admissions Lic. Manuel Perez Rivera, Registrar, Instituto Tecnológico y de Estudios Superiores de Monterrey, Campus Colima, Prolongacion Ignacio Sandoval s/n, Fraccionamiento Jardines de Vista Hermosa, Apartado Postal 190, 28010 Colima, Colima, Mexico. *Phone:* -33-12-53-39. *Web site:* http://www.col.itesm.mx/.

Instituto Tecnológico y de Estudios Superiores de Monterrey, Campus Cuernavaca

Temixco, Mexico

Director of Admissions Lic. Miguel Angel Machua, Registrar, Instituto Tecnológico y de Estudios Superiores de Monterrey, Campus Cuernavaca, Paseo de la Reforma 182-A, Colonia Lomas de Cuernavaca, 62000 Temixco, Morelos, Mexico. *Phone:* -73 18-49-57. *Web site:* http://www.cva.itesm.mx/.

Instituto Tecnológico y de Estudios Superiores de Monterrey, Campus Estado de México

Estado de Mexico, Mexico

Director of Admissions Prof. Jose de Jesus Molina, Registrar, Instituto Tecnológico y de Estudios Superiores de Monterrey, Campus Estado de México, Carretera Lago de Guadalupe Km. 3.5, Atizapan de Zaragoza, Estado de Mexico 52926, Mexico. *Phone:* -5-873-3600. *Web site:* http://www.cem.itesm.mx/.

Instituto Tecnológico y de Estudios Superiores de Monterrey, Campus Guadalajara

Zapopan, Mexico

Director of Admissions Ms. Janet Martell Sotomayor, Registration Director, Instituto Tecnológico y de Estudios Superiores de Monterrey, Campus Guadalajara, Avenida General Ramón Corona 2514, Colonia Nuevo Mexico, 45140 Zapopan, Jalisco, Mexico. *Phone:* -3-669-3006. *Web site:* http://www.gda.itesm.mx/.

Instituto Tecnológico y de Estudios Superiores de Monterrey, Campus Hidalgo

Pachuca, Mexico

Director of Admissions Lic. Lizbet Melo, Registrar, Instituto Tecnológico y de Estudios Superiores de Monterrey, Campus Hidalgo, Boulevard Felipe Angeles s/n al lado de la Unidad Deportiva, Apartado Postal 337, 42090 Pachuca, Hidalgo, Mexico. *Phone:* -714-25-00 Ext. 128. *Web site:* http://www.hgo.itesm.mx/.

Instituto Tecnológico y de Estudios Superiores de Monterrey, Campus Irapuato

Irapuato, Mexico

Director of Admissions Ing. Marcela Beltrán, Registrar, Instituto Tecnológico y de Estudios Superiores de Monterrey, Campus Irapuato, Paseo Mirador del Valle No. 445, Col. Villas de Irapuato, Apartado Postal 568, 36660 Irapuato, Guanajuato, Mexico. *Phone:* -46-230342. *Web site:* http://www.ira.itesm.mx/.

Instituto Tecnológico y de Estudios Superiores de Monterrey, Campus Laguna

Torreón, Mexico

Director of Admissions Ing. Aroldo Camargo Soto, Registrar, Instituto Tecnológico y de Estudios Superiores de Monterrey, Campus Laguna, Paseo del Tecnologico s/n Ampliacion La Rosita, Apartado Postal 506, 27250 Torreón, Coahuila, Mexico. *Phone:* -17-20-66-61 Ext. 23. *Web site:* http://www.lag.itesm.mx/.

Instituto Tecnológico y de Estudios Superiores de Monterrey, Campus León

León, Mexico

Director of Admissions Lic. Eddie Villegas, Registrar, Instituto Tecnológico y de Estudios Superiores de Monterrey, Campus León, Avenida Eugenio Garza Sada s/n Colonia Cerro Gordo, Apartado Postal 872, 37120 León, Guanajuato, Mexico. *Phone:* -47-17-10-00 Ext. 131. *Web site:* http://www.leo.itesm.mx/.

Instituto Tecnológico y de Estudios Superiores de Monterrey, Campus Mazatlán

Mazatlán, Mexico

Director of Admissions Ing. Martin Ley Urias, Registrar, Instituto Tecnológico y de Estudios Superiores de Monterrey, Campus Mazatlán, Carretera Mazatlan-Higueras, Km 3, Camino al Conchi, Apartado Postal 799, 82000 Mazatlán, Sinaloa, Mexico. *Phone:* -69-80-1143. *Web site:* http://www.maz.itesm.mx/.

Instituto Tecnológico y de Estudios Superiores de Monterrey, Campus Monterrey

Monterrey, Mexico

Director of Admissions Lic. Carlos Ordoñez, International Student Advisor, Instituto Tecnológico y de Estudios Superiores de Monterrey, Campus Monterrey, Avenida Eugenio Garza Sada 2501 Sur Colonia Tecnnologico, Sucursal de Correos J, 64849 Monterrey, Nuevo León, Mexico. *Phone:* -52 81 8328 4065 Ext. 3942. *Toll-free phone:* -52-81-83284065 (in-state); -52-81-83593293 (out-of-state). *Web site:* http://www.mty.itesm.mx/.

Instituto Tecnológico y de Estudios Superiores de Monterrey, Campus Querétaro

Santiago de Querétaro, Mexico

Director of Admissions Lic. Marco Vinicio Lopez, Registrar, Instituto Tecnológico y de Estudios Superiores de Monterrey, Campus Querétaro, Avenida Epigmenio González #500, Apartado Postal 37, 76130 Querétaro, Querétaro, Mexico. *Phone:* -42-17-38-25 Ext. 156. *Web site:* http://www.qro.itesm.mx/.

Instituto Tecnológico y de Estudios Superiores de Monterrey, Campus Saltillo

Saltillo, Mexico

Director of Admissions Lic. Esteban Ramos, Registrar, Instituto Tecnológico y de Estudios Superiores de Monterrey, Campus Saltillo, Prolongacion Juan de la Barrera 1241 Ote, Apartado Postal 539, 25270 Saltillo, Coahuila, Mexico. *Phone:* -84-15-06-90 Ext. 12. *Web site:* http://www.sal.itesm.mx/.

Instituto Tecnológico y de Estudios Superiores de Monterrey, Campus San Luis Potosí

San Luis Potosí, Mexico

Director of Admissions Ing. Consuelo Gonzalez, Registrar, Instituto Tecnológico y de Estudios Superiores de Monterrey, Campus San Luis Potosí, Avenida Robles 600, Colonia Jacarandas, Apartado Postal 1473 Suc E, 78140 San Luis Potosí, SLP, Mexico. *Phone:* -48 13-3441 Ext. 14. *Web site:* http://www.slp.itesm.mx/.

Instituto Tecnológico y de Estudios Superiores de Monterrey, Campus Sinaloa

Culiacán, Mexico

Director of Admissions Lic. Hugo Guerrero, Registrar, Instituto Tecnológico y de Estudios Superiores de Monterrey, Campus Sinaloa, Boulevard Culiacán 3773, Apartado Postal 69-F, 80800 Culiacán, Sinaloa, Mexico. *Phone:* -67-14-03-69. *Web site:* http://www.sin.itesm.mx/.

Instituto Tecnológico y de Estudios Superiores de Monterrey, Campus Sonora Norte

Hermosillo, Mexico

Director of Admissions Ing. Victor Eduardo Perez Orozco, Library and Admissions/Registration Director, Instituto Tecnológico y de Estudios Superiores de Monterrey, Campus Sonora Norte, Carretera Hermosillo-Nogales Km 9, Apartado Postal 216, 83000 Hermosillo, Sonora, Mexico. *Phone:* -62-15-52-05 Ext. 131. *Web site:* http://www.her.itesm.mx/.

Instituto Tecnológico y de Estudios Superiores de Monterrey, Campus Tampico

Altimira, Mexico

Director of Admissions Ing. Javier Ponce, Registrar, Instituto Tecnológico y de Estudios Superiores de Monterrey, Campus Tampico, Boulevard Petrocel Km 1.3, Corredor Industrial, Carretera Tampico-Mante, 89120 Altimira, Tamaulipas, Mexico. *Phone:* -126-4-19-79. *Web site:* http://www.itesm.edu/wps/portal?WCM_GLOBAL_CONTEXT=/migration/TAM2/Tampico.

Instituto Tecnológico y de Estudios Superiores de Monterrey, Campus Toluca

Toluca, Mexico

Director of Admissions Ing. Victor M. Martinez Orta, Registrar, Instituto Tecnológico y de Estudios Superiores de Monterrey, Campus Toluca, Ex-hacienda La Pila, 100 metros al norte de San Antonio Buenavista, 50252 Toluca, Estado de Mexico, Mexico. *Phone:* -72-74-11-92. *Web site:* http://www.tol.itesm.mx/.

Instituto Tecnológico y de Estudios Superiores de Monterrey, Campus Zacatecas

Zacatecas, Mexico

Director of Admissions Lic. de Lourdes Zorrilla, Business Affairs Director and Registrar, Instituto Tecnológico y de Estudios Superiores de Monterrey, Campus Zacatecas, Calzada Pedro Coronel #16, Frente al Club Bernades, Municipio de Guadalupe, 98000 Zacatecas, Zacatecas, Mexico. *Phone:* -49 23-00-40. *Web site:* http://www.zac.itesm.mx/.

Universidad de las Americas, A.C.

Mexico City, Mexico

Admissions Office Contact Universidad de las Americas, A.C., Calle de Puebla 223, Col. Roma, 06700 Mexico City, Mexico. *Web site:* http://www.udla.mx/.

Universidad de las Américas–Puebla

Puebla, Mexico

- **Independent** university, founded 1940
- **Suburban** 84-hectare campus with easy access to Puebla
- **Endowment** $38.7 million
- **Coed**
- **Moderately difficult** entrance level

Faculty *Student/faculty ratio:* 11:1.

Academics *Calendar:* semesters. *Degrees:* certificates, diplomas, associate, bachelor's, master's, and doctoral-research/scholarship.

Student Life *Campus security:* 24-hour emergency response devices and patrols.

Standardized Tests *Required for some:* SAT or ACT (for admission).

Costs (2010–11) *One-time required fee:* $630. *Comprehensive fee:* $16,500 includes full-time tuition ($11,200) and room and board ($5300). Full-time tuition and fees vary according to course load, degree level, and program. Part-time tuition: $1150 per course. Part-time tuition and fees vary according to course load, degree level, and program. No tuition increase for student's term of enrollment. *Required fees:* $160 per course part-time. *College room only:* $2950. Room and board charges vary according to housing facility.

Franklin College Switzerland
Sorengo, Switzerland

- **Independent** 4-year, founded 1969
- **Suburban** 10-acre campus with easy access to Milan, Italy
- **Endowment** $2.6 million
- **Coed** 450 undergraduate students, 98% full-time, 65% women, 35% men
- **Moderately difficult** entrance level, 65% of applicants were admitted

Undergraduates 442 full-time, 8 part-time. Students come from 36 states and territories; 62 other countries; 100% are from out of state; 3% transferred in; 81% live on campus. *Retention:* 58% of full-time freshmen returned.
Freshmen *Admission:* 607 applied, 396 admitted, 135 enrolled. *Average high school GPA:* 3.27. *Test scores:* SAT critical reading scores over 500: 95%; SAT math scores over 500: 88%; SAT writing scores over 500: 96%; ACT scores over 18: 100%; SAT critical reading scores over 600: 69%; SAT math scores over 600: 45%; SAT writing scores over 600: 55%; ACT scores over 24: 86%; SAT critical reading scores over 700: 14%; SAT math scores over 700: 4%; SAT writing scores over 700: 13%; ACT scores over 30: 34%.
Faculty *Total:* 50, 50% full-time, 56% with terminal degrees. *Student/faculty ratio:* 11:1.
Academics *Calendar:* semesters. *Degrees:* associate and bachelor's. *Special study options:* accelerated degree program, advanced placement credit, double majors, English as a second language, honors programs, independent study, internships, part-time degree program, study abroad, summer session for credit.
Computers on Campus 137 computers/terminals and 20 ports are available on campus for general student use. Students can access the following: campus intranet, computer help desk, free student e-mail accounts, online (class) grades, online (class) registration, online (class) schedules, Live@EDU sky-drive, Moodle, office on-line collaboration tools, LAN Storage space, student access to academic/financial records and portal available in student lounge and libraries. Campuswide network is available. 100% of college-owned or -operated housing units are wired for high-speed Internet access. Wireless service is available via entire campus.
Student Life *Housing:* on-campus residence required through sophomore year. *Options:* coed, women-only. Campus housing is university owned and leased by the school. Freshman campus housing is guaranteed. *Activities and organizations:* drama/theater group, student-run newspaper, Student Government Association, newspaper, Literary Society, Drama Society, Baobab Initiative. *Campus security:* 24-hour emergency response devices, student patrols, controlled dormitory access, late night patrols by professional security service personnel. *Student services:* health clinic, personal/psychological counseling.
Athletics *Intramural sports:* basketball M(c)/W(c), ice hockey M(c), skiing (downhill) M(c)/W(c), soccer M(c)/W(c), swimming and diving M(c), tennis M(c)/W(c), volleyball M(c)/W(c), water polo M(c).
Standardized Tests *Required:* SAT or ACT (for admission). *Recommended:* SAT Subject Tests (for admission).
Costs (2010–11) *Comprehensive fee:* $46,700 includes full-time tuition ($34,500), mandatory fees ($1400), and room and board ($10,800). Full-time tuition and fees vary according to program. Part-time tuition: $3050 per course. Part-time tuition and fees vary according to program. *Required fees:* $295 per term part-time. *College room only:* $7900. Room and board charges vary according to board plan and housing facility. *Payment plan:* deferred payment. *Waivers:* employees or children of employees.
Financial Aid Of all full-time matriculated undergraduates who enrolled in 2008, 164 applied for aid, 139 were judged to have need, 12 had their need fully met. In 2008, 88 non-need-based awards were made. *Average percent of need met:* 70%. *Average financial aid package:* $17,838. *Average need-based loan:* $4121. *Average need-based gift aid:* $13,717. *Average non-need-based aid:* $5843. *Financial aid deadline:* 3/15.
Applying *Options:* electronic application, early action, deferred entrance. *Application fee:* $90. *Required:* essay or personal statement, high school transcript, minimum 2 GPA, 3 letters of recommendation. *Recommended:* interview. *Application deadlines:* 3/15 (freshmen), 6/15 (transfers), 12/1 (early action). *Notification:* continuous (freshmen), continuous (transfers), 1/15 (early action).
Freshman Application Contact Karen Ballard, Dean of Admissions, Franklin College Switzerland, Franklin College, US Office, The Graybar Building, Suite 2746, 420 Lexington Avenue, New York, NY 10170. *Phone:* 212-922-9650. *Fax:* 212-922-9870. *E-mail:* Info@fc.edu. *Web site:* http://www.fc.edu/.

See page 1300 for the College Close-Up.

Glion Institute of Higher Education
Glion-sur-Montreux, Switzerland

Freshman Application Contact Admissions, Glion Institute of Higher Education, Route de Glion 111, CH-1823 Glion-sur-Montreux, Switzerland.

Phone: 41-0 21 989 26 77. *Fax:* 41-0 21 989 26 78. *E-mail:* info@glion.edu. *Web site:* http://www.glion.edu/.

Les Roches International School of Hotel Management
Bluche, Switzerland

Freshman Application Contact Enrollment Management Department, Les Roches International School of Hotel Management, CH-3975 Bluche, Switzerland. *Phone:* 41-021 989 26 44. *Fax:* 41-021 989 26 45. *E-mail:* info@lesroches.edu. *Web site:* http://www.lesroches.cc/.

TAIWAN

Christ's College
Taipei, Taiwan

Admissions Office Contact Christ's College, 51 Tzu Chiang Road, Tanshui 251 Tapei, Taiwan, Taiwan. *Web site:* http://www.christc.org.tw/.

UNITED ARAB EMIRATES

The American University in Dubai
Dubai, United Arab Emirates

- **Proprietary** comprehensive, founded 1995
- **Urban** campus
- **Coed** 2,449 undergraduate students, 85% full-time, 46% women, 54% men
- **88%** of applicants were admitted

Undergraduates 2,070 full-time, 379 part-time.
Freshmen *Admission:* 1,062 applied, 930 admitted, 394 enrolled.
Faculty *Total:* 167, 63% full-time.
Academics *Calendar:* semesters. *Degrees:* certificates, bachelor's, and master's. *Special study options:* accelerated degree program, advanced placement credit, double majors, English as a second language, honors programs, independent study, internships, part-time degree program, services for LD students, study abroad, summer session for credit.
Computers on Campus 708 computers/terminals are available on campus for general student use. Students can access the following: computer help desk, free student e-mail accounts, online (class) grades, online (class) registration, online (class) schedules. Campuswide network is available. 100% of college-owned or -operated housing units are wired for high-speed Internet access.
Student Life *Housing options:* men-only, women-only. Campus housing is university owned. Freshman campus housing is guaranteed. *Activities and organizations:* drama/theater group, student-run newspaper, Student Government Association, Community Service Club, Drama Club, Music Club, Debate Club. *Campus security:* 24-hour patrols. *Student services:* health clinic, personal/psychological counseling.
Athletics *Intercollegiate sports:* basketball M/W, soccer M/W, tennis M/W, volleyball M/W. *Intramural sports:* basketball M/W, football M/W, soccer M/W, swimming and diving M/W, table tennis M/W, tennis M/W, track and field M/W, volleyball M/W.
Costs (2010–11) *Tuition:* $790 per credit hour part-time. *Waivers:* employees or children of employees.
Applying *Options:* early admission. *Application fee:* 55 United Arab Emirates dirhams. *Required:* high school transcript, minimum 2 GPA, 2 letters of recommendation. *Recommended:* essay or personal statement.
Freshman Application Contact Mrs. Zeina Tannir, Associate Director of Admissions, The American University in Dubai, PO Box 28282, Dubai, United Arab Emirates. *Phone:* -971 4 399 9000 Ext. 171. *Fax:* 971 4 399 8899. *E-mail:* admissions@aud.edu. *Web site:* http://www.aud.edu/.

American University of Sharjah
Sharjah, United Arab Emirates

Director of Admissions Ali Shuhaimy, Vice Chancellor of Enrollment Management, American University of Sharjah, PO Box 26666, Sharjah, United Arab Emirates. *Phone:* -971 6 515-5555. *E-mail:* ashuhaimy@aus.edu. *Web site:* http://www.aus.edu/.

UNITED KINGDOM

American InterContinental University London

London, United Kingdom

Freshman Application Contact American InterContinental University London, 110 Marylebone High Street, London W1U 4RY, United Kingdom. *Phone:* 877-564-6248. *Toll-free phone:* 888-567-5888. *Fax:* 877-564-6248. *Web site:* http://www.aiuniv.edu/.

Hult International Business School

London, United Kingdom

- **Independent** comprehensive, founded 1975
- **Urban** campus with easy access to Boston, San Francisco, London, Dubai and Shanghai
- **Coed**
- **Moderately difficult** entrance level

Academics *Calendar:* semesters. *Degrees:* certificates, diplomas, associate, bachelor's, and master's.

Student Life *Campus security:* 24-hour emergency response devices, controlled dormitory access.

Costs (2010–11) *Tuition:* 14,200 British pounds full-time.

Applying *Options:* electronic application. *Application fee:* 50 British pounds. *Required:* essay or personal statement, high school transcript, minimum 2.5 GPA, 2 letters of recommendation, interview.

Freshman Application Contact Mrs. Anna Frolander, Executive Director of Undergraduate Admissions, Hult International Business School, 46-47 Russell Square, London WC1B 4JP, United Kingdom. *Phone:* -44 207 341 8555. *E-mail:* anna.frolander@hult.edu. *Web site:* http://www.hult.edu/.

Regent's American College London

London, United Kingdom

Director of Admissions Admissions Director, Regent's American College London, Regent's College, Inner Circle, Regent's Park, London NW1 4NS, United Kingdom. *Phone:* 44-0 207 487 7505. *Fax:* 44-0 207 487 7425. *E-mail:* bacl@regents.ac.uk. *Web site:* http://www.bacl.ac.uk/.

Richmond, The American International University in London

Richmond, United Kingdom

Freshman Application Contact Mr. Nick Atkinson, Director of United States Admissions, Richmond, The American International University in London, 343 Congress Street, Suite 3100, Boston, MA 02210-1214. *Phone:* 617-450-5617. *Fax:* 617-450-5601. *E-mail:* us_admissions@richmond.ac.uk. *Web site:* http://www.richmond.ac.uk/.

See page 1528 for the College Close-Up.

Schiller International University

London, United Kingdom

Freshman Application Contact Ms. Kamala Dontamsetti, Associate Director of Admissions, Schiller International University, 300 East Bay Drive, Largo, FL 33770. *Phone:* 727-736-5082 Ext. 239. *Toll-free phone:* 800-336-4133. *Fax:* 727-734-0359. *E-mail:* admissions@schiller.edu. *Web site:* http://www.schiller.edu/.

College Close-Ups

ADELPHI UNIVERSITY

GARDEN CITY, NEW YORK

The University

Adelphi University, founded in 1896, is Long Island's first private coeducational institution of higher learning. A nonsectarian, independent university, Adelphi welcomes men and women of all backgrounds who display intellectual inquisitiveness, academic commitment, and a desire for achievement and purpose in life. The University enrolls 4,939 undergraduates and 2,978 graduate students. Forty-one states and forty-eight countries are represented in its diverse student body. The campus is located on 75 landscaped acres in Garden City, New York, 20 miles east of New York City and easily accessible by public transportation. The University also has three off-campus centers: the Manhattan Center in New York City, the Hauppauge Center on Long Island, and the Hudson Valley Center in Poughkeepsie, New York.

Adelphi University's schools and programs include the College of Arts and Sciences; the Honors College; the Schools of Business, Nursing, and Social Work; the Ruth S. Ammon School of Education; the Gordon F. Derner Institute of Advanced Psychological Studies; and adult academic programs in University College.

The University's six residence halls accommodate more than 1,100 students, and construction is underway on a new residence hall to be completed for fall 2011. The residential life staff at Adelphi is committed to bringing education to the residence halls. A lecture and discussion series brings faculty members together with students to examine events of the day and issues related to the classroom. In addition, about 200 seminars, workshops, and events are offered each year. Faculty and guest lecturers lead discussions on such topics as American and global politics, ethnic diversity, legal affairs, job interviewing, sexual conduct, and AIDS.

Opportunities for enhancing life beyond the classroom abound at Adelphi. Students participate in intramural and intercollegiate athletics (including nationally ranked men's and women's soccer, women's softball, and men's baseball, basketball, and lacrosse), drama productions, and more than eighty student clubs, community-service groups, and organizations. Students take advantage of the thriving cultural arts programs, including plays, art exhibits, concerts, and lectures; the comprehensive sports and fitness services; and the breathtaking campus. Physical education facilities include a swimming pool; basketball courts; weight-training and exercise rooms; a large indoor running track; and fields for baseball, lacrosse, soccer, and softball. In addition, a vast array of activities such as movies, exhibits, cabarets, symposia, and field trips are scheduled every semester.

The Adelphi student newspaper (*Delphian*) and the yearbook (*Oracle*) welcome writers and photographers.

In the Ruth S. Harley University Center (UC)—a central meeting place on campus—Adelphi students browse the full-service bookstore, refresh themselves and relax in one of the Center's lounges (commuter students have a special lounge equipped with lockers), eat in the UC Café, and enjoy a vast array of activities including movies, comedy shows, lectures, dance parties, and musical events. Cultural trips are also offered. The UC also houses Adelphi's numerous student organizations.

Location

Adelphi's main campus is located in Garden City, New York, a village of stately homes, historic buildings, and parks. The cultural and commercial resources of New York City and the recreation and entertainment of Long Island are only a short distance away by public or private transit.

Majors and Degrees

Undergraduate studies leading to the degrees of Bachelor of Arts (B.A.), Bachelor of Business Administration (B.B.A.), Bachelor of Fine Arts (B.F.A.), Bachelor of Science (B.S.), and Bachelor of Social Work (B.S.W.) are offered at Adelphi. Programs of study at Adelphi include: accounting; African, Black, and Caribbean studies; anthropology/forensic anthropology; art, with specializations in art history, fine arts and studio art* (ceramics, painting, photography, printmaking, and sculpture), and graphic design*; biochemistry; biology; business; chemistry; communication sciences and disorders; communications (journalism, media studies, moving image production); computer and management information systems; computer science; criminal justice; dance; economics; education studies, with programs of study in childhood education (STEP) and adolescence education (STEP); English (literature, creative writing); environmental studies; exercise science; finance; French; history; interdisciplinary studies; international studies; languages and international studies (political science, environmental studies, business); Latin American studies; management; marketing; mathematics; music**; music education; nursing; philosophy; physical education; physical education/health education; physics; political science; psychology; social work; sociology; Spanish; sport management; theatre arts** (acting and design technology); undecided arts and sciences; and undecided business. (A * indicates that an art portfolio is required; ** indicates that an audition is required.)

Five-year bachelor's/master's programs are offered in social work and business, as well as the Scholars Teacher Education Program (STEP) in childhood education and adolescence education.

Opportunities for preprofessional studies are available in predental, pre-engineering, prelaw, premedicine, preoptometry, and prephysical therapy/allied health.

Academic Programs

The goal of the academic programs at Adelphi is to provide higher education that cultivates the intellect and prepares students for the future. Consistent with the University's approach to liberal learning, students take part in the University's general education distribution requirements.

A minimum of 120 credits is required for a baccalaureate degree, with a specified number in the chosen major. Double majors and various minors may be elected. Seniors of superior academic ability may be admitted to graduate courses in their major field.

Off-Campus Programs

Adelphi University offers study-abroad programs that can last several weeks or span up to an academic year. Students can participate in Adelphi-run programs in Florence, London, Greece, Poland, and Australia, or join programs run by other educational institutions. Adelphi offers students the opportunity to participate in internship programs that provide access to a variety of industries and locations—in the local Long Island community, the surrounding New York City area, and beyond. Also offered is the Community Fellows Program, which pairs students with nonprofit organizations across Long Island and New York City, for 10-week, paid summer internships.

Academic Facilities

The University Libraries are composed of the Swirbul Library, the Archives and Special Collections, and the libraries at the Manhattan, Hauppauge, and Hudson Valley centers. These libraries contain 593,920 volumes and 806,642 items in microformat, plus 33,256 audiovisual items, 1,203 periodical subscriptions, and access to over 30,000 electronic titles. The University Libraries are fully automated with holdings accessible through ALICAT (the Adelphi Libraries Catalog Online). As an enhancement of the traditional reference services, online access is provided to 195 research databases.

The Swirbul Library is also the center of information technology on campus. Its amenities include a battery of personal computers that are fully networked for student use, a faculty development lab, and a technology infrastructure that reaches into every classroom and every part of the curriculum to provide Web-based learning and other applications of communication and information media.

The new 18,000-square-foot Adele and Herbert J. Klapper Center for Fine Arts has greatly expanded Adelphi's art studio and classroom space and offers greater opportunity for nonmajors to take art courses. This is in addition to the current state-of-the-art digital graphics design studio and faculty offices and the expansion of drawing studios in Blodgett Hall.

In 2006, Adelphi broke ground on an ambitious construction project to expand and enhance academic, cultural, and athletic facilities. Opened in fall 2008, the new Performing Arts Center showcases prestigious programs in acting, design/technical theater, music, and dance together under one roof. The new center features a 500-seat music performance hall, dance and recital rooms, music practice rooms, temperature-controlled instrument storage rooms, and a black box theater.

The Center for Recreation and Sports, which also opened in fall 2008, is the new home of Adelphi's successful athletics programs. The center's three-story, three-court gym, which converts into a 2,200-seat arena for basketball games and other events, accommodates recreational and intercollegiate athletes and health and physical education students, and can host NCAA tournaments and championships.

Costs

The 2010–11 tuition and fees for full-time undergraduates were $27,900. For students living on campus, additional costs included room ($7930 for a typical double room without air conditioning) and board ($2500 for a basic meal plan).

Financial Aid

The Office of Student Financial Services administers federal and New York State programs that provide funds to assist students in pursuing their academic goals. In addition to grants based on need, Adelphi annually offers almost 1,000 of its own scholarships based on merit, talent, and extracurricular excellence. Ninety-five percent of Adelphi freshmen receive some form of financial aid each year. The average financial aid package award for a full-time freshman is approximately $18,475.

Faculty

At Adelphi, the quality of education is entrusted to its distinguished faculty members, who are noted for their serious commitment to students, as well as for their research and professional contributions. Here, professors, not graduate assistants, teach undergraduate courses, and students learn in small, intimate environments.

Student Government

The Student Government Association is the elected student group that represents the opinions of the full-time undergraduate body to the administration and other groups. The Student Government Association hosts speakers, sponsors awareness days, and serves as a voice for student concerns and interests.

Admission Requirements

Recommended admission qualifications include graduation from a four-year public or private high school or equivalent credentials, four years of English, three years of science, three years of mathematics, two to three years of a foreign language or languages, and 4 additional units chosen from the fields mentioned or from history and social studies. Official test results from the SAT or ACT with writing are required.

Personal interviews and campus tours are strongly recommended for all applicants. Arrangements can be made by contacting the Office of Admissions at 516-877-3050.

Application and Information

The following admission credentials should be submitted by applicants: a completed application for admission, the $40 nonrefundable application fee, an official secondary school transcript or GED certificate, official results of the SAT or ACT, and letters of recommendation. Transfer students must submit official transcripts from all colleges previously attended.

Adelphi accepts applications on a rolling basis, with admission twice each year for the semesters beginning in September and January. Freshman filing dates are December 1 for early action, February 1 for priority consideration for joint-degree programs, March 1 for regular admission to the fall semester (applications received later are reviewed on a rolling basis), and November 1 for regular admission for the spring semester (applications received later are reviewed on a rolling basis). The nonbinding early-action plan is available only for the September term. An early-action decision means that applicants who submit their completed applications by December 1 receive an admissions decision by December 31 and that they are considered for scholarships and financial aid.

For more information, students should contact:

University Admissions
Adelphi University
Garden City, New York 11530
Phone: 516-877-3050
       800-ADELPHI (toll-free)
E-mail: admissions@adelphi.edu
Web site: http://www.adelphi.edu

Adelphi University's main campus in historic Garden City, New York.

ALBERTUS MAGNUS COLLEGE
NEW HAVEN, CONNECTICUT

The College

Founded in 1925 by the Dominican Sisters of St. Mary of the Springs, Albertus Magnus College educates men and women to become leaders in all walks of life. The College is committed to providing a liberal arts education rooted in the Dominican tradition of scholarship. Professors at Albertus strive to help their students develop in all areas; as much attention is paid to the nurturing of a student's aesthetic, physical, and moral capacities as to his or her intellectual capabilities. In 1992, the College began offering its first graduate-level course of study through the Master of Arts in Liberal Studies program. More recently, the College has expanded its graduate-level offerings to include the Master of Science in Management, the Master of Arts in Art Therapy, the Master of Arts in Leadership, and the Master of Business Administration.

The traditional undergraduate program has a student body of approximately 500 students, who live and learn on the beautiful 50-acre campus in the Prospect Hill neighborhood of New Haven. Another 1,500 students attend graduate programs or accelerated programs for adults. These students come from various parts of the United States (largely the New England area). About 60 percent of the students live on campus in student dormitories that are renovated mansions from the early 1900s. The housing program fosters a strong sense of community spirit, and students often plan workshops, parties, and other social and learning events in their residence halls.

The Hubert Campus Center is a hub of student activities, such as comedy shows, live music, contests, and other unique functions. The variety of on-campus organizations includes the Student Government Association, the Campus Activities Board, the multicultural student union, a dance team, the Psychology Club, the Art Club, the Environmental Club, the Business Club, and numerous creative writing options, such as *Breakwater* literary magazine and the English Club. Albertus has recently added a new cyber lounge, the Common Ground, where students can check e-mail, work on homework, and enjoy a cup of coffee.

Students may also share in the excitement of live drama through the College's professionally managed ACT 2 Theatre, providing a number of artistic, academic, and recreational possibilities. In addition, students are encouraged to become part of the New Haven community through extracurricular and volunteer activities. The active Campus Ministry provides opportunities to volunteer, organize campus events, and participate in community service projects.

The Cosgrove, Marcus, Messer Athletic Center houses a 25-yard pool, a Jacuzzi, three racquetball courts, a weight and cardio room, a dance studio, and a gymnasium. In addition to this facility, there are soccer and softball fields, an outdoor track, and several tennis courts. Albertus fields intercollegiate athletic teams in baseball, basketball, cross-country, soccer, tennis, and volleyball for men and basketball, cross-country, soccer, softball, tennis, and volleyball for women. Albertus's teams compete in the NCAA Division III/Great Northeast Athletic Conference (GNAC) and the Eastern College Athletic Conference (ECAC). The Athletic Department also offers an intramural program in some sports.

Location

New Haven is a multicultural city with a population of more than 130,000 people. The city hosts approximately 16,000 students attending the seven colleges and universities in the greater New Haven area. This concentration of students creates exciting choices for social, recreational, and cultural activities for Albertus students. The city has some of the finest theaters in the country, including the Long Wharf and Shubert theaters. There are many fantastic art collections, museums, and movie theaters. Large shopping facilities, excellent restaurants, and several recreational areas are only a short distance from the Albertus Magnus College campus.

Majors and Degrees

The Albertus Magnus College traditional undergraduate program confers the Bachelor of Arts (B.A.), Bachelor of Science (B.S.), and Bachelor of Fine Arts (B.F.A.) degrees. The areas of study include accounting, art (history and studio), art therapy, biology, business administration, chemistry, child development and mental health, communications, computer information systems, creative writing, criminal justice, drama, education (grades 4–12), English, finance, general studies, graphic design, history, humanities, human services, industrial and organizational psychology, international business, marketing, mathematics, performing communications, philosophy/religion, photography, physical sciences, political science, prelaw, premedicine, psychology, Spanish, sport management, sports communications, social science, social work, sociology, urban studies, and visual arts.

Academic Programs

Albertus Magnus College is committed to providing a liberal arts education that promotes the pursuit of truth in all its dimensions. The College recognizes the importance of cultivating core competencies and knowledge if students are to meet the challenges and opportunities they encounter in their communities and workplaces. Albertus has recently developed the Insight Program, which serves as the College's core curriculum. Through this program, students build a thinking framework that supports them throughout their lives as they realize their goals. In addition, the Insight Program helps students improve their capabilities in critical and creative thinking; grasp the methods of scientific, quantitative, mathematical, and philosophical reasoning; and appreciate and assess perspectives different from their own. The B.A. and B.S. degrees require 120 credits for graduation and the B.F.A. requires 127 credits. The College's Office of Career Services helps graduating students prepare for career direction and job placement. The Academic Development Center and Writing Center provide personal instruction to students who may benefit from additional help with their schoolwork. The centers also provide services to those students with learning disabilities. Students who show strong academic potential may pursue a course of study through the College's honors program. Students may relate academic study to work experience through a system of academically credited internships. Through the College's system of internships for juniors and seniors, Albertus students have become increasingly involved in the New Haven community and gain valuable, practical, professional training. Often, internships lead to permanent positions with local companies and corporations.

Academic Facilities

Rosary Hall, the College's first building, now houses a library collection of 110,000 volumes, 600 periodicals, 4,400 pieces of microfilm, and full access to the Internet, including LexisNexis, EBSCOhost, and PsycINFO. The interlibrary loan program has access to materials at academic and public libraries across the country. The Media Center has equipment that students may use to produce new materials as well as review older materials. Interlibrary services with other local universities are also available. The New Center for Science, Art and Technology provides the most modern scientific equipment available for students majoring in biological and physical sciences, along with state-of-the-art broadcasting technology for communication students. Aquinas Hall houses the academic computer labs, which are equipped with personal computers, digital scanners, laser printers, and full Internet access. Every classroom in Aquinas Hall is laptop compatible, and the entire campus is engineered for wireless use.

Costs

The costs for the 2010–11 school year were $25,272 for tuition and $10,460 for room and board (nineteen meals per week). Expenses for books, travel, and personal supplies vary.

Financial Aid

Albertus Magnus College offers a variety of merit-based scholarships to students who have achieved high academic standing in high school or in their two-year college programs. Interested students should contact the Office of Admission for specific information regarding scholarship opportunities. Scholarships are awarded to eligible students who apply and are accepted to the College prior to March 15.

Approximately 85 percent of the College's students receive financial aid in some form. The College requires that students file the Albertus Magnus College financial aid application form and the Free Application for Federal Student Aid (FAFSA) to be considered for Albertus scholarships and grants, Federal Perkins Loans, Federal Supplemental Educational Opportunity Grants, and Federal Work-Study Program awards. The College awards financial aid on a rolling basis; however, students who are accepted and submit their FAFSA forms by February 28 are given priority.

Faculty

Faculty members at Albertus come from leading universities in the United States and abroad and are one of the College's greatest assets. Ninety percent of the full- and part-time faculty members hold a Ph.D. or the equivalent. Their primary concern is teaching, although the work of many faculty members has been published. Students find faculty members accessible for academic or personal counseling and for campus sports and activities.

Student Government

Through the Student Government Association (SGA), Albertus students have the primary responsibility for governing their own residential and social life. All full-time matriculated students are members of the SGA and, through its committees and officers, manage student government and social affairs and participate in the campus judicial system. Students serve on faculty committees, the Academic Policy Committee, and the Library Committee.

Admission Requirements

Albertus Magnus College welcomes applications from students of all ages, nationalities, and ethnic, cultural, racial, and religious groups. Applicants may be admitted as freshmen or as transfer, provisional, or special students.

In evaluating freshman candidates, the Office of Admission considers a student's application, counselor recommendation, high school transcript, essay, extracurricular activities, and scores on the SAT or ACT. Emphasis is placed on the student's record of performance rather than on the results of standardized tests.

Transfer students are welcome at the College. They must submit high school records, SAT or ACT scores, and college records for evaluation, in addition to the application and the recommendation. Interviews are recommended for freshman and transfer applicants.

More information is available on the College's Web site, http://www.albertus.edu.

Application and Information

The College accepts students for entrance on a rolling admission basis. Students may also apply online at http://www.albertus.edu. As soon as all of a candidate's admission materials have been received, his or her application is considered and notification is made as soon as a decision has been reached.

Application forms, recommendation forms, and information may be obtained by contacting:

Office of Admission
Albertus Magnus College
700 Prospect Street
New Haven, Connecticut 06511-1189
Phone: 203-773-8501
         800-578-9160 (toll-free)
Fax: 203-773-5248
E-mail: admissions@albertus.edu
Web site: http://www.albertus.edu

Beautiful Rosary Hall.

ALVERNIA UNIVERSITY

READING, PENNSYLVANIA

The University

Alvernia University offers all the best features of an outstanding university—specialized professional programs, experiential learning, internships and a variety of leadership opportunities—in the personal setting of a college environment. Students appreciate the small class sizes and breadth of academic programs offered, all taught by faculty who are experts in their fields and committed foremost to their students' success. Guided by Franciscan ideals that foster each individual's unique gifts and embrace students of diverse backgrounds and beliefs, Alvernia provides an affordable, private education within a caring community. The 121-acre tree-lined campus is located in a secure, residential neighborhood just minutes from the bustle of city life and within easy driving distance of metropolitan centers like New York, Philadelphia and Baltimore.

With a total enrollment of 3,000 men and women (1,500 traditional undergraduate students) Alvernia offers a quality, affordable education in a friendly setting. With a student-faculty ratio of 14:1 and class sizes of fewer than 20, students get the individual attention that can make a difference in their future. This personal approach to learning is a hallmark of an Alvernia education.

Alvernia offers opportunities to achieve athletic and personal goals through NCAA Division III intercollegiate athletics, club sports, and intramural programs. Whether playing among themselves or competing on one of the University's twenty-one varsity teams, students of all interests and abilities discover the benefits of an active lifestyle. Alvernia competes in the highly competitive Commonwealth Conference of the Middle Atlantic States Collegiate Athletic Corporation.

Alvernia encourages students to take advantage of learning opportunities outside the classroom by participating in a growing roster of student events, activities, and organizations. The Student Government Association and the Campus Activities Board plan plenty of on-campus entertainment and social events, including comedians, bands, film series, and other events, as well as discounted trips (transportation included) in and around the region.

A fast-growing Franciscan institution rooted in the Catholic and liberal arts traditions, Alvernia's core institutional values—service, humility, peacemaking, contemplation, and collegiality—have a universal ethical appeal. As part of Alvernia's commitment to those values, students complete 40 hours of volunteer service as a graduation requirement. Depending on their interests, schedules, and talents, students can tutor schoolchildren, shovel sidewalks for the elderly, stock groceries at a food bank, or practice Spanish language skills on alternative spring break mission trips to Ecuador or Santo Domingo. Giving back, pitching in, helping out, getting involved, making a difference—service to others is part of the Alvernia experience.

On-campus housing includes traditional residence halls, apartments, suites and town houses. The newest residence halls, the Village Apartments, were completed in 2009 and offer contemporary housing for juniors and seniors with gas fireplaces in the main lounges and business centers for student use. All of the residential facilities are clean and spacious and equipped with laundry, cable TV, and phones with voice mail. The student center is the hub of campus life, with the newly renovated dining hall and the student-run Crusader Café that offers wireless Internet access and is open 24/7 for late-night study breaks or a quick stop between classes. There is also a lounge with a big-screen television and game room for students to enjoy.

Chartered by the commonwealth of Pennsylvania, fully accredited by the Middle States Association of Colleges and Schools, and sponsored by the Bernardine Franciscan Sisters, Alvernia has been honored by the Templeton Foundation as one of the top 100 character-building colleges in the nation and a model of excellence in education. In addition, the University is regularly named to the President's Higher Education Community Service Honor Roll for its commitment to achievement in community service.

Location

Alvernia offers a setting that is both conducive to learning and conveniently accessible. Situated on a scenic 121-acre suburban campus in Reading, Pennsylvania, the campus is bordered by a park with hiking trails, a picnic grove and a nine-hole disc golf course. Students are minutes away from a mix of attractions such as the GoggleWorks Center for the Arts, outlet shopping, minor league sports, and concerts at the Sovereign Center. The campus is an easy car ride from Philadelphia, New York, Baltimore and Washington, D.C.

Majors and Degrees

Bachelor's degrees are awarded in the following majors: accounting, addiction studies, athletic training, biochemistry, biology, biology–medical technology, business management, chemistry, chemistry–medical technology, communication, criminal justice administration, education (concentrations in early childhood, middle school, secondary, and special education), English, forensic science, general science, history, human resource management, liberal studies, marketing, mathematics, nursing, philosophy, political science, psychology, social work, sport management, theater, and theology. Preprofessional programs are available in dentistry, law, medicine, and veterinary studies. Alvernia also offers minors and certificate programs.

Master's degrees are awarded in occupational therapy, business administration, nursing, community counseling, education, and liberal studies. A Ph.D. program in leadership is also available.

Alvernia has been accredited by the Middle States Association of Colleges and Schools since 1967. The education program for elementary and secondary teachers is approved by the Pennsylvania Department of Education. The occupational therapy program is fully accredited by the American Occupational Therapy Association. The Bachelor of Science in Nursing has approval from the Pennsylvania State Board of Nursing and is accredited by the Commission on Collegiate Nursing Education. The Commission on Accreditation of Allied Health Education Programs accredits the athletic training program in cooperation with the Joint Review Committee on Educational Programs in Athletic Training. The Council on Social Work Education accredits the social work program. The Pennsylvania Certification Board certifies the addiction studies program. The Association of Collegiate Business Schools and Programs accredits the Business Department.

Academic Programs

Alvernia offers a variety of academic programs with a boundary-free learning approach that provides choices and options, yet is grounded in the real world. With more than 600 courses offered in over fifty majors and minors in nearly every field, including preprofessional programs in medicine, dentistry, law, and veterinary medicine, an Alvernia education prepares students for the careers they want.

Study abroad, internships, service projects (domestic and international), the unique Washington Center Experience, and the Holleran Center for Community Engagement are just a few of the opportunities at Alvernia that make classroom learning come alive. Through these hands-on experiences, students are exposed to real-world lessons that help develop successful professionals and engaged global citizens.

The Honors Program is ideal for exceptional students, high achievers, and those considering graduate school. Students who want a greater intellectual challenge find this program gives them the opportunity to pursue academic excellence at the next level while encouraging the exchange of ideas between students with different interests.

Selecting a major can be difficult. The Genesis Experience was created to guide students through the process of selecting a major. This program provides individual advising, access to information and resources, workshops, and a for-credit course to help students learn about themselves and the range of academic options available to them.

In order to earn a bachelor's degree from Alvernia, students must complete a minimum of 123 credits, with 54 credits in the liberal arts. Additional requirements vary by major.

Academic Facilities

Alvernia is currently investing in several multimillion-dollar additions to campus. These include a new laser laboratory to support science programs, state-of-the-art learning suites developed for the criminal justice program, an educational technology center that supports all majors, and a new recital hall and theater.

The newest academic building, the O'Pake Science Center, a $9.3 million state-of-the-art facility, opened in 2006. This facility added 31,582 square feet of classroom, laboratory, and faculty office space to the campus. Each of two floors is equipped with five laboratory/classrooms, all of which have smart capability or Internet access, to bring resources, research, and data into all classrooms.

Alvernia's campus is fully networked. Students have access to the academic information network and the Internet from their residence hall rooms as well as from other campus locations including classrooms, the library, and labs. All students may connect personal computers through a secure system. Network access and Alvernia e-mail accounts are available to all students.

Alvernia's library facility holds more than 100,000 volumes, including reference works, books for general circulation, and bound periodicals. The library currently subscribes to 400 periodicals covering all areas of study taught at the University, and more than 1,440 volumes of back issues are in the microfilm collection. The library also houses the Audio-Visual Center, which has 23,000 pieces of audiovisual material, including more than 4,750 music records and scores.

Costs

For 2011–12, the basic tuition fee is $26,100; room and board are $9510.

Financial Aid

More than 99 percent of the students attending Alvernia receive some type of financial aid, most commonly Pennsylvania Higher Education Assistance Agency grants for Pennsylvania residents, Federal Pell Grants, and numerous scholarships from private sources, as well as grants and scholarships from the University itself. This aid is awarded on the basis of academic performance and financial need. The deadline for application for Alvernia University aid is April 1. Alvernia participates in the federally funded Federal Work-Study Program. Student loans are also available.

Faculty

The dedicated faculty members are accomplished scholars who bring real-world experience into the classroom and are as diversified as the fields of interest that they represent. Alvernia faculty members publish in professional journals and other media; present papers and moderate conferences in the region and as far away as India, Italy, Mexico, and South Africa; and serve on boards and committees of professional associations and corporate and community boards.

Student Government

The Student Government Association (SGA) provides an opportunity for individual leadership and development while also determining, in cooperation with the administration and faculty, suitable standards for University and community life. SGA leaders, elected annually by the student body, are responsible for maintaining the student voice when issues on campus arise. Other duties include activities such as social events, a speaker series, and club activities. The SGA also acts as an intermediary between the administration, the faculty, and the student body and maintains order on campus by proposing rules and regulations for the welfare of the University community. It is composed of a president, vice president, secretary, treasurer, and chief justice elected by the student body and is augmented by 2 representatives from each class.

Admission Requirements

Admission requirements normally include a high school diploma with 16 Carnegie units in the following subjects: English, 4 units; mathematics, 2 units; science, 2 units; social studies, 2 units; and modern languages, 2 units. The remaining units may be made up of academic electives. The University is willing to consider good students whose preparation does not include all of these subjects. Nursing students must fulfill the admission requirements established by the Pennsylvania State Board of Nurse Examiners. The State High School Equivalency Diploma is generally recognized as fulfilling the minimum entrance requirements. Applicants are required to take the SAT; the ACT is also acceptable. Outstanding candidates are considered for entrance to Alvernia at the end of their junior year of high school on the basis of requests made by the candidate and the school. With the approval of their school officials, students may also be admitted to certain courses during their senior year, simultaneously earning credit toward their high school diploma and a college degree.

Application and Information

The welcoming Alvernia attitude makes applying for admission easy. Many factors are considered for admission, including academic performance, standardized test scores, class rank, extracurricular activities, and community involvement. Application and admission notification is on a rolling basis; however, applicants are encouraged to submit the admission application as early as possible. In addition to their transcripts and SAT or ACT scores, nursing applicants must also submit two letters of reference.

Alvernia accepts and/or offers special programs for accelerated high school students, nontraditional students (older than 24), transfer students, students with disabilities, and international students.

Applicants should submit an application for admission and enclose a nonrefundable $25 processing fee. The application form may be obtained from the Office of Admissions or the University's Web site at www.alvernia.edu/admissions/undergraduate/apply.html. Applicants should have an official copy of their high school record sent to the Office of Admissions, along with the official results of the SAT or ACT.

Because Alvernia has a rolling admission policy, the Director of Admissions notifies an applicant of acceptance shortly after the necessary credentials are on file and have been reviewed, generally within one month. To reserve a place in the freshman class, all students must make a $300 deposit by May 1. This deposit is credited to the student's account for the first semester but is not refunded if the student fails to attend. Transfer students should have a grade point average of 2.0 or higher on a 4.0 scale and should be aware that only grades of C or better are eligible for credit transfer. Alvernia accepts a maximum of 75 transfer credits; at least 45 credits that are required for graduation must be earned at Alvernia and must satisfy all graduation requirements. A detailed analysis of credits to be transferred is done only after the University has accepted students.

The best way to get to know Alvernia is through a campus visit and tour. Applicants and those considering the school are strongly encouraged to come for an individual campus visit, which will be personalized to match each student's unique interests. Alvernia also hosts information sessions and open houses throughout the year that allow prospective freshmen or transfers to meet current students, talk to admissions and financial aid counselors, and meet faculty and coaches. Overnight and shadow visits are also available.

For more information or to schedule a visit, students should contact:

Director of Admissions
Alvernia University
Reading, Pennsylvania 19607
Phone: 888-ALVERNIA (258-3764, toll-free)
Fax: 610-790-2873
E-mail: admissions@alvernia.edu
Web site: http://www.alvernia.edu
    http://on.fb.me/Alvernia_University (Facebook)
    http://twitter.com/alverniauniv (Twitter)

Friends outside historic Francis Hall on Alvernia's peaceful, tree-lined campus.

AMERICAN INTERNATIONAL COLLEGE
SPRINGFIELD, MASSACHUSETTS

The College

American International College, founded in 1885, is a master's level university fully committed to its mission of preparing students for personal fulfillment, professional achievement, and civic engagement through educational experiences that transform lives. Today, the College enrolls approximately 3,500 students of whom just over 1,700 are undergraduates. The College's diverse population attracts students from twenty-eight states and twenty-five countries. The undergraduate population is evenly divided between men and women, with about 52 percent residing on campus. Campus housing includes traditional-style residence halls as well as several options for suite- and apartment-style living. Students are engaged in a variety of cocurricular activities reflecting interests that range from volunteer and community service in the surrounding community to theater, student government, hosting a show on the campus radio station, writing for the campus newspaper, and much more. More than forty student clubs and organizations result in a vibrant student life. Additionally, a large number of students have the opportunity to participate in a variety of intramural, club, and intercollegiate athletic programs. Intercollegiate sports teams, which compete at the NCAA Division II level (except ice hockey which is Division I) include men's baseball, basketball, cross-country, football, golf, hockey, indoor and outdoor track, lacrosse, soccer, tennis, and wrestling and women's basketball, cross-country, field hockey, indoor and outdoor track, lacrosse, soccer, softball, tennis, and volleyball. Cheerleading and men's and women's rugby are also offered at the club level.

Location

American International College is located in Springfield, Massachusetts, a city of 165,000 people, which is the seat of Hampden County and the metropolitan center for half a million people. Springfield is also the transportation center of western New England, easily reached by automobile on Interstate 91 and the Massachusetts Turnpike, by rail via major north-south and east-west lines, and by plane via Bradley International Airport. There are many cultural offerings in the area, including the Springfield Symphony, Mass Mutual Center, and City Stage Theatre Company.

Majors and Degrees

At the undergraduate level, the School of Arts, Education, and Sciences offers both Bachelor of Arts and Bachelor of Science degrees. Majors leading to a B.A. include American studies, biology, chemistry, communications, English, history, interdepartmental science, international studies, liberal studies, new media, political science, psychology, and sociology. The B.S. is offered in criminal justice. Five-year entry-level master's degree programs are offered in early childhood education, elementary education, secondary education, and special education. Massachusetts teacher certification requirements mandate that students seeking certification must also complete the requirements of a second major selected from among those offered in the liberal arts and sciences. Preprofessional programs in dentistry, law, medicine, optometry, physical therapy, podiatry, and veterinary science are also available. Minors are available in these disciplines as well as in the fields of journalism, physics, and theater.

The School of Business Administration awards the degree of Bachelor of Science in Business Administration with majors in accounting, economics, finance, health-care management, health-care marketing, international business, management, marketing, and sports and recreation management.

The School of Health Sciences offers majors in nursing, a five-year entry-level master's degree program in occupational therapy, and a six-year entry-level doctoral program in physical therapy.

American International College is accredited by the New England Association of Schools and Colleges, Inc. Additional program accreditations include the Accreditation Council for Occupational Therapy Education of the American Occupational Therapy Association; the Commission on Accreditation in Physical Therapy of the American Physical Therapy Association; the Commission on Collegiate Nursing Education; and the International Assembly for Collegiate Business Education. Additionally, the education preparation programs are approved by the Massachusetts Department of Education for state licensure eligibility.

The occupational therapy program offers an accredited program leading to a combined Bachelor of Science in occupational science/Master of Science in Occupational Therapy (B.S./M.S.O.T.) degree.

The physical therapy program offers an accredited six-year program leading to a doctoral degree in physical therapy.

Academic Programs

Since all programs are founded on the knowledge, skills, and values of the liberal arts, general education requirements are central to all degree programs.

General education requirements include a year of freshman English and literature, an additional literature course, 12 semester hours in the social sciences, 6 in humanities, 8 in a laboratory science, and 3 in a quantitative course as well as one computer-oriented course. To graduate, students are required to complete a minimum total of 120 hours of academic credit with a C average or better.

A special four-year program, the Curtis Blake Center's Supportive Learning Services Program, provides a range of services to students with a diagnosed learning disability.

An honors program is also offered.

Off-Campus Programs

A variety of off-campus learning opportunities are available to students to complement their classroom instruction. Among them are several international experiences ranging from semester-long and yearlong study-abroad programs to short-term study trips focused on a specific discipline or topic.

Nearly 80 percent of the College's students participate in off-campus internships at many local, regional, and national firms such as banks, social service sites, health-care facilities, media outlets, schools, courts, and others. This program is designed to provide all students with an opportunity to gain practical experience in their field of study and is required of the students in many of the business disciplines and in communications, criminal justice, education, human services, nursing, occupational therapy, and physical therapy.

Academic Facilities

James J. Shea Sr. Memorial Library (1980) houses 125,000 volumes, 519 current periodicals, 14,800 bound periodicals, 12,759 units of microfilm, and 3,423 sound recordings and tapes. An area for group study, a media center, and individual study carrels are provided for students. Also located in the library are the Center for Academic Success and the Information Technology offices.

Amaron Hall is the primary facility for liberal arts and business classrooms and includes many smart classrooms and several computer labs. Old Science and the Breck Hall of Science buildings provide classrooms and laboratories for science, mathematics, and preprofessional studies. The Curtis Blake Child Development Center is a community resource that serves the region's school system as a diagnostic center for children with learning difficulties and offers graduate-level courses in special education. The center also provides services for specially selected college-age students with learning disabilities.

Courniotes Hall is the academic center for the physical therapy, occupational therapy, and nursing programs. The 30,000-square-foot facility includes an amphitheater, several laboratories, classrooms, and faculty and administrative offices.

Costs

The comprehensive 2010–11 fee for tuition, room, board, and miscellaneous expenses was approximately $38,700. Books and supplies are approximately $1200. Personal expenses average $1000 per year.

Financial Aid

American International College provides aid from institutional and external sources to assist over 90 percent of the student body. The average financial aid package for the 2010–11 school year was over $19,000. The College participates in the Federal Perkins Loan, Federal Supplemental Educational Opportunity Grant, Federal Pell Grant, and Federal Work-Study programs. Merit-based scholarships are available for eligible freshmen and transfers, and additional College grants are awarded on a need basis. The preferred deadline for applying for financial aid is April 1. Only the Free Application for Federal Student Aid (FAFSA) is required. Students are urged to file the FAFSA online. Further information about financial aid should be obtained from the Financial Aid Office directly. Students should reference the College's Web site (www.aic.edu) to access a scholarship calculator to determine eligibility for merit-based scholarships.

Faculty

The emphasis of the faculty is on teaching and advising. The full-time faculty members number 86, most of whom have terminal degrees. All teach freshman-level courses, and serve as advisers. The student-faculty ratio is 14:1.

Student Government

All students are members of the Student Government Association, and the elected officers play an important role in the administration of the College. Serious disciplinary problems are adjudicated by the various levels of the Student Judicial System as well as by the Vice President of Academic Affairs and the Dean of Students.

In addition, students are largely responsible for planning the various social activities at the College with the Director of Student Activities.

Admission Requirements

Admission decisions are based on an assessment of the applicant's ability to be successful at the college level. That decision is made after a holistic review of the applicant's secondary school record, standardized test scores (SAT I or ACT is required), and letters of recommendation. Students must be graduates of an approved secondary school and must have successfully completed 16 units of study or show evidence of equivalent education. Among subjects that should be a part of a student's secondary program are English (4 units) and a selection from mathematics, science, social studies, and foreign languages. Students are encouraged to apply online (www.aic.edu/apply) but paper applications, which can be obtained from the Admissions Office, are also accepted. Transfer applicants are strongly encouraged; in fact, nearly one third of each year's new students enter as transfers.

An interview at the College is recommended but not required except for those applying to the Supportive Learning Services Program. Guides offer campus tours to all guests; class attendance or an overnight stay may be arranged through the Admissions Office. Admission staff members also visit schools throughout the Northeast each year, and candidates who are unable to visit the campus are urged to meet with staff members or talk with alumni in their home area.

Application and Information

A completed application includes the candidate's high school transcript, SAT or ACT scores, and at least one letter of recommendation. Admission decisions are made on a rolling basis, usually within two to three weeks after the application is completed.

The Admissions staff is glad to advise prospective students who wish to e-mail, write, or call for additional information.

Vice President for Admission Services
American International College
1000 State Street
Springfield, Massachusetts 01109
Phone: 413-205-3201
        800-242-3142 (toll-free)
E-mail: peter.miller@aic.edu
Web site: http://www.aic.edu

Sokolowski Tower, a hub of student activity.

AMRIDGE UNIVERSITY
MONTGOMERY, ALABAMA

The University

Founded in 1967, Amridge University is an independent, coeducational institution dedicated to the spirit of its ideals and Christian heritage. All Amridge University programs are taught from a Christian perspective. Amridge University is one of the nation's leading universities offering distance learning programs and services to adults nationally since 1993. Adding to the prestige of the University is its selection in 1999 by the U.S. Department of Education as one of fifteen initial participants in the Distance Education Demonstration Program. Amridge University worked with the U.S. Department of Education to develop a national model to help chart the future of distance learning.

Accredited by the Southern Association of Colleges and Schools, Amridge University grants associate, bachelor's, master's, and doctoral degrees, all available via a distance learning format. Graduate degrees are awarded in counseling/family therapy, organizational leadership, and religious studies. These degrees foster leadership, counseling and family therapy skills, knowledge, and biblical and Christian ministry skills. The counseling degrees are designed to help prepare students for licensure. Doctoral degrees include Doctor of Ministry and Doctor of Philosophy degrees. These are advanced professional degrees for community organization and church-related vocations, with a concentration designed to prepare participants to counsel families and individuals.

The policy of Amridge University is to provide reasonable accommodation for persons who are handicapped or disabled as designated in Section 504 of the Rehabilitation Act of 1973 and the Americans with Disabilities Act of 1990. Although the Morgan W. Brown building is not equipped with an elevator, the needs of the physically challenged can be met from the first floor. These include registration, counseling, library facilities, classroom facilities, rest rooms, break room facilities, and others. Ample parking is provided.

Location

Amridge University is located in Montgomery, Alabama, the capital city of the state. Strategically located in the central part of the state between Huntsville and Mobile and Atlanta, Georgia, Montgomery is one of the fastest-growing cities in the state and the region. The city is clean and modern, with beautiful residential areas, parks and playgrounds, and fine schools and universities. Students and families can also enjoy its museums, zoo, and facilities of the capitol building.

Montgomery has two major U.S. Air Force installations: Maxwell Air Force Base and Gunter Annex. Maxwell is where the Air War College is located and is a strategic center for education.

The metropolitan area has a population of more than 350,000 citizens. There are many churches and educational institutions. The city has an abundance of good housing in addition to other advantages.

Majors and Degrees

Undergraduate degrees are awarded in Biblical studies, business, homeland security, human development, human resource management, liberal studies, management communication, and public safety and criminal justice. These degrees promote biblical and Christian ministry skills, human development skills, knowledge in the arts, and management communication skills. Amridge University students are fully matriculated students of Amridge University with full student privileges, rights, and responsibilities.

Academic Programs

Amridge University is primarily a distance learning institution, although there are many classes offered on campus. The academic year consists of three semesters: fall, spring, and summer.

A student must fulfill the required semester hours in a major as well as the basic requirements of the core curriculum. All core and major requirements can be received from the University. Amridge University programs have a traditional structure.

Distance education is approved by the Southern Association of Colleges and Schools and the U.S. Department of Education, ensuring that distance education students receive the same high-quality education as on-campus students. Faculty and student services for students on campus are available to distance learners. Amridge University ensures that students have regular contact with faculty and staff members via e-mail and telephone. No residency is required for undergraduates.

In addition to offering distance learning to a diverse array of individuals, Amridge University is a participating member of the GoArmyEd project. This is an online, streamlined process giving soldiers easy access to obtaining funding for their educations.

Academic Facilities

Amridge University sits stately on a 9-acre campus adjoining Interstate 85. A beautiful building houses the administration offices, classrooms, and Library Resource Center.

Costs

Undergraduate tuition per semester hour is $315.

Financial Aid

Aid from institutionally generated funds is provided on the basis of academic merit, financial need, and other criteria. A limited number of scholarships are available. Priority is given to early applicants.

Federal funding available for undergraduates includes Federal Pell Grants, Federal Supplemental Educational Opportunity Grants (FSEOG), the Academic Competitiveness Grant (ACG), the SMART Grant, the Federal Work-Study Program, and direct subsidized and unsubsidized loans. Eighty percent of students receive financial aid.

Faculty

The instructional faculty members total approximately 100. Approximately 65 percent of the full-time faculty members hold doctoral degrees, 100 percent hold master's degrees, and 100 percent hold terminal degrees. Faculty members specialize in their areas and have exceptional training in distance learning delivery.

Student Government

Student volunteers serve as members of the Student Advisory Committee. Volunteers are appointed by the Student Services Team, with recommendations from the deans. The committee meets on a regular basis and is reorganized on an annual basis. Concerns, recommendations, and requests are presented directly from the committee to the appropriate University area.

Admission Requirements

Amridge University is open to all persons who are of good character and who are academically qualified. The University has developed a streamlined admissions process to help potential students complete the process in a timely manner so they can begin their studies. As new technologies and processes become available, Amridge University makes every effort to adopt and use the latest technologies to help the admissions process. Transfer students in good academic standing are invited to apply to Amridge University. Prospective students must submit a $75 nonrefundable fee along with the completed application for admission.

Application and Information

For further information, students may contact:

Carl Byrd
Amridge University
1200 Taylor Road
Montgomery, Alabama 36117
Phone: 334-387-7569
      800-351-4040 Ext. 7569 (toll-free)
Fax: 334-387-3878
E-mail: carlbyrd@amridgeuniversity.edu
Web site: http://www.amridgeuniversity.edu

ANGELO STATE UNIVERSITY

SAN ANGELO, TEXAS

The University

Founded in 1928, Angelo State University (ASU) has been recognized as one of the United States' outstanding regional public universities. A proud member of the Texas Tech University System, ASU maintains one of the lowest tuition and fee schedules in the state. The University aims to create a stimulating educational climate that offers students maximum opportunities for academic achievement and personal growth both in and out of the classroom. With personal attention from a superb faculty and with numerous prospects for practical experience and internships, students enjoy an enhanced undergraduate experience. To achieve this goal, ASU maintains a distinguished student body and a superb faculty. Of the approximately 6,856 students enrolled, 6,155 are undergraduates. This diverse student population is drawn from throughout Texas, forty-one other states, and nineteen countries. Additional information can be found at http://www.angelo.edu.

Location

The 268-acre campus of Angelo State University is in San Angelo, an attractive and progressive community of 100,000 in the heart of Texas at the gateway to the scenic hill country. The attractively landscaped campus is convenient to downtown as well as to entertainment options in suburban areas. The athletic, cultural, and entertainment offerings of the campus are complemented by those of the community, including a symphony orchestra, art and historical museums, popular concerts, two professional sports teams, and a host of special events. The ASU Lake House on Lake Nasworthy, one of three recreational lakes around San Angelo, provides facilities for various university functions as well as picnicking, swimming, fishing, and other water activities.

Majors and Degrees

Angelo State University provides forty-five undergraduate programs leading to seven baccalaureate degrees and one associate degree.

The Bachelor of Arts degree is offered in art, communication, criminal justice, English, French, German, history, mass media, mathematics, music, political science, psychology, sociology, Spanish, and theater. Programs for teacher certification at the elementary level are available as interdisciplinary programs in fine arts, language arts, and social studies. Programs for teacher certification are available in communication, English language arts and reading, fine arts, French, special education, German, history, mass media, social studies, Spanish, and theater.

The Bachelor of Business Administration degree may be earned in accounting, business, computer science, finance, finance with a financial planning option, finance with a real estate option, international business, management, management information systems, and marketing. The University's undergraduate and graduate business programs are accredited by the Association of Collegiate Business Schools and Programs. A five-year integrated undergraduate/graduate program in accounting is designed to fulfill state requirements for eligibility for the Certified Public Accountancy (CPA) examination.

The Bachelor of Music degree is offered in music, and the Bachelor of Fine Arts degree is offered in studio art. A program in teacher certification in music is available.

The Bachelor of Science degree is offered in animal science, applied physics, biochemistry, biology, chemistry, computer science, criminal justice, kinesiology, mathematics, medical technology, physics, psychology, and sociology. Programs for teacher certification are available as interdisciplinary programs in early childhood, math/science, and special learning and development and in the content areas of computer science, kinesiology, life science, mathematics, and physical science.

The University also offers a Bachelor of General Studies degree, a Bachelor of Science in Nursing degree, and an Associate in Applied Science in Nursing degree.

Angelo State's newest degree programs are both bachelor's and master's in border security, cultural competence and security studies, and cultural fluency and security studies. These programs are open to both military personnel and civilians.

In addition, students may pursue courses and advising designed to help them meet entrance requirements to various professional schools, including dentistry, engineering, law, medicine, occupational therapy, pharmacy, physical therapy, and veterinary medicine.

A complete list of majors and degree programs is accessible at http://www.angelo.edu/dept/admissions/degreeprograms.html.

Academic Programs

The academic requirements at ASU are designed to give the student a broad background in the liberal arts and to enhance that foundation with discipline-specific courses. Curricula are continually evaluated to ensure the best and most current educational experience possible. Baccalaureate-seeking students must file a degree plan prior to the first semester of their junior year or the completion of 70 semester hours. Faculty advisers monitor students' progress from the beginning of the academic program until completion.

Two-year and four-year aerospace studies programs for men and women are also available. Completion of these programs leads to a commission in the U.S. Air Force. ASU has one of the nation's most highly decorated detachments and can offer tremendous scholarships.

The college year consists of a long session and a summer session. The long session is divided into fall and spring semesters, each approximately sixteen weeks long. The summer session is divided into two 6-week terms.

Off-Campus Programs

The International Studies Program provides academic study and travel opportunities in Europe and Asia. Study-abroad programs carry college credit. Other off-campus programs include professional internships in education, government, mass media, and public administration and cooperative education programs in nursing and medical technology offered in conjunction with numerous local medical centers.

ASU operates a 4,643-acre multiple-purpose agricultural production and wildlife management area called the Management, Instruction, and Research (MIR) Center. Located near O. C. Fisher Lake and San Angelo, the MIR Center is one of the most complete domestic livestock/range and wildlife management facilities in the Southwest.

Academic Facilities

Attractive and well-maintained academic buildings enable ASU students to study in some of the most pleasant and modern facilities anywhere. Classrooms range from the intimacy of seminar-oriented size to a small number of lecture halls. Specialized and general research laboratories serve many of the University's programs, including the applied sciences, nursing, communication, mass media, kinesiology, education, business, and computer science, among others. The Porter Henderson Library is the focal point of academic life at ASU. Containing more than 1 million holdings in bound volumes, government documents, and microforms made accessible by an online cataloging system, the Henderson Library ranks among the finest libraries in Texas. The West Texas Collection of archival material admirably meets the genealogical and historical interests of students and faculty members desiring to learn more about the distinct West Texas heritage.

There are seven computer labs on campus that are available to all students. One of these labs is open 144 hours per week when classes are in session. The 15:1 student-to-computer ratio is extremely low. A radio/television studio, modular and proscenium theaters, a planetarium, musical rehearsal and recital halls, art studios, recreational facilities, and a Language Learning Center provide ASU students with exceptional opportunities for learning and fun outside the classroom. An extensive network of student-accessible microcomputer laboratories further complements the academic mission of the computer-intensive campus.

Costs

In 2010–11, state residents registered for a normal course load of 15 semester hours (full-time study) paid $3344 per semester for required tuition and fees. Room and board averaged $3635 per semester, depending upon the meal plans and residence hall selected. Tuition and required fees for out-of-state students were $7994 per semester. Books and supplies are estimated to cost about $500 per semester.

Financial Aid

To assist students toward meeting their financial responsibilities, the Office of Student Financial Aid administers a wide variety of programs from funds provided by the federal government and the state of Texas, including funds from the Federal Work-Study, Federal Pell Grant, Federal Supplemental Educational Opportunity Grant, Federal Perkins Loan, Federal Family Education Loan, Texas Public Educational Grant, and State Student Incentive Grant programs. In addition, numerous scholarships are awarded annually through the financial aid office in recognition of academic achievement, outstanding leadership, and exceptional promise or potential. ASU financial aid opportunities are available at http://www.angelo.edu/services/financial_aid.

One of the most distinctive features of the University is the Robert G. Carr and Nona K. Carr Academic Scholarship Program. One of the largest privately endowed academic scholarship programs in the nation, this program provides scholarships ranging in value from $1500 to $5000 annually. Approximately one in five students enrolled at Angelo State University receives these awards. To compete favorably for one of these renewable scholarships, a student must submit test scores of at least 21 on the ACT or at least 990 on the SAT.

Students interested in the University's Air Force ROTC program may also apply for scholarships awarded through the Air Force ROTC detachment. These awards are funded by an endowment established by the late Mr. and Mrs. Robert G. Carr. This unique program provides scholarships ranging in value from $500 to $1500 annually to qualified cadets enrolled in the University's ROTC program.

Faculty

Angelo State University retains a distinguished faculty. A 20:1 student-faculty ratio provides for an intimate classroom setting with 90 percent of the faculty members teaching undergraduate classes. In terms of academic preparation, the faculty ranks near the top of all colleges and universities in the South. More than 60 percent of the faculty members hold earned doctorates in their teaching field. Faculty members are selected with great care, as the University seeks to obtain the services of individuals who are prominent scholars and dedicated teachers who will merit the confidence of the students.

Student Government

The Student Senate is the official representative organization of the Angelo State University student body. As the primary forum for student opinion, the Student Senate provides a mutually beneficial communication link between the student body and administrative officials.

Admission Requirements

High school graduates are admitted to Angelo State University on a competitive basis. Admission to ASU is based on class rank, high school program type, and ACT or SAT scores. Students graduating in the top 10 percent of their high school classes receive automatic admission with no required minimum score on the ACT or SAT. Those graduating in the next 40 percent of their high school classes must submit scores of at least 16 on the ACT or at least 760 on the SAT. Students in the third quarter of their last year in high school must score a minimum at least 23 on the ACT or at least 1030 on the SAT. Those in the last quarter need scores of at least 30 ACT or at least 1270 on the SAT for admission.

Transfer students who have completed 18 or more hours of college-level work are admitted, provided they have maintained at least a 2.0 cumulative GPA. Students with less than 18 college-level hours must also meet the criteria established for high school students. The University welcomes applications from international students, who are considered on the basis of their secondary school record, their ACT or SAT scores, and their Test of English as a Foreign Language (TOEFL) scores (550 minimum).

For more information about ASU admission requirements, visit http://www.angelo.edu/admissions or call 800-946-8627 (toll-free).

Application and Information

High school applicants are required to submit an application for admission, results of the ACT or SAT, appropriate academic transcripts, and a $30 application fee. To request additional information and admission application forms, prospective students should e-mail admissions@angelo.edu.

Office of Admissions
Angelo State University
ASU Station #11014
San Angelo, Texas 76909-1014
Phone: 325-942-2041
      800-946-8627 (toll-free)
E-mail: admissions@angelo.edu
Web site: http://www.angelo.edu
      http://www.facebook.com/angelostateuniversity
      http://twitter.com/AngeloState

Angelo State University Centennial Village.

AQUINAS COLLEGE
GRAND RAPIDS, MICHIGAN

The College

Located on the eastern edge of the city of Grand Rapids, Aquinas enjoys all of the advantages of Michigan's second-largest city and is just a 3-hour drive from Detroit or Chicago. The Aquinas College campus is an interesting blend of early-nineteenth-century architecture coupled with modern-day structures. The campus abounds with natural beauty; it has been called the most beautiful small campus in Michigan. Its ninety species of trees, winding woodland paths, and inviting creeks and ponds create a peaceful 110-acre environment that students of all ages find welcoming. Founded by the Dominican Sisters of Grand Rapids in 1886, Aquinas has a Catholic heritage and a Christian tradition. The Dominican tradition of working and serving remains alive at Aquinas. It is lived out by Aquinas students who volunteer their time and talents in the Grand Rapids community and by those who travel to places such as Oaxaca, Mexico; Appalachia, Kentucky; or any of a dozen other service-learning project sites. An ability to see the world from different perspectives is the hallmark of an Aquinas-educated student. Aquinas, a coeducational liberal arts college, offers an approach to learning and living that teaches students unlimited ways of seeing the world. That is why every Aquinas student enrolls in the humanities program, a two-semester exploration of the best that has been thought, written, composed, and painted. As students find their way in the world of thought, the core curriculum in natural science ensures that they discover the workings of the physical world as well.

An Aquinas education makes graduates more employable. Each year, almost 200 Aquinas students find businesses, government agencies, and other organizations eager to offer field experience and internship opportunities. Students can write press releases, keep sports statistics, and travel around the country with such organizations as Major League Soccer; work on historic preservation projects with the Michigan Bureau of History in Lansing; or learn about politics from the inside as a congressional intern in Washington, D.C. Nine out of 10 applicants recommended by the Aquinas premedical advisory committee are admitted to medical school, and 19 of 20 are accepted into other graduate programs. In all, more than 90 percent of Aquinas seniors find jobs or enroll in graduate school soon after graduation. Aquinas sees a liberal arts education as career preparation. The Aquinas general education plan exposes students to the necessary skills that enable them to become critical thinkers, articulate speakers, strong writers, and effective problem solvers. Aquinas faculty members insist that students carry values as well as skills into the workplace. The College's curriculum, with its more than sixty majors, is designed to provide students with both breadth and depth and to foster a thirst for knowledge and truth and a spirit of intellectual dialogue and inquiry. Coupled with nationally recognized internship programs, it prepares students to both live and work in the rapidly changing world of today and tomorrow.

Arriving from places as near as Grand Rapids, Chicago, and Detroit and as far as Japan and Russia, the 2,300 students include 1,700 full-time, 400 part-time, and 200 graduate students. The Insignis program at Aquinas encourages students of exceptional academic ability to participate in social and intellectual activities such as lectures and receptions for visiting scholars and trips to places of cultural interest. Aquinas offers more than sixty student organizations, ranging from intramural teams and departmental clubs to a wide variety of musical groups, student publications, and service organizations.

In addition to its undergraduate degrees, Aquinas also offers Master in the Art of Teaching, Master in Education, Master in Science Education, Master of Management, and Master of Sustainable Business degrees.

Location

Aquinas' location in Grand Rapids allows students to reap the benefits of west Michigan's economic, educational, and cultural center. The city is one of the fastest-growing areas in the Great Lakes region. Grand Rapids combines big-city excitement and small-town charm. There are cosmopolitan amenities ranging from four-star hotels and restaurants to top-notch cultural facilities and entertainment venues. In addition to established attractions such as the Gerald R. Ford Presidential Museum, the Van Andel Public Museum, an expanded zoo, the 5,500-seat Fifth Third Park stadium for Whitecaps minor-league baseball, and the 70-acre Fredrik Meijer Gardens, recent attractions include the more than 12,000-seat Van Andel Arena, home to the Grand Rapids Griffins AHL hockey team and a venue for nationally known music concerts and performances. These major facilities add to the list of popular points of interest, festivals, and special events. With nearly half a million residents, there are abundant recreation, arts, and cultural opportunities available.

Majors and Degrees

Aquinas College offers the following undergraduate degree programs: Bachelor of Arts, Bachelor of Fine Arts, Bachelor of Arts in general education, Bachelor of Music Education, Bachelor of Science, Bachelor of Science in Business Administration, Bachelor of Science in sustainable business, and Bachelor of Science in international business. A Bachelor of Science in Nursing degree program is offered in collaboration with the University of Detroit Mercy and St. Mary's Health Care. Majors and programs of study are offered in accounting, accounting/business administration, art, art/business administration, art history, biology, business administration, business administration/chemistry, business administration/communication, business administration/music, business administration/sports management, chemical physics, chemistry, communication, community leadership, computer information systems, drawing, economics, education, English, environmental science, environmental studies, French, geography, German, health, history, international studies, Japanese, journalism/publications, learning disabilities, management information systems, mathematics, music, not-for-profit management, organizational communication, painting, philosophy, photography, physical education and recreation, physics, political science, pre-engineering, printmaking, psychology, sculpture, social science, sociology, Spanish, studio art, sustainable business, theater, theology, urban studies, visual arts administration, and women's studies. Preprofessional courses are available in dentistry, law, medicine, and veterinary science.

Associate degrees are also available, including the Associate of Arts and the Associate of Science.

Academic Programs

In addition to their major and minor fields of study, students take an integrated skills course called Inquiry and Expression. This course spans the first semester of the freshman year and has an emphasis on writing integrated with reading critically, oral communication skills, critical thinking, library/electronic research methods, computer utilization, and basic quantitative reasoning. The thematic content is American Pluralism: The Individual in a Diverse America. Sophomores take a yearlong course in the humanities. As juniors, they are required to take 3 hours in

Theological Foundation. Students are also required to be proficient in a second language through the 102 level. There also is a distribution plan in the general education plan covering social science, history/philosophy, natural world, artistic and creative studies, technology, and health, physical education, and recreation. A career/professional development component begins in summer orientation and offers career planning courses and activities over four years; topics include assessment of students' strengths, skills, and interests; development of goals, a learning plan, and setting a direction; focus on the individual—wellness, personal finances, and leadership/team skills; awareness of careers, professions, and graduate study; information on making and maintaining a professional portfolio and resume; participating in a professional/career mentor program; career fairs and networking; and experiential learning (choices include internship, service learning, service trips, and study abroad). The College follows a two-semester calendar with a summer session. Aquinas also accepts credit through CLEP, Advanced Placement, and International Baccalaureate.

Off-Campus Programs

Students have the option of participating in the Dominican College Campus Interchange Program. Cooperating colleges are Barry University in Miami, Florida; Dominican College in San Rafael, California; and St. Thomas Aquinas College in Sparkill, New York. Students can increase their foreign language skills through cultural-immersion programs in Costa Rica, France, Italy, Japan, Spain, or Germany. Two Aquinas faculty members accompany 30 students to Aquinas' study center in Tully Cross, Ireland. Students have the opportunity to earn a full semester of credit, travel abroad, and live in a rural Irish community. The curriculum is centered on several aspects of Irish studies.

Academic Facilities

The newly opened Grace Hauenstein Library is a $6-million facility with resources that include a public access catalog, audiovisual materials, circulation and course reserve materials, reference services, and interlibrary loan services (free access to more than 60 million books and documents from libraries across the country). Students find centrally located PC-based labs having more than 150 Pentium computers, with additional PCs in such areas as residence halls and the Cook Carriage House. The lab technology works in a network environment to allow access to standard applications such as Windows XP, Microsoft Office 2007, and Web-based e-mail, as well as more than eighty-five discipline-specific applications; printing to high-quality multifunction printers; and access to multimedia technology. Labs are open seven days a week and are staffed by trained assistants. Albertus Magnus Hall of Science features the handicapped-accessible Baldwin Observatory and a greenhouse. Other facilities include the Cook Carriage House, a student center, and the modern Art and Music Center, featuring a darkroom, a 200-seat recital hall, an art gallery, and a sculpture studio. The Jarecki Center for Advanced Learning offers network plug-ins every few feet and provides the latest in technology. Four new apartment buildings have opened, providing another housing option. The Aquinas Performing Arts Center is a $7-million facility providing a state-of-the-art theater venue.

Costs

For 2011–12, tuition is $24,106 and room and board are $7438, for a total of $31,544. Other expenses, including books, travel, and personal supplies, average $2000.

Financial Aid

Aquinas College awards both merit-based financial assistance and traditional need-based assistance to qualified students. The Spectrum Scholarship Program was developed to recognize students' achievements in academics, leadership, and service. More than 90 percent of entering freshmen receive some form of financial assistance. The College administers the traditional grant and loan programs, including Federal Direct Loans and Federal PLUS loans. Athletic grants are also available. The College participates in the NBS E-cashier automatic payment program. This plan assists students in paying costs over a period of time. To apply for financial assistance, students must complete the Free Application for Federal Student Aid (FAFSA).

Faculty

Aquinas faculty members are teachers first: while research plays an important part in the Aquinas faculty's development, teaching remains the number-one priority. In addition to teaching, faculty members serve as academic advisers, mentors, and advisers to various clubs and organizations on campus. With a student-professor ratio of 14:1, faculty members give individual attention and assistance to students. All classes and labs are taught by faculty members, not graduate assistants. Approximately 90 percent of Aquinas faculty members have doctoral or terminal degrees.

Student Government

The Student Senate is the governing body of Aquinas students. Senators are chosen by securing twenty-five signatures of students in support of their involvement. These students have both voice and vote on issues facing the College's Academic Assembly. The senate is responsible for many of the academic, social, recreational, and cultural activities that are brought to the campus.

Admission Requirements

Freshman and transfer applications are received on a rolling basis. A candidate for admission to Aquinas is considered on the basis of academic preparation, scholarship, and character. Admission depends on a number of factors, including high school academic record and ACT or SAT test scores. Transfer students must present a minimum 2.0 grade point average on a 4.0 scale. Paper and online applications do not require an application fee. The admissions office reserves the right to review applications on a case-by-case basis. Curriculum, extracurricular activities, and any extenuating circumstances are considered in the decision. Letters of recommendation are encouraged but not required.

Application and Information

For further information, interested students should contact:

Tom Mikowski
Dean of Admissions
Aquinas College
1607 Robinson Road, SE
Grand Rapids, Michigan 49506
Phone: 616-632-2900
        800-678-9593 (toll-free)
E-mail: admissions@aquinas.edu
Web site: http://www.aquinas.edu

The Aquinas campus was once a private country estate.

ARCADIA UNIVERSITY
GLENSIDE, PENNSYLVANIA

The University

Arcadia is a top-ranked private university offering bachelor's, master's, and doctoral degrees. More than 4,000 students choose from among eighty fields of study. *U.S. News & World Report* ranks Arcadia University among the top 30 universities in the North. Arcadia's diverse student population represents a cross section of cultural and socioeconomic backgrounds. Enrollment includes over 2,200 undergraduate and 1,800 graduate students. At present, Arcadia students come from forty-six states and twenty-one other countries, and 80 percent of the full-time undergraduate population resides on campus.

Arcadia was ranked first in the nation for the percentage of undergraduate students studying abroad in the 2010 *Open Doors* report and has an extensive study-abroad program. Students can choose from over 100 programs in sixteen countries.

Campus life, which includes more than ninety clubs and organizations, athletics, and cultural and social events, is rich and varied. Community service is an integral part of the Arcadia University experience. Students volunteer on neighborhood improvement projects, work at literacy or gerontology centers, and assist disadvantaged or disabled children. NCAA Division III intercollegiate competition is offered in basketball, field hockey, lacrosse, soccer, softball, swimming, tennis, and volleyball for women and baseball, basketball, golf, lacrosse, soccer, swimming, and tennis for men. Cheerleading and equestrian are offered as club sports, while intramural sports provide other athletic opportunities.

Arcadia offers master's programs in business administration, counseling psychology, education, English, forensic science, genetic counseling, health education, humanities, international peace and conflict resolution, international relations and diplomacy, physician assistant studies, and public health. A Doctor of Physical Therapy (D.P.T.) and Doctor of Education (Ed.D.) programs in special education and educational leadership are also offered.

Location

Arcadia, located in metropolitan Philadelphia, features a beautiful rolling campus built around the historic landmark Grey Towers Castle. The University is 12 miles from Center City Philadelphia and only 90 minutes from the Jersey shore and Pennsylvania's Pocono Mountains. Students have access to dozens of museums, galleries, performing arts centers, and nightspots; and historic, government, and commercial sites in the metropolitan area.

Majors and Degrees

Arcadia offers Bachelor of Arts degrees in accounting, anthropology (cultural), art and design (B.A. or B.F.A.) (art education, art history, ceramics, graphic design, interior design, metals and jewelry, painting, photography, pre–art therapy, printmaking, studio art), biology (allied health, biological basis of behavior, biomedical, conservation, forensics, molecular), business (economics, international economics, international finance, international human resources, international marketing, marketing), chemistry (biochemistry, chemical professions, forensics, health professions), communications (cinema studies, corporate, international cinema, print, video), computer science, computing technology (design, technical), criminal justice, digital media/global media, education (art education, elementary and early childhood, middle level, secondary, special education), engineering, English (creative writing, professional writing), environmental studies, fashion studies, forensic science, French studies, global legal studies, global security and emergency management, health administration, history, interdisciplinary science, international business and culture, international peace and conflict resolution, international studies (global public health; globalization, development, and human rights; modern Mediterranean world), Italian studies, liberal studies (applied social science for the global citizen, individualized), management information systems, mathematics (actuarial science), media industries, modern languages, optometry, philosophy, physical therapy, physician assistant studies, political science (international politics, prelaw and political theory, U.S. politics and policy), predentistry, premedicine, prenursing, pre–veterinary medicine, psychology (pre–art therapy,

human resources), scientific illustration, sociology (human services), sound and music, Spanish, Spanish cultural studies, special education, sport psychology, sports management, and theater arts and English. A five-year program combines the B.A. in education with a Master of Education in special education.

Bachelor of Science degrees are offered in accounting, business administration, chemistry, chemistry and business, computer science, international finance, management information systems, marketing, and mathematics.

Bachelor of Fine Arts degrees are awarded to students majoring in acting or studio arts with concentrations in ceramics, graphic design, interior design, metals and jewelry, painting, photography, and printmaking. Preparation for certification in art education is offered in conjunction with the B.F.A. program, as is preparation for graduate study in art therapy.

Arcadia's physician assistant studies 4+2 program provides a four-year undergraduate degree in a related field, followed by two years of study in Arcadia's Master of Medical Science: Physician Assistant Program. Arcadia undergraduates who satisfy the prerequisites are assured admission to the program. Arcadia also offers a combined undergraduate and graduate (4+2.5) program leading to the Doctor of Physical Therapy, with assured admission for undergrads who meet established criteria. An accelerated 3+3 program also is offered, combining a bachelor's degree in biology with a doctorate in physical therapy. The International Peace and Conflict Resolution 4+2 Program is a four-year undergraduate degree followed by two years of study in the M.A. degree program; an accelerated 3+2 option is also offered. The forensic science program provides a four-year undergraduate program in a related field followed by two years in the Master of Science in Forensic Science (M.S.F.S.) program. A 3+2 Accelerated Forensic Science Program also is offered, allowing academically talented students to earn a B.A. or B.S. in biology/chemistry and an M.S. in forensic science.

Arcadia also offers accelerated three-year bachelor's degrees in business administration, communications, international business and culture, international studies, and psychology. The format includes one summer of service learning overseas or in the United States and one summer internship at an international or U.S. location.

Arcadia offers several five-year combined programs in education. These include master's degrees in special education, environmental education, literacy education/reading, literacy education/ESL, technology education, and library science.

A dual-degree (3+2) program in engineering is offered in conjunction with Columbia University. An accelerated (3+4) program with Salus University leads to B.A. and Doctor of Optometry degrees. The 3+2 Environmental Studies program leads to a B.A. in biology and an M.A. in education, with certification in environmental education.

Academic Programs

Arcadia's undergraduate curriculum provides a distinctively global, integrative, and personal learning experience that prepares students to contribute and prosper in a diverse and dynamic world. Students are encouraged to design their own path, explore the globe, make intellectual connections, and develop an area of expertise. There are opportunities to study around the world and make connections across disciplines and cultures. Every student pursues a major, participates in cultural experiences, explores areas of inquiry, and develops intellectual practices.

Highly qualified students may enhance their education through the Honors Program, which merges the best of Arcadia's academic traditions with innovative honors courses and features unique leadership and study-abroad opportunities. Admission to the Honors Program may occur at the time of admission to Arcadia or after the student has been enrolled at the University for one or more semesters.

Credit toward graduation is granted for scores of 3 or better on AP exams. Exemption from or credit for courses may also be earned through the College-Level Examination Program (CLEP) and locally administered examinations at the discretion of the department.

Arcadia's academic year is divided into two semesters. Three summer sessions are offered, beginning in May and continuing through early August. Most full-time students carry four academic courses in each regular semester; 128 semester hours are required for graduation.

Off-Campus Programs

Arcadia is top-ranked in the nation by *U.S. News & World Report* for international study. With over 100 programs around the world, the College of Global Studies supports and implements the University's commitment to international education. Students can spend a semester or full year abroad for approximately the same cost as remaining on campus. Many shorter-term options are also available.

Arcadia offers two distinct opportunities for students to study abroad during their first year. The University's Preview program enables first-year students in good academic standing to earn 2 credits while spending their spring break in England, Ireland, Mexico, Scotland, Spain, or other countries. Previews also are offered in Los Angeles and other U.S. cities. The unique First Year Study Abroad Experience (FYSAE) gives select incoming students the chance to spend their first or second semester in London, England, or Stirling, Scotland. Arcadia's FYSAE and Preview programs have been recognized as among the most innovative international programs in the country by the American Council on Education, *U.S. News & World Report,* and the Princeton Review.

Arcadia also offers ten Majors Abroad Programs (MAPs). Students in these majors spend a year (two semesters) abroad, taking general courses as well as major-related courses at an overseas institution.

Off-campus study in the Philadelphia area includes internships and fieldwork in most majors. The University requires students to partake in a global connections experience, which may occur overseas, through a domestic study-away program, or locally.

Academic Facilities

The campus includes historical buildings as well as extensive modern facilities. A prime academic resource on Arcadia's campus is Landman Library, which offers students increased technology and access to resources both on campus and around the globe.

Arcadia's Kuch Athletic and Recreation Center features the Alumni Gymnasium, which seats 1,500 and includes basketball and volleyball courts. The Lenox Pool is a six-lane wave-resistant swimming pool with adjacent Jacuzzi. The Kuch Center also includes an indoor track that overlooks the gym, an aerobics/dance studio, a fitness center, locker rooms, saunas, first aid/training rooms, and the University Bookstore. A new student center, featuring lounges, dining areas, meeting rooms, and more, is scheduled to open in fall 2011.

Wireless Internet access is available everywhere on campus and extends to every room in the residence halls. Computer labs—including a Mac lab—are available for student use.

Costs

For 2010–11, undergraduate tuition was $32,140. Room and board charges were $11,150 per year and annual student fees were $580.

Financial Aid

On average, 98 percent of full-time undergraduates receive financial aid, and 96 percent receive grants and scholarships. Every effort is made to see that students requiring financial assistance are able to attend Arcadia. Aid is awarded on the basis of need, as determined by the Free Application for Federal Student Aid (FAFSA) and the Arcadia University Financial Aid Application, and is available in the form of grants, loans, and part-time campus employment or some combination of the three. Scholarships are presented annually to entering first-year and transfer students who have achieved academic distinction or have been recognized for outstanding extracurricular accomplishments. Distinguished Scholarships, ranging from $60,000 to $82,000 over four years, and Achievement Awards, ranging from $4000 to $58,000 over four years, recognize academic excellence, leadership, and extracurricular accomplishments. A limited number of full-tuition scholarships are available to the top entering first-year undergraduates in the applicant pool. To receive full consideration for financial aid, students should complete their applications and submit the FAFSA and Arcadia's Financial Aid Application by March 1.

Faculty

Arcadia University has a faculty with a primary commitment to teaching. The average class size is 16 students, and the ratio of students to faculty members is 13:1. This fosters an environment in which students and faculty members collaborate on research and writing and engage in informal discussions, field trips, and other activities outside the classroom. Eighty-nine percent of Arcadia faculty members hold doctorates or terminal degrees, and all courses are taught by faculty members, not graduate assistants.

Student Government

Student life is largely self-regulated by the Student Government Organization (SGO) through the Student Senate. Students serve on most major faculty committees, and student leaders attend Board of Trustees meetings.

Admission Requirements

Students are selected on the basis of educational preparation, intellectual promise, and potential. Emphasis is placed on the candidate's academic record, including the type of program followed and the grades and class rank earned. Standardized test scores also carry significant weight. Counselor and teacher recommendations, participation in school and community activities, and other supporting credentials also are strongly considered.

Freshman applicants must submit an official high school transcript, standardized test scores (SAT or ACT), and counselor and teacher recommendations. Applicants should pursue a college-preparatory program consisting of at least 16 academic units. Students are encouraged to visit the campus for a student-guided tour and an information session or one-on-one meeting with an admissions counselor.

Transfer applicants may apply for the fall term or at midyear and must submit official college transcripts. In some cases, transfer applicants are required to submit high school transcripts and SAT or ACT scores.

Application and Information

Students are encouraged to submit their applications as early as possible in the senior year. Admission decisions are made on a rolling basis, and applicants are usually notified within four to six weeks of the date of submission of the completed application. For freshman applicants, the priority admissions application deadline for Distinguished Scholarship consideration—as well as consideration for the Honors Program, First Year Study Abroad Experience, and accelerated degree programs—is January 15. The priority admissions application deadline for Achievement Award consideration is March 1. The admissions application deadline is also March 1. The transfer student deadline for portfolio review, Honors Program, Distinguished Scholarship consideration, and priority admissions is June 15 for fall-term admission.

Requests for further information should be directed to:

Office of Enrollment Management
Arcadia University
450 South Easton Road
Glenside, Pennsylvania 19038-3295

Phone: 215-572-2910
      877-ARCADIA (877-272-2342, toll-free)
E-mail: admiss@arcadia.edu
Web site: http://www.arcadia.edu/pet.asp
      http://www.arcadia.edu/socialmedia

Grey Towers Castle, Arcadia University.

ARGOSY UNIVERSITY

ARGOSY UNIVERSITY.

The University

Argosy University is a postsecondary institution of higher education offering a variety of degree programs that focus on the human side of success alongside professional competence. For students looking for a more personal approach to education, Argosy University may just be the answer. Drawing upon over thirty years of history, Argosy University has developed a curriculum that focuses on interpersonal skills and practical experience alongside academic learning. Argosy's programs are taught by practicing professionals who bring real-world experience into the classroom. Students graduate with both a solid foundation of knowledge and the power to put it to work. To accommodate busy working adults, many programs at Argosy University have a flexible structure, with both campus and online learning, and evening, weekend, and daytime classes. There are also financial aid options available for students who qualify.

Argosy University is a private institution of higher education dedicated to providing quality professional education programs at the doctoral, master's, bachelor's, and associate degree levels as well as continuing education to individuals who seek to enhance their professional and personal lives. The University emphasizes programs in the behavioral sciences (psychology and counseling), business, education, and the health-care professions. A limited number of preprofessional programs and general education offerings are provided to permit students to prepare for entry into these professional fields. The programs of Argosy University are designed to instill the knowledge, skills, and ethical values of professional practice and to foster values of social responsibility in a supportive, learning-centered environment of mutual respect and professional excellence.

With nineteen campuses nationwide, Argosy University provides students with a network of resources found at larger universities, including a career resources office, an academic resources center, and extensive information access for research. The University's innovative programs feature dynamic, relevant, and practical curricula delivered in flexible class formats. Students enjoy scheduling options that make it easier to fit school into their busy lives. They can choose from day and evening courses, on campus or online. Many students find a combination of both to be an ideal way of continuing their education while meeting family and professional demands.

Most students are full-time working professionals who live within driving distance of the campus. The University does not offer or operate student housing.

Argosy University is accredited by the Higher Learning Commission of the North Central Association and is a member of the North Central Association (230 South LaSalle Street, Suite 7-500, Chicago, Illinois 60604-1413; phone: 800-621-7440 (toll-free); Web site: http://ncahlc.org).

Location

Argosy University operates nineteen locations across the U.S. and offers a variety of degree programs online (http://www.argosy.edu). Campus locations include the following:

Atlanta, 980 Hammond Drive, Suite 100, Atlanta, Georgia 30328; phone: 770-671-1200 or 888-671-4777 (toll-free)

Chicago, 225 North Michigan Avenue, Suite 1300, Chicago, Illinois 60601; phone: 312-777-7600 or 800-626-4123 (toll-free)

Dallas, 5001 Lyndon B. Johnson Freeway, Heritage Square, Farmers Branch, Texas 75244; phone: 214-890-9900 or 866-954-9900 (toll-free)

Denver, 7600 E. Eastman Avenue, Denver, Colorado 80231; phone: 303-923-4110 or 866-431-5981 (toll-free)

Hawai'i, 400 ASB Tower, 1001 Bishop Street, Honolulu, Hawaii 96813; phone: 808-536-5555 or 888-323-2777 (toll-free)

Inland Empire, 3401 Centre Lake Drive, Suite 200, Ontario, California 91761; phone: 909-472-0800 or 866-217-9075 (toll-free)

Los Angeles, 5230 Pacific Concourse, Suite 200, Los Angeles, California 90045; phone: 310-866-4000 or 866-505-0332 (toll-free)

Nashville, 100 Centerview Drive, Suite 225, Nashville, Tennessee 37214; phone: 615-525-2800 or 866-833-6598 (toll-free)

Orange County, 601 South Lewis Street, Orange County, California 92868; phone: 714-620-3700 or 800-716-9598 (toll-free)

Phoenix, 2233 West Dunlap Avenue, Phoenix, Arizona 85021; phone: 602-216-2600 or 866-216-2777 (toll-free)

Salt Lake City, 121 Election Road, Suite 300, Draper, Utah 84020; phone: 801-601-5000 or 888-639-4756 (toll-free)

San Diego, 1615 Murray Canyon Road, Suite 100, San Diego, California 92108; phone: 619-321-3000 or 866-505-0333 (toll-free)

San Francisco Bay Area, 1005 Atlantic Avenue, Alameda, California 94501; phone: 510-217-4700 or 866-215-2777 (toll-free)

Sarasota, 5250 17th Street, Sarasota, Florida 34235; phone: 941-379-0404 or 800-331-5995 (toll-free)

Schaumburg, 999 North Plaza Drive, Suite 111, Schaumburg, Illinois 60173-5403; phone: 847-969-4900 or 866-290-2777 (toll-free)

Seattle, 2601-A Elliott Avenue, Seattle, Washington 98121; phone: 206-283-4500 or 888-283-2777 (toll-free)

Tampa, 1403 North Howard Avenue, Tampa, Florida 33607; phone: 813-393-5290 or 800-850-6488 (toll-free).

Twin Cities, 1515 Central Parkway, Eagan, Minnesota 55121; phone: 651-846-2882 or 888-844-2004 (toll-free)

Washington, D.C., 1550 Wilson Boulevard, Suite 600, Arlington, Virginia 22209; phone: 703-526-5800 or 866-703-2777 (toll-free)

Argosy University is certified by SCHEV to operate in Virginia.

Argosy University, Nashville is authorized for operation as a postsecondary educational institution by the Tennessee Higher Education Commission.

Majors and Degrees

Argosy University's College of Undergraduate Studies offers Bachelor of Arts (B.A.) programs in liberal arts and psychology as well as Bachelor of Science (B.S.) programs in business administration and criminal justice. Please note that not all degree programs are offered at all locations.

Academic Programs

The Bachelor of Arts (B.A.) in liberal arts program offers an integrative approach to learning which aims to develop competencies in the basic academic areas and disciplines in higher education. It extends the capacity for intellectual inquiry through the incorporation of courses that develop the individual, prepare them for the workplace, and for constructive participation in a global society. The B.A. in liberal arts gives students the opportunity to integrate real world experience with the critical acquisition of a variety of human knowledge and skills that not only encourages sensitivity to the diversity of human cultures, but also creates a desire to achieve personal and professional excellence.

The Bachelor of Arts (B.A.) in psychology program is designed to prepare students to begin a human services career as an entry-level counselor, case manager, or human resources administrator or in management and business services, as well as for graduate study in fields such as counseling, social work, and marriage and family therapy. The program is flexible enough to allow students to pursue opportunities offered by a number of states for credentialing or certification at the bachelor's level.

The Bachelor of Science (B.S.) in business administration degree program is designed to help students focus their academic and professional development consistent with their career objectives and experiences. In addition to the business core, students complete one of the following concentrations: accounting, finance, health-care management, human resources, international business, marketing, and organizational management. Students may choose one of five optional concentrations: customized professional concentration, finance, health-care management, international business, or marketing.

The Bachelor of Science (B.S.) in criminal justice is a practitioner-oriented program that prepares students to become successful professionals in the fields of law enforcement, corrections, probation and parole, and security. The curriculum provides students with critical thinking, communication, research, and professional skills that contribute to career development. In addition to core course work, students will complete two of seven optional concentrations: corrections, forensic psychology, homeland security, management, police, security management, and substance abuse.

Argosy University's bachelor's degree programs are open to students and working professionals with no college experience and those who have attended a community college, junior college, or other university.

Program offerings vary by school.

Academic Facilities

Argosy University libraries provide curriculum support and educational resources including current text materials, diagnostic training documents, reference materials and databases, journals and dissertations, and major and current titles in program areas. There is an online public-access catalog of library resources available throughout the Argosy University system. Students enjoy full remote access to their campus library database, enabling them to study and conduct research at home. Academic databases offer dissertation abstracts, academic journals, and professional periodicals. All library computers are Internet accessible. Software applications include Word, Excel, PowerPoint, SPSS, and various test-scoring programs.

Costs

Tuition varies by program. Students should contact the Argosy University campus of their choice for tuition information.

Financial Aid

Financial aid options are available to students who qualify. Argosy University offers access to federal and state aid programs, merit-based awards, grants, loans, and a work-study program. As a first step, students should complete the Free Application for Federal Student Aid (FAFSA). Prospective students can apply electronically at http://www.fafsa.ed.gov or at the campus. To receive consideration for financial aid and ensure timely receipt of funds, it is best to submit an application promptly.

Faculty

The Argosy University faculty is composed of working professionals who have a passion to help students succeed. Members bring real-world experience and the latest practice innovations to the academic setting. The diverse faculty is widely recognized for contributions to the field. Most hold doctoral degrees. They provide a substantive education that combines comprehensive knowledge with critical skills and practical workplace relevance. Above all, faculty members are committed to their students' personal and professional development.

Student Government

Argosy University campuses offer unique opportunities for student involvement beyond individual programs of study. Most faculty committees include a student representative. In addition, a student group meets with faculty members and administrators regularly to discuss pertinent campus-related issues.

Admission Requirements

Admission requirements differ depending on the number of college credits completed prior to application.

Students who have earned 12 or fewer semester college credits must provide proof of high school graduation or GED and meet one of the following conditions for admission: ACT composite score of 18 or above, or a combined math and verbal SAT score of 870, or minimum ACCUPLACER scores of 86 in sentence skills and 53 in algebra. Applicants who do not meet any of the above conditions for admission will be admitted with academic support if they provide proof of high school graduation or GED and meet one of the following: ACT composite score of 14 to 17, or a combined math and verbal SAT score of 660 to 869, or minimum ACCUPLACER scores of 54 in sentence skills and 36 in arithmetic.

Applicants who have earned 13 or more semester college credits must provide proof of high school graduation or GED and meet one of the following conditions for admission: cumulative college GPA of 2.0 or above or minimum ACCUPLACER scores of 86 for sentence skills and 53 in algebra. Students who do not meet either of the above criteria will be admitted with academic support if they provide proof of high school graduation or GED and meet the following condition: minimum ACCUPLACER scores of 54 in reading and 36 in arithmetic.

Students admitted with academic support are limited to 12 credit hours of study during their first semester (6 credit hours per session). Students admitted with academic support will be required to complete developmental English and/or math courses unless they meet the following conditions: Writing Review (ENG099)—must meet one of the following: a minimum ACCUPLACER score of 86 in sentence skills, or a minimum ACT verbal score of 18, or a minimum SAT verbal score of 425, or completion of a college-level English composition course with a grade of C or above; Mathematics Review I (MAT096)—must meet one of the following: a minimum ACCUPLACER score of 53 in algebra, or a minimum ACT math score of 18, or a minimum SAT math score of 440, or completion of a college-level English composition course with a grade of C or above.

Other admission requirements may include credit hours of qualified transfer credit with a grade of C- or better from a regionally accredited institution or a nationally accredited institution approved and documented by the faculty and dean of the College of Business, or the College of Professional Psychology, at Argosy University or completion of an Associate of Arts or Associate of Science degree from a regionally accredited institution. A maximum of 78 lower-division or 90 total credit hours may be transferred. A minimum written TOEFL score of 500 (paper-based test), 173 (computer-based test), or 61 (Internet-based test) is required for all applicants whose native language is not English or who have not graduated from an institution in which English is the language of instruction.

Official transcripts from approved postsecondary institutions must include a minimum grade point average of 2.0 (on a scale of 4.0) for all academic work completed. Exceptions may be made for extenuating circumstances. All applications must include a completed application form, proof of high school graduation or successful completion of the GED test, official postsecondary transcripts, and a nonrefundable (except in California) application fee. Additional materials are required prior to matriculation. Some programs have additional application requirements or include exceptions to admission requirements. An admissions representative can provide further information.

Please refer to the University's catalog for additional information.

Application and Information

Argosy University accepts students on a rolling admissions basis year-round, depending on availability of required courses. Applications for admission are available online at http://www.argosy.edu or by contacting one of the campus locations.

Argosy University Administrative Office
Phone: 800-377-0617 (toll-free)
Web site: http://www.argosy.edu

ARGOSY UNIVERSITY, TWIN CITIES
EAGAN, MINNESOTA

The University

Argosy University is an institution of higher education offering a variety of degree programs that focus on the human side of success alongside professional competence. For students looking for a more personal approach to education, Argosy University may just be the answer. Drawing upon over thirty years of history, Argosy University has developed a curriculum that focuses on interpersonal skills and practical experience alongside academic learning. Argosy's programs are taught by practicing professionals who bring real-world experience into the classroom. Students graduate with both a solid foundation of knowledge and the power to put it to work. To accommodate busy working adults, many programs at Argosy University have a flexible structure with both on-campus and online learning, and evening, weekend, and daytime classes. There are financial aid options available for students who qualify.

Argosy University is a private institution of higher education dedicated to providing quality professional education programs at the doctoral, master's, bachelor's, and associate degree levels as well as continuing education to individuals who seek to enhance their professional and personal lives. The University emphasizes programs in the behavioral sciences (psychology and counseling), business, education, and the health-care professions. A limited number of preprofessional programs and general education offerings are provided to permit students to prepare for entry into these professional fields. The programs of Argosy University are designed to instill the knowledge, skills, and ethical values of professional practice and to foster values of social responsibility in a supportive, learning-centered environment of mutual respect and professional excellence.

With nineteen campuses nationwide, Argosy University provides students with a network of resources found at larger universities, including a career resources office, an academic resources center, and extensive information access for research.

The University's innovative programs feature dynamic, relevant, and practical curricula delivered in flexible class formats. Students enjoy scheduling options that make it easier to fit school into their busy lives. They can choose from day and evening courses, on campus or online. Many students find a combination of both to be an ideal way of continuing their education while meeting family and professional demands.

Most students are full-time working professionals who live within driving distance of the campus. The University does not offer or operate student housing.

Argosy University is accredited by the Higher Learning Commission of the North Central Association and is a member of the North Central Association, 230 South LaSalle Street, Suite 7-500, Chicago, Illinois 60604-1413; phone: 800-621-7440 (toll-free); http://ncahlc. org.

Location

Argosy University's Twin Cities location offers academics in a supportive environment. The campus is nestled in a parklike suburban setting within 10 miles of the airport and the Mall of America. Students enjoy the convenience of nearby shops, restaurants, and housing, and easy freeway access. The neighboring Eagan Community Center offers many amenities, including walking paths, a fitness center, meeting rooms, and an outdoor amphitheater. The Twin Cities of Minneapolis and St. Paul have been rated by popular magazines as one of the most livable metropolitan areas in the country. With a population of 2.5 million, the area offers an abundance of recreational opportunities. Year-round outdoor activities; nationally acclaimed venues for theater, art, and music; and professional sports teams attract residents and visitors alike. The Minneapolis–St. Paul metropolitan area offers a diversified economic base fueled by a broad array of companies. Among the numerous publicly traded companies headquartered in the area are Target, UnitedHealth Group, 3M, General Mills, and U.S. Bancorp.

Majors and Degrees

The Bachelor of Arts (B.A.) in liberal arts program offers an integrative approach to learning which aims to develop competencies in the basic academic areas and disciplines in higher education. It extends the capacity for intellectual inquiry through the incorporation of courses that develop the individual, prepare them for the workplace, and for constructive participation in a global society. The B.A. in liberal arts gives students the opportunity to integrate real-world experience with the critical acquisition of a variety of human knowledge and skills that not only encourages sensitivity to the diversity of human cultures, but also creates a desire to achieve personal and professional excellence.

The Bachelor of Arts (B.A.) in psychology program is designed to prepare students to begin a human services career as an entry-level counselor, case manager, or human resources administrator; in management and business services; or for graduate study in fields such as counseling, social work, and marriage and family therapy. The program is flexible enough to allow students to pursue opportunities offered by a number of states for credentialing or certification at the bachelor's level.

The Bachelor of Science (B.S.) in business administration degree program is designed to help students focus their academic and professional development in ways consistent with their career objectives and experiences. In addition to the business core, students complete one of the following concentrations: accounting, finance, healthcare management, human resources, international business, marketing, and organizational management. Students may choose one of five optional concentrations: customized professional concentration, finance, healthcare management, international business, or marketing.

The Bachelor of Science (B.S.) in criminal justice is a practitioner-oriented program that prepares students to become successful professionals in the fields of law enforcement, corrections, probation and parole, and security. The curriculum provides students with critical thinking, communication, research, and professional skills that contribute to career development. In addition to core course work, students will complete two of seven optional concentrations: corrections, forensic psychology, homeland security, management, police, security management, and substance abuse.

The Bachelor of Science (B.S.) in medical technology degree program is designed for individuals who have completed an associate degree in medical laboratory technology. Medical technologists perform the more complex laboratory testing in the clinical lab which requires a higher level of judgment and expertise than that of a medical laboratory technician. Medical technologists write and implement new procedures, evaluate test results, and establish and monitor programs to ensure the accuracy of laboratory testing. Additionally, this program includes coursework designed to help students acquire the knowledge, skills, and competencies they need to seek entry-level management or leadership positions.

Argosy University Twin Cities also offers a variety of associate degree programs in the health sciences discipline.

Academic Programs

Argosy University's bachelor's degree programs are open to students and working professionals with no college experience and those who have attended a community college, junior college, or other university.

Academic Facilities

Argosy University libraries provide curriculum support and educational resources, including current text materials, diagnostic training documents, reference materials and databases, journals and dissertations, and major and current titles in program areas. The University provides an online public-access catalog of library resources throughout the Argosy University system. Students enjoy full remote access to their campus library database, enabling them to study and conduct research at home. Academic databases offer dissertation abstracts, academic journals, and professional periodicals. All library computers are Internet accessible. Software applications include Word, Excel, PowerPoint, SPSS, and various test-scoring programs.

Costs

Tuition varies by program. Students should contact Argosy University's Twin Cities location for tuition information.

Financial Aid

Financial aid options are available to students who qualify. Argosy University offers access to federal and state aid programs, merit-based awards, grants, loans, and a work-study program. As a first step, students should complete the Free Application for Federal Student Aid (FAFSA). Prospective students can apply online at http://www.fafsa.ed.gov or at the campus. To receive consideration for financial aid and ensure timely receipt of funds, it is best to submit an application promptly.

Faculty

The Argosy University faculty is composed of working professionals who are committed to student success. Members bring real-world experience and practice innovations to the academic setting. Argosy's diverse faculty is widely recognized for contributions to the field. Most hold doctoral degrees. They provide a substantive education that combines comprehensive knowledge with critical skills and practical workplace relevance. Above all, faculty members of the College of Health Sciences are committed to their students' personal and professional development.

Student Government

Argosy University campuses offer unique opportunities for student involvement beyond individual programs of study. Most faculty committees include a student representative. In addition, a student group meets with faculty members and administrators regularly to discuss pertinent campus-related issues.

Admission Requirements

Students who have successfully completed a program of secondary education or the equivalent (GED) are eligible for admission to Argosy University's programs. Entrance requirements include either an ACT composite score of 18 or above, a combined math and verbal SAT score of 960 or above, a passing score on the Argosy University Entrance Exam, or a minimum TOEFL score of 550 (paper version), 213 (computer version), or 79 (Internet version) for all applicants whose native language is not English or who have not graduated from an institution in which English is the language of instruction.

All applicants must include a completed application form; proof of high school graduation or successful completion of the GED test; official postsecondary transcripts; SAT, ACT, Argosy University exam, or TOEFL scores; and the nonrefundable application fee. Additional materials are required prior to matriculation. Some programs have additional application requirements. An admissions representative can provide further detailed information.

Application and Information

Argosy University, Twin Cities, accepts students on a rolling admissions basis year-round, depending on availability of required courses. Applications for admission are available online or by contacting the campus, using the information listed in this description.

Argosy University, Twin Cities
1515 Central Parkway
Eagan, Minnesota 55121
Phone: 651-846-2882
Phone: 800-377-0617 (toll-free)
E-mail: auadmissions@argosy.edu
Web site: http://www.argosy.edu/twincities

THE ART INSTITUTE OF ATLANTA

ATLANTA, GEORGIA

A focused education from The Art Institute of Atlanta can help students turn their creative energy into a powerful tool that can make a difference in the world. Students are part of a collaborative and supportive community, where experienced instructors provide the guidance and skills needed to pursue a career in the creative economy.

The school's programs in the areas of design, media arts, fashion, and culinary give students the opportunity to learn by using professional-grade technology and build a portfolio of work to show potential employers after graduation.

The Art Institute of Atlanta, including its branch campuses—The Art Institute of Atlanta–Decatur, The Art Institute of Charleston, The Art Institute of Tennessee–Nashville, The Art Institute of Virginia Beach, The Art Institute of Washington, and The Art Institute of Washington–Northern Virginia—is accredited by the Commission on Colleges of the Southern Association of Colleges and Schools to award associate and baccalaureate degrees. Contact the Commission on Colleges at 1866 Southern Lane, Decatur, Georgia 30033-4097 or call 404-679-4500 for answers to questions about the accreditation of The Art Institute of Atlanta.

The Associate in Arts degree in culinary arts and the Bachelor of Science degree in culinary arts management programs are accredited by the Accrediting Commission of the American Culinary Federation Education Foundation.

The interior design program leading to the Bachelor of Fine Arts degree is accredited by the Council for Interior Design Accreditation, 206 Grandville Avenue, Suite 350, Grand Rapids, Michigan 49503; http://www.accredit-id.org.

The Art Institute of Atlanta is an accredited institutional member of the National Association of Schools of Art and Design (NASAD).

The Art Institute of Atlanta is licensed by the Georgia Nonpublic Postsecondary Education Commission, 2082 East Exchange Place, Suite 220, Tucker, Georgia 30084.

Location

Located in bustling suburban Atlanta, the school is close to public transportation and within walking distance of a shopping center with movie theaters, several restaurants, and stores. One of the city's largest malls is less than a 10-minute drive—or one subway stop from The Art Institute of Atlanta. There are at least thirty restaurants within a 15-minute drive. Students enjoy clubs and concerts, galleries and museums, baseball games, and rollerblading in Piedmont Park. The High Museum of Art, Michael C. Carlos Museum, Atlanta Contemporary Art Center, and dozens of art galleries throughout the city are wonderful resources for creative-minded students.

Programs of Study and Degrees

No matter which course of study a student may choose, the professionals at The Art Institute of Atlanta will guide, support, and help each student as their talents evolve on their journey of personal and professional transformation. Students studying design learn to fine-tune their visual thinking and problem-solving skills, as they create everything from logos to TV ads. Programs in the area of media arts focus on utilizing technology to deliver information and entertainment, while students studying fashion learn to design clothes for the runway or run a retail shop. Culinary programs focus on the fundamental techniques while exposing students to a full menu of international cuisines and management techniques.

Bachelor's degree programs are offered in audio production, culinary management, design and technical graphics, digital filmmaking and video production, fashion and retail management, game art and design, graphic design, interior design, media arts and animation, photography, and Web design and interactive media.

Associate degree programs are offered in baking and pastry, culinary arts, graphic design, restaurant and catering management, and Web design and interactive media.

A diploma program is offered in culinary arts.

Academic Programs

The academic year of The Art Institute of Atlanta is divided into four quarters that begin in January, April, July, and October. Full-time students typically take 16 academic credits per quarter. An associate degree can be earned in as little as six to seven quarters (approximately two years), and a bachelor's degree can be earned in as little as twelve quarters (three to four years). Students may take online classes in order to earn a degree on a flexible schedule, or they may take online classes as a supplement to traditional classroom learning.

Academic Facilities

The Art Institute of Atlanta provides a learning environment with professional-grade technology applicable to each student's course of study. Students have the opportunity to build a portfolio of work that shows potential employers that they are trained to use the software, hardware, or equipment utilized within the industry. Depending upon the course of study, students are immersed in a creative environment—from classrooms to computer labs to studios—focused on relevant, hands-on education designed to prepare students for the real world.

Costs

Tuition cost varies by program. Prospective students should contact the school for current tuition costs. Other charges include a starting kit for all first-quarter students. Kits vary in price depending on the program of study.

Financial Aid

Financial aid is available for those who qualify. Students who require financial assistance should first complete and submit a Free Application for Federal Student Aid (FAFSA) and meet with a financial aid officer.

Faculty

Faculty members are experienced professionals who create a learning environment that is similar to the professional world students will face after graduation. Instructors are focused on helping students develop the skills they need to transform their creative potential into marketable skills.

Student Government

The Student Advisory Assembly, the representative body of students, meets regularly to discuss policy matters and to plan programs to enhance student life. The assembly offers a valuable opportunity for students to learn the principles of leadership as well as communication and human relations skills. Other organizations dedicated to student life include the Housing Council, International Student Association, Student Activities Board, and Student Ambassadors. Students may take part in several student organizations, such as professional organizations for creative artists, which provide networking and other career opportunities.

Admission Requirements

To apply to The Art Institute of Atlanta, students must submit an application for admission, a 150-word essay, a signed notice regarding transferability for credit earned, and high school transcripts or General Educational Development (GED) test scores. Official reports of SAT, ACT, ASSET, or COMPASS scores must also be given to the school. Finally, students are required to complete an interview with an assistant director of admissions and to present a portfolio of their work. There is a $50 application fee.

Admissions decisions are made by the Admissions Committee, which consists of school faculty and staff members. The committee determines whether an applicant has a reasonable chance to be successful at The Art Institute of Atlanta, based upon the applicant's academic record, essay, and the appropriateness of stated career goals as they relate to the chosen program of study.

For the most recent information regarding admission requirements, please refer to the current academic catalog.

Application and Information

To obtain an application, make arrangements for an interview, or tour the school, prospective students should contact:

The Art Institute of Atlanta
6600 Peachtree Dunwoody Road, N.E.
100 Embassy Row
Atlanta, Georgia 30328-1635
Phone: 770-394-8300
         800-275-4242 (toll-free)
Fax: 770-394-0008
Web site: http://www.artinstitutes.edu/atlanta

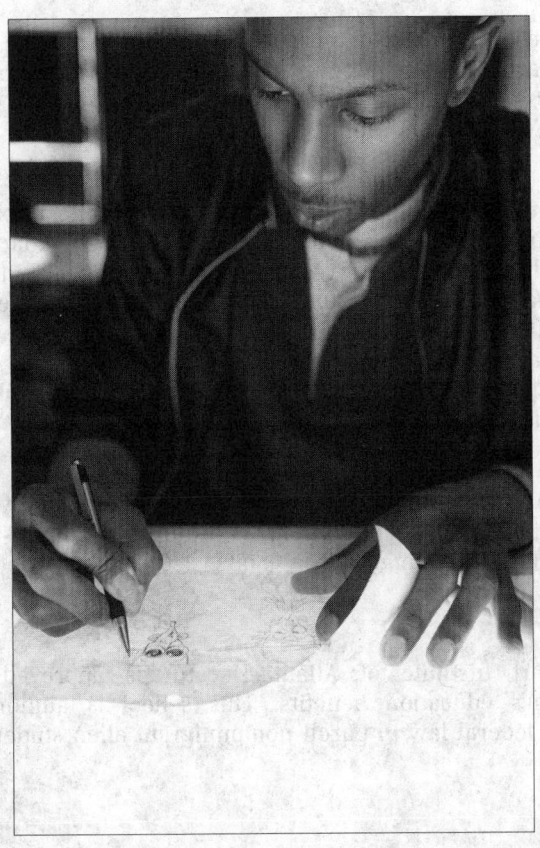

The Art Institute of Atlanta; The Art Institute of Atlanta–Decatur[1]; The Art Institute of Austin[2]; The Art Institute of California–Hollywood; The Art Institute of California–Inland Empire; The Art Institute of California–Los Angeles; The Art Institute of California–Orange County; The Art Institute of California–Sacramento; The Art Institute of California–San Diego; The Art Institute of California–San Francisco; The Art Institute of California–Sunnyvale; The Art Institute of Charleston[1]; The Art Institute of Charlotte; The Art Institute of Colorado; The Art Institute of Dallas[3]; The Art Institute of Fort Lauderdale; The Art Institute of Fort Worth[3]; The Art Institute of Houston; The Art Institute of Houston–North[2]; The Art Institute of Indianapolis[4]; The Art Institute of Jacksonville[5]; The Art Institute of Las Vegas; The Art Institute of Michigan; The Art Institute of New York City; The Art Institute of Ohio–Cincinnati[6]; The Art Institute of Philadelphia; The Art Institute of Phoenix; The Art Institute of Pittsburgh; The Art Institute of Portland; The Art Institute of Raleigh–Durham; The Art Institute of Salt Lake City; The Art Institute of San Antonio[2];The Art Institute of Seattle; The Art Institute of Tampa[5]; The Art Institute of Tennessee–Nashville[1]; The Art Institute of Tucson; The Art Institute of Vancouver; The Art Institute of Virginia Beach[1,7]; The Art Institute of Washington[1,7]; The Art Institute of Washington–Northern Virginia[1,7]; The Art Institute of Wisconsin; The Art Institute of York–Pennsylvania; The Art Institutes International–Kansas City; The Art Institutes International Minnesota; The Illinois Institute of Art–Chicago; The Illinois Institute of Art–Schaumburg; The Illinois Institute of Art–Tinley Park; Miami International University of Art & Design; The New England Institute of Art.

[1]A branch of The Art Institute of Atlanta
[2]A branch of The Art Institute of Houston
[3]A campus of South University
[4]The Art Institute of Indianapolis is regulated by the Indiana Commission on Proprietary Education, 302 West Washington Street, Room E201, Indianapolis, Indiana 46204, AC-0080
[5]A branch of Miami International University of Art & Design
[6]The Art Institute of Ohio–Cincinnati, 8845 Governors Hill Drive, Suite 100, Cincinnati, Ohio 45249-3317, OH Reg. #04-01-1698B
[7]Certified by the State Council of Higher Education to operate in Virginia

THE ART INSTITUTE OF ATLANTA–DECATUR

DECATUR, GEORGIA

A focused education from The Art Institute of Atlanta–Decatur, a branch of The Art Institute of Atlanta, can help students turn their creative energy into a powerful tool that can make a difference in the world. Students are part of a collaborative and supportive community, where experienced instructors provide the guidance and skills needed to pursue a career in the creative economy.

The school's programs in the areas of design, media arts, and fashion give students the opportunity to learn on professional-grade technology and build a portfolio of work to show potential employers after graduation.

The Art Institute of Atlanta–Decatur is a branch campus of The Art Institute of Atlanta. The Art Institute of Atlanta is accredited by the Commission on Colleges of the Southern Association of Colleges and Schools to award associate and baccalaureate degrees. Contact the Commission on Colleges at 1866 Southern Lane, Decatur, Georgia 30033-4097 or call 404-679-4500 for answers to questions about the accreditation of The Art Institute of Atlanta.

The Art Institute of Atlanta–Decatur is licensed by the Georgia Nonpublic Postsecondary Education Commission, 2082 East Exchange Place, Suite 220, Tucker, Georgia 30084.

The Art Institute of Atlanta–Decatur is approved for veteran's education benefits. This school is authorized under federal law to enroll nonimmigrant alien students.

Location

Decatur is a diverse, progressive community that retains a small-town feel, with quiet residential areas and historic districts. Decatur has easy access to the bustling city of Atlanta with its varied and plentiful arts, culture, entertainment, and sports venues.

Programs of Study and Degrees

No matter which course of study a student may choose, the professionals at The Art Institute of Atlanta–Decatur will guide, support, and help each student as their talents evolve on their journey of personal and professional transformation. Students studying design learn to fine-tune their visual thinking and problem-solving skills, as they create everything from logos to TV ads. Programs in the area of media arts focus on utilizing technology to deliver information and entertainment, while students studying fashion learn to design clothes for the runway or run a retail shop.

Bachelor's degree programs are offered in advertising, fashion and retail management, game art and design, graphic design, interior design, media arts and animation, photographic imaging, and Web design and interactive media.

Associate degrees are offered in graphic design and Web design and interactive media.

Diploma programs are available in advertising design, digital design, residential interiors, and Web design.

Academic Programs

The Art Institute of Atlanta–Decatur operates on a year-round, four-quarter system.

Academic Facilities

The Art Institute of Atlanta–Decatur provides a learning environment with professional-grade technology applicable to each student's course of study. Students have the opportunity to build a portfolio of work that shows potential employers that they are trained to use the software, hardware, or equipment utilized within the industry. Depending upon the course of study, students are immersed in a creative environment—from classrooms to computer labs to studios—focused on relevant, hands-on education designed to prepare students for the real world.

Costs

Tuition cost varies by program. Prospective students should contact the school for current tuition costs. Other charges include a starting kit for all first-quarter students. Kits vary in price depending on the program of study.

Financial Aid

Financial aid is available for those who qualify. Students who require financial assistance should first complete and submit a Free Application for Federal Student Aid (FAFSA) and meet with a financial aid officer.

Faculty

Faculty members are experienced professionals who create a learning environment that is similar to the professional world students will face after graduation. Instructors are focused on helping students develop the skills they need to transform their creative potential into marketable skills.

Admission Requirements

Applicants must provide proof of high school graduation or achievement of a General Educational Development (GED) certificate as a prerequisite for admission. In lieu of documenting high school graduation or a GED certificate, applicants may provide proof of attaining an associate degree or higher from an accredited institution. An official transcript indicating date of high school graduation, GED certificate (including test scores), or date of college graduation (including degree granted) is required as proof.

All individuals seeking admission to The Art Institute of Atlanta–Decatur are interviewed in person or by phone by an assistant director of admissions, and each applicant must submit an original essay of at least 150 words stating how an education at The Art Institute of Atlanta–Decatur would help the student to achieve career goals. There is a $50 application fee.

For the most recent information regarding admission requirements, please refer to the current academic catalog.

Application and Information

To obtain an application, make arrangements for an interview, or tour the school, prospective students should contact:

The Art Institute of Atlanta–Decatur
One West Court Square, Suite 110
Decatur, Georgia 30030
Phone: 404-942-1800
   866-856-6203 (toll-free)
Fax: 404-942-1818
Web site: http://www.artinstitutes.edu/decatur

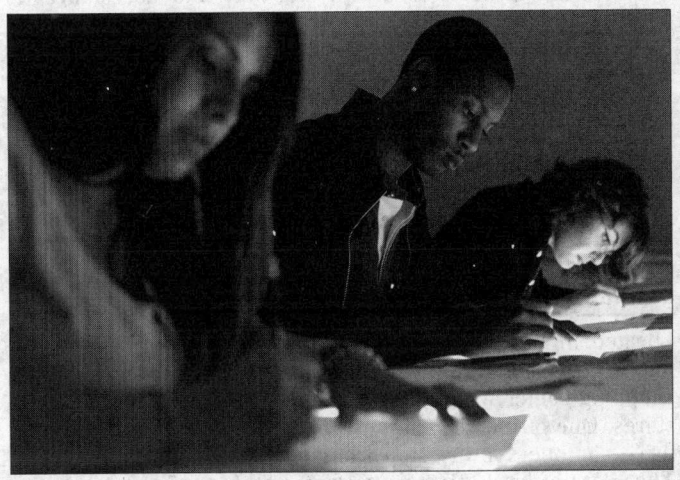

The Art Institute of Atlanta; The Art Institute of Atlanta–Decatur[1]; The Art Institute of Austin[2]; The Art Institute of California–Hollywood; The Art Institute of California–Inland Empire; The Art Institute of California–Los Angeles; The Art Institute of California–Orange County; The Art Institute of California–Sacramento; The Art Institute of California–San Diego; The Art Institute of California–San Francisco; The Art Institute of California–Sunnyvale; The Art Institute of Charleston[1]; The Art Institute of Charlotte; The Art Institute of Colorado; The Art Institute of Dallas[3]; The Art Institute of Fort Lauderdale; The Art Institute of Fort Worth[3]; The Art Institute of Houston; The Art Institute of Houston–North[2]; The Art Institute of Indianapolis[4]; The Art Institute of Jacksonville[5]; The Art Institute of Las Vegas; The Art Institute of Michigan; The Art Institute of New York City; The Art Institute of Ohio–Cincinnati[6]; The Art Institute of Philadelphia; The Art Institute of Phoenix; The Art Institute of Pittsburgh; The Art Institute of Portland; The Art Institute of Raleigh–Durham; The Art Institute of Salt Lake City; The Art Institute of San Antonio[2];The Art Institute of Seattle; The Art Institute of Tampa[5]; The Art Institute of Tennessee–Nashville[1]; The Art Institute of Tucson; The Art Institute of Vancouver; The Art Institute of Virginia Beach[1,7]; The Art Institute of Washington[1,7]; The Art Institute of Washington–Northern Virginia[1,7]; The Art Institute of Wisconsin; The Art Institute of York–Pennsylvania; The Art Institutes International–Kansas City; The Art Institutes International Minnesota; The Illinois Institute of Art–Chicago; The Illinois Institute of Art–Schaumburg; The Illinois Institute of Art–Tinley Park; Miami International University of Art & Design; The New England Institute of Art.
[1]A branch of The Art Institute of Atlanta
[2]A branch of The Art Institute of Houston
[3]A campus of South University
[4]The Art Institute of Indianapolis is regulated by the Indiana Commission on Proprietary Education, 302 West Washington Street, Room E201, Indianapolis, Indiana 46204, AC-0080
[5]A branch of Miami International University of Art & Design
[6]The Art Institute of Ohio–Cincinnati, 8845 Governors Hill Drive, Suite 100, Cincinnati, Ohio 45249-3317, OH Reg. #04-01-1698B
[7]Certified by the State Council of Higher Education to operate in Virginia

COLLEGE CLOSE-UPS

THE ART INSTITUTE OF AUSTIN

AUSTIN, TEXAS

A focused education from The Art Institute of Austin, a branch of The Art Institute of Houston, can help students turn their creative energy into a powerful tool that can make a difference in the world. Students are part of a collaborative and supportive community, where experienced instructors provide the guidance and skills needed to pursue a career in the creative economy.

The school's programs in the areas of design, media arts, fashion, and culinary give students the opportunity to learn by using professional-grade technology and build a portfolio of work to show potential employers after graduation.

The Art Institute of Austin is a branch campus of The Art Institute of Houston. The Art Institute of Houston is accredited by the Commission on Colleges of the Southern Association of Colleges and Schools to award associate and baccalaureate degrees. Contact the Commission on Colleges, 1866 Southern Lane, Decatur, Georgia 30033-4097 or call 404-679-4500 for answers to questions about the accreditation of The Art Institute of Houston.

The Art Institute of Austin holds a certificate of authorization acknowledging exemption from Texas Higher Education Coordinating Board regulations.

Location

Located in bustling suburban Austin, the school is close to public transportation and within walking distance of a shopping center with movie theaters, several restaurants, and stores. One of the city's largest malls is less than a 10-minute drive—or one subway stop from The Art Institute of Austin. There are at least thirty restaurants within a 15-minute drive. Students enjoy clubs and concerts, galleries and museums, baseball games, and rollerblading in Piedmont Park. The High Museum of Art, Michael C. Carlos Museum, Austin Contemporary Art Center, and dozens of art galleries throughout the city are wonderful resources for creative-minded students.

Programs of Study and Degrees

No matter which course of study a student may choose, the professionals at The Art Institute of Austin will guide, support, and help each student as their talents evolve on their journey of personal and professional transformation. Students studying design learn to fine-tune their visual thinking and problem-solving skills, as they create everything from logos to TV ads. Programs in the area of media arts focus on utilizing technology to deliver information and entertainment, while students studying fashion learn to design clothes for the runway or run a retail shop. Culinary programs focus on the fundamental techniques while exposing students to a full menu of international cuisines and management techniques.

Bachelor's degree programs are offered in audio production, culinary management, design and technical graphics, digital filmmaking and video production, fashion and retail management, game art and design, graphic design, interior design, media arts and animation, photography, and Web design and interactive media.

Associate degree programs are offered in baking and pastry, culinary arts, graphic design, restaurant and catering management, and Web design and interactive media.

A diploma program is offered in culinary arts.

Academic Programs

The academic year of The Art Institute of Austin is divided into four quarters that begin in January, April, July, and October. Full-time students typically take 16 academic credits per quarter. An associate degree can be earned in as little as six to seven quarters (approximately two years), and a bachelor's degree can be earned in as little as twelve quarters (three to four years). Students may take online classes in order to earn a degree on a flexible schedule, or they may take online classes as a supplement to traditional classroom learning.

Academic Facilities

The Art Institute of Austin provides a learning environment with professional-grade technology applicable to each student's course of study. Students have the opportunity to build a portfolio of work that shows potential employers that they are trained to use the software, hardware, or equipment utilized within the industry. Depending upon the course of study, students are immersed in a creative environment—from classrooms to computer labs to studios—focused on relevant, hands-on education designed to prepare students for the real world.

Costs

Tuition cost varies by program. Prospective students should contact the school for current tuition costs. Other charges include a starting kit for all first-quarter students. Kits vary in price depending on the program of study.

Financial Aid

Financial aid is available for those who qualify. Students who require financial assistance should first complete and submit a Free Application for Federal Student Aid (FAFSA) and meet with a financial aid officer.

Faculty

Faculty members are experienced professionals who create a learning environment that is similar to the professional world students will face after graduation. Instructors are focused on

helping students develop the skills they need to transform their creative potential into marketable skills.

Student Government

The Student Advisory Assembly, the representative body of students, meets regularly to discuss policy matters and to plan programs to enhance student life. The assembly offers a valuable opportunity for students to learn the principles of leadership as well as communication and human relations skills. Other organizations dedicated to student life include the Housing Council, International Student Association, Student Activities Board, and Student Ambassadors. Students may take part in several student organizations, such as professional organizations for creative artists, which provide networking and other career opportunities.

Admission Requirements

To apply to The Art Institute of Austin, students must submit an application for admission, a 150-word essay, a signed notice regarding transferability for credit earned, and high school transcripts or General Educational Development (GED) test scores. Official reports of SAT, ACT, ASSET, or COMPASS scores must also be given to the school. Finally, students are required to complete an interview with an assistant director of admissions and to present a portfolio of their work. There is a $50 application fee.

Admissions decisions are made by the Admissions Committee, which consists of school faculty and staff members. The committee determines whether an applicant has a reasonable chance to be successful at The Art Institute of Austin, based upon the applicant's academic record, essay, and the appropriateness of stated career goals as they relate to the chosen program of study.

For the most recent information regarding admission requirements, please refer to the current academic catalog.

Application and Information

To obtain an application, make arrangements for an interview, or tour the school, prospective students should contact:

The Art Institute of Austin
101 West Louis Henna Boulevard, Suite 100
Austin, Texas 78728
Phone: 512-691-1707
　　　　866-583-7952 (toll-free)
Fax: 512-691-1790
Web site: http://www.artinstitutes.edu/austin

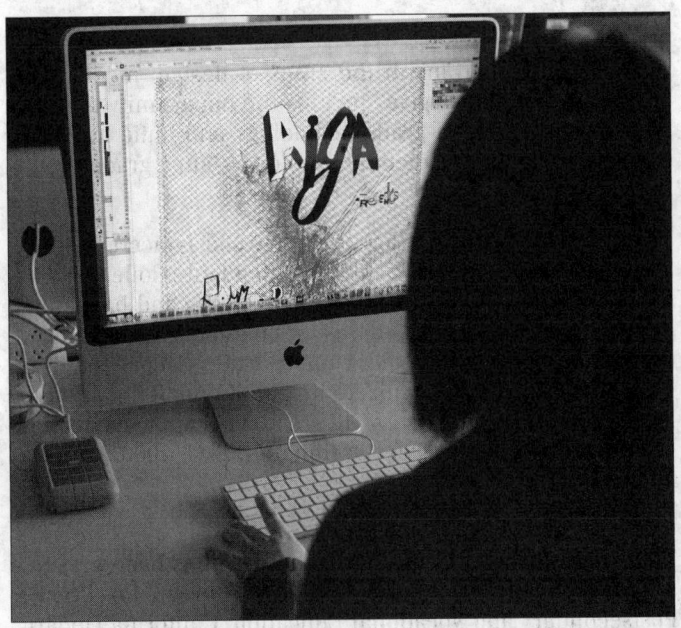

The Art Institute of Atlanta; The Art Institute of Atlanta–Decatur[1]; The Art Institute of Austin[2]; The Art Institute of California–Hollywood; The Art Institute of California–Inland Empire; The Art Institute of California–Los Angeles; The Art Institute of California–Orange County; The Art Institute of California–Sacramento; The Art Institute of California–San Diego; The Art Institute of California–San Francisco; The Art Institute of California–Sunnyvale; The Art Institute of Charleston[1]; The Art Institute of Charlotte; The Art Institute of Colorado; The Art Institute of Dallas[5]; The Art Institute of Fort Lauderdale; The Art Institute of Fort Worth[5]; The Art Institute of Houston; The Art Institute of Houston–North[2]; The Art Institute of Indianapolis[4]; The Art Institute of Jacksonville[5]; The Art Institute of Las Vegas; The Art Institute of Michigan; The Art Institute of New York City; The Art Institute of Ohio–Cincinnati[6]; The Art Institute of Philadelphia; The Art Institute of Phoenix; The Art Institute of Pittsburgh; The Art Institute of Portland; The Art Institute of Raleigh–Durham; The Art Institute of Salt Lake City; The Art Institute of San Antonio[2];The Art Institute of Seattle; The Art Institute of Tampa[5]; The Art Institute of Tennessee–Nashville[1]; The Art Institute of Tucson; The Art Institute of Vancouver; The Art Institute of Virginia Beach[1,7]; The Art Institute of Washington[1,7]; The Art Institute of Washington–Northern Virginia[1,7]; The Art Institute of Wisconsin; The Art Institute of York–Pennsylvania; The Art Institutes International–Kansas City; The Art Institutes International Minnesota; The Illinois Institute of Art–Chicago; The Illinois Institute of Art–Schaumburg; The Illinois Institute of Art–Tinley Park; Miami International University of Art & Design; The New England Institute of Art.

[1]A branch of The Art Institute of Atlanta
[2]A branch of The Art Institute of Houston
[3]A campus of South University
[4]The Art Institute of Indianapolis is regulated by the Indiana Commission on Proprietary Education, 302 West Washington Street, Room E201, Indianapolis, Indiana 46204, AC-0080
[5]A branch of Miami International University of Art & Design
[6]The Art Institute of Ohio–Cincinnati, 8845 Governors Hill Drive, Suite 100, Cincinnati, Ohio 45249-3317, OH Reg. #04-01-1698B
[7]Certified by the State Council of Higher Education to operate in Virginia

THE ART INSTITUTE OF CALIFORNIA–HOLLYWOOD

NORTH HOLLYWOOD, CALIFORNIA

A focused education from The Art Institute of California–Hollywood can help students turn their creative energy into a powerful tool that can make a difference in the world. Students are part of a collaborative and supportive community, where experienced instructors provide the guidance and skills needed to pursue a career in the creative economy.

The school's programs in the areas of design, media arts, fashion, and culinary give students the opportunity to learn by using professional-grade technology and build a portfolio of work to show potential employers after graduation.

The Art Institute of California–Hollywood is accredited by the Accrediting Council for Independent Colleges and Schools (ACICS) to award associate degrees and bachelor's degrees. ACICS is listed as a nationally recognized accrediting agency by the United States Department of Education and is recognized by the Council for Higher Education Accreditation. ACICS can be contacted at 750 First Street NE, Suite 980, Washington, D.C. 20002; phone: 202-336-6780.

The Art Institute of California–Hollywood has been granted approval to operate by the California Bureau for Private Postsecondary and Vocational Education, California Department of Consumer Affairs, 1625 North Market Boulevard, Suite S-308, Sacramento, California 95834; phone: 916-574-8200; www.bppve.ca.gov.

Location

The school is located at the crossroads of California's design, fashion, and entertainment industries. The Art Institute of California–Hollywood is designed with the creative student in mind.

Programs of Study and Degrees

No matter which course of study a student may choose, the professionals at The Art Institute of California–Hollywood will guide, support, and help each student as their talents evolve on their journey of personal and professional transformation. Students studying design learn to fine-tune their visual thinking and problem-solving skills, as they create everything from logos to TV ads. Programs in the area of media arts focus on utilizing technology to deliver information and entertainment, while students studying fashion learn to design clothes for the runway or run a retail shop. Culinary programs focus on the fundamental techniques while exposing students to a full menu of international cuisines and management techniques.

Bachelor's degree programs are offered in culinary management, digital filmmaking and video production, digital photography, fashion design, fashion marketing and management, game art and design, graphic design, industrial design, interior design, media arts and animation, set and exhibit design, visual and game programming, visual effects and motion graphics, and Web design and interactive media.

Associate degree programs are offered in culinary arts, digital photography, fashion design, fashion marketing, graphic design, and Web design and interactive media.

The graphic design and interior design programs are also available in an evening and weekend option format.

Academic Programs

The Art Institute of California–Hollywood operates on a year-round, four-quarter system.

Academic Facilities

The Art Institute of California–Hollywood provides a learning environment with professional-grade technology applicable to each student's course of study. Students have the opportunity to build a portfolio of work that shows potential employers that they are trained to use the software, hardware, or equipment utilized within the industry. Depending upon the course of study, students are immersed in a creative environment—from classrooms to computer labs to studios—focused on relevant, hands-on education designed to prepare students for the real world.

Costs

Tuition cost varies by program. Prospective students should contact the school for current tuition costs. Other charges include a starting kit for all first-quarter students. Kits vary in price depending on the program of study.

Financial Aid

Financial aid is available for those who qualify. Students who require financial assistance should first complete and submit a Free Application for Federal Student Aid (FAFSA) and meet with a financial aid officer.

Faculty

Faculty members are experienced professionals who create a learning environment that is similar to the professional world students will face after graduation. Instructors are focused on helping students develop the skills they need to transform their creative potential into marketable skills.

Admission Requirements

Applicants must provide proof of high school graduation or achievement of General Educational Development (GED) certificate as a prerequisite for admission. In lieu of documenting high school graduation or a GED certificate, applicants may provide proof of attaining an associate degree or higher from an accredited institution. An official transcript indicating date of high school graduation, GED certificate (including test scores), or date of college graduation (including degree granted) is required as proof.

All individuals seeking admission to The Art Institute of California–Hollywood are interviewed in person or by phone by an assistant director of admissions, and each applicant must create an original essay of at least 150 words stating how an education at The Art Institute of California–Hollywood would help the student to achieve career goals. There is a $50 application fee.

For the most recent information regarding admission requirements, please refer to the current academic catalog.

Application and Information

To obtain an application, make arrangements for an interview, or tour the school, prospective students should contact:

The Art Institute of California–Hollywood
5250 Lankershim Boulevard
North Hollywood, California 91601
Phone: 818-299-5100
           877-468-6232 (toll-free)
Fax: 818-299-5150
Web site: http://www.artinstitutes.edu/hollywood

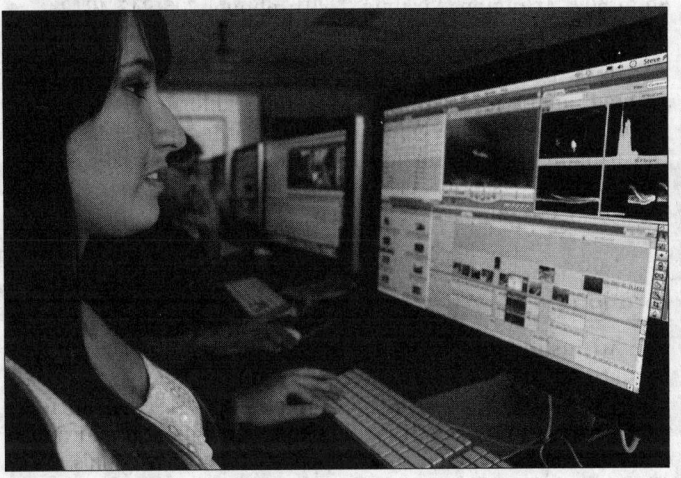

The Art Institute of Atlanta; The Art Institute of Atlanta–Decatur[1]; The Art Institute of Austin[2]; The Art Institute of California–Hollywood; The Art Institute of California–Inland Empire; The Art Institute of California–Los Angeles; The Art Institute of California–Orange County; The Art Institute of California–Sacramento; The Art Institute of California–San Diego; The Art Institute of California–San Francisco; The Art Institute of California–Sunnyvale; The Art Institute of Charleston[1]; The Art Institute of Charlotte; The Art Institute of Colorado; The Art Institute of Dallas[3]; The Art Institute of Fort Lauderdale; The Art Institute of Fort Worth[3]; The Art Institute of Houston; The Art Institute of Houston–North[2]; The Art Institute of Indianapolis[4]; The Art Institute of Jacksonville[5]; The Art Institute of Las Vegas; The Art Institute of Michigan; The Art Institute of New York City; The Art Institute of Ohio–Cincinnati[6]; The Art Institute of Philadelphia; The Art Institute of Phoenix; The Art Institute of Pittsburgh; The Art Institute of Portland; The Art Institute of Raleigh–Durham; The Art Institute of Salt Lake City; The Art Institute of San Antonio[2];The Art Institute of Seattle; The Art Institute of Tampa[5]; The Art Institute of Tennessee–Nashville[1]; The Art Institute of Tucson; The Art Institute of Vancouver; The Art Institute of Virginia Beach[1,7]; The Art Institute of Washington[1,7]; The Art Institute of Washington–Northern Virginia[1,7]; The Art Institute of Wisconsin; The Art Institute of York–Pennsylvania; The Art Institutes International–Kansas City; The Art Institutes International Minnesota; The Illinois Institute of Art–Chicago; The Illinois Institute of Art–Schaumburg; The Illinois Institute of Art–Tinley Park; Miami International University of Art & Design; The New England Institute of Art.
[1] A branch of The Art Institute of Atlanta
[2] A branch of The Art Institute of Houston
[3] A campus of South University
[4] The Art Institute of Indianapolis is regulated by the Indiana Commission on Proprietary Education, 302 West Washington Street, Room E201, Indianapolis, Indiana 46204, AC-0080
[5] A branch of Miami International University of Art & Design
[6] The Art Institute of Ohio–Cincinnati, 8845 Governors Hill Drive, Suite 100, Cincinnati, Ohio 45249-3317, OH Reg. #04-01-1698B
[7] Certified by the State Council of Higher Education to operate in Virginia

THE ART INSTITUTE OF CALIFORNIA–INLAND EMPIRE

SAN BERNARDINO, CALIFORNIA

A focused education from The Art Institute of California–Inland Empire can help students turn their creative energy into a powerful tool that can make a difference in the world. Students are part of a collaborative and supportive community, where experienced instructors provide the guidance and skills needed to pursue a career in the creative economy.

The school's programs in the areas of design, media arts, fashion, and culinary give students the opportunity to learn by using professional-grade technology and build a portfolio of work to show potential employers after graduation.

The Art Institute of California–Inland Empire is accredited by the Accrediting Commission of Career Schools and Colleges (ACCSC) as a branch of The Art Institute of California–San Diego. ACCSC may be contacted at 2101 Wilson Boulevard, Suite 302, Arlington, Virginia 22201; phone: 703-247-4212.

The Art Institute of California–Inland Empire has been granted approval to operate by the California Bureau for Private Postsecondary and Vocational Education, California Department of Consumer Affairs, 1625 North Market Boulevard, Suite S-308, Sacramento, California 95834; phone: 916-574-8200; http://www.bppve.ca.gov.

Location

The Art Institute of California–Inland Empire is located in San Bernardino. Within a short drive from the school, students can enjoy mountains, deserts, Los Angeles, or Mexico. Surfing, water sports, tennis, golf, jogging, mountain biking, and many other outdoor activities are supported by the region's mild climate.

Programs of Study and Degrees

No matter which course of study a student may choose, the professionals at The Art Institute of California–Inland Empire will guide, support, and help each student as their talents evolve on their journey of personal and professional transformation. Students studying design learn to fine-tune their visual thinking and problem-solving skills, as they create everything from logos to TV ads. Programs in the area of media arts focus on utilizing technology to deliver information and entertainment, while students studying fashion learn to design clothes for the runway or run a retail shop. Culinary programs focus on the fundamental techniques while exposing students to a full menu of international cuisines and management techniques.

Bachelor's degree programs are offered in audio production, culinary management, fashion and retail management, fashion design, game art and design, graphic design, interior design, media arts and animation, and Web design and interactive media.

Associate degree programs are offered in baking and pastry, culinary arts, and graphic design.

A diploma program is offered in baking and pastry.

The culinary arts, graphic design, and interior design programs are available in an evening and weekend option format.

Academic Programs

The academic year is divided into four quarters, beginning in January, April, July, and October. Each program is offered on a year-round basis, allowing students to continue to work uninterrupted toward their degrees.

Academic Facilities

The Art Institute of California–Inland Empire provides a learning environment with professional-grade technology applicable to each student's course of study. Students have the opportunity to build a portfolio of work that shows potential employers that they are trained to use the software, hardware, or equipment utilized within the industry. Depending upon the course of study, students are immersed in a creative environment—from classrooms to computer labs to studios—focused on relevant, hands-on education designed to prepare students for the real world.

Costs

Tuition cost varies by program. Prospective students should contact the school for current tuition costs. Other charges include a starting kit for all first-quarter students. Kits vary in price, depending on the program of study.

Financial Aid

Financial aid is available for those who qualify. Students who require financial assistance should first complete and submit a Free Application for Federal Student Aid (FAFSA) and meet with a financial aid officer.

Faculty

Faculty members are experienced professionals who create a learning environment that is similar to the professional world students will face after graduation. Instructors are focused on helping students develop the skills they need to transform their creative potential into marketable skills.

Student Government

The Student Federation is responsible for student government and acts as a liaison between the student body and faculty and staff members.

Admission Requirements

Applicants must provide proof of high school graduation or achievement of a General Educational Development (GED) certificate as a prerequisite for admission. In lieu of documenting high school graduation or a GED certificate, applicants may provide proof of attaining an associate degree or higher from an accredited institution. An official transcript indicating date of high school graduation, GED certificate (including test scores), or date of college graduation (including degree granted), is required as proof.

All individuals seeking admission to The Art Institute of California–Inland Empire are interviewed in person or by phone by an assistant director of admissions, and each applicant must create an original essay of at least 150 words stating how an education at the school would help the student to achieve career goals. There is a $50 application fee.

For the most recent information regarding admission requirements, please refer to the current academic catalog.

Application and Information

To obtain an application, make arrangements for an interview, or tour the school, prospective students should contact:

The Art Institute of California–Inland Empire
674 East Brier Drive
San Bernardino, California 92408-2800
Phone: 909-915-2100
       800-353-0812 (toll-free)
Fax: 909-915-2130
Web site: http://www.artinstitutes.edu/inlandempire

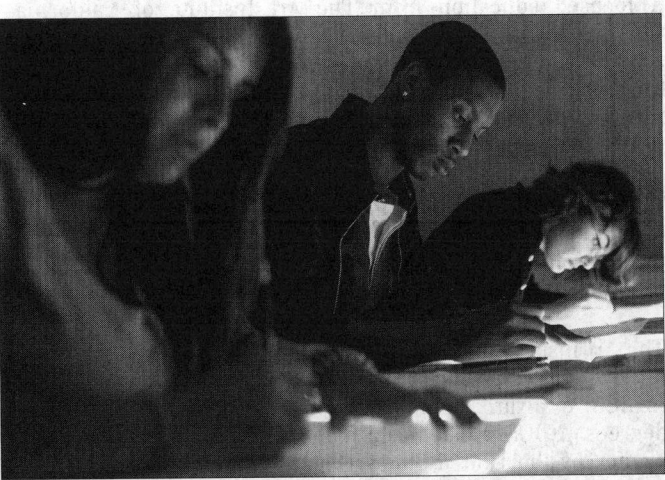

The Art Institute of Atlanta; The Art Institute of Atlanta–Decatur[1]; The Art Institute of Austin[2]; The Art Institute of California–Hollywood; The Art Institute of California–Inland Empire; The Art Institute of California–Los Angeles; The Art Institute of California–Orange County; The Art Institute of California–Sacramento; The Art Institute of California–San Diego; The Art Institute of California–San Francisco; The Art Institute of California–Sunnyvale; The Art Institute of Charleston[1]; The Art Institute of Charlotte; The Art Institute of Colorado; The Art Institute of Dallas[3]; The Art Institute of Fort Lauderdale; The Art Institute of Fort Worth[3]; The Art Institute of Houston; The Art Institute of Houston–North[2]; The Art Institute of Indianapolis[4]; The Art Institute of Jacksonville[5]; The Art Institute of Las Vegas; The Art Institute of Michigan; The Art Institute of New York City; The Art Institute of Ohio–Cincinnati[6]; The Art Institute of Philadelphia; The Art Institute of Phoenix; The Art Institute of Pittsburgh; The Art Institute of Portland; The Art Institute of Raleigh–Durham; The Art Institute of Salt Lake City; The Art Institute of San Antonio[2];The Art Institute of Seattle; The Art Institute of Tampa[5]; The Art Institute of Tennessee–Nashville[1]; The Art Institute of Tucson; The Art Institute of Vancouver; The Art Institute of Virginia Beach[1,7]; The Art Institute of Washington[1,7]; The Art Institute of Washington–Northern Virginia[1,7]; The Art Institute of Wisconsin; The Art Institute of York–Pennsylvania; The Art Institutes International–Kansas City; The Art Institutes International Minnesota; The Illinois Institute of Art–Chicago; The Illinois Institute of Art–Schaumburg; The Illinois Institute of Art–Tinley Park; Miami International University of Art & Design; The New England Institute of Art.

[1] A branch of The Art Institute of Atlanta
[2] A branch of The Art Institute of Houston
[3] A campus of South University
[4] The Art Institute of Indianapolis is regulated by the Indiana Commission on Proprietary Education, 302 West Washington Street, Room E201, Indianapolis, Indiana 46204, AC-0080
[5] A branch of Miami International University of Art & Design
[6] The Art Institute of Ohio–Cincinnati, 8845 Governors Hill Drive, Suite 100, Cincinnati, Ohio 45249-3317, OH Reg. #04-01-1698B
[7] Certified by the State Council of Higher Education to operate in Virginia

THE ART INSTITUTE OF CALIFORNIA–LOS ANGELES

SANTA MONICA, CALIFORNIA

The Art Institute of California–Los Angeles
CREATE TOMORROW

A focused education from The Art Institute of California–Los Angeles can help students turn their creative energy into a powerful tool that can make a difference in the world. Students are part of a collaborative and supportive community, where experienced instructors provide the guidance and skills needed to pursue a career in the creative economy.

The school's programs in the areas of design, media arts, fashion, and culinary give students the opportunity to learn by using professional-grade technology and build a portfolio of work to show potential employers after graduation.

The Art Institute of California–Los Angeles is accredited by the Accrediting Council for Independent Colleges and Schools (ACICS) to award diplomas, associate degrees, and bachelor's degrees. ACICS is listed as a nationally recognized accrediting agency by the United States Department of Education and is recognized by the Council for Higher Education Accreditation. ACICS can be contacted at 750 First Street NE, Suite 980, Washington, D.C. 20002; phone: 202-336-6780.

The Art Institute of California–Los Angeles has been granted approval to operate by the California Bureau for Private Postsecondary and Vocational Education, California Department of Consumer Affairs, 1625 North Market Boulevard, Suite S-308, Sacramento, California 95834; phone: 916-574-8200; http://www.bppve.ca.gov.

The interior design program leading to the Bachelor of Science degree is accredited by the Council for Interior Design Accreditation, 206 Grandville Avenue, Suite 350, Grand Rapids, Michigan 49503; www.accredit-id.org.

Location

Located in Los Angeles, the arts and entertainment capital of the world, The Art Institute of California–Los Angeles is within easy driving distance of the Pacific Coast Highway, Century City, and downtown. The city offers a rich diversity of food, fashion, architecture, entertainment, languages, world views, and religions that are showcased in numerous community and ethnic festivals throughout the year. Leisure activities include hiking on Santa Monica Mountain trails or visits to the Getty Museum, Los Angeles County Museum of Art, or Los Angeles Zoo. Students may also enjoy dining and shopping on Santa Monica's Third Street Promenade or in nearby Westwood Village. Music and theater venues include the Hollywood Bowl, the Greek Theatre, the Music Center, and the Dorothy Chandler Pavilion. Other popular destinations are Watts Towers, the La Brea Tar Pits, Hollywood Boulevard's Walk of Fame, and Mann's Chinese Theater.

Programs of Study and Degrees

No matter which course of study a student may choose, the professionals at The Art Institute of California–Los Angeles will guide, support, and help each student as their talents evolve on their journey of personal and professional transformation. Students studying design learn to fine-tune their visual thinking and problem-solving skills, as they create everything from logos to TV ads. Programs in the area of media arts focus on utilizing technology to deliver information and entertainment, while students studying fashion learn to design clothes for the runway or run a retail shop. Culinary programs focus on the fundamental techniques while exposing students to a full menu of international cuisines and management techniques.

Bachelor's degree programs are offered in audio production, culinary management, digital filmmaking and video production, fashion design, fashion marketing and management, game art and design, game programming, graphic design, interior design, media arts and animation, visual effects and motion graphics, and Web design and interactive media.

Associate degree programs are offered in baking and pastry, culinary arts, graphic design, video production, and Web design and interactive media.

Diploma programs are offered in the art of cooking and baking and pastry.

The culinary arts, culinary management, graphic design, and interior design programs are available in an evening and weekend option format.

Academic Programs

The academic year is divided into four quarters that begin in January, April, July, and October. Associate degree candidates must complete 112 academic credits to graduate, including 28 general education credits. These are generally earned over seven quarters. Bachelor's degree candidates must complete 192 credits, including 56 general education credits. These are generally earned over eleven quarters. All students must complete their programs of study with a minimum 2.0 cumulative GPA to meet graduation requirements.

Academic Facilities

The Art Institute of California–Los Angeles provides a learning environment with professional-grade technology applicable to each student's course of study. Students have the opportunity to build a portfolio of work that shows potential employers that they are trained to use the software, hardware, or equipment utilized within the industry. Depending upon the course of study, students are immersed in a creative environment—from classrooms to computer labs to studios—focused on relevant, hands-on education designed to prepare students for the real world.

Costs

Tuition cost varies by program. Prospective students should contact the school for current tuition costs. Other charges include a starting kit for all first-quarter students. Kits vary in price depending on the program of study.

Financial Aid

Financial aid is available for those who qualify. Students who require financial assistance should first complete and submit a Free Application for Federal Student Aid (FAFSA) and meet with a financial aid officer.

Faculty

Faculty members are experienced professionals who create a learning environment that is similar to the professional world students will face after graduation. Instructors are focused on helping students develop the skills they need to transform their creative potential into marketable skills.

Student Government

The Associated Student Council provides a forum to discuss student issues, facilitates the exchange of ideas and information among students, and acts as a liaison between students and members of the faculty and administration; it also organizes student activities at the school and provides student leadership opportunities. In addition, the Activities and Events Council consists of an elected board, representatives from each student organization, and other interested students.

Admission Requirements

The admission process at The Art Institute of California–Los Angeles includes a student interview with the admissions office (either in person or by phone) and submission of a completed application form, a 150-word essay, high school transcripts or General Educational Development (GED) test scores, and official SAT or ACT scores. There is a $50 application fee.

For the most recent information regarding admission requirements, please refer to the current academic catalog.

Application and Information

To obtain an application, make arrangements for an interview, or tour the school, prospective students should contact:

The Art Institute of California–Los Angeles
2900 31st Street
Santa Monica, California 90405-3035
Phone: 310-752-4700
       888-646-4610 (toll-free)
Fax: 310-752-4708
Web site: http://www.artinstitutes.edu/losangeles

The Art Institute of Atlanta; The Art Institute of Atlanta–Decatur[1]; The Art Institute of Austin[2]; The Art Institute of California–Hollywood; The Art Institute of California–Inland Empire; The Art Institute of California–Los Angeles; The Art Institute of California–Orange County; The Art Institute of California–Sacramento; The Art Institute of California–San Diego; The Art Institute of California–San Francisco; The Art Institute of California–Sunnyvale; The Art Institute of Charleston[1]; The Art Institute of Charlotte; The Art Institute of Colorado; The Art Institute of Dallas[3]; The Art Institute of Fort Lauderdale; The Art Institute of Fort Worth[5]; The Art Institute of Houston; The Art Institute of Houston–North[2]; The Art Institute of Indianapolis[4]; The Art Institute of Jacksonville[5]; The Art Institute of Las Vegas; The Art Institute of Michigan; The Art Institute of New York City; The Art Institute of Ohio–Cincinnati[6]; The Art Institute of Philadelphia; The Art Institute of Phoenix; The Art Institute of Pittsburgh; The Art Institute of Portland; The Art Institute of Raleigh–Durham; The Art Institute of Salt Lake City; The Art Institute of San Antonio[2];The Art Institute of Seattle; The Art Institute of Tampa[5]; The Art Institute of Tennessee–Nashville[1]; The Art Institute of Tucson; The Art Institute of Vancouver; The Art Institute of Virginia Beach[1,7]; The Art Institute of Washington[1,7]; The Art Institute of Washington–Northern Virginia[1,7]; The Art Institute of Wisconsin; The Art Institute of York–Pennsylvania; The Art Institutes International–Kansas City; The Art Institutes International Minnesota; The Illinois Institute of Art–Chicago; The Illinois Institute of Art–Schaumburg; The Illinois Institute of Art–Tinley Park; Miami International University of Art & Design; The New England Institute of Art.
[1]A branch of The Art Institute of Atlanta
[2]A branch of The Art Institute of Houston
[3]A campus of South University
[4]The Art Institute of Indianapolis is regulated by the Indiana Commission on Proprietary Education, 302 West Washington Street, Room E201, Indianapolis, Indiana 46204, AC-0080
[5]A branch of Miami International University of Art & Design
[6]The Art Institute of Ohio–Cincinnati, 8845 Governors Hill Drive, Suite 100, Cincinnati, Ohio 45249-3317, OH Reg. #04-01-1698B
[7]Certified by the State Council of Higher Education to operate in Virginia

THE ART INSTITUTE OF CALIFORNIA–ORANGE COUNTY

SANTA ANA, CALIFORNIA

A focused education from The Art Institute of California–Orange County can help students turn their creative energy into a powerful tool that can make a difference in the world. Students are part of a collaborative and supportive community, where experienced instructors provide the guidance and skills needed to pursue a career in the creative economy.

The school's programs in the areas of design, media arts, fashion, and culinary give students the opportunity to learn by using professional-grade technology and build a portfolio of work to show potential employers after graduation.

The Art Institute of California–Orange County is accredited by the Accrediting Council for Independent Colleges and Schools to award diplomas, associate degrees, and bachelor's degrees. The Accrediting Council for Independent Colleges and Schools (ACICS) is listed as a nationally recognized accrediting agency by the United States Department of Education and is recognized by the Council for Higher Education Accreditation. ACICS can be contacted at 750 First Street NE, Suite 980, Washington, D.C. 20002; phone: 202-336-6780.

The Art Institute of California–Orange County has been granted approval to operate by the California Bureau for Private Postsecondary and Vocational Education, California Department of Consumer Affairs, 1625 North Market Boulevard, Suite S-308, Sacramento, California 95834; phone: 916-574-8200; http:// www.bppve.ca.gov.

The interior design program leading to the Bachelor of Science degree is accredited by the Council for Interior Design Accreditation, 206 Grandville Avenue, Suite 350, Grand Rapids, Michigan 49503; http://www.accredit-id.org.

Location

The Art Institute of California–Orange County is strategically located in the heart of the booming Southern California region that includes the counties of Orange, Los Angeles, San Diego, and Ventura. Southern California is a central hub of the entertainment, advertising, design, aerospace, and culinary industries. Orange County offers 42 miles of beautiful, sandy Pacific Ocean coastline, and wilderness parks are minutes away for camping, hiking, and biking. The area has more than 250 sunny days a year and is home to Disneyland, Knott's Berry Farm, and world-renowned cultural events, including the annual Laguna Beach Festival of the Arts.

Programs of Study and Degrees

No matter which course of study a student may choose, the professionals at The Art Institute of California–Orange County will guide, support, and help each student as their talents evolve on their journey of personal and professional transformation. Students studying design learn to fine-tune their visual thinking and problem-solving skills, as they create everything from logos to TV ads. Programs in the area of media arts focus on utilizing technology to deliver information and entertainment, while students studying fashion learn to design clothes for the runway or run a retail shop. Culinary programs focus on the fundamental techniques while exposing students to a full menu of international cuisines and management techniques.

Bachelor's degree programs are offered in advertising, culinary management, digital filmmaking and video production, fashion design, fashion marketing and management, game art and design, graphic design, industrial design, interior design, media arts and animation, visual and game programming, visual effects and motion graphics, and Web design and interactive media.

Associate degree programs are offered in baking and pastry, culinary arts, digital photography, graphic design, and Web design and interactive media.

Diploma programs are offered in the art of cooking and baking and pastry.

The culinary arts, culinary management, graphic design, and interior design programs are available in an evening and weekend option format.

Academic Programs

A bachelor's degree requires the completion of 192 credits, while an associate degree requires the completion of 112 academic credits. The academic year is divided into four quarters that begin in January, April, July, and October. Each program is offered on a year-round basis, allowing students to continue to work uninterrupted toward their degrees.

The school arranges study trips to local cultural and commercial sites. These visits offer an opportunity for valuable exposure to places and events relating to the student's field of study. In addition, out-of-town seminars and visits may be planned in individual programs.

The Student Tutoring Program is a peer-to-peer tutoring assistance program that is available to all current students. Each tutor has unique qualifications in his or her area of expertise.

Academic Facilities

The Art Institute of California–Orange County provides a learning environment with professional-grade technology applicable to each student's course of study. Students have the opportunity to build a portfolio of work that shows potential employers that they are trained to use the software, hardware, or equipment utilized within the industry. Depending upon the course of study, students are immersed in a creative environment—from classrooms to computer labs to studios—focused on relevant, hands-on education designed to prepare students for the real world.

Costs

Tuition cost varies by program. Prospective students should contact the school for current tuition costs. Other charges include a starting kit for all first-quarter students. Kits vary in price depending on the program of study.

Financial Aid

Financial aid is available for those who qualify. Students who require financial assistance should first complete and submit a Free Application for Federal Student Aid (FAFSA) and meet with a financial aid officer.

Faculty

Faculty members are experienced professionals who create a learning environment that is similar to the professional world

students will face after graduation. Instructors are focused on helping students develop the skills they need to transform their creative potential into marketable skills.

Student Government

The President's Club is a group of students who promote the philosophy of "students helping students." Members act as emissaries for the school and as liaisons between students and faculty and staff members. The club assists new students as well as helping in the organization and promotion of campus activities. Student members must be nominated for the organization by a member of the faculty or staff.

Admission Requirements

Prospective students must hold a high school diploma or General Educational Development (GED) certificate or have earned a bachelor's degree or higher from an accredited institution. High school seniors who have not yet graduated should submit a partial transcript that indicates their expected graduation date. All prospective students are required to submit two essays of approximately one page in length, describing what they expect from the school and how an education at The Art Institute of California–Orange County may help them to reach their career goals. Applicants are interviewed either in person or by telephone by an assistant director of admissions. In addition, other standardized exams, such as the SAT or ACT, may be considered. Prospective students may apply at any time prior to the start of the upcoming quarter, and applications may be submitted online or mailed directly to the school. There is a $50 application fee.

For the most recent information regarding admission requirements, please refer to the current academic catalog.

Application and Information

To obtain an application, make arrangements for an interview, or tour the school, prospective students should contact:

The Art Institute of California–Orange County
3601 West Sunflower Avenue
Santa Ana, California 92704-7931
Phone: 714-830-0200
        888-549-3055 (toll-free)
Fax: 714-556-1923
Web site: http://www.artinstitutes.edu/orangecounty

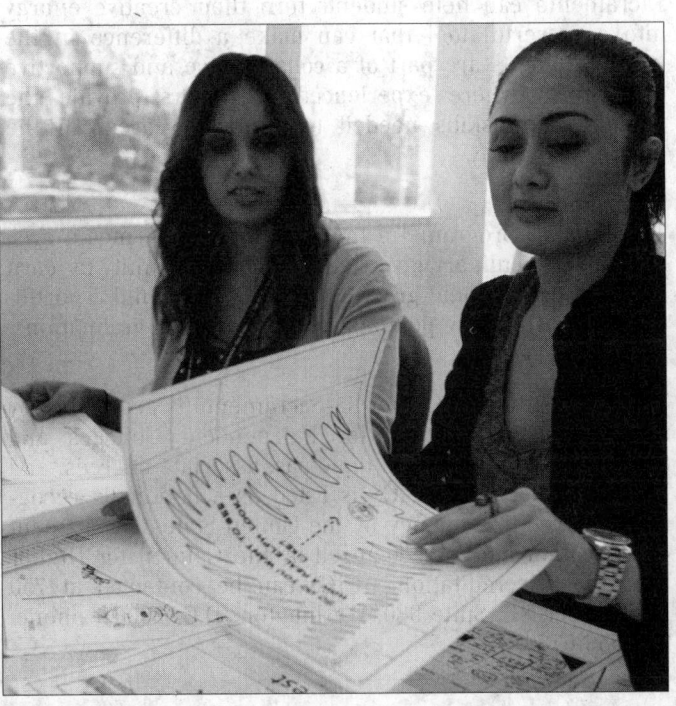

The Art Institute of Atlanta; The Art Institute of Atlanta–Decatur[1]; The Art Institute of Austin[2]; The Art Institute of California–Hollywood; The Art Institute of California–Inland Empire; The Art Institute of California–Los Angeles; The Art Institute of California–Orange County; The Art Institute of California–Sacramento; The Art Institute of California–San Diego; The Art Institute of California–San Francisco; The Art Institute of California–Sunnyvale; The Art Institute of Charleston[1]; The Art Institute of Charlotte; The Art Institute of Colorado; The Art Institute of Dallas[5]; The Art Institute of Fort Lauderdale; The Art Institute of Fort Worth[5]; The Art Institute of Houston; The Art Institute of Houston–North[2]; The Art Institute of Indianapolis[4]; The Art Institute of Jacksonville[5]; The Art Institute of Las Vegas; The Art Institute of Michigan; The Art Institute of New York City; The Art Institute of Ohio–Cincinnati[6]; The Art Institute of Philadelphia; The Art Institute of Phoenix; The Art Institute of Pittsburgh; The Art Institute of Portland; The Art Institute of Raleigh–Durham; The Art Institute of Salt Lake City; The Art Institute of San Antonio[2];The Art Institute of Seattle; The Art Institute of Tampa[5]; The Art Institute of Tennessee–Nashville[1]; The Art Institute of Tucson; The Art Institute of Vancouver; The Art Institute of Virginia Beach[1,7]; The Art Institute of Washington[1,7]; The Art Institute of Washington–Northern Virginia[1,7]; The Art Institute of Wisconsin; The Art Institute of York–Pennsylvania; The Art Institutes International–Kansas City; The Art Institutes International Minnesota; The Illinois Institute of Art–Chicago; The Illinois Institute of Art–Schaumburg; The Illinois Institute of Art–Tinley Park; Miami International University of Art & Design; The New England Institute of Art.

[1]A branch of The Art Institute of Atlanta
[2]A branch of The Art Institute of Houston
[3]A campus of South University
[4]The Art Institute of Indianapolis is regulated by the Indiana Commission on Proprietary Education, 302 West Washington Street, Room E201, Indianapolis, Indiana 46204, AC-0080
[5]A branch of Miami International University of Art & Design
[6]The Art Institute of Ohio–Cincinnati, 8845 Governors Hill Drive, Suite 100, Cincinnati, Ohio 45249-3317, OH Reg. #04-01-1698B
[7]Certified by the State Council of Higher Education to operate in Virginia

THE ART INSTITUTE OF CALIFORNIA–SACRAMENTO

SACRAMENTO, CALIFORNIA

A focused education from The Art Institute of California–Sacramento can help students turn their creative energy into a powerful tool that can make a difference in the world. Students are part of a collaborative and supportive community, where experienced instructors provide the guidance and skills needed to pursue a career in the creative economy.

The school's programs in the areas of design, media arts, fashion, and culinary give students the opportunity to learn by using professional-grade technology and build a portfolio of work to show potential employers after graduation.

The Art Institute of California–Sacramento is accredited by the Accrediting Council for Independent Colleges and Schools (ACICS) to award diplomas, associate degrees, and bachelor's degrees. ACICS is listed as a nationally recognized accrediting agency by the United States Department of Education and is recognized by the Council for Higher Education Accreditation. ACICS can be contacted at 750 First Street NE, Suite 980, Washington, D.C. 20002; phone: 202-336-6780.

The Art Institute of California–Sacramento has been granted approval to operate by the California Bureau for Private Postsecondary and Vocational Education, California Department of Consumer Affairs, 1625 North Market Boulevard, Suite S-308, Sacramento, California 95834; phone: 916-574-8200; http://www.bppve.ca.gov.

Location

Sacramento's metropolitan population of more than 2 million means that students have access to recreation and the arts. In addition to state government, the city is a major transportation and commerce hub linking the east with California's coastal cities.

Programs of Study and Degrees

No matter which course of study a student may choose, the professionals at The Art Institute of California–Sacramento will guide, support, and help each student as their talents evolve on their journey of personal and professional transformation. Students studying design learn to fine-tune their visual thinking and problem-solving skills, as they create everything from logos to TV ads. Programs in the area of media arts focus on utilizing technology to deliver

information and entertainment, while students studying fashion learn to design clothes for the runway or run a retail shop. Culinary programs focus on the fundamental techniques while exposing students to a full menu of international cuisines and management techniques.

Bachelor's degree programs are available in culinary management, digital filmmaking and video production, game art and design, graphic design, interior design, media arts and animation, and Web design and interactive media.

Associate degrees are offered in baking and pastry, culinary arts, graphic design, and Web design and interactive media.

Diploma programs are offered in the art of cooking and baking and pastry.

Academic Programs

The Art Institute of California–Sacramento operates on a year-round, four-quarter system.

Academic Facilities

The Art Institute of California–Sacramento provides a learning environment with professional-grade technology applicable to each student's course of study. Students have the opportunity to build a portfolio of work that shows potential employers that they are trained to use the software, hardware, or equipment utilized within the industry. Depending upon the course of study, students are immersed in a creative environment—from classrooms to computer labs to studios—focused on relevant, hands-on education designed to prepare students for the real world.

Costs

Tuition cost varies by program. Prospective students should contact the school for current tuition costs. Other charges include a starting kit for all first-quarter students. Kits vary in price depending on the program of study.

Financial Aid

Financial aid is available for those who qualify. Students who require financial assistance should first complete and submit a Free Application for Federal Student Aid (FAFSA) and meet with a financial aid officer.

Faculty

Faculty members are experienced professionals who create a learning environment that is similar to the professional world students will face after graduation. Instructors are focused on helping students develop the skills they need to transform their creative potential into marketable skills.

Admission Requirements

Applicants must provide proof of high school graduation or achievement of a General Educational Development (GED) certificate as a prerequisite for admission. In lieu of documenting high school graduation or a GED certificate, applicants may provide proof of attaining an associate degree or higher from an accredited institution. An official transcript indicating date of high school graduation, GED certificate (including test scores), or date of college graduation (including degree granted) is required as proof.

All individuals seeking admission to The Art Institute of California–Sacramento are interviewed in person or by phone by an assistant director of admissions, and each applicant must create an original essay of at least 150 words stating how an education at The Art Institute of California–Sacramento would help the student achieve career goals. There is a $50 application fee.

For the most recent information regarding admission requirements, please refer to the current academic catalog.

Application and Information

To obtain an application, make arrangements for an interview, or tour the school, prospective students should contact:

The Art Institute of California–Sacramento
2850 Gateway Oaks Drive, Suite #100
Sacramento, California 95833
Phone: 916-830-6320
       800-477-1957 (toll-free)
Fax: 916-830-6344
Web site: http://www.artinstitutes.edu/sacramento

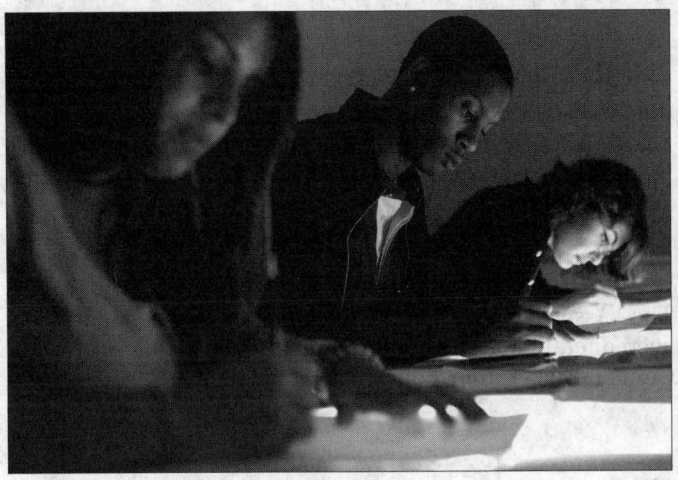

The Art Institute of Atlanta; The Art Institute of Atlanta–Decatur[1]; The Art Institute of Austin[2]; The Art Institute of California–Hollywood; The Art Institute of California–Inland Empire; The Art Institute of California–Los Angeles; The Art Institute of California–Orange County; The Art Institute of California–Sacramento; The Art Institute of California–San Diego; The Art Institute of California–San Francisco; The Art Institute of California–Sunnyvale; The Art Institute of Charleston[1]; The Art Institute of Charlotte; The Art Institute of Colorado; The Art Institute of Dallas[3]; The Art Institute of Fort Lauderdale; The Art Institute of Fort Worth[3]; The Art Institute of Houston; The Art Institute of Houston–North[2]; The Art Institute of Indianapolis[4]; The Art Institute of Jacksonville[5]; The Art Institute of Las Vegas; The Art Institute of Michigan; The Art Institute of New York City; The Art Institute of Ohio–Cincinnati[6]; The Art Institute of Philadelphia; The Art Institute of Phoenix; The Art Institute of Pittsburgh; The Art Institute of Portland; The Art Institute of Raleigh–Durham; The Art Institute of Salt Lake City; The Art Institute of San Antonio[2];The Art Institute of Seattle; The Art Institute of Tampa[5]; The Art Institute of Tennessee–Nashville[1]; The Art Institute of Tucson; The Art Institute of Vancouver; The Art Institute of Virginia Beach[1,7]; The Art Institute of Washington[1,7]; The Art Institute of Washington–Northern Virginia[1,7]; The Art Institute of Wisconsin; The Art Institute of York–Pennsylvania; The Art Institutes International–Kansas City; The Art Institutes International Minnesota; The Illinois Institute of Art–Chicago; The Illinois Institute of Art–Schaumburg; The Illinois Institute of Art–Tinley Park; Miami International University of Art & Design; The New England Institute of Art.

[1] A branch of The Art Institute of Atlanta
[2] A branch of The Art Institute of Houston
[3] A campus of South University
[4] The Art Institute of Indianapolis is regulated by the Indiana Commission on Proprietary Education, 302 West Washington Street, Room E201, Indianapolis, Indiana 46204, AC-0080
[5] A branch of Miami International University of Art & Design
[6] The Art Institute of Ohio–Cincinnati, 8845 Governors Hill Drive, Suite 100, Cincinnati, Ohio 45249-3317, OH Reg. #04-01-1698B
[7] Certified by the State Council of Higher Education to operate in Virginia

THE ART INSTITUTE OF CALIFORNIA– SAN DIEGO

SAN DIEGO, CALIFORNIA

The Art Institute of California™–San Diego

CREATE TOMORROW

COLLEGE CLOSE-UPS

A focused education from The Art Institute of California–San Diego can help students turn their creative energy into a powerful tool that can make a difference in the world. Students are part of a collaborative and supportive community, where experienced instructors provide the guidance and skills needed to pursue a career in the creative economy.

The school's programs in the areas of design, media arts, fashion, and culinary give students the opportunity to learn by using professional-grade technology and build a portfolio of work to show potential employers after graduation.

The Art Institute of California–San Diego is accredited by the Accrediting Commission of Career Schools and Colleges (ACCSC) which may be contacted at 2101 Wilson Boulevard, Suite 302, Arlington, Virginia 22201; phone: 703-247-4212.

The Associate of Science degree in culinary arts is accredited by the Accrediting Commission of the American Culinary Federation Education Foundation.

The Art Institute of California–San Diego has been granted approval to operate by the California Bureau for Private Postsecondary and Vocational Education, California Department of Consumer Affairs, 1625 North Market Boulevard, Suite S-308, Sacramento, California 95834; phone: 916-574-8200; http://www.bppve.ca.gov.

Location

Within a 2-hour drive are mountains, deserts, Los Angeles, Mexico, surfing, water sports, tennis, golf, jogging, mountain biking, and beaches. San Diego offers many regional shopping centers as well as picturesque spots, including the San Diego Zoo, Wild Animal Park, Sea World, Seaport Village, Old Town, Horton Plaza, the Gaslamp District, and La Jolla. The opera, symphony, live theater district, professional and collegiate athletic events, and concerts are also nearby. San Diego's average daytime temperature is 70 degrees, and the city averages 267 sunny days each year.

Programs of Study and Degrees

No matter which course of study a student may choose, the professionals at The Art Institute of California–San Diego will guide, support, and help each student as their talents evolve on their journey of personal and professional transformation. Students studying design learn to fine-tune their visual thinking and problem-solving skills, as they create everything from logos to TV ads. Programs in the area of media arts focus on utilizing technology to deliver information and entertainment, while students studying fashion learn to design clothes for the runway or run a retail shop. Culinary programs focus on the fundamental techniques while exposing students to a full menu of international cuisines and management techniques.

Bachelor's degree programs are offered in advertising, audio production, culinary management, fashion design, fashion marketing and management, game art and design, graphic design, hospitality management, food and beverage management, interior design, media arts and animation, visual and game programming, and Web design and interactive media.

Associate degree programs are available in advertising, baking and pastry, culinary arts, and graphic design.

Diploma programs are offered in the art of cooking and baking and pastry.

The graphic design and interior design programs are also available in an evening and weekend option format.

Academic Programs

The Art Institute of California–San Diego operates on a year-round, four-quarter system.

Academic Facilities

The Art Institute of California–San Diego provides a learning environment with professional-grade technology applicable to each student's course of study. Students have the opportunity to build a portfolio of work that shows potential employers that they are trained to use the software, hardware, or equipment utilized within the industry. Depending upon the course of study, students are immersed in a creative environment—from classrooms to computer labs to studios—focused on relevant, hands-on education designed to prepare students for the real world.

Costs

Tuition cost varies by program. Prospective students should contact the school for current tuition costs. Other charges include a starting kit for all first-quarter students. Kits vary in price depending on the program of study.

Financial Aid

Financial aid is available for those who qualify. Students who require financial assistance should first complete and submit a Free Application for Federal Student Aid (FAFSA) and meet with a financial aid officer.

Faculty

Faculty members are experienced professionals who create a learning environment that is similar to the professional world students will face after graduation. Instructors are focused on helping students develop the skills they need to transform their creative potential into marketable skills.

Admission Requirements

Prospective students must be high school graduates or hold a General Educational Development (GED) certificate. High school seniors who have not yet graduated should submit a partial transcript that indicates their expected graduation date. All prospective students are required to write an essay of approximately 150 words describing how an education at The Art Institute of

California–San Diego will help them to attain their creative goals. An interview, either in person or by telephone, is required. SAT or ACT scores may also be considered. Applications may be submitted online or mailed to the school. There is a $50 application fee.

For the most recent information regarding admission requirements, please refer to the current academic catalog.

Application and Information

To obtain an application or make arrangements for an interview or tour of the school, prospective students should contact:

The Art Institute of California–San Diego
7650 Mission Valley Road
San Diego, California 92108-4423

Phone: 858-598-1200
       866-275-2422 (toll-free)
Fax: 619-291-3206
Web site: http://www.artinstitutes.edu/sandiego

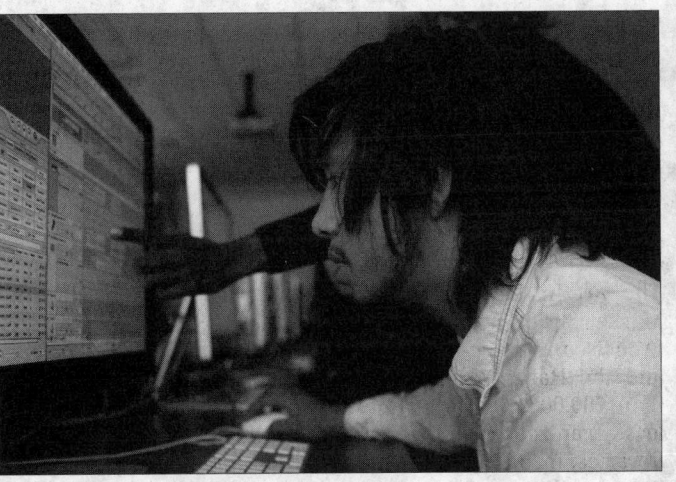

The Art Institute of Atlanta; The Art Institute of Atlanta–Decatur[1]; The Art Institute of Austin[2]; The Art Institute of California–Hollywood; The Art Institute of California–Inland Empire; The Art Institute of California–Los Angeles; The Art Institute of California–Orange County; The Art Institute of California–Sacramento; The Art Institute of California–San Diego; The Art Institute of California–San Francisco; The Art Institute of California–Sunnyvale; The Art Institute of Charleston[1]; The Art Institute of Charlotte; The Art Institute of Colorado; The Art Institute of Dallas[3]; The Art Institute of Fort Lauderdale; The Art Institute of Fort Worth[3]; The Art Institute of Houston; The Art Institute of Houston–North[2]; The Art Institute of Indianapolis[4]; The Art Institute of Jacksonville[5]; The Art Institute of Las Vegas; The Art Institute of Michigan; The Art Institute of New York City; The Art Institute of Ohio–Cincinnati[6]; The Art Institute of Philadelphia; The Art Institute of Phoenix; The Art Institute of Pittsburgh; The Art Institute of Portland; The Art Institute of Raleigh–Durham; The Art Institute of Salt Lake City; The Art Institute of San Antonio[2];The Art Institute of Seattle; The Art Institute of Tampa[5]; The Art Institute of Tennessee–Nashville[1]; The Art Institute of Tucson; The Art Institute of Vancouver; The Art Institute of Virginia Beach[1,7]; The Art Institute of Washington[1,7]; The Art Institute of Washington–Northern Virginia[1,7]; The Art Institute of Wisconsin; The Art Institute of York–Pennsylvania; The Art Institutes International–Kansas City; The Art Institutes International Minnesota; The Illinois Institute of Art–Chicago; The Illinois Institute of Art–Schaumburg; The Illinois Institute of Art–Tinley Park; Miami International University of Art & Design; The New England Institute of Art.

[1]A branch of The Art Institute of Atlanta
[2]A branch of The Art Institute of Houston
[3]A campus of South University
[4]The Art Institute of Indianapolis is regulated by the Indiana Commission on Proprietary Education, 302 West Washington Street, Room E201, Indianapolis, Indiana 46204, AC-0080
[5]A branch of Miami International University of Art & Design
[6]The Art Institute of Ohio–Cincinnati, 8845 Governors Hill Drive, Suite 100, Cincinnati, Ohio 45249-3317, OH Reg. #04-01-1698B
[7]Certified by the State Council of Higher Education to operate in Virginia

THE ART INSTITUTE OF CALIFORNIA–SAN FRANCISCO

SAN FRANCISCO, CALIFORNIA

COLLEGE CLOSE-UPS

A focused education from The Art Institute of California–San Francisco can help students turn their creative energy into a powerful tool that can make a difference in the world. Students are part of a collaborative and supportive community, where experienced instructors provide the guidance and skills needed to pursue a career in the creative economy.

The school's programs in the areas of design, media arts, fashion, and culinary give students the opportunity to learn by using professional-grade technology and build a portfolio of work to show potential employers after graduation.

The Art Institute of California–San Francisco is accredited by the Accrediting Council for Independent Colleges and Schools (ACICS) to award associate and bachelor's degrees. The ACICS is listed as a nationally recognized accrediting agency by the United States Department of Education and is recognized by the Council for Higher Education Accreditation. ACICS can be contacted at 750 First Street NE, Suite 980, Washington, D.C. 20002; phone: 202-336-6780.

The Art Institute of California–San Francisco has been granted approval to operate by the California Bureau for Private Postsecondary and Vocational Education, California Department of Consumer Affairs, 1625 North Market Boulevard, Suite S-308, Sacramento, California 95834; phone: 916-574-8200; http://www.bppve.ca.gov.

Location

The Art Institute of California–San Francisco is located on Market Street, in the center of downtown San Francisco. San Francisco is home to the Golden Gate Bridge, Alcatraz Island, and the Haight-Ashbury district. With a population of more than 700,000, San Francisco has the highest concentration of arts organizations in the world. Students have access to public libraries, including the Center of Performing Arts Library, with its specialized sections on fashion and costuming. Natural attractions include the rolling hills and mountains in nearby wine country and dramatic vistas overlooking the Pacific, which provide options for hiking, biking, and other outdoor activities. Asian, Hispanic, and Italian neighborhoods are within walking distance. Public transportation, including cable cars, is available. The Bay Area and nearby Silicon Valley are home to leading new-media companies.

Programs of Study and Degrees

No matter which course of study a student may choose, the professionals at The Art Institute of California–San Francisco will guide, support, and help each student as their talents evolve on their journey of personal and professional transformation. Students studying design learn to fine-tune their visual thinking and problem-solving skills, as they create everything from logos to TV ads. Programs in the area of media arts focus on utilizing technology to deliver information and entertainment, while students studying fashion learn to design clothes for the runway or run a retail shop. Culinary programs focus on the fundamental techniques while exposing students to a full menu of international cuisines and management techniques.

Bachelor's degree programs are offered in advertising, audio production, culinary management, digital filmmaking and video production, fashion design, fashion marketing and management, game art and design, graphic design, interior design, media arts and animation, visual and game programming, and Web design and interactive media.

Associate degrees are available in baking and pastry, culinary arts, fashion design, fashion marketing, graphic design, and Web design and interactive media.

A diploma program is offered in baking and pastry, and a Master of Fine Arts is offered in computer animation.

Academic Programs

The academic year is divided into four quarters, beginning in January, April, July, and October. A bachelor's degree requires completion of 192 credits. An associate degree requires completion of 112 academic credits.

Academic Facilities

The Art Institute of California–San Francisco provides a learning environment with professional-grade technology applicable to each student's course of study. Students have the opportunity to build a portfolio of work that shows potential employers that they are trained to use the software, hardware, or equipment utilized within the industry. Depending upon the course of study, students are immersed in a creative environment—from classrooms to computer labs to studios—focused on relevant, hands-on education designed to prepare students for the real world.

Costs

Tuition cost varies by program. Prospective students should contact the school for current tuition costs. Other charges include a starting kit for all first-quarter students. Kits vary in price, depending on the program of study.

Financial Aid

Financial aid is available for those who qualify. Students who require financial assistance should first complete and submit a Free Application for Federal Student Aid (FAFSA) and meet with a financial aid officer.

Faculty

Faculty members are experienced professionals who create a learning environment that is similar to the professional world students will face after graduation. Instructors are focused on helping students develop the skills they need to transform their creative potential into marketable skills.

Student Government

The Student Federation is responsible for student government and acts as a liaison between the student body and faculty and staff members.

Admission Requirements

Prospective students must submit an application for admission, record of proof of high school graduation or a General Educational Development (GED) certificate, high school transcripts, and SAT or ACT scores, if available. High school seniors who have not yet graduated should submit a partial transcript that indicates their expected graduation date. Portfolios are welcomed but are not required. Applicants are evaluated on the basis of their previous education, background, and stated or demonstrated interest in the school's programs. Students must be interviewed either in person or via telephone by an assistant director of admissions. Prospective students may apply at any time prior to the start of the upcoming quarter. There is a $50 application fee.

For the most recent information regarding admission requirements, please refer to the current academic catalog.

Application and Information

To obtain an application, make arrangements for an interview, or tour the school, prospective students should contact:

The Art Institute of California–San Francisco
1170 Market Street
San Francisco, California 94102-4928
Phone: 415-865-0198
        888-493-3261 (toll-free)
Fax: 415-865-6344
Web site: http://www.artinstitutes.edu/sanfrancisco

THE ART INSTITUTE OF CALIFORNIA–SUNNYVALE

SUNNYVALE, CALIFORNIA

A focused education from The Art Institute of California–Sunnyvale can help students turn their creative energy into a powerful tool that can make a difference in the world. Students are part of a collaborative and supportive community, where experienced instructors provide the guidance and skills needed to pursue a career in the creative economy.

The school's programs in the areas of design, media arts, fashion, and culinary give students the opportunity to learn by using professional-grade technology and build a portfolio of work to show potential employers after graduation.

The Art Institute of California–Sunnyvale, a branch of The Art Institute of California–Hollywood, is accredited by the Accrediting Council for Independent Colleges and Schools (ACICS) to award associate degrees and bachelor's degrees. ACICS is listed as a nationally recognized accrediting agency by the United States Department of Education and is recognized by the Council for Higher Education Accreditation. ACICS can be contacted at 750 First Street NE, Suite 980, Washington, D.C. 20002; phone: 202-336-6780.

The Art Institute of California–Sunnyvale has been granted temporary approval to operate by the California Bureau for Private Postsecondary and Vocational Education (California Department of Consumer Affairs, 1625 North Market Boulevard, Suite S-308, Sacramento, California 95834; phone: 916-574-8200; http://www.bppve.ca.gov) in order to enable the bureau to conduct a quality inspection of the institution.

Location

Sunnyvale, a town of over 131,000 people, is one of the major cities that make up California's Silicon Valley. It's located between the San Francisco Bay and San Jose, providing easy access to cultural exhibitions, art museums, professional sports, and other entertainment options.

Programs of Study and Degrees

No matter which course of study a student may choose, the professionals at The Art Institute of California–Sunnyvale will guide, support, and help each student as their talents evolve on their journey of personal and professional transformation. Students studying design learn to fine-tune their visual thinking and problem-solving skills, as they create everything from logos to TV ads. Programs in the area of media arts focus on utilizing technology to deliver information and entertainment, while students studying fashion learn to design clothes for the runway or run a retail shop. Culinary programs focus on the fundamental techniques while exposing students to a full menu of international cuisines and management techniques.

Bachelor's degree programs are offered in culinary management, digital filmmaking and video production, fashion marketing and management, game art and design, graphic design, interior design, media arts and animation, and Web design and interactive media.

Associate degrees are offered in culinary arts, graphic design, and Web design and interactive media.

Academic Programs

The Art Institute of California–Sunnyvale operates on a year-round, four-quarter system.

Academic Facilities

The Art Institute of California–Sunnyvale provides a learning environment with professional-grade technology applicable to each student's course of study. Students have the opportunity to build a portfolio of work that shows potential employers that they are trained to use the software, hardware, or equipment utilized within the industry. Depending upon the course of study, students are immersed in a creative environment—from classrooms to computer labs to studios—focused on relevant, hands-on education designed to prepare students for the real world.

Costs

Tuition cost varies by program. Prospective students should contact the school for current tuition costs. Other charges include a starting kit for all first-quarter students. Kits vary in price depending on the program of study.

Financial Aid

Financial aid is available for those who qualify. Students who require financial assistance should first complete and submit a Free Application for Federal Student Aid (FAFSA) and meet with a financial aid officer.

Faculty

Faculty members are experienced professionals who create a learning environment that is similar to the professional world students will face after graduation. Instructors are focused on helping students develop the skills they need to transform their creative potential into marketable skills.

Admission Requirements

Applicants must provide proof of high school graduation or achievement of a General Educational Development (GED) certificate as a prerequisite for admission. In lieu of documenting high school graduation or a GED certificate, applicants may provide proof of attaining an associate degree or higher from an accredited institution. An official transcript indicating date of high school graduation, GED certificate (including test scores), or date of college graduation (including degree granted) is required as proof.

All individuals seeking admission to The Art Institute of California–Sunnyvale are interviewed in person or by phone by an assistant director of admissions, and each applicant must create an original essay of at least 150 words stating how an education at The Art Institute of California–Sunnyvale would help the student to achieve career goals. There is a $50 application fee.

For the most recent information regarding admission requirements, please refer to the current academic catalog.

Application and Information

To obtain an application, make arrangements for an interview, or tour the school, prospective students should contact:

The Art Institute of California–Sunnyvale
1120 Kifer Road
Sunnyvale, California 94086
Phone: 408-962-6400
      866-583-7961 (toll-free)
Fax: 408-962-6498
Web site: http://www.artinstitutes.edu/sunnyvale

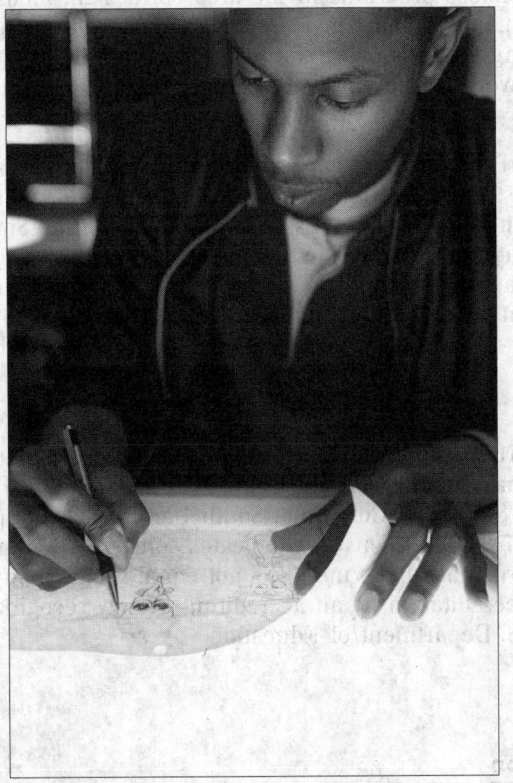

The Art Institute of Atlanta; The Art Institute of Atlanta–Decatur[1]; The Art Institute of Austin[2]; The Art Institute of California–Hollywood; The Art Institute of California–Inland Empire; The Art Institute of California–Los Angeles; The Art Institute of California–Orange County; The Art Institute of California–Sacramento; The Art Institute of California–San Diego; The Art Institute of California–San Francisco; The Art Institute of California–Sunnyvale; The Art Institute of Charleston[1]; The Art Institute of Charlotte; The Art Institute of Colorado; The Art Institute of Dallas[5]; The Art Institute of Fort Lauderdale; The Art Institute of Fort Worth[5]; The Art Institute of Houston; The Art Institute of Houston–North[2]; The Art Institute of Indianapolis[4]; The Art Institute of Jacksonville[5]; The Art Institute of Las Vegas; The Art Institute of Michigan; The Art Institute of New York City; The Art Institute of Ohio–Cincinnati[6]; The Art Institute of Philadelphia; The Art Institute of Phoenix; The Art Institute of Pittsburgh; The Art Institute of Portland; The Art Institute of Raleigh–Durham; The Art Institute of Salt Lake City; The Art Institute of San Antonio[2];The Art Institute of Seattle; The Art Institute of Tampa[5]; The Art Institute of Tennessee–Nashville[1]; The Art Institute of Tucson; The Art Institute of Vancouver; The Art Institute of Virginia Beach[1,7]; The Art Institute of Washington[1,7]; The Art Institute of Washington–Northern Virginia[1,7]; The Art Institute of Wisconsin; The Art Institute of York–Pennsylvania; The Art Institutes International–Kansas City; The Art Institutes International Minnesota; The Illinois Institute of Art–Chicago; The Illinois Institute of Art–Schaumburg; The Illinois Institute of Art–Tinley Park; Miami International University of Art & Design; The New England Institute of Art.

[1] A branch of The Art Institute of Atlanta
[2] A branch of The Art Institute of Houston
[3] A campus of South University
[4] The Art Institute of Indianapolis is regulated by the Indiana Commission on Proprietary Education, 302 West Washington Street, Room E201, Indianapolis, Indiana 46204, AC-0080
[5] A branch of Miami International University of Art & Design
[6] The Art Institute of Ohio–Cincinnati, 8845 Governors Hill Drive, Suite 100, Cincinnati, Ohio 45249-3317, OH Reg. #04-01-1698B
[7] Certified by the State Council of Higher Education to operate in Virginia

THE ART INSTITUTE OF CHARLESTON

CHARLESTON, SOUTH CAROLINA

The Art Institute of Charleston
A branch of The Art Institute of Atlanta
CREATE TOMORROW

A focused education from The Art Institute of Charleston, a branch of The Art Institute of Atlanta, can help students turn their creative energy into a powerful tool that can make a difference in the world. Students are part of a collaborative and supportive community, where experienced instructors provide the guidance and skills needed to pursue a career in the creative economy.

The school's programs in the areas of design, media arts, fashion, and culinary give students the opportunity to learn by using professional-grade technology and build a portfolio of work to show potential employers after graduation.

The Art Institute of Charleston is a branch campus of The Art Institute of Atlanta. The Art Institute of Atlanta is accredited by the Commission on Colleges of the Southern Association of Colleges and Schools to award associate and baccalaureate degrees. Contact the Commission on Colleges at 1866 Southern Lane, Decatur, Georgia 30033-4097 or call 404-679-4500 for questions about the accreditation of The Art Institute of Atlanta.

The Art Institute of Charleston is licensed by the South Carolina Commission on Higher Education, 1333 Main Street, Suite 200, Columbia, South Carolina 29201; phone: 803-737-8860. Licensure indicates only that minimum standards have been met; it is not equal to or synonymous with accreditation by an accrediting agency recognized by the U.S. Department of Education.

Location

The school's Market Street location is close to arts, historical, and cultural organizations, allowing students to experience all that Charleston has to offer.

Programs of Study and Degrees

No matter which course of study a student may choose, the professionals at The Art Institute of Charleston will guide, support, and help each student as their talents evolve on their journey of personal and professional transformation. Students studying design learn to fine-tune their visual thinking and problem-solving skills, as they create everything from logos to TV ads. Programs in the area of media arts focus on utilizing technology to deliver information and entertainment, while students studying fashion learn to design clothes for the runway or run a retail shop.

Culinary programs focus on the fundamental techniques while exposing students to a full menu of international cuisines and management techniques.

Bachelor's degree programs are offered in culinary arts management, digital filmmaking and video production, fashion and retail management, graphic design, interior design, photographic imaging, and Web design and interactive media.

Associate degrees are offered in culinary arts; culinary arts with a concentration in baking and pastry; graphic design; Web design and interactive media; and wine, spirits, and beverage management.

A certificate program is available in culinary arts–skills.

Academic Programs

The Art Institute of Charleston operates on a year-round, four-quarter system.

Academic Facilities

The Art Institute of Charleston provides a learning environment with professional-grade technology applicable to each student's course of study. Students have the opportunity to build a portfolio of work that shows potential employers that they are trained to use the software, hardware, or equipment utilized within the industry. Depending upon the course of study, students are immersed in a creative environment—from classrooms to computer labs to studios—focused on relevant, hands-on education designed to prepare students for the real world.

Costs

Tuition cost varies by program. Prospective students should contact the school for current tuition costs. Other charges include a starting kit for all first-quarter students. Kits vary in price depending on the program of study.

Financial Aid

Financial aid is available for those who qualify. Students who require financial assistance should first complete and submit a Free Application for Federal Student Aid (FAFSA) and meet with a financial aid officer.

Faculty

Faculty members are experienced professionals who create a learning environment that is similar to the professional world students will face after graduation. Instructors are focused on helping students develop the skills they need to transform their creative potential into marketable skills.

Admission Requirements

Applicants must provide proof of high school graduation or achievement of a General Educational Development (GED) certificate as a prerequisite for admission. In lieu of documenting high school graduation or a GED certificate, applicants may provide proof of attaining an associate degree or higher from an accredited institution. An official transcript indicating date of high school graduation, GED certificate (including test scores), or date of college graduation (including degree granted) is required as proof.

All individuals seeking admission to The Art Institute of Charleston are interviewed in person or by phone by an assistant director of admissions, and each applicant must create an original essay of at least 150 words stating how an education at The Art Institute of Charleston would help the student to achieve career goals. There is a $50 application fee.

For the most recent information regarding admission requirements, please refer to the current academic catalog.

Application and Information

To obtain an application, make arrangements for an interview, or tour the school, prospective students should contact:

The Art Institute of Charleston
24 North Market Street
Charleston, South Carolina 29401-2623
Phone: 843-727-3500
       866-211-0107 (toll-free)
Fax: 843-727-3440
Web site: http://www.artinstitutes.edu/charleston

The Art Institute of Atlanta; The Art Institute of Atlanta–Decatur[1]; The Art Institute of Austin[2]; The Art Institute of California–Hollywood; The Art Institute of California–Inland Empire; The Art Institute of California–Los Angeles; The Art Institute of California–Orange County; The Art Institute of California–Sacramento; The Art Institute of California–San Diego; The Art Institute of California–San Francisco; The Art Institute of California–Sunnyvale; The Art Institute of Charleston[1]; The Art Institute of Charlotte; The Art Institute of Colorado; The Art Institute of Dallas[3]; The Art Institute of Fort Lauderdale; The Art Institute of Fort Worth[3]; The Art Institute of Houston; The Art Institute of Houston–North[2]; The Art Institute of Indianapolis[4]; The Art Institute of Jacksonville[5]; The Art Institute of Las Vegas; The Art Institute of Michigan; The Art Institute of New York City; The Art Institute of Ohio–Cincinnati[6]; The Art Institute of Philadelphia; The Art Institute of Phoenix; The Art Institute of Pittsburgh; The Art Institute of Portland; The Art Institute of Raleigh–Durham; The Art Institute of Salt Lake City; The Art Institute of San Antonio[2];The Art Institute of Seattle; The Art Institute of Tampa[5]; The Art Institute of Tennessee–Nashville[1]; The Art Institute of Tucson; The Art Institute of Vancouver; The Art Institute of Virginia Beach[1,7]; The Art Institute of Washington[1,7]; The Art Institute of Washington–Northern Virginia[1,7]; The Art Institute of Wisconsin; The Art Institute of York–Pennsylvania; The Art Institutes International–Kansas City; The Art Institutes International Minnesota; The Illinois Institute of Art–Chicago; The Illinois Institute of Art–Schaumburg; The Illinois Institute of Art–Tinley Park; Miami International University of Art & Design; The New England Institute of Art.

[1]A branch of The Art Institute of Atlanta
[2]A branch of The Art Institute of Houston
[3]A campus of South University
[4]The Art Institute of Indianapolis is regulated by the Indiana Commission on Proprietary Education, 302 West Washington Street, Room E201, Indianapolis, Indiana 46204, AC-0080
[5]A branch of Miami International University of Art & Design
[6]The Art Institute of Ohio–Cincinnati, 8845 Governors Hill Drive, Suite 100, Cincinnati, Ohio 45249-3317, OH Reg. #04-01-1698B
[7]Certified by the State Council of Higher Education to operate in Virginia

THE ART INSTITUTE OF CHARLOTTE

CHARLOTTE, NORTH CAROLINA

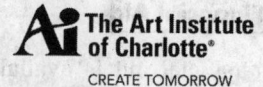

A focused education The Art Institute of Charlotte can help students turn their creative energy into a powerful tool that can make a difference in the world. Students are part of a collaborative and supportive community, where experienced instructors provide the guidance and skills needed to pursue a career in the creative economy.

The school's programs in the areas of design, media arts, fashion, and culinary give students the opportunity to learn by using professional-grade technology and build a portfolio of work to show potential employers after graduation.

The Art Institute of Charlotte is accredited by the Accrediting Council for Independent Colleges and Schools (ACICS) to award certificates, associate degrees, and bachelor's degrees. ACICS is listed as a nationally recognized accrediting agency by the United States Department of Education and is recognized by the Council for Higher Education Accreditation. ACICS can be contacted at 750 First Street NE, Suite 980, Washington, D.C. 20002; phone: 202-336-6780.

The Art Institute of Charlotte is licensed to award certificates by the North Carolina State Board of Community Colleges and is licensed to award associate and bachelor's degrees by the Board of Governors of the University of North Carolina.

Location

Charlotte mixes the characteristics of a large urban center with the charm of suburban life. With a mild climate and central location, Charlotte residents are only 2 hours from the Blue Ridge Mountains and 3 hours from the Atlantic coast. Charlotte is known for its arts community, sports, shopping, and restaurants. More than 300 Fortune 500 companies have offices in Charlotte, the nation's second-largest banking center and fifth-largest urban region, with 6.3 million people living within a 100-mile radius.

Programs of Study and Degrees

No matter which course of study a student may choose, the professionals at The Art Institute of Charlotte will guide, support, and help each student as their talents evolve on their journey of personal and professional transformation. Students studying design learn to fine-tune their visual thinking and problem-solving skills, as they create every-thing from logos to TV ads. Programs in the area of media arts focus on utilizing technology to deliver information and entertainment, while students studying fashion learn to design clothes for the runway or run a retail shop. Culinary programs focus on the fundamental techniques while exposing students to a full menu of international cuisines and management techniques.

Bachelor's degree programs are available in culinary arts management, digital filmmaking and video production, fashion marketing and management, graphic design, interior design, photography, and Web design and interactive media.

Associate degree programs are offered in culinary arts, fashion marketing, graphic design, interior design, and Web design and interactive media.

A certificate program is available in Web design.

Academic Programs

The Art Institute of Charlotte operates on a year-round, four-quarter system.

Academic Facilities

The Art Institute of Charlotte provides a learning environment with professional-grade technology applicable to each student's course of study. Students have the opportunity to build a portfolio of work that shows potential employers that they are trained to use the software, hardware, or equipment utilized within the industry. Depending upon the course of study, students are immersed in a creative environment—from classrooms to computer labs to studios—focused on relevant, hands-on education designed to prepare students for the real world.

Costs

Tuition cost varies by program. Prospective students should contact the school for current tuition costs. Other charges include a starting kit for all first-quarter students. Kits vary in price depending on the program of study.

Financial Aid

Financial aid is available for those who qualify. Students who require financial assistance should first complete and submit a Free Application for Federal Student Aid (FAFSA) and meet with a financial aid officer.

Faculty

Faculty members are experienced professionals who create a learning environment that is similar to the professional world students will face after graduation. Instructors are focused on helping students develop the skills they need to transform their creative potential into marketable skills.

Admission Requirements

Applicants must be high school graduates or have a General Educational Development (GED) certificate. A 150-word written essay is required, as are high school transcripts and any records from other academic institutions attended. All interested students are interviewed in person or over the phone. Following this interview, prospective students complete an application for admission and submit the enrollment fee. Applicants who have taken the SAT or ACT are encouraged to submit their scores to the Admissions Office for evaluation. There is a $50 application fee.

For the most recent information regarding admission requirements, please refer to the current academic catalog.

Application and Information

To obtain an application or make arrangements for an interview or tour of the school, prospective students should contact:

The Art Institute of Charlotte
Three LakePointe Plaza
2110 Water Ridge Parkway
Charlotte, North Carolina 28217-4536
Phone: 704-357-8020
      800-872-4417 (toll-free)
Fax: 704-357-1133
Web site: http://www.artinstitutes.edu/charlotte

The Art Institute of Atlanta; The Art Institute of Atlanta–Decatur[1]; The Art Institute of Austin[2]; The Art Institute of California–Hollywood; The Art Institute of California–Inland Empire; The Art Institute of California–Los Angeles; The Art Institute of California–Orange County; The Art Institute of California–Sacramento; The Art Institute of California–San Diego; The Art Institute of California–San Francisco; The Art Institute of California–Sunnyvale; The Art Institute of Charleston[1]; The Art Institute of Charlotte; The Art Institute of Colorado; The Art Institute of Dallas[3]; The Art Institute of Fort Lauderdale; The Art Institute of Fort Worth[3]; The Art Institute of Houston; The Art Institute of Houston–North[2]; The Art Institute of Indianapolis[4]; The Art Institute of Jacksonville[5]; The Art Institute of Las Vegas; The Art Institute of Michigan; The Art Institute of New York City; The Art Institute of Ohio–Cincinnati[6]; The Art Institute of Philadelphia; The Art Institute of Phoenix; The Art Institute of Pittsburgh; The Art Institute of Portland; The Art Institute of Raleigh–Durham; The Art Institute of Salt Lake City; The Art Institute of San Antonio[2];The Art Institute of Seattle; The Art Institute of Tampa[5]; The Art Institute of Tennessee–Nashville[1]; The Art Institute of Tucson; The Art Institute of Vancouver; The Art Institute of Virginia Beach[1,7]; The Art Institute of Washington[1,7]; The Art Institute of Washington–Northern Virginia[1,7]; The Art Institute of Wisconsin; The Art Institute of York–Pennsylvania; The Art Institutes International–Kansas City; The Art Institutes International Minnesota; The Illinois Institute of Art–Chicago; The Illinois Institute of Art–Schaumburg; The Illinois Institute of Art–Tinley Park; Miami International University of Art & Design; The New England Institute of Art.

[1]A branch of The Art Institute of Atlanta
[2]A branch of The Art Institute of Houston
[3]A campus of South University
[4]The Art Institute of Indianapolis is regulated by the Indiana Commission on Proprietary Education, 302 West Washington Street, Room E201, Indianapolis, Indiana 46204, AC-0080
[5]A branch of Miami International University of Art & Design
[6]The Art Institute of Ohio–Cincinnati, 8845 Governors Hill Drive, Suite 100, Cincinnati, Ohio 45249-3317, OH Reg. #04-01-1698B
[7]Certified by the State Council of Higher Education to operate in Virginia

THE ART INSTITUTE OF COLORADO
DENVER, COLORADO

A focused education from The Art Institute of Colorado can help students turn their creative energy into a powerful tool that can make a difference in the world. Students are part of a collaborative and supportive community, where experienced instructors provide the guidance and skills needed to pursue a career in the creative economy.

The school's programs in the areas of design, media arts, fashion, and culinary give students the opportunity to learn by using professional-grade technology and build a portfolio of work to show potential employers after graduation.

The Art Institute of Colorado is accredited by the Higher Learning Commission and is a member of the North Central Association, 230 South LaSalle Street, Suite 7-500, Chicago, Illinois, 60604-1413; http://www.ncahlc.org.

The Art Institute of Colorado is authorized to award diplomas, associate of applied science degrees, and bachelor of arts degrees by the Colorado Department of Higher Education, Commission on Higher Education, 1380 Lawrence Street, Suite 1200, Denver, Colorado 80202.

The Associate of Applied Science in culinary arts degree program is accredited by the Accrediting Commission of the American Culinary Federation Education Foundation.

The interior design program leading to the Bachelor of Arts degree is accredited by the Council for Interior Design Accreditation, 206 Grandville Avenue, Suite 350, Grand Rapids, Michigan 49503; http://www.accredit-id.org.

The Associate of Applied Science in kitchen and bath design degree program is accredited by the National Kitchen & Bath Association (NKBA). NKBA can be contacted at 687 Willow Grove Street, Hackettstown, New Jersey 07840; phone: 800-THE-NKBA; http://www.nkba.org.

Location

The Art Institute of Colorado is located in Denver, home to many major corporations and high-technology companies. Located near galleries, museums, and theaters, The Art Institute of Colorado provides easy access to music and dance performances at both the Performing Arts Complex and Red Rocks Amphitheater. Denver is a 1-hour drive from world-class skiing and water sports, amid the Rocky Mountains' breathtaking scenery. The city itself offers ample opportunities for biking, hiking, in-line skating, and viewing professional sports.

Programs of Study and Degrees

No matter which course of study a student may choose, the professionals at The Art Institute of Colorado will guide, support, and help each student as their talents evolve on their journey of personal and professional transformation. Students studying design learn to fine-tune their visual thinking and problem-solving skills, as they create everything from logos to TV ads. Programs in the area of media arts focus on utilizing technology to deliver information and entertainment, while students studying fashion learn to design clothes for the runway or run a retail shop. Culinary programs focus on the fundamental techniques while exposing students to a full menu of international cuisines and management techniques.

Bachelor's degrees are offered in culinary management, design and technical graphics, design management, digital filmmaking and video production, fashion design, fashion retail management, food and beverage management, game art and design, graphic design, hospitality management, interior design, media arts and animation, photography, visual effects and motion graphics, and Web design and interactive media.

Associate degree programs are available in baking and pastry, culinary arts, graphic design, kitchen and bath design, photography, video production, and Web design and interactive media.

Diploma programs are offered in baking and pastry, digital image management, fashion retailing, and the art of cooking.

The culinary arts, fashion retail management, interior design, and photography programs are available in an evening and weekend option format.

Academic Programs

The Art Institute of Colorado offers Bachelor of Arts degree programs that are designed to be thirty-six months in length. Associate degree programs are designed to take twenty-one months to complete.

Academic Facilities

The Art Institute of Colorado provides a learning environment with professional-grade technology applicable to each student's course of study. Students have the opportunity to build a portfolio of work that shows potential employers that they are trained to use the software, hardware, or equipment utilized within the industry. Depending upon the course of study, students are immersed in a creative environment—from classrooms to computer labs to studios—focused on relevant, hands-on education designed to prepare students for the real world.

Costs

Tuition cost varies by program. Prospective students should contact the school for current tuition costs. Other charges include a starting kit for all first-quarter students. Kits vary in price, depending on the program of study.

Financial Aid

Financial aid is available for those who qualify. Students who require financial assistance should first complete and submit a Free Application for Federal Student Aid (FAFSA) and meet with a financial aid officer.

Faculty

Faculty members are experienced professionals who create a learning environment that is similar to the professional world students will face after graduation. Instructors are focused on helping students develop the skills they need to transform their creative potential into marketable skills.

Admission Requirements

All applicants are evaluated on the basis of previous education, background, and stated or demonstrated interest in a career program. Applicants must provide high school or college transcripts and an essay of approximately 150 words stating how an education at The Art Institute of Colorado will help them attain their creative goals. Portfolios are welcome but not required. Applicants who have taken the SAT or ACT are encouraged to submit scores for evaluation. There is a $50 application fee.

For the most recent information regarding admission requirements, please refer to the current academic catalog.

Application and Information

To obtain an application, make arrangements for an interview, or tour the school, prospective students should contact:

The Art Institute of Colorado
1200 Lincoln Street
Denver, Colorado 80203-2172
Phone: 303-837-0825
       800-275-2420 (toll-free)
Fax: 303-860-8520
Web site: http://www.artinstitutes.edu/denver

THE ART INSTITUTE OF DALLAS

DALLAS, TEXAS

A focused education from The Art Institute of Dallas, a campus of South University, can help students turn their creative energy into a powerful tool that can make a difference in the world. Students are part of a collaborative and supportive community, where experienced instructors provide the guidance and skills needed to pursue a career in the creative economy.

The school's programs in the areas of design, media arts, fashion, and culinary give students the opportunity to learn by using professional-grade technology and build a portfolio of work to show potential employers after graduation.

The Art Institute of Dallas is a campus of South University. South University is accredited by the Commission on Colleges of the Southern Association of Colleges and Schools to award associate, baccalaureate, master's, and doctoral degrees. Contact the Commission on Colleges at 1866 Southern Lane, Decatur, Georgia 30033-4097 or call 404-679-4500 for questions about the accreditation of South University.

The Art Institute of Dallas holds a certificate of authorization acknowledging exemption from Texas Higher Education Coordinating Board regulations. The Art Institute of Dallas is licensed by the Arkansas State Board of Private Career Education. The Art Institute of Dallas is licensed by the Oklahoma Board of Private Vocational Schools, 3700 North Classen Boulevard, Suite 250, Oklahoma City, Oklahoma 73118; phone: 405-528-3370.

The certificate in art of cooking and the Associate of Applied Science degree in culinary arts programs are accredited by the Accrediting Commission of the American Culinary Federation Education Foundation.

The interior design program leading to the Bachelor of Fine Arts degree is accredited by the Council for Interior Design Accreditation, 206 Grandville Avenue, Suite 350, Grand Rapids, Michigan 49503; http://www.accredit-id.org.

Location

The school is located in the Dallas/Fort Worth area, which has one of the lowest cost-of-living indexes of any major metropolitan area. The Dallas/Fort Worth area offers a diverse range of cultural and recreational activities, including the Dallas Symphony, Mesquite Rodeo, Six Flags, Lone Star Park, concerts in the West End, and national sports teams. Many major employers have relocated to the Dallas/Fort Worth area due to its positive economic environment.

Programs of Study and Degrees

No matter which course of study a student may choose, the professionals at The Art Institute of Dallas will guide, support, and help each student as their talents evolve on their journey of personal and professional transformation. Students studying design learn to fine-tune their visual thinking and problem-solving skills, as they create everything from logos to TV ads. Programs in the area of media arts focus on utilizing technology to deliver information and entertainment, while students studying fashion learn to design clothes for the runway or run a retail shop. Culinary programs focus on the fundamental techniques while exposing students to a full menu of international cuisines and management techniques.

The Art Institute of Dallas offers bachelor's degree programs in advertising design, culinary management, digital filmmaking and video production, fashion and retail management, fashion design, graphic design, interior design, media arts and animation, photography, and Web design and interactive media.

Associate degree programs include baking and pastry, culinary arts, fashion design, graphic design, kitchen and bath design, photography, restaurant and catering management, and video production.

A certificate program is available in the art of cooking.

The culinary arts, graphic design, and interior design programs, as well as the Bachelor of Fine Arts in fashion design program, are available in an evening and weekend option format.

Academic Programs

Associate degree programs can be completed in as little as twenty-one months. Bachelor's degree programs can be completed in as little as thirty-six months.

Academic Facilities

The Art Institute of Dallas provides a learning environment with professional-grade technology applicable to each student's course of study. Students have the opportunity to build a portfolio of work that shows potential employers that they are trained to use the software, hardware, or equipment utilized within the industry. Depending upon the course of study, students are immersed in a creative environment—from classrooms to computer labs to studios—focused on relevant, hands-on education designed to prepare students for the real world.

Costs

Tuition cost varies by program. Prospective students should contact the school for current tuition costs. Other charges include a starting kit for all first-quarter students. Kits vary in price depending on the program of study.

Financial Aid

Financial aid is available for those who qualify. Students who require financial assistance should first complete and submit a Free Application for Federal Student Aid (FAFSA) and meet with a financial aid officer.

Faculty

Faculty members are experienced professionals who create a learning environment that is similar to the professional world

students will face after graduation. Instructors are focused on helping students develop the skills they need to transform their creative potential into marketable skills.

Student Government

The Student Ambassador Organization promotes high-quality representation of the student body. The group provides a channel of communication among students, the administration, and faculty members.

Admission Requirements

Applicants are required to write a paragraph of approximately 300 words stating how The Art Institute of Dallas may help them reach their creative goals. Applicants must present proof of high school graduation or a General Educational Development (GED) certificate as well as their accomplishments and core academic courses. Successful admission depends on QPA, accomplishments, SAT or ACT scores, and a personal interview with admission representatives. Applicants who do not submit a transcript of GED scores are required to take additional testing.

To enroll, students must submit an admission application and an enrollment agreement along with a $50 application fee.

For the most recent information regarding admission requirements, please refer to the current academic catalog.

Application and Information

To obtain an application, make arrangements for an interview, or tour the school, prospective students should contact:

The Art Institute of Dallas
8080 Park Lane, Suite 100
Dallas, Texas 75231-5993
Phone: 214-692-8080
        800-275-4243 (toll-free)
Fax: 214-750-9460
Web site: http://www.artinstitutes.edu/dallas

COLLEGE CLOSE-UPS

THE ART INSTITUTE OF FORT LAUDERDALE

FORT LAUDERDALE, FLORIDA

The Art Institute of Fort Lauderdale®
CREATE TOMORROW

A focused education from The Art Institute of Fort Lauderdale can help students turn their creative energy into a powerful tool that can make a difference in the world. Students are part of a collaborative and supportive community, where experienced instructors provide the guidance and skills needed to pursue a career in the creative economy.

The school's programs in the areas of design, media arts, fashion, and culinary give students the opportunity to learn by using professional-grade technology and build a portfolio of work to show potential employers after graduation.

The Art Institute of Fort Lauderdale is accredited by the Accrediting Council for Independent Colleges and Schools (ACICS) to award diplomas, associate degrees, and bachelor's degrees. ACICS is listed as a nationally recognized accrediting agency by the United States Department of Education and is recognized by the Council for Higher Education Accreditation. ACICS can be contacted at 750 First Street NE, Suite 980, Washington, D.C. 20002; phone: 202-336-6780.

The Art Institute of Fort Lauderdale is licensed by the Commission for Independent Education, Florida Department of Education. Additional information regarding this institution may be obtained by contacting the commission at 325 West Gaines Street, Suite 1414, Tallahassee, Florida 32399-0400; phone: 888-224-6684 (toll-free).

The Associate of Science degree in culinary arts and the Bachelor of Science degree in culinary management are accredited by the Accrediting Commission of the American Culinary Federation Education Foundation.

The interior design program leading to the Bachelor of Science degree is accredited by the Council for Interior Design Accreditation, 206 Grandville Avenue, Suite 350, Grand Rapids, Michigan 49503; http://www.accredit-id.org.

Location

Surrounded by waterways, Fort Lauderdale is known as "The Venice of America." The area has an average temperature of 70 degrees in the winter and offers many opportunities for fun in the sun. The Art Institute of Fort Lauderdale is close to 23 miles of beaches, shopping districts, museums, historical sites, restaurants, and nightclubs. Located between Miami and Palm Beach, Fort Lauderdale's many attractions include its world-famous beach, the picturesque Riverwalk, and Las Olas Boulevard—a centerpiece of fashion, fine dining, and entertainment. Tourists and residents alike enjoy the Broward Center for the Performing Arts, Museum of Discovery and Science, Museum of Art, and Old Fort Lauderdale Village and Museum. Fort Lauderdale also supports a diverse range of industries, including marine, manufacturing, finance, insurance, real estate, high technology, avionics/aerospace, and film and television production.

Programs of Study and Degrees

No matter which course of study a student may choose, the professionals at The Art Institute of Fort Lauderdale will guide, support, and help each student as their talents evolve on their journey of personal and professional transformation. Students studying design learn to fine-tune their visual thinking and problem-solving skills, as they create everything from logos to TV ads. Programs in the area of media arts focus on utilizing technology to deliver information and entertainment, while students studying fashion learn to design clothes for the runway or run a retail shop. Culinary programs focus on the fundamental techniques while exposing students to a full menu of international cuisines and management techniques.

Bachelor's degree programs are offered in advertising, culinary management, digital filmmaking and video production, fashion design, fashion merchandising, game art and design, graphic design, illustration, industrial design, interior design, media arts and animation, photography, visual effects and motion graphics, and Web design and interactive media.

Associate degree programs are offered in baking and pastry, culinary arts, fashion design, graphic design, interior design, photography, video production, and Web design and interactive media.

Diploma programs are offered in art of cooking and residential design.

Academic Programs

The Art Institute of Fort Lauderdale offers Bachelor of Science degree programs, Associate of Science degree programs, and diploma programs.

Academic Facilities

The Art Institute of Fort Lauderdale provides a learning environment with professional-grade technology applicable to each student's course of study. Students have the opportunity to build a portfolio of work that shows potential employers that they are trained to use the software, hardware, or equipment utilized within the industry. Depending upon the course of study, students are immersed in a creative environment—from classrooms to computer labs to studios—focused on relevant, hands-on education designed to prepare students for the real world.

Costs

Tuition cost varies by program. Prospective students should contact the school for current tuition costs. Other charges include a starting kit for all first-quarter students. Kits vary in price depending on the program of study.

Financial Aid

Financial aid is available for those who qualify. Students who require financial assistance should first complete and submit a Free Application for Federal Student Aid (FAFSA) and meet with a financial aid officer.

Faculty

Faculty members are experienced professionals who create a learning environment that is similar to the professional world students will face after graduation. Instructors are focused on helping students develop the skills they need to transform their creative potential into marketable skills.

Student Government

All students have the right to participate and vote in Student Government elections and referenda. The Student Government works with faculty and staff members to provide numerous events, including student socials, community outreach programs, volunteer work, and student service events.

Admission Requirements

Admission to The Art Institute of Fort Lauderdale requires a completed application form, evidence of high school graduation or successful completion of the General Educational Development (GED) test, and an essay on how the school may assist in achieving the applicant's creative goals. Applicants are also required to schedule an interview with an admissions representative and, if financial aid is needed, to complete the FAFSA and PLUS loan forms found in the application packet. There is a $50 application fee.

For the most recent information regarding admission requirements, please refer to the current academic catalog.

Application and Information

To obtain an application, make arrangements for an interview, or tour the school, prospective students should contact:

The Art Institute of Fort Lauderdale
1799 S.E. 17th Street
Fort Lauderdale, Florida 33316-3013

Phone: 954-463-3000
          800-275-7603 (toll-free)
Fax: 954-728-8637
Web site: http://www.artinstitutes.edu/fortlauderdale

The Art Institute of Atlanta; The Art Institute of Atlanta–Decatur[1]; The Art Institute of Austin[2]; The Art Institute of California–Hollywood; The Art Institute of California–Inland Empire; The Art Institute of California–Los Angeles; The Art Institute of California–Orange County; The Art Institute of California–Sacramento; The Art Institute of California–San Diego; The Art Institute of California–San Francisco; The Art Institute of California–Sunnyvale; The Art Institute of Charleston[1]; The Art Institute of Charlotte; The Art Institute of Colorado; The Art Institute of Dallas[3]; The Art Institute of Fort Lauderdale; The Art Institute of Fort Worth[3]; The Art Institute of Houston; The Art Institute of Houston–North[2]; The Art Institute of Indianapolis[4]; The Art Institute of Jacksonville[5]; The Art Institute of Las Vegas; The Art Institute of Michigan; The Art Institute of New York City; The Art Institute of Ohio–Cincinnati[6]; The Art Institute of Philadelphia; The Art Institute of Phoenix; The Art Institute of Pittsburgh; The Art Institute of Portland; The Art Institute of Raleigh–Durham; The Art Institute of Salt Lake City; The Art Institute of San Antonio[2];The Art Institute of Seattle; The Art Institute of Tampa[5]; The Art Institute of Tennessee–Nashville[1]; The Art Institute of Tucson; The Art Institute of Vancouver; The Art Institute of Virginia Beach[1,7]; The Art Institute of Washington[1,7]; The Art Institute of Washington–Northern Virginia[1,7]; The Art Institute of Wisconsin; The Art Institute of York–Pennsylvania; The Art Institutes International–Kansas City; The Art Institutes International Minnesota; The Illinois Institute of Art–Chicago; The Illinois Institute of Art–Schaumburg; The Illinois Institute of Art–Tinley Park; Miami International University of Art & Design; The New England Institute of Art.

[1]A branch of The Art Institute of Atlanta
[2]A branch of The Art Institute of Houston
[3]A campus of South University
[4]The Art Institute of Indianapolis is regulated by the Indiana Commission on Proprietary Education, 302 West Washington Street, Room E201, Indianapolis, Indiana 46204, AC-0080
[5]A branch of Miami International University of Art & Design
[6]The Art Institute of Ohio–Cincinnati, 8845 Governors Hill Drive, Suite 100, Cincinnati, Ohio 45249-3317, OH Reg. #04-01-1698B
[7]Certified by the State Council of Higher Education to operate in Virginia

THE ART INSTITUTE OF FORT WORTH

FORT WORTH, TEXAS

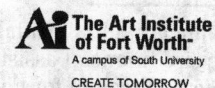

A focused education from The Art Institute of Fort Worth, a campus of South University, can help students turn their creative energy into a powerful tool that can make a difference in the world. Students are part of a collaborative and supportive community, where experienced instructors provide the guidance and skills needed to pursue a career in the creative economy.

The school's programs in the areas of design, media arts, and fashion give students the opportunity to learn by using professional-grade technology and build a portfolio of work to show potential employers after graduation.

The Art Institute of Fort Worth is a campus of South University. South University is accredited by the Commission on Colleges of the Southern Association of Colleges and Schools to award associate, baccalaureate, master's, and doctoral degrees. Contact the Commission on Colleges at 1866 Southern Lane, Decatur, Georgia 30033-4097 or call 404-679-4500 for questions about the accreditation of South University.

The Art Institute of Fort Worth holds a certificate of authorization acknowledging exemption from Texas Higher Education Coordinating Board regulations.

Location

Downtown Fort Worth is known for its art deco style buildings and culture, including theater, museums, and music. The city is also known for the popular Fort Worth Stockyards historic district.

Programs of Study and Degrees

No matter which course of study a student may choose, the professionals at The Art Institute of Fort Worth will guide, support, and help each student as their talents evolve on their journey of personal and professional transformation. Students studying design learn to fine-tune their visual thinking and problem-solving skills, as they create everything from logos to TV ads. Programs in the area of media arts focus on utilizing technology to deliver information and entertainment, while students studying fashion learn to market clothing or run a retail shop.

Bachelor's degree programs are offered in advertising design, fashion and retail management, graphic design, interior design, photography, and Web design and interactive media.

Associate degree programs are offered in graphic design and Web design and interactive media.

Academic Programs

The Art Institute of Fort Worth operates on a year-round, four-quarter system.

Academic Facilities

The Art Institute of Fort Worth provides a learning environment with professional-grade technology applicable to each student's course of study. Students have the opportunity to build a portfolio of work that shows potential employers that they are trained to use the software, hardware, or equipment utilized within the industry. Depending upon the course of study, students are immersed in a creative environment—from classrooms to computer labs to studios—focused on relevant, hands-on education designed to prepare students for the real world.

Costs

Tuition cost varies by program. Prospective students should contact the school for current tuition costs. Other charges include a starting kit for all first-quarter students. Kits vary in price depending on the program of study.

Financial Aid

Financial aid is available for those who qualify. Students who require financial assistance should first complete and submit a Free Application for Federal Student Aid (FAFSA) and meet with a financial aid officer.

Faculty

Faculty members are experienced professionals who create a learning environment that is similar to the professional world students will face after graduation. Instructors are focused on helping students develop the skills they need to transform their creative potential into marketable skills.

Admission Requirements

Applicants must provide proof of high school graduation or achievement of a General Educational Development (GED) certificate as a prerequisite for admission. In lieu of documenting high school graduation or a GED certificate, applicants may provide proof of attaining an associate degree or higher from an accredited institution. An official transcript indicating date of high school graduation, GED certificate (including test scores), or date of college graduation (including degree granted) is required as proof.

All individuals seeking admission to The Art Institute of Fort Worth are interviewed in person or by phone by an assistant director of admissions, and each applicant must create an original essay of at least 150 words stating how an education at The Art Institute of Fort Worth would help the student to achieve career goals. There is a $50 application fee.

For the most recent information regarding admission requirements, please refer to the current academic catalog.

Application and Information

To obtain an application, make arrangements for an interview, or tour the school, prospective students should contact:

The Art Institute of Forth Worth
7000 Calmont Avenue, Suite 150
Fort Worth, Texas 76116
Phone: 817-210-0808
         888-422-9686 (toll-free)
Fax: 817-210-0901
Web site: http://www.artinstitutes.edu/fort-worth

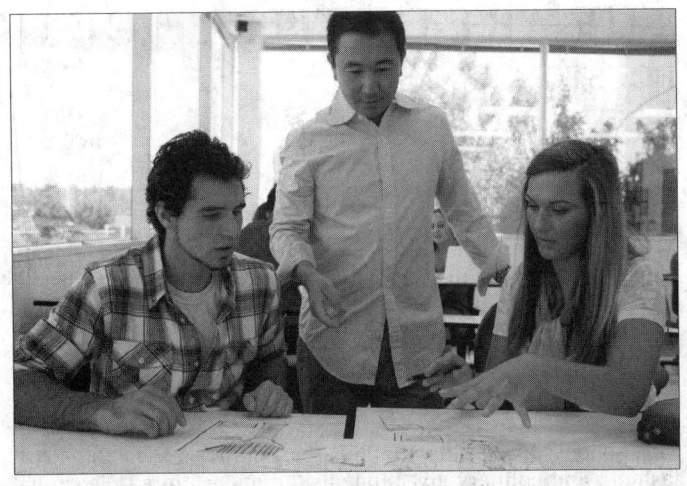

COLLEGE CLOSE-UPS

THE ART INSTITUTE OF HOUSTON

HOUSTON, TEXAS

The Art Institute of Houston
CREATE TOMORROW

A focused education from The Art Institute of Houston can help students turn their creative energy into a powerful tool that can make a difference in the world. Students are part of a collaborative and supportive community, where experienced instructors provide the guidance and skills needed to pursue a career in the creative economy.

The school's programs in the areas of design, media arts, fashion, and culinary give students the opportunity to learn by using professional-grade technology and build a portfolio of work to show potential employers after graduation.

The Art Institute of Houston is accredited by the Commission on Colleges of the Southern Association of Colleges and Schools to award associate degrees and baccalaureate degrees. Contact the Commission on Colleges at 1866 Southern Lane, Decatur, Georgia 30033-4097 or call 404-679-4500 for questions about the accreditation of The Art Institute of Houston.

The diploma program in culinary arts, Associate of Applied Science degree in baking and pastry, Associate of Applied Science degree in culinary arts, and the Bachelor of Science degree in culinary management are accredited by The Accrediting Commission of the American Culinary Federation Education Foundation.

The interior design program leading to the Bachelor of Fine Arts degree is accredited by the Council for Interior Design Accreditation, 206 Grandville Avenue, Suite 350, Grand Rapids, Michigan 49503; http://www.accredit-id.org.

The Art Institute of Houston holds a certificate of authorization acknowledging exemption from Texas Higher Education Coordinating Board Regulations.

Location

The Art Institute of Houston is close to several major art museums, a premier opera, a ballet, a symphony, and live theater companies. Culturally diverse, Houston has several international ethnic communities, great restaurants, and an eclectic nightlife as well as national sports teams. The city features a mild, semitropical climate and sunny beaches in nearby Galveston and Mexico.

Programs of Study and Degrees

No matter which course of study a student may choose, the professionals at The Art Institute of Houston will guide, support, and help each student as their talents evolve on their journey of personal and professional transformation. Students studying design learn to fine-tune their visual thinking and problem-solving skills, as they create everything from logos to TV ads. Programs in the area of media arts focus on utilizing technology to deliver information and entertainment, while students studying fashion learn to design clothes for the runway or run a retail shop. Culinary programs focus on the fundamental techniques while exposing students to a full menu of international cuisines and management techniques.

Bachelor's degree programs are offered in advertising design, audio production, culinary management, design and technical graphics, digital filmmaking and video production, fashion and retail management, fashion design, food and beverage management, game art and design, graphic design, hospitality management, interior design, media arts and animation, photography, visual effects and motion graphics, and Web design and interactive media.

Associate degree programs are available in baking and pastry, culinary arts, graphic design, restaurant and catering management, and Web design and interactive media.

Diploma programs are offered in baking and pastry and culinary arts.

The bachelor's degree programs in culinary management, interior design, and Web design and interactive media, as well as the Associate of Applied Science degree program in culinary arts are available in an evening and weekend option format.

Academic Programs

The academic year is divided into four quarters of approximately eleven weeks each. Students may start their program of study in any quarter. Bachelor's degrees can be earned upon completion of 180 academic credits over approximately twelve quarters. Associate degrees are earned upon completion of 90 to 108 academic credits, depending on the program, and can take seven to eight quarters. Diploma programs require the completion of 61 academic credits. Online programs are offered in two sessions per academic quarter.

Academic Facilities

The Art Institute of Houston provides a learning environment with professional-grade technology applicable to each student's course of study. Students have the opportunity to build a portfolio of work that shows potential employers that they are trained to use the software, hardware, or equipment utilized within the industry. Depending upon the course of study, students are immersed in a creative environment—from classrooms to computer labs to studios—focused on relevant, hands-on education designed to prepare students for the real world.

Costs

Tuition cost varies by program. Prospective students should contact the school for current tuition costs. Other charges include a starting kit for all first-quarter students. Kits vary in price depending on the program of study.

Financial Aid

Financial aid is available for those who qualify. Students who require financial assistance should first complete and submit a Free Application for Federal Student Aid (FAFSA) and meet with a financial aid officer.

Faculty

Faculty members are experienced professionals who create a learning environment that is similar to the professional world students will face after graduation. Instructors are focused on helping students develop the skills they need to transform their creative potential into marketable skills.

Student Government

The Student Government is the primary vehicle for student participation in institutional decision making. The Student Government acts as a voice on behalf of the student body and sponsors speakers, workshops, seminars, and other activities. When students seek change or have a request that affects the student body as a whole, Student Government serves as a forum for discussion and decision making. All students are eligible to belong to Student Government.

Admission Requirements

Admission to The Art Institute of Houston begins with an interview with an assistant director of admissions, either in person or by phone. Upon approval, students submit an application for admission and an enrollment agreement. Prospective students must be high school graduates, hold a General Educational Development (GED) certificate, or have earned an associate degree or higher from an accredited institution. The Art Institute of Houston considers alternative documentation from students who have completed high school or its equivalent but cannot provide the usual documentation. (The president of The Art Institute of Houston must approve all exceptions.) Evaluations are based on an applicant's previous education, background, and stated or demonstrated interest in a particular program. Portfolios are required for admission to the media arts and animation program; they are welcomed for other programs but not required. Applicants who have taken the SAT or ACT are encouraged to submit their scores for evaluation. There is a $50 application fee.

For the most recent information regarding admission requirements, please refer to the current academic catalog.

Application and Information

To obtain an application, make arrangements for an interview, or tour the school, prospective students should contact:

The Art Institute of Houston
1900 Yorktown Street
Houston, Texas 77056-4197
Phone: 713-623-2040
       800-275-4244 (toll-free)
Fax: 713-966-2797
Web site: http://www.artinstitutes.edu/houston

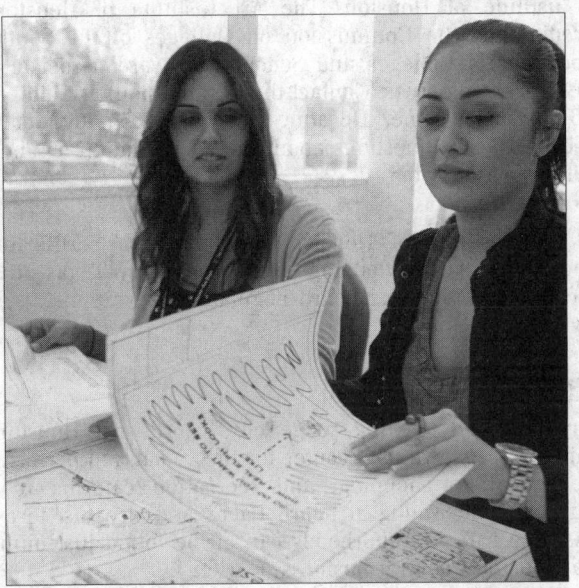

The Art Institute of Atlanta; The Art Institute of Atlanta–Decatur[1]; The Art Institute of Austin[2]; The Art Institute of California–Hollywood; The Art Institute of California–Inland Empire; The Art Institute of California–Los Angeles; The Art Institute of California–Orange County; The Art Institute of California–Sacramento; The Art Institute of California–San Diego; The Art Institute of California–San Francisco; The Art Institute of California–Sunnyvale; The Art Institute of Charleston[1]; The Art Institute of Charlotte; The Art Institute of Colorado; The Art Institute of Dallas[5]; The Art Institute of Fort Lauderdale; The Art Institute of Fort Worth[3]; The Art Institute of Houston; The Art Institute of Houston–North[2]; The Art Institute of Indianapolis[4]; The Art Institute of Jacksonville[5]; The Art Institute of Las Vegas; The Art Institute of Michigan; The Art Institute of New York City; The Art Institute of Ohio–Cincinnati[6]; The Art Institute of Philadelphia; The Art Institute of Phoenix; The Art Institute of Pittsburgh; The Art Institute of Portland; The Art Institute of Raleigh–Durham; The Art Institute of Salt Lake City; The Art Institute of San Antonio[2];The Art Institute of Seattle; The Art Institute of Tampa[5]; The Art Institute of Tennessee–Nashville[1]; The Art Institute of Tucson; The Art Institute of Vancouver; The Art Institute of Virginia Beach[1,7]; The Art Institute of Washington[1,7]; The Art Institute of Washington–Northern Virginia[1,7]; The Art Institute of Wisconsin; The Art Institute of York–Pennsylvania; The Art Institutes International–Kansas City; The Art Institutes International Minnesota; The Illinois Institute of Art–Chicago; The Illinois Institute of Art–Schaumburg; The Illinois Institute of Art–Tinley Park; Miami International University of Art & Design; The New England Institute of Art.

[1]A branch of The Art Institute of Atlanta
[2]A branch of The Art Institute of Houston
[3]A campus of South University
[4]The Art Institute of Indianapolis is regulated by the Indiana Commission on Proprietary Education, 302 West Washington Street, Room E201, Indianapolis, Indiana 46204, AC-0080
[5]A branch of Miami International University of Art & Design
[6]The Art Institute of Ohio–Cincinnati, 8845 Governors Hill Drive, Suite 100, Cincinnati, Ohio 45249-3317, OH Reg. #04-01-1698B
[7]Certified by the State Council of Higher Education to operate in Virginia

THE ART INSTITUTE OF HOUSTON–NORTH

HOUSTON, TEXAS

CREATE TOMORROW

A focused education from The Art Institute of Houston–North, a branch of The Art Institute of Houston, can help students turn their creative energy into a powerful tool that can make a difference in the world. Students are part of a collaborative and supportive community, where experienced instructors provide the guidance and skills needed to pursue a career in the creative economy.

The school's programs in the areas of design, media arts, and fashion give students the opportunity to learn by using professional-grade technology and build a portfolio of work to show potential employers after graduation.

The Art Institute of Houston–North is a branch campus of The Art Institute of Houston. The Art Institute of Houston is accredited by the Commission on Colleges of the Southern Association of Colleges and Schools to award associate and baccalaureate degrees. Contact the Commission on Colleges at 1866 Southern Lane, Decatur, Georgia 30033-4097 or call 404-679-4500 for questions about the accreditation of The Art Institute of Houston.

The Art Institute of Houston–North holds a certificate of authorization acknowledging exemption from Texas Higher Education Coordinating Board Regulations.

Location

A growing and exciting "edge city," northwest Houston is coming into its own as a center for the visual and performing arts, education, shopping, and recreation catering to the young—and the young at heart. Lakes and streams, forested parks, and safe neighborhoods can all be found just minutes from Houston's central business district.

Programs of Study and Degrees

No matter which course of study a student may choose, the professionals at The Art Institute of Houston–North will guide, support, and help each student as their talents evolve on their journey of personal and professional transformation. Students studying design learn to fine-tune their visual thinking and problem-solving skills, as they create everything from logos to TV ads. Programs in the area of media arts focus on utilizing technology to deliver information and entertainment, while students studying fashion learn to market clothing or run a retail shop.

Bachelor's degree programs are offered in fashion and retail management, graphic design, interior design, media arts and animation, photography, and Web design and interactive media.

Associate degree programs are offered in graphic design and Web design and interactive media.

Academic Programs

The Art Institute of Houston–North operates on a year-round, four-quarter system.

Academic Facilities

The Art Institute of Houston–North provides a learning environment with professional-grade technology applicable to each student's course of study. Students have the opportunity to build a portfolio of work that shows potential employers that they are trained to use the software, hardware, or equipment utilized within the industry. Depending upon the course of study, students are immersed in a creative environment—from classrooms to computer labs to studios—focused on relevant, hands-on education designed to prepare students for the real world.

Costs

Tuition cost varies by program. Prospective students should contact the school for current tuition costs. Other charges include a starting kit for all first-quarter students. Kits vary in price depending on the program of study.

Financial Aid

Financial aid is available for those who qualify. Students who require financial assistance should first complete and submit a Free Application for Federal Student Aid (FAFSA) and meet with a financial aid officer.

Faculty

Faculty members are experienced professionals who create a learning environment that is similar to the professional world students will face after graduation. Instructors are focused on helping students develop the skills they need to transform their creative potential into marketable skills.

Admission Requirements

Applicants must provide proof of high school graduation or achievement of a General Educational Development (GED) certificate as a prerequisite for admission. In lieu of documenting high school graduation or a GED certificate, applicants may provide proof of attaining an associate degree or higher from an accredited institution. An official transcript indicating date of high school graduation, GED certificate (including test scores), or date of college graduation (including degree granted) is required as proof.

All individuals seeking admission to The Art Institute of Houston–North are interviewed in person or by phone by an assistant director of admissions, and each applicant must create an original essay of at least 150 words stating how an education at The Art Institute of Houston–North would help the student to achieve career goals. There is a $50 application fee.

For the most recent information regarding admission requirements, please refer to the current academic catalog.

Application and Information

To obtain an application, make arrangements for an interview, or tour the school, prospective students should contact:

The Art Institute of Houston–North
10740 North Gessner Drive, Suite 190
Houston, Texas 77064
Phone: 281-671-3381
      866-830-4450 (toll-free)
Fax: 281-671-3550
Web site: http://www.artinstitutes.edu/houston-north

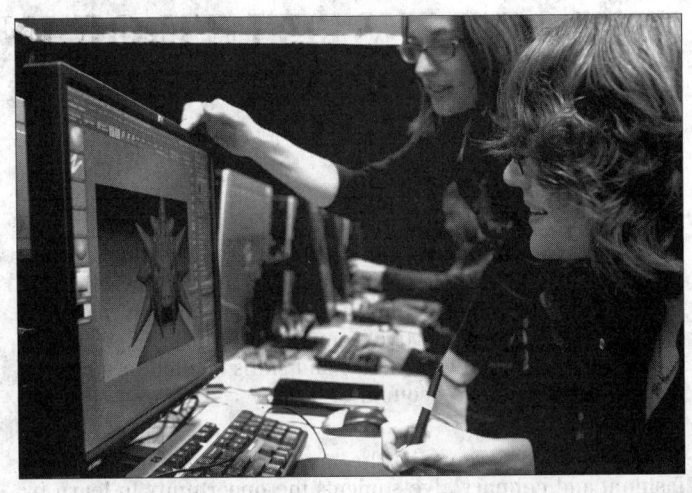

The Art Institute of Atlanta; The Art Institute of Atlanta–Decatur[1]; The Art Institute of Austin[2]; The Art Institute of California–Hollywood; The Art Institute of California–Inland Empire; The Art Institute of California–Los Angeles; The Art Institute of California–Orange County; The Art Institute of California–Sacramento; The Art Institute of California–San Diego; The Art Institute of California–San Francisco; The Art Institute of California–Sunnyvale; The Art Institute of Charleston[1]; The Art Institute of Charlotte; The Art Institute of Colorado; The Art Institute of Dallas[3]; The Art Institute of Fort Lauderdale; The Art Institute of Fort Worth[3]; The Art Institute of Houston; The Art Institute of Houston–North[2]; The Art Institute of Indianapolis[4]; The Art Institute of Jacksonville[5]; The Art Institute of Las Vegas; The Art Institute of Michigan; The Art Institute of New York City; The Art Institute of Ohio–Cincinnati[6]; The Art Institute of Philadelphia; The Art Institute of Phoenix; The Art Institute of Pittsburgh; The Art Institute of Portland; The Art Institute of Raleigh–Durham; The Art Institute of Salt Lake City; The Art Institute of San Antonio[2];The Art Institute of Seattle; The Art Institute of Tampa[5]; The Art Institute of Tennessee–Nashville[1]; The Art Institute of Tucson; The Art Institute of Vancouver; The Art Institute of Virginia Beach[1,7]; The Art Institute of Washington[1,7]; The Art Institute of Washington–Northern Virginia[1,7]; The Art Institute of Wisconsin; The Art Institute of York–Pennsylvania; The Art Institutes International–Kansas City; The Art Institutes International Minnesota; The Illinois Institute of Art–Chicago; The Illinois Institute of Art–Schaumburg; The Illinois Institute of Art–Tinley Park; Miami International University of Art & Design; The New England Institute of Art.

[1]A branch of The Art Institute of Atlanta
[2]A branch of The Art Institute of Houston
[3]A campus of South University
[4]The Art Institute of Indianapolis is regulated by the Indiana Commission on Proprietary Education, 302 West Washington Street, Room E201, Indianapolis, Indiana 46204, AC-0080
[5]A branch of Miami International University of Art & Design
[6]The Art Institute of Ohio–Cincinnati, 8845 Governors Hill Drive, Suite 100, Cincinnati, Ohio 45249-3317, OH Reg. #04-01-1698B
[7]Certified by the State Council of Higher Education to operate in Virginia

THE ART INSTITUTE OF INDIANAPOLIS

INDIANAPOLIS, INDIANA

A focused education from The Art Institute of Indianapolis can help students turn their creative energy into a powerful tool that can make a difference in the world. Students are part of a collaborative and supportive community, where experienced instructors provide the guidance and skills needed to pursue a career in the creative economy.

The school's programs in the areas of design, media arts, fashion, and culinary give students the opportunity to learn by using professional-grade technology and build a portfolio of work to show potential employers after graduation.

The Art Institute of Indianapolis is accredited by the Accrediting Council for Independent Colleges and Schools as a branch of The Art Institute of Phoenix, 2233 West Dunlap Avenue, Phoenix, Arizona 85021-2859; phone: 602-331-7500.

This institution is regulated by the Indiana Commission on Proprietary Education, 302 West Washington Street, Room E201, Indianapolis, Indiana 46204; phone: 800-227-5695 (toll-free) or 317-232-1320. (Indiana advertising code: AC-0080.)

Location

Located in the northwest part of Indianapolis, at the Pyramids, the school is within minutes of a thriving metropolis. The Pyramids are situated on 45 acres, with a 25-acre lake. The Pyramids are adjacent to I-465 for convenient travel to all major thoroughfares.

Programs of Study and Degrees

No matter which course of study a student may choose, the professionals at The Art Institute of Indianapolis will guide, support, and help each student as their talents evolve on their journey of personal and professional transformation. Students studying design learn to fine-tune their visual thinking and problem-solving skills, as they create everything from logos to TV ads. Programs in the area of media arts focus on utilizing technology to deliver information and entertainment, while students studying fashion learn to design clothes for the runway or run a retail shop. Culinary programs focus on the fundamental techniques while exposing students to a full menu of international cuisines and management techniques.

Bachelor's degree programs are offered in culinary management, digital photography, fashion and retail management, fashion design, graphic design, interior design, media arts and animation, and Web design and interactive media.

Associate degree programs are offered in baking and pastry, culinary arts, digital photography, and graphic design.

Certificate programs are available in baking and pastry, culinary arts, and digital design.

Academic Programs

The Art Institute of Indianapolis operates on a year-round, four-quarter system.

Academic Facilities

The Art Institute of Indianapolis provides a learning environment with professional-grade technology applicable to each student's course of study. Students have the opportunity to build a portfolio of work that shows potential employers that they are trained to use the software, hardware, or equipment utilized within the industry. Depending upon the course of study, students are immersed in a creative environment—from classrooms to computer labs to studios—focused on relevant, hands-on education designed to prepare students for the real world.

Costs

Tuition cost varies by program. Prospective students should contact the school for current tuition costs. Other charges include a starting kit for all first-quarter students. Kits vary in price depending on the program of study.

Financial Aid

Financial aid is available for those who qualify. Students who require financial assistance should first complete and submit a Free Application for Federal Student Aid (FAFSA) and meet with a financial aid officer.

Faculty

Faculty members are experienced professionals who create a learning environment that is similar to the professional world students will face after graduation. Instructors are focused on helping students develop the skills they need to transform their creative potential into marketable skills.

Admission Requirements

Applicants must provide proof of high school graduation or achievement of a General Educational Development (GED) certificate as a prerequisite for admission. In lieu of documenting high school graduation or a GED certificate, applicants may provide proof of attaining an associate degree or higher from an accredited institution. An official transcript indicating date of high school graduation, GED certificate (including test scores), or date of college graduation (including degree granted) is required as proof.

All individuals seeking admission to The Art Institute of Indianapolis are interviewed in person or by phone by an assistant director of admissions, and each applicant must create an original essay of at least 150 words stating how an education at The Art Institute of Indianapolis would help the student to achieve career goals. There is a $50 application fee.

For the most recent information regarding admission requirements, please refer to the current academic catalog.

Application and Information

To obtain an application, make arrangements for an interview, or tour the school, prospective students should contact:

The Art Institute of Indianapolis
3500 Depauw Boulevard, Suite 1010
Indianapolis, Indiana 46268-6124

Phone: 317-613-4800
          866-441-9031 (toll-free)
Fax: 317-613-4808
Web site: http://www.artinstitutes.edu/indianapolis

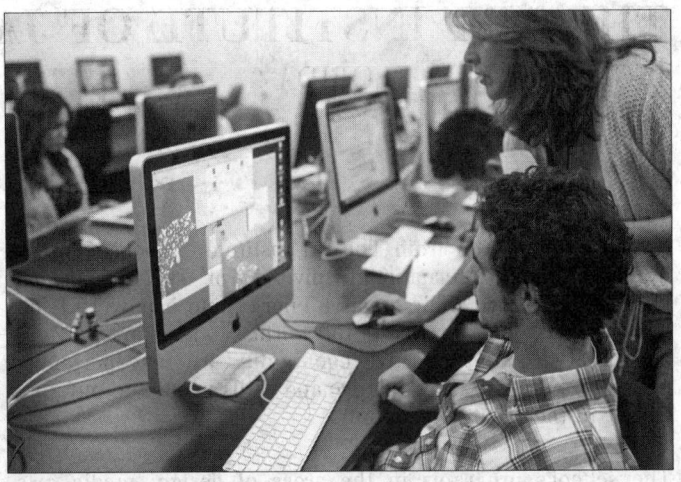

The Art Institute of Atlanta; The Art Institute of Atlanta–Decatur[1]; The Art Institute of Austin[2]; The Art Institute of California–Hollywood; The Art Institute of California–Inland Empire; The Art Institute of California–Los Angeles; The Art Institute of California–Orange County; The Art Institute of California–Sacramento; The Art Institute of California–San Diego; The Art Institute of California–San Francisco; The Art Institute of California–Sunnyvale; The Art Institute of Charleston[1]; The Art Institute of Charlotte; The Art Institute of Colorado; The Art Institute of Dallas[3]; The Art Institute of Fort Lauderdale; The Art Institute of Fort Worth[3]; The Art Institute of Houston; The Art Institute of Houston–North[2]; The Art Institute of Indianapolis[4]; The Art Institute of Jacksonville[5]; The Art Institute of Las Vegas; The Art Institute of Michigan; The Art Institute of New York City; The Art Institute of Ohio–Cincinnati[6]; The Art Institute of Philadelphia; The Art Institute of Phoenix; The Art Institute of Pittsburgh; The Art Institute of Portland; The Art Institute of Raleigh–Durham; The Art Institute of Salt Lake City; The Art Institute of San Antonio[2];The Art Institute of Seattle; The Art Institute of Tampa[5]; The Art Institute of Tennessee–Nashville[1]; The Art Institute of Tucson; The Art Institute of Vancouver; The Art Institute of Virginia Beach[1,7]; The Art Institute of Washington[1,7]; The Art Institute of Washington–Northern Virginia[1,7]; The Art Institute of Wisconsin; The Art Institute of York–Pennsylvania; The Art Institutes International–Kansas City; The Art Institutes International Minnesota; The Illinois Institute of Art–Chicago; The Illinois Institute of Art–Schaumburg; The Illinois Institute of Art–Tinley Park; Miami International University of Art & Design; The New England Institute of Art.

[1] A branch of The Art Institute of Atlanta
[2] A branch of The Art Institute of Houston
[3] A campus of South University
[4] The Art Institute of Indianapolis is regulated by the Indiana Commission on Proprietary Education, 302 West Washington Street, Room E201, Indianapolis, Indiana 46204, AC-0080
[5] A branch of Miami International University of Art & Design
[6] The Art Institute of Ohio–Cincinnati, 8845 Governors Hill Drive, Suite 100, Cincinnati, Ohio 45249-3517, OH Reg. #04-01-1698B
[7] Certified by the State Council of Higher Education to operate in Virginia

THE ART INSTITUTE OF JACKSONVILLE

JACKSONVILLE, FLORIDA

A focused education from The Art Institute of Jacksonville, a branch of Miami International University of Art & Design, can help students turn their creative energy into a powerful tool that can make a difference in the world. Students are part of a collaborative and supportive community, where experienced instructors provide the guidance and skills needed to pursue a career in the creative economy.

The school's programs in the areas of design, media arts, fashion, and culinary give students the opportunity to learn by using professional-grade technology and build a portfolio of work to show potential employers after graduation.

The Art Institute of Jacksonville is a branch of Miami International University of Art & Design. Miami International University of Art & Design and its branch campuses are accredited by the Commission on Colleges of the Southern Association of Colleges and Schools to award diplomas, associate, baccalaureate, and master's degrees. Contact the Commission on Colleges at 1866 Southern Lane, Decatur, Georgia 30033-4097; or call 404-679-4500 for questions about the accreditation of Miami International University of Art & Design.

The Art Institute of Jacksonville is licensed by the Commission for Independent Education, Florida Department of Education. Additional information regarding this institution may be obtained by contacting the Commission at 325 West Gaines St., Suite 1414, Tallahassee, Florida 32399-0400; phone: 888-224-6684 (toll-free).

Location

The Art Institute of Jacksonville is located in Jacksonville, Florida's largest city. With mild winters and warm summers, Jacksonville is a popular tourist destination. The Jacksonville beaches, Florida Theater, and professional sports teams are exciting entertainment options within the region.

Programs of Study and Degrees

No matter which course of study a student may choose, the professionals at The Art Institute of Jacksonville will guide, support, and help each student as their talents evolve on their journey of personal and professional transformation. Students studying design learn to fine-tune their visual thinking and problem-solving skills, as they create everything from logos to TV ads. Programs in the area of media arts focus on utilizing technology to deliver information and entertainment, while students studying fashion learn to design clothes for the runway or run a retail shop. Culinary programs focus on the fundamental techniques while exposing students to a full menu of international cuisines and management techniques.

Bachelor's degrees are offered in culinary management, digital filmmaking and video production, digital photography, fashion and retail management, graphic design, interior design, media arts and animation, and Web design and interactive media.

Associate degrees are offered in culinary arts, graphic design, and Web design and interactive media design.

A diploma program is offered in culinary arts: skills.

Academic Programs

The academic year is divided into four quarters, beginning in January, April, July, and October. Each program is offered on a year-round basis, allowing students to continue to work uninterrupted toward their degrees.

Academic Facilities

The Art Institute of Jacksonville provides a learning environment with professional-grade technology applicable to each student's course of study. Students have the opportunity to build a portfolio of work that shows potential employers that they are trained to use the software, hardware, or equipment utilized within the industry. Depending upon the course of study, students are immersed in a creative environment—from classrooms to computer labs to studios—focused on relevant, hands-on education designed to prepare students for the real world.

Costs

Tuition cost varies by program. Prospective students should contact the school for current tuition costs. Other charges include a starting kit for all first-quarter students. Kits vary in price depending on the program of study.

Financial Aid

Financial aid is available for those who qualify. Students who require financial assistance should first complete and submit a Free Application for Federal Student Aid (FAFSA) and meet with a financial aid officer.

Faculty

Faculty members are experienced professionals who create a learning environment that is similar to the professional world students will face after graduation. Instructors are focused on helping students develop the skills they need to transform their creative potential into marketable skills.

Student Government

The Student Federation is responsible for student government and acts as a liaison between the student body and faculty and staff members.

Admission Requirements

Applicants must provide proof of high school graduation or achievement of a General Educational Development (GED) certificate as a prerequisite for admission. In lieu of documenting high school graduation or a GED certificate, applicants may provide proof of attaining an associate degree or higher from an accredited institution. An official transcript indicating date of high school graduation, GED certificate (including test scores), or date of college graduation (including degree granted) is required as proof.

All individuals seeking admission to The Art Institute of Jacksonville are interviewed in person or by phone by an assistant director of admissions, and each applicant must submit an original essay of at least 150 words stating how an education at the school would help the student to achieve career goals. There is a $50 application fee.

For the most recent information regarding admission requirements, please refer to the current academic catalog.

Application and Information

To obtain an application, make arrangements for an interview, or tour the school, prospective students should contact:

The Art Institute of Jacksonville
8775 Baypine Road
Jacksonville, Florida 32256-8528
Phone: 904-486-3000
      800-924-1589 (toll-free)
Fax: 904-732-9423
Web site: http://www.artinstitutes.edu/jacksonville

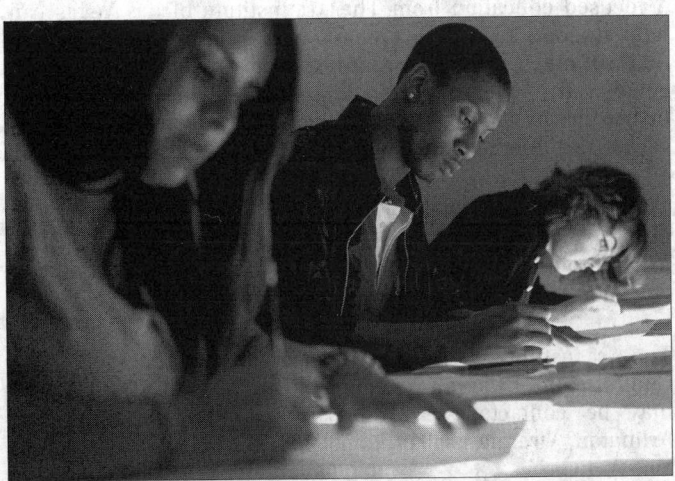

The Art Institute of Atlanta; The Art Institute of Atlanta–Decatur[1]; The Art Institute of Austin[2]; The Art Institute of California–Hollywood; The Art Institute of California–Inland Empire; The Art Institute of California–Los Angeles; The Art Institute of California–Orange County; The Art Institute of California–Sacramento; The Art Institute of California–San Diego; The Art Institute of California–San Francisco; The Art Institute of California–Sunnyvale; The Art Institute of Charleston[1]; The Art Institute of Charlotte; The Art Institute of Colorado; The Art Institute of Dallas[3]; The Art Institute of Fort Lauderdale; The Art Institute of Fort Worth[3]; The Art Institute of Houston; The Art Institute of Houston–North[2]; The Art Institute of Indianapolis[4]; The Art Institute of Jacksonville[5]; The Art Institute of Las Vegas; The Art Institute of Michigan; The Art Institute of New York City; The Art Institute of Ohio–Cincinnati[6]; The Art Institute of Philadelphia; The Art Institute of Phoenix; The Art Institute of Pittsburgh; The Art Institute of Portland; The Art Institute of Raleigh–Durham; The Art Institute of Salt Lake City; The Art Institute of San Antonio[2];The Art Institute of Seattle; The Art Institute of Tampa[5]; The Art Institute of Tennessee–Nashville[1]; The Art Institute of Tucson; The Art Institute of Vancouver; The Art Institute of Virginia Beach[1,7]; The Art Institute of Washington[1,7]; The Art Institute of Washington–Northern Virginia[1,7]; The Art Institute of Wisconsin; The Art Institute of York–Pennsylvania; The Art Institutes International–Kansas City; The Art Institutes International Minnesota; The Illinois Institute of Art–Chicago; The Illinois Institute of Art–Schaumburg; The Illinois Institute of Art–Tinley Park; Miami International University of Art & Design; The New England Institute of Art.

[1]A branch of The Art Institute of Atlanta
[2]A branch of The Art Institute of Houston
[3]A campus of South University
[4]The Art Institute of Indianapolis is regulated by the Indiana Commission on Proprietary Education, 302 West Washington Street, Room E201, Indianapolis, Indiana 46204, AC-0080
[5]A branch of Miami International University of Art & Design
[6]The Art Institute of Ohio–Cincinnati, 8845 Governors Hill Drive, Suite 100, Cincinnati, Ohio 45249-3317, OH Reg. #04-01-1698B
[7]Certified by the State Council of Higher Education to operate in Virginia

THE ART INSTITUTE OF LAS VEGAS

HENDERSON, NEVADA

A focused education from The Art Institute of Las Vegas can help students turn their creative energy into a powerful tool that can make a difference in the world. Students are part of a collaborative and supportive community, where experienced instructors provide the guidance and skills needed to pursue a career in the creative economy.

The school's programs in the areas of design, media arts, fashion, and culinary give students the opportunity to learn by using professional-grade technology and build a portfolio of work to show potential employers after graduation.

The Art Institute of Las Vegas is accredited by the Accrediting Commission of Career Schools and Colleges (ACCSC). ACCSC may be contacted at 2101 Wilson Boulevard, Suite 302, Arlington, Virginia 22201; phone: 703-247-4212.

The Art Institute of Las Vegas is licensed to operate by the Commission on Postsecondary Education, 3663 East Sunset Road, Suite 202, Las Vegas, Nevada 89120; phone: 702-486-7330.

The Bachelor of Arts in interior design degree program is accredited by the National Kitchen & Bath Association (NKBA). NKBA can be contacted at 687 Willow Grove Street, Hackettstown, New Jersey 07840; phone: 800-THE-NKBA, www.nkba.org.

The interior design program leading to the Bachelor of Arts degree is accredited by the Council for Interior Design Accreditation, 206 Grandville Avenue, Suite 350, Grand Rapids, Michigan 49503; www.accredit-id.org.

Location

Las Vegas provides sunny days, museums, libraries, parks, gift shops, and historical sites. Just outside the city are some of the world's most beautiful natural wonders, including the Grand Canyon, Red Rock Canyon, Death Valley, Hoover Dam, and Valley of Fire State Park. Nearly 1.5 million residents live in the Las Vegas metro area.

Programs of Study and Degrees

No matter which course of study a student may choose, the professionals at The Art Institute of Las Vegas will guide, support, and help each student as their talents evolve on their journey of personal and professional transformation. Students studying design learn to fine-tune their visual thinking and problem-solving skills, as they create everything from logos to TV ads. Programs in the area of media arts focus on utilizing technology to deliver information and entertainment, while students studying fashion learn to design clothes for the runway or run a retail shop. Culinary programs focus on the fundamental techniques while exposing students to a full menu of international cuisines and management techniques.

Bachelor's degree programs are offered in audio production, culinary management, digital filmmaking and video production, digital photography, fashion and retail management, food and beverage management, game art and design, graphic design, interior design, media arts and animation, visual effects and motion graphics, and Web design and interactive media.

Associate degree programs are available in baking and pastry, culinary arts, and drafting technology and design.

Academic Programs

To receive an associate degree, a student must complete a minimum of 112 quarter credits, with 28 quarter credits in general education courses and 84 quarter credits in a specialty area. To receive a bachelor's degree, a student must complete a minimum of 192 quarter credits, with 48 quarter credits in general education courses and 114 quarter credits in a specialty area. For both degrees, the student must achieve a cumulative GPA of 2.0 or higher, meet portfolio or other requirements, and satisfy all financial obligations to the school. A limited number of courses are available online for an additional fee per course.

Academic Facilities

The Art Institute of Las Vegas provides a learning environment with professional-grade technology applicable to each student's course of study. Students have the opportunity to build a portfolio of work that shows potential employers that they are trained to use the software, hardware, or equipment utilized within the industry. Depending upon the course of study, students are immersed in a creative environment—from classrooms to computer labs to studios—focused on relevant, hands-on education designed to prepare students for the real world.

Costs

Tuition cost varies by program. Prospective students should contact the school for current tuition costs. Other charges include a starting kit for all first-quarter students. Kits vary in price depending on the program of study.

Financial Aid

Financial aid is available for those who qualify. Students who require financial assistance should first complete and submit a Free Application for Federal Student Aid (FAFSA) and meet with a financial aid officer.

Faculty

Faculty members are experienced professionals who create a learning environment that is similar to the professional world

students will face after graduation. Instructors are focused on helping students develop the skills they need to transform their creative potential into marketable skills.

Admission Requirements

As a prerequisite for admission, a prospective student must be a high school graduate, hold a General Educational Development (GED) certificate, or have earned a bachelor's degree or higher from an accredited institution of postsecondary education. Each prospective student is interviewed, either in person or by telephone, by an assistant director of admissions to determine whether the student and school are a good fit. Portfolios may qualify the student for advanced placement, and applications may be submitted any time prior to the start of the next quarter. There is a $50 application fee.

For the most recent information regarding admission requirements, please refer to the current academic catalog.

Application and Information

To obtain an application, make arrangements for an interview, or tour the school, prospective students should contact:

The Art Institute of Las Vegas
2350 Corporate Circle
Henderson, Nevada 89074-7737

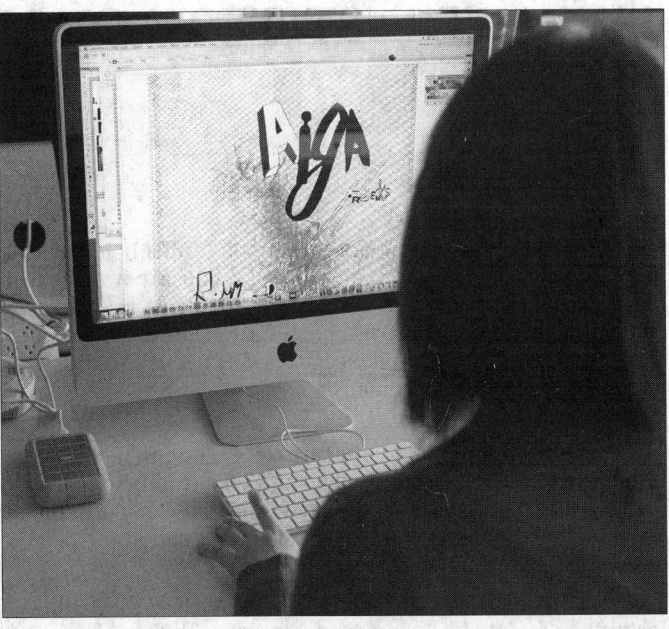

Phone: 702-369-9944
       800-833-2678 (toll-free)
Fax: 702-992-8458
Web site: http://www.artinstitutes.edu/lasvegas

The Art Institute of Atlanta; The Art Institute of Atlanta–Decatur[1]; The Art Institute of Austin[2]; The Art Institute of California–Hollywood; The Art Institute of California–Inland Empire; The Art Institute of California–Los Angeles; The Art Institute of California–Orange County; The Art Institute of California–Sacramento; The Art Institute of California–San Diego; The Art Institute of California–San Francisco; The Art Institute of California–Sunnyvale; The Art Institute of Charleston[1]; The Art Institute of Charlotte; The Art Institute of Colorado; The Art Institute of Dallas[3]; The Art Institute of Fort Lauderdale; The Art Institute of Fort Worth[3]; The Art Institute of Houston; The Art Institute of Houston–North[2]; The Art Institute of Indianapolis[4]; The Art Institute of Jacksonville[5]; The Art Institute of Las Vegas; The Art Institute of Michigan; The Art Institute of New York City; The Art Institute of Ohio–Cincinnati[6]; The Art Institute of Philadelphia; The Art Institute of Phoenix; The Art Institute of Pittsburgh; The Art Institute of Portland; The Art Institute of Raleigh–Durham; The Art Institute of Salt Lake City; The Art Institute of San Antonio[2];The Art Institute of Seattle; The Art Institute of Tampa[5]; The Art Institute of Tennessee–Nashville[1]; The Art Institute of Tucson; The Art Institute of Vancouver; The Art Institute of Virginia Beach[1,7]; The Art Institute of Washington[1,7]; The Art Institute of Washington–Northern Virginia[1,7]; The Art Institute of Wisconsin; The Art Institute of York–Pennsylvania; The Art Institutes International–Kansas City; The Art Institutes International Minnesota; The Illinois Institute of Art–Chicago; The Illinois Institute of Art–Schaumburg; The Illinois Institute of Art–Tinley Park; Miami International University of Art & Design; The New England Institute of Art.

[1]A branch of The Art Institute of Atlanta
[2]A branch of The Art Institute of Houston
[3]A campus of South University
[4]The Art Institute of Indianapolis is regulated by the Indiana Commission on Proprietary Education, 302 West Washington Street, Room E201, Indianapolis, Indiana 46204, AC-0080
[5]A branch of Miami International University of Art & Design
[6]The Art Institute of Ohio–Cincinnati, 8845 Governors Hill Drive, Suite 100, Cincinnati, Ohio 45249-3317, OH Reg. #04-01-1698B
[7]Certified by the State Council of Higher Education to operate in Virginia

THE ART INSTITUTE OF MICHIGAN

NOVI, MICHIGAN

CREATE TOMORROW

A focused education from The Art Institute of Michigan can help students turn their creative energy into a powerful tool that can make a difference in the world. Students are part of a collaborative and supportive community, where experienced instructors provide the guidance and skills needed to pursue a career in the creative economy.

The school's programs in the areas of design, media arts, fashion, and culinary give students the opportunity to learn by using professional-grade technology and build a portfolio of work to show potential employers after graduation.

The Art Institute of Michigan, as a branch of the Illinois Institute of Art, is accredited by the Higher Learning Commission and is a member of the North Central Association (NCA), 230 South LaSalle Street, Suite 7-500, Chicago, Illinois 60604-1413; http://www.ncahlc.org.

The Art Institute of Michigan is licensed under the laws of the Michigan Department of Labor and Economic Growth.

Location

Novi, a town of over 52,000, is a suburb of Detroit. One of the fastest-growing cities in Michigan, Novi is home to the Motorsports Hall of Fame of America and Twelve Oaks Mall and is just a short drive from the cultural, entertainment, and sports facilities of Detroit.

Programs of Study and Degrees

No matter which course of study a student may choose, the professionals at The Art Institute of Michigan will guide, support, and help each student as their talents evolve on their journey of personal and professional transformation. Students studying design learn to fine-tune their visual thinking and problem-solving skills, as they create everything from logos to TV ads. Programs in the area of media arts focus on utilizing technology to deliver information and entertainment, while students studying fashion learn to design clothes for the runway or run a retail shop. Culinary programs focus on the fundamental techniques while exposing students to a full menu of international cuisines and management techniques.

Bachelor's degree programs are offered in culinary management, digital photography, fashion marketing and management, graphic design, interior design, media arts and animation, and Web design and interactive media.

Associate degrees are offered in culinary arts, fashion merchandising, graphic design, interior design, and Web design and interactive media.

A certificate program is offered in professional baking and pastry.

Academic Programs

The Art Institute of Michigan operates on a year-round, four-quarter system.

Academic Facilities

The Art Institute of Michigan provides a learning environment with professional-grade technology applicable to each student's course of study. Students have the opportunity to build a portfolio of work that shows potential employers that they are trained to use the software, hardware, or equipment utilized within the industry. Depending upon the course of study, students are immersed in a creative environment—from classrooms to computer labs to studios—focused on relevant, hands-on education designed to prepare students for the real world.

Costs

Tuition cost varies by program. Prospective students should contact the school for current tuition costs. Other charges include a starting kit for all first-quarter students. Kits vary in price depending on the program of study.

Financial Aid

Financial aid is available for those who qualify. Students who require financial assistance should first complete and submit a Free Application for Federal Student Aid (FAFSA) and meet with a financial aid officer.

Faculty

Faculty members are experienced professionals who create a learning environment that is similar to the professional world students will face after graduation. Instructors are focused on helping students develop the skills they need to transform their creative potential into marketable skills.

Admission Requirements

Applicants must provide proof of high school graduation or achievement of a General Educational Development (GED) certificate as a prerequisite for admission. In lieu of documenting high school graduation or a GED certificate, applicants may provide proof of attaining an associate degree or higher from an accredited institution. An official transcript indicating date of high school graduation, GED certificate (including test scores), or date of college graduation (including degree granted) is required as proof.

All individuals seeking admission to The Art Institute of Michigan are interviewed in person or by phone by an assistant director of admissions, and each applicant must submit an original essay of at least 150 words stating how an education at The Art Institute of Michigan would help the student to achieve career goals.

There is a $50 application fee.

For the most recent information regarding admission requirements, please refer to the current academic catalog.

Application and Information

To obtain an application, make arrangements for an interview, or tour the school, students should contact:

The Art Institute of Michigan
28125 Cabot Drive, Suite 120
Novi, Michigan 48377
Phone: 248-675-3800
       800-479-0087 (toll-free)

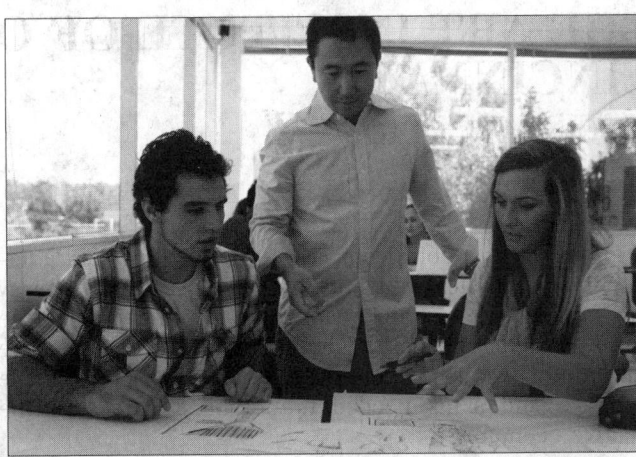

Fax: 248-675-3830
Web site: http://www.artinstitutes.edu/detroit

THE ART INSTITUTE OF OHIO–CINCINNATI

CINCINNATI, OHIO

The Art Institute of Ohio–Cincinnati

CREATE TOMORROW

A focused education from The Art Institute of Ohio–Cincinnati can help students turn their creative energy into a powerful tool that can make a difference in the world. Students are part of a collaborative and supportive community, where experienced instructors provide the guidance and skills needed to pursue a career in the creative economy.

The school's programs in the areas of design, media arts, fashion, and culinary give students the opportunity to learn by using professional-grade technology and build a portfolio of work to show potential employers after graduation.

The Art Institute of Ohio–Cincinnati, as a branch of the Illinois Institute of Art, is accredited by the Higher Learning Commission and is a member of the North Central Association (NCA), 230 South LaSalle Street, Suite 7-500, Chicago, Illinois 60604-1413; phone: 800-621-7440 (toll-free); http://www.ncahlc.org.

The Art Institute of Ohio–Cincinnati holds a provisional certificate of authorization for its academic programs by the Ohio Board of Regents, 30 East Broad Street, Columbus, Ohio 43215; phone: 614-466-6000. The provisional authorization expires on December 31, 2012.

The Art Institute of Ohio–Cincinnati is licensed by the Ohio State Board of Career Colleges and Schools, 35 East Gay Street, Columbus, Ohio 43266-0591; phone: 614-466-2752. OH Reg. # 04-01-1698B.

The Art Institute of Ohio–Cincinnati is regulated by the Indiana Commission on Proprietary Education, 302 West Washington Street, Room E201, Indianapolis, Indiana 46204-2767; phone: 317-232-1320 (in-state) or 800-227-5695 (toll-free). AC0165.

The Associate of Applied Science in culinary arts degree program is accredited by the Accrediting Commission of the American Culinary Federation Education Foundation.

Location

Cincinnati is home to major-league sporting events, concerts, a professional symphony, theater, Kings Island, award-winning restaurants, and downtown entertainment districts that offer exciting nightlife. The city is known for its great beauty, with steep hills, wooded suburbs, a picturesque downtown riverfront, and four distinct seasons.

Programs of Study and Degrees

No matter which course of study a student may choose, the professionals at The Art Institute of Ohio–Cincinnati will guide, support, and help each student as their talents evolve on their journey of personal and professional transformation. Students studying design learn to fine-tune their visual thinking and problem-solving skills, as they create everything from logos to TV ads. Programs in the area of media arts focus on utilizing technology to deliver information and entertainment, while students studying fashion learn to design clothes for the runway or run a retail shop. Culinary programs focus on the fundamental techniques while exposing students to a full menu of international cuisines and management techniques.

Bachelor's degree programs are available in advertising, culinary management, digital filmmaking and video production, fashion marketing and management, interior design, media arts and animation, visual communications, and Web design and interactive media.

Associate degree programs include culinary arts, fashion merchandising, graphic design, interior design, video production, and Web design and interactive media.

A diploma program is offered in professional baking and pastry.

Academic Programs

The Art Institute of Ohio–Cincinnati operates on a year-round, four-quarter system.

Academic Facilities

The Art Institute of Ohio–Cincinnati provides a learning environment with professional-grade technology applicable to each student's course of study. Students have the opportunity to build a portfolio of work that shows potential employers that they are trained to use the software, hardware, or equipment utilized within the industry. Depending upon the course of study, students are immersed in a creative environment—from classrooms to computer labs to studios—focused on relevant, hands-on education designed to prepare students for the real world.

Costs

Tuition costs vary by program. Prospective students should contact the school for current tuition costs. Other charges include a starting kit for all first-quarter students. Kits vary in price, depending on the program of study.

Financial Aid

Financial aid is available for those who qualify.

Faculty

Faculty members are experienced professionals who create a learning environment that is similar to the professional world students will face after graduation. Instructors are focused on helping students develop the skills they need to transform their creative potential into marketable skills.

Admission Requirements

Applicants to The Art Institute of Ohio–Cincinnati must demonstrate proof of high school graduation or its equivalent. An official copy of the high school transcript or General Educational Development (GED) certificate is required. Candidates are interviewed and must write an essay on how an education at The Art Institute of Ohio–Cincinnati can help them reach their career goals.

Each applicant's academic transcript and completed essay are evaluated by the Admissions Acceptance Committee. A separate application and enrollment form must be completed and signed by the applicant and then submitted to The Art Institute of Ohio–Cincinnati. There is an application fee of $50.

For the most recent information regarding admission requirements, please refer to the current academic catalog.

Application and Information

To obtain an application or make arrangements for an interview or tour of the school, prospective students should contact:

The Art Institute of Ohio–Cincinnati
8845 Governors Hill Drive
Cincinnati, Ohio 45249-3317
Phone: 513-833-2400
       866-613-5184 (toll-free)
Fax: 877-477-8486 (toll-free)
Web site: http://www.artinstitutes.edu/cincinnati

The Art Institute of Atlanta; The Art Institute of Atlanta–Decatur[1]; The Art Institute of Austin[2]; The Art Institute of California–Hollywood; The Art Institute of California–Inland Empire; The Art Institute of California–Los Angeles; The Art Institute of California–Orange County; The Art Institute of California–Sacramento; The Art Institute of California–San Diego; The Art Institute of California–San Francisco; The Art Institute of California–Sunnyvale; The Art Institute of Charleston[1]; The Art Institute of Charlotte; The Art Institute of Colorado; The Art Institute of Dallas[3]; The Art Institute of Fort Lauderdale; The Art Institute of Fort Worth[5]; The Art Institute of Houston; The Art Institute of Houston–North[2]; The Art Institute of Indianapolis[4]; The Art Institute of Jacksonville[5]; The Art Institute of Las Vegas; The Art Institute of Michigan; The Art Institute of New York City; The Art Institute of Ohio–Cincinnati[6]; The Art Institute of Philadelphia; The Art Institute of Phoenix; The Art Institute of Pittsburgh; The Art Institute of Portland; The Art Institute of Raleigh–Durham; The Art Institute of Salt Lake City; The Art Institute of San Antonio[2];The Art Institute of Seattle; The Art Institute of Tampa[5]; The Art Institute of Tennessee–Nashville[1]; The Art Institute of Tucson; The Art Institute of Vancouver; The Art Institute of Virginia Beach[1,7]; The Art Institute of Washington[1,7]; The Art Institute of Washington–Northern Virginia[1,7]; The Art Institute of Wisconsin; The Art Institute of York–Pennsylvania; The Art Institutes International–Kansas City; The Art Institutes International Minnesota; The Illinois Institute of Art–Chicago; The Illinois Institute of Art–Schaumburg; The Illinois Institute of Art–Tinley Park; Miami International University of Art & Design; The New England Institute of Art.
[1]A branch of The Art Institute of Atlanta
[2]A branch of The Art Institute of Houston
[3]A campus of South University
[4]The Art Institute of Indianapolis is regulated by the Indiana Commission on Proprietary Education, 302 West Washington Street, Room E201, Indianapolis, Indiana 46204, AC-0080
[5]A branch of Miami International University of Art & Design
[6]The Art Institute of Ohio–Cincinnati, 8845 Governors Hill Drive, Suite 100, Cincinnati, Ohio 45249-3317, OH Reg. #04-01-1698B
[7]Certified by the State Council of Higher Education to operate in Virginia

THE ART INSTITUTE OF PHILADELPHIA
PHILADELPHIA, PENNSYLVANIA

A focused education from The Art Institute of Philadelphia can help students turn their creative energy into a powerful tool that can make a difference in the world. Students are part of a collaborative and supportive community, where experienced instructors provide the guidance and skills needed to pursue a career in the creative economy.

The school's programs in the areas of design, media arts, fashion, and culinary give students the opportunity to learn by using professional-grade technology and build a portfolio of work to show potential employers after graduation.

The Art Institute of Philadelphia is accredited by the Accrediting Council for Independent Colleges and Schools (ACICS) to award diplomas, associate degrees, and bachelor's degrees. ACICS is listed as a nationally recognized accrediting agency by the United States Department of Education and is recognized by the Council for Higher Education Accreditation. ACICS can be contacted at 750 First Street NE, Suite 980, Washington, D.C. 20002; phone: 202-336-6780.

The Art Institute of Philadelphia is authorized by the Pennsylvania Department of Education to confer Bachelor of Science degrees, Associate of Science degrees, and diplomas. The Department of Education can be contacted at Commonwealth of Pennsylvania, Department of Education Office of Postsecondary and Higher Education, 333 Market Street, Harrisburg, Pennsylvania 17126; phone: 717-783-6788.

The Associate of Science in culinary arts degree program is accredited by the Accrediting Commission of the American Culinary Federation Education Foundation.

The Bachelor of Science in interior design degree program is accredited by the National Kitchen and Bath Association (NKBA). NKBA can be contacted at 687 Willow Grove Street, Hackettstown, New Jersey 07840;,phone: 800-THE-NKBA, www.nkba.org.

The interior design program leading to the Bachelor of Science degree is accredited by the Council for Interior Design Accreditation, 206 Grandville Avenue, Suite, 350, Grand Rapids, Michigan 49503; www.accredit-id.org.

Location

Philadelphia is the birthplace of American democracy. The City of Brotherly Love surrounds the largest municipal landscaped park in the world, with tree-lined streets and an elegant blend of contemporary and historic architecture. Philadelphia has a renowned symphony orchestra, theater, film, jazz, and opera. With thirty-two major museums—including the expansive collections at the Museum of Art—the city is also home to fine shopping at locations like the European-style Bourse, with its fifty international boutiques and restaurants, and to sports teams, such as baseball's Phillies, the NFL's Eagles, the NBA's 76ers, and the NHL's Flyers.

Programs of Study and Degrees

No matter which course of study a student may choose, the professionals at The Art Institute of Philadelphia will guide, support, and help each student as their talents evolve on their journey of personal and professional transformation. Students studying design learn to fine-tune their visual thinking and problem-solving skills, as they create everything from logos to TV ads. Programs in the area of media arts focus on utilizing technology to deliver information and entertainment, while students studying fashion learn to design clothes for the runway or run a retail shop. Culinary programs focus on the fundamental techniques while exposing students to a full menu of international cuisines and management techniques.

The Art Institute of Philadelphia offers bachelor's degree programs in advertising, audio production, culinary management, digital filmmaking and video production, fashion design, fashion marketing, graphic design, industrial design technology, interior design, media arts and animation, photography, visual effects and motion graphics, and Web design and interactive media.

Associate degree programs are offered in culinary arts, digital filmmaking and video production, fashion design, fashion marketing, graphic design, interior design, photography, visual merchandising, and Web design and interactive media.

Diploma programs are offered in baking and pastry and culinary arts.

The baking and pastry program and the Associate of Science in culinary arts program are available in an evening and weekend option format.

Academic Programs

School quarters are eleven weeks long, and academic programs are between six and twelve quarters in length. Programs are offered on a year-round basis, allowing for strong continuity and the ability to work uninterrupted toward a degree.

The Art Institute of Philadelphia arranges student trips to local cultural and commercial sites. These visits can be an integral part of each student's learning experience. In addition to local student trips to support the curriculum, out-of-town seminars and visits are planned within individual programs.

Academic Facilities

The Art Institute of Philadelphia provides a learning environment with professional-grade technology applicable to each student's course of study. Students have the opportunity to build a portfolio of work that shows potential employers that they are trained to use the software, hardware, or equipment utilized within the industry. Depending upon the course of study, students are immersed in a creative environment—from classrooms to computer labs to studios—focused on relevant, hands-on education designed to prepare students for the real world.

Costs

Tuition cost varies by program. Prospective students should contact the school for current tuition costs. Other charges include a starting kit for all first-quarter students. Kits vary in price depending on the program of study.

Financial Aid

Financial aid is available for those who qualify. Students who require financial assistance should first complete and submit a Free Application for Federal Student Aid (FAFSA) and meet with a financial aid officer.

Faculty

Faculty members are experienced professionals who create a learning environment that is similar to the professional world students will face after graduation. Instructors are focused on helping students develop the skills they need to transform their creative potential into marketable skills.

Admission Requirements

High school graduation or a General Educational Development (GED) certificate is a prerequisite for admission. All applicants are evaluated on the basis of previous education and their background/interest in the program of interest. Portfolios are welcomed but not required.

The Art Institute of Philadelphia operates on a rolling admissions basis. High school and/or college transcripts must be submitted to The Art Institute of Philadelphia at least one month prior to starting classes. There is a $50 application fee.

For the most recent information regarding admission requirements, please refer to the current academic catalog.

Application and Information

To obtain an application, make arrangements for an interview, or tour the school, prospective students should contact:

The Art Institute of Philadelphia
1622 Chestnut Street
Philadelphia, Pennsylvania 19103-5119
Phone: 215-567-7080
   800-275-2474 (toll-free)
Fax: 215-405-6399
Web site: http://www.artinstitutes.edu/philadelphia

The Art Institute of Atlanta; The Art Institute of Atlanta–Decatur[1]; The Art Institute of Austin[2]; The Art Institute of California–Hollywood; The Art Institute of California–Inland Empire; The Art Institute of California–Los Angeles; The Art Institute of California–Orange County; The Art Institute of California–Sacramento; The Art Institute of California–San Diego; The Art Institute of California–San Francisco; The Art Institute of California–Sunnyvale; The Art Institute of Charleston[1]; The Art Institute of Charlotte; The Art Institute of Colorado; The Art Institute of Dallas[5]; The Art Institute of Fort Lauderdale; The Art Institute of Fort Worth[5]; The Art Institute of Houston; The Art Institute of Houston–North[2]; The Art Institute of Indianapolis[4]; The Art Institute of Jacksonville[5]; The Art Institute of Las Vegas; The Art Institute of Michigan; The Art Institute of New York City; The Art Institute of Ohio–Cincinnati[6]; The Art Institute of Philadelphia; The Art Institute of Phoenix; The Art Institute of Pittsburgh; The Art Institute of Portland; The Art Institute of Raleigh–Durham; The Art Institute of Salt Lake City; The Art Institute of San Antonio[2];The Art Institute of Seattle; The Art Institute of Tampa[5]; The Art Institute of Tennessee–Nashville[1]; The Art Institute of Tucson; The Art Institute of Vancouver; The Art Institute of Virginia Beach[1,7]; The Art Institute of Washington[1,7]; The Art Institute of Washington–Northern Virginia[1,7]; The Art Institute of Wisconsin; The Art Institute of York–Pennsylvania; The Art Institutes International–Kansas City; The Art Institutes International Minnesota; The Illinois Institute of Art–Chicago; The Illinois Institute of Art–Schaumburg; The Illinois Institute of Art–Tinley Park; Miami International University of Art & Design; The New England Institute of Art.
[1]A branch of The Art Institute of Atlanta
[2]A branch of The Art Institute of Houston
[3]A campus of South University
[4]The Art Institute of Indianapolis is regulated by the Indiana Commission on Proprietary Education, 302 West Washington Street, Room E201, Indianapolis, Indiana 46204, AC-0080
[5]A branch of Miami International University of Art & Design
[6]The Art Institute of Ohio–Cincinnati, 8845 Governors Hill Drive, Suite 100, Cincinnati, Ohio 45249-3317, OH Reg. #04-01-1698B
[7]Certified by the State Council of Higher Education to operate in Virginia

THE ART INSTITUTE OF PHOENIX

PHOENIX, ARIZONA

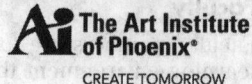

A focused education from The Art Institute of Phoenix can help students turn their creative energy into a powerful tool that can make a difference in the world. Students are part of a collaborative and supportive community, where experienced instructors provide the guidance and skills needed to pursue a career in the creative economy.

The school's programs in the areas of design, media arts, fashion, and culinary give students the opportunity to learn by using professional-grade technology and build a portfolio of work to show potential employers after graduation.

The Art Institute of Phoenix is accredited by the Accrediting Council for Independent Colleges and Schools (ACICS) to award diplomas, associate degrees, and bachelor's degrees. ACICS is listed as a nationally recognized accrediting agency by the United States Department of Education and is recognized by the Council for Higher Education Accreditation. ACICS can be contacted at 750 First Street NE, Suite 980, Washington, D.C. 20002; phone: 202-336-6780.

The Art Institute of Phoenix is authorized by the Arizona State Board for Private Postsecondary Education, 1400 West Washington Street, Room 2560, Phoenix, Arizona 85007; phone: 602-542-5709; http://azppse.state.az.us.

The Associate of Applied Science in culinary arts, the Associate of Applied Science in baking and pastry, and the Bachelor of Arts in culinary management degree programs are accredited by the Accrediting Commission of the American Culinary Federation Education Foundation.

The interior design program leading to the Bachelor of Arts degree is accredited by the Council for Interior Design Accreditation, 206 Grandville Avenue, Suite 350, Grand Rapids, Michigan 49503; http://www.accredit-id.org.

Location

Phoenix is one of the fastest-growing metropolitan areas in the country. Located in the heart of the beautiful Sonoran Desert, Phoenix is the gateway to cool pine forests, the red rock towers of Sedona, and the Grand Canyon. The city offers sun-filled days and a nightlife that ranges from top comedy and music clubs to the Phoenix Art Museum and Phoenix Symphony Orchestra. Professional sports teams include the Diamondbacks, Suns, Cardinals, and Coyotes.

Programs of Study and Degrees

No matter which course of study a student may choose, the professionals at The Art Institute of Phoenix will guide, support, and help each student as their talents evolve on their journey of personal and professional transformation. Students studying design learn to fine-tune their visual thinking and problem-solving skills, as they create everything from logos to TV ads. Programs in the area of media arts focus on utilizing technology to deliver information and entertainment, while students studying fashion learn to design clothes for the runway or run a retail shop. Culinary programs focus on the fundamental techniques while exposing students to a full menu of international cuisines and management techniques.

Bachelor's degree programs are offered in advertising, culinary management, digital filmmaking and video production, digital photography, fashion marketing, game art and design, graphic design, interior design, media arts and animation, visual and game programming, visual effects and motion graphics, and Web design and interactive media.

Associate of Applied Science degree programs are offered in baking and pastry arts, culinary arts, and graphic design.

Diploma programs are offered in baking and pastry and culinary arts.

The culinary management, graphic design, and Web design and interactive media programs, and the Associate of Applied Science in culinary arts program are also available in an evening and weekend option format.

Academic Programs

The Art Institute of Phoenix is in session year-round. Depending on the program, students can graduate in nine to thirty-six months with a diploma, an Associate of Applied Science degree, or a Bachelor of Arts degree in their chosen field.

Academic Facilities

The Art Institute of Phoenix provides a learning environment with professional-grade technology applicable to each student's course of study. Students have the opportunity to build a portfolio of work that shows potential employers that they are trained to use the software, hardware, or equipment utilized within the industry. Depending upon the course of study, students are immersed in a creative environment—from classrooms to computer labs to studios—focused on relevant, hands-on education designed to prepare students for the real world.

Costs

Tuition cost varies by program. Prospective students should contact the school for current tuition costs. Other charges include a starting kit for all first-quarter students. Kits vary in price depending on the program of study.

Financial Aid

Financial aid is available for those who qualify. Students who require financial assistance should first complete and submit a Free Application for Federal Student Aid (FAFSA) and meet with a financial aid officer.

Faculty

Faculty members are experienced professionals who create a learning environment that is similar to the professional world

students will face after graduation. Instructors are focused on helping students develop the skills they need to transform their creative potential into marketable skills.

Student Government

The President's Club is a school organization that promotes the philosophy of students helping students. Those students selected to join the club assist new students with adjusting to life in Phoenix, studies at The Art Institute of Phoenix, and school activities. Criteria for selection into this club are a minimum GPA of 3.0 at The Art Institute of Phoenix, good attendance, completion of at least one full quarter of study, a desire to assist other students, and responsible behavior.

Admission Requirements

Many prospective students meet with an assistant director of admissions to discuss future goals and plan the admissions process. For admission to The Art Institute of Phoenix, students are evaluated on the basis of previous education, background, and a demonstrated interest in the selected program. Portfolio submission is encouraged but not required.

As part of the application process, students must write an essay stating how an education at The Art Institute of Phoenix will help them to attain their creative goals. Successful admission into The Art Institute of Phoenix and a satisfactory program start is dependent upon the essay; grade point average, as evidenced in transcript evaluation; an evaluation of General Educational Development (GED) test scores; a review of nationally based exams (preferred but not required), such as the SAT or ACT; and a personal interview with an assistant director of admissions. There is a $50 application fee.

For the most recent information regarding admission requirements, please refer to the current academic catalog.

Application and Information

To obtain an application, make arrangements for an interview, or tour the school, prospective students should contact:

The Art Institute of Phoenix
2233 West Dunlap Avenue
Phoenix, Arizona 85021-2859

Phone: 602-331-7500
        800-474-2479 (toll-free)
Fax: 602-331-5301
Web site: http://www.artinstitutes.edu/phoenix

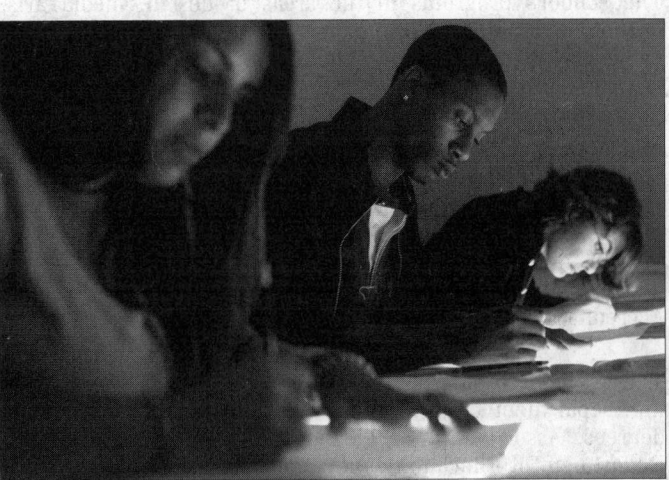

The Art Institute of Atlanta; The Art Institute of Atlanta–Decatur[1]; The Art Institute of Austin[2]; The Art Institute of California–Hollywood; The Art Institute of California–Inland Empire; The Art Institute of California–Los Angeles; The Art Institute of California–Orange County; The Art Institute of California–Sacramento; The Art Institute of California–San Diego; The Art Institute of California–San Francisco; The Art Institute of California–Sunnyvale; The Art Institute of Charleston[1]; The Art Institute of Charlotte; The Art Institute of Colorado; The Art Institute of Dallas[3]; The Art Institute of Fort Lauderdale; The Art Institute of Fort Worth[3]; The Art Institute of Houston; The Art Institute of Houston–North[2]; The Art Institute of Indianapolis[4]; The Art Institute of Jacksonville[5]; The Art Institute of Las Vegas; The Art Institute of Michigan; The Art Institute of New York City; The Art Institute of Ohio–Cincinnati[6]; The Art Institute of Philadelphia; The Art Institute of Phoenix; The Art Institute of Pittsburgh; The Art Institute of Portland; The Art Institute of Raleigh–Durham; The Art Institute of Salt Lake City; The Art Institute of San Antonio[2];The Art Institute of Seattle; The Art Institute of Tampa[5]; The Art Institute of Tennessee–Nashville[1]; The Art Institute of Tucson; The Art Institute of Vancouver; The Art Institute of Virginia Beach[1,7]; The Art Institute of Washington[1,7]; The Art Institute of Washington–Northern Virginia[1,7]; The Art Institute of Wisconsin; The Art Institute of York–Pennsylvania; The Art Institutes International–Kansas City; The Art Institutes International Minnesota; The Illinois Institute of Art–Chicago; The Illinois Institute of Art–Schaumburg; The Illinois Institute of Art–Tinley Park; Miami International University of Art & Design; The New England Institute of Art.

[1]A branch of The Art Institute of Atlanta
[2]A branch of The Art Institute of Houston
[3]A campus of South University
[4]The Art Institute of Indianapolis is regulated by the Indiana Commission on Proprietary Education, 302 West Washington Street, Room E201, Indianapolis, Indiana 46204, AC-0080
[5]A branch of Miami International University of Art & Design
[6]The Art Institute of Ohio–Cincinnati, 8845 Governors Hill Drive, Suite 100, Cincinnati, Ohio 45249-3317, OH Reg. #04-01-1698B
[7]Certified by the State Council of Higher Education to operate in Virginia

THE ART INSTITUTE OF PITTSBURGH
PITTSBURGH, PENNSYLVANIA

CREATE TOMORROW

A focused education from The Art Institute of Pittsburgh can help students turn their creative energy into a powerful tool that can make a difference in the world. Students are part of a collaborative and supportive community, where experienced instructors provide the guidance and skills needed to pursue a career in the creative economy.

The school's programs in the areas of design, media arts, fashion, and culinary give students the opportunity to learn by using professional-grade technology and build a portfolio of work to show potential employers after graduation.

The Art Institute of Pittsburgh is accredited by the Middle States Commission on Higher Education, 3624 Market Street, Philadelphia, Pennsylvania 19104; phone: 267-284-5000. The Middle States Commission on Higher Education is an institutional accrediting agency recognized by the U.S. Secretary of Education and the Council for Higher Education Accreditation.

The Art Institute of Pittsburgh is authorized by the Pennsylvania Department of Education to confer Bachelor of Science degrees, Associate of Science degrees, and diplomas. The Department of Education can be contacted at Commonwealth of Pennsylvania, Department of Education Office of Postsecondary and Higher Education, 333 Market Street, Harrisburg, Pennsylvania 17126; phone: 717-783-6788.

The Associate of Science degree in culinary arts and the Bachelor of Science degree in culinary management are accredited by the Accrediting Commission of the American Culinary Federation Education Foundation.

The interior design program leading to the Bachelor of Science degree is accredited by the Council for Interior Design Accreditation, 206 Grandville Avenue, Suite 350, Grand Rapids, Michigan 49503; http://www.accredit-id.org.

Location

The Art Institute of Pittsburgh is nestled in the heart of downtown Pittsburgh's Golden Triangle. Pittsburgh is a thriving metropolis, sprawling over 55 square miles. It is situated halfway between New York City and Chicago and is within a 2-hour flight or a one-day drive of more than 70 percent of the U.S. population.

Pittsburgh is the international headquarters of many technology-driven businesses. Culture abounds, with summer concerts in the downtown's Market Square at no charge, new theaters, thriving nightlife districts, quaint coffee shops, and retail merchants on every corner. The Pittsburgh Steelers' stadium and the Pirates' waterfront PNC Park adorn the city's North Shore. Pittsburgh is serviced by Greater Pittsburgh International Airport, one of the largest and most retail-developed airports in the country.

Programs of Study and Degrees

No matter which course of study a student may choose, the professionals at The Art Institute of Pittsburgh will guide, support, and help each student as their talents evolve on their journey of personal and professional transformation. Students studying design learn to fine-tune their visual thinking and problem-solving skills, as they create everything from logos to TV ads. Programs in the area of media arts focus on utilizing technology to deliver information and entertainment, while students studying fashion learn to design clothes for the runway or run a retail shop. Culinary programs focus on the fundamental techniques while exposing students to a full menu of international cuisines and management techniques.

The Art Institute of Pittsburgh offers bachelor's degree programs in advertising, culinary management, digital filmmaking and video production, entertainment design, fashion and retail management, fashion design, game art and design, graphic design, hotel and restaurant management, industrial design, interior design, media arts and animation, photography, visual effects and motion graphics, and Web design and interactive media.

Associate of Science degree programs are offered in baking and pastry, culinary arts, digital filmmaking and video production, graphic design, industrial design technology, kitchen and bath design, photography, and Web design and interactive media.

Diploma programs are offered in digital design, residential planning, the art of cooking, and Web design.

Academic Facilities

The Art Institute of Pittsburgh provides a learning environment with professional-grade technology applicable to each student's course of study. Students have the opportunity to build a portfolio of work that shows potential employers that they are trained to use the software, hardware, or equipment utilized within the industry. Depending upon the course of study, students are immersed in a creative environment—from classrooms to computer labs to studios—focused on relevant, hands-on education designed to prepare students for the real world.

Costs

Tuition cost varies by program. Prospective students should contact the school for current tuition costs. Other charges include a starting kit for all first-quarter students. Kits vary in price depending on the program of study.

Financial Aid

Financial aid is available for those who qualify. Students who require financial assistance should first complete and submit a Free Application for Federal Student Aid (FAFSA) and meet with a financial aid officer.

Faculty

Faculty members are experienced professionals who create a learning environment that is similar to the professional world students will face after graduation. Instructors are focused on helping students develop the skills they need to transform their creative potential into marketable skills.

Admission Requirements

A prospective student must be a high school graduate with a high school QPA of 2.0 or higher (2.5 or higher QPA required for admission into game art and design), hold a General Educational Development (GED) certificate, or have a bachelor's degree or higher as a prerequisite for admission. Students who have completed high school or its equivalent but cannot provide the necessary documentation may provide alternate documentation to satisfy this requirement. The president of The Art Institute of Pittsburgh must approve all exceptions. A student who holds a bachelor's degree or higher may submit proof of the degree to satisfy the high school graduation or General Educational Development (GED) requirement. There is a portfolio requirement for media arts and animation and game art and design program candidates.

All applicants are evaluated on the basis of their previous education, background, and stated or demonstrated interest in their program of choice. Applicants who have taken the SAT or ACT are encouraged to submit scores to the Admissions Office for evaluation.

Applications are accepted on a rolling basis. An application for admission must be completed and signed by the applicant and be submitted along with an essay stating how The Art Institute of Pittsburgh can help the student to attain his or her creative goals. There is a $50 application fee.

For the most recent information regarding admission requirements, please refer to the current academic catalog.

Application and Information

To obtain an application, make arrangements for an interview, or tour the school, prospective students should contact:

The Art Institute of Pittsburgh
420 Boulevard of the Allies
Pittsburgh, Pennsylvania 15219-1301
Phone: 412-263-6600
        800-275-2470 (toll-free)
Fax: 412-263-6667
Web site: http://www.artinstitutes.edu/pittsburgh

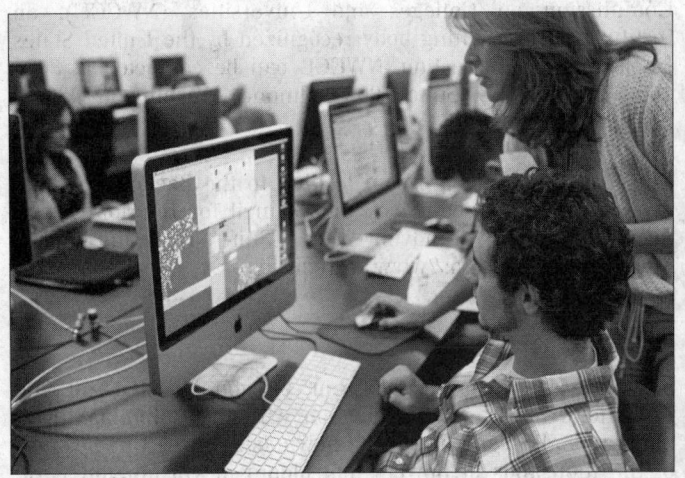

The Art Institute of Atlanta; The Art Institute of Atlanta–Decatur[1]; The Art Institute of Austin[2]; The Art Institute of California–Hollywood; The Art Institute of California–Inland Empire; The Art Institute of California–Los Angeles; The Art Institute of California–Orange County; The Art Institute of California–Sacramento; The Art Institute of California–San Diego; The Art Institute of California–San Francisco; The Art Institute of California–Sunnyvale; The Art Institute of Charleston[1]; The Art Institute of Charlotte; The Art Institute of Colorado; The Art Institute of Dallas[3]; The Art Institute of Fort Lauderdale; The Art Institute of Fort Worth[3]; The Art Institute of Houston; The Art Institute of Houston–North[2]; The Art Institute of Indianapolis[4]; The Art Institute of Jacksonville[5]; The Art Institute of Las Vegas; The Art Institute of Michigan; The Art Institute of New York City; The Art Institute of Ohio–Cincinnati[6]; The Art Institute of Philadelphia; The Art Institute of Phoenix; The Art Institute of Pittsburgh; The Art Institute of Portland; The Art Institute of Raleigh–Durham; The Art Institute of Salt Lake City; The Art Institute of San Antonio[2];The Art Institute of Seattle; The Art Institute of Tampa[5]; The Art Institute of Tennessee–Nashville[1]; The Art Institute of Tucson; The Art Institute of Vancouver; The Art Institute of Virginia Beach[1,7]; The Art Institute of Washington[1,7]; The Art Institute of Washington–Northern Virginia[1,7]; The Art Institute of Wisconsin; The Art Institute of York–Pennsylvania; The Art Institutes International–Kansas City; The Art Institutes International Minnesota; The Illinois Institute of Art–Chicago; The Illinois Institute of Art–Schaumburg; The Illinois Institute of Art–Tinley Park; Miami International University of Art & Design; The New England Institute of Art.
[1]A branch of The Art Institute of Atlanta
[2]A branch of The Art Institute of Houston
[3]A campus of South University
[4]The Art Institute of Indianapolis is regulated by the Indiana Commission on Proprietary Education, 302 West Washington Street, Room E201, Indianapolis, Indiana 46204, AC-0080
[5]A branch of Miami International University of Art & Design
[6]The Art Institute of Ohio–Cincinnati, 8845 Governors Hill Drive, Suite 100, Cincinnati, Ohio 45249-3317, OH Reg. #04-01-1698B
[7]Certified by the State Council of Higher Education to operate in Virginia

THE ART INSTITUTE OF PORTLAND
PORTLAND, OREGON

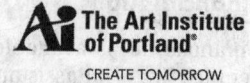
The Art Institute of Portland®
CREATE TOMORROW

A focused education from The Art Institute of Portland can help students turn their creative energy into a powerful tool that can make a difference in the world. Students are part of a collaborative and supportive community, where experienced instructors provide the guidance and skills needed to pursue a career in the creative economy.

The school's programs in the areas of design, media arts, fashion, and culinary give students the opportunity to learn by using professional-grade technology and build a portfolio of work to show potential employers after graduation.

The Art Institute of Portland is accredited by the Northwest Commission on Colleges and Universities (NWCCU), an institutional accrediting body recognized by the United States Department of Education. NWCCU can be contacted at 8060 165th Avenue NE, Suite 100, Redmond, Washington 98052-3981.

The interior design program leading to the Bachelor of Fine Arts degree is accredited by the Council for Interior Design Accreditation, 206 Grandville Avenue, Suite 350, Grand Rapids, Michigan 49503; http://www.accredit-id.org.

Location

Portland is the largest city in Oregon, located on the Willamette River near its junction with the Columbia River. Since 1888, Portland has been known as the Rose City because of the thousands of flowers that bloom in Washington Park. Natural attractions include the Columbia River Gorge's 3,000-foot-high basaltic cliffs, Multnomah Falls, and Mount Hood—the site of America's longest ski season. Portland also has a wide array of coffee shops, Native American art galleries, bookstores, and brew pubs as well as the Oregon Symphony, Tygres Heart Shakespeare Company, Musical Theater Company, Portland Opera, Baroque Orchestra, Northwest Afrikan American Ballet, Oregon Ballet Theatre, and Mount Hood Festival of Jazz.

Portland is home to many large apparel companies—students in the apparel accessory design and the apparel design programs have the advantage of learning from talented professionals in the industry. In addition, The Art Institute of Portland has built valuable relationships with the Oregon Film and Video Office and the Oregon Media Production Association.

Programs of Study and Degrees

No matter which course of study a student may choose, the professionals at The Art Institute of Portland will guide, support, and help each student as their talents evolve on their journey of personal and professional transformation. Students studying design learn to fine-tune their visual thinking and problem-solving skills, as they create everything from logos to TV ads. Programs in the area of media arts focus on utilizing technology to deliver information and entertainment, while students studying fashion learn to design clothes for the runway or run a retail shop. Culinary programs focus on the fundamental techniques while exposing students to a full menu of international cuisines and management techniques.

Bachelor's degrees are available in advertising, apparel accessory design, apparel design, culinary management, design management, design research, design visualization, digital film and video, fashion marketing, game art and design, graphic design, industrial design, interior design, media arts and animation, photography and design, visual and game programming, visual effects and motion graphics, and Web design and interactive media.

Associate degrees are offered in apparel accessory design, apparel design, culinary arts, and graphic design.

Diploma programs are offered in the art of cooking and baking and pastry.

A minor in sustainability is offered with the bachelor's degree programs in apparel accessory design, apparel design, culinary management, design management, design research, fashion marketing, industrial design, and interior design.

Academic Programs

The academic year is divided into four quarters, beginning in January, April, July, and October. To earn a bachelor's degree, students must complete, at minimum, 180 academic credits. To earn an associate degree, students must earn, at minimum, 105 academic credits.

Academic Facilities

The Art Institute of Portland provides a learning environment with professional-grade technology applicable to each student's course of study. Students have the opportunity to build a portfolio of work that shows potential employers that they are trained to use the software, hardware, or equipment utilized within the industry. Depending upon the course of study, students are immersed in a creative environment—from classrooms to computer labs to studios—focused on relevant, hands-on education designed to prepare students for the real world.

Costs

Tuition varies by program. Prospective students should contact the school for current tuition costs. Other charges include a starting kit for all first-quarter students. Kits vary in price depending on the program of study.

Financial Aid

Financial aid is available for those who qualify. Students who require financial assistance should first complete and submit a Free Application for Federal Student Aid (FAFSA) and meet with a financial aid officer.

Faculty

Faculty members are experienced professionals who create a learning environment that is similar to the professional world students will face after graduation. Instructors are focused on helping students develop the skills they need to transform their creative potential into marketable skills.

Admission Requirements

Prospective students must submit an essay of approximately 150 words in which they describe the ways an education at The Art Institute of Portland may help to meet their creative objectives. Portfolios are encouraged but not required. An application for admission and enrollment agreement must be submitted to the school. Applicants who have taken the SAT or ACT should also submit these test scores. Each individual seeking admission is interviewed by an assistant director of admissions in order to explore the applicant's background, interests, and goals. There is a $50 application fee.

For the most recent information regarding admission requirements, please refer to the current academic catalog.

Application and Information

To obtain an application or make arrangements for an interview or tour of the school, prospective students should contact:

The Art Institute of Portland
1122 N.W. Davis Street
Portland, Oregon 97209-2911
Phone: 503-228-6528
          888-228-6528 (toll-free)
Fax: 503-227-1945
Web site: http://www.artinstitutes.edu/portland

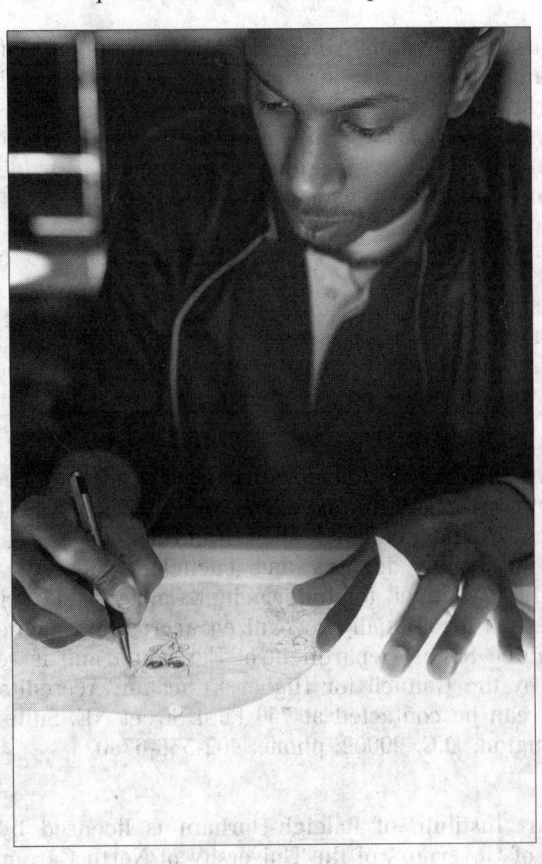

THE ART INSTITUTE OF RALEIGH-DURHAM

DURHAM, NORTH CAROLINA

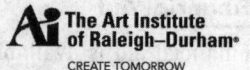

A focused education from The Art Institute of Raleigh-Durham can help students turn their creative energy into a powerful tool that can make a difference in the world. Students are part of a collaborative and supportive community, where experienced instructors provide the guidance and skills needed to pursue a career in the creative economy.

The school's programs in the areas of design, media arts, fashion, and culinary give students the opportunity to learn by using professional-grade technology and build a portfolio of work to show potential employers after graduation.

The Art Institute of Raleigh-Durham, a branch of The Art Institute of Charlotte, is accredited by the Accrediting Council for Independent Colleges and Schools (ACICS) to award associate degrees and bachelor's degrees. The Accrediting Council for Independent Colleges and Schools is listed as a nationally recognized accrediting agency by the United States Department of Education and is recognized by the Council for Higher Education Accreditation. ACICS can be contacted at 750 First Street NE, Suite 980, Washington, D.C. 20002; phone: 202-336-6780.

The Art Institute of Raleigh-Durham is licensed by the Board of Governors of the University of North Carolina to confer Associate of Applied Science and Bachelor of Art degrees.

Location

The Art Institute of Raleigh-Durham is located in the heart of the downtown Durham historical and entertainment district. The metropolitan area of North Carolina is known as the Research Triangle, with a population of over 1.6 million people.

Programs of Study and Degrees

No matter which course of study a student may choose, the professionals at The Art Institute of Raleigh-Durham will guide, support, and help each student as their talents evolve on their journey of personal and professional transformation. Students studying design learn to fine-tune their visual thinking and problem-solving skills, as they create everything from logos to TV ads. Programs in the area of media arts focus on utilizing technology to deliver information and entertainment, while students studying fashion learn to design clothes for the runway or run a retail shop. Culinary programs focus on the fundamental techniques while exposing students to a full menu of international cuisines and management techniques.

Bachelor's degree programs are offered in culinary arts management, fashion marketing and management, game art and design, graphic design, interior design, photography, and Web design and interactive media.

Associate degree programs are offered in culinary arts, fashion marketing, graphic design, and Web design and interactive media.

Academic Programs

The Art Institute of Raleigh-Durham operates on a year-round, four-quarter system.

Academic Facilities

The Art Institute of Raleigh-Durham provides a learning environment with professional-grade technology applicable to each student's course of study. Students have the opportunity to build a portfolio of work that shows potential employers that they are trained to use the software, hardware, or equipment utilized within the industry. Depending upon the course of study, students are immersed in a creative environment—from classrooms to computer labs to studios—focused on relevant, hands-on education designed to prepare students for the real world.

Costs

Tuition cost varies by program. Prospective students should contact the school for current tuition costs. Other charges include a starting kit for all first-quarter students. Kits vary in price depending on the program of study.

Financial Aid

Financial aid is available for those who qualify. Students who require financial assistance should first complete and submit a Free Application for Federal Student Aid (FAFSA) and meet with a financial aid officer.

Faculty

Faculty members are experienced professionals who create a learning environment that is similar to the professional world students will face after graduation. Instructors are focused on helping students develop the skills they need to transform their creative potential into marketable skills.

Admission Requirements

Applicants must provide proof of high school graduation or achievement of a General Educational Development (GED) certificate as a prerequisite for admission. In lieu of documenting high school graduation or a GED certificate, applicants may provide proof of attaining an associate degree or higher from an accredited institution. An official transcript indicating date of high school graduation, GED certificate (including test scores), or date of college graduation (including degree granted) is required as proof.

All individuals seeking admission to The Art Institute of Raleigh-Durham are interviewed in person or by phone by an assistant director of admissions, and each applicant must create an original essay of at least 150 words stating how an education at The Art Institute of Raleigh-Durham would help the student to achieve career goals. There is a $50 application fee.

For the most recent information regarding admission requirements, please refer to the current academic catalog.

Application and Information

To obtain an application, make arrangements for an interview, or tour the school, students should contact:

The Art Institute of Raleigh-Durham
410 Blackwell Street, Suite 200
Durham, North Carolina 27701
Phone: 919-317-3050
        888-245-9593 (toll-free)
Fax: 919-317-3231
Web site: http://www.artinstitutes.edu/raleigh-durham

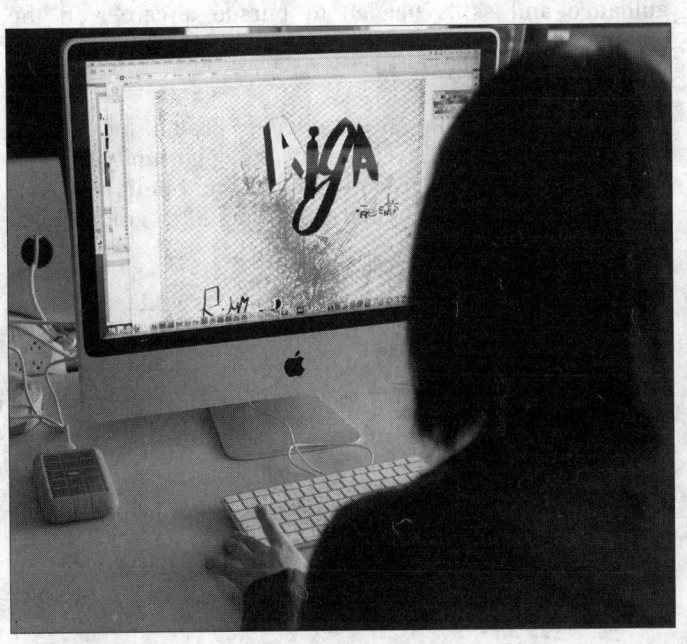

THE ART INSTITUTE OF SALT LAKE CITY

DRAPER, UTAH

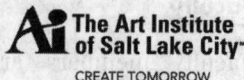

A focused education from The Art Institute of Salt Lake City can help students turn their creative energy into a powerful tool that can make a difference in the world. Students are part of a collaborative and supportive community, where experienced instructors provide the guidance and skills needed to pursue a career in the creative economy.

The school's programs in the areas of design, media arts, fashion, and culinary give students the opportunity to learn by using professional-grade technology and build a portfolio of work to show potential employers after graduation.

The Art Institute of Salt Lake City is accredited by the Accrediting Commission of Career Schools and Colleges (ACCSC) as a branch of The Art Institute of Las Vegas. ACCSC may be contacted at 2101 Wilson Boulevard, Suite 302, Arlington, Virginia 22201; phone: 703-247-4212.

The Art Institute of Salt Lake City is exempt from registration pursuant to the Utah Postsecondary Proprietary School Act. Any questions should be directed to the Utah Division of Consumer Protection (UDCP), 160 East 300 South, Second Floor, Salt Lake City, Utah 84114; phone: 801-530-6601.

Location

Draper is located in the Wasatch Mountains at the south end of the Salt Lake Valley. The city has long been known as a premier hang-gliding destination with breathtaking views. Draper is fast becoming a hub for new development in the Salt Lake and Utah Valleys.

Programs of Study and Degrees

No matter which course of study a student may choose, the professionals at The Art Institute of Salt Lake City will guide, support, and help each student as their talents evolve on their journey of personal and professional transformation. Students studying design learn to fine-tune their visual thinking and problem-solving skills, as they create everything from logos to TV ads. Programs in the area of media arts focus on utilizing technology to deliver information and entertainment, while students studying fashion learn to design clothes for the runway or run a retail shop. Culinary programs focus on the fundamental

techniques while exposing students to a full menu of international cuisines and management techniques.

Bachelor's degree programs are offered in culinary management, digital filmmaking and video production, digital photography, game art and design, graphic design, interior design, media arts and animation, and Web design and interactive media.

Associate degrees are offered in baking and pastry, culinary arts, and graphic design.

Diploma programs are offered in baking and pastry and culinary arts.

Academic Programs

The Art Institute of Salt Lake City operates on a year-round, four-quarter system.

Academic Facilities

The Art Institute of Salt Lake City provides a learning environment with professional-grade technology applicable to each student's course of study. Students have the opportunity to build a portfolio of work that shows potential employers that they are trained to use the software, hardware, or equipment utilized within the industry. Depending upon the course of study, students are immersed in a creative environment—from classrooms to computer labs to studios—focused on relevant, hands-on education designed to prepare students for the real world.

Costs

Tuition cost varies by program. Prospective students should contact the school for current tuition costs. Other charges include a starting kit for all first-quarter students. Kits vary in price depending on the program of study.

Financial Aid

Financial aid is available for those who qualify. Students who require financial assistance should first complete and submit a Free Application for Federal Student Aid (FAFSA) and meet with a financial aid officer.

Faculty

Faculty members are experienced professionals who create a learning environment that is similar to the professional world students will face after graduation. Instructors are focused on helping students develop the skills they need to transform their creative potential into marketable skills.

Admission Requirements

Applicants must provide proof of high school graduation or achievement of a General Educational Development (GED) certificate as a prerequisite for admission. In lieu of documenting high school graduation or a GED certificate, applicants may provide proof of attaining an associate degree or higher from an accredited institution. An official transcript indicating date of high school graduation, receipt of a GED certificate (including test scores), or date of college graduation (including degree granted) is required as proof.

All individuals seeking admission to The Art Institute of Salt Lake City are interviewed in person or by phone by an assistant director of admissions, and each applicant must create an original essay of at least 150 words stating how an education at The Art Institute of Salt Lake City would help the student to achieve career goals. There is a $50 application fee.

For the most recent information regarding admission requirements, please refer to the current academic catalog.

Application and Information

To obtain an application, make arrangements for an interview, or tour the school, prospective students should contact:

The Art Institute of Salt Lake City
121 West Election Road, Suite 100
Draper, Utah 84020-9492
Phone: 801-601-4700
          800-978-0096 (toll-free)
Fax: 801-601-4724
Web site: http://www.artinstitutes.edu/saltlakecity

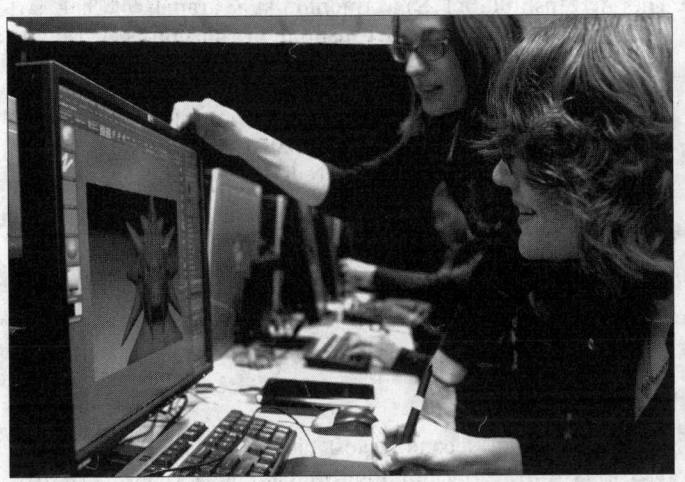

The Art Institute of Atlanta; The Art Institute of Atlanta–Decatur[1]; The Art Institute of Austin[2]; The Art Institute of California–Hollywood; The Art Institute of California–Inland Empire; The Art Institute of California–Los Angeles; The Art Institute of California–Orange County; The Art Institute of California–Sacramento; The Art Institute of California–San Diego; The Art Institute of California–San Francisco; The Art Institute of California–Sunnyvale; The Art Institute of Charleston[1]; The Art Institute of Charlotte; The Art Institute of Colorado; The Art Institute of Dallas[5]; The Art Institute of Fort Lauderdale; The Art Institute of Fort Worth[3]; The Art Institute of Houston; The Art Institute of Houston–North[2]; The Art Institute of Indianapolis[4]; The Art Institute of Jacksonville[5]; The Art Institute of Las Vegas; The Art Institute of Michigan; The Art Institute of New York City; The Art Institute of Ohio–Cincinnati[6]; The Art Institute of Philadelphia; The Art Institute of Phoenix; The Art Institute of Pittsburgh; The Art Institute of Portland; The Art Institute of Raleigh–Durham; The Art Institute of Salt Lake City; The Art Institute of San Antonio[2];The Art Institute of Seattle; The Art Institute of Tampa[5]; The Art Institute of Tennessee–Nashville[1]; The Art Institute of Tucson; The Art Institute of Vancouver; The Art Institute of Virginia Beach[1,7]; The Art Institute of Washington[1,7]; The Art Institute of Washington–Northern Virginia[1,7]; The Art Institute of Wisconsin; The Art Institute of York–Pennsylvania; The Art Institutes International–Kansas City; The Art Institutes International Minnesota; The Illinois Institute of Art–Chicago; The Illinois Institute of Art–Schaumburg; The Illinois Institute of Art–Tinley Park; Miami International University of Art & Design; The New England Institute of Art.
[1]A branch of The Art Institute of Atlanta
[2]A branch of The Art Institute of Houston
[3]A campus of South University
[4]The Art Institute of Indianapolis is regulated by the Indiana Commission on Proprietary Education, 302 West Washington Street, Room E201, Indianapolis, Indiana 46204, AC-0080
[5]A branch of Miami International University of Art & Design
[6]The Art Institute of Ohio–Cincinnati, 8845 Governors Hill Drive, Suite 100, Cincinnati, Ohio 45249-3317, OH Reg. #04-01-1698B
[7]Certified by the State Council of Higher Education to operate in Virginia

THE ART INSTITUTE OF SAN ANTONIO
SAN ANTONIO, TEXAS

A focused education from The Art Institute of San Antonio, a branch of The Art Institute of Houston, can help students turn their creative energy into a powerful tool that can make a difference in the world. Students are part of a collaborative and supportive community, where experienced instructors provide the guidance and skills needed to pursue a career in the creative economy.

The school's programs in the areas of design, media arts, fashion, and culinary give students the opportunity to learn by using professional-grade technology and build a portfolio of work to show potential employers after graduation.

The Art Institute of San Antonio is a branch of The Art Institute of Houston. The Art Institute of Houston is accredited by the Commission on Colleges of the Southern Association of Colleges and Schools to award associate and baccalaureate degrees. Contact the Commission on Colleges at 1866 Southern Lane, Decatur, Georgia 30033-4097 or call 404-679-4500 for questions about the accreditation of The Art Institute of Houston.

The Art Institute of San Antonio holds a certificate of authorization acknowledging exemption from Texas Higher Education Coordinating Board regulations.

Location

San Antonio, the second-largest city in Texas, is one of the fastest growing areas in the United States. There are five Fortune 500 companies in the area, and visitors and locals alike enjoy the River Walk, Majestic Theatre, Alamo complex, and Spanish Governor's Palace.

Programs of Study and Degrees

No matter which course of study a student may choose, the professionals at The Art Institute of San Antonio will guide, support, and help each student as their talents evolve on their journey of personal and professional transformation. Students studying design learn to fine-tune their visual thinking and problem-solving skills, as they create everything from logos to TV ads. Programs in the area of media arts focus on utilizing technology to deliver information and entertainment, while students studying fashion learn to design clothes for the runway or run a retail shop. Culinary programs focus on the fundamental techniques while exposing students to a full menu of international cuisines and management techniques.

Bachelor's degree programs are offered in culinary management, fashion and retail management, graphic design, interior design, media arts and animation, photography, and Web design and interactive media.

Associate degree programs are offered in culinary arts, graphic design, and Web design and interactive media.

Academic Programs

The Art Institute of San Antonio operates on a year-round, four-quarter system.

Academic Facilities

The Art Institute of San Antonio provides a learning environment with professional-grade technology applicable to each student's course of study. Students have the opportunity to build a portfolio of work that shows potential employers that they are trained to use the software, hardware, or equipment utilized within the industry. Depending upon the course of study, students are immersed in a creative environment—from classrooms to computer labs to studios—focused on relevant, hands-on education designed to prepare students for the real world.

Costs

Tuition cost varies by program. Prospective students should contact the school for current tuition costs. Other charges include a starting kit for all first-quarter students. Kits vary in price depending on the program of study.

Financial Aid

Financial aid is available for those who qualify. Students who require financial assistance should first complete and submit a Free Application for Federal Student Aid (FAFSA) and meet with a financial aid officer.

Faculty

Faculty members are experienced professionals who create a learning environment that is similar to the professional world students will face after graduation. Instructors are focused on helping students develop the skills they need to transform their creative potential into marketable skills.

Admission Requirements

Applicants must provide proof of high school graduation or achievement of a General Educational Development (GED) certificate as a prerequisite for admission.

In lieu of documenting high school graduation or a GED certificate, applicants may provide proof of attaining an associate degree or higher from an accredited institution. An official transcript indicating date of high school graduation, GED certificate (including test scores), or date of college graduation (including degree granted) is required as proof.

All individuals seeking admission to The Art Institute of San Antonio are interviewed in person or by phone by an assistant director of admissions, and each applicant must create an original essay of at least 150 words stating how an education at The Art Institute of San Antonio would help the student to achieve career goals. There is a $50 application fee.

For the most recent information regarding admission requirements, please refer to the current academic catalog.

Application and Information

To obtain an application, make arrangements for an interview, or tour the school, prospective students should contact:

The Art Institute of San Antonio
10000 IH-10 West
Suite 200
San Antonio, Texas 78230
Phone: 210-338-7320
Phone: 888-222-0040 (toll-free)

Fax: 210-338-7321
Web site: http://www.artinstitutes.edu/san-antonio

The Art Institute of Atlanta; The Art Institute of Atlanta–Decatur[1]; The Art Institute of Austin[2]; The Art Institute of California–Hollywood; The Art Institute of California–Inland Empire; The Art Institute of California–Los Angeles; The Art Institute of California–Orange County; The Art Institute of California–Sacramento; The Art Institute of California–San Diego; The Art Institute of California–San Francisco; The Art Institute of California–Sunnyvale; The Art Institute of Charleston[1]; The Art Institute of Charlotte; The Art Institute of Colorado; The Art Institute of Dallas[3]; The Art Institute of Fort Lauderdale; The Art Institute of Fort Worth[3]; The Art Institute of Houston; The Art Institute of Houston–North[2]; The Art Institute of Indianapolis[4]; The Art Institute of Jacksonville[5]; The Art Institute of Las Vegas; The Art Institute of Michigan; The Art Institute of New York City; The Art Institute of Ohio–Cincinnati[6]; The Art Institute of Philadelphia; The Art Institute of Phoenix; The Art Institute of Pittsburgh; The Art Institute of Portland; The Art Institute of Raleigh–Durham; The Art Institute of Salt Lake City; The Art Institute of San Antonio[2];The Art Institute of Seattle; The Art Institute of Tampa[5]; The Art Institute of Tennessee–Nashville[1]; The Art Institute of Tucson; The Art Institute of Vancouver; The Art Institute of Virginia Beach[1,7]; The Art Institute of Washington[1,7]; The Art Institute of Washington–Northern Virginia[1,7]; The Art Institute of Wisconsin; The Art Institute of York–Pennsylvania; The Art Institutes International–Kansas City; The Art Institutes International Minnesota; The Illinois Institute of Art–Chicago; The Illinois Institute of Art–Schaumburg; The Illinois Institute of Art–Tinley Park; Miami International University of Art & Design; The New England Institute of Art.

[1]A branch of The Art Institute of Atlanta
[2]A branch of The Art Institute of Houston
[3]A campus of South University
[4]The Art Institute of Indianapolis is regulated by the Indiana Commission on Proprietary Education, 302 West Washington Street, Room E201, Indianapolis, Indiana 46204, AC-0080
[5]A branch of Miami International University of Art & Design
[6]The Art Institute of Ohio–Cincinnati, 8845 Governors Hill Drive, Suite 100, Cincinnati, Ohio 45249-3317, OH Reg. #04-01-1698B
[7]Certified by the State Council of Higher Education to operate in Virginia

THE ART INSTITUTE OF SEATTLE

SEATTLE, WASHINGTON

A focused education from The Art Institute of Seattle can help students turn their creative energy into a powerful tool that can make a difference in the world. Students are part of a collaborative and supportive community, where experienced instructors provide the guidance and skills needed to pursue a career in the creative economy.

The school's programs in the areas of design, media arts, fashion, and culinary give students the opportunity to learn by using professional-grade technology and build a portfolio of work to show potential employers after graduation.

The Art Institute of Seattle is accredited by the Northwest Commission on Colleges and Universities (NWCCU), an institutional accrediting body recognized by the United States Department of Education.

The Art Institute of Seattle is licensed under Chapter 28c.10RCW; inquiries or complaints regarding this or any other private vocational school may be made to the Workforce Training and Education Coordinating Board, 128 10th Avenue SW, P.O. Box 43105, Olympia, Washington 98504-3105; phone: 360-753-5662.

The Associate of Applied Arts in culinary arts degree program is accredited by the Accrediting Commission of the American Culinary Federation Education Foundation.

The interior design program leading to the Bachelor of Fine Arts degree is accredited by the Council for Interior Design Accreditation, 206 Grandville Avenue, Suite 350, Grand Rapids, Michigan 49503; www.accredit-id.org.

Location

The Art Institute of Seattle is located in the city's Belltown district. Founded by Native Americans and traders, the city has retained respect for its different cultures and customs. People from all over the world come to study, work, and live in this city that is known for its friendly people and beautiful natural surroundings.

World-class companies, such as Microsoft, Boeing, Starbucks, Amazon.com, and Nordstrom, make their global headquarters in Seattle. As a gateway to the Pacific Rim, Seattle is a crossroads where creativity, technology, and business meet.

Programs of Study and Degrees

No matter which course of study a student may choose, the professionals at The Art Institute of Seattle will guide, support, and help each student as their talents evolve on their journey of personal and professional transformation. Students studying design learn to fine-tune their visual thinking and problem-solving skills, as they create everything from logos to TV ads. Programs in the area of media arts focus on utilizing technology to deliver information and entertainment, while students studying fashion learn to design clothes for the runway or run a retail shop. Culinary programs focus on the fundamental

techniques while exposing students to a full menu of international cuisines and management techniques.

Bachelor's degree programs are available in audio design technology, culinary arts management, digital filmmaking and video production, fashion design, fashion marketing, game art and design, graphic design, industrial design, interior design, media arts and animation, photography, and Web design and interactive media.

Associate degrees are available in animation art and design, audio production, baking and pastry, culinary arts, fashion design, fashion marketing, graphic design, industrial design technology, interior design, photography, video production, and Web design and interactive media.

Diploma programs are offered in baking and pastry, digital design, residential design, and the art of cooking.

Academic Programs

The Art Institute of Seattle operates on a year-round, quarterly basis. Each quarter totals eleven weeks. Bachelor's degree programs are twelve quarters in length.

Academic Facilities

The Art Institute of Seattle provides a learning environment with professional-grade technology applicable to each student's course of study. Students have the opportunity to build a portfolio of work that shows potential employers that they are trained to use the software, hardware, or equipment utilized within the industry. Depending upon the course of study, students are immersed in a creative environment—from classrooms to computer labs to studios—focused on relevant, hands-on education designed to prepare students for the real world.

Costs

Tuition cost varies by program. Prospective students should contact the school for current tuition costs. Other charges include a starting kit for all first-quarter students. Kits vary in price depending on the program of study.

Financial Aid

Financial aid is available for those who qualify. Students who require financial assistance should first complete and submit a Free Application for Federal Student Aid (FAFSA) and meet with a financial aid officer.

Faculty

Faculty members are experienced professionals who create a learning environment that is similar to the professional world students will face after graduation. Instructors are focused on helping students develop the skills they need to transform their creative potential into marketable skills.

Admission Requirements

A student seeking admission to The Art Institute of Seattle is required to interview with an admissions representative (in person or over the phone). Applicants are required to have a high school diploma or a General Educational Development (GED) certificate and to submit an admissions application and an essay describing how an education at The Art Institute of Seattle may help the student to achieve career goals. For advanced placement, additional information, including college transcripts, letters of recommendation, or portfolio work, may be required. Students may apply for admission online.

The Art Institute of Seattle follows a rolling admissions schedule. Students are encouraged to apply for their chosen quarter early so that they may take advantage of orientation activities. Students may also apply until the actual start date for any given quarter, depending on space availability. There is a $50 application fee.

For the most recent information regarding admission requirements, please refer to the current academic catalog.

Application and Information

To obtain an application, make arrangements for an interview, or tour the school, prospective students should contact:

The Art Institute of Seattle
2323 Elliott Avenue
Seattle, Washington 98121-1642

Phone: 206-448-6600
        800-275-2471 (toll-free)

Fax: 206-269-0275

Web site: http://www.artinstitutes.edu/seattle

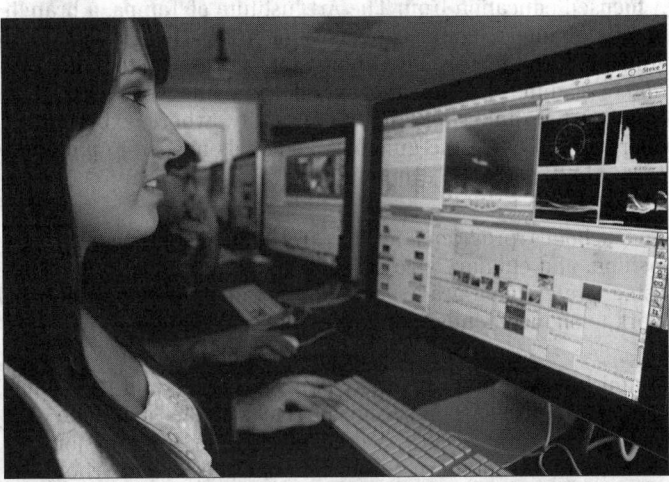

The Art Institute of Atlanta; The Art Institute of Atlanta–Decatur[1]; The Art Institute of Austin[2]; The Art Institute of California–Hollywood; The Art Institute of California–Inland Empire; The Art Institute of California–Los Angeles; The Art Institute of California–Orange County; The Art Institute of California–Sacramento; The Art Institute of California–San Diego; The Art Institute of California–San Francisco; The Art Institute of California–Sunnyvale; The Art Institute of Charleston[1]; The Art Institute of Charlotte; The Art Institute of Colorado; The Art Institute of Dallas[3]; The Art Institute of Fort Lauderdale; The Art Institute of Fort Worth[3]; The Art Institute of Houston; The Art Institute of Houston–North[2]; The Art Institute of Indianapolis[4]; The Art Institute of Jacksonville[5]; The Art Institute of Las Vegas; The Art Institute of Michigan; The Art Institute of New York City; The Art Institute of Ohio–Cincinnati[6]; The Art Institute of Philadelphia; The Art Institute of Phoenix; The Art Institute of Pittsburgh; The Art Institute of Portland; The Art Institute of Raleigh–Durham; The Art Institute of Salt Lake City; The Art Institute of San Antonio[2];The Art Institute of Seattle; The Art Institute of Tampa[5]; The Art Institute of Tennessee–Nashville[1]; The Art Institute of Tucson; The Art Institute of Vancouver; The Art Institute of Virginia Beach[1,7]; The Art Institute of Washington[1,7]; The Art Institute of Washington–Northern Virginia[1,7]; The Art Institute of Wisconsin; The Art Institute of York–Pennsylvania; The Art Institutes International–Kansas City; The Art Institutes International Minnesota; The Illinois Institute of Art–Chicago; The Illinois Institute of Art–Schaumburg; The Illinois Institute of Art–Tinley Park; Miami International University of Art & Design; The New England Institute of Art.

[1]A branch of The Art Institute of Atlanta
[2]A branch of The Art Institute of Houston
[3]A campus of South University
[4]The Art Institute of Indianapolis is regulated by the Indiana Commission on Proprietary Education, 302 West Washington Street, Room E201, Indianapolis, Indiana 46204, AC-0080
[5]A branch of Miami International University of Art & Design
[6]The Art Institute of Ohio–Cincinnati, 8845 Governors Hill Drive, Suite 100, Cincinnati, Ohio 45249-3317, OH Reg. #04-01-1698B
[7]Certified by the State Council of Higher Education to operate in Virginia

THE ART INSTITUTE OF TAMPA

TAMPA, FLORIDA

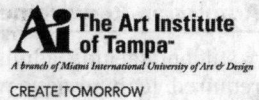

CREATE TOMORROW

A focused education from The Art Institute of Tampa, a branch of Miami International University of Art & Design, can help students turn their creative energy into a powerful tool that can make a difference in the world. Students are part of a collaborative and supportive community, where experienced instructors provide the guidance and skills needed to pursue a career in the creative economy.

The school's programs in the areas of design, media arts, fashion, and culinary give students the opportunity to learn by using professional-grade technology and build a portfolio of work to show potential employers after graduation.

Miami International University of Art & Design and its branch campuses, The Art Institute of Jacksonville and The Art Institute of Tampa, are accredited by the Commission on Colleges of the Southern Association of Colleges and Schools to award diplomas, associate, baccalaureate, and master's degrees. Contact the Commission on Colleges at 1866 Southern Lane, Decatur, Georgia 30033-4097; or call 404-679-4500 for questions about the accreditation of Miami International University of Art & Design.

The Art Institute of Tampa is licensed by the Commission for Independent Education, Florida Department of Education. Additional information regarding this institution may be obtained by contacting the commission at 325 West Gaines Street, Suite 1414, Tallahassee, Florida 32399-0400; phone: 888-224-6684 (toll-free).

The Associate of Arts in culinary arts and the Bachelor of Arts in culinary management degree programs are accredited by the Accrediting Commission of the American Culinary Federation Education Foundation.

Location

Located in Tampa's bustling business district, The Art Institute of Tampa is situated across from Raymond James Stadium and Al Lopez Park, comprising 126 acres of Florida's fauna and flora. Tampa's balmy climate makes the outdoors enjoyable year-round. Residents enjoy bicycling, jogging, sunbathing, walking, in-line skating, swimming, sport fishing, scuba diving, and snorkeling. Gyms and dance studios offer opportunities for aerobics, weight lifting, ballet, kickboxing, and the martial arts. Local attractions include Busch Gardens, the Florida Aquarium, Lowry Park Zoo, the Tampa Museum of Art, Shakespeare in the Park, the Clearwater Jazz Festival, and the world-renowned Salvador Dalí Museum. Sports fans follow the Tampa Bay Buccaneers, Devil Rays, or Lightning, and popular nightlife spots include Channelside, Bay Street, and Ybor City, the center of the city's bustling music scene. Theater, symphony, and dance performances; museums; and a diverse range of art galleries showcase some of the world's greatest talent. Situated on the west coast of Florida, the Tampa Bay area has grown to become one of the most populous and affluent regions in Florida. With its unique blend of urban excitement and natural beauty, there really is something for everyone who lives in the beautiful, diverse communities connected by green spaces and waterways.

Programs of Study and Degrees

No matter which course of study a student may choose, the professionals at The Art Institute of Tampa will guide, support, and help each student as their talents evolve on their journey of personal and professional transformation. Students studying design learn to fine-tune their visual thinking and problem-solving skills, as they create everything from logos to TV ads. Programs in the area of media arts focus on utilizing technology to deliver information and entertainment, while students studying fashion learn to design clothes for the runway or run a retail shop. Culinary programs focus on the fundamental techniques while exposing students to a full menu of international cuisines and management techniques.

Bachelor's degrees are offered in culinary management, digital filmmaking and video production, digital photography, fashion and retail management, game art and design, graphic design, interior design, media arts and animation, visual effects and motion graphics, and Web design and interactive media.

Associate degrees are available in baking and pastry, culinary arts, and graphic design.

A diploma is available in baking and pastry.

Academic Programs

The academic year is divided into four quarters, beginning in January, April, July, and October. Bachelor's degrees require the completion of 192 credits, and associate degrees require completion of 112 academic credits.

Academic Facilities

The Art Institute of Tampa provides a learning environment with professional-grade technology applicable to each student's course of study. Students have the opportunity to build a portfolio of work that shows potential employers that they are trained to use the software, hardware, or equipment utilized within the industry. Depending upon the course of study, students are immersed in a creative environment—from classrooms to computer labs to studios—focused on relevant, hands-on education designed to prepare students for the real world.

Costs

Tuition cost varies by program. Prospective students should contact the school for current tuition costs. Other charges include a starting kit for all first-quarter students. Kits vary in price, depending on the program of study.

Financial Aid

Financial aid is available for those who qualify. Students who require financial assistance should first complete and submit a Free Application for Federal Student Aid (FAFSA) and meet with a financial aid officer.

Faculty

Faculty members are experienced professionals who create a learning environment that is similar to the professional world students will face after graduation. Instructors are focused on helping students develop the skills they need to transform their creative potential into marketable skills.

Student Government

Student leadership is fundamental to academic success and is a way to network with and meet other students. Student leaders serve as role models for peers and act as student advocates for the school. Student leadership programs at The Art Institute of Tampa are designed to support the mission of the school, help students refine interpersonal skills, implement positive change for the student body, and promote school and community spirit. Students may become active members of The Art Institute of Tampa Student Government, start or join a university club, or attend school-sponsored seminars designed to improve leadership skills.

Admission Requirements

Applicants must demonstrate proof of high school graduation or its equivalent in order to receive final acceptance. An official copy of a high school transcript or General Educational Development (GED) transcript is required. Applicants are also required to interview with the school (either in person or by telephone) and write an essay of approximately 150 words in length describing how an education at The Art Institute of Tampa will help them attain creative goals. The Admissions Acceptance Committee determines the compatibility of the applicant with the school and reserves the right to request the results of the SAT or ACT exam and other additional information. A separate application and enrollment form must be completed and signed by the applicant. Prospective students may apply at any time of the year. Applications may be submitted online or mailed to the school. There is a $50 application fee.

For the most recent information regarding admission requirements, please refer to the current academic catalog.

Application and Information

To obtain an application, make arrangements for an interview, or tour the school, prospective students should contact:

The Art Institute of Tampa
Parkside at Tampa Bay Park
4401 North Himes Avenue, Suite 150
Tampa, Florida 33614-7086
Phone: 813-873-2112
       866-703-3277 (toll-free)
Fax: 813-873-2171
Web site: http://www.artinstitutes.edu/tampa

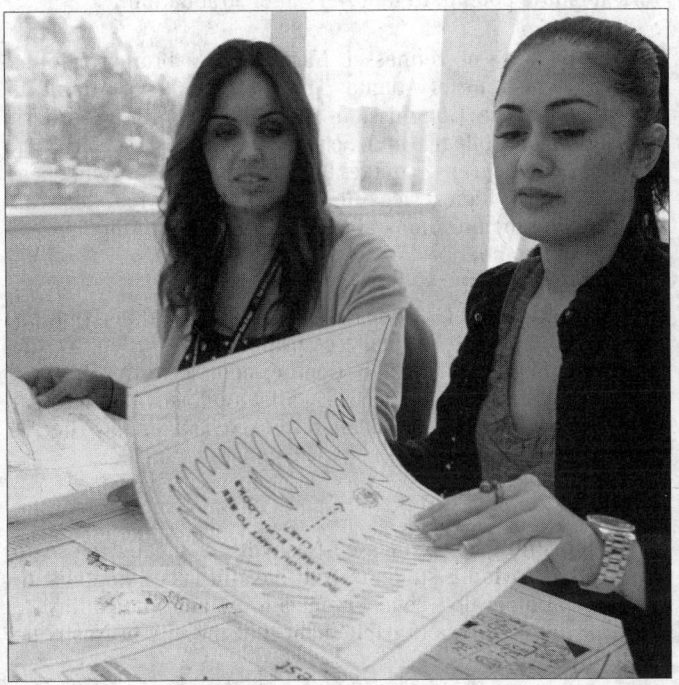

THE ART INSTITUTE OF TENNESSEE–NASHVILLE

NASHVILLE, TENNESSEE

A focused education from The Art Institute of Tennessee–Nashville, a branch of The Art Institute of Atlanta, can help students turn their creative energy into a powerful tool that can make a difference in the world. Students are part of a collaborative and supportive community, where experienced instructors provide the guidance and skills needed to pursue a career in the creative economy.

The school's programs in the areas of design, media arts, fashion, and culinary give students the opportunity to learn by using professional-grade technology and build a portfolio of work to show potential employers after graduation.

The Art Institute of Tennessee–Nashville is a branch campus of The Art Institute of Atlanta. The Art Institute of Atlanta is accredited by the Commission on Colleges of the Southern Association of Colleges and Schools to award associate and baccalaureate degrees. Contact the Commission on Colleges at 1866 Southern Lane, Decatur, Georgia 30033-4097 or call 404-679-4500 for questions about the accreditation of The Art Institute of Atlanta.

The Art Institute of Tennessee–Nashville is authorized for operation as a postsecondary educational institution by the Tennessee Higher Education Commission, Parkway Towers, Suite 1900, 404 James Robertson Parkway, Nashville, Tennessee 37243; phone: 615-741-6230; http://www.state.tn.us/thec.

Location

The Art Institute of Tennessee–Nashville is located close to downtown, providing students with ease of access, opportunities to volunteer for civic organizations, and the ability to enjoy all the culture and excitement that the city of Nashville has to offer.

Programs of Study and Degrees

No matter which course of study a student may choose, the professionals at The Art Institute of Tennessee–Nashville will guide, support, and help each student as their talents evolve on their journey of personal and professional transformation. Students studying design learn to fine-tune their visual thinking and problem-solving skills, as they create everything from logos to TV ads. Programs in the area of media arts focus on utilizing technology to deliver information and entertainment, while students studying fashion learn to design clothes for the runway or run a retail shop. Culinary programs focus on the fundamental techniques while exposing students to a full menu of international cuisines and management techniques.

Bachelor's degrees are offered in advertising, audio production, culinary arts management, digital filmmaking and video production, fashion and retail management, graphic design, interior design, media arts and animation, photographic imaging, and Web design and interactive media.

Associate degrees are available in baking and pastry, culinary arts, graphic design, video production, and Web design and interactive media.

Diploma programs are offered in culinary arts–baking and pastry and culinary arts–skills.

The diploma in culinary arts–skills program is also available in an evening and weekend option format.

Academic Programs

The academic year is divided into four quarters, beginning in January, April, July, and October. Each program is offered on a year-round basis, allowing students to continue to work uninterrupted toward their degrees.

Academic Facilities

The Art Institute of Tennessee–Nashville provides a learning environment with professional-grade technology applicable to each student's course of study. Students have the opportunity to build a portfolio of work that shows potential employers that they are trained to use the software, hardware, or equipment utilized within the industry. Depending upon the course of study, students are immersed in a creative environment—from classrooms to computer labs to studios—focused on relevant, hands-on education designed to prepare students for the real world.

Costs

Tuition cost varies by program. Prospective students should contact the school for current tuition costs. Other charges include a starting kit for all first-quarter students. Kits vary in price, depending on the program of study.

Financial Aid

Financial aid is available for those who qualify. Students who require financial assistance should first complete and submit a Free Application for Federal Student Aid (FAFSA) and meet with a financial aid officer.

Faculty

Faculty members are experienced professionals who create a learning environment that is similar to the professional world students will face after graduation. Instructors are focused on helping students develop the skills they need to transform their creative potential into marketable skills.

Student Government

The Student Federation is responsible for student government and acts as a liaison between the student body and faculty and staff members.

Admission Requirements

Applicants must provide proof of high school graduation or achievement of a General Educational Development (GED) certificate as a prerequisite for admission. In lieu of documenting high school graduation or a GED certificate, applicants may provide proof of receiving an associate degree or higher from an accredited institution. An official transcript indicating date of high school graduation, receipt of a GED certificate (including test scores), or date of college graduation (including degree granted) is required as proof.

All individuals seeking admission to The Art Institute of Tennessee–Nashville are interviewed in person or by phone by an assistant director of admissions, and each applicant must write an original essay of at least 150 words stating how an education at the school would help the student achieve career goals. There is a $50 application fee.

For the most recent information regarding admission requirements, please refer to the current academic catalog.

Application and Information

To obtain an application, make arrangements for an interview, or tour the school, prospective students should contact:

The Art Institute of Tennessee–Nashville
100 Centerview Drive, Suite 250
Nashville, Tennessee 37214-3439
Phone: 615-874-1067
      866-747-5770 (toll-free)
Fax: 615-874-3530
Web site: http://www.artinstitutes.edu/nashville

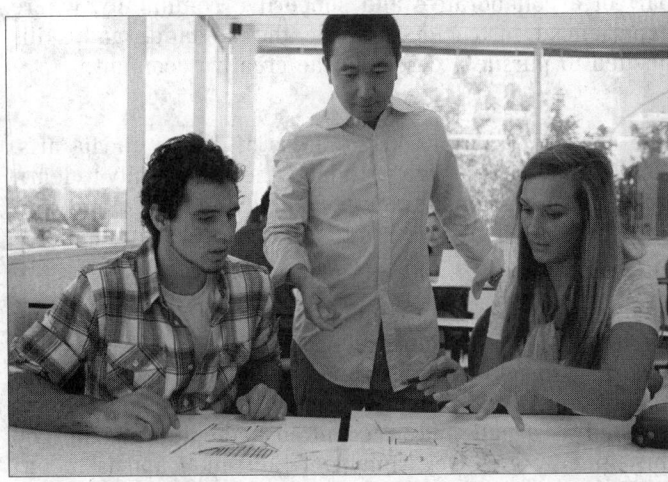

COLLEGE CLOSE-UPS

THE ART INSTITUTE OF TUCSON

TUCSON, ARIZONA

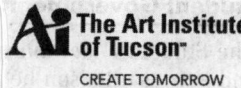

A focused education from The Art Institute of Tucson can help students turn their creative energy into a powerful tool that can make a difference in the world. Students are part of a collaborative and supportive community, where experienced instructors provide the guidance and skills needed to pursue a career in the creative economy.

The school's programs in the areas of design, media arts, fashion, and culinary give students the opportunity to learn by using professional-grade technology and build a portfolio of work to show potential employers after graduation.

The Art Institute of Tucson is accredited by the Accrediting Council for Independent Colleges and Schools (ACICS) to award associate degrees and bachelor's degrees. The Accrediting Council for Independent Colleges and Schools is listed as a nationally recognized accrediting agency by the United States Department of Education and is recognized by the Council for Higher Education Accreditation. ACICS can be contacted at 750 First Street NE, Suite 980, Washington, D.C. 20002; phone: 202-336-6780.

The Art Institute of Tucson is licensed, approved, and regulated by the Arizona State Board for Private Postsecondary Education.

Location

Tucson is a fast-growing, progressive metropolitan area with an incredibly rich cultural heritage. Arizona, also known as the Grand Canyon state, today combines the cultures of the United States and Mexico with continued influence from past settlement by Native Americans, Spanish explorers, and Anglo frontiersmen. The result is a diverse mix of people, architecture, food, and communities that can serve as a catalyst for inspiring our students' creativity.

Programs of Study and Degrees

No matter which course of study a student may choose, the professionals at The Art Institute of Tucson will guide, support, and help each student as their talents evolve on their journey of personal and professional transformation. Students studying design learn to fine-tune their visual thinking and problem-solving skills, as they create everything from logos to TV ads. Programs in the area of media arts focus on utilizing technology to deliver information

and entertainment, while students studying fashion learn to design clothes for the runway or run a retail shop. Culinary programs focus on the fundamental techniques while exposing students to a full menu of international cuisines and management techniques.

Bachelor's degree programs are offered in advertising, culinary arts, digital filmmaking and video production, digital photography, fashion design, fashion marketing, graphic design, interior design, media arts and animation, and Web design and interactive media.

Associate degree programs are offered in baking and pastry, culinary arts, and graphic design.

A diploma program is offered in baking and pastry.

Academic Programs

The Art Institute of Tucson operates on a year-round, four-quarter system.

Academic Facilities

The Art Institute of Tucson provides a learning environment with professional-grade technology applicable to each student's course of study. Students have the opportunity to build a portfolio of work that shows potential employers that they are trained to use the software, hardware, or equipment utilized within the industry. Depending upon the course of study, students are immersed in a creative environment—from classrooms to computer labs to studios—focused on relevant, hands-on education designed to prepare students for the real world.

Costs

Tuition cost varies by program. Prospective students should contact the school for current tuition costs. Other charges include a starting kit for all first-quarter students. Kits vary in price depending on the program of study.

Financial Aid

Financial aid is available for those who qualify. Students who require financial assistance should first complete and submit a Free Application for Federal Student Aid (FAFSA) and meet with a financial aid officer.

Faculty

Faculty members are experienced professionals who create a learning environment that is similar to the professional world students will face after graduation. Instructors are focused on helping students develop the skills they need to transform their creative potential into marketable skills.

Admission Requirements

Applicants must provide proof of high school graduation or achievement of a General Educational Development (GED) certificate as a prerequisite for admission.

In lieu of documenting high school graduation or a GED certificate, applicants may provide proof of attaining an associate degree or higher from an accredited institution. An official transcript indicating date of high school graduation, GED certificate (including test scores), or date of college graduation (including degree granted) is required as proof.

All individuals seeking admission to The Art Institute of Tucson are interviewed in person or by phone by an assistant director of admissions, and each applicant must create an original essay of at least 150 words stating how an education at The Art Institute of Tucson would help the student to achieve career goals. There is a $50 application fee.

For the most recent information regarding admission requirements, please refer to the current academic catalog.

Application and Information

To obtain an application, make arrangements for an interview, or tour the school, students should contact:

The Art Institute of Tucson
5099 East Grant Road
Suite 100
Tucson, Arizona 85712
Phone: 520-318-2700
      866-690-8850 (toll-free)
Fax: 520-881-4794
Web site: http://www.artinstitutes.edu/tucson

The Art Institute of Atlanta; The Art Institute of Atlanta–Decatur[1]; The Art Institute of Austin[2]; The Art Institute of California–Hollywood; The Art Institute of California–Inland Empire; The Art Institute of California–Los Angeles; The Art Institute of California–Orange County; The Art Institute of California–Sacramento; The Art Institute of California–San Diego; The Art Institute of California–San Francisco; The Art Institute of California–Sunnyvale; The Art Institute of Charleston[1]; The Art Institute of Charlotte; The Art Institute of Colorado; The Art Institute of Dallas[5]; The Art Institute of Fort Lauderdale; The Art Institute of Fort Worth[3]; The Art Institute of Houston; The Art Institute of Houston–North[2]; The Art Institute of Indianapolis[4]; The Art Institute of Jacksonville[5]; The Art Institute of Las Vegas; The Art Institute of Michigan; The Art Institute of New York City; The Art Institute of Ohio–Cincinnati[6]; The Art Institute of Philadelphia; The Art Institute of Phoenix; The Art Institute of Pittsburgh; The Art Institute of Portland; The Art Institute of Raleigh–Durham; The Art Institute of Salt Lake City; The Art Institute of San Antonio[2];The Art Institute of Seattle; The Art Institute of Tampa[5]; The Art Institute of Tennessee–Nashville[1]; The Art Institute of Tucson; The Art Institute of Vancouver; The Art Institute of Virginia Beach[1,7]; The Art Institute of Washington[1,7]; The Art Institute of Washington–Northern Virginia[1,7]; The Art Institute of Wisconsin; The Art Institute of York–Pennsylvania; The Art Institutes International–Kansas City; The Art Institutes International Minnesota; The Illinois Institute of Art–Chicago; The Illinois Institute of Art–Schaumburg; The Illinois Institute of Art–Tinley Park; Miami International University of Art & Design; The New England Institute of Art.

[1]A branch of The Art Institute of Atlanta
[2]A branch of The Art Institute of Houston
[3]A campus of South University
[4]The Art Institute of Indianapolis is regulated by the Indiana Commission on Proprietary Education, 302 West Washington Street, Room E201, Indianapolis, Indiana 46204, AC-0080
[5]A branch of Miami International University of Art & Design
[6]The Art Institute of Ohio–Cincinnati, 8845 Governors Hill Drive, Suite 100, Cincinnati, Ohio 45249-3317, OH Reg. #04-01-1698B
[7]Certified by the State Council of Higher Education to operate in Virginia

THE ART INSTITUTE OF VIRGINIA BEACH

VIRGINIA BEACH, VIRGINIA

A focused education from The Art Institute of Virginia Beach, a branch of The Art Institute of Atlanta, can help students turn their creative energy into a powerful tool that can make a difference in the world. Students are part of a collaborative and supportive community, where experienced instructors provide the guidance and skills needed to pursue a career in the creative economy.

The school's programs in the areas of design, media arts, fashion, and culinary give students the opportunity to learn by using professional-grade technology and build a portfolio of work to show potential employers after graduation.

The Art Institute of Virginia Beach is a branch campus of The Art Institute of Atlanta. The Art Institute of Atlanta is accredited by the Commission on Colleges of the Southern Association of Colleges and Schools to award associate and baccalaureate degrees. Contact the Commission on Colleges at 1866 Southern Lane, Decatur, Georgia 30033-4097 or call 404-679-4500 for questions about the accreditation of The Art Institute of Atlanta.

The Art Institute of Virginia Beach, a branch of The Art Institute of Atlanta, is certified to operate in Virginia by the State Council of Higher Education for Virginia, James Monroe Building, 101 North Fourteenth Street, Richmond, Virginia 23219; phone: 804-225-2600.

Location

Virginia Beach gives students easy access to cultural and recreational opportunities. Located at the mouth of the Chesapeake Bay, Virginia Beach is home to nearly 450,000 people, miles of beach, and many historic sites.

Programs of Study and Degrees

No matter which course of study a student may choose, the professionals at The Art Institute of Virginia Beach will guide, support, and help each student as their talents evolve on their journey of personal and professional transformation. Students studying design learn to fine-tune their visual thinking and problem-solving skills, as they create everything from logos to TV ads. Programs in the area of media arts focus on utilizing technology to deliver information and entertainment, while students studying fashion learn to design clothes for the runway or run a retail shop. Culinary programs focus on the fundamental

techniques while exposing students to a full menu of international cuisines and management techniques.

Bachelor's degree programs are offered in advertising, culinary arts management, fashion and retail management, graphic design, interior design, media arts and animation, photographic imaging, and Web design and interactive media.

Associate degree programs are offered in culinary arts, graphic design, and Web design and interactive media.

Academic Programs

The Art Institute of Virginia Beach operates on a year-round, four-quarter system.

Academic Facilities

The Art Institute of Virginia Beach provides a learning environment with professional-grade technology applicable to each student's course of study. Students have the opportunity to build a portfolio of work that shows potential employers that they are trained to use the software, hardware, or equipment utilized within the industry. Depending upon the course of study, students are immersed in a creative environment—from classrooms to computer labs to studios—focused on relevant, hands-on education designed to prepare students for the real world.

Costs

Tuition cost varies by program. Prospective students should contact the school for current tuition costs. Other charges include a starting kit for all first-quarter students. Kits vary in price depending on the program of study.

Financial Aid

Financial aid is available for those who qualify. Students who require financial assistance should first complete and submit a Free Application for Federal Student Aid (FAFSA) and meet with a financial aid officer.

Faculty

Faculty members are experienced professionals who create a learning environment that is similar to the professional world students will face after graduation. Instructors are focused on helping students develop the skills they need to transform their creative potential into marketable skills.

Admission Requirements

Applicants must provide proof of high school graduation or achievement of a General Educational Development (GED) certificate as a prerequisite for admission.

In lieu of documenting high school graduation or a GED certificate, applicants may provide proof of attaining an associate degree or higher from an accredited institution. An official transcript indicating date of high school graduation, GED certificate (including test scores), or date of college graduation (including degree granted) is required as proof.

All individuals seeking admission to The Art Institute of Virginia Beach are interviewed in person or by phone by an assistant director of admissions, and each applicant must create an original essay of at least 150 words stating how an education at The Art Institute of Virginia Beach would help the student to achieve career goals. There is a $50 application fee.

For the most recent information regarding admission requirements, please refer to the current academic catalog.

Application and Information

To obtain an application, make arrangements for an interview, or tour the school, prospective students should contact:

The Art Institute of Virginia Beach
Two Columbus Center
4500 Main Street, Suite 100
Virginia Beach, Virginia 23462
Phone: 757-493-6700
          877-437-4428 (toll-free)
Fax: 757-493-6800
Web site: http://www.artinstitutes.edu/virginia-beach

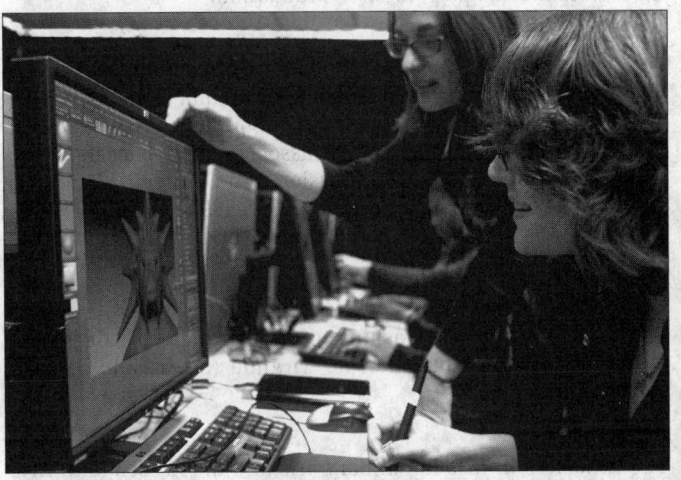

The Art Institute of Atlanta; The Art Institute of Atlanta–Decatur[1]; The Art Institute of Austin[2]; The Art Institute of California–Hollywood; The Art Institute of California–Inland Empire; The Art Institute of California–Los Angeles; The Art Institute of California–Orange County; The Art Institute of California–Sacramento; The Art Institute of California–San Diego; The Art Institute of California–San Francisco; The Art Institute of California–Sunnyvale; The Art Institute of Charleston[1]; The Art Institute of Charlotte; The Art Institute of Colorado; The Art Institute of Dallas[5]; The Art Institute of Fort Lauderdale; The Art Institute of Fort Worth[3]; The Art Institute of Houston; The Art Institute of Houston–North[2]; The Art Institute of Indianapolis[4]; The Art Institute of Jacksonville[5]; The Art Institute of Las Vegas; The Art Institute of Michigan; The Art Institute of New York City; The Art Institute of Ohio–Cincinnati[6]; The Art Institute of Philadelphia; The Art Institute of Phoenix; The Art Institute of Pittsburgh; The Art Institute of Portland; The Art Institute of Raleigh–Durham; The Art Institute of Salt Lake City; The Art Institute of San Antonio[2];The Art Institute of Seattle; The Art Institute of Tampa[5]; The Art Institute of Tennessee–Nashville[1]; The Art Institute of Tucson; The Art Institute of Vancouver; The Art Institute of Virginia Beach[1,7]; The Art Institute of Washington[1,7]; The Art Institute of Washington–Northern Virginia[1,7]; The Art Institute of Wisconsin; The Art Institute of York–Pennsylvania; The Art Institutes International–Kansas City; The Art Institutes International Minnesota; The Illinois Institute of Art–Chicago; The Illinois Institute of Art–Schaumburg; The Illinois Institute of Art–Tinley Park; Miami International University of Art & Design; The New England Institute of Art.

[1]A branch of The Art Institute of Atlanta
[2]A branch of The Art Institute of Houston
[3]A campus of South University
[4]The Art Institute of Indianapolis is regulated by the Indiana Commission on Proprietary Education, 302 West Washington Street, Room E201, Indianapolis, Indiana 46204, AC-0080
[5]A branch of Miami International University of Art & Design
[6]The Art Institute of Ohio–Cincinnati, 8845 Governors Hill Drive, Suite 100, Cincinnati, Ohio 45249-3317, OH Reg. #04-01-1698B
[7]Certified by the State Council of Higher Education to operate in Virginia

THE ART INSTITUTE OF WASHINGTON
ARLINGTON, VIRGINIA

The Art Institute
of Washington™
A branch of The Art Institute of Atlanta
CREATE TOMORROW

A focused education from The Art Institute of Washington, a branch of The Art Institute of Atlanta, can help students turn their creative energy into a powerful tool that can make a difference in the world. Students are part of a collaborative and supportive community, where experienced instructors provide the guidance and skills needed to pursue a career in the creative economy.

The school's programs in the areas of design, media arts, fashion, and culinary give students the opportunity to learn on professional-grade technology and build a portfolio of work to show potential employers after graduation.

The Art Institute of Washington is a branch campus of The Art Institute of Atlanta. The Art Institute of Atlanta is accredited by the Commission on Colleges of the Southern Association of Colleges and Schools to award associate and baccalaureate degrees. Contact the Commission on Colleges at 1866 Southern Lane, Decatur, Georgia 30033-4097 or call 404-679-4500 for questions about the accreditation of The Art Institute of Atlanta.

The Art Institute of Washington is certified by the State Council of Higher Education for Virginia (SCHEV) to operate in Virginia.

The Associate in Arts in culinary arts and the Associate in Arts in culinary arts with a concentration in baking and pastry degree programs are accredited by the Accrediting Commission of the American Culinary Federation Education Foundation.

The interior design program leading to the Bachelor of Fine Arts is accredited by the Council for Interior Design Accreditation, 206 Grandville Avenue, Suite 350, Grand Rapids, Michigan 49503; http://www.accredit-id.org.

Location

Located in Arlington, Virginia, directly across the Potomac River from Washington, D.C., The Art Institute of Washington occupies the ground floor and the ninth through twelfth floors of the Ames Center. The area is home to a variety of activities, including professional sports, first-rate theatrical and musical entertainment, beautiful parks, and cultural events. Some of the most popular places to visit are the Washington Monument, Lincoln Memorial, Vietnam and Korean War Memorials, Arlington National Cemetery, Smithsonian Institution and Museums, and Capitol Building. The Arlington community is home to the Fashion Center at Pentagon City, with its more than 150 stores, and the Crystal City Underground and Plaza Shops, which hosts more than 120 retail shops. In addition, Arlington has more than 170 county parks and playgrounds, including over 80 miles of bicycle routes and jogging trails.

Programs of Study and Degrees

No matter which course of study a student may choose, the professionals at The Art Institute of Washington will guide, support, and help each student as their talents evolve on their journey of personal and professional transformation. Students studying design learn to fine-tune their visual thinking and problem-solving skills, as they create everything from logos to TV ads. Programs in the area of media arts focus on utilizing technology to deliver information and entertainment, while students studying fashion learn to design clothes for the runway or run a retail shop. Programs in the culinary area focus on the fundamental techniques while exposing students to a full menu of international cuisines and management techniques.

Bachelor's degrees are available in advertising, audio production, culinary arts management, digital filmmaking and video production, fashion and retail management, food and beverage management, game art and design, graphic design, interior design, media arts and animation, photographic imaging, visual and game programming, visual effects and motion graphics, and Web design and interactive media.

Associate degrees are offered in culinary arts; culinary arts with a concentration in baking and pastry; graphic design; photographic imaging; video production; Web design and interactive media; and wine, spirits, and beverage management.

Diploma programs are available in advertising design, commercial photography, culinary arts–baking and pastry, culinary arts–skills, digital design, video skills, and Web design.

The culinary arts and associate in graphic design programs are available in an evening and weekend option format.

Academic Programs

The academic year is divided into four quarters, beginning in January, April, July, and October. Students may begin their program of study during any quarter. Bachelor's degrees require the completion of 192 credit hours, and associate degree programs require completion of 96 to 112 credit hours.

Academic Facilities

The Art Institute of Washington provides a learning environment with professional-grade technology applicable to each student's course of study. Students have the opportunity to build a portfolio of work that shows potential employers that they are trained to use the software, hardware, or equipment utilized within the industry. Depending upon the course of study, students are immersed in a creative environment—from classrooms to computer labs to studios—focused on relevant, hands-on education designed to prepare students for the real world.

Costs

Tuition cost varies by program. Prospective students should contact the School for current tuition costs. Other charges include a starting kit for all first-quarter students. Kits vary in price, depending on the program of study.

Financial Aid

Financial aid is available for those who qualify. Students who require financial assistance should first complete and submit a Free Application for Federal Student Aid (FAFSA) and meet with a financial aid officer.

Faculty

Faculty members are experienced professionals who create a learning environment that is similar to the professional world students will face after graduation. Instructors are focused on helping students develop the skills they need to transform their creative potential into marketable skills.

Admission Requirements

Prospective students must interview, either by telephone or in person, with a member of the admissions staff in order to explore the student's background and interests and how they relate to The Art Institute of Washington's programs. To apply, students must submit a completed application for admission, including an essay, high school transcripts or General Educational Development (GED) test scores, SAT or ACT scores, and a $50 nonrefundable application fee. Prospective students may apply at any time of the year. Applications may be submitted online or mailed to the School.

For the most recent information regarding admission requirements, please refer to the current academic catalog.

Application and Information

To obtain an application, make arrangements for an interview, or tour the school, prospective students should contact:

The Art Institute of Washington
1820 North Fort Myer Drive
Arlington, Virginia 22209-1802
Phone: 703-358-9550
      877-303-3771 (toll-free)
Fax: 703-358-9759
Web site: http://www.artinstitutes.edu/arlington

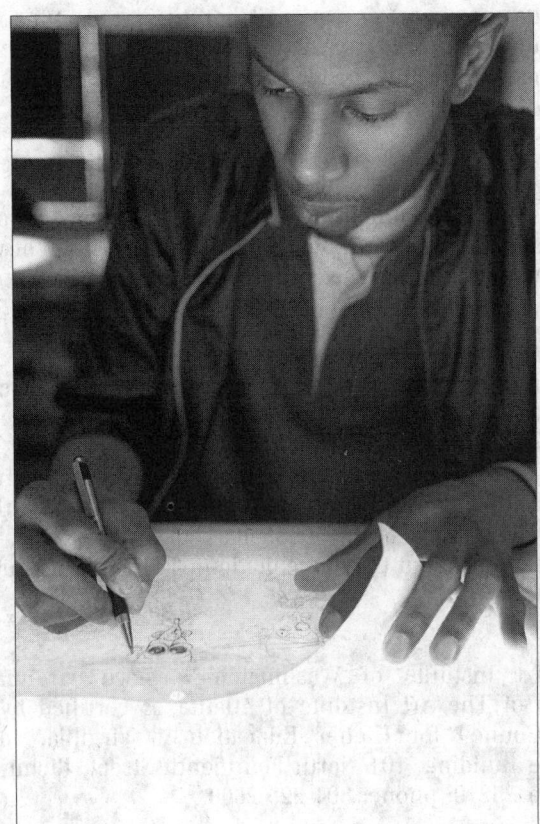

The Art Institute of Atlanta; The Art Institute of Atlanta–Decatur[1]; The Art Institute of Austin[2]; The Art Institute of California–Hollywood; The Art Institute of California–Inland Empire; The Art Institute of California–Los Angeles; The Art Institute of California–Orange County; The Art Institute of California–Sacramento; The Art Institute of California–San Diego; The Art Institute of California–San Francisco; The Art Institute of California–Sunnyvale; The Art Institute of Charleston[1]; The Art Institute of Charlotte; The Art Institute of Colorado; The Art Institute of Dallas[3]; The Art Institute of Fort Lauderdale; The Art Institute of Fort Worth[3]; The Art Institute of Houston; The Art Institute of Houston–North[2]; The Art Institute of Indianapolis[4]; The Art Institute of Jacksonville[5]; The Art Institute of Las Vegas; The Art Institute of Michigan; The Art Institute of New York City; The Art Institute of Ohio–Cincinnati[6]; The Art Institute of Philadelphia; The Art Institute of Phoenix; The Art Institute of Pittsburgh; The Art Institute of Portland; The Art Institute of Raleigh–Durham; The Art Institute of Salt Lake City; The Art Institute of San Antonio[2];The Art Institute of Seattle; The Art Institute of Tampa[5]; The Art Institute of Tennessee–Nashville[1]; The Art Institute of Tucson; The Art Institute of Vancouver; The Art Institute of Virginia Beach[1,7]; The Art Institute of Washington[1,7]; The Art Institute of Washington–Northern Virginia[1,7]; The Art Institute of Wisconsin; The Art Institute of York–Pennsylvania; The Art Institutes International–Kansas City; The Art Institutes International Minnesota; The Illinois Institute of Art–Chicago; The Illinois Institute of Art–Schaumburg; The Illinois Institute of Art–Tinley Park; Miami International University of Art & Design; The New England Institute of Art.

[1] A branch of The Art Institute of Atlanta
[2] A branch of The Art Institute of Houston
[3] A campus of South University
[4] The Art Institute of Indianapolis is regulated by the Indiana Commission on Proprietary Education, 302 West Washington Street, Room E201, Indianapolis, Indiana 46204, AC-0080
[5] A branch of Miami International University of Art & Design
[6] The Art Institute of Ohio–Cincinnati, 8845 Governors Hill Drive, Suite 100, Cincinnati, Ohio 45249-3317, OH Reg. #04-01-1698B
[7] Certified by the State Council of Higher Education to operate in Virginia

THE ART INSTITUTE OF WASHINGTON–NORTHERN VIRGINIA
DULLES, VIRGINIA

A focused education from The Art Institute of Washington–Northern Virginia, a branch of The Art Institute of Atlanta, can help students turn their creative energy into a powerful tool that can make a difference in the world. Students are part of a collaborative and supportive community, where experienced instructors provide the guidance and skills needed to pursue a career in the creative economy.

The school's programs in the areas of design, media arts, and fashion give students the opportunity to learn by using professional-grade technology and build a portfolio of work to show potential employers after graduation.

The Art Institute of Washington–Northern Virginia is a branch campus of The Art Institute of Atlanta. The Art Institute of Atlanta is accredited by the Commission on Colleges of the Southern Association of Colleges and Schools to award associate and baccalaureate degrees. Contact the Commission on Colleges at 1866 Southern Lane, Decatur, Georgia 30033-4097 or call 404-679-4500 for questions about the accreditation of The Art Institute of Atlanta.

The Art Institute of Washington–Northern Virginia, a branch of The Art Institute of Atlanta, is certified by the State Council for Higher Education in Virginia, James Monroe Building, 101 North Fourteenth Street, Richmond, Virginia 23219; phone: 804-225-2600.

Location

Dulles is part of the Washington D.C. metropolitan area, with a regional population of 5.3 million people. Several large corporations, including MCI and AOL, are based here. The close proximity of Dulles to the nation's capital provides students the opportunity to experience the arts, museums, and national monuments. Students can enjoy performances by the National Symphony Orchestra, Washington National Opera, or the Washington Ballet at the John F. Kennedy Center for the Performing Arts. The area also offers five professional sports teams: the Wizards, Capitals, Nationals, D.C. United, and Redskins.

Programs of Study and Degrees

No matter which course of study a student may choose, the professionals at The Art Institute of Washington–Northern Virginia will guide, support, and help each student as their talents evolve on their journey of personal and professional transformation. Students studying design learn to fine-tune their visual thinking and problem-solving skills, as they create everything from logos to TV ads. Programs in the area of media arts focus on utilizing technology to deliver information and entertainment, while students studying fashion learn to market and merchandise clothing.

Bachelor's degree programs are offered in advertising, fashion and retail management, graphic design, interior design, media arts and animation, photographic imaging, and Web design and interactive media.

Associate degree programs are offered in graphic design and Web design and interactive media.

Academic Programs

The Art Institute of Washington–Northern Virginia operates on a year-round, four-quarter system.

Academic Facilities

The Art Institute of Washington–Northern Virginia provides a learning environment with professional-grade technology applicable to each student's course of study. Students have the opportunity to build a portfolio of work that shows potential employers that they are trained to use the software, hardware, or equipment utilized within the industry. Depending upon the course of study, students are immersed in a creative environment—from classrooms to computer labs to studios—focused on relevant, hands-on education designed to prepare students for the real world.

Costs

Tuition cost varies by program. Prospective students should contact the school for current tuition costs. Other charges include a starting kit for all first-quarter students. Kits vary in price depending on the program of study.

Financial Aid

Financial aid is available for those who qualify. Students who require financial assistance should first complete and submit a Free Application for Federal Student Aid (FAFSA) and meet with a financial aid officer.

Faculty

Faculty members are experienced professionals who create a learning environment that is similar to the professional world students will face after graduation. Instructors are focused on helping students develop the skills they need to transform their creative potential into marketable skills.

Admission Requirements

Applicants must provide proof of high school graduation or achievement of a General Educational Development (GED) certificate as a prerequisite for admission.

In lieu of documenting high school graduation or a GED certificate, applicants may provide proof of attaining an associate degree or higher from an accredited institution. An official transcript indicating date of high school graduation, GED certificate (including test scores), or date of college graduation (including degree granted) is required as proof.

All individuals seeking admission to The Art Institute of Washington–Northern Virginia are interviewed in person or by phone by an assistant director of admissions, and each applicant must create an original essay of at least 150 words stating how an education at The Art Institute of Washington–Northern Virginia would help the student to achieve career goals. There is a $50 application fee.

For the most recent information regarding admission requirements, please refer to the current academic catalog.

Application and Information

To obtain an application, make arrangements for an interview, or tour the school, prospective students should contact:

The Art Institute of Washington–Northern Virginia
The Corporate Office Park at Dulles Town Center
21000 Atlantic Blvd., Suite 100
Dulles, Virginia 20166

Phone: 571-449-4400
        888-627-5008 (toll-free)
Fax: 571-449-4500
Web site: http://www.artinstitutes.edu/northern-virginia

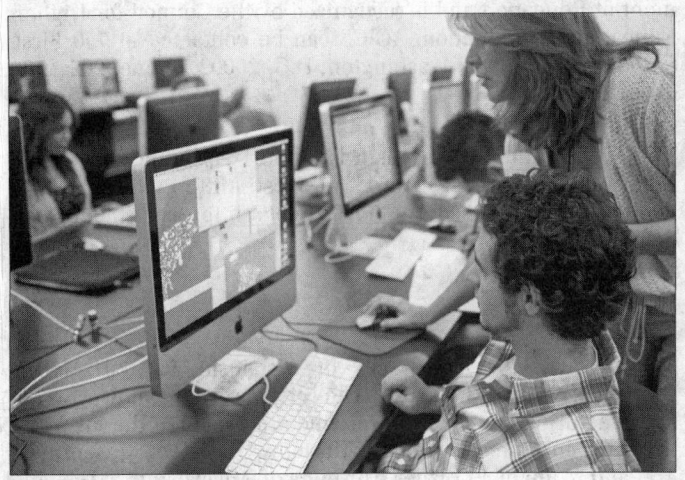

The Art Institute of Atlanta; The Art Institute of Atlanta–Decatur[1]; The Art Institute of Austin[2]; The Art Institute of California–Hollywood; The Art Institute of California–Inland Empire; The Art Institute of California–Los Angeles; The Art Institute of California–Orange County; The Art Institute of California–Sacramento; The Art Institute of California–San Diego; The Art Institute of California–San Francisco; The Art Institute of California–Sunnyvale; The Art Institute of Charleston[1]; The Art Institute of Charlotte; The Art Institute of Colorado; The Art Institute of Dallas[3]; The Art Institute of Fort Lauderdale; The Art Institute of Fort Worth[3]; The Art Institute of Houston; The Art Institute of Houston–North[2]; The Art Institute of Indianapolis[4]; The Art Institute of Jacksonville[5]; The Art Institute of Las Vegas; The Art Institute of Michigan; The Art Institute of New York City; The Art Institute of Ohio–Cincinnati[6]; The Art Institute of Philadelphia; The Art Institute of Phoenix; The Art Institute of Pittsburgh; The Art Institute of Portland; The Art Institute of Raleigh–Durham; The Art Institute of Salt Lake City; The Art Institute of San Antonio[2]; The Art Institute of Seattle; The Art Institute of Tampa[5]; The Art Institute of Tennessee–Nashville[1]; The Art Institute of Tucson; The Art Institute of Vancouver; The Art Institute of Virginia Beach[1,7]; The Art Institute of Washington[1,7]; The Art Institute of Washington–Northern Virginia[1,7]; The Art Institute of Wisconsin; The Art Institute of York–Pennsylvania; The Art Institutes International–Kansas City; The Art Institutes International Minnesota; The Illinois Institute of Art–Chicago; The Illinois Institute of Art–Schaumburg; The Illinois Institute of Art–Tinley Park; Miami International University of Art & Design; The New England Institute of Art.

[1] A branch of The Art Institute of Atlanta
[2] A branch of The Art Institute of Houston
[3] A campus of South University
[4] The Art Institute of Indianapolis is regulated by the Indiana Commission on Proprietary Education, 302 West Washington Street, Room E201, Indianapolis, Indiana 46204, AC-0080
[5] A branch of Miami International University of Art & Design
[6] The Art Institute of Ohio–Cincinnati, 8845 Governors Hill Drive, Suite 100, Cincinnati, Ohio 45249-3317, OH Reg. #04-01-1698B
[7] Certified by the State Council of Higher Education to operate in Virginia

THE ART INSTITUTE OF WISCONSIN

MILWAUKEE, WISCONSIN

A focused education from The Art Institute of Wisconsin can help students turn their creative energy into a powerful tool that can make a difference in the world. Students are part of a collaborative and supportive community, where experienced instructors provide the guidance and skills needed to pursue a career in the creative economy.

The school's programs in the areas of design, media arts, and fashion give students the opportunity to learn by using professional-grade technology and build a portfolio of work to show potential employers after graduation.

The Art Institute of Wisconsin is accredited by the Accrediting Council for Independent Colleges and Schools to award bachelor's and associate degrees. The Accrediting Council for Independent Colleges and Schools is listed as a nationally recognized accrediting agency by the United States Department of Education and is recognized by the Council for Higher Education Accreditation. ACICS can be contacted at 750 First Street NE, Suite 980, Washington, D.C. 20002; phone: 202-336-6780.

The Art Institute of Wisconsin is authorized by the Wisconsin Educational Approval Board, 30 West Mifflin Street, Ninth floor, Madison, Wisconsin 53708-8696; http://eab.state.wi.us/default.asp.

Location

Milwaukee is the largest city in Wisconsin, located on the shores of Lake Michigan. The city is well known as a manufacturing center. Cultural amenities include the Milwaukee Art Museum, Grohmann Museum, Haggerty Museum of Art, and William F. Eisner Museum of Advertising & Design, as well as the Milwaukee Symphony Orchestra, Marcus Center for the Performing Arts, and Milwaukee Ballet.

Programs of Study and Degrees

No matter which course of study a student may choose, the professionals at The Art Institute of Wisconsin will guide, support, and help each student as their talents evolve on their journey of personal and professional transformation. Students studying design learn to fine-tune their visual thinking and problem-solving skills, as they create everything from logos to TV ads. Programs in the area of media arts focus on utilizing technology to deliver information and entertainment, while students studying fashion learn to market and merchandise clothing.

Bachelor's degree programs are offered in advertising, digital filmmaking and video production, fashion marketing, graphic design, interior design, media arts and animation, and web design and interactive media.

An associate degree program is offered in graphic design.

Academic Programs

The Art Institute of Wisconsin operates on a year-round, four-quarter system.

Academic Facilities

The Art Institute of Wisconsin provides a learning environment with professional-grade technology applicable to each student's course of study. Students have the opportunity to build a portfolio of work that shows potential employers that they are trained to use the software, hardware, or equipment utilized within the industry. Depending upon the course of study, students are immersed in a creative environment—from classrooms to computer labs to studios—focused on relevant, hands-on education designed to prepare students for the real world.

Costs

Tuition cost varies by program. Prospective students should contact the School for current tuition costs. Other charges include a starting kit for all first-quarter students. Kits vary in price, depending on the program of study.

Financial Aid

Financial aid is available for those who qualify. Students who require financial assistance should first complete and submit a Free Application for Federal Student Aid (FAFSA) and meet with a financial aid officer.

Faculty

Faculty members are experienced professionals who create a learning environment that is similar to the professional world students will face after graduation. Instructors are focused on helping students develop the skills they need to transform their creative potential into marketable skills.

Admission Requirements

Applicants must provide proof of high school graduation or achievement of a General Educational Development (GED) certificate as a prerequisite for admission. In lieu of documenting high school graduation or a GED certificate, applicants may provide proof of attaining an associate degree or higher from an accredited institution. An official transcript indicating date of high school graduation, GED certificate (including test scores), or date of college graduation (including degree granted) is required as proof.

All individuals seeking admission to The Art Institute of Wisconsin are interviewed in person or by phone by an assistant director of admissions, and each applicant must create an original essay of at least 150 words stating how an education at The Art Institute of Wisconsin would help the student to achieve career goals. There is a $50 application fee.

For the most recent information regarding admission requirements, please refer to the current academic catalog.

Application and Information

To obtain an application, make arrangements for an interview, or tour the school, prospective students should contact:

The Art Institute of Wisconsin
320 East Buffalo Street
Suite 100
Milwaukee, Wisconsin 53202
Phone: 414-978-5000
        877-285-4234 (toll-free)
Fax: 414-978-5182

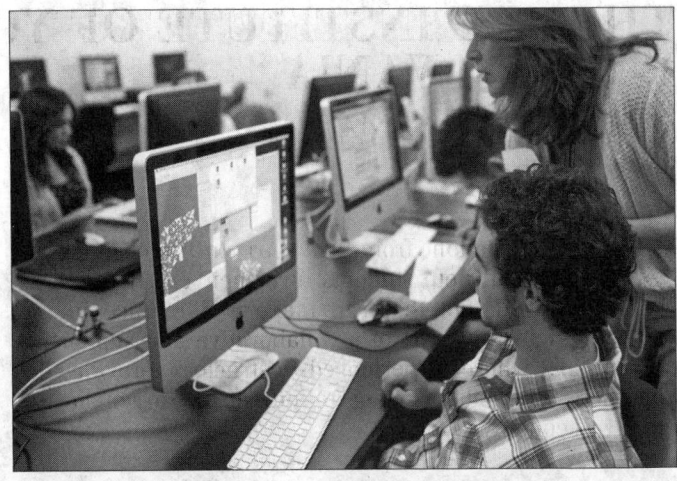

Web site: http://www.artinstitutes.edu/milwaukee

The Art Institute of Atlanta; The Art Institute of Atlanta–Decatur[1]; The Art Institute of Austin[2]; The Art Institute of California–Hollywood; The Art Institute of California–Inland Empire; The Art Institute of California–Los Angeles; The Art Institute of California–Orange County; The Art Institute of California–Sacramento; The Art Institute of California–San Diego; The Art Institute of California–San Francisco; The Art Institute of California–Sunnyvale; The Art Institute of Charleston[1]; The Art Institute of Charlotte; The Art Institute of Colorado; The Art Institute of Dallas[3]; The Art Institute of Fort Lauderdale; The Art Institute of Fort Worth[3]; The Art Institute of Houston; The Art Institute of Houston–North[2]; The Art Institute of Indianapolis[4]; The Art Institute of Jacksonville[5]; The Art Institute of Las Vegas; The Art Institute of Michigan; The Art Institute of New York City; The Art Institute of Ohio–Cincinnati[6]; The Art Institute of Philadelphia; The Art Institute of Phoenix; The Art Institute of Pittsburgh; The Art Institute of Portland; The Art Institute of Raleigh–Durham; The Art Institute of Salt Lake City; The Art Institute of San Antonio[2];The Art Institute of Seattle; The Art Institute of Tampa[5]; The Art Institute of Tennessee–Nashville[1]; The Art Institute of Tucson; The Art Institute of Vancouver; The Art Institute of Virginia Beach[1,7]; The Art Institute of Washington[1,7]; The Art Institute of Washington–Northern Virginia[1,7]; The Art Institute of Wisconsin; The Art Institute of York–Pennsylvania; The Art Institutes International–Kansas City; The Art Institutes International Minnesota; The Illinois Institute of Art–Chicago; The Illinois Institute of Art–Schaumburg; The Illinois Institute of Art–Tinley Park; Miami International University of Art & Design; The New England Institute of Art.

[1] A branch of The Art Institute of Atlanta
[2] A branch of The Art Institute of Houston
[3] A campus of South University
[4] The Art Institute of Indianapolis is regulated by the Indiana Commission on Proprietary Education, 302 West Washington Street, Room E201, Indianapolis, Indiana 46204, AC-0080
[5] A branch of Miami International University of Art & Design
[6] The Art Institute of Ohio–Cincinnati, 8845 Governors Hill Drive, Suite 100, Cincinnati, Ohio 45249-3317, OH Reg. #04-01-1698B
[7] Certified by the State Council of Higher Education to operate in Virginia

THE ART INSTITUTE OF YORK–PENNSYLVANIA

YORK, PENNSYLVANIA

A focused education from The Art Institute of York–Pennsylvania can help students turn their creative energy into a powerful tool that can make a difference in the world. Students are part of a collaborative and supportive community, where experienced instructors provide the guidance and skills needed to pursue a career in the creative economy.

The school's programs in the areas of design, media arts, and fashion give students the opportunity to learn by using professional-grade technology and build a portfolio of work to show potential employers after graduation.

The Art Institute of York–Pennsylvania is accredited by the Accrediting Commission of Career Schools and Colleges (ACCSC). ACCSC may be contacted at 2101 Wilson Boulevard, Suite 302, Arlington, Virginia 22201; phone: 703-247-4212.

The Art Institute of York–Pennsylvania is authorized by the Pennsylvania Department of Education to confer the Bachelor of Science degrees and Associate of Science degrees. The Department of Education can be contacted at the Commonwealth of Pennsylvania, Department of Education Office of Postsecondary and Higher Education, 333 Market Street, Harrisburg, Pennsylvania 17126; phone: 717-783-6788.

Location

The Art Institute of York–Pennsylvania is located in York, a suburban area in south-central Pennsylvania. Surrounded by sprawling hills and Amish farmlands, York offers visitors an abundance of shopping areas and museums and three centuries of American history, including battlefields from the Revolutionary and Civil wars. York is a 30-minute drive from Hershey and Harrisburg, Pennsylvania; approximately a 90-minute drive from Philadelphia; and a 1-hour drive from Baltimore, Maryland.

Programs of Study and Degrees

No matter which course of study a student may choose, the professionals at The Art Institute of York–Pennsylvania will guide, support, and help each student as their talents evolve on their journey of personal and professional transformation. Students studying design learn to fine-tune their visual thinking and problem-solving skills, as they create everything from logos to TV ads. Programs in the area of media arts focus on utilizing technology to deliver information and entertainment, while students studying fashion learn to market and merchandise clothing.

Bachelor's degree programs are offered in fashion and retail management, graphic design, interior design, media arts and animation, and Web design and interactive media.

Associate degrees are offered in graphic design and kitchen and bath design.

Academic Programs

The Art Institute of York–Pennsylvania operates on a year-round, four-quarter system.

Academic Facilities

The Art Institute of York–Pennsylvania provides a learning environment with professional-grade technology applicable to each student's course of study. Students have the opportunity to build a portfolio of work that shows potential employers that they are trained to use the software, hardware, or equipment utilized within the industry. Depending upon the course of study, students are immersed in a creative environment—from classrooms to computer labs to studios—focused on relevant, hands-on education designed to prepare students for the real world.

Costs

Tuition cost varies by program. Prospective students should contact the school for current tuition costs. Other charges include a starting kit for all first-quarter students. Kits vary in price depending on the program of study.

Financial Aid

Financial aid is available for those who qualify. Students who require financial assistance should first complete and submit a Free Application for Federal Student Aid (FAFSA) and meet with a financial aid officer.

Faculty

Faculty members are experienced professionals who create a learning environment that is similar to the professional world students will face after graduation. Instructors are focused on helping students develop the skills they need to transform their creative potential into marketable skills.

Admission Requirements

The Art Institute of York–Pennsylvania encourages interested students to apply early. To apply, students must possess a high school diploma or General Educational Development (GED) certificate and a minimum SAT score of 800 (at least 400 math and 400 verbal) or a minimum ACT score of 16. A portfolio review may be required. There is a $50 application fee.

For the most recent information regarding admission requirements, please refer to the current academic catalog.

Application and Information

To obtain an application or make arrangements for an interview or tour of the school, prospective students should contact:

The Art Institute of York–Pennsylvania
1409 Williams Road
York, Pennsylvania 17402-9012

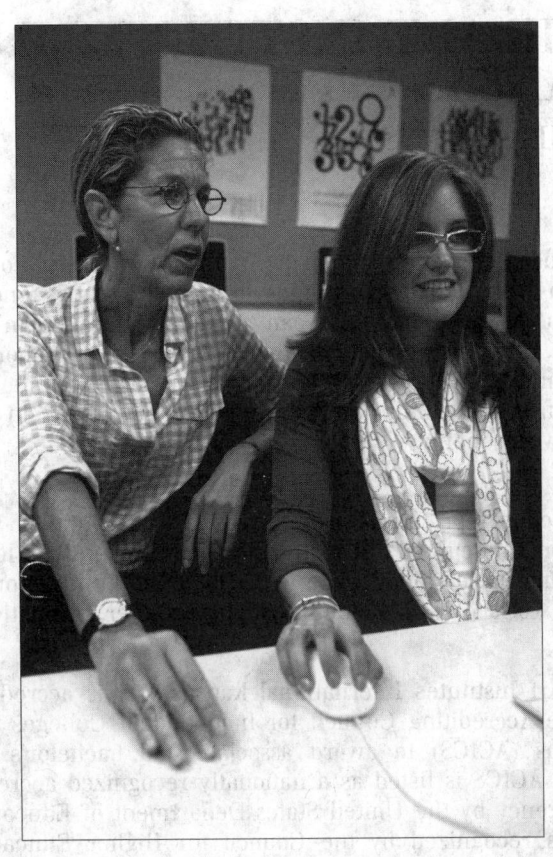

Phone: 717-755-2300
       800-864-7725 (toll-free)
Fax: 717-840-1951
Web site: http://www.artinstitutes.edu/york

The Art Institute of Atlanta; The Art Institute of Atlanta–Decatur[1]; The Art Institute of Austin[2]; The Art Institute of California–Hollywood; The Art Institute of California–Inland Empire; The Art Institute of California–Los Angeles; The Art Institute of California–Orange County; The Art Institute of California–Sacramento; The Art Institute of California–San Diego; The Art Institute of California–San Francisco; The Art Institute of California–Sunnyvale; The Art Institute of Charleston[1]; The Art Institute of Charlotte; The Art Institute of Colorado; The Art Institute of Dallas[3]; The Art Institute of Fort Lauderdale; The Art Institute of Fort Worth[3]; The Art Institute of Houston; The Art Institute of Houston–North[2]; The Art Institute of Indianapolis[4]; The Art Institute of Jacksonville[5]; The Art Institute of Las Vegas; The Art Institute of Michigan; The Art Institute of New York City; The Art Institute of Ohio–Cincinnati[6]; The Art Institute of Philadelphia; The Art Institute of Phoenix; The Art Institute of Pittsburgh; The Art Institute of Portland; The Art Institute of Raleigh–Durham; The Art Institute of Salt Lake City; The Art Institute of San Antonio[2];The Art Institute of Seattle; The Art Institute of Tampa[5]; The Art Institute of Tennessee–Nashville[1]; The Art Institute of Tucson; The Art Institute of Vancouver; The Art Institute of Virginia Beach[1,7]; The Art Institute of Washington[1,7]; The Art Institute of Washington–Northern Virginia[1,7]; The Art Institute of Wisconsin; The Art Institute of York–Pennsylvania; The Art Institutes International–Kansas City; The Art Institutes International Minnesota; The Illinois Institute of Art–Chicago; The Illinois Institute of Art–Schaumburg; The Illinois Institute of Art–Tinley Park; Miami International University of Art & Design; The New England Institute of Art.
[1]A branch of The Art Institute of Atlanta
[2]A branch of The Art Institute of Houston
[3]A campus of South University
[4]The Art Institute of Indianapolis is regulated by the Indiana Commission on Proprietary Education, 302 West Washington Street, Room E201, Indianapolis, Indiana 46204, AC-0080
[5]A branch of Miami International University of Art & Design
[6]The Art Institute of Ohio–Cincinnati, 8845 Governors Hill Drive, Suite 100, Cincinnati, Ohio 45249-3317, OH Reg. #04-01-1698B
[7]Certified by the State Council of Higher Education to operate in Virginia

THE ART INSTITUTES INTERNATIONAL– KANSAS CITY

LENEXA, KANSAS

A focused education from The Art Institutes International– Kansas City can help students turn their creative energy into a powerful tool that can make a difference in the world. Students are part of a collaborative and supportive community, where experienced instructors provide the guidance and skills needed to pursue a career in the creative economy.

The school's programs in the areas of design, media arts, fashion, and culinary give students the opportunity to learn by using professional-grade technology and build a portfolio of work to show potential employers after graduation.

The Art Institutes International–Kansas City is accredited by the Accrediting Council for Independent Colleges and Schools (ACICS) to award associate and bachelor's degrees. ACICS is listed as a nationally recognized accrediting agency by the United States Department of Education and is recognized by the Council for Higher Education Accreditation. ACICS can be contacted at 750 First Street NE, Suite 980, Washington, D.C. 20002; phone: 202-336-6780.

The Kansas Board of Regents has approved The Art Institutes International–Kansas City to operate in the state of Kansas. The Kansas Board of Regents may be contacted at the following address: Kansas Board of Regents, Private Postsecondary Education Division, 1000 SW Jackson Street, Suite 520, Topeka, Kansas 66612-1368; phone: 785-296-0911; fax: 785-296-4526.

Location

Lenexa is part of the Kansas City metropolitan area of nearly two million people. Kansas City's contributions to jazz and the blues are well known. The city is also home to over 200 fountains and more boulevards than any city besides Paris.

Programs of Study and Degrees

No matter which course of study a student may choose, the professionals at The Art Institutes International–Kansas City will guide, support, and help each student as their talents evolve on their journey of personal and professional transformation. Students studying design learn to fine-tune their visual thinking and problem-solving skills, as they create everything from logos to TV ads. Programs

in the area of media arts focus on utilizing technology to deliver information and entertainment, while students studying fashion learn to design clothes for the runway or run a retail shop. Culinary programs focus on the fundamental techniques while exposing students to a full menu of international cuisines and management techniques.

Bachelor's degree programs are offered in advertising, culinary arts, digital filmmaking and video production, fashion marketing, graphic design, interior design, photography, and Web design and interactive media.

Associate degree programs are offered in baking and pastry arts, culinary arts, and graphic design.

Diploma programs are offered in baking and pastry and culinary arts.

Academic Programs

The Art Institutes International–Kansas City operates on a year-round, four-quarter system.

Academic Facilities

The Art Institutes International–Kansas City provides a learning environment with professional-grade technology applicable to each student's course of study. Students have the opportunity to build a portfolio of work that shows potential employers that they are trained to use the software, hardware, or equipment utilized within the industry. Depending upon the course of study, students are immersed in a creative environment—from classrooms to computer labs to studios—focused on relevant, hands-on education designed to prepare students for the real world.

Costs

Tuition cost varies by program. Prospective students should contact the School for current tuition costs. Other charges include a starting kit for all first-quarter students. Kits vary in price depending on the program of study.

Financial Aid

Financial aid is available for those who qualify. Students who require financial assistance should first complete and submit a Free Application for Federal Student Aid (FAFSA) and meet with a financial aid officer.

Faculty

Faculty members are experienced professionals who create a learning environment that is similar to the professional world students will face after graduation. Instructors are focused on helping students develop the skills they need to transform their creative potential into marketable skills.

Admission Requirements

Applicants must provide proof of high school graduation or achievement of a General Educational Development (GED) certificate as a prerequisite for admission. In lieu of documenting high school graduation or a GED certificate, applicants may provide proof of attaining an associate degree or higher from an accredited institution. An official transcript indicating date of high school graduation, GED certificate (including test scores), or date of college graduation (including degree granted) is required as proof.

All individuals seeking admission to The Art Institutes International–Kansas City are interviewed in person or by phone by an assistant director of admissions, and each applicant must create an original essay of at least 150 words stating how an education at The Art Institutes International–Kansas City would help the student to achieve career goals. There is a $50 application fee.

For the most recent information regarding admission requirements, please refer to the current academic catalog.

Application and Information

To obtain an application, arrange for an interview, or tour the school, prospective students should contact:

The Art Institutes International–Kansas City
8208 Melrose Drive
Lenexa, Kansas 66214
Phone: 913-217-4600
          866-530-8508 (toll-free)
Fax: 913-217-4690
Web site: http://www.artinstitutes.edu/kansascity

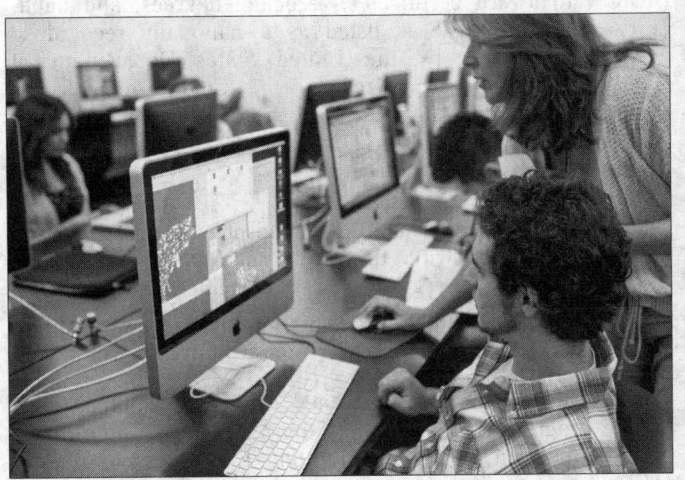

The Art Institute of Atlanta; The Art Institute of Atlanta–Decatur[1]; The Art Institute of Austin[2]; The Art Institute of California–Hollywood; The Art Institute of California–Inland Empire; The Art Institute of California–Los Angeles; The Art Institute of California–Orange County; The Art Institute of California–Sacramento; The Art Institute of California–San Diego; The Art Institute of California–San Francisco; The Art Institute of California–Sunnyvale; The Art Institute of Charleston[1]; The Art Institute of Charlotte; The Art Institute of Colorado; The Art Institute of Dallas[5]; The Art Institute of Fort Lauderdale; The Art Institute of Fort Worth[3]; The Art Institute of Houston; The Art Institute of Houston–North[2]; The Art Institute of Indianapolis[4]; The Art Institute of Jacksonville[5]; The Art Institute of Las Vegas; The Art Institute of Michigan; The Art Institute of New York City; The Art Institute of Ohio–Cincinnati[6]; The Art Institute of Philadelphia; The Art Institute of Phoenix; The Art Institute of Pittsburgh; The Art Institute of Portland; The Art Institute of Raleigh–Durham; The Art Institute of Salt Lake City; The Art Institute of San Antonio[2];The Art Institute of Seattle; The Art Institute of Tampa[5]; The Art Institute of Tennessee–Nashville[1]; The Art Institute of Tucson; The Art Institute of Vancouver; The Art Institute of Virginia Beach[1,7]; The Art Institute of Washington[1,7]; The Art Institute of Washington–Northern Virginia[1,7]; The Art Institute of Wisconsin; The Art Institute of York–Pennsylvania; The Art Institutes International–Kansas City; The Art Institutes International Minnesota; The Illinois Institute of Art–Chicago; The Illinois Institute of Art–Schaumburg; The Illinois Institute of Art–Tinley Park; Miami International University of Art & Design; The New England Institute of Art.

[1]A branch of The Art Institute of Atlanta
[2]A branch of The Art Institute of Houston
[3]A campus of South University
[4]The Art Institute of Indianapolis is regulated by the Indiana Commission on Proprietary Education, 302 West Washington Street, Room E201, Indianapolis, Indiana 46204, AC-0080
[5]A branch of Miami International University of Art & Design
[6]The Art Institute of Ohio–Cincinnati, 8845 Governors Hill Drive, Suite 100, Cincinnati, Ohio 45249-3317, OH Reg. #04-01-1698B
[7]Certified by the State Council of Higher Education to operate in Virginia

THE ART INSTITUTES INTERNATIONAL MINNESOTA

MINNEAPOLIS, MINNESOTA

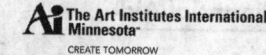

A focused education from The Art Institutes International Minnesota can help students turn their creative energy into a powerful tool that can make a difference in the world. Students are part of a collaborative and supportive community, where experienced instructors provide the guidance and skills needed to pursue a career in the creative economy.

The school's programs in the areas of design, media arts, fashion, and culinary give students the opportunity to learn by using professional-grade technology and build a portfolio of work to show potential employers after graduation.

The Art Institutes International Minnesota is accredited by the Accrediting Council for Independent Colleges and Schools (ACICS) to award certificates, associate degrees, and bachelor's degrees. ACICS is listed as a nationally recognized accrediting agency by the United States Department of Education and is recognized by the Council for Higher Education Accreditation. ACICS can be contacted at 750 First Street NE, Suite 980, Washington, D.C. 20002; phone: 202-336-6780.

The Art Institutes International Minnesota is registered as a private institution with the Minnesota Office of Higher Education (1450 Energy Park Drive, Suite 350, St. Paul, Minnesota 55108; phone: 651-642-0567; http://www.ohe.state.mn.us) pursuant to sections 136A.61 to 136A.71.

The Associate in Applied Science degree in culinary arts degree program is accredited by the Accrediting Commission of the American Culinary Federation Education Foundation (ACF).

Location

Minneapolis is a thriving environment for creative minds; home to culture, arts, and entertainment. The Twin Cities region has many Fortune 500 companies, including Target, Best Buy, 3M, and General Mills. The area is also home to a top design and advertising market and is a major U.S. business hub.

Programs of Study and Degrees

No matter which course of study a student may choose, the professionals at The Art Institutes International Minnesota will guide, support, and help each student as their talents evolve on their journey of personal and professional transformation. Students studying design learn to fine-tune their visual thinking and problem-solving skills, as they create everything from logos to TV ads. Programs in the area of media arts focus on utilizing technology to deliver information and entertainment, while students studying fashion learn to design clothes for the runway or run a retail shop. Culinary programs focus on the fundamental techniques while exposing students to a full menu of international cuisines and management techniques.

Bachelor's degree programs are offered in advertising, audio production, culinary management, design management, digital film and video production, fashion and retail management, graphic design, hospitality management, interior design, media arts and animation, photography, visual effects and motion graphics, and Web design and interactive media.

Associate degree programs are offered in baking and pastry, culinary arts, graphic design, interior design, interior planning with AutoCAD, and Web design and interactive media.

Diploma programs are offered in baking and pastry and the art of cooking.

The programs in culinary arts, culinary management, graphic design, and Web design and interactive media are available in an evening and weekend option format.

Academic Programs

The Art Institutes International Minnesota operates on a year-round, four-quarter system.

Academic Facilities

The Art Institutes International Minnesota provides a learning environment with professional-grade technology applicable to each student's course of study. Students have the opportunity to build a portfolio of work that shows potential employers that they are trained to use the software, hardware, or equipment utilized within the industry. Depending upon the course of study, students are immersed in a creative environment—from classrooms to computer labs to studios—focused on relevant, hands-on education designed to prepare students for the real world.

Costs

Tuition cost varies by program. Prospective students should contact the school for current tuition costs. Other charges include a starting kit for all first-quarter students. Kits vary in price depending on the program of study.

Financial Aid

Financial aid is available for those who qualify. Students who require financial assistance should first complete and submit a Free Application for Federal Student Aid (FAFSA) and meet with a financial aid officer.

Faculty

Faculty members are experienced professionals who create a learning environment that is similar to the professional world students will face after graduation. Instructors are focused on

helping students develop the skills they need to transform their creative potential into marketable skills.

Admission Requirements

Applicants must provide proof of high school graduation or achievement of a General Educational Development (GED) certificate as a prerequisite for admission. In lieu of documenting high school graduation or a GED certificate, applicants may provide proof of attaining an associate degree or higher from an accredited institution. An official transcript indicating date of high school graduation, GED certificate (including test scores), or date of college graduation (including degree granted) is required as proof.

All individuals seeking admission to The Art Institutes International Minnesota are interviewed in person or by phone by an assistant director of admissions, and each applicant must create an original essay of at least 150 words stating how an education at The Art Institutes International Minnesota would help the student to achieve career goals. There is a $50 application fee.

For the most recent information regarding admission requirements, please refer to the current academic catalog.

Application and Information

To obtain an application, arrange for an interview, or tour the school, prospective students should contact:

The Art Institutes International Minnesota
15 South 9th Street
Minneapolis, Minnesota 55402-3105
Phone: 612-332-3361
        800-777-3643 (toll-free)
Fax: 612-332-3934
Web site: http://www.artinstitutes.edu/minneapolis

The Art Institute of Atlanta; The Art Institute of Atlanta–Decatur[1]; The Art Institute of Austin[2]; The Art Institute of California–Hollywood; The Art Institute of California–Inland Empire; The Art Institute of California–Los Angeles; The Art Institute of California–Orange County; The Art Institute of California–Sacramento; The Art Institute of California–San Diego; The Art Institute of California–San Francisco; The Art Institute of California–Sunnyvale; The Art Institute of Charleston[1]; The Art Institute of Charlotte; The Art Institute of Colorado; The Art Institute of Dallas[3]; The Art Institute of Fort Lauderdale; The Art Institute of Fort Worth[3]; The Art Institute of Houston; The Art Institute of Houston–North[2]; The Art Institute of Indianapolis[4]; The Art Institute of Jacksonville[5]; The Art Institute of Las Vegas; The Art Institute of Michigan; The Art Institute of New York City; The Art Institute of Ohio–Cincinnati[6]; The Art Institute of Philadelphia; The Art Institute of Phoenix; The Art Institute of Pittsburgh; The Art Institute of Portland; The Art Institute of Raleigh–Durham; The Art Institute of Salt Lake City; The Art Institute of San Antonio[2];The Art Institute of Seattle; The Art Institute of Tampa[5]; The Art Institute of Tennessee–Nashville[1]; The Art Institute of Tucson; The Art Institute of Vancouver; The Art Institute of Virginia Beach[1,7]; The Art Institute of Washington[1,7]; The Art Institute of Washington–Northern Virginia[1,7]; The Art Institute of Wisconsin; The Art Institute of York–Pennsylvania; The Art Institutes International–Kansas City; The Art Institutes International Minnesota; The Illinois Institute of Art–Chicago; The Illinois Institute of Art–Schaumburg; The Illinois Institute of Art–Tinley Park; Miami International University of Art & Design; The New England Institute of Art.

[1]A branch of The Art Institute of Atlanta
[2]A branch of The Art Institute of Houston
[3]A campus of South University
[4]The Art Institute of Indianapolis is regulated by the Indiana Commission on Proprietary Education, 302 West Washington Street, Room E201, Indianapolis, Indiana 46204, AC-0080
[5]A branch of Miami International University of Art & Design
[6]The Art Institute of Ohio–Cincinnati, 8845 Governors Hill Drive, Suite 100, Cincinnati, Ohio 45249-3317, OH Reg. #04-01-1698B
[7]Certified by the State Council of Higher Education to operate in Virginia

ASSUMPTION COLLEGE
WORCESTER, MASSACHUSETTS

The College

Assumption College, established in 1904 by the Augustinians of the Assumption, is a coeducational institution known for its classic liberal arts curriculum and strong academic programs in business and professional studies. The College's 2,000 undergraduates choose among forty majors and forty-four minors, gaining a depth and breadth of knowledge that is the foundation of lifelong success. Their educational experience is grounded in the rich Catholic intellectual tradition, which cultivates both the intellect and personal values students need to meet the demands of a constantly changing world. Undergraduates and graduate students interact closely with faculty members and staff in a thriving community that develops graduates known for critical intelligence, thoughtful citizenship, and compassionate service.

The academic atmosphere is marked by individual attention and the quest for personal excellence. With a student-faculty ratio of just 11:1, Assumption's professors serve as mentors, who challenge students to ask questions, find their own answers, and grow—intellectually, socially, and spiritually. Students are encouraged to gain hands-on experience at internships and to participate in individual research projects. The result is that 97 percent of the graduates who a survey six months after graduation are either employed or in graduate school.

At Assumption, 90 percent of the undergraduates live on campus and housing is guaranteed for all four years. The campus is lively seven days a week with academic programming, activities sponsored by student clubs and organizations, community service opportunities, campus ministry programs, and intercollegiate, intramural, and club sports. The College's state-of-the-art recreation center supports the well-being of all students.

Location

Spreading across 185 acres, the College's beautiful campus is situated in a residential neighborhood just minutes from downtown Worcester, Massachusetts. Worcester, the second largest city in New England, is a vibrant college town, home to 30,000 students. The city offers extensive opportunities for entertainment, internships, and community service. Great restaurants, cultural venues and programs, retail and entertainment options, and professional sports teams provide students with many off-campus activities. Worcester is also centrally located, with Boston, Providence, Rhode Island, and Hartford, Connecticut, each an hour's drive away. There is regular commuter rail service to Boston.

Majors and Degrees

The College offers Bachelor of Arts degrees. The most popular majors include English (concentrations in literature or writing and mass communications), history, political science, psychology, the natural sciences (biology, biotechnology and molecular biology, chemistry, and environmental science), education, human services and rehabilitation studies, and business disciplines such as accounting, international business, management, marketing, and organizational communication. Minors are offered in forty-four areas.

The College offers graduate degrees in business, special education, school counseling, counseling psychology, and rehabilitation counseling. The College also has agreements with a number of highly regarded institutions so that students can continue their education in medical technology, physical therapy, engineering (a 3-2 program with University of Notre Dame), and law

(3-3 programs with Duquesne, Vermont, and Western New England Law Schools). Joint seven-year programs are also available for those interested in podiatry or optometry.

Preprofessional preparation is available for dentistry, medicine, and law.

Academic Programs

The College's classic liberal arts curriculum promotes the lively discussion of the books, ideas, people, and events that have shaped civilization. Faculty members and students explore the rich Catholic intellectual tradition as they seek truth and the nature of the world.

Assumption also offers academic programs and courses that help students achieve their full potential. The College's first-year program engages new students with linked courses from two disciplines and coordinated activities that complement classroom experiences. The same 20 students take courses in the fall and spring semesters, enabling them to make important intellectual connections, while getting to know other students. The honors program and the Fortin and Gonthier Foundations of Western Civilization Program encourage students to challenge themselves intellectually. Air Force and Army ROTC are also available.

Assumption College follows a traditional two-semester calendar, from late August to mid-May, as well as an optional January intersession. The Graduate School and the Center for Continuing and Career Education also offer two summer sessions for students.

Undergraduates complete a core curriculum that provides a strong foundation in the liberal arts. Students must complete 120 credit hours in all the academic programs to earn a degree.

Off-Campus Programs

The College and twelve other institutions of higher learning created the Colleges of Worcester Consortium to offer the 30,000 college students in the area even greater academic and social opportunities. Assumption students may cross-register for academic credit at any of the participating colleges and enjoy their social and cultural events. Free transportation to many other participating institutions is available.

Eligible students may choose to spend a semester or a year abroad. The College's students have studied abroad in Australia, Austria, Chile, China, Costa Rica, the Czech Republic, England, France, Germany, Greece, Ireland, Italy, Japan, the Netherlands, Spain, and other locations. There are also numerous one- and two-week international experiences led by Assumption faculty.

Students explore their professional choices and broaden their workplace skills at local, regional, national, and international internships. In recent years, they have interned at PBS, the U.S. House of Representatives, Ralph Lauren, the Hungarian Embassy, Smith Barney, Fidelity, *The Daily Show with Jon Stewart*, ABC News, Dean Witter Reynolds, AT&T, and Sony Japan.

Academic Facilities

The College has invested more than $80 million to enhance the campus facilities. Nearly the entire campus is wireless.

The Testa Science Center houses the Department of Natural Sciences and features multiuse classrooms with state-of-the-art technology, ten teaching laboratories, seven laboratories dedicated for faculty and student research, a working greenhouse, conference rooms, and student lounge areas.

The Information Technology Center houses computer labs, technology-rich classrooms, and experienced support staff. Students can learn Web authoring, graphics and animation, digital video, and multimedia production. The digital audio studio is available for all students and faculty members.

Assumption offers a variety of housing options to accommodate the 90 percent of students who live on campus. There are traditional residence halls, suites, a living and learning residence, and apartments. All resident students have individual hard-wired and wireless Internet access in their rooms. The outstanding stadium and athletic facilities support the College's twenty-three NCAA Division II intercollegiate teams, many recreational programs, and the physical well-being of the entire campus community.

Costs

For 2010–11, tuition was $30,940; room and board were $10,260. The board plan is required for all first-year students. Student fees totalled $365. The total for tuition, room and board, and fees was $41,565.

Financial Aid

The College offers financial aid based on demonstrated need and scholastic achievement. The College requires that students submit the Free Application for Federal Student Aid (FAFSA), which is available on January 1. This form should be filed by February 1, so that the College can consider the information as it makes financial aid awards.

All applicants for admission are considered for merit awards up to $20,000 per year. Funds awarded through this program reflect the College's commitment to academic excellence and student leadership.

Faculty

Approximately 90 percent of the Assumption College faculty members hold the doctoral or highest degree in their field. They are active scholars presenting their ideas and research at professional conferences, writing books and articles, and publishing in journals. With a student-to-faculty ratio of 11:1, professors get to know the students—to mentor, encourage, and help students succeed. Professors work closely with students and challenge them to explore new paths of knowledge and make their own discoveries. All of Assumption's academic advisors are full-time faculty members.

Student Government

There are more than sixty clubs and organizations on campus, offering students opportunities in community service, sports, academics, leadership, and special interests. The Student Government Association (SGA), the elected representatives of the student body, coordinates official communication between the student community and the College administration and officially recognizes student clubs and activities.

Admission Requirements

All applicants must graduate from an accredited secondary school with a minimum of 18 academic units. These units should include 4 years of English, 3 years of mathematics, 2 years of a foreign language, 2 years of history, 2 years of science, and 5 additional academic units.

Admission to Assumption is test-score optional. When submitting an application an essay and recommendations are required. Interviews are recommended, but not required.

The number of solid academic courses, including the number of honors-level or Advanced Placement–level courses, is considered during the application review process.

The Admissions Committee understands that grading standards vary from school to school or from one course to another. Class rank provides some context within which to place the grades of students applying from a given school. Some schools also provide grade distribution charts. The Committee also considers whether the applicant's grade point average or rank in class is weighted or unweighted.

Application and Information

Campus visits are strongly recommended. Appointments can be scheduled Monday through Friday. Group Information Sessions are held most Saturdays in the fall.

Applicants must submit a completed application, a $50 application fee, official transcripts, a recommendation, and an essay. Applications for early action must be received by November 15. The deadline for regular admission is February 15. To apply, students may complete the College's application online at http://www.assumption.edu/apply or the Common Application and Supplement at http://www.commonapp.org.

For more information, students should contact:

Office of Admissions
Assumption College
500 Salisbury Street
P.O. Box 15005
Worcester, Massachusetts 01609-1296
Phone: 508-767-7285
       866-477-7776 (toll-free)
E-mail: admiss@assumption.edu
Web site: http://www.assumption.edu

The flagship of Assumption's $80-million physical plant expansion program is the Testa Science Center.

AURORA UNIVERSITY
AURORA, ILLINOIS

AURORA UNIVERSITY

The University

Aurora University was founded in 1893. The school has grown substantially over the years and has taken on many new challenges. In 1938, it was one of the first small colleges to achieve regional accreditation. In 1947, the college's evening program was instituted—one of the nation's first adult education programs at a liberal arts college. In 1985, Aurora College was reorganized as Aurora University, reflecting both the increased size of the institution and the needs associated with its many new programs. In addition to the College of Arts and Sciences, the University comprises the College of Education (including health and physical education) and the College of Professional Studies (social work, nursing, criminal justice, and business). Today, the University enrolls 4,300 students in more than forty undergraduate programs and thirteen graduate degree programs in business, criminal justice, education, nursing, and social work. Also offered are the Doctor of Education (Ed.D.) degree in educational leadership and the Doctor of Social Work (D.S.W.) degree.

Undergraduate degree programs are also offered on the shores of Geneva Lake in Williams Bay, Wisconsin at George Williams College of Aurora University (GWC). Undergraduate degree programs at GWC include elementary education, parks and recreation, social work, and the R.N. to B.S.N. adult degree-completion program. In addition, GWC offers nine graduate degree programs in the areas of education, recreation administration, and social work; the Doctor of Education (Ed.D.) degree in educational leadership; and the Doctor of Social Work (D.S.W.) degree.

The newest educational facility for Aurora University is Woodstock Center in Woodstock, Illinois. Woodstock offers three degree-completion programs: business, criminal justice, and the R.N. to B.S.N. Graduate programs are offered in education, an M.B.A. in leadership, and the M.S.N.

The University's student body includes 675 on-campus, traditional-age students, 1,400 undergraduate commuters, 1,900 graduate students on the Aurora campus, and more than 400 students at the George Williams College campus and Woodstock Center. The majority of Aurora's students come from the upper-Midwest region, but twenty states are also represented.

Social life is based on campus, and most activities are campuswide. The Aurora campus has more than fifty musical, literary, religious, social, and service clubs and organizations. There are also opportunities to be involved in theater and the highly regarded University Chorale. Aurora University has a long history of excellence in both intercollegiate and intramural athletics. A member of the NCAA Division III, Aurora fields intercollegiate teams in baseball, basketball, cross-country, football, golf, lacrosse, soccer, softball, tennis, track (indoor and outdoor), and volleyball, often with championship results.

Aurora University is accredited at the bachelor's, master's, and doctoral degree levels by the Higher Learning Commission of the North Central Association of Colleges and Schools, and its programs are accredited by the Commission on Collegiate Nursing Education, Illinois Department of Professional Regulation, Council on Social Work Education, and the National Recreation and Park Association/American Association of Leisure and Recreation. The College of Education is also accredited by the National Council for Accreditation of Teacher Education.

Location

Aurora University's Aurora campus is located in an attractive residential neighborhood on the southwest side of Aurora, Illinois, which has a population of more than 170,000 and is the state's second-largest city. The 32-acre main campus is located only minutes from the Illinois Research and Development Corridor, the site of dozens of nationally and internationally based businesses and industries. Aurora is also within an hour's drive or train ride of Chicago, one of the most vibrant cities in the world.

The University's George Williams College campus and conference center is 70 miles to the north, along the shores of Geneva Lake in Wisconsin. The Woodstock Center is located approximately 1 hour north of the Aurora campus, just off the square in downtown Woodstock, Illinois.

Majors and Degrees

The Bachelor of Arts degree is awarded in accounting, art, biology, business administration, business and commerce, coaching and youth sport development, communication, computer science, criminal justice, elementary education, English, finance, history, management information technology, marketing, organizational management, physical education (K–12 teacher certification), political science, psychology, religion, sociology, Spanish, special education, and theater. The Bachelor of Science degree is awarded in accounting, actuarial science, athletic training, biology, business administration, business and commerce, computer science, finance, health science (allied health, predentistry, premedicine, and pre–veterinary studies), management information technology, marketing, mathematics, organizational management, physical education (fitness and health promotion), and parks and recreation. The Bachelor of Science in Nursing and the Bachelor of Social Work are also offered. The University offers supplemental majors in prelaw and secondary education.

Academic Programs

Aurora University prides itself on its first-year program, which ensures that entering students make a successful transition to college. The only private college in Illinois selected to be part of a national project to create a model of excellence for the first college year, Aurora University recognizes the unique needs of freshmen.

Aurora University offers academic programs combining a liberal arts foundation with majors emphasizing career preparation and selected concentrations. Graduates are educated to be purposeful, ethical, and proficient—equipped for worthwhile careers and productive lives and for venturing forth into a changing world.

To earn a bachelor's degree, students are required to fulfill the general education core curriculum of the University and the major requirements for an approved major; complete at least 120 semester hours with a GPA of at least 2.0 on a 4.0 scale, including at least 52 semester hours at a senior college; and complete at least 30 semester hours, including the last 24 for the degree and at least 18 in the major, at Aurora University.

Entering freshmen who qualify and are highly motivated are invited to join the Honors Program. Students with an ACT score of 26 or above and a high school GPA of at least 3.25 on a 4.0 scale are invited to join. Those in the program participate in innovative seminars, service learning, advanced course work, and other special and cultural events.

Aurora University accepts credits earned through APP, CLEP, and DANTES. In addition, credit based on portfolio assessment is available to students who have significant prior learning from career experience or individual study.

The University observes a semester calendar (two 16-week semesters), with classes beginning in late August and concluding in early May. A three-week May Term offers exciting course work, including international study/travel and unique intensive courses.

Off-Campus Programs

Aurora University offers travel-study programs abroad and within the United States. Recent travel/study destinations included Africa,

China, Costa Rica, England, France, Greece, Honduras, Italy, and Puerto Rico. The University also has off-campus classes in various locations in Illinois and Wisconsin.

Academic Facilities

The major buildings at Aurora are marked by the distinctive, red-tiled roofs specified by Charles Eckhart in his donation for the original campus. Dunham Hall houses state-of-the-art computer facilities as well as the Schingoethe Center for Native American Cultures. The newest classroom building houses the Institute for Collaboration, which brings together education, health and human services, business, and government to facilitate the development of collaborative leadership. Other facilities include the fully equipped Perry Theatre, the Parolini Fine Arts Center, science labs, a flora-fauna complex, and the College Commons. Music practice rooms, piano labs, and a spacious art studio are housed in the Parolini Music Center.

The Phillips Library of Aurora University has almost 90,000 volumes and approximately 7,000 multimedia materials. It belongs to a consortia of seventy-six academic and research libraries in the state of Illinois which provides access to the materials of those libraries as well through a resource-sharing program. The library subscribes to more than 70 databases that provide full-text electronic access to over 30,000 journals and other periodicals. Almost 50 online subject research guides are available through the library's Web site. The library is open 102 hours a week and provides reference service for 81 of those hours. Reference service is available in person, by telephone, by e-mail, by live chat instant messaging, or by SMS text messaging.

Costs

Tuition for the 2011–12 school year is $19,250 for full-time students (24–34 semester hours per year), and yearly room and board costs average $8460.

Financial Aid

Aurora University's financial aid program has been designed to make it possible for any academically qualified student to afford the benefits of a private education. The University works with students to determine the amount of their costs and to identify all available resources so students can meet these expenses. Financial aid is awarded based on financial need as reported on the FAFSA. In addition to need-based financial aid, Aurora University offers academic scholarships, including the T. P. Stephens Scholarship, Board of Trustees Scholarship, Crimi Scholarship, Deans' Scholarship, Aurora University Opportunity Grant, and transfer scholarships.

Faculty

The favorable student-faculty ratio of 15:1 ensures that students receive plenty of individual attention in class. Instructors also make time for students outside of class, acting as mentors and advisers, and they are eager to answer questions and join students in campus activities.

Student Government

The student body is represented by the Aurora University Student Association (AUSA), which provides funding for over fifty student groups on campus. Students are also active members of committees ranging from faculty searches to ad hoc task forces and are provided with certain voting privileges.

Admission Requirements

The Aurora University Committee on Admission considers the complete record of a candidate for admission. The University seeks qualified students from varied geographical, cultural, economic, racial, and religious backgrounds. Admission requirements include an ACT score of 19 or above, a high school GPA of 2.5 or above, and a college-preparatory curriculum. Two general qualities are considered in each candidate: academic ability, enabling the student to benefit from a high-quality academic program, and a diversity of talents and interests that can contribute to making the campus community a better and more interesting place for learning. An application for admission to Aurora University is considered on the basis of the academic ability, achievements, activities, and motivation of the student. Candidates for the Honors Program must have an ACT score of 26 or higher and a high school GPA of at least 3.25 on a 4.0 scale. Transfer students with fewer than 30 semester hours of credit should apply in the same manner as freshman applicants. Transfer students with more than 15 semester hours may be admitted to Aurora University if they have a transferable overall GPA of 2.0 or higher. Aurora accepts a maximum of 90 semester hours of transfer credits from a combination of two- and four-year schools. A maximum of 68 semester hours may be transferred from two-year schools. For further information, students should contact a transfer representative in the Office of Admission and Financial Aid.

Application and Information

To apply for admission to Aurora University, the following items should be sent to the Office of Admission and Financial Aid: a completed application form (may be completed online at www.aurora.edu/auapply), an official transcript from the guidance counselor, and official ACT or SAT scores. Transfer students should submit official transcripts from each college or university attended, along with the completed application.

For applications and further information, students may contact:

Office of Admission and Financial Aid
Aurora University
347 South Gladstone Avenue
Aurora, Illinois 60506
Phone: 630-844-5533
       800-742-5281 (toll-free)
E-mail: admission@aurora.edu
Web site: http://www.aurora.edu

A view of Eckhart Hall at Aurora University in Aurora, Illinois.

AUSTIN COLLEGE
SHERMAN, TEXAS

The College

One of the finest selective liberal arts and sciences colleges in the nation, Austin College seeks students with evidence of academic ability and achievement, an eagerness for intellectual challenge and self-exploration, and a value-centered approach to their involvement. The learning environment is well suited to students who want to be known and challenged by faculty members and peers alike. The majority of students live on campus, creating a dynamic living and learning environment. Founded in 1849, Austin College is affiliated through a covenant relationship with the Presbyterian Church (U.S.A.). The liberal arts and sciences foundation develops lifelong learning abilities, such as thinking critically, solving problems, and communicating with others, and nurtures the whole person through academic, cocurricular, and social involvement.

International education and global awareness are priorities of the College, and more than 70 percent of Austin College graduates spend at least one month in international study during their college experience. During the past ten years, students have visited ninety-nine countries on six continents.

Austin College has an enrollment of approximately 1,350 students. The students are predominantly 18–21 years old, come from thirty-six states and sixteen countries, and represent a diversity of ethnicity, religion, and experience.

Opportunities for involvement include more than sixty student organizations, ranging from academic to special interest to local fraternities and sororities. Involvement in music, theater, and art programs is available to all students regardless of major. Intercollegiate athletics through membership in the Southern Collegiate Athletic Conference include six sports for men and six for women, and many students take part in intramural activities. The College maintains a 29-acre recreational area on Lake Texoma, about 20 minutes from the campus. All students are encouraged to participate in volunteer service and be involved in the community, with students providing more than 12,000 service hours per year.

Austin College offers guidance to students through Career Services, the Academic Skills Center, and Health Services. The campus dining service offers many food options for students each day. The campus offers coed and single-sex residence halls as well as apartments, cottages, and suites that are available to juniors and seniors. Students of German, French, Japanese, Chinese, and Spanish may choose to live in the language residence, where the target languages are spoken in common areas.

Many students continue on to graduate and professional study and enjoy successful acceptance rates at these institutions. Austin College graduates can be found around the world in exciting and successful careers, and graduates regularly earn prestigious national honors.

Location

Austin College is located in Sherman, Texas, just north of Dallas. Sherman is a small city of approximately 35,000 that *Money* magazine ranks in the top 15 percent of its list of the 300 most livable small cities in the U.S. Sherman offers students plenty of cultural, religious, and social opportunities, and nearby Lake Texoma offers many additional recreational opportunities. For those seeking "big-city" excitement, the Dallas–Fort Worth metroplex is a quick drive south on U.S. Highway 75.

Majors and Degrees

The Bachelor of Arts degree is offered in American studies, art, Asian studies, biochemistry, biology, business administration, chemistry, classical civilization, classics, communication studies (media studies, speech and social interaction, or theater emphasis), computer science, economics, education (through the master's program), English, environmental studies, French, German, history, international economics and finance, international relations, Japanese, Latin, Latin American and Iberian studies, mathematics, music, philosophy, physics, political science, psychology, religious studies, sociology, and Spanish. Minors and interdisciplinary majors are also available in anthropology, art history, cognitive science, community service and policy, educational psychology, ethics, exercise and sport science, film studies, gender studies, Southwestern and Mexican studies, and Western intellectual tradition. In addition, the Special Degree Program allows students to design an individualized major incorporating various interests.

Through the Austin Teacher Program, a special five-year teacher education program, a student earns both the Bachelor of Arts degree in a major of choice and the Master of Arts in Teaching degree.

Austin College also has preprofessional programs in engineering, health sciences, law, and theology.

Academic Programs

Making connections across disciplines and discovering the bigger picture bring learning to life. The Austin College curriculum emphasizes both depth and breadth of study. In the fall of the freshman year, all students take a seminar course that introduces them to the inquisitive learning style that defines Austin College. Instead of requiring every student to take a prescribed list of general education courses, Austin College uses a more flexible system that gives students control over their learning experience. Students fulfill the depth dimension by completing a major in a field of specialization plus a minor (or second major) in another field. The breadth dimension offers students the opportunity to explore across the disciplines in areas of personal interest. By careful selection of a minor, students may meet the goals of the breadth dimension while achieving some depth of study in a second field.

Students seeking a nontraditional major or minor may pursue the Special Program Option, in which study is individually designed. The program is particularly adaptable to the needs of students interested in studying interdisciplinary subject areas or in preparing for unique career fields.

Austin College has a 4-1-4 calendar year. Four courses are taken in the fall and spring terms, and one course is completed during the January term. Summer courses also are available. The January term offers an opportunity for in-depth study of one academic or special interest, travel courses, internships, and individualized study.

The College also offers the four-year Posey Leadership Institute, which combines course work, international study, volunteer service, an internship, involvement with a community mentor, and interaction with national and international leaders to develop awareness of leadership skills and styles.

Off-Campus Programs

Students have opportunities for study around the globe through approved programs of the college's Center for Global Studies. Students have a long history of success in Model United Nations programs across the country and internationally, recently competing in China and in the Czech Republic. Students also can become involved in field study through the social sciences laboratory or individually arranged programs. The Global Outreach

Program funds experiential servant leadership opportunities around the world in areas of community development and humanitarian efforts.

Academic Facilities

The College's facilities include the Robert J. and Mary Wright Campus Center, science classrooms and laboratories, a computer center, the Forster Art Studio Complex, two theaters, the Robert T. Mason Athletic-Recreation Complex, and the Jordan Family Language House, which offers a residential language immersion program in Chinese, French, German, Japanese, and Spanish. Abell Library Center includes more than 300,000 volumes and 900 periodicals to maximize research and learning opportunities. Wireless access connects the community to on-campus resources and the Internet. Five environmental research areas are within a short drive of the campus.

Costs

The basic tuition and fees charge for students entering in 2010–11 was $29,260 and room and board charges were $9599, for a total of $38,859.

Financial Aid

Assistance is given in three forms: grants and/or scholarships, loans, and on-campus jobs. More than 90 percent of students receive some type of financial aid. Students applying for need-based financial aid should submit the Free Application for Federal Student Aid (FAFSA) by April 1 for priority consideration.

Austin College offers a number of general academic awards based on merit rather than financial need. Typically, 75 percent of students receive Austin College merit-based scholarships. Awards also are made to students for involvement in the Presbyterian Church (U.S.A.) and for achievement in theater, art, and music.

Faculty

Of the 104 full-time faculty members, 97 percent hold terminal degrees. Faculty members holding earned doctorates teach at all levels. In addition to carrying out their academic and professional responsibilities, faculty members participate in the governance of the College, serve as students' mentors, and regularly work with students in research and exploration. With a student-faculty ratio of 12:1 and an average class size of 23, Austin College emphasizes excellence in learning and teaching.

Student Government

Under a community-government partnership plan, in which students and members of the faculty and administration are all participants, student involvement and leadership are important aspects of College governance. The College is committed to high principles in scholarship and general behavior.

Admission Requirements

Admission is competitive, with many more applicants than places in the freshman class. Transfer students are subject to the same rigorous standards required of freshman applicants. Students who cannot fulfill these requirements are considered on an individual basis. All admission credentials for fall freshman applicants must be received by the Office of Admission by one of the following deadlines: December 1 for Early Action I applicants (and scholarship applicants), January 15 for Early Action II applicants, and March 1 for regular decision applicants. Students who apply for admission after March 1 are considered on a space-available basis. To reserve a place in the entering class, a $350 deposit is required by May 1. The College's early admission program allows qualified students to enroll after their junior year of high school. Admission to Austin College is on an equal basis, regardless of age, color, disability, race, sex, sexual orientation, religion, national origin, or status as a veteran.

Application and Information

Austin College accepts the Common Application. Prospective students may apply online or download a copy at http://www.commonapp.org. Students also may obtain a copy from their high school guidance counselor or by calling Austin College. The Common Application Supplement for Austin College also is required. A completed application form, SAT Reasoning Test or ACT with writing scores, two letters of reference, and a transcript from each high school and college attended must be submitted to Austin College.

For more information, students should contact:

Office of Admission
Austin College
900 North Grand Avenue, Suite 6N
Sherman, Texas 75090
Phone: 903-813-3000
       800-KANGAROO (800-526-4276, toll-free)
Fax: 903-813-3198
E-mail: admission@austincollege.edu
Web site: http://www.austincollege.edu
       http://www.austincollege.edu/apply
       http://www.austincollege.edu/visit
       http://www.austincollege.edu/scholarships
       http://tour.austincollege.edu (virtual tour)

Austin College's tree-lined walkways, landscaped plazas, and green expanses provide a backdrop for the mixture of historical and modern buildings on the campus of the 162-year-old college.

AVE MARIA UNIVERSITY
AVE MARIA, FLORIDA

The University

As the first new Catholic university in forty years, Ave Maria University exists to further teaching, research, and learning in the abiding tradition of Catholic thought in both national and international settings. The University sponsors a liberal arts education curriculum dedicated to the advancement of human culture, the promotion of dialogue between faith and reason, and the formation of men and women in the intellectual and moral virtues of the Catholic faith.

The University began as Thomas S. Monaghan's dream to build an institution that would be faithful to the Magisterium and could produce faithful educators, leaders, and mentors. Through his initial financial donation, the University opened its doors in August 2003 with 100 students; the enrollment as of fall 2010 was 709.

In addition to its undergraduate degree programs, the University's graduate department offers an M.T.S. in pastoral theology and a Master of Arts and Ph.D. in theology.

The Office of Campus Ministry, in conjunction with Student Life, organizes retreats for students throughout the year. The University also encourages students to find opportunities to serve the poor, the infirm, and the elderly in the local community.

Ave Maria University recognizes the important role that athletics play in forming the whole person. To that end, club and intramural-level sports are offered in a variety of sports. In addition, the University was accepted into the National Association of Intercollegiate Athletics (NAIA) in February 2008. NAIA division sports for fall 2010 included men's baseball and football; men's and women's basketball, cross-country, golf, indoor track, outdoor track and field, soccer, and tennis; and women's cheerleading, rowing, softball, and volleyball.

Full-time students are required to live on campus, unless they are living at home with their parents. However, students who are 23 or older may only live on campus with permission of the Dean of Students (excepting those discerning a religious vocation). Each residence hall includes a live-in adult residence director and a student resident assistant on each floor. Each hall provides students with common areas, kitchen and laundry facilities, meeting rooms, and a chapel. Choice of housing on campus is granted each year primarily, though not exclusively, on the basis of academic seniority. The University has a private dining area in the Student Union. Breakfast, lunch, and dinner are served Monday through Friday. Brunch and an evening meal are served on Saturdays and Sundays.

Location

Ave Maria University's permanent campus currently occupies 100 acres of land approximately 20 miles northeast of the city of Naples. The town of Ave Maria, adjoining the University, provides not only residences but a thriving town center, La Piazza, which is home to restaurants, coffee shops, the University Bookstore, and other vendors. Naples, nestled near the beaches of the Gulf of Mexico, is known for world-class shopping, dining, and more than thirty-five golf courses. It is only steps away from the Everglades and boasts one of the nation's best beaches and calmest seas. Art lovers can spend an evening at the Philharmonic Center for the Arts or the popular Dinner Theater or visit local art galleries and historic sites around the city. The many nearby parks and nature preserves feature rare species of flora and fauna indigenous to the state.

Majors and Degrees

Ave Maria University offers a strong classical liberal arts core curriculum as well as an opportunity for students to choose one of the following majors: biology, business, classics, economics, history, literature, math, music, philosophy, politics, psychology, and theology. The University also offers three preprofessional programs: prelaw, premed, and a certificate of business.

Academic Programs

The University's core curriculum requires students to take specific courses in the liberal arts, thus acquiring the indispensable foundation for a lifetime of learning. Of the 128 credits required to earn a bachelor's degree, the core curriculum comprises one half, or 64 credits. The major of study comprises another 32 to 40 credits, and general electives comprise the final 24 to 32 credits. Students are required to take two noncredit practicums in the fine arts, the first being an introduction to Gregorian chant and the second in chorus, instrumental music, studio art, or theater. Other core courses include three courses each in theology and philosophy; two courses each in history, literature, Latin, and the natural sciences; and one course each in American civilization and mathematics. Some requirements may be met through CLEP, Advanced Placement (with an exam score of 4), and military service.

Off-Campus Programs

The University offers study-abroad programs at Ave Maria University–Latin America Campus, located in San Marcos, Nicaragua, and in Gaming, Austria. Students may enroll in the program for one semester. Courses are taught in English and correspond to the requirements of the degree programs at the University. The cost for each program is the regular University cost of attendance, although students are expected to cover their travel expenses. Participants in the Austria program are also required to pay a nominal Austria fee. Students must have at least sophomore status to enter the programs. Transfer students must have spent at least one full semester at the Ave Maria Florida campus before they are eligible to apply.

Academic Facilities

Ave Maria University's Canizaro Library has 4 librarians and a support staff of 10 members. With more than 190,000 volumes, the Canizaro Library has one of the largest permanent collections in the region. In addition to its impressive open-stack collection, the Canizaro Library has interlibrary loan privileges with university libraries throughout the United States and belongs to the Southwest Florida Library Network consortium. To supplement its print resources, the Canizaro Library provides students and faculty and staff members with access to several electronic databases for research purposes. These can be accessed from any network computer. Computer workstations located throughout the campus are connected to the campus network and include the most up-to-date software. All computer stations are equipped with printers and Internet access. Scanners for photos and graphics are also available. Facilities for viewing audiovisual materials are located throughout the campus. A writing lab program provides students with the opportunity to familiarize themselves with accepted standards for expository writing as well as the institutional style and research conventions.

Costs

For the 2011–12 academic year, undergraduate tuition and fees are $10,045 per semester or $20,090 for the year. Other costs per semester include $2397 for housing and $1812 for meals. The total cost of attendance is $14,255 per semester or $28,510 per academic year.

Financial Aid

Approximately 90 percent of students receive financial assistance. Ave Maria University is Title IV eligible, allowing students to participate in federal student financial aid programs. In addition to federal aid, institutional grants are offered. The Ave Maria University Grant is awarded to students who demonstrate considerable financial need. All financial aid decisions are based on the Free Application for Federal Student Aid (FAFSA). Ave Maria University also offers scholarships to students based on prior academic achievement, ACT or SAT scores, and leadership factors; those interested in a scholarship should apply early (early action deadline is November 15). On-campus employment opportunities are also available. The University offers the option of paying over a five- or ten-month period.

Faculty

The faculty consists of 59 professors, 92 percent of whom hold the terminal degree (Ph.D. or equivalent) in their fields of study. Faculty members are carefully chosen for a clear and strong commitment to Catholic education, and professors of philosophy and theology annually make the Profession of Faith and renew their Oath of Fidelity to the Magisterium of the Catholic Church.

Student Government

The student body is represented by a president, a vice president, a secretary, a treasurer, and 2 elected representatives from each class. The student representatives are responsible for hosting a number of student activities and programs and for setting the budget for other student organizations.

Admission Requirements

Prospective students are required to have completed at least 15 high school credits with a minimum GPA of 2.8 on a 4.0 scale and have a minimum ACT composite score of 22 or SAT score of 1580 (critical reading, math, and writing). Transfer students must have a college GPA of at least 2.4 and at least 24 credit hours at the college level. In order to be admitted, applicants must submit a completed application form, official SAT or ACT scores, high school and college transcripts, two letters of recommendation, a list of extracurricular activities and other high school achievements, and an essay (prospective students should visit the Web site for essay parameters).

Application and Information

There is no fee to apply to Ave Maria University. The early action deadline is November 15. Applications are evaluated on a rolling admissions basis. Applications may be submitted online or mailed to:

Office of Admissions
Ave Maria University
5050 Ave Maria Boulevard
Ave Maria, Florida 34142-9505
Phone: 239-280-2556
         877-283-8648 (toll-free)
Fax: 239-280-2559
Web site: http://www.avemaria.edu

Aerial view of Ave Maria University. The library is in the foreground, the oratory and Ave Maria downtown piazza are the middle, and the Ave Maria K–12 Academy is in the distance.

BABSON COLLEGE
WELLESLEY, MASSACHUSETTS

The College

Since its founding in 1919, Babson College has focused on educating business leaders capable of initiating and managing change, navigating ethical choices, and solving the problems of today and tomorrow. Students are immersed in an enriching environment that fosters leadership, teamwork, creativity, communication, diversity, and ethics. The 2010–11 undergraduate enrollment was 833 women and 1,123 men. An independent, coeducational institution, Babson is accredited by AACSB International–The Association to Advance Collegiate Schools of Business, the New England Association of Schools and Colleges, and the European Quality Improvement System (EQUIS).

Babson is a residential college and is a 24-hours-a-day, seven days-a-week community alive with intellectual, cultural, athletic, and social activities. Approximately 85 percent of the undergraduate student body lives on campus in fourteen residence halls. Housing options include coed residence halls, fraternity and sorority housing, and substance-free, multicultural, entrepreneurial, and other specialty-themed housing.

Babson College is an NCAA Division III school. Most of the College's intercollegiate teams compete in the New England Women's and Men's Athletic Conference (NEWMAC). There are twenty-two men's and women's varsity sports teams, with additional club and intramural sports available to all students. More information is available at http://www.babsonathletics.com.

The Webster Center features an indoor, 200-meter, six-lane track; a field house; a gymnasium with three basketball courts; a racquetball court; a 25-yard, six-lane pool with 1- and 3-meter diving boards; a fitness center; squash courts; and a dance/aerobics studio. The Babson Skating Center features a 600-seat skating arena. Outdoor facilities include eight tennis courts, a new AstroTurf field, a game field, a renovated softball diamond, a baseball field, two sand-based varsity fields, and a club rugby field.

Location

Babson's beautiful 370-acre campus is in Wellesley, Massachusetts, 14 miles west of Boston, a city renowned for its cultural and recreational opportunities. More than sixty colleges and universities bring more than 250,000 college students to the Boston area, making it one of the world's best college towns for cultural exchange and research.

Majors and Degrees

Babson offers a Bachelor of Science degree, a Master of Business Administration degree, three Master of Science degree programs, and executive education programs for business professionals.

Academic Programs

The curriculum breaks down the artificial barriers between disciplines by emphasizing an integrated, holistic approach to learning. The curriculum integrates core competencies, key business disciplines, and the liberal arts into foundation, intermediate, and advanced programs. Babson's core competencies include rhetoric, quantitative analysis, entrepreneurial and creative thinking, global and multicultural perspectives, ethics and social responsibility, leadership and teamwork, and critical and integrative thinking.

These learning outcomes are introduced and reinforced as students' progress through the undergraduate curriculum. The Foundation Program lays the groundwork, raising students' abilities to formulate, explore, and reflect critically. In the second year, students proceed to the Intermediate Program, which adds breadth, elaborates issues, and exposes them to more disciplinary and interdisciplinary analyses. The Advanced Program challenges students to think about issues with increased confidence, independence, and creativity.

Foundation Program courses may include quantitative methods with calculus, probability and statistics, financial accounting, rhetoric, arts and humanities, history and society, business law, science, and Foundations of Management and Entrepreneurship (FME), a year-long immersion into the world of start-ups, where student teams actually create their own businesses, receiving grants of up to $3000 to cover costs. Babson is the only U.S. school to teach the management core curriculum as an integrated three-semester course where all aspects of business are covered, including accounting, marketing, finance, management operations, strategy, organizational behavior, IT sales, and economics.

In the Advanced Program, students are free to expand and fine-tune core competencies as they reflect on their own career and life goals. During this time, students take courses in advanced management and liberal arts electives. Babson offers twenty-five optional concentrations in both business and liberal arts disciplines and descriptions can be found at http://www.babson.edu/concentrations. This way, students may further plan their own course of study by focusing on certain areas of interest while continuing to benefit from Babson's interdisciplinary approach to learning. Students also have the opportunity to participate in field-based experiences such as an internship or consulting experience. Special programs, such as the Weissman program, the Honors Program, the Women's Leadership Program, the Management Consulting Field Experience, the Babson College Fund (student-managed endowment), Master of Science in Accounting (M.S.A.), and Independent Research allow students to take advantage of customized learning opportunities at Babson.

Babson's flexible curriculum allows students to pursue courses that appeal to them and align with their goals. To aid in the decision-making process, students receive guidance from faculty mentors and professional staff throughout their four years.

To earn the Bachelor of Science degree, students are required to complete a minimum of 126 semester hours with a C average or better, with a minimum of 63 credits in the liberal arts (including 20 credits in advanced liberal arts). Transfer students must complete a minimum of 64 semester hours at Babson. Once a student has earned 96 credits, all remaining credits must be earned at Babson, at a Babson-approved cross-registration program, or at a Babson-affiliated study abroad program.

Entering students may be granted credit or advanced course placement for successful scores on Advanced Placement (AP) examinations administered by the College Board as well as some courses in the International Baccalaureate (IB) curriculum.

The College operates on a two-semester academic calendar. Semesters run from September to December and from late January through May. An optional credit-bearing three-week winter session is offered in January, and two summer sessions are offered—one from late May to early July and one from mid-July to mid-August.

Off-Campus Programs

In addition, Babson has a partnership with Wellesley College and the Franklin W. Olin College of Engineering, an independent institution that opened in 2001, and is located on a 70-acre site adjacent to Babson. Babson, Olin, and Wellesley are collaborating academically and cocurricularly in order to provide extraordinary opportunities in all aspects of the student experience, including joint academic and research programming, student life programming, and lecture series.

Babson students can also take a course each semester at one of the other area colleges, including Brandeis University and Regis College, for full academic credit. These off-campus programs offer greater access to liberal arts courses, including a wide range of foreign languages.

Babson's vibrant study abroad program enables students to spend either a summer or one or both semesters of their junior year overseas at a college or university. Currently, forty-seven programs are offered in twenty-six countries, and full academic credit is given for approved management and liberal arts courses.

Academic Facilities

Horn Library houses an extensive business collection of print, media, and computerized information resources. Students have campuswide access to newspapers, journals, investment analyst reports, corporate records, directories, and international information. They also benefit from numerous electronic research and news services that supplement a selection of the best business and liberal arts books, newspapers, journals, CD-ROMs, audiocassettes, videocassettes, and videodiscs.

Horn Computer Center is equipped with a lab that remains open 24 hours a day. Wireless access is available throughout the campus. Every incoming Babson undergraduate student receives a leased laptop computer with integrated Wi-Fi wireless technology.

Other facilities are the Donald W. Reynolds Campus Center, the Richard W. Sorenson Family Visual Arts Center, the Richard W. Sorenson Center for the Arts, the Stephen D. Culter Center for Investments and Finance, the Glavin Family Chapel, and the Arthur M. Blank Center for Entrepreneurship.

Costs

For 2010–11, tuition and fees were $39,040. The total estimated cost for a residential student was $51,916.

Financial Aid

Babson is committed to educating students from diverse backgrounds. Applying for financial aid does not affect a student's chances of being admitted to Babson College. Financial assistance is awarded on merit and demonstrated financial need. Assistance for students begins with consideration for student loans and work-study. Those with need beyond the loan and work-study amounts are also considered for Babson grants.

In 2009–10, over 40 percent of all first-year students received need-based Babson grants. Nearly half of Babson students receive some form of financial assistance. Students should note that need-based financial assistance is available to U.S. citizens and permanent residents of the United States. Babson's merit scholarships include Weissman Scholarships, Presidential Scholarships, the Women's Leadership Awards, and the Diversity Leadership Awards. Application for aid is made by submitting the Free Application for Federal Student Aid (FAFSA) and the Financial Aid PROFILE of the College Scholarship Service. The application deadline for first-year undergraduate students is January 15. For transfer students and September enrollment, the deadline is April 1, and November 1 for January enrollment.

Faculty

Because of Babson's close-knit community, students are able to form close relationships with the faculty. Of the 262 faculty members, 171 are full-time, and 88 percent of the full-time faculty members hold a doctoral degree or its equivalent. Faculty members are accomplished entrepreneurs, executives, scholars, authors, researchers, poets, and artists who bring an intellectual diversity that adds depth to Babson's educational programs and offers students a rich, challenging experience. Babson's student-faculty ratio is 14:1, with an average class size of 29. Most importantly, faculty members teach 100 percent of the courses. More information can be found at http://www.babson.edu/ugradfaculty.

Student Government

Students are encouraged to take an active role in campus activities and student government. The Student Government Association promotes students' interests; allocates funds to campus organizations for academic, social, and recreational activities; licenses student-run businesses; and helps formulate and maintain student regulations. There are over seventy student clubs and organizations currently on campus.

Admission Requirements

In selecting new students, the admission office considers each candidate's biographical data, transcripts, test scores, personal statements, and references. Evaluation is based upon comparisons of the qualifications of those who apply. The degree of competition is set by the caliber of the applicants themselves. Consideration is given to the depth and rigor of each candidate's academic program, academic motivation and achievement, and progress from one year to the next. Prospective students are strongly encouraged to have completed or be currently enrolled in a precalculus math class.

The Admission Committee carefully reviews courses taken, math aptitude, and standardized test scores. Reading and writing skills as well as verbal expression are measured using English grades, essays, and standardized test scores. Intangible personal qualities are also important—leadership, creativity, enthusiasm, and an overall good fit with Babson that includes a willingness to contribute to the community in meaningful and positive ways. There is no standard format for submitting this information, so Babson relies on letters of recommendation, references, and personal statements. In addition, the College evaluates extracurricular activities and work experience, seeking candidates who have exceptional leadership qualities and have participated in activities that have potential carryover to college. Efforts are made to enroll students with diverse backgrounds and experiences.

The College offers three application plans: regular decision, early decision, and early action. For more information about these plans and their deadlines, prospective students should visit the College's Web site (http://www.babson.edu/ugrad). Campus visits and group information sessions with an admission counselor are strongly recommended.

Application and Information

For further information or application forms, students should contact:

Lunder Undergraduate Admission Center
Babson College
Babson Park, Massachusetts 02457-0310
Phone: 781-239-5522
      800-488-3696 (toll-free)
Fax: 781-239-4006
E-mail: ugradadmission@babson.edu
Web site: http://www.babson.edu/ugrad
    http://www.facebook.com/babsoncollege
    http://twitter.com/babsoncollegeUG

Babson College's Tomasso Hall.

BALDWIN-WALLACE COLLEGE

BEREA, OHIO

The College

Founded in 1845, Baldwin-Wallace College (B-W) in Berea, Ohio, is an accredited institution affiliated with the United Methodist Church that blends the hallmarks of a traditional liberal arts education with an emphasis on professional preparation. Baldwin-Wallace has a long history of diversity, as it was one of the first institutions of higher learning in Ohio to admit students without regard to race or gender. That spirit of inclusiveness has flourished and evolved into a personalized approach to education—one that stresses individual growth as students learn to learn, respond to new ideas, adapt to new situations, and prepare for the certainty of change.

With an enrollment of approximately 3,100 full-time undergraduate students, B-W offers unique opportunities for engaged, transformative learning. The student profile shows that 25 percent of incoming first-year students come from the top 10 percent of their high school classes, with more than 50 percent in the top quarter. In addition to the traditional-aged college student, Baldwin-Wallace has helped adult learners for more than fifty years to develop skills, redirect careers, and enhance lives. Today, 500 adult learners of all ages participate in evening and weekend classes in a variety of programs that are designed to accommodate the varying learning styles and schedules of busy adult learners. Another 700 students are enrolled in part-time graduate programs in education and business administration.

Experiential learning is the product of the Baldwin-Wallace education. An experienced and proven commitment to the liberal arts and sciences—characterized by excellence in teaching and learning—provides a strong foundation for internships, faculty-directed research, and service-learning programs. Students work closely with their faculty adviser to develop a personal Action Plan that combines these opportunities in a way that stresses the importance of lifelong learning and fully prepares graduates for success after college.

Over 80 percent of B-W students who graduated in 2008 were employed in rewarding positions (with an average starting salary of over $40,000) or admitted to graduate school within nine months of receiving their diplomas. In addition, two thirds of B-W graduates attend graduate or professional school at some point in their lives. B-W students are accepted into graduate programs at a rate 10 to 20 percent higher than graduates of similar colleges and universities. Some programs—including athletic training, communication disorders, and neuroscience—have close to 100 percent acceptance rates.

Baldwin-Wallace is also home to a world-renowned Conservatory of Music. The undergraduate-only nature of the conservatory offers collaborative mentoring opportunities with a faculty of accomplished artists and extraordinary opportunities for performance in a variety of ensembles. In addition to hosting the country's oldest collegiate Bach Festival, the conservatory serves over 2,000 community members each year through outreach initiatives.

A Sustainable Future: B-W embraces practices and principles that demonstrate its commitment to the environment. An undergraduate major in sustainability—the first of its kind in Ohio—offers students the opportunity to lead in the twenty-first century. The campus community continues to reduce its environmental footprint through significant recycling efforts, the addition of a wind turbine and food composter, and the use of geothermal heating and cooling systems in three green campus complexes.

Location

B-W students enjoy the best of both worlds. Berea, Ohio, with its tree-lined streets, picturesque homes, and population of 19,000, is an ideal college town. At the same time, students are only 20 minutes from the heart of Cleveland, which is home to Fortune 500 companies as well as unique recreational and cultural opportunities.

Cleveland is home to outstanding museums and galleries, professional sporting events, a world-class orchestra, exciting nightlife, and an extensive park system.

Approximately 1,900 B-W students live on campus in a variety of settings, ranging from residence halls exclusively housing first-year students to the Carmel Living Learning Center, where students enroll in shared classes taken in the residence hall. Other opportunities include residential learning communities and College-owned apartments for upperclassmen. All full-time students are required to live on campus during their first and second years at Baldwin-Wallace, with residency exemptions available for commuting students who live with their families. Residence halls provide students with social and educational programming, a diverse living environment, and leadership opportunities.

Majors and Degrees

Baldwin-Wallace offers the Bachelor of Arts (B.A.), Bachelor of Science (B.S.), Bachelor of Science in Education (B.S.E.), Bachelor of Music (B.M.), and Bachelor of Music in Education (B.M.E.) degrees. Majors and programs include accounting, art history, art studio, arts management, athletic training, biology, broadcasting and mass communication, business, chemistry, communication disorders, communication studies, computer information systems, computer science, criminal justice, digital media and design, economics, education, English, exercise science, film studies, finance, French, German, health-care management, health promotion and education, history, human resource management, international business, international studies, management, marketing, mathematical economics, mathematics, medical technology, neuroscience, philosophy, physical education, physics, political science, pre-engineering, prepharmacy, pre–physical therapy, psychology, public health, public relations, religion, sociology, Spanish, sport management, sustainability, and theater. The Conservatory of Music offers majors in music composition, music education, music history and literature, music in the liberal arts, music management, music performance, music theater, music theory, and music therapy.

Academic Programs

More than fifty majors and several 3-2 cooperative and pre-professional programs are available to traditional B-W undergraduates. Evening and weekend programs include thirteen majors and six certificate programs.

Off-Campus Programs

Baldwin-Wallace College has institutional partnerships with several other universities around the globe, some of which include Edge Hill College (England), University of the Sunshine Coast (Australia), Ewha University (Korea), Bohme Jesus (Brazil), University of Osnabrück (Germany), Kansai Gaidai University (Japan), Hong Kong Baptist University (China), University of Hull (England), Athlone Institute of Technology (Ireland), Galway Mayo Institute of Technology (Ireland), American Business School in Paris, York St. John University (England), Washington Center, New York Media Institute at Marist College, Christ College (India), and American University (Washington, D.C.).

In addition to traditional study-abroad programs, with students studying and living on a particular campus for the semester, B-W features a series of focused-study tours that are led by B-W faculty and staff members and examine specific topics or geographic regions. Some programs involve homestays, while others use hostels and hotels. Quite literally, students learn while on the road. Study tours are offered in alternating academic years.

B-W often sponsors faculty-led two- to three-week seminars for credit in May, which are perfect for students who seek an international experience but do not want to be away for extended periods.

Destinations have included Vienna, Prague, and Budapest. Recent spring trips have included India and China, and there was a seminar in Europe as well as an environmental excursion to Ecuador. Most locations for study-abroad programs offered during the academic year—such as Australia, China, England, Korea, and Spain—are also offered during the summer term. The Semester at Sea program sends students to ten different countries—such as Brazil, Egypt, India, Japan, and Vietnam—aboard a 23,000-ton ship with 600 other college undergraduates.

Academic Facilities

Baldwin-Wallace continues to invest in facilities for student learning. In August 2010, the College completed the $29-million renovation and expansion of the Thomas Family Center for Science and Innovation, a facility featuring a combined 100,000-square-feet of comprehensive laboratory, research, and study space. This new complex includes the Center for Innovation and Growth, a facility that reflects the synergy of B-W's cross-curricular academic offerings through entrepreneurial study and innovation.

In addition, construction is under way on the renovation and expansion of the Conservatory of Music facilities, which will provide students with additional, improved rehearsal and performance spaces. The conservatory will remain home to the Jones Music Library and the Riemenschneider Bach Institute, where priceless Bach-related manuscripts and first editions are stored.

These new facilities complement the extensive offerings already available to students, including twenty campus computer labs; a 4,000-watt campus radio station; recently renovated recreation facilities; an on-campus gallery showcasing the work of student, faculty, and area artists; and the Burrell Memorial Observatory.

Costs

Baldwin-Wallace's tuition ranks among the lowest and most affordable of private colleges in Ohio. In 2010–11, full-time (12–18 credit hours) liberal arts students paid $33,560 per academic year in tuition, room, board, and fees. Conservatory students paid $35,664 per academic year.

Financial Aid

To help students and their families meet the cost of a high-quality education, B-W awards more than $50 million annually to students in the form of scholarships, grants, loans, and work-study opportunities. B-W is committed to working with students and their families to offer financial support. Nearly all Baldwin-Wallace students receive some sort of financial assistance.

Renewable merit scholarships ranging from $1000 to $13,000 are awarded to academically exceptional incoming freshmen. The College also offers special and competitive awards, ranging from $1000 to $4000, as well as scholarships for transfer students.

Faculty

Close relationships are at the heart of the B-W experience. Most classes average only 19 students, and the student-faculty ratio is 15:1. Professors share their wisdom and experience on a one-to-one basis, helping students choose classes or assisting students in their search for the perfect internship. Faculty members regularly give out their home phone numbers. From corporate executives and lifelong educators to environmentalists and practicing psychologists, B-W's more than 300 full-time and part-time faculty members bring impressive credentials from their fields. Nearly 80 percent have earned the highest degree in their field. They are dedicated and talented teachers who want to provide an educational experience that goes well beyond the textbook.

Student Government

Student Government consists of three branches—the legislative, the executive, and the judicial. The Student Senate is the official representative body of the students of Baldwin-Wallace College. All meetings are open, and all students are welcome to participate. The president and vice president of the student body lead the executive branch and work closely with the Senate to express student body views to the College faculty and administration. The judicial branch of Student Government consists of the supreme court of the student body, which hears cases pertaining to Student Government and the clubs it funds. Elections for student body government occur each February.

Admission Requirements

Applicants must submit the completed application (electronic or paper), a high school transcript, a teacher recommendation, the Secondary School Record Request Form, and the $25 application fee (waived if applying online). SAT and ACT results are optional. (In lieu of standardized test results, students must submit a graded writing sample.) Transfer applicants also must submit college or university transcripts. Candidates applying to the Conservatory of Music also must complete the Conservatory Audition Portfolio.

Application and Information

The deadline for undergraduate admission is May 1. The priority admission deadline is March 1. Applicants are notified, beginning November 1, on a rolling basis within four to six weeks of receipt of a completed application.

Office of Admission
Baldwin-Wallace College
275 Eastland Road
Berea, Ohio 44017-2088
Phone: 440-826-2222
        877-BW-APPLY (toll-free)
Fax: 440-826-3830
E-mail: admission@bw.edu
Web site: http://www.bw.edu/admission

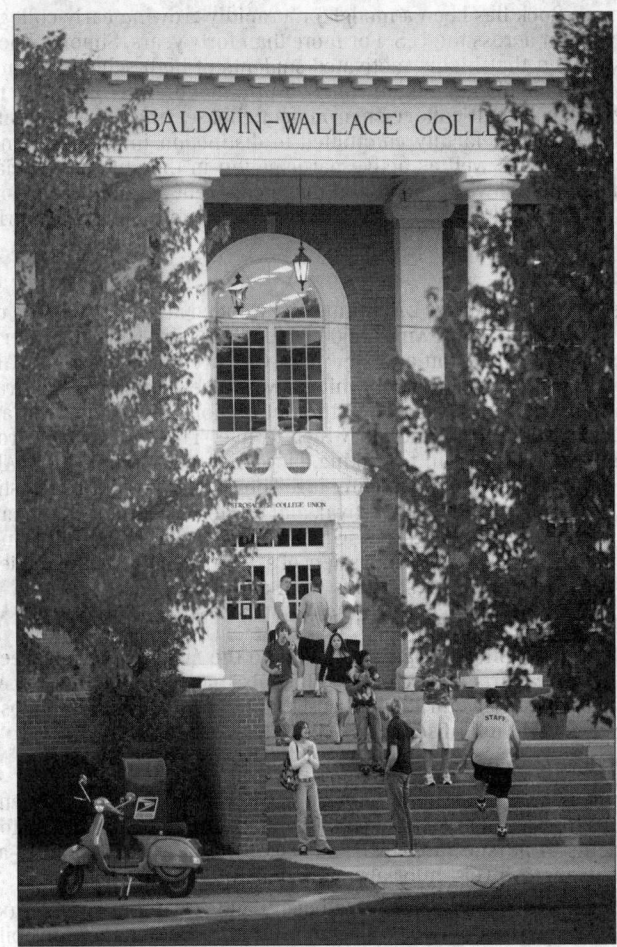

Baldwin-Wallace College is located in suburban, tree-lined Berea, Ohio, but is just 20 minutes from the heart of Cleveland and its cultural, educational, and recreational resources.

BARD COLLEGE AT SIMON'S ROCK

GREAT BARRINGTON, MASSACHUSETTS

The College

Simon's Rock is the only four-year residential college of the liberal arts and sciences specifically designed to provide bright, highly motivated students with the opportunity to begin college after the tenth or eleventh grade. Students who successfully complete the requirements receive the Associate of Arts (A.A.) degree after two years of study and the Bachelor of Arts (B.A.) degree after four. Full- and partial-tuition scholarships are available. The average age of entering students is 16.

Simon's Rock challenges the traditional assumption that students must be 18 before they can be asked to develop seriously their intelligence, imagination, and self-discipline. Students at Simon's Rock pursue an academic program that enables them to fulfill their potential at an age when their interest, energy, and curiosity are at a peak.

The College was founded in 1964 by Elizabeth Blodgett Hall and first admitted students in 1966. In 1979, Simon's Rock became a part of Bard College, located 50 miles away at Annandale-on-Hudson, New York.

Simon's Rock has been a model for a rapidly growing early college movement across the U.S. For more than forty years, Simon's Rock has proven that highly motivated students of high school age are fully capable of engaging in college work; that they are best able to develop in a small-college environment; that serving these students well requires a faculty committed to distinction in teaching and scholarship, as well as active participation in the students' social and personal development; and that a coherent general education in the liberal arts and sciences should be the foundation for early college students.

Location

The College is built on 275 rolling and wooded acres just outside of Great Barrington, a town of 8,500, in the Berkshire Hills of western Massachusetts. Boston and New York City are 2½ hours away; Albany and Springfield are 40 miles away. The Berkshires' natural beauty and wide variety of cultural attractions make the area an unusually attractive place in which to live. The countryside provides excellent terrain for hiking, bicycling, cross-country and Alpine skiing, canoeing, and climbing. The Tanglewood Music Festival, Jacob's Pillow Dance Festival, and numerous summer theaters are located in nearby towns. Great Barrington itself is a thriving business community with a variety of schools and service agencies in which Simon's Rock students work and volunteer.

Majors and Degrees

Simon's Rock offers programs leading to the A.A. and B.A. degrees in the liberal arts and sciences. Students may complete their B.A. studies with a concentration in most traditional disciplines or choose one of several interdisciplinary concentrations.

Academic Programs

The academic program at Simon's Rock combines a core curriculum in the liberal arts and sciences with extensive opportunities for students to pursue their own interests through electives, and—at the advanced level—tutorials and independent studies.

Because Simon's Rock students begin college without completing high school, the College is particularly conscious of its responsibility to ensure that all students develop the skills and knowledge expected of an educated person. The core curriculum comprises approximately half of students' total academic load during their first two years. Requirements include a writing and thinking workshop, which new students attend during the week before the regular semester begins; first-year, sophomore, and cultural perspectives seminars; and courses in the arts, mathematics, natural science, and foreign language. The College also requires that students participate in a recreational athletics program and attend a series of health and wellness programs.

All new students are assigned a faculty adviser, who meets with them weekly during their first semester and regularly throughout the rest of their career at Simon's Rock. Classes are small, faculty members are accessible, and the opportunities for students to pursue diverse interests are extensive.

The curriculum of the first two years at Simon's Rock leads to the A.A. in liberal arts. Students who successfully complete the A.A. requirements may continue at Simon's Rock for a B.A. or transfer to another college or university to complete their baccalaureate degree. Close to half of each sophomore class remains to complete a B.A. at Simon's Rock in one of approximately forty concentrations; the remainder of the students transfer. Through the sophomore planning process, students receive individualized guidance from staff in the Win Student Resource Commons and their faculty as they explore options for their last two years of undergraduate study.

Students wishing to stay at Simon's Rock for a B.A. must apply for admission to a concentration through a process called Moderation. Each student meets with a group of faculty in his or her area(s) of interest to review the student's accomplishments and together plan the remainder of the student's education at Simon's Rock. Students suggest and are advised of junior- and senior-year opportunities. These traditionally include advanced seminars, independent study involvement in faculty research projects, specialized tutorials, internships, courses at Bard, and a possible semester or full year of study abroad.

The senior thesis is the focus of each B.A. student's final year. Drawing on the skills in analysis and synthesis acquired during the previous three years, students devote themselves wholeheartedly to the project, which is personally defined and developed under the guidance of 2 or more faculty members. Recent theses have taken many forms: critical studies in literature, psychological research, musical compositions, creative fiction, translations, scientific experiments, mathematical problem solving, artistic exhibitions and performances, and various combinations of these forms.

The regular academic program is supplemented by a number of signature programs. The Simon's Rock/Columbia University Engineering Program offers three years at Simon's Rock and two years in the engineering school at Columbia University in New York, at the end of which students receive both a B.A. from Simon's Rock and a B.S. from Columbia's School of Engineering and Applied Science. Simon's Rock also offers a similar arrangement with the engineering school at Dartmouth University.

Through Simon's Rock Scholars at Oxford, a select group of Simon's Rock students are admitted to spend their junior year at Lincoln College of the University of Oxford in England each year. Founded in 1427, Lincoln College is one of the oldest and most esteemed of the Oxford Colleges. Simon's Rock Scholars at Oxford are full members of Lincoln College, live on the grounds at Lincoln, are taught by the regular faculty members at Oxford, and have access to the rich resources and facilities of the University.

Simon's Rock has a program in creative writing through which students are able to spend up to a full year at the Centre for New Writing at the University of Manchester in the UK. Launched in September 2007, the Centre was designed to develop and refine the creative and critical work of its students, explore and research collaboration between creative and critical writing, and broaden access to literature and writers in the region. Founded on the principle that good reading and good writing naturally go together, the Centre's goal is to be a place where the best, most interesting contemporary literature is both written and written about.

The proseminar in Social Scientific Inquiry, an in-house program first introduced in the 2008–09 academic year, provides students with an opportunity for immersion in social theory, social research, and social action through intensive interaction with scholars active across the broad spectrum of the disciplines. The Arts Bridges Program offers a similar program of study with visiting artists.

Simon's Rock students also have the opportunity to study at Bard College at Annandale. Upper-college (B.A.) students can take classes at Bard's campus in Annandale-on-Hudson, New York, or spend a semester in residence at the Annandale campus. Students can also take advantage of Bard's study-abroad programs; its groundbreaking Manhattan-based Globalization and International Affairs Program; and the Bard Rockefeller Program, a collaborative venture with Rockefeller University offering advanced research opportunities in medicine and the sciences.

Off-Campus Programs

Students pursue a variety of study-abroad programs and options. The Simon's Rock Win Resource Commons works with students to find study-abroad opportunities suited to their goals and interests. They use established independent programs (the School for Field Studies, SEA Semester, Global Routes), programs through other schools (Oxford University, the Sorbonne, Bogazici University in Istanbul, Turkey), and special Simon's Rock programs (fieldwork in geography in China). The result is something very different from the standard tour of famous sites. Students have recently taken intensive math instruction at Central European University in Budapest, Hungary; helped build a school in a remote village in northern Thailand; and served as apprentices to dancers, drummers, mask carvers, and batik artists in Bali. Students can also take advantage of Bard's study-abroad and international programs, including special arrangements with universities in Germany, Russia, and South Africa and intensive language immersion programs in China, France, Germany, Italy, Japan, Morocco, Mexico, and Russia. Programs can last for a semester, a full academic year, or shorter periods during the breaks.

Academic Facilities

The Fisher Science and Academic Center houses the College's biology, chemistry, ecology, and physics laboratories; research labs for faculty members and students; classrooms and tutorial rooms; a sixty-seat lecture center; and faculty offices. The Daniel Arts Center, which opened in the fall of 2004, incorporates a 350-seat theater and concert hall, a black box theater, a dance studio, and rehearsal facilities; painting, drawing, photography, ceramics, metalworking, printmaking, 3-D, video production, and digital arts studios; exhibition areas; and spaces for large-scale art and set construction. A music hall, a recording studio, and music practice rooms are also available to students in the arts. The campus library houses 68,000 volumes and collections of recordings and periodicals, a listening room, and a language laboratory. Simon's Rock students also have access to the Bard College library. An interlibrary loan system provides access to other college and university collections. The Kilpatrick Athletic Center includes squash courts, a basketball court, an elevated track, a swimming pool, and a full-service fitness center.

The Liebowitz International Center, scheduled to open in fall 2011, will house faculty and programs focused on global issues, as well as two state-of-the-art classrooms.

Costs

For 2010–11, tuition and fees were $41,160, and room and board were $11,450. For first-year students, there is also an orientation fee.

Financial Aid

Simon's Rock is committed to making an early college education available to a diverse group of highly motivated, academically qualified students. U.S. citizens and permanent residents are eligible to apply for federal and state financial assistance programs as well as institutional scholarships and grants. International students are eligible to receive Simon's Rock scholarships and grants. Approximately 85 percent of students receive some form of financial aid.

Applicants wishing to be considered for an Acceleration to Excellence Program merit scholarship must submit their applications by February 1.

Faculty

The College has approximately 40 full-time faculty members, all of whom hold either a doctorate or an equivalent terminal degree in their field. Simon's Rock supplements this full-time faculty with visiting scholars, regular adjunct faculty members in music and studio arts, and part-time faculty members in other areas as needed. Faculty members are distinguished not only by their excellence in teaching and advising but also by their sensitivity to the particular developmental needs of the College's younger students.

Student Government

Students at Simon's Rock participate in the decision making and governance of the community through elected and appointed positions on College committees that oversee academic and social life. The campus is characterized by respect for individual rights and a strong sense of community.

Admission Requirements

Simon's Rock seeks students who are smart, independent-minded, self-directed, creative, and passionate about learning. The admission staff recognizes its special responsibility to work closely with prospective students and their parents to ensure that the decision to enter Simon's Rock is the right one. For this reason, a personal interview is required of each applicant. The application also requires an official high school transcript, three letters of recommendation, writing samples, and a parent's statement. Standardized test scores are optional for most applicants; however, international students for whom English is not a first language must submit TOEFL scores.

Application and Information

Candidates should submit their materials by May 31 for fall admission. Applications are reviewed on a rolling basis year-round, and early application is strongly encouraged. Applicants are generally notified as to the Admission Committee's decision within several weeks of the time they complete their applications. The application fee is $50.

Bard College at Simon's Rock is on Facebook (http://www.facebook.com/simonsrock) and Twitter (http://twitter.com/SimonsRock).

To schedule an interview or request further information, students should contact:

Office of Admission
Bard College at Simon's Rock
84 Alford Road
Great Barrington, Massachusetts 01230-2499

Phone: 800-235-7186 (toll-free)
Fax: 413-541-0081
E-mail: admit@simons-rock.edu
Web site: http://www.simons-rock.edu

"I have met so many different people from so many different places and different countries—everybody brings something different, says something different," student, Abdul Samad Sadri.

BARNARD COLLEGE

NEW YORK, NEW YORK

The College

Barnard College was among the pioneers in the late nineteenth-century crusade to make higher education available to young women. Founded in 1889 and formally partnered with Columbia University since 1900, today Barnard serves 2,390 students from almost every state and nearly fifty countries. It remains a partner of the university, and students at the two schools regularly cross-register for courses at either institution. Barnard students have access to Columbia University libraries, and graduates receive their degree from the university. Despite this close connection, Barnard College remains a small, independent liberal arts college, devoted solely to the undergraduate education of women. The College maintains its own Board of Trustees, faculty, and administrative staff; its own endowment; an independent admissions process; and sole ownership of its property and physical plant. It offers the intimacy of a small college with all the added advantages of a major university.

The self-contained Barnard campus occupies 4 acres of urban property along Broadway between 116th and 120th streets. Barnard Hall, home of the Ethel S. LeFrak '41 and Samuel J. LeFrak Gymnasium, the Barnard Center for Research on Women, the Athena Center for Leadership Studies, and the Julius S. Held Lecture Hall, stands opposite the main gates of the College. The south end of the campus, referred to as the Quad, contains the Brooks, Reid, Hewitt, and Sulzberger residence halls complex; first-year students are housed in three of the four buildings in the Quad. Additional housing is located nearby, and options for coed housing with Columbia are available. Students are guaranteed housing for all four years at Barnard. The latest addition, the Diana Center, a 70,000-square-foot modern student center, adds a new element of design to an amalgam of architectural styles. Its seven-story glass structure stretches across campus, linking the historic gates of the entrance at the south end of campus to one of the original campus buildings, Milbank Hall, to the north.

Location

Barnard is located on the upper west side of Manhattan, in the safe and student-friendly Morningside Heights neighborhood, directly across from Columbia University. Abounding with cultural, educational, internship, and professional opportunities and more than 600,000 college students, New York is Barnard's laboratory.

Majors and Degrees

Students can earn a Bachelor of Arts in the following subjects: Africana studies, American studies, ancient studies, anthropology, architecture, art history, Asian and Middle Eastern cultures, astronomy, biochemistry, biological sciences, chemistry, classics (Greek and Latin), comparative literature, computer science, dance, economics, education, English, environmental biology, environmental science, European studies, film studies, French, German, history, human rights studies, Italian, Jewish studies, mathematics and applied mathematics, medieval and Renaissance studies, music, neuroscience, philosophy, physics, political science, psychology, religion, Russian and Slavic studies, sociology, Spanish and Latin American cultures, statistics, theater, urban studies, and women's studies. The College provides an excellent education program, leading to certification and available to Barnard and Columbia students, and prepares students for programs in health and medicine, law, and business.

Barnard College also offers double- and joint-degree programs in cooperation with other schools within the Columbia University community. These include a five-year (3-2) program offered in conjunction with the School of International and Public Affairs, in which a student earns both an A.B. degree and a Master in International Affairs (M.I.A.) or a Master of Public Administration (M.P.A.). In cooperation with the School of Law, Barnard offers an accelerated program in interdisciplinary legal education, whereby selected students can begin their legal studies after three years of undergraduate course work. Through the School of Engineering and Applied Science, Barnard students can pursue a five-year (3-2) program in all branches of engineering, including aerospace, civil, and electrical engineering, leading to both an A.B. and a B.S. degree. In cooperation with the School of Dentistry, a limited number of students may enter the Columbia University School of Dental and Oral Surgery after three years of undergraduate work at Barnard. Outside the university, a student can earn both an A.B. degree and a Master of Music (M.M.) in a five-year (3-2) program with the Juilliard School. Through an agreement with List College of the Jewish Theological Seminary, students can earn an A.B. degree from Barnard and a bachelor's degree in Hebrew literature.

Academic Programs

Two required courses, First-Year Seminar and First-Year English, set the foundation for a Barnard education with small seminar classes limited to 16 students. General education requirements are organized around Nine Ways of Knowing which reflect the breadth and depth of a true liberal arts education while building the skills of analysis, independent thought, and self-expression. The Ways of Knowing offer a flexible structure and a wide array of courses under the following categories: ethics and values, social analysis, cultures in comparison, language, laboratory science, quantitative and deductive reasoning, historical studies, literature, and visual and performing arts.

Advanced placement and I.B. credit are available. Barnard operates on a two-semester calendar, with classes beginning in early September. The fall semester ends in mid-December; classes resume for the spring semester in mid-January and end in mid-May.

Off-Campus Programs

As an independent partner of Columbia University, Barnard offers students open access to courses, libraries, and other facilities of Columbia. With special permission, students may register for selected classes in Columbia's graduate and professional schools. A program offered in cooperation with the Jewish Theological Seminary, located two blocks north of Barnard, allows qualified students to take courses for credit. In a similar exchange with both the Juilliard School and the nearby Manhattan School of Music, qualified Barnard students may take music lessons in a conservatory setting.

Barnard has a rich history and tradition of study abroad dating back to the 1930s. Today, qualified students are eligible to study in nearly 150 programs in more than fifty countries worldwide and more than a third of Barnard students spend a semester or year abroad. Students are currently studying in Argentina, Australia, Austria, Bolivia, Brazil, British West Indies, Chile, China, Costa Rica, Czech Republic, Denmark, Dominican Republic, Ecuador, England, France, Germany, Greece, Hungary, Ireland, Israel, Italy, Japan, Jordan, Kenya, Madagascar, Netherlands, New Zealand, Panama, Peru, Russia, Scotland, Senegal, South Africa, Spain, Switzerland, and Syria. Students may also participate in domestic exchange programs with Spelman College in Atlanta and Howard University in Washington, D.C.

Barnard's metropolitan location offers its students a variety of work experiences through its extensive program of more than 2,500 internships. More than two thirds of Barnard students participate in internships throughout the academic year and summer; nearly one third of these internship opportunities receive stipends.

Academic Facilities

Historic Milbank Hall anchors the north end of campus, topped by the 2,500-square-foot Arthur Ross Greenhouse, and housing administrative and faculty offices in addition to the Minor Latham Playhouse. Sulzberger Tower and the residential quadrangle secure the south end of campus where more than 90 percent of Barnard students reside.

There are over 300,000 volumes in the library in Lehman Hall (and nearly another 10 million in the University Library System); dance studios and classrooms in Barnard Hall and the Barnard Hall Annex; state-of-the-art science labs in the fourteen-story Altschul Hall; and architecture classrooms with a view in the Diana Center, with its terra-cotta glass façade, black box theatre, and art gallery, among other remarkable features. At the heart of it all is the welcoming beauty of Barnard's beloved Lehman Lawn.

Costs

Tuition and fees for 2010–11 were $40,546. Room and board costs were $12,950.

Financial Aid

Financial aid at Barnard is awarded based upon demonstrated need. Federal funds and institutional grants are administered as determined by federal and institutional methodology, assuming College aid is supplementary to family resources. Barnard gives no merit or athletic scholarships. Once need has been established, Barnard is committed to covering 100 percent of demonstrated need for U.S. citizens and permanent residents through a combination of grants, loans, and work-study. Approximately 51 percent of the students at Barnard receive some form of financial aid. A limited number of scholarships are available to international citizens.

Barnard College has a need-blind admission policy in which all applications are judged on merit without reference to the applicant's financial circumstances.

Faculty

Barnard College employs 361 teaching faculty members. The student-faculty ratio is 7:1 (9:1 FTE). The faculty includes editors of leading scholarly journals, prize-winning novelists and translators, and frequent winners of awards from respected foundations, corporations, and government agencies. They are actively engaged in research and publication in their respective fields, but they regard teaching as their primary commitment. From the start of their time at the College, all students have faculty advisers who assist them in selecting courses and designing individual academic programs.

Student Government

Barnard women have access to more than eighty clubs and organizations on the College campus alone. Add to this list the hundreds of additional dually recognized clubs with members from both the Barnard and Columbia campuses provided for through Barnard's longstanding partnership with the University, and the friendships developed among students on either side of Broadway. Student groups include theatre and vocal music groups, academic and preprofessional organizations, ethnic and cultural organizations, language clubs, community service groups, and yearbook and literary magazine staffs. The Barnard student newspaper, the *Barnard Bulletin*, is published biweekly. Cooperation between Barnard and Columbia groups is quite common and virtually seamless, with Barnard women regularly joining and leading a variety of Columbia University organizations. Students, faculty members, and administrators also serve on tripartite committees and share responsibility for policy recommendations on curriculum, housing, financial aid, orientation, and the library.

Admission Requirements

The Committee on Admissions selects young women of proven academic strength who exhibit the potential for further intellectual growth. Careful consideration is given to candidates' high school records, recommendations, writing skills, standardized test scores, and special abilities and interests. While admission is highly selective, no one criterion determines acceptance. Each applicant is considered in terms of her individual qualities of mind and spirit and her potential for successfully completing her program of study at Barnard.

Candidates for admission to the first-year class must have taken a college-preparatory program at an approved secondary school or have an equivalent level of education. A recommended program, at minimum, comprises 4 years of work in English, 3 or more years in mathematics, 3 or more years in a foreign language, 3 or more years in science (with laboratory), and 3 or more years in history. Barnard also requires candidates to submit scores from the SAT Reasoning Test, along with two SAT Subject Tests. Alternatively, students may submit scores from the ACT with writing in place of the SAT and subject tests. Students educated in a non-English-speaking setting or who have studied in English for less than five years should take the TOEFL or IELTS exam as well. An interview is recommended for first-year students, but is not required.

Application and Information

Applicants for first-year admission should apply to Barnard in the fall of their senior year of high school. Applications must be received by January 1 and should be accompanied by a nonrefundable fee of $55. Students are notified of the admission decision in late March. Well-qualified high school seniors who have selected Barnard as their first-choice college may apply under the binding early decision plan. Early decision applications must be submitted by November 15. Barnard accepts transfer students to the sophomore and junior classes. Transfer applications must be submitted by March 15 for consideration for September enrollment and by November 1 for consideration for January enrollment.

For more information about Barnard College, students should contact:

Jennifer Gill Fondiller
Dean of Admissions and Financial Aid
Barnard College
3009 Broadway
New York, New York 10027

Phone: 212-854-2014
Fax: 212-854-6220
E-mail: admissions@barnard.edu
Web site: http://www.barnard.edu
http://www.facebook.com/barnardadmissions

A view of Milbank Hall from the Diana, Barnard's new student center.

BARRY UNIVERSITY
MIAMI SHORES, FLORIDA

The University

Barry University in Miami Shores, Florida, is the second-largest private, Catholic university in the southeastern United States. Founded in 1940 by the Dominican Sisters of Adrian, Michigan, the University provides a multicultural student body with a high-quality education; a caring environment; and a religious dimension, which encourages a commitment to social justice and community service. Classes are small, so students receive personal attention from distinguished faculty members and advisers. The student-faculty ratio is 14:1.

The palm-tree lined main campus is in Miami Shores, but the University also offers adult and continuing education programs at more than twenty additional sites from South Miami to Tallahassee. Students come from all compass points, age groups, ethnicities, and faith perspectives, representing nearly all fifty states and close to 120 countries. Of the nearly 9,000 students enrolled, more than 3,000 are traditional undergraduate students and nearly 5,500 are graduate and continuing education students.

Barry offers more than 100 bachelor's, master's, and doctoral degree programs in the arts and sciences, business, education, health sciences, human performance and leisure sciences, law, podiatric medicine, and social work. Some are five-year bachelor's-to-master's programs. Students can also gain hands-on professional experience before graduation through internships.

Resident students live in eight air-conditioned residence halls and three apartment buildings. Each room includes cable and high-speed Internet access. All students may keep cars on campus. The University's Department of Commuter Affairs serves as a resource center for students who live off campus.

Barry holds membership in twenty honor societies and hosts more than sixty student organizations, including the dance club, gospel choir, Campus Activities Board, and WBRY student radio station, as well as fraternities and sororities. Barry also promotes community service through organizations including Best Buddies, Habitat for Humanity, Alternative Spring Break, and Pals-4-Paws animal rescue.

The 78,000-square-foot R. Kirk Landon Student Union houses the offices of student services and student organizations as well as a bookstore, dining room, snack bar, game room, and more. A fully equipped fitness center features weight and cardio equipment.

The University fields twelve intercollegiate athletic teams that participate in the NCAA Division II and the Sunshine State Conference. The Buccaneers have won eight national championships. Nearly 60 percent of Barry's student-athletes achieve grade point averages above 3.0. Intramural sports include basketball, flag football, soccer, softball, and table tennis.

The University is accredited by the Southern Association of Colleges and Schools to award bachelor's, master's, specialist, and doctoral degrees. Barry also holds a number of accreditations from professional organizations for specific programs.

Location

Barry University is located in sunny Miami Shores, Florida, just 5 miles from the ocean and minutes from the dynamic city of Miami. South Florida is a center for international business, tourism, and entertainment, providing a wide range of internship options and a vibrant cultural scene. Highlights include Urban Beach Week, the Calle Ocho street festival, the Miami International Book Fair, and the Art Basel Miami Beach contemporary art festival. The New World Symphony, the Miami International Film Festival, and the Miami City Ballet provide a full season of performances. South Florida also hosts the Miami Dolphins football team, the Miami Heat basketball team, the Florida Marlins baseball team, and the Florida Panthers hockey team. The hospitable climate allows for swimming, sailing, scuba diving, golf, tennis, soccer, and other outdoor activities year-round, and the natural beauty of the Florida Keys, Everglades, and coral reefs are just a day trip away.

Majors and Degrees

Barry University offers the Bachelor of Arts degree in advertising, art (art history, ceramics, graphic design, and painting and/or drawing), broadcast communication, communication studies, English (literature and professional writing), history, international studies, music, philosophy, photography (biomedical/forensic), prelaw, public relations, Spanish (language and literature and translation and interpretation), theater (acting, dance theater, technical theater), and theology.

The Bachelor of Science degree is offered in accounting, athletic training (premedicine and pre–physical therapy specializations and a five-year seamless B.S. to M.S.), biology (clinical, marine, and preprofessional), cardiovascular perfusion, chemistry (biochemistry, environmental chemistry, predental, premedical, prepharmacy, and pre-veterinary), computer information sciences, computer science, criminology, elementary education (ESOL, autism, gifted, and reading endorsements), exercise science (premedical and pre–physical therapy specializations and a five-year seamless B.S. to M.S.), exceptional student education (ESOL endorsement), finance, international business, management, marketing, mathematical sciences (computational, general, and statistics/actuarial science), physical education (grades K–12), political science, psychology (industrial/organizational), sociology, and sport management (diving industry, golf industry, and five-year seamless B.S. to M.S.). There is also a five-year seamless B.S. to M.S. degree in education, with three specializations: infancy through early childhood (birth–grade 3), early and middle childhood (K–6), and special education (K–12).

The University also offers the Bachelor of Science in Nursing, the Bachelor of Fine Arts (art and photography), the Bachelor of Music (instrumental performance; sacred music; and voice, opera, and musical theater), and the Bachelor of Social Work.

Minor concentrations are available in specific subject areas as well as in the interdisciplinary areas of Africana studies, film studies, journalism, peace studies, social sciences, and women's studies.

Accelerated undergraduate degree programs are offered for working adults through Barry's evening and weekend programs.

Academic Programs

The University operates on a semester plan. The first semester extends from the end of August to mid-December, and the second semester extends from mid-January to early May. Two 6-week sessions are offered during the summer. Students must maintain a minimum cumulative grade point average of 2.0 (or C) and earn a minimum of 120 credits for a degree. Of these 120 credits, 9 must be in philosophy and theology, 9 in communication—oral and written, 9 in humanities and arts, 9 in physical or natural sciences and mathematics, and 9 in social and behavioral sciences. The traditional full-time academic load is 12 to 18 credits each semester and 6 credits each summer term. Candidates for degree programs may elect a major and area of specialization and must satisfy all requirements of the program that they choose to follow, including all professional preparation requirements. Internships are required for many majors.

An ELS Language Centers program is available to international students who need to increase language proficiency. The Center for Advanced Learning offers a program designed to assist students with learning disabilities who have the intellectual potential and motivation to complete a four-year degree.

The Honors Program offers an active, interdisciplinary honors curriculum designed to add breadth and depth to the educational experience.

Off-Campus Programs

Barry University offers summer programs abroad in places such as Europe and China. Barry is also a member of the College Consortium for International Studies, enabling students to participate in programs offered by member colleges and universities in more than thirty countries. Barry University students may enroll in Air Force ROTC courses through cross-registration at a nearby university.

Academic Facilities

At Barry, students find the high-quality resources they need to support their education. Campus facilities include the Monsignor William Barry Memorial Library, an extensive library network, the Glenn Hubert Learning Center, photography and digital imaging labs, a human performance lab, an athletic training room, a biomechanics lab, a full-service digital television production studio, an academic computing center, multimedia business classrooms, art studios, a performing arts center, a nursing lab and resource center, and several other labs dedicated to Barry's health, science, and education programs.

Costs

For 2010–11, tuition for full-time undergraduate students for the academic year was $27,200. Student services fees are included in tuition. Room and board costs averaged $9000, based on a double-occupancy room. Expenses such as books, supplies, laboratory or other special fees, and transportation are not included in these costs.

Financial Aid

Close to 90 percent of all undergraduate students at Barry University receive some form of financial aid. Barry participates in the full array of federal and state of Florida financial aid programs. Barry also offers an excellent scholarship program, awarding aid each year to students who have demonstrated academic success and promise. These scholarships may be renewed for up to four years as long as the student meets the renewal criteria. Athletic scholarships are also available.

To be considered for financial assistance, applicants must submit the Free Application for Federal Student Aid (FAFSA). Additional information may be obtained by calling the Office of Financial Aid at 305-899-3673 or 800-695-2279 (toll-free) or by e-mail at finaid@mail.barry.edu.

Faculty

Faculty members are easily accessible to students and are committed to providing personal attention. More than 80 percent of faculty members hold a Ph.D. or terminal degree in their field of study. The student-faculty ratio is 14:1.

Student Government

The Student Government Association serves as a liaison between the student body and the administration and faculty. All undergraduate students are members of the association, which is governed by an Executive Board comprising 4 members, and the Senate, which consists of 7 elected representatives. Unless otherwise specified, Senate meetings are open, and students are invited and encouraged to attend the weekly sessions.

Admission Requirements

In reviewing the credentials of students seeking admission, Barry University considers an applicant's composite efforts. Candidates must present the following materials: the completed application form, official high school or college transcripts, and the results of the SAT or ACT.

Application and Information

The University reviews applications as they are completed. Students are advised of their acceptance once the admissions staff has reviewed all required documents. Students may apply any time after completion of their junior year in high school. It is advisable to apply early. The student's completed application form and supporting credentials should be sent to the Office of Admissions. Students may also apply online at http://www.barry.edu/mybarry.

Ms. Magda Castineyra
Director of Undergraduate Admissions
Barry University
Division of Enrollment Services
11300 Northeast Second Avenue
Miami Shores, Florida 33161-6695
Phone: 305-899-3100
            800-695-2279 (toll-free)
Fax: 305-899-2971
E-mail: admissions@mail.barry.edu
Web site: http://www.barry.edu
            http://twitter.com/BarryUniversity (Twitter)

Barry's tropical, palm-tree lined main campus is just a few miles from the dynamic city of Miami.

BARTON COLLEGE
WILSON, NORTH CAROLINA

The College

Founded in 1902 as the first degree-granting institution in eastern North Carolina, Barton College opened its doors to 107 students with one building on 5 acres of campus. Today, Barton welcomes approximately 1,200 students from twenty-four states and nine countries to a campus of twenty-six buildings on 65 acres.

The College offers several avenues of assistance for students, especially during the freshman year, including an innovative freshman advising program designed to assist students in making the transition from home and high school to college and residence hall life. All freshmen meet with their adviser three times a week in a classroom seminar setting. Outside the classroom experience, the First-Year Seminar program also offers exposure to a variety of cultural and social events, including concerts, lectures, art exhibits, theater productions, and sports events. Inside the classroom, Barton's student-centered core curriculum enhances academic success and provides students with an outstanding foundation from which the total liberal arts experience is achieved.

Barton's Student Affairs Program includes residence life programs, special activities, fellowship programs, and counseling services that provide for the students' cultural, social, spiritual, and emotional development. In addition, Barton has fifty clubs and organizations in which students can be involved, including academic organizations, specialty clubs, fraternities, and sororities. Another vital component of student life is the Career Services Center. The center provides a vigorous on-campus recruiting program that brings approximately 100 recruiters to Barton's campus annually, representing corporations, government, and educational areas. In addition, several hundred other employers seek to hire Barton students each year. Barton's graduates rank exceptionally well in obtaining employment in their chosen field of study, and their salaries are competitive with those of students from other North Carolina colleges and universities.

On-campus housing is provided in five residence halls: East Campus Suites, Hilley, Hackney, Waters, and Wenger. All five facilities feature cable television and Internet access in each room. East Campus Suites is Barton's newest residence hall for juniors and seniors and offers additional amenities and more independence.

Offering a strong, competitive sports program, Barton College's Bulldogs compete in the NCAA Division II and the Conference Carolinas. The intercollegiate sports program includes women's basketball, cross-country, fast-pitch softball, soccer, tennis, track and field, and volleyball; and men's baseball, basketball, cross-country, golf, soccer, tennis, and track and field. Beginning in fall 2011, Barton will also offer women's golf and men's volleyball. In 2007, the Barton College men's basketball team won the NCAA Division II National Championship. Also, in recent years, Barton has won the Joby Hawn Award multiple times, recognizing the College as having the best overall athletics program within the Conference Carolinas. A wide variety of intramural sports are also offered to the entire campus community. All students and especially those involved in Barton's intramural, physical education, and athletic programs benefit from the Kennedy Recreation and Intramural Center that features an indoor swimming pool, walking/jogging areas, an auxiliary gym, and a weight/fitness room. Barton also has a twelve-court tennis complex to add to its outstanding facilities package.

The 30-acre Barton College Athletic Complex includes the award-winning Nixon Baseball Field, the Jeffries Softball Field, and a newly lighted soccer field, in addition to several practice fields and the Scott Davis Field House.

Location

Wilson is in the coastal plain region of eastern North Carolina. The city provides an excellent home for the College and is within easy driving distance of several metropolitan areas and scenic attractions. The state capital of Raleigh is a 35-minute drive to the west; to the north, Richmond, Virginia, is 2 hours away and Washington, D.C., is 4 hours away. The beautiful Atlantic coast of North Carolina is 100 miles from the campus, and the scenic Blue Ridge Mountains are easily accessible. Located on Interstate 95, Wilson is also accessible by U.S. Routes 264, 117, and 301 and North Carolina Routes 42 and 58. Wilson is 45 minutes from Raleigh/Durham International Airport. Amtrak has daily service with one northbound and one southbound departure.

The College's historic neighborhood is just a few minutes from busy downtown Wilson. Banks, theaters, shopping centers, and restaurants are close by. Many of Wilson's arts and cultural events take place on the College campus. The Wilson community (approx. population 50,000) enjoys a mild climate that has an average annual temperature of 65 degrees.

Majors and Degrees

Barton College offers six baccalaureate degrees: Bachelor of Arts, Bachelor of Science, Bachelor of Fine Arts, Bachelor of Nursing, Bachelor of Social Work, and Bachelor of Liberal Studies. A new graduate degree program, the Master of Education in elementary education, is also offered. These degrees are administered by five schools.

The School of Arts and Sciences offers programs in art education (K–12), art and design (with concentrations in ceramics, graphic design, painting, and photography), athletic training, biology, (preprofessional programs in dentistry, medical technology, medicine, physical therapy, and veterinary medicine), chemistry (preprofessional program in pharmacy), criminal justice and criminology, English*, fitness management, health and physical education (with teacher licensure), history, mass communications (concentrations include audio recording technology, broadcast/video production, journalism, and public relations), mathematics (preprofessional program in engineering), political science (concentrations include business and prelaw), psychology, religion and philosophy, social studies secondary education, Spanish*, sport management, and theater (concentrations include design, management, and performance).

The School of Social Work offers a program in social work.

The School of Business offers programs in accounting, business management, economics, and management of human resources.

The School of Education offers programs in education of the deaf and hard of hearing (K–12), elementary education (K–6), middle school education (6–9), and special education: general curriculum (K–12), as well as a Master of Education degree in elementary education.

The School of Nursing offers programs in nursing and gerontology.

*Programs indicated with an asterisk (*) are available with or without a teacher licensure program.

Minors can be earned in accounting, American studies, art and design, biology, business administration, chemistry, computer information systems, criminal justice and criminology, economics, English, finance, geography, gerontology, history, international business, management, mass communications, mathematics, political science, psychology, religion and philosophy, Spanish, strength and conditioning, theater, and writing.

Academic Programs

Barton College offers a strong liberal arts tradition, and students follow a core curriculum during their freshman and sophomore years. Through a carefully guided advising program they declare a major area of study at the end of their freshman year or at the beginning of their sophomore year. At that point, they begin an intense and challenging program of study in their chosen field while completing general college requirements.

Barton College's athletic training education, nursing, education, and social work programs are nationally accredited programs. The School of Business majors continue to be popular areas of study. Barton is one of the few colleges on the East Coast to offer a program for the education of the deaf and the hard of hearing. Also unique is the audio recording technology program, which features a 32-track digital recording studio. Theater majors benefit from the new Lauren Kennedy and Alan Campbell Theatre, a state-of-the art black-box theater facility.

Off-Campus Programs

Each year students participate in faculty-led trips to different areas of the world. Students recognize this travel as an excellent opportunity to enrich their college experience. Depending on the nature and destination of the travel, students may obtain college credit for their participation. Barton also has exchange agreements with colleges in Europe and Asia for extended overseas study offered in conjunction with a global focus emphasis.

Academic Facilities

Barton College has a fiber-optic underground network that includes an infrastructure of data, voice, and video wiring across campus. The Willis N. Hackney Library is open 87.5 hours per week to serve the College community. The library's offerings include over 152,000 volumes, more than 24,460 electronic books, and a substantial collection of non-print materials. It subscribes to approximately 355 periodicals and newspapers in print and microform format and provides full-text access to over 19,000 periodicals in online databases, which are accessible to Barton users both on and off campus. The curriculum lab, located on the second floor of Hackney Library, includes copies of textbooks and other resource materials used in the North Carolina public schools. Hackney Library is also a depository for selected U.S. government documents and offers Internet access to a wide variety of resources. The library has an automated cataloging system that is accessible via the Internet. Computers for research and other uses are available at the library to both the Barton community and the public. A wireless computer network and loaner wireless laptops are also available to Barton students.

The newest teaching facility is the Lauren Kennedy and Alan Campbell Theatre, which opened in 2009. This innovative black box theater provides a flexible and adaptable space for teaching and performance.

Located on the first floor of J. W. Hines Hall are two computer labs for classes and individual student use. Computer labs are also available for student use in the Nixon Nursing Building, the Belk Education Building, Hamlin Student Center, and Moye Science Hall. Belk Education Building houses the Merck Science and Mathematics Instructional Lab. The Sam and Marjorie Ragan Writing Center supplements Barton's commitment to language and writing as vital components of the liberal arts curriculum.

WEDT-TV, a local cable television station operated by Barton College and staffed by Barton students, is located in the Roma Hackney Music Building. The TV studio provides equipment and facilities for study and use in video and audio production. The Hackney Music Building also houses classrooms, the College's library for recordings and musical scores, and the Sara Lynn Kennedy Recording Studio. Moye Science Hall provides classrooms, laboratories, a greenhouse, and research-related study areas for students. The Nixon Nursing Building houses classrooms and a laboratory for the nursing program, as well as a multimedia center with a projection system used for a broad range of lecture and teaching purposes. Case Art Building provides classrooms, class studios, and two art galleries for Barton's permanent art collection and visiting exhibits. The art building also houses computer graphics, digital imaging, and darkroom labs.

Costs

Expenses for the 2010–11 year included tuition, $20,150; room, $3344; board plan, $3972; and combined fees, $1634. These totaled $29,100 for the year. The estimated cost of books per semester is $600. Rates for East Campus Suites are not listed because of limited availability; this facility is reserved for juniors and seniors.

Financial Aid

The objective of the financial aid program at Barton College is to provide financial assistance to qualified students who would not otherwise be able to begin or continue their college education. Financial aid is awarded on the basis of need. (Financial need exists when the total cost of education exceeds the amount of money a student and family can reasonably make available from income and assets.) Barton College requires that all applicants for financial aid complete the Free Application for Federal Student Aid (FAFSA) as a means of determining financial need. Approximately 90 percent of Barton students receive financial aid. Aid comes from federal, state, and institutional resources and may be awarded as scholarships, grants, loans, or work-study. In addition, many students apply for part-time jobs on campus or in the community.

Students are encouraged to apply early for financial aid and should have their completed application in the Financial Aid Office by June 1 in order to ensure receipt of awards by the beginning of the fall semester. Every effort is made to process completed applications received after this date; however, earlier applications receive top priority in the awards process.

Faculty

Faculty members at Barton College recognize the importance of personalized attention for the students' learning experience. Because of the 11:1 student-faculty ratio, professors at Barton are able to teach small classes and have the opportunity to meet and to get to know their students as individuals. Faculty members make every effort to be accessible to students between classes and during regularly scheduled office hours. Professors at Barton are committed to the success of their students.

Student Government

The Student Government Association (SGA) of Barton College provides students with opportunities to express themselves on issues of concern. Student government also provides a setting for studying the democratic process. The officers of the SGA are elected by the members of the student body, and the president of the SGA serves as an ex officio member of the College Board of Trustees.

Admission Requirements

To be considered for admission to Barton College, a student must have a high school diploma or its equivalent with a minimum total of 13 college-preparatory units. The following courses are recommended: English, 4 units; mathematics, 3 or more units (algebra I, geometry, and algebra II are required); natural sciences, 2 or more units (one lab science is required); social sciences, 3 or more units; and foreign language, 2 or more units (encouraged, but not required). A student applying for admission must also take the SAT or ACT and achieve a score that, when considered along with the high school record, predicts probable success in college. Students interested in transferring to Barton College should contact the Office of Admissions for requirements.

Application and Information

To apply for admission to the College, a student must submit a completed application, a nonrefundable $25 application fee ($50 for international students), and an official transcript of high school credits. A copy of SAT or ACT scores should be sent to the Office of Admissions by the testing agency. International applicants whose native language is not English must also submit the results of the Test of English as a Foreign Language (TOEFL). Students are encouraged to apply early and are usually notified of a decision within two weeks of the admission office's receipt of the completed application and information.

For further information, students may contact:

Office of Admissions
Barton College
Box 5000
Wilson, North Carolina 27893-7000
Phone: 252-399-6317
      800-345-4973 (toll-free)
Fax: 252-399-6572
E-mail: enroll@barton.edu
Web site: http://www.barton.edu
     http://on.fb.me/Barton_Coll (Facebook)
     http://twitter.com/bartonadmission
     http://www.youtube.com/bartoncollege

BASTYR UNIVERSITY

KENMORE, WASHINGTON

The University

An undergraduate education at Bastyr University is the first step on a path leading to a richly rewarding future in the dynamic field of science-based natural health. Bastyr's unparalleled programs are based on a mind-body-spirit approach to wellness, with a challenging curriculum that prepares students to further their goals in scientific, medical, and wellness-related fields. Expertise in natural and holistic healing is increasingly in demand, so graduates with degrees in the natural health sciences fulfill an important role in the marketplace.

Bastyr University is a world-renowned institution of natural health arts and sciences, with a reputation as a leader and innovator in the field. Founded as a naturopathic medical college in 1978, Bastyr has since expanded its offerings to become a multidisciplinary university with a wide range of graduate and undergraduate educational opportunities. The foundation of Bastyr University's entire curriculum rests on the integration of modern science with traditional healing methods.

As a small independent university, Bastyr offers students a strong sense of community with abundant academic and personal support. Undergraduate students enjoy a collegial relationship with graduate students as well as with faculty and staff members.

Bastyr undergraduate students are goal-oriented individuals who bring a passionate interest and intense focus to their areas of study. They thrive on diversity and individual expression, and they continually seek out opportunities to grow both intellectually and personally.

As part of its mission to improve the well-being of the human community, Bastyr University conducts research studies at its research institute and delivers premier care at its natural health care clinic. The Bastyr University Research Institute is devoted to the evaluation of natural medicine practices and the exploration of natural therapies for serious chronic diseases. Participation in research projects is available to a select number of students. The University's teaching clinic in Seattle, Bastyr Center for Natural Health, is the largest natural health clinic in the Northwest and provides the main venue for graduate students' clinical training.

In 1989, Bastyr University became the first naturopathic school to achieve accreditation and is accredited by the Northwest Commission on Colleges and Universities.

Location

The Bastyr University campus is located in Kenmore, Washington, just north of Seattle, in the heart of the picturesque Pacific Northwest. Bastyr's inviting campus environment is a strong attraction for students, who find it uniquely suited to the study of healing practices. Adjacent to the University's 51 acres of fields and gardens are miles of wooded trails winding through the 316-acre St. Edward State Park on the northeast shore of Lake Washington. The park also features a public swimming pool, outdoor volleyball courts, tennis courts, and playfields, which are available to Bastyr students.

Seattle is one of the most attractive cities in the Pacific Northwest and has easy access to mountains, ocean beaches, lakes, and numerous national, state, and city parks. Several ski areas are within an hour's drive, and there are plentiful opportunities for hiking, camping, and other outdoor recreation. The city offers a full range of museums, theaters, fine restaurants, a major opera company, a symphony orchestra, major-league sports, and outdoor activities.

Majors and Degrees

Bastyr University offers several two-year, upper-division programs that lead to Bachelor of Science degrees. Undergraduates may choose majors in exercise science and wellness, health psychology, herbal sciences, integrated human biology, nutrition, nutrition and culinary

arts, nutrition and exercise science, or a combined B.S./M.S. program in acupuncture and Oriental medicine (AOM) that is designed to meet the requirements for national licensure in acupuncture. Students can also choose a double major.

Academic Programs

In each degree program at Bastyr, students learn to integrate the pursuit of physical health with the mental, spiritual, and environmental factors involved in wellness.

The Bachelor of Science with a major in nutrition provides students with a comprehensive education that merges the science of nutrition with a broader view of wellness, community and the environment. Bastyr's experienced faculty guides students through the physiological, biochemical, socioeconomic, political, and psychological aspects of human nutrition. This B.S. degree program can be combined with the Didactic Program in Dietetics for those interested in becoming registered dietitians (RD). Bastyr University's Didactic Program in Dietetics has been approved by the American Dietetic Association Council on Education.

The Bachelor of Science with a major in nutrition and culinary arts is one of the nation's first degree programs of its kind, combining the rigorous sciences of human metabolism, nutrition, and food with a full spectrum of culinary skill development. With a whole food philosophy at its core, this innovative degree will prepare graduates for enhanced career opportunities in areas that require knowledge of both nutrition and the culinary arts.

The Bachelor of Science with a major in nutrition and exercise science integrates the University's unique whole-food approach with exercise physiology and holistic health and wellness. Students learn about the impact that nutrition and physical activity have on health and wellness. Graduates may develop careers in the areas of community health and fitness or disease prevention and health promotion, including strength and conditioning coaches and personal trainers. This degree also prepares students for graduate work in related health science fields.

The Bachelor of Science with a major in exercise science and wellness combines a rigorous, in-depth study of the body's physiology and mechanics with a focus on nutrition, stress management, and holistic wellness. Graduates are prepared to work in the fitness and wellness industry and possess the educational requirements needed to achieve exercise certification from the American College of Sports Medicine and other professional exercise affiliates.

The Bachelor of Science with a major in health psychology offers a solid foundation in core psychology with a progressive focus on the relationship between health and the body, mind, and spirit. Students learn the tools to improve people's quality of life and to address systemic problems in society and social institutions. Students may enroll in one of two tracks: health psychology, or psychology and human biology (psychology premed).

The Bachelor of Science with a major in herbal sciences provides a thorough and scientifically rigorous introduction to herbal medicine, including plant identification and pharmacology. The program also imparts real-world skills and expertise in the herbal products industry and introduces the student to concepts of disease prevention and health maintenance using medicinal herbs.

The Bachelor of Science with a major in integrated human biology serves as excellent preparation for a career as a twenty-first-century health practitioner or biomedical researcher. With a focus on hands-on scientific research, this progressive program connects concepts from physiology, anatomy, cell biology, biochemistry, and genetics. Graduates are prepared to pursue a range of professional degrees (naturopathic doctor, medical doctor, dentist, pharmacist), allied health degrees (physician's assistant, nurse, physical therapist), and graduate studies in biological sciences.

Bastyr's acupuncture and Oriental medicine program combines the ancient wisdom and time-honored traditions of Oriental medicine with the rigors of contemporary medical science. The combined B.S./M.S. option in acupuncture and Oriental medicine is generally a 3.5 year program. A certificate program for additional study in Chinese herbal medicine is also offered. The University's acupuncture and Oriental medicine programs are accredited by the Accreditation Commission for Acupuncture and Oriental Medicine (ACAOM) and meet the requirements of the national certification exam.

In addition to its undergraduate programs, the University offers master's programs in nutrition and in acupuncture as well as doctoral programs in naturopathic medicine and in acupuncture and Oriental medicine.

Academic Facilities

The University's 186,000-square-foot facility houses a wealth of resources dedicated to students, including a comprehensive bookstore, numerous scientific laboratories, a whole-food nutrition kitchen, research facilities, a gourmet vegetarian cafeteria, dormitory space, and wireless Internet access and computer labs.

The University also maintains a medical library with extensive resources for conventional and natural medicine. These include more than 19,000 volumes; 250 journal subscriptions; special collections in the areas of nutrition, herbal sciences, psychology, and exercise science; and access to many health and natural medicine databases. Students at Bastyr University are also eligible to use the Health Sciences Library at the University of Washington.

Costs

Tuition for the 2010–11 academic year was $528 per credit for 1 to 11.5 credits and $6325 per quarter for 12–16 credits; the cost for each additional credit over 16 was $335. The total cost of tuition and fees for a full-time student for the academic year was $19,995 ($24,431 for the combined B.S./M.S. AOM program), depending on the number of credits needed to complete a program. Students can expect to spend approximately $1125 per year on books and supplies ($1950 for the combined B.S./M.S. program).

Bastyr's new Student Village housing complex is eco-friendly and LEED-certified Platinum. Opened in summer 2010, the village includes eleven cottage-style buildings and can house up to 132 students in individual rooms. The three-story cottages connect to a series of garden paths, courtyards, and outdoor living spaces designed to be energy efficient.

Many students also live in shared housing facilities off campus; the average rent per person ranges from $400 to $900 per month. The Office of Student Affairs maintains listings of available housing, which are also listed on Bastyr's Web site at http://www.bastyr.edu/housing. The Washington Financial Aid Association estimates that living expenses for nine months, including transportation and personal expenses, average $1405 per month.

Financial Aid

Students are eligible to participate in state and federal financial aid programs, including the Washington State Need Grant, Washington State Education Opportunity Grant, Federal Pell Grant, Federal Supplemental Educational Opportunity Grant (FSEOG), Federal Stafford Student Loan, Federal Perkins Loan, and the Federal Work-Study Program. Applicants seeking financial aid should complete the application process by May 15. Financial aid information is provided by the University on request.

Faculty

Bastyr University students enjoy a 9:1 student-faculty ratio with professors who are approachable and accessible. There are 49 core and 95 adjunct faculty members, many of whom teach in both the undergraduate and graduate programs. More than 80 percent hold advanced or doctoral degrees. All faculty members are involved in teaching and are dedicated to providing students with programs of the highest quality.

Student Government

Students have a variety of opportunities for contributing to the operation of the Bastyr community. The Student Council makes decisions about social activities, school policies, and budget items affecting students. Each class and program is represented on the council. Students also serve on the Curriculum Review, Library, and Resident Selection committees; the Appeals Board; and ad hoc committees.

Admission Requirements

Admission is based on academic achievement, personal and social development, and demonstrated humanistic qualities. Credentials to be submitted include all official transcripts, a completed application form, and a $60 application fee. The minimum prerequisite for the bachelor's programs is two years of college-level general education (90 quarter or 60 semester credits), including those distribution and course requirements described below. Students must take the following distribution of general education courses, which are not counted toward any other requirements: arts and humanities, 15 quarter credits; social sciences, 15 quarter credits; and natural sciences and mathematics, 12 quarter credits. In addition, specific required courses include 9 quarter credits of English composition and/or literature, 4 quarter credits of intermediate algebra, 8 quarter credits of general chemistry (science-major level, with lab), 4 quarter credits of general biology (with lab), 3 quarter credits of general psychology, and 3 quarter credits of public speaking. Nutrition majors are required to have taken 5 quarter credits of introductory nutrition. Herbal sciences majors are required to have 3 quarter credits of botany. A minimum 2.25 overall GPA and a C or better in all basic proficiency and science requirement courses are needed.

Application and Information

Applications should be submitted to the University by March 15 for priority consideration for fall admission. Late applications are considered if space is available. Application may be made by submitting the Bastyr University undergraduate application with a $60 nonrefundable fee and all official transcripts. Online applications are also available and can be accessed at http://www.bastyr.edu/admissions.

Prospective students are encouraged to visit the campus or attend recruiting events in their region. For further information, students should contact:

Admissions Office
Bastyr University
14500 Juanita Drive NE
Kenmore, Washington 98028
Phone: 425-602-3330
E-mail: admissions@bastyr.edu
Web site: http://www.bastyr.edu/sub/adtrack.asp?adid=pe01

Students on the Bastyr Kenmore campus.

BAY STATE COLLEGE
BOSTON, MASSACHUSETTS

The College

Founded in 1946, Bay State College is a private, independent coeducational institution located in Boston's historic Back Bay. Since its founding, Bay State College has been preparing graduates for outstanding careers and continued education.

The College primarily offers associate degrees and has expanded into bachelor's degree offerings. The educational experience offered through the variety of associate and bachelor's degree programs prepares students to excel in the career of their choice. Personalized attention is the cornerstone of a Bay State College education. Through the transformative power of its core values of quality, respect, and support, Bay State College has been able to assist students with setting and achieving goals that prepare them for careers and continued education. In fact, with its First-Year Experience, a 1-credit course all students must complete, Bay State College students are exposed to the concept of "action planning." The Bay State College action plan is designed to help students identify their goals and set about a course of action to achieve those goals. Students review their action plan each semester with their academic adviser and evaluate how they are progressing on their plan. This is just one method Bay State College graduates apply to their lives beyond college. The ability to identify, set, and achieve goals is a trait all people aspire to master.

Recognizing that one of the most important aspects of college is life outside the classroom, the Office of Student Affairs seeks to provide services to Bay State College students from orientation through graduation and beyond. There are many clubs and organizations on campus, such as the Criminal Justice Society, the Early Childhood Education Club, the Student Government Association, and the Entertainment Management Association. Bay State College students enjoy the opportunity to create clubs and organizations that meet their interests. Special events throughout the year include a fashion show and a host of events produced by the Entertainment Management Association. Students also enjoy professional sports teams such as the Boston Celtics and the Boston Red Sox.

To support the overall wellness of the student body, Bay State has partnered with the Body Evolver Fitness Club, where students can take advantage of a wide variety of fitness equipment and classes at a discounted rate.

One of the unique aspects of living at Bay State College is the residence halls. With their location in the historic Back Bay, the buildings are original Victorian town houses and brownstones. Each building has its own character and charm, making living on campus a distinctive experience. Each building has a computer lab with free Internet access, coin-operated laundry, vending machines, a house phone with free local calling, and a social lounge that includes cable television and a microwave oven. Each student room has basic cable service and access to a wireless Internet network.

The Career Services office offers lifetime career assistance to both current students and alumni, continuing to provide assistance and support to them throughout their careers, with career-management counseling, workshops, career panels, guest speakers, resume and cover letter reviews, interview preparation, and job listings.

Bay State College is accredited by the New England Association of Schools and Colleges; is authorized to award the Associate in Science, Associate in Applied Science, and three Bachelor of Science degrees by the commonwealth of Massachusetts; and is a member of several professional educational associations. The College's medical assisting program is accredited by the Accrediting Bureau of Health Education Schools (ABHES). The College's nursing program has been given pre-approval by the Massachusetts Board of Registration of Nursing (BORN) and will have the National League of Nursing accreditation survey in the spring of 2012. The physical therapist assistant studies program is accredited by the Commission on Accreditation in Physical Therapy Education (CAPTE) of the American Physical Therapy Association (APTA).

Location

Located in the historic city of Boston, Massachusetts, and surrounded by dozens of colleges and universities, Bay State College is an ideal setting in which to pursue a college degree. Tree-lined streets around the school are mirrored in the skyscrapers of the Back Bay. The College is located within walking distance of several major-league sports franchises, concert halls, museums, the Freedom Trail, Boston Symphony Hall, the Boston Public Library, and the Boston Public Garden. World-class shopping and major cultural and sporting events help make college life an experience that students will always remember. The College is accessible by the MBTA, commuter rail, and bus and is near Boston Logan International Airport.

Majors and Degrees

Bay State College is continually reviewing, enhancing, and adding new programs to help graduates remain industry-current in their respective fields.

Bachelor's degrees are offered in criminal justice, entertainment management, fashion merchandising, and management.

Associate degrees are offered in business administration, criminal justice, early childhood education, entertainment management (with a concentration in recording arts production), fashion design, fashion merchandising, health studies, medical assisting, nursing, physical therapist assistant studies, retail business management, and travel and hospitality management.

Academic Programs

Bay State College operates on a semester calendar. The fall semester runs from early September to late December. The spring semester runs from late January to mid-May. A satellite campus is located in Middleborough, Massachusetts.

Bay State College also offers courses on-ground and online to working adults in its Evening & Online Division. The courses, offered in eight-week sessions, allow more flexibility for students who must balance work and family commitments while pursuing their education.

Off-Campus Programs

The internship program, available in all major areas of study, provides students with practical field experience, enabling them to hone their skills and gain insight into the various technologies employed in their respective fields. Fieldwork is a requirement for many majors and is a great opportunity for students to build resumes, apply what they have learned in the classroom, and gain a competitive advantage in the job market.

Students from Bay State College are among the 250 students participating in the Walt Disney World College Program. During their stay at Walt Disney World, students receive on-the-job training and classroom experience. This is just one of the many internship possibilities for students each year at Bay State College.

Academic Facilities

The library has a combined book collection of approximately 5,300 books. In addition, Bay State College has 100 periodicals and 200 audiovisual titles. The College's sixty computers have access to the Internet and several databases for magazine and journal articles, including ProQuest Academic, LexisNexis Academic, JSTOR, Infotrac, Newsbank, EBSCO, the Internet Public Library, and the Library of Congress Research Tools. The library also participates in an interlibrary-loan program with the Boston Regional Library System.

Costs

Tuition for 2011–12 for full-time students is $21,930 per year. Room and board for 2011–12 are $11,800 per year; application fee, $40; student services fee, $375; and student activity fee, $50. The cost of books and additional fees varies by major. A residence hall security deposit of $300 and a technology fee of $250 are required of all resident students.

Financial Aid

Bay State College offers the following financial aid programs to qualified students: Bay State College grant, which ranges from $500 to $4000; Federal Pell Grant; MASSGrant/State Scholarship; Federal Supplemental Educational Opportunity Grant; Massachusetts No Interest Loan; Federal Perkins Loan; and Federal Direct Stafford/Ford Loan. The College also offers numerous part-time employment and work-study opportunities during the academic year.

Faculty

There are 41 faculty members, with the majority holding advanced degrees and several holding doctoral degrees. The student-faculty ratio is 15:1.

Student Government

The Student Association serves as the voice of the Bay State College student body. It consists of a group of elected student representatives from the various academic programs. Roles and responsibilities of Student Association members include providing input on College policies and procedures, assuming leadership roles on campus, acting as a voice of the student body, and planning activities and events.

Elections are held every fall, and all students are encouraged to vote. The group comprises representatives from each College department, club, and organization, and membership spans all four class years.

Admission Requirements

An applicant to Bay State College must be a high school graduate, a current high school student working toward graduation, or a recipient of a GED certificate. The Office of Admissions recommends that applicants to the associate degree programs have a minimum 2.0 GPA on a 4.0 scale; if available, applicants may submit SAT or ACT scores. Applicants must receive the recommendation of a Bay State College admissions officer. Applicants to the bachelor's degree programs must have a minimum 2.3 GPA on a 4.0 scale and must also submit SAT or ACT scores. A personal interview is highly recommended for all students, and parents are encouraged to attend. Students are responsible for arranging for their official high school transcripts, test scores, and letters of recommendation to be submitted to Bay State College. International applicants must also submit high school transcripts translated into English with an explanation of the grading system, a TOEFL score of at least 500 on the paper-based exam or 173 on the computer-based exam if English is not the native language, and financial documentation. The physical therapist assistant studies program and Evening Division have different or additional admission requirements. For more information about these programs, students should visit the Web site at http://www.baystate.edu.

The Bay State College Admissions Office notifies applicants of a decision within three weeks of receipt of the transcript and other required documents. When a student is accepted to Bay State College, there is a $100 nonrefundable tuition deposit required to ensure a place in the class, which is credited toward the tuition fee. Deposits are due within thirty days of acceptance. Once a student is accepted, a Bay State College representative creates a personalized financial plan that provides payment options for a Bay State College education.

Application and Information

Applications are accepted on a rolling basis. A $40 application fee is due with the application. The fall tuition payment due date is July 1; the spring tuition payment due date is December 1.

Applications should be submitted to:

Admissions Office
Bay State College
122 Commonwealth Avenue
Boston, Massachusetts 02116

Phone: 800-81-LEARN (toll-free)
Fax: 617-536-1735
E-mail: admissions@baystate.edu
Web site: http://www.baystate.edu
http://www.facebook.com/baystatecollege
http://twitter.com/baystatecollege

BEACON COLLEGE
LEESBURG, FLORIDA

The College

The mission of Beacon College is to offer academic degree programs exclusively for students with learning disabilities (LD), attention-deficit hyperactivity disorder (ADHD), or gifted LD. Students are not defined by their learning disabilities—they are people with interests, concerns, and wishes about what they want to do during their college years and beyond. Beacon offers a fun, supportive, collegiate atmosphere that facilitates academic success, recognizes personal accomplishments, and fosters lifelong friendships.

Beacon College takes seriously its responsibility to assist students in determining realistic goals, discovering personal abilities and interests, and realizing their potential. Beacon combines educational support services with a student life program that contributes to the cultural, social, and intellectual development of all students. New technologies enable students to learn to manage many problems inherent with learning disabilities. Students receive intensive and proactive academic mentoring, appropriate test accommodations, and classroom instruction in a variety of learning modalities. The College also provides support services outside the classroom through the Writing Center and academic mentoring, field placement opportunities in all majors, an emphasis on small classes and supplemental instruction, an outstanding faculty, and academic advisers who have the education and/or training needed to facilitate the growth of students with learning differences.

Out-of-the-classroom experiences are invaluable in the personal development of well-rounded students. Activities include involvement in global/cultural awareness events, social outings, health and wellness programs, leadership education, and community service. The College hosts a variety of on- and off-campus activities that include outdoor/nature experiences, sporting events, cultural/ethnic festivals, musical and arts entertainment, relationship and leadership building, and health education and fitness programs.

The Beacon Activities Council, along with the support and advisement of the Coordinator of Student Activities, plan, schedule, and carry out college-sponsored cocurricular activities. The activities calendar is available online and updated regularly with descriptions of each event. In addition, the Student Services Office maintains an up-to-date list of all student-run organizations and encourages the initiation of new clubs and organizations.

Residential life plays a key part in student development, offering a supportive living environment that fosters interpersonal skills and positive life experiences. The Director of Student Life and the residential assistants (RAs) are trained professionals who provide guidance, support, and assistance. This unique and rewarding housing system allows students to live in apartment-style facilities and develop independent living skills while attending college. The Beacon Village Apartments are equipped with a full-size kitchen (including a dishwasher, a self-cleaning oven, and a refrigerator), a washer/dryer, basic cable television, Internet access, and ceiling fans throughout. The complex is within walking distance of the education building and all campus buildings. Recreational highlights include a swimming pool, a basketball court, a tennis/volleyball court, and a gazebo area.

Location

Situated in the city of Leesburg, Beacon College is approximately 50 miles northwest of Orlando in central Florida, and the Orlando International Airport is about an hour's drive from campus. Central Florida is one of the most beautiful, versatile, and popular vacation destinations in the state—an area of unmatched natural beauty and old Florida charm, all within minutes of the theme park thrills of nearby Orlando and Tampa and the glorious sands of both coasts. Central Florida is also known for its outdoor activities and wildlife, with more than 550 freshwater lakes, making it an ideal spot for anglers,

boaters, water-skiers, bicyclists, hikers, bird watchers, and nature enthusiasts. Leesburg has devoted 15 percent of its land area to parks and recreational activities. Local organizations in Mount Dora, Eustis, and Leesburg sponsor outstanding art and theater productions, festivals, and community events. There are quaint downtown streets with period architecture and recreational opportunities, as well as shopping in numerous discount and factory outlets and several upscale malls.

Majors and Degrees

Beacon College offers the Associate of Arts (A.A.) and Bachelor of Arts (B.A.) degrees in three majors—computer information systems (CIS), human services (HS), and liberal studies (LS).

Academic Programs

The computer information systems program offers students the opportunity to learn about the latest technology used in the marketplace and explore a vast number of career choices. Students can choose one of the two tracks to meet their specific career goals: information systems or Web and digital media. The former provides students with a thorough background of incorporating technology into the corporate world, while the latter gives students a basic understanding of creating professional digital media and Web pages.

A career in human services involves helping people to adapt, change, and cope with physical and social conditions in their environment. The HS program provides a comprehensive knowledge of the theoretical foundations of the social sciences and offers practical experience in the professional fields associated with public and community services. This major field of study focuses on psychological and sociological approaches to understanding the holistic development of individuals, families, and communities. Through field placements, students gain work experience designed to facilitate employment in the human services field or further study in a graduate degree program.

The liberal studies program provides a broad-based liberal arts education for students seeking intellectual and personal change. Through LS, students are exposed to a variety of subjects designed to establish a basis for effective lifelong learning and attainment of personal goals. Students learn communication and critical-thinking skills and how to interpret human experience through studies of aesthetic, historical, ethical, and cultural foundations. Students help design their degree by choosing courses in areas of emphasis and minors and by completing internship hours directed toward employment or continuing education.

Students must complete at least 60 credit hours to earn an A.A. degree and 120 credit hours to earn a B.A. degree with a minimum cumulative GPA of 2.0. The general education requirement for all students is 36 credit hours: 9 credit hours in English and communication, 6 in computer information systems, 6 in the humanities and fine arts, 6 in mathematics and natural science, 6 in the social/behavioral sciences, and 3 in critical thinking.

The HS and LS programs require a minimum number of credit hours in the major: 18 credit hours for the associate degree and 36 credit hours for the bachelor's degree. The CIS major requires 21 credit hours in a CIS sequence for the A.A. degree or 36 credit hours for the B.A degree. Students may also choose a minor concentration, which requires at least 18 credit hours, in areas of business management, computer information systems, education, English/literature, history, psychology, and Web and digital media.

Off-Campus Programs

During the summer, Beacon College offers an international cultural studies program, building upon the current requisite global-learning perspective and affording each student a life-changing experience. Programs have included such countries as Australia,

England, France, Germany, Greece, Ireland, Italy, New Zealand, Russia, Spain, Sweden, and Switzerland.

Students gain valuable work experience that focuses on defining career goals through internships in the community. In the Field Placement Program, students develop a transitional plan while taking courses in the psychology and the culture of the workplace.

Academic Facilities

The Beacon College Learning Resource Center (LRC) provides access to the library, the Writing Center, and academic mentoring offices. Dedicated to providing flexible, diverse, and user-centered information services and technology, the Beacon College Library is the focal point of academic life on campus. The library staff has created an inviting environment open to innovation and focused on continuous improvement in resources and accommodations. The library's collection includes more than 23,000 volumes, 38,000 electronic book titles, 100 periodicals in print, 65 full-text databases, 1,000 audiovisual materials, and more than 600 items in its specialized learning disabilities collection. The collection is curriculum based and supports students and faculty in their research efforts. Supplemental materials can be requested through interlibrary loan or acquired through the College's cooperative agreements with local libraries.

The Writing Center offers assistance and support for every phase of the writing process, helping all students develop their critical-thinking skills through a focus on the reading and writing processes necessary for the successful completion of college-level writing for both the advanced and struggling writer.

The College's computer center is equipped with multimedia technology and networked computer workstations. In addition to word processing, e-mail, and Web access, the computer center provides page scanners, voice-activated dictation software, and computerized reading programs to enhance and support the learning process of all students. Individual workstations ensure ready access to systems technology, including technology that assists students with specific learning disabilities.

Costs

In 2010–11, full-time tuition was $27,810 for the academic year. Room and board totaled $8150 per academic year (two semesters).

Financial Aid

The Office of Financial Aid makes a variety of scholarships, grants, work opportunities, and loans available to eligible students. Many students qualify for some form of financial aid and are encouraged to apply for aid by completing the Beacon College financial aid application and the Free Application for Federal Student Aid (FAFSA) at http://www.fafsa.ed.gov.

Faculty

The Beacon College faculty is committed to helping students achieve individual success. Faculty members facilitate instruction by designing appropriate learning opportunities that reflect an understanding of different learning styles and a variety of learning differences. Team meetings allow faculty to discuss teaching methods and effective intervention techniques, while assessing student progress. An emphasis on self-awareness and critical thinking focused on strategies for lifelong learning are facilitated by faculty and students working together. A low student-faculty ratio provides the opportunity for individual attention, while fostering the competencies necessary for success. The average class size is 12 students. About 80 percent of full-time faculty members hold terminal master's or doctoral degrees.

Student Government

The Student Government Association is dedicated to improving student life and campus involvement through student-led initiatives.

Admission Requirements

To give each candidate full consideration, the Beacon College admissions committee evaluates applicant files only when they are deemed complete. Applicants must submit the completed application, the nonrefundable $50 application fee, a college essay, a recent educational evaluation, official high school transcripts, and three letters of recommendation. Transfer credits are considered based upon official transcripts from an accredited college/university. Official ACT or SAT scores are not mandatory.

The educational evaluation must include a clear diagnosis of learning disability or ADD/HD, or LD Gifted; Wechsler scales (preferably WAIS-IV), with full-scale, cluster, and subtest scores; and achievement assessments (such as Woodcock Johnson or WIAT), with grade-equivalence reporting in reading, writing, or mathematics. An interview may be required. Though not mandatory, it is highly recommend that all candidates visit the campus to fully evaluate the College's academic and student life.

Beacon College accepts applications from English-speaking nonimmigrant students. All accepted international students are required to purchase an insurance policy before the I-20 is issued. All guidelines and application requirements are outlined in the application packet (available online).

Application and Information

Beacon College accepts students on a rolling basis, but the preferred application deadlines are May 1 and November 1 for the fall and spring semesters, respectively. Candidates who apply after the priority deadline are processed on a space-available basis. Candidates are encouraged to apply after the deadline dates until spaces are filled. A $750 nonrefundable deposit is due upon receipt of enrollment contract and is applied to first semester fees.

Office of Admissions
Beacon College
105 East Main Street
Leesburg, Florida 34748
Phone: 352-638-9731
Fax: 352-787-0796
E-mail: admissions@beaconcollege.edu
Web site: http://www.beaconcollege.edu/
    http://on.fb.me/Beacon_Coll (Facebook)

Beacon College students head back to Beacon Village Apartments after class.

BELMONT UNIVERSITY

NASHVILLE, TENNESSEE

The University

Nationally recognized programs thrive on the Belmont University campus, which is located in the heart of the state capital, known both as Music City, U.S.A., and the Athens of the South (for its many educational institutions). Nashville offers big-city advantages with small-town charm.

Belmont's vision is to be a leader among teaching universities, bringing together the best of liberal arts and professional education in a Christian community of learning and service. Central to the fulfillment of that vision are faculty members who have a passion for teaching and the belief that premier teaching is interactive, technology-supported, motivational, creative, and exciting.

With an enrollment of approximately 5,900 students, Belmont is the second-largest of Tennessee's private colleges and universities.

In addition to the twenty-five international countries represented in the student body, Belmont University attracts students from every state in the United States. The culturally diverse institution is committed to listening and learning from everyone. Students of today are helping shape the way students of tomorrow will be educated.

Belmont's beautiful, antebellum campus reflects a long, rich history that dates back to the nineteenth century, when the grounds were Adelicia Acklen's Belle Monte estate. University buildings that were erected over the past 110 years flank the Italianate mansion, which is still used by the campus. On the way to classes that prepare them for the twenty-first century, students enjoy Victorian gardens, statuary, and gazebos that recall a treasured past.

Two prestigious women's schools preceded the comprehensive liberal arts institution: the original Belmont College (1890–1913) and Ward-Belmont (1913–1951). In 1951, the Tennessee Baptist Convention founded the second Belmont College (1951–1991), with an initial coeducational enrollment of 136 students. Soon after celebrating 100 years of education on the same campus, the institution became a university in 1991, culminating a decade of dramatic growth and progress.

In addition to seven baccalaureate degrees, Belmont University offers thirteen graduate and doctoral degree programs: the Master of Accountancy, the Master of Arts in Teaching, the Master of Business Administration, the Master of Sport Administration, the Master of Arts in English, the Master of Music, the Master of Education, the Master of Science in Nursing, the Master of Science in Occupational Therapy, the Master of Arts in Special Education, the Doctor of Occupational Therapy, the Doctor of Pharmacy, and the Doctor of Physical Therapy. In the fall of 2011, Belmont is slated to open a College of Law to offer the Juris Doctor.

Location

Belmont University occupies a 75-acre campus in southeast Nashville. With a metropolitan area of roughly a million residents, Nashville is a cultural, educational, health-care, commercial, and financial center in the mid-South. Practical educational opportunities, offered through diverse curriculums, provide students with the hands-on experience they need in preparation for a meaningful career. The city's location halfway between the northern and southern boundaries of the United States, with three intersecting interstate highways and an international airport, makes it accessible to students from across the country.

Majors and Degrees

Belmont University is accredited by the Commission on Colleges of the Southern Association of Colleges and Schools to award baccalaureate, master's, and doctoral degrees. Belmont grants seven undergraduate degrees: the Bachelor of Arts, the Bachelor of Business Administration, the Bachelor of Fine Arts, the Bachelor of Music, the Bachelor of Science, the Bachelor of Science in Nursing, and the

Bachelor of Social Work. Majors or concentrations are offered in accounting, applied discrete mathematics, art (art education, art history, design communications, and studio art), Asian studies, audio and video production, audio engineering technology, biblical languages, biblical studies, biochemistry and molecular biology, biology, business administration, chemistry, Christian ethics, Christian leadership, classics, communication studies, computer science, early childhood education, economics, engineering physics, English, entertainment industry studies, entrepreneurship, environmental science, European studies, exercise science, finance, French, German, health, history, information systems management, international business, international economics, international politics, journalism, management, marketing, mass communication, mathematics, medical imaging technology, medical physics, medical technology, middle school education, music (church music, commercial music, music composition, music education, music with an outside minor, musical theater, music performance, piano pedagogy, music theory), music business, neuroscience, nursing, organizational and corporate communications, pharmaceutical studies, philosophy, physical education and health, physics, politics and public law, political science, psychology, public relations, religion and the arts, religious studies, science and engineering management, social entrepreneurship, social work, sociology, songwriting, Spanish, theater and drama, video production, and Web programming and development.

Academic Programs

Uniquely positioned to provide the best of liberal arts and professional education, Belmont University offers celebrated professional programs structured to provide an academically well-rounded education. Belmont University operates on a two-semester schedule with classes beginning in late August and ending in early May. Two summer sessions are also offered. The academic program is arranged by school: the College of Arts and Sciences, the College of Business Administration, the Gordon E. Inman College of Health Sciences and Nursing, the College of Visual and Performing Arts, the Mike Curb College of Entertainment and Music Business, and the School of Religion.

In addition to the degrees offered through the schools, Belmont University offers an honors program, which was created to provide an enrichment opportunity for students who have potential for superior academic performance and who seek added challenge and breadth to their studies. Students enrolled in the honors program are led in designing and working through a flexible, individual curriculum and interdisciplinary general education curriculum by a private tutor who is an honors faculty member.

The University's advancements in undergraduate research are credited to a faculty committed to helping students practice their disciplines. The annual Belmont Undergraduate Research Symposium puts Belmont at the forefront of this national movement by providing a public forum for in-depth research at the undergraduate level.

Off-Campus Programs

Belmont University has contracts for dual-degree programs with Auburn University and University of Tennessee, Knoxville. These programs require three years of study at Belmont University followed by approximately two years of study at one of the above institutions. The course of study at Belmont must be mathematics, physics, or chemistry. Following completion of the academic requirements at both institutions, a student is awarded a Bachelor of Science degree from Belmont University and the appropriate degree from the second institution.

Several programs at Belmont have agreements with area organizations to provide students practical training. Nursing students gain clinical experience at all fourteen local area hospitals and other clinical agencies. Education students gain classroom experience in Metro-Davidson County Schools. Music business students gain real-world experience through internships in the Nashville music industry and in Los Angeles and New York City through the Belmont West and East (respectively) programs of study and internships.

Through a wide variety of international study programs on the six populated continents, Belmont offers students the opportunity to broaden and deepen their education while earning credit hours toward their degrees. These programs, which range in duration from two weeks to a year, are available in Australia, the Bahamas, China, Costa Rica, England, France, Germany, Hong Kong, Ireland, Italy, Mexico, New Zealand, Russia, Scotland, South Africa, and Spain.

Academic Facilities

Belmont offers a quiet, secluded environment, and classes are held in nine buildings with the library and other facilities located in proximity to those classrooms.

The Lila D. Bunch Library includes a microcomputer center, multimedia room, and group study rooms. Adjacent to it is the 3,000-square-foot Leu Art Gallery. Located next to the library is the Leu Center for the Visual Arts, featuring state-of-the-art studios with natural lighting and spacious work areas.

The Sam A. Wilson School of Music Building houses classrooms, a resource room, seminar rooms, studio/offices, music practice rooms, a piano lab, and a music technology lab.

The Jack C. Massey Business Center provides classrooms, office space, study lounges, seminar and conference rooms, a copy center, a post office, and a convenience store. A state-of-the-art learning center includes five computer labs. In addition, Massey Business Center houses the 9,000-square-foot Center for Music Business, which provides classrooms, an academic resource center, two state-of-the-art recording studios and control rooms, four isolation booths, a MIDI pre–postproduction room, and an engineering repair shop.

The recently opened Gordon Inman Center for Health Sciences and Nursing houses Belmont's nursing, social work, and occupational therapy programs. Students train in state-of-the-art labs and classrooms that include lift equipment to teach student safety, simulated mannequins that respond to basic stimuli, and apartments to teach social work students how to work with clients with special needs.

Costs

Belmont's tuition and fees were $23,680 per academic year in 2010–11. Room and board in campus residence halls were $9030.

Financial Aid

More than 75 percent of Belmont's students receive some type of financial assistance. The financial aid program at Belmont combines merit-based assistance with need-based assistance to make the University program affordable. Institutional merit awards range from full tuition Presidential Scholarships to performance scholarships. Also included are many levels of academic merit awards. Belmont University also administers traditional state and federal need-based programs, including the Federal Pell Grant, Federal Stafford Student Loan, Federal Perkins Loan, Federal PLUS loan, and Tennessee Student Assistance Grants and Scholarships. Campus employment is available. Parents may arrange monthly tuition payments through an outside vendor. To apply for assistance, the student must complete the Free Application for Federal Student Aid (FAFSA).

Faculty

A highly competent faculty is the paramount attribute of a strong institution of higher education. Belmont University has faculty members who are dedicated to their profession and to the University. Of the more than 200 full-time faculty members, 65 percent hold terminal degrees. Another 30 percent of faculty members have completed formal studies beyond the master's degree.

The influence of the Belmont University faculty is felt beyond the campus. Faculty members are active in church, civic, professional, and academic associations; frequently speak to various groups; and often write for denominational and secular publications. Most faculty members have traveled extensively and many have experienced life in other regions of the United States and abroad.

Student Government

A liaison between the University and student body, the Student Government Association seeks to address educational, social, and spiritual needs of students. As a service organization for the student body, it offers opportunity for campus involvement, acts as the coordinating body for all student organizations, serves as a resource for the campus community, and represents student interests to the faculty and administration.

Admission Requirements

Applicants are considered based on the total picture a student's credentials present. High school students are considered competitive for admission if they present a rigorous course of college-preparatory academic studies. Students should have an above-average academic and cumulative grade point average and rank in the top half of their graduating class. Any college-level work is also expected to be at the above-average level. A strong correlation between high school grades and entrance examination scores is expected. The personal supplement information, a resume of activities, and recommendations are also strongly considered as positive indicators of success at Belmont. Additional requirements, such as portfolios or auditions, are considered in conjunction with the academic credentials for those programs that require them. Each application is considered on an individual basis. No two applicants present the same credentials or the same degree of "fit" with the University. The University desires to work with each student to determine the likelihood for that student to enroll, graduate, and benefit from the Belmont educational experience.

Application and Information

Further information and application materials may be obtained by contacting:

Office of Admissions
Belmont University
1900 Belmont Boulevard
Nashville, Tennessee 37212
Phone: 615-460-6785
        800-56ENROLL (toll-free)
Fax: 615-460-5434
E-mail: admissions@belmont.edu
Web site: http://www.belmont.edu
         http://www.facebook.com/BelmontUniversity
         http://www.twitter.com/BelmontUniv

Belmont University students enjoy a beautiful antebellum campus located in thriving metropolitan Nashville.

BELOIT COLLEGE
BELOIT, WISCONSIN

The College

Beloit College is a private, independent, residential college which engages its students' curiosity and intelligence by bringing the liberal arts to life. Beloit's focus is on teaching and on the close collaboration that takes place among students and faculty members in small classroom and lab settings. Undergraduates learn to approach problems ethically and thoughtfully in an academic community that places a high premium on international and interdisciplinary perspectives. Active learning is key to the college's educational experience; students are expected to think on their feet, learn outside of the classroom and put the liberal arts into practice.

Beloit is Wisconsin's first college, founded by New Englanders on the Midwestern frontier in 1846. Today, a geographically diverse population of 1,250 students is drawn to Beloit's residential campus from nearly all North American states and more than forty other countries. Eight percent come from countries outside the United States, 15 percent of U.S. students are non-Caucasian, and many religious orientations and socioeconomic backgrounds are represented on campus. Beloit students are equally diverse in their academic choices; no more than 10 percent of the seniors are represented in any one of more than fifty majors available.

Beloit students are informed about and active in political and social issues, and they value individual expression. Beloit students serve on College governance committees, create new clubs, manage an annual music festival, and host their own radio and cable TV shows. In a given week, students may have the choice of attending (or organizing) a lecture series, a movie, music performances, a poetry reading, or an environmental debate. Seventy percent of Beloit's students participate in some form of athletics—club, intramural, or varsity. Those who live on campus (most do) may choose to live on quiet or substance-free floors, in one of three fraternity houses or three sorority houses, or in one of the special-interest houses, such as those formed around particular languages, gay and lesbian issues, anthropology, the arts, black student issues, faith and spirituality, music, the environment, peace and justice issues, science fiction and fantasy, Latino student issues, and women's issues. Two town-house complexes have been constructed in the past ten years and offer roomy, apartment-style living for juniors and seniors. Meals, served in two locations on campus, include organic, vegetarian, and vegan meal options.

New students quickly become part of this active and diverse environment through the Beloit Initiatives Program which places new students in interdisciplinary seminars taught by experienced professors and staff members. These seminars begin the day students arrive on campus and provide an academic grounding and a social network. They also begin two years of faculty advising, designed to help students transition to Beloit and focus on developing skills and perspectives that will help them put theory into practice through study abroad, community-based learning, internships, and more.

From Beloit College, students can see the world. Learn how at the College's YouTube channel at http://bit.ly/YouTube_Beloit.

Location

Beloit's 40-acre campus is located on the border between Wisconsin and Illinois, 90 miles northwest of Chicago, 50 miles south of Madison, and 70 miles southwest of Milwaukee, in a small, diverse city of 36,000 that Margaret Mead once called "American society in a microcosm." Students may take advantage of the resources of the three major metropolitan areas, and Beloit's businesses and civic and service organizations provide numerous internship, job shadowing, and community outreach opportunities. Beloit's academic buildings are clustered around lawns dotted with ancient North American Indian mounds, while residence halls on the other side of campus provide the base of the College's social scene. A 25-acre athletic field and Strong Memorial Stadium are located a few blocks east of campus.

Majors and Degrees

Beloit awards Bachelor of Arts and Bachelor of Science degrees in nineteen departments and more than fifty fields of study. In natural sciences and mathematics, students may choose majors from the departments of biology, biochemistry, chemistry, environmental studies, geology, mathematics and computer science, and physics. In social sciences, students may choose majors from the departments of anthropology, economics and management, education and youth studies, political science and international relations, psychology, and sociology. In arts and humanities, majors are offered in the departments of art and art history, classics, English, history, modern languages and literatures, music, philosophy and religious studies, theater arts, and women's and gender studies. Students often create a unique interdisciplinary major or minor. The College offers departmental minors in anthropology, studio art and art history, biology and society, chemistry, computer science, English, geology, history, integrative biology, international economics, management, mathematics, music, philosophy, physics, political economy, political science, and religious studies. Permanent interdisciplinary minors include African studies, American studies, ancient Mediterranean studies, Asian studies, computational visualization and modeling, environmental studies, European studies, health and society, interdisciplinary studies, journalism, Latin American studies, legal studies, medieval studies, museum studies, peace and justice studies, performing arts, Russian studies, and women's and gender studies.

Beloit offers 3-2 cooperative programs in engineering and environmental management and forestry and preprofessional programs in dentistry, law, medicine, and nursing. These programs, which have strong advisory and internship components, complement a major in an appropriate discipline. Beloit students may also earn teaching certification.

Academic Programs

Beloit's academic calendar consists of two 14-week semesters with one-week midterm breaks. At the end of the sophomore year, students are required to declare a major and may add a second major, a minor, or teaching certification. Sophomore students work with faculty advisers to define academic and personal goals, including completion of graduation requirements and the declaration of majors, and develop a plan—including internships, independent research, or study abroad—for accomplishing them. In addition, Beloit requires completion of five breadth requirements, a senior-year capstone experience, an experience outside the classroom which puts the liberal arts into practice, three writing-intensive courses, and significant contact with a culture not one's own. Thirty-one units are required for graduation, each unit representing the equivalent of a course of study involving 4 hours of class time a week per semester.

Off-Campus Programs

Beloit has a century-old tradition of domestic and international off-campus study opportunities, and more than half of new Beloit graduates will have studied and/or conducted research in such a program. Domestic programs include an opportunity to study at the Marine Biological Laboratory at Woods Hole in Massachusetts; a science semester at the Oak Ridge National Laboratory in Knoxville, Tennessee; a semester in the arts, an urban studies program, and a Newberry Library semester in the humanities, all in Chicago; and a Washington Semester at American University in Washington, D.C. Internships, field terms in the humanities and sciences, and summer employment opportunities are arranged through the Liberal Arts in Practice Center.

At Beloit College, study abroad is more of an expectation than a luxury. Whether through Beloit's own extensive programs or the Associated Colleges of the Midwest (ACM) and independent programs, Beloit students have studied in more than forty countries worldwide, from Australia to Zimbabwe.

Academic Facilities

Beloit's historic brick and stone buildings coexist with innovative contemporary structures such as the Center for the Sciences. Completed in 2008, the 117,000-square-foot center is LEED-certified Platinum and includes a vegetated roof, high recycled/reused content, water management systems, and other sustainable features. Platinum is the highest rating offered by the U.S. Green Building Council. The College's newest facility, the Hendricks Center for the Arts, opened in the fall of 2010 in downtown Beloit, in a building that formerly housed the city's public library. The 48,000-square-foot building provides a centralized home to the College's dance and music programs, and features four studio classrooms, a state-of-the-art film classroom, faculty offices, rehearsal rooms, and design and staging labs. The Logan Museum of Anthropology and the Wright Museum of Art are highly regarded teaching museums that offer students excellent resources for research and work experience. The Neese Performing Arts Theatre complex features a large thrust stage theater, a black-box theater, a scenic design studio, and a complete costume shop. The World Affairs Center is the hub of language and literature study. Nearly 250 student-accessible computer workstations are located throughout campus, with a combination of wireless and wired network Internet access in academic buildings. Residence halls have a wired Internet connection for every student. Beloit's library collection is in excess of half a million holdings and provides individual and group study areas, computer labs, and extensive listening and viewing areas for the use of audiovisual materials. A 6,000-square-foot center for entrepreneurship in downtown Beloit provides physical space, office resources, and a recording studio where students can put venture plans of their own design into action.

Costs

Tuition for the 2011–12 academic year is $36,444, fees are $230, a double room is $3678, and board (twenty-meal plan) is $3824, for a total comprehensive fee of $44,176. While the cost of books and incidental expenses varies, it totals about $1500.

Financial Aid

Beloit College is committed to making the Beloit experience affordable to all qualified students. The financial aid program recognizes two criteria—scholastic ability and financial need—that may qualify students for awards. During the 2010–11 academic year, more than 85 percent of first-year students received financial assistance through grants, loans, or work-study.

In 2010, new students from families with incomes below $50,000 received an average grant of $29,000; qualifying students from families with incomes above $100,000 received an average grant of $19,500. Beloit's attention to providing students high value has won the College recognition in the Princeton Review's guides, the *Fiske Guide to Colleges,* and *U.S. News & World Report* as among the nation's best buys in top colleges.

Faculty

The focus of Beloit's faculty is great teaching. Beloit professors are committed to an educational environment that emphasizes discussion and collaborative learning in small classes. Of the 123 full-time faculty members, 94 percent hold the highest academic degree in their field. All classes are taught by professors. In classrooms, it is easy for students and faculty members to become immersed in their work, since the student-faculty ratio is 11:1 and the average class size is 15 students. All Beloit professors are also academic advisers who are involved in students' academic concerns as well as their adjustment to life at the College. Discussions begun in the classroom are often continued in an informal setting, such as at a basketball game or over dinner at a professor's house.

Student Government

Students at Beloit are actively involved in the governance of the College. The Beloit Student Congress is the College's student government. Its committees (Governance Committee, Publicity Committee, Food Committee, Organization Task Force, and Programming Board) allow the congress to focus on representing the student body and meeting its goals. In addition to this entirely student-run governing body, students are elected to the College's Academic Senate and serve as voting members of major College committees. Students also sit on all academic search committees.

Admission Requirements

Admission to Beloit is selective. Beloit seeks applicants with special qualities and talents, as well as those from diverse ethnic, geographic, and economic backgrounds. When reviewing applications, the transcript is the most important element. Beloit has no absolute secondary school requirements but recommends a rigorous college-preparatory program. This includes 4 years of English, 4 years of college-preparatory mathematics, 4 years of laboratory science, 4 years of history or social science, and 4 years of a foreign language. Seventh-semester grades may be required. A counselor recommendation is a required part of the application. One teacher recommendation is also required. The essay component of Beloit's application is critical. There is no required topic, so students should write about a topic they believe will represent them well. Either SAT or ACT test scores are required, but they are the least important part of the application. Beloit does not consider the SAT or ACT writing exam for purposes of admission. Interviews are not required for admission but are encouraged. Off-campus alumni interviews can be arranged if a student would like to interview but cannot travel to the campus. Transfer applications are considered for August or January entrance. Applicants must hold at least a B average at an accredited college or university.

Application and Information

Beloit has modified rolling admissions, so students may apply at any time. For priority consideration, both in admissions and in financial aid, however, students should file their applications by January 15. Students who apply by this date are mailed notification by early March. Early Action 1 applications are due November 1, with notification December 15; Early Action 2 applications are due December 1, with notification January 15. Students who wish to be considered for merit scholarships are strongly encouraged to apply under the Early Action plan. Transfer applications for the fall term are due by March 15 and for the spring term, by November 1. Notification for transfer applications is rolling. For more information, students should contact:

Admissions Office
Beloit College
700 College Street
Beloit, Wisconsin 53511

Phone: 608-363-2500
      800-9-BELOIT (toll-free)
Fax: 608-363-2075
E-mail: admiss@beloit.edu
Web site: http://www.beloit.edu
      http://www.facebook.com/BeloitCollege
      http://twitter.com/#!/beloit_college

Beloit College Spanish Professor Sylvia Lopez leads a class discussion in the World Affairs Center. At Beloit, professors engage students and encourage them to share their ideas.

BENTLEY UNIVERSITY
WALTHAM, MASSACHUSETTS

The University

Bentley University is a national leader in business education. Centered on education and research in business and related professions, Bentley blends the breadth and technological strength of a university with the values and student focus of a small college. A Bentley education is an unparalleled fusion of business and the arts and sciences that allows students to truly customize their learning; this includes a unique liberal studies double-major program. Bentley also stresses the benefits of hands-on learning through internships, service learning, study abroad, and corporate partnerships.

In 2010, Bentley was ranked sixth in the nation by the Princeton Review for best career services. The Miller Center for Career Services (CSS) offers resources including an on-campus recruiting program involving 1,000 national and international companies, an on-line job and internship database for Bentley students and alumni, career fairs, and insightful workshops such as From Backpack to Briefcase and How to Ace the Interview.

In addition, each student can develop a customized four-year development plan, an asset that contributes to the University's outstanding placement rates. In 2010, 99 percent of Bentley students found employment or enrolled in graduate school within six months of graduation. Their median annual salary was over $50,000.

Approximately 98 percent of freshmen live on campus. Twenty-three residence halls provide a range of housing options: traditional dorms, suites, and apartments. Housing is provided to students for all four years. All residence halls are air-conditioned and typically include study lounges, exercise facilities, TV lounges, and game rooms. In 2010, the Princeton Review ranked Bentley eighteenth on its list of dorms like palaces.

Students live and learn in a multicultural environment that reflects and prepares them to thrive in today's diverse work world. International students representing more than eighty countries are part of the Bentley community.

Supporting Bentley's commitment to diversity are offices such as the Multicultural Center, Spiritual Life Center, Center for International Students and Scholars, and the Women's Center.

The Student Center is the hub of campus activity and is home to Seasons Dining Room and Mongolian Grill, the Mad Falcon, Harry's Pub, and more than 100 student clubs and organizations. These groups represent academic interests as well as the performing arts, campus media, fraternity and sorority life, and cultural organizations.

Extensive athletic programs are a Bentley hallmark and include intramurals, recreational sports, and twenty-three varsity teams in NCAA Divisions I and II. The Dana Athletic Center houses a weight and fitness complex, full-service food court, locker rooms, a gym, a basketball court, volleyball and racquetball courts, a competition-size pool with a diving tank, and saunas. Outdoor facilities include soccer and baseball fields, a track, lighted tennis courts, and other fields.

Location

Bentley's location in Waltham, Massachusetts—just minutes west of Boston—puts the city's many resources within easy reach. As the country's ultimate university town, Boston's options range from theater to art exhibits, dance clubs to alternative rock concerts, and championship sports to world-class shopping. Bentley's free shuttle makes regular trips to Harvard Square in Cambridge, just a subway ride from the heart of Boston. Boston also offers students many opportunities for internships and jobs after graduation.

Majors and Degrees

Bentley's strong curriculum, focusing on business, technology, and the liberal arts, provides students with options for shaping an academic program that fits their skills, interests, and career goals.

Bachelor of Science (B.S.) degree programs enable students to gain in-depth knowledge and skills in specific business disciplines: accountancy, computer information systems, corporate finance and accounting, economics–finance, finance, information design and corporate communication, information systems audit and control, management, managerial economics, marketing, and mathematical sciences.

Bentley also offers Bachelor of Arts (B.A.) degree programs with majors in global studies, history, liberal arts, media and culture, and philosophy. Additionally, students can choose from a number of minors and concentration programs including topics such as entrepreneurial studies, law, and sports management.

The Liberal Studies Major (LSM), an optional double major for business students, can be combined with any business program. It provides students with a competitive edge by building meaningful connections across and within disciplines. Students take the same number of courses but add another credential to their degree, helping them stand out to employers. LSM concentrations include American perspectives; earth, environment, and global sustainability; ethics and social responsibility; global perspectives; health and industry; media arts and society; and quantitative perspectives.

Academic Programs

The Bentley curriculum is an integration of business and the liberal arts. The University's 4,200 undergraduates benefit from an incredible breadth of programs and the ability to specialize and combine subjects to best fit their interests. Whether students are interested in creating ad campaigns, managing a health-care organization, or working on Wall Street, Bentley gives them the tools to prepare them for their careers.

The curriculum is supported by an emphasis on technology in state-of-the-art labs. A Bentley education also focuses on gaining hands-on experience in the classroom. Students benefit from classes where they partner with outside companies to solve current business problems. Whether it's a national footwear company seeking to learn more about its customer base or a nonprofit that needs help developing a business plan, students work in teams to develop a solution that they present directly to company executives. Bentley also offers top applicants a chance to enroll in the University's honors program. Participants select honors-level courses each semester that offer an extra intellectual challenge in an intimate, seminar atmosphere.

The Five-Year Master's Candidate program enables students to earn a Bachelor of Business Administration degree and either a Bentley M.B.A. or Master of Science (M.S.) degree.

Off-Campus Programs

Hands-on experience is emphasized across the Bentley curriculum. Internships, study abroad, service-learning assignments, and other opportunities allow students to apply classroom theory in the workplace and community.

Each year, more than 90 percent of Bentley students complete at least one internship, building useful work experience and valuable networking connections. Some of the top internship employers include Fidelity Investments, The TJX Companies, Liberty Mutual, Bain & Company, and all of the Big Four accounting firms.

Bentley students can gain valuable insight into different countries and cultures by studying abroad. Programs take place in more than twenty-six countries and vary in length from one week to a full academic year.

Through Bentley's Service-Learning Center, students build valuable skills in business, communication, and teamwork while assisting nonprofit and community-based organizations both locally and internationally.

Academic Facilities

Concepts and theories taught in the classroom are put to use in several high-tech learning laboratories.

Bentley's financial trading room—one of the first in higher education—combines state-of-the-art technology and real-time data to offer first-hand exposure to financial concepts in simulated trading sessions. Resources include Bloomberg, FactSet, Datastream, Wonda, and Thomson One Analytics.

The Center for Marketing Technology plays an integral role in marketing programs at Bentley. Students gain a full grasp of software options, familiarity with research tools and techniques, and knowledge of the new digital marketing frameworks.

The Accounting Center for Electronic Learning and Business Management (ACELAB) introduces cutting-edge tools and technologies that are reshaping the accounting profession. Students have access to auditing and tax preparation software as well as other professional applications and software from industry leaders such as SAP and Oracle.

The Center for Languages and International Collaboration (CLIC) is a key resource for language courses, international studies majors, and students with an interest in global issues. The center promotes collaboration among Bentley students and their counterparts overseas.

The Media and Culture Labs and Studio feature state-of-the-art resources for video production and editing as well as digital photography. The lab also provides students with industry-standard software programs for screenwriting, sound mixing, graphic design, and DVD authoring.

The Design and Usability Center (DUC) features labs ideal for usability testing. Students use the applications employed by technical communicators, Web developers, user-interface designers, and usability specialists.

The Bentley Library is outfitted with computer workstations, group study rooms, and wireless network access. It also has an exceptional number of online database resources. In 2010, Bentley was ranked 14th on the Princeton Review's list of best college libraries.

Costs

Tuition for resident and nonresident students during the 2011–12 academic year is $36,840. Room and board (double room, meal plan) costs are $12,520. Additional expenses include books, supplies, laptop computer, and personal and travel expenses.

Financial Aid

Bentley administers approximately $100 million in undergraduate financial aid every year to ensure that all academically qualified students have access to educational choices regardless of financial resources. Currently, more than 70 percent of Bentley's undergraduates receive some form of financial assistance in the form of grants, scholarships, loans, and/or work eligibility.

Faculty

Bentley faculty members are teacher-scholars known for their classroom skills and cutting-edge research. They bring practical, real-world experience to the classroom, based on years of professional involvement in their fields. Faculty research focuses on issues of prime importance to current business practice. Much of the research is conducted in partnership with leading organizations. A student-faculty ratio of 14:1 and average class size of 24 ensure a personal experience for Bentley students. All courses are taught by professors; there are no teaching assistants. Students often note that professors are accessible to them outside of the classroom.

Student Government

Bentley has a number of student governing associations, including the Student Government Association, Greek Council, Residence Hall Association, and the Graduate Student Association.

Admission Requirements

Students applying for admission are encouraged to complete a competitive university preparatory program. Recommendations include 4 years of English, 4 years of mathematics (preferably algebra I and II, geometry, and precalculus or its equivalent), and 3 to 4 years each of history, laboratory science, and a foreign language.

Along with the application, students must submit a secondary school transcript, letters of recommendation from a teacher and a counselor, and official scores of either the SAT or ACT, including the ACT writing test. The University has special applications for international students and transfer students. Applicants who are nonnative speakers of English must also supply official scores of the Test of English as a Foreign Language (TOEFL).

Application and Information

Bentley University accepts the Common Application. The application deadline for students planning to enter in September is January 15. For students planning to begin study in January, the deadline is November 1. Candidates for the fall semester are notified by April 1; spring semester candidates are notified on a rolling basis.

The early decision program is designed for academic achievers for whom Bentley is their first choice. Students who are admitted through this binding program agree to withdraw any applications submitted to other universities. The early decision application deadline is November 1.

The early action program is designed for students who are seriously considering Bentley but are not prepared to commit through the early decision program. This program provides students with an earlier admission decision but gives them the ability to consider other options. The application deadline is November 15.

The regular decision program offers students more time to prepare their application and gives them the opportunity to provide Bentley with their senior year first-term grades. The application deadline is January 15.

For more information, students should contact:

Office of Undergraduate Admission
Bentley University
175 Forest Street
Waltham, Massachusetts 02452-4705
Phone: 781-891-2244
        800-523-2354 (toll-free)
Fax: 781-891-3414
E-mail: ugadmission@bentley.edu
Web site: http://www.bentley.edu
       https://www.facebook.com/bentleyadmission
       http://twitter.com/bentleyu

The Bentley Library—the hub of the academic campus.

BERKLEE COLLEGE OF MUSIC
BOSTON, MASSACHUSETTS

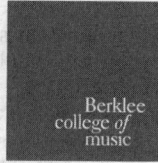
Berklee college of music

The College

Berklee College of Music was founded on the revolutionary principle that the best way to prepare students for careers in music is through the study and practice of contemporary music. For more than half a century, the college has evolved to reflect the state-of-the-art of music and the music business. With more than a dozen performance and non-performance majors, a diverse and talented student body of 4,000 students representing more than seventy countries, and a music industry "who's who" of alumni, Berklee is the world's premier learning lab for the music of today—and tomorrow.

Berklee has proven its commitment to this approach by wholeheartedly embracing change. The musical landscape looks nothing like it did when Berklee was founded in 1945, but the college has remained current by supplementing its core curriculum with studies in emerging musical genres and indispensable new technology. Berklee also has responded to important developments in music education and music therapy, making good on its promise to improve society through music.

At Berklee, students acquire a strong foundation of contemporary music theory and technique, then build upon that foundation by learning the practical, professional skills needed to sustain a career in music. Majors such as music production and engineering, film scoring, music business/management, electronic production and design, songwriting, and music therapy, as well as traditional mainstays of performance and composition, lead toward either a fully accredited four-year baccalaureate degree or a professional diploma. Perhaps more importantly, they prepare students for employment in the music industry.

Berklee attracts a diverse range of students who reflect the multiplicity of influences in today's music, be it jazz, rock, hip-hop, country, gospel, electronica, Latin, or funk. The college is a magnet for aspiring musicians from every corner of the earth, which gives the school a uniquely international flavor. Of all U.S. colleges and universities, Berklee has one of the largest percentages of undergraduates from outside the United States—25 percent. Reflecting the interplay between music and culture, Berklee creates an environment where aspiring music professionals learn how to integrate new ideas and showcase their distinctive skills in an evolving community.

The College's alumni form an ever-widening network of industry professionals who use their openness, virtuosity, and versatility to take music in surprising new directions. Notable alumni include Gary Burton, Terri Lyne Carrington, Bruce Cockburn, Juan Luis Guerra, Roy Hargrove, Quincy Jones, Diana Krall, Aimee Mann, Arif Mardin, Branford Marsalis, Danilo Perez, John Scofield, Howard Shore, Alan Silvestri, Esperanza Spalding, Susan Tedeschi, and Gillian Welch.

Location

Berklee College of Music is located in Boston's Fenway Cultural District. An international hub of intellectual and creative exploration, the neighborhood includes treasure-filled museums and galleries and world-class performing arts centers such as Symphony Hall and the Wang Center. Great performers appear at the Berklee Performance Center; the College's student-run, all-ages venue Cafe 939 highlights up-and-coming international performers in all genres. Boston is also home to many of the world's other great colleges and universities. In addition to the music made at Berklee, there is a lively club and concert scene in the area with coffee houses featuring folk and bluegrass music; neighborhood clubs offering jazz, reggae, and world music; and clubs specializing in rock, blues, dance, urban, and country music.

Berklee students participate in intramural sports and fitness programs at nearby institutions; watch Boston's professional sports teams play in the TD Garden or at Fenway Park or other area sports venues; attend theater, club, and concert hall events year-round throughout the city; and walk, skate, or bike through the city's many scenic parks and public gardens. The College is on Boston's public transportation system, allowing students to take advantage of all that Boston has to offer.

Majors and Degrees

Berklee offers a Bachelor of Music (B.M.) degree program and a four-year program leading to a professional diploma. Students may choose to major in composition, contemporary writing and production, electronic production and design, film scoring, jazz composition, music business/management, music education, music production and engineering, music therapy, performance, professional music, and songwriting. In addition, students may choose from nine minors: acoustics, conducting, drama, English, Latin music performance, music and society, psychology, video game scoring, and visual culture/new media studies. The College also offers a five-year, dual-major option in which students graduate with an even more marketable education that expands their career options in the music industry.

Academic Programs

The Bachelor of Music program offers a complete music curriculum combined with liberal arts courses such as English, history, languages, mathematics, philosophy, and physical or social science. Intensive concentration in music subjects provides students with the necessary tools for developing their musical talents to the fullest and preparing for the multifaceted and ever-changing demands of today's professional music. The degree program is especially appropriate for students who wish to earn a formal degree; are interested in pursuing a career in music education, music therapy, or music business/management; or want to continue their studies at the graduate level.

The diploma is designed for students who want to focus exclusively on contemporary music studies and still get the benefits of a Berklee experience, as well as students who have already earned a bachelor's degree at another institution.

All students must complete the core music curriculum, which consists of harmony, arranging, ear training, and introduction to music technology; instrumental studies; ensembles and instrumental labs; and the concentrate courses designated for each major. All degree candidates must complete the general education curriculum and traditional music studies courses.

Off-Campus Programs

Through the Professional Arts Consortium (ProArts), an association of six area institutions of higher education dedicated to the performing and visual arts, Berklee students can take courses at leading Boston area arts institutions in such areas as communications, modern dance, visual arts, ballet, architectural and graphic design, theater arts, and liberal arts. The other members of the consortium are Boston Architectural Center, the Boston Conservatory, Emerson College, Massachusetts College of Art, and the School of the Museum of Fine Arts.

Students who major in music business/management may be eligible to receive credit for their Berklee course work toward an M.B.A. from Suffolk University.

The Berklee International Network is a shared endeavor designed to promote the effectiveness of contemporary music education among members and to advance the value of contemporary music education internationally. Berklee faculty and staff members visit network member schools annually to conduct workshops and clinics and to audition students for scholarships for full-time study at Berklee. There are currently thirteen members of the network: Fundacio L'Aula de Musica Moderna i Jazz in Barcelona, Spain; Rimon School of Jazz and Contemporary Music in Ramat Hasharon (Tel Aviv), Israel; Phillipos Nakas Conservatory in Athens, Greece; Music Academy International in Nancy, France; Instituto de Musica Contemporanea Universidad San Francisco de Quito in Quito, Ecuador; Pop and Jazz Conservatory in Helsinki, Finland; Koyo Conservatory in Kobe, Japan; Jazz and Rock Schule in Freiburg, Germany; International College of Music in Kuala Lumpur, Malaysia; Conservatorio Souza Lima in São Paulo, Brazil; Seoul Jazz Academy in Seoul, Korea; Metropolia University of Applied Sciences in Helsinki, Finland; and the Newpark Music Centre in Dublin, Ireland.

The College has a robust internship program, with students learning in music companies in Los Angeles, New York, Nashville, London, and beyond, as well as semester-long study-abroad programs at the Phillipos Nakas Conservatory in Athens, Greece and the Jazz and Rock Schule in Freiburg, Germany.

Academic Facilities

Berklee students have the opportunity to work in the College's state-of-the-art music technology facilities, using some of the most sophisticated recording and synthesis equipment currently available, in addition to facilities specifically designed for the areas of composition, arranging, and film scoring. The facilities at Berklee are furnished with the instruments and equipment that are being used in the world beyond the classroom. Berklee's performance facilities include the Berklee Performance Center, a 1,200-seat concert hall hosting more than 300 student, faculty, and other concerts each year; Cafe 939, a state-of-the-art, all-ages, student-run music venue and coffee house; four recital halls equipped with a variety of sound reinforcement systems; more than forty ensemble rooms; over eighty private instruction studios; about 300 private practice rooms; and an outdoor concert pavilion.

Technological facilities include the Recording Studio Complex, consisting of thirteen studio facilities that include 8-, 16-, and 24-track digital and analog recording capability; synthesis labs, featuring more than 250 MIDI-equipped synthesizers, drum machines, sequencers, and computers, including hard-disk recording; the Learning Center, equipped with forty computer-based MIDI workstations; the Professional Writing Division MIDI Lab; and film scoring labs, providing professional training in the areas of film music composition, editing, sequencing, and computer applications.

Costs

Tuition for the 2011–12 year is $33,460. For more information on costs, visit http://www.berklee.edu/tuition.

Financial Aid

A very large percentage of the student body receives some form of financial aid, so no student should allow financial barriers to stop him or her from applying to the College. Funds are available from many different sources, including Berklee and federal and state programs. Students are eligible for merit-based scholarships and, in cases of demonstrated need, federal assistance is provided. Subsidized loans, a tuition-installment plan, and campus employment are also available. Financial aid counselors are available to students and their families to discuss the various options available to them. Students should be aware that there are specific deadlines for federal and state fund applications and for scholarships. Berklee awards over $30 million in scholarships each year to students from all over the world who demonstrate the potential to succeed in today's music industry.

Berklee's Office of Scholarships and Student Employment provides extensive opportunities for both domestic and international students to apply for merit-based scholarships via audition (entering students) or submission of an achievement portfolio (continuing and returning students who have successfully completed a minimum of two semesters).

Faculty

The personal attention students receive from teachers at Berklee guides them beyond the theoretical so that they can apply what they've learned in their next ensemble rehearsal, evening jam session, or gig. All instruction is administered by Berklee's more than 500 faculty members. Teachers are talented artists who demonstrate their commitment to music education in the classroom and beyond. Most faculty members also write and arrange music, perform in concert halls and clubs, make recordings, or perform on television and radio, and some do it all. All faculty members bring to the classroom knowledge of music and the wisdom that comes from professional music experience.

Student Government

Berklee's broad-based system of governance relies on participation from all areas of the college community. The Council of Students represents the voice and perspectives of students regarding all of the issues reviewed by the College. Students are also asked to serve on a wide variety of College committees that advise administrators on such topics as the College's master plan, honorary degree recipients, Web site, and academic and student policies. And many of Berklee's student leaders have opportunity to meet with the president, vice presidents, and trustees during the academic year to discuss current issues, concerns, and institutional activities.

Admission Requirements

Berklee's board of admissions seeks students who show high potential; who are creative, collaborative, and who have something extra that sets them apart. The College considers every aspect of an applicant's strengths and looks for candidates who reflect the rich diversity of Berklee's curriculum, with high musical aptitude as players or writers; or in business, production, music therapy, or music education.

The College takes into consideration both academics as well as musical aptitude. Berklee does not have specific GPA or test score requirements, nor does it have any specific class ranking requirements. The audition and interview process, along with a comprehensive and holistic evaluation of each applicant, provides the College with a wealth of information to assess students' ability to succeed at Berklee.

Application and Information

Berklee uses fixed application deadlines for each semester of entry. Applying to the College is a three-step process. All applicants must submit an online application, participate in a live audition and interview, and mail in the appropriate transcripts to be considered for full-time enrollment at the College.

The online application asks that students provide their personal contact information, including whether they are a vocalist or instrumentalist; their preferred audition location; and responses to fourteen questions that will be used in their interview. A live audition and interview is required as part of the application. A complete listing of audition dates, deadlines, and locations throughout the world is available on Berklee's Web site.

The College also asks that students provide information about their musical and academic background. All supporting materials must be postmarked by the posted deadline date. To learn more about how to apply to the College, and information about the audition and interview experience, students should take Berkelee's online tour at http://www.berklee.edu/campustour/index.html.

For further information, students should contact:

Office of Admissions
Berklee College of Music
1140 Boylston Street
Boston, Massachusetts 02215

Phone: 617-266-2222 (worldwide)
       800-BERKLEE (toll-free in the U.S. and Canada)
Fax: 617-747-2047
E-mail: admissions@berklee.edu
Web site: http://www.berklee.edu
       http://www.facebook.com/berkleecollege
       http://twitter.com/BerkleeCollege
       http://www.youtube.com/berkleecollege

Berklee College of Music student using state-of-the-art music technology.

BIRMINGHAM–SOUTHERN COLLEGE

BIRMINGHAM, ALABAMA

The College

Birmingham-Southern College (BSC) was created through a merger of Southern University (established in 1856) and Birmingham College (established in 1898). Since 1959, when *Harper's Magazine* called it "one of the leading small colleges in the South," Birmingham-Southern continues to be recognized nationally for its quality academics, its value, and its safety preparedness. In 2010, *Kiplinger's Personal Finance* magazine listed Birmingham-Southern as one of America's best values for providing a "higher-quality education at an affordable price." Loren Pope's *Colleges That Change Lives* includes BSC as one of forty colleges and universities that are "outdoing the Ivy League schools and the major universities in producing winners." The Princeton Review has listed Birmingham-Southern in *The Best 373 Colleges* as well as among America's Best Value Colleges and America's Greenest Colleges. The only institution of higher learning in Alabama to receive an "A" for safety preparedness in a recent *Reader's Digest* survey, BSC was ranked ninth in the nation overall, making it the top-ranked liberal arts college in America. In the past decade, three of Alabama's best professors, as determined by the Council for Advancement and Support of Education and the Carnegie Foundation, teach at BSC. The College is also on the President's Higher Education Community Service Honor Roll for helping to build a culture of service and civic engagement in the nation.

Birmingham-Southern is accredited by AACSB International— The Association to Advance Collegiate Schools of Business and is a Phi Beta Kappa institution.

Each year, Birmingham-Southern ranks first in Alabama and among the nation's best in percentage of all graduates accepted to medical, dental, or health career programs; the College also ranks high nationally in graduates accepted to law school.

Birmingham-Southern competes in NCAA Division III athletics and supports twenty-one varsity sports. New sports include football, men's and women's indoor and outdoor track and field, and men's and women's lacrosse. The College has more than eighty clubs and organizations and intramural sports. Its enrollment has grown to more than 1,500 students per year.

Location

Located on a 197-acre hilltop campus in western Birmingham, the College is just 3 miles via I-59/20 from the downtown business district. Birmingham, which is Alabama's largest city, has been honored by the U.S. Conference of Mayors as the most livable city in America and offers fine restaurants, museums, city and state parks, and theater. Its offerings are supplemented by the activities of four other Birmingham colleges. Birmingham's 17,000-seat Civic Center is the setting for many outstanding cultural and athletic events.

Majors and Degrees

Birmingham-Southern offers the undergraduate degrees of Bachelor of Arts, Bachelor of Science, Bachelor of Music, Bachelor of Music Education, and Bachelor of Fine Arts. Departmental majors include art, art history, biology, business administration, chemistry, economics, education, engineering (3-2 program), English, environmental studies (3-2 program), history, mathematics, music, nursing (3-2 program), philosophy, physics, political science, psychology, religion, sociology, Spanish, and theater arts.

Individualized and interdisciplinary majors are also available, including new majors in media and film studies and urban environmental studies.

Academic Programs

The College operates on a 4-1-4 calendar. Thirty-six units are required for the bachelor's degree; these comprise 32 regular term units and 4 Interim Term units. The minimum residence requirement is two years. In addition to its traditional liberal arts programs, Birmingham-Southern offers a number of individualized learning opportunities to meet students' special needs and career goals. These are the Honors Program, the Mentor Program, leadership studies, independent study, the student internship program, individualized majors, and the Interim Term. The College emphasizes international opportunities for students through course offerings, visitors to the campus, and international travel/study programs. Through the Associated Colleges of the South, the College offers international programs in England, Brazil, and Central Europe.

Credit is available through Advanced Placement tests and also may be earned through a College-approved internship program.

Birmingham-Southern offers several special programs including a dual-enrollment program that enables high school seniors to take college-credit courses.

Off-Campus Programs

The College sponsors an internship program, through which students may earn credit for actual work experience. Depending on their major, students may be assigned positions in business, government, industry, human services, or other preprofessional areas of interest. In addition, students may take part in a cooperative exchange program that enables them to take courses at the University of Alabama at Birmingham, Miles College, or Samford University. They also may participate in Army ROTC at the University of Alabama at Birmingham or Air Force ROTC at Samford University.

Academic Facilities

Birmingham-Southern College features several modern facilities constructed within the last few years, including the Norton Campus Center, the Striplin Physical Fitness Center, the Stephens Science Center, the Admission Welcome Center, the Athletics Complex, and the Urban Environmental Park. The only split-revolve-lift stage in the country is housed in the College Theatre. Six fraternity houses on fraternity row recently opened, a major renovation to Daniel Men's Residence Hall resulted in suite-style living, and two new ecofriendly, suite-style residence halls for men and women opened in fall 2010. A newly renovated Humanities Center also opened recently.

Costs

Tuition at BSC for 2010–11 was $26,900, and room and board fees averaged $8200. There is a $410 student activity fee and $580 IT fee. Estimated expenses for books and supplies are $1260. Transportation and personal expenses are additional costs.

Financial Aid

Birmingham-Southern feels strongly that well-qualified students should have an opportunity for a college education regardless of economic circumstances. More than 97 percent of the College's students receive financial aid of some kind. Birmingham-Southern students received more than $25 million in aid last year. Scholarships and grants range from $1000 to full tuition and may be renewed annually. Each student requesting financial assistance must submit the Free Application for Federal Student Aid (FAFSA). With the exception of the College's competitive scholarship programs and the Alabama Student Grant, all financial assistance awarded through the Office of Financial Aid is based on a demonstrated need determined from the required forms. Preference is given to those students who file by the March 1 priority deadline. In addition to the need-based programs, Birmingham-Southern awards more than $1.5 million in merit-based scholarships through a scholarship competition that is held in the spring.

Faculty

The faculty is composed of 104 full-time and 31 part-time teaching members; approximately 95 percent hold a Ph.D. degree or the terminal degree in their field. In addition to teaching, the faculty's major responsibility is advising students. Faculty members are actively involved in cocurricular activities that are planned primarily for students, and all are assigned a limited number of student advisees. They work closely with these students in planning and developing individual programs to fulfill the students' career interests. The student-faculty ratio is 13:1, and no freshman English class has more than 16 students.

Student Government

The Student Government Association of the College is chartered to operate under a constitution developed by the students, faculty members, and administration. Through a large measure of self-government, this organization helps provide a well-balanced intellectual, educational, and social cocurricular program for all students. The Honor Code makes each student responsible for upholding the social and academic standards of the College. Students serve on numerous College committees.

Admission Requirements

The College enrolled four of its largest freshman classes in the past five years. Students are selected on the basis of high school record, ACT or SAT scores, academic courses attempted, an admission essay, an interview, and recommendations of school officials. Applicants are expected to have completed at least 16 units

of course work, 12 of which must be in academic subjects. Four units of English and at least 2 units each of mathematics, history, science, and social sciences are required, and 2 units of a foreign language are recommended. Students are encouraged to take more than the minimum units required in academic subjects.

Although an interview is not required except in the case of early admission, each applicant is encouraged to visit the campus and talk with an admission counselor or the Dean of Enrollment Management.

Transfer applicants must have at least a C average (2.0 on a 4.0 scale) on a full schedule of courses that are acceptable to Birmingham-Southern and a status of good standing with a clear academic and social record from the last college attended. If the applicant has attended more than one college, his or her overall average at these schools must meet the minimum academic year grade point average required at Birmingham-Southern. Transfer students may enroll at the beginning of any term.

Application and Information

The College considers applications on a rolling admission basis. The priority deadline for scholarship applications is a January 1 postmark.

Preview Days are held in September, October, November, and April, and the College offers two Preview Days during the summer.

Inquiries concerning admission should be addressed to:

Sheri S. Salmon
Dean of Enrollment Management
Birmingham-Southern College
900 Arkadelphia Road
Box 549008
Birmingham, Alabama 35254
Phone: 205-226-4696
      800-523-5793 (toll-free)
E-mail: admission@bsc.edu
Web site: http://www.bsc.edu
      http://on.fb.me/bsc_admissions (Facebook)
      http://twitter.com/FromTheHilltop

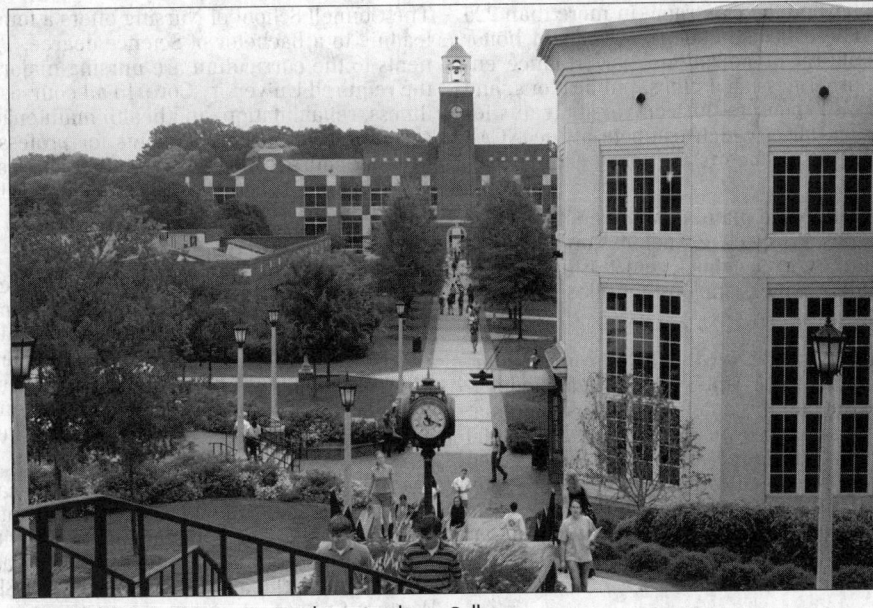

A view of the campus at Birmingham-Southern College.

BOSTON COLLEGE
CHESTNUT HILL, MASSACHUSETTS

The University

Boston College (BC) was founded in 1863 by the Jesuits to serve the sons of Boston's Irish immigrants. Today a coeducational university on more than 207 acres in Chestnut Hill, BC may seem a world apart from the small school in the crowded heart of Boston that was its first home. Through more than fourteen decades of growth and change, however, BC has held fast to the Jesuit ideals that inspired its founders. A Jesuit education today, as a century ago, is grounded in the liberal arts and in a commitment to the service of others.

Undergraduates may enroll in the College of Arts and Sciences, the Wallace E. Carroll School of Management, the Connell School of Nursing, or the Lynch School of Education.

BC's approximately 9,000 undergraduates come from many backgrounds. The university draws from nearly all fifty states and more than fifty countries. Students' religious and cultural backgrounds are similarly diverse. Today, the university's AHANA (African American, Hispanic, Asian, and Native American) and international students make up 25 percent of the undergraduate student body.

In today's complex and increasingly diverse world, the university believes that the best education is one that broadens a student's capacity to reason, think, and make critical judgments in a wide range of areas. Thus, each BC student fulfills a core of liberal arts courses from which he or she can pursue degrees in more than fifty areas of study and choose from more than 1,400 course offerings throughout the university.

According to several recent national publications, BC is in the top tier of the nation's colleges and universities. The foundation for that achievement is the university's scholars and researchers—725 full-time professionals who make up the faculty. The kinship between teachers and students is one of the hallmarks of a BC education; that relationship is nurtured by a student-teacher ratio of 13:1. The median class size at the university is 20 students.

At BC, learning continues beyond the classroom in more than 225 student-run organizations. These include student government, honor societies, language and cultural organizations, performance ensembles, political groups, preprofessional clubs, publications, and service organizations. BC also sponsors thirteen varsity teams for men and sixteen for women, all of which compete at the NCAA Division I level. The College also supports over sixty club and intramural sports.

Boston College's public affairs office maintains university profiles on two social networking sites. Prospective students can become a fan of BC on Facebook (http://www.facebook.com/BostonCollege) or follow BC on Twitter (http://twitter.com/BostonCollege).

Location

Located in the Chestnut Hill section of Newton, BC sits on the doorstep of one of America's great cities, a center of culture and education for more than three centuries. It is an energetic, cosmopolitan city that draws life and enthusiasm from the more than 200,000 college students in residence during the academic year. Located just 6 miles from downtown Boston and with easy access to the city via the trolley system that stops at the foot of the campus, BC offers the best of both worlds: a scenic suburban setting neighboring an exciting metropolitan center.

Majors and Degrees

The College of Arts and Sciences (A&S) is the oldest and largest of the four undergraduate schools at BC. A&S students must complete thirty-eight 1-semester courses, thirty-two of which are in A&S departments. The normal course load is five courses per semester for the first three years and four courses per semester during the senior year. The undergraduate curriculum includes the university Core Curriculum and ten to twelve courses in the major field, with the remainder of courses chosen as electives. A&S offers degrees in the following areas: art history, biochemistry, biology, chemistry, classical studies, communication, computer science, economics, English, environmental geosciences, film studies, French, geology, geological studies, geophysics, German studies, Hispanic studies, history, independent major, international studies, Islamic civilizations and societies, Italian, linguistics, mathematics, music, philosophy, physics, political science, psychology, Russian, Slavic studies, sociology, studio art, theater, and theology. Preprofessional advisement is also available in medical, dental, veterinary, and legal programs. Students can also select from twenty-one departmental minors, or seventeen interdisciplinary minors.

The Carroll School of Management educates students to be leaders in business and industry and in public agencies, educational institutions, and service organizations. The Carroll School offers concentrations in accounting, accounting information systems, computer science, corporate reporting and analysis, economics, finance, general management, human resource management, information systems, management and leadership, marketing, and operations and strategic management.

The Lynch School of Education prepares students for education and human services professions. Programs provide a general education, professional preparation, and specialized education in the major field. Fieldwork in area schools is closely linked to course work in each specialization. The Lynch School awards degrees upon completion of thirty-eight courses, including the University Core, a major field of study in education, and a second major in a subject field or an interdisciplinary area in A&S that complements the student's program. Areas of specialization include early childhood education, elementary education, human development, and secondary education. The Lynch School also offers interdisciplinary majors in American heritages, general science, mathematics/computer science, and perspectives on Spanish America.

The Connell School of Nursing offers a four-year program of study leading to a Bachelor of Science degree. The three major components to the curriculum are nursing major courses, electives, and the required University Core. In all courses, principles of wellness, illness, rehabilitation, and health maintenance serve as a theoretical basis in preparing students for professional nursing practice. Nursing courses include traditional classes, simulated and audiovisual laboratory activities on campus, and clinical learning activities in health-care settings.

Academic Programs

Every BC education is centered on a core curriculum—a set of required courses. BC offers a core curriculum because it believes in the unity of knowledge. While the core, which is continually reviewed by a committee of faculty members, varies somewhat by school, its common elements include literature, natural science, writing, philosophy, theology, social science, modern European history, mathematics, fine arts, and the study of a non-European culture.

There is a wide variety of extraordinary academic programs available to BC students to enhance their educational experience. They include, among others, honors programs within each of the university's four undergraduate schools, Undergraduate Faculty Research Fellows, the Scholar of the College, PULSE, and Perspectives on Western Culture.

Off-Campus Programs

BC encourages all students to take part in internship programs. More than half of BC undergraduates participate in at least one internship or prepracticum placement during their college years. Internships can be paid or unpaid and may take place during the academic year or the summer; some carry academic credit.

BC students may take on the challenge of international study in more than sixty programs administered by BC at universities in more than forty countries. BC students who study abroad typically do so in their junior year, but there is also a range of full-year and summer-abroad opportunities. The Office of International Programs helps students with program selection and applications and maintains a library of reference books and professional evaluations of international study programs.

Academic Facilities

BC's eight libraries contain more than 2.5 million printed volumes, over 4.2 million items in microform, 304,701 e-books, 219,174 government documents, 6,762 serial subscriptions, and a wide collection of films and archival items. The resources of the library system range from some of Europe's earliest printed books to hundreds of computerized databases. Students with personal computers have dorm-room access to these databases as well as to Quest and other library information sources through Agora, the campus information network. BC also offers a 24/7 "Ask a Librarian" e-mail service and the capability to text questions to a librarian. In addition, all of BC's libraries and classrooms offer a wireless network that provides access to these resources and the Internet.

Research laboratories in the state-of-the-art science facilities have been specially designed to accommodate the advanced instrumentation required for modern science and to provide flexibility for accommodating new equipment. The $85-million expansion to the Higgins Biology and Physics Center was carefully designed to place classrooms, laboratories, computer facilities, and office space in proximity and to facilitate interaction among faculty members, researchers, and students. In addition to the Center's seventeen new teaching laboratories, special working labs are designed and outfitted for research and teaching in the fields of biology and physics.

Costs

Tuition for the 2010–11 academic year was $40,542, which included a student activity fee and campus health fee. The total for room and board was $12,082, which includes the board plan. Freshman mandatory fees include a one-time required charge of $430 for first year orientation and student identification.

Financial Aid

BC maintains a financial aid program to assist deserving and qualified students who might otherwise not be able to attend the university. Boston College is committed to providing funds to meet the full demonstrated need of every admitted student who applies for financial aid. Overall, 69 percent of students receive some form of financial aid. Assistance for freshmen alone included more than $19 million in need-based grants. The university offers financial aid to students based on need as demonstrated by completion of the College Scholarship Service's Financial Aid PROFILE and the Free Application for Federal Student Aid (FAFSA). All requirements and deadlines and complete instructions are available in BC admission literature. An application for financial aid in no way affects a decision on admission.

Each year, BC chooses 15 incoming freshmen as Presidential Scholars to receive merit-based, full-tuition scholarships. Students are selected from all candidates who apply through the Early Action program.

Faculty

BC has 725 full-time faculty members. Of these faculty members, 98 percent hold doctoral degrees. Approximately 100 Jesuits live on the BC campus and make up one of the largest Apostolic Jesuit communities in the world. Nearly half of these members are active in the College's administration and teaching.

Student Government

The Undergraduate Government of Boston College (UGBC), formed in 1968, is led by the president and vice president, who are elected in the spring of each year by the entire student body. UGBC's goal is to serve the students by providing services and opportunities and by representing them in the best manner possible to the university community. To accomplish this goal, UGBC provides many educational, social, and cultural programs, such as concerts, lectures, roundtables, and more.

Admission Requirements

The undergraduate admission staff pays particular attention to students who have done well in a demanding college-preparatory curriculum, including Advanced Placement (AP) and honors courses when available. For the class of 2014, there were 29,933 applications for 2,359 places. The majority of incoming freshmen ranked comfortably in the top 10 percent of their high school class. The SAT scores of the middle half of admitted freshmen were 1880–2150. On the ACT, scores of the middle half were between 29 and 32.

Application and Information

Students applying to Boston College for a place in the freshman class must complete both the Common Application and the Boston College Supplemental Application. All applicants should submit the BC Supplemental Application as soon as they have decided to apply to Boston College. Students are encouraged to apply via BC's Web site at http://www.bc.edu/applications but may also apply at http://www.commonapp.org.

Students applying through the regular admission program must submit the Common Application and all other required forms, along with the $70 application fee, by January 1. Candidates are notified of action taken on their application in early April. Admitted students intending to matriculate are required to forward a confirmation fee to the Admission Office postmarked by May 1.

Students with superior academic credentials who view Boston College as a top choice may apply through the nonbinding early action program. These applicants must submit both application forms, along with the $70 application fee, by November 1. Candidates learn of their admission decision before December 25 but have the standard deadline (May 1) to reserve their places as freshmen. Boston College does not permit students to apply under early action if they have applied to an early decision college.

BC accepts transfer applicants each semester. Transfer candidates should request applications for transfer admission from the Office of Undergraduate Admission or via the Web site at http://www.bc.edu/transfer. In addition to high school records and standardized test results, transfer applicants must furnish transcripts from all postsecondary institutions they have attended.

For more information, students should contact:

Office of Undergraduate Admission
Devlin Hall 208
Boston College
Chestnut Hill, Massachusetts 02467
Phone: 617-552-3100
   800-360-2522 (toll-free)
Fax: 617-552-0798
Web site: http://www.bc.edu

Located just 6 miles from downtown Boston, Boston College offers the best of both worlds: a scenic suburban setting neighboring an exciting metropolitan center.

BOSTON UNIVERSITY

BOSTON, MASSACHUSETTS

The University

Boston University (BU) offers a potent array of academic offerings, research opportunities, and extracurricular activities, all in the exciting city of Boston.

BU has more than 250 programs of study, but students aren't required to declare a major until the end of their sophomore year. This gives them the opportunity to try out classes in subjects as varied as biology, broadcast journalism, business, computer engineering, elementary education, film, international relations, physical therapy, psychology, theater, and more.

There are more than 2,000 laboratories on campus and hundreds of hands-on research opportunities across all areas of study, even for freshmen. The BU faculty includes Pulitzer Prize winners, Nobel Laureates, Fulbright Scholars, and MacArthur Fellows. The 13:1 student-faculty ratio and classes with an average size of 28 make it likely that instructors know students by name and are genuinely interested in what they have to say.

BU welcomes students who are original thinkers and who embrace academic challenges. But the University seeks to engage students beyond the classroom as well, with thousands of extracurricular and social opportunities available.

Location

Boston is an international center of cultural and intellectual activity, with a concentration of institutions for higher education unrivaled throughout the world. Home to world-renowned medical facilities, several outstanding museums, baseball's Fenway Park, an active theater district, and the Boston Symphony Orchestra, the city has a vibrant energy all its own. Opportunities for internships and part-time jobs that relate to the student's major or interests are plentiful.

Majors and Degrees

Boston University grants the B.A., B.S., B.S.B.A., B.L.S., Mus.B., and B.F.A. undergraduate degrees. Of the University's seventeen schools and colleges, nine offer opportunities for undergraduate study. The following lists indicate the range of undergraduate programs available.

Students in the College of Arts and Sciences(CAS) may concentrate in American studies; ancient Greek; ancient Greek and Latin; anthropology; anthropology and religion; archaeology; architectural studies; astronomy; astronomy and physics; biochemistry and molecular biology; biology; biology with a specialization in behavioral biology; biology with a specialization in cell biology, molecular biology, and genetics; biology with a specialization in ecology and conservation biology; biology with a specialization in neurobiology; biology with a specialization in quantitative biology; chemistry; chemistry with specialization in biochemistry; chemistry with specialization in teaching; Chinese language and literature; classical civilization; classics and philosophy; classics and religion; comparative literature; computer science; earth sciences; East Asian studies; economics; economics and mathematics; English; environmental analysis and policy; environmental science; French language and literature; geography with a specialization in human geography; geography with a specialization in physical geography; geophysics and planetary sciences; German language and literature; Hispanic language and literatures; history; history of art and architecture; international relations; Italian studies; Japanese language and literature; Latin; Latin American studies; linguistics; linguistics and philosophy; marine science; mathematics; mathematics and computer science; mathematics and mathematics education; mathematics and philosophy; music (nonperformance); neuroscience; philosophy; philosophy and physics; philosophy and political science; philosophy and psychology; philosophy and religion; physics; political science; predentistry; prelaw; premedicine; pre–veterinary

medicine; psychology; religion; Russian language and literature; Russian/East European studies; and sociology. Special curricula include seven-year accelerated programs in liberal arts and medicine and liberal arts and dentistry; the Modular Medical Integrated Curriculum; the BU Dual Degree program; and various combined B.A./M.A. degree programs.

The College of Fine Arts (CFA) offers programs in the School of Music (composition, music education, musicology, and performance), the School of Theater (acting, design, management, production, and theater arts), and the School of Visual Arts (art education, graphic design, painting, and sculpture). There is also a five-year B.F.A./B.A. Double Degree Program which allows students to earn degrees simultaneously in the College of Fine Arts and the College of Arts and Sciences.

The College of General Studies (CGS) offers a two-year liberal-arts-based program that features a core curriculum and intensive team teaching. It is designed so that students can continue as juniors in the degree-granting schools and colleges of the University and earn a bachelor's degree at the end of their senior year.

The College of Communication (COM) offers major programs of undergraduate study in film, television, journalism (with specialization available in broadcast journalism, magazine journalism, news-editorial journalism, and photojournalism), mass communication, advertising, and public relations.

Majors in the College of Engineering (ENG) include biomedical engineering, computer engineering, electrical engineering, mechanical engineering, mechanical engineering with specialization in aerospace, and mechanical engineering with specialization in manufacturing.

The College of Health and Rehabilitation Sciences: Sargent College (SAR) offers programs in athletic training; health science; human physiology; nutrition; and speech, language, and hearing sciences as well as a five-year combined B.S./M.S. degree program in occupational therapy, a six-year B.S./D.P.T. program in physical therapy, and a six-year B.S. in athletic training/D.P.T. in physical therapy program.

Areas of concentration in the School of Education (SED) include bilingual education, deaf studies, early childhood education, elementary education, English education, Latin and classical studies education, mathematics education, modern foreign language education, science education, social studies education, and special education.

The School of Hospitality Administration (SHA) offers a rigorous program in the management of hotels, restaurants, food and beverage service, travel and tourism, and entertainment.

Concentrations in the School of Management (SMG) include accounting, business law, entrepreneurship, finance, general management, international management, management information systems, marketing, operations and technology management, and organizational behavior.

Academic Programs

A Boston University education combines the elements of a traditional liberal arts education with training for the professions. There are 250 programs of study to choose from, including BU's top-ranked biomedical engineering, occupational therapy, deaf studies, international relations, management information systems, journalism, theater, and archeology programs. Highly qualified freshmen may also be invited to participate in the prestigious University Honors College.

Boston University has more than ninety programs that take students around the world. Internships, fieldwork, and study-abroad opportunities are offered on six continents within twenty-five countries, including the U.S. BU has a series of programs and internships in a variety of locations, including Auckland, Beijing, Dresden, Dublin, Geneva, Haifa, London, Los Angeles, Madrid, Paris, Sydney, and Washington, D.C. Programs offered include studies in art/architecture, business/economics, engineering, health and human services, journalism/communications, visual/performing arts, and many more. Fieldwork programs may be found in locations that include Ecuador and Spain, with study-abroad options that include programs in Burgos, Grenoble, Padova, Quito, and Venice. Summer study programs exist in Argentina, Australia, China, England, France, Ireland, Italy, Peru, Spain, Syria, and the United States.

Boston University operates on a calendar of two semesters and two summer terms. Students generally take four courses each semester; thirty-two courses are required for graduation. Most degree programs are built around a core of humanities and social and natural sciences. Concentrations require eight to thirteen courses. Electives generally total 30–40 percent of the courses taken, allowing for interdisciplinary study.

Academic Facilities

Construction has recently started on a new 106,000 square-foot student center on Boston University's East Campus. This building will be home to BU's Center for Career Development, Educational Resource Center, and several student dining and common areas. Three facilities on campus were recently completed: the School of Hospitality Administration Building, a facility with dedicated space for student activities and career recruitment and a hospitality library; the Agganis Arena; and the Fitness and Recreation Center. BU also has a life science and engineering facility with 187,000 square feet of laboratory and research space for the biology, bioinformatics, chemistry, and bioengineering departments. Boston University's state-of-the-art Photonics Center features classroom and laboratory space for the College of Engineering as well as labs designed to support industry partners who seek to develop new photonics-based products. The School of Management building represents one of the most technologically advanced educational facilities in the country, with a dedicated career center and management library.

Through Boston University Information Services and Technology, students have access to public computing facilities equipped with workstations, terminals, and laser printers as well as a high-speed campus network interconnecting all computer resources and linking them to the Internet. An 890-seat proscenium theater, studio space for visual arts students, practice rooms for music, and a 575-seat music performance center are indicative of Boston University's support for the arts. More than 2.8 million library volumes and more than 4.7 million microform units are contained in Mugar Memorial Library, where the Twentieth-Century Archives are held, including the papers of Martin Luther King Jr., Theodore Roosevelt, Robert Frost, and Bette Davis.

Costs

Tuition for 2010–11 was $39,314; estimated room and board costs were $12,260. University and college fees were $550. These costs are exclusive of books, supplies, travel, and personal expenses.

Financial Aid

The Boston University Financial Assistance office offers a variety of grants, scholarships, student loans, and student employment opportunities available to those who request help in meeting the expenses of attending Boston University. Information about credit-based financing options is also provided to students and parents. Need-based aid is offered to eligible students who apply by established deadlines. Merit awards are offered to selected students.

Financial aid offered on the basis of calculated financial eligibility may include Boston University grants, state and federal grants, loans, Federal Work-Study, and other part-time employment. Boston University makes every effort to assist students with calculated financial eligibility, however, funds are limited and it is not possible to meet the eligibility of all financial aid applicants. Priority for a Boston University grant is given to those students with the strongest academic records. Nevertheless, all applicants who anticipate the need for financial aid are encouraged to apply. Boston University believes in recognizing and rewarding outstanding students for their academic and extracurricular accomplishments. The University is therefore committed to offering a variety of merit awards.

Faculty

Students are taught by faculty members who distinguish themselves through their ability, experience, research, and publications. Seventy-eight percent of BU faculty members have a Ph.D. or equivalent and include Nobel Prize winners, a former U.S. Poet Laureate, Pulitzer Prize winners, Guggenheim scholars, Emmy Award winners, MacArthur Fellows, and Sloan Research Fellows. In addition to fulfilling their classroom responsibilities, faculty members are accessible as academic and career advisers who assist students in obtaining internships as well research opportunities.

Student Government

Each school and college has its own student government, which regulates student affairs within the school or college. The University-wide student governing body, the Student Union, has representation from all University schools and colleges. Each residence also has its own student government, composed of elected representatives.

Admission Requirements

The Board of Admissions considers each candidate individually. Primary emphasis is placed on the strength of the secondary school record, but required test scores (SAT or ACT), character, breadth of interest, school recommendations, and other personal qualifications are also carefully evaluated. Students are required to submit the SAT or the ACT (with writing test). Most programs require students to submit the results of two SAT Subject Tests in different subject areas. Students taking the ACT (with writing test) do not need to submit Subject Tests. Prospective students should see the Requirements and Standards chart at http://www.bu.edu/admissions/apply/ freshman/program-requirements for a full listing of the standardized testing requirements. Secondary school graduation or an equivalency diploma is required of all candidates; for the College of Fine Arts, a prescreening, audition, or a portfolio may be required depending on the program of interest. For certain programs, interviews and additional SAT Subject Test scores are required.

Transfer applicants are considered for September or January entrance. Transfer students are not eligible for admission to the Accelerated Liberal Arts Medical or Dental Programs. January admission to the College of Fine Arts School of Theatre is also not available to transfer students. Boston University offers programs of early decision (binding agreement), early admission, and deferred admission.

Boston University admits qualified students regardless of their race, color, national origin, religion, sex, age, or disability to all its programs and activities.

Application and Information

Boston University requires the Common Application and the Boston University Supplement. Information on applying is available online at http://www.bu.edu/admissions/apply. The deadline for applications is January 1. Applicants for Early Decision must apply by November 1. Accelerated program applicants, Trustee Scholar nominees, Dr. Martin Luther King Jr. Scholarship nominees, and Alexander Graham Bell Scholarship nominees must file by December 1. Candidates for financial aid should complete the College Scholarship Service (CSS) Financial Aid PROFILE and the Free Application for Federal Student Aid (FAFSA) by February 15. Transfer students applying for September admission should submit their applications, CSS/Financial Aid PROFILE forms, and Free Application for Federal Student Aid (FAFSA) forms by April 1 or by November 1 for January admission.

Boston University Admissions
121 Bay State Road
Boston, Massachusetts 02215

Phone: 617-353-2300
E-mail: admissions@bu.edu
Web site: http://www.bu.edu/admissions

BOWIE STATE UNIVERSITY

BOWIE, MARYLAND

Prepare for Life

The University

Bowie State University began as a normal school in the city of Baltimore in 1865, and it has evolved over the years into a four-year, coeducational, liberal arts institution. It is currently situated on a beautiful 500-acre campus in Prince Georges County, Maryland, and offers both graduate and undergraduate programs of study. Teacher education programs were established in 1925; in 1935, with state authorization, a four-year program for the training of elementary school teachers was begun and the school became the Maryland State Teachers College at Bowie. In 1951, with the approval of the State Board of Education, its governing body at the time, the college established a teacher-preparation curriculum for the training of teachers for the core program in the junior high schools. Ten years later, permission was granted to institute a teacher-training program for secondary education. A liberal arts program was established in 1963, and the institution's name was changed to Bowie State College. In 1988, Bowie State achieved university status and joined the University System of Maryland (USM).

Bowie State University's physical plant is valued at more than $225 million, and its current enrollment is 5,578 students, 1,217 of whom are in the Graduate School. The University has twenty-two buildings on campus with the addition of the $21-million state-of-the-art Center for Learning and Technology that opened in 2000, the $11.8-million Computer Science Center that opened in 2002, and the new $19-million Center for Business and Graduate Studies opened in 2007. Two of the buildings, the Communication Arts Center and the physical education complex, were completed in 1973, and an administration building opened in 1977. Seven residence halls, including Goodloe Hall and Alex Haley Hall, a state-of-the-art residence hall that houses honors students, house approximately 850 students. In addition, a 460-bed apartment-style residence hall, Christa McAuliffe, was completed in 2004. The $2.6-million physical education complex houses a 3,000-seat basketball arena, an Olympic-size swimming pool with underwater viewing windows and facilities for 200 spectators, an apparatus gymnasium, a dance studio, a wrestling room, a weight-training room, eight handball/squash courts, a therapy room, and offices for instructors and coaches. The $5.5-million University Activities Center includes a cafeteria. Bowie State has broken ground for its new $79 million Fine and Performing Arts Center. The 123,000-square-foot building will include a 400-seat main theater, a 200-seat black box theater, a 200-seat recital hall, an art gallery, classrooms, labs, and offices.

Bowie State University considers the student activities program a vital part of the total educational program. Students have access to more than forty different activities. These include student government, the student union, intercollegiate athletics, eight fraternities and sororities, numerous departmental clubs and preprofessional organizations, and music and drama organizations.

The Graduate School grants the Master of Arts in counseling psychology, English, human resource development, mental health counseling, organizational communications, school psychology, and teaching (M.A.T.); the Master of Business Administration; the Master of Education in elementary education, reading education, school administration and supervision, school counseling, secondary education, and special education; the Master of Public Administration; and the Master of Science in applied computational mathematics, computer science, management information systems, and nursing. The Doctor of Education is granted in educational leadership and the Applied Doctor of Science is granted in computer science. The Adler-Dreikurs Institute of Human Relations at Bowie State University is the first fully accredited master's-degree-granting Adlerian institute in the United States.

Bowie State University admits students without regard to sex, religion, or nationality, and the University does not discriminate on the basis of race, creed, color, national or ethnic origin, age, sex, or handicap. The University is accredited by the Middle States Association of Colleges and Schools and approved by the Maryland State Department of Education. Its programs in teacher education, social work education, nursing, business, and computer science are accredited by the National Council for Accreditation of Teacher Education, the National Council on Social Work Education, the National League for Nursing Accrediting Commission, the Maryland Board of Nursing, the Association of Collegiate Business Schools and Programs, and the Computer Science Accreditation Commission of the Computing Sciences Accreditation Board, respectively.

Location

Bowie, Maryland, is in a triangle formed by Annapolis (20 miles east), Baltimore (25 miles north), and Washington, D.C. (17 miles southwest). The suburban setting provides an ideal, safe environment for students and scholars, with access to all of the important cultural, governmental, and business activities in any of the three metropolitan areas.

Majors and Degrees

Bowie State University offers the Bachelor of Arts or Bachelor of Science degree with majors in bioinformatics, biology, business administration, communications media, computer science, computer technology, early childhood education, elementary education, English, English education, fine art, government, history, mathematics, nursing, child and adolescent studies, psychology, science education, social work, sport management, sociology/criminal justice, and technology. A dual-degree program is offered in engineering.

Academic Programs

The University operates on a semester calendar. Academic offerings are housed under four schools (School of Arts and Sciences, School of Education, School of Professional Studies, and the new School of Business) and can be divided into four main areas: humanities, science and mathematics, social sciences, and education. To receive a bachelor's degree, a student must earn a minimum of 120 semester hours with a cumulative grade point average of 2.0 or better. Students are provided the opportunity to complete the General Education Program, acquire lifelong learning skills for a competitive world, and make a successful transition into their junior year. General studies requirements include communication skills, 9 hours; humanities, 9 hours; social sciences, 18 hours; science and mathematics, 9 hours; and physical education, 2 hours. The remaining credit hours can be electives or from major and minor areas of interest. Students must also pass the test of Proficiency in the English Language and must take the national standardized test in their major area.

The Honors Program is designed for students with outstanding academic records and potential and provides a special educational opportunity for young adults with exceptional talent. The program is comprehensive and multidisciplinary in structure and interdisciplinary in application. It has been designed to provide a creative approach to the teaching/learning process and to present activities that encourage the shaping of students' own experiences.

The Special Services Project is a federally funded program designed to retain and graduate first-generation, low-income, and disabled students who have been admitted to Bowie State University. The purpose of the project is to help students overcome academic and nonacademic barriers to academic success, through participation in specially designed activities, including counseling, tutoring, and workshops on test taking and study skills.

Through the Cooperative Education Program, a student may choose either the alternate or parallel programs of study and work in business, industry, government, or a social-service agency. This program is open to Bowie State students who have completed at least one academic year with a minimum cumulative grade point average of 2.0.

The University participates in the College-Level Examination Program (CLEP), administered by the Educational Testing Service for the College Board, and in the Defense Activity for Non-Traditional Education Support (DANTES) program. The University also has a program for awarding students credit for learning acquired through life and work experience. Under this program, students document their backgrounds in a portfolio, which is reviewed by the faculty. Through all of these programs, qualified students may receive up to 30 credit hours toward their degree. In addition, the University offers an Army ROTC program. Two-year and three-year scholarships are available.

Academic Facilities

The Communication Arts Center, a $6.5-million building that houses the humanities division, contains classrooms, offices, conference rooms, and studio-laboratories and seats approximately 1,000 patrons. The $8.8-million, 345,514-volume Thurgood Marshall Library is centrally located on campus and provides excellent equipment and reference departments for the student body. The microfilm file contains 474,196 items; periodicals number 767. Campus research facilities include science laboratories, television and radio studios, language laboratories, and the Adler-Dreikurs Institute. Access to the library collection is provided through Victor Web, the electronic catalog that also links users to millions of USM volumes. The new Center for Learning and Technology, the main classroom building, features a new supercomputer (one of the fastest computers in the world), fourteen electronic classrooms, two interactive lecture halls, three computer labs, one speech lab, and a 300-seat auditorium and conference center. In addition, the new Computer Science Center has five classrooms and thirteen labs. Finally, the Center for Business and Graduate Studies, which opened in 2007, provides modern classrooms, labs, study space, offices, and administrative support space for the School of Business and the Division of Graduate Studies.

Costs

In 2010–11, the annual cost of tuition, fees, board, and room for a freshman who is a Maryland resident averaged $13,000; for a non-Maryland resident, the cost averaged $25,000. The annual cost for a commuting student who is a Maryland resident was about $7000; the cost for a commuting student who is not a Maryland resident was about $17,000.

Financial Aid

Federal Pell Grants, Supplemental Grants, Work-Study, Perkins Loans, and Direct Loans are available. University scholarships, tuition waivers, and diversity grants are awarded. Most awards are based on need. Academic scholarships could be offered to students with cumulative weighted grade point averages of at least 3.3 and minimum SAT (reading and math) scores of 1100. In addition, merit awards are given for athletics, music and fine arts, and ROTC. More than 77 percent of all undergraduate students receive some form of financial aid. Deadlines are March 1 for the fall semester and November 15 for the spring semester.

Faculty

More than 60 percent of the 160 full-time faculty members have earned doctoral degrees. The faculty-student ratio is 1:16.

Student Government

All students are members of the Student Government Association, which, in cooperation with the administration, sets the standards for student life. Students are encouraged to assume leadership roles and to participate in the various programs and activities of the University. The Residence Hall Council provides opportunities for students to participate in the administration of residence life and in the cultural growth of the campus community.

Admission Requirements

Maryland residents applying for admission should have a minimum cumulative grade point average in their core high school courses of 2.0 (on a 4.0 scale) and a minimum SAT (reading and math only) score of 900 (or a minimum ACT score of 19). A sliding scale is used for students who have higher grade point averages or SAT scores. Conditional admission may be offered to students with a minimum cumulative grade point average of 2.0 and minimum SAT (reading and math only) scores of 830 to 899 (or a minimum ACT score of 17). Applicants must have earned a high school diploma or a GED certificate. The following courses are required: English, 4 credits; social science/history, 3 credits; mathematics (algebra I, algebra II, and geometry), 3 credits; laboratory sciences, 2 credits; foreign language, 2 credits; and electives, 6 credits. A $40 application fee is charged, and a health certificate must be submitted before entering the University.

Transfer students must have a minimum 2.0 cumulative grade point average for a minimum of 24 transferable credits, or SAT scores are required. International students and mature adults are encouraged to apply.

Application and Information

The application deadline is April 1 for the fall semester and November 1 for spring. Students should apply online at http://www.bowiestate.edu/apply.

Admissions Office
Bowie State University
Bowie, Maryland 20715-9465
Phone: 301-860-3415
    410-880-4100 Ext. 3415 (from the
       Baltimore-Columbia area)
    877-77-BOWIE (toll-free)
Fax: 301-860-3518
E-mail: undergradadmissions@bowiestate.edu
Web site: http://www.bowiestate.edu
      http://www.facebook.com/bowiestate
      http://twitter.com/bowiestate

Flags representing the international student population of Bowie State University frame the entrance to the 500-acre campus.

BOWLING GREEN STATE UNIVERSITY

BOWLING GREEN, OHIO

The University

Bowling Green State University (BGSU) is a vibrant university that engages, challenges, and prepares students for meaningful futures. At BGSU, students enjoy an education that integrates personal growth, academic excellence, and an environment that expands their thinking and potential. Students will find a campus with diverse activities, innovative academic programs, and a dynamic mix of learning opportunities on campus and beyond. BGSU has earned national recognition for its residential learning communities and student success initiatives, which help ease the transition to college life.

BGSU has approximately 21,000 students who are challenged to stay curious, think critically, and keep learning. With more than 200 undergraduate majors and programs, BGSU's learning community provides high-quality faculty members who care about their students, an appreciation for diversity, and the latest in information technology. About 7,000 students live on campus. BGSU attracts students who balance academic excellence with involvement in more than 300 student organizations. Committed to ensuring that every student succeeds, Bowling Green challenges and supports students, both in and out of the classroom.

BGSU offers a physically compact campus located within the Bowling Green community. New construction on campus is slated to add new residence halls and dining centers, a new convocation center, and a new center for the arts during the 2011–12 academic year. Most restaurants and businesses are within walking or biking distance of residence halls. All students are permitted to have cars.

Combined enrollment at Bowling Green's main campus and the BGSU–Firelands regional campus is approximately 21,000 students, including 3,000 graduate students. The total University population includes students from forty-nine states and eighty-two nations. In addition, the University's diverse population includes 19 percent who are students of color. Students are actively involved outside of class, participating in student organizations, service learning opportunities, and the more than 400 cultural and special events that are offered each year.

Residence halls reinforce the learning environment with a computer laboratory for each residence complex and one personal computer available for every 23 resident students. Every residence hall room has high-speed Ethernet connections to the University's computing backbone.

BGSU's Graduate College offers a broad range of doctoral and master's degree programs and specialist and certificate programs. BGSU Firelands also has an array of programs, from one-year certificate and two-year associate degree programs to bachelor's and master's degree programs.

The University is fully accredited by the Higher Learning Commission and is a member of the North Central Association of Schools and Colleges (30 LaSalle Street, Suite 3400, Chicago, Illinois 60602-2504; telephone: 800-621-7440, toll-free).

Location

The city of Bowling Green, Ohio, population 30,028, is located in northwest Ohio, about 20 miles south of Toledo. It is within comfortable driving distance of all major cities in Ohio and is an easy commute from nearby towns.

Majors and Degrees

BGSU offers more than 200 undergraduate majors and programs in seven undergraduate colleges: Arts and Sciences, Business Administration, Education and Human Development, Health and Human Services, Musical Arts, Technology, and BGSU–Firelands, the regional campus in Huron, Ohio. Numerous programs within these colleges are accredited by their respective national accrediting agencies.

Majors (and specializations) within the Bachelor of Arts degree include Africana studies, American culture studies, art, art history, Asian studies, classical civilization, communication, computer science (business systems, geographic information systems), economics, English, environmental policy and analysis, ethnic studies, film (film production,

film studies), French, geography, geology, German, history, international studies, Latin, mathematics (actuarial science), music, philosophy, political science, popular culture, preprofessional programs, psychology, Russian, scientific and technical communication, sociology, Spanish (Latin American culture studies), statistics, theater, and women's studies.

Within the Bachelor of Arts in Communication, students can choose majors (and specializations) in communication, telecommunications, and theater (acting/directing, design/technical theater, musical theater, performance studies, youth theater/puppetry).

Majors (and specializations) within the Bachelor of Fine Arts include art education (three-dimensional studies, two-dimensional studies), creative writing, digital arts, graphic design, three-dimensional studies, and two-dimensional studies.

Within the Bachelor of Science degree, students can choose majors (and specializations) in biology, chemistry (biochemistry), computer science (business systems, geographic information systems), environmental science, geology (geochemistry, geophysics), gerontology (long-term-care administration), mathematics (actuarial science, applied mathematics), microbiology, neuroscience, physics (applied physics), psychology, scientific and technical communication, and statistics.

Students can choose from among three specializations in the Bachelor of Science degree in journalism: broadcast journalism, print journalism, and public relations.

The Bachelor of Science in Business Administration degree offers the following specializations: accounting, business prelaw, economics, finance, financial economics, general business, information systems auditing and control, international business, management information systems, marketing, public policy and administration, and supply chain management.

The Bachelor of Science in Education offers majors (and specializations) that include the teaching areas of adolescent/young adult education (secondary education), including integrated language arts, mathematics, and social studies; single and double field sciences in earth sciences, life sciences, and physical sciences in chemistry and physics; foreign language (French, German, Latin, Russian, and Spanish); intervention specialist (deaf/hard of hearing, dual mild/moderate and moderate/intensive, mild/moderate and moderate/intensive); middle childhood studies; physical education teacher education; and marketing education.

The human development programs include apparel merchandising; athletic training/clinic management; human development and family studies; dance; developmental disabilities and habilitation; dietetics; exercise science; human movement science; interior design; nutrition science; recreation; sport management; and tourism, leisure, and event planning.

The Bachelor of Applied Health Science offers specializations in allied health, applied microbiology, health science, and pre–physical therapy.

The Bachelor of Music offers majors (and specializations) in jazz studies, music composition, music education (choral, classroom/general music, instrumental), music history and literature, music performance (church music, guitar: jazz and classical emphasis, harpsichord, instrumental, keyboard/accompanying, keyboard/literature, keyboard/pedagogy, organ, vocal pedagogy, voice, voice/musical theater, woodwind specialist), and world music.

The Bachelor of Science in Technology offers majors (and specializations) in advanced technological education, architecture and environmental design, aviation studies (aviation management and operations, aviation technical management, flight technology and operations), construction management and technology, electronics and computer technology, mechanical design, technology education, and visual communication technology.

The following degrees are offered without separately identified majors within the degree: Bachelor of Liberal Studies, Bachelor of Science in apparel merchandising and product development, Bachelor of Science in communication disorders, Bachelor of Science in criminal justice, Bachelor of Science in dietetics, Bachelor of Science in economics, Bachelor of Science in environmental health, Bachelor of Science in interior design, Bachelor of Science in medical technology, Bachelor of Science in nursing, Bachelor of Science in nutrition sciences, and Bachelor of Science in social work.

BGSU–Firelands offers fourteen programs that lead to associate degrees in applied business, applied sciences, nursing, science, and technical study, plus eight bachelor's degree programs.

Every entering student has the option of enrolling in an undergraduate college with a declared major or enrolling as an undecided student. Students who are undecided about a college begin their studies in premajor advising.

Academic Programs

The academic program at BGSU is designed to help students achieve their full potential. All students, regardless of their major, take a core group of general education courses.

Classroom work is closely integrated with out-of-class experiences in the residence halls and off campus. Students can choose one of fourteen smaller residential learning or theme communities. *U.S. News & World Report*'s "America's Best Colleges for 2011" includes BGSU's learning communities and first-year programs in "Strong Focus on Student Success." The report states, "Some schools are much more determined than others to provide freshmen and all undergrads with the best possible experience recognizing that certain enriched offerings, from service learning to learning communities to study abroad, are linked to student success." BGSU has been at the forefront of the learning community movement in the country and has been noted for its communities in the *U.S. News & World Report* multiple times, beginning in 2003. BGSU has a number of these learning communities, ranging from those in which students share a common major, such as health science or urban education, to those in which they share a commitment to an area of interest, such as global connections or appreciation of the arts. Within the learning communities, professors teach classes and have offices in the residence halls, and extend experiential and service learning beyond the classroom.

Bowling Green offers a challenging honors program, honors housing, and the opportunity to complete a senior honors project for graduation with University or departmental honors. All students receive academic advising, and tutoring services are available. Bowling Green has Army and Air Force ROTC programs.

Off-Campus Programs

Education-abroad programs range from a full academic year to a few weeks and are available at thirty sites in twenty countries.

Every Bowling Green student can take advantage of at least one opportunity to gain practical experience related to his or her major. Cooperative education, an earn-while-you-learn program, allowed more than 700 students from approximately seventy majors to gain practical experience during 2009–10, earning an average of $12.20 an hour. More than 250 employers in forty-five different industries hired BGSU co-op and intern students. The University's co-op program ranks in the top 10 percent in the country for number of placements and is open to all students in all majors.

Academic Facilities

Extensive state-of-the-art facilities support the work of faculty members and students at Bowling Green. BGSU Libraries provide a gateway to several million items on site and online, including resources of the Music Library and Sound Recordings Archives, Popular Culture Library, Curriculum Resource Center, and Center for Archival Collections. The libraries are linked to the resources of all major colleges and universities in Ohio and can locate materials worldwide.

Far-reaching access to information and the latest technological learning and teaching resources are a staple of the BGSU campus, from digital media, digital textbooks, and satellite links to high-speed Internet access in every residence hall room, online courses, and numerous labs with highly specialized hardware and software for individual disciplines.

Olscamp Hall, a classroom building with seating for 2,000, is equipped for teleteaching/distance learning. BGSU has a modern physical sciences laboratory building and planetarium, a renovated fine arts center, and outstanding music facilities.

Costs

A full-time first-year student from Ohio living on campus in standard housing and with the limited meal plan paid $17,214 in 2010–11. Out-of-state students paid a surcharge of $7308, for a total of $24,522. Students are encouraged to budget about $800 to $1200 a year for books and supplies, and an additional $2600 for other expenses, such as entertainment, clothing, transportation, and laundry.

Financial Aid

About 73 percent of all BGSU undergraduates receive an average financial aid package of $9000. In addition, BGSU awards more than $20 million in scholarships each year. BGSU offers automatic and renewable scholarships (from $1000 to $5000) to students who have a minimum 3.0 grade point average and a minimum 20 ACT or 920 SAT score; credentials must be submitted to the Office of Admissions by January 15. Students who qualify for the $5000 award may also be considered for a scholarship of up to full in-state fees, currently $9140. All awards are renewable for three additional years, provided the student maintains a 2.75 minimum cumulative grade point average. Academically qualified nonresidents are eligible for the BG Success Scholarship, which covers half of the nonresident surcharge, currently $3654. Student employment, grants, and loans are other options available. BGSU employs about 4,500 students annually. Students apply for aid by completing the Free Application for Federal Student Aid (FAFSA). Prospective students should contact the Office of Admissions for additional information.

Faculty

At the heart of Bowling Green State University are 921 full-time faculty members who devote their energies to teaching, research, and working closely with students; 75 percent have the highest degree in their field. Their reputations as scholars, authors, and teachers complement the faculty's role as people who care about students and the future of the University. The personal attention students receive from the faculty and support staff contributes to the small-college atmosphere that is distinctive at BGSU.

Student Government

The Undergraduate Student Government (USG) is the representative body for Bowling Green's undergraduate students. Leaders and delegates are elected by the entire student body and carry the students' voice to both the University Board of Trustees and the Faculty Senate. Each year, the governor appoints an undergraduate and a graduate student to the University Board of Trustees.

Admission Requirements

High school students are encouraged to apply for admission beginning May 1 between their junior and senior years. Admission to the fall semester is competitive. Nonresidents of Ohio are considered for admission on the same basis as in-state students. An applicant is considered on the basis of high school course work, cumulative GPA, official ACT or SAT results, and class rank. The University also considers the diversity of the student body and applicants' special abilities, talents, and achievements in making admission decisions.

Admission to the University for transfer students is determined by their college academic credentials. Several academic majors and programs have specific requirements for transfer students, but, in general, a minimum 2.0 GPA is required for students who have earned at least 60 semester hours; a minimum 2.5 GPA is required for students who have earned fewer than 60 semester (90 quarter) hours.

Application and Information

Prospective students are encouraged to have all admission credentials complete before February 1 of the year they intend to enroll. Notification of admission decisions begins on September 1 for those who have submitted all credentials and continues on a rolling basis. Bowling Green does not discriminate in admission on the basis of race, sex, sexual orientation, color, national origin, religion, creed, age, marital status, mental or physical disability, or veteran status. Students are encouraged to apply online at BGSU's Web site or obtain an application for admission by contacting:

Gary D. Swegan
Assistant Vice Provost and Director of Admissions
110 McFall Center
Bowling Green State University
Bowling Green, Ohio 43403-0085
Phone: 419-372-BGSU
      866-CHOOSE-BGSU (toll-free)
Fax: 419-372-6955
E-mail: choosebgsu@bgsu.edu
Web site: http://www.bgsu.edu

BROOKLYN COLLEGE OF THE CITY UNIVERSITY OF NEW YORK

BROOKLYN, NEW YORK

Brooklyn College The City University of New York

The College

You have a purpose. Brooklyn College has a program.

You want to be a doctor, a lawyer, a financial advisor. You want to teach physical education or coach a school athletics team. You have always wanted to be an artist or a writer; a professional musician, a singer, or an actor. Most of all, you want focus in life and preparation for a career. You will find that and more at Brooklyn College.

Since its founding in 1930, Brooklyn College has distinguished itself as one of the nation's leading public institutions. It plays an important role in the borough's vibrant cultural life and is very much a part of its ethnically diverse communities.

Faculty members at Brooklyn College take advantage of the College's location to utilize New York City as an extension of their classrooms, allowing students to benefit from the dynamic cultural, social, and economic resources beyond the campus.

More than 17,000 undergraduate and graduate students are currently enrolled in 125 programs leading to bachelor's and master's degrees or advanced certificates in business and education, across the sciences and social sciences, and in the arts and humanities. The School of Education is rated among the top 20 education programs in the country, and the College's Master of Fine Arts (M.F.A.) program was recently rated fifteenth in the country—above highly regarded programs at Columbia University and Sarah Lawrence College.

One of the best resources Brooklyn College offers is the Magner Center for Career Development and Internships. The Center helps students explore career options through internship opportunities at more than 700 companies throughout the city. Students are able to build an impressive resume even before they graduate and make valuable connections from employers in almost every field—from major media outlets to medical centers and from government offices to prestigious financial institutions.

Brooklyn college students participate in a lively student community, where there are many activities to choose from. There are fraternities and sororities; two student newspapers and a student-run radio station; community service opportunities; student government; the Hillel Foundation, Intervarsity Christian Fellowship, and the Newman Center; intramural and NCAA Division III sport teams; and 140 clubs and organizations.

Location

Brooklyn College is located in the residential Midwood section of Brooklyn, a short subway ride from Manhattan. The many different cultures of Brooklyn contribute to the wide ethnic diversity of the College's student and teacher population. Subway and bus transportation to all points inside and outside the borough is easily accessible from the College.

Majors and Degrees

Brooklyn College awards the Bachelor of Arts (B.A.), Bachelor of Science (B.S.), Bachelor of Music (B.Mus.), Bachelor of Fine Arts (B.F.A.), Bachelor of Science/Master of Professional Studies (B.S./M.P.S.), and Bachelor of Business Administration (B.B.A.) degrees.

Majors are available in the following areas: accounting; Africana studies; American studies; anthropology; art; art history; art studio; biology; broadcast journalism; business administration; business, finance, and management; business information systems; Caribbean studies; chemistry; children's studies; classics; communication; comparative literature; computer science; creative writing; economics; education (childhood education, early childhood education, secondary education with certification in eleven subject areas); English; environmental studies; film; French; geology; health and nutrition sciences; history; information systems; Italian; journalism;

Judaic studies; linguistics; mathematics; mathematics-computational; media studies; multimedia computing; music; music composition; music performance; philosophy; physical education; physics; political science; psychology; Puerto Rican and Latino studies; religion; Russian; sociology; Spanish; speech; speech-language pathology, audiology, speech and hearing science; television and radio; theater; and women's studies.

Certificate programs are offered in accounting, computers and programming, and film; credits earned in these programs are also applicable toward a baccalaureate degree.

A 4½-year Business Information Systems program leads to Bachelor of Science and Master of Professional Studies (B.S./M.P.S.) degrees.

An eight-year coordinated honors program with SUNY's Brooklyn Health Science Center leads to B.A. and M.D. degrees and is limited to 15 students per year who are admitted in the fall following their high school graduation.

A two-year coordinated engineering program includes attending Brooklyn College for two years of pre-engineering studies and then transferring to Polytechnic University, City College, or the College of Staten Island for an additional two years of study to fulfill the B.S. degree requirements in a specific engineering field.

Qualified students can earn a Brooklyn College B.A. or B.S. degree by satisfactorily completing all requirements for graduation except 30 elective credits, and also satisfactorily completing at least one year's work in an accredited dental, engineering, law, medical, optometry, podiatry, or veterinary school.

Academic Programs

The College-wide core curriculum provides a diverse educational experience in the liberal arts and sciences for all students; major studies, which comprise specialized, intensive study in one discipline or an interdisciplinary program; and elective courses, selected from more than seventy-five areas. Students pursuing a bachelor's degree must successfully complete a minimum of 120 credits.

The academic calendar consists of a fall and a spring semester. Two summer sessions and a January intersession are available. Classes are offered in day, evening, and weekend sessions.

The Honors Academy includes the William E. Macaulay Honors College Program, which consists of an energetic honors curriculum and cultural experiences, as well as a full-tuition scholarship, internship opportunities, and an academic expense account; the Scholars Program, offering students who combine academic excellence with initiative and inquisitiveness the opportunity to take classes and courses that are only for members of the program; the Coordinated B.A./M.D. Program, which gives students who are interested in medical careers the necessary foundation in the sciences and guarantees admission to SUNY Downstate College of Medicine; the Mellon Mays Undergraduate Fellowship, a two-year program for members of minority groups who are considering scholarly study in the humanities; the Minority Access Research Careers Program; and the Coordinated Engineering Honors Program.

Students who have completed college-level courses in high school may be considered for exemption, with or without credit, from equivalent college courses on the basis of Advanced Placement tests given by the College Board. Brooklyn College gives exemption examinations in subjects not offered by the College Board. Students completing three years of foreign language in high school are exempt from the College's language requirement.

Academic Facilities

The College is currently in a period of expansion. A new performing arts center is being constructed for the Department of Theater and the Conservatory of Music, and plans are on the drawing board for an ambitious new science complex.

The College's magnificent library is much more than a traditional academic library—it is a comprehensive information center with extensive physical and digital collections, the College archives, a new media center, and both academic and administrative computing. The library's growing collections include approximately 15,000 electronic subscriptions and works of reference; 50,000 electronic books; 1.3 million volumes; 1.6 million microfilms; 50,000 serials; and 25,000 rich media items (sound recordings, videotapes, and DVDs). The library's twenty-two group-study rooms, five computer classrooms, and over 600 computers make it the campus's premier study and research space.

Students have access to over 1,000 computers with the latest software in various public computer labs, each with extensive operating hours, including the Library Café that offers a Starbucks bar with 24/7 computer availability. Scores of department computer labs and high-tech learning spaces throughout the campus support the College's many programs.

The year-old West Quad Center includes extensive state-of-the-art physical education and recreation facilities and a huge consolidated student services center offering one-stop service for most student administrative transactions.

Other special facilities include a walk-in learning and tutoring center, a language laboratory, art studios, an advanced color television production studio, a fully operational advanced radio station, a working journalism newsroom, film production and editing facilities, a speech and hearing clinic, psychological laboratories, laser laboratories, an aquatic research center whose projects were aboard the space shuttle, a nuclear physics laboratory, and much more.

The Brooklyn Center for the Performing Arts at Brooklyn College presents music, dance and theater productions. It includes a 2,500-seat auditorium, a theater, a recital hall, and a workshop theater. Construction is beginning on a new $50 million center for the performing arts, which will serve the Conservatory of Music, the Department of Theater, and related disciplines.

Costs

In 2010–11, New York State residents paid tuition of $2300 per semester for full-time students, $195 per credit for part-time students, and $285 per credit for non-degree resident students. Non–New York State residents and international students paid tuition of $415 per credit (both full- and part-time students) or $610 per credit (non-degree students). All students pay per credit for summer session and intersession courses. The College is an easily accessible commuter institution with many housing options nearby, including a new residence hall, which opened at the beginning of the fall 2010 semester.

Financial Aid

Admission, financial aid, and scholarship decisions are made independently of each other, and an application for aid does not hinder a student's opportunity for admission. Financial assistance is available for eligible students through state and federal grant, loan, and work-study programs.

New students, especially those with strong high school or college academic records and SAT scores, are encouraged to apply for annual scholarships. Continuing students may qualify for one of the more than 400 scholarships, prizes, and awards that are given each year to Brooklyn College students. The requirements vary for each award, but recipients are chosen based on academic performance, financial need, and other criteria that may be stipulated by the donors. Scholarships range from $100 to $4000 per year.

Faculty

The College has an outstanding faculty (537 full-time and 837 part-time). Among the faculty members are Fulbright, Guggenheim, and MacArthur Foundation fellows; Obie Award-winning playwrights; Pulitzer Prize and National Book Award recipients; and Grammy-nominated musicians. The College's scientists receive substantial research grants from such competitive sources as the National Institute of Science and the National Science Foundation, whose members have demonstrated excellence in teaching and scholarly re-

search. Faculty members assist in the academic advisement of entering students and provide counseling to students majoring in their department. They also hold regular office hours and are generally available to support student activities.

Student Government

Brooklyn College has three student government organizations on campus: one for undergraduate day students, one for undergraduate evening students, and one that represents graduate students. Student government is expected to advocate for the interests of the student body, provide a venue for making decisions that can shape students' academic futures, and help improve campus life by creating and maintaining student services. Students also serve on the Policy Council, the major College-wide governing body.

Admission Requirements

Brooklyn College admits freshmen and transfers for both the fall and spring semesters. Regular freshman admission is based on the student having a minimum of an 81 average in their academic subjects and a minimum SAT of 1000 or the equivalent ACT scores. Freshman students should demonstrate successful completion of at least 12 or more high school academic units (of which at least 5 units must include 2 or more years of English and 2 or more years of math). The recommended high school preparation for the College's curriculum is 4 years of English, 4 years of social studies, 3 years of mathematics, 3 years of science, and 3 years of a foreign language. Highly qualified high school juniors may apply for early admission directly at the Admissions Office of the College.

The Search for Education, Elevation, and Knowledge (SEEK) Program at Brooklyn College is committed to helping students from educationally and financially disadvantaged backgrounds meet their educational goals through tutoring and mentoring. Students must fill out a separate section on the CUNY application for the SEEK Program.

Freshmen seeking admission to the Brooklyn College Honors Academy—which includes the Scholars Program, the Macaulay Honors College Program, and the B.A./M.D. Program—must present a high school average of 90 or better, exceptional SAT or ACT scores, letters of recommendation, an essay, and a personal interview.

Transfer students are admitted to the College with a minimum of a 2.3 cumulative average on prior course work. In addition, students with fewer than 25 credits completed must also meet the regular freshman requirements.

Application and Information

Application for admission to the undergraduate programs for the fall or spring semester should be made online via the College's Web site at http://www.brooklyn.edu/pug. Some honors programs, fellowships, and coordinated programs have special applications or application requirements, which can be obtained at the College's Web site. Undergraduate applications are processed by the City University of New York's central processing center (University Applications Processing Center–UAPC), and although applications for admission are processed on a rolling basis, applicants who apply by February 1 for fall admission and by September 15 for spring have the best opportunity for admission consideration, comprehensive advisement, and course registration. The CUNY Macaulay Honors College applicants are required to apply by December 1 for fall admission.

For additional information or to arrange to meet with an admissions counselor, please visit the College's Web site.

Office of Admissions
Brooklyn College
222 West Quad Center
2900 Bedford Avenue,
Brooklyn, New York 11210
Phone: 718-951-5001
E-mail: adminqry@brooklyn.cuny.edu
Web site: http://www.brooklyn.edu/pug
　　　　http://on.fb.me/brooklyncoll_cuny (Facebook)
　　　　http://twitter.com/bklyncollege411 (Twitter)

BROWN MACKIE COLLEGE–ALBUQUERQUE

ALBUQUERQUE, NEW MEXICO

The College

Brown Mackie College–Albuquerque is one of over twenty-five locations in the Brown Mackie College system of schools (www.brownmackie.edu), which is dedicated to providing educational programs that prepare students to pursue entry-level positions in a competitive, rapidly changing workplace. Brown Mackie College schools offer bachelor's degree, associate degree, certificate, and diploma programs in health sciences, business, information technology, legal studies, and design to over 20,000 students in the Midwest, Southeast, Southwest, and Western United States.

Brown Mackie College was originally founded and approved by the Board of Trustees of Kansas Wesleyan College in Salina, Kansas on July 30, 1892. In 1938, the College was incorporated as the Brown Mackie School of Business under the ownership of Perry E. Brown and A.B. Mackie, former instructors at Kansas Wesleyan University in Salina, Kansas. Their last names formed the name of Brown Mackie. By January 1975, with improvements in curricula and higher degree-granting status, the Brown Mackie School of Business became Brown Mackie College.

Brown Mackie College–Albuquerque is accredited by the Accrediting Council for Independent Colleges and Schools (ACICS) to award bachelor's degrees, associate degrees, and diplomas. The Accrediting Council for Independent Colleges and Schools is listed as a nationally recognized accrediting agency by the United States Department of Education and is recognized by the Council for Higher Education Accreditation. ACICS can be contacted at 750 First Street NE, Suite 980, Washington, D.C. 20002; phone: 202-336-6780.

The occupational therapy assistant program is accredited by the Accreditation Council for Occupational Therapy Education (ACOTE) of the American Occupational Therapy Association (AOTA), located at 4720 Montgomery Lane, P.O. Box 31220, Bethesda, Maryland 20824; phone: 301-652-AOTA.

Location

Brown Mackie College–Albuquerque is conveniently located at 10500 Copper Avenue NE, in Albuquerque, New Mexico. The College has a generous parking area and is easily accessible by public transportation.

Programs of Study and Degrees

Brown Mackie College–Albuquerque provides higher education to traditional and nontraditional students through bachelor's degree, associate degree, and diploma programs that assist in enhancing their career opportunities, broadening their perspectives through appropriate general education courses, thinking independently and critically, and improving problem-solving abilities. The College strives to develop within its students the desire for lifelong and continued education.

The Bachelor of Science degree is awarded in business administration, criminal justice, healthcare management, and legal studies.

The Associate of Applied Science degree is awarded in accounting technology, architectural design and drafting technology, business management, criminal justice, healthcare administration, information technology, medical assisting, occupational therapy assistant, paralegal, pharmacy technology, surgical technology, and veterinary technology.

The College offers diploma programs in accounting, business, criminal justice, medical assistant, and paralegal assistant.

Academic Programs

Each College quarter comprises twelve weeks. Bachelor's degree programs require a minimum of sixteen quarters to complete. Associate degree programs require a minimum of eight quarters to complete. Programs are offered on a year-round basis, providing students with the ability to work uninterrupted toward completion of their programs. The College offers all programs in a unique One Course a Month format. This allows students to focus studies on only one course for four weeks. This schedule has proven convenient for students with multiple obligations such as jobs and family.

Academic Facilities

A modern facility, Brown Mackie College–Albuquerque offers more than 35,000 square feet. The College is equipped with multiple computer labs, housing over 100 computers. High-speed access to the Internet and other online resources are available to students and faculty. Multimedia classrooms are outfitted with overhead projectors, VCR/DVD players, and computers.

The campus is nonresidential; public transportation and ample parking at no cost are available. The campus is a smoke-free facility.

Costs

Tuition in the 2010–11 academic year for all bachelor's and associate degrees and certificates was $295 per credit hour; fees were $20 per credit hour. Tuition for the occupational therapy assistant program was $325 per credit hour; fees were $20 per credit hour. Tuition for the surgical technology program was $310 per credit hour; fees were $20 per credit hour. The cost of textbooks and other instructional materials varies by program.

Financial Aid

Financial aid is available for those who qualify. The College maintains a full-time staff of financial aid professionals to assist qualified students in obtaining the financial assistance they require to meet their educational expenses. Available resources include federal and state aid, student loans from private lenders, and Federal Work-Study opportunities, both on and off college premises.

Each year, the College makes available scholarships of $1000 each to qualifying seniors from area high schools. No more than one scholarship is awarded per high school. In order to qualify, a senior must have graduated from a participating high school, must have maintained a cumulative grade point average of at least 2.0, and submitted a brief essay. The student's extracurricular activities and community service are also considered. These scholarships are available only to students enrolling in one of the College's degree programs. Students awarded the scholarship must enroll at Brown Mackie College–Albuquerque between June and September immediately following their high school graduation. Applications for these scholarships can be obtained from the guidance departments of participating high schools. These applications must be completed and returned to the College by March 31.

Faculty

Experienced faculty members provide academic support and are committed to the academic and technical preparation of their students. The College has both full-time and part-time instructors, with a student-faculty ratio of 15:1.

Admission Requirements

Each applicant for admission is assigned an Assistant Director of Admissions who directs the applicant through the steps of the admissions process. They provide information on curriculum, policies, procedures, and services and assist the applicant in setting necessary appointments and interviews. To qualify for admission, each applicant must provide documentation of graduation from an accredited high school or from a state-approved secondary education curriculum or provide official documentation of high school graduation equivalency. All transcripts become the property of the College. Admission to the College is based on the applicant meeting the stated requirements, a review of the applicant's previous educational records, and a review of the applicant's career interests. If previous academic records indicate the College's education and training programs would not benefit the applicant, the College reserves the right to advise the applicant not to enroll. Special requirements for enrollment into certain programs are discussed in the descriptions of those programs.

For the most recent information regarding admission requirements, prospective students should refer to the current academic catalog.

Application and Information

Applicants must complete and submit an application form, along with documentation of graduation from an accredited high school or state-approved secondary education curriculum or official documentation of high school graduation equivalency.

For additional information, prospective students should contact:

Director of Admissions
Brown Mackie College–Albuquerque
10500 Copper Avenue
Albuquerque, New Mexico 87123

Phone: 505-559-5200
      877-271-3488 (toll-free)
Fax: 505-559-5222
E-mail: bmcalbadm@brownmackie.edu
Web site: http://www.brownmackie.edu/Albuquerque

BROWN MACKIE COLLEGE–BIRMINGHAM

BIRMINGHAM, ALABAMA

The College

Brown Mackie College–Birmingham is one of over twenty-five locations in the Brown Mackie College system of schools (www.brownmackie.edu), which is dedicated to providing educational programs that prepare students to pursue entry-level positions in a competitive, rapidly changing workplace. Brown Mackie College schools offer bachelor's degree, associate degree, certificate, and diploma programs in health sciences, business, information technology, legal studies, and design to over 20,000 students in the Midwest, Southeast, Southwest, and Western United States.

Brown Mackie College was originally founded and approved by the Board of Trustees of Kansas Wesleyan College in Salina, Kansas on July 30, 1892. In 1938, the College was incorporated as the Brown Mackie School of Business under the ownership of Perry E. Brown and A.B. Mackie, former instructors at Kansas Wesleyan University in Salina, Kansas. Their last names formed the name of Brown Mackie. By January 1975, with improvements in curricula and higher degree-granting status, the Brown Mackie School of Business became Brown Mackie College.

Brown Mackie College–Birmingham is accredited by the Accrediting Council for Independent Colleges and Schools (ACICS) to award bachelor's degrees, associate degrees, and diplomas. The Accrediting Council for Independent Colleges and Schools is listed as a nationally recognized accrediting agency by the United States Department of Education and is recognized by the Council for Higher Education Accreditation. ACICS can be contacted at 750 First Street NE, Suite 980, Washington, D.C. 20002; phone: 202-336-6780.

Location

Brown Mackie College–Birmingham is conveniently located at 105 Vulcan Road, in Birmingham, Alabama. The College has a generous parking area and is easily accessible by public transportation.

Programs of Study and Degrees

Brown Mackie College–Birmingham provides higher education to traditional and nontraditional students through bachelor's degree, associate degree, and diploma programs that assist in enhancing their career opportunities, broadening their perspectives through appropriate general education courses, thinking independently and critically, and improving problem-solving abilities. The College strives to develop within its students the desire for lifelong and continued education.

The Bachelor of Science degree is awarded in business administration, healthcare management, and legal studies.

The Associate of Applied Science degree is awarded in accounting technology, architectural design and drafting technology, biomedical equipment technology, business management, graphic design, healthcare administration, information technology, medical assisting, paralegal, and surgical technology.

The College offers diploma programs in accounting, business, dental assistant, healthcare administrative specialist, medical assistant, and paralegal assistant.

Academic Programs

Each College quarter comprises twelve weeks. Bachelor's degree programs require a minimum of sixteen quarters to complete. Associate degree programs require a minimum of eight quarters to complete. Programs are offered on a year-round basis, providing students with the ability to work uninterrupted toward completion of their programs. The College offers all programs in a unique One Course a Month format. This allows students to focus studies on only one course for four weeks. This schedule has proven convenient for students with multiple obligations such as jobs and family.

Academic Facilities

A modern facility, Brown Mackie College–Birmingham offers approximately 35,000 square feet of classroom, computer and allied health labs, library, and office space. The College is equipped with multiple computer labs, housing over 100 computers. High-speed access to the Internet and other online resources are available to students and faculty. Multimedia classrooms are outfitted with overhead projectors, VCR/DVD players, and computers.

The campus is nonresidential; public transportation and ample parking at no cost are available. The campus is a smoke-free facility.

Costs

Tuition in the 2010–11 academic year for all bachelor's and associate degrees and certificates was $295 per credit hour; fees were $15 per credit hour. Tuition for the surgical technology program was $330 per credit hour; fees were $15 per credit hour. The cost of textbooks and other instructional materials varies by program.

Financial Aid

Financial aid is available for those who qualify. The College maintains a full-time staff of financial aid professionals to assist qualified students in obtaining the financial assistance they require to meet their educational expenses. Available resources include federal and state aid, student loans from private lenders, and Federal Work-Study opportunities, both on and off college premises.

Each year, the College makes available scholarships of $1000 each to qualifying seniors from area high schools. No more than one scholarship is awarded per high school. In order to qualify, a senior must have graduated from a participating high school, must be maintained a cumulative grade point average of at least 2.0, and submitted a brief essay. The student's extracurricular activities and community service are also considered. These scholarships are available only to students enrolling in one of the College's degree programs. Students awarded the scholarship must enroll at Brown Mackie College–Birmingham between June and September immediately following their high school graduation. Applications for these scholarships can be obtained from the guidance departments of participating high schools. These applications must be completed and returned to the College by March 31.

Faculty

Experienced faculty members provide academic support and are committed to the academic and technical preparation of their students. The College has both full-time and part-time instructors, with a student-faculty ratio of 15:1.

Admission Requirements

Each applicant for admission is assigned an Assistant Director of Admissions who directs the applicant through the steps of the admissions process. They provide information on curriculum, policies, procedures, and services and assist the applicant in setting necessary appointments and interviews. To qualify for admission, each applicant must provide documentation of graduation from an accredited high school or from a state-approved secondary education curriculum or provide official documentation of high school graduation equivalency. All transcripts become the property of the College. Admission to the College is based on the applicant meeting the stated requirements, a review of the applicant's previous educational records, and a review of the applicant's career interests. If previous academic records indicate the College's education and training programs would not benefit the applicant, the College reserves the right to advise the applicant not to enroll. Special requirements for enrollment into certain programs are discussed in the descriptions of those programs.

For the most recent information regarding admission requirements, prospective students should refer to the current academic catalog.

Application and Information

Applicants must complete and submit an application form, along with documentation of graduation from an accredited high school or state-approved secondary education curriculum or official documentation of high school graduation equivalency.

For additional information, prospective students should contact:

Director of Admissions
Brown Mackie College–Birmingham
105 Vulcan Road
Suite 100
Birmingham, Alabama 35209

Phone: 205-909-1500
       888-299-4699 (toll free)
Fax: 205-909-1588
E-mail: bmbirmadm@brownmackie.edu
Web site: http://www.brownmackie.edu/Birmingham

BROWN MACKIE COLLEGE–BOISE

BOISE, IDAHO

BROWN MACKIE COLLEGE
BOISE™

The College

Brown Mackie College–Boise is one of over twenty-five locations in the Brown Mackie College system of schools (www.brownmackie.edu), which is dedicated to providing educational programs that prepare students to pursue entry-level positions in a competitive, rapidly changing workplace. Brown Mackie College schools offer bachelor's degree, associate degree, certificate, and diploma programs in health sciences, business, information technology, legal studies, and design to over 20,000 students in the Midwest, Southeast, Southwest, and Western United States.

Brown Mackie College–Boise is accredited by the Accrediting Council for Independent Colleges and Schools to award bachelor's degrees, associate degrees, and diplomas. The Accrediting Council for Independent Colleges and Schools is listed as a nationally recognized accrediting agency by the United States Department of Education and is recognized by the Council for Higher Education Accreditation. ACICS can be contacted at 750 First Street NE, Suite 980, Washington, D.C. 20002; phone: 202-336-6780.

The occupational therapy assistant program is accredited by the Accreditation Council for Occupational Therapy Education (ACOTE) of the American Occupational Therapy Association (AOTA), 4720 Montgomery Lane, P.O. Box 31220, Bethesda, Maryland 20824-1220; phone: 301-652- AOTA.

The Associate of Applied Science in Veterinary Technology program at Brown Mackie College–Boise is accredited by the American Veterinary Medical Association (AVMA) as a program for educating veterinary technicians. The American Veterinary Medical Association can be contacted at 1931 North Meacham Road, Suite 100, Schaumburg, Illinois 60173-4360; phone: 800-248-2862.

Location

Brown Mackie College–Boise is conveniently located at 9050 West Overland Road in Boise, Idaho. The College has a generous parking area and is easily accessible by public transportation.

Programs of Study and Degrees

Brown Mackie College–Boise provides higher education to traditional and nontraditional students through bachelor's degree, associate degree, and diploma programs that assist in enhancing their career opportunities, broadening their perspectives through appropriate general education courses, thinking independently and critically, and improving problem-solving abilities.

The Bachelor of Science degree is awarded in business administration, criminal justice, healthcare management, and legal studies.

The Associate of Science degree is awarded in accounting technology, bioscience laboratory technology, business management, criminal justice, healthcare administration, information technology, medical assisting, paralegal, and surgical technology.

The Associate of Applied Science degree is awarded in architectural design and drafting technology, occupational therapy assistant, and veterinary technology.

The College offers a diploma program in accounting, business, criminal justice, medical assistant, and paralegal assistant.

Academic Programs

Each College quarter comprises twelve weeks. Bachelor's degree programs require a minimum of sixteen quarters to complete. Associate degree programs require a minimum of eight quarters to complete. Programs are offered on a year-round basis, providing students with the opportunity to work uninterrupted toward completion of their programs. The College offers all programs in a unique One Course a Month format. This allows students to focus studies on only one course for four weeks. This schedule has proven convenient for students with multiple obligations such as jobs and family.

Academic Facilities

Opened in 2008, this modern facility offers more than 40,000 square feet of tastefully decorated classrooms, laboratories, and office space designed to specifications of the College for its business, medical, and technical programs. Instructional equipment is comparable to current technology used in business and industry today. Modern classrooms for special instructional needs offer multimedia capabilities with surround sound and overhead projectors accessible through computer, DVD, or VHS. Internet access and instructional resources are available at the College's library. Experienced faculty members provide academic support and are committed to the academic and technical preparation of their students.

The campus is nonresidential; public transportation and ample parking at no cost are available.

Costs

Tuition for programs in the 2010–11 academic year was $295 per credit hour, with a $15 per credit hour general fee applied to instructional costs for activities and services. Textbooks and other instructional materials vary by program. Tuition for the occupational therapy assistant courses was $390 per credit hour with a $15 per credit fee applied to instructional costs for activities and services. Tuition for the surgical technology program was $330 per credit hour with a $15 per credit fee applied to instructional costs for activities.

Financial Aid

Financial aid is available for those who qualify. The College maintains a full-time staff of financial aid professionals to assist qualified students in obtaining financial assistance. The College participates in several student aid programs. Forms of financial aid available through federal resources include the Federal Pell Grant Program, Federal Supplemental Educational Opportunity Grant (FSEOG) Program, Federal Work-Study Program, Federal Perkins Loan Program, Federal Stafford Student Loan Program (subsidized and unsubsidized), and the Federal PLUS Loan Program.

Each year, the College makes available President's Scholarships of $1000 each to qualifying seniors from area high schools. No more than one scholarship is awarded per high school. In order to qualify, a senior must be graduating from a participating high school, must be maintaining a cumulative grade point average of at least 2.0, and must submit a brief essay. The student's extracurricular activities and community service are also considered. The President's Scholarship is available only to students enrolling in one of the College's degree programs. Students awarded the scholarship must enroll at Brown Mackie College–Boise between June and September immediately following their high school graduation. Applications for these scholarships can be obtained from the guidance departments of participating high schools. These applications must be completed and returned to the College by March 31.

Faculty

There are 17 full-time and 34 part-time faculty members at the College. The average student-faculty ratio is 15:1. Each student is assigned a program department chair as an adviser.

Admission Requirements

Each applicant for admission is assigned an Assistant Director of Admissions who directs the applicant through the steps of the admissions process. They provide information on curriculum, policies, procedures, and services, and assist the applicant in setting necessary appointments and interviews. To qualify for admission, each applicant must provide documentation of graduation from an accredited high school or from a state-approved secondary education curriculum or provide official documentation of high school graduation equivalency. All transcripts become the property of the College.

As part of the admission process, students are given an assessment of academic skills. Although the results of this assessment do not determine eligibility for admission, they provide the College with a means of determining the need for academic support as well as a means by which the College can evaluate the effectiveness of its educational programs. All new students are required to complete this assessment, which is readministered at the end of the student's program so results may be compared with those of the initial administration.

In addition to the College's general admission requirements, applicants enrolling in the occupational therapy assistant program must document one of the following: a high school cumulative grade point average of at least 2.5, a score on the GED examination of at least 57 (557 if taken on or after January 15, 2002), or completion of 12 quarter-credit hours or 8 semester-credit hours of collegiate course work with a grade point average of at least 2.5. Credit hours may not include Professional Development (CF 1100), the Brown Mackie College–Boise course. Students entering the program must also have completed a biology course with a grade of at least a C (or an average of at least 2.0 on a 4.0 scale).

For the most recent information regarding admission requirements, prospective students should refer to the current academic catalog.

Application and Information

Applicants must complete and submit an application form, along with documentation of graduation from an accredited high school or state-approved secondary education curriculum or official documentation of high school graduation equivalency.

For additional information, prospective students should contact:

Director of Admissions
Brown Mackie College–Boise
9050 W. Overland Road, Suite 100
Boise, Idaho 83709
Phone: 208-321-8800
      888-810-9286 (toll-free)
Fax: 208-375-3249
E-mail: bmcboiadm@brownmackie.edu
Web site: http://www.brownmackie.edu/Boise

BROWN MACKIE COLLEGE–FORT WAYNE

FORT WAYNE, INDIANA

The College

Brown Mackie College–Fort Wayne is one of over twenty-five locations in the Brown Mackie College system of schools (www.brownmackie.edu), which is dedicated to providing educational programs that prepare students to pursue entry-level positions in a competitive, rapidly changing workplace. Brown Mackie College schools offer bachelor's degree, associate degree, certificate, and diploma programs in health sciences, business, information technology, legal studies, and design to over 20,000 students in the Midwest, Southeast, Southwest, and Western United States.

Brown Mackie College–Fort Wayne is one of the oldest institutions of its kind in the country and the oldest in the state of Indiana. Established in 1882 as the South Bend Commercial College, the school later changed its name to Michiana College. In 1930, the College was incorporated under the laws of the state of Indiana and was authorized to confer associate degrees and certificates in business. In 1992, the College in South Bend added a branch location in Fort Wayne, Indiana. In 2004, Michiana College changed its name to Brown Mackie College–Fort Wayne. Brown Mackie College–Fort Wayne is owned and operated by Education Management Corporation (EDMC), 210 Sixth Avenue, 33rd Floor, Pittsburgh, Pennsylvania 15222-2603. EDMC has been in business for over forty years and is one of the largest providers of private post-secondary education in North America with eighty-nine campus locations in twenty-eight states and Canada.

Brown Mackie College–Fort Wayne is accredited by the Accrediting Council for Independent Colleges and Schools to award bachelor's degrees, associate degrees, diplomas, and certificates. The Accrediting Council for Independent Colleges and Schools is listed as a nationally recognized accrediting agency by the United States Department of Education and is recognized by the Council for Higher Education Accreditation. ACICS can be contacted at 750 First Street NE, Suite 980, Washington, D.C. 20002; phone: 202-336-6780.

The occupational therapy assistant program is accredited by the Accreditation Council for Occupational Therapy Education (ACOTE) of the American Occupational Therapy Association (AOTA), 4720 Montgomery Lane, P.O. Box 31220, Bethesda, Maryland 20824-1220; phone: 301-652-AOTA. In order to practice as occupational therapy assistants, graduates must pass the certification examination for the certified occupational therapy assistant. Application for such examination is arranged through the National Board for Certification in Occupational Therapy, Inc. (NBCOT). Graduates may request application materials and the candidate handbook from NBCOT or apply online. For further information, graduates should contact NBCOT, 800 South Frederick Avenue, Suite 200, Gaithersburg, Maryland 20877-4150; phone: 301-990-7979; Web site: www.nbcot.org. To practice as an occupational therapy assistant in Indiana, a graduate must be certified by the state. Graduates may apply for a temporary permit to work between graduation and successful completion of certification examination. For information on application procedures for either a temporary permit or permanent state endorsement, graduates should contact the Occupational Therapy Committee, Health Professions Bureau, Indiana Government Center South, 402 West Washington Street, Room 041, Indianapolis, Indiana 46204; phone: 317-232-2960; Web site: www.in.gov/hpb/boards/otc/; hbp6@hpb.state.in.us.

The College's diploma program in practical nursing is accredited by the Indiana State Board of Nursing, 402 West Washington Street, Room W066, Indianapolis, Indiana 46204; phone: 317-234-2043. Graduates are eligible to complete two applications: the National Council Licensure Examination (NCLEX) and the Indiana licensure application. Indiana applications for licensure by examination must be completed by each candidate and be submitted to the Health Professions Bureau. Registration with NCLEX must be completed

according to the instructions in the NCLEX Candidate Bulletin. Both the Indiana licensure application and the NCLEX registration process must be completed before eligibility to take the examination can be granted by the Indiana Board of Nursing. Graduates may obtain further information by contacting the Indiana State Board of Nursing, 402 West Washington Street, Room W066, Indianapolis, Indiana 46204; phone: 317-234-2043; Web site: www.ai.org/hpb.

The surgical technology program is accredited by the Accrediting Bureau of Health Education Schools (ABHES). Graduates of this program are eligible at their option to sit for the CST Certification Examination of Surgical Technologists. Graduates who pass this examination are awarded the Certified Surgical Technologist (CST) credential. A CST must be recertified every four years through continuing education or reexamination. Further information can be obtained by contacting the Surgical Technology Program Director or by contacting the ABHES, 7777 Leesburg Pike, Suite 314 North, Falls Church, Virginia 22043; phone: 703-917-9503; Web site: www.abhes.org.

The College is licensed and regulated by the Indiana Commission on Proprietary Education, 302 West Washington Street, Room E201, Indianapolis, Indiana 46204; phone: 800-227-5695 (toll-free) or 317-232-1320. (Indiana advertising code: AC-0109.)

Location

Brown Mackie College–Fort Wayne is located at 3000 East Coliseum Boulevard in Fort Wayne, Indiana. The College facility is accessible by public transportation. Ample parking is provided at no additional charge. For added convenience, the College also operates a learning site at 2135 South Hannah Drive in Fort Wayne.

Programs of Study and Degrees

Brown Mackie College–Fort Wayne provides higher education to traditional and nontraditional students through bachelor's degree, associate degree, diploma, and certificate programs that assist them in enhancing their career opportunities, broadening their perspectives through appropriate general education courses, thinking independently and critically, and improving problem-solving abilities. The College strives to develop within its students the desire for lifelong and continued education.

The Bachelor of Science degree is awarded in business administration, criminal justice, healthcare management, and legal studies.

The Associate of Science degree is awarded in accounting technology, business management, criminal justice, healthcare administration, medical assisting, office management, paralegal, and surgical technology.

The Associate of Applied Science degree is awarded in biomedical equipment technology, dietetics technology, health and fitness training, health and therapeutic massage, nursing, occupational therapy assistant, physical therapist assistant, and veterinary technology.

A diploma is awarded in practical nursing.

The College offers certificate programs in accounting, business, criminal justice, fitness trainer, medical assistant, and paralegal assistant.

Academic Programs

Each College quarter comprises twelve weeks. Bachelor's degree programs require a minimum of sixteen quarters to complete. Associate degree programs require a minimum of eight quarters to complete. Programs are offered on a year-round basis, providing students with the ability to work uninterrupted toward their degrees. The College offers all programs in a unique One Course a Month format. This allows students to focus studies on only one course for four weeks. This schedule has proven convenient for students with multiple obligations such as jobs and family.

Academic Facilities

In 2005, the campus located in a 75,000-square-foot facility at 3000 East Coliseum Boulevard. Record enrollment allowed the institution to triple in size in less than one year. The three-story building offers a modern, professional environment for study. Ten classrooms are outfitted as "classrooms of the future," with an instructor workstation, full multimedia capabilities, a surround sound system, and projection screen that can be accessed by computer, DVD, or VHS equipment. The Brown Mackie College–Fort Wayne facility includes a criminal justice lab, surgical technology labs, medical labs, computer labs, and occupational and physical therapy labs, as well as a library and bookstore. The labs provide students with hands-on opportunities to apply knowledge and skills learned in the classroom. Students are welcome to use the labs when those facilities are not in use for scheduled classes.

The College is nonresidential; public transportation and ample parking at no cost are available. The campus is a smoke-free facility.

Costs

Tuition in the 2010–11 academic year was $285 per credit hour with fees of $15 per credit hour for all programs except nursing, practical nursing, surgical technology, personal fitness training, occupational therapy assistant studies, and physical therapist assistant studies. Textbooks and other instructional materials vary by program. For the nursing program, tuition was $390 per credit hour; fees were $25 per credit hour. For the practical nursing program, tuition was $350 per credit hour; fees were $25 per credit hour. For the surgical technology program, tuition was $330 per credit hour; fees were $15. Tuition for the personal fitness training programs was $295 per credit hour; fees were $25 per credit hour. Textbook expenses are estimated at $400 for the first term, $600 for the second term, and $100 for the third, fourth, and fifth terms. For certain courses in the occupational therapy assistant studies and physical therapist assistant studies programs, tuition was $350 per credit hour; fees were $15 per credit hour. Textbook expenses are estimated at $370 per quarter for the first six terms and $460 for the seventh term.

Financial Aid

The College maintains a full-time staff of financial aid professionals to assist qualified students in obtaining financial assistance. The College participates in several student aid programs. Forms of financial aid available through federal resources include the Federal Pell Grant Program, Federal Supplemental Educational Opportunity Grant (FSEOG) Program, Federal Work-Study Program, Federal Perkins Loan Program, Federal Stafford Student Loan Program (subsidized and unsubsidized), and the Federal PLUS Loan Program. Eligible students may apply for Indiana state awards, such as the Frank O'Bannon Grant Program (formerly the Indiana State Grant Program), the Higher Education Award, and Twenty-First Century Scholarships for high school students; for the Core 40 awards; and for veterans' educational benefits. For further information, students should contact the College Student Financial Services Office.

Each year, the College makes available President's Scholarships of $1000 each to qualifying seniors from area high schools. No more than one scholarship is awarded per high school. In order to qualify, a senior must have graduated from a participating high school, maintained a cumulative grade point average of at least 2.0, and submitted a brief essay. The student's extracurricular activities and community service are also considered. The President's Scholarship is available only to students enrolling in one of the College's degree programs. Students awarded the scholarship must enroll at Brown Mackie College–Fort Wayne between June and September immediately following their high school graduation. Applications for these scholarships can be obtained from the guidance departments of participating high schools. These applications must be completed and returned to the College by March 31.

Faculty

The College has 45 full-time and 80 part-time instructors, with a student-faculty ratio of 15:1. Each student is assigned a faculty adviser.

Admission Requirements

Each applicant for admission is assigned an Assistant Director of Admissions, who directs the applicant through the steps of the admissions process, providing information on curriculum, policies, procedures, and services and assisting the applicant in setting necessary appointments and interviews. To qualify for admission, each applicant must provide documentation of graduation from an accredited high school or from a state-approved secondary education curriculum or provide official documentation of high school graduation equivalency. All transcripts become the property of the College. Admission to the College is based on the applicant meeting the stated requirements, a review of the applicant's previous educational records, and a review of the applicant's career interests. If previous academic records indicate the College's education and training programs would not benefit the applicant, the College reserves the right to advise the applicant not to enroll. Special requirements for enrollment into certain programs are discussed in the descriptions of those programs.

In addition to the College's general admission requirements, applicants enrolling in the practical nursing program must document the following, which must be completed and a record of proof must appear in the student's file prior to the start of the nursing fundamentals course. No student will be admitted to a clinical agency unless all paperwork is completed. This paperwork is a requirement of all contracted agencies. This paperwork includes records of (1) a complete physical, current to within six months of admission; (2) a two-step Mantoux test that is kept current throughout schooling; (3) a hepatitis B vaccination or signed refusal; (4) up-to-date immunizations, including tetanus and rubella; (5) a record of current CPR certification that is maintained throughout the student's clinical experience; and (6) hospitalization insurance or a signed waiver.

Application and Information

Applicants must complete and submit an application form, along with documentation of graduation from an accredited high school or state-approved secondary education curriculum or official documentation of high school graduation equivalency.

For additional information, prospective students should contact:

Director of Admissions
Brown Mackie College–Fort Wayne
3000 East Coliseum Boulevard
Fort Wayne, Indiana 46805
Phone: 260-484-4400
      866-433-2289 (toll-free)
Fax: 260-484-2678
E-mail: bmcfwaadm@brownmackie.edu
Web site: http://www.brownmackie.edu/FortWayne

BROWN MACKIE COLLEGE–GREENVILLE
GREENVILLE, SOUTH CAROLINA

The College

Brown Mackie College–Greenville is one of over twenty-five locations in the Brown Mackie College system of schools (www.brownmackie.edu), which is dedicated to providing educational programs that prepare students to pursue entry-level positions in a competitive, rapidly changing workplace. Brown Mackie College schools offer bachelor's degree, associate degree, and certificate programs in health sciences, business, information technology, and legal studies to over 20,000 students in the Midwest, Southeast, Southwest, and Western United States.

Brown Mackie College was originally founded and approved by the Board of Trustees of Kansas Wesleyan College in Salina, Kansas on July 30, 1892. In 1938, the College was incorporated as The Brown Mackie School of Business under the ownership of Perry E. Brown and A.B. Mackie, former instructors at Kansas Wesleyan University in Salina, Kansas. Their last names formed the name of Brown Mackie. By January 1975, with improvements in curricula and higher degree-granting status, The Brown Mackie School of Business became Brown Mackie College.

Brown Mackie College–Greenville is accredited by the Accrediting Council for Independent Colleges and Schools to award certificates, associate degrees, and bachelor's degrees. The Accrediting Council for Independent Colleges and Schools is listed as a nationally recognized accrediting agency by the United States Department of Education and is recognized by the Council for Higher Education Accreditation. ACICS can be contacted at 750 First Street NE, Suite 980, Washington, D.C. 20002; phone: 202-336-6780.

The occupational therapy assistant program has applied for accreditation by the Accreditation Council for Occupational Therapy Education (ACOTE) of the American Occupational Therapy Association (AOTA), located at 4720 Montgomery Lane, P.O. Box 31220, Bethesda, Maryland 20824; phone: 301-652-AOTA.

Location

Brown Mackie College–Greenville is conveniently located at Two Liberty Square, 75 Beattie Place, Suite 100, in Greenville, South Carolina. The College has a generous parking area and is easily accessible by public transportation.

Programs of Study and Degrees

Brown Mackie College–Greenville provides higher education to traditional and nontraditional students through bachelor's degree, associate degree, and certificate programs that assist in enhancing their career opportunities, broadening their perspectives through appropriate general education courses, thinking independently and critically, and improving problem-solving abilities. The College strives to develop within its students the desire for lifelong and continued education.

The Bachelor of Science degree is awarded in business administration, criminal justice, healthcare management, and legal studies.

The Associate of Applied Science degree is awarded in accounting technology, business management, criminal justice, healthcare administration, information technology, medical assisting, occupational therapy assistant, office management, paralegal, and surgical technology.

The certificate is awarded in accounting, business, criminal justice, medical assistant, and paralegal assistant.

Academic Programs

Each College quarter comprises twelve weeks. Bachelor's degree programs require a minimum of sixteen quarters to complete. Associate degree programs require a minimum of eight quarters to complete. Programs are offered on a year-round basis, providing students with the ability to work uninterrupted toward completion of their degrees. The College offers all programs in a unique One Course a Month format. This allows students to focus studies on only one course for four weeks. This schedule has proven convenient for students with multiple obligations such as jobs and family.

Academic Facilities

A modern facility, Brown Mackie College–Greenville offers more than 40,000 square feet. The College is equipped with multiple computer labs housing over one hundred computers. High-speed access to the Internet and other online resources are available for students and faculty. Multimedia classrooms are outfitted with overhead projectors, VCR/DVD players, and computers.

The campus is nonresidential; public transportation and ample parking at no cost are available. The campus is a smoke-free facility.

Costs

Tuition in the 2010–11 academic year for most bachelor's and associate degrees and certificates was $285 per credit hour; fees were $15 per credit hour. Tuition for the occupational therapy assistant program was $350 per credit hour; fees were $15 per credit hour. Tuition for the surgical technology program was $330 per credit hour; fees were $15 per credit hour. The cost of textbooks and other instructional expenses vary by program.

Financial Aid

Financial aid is available for those who qualify. The College maintains a full-time staff of financial aid professionals to assist qualified students in obtaining the financial assistance they require to meet their educational expenses. Available resources include federal and state aid, student loans from private lenders, and Federal Work-Study opportunities, both on and off college premises.

Each year, the College makes available President's Scholarships of $1000 each to qualifying seniors from area high schools. No more than one scholarship is awarded per high school. In order to qualify, a senior must have graduated from a participating high school, maintained a cumulative grade point average of at least 2.0, and submitted a brief essay. The student's extracurricular activities and community service are also considered. The President's Scholarship is available only to students enrolling in one of the College's degree programs. Students awarded the scholarship must enroll at Brown Mackie College–Greenville between June and September immediately following their high school graduation. Applications for these scholarships can be obtained from the guidance departments of participating high schools. These applications must be completed and returned to the College by March 31.

Faculty

Experienced faculty members provide academic support and are committed to the academic and technical preparation of their students. The College has 9 full-time and 30 part-time instructors, with a student-faculty ratio of 24:1. Each student is assigned a faculty adviser.

Admission Requirements

Each applicant for admission is assigned an Assistant Director of Admissions who directs the applicant through the steps of the admissions process. They provide information on curriculum, policies, procedures, and services and assist the applicant in setting necessary appointments and interviews. To qualify for admission, each applicant must provide documentation of graduation from an accredited high school or from a state-approved secondary education curriculum or provide official documentation of high school graduation equivalency. All transcripts become the property of the College. Admission to the College is based on the applicant meeting the stated requirements, a review of the applicant's previous educational records, and a review of the applicant's career interests. If previous academic records indicate the College's education and training programs would not benefit the applicant, the College reserves the right to advise the applicant not to enroll. Special requirements for enrollment into certain programs are discussed in the descriptions of those programs.

For the most recent information regarding admission requirements, prospective students should refer to the current academic catalog.

Application and Information

Applicants must complete and submit an application form along with documentation of graduation from an accredited high school or state-approved secondary education curriculum or official documentation of high school graduation equivalency.

For additional information, prospective students should contact:

Director of Admissions
Brown Mackie College–Greenville
Two Liberty Square
75 Beattie Place, Suite 100
Greenville, South Carolina 29601
Phone: 864-239-5300
       877-479-8465 (toll-free)
Fax: 864-232-4094
E-mail: bmcgrweb@brownmackie.edu
Web site: http://www.brownmackie.edu/greenville

BROWN MACKIE COLLEGE–INDIANAPOLIS

INDIANAPOLIS, INDIANA

The College

Brown Mackie College–Indianapolis is one of over twenty-five locations in the Brown Mackie College system of schools (http://www.brownmackie.edu), which is dedicated to providing educational programs that prepare students to pursue entry-level positions in a competitive, rapidly changing workplace. Brown Mackie College's system of schools offer bachelor's degree, associate degree, certificate, and diploma programs in health sciences, business, information technology, legal studies, and design to more than 20,000 students in the Midwest, Southeast, Southwest, and Western United States.

Brown Mackie College–Indianapolis was founded in 2007 as a branch of Brown Mackie College–Findlay, Ohio.

Brown Mackie College–Indianapolis is accredited by the Accrediting Council for Independent Colleges and Schools (ACICS) to award bachelor's degrees, associate degrees, and certificates. ACICS is listed as a nationally recognized accrediting agency by the United States Department of Education and is recognized by the Council for Higher Education Accreditation. ACICS can be contacted at 750 First Street NE, Suite 980, Washington, D.C. 20002; phone: 202-336-6780.

The occupational therapy assistant program is accredited by the Accreditation Council for Occupational Therapy Education (ACOTE) of the American Occupational Therapy Association (AOTA), 4720 Montgomery Lane, P.O. Box 31220, Bethesda, Maryland 20824-1220; phone: 301-652-2682.

Brown Mackie College–Indianapolis is licensed and regulated by the Indiana Commission on Proprietary Education, 302 West Washington Street, Indianapolis, Indiana 46204; phone: 317-232-1320 or 800-227-5695 (toll-free). (Indiana advertising code: AC-0078.)

Location

Brown Mackie College–Indianapolis is conveniently located at 1200 North Meridian Street in Indianapolis, Indiana. The College has a generous parking area and is easily accessible by public transportation.

Programs of Study and Degrees

Brown Mackie College–Indianapolis provides higher education to traditional and nontraditional students through bachelor's degree, associate degree, diploma, and certificate programs that assist them in enhancing their career opportunities, broadening their perspectives through appropriate general education courses, thinking independently and critically, and improving problem-solving abilities. The College strives to develop within its students the desire for lifelong and continued education.

The Bachelor of Science degree is awarded in business administration, criminal justice, and legal studies.

The Associate of Science degree is awarded in business management, criminal justice, healthcare administration, medical assisting, and paralegal. The Associate of Applied Science degree is awarded in occupational therapy assistant.

A diploma program in practical nursing is offered.

The College offers certificate programs in business and medical assistant.

Academic Programs

Each College quarter comprises twelve weeks. Bachelor's degree programs require a minimum of sixteen quarters to complete. Associate degree programs require a minimum of eight quarters to complete. Programs are offered on a year-round basis, providing students with the ability to work uninterrupted toward their degrees. The College offers all programs in a unique One Course a Month format. This allows students to focus studies on only one course for four weeks. This schedule has proven convenient for students with multiple obligations such as jobs and family.

Academic Facilities

Opened in January 2008, this modern facility offers more than 22,000 square feet of tastefully decorated classrooms, laboratories, and office space designed to the specifications of the College for its business, health-care, and technical programs. Instructional equipment is comparable to current technology used in business and industry today. Modern classrooms for special instructional needs offer multimedia capabilities with surround sound and overhead projectors accessible through computer, DVD, or VHS. Internet access and instructional resources are available at the College's library. Experienced faculty members provide academic support and are committed to the academic and technical preparation of their students.

The campus is nonresidential; public transportation and ample parking at no cost are available.

Costs

Tuition for most programs in the 2010–11 academic year was $303 per credit hour with a $15 per credit hour general fee. Tuition for the practical nursing diploma program was $350 per credit hour with a $25 per credit hour general fee applied to instructional costs for activities and services. For the occupational therapy assistant program the tuition was $350 per credit hour with a $15 per credit hour general fee.

Financial Aid

Financial aid is available to those who qualify. The College maintains a full-time staff of financial aid professionals to assist qualified students in obtaining the financial assistance they require to meet their educational expenses. Available resources include federal and state aid, student loans from private lenders, and federal work-study opportunities, both on and off college premises.

Each year, the College makes available scholarships of $1000 each to qualifying seniors from area high schools. No more than one scholarship is awarded per high school. In order to qualify, a senior must be graduating from a participating high school, must be maintaining a cumulative grade point average of at least 2.0, and must submit a brief essay. The student's extracurricular activities and community service are also considered. These scholarships are available only to students enrolling in one of the College's degree programs. Students awarded the scholarship must enroll at Brown Mackie College–Indianapolis between June and September immediately following their high school graduation. Applications for these scholarships can be obtained from the guidance departments of participating high schools. These applications must be completed and returned to the College by March 31.

Faculty

The College has 24 full-time instructors, 77 adjunct instructors, and 16 lab assistants, with a student-faculty ratio of 12:1. Faculty members provide tutoring and additional academic services to students as needed.

Admission Requirements

Each applicant for admission is assigned an Assistant Director of Admissions, who directs the applicant through the steps of the admissions process, providing information on curriculum, policies, procedures, and services and assisting the applicant in setting necessary appointments and interviews. To qualify for admission, each applicant must provide documentation of graduation from an accredited high school or from a state-approved secondary education curriculum or provide official documentation of high school graduation equivalency. All transcripts become the property of the College. Admission to the College is based on the applicant meeting the stated

requirements, a review of the applicant's previous educational records, and a review of the applicant's career interests. If previous academic records indicate the College's education and training programs would not benefit the applicant, the College reserves the right to advise the applicant not to enroll. Special requirements for enrollment into certain programs are discussed in the descriptions of those programs.

In addition to the College's general admission requirements, applicants enrolling in the practical nursing program must document the following: fulfillment of Brown Mackie College–Indianapolis general requirements; complete physical (must be current to within six months of admission); two-step Mantoux TB skin test (must be current throughout schooling); hepatitis B vaccination or signed refusal; up-to-date immunizations, including tetanus and rubella; record of current CPR certification (certification must be current throughout the clinical experience through health-care provider certification or the American Heart Association); and hospitalization insurance or a signed waiver.

For the most recent information regarding admission requirements, please refer to the current academic catalog.

Application and Information

Applicants must complete and submit an application form, along with documentation of graduation from an accredited high school or state-approved secondary education curriculum or official documentation of high school graduation equivalency.

For additional information, prospective students should contact:

Senior Director of Admissions
Brown Mackie College–Indianapolis
1200 North Meridian Street, Suite 100
Indianapolis, Indiana 46204
Phone: 866-255-0279 (toll-free)
Fax: 317-632-4557
E-mail: bmcindadm@brownmackie.edu
Web site: http://www.brownmackie.edu/Indianapolis

BROWN MACKIE COLLEGE–LOUISVILLE

LOUISVILLE, KENTUCKY

The College

Brown Mackie College–Louisville is one of over twenty-five locations in the Brown Mackie College system of schools (www.brownmackie.edu), which is dedicated to providing educational programs that prepare students to pursue entry-level positions in a competitive, rapidly changing workplace. Brown Mackie College schools offer bachelor's degree, associate degree, certificate, and diploma programs in health sciences, business, information technology, legal studies, and design to over 20,000 students in the Midwest, Southeast, Southwest, and Western United States.

Brown Mackie College–Louisville opened in 1972 as RETS Institute of Technology. The first RETS school was founded in 1935 in Detroit in response to the rapid growth of radio broadcasting and the need for qualified radio technicians. The RETS Institute changed its name to Brown Mackie College–Louisville in 2004.

Brown Mackie College–Louisville is accredited by the Accrediting Council for Independent Colleges and Schools (ACICS) to award bachelor's degrees, associate degrees, certificates, and diplomas. The Accrediting Council for Independent Colleges and Schools is listed as a nationally recognized accrediting agency by the United States Department of Education. Its accreditation of degree-granting institutions is recognized by the Council for Higher Education Accreditation. ACICS can be contacted at 750 First Street NE, Suite 980, Washington, D.C. 20002; phone: 202-336-6780.

Brown Mackie College–Louisville is licensed by the Kentucky Council on Postsecondary Education for all programs offered by the College. The council is located at 1024 Capital Center Drive, Suite 320 Frankfort, Kentucky 40601.

Brown Mackie College–Louisville is regulated by the Indiana Commission on Proprietary Education, 302 West Washington Street, Indianapolis, Indiana 46204; phone: 317-232-1320 or 800-227-5695 (toll-free). (Indiana advertising code: AC-0045).

The Brown Mackie College–Louisville's Associate of Applied Science degree in surgical technology is accredited by the Accrediting Bureau of Health Education Schools, 7777 Leesburg Pike, Suite 314N, Falls Church, Virginia 22043; phone: 703-917-9503.

The occupational therapy assistant program is accredited by the Accreditation Council for Occupational Therapy Education (ACOTE) of the American Occupational Therapy Association (AOTA), located at 4720 Montgomery Lane, P.O. Box 31220, Bethesda, Maryland 20824; phone: 301-652-AOTA.

The veterinary technology program is accredited as a program for educating veterinary technicians by the American Veterinary Medical Association (AVMA), 1931 North Meacham Road, Suite 100, Schaumburg, Illinois 60173.

Location

Brown Mackie College–Louisville is conveniently located at 3605 Fern Valley Road in Louisville, Kentucky. The College has a generous parking area and is easily accessible by public transportation.

Programs of Study and Degrees

Brown Mackie College–Louisville provides higher education to traditional and nontraditional students through bachelor's degree, associate degree, and diploma programs that assist in enhancing their career opportunities, broadening their perspectives through appropriate general education courses, thinking independently and critically, and improving problem-solving abilities.

The Bachelor of Science degree is awarded in business administration, criminal justice, healthcare management, and legal studies.

The Associate of Applied Business degree is awarded in accounting technology, business management, computer networking and applications, criminal justice, graphic design, and paralegal.

The Associate of Applied Science degree is awarded in biomedical equipment technology, electronics, healthcare administration, medical assisting, occupational therapy assistant, pharmacy technology, surgical technology, and veterinary technology.

The College offers a diploma program in practical nursing.

The College offers a certificate program in computer networking.

Academic Programs

Each College quarter comprises twelve weeks. Bachelor's degree programs require a minimum of sixteen quarters to complete. Associate degree programs require a minimum of eight quarters to complete. Programs are offered on a year-round basis, providing students with the ability to work uninterrupted toward completion of their programs. The College offers all programs in a unique One Course a Month format. This allows students to focus studies on only one course for four weeks. This schedule has proven convenient for students with multiple obligations such as jobs and family.

Academic Facilities

Brown Mackie College–Louisville has more than 69,000 square feet of multipurpose classrooms, including networked computer laboratories, electronics laboratories, veterinary technology labs, medical labs, nursing labs, a resource center, and offices for administrative personnel as well as for student services such as admissions, student financial services, and career-services assistance. In 2009, 6,000 square feet was opened at the Louisville location. Included in this build-out are an occupational therapy lab, a criminal justice lab, additional classrooms, and faculty space. In 2010, 25,000 square feet opened at this location. This build-out included a biomedical equipment lab, additional classrooms, a career services center, and additional faculty/administration space.

The College is nonresidential; ample parking at no cost is available. The campus is a smoke-free facility.

Costs

Tuition for most programs in the 2010–11 academic year was $285 per credit hour, and the general fees were $15 per credit hour. The practical nursing diploma program was $350 per credit hour, and the general fees were $25 per credit hour. The surgical technology program was $330 per credit hour, and the general fees were $15 per credit hour. The occupational therapy program was $350 per credit hour, and the general fees were $15 per credit hour. The computer networking certificate program was $300 per credit hour, and the general fees were $25 per credit hour. The length of the program determines total cost. The cost of textbooks and other instructional materials varies by program.

Financial Aid

Financial aid is available for those who qualify. The College maintains a full-time staff of financial aid professionals to assist qualified students in obtaining financial assistance. The College participates in several student aid programs. Forms of financial aid available through federal resources include the Federal Pell Grant Program, Federal Supplemental Educational Opportunity Grant (FSEOG) Program, Federal Work-Study Program, Federal Perkins Loan Program, Federal Stafford Student Loan Program (subsidized and unsubsidized), and the Federal PLUS Loan Program.

Each year, the College makes available President's Scholarships of $1000 each to qualifying seniors from area high schools. No more than one scholarship is awarded per high school. In order to qualify, a senior must have graduated from a participating high school, maintained a cumulative grade point average of at least 2.0, and submitted a brief essay. The student's extracurricular activities and community service are also considered. The President's Scholarship is available only to students enrolling in one of the College's degree programs. Students awarded the scholarship must enroll at Brown Mackie College–Louisville between June and September immediately following their high school graduation. Applications for these scholarships can be obtained from the guidance departments of participating high schools. These applications must be completed and returned to the College by March 31.

Faculty

There are 45 full-time and over 100 part-time faculty members at the College. The average student-faculty ratio is 20:1.

Admission Requirements

Each applicant for admission is assigned an Assistant Director of Admissions, who directs the applicant through the steps of the admissions process, providing information on curriculum, policies, procedures, and services and assisting the applicant in setting necessary appointments and interviews.

To qualify for admission, each applicant must provide documentation of graduation from an accredited high school or from a

state-approved secondary education curriculum or provide official documentation of high school graduation equivalency. All transcripts become the property of the College. Admission to the College is based on the applicant meeting the stated requirements, a review of the applicant's previous educational records, and a review of the applicant's career interests. If previous academic records indicate the College's education and training programs would not benefit the applicant, the College reserves the right to advise the applicant not to enroll. Special requirements for enrollment into certain programs are discussed in the descriptions of those programs.

In addition to the College's general admission requirements, applicants enrolling in either the occupational therapy assistant program or the surgical technology program must document one of the following: a high school cumulative grade point average of at least 2.5, a score on the GED examination of at least 57 (557 if taken on or after January 15, 2002), or completion of 12 quarter-credit hours or 8 semester-credit hours of collegiate course work with a grade point average of at least 2.5. Credit hours may not include Professional Development (CF 1100), the Brown Mackie College–Louisville course. Students entering the program must also have completed a biology course with a grade of at least a C (or an average of at least 2.0 on a 4.0 scale).

In addition to the College's general admission requirements, applicants enrolling in the practical nursing program must document the following, which must be completed and a record of proof must appear in the student's file prior to the start of the nursing fundamentals course. No student will be admitted to a clinical agency unless all paperwork is completed. The paperwork is a requirement of all contracted agencies. This paperwork includes records of (1) a complete physical, current to within six months of admission; (2) a two-step Mantoux test that is kept current throughout schooling; (3) a hepatitis B vaccination or signed refusal; (4) up-to-date immunizations, including tetanus and rubella; (5) a record of current CPR certification that is maintained throughout the student's clinical experience; and (6) hospitalization insurance or a signed waiver.

For the most recent information regarding admission requirements, prospective students should refer to the current academic catalog.

Application and Information

Applicants must complete and submit an application form along with documentation of graduation from an accredited high school or completion of state-approved secondary education curriculum or provide official documentation of high school graduation equivalency.

For additional information, prospective students should contact:

Director of Admissions
Brown Mackie College–Louisville
3605 Fern Valley Road
Louisville, Kentucky 40219
Phone: 502-968-7191
        800-999-7387 (toll-free)
Fax: 502-357-9956
E-mail: bmcloadm@brownmackie.edu
Web site: http://www.brownmackie.edu/Louisville

BROWN MACKIE COLLEGE–MERRILLVILLE
MERRILLVILLE, INDIANA

BROWN MACKIE COLLEGE
MERRILLVILLE™

The College

Brown Mackie College–Merrillville is one of over twenty-five locations in the Brown Mackie College system of schools (www.brownmackie.edu), which is dedicated to providing educational programs that prepare students to pursue entry-level positions in a competitive, rapidly changing workplace. Brown Mackie College schools offer bachelor's degree, associate degree, certificate, and diploma programs in health sciences, business, information technology, legal studies, and design to over 20,000 students in the Midwest, Southeast, Southwest, and Western United States.

Founded in 1890 by A. N. Hirons as LaPorte Business College in LaPorte, Indiana, the institution later became known as Commonwealth Business College. In 1919, ownership was transferred to Grace and J. J. Moore, who successfully operated the College under the name of Reese School of Business for several decades. In 1975, the College came under the ownership of Steven C. Smith as Commonwealth Business College. A second location, now known as Brown Mackie College–Merrillville, was opened in 1984 in Merrillville, Indiana.

Brown Mackie College–Merrillville is accredited by the Accrediting Council for Independent Colleges and Schools (ACICS) to award bachelor's degrees, associate degrees, diplomas, and certificates. The Accrediting Council for Independent Colleges and Schools is listed as a nationally recognized accrediting agency by the United States Department of Education and is recognized by the Council for Higher Education Accreditation. ACICS can be contacted at 750 First Street NE, Suite 980, Washington, D.C. 20002; phone: 202-336-6780.

The College is licensed and regulated by the Indiana Commission on Proprietary Education, 302 West Washington Street, Indianapolis, Indiana 46204; phone: 800-227-5695 (toll-free) or 317-232-1320. (Indiana advertising code: AC-0138.)

The surgical technology Associate of Science degree is accredited by the Commission on Accreditation of Allied Health Education Programs (www.caahep.org) upon the recommendation of the Accreditation Review Committee on Education in Surgical Technology of the Commission on Accreditation of Allied Health Education Programs, 1361 Park Street, Clearwater, Florida 33756; phone: 727-210-2350.

The occupational therapy assistant Associate of Applied Science degree is accredited by the Accreditation Council for Occupational Therapy Education (ACOTE) of the American Occupational Therapy Association (AOTA), 4720 Montgomery Lane, P.O. Box 31220, Bethesda, Maryland 20824-1220; phone: 301-652-2682.

The College is a nonresidential, smoke-free institution.

Location

Brown Mackie College–Merrillville is conveniently located in northwest Indiana at 1000 East 80th Place, Merrillville, in the Twin Towers business complex just west of the intersection of U.S. Route 30 and Interstate 65. A spacious parking lot provides ample parking at no additional charge.

Programs of Study and Degrees

Brown Mackie College–Merrillville provides higher education to traditional and nontraditional students through bachelor's degree, associate degree, diploma, and certificate programs that assist in enhancing their career opportunities, broadening their perspectives through appropriate general education courses, thinking independently and critically, and improving problem-solving abilities. The College strives to develop within its students the desire for lifelong and continued education.

The Bachelor of Science degree is awarded in business administration, criminal justice, healthcare management, and legal studies.

The Associate of Science degree is awarded in accounting technology, administration in gerontology, business management, computer software technology, criminal justice, medical assisting studies, medical office management, paralegal, and surgical technology.

The Associate of Applied Science degree is awarded in biomedical equipment technology and occupational therapy assistant.

A diploma program in practical nursing is offered.

The College offers certificate programs in accounting, business, computer software applications, criminal justice, medical assistant, and paralegal assistant.

Academic Programs

Each College quarter comprises ten to twelve weeks. Bachelor's degree programs require a minimum of sixteen quarters to complete. Associate degree programs require a minimum of eight quarters to complete. Programs are offered on a year-round basis, providing students with the ability to work uninterrupted toward completion of their programs. The College offers all programs in a unique One Course a Month format. This allows students to focus on only one course for four weeks. This schedule has proven convenient for students with multiple obligations such as jobs and family.

Academic Facilities

Occupying 26,000 square feet, Brown Mackie College–Merrillville was opened to students in October 1998 in the Twin Towers complex of Merrillville and comprises several instructional rooms, including five computer labs with networked computers and four medical laboratories. The administrative offices, college library, and student lounge are all easily accessible to students. The College bookstore stocks texts, courseware, and other educational supplies required for courses at the College. Students also find a variety of personal, recreational, and gift items, including apparel, supplies, and general merchandise incorporating the College logo. Hours are posted at the bookstore entrance.

Costs

Tuition for most programs in the 2010–11 academic year was $285 per credit hour and fees were $15 per credit hour, with some exceptions. For the practical nursing diploma program, tuition was $350 per credit hour and fees were $25 per credit hour. For the surgical technology program, tuition was $330 per credit hour and fees were $15 per credit hour. For the occupational therapy assistant program, tuition was $350 per credit hour and fees were $15 per credit hour. The length of the program determines total cost. Textbook fees vary according to program.

Financial Aid

Financial aid is available to those who qualify. The College maintains a full-time staff of financial aid professionals to assist qualified students in obtaining financial assistance. The College participates in several student aid programs. Forms of financial aid available through federal resources include the Federal Pell Grant Program, Federal Supplemental Educational Opportunity Grant (FSEOG) Program, Federal Work-Study Program, Federal Perkins Loan Program, Federal Stafford Student Loan Program (subsidized and unsubsidized), and the Federal PLUS Loan Program. Eligible students may apply for Indiana state awards, such as the Higher Education Award and Twenty-First Century Scholarships for high school students, the Core 40 awards, and veterans' educational benefits. Students with physical or mental disabilities that are a handicap to employment may be eligible for training services through the state's Bureau of Vocational Rehabilitation. For further information, students should contact the College's Student Financial Services Office.

Each year, the College makes available scholarships of $1000 each to qualifying seniors from area high schools. No more than one scholarship is awarded per high school. In order to qualify, a senior must be graduating from a participating high school, must be maintaining a cumulative grade point average of at least 2.0, and must submit a brief essay. The student's extracurricular activities and community service are also considered. These scholarships are available only to students enrolling in one of the College's degree programs. Students awarded the scholarship must enroll at Brown Mackie College–Merrillville between June and September immediately following their high school graduation. Applications for these scholarships can be obtained from the guidance departments of participating high schools. These applications must be completed and returned to the College by March 31.

Faculty

There are approximately 60 full-time and 25 part-time faculty members at the College, practitioners in their fields of expertise. The average student-faculty ratio is 17:1.

Admission Requirements

Each applicant for admission is assigned an Assistant Director of Admissions who directs the applicant through the steps of the admissions process, providing information on curriculum, policies, procedures, and services and assisting the applicant in setting necessary appointments and interviews. To qualify for admission, each applicant must provide documentation of graduation from an accredited high school or completion of a state-approved secondary education curriculum or provide official documentation of high school graduation equivalency. All transcripts become the property of the College.

As part of the admission process, students are given an assessment of academic skills. Although the results of this assessment do not determine eligibility for admission, they provide the College with a means of determining the need for academic support as well as a means by which the College can evaluate the effectiveness of its educational programs. All new students are required to complete this assessment, which is readministered at the end of the student's program so results may be compared with those of the initial administration.

In addition to the College's general admission requirements, applicants enrolling in the practical nursing program must document the following, which must be completed, and a record of proof must appear in the student's file prior to the start of the nursing fundamentals course. No student will be admitted to a clinical agency unless all paperwork is completed. The paperwork is a requirement of all contracted agencies. This paperwork includes records of (1) a complete physical, current to within six months of admission, (2) a two-step Mantoux test that is kept current throughout schooling, (3) a hepatitis B vaccination or signed refusal, (4) up-to-date immunizations, including tetanus and rubella, (5) a record of current CPR certification that is maintained throughout the student's clinical experience, and (6) hospitalization insurance or a signed waiver.

For the most recent information regarding admission requirements, please refer to the current academic catalog.

Application and Information

Applicants must complete and submit an application form along with documentation of graduation from an accredited high school or completion of state-approved secondary education curriculum or provide official documentation of high school graduation equivalency. For additional information, prospective students should contact:

Brown Mackie College–Merrillville
1000 East 80th Place, Suite 205S
Merrillville, Indiana 46410
Phone: 219-769-3321
        800-258-3321 (toll-free)
Fax: 219-738-1076
E-mail: bmcmeadm@brownmackie.edu
Web site: http://www.brownmackie.edu/Merrillville

BROWN MACKIE COLLEGE–MIAMI

MIAMI, FLORIDA

The College

Brown Mackie College–Miami is one of over twenty-five locations in the Brown Mackie College system of schools (www.brownmackie.edu), which is dedicated to providing educational programs that prepare students to pursue entry-level positions in a competitive, rapidly changing workplace. Brown Mackie College schools offer bachelor's degree, associate degree, certificate, and diploma programs in health sciences, business, information technology, legal studies, criminal justice, early childhood education, and design to over 20,000 students in the Midwest, Southeast, Southwest, and Western United States.

Brown Mackie College–Miami, Florida is accredited by the Accrediting Council for Independent Colleges and Schools (ACICS) to award bachelor's degrees and associate degrees. The Accrediting Council for Independent Colleges and Schools is listed as a nationally recognized accrediting agency by the United States Department of Education and is recognized by the Council for Higher Education Accreditation. ACICS can be contacted at 750 First Street NE, Suite 980, Washington, D.C. 20002; phone: 202-336-6780.

The College is a nonresidential, smoke-free institution.

Location

Brown Mackie College–Miami occupies space within the newly renovated One Herald Plaza in Miami, Florida. It is conveniently located adjacent to the OMNI Metro Mover and bus stop, with access to Metro Rail and Florida's regional Tri-Rail system. Ample parking is also available.

Programs of Study and Degrees

Brown Mackie College–Miami provides higher education to traditional and nontraditional students through bachelor's degree and associate degree programs that assist them in enhancing their career opportunities, broadening their perspectives through appropriate general education courses, thinking independently and critically, and improving problem-solving abilities. The College strives to develop within its students the desire for lifelong and continued education.

The Bachelor of Science degree is awarded in business administration, criminal justice, healthcare management, and information technology.

The Associate of Science degree is awarded in accounting technology, architectural design and drafting technology, biomedical equipment technology, business management, criminal justice, early childhood education, healthcare administration, information technology, medical assisting, and paralegal.

Academic Programs

Each College quarter comprises twelve weeks. Bachelor's degree programs require a minimum of sixteen quarters to complete. Associate degree programs require a minimum of eight quarters to complete. Programs are offered on a year-round basis, providing students with the ability to work uninterrupted toward their degrees. The College offers all programs in a unique One Course a Month format. This allows students to focus studies on only one course for four weeks. This schedule has proven convenient for students with multiple obligations such as jobs and family.

Academic Facilities

Brown Mackie College–Miami is conveniently located at One Herald Plaza, Miami, Florida 33132. The College occupies 50,000 square feet on the top floor of the Miami Herald building, which sits on beautiful Biscayne Bay and offers a clear view of Miami and the Miami Beach skylines.

The College—owned and operated by Pittsburgh-based Education Management Corporation (EDMC)—offers hands-on experiences in its many labs including a criminal justice lab featuring facial recognition software along with a multitude of forensic equipment. The computer networking lab as well as multiple computer classrooms offers students a modern and professional environment for study. Four medical labs are used to instruct clinical medical skills as well as biomedical equipment use and repair. Each student has access to the technology, tools, and facilities needed to complete projects in each subject area. Students are welcome to use the labs when they're not being used for scheduled classes.

The College features a comfortable student lounge as well as an on-site eatery available during all class shifts. The college bookstore offers retail items including textbooks, kits specific to programs of study, and college apparel. The on-site library offers multi-media resources including books, periodicals, and electronic resources specific to all academic programs offered. Course delivery at Brown Mackie College–Miami includes on-ground as well as blended courses.

Costs

Tuition in the 2010–11 academic year for all programs was $360 per credit hour; fees were $15 per credit hour. Textbooks and other instructional materials vary by program.

Financial Aid

Financial aid is available for those who qualify. The College maintains a full-time staff of financial aid professionals to assist qualified students in obtaining financial assistance. The College participates in several student aid programs. Forms of financial aid available to qualified students through federal resources include the Federal Pell Grant Program, Federal

Supplemental Educational Opportunity Grant (FSEOG) Program, Federal Work-Study Program, Federal Perkins Loan Program, Federal Stafford Student Loan Program (subsidized and unsubsidized), Federal PLUS loan program, and Florida State grant program. Eligible students may apply for veterans' educational benefits. Students with physical or mental disabilities that are a handicap to employment may be eligible for training services through the state Agency for Vocational Rehabilitation. For further information, students should contact the College Student Financial Services Office.

Each year, the College makes available President's Scholarships of $1000 each to qualifying seniors from area high schools. No more than one scholarship is awarded per high school. In order to qualify, a senior must be graduating from a participating high school, must be maintaining a cumulative grade point average of at least 2.0, and must submit a brief essay. The student's extracurricular activities and community service are also considered. The President's Scholarship is available only to students enrolling in one of the College's degree programs. Students awarded the scholarship must enroll at Brown Mackie College–Miami between June and September immediately following their high school graduation. Applications for these scholarships can be obtained from the guidance departments of participating high schools. These applications must be completed and returned to the College by March 31.

Faculty

There are 15 full-time and 27 adjunct faculty members at the College. The average student-faculty ratio is 20:1.

Admission Requirements

Each applicant for admission is assigned an Assistant Director of Admissions, who directs the applicant through the steps of the admissions process, providing information on curriculum, policies, procedures, and services and assisting the applicant in setting necessary appointments and interviews. To qualify for admission, applicants must be a graduate of a public or private high school or a correspondence school or education center that is accredited by an agency that is recognized by the U.S. or State of Florida Department of Education or any of its approved agents. As part of the admissions process, applicants must sign a document attesting to graduation or completion and containing the information to obtain verification of such. Verification must be obtained within the first term. All transcripts become the property of the College. Admission to the College is based on the applicant meeting the stated requirements, a review of the applicant's previous educational records, and a review of the applicant's career interests. If previous academic records indicate the College's education and training programs would not benefit the applicant, the College reserves the right to advise the applicant not to enroll. Special requirements for enrollment into certain programs are discussed in the descriptions of those programs.

Students are given an assessment of academic skills during the first two weeks of class. Although the results of this assessment do not determine eligibility for admission, they provide the College with a means of determining the need for academic support as well as a means by which the College can evaluate the effectiveness of its educational programs. All new students are required to complete this assessment.

For the most recent information regarding admission requirements, please refer to the current academic catalog.

Application and Information

Applicants must complete and submit an application form.

Director of Admissions
Brown Mackie College–Miami
One Herald Plaza
Miami, Florida 33132-1418
Phone: 305-341-6600
        866-505-0335 (toll-free)
Fax: 305-373-8814
E-mail: bmmiaadm@brownmackie.edu
Web site: http://www.brownmackie.edu/Miami

BROWN MACKIE COLLEGE–MICHIGAN CITY

MICHIGAN CITY, INDIANA

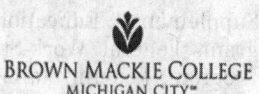

The College

Brown Mackie College–Michigan City is one of over twenty-five locations in the Brown Mackie College system of schools (www.brownmackie.edu), which is dedicated to providing educational programs that prepare students to pursue entry-level positions in a competitive, rapidly changing workplace. Brown Mackie College schools offer bachelor's degree, associate degree, certificate, and diploma programs in health sciences, business, information technology, legal studies, and design to over 20,000 students in the Midwest, Southeast, Southwest, and Western United States.

Founded in 1890 by A. N. Hirons as LaPorte Business College in LaPorte, Indiana, the institution later became known as Commonwealth Business College. In 1919, ownership was transferred to Grace and J. J. Moore, who successfully operated the College under the name of Reese School of Business for several decades. In 1975, the College came under the ownership of Steven C. Smith as Commonwealth Business College. In 1997, the College relocated to its present site in Michigan City, Indiana. The College was acquired by Education Management Corporation (EDMC) on September 2, 2003, and changed its name to Brown Mackie College–Michigan City in November 2004.

Brown Mackie College–Michigan City is accredited by the Accrediting Council for Independent Colleges and Schools (ACICS) to award bachelor's degrees, associate degrees, and certificates. The Accrediting Council for Independent Colleges and Schools is listed as a nationally recognized accrediting agency by the United States Department of Education and is recognized by the Council for Higher Education Accreditation. ACICS can be contacted at 750 First Street NE, Suite 980, Washington, D.C. 20002; phone: 202-336-6780.

The College is regulated by the Indiana Commission on Proprietary Education, 302 West Washington Street, Indianapolis, Indiana 46204; phone: 317-232-1320 or 800-227-5695 (toll-free). The Indiana advertising code for Brown Mackie College–Michigan City is AC-0138.

The College's medical assisting degree program is accredited by the Accrediting Bureau of Health Education Schools (ABHES), 7777 Leesburg Pike, Suite 314 N, Falls Church, Virginia 22043; phone: 703-917-9503.

The College's surgical technology program is accredited by the Commission on Accreditation of Allied Health Education Programs (CAAHEP), 1361 Park Street, Clearwater, Florida 33756; phone: 727-210-2350.

The College's veterinary technology degree program is accredited by the American Veterinary Medical Association (AVMA), Committee on Veterinary Technician Education and Activities (CVTEA), 1931 North Meacham Road, Suite 100, Schaumberg, Illinois 60173; phone: 800-248-2862.

The College is a nonresidential, smoke-free institution.

Location

Brown Mackie College–Michigan City is conveniently located in northwest Indiana, at 325 East U.S. Highway 20, Michigan City, 1 mile north of Interstate 94, near the intersection of routes 20 and 421.

Programs of Study and Degrees

Brown Mackie College–Michigan City provides higher education to traditional and nontraditional students through bachelor's degree, associate degree, and certificate programs that assist in enhancing their career opportunities, broadening their perspectives through appropriate general education courses, thinking independently and critically, and improving problem-solving abilities. The College strives to develop within its students the desire for lifelong and continued education.

The Bachelor of Science degree is awarded in business administration, criminal justice, and legal studies.

The Associate of Science degree is awarded in accounting technology, business management, computer software technology, criminal justice, early childhood education, health and therapeutic massage, healthcare administration, medical assisting, medical office management, paralegal, surgical technology, and veterinary technology.

The College offers certificate programs in accounting, business, computer software applications, criminal justice, medical assistant, medical coding and billing, and paralegal assistant.

Academic Programs

Each College quarter comprises twelve weeks. Bachelor's degree programs require a minimum of sixteen quarters to complete. Associate degree programs require a minimum of eight quarters to complete. Programs are offered on a year-round basis, providing students with the ability to work uninterrupted toward their degrees. The College offers all programs in a unique One Course a Month format. This allows students to focus studies on only one course for four weeks. This schedule has proven convenient for students with multiple obligations such as jobs and family.

Academic Facilities

In 2002, the College underwent a major renovation and added 3,360 square feet, for a total of 10,338 square feet of occupancy. An additional medical laboratory, a larger library, new classrooms, and a bookstore were added. All classrooms and the library are equipped with new technology, including multimedia projectors, surround-sound audio systems, VCRs, and DVD players. Five of the ten new classrooms are equipped with networked computer systems. The two medical laboratories contain newly acquired medical equipment and instructional tools and supplies. Administrative offices are easily accessible to students. In 2008, a learning site was opened at 1623 South

Woodland Avenue, Michigan City, Indiana. Of approximately 6,500 square feet, this site is conveniently located within a mile of the main campus.

Costs

Tuition in the 2010–11 academic year was $285 per credit hour and fees were $15 per credit hour. For the surgical technology program, the tuition was $330 per credit hour and fees were $15 per credit hour. Textbook fees vary according to the program.

Financial Aid

The College maintains a full-time staff of financial aid professionals to assist qualified students in obtaining financial assistance. The College participates in several student aid programs. Forms of financial aid available to qualified students through federal resources include the Federal Pell Grant Program, Federal Supplemental Educational Opportunity Grant (FSEOG) Program, Federal Work-Study Program, Federal Stafford Student Loan Program (subsidized and unsubsidized), and Federal PLUS loan program.

Eligible students may apply for Indiana state awards, such as the Higher Education Award and Twenty-First Century Scholarships for high school students, the Core 40 awards, and veterans' educational benefits. Students with physical or mental disabilities that are a handicap to employment may be eligible for training services through the state's Bureau of Vocational Rehabilitation. For further information, students should contact the College Student Financial Services Office.

Each year, the College makes available scholarships of $1000 each to qualifying seniors from area high schools. No more than one scholarship is awarded per high school. In order to qualify, a senior must be graduating from a participating high school, must be maintaining a cumulative grade point average of at least 2.0, and must submit a brief essay. The student's extracurricular activities and community service are also considered. These scholarships are available only to students enrolling in one of the College's degree programs. Students awarded the scholarship must enroll at Brown Mackie College–Michigan City between June and September immediately following their high school graduation. Applications for these scholarships can be obtained from the guidance departments of participating high schools. These applications must be completed and returned to the College by March 31.

Faculty

There are 9 full-time and 31 part-time faculty members at the College. The average student-faculty ratio is 13:1. Each student is assigned a department chair.

Admission Requirements

Each applicant for admission is assigned an Assistant Director of Admissions, who directs the applicant through the steps of the admissions process, providing information on curriculum, policies, procedures, and services and assisting the applicant in setting necessary appointments and interviews. To qualify for admission, each applicant must provide documentation of graduation from an accredited high school or completion of a state-approved secondary education curriculum or provide official documentation of high school graduation equivalency. All transcripts become the property of the College.

As part of the admission process, students are given an assessment of academic skills. Although the results of this assessment do not determine eligibility for admission, they provide the College with a means of determining the need for academic support, as well as a means by which the College can evaluate the effectiveness of its educational programs. All new students are required to complete this assessment.

For the most recent information regarding admission requirements, please refer to the current academic catalog.

Application and Information

Applicants must complete and submit an application form along with documentation of graduation from an accredited high school or completion of a state-approved secondary education curriculum or provide official documentation of high school graduation equivalency. For additional information, prospective students should contact:

Director of Admissions
Brown Mackie College–Michigan City
325 East U.S. Highway 20
Michigan City, Indiana 46360
Phone: 219-877-3100
      800-519-2416 (toll-free)
Fax: 219-877-3110
E-mail: bmcmcadm@brownmackie.edu
Web site: http://www.brownmackie.edu/MichiganCity

BROWN MACKIE COLLEGE–NORTHERN KENTUCKY

FORT MITCHELL, KENTUCKY

The College

Brown Mackie College–Northern Kentucky is one of over twenty-five locations in the Brown Mackie College system of schools (www.brownmackie.edu), which is dedicated to providing educational programs that prepare students to pursue entry-level positions in a competitive, rapidly changing workplace. Brown Mackie College's system of schools offer bachelor's degree, associate degree, certificate, and diploma programs in health sciences, business, information technology, legal studies, and design to more than 20,000 students in the Midwest, Southeast, Southwest, and Western United States.

The College was founded in Cincinnati, Ohio, in February 1927 as a traditional business college. In May 1981, the College opened a branch location in northern Kentucky, which moved in 1986 to its current location in Fort Mitchell.

Brown Mackie College–Northern Kentucky is accredited by the Accrediting Council for Independent Colleges and Schools (ACICS) to award bachelor's degrees, associate degrees, and diplomas. The Accrediting Council for Independent Colleges and Schools is listed as a nationally recognized accrediting agency by the United States Department of Education and is recognized by the Council for Higher Education Accreditation. ACICS can be contacted at 750 First Street NE, Suite 980, Washington, D.C. 20002; phone: 202-336-6780.

Brown Mackie College–Northern Kentucky is regulated by the Indiana Commission on Proprietary Education; 302 West Washington Street, Room E201, Indianapolis, Indiana 46204; phone: 317-232-1320 or 800-227-5695 (toll-free). (Indiana Advertising Code: AC-0150.)

The College is licensed by the Ohio State Board of Career Colleges and Schools, 35 East Gay Street, Suite 403, Columbus, Ohio 43215; phone: 614-466-2752. (Ohio registration number: 06-03-1781T.)

The occupational therapy assistant program is accredited by the Accreditation Council for Occupational Therapy Education (ACOTE) of the American Occupational Therapy Association (AOTA), located at 4720 Montgomery Lane, P.O. Box 31220, Bethesda, Maryland 20824; phone: 301-652-AOTA.

The Associate of Science degree in surgical technology is accredited by the Commission on Accreditation of Allied Health Education Programs (http://www.caahep.org) upon the recommendation of the Accreditation Review Council on Education in Surgical Technology and Surgical Assisting (ARC/STSA).

Location

Brown Mackie College–Northern Kentucky is conveniently located at 309 Buttermilk Pike in Fort Mitchell, Kentucky. A spacious parking lot provides ample parking at no additional charge.

Programs of Study and Degrees

Brown Mackie College–Northern Kentucky provides higher education to traditional and nontraditional students through bachelor's degree, associate degree, and diploma programs that assist them in enhancing their career opportunities, broadening their perspectives through appropriate general education courses, thinking independently and critically, and improving problem-solving abilities. The College strives to develop within its students the desire for lifelong and continued education.

The Bachelor of Science degree is awarded in business administration, criminal justice, healthcare management, and legal studies.

The Associate of Applied Business degree is awarded in accounting technology, business management, computer software technology, criminal justice, healthcare administration, information technology, and paralegal.

The Associate of Applied Science degree is awarded in computer-aided design and drafting technology, medical assisting, occupational therapy assistant, pharmacy technology, and surgical technology.

The College offers a diploma program in accounting, business, computer applications, computer software applications, medical assistant, and practical nursing.

Academic Programs

Each College quarter comprises ten to twelve weeks. Bachelor's degree programs require a minimum of sixteen quarters to complete. Associate degree programs require a minimum of eight quarters to complete. Programs are offered on a year-round basis, providing students with the ability to work uninterrupted toward their degrees. The College offers all programs in a unique One Course a Month format. This allows students to focus studies on only one course for four weeks. This schedule has proven convenient for students with multiple obligations such as jobs and family.

Academic Facilities

Brown Mackie College–Northern Kentucky offers media presentation rooms for special instructional needs and a library that provides instructional resources and academic support for both faculty members and students.

The campus is nonresidential; public transportation and ample parking at no cost are available. The campus is a smoke-free facility.

Costs

Tuition for the 2010–11 academic year was $285 per credit hour and general fees were $15 per credit hour, with some exceptions. The practical nursing program tuition was $350 per credit hour and general fees were $25 per credit hour. The surgical technology tuition was $330 per credit hour. Tuition for the occupational therapy assistant program was $350 per credit hour and general fees were $15 per credit hour. The cost of textbooks and other instructional materials varies by program.

Financial Aid

Financial aid is available to those who qualify. The College maintains a full-time staff of financial aid professionals to assist qualified students in obtaining financial assistance. The College participates in several student aid programs. Forms of financial aid available through federal resources include Federal Pell Grants, Federal Supplemental Educational Opportunity Grants (FSEOG), Federal Work-Study Program awards, Federal Perkins Loans, Federal Stafford Student Loans (subsidized and unsubsidized), and Federal PLUS loans. Eligible students may apply for veterans' educational benefits. Students with physical or mental disabilities that are a handicap to employment may be eligible for training services through the state Vocational Rehabilitation Agency. For further information, students should contact the College Student Financial Services Office.

Each year, the College makes available President's Scholarships of $1000 each to qualifying seniors from area high schools. No more than one scholarship is awarded per high school. In order to qualify, a senior have graduated from a participating high school, maintained a cumulative grade point average of at least 2.0, and submitted a brief essay. The student's extracurricular activities and community service are also considered. The President's Scholarship is available only to students enrolling in one of the College's degree programs. Students who receive the scholarship must enroll at Brown Mackie College–Northern Kentucky between June and September immediately following their high school graduation. Applications for these scholarships can be obtained from the guidance departments of participating high schools. These applications must be completed and returned to the College by March 31.

Faculty

There are 11 full-time and 30 adjunct faculty members. The student-faculty ratio is 15:1.

Admission Requirements

Each applicant for admission is assigned an Assistant Director of Admissions, who directs the applicant through the steps of the admissions process, providing information on curriculum, policies, procedures, and services and assisting the applicant in setting necessary appointments and interviews. To qualify for admission, each applicant must provide documentation of graduation from an accredited high school or from a state-approved secondary education curriculum or provide official documentation of high school graduation equivalency. All transcripts become the property of the College. Admission to the College is based upon the applicant meeting the stated requirements, a review of the applicant's previous education records, and a review of the applicant's career interests. If previous academic records indicate the College's education and training programs would not benefit the applicant, the College reserves the right to advise the applicant not to enroll. Special requirements for enrollment into certain programs are discussed in the descriptions of those programs.

In addition to the College's general admission requirements, applicants enrolling in the practical nursing program must document the following, which must be completed, and a record of proof must appear in the student's file prior to the start of the nursing fundamentals course. No student will be admitted to a clinical agency unless all paperwork is completed. The paperwork is a requirement of all contracted agencies. This paperwork includes records of (1) a complete physical, current to within six months of admission; (2) a two-step Mantoux test that is kept current throughout schooling; (3) a hepatitis B vaccination or signed refusal; (4) up-to-date immunizations, including tetanus and rubella; (5) a record of current CPR certification that is maintained throughout the student's clinical experience; and (6) hospitalization insurance or a signed waiver.

For the most recent information regarding admission requirements, prospective students should refer to the current academic catalog.

Application and Information

Applicants must complete and submit an application form, along with documentation of graduation from an accredited high school or state-approved secondary education curriculum or official documentation of high school graduation equivalency.

For additional information, prospective students should contact:

Director of Admissions
Brown Mackie College–Northern Kentucky
309 Buttermilk Pike
Fort Mitchell, Kentucky 41017
Phone: 859-341-5627
Fax: 859-341-6483
E-mail: bmcnkadm@brownmackie.edu
Web site: http://www.brownmackie.edu/NorthernKentucky

BROWN MACKIE COLLEGE–PHOENIX

PHOENIX, ARIZONA

The College

Brown Mackie College–Phoenix is one of over twenty-five locations in the Brown Mackie College system of schools (www.brownmackie.edu), which is dedicated to providing educational programs that prepare students to pursue entry-level positions in a competitive, rapidly changing workplace. Brown Mackie College schools offer bachelor's degree, associate degree, certificate, and diploma programs in health sciences, business, information technology, legal studies, and design to over 20,000 students in the Midwest, Southeast, Southwest, and Western United States.

Brown Mackie College–Phoenix was founded in 2009 as a branch of Brown Mackie College–Tucson, Arizona.

Brown Mackie College–Phoenix is accredited by the Accrediting Council for Independent Colleges and Schools (ACICS) to award bachelor's degrees, associate degrees, certificates, and diplomas. The Accrediting Council for Independent Colleges and Schools is listed as a nationally recognized accrediting agency by the United States Department of Education and is recognized by the Council for Higher Education Accreditation. ACICS can be contacted at 750 First Street NE, Suite 980, Washington, D.C. 20002; phone: 202-336-6780.

The occupational therapy assistant program is accredited by the Accreditation Council for Occupational Therapy Education (ACOTE) of the American Occupational Therapy Association (AOTA), located at 4720 Montgomery Lane, P.O. Box 31220, Bethesda, Maryland 20824-1220; phone: 301-652-2682.

The surgical technology program is accredited by the Accrediting Bureau of Health Education Schools (ABHES), 7777 Leesburg Pike, Suite 314 North Falls Church, Virginia 22043; phone 703-917-9503.

This institution is licensed by the Arizona State Board for Private Postsecondary Education, 1400 West Washington Street, Room 2560, Phoenix, Arizona 85007; phone: 602-542-5709.

The College is a nonresidential, smoke-free institution.

Location

Brown Mackie College–Phoenix is conveniently located at 13430 North Black Canyon Highway, Suite 190, in Phoenix, Arizona. The College has a generous parking area and is easily accessible by public transportation.

Programs of Study and Degrees

Brown Mackie College–Phoenix provides higher education to traditional and nontraditional students through bachelor's and associate degree programs that assist in enhancing their career opportunities, broadening their perspectives through appropriate general education courses, thinking independently and critically, and improving problem-solving abilities. The College strives to develop within its students the desire for lifelong and continued education.

The Bachelor of Science degree is awarded in business administration, criminal justice, healthcare management, and legal studies.

The Associate of Science degree is awarded in accounting technology, business management, criminal justice, healthcare administration, information technology, medical assisting, paralegal, and surgical technology.

The Associate of Applied Science degree is awarded in nursing and occupational therapy assistant.

Academic Programs

Each College quarter comprises twelve weeks. Bachelor's degree programs require a minimum of sixteen quarters to complete. Associate degree programs require a minimum of eight quarters to complete. Programs are offered on a year-round basis, providing students with the ability to work uninterrupted toward completion of their programs. The College offers all programs in a unique One Course a Month format. This allows students to focus studies on only one course for four weeks. This schedule has proven convenient for students with multiple obligations such as jobs and family.

Academic Facilities

Brown Mackie College–Phoenix has a variety of classrooms including computer labs housing the latest technology in the industry. High-speed access to the Internet and other online resources are available for students and faculty. Multimedia classrooms provide a learning environment equipped with overhead projectors, TVs, DVD/VCR players, computers, and sound systems.

Costs

Tuition for programs in the 2010–11 academic year was $285 per credit hour, with a $15 per credit hour general fee applied to instructional costs for activities and services. For the surgical technology program, the tuition was $330 per credit hour with a $15 per credit hour general fee applied to instructional costs for activities. For the occupational therapy assistant program, the tuition was $350 per credit hour with a $15 per credit hour general fee applied to instructional costs for activities. For the nursing program, the tuition was $390 per credit hour with a $25 per credit hour general fee applied to instructional costs for activities. Textbooks and other instructional materials vary by program.

Financial Aid

Financial aid is available for those who qualify. The College maintains a full-time staff of financial aid professionals to assist qualified students in obtaining financial assistance. The College participates in several student aid programs. Forms of financial aid available to those who qualify through federal resources include the Federal Pell Grant Program, Federal Supplemental Educational Opportunity Grant (FSEOG) Program, Federal

COLLEGE CLOSE-UPS

Work-Study Program, Federal Perkins Loan Program, Federal Stafford Student Loan Program (subsidized and unsubsidized), and the Federal PLUS Loan Program.

Each year, the College makes available President's Scholarships of $1000 each to qualifying seniors from area high schools. No more than one scholarship is awarded per high school. In order to qualify, a senior must be graduating from a participating high school, must be maintaining a cumulative grade point average of at least 2.0, and must submit a brief essay. The student's extracurricular activities and community service are also considered. The President's Scholarship is available only to students enrolling in one of the College's degree programs. Students awarded the scholarship must enroll at Brown Mackie College–Phoenix between June and September immediately following their high school graduation. Applications for these scholarships can be obtained from the guidance departments of participating high schools. These applications must be completed and returned to the College by March 31.

Faculty

Experienced faculty members provide academic support and are committed to the academic and technical preparation of their students. The College has both full- and part-time faculty members. The average student-faculty ratio is 14:1. Each student is assigned a program director as an adviser.

Admission Requirements

Each applicant for admission is assigned an Assistant Director of Admissions, who directs the applicant through the steps of the admissions process, providing information on curriculum, policies, procedures, and services and assisting the applicant in setting necessary appointments and interviews. To qualify for admission, each applicant must provide documentation of graduation from an accredited high school or from a state-approved secondary education curriculum or provide official documentation of high school graduation equivalency. All transcripts become the property of the College.

For the most recent information regarding admission requirements, please refer to the current academic catalog.

Application and Information

Applicants must complete and submit an application form, along with documentation of graduation from an accredited high school or state-approved secondary education curriculum or official documentation of high school graduation equivalency.

For additional information, prospective students should contact:

Director of Admissions
Brown Mackie College–Phoenix
13430 N. Black Canyon Highway, Suite 190
Phoenix, Arizona 85029
Phone: 602-337-3044
        866-824-4793 (toll-free)
Fax: 480-375-2450
E-mail: bmcpxadmn@brownmackie.edu
Web site: http://www.brownmackie.edu/Phoenix

BROWN MACKIE COLLEGE–ST. LOUIS
FENTON, MISSOURI

The College

Brown Mackie College–St. Louis is one of over twenty-five locations in the Brown Mackie College system of schools (www.brownmackie.edu), which is dedicated to providing educational programs that prepare students to pursue entry-level positions in a competitive, rapidly changing workplace. Brown Mackie College schools offer bachelor's degree, associate degree, certificate, and diploma programs in health sciences, business, information technology, legal studies, and design to over 20,000 students in the Midwest, Southeast, Southwest, and Western United States.

Brown Mackie College was originally founded and approved by the Board of Trustees of Kansas Wesleyan College in Salina, Kansas on July 30, 1892. In 1938, the College was incorporated as The Brown Mackie School of Business under the ownership of Perry E. Brown and A.B. Mackie, former instructors at Kansas Wesleyan University in Salina, Kansas. Their last names formed the name of Brown Mackie. By January 1975, with improvements in curricula and higher degree-granting status, The Brown Mackie School of Business became Brown Mackie College.

Brown Mackie College–St. Louis is accredited by the Accrediting Council for Independent Colleges and Schools (ACICS) to award bachelor's degrees, associate degrees, and diplomas. The Accrediting Council for Independent Colleges and Schools is listed as a nationally recognized accrediting agency by the United States Department of Education and is recognized by the Council for Higher Education Accreditation. ACICS can be contacted at 750 First Street NE, Suite 980, Washington, D.C. 20002; phone: 202-336-6780.

The occupational therapy assistant program has applied for accreditation by the Accreditation Council for Occupational Therapy Education (ACOTE) of the American Occupational Therapy Association (AOTA), located at 4720 Montgomery Lane, P.O. Box 31220, Bethesda, Maryland 20824-1220; phone: 301-652-AOTA.

Location

Brown Mackie College–St. Louis is conveniently located at #2 Soccer Park Road in Fenton, Missouri. The College has a generous parking area and is easily accessible by public transportation.

Programs of Study and Degrees

Brown Mackie College–St. Louis provides higher education to traditional and nontraditional students through bachelor's and associate degree programs that assist in enhancing their career opportunities, broadening their perspectives through appropriate general education courses, thinking independently and critically, and improving problem-solving abilities. The

College strives to develop within its students the desire for lifelong and continued education.

The Bachelor of Science degree is awarded in business administration, criminal justice, healthcare management, and legal studies.

The Associate of Applied Science degree is awarded in accounting technology, architectural design and drafting technology, business management, criminal justice, healthcare administration, information technology, medical assisting, occupational therapy assistant, office management, paralegal, pharmacy technology, surgical technology, and veterinary technology.

The College offers diploma programs in accounting, business, criminal justice, medical assistant, and paralegal assistant.

Academic Programs

Each College quarter comprises twelve weeks. Bachelor's degree programs require a minimum of sixteen quarters to complete. Associate degree programs require a minimum of eight quarters to complete. Programs are offered on a year-round basis, providing students with the ability to work uninterrupted toward completion of their programs. The College offers all programs in a unique One Course a Month format. This allows students to focus studies on only one course for four weeks. This schedule has proven convenient for students with multiple obligations such as jobs and family.

Academic Facilities

A modern facility, Brown Mackie College–St Louis offers more than 30,000 square feet. The College is equipped with multiple computer labs, housing over 200 computers. High-speed access to the Internet and other online resources are available for students and faculty. Multimedia classrooms are outfitted with overhead projectors, VCR/DVD players, and computers.

The campus is nonresidential; public transportation and parking at no cost are available. The campus is a smoke-free facility.

Costs

Tuition in the 2010–11 academic year for all bachelor's and associate degrees and diploma programs was $260 per credit hour; fees were $15 per credit hour. Tuition for the surgical technology program was $310 per credit hour; fees were $15 per credit hour. Tuition for the occupational therapy assistant program was $325 per credit hour; fees were $15 per credit hour. The cost of textbooks and other instructional materials varies by program.

Financial Aid

Financial aid is available for those who qualify. The College maintains a full-time staff of financial aid professionals to assist qualified students in obtaining the financial assistance they require to meet their educational expenses. Available resources include federal and state aid, student loans from private lenders, and Federal Work-Study opportunities, both on and off college premises.

Each year, the College makes available scholarships of $1000 each to qualifying seniors from area high schools. No more than one scholarship is awarded per high school. In order to qualify, a senior must have graduated from a participating high school, maintained a cumulative grade point average of at least 2.0, and submitted a brief essay. The student's extracurricular activities and community service are also considered. These scholarships are available only to students enrolling in one of the College's degree programs. Students awarded the scholarship must enroll at Brown Mackie College–St. Louis between June and September immediately following their high school graduation. Applications for these scholarships can be obtained from the guidance departments of participating high schools. These applications must be completed and returned to the College by March 31.

Faculty

Experienced faculty members provide academic support and are committed to the academic and technical preparation of their students. The College has 3 full-time and 3 part-time instructors, with a student-faculty ratio of 20:1.

Admission Requirements

Each applicant for admission is assigned an Assistant Director of Admissions who directs the applicant through the steps of the admissions process. They provide information on curriculum, policies, procedures, and services and assist the applicant in setting necessary appointments and interviews. To qualify for admission, each applicant must provide documentation of graduation from an accredited high school or from a state-approved secondary education curriculum or provide official documentation of high school graduation equivalency. All transcripts become the property of the College. Admission to the College is based on the applicant meeting the stated requirements, a review of the applicant's previous educational records, and a review of the applicant's career interests. If previous academic records indicate the College's education and training programs would not benefit the applicant, the College reserves the right to advise the applicant not to enroll. Special requirements for enrollment into certain programs are discussed in the descriptions of those programs.

For the most recent information regarding admission requirements, prospective students should refer to the current academic catalog.

Application and Information

Applicants must complete and submit an application form, along with documentation of graduation from an accredited high school or state-approved secondary education curriculum or official documentation of high school graduation equivalency.

For additional information, prospective students should contact:

Director of Admissions
Brown Mackie College–St. Louis
2 Soccer Park Road
Fenton, Missouri 63026
Phone: 636-651-3290
        888-874-4375 (toll-free)
Fax: 636-651-3349
E-mail: bmcstladm@brownmackie.edu
Web site: http://www.brownmackie.edu/StLouis

BROWN MACKIE COLLEGE–SAN ANTONIO

SAN ANTONIO, TEXAS

The College

Brown Mackie College–San Antonio is one of over twenty-five locations in the Brown Mackie College system of schools (www.brownmackie.edu), which is dedicated to providing educational programs that prepare students to pursue entry-level positions in a competitive, rapidly changing workplace. Brown Mackie College schools offer bachelor's degree, associate degree, certificate, and diploma programs in health sciences, business, information technology, legal studies, and design to over 20,000 students in the Midwest, Southeast, Southwest, and Western United States.

Brown Mackie College was originally founded and approved by the Board of Trustees of Kansas Wesleyan College in Salina, Kansas on July 30, 1892. In 1938, the College was incorporated as the Brown Mackie School of Business under the ownership of Perry E. Brown and A. B. Mackie, former instructors at Kansas Wesleyan University in Salina, Kansas. Their last names formed the name of Brown Mackie. By January 1975, with improvements in curricula and higher degree-granting status, the Brown Mackie School of Business became Brown Mackie College.

Brown Mackie College–San Antonio is accredited by the Accrediting Council for Independent Colleges and Schools (ACICS) to award bachelor's degrees and associate degrees. The Accrediting Council for Independent Colleges and Schools is listed as a nationally recognized accrediting agency by the United States Department of Education and is recognized by the Council for Higher Education Accreditation. ACICS can be contacted at 750 First Street NE, Suite 980, Washington, D.C. 20002; phone: 202-336-6780.

Location

Brown Mackie College–San Antonio is conveniently located at 4715 Fredericksburg Road in San Antonio, Texas. The College has a generous parking area and is easily accessible by public transportation.

Programs of Study and Degrees

Brown Mackie College–San Antonio provides higher education to traditional and nontraditional students through bachelor's degree and associate degree programs that assist in enhancing their career opportunities, broadening their perspectives through appropriate general education courses, thinking independently and critically, and improving problem-solving abilities. The College strives to develop within its students the desire for lifelong and continued education.

The Bachelor of Science degree is awarded in business administration, criminal justice, healthcare management, and legal studies.

The Associate of Applied Science degree is awarded in accounting technology, architectural design and drafting technology, business management, criminal justice, healthcare administration, information technology, medical assisting, paralegal, pharmacy technology, and surgical technology.

Academic Programs

Each College quarter comprises twelve weeks. Bachelor's degree programs require a minimum of sixteen quarters to complete. Associate degree programs require a minimum of eight quarters to complete. Programs are offered on a year-round basis, providing students with the ability to work uninterrupted toward completion of their programs. The College offers all programs in a unique One Course a Month format. This allows students to focus studies on only one course for four weeks. This schedule has proven convenient for students with multiple obligations such as jobs and family.

Academic Facilities

A modern facility, Brown Mackie College–San Antonio offers more than 35,000 square feet. The College is equipped with multiple computer labs, housing over 100 computers. High-speed access to the Internet and other online resources are available to students and faculty. Multimedia classrooms are outfitted with overhead projectors, VCR/DVD players, and computers.

The campus is nonresidential; public transportation and ample parking at no cost are available. The campus is a smoke-free facility.

Costs

Tuition in the 2010–11 academic year for all bachelor's and associate degrees was $295 per credit hour; fees were $15 per credit hour. Tuition for the surgical technology program was $330 per credit hour; fees were $15 per credit hour. The cost of textbooks and other instructional materials varies by program.

Financial Aid

Financial aid is available for those who qualify. The College maintains a full-time staff of financial aid professionals to assist qualified students in obtaining the financial assistance they require to meet their educational expenses. Available resources include federal and state aid, student loans from private lenders, and Federal Work-Study opportunities, both on and off college premises.

Each year, the College makes available scholarships of $1000 each to qualifying seniors from area high schools. No more than one scholarship is awarded per high school. In order to qualify, a senior must have graduated from a participating high school, must be maintained a cumulative grade point average of at least 2.0, and submitted a brief essay. The student's extracurricular activities and community service are also considered. These scholarships are available only to students enrolling in one of the College's degree programs. Students awarded the scholarship must enroll at Brown Mackie College–San Antonio between June and September immediately following their high school graduation. Applications for these scholarships can be obtained from the guidance departments of participating high schools. These applications must be completed and returned to the College by March 31.

Faculty

Experienced faculty members provide academic support and are committed to the academic and technical preparation of their students. The College has both full-time and part-time instructors, with a student-faculty ratio of 15:1.

Admission Requirements

Each applicant for admission is assigned an Assistant Director of Admissions who directs the applicant through the steps of the admissions process. They provide information on curriculum, policies, procedures, and services and assist the applicant in setting necessary appointments and interviews. To qualify for admission, each applicant must provide documentation of graduation from an accredited high school or from a state-approved secondary education curriculum or provide official documentation of high school graduation equivalency. All transcripts become the property of the College. Admission to the College is based on the applicant meeting the stated requirements, a review of the applicant's previous educational records, and a review of the applicant's career interests. If previous academic records indicate the College's education and training programs would not benefit the applicant, the College reserves the right to advise the applicant not to enroll. Special requirements for enrollment into certain programs are discussed in the descriptions of those programs.

For the most recent information regarding admission requirements, prospective students should refer to the current academic catalog.

Application and Information

Applicants must complete and submit an application form, along with documentation of graduation from an accredited high school or state-approved secondary education curriculum or official documentation of high school graduation equivalency.

For additional information, prospective students should contact:

Director of Admissions
Brown Mackie College–San Antonio
4715 Fredericksburg Road, Suite 100
San Antonio, Texas 78229
Phone: 210-428-2210
       877-460-1714 (toll-free)
Fax: 210-428-2265
E-mail: bmsanadm@brownmackie.edu
Web site: http://www.brownmackie.edu/San Antonio

BROWN MACKIE COLLEGE–SOUTH BEND

SOUTH BEND, INDIANA

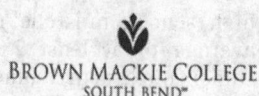

The College

Brown Mackie College–South Bend is one of over twenty-five locations in the Brown Mackie College system of schools (www.brownmackie.edu), which is dedicated to providing educational programs that prepare students to pursue entry-level positions in a competitive, rapidly changing workplace. Brown Mackie College schools offer bachelor's degree, associate degree, certificate, and diploma programs in health sciences, business, information technology, legal studies, and design to over 20,000 students in the Midwest, Southeast, Southwest, and Western United States.

The College is one of the oldest institutions of its kind in the country and the oldest in the state of Indiana. Established in 1882 as the South Bend Commercial College, the school later changed its name to Michiana College. In 1930, the school was incorporated under the laws of the state of Indiana and was authorized to confer associate degrees and certificates in business. The College relocated to East Jefferson Boulevard in 1987. In September 2009, Brown Mackie College–South Bend officially opened a new 46,000-square-foot facility at 3454 Douglas Road in South Bend, Indiana.

Brown Mackie College–South Bend is accredited by the Accrediting Council for Independent Colleges and Schools (ACICS) to award bachelor's degrees, associate degrees, diplomas, and certificates. ACICS is listed as a nationally recognized accrediting agency by the United States Department of Education and is recognized by the Council for Higher Education Accreditation. ACICS can be contacted at 750 First Street NE, Suite 980, Washington, D.C. 20002; phone: 202-336-6780.

Brown Mackie College–South Bend is regulated by the Indiana Commission on Proprietary Education, 302 West Washington Street, Indianapolis, Indiana 46204; phone: 317-232-1320 or 800-227-5695 (toll-free). (Indiana advertising code AC-0110.)

The Brown Mackie College–South Bend medical assisting Associate of Science degree program is accredited by the Commission on Accreditation of Allied Health Education Programs (www.caahep.org) upon the recommendation of the Curriculum Review Board of the American Association of Medical Assistants Endowment (AAMAE).

The occupational therapy assistant program is accredited by the Accreditation Council for Occupational Therapy Education (ACOTE) of the American Occupational Therapy Association (AOTA), located at 4720 Montgomery Lane, P.O. Box 31220, Bethesda, Maryland 20824-1220; phone: 301-652-2682.

The physical therapist assistant program at the South Bend location is accredited by the Commission on Accreditation in Physical Therapy Education (CAPTE) of the American Physical Therapy Association (APTA), 1111 North Fairfax Street, Alexandria, Virginia 22314; phone: 703-706-3241.

The practical nursing program is accredited by the Indiana State Board of Nursing, 402 West Washington Street, Room W066, Indianapolis, Indiana 46204; phone: 317-234-2043.

The College is a nonresidential, smoke-free institution.

Location

Brown Mackie College–South Bend is conveniently located at 3454 Douglas Road in South Bend, Indiana. The College has a generous parking area and is also easily accessible by public transportation.

Programs of Study and Degrees

Brown Mackie College–South Bend provides higher education to traditional and nontraditional students through bachelor's degree, associate degree, diploma, and certificate programs that assist in enhancing their career opportunities, broadening their perspectives through appropriate general education courses, thinking independently and critically, and improving problem-solving abilities.

The Bachelor of Science degree is awarded in business administration, criminal justice, healthcare management, and legal studies.

The Associate of Science degree is awarded in accounting technology, business management, computer software technology, criminal justice, health and therapeutic massage, healthcare administration, information technology, medical assisting, paralegal, and veterinary technology.

The Associate of Applied Science degree is awarded in occupational therapy assistant and physical therapist assistant.

The College offers a diploma program in practical nursing.

The College offers the following certificate programs: accounting, business, computer software applications, criminal justice, medical assistant, and paralegal assistant.

Academic Programs

Each College quarter comprises twelve weeks. Bachelor's degree programs require a minimum of sixteen quarters to complete. Associate degree programs require a minimum of eight quarters to complete. Programs are offered on a year-round basis, providing students with the ability to work uninterrupted toward completion of their programs. The College offers all programs in a unique One Course a Month format. This allows students to focus studies on only one course for four weeks. This schedule has proven convenient for students with multiple obligations such as jobs and family.

Academic Facilities

Brown Mackie College–South Bend's new location has a generous parking area and is easily accessible by public transportation. The College's smoke-free, three-story 46,000 square foot building offers a modern, professional environment for study. The facility offers "classrooms of the future," with instructor workstations and full multimedia capabilities that include surround sound and projection screens that can be accessed by computer, DVD, and VHS machines. The new facility includes medical, computer, and occupational and physical therapy labs, as well as a library and bookstore. The labs provide students with hands-on opportunities to apply knowledge and skills learned in the classroom. The veterinary technology lab is 2,600 square feet and includes surgery areas, treatment areas, and kennels.

Costs

Tuition for programs in the 2010–11 academic year was $285 per credit hour, with a $15 per credit hour general fee applied to instructional costs for activities and services. Textbooks and other instructional materials vary by program. Tuition for the practical nursing program was $350 per credit hour, with a $25 per credit hour general fee applied to instructional costs for activities and services. Tuition for the physical therapist assistant program was $350 per credit hour. Tuition for the occupational therapy assistant program was $350 per credit hour.

Financial Aid

Financial aid is available for those who qualify. The College maintains a full-time staff of financial aid professionals to assist qualified students in obtaining financial assistance. The College participates in several student aid programs. Forms of financial aid available through federal resources include the Federal Pell Grant Program, Federal Supplemental Educational Opportunity Grant (FSEOG) Program, Federal Work-Study Program, Federal Perkins Loan Program, Federal Stafford Student Loan Program (subsidized and unsubsidized), and the Federal PLUS Loan Program.

Eligible students may apply for Indiana state awards, such as the Frank O'Bannon Grant Program (formerly the Indiana Higher Education Grant) and Twenty-First Century Scholars Program for high school students, the Core 40 awards, and veterans' educational benefits. Students with physical or mental disabilities that are a handicap may be eligible for training services through the state's Bureau of Vocational Rehabilitation. For further information, students should contact the College Student Financial Services Office.

Each year, the College makes available President's Scholarships of $1000 each to qualifying seniors from area high schools. No more than one scholarship is awarded per high school. In order to qualify, a senior must be graduating from a participating high school, must be maintaining a cumulative grade point average of at least 2.0, and must submit a brief essay. The student's extracurricular activities and community service are also considered. The President's Scholarship is available only to students enrolling in one of the College's degree programs. Students awarded the scholarship must enroll at Brown Mackie College–South Bend between June and September immediately following their high school graduation. Applications for these scholarships can be obtained from the guidance departments of participating high schools. These applications must be completed and returned to the College by March 31.

Faculty

There are 29 full-time and 46 part-time faculty members at the College. The average student-faculty ratio is 12:1. Each student is assigned a program director as an adviser.

Admission Requirements

Each applicant for admission is assigned an Assistant Director of Admissions, who directs the applicant through the steps of the admissions process, providing information on curriculum, policies, procedures, and services; and assisting the applicant in setting necessary appointments and interviews. To qualify for admission, each applicant must provide documentation of graduation from an accredited high school or from a state-approved secondary education curriculum or provide official documentation of high school graduation equivalency. All transcripts become the property of the College.

Admission to the College is based on the applicant meeting the stated requirements, a review of the applicant's previous educational records, and a review of the applicant's career interests. If previous academic records indicate the College's education and training programs would not benefit the applicant, the College reserves the right to advise the applicant not to enroll. Special requirements for enrollment into certain programs are discussed in the descriptions of those programs.

In addition to the College's general admission requirements, applicants enrolling in the occupational therapy assistant (OTA) program must also meet some additional requirements. They must complete COMPASS assessment before the first course is scheduled to determine if transitional courses are needed (minimal scores: reading 75, writing 60, math 51). If minimum scores or better are attained on all three sections the student is scheduled in CF1000–Professional Development. If the student's scores are below the minimum on any of the sections, the student is advised that they will be placed in transitional course(s). After successful completion of all the required transitional courses, the student will have one opportunity to retake the COMPASS assessment and achieve the minimum score(s). If the student does not successfully obtain the minimum scores in all three sections on the second attempt, the student will not be allowed to continue in the OTA program, but can be considered for another program at Brown Mackie College.

In addition to the College's general admission requirements, applicants enrolling in the physical therapist assistant program must document the following: a minimum high school cumulative grade point average of 3.0 on a 4.0 scale or minimum score of 600 on the GED examination (if taken on or after January 15, 2002) or 60 (if taken before January 15, 2002); a minimum of 12 quarter-credit hours or 9 semester-credit hours of consecutive collegiate coursework with a minimum GPA of 3.0 on a 4.0 scale (may be completed at Brown Mackie College); a biology course in high school or college with a minimum grade of a B (3.0 on a 4.0 scale); and 20 hours (total) of documented observation, volunteer, or employment hours in at least two different physical therapy settings with no less than 8 hours in one setting completed within the past three years.

In addition to the College's general admission requirements, applicants enrolling in the practical nursing program must document the following: fulfillment of Brown Mackie College–South Bend general requirements; complete physical (must be current to within six months of admission); two-step Mantoux TB skin test (must be current throughout schooling); hepatitis B vaccination or signed refusal; up-to-date immunizations, including tetanus and rubella; record of current CPR certification (certification must be current throughout the clinical experience through health-care provider certification or the American Heart Association); and hospitalization insurance or a signed waiver.

For the most recent administration regarding admission requirements, please refer to the current academic catalog.

Application and Information

Applicants must complete and submit an application form, along with documentation of graduation from an accredited high school or state-approved secondary education curriculum or official documentation of high school graduation equivalency.

For additional information, prospective students should contact:

Director of Admissions
Brown Mackie College–South Bend
3454 Douglas Road
South Bend, Indiana 46635
Phone: 574-237-0774
      800-743-2447 (toll-free)
Fax: 574-237-3585
E-mail: bmcsbadm@brownmackie.edu
Web site: http://www.brownmackie.edu/SouthBend

BROWN MACKIE COLLEGE–TUCSON

TUCSON, ARIZONA

The College

Brown Mackie College–Tucson is one of over twenty-five locations in the Brown Mackie College system of schools (www.brownmackie.edu), which is dedicated to providing educational programs that prepare students to pursue entry-level positions in a competitive, rapidly changing workplace. Brown Mackie College schools offer bachelor's degree, associate degree, and diploma programs in health sciences, business, information technology, legal studies, and design to over 20,000 students in the Midwest, Southeast, Southwest, and Western United States.

Brown Mackie College was originally founded and approved by the Board of Trustees of Kansas Wesleyan College in Salina, Kansas on July 30, 1892. In 1938, the College was incorporated as The Brown Mackie School of Business under the ownership of Perry E. Brown and A. B. Mackie, former instructors at Kansas Wesleyan University in Salina, Kansas. Their last names formed the name of Brown Mackie. By January 1975, with improvements in curricula and higher degree-granting status, The Brown Mackie School of Business became Brown Mackie College.

Brown Mackie College entered the Arizona market in 2007 when it purchased a school that had been previously established in the Tucson area. That school had an established history in the community and was converted into what is now known as Brown Mackie College–Tucson. The historical timeline of Brown Mackie College–Tucson started in 1972 when Rockland West Corporation first formed a partnership with Lamson Business College. At that time the school was a career college that offered only short-term programs focusing on computer training and secretarial skills. In 1994 the College became accredited as a junior college and began offering associate degrees in academic subjects. The mission was then modified to include the goal of instilling in graduates an appreciation for lifelong learning through the general education courses that became a part of every program.

In 1996 the College applied for and received status as a senior college by the Accrediting Commission of Independent Colleges and Schools. This gave the school the ability to offer course work leading to a Bachelor of Science degree in business administration. Since then the program offerings for bachelor's and associate degrees have expanded.

In 1986, the campus moved from 5001 East Speedway to the 4585 East Speedway location where it remains today. In 2008, two of the College's three buildings were remodeled which resulted in updated classrooms; networked computer laboratories; new medical, surgical technology ,and forensics laboratories; a larger library and offices for student services such as academics, admissions, and student financial services; and a full-service college store. In 2009, the third building was remodeled and provides newer classrooms and a new career services department.

Brown Mackie College–Tucson, Arizona is accredited by the Accrediting Council for Independent Colleges and Schools (ACICS) to award bachelor's degrees, associate degrees, and certificates. The Accrediting Council for Independent Colleges and Schools is listed as a nationally recognized accrediting agency by the United States Department of Education and is recognized by the Council for Higher Education Accreditation. ACICS can be contacted at 750 First Street NE, Suite 980, Washington, D.C. 20002; phone: 202-336-6780.

This institution is licensed by the Arizona State Board for Private Postsecondary Education, 1400 West Washington Street, Room 2560, Phoenix, Arizona 85007; phone: 620-542-5709.

The occupational therapy assistant program is accredited by the Accreditation Council for Occupational Therapy Education (ACOTE) of the American Occupational Therapy Association (AOTA), located at 4720 Montgomery Lane, P.O. Box 31220, Bethesda, Maryland 20824; phone: 301-652-AOTA.

The surgical technology program is accredited by the Accrediting Bureau of Health Education Schools (ABHES).

Location

Brown Mackie College–Tucson is conveniently located at 4585 East Speedway Boulevard in Tucson, Arizona. The College has a generous parking area and is also easily accessible by public transportation.

Programs of Study and Degrees

Brown Mackie College–Tucson provides higher education to traditional and nontraditional students through bachelor's degree, associate degree, and diploma programs that assist in enhancing their career opportunities, broadening their perspectives through appropriate general education courses, thinking independently and critically, and improving problem-solving abilities. The College strives to develop within its students the desire for lifelong and continued education.

The Bachelor of Science degree is awarded in accounting, business administration, criminal justice, healthcare management, information technology, and legal studies.

The Associate of Science degree is awarded in accounting technology, business management, computer networking and security, criminal justice, early childhood education, graphic design, healthcare administration, information technology, medical assisting, paralegal, and surgical technology.

The Associate of Applied Science degree is awarded in biomedical equipment technology, health and fitness training, and occupational therapy assistant.

A diploma is awarded in the fitness trainer program.

Academic Programs

Each College quarter comprises twelve weeks. Bachelor's degree programs require a minimum of sixteen quarters to complete. Associate degree programs require a minimum of eight quarters to complete. Programs are offered on a year-round basis, providing students with the ability to work uninterrupted toward their degrees. The College offers all programs in a unique One Course a Month format. This allows students to focus studies on only one course for four weeks. This schedule has proven convenient for students with multiple obligations such as jobs and family.

Academic Facilities

A modern facility, Brown Mackie College–Tucson offers more than 31,000 square feet. The College is equipped with multiple computer labs housing over 200 computers. High-speed access to the Internet and other online resources are available for students and faculty. Multimedia classrooms are outfitted with overhead projectors, VCR/DVD players, and computers. The campus is nonresidential; public transportation and parking at no cost are available.

Costs

Tuition in the 2010–11 academic year for most bachelor's, associate, and diploma programs was $315 per credit hour; fees were $15 per credit hour. Tuition for the surgical technology program was $330 per credit hour; fees were $15 per credit hour. Tuition for the occupational therapy assistant program was $350 per credit hour; fees were $15 per credit hour. Textbook and other instructional expenses vary by program.

Financial Aid

Financial aid is available for those who qualify. The College maintains a full-time staff of financial aid professionals to assist qualified students in obtaining the financial assistance they require to meet their educational expenses. Available resources include federal and state aid, student loans from private lenders, and Federal Work-Study opportunities, both on and off college premises.

Each year, the College makes available scholarships of $1000 each to qualifying seniors from area high schools. No more than one scholarship is awarded per high school. In order to qualify, a senior must be graduating from a participating high school, must be maintaining a cumulative grade point average of at least 2.0, and must submit a brief essay. The student's extracurricular activities and community service are also considered. These scholarships are available only to students enrolling in one of the College's degree programs. Students awarded the scholarship must enroll at Brown Mackie College—Tucson between June and September immediately following their high school graduation. Applications for these scholarships can be obtained from the guidance departments of participating high schools. These applications must be completed and returned to the College by March 31.

Faculty

Experienced faculty members provide academic support and are committed to the academic and technical preparation of their students. The College has 15 full-time and 35 part-time instructors, with a student-faculty ratio of 12:1. Each student is assigned a faculty adviser.

Admission Requirements

Each applicant for admission is assigned an Assistant Director of Admissions who directs the applicant through the steps of the admissions process. They provide information on curriculum, policies, procedures, and services and assist the applicant in setting necessary appointments and interviews. To qualify for admission, each applicant must provide documentation of graduation from an accredited high school or from a state-approved secondary education curriculum or provide official documentation of high school graduation equivalency. All transcripts become the property of the College. Admission to the College is based on the applicant meeting the stated requirements, a review of the applicant's previous educational records, and a review of the applicant's career interests. If previous academic records indicate the College's education and training programs would not benefit the applicant, the College reserves the right to advise the applicant not to enroll. Special requirements for enrollment into certain programs are discussed in the descriptions of those programs.

For the most recent information regarding admission requirements, please refer to the current academic catalog.

Application and Information

Applicants must complete and submit an application form, along with documentation of graduation from an accredited high school or state-approved secondary education curriculum or official documentation of high school graduation equivalency.

For additional information, prospective students should contact:

Senior Director of Admissions
Brown Mackie College–Tucson
4585 East Speedway Boulevard, Suite 204
Tucson, Arizona 85712
Phone: 520-319-3300
Fax: 520-325-0108
E-mail: bmctuadm@brownmackie.edu
Web site: http://www.brownmackie.edu/Tucson

BRYN MAWR COLLEGE
BRYN MAWR, PENNSYLVANIA

BRYN MAWR

The College

Bryn Mawr women share an intense intellectual commitment, a purposeful vision of their lives, and a common desire to make a meaningful contribution to the world.

Every year 1,300 undergraduate women and 400 graduate students from around the world gather on the College's historic campus to study with leading scholars, conduct advanced research, and expand the boundaries of what's possible.

The undergraduate college is known as one of the most academically rigorous liberal arts colleges in the nation and consistently ranks among the top feeder schools to the world's premier graduate programs and professional schools.

Bryn Mawr's Katherine Houghton Hepburn Center, Office of Civic Engagement, and the Praxis Program, which integrates fieldwork with theoretical study, provide students with extensive opportunities for internships in Philadelphia, where they may apply knowledge far beyond the classroom. Many students pursue independent and interdepartmental majors with faculty permission. Joint academic programs also exist with Haverford, Swarthmore, and the University of Pennsylvania.

Through advanced research projects, summer internships, and collaborative research with faculty members, students are involved in the local, national, and global communities.

Bryn Mawr's prestigious alumnae include the first woman to be president of Harvard University, one of the first women to receive the Nobel Peace Prize, the first woman neurosurgeon, and the first and only woman to receive four Academy Awards.

Diversity is central to Bryn Mawr's mission as an extraordinary liberal arts college, improving the academic experience and enriching the campus community. Students of color and international students make up nearly 40 percent of the undergraduate enrollment. Bryn Mawr's student body is composed of women from forty-seven states and sixty-two other countries.

Above all else, Bryn Mawr women share a tremendous respect for individual differences, not merely a passive tolerance of other lifestyles and points of view. The result is a community that resounds with the energy, healthy friction, and range of perspectives that can only come from true cultural and ideological diversity.

The diversity that Bryn Mawr students experience, in and out of the classroom, helps prepare them to be confident global citizens and leaders.

Bryn Mawr women share a commitment to a community that is based on inclusion and support, reinforced by the College's Honor Code, a set of principles stressing personal integrity and mutual respect. In the words of one graduating senior, "This is a place where being yourself makes you feel part of something larger than yourself. A strong sense of self is what we all have in common."

Bryn Mawr is a charter member of the Centennial Conference and is home to twelve NCAA varsity athletic teams. Students may compete in badminton, basketball, crew, cross-country, field hockey, lacrosse, soccer, swimming, tennis, indoor track and field, outdoor track and field, and volleyball. The newly-renovated Bern Schwartz Fitness and Athletic Center offers enhanced spaces for training, fitness, and aquatics.

Renovation and improvement of Goodhart Hall was completed in the fall of 2009, with major upgrades to accommodate student interest in performing arts.

Bryn Mawr students participate in more than 100 active student organizations. The tricollege community of Haverford, Swarthmore, and Bryn Mawr Colleges also sponsors many student groups and activities.

Location

Students at Bryn Mawr have the best of it all in terms of location. The campus itself is such a picture-perfect example of Collegiate Gothic that it has been used as the backdrop for many motion pictures. A quick 5-minute walk into the suburban town of Bryn Mawr finds an eclectic mix of funky independent and favorite franchise coffee shops, eateries, and retailers; an historic movie theater; and a commuter train that can take students to the heart of Philadelphia in less than 20 minutes.

Philadelphia has a bustling arts scene and nightlife and is home to more than 250,000 college students. Bryn Mawr women enjoy a rich academic and social life on their own campus and at neighboring tricollege partners, Haverford and Swarthmore Colleges, as well as the University of Pennsylvania.

Bryn Mawr's relationship with Haverford College is particularly close and students participate in many bicollege extracurricular activities, including the orchestra, the chorus, the drama program, and a bicollege newspaper. A 20-minute walk or a 5-minute ride on the bicollege Blue Bus brings students from one campus to the other.

Almost all students live on campus in one of thirteen main residence halls. Two of the buildings are listed on the National Register of Historic Places, and one is also a National Historic Landmark. Several residence halls house students with shared interests in topics including sustainability and foreign languages and cultures.

Majors and Degrees

Bryn Mawr College grants the Bachelor of Arts (A.B.) degree with majors, minors, and concentrations in more than forty areas: Africana studies, anthropology, astronomy, biology, chemistry, classical and Near Eastern archaeology, classical languages, classical studies, comparative literature, computational methods, computer science, creative writing, dance, East Asian studies, economics, education, English, environmental studies, film studies, fine arts, French and French studies, gender and sexuality, geology, German and German studies, Greek, growth and structure of cities, Hebrew and Judaic studies, history, history of art, international studies, Italian, Latin, Latin American, Latino and Iberian people and cultures, linguistics, mathematics, Middle East studies, music, neural and behavioral sciences, peace and conflict studies, philosophy, physics, political science, psychology, religion, Romance languages, Russian, sociology, Spanish, and theater and theater studies.

There are nearly 3,000 course exchanges between Bryn Mawr and Haverford each year, selected from a jointly published course list. Bryn Mawr students may major in any of Haverford's coordinate departments or in astronomy, classics, music, or religion while earning a Bachelor of Arts degree from Bryn Mawr. A new major in linguistics offered through Swarthmore College is also available. Finally, Haverford, Swarthmore, and Bryn Mawr have joined together to form the Middle East Studies program.

Academic Programs

The Bryn Mawr curriculum is designed to encourage breadth of learning and training in the fundamentals of scholarship. At some point during their first three years at Bryn Mawr, students are required to complete Approaches to Inquiry, a curriculum designed to introduce possibilities and problems in scientific investigation, critical interpretation, cross-cultural analysis, and inquiry into the past. Many options are available to fulfill these requirements and students are encouraged to explore. Innovative curricular options include the Growth and Structure of Cities program; the Middle East Studies program; 360°, an in-depth, semester-long, multidisciplinary, cohort-based approach to a problem or discovery; and Quarter Courses, demanding, half-semester courses that may ignite a new intellectual passion. Mature, sophisticated, in-depth study in a major program during the last two years is designed to prepare students for the lifelong pleasure and responsibility of educating themselves and playing an active role in contemporary society. The curriculum encourages independence within a rigorous but flexible framework. Each student chooses and plans her major in consultation with her dean and faculty adviser. Some students take advantage of this freedom to design an independent major, while others fashion their own intellectual perspectives by enrolling in courses that span academic fields or assisting with a faculty member's research project.

With certain restrictions, full-time Bryn Mawr students may also take courses at Swarthmore College, the University of Pennsylvania, and Villanova University during the academic year without paying additional fees.

Off-Campus Programs

Bryn Mawr is only 20 minutes by car or seven short stops by train from the vast cultural and professional resources of Philadelphia, the nation's sixth-largest city. Philadelphia is an incredible resource for Bryn Mawr—a truly accessible city, rich with cultural and professional opportunities, including the Philadelphia Museum of Art, the Philadelphia Orchestra, the Pennsylvania Ballet, numerous theaters, professional sports teams, and some of the nation's most important historic sites, as well as internship opportunities in Center City law firms, art galleries, government agencies, hospitals, TV studios, banks, and schools. When Philadelphia seems too small, 1 in 3 Bryn Mawr students participate in one of more than seventy study-abroad programs from Stockholm to South Africa.

Academic Facilities

Bryn Mawr ranks among the top 10 of all U.S. colleges and universities in the percentage of graduates going on to earn a Ph.D. Bryn Mawr students have unlimited access to libraries and laboratories equal to those of many graduate programs, allowing students to pursue independent research at a level unavailable at most undergraduate institutions. These resources include an extensive array of laboratory equipment for the study of science, such as a robotics lab, laser with rangefinder, DNA analyzers, and a geological subsurface profiling system. More than 1 million volumes in a network of open-stack libraries are available to Bryn Mawr students, as well as access to the libraries of both Haverford and Swarthmore Colleges via the Tripod Library System.

In addition, the College has recently enhanced several of its buildings to support student inquiry in all of the liberal arts, including a $19-million renovation of the Marjorie Goodhart Theater which consists of a new state-of-the-art theater, practice rooms, a teaching theater, and scene shop; the upgrade of Dalton Hall, home to Bryn Mawr's social science labs and classrooms; and Bettws-y-Coed, a center for the study of psychology complete with new labs, faculty offices, and meeting rooms. Four former faculty residences have also been renovated to house the student activities village, Cambrian Row.

Costs

In 2011–12, Bryn Mawr tuition, room and board, and fees totaled $53,714.

Financial Aid

To apply for financial aid, students must submit the Free Application for Federal Student Aid (FAFSA), the College Scholarship Service (CSS) PROFILE form, and if applicable, the CSS Noncustodial Parent PROFILE. The College also requires a signed copy of the custodial and noncustodial parents' and student's most recent federal income tax returns, including W-2 forms, and all schedules and attachments. Tax returns must be submitted to The College Board's Institutional Documentation Service (IDOC). Applicants who are not citizens of the U.S. may file the (CSS) PROFILE or may instead submit the International Student Financial Aid Application directly to the Financial Aid Office. Non–U.S. citizens must also submit letters (in English) from their parents' employers stating gross income and the value of any perquisites, subsidies, and benefits directly to the Financial Aid Office. Prospective freshmen are notified of the admission and financial aid decisions at the same time.

Faculty

The Bryn Mawr faculty has 158 full-time members, of whom 49 percent are women and 15 percent are professors of color. The College's student-faculty ratio is 8:1. Few colleges or universities can genuinely claim the intellectual curiosity, intensity, and passion found at Bryn Mawr. Classes are small (many have fewer than 15 students), and faculty members come to know their students as individuals. That means more than just being on a first-name basis. In fact, Bryn Mawr

faculty members, world-renowned leaders in their fields, regard their students as junior colleagues, fully capable of working at a high level, developing their own ideas, and making important contributions. It is in this way that, perhaps more than at any other school, Bryn Mawr feels like a graduate school on an undergraduate level.

Student Government

Bryn Mawr's culture of innovative leadership dates back to 1892 and the founding of the Student Self-Government Association (SGA), the oldest undergraduate governing body in the country. SGA gives Bryn Mawr students the responsibility of running many campus organizations and activities and participating in discussion and resolution of important issues, such as curriculum and faculty appointments.

Admission Requirements

Every year, Bryn Mawr receives many more outstanding applications for admission than can be admitted into the first-year class of about 360 students. As members of the Common Application, Bryn Mawr practices holistic review, with admission decisions based on a number of factors. Strength of the applicant's high school curriculum within the context of the high school and academic performance are of significant importance. Other factors considered are a student's writing, recommendations from the high school counselor and academic teachers, testing, involvement in school and community, and diverse or unique perspectives and talents a student might bring to the Bryn Mawr community.

Basic high school academic requirements include 4 years of English, 3 years of mathematics, at least 1 year each of a laboratory science and history, and a solid foundation in at least one foreign language. However, most applicants are well prepared for the academic rigor of Bryn Mawr and have taken at least three lab science courses as well as mathematics courses that include trigonometry.

Bryn Mawr has adopted a test-flexible admissions policy which allows students to submit a combination of the SAT, SAT Subject Tests, the ACT, and AP exam scores. Complete details on the test-flexible policy may be found on the Bryn Mawr Web site. For tests scores to be considered in the application process, tests must be taken by November of the senior year for early decision applicants and January for regular decision applicants.

An interview, either at the College or with a local alumnae representative, is also strongly recommended.

Bryn Mawr exclusively accepts the Common Application and waives the $50 application fee when students apply online. Application forms should be submitted by November 15 for fall early decision applicants, by January 1 for winter early decision applicants, and by January 15 for regular decision applicants.

Transfer students must complete a minimum of two years of work at Bryn Mawr to qualify for the A.B. degree.

Application and Information

The Admissions Office is open from 9 a.m. to 5 p.m. on weekdays and, some Saturdays throughout the year. Please visit the College Web site http://www.brynmawr.edu/admissions/ to plan a visit. Bryn Mawr accepts the Common Application, which can be found online (http://www.commonapplication.org). For further information, an application form, or the name of a local alumnae representative, prospective students should contact:

Bryn Mawr College Office of Admissions
101 North Merion Avenue
Bryn Mawr, Pennsylvania 19010-2899

Phone: 610-526-5152
Fax: 610-526-7471
E-mail: admissions@brynmawr.edu
Web site: http://www.brynmawr.edu
　　　　 http://www.brynmawr.edu/admissions/
　　　　 http://www.facebook.com/BrynMawrCollege
　　　　 http://twitter.com/BrynMawrCollege

BUCKNELL UNIVERSITY
LEWISBURG, PENNSYLVANIA

The University

Bucknell University offers a personalized and comprehensive liberal arts education to exceptionally talented students from across the U.S. and around the world. With academic programs in the arts, engineering, humanities, management, and social and natural sciences, and broad opportunities outside of class, Bucknell is a place that prepares students for success in an increasingly complex and interconnected global society.

Bucknell's 3,500 undergraduates can choose from more than fifty majors and sixty minors. Opportunities abound—students build robots, write and perform in their own plays, or debate solutions to the crisis in Sudan; engineers make art; artists analyze DNA; and philosophers make music. Each student chooses his or her own pathway, but what unites everyone is a shared passion for learning and a desire to achieve deeper levels of understanding about life and the world.

Bucknell's faculty creates an environment of free-flowing ideas and stimulating discussions. Professors teach every class, getting to know students personally and challenging them to do their best. The professors are also dedicated scholars who frequently receive awards and grants for their work. Often, they engage students in research and creative projects outside of class. By doing so, they provide students with mentorship and guidance for the future.

Outside of class, students participate in myriad activities. Bucknell offers Division I athletics along with intramural and club sports, Greek life, and more than 150 student-run clubs and organizations. These organizations focus on anything from social and environmental causes to cultural awareness, poetry slams, volunteering and service, or politics. Students can enrich their religious and spiritual lives through multiple University and student-led faith organizations.

The University is a residential campus, requiring nearly all of its undergraduates to live on campus. Living on campus does not, however, mean students are isolated from the "real" world—quite the opposite is true. Visiting scholars and speakers come to Bucknell nearly every week, and much of the curriculum focuses on cultures, societies, and economies around the globe. Learning happens off campus, too. Students frequently perform service work in places as close as the local nursing home and as far away as Nicaragua or Uganda. They secure summer internships with nonprofit organizations and corporations. They study abroad through one of University's own "in" programs or 130 other approved programs in Africa, Asia, Europe, and South America. And after they graduate, they live and work all over the world.

Alumni of Bucknell succeed in their careers because they offer a combination of skills, knowledge, and flexibility of mind that employers seek. To prepare students, the University offers career services including advising, networking, mock interviews, internship and externship support, and employer fairs to students throughout their four years at Bucknell. The placement rate is consistently high: 95 percent of the class of 2009 was employed, in graduate school, traveling, or volunteering within nine months of graduation. In 2011, PayScale Inc. included Bucknell on its list of colleges whose graduates earn the highest paychecks.

Location

With its green spaces, red brick buildings, and striking vistas, Bucknell's campus is a quintessential college environment in the heart of scenic central Pennsylvania. The shops of historic downtown Lewisburg, including the new Barnes & Noble at Bucknell University bookstore, lie within walking distance of campus. The University is located within a 3- to 4-hours' drive of most of the major Eastern cities, including New York City; Washington, D.C.; Philadelphia; and Pittsburgh.

Majors and Degrees

Bucknell provides students with a choice of more than fifty majors in a variety of liberal arts and professional fields. Bachelor of Arts degrees are available in animal behavior, anthropology, art, art history, biology, chemistry, classics (Greek or Latin concentrations),

comparative humanities, computer science, East Asian studies (China or Japan concentrations), economics, education, English (creative writing or film/media studies concentrations), environmental geology, environmental studies, French, geography, geology, German, history, international relations (Africa, Europe, East Asia, Latin America, Middle East, North America, or Russia concentrations), Latin American studies, mathematics (general, pure mathematics, or statistics concentrations), music, philosophy, physics, political science, psychology, religion, Russian, sociology (general, human services, or legal studies concentrations), Spanish, theater, and women's and gender studies.

The music program offers a Bachelor of Music degree with majors in music composition, music education, music history, and performance.

Bachelor of Science degrees are available in animal behavior, biology, cell biology and biochemistry, chemistry, computer science, engineering (in the disciplines of biomedical, chemical, civil, computer, electrical, and mechanical engineering as well as a degree in computer science and engineering), environmental geology, environmental studies, geology, interdisciplinary studies in economics and mathematics, mathematics (general, pure mathematics, or statistics concentrations), neuroscience, and physics.

Bachelor of Science in Business Administration degrees are available in four new majors: accounting and financial management; global management; managing for sustainability; and markets, innovation, and design.

Bachelor of Science in Education degrees are available in early childhood development and elementary education.

In consultation with an academic adviser, students also may design their own major based around their individualized educational goals. Select engineering students also have the option of completing one of two five-year interdisciplinary programs; these programs lead to a B.S. in an engineering field and either a B.A. in another discipline or a specially designed Bachelor of Management for Engineers degree.

Academic Programs

Requirements for each degree program vary, but all students are required to complete three writing courses. Special programs are offered to encourage each student's personal and intellectual development. Examples include the first-year foundation seminars, an introductory engineering course open to students in the College of Arts and Sciences, and Bucknell's Residential College living-learning community program. These living-learning communities are theme-based options for first-year students that combine classroom and out-of-class activities into a living and learning experience. The themes are the arts, environmental issues, global affairs, humanities, languages and cultures, social justice, and society and technology.

Off-Campus Programs

Bucknell University's Office of International Education offers one of the largest study-abroad programs available at an undergraduate liberal arts institution. More than 45 percent of Bucknell's students study abroad for a year, a semester, and/or a summer. Bucknell sponsors four of its own semester-long "Bucknell In" programs: Bucknell in Barbados, Bucknell in London, Bucknell en France, and Bucknell en España. During the summer, the University offers "Bucknell In" programs in Barbados, Northern Ireland, Nicaragua, and the Virgin Islands.

In addition to Bucknell-run programs, the University is affiliated with 130 other programs worldwide. Shorter-term service and learning programs are also available, along with internship programs in Philadelphia or Washington, D.C. Financial aid, grants, and scholarships apply toward study abroad.

Academic Facilities

Bucknell's 450-acre campus includes facilities for art, engineering, music, the sciences, theater, and dance and a 1,200-seat performance hall. Bertrand Library holds 833,000 volumes, provides access to more than 26,000 periodicals, and offers thousands of audiovisual materials. Computer labs are available across campus, and most of campus is wireless-accessible. Classrooms are equipped with projectors and computers, some with computers for each student. All student residences are connected to the residential network, featuring a high-speed data connection for each student. Science and engineering programs have sophisticated instrumentation available for student use.

Costs

The cost of tuition and fees for 2010–11 was $52,280, including $42,112 for tuition, $9938 for room and board, and $230 for student fees.

Financial Aid

About 50 percent of students receive financial aid from the University, and 62 percent receive financial aid of some form, including need-based scholarships, loans, work-study, and a limited amount of merit scholarships. In 2010–11, Bucknell budgeted over $42 million toward scholarship aid for undergraduates. Another $16 million was awarded in student loans, $3 million in work-study, and $2.5 million in federal and state grants. The average total financial aid package in the fall of 2010 for first-year students with financial need was about $25,500. The average student loan debt upon graduation is about $20,000.

Arts merit scholarships are available in the areas of art and art history, creative writing, dance, music, and theater (design and technology, performance).

If prospective students and their families believe they will need financial aid, they must file the Financial Aid PROFILE with the College Scholarship Service before January 15.

Faculty

Bucknell has more than 330 full-time faculty members; 97 percent of them hold doctorates or appropriate terminal degrees. The student-faculty ratio is 10:1.

Bucknell's professors uphold the teacher-scholar ideal, through which they are committed to providing an excellent undergraduate education and also actively pursuing their scholarly work. Many students collaborate with faculty members in research, and projects regularly lead to joint publications or presentations at professional meetings.

Student Government

The Bucknell Student Government serves as the official voice of Bucknell's students. It dispenses funds for most student clubs and organizations, and its representatives serve on standing committees of the Board of Trustees and other University governance groups.

Admission Requirements

Admission decisions focus on intellectual ability; quality of preparation as demonstrated by achievement in rigorous high school courses and SAT or ACT scores; special talent; significant contribution to school or community; and evidence of strong character and integrity. Well-written essays weigh heavily in the admissions process. The University seeks qualified students from all backgrounds throughout the United States and abroad.

Application and Information

Regular Decision applications should be filed before January 15 of the senior year in high school for notification by April 1. SAT and/or ACT results must be submitted before March 1. Early Decision candidates may apply for Early Decision–Round One consideration by November 15 or Early Decision–Round Two consideration by January 15. Applications for transfer students should be submitted by March 15 for studies beginning the following fall and by November 1 for the spring semester.

Robert G. Springall
Dean of Admissions
Bucknell University
Lewisburg, Pennsylvania 17837
Phone: 570-577-1101
Fax: 570-577-3538
E-mail: admissions@bucknell.edu
Web site: http://www.bucknell.edu
    www.facebook.com/BucknellU
    www.facebook.com/BucknellAdmissions

The Academic Quad is the hub of campus, where students and faculty members greet each other between classes and soak up the sun on warm days. The tower of Bertrand Library is both a landmark and a symbol of University life.

BURLINGTON COLLEGE
BURLINGTON, VERMONT

The College

Founded in 1972, Burlington College is a small progressive private College in the heart of Burlington, Vermont. The 32-acre campus overlooks Lake Champlain and the Adirondack Mountains.

Burlington College is accredited by the New England Association of Schools and Colleges (NEASC) to offer undergraduate and graduate degrees. The following information applies to the College undergraduate program only.

A unique college experience—Burlington College invites students to be partners in planning their academic career. Students are encouraged to take courses in a variety of subjects and develop their own vision. Working in small discussion-centered classes of between 6 and 15 members, students come to know each other and themselves well. Lead by knowledgeable and dedicated faculty, these stimulating classes can take on lives of their own as students make contributions to the discussions, and instructors, at times, become equal observer-learners in the process.

An integral part of Burlington College's progressive education is the collaboration between students and instructors, setting the goals and expectations for the semester. During evaluation week, both students and instructors provide written evaluations of progress made toward the agreed upon goals. Thus, the evaluation period becomes a time for reflection on what a student has learned and what they need to do moving forward to achieve their larger goals.

Location

Just a short walk from campus is Burlington's famous Church Street, a pedestrian mall with numerous outdoor cafes, eateries, coffee shops, and a Ben & Jerry's Ice Cream scoop shop.

Students can enjoy the things that have won Burlington the title of "Most Livable City in America." There is a wide array of festivals including the South End Art Hop, the Vermont International Film Festival, the Discover Jazz Festival, the Festival of Fools, and Winter Festival just to name a few. The music scene is vibrant with many local performance venues: Higher Ground, Champlain Valley Expo, the Flynn Center, Red Square and Nectar's—where the band Phish got its start.

The options are limitless when it comes to how one can enjoy Vermont's extraordinary outdoors. Burlington College is just 45 minutes from the snowy slopes where the founder of Burton Snowboards, Jake Burton Carpenter, invented the snowboard and perfected his ride.

During the warmer months, students can stroll down to the College's sandy beach and swim in Lake Champlain or hop on the bike path that passes through the campus and runs along the shoreline. For adventurous spirits, the Green Mountain state offers an abundance of outdoor activities, such as hiking the Long Trail, scuba diving at shipwrecks, and some of the best wind-surfing in the northeast.

Burlington College is 2 hours south of Montreal, 4 hours northwest of Boston, and about 5½ hours from New York City.

Majors and Degrees

Burlington College provides a rare opportunity for students to self-design their major in the Individualized Studies program. This allows for interdisciplinary studies and enables students to explore their areas of interests more freely.

A Bachelor of Fine Arts degree is offered in craftsmanship and design, cinema studies and film production, graphic design, and photography.

A Bachelor of Arts is offered in fine arts, photography, cinema studies and film production, documentary studies, expressive arts, human services, individualized major, integral psychology, inter-American studies, international relations and diplomacy, legal and justice studies, media activism, psychology, transpersonal psychology, and writing and literature.

An Associate of Arts degree is offered in craftsmanship and design, film studies, and liberal studies. The College has certificate programs in Cuban studies (with a semester of study in Cuba), documentary filmmaking, film production, paralegal studies, screenwriting, peace-building and woodworking and fine-furniture making, as well as an advanced certificate in fine-furniture making.

Other opportunities for course work are available through the three-college consortium with Champlain College and St. Michael's College and the College's partnership with Vermont Law School.

Academic Programs

Burlington College's founders intended to create an undergraduate institution firmly rooted in a concern for, and interaction with, the greater Burlington community. The College continues to offer rich and diverse opportunities for its students to participate in arts-related events, the natural environment, and civic and humanitarian projects. The College's mission gives direction to a program of education that addresses learners as individuals and helps them increase their awareness, knowledge, and competence. Students are actively engaged in the planning and implementation of their education in an atmosphere of open communication and shared responsibility.

Off-Campus Programs

Burlington College Distance Learning is a mode of instruction that meets the needs of students who want to earn their bachelor's degree in courses outside the typical classroom environment. This personalized program offers flexibility for creative, self-directed, and mature individuals. Applicants must be experienced students who have already earned at least 30 college credits from one or more accredited college programs. Once accepted, students are assigned an academic adviser who assists with the planning and development of their major. In addition to online classes, individual instructors are selected to work with each student on a semester-to-semester basis.

Distance-learning students must attend at least one residency at the College per year. These residencies take place biannually over a long weekend at the start of the fall and spring semesters. During the residency, students meet with their adviser, faculty members, and College staff. Distance-learning students are encouraged and expected to connect with the on-campus community. They are invited to attend seminars, courses, workshops, and events.

Academic Facilities

Burlington College is committed to providing students with resources they need throughout their educational journey and has many academic resources on campus. The city of Burlington has much to offer when it comes to the arts, museums, community organizations, and educational resources. Much like its classrooms, which break through conventional boundaries and extend into the community itself, Burlington College regularly reaches out to the community for resources for its students' individualized studies. On-campus resources include event spaces, a library, galleries, lounges, and a café. In addition, students have access to several local resources, such as the University of Vermont's lending library and the local YMCA.

Costs

For the 2011–12 academic year, full-time tuition (12–15 credits per semester) is $ 22,410 per year/$11,205 per semester. For more than 15 credits, $740 is charged per additional credit. Three-quarter-time tuition (9–11 credits per semester) costs $17,100 per year/$8550 per semester, and half-time tuition (6–8 credits per semester) costs $11,600 per year/$5800 per semester. The per credit charge for less than half time (up to 5 credits) is $740 per credit.

Costs for housing are as follows: single-occupancy bedroom—$7450; double-occupancy bedroom—$6670; triple-occupancy bedroom—$6300; and premium bedroom—$7980.

Occasionally, courses and other learning activities may have additional charges. Students should see the course descriptions for any exceptions. All charges are subject to change without notice.

Financial Aid

The Financial Aid Office is available to assist students in navigating the variety of financial aid programs offered. Burlington College is a Yellow Ribbon School and works with veterans to maximize the benefits and minimize out-of-pocket expenses. Prospective students may contact the Financial Aid Office for more information at 800-862-9616 (toll-free).

Faculty

Burlington College students cite the small class sizes, personal attention, and academic freedom as their reason for selecting the College. The student body is under 200 students, and the faculty ratio is about 6 to 1.

Student Government

The student government meets with the College President to exchange ideas, share information, and address concerns. Members organize some of the student activities on campus.

The Student Judiciary Board is a panel made up of students, faculty members, and advisers. They determine sanctions when there is a serious infraction by a student of policies detailed in the student handbook.

Admission Requirements

Burlington College seeks students who are independent thinkers and share a commitment to collaborative learning. Burlington College's application process is highly personalized and holistic. Students must have a minimum of a high school diploma or GED in order to apply. The College selects students by reviewing their admission essay, academic track record, letters of recommendation, as well as through meaningful communication between the student and the Admissions Office.

Application and Information

Burlington College accepts applications on a rolling basis. This means that an application is evaluated and a decision is made within two weeks of the application being received. Freshman and transfer applicants are considered for both the fall and spring semesters. In some cases, summer start dates may be an option. There is no official deadline for the submission of applications. However, scholarships, College financial aid, and spaces in each class are limited, so students are encouraged to apply by May 1 for the fall semester and December 15 for the spring semester. An application for admission is required of anyone who wishes to matriculate and enroll in a program of study leading to an academic degree or certificate.

Admissions Office
Burlington College
351 North Avenue
Burlington, Vermont 05401

Phone: 800-862-9616 (toll-free)
E-mail: admissions@burlington.edu
Web site: http://www.burlington.edu/

Students enjoying campus life at Burlington College in Vermont.

BUTLER UNIVERSITY
INDIANAPOLIS, INDIANA

The University

Butler University has a proud tradition of excellence and innovation. Challenging and enabling students to meet their personal and professional goals has guided the University since 1855. Today, Butler is a nationally recognized comprehensive university with a total undergraduate enrollment of more than 4,050 students. Butler is accredited by the Higher Learning Commission of the North Central Association of Colleges and Schools.

Butler students represent almost every state in the nation and fifty countries, reflecting a diversity of cultures, interests, aspirations, personalities, and experiences. Students can choose from a number of housing options, including an upperclass residential apartment village, an apartment-style residence hall, one all-women residence hall with an optional living-learning center, two coeducational residence halls with optional living-learning centers, fraternities, and sororities. A health and recreation complex is equipped with recreation courts, an indoor jogging track, an aquatics area, a weight and fitness space, a lounge, and a juice bar.

There are more than 140 official student organizations, fourteen Greek organizations, and nineteen Division I varsity athletic teams. Students take advantage of Broadway shows at Butler's Clowes Memorial Hall, the city's premier performing arts center. Basketball fans cheer on the Bulldogs at the 10,000-seat historic Hinkle Fieldhouse, where the final game in the movie *Hoosiers* was filmed.

Graduate degrees include accounting, business administration, creative writing, dance, education administration (EPPSP), effective teaching and leadership, English, history, music conducting, music composition, music education, music history, music theory, music performance, piano pedagogy, pharmaceutical science, physician assistant studies, and school counseling. In addition, Butler offers a doctor of pharmacy (Pharm.D.) program. A dual Pharm.D./M.B.A. program allows pharmacy students to develop management skills and entrepreneurial capabilities in conjunction with pharmacy experience while earning both a Pharm.D. and an M.B.A. in six years.

Location

Butler University is located on 290 acres of Indianapolis' historic Butler-Tarkington neighborhood, which is also home to Indiana's governor. Most of the University's full-time students live on campus and enjoy a nature preserve, prairie, historical canal, formal botanical garden, an observatory, and jogging paths.

Just 5 miles from downtown Indianapolis, Butler's urban location offers internship opportunities that provide excellent graduate school and career preparation. Indianapolis, Indiana's state capital and the thirteenth-largest city in the nation, boasts a variety of cultural activities, including the Indianapolis Symphony Orchestra, the Indiana Repertory Theatre, the Indianapolis Museum of Art (just two blocks from campus), the Indiana State Museum, and the world's largest children's museum.

The Indianapolis Motor Speedway is the anchor of Indianapolis' professional sports, while basketball, football, hockey, and baseball have homes in three major sports arenas. Indianapolis is home to the NCAA headquarters. In 2012, Indianapolis will host the Super Bowl.

Butler has been the proud co-host of the NCAA Final Four championship in 1991, 1997, 2000, 2006, and 2010.

Majors and Degrees

As a comprehensive university with a strong liberal arts foundation, Butler is committed to graduating students who have a well-rounded yet focused education. A core curriculum affords students the opportunity to gain knowledge in the humanities, the arts, social sciences, natural sciences, and mathematics.

Baccalaureate degrees are offered through Butler's six colleges. Unique programs include the engineering dual-degree program, offered jointly by Butler University and the Purdue School of Engineering and Technology at Indianapolis. Students receive both a Butler Bachelor of Science degree in a selected liberal arts and sciences major and a Purdue Bachelor of Science degree in biomedical, computer, electrical, or mechanical engineering.

For students who are undecided about their major field of study, there is an Exploratory Studies Program.

The College of Education is dedicated to preparing outstanding teachers. The administration and the faculty and staff members of the College of Education are committed to providing the best possible learning experience for students. For the past nine years, the College has experienced a 99 percent (or above) placement rate for its students, an indicator that Butler students place first in education. Undergraduate majors offered through the College are early and middle childhood education and middle and secondary education.

The College of Liberal Arts and Sciences creates lifelong learners. The College affirms the central role of liberal arts education while offering opportunities for specialization. Majors include actuarial science, anthropology, anthropology and psychology, biology, chemistry, classical studies, computer science, economics, English literature and writing, French, French and business studies, German, German and business studies, history, history and anthropology, individualized major, mathematics, philosophy, philosophy and religion, physics, political science, psychology, psychology and journalism, psychology and political science, public and corporate communications, religion, sociology, sociology and psychology, sociology and criminology, software engineering, Spanish, Spanish and business studies, and urban affairs.

The College of Business' motto is "Real Life. Real Business." and that's the mindset as students are prepared to be tomorrow's business leaders. Students receive hands-on, experiential learning and have two required internships. A unique program in the College—the Butler Business Accelerator—allows students to serve as consultants for central Indiana businesses. Majors in the College include accounting, economics, finance, international business, management, management information systems, and marketing.

Butler University's College of Communication prepares students for success in a digital and global society. Students will develop the ability to analyze and synthesize human and mediated communication, and learn to speak, write, and create responsible messages across dynamic communication contexts and digital media platforms. Majors offered in this communication-centered curriculum include digital media production, electronic media, integrated communications, journalism, public and corporate communications, public relations, recording industry studies, communication studies, and communication sciences and disorders.

The Jordan College of Fine Arts integrates intensive conservatory training with broad objectives and a strong academic curriculum. The College is well respected for its tradition of educating students as emerging professionals in the arts. Majors offered are applied composition, arts administration, dance, electronic media studies–journalism, electronic media studies–video, multimedia studies, music, music history, music theory, music education, piano pedagogy, recording industry studies, and theater.

College of Pharmacy and Health Sciences graduates serve society as caring, ethical health professionals and community leaders. The College's professional programs combine intensive classroom education with clinical experiences in the professional phases of the degrees. Majors offered are prepharmacy and health sciences.

Academic Programs

All candidates for the baccalaureate degree must complete the University core requirements and at least 45 semester hours of work. Thirty of the 45 hours must be in the college granting the degree. Eligible students may participate in the honors program. By the end of the sophomore year, honors course work is generally completed. Students then begin the next phase, an independent study to help them research, write, and eventually present their honors thesis. Butler is a sponsoring institution for the National Merit Scholarship Program. Butler also offers advanced placement with appropriate academic credit in most subjects covered by either the AP examinations or the CLEP tests. Students may choose to enroll in Air Force and Army ROTC programs.

Butler students have the chance to originate research projects and participate in them with faculty members and then develop these projects into professional presentations and publications. Hundreds of Butler students present their projects at the Undergraduate Research Conference, hosted by Butler every April. In addition, the Butler Summer Institute awards accepted students a $2000 grant plus housing while they work on summer research projects with faculty members.

Off-Campus Programs

Butler offers more than 110 study abroad programs in over forty countries to meet the diverse needs of the student population. Butler students have studied in Argentina, Australia, Chile, Costa Rica, England, Ireland, Mexico, New Zealand, Northern Ireland, and Scotland. Students can choose to study for a semester, academic year, or summer term.

Academic Facilities

Butler's academic facilities include the latest technology. These include Mac and PC computers, wireless and Ethernet connections in every residence hall room and all classrooms, multimedia classrooms, language labs, international studies center, electronic card access into most buildings, access to Internet2, e-portfolios, and four 24-hour campus computer labs plus one in each residence hall.

The Richard M. Fairbanks Center for Communication and Technology includes state-of-the-art classrooms, laboratories, conference rooms, television studios, graphics production and editing facilities, recording studios, student newspaper offices, online magazine production space, and speaker labs.

Many student performances, including theater, dance, and music, can be seen in Butler's 2,200-seat Clowes Memorial Hall and the 140-seat Eidson-Duckwall Recital Hall. The Holcomb Observatory and Planetarium houses the largest telescope in the state of Indiana, a 38-inch Cassegrain reflector. Butler's libraries house approximately 250,000 monograph volumes, 110,000 government documents, 1,500 current journal subscriptions, 14,000 audiovisual materials, and more than 17,000 musical scores. The library system also features a searchable computer database, rare books collection, archives, online catalog access, and research tools.

Costs

For the 2010–11 academic year, tuition was $29,740 for full-time undergraduate students. Average room and board were $9620 per year. Books are estimated at $800 per semester, and other fees are estimated at $800. Tuition for the professional pharmacy program was $32,170 and $35,670 for the sixth year. Tuition for the professional health sciences program was $32,170 and $460 per hour for the fifth year master of physician assistant program.

Financial Aid

Butler University offers a variety of financial assistance programs based on the demonstration of academic excellence, performance talent, or financial need. Butler awards merit-based academic scholarships to students who have displayed outstanding high school achievement and have excelled in leadership and community service. Performance awards are available in the areas of music, dance, theater, and athletics. Scholarships are also offered in selected majors. On-campus employment and work-study programs are also available. All students who seek need-based financial assistance are required to file the Free Application for Federal Student Aid (FAFSA).

The University offers National Merit, National Achievement, and National Hispanic Recognition Program scholarships. Semifinalists in these programs are guaranteed a minimum Freshman Academic Scholarship. However, based on academic screening, these students may qualify for a higher award. Finalists in these programs who designate Butler as their sponsor and file their FAFSA by March 1 are eligible for an additional award that ranges from $750 to $2000.

The University also offers Dr. John Morton-Finney Leadership Program Awards to students who exhibit leadership and a commitment to diversity in their high schools and communities. Awards are based on class rank, SAT/ACT scores, leadership roles in school and the community, and an on-campus interview. These awards include an expectation of continued campus and community leadership while at Butler.

Faculty

Teaching is the top priority for Butler's 328 full-time faculty members; 81 percent hold the highest (terminal) degree in their fields. Many are active in national research programs, write for publications, counsel in government and business, and participate in the arts. With a comfortable teaching load, Butler's faculty members have time to work with students individually. The student-faculty ratio is 11:1. All classes are taught by professors; there are no teaching assistants.

Student Government

As the official student governing body, Student Government Association (SGA) is the liaison between faculty and administration members. The organization is also responsible for budgeting funds from the student activity fee. These funds promote SGA's Program Board activities, including the film series, concerts, and all campus special events as well as the purchase of the Butler yearbook, *The Drift*.

Admission Requirements

Applicants are expected to complete a minimum of 14 academic units in high school, including 4 years of English, 3 years each of laboratory sciences (must include biology and chemistry), 3 years of mathematics (must include algebra 1, geometry, and algebra 2), 2 years each of history or social studies, and 2 years of the same foreign language. A candidate for admission typically ranks in the upper third of his or her high school class and should submit satisfactory results of the SAT or the ACT, including the optional Writing Test. The Jordan College of Fine Arts requires an audition. In addition to these factors, the Admission Committee considers the applicant's leadership skills, course selection, academic performance, and a writing sample. Students who wish to transfer from another regionally accredited college or university are considered if they are in good standing and have a grade point average of 2.0 or better in their previous academic work. Transfer students must submit official transcripts of all college work.

Application and Information

Butler offers three nonbinding admission programs: early action, November 15; early action II, January 15; and regular decision, February 15.

Campus visits are strongly recommended, though not required, and are arranged on a daily basis. Several open-house programs are also scheduled throughout the year. Interested students and their families are encouraged to visit http://go.butler.edu to make arrangements for campus visits.

Office of Admission
Butler University
4600 Sunset Avenue
Indianapolis, Indiana 46208-3485
Phone: 317-940-8100
      888-940-8100 (toll-free)
Fax: 317-940-8150
E-mail: admission@butler.edu
Web site: http://go.butler.edu

Butler students make the short walk to class from their residence halls.

CALIFORNIA COLLEGE OF THE ARTS

SAN FRANCISCO AND OAKLAND, CALIFORNIA

The College

California College of the Arts (CCA) (www.cca.edu), founded in 1907, offers studies in twenty-one undergraduate and seven graduate majors in the areas of fine arts, architecture, design, and writing at its two campuses in San Francisco and Oakland. Students and faculty members create a supportive community of friends, colleagues, and mentors in an intimate, private-college environment. Students discover their creative passions and develop their individual points of view, and they are particularly encouraged to experiment across disciplines. CCA welcomes students who want to make art that matters.

CCA alumni have been at the forefront of nearly every major art movement of the past century. Noted alumni include the designers Lucille Tenazas and Michael Vanderbyl; the painters Nathan Oliveira and Raymond Saunders; the conceptual artists David Ireland and Dennis Oppenheim; the ceramicists Robert Arneson, Viola Frey, and Peter Voulkos; and the filmmaker Wayne Wang.

CCA students begin making their mark well before graduation. They have won the Adobe Design Achievement Award, the James Dyson Award in industrial design, and awards from the Art Directors Club, STEP Inside Design, the Type Directors Club, and *ID* magazine. Their work has been featured in the Cannes Film Festival, the Slamdance Film Festival, the Milan Furniture Fair, the International Contemporary Furniture Fair, and the International Home and Housewares Show

Architecture students, together with students from numerous other programs (from interior design to glass to ceramics) participated in the 2009 international Solar Decathlon competition. Their multi-year effort culminated in a high-profile event on the National Mall in Washington, D.C., a first-place win in the architecture category, and a third-place win overall.

Additional CCA student achievements within the last year include the following: An industrial design student signed a contract with Universal Toys to manufacture a toy he first conceived as a freshman-year class project. Two jewelry/metal arts students received the coveted $15,000 Windgate fellowship. A graphic design student had his portfolio selected as the best of 145 entries at the AIGA SF student portfolio competition and won a major scholarship award. Six illustration students placed in the New York Society of Illustrators student scholarship competition. Two interior design students received major scholarship awards from the Northern California chapter of the International Interior Design Association (IIDA). And an animation student was hired full-time at Pixar Animation Studios—in 2008, he was one of only 12 selected (out of 2,500 applicants) for Pixar's prestigious animation internship.

BusinessWeek magazine named CCA one of the world's best design schools in 2009. CCA is accredited by the Western Association of Schools and Colleges, the National Association of Schools of Art and Design, the National Architectural Accrediting Board, and the Council for Interior Design Accreditation.

CCA has approximately 1,400 undergraduate and 500 graduate students. In the undergraduate population, 60 percent are women, 40 percent are men, 17 percent are from underrepresented populations, and 11 percent are international students.

Of the entering class, 55 percent are first-time freshmen and 45 percent are transfer and second-degree students. About 38 percent come from out of state.

About 80 percent of first-year students live on campus. Throughout the year, the residential-life staff hosts social and educational programs ranging from movie nights to museum trips and professional lectures.

Students are encouraged to join existing clubs and organizations or to form new ones. They are active in preprofessional groups, including the American Institute of Architecture Students (AIAS), American Institute of Graphic Arts (AIGA), Industrial Designers Society of America (IDSA), and International Interior Design Association (IIDA).

Location

The San Francisco Bay Area is known for creative and technological innovation, environmental leadership, and thriving art and design communities. It is home to world-class museums and alternative galleries as well as active endeavors in theater, music, dance, film, and literature. Beaches, the Napa Valley, Santa Cruz, Monterey, Lake Tahoe, and Yosemite are all close by.

CCA's San Francisco campus spans a city block in the Potrero Hill neighborhood, near the design district. The Oakland campus occupies 4 acres in the Rockridge neighborhood, 3 miles from the University of California, Berkeley. A free shuttle connects the campuses and residence halls. Both campuses are easily accessible via public transportation.

Majors and Degrees

CCA offers the Bachelor of Fine Arts (B.F.A.) degree in animation, ceramics, community arts, fashion design, film, furniture, glass, graphic design, illustration, industrial design, interaction design, interior design, jewelry/metal arts, painting/drawing, photography, printmaking, sculpture, and textiles. The College offers the Bachelor of Arts (B.A.) degree in visual studies and writing and literature. CCA also offers a bachelor of architecture (B.Arch.) degree, a five-year program. For more information, visit http://www.cca.edu/academics.

CCA offers the M.F.A. in design, fine arts, and writing; the M.A. in curatorial practice and visual and critical studies; the M.Arch. and M.A.A.D. in architecture; and the M.B.A. in design strategy. Graduate fine arts media areas include ceramics, film, furniture, glass, jewelry/metal arts, painting/drawing, photography, printmaking, sculpture, and textiles.

Academic Programs

The B.F.A. requires the completion of 126 semester units (75 in studio work and 51 in humanities and sciences). The B.A. requires 126 semester units (51 in humanities and sciences, 36 in the major, and 39 in studio work). The B.Arch. requires 165 semester units, including the core program and a 9-semester major program. For details, visit http://www.cca.edu/academics.

Undergraduates begin with a core curriculum, which covers a variety of artistic media, principles, and processes as well as writing, literature, art history, and critical theory.

CCA operates on a two-semester academic calendar with a six-week summer session. Summer programs include the Pre-College Program for high school students (participants earn college credit). Continuing education programs are offered throughout the year.

Off-Campus Programs

Qualified upper-division students may spend a semester at one of thirty-two other U.S. art schools through the Association of Independent Colleges of Art and Design (AICAD). Students may cross-register at Mills College or Holy Names University, both in Oakland.

Through the International Exchange Program, students may spend a semester at one of more than thirty colleges of art and design around the world. CCA also offers summer study-abroad courses.

Academic Facilities

The Oakland campus is home to the first-year program and the programs in animation, ceramics, community arts, glass, jewelry/metal arts, photography, printmaking, sculpture, textiles, visual studies, and writing and literature. Animation students have dedicated studios and equipment for digital video, film, and sound production. The ceramics facilities include numerous gas and electric kilns. Sculpture facilities include a bronze foundry, a waxworking area, a plaster and mold-making room, a metal fabrication studio, and a woodshop. Textiles facilities include a computerized weaving lab, a digital Jacquard TC-1 loom, and a fiber sculpture studio. For printmaking there are lithography presses, a 40x60 American French Tool etching press, a silkscreening and papermaking complex, and a letterpress lab. The two-floor photography center has darkrooms for black-and-white and color printing, a 42-inch RA4 color processor, a mural printing room, a digital lab, and an alternative processes room.

The San Francisco campus houses the programs in architecture, fashion design, film, furniture, graphic design, illustration, industrial design, interaction design, interior design, and painting/drawing as well as all of the graduate programs. There is a state-of-the-art digital production facility and stage. The studio and shop facilities include a furniture studio, a model making studio, an alternative materials studio, a rapid prototyping studio, a welding studio, a plaster room, a sanding room, and a spray booth. Seniors in the painting/drawing program have individual studios, as do all fine arts graduate students.

Media centers offer equipment for checkout. The fourteen dedicated computer labs are available to all students 16 to 24 hours daily, whenever they are not being used for classes. The labs have Intel-based Macintosh computers and a complete range of software. Available hardware includes slide and flatbed scanning devices, Cintiq displays, audio/video decks, graphics tablets, CD/DVD burners, and large-format color printers. There is a rapid prototyping studio for 3-D printing.

CCA's libraries hold more than 60,000 titles. They subscribe to approximately 300 hard-copy periodicals and more than 2,500 full-text online periodicals. On the San Francisco campus there is also an extensive materials library.

The campuses have several spaces for student exhibitions. The CCA Wattis Institute for Contemporary Arts, on the San Francisco campus, presents exhibitions of internationally prominent contemporary artists.

Costs

Tuition for the 2010–11 year was $34,872 for full-time undergraduates and $1371 per unit for part-time students.

Tuition is the same for California and out-of-state residents. Campus housing costs an additional $7000. Total costs for 2010–11 were $50,022, which includes $35,222 in tuition and fees, $9850 for room and board, $1500 for books and supplies, and $3450 for miscellaneous expenses. For more information, visit http://www.cca.edu/students/handbook/tuition_fees.

Financial Aid

In 2010–11, 88 percent of CCA students received financial aid from some source. Approximately 79 percent received CCA scholarships. The college offers financial aid in the form of scholarships, grants, loans, and work-study programs. There are both need- and merit-based awards. For details, visit http://www.cca.edu/admissions/financialaid.

Students seeking merit scholarships must submit their admissions application by February 1. Students applying for financial assistance in 2011–12 should submit the FAFSA by March 1. CCA continues to award aid after March 1 as funding permits. Students can apply for grants and loans throughout the year. CCA is approved for veterans who wish to attend under the Veterans Administration Educational Benefits Program. CCA offers an interest-free payment plan.

Faculty

CCA's faculty includes 500 artists, architects, designers, writers, and scholars, most of whom combine teaching with professional work in their respective fields. The average class size is 18. Faculty members serve as advisers to first-year students. (http://www.cca.edu/academics/faculty)

Student Government

The Student Council includes students from all areas of CCA and sponsors extracurricular activities, including films, receptions, and gallery excursions.

Admission Requirements

Admitted undergraduates must have a high school diploma or equivalent. Applications are reviewed on an individualized basis, taking into account academic achievements, creative abilities, individual achievements and activities, a personal essay, recommendations, and a portfolio. For more information, visit http://www.cca.edu/admissions.

Application and Information

For undergraduates, there are two priority deadlines for fall admission: February 1 and March 1. Those interested in applying for merit scholarships should submit their applications by February 1. The priority deadline for spring undergraduate applicants is October 1. Students who meet the admissions priority deadlines receive first consideration for housing, financial aid, and course selection. Applications are reviewed in the order they are received. There is a nonrefundable application fee of $60. It is possible to register for courses as a nondegree student (on a space-available basis).

Students may apply online at http://www.cca.edu/admissions. To request forms and brochures, the college viewbook, or any additional information, please contact:

Office of Enrollment Services
California College of the Arts
1111 Eighth Street
San Francisco, California 94107-2247

Phone: 800-447-1ART (toll-free)
Fax: 415-703-9539
Web site: http://www.cca.edu
http://www.facebook.com/CaliforniaCollegeoftheArts
http://twitter.com/CACollegeofArts

CALIFORNIA INSTITUTE OF THE ARTS

VALENCIA, CALIFORNIA

The Institute

CalArts educates professional artists in a unique learning environment founded on the principles of art-making excellence, experimentation, critical reflection, and independent inquiry. Throughout its history, CalArts has sought to advance the practice of art and promote its understanding in a broad social, cultural, and historical context. CalArts offers students the knowledge and expertise of leading professional artists and scholars and a full complement of art-making tools. In return, it asks for the highest artistic and academic achievement. Reflecting its longstanding commitment to new forms and expressions in art, CalArts invites creative risk-taking and urges active collaboration and exchange among artists, artistic disciplines, and cultural traditions.

CalArts is the first higher educational institution in the United States to offer undergraduate and graduate degrees in both visual and performing arts. It was established in 1961 by Walt and Roy Disney through the merger of two professional schools, the Los Angeles Conservatory of Music and the Chouinard Art Institute.

Since its founding, CalArts has been recognized internationally as a leader in every discipline in which it provides instruction. Its artists and alumni have defined, and continue to extend, the very forefront of creative practice as we know it today.

At the graduate level, the Institute grants the Master of Fine Arts (M.F.A.) degree in art, dance, film/video, theater, and writing and the Master of Arts (M.A.) degree in aesthetics and politics, and a Doctor of Musical Arts (D.M.A.) degree in performer-composer. Graduate programs take one, two, or three years to complete, depending on the individual program. Certificates and advanced certificates are also offered.

The total enrollment of the Institute is approximately 1,454 men and women, of whom 895 are undergraduates. The student body is gender balanced and geographically diverse, with students hailing from fifty states and thirty-one different countries.

Location

Thirty miles north of downtown Los Angeles, CalArts occupies 60 acres on hills overlooking the incorporated city of Santa Clarita. Rapid development in this peaceful suburban area has resulted in new residential communities and an ever-increasing population of more than 150,000. Los Angeles, the second-largest city in the United States and an important international hub for the arts, offers a vast array of professional and cultural resources.

Majors and Degrees

California Institute of the Arts grants the Bachelor of Fine Arts (B.F.A.) degree in art, dance, film/video, music, and theater; the Master of Fine Arts (M.F.A.) degree in art, dance, film/video, theater, and writing; the Master of Arts (M.A.) degree in aesthetics and politics; and the Doctor of Musical Arts (D.M.A.) degree in performer-composer.

Academic Programs

Students must apply to and enroll in a specific program within a particular school. A modified, nontraditional grading system is utilized, with each school's curriculum being determined by the special demands of the discipline. Instruction proceeds according to the student's preparation and need, with the student receiving guidance from a faculty mentor.

Undergraduate programs take four years or eight semesters and a minimum of 120 semester units to complete. All undergraduate students must fulfill the Critical Studies Requirements (40 percent of the total curriculum), which include courses in the humanities, social sciences, cultural studies, and natural sciences. These courses are intended to inform and influence each student's artistic practice.

Academic Facilities

Open 24 hours a day, the campus houses classrooms, art studios, animation studios, rehearsal rooms, and dance studios; galleries; theaters for drama, dance, and film; a music performance hall; costume, scenery, and machine shops; photo labs; computer and media labs; editing suites for film and video; and digital recording studios.

CalArts students also take advantage of a variety of special initiatives designed to respond to the realities of the social and cultural world today. These range from the Community Arts Partnership (CAP), which offers students a chance to teach in community and public school settings to the Cotsen Center for Puppetry and the Arts, which allows students to explore the potential of puppetry in their art-making and from the groundbreaking Center for New Performance, the professional wing of CalArts' Schools of Performance where students and faculty members collaborate on professionally presented performances, to the Institute's contemporary art journal *Afterall,* copublished with London's Central Saint Martins College of Art and Design, and the literary magazine *Black Clock*, published in association with CalArts' M.F.A. Writing Program.

The most momentous of these initiatives is the Roy and Edna Disney/CalArts Theater, or REDCAT, part of the Walt Disney Concert Hall complex in downtown Los Angeles. Designed by Frank Gehry, REDCAT includes a state-of-the-art, flexible performance space, a 3,000-square-foot gallery, and a café. REDCAT plays host to the most interesting new experimental theater, dance, music, art, film and video, and literature from Southern California, the nation, and the world. In the process, CalArts brings new resources to its students' education through performances, master classes, and residencies by visiting artists and helps its students make a seamless transition into the local, national, and international arts communities.

The library contains a collection designed especially for the visual and performing arts. In addition to holding more than 95,000 volumes, the library includes musical scores, sound recordings, films, videotapes, and slides that enable students to progress on their own in obtaining knowledge relevant to their specific studies.

Costs

Tuition for 2010–11 was $37,684 for the academic year. Room charges ranged from $4100 to $7970 per year, and board cost between $3710 and $4265. The cost of books and supplies varies according to major.

Financial Aid

The Financial Aid Office at CalArts is dedicated to helping students meet the cost of attendance at the Institute. Funds made available through the Financial Aid Office are awarded on a combination of need and artistic merit. Need is determined by completing and submitting the FAFSA (Free Application for Federal Student Aid). CalArts offers a limited number of merit-only awards; however, to be considered for these awards, students must have completed the FAFSA.

CalArts offers the following financial aid programs: Institute scholarships and grants, Federal Pell Grants, Federal Supplemental Educational Opportunity Grants, Federal Work-Study Program awards, Federal Perkins Loans, Federal Stafford Loans, and Cal Grants. Details of these financial aid programs are available from the Financial Aid Office.

Faculty

The faculty numbers approximately 300, including both full- and part-time members. The student-faculty ratio is approximately 7:1. Faculty members maintain active, often prolific, careers in their respective disciplines. Their approach to teaching combines rigorous instruction with careful guidance and individualized attention, a process that empowers students to define their own artistic objectives. Every student works closely with an assigned faculty mentor.

Student Government

Student government is conducted through the Student Council, whose members are elected by the student body. In addition, students are active participants in a variety of Institute-wide standing committees, the composition of which also includes a Board of Trustees, faculty members, and staff members.

Admission Requirements

CalArts welcomes application for admission from any individual engaged in the visual and performing arts. The main criterion for admission is artistic merit, as assessed by the faculty of the individual programs. An artist statement, letters of recommendation, and school transcripts are also required.

Application and Information

For application forms and additional information, prospective students should visit http://calarts.edu/applycalart or contact:

Office of Admissions
California Institute of the Arts
24700 McBean Parkway
Valencia, California 91355

Phone: 661-255-1050
E-mail: admissions@calarts.edu
Web site: http://www.calarts.edu

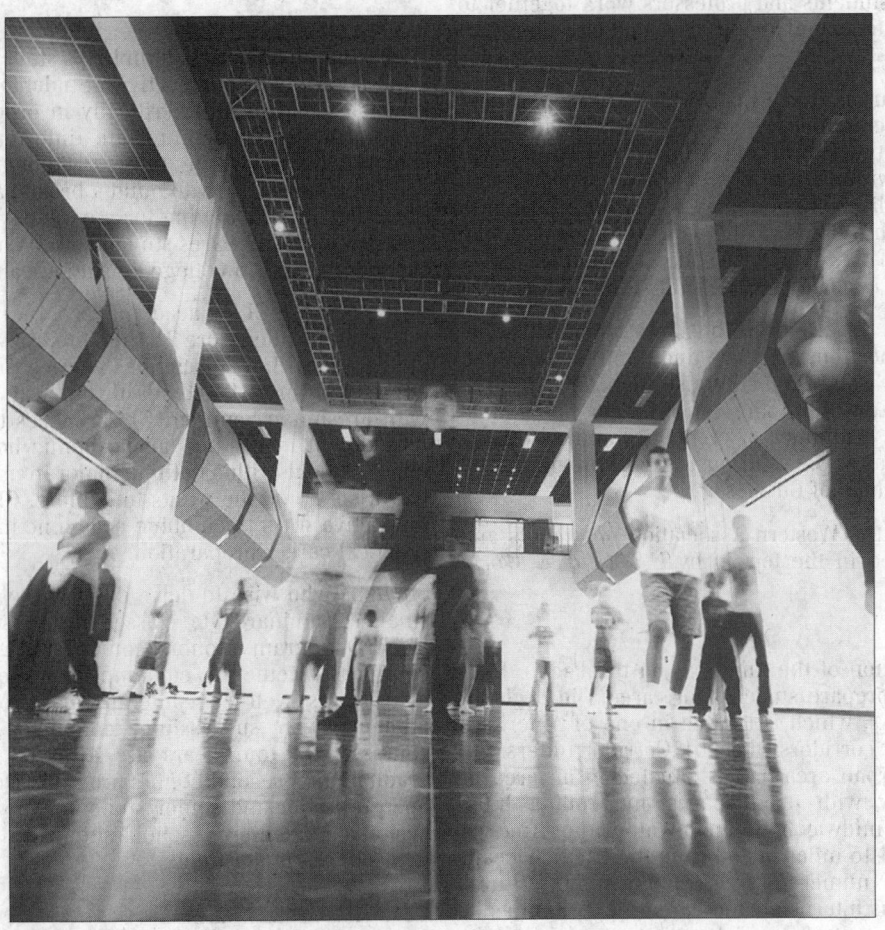

CalArts has extensive facilities for all the visual and performing arts.

CALIFORNIA LUTHERAN UNIVERSITY

THOUSAND OAKS, CALIFORNIA

The University

California Lutheran University (CLU) was founded in 1959, but its history goes back much farther than that. CLU is part of a 500-year-old tradition of Lutheran higher education—a tradition begun on a university campus as a teaching and reforming movement, a tradition of thoughtful investigation and bold discovery.

Following in this tradition, CLU insists on wide-ranging, critical inquiry into matters of both faith and reason. Students are encouraged to investigate personal beliefs that impact their educational and career choices and are asked to reflect on how their intellectual and spiritual convictions come together to define them as a whole person. Ultimately, the goal of CLU is to educate leaders for a global society who are strong in character and judgment, confident in their identity and vocation, and committed to service and justice. The individual exploration of truth is only a starting point for the whole educational experience by which students and professors work together to seek answers to the intellectual and professional questions that face world citizens.

CLU's 225-acre campus is home to 2,545 undergraduate and 1,362 graduate students that represent a diversity of faiths and cultures from across the nation and around the world. CLU provides access to a wide variety of organizations, sports, and other activities, providing ample opportunities for students to develop their leadership skills. KCLU-FM, a National Public Radio affiliate on the CLU campus, provides a valuable service to the community and a learning opportunity for students.

Master's degrees are awarded in business administration, computer science, education, marriage and family counseling, psychology, and public policy and administration. The NCATE-accredited School of Education offers an Ed.D. in educational leadership as well as a number of credential and certificate programs. International M.B.A. and post-M.B.A. programs are offered through the School of Business.

CLU is accredited by the Western Association of Schools and Colleges and is ranked in the top 20 by *U.S. News & World Report.*

Location

Poised at the intersection of the Americas on the Pacific Rim, CLU's location helps prepare students for careers in a global society. Thousand Oaks, which is located in one of America's significant technology corridors, the 101 Corridor, offers the conveniences of an urban area, but is situated in an area of scenic natural beauty with open spaces and rolling hills. Because of its location midway between downtown Los Angeles and Santa Barbara and 15 miles inland from the Pacific Ocean, CLU offers students numerous recreational and cultural opportunities as well as internship and career opportunities in government, entertainment, and social services.

Majors and Degrees

CLU offers thirty-six majors within the College of Arts and Science, the School of Business, and the School of Education. In addition, undergraduate pre-professional preparation is available in law, medicine, and health-related fields. Undergraduate degrees are offered in accounting, art, biochemistry and

molecular biology, bioengineering, biology, business administration, chemistry, communication, computer information systems, computer science, criminal justice, economics, English, environmental science, exercise science and sports medicine, French, geology, German, history, interdisciplinary studies, international studies, liberal studies (education), marketing communication, mathematics, multimedia, music, philosophy, physics, political science, psychology, religion, social science, sociology, Spanish, and theater arts. Minors are offered in art, bioengineering, biology, business administration, chemistry, church music, communication, computer science, economics, English, environmental studies, ethnic studies, French, gender and women's studies, geography, geology, German, Greek, history, international business, international studies, legal studies, mathematics, multimedia, music, philosophy, physics, political science, psychology, religion, religion minor with church vocations, religion minor with youth ministry, sociology, Spanish, and theater arts.

Academic Programs

CLU's integrated curriculum helps students comprehend issues from a variety of perspectives. Students learn to ask the right questions and to think critically in order to analyze, process, transform, and communicate information. With thirty-six majors and thirty-one minors, students are encouraged to sample classes widely to build a broad base of knowledge. CLU feels that while planning for a career is important, the type of education that prepares students for a changing world is one of the greatest gifts a college education can provide.

At the heart of CLU's academic program is a general education curriculum called Core 21. Students' views of the world expand as they learn how disciplines connect in this interdisciplinary approach. Core 21 extends through all four years, beginning with Freshman Seminar. CLU realizes that students' interests may not fit neatly into an academic box. Whether a student enters college with a definite major in mind or an awareness of the areas he or she wants to explore, CLU's curriculum offers distinctive ways to combine academic interests and goals with practical career preparation.

Students who wish to delve deeper into the life of the mind in smaller, seminar-style classes may also have access to the Honors Program. Honors courses bring students and faculty members together to contemplate issues of enduring human concern as well as contemporary problems facing society. Students who successfully complete the requisite honors courses over four years are awarded University Honors at graduation. A second honors program, Departmental Honors, is open to junior and senior students who wish to participate in prolonged, mentored scholarship with a faculty member in their chosen major field.

Off-Campus Programs

Students may take courses abroad while maintaining their student status at CLU by enrolling in one of the more than forty study-abroad programs offered. The University offers ongoing study, internship, and exchange programs in Austria, Belgium, Germany, Hong Kong, India, Mexico, Sweden, Tanzania, and Thailand. CLU also offers a Washington, D.C., semester for students in every field of study. This program allows students to live, study, and work in the nation's capital while earning a full semester of academic credit. While completing their professional internship and taking two academic courses, they also participate in orientation sessions, field trips, meetings with experts, and seminars on current events. Students are housed in furnished condominiums across the Potomac River in Arlington, Virginia.

Academic Facilities

The most recent addition to the CLU campus is the Swenson Center, CLU's first LEED-certified building, that houses nine classrooms, forty-three offices, two computer labs, a psychology lab, a conference room, and a faculty/staff lounge.

Several new athletic arenas have been added to the north side of the campus in recent years, including the 96,000-square-foot Gilbert Sports and Fitness Center, featuring two gymnasiums, an events center, fitness and strength conditioning centers, dance studios, and a Hall of Fame; the Samuelson Aquatics Center, the George "Sparky" Anderson baseball field at Ullman Stadium; and the Hutton softball field.

The campus is distinctive in its combination of mid-century modern and classic-contemporary architecture. The 600-seat Samuelson Chapel, with its towering wall of stained glass, mahogany carvings, and handcrafted Steiner-Reck organ, anchors the campus, which also includes the state-of-the-art Ahmanson Science Center, Pearson Library, and Soiland Humanities Center. The Preus-Brandt Forum is a 250-seat lecture/performance center equipped with modern sound and lighting equipment.

Costs

Tuition for the 2010–11 academic year is $32,600 (12–18 credits per semester). Room and board for the year is $11,070. Student fees are $250 per year.

Financial Aid

Available assistance includes need-based and non-need-based University scholarships; low-interest, long-term loans from external sources; Federal Supplemental Educational Opportunity Grants; Federal Pell Grants; and Federal Work-Study Program positions. Part-time jobs are available both on and off campus. Applicants for aid should submit the Free Application for Federal Student Aid (FAFSA). The parents' and/or student's most recent IRS 1040 form must also be submitted. The priority application deadline is March 1. CLU scholarships are awarded on the submission of a completed application.

Faculty

At CLU, professors care passionately about teaching and students. CLU's average class size of 22 students enables faculty members to know their students and enables students to develop relationships with mentors. Students have lively, in-depth discussions with the highly trained faculty members who teach their classes. Eighty-one percent of the full-time faculty members have earned their doctoral or terminal degree. They bring a depth of intellectual expertise and academic curiosity to the classroom. Among the faculty members are a former senior economist of the United Nations Development Programme (UNDP), as well as master scholars in everything from media law and Mexican narrative to artificial intelligence and classical and quantum chaos. The list of their areas of research and interests—the social psychology of moral development, molecular evolution, economic and business forecasting models, and politics in movies, to name a few—brings a broad and beneficial foundation to students' liberal arts experience.

Student Government

All undergraduate students carrying 9 or more units are automatically members of the Associated Students of California Lutheran University by virtue of their enrollment in the University. Student governance, including allocation of the student activity fee, is conducted by student body–elected officials.

Admission Requirements

Applicants for admission must complete the application form (the CLU application or the Common Application may be used) and submit a high school transcript, SAT or ACT scores, one recommendation, an essay/personal statement, and a $45 non-refundable application fee ($25 for online applications). An interview is not required but is strongly recommended. International students whose native language is not English must also submit TOEFL or IELTS scores. All students are expected to have followed the most competitive college-prep curriculum available to them at their high school. Transfer students must also send a transcript of all completed college work (if more than 28 semester units of college work have been completed, SAT/ACT scores are not required).

Application and Information

The Early Action (EA) deadline is November 15. The Regular Decision Round 1 deadline is January 15, and the Regular Decision Round 2 deadline is March 15. For additional information, interested students should contact:

Office of Undergraduate Admission
California Lutheran University
60 West Olsen Road #1350
Thousand Oaks, California 91360-2700
Phone: 805-493-3135
      877-CLU-FOR-U (toll-free)
Fax: 805-493-3114
E-mail: admissions@callutheran.edu
Web site: http://www.callutheran.edu
      http://www.facebook.com/callutheran
      http://twitter.com/callutheran

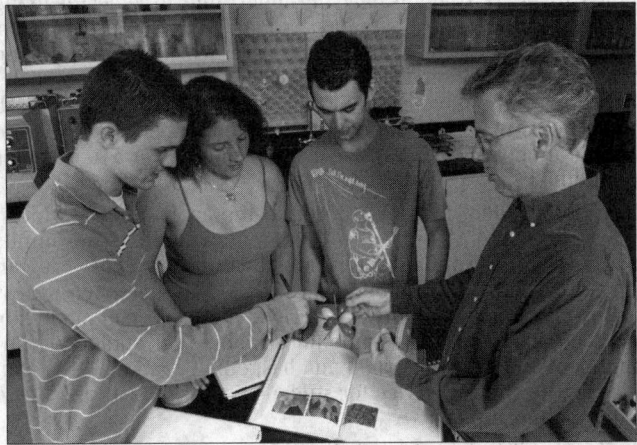

At CLU, professors care passionately about teaching and students.

CALIFORNIA UNIVERSITY OF PENNSYLVANIA

CALIFORNIA, PENNSYLVANIA

The University

California University of Pennsylvania, a member of Pennsylvania's State System of Higher Education, traces its origin to the establishment of an academy in the town of California, Pennsylvania, in 1852. It has as its mission "Building character and building careers." California University began as a teacher-preparation school and has evolved into a multifaceted university that grants both undergraduate and graduate degrees.

Since 2006, California has been included annually in the Princeton Review's *Best Northeastern Colleges.* California University was also included in the *Templeton Guide to Character Building Colleges* and the *Making a Difference College and Graduate Guide,* the distinctive guide for students who want to use their education to make a better world. The University adopted integrity, civility, and responsibility as its core values in 1998 and encourages all members of the community to aspire to these high ideals in order to make the University community, and the world, a better place.

The campus consists of 294 acres with forty-six primary buildings, nestled on a bend of the Monongahela River. The Natali Student Center, which is located in the center of the main campus, houses the student information center, dining facilities, movie theater, convenience store, food court, bookstore, ATM machine, and a variety of student organizations, including the Commuter Center and the University radio (WCAL) and television (CUTV) stations. The south campus is located less than 1½ miles from the main campus. Tennis courts; running tracks; picnic areas; baseball, softball, rugby, and soccer fields; and the football stadium are located there, along with a farmhouse that is slated to be used for meetings of student groups.

The current enrollment is 7,419 undergraduate and 1,981 graduate students. About 4,000 undergraduate students commute, 1,500 live on campus in six recently completed air-conditioned residence halls, 768 live off campus in a garden-style apartment complex that is affiliated with the University, and the rest live in off-campus fraternity or sorority houses, rental units, or private homes.

At the University, students have the opportunity to select the living arrangement that best fits their personal needs and preferences. Residence halls on the main campus are near all academic and recreational activities. On-campus living also provides a structured environment, convenient to classrooms, dining, the Natali Student Center, and Manderino Library. A variety of room configurations allow students to choose from 1, 2, or 3 roommates or suitemates.

More independent living is offered in the apartments at Vulcan Village, less than 1½ miles from the main campus. These units have a variety of configurations, most with private baths. Vulcan Village also provides a clubhouse with a fully equipped fitness center, a recreation room with various games, a computer lab, and a media room. Other amenities include an outdoor swimming pool and sand volleyball and basketball courts. The Vulcan Flyer, a free shuttle service for students, connects Vulcan Village to the main campus.

The University offers students the convenience of an on-campus Health and Wellness Center, which is staffed by registered nurses and a nurse practitioner. A medical director/physician has regularly scheduled office hours.

The Counseling Center, also staffed by professionals, is available to all students and provides psychological services. The University also offers drug and alcohol education programs that include consultation, intervention, counseling, education, awareness programs, and substance-free activities.

Location

The campus is located in the borough of California, Pennsylvania, a community of approximately 6,000 people. It is about 35 miles south of Pittsburgh in the foothills of the Allegheny Mountains, near Pennsylvania's Laurel Highlands recreational area. Professional baseball, football, and hockey, as well as a variety of cultural activities, are available in Pittsburgh. The region has a number of significant historical sites related to the pre–Revolutionary War era. The University also offers students the option of off-campus classes in Canonsburg at the Southpointe Technology Park.

Majors and Degrees

California University of Pennsylvania offers the following baccalaureate degree programs: Bachelor of Arts, Bachelor of Fine Arts, Bachelor of Science, Bachelor of Science in Athletic Training, Bachelor of Science in Education, Bachelor of Science in Nursing, and Bachelor of Science in Sports Management. Associate of Arts, Associate of Science, and Associate of Applied Science degrees are also offered.

The liberal arts majors include art, commercial music technology, communication studies (language and literacy, public relations, radio/television, and speech concentrations available), criminal justice, English (creative writing, journalism, and literature concentrations available), French, graphic design, history, international studies (business and economics, geography, modern languages, and political science concentrations available), philosophy, political science (campaign management, prelaw, and public policy concentrations available), psychology (industrial-organizational psychology concentration available), sociology (applied sociology concentration available), Spanish, and theater.

The Bachelor of Science in Education includes majors in athletic training, communication disorders, early childhood education, elementary education, secondary education (art, biology, chemistry, communication, comprehensive social sciences, earth and space science, English, French, mathematics, physics, and Spanish), special education, and technology education. Dual majors are available in many education programs. The College of Education and Human Services also offers bachelor's degrees in gerontology, social work, and sport management, with concentrations in professional golf management and wellness and fitness.

The Eberly College of Science and Technology offers majors in the areas of administration and management, biology, business administration (accounting, business administration, business economics, computer-based systems management, finance, human resources management, management, and marketing), computer information systems, computer science, earth science, electrical engineering technology, environmental earth science, environmental studies (ecology, environmental science, and fisheries and wildlife concentrations) geography (geographic information systems and travel and tourism concentrations), geology, graphic communication technology, natural sciences (biology, chemistry, earth science, geology, mathematics, natural sciences interdisciplinary, and physics), parks and recreation management, and pre–health professions (pre–chiropractic medicine, predentistry, premedicine, pre–mortuary science, preoptometry, pre–osteopathic medicine, prepharmacy, pre–podiatric medicine, and pre–veterinary medicine). A cooperative nursing program is offered with the Community College of Allegheny County. The University offers an upper-division Bachelor of Science in Nursing degree program for students who have completed an RN program.

Academic Programs

Each bachelor's degree requires a minimum of 120 semester hours of credit. A general education requirement of 51 credits is distributed among the following areas: building a sense of community (1 credit), communication skills (9 credits), critical-thinking skills (3 credits), fine arts (3 credits), health and wellness (3 credits), humanities (3 credits), mathematics (3 credits), multicultural awareness (3 credits), natural sciences (8 credits), social sciences (6 credits), technological literacy (6 credits), and values (3 credits). An honors program provides an opportunity for an enhanced educational experience to students who meet the criteria. Honors students have the option of living in the Honors Residence Hall, which offers numerous outstanding amenities, including a private library. Wireless Internet connections are available throughout campus. Applications of all incoming first-year and transfer students are reviewed, and those with the highest indicators of past and future academic success are invited to participate in the honors program.

Academic Facilities

The University has traditional library holdings of more than 360,000 volumes, more than 1 million microfilm units, nearly 1,500 periodical titles, and U.S. government documents. It is a member of the Keystone Library Network, which provides access to library holdings, databases, and electronic resources among fourteen State System of Higher Education libraries. This virtual library electronically links users to a variety of information sources and delivers both text and multimedia resources immediately and seamlessly from any location. The 80,400-square-foot Eberly Science and Technology Center features state-of-the-art science and computer laboratories and is one of the premier teaching facilities on campus. Every residence hall room is wired with fiber optics so that students can bring computers, plug them in, and have immediate access to the Internet and all its resources. For students who do not have computers of their own, there is a computer lab on every floor of the residence halls. Numerous specialized computer facilities are available across the campus, including ones devoted to meteorology, math and computer science, word processing, accounting, CAD-CAM, robotics, teacher education, art, and chemistry.

Costs

The 2010–11 tuition for a resident of Pennsylvania attending full-time (12 to 18 credits) was $2902 per semester. For a full-time nonresident, tuition was $4644 per semester. Room costs for 2010–11 ranged from $2960 to $4318. Board prices ranged from $1260 to $1713. Based on a full-time schedule, fees for 2010–11 included a $116 technology fee, an $85 service fee, a $265 Student Association fee, an $81 student union building fee, an $84 student center operations and maintenance fee, and a $290 academic support fee. The cost of books, materials, and supplies varies with each program.

Financial Aid

California University of Pennsylvania has available a number of types of financial aid, including student employment, grant and scholarship aid through the Pennsylvania Higher Education Assistance Agency, federal grants, and student loans. A number of non-need-based academic scholarships are available for talented students. All students must complete the Pennsylvania State Grant and federal financial aid application for need-based aid. The director of financial aid at the University administers all student aid. Overall, 98 percent of student need is met for students who are awarded need-based aid.

Faculty

Classes are taught by nearly 300 full-time faculty members; no classes are taught by graduate assistants. Terminal degrees are held by 80 percent of the full-time faculty members. Faculty advisers are assigned based on the student's major, department, or school.

Student Government

Student government at California University of Pennsylvania regulates cocurricular activities. It furthers the quality of student life by encouraging and funding diverse student activities, providing experiences in the principles and practices of democratic government, supplying a forum for general student interest, and improving and promoting the cultural standards of the University. Students sit on many important University committees, including the University Forum, and have a voice in most policy decisions.

Admission Requirements

California University of Pennsylvania welcomes applications from all qualified persons. Admission standards have been established by California University of Pennsylvania for the purpose of ascertaining which prospective students are most likely to succeed at the University. An applicant for admission should have graduated from an accredited four-year high school or should possess an equivalency diploma issued by a state department of education. All applicants should submit to the University evidence of their ability to do college-level work, as indicated by such tests as the College Board's SAT. All applicants are required to have a Social Security number.

Application and Information

Prospective students should obtain, complete, and return an application form, along with the Secondary School Record (which is completed by the high school guidance counselor). A nonrefundable application fee of $25 must accompany the application. Students can apply and pay online at the University's Web site. A student who would like to transfer to California University of Pennsylvania should complete the application form (hard copy or online) and forward it to the Admissions Office with a nonrefundable check or money order for $25 or pay online. Official transcripts from all colleges and universities attended must be sent to the Admissions Office.

For additional information regarding admission, students should contact:

Dr. William Edmonds
Director of Admissions
California University of Pennsylvania
250 University Avenue
California, Pennsylvania 15419
Phone: 724-938-4404
      888-412-0479 (toll-free)
E-mail: inquiry@calu.edu
Web site: http://www.calu.edu

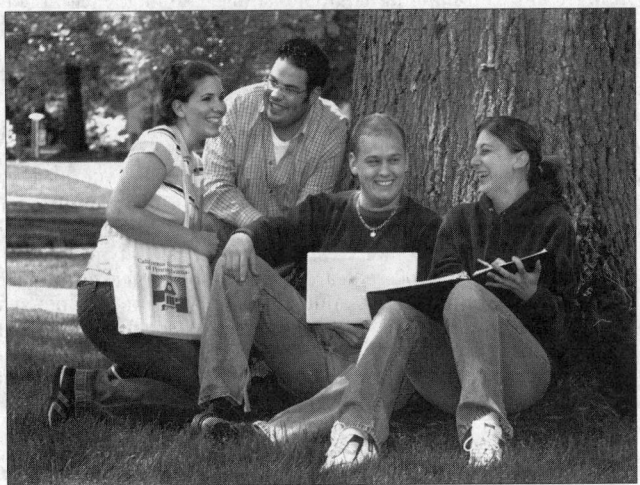

Students on the campus of California University of Pennsylvania.

CALVIN COLLEGE
GRAND RAPIDS, MICHIGAN

The College

Calvin College is an institution that values both intellect and faith. In every aspect of college life—teaching and learning, athletics and the arts, campus life and community activities—the Calvin community aims to live *coram Deo*, before the face of God.

Calvin is one of the nation's largest and most respected Christian colleges. With 3,991 students and 319 full-time professors, learning is a collaborative adventure. Named for John Calvin, the sixteenth-century Protestant reformer, Calvin maintains a strong affiliation with the Christian Reformed Church. But students from more than fifty other church denominations across North America and around the world also choose Calvin for its unique curriculum and faith-based mission.

Students come from nearly every state and forty-eight countries. Most are between 18 and 22 years old; however, those pursuing the Master of Education (M.Ed.) add to the age diversity on campus.

Calvin helps students develop the faith, knowledge, and skills to walk confidently into careers—and into life. When members of the class of 2009 were surveyed, results indicated that 76 percent are employed and 24 percent are pursuing graduate education. Career Development assists students with career counseling and services, equipping them for interviews, internships, and the search for full-time employment upon graduation. Over 80 percent of recent graduates reported having at least one internship or practicum while at Calvin. The Broene Counseling Center offers individual and group counseling.

Academic work isn't the only thing shaping the student experience at Calvin. New friends in every class; over seventy-five student organizations; seventeen sports teams; dozens of concerts, films, and theater productions; service-learning projects; and even part-time jobs help students think more deeply and more wholly about what God is calling them to do in this world.

Calvin is an NCAA Division III school and participates in the Michigan Intercollegiate Athletic Association; Calvin's athletic teams are regularly ranked nationally in Division III. The women's volleyball team won the national championship in 2010; the men's basketball team won the national championship in 1992 and 2000; and the women's cross-country team captured the national championship in 1998 and 1999. In 2000, 2003, 2004, and 2006, the men's cross-country team won national championships. The men's ice-hockey club won the 2004 ACHA DIII national championship. Fourteen teams have finished as national runners-up. Calvin ranks fourth among DIII schools in the number of Academic All-American student-athletes since 2000.

The 400-acre campus is a modern, well-planned community; its oldest academic building was erected in 1960. Fifteen residence halls, eleven apartment buildings, and two spacious dining halls accommodate 2,600 resident students. High-speed computing is available throughout the campus, and wireless service is offered in the residence halls and many campus locations. Calvin's athletic complex features a 5,000-seat arena, an indoor track and tennis center, a health center, and an aquatics center with an Olympic-size pool. Calvin's outdoor athletic sites include baseball and softball diamonds, a premier soccer field with seating for 1,500 and two practice fields, an eight-lane track, a six-court tennis facility, a paved jogging path, and two sand volleyball courts.

Location

Calvin's beautifully wooded campus, which includes a 100-acre ecosystem preserve, is located in Grand Rapids, Michigan, a metropolitan area of more than 600,000 people. Here, Calvin students find every urban amenity. Hundreds of restaurants, dozens of theaters, seven shopping malls, and a fine selection of museums and parks are within a short drive. Lake Michigan beaches, ski areas, parks, and trails are within a 40-minute drive. Premed and nursing students take advantage of the Medical Mile, a street running through the core of the city that is flanked with new medical and scientific research facilities.

Majors and Degrees

The Bachelor of Arts and Bachelor of Science degrees are offered, with major concentrations in accounting, art, art history, Asian studies, biochemistry, biology, biotechnology, business, chemistry, Chinese, classical studies, communication arts and sciences, computer science, digital communications, Dutch, early childhood education, economics, elementary and secondary education, engineering, English, environmental science, environmental studies, exercise science, film studies, French, geography, geology, German, Greek, history, information systems, international development studies, international relations, Japanese, Latin, linguistics, literature, mathematics and statistics, media production, media studies, music, nursing, philosophy, physical education, physics/astronomy, political science, psychology, public health, recreation, religion, social work, sociology, Spanish, special education, speech pathology and audiology, sport management, theater, and writing.

Professional programs include engineering (chemical, civil/environmental, electrical/computer, mechanical); natural resources; architecture (minor); predentistry; prelaw; premedicine; prepharmacy; pre–physical therapy; pre–seminary studies; social work; and elementary, secondary, and special education. Minor concentrations are available in African and African diaspora studies, archaeology, astronomy, coaching, congregational studies, dance, English as a second language, gender studies, health education, journalism, medieval studies, ministry studies, missions, urban studies, and youth ministry leadership. Calvin offers a Master of Education degree and a master of speech pathology program.

Academic Programs

Calvin College maintains a strong commitment to a multifaceted liberal arts curriculum as an integral way to help students connect the way they think with the way they live. The College follows a 4-1-4 academic calendar, consisting of two four-month semesters with a three-week January Interim term. Graduation requires the successful completion of 124 semester hours.

Calvin's core curriculum begins with a first-year gateway course, Developing a Christian Mind, and ends with a capstone course in the senior year. Core curriculum requirements include foreign language, history, literature and arts, mathematics, natural sciences, philosophy, physical education, religion, social sciences, and written and spoken rhetoric. Some requirements can be satisfied by advanced high school work. Qualified students can earn course exemption and/or credit by completing college-level work in high school or by examination. Satisfactory scores on Advanced Placement (AP), International Baccalaureate (I.B.), and/or CLEP exams are also accepted.

Incoming students with an ACT composite of at least 29 who are interested in nursing and meet other admissions requirements will receive automatic admission to Calvin's nursing program. Incoming students with an ACT composite of at least 29 are invited to participate in the honors program, which offers advanced-level courses and cocurricular opportunities. The Office of Student Academic Services provides academic counseling, tutoring, training in study skills, and review courses in key subjects for all students.

Off-Campus Programs

Semester-long study-abroad programs are offered in Britain, China, France, Ghana, Honduras, Hungary, the Netherlands, Peru, Spain, Thailand, and a U.S.-based program in New Mexico. Students register for courses in various subjects, and the credits earned are applied toward graduation requirements. Calvin offers many other programs in cooperation with other colleges, including programs of the Council for Christian Colleges and Universities in Washington, D.C., Central America, Hollywood, Egypt, and Moscow. Some students may fulfill their foreign language requirement through study-abroad programs. Many courses offered during the January Interim are also taught abroad.

Academic Facilities

The four-floor Science Complex features a center core of laboratories, an atom trapper, and an observatory. The Engineering Building provides space for engineering students and faculty members to do research, design work and project construction. The DeVries Hall of Science includes medical research laboratories and classrooms. The Spoelhof College Center houses administrative offices, a social research center, an art gallery, six art studios, and a 340-seat auditorium. The renovated Covenant Fine Arts Center features a 1,100-seat auditorium, a second art gallery, a 240-seat recital hall, classrooms, and music suites.

The Hekman Library includes a five-level, computerized library containing more than 800,000 bound volumes, 2,750 periodicals, an extensive collection of microfiche, records and tapes, and government publications; more than 1,500 students can be comfortably seated at study carrels and tables. The complex also houses the Information Technology Center, the Calvin Center for Christian Scholarship, the Meeter Center for Calvinism Studies, a distance-learning classroom, a graphics production lab, and a curriculum center for teacher education students. The 55,000-square-foot De-Vos Communications Center is home to a 150-seat video theater, a television studio, an audio studio, digital audio and video editing labs, and a speech pathology and audiology clinic. The Prince Conference Center houses seminars, meetings, retreats, and hotel rooms.

Costs

Tuition and fees for 2010–11 were $24,645; tuition for the Interim was free for full-time students enrolled for at least one semester. Room and board charges were $8525 for resident students with a twenty-one-meal-per-week plan (ten- and fifteen-meal-per-week plans are also available). About $800 is needed for textbooks.

Financial Aid

Over 75 percent of first-year students are awarded an academic scholarship in amounts ranging from $10,000 to $1,000. Sixty percent of Calvin students receive need-based financial aid; demonstrated need is the most important criterion in determining eligibility. Students wishing to be considered for financial aid must be admitted to the College and must submit the Free Application for Federal Student Aid (FAFSA) and Calvin's Supplemental Application for Financial Aid. February 15 is the filing deadline for maximum consideration. Financial awards to eligible applicants consist of state and federal grants, loans, Federal Work-Study Program funds, and institutional grants and scholarships. Part-time employment is available on campus, and placement preference is given to students with financial need. Calvin's Student Employment Office also helps students find off-campus employment.

Faculty

Calvin's outstanding faculty members have distinguished themselves through publication and research, yet each is available 10–15 hours per week outside of class. More than 82 percent have earned the highest academic degree in their field. Each faculty member is a professing Christian, committed to the integration of his or her personal faith and discipline. There are over 319 full-time and 69 part-time faculty members; the faculty-student ratio is 1:11.

Student Government

The 27-member Student Senate supervises most student activities and oversees the budgets for student publications, homecoming, the film arts, and the Service-Learning Center. Student members serve on most faculty committees governing the College. Each residence hall has its own governing council and judiciary committee. Campus rules are designed to build a Christian academic community. Calvin attempts to aid student development and responsible action by clearly expressing its expectations and de-emphasizing regulations.

Admission Requirements

Applicants should be graduates of an accredited high school program and should have completed satisfactorily at least 15 units of college-preparatory work, including 3 in English and 3 in algebra and geometry. Applicants with high school averages of C+ (2.5) or higher who score above 20 on the ACT composite or above 470 on both the math and critical reading sections of the SAT are normally given regular admission. Applicants with lower grades and scores, or those with deficiencies in their high school preparation, may be admitted under special conditions. International students should refer to http://www.calvin.edu/international for application procedures. Students who come from a non-English-speaking culture must submit results of the TOEFL or IELTS or provide other documentation of English-language proficiency.

Application and Information

Applicants must submit a completed application form, a high school or college transcript, results of either the ACT or SAT, and an educational recommendation completed by a teacher or counselor. Admission decisions are made on a rolling basis beginning in mid-October. Applicants for fall admission are urged to complete their file before February 1; the deadline for admission is August 15 for U.S. and Canadian applicants and April 1 for international applicants, as long as space is available. Students and parents are strongly encouraged to visit the campus. The Fridays at Calvin campus visit program provides an excellent opportunity to experience life at Calvin firsthand. For more information about Calvin or to register for a visit, students should contact:

Office of Admissions and Financial Aid
Calvin College
3201 Burton Street, SE
Grand Rapids, Michigan 49546
Phone: 616-526-6106 (admissions)
      616-526-6134 (financial aid)
      616-526-8480 (TTY)
      800-688-0122 (toll-free in North America)
Fax: 616-526-6777
E-mail: admissions@calvin.edu
      finaid@calvin.edu
Web site: http://www.calvin.edu
      http://www.facebook.com/calvincollege
      http://twitter.com/calvincollege

Recognized as one of the finest research libraries in western Michigan, the Hekman Library is a hub of student and faculty activity on the Calvin College campus.

CANISIUS COLLEGE
BUFFALO, NEW YORK

The College

Canisius College offers an exceptional liberal arts education based on high-quality academic programs taught by outstanding faculty members who are leaders in their fields. In fact, 95 percent of Canisius faculty members hold Ph.D.'s or terminal degrees in their fields. With more than seventy-five distinct majors, minors, and special programs and an exciting urban location to support internships, research opportunities, and service-based learning experiences, Canisius College prepares students for success. Canisius is a place where leaders are made.

Canisius College offers a state-of-the-art campus with enhanced technology in academic and living facilities. Canisius housing is like a home away from home, not just a temporary living accommodation. Bosch and Frisch Residence Halls, which were recently renovated, and Dugan Hall, which opened in 2005, are the primary residences for first-year students at Canisius. Apartment-style living is available to sophomores, juniors, and seniors in one of the many town-house complexes and apartment buildings on campus. Specialty housing options include George Martin Honors Hall, available to students in the All-College Honors Program, and the Intercultural Living Center, a learning community residence for international and U.S. students. All campus housing is equipped with high-speed, wireless Internet access and cable television.

Students have opportunities to develop leadership skills through involvement in student clubs and organizations, research, and service learning. There is something for everyone at Canisius. There are more than 100 college-sponsored student clubs and organizations and a wide range of athletic teams. The students are not only leaders in the classroom but also on the NCAA Division I athletic field. Most of the sixteen Golden Griffin teams compete in the Metro Atlantic Athletic Conference (MAAC), in which a majority of the champions receive an entry into their respective NCAA tournaments. Since joining the MAAC in 1989, men's basketball, baseball, women's cross-country, men's lacrosse, men's soccer, and softball have claimed conference titles.

Location

Canisius College's urban setting is a significant advantage for students seeking internship, research, and service learning opportunities because of the proximity to a wide range of businesses and organizations. Many of Canisius' vast network of 40,000 alumni live and work in the Buffalo area as leaders in their businesses and community.

Canisius is located on 62 acres in a residential neighborhood in north-central Buffalo. Buffalo is a great college town that has it all—professional sports teams, a world-renowned art gallery, historic architecture, and scenic parks and waterways—all within minutes from campus. Buffalo is located in close proximity to the U.S.-Canadian border, offering students international experience through internships, research, and travel.

The internationally known Albright-Knox Art Gallery holds one of the world's finest collections of nineteenth- and twentieth-century American and European works of art. Buffalo is also home to the Buffalo Philharmonic Orchestra and Shea's Performing Arts, which provides a wide variety of theater experiences, including a Broadway series.

The Metro Rail rapid transit system connects the College with some of Buffalo's most exciting venues, including HSBC Arena, home of the National Hockey League's Buffalo Sabres. The arena also hosts college basketball with Canisius' Golden Griffins as well as major popular and rock music concerts. During the summer, students can catch Buffalo Bisons Triple-A baseball games at Coca-Cola Field. At Ralph Wilson Stadium, in Orchard Park, the Buffalo Bills are a focal point throughout the football season.

The Buffalo Zoo and Delaware Park, a 350-acre park with a lake and a golf course, are located less than a mile from the campus.

Majors and Degrees

The College of Arts and Sciences is the largest and most diverse of Canisius' three academic divisions, with majors in the natural and social sciences, humanities, and preprofessional studies. It also houses the core curriculum, which strengthens fundamental critical thinking, oral, and written communication skills and helps enhance students' understanding of other cultures. The College of Arts and Sciences offers programs leading to bachelor's degrees in anthropology, art history, biochemistry, bioinformatics, biology, chemistry, clinical laboratory science, communication studies, computer science, criminal justice, digital media arts, economics, English, environmental science, European studies, history, international relations, mathematics and statistics, modern languages (French, German, and Spanish), music, philosophy, physics, political science, psychology, religious studies and theology, sociology, and urban studies.

The Richard J. Wehle School of Business offers a well-rounded business curriculum to complement the liberal arts courses in the major, which gives the student an understanding of the broad and interrelated nature of business issues. There are programs leading to the B.S. degree in accounting, accounting information systems, economics, entrepreneurship, finance, information systems, international business, management, and marketing. All the business programs are accredited by the AACSB International—The Association to Advance Collegiate Schools of Business.

The School of Education and Human Services offers degrees that lead to teacher certification at the early childhood, childhood, middle childhood, or adolescent level, such as adolescence education, athletic training/sports medicine, childhood education, early childhood education, physical education, and special education. All programs are accredited by the National Council for Accreditation of Teacher Education (NCATE).

Canisius also offers diverse and flexible academic programs, such as fashion merchandising (in conjunction with the Fashion Institute of Technology), fine arts, and military science, and certification programs in gerontology and women's studies. Preprofessional programs are available in dentistry, engineering, law, medicine, pharmacy, and veterinary medicine. Canisius also has an early assurance of admission agreement for New York State residents, with the Schools of Medicine and Dental Medicine of SUNY at Buffalo and SUNY Medical School at Syracuse. In fact, Canisius has a 90 percent acceptance rate for students applying to medical school—that's twice the national average.

Seven-year joint-degree programs exist between Canisius and the SUNY Buffalo School of Dental Medicine, the Ohio College of Podiatric Medicine, the New York College of Podiatric Medicine, the SUNY College of Optometry, and the Lake Erie College of Osteopathic Medicine. A new five-year engineering degree program with SUNY at Buffalo and Penn State Behrend allows students to get a bachelor's degree from Canisius and the other institution, and a five-year combined degree program leads to the B.A. in a major in one of the liberal arts disciplines and a Master of Business Administration degree.

Academic Programs

To earn a bachelor's degree from Canisius College, students must complete forty courses and a minimum of 120 credit hours. Within each curriculum, the courses are distributed into three areas: core curriculum, major field requirements, and free electives. The College requires that students complete a rounded program of humanistic studies embracing literature, the physical and social sciences, oral and written communication, philosophy, history, and religious studies.

The All-College Honors Program is available for qualified students. This program includes rigorous exploration of the arts and sciences in an enriched curriculum with close faculty supervision and small classes. Students may also obtain college credit through the Advanced Placement Program of the College Board, the International Baccalaureate Program or through college courses offered in their high schools. Students with scores of 3 or better on Advanced Placement tests, 4 or better on International Baccalaureate tests or grades of C or better in college-level courses are considered for credit and advanced standing.

Off-Campus Programs

Many Canisius students choose to spend a semester or a year studying abroad, improving their fluency in another language, and opening the doors to exciting personal and professional opportunities. Canisius administers semester-abroad programs in Australia, Belgium, China, El Salvador, England, France, Germany, Ireland, Italy, Japan, Puerto Rico, Spain, and Sweden. Service immersion experiences also allow students to gain community service experience in the Appalachia region, Jamaica, El Salvador, India, Mexico, New York City, and Poland. The Office of International Student Programs assists students in selecting a study-abroad program, organizes a predeparture orientation, and assists students upon their return to the United States. Canisius also partners with the twenty-seven other Jesuit institutions across country for over 700 international programs to choose from.

Students majoring in international relations and political science may participate in programs in Washington, D.C., or Albany, New York, which have been designed to give students practical experience in their fields.

Academic Facilities

Canisius has invested nearly $120 million over the last thirteen years to create state-of-the-art technology classrooms, residence halls, and cultural and recreational spaces. In addition, the campus provides wireless access in every building and residence hall. Instructional computing facilities include dual-platform computers located in general-purpose labs and teaching labs. The College offers fifty laptops students can check out for use within the library as well as e-mail and Internet stations at various convenient locations on campus.

Costs

For the academic year 2010–11, tuition and fees were $30,077, and room and board were $10,980. Books and supplies were estimated to cost $700. An additional $1130 per year was recommended for travel and personal expenses. Students are automatically considered for merit scholarships up to $18,000 upon application.

Financial Aid

Of the class of 2014, 98 percent receive some form of financial aid, and the average award is $29,202. This aid includes Canisius College scholarships and grants, state grants, state and federal loans, federal grants, and Federal Work-Study Program awards. Applications for financial aid should be completed by February 15. The Free Application for Federal Student Aid (FAFSA) and the TAP application (New York State residents only) must be filed before consideration can be given to applicants.

Faculty

The Canisius College faculty consists of 226 full-time teachers, including Jesuits and laymen and women. More than 95 percent hold doctorates or other terminal degrees. The primary emphasis of the faculty members is teaching, and many serve as academic advisers. The student-faculty ratio is 11:1.

Student Government

The Undergraduate Student Association comprises the entire undergraduate student body and is represented by elected officers who serve on the Student Senate. The senate assists and supervises student activities and advocates on behalf of the students, presenting their views to the College administration. In addition, students serve on many College committees.

Admission Requirements

Students' applications for admission are evaluated on a combination of factors, including a student's academic ability, strength of character, high school record, rank in class, an essay, aptitude tests (SAT or ACT), extracurricular activities, and recommendations. An applicant to the College is encouraged to pursue a challenging college-preparatory program in high school. This program of studies should include a minimum of 16 units of credit in the academic subjects of English, foreign language, mathematics, science, and social studies. Recommendations from teachers or school counselors are strongly encouraged. They are considered in reviewing applications for admission. Campus interviews are strongly recommended and in some cases may be required.

Transfer students are welcome and are admitted to Canisius in the fall and spring semesters. In addition to meeting the academic standards required of all entering students, transfer students are considered for admission if they have a minimum 2.0 cumulative quality point average when transferring from either a two-year or a four-year accredited institution.

Canisius College does not discriminate on the basis of age, race, religion or creed, color, sex, national or ethnic origin, sexual orientation, marital status, veteran's status, genetic predisposition or carrier status, or disability in administration of its educational policies, employment practices, admissions policies, scholarship and loan programs, and athletic and other school-administered programs.

Application and Information

Students are encouraged to submit their applications for admission in the fall of their senior year in high school. Application forms are available from the Office of Admissions, or fee-waived applications can be found on the Web at http://www.canisius.edu/admissions. Students may also apply using the Common Application. The completed application form should be presented to the high school counselor, to be forwarded to the Office of Admissions with an official high school transcript, SAT or ACT scores, and any letters of recommendation. Arrangements for interviews may be made by contacting the Office of Admissions at least one week in advance of the desired date for a visit.

Canisius considers applications under a rolling admission policy. Students applying by November 15 are notified of admission decision by December 15, along with scholarship notification. Students are encouraged to apply no later than March 1 for full and equal consideration.

For application forms and additional information, students should contact:

Admissions Office
Canisius College
2001 Main Street
Buffalo, New York 14208
Phone: 716-888-2200
       800-843-1517 (toll-free)
Fax: 716-888-3230
E-mail: admissions@canisius.edu
Web site: http://www.canisius.edu/admissions
      http://www.facebook.com/canisius.admissions
      http://twitter.com/CanisiusAdmiss

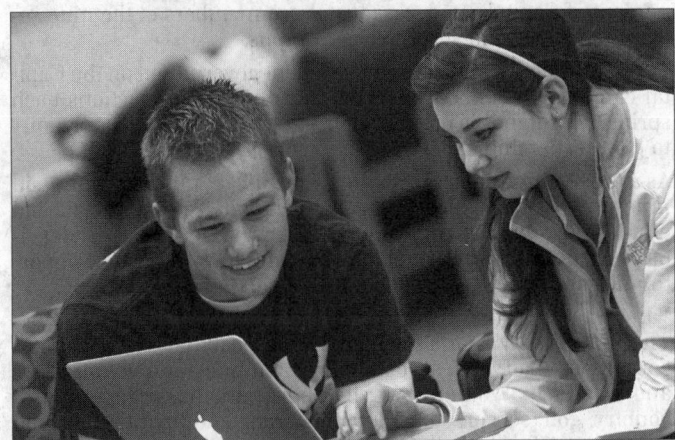

Canisius College students receive an exceptional liberal arts education at Western New York's only private institution.

CAPITAL UNIVERSITY

COLUMBUS, OHIO

The University

Since its founding in 1830 by the Lutheran Church, Capital University has earned a reputation for academic excellence and affordability, an accomplishment that earned Capital recognition as one of the top regional universities by *U.S. News & World Report*. The University's undergraduate and graduate programs combine personal attention with a balanced liberal arts and professional studies education to prepare students for lifelong learning, leadership, and service. Students also benefit from the attention faculty and staff members pay to their moral, social, and ethical development. Students at Capital are part of the "Capital Family," a family that cares about the total growth and well-being of each of its members.

Five schools comprise The College at Capital University: the Conservatory of Music and School of Communication; the School of Humanities; the School of Management and Leadership; the School of Natural Sciences, Nursing, and Health; and the School of Social Sciences and Education. In addition to the sixty majors and forty minors available to undergraduates, graduate students can earn master's degrees in business, music education, and nursing; the Capital University Law School offers the Juris Doctor and four other advanced degrees. The University also offers adult learners an opportunity to balance their lives and their goals as they complete their undergraduate degree through the Adult and Continuing Education Program. Of the approximately 3,600 students enrolled at Capital, more than 1,800 are traditional undergraduates. Approximately 65 percent of these students reside on campus in the University's six residence halls, including suite-style housing and apartments for upperclass students.

There are more than seventy student organizations, including a number of musical groups that are open to music and nonmusic majors alike. Other opportunities for involvement include preprofessional groups, theater, the student newspaper, departmental organizations, and the debate team. Numerous opportunities for volunteerism and service projects also exist. Approximately 20 percent of Capital's undergraduates are members of the nine social fraternities and sororities on campus.

There is an active and influential student government on the Capital campus. Students are elected in campuswide elections each spring. Through this organization, students have the opportunity to gain leadership experiences.

As a university affiliated with the Evangelical Lutheran Church in America, Capital believes that the religious, social, racial, and ethnic diversity found on campus enhances each student's development. In this spirit, worship, study, and extracurricular opportunities are offered in a cooperative, ecumenical way.

Varsity and intramural athletics are offered for men and women. The nine varsity sports for men are baseball, basketball, cross-country, football, golf, soccer, tennis, and track and field (indoor and outdoor). Women's varsity sports are basketball, cross-country, golf, soccer, softball, tennis, track and field (indoor and outdoor), and volleyball. Capital's sports teams are sanctioned by the National Collegiate Athletic Association Division III, and the University is a member of the Ohio Athletic Conference. Intramural sports are also a big part of campus life. In addition, Capital's fitness rooms and activities such as aerobics provide options for students who want to develop their own individual fitness programs.

Location

Capital is located in the Columbus suburb of Bexley, which is primarily a residential community with a number of small shops and restaurants. Downtown Columbus is just 4 miles from campus and easily reached by city buses. As the sixteenth-largest city in the country and part of a major metropolitan area, Columbus offers a wide variety of social and cultural opportunities. Students can enjoy performances by BalletMet, Opera Columbus, or the Columbus Jazz Orchestra, or they may visit the more than fifty art galleries in the area. Students may follow professional sports by attending the games of the Columbus Crew (Major League Soccer), the Columbus Blue Jackets (National Hockey League), or the Columbus Clippers (AAA franchise of the Cleveland Indians). There is also an expansive network of parks and recreation facilities, bike trails, and the Columbus Zoo. Many of the city's attractions are free or offer substantial student discounts. In addition, as Ohio's capital and largest city, Columbus is the home of many national and international corporations. These companies offer Capital students unlimited opportunities for internships and employment after graduation.

Majors and Degrees

Capital University offers the Bachelor of Arts degree in art, art therapy, athletic training, biochemistry, biology, business (accounting, financial economics, leadership and management, and marketing), chemistry (major approved by the American Chemical Society), communication, computer science, criminology, economics, education, electronic media and film, English (literature, creative writing, and professional writing), environmental science, exercise science, health and fitness management, history, interdisciplinary studies, international studies, mathematics, modern languages (French and Spanish), organizational communication, philosophy, political science, psychology, public administration, public relations, religion (worship ministry and youth ministry), sociology, and theater studies. Preparation for professional programs is available in dentistry, medicine, occupational therapy, optometry, pharmacy, physical therapy, physician assistant studies, podiatry, public health, and veterinary medicine. Prelaw and preseminary studies help prepare students for graduate studies in the legal profession and religion.

Capital also offers the Bachelor of Science in Nursing (approved by the National League for Nursing Accrediting Commission) and Bachelor of Social Work (approved by the Council on Social Work Education). For music students, Capital offers a Bachelor of Music in composition, jazz studies, keyboard pedagogy (church music, organ, and piano), music education (vocal and instrumental), music industry, music media, music merchandising, music technology, and performance (instrumental, organ, piano, and vocal). The Bachelor of Arts in music is also offered.

A program in engineering, which leads to dual degrees, is offered in cooperation with Washington University in St. Louis and Case Western Reserve University in Cleveland. A similar dual-degree program in pre–occupational therapy is also offered in conjunction with Washington University and the University of Indianapolis.

Academic Programs

The academic year consists of two semesters, the first of which begins in late August and ends in December. The second semester begins in early January and ends in early May. Summer classes are available.

In addition to taking courses related to their field of study, all undergraduate students take courses that fulfill a set of general education goals and bring together the University's academic, scientific, religious, and artistic disciplines.

Learning is not confined to the classroom at Capital. All undergraduate students, regardless of their major, may participate in internships that allow them to apply newly learned skills to on-the-job situations.

Faculty advisers help students select a major, choose appropriate classes, and suggest career options. In addition, staff members in Capital's Career Development Office help students plan careers, provide instruction in resume writing and interviewing, and share information about graduate schools. On-campus recruiting sessions and a job-referral service also enhance employment opportunities.

Off-Campus Programs

At Capital, one way students learn more about other cultures and countries is through international study.

Capital is the only school in the country that offers a semester of undergraduate study at the Zoltán Kodály Pedagogical Institute of Music in Hungary for students in the Conservatory of Music.

In addition, Capital's International Education Office offers overseas study opportunities in countries around the world, including China, Ecuador, France, Germany, Israel, the Netherlands, Spain, and Tanzania.

Closer to home, students may participate in a semester internship in one of thousands of organizations in the nation's capital through an arrangement with the Washington Center. In addition, cross-registration for enrolled students is available with Columbus College of Art and Design, Columbus State Community College, Franklin University, Ohio Dominican University, The Ohio State University, Otterbein University, and other area colleges and universities.

Academic Facilities

Capital's campus consists of twenty-four buildings. Through CAP-Net, Capital's campuswide voice, data, and video network, every residence hall room, classroom, and office is connected to the Internet and the Web. Through the library's connection to OhioLINK, students have access to more than 10 million items held by fifty libraries throughout the state. Information Technology provides a television studio and computer labs for student use. The Advanced Computational Studies Laboratory includes an array of computer hardware that allows students to access an extensive collection of scientific software and to simulate a parallel computing environment. A state-of-the-art technology classroom and language lab enhance teaching and learning. Nursing students may also use the microcomputers and instructional software contained in the School of Nursing's Helene Fuld Health Trust Learning Resources Laboratory. For the art lover, Chagall, Picasso, and Warhol are as close as Capital's Blackmore Library, which houses the University's Schumacher Gallery and its 2,500-piece collection.

Costs

In 2010–11, tuition and fees were $29,310. Room and board charges were $7864.

Financial Aid

Approximately 99 percent of Capital's undergraduate students receive some form of financial assistance. To apply, a student must file the Free Application for Federal Student Aid (FAFSA).

University scholarships are awarded to incoming freshmen and transfer students on the basis of academic achievement (and standardized test scores for freshmen). Full-tuition scholarships (Collegiate Fellowships) are awarded to incoming freshmen based on academic achievement and an on-campus competition. Music scholarships and participation awards are granted based on music ability as demonstrated during an audition. Additional grants are available for leadership, underrepresented or disadvantaged students, and out-of-state residents.

Faculty

The University has 230 full- and part-time faculty members for its undergraduate programs. The student-faculty ratio is 11:1.

Admission Requirements

Capital University admits qualified students regardless of race, color, religion, gender, age, disability, or national or ethnic origin to all the rights, privileges, programs, and activities generally accorded or made available to the students at the University.

To be considered for admission to any of the undergraduate programs, students must submit copies of their high school transcript, ACT or SAT scores, and a counselor recommendation. Applicants to the Conservatory of Music must also arrange for an audition, either in person or by videotape. There are special admission requirements for the Department of Nursing, and students should contact the Admission Office for details. Scores on Advanced Placement tests and College-Level Examination Program subject examinations are accepted as additional indicators of an applicant's ability, and course credit may be awarded for satisfactory scores on these examinations. Campus visits are encouraged. Arrangements for a tour of the campus and an interview, class visits, and appointments with professors may be made through the Admission Office. When an admission representative visits high schools, interested students in the area are notified and encouraged to meet with the representative. Transfer applicants must be in good social and academic standing and have a minimum grade point average of 2.25 at the institutions they attended previously. International applicants must submit official secondary school transcripts and photocopies of school-leaving certificates, TOEFL scores, SAT scores if available, and recommendation letters from a guidance counselor or headmaster and from a teacher.

Application and Information

Applications for admission may be submitted starting September 1 for the following year. Applicants are notified of their status as soon as their application is complete. The priority application deadline for the fall semester is April 15. Applications received after April 15 are reviewed on a space-available basis. For more information, visit http://www.capital.edu.

Director of Admission
Capital University
1 College and Main
Columbus, Ohio 43209-2394
Phone: 614-236-6101
       866-544-6175 (toll-free)
Fax: 614-236-7947
E-mail: admission@capital.edu
Web site: http://www.capital.edu

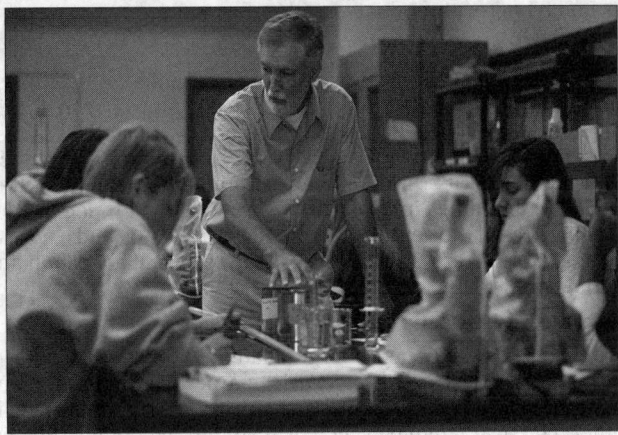

Undergraduate students at Capital University are encouraged to explore original research projects, independently or with other students and faculty members, and then present their findings at local, national, and international conferences.

CARLETON COLLEGE
NORTHFIELD, MINNESOTA

The College

Since its inception in 1866, Carleton College has been a coeducational, residential, liberal arts college. Sponsored initially by the Congregationalists, Carleton opened its doors in 1867 as Northfield College. Four years later, William Carleton of Charlestown, Massachusetts, donated $50,000 to the fledgling college, the result of which was the change of name from Northfield to Carleton. Binding church ties were dropped long ago, and the College continues to welcome students from a kaleidoscope of races, religions, and cultures.

Today, first-year classes number about 490 to 510, and the student body is approximately 50 percent men. The on-campus enrollment of about 1,800 includes students from virtually every state and about forty other countries. About a fifth are from Minnesota, and the next most represented states are Illinois, California, Wisconsin, New York, Massachusetts, and Washington. About 20 percent are students who are members of minority groups, and about 10 percent are the first generation of their families to attend college.

All first-year students take a first-year seminar, some of which deal with contemporary problems or concerns, others with more esoteric material. Many upperclass students do at least some independent study in their major, and a significant number of students take advantage of internship and work experience.

Though academic work takes top priority, Carleton students are actively involved in over 130 organizations, clubs, and other activities, ranging from the Quiz Bowl team (which won the nationals in 2007), and the improvisational comedy troupe Cujokra to Ultimate (Frisbee) (Carleton's women's team won the national intercollegiate championship in 2000, and the men's team won in 2009) and one of the top Model United Nations teams in the country. Musicians can play in the orchestra or smaller ensembles or sing in the choir, the Carleton Singers, or the a cappella groups. Athletes can participate in one of twenty varsity sports for men and women, one of twenty competitive club teams, or any of fifteen intramural sports.

Normally, 96 percent of Carleton first-year students return for their sophomore year. The most recent figures available show that 89 percent of first-year students graduated in four years or less and 93 percent graduated within five years.

Location

Northfield is about 35 miles from the Minneapolis–St. Paul International Airport and 40 miles from the downtown Twin Cities. Once a traditional small agrarian community, Northfield is also the home of St. Olaf College and several multinational businesses, and a number of its residents now commute to the Twin Cities. Most of the buildings in downtown Northfield look much as they did at the turn of the century. A revitalized riverbank and a core of downtown businesses and shops make for pleasant afternoon and evening strolls.

Majors and Degrees

Carleton grants only one undergraduate degree, the Bachelor of Arts. Majors offered are African/African American studies, American studies, art history, biology, chemistry, cinema and media studies, classical languages, classical studies, computer science, economics, English, environmental studies, French, French and Francophone studies, geology, German, Greek, history, international relations, Latin, Latin American studies, linguistics, mathematics, music, philosophy, physics, political science, psychology, religion, Romance languages, Russian, sociology and anthropology,

Spanish, studio art, theater arts, and women's studies. Students may also self-design their own majors.

In addition to a major, students may elect to study one of fifteen concentrations, integrated interdisciplinary programs that cut across traditional boundaries of academic disciplines and serve to both strengthen and complement the major: African/African American studies, archaeology, biochemistry, cognitive studies, cross-cultural studies, East Asian studies, educational studies, environmental studies, French and Francophone studies, Latin American studies, media studies, medieval and Renaissance studies, political economy, Russian studies, South Asian studies, and women's studies.

Special programs are available in dance, Hebrew/Judaic studies, Arabic, and literary and cultural studies. Carleton offers a teacher education program leading to a secondary teaching license in art, English, French, German, mathematics, Russian, science, social studies, or Spanish. Elementary licensure is available only in art and world languages, French, German, and Spanish. The joint liberal arts–engineering program, commonly known as the 3-2 program, is offered in conjunction with either Columbia University or Washington University (St. Louis).

Academic Programs

Carleton's avowed purpose is to provide a liberal arts education of the highest quality. The College teaches the basic skills upon which all higher achievements rest: to read perceptively, to write and speak clearly, and to think analytically. The Carleton education aims to nurture a sense of curiosity and intellectual adventure, an awareness of method and purpose in a variety of fields, and an affinity for quality and integrity wherever they may be found. These values prepare Carleton graduates to lead fully realized lives in a diverse and changing world.

To this end, the Carleton curriculum balances a traditional emphasis upon classic fields of study, or disciplines, with a complementary offering of distribution courses, electives, and interdisciplinary programs. To be awarded the Bachelor of Arts degree, a student must take at least thirty-five courses, six of which are in varied disciplinary fields like humanities, social science, and arts. In addition, all students must also satisfy three proficiency requirements: the writing of English, skill in quantitative reasoning, and courses in international understanding, which includes the learning of a second language.

Carleton students normally choose a major during the spring term of their sophomore year. In any given year, 12–18 students graduate with double majors, and about 15 graduate with special majors. All students must complete an integrative exercise, which could include a comprehensive examination, an extensive research project, a major paper, or a public lecture, in their major field, usually in the senior year. Carleton's academic year is composed of three 10-week-long terms: fall, winter, and spring.

Off-Campus Programs

Two thirds of Carleton students spend at least one term completing an off-campus program. During any one academic year, more than 350 students are involved in off-campus study in locations such as Australia, Japan, China, England, India, Mexico, Costa Rica, Western Africa, and Washington, D.C. Each year the College sponsors as many as ten faculty-led off-campus seminars for Carleton students. Through membership in a number of consortia, Carleton students may participate in more than twenty additional international programs lasting from a semester to a full year. Students may also select from a list of programs sponsored by other institutions, consortia, and agencies that Carleton has evaluated and approved for academic credit, or they can request approval of a program that they and their academic advisers believe will further their educational goals.

Academic Facilities

The Carleton campus consists of almost 1,000 acres of land, about 880 of which are the Arboretum, a game and nature preserve used regularly as an outdoor laboratory for biology, chemistry, and geology as well as a recreational area. Twenty miles of running and skiing trails crisscross the "arb," which *Runner's World* has named the best place to run in the state of Minnesota.

Approximately forty buildings are found on the College's main campus of nearly 100 acres. Eleven are student residence halls ranging in capacity from 90 to 205. New in 2011, the Weitz Center for Creativity is home to a new digital resource center, a 250-seat cinema, a flexible design theater, and a teaching museum. The Music and Drama Center offers a 500-seat concert hall joined by a gallery, ensemble rooms, practice rooms, and dressing rooms. Three buildings are devoted to the sciences: Olin (physics and psychology), Mudd (chemistry and geology), and Hulings (biology). Goodsell Observatory houses a 16-inch visual refractor telescope and an 8-inch photographic refractor telescope. The four-story Center for Mathematics and Computing (CMC) offers computer labs open around-the-clock. Along with six other labs distributed around campus, they provide easy access to a wide range of applications, free printing, and specialized multimedia equipment. The campus has more than 600 advanced workstations and personal computers, all of which are linked to the high-speed campus network and Internet2. In the residence halls, every room provides Internet connections, allowing students to plug in their own computers for access to the campus network. Wireless networks are also available in many locales.

Costs

For 2011–12, tuition is $42,690; fees, $252; and room and board, $11,238. Travel costs vary. Books, supplies, and personal expenses are estimated to be about $1460.

Financial Aid

Carleton meets the full demonstrated financial need of every student admitted to the College and continues meeting each student's need for four years or until graduation. An on-campus job of 8 to 10 hours per week and a loan opportunity are included in nearly every financial aid package. In 2009–10, about 80 percent of Carleton students received a total of more than $30 million in financial aid or scholarships from all sources. Fifty-five percent received grant assistance; the average need-based award was $35,273. The only non-need scholarships the College offers are sixty-five to seventy-five Carleton-sponsored National Merit, National Achievement, and National Hispanic Scholarships.

Faculty

All Carleton classes are taught by faculty members rather than graduate students or teaching assistants. Of the 235 faculty members, 188 are full-time, resulting in a student-faculty ratio of 9:1. Of those full-time faculty members, 95 percent hold the highest degree in their academic field. The average class size is about 18, and the average lab size is 16. Most faculty members also serve as academic advisers.

Student Government

Students are actively involved in the governance of the College. Directly below the Board of Trustees is the College Council, chaired by the President, which is composed of 5 faculty members, 5 students, 5 staff members, 1 trustee, and 1 alumnus. The three major policy committees, Education and Curriculum, Student Life, and the Budget Committee, are also made up of faculty members, students, and staff members. Every student is a member of the Carleton Student Association (CSA). Three officers and 16 senators are elected annually to serve as the CSA Senate, which, among other duties, manages the student activities budget.

Admission Requirements

Carleton normally receives about 4,900 applications for the approximately 500 places available in the first-year class. Admission is based on several considerations: superior academic achievement, personal qualities and interests, participation in extracurricular activities, and potential for development as a student and a graduate of the College. The Admissions Committee weighs all factors to ensure that those students offered admission are not only adequately prepared for the academic work but also will benefit from their total experience at Carleton and are likely to add significantly to the College through their individual talents and personal qualities.

Application and Information

Students interested in applying for admission should go to the Web site at http://apps.carleton.edu/admissions/apply/ or contact the Office of Admissions. Interviews, with either a staff member or an alumni admissions representative, are recommended but not required. A visit to the campus is strongly encouraged. During the academic year, overnight stays, interviews, and class visits are usually available but must be scheduled in advance.

Students who decide that Carleton is their first-choice college are encouraged to apply for early decision by November 15, first round, or by January 15, second round. The application deadline for regular decision is January 15. Regular decision candidates are notified before April 15, and the candidate's reply date is May 1. For more information, prospective students should contact:

Office of Admissions
Carleton College
100 South College Street
Northfield, Minnesota 55057

Phone: 507-222-4190
      800-995-2275 (toll-free)
Fax: 507-222-4526
E-mail: admissions@carleton.edu
Web site: http://www.carleton.edu
     http://go.carleton.edu/admissions
     http://go.carleton.edu/apply
     http://www.facebook.com/CarletonCollege
     http://twitter.com/carletoncollege
     http://www.youtube.com/user/carletoncollege

An aerial view of the Carleton College campus.

CARLOS ALBIZU UNIVERSITY

MIAMI, FLORIDA

The University

Carlos Albizu University (CAU) is a university system with campuses in San Juan, Puerto Rico and Miami, Florida. CAU is dedicated to the study and understanding of human endeavors from a holistic, dynamic, and integrated perspective. The University's programs have produced culturally sensitive professionals who are capable of serving the diverse and multicultural population of the global community. It is accredited by the Middle States Commission of Higher Education and American Psychological Association (APA) and is licensed by the Florida Department of Education Commission for Independent Education.

The University was founded in San Juan, Puerto Rico in 1966 by Dr. Carlos Albizu-Miranda as the Caribbean Center for Advanced Studies, a private nonprofit university. The Miami campus was established in 1980 as Miami Institute of Psychology. In 2000, the two-campus institution was renamed Carlos Albizu University as a posthumous honor to its founder, making it the only fully accredited secular university in the United States named in honor of a Hispanic. CAU proudly recognizes Dr. Albizu's distinguished career as a professor of psychology and his service as the first president of the National Hispanic Psychological Association.

The University's mission is achieved through advanced training, research, the dissemination of scientific and cultural information, and the provision of professional services with sensitivity toward culturally diverse constituencies. Through its expert faculty, CAU offers exciting and challenging programs to more than 2,000 students, who represent more than forty countries. Classes are small, with flexible schedules to meet the students' needs.

In addition to its undergraduate programs in psychology, education, and business administration, the University also offers the following master's degree programs: an accelerated, 15-month Master of Business Administration (M.B.A.); a Master of Science in psychology with majors in marriage and family therapy, mental health counseling, and school counseling; and a Master of Science in industrial and organizational psychology (ranked third in the nation and the top program of its kind in the Eastern U.S. by independent researchers). CAU also offers Master of Science degree programs in exceptional student education (ESSE) and in teaching English to speakers of other languages (TESOL). The APA-accredited Doctor of Psychology (Psy.D.) program offers concentrations in child psychology, clinical neuropsychology, forensic psychology, and general psychology. CAU is approved to provide the course work leading to state certification in early childhood education, English for speakers of other languages (ESOL), and for reading endorsement in elementary education.

CAU was ranked by *The Hispanic Outlook in Higher Education Magazine* as one of the 100 best universities in the United States for Hispanic students and was also ranked twelfth in granting doctoral degrees to Hispanic students and eighty-sixth in master's degrees programs.

CAU was founded in 1966 in Puerto Rico with the specific objective of offering a Master of Science degree in clinical psychology. At that time, very few mental health professionals worked on the island, and most of them received their professional education outside of Puerto Rico. CAU enabled these professionals to receive training that was specifically adapted to Puerto Rican sociocultural realities. The University is now a thriving and modern $14-million campus with 240,000 square feet of facilities that include the Goodman Psychological Services Center that has provided direct mental health services to over 10,000 members of the South Florida community, an auditorium/lecture hall with more than 300 seats, and parking space for 554 cars.

Location

The University is located in the new city of Doral in Miami-Dade County, Florida. Multiple dining, an international airport, shopping, and entertainment venues are located just around the corner from the Miami campus, and the world-famous art deco district of Miami Beach is only 25 minutes away. In addition, many national and international companies have their headquarters in the area neighboring the campus. Rich in multicultural diversity and laden with the complex socioeconomic and psychosocial realities that accompany such diversity, Miami has become a multicultural and international center as well as the home of many who have moved to the U.S. from Latin America and the Caribbean.

Majors and Degrees

At the Miami campus, the University offers the following undergraduate programs: a Bachelor of Science (B.S.) degree in psychology, a Bachelor of Business Administration (B.B.A.) degree, a Bachelor of Arts (B.A.) in elementary education, and certificate programs in early childhood education (ECE) and in English for speakers of other languages (ESOL).

Academic Programs

A bachelor's degree requires completion of 120 to 124 credits, including 48 to 60 credits in foundation courses, 43 to 48 credits in core major courses, and the rest in concentrations or electives. The B.S. in psychology and the B.A. in elementary education may receive a maximum of 90 transfer credits from an accredited institution of higher learning. The Bachelor of Business Administration may receive a maximum of 72 transfer credits. Students must have an overall grade point average (GPA) of at least 2.0 in order to be admitted; the GPA within the program of study must be maintained at 2.25 to 2.5, depending on the program.

Independent study allows students to take a regular course from an instructor on an individual or small-group basis rather than in a classroom setting. With the approval of a professor and the program director, a student may take a maximum of 9 hours of independent study after competing at least 24 hours of traditional study. Special project courses allow students to design courses to fit their particular interests and needs, including online, Saturday, and afternoon courses, among others.

The academic year is divided into three 15-week academic terms: spring (January to April), summer (May to August), and fall (September to December).

Academic Facilities

The Albizu Library's collection includes printed and nonprinted materials in the behavioral sciences, psychology, psychiatry, and mental health. The collection also includes a number of volumes and resources on business, management, marketing, economics, accounting, and finance, as well as subscriptions to the leading management journals and publications. Additional resources are offered in the areas of curriculum development, elementary education, special education, and classroom management. CAU students have access to the leading online databases, such as EBSCO and ProQuest. A special collection of materials on cross-cultural topics is also housed in the library, and there is a collection of testing materials for different disciplines.

The CAU campus offers it students many facilities and features similar to those offered at a larger university while also providing the personal attention afforded by a small university. The University features five computer labs, a student lounge, cafeteria, indoor and outdoor study areas, and the Albizu Library. The University has wireless Internet connections available throughout the campus and has technologically equipped classrooms.

CAU is home to the Goodman Psychological Services Center. This is a unique resource to both the students training to become practitioners in the field of psychology and to the community. The students are given the opportunity to hone clinically acquired skills while providing supervised mental health services to CAU's local community. Since 1980, the Goodman Center has provided services to more than ten thousand members of the community and continues to contribute to the availability of affordable mental health care to underserved populations.

Costs

Undergraduate tuition for 2010–11 was $314 per credit ($397 per credit for the fast-track business administration program). Other expenses include a global fee of $248 per session.

Financial Aid

More than 75 percent of CAU's students receive financial aid. Recipients must be U.S. citizens or eligible noncitizens who are enrolled for at least 6 credits. In addition, students must not be in default or owe repayment on a grant. Financial aid applications must be received by June 1 for fall enrollment, October 1 for spring enrollment, and March 1 for summer enrollment. In accordance with Title IV regulations, an undergraduate student is considered to be full-time when enrolled in 12 or more credits and part-time when enrolled in 6 to 11 credits of study. Available grants include the Federal Pell Grant, the Federal Supplemental Opportunity Educational Grant, the Florida State Assistance Grant, and the Florida Bright Futures Scholarship. Fifteen $1000 Albizu Scholarships are offered each term. Tuition assistance of 20 percent is available to government employees for qualifying programs. Federal Stafford Student Loans and Federal PLUS loans are available with interest rates that do not exceed 9 percent.

Faculty

The faculty consists of approximately 100 full-time and part-time instructors, all of whom have advanced degrees (master's or higher) in their respective programs of study and are members of professional organizations related to their fields of interest and research.

Student Government

The Student Council seeks to promote communication, cooperation, and understanding among students and members of the faculty and administration and suggests ways to promote the best interests and objectives of the academic community. The Student Council's functions are regulated by the applicable dispositions of the General Regulations for Students of the CAU.

Admission Requirements

Undergraduate applicants must submit the following items to be considered for admission: a completed and signed application form; official transcripts from all high schools, colleges, or universities previously attended; letters of recommendation; a resume; and a $25 application fee. Undergraduate applicants must present a GPA of 2.0 or higher to be considered for admission. Graduate degree programs follow different admission standards and procedures.

International students applying for admission must comply with current immigration regulations and submit their academic records to authorized agencies for verification of their equivalency to course work offered in the United States. In addition, they should have all admission credentials on file at least ninety days prior to the beginning of the term of expected enrollment.

Transfer students may transfer credits earned from an accredited college or university. Education and training must have been received in an accredited institution of higher education that at the time of training was accredited by an accrediting organization recognized by the U.S. Department of Education. Students may apply for prior learning credits for college-level course work, work experience, military service, or analogous learning outside of the traditional classroom.

After all materials have been received, the applicant's completed file is forwarded to the appropriate undergraduate program and reviewed by a faculty member. At the discretion of the director of the undergraduate program, the applicant is scheduled for an interview. Upon admission to the program, a faculty adviser is assigned to the prospective student.

CAU does not discriminate against any student with special needs and/or conditions who is otherwise eligible and who meets program and professional performance standards and expectations.

Application and Information

Applications must be received prior to the beginning of the term of enrollment for which the applicant is requesting admission. Out-of-state and international applicants should submit all admission documents at least ninety days prior to the beginning of the term of expected enrollment. Applications may be submitted online at www.mia.albizu.edu or mailed to:

Miami Campus
Carlos Albizu University
2173 Northwest 99th Avenue
Miami, Florida 33172
Phone: 305-593-1223 Ext. 137
      888-GO-TO-CAU (toll-free)
Phone: 888-468-6228 (toll-free)
Fax: 305-593-1854
Web site: http://www.mia.albizu.edu

CAU is a federally designated Hispanic Serving Institution with a multicultural emphasis integrated into its programs and courses to enhance students' knowledge, skills, and abilities in working within multicultural settings. The diversity of the student body is represented by students from sixty-five countries seeking a degree to advance professionally.

CARLOW UNIVERSITY
PITTSBURGH, PENNSYLVANIA

The University

Carlow University was founded in 1929 in response to a local need for a Catholic women's college. The mission of the University is to involve people, primarily women, in a process of self-directed lifelong learning that frees them to think clearly and creatively, to discover and to challenge or affirm cultural and aesthetic values, to respond reverently to God and others, and to render competent and compassionate service in personal and professional life. Although Carlow makes explicit its strong continuing commitment to the education of women, it welcomes men. The University's mission has been confirmed over the years by the growing number of students who come seeking a solid liberal arts education as well as strong career preparation. In addition to its undergraduate programs, the University offers an M.B.A., an M.F.A., a Master of Science in Fraud and Forensics, and other graduate degrees.

Current enrollment exceeds 2,300 students. Carlow's students have various backgrounds and come mainly from the Middle Atlantic states; the majority are from western Pennsylvania.

Placement and career counseling, free professional and peer tutorial services, the Center for Academic Achievement, the Disabilities Service Office, student health, personal counseling programs, and campus ministry are support services available to students.

Cocurricular organizations include the Student Government Association, the Commuter Student Association, the International Student Association, the *Purple Menace* newspaper, and United Black Students, among many others.

The University has a large group of students involved in community service and volunteerism. Spring break service projects have taken students to Jamaica, the Virgin Islands, Arizona, Arkansas, Texas, Ireland, and many other locations. Academic- or career-oriented organizations include Alpha Phi Omega (national service/honor society), American Chemical Society, Beta Beta Beta (biology club), Business Leaders of Carlow, the Council for Exceptional Children, Kappa Delta Epsilon (for education majors), Social Work Organization, Student Nurses Association of Pennsylvania, Phi Chi Theta (business fraternity), and the Psychology Club. Special-interest groups include Blessed, the Gospel choir; the Environmental Clean-up Organization; Pep Band; Spirit; Student Athlete Association; Theater Group; and Women in Communication (WIC).

The athletic program includes women's intercollegiate basketball, soccer, softball, tennis, and volleyball as well as a selection of physical education courses, including aerobics, fitness and weight control, martial arts/self-defense, modern dance, water aerobics, weight training, and yoga. Wellness and fitness services include individual health assessment, fitness programming, and nutrition counseling.

Popular campus events include entertainment, film series, carnivals, Homecoming, Mercy Founders Week, a St. Patrick's Day celebration and parade, the International Festival, Black History Month events, Women's History Month events, and theater productions.

The University's central location gives students opportunities for internships in various businesses and agencies. Students in health-related fields complete their clinical experiences in the many fine teaching hospitals and private health-care facilities in the city of Pittsburgh. City buses stop in front of the campus, and campus parking is available for commuting students.

Location

Carlow University is located on a 15-acre campus in the heart of Oakland, one of the nation's biggest college towns and the educational, cultural, and medical center of Pittsburgh. Nine other colleges and universities at which students can cross-register are within walking distance or just minutes away by bus. Schenley Park, Carnegie Library and Museums, Phipps Conservatory, Carnegie Music and Lecture Halls, and the Oakland shopping district are all a short walk from the campus. Downtown Pittsburgh is only a 10-minute bus ride away. Greater Pittsburgh International Airport is a 30-minute drive from the Carlow campus.

Majors and Degrees

Carlow University grants the undergraduate degrees of Bachelor of Arts, Bachelor of Science, Bachelor of Science in Nursing, and Bachelor of Social Work. Programs include accounting, art, art/art education, art/art history, art/ceramics, art/graphic design, art/interactive media design, art/painting and drawing, art/photography, art with a certificate in art therapy preparation, biology (with concentrations in forensic medical and legal investigations/autopsy specialization, human biology, molecular cell and biotechnology, and organismal/ecological biology), business management, business management/communication, chemistry, communication studies, creative writing, early childhood education, elementary education, English, forensic accounting, health science (available to students who have previously earned an associate degree), history, human resource management and technology, information systems management, liberal studies, marketing, mathematics, nursing, philosophy, political science, professional writing, professional writing/business, psychology, public policy and leadership, scientific/medical marketing, social work, sociology, sociology/criminal justice, Spanish, special education, and theology. An independent major, designed by the student, may also be arranged.

Certification programs are offered in forensic accounting, perfusion technology (biology majors only) and secondary education (biology, chemistry, English, general science, mathematics, and social studies).

The University offers 3-2 programs in engineering in three areas: biology/environmental engineering, chemistry/chemical engineering, and mathematics/engineering. In addition, there is a 3-2 program in environmental science.

Academic Programs

Carlow's primary concern is the development of the student as a lifelong learner. To this end, members of the Carlow community—students, faculty, and staff—recognize the integrity and value of each person in the daily life and work of the University. The academic programs are broad and flexible, including opportunities for double majors, single majors with certification in education, minors, certificate programs, and changes of major. Transfer students are warmly welcomed.

The University operates on the two-semester system, August to December and January to May. Summer sessions, a variable number of weeks in length, are offered every year. Most courses carry 3 credits (laboratory courses, among others, carry 4 credits). Students normally take five courses each semester. Each student must demonstrate basic competence in English composition, speech and interpersonal communication, reading comprehension, and mathematics. Required of all students is one course each in a lab science, history, literature, mathematics, social/behavioral science (such as psychology or sociology), theology, fine arts, philosophy, women's studies, and political science or economics, as well as one global perspective course. Students are also required to take an interdisciplinary course, which is selected from a variety of subject areas. Students in nursing, education, social work, psychology, management, and perfusion technology are required to do fieldwork as part of their program. Field placements and internships are guaranteed and encouraged in all areas of study. An honors program is open to eligible students. After the first semester of the first year, one course per semester (outside of the major) may be taken on a pass-fail basis. Some courses may be challenged, for credit or exemption, by passing an examination. CLEP general exam credits may be used for this purpose as well.

The University gives women and men the opportunity to return to the classroom at various stages of their lives. Adult learners may enroll in full-time and part-time degree programs, noncredit enrichment courses, seminars, and workshops. Scheduling options include day, evening, accelerated, weekend, and online courses.

Academic Facilities

Grace Library, a five-level multipurpose learning center in the heart of the campus, currently contains more than 100,000 books, subscribes to over 350 print journals, and offers access to more than 4,500 online journals. The library houses the offices of the President and Provost. The Center for Academic Achievement, the mail room, the bookstore, Academic Affairs, the Center for Career Enrichment, Printing Services, the International Poetry Forum, University Archives, and computer laboratories are also located here. Kresge Theatre, a 300-seat auditorium, is located on the fifth level as well.

Curran Hall houses the School of Nursing and includes a state-of-the-art nursing skills lab and conference and seminar rooms. Frances Warde Hall is a residence hall that also houses the School of Education, art labs, student affairs offices, and the campus café. Antonian Hall houses the 1,000-seat Sister Rosemary Heyl Theatre, the School for Social Change, the fine arts department, and classrooms as well as administrative offices for admissions, financial aid, advising, the registrar, and student accounts.

The cafeteria and the Campus School of Carlow University (kindergarten through grade 8) are located in Tiernan Hall. St. Joseph Hall contains the gymnasium, fitness center, and swimming pool, and Aquinas Hall houses classrooms, the humanities division, the International Student Center, and faculty and staff offices.

Carlow's A. J. Palumbo Hall of Science and Technology houses state-of-the-art teaching/research laboratories in physics, organic and advanced chemistry, genetics, cell biology, and gross anatomy; a herbarium to store dry plant specimens; a greenhouse; an amphitheater for scientific presentations; and the Bayer Children's Science Learning Laboratory.

Carlow University's campus computer network features Internet accounts and e-mail, network and Internet access from any location on campus. There is one network port per pillow in the residence halls.

Costs

Tuition for 2011–12 is $23,504 for full-time students. Room and board charges for the year are $9256 for double occupancy.

Financial Aid

Financial aid in the form of grants, scholarships, loans, and student employment is available to eligible applicants. More than 90 percent of all full-time students receive some type of financial assistance. The University expects that most aid recipients assume a portion of their expenses through loans and/or part-time employment. Job opportunities are available on campus in a wide variety of positions, and students are placed, whenever possible, in positions that coincide with their skills and interests. Basketball, soccer, softball, tennis, and volleyball scholarships are also available.

Faculty

Carlow's student-faculty ratio is 12:1, and faculty members are readily available to help plan individualized programs of study, to provide assistance relating to field placements and internships, and to assist in career preparation. The student's major adviser is normally a faculty member in the department.

Student Government

All registered students are members of the Student Government Association (SGA). Through the SGA, students act as equal participants with the administration, faculty, and staff in general governance. The SGA promotes the general welfare of the students and is the advocate to ensure that the academic, social, and spiritual needs of students are met. SGA is empowered to charter all student organizations.

Admission Requirements

Applicants are evaluated on the basis of their secondary school record, class rank, and scores on the SAT or ACT. The Committee on Admissions recognizes that school curricula vary greatly and always gives careful consideration to the application of an able student whose course work or grading scale is more challenging or whose preparation differs from the traditional program. A personal interview is strongly recommended but not required. Overnight visits, a day of classes, campus tours, and meals are available and are strongly encouraged. Throughout the year, the University sponsors programs that give candidates the opportunity to tour the campus and meet faculty and staff members and Carlow students.

Application and Information

Although Carlow subscribes to the rolling admission plan, high school students are encouraged to submit an application early in the first semester of the senior year. Students interested in early notification should apply by September 30. The University's priority admission and scholarship deadline is February 15.

Students may apply online or request an application form by contacting:

Office of Admissions
Carlow University
3333 Fifth Avenue
Pittsburgh, Pennsylvania 15213
Phone: 412-578-6059
        800-333-2275
E-mail: admissions@carlow.edu
Web site: http://www.carlow.edu

CARNEGIE MELLON UNIVERSITY

PITTSBURGH, PENNSYLVANIA

Carnegie Mellon

The University

Since its beginning more than 100 years ago, Carnegie Mellon has evolved into an institution consistently ranked in the top 25 for its unique approach to education and research. Students become experts in fields ranging from business, the fine arts, and computer science to humanities, the sciences, and engineering—far more than steel magnate and philanthropist Andrew Carnegie first envisioned when he founded Carnegie Mellon as a technical school in 1900.

Carnegie Mellon is world renowned for its left-brain and right-brain thinking that unite within the University's collaborative culture and are the foundation of learning at Carnegie Mellon. Students acquire a depth and breadth of knowledge while sharpening problem-solving, critical-thinking, creative, and quantitative skills. The University's unique approach to education develops sound critical judgment, resourcefulness, and professional ethics through interdisciplinary and hands-on experiences. Graduates go on to become the innovative leaders and problem solvers of tomorrow.

Students in this private coeducational university come from all fifty states and more than forty countries. Each year, Carnegie Mellon enrolls a diverse freshman class of approximately 1,450 students from a variety of social and cultural backgrounds with a wide range of academic and artistic interests. The total undergraduate population is 5,950. Approximately 14 percent of the student body identifies with an ethnic minority population such as African American, Hispanic/Latino American, or Native American. The international student population makes up 14 percent of the student body.

Carnegie Mellon spans the best of both worlds; its traditional 150-acre campus is located minutes from downtown Pittsburgh, yet it is surrounded by residential neighborhoods. Student activities include more than 225 clubs and organizations, varsity and intramural sports, fraternities and sororities, and student government. Off campus, students can take advantage of three culturally active neighborhoods (all within walking distance), the largest public park in Pittsburgh, urban and suburban shopping, excellent sightseeing, professional sports, museums, art galleries, and amusement parks.

Approximately 70 percent of students live in University housing, which is guaranteed for all four years, provided students remain in the housing system, and ranges from traditional residence halls, special-interest housing, and apartment buildings to fraternity and sorority housing. Freshmen are required to live in University housing.

Carnegie Mellon students come away from their undergraduate experience poised to be trendsetters, whether in the business world, the art community, or graduate school. Students not only gain the knowledge necessary to succeed professionally, they also learn how to maximize their creativity, intellectual playfulness, and analytical skills in order to survive in an ever-changing global environment. The University strives to produce graduates who are adaptable, resourceful, and independent—graduates who communicate effectively, strive to be leaders, and understand their professional and social responsibilities.

High school juniors can participate in Carnegie Mellon's six-week summer Pre-College programs, in which students have the opportunity to take college course work, meet people from all over the country, live like true college students, and explore the city of Pittsburgh. Students can take two regular Carnegie Mellon courses for full credit in disciplines such as engineering, humanities, computer science, or the sciences; immerse themselves in the fine arts studio or conservatory-based courses to determine their level of interest for study at the college level in architecture, art and design, drama, or music; or attend the National High School Game Academy, in which students learn interactive digital game development through hands-on experience.

In addition to bachelor's degrees, Carnegie Mellon offers master's and doctoral degrees.

Location

Carnegie Mellon is located 5 miles from the downtown area in the Oakland neighborhood of Pittsburgh. Home to several of the city's colleges, universities, museums, and hospitals, Oakland offers many activities and resources to area students. Although Carnegie Mellon has the collegiate feel of a suburban campus, the surrounding Pittsburgh community provides all of the cultural and social advantages of a big city. The University is approximately 1 hour from some of the best skiing in the East and is only a short plane ride from many major metropolitan areas, including Boston, New York City, Chicago, Philadelphia, and Washington, D.C.

Majors and Degrees

Undergraduate majors at Carnegie Mellon include business administration, computer science, engineering (biomedical engineering*, chemical engineering, civil and environmental engineering, electrical and computer engineering, engineering and public policy*, materials science engineering, and mechanical engineering), fine and performing arts (architecture, art, design, drama, and music), information systems, liberal arts and professional studies (economics, English, history, information systems, modern languages, philosophy, psychology, social and decision sciences, and statistics), and the sciences (biological sciences, chemistry, mathematical sciences, and physics). The Bachelor of Humanities and Arts (B.H.A.), Bachelor of Science and Arts (B.S.A.), and Bachelor of Computer Science and Arts (B.C.S.A.) degree programs are also available, as are many interdepartmental majors. (* indicates double majors only.)

Academic Programs

There is no core curriculum at Carnegie Mellon. The only required classes are Computing@CarnegieMellon (C@CM) and a first-year writing course. Each college has its own requirements for graduation.

Students at Carnegie Mellon have the freedom to design courses of study that cross over majors and disciplines. In fact, some students have double majors, minors, or concentrations in areas other than their principal major. It is not unusual to find an engineering student with a double major in music or an English major with a minor in business administration.

The Bachelor of Humanities and Arts, Bachelor of Science and Arts, and Bachelor of Computer Science and Arts degree programs are unique, nonperformance-based programs that allow students to pursue interdisciplinary programs in the fine arts and either computer science, humanities and social sciences, or the pure sciences. Other special programs include Army, Navy, and Air Force ROTC; self-defined majors and interdepartmental major options in the College of Humanities and Social Sciences; prelaw and premedicine advising programs; and five-year combined bachelor's/master's degree programs.

Carnegie Mellon has nearly unlimited opportunities for students to participate in undergraduate research, sometimes as early as the second semester of the freshman year. Many departments offer research training courses and research programs during the academic year and summer. Students can work on research in groups, individually with a professor, or independently through Carnegie Mellon's Small Undergraduate Research Grant (SURG) program.

Off-Campus Programs

Carnegie Mellon students can take one course per semester at any of the following colleges and universities in Pittsburgh for full credit: the University of Pittsburgh, Carlow College, Chatham University, Duquesne University, La Roche College, Point Park University, Robert Morris University, Pittsburgh Theological Seminary, and the Community College of Allegheny County.

Carnegie Mellon has numerous study-abroad programs, including university exchange programs in Chile, Singapore, Mexico, Japan, and Switzerland. More than 480 students take advantage of study abroad each year. Students may also take advantage of study-abroad opportunities through their department or another university.

Academic Facilities

Carnegie Mellon has a 150-acre main campus with a few outlying research buildings. The campus contains more than fifty academic and administrative buildings and three libraries. The Hunt, Engineering and Science, and Mellon Institute Libraries contain more than 1 million volumes and thousands of periodicals. An international online resource sharing system and reciprocal borrowing between Carnegie Mellon and other local universities provide students with almost unlimited library resources.

A wireless network spans all academic, administrative, and residence hall buildings as well as key outdoor areas across campus. Public computing labs, known as clusters, offer more than 400 Macintosh, Windows, and Linux workstations.

All of the residence hall rooms are wired to the Andrew network—Carnegie Mellon's high-speed computer network that links the campus and provides access to the outside world. Carnegie Mellon was the first university campus to offer wireless networking.

In addition to academic facilities, Carnegie Mellon features the University Center—a centralized building with eateries and recreational facilities, the historic Kresge Theater for Performing Arts, studio and black-box theaters, art galleries, abundant studio and rehearsal space, a gymnasium, and numerous research laboratories.

Costs

Carnegie Mellon's costs for the 2010–11 academic year included tuition and fees of $41,500 and room and board of $10,750. Books, supplies, and personal expenses were estimated at $2400. The total cost was approximately $55,286. International students also paid an additional $1000 for required health insurance.

Financial Aid

Carnegie Mellon is a need-blind institution, meaning that students' personal financial information is not considered in the admission process. Approximately 56 percent of the freshman class receives financial aid (U.S. citizens and eligible noncitizens).

Carnegie Mellon uses Federal Methodology to determine financial aid eligibility. The forms required to apply for financial assistance are the Free Application for Federal Student Aid (FAFSA), the College Scholarship Service Financial Aid PROFILE, parental W-2s, and both parental and student tax returns. Financial aid packages usually include a combination of loans, grants, and work-study allowances.

Carnegie Mellon also offers the Carnegie Scholarship, a need- and merit-based scholarship, awarded to academically and artistically talented middle-income students who qualify for little to no need-based financial aid. Carnegie Scholarships are open to all qualified U.S. citizens and permanent residents, regardless of race or national origin. In order to be considered for the Carnegie Scholarship, students must file the FAFSA. Students are also encouraged to apply for outside scholarships as a source of aid.

Faculty

Carnegie Mellon has more than 1,200 teaching and research faculty members and a student-faculty ratio of 12:1. The average class size is 25 to 35 students. Faculty members are practicing professionals at the forefront of their respective fields who often teach both undergraduate and graduate courses. Carnegie Mellon's classes are taught by faculty members, not teaching assistants. Professors, instructors, and lecturers are in the classroom, lab, studio, or workplace creating new knowledge on a daily basis and passing that knowledge on to their students. Undergraduates have the opportunity to work on groundbreaking research projects with award-winning faculty members, many times one-on-one, through assistantships, internships, work-study positions, and extracurricular organizations.

Student Government

Carnegie Mellon's Student Senate is composed of representatives from each college at Carnegie Mellon and exists to promote the welfare of the campus community, distribute budget funds to student groups, provide a liaison between students and the administration, and inform the student body of proposals and changes.

Admission Requirements

Carnegie Mellon looks for strong students, both academically and socially, who have a wide range of interests and activities. There are no minimum grade requirements or standardized test scores, although most of Carnegie Mellon's students tend to have strong test scores and are at the top of their classes. The University uses standardized test scores, including the SAT Reasoning Test or ACT with Writing Test and SAT Subject Tests; high school performance; evidence of leadership; honors and awards earned; and extracurricular activities to make admission decisions. Recommendations from a guidance counselor and a teacher are required along with a personal statement and essay. Interviews with admission counselors are recommended but not required.

Carnegie Mellon also requires the TOEFL or IELTS if the student's native language is not English. Carnegie Mellon requires TOEFL scores of 250 or better on the CBT TOEFL, 600 or better on the pencil and paper TOEFL, 102 or better on the Internet-based TOEFL, or an IELTS score of 7 or above.

Carnegie Mellon strives to build a class of students that is racially, socially, economically, and geographically diverse. The University is committed to recruiting students from traditionally underrepresented backgrounds, including African Americans, Hispanic/Latino Americans, and Native Americans. Transfer students are also welcome.

Application and Information

Carnegie Mellon has three types of decision plans: early admission, early decision, and regular decision.

Early admission is for high school juniors who wish to skip their senior year to go directly to college. In addition to academic strength, early admission candidates must display maturity and have strong teacher and guidance counselor recommendations. The application deadline for early admission is January 1 (December 1 for fine arts), and candidates are notified between March 15 and April 15.

Early decision is offered for students who declare Carnegie Mellon as their first choice. Early decision is a binding agreement; if admitted, students are expected to enroll. The University offers two early decision plans. The deadline for Early Decision I is November 1 (there is no Early Decision I for acting, music, theater, directing, composition, voice, flute, music technology, or B.C.S.A./B.H.A./B.S.A.), and candidates are notified of a decision by December 15. The deadline for Early Decision II is December 1 (there is no Early Decision II for architecture, art, design, drama, music, or B.C.S.A./B.H.A./B.S.A.), and candidates are notified by January 15.

Regular decision is the most popular plan. Applications are due by January 1 (December 1 for fine arts), and notification occurs between March 15 and April 15.

Students interested in learning more about Carnegie Mellon can arrange to visit the campus. Throughout most of the year, the University offers group information sessions, campus tours, and personal interviews, which are recommended, but not required, for admission.

Group information sessions and hometown or alumni interviews are available for students who cannot come to Pittsburgh. University representatives travel across the United States during the fall of every year. Students should visit http://www.cmu.edu/admission to see the current travel schedule.

For more information, students should contact:

Carnegie Mellon Office of Admission
5000 Forbes Avenue
Pittsburgh, Pennsylvania 15213-3890

Phone: 412-268-2082
Fax: 412-268-7838
E-mail: undergraduate-admissions@andrew.cmu.edu
Web site: http://www.cmu.edu/admission/
http://www.facebook.com/CarnegieMellonAdmission
http://twitter.com/CM_Admission

Carnegie Mellon University, located in Pittsburgh, Pennsylvania, is one of America's leading universities.

CARROLL COLLEGE

HELENA, MONTANA

The College

Student-centered and affordable, Carroll College is a private, four-year Catholic college located in Montana's state capital that offers a firm track record of proven success for its graduates. In the sciences, Carroll premed students have a consistent average medical school acceptance rate to top medical schools of around 85 percent—the national average is around 50 percent. Carroll's premed graduates are practicing medicine all over the world and performing cutting-edge medical research into curing cancer and other human diseases. Also much higher than the national average is the 95 percent first-time pass rate Carroll's nursing graduates earn on their professional RN examination and subsequent success in obtaining the best nursing jobs nationwide and internationally. Carroll's civil engineering majors have a 90 percent first-time pass rate on the national Engineer-in-Training exam and have jobs or graduate school acceptances in their fields within weeks of earning their degrees.

The Carroll educational experience also includes the opportunity for students to have fun while they are preparing for the professional world. Carroll students enjoy access to internships in their chosen fields so they can experience what it might be like to work in the legal profession, as an accountant, or as a business owner; they can test-drive a career in health care, government, politics, teaching, or the nonprofit arena. Because Carroll is small, with an enrollment of 1,450, students don't have to stand in line for professional opportunities—they're available for anyone with the motivation and the desire.

On campus, there are opportunities to explore future careers in science by becoming a student researcher for one of Carroll's biology or chemistry professors. Carroll students are currently researching chronic wasting disease and the West Nile Virus in outstanding, grant-funded laboratory facilities. For a small school, Carroll has earned big national recognitions. Three times since 2003, Carroll math students have won the world's top prize in the Interdisciplinary Contest in Modeling and the Mathematical Contest in Modeling. Carroll students won their latest best-in-the-world math contest award in 2010—and the winning team was led by a female math student, one of the few women worldwide ever to take the top prize in this competition. The Carroll Talking Saints forensics team—which combines speech, debate, politics, and acting skills—finished last season ranked in the top 10 of all colleges and universities nationwide and is in the running for its twenty-first straight year as Northwest regional champions. In athletics, Carroll's Fighting Saints football team reigns as the current and six-time NAIA national champions.

Distinctive to Carroll is its dedication to service learning and social justice. Starting from the first semester of freshman year, students embark on professor-led projects to help underserved people while examining the deeper issues involved. These projects take students into the community, where they offer volunteer hours and research expertise to organizations such as the local food bank, homeless shelter, and schools. Service abroad is available several times a year to Carroll students. Recent trips include student journeys to Haiti, Honduras, and Columbia to provide medical care. Carroll's student chapter of Engineers Without Borders constructed an integrated sewer, farm irrigation, fish hatchery, and spice farm system at a Mexican orphanage and are now designing and building water and wastewater engineering projects for a Guatemalan school and clinic. Carroll students can also create their own social justice project. As an example, for four years, students have led an award-winning campaign to benefit St. Jude Children's Research Hospital and raised over $100,000.

Founded in 1909, Carroll College is accredited by the Northwest Association of Schools and Colleges. The College is a member of the National Association of Independent Colleges and Universities, the American Council on Education, the Council of Independent Colleges, the Association of Catholic Colleges and Universities, and the Western Independent College Fund.

Location

Helena, the state capital, nestles in the heart of southwestern Montana's Rocky Mountains and is a wonderland for hikers, mountain bikers, climbers, skiers and boarders, kayakers, and enthusiasts of almost every outdoor sport. The city offers cultural, arts, and entertainment opportunities year-round, and the local business community and state government provide Carroll students outstanding internship and job opportunities. Helena has city amenities without the drawbacks; getting around is easy and quick, with no traffic congestion and a downtown within walking distance. Friendly and welcoming, Helena has a consistently low crime rate and high quality of life.

Majors and Degrees

Carroll College offers a four-year Bachelor of Arts degree program. Its majors and areas of concentration include accounting; biology; biochemistry-molecular biology; business administration (with concentrations in economics, finance, international business, management, and marketing); chemistry; civil engineering; civil engineering with a concentration in environmental engineering; classical studies; communication studies; community health; computer information systems (CIS); computer science; elementary education; engineering (3-2 and 4-2 programs); engineering mechanics; English literature; English writing; environmental studies (with concentrations in biology, chemistry, community formation, culture integration, and public policy and management); ethics and values studies; French; health and physical education (with concentrations in K–12 and sport management); health science; history; international relations; mathematics (with a cognate concentration); nursing; philosophy; political science; psychology; public administration; public relations (with concentrations in marketing, print journalism, and TV production); secondary education (with concentrations in biology, chemistry, communication studies, English, history, mathematics, political science, and social studies); sociology; Spanish; Spanish education (K–12); theater (with concentrations in acting/directing and design/stagecraft); and theology (with concentrations in contextual and systematic).

Under the 3-2 engineering program, students attend Carroll for three years and then transfer to an affiliate school to complete their studies in a specialized engineering field (mechanical, electrical, chemical, etc). Upon completion, students receive two bachelor's degrees, one from Carroll in engineering mathematics, and one from the affiliate school in their chosen specialty field. Affiliate schools are Columbia, Gonzaga, Montana State, Montana Tech, the University of Minnesota, Notre Dame, and USC.

Carroll offers preprofessional programs in dentistry, law, medicine, optometry, pharmacy, physical therapy, physician's assistant studies, seminary, and veterinary medicine. Carroll also offers various two-year Associate of Arts degrees.

Academic Programs

The academic year consists of fall and spring semesters and a limited summer term. Carroll's Bachelor of Arts degree program requires that all students study the arts, sciences, humanities, and social sciences for at least four of their eight semesters at Carroll. A Bachelor of Science in Nursing is also available.

Minors and special course offerings include anthropology, arts management and administration, community health, dance, economics, education abroad, European studies, gender studies, geographic information system (GIS) certification, the Honors Scholars Program, human-animal bond, languages (including French, German, Greek, Latin, linguistics, and Spanish), Latin American studies, military science (ROTC), music, physics, special education, project management certification, television production, and visual arts.

Off-Campus Programs

Nearly 90 percent of all academic disciplines at Carroll offer professional internship opportunities to give students real-world experience in their future careers. Education-abroad opportunities round out Carroll's academic offerings. Carroll has provided students professor-led programs on every continent except Antarctica. Carroll's Study Abroad Office also arranges for students to enter exchange programs and to perform independent study at colleges and universities worldwide.

Academic Facilities

Carroll College offers comfortable and welcoming learning facilities equipped with the latest technology. The Fortin Science Center provides outstanding chemistry and biology laboratories where students perform real-world, published scientific research. As part of Carroll's centennial capital campaign, biology and chemistry labs were extensively remodeled to create an updated undergraduate research center and allow Carroll to launch a new biochemistry–molecular biology major. The Nursing Department's training facility is the regional leader, with a realistic ER triage unit and an extensive array of the most advanced patient-simulation equipment available, including SimMan and SimBaby. The Civil Engineering Laboratory houses professional-grade machinery and materials, including hydraulics-, machinery-, and structures-testing capabilities and a model water-treatment plant. Carroll's four coed residence halls provide classrooms, computer labs, chapels, a performing arts center, and art studios and galleries. Nelson Stadium and the Carroll PE Center are home to the six-time national football champions, the Fighting Saints, and to Carroll's other athletic teams (soccer, volleyball, men's and women's basketball, cross-country, golf, and track and field), which regularly win Frontier Conference honors and championships.

Costs

For the 2010–11 academic year, Carroll's tuition and fees totaled $23,144; room and board fees were $7518 and the technology and activities fee was $450. Other general personal expenses included books, supplies, and transportation. Generous financial aid provides substantial discounts to almost all students (see Financial Aid below).

Financial Aid

Because of the Carroll's generous financial aid packages and the likelihood of graduating in four years, students matriculate with about the same debt as state-school alumni. In the 2009–10 academic year, Carroll awarded an average of $20,415 in financial aid packages to freshmen. Ninety-five percent of Carroll's full-time degree-seeking students receive College-sponsored, state, and federal financial aid. Merit scholarships range from $7000 to $13,000 annually.

Almost 80 percent of Carroll graduates earn their degrees in four years or fewer, which can lower graduates' debts and improve their lifetime earning potential. Because of these factors—the four-year graduation rate, overall affordability, generous financial aid, debt counseling for students, and its graduates' success in obtaining well-paying jobs—Carroll's student loan repayment default rate is zero, making it one of the most successful in the nation.

More information on Carroll scholarships is available at the College Web site at http://www.carroll.edu/finaid/. To receive priority consideration for scholarships, students must have a complete admission file by February 15. Carroll requires students interested in need-based financial assistance to submit the Free Application for Federal Student Aid (FAFSA), available from high school counselors or at http://www.fafsa.ed.gov, as early as possible after January 1.

Faculty

Carroll's 81 full-time and 64 adjunct faculty members are expert teachers and experts in their fields, with almost all holding doctorate or terminal degrees. Professors, not graduate students, instruct all courses.

Carroll's faculty members are consistently recognized for their excellence, earning Fulbright Scholarships and winning National Endowment for the Arts and National Endowment for the Humanities grants and awards for leadership and scholarship in their fields. In the sciences, Carroll professors perform groundbreaking research across the globe and lead student research in biology, chemistry, history, psychology, and many other disciplines. Widely published in the humanities and sciences, Carroll professors are also student-centered, placing a particular emphasis on mentoring students.

Student Government

The Associated Students of Carroll College helps students communicate with the administration and make decisions about campus activities and student life. All students vote to elect the campus president, vice president, executive secretary and treasurer, and each class (freshman, sophomore, junior, and senior) elects 4 student senators to represent them. Carroll's House of Representatives includes leaders of each campus club. The Carroll Activities Board assists students in starting their own clubs and leading their own projects, including a variety of campus events such as concerts, film festivals, comedy nights, and charity fund-raisers. Students are always welcome to write for Carroll's student newspaper, literary magazine, and yearbook; be

a DJ on Carroll KROL-FM radio; film and report news as an intern reporter/anchor at Saints TV (aired on our NBC affiliate station on campus); and make indie movies for the annual Carroll film festival. Campus clubs include those devoted to service work; faith; social justice activism; professions like engineering, psychology, health care, and education; the environment and recycling; outdoor adventure; politics; international students; dance; rodeo; and astronomy.

Admission Requirements

Degree candidates are those who have applied through the Office of Admission for a course of study leading to the Bachelor of Arts degree. Degree candidates may be enrolled on a full- or part-time basis. Admission decisions are based upon a student's high school performance, personal essay, a secondary school report, letters of recommendation, demonstrated commitment to intellectual achievement, and performance on standardized college entrance exams.

When applying for admission, candidates must submit the application form, official transcripts from the high school and all colleges previously attended, a secondary school report and/or a letter of recommendation, ACT or SAT scores, and a $35 nonrefundable application fee. There is no fee for online applications at http://www.carroll.edu/admission/apply or through the Common Application at https://www.commonapp.org/. Transfer students who have successfully completed more than 24 college semester credits with at least a C (2.5) grade average are not required to submit high school transcripts or ACT or SAT scores.

Application and Information

Carroll College has a rolling admission policy. Deadlines for incoming freshmen are: early action, November 1 and December 1; regular admission, February 15; and rolling admission, May 1. Transfer applicants have a regular admission deadline of March 15. Students should apply early to take advantage of financial aid awards and course registration. Students can apply online at the Carroll Web site or through the Common Application Web site.

For application forms or more information, students should contact:

Director of Admission
Carroll College
1601 North Benton Avenue
Helena, Montana 59625-0002
Phone: 406-447-4384
      800-992-3648 (toll-free)
E-mail: admission@carroll.edu
Web site: http://www.carroll.edu
      http://www.facebook.com/carrollcollege
      http://twitter.com/carrollcollege

Carroll College's St. Charles Hall.

CARROLL UNIVERSITY
WAUKESHA, WISCONSIN

The University

Carroll University was chartered by the territorial legislature of Wisconsin in 1846. Carroll University is affiliated with the Presbyterian Church (U.S.A.) but is nonsectarian and ecumenical.

The University realizes that personalized education is the special province of a small college and recognizes the variety of students' individual needs and preferences. Carroll's student body is diverse, with representation from twenty-five states and thirty-three countries. The campus has more than 2,600 full-time men and women, as well as more than 450 part-time students. In addition, there are more than 250 graduate students on the Carroll campus.

Many opportunities exist for co-curricular involvement. Three fraternities and four sororities draw participation from about 13 percent of the students. A broad variety of special interest organizations provide a full program of campus activities in addition to the all-campus social, intellectual, and athletic events that are scheduled throughout the year. The University's facilities for recreation and athletics include the Van Male Fieldhouse, which has a basketball court; an indoor track; indoor facilities for badminton, tennis, and volleyball; and a pool. The adjacent Ganfield Gymnasium provides additional space for athletics and recreation. A football field, soccer field, outdoor track, and softball diamond are also available.

In addition to the bachelor's degrees Carroll offers, the University also grants the master's degree in education, software engineering, business, and physician assistant studies as well as a clinical doctorate in physical therapy.

Location

The University is located in the city of Waukesha, a residential community of 68,000 people, which is 18 miles west of Milwaukee and 100 miles north of Chicago. The University's proximity to these two major urban centers and to the settings associated with Wisconsin's famous outdoor sports and leisure activities provides Carroll students with numerous opportunities for recreation, entertainment, and enrichment.

Majors and Degrees

Carroll University grants the B.A., B.S., B.M.E. (Bachelor of Music Education), and B.S.N. (Bachelor of Science in Nursing) degrees. Areas of study include accounting; actuarial science; applied physics; art; athletic training; biochemistry; biology; book art; business administration (entrepreneurship, finance, human resources, management, marketing); chemistry; communication; computer science (information systems, software engineering); criminal justice; diagnostic medical sonography; education (adaptive, early childhood, elementary, secondary); English; environmental science; European studies; exercise science; forensic science; global studies; graphic communication; history; information technology (Web application development, business and social applications); journalism; marine biology; mathematics; music; music education; nursing; oceanography; organizational leadership; philosophy, politics, and economics; photography; physical education; physical therapy; politics; psychology; public relations; radiologic technology; recreation management; religious studies; self-designed major; sociology; Spanish; theater arts; and writing.

Academic Programs

The University currently operates on a semester calendar. All students must complete 128 credits with a C average or better. A major, generally consisting of 40 credits, must be completed. General education requirements include the Cultural Seminar, English, liberal studies distribution courses, a cross-cultural experience, and a Global Perspectives Colloquium. B.A. students must take two years of a modern language or the equivalent. B.S. students must take mathematics and either a computer science or logic course. Students may also select a second major or they may select a minor, which generally requires 16 to 28 credits. The honors program offers intensive sections of courses in the arts and sciences for academically talented students.

Advanced placement or credit may be granted to students who have completed the appropriate College Board Advanced Placement examinations. Credit may be granted for a score at or above the 75th percentile on the humanities, natural science, or social science general examination of the College-Level Examination Program (CLEP). Scores on CLEP subject examinations may also qualify to be approved for credit. A total of not more than 48 credit hours may be awarded through CLEP general and subject examinations.

Off-Campus Programs

The New Cultural Experiences Program gives all Carroll students the opportunity to study in a different cultural setting. Students may plan an individual program or participate in a planned group experience involving other students and Carroll faculty members. Group experiences are offered in locations such as Australia, Belize, England, and Japan and countries in Europe and Africa. Other off-campus programs include the Washington Semester, the United Nations Semester, and the Junior Year Abroad. In addition, career internships are provided in the Milwaukee-Waukesha area for students interested in gaining practical work experience in their proposed career field. All of these programs carry degree credit; the amount depends upon the nature and duration of the experience.

Academic Facilities

The University library houses more than 150,000 volumes, 18,000 microforms, and 400 periodicals. The Department of Education is in the Barstow Building with the Modern Language and Communication Departments. Rankin Hall houses the Departments of Biology, Psychology, and Religious Studies, as well as the psychology laboratories. Maxon Hall houses the Departments of Geography and Mathematics. It also contains the laboratories for advanced chemistry; the geography laboratory, with independent-study booths and audiovisual instruments; a darkroom; a cartography laboratory; a map library; and a National Weather Service observation station. The chemistry and physics laboratories are in Lowry Hall. All science laboratories are provided with up-to-date equipment. Main Hall houses classrooms for all academic areas. MacAllister Hall is home to the Departments of English, History, Politics, and Philosophy.

The Shattuck Music Center houses a recital hall that seats 150, an auditorium that seats 1,350, and a Schantz seventy-two-stop pipe organ. The Department of Music has a large band-practice room, teaching studios, a multisensing room, a computerized music laboratory, and classrooms. The Humphrey Building houses the Art Department and Humphrey Memorial Chapel. The University's physical therapy program is located adjacent to the University's athletic complex. A state-of-the-art nursing lab is found in the lower level of the Theatre Arts Building.

Costs

For 2010–11, the tuition was approximately $23,582 and room and board were $7371.

Financial Aid

Approximately 98 percent of Carroll's students receive some form of financial aid. Aid is based on need, as determined by the U.S. Department of Education's Free Application for Federal Student Aid (FAFSA), as well as on scholastic ability and achievement. Generally, students receive a package consisting of a scholarship, a grant, a loan, and/or campus employment.

Various merit scholarships are available to students. Merit scholarships range from $34,000 to $54,000 over four years and are determined by a student's ACT or SAT scores and class rank. Students who attend high schools that do not rank are not excluded from consideration for any academic scholarships. Additional scholarships are awarded to qualified students who are interested in music, theater, history, art, math, or the sciences. Students should contact the Office of Admission for details.

Faculty

The student-faculty ratio at Carroll is approximately 16:1. More than 85 percent of faculty members hold a doctorate in their specialized area of study. There are more than 100 full-time faculty members at Carroll.

Student Government

Through election to the Student Senate and College Activities Board, students have responsibility for nonacademic matters affecting their lives at the University. In addition, there is voting student representation on all University committees, and there are student observers on the Board of Trustees.

Admission Requirements

Carroll's admission procedure is intended to ensure academic and personal success for accepted students. Each candidate is evaluated individually; evidence of the interest in and ability to do college-level work is important. The University exercises careful selection, but no candidate is disqualified because of race, color, religion, sex, national origin, age, disability, sexual orientation, or veteran status.

Application and Information

To be considered, each candidate for freshman admission must submit the following materials: a completed application for admission, a transcript from an accredited high school showing progress toward or completion of 15 units of work and graduation, a satisfactory personal evaluation from the high school, and scores on the SAT or ACT. Transfer students must submit a transcript from every college attended previously and a statement of good standing. Admission decisions are made on a rolling basis until the class is filled. There are no deadlines, but early application is recommended.

Admission to the University may be granted following the completion of three years of high school work, provided that the high school indicates that this is in the applicant's best interest. The candidate may or may not have completed the course work required for high school graduation at the time of admission, but he or she must show unusual promise and achievement.

For more information about Carroll University, prospective students should contact:

Admission Office
Carroll University
100 North East Avenue
Waukesha, Wisconsin 53186
Phone: 262-524-7220
        800-CARROLL (toll-free)
E-mail: info@carrollu.edu
Web site: http://www.carrollu.edu
          http://on.fb.me/carroll_univ (Facebook)
          http://twitter.com/carrollu (Twitter)

CARSON-NEWMAN COLLEGE
JEFFERSON CITY, TENNESSEE

The College

Founded in 1851 by Tennessee Baptists, Carson-Newman (C-N) is a private, coeducational, Christian liberal arts college. The College has an enrollment of approximately 2,000 undergraduate and over 150 graduate students. The average class size is 16 students, and the student to faculty ratio is 13:1. Each fall, Carson-Newman enrolls approximately 450 new undergraduate students. While most states are represented, students come primarily from the Southeastern U.S., with Tennessee accounting for 57 percent of C-N students.

In addition to its outstanding academics, C-N also provides many opportunities for student involvement in various clubs and organizations, nationally recognized varsity athletics, intramural athletics, music and drama groups, an award-winning forensics team, and many other extracurricular activities. The majority of C-N students live on campus in one of the five residence halls or two apartment complexes.

Carson-Newman also offers twelve graduate programs including master's degrees in education and teaching (educational leadership, education/curriculum and instruction, teaching/curriculum and instruction, and English as a second language), counseling (counseling, school counseling, and spiritual guidance and care), business (business administration), nursing (RN to M.S.N., family nurse practitioner, and nurse educator), and religion (applied theology).

Location

C-N is conveniently located in eastern Tennessee, just 30 miles from Knoxville, which has a population of 450,000, and 45 miles from Gatlinburg, the gateway to the Great Smoky Mountains. Students appreciate the diverse opportunities available in the city and in the outdoor areas. Shopping, dining, and entertainment opportunities are available near the College.

Majors and Degrees

The nine schools of the College are Business, Education, Family and Consumer Sciences, Fine Arts, Humanities, Natural Sciences and Mathematics, Nursing and Behavioral Health, Religion, and Social Sciences. C-N awards Bachelor of Arts, Bachelor of Music, Bachelor of Science, and Bachelor of Science in Nursing degrees. In addition, an Associate of Arts in Christian ministries degree is also offered.

Majors are available in art (art, photography), athletic training, business (accounting, business administration, international economics, general business, management), church recreation, communication studies and theater (advertising/public relations, journalism, media ministry, radio/television/film, speech), computer information systems (computer studies, data processing), education (athletic coaching, elementary education, physical education/health, secondary certification, special education), English (creative writing, literature), family and consumer sciences (child and family studies, consumer services, fashion design and merchandising, foods and nutrition, interior design, and retail), early childhood education, foreign language (biblical languages, French, Spanish), general studies, history, human services, mathematics, music (church music, music composition, music education, music theory, music with an outside field, piano and organ performance, vocal performance), natural and physical science (biochemistry, biology,

chemistry, physics), nursing, philosophy (philosophy, philosophy/religion), political science, psychology (applied psychology, social entrepreneurship), religion, sociology, and sport science (exercise science).

The College offers extremely strong curricula in preprofessional programs and health professions. Preprofessional programs are offered in dentistry, health information management, law, medicine, occupational therapy, optometry, physical therapy, and veterinary medicine. In cooperation with several other institutions, C-N offers binary degrees (2-3 and 3-2 programs) in medical technology, pharmacy, and physician assistant studies.

Academic Programs

The College operates on a traditional semester system. May term is a three-week intensive period of study giving students the opportunity to earn 3 credit hours. Summer terms are also offered.

All baccalaureate degrees require completion of 128 semester hours. Students must complete the C-N liberal arts core requirements and a total of 36 semester hours at the junior/senior level. Specific course requirements vary depending on major and degree program. Honors courses, independent study, and internships are available to students who qualify. Advanced credit is available for students who achieve required scores on AP exams, CLEP tests, and C-N departmental examinations.

New students are assigned a faculty adviser, who assists with course selection and student concerns. Career planning and tutoring services are also available through the Life Directions Center. The College's exceptionally high placement rate in professional programs in medicine, law, business, and theological study is testimony to the excellence of its rigorous academic program.

Off-Campus Programs

Students have the opportunity to spend an entire semester abroad by participating in the London Semester and other study-abroad opportunities. C-N, along with International Enrichment, Inc., provides all academic and nonacademic support services.

The Washington Semester is available as an internship program primarily for political science and prelaw majors. Through the program, students earn credit for work in the nation's capital. Art and foreign language majors may earn credit while studying and traveling throughout Europe during the three-week May term.

Academic Facilities

C-N offers the facilities and resources necessary for the enrichment of each student's education. Facilities include numerous computer labs; a campuswide computer network; a media service center; two theaters for drama production; Thomas Recital Hall, which is one of the finest music facilities in the Southeast; two art galleries and twenty-three individual art studios; the Stephens-Burnette Library, with more than 500,000 volumes; and an award-winning 96,000-square-foot Student Activities Center. The new family and consumer science building, Blye-Poteat Hall, opened in 2007, and the new business building, Ted Russell Hall, opened in 2009.

Costs

The annual cost at Carson-Newman, including room, board, and tuition, is well below the national average for four-year private colleges. Tuition for 2010–11 was $19,628, room averaged $2400, board averaged $3050, the student activity fee was approximately $460, and the technology fee was approximately $460. Students should allow approximately $800 for books per year.

Financial Aid

Carson-Newman allocates thousands of dollars each year to help supplement the resources of families. Financial aid awards are tailored to meet students' economic needs. Carson-Newman participates in all state and federal aid programs and awards aid based on demonstrated need as documented by a need analysis form, such as the Free Application for Federal Student Aid (FAFSA). Carson-Newman also awards academic scholarships based on achievement. The priority deadline for filing financial assistance forms is March 1. Additional information is available at http://admissions.cn.edu/admissions/finaid/default.asp.

Faculty

C-N faculty members are known for their interaction with students both inside and outside of classes. The student-faculty ratio at C-N is 13:1, so students are sure to receive individual attention. Faculty members are involved in scholarly pursuits such as authoring books, leading national scholastic organizations, and research, but their primary focus is teaching.

Student Government

The Student Government Association (SGA) represents the entire student body by voicing student concerns in campus affairs. The purpose of SGA is to promote the welfare of every student through justice, to protect individual rights and freedoms, to encourage high standards of conduct, and to train students in the general principles of self-government.

Admission Requirements

Carson-Newman College seeks applicants who demonstrate academic preparation and who possess an appreciation of and sensitivity to a Christian education and a liberal arts curriculum. Carson-Newman accepts applications for freshman and transfer admission for each term of enrollment (fall, spring, and summer). Prospective students can obtain additional information on admission requirements on the Carson-Newman College Office of Admissions Web pages at http://admissions.cn.edu/admissions/default.asp.

Application and Information

Applicants must submit all required application materials (application, application fee, official transcripts, test scores, and the C-N recommendation form) in order to be considered for admission. Admission decisions are made on a rolling basis, and students are notified within two weeks of receipt of all required documents. The application deadline is May 1 for the fall semester or December 1 for the spring semester. Applicants who wish to be considered for merit scholarships should apply by December 31.

For additional information, students should contact the Office of Undergraduate Admissions at 865-471-3223, admitme@cn.edu or visit http://www.cn.edu. Students may also follow C-N admissions on Facebook (http://www.facebook.com/Carson.Newman) or Twitter (http://twitter.com/cnadmissions).

Office of Undergraduate Admissions
Carson-Newman College
Jefferson City, Tennessee 37760
Phone: 865-471-3223
      800-678-9061 (toll-free)
E-mail: admitme@cn.edu
Web site: http://www.cn.edu
      http://www.facebook.com/Carson.Newman
      http://twitter.com/cnadmissions

Students on the Carson-Newman campus.

CASE WESTERN RESERVE UNIVERSITY
CLEVELAND, OHIO

The University

Ranking consistently among the top private universities in the United States, Case Western Reserve University (CWRU) offers unlimited opportunities for motivated students. Its faculty members challenge and support students to help them flourish, and its partnerships with world-class cultural, educational, and scientific institutions ensure that undergraduate education extends beyond the classroom.

Challenging and innovative academic programs and experiential learning opportunities are at the core of the undergraduate experience. Case Western Reserve's 9:1 student-faculty ratio allows students to have close interaction with professors. Co-ops, internships, study abroad, and other experiential learning opportunities bring theory to life in amazing settings, and nearly every student participates in research or independent study.

Although Case Western Reserve was formed in 1967 by the merger of Western Reserve University and Case Institute of Technology, it traces its roots back to the 1826 founding of Western Reserve College, making Case Western Reserve both a young university and one of the oldest private colleges in the nation. Currently, more than 4,200 undergraduates are enrolled in programs in engineering, natural sciences, management, nursing, the arts, the humanities, and the social and behavioral sciences. Students access CWRU's graduate and professional schools in applied social sciences, dental medicine, graduate studies, law, management, medicine, and nursing. Several undergraduate programs and majors combine undergraduate and graduate and professional degrees and resources. Examples are five-year B.A./M.A. or B.S./M.S. degrees, including a five-year B.S./M.S. degree in engineering and management, and dual admission to undergraduate and professional school. In addition, collaborative arrangements with neighboring cultural and health-care institutions enable the University to provide special opportunities in other fields, such as art history, offered in conjunction with the renowned Cleveland Museum of Art.

Nearly every type of student interest group, from political organizations to multiethnic student unions, is represented on campus. Campus Greek life consists of sixteen national fraternities and seven sororities, with approximately 30 percent of undergraduate students participating. Residence halls are coeducational, and over 80 percent of the students reside on campus.

A charter member of the University Athletic Association, an NCAA Division III conference, CWRU has won championships in cross-country, football, softball, track and field, and wrestling. Twenty percent of undergraduates wear the blue-and-white varsity uniform, and 70 percent join an intramural team. Club sports include fencing, golf, ice hockey, skiing, and Ultimate (Frisbee).

Location

CWRU is located in University Circle, a unique cultural district comprising 550 acres of parks, gardens, museums, schools, hospitals, churches, and human service institutions. The Cleveland Museum of Art, the Cleveland Museum of Natural History, and Severance Hall, home of the Cleveland Orchestra, are within walking distance; downtown Cleveland is 10 minutes away by car or public transportation. Partnerships in education and research among University Circle institutions enable students to make full use of resources beyond those of the University itself, and students receive free access to these and other local institutions, including the downtown Rock and Roll Hall of Fame and Museum.

Majors and Degrees

CWRU has a single-door admission policy—once students are admitted, they can pursue any major(s) they wish. Programs of study leading to the Bachelor of Arts degree include anthropology, art history (joint program with the Cleveland Museum of Art), Asian studies, astronomy, biochemistry, biology, chemistry, classics, cognitive science, communication sciences (collaborative program with the Cleveland Hearing and Speech Center), computer science, dance, economics, English, environmental geology, environmental studies, French, French and Francophone studies, geological sciences, German, German studies, history, history and philosophy of science, international studies, Japanese studies, mathematics, music (joint program with the Cleveland Institute of Music), nutrition, nutritional biochemistry and metabolism, philosophy, physics, political science, psychology, religious studies, sociology, Spanish, statistics, theater, and world literature. The following B.A. programs are available as a second major only: American studies, evolutionary biology, gerontological studies, natural sciences, prearchitecture, teacher education, and women's studies.

Bachelor of Science degrees are offered in the following fields: accounting, aerospace engineering, applied mathematics, art education (joint program with the Cleveland Institute of Art), astronomy, biochemistry, biology, biomedical engineering, chemical engineering, chemistry, civil engineering, computer engineering, computer science, electrical engineering, engineering physics, geological sciences, management (business), materials science and engineering, mathematics, mathematics and physics (combined major), mechanical engineering, music education, nursing, nutrition, nutritional biochemistry and metabolism, physics, polymer science and engineering, statistics, systems and control engineering, systems biology, and an undesignated engineering major.

Minor areas of concentration include artificial intelligence, art studio, childhood studies, Chinese, electronics, entrepreneurship, ethnic studies, finance, history of science and technology, Italian, Japanese, Judaic studies, management information and decision systems, marketing, photography, public policy, Russian, sports medicine, and teacher licensure. In addition, most major subjects are available as minors. A minor in electrical engineering is available to students pursuing any other engineering major.

Students may work toward a combined B.A./B.S. degree or integrate undergraduate and graduate studies to complete both the bachelor's and master's degrees in five years or less. Students who are interested in both the liberal arts and engineering can benefit from the 3–2 Engineering Program. Students spend three years at one of forty participating liberal arts colleges and then spend two years at CWRU studying engineering or a related field. Graduates of this program receive both a B.A. and a B.S. degree.

Academic Programs

Students in all majors participate in SAGES, the Seminar Approach to General Education and Scholarship program. SAGES consists of four innovative and engaging seminars that emphasize written and verbal communication skills and concludes with a Senior Capstone project. As a result, all CWRU students benefit from building on these important skills throughout their undergraduate education. Through a combination of core curricula, major requirements, and minors or approved course sequences, all undergraduates receive a broad educational base as well as specialized knowledge in their chosen fields.

The University offers students opportunities for independent research and internships in business, health care, government, and the arts. A co-op option providing two 7-month work periods in industry or government is available for majors in engineering, science, management, accounting, and computer science.

High school seniors who are exceptionally well qualified in specific fields are eligible for the Pre-professional Scholars Program (PPSP), which is offered in association with the Schools of Applied Social Sciences, Dental Medicine, Law, and Medicine. Each PPSP student is awarded admission to CWRU as an undergraduate and conditional admission to the appropriate professional school upon completion of the entrance requirements set by each school.

The University has two 4-month semesters and one 4- to 8-week summer session.

Off-Campus Programs

Selected students may enroll as juniors and seniors in the Washington Semester program, which is conducted each spring at American University. Students with a B average or higher may participate in the Junior Year Abroad program. Up to 36 hours of credit may be granted for study at an international university. Engineering students can participate in a Global Exchange with universities such as Waseda in Tokyo, Japan. Students may also cross-register at other Cleveland-area colleges and universities for one course per semester.

Academic Facilities

The $30-million Kelvin Smith Library is located in the heart of the campus. Through reciprocal borrowing arrangements, CWRU students have access to the holdings of the Cleveland Public Library as well as the libraries of five University Circle institutions; the members of OhioLINK, a network that includes state colleges and universities; the State Library of Ohio; and several private institutions. CWRU is classified by the Carnegie Foundation as a university with very high research activity (RU/VH), and its lab facilities are state of the art. The University operates two astronomical observatories, a biological field station, a $6-million undergraduate engineering lab, and nearly 100 other designated research centers and laboratories. The University's high-speed communications network links every residence hall room with computing centers, libraries, and databases on and off campus. CWRU's wireless network is one of the largest in the U.S. Other computer facilities on campus offer various models of computers and a wide variety of software programs, available free of charge to CWRU students.

The University Farm, located in nearby Hunting Valley, Ohio, offers educational opportunities in natural settings. Its 389 acres encompass a variety of deciduous forests, ravines, waterfalls, meadows, ponds, and a self-contained natural watershed.

Costs

For 2011–12, tuition and compulsory health and laboratory fees total $38,760. Room and board cost an average of $11,940.

Financial Aid

Financial aid consisting of grants, loans, and work assistance is awarded on the basis of a student's need. Applicants must file the Free Application for Federal Student Aid (FAFSA). Students are automatically considered for merit-based scholarships when they apply to the University; these awards typically range from $10,000 to $20,000.

Faculty

The undergraduate student-faculty ratio at CWRU is 9:1. Ninety-five percent of credit hours are taught by faculty members, not graduate students. Each college provides counselors who are available for both academic and personal advice. Once a major has been chosen, a member of the department in which the student is majoring acts as his or her academic adviser.

CWRU counts 14 Nobel laureates among its alumni and current and former faculty members, including the first American scientist ever to receive the prize. Undergraduate students have several opportunities to partner with faculty members on research or special projects, allowing for valuable learning opportunities, mentoring, networking, and personal development.

Student Government

CWRU's Undergraduate Student Government represents all undergraduate students. The assembly acts as a liaison between undergraduate students and the faculty, administration, and other groups; grants recognition to undergraduate organizations; and has the responsibility and authority to allocate funds from student activity fees to student organizations. The Residence Hall Association is a governing body for on-campus living, the University Program Board plans special events, and the Interfraternity Congress and Panhellenic Council govern the Greek community.

Admission Requirements

It is recommended that students pursue 4 units of English, 3 units of math, 3 units of science (2 of which must be laboratory science), 3 units of social studies, and 2 units of foreign language. The University recommends that applicants interested in engineering and the sciences have an additional unit of math and laboratory science. For students interested in the liberal arts, it is recommended that students take an additional unit of social studies and foreign language. An interview is not a required part of the admission process, but it is strongly recommended. To receive full consideration for admission and scholarships, students must take the SAT or ACT prior to their selected application deadline.

Application and Information

The application deadline is January 15 for notification by April 1. Application deadlines for transfer students are May 15 for fall admission and October 15 for spring admission. The application deadline for the Pre-professional Scholars Program (medicine, dentistry, law, or social work) is December 1. Students can apply to CWRU via the online Common Application. The fall semester begins in late August.

Interviews with admission professionals, campus visits, group information sessions, and other resources are available to all prospective students. For more information, students should contact:

Office of Undergraduate Admission
Case Western Reserve University
10900 Euclid Avenue
Cleveland, Ohio 44106-7055

Phone: 216-368-4450
E-mail: admission@case.edu
Web site: http://admission.case.edu
http://on.fb.me/CWRU_ugadm (Facebook)
http://twitter.com/swruadmission

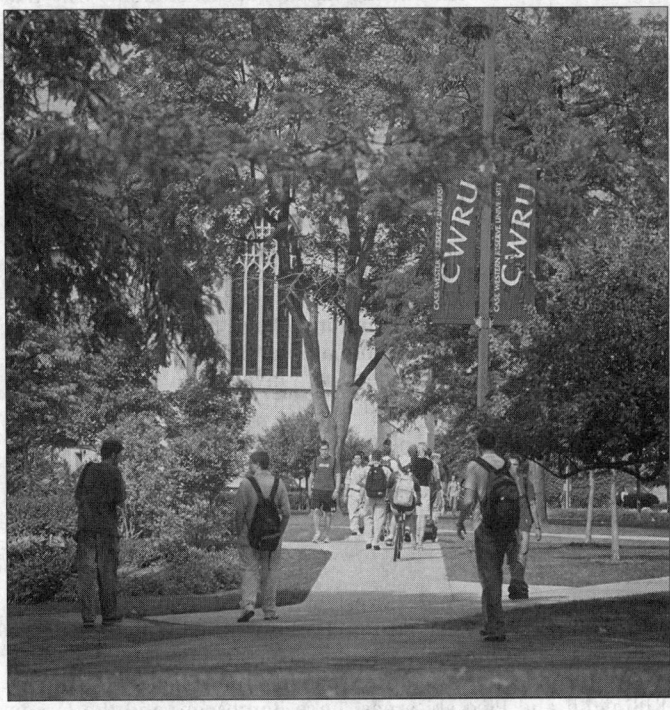

Case Western Reserve University students on campus.

CASTLETON STATE COLLEGE

CASTLETON, VERMONT

The College

Castleton State College was founded in 1787; it was the first institution of higher learning in Vermont and the eighteenth in the United States. The 165-acre campus is located in Castleton, a historic Vermont village. Sixty-five percent of the 1,900 full-time undergraduate students at the College are Vermonters; the balance of the student population comes from New England and the Middle Atlantic states.

Castleton is committed to providing an undergraduate education in which the liberal arts and career preparation complement each other. Through an innovative program called Soundings, freshmen earn academic credit by attending a series of special events that include theater, music, dance, film, debate, and opinion from influential people. New students also participate in the First-Year Seminar, giving them the opportunity to develop the skills of a successful college student. First-year students may apply for the College's Honors Program. Community service and internships play an important role in a Castleton education.

There are ten major residence halls. Together, the residences accommodate nearly 900 students. Each residence hall room is equipped with at least two Internet hookups and wireless access, which give each student the opportunity to access the Web and e-mail using their own personal computer. There is no additional charge for this service. Each room is also equipped with cable TV connections. Off-campus housing is available in the Castleton, Fair Haven, and Rutland areas. Students who live on campus eat in Huden Dining Hall. All students are allowed to have automobiles on campus.

More than forty clubs and organizations provide a wide variety of student activities that include club sports, an FM radio station, the student newspaper, and an active outing club. Other clubs relate to college majors and future careers; still others serve the College or local community. Castleton is a member of the North Atlantic Conference of NCAA Division III. Castleton offers twenty intercollegiate sports. Men compete in baseball, basketball, cross-country running, football, golf, ice hockey, lacrosse, skiing, soccer, and tennis. Women compete in basketball, cross-country running, field hockey, ice hockey, lacrosse, skiing, soccer, softball, tennis, and volleyball. A majority of Castleton's students are involved in the intramural and recreational sports program.

Castleton recently completed a $25.7-million project which included renovation and expansion of the Campus Center and the gymnasium, construction of a stadium, and improvements to the athletic fields.

Location

The campus is 12 miles west of Rutland, one of Vermont's largest cities. Montreal, Boston, Hartford, Albany, and New York City are all within easy driving distance. Amtrak passenger trains to and from New York City stop in the village of Castleton. Killington and Pico ski areas, Lake Bomoseen, and the Green Mountains provide excellent recreational opportunities and an exceptional living and learning environment.

Majors and Degrees

Castleton State College offers B.A. or B.S. degrees in more than thirty areas of study: accounting, American literature, art,

athletic training, biology, children's literature, computer information systems, communication, criminal justice, digital media, elementary education, environmental science, exercise science, forensic psychology, geology, health science, history, journalism, management, marketing, mass media, mathematics, music, music education, nursing, physical education, psychology, public relations, secondary education, social work, sociology, Spanish, special education, sports administration, theater arts, and world literature. Associate degrees can be earned in business, communication, computer programming, criminal justice, general studies, or nursing.

Academic Programs

The Castleton curriculum is designed to provide the student with a strong liberal arts background plus the opportunity for career preparation in a specific area. All four-year students are required to complete a core of general education requirements during the four-year degree program. The first year of study can be used by the undecided student to explore various areas of interest. The student with a specific career interest may begin study in the major field as a freshman, although four-year students are not required to formally declare their major until the end of the sophomore year.

Castleton students typically enroll in five courses each semester. The academic calendar consists of two 15-week semesters and three 4-week summer sessions. Grading is traditional, and a pass/no-pass option is available. Internships and field experiences complement many of the academic programs at Castleton and are required in the communication, criminal justice, social work, and education programs.

Students may transfer internally from two-year to four-year programs in business, communication, computer information systems, criminal justice, and general studies. Students who transfer to Castleton after graduating from an accredited two-year college are granted full transfer credit for all academic work up to 64 credits or the number required for the associate degree.

Freshman students achieving at least a 3.5 grade point average in their first year at Castleton are recognized by the Castleton Chapter of Phi Eta Sigma, a national honor society that recognizes freshman scholastic achievement in colleges throughout the country. Outstanding junior and senior scholars are recognized by the Castleton Chapter of Alpha Chi. Pinnacle, the honor society for nontraditional students, honors qualified candidates. There are honor societies in theater arts, education, psychology, and Spanish. Students who have achieved a 4.0 grade point average are named to the President's List of Outstanding Students and those with a 3.5 grade point average or better to the Dean's List.

Academic Facilities

The Calvin Coolidge Library houses a collection of more than 500,000 books, periodicals, microforms, and nonprint media. Access to Castleton's library resources and outside scholarly sources is made possible through numerous online and CD databases; a sophisticated, networked electronic library system; the Internet; and strong consortial relationships within the state of Vermont. An audiovisual media facility provides a wide range of audiovisual equipment, including digital video editing, digital cameras, and presentation equipment.

Castleton's Stafford Academic Center houses the Computing Center, a high-tech multimedia lecture hall, distance learning classrooms, and the Departments of Education, Mathematics, and Nursing.

The Spartan Athletic Complex houses Glenbrook Gymnasium, the athletic training room, a swimming pool, two racquetball courts, a new fitness center, and a large indoor activity area.

The Fine Arts Center contains a 500-seat auditorium; facilities for art, drama, dance, and music. A new television studio opened in 2010 as part of an addition to Leavenworth Hall.

The Jeffords Center, which was renovated and expanded in the spring and summer of 2007, houses science classrooms and laboratories, a state-of-the-art auditorium, laboratories for faculty and student research projects, and a greenhouse. An astronomical observatory is a short walk away.

There are more than 225 personal computers designated for student use located in labs across the campus.

Costs

Costs for 2011–12 are as follows: tuition for Vermont residents, $8568, and for nonresidents, $20,112. Room and board expenses total $8446. Annual fees are $828. The orientation and registration for new students is $200.

Financial Aid

Eighty percent of Castleton's full-time undergraduate students receive financial assistance from federal, state, College, or other sources. Grants, loans, and work-study jobs are available for qualified students. Applicants for financial aid should file the Free Application for Federal Student Aid (FAFSA) form by April 1 of the senior year in high school. All financial aid awards are based on need.

Most Castleton scholarships are awarded as part of the College's Honors Scholarship Program. Amounts range from $1000 to $6000 per year. First-year students who have a combined critical reading and math SAT score of at least 1100 and have a GPA of at least 3.3 on a 4.0 scale are eligible for one of these scholarships. Additional scholarships are available to new students based on certain academic credentials, service to their community, and financial need. There are also special scholarships for students wishing to study music or Spanish.

Faculty

The full-time faculty at Castleton consists of 90 men and women, 96 percent of whom hold terminal degrees in their field. Adjunct faculty members, many of them local business-people and members of the professions, complement the efforts of the full-time faculty. The student-faculty ratio is 14:1. Each student has a faculty member as an adviser.

Student Government

The Student Association is the chief vehicle of student government. All students who are registered for 8 or more credit hours are members. Elected representatives hold membership on most College committees, including the Curriculum and Cultural Affairs Committees. Students are also able to develop leadership qualities by participating in the various clubs and other organizations on campus.

Admission Requirements

Applicants are evaluated on the basis of their secondary school records, standardized test scores, and recommendations. Admission is granted to those applicants who have demonstrated their ability and potential to meet the challenges of a postsecondary learning experience.

Application and Information

Students may apply for admission through the Castleton Web site. Under Castleton's rolling admission policy, applications are processed throughout the year, and candidates are notified of the admission decision as soon as their folders are complete. Students are admitted in the fall and spring semesters.

For more information about Castleton State College or to arrange a campus visit, students should contact:

Office of Admissions
Castleton State College
Castleton, Vermont 05735
Phone: 802-468-1213
      800-639-8521 (toll-free)
Fax: 802-468-1476
E-mail: info@castleton.edu
Web site: http://www.castleton.edu
      http://tiny.cc/nhamg (Facebook)

On the grounds of Castleton State College.

CEDAR CREST COLLEGE
ALLENTOWN, PENNSYLVANIA

The College

Cedar Crest College was founded in 1867 and for more than 142 years has taken a bold approach to education by providing women with the competitive edge needed to succeed. A liberal arts college by design, Cedar Crest prepares women to lead in a global society. Approximately 1,400 students attend the College annually, representing twenty-seven states and twenty countries. Current students, alumnae, and future students maintain an active presence on the Cedar Crest Twitter and Facebook pages.

Cedar Crest College has more than thirty academic programs and faculty members who put a unique spin on traditional majors such as business and marketing, communication, English, and performing arts. In addition, Cedar Crest College has renowned programs in forensic science (one of fourteen accredited programs in the country and the only one affiliated with a women's college), social work (the only accredited program in the Lehigh Valley), and genetic engineering (one of the oldest programs in the country).

The College's health and wellness program has received a gold award for student health, wellness, and counseling from the National Association of Student Personnel Administrators. Their health and wellness initiative includes personal sports training; nutrition counseling; and a full schedule of dance, yoga, and aerobics classes. The Rodale Aquatic Center for Civic Health, a state-of-the-art, two-pool complex, offers health and fitness opportunities for the entire campus community. The campus also has tennis courts; regulation fields for field hockey, lacrosse, soccer, and softball; and a fitness center.

Cedar Crest students participate in eight NCAA Division III intercollegiate sports: basketball, cross-country, field hockey, lacrosse, soccer, softball, tennis, and volleyball. The College athletic department also supports club sports including equestrian, swimming, and cheerleading. The Falcons belong to the Colonial States Athletic Conference (CSAC) and compete against institutions in Pennsylvania, New Jersey, and Delaware. Cedar Crest student-athletes are held to high academic standards and have proven that it's possible to succeed both on the court and in the classroom. The CSAC recently awarded Cedar Crest student-athletes the first institutional achievement award for earning the highest grade point average in the Conference, and Cedar Crest teams have won several national academic awards. In 2011, basketball center Lizzy Sunderhause was recognized with the Jostens Trophy, awarded for excellence on the court and in the classroom and community.

Cedar Crest students hold leadership positions in more than forty clubs and organizations on campus. Student clubs range from the Student Government Association and Student Activities Board to the Literary Club and Biology Club. The College prepares women to lead in their future careers, community, and in life. Leadership retreats and community service opportunities are held throughout the year. The campus completes more than 20,000 hours in community service annually. Service opportunities are available throughout the Lehigh Valley at schools, hospitals, animal shelters, and Habitat for Humanity. At Cedar Crest, students serve early and often.

Cedar Crest upperclass students have the opportunity to live and learn together in the College's living-learning communities.

These communities focus on a variety of relevant and timely topics such as global social justice, environmental ethics, entrepreneurship, and the arts. They bring together students who share a common interest, regardless of major or career focus. Sharing perspectives and lifestyles in this group setting enhances the students' educational journey as they gain intellectual appreciation and global awareness, apply and hone leadership skills, and make a difference locally and globally. These communities are the epitome of the seamless college experience as students live together, take a house class together, travel together, and develop close relationships with a faculty member affiliated with the community.

Through the Career Planning Office, students are placed in competitive internships near the campus and in major cities.

Cedar Crest's academic programs are fully accredited by the Middle States Association of Colleges and Schools and, where appropriate, by the American Academy of Forensic Science, American Medical Association, American Dietetic Association, American Bar Association, National League for Nursing Accrediting Commission, National Council on Social Work Education, and the Departments of Education of New York, New Jersey, and Pennsylvania. The College offers master's degrees in three fields: education, forensic science, and nursing.

Location

Students enjoy Cedar Crest's parklike campus, nestled in the heart of the Lehigh Valley in the West End of Allentown, Pennsylvania. The campus is a beautiful 84-acre nationally registered arboretum with more than 130 species of trees. The College is within easy distance of the extensive Allentown park system, high-end retail shopping, well-known restaurants, cultural activities, and the Pocono ski and outdoor resorts.

Cedar Crest is located in College Valley, home to more than 32,000 students at eight colleges within 20 minutes of campus. Students can participate in student- and faculty-led trips to nearby Philadelphia (less than 1 hour from campus) and New York City (less than 2 hours away). Students can explore the metropolitan areas of the East Coast, including Washington, D.C., Baltimore, and Boston, while enjoying the benefits of a small, suburban campus.

Majors and Degrees

Cedar Crest offers more than thirty fields of study in the arts, humanities, social sciences, business, and sciences. The combination of majors and course offerings provides students with a strong liberal arts background. The College also offers preprofessional programs in dentistry, law, medicine, and veterinary medicine. These well-respected academic programs provide individual support for students as they create an academic experience that is both personal and practical. Students are expected to be involved in planning their academic pathway from the very beginning.

Academic Programs

Self-designed majors, double majors, minors, and individual and group research projects are available and reflect the academic emphasis at the undergraduate level. Students may begin conducting research as early as their first year on campus. Students can also begin writing for the campus newspaper or hosting their own radio shows early in their college career.

The Honors Program at Cedar Crest is cross-disciplinary and designed for women who have demonstrated a record of high academic achievement. The Honors Program offers students a unique opportunity for growth and enrichment. Honors courses are marked by their engaging classroom environment, diverse and challenging coursework, and graduate-level research experiences.

Through a consortium with the Lehigh Valley Association of Independent Colleges, Cedar Crest upperclass students may cross-register and take courses at Lehigh and DeSales Universities and Lafayette, Moravian, and Muhlenberg Colleges at no additional cost.

Off-Campus Programs

Cedar Crest students are encouraged to pursue internships in their area of study. Internships enable students to gain practical experience at major corporations, small businesses, national nonprofit organizations, and top health-care facilities. Cedar Crest students have served internships with CNN, as a foreign correspondent with the United Nations, and with the FBI, working on a database for DNA fingerprinting.

The College stresses the importance of global awareness and encourages students to take advantage of study-abroad opportunities. Cedar Crest also offers courses with a short "trip abroad" component lasting one to two weeks.

Academic Facilities

Learning spaces include hospital simulation labs, a ceramic studio, a state-of-the art nutrition laboratory, music practice rooms, *The Crestiad* newsroom, dance and art studios and workshops, theaters, genetic engineering laboratories, forensic science laboratories, a papermaking studio, and a greenhouse.

Cedar Crest students socialize and dine in the Tompkins College Center, the hub of student activity. The center is home to Samuels Theatre, club meeting rooms, the dining hall, and the Falcon's Nest café.

Costs

For 2010–11, tuition was $28,567; room and board were $9540.

Financial Aid

Student applications are reviewed for scholarship eligibility at the time of acceptance. The College's scholarships are awarded based on high school merit, leadership, and service. The College also holds an annual scholarship competition that awards one high-achieving student a full tuition scholarship for four years.

The financial aid program at Cedar Crest is based on financial need and includes grants, loans, and employment. Students applying for need-based financial aid should file the Free Application for Federal Student Aid (FAFSA).

Students are encouraged to use Cedar Crest's student aid calculator to receive a fast, accurate estimate of their financial aid package, including scholarships, grants, and loans. This calculator is available at http://www.cedarcrest.edu/calculator.

Faculty

Cedar Crest faculty members demand excellence, creating a challenging and supportive environment that allows students to grow and thrive. Faculty members are working artists, published writers, accomplished actors, international business professionals, and scientists making discoveries that will impact us all. They strive to ensure that student learning extends beyond the classroom.

Cedar Crest students meet one-on-one with a faculty mentor to build course schedules and discuss future plans. Students also work closely with faculty on groundbreaking research in all disciplines. This research can lead to national presentations and professional publications.

Admission Requirements

Cedar Crest welcomes applications from first-year students entering after high school and those seeking to transfer from another college or university. The admissions process looks at the entire student, from academic course work and standardized test scores to leadership potential, volunteer service, employment, and special talents.

Application and Information

Students are encouraged to visit the campus as they begin the application process, and can register for a visit at http://www.cedarcrest.edu/visit. Applications are reviewed on a rolling basis, so they are processed and evaluated as soon as all materials have been received. Applicants are notified of their admissions decision beginning September 15 for the following fall semester. The priority deadline to apply for scholarship review is February 15.

Students can apply online at http://www.cedarcrest.edu/apply or through the Common Application at https://www.commonapp.org.

Vice President for Enrollment Management
Cedar Crest College
100 College Drive
Allentown, Pennsylvania 18104-6196

Phone: 800-360-1222 (toll-free)
Fax: 610-606-4647
E-mail: admissions@cedarcrest.edu
Web site: http://www.cedarcrest.edu
　　　　http://on.fb.me/CedarCrest (Facebook)
　　　　http://twitter.com/cedarcrestcolle

Cedar Crest College is a great place to live and learn! The campus community comprises smart, creative women who will shape the world in which we live.

CHAPMAN UNIVERSITY
ORANGE, CALIFORNIA

The University

During its 150-year history, Chapman has evolved from a small, traditional liberal arts college that was founded in 1861 by members of the First Christian Church (Disciples of Christ) into a midsized comprehensive liberal arts and sciences university that is distinguished for its nationally recognized programs in film and television production, business and economics, theater, dance, music, education, and the natural and applied sciences. The mission of Chapman University is to provide personalized education of distinction that leads to inquiring, ethical, and productive lives as global citizens.

Chapman's parklike ivy-covered, tree-lined campus features a blending of fully refurbished historic structures with the newest in state-of-the-art Internet and satellite-connected learning environments. Six residence halls and six on-campus apartment buildings are conveniently located on the edge of the campus. Prominent in the center of the campus is Liberty Plaza, featuring a raised replica of a Lincoln chair viewing a 5-ton section of the Berlin Wall.

Chapman University's academic structure includes the Wilkinson College of Humanities and Social Sciences, the Dodge College of Film and Media Arts, the AACSB International–accredited Argyros School of Business and Economics, the CTC-approved College of Educational Studies, the ABA-accredited School of Law, the Schmid College of Science, and the College of Performing Arts, which includes the NASM-accredited Conservatory of Music, the NAST-accredited Department of Theatre, and the NASD-accredited Department of Dance. Other nationally accredited programs include the APTA-accredited Doctor of Physical Therapy program. Chapman has been further recognized by the Templeton Foundation as one of only 100 colleges nationally to be designated as a Templeton Foundation "Character-Building College" for its emphasis on global citizenry and for student involvement in community action and stewardship activities.

With just over 6,500 undergraduate, graduate, and professional school students enrolled, the University environment is electric, involving, and outdoor-oriented. Along with the obvious benefits associated with the southern California climate, Chapman students enjoy a dynamic and involving student activities program. Although predominantly from California, Chapman students come from all fifty states; in addition, approximately 10 percent of its students come from thirty-four other countries. Over the past five years, Chapman students have been named Truman Scholars, Coro Fellows, *USA Today* All-USA College Academic Team members, NCAA All-Americans, and NCAA Academic All-Americans. Chapman's long and distinguished heritage in intercollegiate athletics includes five NCAA national championships in baseball, tennis, and softball. Chapman competes as an independent in the NCAA Division III level and fields teams in baseball, basketball (m/w), crew (m/w), cross-country (m/w), football, golf, lacrosse (m/w), soccer (m/w), softball, swimming (w), tennis (m/w), track and field (w), volleyball (w), and water polo (m/w). Approximately 20 percent of Chapman's student body participates in intercollegiate athletics. In 2009–10, 5 student-athletes were named as NCAA All-Americans and 8 as NCAA Academic All-Americans.

More than ninety clubs and organizations are recognized on campus, many with commitments to a wide range of community service efforts. Chapman's Greek system includes seven nationally chartered fraternities for men and seven nationally chartered sororities for women. A comprehensive intramural sports program involves myriad sports activities for all campus community members throughout the school year. On-campus intercollegiate athletic events as well as music, art, and theater productions provide students with extensive extracurricular activity options. Chapman's proximity to area recreational and cultural opportunities allows Chapman students to enjoy the essence of what makes Orange County's south coast area an enviable environment in which to live and learn.

Prominent Chapman alumni include the Honorable Loretta Sanchez '88, member of Congress; the Honorable David Bonior '72, member of Congress; CNBC World anchorwoman, Bettina Chua '88; television and film producers John Copeland '73, Jon Garcia '93, and John David Currey '98; cinematographer Gene Jackson '70; St. John's University basketball coach Steve Lavin '88; major-league baseball executive Gordon Blakely '76; major-league baseball Cy Young Award winner Randy Jones '72; Tony Award nominee and star of Broadway's *Showboat*, Michel Bell '68; resident tenor at the Staatsoper-Vienna John Nuzzo '91; and former U.S. Ambassador to Spain and philanthropist George L. Argyros '65.

Location

Orange County, California, has been rated by *Places Rated Almanac* as "the #1 place to live in North America," citing superior climate, cultural, recreational, educational, and career-entree opportunities. Los Angeles is 35 miles to the north, and San Diego is 80 miles to the south. Nearby entertainment venues include Disneyland, Knott's Berry Farm, the Orange County Performing Arts Center, Major League Baseball's Los Angeles Angels of Anaheim, and the National Hockey League's Anaheim Ducks. Pristine West Coast beaches are less than 10 miles from the campus, and seasonal snow skiing is 90 minutes away. The average year-round temperature on campus is 71°F, and the daily breeze coming off the nearby Pacific Ocean keeps the air clean and smog free.

Majors and Degrees

Chapman awards the Bachelor of Arts degree in the fields of art, art history, communication studies, dance, economics, English, film studies, French, history, integrated educational studies (teaching), music, peace studies, philosophy, political science, psychology, public relations and advertising, religious studies, screenwriting, sociology, Spanish, and theater. The Bachelor of Fine Arts degree is offered in creative producing, creative writing, dance performance, digital arts, film production, graphic design, screen acting, studio art, television and broadcast journalism, and theater performance. The Bachelor of Science degree is offered in accounting, athletic training, biochemistry, biological sciences, business administration, chemistry, computer information systems, computer science, environmental science and policy, health sciences, mathematics, and physics and computational sciences. The Bachelor of Music degree is granted in composition, performance, and music education (precertification). Preprofessional or prevocational programs are offered in dentistry, law, medicine, physical therapy, social service, teaching, theology, and veterinary medicine.

Academic Programs

Chapman's Academic Advising Center offers advising services for all students, supports them in formulating their educational goals, and encourages them to develop individualized plans to realize those goals. The Center advises in all majors and serves all undeclared students; offers general academic counseling and placement testing services; advises students on academic probation; and serves as an information, resource, and referral center for all students who need current information about general education, degree requirements, and academic policies. Individual appointments, drop-in hours, online resources, and advising workshops are available. Also associated with the Academic Advising Center is the Tutoring, Learning, and Testing Center, which provides students with peer tutoring, study technique development, and advocacy services.

A wide variety of study and research opportunities are available through Chapman's academic and research centers. These include the A. Gary Anderson Center for Economic Research; the Albert Schweitzer Institute; the Rodgers Center for Holocaust Education;

the Center for Educational and Social Equity; the John Fowles Center for Creative Writing; the Leatherby Center for Entrepreneurship and Business Ethics; the Walter Schmid Center for International Business; the C. Larry Hoag Center for Real Estate and Finance; the Institute for the Study of Media and the Public Interest; the Center for Global Trade and Development; the Economic Science Institute; the Center of Excellence in Applied, Fundamental, and Computational Sciences; the Center for Media and Public Affairs; and the Center for the Economic Study of Religion.

Requirements for graduation are commensurate with the liberal arts philosophy of education maintained by Chapman. The program of studies is designed to ensure a breadth of subject matter selection in the liberal arts as well as depth of preparation in the student's major field. The minimum graduation requirements include successful completion (C average) of 124 semester credits, of which 36 must be earned in the upper division. Competence in reading, written communication, oral communication, computation, and library usage is required of all students. Chapman's general education sequence provides a broad introduction to the humanities, social sciences, and natural sciences. Students select general education classes with the guidance of their faculty adviser. A maximum of 32 semester credits may be gained through Advanced Placement (AP), College-Level Examination Program (CLEP), and departmental examinations.

Chapman's academic year operates on a 4-1-4 modified semester system. January is reserved for an optional four-week Interterm when students can take a traditional course in an accelerated time frame, or take advantages of experiential opportunities such as travel-study courses or travel abroad.

Ample opportunities are available for alternative learning experiences. Internships and cooperative education programs are recommended. Students may also undertake in-depth individual study or research in their major field in conjunction with a faculty member.

Academic Facilities

Major facilities additions to the Chapman campus over the past few years include the completion of the 100,000-square-foot Leatherby Libraries complex, which houses eight discipline-specific individual libraries, a sculpture garden, a cyber courtyard, and a 24-hour study commons and coffee bar. The Conservatory of Music's 24,000-square foot Oliphant Hall addition features fourteen teaching studios, a sixty-seat lecture hall, music therapy laboratory, and orchestra hall. The Fish Interfaith Center includes the 12,500-square-foot Wallace All-Faiths Chapel, recognized by *Architectural Digest* magazine for innovation in design. The recently completed 200,000-square-foot Sandhu Residence and Conference Center houses the primary on-campus dining facility for resident students, as well as a conference center and residence hall. The 90,000-square-foot Argyros Forum provides additional campus dining options, as well as conference and classroom facilities. The 1,000-seat Memorial Auditorium is the primary performance and assembly venue on campus and is listed on the National Register of Historic Places. Athletic facilities include the 2,500-seat Hutton Sports Center arena, four championship tennis courts, and training and fitness facilities for the campus and surrounding community. Recent additions to the athletic complex include the new 2,000-seat Ernie Chapman Stadium (for football, lacrosse, and soccer) and the 500-seat Zee Allred Aquatics Center and Olympic pool. Arnold Beckman Hall is the center for business and information technology, including the Argyros School of Business and Economics, and the Hobbs Institute for Real Estate, Law, and Environmental Studies. In addition to the Conservatory of Music's Bertea and Oliphant Halls, the College of Performing Arts utilizes the Moulton Fine Arts Complex, with the 250-seat repertory-style Waltmar Theatre, a black box theater, and the Guggenheim Art Gallery. The Hashinger Science Center features laboratories for nuclear science, radiation, crystallography, genetics, food science, and physics and computational science.

Costs

For the 2010–11 academic year, full-time tuition and fees (including accident and health services fee and associated student membership fee) were $37,864. Annual room and board costs averaged $13,000. The estimated cost for books was $1000 per year.

Financial Aid

More than 85 percent of Chapman students benefit from some form of financial aid or scholarship assistance. Need-based financial awards include a combination of grants, scholarships, loans, and work-study jobs on campus. Awards are renewable, assuming that students complete the annual application process on time. By using a combination of Chapman's internal resources and federal and state funding, an individual financial aid package can be tailored in an attempt to meet the student's financial need. Merit and talent scholarship awards, regardless of financial need, round out the types of financial assistance that Chapman offers.

Faculty

The University's faculty is composed of 280 full-time and 258 part-time members, more than 80 percent of whom hold doctoral or other terminal degrees. Their primary commitment is to undergraduate teaching, although most are also actively involved in scholarly research and publication. Many faculty members teach both undergraduate and graduate courses. Teaching assistants or graduate assistants are not used for the instruction of undergraduate classes. Chapman's favorable student-faculty ratio of 16:1 allows extensive interaction between the faculty members and students.

Student Government

Chapman has an associated student government that actively participates in the administration of the University.

Admission Requirements

Admission to Chapman is selective. In 2010, admission was granted to 47 percent of the applicant pool. The University is interested in admitting students whose prior records indicate that they will be successful in a competitive collegiate environment. Freshman applicants are considered for admission based primarily on the nature and sequence of their high school course work, the grade point average they achieved, their results on either the SAT or ACT examination, cocurricular activities, and personal characteristics. Transfer candidates are considered for admission on the basis of their course work and cumulative grade point average earned at other regionally accredited postsecondary institutions, their cocurricular involvement, and personal characteristics.

Application and Information

Chapman University is an exclusive user of the Common Application (http://www.commonapp.org), but applicants must also submit a Chapman-specific supplement and a departmental application for those applying to art, dance, film, music, or theater programs. Candidates are strongly encouraged to visit and tour the campus and participate in an information session led by an admission officer. Arrangements for a group information session and campus tour can be made through the Office of Admission. Freshman applicants can choose either a nonbinding November 15 early action application deadline or the January 15 regular application deadline. Transfer applicants must apply before the March 15 transfer deadline. Freshman candidates who apply after January 15 and transfer candidates who apply after March 15 are considered on a space-available basis. For further information, students should contact:

Office of Admission
Chapman University
One University Drive
Orange, California 92866
Phone: 714-997-6711
      888-CUAPPLY (toll-free)
Fax: 714-997-6713
E-mail: admit@chapman.edu
Web site: http://www.chapman.edu
    http://www.facebook.com/ChapmanUniversity

CHATHAM UNIVERSITY
PITTSBURGH, PENNSYLVANIA

chatham
UNIVERSITY

The University

Founded in 1869, Chatham University is a coed university with a women's college at its historic heart. Chatham University provides students with a solid education built upon strong academics, public leadership, and global understanding. Chatham's Shadyside Campus is located on historic Woodland Road in Pittsburgh's Shadyside neighborhood, while its Eden Hall Campus is located 45 minutes north in Richland Township.

The University houses three distinctive colleges. Chatham College for Women provides academic and cocurricular programs for undergraduate women and embodies the traditions and rituals of one of the nation's oldest colleges for women. The College for Graduate Studies offers women and men both master's and doctoral programs. The College for Continuing and Professional Studies provides online and hybrid undergraduate and graduate degree programs for women and men, certificate programs, and community programming.

The University's total student body of almost 2,300 represents forty-four states and twenty-six other countries. Members of minority groups and international students compose 14 percent of the total student body. Resident and commuting students participate actively in the numerous professional, academic, social, and special-interest organizations at the University. Each year, Chatham students complete thousands of hours of community service with organizations throughout the region.

Chatham College for Women offers NCAA Division III intercollegiate competition in basketball, cross-country, ice hockey, soccer, softball, swimming and diving, tennis, volleyball, and water polo, as well as intramural and recreational competition in other sports. Chatham's Athletic and Fitness Center includes an eight-lane competition pool, a gymnasium, squash courts, cardio rooms, a climbing wall, a running track, and exercise and dance studios.

All incoming undergraduate students receive an Apple MacBook Pro that can access the University's wireless network and are incorporated into the curriculum for in-class note-taking, research, and on-line learning. Students are assessed a technology fee each year to lease the computers, which they own upon graduation.

All residence halls have computer labs and high-speed network printers as well as network ports in each room. Central computer equipment supports e-mail, computer-mediated courseware, personal Web pages, and file and print servers. Chatham participates in campuswide software license agreements that permit students to install select productivity software on their personal machines at no additional cost.

Location

Chatham's suburban, historic Shadyside Campus is located minutes from downtown Pittsburgh and features towering trees, wandering paths, and century-old mansions that serve as residence halls. The Shadyside Campus includes Chatham Eastside, a new LEED Silver facility that houses the University's interior architecture, landscape architecture, occupational therapy, physical therapy, and physician assistant studies programs. The University's new 388-acre Eden Hall Campus is located north of the city in Richland Township and is the home of Chatham's new School of Sustainability and the Environment.

Pittsburgh is one of the safest and most dynamic green cities in the country and is headquarters to major businesses and industries in finance, health care, and technology. Eclectic neighborhoods reflect Pittsburgh's historic qualities and appeal to a wide audience. Students may ride public transportation free within Allegheny County simply by presenting their Chatham ID. Arts and entertainment options range from the Pittsburgh Symphony to world-renowned opera, ballet, and theater companies and museums. For sports enthusiasts, Pittsburgh offers the Penguins, Pirates, and Steelers professional ice-hockey, baseball, and football teams. Pittsburgh has also been rated America's Most Livable City by *Places Rated Almanac* and Most Livable City in the U.S. and twenty-ninth Most Livable City Worldwide by *The Economist*. Bus, rail, and air connections are available to and from most major cities. For more information, students should visit http://www.pittsburghregion.org.

Majors and Degrees

Chatham University offers the following majors leading to a Bachelor of Arts or Bachelor of Science degree: accounting, art history, arts management, biochemistry, biology, business, business economics, chemistry, creative writing, cultural studies, economics, education (elementary, early childhood, secondary, environmental science, visual arts), engineering (3-2 program), English, environmental science (B.A. or B.S.), environmental studies, exercise science, film and digital videomaking, forensics, government, history, interior architecture, international business, international studies, landscape studies certificate, management, marketing, mathematics, music, nursing, physics, political science, policy studies (global or public), professional communication (broadcast journalism, print journalism, professional writing, public relations), psychology, social work, Spanish and Hispanic studies, visual arts (emerging media, photography or studio arts), and women's studies. Students may choose a traditional major, an interdisciplinary major, a double major, or a self-designed major.

Preprofessional programs are offered in education and law, medicine and health professions, physical therapy, teaching certification, and veterinary medicine. A joint-degree engineering program is offered with Carnegie Mellon University and the University of Pittsburgh. Teacher certification is available through the education program in early childhood, elementary, environmental, school counseling, secondary education, and special education.

The Accelerated Graduate Program enables qualified undergraduate students to become candidates for admission to one of the University's graduate programs during their junior year, enabling them to earn both a bachelor's and master's degree in as little as five years. The following degree programs are included: Master of Accounting, Master of Arts (M.A.) in food studies, M.A. in landscape studies, M.A. in Teaching, Master of Business Administration, Master of Fine Arts (M.F.A.) in film and digital technology, M.F.A. in creative writing, Master of Occupational Therapy, Master of Physician Assistant Studies, Master of Science (M.S.) in biology, and M.S. in counseling psychology. Chatham also offers its Accelerated Graduate Program with the prestigious H. John Heinz III School of Public Policy at Carnegie Mellon University. Students may apply during their junior year to one of the following Heinz School programs: Master of Arts Management, Master of Information Systems Management, M.S. in Healthcare Policy and Management, and M.S. in Public Policy and Management. Accepted students take courses at both Chatham and the Heinz School during their senior year and earn a bachelor's degree from Chatham and a master's degree from Carnegie Mellon. Beginning in 2011, students may apply during their junior year to one of the following Duquesne University programs: M.S. in biotechnology, M.S. in computational mathematics, or M.S. in forensic science and law.

Academic Programs

Chatham's general education curriculum includes six required interdisciplinary courses, plus analytical reasoning, an international or intercultural experience, and wellness courses. Graduation requirements include the general education courses, a major, and the Senior Tutorial—an original research/capstone project. Students are mentored one-on-one by a faculty member throughout the tutorial process. The project provides an excellent bridge to graduate and professional schools and strong preparation for law and medical schools.

The University's 4-4-1 academic calendar consists of fall and spring terms plus a three-week "Maymester," which features study abroad, concentrated study, experimental projects, travel and field experiences, internships, interdisciplinary study, and student exchanges with other institutions.

The First-Year Student Sequence introduces students to the faculty and the University community and its culture and provides opportunities to learn about the resources of the urban environment and study issues of concern to women. Interactive seminar courses provide students with the analytical and communication skills essential for successful academic performance.

Chatham's Programs for Academic Success, Career Development, and Educational Enrichment (PACE) offers students a comprehensive approach to academic and career planning as well as an academic support network designed to maximize each student's academic success. Career services include counseling for undecided students, student internships, placement, workshops, recruitment, and mentor programs.

The Rachel Carson Institute honors Chatham's 1929 alumna and her commitment to the environment. The Pennsylvania Center for Women, Politics, and Public Policy introduces students to the world of politics, public policy, and civic engagement. The Center for Women's Entrepreneurship provides support for women entrepreneurs in the Pittsburgh region.

Off-Campus Programs

Chatham students may register at no additional cost for classes at any of Pittsburgh's eight other colleges and universities, including Carnegie Mellon and the University of Pittsburgh, both of which are within walking distance of the campus and accessible via free shuttle service. Chatham Abroad is a three-week travel experience with faculty members during the sophomore year Maymester (for an additional fee); past trips featured Belize, Egypt, England, France, the Galapagos Islands, Ireland, Italy, Morocco, Russia, and Spain.

Chatham students may participate in up to six internships related to their major and career goal. Recent examples include American Cancer Society, Children's Institute, East End Cooperative Ministry, Greater Pittsburgh Community Food Bank, Pittsburgh Action Against Rape, Race for the Cure, Sojourner House, Womansplace, Women and Girls Foundation of Southwest Pennsylvania, YWCA, and various corporate, nonprofit, government, health-care, and communications sites.

Academic Facilities

The Jennie King Mellon (JKM) Library serves the Chatham community as a primary research, study, and resource center. Students may access the Library's books, current print journals, full-text electronic journals, and online databases through the library's Web page. Librarians are available for research assistance. Individual study rooms, special seminar rooms, and a 24/7 study room are also offered. Through consortium memberships, the library provides access to materials from hundreds of academic libraries nationwide.

The Science Laboratory Complex houses state-of-the-art laboratories and individual lab units. Psychology and language labs and audiovisual facilities are also available. The Broadcast Studio contains sophisticated audio- and video-editing technology, including Macintosh G5 computers, as well as a multifunctional studio. Chatham's Art and Design Center features fine and applied art studios, a computer lab, and classroom space as well as gallery and student exhibition space.

Costs

For 2010–11, full-time tuition was $28,088 per year, and room and board were approximately $8900. A one-time deposit of $150 for tuition and $150 for on-campus housing is paid by newly admitted students and is applied to first-semester charges. Regularly enrolled full-time students pay no additional costs for Maymester courses, except for special supplies or travel. Music lessons and art supplies are additional. Students must have health and accident insurance. A technology fee is assessed for the MacBook program.

Financial Aid

Financial aid is awarded on the basis of an individual's financial need, as determined through the Free Application for Federal Student Aid (FAFSA). The awards combine grants, loans, and employment. The priority financial aid deadline is March 15. Sources of financial aid include Chatham University grants and scholarships, state grants, Federal Pell Grants, Federal Supplemental Educational Opportunity Grants, Direct Loans, and employment under the Federal Work-Study Program, as well as positions through the University. Chatham Merit scholarships for entering students are awarded without regard to need on the basis of high academic achievement and an on-campus interview. Scholarships begin at approximately $4000 and continue up to full tuition, room and board, and fees. Scholarships are awarded based on the student's match with Chatham's mission as well as the academic merits on her application for admission. Chatham also offers scholarships on the basis of music, art, leadership, interior architecture, Girl Scout participation, Rotary, and Phi Theta Kappa membership. Approximately 98 percent of undergraduate students receive aid administered by the University.

Faculty

The undergraduate student-teacher ratio of 9:1 ensures individual consideration and interaction between students and faculty members. Each student is assigned a faculty member who serves as her adviser through the completion of her degree program, including the Senior Tutorial capstone project. Ninety-eight percent of all undergraduate faculty members hold terminal degrees.

Admission Requirements

Evaluation is made on the basis of the prospective student's academic record, recommendations, essay, involvement in activities, and other submitted material. Chatham seeks to enroll students representing a variety of cultural, geographical, racial, religious, and socioeconomic backgrounds, with diverse talents in academic and creative areas. The admissions requirements now include a Standardized Test–Optional Policy. Applicants may choose to submit a graded writing sample and resume or a list of curricular and cocurricular activities as well as a portfolio or special project/activity in lieu of SAT or ACT scores. These materials are reviewed by Chatham faculty members and may be applied toward the scholarship review process.

Early action at Chatham University is a nonbinding admission option for first-year students who have completed their college search and know that Chatham is their first choice. Applicant deadline for early action is November 1 at midnight (Eastern time).

Admission decisions are provided within two weeks of receipt of a completed application. Applicants who apply early action will receive their merit scholarship award at the time of admission. They will also receive priority registration for housing and for the World Ready Women scholarship event in December. An estimated financial aid award is also provided in December for those who are admitted.

Applicants choosing to apply early action may apply for regular decision admission at any number of colleges and universities. Applicants who are admitted have until May 1 to respond to the admission offer.

It is strongly recommended that candidates arrange to visit the Chatham for a personal appointment, a student-guided campus tour, observation of one or more classes, and conversations with faculty and staff members and students. Early entrance is available for well-qualified and mature students who wish to begin at the end of their junior year in high school; candidates must have an on-campus interview. Chatham welcomes the opportunity to discuss future educational plans with transfer candidates in good academic standing, including junior college and community college graduates. Chatham grants college course credit for grades of 4 or 5 on Advanced Placement (AP) exams. Certain course prerequisites may be fulfilled by attaining scores of 3, 4, or 5.

Application and Information

Candidates for admission must file an application with the Admissions Office, together with a $35 nonrefundable processing fee. A free online application is available on the University's Web site. Applications are accepted on a rolling basis.

Vice President of Admissions and Financial Aid
Office of Admissions
Chatham University
Woodland Road
Pittsburgh, Pennsylvania 15232
Phone: 412-365-1290
   800-837-1290 (toll-free)
Fax: 412-365-1609
E-mail: admission@chatham.edu
Web site: http://www.chatham.edu
   http://www.facebook.com/chathamu

A view of the Chatham University campus.

CHEYNEY UNIVERSITY OF PENNSYLVANIA

CHEYNEY, PENNSYLVANIA

The University

Founded in 1837 by Richard Humphreys, a Philadelphia Quaker, Cheyney University is America's oldest historically Black institution of higher education. Today it leverages that rich history of providing access to higher education for all students by producing visionary leaders and responsible citizens. Cheyney graduates are successful, talented individuals; some of the best-known include *60 Minutes* journalist Ed Bradley, *Philadelphia Tribune CEO* Robert W. Bogle, NBC news anchor Jim Vance, and Comcast Network TV personality Robert Traynham. Cheyney University is in the business of developing human potential and talent, and does so through an intellectually challenging environment and personal attention to every student—a hallmark of the Cheyney experience.

The University's 275-acre campus on the rolling hillsides of southeastern Pennsylvania is located only 25 miles from Philadelphia. The heart of the campus is its historic quadrangle with buildings dating back to the early 1900s. The campus offers five residence halls, including a new 400-bed suite-style residence hall. The newly established Center of Excellence in Communications Media, Fine Arts, and Entertainment Arts includes two theaters for the performing arts—Dudley Theatre and the recently renovated Marian Anderson Music Center—as well as a state-of-the art graphic design lab. The University is complemented by a library, an aquaponics greenhouse, dining hall, snack bar, fitness center, student union, and multiple athletic facilities. A new science center is scheduled to open in 2012. Cheyney University also has a location in downtown Philadelphia, which primarily houses the University's graduate degree programs.

Approximately 1,400 students choose from more than thirty undergraduate and graduate degree programs and participate in more than forty clubs, societies, and student organizations. Further, the University has implemented the University College Model for freshmen and sophomore students, enhancing student engagement and establishing a critical link between residence life and academics. The model carefully monitors students' academic progress, social skills, and social maturity via appropriately arranged advising, mentoring, counseling, and career services.

The University is an NCAA Division II institution with twelve intercollegiate sports teams. The campus includes two training facilities, O'Shields Stevenson Stadium (football and track) and Cope Hall (volleyball, basketball, and swimming). Cheyney's student-athletes will be viewed as students first, and only then as athletes. The department's focus is on developing graduates who are successful, well-rounded, and prepared to make positive contributions to society. Academic achievements in the classroom, combined with the development of character, individual and team skills, the will to win, and a sense of fair play and sportsmanship in athletic competition determine distinction in intercollegiate athletics programs.

Cheyney University is part of the Pennsylvania State System of Higher Education and is regionally accredited by the Middle States Commission on Higher Education.

Location

Cheyney University's main campus is 25 miles west of Philadelphia. SEPTA bus service is available between the campus, Center City Philadelphia, Chester, and several sites in Delaware County. Lancaster is 1½ hours away, and Harrisburg is 2 hours from Cheyney. Wilmington, Delaware is 15 miles south of Cheyney; both New York City and Washington, D.C., are 2 hours away. The campus is easily accessible via the Pennsylvania Turnpike and Interstate 95.

Cheyney University Center City (CUCC) is located at 701 Market Street in downtown Philadelphia.

Majors and Degrees

Undergraduate degrees conferred from the School of Education and Professional Studies and the School of Arts and Sciences are the Bachelor of Arts, Bachelor of Science, and Associate in Science. Graduate degrees conferred are the Master of Education, Master of Science, Master of Arts in Teaching, and Master of Public Administration. A complete list of academic majors is available on the University's Web site.

Academic Programs

The completion of 120 semester hours is required for a bachelor's degree. Of the 120 hours, 40 percent are in general education and 60 percent in humanities, social sciences, natural sciences, mathematics, health and physical education, and electives.

Cheyney's Keystone Honors Academy is a learning community of high-achieving students. The academy offers its members study-abroad opportunities, internship experiences, professional development, and graduate school preparation.

The University College Model is a unique program for freshmen and sophomores that helps students mature academically and socially. The model combines targeted advising, mentoring, counseling, and career services to help in the maturation and graduation process.

The Academic Success Center provides tutors and counselors for students who seek academic support.

The University's graduate degree program offers programs in education, educational leadership, and public administration.

Academic Facilities

The Leslie Pinckney Hill Library houses approximately 200,000 books plus a periodical collection of more than 23,000 bound volumes and 1,100 current subscriptions. Audiovisual media, CD-ROM full-text/image databases, and Internet access are available. The library also houses the famed Schomburg Collection of African-American History and Culture on microfilm.

The Center of Excellence in Communications Media, Fine Arts, and Entertainment Arts is complemented by the Marian Anderson Music Center which recently underwent a $3.2-million restoration. The Center also features a state-of-the art graphic design lab; a newly refurbished radio broadcast studio; and the telecommunications center, which includes a 240-seat auditorium with state-of-the-art satellite television capabilities, a cable television control facility, a television studio, and the AT&T Distance Learning and Teleconferencing Center, equipped with twenty computers and teleconference network access.

The Vaux-Logan Auditorium supports academics and the University College Model, and features newly enhanced lighting, sound, and projection technology; upgraded seating; and new stage flooring.

The Aquaponics Greenhouse Center is a 12,000-square-foot learning lab for biology, marketing, and business students, as well as a commercial production facility for wholesale basil and tilapia, which are sold to benefit the University.

The new science center (slated to open in 2012) is a 40,000-square-foot sustainable LEED-certified facility being built with recycled and local building materials. It is designed to house a planetarium; chemistry, biology, computer science, and physics labs; faculty offices; and seminar and lecture halls. Plans also include a demonstration green roof and rain/gray water reuse and recycling system.

Costs

For the 2010–11 academic year, tuition for Pennsylvania residents for 12–18 credits was $7718 for full-time students. For residents of Delaware, Maryland, New Jersey, and New York, tuition for 12–18 credits was $13,640. For other states and international students, tuition was $16,542. Room and board, based on double occupancy and a nineteen-meal plan, totaled $8486.

Financial Aid

The University makes every possible effort to enable interested and qualified students to take advantage of its educational opportunities. Financial assistance may be available in the form of academic scholarships, grants, loans, and the Federal Work-Study Program. Financial aid packages are developed for qualified students based on individual student need. Students wishing to apply for financial aid must complete the Free Application for Federal Student Aid (FAFSA). Students should pay strict attention to all state and federal application deadlines. About 95 percent of all full-time undergraduate students receive some sort of aid.

Faculty

Cheyney University has over 145 full- and part-time faculty members. The student to faculty ratio is approximately 10:1 and each student has a faculty adviser.

Student Government

All students are members of the Student Government Cooperative Association (SGCA), which sponsors many cultural, educational, and social events and brings speakers and performers to the campus. SGCA and other student representatives sit on all University committees. A student representative is also selected to serve on the University's Council of Trustees.

Admission Requirements

Applicants to Cheyney University are evaluated on the following criteria: GPA; SAT or ACT scores; class rank; and academic curriculum. Letters of recommendation and an essay are encouraged. Admission requirements include graduation from an approved secondary school or a General Education Development (GED) certificate from an approved agency. A campus visit and an admission interview are encouraged. Transfer students in good standing with a minimum 2.0 grade point average may apply for admission; those who have completed 12 credits or more are not required to have taken the SAT or ACT.

Application and Information

Students are admitted for the fall or spring semester and can apply online. Along with a completed application, the University must receive an official, final copy of the high school transcript, SAT or ACT scores, and a nonrefundable application fee. Transfer students are required to submit official transcripts from all colleges or universities previously attended.

For additional information contact:

Office of Admissions
Cheyney University of Pennsylvania
1837 University Circle
P.O. Box 200
Cheyney, Pennsylvania 19319-0200
Phone: 610-399-2275
       800-CHEYNEY (toll-free)
       admissions@cheyney.edu
Web site: http://www.cheyney.edu

Cheyney University is located on a beautiful 275-acre campus, located in Southeastern Pennsylvania, 25 miles outside of Philadelphia, within a few hours of Baltimore and Washington, D.C.

CHRISTOPHER NEWPORT UNIVERSITY

NEWPORT NEWS, VIRGINIA

The University

Christopher Newport University (CNU) was founded in 1960 and enrolls 4,800 students in more than seventy areas of study (including three 5-year master's degree programs). The University takes pride in its "student-first, teaching-first" community. Small classes taught by veteran faculty members, a beautiful and safe campus, and one of the nation's finest sports programs make CNU a distinctive choice among Virginia's public universities.

At CNU, students are challenged to thrive academically. Each fall, the President's Leadership Program accepts approximately 300 high-achieving freshmen who have exhibited leadership characteristics in their schools and communities. Through the four-year Honors Program, academically talented students enjoy a rich educational experience, participating in challenging courses and cultural/intellectual activities. CNU students also actively participate in community service and service learning, hallmarks of the University.

Location

CNU ranks as one of the safest midsize campuses in Virginia. Its picturesque 260-acre campus and superb residential facilities receive high praise from students and visitors alike. The University is located on the Virginia Peninsula in suburban Newport News. It is adjacent to Mariners' Museum Park, a pristine 550-acre nature preserve with miles of jogging trails around Lake Maury and along the James River.

CNU is 35 miles from the pounding surf and rolling dunes of Virginia Beach, 25 miles from historic Williamsburg, 75 miles from Richmond, and 150 miles from Washington, D.C. Students enjoy the year-round moderate climate, the short driving distance to the beach, and the region's diverse recreational opportunities.

Majors and Degrees

CNU's academic programs fall within three colleges: the College of Arts and Humanities, the College of Natural and Behavioral Sciences, and the College of Social Sciences (which includes the Joseph W. Luter III School of Business). CNU offers the Bachelor of Arts degree in American studies (concentrations in humanities and social science), communication studies, English (concentrations in film studies, literature, and writing), fine arts (concentrations in art history and studio art), foreign language (majors in French, German, and Spanish), history (interdisciplinary prelaw program available), interdisciplinary studies, philosophy (concentrations in preseminary studies and religious studies), political science, psychology, and sociology (social work major and concentrations in anthropology, criminology, and education and socialization).

Students may choose the Bachelor of Music degree (concentrations in performance, theory/composition, choral music education, and instrumental music education) or the Bachelor of Science degree in interdisciplinary studies. A special curriculum is offered in jazz studies. A Bachelor of Arts in theater is offered (concentrations in acting, arts administration, design/technology, directing and dramatic literature, music theater/dance, and theater studies).

Minors are available in American studies, anthropology, art history/studio art, childhood studies, civic engagement and social entrepreneurship, classical civilization, communication studies, film studies, French, German, gerontology, history, journalism, Latin classical studies, leadership studies, music, philosophy and

religious studies, political science, psychology, sociology, Spanish, theater arts, women's and gender studies, U.S. national securities studies, and writing.

Also offered in the sciences are the Bachelor of Arts degree in biology, interdisciplinary studies, and mathematics; and the Bachelor of Science degree in applied physics, biology (preprofessional programs in dental, medical, and veterinary studies), chemistry, computer engineering, computer science, environmental science, information systems, interdisciplinary studies, mathematics, and psychology. Minors are available in applied physics, biology, chemistry, computer science, and mathematics.

The Luter School of Business, accredited by AACSB International—The Association to Advance Collegiate Schools of Business, offers the Bachelor of Science in Business Administration degree, with majors in accounting, economics, finance, management, and marketing and minors in business administration and economics.

Academic Programs

To be eligible for an undergraduate degree, students must successfully complete 120 academic semester hours. The last 45 semester hours of credit must be taken in residence.

The first two years of all students' academic programs require successful completion of the Liberal Learning Core requirements in such areas as English (writing), foreign language, humanities, laboratory science, mathematics, social science, and various areas of inquiry. New, innovative freshman seminars allow students to explore unique interdisciplinary courses.

At CNU, students also enjoy unique opportunities for specialized study. The premed and prehealth program includes academic and career advising, mentoring, clinical internships, and expert guidance throughout the application process. Through an agreement between CNU and Eastern Virginia Medical School (EVMS), selected students may receive early assurance of a position in medical school at EVMS upon satisfactory completion of their undergraduate degree program and their continued high academic achievement.

With the Master of Arts in Teaching (M.A.T.), students major in a specific content area, receiving a bachelor's degree after four years. In the fifth year they complete graduate-level professional courses and a semester of student teaching.

Students interested in attending law school reap the benefits of hands-on advising and mentoring provided by the prelaw program. While not a degreed program, it prepares students in departments across campus for law school admittance and success.

First-year students may participate in Learning Communities. Students in these groups live together, take classes together, and are guided by an upper-class student dedicated to their academic success.

Off-Campus Programs

The University actively supports study abroad for all its students and sponsors a variety of international study programs each year that promote cross-cultural education and growth. Students have recently participated with faculty members in study-abroad programs in Belgium, China, England, France, Germany, Holland, Ireland, Italy, Kenya, Morocco, and Spain. CNU offers top students the opportunity to study at Oxford University each summer. CNU provides up to $5000 for international study to students who participate in the President's Leadership Program. Students may also travel to Europe with the CNU Chamber Singers or worldwide with CNU's award-winning Model U.N. Club.

Students also broaden their education through internships. Each year they receive opportunities with prominent organizations like NASA; the Thomas Jefferson National Laboratory; the Secret Service; and countless media, health-care, education, and social-service firms and agencies, among others.

Academic Facilities

CNU's academic buildings contain a variety of small classrooms and auditoriums, computer laboratories, specialty laboratories, an instructional technology center, and a greenhouse/herbarium.

Students have access to more than 1,200 computer workstations on campus as well as e-mail and Internet access in the residential facilities. Wireless access is available in all public areas. Top-rated, state-of-the-art residence halls and upperclass apartments accommodate 3,000 students on campus.

In 2010, CNU celebrated the opening of a new academic home for all of the liberal arts, the Lewis Archer McMurran Jr. Hall, which provides more than 82,000 square feet of teaching and learning spaces. A new $80-million integrated science center is under construction.

The University has completed $500 million in new facilities over the past decade, creating an impressive and appealing "home" for its students and faculty. An additional $500 million in capital construction is scheduled to take place by 2020.

The dazzling Paul and Rosemary Trible Library opened in 2008 with more than 100,000 square feet for information technology and traditional library collections. As the intellectual center of the campus, the library features a fourteen-story tower, lighted day and night, and a 1,600-square-foot coffee shop with adjacent study rooms. The stunning rotunda in the Trible Library and its many elegant study spaces have created an outstanding academic home for study.

CNU is home to the $16-million Freeman Sports and Convocation Center, the $64-million Ferguson Center for the Arts (designed by I. M. Pei), and the $35-million David Student Union. At the Ferguson Center, CNU hosts internationally recognized performers like Andrea Bocelli, David Copperfield, Whoopi Goldberg, and B.B. King, among others. Students may attend these performances for between $5 and $15.

Costs

In-state tuition for full-time students for the spring 2011 semester was $4625; nonresident tuition for full-time students for the spring 2011 semester was $8996. Books and supplies average $750–$1000 per year. The room and board rate for the spring 2011 semester was $4670.

Financial Aid

The University's financial aid programs serve approximately 50 percent of the student body. CNU offers every form of federally funded financial aid and more than 200 renewable merit scholarships for freshmen. The President's Leadership Program offers a minor in leadership studies and up to $5000 per year for academically superior students, regardless of need. The Honors Program offers scholarships of up to $5000 per year and gives students priority registration and the opportunity to develop their own path of courses instead of being tied to core requirements.

Faculty

Nearly 90 percent of CNU faculty members hold the highest degree in their professional field. Faculty members are chosen at CNU only if teaching is their top priority. They are advisers, mentors, and friends to their students, placing great emphasis on undergraduate research and preparation for graduate school.

Student Government

With more than 100 student clubs and organizations, students find no shortage of opportunities for campus involvement.

The University also encourages students to participate in the formulation of rules, regulations, and policies directly affecting student life. Students may get involved with the University's committees and councils. CNU is a community of honor, and all freshmen take an honor pledge during their Welcome Week orientation activities.

Admission Requirements

CNU welcomes applications from Virginia residents and out-of-state students whose education includes a strong college-preparatory curriculum and a record of success. Of the students accepted into the freshman class, the midrange (middle 50 percent) SAT score was 1100 to 1280 (critical reading and math); the average GPA was 3.6 on a 4.0 scale. CNU applicants may also submit the ACT exam, with or without the writing sample. Superior students with a GPA of 3.5 or better may apply to the University without submitting an SAT or ACT score.

Application and Information

Applications, viewbooks, and additional information may be obtained from the University's Web site or by contacting:

Christopher Newport University
Admissions Office
1 University Place
Newport News, Virginia 23606-2998
Phone: 757-594-7015
       757-594-7938 (TDD)
       800-333-4CNU (toll-free)
E-mail: admit@cnu.edu
Web site: http://www.cnu.edu

Trible Library is the intellectual center of Christopher Newport University.

CLARKSON UNIVERSITY
POTSDAM, NEW YORK

The University

Founded in 1896, Clarkson stands out among America's private, nationally ranked research institutions because of its dynamic collaborative learning environment, innovative degree and research programs, and unmatched record of accomplishment for producing leaders and innovators.

The University attracts 3,000 enterprising students from diverse backgrounds (including some 400 graduate students) who thrive in rigorous programs in engineering, arts, sciences, business, and health sciences and in the University's close-knit, residential learning/living community. Clarkson defies convention in the classroom, in its laboratories, and by the impact its graduates have in the world. The University is New York State's highest-ranked small research institution. However, size is Clarkson's advantage—fostering leadership and problem-solving skills and readily affording students and faculty members the flexibility to span the boundaries of traditional academic areas.

Clarkson students also enjoy extraordinary opportunities to pursue faculty-mentored research. They gain professional experience through internships and co-ops with corporations and government organizations and can broaden their perspectives through a wide range of study-abroad opportunities.

Top graduate schools welcome Clarkson graduates to study medicine, law, and other professions. Johns Hopkins, MIT, Princeton, Yale, Caltech, Rice, and Stanford are just some of the schools chosen by Clarkson students.

Clarkson's 98 percent placement rate is among the nation's highest, with the most recent starting salaries averaging nearly $51,000. Clarkson is a key recruitment source for many of America's industry leaders, including General Electric, Alcoa, Xerox, Accenture, IBM, and Procter & Gamble. In fact, 1 in 6 Clarkson alumni is already a CEO, president, vice president, or company owner.

Clarkson's active campus also offers a wide variety of extracurricular activities, including more than eighty clubs and interest groups. Students publish a lively campus newspaper and run campus radio and television stations. Active professional and honor societies enrich the campus experience.

There are Division I men's and women's hockey teams, as well as, seventeen Division III intercollegiate athletic teams for women and men. Recreational facilities include a field house and gym with racquetball, basketball, and indoor tennis courts; a state-of-the-art fitness center; and a swimming pool.

Location

Clarkson is located in Potsdam, the quintessential "college town," nestled in the foothills of the northern Adirondack region of New York. The beautiful Northeast corner of the state is the home of the 6-million-acre Adirondack Park. Lake Placid and the cosmopolitan Canadian cities of Montreal and Ottawa are less than 2 hours from the campus.

Majors and Degrees

Undergraduate degree programs offered are aeronautical engineering, American studies, applied mathematics and statistics, Areté (liberal arts/business), biology, biomolecular engineering, biomolecular science, chemical engineering, chemistry, civil engineering, communication, computer engineering, computer science, digital arts and sciences, electrical engineering, engineering and management, environmental engineering, environmental health science, environmental science and policy, financial information and analysis, global supply chain management, history, humanities, information systems and business processes,
innovation and entrepreneurship, liberal studies, mathematics, mechanical engineering, physician assistant studies (pre– physician assistant studies leading to a master's degree), physical therapy (pre–physical therapy leading to a doctorate), physics, political science, psychology, social documentation, social sciences, and software engineering.

First-year students who are still deciding on a major may begin in a general program in business studies, engineering studies, science studies, or university studies.

Clarkson offers a University honors program, a three-year bachelor's degree option, a five-year B.S./M.S. in chemistry/biochemistry, a five-year B.S./M.B.A., and preprofessional programs in dentistry, law, medicine, physical therapy, and veterinary science.

Academic Programs

Clarkson's historic strengths in business, engineering, liberal arts, and science remain at the core of the curriculum. These programs have also been combined into cutting-edge, cross-disciplinary majors, including biomolecular science, digital arts and sciences, environmental science and policy, engineering and management, and software engineering.

A dynamic, hands-on approach to learning is one of the hallmarks of a Clarkson education. Clarkson students learn about business by actually starting a business. They conduct scientific research alongside distinguished faculty mentors in state-of-the-art laboratories. The University's undergraduate research program has produced 25 Goldwater Scholars since the highly competitive national scholarship program was launched in 1986.

Students can also take advantage of educational initiatives and research opportunities through the Institute for a Sustainable Environment, the Center for Sustainable Energy Systems, the Shipley Center for Innovation, the Center for Entrepreneurship, the Center for Rehabilitation Engineering and Science (CREST), and the Center for Air Resources Engineering and Sciences (CARES), among others.

In 2011, *Bloomberg Businessweek* placed Clarkson twentieth on its list of Fifty Affordable Colleges with the Best Return on Investment.

National rankings and honors include the following: among the 125 Best National Universities–Doctoral, *U.S. News & World Report*, 2010; among the Best Undergraduate Engineering Programs, *U.S. News & World Report*, 2010; among the best undergraduate business programs in the nation, *Bloomberg Businessweek* 2011; and among *The Best 373 Colleges*, the Princeton Review, 2011.

The supply chain management program is ranked fourteenth in the nation by *U.S. News & World Report*, 2011; and in the top 20 in the nation for production/operations management by *U.S. News & World Report*, in "America's Best Colleges," 2010.

The digital arts and sciences major at Clarkson was named the most innovative program in North America by the International Digital Media and Arts Association (iDMAa), November 2010.

Clarkson was also ranked among the top 100 graduate schools in environmental engineering and civil engineering by *U.S. News & World Report's* "Best Graduate Programs," 2009.

ROTC service at Clarkson ranked second in the nation by *Washington Monthly* magazine in 2010. Clarkson was rated among the nation's most environmentally-focused colleges in the Princeton Review's *Guide to 311 Green Colleges*.

In addition, Clarkson's award-winning Student Projects for Engineering Experience and Design (SPEED) program promotes multidisciplinary, project-based extracurricular learning opportunities for more than 400 undergraduates annually. Some fifteen design teams compete in national and regional collegiate competitions that involve design and analysis, teamwork, and communication skills.

Off-Campus Programs

Students benefit from the resources of the Associated Colleges of the St. Lawrence Valley, which comprises Clarkson University, St. Lawrence University, SUNY Canton, and SUNY Potsdam. Benefits for students include opportunities to participate in activities ranging from clubs to concerts, interlibrary exchange, and cross-registration that allows students to pursue two courses per year at member colleges at no extra cost.

Academic Facilities

The University's 640-acre wooded campus is the site of forty-six buildings that comprise more than 1.2-million square feet of assignable space. Dedicated exclusively to instructional programs are more than 375,000 square feet, including some 54,000 square feet of traditional classrooms and more than 168,000 square feet assigned as laboratory areas. In the Center for Advanced Materials Processing (a New York State Center for Advanced Technology), there are seventy state-of-the-art research labs, including many related to nanotechnology and environmental research. Others include a multidisciplinary engineering and project laboratory for team-based projects, such as the mini-Baja and Formulae SAE racers, a robotics laboratory, a high-voltage lab, electron microscopy, a Class 10 clean room, a polymer fabrication lab, crystal growth labs, and a structural testing lab. School of Arts and Sciences facilities include a virtual-reality laboratory, the Clarkson Open Source Institute, a molecular design laboratory, a human brain electrophysiology laboratory, and other specialized facilities. In 2008, a 16,000-square-foot Technology Advancement Center was opened.

Bertrand H. Snell Hall houses the School of Business and the School of Arts and Sciences administrative offices as well as fully networked classrooms and study spaces and collaborative centers that feature wireless network access and videoconferencing capabilities. The facility includes three academic centers, which are available to all students: the Shipley Center for Innovation, the Center for Global Competitiveness, and the Eastman Kodak Center for Excellence in Communication. The Center for Health Sciences at Clarkson is a regional center of excellence for education, treatment, and research in physical rehabilitation and other health sciences.

Costs

Tuition was $34,070 for the 2010–11 year, room (2-person) was $6126, and the meal plan was $5438. Student fees totaled $690. In addition, students usually spend about $2000 annually on books, supplies, travel, and personal expenses.

Financial Aid

The University offers a variety of scholarships and loans, including state and federal student loans, state scholarships and awards, individual scholarships, federal grants, and federal work-study programs.

Faculty

Clarkson's 190 full-time faculty members teach undergraduate and graduate classes, with graduate students assisting only in undergraduate lab sciences. With an excellent student-faculty ratio of 15:1, undergraduates benefit from regular interaction with the school's faculty members and small class sizes (especially at the upper levels). The University attracts teacher/scholars who are also highly regarded scholars in their fields. 96 percent hold a doctorate.

Student Government

The Student Senate and the Interfraternity Council combine to form the student government at Clarkson University. The former supervises all extracurricular activities (except athletics) and has responsibility for the allocation of student activity funds and for other appropriate business. The latter prescribes standards and rules for fraternities. Students are involved in the formation of University policies through membership, with faculty and staff representatives, on all important committees.

Admission Requirements

Clarkson recommends that prospective students follow a challenging secondary school curriculum that includes mathematics, science, and English. Candidates for entrance to the Wallace H. Coulter School of Engineering or students pursuing a degree in the sciences or an engineering and management degree should have successfully completed secondary school courses in physics and chemistry. All candidates for admission are required to take the SAT or ACT. SAT Subject Tests are optional. The high school record is the most important factor in an admission decision. International students for whom English is a second language must submit a minimum TOEFL score of 550 (paper-based) or 212 (computer-based). All applicants must include a personal statement of 250 to 500 words.

Students achieving scores of 4 or better on the College Board's Advanced Placement examinations are considered for advanced placement and credit in virtually all academic areas.

An early decision plan is offered on a first-choice basis; this plan does not prohibit the student from making other applications, but it does commit the student to withdrawing other applications if accepted at Clarkson.

Although not required, a personal interview with a member of the Office of Admission is highly recommended, especially for early decision candidates. Interviews on campus should be arranged by letter or telephone at least one week prior to the intended visit. The Office of Admission is open Monday through Friday, from 8 a.m. to 4:30 p.m., and Saturday by appointment. The University welcomes visitors to the campus and makes arrangements, as requested, for families to tour and meet with academic and other departments on campus.

Application and Information

Office of Undergraduate Admission
Holcroft House
Clarkson University
P.O. Box 5605
Potsdam, New York 13699-5605
Phone: 315-268-6480
   800-527-6577 (toll-free)
Fax: 315-268-7647
E-mail: admission@clarkson.edu
Web site: http://www.clarkson.edu

Clarkson is a leader in project-based learning, providing students with strong problem-solving and leadership skills.

CLARK UNIVERSITY
WORCESTER, MASSACHUSETTS

CLARK UNIVERSITY 1887
CHALLENGE CONVENTION.
CHANGE OUR WORLD.

The University

Founded in 1887, Clark is a private, liberal arts-based research university committed to scholarship that addresses social imperatives in a global context. Clark enrolls approximately 2,200 undergraduate and 1,000 graduate students. Undergraduates are offered a broad and deep liberal arts education that enables them to address the complex scientific, social, and economic challenges facing the world through hands-on research, in-depth exploration, and practical problem solving. Clark's focused areas of research excellence are backed by strong Ph.D. and master's-degree programs that engage graduate students from around the world in relevant, challenging, and innovative research that transforms communities. Research is a central component of Clark's mission, and the University has a tradition of challenging convention in the quest for new knowledge. Today, Clark continues this legacy of innovation with a research program that focuses on such areas as urban education, environmental issues and policies, management, health care, child and family welfare, holocaust and genocide studies, and international development and social change, generating findings and insights that directly benefit the communities the University serves.

Of the undergraduate students, about 60 percent are women, 8 percent are international students, and 70 percent live on campus. Students are guaranteed housing in one of nine residence halls for their first two years at Clark. Students can live with other freshmen in one of Clark's three First-Year Experience residence halls, or with upperclass students in one of the mixed-class residence halls. Housing options for upperclass students include suites (which resemble an apartment with a separate entry door, living room, and bathroom).

Clark's students are passionate about ideas, causes, and events beyond themselves; and are empowered to seek out and become involved in the many cocurricular opportunities available both on campus and off. Students can participate in more than 120 clubs and organizations.

Clark University is a Division III member of the National Collegiate Athletic Association and maintains highly competitive varsity athletic teams in a variety of sports. Men compete in baseball, basketball, cross-country, lacrosse, rowing, soccer, swimming and diving, and tennis. Women compete in basketball, cross-country, field hockey, rowing, soccer, softball, swimming and diving, tennis, and volleyball. Sixty-five percent of undergraduate students participate in intercollegiate, intramural, club, wellness, or recreational programs.

Clark's intramural program gives students the opportunity to compete and have fun without the demands of varsity athletics. Approximately half of the student body participates in the intramural program, which also encourages participation by Clark's faculty, staff, and alumni.

Location

Located in the heart of New England and about 40 miles west of Boston, Worcester (pronounced "wooster") is within easy reach of many cultural and recreational opportunities. With a population of approximately 175,000, the city is home to a broad mix of immigrants, from Armenian to French-Canadian to Vietnamese, who have lent their distinctive cultures to Worcester neighborhoods, restaurants, and places of worship. Worcester is also recognized as one of the ten most livable cities in the U.S. by *Forbes* magazine. Nearby attractions include Old Sturbridge Village and the Worcester Horticultural Society's Tower Hill Botanical Garden. Wachusett Mountain provides opportunities for skiing and hiking.

Majors and Degrees

Bachelor's degrees are offered in ancient civilization, art history, Asian studies, biochemistry/molecular biology, biology, business management, chemistry, communication and culture, comparative literature, computer science, economics, English, environmental science, foreign languages and literatures, French, geography, global environmental studies, history, international development and social change, mathematics, music, philosophy, physics, political science, psychology, screen studies, sociology, Spanish, studio art, theater arts, and women's and gender studies. Students can also design their own major.

Academic Programs

Clark's challenging liberal arts curriculum encourages students to think critically, comprehend major global challenges, and develop the breadth of capabilities necessary for success in career and citizenship. Clark provides students many of the benefits typically associated with an excellent liberal arts college, including small classes, a strong sense of community, extensive cocurricular opportunities, and faculty members passionate about teaching and mentoring students. In addition, as a research university, Clark offers students the opportunity to participate in cutting-edge scholarship and creative work, working side-by-side with faculty members and graduate students, many of whom are international leaders in their fields. The smaller scale of the institution fosters close, active collaborations among faculty members, graduate students, and undergraduates. The University's dynamic learning environment and social values encourage students to seek out innovative solutions to real-world problems and create positive change in the community and the world.

Clark University's Program of Liberal Studies introduces students to the ways in which different fields and disciplines organize ideas and address questions. Students have the opportunity to engage in original research and creative work and present their results at campuswide celebrations of student accomplishments. Other academic opportunities include a university-wide innovation and entrepreneurship program, a rich array of internship and study-abroad options, and a variety of summer research opportunities. The International Studies Stream provides a broad-based international experience for students through courses, speakers, programs, internships, and study-abroad opportunities.

Clark has received national attention for its accelerated degree program that allows students to complete both a bachelor's degree and a master's degree in five years, with fifth-year tuition waived for eligible students.

Off-Campus Programs

Studying abroad can enrich and strengthen students' academic program, help perfect their language skills, and broaden their horizons. Clark offers more than thirty opportunities to study abroad in both foreign-language and English-language programs. Students must declare a major before choosing a program.

An academic internship is a credit-bearing, career-related work experience of limited duration in which an individual takes on responsible roles outside the traditional university environment in a nonprofit organization, government office, or for-profit business. The Clark Recruiter, an online career management system, typically lists more than 300 internships every year. For assistance, students can make a one-on-one appointment with a counselor in the Office of Career Services.

Academic Facilities

In the past decade, Clark has made major investments in facilities to support student and faculty scholarship, including the Traina Center for the Arts, the Lasry Center for the Biosciences, and the Academic Commons at Goddard Library. The University's main library, Goddard, is a cutting-edge facility for research, teaching, and learning. In addition to the archives and special collections, traditional and electronic resources are available, including Goddard's collection of more than 375,000 volumes, 275,000 monographs, subscriptions to 1,500 periodicals, full Internet access, nearly 50 subject-specific databases, and a public online catalog available 24 hours a day. Clark students and faculty also have access to the library collections of thirteen other colleges and universities in the Worcester Consortium.

Clark's research institutes and centers—which include the Mosakowski Institute for Public Enterprise, the George Perkins Marsh Institute, the Clark Labs for Cartographic Analysis, the Jacob Hiatt Center for Urban Education, the Heinz Werner Institute for Development Analysis, and the Strassler Center for Holocaust and Genocide Studies—build on a foundation of interdisciplinary scholarship, with faculty and students working across boundaries to develop innovative solutions to a wide range of contemporary challenges.

Costs

For the 2011–12 academic year, tuition is $37,000, and the student activity fee is $320. Housing varies between $4000 and $7500; meal plans range between $2600 and $3100.

Financial Aid

The Office of Financial Assistance works closely with families to explore a range of financial options. A financial aid package usually comprises grants, loans, and employment. Around 85 percent of students receive some form of financial assistance. In 2010, Clark awarded approximately $45 million in financial assistance. Merit-based scholarships are available, and eligible students can receive scholarships of up to $18,000. Seventy-nine percent of the most recent incoming first-year class received University scholarships.

Faculty

Faculty members take pride in serving as scholars, teachers, and mentors. There are 187 full-time faculty members, 96 percent of whom hold a doctorate or terminal degree in their field. The student-to-faculty ratio is 10:1. All undergraduate courses are taught by the faculty members, not graduate students.

Student Government

The Student Council advances the interests of students and ensures that students play a vital role in decisions at the University. Student Council members, elected every semester, work to maximize student influence at Clark.

Admission Requirements

The admissions committee recommends that applicants have a strong senior year course load (at least four, preferably five, solid academic courses). In addition, students should have taken, at minimum, 4 years of English, 3 of mathematics, 3 of science, 2 of social science, and 2 of a foreign language, as well as other electives, including the arts.

Students must submit the completed application, the $55 nonrefundable application fee, transcripts of all high school and college work completed, official ACT or SAT scores, and two letters of recommendation. Transfer students should also include a statement explaining why they wish to attend Clark University. All students whose native language is not English are encouraged to take the TOEFL. Students can apply online using the common or the universal application; paper applications are also accepted.

Application and Information

The regular decision deadlines for the fall and spring semesters are January 15 and November 1 for first-year students, April 1 and November 1 for transfer students, and January 15 for international students. First-year students may apply early action for the fall semester. The early action deadline is November 15.

Office of Admissions
Clark University
950 Main Street
Worcester, Massachusetts 01610
Phone: 508-793-7431
      800-462-5275 (toll-free)
Fax: 508-793-8821
E-mail: admissions@clarku.edu
Web site: http://www.clarku.edu
      http://www.facebook.com/lewisandclarkcollege
      http://twitter.com/lcadmissions (Twitter)

CLEMSON UNIVERSITY
CLEMSON, SOUTH CAROLINA

The University

One of the country's most selective public research universities, Clemson was founded in 1889 with a mission to be a "high seminary of learning" dedicated to teaching, research, and service. Today, these three concepts remain at the heart of the University and provide the framework for an exceptional educational experience.

At Clemson University, professors take the time to get to know students and explore innovative ways of teaching. Exceptional teaching is one reason Clemson's retention and graduation rates rank among the highest in the country for public universities.

Exceptional teaching is also why Clemson continues to attract an increasingly talented student body. In 2010, roughly half of the entering freshmen were ranked in the top 10 percent of their high school classes, and the freshman class averaged 1231 on the critical reading and math sections of the SAT—one of the highest averages among the nation's public research universities.

Clemson is committed to world-class research. With more than $187 million in sponsored research support annually, undergraduates have the opportunity to work closely with faculty members on exciting and challenging research projects.

The University also encourages faculty members to engage their classes through service learning. One example of this is the Clemson Elementary Outdoors project, in which more than 750 Clemson students from a broad range of disciplines researched and designed outdoor learning areas for the city's elementary school. Clemson has received national recognition for its innovative Communication-Across-the-Curriculum (CAC) program, in which professors focus on providing real-life challenges that require students to think and communicate effectively. At Clemson, CAC has become a standard teaching method used in nearly every department.

From cheering the Tigers at a football game to socializing at the Hendrix Student Center, Clemson students can participate in a wide variety of activities outside the classroom. The more than 325 campus clubs and organizations include fraternities and sororities, as well as honorary, international, military, performing arts, political, professional, religious, service, social interest, special interest, sports and fitness, student media, and union programs and activities.

With nineteen intercollegiate sports, Clemson offers exciting spectator sports year-round. Clemson is a charter member of the Atlantic Coast Conference and is an NCAA Division I school. Admission to regular-season home events is included in University fees for full-time students.

Clemson University is accredited by the Commission on Colleges of the Southern Association of Colleges and Schools to award bachelor's, master's, specialist, and doctoral degrees. Contact the Commission on Colleges at 1866 Southern Lane, Decatur, Georgia 30033-4097 or call 404-679-4500 for questions about the accreditation of Clemson University.

Location

Approximately midway between Charlotte, North Carolina, and Atlanta, Georgia, Clemson University is located on 1,400 acres in the foothills of the Blue Ridge Mountains and along the shores of Lake Hartwell. Great weather and proximity to natural wonders and large cities offer year-round recreational opportunities.

The University's enrollment of more than 19,000 undergraduate and graduate students makes it a defining presence in Clemson, South Carolina, a town of about 12,000. Students may live on campus in one of the twenty-one residence halls and four apartment complexes, most of which are within a 10-minute walk to class or downtown.

Majors and Degrees

Clemson offers approximately eighty undergraduate and 110 graduate degree programs through five academic colleges: Agriculture, Forestry, and Life Sciences; Architecture, Arts, and Humanities; Business and Behavioral Science; Engineering and Science; and Health, Education, and Human Development. Undergraduate students can earn B.A., B.S., or preprofessional degrees in accounting; agricultural education; agricultural mechanization and business; animal and veterinary sciences; architecture; biochemistry; biological sciences; biosystems engineering; ceramic and materials engineering; chemical engineering; chemistry; civil engineering; communication studies; computer engineering; computer information systems; computer science; construction science and management; early childhood education; economics; electrical engineering; elementary education; English; environmental and natural resources; financial management; food science; forest resource management; genetics; geology; graphic communications; health science; history; horticulture; industrial engineering; landscape architecture; language and international health; language and international trade; management; marketing; mathematical sciences; mathematics teaching; mechanical engineering; microbiology; modern languages; nursing; packaging science; parks, recreation, and tourism management; philosophy; physics; political science; polymer and fiber chemistry; preprofessional health studies; prepharmacy; pre–rehabilitation sciences; pre–veterinary medicine; production studies in performing arts; psychology; science teaching; secondary education; sociology; soils and sustainable crop systems; special education; turfgrass; visual arts; and wildlife and fisheries biology.

Academic Programs

Clemson's academic year is divided into two semesters. The fall semester begins in mid-August and the spring semester starts in early January. Three summer sessions and four mini-semesters are also available. Students average 16 credit hours per semester, and Clemson requires all students to complete some general education classes specified by the University before graduation. The number of completed credit hours required for graduation varies, depending on the major.

Calhoun Honors College is a University-wide program that combines the strengths of a public, land-grant university with those of a highly selective small college. Calhoun Scholars may choose to pursue departmental honors within their specific academic discipline. In addition, EUREKA! (Experiences in Undergraduate Research, Exploration, and Knowledge Advancement) is a unique and exciting program that enables honors students to pursue research and scholarly activities with faculty members across all disciplines. The advantages of membership in the Honors College include priority registration, extended library loan privileges, honors research grants, and honors housing.

The National Scholars Program is a highly selective program for exceptional students who strive to meet their highest intellectual potential. One of its goals is to develop the interests and talents students need to compete for Rhodes, Marshall, and Truman scholarships; Fulbright Grants; National Science Foundation Graduate Fellowships; and other prestigious international fellowships.

Clemson's nationally recognized Programs for Educational Enrichment and Retention (PEER) is committed to improving the academic performance of underrepresented students in engineering and science. Today, thanks in large part to PEER, the six-year graduation rate for African American first-time freshmen is above the national average.

The Women in Science and Engineering (WISE) program focuses on recruiting women into science and engineering majors and helping them succeed in college and their careers. WISE offers support activities such as mentoring programs, career planning, and study groups.

Tutoring, supplemental instruction, academic skills workshops, and academic counseling are also available free to all Clemson students through the Academic Support Center.

Off-Campus Programs

Clemson's study-abroad and off-campus programs give students the opportunity to study almost anywhere in the world. The International Student Exchange Program and the Clemson Exchange Program allow students to enroll for a summer, semester or full academic year at one of more than 100 universities throughout the world. About 28 percent of the student body enriched their education through study abroad last year. Students in a variety of majors have opportunities at the Archbold Center in Dominica; the Daniel Center in Genoa, Italy; the Clemson University Brussels Center in Belgium; and other locations.

The Cooperative Education program provides an opportunity for students to alternate periods of academic study with semesters of paid, career-related, engaged-learning experiences to bridge the gap between academic study and its application in professional practice.

Academic Facilities

The Clemson campus is home to a blend of historic buildings and advanced research facilities surrounded by stately trees and lush greenery.

The libraries and the computing and information technology department are committed to providing students and faculty members with the latest ways to access information. Clemson's main library, the Robert M. Cooper Library, is located at the center of campus and provides a variety of services and up-to-date collections. The University's wireless networking capability lets students communicate with professors and classmates, read online course materials, check e-mail, and conduct research—all from their own laptops. Students are required to complete an electronic portfolio prior to graduation, allowing them the opportunity to present themselves through a creative venue to prospective employers and graduate schools.

The campus offers an array of facilities and programs designed to enhance a student's entire educational experience. These include the Pearce Center for Professional Communication, Class of 1941 Studio for Student Communication, Rutland Center for Ethics, and the Academic Support Center.

Clemson real estate holdings also include more than 32,000 acres of forestry and agricultural lands throughout the state, the majority of which are dedicated to the University's research and service missions.

Costs

For the 2010–11 academic year, undergraduate tuition and fees were $12,346 for South Carolina residents and $27,858 for out-of-state residents. Room and board costs were approximately $7034, and books and supplies were $940. The one-time laptop computer cost was about $1300.

Financial Aid

Financial aid is usually awarded on the basis of need to supplement the amount students and their parents can contribute to college expenses. The University also awards some scholarships based entirely on academic merit. Clemson offers financial aid in the form of grants, scholarships, loans, and part-time employment.

Entering freshmen are evaluated on a competitive basis for scholarships using the admission application. There is no separate scholarship application. For academic recruiting scholarships, selection is based on test scores, high school rank-in-class, and other academic factors. In past years, students offered one of these merit scholarships normally had a minimum SAT score of 1401 (combined score from critical reading and mathematics sections), or an ACT of at least 32, and were ranked no lower than the top 10 percent of their senior class. Stipends for in-state residents range from $500 per year to the full cost of attendance. Merit scholarships for out-of-state students range from $2500 per year to the full cost of attendance. Academic recruiting scholarships are available only to entering freshmen and are renewable for three additional years provided that the minimum standards are maintained. The application for admission is the first step for prospective freshmen to be considered for merit awards.

General scholarships are awarded to both entering freshmen and upperclassmen. To be considered for scholarships, upperclassmen must have a minimum cumulative GPR of at least 2.5. These scholarships may have special criteria set up by the donor, such as a certain residency, major, or career interest. Because of the restrictions on many of these scholarships, it is impossible to predict the recipients. However, the scholarship selection process is very competitive. Stipends range from $250 to $7500.

Faculty

Clemson has more than 1,300 full-time faculty members, of whom 82 percent hold a Ph.D. or terminal degree in their fields. In addition, the University has more than 240 part-time faculty members. Faculty honors include the Fulbright Scholarship, Guggenheim Fellowship, National Science Foundation CAREER Award, National Institutes of Health Senior Scientist Award, and American Academy of Arts and Sciences membership. The average class size is 31, and the student-to-faculty ratio is 16:1.

Admission Requirements

Each year, the University receives about 17,000 applications for a fall freshman class of 3,000. Transfer applications are received from about 2,200 students, of whom Clemson enrolls 900. Undergraduate applications are available online at http://www.clemson.edu/admissions.

For freshman applicants, the following factors are considered: class standing, standardized test scores (SAT or ACT), high school curriculum, grades, and choice of major. All entering freshmen must have completed 4 credits of English, 3 credits of mathematics, 3 credits of laboratory science, 3 credits of a foreign language (in the same language), 3 credits of social sciences, 2 credits in other areas, and 1 credit of physical education.

To be considered for transfer admission, candidates must have completed a full year of college study (a minimum of 30 semester hours or 45 quarter hours of transferable work), earned a cumulative grade point average of at least 2.5 on a 4.0 scale (3.0 preferred), and completed freshman-level courses in English, science, and mathematics for their intended major at Clemson.

Application and Information

Application deadlines for freshman admissions are December 1 (priority date for fall semester), May 1 (fall semester), and December 15 (spring semester). For transfer admissions, the application deadlines are July 1 (fall semester) and December 15 (spring semester).

Office of Admissions
Clemson University
105 Sikes Hall, Box 345124
Clemson, South Carolina 29634-5124

Phone: 864-656-2287
Fax: 864-656-2464
E-mail: cuadmissions@clemson.edu
Web site: http://www.clemson.edu/admisions
       http://twitter.com/BeAClemsonTiger (Twitter)

Clemson's campus includes 1,400 acres, yet the residence halls and classroom buildings are an easy 10-minute walk from each other.

CLEVELAND INSTITUTE OF MUSIC

CLEVELAND, OHIO

The Institute

The mission of the Cleveland Institute of Music (CIM) is to provide exceptionally talented students from around the world an outstanding, thoroughly professional education in the art of music performance and related musical disciplines. The Institute embraces the legacy of the past and promotes the continuing evolution of music within a supportive and nurturing environment. The Institute also provides rigorous training in programs for gifted precollege musicians and serves as a resource for the community, with training for individuals of all ages and abilities.

A guiding principle at the Institute maintains that a liberal arts education contributes to a broad, humanistic perspective and is a vital component of the undergraduate curriculum. Equally important is the faculty's commitment to incorporating new technologies to complement and enhance the educational program.

The distinguished faculty of the Institute aims to develop the full artistic potential of all of its students. Through performance and teaching, the faculty and administration are dedicated to passing along their knowledge and love for this great art and to providing the bridge to an exciting and fulfilling career.

Founded in 1920, the Cleveland Institute of Music maintains its current size of approximately 450 undergraduate and graduate students and 90 full- and part-time faculty members by controlling the enrollment through carefully balanced admission policies, thus ensuring personal, individual attention for each student. In admitting the optimum number of students to each performance area rather than an unlimited number, CIM maximizes the performance experiences of its students so that they are well prepared to meet the challenges of professional life. The achievements of the Cleveland Institute of Music's alumni throughout the world are indicative of the Institute's commitment to high quality and professionalism. The distinguished-artist faculty includes the principals and other section players of The Cleveland Orchestra, a neighboring institution with which the Institute has a close relationship. All collegiate-level instruction is conducted by members of the CIM faculty and not by teaching assistants.

About 25 percent of CIM's students are in residence at Cutter House, the Institute's residence hall, which is adjacent to the school's main building. In addition to having the usual amenities, each room is connected to the computer network operated by Case Western Reserve University (CWRU), whose campus borders that of CIM. Since all residents are CIM students, practice is permitted in the rooms of Cutter House. Residence hall accommodations are required for freshmen and sophomores.

In addition to the programs of study listed under the Majors and Degrees section, the Cleveland Institute of Music offers programs leading to the following graduate degrees and diplomas: Master of Music, Doctor of Musical Arts, Artist Diploma, and Professional Studies.

Location

CIM is located in University Circle, a cultural, educational, and scientific center situated approximately 4 miles east of downtown Cleveland. University Circle comprises more than thirty institutions that together constitute one of the largest diversified cultural complexes in the world. The complex includes museums, libraries, concert halls, colleges and universities, hospitals, gardens, churches, and temples. Occupying 500 acres in one of the most beautiful areas in the city, the facilities of University Circle offer extensive opportunities for serious study in many fields.

Located within easy walking distance of CIM are Case Western Reserve University, with which CIM cooperates in the Joint Music Program, and Severance Hall, the spectacularly restored home of The Cleveland Orchestra, whose rehearsals are open to CIM students by special arrangement. Students may also visit the Cleveland Museum of Art and enjoy its world-famous collections as well as its annual concert series, featuring world-renowned performers. Easily accessible to Institute students are numerous other University Circle institutions, such as the Cleveland Institute of Art, the Cleveland Play

House, the Cleveland Museum of Natural History, the Western Reserve Historical Society, the Crawford Auto-Aviation Museum, and the Cleveland Botanical Garden.

Majors and Degrees

Students may major in audio recording, bassoon, bass trombone, cello, clarinet, collaborative piano, composition, double bass, eurhythmics, flute, guitar, harp, harpsichord, horn, oboe, orchestral conducting, organ, piano, Suzuki cello pedagogy, Suzuki violin pedagogy, timpani and percussion, trombone, trumpet, tuba, viola, violin, and voice.

Through the Joint Music Program with Case Western Reserve University, five-year double-degree programs are available to CIM students. Of the two degrees earned by students in these programs, the Bachelor of Music is one component. Both B.M./B.A. and B.M./B.S. programs may be structured within music or with the CWRU component in a nonmusic field.

Academic Programs

CIM programs offer intensive and comprehensive preparation for professional careers in music. All courses at the school revolve around a core of studies in theory, music history, and literature; the core is designed to provide a thorough musical education. At the undergraduate level, additional educational breadth is provided by required liberal arts courses.

An unusually intense performance environment involves students in a wide repertoire, including solo, chamber, orchestral, and operatic literature.

The development of the disciplines and skills required of a solo performer is an integral part of a student's training at CIM. This training, involving access to faculty members and visiting artists who are practicing professionals, is augmented by the many master classes, repertoire classes, and recitals offered annually. A concerto competition is held each semester, and approximately 6 to 8 students are selected for either public performances or readings with orchestra.

The orchestral training programs are designed to develop and maintain the disciplines and skills essential in making the smoothest possible transition from school to professional life. Sectional rehearsals and orchestral repertoire classes are conducted by principals of The Cleveland Orchestra. CIM's two symphony orchestras present approximately twenty concerts during the academic year, including multiple performances of two fully staged operas. The orchestras also provide a vehicle by which students in the Composition Department may hear and record readings of their works.

The sequence of opera courses is devoted to the principles of theory and practice of the various arts that combine to create an operatic performance. Emphasis is placed on vocal, musical, stylistic, linguistic, and dramatic techniques. Study stresses the application of these elements to role preparation for operas of different historical periods.

Started in 1969, the Joint Music Program between CWRU and CIM represents one of the strongest and most successful academic alliances in the U.S. It is a formal agreement for degree study at both the undergraduate and graduate levels. Each institution focuses on its strengths, which complement those of the partner institution. CIM concentrates on the education and training of professionals skilled in the art of performance, composition, and other related disciplines. CWRU concentrates on the fields of music history, musicology, music education, and early music performance.

Campuses for each institution are adjacent, allowing for easy access to classes and lessons and providing opportunities for regular exchanges of ideas for joint projects.

At its simplest level, the Joint Music Program provides CWRU music majors with instrumental, vocal, and composition lessons, as well as theory classes at CIM. It provides CIM students with music history and general education classes at CWRU. The program also provides a shared Audio Recording Degree Program; a partnership between CIM's library and CWRU's Kulas Music Library, with each collection complementing the other; academic advisement for D.M.A. candidates; and distance learning partnerships, with CIM adding an arts focus to CWRU's advanced Internet2 network.

CIM operates on a two-semester calendar, with fall examinations preceding the Christmas holiday recess.

Academic Facilities

CIM recently completed a $40-million expansion project that adds practice, teaching, and performance space to its facility. The project provides two major additions, including a new state-of-the-art recital hall and new façade at its main entrance. The recital hall seats 250 in a visually and acoustically outstanding space for recitals and chamber music. Another addition at the rear of the main building includes practice rooms, teaching studios, audio recording and distance learning studios, administrative space, a new student lounge, and an outdoor patio.

Cleveland Institute of Music's main building includes a concert hall, classrooms, teaching studios, practice rooms, a library, a eurhythmics studio, an orchestra library, an opera theater workshop and studio, and a music store. Through connection of the entire facility to Case Western Reserve University's computer network, CIM also provides wireless Internet access as well as a Technology Learning Center that enables students to become aware of and accustomed to the ways in which music and technology go hand in hand.

CIM's Robinson Music Library holds excellent print collections in all areas of study at the Institute, with emphasis on performance editions of solo, chamber, and orchestral music and books focusing on Western classical music. It also has a growing collection of electronic resources, including streamed audio subscriptions. The Library Media Center provides distributed sound access to the extensive audiovisual collection, enabling simultaneous listening possibilities in its multimedia carrels and group multimedia rooms. A shared online system with Case Western Reserve University permits the viewing of CWRU library holdings from online public catalogs in the CIM library. There is also wireless computer access in the library.

The residence hall, Cutter House, is adjacent to CIM's main building. In addition to the usual amenities, each room has fiber-optic computer access. Also adjacent to CIM's main building is the Hazel Road Annex, an additional facility for individual practice, chamber music, rehearsal and coaching, master classes, and class recitals.

Costs

A comprehensive catalog, including information on costs as well as other areas of vital interest, is available on CIM's admission Web page (http://www.cim.edu/admission).

Financial Aid

The Cleveland Institute of Music offers outstanding professional training for talented musicians. While such training can be costly, CIM provides many forms of financial assistance, including scholarships, fellowships, work-study awards, and loans. Awards are available to full-time students and are based upon both musical capability and financial need. Entrance auditions as well as financial need serve as the basis for determining the eligibility of new students. More than 95 percent of CIM students receive some form of financial assistance. Further information is available by contacting the Institute's Director of Financial Aid.

Faculty

The distinguished faculty of performers, composers, and teachers, led by CIM's President, Joel Smirnoff, includes more than 40 members of the renowned Cleveland Orchestra and many other outstanding musicians. All liberal arts course offerings are taught by members of the faculty of Case Western Reserve University.

Student Government

The Student Government is the representative organization of the student body. Members are elected annually by the students. The organization carries on an active dialogue with the administration and addresses the daily and long-term needs of currently enrolled students.

Admission Requirements

Acceptance for study at the Cleveland Institute of Music is determined by musical talent, achievement, and academic performance. The Institute expects applicants to have achieved a sufficient musical and academic background demonstrating their potential for successful completion of the intended course of study. Audition appointments are scheduled through the Admission Office upon receipt of application. Candidates are required to submit two letters of recommendation from appropriate musically qualified individuals as well as all appropriate academic transcripts. Freshman applicants who are U.S. citizens or permanent residents must also submit scores on either the SAT or ACT. International applicants for whom English is a second language must submit scores on the Test of English as a Foreign Language (TOEFL); the minimum TOEFL score requirement for degree study is 79 (iBT).

CIM does not discriminate on the basis of race, color, national or ethnic origin, citizenship, religion, age, sex, sexual orientation, or disability in its admission and scholarship policies, in the educational programs or activities it operates, or in employment.

Application and Information

The application deadline is December 1. An appointment for an entrance audition and the required admission examinations is scheduled by the Admission Office upon receipt of application. The application process must be completed online. There is a $100 application fee.

Director of Admission
Cleveland Institute of Music
11021 East Boulevard
Cleveland, Ohio 44106
Phone: 216-795-3107
Web site: http://www.cim.edu
http://www.facebook.com/ClevelandInstituteofMusic
http://twitter.com/cim_edu

CIM production of Mozart's *The Magic Flute.*

COLBY–SAWYER COLLEGE
NEW LONDON, NEW HAMPSHIRE

The College

Colby-Sawyer College, a coeducational, residential, undergraduate college founded in 1837, evolved from the New England academy tradition and has been engaged in higher education since 1928. The College provides programs of study that innovatively integrate the liberal arts and sciences with professional preparation. Through all of its programs, the College encourages students of varied backgrounds and abilities to realize their full intellectual and personal potential so they may gain understanding about themselves, others, and the major forces shaping our rapidly changing world. At present, students come from all over the United States and eight other countries, with nearly 70 percent of the students coming from outside of New Hampshire. Within the last ten years, two suite-style residence halls have been built to accommodate the College's steady growth in enrollment.

Student athletic involvement occurs at the varsity, club, intramural, and recreational levels. There are eleven varsity sports for women (NCAA Division III basketball, cross-country, field hockey, lacrosse, soccer, swimming and diving, tennis, track and field, and volleyball; ECSC Alpine ski racing; and IHSA riding) and nine for men (NCAA Division III baseball, basketball, cross-country, soccer, swimming and diving, tennis, and track and field; ECSC Alpine ski racing; and IHSA riding). Athletic successes include a men's basketball team that competed in the NCAA tournaments from 2001 to 2003; a track and field team that produced 2 All-Americans in 2004 and 2005 and sent individual qualifiers to the NCAA Championships in 2000, 2002, 2004, 2005, and 2006; and conference championships for men's baseball in 1998 and 1999, men's basketball in 2001–03, women's volleyball in 1999, 2003, and 2005, and women's basketball in 1997–99, 2005–06, and 2008. The women's basketball team also competed in the 2001–04 ECAC tournaments as well as the NCAA tournaments in 1997–99, 2005, and 2008. The women's volleyball team also made appearances at the NCAA tournaments in 1999, 2003, and 2005. Colby-Sawyer's equestrian team was the national champion in 1989 and 1994 as well as the reserve national champion in 1998 and has sent riders to the IHSA national team every year since 1987. For the past ten seasons, the Alpine ski racing team has competed in the USCSA National Championships, where, in 2009, the men's team won the national championship and the women's team finished third. In 2005, they placed both teams within the top three. The women's team finished second in 2008. The Alpine ski racing team has produced 100 All-American citations since 1988. The Colby-Sawyer Chargers compete as a member of the Commonwealth Coast Conference.

The College is accredited by the New England Association of Schools and Colleges, and professional programs also carry the appropriate accreditations. Colby-Sawyer has consistently received recognition as one of the top colleges in its category.

Location

Colby-Sawyer's 200-acre campus is located on the crest of a hill in New London, New Hampshire. Its beautifully maintained grounds and stately Georgian architecture create a picturesque and safe environment that is conducive to learning. The College is located in the heart of the Dartmouth–Lake Sunapee region, a four-season recreational and cultural community known for the natural beauty of its lakes and mountains. Boston is only 1½ hours south and Montreal is 3½ hours north. Students have access to major cities by College van or public bus. The nearby seacoast at Portsmouth, and surrounding lakes, mountains, and state parks provide opportunities for biking, camping, canoeing, golf, hiking, ice skating, Nordic and Alpine skiing, swimming, and tennis. Arts and cultural opportunities can be found in New London as well as in nearby Concord, the state capital, and Hanover, the home of Dartmouth College.

Majors and Degrees

Colby-Sawyer offers bachelor's degrees in many fields. Majors include art history; art-graphic design; art-studio art; biology; business administration; child development; communication studies; creative writing; English; environmental sciences; environmental studies; athletic training; exercise science; sport management; history, society, and culture; nursing; philosophy; psychology; and sociology. Other programs include a coaching certificate program, and prelaw, premedicine, pre–physical therapy, and preveterinary tracks.

Academic Programs

Colby-Sawyer College faculty and staff are excellent at working with students who are undecided on a major and they are highly qualified to help students explore their values, talents, and academic and career interests. At Colby-Sawyer College, it is believed that knowledge and experience nurture each other. Therefore, the combination of classroom learning and professional experience is an integral part of each student's education.

All students begin their liberal education at Colby-Sawyer by selecting a Pathway Seminar. Students choose a topic they are interested in learning more about, pose questions that are personally relevant, and search for answers through experiences in several liberal arts areas. They return to these themes in a seminar in their sophomore year, applying all they have learned to answer their own questions and share insights with classmates on such topics as "Sound: From Physics to Fantasia" and "Rituals, Excellence, and Challenge: The Ancient and Modern Games."

Colby-Sawyer's Wesson Honors Program offers an environment conducive to intellectual exploration and creativity beyond that which is available in the general curriculum. This program is carefully designed to advance and polish critical skills of each participating student.

Through a carefully crafted program offered by the Harrington Center for Career Development, all students are encouraged throughout their four years of study to continue to clarify their interests and goals and to gain practical experiences through student employment, internships, and voluntary service to the community.

Internships are a key element in career development and are required for almost all majors. Colby-Sawyer has an impressive roster of internship opportunities available, and through the internship experience, students often receive their first offer of a permanent position. During the internship, students have an opportunity to work directly with professionals in their field of study while developing valuable contacts who can serve as references and career mentors. Organizations that have recently accepted Colby-Sawyer interns include Merrill Lynch, the Minnesota Twins, Continental Cable, Beth Israel Hospital, Blue Cross/Blue Shield, Harvard University Athletic Department, the Buffalo Bisons, the New England Patriots, Nantucket Nectars, the Currier Gallery of Art, the Basketball Hall of Fame, the Olympic Regional Development Authority, Channel 7 (Boston), the Appalachian Mountain Club, and CNN.

Off-Campus Programs

Colby-Sawyer encourages students to study abroad for a semester or a year. The study-abroad adviser works closely with students to select an experience and a school best suited to their individual needs and interests. Students have studied in England, Poland, Australia, Spain, New Zealand, France, Italy, Ireland, Scotland, Switzerland, and many other countries.

Additionally, Colby-Sawyer offers an innovative program for students interested in studying abroad called Global Explorations. Global Explorations is a study-abroad program designed for students seeking international travel and cultural exploration. This adventurous program combines the traditional Colby-Sawyer educational experience, as accompanying Colby-Sawyer professors teach classes, with the benefits of cultural immersion. Past locations for Global Beginnings have included Paris/Strasbourg, France and Florence, Italy.

Colby-Sawyer's membership in the fourteen-college New Hampshire College and University Council (NHCUC) allows students to enroll in other NHCUC institutions for a course or for an entire semester.

Academic Facilities

The Susan Colgate Cleveland Library/Learning Center is housed in a unique five-level structure constructed from two pre–Civil War dairy barns masterfully transformed into a warm and inviting facility that has won regional and national architectural awards. Housed in the Library/Learning Center, the Academic Development Center provides academic support services for all students. The staff consists of faculty members, learning specialists, and student academic counselors who work with students to strengthen their writing, math, and research skills, as well as their study skills, such as time management, note-taking, and exam preparation. Colby-Sawyer's English Language and American Culture Program provides support for international students and others whose first language is not English. Among the services available to students with diagnosed learning differences are classroom modifications, personal counseling, and professional as well as peer tutoring. The Library/Learning Center also houses a curriculum lab, an audiovisual room, thirty PC workstations for Internet and library database access, a twelve-station wireless lab, and a networked computer classroom with twenty-five PCs and interactive multimedia teaching equipment. Interlibrary loan service provides access to an extensive array of library holdings throughout New England and the nation.

The magnificent 63,000-square-foot Dan and Kathleen Hogan Sports Center was designed to meet the athletic and recreational needs of Colby-Sawyer College students and members of the local community. This sports center contains a large field house with newly installed maple-wood floors; a suspended walking/jogging track; a six-lane, competition-size swimming pool; and a fitness center furnished with equipment such as StairMasters, Body Master stations, treadmills, rowing ergometers, Nordic cross-country skiing tracks, a Universal gym, stationary bicycles, and a complete selection of free weights. The Hogan Center also houses the Sports Medicine Clinic, which is fully equipped with the latest technology to support the Exercise and Sport Sciences Program.

Opened in 2004, the Curtis L. Ivey Science Center is one of Colby-Sawyer's finest academic facilities and houses the Natural Science and Environmental Studies Programs. Set against nearby Mt. Kearsarge, this beautiful two-story, 33,000-square-foot building consists of a variety of classrooms, laboratories, and offices as well as a 180-seat lecture hall. One of these laboratories focuses on spatial ecology and performs grant-funded research utilizing Geographic Information Systems (GIS) and Global Positioning Systems (GPS) technology.

The nursing program features a Nursing and Health Laboratory containing resources that simulate clinical practice settings. Students also have access to a computer laboratory with software that helps to prepare them for clinical experiences. The nursing program is enriched by its relationship with Dartmouth Hitchcock Medical Center, one of the most well-equipped and technologically advanced teaching hospitals in North America.

The Colby-Sawyer campus computing array includes a campus network with wireless Internet access, five computer laboratory/classrooms, and six mobile multimedia teaching stations, which provide computer graphics, audio, and video capabilities employing the latest digital technology. Computing facilities are equipped with the latest Microsoft Windows applications and laser printers for student use. The College now has a 5:1 student-computer ratio.

The Frances Lockwood Bailey Graphic Design Studios are the center of the graphic design facilities. These studios are equipped with computers loaded with the latest versions of graphic design software programs and desktop publishing capability. Students create graphic images while working with digital scanning and optical character recognition, still-video photography, and VCR, video camera, and other state-of-the-practice images. Advanced student projects are sent to professional imaging centers to create high-resolution hard copy.

Costs

Tuition, room, and board for 2010–11 were $45,810. Approximately $1750 should be allowed for books, supplies, personal expenses, and travel, depending on where students live.

Financial Aid

Through its Financial Aid Program, Colby-Sawyer encourages the attendance of students from a variety of ethnic and cultural backgrounds, economic levels, and geographic regions. Currently, 91 percent of the students receive some form of financial assistance, and Colby-Sawyer provides more than $9 million a year in financial aid and scholarships. Both need-based and merit awards are available, including merit awards for outstanding academic achievement, community service, student leadership, and special talent in art, creative writing, or original research. Each applicant for need-based aid must submit the Free Application for Federal Student Aid (FAFSA). Priority is given to students whose completed forms are received before March 1. Financial assistance is available for international students.

Faculty

Colby-Sawyer has a distinguished faculty and staff dedicated to undergraduate teaching, and a personalized education is ensured by a 12:1 student-faculty ratio and average class size of 16. At Colby-Sawyer, senior faculty members teach first-year students as well as students in the upper classes.

Student Government

The Student Government Association (SGA) is structured to provide considerable interaction among students, faculty members, and staff, and the SGA allocates the resources that fund a multitude of involvement and leadership opportunities outside the classroom. Campus activities include the Campus Activities Board, Dance Club, Alpha Chi Honor Society, yearbook, radio station (WSCS 90.9 FM), Drama Club, Admissions Key Association, Art Students Society, Student Nurses Association, *The Courier* (student newspaper), community service, and numerous clubs and intramural teams.

Admission Requirements

The College requires prospective students to present at least 15 units of college-preparatory work. This would usually include 4 years of English, 3 years of mathematics, 3 or more years of social studies, 2 years of a foreign language, and 2 or more years of a laboratory science.

While an admissions interview is not required, every applicant is strongly encouraged to visit Colby-Sawyer for a tour and interview. Interviews often play an important part in the final admissions decision.

Application and Information

Colby-Sawyer College receives and considers applications throughout the year. Beginning in September, applications are reviewed as soon as they become complete, and candidates are notified as soon as the admissions decision is finalized. A completed application includes a transcript of the candidate's high school work (including first-quarter grades for the senior year), one letter of recommendation (from a teacher or a guidance professional), and a personal statement. SAT or ACT scores may be submitted, but are not required. Colby-Sawyer College uses the Common Application found at https://www.commonapp.org.

Office of Admissions
Colby-Sawyer College
541 Main Street
New London, New Hampshire 03257
Phone: 603-526-3700
        800-272-1015 (toll-free)
Fax: 603-526-3452
E-mail: admissions@colby-sawyer.edu
Internet: http://www.colby-sawyer.edu

THE COLLEGE OF MOUNT ST. JOSEPH

CINCINNATI, OHIO

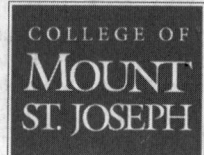

The College

The College of Mount St. Joseph offers a variety of academic programs, a faculty known for high standards of excellence and innovation, and student activities that include twenty-two NCAA Division III sports teams. Small class sizes and individual attention, as well as opportunities for leadership and service learning, contribute to a positive college experience and student success. Founded in 1920 by the Sisters of Charity, the Mount is a private, Catholic college that emphasizes values, integrity, and social responsibility.

Specialized services are also part of a Mount education and include renewable scholarships, financial aid, cooperative education, multicultural programs, the Wellness Center, child-care services for students with children, and on-campus housing. The newly expanded Academic Advising Resource Center offers ongoing advising support to students, and the Success Coaching Program provides first-year students with guidance from an assigned professional staff member trained to help them address first-year challenges and achieve their goals.

A wireless network enables students to e-mail faculty members, check grades, complete research, and register for classes anytime, from anywhere. Spacious rooms are available in the newly renovated Seton Center Residence Hall, with some offering private bedrooms, a bath, and a shared living area for studying and socializing. Resident students may keep cars on campus. The close-knit campus community is part of a living and learning environment that encourages and nurtures the personal and academic growth of each student.

The undergraduate student body consists of students from seventeen states and four countries. Fifty-four percent of undergraduate students are women, and 10 percent are members of minority groups. The average freshman has an ACT score of 21.5 and/or a combined SAT score of 971 and a high school GPA of 3.24. Sixty-eight percent of freshman students attended a public high school. Sixty-seven percent of freshman applicants are accepted.

There are more than thirty clubs and organizations at the College. These include student government, the student newspaper, academic honor societies, environmental clubs, social clubs, symphonic and community concert bands, jazz and percussion ensembles, chorale groups, theater/drama clubs, political clubs, and intramural athletics. Events and activities include Homecoming, spring break service trips, Exam Jam, and Little Sibs Weekend.

The Mount offers a full intercollegiate athletic program for men and women. Women's programs include basketball, cheerleading, cross-country, dance, golf, lacrosse, soccer, softball, tennis, track and field, and volleyball. Programs for men include baseball, basketball, cross-country, football, golf, lacrosse, soccer, tennis, track and field, volleyball, and wrestling. The Mount Lions compete in the NCAA Division III as a member of the Heartland Collegiate Athletic Conference. See http://www.msjsports.com.

The Mount is fully accredited by the Higher Learning Commission of the North Central Association of Colleges and Schools. The College is consistently ranked among the top Midwest regional universities for quality and value by *U.S. News & World Report* in its guide to America's Best Colleges.

The Mount maintains a presence on Facebook (http://www.facebook.com/MountStJoseph) and Twitter (http://twitter.com/mount_news). For more information about the College, visit http://www.msj.edu/about.

Location

Located 15 minutes from downtown Cincinnati, the College is situated on a 92-acre suburban campus overlooking the Ohio River and is easily accessible from the airport, bus terminal, railway station, and interstate. Well known for its scenic and rolling hills, greater Cincinnati offers numerous parks, cultural and arts events, museums, theaters, professional athletics, shopping areas, and a wide assortment of fine restaurants. Mount students often join other students attending colleges and universities in and around Cincinnati to participate in social and service activities. See http://www.msj.edu/visit.

Majors and Degrees

The Mount awards bachelor's degrees in the following areas: accounting, art, art education, art history, athletic training, biochemistry, biology, business administration, business administration/mathematics, chemistry, chemistry/mathematics, communication studies, computer information systems, criminology/sociology, English, fine arts, general studies, graphic design, history, inclusive early childhood education, interactive media design and computing, interdisciplinary liberal studies, interior architecture and design, mathematics, mathematics/business administration, mathematics/chemistry, middle childhood education, music, natural science, nursing, paralegal studies, psychology, religious education, religious pastoral ministry, religious studies, social work, sociology, special education, and sport management.

Preprofessional studies are offered in a number of areas, including prehealth, premedicine, pre–art therapy, and prelaw.

Associate degrees are offered in accounting, art, business administration, communication studies, computer information systems, general studies, graphic design, interior design, and paralegal studies.

Certificate programs in gerontology, iDesign (Web and interactive design), nonprofit leadership, and paralegal studies are available, as are teacher licensure programs.

For the state of Ohio licensure in education, the Mount offers programs in adolescent and young adults, inclusive early childhood, middle childhood, multiage, and intervention specialist/special education. Licensure programs for other states are also available.

For more information, visit http://www.msj.edu/academics.

Academic Programs

To help students explore options in choosing a major, the Academic Exploration Program provides advising, career counseling, and the opportunity to attend linked courses with classmates who are also undecided.

In recognition of its commitment to provide cooperative education experiences in all baccalaureate majors, the Mount's program has received top honors from the Ohio Cooperative Education Association. Students may participate as early as the second semester of their sophomore year and gain paid work experience in their field of study. More than 100 local corporations, businesses, health-care facilities, schools, and nonprofits hire co-ops from the Mount. Other opportunities for practical experience and career development are available through the Career and Experiential Learning Center, on-campus recruiting programs, networking opportunities, and resume services.

In compliance with Section 504 of the Rehabilitation Act of 1973, the Mount provides academic adjustments and auxiliary aids for students with physical or mental impairments that substantially limit or restrict one or more of such major life activities as walking, seeing, hearing, or learning.

The College provides these reasonable academic adjustments and auxiliary aids to eligible students at no charge, according to students' individual needs. Advocacy assistance on disability-related issues is also provided. Eligibility depends on the nature of the impairment and its impact on the particular individual, and is based on documentation from a qualified professional.

Students whose primary disability is a specific learning disability and/or ADHD may apply to Project EXCEL, which addresses the needs of this specific group of students through a comprehensive academic support system. Project EXCEL is a fee-for-service program. Students must be admitted to the College of Mount St. Joseph before applying for Project EXCEL.

All majors are backed by a strong liberal arts curriculum that encourages students to develop skills in analytical thinking, problem solving, decision making, and communication. Students must earn 128 credit hours for a bachelor's degree, with 52 of those credits from the liberal arts and sciences core. For an associate degree, students must earn 64 credit hours, with 27 to 28 of those credits from the liberal arts and sciences core.

The academic year has fall and spring semesters and two summer terms. Classes are held during the day, evening, or weekends. See http://www.msj.edu/academics and http://www.msj.edu/services.

Off-Campus Programs

Study abroad programs are available in London, England. Travel study programs to Africa, Eastern Europe, Egypt, England, Greece, Ireland, Italy, and Japan are also offered. Immersion courses introduce students to the cultures and histories of Pine Ridge Indian Reservation, South Dakota; Tierra Madre Mission, New Mexico; and Appalachia. For more information, visit http://www.msj.edu/travel-study.

Academic Facilities

The Mount's campus features a wireless environment as well as up-to-date facilities, including electronic classrooms. Access is provided to IBM and Macintosh systems that support more than 500 different software packages. Students in health sciences learn in laboratories on the campus, including the new two-level Nursing Learning Lab, and benefit from the College's partnerships with nearby hospitals and clinics.

The Mount's Learning Center, which includes a math center and a writing center, offers peer and professional tutoring as well as diagnostic testing.

The Archbishop Alter Library is home to more than 96,000 volumes of books, journals, videotapes, DVDs, and CDs. Patrons have access to more than 140 databases, thousands of electronic books, and hundreds of Web sites specifically chosen for students, faculty, and staff. Through its wide variety of services, the library plays an active role in the College's educational process. Some of these services include interlibrary loan, in-person and online research help, traditional and electronic course reserves, instructional sessions designed for specific courses, a group study room, and full Internet access. See http://www.msj.edu/services and http:www.msj.edu/learningcenter.

Costs

For the 2010–11 academic year, full-time tuition was $22,750. Part-time tuition (less than 12 hours) was $475 per hour. Room costs ranged from $3646 to $6180 a year, and costs for board ranged from $3546 to $3746 a year. The College offers private and semiprivate housing accommodations and a variety of meal plans. A general fee of $800 a year covers student activities, technology, counseling, student and academic support services, and logistical services. The cost of books varies, depending on course load and major. For more information, see http://www.msj.edu/financial-aid.

Financial Aid

The Mount offers academic scholarship programs in the areas of scholastic achievement and leadership, based on merit or on a combination of merit and need. Many scholarships are renewable each year. Ninety-nine percent of traditional freshman receive some form of gift aid, and the average gift aid package is $16,851. The most common are federal, state, or College grants; work-study awards; and loans. Part-time employment may be available on the campus or in the metropolitan area. Interested students should inquire early in their senior year of high school.

Students needing financial support must submit the Free Application for Federal Student Aid (FAFSA) no later than April 15 prior to the fall semester. Most College-sponsored scholarships are awarded on a rolling basis. See http://www.msj.edu/financial-aid.

Faculty

There are 120 full-time professors at the College. Faculty members have been recognized regionally and nationally for their research and expertise outside the classroom as well as for their contributions as teachers, particularly in the fields of art, science, math, sociology, and education. The student-faculty ratio of 12:1 encourages personal interaction between students and professors. For more information, visit http://www.msj.edu/faculty.

Student Government

All matriculated students at the Mount are members of the Student Government Association (SGA). Its purpose is to help students understand their rights, privileges, and responsibilities, as well as maintain effective communication with the faculty, staff, and administration.

The SGA encourages students to participate in College governance through active membership on College committees and by assisting in the development of policies that affect student life.

Programs and activities sponsored by SGA include Campus Fair, community service projects, fund-raising events, and social activities such as movies and dances. See http://www.msj.edu/life.

Admission Requirements

The Mount reviews every candidate's request for admission. Credentials should include evidence of a college-preparatory high school curriculum, grade point average, standardized test scores, leadership, and extracurricular activities. In addition, personal background and attributes as well as life circumstances are taken into consideration. See http://www.msj.edu/admission.

Application and Information

Decisions on offers of admission are generally made within two weeks of the date the application process is completed. The application fee is $25, which is not refundable and does not apply toward tuition. Students who want to learn more about the Mount may arrange a visit by contacting the Office of Admission. In addition to individual appointments, the College schedules Get Acquainted Days and Discovery Days throughout the year, giving students and their parents the opportunity to visit the campus, explore academic programs, and take a tour. For admission details, see http://www.msj.edu/admission. Students planning a visit should go online to http://www.msj.edu/visit.

Office of Admission
College of Mount St. Joseph
5701 Delhi Road
Cincinnati, Ohio 45233-1672
Phone: 513-244-4531
        800-654-9314 (toll-free)
Web site: http://www.msj.edu/admission

The College of Mount St. Joseph provides a liberal arts and professional education that integrates learning and life through academic excellence, respect for others, and service.

THE COLLEGE OF NEW JERSEY
EWING TOWNSHIP, NEW JERSEY

The College

The College of New Jersey (TCNJ) welcomes students who have the talent and motivation to succeed in a highly rigorous academic environment. A public institution founded in 1855, the College enrolls about 5,600 full-time undergraduates, two thirds of whom reside on campus. Today it is heralded by *U.S. News & World Report* as well as *Barron's* as one of the most competitive schools in the nation, public or private. TCNJ serves a diverse student body, preparing graduates to be leaders in their chosen fields.

TCNJ has set the standard for public higher education. Students report they find TCNJ large enough to provide a full range of academic and extracurricular choices, yet small enough to be a genuine residential community of friends and fellow learners. With professors easily available in and out of class and facilities of enviable quality, TCNJ today represents an exceptional value in higher education.

The College of New Jersey's academic approach combines those of both traditional liberal arts schools and professional schools. A liberal learning curriculum ensures that all students are grounded in the beliefs and values of a civic responsibility and intellectual and scholarly growth and that they receive a well-rounded education in the liberal arts. Interdisciplinary studies, internships, research, and faculty mentoring all are part of an educational approach designed to produce successful leaders. While a very high percentage of graduates find immediate employment related to their fields of study, more than 20 percent go directly into graduate schools across the country.

All first- and second-year students are guaranteed on-campus housing, and most juniors and seniors continue to live on campus. Rooming arrangements are quite flexible, from doubles in freshman residence halls to suites and single rooms in campus town houses or apartments for upperclass students. A nationally recognized residence life program and more than 150 student organizations offer numerous opportunities for friendship, personal growth, and leadership. An exceptional 96 percent of first-year students return for their sophomore year.

The arts flourish in two theaters, a recital hall, an art gallery, and numerous other campus venues. Student performances, professional groups on tour, and a large variety of films, lectures, local bands, and solo entertainers fill the academic year with cultural options—many of them free, the rest at low cost.

Student wellness has a high priority, with many facilities for recreation and physical conditioning. In Packer Hall, the campus has access to a larger fitness center, a 25-meter swimming and diving pool, and a basketball court. The Student Recreation Center offers racquetball courts, four tennis courts that are convertible to basketball or volleyball use, a weight room, and an indoor track. Other facilities include a lighted Astroturf field, eight lighted outdoor tennis courts, an outdoor "beach" volleyball court, and numerous athletic fields.

As a Division III member of the National Collegiate Athletic Association, TCNJ offers twenty-one sports: eleven for men and ten for women. Since 1979, TCNJ student-athletes have amassed thirty-six national championships and twenty-nine runner-up awards, more than any other Division III institution in the country. In addition to its NCAA athletics, TCNJ offers a wide variety of recreation programs for intramural competition and self-governing sports clubs. More than 3,500 students play with these less demanding, but spirited and competitive teams, each year, some of which have intercollegiate schedules.

The College's undergraduate programs are accredited by the Middle States Association of Colleges and Schools and by professional associations in business, chemistry, computer science, education, education of the deaf, engineering, music, and nursing.

Location

The College of New Jersey is set on 289 acres in suburban Ewing Township, approximately 15 minutes from downtown Princeton; 10 minutes from Bucks County, Pennsylvania; and 5 miles from the state capital of Trenton. Woodlands and lakes surround the thirty-nine major academic and residential buildings. The campus is 30 miles from the theaters and museums of Philadelphia and 60 miles from those in New York City.

Majors and Degrees

The College of New Jersey offers programs leading to the Bachelor of Arts, Bachelor of Fine Arts, Bachelor of Music, Bachelor of Science, Bachelor of Science in Engineering, and Bachelor of Science in Nursing degrees.

The B.A. is awarded in art education; art history; communication studies; economics; English, including journalism and professional writing options; history; interactive multimedia; international studies; mathematics and statistics; philosophy; political science; psychology; sociology; Spanish; and women's and gender studies. The B.F.A. is awarded in digital arts, and fine art and graphic design. The B.M. is awarded in music (performance and education). The B.S. is granted in accountancy, biology, biomedical engineering, business administration (finance, general business, information systems management, international business, management, and marketing), chemistry, computer engineering, computer science, early childhood education, economics, education for the hearing-impaired, electrical engineering, elementary education, engineering science, health and physical education, law and justice, mechanical engineering, physics, special education, and technology education. Teacher preparation is available in many arts and science majors.

TCNJ offers a five-year combined Master of Arts in Teaching degree with dual certification in deaf and hard-of-hearing and elementary education. Students may also enroll in a seven-year B.S./M.D. degree program with UMDNJ—New Jersey Medical School (Newark) or a seven-year B.S./O.D. degree program with the State University of New York College of Optometry. Students may apply to TCNJ for a 4½-year combined B.S./M.A. program in law and justice with Rutgers, The State University of New Jersey (Newark). The College also offers a Medical Careers Advisory Committee for premed students and a Pre-Law Advisement Committee for students planning a career in law.

Academic Programs

All academic courses contain a significant out-of-class requirement and provide for even more student-faculty interaction. All baccalaureate degrees require at least thirty-two courses, including a core curriculum in the traditional arts and sciences.

The thirty-week year is divided into fall and spring semesters; the summer session offers courses in two 5-week sessions and one 6-week session. The average class size for freshman-level lectures is 24 students and for upper-division lectures, 22 students.

All first-year students participate in a program linking residential learning in small classes taught by full-time faculty members. Seminars, independent studies, and capstone courses give many students the opportunity for challenging advanced study in close collaboration with faculty members. TCNJ students publish the results of these endeavors or present them at national and regional conferences.

The honors program offers students the particularly challenging academic experiences that allow normal progress toward the degree. Whenever possible, honors courses have an interdisciplinary perspective and curriculum, concentrating on central themes within significant periods in the cultural development of civilization. Honors courses in the major consist of either specially designated sections or independent study. All honors classes are small, personal, and stimulating.

Off-Campus Programs

TCNJ offers students a variety of full-year and one-semester programs of study abroad as well as study at other state colleges and universities within the United States. Exchange programs are available in Australia, Austria, Canada, Denmark, France, Germany, Greece, Israel, Japan, Mexico, the United Kingdom, and twenty-three other countries. National exchanges are available at more than 130 participating institutions in the United States, the U.S. Virgin Islands, Puerto Rico, and Guam. The College of New Jersey hosts the New Jersey State Consortium for International Studies.

Academic Facilities

TCNJ has been nationally recognized as one of the most beautiful campuses in the nation. Within the past several years, TCNJ has built and opened a Science Complex, Biology Building, Social Science Building, College Spiritual Center, Art and Interactive Media Building, student apartments, and a state-of-the-art library, which serves as the intellectual and social hub of the campus. Campuswide networking provides full Internet accessibility from all residence hall rooms and more than twenty student computing laboratories.

Costs

Costs are relatively low because of state funding. For 2010–11, full-time undergraduate tuition and fees were $13,000 for New Jersey residents and $22,000 for out-of-state students. Room and board charges for the academic year, with a middle meal plan, averaged $9612.

Financial Aid

Approximately half of the full-time undergraduates receive some form of financial aid, such as federal, state, and institutional grants; merit scholarships; student employment; and loan assistance. The Free Application for Federal Student Aid (FAFSA) or Renewal FAFSA is used to apply for all types of aid.

Scholarships and grants include The College of New Jersey Merit Scholars Program, Bonner Scholars, Chairman of the Board Merit Scholars, the New Jersey Tuition Aid Grant, Federal Pell Grants, Federal Supplemental Educational Opportunity Grants (FSEOG), Educational Opportunity Fund (EOF) Promise Award, and Army and Air Force ROTC Scholarships, as well as other institutional scholarships. Loans include the Federal Subsidized and Unsubsidized Stafford Loans, the Federal Perkins Loan, the Federal Parent Loan for Undergraduate Students (PLUS), the New Jersey CLASS Loan, nursing loans, and short-term emergency loan funds. Student employment options include the need-based Federal Work-Study Program (on- and off-campus positions) as well as institutionally supported campus jobs.

Faculty

The approximately 335 full-time members of the College of New Jersey faculty are teachers and scholars. While teaching is their primary commitment, they are also active researchers, authors, artists, performers, and regular contributors in their academic disciplines. No classes are taught by graduate assistants. The student-faculty ratio is 12:1. From their first day, students study with faculty members who may be researching new ways to use solar energy; writing a new text, play, or novel; or investigating the life cycle of desert ferns. Members of the faculty have attracted many significant grants, fellowships, and awards, including the Bancroft Prize in history, Fulbright Scholarships, and grants from the National Science Foundation, the National Institute for Advanced Study, the Guggenheim Foundation, and the National Endowment for the Humanities. Faculty members mentor their students, preparing them for careers, graduate and professional schools, and prestigious fellowships such as the Fulbright, Truman, and Marshall Fellowships recently awarded to TCNJ students.

Student Government

The Student Government Association, comprising all undergraduate students at the College, is governed by elected representatives. The Residence Hall Association provides the mechanism for student input into campus housing policies, and members of the Student Finance Board oversee and administer approximately $500,000 in student funds. The College Union Board sponsors a wide range of special events, including visits by John Leguizamo, Cornel West, and George Carlin.

Admission Requirements

The College of New Jersey seeks students who can succeed in a highly selective academic program and who show intellectual curiosity, academic talent, and the potential to contribute to the life of the College. The College is committed to attracting students from diverse economic, racial, social, and geographic backgrounds. A high school record of at least 16 college-preparatory credits, high school class rank, SAT scores, and special interests, skills, and qualities of all kinds can be influential. Certain departments, such as art and music, use additional criteria to evaluate candidates seeking admission into their programs. The College of New Jersey reviews candidates holistically and takes into consideration the variations in high schools and communities in which the applicants reside.

Application and Information

The College of New Jersey is a member of the Common Application. The deadline for applications for January admission is November 15 and for September admission, January 15. There is a $75 application fee. Candidates who apply only to the College of New Jersey under the early decision plan may apply before November 15 and will be notified on or before December 15. Students applying in to the seven-year medical program or as a biology major must apply by January 1. For September admission, the College subscribes to the candidates' reply date of May 1 for payment of $300.

For more information, students should contact:

Dean of Admissions
The College of New Jersey
P.O. Box 7718
Ewing, New Jersey 08628-0718
Phone: 609-771-2131
Web site: http://www.tcnj.edu

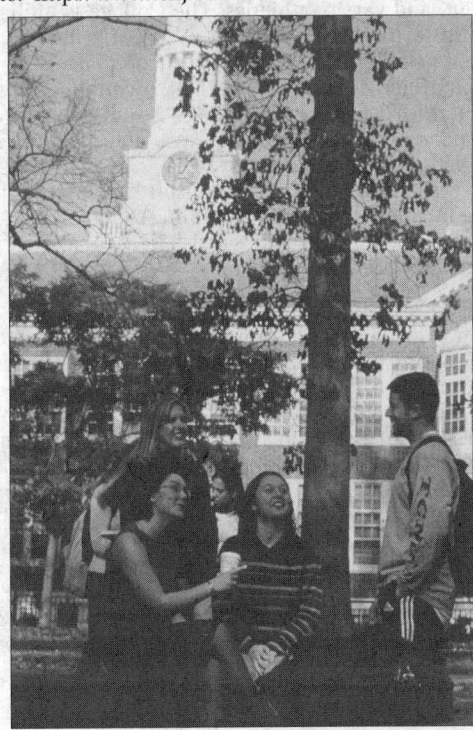

Students take a break in front of Green Hall.

COLLEGE OF SAINT ELIZABETH
MORRISTOWN, NEW JERSEY

The College

The College of Saint Elizabeth (CSE), which celebrated its 110th anniversary in 2009, is the oldest college for women in New Jersey. In addition, CSE is one of the first Catholic colleges in the U.S. to award degrees to women. A Catholic institution in the liberal arts tradition, CSE includes a women's college, coeducational adult undergraduate and graduate degree programs, and one doctoral program. An enrollment of more than 2,100 students fosters considerable student-faculty interaction and a spirit of campuswide encouragement and support. An emphasis is placed on opportunities for individual growth through academic, spiritual, cultural, leadership, and civic experiences.

Located on a 200-acre campus, CSE's buildings command a wide view of the surrounding hills. Although a majority of students belong to New Jersey, more than twenty countries and other states are represented at CSE. Two attractive residence halls provide ample private and double rooms. Each residence hall has kitchenettes, laundry facilities, a mailroom, lounges, and conference rooms. The student center contains a swimming pool, a gymnasium, a fitness center, a dining room, a newly renovated lounge area, and the College store. The Annunciation Center, a multipurpose arts and education facility, houses state-of-the-art music, drama, and art studios and a 560-seat performance center.

Students may belong to extracurricular organizations associated with their academic interests, which include a number of Greek-letter honor and professional societies and student affiliates of the American Chemical Society. In addition, CSE has a variety of organizations such as the Elizabeth Singers, the International/Intercultural Club, the College Activities Board, Campus Ministry, the Students Take Action Committee, Volunteer Services, Student Government, and varsity athletics. The College is affiliated with the North Eastern Athletic Conference (NEAC), the Eastern Colleges Athletic Conference (ECAC), and competes in basketball, cross-country, lacrosse, soccer, softball, swimming, tennis, and volleyball at the NCAA Division III level. A rich calendar of social, cultural, and recreational events is available at the College of Saint Elizabeth. Students frequently socialize with their peers from Drew University and Fairleigh Dickinson University (FDU), two nearby coeducational institutions within walking distance of the campus. Career Services provides assistance with career preparation, internships, and graduate study.

Location

Morristown is located in the rapidly growing corporate center of historical Morris County. Neighboring towns and cities, only minutes from the campus, offer facilities for shopping and recreation. The College is an hour from the cultural and social opportunities of New York City by car, train, or bus and is near the campuses of Fairleigh Dickinson, Seton Hall, Drew, and the County College of Morris. Newark Liberty International Airport is approximately 30 minutes and two New York airports are approximately 1 hour from the campus. Local bus routes are easily accessible, and New Jersey Transit, which has a stop at the campus gate, provides excellent rail commuter service from New York City, Hoboken, Newark, the Oranges, Short Hills, Maplewood, Millburn, Summit, Chatham, Madison, and Dover. Routes 287, 80, 280, 46, 78, 24, and 10 are located close by.

Majors and Degrees

The Bachelor of Arts is offered in allied health studies, American studies, art, biology, chemistry, communications, computer information systems, education (early childhood/elementary), English, global studies, history, individualized major, justice studies, mathematics, music, philosophy, psychology, sociology, Spanish, theology, and women's studies. The Bachelor of Science is offered in biochemistry, biology, business administration, chemistry, clinical laboratory sciences (with University of Medicine and Dentistry of NJ), computer science, and foods and nutrition. The Bachelor of Science in Nursing degree is offered as an upper-division nursing program. In addition to CSE's combined B.A./M.A. degrees in business administration and justice studies, and the B.S./M.S. in Foods and Nutrition, the College offers a combined B.S./M.S. physician assistant degree as a joint program with Seton Hall University.

In addition to the undergraduate majors and degrees listed, the College offers the M.A. degree in counseling psychology, education, educational leadership, forensic psychology and counseling, justice administration and public service, and theology; the M.S. degree in health-care management, management, nursing, and nutrition; and the Ed.D. degree in educational leadership.

Seven-week courses are offered in the evenings. Courses are also given during the summer and winter intersession. Adult undergraduate degree programs are offered in business administration (human resources management, management, or marketing), computer science, foods and nutrition, justice studies, nursing, psychology, and theology.

Academic Programs

The requirements for a B.A., B.S., or B.S.N. degree are 128 semester hours of academic credit, competency in writing, First Year Seminar (not required of adult students), 2 credits in fitness/wellness, and successful completion of the comprehensive examination in the major subject. A minimum of 32 credits is required in the major. The core curriculum requires that students take between 36 and 44 credits distributed among five cluster areas: Literature/Fine Arts/Language; Social and Behavioral Sciences; Natural and Physical Sciences and Mathematics and Computer Science; Philosophy, Theology, and History; and Perspectives on an Interdependent World. The remaining courses are free electives.

Career preparation includes studies in business management, computer information systems, computer science, criminal justice and legal studies, foods and nutrition, gerontology, human resource management, management, marketing, premedicine, preveterinary studies, secondary education, and social work. Education majors may obtain state certification and/or endorsement in early childhood or special education. In addition, the College has a highly successful leadership program, which prepares students for postgraduate success.

Students interested in becoming registered dietitians may enroll in the dietetic internship program if they hold a baccalaureate degree and meet the current American Dietetic Association course work requirements.

Independent study, field experience, internships, study-abroad opportunities, honors, leadership, and accelerated programs, minors, and double majors are available for qualified students. Successful scores on Advanced Placement tests are honored for placement or credit. Credit is given for successful scores on CLEP subject examinations with essays; on the Thomas Edison College Examination Program (TECEP) examinations; on the Regents College Examination in nursing, DANTES, and ACE College Credit Recommendation; and on portfolio assessment of prior learning.

Off-Campus Programs

A cross-registration policy exists with nearby Fairleigh Dickinson and Drew Universities. Qualified students may study abroad during the junior year or in the summer. A January intersession program and summer sessions provide opportunities for short-term courses and off-campus experiences. Students have opportunities in Morris County for volunteer service, field experience, and internships in local agencies, institutions, and the corporate headquarters of numerous multinational corporations.

Academic Facilities

Students majoring in biology and chemistry conduct independent research projects under the guidance of highly qualified professors and in conjunction with local research companies. The College has several well-equipped microcomputer laboratories and extensive software. In addition, approximately 5,000 square feet of the chemistry labs has been newly renovated with modern casework, fume hoods, and SMART technology. Mahoney Library is an air-conditioned facility that provides group and individual study areas. The library's collection includes 165 databases, 374 print journals, 45,532 electronic journals, 1,920 DVDs and videos, and 124,266 monographs. The Phillips Library of Rare Books and Manuscripts houses a variety of special collections. Seventeen Internet workstations provide access to the Internet and a classroom area to provide library and information literacy classes year-round. The library's Web page provides a portal for all services, including a shared online catalog with Fairleigh Dickinson University's library. In addition, there are reciprocal borrowing privileges between FDU and CSE. Media Services provides academic support services to the CSE community in all areas of traditional/non-traditional audio-visual equipment, video conferencing distance education, video/television projects, and stage performance. A TV production studio, an editing suite, and a videoconferencing classroom are housed in the Media Services area.

Costs

Tuition and fees in 2010–11 for incoming full-time freshmen were $25,180 and room and board were $11,340. Part-time undergraduate students paid $670 per credit.

Financial Aid

Approximately 95 percent of full-time undergraduate students at the College of Saint Elizabeth receive financial aid. Aid is available from the College itself in the form of scholarships, grants-in-aid, and campus employment and from the federal and state governments in the form of scholarships, grants, loans, and employment. Students who wish to be considered for grants, loans, and campus employment should apply to the College by March 1 for the fall semester and by November 1 for the spring semester. Campus employment is available in the residence halls, laboratories, the library, and College offices, and a limited number of work-study opportunities for qualified students are available both on and off campus. Transfer scholarships are also available.

Faculty

The faculty-student ratio is 1:11. Eighty-six percent of the full-time instructional faculty members for 2009–10 had the highest degree in their field. Several faculty members hold additional professional credentials. The goals of the faculty are to teach effectively, to be readily available to students, and to pursue research.

Student Government

Students participate in the governance of the College through the Student Organization. The Student Organization elects members to the student government, which serves as the student executive branch. Student views on student activities, clubs, and organizations are expressed and acted on through a committee structure. The academic life, student life, and lectures and concerts committees of the College are composed of both faculty members and students and are engaged in determining methods of implementing institutional goals and increasing student satisfaction with campus life. Students are encouraged to participate fully in the academic community and to exercise considerable influence in social and extracurricular activities. There is an open atmosphere on campus, and students have access to the deans and the president.

Admission Requirements

The College looks for students whose aptitude and academic record demonstrate the ability to meet academic challenges. Normally, a student interested in admission to the College should complete 16 academic units by the end of her senior year, including 3 years of English; 2 years of college-preparatory mathematics, including algebra; 2 years of the same foreign language; 1 year of U.S. history; 1 unit of laboratory science and 1 additional unit of science; and six upper-level academic electives. Applicants must submit either SAT or ACT scores. International students must send scores on the Test of English as a Foreign Language (TOEFL). Students applying to the College should submit a secondary school transcript, including courses currently in progress, plus two letters of recommendation from persons who can attest to their academic potential. Students are encouraged to have an on-campus interview and visit the campus. Open houses are held each spring and fall. Well-qualified students who are recommended by their high school principals may be accepted after three years of high school. Transfers from two- and four-year colleges are accepted for the fall and spring semesters. Through articulation agreements, an applicant who has earned an A.A. degree in a transfer program at an accredited two-year college is eligible for admission with junior-class standing. Adult students must submit secondary and previous college transcripts (if any) in addition to the application.

Application and Information

For further information, students may contact:

College of Saint Elizabeth
2 Convent Road
Morristown, New Jersey 07960-6989

Phone: 800-210-7900 (toll-free)
Fax: 973-290-4710
E-mail: apply@cse.edu
Web site: http://www.cse.edu
        http://www.facebook.com/CollegeOfSaintElizabeth

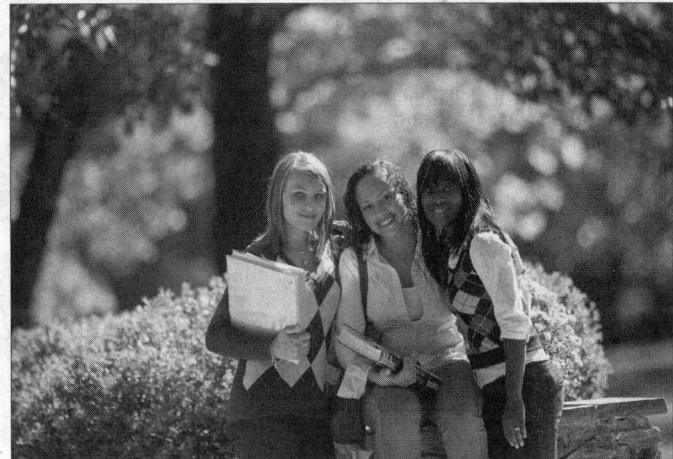

Students at the College of Saint Elizabeth.

THE COLLEGE OF SAINT ROSE

ALBANY, NEW YORK

The College

The College of Saint Rose is an independent, residential, coeducational institution where academics and career preparation are top priorities. The College's progressive liberal education core prepares students to dive into one of the College's sixty-six undergraduate fields of study, most of which incorporate a field experience or internship component. The College offers small class sizes, with a student-faculty ratio of 14:1 and an experienced, mentoring faculty. *Money* magazine and *U.S. News & World Report* have ranked Saint Rose as one of the top colleges in the Northeast and the nation, based on such factors as affordability and high academic quality. With the capital of New York as its convenient location and a distinctly personal learning atmosphere on campus, the College of Saint Rose is a place where students realize they will be challenged intellectually and have the ability to change the world.

Saint Rose was founded in 1920 by the Sisters of Saint Joseph of Carondelet and is a distinguished college interwoven within a remarkable city. The campus is part of the fabric of the city and the students and faculty members the threads that make it whole. The College is located in an area that gives it a distinct educational advantage and a college dedicated to cultivating intellectual dynamic leaders appreciative of diversity and active citizenship. The College encompasses eighty buildings, including the new Massry Center for the Arts, the Thelma P. Lally School of Education, a state-of-the-art Science Center, a high-tech music studio, and the Hubbard Interfaith Sanctuary.

Saint Rose students make up a community of leaders. Most of the 3,000 undergraduates at Saint Rose come from twenty-two states and sixteen different countries. The College of Saint Rose actively seeks to enroll students of all backgrounds who can contribute to and benefit from the experience of shared learning and academic success.

Campus housing includes traditional and suite-style residence halls and town houses as well as more than thirty Victorian homes. Each house has its own history and character, with unique wraparound porches and stained-glass windows.

Students participate in organized social activities as well as ten associations related to academic majors. The College of Saint Rose is a member of the National Collegiate Athletic Association (NCAA) Division II and the Northeast-10 Conference. Intercollegiate teams include men's baseball and golf; men's and women's basketball, cross-country, soccer, swimming, tennis, and track and field; and women's softball and volleyball.

Although students ultimately attend Saint Rose to receive a superior education, they also participate in organized social activities that enhance the Saint Rose experience. Saint Rose students belong to more than thirty groups that include academic-related clubs as well as special-interest clubs. They also play in ten to fifteen intramural programs and produce three publications—the award-winning *Chronicle* weekly student newspaper, the *Sphere* literary magazine, and *Reflections*, the College's yearbook.

Location

Saint Rose is located in the historic Pine Hills neighborhood of Albany. With more than 60,000 college students in the area, there are always things to do and people to meet. A wide variety of restaurants, shops, museums, malls, and theaters are within walking distance or are easily accessible by buses that stop at Saint Rose.

Majors and Degrees

The College of Saint Rose offers programs of study in the fields of accounting, American studies, art education (K–12), biochemistry, biology, biology education (7–12), biology/cytotechnology, bioinformatics, business administration, chemistry, chemistry education (7–12), childhood education, childhood education/special education, communication sciences and disorders, communications, computer information systems, computer science, criminal justice, early childhood education, early childhood/special education, earth science (7–12), English, English education (7–12), environmental affairs, exploratory, forensic science, forensic psychology, geology, graphic design, history, history/political science, mathematics, mathematics education (7–12), medical technology, music education (K–12), music industry, political science, prelaw, premedicine, preveterinary studies, psychology, religious studies, social studies education (7–12), social work, sociology, Spanish, Spanish education (7–12), sport management, studio art, technology education, and women's studies.

Academic Programs

The College offers qualified students the opportunity to pursue accelerated bachelor's/master's degrees in approximately five years of study. The College offers these options in accounting, business, communications sciences and disorders (speech therapy), computer information systems, computer science, English, history, and M.B.A.

Qualified students may also participate in other special programs: a 3+3 option with Albany Law School, a 3+1 medical technology option with Albany College of Pharmacy or Rochester, and a 3+2 engineering option with Union College, Clarkson University, Rensselaer Polytechnic Institute, or Alfred University. Students in these programs complete selected bachelor's degree programs at Saint Rose in three years and transfer to the cooperating institution to finish the professional program.

Students are provided with assistance in planning their programs of study by faculty advisers in their major areas and by the Office of Academic Advisement. They may elect double majors or minors or may design their own programs within the guidelines set by the interdepartmental studies major.

To earn a bachelor's degree, a student must complete a minimum of 122 credits, including, for most majors, the liberal education curriculum requirement of 42 credits, two courses in physical education, and the major requirements as specified. A minimum of 60 credits must be earned on the Saint Rose campus or at one of the colleges in the Hudson-Mohawk Association of Colleges and Universities through cross-registration.

The College operates on a semester calendar, with a fall term extending from August to December and a spring term from January to May. Two summer session programs offer undergraduate and graduate evening courses.

Off-Campus Programs

Saint Rose students can study in one of more than thirty countries, which is made possible by the school's affiliations with the College Consortium for International Studies, Regent's College in London, and the Center for Cross-Cultural Study. All study-abroad opportunities are offered at the same price as Saint Rose tuition (plus airfare and personal expenses), including the Saint Rose financial aid package. All credits count toward the student's degree.

Academic Facilities

The College has invested more than $2.5 million to create the Christian Plumeri Sports Complex with a baseball field, softball field, and an artificial turf soccer/lacrosse field as well as a natural grass practice field. These fields are home to the Saint Rose Golden Knights, who have regularly won bids to Northeast-10 conference and Division II national tournaments, as well as for the College's intramural and club sports.

The College's new $14-million Massry Center for the Arts is a distinctive facility that not only provides a learning environment for music and art but also gives musical and visual artists a prime location to showcase their work to the College community and the public. The 46,000-square-foot facility features a state-of-the-art performance hall, acoustically congruent and separate instrumental and choral rehearsal suites, applied teaching studios, piano keyboard laboratories, smart classrooms, and an art gallery.

The new $7-million Center for Communications and Interactive Media opened in 2010. This 20,000 square foot facility houses new TV and radio studios, a live recording studio, a video and film viewing room, multimedia computer labs, and offices for the College's communications and music industry faculty. It joins the Massry Center for the Arts and the Campus Theatre to form an arts and communications section of the Saint Rose campus.

A recent partnership with IBM and a $7-million technology upgrade greatly enhanced the speed and performance of the College's network, providing the infrastructure for wireless networking, videoconferencing, streaming media, and Blackboard, the Web-based instruction tool. The campuswide network provides wireless access across the campus including the campus center, the library, and all of the residence halls.

The Center for Art and Design houses the student art gallery as well as extensive photography labs, graphic design computers, and one of the largest screen-printing facilities in the state of New York. The College's Music Center features the Saints and Sinners Sound Studio, a music library, a performance hall, and practice rooms. Science and mathematics majors have access to the latest equipment and research facilities in the College's 27,000-square-foot Science Center.

The $15-million, 56,000-square-foot Thelma P. Lally School of Education features a multimedia education forum, classrooms, computer labs, offices, an education and curriculum library, a laboratory nursery school, and a multidisciplinary services clinic. The school provides a learning and teaching environment in which technology plays a critical role and where teachers, parents, and students exchange ideas on how to make the American education system second to none.

With the creation of the $7.5-million Events and Athletics Center, the College of Saint Rose provides an on-campus venue worthy of welcoming best-selling authors, Nobel Prize winners, and world-famous performers. This space is also designed to serve as a unique collegiate basketball venue in the Capital Region, large enough to accommodate the Golden Knights' loyal fan base. In addition, Saint Joseph's Hall, one of Saint Rose's original buildings, received a $5.5-million renovation, turning the building into a student service hub centralized around the College's Student Solution Center.

Costs
Tuition for 2010–11 was $23,330. Room and board costs averaged $9880 per year, depending on the meal plan chosen by the student. Estimated annual costs for books and personal expenses are $1000 and $1400, respectively.

Financial Aid
More than 95 percent of the students receive scholarships and financial assistance. The College of Saint Rose participates in the Federal Pell Grant, FSEOG, TAP, and Federal Work-Study programs and in the Federal Perkins Loan and Federal Stafford Loan Programs. The College provides ample aid in the form of grants, service awards, and scholarships for need or academic achievement. Candidates for financial assistance must file the Free Application for Federal Student Aid. ISIR and SAR forms should be on file in the Financial Aid Office by March 1. Students interested in being considered for academic scholarships must apply to the College by February 1.

Faculty
Saint Rose has a full-time faculty of 207 members, with a student-faculty ratio of 14:1. The average class size is 20–25 students, with more than 55 percent of classes having less than 20 students.

Student Government
The Student Association (SA) consists of elected students who want to make life at the College as enjoyable, interesting, and meaningful as possible. It budgets student funds, appoints representatives to College policymaking committees, and assists individual students and clubs in planning and carrying out projects. It also provides an organ of self-government, promotes an exchange of ideas within the College community, fosters opportunities beyond those offered in the formal curriculum, and advances the welfare of the entire College community. SA also oversees the College's thirty clubs and organizations.

Admission Requirements
The College wishes to admit students who show evidence of strong academic motivation and the ability to benefit from a challenging liberal and professional education. Admission decisions are made after careful study of all the data available for each candidate. Interviews are strongly recommended but not required. Freshman applicants should submit a high school transcript, a letter of recommendation from a teacher or guidance counselor, and scores on the SAT or ACT.

Transfer applicants must submit high school and college transcripts, a letter of recommendation from a college instructor, and a written statement of the reasons for transfer.

Application and Information
The College has an early action (nonbinding) application deadline of December 1. Students are accepted for admission for the fall and spring semesters on a rolling admissions basis. Interested students must apply by February 1 to be considered for academic scholarships ranging from $5000 to $14,000 for each undergraduate year. New students who are accepted for admission are asked to submit a $300 enrollment deposit to secure their place in the new class. Information on all aspects of the campus and the academic programs can be obtained by contacting the Office of Admissions; this office also can arrange personal interviews, campus tours, classroom visits, and overnight accommodations.

Office of Undergraduate Admissions
The College of Saint Rose
432 Western Avenue
Albany, New York 12203
Phone: 518-454-5150
      800-637-8556 (toll-free)
Fax: 518-454-2013
E-mail: admit@strose.edu (admissions)
      finaid@strose.edu (financial aid)
Web site: http://www.strose.edu
      http://on.fb.me/college_saint_rose (Facebook)

Located in the historic Pine Hills neighborhood of Albany, New York, the Saint Rose campus features a mix of classic brick buildings and new stone and glass structures, with the Campus Green at its center. The border of the campus is outlined by more than thirty restored historic Victorian houses featuring wraparound porches and stained-glass windows.

COLLEGE OF STATEN ISLAND OF THE CITY UNIVERSITY OF NEW YORK

STATEN ISLAND, NEW YORK

The College and The University

Founded in 1976 from the merger of two existing colleges, the College of Staten Island (CSI) is a four-year senior college within the City University of New York (CUNY) and is Staten Island's only public institution of higher learning. CSI is dedicated to both access and excellence and currently serves over 13,500 students.

The College of Staten Island was established through the union of Staten Island Community College (CUNY's first community college, founded in 1955) and Richmond College (CUNY's first upper-division college, founded in 1965).

The College ensures that students receive a thorough liberal arts education through core requirements which include classes in the arts and humanities, mathematics, science, and social sciences. Requirements for the associate degree provide a curriculum based on study in a specific area which is often directed toward a career. Requirements for the bachelor's degree provide disciplined and cumulative programs of study in fifty-three majors.

The Campus Center incorporates cocurricular activities for a complete personal growth experience. The two-story rotunda space at the heart of the structure contains the main dining facilities, the College's health services, a bookstore, offices for student organizations, study and sleep lounges, a small performance/cafe space, game rooms with the latest game consoles, and the state-of-the-art studios of WSIA, the student-operated FM radio station.

Location

CSI is located on a sprawling 204-acre campus located in the heart of Staten Island. The campus is the largest site for a college (public or private) within New York City and with its scenic landscape; the grounds and facilities create a rural oasis in an urban setting. Classrooms and academic offices are located in fourteen neo-Georgian buildings which form two quadrangles connected by the campus walk, which extends between the library and the Campus Center. Five well-built and equipped buildings—the library, the Campus Center, the Biological Sciences/Chemical Sciences building, the Center for the Arts, and the Sports and Recreation Center—provide outstanding facilities for scholastic and community-based activities.

CSI's location offers students the best of two worlds, with Staten Island providing a suburban environment with some of the most interesting landscapes in the metropolitan area; while Manhattan, the center of cultural and social life of the city, is only 25 minutes from the island by ferry. The Verrazano-Narrows Bridge provides direct access to Staten Island from Brooklyn.

Majors and Degrees

CSI offers an Associate in degree in liberal arts and science. The Associate in Science degree is offered in liberal arts and science. The Associate in Applied Science degree is offered in business, computer technology, and nursing.

The Bachelor of Arts degree is conferred in African American studies; American studies; art; art with a studio art or art history concentration; cinema studies; economics; English; English with a writing, linguistics, literature, and dramatic literature concentration; history; international studies; Italian studies (new); modern languages; music; philosophy; political science; psychology; science, letters, and society; sociology-anthropology; social work; Spanish; and women's, gender, and sexuality studies.

The Bachelor of Science degree is offered in accounting; art with a photography concentration; biochemistry; bioinformatics; biology; business; business with a finance, international business management, or marketing concentration; chemistry; communications with a journalism, media studies, design and digital media, or corporate communications concentration; computer science; computer science/mathematics; dramatic arts; economics; economics with a business or finance specialization; engineering science with a computer, electrical, or mechanical specialization; information systems; mathematics; medical technology; music; music with an electronics concentration; nursing (upper-division program); preprofessional studies in dentistry, medicine, optometry, podiatry, and law; and physics.

In addition to the exciting array of undergraduate degrees and majors available, CSI also awards the Master of Arts degree in cinema and media studies, English, environmental science, history, and liberal studies; the Master of Science degree in biology, computer science, neuroscience, mental retardation and developmental disabilities, and nursing: adult health and nursing: gerontological; and the Master of Science in Education degree in childhood education, adolescence education, and special education in a selection of concentrations. Post-master's advanced certificates are offered in leadership in education, nursing: nursing education, and nursing: nursing cultural competence.

The graduate teacher education program prepares students to teach at the early childhood, elementary, and secondary levels. The academic work and field experience meet the requirements for the certification and licensing examinations given by the state and city of New York.

Further, CSI offers doctoral programs jointly with the CUNY Graduate School in biochemistry, biology, polymer chemistry, computer science, physical therapy, and physics.

Academic Programs

CSI offers two-year programs in career areas and in liberal arts and sciences and four-year programs with majors in the traditional fields of study. General education requirements have been established for all degrees. The associate degree programs require 60–64 credits, depending on the field; the bachelor's degree programs require 120 credits, with a few exceptions. Credit may be awarded for internships and independent study, and may be earned for experiential learning and by examination. Minors may be taken in several fields, and double majors are permitted. Students may graduate with honors in their field of study in most bachelor's degree majors.

The College follows a two-semester calendar, with classes scheduled both day and evening. The Office of Weekend and Evening Services offers a variety of course combinations leading to associate and bachelor's degrees, providing opportunities for nontraditional students with weekday career commitments to pursue a college education at more convenient times. Intensive summer and winter sessions are also offered to students who would like to accelerate their degrees.

Off-Campus Programs

The College gives a number of courses for credit at off-campus locations throughout the city through internships at major corporations and other fieldwork. Exceptional study-abroad opportunities are available through CSI's Center for International Service which offers students the option of earning academic credit for study in China, Denmark, Ecuador, England, Greece, Italy, Spain, or South Africa.

Academic Facilities

The academic buildings are designed to house approximately 300 modern laboratories and classrooms. Each also houses a study lounge for students, departmental and program offices, and offices for faculty members. Academic and research programs are served by a computer network that allows students and faculty members full access to specialized software, the Internet, online library resources, and e-mail. All major computer languages and software packages are supported. The College is a wireless campus, and its network is available to all students.

The Center for the Arts complex provides facilities for teaching in the instructional wing and areas of public assembly in the public wing. The complex of public facilities includes a 900-seat auditorium, a 450-seat fully equipped theater, a recital hall, an experimental theater, art galleries, and a conference center. Classrooms, lecture halls, studios, and offices for faculty members are located in the instructional wing.

The CSI Library is staffed with 14 full-time librarians and 7 adjunct librarians who hold faculty status and rank. In addition, the library also has 40 support staff members. The library's total collection consists of approximately 300,000 books; 900 print journal subscriptions; 77 electronic databases with more than 26,000 full-text journals; 3,000 videos and films; and more than 4,000 sound recordings. The library's online catalog, CUNY+Plus, provides complete access to the collections, including access to holdings of other CUNY libraries. Students also have round-the-clock access to online database and research tools via the Internet. In addition, the library maintains a collection of current textbooks donated by the CSI Student Government. These and other course materials are available at the Reserve Desk. Wireless laptops are loaned to students for use throughout the library. The library building also houses the Office of Instructional Support and the Cybercafé, which offers Starbucks coffee.

The laboratory science building provides facilities for teaching and for two research centers: the Center for Environmental Science and the Center for Developmental Neuroscience and Developmental Disabilities. It consists of a research wing and an instructional wing. State-of-the-art laboratories serve students and faculty members in their teaching and research.

The CSI Astrophysical Observatory is a world-class resource which has been recognized by the International Astronomical Union as an official asteroid tracking station.

The Sports and Recreation Center is a 77,000-square-foot multipurpose facility providing basketball, handball/paddleball, racquetball, and volleyball courts; locker rooms; a gym; instructional areas; an indoor eight-lane 25-meter swimming pool; and offices for faculty members. Recreational fields occupy the meadows in the northwest quadrant of the campus, providing a green and landscaped open area at the main approach to the campus that includes a running track, indoor and outdoor tennis courts, a soccer field, handball/paddleball courts, softball fields, and a semiprofessional baseball field (original home field to the Staten Island Yankees minor-league baseball team).

Costs

For 2010–11, undergraduate tuition for New York State (NYS) residents was $205 per credit for part-time matriculated students, $2415 per semester for full-time matriculated students, and $300 per credit for nondegree students. Nonresident full- and part-time students were charged $435 per credit, and nondegree students were charged $640 per credit. Graduate NYS resident tuition was $3865 per semester for students attending the College full time and $325 per credit for part-time students. Nonresidents were charged $605 per credit for full- and part-time attendance.

Financial Aid

Financial aid is available through state and federal programs and includes the New York State Tuition Assistance Program (TAP) awards, Federal Pell Grants, Federal Supplemental Educational Opportunity Grants (FSEOG), Search for Elevation and Education through Knowledge (SEEK) awards, scholarships, Federal Work-Study Program awards, and student loan programs. Information about programs, application procedures, and deadlines is available from the Financial Aid Office.

CSI Presidential Scholarships are awarded annually to full-time students based on academic merit and service. In addition, endowments have been established for scholarships in a number of fields. Further information about scholarships is available from the Career and Scholarship Center.

Faculty

The College has a full-time faculty of 300, of whom approximately 80 percent hold a doctoral degree or the equivalent. These faculty members have made significant contributions in many areas of scholarship, creativity, and public service. Numerous faculty members have received prestigious grants and awards, and more than 30 serve as members of CUNY's doctoral faculty.

Student Government

A single body (Senate) comprised of 25 elected students represents the interests of the College's students, serving as liaison to faculty and administrators. The Senate derives funding from the student activity fee and through its various commissions and committees, the student government sponsors many academic and nonacademic programs.

Admission Requirements

A freshman or transfer student applying for admission to a bachelor's degree program must pass the CUNY Assessment Tests (CATs) in reading, writing, and mathematics unless he or she qualifies for exemption based on a satisfactory performance on the SAT or ACT standardized tests or Regents Examinations. Admission to a bachelor's degree program is determined by an applicant's score on the College's admissions index. The index is based on the applicant's high school courses and academic average and the combined verbal and mathematics SAT scores. An applicant whose score reaches or exceeds the College's minimum index number is admitted to a bachelor's degree program. A faculty admissions committee may consider the admission of applicants whose scores approach the College's minimum index number. Students transferring to baccalaureate programs who have fewer than 25 credits must have a GPA of at least 2.0 and must meet freshman entrance criteria.

Entering first-year students may be admitted to two-year programs if they have graduated from an accredited high school or have earned an equivalency diploma (GED) with a satisfactory score.

The College requires a grade point average equivalent of 2.0 for transfer as a matriculated student into a two-year degree program.

Application and Information

Requests for further information and application materials should be directed to:

College of Staten Island
The City University of New York
Office of Recruitment and Admissions
Building 2A, Room 103
Staten Island, New York 10314

Phone: 718-982-2010
E-mail: admissions@csi.cuny.edu
Web site: http://www.csi.cuny.edu
http://www.facebook.com/CollegeOfStatenIsland

College of Staten Island's library offers students the resources to learn and explore in a quiet, comfortable setting.

THE COLLEGE OF WOOSTER
WOOSTER, OHIO

The College

The College of Wooster is a community of independent minds, working together to prepare students to become leaders of character and influence in an interdependent global community.

Founded as a Presbyterian college in 1866, Wooster has been an independent, residential college of the liberal arts and sciences since 1969. With small classes (61 percent have fewer than 20 students) and an 11:1 student-faculty ratio, students receive close attention both in and out of the classroom. More information can be found at http://www.wooster.edu/About-Wooster.

Wooster's nearly 2,000 students come from forty-five states and twenty-six countries from all backgrounds and life experiences.

Ninety-eight percent of Wooster students live on campus. First-year students can choose to live with their First-Year Seminar classmates or a mix of students from all years. After the first year, the options multiply. Wooster's program houses allow students to live with a group of 7 to 14 others who share their interests. Together, they work on a service project in the community throughout the year, from Habitat for Humanity to the Humane Society. For more information, visit http://www.wooster.edu/Student-Life/Residence-Life.

Close to a third of Wooster students follow their passion for making music through three choirs, a symphony orchestra, symphonic and marching bands, a jazz ensemble, four a cappella groups, and other ensembles (http://www.wooster.edu/Music-and-the-Arts). Another third participate in intercollegiate athletics. Wooster has produced 45 All Americans in eleven sports in the past six years and won sixty-seven NCAC championships since 1985. To learn more about the athletics program, visit http://www.woosterathletics.com/landing/index.

From the improv group Don't Throw Shoes, to the student-run investment club (managing a $2-million portfolio for the College's endowment), and the cricket team to the radio station, there is something for just about every interest.

Location

The College is located in Wooster, Ohio, a city of approximately 26,000. Wooster is 55 miles southwest of Cleveland and 30 miles southwest of Akron. An unusually close relationship exists between the College and the community. The economically diverse and vibrant city of Wooster provides activities that include, for example, the Wooster Symphony, the Ambassadors Program, and a variety of volunteer and internship experiences.

Students appreciate how very safe the area is, as also the great restaurants and shopping close to the College.

Majors and Degrees

The College of Wooster offers the degrees of Bachelor of Arts, Bachelor of Music, and Bachelor of Music Education (http://www.wooster.edu/Academics/Areas-of-Study). A student may choose from more than fifty majors and programs of study, including Africana studies; anthropology; archaeology; art history; art–studio; biochemistry and molecular biology; biology; business economics; chemical physics; chemistry; classical studies (Greek, Latin, classical civilization); communication sciences and disorders; communication studies; comparative literature; computer science; cultural area studies (African studies, East Asia Studies, Latin American studies, modern Western Europe, Russia and East Europe studies, and South Asia studies), economics; English; French; geology; German (language, literature, culture); history; international relations; mathematics; music; music education; music history and literature; music performance; music theory–composition; music therapy; neuroscience; philosophy; physics; political science; psychology; religious studies; Russian studies; sociology; Spanish; student-designed major (e.g., journalism, sports medicine); theater and dance; urban studies; and women's, gender, and sexuality studies. In addition, minors are available in most areas as well as Chinese, education (with licensure in elementary or secondary teaching), environmental studies, film studies, international business, and physical education.

Wooster offers dual-degree programs in cooperation with other institutions; such programs lead to either two bachelor's degrees (one from each institution) or a bachelor's degree from Wooster and a master's from the cooperating institution. The dual-degree programs are in the areas of architecture, dentistry, engineering, forestry and environmental studies, nursing, polymer science, and social work.

The College also offers a preprofessional advising program to support those students who want to combine the study of liberal arts with preparation for a specific profession. The preprofessional advising programs provide students with advice on the development of an appropriate academic program, cocurricular and volunteer experiences, guidance on summer research opportunities, lectures by leaders in the various professions, and information about the process of selecting and applying to graduate and professional schools. Wooster's preprofessional programs are in the areas of architecture, business, engineering, forestry and environmental studies, heath professions, law, seminary studies, and social work.

Academic Programs

Students begin their academic journey begins with First-Year Seminar, a writing-intensive course that exercises their intellect and sharpens their critical faculties (http://www.wooster.edu/Academics). In a class of no more than 15, with a professor who is also their academic adviser, students approach a wide range of texts, questioning and analyzing them to tease out meaning and then formulating arguments through extensive writing and discussion.

To ensure that they are conversant with forms of inquiry and discourse in a range of disciplines, students select courses in each of three areas: arts and humanities, history and social sciences, and mathematical and natural sciences. They also gain insight into other cultures through a course in global and cultural perspectives and another in religious perspectives.

Once a major is selected, students engage with the scholarship of that field, master its particular methodologies, and have numerous opportunities to work with faculty members on research projects (as early as the second semester of the first year), participate in internships, or study abroad.

It all culminates in the senior Independent Study (I.S.) project. Working one-on-one with a faculty adviser over the course of a year, students conduct research, create art, or shape a performance that demonstrates their understanding of a discipline and their ability to communicate that knowledge to others. Although called Independent Study, it is a deeply collaborative journey that the student and the faculty adviser take together. In effect, students are guaranteed a 1:1 student-faculty ratio for one class each semester of their senior year. In weekly one-on-one meetings, the adviser helps refine and focus the topic, suggests areas for exploration, asks questions that provoke thought and creativity, and evaluates progress. Students, in turn, review and synthesize literature related to the subject, plan and conduct research in the lab, or work to realize a creative vision in the studio, recital hall, or theater. Students present drafts of their work to their advisers, who offer extensive thoughtful feedback as close collaborators. For more information, visit http://www.wooster.edu/Academics/Areas-of-Study/Philosophy/Independent-Study.

If the I.S. project requires travel or special equipment or supplies, the College's Henry J. Copeland Fund for Independent Study can help. In a typical year, the fund disburses almost $100,000 to support a diverse array of student projects, from studying the lives of West African immigrants in Paris or producing a documentary on survivors of Hiroshima to researching ways to purify methane gas to permit its use as a renewable energy source. When the I.S. is complete, students may find themselves presenting the results at a national conference in their discipline or coauthoring papers with their advisers. (Geology professor Mark Wilson has published articles with more than 40 student coauthors.)

Throughout the I.S. project, students learn not just about a specific topic but also about how to break down any complex project into manageable pieces, develop a plan of action, and follow it through.

Students learn how to analyze a problem, gather and evaluate information, propose a solution, test its validity, and communicate the results clearly and persuasively. The completed I.S. gives employers tangible proof of resourcefulness, creativity, and communication skills. It also marks the student as an independent scholar who is ready to take on graduate-level research wherever his or her interests lead, which is why Wooster ranks twenty-ninth overall among all liberal arts colleges for graduates who have gone on to earn a Ph.D., sixth in chemistry, ninth in the physical sciences, fifteenth in political science and public administration, and eighteenth in history.

To get a full sense of the range of possibilities, students should check out the I.S. database or listen to Wooster students talk about their projects. Go to http://www.wooster.edu/ and click on Independent Study.

Off-Campus Programs

Students who wish to enrich their undergraduate experience by overseas study may choose from a variety of fully accredited programs (http://www.wooster.edu/Academics/Areas-of-Study/Philosophy/Off-Campus-Study). Wooster sponsors a number of its own off-campus programs in the United States and abroad, and through its membership in the Great Lakes Colleges Association and its affiliations, offers off-campus study opportunities in more than fifty countries spanning the globe.

A variety of off-campus opportunities within the United States provide both academic and internship experiences. The Washington Semester and the Semester at the United Nations offer extensive possibilities in national and international government. There is also a fine-arts semester in New York City. Other internship possibilities exist in business, the humanities, the natural sciences, and psychology.

Academic Facilities

The College libraries consist of the Andrews Library, the adjacent Flo K. Gault Library for Independent Study, and the nearby Timken Science Library in Frick Hall. Together, they contain more than 1 million books, periodicals, microforms, electronic journals, videotapes, and audio recordings. As a member of CONSORT and OhioLINK, the libraries can provide almost any book from Ohio's academic libraries within two to three days. The libraries subscribe to a wide variety of electronic databases and to some 5,000 periodicals in electronic form, all available campuswide via the computing network. The libraries house more than 300 study carrels, each of which is equipped with electrical and data connections.

All academic buildings and residence hall rooms are connected to the campus network, and secure wireless service is available throughout campus. The Taylor Hall computer center houses fifty-two terminals for student use while the Wired Scot, a cyber café, features twenty-two PC workstations with Internet access and two large plasma-screen TVs.

The College's science facilities contain the most up-to-date laboratory equipment, libraries, technology, and instrumentation, including ultraviolet, visible, fluorescence, and infrared spectrometers; a scanning electron microscope; an atomic force microscope; a nuclear magnetic resonance spectrometer; a mass spectrometer; an X-ray diffractometer; and various chromatographs.

Wooster's Learning Center provides academic support for students, and priority is given to students with identified learning disabilities. Professional staff work with individual students on time management, organization skills, and effective study strategies. The Writing Center provides writing assistance through one-to-one tutorial sessions and group workshops covering all aspects of the writing process.

The Freedlander Theatre complex contains excellent technical equipment and a separate theater for students' experimental productions. The speech facility houses a radio station and a speech and hearing clinic that also serves the community.

The Scheide Music Center, a 35,000-square-foot complex, contains five classrooms, eleven teaching studios, twenty-three soundproof practice rooms, a music library, and a listening lab. The Timken Rehearsal Hall and the acoustically balanced Gault Recital Hall are "tunable" so that the halls can be rendered "live" to greater or lesser degrees.

The Ebert Art Center has expansive space for studio art and art history. The building includes classrooms, individual studios for senior studio art majors, and the Sussel and Burton D. Morgan Art Galleries.

Costs

The comprehensive fee (room, board, tuition, and fees) for 2010–11 was $45,668. More information is available at http://www.wooster.edu/Admissions-and-Financial-Aid/Tuition-and-Fees.

Financial Aid

Financial assistance is awarded on merit and/or need (http://www.wooster.edu/Admissions-and-Financial-Aid/Financial-Aid). Need-based aid is determined by the Free Application for Federal Student Aid (FAFSA). Merit aid is awarded when students are admitted to the College (http://www.wooster.edu/Admissions-and-Financial-Aid/Merit-Scholarships). Applications for need-based aid should be submitted by February 15.

The College of Wooster believes in recognizing individual talent and hard work. Thus, Wooster offers merit-based scholarships that range from $2000 to $24,000 in a number of academic, performance, and leadership areas. All scholarship awards are applicable only toward tuition and are renewable for four years. In all, the College awards more than $32 million in merit and need-based aid to admitted students each year. Students should contact the Office of Admissions to request detailed information about scholarship opportunities.

Faculty

Faculty members, 98 percent of whom hold a doctoral degree or terminal degree in their field, are dedicated to meeting the educational needs of individual students; they strive to help them realize their inherent potential. The student-faculty ratio is 11:1.

Student Government

The Campus Council, which consists of representatives from the student body, faculty, and administration, is the main legislative body in the areas of student life and cocurricular affairs. The Student Government Association, the Black Students Association, and the International Student Association also contribute to policymaking at Wooster. Students may attend open meetings of the faculty and are represented on several faculty committees.

Admission Requirements

A candidate for admission to the College should have earned a minimum of 16 academic units in high school, with emphases in English, foreign language, mathematics, natural science, and social studies. The student must present satisfactory scores on either the SAT or the ACT. No College Board Subject Test scores are required.

The deadline for regular admission is February 15. Students are notified of the decision by April 1 and must reply by May 1. Early decision applicants must apply by November 15 and are notified on December 15. Early action candidates must apply by December 15 and are notified by February 1. For more information, visit http://www.wooster.edu/Admissions-and-Financial-Aid/How-to-Apply. Students are encouraged to visit the campus and have a personal interview. To learn more, go online to http://www.wooster.edu/Admissions-and-Financial-Aid/Visiting-the-Campus.

The College of Wooster does not discriminate on the basis of age, sex, race, creed, national origin, handicap, sexual orientation, political affiliation, or veteran or military status in the admission of students or in their participation in College educational programs, activities, financial aid, or employment.

Application and Information

Office of Admissions
The College of Wooster
Wooster, Ohio 44691
Phone: 330-263-2000 Ext. 2270 or 2322
   800-877-9905 (toll-free)
Fax: 330-263-2621
E-mail: admissions@wooster.edu
Web site: http://www.wooster.edu
   http://www.facebook.com/#!/CollegeofWooster
   http://twitter.com/woosteredu

COLUMBIA UNIVERSITY
Columbia College/The Fu Foundation School of Engineering and Applied Science

NEW YORK, NEW YORK

The University

In 1754, King George II granted a charter to a group of New York citizens to found King's College, dedicated to instruction in "the Learned Languages and the Liberal Arts and Sciences." In its early days, King's College taught such students as Alexander Hamilton, John Jay, Robert Livingston, and Gouverneur Morris. After the Revolution, New York State issued the college a new charter with a more patriotic name—Columbia. In 1897, Columbia moved to a new site in Morningside Heights on the Upper West Side of Manhattan. The architectural firm of McKim, Mead and White, the preeminent architects of their day, designed an open central enclave six blocks long, with a majestic domed and colonnaded library at the center. To this day, it remains one of New York's most impressive settings.

Today, Columbia College and The Fu Foundation School of Engineering and Applied Science (Columbia Engineering) offer their students unique advantages; they are at the same time small, selective colleges and integral components of a major research university.

The College enrolls approximately 4,200 students; the Columbia Engineering student body is roughly 1,400. Students come from all fifty states and over ninety countries. They represent a dazzling array of ethnic, social, economic, cultural, religious, and geographic backgrounds. The diversity of Columbia's student body reflects the diversity of New York City, the world's most international city.

Columbia guarantees four years of on-campus housing to all entering first-year students. Ninety-five percent of undergraduates remain in University residence halls for all four years.

Columbia students take part in extracurricular groups of all kinds: artistic (theater, musical, and dance), athletic (thirty-one Division I varsity sports and dozens of club and intramural sports), communications (the *Columbia Daily Spectator,* the *Columbia Journal of Literary Criticism,* WKCR-FM, a campus television station, and many others), community service (Amnesty International, Big Brother/Big Sister programs, after-hours tutoring programs, a volunteer ambulance squad, and partnerships with dozens of hospitals, soup kitchens, and homeless shelters), and preprofessional (the Charles Drew Pre-Medical Society and the National Society of Black Engineers). Other groups represent students' ethnic, religious, political, and gender identities. There are thirty-three fraternities and sororities. Alfred Lerner Hall houses office and meeting space for student organizations, a theater, a cinema, the Center for Student Advising, and many dining options.

Location

Columbia shares its Morningside Heights neighborhood with a number of other famous institutions: Barnard College, the Cathedral of St. John the Divine, Union Theological Seminary, Jewish Theological Seminary, and the Manhattan School of Music, to name a few. Most of the faculty members from Columbia and the other surrounding schools make their homes in the neighborhood. Morningside Heights is an area known for bookstores, wonderfully varied restaurants, and merchants that cater to student tastes, student budgets, and student hours.

Students are encouraged and assisted in making full use of New York's breathtaking variety of cultural, recreational, and professional resources. Through the Columbia University Arts Initiative, students can receive discounted tickets to Broadway shows, film screenings, art galleries, and a multitude of cultural events in New York City. Passport to NYC offers students free access to thirty museums throughout the city. Columbia students can be found any day of the week exploring the Metropolitan Museum of Art, the Museum of Modern Art, the Guggenheim Museum, the Museum of African Art, the Museo del Barrio, the Asia Society, or any other of the city's hundreds of museums and galleries. Any evening, they might be discovering the theatrical offerings on, off, or "off-off" Broadway (or on campus); attending the opera, ballet, or symphony at Lincoln Center; taking in a movie on campus or in one of New York's 400-plus cinemas; enjoying jazz in Greenwich Village or blues at the Apollo; sampling *pai gwat* in Chinatown; or biking or boating in Central Park. Columbia's internship programs offer students opportunities to explore a career possibility in depth; nowhere else in the world does the concentration of industries allow such a range of possibilities. New York's public transportation system puts the entire city within easy reach of Columbia students; the campus is directly served by a subway line and five bus routes.

Majors and Degrees

Columbia College grants the B.A. degree in approximately ninety programs of study in the humanities, social sciences, and pure sciences, including many interdisciplinary majors. Columbia Engineering grants the B.S. degree in more than fifteen engineering fields. A five-year program that begins in either school allows students to receive both a B.A. from Columbia College and a B.S. from Columbia Engineering.

Joint degree programs offer selected students the opportunity to combine their undergraduate work with study in Columbia University's schools of law and international affairs and with the Juilliard School.

Academic Programs

Columbia has maintained a coherent and relevant curriculum since the time of the First World War, when it introduced the renowned Core Curriculum, a program of general education that has served as a model for hundreds of colleges around the country. One of the two oldest courses in the core is Contemporary Civilization, a year-long historical survey of Western Civilization's religious, political, and moral philosophies; the second is Literature Humanities, a year-long introduction to western culture's most seminal and meaningful literary works. A second year of humanities offers a semester each of music and art appreciation, encouraging students to experience the cultural treasures of New York City. The Global Core requirement enlarges the scope of inquiry beyond the Western focus in order to promote learning and thought about the variety of cultures and the diversity of traditions that interact in the United States and the world today. The Frontiers of Science course outlines the approaches that scientists take to answer interesting problems in the natural world and introduces students to scientific research methods. The Core Curriculum exposes Columbia's multicultural student body to a variety of disciplines, preparing them for the complex questions and issues of modern society.

The strength of Columbia Engineering education is in its uniquely broad curriculum, preparing students not only to be world-class engineers, but also to be global leaders across industries. In addition to taking rigorous math and science courses typically offered at top undergraduate programs, Columbia Engineering students are also required to take courses in the liberal arts alongside their college counterparts, providing them with interdisciplinary tools for real-world problem solving. This type of broad academic exposure is what alumni often cite as the foundation of their later academic and professional success. Another hallmark of the Columbia Engineering education is the first-year design class, the country's only required, hands-on, community-based learning course. Teams of students work with nonprofit and community organizations to solve actual engineering design problems, both locally and around the globe. For example, first-year students have worked at a New York City nursing home to design a non-weight-bearing walker for its residents and in Guatemala to design a wind turbine system.

Off-Campus Programs

Columbia students, with the help of an adviser, may choose from 150 study-abroad programs on every continent, many of which are Columbia-specific programs.

Columbia maintains several undergraduate programs at Reid Hall, its Paris campus. Courses at Reid Hall are quite varied, permitting students to work not only in the areas of French language, literature, and culture but also in several other fields throughout the range of the humanities and social sciences. In addition, a yearlong program includes course work in the French university system.

Columbia was the first U.S. college to offer an integrated year-abroad program with the Universities of Oxford and Cambridge. Other programs allow students to work at the University of Kyoto in Japan or at the Free University of Berlin in Germany.

Academic Facilities

Columbia has the eighth-largest research library system in North America, consisting of 9.5 million volumes and 26 million manuscripts within 3,000 collections. Included in the twenty-five libraries are collections of particular significance, such as those of the Avery Architectural and Fine Arts Library, the Starr East Asian Library, the Rare Book and Manuscript Library, and the Burke Library of Union Theological Seminary. All divisions are open to Columbia undergraduates. Columbia University Information Technology has five mainframe computers used for academic research and instruction as well as clusters of microcomputers, terminals, and printers; it has remote units and terminals all over campus, including in residence halls, to guarantee accessibility. The brand-new Northwest Corner Building houses cutting-edge labs that bring together researchers in biology, chemistry, physics, and engineering, as well as a science library, lecture hall, and café. Students may also make use of an electronic music lab, a cyclotron, an oral history collection, the facilities and programs of the Lamont-Doherty Earth Observatory, and oceanographic research ships. Construction recently began on the new Interdisciplinary Science Building, fourteen stories housing classrooms, research space, a café, and a new science library.

Costs

Tuition for the 2010–11 academic year was $41,160. Room and board for all first-year students were $10,570. With typical fees, books, and supplies, the total cost of a year at Columbia was approximately $57,192.

Financial Aid

All first-year candidates who are U.S. citizens or have U.S. permanent resident or political refugee status, are considered for admission without regard to their financial need. International students who do not fit into the above categories should be aware that their admissions process is not need-blind; their financial need is taken into account at the time of admission. Regardless of citizenship, Columbia meets the full demonstrated need of every student admitted as a first-year for all four years of study. Columbia has eliminated loans for all students receiving financial aid and replaced them with University grant money. Parental contributions have also been significantly reduced for a large portion of students receiving financial aid. Prospective students should go to http://www.studentaffairs.columbia.edu/finaid/ for information on specific requirements and deadlines. All financial aid at Columbia is based on need; no aid is given in the form of academic, athletic, artistic, or other merit awards. The Office of Financial Aid and Educational Financing believes that cost should not be a barrier to students pursuing their educational dreams.

Faculty

The student-to-faculty ratio is 6:1. Core curriculum classes are capped at 22 students, and almost 80 percent of classes have 20 students or less. The Columbia faculty is committed to both teaching and research, and all faculty members teach undergraduates, even the president of the University. All faculty members maintain office hours, and each student receives a faculty adviser from the department that he or she chooses as a major.

Student Government

Each undergraduate division has its own student council and elects representatives to the Columbia University Senate.

Admission Requirements

The Columbia first-year class of 1,389 students is selected from a much larger pool of applicants through a holistic, committee-based review process. Candidates for admission are expected to demonstrate the necessary ability and interest to do successful college work in a variety of disciplines as required for the Columbia degree. The following secondary school preparation is recommended: 4 years of English, including meaningful work in literature and writing; 3 (preferably 4) years of mathematics, including precalculus and calculus where offered; 3 (preferably 4) years of history and social studies; 3 or more years of the same foreign language; and 3 (preferably 4) years of laboratory science (including chemistry and physics where available). The Admissions Committee recognizes that secondary schools vary in offerings and standards; consideration is given to applicants whose preparations differ from the recommended course of study but have taken advantage of what their schools offer.

Standardized tests are required for admission, according to the following guidelines. Students may take the SAT, which consists of three sections, each graded on an 800-point scale. Students who take the test more than once are evaluated on the highest score they receive in any individual section. Applicants may alternately take the ACT, which is graded on a 36-point scale. Students taking the test more than once are evaluated on the highest composite score they receive. The writing component of the ACT is mandatory for candidates for Columbia.

In addition to either the SAT or ACT, students must also take two SAT Subject Tests. For Columbia College, they may take any two tests; for The Fu Foundation School of Engineering and Applied Science, they must take any mathematics test and either the physics or the chemistry test.

Students who attend a school that does not give conventional grades or who are homeschooled must take two additional SAT Subject Tests in addition to all requirements outlined above for Columbia College or The Fu Foundation School of Engineering and Applied Science.

It is absolutely imperative that applicants have the testing service report their standardized test scores directly to either Columbia College (SAT code 2116, ACT code 2717) or The Fu Foundation School of Engineering and Applied Science (SAT code 2111, ACT code 2719), as appropriate.

Transfer students may enter Columbia in September only.

The College has a Visiting Students Program, which allows students to attend for one or both semesters of their sophomore, junior, or senior year.

Application and Information

Columbia utilizes the Common Application and requires the Columbia University Supplement. The postmark deadline for regular decision applications is January 1. Candidates are notified of the Admissions Committee's decisions on or about April 1. Admitted candidates must respond to Columbia's offer of admission by May 1. Candidates for whom Columbia is their definite first choice may apply under the early decision plan; the deadline is November 1 for all application material, and a decision is rendered by December 15. Candidates admitted to Columbia under early decision are required to withdraw their applications to other colleges. The application fee is $80. The fee may be waived if a school official testifies that the fee would cause the candidate's family financial hardship. For further information, interested students should contact:

Office of Undergraduate Admissions
Columbia University
1130 Amsterdam Avenue, MC2807
New York, New York 10027
Phone: 212-854-2522
Fax: 212-854-1209
E-mail: ugrad-ask@columbia.edu
Web site: http://www.studentaffairs.columbia.edu/admissions
http://www.facebook.com/columbiaadmissions

COLUMBIA UNIVERSITY, SCHOOL OF GENERAL STUDIES

NEW YORK, NEW YORK

The University and The School

The School of General Studies (GS) of Columbia University is one of the finest liberal arts colleges in the United States created specifically for returning and nontraditional students seeking a rigorous, traditional, Ivy League undergraduate degree full- or part-time. Most students at GS have, for personal or professional reasons, interrupted their education, never attended college, or are only able to attend part-time. GS is unique among colleges of its type, because its students are fully integrated into the Columbia undergraduate curriculum: they take the same courses with the same faculty members and earn the same degree as all other Columbia undergraduates.

GS students come from varied backgrounds and all walks of life. Many students work full-time while pursuing a degree, and many have family responsibilities; others attend classes full-time and experience Columbia's more traditional college life. In the classroom, the diversity and varied personal experience of the student body promote discussion and debate, fostering an environment of academic rigor and intellectual development. GS has approximately 1,400 undergraduate degree candidates and more than 400 premedical students. The average age of a GS student is 29. More than 60 percent of GS students attend classes full-time.

In addition to its bachelor's degree program, GS offers combined undergraduate/graduate degree programs with Columbia's Schools of Social Work, International and Public Affairs, Law, Business, Dental Medicine, Teachers College, and the College of Physicians and Surgeons. More than 70 percent of the students go on to earn advanced degrees after graduation.

GS is home to the oldest and largest postbaccalaureate premedical program in the United States. In recent years, the acceptance rate for GS Postbaccalaureate Premedical program students applying to U.S. medical schools is up to 90 percent.

Location

Columbia University is located in Morningside Heights, on the Upper West Side of Manhattan. The University's neighbors include the Union Theological Seminary, the Jewish Theological Seminary, the Manhattan School of Music, St. Luke's Hospital, Riverside Church, and the Cathedral of St. John the Divine. The diversity of intellectual and social activities offered by these institutions is one of Columbia's great assets as a university; another is New York City itself, which offers Columbia students a rich and almost boundless variety of social, cultural, and recreational opportunities that are themselves an education.

Majors and Degrees

The School of General Studies grants the B.A. and B.S. degrees and offers more than seventy majors and concentrations, which include: African studies; African American studies; American studies; ancient studies; anthropology; applied mathematics; archaeology; architecture; architecture, history and theory; art history; art history–visual arts; Asian American studies; astronomy; astrophysics; biochemistry; biology; biophysics; chemical physics; chemistry; classical studies; classics; comparative ethnic studies; comparative literature and society; computer science; computer science–mathematics; creative writing; dance; drama and theater arts; earth science; East Asian studies; East Central European studies; economics; economics–mathematics; economics–operations research; economics–philosophy; economics–political science; economics–statistics; English and comparative literature; environmental biology; environmental chemistry; environmental science; evolutionary biology of the human species; film studies; financial economics; French; French and Francophone studies; German literature and cultural history; Hispanic studies; history; information science; Italian cultural studies; Italian literature; Latin American and Caribbean studies; Latino studies; mathematics; mathematics–statistics; Middle

Eastern, South Asian, and African studies; music; neuroscience and behavior; philosophy; physics; political science; political science–statistics; psychology; regional studies; religion; Russian language and culture; Russian literature and culture; Slavic studies; sociology; statistics; urban studies; visual arts; women's and gender studies; and Yiddish studies. Individually designed majors are also available.

In addition, Columbia University School of General Studies offers undergraduate dual-degree programs with the Columbia School of Engineering and Applied Science, the Jewish Theological Seminary, and the Dual B.A. program between the French university Sciences Po and Columbia University. The Dual B.A. program is an intensive, transatlantic course of study; undergraduate students earn a Bachelor of Arts from Sciences Po and Columbia University. Students will spend two years at one of three Sciences Po campuses, each of which is devoted to a particular region of the world and offers a heavy linguistic and cultural focus. After two years, students will matriculate at Columbia University School of General Studies in New York City to complete the interdisciplinary liberal arts curriculum. Admission to the program is highly competitive, and high school seniors are eligible to apply.

Academic Programs

The School of General Studies offers a traditional liberal arts education designed to provide students with the broad knowledge and intellectual skills that foster continued education and growth in the years after college as well as providing a sound foundation for positions of responsibility in the professional world.

Requirements for the bachelor's degree comprise three elements: (1) core requirements, intended to develop in students the ability to write and communicate clearly; to understand the modes of thought that characterize the humanities, social sciences, and sciences; to gain familiarity with central cultural ideas through literature, fine arts, and music; and to acquire a working proficiency in a foreign language; (2) major requirements, designed to give students sustained and coherent exposure to a particular discipline in an area of strong intellectual interest; and (3) elective courses, in which students pursue particular interests and skills for their own personal growth or for their relationship to future professional or personal objectives. Students are required to complete a minimum of 124 credits for the bachelor's degree; 60 of these may be in transfer credit, but at least 64 credits (including the last 30 credits) must be completed at Columbia. In addition to the usual graduation honors (cum laude, magna cum laude, and summa cum laude), honors programs for superior students are available in a majority of the University's departments.

Off-Campus Programs

Columbia students may enhance their academic experiences through various study-abroad programs around the world. For example, students may spend a term at the Reid Hall Program in the Montparnasse district of Paris, the Berlin Consortium for German Studies, the Kyoto Consortium for Japanese Studies, or the Language Program in Beijing, China. In addition, students may apply to participate in one of the Columbia-approved study-abroad programs located in countries around the world.

Academic Facilities

The Columbia University Libraries constitute the nation's sixth-largest academic library system, with a collection of more than 10.4 million volumes, more than 6 million microform pieces, 26 million manuscript items, and 900,000 rare books. Of the twenty-two libraries in the system, five are designated Distinctive Collections because of their unusual depth and nationally recognized excellence. All library divisions are available to GS students. The University's Computer Center is one of the largest and most powerful university installations in the world and has remote units and terminals in several parts of the campus to enhance its accessibility. The Fairchild Life Sciences Building houses research facilities, laboratories, electron microscopes, and a vast amount of biochemical equipment used for teaching and research. The University's physics building has been the scene of many important developments in the recent history of physics, including the invention of the laser and the first U.S. demonstration of nuclear fission.

Costs

For the 2010–11 academic year, tuition was $1330 per credit, and annual living (room and board) and personal expenses (books, local commuting costs, and miscellaneous expenses) were $20,985.

Financial Aid

The School of General Studies awards financial aid based upon need and academic ability. Approximately 70 percent of GS degree candidates receive some form of financial aid, including Federal Pell Grants, New York State TAP Grants, Federal Stafford and unsubsidized Stafford Loans, Federal Perkins Loans, General Studies Scholarships, and Federal Work-Study Program awards. Priority application deadlines for new students are June 1 for the fall semester and October 15 for the spring semester. The average scholarship award ranges from $6500 to $8000 for first-year students.

Faculty

Students in the School of General Studies take courses with professors who are members of the Columbia University Faculty of Arts and Sciences. These distinguished scholars in virtually every discipline also teach in Columbia College, the Graduate School of Arts and Sciences, and the School of International and Public Affairs. Full-time and part-time students have many opportunities to work closely with faculty members, both in small classes and in research projects. Faculty members also serve as advisers to students majoring in their area of study and maintain regular office hours to see students.

Student Government

One student of the School represents GS students in the University Senate, a decision-making body comprising students, faculty members, and administrative staff members from each division of the University. In addition, 2 GS students sit as voting members on the Committee on Instruction, which oversees the curriculum of the School. The General Studies Student Council elects officers each year and sponsors activities for students. *The Observer*, the School's student-run magazine, is published several times each year. The Premedical Association (PMA) sponsors events related to the medical school admissions process.

Admission Requirements

The GS admission policy is geared to the maturity and varied backgrounds of its students. Aptitude and motivation are considered along with past academic performance, standardized test scores, and employment history. The School's admission decisions are based on a careful review of each application and reflect the Admissions Committee's considered judgment of the applicant's maturity, academic potential, and present ability to undertake course work at Columbia.

Admission requirements include a completed application form; a 1,500- to 2,000-word autobiographical statement describing the applicant's past educational history and work experience, present situation, and future plans; two letters of recommendation from academic or professional evaluators; an official high school transcript; official transcripts from all colleges and universities attended; official SAT or ACT scores (applicants may take the General Studies Admissions Examination); and a nonrefundable application fee of $75.

Students from outside the United States may apply to the School of General Studies to start or complete a baccalaureate degree. In addition to the materials described above, international applicants must submit official TOEFL scores or take the Columbia University American Language Program Essay Exam.

Application and Information

Application deadlines are March 1 for early action (nonbinding), and June 1 for the fall semester, October 1 for early action (nonbinding), and November 1 for the spring semester, and April 1 for the summer semester. Applicants from countries outside the U.S. are urged to apply by August 15 for the spring semester and April 1 for the fall semester. Applications are reviewed as they are completed, and applicants are notified of decisions shortly thereafter.

For more information, students should contact:

Curtis M. Rodgers, Dean of Enrollment Management
Office of Admissions and Financial Aid
School of General Studies
408 Lewisohn Hall
2970 Broadway
Columbia University, Mail Code 4101
New York, New York 10027

Phone: 212-854-2772
E-mail: gsdegree@columbia.edu
Web site: http://www.gs.columbia.edu
    http://facebook.com/ColumbiaGS
    http://www.twitter.com/ColumbiaGS
    http://www.youtube.com/GSColumbia

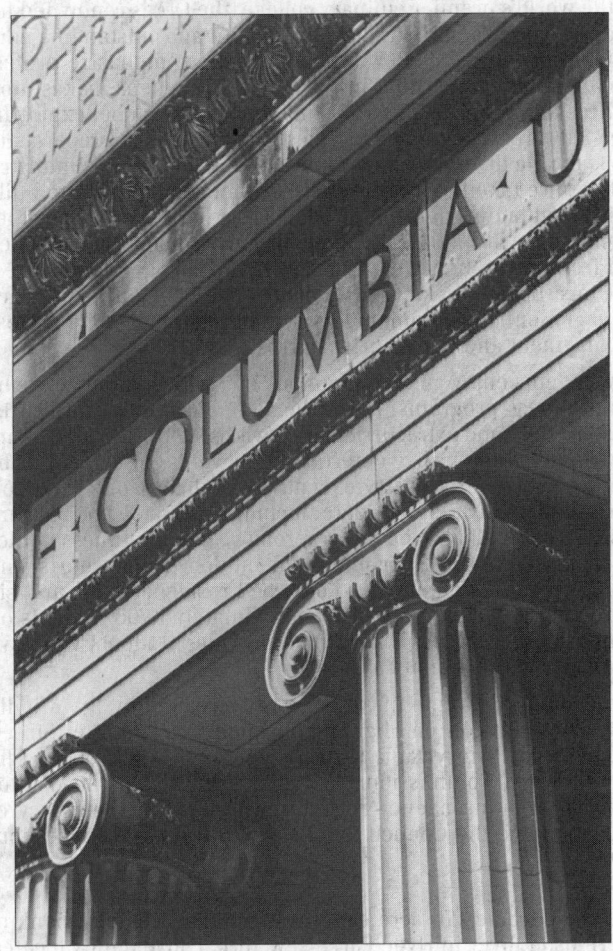

The Low Memorial Library/Visitors Center.

THE CULINARY INSTITUTE OF AMERICA

HYDE PARK, NEW YORK

THE WORLD'S PREMIER
CULINARY COLLEGE

The Institute

The Culinary Institute of America (CIA) is a private, not-for-profit college dedicated to providing the world's best undergraduate education in culinary arts and baking and pastry arts. Guided by its core values of excellence, leadership, professionalism, ethics, and respect for diversity, the CIA strives to foster an atmosphere where students can develop both professionally and personally. At the CIA, aspiring culinarians gain the general knowledge and specific skills they need to grow into positions of leadership in the foodservice and hospitality industry, the largest private employer in the United States.

Founded in 1946, The Culinary Institute of America today enrolls more than 2,800 students from virtually every state and thirty countries around the world, all united by their shared passion for food. The CIA student body has a balance of recent high school graduates and adults returning to higher education.

As the world's premier culinary college, the CIA is renowned for its degree programs, extraordinary faculty, and outstanding educational facilities. All CIA degree programs emphasize professional, hands-on learning in the college's kitchens, bakeshops, and restaurants. CIA classes span the culinary globe, exploring great cultures, cooking techniques, and cuisines to prepare students for the diversity and creativity of the foodservice industry. Classes are taken in a progressive sequence optimized to build skills, food knowledge, and production experience. These studies culminate in operations courses that give students both kitchen and front-of-the-house experiences in the college's famous restaurants. Bachelor's degree students also focus on foodservice management development, with a broad range of business management and liberal arts courses.

CIA students enjoy an active campus life, with a variety of year-round fitness programs, intercollegiate and intramural sports, student clubs, and extracurricular activities such as ski and camping trips, on-campus live entertainment events, presentations by leading chefs and industry executives, and cook-offs. The college's Student Recreation Center includes a six-lane pool, a gymnasium, racquetball courts, an aerobics studio, a fitness center and free-weight room, a game room, outdoor tennis courts, and the Courtside Café and Pub. Four coed residence halls and six Adirondack-style lodges house approximately 1,700 students on campus. The college's dining plan provides students with two meals per instructional day.

The Culinary Institute of America is accredited by the Middle States Commission on Higher Education, 3624 Market Street, Philadelphia, Pennsylvania 19104 (telephone: 215-662-5000). The Middle States Commission on Higher Education is an institutional accrediting agency recognized by the U.S. Secretary of Education and the Council for Higher Education Accreditation.

Location

The CIA's scenic 170-acre campus is set along the east bank of the Hudson River in Hyde Park, New York, conveniently located 1½–2 hours from New York City and Albany.

The Mid-Hudson region's attractions and recreational opportunities offer something for everyone in both rural and urban settings. There are a number of state parks and historic sites throughout the area. Students can taste wines at local vineyards, visit farmer's markets, and pick apples at nearby orchards. To the west lie the Catskill and Shawangunk Mountains, with many opportunities for hiking, skiing, rock climbing, mountain biking,

and sightseeing. Concerts, plays, films, and other cultural and special events are offered regularly at the many colleges, theaters, and community facilities throughout the Hudson Valley and Catskill regions. In addition, students can take advantage of the campus's proximity to New York City to experience the culture, arts, and nightlife of this exciting city and food mecca.

Majors and Degrees

The Culinary Institute of America awards the degree of Bachelor of Professional Studies (B.P.S.) in baking and pastry arts management and in culinary arts management, as well as the degree of Associate in Occupational Studies (A.O.S.) in baking and pastry arts and in culinary arts.

Academic Programs

At the core of The Culinary Institute of America's curriculum lies more than 1,300 hours of hands-on instruction in its kitchens and bakeshops as well as classes developing the managerial skills and creative thinking that today's culinary professional requires. Students learn about foods, cooking and baking techniques, cuisines, and business fundamentals while advancing through skills and production kitchens. They also gain invaluable experience in a paid externship program and by cooking and serving in the college's bakery café or in some of the four fine-dining public restaurants on campus. Bachelor's degree students also take courses in marketing, communications, psychology, foreign languages and cultures, accounting and the use of computers in the food business, and financial and human resources management.

Students must earn 132 total credits in culinary arts management or in baking and pastry arts management to graduate with a bachelor's degree. Students must earn 69 total credits in culinary arts or in baking and pastry arts to graduate with an associate degree.

Off-Campus Programs

All students work in externships for a minimum of eighteen weeks (600 hours). These externships provide students with valuable on-the-job experience at one of more than 1,200 top foodservice and hospitality properties—such as hotels, restaurants, and resorts—around the world. Bachelor's degree students also participate in a travel seminar to one of a number of exciting destination choices—Northern and Southern California, the Pacific Northwest, Spain, Italy, China, and France—where they can learn from local purveyors and visit area restaurants, wineries, and vineyards.

Academic Facilities

CIA students learn the fundamentals of the culinary and baking and pastry arts in the college's forty-one professionally equipped production kitchens and bakeshops and five student-staffed public restaurants on campus—the American Bounty Restaurant, Escoffier Restaurant, Ristorante Caterina de' Medici, St. Andrew's Café, and Apple Pie Bakery Café. Classes are centered in the college's main building, Roth Hall, as well as in the Shunsuke Takaki School of Baking and Pastry, General Foods Nutrition Center, and Colavita Center for Italian Food and Wine. The CIA regularly hosts world-renowned chefs for lectures, cooking demonstrations, and discussions with students in its Danny Kaye Theatre, Anheuser-Busch Theatre, and Ecolab Theatre. Other valuable academic resources include the 84,000-volume Conrad N. Hilton Library, which contains the largest culinary collection of any culinary school; audiovisual programs to supplement course work; computer labs and workstations; and a wireless network that allows students to access online resources from almost anywhere on campus.

Costs

Freshman tuition for academic year 2011–12 is $24,990. Board is $1295 per semester, which includes two meals per instructional day. Housing costs range from $2165 to $3800 per semester, depending on the room to which the student is assigned.

Additional required fees for the freshman year include a confirmation fee of $100, equipment fees of $1780 for culinary supplies or $1680 for baking and pastry supplies, and a general fee of $595 per semester, which includes student activity and exam fees, as well as secondary student accident insurance. The CIA offers students a tuition installment plan. Details are available from the college's Bursar's Office.

Financial Aid

Approximately 90 percent of the CIA's students receive financial aid in the form of scholarships, grants, loans, and work-study. Federal programs offered at the college include the Federal Pell Grant, Federal Supplemental Educational Opportunity Grant (FSEOG), Federal Subsidized Stafford Loan, Federal Unsubsidized Stafford Loan, Federal Perkins Loan, Federal Work-Study Program (which provides a variety of on-campus and community service jobs to eligible students), Federal PLUS, and veterans' benefits. Students should also investigate their own state's programs and apply if those grants or scholarships can be used in New York State.

Students who have applied for admission or who are currently enrolled at the CIA may apply for scholarships offered by various organizations in the foodservice industry. A list of these scholarships, which are administered by the college, is available from the Financial Aid Office.

Faculty

The college's faculty is composed of more than 140 chefs and instructors from sixteen countries whose credentials and industry experience are unmatched in culinary education. The 18:1 student-faculty ratio in hands-on classes provides student support and mentoring, while giving students the opportunity to work in an environment closely representative of the foodservice industry.

Student Government

All students in good standing are members of the Student Government Association (SGA). The association's Executive Board acts as a liaison between students and the administration. The SGA helps support student activities and funds all student clubs and committees.

Admission Requirements

The Admissions Committee seeks candidates who have demonstrated a commitment to a culinary career and who have the personal initiative, confidence, and motivation to succeed. The basic requirements are successful completion of a secondary school education or its equivalent and some experience in the foodservice and hospitality industry. The applicant's educational record is evaluated on the basis of overall performance and the type of program taken. Academics and leadership ability are key requirements for the bachelor's degree program. SATs or ACTs are strongly recommended but not required.

Preference is given to candidates who have worked in foodservice, particularly in a kitchen that offers a varied menu. Before entering the program, students should have had six months of hands-on food preparation experience in a professional kitchen or bakery working with fresh ingredients, for at least 10–15 hours a week. Candidates do not need this experience to apply for admission—the requirement must be met before they enter the CIA.

Applicants must submit a formal application for admission, a nonrefundable $50 application fee, an official secondary school transcript (not a student copy), an essay of between 400 and 500 words, and an official college transcript, if applicable. Students applying directly from high school may include an optional secondary school report. In addition, associate-degree candidates must provide one recommendation, and bachelor's applicants must provide two. Bachelor's degree candidates must also participate in an on-campus or telephone interview.

Application and Information

Students may apply for admission to the CIA year-round, as the college offers multiple enrollment seasons from which to choose. Applicants should submit their materials according to the enrollment schedule (available at the Web site listed below) that corresponds to the season they are interested in beginning the degree program. Students are notified of an admission decision according to that schedule. For information, to schedule a tour, or to participate in an Open House program, students should contact:

Admissions Office
The Culinary Institute of America
1946 Campus Drive
Hyde Park, New York 12538-1499

Phone: 800-CULINARY (toll-free)
E-mail: admissions@culinary.edu
Web site: http://www.ciachef.edu

Set along the banks of the Hudson River, The Culinary Institute of America campus lies on 170 scenic acres in historic Hyde Park, New York.

CURRY COLLEGE
MILTON, MASSACHUSETTS

The College

The mission of Curry College, a private institution, is to develop liberally educated persons who are able to gain and to apply knowledge humanely, intelligently, and effectively in a complex, changing world. To achieve its mission, Curry College promotes individual intellectual and social growth by engaging its students in achieving these educational goals: thinking critically, communicating effectively, understanding context, appreciating aesthetic experience, defining a personal identity, examining value systems, and adapting and innovating. The College's curriculum and programs focus on the two hallmarks of the Curry education: a high respect for the individuality of every student and a developmental approach to learning that maximizes opportunities for achievement. One-on-one faculty-student relationships provide many opportunities for personalized instruction and close interaction. Full student counseling and other support services are provided.

The current undergraduate enrollment is 2,000 men and women. Curry students have access to a wide range of cocurricular activities, including the Student Government Association, the student-run newspaper, the yearbook, the *Curry Arts Journal,* several organizations for the performing arts, and the award-winning, student-run radio station. The Office of Student Activities and the Campus Activities Board provide a variety of special events. A full schedule of men's and women's Division III and intramural sports is also provided. Varsity sports for men are baseball, basketball, football, ice hockey, lacrosse, soccer, and tennis; women's varsity sports are basketball, cross-country, lacrosse, soccer, softball, and tennis.

Now well into its second century of providing distinguished educational service, Curry College was founded in Boston in 1879. It was named in honor of its founders, Samuel Silas Curry and Anna Baright Curry. The College moved to its present site in Milton in 1952. In 1974, it absorbed the Perry Normal School, and, in 1977, it entered into a collaborative relationship with Children's Hospital Medical Center, which resulted in the establishment of Curry's Division of Nursing Studies. Curry College is accredited by the New England Association of Schools and Colleges; the nursing program is accredited by the National League for Nursing Accrediting Commission. Curry also offers four masters degree programs, which include a Master of Education (M.Ed.), an M.A. in criminal justice, an M.S. in nursing and a Master of Business Administration (M.B.A.).

Location

Curry is ideally situated in Milton, Massachusetts, a largely residential suburb located near the exceptional resources of Boston. The greater Boston area provides students with a diversity of cultural, educational, recreational, and sports activities. A wide variety of corporations, hospitals, agencies, broadcasting stations, and schools provide excellent internship and job opportunities for Curry students. The College operates a shuttle bus to the MBTA trains, which provide easy access to Boston. Curry students have the benefit of a traditional, wooded New England campus and access to the excitement of a large city.

Majors and Degrees

Curry College awards the following Bachelor of Arts (B.A.) degrees : biology; child, youth, and community education; communication (with concentrations in corporate communication, film studies, journalism, public communication, public relations, radio broadcasting, relational communication, television/digital video, and theater); criminal justice; early childhood education; elementary education; English (with concentrations in American studies, creative writing, literary genre and movements, traditional literary heritage, journalism, professional writing, and women in literature); environmental science; graphic design; information technology; management (with concentrations in accounting, entrepreneurship, finance,

human resources, marketing, residential property management, and sports management); philosophy; politics and history; psychology (with a concentrations in counseling, developmental psychology, gerontology, health, and substance-abuse counseling); sociology (with concentrations in ethnic and gender studies and service in the community); special education; and visual arts (with a concentration in studio arts). Curry College awards the following Bachelor of Science (B.S.) degrees: health and nursing. Special minors are available in numerous areas, including applied computing, dance, music, religion, Spanish, Web development, women's studies, and writing to name a few. Provision is also made for students to design majors in areas in which they have a special interest.

Academic Programs

A central liberal arts curriculum, which is required for all students, incorporates a variety of academic disciplines into every student's plan of study. Curry's programs also integrate theoretical classroom learning with a wide variety of field internships in the greater Boston area.

Curry College operates on a two-semester calendar with a summer session. To graduate, students must complete at least 120 credit hours for a B.A. degree or B.S. degree. In both cases, a minimum 2.0 cumulative average must be achieved.

Curry allows students to gain advanced standing in a variety of ways: through successful scores on College-Level Examination Program (CLEP) tests, through credit earned at other accredited colleges and universities, and through end-of-course proficiency examinations. Credit may also be granted for experiential education, such as internships, that have occurred outside the traditional academic environment.

Many academic programs enrich and facilitate the Curry education. The First Year Seminar, the Honors Program, the Women's Studies Program, the Essential Skills Center, and the Field Experience Program are representative of that focus on special interests and diverse learning needs.

The Program for Advancement of Learning (PAL) is a credited program designed to help intelligent, motivated, language-based learning-disabled students to achieve at the college level. PAL provides individual or small-group instruction, textbooks on tape, and untimed examinations, as well as a variety of other applied technologies. Students must apply to the PAL program in order to take advantage of PAL's services. Students receive credit for enrollment in the program for the first year and are able to continue in the program as long as needed.

Off-Campus Programs

Curry students may earn up to 30 credit hours for field internships with outside firms, agencies, radio stations, hospitals, schools, or similar organizations. In consultation with faculty members, students develop learning contracts that articulate their educational and personal goals and establish criteria for the evaluation of their field experience. Students may also arrange to study abroad or at another institution within the United States while enrolled at Curry.

Academic Facilities

The Levin Memorial Library houses more than 110,000 volumes, 650 periodicals, and 10,000 microforms. It is a designated depository for U.S. government documents. The library also houses the Essential Skills Center, where students may secure assistance in reading, writing, mathematics, and the development of study skills. Three computer laboratories contain more than 100 Macintosh and IBM computers, laser printers, color printers, and state-of-the-art optical scanning equipment. The entire campus is networked and linked to the Internet. The library is also home to the Educational Technology Center, which is a host of resources and materials for all of the Education students.

The Science Building includes five laboratories while the Kennedy Academic Center houses a simulated hospital room for use as a nursing laboratory; the Nursing Resource Center, which is equipped with an interactive video lab; and a laboratory for experimental psychology equipped with biofeedback, computer control, and animal and human learning facilities. The Learning Center, with its own computer lab, maintains a complete tape library of all textbooks used at the College. The Hafer Academic Center houses the Experiential Education Office; the Career Planning and Placement Office; the Academic Advising Office; the Hirsh Communication Center, which features a state-of-the-art television studio; and the Parent's Lounge, which hosts student art exhibits. In addition, Curry students operate and maintain WMLN-FM, the College's 172-watt radio station.

The Academic and Performance Center is a three-story, 30,000-square-foot facility that features a 250-seat multipurpose auditorium, state-of-the-art classrooms equipped with wireless laptop connectivity and Smart Board technology, breakout conference rooms, a stock-trading classroom, and a café-style food court in the main atrium.

In the fall of 2009, Curry College opened a new student center. The 84,000-square-foot facility is full of state-of-the-art areas for dining, studying, athletics, student activities, or simply lounging around. The student center has become a place to study between classes, to meet up with friends for dinner, work out, or even take on your roommate in a game of billiards or foosball.

Costs

Tuition for the 2011–12 academic year is $30,700. Room and board are $12,285 (based on a fourteen-meal plan). The cost of the Program for Advancement of Learning (PAL) is $6550. The cost of books, supplies, and personal expenses varies from $900 to $1200.

Financial Aid

Curry provides financial assistance for students who need funding in order to attend college. The financial aid program consists of federal, state, and Curry College scholarships, grants, work-study awards, student assistant jobs, and loans. Approximately 70 percent of the student body receives financial aid. All students applying for financial aid must submit the Free Application for Federal Student Aid (FAFSA) by March 1. Students applying for financial aid should contact the financial aid office.

Faculty

There are 113 full-time faculty members at Curry, about half of whom hold earned doctoral degrees. In addition, each year the College hires highly qualified part-time faculty members and visiting lecturers to augment its teaching staff. Although primarily a teaching faculty, many of Curry's faculty members are engaged in writing, research, and consulting.

Student Government

The general purpose of the Student Government Association (SGA) is the advancement of the College community and the promotion of the general welfare of the students. The SGA seeks to increase student involvement in the formulation of College policies, communicate effectively with all constituencies of the College, and promote student participation within the institution. Members of the SGA serve on the Joint Committee on Communication of the Board of Trustees.

Admission Requirements

Curry College accepts all students who have the necessary preparation and educational background to meet the requirements of the College, regardless of race, religion, national or ethnic origin, age, sex, sexual orientation, or physical handicap. Freshman students are selected on the basis of a combination of the following: secondary school record, scores on the SAT or ACT, recommendation of the secondary school, and the candidate's readiness for college. To be considered for admission, students must generally present at least 16 units of high school work, preferably at the college preparatory level, from an approved secondary school. A recommended program of studies includes: 4 years of English, at least 3 years of mathematics, 2 years of a foreign language, 2 years of science (including at least 1 of a laboratory science), and 2 years of social studies. Applicants should contact the Admission Office to discuss any possible exceptions to these requirements. A GED certificate is acceptable in lieu of a high school diploma. Curry College seeks well-rounded students who can contribute to the Curry community in athletic, artistic, and social endeavors as well as in the academic sphere.

Application and Information

Curry's recommended application deadline is April 1; however, Curry operates on a rolling admission basis. Admission options, such as early decision, deferred entrance, and advanced placement, are also available. Students may apply for September or January entrance. Applicants for the nursing program may only apply for the fall semester. Applicants must submit an application and fee, an official high school transcript, scores from the SAT or ACT, and a counselor's recommendation. In addition, transfer students must submit official college transcripts, along with a College Official's Report form. If English is not the primary language of the applicant, then results of the Test of English as a Foreign Language (TOEFL) must be submitted. An interview is optional but not required. The Admission Committee evaluates each application as soon as all required credentials are received, beginning in January.

Applicants to the Program for Advancement of Learning (PAL) must submit a completed application by March 1. In addition to the criteria listed above, PAL applicants must submit the results of a recently administered Wechsler Adult Intelligence Scale (WAIS-R) test. Achievement testing in reading comprehension, written language, and math must also be submitted. The SAT or ACT requirement is waived for PAL applicants. Final decisions on admission to the program are made once all credentials are complete.

For more information about Curry College, students should contact:

Jane Patricia Fidler
Dean of Admission
Curry College
Milton, Massachusetts 02186
Phone: 617-333-2210
      800-669-0686 (toll-free)
Fax: 617-333-2114
E-mail: curryadm@curry.edu
Web site: http://www.curry.edu
      http://on.fb.me/CurryColl_adm
      http://twitter.com/CurryAdmission

The suburban campus of Curry College is only minutes from the city of Boston.

DAEMEN COLLEGE
AMHERST, NEW YORK

The College

Daemen College is a private college established by the Sisters of St. Francis of Penance and Christian Charity as Rosary Hill College in 1947 (a liberal arts college for women). The College became coeducational in 1971. In 1976, it became independent and nonsectarian, changing its name to Daemen College.

The goal at Daemen is to offer the best integrated learning experience possible. The College cultivates minds that embrace connections, welcome challenges, and celebrate innovation. It equips students with invaluable skills that will benefit them and their communities for the rest of their lives.

Daemen has approximately 2,000 undergraduates and 900 graduate students. Students come from all over New York and the United States, as well as from other countries. Small class sizes and a 15:1 student-faculty ratio ensure that students will have an engaging and interactive classroom experience.

Fifty student organizations, themed dinners, movie nights, internationally famous speakers, and more contribute to a dynamic campus life.

Location

Daemen's beautiful suburban 39-acre campus is located in Amherst, New York. Daemen is just minutes away from the city of Buffalo, which has been named a top collegiate destination by the American Institute for Economic Research. Buffalo is renowned for the arts, offering exceptional theater, music, art, restaurants, and major league sports; it is also very close to scenic Niagara Falls and Canada. The campus is easily accessible by the major rail, plane, and motor routes that serve Buffalo.

Majors and Degrees

Daemen's Division of Arts and Sciences is well-suited for students who are interested in becoming anything from a novelist to an occupational psychologist. In Daemen's Visual and Performing Arts program, students learn how to take their talents and skills to the professional level, in a myriad of creative outlets: Web sites, children's books, intensive studio experience, and more. Daemen's modern language students get personalized instruction and become fluent in French, Spanish, or Chinese. The history and government major examines everything from ancient history to the politics of globalization, leading to careers in public affairs, foreign correspondence, law, and more. English majors become acquainted with everything from syntax to Shakespeare, and may move on to careers such as a magazine journalist or high school teacher. A math degree can lead to careers in teaching, research, architecture, meteorology, and banking, among others. Those studying natural sciences will major in biochemistry, biology, or natural science; a chemistry minor is also available. Biology students can specialize in environmental studies, while other specializations include forensic science, health science, and individual studies. Students can explore Christianity, Buddhism, Judaism, and more in the philosophy and religion studies program. Students who choose psychology embrace everything from neuropsychology to human sexuality, in preparation for careers in family therapy, school counseling, law enforcement, or other challenging areas.

Daemen's Division of Health and Human Services is designed to provide students for many career paths with a common destination: a professional orientation toward dedication to others—from special education teachers to athletic trainers, tax accountants to parole officers. Accounting/information systems majors crunch numbers but also consider global issues, to become financial analysts, company comptrollers, tax accountants and more. A Master of Science in athletic training is a five-year program that incorporates both the B.S. and M.S. Business administration majors focus on economics, accounting, marketing, diversity and global management, and more. Future teachers in the education program study childhood/early childhood, special education, and visual arts education with certification opportunities in several areas and the potential for extensive service learning experiences. Health-care studies covers all aspects of practical health care delivery. Students may choose from concentrations in community health, health and fitness training, and complementary and alternative health-care practices. The nursing partner curriculum program allows future nurses to earn both their associate degree (from a partner school) and a bachelor's degree in just four years. Physical therapy at Daemen is nationally recognized, and the Doctorate in Physical Therapy is obtained after six years. Daemen was the first small liberal arts college in New York State accredited to offer the D.P.T. Studies span orthopedics, pediatrics, geriatrics, tissue mechanics, sports medicine, wound healing, and more. Daemen's physical therapy students have a first-time pass rate on the National Physical Therapy Examination above both New York State and national averages, with a current three-year weighted average ultimate pass rate of 100 percent. Daemen's physician assistant studies program prepares students to become licensed to practice medicine with physician supervision. Strong growth is projected in this profession. Physician assistants do everything from writing prescriptions to assisting in surgery. The program is one of only 149 in the country to be accredited. Extensive service-learning opportunities include an annual trip to the Dominican Republic. As many as 98 percent of Daemen students in this program pass the NCCPA Certification exam on the first attempt, compared to 90–92 percent nationally. Students interested in shaping communities will find Daemen's social work program ideal. Practical opportunities abound, including participation in the Seneca Babcock Community Initiative. Graduates enjoy careers as counselors, therapists, probation/parole officers, school social workers, and other human service professionals.

Majors at Daemen include: accounting (B.S./M.S.); art, with an emphasis in applied design/printmaking, drawing/illustration, graphic design, illustration, painting/sculpture, or visual arts education K–12; arts administration, with an emphasis in comprehensive arts, fine arts, or theater; athletic training (B.S./M.S.); biology, with an emphasis available in adolescence education 7–12 or environmental studies; biochemistry, with several preprofessional programs available; business administration, with an emphasis available in human resource management, international business, management information systems, marketing, or sports management; education, with an emphasis in childhood education 1–6, childhood education/special education 1–6, or early childhood education/special education B–2; English, with an emphasis available in adolescence education 7–12 or communication/public relations; French, with an emphasis available in adolescence education 7–12; health-care studies, with an emphasis available in community health, complementary and alternative health-care practices, or health and fitness training; history; history and government, with an emphasis available in adolescence education 7–12 or environmental studies; mathematics, with an emphasis available in adolescence education 7–12; natural sciences, with an emphasis available in environmental studies, forensic science, health science, or individualized studies; nursing; paralegal studies; physical therapy (B.S.N.S./D.P.T.); physician assistant studies (B.S./M.S.); political science; psychology; religious studies; social work; and Spanish, with an emphasis available in adolescence education 7–12. Preprofessional programs are available in predentistry, prelaw, premedicine, and pre–veterinary science.

Academic Programs

Daemen has been named a College of Distinction for its exemplary commitment to engaged students, great teaching, vibrant communities, and successful outcomes.

Daemen College recognizes that education needs to prepare students for professional, intellectual, and civic leadership. The key to fostering the development of these skills is the core curriculum—a common educational experience for all students, regardless of major. The Daemen College core is designed to strengthen students' abilities to become intellectually curious, acquire professional rewards, become responsible citizens, and deal with change. The core experience consists of seven competencies identified as essential. These competencies are introduced at the freshman level, and are emphasized across the entire curriculum so that students develop a greater understanding of, appreciation for, and practice of these important life skills through their academic work. As students complete the core they acquire the ability to think, adapt, and act in a multicultural environment in which the pace and complexity of change are escalating.

Research is carried out on a host of different fronts, from an innovative student/faculty think tank, to a high-profile wound therapy initiative. General research projects that include an enormous diversity of interests are showcased annually in the College's increasingly popular Academic Festival, held each spring.

The honors program meets the intellectual needs of the best students, ensuring that the Damien experience challenges their minds and fosters their potential to contribute both to the community and to society at large.

The Center for Veterans and Veteran Family Services at Daemen provides a comprehensive support system for postsecondary education.

Daemen has a close professional and collaborative association among all members of the College's community while maintaining a student-centered atmosphere.

Off-Campus Programs

Alongside the outstanding and innovative courses that provide the academic foundation at Daemen, there are many other opportunities to enhance a student's education, such as internships, global education programs, and service-learning projects.

Daemen's Co-op and Career Development Office helps students to find an internship or co-op position so they can gain real-world experience in their area of interest. Daemen students say this chance to gain more insight into their fields prepares them better for employment after graduation. Internships are available in a wide range of fields, including business, the sports industry, the arts, industry, government, health-related entities, nonprofit organizations, educational institutions, and cultural organizations. These can be local, national, or international and include excellent opportunities with the Washington Internship Institute.

Daemen's Office of Global Programs coordinates distinctive international programs designed to facilitate students' professional aspirations. In today's global economy, it is vital that students learn about different cultures, political systems, and histories. International study is a staple of the Daemen experience and the College offers semesters abroad, summer programs, and accelerated January term trips.

Daemen believes strongly in learning through service. During their time at Daemen, all undergraduate students engage in various service learning activities. Students participate as individuals or groups in short- and long-term projects or assignments that benefit the local, national, or global communities. Daemen students work with environmental organizations; assist refugee groups; help with programs to benefit the needy; serve residents of nursing homes, hospitals, and clinics; mentor in city schools; and work on other service projects in various cities throughout the city and the world.

Daemen has been named to the President's Higher Education Community Service Honor Roll for the past three years. Daemen founded and operates the Center for Sustainable Communities and Civic Engagement and is founder and headquarters for the Western New York Service Learning Coalition.

Academic Facilities

Modern apartment-style residence halls provide separate housing for men and women, in addition to the existing five-story residence hall for freshmen. Full-service meals are served in the main dining hall in the WICK Student Center.

The Research and Information Commons, a green building, is a technological showcase—a hub of academic research, as well as the academic and social heart of the campus.

Costs

For the 2010–11 academic year, tuition and fees were $21,460, and room and board were $9850.

Financial Aid

Daemen creates individualized financial aid packages. Generous scholarships make attending the College very affordable. Over 90 percent of full-time undergraduates received some kind of financial assistance. The average award made to full-time undergraduates is approximately $21,100.

Faculty

Daemen has approximately 260 faculty members (full- and part-time).

Student Government

All students are members of the Student Association. The controlling body, or Senate, is comprised of an executive board of officers and representatives who are elected each year. A Programming Board works with the Student Activities Director to plan several special events. Students also serve on many institutional committees.

Admission Requirements

Daemen offers a rolling admissions policy. The average student enrolled has a 91 GPA and 1060 SAT. Daemen also has a test-optional policy which provides students with a choice regarding the submission of standardized test scores.

The admissions staff helps guide students through the process from start to finish. Students can create their own personalized Daemen Connection web page at http://www.daemen.edu/admissions.

Application and Information

Prospective students can apply online at http://www.daemen.edu (free) or https://www.commonapp.org/. Call Daemen with any questions at 716-838-8225 or 800-462-7652 (toll-free).

Daemen College
4380 Main Street
Amherst, New York 14226
Phone: 716-839-8225
       800-462-7652 (toll-free)
E-mail: admissions@daemen.edu
Web site: http://www.daemen.edu/admissions
          http://www.facebook.com/DaemenCollege
          http://twitter.com/#!/daemencollege
          http://www.youtube.com/daemencollege

Visit Daemen—that's the best way to really get a feel for what the College has to offer.

No person shall, on the basis of sex, race, color, ethnic and national origin, handicap, religion, or age, be denied admission or be subjected to discrimination in admission to Daemen College.

DELAWARE VALLEY COLLEGE

DOYLESTOWN, PENNSYLVANIA

The College

Founded in 1896, Delaware Valley College (DelVal) is a private, coeducational four-year college enrolling approximately 1,700 full-time undergraduate students. The College concentrates on producing graduates who can fill employers' needs. DelVal is known for its experiential learning philosophy which combines theory with practice. The College is growing and continuing to expand opportunities for experience-based, cross-disciplinary learning.

DelVal tends to attract pre–veterinary science students; some of its most popular majors are small animal science, equine science, and conservation and wildlife management. Other science offerings include chemistry, environmental design, food science, microbiology and biotechnology, and zoology. The College also offers strong programs in business, criminal justice, counseling psychology, and media and communications. DelVal offers master's programs and extensive course offerings in continuing education, including a curriculum that provides adult learners with teacher certification.

Students attend Delaware Valley College, first and foremost, to prepare to enter professional careers. DelVal has an excellent record when it comes to job placement, proving that the time-honored educational philosophy of "scholarship with applied experience" is successful. A high percentage of graduates find employment in their field of study or enter graduate school within six months of graduation.

In addition to its academic programs, the College offers a wide range of extracurricular activities and events. DelVal has more than fifty clubs and organizations, many of which are linked with a specific major. Student publications include the weekly *Ram-Pages* (newspaper), the *Cornucopia* (yearbook), and the *The Gleaner* (literary magazine). The College band and chorale give students the chance to demonstrate their musical talents. There are active minority and international clubs on campus. DelVal students are connected to the community in a variety of ways that are relevant to their majors. A-Day, the student-run campuswide fair, annually attracts 50,000 visitors who enjoy the festival, the entertainment, and the academically oriented projects.

Approximately 64 percent of students live on campus in ten residence halls. A full range of intercollegiate and intramural athletics programs (NCAA Division III, ECAC, and MAC) for both women and men is offered. All elements of the College's educational and recreational programs are in place to develop students as open-minded professionals who are capable of expanding their horizons in a future of unlimited possibilities.

DelVal offers graduate programs in general business, educational leadership, food and agribusiness, and accounting. The College also offers an online master's program in global leadership.

DelVal is officially recognized by the Middle States Commission on Higher Education.

Location

The College is located in historic Bucks County, Pennsylvania, approximately 30 miles north of Philadelphia and 70 miles southwest of New York City. Bucks County is one of the fastest-growing areas in the United States, yet it maintains its rich historical and agricultural heritage. The Doylestown area, where DelVal's campus is located is rich in educational and cultural resources, including museums, a county courthouse, and a library which further enhance the educational opportunities available to students.

The Pennsylvania and New Jersey Turnpikes provide quick access to the College. A commuter railway system links the College with Philadelphia, providing daily scheduled arrivals and departures, right on campus. The College enjoys a relationship with its surrounding community that is mutually beneficial. Many students find convenient employment opportunities with local businesses, and the community benefits from the many events and activities that are held on campus.

Majors and Degrees

Delaware Valley College offers a variety of strong programs and is particularly strong in the life sciences. The College offers more than twenty-seven majors and specializations including biology (with programs in botany, environmental biology, microbiology/biotechnology, preprofessional biology, and zoology); business administration (with programs in accounting, financial services, general business administration, entrepreneurship, management, marketing, and sports management); chemistry and biochemistry; counseling psychology; English; media and communication; secondary education (with programs in agriculture, biology, business, chemistry, English, general science, and social studies); agribusiness; animal biotechnology (with programs in conservation and wildlife management, small animal science, and zoo science); animal science (with programs in equine science and management, livestock science and management, and science); dairy science; equine studies (with programs in equibusiness and equine training); food science, nutrition, and management (with programs in food science, food technology, nutrition science and restaurant and food service management); agronomy and environmental science (with programs in crop science, environmental science, and turf management); horticulture (with programs in commercial crop production and marketing/plant health management, hydroponic crop science, and plant sciences and biotechnology); and ornamental horticulture (with programs in environmental design, floriculture and nursery production and marketing, and landscape contracting and management).

The College also offers preprofessional preparation in dentistry, law, medicine, optometry, and veterinary medicine.

For students interested in applying to veterinary school in their third year, Delaware Valley College offers the 3+1 Program, where a contract is completed prior to May of the sophomore year. The program allows the student to enter veterinary school after three years (96 credits). After acceptance and verified completion of the first full academic year at a nationally accredited professional school, DelVal will confer the Bachelor of Science degree to the student.

Academic Programs

All courses are taught from a liberal arts perspective, which broadens the students' appreciation of cultural heritage. The College is committed to producing graduates who are both highly competent in their areas of study and skilled in more general areas such as communication, mathematics, and computers. Academic programs at DelVal combine theory with practice and students leave with valuable work experience. The College stresses a practical, hands-on approach to learning. The Employment Program, required for graduation, stipulates that students complete 500 hours working in their chosen fields. The program fosters the integration of theory and practice throughout the students' educational continuum and helps students build relationships with professionals in their various fields of study.

The academic calendar consists of two 15-week semesters, with an optional January term, and two optional summer sessions.

Off-Campus Programs

Students can earn credit by studying abroad. DelVal has programs that take students to the Hartpury College in the United Kingdom and the University of Podlasie in Poland. The Polish exchange program is free for students and is funded by the Copernicus Society of America.

Academic Facilities

Many of the courses taught at Delaware Valley College are laboratory or field oriented. The 571-acre campus includes classrooms, modern laboratories, greenhouses, an arboretum, a library, livestock and dairy farms, an equestrian center, 400 acres of agricultural land, and 60 acres of horticultural land. Approximately 225 acres are dedicated to field crops for dairy and livestock operations, which include beef and dairy cattle, sheep, swine and standard-bred horses. Approximately 60 acres are used for horticulture (including plantings of apples, peaches and various fruits, vegetables, and nuts). DelVal also maintains an apiary for beekeeping programs.

These facilities serve just one purpose: to support the education and experience students need to succeed. Even buildings off the traditional main campus, such as the College's Roth Living Museum and the Montgomery County farm, provide extensive opportunities for students. The DelVal philosophy is that students learn best when classroom learning and hands-on experience are combined. The facilities are designed with that goal in mind, and the faculty and staff utilize every building on campus in pursuit of the mission of preparing students for careers and future studies.

These facilities serve just one purpose: to support the education and experience students need to succeed. Even buildings off the traditional main campus, such as the College's Roth Living Museum and the Montgomery County farm, provide extensive opportunities for students. The DelVal philosophy is that students learn best when classroom learning and hands-on experience are combined. The facilities are designed with that goal in mind, and the faculty and staff utilize every building on campus in pursuit of the mission of preparing students for careers and future studies.

DelVal students benefit from the low student-laboratory ratio. This enables ready access to equipment, which is imperative to learning. Specifically, the College utilizes biology, chemistry, physics, plant science, and animal science laboratories. Facilities include a tissue culture laboratory, a food processing plant, a greenhouse-laboratory complex, a dairy, a small-animal science center, equine breeding barns, and an indoor equestrian center. The campus is itself a recognized arboretum that is managed by students and faculty members. These facilities are all supported by the Krauskopf Memorial Library, which houses some 80,000 publications.

Costs

Estimated costs for the 2010–11 were: tuition $27,234, fees $2050, room $4682, residential meal plan $5444, and books and supplies $1000 (if purchasing new books). However, DelVal offers a textbook rental program which allows students to rent textbooks for one semester for 35 percent of the cost of a new book. To keep a book for two semesters students pay 54 percent of the cost of a new book. This program significantly reduces student costs. A student who would spend $1000 annually purchasing new books at another institution would spend just $350 annually if they rented all of their books at DelVal.

Financial Aid

The College is committed to providing financial assistance so that every student is able to meet the costs of obtaining a college education. Approximately 95 percent of full-time undergraduates receive some type of financial aid. The College offers scholarships and grants for students with exceptional academic promise and participates in federal government programs such as Federal Pell Grants, Federal Supplemental Educational Opportunity Grants, Federal Perkins Loans, Federal Work-Study, Federal Academic Competitiveness grants, Federal SMART grants, and Federal TEACH grants. Students can borrow under the Federal Stafford Direct Loan program and parents can borrow under the Federal Parent Direct Loan program. Residents of Pennsylvania can also apply state grants through PHEAA.

Faculty

All courses at DelVal are taught by faculty members, not graduate students. The College's faculty is made up of dedicated professors who combine professional experience with deep theoretical knowledge. The faculty includes 82 full-time members as well as additional part-time instructors, who are friendly and accessible and always ready to help individual students make the most of the educational opportunities offered by the College. Approximately 60 percent of DelVal professors hold the highest degree available in their fields. The student-faculty ratio is 15:1.

Student Government

Students are encouraged to make the most of extracurricular activities to ensure that their education includes as many different experiences as possible. The student government acts to coordinate the activities of all organizations on campus and sponsors a variety of mixers, movies, concerts, and speakers.

Admission Requirements

The College seeks to recruit a diverse population of talented, motivated, and promising students, and draws them from across the nation. Criteria for admission include academic transcripts, class rank, SAT or ACT scores, letters of recommendation, and a personal interview (recommended). While DelVal has a rolling admission period, applications should be submitted as early as possible in the senior year of high school, preferably by the end of the first marking period.

Application and Information

For more information about Delaware Valley College and its academic, athletic, and financial aid programs, students should contact:

Office of Admissions
Delaware Valley College
700 East Butler Avenue
Doylestown, Pennsylvania 18901-2697
Phone: 215-489-2211
      800-2DELVAL (toll-free)
Fax: 215-230-2968
E-mail: admitme@delval.edu
Web site: http://www.delval.edu
      http://www.facebook.com/delval
      http://twitter.com/delvalcollege

Delaware Valley College is located in Doylestown, Pennsylvania, about 30 miles north of Philadelphia and 70 miles south of New York City.

DENISON UNIVERSITY

GRANVILLE, OHIO

The University

Denison University is a highly selective, four-year, independent residential college of liberal arts and sciences for men and women. Founded in 1831, it is steeped in tradition and focused on the success of its approximately 2,100 students, who are educated to be curious, resourceful, and reflective. The student body is geographically diverse, representing fifty states and U.S. territories. The University welcomed 623 members to the class of 2014, 49 percent of whom were in the top 10 percent of their graduating class.

Denison has achieved a national reputation based on its lengthy cultural heritage, the vitality of its intellectual and ethical concerns, and the performance of its graduates. Denison has more than 31,360 alumni and, as of June 2010, an endowment of $585 million. The Denison Annual Fund received more than $5 million in gifts from alumni, parents, and friends during fiscal year 2009–10.

The recently renovated Bryant Arts Center was awarded the U.S. Green Building Council's LEED Gold certification. It houses both the studio art and art history departments and offers state-of-the-art facilities for ceramics, painting, printmaking, photography, and digital media.

Ebaugh Laboratories, home to the chemistry and biochemistry departments, is being renovated and expanded by 19,000 feet and is expected to be ready for classes in fall 2011. The $38.5-million renovation of the Mitchell Recreation and Athletics Center is also under way and includes a new natatorium with an Olympic-size pool. The renovation will provide outstanding training facilities for varsity athletes and modern recreational facilities for students, faculty, staff, and community members. Both projects are being built according to LEED standards.

Ninety percent of students take advantage of the career and professional-school counseling available from Career Services. Each year, approximately 300 Denison students take part in the University's summer internship programs. More than half of Denison's graduates enroll in graduate or professional schools within ten years of graduation. Denison students are consistent finalists for a number of postgraduate awards, including the Rhodes and Marshal scholarships. The University has had 12 National Science Foundation fellows, 11 Goldwater Science scholars, 2 Truman scholars, 1 Udall fellow, 1 Charles B. Rangel International Affairs fellowship, and 58 Fulbright scholarship winners in the last twenty-one years. In 2011, 26 Denison students have applied for Fulbright scholarships.

As a residential college, Denison requires its students to live in University housing all four years and offers a variety of housing options in its thirty-five residence halls. A full slate of social and cultural events is scheduled each semester. Thirty-seven percent of the students join the sixteen fraternities and sororities present on campus. The Denison International Student Association, the Black Student Union, the Asian-American Student Union, and La Fuerza Latina help to enrich the campus community.

Twenty-three intercollegiate sports for men and women and a wide variety of club sports are available. More than 75 percent of students participate in athletics or recreational activities. Denison's varsity teams have won a record eleven North Coast Athletic Conference All-Sports titles and have captured 112 conference championships since 1984, the founding year of the conference.

Location

The 900-acre Denison campus is located on a ridge overlooking the village of Granville, in central Ohio. Founded in 1805 by settlers from Massachusetts, Granville bears a marked resemblance to a New England village. Columbus, the state capital and sixteenth-largest U.S. city, 27 miles to the west, is the nearest major city and is served by numerous national airlines. Newark, 7 miles to the east, is an industrial city of 50,000 people. Granville has several fine restaurants and some shopping facilities, but those seeking the larger department stores go to nearby Easton Town Center or downtown Columbus. The University is a cultural and recreational center for the local community. More than 80 percent of the students contributed over 45,000 hours of community service during the 2009–10 school year. State parks, lakes, bike trails, and ski areas are nearby.

Majors and Degrees

Denison offers Bachelor of Arts, Bachelor of Science, and Bachelor of Fine Arts degrees. Departmental, interdepartmental, and individually designed majors, as well as concentrations within departments, are available within the degree programs. The B.A. can be earned through departmental programs in art (history or studio), biology, chemistry, cinema, communication, computer science, dance, economics, English (literature or writing), environmental studies, geosciences, history, international studies (as a double major), Latin, mathematics, modern languages (French, German, and Spanish), music, philosophy, physics, political science, psychology, religion, sociology/anthropology, and theater. The B.A. can also be earned through interdepartmental programs in black studies; East Asian studies; educational studies; philosophy, politics, and economics (PPE); and women's studies. The B.S. is offered in biochemistry, biology, chemistry, computer science, geosciences, mathematics, physics, and psychology. The B.F.A. major is art (studio).

Preprofessional preparation is available in business, dentistry, engineering, environmental management, forestry, law, medical technology, medicine, nursing, occupational therapy, and veterinary science. Denison offers 3–2 programs in engineering with Rensselaer Polytechnic Institute, Washington University in St. Louis, Case Western Reserve University, and Columbia University; in forestry and environmental management with Duke University; and in medical technology with Rochester General Hospital. Also available are a 3–4 program in dentistry with Case Western Reserve Dental School and a cooperative program with Case Western's Weatherhead School of Management for entrance into a year-long M.S. program.

Academic Programs

Denison expects its students to benefit from exposure to a broad liberal arts education and to achieve proficiency in a major field. University degree requirements include successful completion of approximately thirty-five courses (127 semester hours) with a 2.0 or better average, both overall and in the major and minor fields; fulfillment of all general education requirements; passing comprehensive examinations if required in the major; and fulfillment of minimum residence requirements. Approximately one third of a student's course work (thirteen courses) must be chosen from core course offerings in the humanities, sciences, social sciences, and fine arts. Another third is in the major field of study, and the remainder is in electives. There are opportunities for directed and independent study. Students may receive advanced placement or credit through College Board Advanced Placement (AP) tests or International Baccalaureate higher level examinations. Credit is given for an AP score of 4 or 5. Denison's academic calendar consists of two semesters and an optional summer internship program, which includes internships and travel seminars. The academic year begins in late August and ends in early May.

Off-Campus Programs

Off-campus study acts as a catalyst in a Denison education. Its purposeful combination of classroom and experiential learning gives students the opportunity to hone the analytical literacy and capacity for informed judgment and constructive social engagement that are associated with a liberal arts education.

More than half of Denison students participate in off-campus study during their undergraduate career. The Denison list of accepted off-campus study programs includes over 150 domestic and international opportunities to meet the diverse educational interests of the student body. Through extensive advising and support, the off-campus study program invites students to explore these program possibilities in depth and to imagine how they can seek to engage the world as part of their Denison education.

Academic Facilities

Denison's William Howard Doane Library offers a full range of traditional and online services and collections. Liaison librarians for fine arts, humanities, natural sciences, and social studies collaborate with faculty and students in their respective divisions of the college. The online catalog CONSORT offers access to 4.17 million volumes. As a member of the OhioLINK institutions and the Five Colleges of Ohio, library users also have ready access to more than 48 million volumes. The library is one of thirteen academic and administrative buildings on the academic and science quadrangles.

More than 650 Macintosh and Dell personal computers are available for student use in forty-three public and departmental labs and student clusters. A network dataport is available to every student living in a residence hall and wireless networking covers most of the campus. Laptops may be used online almost anywhere on campus, indoors or outdoors. For more information, students should refer to the library or computing links on the home page of the Denison Web site, listed at the end of this description.

Samson Talbott Hall of Biological Science features flexible teaching labs and interactive lecture and seminar rooms crowned by a spectacular greenhouse. The Chemistry Center contains well-equipped laboratories and a 292-seat circular auditorium. Features of the $7.2-million F. W. Olin Science Hall include a forty-two-seat planetarium with a Zeiss Skymaster projector, a laser spectrometer, and computer-based learning centers for physics and astronomy, geology and geography, and mathematics and computer science. The fine arts quadrangle on the lower campus is made up of six buildings with classrooms and performance facilities for art, music, theater and cinema, and dance. Burke Hall features a recital hall, a theater workshop, and the Denison Museum. Other buildings are the Theatre Arts Building; the Doane Dance Building; Burton Hall, which houses the Department of Music; the newly dedicated Bryant Arts Center; and the Cinema Building, the center of Denison's nationally recognized cinematography program.

Costs

Annual charges for the 2011–12 academic year are as follows: tuition, $39,330; room and board, $9960; and student fees, $880, for a total of $50,170.

Financial Aid

In 2009–10, Denison students received more than $60 million in financial assistance. More than 67 percent was awarded from Denison funds. Financial aid packages based on need are comprised of grants, loans, and employment on campus. Applicants for both federal and Denison grant aid must complete a Free Application for Federal Student Aid (FAFSA) as early as possible after January 1 and request that the information be sent to Denison. In addition to the institutional need-based grants, Denison offers more than 1,000 merit-based scholarships to first-year students, which range from $8000 to $35,000. Denison awards up to twenty Paschal Carter scholarships for selected first-year applicants who earn National Merit Finalist status as determined by the National Merit Scholarship Corporation. It approximates full tuition, and the amount of the award stays constant during a student's enrollment at Denison. Alumni awards in the amounts of $14,000 and $8000, recognizing academic achievement, leadership, and talent, are also offered. The financial aid decision is entirely separate from the admission decision. For more information, students should write to Denison's Office of Financial Aid and ask for the financial aid brochure.

Faculty

Denison's 203 full-time faculty members are deeply committed to teaching and to students. Many have national reputations in their fields; each year faculty members win national awards for teaching excellence. One hundred percent of faculty members have an earned doctorate or terminal degree in their fields. The faculty-student ratio is 1:10. Small classes (average class size is 19) and unique opportunities for one-on-one research with a faculty member encourage active learning. In 2010, 147 summer scholars did research with their professors on campus. All incoming first-year students are assigned a faculty adviser to assist with course selection and to ease the transition to college life.

Student Government

Through the Denison Campus Governance Association, students budget and direct such campus organizations as the Student Senate, FM radio station, Denison Film Society, and campus newspaper. Students are strongly represented on the governance councils of the University.

Admission Requirements

Entering first-year students must have earned at least 16 academic credits in secondary school, including 4 years of college-preparatory English. Strongly recommended are 3 years each of mathematics, science, foreign language, and social studies. A candidate for admission must file a formal application and an essay. Submission of the results of the SAT or the ACT is optional. SAT Subject Tests are not required, although students may provide these scores as additional information in support of their application for admission. International applicants must submit the results of the Test of English as a Foreign Language (TOEFL) or the results of the SAT. The Admissions Committee is particularly interested in the rigor of the academic program and the grade point average. Other selection criteria are written references from a college adviser and an academic teacher, extracurricular and personal accomplishments, and the student's essay on the application. An interview is strongly encouraged. It is Denison's goal to enroll academically talented students. Denison University admits students of any race, color, religion, age, personal handicap, sex, sexual orientation, veteran status, and national or ethnic origin.

Application and Information

First-choice early decision candidates should apply by November 15 or January 15, and will be notified of a decision on a rolling basis. All admitted early decision candidates must send an enrollment deposit within two weeks of notification of acceptance. Students interested in applying for admission under regular application status and for merit-based scholarship consideration must apply by January 15. Those deferred under early decision and all regular applicants are given a final decision by mid-March. Admitted candidates must respond to the admission offer by May 1.

Director of Admissions
Denison University
Box 740
Granville, Ohio 43023-0740
Phone: 740-587-6276
       800-336-4766 (toll-free)
E-mail: admissions@denison.edu
Web site: http://www.denison.edu
Web site: http://www.facebook.com/denisonuniversity
Web site: http://twitter.com/denisonu

Denison—preparing students for a lifetime of leadership and learning.

DePaul University

CHICAGO, ILLINOIS

The University

DePaul University is nationally recognized for its innovative, academically rigorous programs that use an urban, multicultural perspective to prepare students for their careers and lives. DePaul provides an interactive learning environment through expert instruction, small classes, and an emphasis on service learning, undergraduate scholarship, and research. Located in the heart of Chicago, DePaul University offers students unparalleled access to internships and real world experiences.

In fall 2010, DePaul enrolled 25,145 students, retaining its place as the nation's largest Catholic university. Of the 16,052 undergraduates, 2,241 were freshmen. About one third of all undergraduates are students of color. The average high school GPA of incoming freshmen is 3.55; more than 20 percent graduated in the top 10 percent of their class. The mid-range is 22–27 for the ACT and 1060–1255 for the SAT.

DePaul sponsors more than 200 student organizations that provide opportunities for leadership, service, professional development, socializing, recreation, and special interests. The DePaul Blue Demons participate in NCAA Division I sports as part of the Big East Conference. Intramural sports programs and club athletics also are available.

DePaul has more than 140,000 alumni, 97,000 of whom reside in the Chicago metropolitan area, providing students with a network locally, nationally, and abroad.

Location

DePaul has two primary campuses. The Loop Campus is blocks from Chicago's business district, the Art Institute, Orchestra Hall, Millennium Park, and Lake Michigan. The 40-acre Lincoln Park Campus, 5 miles north of the Loop Campus, provides a quintessential residential-college experience surrounded by an urban assortment of stores, theaters, restaurants, and music clubs. From either campus, a short walk or ride on public transit enables students to browse unique shops or visit museums, the zoo, cultural neighborhoods, and professional sports arenas, such as Wrigley Field and the United Center.

Majors and Degrees

Bachelor of Arts, Bachelor of Fine Arts, Bachelor of Music, Bachelor of Science, Bachelor of Science in Commerce, and Bachelor of Science in Physical Education degrees are offered through DePaul's undergraduate colleges. More than 150 undergraduate majors and nearly 100 minors are available. Double majors and minors may be taken in numerous areas of study.

The College of Liberal Arts and Sciences offers programs in African and Black Diaspora studies; allied health technologies; American studies; anthropology; Arabic studies; art, media, and design; Asian American studies; biological sciences; Catholic studies; chemistry; Chinese studies; cities; community service studies; comparative literature; economics; English; environmental science; environmental studies; French; geographic information systems; geography; German; health sciences; history; history of art and architecture; international studies; Irish studies; Islamic world studies; Italian; Japanese studies; Latin American and Latino studies; LGBTQ studies; mathematical sciences; mathematics and computer science; peace, justice, and conflict studies; philosophy; physics; political science; professional writing; psychology; public policy; religious studies; scientific data analysis and visualization; sociology; Spanish; women's and gender studies; and writing, rhetoric, and discourse.

The College of Computing and Digital Media offers programs in animation, computer game development, computer graphics and motion technology, computer science, digital cinema, graphic design,

interactive media, information assurance and security engineering, information systems, information technology, mathematics and computer science, and network technology.

The College of Education offers programs in early childhood education, elementary education, music education (joint program with the School of Music), physical education, secondary education, and world languages education.

The College of Commerce offers programs in accountancy, business administration, e-business, economics, finance, hospitality leadership, management, management information systems, marketing, and real estate.

The College of Communication offers programs in communication and media, communication studies, public relations and advertising, media and cinema studies, and journalism.

The School of Music offers programs in composition, jazz studies, music education, music performance, performing arts management, and sound recording technology.

The Theatre School offers programs in acting, costume design, costume technology, dramaturgy/criticism, lighting design, playwriting, scenic design, sound design, stage management, theater arts, theater management, and theater technology.

Students interested in engineering may complete a five-year joint program with the Illinois Institute of Technology (IIT). This dual-degree program includes three years of study at DePaul and two years at IIT's School of Engineering.

Academic Programs

Each college follows the liberal studies program, which includes the common core and learning domains. The core emphasizes communication, quantitative skills, and intellectual abilities and introduces the University's small-group, interactive educational approach. Learning domains comprise the classic liberal arts and sciences curriculum: arts and literature; philosophical inquiry; religious dimensions; scientific inquiry; self, society, and the modern world; and understanding the past.

The liberal studies curriculum is integrated into each year of study at DePaul. As freshmen, students take either Explore Chicago or Discover Chicago, which introduces them to the intellectual resources of the city, emphasizes DePaul's roles and missions in the city, and demonstrates how DePaul connects classroom learning with persons, communities, and institutions in Chicago. Students then complete a sophomore multiculturalism seminar, a junior experiential learning requirement, and senior capstone course.

The academic year comprises three quarters. Incoming freshmen may enter with previously earned credit from Advanced Placement, CLEP, or International Baccalaureate. Incoming transfer students may combine earned credit through credit by exam and transferable credit hours from two-year institutions (up to 99 quarter hours/66 semester hours) and from four-year institutions (up to 132 quarter hours/88 semester hours). In some cases, degree requirements can be completed in three years. Advanced undergraduates may take graduate courses. Undergraduates in any college may apply to the University Honors Program, which emphasizes cross-cultural and interdisciplinary perspectives through a challenging curriculum that satisfies the required liberal studies core. (Program participation is noted on the students' transcripts.) College-specific honors programs also are offered in accountancy, computer science, finance, and marketing.

Off-Campus Programs

DePaul University sponsors short-term and full-year study-abroad programs in more than forty locations throughout the world to accommodate students' interests and academic program requirements.

Academic Facilities

The DePaul Center, a teaching, research, and student services complex, is the cornerstone of the six-building Loop Campus. The CDM Center, home of the College of Computing and Digital Media, offers more than a dozen specialized labs as well as a digital animation studio. The College of Communication includes a converged newsroom and a performance laboratory. The Merle Reskin Theatre provides a 1,400-seat space for theater and music school performances.

Notable new buildings on the 40-acre Lincoln Park Campus include the student center, Ray Meyer Fitness and Recreation Center, Richardson Library, and Sullivan Athletic Center. Two new state-of-the-art science buildings include classrooms, laboratories, faculty research suites, and a greenhouse. A new classroom building is scheduled to open in January 2012.

Costs

For the 2010–11 academic year, full-time tuition for the College of Liberal Arts and Sciences, the College of Commerce, the College of Communication, the College of Computing and Digital Media, and the College of Education was $28,240. Tuition for the School of Music and The Theatre School was $30,665 and is guaranteed for four years. Average room and board costs for 2010–11 were $10,500.

Financial Aid

DePaul's financial aid program is designed to assist as many students as possible. Scholarships, grants, loans, and work-study opportunities often are combined in a financial aid package to meet demonstrated financial need. About 70 percent of full-time DePaul undergraduate students receive some form of financial aid. Merit scholarships for freshmen and transfer students are based on academic and extracurricular accomplishments. Institutional scholarships for freshmen, with values ranging from $3000 to $15,500 per year for four years, are based on academic merit, without regard to need. Select freshmen admitted for the fall term are invited to apply for service and leadership scholarships ranging from $8500 to $15,500. Institutional scholarships for transfer students range from $2000 to $7000 and may be awarded to students with a cumulative GPA of 3.5 or above and a minimum of 30 semester (44 quarter) hours of transferable credit. All other financial aid programs, except art, athletic, music, and theater talent awards, are based primarily on need.

To apply for aid, students must complete the Free Application for Federal Student Aid (FAFSA). Application and notification of aid decisions are on a rolling basis. Students are encouraged to apply and file their FAFSA before February 15 to receive maximum consideration.

Faculty

In fall 2010, about 88 percent of the full-time faculty members held a doctoral degree or terminal degree in their field. Faculty members are selected for their teaching ability and conduct 98 percent of all university classes. In addition to teaching, DePaul's faculty members engage in research and publish in their fields of expertise. Professors have long-lasting professional relationships with corporations, government agencies, cultural and civic organizations, and a wide array of nonprofits. Students tap into these connections for internships, mentors, class projects, professional contacts, and more.

Admission Requirements

Current high school students are considered for admission on the basis of six or more semesters of high school work. At enrollment, students must have graduated from an accredited secondary school with a minimum of 16 high school units. These should include 4 units in English, 3 in mathematics, 2 in laboratory science plus one additional science, 2 in social sciences, and 4 additional units in college-preparatory subjects. Applicants should have a solid GPA. ACT or SAT scores are optional; students who choose not to provide test scores must complete several short-answer admission essays. Applicants must submit a high school counselor's recommendation. The School of Music and The Theatre School require auditions or interviews for admission.

Transfer students are welcome. To be considered for admission, transfer students must be in good standing (eligible to enroll) at the last college/university attended and must have earned a minimum cumulative GPA of 2.0 (C average). College of Commerce, College of Education, and School of Music applicants must have a cumulative GPA of 2.5 or better. Transfer students who have completed fewer than 30 semester hours (44 quarter hours) of transferable credit need to submit an official high school transcript and ACT or SAT scores.

Application and Information

To receive strongest consideration for merit scholarships as well as priority registration for orientation and housing, freshmen applicants should apply by the non-binding early action deadline of November 15. Applicants who are admitted under the early action program receive their decision by January 15. The application deadline for regular notification is February 1, and students receive an admission decision by March 15. After February 1, applications are considered on a space-available basis.

The Theatre School and School of Music applicants are not eligible to participate in the early action program. Application materials to the School of Music and The Theatre School must be received by January 15. Admission decisions are made by April 1.

Application deadlines for transfer students vary by start term: August 1 for Autumn Quarter (September), November 1 for Winter Quarter (January), March 1 for Spring Quarter (March), and May 1 for Summer Quarter (June). Students who apply for admission after the deadlines will have their application considered on a space-available basis.

Campus visits and overnight stays are available for applicants. Interested students and their families are encouraged to call the admission office to arrange a visit.

For further information, prospective students should contact:

Office of Admission
DePaul University
1 East Jackson Boulevard
Chicago, Illinois 60604-2287
Phone: 312-362-8300
        800-4DEPAUL (toll-free outside Illinois)
E-mail: admission@depaul.edu
Web site: http://www.depaul.edu
          http://www.facebook.com/depaulundergradadmission

DePaul University. *(Photo by Flip Chalfant)*

DeSALES UNIVERSITY

CENTER VALLEY, PENNSYLVANIA

The University

DeSales University is a private, four-year Catholic university for men and women that is administered by the Oblates of St. Francis de Sales. Its mission is to provide high-quality higher education according to the philosophy of Christian humanism. The University imparts knowledge about, and develops talents for, personal, familial, and societal living, enriching the human community and enhancing the dignity of the individual through its educational endeavors. The University is accredited by the Middle States Association of Colleges and Schools.

In 1961, Joseph McShea was appointed Bishop of the new Allentown Diocese. At the time, the Diocese did not include a Catholic college for men. At the request of Bishop McShea, the Oblates of St. Francis de Sales agreed to assume responsibility for establishing a liberal arts college to serve this need. Allentown College of St. Francis de Sales received a charter to grant bachelor's degrees in 1964, and the first classes began in 1965. The College became coeducational in 1970; throughout the 1980s and 1990s, it began to offer graduate and cooperative education programs. These changes led to the college attaining university status, and it was renamed DeSales University in 2001.

Today, DeSales is home to more than 2,500 undergraduate and graduate students. Life on campus best illustrates DeSales' identity as a Christian humanist institution. Approximately 70 percent of the University's 1,600 undergraduate students live on campus and take full advantage of the rich opportunities provided. Students participate in more than forty clubs and organizations that encompass art, politics, and intramural sports; fourteen athletic teams competing in the NCAA Division III, including basketball, soccer, field hockey, and lacrosse; social outreach; student activities; and a Campus Ministry that enables students to participate in retreats and social justice groups. Billera Hall houses facilities for intercollegiate and intramural sports and fitness activities. The McShea Student Union contains health services and counseling offices. The Labuda Center for the Performing Arts houses the largest department in the University and is proud of its thirty-five-year history of success. The newly expanded University Center includes the University bookstore and expanded meeting space in addition to the food court, student dining facility, and student lounge. Eight suite-style residence halls offer a range of living options, including living-learning communities, which allows students with common interests to live together.

Location

The Lehigh Valley contains three cities, including Allentown, the third-largest city in Pennsylvania; Bethlehem; and Easton. The region offers a wide range of year-round recreational activities, from skiing and skating in the winter to golf and swimming in the summer, and theater, dance, fine dining, shopping, and music year-round.

The Lehigh Valley has a wide variety of museums, art galleries, and concert venues for every taste and age group, while farmers' markets are a common sight throughout the region. Amusement parks like Dorney Park and Wildwater Kingdom and the Crayola Factory are nearby, as are Kutztown Festival and other annual celebrations. The Promenade Shops at Saucon Valley offer more than sixty-five stores and restaurants and a state-of-the-art movie theater. For those wanting to travel beyond the region, the Lehigh Valley is less than 2 hours from New York City and 1 hour from Philadelphia.

Majors and Degrees

The University offers undergraduate degrees in more than thirty programs, including accounting, biochemistry, biology, business, chemistry, communications, computer science, criminal justice, dance, digital art, elementary education, English, finance, history, international business, law and society, liberal studies, management, management of information technology, marketing, marriage and family studies, mathematics, media studies, nursing, pharmaceutical marketing, philosophy, physician assistant studies, political science, premedicine, psychology, Spanish, sport and exercise science, sport management, television and film, theater, and theology.

Academic Programs

Students must complete forty courses with a minimum GPA of 2.0 to earn a bachelor's degree. Each degree program has three components. The General Education Core requires completion of sixteen courses, including two courses in English; three physical education courses; two courses in a foreign language or world cultures; two courses in history or political science; one course in art or music; one course in literature; five courses in modes of thinking, concentrating on literature, mathematics, natural science, philosophy, and social science; and three courses in theology. The major provides a thorough and systematic study of one subject area. The major requires completion of sixteen courses. As an alternative, a student may choose to enroll in a special degree program, which may extend the number of required courses. Electives comprise the remaining eight course requirements. Electives provide opportunities for learning in areas of special interest outside the student's major. Some students may want to consider a dual major, in which case the student must complete the requirements of both fields of study. Students who wish to complete a minor must take six courses within that field of study.

Off-Campus Programs

DeSales encourages qualified students to study abroad during the summer and/or the academic year. Through an affiliation with the Lehigh Valley Association of Independent Colleges, the University offers qualified students in a number of disciplines the opportunity to spend a summer or semester in

Germany, Italy, Mexico, Spain, or other countries. Shorter, more intensive trips are offered to all students through a variety of clubs, organizations, and academic programs. Recent trips have taken DeSales students to South Africa, India, Peru, Romania, and other countries.

Academic Facilities

The campus contains twenty-four buildings. A state-of-the-art 37,000-square-foot Science Center houses classrooms and laboratories for the natural sciences. Trexler Library contains more than 550,000 items, including 132,000 volumes and 40,000 electronic books, more than 12,000 electronic journals and newspapers, and 400,000 microfiche items. The periodical collection includes 550 paper and microform subscriptions. Collections of the other five independent colleges of the Lehigh Valley, totaling more than 1 million volumes, are available through an interlibrary loan system.

The University maintains ten computing laboratories or classrooms. The Academic Computing Center contains approximately sixty PCs in its main area, while ACC Computing Classroom houses twenty-three systems. Dooling Hall has three dedicated computing classrooms, each containing approximately twenty-five workstations. Trexler Technology Center contains forty-nine PC systems for both public use and classroom support. Each computing area is supported by at least one high-volume laser printer. All systems have Internet access and contain a suite of both application and network software.

Costs

In 2010–11, full-time tuition was $27,000 per academic year. Other annual fees included a Student Center fee and a technology fee totaling $1294. For students living on campus, room and board cost $10,130 per year.

Financial Aid

Nearly 90 percent of incoming students receive some form of financial aid. Students must complete the Free Application for Federal Student Aid and mail it to the processing center indicated on the form with DeSales University's Title IV code number, which is 003986, after January 1 of the student's senior year. The Office of Financial Aid processes requests for assistance on both a date priority and a financial need basis. The types and amounts of assistance a student will receive are specified in an award letter. The package also provides students and parents with a payment options letter, which outlines the three ways a student can finance the remaining cost of education. Parents may apply for a Federal Parent Loan for Undergraduate Students, students may apply for an alternative loan, or they may take advantage of a monthly billing plan.

All applicants are automatically considered for merit scholarships, which are awarded to incoming first-year students based upon academic achievement. Priority consideration is given to students who apply by December 1 of their senior year. Scholarships include Presidential Scholarships, which can award up to full tuition to students who earn a combined SAT score (math and critical reasoning sections) of at least 1300 (29 ACT) and rank in the top 5 percent of their high school class; Trustee Scholarships of $6000 to $10,000 for students who achieve a combined SAT score (math and critical reasoning sections) of at least 1200 (27 ACT) and rank in the top 15 percent of their high school class; and DeSales Scholarships of $4000 for students who achieve a combined SAT score (math and critical reasoning sections) of at least 1100 (24 ACT) and rank in the top 25 percent of their high school class. Department Scholarships are awarded to students who attend scholarship day and demonstrate excellence in their field of study.

Faculty

There are 103 full-time faculty members teaching at the University. Eighty-five percent of the professors have a doctorate or the highest degree in their specialty. The average class size is 18 students, and the student-faculty ratio is 15:1. Students are assigned a faculty member from their chosen field of study to serve as an academic adviser; undeclared students are assigned to a faculty member who assists them in planning courses, deciding upon a major, and moving toward declaring a major.

Student Government

The Student Government Association is the liaison between the students and the administration. The Executive Board and each of the four undergraduate classes elect a president, vice president, secretary, and treasurer, for a total of 20 officers.

Admission Requirements

Admission is based on past academic achievement, particularly within a college-preparatory course of study, as well as the student's potential for future growth. Preferably, this includes four years of English; three to four years of college-preparatory mathematics; two years of modern, foreign, or classical language; and at least two laboratory science courses. Quality of academic performance is the single most important factor in the decision-making process.

Application and Information

DeSales University uses a rolling admissions process; the school notifies applicants of their admission status within four weeks of receiving all application materials. To apply, students must submit a completed application, official high school or home school transcripts, official SAT or ACT scores, two letters of recommendation, and the $30 application fee. An on-campus interview is recommended but not required. For maximum consideration for scholarships, students are encouraged to apply by December 1.

Prospective students may direct their applications or requests for additional information to:

Admissions Office
DeSales University
2755 Station Avenue
Center Valley, Pennsylvania 18034-9568
Phone: 610-282-1100
E-mail: admiss@desales.edu
Web site: http://www.desales.edu

DOMINICAN UNIVERSITY OF CALIFORNIA

SAN RAFAEL, CALIFORNIA

The University

Dominican University of California is an independent, international, learner-centered university of Dominican heritage. It offers a beautiful setting, a close-knit community of over 2,000 students, and an intimate social environment that is an important context for academic goals and personal development.

The University offers many services that support its educational programs. It provides tutoring, career, and personal counseling without charge to Dominican students; offers housing, health, and job placement services; and helps students make the most of their college experience by its readiness to assist them in resolving problems.

The University and the Associated Students of Dominican University sponsor a number of campus activities each year for both resident and nonresident students. Dominican supports twelve intercollegiate teams that compete in the NCAA's Pacific Western Conference: men's and women's basketball, golf, cross-country, and soccer; men's lacrosse; and women's softball, tennis, and volleyball. Students can participate in the chorus, drama group, literary magazine, campus newspaper, campus ministry activities, special interest clubs, dances, and other social events.

Campus Ministry responds to the spiritual needs of Catholic and non-Catholic members of the University community. Catholic liturgies, ecumenical activities for students of all faiths, and community service projects are scheduled throughout the year.

Graduate degrees (M.A., M.S., M.S.N., M.S.O.T., M.F.T., and M.B.A.) are granted in biological sciences, counseling psychology, education, global management, humanities, nursing, occupational therapy, strategic leadership, and sustainable enterprise (Green MBA®).

The University is approved by the California Commission on Teacher Credentialing to prepare and recommend candidates for credentials in elementary, secondary, and special education.

Four residence halls of varied architecture accommodate more than 600 students; there is a dining hall for resident students and others who wish to purchase meals on campus. Forest Meadows, which comprises approximately 25 acres, is the site of the Conlan Recreation Center, a soccer field, tennis courts, and an outdoor amphitheater, where commencement exercises are held. The Recreation Center features regulation basketball and volleyball courts, two cross-courts for volleyball and basketball, and 1,285 spectator seats. It also features a weight-training and fitness room, a multipurpose room, lockers, athletic department offices, and conference rooms. Outside are a six-lane, recreational swimming pool and grassy patio area.

Location

The University is located on 80 wooded acres in scenic Marin County, which is 12 miles north of San Francisco and within a half hour's drive of Pacific Ocean beaches.

Majors and Degrees

A broad range of degrees and certificate and credential programs are offered in letters, the arts and sciences, and professional and preprofessional disciplines.

Undergraduate degrees (B.A., B.S., B.S.N., and B.F.A.) are awarded in the academic areas of art, art history, biological sciences (with concentrations in ecology, environmental science, general biology, molecular cell biology, and premedical studies), business administration (with concentrations in accounting, finance, international business, management, management information systems, and marketing), chemistry, communications and media studies (with concentrations in broadcast media, cinema, journalism, and print), dance (LINES ballet), English, English with a writing emphasis, health science (pre–occupational therapy), history, humanities, interdisciplinary studies, international studies, liberal studies (elementary teacher education), music, music with a performance concentration, nursing, political science, psychology, religion, and women and gender studies.

Minors are offered in environmental studies, Latin American studies, leadership studies, mathematics, philosophy, prelaw, and sports management.

Academic Programs

The General Education Program offers more than a brief exposure to the major areas of knowledge in the humanities, arts, and natural and social sciences. It is designed to provide a sequence of courses with a thematic focus that integrates the wisdom and perspectives of several disciplines. The focus assists students in discovering relationships between areas of knowledge, beliefs, cultures, and peoples that differ globally and historically, as well as in acquiring an awareness of tradition, a love of discovery, a respect for the diversity of the human condition, and a realization of human interdependence. Courses within the General Education Program also expose students to a variety of learning experiences, including discussion, lectures, seminars, simulations, practicums, and quiet reflection.

A strong internship program offers students job experience in areas of their choice.

An evening bachelor's degree–completion program (Pathways) for nontraditional learners is also available.

The ELS Language Centers program provides intensive, high-quality English instruction to prepare international students to enter American colleges and universities. Completion of the ELS Language Centers Program level 112 satisfies Dominican's English requirement for admission for international students.

Off-Campus Programs

Dominican offers exchange programs with Aquinas College, Grand Rapids, Michigan; Barry University, Miami, Florida; the College of New Rochelle, New Rochelle, New York; and St. Thomas Aquinas College, Sparkill, New York. These programs enable students matriculated at any one of the five colleges to spend a semester on a campus in a different part of the country, taking advantage of its location and programs. Students pay tuition on their home campus and room and board on the host campus. Further information about the program, which is recommended for students in the sophomore or junior year, is available in the Academic Advising Office.

Individualized programs for study in other countries may be planned in consultation with the Office of International Studies, the student's academic adviser, and the transcript evaluator. Dominican grants credit for international study only after a student who obtained prior approval of the program of study has returned to the campus and enrolled for the following year.

Academic Facilities

Archbishop Alemany Library houses more than 100,000 volumes in open stacks; 3,200 reels of microfilm; 775 videocassettes, 225 audiocassettes, and compact discs; and subscriptions to 375 periodicals in print and another 19,000 periodical titles in full text online. Reference services, including access to a variety of computerized databases and indexes, and multimedia facilities are provided to assist students with their studies and assignments. The library also houses the Fletcher Jones Computer Laboratory, an art gallery, a listening room, and a fireplace corner.

Guzman Hall, Albertus Magnus Hall, Bertrand Hall, and the San Marco Art Studios together house faculty offices, science laboratories, lecture halls, a computer center, art galleries and studios, and classrooms. Angelico Hall houses an 850-seat concert auditorium and theater, music studios and practice rooms, and faculty offices.

In 2005, ground was broken on a new $20-million, 35,000-square-foot science and technology facility. The Science Center opened for the fall 2007 classes, featuring more than thirty teaching, research, and computer technology labs.

Costs

Undergraduate full-time tuition (12–17 units per semester) was $33,270 per year for 2010–11. Fees were $300; room and board (a fourteen-meal-per-week plan) cost approximately $12,000 for the year.

Financial Aid

Financial aid is awarded on the basis of need and merit. Merit awards are available for both freshmen and transfer students based on academic achievement. Dominican University of California participates in various federal and state need-based financial aid programs and also has its own financial aid funds, donated by generous alumni and friends, available to help meet University costs.

Need-based financial aid comes in the form of scholarships, grants, part-time employment, and loans. The federal and state financial aid programs are the Federal Supplemental Educational Opportunity Grant, Federal Pell Grant, Federal Work-Study Program, Federal Stafford Student Loan, CLAS/PLUS loan, and Cal Grants A and B. Eligibility for need-based aid is determined after the student, who must be a citizen or permanent resident of the United States, files the Free Application for Federal Student Aid (FAFSA). The need-based financial aid deadline for first-priority consideration is March 2, although late applications are accepted. Student assistantship positions are also available for graduate students.

Faculty

Students find themselves intellectually challenged by the faculty members, who hold degrees from colleges and universities throughout the world and who are committed to individualized teaching and careful supervision of students' development. Seventy-nine percent of Dominican University's full-time faculty members have terminal degrees (the highest obtainable degree in their field). The student-faculty ratio is 11:1.

Student Government

The primary vehicle through which students plan and provide activities, distribute activity funds, and represent themselves to the University's administration and broader community is ASDU—the Associated Students of Dominican University. ASDU is the student association and the student government body. Through elected and appointed representatives to various Dominican committees and governing groups, students may voice their opinions on institutional matters.

Admission Requirements

Dominican University of California welcomes applications from prospective students of all ages, religions, races, and national origins. The University believes that academic potential is measured by more than grades alone. Each candidate for admission is given individual consideration and is evaluated by the Admissions Office on the basis of the student's past scholastic record, present motivation, and potential intellectual development, as indicated by all of the admission materials submitted.

Recommended for undergraduate admission is graduation from an accredited high school with a total of at least 15 units in college-preparatory subjects, to include the following: 4 years of English, 2 years of the same foreign language, 2 years of college-preparatory mathematics (algebra, geometry, algebra 2/trigonometry), 2 years of laboratory sciences to be taken in grades 10–12, and 1 year of U.S. history (1 year of world history or Western civilization is an acceptable alternative for international students). The University encourages students to choose additional courses in at least two of the following areas: English, history, foreign language, social science, advanced mathematics, laboratory science, music, art, and computer science.

Dominican University of California admits highly qualified students after the completion of their junior year in high school if they have fulfilled all admission requirements for freshman standing or passed an equivalency exam and arranged a conference with a member of the admission staff prior to acceptance.

High school seniors wishing to take up to two Dominican courses per semester to meet high school graduation requirements may do so with the written permission of their high school principal or counselor. Arrangements must be made through Academic Advising and Support Services.

Application and Information

The Admissions Office makes its decision on each freshman candidate after receiving his or her completed application form with a $40 nonrefundable fee; an official high school transcript to date; one recommendation from a teacher, administrator, or counselor; scores from either the SAT or the ACT; and a personal essay, as described in the application. For information about the SAT, students should write to Educational Testing Service, 1947 Center Street, Berkeley, California 94704 or P.O. Box 592, Princeton, New Jersey 08541. For information about the ACT, students should write to American College Testing Program, Operations Division, P.O. Box 168, Iowa City, Iowa 52243.

Transfer students must also submit the application form, a $40 fee, and their high school transcript and official test scores if they have fewer than 24 transfer units. In addition, they must send official college transcripts to date; a personal essay, as described in the application; proof of high school graduation; and one academic letter of recommendation or one professional letter of reference.

International students should fulfill the admission requirements for native students; however, an SAT or ACT score is not required. Passing scores for the Test of English as a Foreign Language (TOEFL) of at least 550 (paper-based) or 80 (Internet-based) or official certification of achieving level 112 in the ELS program may be submitted in lieu of SAT or ACT scores. All transcripts must be translated into English and evaluated by an accredited evaluation agency. In addition, a notarized declaration of finances in U.S. dollars must be submitted.

An interview with a member of the admission staff is strongly recommended to enable the candidate and the University to become acquainted with one another.

Students may apply online at the University's Web site, or they may obtain application forms and information by contacting:

Office of Admissions
Dominican University of California
50 Acacia Avenue
San Rafael, California 94901-2298
Phone: 415-485-3204
       888-323-6763 (toll-free)
Fax: 415-485-3214
E-mail: enroll@dominican.edu
Web site: http://www.dominican.edu

DREXEL UNIVERSITY
PHILADELPHIA, PENNSYLVANIA

The University

Drexel University is a private, nonsectarian, coeducational university that has maintained a reputation for academic excellence since its founding in 1891. The University's technologically focused approach to learning prepares undergraduates for graduate school and a variety of careers. Full-time work experience through the cooperative education program is a vital part of a Drexel education. Students gain professional experience in jobs related to their career interests by alternating classroom study with periods of full-time employment. Drexel University grants bachelor's, master's, and doctoral degrees. Last year's undergraduate enrollment numbered 11,517 full-time students representing forty-two states and fifty-eight other countries.

Nine residential halls house almost 4,000 students on campus. In conjunction with Drexel's fourteen fraternities and ten sororities, the Campus Activities Board (CAB) sponsors events such as dances, lectures, excursions, community service projects, and films. Students can also take part in a variety of extracurricular activities, including musical groups, a recording studio, MAD Dragon Records, dance ensembles, theatrical productions, a student-run newspaper, a radio station, and a cable TV station. Drexel offers sixteen NCAA Division I varsity athletic programs, competes in the Colonial Athletic Association Conference, and produces some of the nation's top student athletes in both the academic and athletic arenas. The University sponsors intramural and club sports.

Drexel is committed to expanding its already vast educational opportunities. In 2006, Drexel admitted 181 students to the Earle Mack School of Law. The School of Law was the first law school to be founded by a major research university in thirty years. In January 2009, Drexel opened the Sacramento Center for Graduate Studies in Sacramento, California, which offers graduate degrees in both online and traditional classroom formats.

Location

Drexel is located near the heart of the nation's fifth-largest metropolitan area. Philadelphia has the highest concentration of colleges and universities in the country. Drexel shares its University City neighborhood with the University of Pennsylvania and the University of the Sciences. With thousands of student residents, University City is a great place for students to spend their college years. Philadelphia is home to some of the nation's best historical and cultural attractions. The region also offers all the amenities of a first-class city, with vibrant nightlife, great restaurants, and major league athletics. Drexel's location offers access to the city's numerous bus, trolley, and subway stops. The Drexel shuttle makes transportation between campuses easy. Amtrak's 30th Street Station is a short walk from Drexel's campus. From 30th Street, students can take trains to the Philadelphia suburbs, New York City, Washington D.C., and beyond.

Majors and Degrees

From engineering to the design arts to health sciences to business, whatever their interest, students at Drexel are at the forefront of their fields. Offering more than seventy undergraduate majors, Drexel is comprised of thirteen colleges and schools, including the Pennoni Honors College. Academic majors and concentrations include accounting, animation and visual effects, anthropology, architectural engineering, architecture, behavioral health counseling, biological sciences, biomedical engineering, business administration, business and engineering, chemical engineering, chemistry, civil engineering, communication, computer engineering, computer science, construction management, criminal justice, culinary arts, culinary science, custom-designed major, dance, design and merchandising, economics, education, electrical engineering, engineering, engineering for Still-Deciding Students®, engineering technology, English, entertainment and arts management, entrepreneurship, environmental engineering, environmental science, fashion design, film and video, finance, game art and production, general business for Still-Deciding Students®, general humanities and social sciences for Still-Deciding Students®, graphic design, health services administration, history, hospitality management, information systems, information technology, interior design, international area studies, international business, invasive cardiovascular technology, legal studies, management information systems, marketing, materials engineering, mathematics, mechanical engineering, media arts and design for Still-Deciding Students®, music industry, nursing, nutrition and foods, operations management, pathway to health professions, philosophy, photography, physics, political science, product design, psychology, radiologic technology, science for Still-Deciding Students®, screenwriting and playwriting, sociology, software engineering, sport management, television, and Web development.

Drexel applicants can pursue an accelerated degree program, which allows students to earn more than one degree in a shortened period of time. Accelerated degree options include the B.A./B.S./J.D. in law; B.S./D.P.T. in physical therapy; B.S./M.P.H. in public health; B.S./M.B.A. in business, culinary arts, culinary science, design and merchandising, entertainment and arts management, hospitality management, and music industry; B.A./B.S./M.D. in medicine; B.S./M.H.S. for physician assistant studies; B.S./M.S. programs in biomedical engineering, communications, education, engineering, information systems, psychology, physics, and majors within the information science and technology school; and B.S./Ph.D. in engineering.

Academic Programs

Qualified students can apply to the Pennoni Honors College, which is open to students in every academic discipline. Honors sections of general and required courses and honors colloquia and seminars are available. Special living communities designed for the exceptional student and independent projects characterize the program.

At Drexel, students have opportunities to conduct research. The STAR (Students Tackling Advanced Research) program allows students to participate in research projects in their field as early as the freshman year. Students who take part in these research opportunities may be eligible for stipends or academic credit for their work.

Off-Campus Programs

Classroom study is essential, but experience makes all the difference. Drexel Co-op allows students to alternate periods of full-time work experience with periods of classroom study. Through Drexel Co-op, students have the opportunity to test-drive their degree in a professional setting. Fortune 500 companies, major pharmaceutical companies, and top design firms are among the workplaces where students can earn up to eighteen months of experience before graduation. More than 2,200 employers from forty-one states and fifteen other countries participate in the Drexel Co-op program.

Drexel has an active study-abroad program that allows students to spend a term or several terms studying abroad, earning credit toward their degree and gaining valuable international experience. With any Drexel-sponsored program, students pay Drexel tuition rates and receive financial aid while abroad.

Academic Facilities

Drexel has four campus locations: the University City Main Campus, Hahnemann Center City Campus, Queen Lane Medical Campus, and the Sacramento Center for Graduate Studies. The University's library system is comprised of the W. W. Hagerty Library on the University City Main Campus and three health sciences libraries. The W. W. Hagerty Library, the University's central library, houses 1.4 million volumes and maintains subscriptions to nearly 12,000 electronic journals. The library provides access via its Web site to academic journals and 200 databases. Students may borrow laptops for use on the campus wireless network. The additional libraries on the health sciences campuses provide study space, 75,000 books, and network access to the same set of online journals and databases.

The University is expanding through the addition of several new, state-of-the-art buildings. The Edmund D. Bossone Research Enterprise Center, a $37-million, 155,000-square-foot, multistory facility strengthens the research capabilities of faculty members and students in the engineering and biomedical engineering fields. Millennium Hall is a seventeen-story, green-certified residence hall that serves as home to students in the Pennoni Honors College. Construction is under way on the URBN Center, which will house many academic programs of the Westphal College of Media Arts & Design. The Papadakis Integrated Sciences Building is slated to open in 2011 and will feature classroom and research facilities.

Costs

Students enrolling at Drexel must choose a co-op plan. The number of co-op experiences required for graduation is determined by the chosen academic course of study. The Three Co-op Option includes three six-month periods of full-time employment. This plan takes five years to complete. The One Co-op Option includes just one six-month period of full-time employment and takes four years to complete. The full-time undergraduate tuition for the 2011–12 academic year is $32,300 for a student in the five-year program and $39,700 for a student in the four-year program. Costs for on-campus housing and the campus meal plan average $14,362 per year. Fees are approximately $2510 per year, depending on the degree program.

Financial Aid

Approximately 90 percent of all freshmen receive financial aid. The aid package may contain academic, athletic, or performing arts scholarships; grants; loans; or part-time employment. Federal programs are also included. All incoming students are encouraged to submit the Free Application for Federal Student Aid (FAFSA) by March 1. Notification to incoming freshmen and transfer students begins mid-March. Drexel offers a unique achievement-based award, the A. J. Drexel Scholarship, to all qualified incoming freshmen and transfer students. With an annual award value of up to $27,000, the A. J. Drexel Scholarship is renewable on a yearly basis, provided the student maintains at least a 3.0 GPA and full-time status. Criteria include a strong academic record and involvement in extracurricular and community service activities.

Faculty

Approximately 94 percent of Drexel's full-time faculty members hold a Ph.D. or the terminal degree in their field. The University requires faculty members engaged in research and graduate-level teaching to also teach at the undergraduate level. Thus, the undergraduate student benefits from the research activities of the faculty. Specially selected faculty members serve as advisers for freshmen. The student-faculty ratio is 10:1.

Admission Requirements

All colleges within the University require completion of a college-preparatory program in high school that includes at least 3 years of mathematics and 1 year of laboratory science. Students applying to major in engineering, the sciences, and business and engineering are required to take 4 years of mathematics (through trigonometry) and 2 years of laboratory science. Engineering requires four years of mathematics (through trigonometry and precalculus), chemistry, and physics. The quality of academic performance is more important than merely meeting minimum requirements. The strength of preparation is judged primarily by rank in class or relative grade point average, by the degree of improvement in the quality of the academic record, and by the comments and recommendations from principals, guidance counselors, or teachers. Freshman applicants are required to take the SAT or the ACT. An essay or personal statement is required, with its subject dependent on the major and program. Students who were accepted and enrolled in the fall of 2010 had an average unweighted GPA of 3.4 on an 4.0 scale and an average SAT of 1200 out of 1600, including the math and critical reading sections. Transfer applicants must have a minimum 2.5 cumulative average (2.75 for engineering, information systems, information technology; and a 3.0 GPA for nursing) for consideration and generally are expected to complete at least 24 credits at a regionally accredited four-year college or two-year community college in a program of study comparable to the one being sought at Drexel.

Application and Information

Applications to Drexel are available online (http://www.drexel.edu/apply) or from the address listed. The Common Application and the Universal Application are accepted as well. Each application must be accompanied by a nonrefundable application fee of $75; however, the fee is waived for online applications or if submitted during a campus visit. Applications for regular full-time undergraduate status are accepted throughout the senior year until March 1. Applications for Drexel's premier scholarship program—the A. J. Drexel Scholarship—are due on January 15. Applications for accelerated degree options are due on December 1. Applications for the Westphal College of Media Arts & Design's early decision program are due November 15. Early decision for the Westphal College is binding; students admitted through the early decision process are required to confirm their intention to enroll by February 1. Drexel subscribes to the College Board's Candidates Reply Date of May 1. Transfer students should apply at least three months before the beginning of the term in which they wish to enroll.

Undergraduate Admissions
Drexel University
3141 Chestnut Street
Philadelphia, Pennsylvania 19104-2876

Phone: 215-895-2400
    800-2-DREXEL (toll-free)
      http://www.drexel.edu/admissions (Admissions)
      http://www.drexel.edu/apply (Application)
      http://www.facebook.com/drexeladmission
        (Facebook)
      http://twitter.com/DrexelAdmission (Twitter)

Ms. Joan McDonald
Senior Vice President of Enrollment Management
Drexel University
Phone: 800-2-DREXEL (toll-free)
Fax: 215-895-1285
E-mail: enroll@drexel.edu

DUKE UNIVERSITY
DURHAM, NORTH CAROLINA

The University

Duke University is an independent, comprehensive, coeducational research university that traces its roots to 1838, when it was established as Union Institute in Randolph County, North Carolina. Renamed Trinity College twenty-one years later, the school moved to Durham in 1892. In recognition of its primary benefactors, the Duke family, Trinity College became Duke University in 1924.

Duke offers a variety of outstanding undergraduate programs in two schools—Trinity College of Arts and Sciences and the Pratt School of Engineering. At the graduate level, the master's and doctoral programs in these schools (as well as the University's professional schools in business administration, divinity, the environment, law, medicine, nursing, and public policy) consistently rank at or near the top of their fields.

With a limited enrollment of 14,248 full-time students, Duke is among the smallest of the nation's major universities. Of these, 6,504 are undergraduates—5,306 in arts and sciences and 1,198 in engineering. Because of its size and the emphasis on meeting the needs of a diverse student body, the University maintains a commitment to individual education. At Duke, learning is a priority and teaching is personal. As a result, the student body, as a whole, reflects a quality of creativity and mental restlessness that goes far beyond excellent grades and testing. The University attracts students from all fifty states as well as eighty-five other countries, and about 85 percent of Duke's undergraduates come from states other than North and South Carolina.

Duke believes that to build a strong community students must live together. For this reason, all undergraduates are guaranteed housing as long as space remains available and are required to live on campus for their first three years. To accommodate students' widely varying interests, the residence halls provide diverse living styles, including single-sex or coed dorms, unique academic environments, and theme houses or other selective living groups. About 85 percent of undergraduates live on campus. All first-year students live on East Campus in a community designed to support the academic, residential, and recreational needs and interests of new students, and all sophomores live on West Campus. About 36 percent of undergraduates belong to fraternities or sororities. In addition to a rich campus living environment, students can enjoy a full calendar of activities through the University Union, the University-sponsored Artists Series, the Broadway at Duke Series, and nearly 400 clubs and organizations based on diverse political, cultural, social, arts, health, recreational, service, academic, and religious interests as well as intramural sports.

Location

Durham, located about 450 miles from Atlanta and 250 miles from Washington, D.C., is a city of about 240,000 with active research, medical, and arts communities. Together, Durham and nearby Raleigh and Chapel Hill, with a combined population of around 1.5 million, compose the Research Triangle, one of the nation's foremost centers for research and high-tech industry. The Research Triangle has one of the highest concentrations of Ph.D.'s and M.D.'s in the world. Two interstates and the Raleigh-Durham International Airport, only 20 minutes from campus, make Durham easily accessible.

Majors and Degrees

Duke offers both a rigorous academic program and considerable flexibility in course selection and degree programs. Undergraduates can choose courses in nearly 100 different programs in the humanities, social sciences and natural sciences, mathematics, and engineering. Forty-six majors are offered in Trinity College of Arts and Sciences, and students with interests that cannot be met within an established major are able to design their own curriculum with

the help of a faculty adviser. In addition, students may pursue dual degrees, minors in most fields, and any of the University's twenty-four certificate programs.

Trinity College of Arts and Sciences offers programs leading to the A.B. degree or the B.S. degree in African and African American studies, art history, Asian and Middle Eastern studies, biology, biophysics, Canadian studies, chemistry, classical studies, computer science, cultural anthropology, dance, earth and ocean sciences, economics, English, environmental sciences, environmental science and policy, evolutionary anthropology, French studies, German, history, international comparative studies, Italian studies, linguistics, literature, mathematics, medieval and Renaissance studies, music, neuroscience, philosophy, physics, political science, psychology, public policy studies, religion, Russian, Slavic and Eurasian studies, sociology, Spanish, statistical science, theater studies, visual arts, and women's studies.

Interdisciplinary nonmajor certificate programs are available in aerospace engineering; architectural engineering; arts of the moving image; children in contemporary society; documentary studies; early childhood education studies; East Asian studies; energy and the environment; genome sciences and policy; global health; human development; information sciences and information studies; Islamic studies; Jewish studies; Latino/Latina studies; marine science and conservation leadership; markets and management studies; modeling biological systems; neurosciences; policy journalism and media studies; politics, philosophy, and economics; study of ethics; and study of sexualities.

The Pratt School of Engineering offers accredited four-year programs leading to the B.S.E. in biomedical engineering, civil and environmental engineering, electrical and computer engineering, and mechanical engineering and materials science.

Academic Programs

The year is divided into two semesters with two optional summer terms; first-semester exams fall before the winter break. Students in the liberal arts plan their own courses of study, with the help of an adviser, according to guidelines rather than specific course requirements. Academic Writing, a one-semester class in expository writing, is the only course required of undergraduates. The Trinity College liberal arts curriculum of approximately 15 semester courses encompasses five areas of knowledge: arts, literatures, and performance; civilizations; social sciences; natural sciences; and quantitative studies. As students take courses in these areas, the curriculum provides significant exposure to cross-cultural and ethical inquiry, methods of analysis and reasoning, foreign language, writing, research, and the relationships between science, technology, and society. Thirty-four courses are required for graduation.

First-year students are encouraged to participate in the Focus Program, consisting of about a dozen clusters of interrelated seminars spanning topics such as Evolution and Humankind, Engineering Frontiers: Living Systems for a Living Planet, Exploring the Mind, The Faces of Science, The Power of Ideas, and Visions of Freedom. Students in each Focus Cluster live together to expand the opportunities for discussion and learning. Also, in more than forty-five first-year seminars, offered in nearly every department, professors chosen for their outstanding undergraduate teaching lead classes of 15 or fewer students. In general, other than the occasional large lecture hall, classes at Duke contain between 16 and 35 students.

When students declare a major—no later than the end of the sophomore year in Trinity College and the end of the first year in the Pratt School of Engineering—a faculty member from the major department becomes their adviser. Students who plan to continue their study in a professional school also work with career-specific advisers to plan a program of study that provides the appropriate foundation for advanced work and meets their unique interests.

Off-Campus Programs

Through internships and study-abroad programs, students are encouraged to take advantage of nearly 150 Duke-affiliated off-campus study opportunities. These range from oceanographic studies at the Duke Marine Laboratory in Beaufort, North Carolina, and arts programs in New York or Los Angeles to a variety of overseas programs. Through the Office of Study Abroad, students can choose international programs from four weeks to a full year in length. In most cases, scholarship aid can be applied to study abroad. Approximately 50 percent of each graduating class studies away from campus on nearly every continent in the world. DukeEngage provides funding and faculty support for any undergraduate student who wishes to pursue a summer or semester-long service project.

Academic Facilities

With more than 5 million volumes, 17 million manuscripts, 1.4 million public documents, 3.9 million microforms, and tens of thousands of films, video recordings, and serials, Duke University's library holdings are among the most extensive in the nation. The University's most sophisticated teaching and research facilities—including the Fitzpatrick Center for Interdisciplinary Engineering, Medicine, and Applied Sciences and the Bostock Library—are available to undergraduates as they work with faculty mentors on various research projects.

All students have access to extensive computing facilities and services supported by the Office of Information Technology. Services include free accounts on Duke's main computer system, which provide access to high-speed Internet and e-mail as well as access to the twenty-three campus computer labs, which provide computers, printers, and access to DukeNet, the campuswide fiber-optic network. All undergraduate residence hall rooms are wired for DukeNet access.

Costs

For 2010–11, a year in Trinity College or the Pratt School of Engineering cost $55,690, with $40,575 allotted for tuition and fees, and an average of $11,830 for room and board (although costs vary with accommodations). The total yearly estimate included $3285 for books and miscellaneous expenses. All fees are subject to change, and up-to-date information is available through the Office of Undergraduate Financial Aid.

Financial Aid

Duke University believes that access to a high-quality private education should depend on a student's qualifications, not his or her family's financial strength. Admission to Duke is need-blind for U.S. citizens and permanent residents. Ability to pay is not considered in the admission decision.

All admitted students who apply for financial aid receive 100 percent of their demonstrated financial need for all four years of undergraduate study.

With Duke's new financial aid initiatives, parents whose incomes total $60,000 or less no longer have to contribute financially to their child's education. In addition, student loans have been eliminated for families whose incomes total $40,000 or less, and reduced for families with incomes up to $100,000.

The University also makes need-based financial aid available for a limited number of students who are not U.S. citizens or permanent residents. Duke will also meet the full demonstrated financial need for these students; however, financial need is a factor in the admissions decision for foreign citizens applying for financial aid.

The aid program includes honorary and need-based scholarships, grants, federal and institutional college work-study program awards, Federal Perkins Loans and Stafford Student Loans, and University-sponsored internships. Limited merit, ROTC, and athletic scholarships are available, and all admitted students are automatically considered for all appropriate merit scholarships.

U.S. citizens and permanent residents applying for financial aid should submit the PROFILE application provided by the College Scholarship Service, the Free Application for Federal Student Aid (FAFSA), and a copy of their family's most recently filed tax forms.

Financial aid applicants who are citizens of other countries should submit the College Board's International Student Financial Aid Application along with a copy of their family's most recent national tax forms. Also, their parents' employers must provide, in English, statements that outline annual income and benefits received in connection with their current employment. Further information is available through the Office of Undergraduate Financial Aid.

Faculty

Duke has a faculty of 3,138 full-time and part-time members in its undergraduate, graduate, and professional schools, 832 of whom teach undergraduates, making the student-faculty ratio 8:1. More importantly, people of national or international prominence, members of major academic societies, state and national advisers, and faculty chairs honoring professors of extraordinary ability are found in every department or division. About 90 percent of tenured or tenure-track faculty members teach undergraduates, and many serve as first-year student and departmental advisers.

Student Government

Students at Duke are considered mature individuals capable of governing their own actions, while furthering the best interests of the broader University community. The Duke Student Government and various student-faculty-administration committees provide diverse avenues for student interaction with professors and administrators. In addition, the Duke Student Government supports students who want to start their own campus organizations. Undergraduates also serve as voting members of the University's Board of Trustees.

Admission Requirements

The Committee on Admissions selects students on the basis of their academic record and quality of their secondary school program, recommendations from teachers and counselors, extracurricular activities and accomplishments, the application essay, and standardized test scores. The University does not discriminate on the basis of race, color, national or ethnic origin, gender, handicap, sexual orientation, or age in its admission policies. No geographic quotas are imposed. Applicants should have at least four years of English and at least three of mathematics, natural science, foreign language, and social studies. Engineering applicants are strongly advised to take four years of mathematics and four years of science, including physics and chemistry. Engineering applicants must have taken calculus before they enroll. Students are encouraged to enroll in advanced-level work as preparation for the Duke curriculum.

Duke accepts both ACT and SAT scores. Students should take either the ACT including writing or the three-part SAT Reasoning and SAT Subject Tests in two areas. Engineering applicants who submit SAT scores must take the SAT Subject Test in mathematics. Personal interviews in the applicants' local areas by members of the Alumni Admissions Advisory Committee are recommended but not required.

Application and Information

Application deadlines for first-year students are November 1 for early decision and January 2 for regular decision. Duke accepts the Common Application or the Universal College Application plus the Duke Student Supplement. Students who want to arrange an alumni interview should file either their application or the Duke Student Supplement of their application by October 19 for early decision or by December 10 for regular decision. For transfer students, the application deadline for fall admission is March 15. Students must apply either to Trinity College of Arts and Sciences or the Pratt School of Engineering at the time of application. Required tests should be taken by January of the senior year or by October for early decision applicants. For additional information, students should contact:

Office of Undergraduate Admissions
Duke University
2138 Campus Drive, Box 90586
Durham, North Carolina 27708-0586

Phone: 919-684-3214
Fax: 919-681-8941
Web site: http://www.admissions.duke.edu/

D'YOUVILLE COLLEGE

BUFFALO, NEW YORK

The College

D'Youville College is a leading institution of higher learning for traditional and nontraditional undergraduate, master's, and doctoral level students from around the world. A significant number of the students come from Western New York and Canada. Students receive a well-rounded general education and specific training and experiences to improve the quality of life across the globe. D'Youville is a nurturing community that seeks to ensure the success of each student in diverse fields such as health care, education, and business. D'Youville offers the diversity and academic excellence of a large school, and the attention and sincerity of a small one.

D'Youville is a private, coeducational, liberal arts and professional college that has offered students an education of high quality since 1908. The College was the first in western New York to offer baccalaureate degrees to women. Its current enrollment is 3,100 men and women. Students may choose from thirty undergraduate and graduate degree programs that are enhanced by a 14:1 student-faculty ratio. The College is committed to helping its students to grow not only in academics but also in the social and personal areas of their college experience.

Students residing in Marguerite Hall or the new student apartment complex have a scenic view of the Niagara River and Lake Erie, which separate the U.S. and Canadian shorelines. The Koessler Administration Building, which once housed the entire college, now contains administrative offices, the chapel, Kavinoky Theatre, and the Learning Center. The Student Center, the focal point of leisure and extracurricular activities, has a new gymnasium, a swimming pool, fitness and wellness area, a training room, a dance studio, a general recreation center, and the main dining facilities. Student organizations and regularly scheduled activities, including intramural sports, NCAA Division III intercollegiate sports (baseball, basketball, crew, volleyball, golf, cross-country, soccer, and softball), a ski club, the College newspaper, the yearbook, and social organizations, as well as academic programs, all help to make up an active campus life.

Location

D'Youville is situated on Buffalo's residential west side. The College is within minutes of many local attractions, including the downtown shopping center, the Kleinhans Music Hall, the Albright-Knox Art Gallery, two museums, and several theaters that offer stage productions. Seasonal changes in the area offer a variety of recreational opportunities. Buffalo is only 90 miles from Toronto and 25 minutes from Niagara Falls, making it a gateway to recreation areas in western New York and Ontario. Holiday Valley, a skier's paradise, is an hour's drive away. The city is served by the New York State Thruway, Amtrak, Greyhound and Trailways bus lines, and most major airlines.

D'Youville enjoys a diversified interchange with the community due to its affiliations with schools, hospitals, and social agencies in the area. College students in the Buffalo area number more than 60,000.

Majors and Degrees

D'Youville offers the degrees of Bachelor of Arts (B.A.), Bachelor of Science (B.S.), and Bachelor of Science in Nursing (B.S.N.). Majors include accounting, biology, business management, chemistry, chiropractic, dietetics, education (elementary, secondary, and special), English, exercise and sports studies, global studies, health services management, history, information technology, international business, mathematics, nursing, occupational therapy, pharmacy, philosophy, physical therapy, physician assistant studies, preprofessional studies (dental, law, medicine, and veterinary studies), psychology, and sociology. Five-year combined bachelor's/master's (B.S./M.S.) programs are offered in accounting, dietetics, education, information technology (B.S.)/international business (M.S.), international business, nursing, occupational therapy, and physician assistant studies. A six-year B.S./D.P.T. program is offered in physical therapy. A seven-year B.S./D.C. program is offered in chiropractic studies. The Doctor of Pharmacy program began in 2010 with an early assurance program for prepharmacy students.

Academic Programs

The area of concentration recognizes individual differences and varying interests but still provides sufficient specialization in one discipline to form a foundation for graduate studies and professional careers. Students attending D'Youville are expected to complete the requirements of their chosen concentration while earning a minimum of 120 credit hours. Core requirements include humanities, 24 hours; social science, 12 hours; science, 7 hours; mathematics/computer science, 6 hours; and electives, 9 hours. A cumulative average of at least 2.0 must be maintained to meet graduation requirements. Sixteen credit hours, or five or six courses per semester, are considered a normal workload. Internships to meet specific career goals may be arranged in any major.

The College offers a Career Discovery Program that was purposely designed for the undecided student. This program, which can last for two years, offers credit courses and internships meeting two years of study in any major.

The academic year is composed of two semesters, each lasting approximately fifteen weeks. The first semester, including final examinations, ends before the Christmas holidays. During the eight-week summer sessions, programs of selected courses are given at all levels on a daily basis.

Off-Campus Programs

The baccalaureate program in nursing is affiliated with thirteen area hospitals and public health agencies. The education program is affiliated with local elementary, junior high, and secondary schools and with special education centers in the area for purposes of student teaching. The occupational therapy, physical therapy, and physician assistant programs are affiliated with appropriate clinical settings throughout the United States.

Academic Facilities

D'Youville's modern Montante Family Library offers state-of-the-art computer reference capabilities for both in-house and off-site users, including access to over seventy online databases. The multimillion-dollar Alt Health Science Building houses laboratories, including those for anatomy, organic chemistry, and gross anatomy; activity and daily living labs for the health professions; and additional laboratories for physics, chemistry, quantitative analysis, and computer science. It also houses classrooms, faculty member offices, and development centers, including one for career development. This is augmented by the modern Bauer Family Academic Center, which provides state-of-the-art classrooms, laboratories, and faculty offices.

Costs

For 2011–12, tuition is $10,725 per semester, and room and board cost $4900 per semester. A general college fee is required and is based on credit hours taken; a Student Association fee of $40 per semester is applied toward concerts, yearbooks, activities, and guest lectures. A $100 deposit ($150 for dietetics, physician assistant studies, occupational therapy, and physical therapy programs), credited toward tuition, must be submitted by all candidates who accept an offer of admission.

Financial Aid

D'Youville attempts to provide financial aid for students who would not otherwise be able to attend. Determination of aid is based on the Free Application for Federal Student Aid. Aid is available in the form of grants, loans, and employment on campus. D'Youville automatically offers scholarships for academic achievement to all eligible incoming students.

All students may qualify for D'Youville's Academic Scholarship Program, which offers scholarships with total values up to $66,000. Students who apply, are accepted, and meet the criteria instantly qualify for one of these scholarships, all of which are renewable annually. These scholarships are not based on need. The three scholarship programs are the Honors Scholarship, the Academic Distinction Scholarship, and the Achievement Scholarship. The Honors Scholarship requires an 85 academic average, a minimum SAT score of 1100 (math and critical reading) or an ACT score of at least 24, and awards 50 percent of tuition and 25 percent of room and board costs. The Academic Distinction Scholarship requires SAT scores of at least 1000 (math and critical reading) or ACT scores of 21 to 23 and an academic average of at least 85. It awards 25 percent of tuition and 50 percent of room and board costs. The Achievement Scholarship criteria include SAT scores of 900 to 1090 (math and critical reading) or ACT scores of 19 to 23 and an academic average of 80 to 84. This scholarship awards $1000–$5000. The Transfer Honors Scholarship is based on a starting GPA of 2.75. This scholarship's award ranges from $1000 to $5000.

Faculty

The ratio of faculty members to students is 1:14. All members of the full-time instructional staff hold a doctorate or another advanced degree. Faculty members act as advisers and are available for consultation with students.

Student Government

The Student Association (SA), a representative form of student self-government, seeks to inspire in its members dedication to the intellectual, social, and moral ideals of the College and works closely with the administration and faculty. All students of D'Youville are considered members of the SA and may be elected to the executive council and the student senate. There are seventeen academic and social clubs affiliated with the SA.

Admission Requirements

An applicant must be a high school graduate or have a high school equivalency diploma before matriculating. The applicant should have a college-preparatory background, including required English and history courses and a sequence in either mathematics or science. Scores on the SAT or the ACT are also required for admission. High school advanced placement credit is acceptable and transferable. The admission decision is based on high school grade point average, rank in class, and scores on the SAT or ACT. Students who have difficulty meeting normal admission standards may be admitted with a reduced academic load.

The College Learning Center offers academic assistance to students whose education has been interrupted or has not prepared them adequately for college courses. The Tutor Bank, a system of peer tutoring, offers the assistance of qualified students to those who need help in specific academic disciplines.

Application and Information

D'Youville admits students on a rolling admission basis; therefore, applications are reviewed as they are received by the admissions office. Transfer students who have a quality point average of at least 2.0 are encouraged to apply by December 1 for the spring semester and by July 1 for the fall semester. A brochure listing course offerings and giving details about costs and room and board is available upon request.

Steve Smith
Director of Admissions
D'Youville College
One D'Youville Square
320 Porter Avenue
Buffalo, New York 14201-1084

Phone: 716-829-7600
          800-777-3921 (toll-free)
Fax: 716-829-7900
E-mail: admissions@dyc.edu
Web site: http://www.dyc.edu
            http://www.dyc.edu/facebook
            http://www.dyc.edu/twitter

EASTERN CONNECTICUT STATE UNIVERSITY
WILLIMANTIC, CONNECTICUT

The University

Eastern Connecticut State University, Connecticut's public liberal arts university, offers thirty-five undergraduate majors and graduate degrees in education and organizational management. Eastern has all the advantages of a private liberal arts college combined with public-university resources and cost. The University's public liberal arts focus and concern for the individual student, along with its small classes, personalized counseling, and independent-study opportunities, encourage involvement and engagement as well as intellectual and personal growth and development. The student body (4,417 full-time undergraduates) is remarkably diverse and includes students from various ethnic, geographic, and socioeconomic backgrounds. Students attending Eastern come from 164 of Connecticut's 169 towns, twenty-four states, and forty-eight countries. Eastern is a residential liberal arts campus. The residence life component is considered integral to students' overall liberal arts education. Most full-time students, including 90 percent of the freshmen, reside on campus. There are seven residence halls and five apartment complexes on campus. Hurley Hall, the University's main food court-style dining area, offers unlimited dining during operational hours. On-campus parking is available to students, except incoming freshmen living on campus. There are more than seventy special interest clubs and organizations on campus, as well as a student newspaper, a yearbook, and a literary and arts magazine. Extracurricular events include concerts, an art and lecture series, dances, films, intramural sports, musical and dramatic productions, and bus trips to Boston and New York City. Varsity sports for men include baseball, basketball, cross-country, lacrosse, soccer, and track. Women participate in intercollegiate basketball, cross-country, field hockey, lacrosse, soccer, softball, swimming, track, and volleyball. Sports facilities include an athletic center with a 2,800-seat gymnasium for badminton, basketball, tennis, and volleyball; a six-lane swimming pool; handball and squash courts; saunas; a fitness center and rooms for physical conditioning, modern dance, and gymnastics; and an outdoor athletic complex that includes a state-of-the-art baseball field with a 1,500-seat grandstand; an eight-lane, all-purpose running track; and field hockey and multipurpose fields. The University's impressive Student Center includes ample meeting space, a theater, multipurpose room, game area, expansive food court, and a glass-enclosed exercise room.

Location

Willimantic, Connecticut, a small city of diversified interests and many styles of living, has a population of 22,000. It has convenient shopping centers and a growing community of ambitious and ecology-minded individuals who are concerned with the city's future. The eastern Connecticut region is famous for its rolling hills, forests, state recreational areas, nature trails, clear lakes and streams, and beaches. Skiing areas are nearby. Hartford is 40 minutes away, Providence is an hour from campus, and New York City and Boston are both less than 2 hours from Willimantic by car.

Majors and Degrees

Eastern offers four undergraduate degrees: the Bachelor of Arts, the Bachelor of General Studies, the Bachelor of Science, and the Associate in Science. The Bachelor of Arts degree is awarded with majors in economics, English, history, history and social sciences, labor relations and human resource management, music, political science, psychology, social work, sociology, Spanish, theater, and visual arts (academic tracks in art history, digital art and design, printing and drawing, and sculpture). The Bachelor of

Science degree programs include accounting, biochemistry, biology (academic tracks in premedicine, predentistry, pre-veterinary studies, and ecology), business administration (concentrations in the areas of finance, human resource management, international business, management, and marketing), business information systems, communication, computer science, early childhood education, elementary education, English, environmental earth science, mathematics, physical education, secondary education, and sport and leisure management. Eastern also offers an individualized major option for students who wish to customize their degree to reflect specific interests. Certification in secondary education is available in biology, English, environmental earth science, history, and mathematics. The associate degree program is available in the arts and sciences. The Bachelor of General Studies is a flexible degree program for adults who are 25 or older. Students may design a program integrating life experience into major or minor concentrations through a learning contract developed with their academic adviser.

Academic Programs

The graduation requirements for a bachelor's degree embrace the University's liberal arts mission and require a minimum of 120 hours of credit and completion of a major program of study. All degree candidates must take a freshman English composition course and fulfill specified course requirements in a three-tier liberal arts core. The tier system includes study in methods and concepts, synthesis and application, and independent inquiry. The University operates on a two-semester system. The fall semester usually starts the first week in September and ends in mid-December; the spring semester, which includes a one-week break in March, runs from mid-January to mid-May. One 6-week and two 3-week sessions are offered during the summer. An Inter-session program is offered in January of each year.

Eastern offers an honors program for academically talented students. This highly competitive program emphasizes scholarly activity, independent study, and special courses and offers tuition scholarships. The Contract Admissions Program (CAP) is an educational support service that offers counseling, tutoring, developmental courses, and financial assistance to highly motivated students who might otherwise have been denied admission on the basis of traditional criteria. Cooperative education (co-op) is an optional work-study program; students may choose to participate in the program for one or more periods.

The University grants credit for Advanced Placement Program examination in all the subject areas tested and accepts up to 60 credit hours earned through the College-Level Examination Program (CLEP). Persons with a minimum of five years of successful work experience in areas of specialization taught by the University may qualify for advanced placement through credit for life experience and learning.

U.S. Army and Air Force ROTC programs, which are offered by the University of Connecticut at Storrs, are available to qualified Eastern students.

Off-Campus Programs

Eastern offers a number of opportunities for off-campus study for college credit. These include off-campus internships, study abroad, and consortium arrangements. Internships are available in the academic areas of biology, business administration, communication, computer science, economics, education, environmental earth science, psychology, public policy and government, sociology, and Spanish. Biology majors may study in Belize or Bermuda through the tropical biology program. There are also opportunities to join international study groups for one semester, one academic year, or a summer session. Eastern also participates in the National Student Exchange (NSE) program, which allows students to attend other public colleges and universities across the United States while still paying tuition and fees to Eastern.

Academic Facilities

The J. Eugene Smith Library contains more than 500,000 volumes and 127,000 square feet of educational learning space. The Media Building contains a color television studio, a recording studio, an FM radio station, an electronic auditorium, a computer center, darkrooms, and graphic arts areas and serves as the hub of the audiovisual distribution system. The planetarium contains two electron microscopes and a geology laboratory. The new LEED-approved Science Building provides modern, well-equipped laboratories for biology, chemistry, and physics. A four-story, 72,000 square-foot classroom building and the library and clock tower serve as the main academic areas of the campus. The Childhood and Family Resource Center, with state-of-the-art classroom and teaching space, meeting facilities, and a full-service day-care center, serves as a model facility for its resources. A new Performing Arts Centers is in the planning stages.

Costs

For 2010–11, tuition and fees for a Connecticut resident were $8350, and nonresident tuition and fees were $18,715 on an annual basis. The fees include a required non-refundable tuition deposit of $200, which is required to secure a place in the University, and a non-refundable $250 housing deposit. Room was estimated at $5674 and board at $4374 for two semesters. Books and supplies average $1000 per year. Tuition and fees are subject to change as warranted and are itemized on the University's Web site.

Financial Aid

Financial aid includes grants and scholarships, low-interest loans, student employment opportunities, and special programs for veterans and their families. The University participates in the Federal Perkins Loan, Federal Pell Grant, Federal Supplemental Educational Opportunity Grant, and Federal Work-Study programs. In addition, it provides aid through alumni funds and other resources of its own. Approximately two thirds of all Eastern students receive financial aid. Awards are based primarily on demonstrated financial need. All students who wish to apply for financial assistance are required to complete the Free Application for Federal Student Aid (FAFSA) and send it to the processing agency by March 15 for the fall semester or by November 15 for the spring semester.

Faculty

The friendliness and approachability of the University's professors are usually noted by the students enrolled at Eastern. While faculty members are focused primarily on quality teaching and the full development of students enrolled, many write and conduct significant research. Faculty members hold advanced degrees from leading American and international colleges and universities; 95 percent hold terminal degrees. Faculty members serve as academic counselors and mentors for students. Full-time advisers and counseling services are available to assist students in matters of personal and academic concern. The student-faculty ratio at Eastern is 16:1. The average class size is 24.

Student Government

An organized plan of student government and student representation on University committees permits students to be actively involved with important issues and develop basic policies for student life. The Student Senate is the governing body; it supervises and coordinates all student activities and serves as a liaison with the faculty, administration, and Board of Trustees.

Admission Requirements

Eastern is considered selective in admission. Applicants are considered on an individual basis, with emphasis placed on the applicant's secondary school record, satisfactory SAT or ACT scores, rank in the high school graduating class, personal accomplishments and motivation, and teachers' or guidance counselors' recommendations. Applicants' complete requirements for secondary school graduation or its equivalent should include 16 academic units of college-preparatory work, with the following divisions: English, 4 years; mathematics, 3 years (4 years preferred); science, 2 years (including 1 year of laboratory science); social sciences, 2 years (including U.S. history); and foreign language, 2 years (3 years preferred). Students who are admitted without having fulfilled the language requirement must complete one year of a foreign language (6 credits) at Eastern. Deferred admission is also available. A campus visit is strongly suggested, although not required. A limited number of highly motivated students who do not qualify for admission if traditional criteria are used may be admitted to the University by successfully completing the Summer Transition Experience Program/Contract Admission Program or the Summer Proof of Ability Option. Students should contact the Office of Admissions for more information on special admission options.

Application and Information

Eastern reviews completed applications for admission on a rolling basis. Offers of admission are made and deposits accepted until the University reaches its enrollment capacity. Students are encouraged to apply early in their senior year. Tuition and housing deposits are due upon admission. Applications for the fall semester can be submitted after the first quarter of the senior year of high school. Freshman applicants must submit an admission application; a $50 nonrefundable application fee; a complete transcript of high school grades and rank in class; an essay explaining why Eastern, Connecticut's public liberal arts college, is the right college choice for the applicant; two recommendations from guidance counselors or teachers; and an official copy of their SAT or ACT score report. Applicants are usually notified of the admission decision within one month after the application is complete. Applicants are encouraged to apply online at http://www.easternct.edu. Application forms and information may be requested from:

Christopher Dorsey
Interim Director of Admissions and Enrollment Management
Eastern Connecticut State University
83 Windham Street
Willimantic, Connecticut 06226

Phone: 860-465-5286
Fax: 860-465-5544
E-mail: admissions@easternct.edu
Web site: http://www.easternct.edu
http://on.fb.me/EasternCT_StateU (Facebook)

Eastern's J. Eugene Smith Library, with more than 500,000 volumes and 127,000 square feet of educational space, serves as the academic hub of the campus.

EASTERN UNIVERSITY

ST. DAVIDS, PENNSYLVANIA

The University

Prospective students can connect with Eastern University on Facebook at http://www.facebook.com/easterneagle.

Eastern University (EU) is a Christian university committed to the integration of faith, reason, and justice. In all of its undergraduate, graduate, professional, doctoral, and international programs, the University's mission is to produce Christians who are capable of confronting injustice and indifference. Viewing education through the lens of a Christian worldview, Eastern challenges students to look outside themselves and strive to change the world that is into the world that ought to be.

Eastern University values its affiliation with the American Baptist Churches USA and also welcomes an interdenominational student body, faculty, and campus community. Classes are taught from a Christian worldview by faculty from all ends of the evangelical spectrum. As a result, everyone at the University can actively pursue the full dynamic of abundant Christian life with freedom and confidence.

The academic curriculum at Eastern University emphasizes the liberal arts and sciences while helping a student pursue a major field of study. Classroom experience is intellectually rigorous and practical experience is gained through a variety of internships, practicums, observations, and service learning opportunities.

More than 1,700 full-time undergraduates are enrolled at Eastern in the College of the Arts and Sciences. The total enrollment at the University, including adult education, seminary, and graduate programs, is approximately 3,700 students. These programs take place in the Campolo College for Graduate and Professional Studies, Esperanza College, and Palmer Theological Seminary.

On-campus housing at the St. Davids campus accommodates more than 1,200 students in eight residence halls. Rooms are structured as singles, doubles, triples, quads, suites, and apartments. The entire St. Davids campus is wireless, including dorms and living areas.

Athletics at Eastern University are NCAA Division III and the teams compete in the MAC Freedom Conference. Intercollegiate teams for men are fielded in baseball, basketball, cross-country, Frisbee (club), golf, lacrosse, soccer, swimming (club), tennis, and volleyball (club). The intercollegiate program for women offers basketball, cheerleading (club), cross-country, field hockey, Frisbee (club), lacrosse, soccer, softball, swimming (club), tennis, and volleyball. An intramural program also offers numerous opportunities for students to actively participate in sports.

Eastern provides students with a well-developed Student Ministry Program that challenges students and helps them grow in their faith. With over forty different clubs and ministries, students are bound to find something to be involved in. Student ministries include weekly chapel, "Sunday Night Live" worship led by students, grow groups, Bible studies, and student chaplains. Among the outreach opportunities available are Evangelicals for Social Action, Fellowship of Christian Athletes (FCA), Youth Against Complacency and Homelessness Today (YACHT), Young Life, Christ Hands In Action (CHIA), and Habitat for Humanity. Although it is an independent mission organization, the Evangelical Association for the Promotion of Education (EAPE) works closely with the Student Ministry Program and welcomes Eastern student volunteers to staff its programs in inner-city Philadelphia and Camden. These are just a few of the clubs and ministries offered at EU.

Location

Eastern University is located 25 minutes west of Philadelphia, Pennsylvania, and within 2½ hours of New York City; Washington, D.C.; and Baltimore, Maryland. Sitting in the historic Main Line in the town of Wayne, Eastern's convenient suburban setting provides easy access to Philadelphia via SEPTA trains that run every half hour from the St. Davids station.

Eastern University has one of the most picturesque campuses in America, with its three lakes, wooded walking trails, historic buildings, and working waterwheel. Besides major metropolitan centers, the campus is also within an hour of Lancaster, Pennsylvania, the Jersey Shore, and the Pocono Mountains and within 20 minutes of Valley Forge National Park. The campus is also just 6 minutes from the second-largest mall on the East Coast, King of Prussia.

Majors and Degrees

Undergraduate degrees include the Bachelor of Arts, Bachelor of Science, Bachelor of Science in Nursing, and Bachelor of Social Work degrees. Majors are offered in accounting and finance, athletic training, biblical studies (biblical languages/without biblical languages), biochemistry, biokinetics (exercise science, sports medicine, pre–occupational/pre–physical therapy), biological studies, biology, chemistry, chemistry business, communication studies (interpersonal/organizational, media, rhetoric), dance, economic development, elementary education (early childhood, special education), engineering (3+2 with Villanova), English (journalism, literature, writing), environmental studies, entrepreneurial studies, history, individualized, international area studies and business, management, marketing, mathematics, missions and anthropology, music (church music, composition/electronic music, performance, teaching), nursing, political science, psychology, secondary education (five-year M.Ed. option), social work, sociology, Spanish, theological studies, and youth ministry.

Minors are offered in accounting, American history, anthropology, astronomy, biblical studies, biology, chemistry, communication studies, dance, English (journalism, literature, writing), environmental studies, European history, finance, fine arts, French, gender studies, Latin American studies, legal studies, management, marketing, mathematics, missions, music, nonprofit administration, philosophy, political science, psychology, social welfare, sociology, Spanish, sport and coaching, and theological studies. Preprofessional programs are offered in dentistry, law, medicine, occupational therapy, and physical therapy.

Academic Programs

In the core curriculum, students take courses designed to fulfill the basic mission of Eastern: to provide a biblical foundation for all learning and action, to ensure the acquisition of basic skills, and to broaden the student's view of the world. The central themes of the Christian faith are integrated into the course content of the core curriculum, which includes courses such as Justice in a Pluralistic Society and Science, Technology, and Values. Other core classes include a life fitness course, college writing, and Western civilization.

The Templeton Honors College, "a college within the University," offers a rigorous, classically oriented curriculum designed to challenge academically gifted students and prepare them for leadership and service in all areas of culture and society. The honors college includes special events and a required study-abroad, study-away semester. Enrollment in the honors college is highly competitive and limited to 24 to 35 new students each academic year. Students qualify to apply to the Templeton Honors College by achieving a combined score of 1350 or higher on the SAT or 30 or higher on the ACT or by ranking in the top 9 percent of their high school class. While these areas are important, an interview is required and is often the deciding factor on acceptance to the honors college.

Off-Campus Programs

Eastern students are encouraged to study abroad or participate in special programs recognized by the University. Academic study abroad is required of language majors. Non–language majors may select from many options, including (but not limited to) Austria, Canada, England, Israel, Kenya, Peru, South Africa, and Uganda. At the AuSable Institute in Michigan, students may apply for certificate programs leading to the designation of naturalist, land resources analyst, water resources analyst, or environmental analyst.

The American Studies Program, sponsored by the Coalition of Christian Colleges and Universities, provides an opportunity for students to study or serve as interns in Washington, D.C., with the nation's leaders. In the Latin American Studies Program, students live with native families; study Spanish and the local culture, history, politics, economics, and religious life; participate in service projects; and travel in Central America. The coalition also operates a film-study center in California and offers Russian and Middle East studies programs.

The Oregon Extension offers a semester of community living and liberal arts studies in the Cascade Mountains of southern Oregon. The Honors Research Program at the Argonne National Laboratory in Chicago provides juniors and seniors majoring in biology, chemistry, and math an opportunity for advanced research at a nationally recognized laboratory. Through the Goshen Study Service Trimester, students and faculty members study the history and culture of Caribbean nations and engage in a service project. Exchange programs with selected American Baptist colleges allow upperclassmen to spend a semester or a year at another college. May Term opportunities include special courses, semesters, and study tours. Eastern Baptist Theological Seminary offers students the chance to take selected course work.

Academic Facilities

Of Eastern's twenty-six buildings, the primary academic facility is the McInnis Learning Center. In addition to classrooms and offices for faculty members and administrators, the main floor includes a 300-seat auditorium and several music practice rooms. Other features are the biology center; a highly regarded curriculum laboratory for those preparing to be teachers; a technology classroom for distance learning; the Julia Fowler Planetarium, containing a digital projector "Scidome" powered by Starry Night; a media services center; a computer-assisted language laboratory; fully equipped "smart" classrooms; and three student computer centers. The state-of-the-art Bradstreet Observatory is located on the roof of the McInnis Learning Center.

Heritage House offers an acoustically designed Great Room for music performances as well as smart classrooms with the latest computer technology.

The recently constructed Harold Howard Center is a 25,000-square-foot addition to the Warner Library. In addition to more space for the library, the addition features wireless technology, smart classrooms, and more study and office space. Eastern students have direct access to libraries throughout the region and around the world via the computer and more than fifty electronic databases.

Facilities for chemistry, physics, and computer science are located in Andrews Hall. In addition to offices and classroom space, Andrews houses six teaching laboratories, a computer center, and scientific equipment generally found only at larger colleges and universities. Instrumentation includes 300 MHz FT-NMR, FT-IR, GC-MS, AAS, Diode-array UV-Vis, HPLC, PCR, 96-well microplate reader, and molecular modeling.

Costs

Tuition for the 2010–11 academic year was $24,550 and room and board costs were $9090, for a total of $33,640. However, it is rare that any student pays that amount. Once accepted, a student is generally given an academic/merit scholarship or grants ranging from $3,500 to $11,000.

Financial Aid

Eastern is committed to providing education to qualified students regardless of their means. The financial aid program offers scholarships, grants, loans, and employment. The University utilizes the Pennsylvania Higher Education Assistance Agency (PHEAA) for needs analysis forms processing. The student is required to complete the Free Application for Federal Student Aid (FAFSA) to determine financial aid eligibility.

Overall, the University views financial assistance to students as a cooperative investment. If parents contribute to the maximum of their ability and the student contributes a fair share through earnings and personal savings, the University attempts to complete the partnership.

Non-need academic scholarships ranging from $500 to full tuition are available. These scholarships are awarded on the basis of SAT or ACT scores and high school class rank information. Music, leadership, Templeton Honors College, FCA, Young Life, and church matching grants are other University-based grant programs.

Faculty

Eastern University employs more than 125 full- and part-time faculty members. Eighty-seven percent have earned doctorates. With an emphasis on teaching and a commitment to research, faculty members have authored more than 300 scholarly publications. Some faculty members teach both graduate and undergraduate courses, and almost all serve as academic advisers. Classes are kept small, with a student-faculty ratio of 12:1.

Admission Requirements

The University seeks applicants who present acceptable academic records. The average applicant has a GPA of 3.2 and a score of 1100 out of 1600 on the SAT. A campus visit and interview are recommended. Transfer applicants are welcome.

Application and Information

Applications are generally accepted until the beginning of each term. Admission decisions are made on a rolling basis. For more information, students should visit Eastern's Web site at http://www.eastern.edu. Students should contact:

Michael Dziedziak, M.B.A.
Director of Undergraduate Admissions
Eastern University
1300 Eagle Road
St. Davids, Pennsylvania 19087-3696

Phone: 800-452-0996 (toll-free)
E-mail: ugadm@eastern.edu
Web site: http://www.eastern.edu
          http://www.facebook.com/easterneagle

ELMHURST COLLEGE
ELMHURST, ILLINOIS

The College

Elmhurst is a four-year comprehensive college in the liberal arts tradition. Founded in 1871, the College has a long history of preparing students for lifetimes of professional and personal achievement. Elmhurst is affiliated with the United Church of Christ.

The College has developed a contemporary framing of liberal learning that it calls the Elmhurst Experience. One hallmark is student self-formation, in which students, through study, reflection, and collective action, decide who they will be and what they will stand for. The other is early professional preparation, in which students are exposed early to professional options, so that their career choice is informed by real-world experiences. This way, students will be prepared for meaningful work in a complex and competitive global society.

The College offers more than fifty majors, four accelerated majors for adults, fifteen preprofessional programs, and nine graduate programs. The honors program provides extra opportunities for students who are especially talented, curious, and motivated.

Elmhurst ranks in the top tier of Midwest colleges and universities with master's programs, according to *U.S. News & World Report*'s "America's Best Colleges" issue. The Princeton Review also lists Elmhurst among the region's premier institutions of higher learning. Students come to Elmhurst from many states and countries and from nearly every religious, racial, and ethnic background.

The student body comprises about 2,800 traditional undergraduate students, 350 adults pursuing an undergraduate degree, and nearly 300 graduate students. Students participate in more than 100 activities, including theater, music, social action, and student government. More than half play intramurals or participate in one of eighteen NCAA Division III varsity teams. Six residence halls and a variety of apartment-style housing options are available for students who want to live on campus.

Location

Elmhurst, Illinois, a quiet suburb of Chicago, is filled with family-owned stores and restaurants, as well as theater, music, art museums, and other recreational activities.

The beautiful 38-acre campus looks like a college should look: big trees, broad lawns, and twenty-four stately redbrick buildings. With more than 600 varieties of trees and shrubs, the Elmhurst campus is an arboretum; with modern facilities, top-notch faculty members, and a great geographical location, it's an excellent place to get an education.

Just 16 miles away (30 minutes by train), Chicago has something for everyone. Sports fans can enjoy watching the Bears, Bulls, Cubs, or White Sox in action, or play sports in Millennium Park or along the waterfront. Students who are interested in art or culture can visit the Art Institute of Chicago, the Field Museum, and the Shedd Aquarium. The city has a world-class theater scene and is renowned for its architecture. Chicago also features lots of shopping, dining, and nightlife.

Majors and Degrees

The College offers bachelor's degrees in accounting, American studies, art, art business, art education, biology, business administration, chemistry, communication studies, computer game and entertainment technology, computer science, criminal justice, early childhood education, economics, elementary education, English, exercise science, finance, French, geography, German, history, information systems, interdisciplinary communication studies, international business, jazz studies, logistics and supply chain management, management, marketing, mathematics, multi-language, music, music business, music education, musical theater, nursing, organizational communication, philosophy, physical education, physics, political science, psychology, religion and service, religious studies, secondary education, sociology, Spanish, special education, speech-language pathology, theater, theater arts education, theological studies and Christian ministry, and urban studies. Students also may design their own interdepartmental major.

Preprofessional programs are available in actuarial science, allied health sciences, dentistry, engineering, law, library science, medicine, seminary studies, and veterinary medicine.

Academic Programs

Elmhurst College confers five undergraduate degrees: Bachelor of Arts, Bachelor of Fine Arts, Bachelor of Science, Bachelor of Music, and Bachelor of Liberal Studies. While requirements for each degree vary, all require a minimum of 128 semester hours of credit. The academic program consists of three interrelated parts: courses that meet the general education requirements, courses that fulfill requirements of the major, and elective courses that students select to satisfy intellectual curiosity or to enhance the breadth of their academic programs.

The Elmhurst College Integrated Curriculum (General Education Program) seeks to educate in three ways: exposing students to nine areas of knowledge; requiring practice/proficiency within certain skill sets; and developing values through off-campus experiences. The areas of knowledge in which students will complete a course in each category are inquiry into ethics and justice, religious studies in context, literature, fine arts, historical analysis, social and political analysis, cognitive and behavioral studies, physical science, and life science. Students will also demonstrate proficiencies in writing, math, computer technology, and foreign languages while developing values in civic matters such as global engagement and social responsibility.

Beyond the general education requirements, major-course requirements, and courses taken to fulfill elective requirements, students earning the Bachelor of Science must complete an additional 8 semester hours in mathematics; students earning the Bachelor of Music must complete at least 64 semester hours in music (specific courses are determined by the Department of Music); and students earning the Bachelor of Liberal Studies must complete 32 to 48 semester hours in two areas of concentration (rather than a traditional major). Students are expected to declare their major field of study prior to completion of the sophomore year. Students may also select a maximum of two minors.

Off-Campus Programs

Elmhurst encourages first-, second-, and third-year students to pursue international education programs by going abroad for a month, a term, or a year. Through a range of opportunities to study and work abroad, students refine their language skills, challenge their cultural assumptions, grow as individuals, better understand themselves and their countries, and gain a greater respect for other cultures.

During the January and summer terms, Elmhurst faculty members teach in such places as Costa Rica, England, Germany, Jamaica, and Morocco through the Elmhurst College Abroad program.

In addition to sponsoring its own courses abroad, the College offers programs through a consortium of colleges and through two partnership programs. For example, students can combine classes with internships in Australia, Belgium, France (Paris), Germany, and Spain; students can earn academic credit for participating in service-learning and academic courses in the Czech Republic, Ecuador, India, Mexico, the Philippines, and Scotland; and other programs take students to Austria, China, England, Italy, Ireland, and New Zealand.

Academic Facilities

The A. C. Buehler Library provides a variety of services for Elmhurst students. Books, periodicals, and audiovisual materials are available, along with interlibrary loan services, databases, electronic journals, and other electronic resources.

Three centers for professional development help students explore their interests and assess career options. The Center for Professional Excellence helps students explore their interests and assess career possibilities through internships, mentoring, and shadowing programs. The Patterson Center for the Health Professions offers advising and programs for students considering careers in the health professions. The Niebuhr Center offers programs for students interested in ministry and service.

The Elmhurst College Learning Center helps students succeed as independent learners. Students can receive one-on-one tutoring in math, reading, writing, and study-skills areas or attend test preparation workshops.

Costs

Full-time tuition for 2010–11 was $28,600. Part-time tuition was $3104 per full course ($776 per credit hour). Other costs included a matriculation fee of $125 ($50 for transfer students), an academic technology fee of $30 per term, and a residential network fee of $50 per term. Students living on campus can expect to pay $4956 for a double-occupancy room and $3260 for a standard meal plan.

Financial Aid

Financial aid is awarded to approximately 98 percent of entering students. Entering freshmen are eligible for renewable scholarships based on grade point average and composite ACT scores or combined SAT scores. Students should apply for admission by February 15 for scholarship consideration. Other Elmhurst scholarships are awarded based on grade point average, program of study, financial need, and other criteria. Awards range from $1000 to $21,000 per academic year. The average financial aid package is $19,600 per year. Elmhurst need-based grants are available for eligible full-time students.

The Illinois Student Assistance Commission administers grants of $496 to $4968 per year to eligible Illinois residents. The Department of Education awards Federal Pell Grants of $976 to $5350 per year. Pell recipients may also be eligible for Supplemental Educational Opportunity Grants of $100 to $4000 a year.

Student loans include the Federal Direct Loan, Federal Perkins Loan, and Federal PLUS Program. Alternative loans may be available from private lenders.

Faculty

Elmhurst provides superior teaching on a personal scale. All classes are taught by professors, not teaching assistants. About 84 percent of the College's 136 full-time faculty members hold a Ph.D. or other terminal degree in their field. The student-faculty ratio of 13:1 is among the best in higher education. The average class has 18 students.

Student Government

The Student Government Association (SGA) consists of 21 students elected by the student body, 3 members of the faculty elected by the faculty, and 3 administrators selected by the student members. The SGA serves as the major policy-recommending body to the President and Trustees on issues of student and campus life. The Elmhurst College Union Board and its committees serve as the primary student programming organization on campus.

Admission Requirements

Elmhurst seeks students who show evidence of their ability to complete college-level work based on high school performance. Preference is given to students who have completed 16 academic units, including 3 units of English; 2 units each of mathematics, laboratory science, and social studies; and 7 units in additional college-preparatory subjects.

Application and Information

In order to apply, prospective students are required to submit an application for admission. Applications may be completed online, or paper copies can be downloaded or requested from the Office of Admission and Financial Aid. Students must also submit official high school transcripts or GED results, official SAT or ACT scores, and a teacher recommendation. Elmhurst College's ACT code is 1020. An interview and essay are recommended but not required. Applications are accepted on a rolling basis. Application review begins October 1.

Prospective students can arrange an individual visit, which might include an overnight stay and meetings with faculty members, or come for a Preview Day.

Further information about the College, the application process, and campus visits can be obtained from:

Office of Admission
Elmhurst College
190 Prospect Avenue
Elmhurst, Illinois 60126-3296
Phone: 630-617-3400
      800-697-1871 (toll-free)
E-mail: admit@elmhurst.edu
Web site: http://www.elmhurst.edu/
      http://on.fb.me/ElmhurstCollege (Facebook)
      http://twitter.com/elmhurstcollege
      http://www.youtube.com/user/ECvids#p/p

ELMIRA COLLEGE
ELMIRA, NEW YORK

The College

Elmira College is a small, private, coeducational college that is recognized for its emphasis on education of high quality in the liberal arts and preprofessional programs. One of the oldest colleges in the United States, Elmira was founded in 1855. The College has always produced graduates interested in both community service and successful careers. Friendliness, personal attention, strong college spirit, and support for learning beyond the classroom help to make Elmira a unique community. Elmira College is one of only 270 colleges in the nation to be granted a chapter of the prestigious Phi Beta Kappa honor society.

The full-time undergraduate enrollment is about 1,200 men and women. The students at Elmira represent more than thirty-five states, primarily those in the Northeast, with the highest representation coming from New York, New Jersey, Massachusetts, Connecticut, Maine, and Pennsylvania. International students from thirty-one countries were enrolled in 2010. Ninety-three percent of the full-time undergraduates live in College residence halls, and dormitory rooms are equipped to provide direct access to the Internet. Wireless access is also available in the library, Campus Center, and other hot spots campuswide.

The intercollegiate sports program includes men's and women's basketball, golf, ice hockey, lacrosse, soccer, and tennis and women's cheerleading, field hockey, softball, and volleyball. Intramural programs are also available. Emerson Hall houses the student fitness center, a pool, and a gym capable of seating 1,000, as well as the Gibson Theatre, which has a state-of-the-art sound and lighting system. Professional societies; clubs; music, dance, and drama groups; a student-operated FM radio station; and the student newspaper, yearbook, and literary magazine also provide numerous opportunities for extracurricular activity.

Location

Elmira College is located in the city of Elmira, which has a population of 35,000, in the Finger Lakes region of New York. The campus is a 10-minute walk from downtown Elmira. The relationship between the College and the local community is excellent, and numerous community activities and facilities are open to students, including the Elmira Symphony and Choral Society, the Elmira Little Theatre, clubs and civic groups, museums, movies, and a performing arts center. Excellent recreational areas are available in upstate New York and nearby Pennsylvania.

Majors and Degrees

Elmira College offers programs leading to the bachelor's degree in more than thirty-five majors, including accounting, American studies, art, art education, biology, biology-chemistry, business administration, chemistry, classical studies, clinical laboratory science, criminal justice, economics, childhood and adolescent education, English literature, environmental studies, French, history, human services, individualized studies, international business, international studies, mathematics, music, nursing, philosophy and religion, political science, psychology, public affairs, social studies, sociology and anthropology, Spanish, speech and hearing, and theater. Secondary teaching certification

is offered in several areas. A 3-2 program in chemical engineering with Clarkson University is available, and 4-1 M.B.A. programs are available at Alfred University, Clarkson University, Rochester Institute of Technology, and Union College. Army and Air Force ROTC are available through respective units at Cornell University.

Preprofessional preparation is offered in education, medical technology, nursing, and speech pathology and audiology. Faculty advisers assist those who seek preparation for graduate study in dentistry, law, or medicine in choosing appropriate course work. Nearly 45 percent of Elmira graduates pursue graduate study.

Academic Programs

The College's calendar is composed of two 12-week terms followed by a six-week term in the spring. Students enroll for four subjects during the twelve-week terms, completing the first term by mid-December and the second during the first week of April. Term III, the six-week term, running from mid-April through May, may be devoted to a particular project involving travel, internship, research, or independent study. Students are required to participate in internships in order to gain practical and meaningful experience related to their program of study. Credit is awarded for these experiences. Forty percent of Elmira College students study abroad at least one time during their four years of study.

Special opportunities for outstanding students include participation in thirteen national honorary societies on campus and a chance to assist faculty members in research. The College also offers an accelerated three-year graduation option for outstanding students, and an Advanced Placement Program is available.

Army ROTC and Air Force ROTC are available.

Off-Campus Programs

Through the study-abroad programs, students may study in the United Kingdom, France, Spain, and Japan, as well as in other countries throughout Europe and Asia. Students from Elmira may spend Term III studying marine and island ecology or doing sociological research on the island of San Salvador in the Bahamas. The six-week Term III permits students in any major to study abroad, and students are able to participate in this program starting in their freshman year. Students have the opportunity to spend their junior year abroad studying for either one term or three years in any foreign country.

Academic Facilities

The Elmira campus offers exceptional academic facilities in a beautiful setting. The modern Gannett-Tripp Library houses more than 391,000 volumes, receives 2,500 periodicals, and includes a special Mark Twain collection room and photography and audiovisual facilities.

The College Computer Center offers four PC and Apple Macintosh microcomputer labs for student use.

A Center for Mark Twain Studies has been established at Quarry Farm, the author's summer home, which is located only a few miles from campus. The College also operates a Speech and Hearing Clinic on campus, which serves the public and provides valuable clinical experience for undergraduate students. Excellent facilities for drama and music are available.

Costs

Tuition for 2010–11 was $34,500, room was $6100, board was $5050, and fees were $1400.

Financial Aid

Financial aid is available for both freshmen and transfer students. Awards are based upon the Free Application for Federal Student Aid (FAFSA) as well as the student's past academic performance. Types of aid include grants, scholarships, loans, and work opportunities. Sources of aid include college, federal, state, and private dollars. In addition, superior students may qualify for non-need based Elmira College Honors Scholarships, which are available to both freshmen and transfer students and range from $10,000 to full tuition per year, renewable throughout four years. About 75 percent of the full-time undergraduates receive need-based financial aid. Twenty percent of students receive non-need merit aid.

Faculty

Members of the faculty are chosen for their ability in and dedication to teaching. All full-time faculty members serve as advisers. Currently, the full-time faculty consists of 10 full professors, 28 associate professors, 30 assistant professors, and 12 instructors. One hundred percent of the full-time faculty hold the Ph.D. or highest degree necessary to teach undergraduate students in their field.

Student Government

Student government, an important part of the educational system at Elmira College, prepares students for active and responsible citizenship in society. Student government organizations include the Student Senate, the Judicial Board, and the Student Activities Board.

Admission Requirements

The Office of Admissions at Elmira College uses a rolling admission system. Each applicant is evaluated individually on the basis of his or her total application, including academic record, rank in class, SAT or ACT scores, essay, activities, letters of recommendation, and goals. The College strongly advises a personal interview. The recommendations of teachers and guidance counselors are also important. Special consideration is given to applicants from distant states and other countries, applicants with special skills, and applicants who are prepared to become actively involved in the campus community.

Elmira has two early decision programs available to students.

Application and Information

For further information, applicants should contact:

Director of Admissions
Elmira College
Elmira, New York 14901
Phone: 800-935-6472 (toll-free)
E-mail: admissions@elmira.edu
Web site: http://www.elmira.edu

The Mark Twain Study is one of the most famous literary landmarks in America.

EMBRY-RIDDLE AERONAUTICAL UNIVERSITY

DAYTONA BEACH, FLORIDA

EMBRY-RIDDLE
Aeronautical University

The University

Embry-Riddle Aeronautical University's reputation as the leader in aviation and aerospace education is recognized worldwide. The University's history and legacy date back almost to the time of the Wright brothers, and in 2009 the University introduced the nation's first and only Ph.D. program in aviation. Embry-Riddle is an independent, non-sectarian, not-for-profit, coeducational university serving culturally diverse students seeking careers in aviation, aerospace, engineering, business, and related fields. Residential campuses in Daytona Beach, Florida, and Prescott, Arizona, provide education in a traditional setting, while the Worldwide Campus provides instruction through more than 170 centers in the United States, Europe, Canada, and the Middle East and through online learning.

Approximately 4,500 undergraduate students and 500 graduate students are currently enrolled at the 185-acre Daytona Beach residential campus. Students come from all fifty states, and nearly 100 countries are represented, making Embry-Riddle truly an international university.

More than twenty undergraduate degree programs, six graduate programs, and one doctoral program are offered at the Daytona Beach campus. Embry-Riddle's premier aeronautical science (professional pilot) program and award-winning aerospace engineering program are the largest on campus and among the largest of their type in the nation.

Embry-Riddle conducts applied research valued at approximately $30 million per year, and is leading the development of the Next Generation Air Transportation System along with the Federal Aviation Administration, Lockheed Martin, Boeing, and other high-tech organizations. Alumni are leaders in every facet of the aviation and aerospace industries and serve as a strong network and resource for students.

Students at the Daytona Beach campus enjoy a wide array of activities and clubs, many focused on aviation and aerospace, as well as fraternities, sororities, and recreational opportunities. Forty-three percent of students live on campus.

Embry-Riddle's award-winning precision flight demonstration teams offer students the opportunity to compete nationally in air and ground events. Embry-Riddle also has the largest all-volunteer Air Force ROTC detachment in the country and among the fastest-growing Navy ROTC units and Army ROTC battalions. Embry-Riddle athletes participate in intercollegiate and intramural competitions in many sports, including baseball, basketball, crew, cross-country, golf, soccer, tennis, track, volleyball, and ice hockey.

The 68,000-square-foot ICI Center contains two full-size NCAA basketball courts, a fitness center, and a weight room. The ICI Center provides a place to host sporting events and assemblies. The University sports complex also includes a soccer field, the Sliwa Stadium ballpark, the Ambassador William Crotty Tennis Center, and the Track and Field Complex. The Tine Davis Fitness Center is adjacent to the pool and features comprehensive fitness services and wellness programs.

The 5,300-square-foot interfaith chapel accommodates the variety of faiths represented by the student body of Embry-Riddle. It consists of a 140-seat nondenominational worship area and four prayer rooms (Catholic, Jewish, Muslim, and Protestant).

Location

The year-round clear flying weather and the resort communities surrounding Embry-Riddle's residential campus in Daytona Beach, Florida, offer students an excellent environment in which to study, fly, and enjoy recreational activities. The campus, which is located adjacent to the Daytona Beach International Airport, is only 3 miles from what is called the world's most famous beach. The high-technology industries located in nearby Orlando provide the University with an outstanding support base. In addition, the Kennedy Space Center is less than a 2-hour drive away.

Majors and Degrees

The Daytona Beach campus of Embry-Riddle awards undergraduate degrees at the baccalaureate and associate level. Bachelor of Science degrees are offered in a variety of areas, each with a focus on the aviation and aerospace industries. In engineering, students can pursue a Bachelor of Science degree in aerospace engineering, civil engineering, computer engineering, electrical engineering, engineering physics, mechanical engineering, and software engineering. Students who are interested in business administration may elect to major in management or air transportation. The College of Aviation awards degrees in aeronautical science (professional piloting), air traffic management, applied meteorology, aviation maintenance science, and safety science. Other majors include interdisciplinary studies (design your own major), communication, computational mathematics, homeland security, human factors psychology, and space physics. Students entering Embry-Riddle with an undecided major have the opportunity to explore a variety of academic pursuits before making a commitment to a specific track.

Academic Programs

Even a field as specialized as aviation requires a broad educational background. General education courses required of all students who are pursuing a baccalaureate program include communication skills, such as English composition, literature, and technical report writing; humanities; social sciences; mathematics; physical science; economics; and computer science. To ensure academic success, Embry-Riddle provides free tutorial services.

The academic year is divided into two semesters of fifteen weeks each, with the summer session divided into two terms. The average course load for each fall or spring semester is 15 credit hours.

Academic Facilities

The College of Aviation building at the Daytona Beach campus provides an unsurpassed environment for aviation education and research. The multimillion-dollar simulation laboratories duplicate the components and functions in the national airspace system, including capabilities to replicate actual weather reporting, airports, airways, air traffic control, flow control, and pilot and aircraft performance as found in the national air transportation system. The simulator building, which is located in the greater College of Aviation complex, contains highly sophisticated flight training devices (FTDs) that provide realistic training in aircraft used in flight training as well as the major airlines. Flight instruction is provided in the Embry-Riddle fleet of sixty-plus aircraft and a wide array of flight training devices. Aircraft are equipped with Automatic Dependent Surveillance-Broadcast (ADS-B) technology that decreases hazards associated with traffic, weather, and terrain. The High-Altitude Normobaric Lab allows students to experience the symptoms of high-altitude hypoxia to better enable them to recognize and recover from this threat. Embry-Riddle is the first university in the nation to acquire this technology.

The Advanced Flight Simulation Center gives Embry-Riddle students the opportunity to train in world-class simulators. The center, with more than 20,000 square feet of space and four high bays, currently houses two advanced aviation training devices (AATDs), eight Cessna 172S NAVIIIs (Skyhawk), two Diamond DA42 TAE Twin Stars, two Diamond DA42 L360s, and one Canadair Regional Jet (CRJ-200). These devices duplicate the actual cockpit, adverse weather conditions, a full range of emergency situations, and virtually any flight pattern and complement flight training done in actual aircraft. Flight simulation enables students to learn aircraft performance, experience aerodynamic effects, and perform flight maneuvers immediately and without risk. Qualified to Level 6, the University's devices faithfully reproduce Embry-Riddle's fleet of single-engine and multiengine aircraft and are equipped with 220-degree panoramic visual theaters. In addition, the Aviation Building houses air traffic control and tower simulators, one motion-based disorientation trainer, and six basic aviation training devices (BATDs).

Construction of the James Hagedorn Aviation Complex is scheduled to be completed in the fall of 2011. This expansion of the aviation complex will include 96,000 square feet in a three-building facility that will become the home of flight training operations, aircraft maintenance training, and a fleet maintenance hangar. The Emil Buehler Aviation Maintenance Science building is slated to house cutting-edge labs dedicated to aircraft systems, turbine engines, metallic and composite materials, avionics, and avionics electronics. The facility is designed to include classrooms, a licensed engine-repair station, a machine shop, offices, and a third-floor observation deck overlooking the Daytona Beach International Airport runways.

The facilities in the Lehman Engineering and Technology Center serve academic departments including Human Factors and Systems, Engineering Physics and Space Physics, Mathematics and Computer Science, and all the engineering disciplines. Labs include the atmospheric physics research lab, flight dynamics and simulation lab, materials testing lab, structures lab, aerospace composites lab, real time lab, aerospace engineering and design lab, wind tunnels, airport noise abatement lab, electronic communications and microwave lab, microcomputer and digital lab, circuits and power lab, electricity and magnetism thermo lab, human factors research lab, and many more. Students use the labs to work in teams to develop hands-on projects. Research is conducted by faculty members and graduate and undergraduate students.

The 18,500-square-foot Capt. Willie Miller Instructional Center, a lecture auditorium and classroom complex, provides space for large audience events, including presentations by distinguished lecturers and speakers.

The College of Business academic building features the aviation operations simulation lab, which is used to develop and evaluate aviation/airline operational strategies and processes. In addition, the College's Teaching Airport, a partnership between Embry-Riddle and Daytona Beach International Airport, is focused on teaching, research, and public outreach.

The Jack R. Hunt Memorial Library is a 49,000-square-foot facility with a seating capacity of 800. The library houses more than 230,000 volumes and book titles, and more than 340,000 items of microfiche, periodicals, documents, newspapers, and media programs. Among the library's resources is a historical aviation collection donated by the Manufacturers Aircraft Association (MAA) in 1976. This collection includes a continuous run of *Aviation Week & Space Technology* dating from 1916 to the present and a complete set of *Jane's All the World's Aircraft* dating from 1909 to the present. The library provides rapid interlibrary loan service and wireless access points as well as computer terminals for research.

Costs

The 2010–11 tuition was $14,040 per semester. Flight fees are charged in addition to tuition. On-campus room and board costs were approximately $4400 per semester. Personal expenses, books, and fees are in addition to the above. Costs are subject to change.

Financial Aid

Applicants for financial aid are required to complete the Department of Education's Free Application for Federal Student Aid (FAFSA) and any other documents requested by the University. Students are encouraged to apply early if they wish to be considered for all types of programs. Florida residents may also apply for several additional programs that are available through the state.

Faculty

The faculty members provide an excellent balance of professional experience and academic achievement. There is also a healthy balance between maturity and youth among the faculty. Faculty members who teach in the specialized and major programs have had professional experience in their areas of instruction. The student-faculty ratio is 16:1, and the average class size is 25. The primary concern of each faculty member is personalized teaching in classrooms and laboratories, on the flight line, and in student advising.

Student Government

The University places great emphasis on student self-government. The Student Government Association supports publication of the weekly newspaper and oversees the Touch 'n Go Office that organizes campus entertainment and broadcast of the student radio station, Eagles FM. In addition, the president of the Student Government Association is a voting member of the University's Board of Trustees.

Admission Requirements

Admission is open to any qualified applicant, regardless of creed, sex, race, national origin, handicap, or geographical location. Admission decisions are based on high school grades and course load, college courses attempted, SAT or ACT scores, and letters of recommendation. Embry-Riddle encourages every student to visit the campus before making the decision to attend the University.

Transfer students are required to submit transcripts from all colleges and universities attended. High school transcripts are not required if the student has earned 30 college credits or more.

Application and Information

Embry-Riddle requires each applicant to submit an application form and fee, SAT or ACT scores, two letters of recommendation, and an official high school/college transcript. Flight students must provide an FAA Class I or Class II medical certificate. When a student is accepted for admission, tuition and housing deposits are required by May 1.

University Admissions
Embry-Riddle Aeronautical University
P.O. Box 11767
Daytona Beach, Florida 32120-1767
Phone: 386-226-6100
           800-862-2416 (toll-free nationwide)
E-mail: dbadmit@erau.edu
Web site: http://www.erau.edu/db
              http://twitter.com/ERAUniv
              http://www.youtube.com/EmbryRiddleUniv

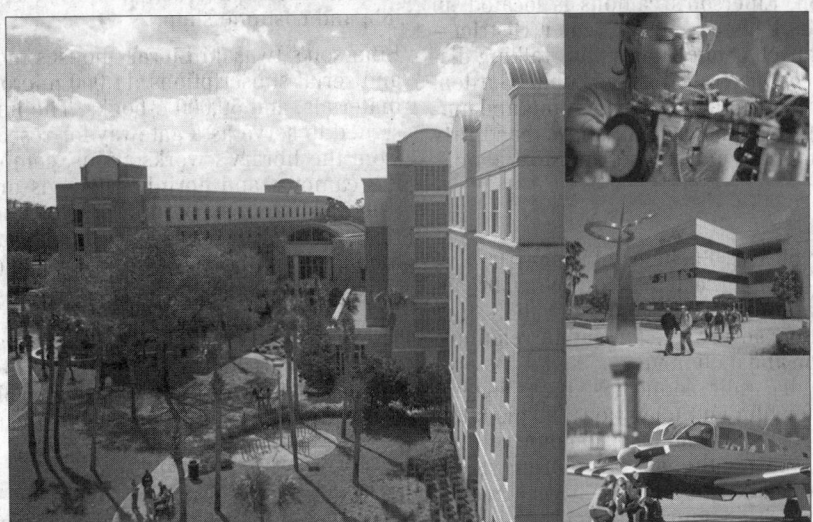

Embry-Riddle Aeronautical University's Daytona Beach, Florida, campus.

EMERSON COLLEGE

BOSTON, MASSACHUSETTS

The College

Founded in 1880, Emerson is one of the premier colleges in the United States for the study of communication and the arts. Students may choose from more than two dozen undergraduate and graduate programs supported by state-of-the-art facilities and a nationally renowned faculty. The campus is home to WERS-FM, the oldest noncommercial radio station in Boston; the historic 1,200-seat Cutler Majestic Theatre; and *Ploughshares*, the award-winning literary journal for new writing.

A pioneer in the fields of communication and performing arts, Emerson was one of the first colleges in the nation to establish a program in children's theater (1919), an undergraduate program in broadcasting (1937), professional-level training in speech pathology and audiology (1935), educational FM radio (1949), closed-circuit television (1955), and a B.F.A. degree program in film as early as 1972. In 1980, the College created the country's first graduate program in professional writing and publishing.

Today, Emerson's 3,600 undergraduate and 850 graduate students come from across the country and more than forty other countries. Approximately 1,900 students live on campus, some in special learning communities, such as the Writers' Block and Digital Culture Floor. All of the College's residence halls are air conditioned with cable television and Internet access. Wireless service is available in several campus locations. There is a fitness center, athletic field, and a brand-new facility that houses two theaters, multiple rehearsal spaces, a professional sound stage, and a fully functional scene shop.

Emerson College is fully accredited by the New England Association of Schools and Colleges.

In addition to its undergraduate programs, Emerson College offers more than a dozen master's degree programs for its graduate students.

Location

With dozens of institutions of higher learning, Boston is considered one of the country's best-known college towns. The city contains a wealth of diversions ranging from scenic harbor cruises and Boston Pops concerts to baseball's Fenway Park and the legendary Boston Marathon. Emerson's campus is located on Boston Common in the heart of the city's Theater District—within sight of the Massachusetts State House and walking distance from the historic Freedom Trail, Boston Public Garden, Chinatown, financial district, and numerous restaurants and museums. Boston is also an international city with more than thirty foreign consulates, a busy international airport, and several multinational corporations.

Majors and Degrees

Emerson confers Bachelor of Arts, Bachelor of Fine Arts, and Bachelor of Science degrees. Students can major in acting; broadcast journalism; communication disorders; communication studies; marketing communication: advertising and public relations; media production (animation and motion media, digital postproduction, film, interactive media, radio, sound design, studio television production, writing for film and television); media studies; musical theater; political communication: leadership, politics, and social advocacy; print and multimedia journalism; stage/production management; theater design/technology; theater education; theater studies; and writing, literature, and publishing. Popular minors include business studies and entrepreneurship. Interdisciplinary and self-designed majors, as well as an honors

program, are available through the College's Institute for Liberal Arts and Interdisciplinary Studies.

Academic Programs

Emerson's academic calendar consists of two fifteen-week semesters, plus two six-week sessions during the summer months. The requirements for graduation combine general education and liberal arts courses with advanced, specialized classes that are specific to individual departments and majors. Internships for academic credit are available in almost every major and the Institute for Liberal Arts and Interdisciplinary Studies offers exciting first-year seminars, independent study options, and innovative courses that cut across academic disciplines.

Off-Campus Programs

Internships are popular with Emerson students. Hundreds of placements exist throughout Boston and in major cities across the country, including the College's Los Angeles Center—a residential study and internship program in the heart of the world's entertainment capital.

Emerson also sponsors a semester-long study program in Washington, D.C., the Netherlands, and Taiwan. In addition, there is a summer film program in Prague and course cross-registration with the six-member Boston ProArts Consortium, whose members include the Berklee College of Music, the Boston Conservatory, Boston Architectural Center, Emerson, the School of the Museum of Fine Arts, and Massachusetts College of Art.

Academic Facilities

Emerson possesses the highest quality visual and media arts equipment, including sound-treated television studios, digital editing labs, audio postproduction suites with analog and digital peripherals, industry-standard software, and a professional marketing-research suite/focus room. In fact, more than half of Emerson's campus has been built new or completely refurbished since 2002. There are two radio stations, an on-campus clinic to observe speech and hearing therapy, and an integrated digital newsroom for aspiring journalists. The eleven-story Tufte Performance and Production Center houses expanded performance and rehearsal space, a theater design/technology center, makeup lab, and costume shop.

Emerson's Iwasaki Library houses more than 175,000 volumes and serial subscriptions, 11,000 microforms, 9,000 audio/visual materials, and 30,000 e-books. The library's Web pages are designed to serve as a gateway for research and can be accessed from the library's workstations, computers located throughout the campus, and dormitory rooms or off-campus apartments, using a student account. Emerson students can also access the resources of a dozen cooperating libraries through the College's membership in the Fenway Library Consortium.

Costs

The basic expenses related to attending Emerson College for the 2010–11 academic year were $30,752 for tuition and $12,881 for room and board. Approximately $3200 should be allotted for books and supplies, fees, health insurance, and personal expenses, including travel.

Financial Aid

Each year, more than two thirds of Emerson's student body receives some form of financial assistance, packaged in awards that typically combine grant and scholarship, loan, and College work-study. Academic scholarships ranging from $10,000 to half-tuition are awarded on a limited basis to students who meet high academic standards. Special performance-based scholarships, averaging $4000, are available to exceptional students in the performing arts.

In order to apply for financial assistance, students must complete the Free Application for Federal Student Assistance (FAFSA) and CSS PROFILE form. Deadlines are March 1 for September admission or November 15 for January admission. More information about financial assistance at Emerson can be found online at http://www.emerson.edu/financial_services or by contacting the Office of Student Financial Services at 617-824-8655 or finaid@emerson.edu.

Faculty

With a student-teacher ratio of 13:1, students at Emerson develop close relationships with remarkably talented and active instructors. Faculty members are nationally recognized and award-winning authors, directors, producers, consultants, playwrights, and editors. The vast majority of the faculty members have earned doctorates or the highest degree obtainable in their field.

Student Government

Emerson has more than eighty student organizations and performance groups, fourteen NCAA intercollegiate teams, and several student publications and honor societies. The Student Government Association, in cooperation with the Office of Student Affairs staff, plans and executes student activities, allocates and supervises funding for clubs, and serves as a liaison between the student body and the College administration.

Admission Requirements

Emerson accepts the Common Application and Application Supplement. Students whose interests and abilities are compatible with the College's specialty in communication and the arts are welcome to apply. Admission is competitive. Each year, more than 7,000 applications are received for a class of around 800. Selection is based on academic promise as indicated by secondary school performance, recommendations, writing competency, and SAT or ACT scores (or TOEFL if English is not the first language). The College also considers personal qualities as seen in extracurricular activities, community involvement, and demonstrated leadership.

The academic preparation for successful candidates should include 4 years of English and 3 years each of mathematics, science, social science, and a single foreign language. Candidates for programs offered by the Department of Performing Arts are asked to fulfill additional requirements (a theatrical resume and one of the following: audition, interview, portfolio, or essay) found on a dedicated Web site, http://stagedoor.emerson.edu. Applicants for the film program must submit a sample of creative work: either a five-to-ten page script or 5–7 minute video.

Application and Information

First-year candidates for September admission should file their application by January 5. Early action applications are due November 1. The regular admission deadline for January admission is November 1.

Transfer students should submit their applications and supporting credentials by March 15 for September admission or November 1 for January admission.

Office of Undergraduate Admission
Emerson College
120 Bolyston Street
Boston, Massachusetts 02116-4624

Phone: 617-824-8600
Fax: 617-824-8609
E-mail: admission@emerson.edu
Web site: http://www.emerson.edu
http://www.facebook.com/emersoncollege
http://www.twitter.com/emersoncollege

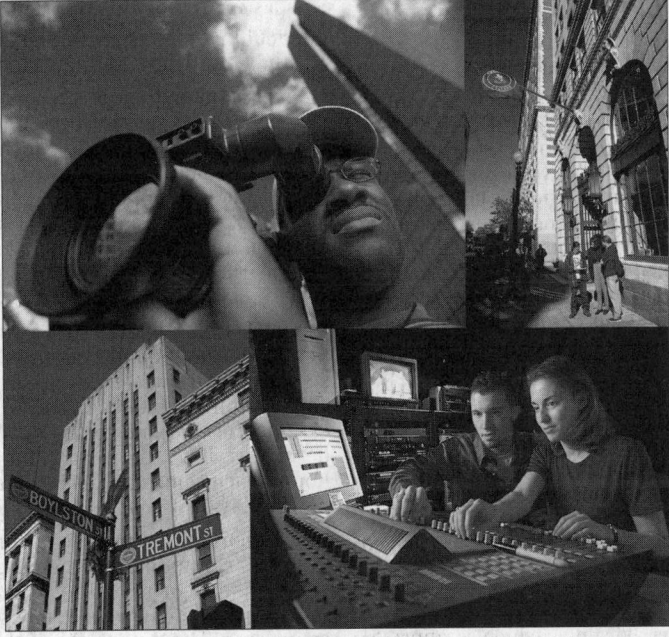

Emerson College: Bringing innovation to communication and the arts.

EMORY & HENRY COLLEGE
EMORY, VIRGINIA

The College

Emory & Henry College is a transformative academic community. The education it offers is distinguished by progress—sometimes sudden, sometimes gradual—toward an expanded sense of personal potential and an enlightened sense of civic responsibility. This transformation, this increase in excellence, is the foundation of the Emory & Henry campus culture. Its impact is lasting and profound.

The College supports a strong research program in the arts and sciences, explicitly designed to encourage student collaboration and initiative. The faculty is committed to teaching as a transformative practice, an opportunity to inspire students to reimagine the nature and purpose of their education.

Emory & Henry claims a proud heritage of enlightened civic activity. A hallmark of the College's civic engagement is its leadership in advancing a pragmatic understanding of sustainable communities and practices.

With an emphasis on service, excellence, and action, Emory & Henry encourages students to envision the world in which they would like to live and then challenges them to create it. Founded in 1836, the College is named for two men who symbolize this dual emphasis on thought and action—Bishop John Emory, an eminent Methodist church leader at the time the College was founded, and Patrick Henry, a famous orator of the American Revolution and Virginia's first governor.

Emory & Henry graduates have found tremendous personal success, which they have used to improve the world around them. Through its comprehensive, four-year liberal arts education, Emory & Henry has produced leading scientific researchers, NASA engineers, well-known writers, and successful physicians, ministers, lawyers, educators, and businesspeople. Emory & Henry provides innovative programs in public policy and community service as well as international studies and environmental science.

Students have opportunities for involvement in a variety of campus activities: service clubs, fraternities, sororities, sports clubs, honor groups, religious life, and multicultural groups. Student staffs produce a yearbook, an online magazine, and a literary magazine; others operate an educational FM radio station. Musically talented students have opportunities to participate in a choral program and a pep band. The prestigious Concert Choir has toured throughout the United States and in parts of Europe. The Barter Theatre, a professional theater in nearby Abingdon, works with Emory & Henry College to provide a theater education program that integrates college-level drama study with the benefits of experience on a professional stage. The Appalachian Center for Community Service is available for students committed to community service and integrates service learning into many classes. The King Health and Physical Education Center includes a state-of-the-art fitness center and enhances the College athletics program. Varsity sports for men are baseball, basketball, cross-country, football, golf, soccer, and tennis; women compete in basketball, cross-country, soccer, softball, swimming, tennis, and volleyball. Several sports are also played on either a club or an intramural basis.

Location

Emory & Henry is located in Emory, Virginia, which is approximately 25 miles north of Bristol, a city that offers large shopping areas, movies, and restaurants. The area surrounding Emory is known for its scenic beauty, recreational opportunities, and talented artisans. Within an hour's drive are slopes for snow skiing, lakes for waterskiing, the Appalachian Trail for hiking, and locations for horseback riding, canoeing, and many other sports. The historic town of Abingdon, Virginia, which lies just 7 miles south of Emory, is the home of the renowned Barter Theatre, the oldest professional theater in the United States. Abingdon's downtown

district includes shopping areas, movie theaters, restaurants, and museums. The town also hosts the annual Virginia Highlands Festival, bringing together musicians, artists, and craftsmen for exhibitions and competition.

Majors and Degrees

Emory & Henry College offers programs of study in art, athletic training, biology, business administration, chemistry, computer information management, economics, education (early childhood through high school, including many subject-area options), English, environmental studies, geography, history, international studies (East Asia, European community, or Middle Eastern and Islamic studies), languages, mass communications, mathematics, music, philosophy, physical education, physics, political science, psychology, public policy and community service, religion, sociology, and theater. Preprofessional preparation in dentistry, law, medicine, and veterinary medicine may be completed within several of the programs.

The Bachelor of Arts degree is awarded in all programs of study and the Bachelor of Science degree in selected areas. Individualized programs of study may be developed in consultation with a faculty adviser.

Academic Programs

Emory & Henry offers a liberal arts program with an emphasis on writing, ethical reasoning, critical thinking, and knowledge of global concerns, as well as a broad introduction to liberal arts subjects. All students complete a core curriculum, which requires students to integrate their classroom work with study and research beyond the classroom and the campus, in order to acquire a deep understanding of regional and cultural differences and challenges. The new curriculum emphasizes foreign language and study abroad, as well as study elsewhere in the United States.

Undergraduate programs of study include art, athletic training, biology, business administration, chemistry, computer information management, economics, education, English, geography, history, languages, mass communications, mathematics, music, philosophy, physical education, physics, political science, psychology, religion, sociology, and theater. Special and interdisciplinary programs of study offered are environmental studies, international studies, preengineering, prelaw, premedicine, and public policy and community service.

Emory & Henry operates on a semester calendar from late August to mid-December and from mid-January to mid-May. Two summer sessions run from late May to early July. First-year students typically carry a four-course load of 13 to 14 credit hours per semester, including the yearlong course on Western Tradition. Upperclass students carrying a full load complete five courses (14 to 15 credit hours) each semester. Classes meet on Monday-Wednesday-Friday or Tuesday-Thursday schedules.

One important feature of the Emory & Henry curriculum is the College's commitment to helping students achieve a smooth transition from high school to college. The Powell Resource Center provides academic support, advising, career services, and personal counseling. The Writing Center helps students in every department to use writing for effective communication.

Off-Campus Programs

Many faculty members encourage students to get involved in community projects or research that benefit the region. Internship opportunities are available for students in most of the College's programs, providing academic credit for off-campus work in community agencies and businesses. Many students have completed internships in the surrounding communities, while others have opted for internships outside the region, including several in Washington, D.C., in positions related to the Congress or the federal government.

Emory & Henry students participate in a wide variety of study-abroad programs. From Rome to Beijing and from Eastern Europe to East Asia, Emory & Henry students experience cultures and people in a way that enriches their perspective on their studies, their lives, and their futures. Emory & Henry helps students prepare for these experiences through language study and with courses offered through a comprehensive international studies program and an international studies and business program. The College has exchange agreements with colleges and universities in Asia, Europe, and Central and South America. Students who desire other types of travel/study are assisted by faculty and staff members in locating suitable programs.

Academic Facilities

McGlothlin-Street Hall is a 70,000-square-foot academic center that houses the Departments of Biology, Business, Chemistry, Education, Environmental Studies, Geography, International Studies, and Psychology, along with a 104-seat auditorium and a tiered sixty-seat auditorium. Classrooms and laboratories in McGlothlin-Street Hall are equipped with the most current technological equipment. Miller Hall contains computerized classrooms used for instruction in such fields as accounting and computer science. Science departments located in Miller and McGlothlin-Street Halls feature a variety of equipment, such as a microcomputer-based laboratory for physics students, computerized chromatography for chemistry students, a DNA sequencer in the biology department, and biofeedback equipment. Art students have access to studios, an exhibition area, and printing equipment, and music students make use of practice rooms and a recital hall.

The historic Byars Hall, which recently underwent massive renovations, is home to the College's Division of Visual and Performing Arts. The building includes choir and ensemble rehearsal halls, a digital art lab, two large art studios, practice rooms for instrumental music, a large piano lab, and a theater support room. In addition the College has renovated Wiley Hall, its historic administrative building, and is in the midst of two major fund-raising projects that will increase and enhance student involvement within fine arts and athletics.

Costs

For 2010–11, resident students paid a comprehensive fee of $34,560, which included tuition, room, and board.

Financial Aid

Forms of aid include need-based and non-need-based scholarships, loans, and part-time jobs. A Bonner Scholars program provides substantial scholarships for selected students who do volunteer work in the surrounding region. Virginia residents are eligible for a special residency grant. Merit-based scholarships are awarded based on academic performance, and many can be renewed based on continued academic success. The average first-year student received an aid package (grants and scholarships) worth $24,775 in recent years. The priority application deadline for financial aid is April 1.

Faculty

Emory & Henry professors are among the best in the nation. Over the last seventeen years, Emory & Henry has received the Carnegie Foundation Virginia Professor of the Year Award six times—more than any other college or university in Virginia. The College's professors are also five-time recipients of the Virginia Outstanding Faculty Award, given by the State Council for Higher Education. Emory & Henry has 75 full-time faculty members, and the current faculty-student ratio is 1:11. The majority of the faculty members hold terminal degrees. Every student is provided with a faculty adviser, who assists in the selection of courses. While the faculty members are encouraged to continue study and research, their primary function is teaching. Many professors live near the campus, and they make their homes open to students for special events, informal class meetings, or other activities.

Student Government

Students at Emory & Henry are encouraged to take part in campus decision making. They have voting representatives on nearly every faculty committee and on the Board of Trustees. The central body in campus government is the Student Senate, which brings together representatives of the student body, faculty, and administration.

Admission Requirements

Admission to Emory & Henry is determined on the basis of both academic achievement and personal qualifications. An applicant's secondary school preparation must include the following: 4 years of English, 3 years of mathematics (algebra I, algebra II, and geometry), 2 years of laboratory sciences, 2 years of a single foreign language, and 2 years of social studies. Strong emphasis is also placed on involvement and leadership in extracurricular and community activities, in addition to consistency and improvement surrounding academic progress.

Application and Information

To apply for admission, students should submit the basic application form, a copy of the high school transcript, scores from either the SAT or the ACT, at least one recommendation letter, and a non-refundable $30 application fee. While not required, an essay/personal statement is strongly recommended.

Transfer applicants must submit an application and a transcript from any college previously attended, along with a completed Dean's Certificate for Transfer Students. A rolling admissions policy allows notification of a decision within two to four weeks after a file has been completed.

In addition to its rolling admissions policy, Emory & Henry College also welcomes interested applicants under the Early Application program. This program offers a nonbinding decision made on completed applications and aforementioned materials received by December 1. Not only does the College guarantee a decision by December 15, but a tentative financial aid package (with necessary materials) is offered to these students prior to January 1. Like rolling admissions decisions, students receiving acceptance under Early Application have until May 1 to make their final decision.

Application forms and other information may be obtained by contacting:

Office of Admissions
Emory & Henry College
P.O. Box 10
Emory, Virginia 24327-0947
Phone: 276-944-6133
   800-848-5493 (toll-free)
Fax: 276-944-6935
E-mail: ehadmiss@ehc.edu
Web site: http://www.ehc.edu
   http://www.facebook.com/emoryandhenry
   http://twitter.com/emoryandhenry

Wiley Hall.

EUGENE LANG COLLEGE
THE NEW SCHOOL FOR LIBERAL ARTS

NEW YORK, NEW YORK

The College

Eugene Lang College is the undergraduate liberal arts division of The New School, a leading university in New York City with a tradition of innovative learning. Eugene Lang College offers all the benefits of a small and supportive college as well as the full range of opportunities found in a university setting. At Lang, rigorous academic programs are closely connected with all that New York City has to offer: its wealth of music, theater, and arts; its vibrant international community; its history; and its energy.

Eugene Lang students are encouraged to participate in the creation and direction of their education. The desire to explore and the freedom to imagine shared by students and faculty members contribute to a distinctive academic community.

Eugene Lang College students currently come from thirty-five states and ten countries. The ratio of men to women is approximately 2:3. About 45 percent of the College's 1,425 students come from outside the New York metropolitan area; 5 percent hold foreign citizenship and 27 percent are members of minority groups. The student body is composed of both residential and day students. The university operates residence halls within walking distance of classes; incoming freshmen and transfer students are given housing priority within these facilities, and housing is guaranteed for the first year for new students. Great diversity in interests and aspirations is found among the students. Through the Office of Student Services, students produce a student newspaper and an award-winning literary magazine. They organize and participate in dramatic, musical, and artistic events through the "Lang in the City Program," as well as numerous political, social, and cultural organizations at the university and throughout New York City.

The New School was founded in 1919 by such notable scholars and intellectuals as John Dewey, Alvin Johnson, and Thorstein Veblen. It has long been a home for leading artists, educators, and public figures. For example, the university was the first institution of higher learning to offer college-level courses in fields such as black culture and race, taught by W. E. B. DuBois, and psychoanalysis, taught by Freud's disciple Sandor Ferenczi. Among the world-famous artists and performers who have taught at The New School are Martha Graham, Aaron Copland, and Thomas Hart Benton. Today, noted scholars and artists are among the hundreds of university faculty members accessible to Eugene Lang College students.

The other divisions of the university are The New School for General Studies, which offers nearly 1,000 credit and noncredit courses to students each semester and awards the B.A., B.S., M.A., M.S., and M.F.A. degrees; The New School for Social Research, which grants M.A. and Ph.D. degrees; Milano The New School for Management and Urban Policy, which awards the M.S. and Ph.D. degrees; Parsons The New School for Design, one of the oldest and most influential art schools in the country; Mannes College The New School for Music, a renowned classical conservatory; The New School for Jazz and Contemporary Music; and The New School for Drama. The total university enrollment in 2009–10 was approximately 10,260 degree-seeking students.

Location

The university is located in New York City's Greenwich Village, which historically has been a center for intellectual and artistic life. This legendary New York City neighborhood of town houses and tree-lined streets offers students a friendly and stimulating environment. Over and above the resources of Greenwich Village, New York City offers virtually unlimited cultural, artistic, recreational, and intellectual resources that make it one of the world's great cities.

Majors and Degrees

Eugene Lang College awards the Bachelor of Arts degree in the arts (dance, music, theater, visual arts, and arts in context), culture and media, economics, environmental studies, history, interdisciplinary science, literary studies, philosophy, psychology, urban studies, and liberal arts. Within the liberal arts major, students may complete interdisciplinary programs of study in education studies, religious studies, and social inquiry. They may also elect a self-designed program of study. Students may supplement their course of study by taking advantage of Lang's new cluster offerings. These interdisciplinary options draw on courses offered across the university. Clustered courses, which may also be used as part of the self-designed liberal arts major, include civic engagement, gender studies, Jewish studies, ethnicity and race, and foreign languages. In addition, students are encouraged to pursue an internship, where appropriate.

Students may apply to a five-year, dual-degree B.A./B.F.A. program in conjunction with Parsons The New School for Design or The New School for Jazz and Contemporary Music. Students may also apply for the accelerated B.A./M.A. option offered in conjunction with the university's graduate divisions.

Academic Programs

By actively participating in the process of their education, Eugene Lang College students gain the knowledge to make informed choices about the direction of their studies with the help of their advisers and peers.

Small seminar classes serve as the focus of the academic program at the College. The maximum class size is 20 students. Classes are in-depth, interdisciplinary inquiries into topics or issues selected each semester by the College's outstanding faculty. Most important, the classes engage participants in the study of primary texts, rather than textbooks, and emphasize dialogue between teacher and student as a mode of learning. Here, not only is intellectual curiosity fostered by the small classes, but a genuine sense of community develops as well.

Freshmen are required to take one writing course and three other seminars of their choice in each of their first two semesters at the College. Upper-level students create their programs by selecting seminars from the College's curriculum, or they may combine offerings of the College with courses and workshops offered by The New School for General Study, The New School for Social Research, Milano The New School for Management and Urban Policy, and Parsons The New School for Design.

The College operates on a semester calendar; the first semester runs from September through mid-December, and the second runs from late January through mid-May. Students generally earn 16 credits per semester; a minimum of 120 credits is required for graduation.

Off-Campus Programs

Eugene Lang College recognizes the immense value of work undertaken beyond the classroom. The College arranges appropriate projects—internships with private and nonprofit organizations—that serve to strengthen the connection between theoretical work in the classroom and practical work on the job.

Sophomores and juniors have the option of spending a year on a sponsored exchange with Sarah Lawrence College and the University of Amsterdam. Other exchanges, both in the United States and abroad, are available.

Academic Facilities

Eugene Lang College is located on 11th Street between Fifth and Sixth Avenues in Greenwich Village. The university includes twelve academic buildings, including a student center, the University Computing Center with IBM and Macintosh stations, a 500-seat auditorium, art galleries, studios for the fine arts, classrooms, a writing center, and faculty offices. Eugene Lang College students have full and easy access to the Raymond Fogelman Library and the Adam and Sophie Gimbel Design Library. In addition, the university participates in the South Manhattan Library Consortium. Together, the libraries in the consortium house approximately 3 million volumes covering all the traditional liberal arts disciplines and the fine arts.

Costs

Tuition and fees for the 2010–11 academic year were $36,350 plus $1817 for student health insurance. Room and board cost approximately $15,260, depending upon the student's choice of specific meal plan and dormitory accommodations.

Financial Aid

Students are encouraged to apply for aid by filing the Free Application for Federal Student Aid (FAFSA) and requesting that a copy of the need analysis report be sent to The New School (FAFSA code number 002780). Qualified College students are eligible for all federal and state financial aid programs in addition to university gift aid. University aid is awarded on the basis of need and merit and is part of a package consisting of both gift aid (grants and/or scholarships) and a self-help component (loans and Federal Work-Study Program awards). Aid is renewable each year as long as need continues and students maintain satisfactory academic standing at the College. Special attention is given to continuing students who have done exceptionally well.

Faculty

At Eugene Lang College, the faculty-student ratio is 1:10. Class size ranges from 10 to 20 students. Faculty members are graduates of outstanding colleges and universities and represent a wide variety of academic disciplines; 95 percent hold Ph.D.'s. College faculty members also serve as academic advisers, who are selected carefully in order to ensure thoughtful supervision of students' programs and academic progress.

Well-known faculty members from other divisions of the university teach at the College on a regular basis. In addition, every semester, the College hosts distinguished scholars and writers as visiting faculty and guest lecturers who further enrich the academic program of the College and the university.

Student Government

There is a student union at the College, which is an organized vehicle for student expression and action as well as a means of funding student projects and events. Students are encouraged to express their views and concerns about academic policies and community life through regular student-faculty member meetings.

Admission Requirements

Eugene Lang College welcomes admission applications from students of diverse racial, ethnic, religious, and political backgrounds whose past performance and academic and personal promise make them likely to gain from and add to the College community. The College seeks students who combine inquisitiveness and seriousness of purpose with the ability to engage in a distinctive, rigorous liberal arts program. Each applicant to the College is judged individually; the Admissions Committee, which renders all admission decisions, considers both academic qualifications and the personal, creative, and intellectual qualities of each applicant. A strong academic background, including a college-preparatory program, is recommended. An applicant's transcript; teacher and counselor recommendations; SAT, ACT, or SAT Subject Test scores; and personal essays are all taken into consideration. In addition, an interview, a tour of university facilities, and a visit to Eugene Lang College seminars are optional but highly recommended.

High school students for whom the College is their first choice are strongly encouraged to apply as early decision candidates and are notified early of an admission decision. Early entrance is an option for qualified high school juniors who wish to enter college prior to high school graduation. Candidates for early entrance must submit two teacher recommendations.

Students who have successfully completed one full year or more at another accredited institution may apply as transfer candidates. If accepted, transfer students may enter upper-level seminars and pursue advanced work. International students may apply for admission as freshmen or transfers by submitting a regular application to the College. If English is spoken as a second language, TOEFL scores are required. The New York Connection Program invites students from other colleges to Eugene Lang College for a semester and incorporates an internship into their studies.

Students interested in applying for the combined B.A./B.F.A. degree program in fine arts or jazz studies are encouraged to apply for admission as freshmen to these special five-year programs. In addition to the admission requirements outlined above, a home exam and a portfolio are required for fine arts, and an audition is required for jazz studies.

Application and Information

Freshmen, transfers, and visiting students may apply for either the September (fall) or January (spring) semester. To apply for admission to the College, students must request an application packet and submit the required credentials and a $50 application fee by the appropriate deadline. The application fee may be waived in accordance with the College Board's Fee Waiver Service. For the semester beginning in January, the required credentials must be submitted by November 15, with notification by December 15. For the September semester, early decision candidates must submit the required credentials by November 15, with notification by December 15. For freshman candidates applying for general admission and freshman early entrants, the deadline is February 1, with notification by April 1. For transfers and visiting students, the deadline is rolling to May 15, with notification rolling until July 1. For further information, students should contact:

Karen Williams
Director of Admissions
Eugene Lang College The New School for Liberal Arts
72 Fifth Avenue, Second Floor
New York, New York 10011

Phone: 212-229-5665
Fax: 212-229-5355
E-mail: lang@newschool.edu
Web site: http://www.newschool.edu/lang

FASHION INSTITUTE OF TECHNOLOGY
State University of New York
NEW YORK, NEW YORK

The College

The Fashion Institute of Technology (FIT) is New York City's celebrated urban college for creative and business talent. A selective State University of New York (SUNY) college of art and design, business, and technology, FIT is a creative mix of innovative achievers, original thinkers, and industry pioneers, with nearly forty programs of study leading to the A.A.S., B.F.A., and B.S. degrees. The School of Graduate Studies offers seven programs leading to a Master of Arts (M.A.), Master of Fine Arts (M.F.A.), or Master of Professional Studies (M.P.S.) degree. The college is accredited by the Middle States Association of Colleges and Schools, National Association of Schools of Art and Design, and Council for Interior Design Accreditation.

FIT serves approximately 10,000 students from the greater metropolitan area, New York State, across the country, and around the world, offering full- and part-time study options, evening/weekend degree programs, and online studies. The School of Art and Design enrolls 55 percent of degree-seeking students. Another 42 percent are enrolled in the Baker School of Business and Technology. Forty-five percent of FIT's students are New York City residents, 23 percent are New York State (non–New York City) residents, and 32 percent are out-of-state residents or international residents. The ethnic/racial makeup of the student body is approximately 0.16 percent American Indian or Alaskan, 11.56 percent Asian, 8.8 percent black, 16.52 percent Hispanic, 3.22 percent multiracial, 0.66 percent Native Hawaiian or Pacific Islander; and 59.08 percent white.

The college provides a singular approach to higher education—balancing a real-world-based curriculum and hands-on instruction with a rigorous liberal arts foundation, marrying design and business, supporting individual creativity in a collaborative environment, and encouraging faculty members to match teaching expertise with professional experience. FIT's mission is to produce well-rounded graduates: doers and thinkers who raise the professional bar to become the next generation of business pacesetters and creative icons. It offers a complete college experience with a vibrant student and residential life.

FIT's four residence halls house 2,300 in fully furnished single-, double-, triple-, and quad-occupancy rooms and apartments. All students taking 12 or more credits are eligible for FIT housing, and students may apply for housing no matter where they live. Kaufman Hall also provides an on-site fitness center. Students have the option of either traditional (meal plan required) or apartment-style accommodations. Various dining options and meal plans are available. Counselors and student staff members live in the halls, helping students adjust to college life and New York City.

The college is home to more than seventy clubs, societies, athletic teams, major-related organizations, and hobby groups. Each organization is open to all students who have paid their activity fee. Concerts, dances, field trips, films, flea markets, and other events are regularly scheduled. Student-run publications include a campus newspaper, a literary and art magazine, and the FIT yearbook.

FIT has intercollegiate teams in cheerleading, cross-country, half marathon, outdoor track, dance, table tennis, tennis, soccer, swimming and diving, and volleyball. Athletics and Recreation offers group fitness classes at no extra cost to students. Open gym activities allow students to participate in team and individual sports.

Throughout the David Dubinsky Student Center are lounges, a game room, a dining hall, a student radio station, a FIT student-run boutique, student government and club offices, health services, two gyms, a dance studio, a fitness center, a counseling center, and laboratories and studios.

Location

Occupying an entire block in Manhattan's Chelsea neighborhood, FIT's campus places students at the heart of the fashion, advertising, visual arts, design, business, and communications industries. Students gain unparalleled exposure to their field through internship opportunities and professional connections. A wide range of cultural and entertainment options—from dining to galleries to theater—are available within walking distance of the campus, as is convenient access to several subway and bus routes and the city's major rail and bus transportation hubs.

Majors and Degrees

FIT offers fifteen Associate in Applied Science (A.A.S.) and twenty-four baccalaureate programs. All students complete a two-year A.A.S. program in their major area of study and the liberal arts and then typically continue in a related, two-year Bachelor of Fine Arts (B.F.A.) or Bachelor of Science (B.S.) program. If students choose, they may begin their careers with the A.A.S. degree, which qualifies them for entry-level positions in their chosen field.

The School of Art and Design offers eleven A.A.S. and thirteen B.F.A. programs, the Jay and Patty Baker School of Business and Technology offers four A.A.S. and ten B.S. programs, and the School of Liberal Arts offers one B.S. program.

The fifteen A.A.S. programs, all of which provide the foundation for one or more corresponding baccalaureate-level programs, are accessories design*, advertising and marketing communications*, communication design foundation*, fashion design*, fashion merchandising management* (with an online option), fine arts, illustration, interior design, jewelry design*, menswear; photography, production management: fashion and related industries, textile development and marketing*, textile/surface design*, and visual presentation and exhibition design. Programs with an * are also available in a one-year format for students with acceptable transferable credits, and the one-year Fashion Merchandising Management A.A.S. program is offered fully online.

The thirteen B.F.A. programs are accessories design and fabrication; advertising design; computer animation and interactive media; fabric styling; fashion design (with specializations in children's wear, fashion design, intimate apparel, and knitwear); fine arts; graphic design; illustration; interior design; packaging design; photography and the digital image; textile/surface design; and toy design.

The eleven B.S. programs are advertising and marketing communications, art history and museum professions, cosmetics and fragrance marketing, direct and interactive marketing, entrepreneurship for the fashion and design industries, fashion merchandising management, home products development, international trade and marketing for the fashion industries, production management: fashion and related industries, technical design, and textile development and marketing.

For those students looking to balance the demands of career or family with their education, FIT offers nine degree programs available through evening/weekend study that include advertising and marketing communications (A.A.S. and B.S.), communication design foundation (A.A.S.), fashion design (A.A.S.), fashion merchandising management (A.A.S. and B.S.), graphic design (B.F.A.), illustration (B.F.A.), and international trade and marketing for the fashion industries (B.S.).

Academic Programs

Each undergraduate program includes a core of traditional liberal arts courses, providing students with a global perspective, critical-thinking skills, and the ability to communicate effectively. The School of Liberal Arts offers FIT students the opportunity to minor in a variety of liberal arts areas in two forms: traditional subject-based minors and interdisciplinary minors unique to the FIT liberal arts curriculum. Selected minors include film and media, economics, Latin American studies, and sustainability.

All degree programs are designed to prepare students for creative and business careers. The college's Career and Internship Center, which offers lifetime placement, reports a graduate employment rate of 90 percent. Internships are a required element of most programs and are available to all students. Nearly one-third of FIT student internships result in employment offers from the sponsoring organization.

The Presidential Scholars honors program, available to academically exceptional students in all disciplines, offers special liberal arts courses, projects, colloquiums, extracurricular activities, and off-campus visits designed to broaden horizons and stimulate discourse. Presidential Scholars are also awarded priority course registration and an annual merit stipend.

Precollege programs (Saturday and Sunday/Summer Live) are available to high school and middle school students during the fall, spring, and summer. More than sixty courses provide the chance to learn in an innovative environment, to develop art and design portfolios, to explore the business and technological sides of a wide range of creative careers, and to discover natural talents and abilities.

The School of Continuing Education and Professional Studies provides convenient evening and weekend credit and noncredit classes to students and working professionals who are interested in pursuing a degree or certificate or furthering their knowledge and expertise in a particular industry.

Off-Campus Programs

The study-abroad experience provides students with the opportunity to immerse themselves in diverse cultures and prepares them to live and work in a global community. Australia, China, England, France, and Mexico are some of the countries where FIT semester study-abroad courses are offered. Students can also study abroad during the winter or summer sessions, or for a semester or a full academic year concentrating in fashion design or fashion merchandising management in Italy.

Academic Facilities

FIT provides its students with an urban campus of classrooms, laboratories, and studios that reflects the most advanced educational and professional practices. The Fred P. Pomerantz Art and Design Center houses studios; a printmaking room; display and exhibit design rooms; a model-making workshop; and a graphics printing service bureau. The Peter G. Scotese Computer-Aided Design and Communications Facility allows students to explore the latest advancements in technology and their integration in design, photography, and computer graphics and animation. The fragrance studio, a professionally equipped fragrance development laboratory, is the only one of its kind on a U.S. college campus. Cutting and sewing laboratories offer the most advanced design and cutting machinery among educational facilities in the U.S. The lighting laboratory, an educational and professional development facility features more than 400 commercially available lighting fixtures. Other college facilities include a broadcasting studio, knitting and weaving labs, a multimedia foreign language laboratory, and twenty-three computer labs containing nearly 700 Mac and PC workstations, in addition to several additional labs with computers reserved for students in specific programs.

The Museum at FIT is New York City's only museum dedicated to fashion. Students, designers, and historians use it for research and inspiration. The museum operates year-round, and its exhibitions are free and open to the public. The Gladys Marcus Library provides more than 300,000 volumes of print, nonprint, and electronic materials. The newspaper and periodicals collection includes 500 current subscriptions. Online resources include more than 90 searchable databases. The library also offers specialized resources, such as clipping files, fashion and trend forecasting services, and sketch collections.

Also on campus are three multimedia venues—the Katie Murphy Amphitheatre, the Morris W. and Fannie B. Haft Auditorium, and the John E. Reeves Great Hall—used for student presentations, industry panels, conferences, and special events.

Costs

For 2010–11, the associate-level tuition per semester was $1857 for in-state residents and $5571 for nonresidents. Baccalaureate-level tuition per semester was $2584 for in-state residents and $6775 for nonresidents. Housing costs ranged from $5685 to $5850 per semester for traditional residence hall accommodations with mandatory meal plan and from $4825 to $8760 for apartment-style accommodations. Meal plans varied from $1555 to $1995 per semester. Textbook costs and other nominal fees such as locker rental or laboratory use vary per program. All costs are subject to change.

Financial Aid

FIT attempts to remove financial barriers to college entrance by providing scholarships, grants, loans, and work-study employment for students in financial need. Nearly all full-time, matriculated students who complete the financial aid application process receive some type of assistance. The college directly administers its own institutional grants and scholarships, which are provided by The Educational Foundation for the Fashion Industries.

College-administered federal funding includes Federal Pell Grants, Federal Perkins Loans, Federal Supplemental Educational Opportunity Grants, Federal Work-Study awards, and Federal Family Educational Loans, which include student and parent loans. New York State residents who meet state guidelines for eligibility may also receive Tuition Assistance Program (TAP) and/or Educational Opportunity Program (EOP) grants. Financial aid applicants must file the Free Application for Federal Student Aid (FAFSA), through which they apply for the Federal Pell Grant. They should also apply for all available outside sources of aid. Additional documentation may be requested by the Financial Aid Office. Applications for financial aid should be completed prior to February 15 for fall admission or prior to November 1 for spring admission.

Faculty

FIT's faculty is drawn from top professionals in academia, art, and business who bring their experience to the classroom and introduce students to the real-life opportunities and challenges of their disciplines through field trips, guest lectures, and sponsored competitions. Academic departments consult with industry advisory boards of noted experts in their fields, ensuring that the curriculum and classroom technology reflect evolving industry practices. Student-instructor interaction is encouraged, with a maximum class size of 25, and courses are structured to foster participation, independent thinking, and self-expression.

Student Government

The Student Council, the governing body of the FIT Student Association, gives all students the privileges and responsibilities of citizens in a self-governing college community. Many faculty committees include student representatives, and the president of the student government sits on FIT's Board of Trustees.

Admission Requirements

Applicants for admission must be either candidates for or recipients of a high school diploma or a General Educational Development (GED) certificate. Admission is based on class rank, strength and performance in college-preparatory course work, and the student essay. A portfolio evaluation is required for art and design majors. Specific portfolio requirements are explained on FIT's Web site. SAT and ACT scores are required for placement in math and English classes and they are required for students applying to the Presidential Scholars honors program. Letters of recommendation are not required.

Transfer students from regionally accredited colleges must submit official transcripts for credit evaluation. Students may qualify for the one-year A.A.S. option if they hold a baccalaureate degree from an accredited college or if they have a minimum of 30 transferable credits from an accredited college, including 24 credits that are equivalent to FIT's liberal arts requirements and at least one semester of physical education.

Students seeking admission to a B.F.A. or B.S. program must hold an A.A.S. degree from FIT or an equivalent degree from an accredited and approved college. They must also meet the appropriate prerequisites for the specific major and must have completed FIT's liberal arts requirements. Further requirements may include an individual interview with a departmental committee, review of academic standing, and a portfolio review (for applicants to B.F.A. programs). Any student who applies for transfer to FIT from a four-year program must have completed a minimum of 60 credits, including the requisite art or technical courses and the liberal arts requirements.

Application and Information

Students wishing to visit FIT are encouraged to attend a group information session and take a tour of FIT's campus. The visit schedule is available online at http://www.fitnyc.edu/visitfit.

Interested candidates may apply online at http://www.fitnyc.edu/admissions. For more information, students should contact:

Admissions
Fashion Institute of Technology
227 West 27 Street, Room C139
New York, NY 10001-5992
Phone: 212-217-3760
     800-GO-TO-FIT (toll-free)
E-mail: fitinfo@fitnyc.edu
Web site: http://www.fitnyc.edu
     http://www.facebook.com/FashionInstituteofTechnology

FELICIAN COLLEGE

LODI, NEW JERSEY

The College

Felician College is a Catholic/Franciscan college serving more than 2,000 men and women. Its mission is to create a close-knit nurturing community committed to putting students first and enabling every student's full potential. Felician provides a solid and supportive foundation within a liberal arts framework, which allows students to meet the challenges of the new century with informed minds and understanding hearts. The College is accredited by the Middle States Association of Colleges and Schools, and carries program accreditation from the Commission on Collegiate Nursing Education, Teacher Education Accreditation Council, and the International Assembly for Collegiate Business Education.

In addition to its undergraduate degree programs, Felician College offers the Master of Science in Nursing (M.S.N.), Master of Business Administration (M.B.A.), Master of Arts in Religious Education, and Master of Arts in Teacher Education.

Felician College competes in Division II of the National Collegiate Athletic Association (NCAA). The Felician teams, called the Golden Falcons, compete in men's baseball, men's and women's basketball, men's and women's soccer, men's and women's cross-country, men's golf, and women's softball and volleyball. The Athletic Department also sponsors numerous intramural sports activities, such as indoor soccer, faculty-student softball and volleyball games on the quad.

Students may elect to reside in one of the spacious suites in Elliott Hall or Milton Court Residence, both located on the Rutherford Campus, a 10-minute shuttle bus ride from the campus in Lodi. The campuses offer comfortable student lounge areas, student meeting rooms, dining halls, a gymnasium, a fitness center, and grassy areas for outdoor recreation.

Location

Felician College is located on two beautifully landscaped campuses in Lodi and Rutherford, in Bergen County, in northern New Jersey. Both campuses, nestled in suburban towns, are 12 miles from New York City and a few miles from the New Jersey Meadowlands sports complex.

Majors and Degrees

Felician College offers programs of study in the arts and sciences, business and management sciences, nursing and health management, and teacher education.

A liberal arts program leading to the Bachelor of Arts, Bachelor of Science, Bachelor of Science in Nursing, or Associate in Arts degree is designed to provide students with a broad general education and concentrated preparation in a major area. For the B.A. degree, a student may choose a departmental major in art, biology, communications, computer information systems, English, history, mathematics, music, philosophy, psychology, or religious studies. A student may choose an interdisciplinary major in one of three liberal arts areas: humanities, natural sciences and mathematics, or social and behavioral sciences. Concentrations are available in digital video production, fine arts, general science, global peace and justice, graphic design, international education and foreign languages, journalism, mathematical sciences, political science, sociology, and theater arts. Bachelor of Arts degree programs are available in

elementary education (K–5), early childhood education (P–3 and K–5), elementary education with content area specializations (5–8), special education (K–5, dual certification), teacher of students with disabilities (K–12), and secondary education (art, English, history, math, and science).

The Bachelor of Science degree is offered in accounting, business administration, criminal justice, management, marketing, and nursing. A program leading to the Bachelor of Science degree in clinical laboratory science and eligibility for national certification is offered in collaboration with the University of Medicine and Dentistry of New Jersey's School of Health-Related Professions (UMDNJ–SHRP). For this degree, a student may concentrate in cytotechnology or medical technology. Also offered in conjunction with UMDNJ–SHRP is a Bachelor of Science program in allied-health technology. Students may study medical sonography, nuclear medicine technology, respiratory care, or vascular technology. Joint degree programs that lead to a master's or doctoral degree are offered for the following preprofessional programs: audiology, chiropractic studies, medicine, occupational therapy, optometry, physical therapy, physician assistant studies, and podiatry.

Two-year programs are offered leading to the Associate in Arts degree in liberal arts, with a concentration in business.

Academic Programs

A candidate for the B.A. in liberal arts is required to complete an organized program of study comprising a minimum of 120 semester hours distributed among prescribed and elective courses. Four interdisciplinary courses in the College's Core Curriculum are mandatory for all students. Each baccalaureate degree student in arts and sciences is required to prepare a written and oral senior research project. A minimum of 30 credit hours must be earned at the College. A student who pursues an A.A. degree is required to complete 64 to 66 credits in an approved program of study.

A candidate for the B.A. in elementary or special education is required to complete a program of 126 to 131 semester hours, including credits in general education, professional education, and a major in the arts and sciences. Field experience begins in the freshman year, students participate in a practicum in the junior year, and there is supervised teaching during the senior year in a public elementary school. The education programs are accredited by the Teacher Education Accreditation Council.

Evening and weekend classes provide adults with the opportunity to earn associate and baccalaureate degrees offered at Felician College. Students may take courses through the traditional semester format and through an accelerated trimester format. Distance learning courses are also offered.

The Honors Program, for students with strong academic records, provides an opportunity to conduct scholarly research and develop leadership skills through service learning. Upon successful completion of the program students graduate as Honors Scholars.

The Service Learning Program allows students to be of service to others while learning the value of citizenship and responsibility through action and reflection.

Academic Facilities

Seminar rooms, multimedia and learning resource centers, and laboratories in accounting, computers, psychology, science, and writing are updated annually the latest instructional technology. Through the Internet Laboratories, all students have access to e-mail and the World Wide Web. The College auditorium comfortably seats 1,500 people; its large stage with modern theatrical features hosts performing groups from all parts of the country. The College library has a selective collection of more than 110,000 volumes, as well as periodicals, cassettes, records, microfilms, and ultrafiche. A curriculum library serves as a resource center for the teacher education programs. The Nursing Skills Laboratory, located on the Lodi campus, furnishes convenient facilities for observation, application of learning, and field experiences.

Costs

Undergraduate tuition in 2009–10 is $23,650 per year for full-time students. The annual cost of room and board is $9700 (double occupancy). There are additional student fees, commuter fees, and resident fees.

Financial Aid

Felician College participates in federal, state, and institutional programs of financial assistance. To determine the amount and type of aid needed, applicants must file a Free Application for Federal Student Aid (FAFSA) with the Department of Education. The College participates in the Federal Work-Study, Federal Pell Grant, Academic Competitiveness Grant, and Federal Supplemental Educational Opportunity Grant programs. Students from New Jersey may be considered for New Jersey tuition aid grants. Through a state-guaranteed loan program, students may also take out low-interest bank loans. A number of institutional scholarships are available for qualified students in need of financial assistance. The Office of Undergraduate Admission also awards merit-based scholarships to those who are eligible, regardless of need. Monies range from $4000 to full tuition based on GPA and SAT scores. To take advantage of federal financial aid programs exclusively for veterans, a certificate of eligibility should be submitted to the director of financial aid at Felician College. More than half of the students attending Felician receive some form of financial aid.

Faculty

All courses are taught by fully qualified faculty members with advanced degrees, who are dedicated primarily to teaching, advising, and continued involvement in their disciplines. The student-faculty ratio of 10:1 facilitates a close working relationship, as well as individualized programs of instruction. The faculty members are dedicated to supporting student growth and development in a supportive, learner-centered environment designed to help students reach their highest potential.

Student Government

All students participate in the Student Government Organization (SGO). The governing body of the SGO, composed of elected representatives from various student groups, coordinates activities on and off campus, including community service, campus ministry, and social, cultural, civic, and athletic events. Student representatives also serve on College committees with faculty members and administrators.

Admission Requirements

Applicants must be graduates of an accredited high school or have the high school equivalency certificate and satisfactory SAT or ACT scores. A personal essay and interview are strongly recommended.

Students graduating with an associate degree from a recognized junior college are eligible for admission into the upper division of Felician College. Applications for transfer are considered for both fall and spring semesters. Admission requirements may be adjusted for adults on the basis of maturity and experience.

Felician College offers credit and advanced placement of up to 90 credits for coursework from accredited colleges as well as for acceptable scores on the College Board Advanced Placement tests and the College-Level Examination Program tests.

Application and Information

Applications, accompanied by a $30 fee, should be submitted during the fall of the senior year. The Office of Undergraduate Admission evaluates applicants' credentials on a rolling basis. However, applicants for the fall semester are strongly encouraged to apply before April 15.

Office of Undergraduate Admission
Felician College
262 South Main Street
Lodi, New Jersey 07644
Phone: 201-559-6131
Fax: 201-559-6138
Web site: http://www.felician.edu

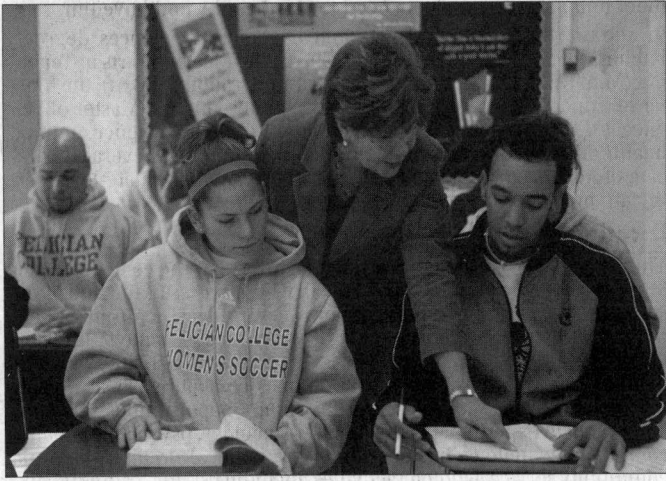

Felician College offers small class size and personal attention to help students achieve academic success.

FITCHBURG STATE UNIVERSITY
FITCHBURG, MASSACHUSETTS

The University

Fitchburg State University is a public liberal arts institution, dedicated to teaching, with thriving career-oriented and professional education programs. The University prepares its graduates for jobs in their fields and continues to place more than 70 percent of its graduates in their chosen professions within six months of graduation.

Fitchburg State's excellent academic reputation and graduate placement can be attributed to a nationally recognized faculty and a strong commitment to teaching. The University enrolls approximately 3,500 undergraduate students in its day and evening divisions and another 3,500 students in its graduate and continuing education programs. The average undergraduate class size is 21, and the overall student-teacher ratio remains low at 17:1. Each student is assigned to an academic adviser to assist with the planning of a program of study. In addition, each department has access to state-of-the-art equipment and an internship network that spreads throughout New England and across the country.

Student life at Fitchburg State is friendly, fun, and informal. There are numerous and varied opportunities for student leadership and involvement. There are more than sixty student-run clubs and organizations, including academic, cultural and ethnic; profession-oriented; performance; sports and fitness; social and volunteer; fraternities and sororities; student government; and academic honor societies. Hundreds of popular and well-attended activities take place during the year, including films, lectures, concerts, seminars, coffeehouses, pub entertainment, recreational tournaments, a performing arts series, and visual arts exhibits. The University participates in Division III athletics, offering sixteen intercollegiate varsity sports teams for both men and women. There is a variety of intramural sports for all students. The beautiful, well-equipped Recreation Center has all the equipment and activities students need to stay healthy and have fun.

In addition to Bachelor of Arts and Bachelor of Sciences degrees, Fitchburg State confers the Master of Arts; the Master of Arts in Teaching (M.A.T.); the Master in Business Administration (M.B.A.); the Master of Education (M.Ed.) in several disciplines; and the Master of Science (M.S.) in applied communication, computer science, mental health and school counseling, and forensic nursing. Several Certificate of Advanced Graduate Studies (C.A.G.S.) and graduate-level certificate programs are available as well.

Location

The University is located in a residential area near the center of Fitchburg, a city with a population of 41,000, which serves as the hub of the commercial and industrial life of north-central Massachusetts. Fitchburg State owns the Wallace Civic Center which is home to the University's ice hockey team and provides a variety of activities, such as exhibits, fairs, performances, free public ice skating, local hockey events, and lectures. Fitchburg offers many opportunities for study and practical experience in the areas of sociology, psychology, health, computer technology, business, industry, political organization, and community service. Outdoor activities, including skiing, camping, hiking, canoeing, and fishing, are just minutes from the campus.

The historic and literary centers of Lexington and Concord and the city of Boston are only about an hour from the University. It's very easy to get to Boston—the commuter rail station is right on the edge of campus. The city of Worcester, the third largest in New England, is a half hour to the south. Fitchburg offers students the convenience of a residential campus with easy access to all that the surrounding area offers.

Majors and Degrees

Fitchburg State University offers the Bachelor of Arts, Bachelor of Science, and Bachelor of Science in Education degrees and offers the following undergraduate programs: accounting; architectural technology; biology; biotechnology; business administration; clinical exercise physiology; communications media studies; computer information systems; computer science; construction technology; criminal justice; developmental psychology; earth science; economics;

education, with teacher education programs available in early childhood education, elementary education, middle school education, secondary education (with emphases in biology, English, history, and mathematics), special education with emphases in severe disabilities (all levels) and moderate disabilities (pre-K–8 and 5–12), and technology education; electronics engineering technology; English; environmental science; exercise and sport science; energy management; film/video production; fitness management; geography; geo/physical sciences; graphic design; history; human services; industrial and organizational psychology; interactive media; humanities–interdisciplinary studies; industrial technology; international business and economics; literature; management; manufacturing engineering technology; marketing; mathematics; nursing; photography; political science; professional communication; professional writing; psychology; sociology; technical theater; theater; undeclared/premajor; and the following preprofessional programs: dentistry, law, medicine, and veterinary medicine.

Academic Programs

The University's undergraduate programs operate on a two-semester calendar. The first semester begins in early September and ends in mid-December, and the second semester begins in mid-January and ends in mid-May.

The curriculum has a strong liberal arts and sciences requirement, providing a solid foundation for either further academic study or a career. Students may obtain practical experience through numerous internships in social agencies, government offices, hospitals, and corporations related to their interests. Some major programs require an extensive supervised practicum to complete degree requirements. For education and nursing majors, a broad spectrum of student-teaching and clinical experience is incorporated into their respective programs of study. The Leadership Academy (the University's four-year honors program) culminates in a senior thesis or project.

Off-Campus Programs

Fitchburg State is one of nine state universities under the jurisdiction of the Massachusetts Department of Higher Education. Through this affiliation, students may participate in the College Academic Program Sharing program, which allows study for a semester or a year at another university. The Office of International Education at Fitchburg State provides undergraduate students with the opportunity to study abroad at a variety of colleges and universities all over the world. Programs vary in length from a few weeks to as long as a semester or a year. Some of the locations in the exchange program include Australia, Canada, China, England, France, Ireland, Italy, Japan, New Zealand, Russia, Scotland, Spain, and Sweden.

Academic Facilities

The University has a number of special facilities. A well-equipped Academic Success Center includes offices for academic advising, career services, disability services, math and writing centers, multicultural student services, and peer tutoring. The McKay Campus School is a pre-K through fourth grade elementary school located on campus, which gives education majors direct experience in an operating school. An Instructional Media Center has extensive, modern, well-equipped facilities which support the industrial education and industrial technology programs. The nursing program utilizes an on-campus clinical lab that simulates a hospital setting with computerized training models: SimMan, SimBaby, and SimNewB. The communications media program owns a full range of the latest equipment, such as media/film composers, digital audio workstations, a full-color dye-sublimation printer, CD recording and slide-scanning equipment, multiple editing rooms, a production studio, darkrooms, and graphic design computer labs. Communication students at Fitchburg State have access to many of the labs and facilities as early as their freshman year.

Costs

Annual tuition for residents of Massachusetts was $970 per year in 2010–11; out-of-state tuition was $7050. Required annual fees in 2010–11 totaled $6830. The estimated annual total for a full-time, on-campus student from Massachusetts was $15,860 and for an out-of-state student it was $21,940. Fees are subject to change.

Financial Aid

Many sources of financial aid are available to Fitchburg State students. The University participates in federal and state programs. Packages consisting of grants, loans, work-study awards, and scholarships are given to students demonstrating financial need and academic merit. All students who submit a completed application for admission by February 1 will automatically be considered for all available merit scholarships for the fall semester. Financial aid applications (including the FAFSA) for the fall semester must be completed by the preceding March 1 to be given priority consideration. Over $23 million in financial aid is granted annually to approximately 80 percent of Fitchburg State students.

Faculty

More than 92 percent of Fitchburg State's 192 full-time faculty members hold earned doctoral or other terminal degrees. Full professors teach freshman sections as well as advanced courses and serve as academic advisers to students majoring in their respective programs. Faculty members are accessible, engaging, and available to teach and advise students throughout their four years at the University.

Student Government

All full-time undergraduate students are members of the Student Government Association (SGA). The purpose of the SGA is to encourage responsibility and cooperation in democratic self-government; to form an official body for expressing the judgments of students and fostering activities and matters of general student interest; and to promote full understanding and cooperation among the students, the faculty members, and the administration in order to further the welfare of the University.

The governing body of the SGA consists of 6 SGA officers and a General Council, which includes these officers and 55 elected representatives of classes and residence halls, as well as the commuter student body. The SGA operates through a number of standing and ad hoc committees, membership on which is open to all students.

A 14-member All-University Committee, representing students, the faculty, and the administration, makes recommendations to the president of the University concerning matters of campuswide policy.

Admission Requirements

As part of the Massachusetts State University system, Fitchburg State evaluates each applicant from any state, based on standards set by the Massachusetts Department of Higher Education and the University. The University considers high school curriculum, grade point average, SAT and/or ACT scores, school and community service, recommendations, application essay, life experience, special talents, and learning styles. The state admissions standards place significant attention on the student's high school record and SAT or ACT scores. The record of achievement in high school is the single most important item in the applicant's academic credentials. Freshman applicants should have completed a college-preparatory program that includes 16 college-preparatory units, with 4 units in English, 2 units in the same foreign language, 2 units in social studies, 3 units in mathematics (algebra I and II and geometry), 3 units in the natural sciences (2 of which must be laboratory courses), and 2 college-preparatory electives.

An essay is required; however, interviews are not required. Applicants who have questions about the programs and admission procedures at the University are encouraged to contact the Admissions Office to speak with a counselor.

Transfer students are encouraged to apply to Fitchburg State. An official transcript from each college previously attended must be submitted along with the application for admission.

International students are encouraged to apply. Scores on the Test of English as a Foreign Language (TOEFL), evaluations of all international transcripts, and translations of international transcripts must be submitted in addition to the application for admission. Additional information for international students is available on the University's Web site.

Application and Information

Fitchburg State University reviews applications on a rolling basis, sending its first set of admission decisions for the fall semester by mid-December. The priority deadline for applications is March 1. Applicants to the communications media and nursing programs are reviewed against a higher set of admissions standards and are strongly encouraged to submit their applications by the January 1 priority deadline. In addition, applicants who wish to be considered for merit scholarships and the Leadership Academy must complete their admission and financial aid application process (i.e., submit all required materials) by February 1.

Transfer applicants are encouraged to apply by April 15 for the fall and by November 1 for the spring semester. International applicants applying for the fall semester must complete the application process by March 15 if they require on-campus housing and by July 15 if they are not in need of campus housing. Applicants for the spring semester must file their application for admission by December 1.

For further information, students should contact:

Admissions Office
Fitchburg State University
160 Pearl Street
Fitchburg, Massachusetts 01420

Phone: 800-705-9692 (toll-free)
Fax: 978-665-4540
E-mail: admissions@fitchburgstate.edu
Web site: http://www.fitchburgstate.edu
 http://on.fb.me/FitchburgState (Facebook)
 http://twitter.com/FITCHBURG_STATE

A student works on a laptop in Edgerly Hall at Fitchburg State University. The University requires all incoming freshmen to purchase laptops.

FIVE TOWNS COLLEGE
DIX HILLS, NEW YORK

The College

Located on Long Island's North Shore, Five Towns College offers students the opportunity to study in a suburban environment that is close to New York City. Founded in 1972, Five Towns College is an independent, nonsectarian, coeducational institution that places its emphasis on the student as an individual. Many students are drawn to the College because of its strong reputation in music, media, education, and the performing arts. The College offers associate and bachelor's degrees. The College also offers programs leading to the Master of Music (M.M.) degree in jazz/commercial music and in music education as well as a Master of Science in Education (M.S.Ed.) and a Doctor of Musical Arts (D.M.A.).

From as far away as England and South Korea and from as close as Long Island and New York City, the 1,100 undergraduate and graduate students reflect a rich cultural diversity. The College's enrollment is 55 percent men and 45 percent women, with a minority population of approximately 30 percent. The College's music programs are contemporary jazz in nature, although classical musicians are also part of this creative community. The most popular programs are audio recording technology, broadcasting, journalism, music performance, music business, music and elementary teacher education, theater, and film/video production.

Coeducational living accommodations are available on campus. The Five Towns College Living/Learning Center is a new complex containing four modern life residence halls. Each residence hall contains single- and double-occupancy rooms equipped with private bathrooms, broadband Internet access, cable television, and other amenities.

Location

The College's beautiful 35-acre campus, located in the wooded countryside of Dix Hills, New York, provides students with a quiet college setting to pursue their studies. Just off campus is Long Island's bustling Route 110 corridor, home to numerous national and multinational corporations. New York City, with everything from Lincoln Center to Broadway, is just a train ride away and provides students with some of the best cultural advantages in the world.

Closer to the campus, the many communities of Long Island abound with cultural and recreational opportunities. The College is located within the historic town of Huntington, which is home to the Cinema Arts Center, Hecksher Museum, Vanderbilt Museum, and numerous restaurants, coffeehouses, and quaint shops. The nearby shores of Jones Beach State Park and the Fire Island National Seashore are world renowned for their white, sandy beaches.

Majors and Degrees

Five Towns College offers the Associate in Arts (A.A.) degree in liberal arts, with concentrations in teaching assistant studies and literature; the Associate in Science (A.S.) degree in business administration; and the Associate in Applied Science (A.A.S.) degree in business management and in jazz commercial music, with concentrations in audio recording technology and music business.

The College offers the Bachelor of Music (Mus.B.) degree in music education and in jazz/commercial music, with concentrations in audio recording technology, composition/songwriting, music business, musical theater, and performance; the Bachelor of Fine Arts (B.F.A.) degree in theater or film/video arts; the Bachelor of Professional Studies (B.P.S.) degree in business management, with concentrations in audio recording technology and music business; the Bachelor of Science (B.S.) degree in childhood education; and the B.S. in mass communication, which features broadcasting and journalism concentrations.

Academic Programs

The following describes some of the more popular programs at Five Towns College. For a complete description of the College's academic program, students should visit the Five Towns College Web site at http://www.ftc.edu.

The music education program is designed for students interested in a career as a teacher of music in a public or private school. The undergraduate program leads to New York State provisional certification. The course work provides professional training and includes a student-teaching experience. The audio recording technology concentration is designed to provide students with the tools needed to succeed as professional studio engineers and producers in the music industry. The music business concentration is designed for students interested in a career in entertainment-related business fields. The course work includes the technical, legal, production, management, and merchandising aspects of the music business. The composition/songwriting concentration provides intensive instruction in a core of technical studies in harmony, orchestration, counterpoint, MIDI, songwriting, form and analysis, arranging, and composition for those who intend to pursue careers as composers, arrangers, and songwriters. The performance concentration includes a common core of technical studies and a foundation of specialized courses, such as music history, harmony, counterpoint, improvisation, ensemble performance, and private instruction. The theater arts program is designed for students interested in careers as actors, entertainers, scenic designers, directors, stage managers, and lighting or sound directors. The film/video program includes extensive technical preparation in videography, filmmaking, linear and nonlinear editing, storyboarding, scriptwriting, producing, and directing for filmmakers and videographers. Elementary education students are prepared as teachers for grades 1–6, while those interested in journalism and broadcasting are prepared for careers in radio, television, newspaper, or editorial writing.

To earn a bachelor's degree, students must accumulate between 122 and 130 credits, depending on the program of study, with a proper distribution of courses and a GPA of a minimum of 2.0. To earn an associate degree, students must accumulate between 62 and 66 credits.

Off-Campus Programs

Off-campus internship opportunities are available to Five Towns College students who have fulfilled the necessary prerequisites, including a cumulative grade point average of at least 2.5, with a 3.0 in their major. In recent semesters, students have interned for major corporations such as MTV, Atlantic Records, Polygram Records, CBS, ABC, EMI Records, MCA Records, Sony Records, The Power Station, Universal Mastering Studios, Channel 12 News, and many others.

Academic Facilities

Five Towns College occupies a multiwinged facility that comprises approximately 120,000 square feet and includes a 500-seat auditorium, production studios, athletic and dining facilities, classrooms, PC and Mac computer labs, and a student center. T-3 lines connect the College's completely fiber-optic computer network to the Internet. All students have access to this network and are provided with an e-mail account.

The Five Towns College Library has more than 50,000 print and nonprint materials. These include nearly 32,000 books and print items, 450 periodical subscriptions, and approximately 5,000 records, 2,600 DVDs, and more than 4,300 CDs. Through its membership in the Long Island Library Resource Council (LILRC), students have access to other libraries around the country.

The John Lennon Center for Music and Technology at Five Towns College houses state-of-the-art audio recording studios and a fully loaded electronic music/MIDI computer lab. The studios and lab feature industry-standard recording equipment and software programs that rival major recording facilities around the world, such as a 72-channel SSL 9000J and Neve Genesys mixing console; Telefunken, Neumann, AKG, Royer, Blue, and other microphones; outboard gear such as Manley, API, Chandler Limited, Lexicon, Universal Audio, and Apogee; and the latest versions of Pro Tools, Logic, Reason, and Sibelius. The film/video division uses Sony PMW-EX3 XD cameras with SxS cards, Canon 5D Mark II cameras, and Arriflex Super 16-mm film cameras. Editing suites offer Final Cut Pro and Adobe CS4 Creative Suite on iMac computers. Students utilize these facilities to develop their skills while creating professional-quality productions, both in the studio and on location under the supervision of industry professionals. Student productions include short films, music videos, documentaries, public service announcements, commercials, and live events, among many others.

The Dix Hills Center for Performing Arts at Five Towns College is an acoustically "perfect" venue, with digital lighting systems, digital sound reinforcement for concert production, and a Barco 6300 digital projection system for multimedia productions. The professional stage is 60 feet wide, with a proscenium opening of 16 feet and 32 feet of fly space. Students utilize this facility to produce live concerts, plays, musicals, and other performances and special presentations.

Costs

The tuition for 2010–11 was $18,400 per year. Miscellaneous fees total approximately $400, and books cost about $500. Private instruction fees for performing music students are $775 per semester.

Financial Aid

The annual tuition at Five Towns College is among the lowest of all the private colleges in the region. Nevertheless, approximately 82 percent of all students receive some form of financial assistance. Need-based and/or merit-based grants, scholarships, loans, and work-study programs are available to qualified recipients, including transfer students. Prospective students are urged to contact the Financial Aid Office as early as possible.

Faculty

The College's growing faculty consists of 120 full- and part-time members. The student-faculty ratio is 14:1. While the faculty is more strongly committed to teaching than to research, many members continue to be active in their respective areas of expertise.

Student Government

Student Government Association (SGA) serves as a voice of the students to the faculty and administration. Students can get involved through organizations and committees. All recognized organizations and committees fall under the jurisdiction of the SGA. The SGA is the elected representative student body of the campus and is responsible for creating many of the policy-making decisions that affect organizations and student life.

There are several media clubs and organizations for students. They include *Keynotes* (the College yearbook), *The Record* (the student newspaper), and WFTU (the College radio station).

Admission Requirements

The College encourages applications from students who will engage themselves in its creative community. Students applying to the College should have attained a minimum high school average grade of 78 percent. The SAT or ACT exam is required for all freshmen. Transfer students must also submit official transcripts of all college-level work as well as their high school transcripts. International students from non-English-speaking countries must submit a TOEFL Internet score of at least 80 or its equivalent. The College does not accept students on an early admissions basis, although early decision is available. Candidates for admission must submit a completed Application for Undergraduate Admission, official high school transcripts, at least two letters of recommendation, and a personal statement. International students must submit their TOEFL scores, financial documentation and sponsor information.

Application and Information

Admission into any music program is contingent upon passing an audition demonstrating skill in performance on a major instrument or vocally. Admission into any theater program is also contingent upon passing an audition. In some cases, the Admissions Committee may request an on-campus interview with an applicant. Music, theater, and film/video students are encouraged to submit an electronic portfolio or DVD, if available.

Except for applicants applying on an early decision basis, new students are accepted on a rolling basis, with decisions for the fall and spring semesters mailed starting February 15 and December 1, respectively. There is an application fee of $35.

For further information, students should contact the Admissions Office at 631-656-2110 or admissions@ftc.edu.

Director of Admissions
Five Towns College
305 North Service Road
Dix Hills, New York 11746-5871
Phone: 631-656-2110
Fax: 631-656-3199
E-mail: admissions@ftc.edu
Web site: http://www.ftc.edu

FLORIDA ATLANTIC UNIVERSITY
BOCA RATON, FLORIDA

The University

Florida Atlantic University (FAU) is a midsize comprehensive university that serves more than 28,000 students on seven campuses throughout South Florida. FAU was established in 1961, making it the fifth-oldest university in the state system. As an upper-division and graduate state university, FAU admitted its first students in September 1964. Enrollment has increased from 867 in the first year to more than 28,000 in the 2010–11 academic year.

Since the original Boca Raton campus was founded in 1964, the University has expanded to six other campuses in South Florida: Dania Beach, Davie, Fort Lauderdale, Jupiter, and Treasure Coast. Admission to incoming freshman students is limited to the Boca Raton campus and the Harriet L. Wilkes Honors College.

The Boca Raton campus provides an exciting and supportive learning environment for students. The University Center hosts student activities and meetings. In addition, its 2,400-seat auditorium enables students to enjoy a wide variety of musical performances.

The Boca Raton campus is also the home of FAU's Division I intercollegiate athletics program and facilities. A new 30,000-seat football stadium is under construction and slated to open by fall 2011. It will feature such state-of-the-art amenities as 6,000 premium seats, including suites, priority club seating, and a student and band-only section in the south end zone.

FAU's new recreation and fitness center includes an aquatic center, gymnasium, treadmill and elliptical area, and personal trainers. The recreation and wellness complex includes tennis courts, a track, and a variety of fields for club and intramural sports competition. The five-story S. E. Wimberly Library houses a large collection of monographs, serials, and other academic resources. Computer labs, study lounges, a media center, and tutoring services also provide valuable academic support for students.

One of FAU's newest campuses is Dania Beach, also known as SeaTech. This is FAU's Institute for Ocean and Systems Engineering, located on 8 acres between the Atlantic Ocean and the Intracoastal Waterway, with valuable access to the ocean and seawater.

FAU's Davie campus is located on 38 acres in western Broward County and is FAU's second-largest campus. The Davie campus has served FAU students since 1990 with 2+2 programs in partnership with Broward Community College.

The Fort Lauderdale campus in downtown Fort Lauderdale takes advantage of its unique urban setting to serve as a center for FAU programs in creative industries and urban affairs. The campus is part of Fort Lauderdale's evolving, dynamic urban community and provides a laboratory for students in business, computer arts, graphic arts, multimedia communication, architecture, urban and regional planning, and public administration.

The John D. MacArthur Campus presently enrolls more than 2,000 students and offers a wide range of upper division and graduate programs. It is home to the Harriet L. Wilkes Honors College, the Center for Environmental Studies, the Hibel Museum of Art, the new research facility for Scripps Florida, and the future site of the Max Planck Florida Institute.

In 2006, FAU opened the FAU/Harbor Branch Marine Sciences Building—a 40,000-square-foot, joint-use facility housing specially equipped marine science labs, classrooms and video-conferencing equipped meeting rooms—at the Harbor Branch Oceanographic Institution's 600-acre site in Fort Pierce.

The Treasure Coast Campus is conveniently situated in St. Lucie West, part of the city of Port St. Lucie. It offers upper-division degree programs to transfer and graduate students in disciplines such as nursing, education, computer science, and geomatics engineering.

The FAU/Harbor Branch Oceanographic Institution Marine Science Partnership Building in Fort Pierce is a new FAU location on the Treasure Coast. This state-of-the-art facility provides an ideal setting for marine science research and teaching.

Through its partnerships with other educational institutions, local businesses, industries, and civic and cultural organizations, FAU enhances the economic, human, and cultural development of the surrounding communities and beyond. Students at FAU may participate in a work-study program that combines their classroom learning with hands-on experience.

The University's Charles E. Schmidt College of Medicine has been granted preliminary accreditation by the Liaison Committee on Medical Education (LCME) and has started recruiting students for the College's charter medical school class that begins fall 2011. It also is partnering with FAU's Wilkes Honors College to offer select students early provisional admission to medical school, making it possible to receive both a bachelor's degree and an M.D. from FAU in only seven or eight years. Incoming freshmen who are accepted into the new Wilkes Medical Scholars Program will begin their undergraduate programs already assured of a spot in FAU's new medical school, provided they complete all program requirements and score at least 29 on the MCAT. To learn more, visit: http://www.fau.edu/divdept/honcol/admissions_med.htm.

The University has developed a partnership with Broward College and Palm Beach State College called the Link Program. Through this program, students are prepared for guaranteed admission to FAU upon successful completion of their Associate in Arts degree.

Florida Atlantic University is accredited by the Commission on Colleges of the Southern Association of Colleges and Schools to award associate, bachelor's, master's, and doctoral degrees. In addition, it is accredited by fourteen professional agencies. FAU is also a member of the National Association of State Universities and Land-Grant Colleges and the Council of Graduate Schools in the United States.

Location

FAU's main campus in Boca Raton is on an 850-acre site located only 3 miles from the Atlantic Ocean. The campus is conveniently located halfway between Palm Beach and Fort Lauderdale and offers a broad range of academic programs, activities, and services.

South Florida's climate is subtropical, with an average year-round temperature of 75 degrees. FAU's campuses are within easy driving distance of some of the most beautiful beaches and recreational facilities to be found anywhere.

Majors and Degrees

FAU offers programs leading to the Bachelor of Arts (B.A.), Bachelor of Science (B.S.), and specialized bachelor's degrees. A minimum of 120 credit hours is required for a bachelor's degree.

The College for Design and Social Inquiry offers majors in architecture, criminal justice, public management, social work, and urban and regional planning.

The Dorothy F. Schmidt College of Arts and Letters offers a general college major and majors in anthropology, art, Caribbean and Latin American studies, English, history, Jewish studies, languages and linguistics (French, German, Italian, Japanese, and Spanish), music, philosophy, political science, social science, sociology, and theater.

The College of Business offers majors in accounting, economics, finance, hospitality management, insurance, international business, management, management information systems, and marketing.

The Harriet L. Wilkes Honors College in Jupiter offers a liberal arts and sciences education in a highly selective environment. Concentrations include American studies, anthropology, biological sciences/pre-med, chemistry, economics, English literature, environmental studies, history, international studies, Latin American studies, law and society, marine biology, math and science, mathematics, philosophy, physics, political science, psychology, Spanish, and women's studies.

The University Honors Program at the Boca Raton Campus provides students with exceptional and rewarding learning opportunities through special honors seminars. Learn more at http://www.fau.edu/divdept/honorsboca/faq.htm.

The College of Education offers majors in elementary education, exceptional student education, and exercise science and wellness education. Secondary certification is also available.

The College of Engineering and Computer Science offers majors in computer science as well as civil, computer, electrical, mechanical, and ocean engineering. FAU established the nation's first ocean engineering degree program in 1965 and now conducts millions of dollars in research annually.

The Christine E. Lynn College of Nursing offers a B.S. in Nursing degree and is nationally and internationally known for developing innovative approaches to nursing education within a caring philosophy.

The Charles E. Schmidt College of Science has majors in biological science (biotechnology, ecology and organismic biology, marine biology, microbiology, and molecular biology), chemistry, geography, geology, mathematical sciences, physics, psychology, and social psychology.

Academic Programs

Florida Atlantic University prepares its undergraduate students to be productive and thoughtful citizens by offering a broad liberal education coupled with the development of competency in fields of special interest. FAU encourages students to think creatively and critically and provides the intellectual tools needed for lifelong learning.

Off-Campus Programs

While there is no substitute for the dynamic synergy created in the classroom, FAU faculty and students seek out real-world experiences that enhance the classroom experience, such as internships, hands-on research, and study-abroad opportunities. FAU has exchange agreements with international schools in locations ranging from China to Germany. Arrangements can be made through the Office of International Programs (http://www.fau.edu/goabroad).

Academic Facilities

The Boca Raton campus resources feature the S. E. Wimberly Library, with more than 1 million holdings. The Dorothy F. Schmidt College of Arts and Letters features a 75,000-square-foot, three-building complex encompassing a performance arts center, an art gallery, an experimental theater, a visual arts center, lecture halls, classrooms, and offices. The College of Business occupies a four-story building including wireless classrooms with a simulated trading room floor. The College of Education's four-story, 90,000-square-foot facility houses its five academic departments and offers a teaching gymnasium, an early childhood center, and the A. D. Henderson University School operated by the College of Education. There is also a marine sciences center, Gumbo Limbo, located between the Intracoastal Waterway and the Atlantic Ocean; it provides teaching and research facilities. The Christine E. Lynn College of Nursing is housed in a state-of-the-art building which is a LEED-certified Gold.

FAU continues to enhance the campus environment with many new facilities under construction. Recently completed projects on the Boca Raton campus include the Marleen and Harold Forkas Alumni Center; the College of Engineering and Computer Science facility, which is designed to achieve LEED Platinum certification; and the new Culture and Society building that includes the Living Room Theaters, a 200-seat digital movie complex.

Expansions are under way across all of FAU's seven campuses. On the Davie campus, a new student activity center was recently completed. The Treasure Coast campus has added additional classroom facilities to accommodate its growing student body.

Costs

For the 2010–11 academic year, in-state tuition was $159.81 per credit hour and out-of-state tuition was $604.39 per credit hour. Average room and board costs are $9690. Approximate expenses are $924 for books, $1652 for personal items, and $2815 for transportation for off-campus students. Fees are subject to change.

Financial Aid

Approximately $154 million in financial aid is awarded each year. A comprehensive program of student financial aid includes scholarships, grants, loans, and work-study that may provide assistance from initial enrollment through graduate study. As a member of the College Scholarship Service of the College Board, the University is guided by the principles and policies of that organization. Students who are interested in applying for need-based aid must complete the Free Application for Federal Student Aid (FAFSA), which is available online at http://www.fau.edu/finaid and at all U.S. high schools, colleges, and universities. Students are strongly encouraged to complete the FAFSA

in January for fall admission. The process of applying for aid normally takes six to eight weeks. The priority deadline is March 1.

There are a variety of scholarships for academic, athletic, or artistic talent. Students should visit the Admissions Web site at http://www.fau.edu/admissions for more information on academic scholarships and should check with individual departments for information on athletic or artistic scholarships.

Faculty

Recognizing that the excellence of its faculty is the true measure of the worth of a university, FAU has brought together a distinguished group of scholars who hold a balanced dedication to both teaching and research. Faculty members come from more than thirty states and several countries. The majority hold a doctorate or professional degree. They all represent a high level of professional experience and academic attainment and are committed to the development of a vigorous educational program of high caliber. The FAU community has benefited from the presence of 12 Eminent Scholars, distributed over seven colleges. In addition, two Endowed Chairs have been fully funded and five others partially funded. The presence of these distinguished scholars and researchers has greatly enhanced the academic climate of the University and has provided focal points for the development of new programs, particularly at the graduate level.

Student Government

FAU gives students an active role on virtually all University and faculty committees, including the Curriculum Committee. They serve on the Board of Trustees and college advisory councils and operate the Student Government Association and Residence Hall Councils as well as the interclub, interfraternity, and Panhellenic groups. Students also serve on the University Senate along with faculty and staff members.

Admission Requirements

Admission to the University is limited to applicants who have graduated from regionally accredited high schools or who hold a GED certificate. Evaluation is based on the academic course grade point average and rigor of curriculum combined with acceptable results on the SAT or ACT. Candidates for admission should have 18 academic high school units, including 4 units of English, 4 units of mathematics (algebra I and above), 3 units of natural science (2 with labs), 3 units of social science, 2 units of foreign language in sequence, and 2 academic electives. Applicants who have completed the GED test should request official high school transcripts (if applicable) and an official GED score report from the Department of Education.

Admission for freshman students requires an application for admission, a nonrefundable $30 application fee, official transcripts from an accredited high school, and the official results of the SAT or ACT. Admitted freshmen must confirm their intention to enroll and secure their place with the freshman class by submitting a nonrefundable $200 deposit, which is applied to the student's tuition and other expenses for the term in which they have been admitted to FAU.

Undergraduate students who wish to transfer to FAU must be in good academic standing at their previous college or university and have a minimum 2.5 GPA. Students with fewer than 60 transferable credits should submit an application for admission, a nonrefundable $30 application fee, official transcripts from high school and previously attended colleges or universities, and acceptable SAT or ACT scores. Students with 60 or more transferable credits must submit an application for admission, a nonrefundable $30 application fee, and official transcripts from each previously attended college or university.

Students who have completed all or part of their education abroad are required to have their foreign credentials evaluated by an independent evaluation service. International students must also furnish evidence of proficiency in English by submitting TOEFL scores. For additional requirements, students should visit http://www.fau.edu/admissions.

Application and Information

Office of Undergraduate Admissions
Florida Atlantic University
777 Glades Road
Boca Raton, Florida 33431
Phone: 561-297-3040
        800-920-8705 (Honors College, toll-free)
E-mail: admissions@fau.edu
        hcadmissions@fau.edu (Honors College)
Web site: http://www.fau.edu

FLORIDA SOUTHERN COLLEGE
LAKELAND, FLORIDA

The College

The oldest private college in the state, Florida Southern College was chartered in 1885 and settled on the shores of spectacular Lake Hollingsworth in Lakeland in 1922.

Florida Southern today is a nationally ranked, residential, coeducational, and comprehensive college. Its 2,200 students represent forty-four states and more than forty countries. Students choose Florida Southern because of its national reputation for dynamic, hands-on learning that features guaranteed internships and study abroad. The atmosphere is friendly and personal, fostering a close-knit student body and faculty.

All members of the academic community take pride in the beautiful campus, a historic landmark and home to the world's largest single-site collection of buildings designed by renowned architect Frank Lloyd Wright.

Students, whether members of fraternities and sororities or as independents, live in a variety of contemporary on-campus accommodations, including the new state-of-the-art Barnett Residential Life Center, which features stunning views of the lake, contemporary student lounges, modern kitchens and bathrooms, and wireless Internet access.

The George Jenkins Field House, which seats 3,000, includes a three-court gymnasium, a weight room, and an athletic training room. Facilities for tennis, racquetball, dance, swimming, and waterskiing are available at the popular Nina B. Hollis Wellness Center, which offers a fully equipped fitness center, an aerobics/dance studio, an intramural gymnasium, an Olympic swimming pool, and a wide-screen TV/lounge area.

There are branches of seven national Greek fraternities and seven national Greek sororities on campus. Popular student activities include intercollegiate and intramural sports, drama and music groups, publications, and more than seventy clubs and organizations related to academic, political, religious, and social interests. A high percentage of students are involved in volunteer programs and internships in the surrounding community, statewide, and internationally.

Location

Florida Southern's campus consists of approximately 100 acres on the shore of Lake Hollingsworth in Lakeland, Florida, a dynamic suburban community of about 120,000 residents in the heart of Florida's high-tech corridor. The campus is within walking or biking distance of Lakeland's historic downtown, and Lakeland is just 45 minutes from Tampa and an hour from Orlando. Within an hour's drive of the state's major recreational attractions, including Walt Disney World and award-winning beaches, the College is ideally situated for internships and job opportunities with leading corporations that tap into one of the largest markets in the U.S. Students enjoy Festival of Fine Arts series performances in music, dance, and drama; distinguished speakers; and exciting College and business symposiums. The Lakeland Center also offers many cultural and entertainment opportunities.

Majors and Degrees

Florida Southern College offers Bachelor of Arts, Bachelor of Fine Arts, Bachelor of Music, Bachelor of Music Education, Bachelor of Science, and Bachelor of Science in Nursing degrees in more than fifty majors including accounting, art (art education, art history, graphic design, and studio art), athletic training, biochemistry and molecular biology, biology, business administration (concentrations in finance, international business, management, and marketing), chemistry, citrus, communication (advertising, broadcast journalism, print journalism, and public relations), criminology, economics, education (elementary education), English, history, horticultural science, mathematics, mathematics/computer science, music (music composition, music education, and music performance), nursing, philosophy, physical education, political science, psychology, religion, sociology, Spanish, theater arts (performance and technical), and youth ministry. Divisional majors are available in humanities and social science.

Preprofessional programs are offered in dentistry, engineering, law, medicine, pharmacy, physical therapy, theology, and veterinary medicine. Interdisciplinary professional programs include music management and sport management. Programs in environmental horticulture include recreational turfgrass management as well as landscape design. Students who wish to teach at the secondary level choose a major in a subject area and complete the requirements for secondary education certification by the state of Florida.

An honors program provides special opportunities for a select group of entering freshmen to explore topics of common interest in an integrated and interdisciplinary fashion.

Academic Programs

All degree programs require the satisfactory completion of a minimum of 128 semester hours with a minimum grade point average of 2.0. Students and professors work together in discussion-based classes featuring debate, collaborative projects, and other forms of engaged learning. The College operates on the semester system, with two 15-week semesters, a three-week May term, and three 4-week summer sessions. The average course load is 16 hours per semester. Students are required to complete a general education curriculum designed to help develop knowledge, skills, and attitudes for lifelong success, in addition to their major course work. Credit by examination is awarded on the basis of successful scores on Advanced Placement tests, the International Baccalaureate (I.B.), and College-Level Examination Program (CLEP) tests.

Florida Southern has a Career Center that assists students in clarifying their career and life goals and provides opportunities for them to explore these goals. Approximately 20 percent of Florida Southern graduates go immediately to graduate school, and some FSC signature programs, such as premedicine, have a 100 percent placement rate.

Florida Southern guarantees every student an internship, and those real-world experiences help to place the vast majority of graduates in jobs in their chosen fields. Ninety-four percent of graduates report having a great job or being enrolled in graduate school within three months of graduation.

Off-campus Programs

The College sponsors a number of popular study-abroad opportunities, including May Option experiences in Harlaxton Manor (England), Cuernavaca (Mexico), and Salamanca and Alicante (Spain). Beginning with students entering in fall 2010, all students will be guaranteed a domestic or international travel experience in their junior or senior year at no charge other than the usual course credit fees.

Other study-abroad options include Angers (France) and semester or yearlong programs in England, Northern Ireland, Central and South America, or a vast array of additional options through one of the College's consortium programs.

Florida Southern College recently affiliated with the highly regarded, nonpartisan Washington Center (TWC), an internship provider with international scope. Florida Southern College is the only private institution of higher education in the state of Florida to affiliate with The Washington Center. This affiliation allows FSC students to access prestigious and valuable field experiences as part of their undergraduate studies. Programs range from tailored internships that are academic and work-experience based for governmental, international, corporate, and nonprofit organizations, to intensive-learning academic seminars focused on timely topics.

Academic Facilities

The College recently opened the new Marshall and Vera Lea Rinker Technology Center, which is equipped with the latest technology and Wi-Fi, as are other computer labs on campus, such as the popular new TûTû's Cyber Café in the library.

There are several new academic buildings on campus, including the state-of-the-art Joe K. and Alberta Blanton Nursing Building, home to the College's growing School of Nursing; and the Dr. Marcene H. and

Robert E. Christoverson Humanities Building, which features contemporary classrooms, a modern language lab, film studies center, and art gallery.

Florida Southern's Roux Library houses a collection of 175,213 volumes; more than 650 periodical subscriptions; access to more than 2,000 full-text electronic periodicals and more than 72,000 electronic books; a 5,700-item media collection that includes videocassettes, CDs, DVDs, and CD-ROMs; a substantial microforms collection; and seating for more than 350 students. The new, adjacent Sarah D. and L. Kirk McKay Jr. Archives Center houses records from the Florida Conference of the United Methodist Church; Frank Lloyd Wright drawings and documents; the Lawton M. Chiles Center for Florida History; and the Florida Citrus Archives.

In addition, the Branscomb Memorial Auditorium seats 1,800 and is nationally known for its perfect acoustics. The Ludd M. Spivey Fine Arts Center comprises the Marjorie M. McKinley Music Building, the Melvin Art Gallery, and the Loca Lee Buckner Theater, which seats 350. The Polk Science Building houses the College's state-of-the-art science laboratories and planetarium. The on-campus Preschool provides an opportunity for students majoring in elementary education to observe and teach preschoolers.

Costs

The comprehensive cost for 2011–12 is $34,920 ($26,112 for tuition and standard fees and $8808 for room and board). There are additional fees for individual music instruction and the use of practice rooms. FSC estimates that another $1150 is adequate for books and supplies, and $1500 should cover personal expenses, exclusive of travel to and from home.

Financial Aid

The Student Financial Aid Office offers students its counsel and assistance in meeting their educational expenses. Aid is awarded on the basis of an applicant's need, academic performance, and promise. Ninety-six percent of the students at Florida Southern receive financial assistance. To demonstrate need, an applicant is required to file the Free Application for Federal Student Aid (FAFSA). Various forms of aid, such as scholarships, grants, loans, and campus employment, are used to help meet students' needs. Merit scholarships are available, and awards are based on academic promise; performance ability in music, theater, or art; or athletic ability in baseball, basketball, cross-country, golf, soccer, softball, swimming, tennis, volleyball, or lacrosse. Applicants for aid must reapply each year. Florida Southern participates in the Federal Perkins Loan, Federal Supplemental Educational Opportunity Grant, and Federal Work-Study college-based programs. All applicants are expected to apply for any entitlement grant for which they are eligible, such as a Federal Pell Grant and, for Florida residents, the Florida Student Assistance Grant. The Federal Stafford Direct Student Loan Program is also available. The completed FAFSA and the College's financial aid application must be filed with the Student Financial Aid Office by April 1. Early application is encouraged for students seeking academic scholarships.

Faculty

Ninety percent of Florida Southern's faculty members have doctoral or other terminal degrees in their fields. The faculty is devoted to teaching and the success of students; all faculty members have posted office hours and are available for consultation and advising. Faculty members are selected not only for their teaching ability but also for their ability to relate to the needs and concerns of college students. The student-faculty ratio is 14:1.

Student Government

The Student Government Association represents the student body in matters involving the College administration, faculty, and student body and is responsible for coordinating student government. Each full-time student is a member of the association and has a vote in its affairs. The subsidiaries of the association are the Association of Campus Entertainment (ACE), the House of Representatives, the Student Senate, and the four classes: freshman, sophomore, junior, and senior.

Admission Requirements

Florida Southern looks for two things in applicants: performance and promise. The majority of applicants who have been admitted as freshmen have had a grade of B or better in college-preparatory courses (including four courses in English, three in mathematics, and the balance divided among science, foreign language, and social science); and have earned minimum scores of 500 on each of the verbal and math portions of the SAT or a composite score of at least 23 on the ACT. The Admissions Office is committed to reviewing individual applicants on their own merits, based on the level of challenge attempted, patterns of grades over time, recommendations from references, and an applicant's own assessment of the learning environment best suited to his or her needs. Evidence of leadership and community service also are typical attributes of a successful applicant.

Applicants must graduate from an accredited high school with a minimum of 19 credits, 16 of which must be academic. Qualified high school juniors may apply for early admission if they have the recommendation of their secondary school and have had a personal interview with the Director of Admissions. Applications from transfers are welcome, as are those from students resuming their education and from older students who have delayed their entrance into college. Transfer applicants should have a minimum 2.5 grade point average and be graduates of or be eligible to return to their former institutions. Transfer students with fewer than 25 semester hours must submit high school transcripts and standardized test scores. Applicants who hold Associate of Arts degrees from regionally accredited two-year institutions are typically granted junior standing. All applicants are encouraged to interview; an interview may be required for some candidates.

Application and Information

An application is considered by the Admissions Committee when it has been received with the $30 application fee, required test scores and references, and transcripts from each school attended. Because all students are required to live on campus unless they are seniors, married, or living with their parents, early application is desirable to ensure that housing is available. The freshman application priority date is March 1. The deadline for early decision applicants is December 1.

For more information about Florida Southern College, prospective students should contact:

Office of Admissions
Florida Southern College
111 Lake Hollingsworth Drive
Lakeland, Florida 33801-5698

Phone: 800-274-4131 (toll-free)
E-mail: fscadm@flsouthern.edu
Web site: http://www.flsouthern.edu

Students walk alongside the Frank Lloyd Wright Water Dome.

FORDHAM UNIVERSITY
NEW YORK, NEW YORK

The University

Fordham, the Jesuit University of New York, offers a distinctive educational experience that is rooted in the nearly 500-year-old Jesuit tradition of intellectual rigor and personal respect for the individual. A Fordham education blends a challenging curriculum with the resources, culture and energy of New York City—a unique combination by any measure.

The University enrolls approximately 15,158 students, of whom 8,220 are undergraduates. Fordham has four undergraduate colleges and six graduate and professional schools. In addition to its full-time undergraduate programs, the University offers part-time undergraduate study at Fordham College of Liberal Studies and through two summer sessions.

Fordham offers two residential campuses: Rose Hill, on 85 green, leafy acres adjacent to the New York Botanical Garden and the Bronx Zoo; and Lincoln Center, a cosmopolitan campus in the cultural heart of Manhattan, which features a twenty-story complex that provides apartment-style living and great city views. Both campuses are easily accessible by public and private transportation. Enjoying the academic and student life of both is convenient with the University's Ram Van service, which operates between the two campuses.

The University has an extensive athletics program consisting of twenty-three varsity sports and numerous club and intramural sports. Murphy Field is the heart of intramural and recreational sports at Fordham, hosting softball, soccer, and flag football games. The Vincent T. Lombardi Memorial Center provides facilities for basketball, squash, swimming and diving, tennis, track, and water polo.

Location

As the Jesuit University of New York, Fordham offers its students the unparalleled academic, cultural, and recreational advantages of one of the world's great cities. Fordham draws students from across the country who want to live and learn while immersed in the diversity and opportunity of a global capital. More than 2,600 corporations and organizations—from the United Nations to Fortune 500 companies—offer valuable work experience to Fordham interns. New York City not only provides extraordinary internship possibilities and career advantages, but also a never-ending list of things to see and do—from Broadway theater, museums and music to major league sports or a bike ride through Central Park.

Majors and Degrees

Fordham offers undergraduates more than fifty majors, minors, and certificates. Fordham College at Rose Hill provides programs of study in African and African American studies, American Catholic studies, American studies, anthropology, art history, biological sciences, chemistry, classical civilization, classical languages (Latin and Greek), communication and media studies, comparative literature, computer sciences, economics, engineering physics, English, environmental policy, environmental science, French language and literature, French studies, general science, German language and literature, German studies, history, information science, international political economy, Italian language and literature, Italian studies, Latin American and Latino studies, mathematics, mathematics/economics, medieval studies, Middle East studies,

music, Orthodox Christian studies, peace and justice studies, philosophy, physics, political science, psychology, religious studies, social work, sociology, Spanish language and literature, Spanish studies, theology, urban studies, visual arts, and women's studies.

Also located at the Rose Hill campus, the Gabelli School of Business offers programs leading to majors, minors, concentrations, or specializations in accounting, accounting information services, applied accounting and finance, business administration, business economics, business law and ethics, communication and media management, e-business, entrepreneurship, finance, human resource management, information systems, management of information and communication systems, management systems, marketing, and public accountancy. The G.L.O.B.E. Program (Global Learning Opportunities and Business Experiences) provides business students with an international study option that incorporates course offerings in language, culture, and history with business.

Special programs at Rose Hill include a cooperative engineering program, double majors or individualized majors, interdisciplinary studies, a B.S./M.B.A. program, numerous joint master's degree programs (dual degree), 3-3 law and honors programs. Preprofessional programs are offered in architecture, law, medicine, and health professions; a program for teacher certification is offered in elementary and secondary education.

At Fordham College at Lincoln Center students choose from African and African American studies, American Catholic studies, American studies, anthropology, art history, bioinformatics, business, classical civilization, classical languages (Latin and Greek), communication and media studies, comparative literature, computer science, dance, economics, English, environmental policy, environmental science, French language and literature, French studies, German language and literature, German studies, history, information science, international studies, Irish studies, Italian language and literature, Italian studies, Latin American and Latino studies, mathematics, mathematics/economics, medieval studies, Middle East studies, music, natural science, Orthodox Christian studies, peace and justice studies, philosophy, political science, psychology, religious studies, social work, sociology, Spanish language and literature, Spanish studies, theater, theology, urban studies, visual arts, and women's studies. Special programs at Fordham College at Lincoln Center include options in the performing arts (including a B.F.A. in dance with The Ailey School), creative writing, double majors or individualized majors, independent study, an honors program, and interdisciplinary studies. Preprofessional studies are offered in architecture, engineering, health professions, and law. A teacher certification program is offered in elementary and secondary education.

Academic Programs

Students in all undergraduate colleges pursue a common core curriculum designed to provide them with the breadth of knowledge that marks the educated person. The core involves foundational courses chosen from groups of academic disciplines: history, philosophy, theology, natural sciences, social sciences, languages, and literature. In every core course, students think, speak, write, and act in fundamentally new ways, with a broadened appreciation of human values and a deepened commitment to the human community.

Off-Campus Programs

Reflecting the values-centered education that is a Fordham hallmark, more than 1,300 students engage in community service each year, locally and in distant corners of the world. The Global Outreach program is an ambitious international service program designed for students to live and work in communities of need. The University also provides access to yearlong, semester-long and summer study-abroad programs in more than fifty countries on six continents including La Sorbonne in Paris and American University in Cairo.

Academic Facilities

The outstanding libraries on the two campuses have combined holdings of more than 2.28 million volumes and more than 40,476 electronic and print periodicals. On the Rose Hill campus, the William D. Walsh Family Library, which serves the entire Fordham community, has seating for more than 1,500 and a state-of-the-art Electronic Information Center, as well as media production laboratories, studios, and an auditorium. Students also have access to the vast library facilities of New York City, neighboring universities, and the various specialized collections maintained by numerous local museums and other institutions. Among laboratory facilities utilized by undergraduates are Mulcahy Hall (chemistry), Larkin Hall (biology), and Freeman Hall (physics and biology). The University has more than forty buildings that provide ample space for smart classrooms, science laboratories, theaters, and athletic facilities.

Costs

At the Rose Hill and Lincoln Center campuses, undergraduate costs for the 2011–12 academic year are $40,292 for tuition and fees, and an average of $15,005 for room and board. Chemistry, physics, and biology fees were approximately $50 per laboratory course. Nominally priced meals are available in cafeterias on each campus. Such incidentals as transportation and laundry vary in cost. There is no difference in fees for out-of-state students.

Financial Aid

More than 90 percent of the entering students enroll with aid from Fordham as well as from outside sources. Among the major aid programs are Federal Pell Grants, Federal Supplemental Educational Opportunity Grants, Federal Perkins Loans, work grants sponsored by both the government and the University, and University grants-in-aid. Outside sources of aid include state scholarships, the New York State Tuition Assistance Program (TAP), privately sponsored scholarships, state government loan programs, and deferred-payment programs. The University also offers academic merit scholarships ranging from $10,000 to the full cost of tuition and room. Applicants for aid must submit the Free Application for Federal Student Aid (FAFSA) and the College Scholarship Service (CSS) PROFILE. Please direct inquiries to Fordham's Office of Undergraduate Admission or Office of Student Financial Services.

Faculty

The University has a full-time faculty of 699 and a student-faculty ratio of 13:1. Most members of the undergraduate faculty also teach at the graduate level, and 95 percent of the full-time faculty members hold doctoral or other terminal degrees.

Student Government

The traditional student governing body at Fordham has been the United Student Government, composed of undergraduates attending the University.

Admission Requirements

Admission is based on academic performance, class rank (if available), secondary school recommendations, and SAT or ACT scores. Extracurricular activities and essays are also factors in the evaluation process. Religious preference, physical handicap, race, or ethnic origin is not considered. Out-of-state students are encouraged to apply. More than 85 percent of the students accepted for the freshman class ranked in the top quarter of their secondary school class. The middle 50 percent combined SAT score for students accepted in fall 2010 was 1810–2020. Recommended are 22 high school units, including 4 in English, 3 in mathematics, 3 in science, 2 in social studies, 2 in foreign language, 2 in history, and 6 electives. For regular admission, the SAT or the ACT should be taken no later than the January preceding entrance. Candidates for early action should complete the examinations by October of their senior year. The University participates in the College Board's Advanced Placement Program. Personal interviews are not required.

Application and Information

Application may be made for either September or January enrollment. The regular decision application deadline is January 15 for fall admission. The completed application, the secondary school report, the results of the SAT or ACT, and an application fee of $50 (check or money order made payable to Fordham University) should be submitted by this date. All financial aid forms are due by February 1. Students are notified on or about April 1. Candidates for Early Action should apply by November 1 and receive notification by December 25. Transfer students must apply by December 1 for spring admission or by June 1 for fall admission.

For additional details and application forms, students should contact:

Peter Farrell
Director of Admission
Fordham University
Duane Library
441 East Fordham Road
Bronx, New York 10458

Phone: 800-FORDHAM (367-3426)
E-mail: enroll@fordham.edu
Web site: http://www.fordham.edu

Members of a recent graduating class join Fordham's distinguished alumni family of more than 120,000.

FRAMINGHAM STATE UNIVERSITY
FRAMINGHAM, MASSACHUSETTS

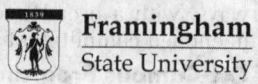

The University

Framingham State University offers small, personalized classes to 6,000 undergraduate and graduate students on a traditional, New England campus. Student success is central to the mission of the University. Many options are available for student support, including programs to help freshmen transition into college. The University also has a robust honors program for exceptional students.

The breadth of programs offered by Framingham State University reflects the expertise of the faculty. Although the University's original focus was teacher education, the majority of students today major in fields ranging from business to the sciences to fashion design and retailing, along with a significant number who continue to major in education. The University offers twenty-five majors and many career-related concentrations.

In addition to its undergraduate program, Framingham State University graduates approximately 500 master's students each year. In 2008, the University added an M.S.N. program to its graduate program mix. In addition, the University is a pioneer in undergraduate and graduate online education, having offered online courses since 1998.

Traditional college-age students, as well as nontraditional students seeking higher education on either a full- or part-time basis, have opportunities to participate in campus life through a variety of cocurricular programs and activities and to develop the knowledge and skills needed to compete in a global and technological society.

Framingham State University offers residential housing to more than 1,500 students in six residence halls. Resident students are required to purchase a meal plan. Both the Dining Commons and the State Street Grille are located in the McCarthy Center, the hub of all student activities. The newly renovated McCarthy Center is the home for the campus art gallery, game room, meeting rooms, radio station, newspaper, club and organization offices, and offices for student services and student activities.

The Student Union Activities Board (SUAB), one of the largest and most active clubs on campus, plans the majority of campus events, including concerts, films, special social programs, recreation, concerts, dances, lectures, films, spring break events, cultural activities, and much more. SUAB also sponsors the Annual Semi-Formal, Spring Show, and the Sandbox Carnival.

The University competes in NCAA Division III athletics for men and women, including baseball, basketball, cross-country, field hockey, football, ice hockey, lacrosse, soccer, softball, and volleyball. Intramural sports are also offered, including cheerleading and rugby. A 65,000-square-foot athletic facility opened in 2001.

Location

The University is located just 20 miles west of Boston. It is the only public four-year college between Route 495 and Route 128, close to the heart of the high-technology industry and within reach of hundreds of professional companies and businesses. The 73-acre campus offers students a small- to medium-sized suburban campus with access to the cultural, recreational, educational, and career opportunities of Boston and New England.

Majors and Degrees

Framingham State University confers the Bachelor of Arts, Bachelor of Science, and Bachelor of Science in Education degrees. Undergraduate majors are offered in art history, art studio, biology, business administration, business and information technology, chemistry, communication arts, computer science, criminology, early childhood education, economics, elementary education, English, environmental science, fashion design and retailing, food and nutrition, food science, geography, health and consumer sciences, history, liberal studies, mathematics, modern languages, nursing (post-RN program), political science, psychology, and sociology. Within the twenty-five major programs are a variety of concentrations and minors. Pre-engineering, prelaw, and premedical professional programs are also offered.

Academic Programs

The mission of Framingham State University is to offer a dynamic and affordable program of educational excellence to its students. The University emphasizes a broad curriculum that blends liberal arts and sciences with several professional fields.

Each student must satisfy a thirty-two-course requirement for completion of any degree program. Up to twenty courses form the basis of a student's major area of study. The remaining twelve courses are used to fulfill the general education requirement, which encompasses writing, mathematics, humanities, social sciences, physical and life sciences, foreign language, and the study of federal and state constitutions. The general education requirement ensures that students experience the benefits of a liberal arts education through familiarity with a variety of curricula. Each student is assigned a faculty member in his or her major as an academic adviser. Undeclared students are assigned advisers through the Center for Academic Support and Advising (CASA). Selected students may participate in departmental and University-wide honors programs.

The University operates on the traditional two-semester calendar, with two optional summer sessions as well as a winter intersession.

Off-Campus Programs

Framingham State University students may choose to participate in one or several college-affiliated programs, allowing them to take credit-bearing courses outside of the University. Among the most popular are internships, the College Academic Program Sharing (CAPS) program, the Massachusetts Bay Marine Studies Consortium, and study abroad.

Internships are available in most majors. Annually, hundreds of Framingham State University students serve as interns in the Massachusetts State House, town and city governments, museums, and a variety of businesses and high-technology firms in the greater Boston area. Internships allow students the opportunity to gain direct, practical experience while applying the knowledge and skills they have acquired in the classroom.

Through the CAPS program, Framingham State University students may take up to 30 semester hours of college credit at one of the seven other Massachusetts state universities. Students who participate in the Massachusetts Bay Marine Studies Consortium may also attend a variety of credit-bearing classes and symposia at other schools.

Students who seek an international dimension to enhance their undergraduate program can study abroad for a summer, semester, or academic year. In the past, students have studied in Australia, Canada, England, France, Ireland, Italy, Mexico, New Zealand, and Spain.

Academic Facilities

The Henry Whittemore Library houses more than 200,000 bound volumes, 600,000 volume equivalents in microforms, and 1,600 current periodicals in subscriptions. Electronic databases supplement the library's in-house journal collection, and students have access to a variety of materials shared within the Minuteman Library Network. The University provides extensive computing capabilities for its students, including a wireless network across the campus.

A child-development center, planetarium, and greenhouse provide students with the opportunity to gain practical experience in related studies. Likewise, the radio station and television studios serve as forums to apply textbook knowledge.

The Challenger Learning Center, established in memory of Christa Corrigan McAuliffe, the nation's first teacher astronaut and a 1970 graduate of the University, is located on campus. The center provides a unique hands-on learning experience designed to foster interest in mathematics, science, and technology.

Costs

Tuition and fees for the 2010–11 academic year were $7065 for in-state students and $13,145 for out-of-state students. Yearly residence hall charges were $5600, and the yearly meal plan was $3000. Students should anticipate additional expenses for books, a laptop computer, supplies, transportation, and personal items. All costs are subject to change.

Financial Aid

Sources of financial aid available to Framingham State University students include federal, state, and institutional programs. Framingham State University students were the recipients of more than $24.5 million last year in loans, scholarships, grants, and work-study.

Federal programs include the Federal Work-Study Program, the Federal Pell Grant, Federal Supplemental Educational Opportunity Grant, the Federal Perkins Loan, and both subsidized and unsubsidized Federal Stafford Student Loans. State-funded aid includes state scholarship grants and a no-interest loan program. Institutional funds mainly provide merit and need-based scholarships.

All students applying for financial aid must file the Free Application for Federal Student Aid (FAFSA), designating Framingham State University as the recipient. Transfer students must submit financial aid transcripts documenting all previous aid received. The priority filing deadline for fall entrance is March 1.

Faculty

One hundred sixty-four full-time faculty members are dedicated to upholding the undergraduate mission of the University. More than 86 percent of the faculty members hold the terminal degree in their field. The active involvement of many professors in research and writing complements their primary commitment and dedication to teaching excellence at the undergraduate level. With an impressive student-faculty ratio of 17:1, Framingham State University is able to offer a variety of programs in a challenging academic atmosphere.

Student Government

The Student Government Association (SGA) is the center of all political and social activity of the students of Framingham State University. The primary duties of SGA are to provide funding for more than fifty organizations through the student activity fee, to ensure representation of Framingham State University students, and to act on all other matters that concern the students of the University. SGA also plays a major role in the formulation of University policies that are of mutual concern to the students, the faculty, and the administration.

Admission Requirements

Framingham State University seeks to enroll students with a strong academic background who possess the necessary skills to succeed in college. Admission decisions are based primarily on the strength of the high school record and test scores. Secondary school students are required to pass 16 college-preparatory units: 4 years of English; 3 years of math, including algebra I and II and geometry; 3 years of science, including 2 years of laboratory science; 2 years of history/social science, including 1 year of U.S. history; 2 years of the same foreign language; and two college-preparatory-level electives. High school students are encouraged to elect additional courses in music, art, and computer science.

Students in the upper 50 percent of their class with a B average or higher are encouraged to apply. An essay and at least one recommendation are required as part of the application. International and transfer students, as well as adults returning to college, are also encouraged to apply.

Application and Information

To be considered for admission to a degree program at the University, all applicants must submit a completed application along with the application fee, an official high school transcript, and official complete SAT scores. Transfer students must submit official transcripts from all colleges previously attended.

It is recommended that students apply by the preferred filing date of February 15 for fall admission and December 1 for spring admission. Students are encouraged to attend an admissions information session and tour. The information sessions are presented by a member of the admissions staff and are followed by a tour of the campus conducted by a student admissions representative. Students should call the Office of Undergraduate Admissions to arrange an appointment.

For further information and application materials or to schedule a campus visit, students should contact:

Office of Undergraduate Admissions
Framingham State University
100 State Street
P.O. Box 9101
Framingham, Massachusetts 01701-9101
Phone: 508-626-4500
E-mail: admissions@framingham.edu
Web site: http://www.framingham.edu
http://on.fb.me/FraminghamStateU (Facebook)
http://twitter.com/fsusild

FRANKLIN COLLEGE

FRANKLIN, INDIANA

The College

As an innovative scientist, diplomat, thinker, writer, and leader, Benjamin Franklin's remarkable life and accomplishments left a mark on not only a young nation, but also the world. Named in the spirit of this extraordinary American icon, Franklin College continues his legacy of exploration and knowledge.

Since its founding in 1834, Franklin College has a long history of preparing students for lives committed to excellence, leadership, and service. With a comprehensive liberal arts curriculum combined with a leading-edge Professional Development Program, Franklin College provides an education that blends thinking with doing, reasoning with acting, and discovering with challenging.

Small classes and dedicated faculty members ensure that students get the attention needed to succeed, and Franklin's career and graduate school admission rates prove this.

Franklin combines liberal arts training with preprofessional development like no other college. Students can develop the competencies and resources necessary to be successful in their personal and professional lives through Franklin's innovative Professional Development Program (PDP). This exciting program gives them the opportunity to dine with corporate executives, network with national and community leaders, learn the finer points of corporate communication, and develop a level of polish and sophistication that sets them apart from other college graduates.

Location

Located in the heart of the Midwest, Franklin College offers students the best of both a small community and a big city's excitement.

Franklin, Indiana, only 20 miles south of Indiana's capital city Indianapolis, is the thirteenth largest city in the U.S. It offers a wide variety of internship opportunities, as well as athletic, cultural, and entertainment events that appeal to all students.

Majors and Degrees

Flagship programs at Franklin College include athletic training, business, journalism, pre-med, and education. The Pulliam School of Journalism is one of a few comprehensive journalism schools housed at a small liberal arts institution. Student media opportunities include a student-run PR agency and a student newspaper, magazine, and radio show. After graduation, education majors are placed at 97 percent or higher in the classroom, while business students repeatedly score in the top 5 percent on the National College Business Examination. One hundred percent of athletic training majors are employed six months after graduation. Preparation for graduate school is exceptional, with 85 percent of students gaining admission to medical school and 90 percent of applicants accepted to law school.

Franklin College confers more than twenty-five Bachelor of Arts degrees in the following areas: accounting, American studies, art, (art history and studio art), biology, business (finance, general, international business, management/industrial relations, and marketing), Canadian studies, chemistry, computing/computer information systems, economics, education (elementary, middle school, and secondary), English, French, history, journalism (advertising/public relations, broadcasting, and news-editorial), mathematics, music (instrumental and vocal), philosophy, physical education, political science, psychology,

recreation, religious studies, sociology (criminal justice and social work), Spanish, and theater. Minors are also offered in many of these areas, including fine arts, leadership, and physics.

Engineering is offered as a 3+2 program. Students earn a Bachelor of Arts degree from Franklin College and a Bachelor of Science degree in one of the engineering disciplines from the Purdue School of Engineering and Technology (IUPUI).

Students considering a career in dentistry, forestry, medical technology, medicine, optometry, physical therapy, or veterinary medicine arrange their program with the advice of the preprofessional adviser of the science division. Students seeking a career in law plan their program in consultation with prelaw advisers. Students planning a career in secondary education may elect an academic area of concentration that will satisfy the state requirements for a teaching major. The education department is endorsed and approved by the Indiana Professional Standards Board and the National Council for Accreditation of Teacher Education (NCATE).

Academic Programs

The current academic program is the result of the faculty's plan to meet the express needs of students; the primary emphasis is on the unity of knowledge. Franklin believes in the importance of providing students with a liberal arts background while they develop talents for a particular professional career. Approximately one third of each student's total course work is composed of the prescribed and exploratory courses that make up the general education core curriculum.

All of Franklin's academic departments offer individualized study, allowing a student to pursue his or her field of interest in depth. Students interested in pursuing a major not offered at Franklin may submit a proposal for their individualized major.

As part of the 4-1-4 calendar, students complete up to 8 hours of credit in a special four-week winter-term program in January. The winter term is designed to allow students to study in areas of particular interest to them, either within or outside their major field of study. Some January classes offer students the opportunity to travel to locations such as Belize, England, France, Italy, and Mexico.

A large number of internships are available during the winter term and the summer, offering practical experience under the supervision of a professional. The fall semester ends before Christmas; the spring semester begins in February and ends in May. An eight-week summer session beginning in mid-June allows students to take up to 9 additional credit hours. Ninety-five percent of Franklin College students complete an internship prior to graduation.

Franklin gives credit in seventeen academic areas for successful scores on CLEP subject examinations; credit is also granted for successful scores on the Advanced Placement tests of the College Board. The Running Start Program enables talented high school students to get an early start on their college education.

Study-Abroad Programs

Franklin College students participate in a variety of international study opportunities, including a year or a semester of study through Acadia University of Nova Scotia, Telemark University of Norway, and Hong Kong Baptist University. Other off-campus study programs include the American University Washington Semester; a junior year abroad; programs at Harlaxton College in England, Franklin College of Switzerland, and Brethren Colleges Abroad; and specific exchange programs in Japan and Taiwan. Students may also participate in a Semester at Sea program sponsored by the University of Pittsburgh.

Academic Facilities

Franklin College has two campus buildings listed on the National Historic Register. Old Main, the original home of the College, and Shirk Hall, home of the Pulliam School of Journalism, are footholds of the rich past and recent renovation of the Franklin College campus. Classrooms and administrative, business, and professorial offices, along with computer laboratories, occupy Old Main; Shirk Hall also houses classrooms and the radio station.

A. A. Barnes Science Building houses all physics, biology, and chemistry department classrooms and laboratories. The Spurlock Center gymnasium and fitness center provides workout and weight equipment to students in order to maintain a healthy lifestyle.

The Dietz Center for Professional Development is the home of the Professional Development Program. State-of-the-art conference rooms and computer facilities enhance Franklin's career programming commitment to its students.

The B. F. Hamilton Library, containing more than 117,000 volumes and collections of microfilm, slides, art reproductions, recordings, and periodicals, is a member of P.A.L.N.I. (Private Academic Library Network of Indiana). The Johnson Center for Fine Arts provides classrooms and practice and performance accommodations, and it houses the facilities and meeting rooms for the Leadership Program.

Costs

The direct cost for the 2011–12 academic year is $33,840. This amount is derived from tuition, which is $25,680; residence hall, which is $4540; student fees of $185; and Winter Term meal fees of $325 plus the meal plan, which is $3110.

Financial Aid

The Franklin College financial aid program assists students who might not otherwise be able to attend college and rewards applicants for excellent academic achievement in high school. Awards are based on scholarship, curricular and extracurricular activities, and financial need. Aid involving financial need includes Franklin College grants, loans, and employment. Franklin participates in the Federal Stafford Student Loan and Federal Work-Study programs. Merit-based scholarships ranging from $5500 to full tuition are awarded to students based on academic performance, activities, and standardized test scores. In addition, students identified by the state of Indiana as Twenty-first Century Scholars will be awarded full tuition scholarships, if they are eligible for the Pell Grant. Twenty-first Century Scholars who are not eligible for the Pell Grant will be awarded half tuition scholarships. Scholarships are renewable for each of the recipient's four academic years at Franklin, provided students maintain specific GPA requirements and advance in class status each year. The Free Application for Federal Student Aid (FAFSA) is required.

Faculty

The 16:1 student-faculty ratio allows Franklin faculty members to provide excellent instruction in small classes that promote participatory learning. Eighty-three percent of current faculty members have obtained the highest degree in their field. Faculty members serve as advisers and provide supplemental attention outside the classroom. While many faculty members carry on research and publish their work, their main emphasis is teaching. No classes are taught by graduate students or teaching assistants.

Student Organizations

Franklin College offers more than sixty clubs and organizations such as Student Congress, Black Student Union, Greek Life, and Student Entertainment Board. These organizations allow students to plan on-campus concerts/events, represent the student body to change campus policies, and volunteer their time with the College's Habitat for Humanity programs from the first year. In addition to the existing organizations, the College allows students to set up new groups of their interests.

Admission Requirements

Applications for admission to Franklin College are evaluated on an individual basis. A student's potential academic and personal contributions to the College, recommendations, school and community activities, academic record, and standardized test scores are taken into consideration by the Admissions Committee. A student should complete a strong college-preparatory program. Candidates for admission are urged to visit the campus in order to experience the College community. The College offers different visit opportunities—from personal visits to open houses, all provide opportunities to meet current students, professors, and coaches, and to take a campus tour.

Application and Information

To be considered for admission, an applicant must submit a completed application (paper or online), a transcript of all secondary school and college work attempted, and either SAT or ACT scores. A decision regarding acceptance is made after the College receives all necessary credentials. Notification is sent immediately after the Enrollment Committee has acted.

Office of Admission
Franklin College
101 Branigin Boulevard
Franklin, Indiana 46131
Phone: 317-738-8062
   888-852-6471 (toll-free)
Fax: 317-738-8274
E-mail: admissions@franklincollege.edu
Web site: http://admissions.franklincollege.edu
   http://www.facebook.com/fcadmissions

Old Main is the oldest academic building on the Franklin College campus.

FRANKLIN COLLEGE SWITZERLAND

LUGANO, SWITZERLAND

The College

Franklin College Switzerland, named for the United States' first and most illustrious ambassador to Europe, was founded in 1969 as a nonprofit, independent, postsecondary institution. It takes as its cornerstone Benjamin Franklin's vigorous support of intellectual interchange between nations. An American liberal arts institution in an international environment, Franklin is fully accredited in the United States by the Commission on Higher Education of the Middle States Association of Colleges and Schools and in Switzerland by the Swiss University Conference.

Franklin College places a strong emphasis on cross-cultural perspectives, advocating that international studies should be an integral part of a college education, as a prelude to, and basis for, a student's commitment to a major field of study. Franklin defines higher education from its beginning as the experience of thinking internationally. Its emphasis, both academic and social, on global perspectives is designed to affect the direction and meaning of a student's college experience, life, and career.

The essence of a Franklin College education is the exposure of its students to cultures other than their own, providing them with a better understanding of others, the world, and their place in the world. The College's location in Lugano, a vibrant Swiss city that is part of the cultural milieu of northern Italy, ensures a constant commingling of cultures in a quadrilingual nation. Students and faculty members, many who have a cross-cultural background, come to Franklin College from every corner of the globe, further strengthening international study and international experiences.

Approximately 60 percent of the students come from the United States; 40 percent are from Europe, Asia, Africa, South America, and the Middle East. Bringing diverse experiences and perspectives to college life, they live in College residences both on and near the campus. These apartments all have kitchens available, and two campus dining facilities provide regular meal service and a meal plan. There are residence supervisors for each of the ten buildings.

Campus activities are varied. Franklin's Student Government Association (SGA) promotes a student newspaper; a literary magazine; a drama society; cultural, language, and sports clubs; and numerous social events that take advantage of southern Switzerland's extensive recreational resources. There are competitive College sports teams in men's and women's soccer, and intramural teams include basketball, soccer, and volleyball. In addition, the Athletic Director enrolls interested students in a considerable number of local Swiss clubs and teams that welcome newcomers—basketball, ice hockey, soccer, and volleyball teams, as well as clubs for crew, fencing, flying, golf, hang gliding, ice skating, judo, parachuting, riding, rock climbing, sailing, swimming, tennis, track, and windsurfing. By joining these local groups, Franklin students become part of the region's life; they are themselves essential to the cross-cultural learning the College promotes.

Location

Franklin College's campus is in the community of Sorengo, a section of the city of Lugano, southern Switzerland's principal business, banking, medical, and cultural center. Easily accessible from the campus either by public transportation or on foot, downtown Lugano and its surrounding lakeside villages are renowned for their scenic beauty and Mediterranean climate. Palm trees line lakefront piazzas, and an outdoor lifestyle is typical of Ticino, the Italian-speaking canton of Switzerland that best exemplifies Swiss versatility in all three of the national languages—Italian, German, and French.

Throughout the year, Lugano features outstanding cultural activities at the world-famous Thyssen art collection, the Swiss-Italian radio station with its own permanent symphony orchestra, and the International Convention Center, which attracts guest performers from around the world. Nine public museums, many art galleries, several movie houses, and a multitude of restaurants and discotheques make for a range of recreational choices normally found only in a large city. A covered ice rink, swimming pools, and a wide range of other sports facilities are maintained by local sports clubs; Lugano and the southern part of Switzerland offer access to an extraordinary variety of sports activities. In the spring and fall, Ticino's most popular recreation is hiking. In winter, skiing is available in San Bernardino and Andermatt, about an hour from the campus, or in the fabled St. Moritz, Davos, Klosters, and Zermatt.

Majors and Degrees

The Bachelor of Arts program offers majors in art history, comparative literary and cultural studies, environmental studies, history, international banking and finance, communication and media studies, international economics, international management, international relations, literature, French studies, Italian studies, and visual and communication arts, with combined and double majors in a number of study areas. The Associate in Arts degree program provides a strong liberal arts foundation for students who usually continue their education in a baccalaureate degree program.

Academic Programs

Franklin's curricula promote international awareness and critical thinking, while being interdisciplinary in the highest tradition of liberal education. The courses of study explore the diverse disciplines that enlighten an educated human being. Students must complete at least 125 credit hours to be eligible for the B.A. degree and 64 for the A.A. degree, while maintaining a minimum cumulative grade point average of 2.0 on a 4.0 scale.

As an integral credit-bearing part of the academic program, twice a year (in mid-October and mid-March) students participate in faculty-led academic travel programs to various destinations in Eastern and Western Europe, Africa, Asia, Latin America, and North America.

All degree candidates must demonstrate a foreign language proficiency in a language other than their mother tongue equivalent to three years of university-level instruction in one of the languages taught at Franklin. This requirement is met by successfully completing appropriate courses at Franklin or by passing an equivalency test administered by the language department.

In addition to their major field of study, students may add courses within another discipline to form a minor. The number of credit hours (12 to 15) and the program of courses are subject to departmental approval.

The College operates on a two-semester calendar, with classes starting in late August and mid-January; two 3-week summer sessions and one concurrent 6-week summer session are also available. A required orientation program for all new students is held in August and mid-January.

Off-Campus Programs

Franklin's renowned Academic Travel Program is a fully integrated part of the regular curriculum. Each semester, students participate in two weeks of faculty-led academic travel. More than any other program of study, it gives students an opportunity to learn through experience. Travel destinations for 2010–11 included Austria, Brazil, Croatia, Dominican Republic, Egypt, England, France, Germany, Greece, Hungary, Iceland, Ireland, Italy, Japan, Morocco, Poland, Russia, Scotland, Serbia, Slovakia, Slovenia, Spain, Turkey, Ukraine, and the United States.

Internships are also available. Students with academic interest in any area may apply for an internship after two semesters of residence at Franklin, either by asking to be considered for one of the internships provided by the College or by arranging for an appointment themselves. The Dean of Intercultural Engagement and Learning coordinates the internship program; a student may earn a maximum of 3 credit hours in an assignment.

Students in good standing who major in modern languages are eligible for study in a country where the target language is spoken; such study is limited to one semester at an approved institution.

Academic Facilities

The Franklin College Library contains 38,000 volumes and offers numerous English and foreign-language periodicals. The library also participates in the Swiss interlibrary loan system linking major Swiss university libraries. In addition to the print and AV collections, the library subscribes to many indexes and full-text databases, including ProQuest resources, EBSCO resources, Lexis-Nexis Academic Universe, MarketWatch, Earthscape, Columbia International Affairs Online (CIAO), and National Bureau of Economic Research. Three computer labs with Internet access are available for student use.

Costs

The comprehensive fee for the 2010–11 academic year was $46,800. This figure includes the cost of tuition, room and board, academic travel, and student fees. The estimated cost of personal expenses and incidentals, including textbooks, is $6500 per year. The estimated cost range to fly round-trip from the United States is from $1100 to $1400.

Financial Aid

Franklin College offers academic merit awards and need-based financial aid to qualified students. U.S. applicants for financial aid must submit the FAFSA for evaluation. Veterans' and Social Security benefits are also available to eligible students. Federal Stafford Student Loans and PLUS loans may be obtained through the Department of Education's Direct Loan Program. International students must submit the International Student Financial Aid Form. Campus internships are also available. Students interested in applying for one can do so by requesting information about available Life Long Learning Scholarships through the Office of Student Life at the beginning of each semester.

Faculty

Franklin College has 50 full-time and part-time professors, approximately half of whom are American or British; the other half are of various nationalities. The majority of them have advanced degrees from prestigious American universities, the others from highly recognized British and Continental universities; most have lived, studied, and taught in a variety of countries. The teaching staff characterizes the cross-cultural essence of the College. Professors are committed to both the European and global arenas of study; are knowledgeable about particular countries enough to organize and lead rewarding academic travels; are competent in more than one language; and are dedicated to the personal, discursive style of teaching required by a small liberal arts college with small classes. The faculty members also advise the various student activities, lead local excursions, and regularly contribute to the College's cocurricular program of lectures. In addition, each faculty member acts as academic counselor to a number of students. The faculty-conducted Academic Travel Program promotes the intellectual friendship between teacher and student essential to a liberal arts education. Franklin's student-faculty ratio is approximately 10:1.

Student Government

The student body elects the members of the Student Government Association (SGA). In addition to sponsoring interest groups and arranging social events, the SGA is actively involved in campus governance by appointing members to participate in meetings of the Curriculum Committee, Faculty Assembly, and the Appeals Board.

Admission Requirements

Franklin College seeks students who are eager to meet the challenge of studying and living in Europe, serious about undertaking college-level learning, and prepared to contribute positively to the intellectual life of the College. To identify such students, and also to ensure a diverse student population, the College Admissions Committee considers both academic and personal facts, including the student's academic record, evaluations by teachers and counselors, standardized test scores, extracurricular interests and talents, and academic distinctions. Admission to the College is limited and therefore competitive. To achieve the best match between the student and Franklin, a personal interview is strongly recommended; one can be arranged by contacting the Admissions Office in Lugano or New York. Applicants to the freshman class must submit a completed application form and a nonrefundable fee of $90; an official transcript of their secondary school record; SAT or ACT scores, either included on transcripts or forwarded by the testing service to Franklin College (CEEB code number 0922; ACT code number 5223); and three letters of academic evaluation. Applicants whose first language is not English must submit their score on the Test of English as a Foreign Language (TOEFL); a score of at least 79 iBT, or 550 PBT is required. Transfer applicants and institute applicants are required to submit a completed application and a nonrefundable application fee of $90, an official transcript of their college record, a dean's report from the dean of students, and one letter of academic recommendation.

Application and Information

The priority application deadline for fall entry is March 15 for applicants to the freshman class and June 15 for transfer and institute applicants. The application deadline for the spring semester is November 15. Admission decisions are made on a rolling basis. Applicants can usually expect a decision within three weeks from the time their application is completed. All inquiries and applications should be directed to the nearest Admissions Office.

Franklin College Switzerland
US Office, Suite 2746
420 Lexington Avenue
New York, NY 10170
Phone: 212-922-9650
Fax: 212-922-9870
E-mail: info@fc.edu

Karen Ballard
Dean of Admissions
Franklin College Switzerland
Via Ponte Tresa, 29
6924 Sorengo/Lugano
Switzerland
Phone: 41-91-986-3613
Fax: 41-91-993-3906
E-mail: info@fc.edu
Web site: http://www.fc.edu

FULL SAIL UNIVERSITY
WINTER PARK, FLORIDA

The College

Since 1979, Full Sail University, located outside of Orlando, Florida, has been an innovative educational leader for those pursuing careers in the entertainment industry. With over 34,500 alumni, graduate credits include work on OSCAR®-, Emmy®-, and GRAMMY®-winning projects; best-selling video games; and the top-grossing U.S. concert tours. Full Sail's 191-acre campus and online education platform proudly welcomes more than 12,400 students from fifty states and forty-nine countries.

The world of entertainment media is constantly innovating, and so is Full Sail University. All of the degree programs at Full Sail are built to reflect the needs of the entertainment media industry, so students can develop their skills working on real projects, using industry-standard workflows and processes—from conception and planning through production and delivery.

The Full Sail campus is equipped with industry-standard technology, and instructors and faculty members all have experience working in the fields they teach. Full Sail's accelerated degree programs not only get students out into the industry in half the time of traditional schools, but by using 40-hour weeks and 24-hour schedules, the programs prepare students for the entertainment field's tough deadlines and intense creative demands.

Full Sail does not offer on-campus housing, but students can find information from the Housing Department about affordable accommodations in the many apartment complexes near the school.

Full Sail University is accredited by the Accrediting Commission of Career Schools and Colleges (ACCSC), and is licensed by the Commission for Independent Education (CIEICU), Florida Department of Education.

Location

Full Sail's college campus is situated in a beautiful area of central Florida in Winter Park. The school is 20 minutes from downtown Orlando, 35 minutes from Disney and Universal Studios, 1 hour from Cape Canaveral and the Atlantic beaches, and 2 hours from the Gulf of Mexico.

Majors and Degrees

Full Sail currently offers a total of thirty-three campus (http://www.fullsail.edu/degrees) and online degree (http://online.fullsail.edu/degrees) programs.

Academic Programs

The following are Full Sail's bachelor's degree programs:

Learn the tools and processes to bring amazing new worlds and characters to life. Full Sail's **Computer Animation** program instructs in the creation of 3-D computer graphics, emphasizing the techniques used throughout the entertainment media industry in feature-length films, visual effects, commercials, and video games. Students learn the entire animation process starting with storyboards and computer-generated models. These concepts are then fully developed into animation projects that culminate with the creation of the student's professional demo reel. This degree is offered on campus and online.

Creative writers are in high demand within the entertainment industry, and Full Sail's online **Creative Writing for Entertainment** program provides a challenging curriculum to help students perfect their writing and editorial skills by emphasizing visual storytelling, narrative structures, character development, scriptwriting, and storyboarding. Students write and workshop their writing in a variety of formats and genres including horror, science fiction, mystery, comedy, and suspense. This degree is offered online.

For students who envision designing the elements of tomorrow's media, Full Sail's **Digital Arts & Design** program delivers a comprehensive multimedia education that combines art and technology. Students receive a solid grounding in graphic design fundamentals and print work and then create projects in a multitude of digital and multimedia platforms. Students work with the latest industry software and leave the program with a cohesive demo reel to showcase their talent to prospective employers. This degree is offered on campus.

With the impact of viral videos, streaming-video options, and growth of independent films, applications of digital video and demand for high-quality projects are crucial. Full Sail's online **Digital Cinematography** program explores how these new technologies can create inspiring cinematic and commercial works. Students learn the creative process within the context of the film industry—from lighting, scripting, and HD video production to shooting in a variety of styles.

Full Sail University's **Entertainment Business** program combines fundamental business courses with relevant industry insight. Students learn the basics of business management for music, television, and advertising. As they sharpen their writing skills, students also develop a deep understanding of the dynamics and economics of entertainment production. Students build their network by sharing ideas with peers and instructors who share the same passion for the industry. The final project is a complete business proposal unique to the student's interests. This degree is offered on campus and online.

The **Film** program teaches students the skills and provides the experience to pursue a career in the film, TV, and postproduction job markets. Students learn how to execute every role on a film set, from directing to cinematography to lighting and set design. Students make films using industry-standard cameras, equipment, and software on Full Sail's professional-level soundstages and backlot. This degree is offered on campus.

As gaming design technology evolves, Full Sail's **Game Art** program teaches students to develop specialized, realistic elements for breathtaking game experiences. The program's course work focuses on 3-D art and content creation, with a heavy emphasis on character development, shading and lighting, texturing, and modeling. Game Art students work with students in the Game Development program in a real-world production setting, creating a playable game from start to finish. This degree is offered on campus and online.

In the online **Game Design** program, students learn how to develop a game from concept to completion using the processes used by the world's top studios. The specialized curriculum teaches the elements of game development—from storytelling and narration to technology and production to leadership and project management. Using Full Sail's unique online platform, students can engage in the same interaction that exists between professional developers and artists.

The **Game Development** program teaches students about the game creation process from start to finish. Courses encompass preproduction and how to create game docs, programming and implementation, and game play and level design. Working in a production environment with a team of programmers, artists, and designers, students develop a playable video game. Students who complete the Entertainment Business degree program along with this degree earn a Master of Science degree. This degree is offered on campus.

Full Sail's online **Graphic Design** program gives students an in-depth look at the world of design. From print publishing to package design to Web site interfaces, the demand for well-designed graphics of all types has never been so high. Students are prepared to enter the industry with the ability to meet client demands and work under hard deadlines while still producing creative results.

The online **Internet Marketing** program explores the constantly evolving world of integrated marketing and its role in steering the online power of successful businesses in the 21st century. The curriculum prepares students for the changing field of online branding, e-commerce, search engine optimization (SEO), and the psychology of the online consumer. In the final capstone project, students create and produce their own Internet marketing campaign.

Growing technology options for mobile and Web-based applications have created an increased demand for skilled designers and developers. Full Sail's online **Mobile Development** program offers a cutting-edge curriculum with usability and design principles, software development and management, and application production for cell phones, iPads, Web sites, handheld games, and other devices.

Students learn what it takes to build a career in one of entertainment's most exciting industries through Full Sail's **Music Business** program. They learn fundamentals such as marketing, human relations, finance, and accounting, as well as unique music industry topics like artist development, music distribution, record label development, and the negotiation process. This degree is offered on campus and online.

The online **Music Production** program gives students the tools needed to pursue a career in writing, producing, and recording music for all types of media. Classes focus on the music-making process, from music composition and arranging to theory and ear training. Students use various software and hardware technologies and develop a digital portfolio showcasing their work.

For students who dream of being the production mastermind behind the next great recording, Full Sail's **Recording Arts** program lays the groundwork for this career. Students learn tracking and mixing techniques that can be applied to sound design and post-production for film, television, video games, and multimedia applications in the same kind of recording studios and on the same kind of production gear used by today's professionals. This degree is offered on campus.

In Full Sail's **Show Production** program, students master the techniques and equipment used in dynamic live productions while learning essential career skills. Students are immersed in the technology and tools at Full Sail Live—a custom-designed concert-venue environment—gaining the practical experience needed to hit the road with touring bands, run lights and sound at world-class performing arts halls, and take multimedia presentations to the next level. This degree is offered on campus.

The sports world is a business both on and off the field. Qualified professionals are needed to create new content, generate revenue, and establish fan branding within an evolving media landscape. Full Sail's online **Sports Marketing and Media** program covers concepts such as business principles, legal and ethical issues, public relations, and leadership. Students are prepared for positions where digital art and design, communication, distribution, game operations, and marketing all intersect.

Students can explore all aspects of Web site creation through Full Sail's on-campus and online **Web Design & Development** program. As the Internet emerges as the epicenter of communication, experienced professionals are needed to develop, implement, and maintain effective Web sites and databases. Students learn front-end design, back-end development, and client-side scripting development and deployment, and they are well-versed in coding formats like XHTML, CSS, and XML as well as Flash and ActionScript.

Academic Facilities

As part of the University's commitment to provide students with facilities that mirror the experience of working in entertainment and media, Full Sail recently unveiled its latest on-campus expansion—a 2.2-acre project more than five years in the making, Full Sail Studios. It comprises the new Live Venue, a recording studio, a game production studio, an outdoor plaza courtyard, and an expansion to the school's on-campus film studio backlot.

Live Venue: This facility can accommodate live musical performances, monthly graduations, open-house events, multi-visual presentations, guest lectures, movie screenings, trade shows, and more.

Recording Studio: This new studio employs industry-current recording technology within a carefully crafted acoustical environment.

Guests can view the recording process through oversized, acoustically treated windows that line the building's hallways.

Game Production Studio: This new game studio offers Game Development and Game Art students the perfect professional game studio environment to create and finish final projects. The studio has areas specifically designed for audio, graphics, and technical development.

Backlot and Courtyard: An illuminated archway leads to a production area complete with nineteen distinct scenic environments to accommodate students in the Film program. Amid the two newly constructed buildings is a spacious common area with seating areas and Wi-Fi to serve as a networking hub for students and faculty.

Costs

Tuition costs vary depending on the program, ranging from $30,380 to $77,500. The cost includes expenses such as textbooks, manuals, media, production materials, lab fees, technology fees, career-development assistance, and lifetime auditing. There is an additional fee for a computer and software; the primary component of this fee is Project LaunchBox, which provides students with a laptop computer and media creation software at a deep institutional discount.

Financial Aid

Each financial aid package is unique. Financial aid advisers work to ensure that students have the information they need to make decisions that will enable them to attend Full Sail. Since Full Sail is an accredited school, there are a number of packages consisting of grants and loans that are available to those who qualify and are tailored to each student's financial need.

Faculty

Full Sail's teachers are veterans of the industry and often work on professional projects as they teach, bringing to the classroom a wealth of techniques and tips learned from years of creating movies, music, games, and more.

Admission Requirements

Admission requirements vary depending on the degree program. Associate and bachelor's degree applicants must submit a high school diploma or GED equivalent, with official high school transcripts and one recommendation letter. Acceptance to Full Sail's undergraduate degrees is not based on grade point average, SAT scores, or other standardized test scores.

Application and Information

For details concerning applications and deadlines, contact a Full Sail Admissions Representative.

Full Sail University
3300 University Boulevard
Winter Park, Florida 39792-7429

Phone: 407-679-6333
       800-226-7625 (toll-free)
E-mail: admissions@fullsail.com
Web site: http://www.fullsail.edu
       http://www.facebook.com/FullSailUniversity
       http://twitter.com/fullsailupdate

Full Sail Studios and Live Venue.

GANNON UNIVERSITY

ERIE, PENNSYLVANIA

Believe in the possibilities.

The University

Gannon University, which is consistently named one of America's Best Colleges by *U.S. News & World Report*, is dedicated to excellence in holistic education. The oldest part of the University is Villa Maria College, which was founded in 1925 by the Sisters of St. Joseph. In 1933, Archbishop John Mark Gannon established Cathedral College, a two-year institution, which by 1941 had evolved into a four-year college, the Gannon School of Arts and Sciences. The name Gannon College was adopted in 1944, and Gannon achieved university status in 1979. Villa Maria College subsequently merged with Gannon University in 1989.

Gannon's campus is located in the heart of downtown Erie, giving students the benefit of internships with businesses, law and law-enforcement agencies, health-care facilities, industries, and social service organizations. It is within walking distance of stores, shops, restaurants, and theaters. The campus consists of forty-six buildings located within six city blocks. Among these buildings is the Carneval Athletic Pavilion, which has a pool; three gyms; a running track; a weight room; courts for racquetball, handball, volleyball and basketball; and other facilities. Also on campus are three residence halls, nine apartment buildings, classroom and faculty office buildings, an administration building, and a multi-purpose chapel building. The Waldron Campus Center is a focal point that gives students the opportunity to meet and socialize between classes with faculty members and other students.

Gannon offers students a broad intramural sports program that runs throughout the entire year. In Division II intercollegiate athletics, Gannon offers men's baseball, basketball, cross-country, football, golf, soccer, swimming and diving, water polo, and wrestling and women's basketball, cross-country, golf, lacrosse, soccer, softball, swimming and diving, volleyball, and water polo. Gannon's athletes utilize the Gannon University Field, a multi-purpose athletic facility that is conveniently located on campus.

There are over 4,200 students at Gannon, more than 2,900 of whom are undergraduates. The ratio of commuters to resident students is approximately 1:4. To assist in internship placement, career development and employment, and tutoring services, students will find the Student Success Center a must to visit when on campus.

Location

Erie is Pennsylvania's fourth-largest city and is located in the northwestern corner of the state on the shore of Lake Erie. Erie is approximately 120 miles north of Pittsburgh, Pennsylvania; 90 miles east of Cleveland, Ohio; and 90 miles southwest of Buffalo, New York. The campus is within 5 miles of Interstates 79 and 90 and 5 miles from Erie International Airport. Erie is also serviced by rail and bus transportation.

Majors and Degrees

The College of Humanities, Education, and Social Sciences awards the Bachelor of Arts and Bachelor of Science degrees.

In the College of Humanities, Education and Social Sciences, the areas of study from which students may select a major are communication arts, criminal justice, English (with concentrations in applied communications, literature, and writing), foreign language and international studies, foreign language and literature, foreign language teaching (Spanish only), history, international studies, journalism communications, legal studies, liberal arts, mortuary science, philosophy, political science, prelaw, a 3+3 prelaw program that includes early admission to Duquesne University, psychology, social work, theater, theater and communication arts, and theology.

In the School of Education, the areas of study from which students may select a major are early childhood education Pre-K–4, early childhood education PreK–4/special education PreK–8, middle level education 4–8, middle level education 4–8/special education PreK–8, secondary education (in biology, English, foreign language (Spanish only), mathematics, and social studies).

The Morosky College of Health Professions and Sciences offers degrees in the health professions and sciences. The degrees offered in the health professions include medical technology, nursing, nutrition and human performance, occupational therapy, physical therapy, physician assistant, radiologic sciences, respiratory care, sport and exercise science, and undecided health science.

The School of Sciences offers degrees in bioinformatics, biology, chemistry, environmental science, mathematics, and science. Also offered are preprofessional programs for students who wish to enter medical, dental, or veterinary school, as well as accelerated and cooperative medical programs in allopathy, osteopathy, optometry, podiatry, and pharmacy.

The Morosky College of Health Professions and Sciences recently relocated to the Robert H. Morosky Academic Center. This 99,000-square-foot facility includes classrooms, labs, and faculty offices. It also includes a 5,800-square-foot state-of-the-art Patient Simulation Center.

The College of Engineering and Business offers degrees in a variety of areas. Students may choose from majors in bioinformatics, biomedical engineering, chemical engineering (cooperative program), computer science, electrical engineering, electrical engineering (five-year co-op program), environmental engineering, information systems, mechanical engineering, mechanical engineering (five-year co-op program), and software engineering. Business majors include accounting, advertising communications, business administration, entrepreneurship, finance, international business, management, marketing, risk management and insurance, and sports management and marketing. All business students are required to participate in an internship before graduation.

The associate degree program offers Associate of Science and Associate of Arts degrees. Areas of study in which students may major are accounting, business administration, criminal justice, early childhood education, legal studies, radiologic sciences, and respiratory care.

Academic Programs

Each undergraduate program has its own sequence of requirements. Students in all programs must complete credits in liberal studies. A faculty adviser is assigned to each student to assist with academic planning. A department chairperson and faculty adviser also assist each student in selecting courses that fulfill requirements and best meet the student's desired career objectives. The basic graduation requirements for bachelor's degree candidates are 128 credit hours, including completion of requirements for their major and the liberal studies program. To earn an associate degree, students must usually complete 60 to 68 credit hours, depending on the program. Students may receive credit through the Advanced Placement Program.

Gannon offers a program for students with learning disabilities (PSLD) and an Army ROTC program that is open to interested students.

Gannon's academic calendar consists of two full semesters, running from August to December and from January to May. There are also optional summer classes.

Academic Facilities

The Nash Library contains over 265,000 books, 4,000 audiovisual items, and 300 periodicals (along with online subscriptions to over 58,000 more). Special collections include University Archives, the curriculum library, and entertainment DVDs (over 1,000 and growing). Interlibrary loan is available for items not owned by Nash. Additionally, reference service and information literacy instruction are integral components of the library's educational mission. The library is open 97 hours per week during fall and spring semesters and provides a variety of spaces for study including tables, lounge-type furniture, private study carrels, and group study rooms. There are several computer workstations with Internet and Microsoft Office access, and the entire building is covered by Gannon's wireless network. Laptop computers are available for in-library use.

The A. J. Palumbo Academic Center houses the College of Humanities, Education and Social Sciences. It offers some of the finest laboratories, technology, and classrooms available today. From education to criminal justice and foreign language programs, the faculty members and facilities in Palumbo provide high-quality education. The University's Honors Program also has a home in the Palumbo Center.

The Zurn Science Center has laboratories for research in biology, anatomy, physics, chemistry, and engineering. The building also houses an open engineering computer lab as well as additional computer labs for student use. There are numerous classrooms and two auditoriums in the building. Among other University facilities are additional classroom buildings, a radio station, and a theater. All academic buildings are wireless.

Costs

For 2010–11, full-time tuition was $12,490 per semester ($13,245 for engineering and health sciences), or $24,980 per academic year ($26,490 for engineering and health sciences). Tuition for part-time students was $775 per credit hour. Room and board were approximately $4950 per semester. The total cost for the academic year at Gannon was between $25,092 and $26,602 for commuting students and $34,992 and $36,502 for resident students, depending on the program of study.

Financial Aid

In order to bring a Gannon education to qualified students who could not otherwise afford it, the University offers an integrated financial aid program of scholarships, grants, loans, and employment. Gannon's financial aid program is open to all full-time students attending classes during the period from August to May. It is highly recommended that all students seeking financial aid should file the admissions and financial aid applications no later than March 15. Numerous scholarship opportunities are available to qualified students. Each year the University offers its top incoming freshmen the ability to compete for full tuition scholarships. Application deadline for this competition is December 31 with on-campus competition taking place in late January.

Faculty

Gannon's faculty consists of 200 lay and religious men and women, and 72 percent of the full-time faculty members have either doctoral or terminal degrees. The student-faculty ratio is about 13:1, and average class size is approximately 25 students in each class. Most faculty members assist in the faculty adviser program, giving each student individual attention and counseling on academic and personal matters.

Student Government

The Student Government Association (SGA) is composed of students elected by members of their class. Through the SGA, students can play a responsible role in the planning and working of the University. SGA has voting representatives on all of the standing committees of the University. Members of the SGA not only research existing policies and problems, they also look for new ways to improve the academic life of students. The SGA also plans social events for the student body.

Admission Requirements

Gannon University actively recruits students of all races, creeds, and ages from all geographic regions. Transfer and international students are encouraged to seek admission. Applicants are required to submit scores (including senior-year scores) on either the SAT or ACT; an up-to-date transcript of the high school record, showing rank in class (plus a college transcript for transfer applicants); a completed application form; and a nonrefundable $25 fee. Admission decisions are based upon numerous factors, central of which is the strength of the high school record, as demonstrated through grades and relative class standing and SAT and/or ACT scores and other test scores that may be available. Recommendations and personal statements also affect admission decisions. Transfer and international students should check with the admissions office for special application procedures.

Application and Information

Students applying for admission in the fall semester should start the application process at the beginning of their senior year in high school. Gannon operates on a rolling admissions basis, which means that there is no deadline for filing applications, with the exceptions of the LECOM (Lake Erie College of Osteopathic Medicine) and PCOM (Philadelphia College of Osteopathic Medicine) 4+4 Medical Programs and the accelerated pharmacy options, which have a deadline of January 15 for the fall semester. Due to the competitiveness of the program, students who are interested in the physician assistant studies or nursing programs are highly encouraged to file their applications in September. Early applications are recommended, as are enrollment deposits.

For further information, students should contact:

Office of Admissions
Gannon University
109 University Square
Erie, Pennsylvania 16541
Phone: 814-871-7240
      800-GANNON-U (426-6668, toll-free)
Fax: 814-871-5803
E-mail: admissions@gannon.edu
Web site: http://www.gannon.edu

A *U.S. News & World Report* Best College for 2011.

THE GEORGE WASHINGTON UNIVERSITY

WASHINGTON, D.C.

THE GEORGE
WASHINGTON
UNIVERSITY
WASHINGTON DC

The University

Located just four blocks from the White House, The George Washington University (GW) is the largest institution of higher education in the nation's capital. Founded in 1821 by an Act of Congress, GW is a private nonsectarian coeducational institution accredited by the Middle States Association of Colleges and Universities. GW prides itself in being at the forefront of major research endeavors, while providing a stimulating intellectual environment for its diverse students and faculty members.

The student population at GW consists of approximately 9,500 undergraduates and 7,000 graduates. Undergraduates hail from all fifty states, the District of Columbia, Puerto Rico, the Virgin Islands, and 125 countries. The undergraduate student body is 10 percent Asian American, 7 percent African American, 7.2 percent Hispanic American, and 6.7 percent international.

Both the Foggy Bottom and Mount Vernon campuses are located in historical and prestigious D.C. neighborhoods. The Foggy Bottom campus is situated in the heart of downtown D.C., neighbored by the Kennedy Center, the Watergate complex, the State Department, and the White House. The 26-acre Mount Vernon campus is home to athletic facilities and is surrounded by embassy and diplomatic residences. Both campus communities offer vibrant and distinctive residential options to freshmen and continuing students.

GW guarantees housing for entering freshmen and sophomores and houses more than 70 percent of undergraduates in thirty-one residence halls. GW offers a number of living arrangements, including apartment-style living for upperclassmen and residential town houses. GW's community living and learning philosophy guarantees that residence hall life is a valuable extension of the undergraduate experience. With nearly 100 percent of the entering class living in University housing, the atmosphere proves to be academically as well as socially stimulating.

GW hosts a strong intercollegiate varsity athletic program with twenty-two teams participating in the NCAA Division I and Atlantic 10 Conference. They include men's baseball, basketball, crew, cross-country, golf, soccer, swimming, tennis, and water polo, and women's basketball, crew, cross-country, gymnastics, soccer, swimming and diving, tennis, volleyball, and water polo. Students interested in playing sports, but not quite up to the varsity level, may join a number of University-supported club and intramural sports.

There are more than 400 student-created and student-run organizations at GW. These organizations run the spectrum from academic to cultural, spiritual to recreational, and political to artistic. In addition to these special-interest organizations, GW is home to twenty-six national sororities and fraternities and nineteen honor societies, the Student Association (details in the Student Government section), the Program Board, the *Hatchet* (GW's independent newspaper), and WRGW (the campus radio station). The Student Activities Center plans large-scale events for students on campus, ranging from Welcome Week to Excellence in Student Life Awards to Fall Fest and Fountain Fling.

Location

Many students at GW also choose to immerse themselves in the excitement of Washington, which has been called the most livable city on the East Coast. Washington, D.C., offers an infinite array of internships and cooperative education experiences, allowing GW students to explore their career aspirations outside of the four walls of the classroom. GW students have interned at the White House, the World Bank, IBM, the U.S. House of Representatives and Senate, NASA, the National Zoo, and CNN, among many other world famous organizations.

The hordes of tourists that flock to Washington, D.C., every year experience the vibrant college town and young professional social scene in the nation's capital. There are more than 50,000 college students in the D.C. metropolitan area.

Majors and Degrees

GW offers a wide range of undergraduate programs in six undergraduate schools: the Columbian College of Arts and Sciences, the Elliott School of International Affairs, the School of Business, the School of Engineering and Applied Science, the School of Medicine and Health Sciences, and the School of Public Health and Health Services.

GW offers eighty-eight majors, more than 2,000 courses, and yet, the average class size is only 28. Students may earn an undergraduate degree in a single field of study, or they may choose to double major, major in one field and minor in another, participate in an interdisciplinary program, or create their own individualized field of study.

The University awards an array of bachelor's degrees, including Bachelor of Arts (B.A.), Bachelor of Science (B.S.), Bachelor of Accountancy (B.Accy.), and Bachelor of Business Administration (B.B.A.).

Several joint-degree programs are available to undergraduates. In addition to a seven-year B.A/M.D. program, the University offers seventeen 5-year B.A./M.A. programs.

Academic Programs

Most undergraduate students must complete 120 credit hours to be eligible for graduation, which means that the average student carries 15 credit hours (five courses) per semester. All students at GW are required to participate in the University's writing program. In addition, each school has general curriculum requirements, ranging from 17 to 45 credit hours.

GW is home to nineteen honor societies, including Phi Beta Kappa and Golden Key National Honor Society. GW offers a variety of specialized academic programs. The University Honors Program, which does not replace a regular program of study but rather enhances it with intellectually challenging analysis and discussion, consists of approximately 500 undergraduates.

The seven-year Integrated B.A./M.D. Program is designed for students who wish to obtain a strong foundation in the liberal arts prior to becoming physicians, enabling them to accomplish that goal in a shorter amount of time than a traditional program of study.

Off-Campus Programs

GW students are encouraged to study abroad in order to expand their world view and their educational opportunities. GW offers study abroad centers in Madrid, Paris, England, and Latin America (Chile, Costa Rica, and Argentina), as well as affiliated and exchange programs. Each year, more than 1,100 GW undergraduates study abroad in nearly sixty countries.

Many GW students also take advantage of cooperative education (co-op), which provides students with an opportunity to gain valuable paid work experiences directly related to their major. The Career Center manages the program, in partnership with area employers, to ensure that co-op experiences are substantive and well-supervised. Similarly, most GW students engage in internships, which serve as a means for students to gain practical, professional experience and to augment their academic knowledge. Internships can be paid or unpaid, offered for academic credit, and can last for as long (or short) as the student and employer choose. The Career Center also acts as a clearinghouse for internship positions.

Academic Facilities

The Gelman Library houses more than 2 million volumes and, as a member of the Washington Research Library Consortium (WRLC), offers GW students access to more than 6 million volumes at eight area universities. Gelman Library is open 168 hours per week offering 24-hour study lounges, group discussion rooms, computer labs, walk-up reference consultation, and an interlibrary loan service. GW provides on-site and remote access to ALADIN, the shared online catalogue of WRLC libraries, plus databases indexing periodical articles and some full-text journals. GW is also home to the Eckles Library, the Jacob Burns Law Library, and the Himmelfarb Health Sciences Library.

GW is infused with the latest, state-of-the-art facilities enhancing campus life. Completed and planned projects include a new hospital, the Elliott School of International Affairs classroom and residential complex, the School of Business, the stunning 400-bed Ivory Tower residence hall, Potomac House, a 700-bed freshman residence hall, the Science and Engineering Complex, and West Hall, a 287-bed suite-style residence hall for first-year and upperclass students with multimedia studios, a black box theater, and a fitness center.

Costs

In response to family concerns about paying for college, GW has instituted a fixed tuition plan. Under this plan, the tuition remains the same each year for students who remain enrolled in full-time status during their undergraduate programs. Therefore, except for marginal increases in housing costs, cost of attendance will not rise. Students who entered in fall 2010 have tuition costs of $42,860 per year for four years. Room and board costs are approximately $10,120.

Financial Aid

The ability to finance a GW education is a priority, so the Office of Student Financial Assistance seeks to assist students and their families in meeting the costs to attend the University. The University budgets more than $150 million for undergraduate financial assistance, which includes scholarships and need-based assistance. In addition, GW offers families the opportunity to participate in a number of payment plans.

By applying for admission, students with outstanding academic credentials are automatically considered for Presidential Academic Scholarships. Approximately 20 percent of freshmen receive merit-based financial assistance. In addition, approximately 65 percent of GW's students receive need-based assistance with an average package of over $35,926.

The Presidential Scholars in the Arts Program awards scholarships to, and encourages the work of, entering freshmen who have shown promise in the fine arts (ceramics, design, drawing, painting, photography, and sculpture), music, theater, technical theater, directing, dance, and choreography.

More information about financial aid at GW can be obtained online at http://www.gwu.edu. Both merit scholarships and a portion of need-based financial aid are guaranteed for all four years for students who remain enrolled in full-time status during their undergraduate program.

Faculty

There is 1 faculty member for every 14 students at GW. Ninety-two percent of GW's full-time faculty members hold a doctoral degree. Part-time and adjunct faculty members are often leaders in their fields of expertise. GW professors are engaging, eminently qualified, and well connected, which allows for a robust intellectual community.

Student Government

The Student Association (SA) is an organization chartered by GW's Board of Trustees to represent students and their concerns. Any person registered for any academic credit at GW is a member of the SA. The SA undertakes initiatives related to academics, community service, neighborhood relations, and student activities.

Admission Requirements

GW receives approximately 21,500 applications for freshman admission and aims to recruit a class of 2,350. Admitted students have strong academic records and the demonstrated ability to achieve success in their college endeavors. To be considered for admission, applicants must submit the following credentials: application and fee, high school transcripts, essay, letters of recommendation from a teacher and a guidance counselor, and either SAT or ACT scores. Details can be obtained online at http://www.gwu.edu. GW also accepts the Common Application, with the GW supplement to the Common Application. Freshman interviews are not required, but may be helpful.

Application and Information

GW has a number of application options: regular decision, early decision I, and early decision II. Prospective students should consult the Web site (http://www.gwu.edu) for the application and deadlines.

Office of Admissions
The George Washington University
2121 I Street, NW, Suite 201
Washington, D.C. 20052
Phone: 202-994-6040
E-mail: gwadm@gwu.edu
Web site: http://www.gwu.edu

Students on campus at The George Washington University.

GEORGIAN COURT UNIVERSITY

LAKEWOOD, NEW JERSEY

The University

Georgian Court University (GCU) was founded in 1908 by the Sisters of Mercy, and for more than 100 years has helped students of all faiths and backgrounds realize their dreams of a high-quality, affordable private education. Georgian Court, the only Mercy University in New Jersey and one of only two Catholic universities in the state, incorporates the Mercy core values of respect, integrity, compassion, service, and justice in every aspect of the student experience. Mercy values are a distinctive part of a Georgian Court University education.

Georgian Court University's strong liberal arts foundation offers students a personalized and supportive learning environment within a technologically advanced university setting. With a student body of nearly 3,000 and an average class size of just 14, GCU students are able to work closely with faculty members who are leaders in their respective fields, including neurobiology, biochemistry, school administration, music, business and industry, criminal justice, and history.

A National Historic Landmark, the stunning 156-acre campus borders Lake Carasaljo in suburban Lakewood, New Jersey, and is distinguished by impressive Georgian architecture, prompting its name, Georgian Court. With magnificent statuary, lush gardens, and close proximity to the popular Jersey Shore, GCU is truly an inspiring place to learn, study, and live.

Georgian Court University students can choose from among thirty-one undergraduate programs—including new majors in dance; exercise science, wellness, and sports; and nursing—offered through GCU's two highly regarded colleges, the Women's College and University College.

The Women's College at Georgian Court University is dedicated to the success of women, both personally and professionally. The college offers a comprehensive liberal arts education with an emphasis on building strong women leaders who excel in their careers; contribute to the greater good of their communities, state, and nation; and can approach any obstacle with confidence. Studies show that students at women's colleges like GCU develop high self-esteem, participate fully in and out of the classroom, and enjoy success in their careers. The Women's College is open to both residential and commuter students.

University College encompasses GCU's coeducational, nonresidential graduate programs and certificates, as well as more than sixteen undergraduate programs geared to nontraditional learners—students whose family obligations, hectic employment schedules, and other commitments leave them limited time to attend class. University College features flexible scheduling, technology-enhanced courses, and convenient locations, while upholding the high caliber of education expected of GCU. University College programs are offered in the evening at the GCU main campus in Lakewood and during the day and evening at GCU at Woodbridge, GCU at Cumberland County College, and GCU at the New Jersey Coastal Communiversity in Wall. Select courses, offered on weekends or online, give students added flexibility.

Residents and commuters alike enjoy a variety of activities, including trips to museums, theater events, and concerts. GCU offers a wide variety of clubs and special interest organizations, in addition to the Student Government Association, and seventeen academic honor societies. GCU's Learning-Living Communities bring together students who are interested in a special topic—international cultures, the arts, sustainability, outdoor adventures—for discussion groups, lectures, and off-campus experiences.

Committed to empowering students through education, GCU fosters academic leadership through the honors program, while professional growth is nurtured through Women in Leadership Development (WILD), an innovative four-phase program that cultivates the students' professional skills through hands-on workshops and seminars led by notable professional women who are leaders in business, education, and government.

Georgian Court University also participates in eight NCAA Division II sports: basketball, cross-country, lacrosse, soccer, softball, tennis, track and field, and volleyball.

Students enjoy using the University's new $26-million Wellness Center. The 64,000-square-foot, eco-friendly center has a 1,200-seat arena to support GCU's basketball, volleyball, and physical education programs; an exercise science laboratory and offices to support the new exercise science, wellness and sports major; professional dance studios to support the new dance major; a fitness center, a fifty-seat classroom, and the GCU bookstore. Outside the Wellness Center are state-of-the-art athletic fields that serve GCU's championship softball, soccer, and lacrosse teams, and an eight-lane track and tennis courts.

There are three residence halls on campus: Maria Hall, St. Joseph Hall, and St. Catherine Hall, as well as a new chapel, a residence hall for visiting faculty members and Sisters of Mercy, and the 1896 Gilded Age mansion, now home to a series of interactive history theater productions.

Location

Georgian Court University is located in Lakewood, New Jersey, a suburban town midway between the urban excitement of New York City and Philadelphia, and only minutes from the spectacular beaches of the Jersey Shore. The campus is easily accessible from Route 9, the Garden State Parkway, and Interstate 195. New Jersey Transit bus access is within walking distance, giving students quick, inexpensive transportation to points of interest throughout the tristate area.

Majors and Degrees

The three prestigious schools of Georgian Court University—the School of Arts and Sciences, the School of Business, and the School of Education—are seamlessly integrated into both the Women's College and University College. GCU regularly reviews its academic offerings, based on recommendations from faculty members, students, and industry and community leaders.

The Bachelor of Arts is awarded in applied arts and sciences, art, biology, chemistry, communications, criminal justice, dance, elementary education, English, history, humanities, mathematics, music, physics, psychology, sociology, and Spanish. The Bachelor of Science is awarded in accounting; allied health technologies; biochemistry; biology; business administration; chemistry; clinical laboratory sciences; exercise science, wellness, and sports; natural sciences; nursing; tourism, hospitality, and recreation management; and physics. Students planning a career in social work may earn a Bachelor of Social Work, and future fine and graphic artists may participate in the Bachelor of Fine Arts program.

GCU keeps pace with changing needs in the workforce. The University recently developed a new B.S. in psychiatric rehabilitation and psychology (offered jointly with the University of Medicine and Dentistry of New Jersey), and new programs in homeland security and applied behavior analysis—all reflective of the demands in today's job market.

There are more than fifty minor field sequences, certification programs, and concentrations available, including anthropology, bilingual/bicultural studies, coaching women athletes, communications, criminal justice, economics, English as a second language, general fine art, gerontology, graphic design/illustration, holistic health, human resource management, marketing, medical technology, nuclear medicine technology, philosophy, political science, pre–physical therapy, sports management toxicology, and more. Preprofessional programs include chiropractic, dentistry, law, medicine, and veterinary medicine. Interdisciplinary minors are offered in international area studies, Latin American studies, and women's studies. Internships and practicums are offered in most majors, and independent study is available. By the time GCU students graduate, more than 64 percent of them have worked in their chosen fields.

Academic Programs

A Georgian Court University education is holistic, developing students in mind, body, and spirit. A well-rounded, wide-ranging liberal arts education is intellectually rigorous, and participating in service learning develops the spirit. With this dual approach, GCU graduates become successful professionals as well as compassionate neighbors, concerned citizens, and ethical civic leaders.

The undergraduate curriculum is designed to capitalize on the student's college preparation as well as embrace the aptitudes, talents, and interests of the individual. Service learning opportunities, such as working hand in hand with Honduran villagers to build a new school, or helping disadvantaged women in Peru, challenge GCU students to put classroom learning into action.

Candidates for a bachelor's degree at Georgian Court must complete 120 credit hours. With departmental approval, students may elect a second major. Elementary education majors are required to choose a second liberal arts major. A minimum cumulative GPA of 2.0 and a minimum cumulative major GPA of 2.5 are required for graduation.

Georgian Court University hosts more than seventeen chapters of national honor societies in biology, business administration, chemistry, education, English, mathematics, physics, psychology, social work, and sociology.

Off-Campus Programs

In addition to offering students opportunities to study abroad, Georgian Court University offers joint-degree programs allowing students to take courses at GCU and at a partner institution, such as the University of Medicine and Dentistry of New Jersey.

Academic Facilities

The Arts and Science Center is Georgian Court's largest academic building, providing classrooms, seminar rooms, offices, art studios, and a computer lab. The state-of-the-art Audrey Birish George Science Center offers the latest laboratory and instruction space for scientific study.

Other campus buildings include the Sister Mary Joseph Cunningham Library, the Raymond Hall Complex, which houses the School of Education, the Raymond Hall Computer Center, and the GCU Dining Hall. The School of Business and the Department of Psychology reside in Farley Center, which includes a computer lab, student lounge, and conference center. The newest building on campus is the Wellness Center, which offers state-of-the-art spaces for hands-on learning.

Costs

Full-time tuition for the 2010–11 academic year was $24,932. Residence and board for the Women's College were $9856. Full-time undergraduate fees were $1244. Instructional materials (textbooks and other items) cost extra and vary depending on the course.

Financial Aid

As a private university, Georgian Court strives to keep the cost of attendance affordable. Ninety-nine percent of first-year, full-time students at GCU receive financial aid in the form of scholarships, grants, loans, and work-study. The average financial aid package for a first-year student is $27,566. GCU also offers the Women's Leadership Award, a $2500 grant given to qualified full-time resident students in recognition of outstanding leadership and service to school, community, or church. It also participates in the New Jersey Educational Opportunity Fund. To be considered for financial aid, candidates must submit a Free Application for Federal Student Aid (FAFSA) to the Office of Financial Aid online at http://www.fafsa.ed.gov.

Faculty

At GCU, 90 percent of the full-time faculty members hold doctoral degrees. From the freshman year on, students have the opportunity to take classes taught by department chairs, even school deans. Georgian Court features a student-faculty ratio of 14:1 and an average class size of 14, which promotes individual attention and open, thoughtful discourse among students and professors. All students receive individual counseling by a faculty adviser.

Student Government

The Student Government Association, composed of elected students, organizes extracurricular activities, charity fund-raisers, and other events. Through the student government structure, students take leadership roles in shaping student life and participate in all major University committees, alongside members of the faculty and administration.

Admission Requirements

Georgian Court University welcomes applications from qualified students of all faiths and backgrounds who desire a liberal arts education. The University strives to enroll students who can benefit most from its academic program. Entrance is based on individual merit.

The high school record of achievement is of primary importance and must reflect solid performance. Candidates for admission must have completed 16 academic (Carnegie) units. The majority of students at Georgian Court ranked in the upper half of their senior high school class.

Further consideration is given to the applicant's extracurricular activities and the letters of recommendation submitted by teachers, counselors, employers, or similarly qualified people. A campus interview is highly recommended, and a guided tour of the campus is available at the interview.

Qualified applicants whose first choice is Georgian Court University and who apply no later than November 15 may be considered for early decision. A mature, well-qualified student who wishes to enter the University after three years of high school may apply for early entrance.

Transfer students are accepted into the freshman, sophomore, and junior classes for fall and spring semesters. All transfer applicants must be in good standing at their previous college. Applicants with fewer than 24 credits must fulfill all requirements for admission to the freshman class. International students in need of a student visa must present official documents at least six months prior to the semester start and must have a minimum TOEFL score of 550 on the paper-based test or 213 on the computer-based test. International students must also complete a GCU financial support form and should be prepared to assume full financial responsibility for their educational and personal expenses in the United States.

Application and Information

To apply for admission, first-time freshman applicants should send an application, high school transcript, and nonrefundable $40 application fee payable to Georgian Court University to the Office of Admissions. Transfer students should submit those materials as well as transcripts from all colleges previously attended. Freshman applicants are urged to submit an application as early as possible during their senior year of high school. Completed applications must be received by August 1 for the fall semester and December 15 for the spring semester. Printable and electronic applications are available at http://www.georgian.edu. Schedules and registration for campus visits are available at http://www.georgian.edu/admissions. Interested students can also learn more by contacting GCU admissions counselors on Facebook, by following @GCUAdmissions on Twitter, or by watching GCU students talk about their experiences on GeorgianCourtU-Tube, the University's YouTube channel.

For further information, prospective students should contact:

Office of Admissions
Georgian Court University
900 Lakewood Avenue
Lakewood, New Jersey 08701-2697
Phone: 732-987-2760
        800-458-8422 Ext. 2760 (toll-free)
Fax: 732-987-2000
E-mail: admissions@georgian.edu
Web site: http://www.georgian.edu/admissions

Nearly 3,000 students attend Georgian Court University, located in Lakewood, New Jersey, just minutes away from the Jersey Shore and about an hour from Philadelphia and New York.

GONZAGA UNIVERSITY

SPOKANE, WASHINGTON

The University

Founded in 1887, Gonzaga is an independent, comprehensive university with a distinguished background in the Catholic, Jesuit, and humanistic tradition. Gonzaga emphasizes the moral and ethical implications of learning, living, and working in today's global society. As a testament to this educational approach, Gonzaga's first-to-second-year retention rate tops 90 percent. Through the University Core Curriculum, each student develops a strong liberal arts foundation, which many alumni cite as a valuable asset. In addition, students choose from more than seventy-five academic areas of study in which to specialize.

Gonzaga's 120-acre campus is characterized by sprawling green lawns and majestic evergreen trees. Towering above the campus are the stately spires of St. Aloysius Church, the well-recognized landmark featured in the University logo.

Because personal growth is as important as intellectual development, Gonzaga places great emphasis on student life outside the classroom. Ranging in population size from 35 to 361 students and offering both coed and single-sex living, Gonzaga's eighteen residence halls and seven apartment complexes offer an intimate atmosphere and a lively campus experience. Each hall has one or more Residence Assistants and a chaplain or a resident Jesuit. While freshmen and sophomores are required to live on campus, 40 percent of the upperclass students also reside in Gonzaga's halls and apartments. Campus-based activities ranging from residence hall government to current affairs symposiums to intramural sports keep students informed and entertained. Students in all academic majors integrate with the Spokane community through a variety of activities, such as volunteer opportunities and internships at numerous businesses and agencies. Gonzaga provides both career and counseling centers.

Gonzaga enrolls 7,837 students, of whom 4,805 are undergraduates. About 46 percent of the students come from Washington State, with forty-seven other states and forty-six other countries also represented. In addition to its undergraduate colleges and schools, Gonzaga University offers about twenty master's programs, a doctoral program in leadership studies, and a School of Law.

Location

Located along the banks of the Spokane River in a quiet, turn-of-the-century neighborhood, Gonzaga University is just a 15-minute walk from downtown Spokane, a city with a metropolitan-area population of 468,684. Spokane's beautiful 125-acre Riverfront Park, in the heart of downtown, lies near the INB Performing Arts Center, Spokane Convention Center, and Spokane Arena. Fine restaurants, a twenty-screen AMC movie theater, and an assortment of shops and department stores, many of which can be reached through a convenient, weatherproof skywalk system, are also in the city's core. For mall shoppers, the Northtown Mall is a 10-minute drive from the campus. Easily accessible outdoor recreation activities, such as skiing, golfing, hiking, biking, camping, and rock climbing, add excitement for the avid outdoor enthusiast.

Majors and Degrees

Gonzaga's undergraduate school awards the B.A., B.B.A., B.E., B.Ed., B.S., B.S.C.E., B.S.Cp.E., B.S.G.E., B.S.E.E., B.S.M.E., and B.S.N. degrees. Majors offered in the College of Arts and Sciences are applied communication studies, art, biochemistry, biology (research option), broadcast and electronic media studies, chemistry, classical civilizations, criminal justice, economics, English (writing track option), environmental studies, French, history, integrated studies, international studies (including international relations and Asian, European, and Latin American studies), Italian studies, journalism, mathematics, mathematics/computer science, music (including composition, conducting, education, general studies, jazz, and performance), philosophy (Kossel track option), physics, political science, psychology, public relations, religious studies, sociology, Spanish, and theater arts.

The School of Business Administration, which is accredited by AACSB International–The Association to Advance Collegiate Schools of Business, offers a Bachelor of Business Administration degree with a major in accounting or a major in business administration, with concentrations in economics, entrepreneurship, finance, human resource management, individualized study, international business, law and public policy, management information systems, marketing, and operations and supply chain management.

As well as granting teacher certification on both the elementary and secondary levels, the School of Education offers degrees in physical education, special education, and sport management.

The School of Engineering and Applied Science awards Bachelor of Science degrees in civil, computer, electrical, and mechanical engineering, as well as computer science and engineering management. The engineering management program includes numerous business courses and also allows attainment of the M.B.A. in five years of study. The civil, computer, electrical, and mechanical programs are accredited by the Engineering Accreditation Commission of the Accreditation Board for Engineering and Technology, Inc. (EAC/ABET).

The School of Professional Studies offers degrees in human physiology and nursing.

Academic Programs

Gonzaga University believes that all students, regardless of their chosen major or profession, benefit from attaining an education that goes beyond specialization. Therefore, all students receive a strong liberal arts background as well as depth in their majors. The Core Curriculum is a very important component of the minimum 128 semester units a student must earn for graduation.

The Honors Program challenges exceptional students with an integrated curriculum that is compatible with any major and most double majors. Motivated and imaginative students in all majors create new ventures and seek to make a difference in the world through the Hogan Entrepreneurial Leadership Program. The Comprehensive Leadership Program, which is also open to students from all majors, allows students to fine-tune their leadership skills and knowledge while completing an academic leadership concentration. All three programs require separate applications. The Gonzaga University Summer Term (GUST) offers motivated high school students intensive course work in a variety of academic disciplines. Academic and co-curricular activities are included in the six-week session.

Credits earned through the Washington State Running Start Program or International Baccalaureate (I.B.) program are accepted on a class-by-class basis. College credit is given for certain test scores in most Advanced Placement (AP) subjects. (Please see Gonzaga's website for the most current policy.) The academic year follows a two-semester system, beginning in late August. Two summer sessions are also available.

Off-Campus Programs

Gonzaga University offers qualified students the opportunity to study abroad through programs in Australia, Benin, China, Costa Rica, Ecuador and the Galapagos Islands, El Salvador, England, France, Ireland, Italy, Japan, Mexico, the Netherlands, Scotland, Spain, Turks & Caicos, and Zambia (see http://www.GoAbroadZAGS.org for more details). As the largest and most popular program, Gonzaga-in-Florence allows approximately 330 students the opportunity to live in Italy for a year, a semester, or a summer; and to travel to many other countries and continents.

Academic Facilities

Gonzaga's "library of the future," the Ralph E. and Helen Higgins Foley Center, is a $20-million window to worldwide information resources. The library features more than 300 specialized databases, satellite capabilities, an advanced computer-controlled video editing system, a rare book room, computerized retrieval services, a wireless Internet connection, and beautiful views.

Foley Center holdings include 782,000 volumes and microform titles, with two special collections of materials that are especially rich in the areas of philosophy and classical civilization. The Foley Center also has the nation's most extensive collection of works by the famous Jesuit poet Gerard Manley Hopkins. The School of Law maintains its own library of 130,000 volumes. The historic College Hall houses the Harry & Colleen Magnuson Theatre, a 24-hour computer lab, the University Chapel, and the main administrative offices and classrooms. A student-operated FM radio station, a state-of-the-art television broadcasting studio, and the offices of the *Bulletin*, a weekly student-published newspaper, reside in the newly renovated Communications Building.

Campus computing services include more than 700 Windows and Macintosh computers dispersed throughout approximately twenty computer labs. Public access workstations are located throughout the Foley Center Library and students can also check out laptop computers for use in the Foley Center. Technology-equipped group study and collaboration spaces are located in multiple locations across the campus. All campus classrooms are equipped with sophisticated presentation and learning technologies. Student e-mail service is provided by Google and students may retain their e-mail address for life. Students have high-speed Ethernet access to campus academic and administrative services and more than 400 megabits of Internet service from their dorm rooms and other University facilities. High-speed wireless network access is available in all buildings on campus and from many outdoor spaces.

The Herak Center for Engineering and the PACCAR Center for Applied Science house a CAD/CAE center, general-purpose computer facilities, a computer cluster network array, electronics and mechanical calibration rooms, and laboratories for physics, electronics, digital electronics/circuits, microprocessors, communications/controls, computer analysis, automation and embedded systems, power, mechanical design, mechanical engineering, materials testing, manufacturing engineering, rapid prototyping, water/wastewater, geotechnical engineering, and hydrology/hydraulics. The centers also contain a large Fabrication Facility, extensive areas for the design and construction of student projects, a sensor networks and robotics lab, and a transmission and distribution electric utility lab.

Hughes Hall Life Sciences Building offers lab and classroom space for a program that is especially rich in environmental biology and student research opportunities, some of which are funded by a grant from the Howard Hughes Medical Institute. The Martin Athletic Centre provides a 13,000-square-foot fitness center, and the 6,000-seat McCarthey Athletic Center hosts basketball games and concerts. The Patterson Baseball Complex and Washington Trust Field is located on the south side of campus. A 23,000-square-foot addition to the Jepson Center for Business Administration houses additional classrooms, computer labs, the Ethics Institute, the Hogan Entrepreneurial Leadership Program, and a student lounge and café.

Costs

Tuition for the 2010–11 academic year was $30,440. Average room and board costs were $8300 for the year.

Financial Aid

Gonzaga University offers many different types of financial aid to qualified students, including scholarships, Federal Pell Grants, Federal Supplemental Educational Opportunity Grants, work-study jobs, Federal Perkins Loans, Federal Stafford Student Loans, and on- and off-campus employment. In order to apply for financial aid awards, a student must first be accepted by the University and must submit the Free Application for Federal Student Aid (FAFSA) by February 1. After this date, awards are made on a funds-available basis. Approximately 98 percent of the students at Gonzaga receive financial assistance, and the average award for this group (for the 2009–10 year) is $23,265 (includes all types of aid). On average, 85 percent of need was met using FAFSA information.

Faculty

The student-faculty ratio is 11:1, and the average class size is 22, allowing close, mentoring relationships to develop. All classes at Gonzaga are taught by faculty members, and faculty members also serve as academic advisers. Eight percent of the faculty members are Jesuits, and 87 percent of the 395 full-time faculty members hold the highest degree in their fields.

Student Government

The Gonzaga Student Body Association provides the means for students to participate in making decisions about student life at Gonzaga. The Executive Council, an elected board of students that administers and initiates programs, also serves as a liaison between the administration and the students. The Student Senate, a legislative body consisting of 26 senators, is responsible for sounding out the needs of the student body and directing this information to the Executive Council. Students also serve on the Board of Regents, search committees, the budget committee, and many other University committees.

Admission Requirements

Gonzaga expects freshman applicants to have taken a challenging college-preparatory curriculum and to submit strong test scores on the ACT or SAT. Transfer students who have earned at least 30 semester credits or 45 quarter credits do not need to submit a high school transcript or test scores. The admission process is selective, and freshman applicants are considered through a pooling process. The Admissions Committee seeks motivated, well-rounded students and considers the rigor of academic study in high school in addition to grades and test scores, as well as personal characteristics, awards and activities, and an essay.

Application and Information

Gonzaga University's nonbinding Early Action deadline for admission applications is November 15. Students who meet this deadline with a complete application are notified of an admission decision by January 15. The final deadline for freshmen to apply for admission under Regular Decision is February 1. Regular Decision applicants receive an admission decision by the middle of March. Transfer students are admitted on a rolling admission basis. Transfer students seeking financial aid are encouraged to apply for admission by March 1. Otherwise, to ensure a smooth transition to Gonzaga, transfer students should apply by June 1. After June 1, the University accepts transfer applicants only if space is available. Freshman and transfer students apply by using the Common Application. For priority financial aid, all students are encouraged to submit the FAFSA by February 1.

All requests for further information or materials should be addressed to:

Julie McCulloh
Dean of Admission
Gonzaga University
502 E. Boone Ave.
Spokane, Washington 99258-0102
Phone: 800-322-2584 (toll-free)
E-mail: admissions@gonzaga.edu
Web site: http://www.gonzaga.edu
http://www.facebook.com/GonzagaUniversity
http://twitter.com/GonzagaU

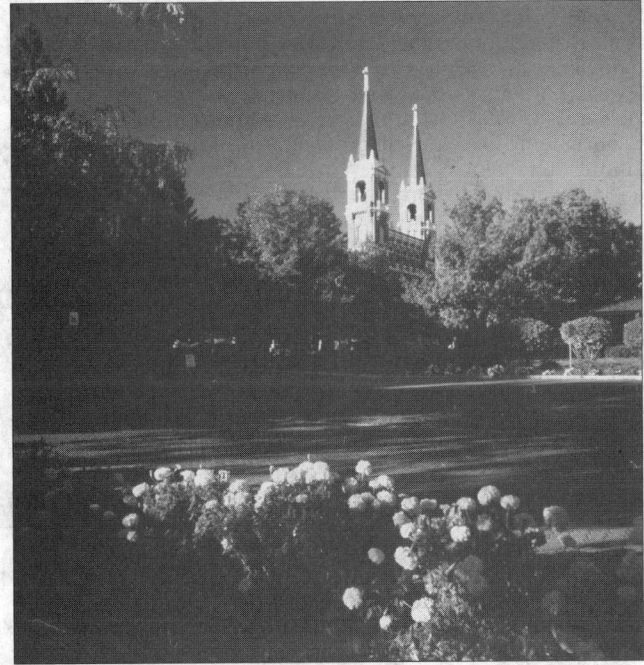

Gonzaga University: Education that inspires mind, body, and spirit.

GRACELAND UNIVERSITY

LAMONI, IOWA

GRACELAND
UNIVERSITY

The University

Graceland University (GU) provides challenging academic programs rooted in the liberal arts tradition, with a strong emphasis on career preparation. Since 1895, the University has maintained a tradition of academic excellence based on the Christian view of wholeness, worth, and dignity for every person. The 2010–11 class hailed from forty states and forty countries; seventeen percent of the 1,000 students on Graceland's Lamoni, Iowa campus are international students.

The Graceland experience combines a personalized education and an ongoing adventure, intended to last throughout the student's lifetime. Graduates go on to careers in the sciences, arts, nursing, education, business, athletics, and humanitarian service. Alumni say that Graceland helped focus their passions and shape their futures.

Graceland's house residential system makes students feel instantly at home. Residence halls are divided into floors known as houses, where students live with friends from day one through graduation. Each house has its own traditions and every student becomes a part of the traditions of tomorrow. Members of each house elect a council to plan social, intramural, religious, and academic-support activities.

Leadership is defined in many ways at Graceland. Hands-on experiences allow students to cultivate skills and prepare for future leadership positions. Students hold 200 leadership posts on campus that provide skills for an added edge in the job market and graduate school. Graceland was named a 2011 Best College in the Midwestern Region by the Princeton Review and a first-tier university by *U.S. News & World Report*, which serves as evidence of the University's leadership in higher education today.

Location

Lamoni is located in the rolling hills of south-central Iowa on Interstate 35, halfway between Des Moines and Kansas City. Shops, restaurants, a vintage theater, a cozy downtown district, and a scenic bike trail are all within walking or biking distance. It is a safe, friendly, small town where students always feel welcome. Graceland also has a stunning urban campus in Independence, Missouri, home to a wide array of online programs and its award-winning School of Nursing. The Graceland Web site (www.graceland.edu) offers more information about the students, alumni, the university, and the welcoming community. The University's Facebook page (www.facebook.com/GracelandUniversity) is another way to connect with Graceland.

Majors and Degrees

GU offers more than fifty academic majors and programs. Students work closely with professors—the student-faculty ratio is 15:1—who are both teachers and scholars. Students may participate in summer internships in their fields and travel abroad during Winter Term service-learning ventures to places like Zambia, Nicaragua, China, Hungary, and Italy.

Graceland awards the Bachelor of Arts, Bachelor of Science, and Bachelor of Science in Nursing degrees. Concentrations in the arts include accounting; agricultural business; athletic training; business administration; communications; criminal justice; economics; elementary education; English; film, theater, and performance studies; health; history; human services; liberal studies; mathematics; music; physical education; psychology; recreation; religion and philosophy; sociology; sport management; and visual art. The first two years of the Bachelor of Science in nursing program are offered on the Lamoni campus, while the junior and senior years are on the Independence, Missouri campus. Bachelor

of Science programs and majors include biology, chemistry, computer science, and preprofessional programs.

Graceland also offers degree programs at satellite campus locations. Through a partnership with North Central Missouri College in Trenton, Missouri, Graceland offers undergraduate degrees in liberal studies and elementary education. Through a partnership with Indian Hills Community College in Centerville, Iowa, Graceland offers an undergraduate degree in elementary education. The undergraduate elementary education program is also offered at the Independence campus.

Graduate programs include the Master of Arts in Christian Ministries, Master of Arts in Religion, Master of Education, and Master of Science in Nursing. Post-master's certificates are offered in family nurse practitioner, nurse educator, and health-care administration.

Graceland offers many options for distance learners. Programs offered online by the School of Nursing include a bachelor's degree in health-care management, RN-B.S.N., RN-M.S.N., and M.S.N. programs. The M.S.N. program has three tracks: family nurse practitioner, nurse educator, and health-care administrator.

The Edmund J. Gleazer School of Education offers a Master of Education degree with an emphasis in special education or collaborative learning and teaching. The Master of Education program is offered in Cedar Rapids, Des Moines, and Lamoni, Iowa; Independence, Missouri; and online.

The Community of Christ Seminary at Graceland offers the Master of Arts in Religion and Master of Arts in Christian Ministries degrees for distance learners in blended-delivery systems.

Graceland University is a member of the North Central Association of Colleges and Schools (NCA) and is accredited by the Higher Learning Commission (30 North LaSalle Street, Suite 2400, Chicago, Illinois 60602-2504; 800-621-7440 (toll-free); http://www.ncahigherlearningcommission.org). All teacher-education programs at GU are approved by the Iowa Department of Education. The Bachelor of Arts (B.A.) in education and Master of Education (M.Ed.) programs in collaborative teaching and learning, quality education, and special education are accredited by the National Council for Accreditation of Teacher Education (NCATE; 2010 Massachusetts Avenue NW, Suite 500, Washington, D.C. 20036; 202-466-7496; http://www.ncate.org). All GU nursing programs are accredited by the Iowa and Missouri Departments of Education and the Commission on Collegiate Nursing Education (CCNE; One Dupont Circle NW, Suite 530, Washington, D.C. 20036; http://www.aacn.nche.edu). The athletic training program is accredited by the Commission on Accreditation of Athletic Training Education Programs (CAATE; 2201 Double Creek Drive, Suite 5006, Round Rock, Texas 78664; 512-733-9700; http://www.caate.net). These academic standards ensure that a degree from Graceland University is recognized by educational, business, and professional communities.

Academic Programs

Graceland is committed to helping develop the lives of its students—intellectually, socially, physically, and ethically—through a curriculum that is strongly rooted in the liberal arts. General education requirements are based on ten core competencies and can be satisfied by course selections, internships, portfolios, proficiency exams, work experience, independent studies, performance, and achievement. Graceland programs foster conceptual thinking, encourage team building, develop communication skills, and accommodate growth and enrichment.

Two programs at Graceland provide attention to special needs of students. The honors program is designed for highly motivated students who want to expand their learning beyond traditional academic curriculum by developing and completing honors theses or projects. Chance is a program for students who clearly have the aptitude for university education but have experienced learning challenges and may benefit from individual attention.

Off-Campus Programs

The University operates on a 4-1-4 academic calendar. The regular semesters are separated by a one-month Winter Term in January. Full tuition for either the fall or the spring semester includes Winter Term, a program geared to innovative and exceptional approaches to learning and action-oriented learning experiences. On-campus Winter Terms include a variety of options, from yoga to science fiction writing to explorations in the sciences. Off-campus Winter Term experiences range from scuba diving and marine-life exploration in Grand Cayman to touring the great art museums of France to humanitarian work in Zambia. Winter Term is also an opportune time for students to explore career interests through internships and job shadowing.

Students who major in a foreign language may study abroad during their junior or senior year under the auspices of a recognized academic program. Graceland sponsors an International Health Center that provides opportunities for students to interact with health workers in villages in Africa and Asia. School of Nursing and School of Education students may participate in international humanitarian aid missions during Winter Term.

Academic Facilities

The Resch Science and Technology Hall was completed in 2009 and provides superb infrastructure and industry-standard lab equipment. The beautiful facility offers Graceland students some of the best science, math, and technology facilities in the Midwest.

The Helene Center for the Visual Arts includes 29,000 square feet of classrooms, galleries, and numerous studios. It includes large, north-facing windows to allow optimum light for artists.

The Shaw Center has a 750-seat performance auditorium, a 150-seat studio theater, a world-class Casavant pipe organ, an art gallery, and a scene-and-wardrobe shop. The Shaw Center is scheduled to undergo an extensive makeover in 2011–12. Plans call for a beautiful new recital hall, a black box experimental theater, a new gallery, and a stunning new, glass-front atrium and student gathering area to be added.

The Eugene E. and Julia Travis Closson Physical Education Center includes an indoor pool; indoor track; weight and training room; new locker rooms; and basketball, tennis, volleyball, and racquetball courts. The Bruce Jenner Sports Complex includes a new outdoor track, a new $1-million artificial-turf football field, and three outstanding soccer fields. The campus borders a nine-hole golf course and has a highly-regarded disc golf course where Midwest tournaments are held.

Costs

Full-time tuition for 2011–12 is $21,490, making Graceland one of the most affordable private universities in the Midwest.

Financial Aid

Graceland students receive academic and athletic scholarships, performance grants, work-study opportunities, federal and state grants, and government loans. Grants are available for achievement in athletics and performing arts, and for international students. The University offers significant scholarships to members of its sponsoring church, the Community of Christ.

Faculty

The majority of Graceland faculty members have earned a doctorate or the highest degree in their field. They are experts, by experience and education. Their passion is to share their knowledge with students. Faculty members are active in their professional fields but consider teaching their primary responsibility.

Student Government

Students are actively involved in the decision-making process of the University. Student-elected executive members of the Graceland Student Government attend faculty meetings and participate with voice and vote. Each academic department has student representatives who participate in business sessions and serve on faculty search committees. Students provide leadership for Graceland's house residential and campus social programs. There are numerous ways for students to gain practical leadership experience.

Admission Requirements

High school graduates must meet two of the following criteria: rank in the upper 50 percent of their class, have a minimum 2.5 GPA, or have either a minimum composite ACT score of 21 or a minimum SAT combined score of 960.

Application and Information

Interested students can request additional admissions information online at www.graceland.edu/requestinformation or www.graceland.edu/apply.

Admissions Office
Graceland University
1 University Place
Lamoni, Iowa 50140
Phone: 641-784-5196
          866-GRACELAND (toll-free in the U.S. and
               Canada)
Fax: 641-784-5480
E-mail: admissions@graceland.edu
Web site: http://www.admissions.graceland.edu

Higdon Administration Building on Graceland's Lamoni Campus.

GRAND VIEW UNIVERSITY

DES MOINES, IOWA

The University

Grand View is a liberal arts institution affiliated with the Evangelical Lutheran Church in America. Founded more than 100 years ago, Grand View offers a high-quality education to a diverse student body in a career-oriented, liberal arts–grounded curriculum at two campus locations in greater Des Moines. Grand View welcomes traditional students and adult learners representing a wide range of religious and cultural backgrounds.

At Grand View University, students find a winning combination of high-quality programs, experienced professors, and caring individuals. With 2,000 students and an average class size of 16, students get to know their professors and other students well. They learn independence and seek responsibility in Grand View's educational environment. Learning is an interactive process at Grand View—students engage in lively discussions, work on real-world projects, and participate in career-related work experiences.

Grand View University stands out from other universities because of its partnerships with leading businesses and organizations in Des Moines, which has led to challenging internships and to nearly 100 percent of students finding jobs right after graduation or continuing their education every year for more than a decade and a half. Grand View is known for its ability to connect students with exciting and challenging career opportunities.

Students are encouraged to develop leadership and team skills through involvement in campus organizations, which include intercollegiate and intramural athletics, speech and theater groups, major department clubs, student government, and musical ensembles. Active honorary societies include Alpha Chi, Alpha Mu Gamma, Alpha Psi Omega, Alpha Sigma Lambda, Beta Beta Beta, Phi Eta Sigma, Sigma Theta Tau, and Theta Alpha Kappa. Grand View's student leadership program provides opportunities for students without leadership experience to seek and develop critical thinking, interpersonal, and networking skills.

Student athletes compete in men's baseball, basketball, bowling, cross-country, football, golf, soccer, tennis, track and field, and wrestling and women's basketball, bowling, cheerleading, competitive dance, cross-country, golf, soccer, softball, tennis, track and field, and volleyball. Grand View participates in the Midwest Collegiate Conference of the National Association of Intercollegiate Athletics. Athletic scholarships are available.

Two locations offer Grand View students convenient scheduling options for their program of study. Weekend and evening classes are offered at the main campus in Des Moines and at Grand View's campus in Johnston, Iowa. For motivated students seeking to complete their degree quickly, accelerated schedules are offered for several of sixteen evening majors.

Location

Grand View is located in Des Moines, a metropolitan area of more than half a million people in central Iowa. Des Moines is the state capital and serves as the communications hub for Iowa. Nationally recognized organizations that have their corporate offices in Des Moines include Pioneer Hi-Bred International, Inc.; the Principal Financial Group; Meredith Corporation; and the *Des Moines Register*.

In essence, Grand View's campus is the entire city of Des Moines—as part of the Grand View community, students are not limited by the confines of a small school or small town. In a given day, students can catch an Iowa Cubs professional baseball doubleheader, head down to the Court Avenue district for great food and nightlife, or take in a rock concert at Wells Fargo Arena.

A thriving arts program in Des Moines features the Des Moines Metro Opera, Ballet Iowa, the Des Moines Symphony, the Des Moines Art Center, and the Des Moines Playhouse. The summer Des Moines Art Festival is ranked third in the nation.

Des Moines features four distinct and beautiful seasons. Except for a month or so of bundle-up, see-your-breath weather, the climate is ideal for outdoor activities. Grand View students can take advantage of terrific recreational opportunities, including several golf courses, Saylorville Lake, and many city parks and state forests.

Easily accessible from Interstates 35 and 80, Grand View is 4 hours from Minneapolis, 6 hours from Chicago, and 3 hours from Kansas City.

Majors and Degrees

Grand View University grants the Bachelor of Arts degree and offers thirty-eight majors in areas such as accounting, art education, biology, broadcast, business administration (with concentrations in agricultural business, finance, human resource management, management, marketing, and real estate), computer science, criminal justice, elementary education, English, general studies–liberal arts, graphic design, graphic journalism, health promotion, history, human services, individualized major, journalism, management information systems, mass communication, math, music, music education, organizational studies, paralegal studies, physical science, political studies (prelaw or public administration), psychology, religion, secondary education, service management, sociology–liberal arts, Spanish for careers and professionals, theater arts, and visual arts. Grand View also offers a Bachelor of Science degree in nursing, as well as an RN to B.S.N. program. In addition, the University offers certificate programs in art therapy, entrepreneurship, human resource management, in-house communication, real estate, Spanish essentials, and sport management, as well as postbaccalaureate certificates in accounting and management in accounting.

The Master of Science in innovative leadership program is an interdisciplinary advanced degree with tracks in business, education, and nursing. This cutting-edge, 40-credit-hour program qualifies graduates as organizational leaders, clinical nurse leaders, and teacher leaders.

Academic Programs

Grand View operates on a 4-4-1 academic calendar. The first semester runs from September to December. The second semester begins in early January and ends in late April. Three 1-month summer sessions are offered in May, June, and July, as is a summer trimester evening program.

Grand View University has adopted a competency-based General Education Core. Requirements for the core are defined in student learning goals. Completion of the educational core enables students to achieve a measurable level of competency in key skill and knowledge areas, such as writing, critical analysis, oral communication, and computer proficiency.

The Logos Honors Program provides an alternative to the General Education Core. By invitation, freshman and sophomore students enrolled in this program complete a series of courses designed to challenge exceptional students.

The Expressions honors program for business and accounting students offers a three-year accelerated option. And the *ALT* honors magazine offers invited students an opportunity to design, write, and produce an award-winning publication.

An active study-abroad program gives students opportunities to learn in an international setting, particularly through a partnership with the Danish Institute for Study Abroad.

The Grand View academic mission is to provide a diverse student body with an academically rigorous education. In order to meet this commitment, Grand View provides a variety of learning environments and teaching techniques. The University's academic support programs and services were lauded as a national model by the examining team from the North Central Association of Colleges and Schools during reaccreditation in 2005, when the University received complete ten-year accreditation with no follow-up required.

Costs

For 2010–11, the comprehensive cost for freshmen living on campus was approximately $27,124, which included tuition, an activity fee, a technology fee, a parking fee, and room and board. Students have several residential and meal plan options that affect cost. Health services and Internet access are also included in the comprehensive fee.

Financial Aid

Typically, most full-time Grand View students received financial assistance. The average freshman full-time award package is usually around $23,000 with about $14,000 in grants and scholarships and the remainder in work-study and student loans. The amount of aid is determined through a combination of merit and analysis of need as determined through the Free Application for Federal Student Aid. The priority deadline for financial aid is March 1. Students receive notification of financial aid packages following acceptance of admission to the University and receipt of their financial aid analysis of need.

Faculty

There are approximately 90 full-time faculty members and 90 part-time faculty members. More than fifty percent hold terminal degrees. All classes are taught by professors; no graduate or teaching assistants instruct Grand View classes.

Student Government

Students participate in University governance. The Student Activities Council and Viking Council plan student activities that promote educational, social, cultural, and recreational aspects of student life. Students serve as representatives on faculty and staff search committees, programming committees, and student life committees.

Admission Requirements

Applicants' files are reviewed to determine their preparedness for a Grand View education. Official high school transcripts and submission of ACT or SAT scores are required for applicants with less than 24 semester hours of college credit. Applicants transferring from another college are required to submit official transcripts from all colleges previously attended.

Application and Information

For more information about Grand View, students should contact:

Admissions Office
Grand View University
1200 Grandview Avenue
Des Moines, Iowa 50316
Phone: 515-263-2810
      800-444-6083 (toll-free)
Fax: 515-263-2974
E-mail: admissions@grandview.edu
Web site: http://www.admissions.grandview.edu
    http://on.fb.me/aGuPhF (Facebook)

Grand View students chat with a professor on their way to class.

GREENSBORO COLLEGE
GREENSBORO, NORTH CAROLINA

The College

Established in 1838, Greensboro College is a four-year coeducational liberal arts college affiliated with the United Methodist Church. It is located in the College Hill Historic District of Greensboro, North Carolina. With an enrollment of approximately 1,200 men and women, the College enjoys a small-community atmosphere and maintains a student-faculty ratio of 13:1.

The 60-acre campus is located in the College Hill Historic District, only six blocks from downtown Greensboro. Its architecture is in the traditional Georgian style. The buildings include an indoor athletic center, four residential halls, classroom buildings, a chapel, a performing arts center, a library, and a main administrative building.

At the Royce Reynolds Family Student Life Center, students enjoy squash, racquetball, and basketball courts; a fitness facility; an indoor pool; an aerobics room; a Jacuzzi; a steam room; and a sauna. Intercollegiate sports include baseball, basketball, cross-country, football, golf, lacrosse, soccer, swimming, and tennis for men as well as basketball, cross-country, lacrosse, soccer, softball, swimming, tennis, golf, and volleyball for women. Greensboro College is a member of the NCAA Division III and competes in the U.S.A. South Athletic Conference. An intramural program is also offered for students.

There is cultural, religious, and ethnic diversity at Greensboro College, where students come from more than thirty states and twenty-four nations. Many graduates have earned distinction in graduate and professional schools in all parts of the United States and abroad. Recent Greensboro College graduates have been accepted into the graduate schools of the College of William and Mary as well as Duke, Emory, Georgetown, Johns Hopkins, North Carolina at Chapel Hill, North Carolina State, Princeton, St. Andrews (Scotland), Temple, Vanderbilt, and Wake Forest Universities and the Eastman School of Music. Most graduates pursue careers in business, education, health care, and the arts.

Extracurricular activities are designed to supplement and reinforce academic study at the College. More than 100 student leadership positions are available in more than thirty different student organizations, enabling most students to be as active in campus life as they wish.

In addition to its undergraduate programs, Greensboro College offers the Master of Education degree.

Location

The city of Greensboro, which is located near the center of North Carolina, offers major industries, including insurance companies and textile manufacturers, and many cultural, social, and athletic opportunities. With a population of more than 1 million people in the Triad region, the city is a thriving business center that offers excellent internship opportunities. More than 45,000 students study at the seven colleges and universities within the city. Greensboro College is at the heart of this community.

Majors and Degrees

Greensboro College awards the Bachelor of Arts (B.A.), Bachelor of Science (B.S.), and Bachelor of Business Administration degrees. Students can major in the following areas: accounting, art, athletic training, biology, birth-through-kindergarten teacher education, business administration, business administration and economics, chemistry, criminal justice, elementary education, English, English and communications, exercise and sport studies, French, health and physical education, history, history and political science, liberal studies, mathematics, mathematics education, middle grades education, music, music education, political science, psychology, religion, secondary education, sociology, Spanish, special education, theater, and urban ecology. Minors are available in child and family studies, Christian education, computer information systems, computer science, dance, ethics, interdisciplinary studies, international studies, legal administration, women's studies, and other areas in which majors are offered. Combined-degree programs are offered in medical technology and radiological technology.

Academic Programs

All students are required to take courses in the humanities, the natural sciences, the social sciences, and the arts. The general education requirements for both the B.A. and B.S. degrees total 52 semester hours. Graduation requires the completion of 124 semester hours.

Greensboro College offers an honors program for superior students who qualify on the basis of SAT or ACT scores, high school grade point averages, or AP examination results. Students enrolled in the program must complete requirements in addition to those expected of students in the regular B.A. and B.S. degree programs.

Because Greensboro College recognizes that people must learn not only how to live but also how to make a living, the liberal arts curriculum and setting provide the context for a variety of professional programs, including accounting, business, and legal administration, as well as preprofessional programs in law, medicine, and theology. Besides providing career and academic counseling, the College seeks to ensure that its graduates acquire the basic intellectual and communications capabilities to cope with the changing demands of any career. An internship program during the junior and senior years places students in business and agency settings that are related to their major and career aspirations. The College also seeks to develop in its graduates a philosophy of life and an appreciation of Judeo-Christian values that transcend particular vocational skills.

Off-Campus Programs

Greensboro College is a member of the Greater Greensboro Consortium and the Piedmont Independent Colleges Association, which provide for arrangements with Bennett College, Elon University, Guilford College, Guilford Technical Community College, High Point University, North Carolina Agricultural and Technical State University, Salem College, and the University of North Carolina at Greensboro. With permission from the academic dean, students at Greensboro College may take courses offered at any of the other campuses. Library resources are shared.

Academic Facilities

The James Addison Jones Library has approximately 112,000 volumes, periodicals, CD-ROMs, and microfilm reels. The computerized card catalog system allows students to access the holdings of other area colleges. Interlibrary loan among the colleges is permitted. There are reading rooms, periodical and browsing rooms, and a multipurpose meeting room.

One of the College's goals is to ensure that every student develops a broad range of technical skills in order to flourish in the twenty-first century. State-of-the-art computer labs are available for all students, and students can access the Internet and World

Wide Web from most points on campus. All dorm rooms provide high-speed access to the Internet.

Other facilities include a computerized writing laboratory, natural science laboratories, the Annie Sellars Jordan Parlor Theater, and the Gail Brower Huggins Performance Center, one of the most elegant and state-of-the-art performance facilities in the area. Music facilities include a computerized music laboratory, practice rooms, two recital areas, thirty-nine pianos (including a 9-foot concert grand), and a concert stage. In addition, Greensboro College is one of only three colleges in the state to have a Fisk organ. There are two large art studios, one for the teaching of two-dimensional media and one for the teaching of three-dimensional media. Students in the education department are served by the Curriculum Materials Center, which contains audiovisual equipment, books, teaching kits, and a variety of other special supplies.

Costs

For 2011–12, the total cost of tuition, fees, room, and board is $34,100. Greensboro College estimates that $800 to $1600 is adequate for books, clothing, entertainment, and other incidental expenses.

Financial Aid

Greensboro College participates in many federal programs of student aid, including the Federal Pell Grant, Federal Work-Study, Federal Perkins Loan, Federal Supplemental Educational Opportunity Grant, Federal Parent Loan for Undergraduate Students, and Federal Stafford Student Loan programs. Authorized state programs include North Carolina Legislative Tuition Grants, the State Contractual Scholarship Fund, North Carolina Prospective Teacher's Scholarships/Loans, and North Carolina Student Incentive Grants. Institutional programs funded by Greensboro College include the College work-study program, grants, scholarships, and loans. Full- and partial-tuition scholarships are awarded to students based on academic profile. United Methodist Church scholarships and grants, which are based on both financial need and merit, are available. Full Tuition Presidential Scholarships, valued at more than $100,000 each, are available. Approximately 92 percent of the students at Greensboro College receive some form of financial assistance. All students are encouraged to apply for financial aid, and the College accepts the Free Application for Federal Student Aid (FAFSA). Applications for United Methodist Church scholarships and grants are available from the financial planning office. A career-development office on campus is available to aid all students seeking a part-time job, regardless of their financial need.

Faculty

Greensboro College has 59 full-time faculty members. All of the full-time faculty members hold the highest degree in their areas of study. Although some faculty members have distinguished themselves by their research, scholarship, and creativity, all are deeply and primarily committed to undergraduate teaching and the personal welfare of the students. Every student has a faculty adviser; the average class size is 18, and there is a favorable student-faculty ratio of 13:1.

Student Government

The College's Student Government Association (SGA), acting within the policies and regulations of the College, is the main representative voice of the students. The SGA addresses various policy decisions that affect the students and acts as a sounding board for student opinions. The SGA is the communication link between student organizations, the student body, the administration, the staff, and the faculty. The Campus Activities Board plans and executes student events on campus.

Admission Requirements

Admission decisions are based on all available information. Although applicants are asked to submit scores from the SAT and/or ACT, the high school record is actually the most important single factor. No exact formula can be applied to all applications, but acceptable scores on the SAT or ACT, rank in class, grade point average, and high school program form the basis for evaluation. Candidates for admission should demonstrate academic achievement in a select academic program in high school, although completion of a given program of study is not as important as evidence of intellectual curiosity and emotional and social maturity. A curriculum that provides good preparation for Greensboro College might include 4 units of English, 3 units of college-preparatory math (algebra I and II and geometry), 2 units of science (including one laboratory science), 2 units of history, 2 units of the same foreign language, and electives chosen from art, music, physical education, and social science. An interview on campus is very helpful to the student and to the College. Arrangements may be made for the interview at the student's convenience.

Greensboro College accepts transfer credits on a case-by-case basis. Credit is given for courses that have been successfully completed at accredited universities, senior colleges, junior colleges, community colleges, and technical colleges.

Application and Information

Students should submit an application for admission and immediately ask high schools and any colleges they have attended to forward official transcripts to Greensboro College. SAT or ACT scores should be forwarded to the College by the testing agency or the student's high school. Reference letters may be requested by the Admissions Committee, which reviews all applications on a rolling basis. As soon as a decision is reached, the student is notified. Greensboro College has no closing date for applications, but those received before March 31 are given priority.

For inquiries and application materials, students should contact:

Office of Admissions
Greensboro College
815 West Market Street
Greensboro, North Carolina 27401-1875

Phone: 800-346-8226 (toll-free)
Fax: 336-378-0154
E-mail: admissions@greensborocollege.edu
Web site: http://www.greensborocollege.edu

Greensboro College students frequently gather near the historic Main Building.

GROVE CITY COLLEGE
GROVE CITY, PENNSYLVANIA

The College

The beautifully landscaped campus of Grove City College (GCC) stretches more than 150 acres and includes twenty-seven neo-Gothic buildings valued at more than $100 million. The campus is considered one of the loveliest in the nation. While the College has changed to meet the needs of the society it serves, its basic philosophy has remained unchanged since its founding in 1876. It is a Christian liberal arts and sciences institution of ideal size and dedicated to the principle of providing the highest-quality education at the lowest possible cost. Wishing to remain truly independent and to retain its distinctive qualities as a private school governed by private citizens (trustees), it is one of the very few colleges in the country that does not accept any state or federal monies. It is informally affiliated with the Presbyterian Church (U.S.A.) but not narrowly denominational; the College believes that to be well educated a student should be exposed to the central ideas of the Christian faith. A 20-minute chapel program offered Tuesday and Thursday mornings, along with a Sunday evening worship service, challenges students in their faith. Sixteen chapel services per semester are required out of fifty opportunities. Religious organizations and activities exist to provide fellowship and spiritual growth.

Grove City attracts students from all over the United States. While most come from Pennsylvania, Ohio, New Jersey, Virginia, and New York, forty-five states and nine other countries were represented in 2010–11. Seventy-seven percent of the women and 58 percent of the men in the most recent freshman class ranked in the top fifth of their high school class. Their average SAT combined score was 1246 (combining only the critical reading and math scores); the average ACT composite score was 28.

Ninety-four percent of the 2,500 students live in separate men's and women's residence halls. All others are regular commuters or married students. A full program of cultural, professional, athletic, and social activities is offered. An arena, Crawford Auditorium, and the J. Howard Pew Fine Arts Center are used for athletics, concerts, movies, plays, and lectures. The Physical Learning Center is one of the finest among the nation's small colleges and includes an eight-lane bowling alley, two swimming pools, handball/racquetball courts, playing surfaces, fitness rooms with free weights, aerobic equipment and Cybex machines, an indoor three-lane running track, and the basketball arena. The Breen Student Union provides an eatery; mailroom; bookstore; commuters' lounge; and a commons area for dining, studying, and socializing. The Ketler and South Hall Recreation Lounge are also available for cooking, games, and socializing. There are more than 130 organizations and special interest groups, including local fraternities and sororities. No alcohol or drugs are permitted on campus. The athletic activities include extensive intramural, club, and varsity sports programs that provide nineteen intercollegiate teams that compete at the NCAA Division III level for men and women.

The College's well-established placement services, ranked recently by *The Princeton Review* among the top 20 in the nation, are used constantly by students who are interested in business and industrial employment and by those seeking educational positions in the teaching field. A complete file of personal data, scholastic records, and recommendations is prepared for each registrant. These files are available to the scores of prospective employers who visit the campus annually to interview the graduating seniors. One of Grove City's strengths is placing students in business, industrial, and teaching positions, as well as in professional institutions such as medical schools.

Prospective students can check out Grove City's Facebook page at http://on.fb.me/grovecity_coll.

Location

Grove City, a town of 8,000 people, is 60 miles north of Pittsburgh and is located 4 miles from restaurants, hotels, and a 140-store outlet mall. Convenient to I-79 and I-80, Grove City is only a day's drive from Chicago, New York City, Toronto, and Washington, D.C. The municipal airport has a 3,500-foot runway, and there is bus service to Pittsburgh.

Majors and Degrees

Grove City College offers undergraduate degrees in liberal arts, sciences, engineering, and music. The Bachelor of Arts is offered with majors in Christian thought, communication studies, economics, English, history, modern language (French and Spanish), philosophy, political science, psychology, secondary education, and sociology. Preprofessional students in law or theology usually earn the B.A. degree. Interdisciplinary major programs are also available for qualified students.

The Bachelor of Science is granted with majors in accounting, applied physics, applied physics/computer, biochemistry, biology, business management, chemistry, computer information systems, computer science, early childhood education, elementary education, entrepreneurship, exercise science, financial management, industrial management, international business, marketing management, mathematics, molecular biology, psychology, and special education. Preprofessional students often select one of these majors for dentistry, medicine, or other health fields.

The Bachelor of Science in Electrical and Computer Engineering degree is also offered. The Bachelor of Science in Mechanical Engineering major provides for mechanical systems design and/or thermal systems design. The electrical and computer and mechanical engineering programs are accredited by the Engineering Accreditation Commission of the Accreditation Board for Engineering and Technology, Inc. (ABET).

The Bachelor of Music degree is awarded to those who major in music. Programs may also include concentrations in business, education, performing arts, or religion.

Academic Programs

Grove City College's goal is to assist young men and women in developing as complete individuals—academically, spiritually, and physically. The general education requirements provide all students with a high level of cultural literacy and communication skills. They include 46 semester hours of courses with emphases in the humanities, social sciences, and natural sciences; in quantitative and logical reasoning; and in science, faith, and technology, as well as a language requirement for all majors except engineering and science. Degree candidates must also complete the requirements in their field of concentration, physical education, electives, and convocation. To graduate, a student must have completed 128 semester hours (132 hours for electrical engineering) plus 4 convocation credits. Seventy-eight percent of those entering as freshmen stay and receive a diploma in four years.

A distinctive liberal arts–engineering program includes engineering courses plus courses in the humanities to provide students with a well-grounded preparation for entering the engineering field, as well as the civic and cultural life of society. The Austrian economics program exposes students to all economic philosophies, yet strongly advocates economic freedoms and free markets.

Grove City follows the early semester calendar plan. Academic credit may be granted to incoming freshmen on the basis of scores on appropriate Advanced Placement tests, International Baccalaureate tests, or College-Level Examination Program tests. Honors courses, independent study, seminars, and the opportunity for juniors to study abroad for credit are also offered.

Academic Facilities

The Hall of Arts and Letters opened in 2003. This state-of-the-art teaching facility features a 200-seat lecture hall, forty classrooms (including multimedia-equipped rooms and tiered "case study" rooms), eighty faculty offices, the Early Education Center, the Curriculum Library, and language, computer, and video production labs.

The College library houses 135,100 books and 13,250 microform units; 2,905 audio/video tapes, CDs, and DVDs; and 36,992 periodical subscriptions. Modern, well-equipped laboratories for biology, chemistry, engineering, and physics are available, as are facilities for language and piano studies.

The College recently acquired an observatory and the remote structure will be utilized for astronomy classes as well as faculty and student research.

The Weir C. Ketler Technological Learning Center consists of forty microcomputers and three big-screen projection systems and houses the help desk and repair center that support the student technology initiative. All freshmen receive their own tablet PC and color printer/scanner/copier.

The J. Howard Pew Fine Arts Center has art, photography, and music studios; a rehearsal hall; a little theater; a museum; an art gallery; music practice rooms; and an auditorium and stage large enough to accommodate the most elaborate drama productions and concerts. An addition completed in 2002 contains additional classrooms, practice rooms, and a 188-seat recital hall.

Costs

As a relatively small, financially sound college, Grove City is able to charge an unusually low tuition in comparison to other independent institutions of similar quality. The 2010–11 annual tuition charge was $13,088 for all degrees. The cost of a tablet PC for all freshmen is included in the tuition fees. There is no comprehensive fee. Part-time tuition was $410 per credit. Room and board were $7132. Expenses for books, laundry, transportation, and personal needs vary considerably with the lifestyle of the individual.

Financial Aid

Because the College's tuition charges are low, every student, in effect, receives significant financial assistance. Forty-four percent of the freshmen receive additional aid from GCC. Students applying for financial assistance must complete Grove City College's financial aid form. Job opportunities are available both on and off campus.

Faculty

The focus of the Grove City faculty members is on teaching students, although many members are involved with research and writing. Ninety-five percent of the faculty members hold doctorates. Most of the administrative staff members also teach part-time in various departments. The student-faculty ratio is approximately 16:1. Faculty members emphasize teaching and attention to the students' individual needs; they also participate extensively in the College's extracurricular programs.

Student Government

The Student Government Association provides an opportunity for direct student interaction with the faculty members and administration in matters relating to campus activities. Students serve on regular College committees (library, publications, religious activities, and student activities) and also on the Men's and Women's Governing Board and the Discipline Committee.

Admission Requirements

The College seeks academically qualified students without regard to race, color, sex, religion, or national or ethnic origin. An applicant for admission should be a high school graduate with the following recommended units: English, 4; foreign language, 3; mathematics, 3; history, 2; and science, 2. Engineering, science, and mathematics majors should have 4 units each in both mathematics and science. Auditions are required for music majors. An interview is highly recommended, especially for those who live within a day's drive (400 miles).

Transfer students may receive advanced standing if they have been in good standing at their previous institutions and have maintained a minimum grade point average of 2.0 (on a 4.0 scale).

Application and Information

A regular admission applicant should take the SAT or ACT by October or November of the senior year in high school. The application should include scores on the SAT (preferred) or the ACT, a high school transcript, references, a recommendation from the student's principal or counselor, and a nonrefundable application fee of $50. An application may be submitted after the eleventh grade. An early decision applicant should take the entrance test in the eleventh grade, visit the College for an interview, and submit the application by November 15; notification of the admission decision is mailed on December 15. Approved early decision applicants must accept by January 15 and submit a nonrefundable deposit of $250.

Applicants seeking regular decision must submit the completed application and supporting documents by February 1 of their senior year. Notification of the admission decision is mailed on March 15. Students who are offered admission should reply as soon as possible, but no later than May 1, and include a nonrefundable deposit of $250. Applications received after February 1 are considered as space permits. The College receives nearly three applications for every freshman vacancy.

Additional information may be obtained from:

Jeffrey C. Mincey
Director of Admissions
Grove City College
100 Campus Drive
Grove City, Pennsylvania 16127-2104

Phone: 724-458-2100
Fax: 724-458-3395
E-mail: admissions@gcc.edu
Web site: http://www.gcc.edu
　　　　http://on.fb.me/grovecity_coll (Facebook)

A view of the campus at Grove City College.

GUILFORD COLLEGE
GREENSBORO, NORTH CAROLINA

The College

Founded in 1837 as the Quaker New Garden Boarding School, Guilford College, (www.guilford.edu) is located on 340 wooded acres in Greensboro, North Carolina. Guilford is among the oldest coeducational colleges in the nation and has a long-standing history of commitment to the individual student and to Quaker values. Guilford College draws on Quaker and liberal arts traditions to prepare men and women for a lifetime of learning, work, and social responsibility dedicated to the betterment of the world.

Guilford's 2,688 students, aged 16 to 72, come from more than forty-five states and nineteen countries. The College's size ensures the academic community's commitment to personalized education (95 percent of classes have fewer than 30 students) while embracing academic diversity. Students are encouraged to take an active part in extracurricular activities on campus, including seminars and lecture series, interest and service clubs, and wide-ranging cultural opportunities, as well as a program of intercollegiate athletics and intramurals for both men and women. The Student Union, a student organization, sponsors many of the social, recreational, and cultural programs offered at the College. Many students participate in a variety of community service projects and volunteer programs.

The Bryan Distinguished Visiting Professorship in the Arts, Humanities, and Public Affairs at Guilford College (www.guilford.edu/bryanseries) brings to campus individuals who are widely regarded as experts in their field. Past speakers include former President Bill Clinton, Mikhail Gorbachev, Madeleine Albright, Cokie Roberts, Archbishop Desmond Tutu, David Gregory, and Sidney Poitier, among others. Guilford College students attend Bryan Series lectures free of charge.

Guilford's intercollegiate athletic teams (www.guilford.edu/athletics) compete at the NCAA Division III level and in the Old Dominion Athletic Conference (ODAC). The sports include women's basketball, cross-country, lacrosse, soccer, softball, swimming, tennis, track, and volleyball, as well as men's baseball, basketball, cross-country, football, golf, lacrosse, soccer, tennis, and track. Sports programs are coupled with special academic opportunities in sports medicine, sport management, and physical education. Guilford's athletic facilities include basketball courts, cardio and weight-training facilities, racquetball courts, and additional multipurpose courts.

At Guilford College, the commitment to sustainability is woven into the fabric of the institution. Guildford believes it is important not only to conserve energy and resources, but also to educate the community as to how it can integrate green practices into every aspect of life. The College leads by example to ensure that every student has a lifelong appreciation for environmental stewardship.

Location

A city of 245,000 people, Greensboro is located midway between Washington, D.C., and Atlanta, Georgia. The greater metropolitan area has a population of approximately 1.3 million. Greensboro is the home of six colleges and universities, with a total student enrollment of approximately 40,000. Guilford participates in an academic consortium with the other institutions. Two interstate highways serve the city, and the Piedmont Triad International Airport is less than 5 miles from campus. Numerous historic sites as well as local, state, and national parks are within day-trip distance of the College. Greensboro's central location in the state allows easy access to the state's beautiful beaches and to several major ski areas in the mountains. The amenities of life in the Southeast—climate, pace, and friendliness—coupled with rich cultural opportunities and sound economic growth make the Sun Belt an attractive area in which to study and live.

Majors and Degrees

Guilford College offers B.A. or B.S. degrees (www.guilford.edu/academics) in accounting, African-American studies, art, biology, business management, chemistry, community and justice studies, computer information systems, computing and information technology, criminal justice, economics, education studies, English, environmental studies, exercise and sports studies, forensic biology, French, forensic accounting, geology and earth sciences, German, German studies, health sciences, history, integrative studies, international studies, life sciences, mathematics, music, peace and conflict studies, philosophy, physics, political science, psychology, religious studies, sociology/anthropology, Spanish, sport management, sports medicine, theater studies, and women's studies. The B.F.A. degree is offered in art. Also offered is a Bachelor of Music degree.

Concentrations are available in accounting, African-American studies, African studies, anthropology, applied ethics, astronomy, business, business law, chemistry, communications, community studies, computing and information technology, criminal justice, dance, earth science, East Asian studies, economics, education studies, English, environmental studies, field biology, forensic science, French language and society, German language and society, history, human resource management, integrated science, international business management, international political economy, interpersonal communication, Japanese language and society, Latin American studies, mathematics for the sciences, medieval/early modern studies, money and finance, music, nonprofit management, organizational communication, peace and conflict studies, philosophy, philosophy of mathematics, physics, political science, psychology, Quaker studies, religious studies, sociology, Spanish language and society, sport administration, sport marketing, theater studies, visual arts, and women's studies.

Most recently, Guilford College has entered into an agreement with University of North Carolina at Greensboro to offer an accelerated Master of Business Administration (M.B.A.) degree. Preprofessional programs are offered in dentistry, law, medicine, ministry, and veterinary science.

Academic Programs

Each student works closely with a faculty adviser to select courses that meet individual educational and career goals. Thirty-two semester courses are required for graduation, eight of which are generally in the major field of study. Required courses are few but represent a distribution over the principal fields of the arts and sciences. Flexible requirements allow for interdisciplinary and double majors.

Incoming first-year students and transfer students participate in an orientation program that includes computer training, learning skills, academic advising, self-awareness workshops, and outdoor experiences.

Independent studies, off-campus internships, and off-campus seminars are open to all students. An expanded honors program includes a variety of honors courses for students with exceptional academic credentials and motivation. One pass/fail elective course may be taken each semester.

Entering students may waive courses through Advanced Placement (AP) examinations in English, history, laboratory science, mathematics, and foreign languages. Advanced placement requires an AP score of 3 or better or a general CLEP score of 500 or better; credit requires an AP score of 4 or better or a general CLEP score of 550 or better. Subject CLEP scores must be at least 50 for advanced placement and at least 55 for credit.

Guilford College has a two-semester calendar. The first semester ends before winter break and the second semester ends in early May.

Off-Campus Programs

Semester abroad programs (www.guilford.edu/studyabroad) enable students to study in China, England, France, Germany, Ghana, Greece, Ireland, Italy, Japan, Mexico, the Netherlands, Scotland, Spain, and Wales, as well as a variety of other locations. Students can choose Guilford-led programs or those managed by affiliated partners like the School for Field Studies, the Foundation for International Education, or the School for International Training. A full year of academic credit for study in Japan is available through a cooperative program with International Christian University in Tokyo.

Guilford participates in two consortia that allow open registration in eight area colleges and universities without additional fees. Other member schools are Bennett College, Elon University, Greensboro College, Guilford Technical Community College, High Point University, North Carolina A&T State University, and the University of North Carolina at Greensboro.

An on-campus program director assists students who wish to study abroad. An internship director helps place students who wish to study elsewhere in the United States. Course credit is given for all approved off-campus study. The Washington Semester in Washington, D.C., supplements the academic program and helps students develop professional skills and career potential through internships with the federal government, lobbying organizations, or public agencies.

Internships may be done in any discipline. Locally, students may pursue internships as part of their academic and career development in business, education, government, health services, law, medicine, scientific research, and social services. In addition, the Guilford College Career Development Office is focused on assisting graduates as they pursue internships, jobs, and graduate school. Career Development services are a lifetime benefit for alums.

Academic Facilities

Guilford's stately Georgian-style buildings house classrooms, a spacious auditorium, the library, student center, administrative offices, and residence halls. The state-of-the-art 65,000-square-foot Frank Family Science Center features fourteen laboratories (with twenty-four workstations each), 1,600 computer connections, a rooftop observatory with a computer-driven telescope, and a 150-seat multipurpose auditorium/planetarium. Multiple studio spaces are available to students in the fine arts.

Guilford's Hege Library is one of the three largest private libraries in North Carolina. The library contains 250,000 volumes and includes an art gallery, a media center, and the only Friends Historical Collection in the Southeast. Hege Library is fully automated and is linked to buildings across the entire campus. Students also have library privileges at six colleges within 20 miles that have an additional 1.3 million volumes.

Bauman Telecommunications Center houses two computer-equipped classrooms, faculty offices, and three computer labs with ninety-one personal computers. In addition, there are 200 public terminals in the Center and other terminals in academic buildings around the campus. Guilford's campus is completely wireless. In addition, satellite connections make it possible to bring in foreign language programming from around the world. Guilford offers state-of-the-art computers in its multimedia learning center for cultures and languages. Most residential students have PCs in their rooms connected to the College network.

Costs

Basic expenses for the 2011–12 academic year are $30,430 for tuition and fees, and $8270 for room and board. Personal expenses, book costs, and transportation expenses vary according to individual need.

Financial Aid

Guilford College tries to meet the demonstrated financial need (www.guilford.edu/finaid) of all students, as determined by the Free Application for Federal Student Aid (FAFSA). More than $32 million in scholarships, loans, grants, and work-study opportunities was awarded to students last year. Academic scholarships are awarded on a competitive basis. Guilford offers several academic merit-based and special-interest scholarship programs. Approximately 90 percent of last year's student body received some form of merit-based or need-based assistance. The average need-based award was more than $25,416 a year per recipient. The average merit-based award was $6820.

Faculty

Guilford has 136 full-time faculty members. The College seeks faculty members who value the sense of community and concern for individuals that are part of Guilford's heritage. The student-faculty ratio is currently 16:1. The average class size is 19.

Student Government

Guilford entrusts its students with responsibility for governing their own actions and furthering the best interests of the entire College community. The student Community Senate is composed of representatives from residence halls and the day-student organization, a member of the administration, and 2 faculty members. Students serve on all faculty and administrative committees and on the College's Board of Trustees and Alumni Board.

Admission Requirements

As one of the oldest coeducational institutions in the nation, Guilford takes the commitment to academics and the liberal arts seriously. To that end, the Admission Committee (www.guilford.edu/admission) uses a holistic method of application evaluation. Each applicant is considered on an individual basis. Students are encouraged to challenge themselves within their high school environment, both in and out of the classroom. While the majority of applicants submit some form of standardized test scores (ACT or SAT), students have the option of submitting a portfolio of written work in lieu of standardized test scores. The Guilford College community is full of active and involved citizens. The evaluation process seeks to continue to admit students that bring a diverse variety of backgrounds and interests to the College. Interviews, although not required, are available so that the applicant can become better acquainted with Guilford and so that the admission staff can better evaluate the candidate. Guilford is competitive with respect to admissions.

Application and Information

Admission plans (www.guilford.edu/apply) include early action and regular decision. Early action I applicants must apply by November 15 and are notified by December 15. Early action II applicants must apply by January 15 and are notified by February 15. The regular decision priority deadline is February 15, and applicants are notified by April 1. After February 15, applications are considered on a space-available basis. Candidates admitted for both early action and regular decision must reply to their offers of admission by May 1.

Early entrance applicants are considered after their junior year of high school. They must have an outstanding academic record and must be sufficiently mature socially to adjust to college life.

Transfer candidates should apply for admission by December 1 for the spring semester and by June 1 for the fall semester.

The priority deadline for applying for financial aid is March 1.

The Admission Office is open for visits (www.guilford.edu/visit) Monday through Saturday during the academic year. During the summer, the Admission Office is open for visits Monday through Friday. Guilford College encourages students to visit for a campus tour. More than a classroom education, the Guilford experience is designed to stimulate the whole person and provide the critical thinking that will help today's students take their place as leaders who will guide tomorrow.

For further information and application forms for admission and financial aid, students should contact:

Admission Office
Guilford College
5800 West Friendly Avenue
Greensboro, North Carolina 27410
Phone: 336-316-2100
      800-992-7759 (toll-free)
E-mail: admission@guilford.edu
Web site: http://www.guilford.edu

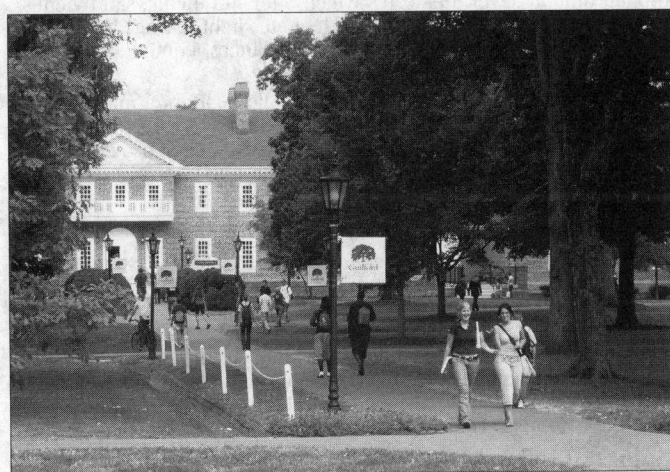

The Quad at Guilford College.

GWYNEDD-MERCY COLLEGE
GWYNEDD VALLEY, PENNSYLVANIA

Gwynedd-Mercy College
BRINGING *FUTURES* INTO *FOCUS*

The College

Founded by the Sisters of Mercy, Gwynedd-Mercy College (GMC) is a Catholic college offering a strong foundation in the liberal arts. For more than sixty years, Gwynedd-Mercy College has been "Bringing Futures Into Focus" by preparing students to become top professionals in the fields of allied health professions, arts and sciences, business, education, and nursing. GMC offers more than forty associate, bachelor's, and master's degree programs on a full- and part-time basis. GMC's academic distinction lies in the intersection of excellent programs in health care, education, and business administration, which prepare students to become leaders in the region's powerful and growing life sciences industry.

Located just 30 minutes from Philadelphia and with an enrollment of nearly 2,700 students, Gwynedd-Mercy College is large enough to offer a vibrant campus life but small enough that professors can develop mentoring relationships with students. The College educates students in the Mercy tradition of service to society, preparing graduates who not only are recruited for jobs but also create lives and careers with deep meaning. In the 2001 edition of *U.S. News & World Report*'s "Best Colleges," Gwynedd-Mercy College ranked in the first tier of its category, in part because of its high graduation and retention rates.

Gwynedd-Mercy College has nineteen NCAA Division III athletic teams, including baseball, basketball, cheerleading, cross-country, field hockey, indoor/outdoor track and field, lacrosse, soccer, softball, tennis, and volleyball. The men's baseball and men's and women's basketball teams have won various championships. The College also offers a variety of intramural sports. The field hockey, soccer, lacrosse, and track and field teams compete at the College's new Outdoor Athletic Complex, which offers a turf field and Olympic-size track.

Students are encouraged to participate in activities and student government so that they can socialize with friends, develop talents, and build leadership skills. The College offers more than thirty clubs and organizations, including the drama club, campus ministry, a nationally renowned choir, the yearbook staff, and social committees. Students can write for the College newspaper, the *Gwynmercian*, which has received a first-place rating with special merit from the American Scholastic Press Association. Through the on-campus chapter of the Mercy Works Program, students can help the poor with fund-raising efforts and adopt-a-family programs at the Thanksgiving and Christmas holidays. Some students decide to give a year of service after graduation to Mercy Volunteer Corps' nationwide outreach program.

On campus, students can choose from four residence halls for rooming and dine at several eateries which offer full meals, sandwiches, pizza, salads, breakfast and coffee. The Late Night Lounge has events every weekend, including movie nights, dances, comedians, bingo, rock band competitions, and game parties.

At the graduate level, Gwynedd-Mercy College offers a master's degree program in education (educational administration, reading, school counseling, special education, and a Master Teacher program) and nursing (nurse educator, nurse practitioner, and clinical nurse specialist).

Location

Gwynedd-Mercy's idyllic 160-acre campus is located in Gwynedd Valley, Pennsylvania, a suburb 20 miles from downtown Philadelphia. Old City, South Street, and sports arenas are a 25- to 30-minute car or train ride from the campus. The College is situated just minutes from several major highways, including the Pennsylvania Turnpike. In addition to the vibrant city life of Philadelphia, students can travel to the New Jersey beaches or the Pocono Mountains, which are only 2 hours from the campus.

Majors and Degrees

Gwynedd-Mercy offers baccalaureate degrees in accounting, behavioral/social gerontology, biology, business administration, business education, communication, computer information technology, criminal justice, elementary education, English, history, human services,

mathematics, nursing, psychology, sociology, and special education. Seven certification options are available through the School of Education.

Associate in Science degrees are awarded in the allied health fields of cardiovascular technology, health information technology, and respiratory care. Associate degrees are also granted in accounting, business administration, computer programming, liberal studies, natural science, and nursing.

Academic Programs

The school year is divided into two semesters, and most baccalaureate degree programs require the completion of a minimum of 125 credit hours. GMC maintains a strong liberal arts component in all of its degree programs. Whether the student chooses to major in one of the liberal arts or to pursue a professionally oriented degree, courses are required in language, literature and the fine arts, humanities, and behavioral, social, and natural sciences. Students have access to the Academic Resource Center for free class tutoring and assistance with improving their writing skills.

Individualized internships and work-experience programs are available and recommended in all majors to give students firsthand experience in their chosen major. Nearby Fortune 500 companies offer a variety of experiences to students in business and accounting. TAP, the Teacher Assistant Program, places every education major in the classroom one day a week beginning in the freshman year. All allied health and nursing programs require clinical experience. The 2-2 programs—those with an associate degree to bachelor's degree progression—offer allied health and nursing students the opportunity to gain employment in their field while continuing toward the baccalaureate degree. The School of Business maintains a successful work-experience semester. Through this paid internship, students earn credit while gaining valuable experience in challenging positions.

Students are encouraged to develop a global perspective through various study-abroad opportunities. In June of 2010, the College launched a study-abroad program to Brescia, Italy. During the month-long program, students took courses in Italian language, culture, and philosophy; rode bikes to get around town; and toured Italy on weekends.

Off-Campus Programs

The excellent on-campus laboratory facilities are extended by affiliations with more than 200 hospitals and health-care agencies in Pennsylvania, New Jersey, and Delaware, where students may complete their clinical experience. Merck provides a one-semester industrial laboratory experience for qualified biology majors. Gwynedd-Mercy College maintains a close relationship with nearby companies, including Johnson & Johnson, McNeil, and Sun Company, for work-experience programs.

Academic Facilities

Gwynedd-Mercy has expanded its physical facilities as its student enrollment has increased. The Sister Isabelle Keiss Center for Health and Science houses the Schools of Nursing and Allied Health Professions and the Division of Natural Sciences. The 50,000-square-foot state-of-the-art facility offers laboratories for areas such as nursing skills, respiratory care, cardiovascular technology, radiation therapy, health information technology, organic chemistry, and microbiology. The College's Griffin Complex houses the College's Student Union—which is equipped with a game room, full gymnasium and track, racquetball court, and weight room. The College offers four residence halls that house 40 percent of the school population. Theaters include the Julia Ball Auditorium, a small in-the-round theater, and a TV production studio. The Student Technology Center is equipped with personal computers and printers and the latest software for student use. The Valie Genuardi Hobbit House, a private school for preschoolers where students in the School of Education are trained, is situated on campus.

Costs

The 2010–11 academic-year tuition (two semesters) for full-time students (12 to 18 credits per semester) was $25,160. The tuition for allied health and nursing students was $26,660. Room and board were, on average, $9400. Professional liability fees for students enrolled in clinical components and lab fees are extra.

Financial Aid

Gwynedd-Mercy's financial aid program is designed to provide financial assistance to academically qualified students whose resources are inadequate to meet the costs of attending the College. The student Financial Aid Committee endeavors to assist as many students as possible, using Gwynedd-Mercy funds as well as federal, state, and other available funds. Aid is awarded on the basis of demonstrated financial need, academic proficiency, and responsible campus citizenship.

A financial aid packet is sent, with instructions, to those who request it on their application form. High school students should request the Free Application for Federal Student Aid (FAFSA) from their guidance office. In 2010–11, 91 percent of Gwynedd-Mercy College full-time students received some form of financial aid. March 15 is the deadline for freshmen entering in the fall semester. The deadline for Academic Scholarships is February 15.

Faculty

The student-faculty ratio is 13:1, allowing for personal contact, advising, and after-class instruction. This is a widely acknowledged strength of the GMC experience. For nursing students in the clinical setting, there are never more than 8 students to 1 clinical adviser; in the allied health programs, there often is one-to-one instruction. The quality of teaching is enhanced by the diversified interests of the faculty. The 181 faculty members teach both day and evening classes, allowing students the greatest flexibility in scheduling. Free tutoring is available in all disciplines.

Student Government

All students are encouraged to take part in the responsibilities of student government. This student participation and shared responsibility for the welfare of the College are promoted through a framework of committees. The student government president and 3 other students are members of the College Council, which is responsible for the continuing self-evaluation of the College and policy formation. In addition, students share membership in the Educational Planning Committee, Faculty/Student Committee, Financial Aid Committee, and Library Committee.

Admission Requirements

Admission to Gwynedd-Mercy College is based on a student's high school record, rank in class, SAT or ACT scores, counselor's recommendation, and choice of major. Entrance requirements vary with the program. The rolling admission policy allows the student to be informed of the admission decision within two to three weeks after submitting their application.

GMC awards College credit for satisfactory completion of Advanced Placement courses. The exam score must be 3 or above.

A minimum 2.0 grade point average (on a 4.0 scale) is generally required to transfer from another college. Gwynedd-Mercy College does, however, retain the right to require a higher GPA for admission to some programs.

GMC selects all students on the basis of academic achievement and does not discriminate on the basis of race, religion, gender, handicap, or sexual orientation.

Application and Information

All prospective applicants are urged to visit the campus to meet and talk with an admission counselor, a dean, or a program director. To apply for admission, applicants should complete an application form and submit it to the admissions office along with the required nonrefundable $25 application fee. The fee is waived for students who apply online at http://www.gmc.edu. First-time freshmen must also submit an official high school transcript or equivalency certificate; a written recommendation from a principal, teacher, guidance counselor, or employer; and results of the SAT or ACT (for recent high school graduates). All applicants should verify that they meet the specific requirements and have the necessary high school prerequisites for admission.

Students who wish to transfer to Gwynedd-Mercy College should complete the application form and submit it to the admissions office along with the required nonrefundable $25 application fee, high school and college transcripts, and a letter of recommendation.

For additional information or to schedule campus tours and visits, students are encouraged to contact the Campus Guest Program Office at campusguestprogram@gmc.edu or 215-641-5514.

Office of Admissions
Gwynedd-Mercy College
1325 Sumneytown Pike
P.O. Box 901
Gwynedd Valley, Pennsylvania 19437-0901

Phone: 800-DIAL-GMC (toll-free)
E-mail: admissions@gmc.edu
Web site: http://www.gmc.edu
http://twitter.com/gwyneddmercycol

Students enjoy the beautiful spring weather on campus between classes.

HAWAI'I PACIFIC UNIVERSITY

HONOLULU, HAWAI'I

The University

Hawai'i Pacific University (HPU) is a private, nonprofit university with a student population of approximately 8,200. HPU is one of the most culturally diverse universities in America with students from all fifty U.S. states and more than 100 countries. Founded in 1965, HPU prides itself on maintaining strong academic programs, small class sizes, individual attention to students, and a diverse faculty and student population. HPU offers more than fifty acclaimed undergraduate programs and thirteen distinguished graduate programs. HPU is recognized as a Best in the West college by the Princeton Review and a Best Buy by *Barron's* business magazine. HPU is accredited by the Western Association of Schools and Colleges, the National League for Nursing Accrediting Commission, and the Council on Social Work Education, to name a few.

The diversity of the HPU student body stimulates learning about other cultures firsthand, both inside and outside of the classroom. There is no majority population at HPU. Students are encouraged to examine the values, customs, traditions, and principles of others to gain a clearer understanding of their own perspectives. HPU students develop friendships with students from throughout the United States and the world and form important connections for success in the global economy of the twenty-first century.

HPU has NCAA Division II intercollegiate sports. Men's athletic programs include baseball, basketball, cross-country, golf, soccer, and tennis. Women's athletics include basketball, cross-country, soccer, softball, tennis, and volleyball.

The housing office at HPU offers many services and living options for students. Residence halls with cafeteria service are available on the windward Hawai'i Loa campus, while off-campus apartments are available in the Honolulu and Waikiki areas for those seeking more independent living arrangements.

Location

Hawai'i Pacific University's main campus in downtown Honolulu provides a fast-paced, exciting urban environment in the heart of the business community. The downtown campus comprises six buildings in the center of Honolulu's business district, and is home to the College of Business Administration and the College of Humanities and Social Sciences. The campus location makes it easy for students to commute to and also find and maintain internship opportunities at neighboring businesses.

Eight miles away, the 135-acre windward Hawai'i Loa campus, which is set in the lush foothills of the Ko'olau mountains, is home to the College of Nursing and Health Sciences and the College of Natural and Computational Sciences. The Hawai'i Loa campus has residence halls, dining commons, the Educational Technology Center, a student center, and outdoor recreational facilities, including a soccer field, tennis courts, a softball field, and an exercise room.

HPU is also affiliated with the Oceanic Institute, a 56-acre aquaculture research facility located at Makapu'u Point on the southeastern coast of O'ahu, Hawai'i. At the facility, undergraduate and graduate students are able to get hands-on experience in marine science. All three sites are conveniently linked by a free shuttle.

Majors and Degrees

Hawai'i Pacific University offers programs that lead to the undergraduate degrees of Bachelor of Arts (B.A.), Bachelor of Science (B.S.), Bachelor of Science in Business Administration (B.S.B.A.), Bachelor of Science in Nursing (B.S.N.), and Bachelor of Social Work (B.S.W.).

Undergraduate majors include accounting, advertising/public relations, anthropology, Asian studies, biochemistry, biology, business (general), business economics, chemistry, communication, computer information systems, computer science, diplomacy and military studies, economics, 4+1 secondary education, elementary education, English, entrepreneurial studies, environmental science, environmental studies, finance, health science, history, human resource development, human resource management, humanities, international business, international relations, international studies, journalism, justice administration, management, marine biology, marketing, mathematics (concentrations in applied math, engineering (3-2), mathematics education, and pure math), multimedia cinematic production, integrated multimedia, nursing, oceanography, political science, prechiropractic, prelaw program, premedical studies, pre–physical therapy, psychology, public administration, social science, social work, sociology, teaching English to speakers of other languages, and travel industry management.

In addition to the undergraduate programs, HPU offers thirteen graduate programs. The Master of Arts (M.A.) is offered in communications, diplomacy and military studies, global leadership and sustainable development, human resource management, organizational change, and teaching English as a second language. The Master of Business Administration (M.B.A.) is available in accounting, e-business, economics, finance, human resource management, information systems, international business, management, marketing, and travel industry management. Other graduate programs include Master of Education in Secondary Education and the Master of Education in Elementary Education (M.Ed.), Master of Science in Information Systems (M.S.I.S.), Master of Science in Marine Science (M.S.M.S.), Master of Science in Nursing (M.S.N.), and Master of Social Work (M.S.W.)

Academic Programs

The baccalaureate student must complete at least 124 semester hours of credit. Forty-five of these credits provide the student with a strong foundation in the liberal arts, while the remaining credits are composed of appropriate upper-division classes in the student's major and related areas. The academic year operates on a semester system, with regular fall and spring semesters as well as shorter sessions, including one winter and three summer sessions. By attending the supplemental summer and winter sessions, a student may complete the baccalaureate degree program in three years. A five-year B.S.B.A./M.B.A. program is also available.

Off-Campus Programs

As part of its emphasis on international education and global citizenship, Hawai'i Pacific University offers study-abroad opportunities that complement and enhance students' academic experience. Study-abroad opportunities are available in Australia, Austria, Brazil, China, France, Germany, Great Britain, Italy, Spain, Sweden, Taiwan, and Thailand. HPU undergraduates and graduates who have completed at least one semester of studies at HPU and intend to complete a degree at HPU are eligible to apply.

The Career Services Center offers a comprehensive education/internship program to further develop students' studies and elevate their career-related position through experience. HPU intertwines academic and cocurricular programs with the world of work so students gain academic credit, work experience, and a salary. HPU students have done co-ops and internships at some of the world's best-known companies and organizations, including American Express Financial Advisors; Deloitte & Touche, LLP; the FBI; Hilton Hotels; Microsoft; Oceanic Institute; Polo Ralph Lauren; and Walt Disney World. The staff at the Career Services Center continues to work with students before and after graduation, assisting with everything from resume writing to job interview preparation.

Academic Facilities

The downtown campus comprises six buildings in the center of Honolulu's business district. One of these buildings is the HPU Frear Center, which houses state-of-the-art classrooms, a communication lab, and a high-tech information systems classroom. HPU's Meader Library provides a multitude of general and specialized resources, including a business reference collection, a National Endowment for the Humanities (NEH) collection, and many online databases and journals. The circulating book collections support communications, computer studies, education, literature, social sciences, and other curriculum areas. Also available are study areas, group study rooms, computer workstations, and wireless Internet. The Tutoring and Testing Center provides free tutoring in all core subjects. The expanded downtown computer lab includes more than 420 computers for student use.

On the suburban and residential windward Hawai'i Loa campus, academic life revolves around the Amos N. Starr and Juliette Montague Cooke Academic Center (AC). The AC houses classrooms; organic chemistry, nuclear magnetic resonance, and regular laboratories; faculty and staff offices; a theater; an art gallery; and the Atherton Library, which includes circulating and reference book collections in the areas of art, history, marine science, nursing, and Hawai'i and the Pacific. Additionally, the library provides access to electronic books (e-books), databases, study rooms, IBM computers, and wireless Internet. Computers are also available for library research, e-mail, and word processing.

HPU is also affiliated with the Oceanic Institute, a major research center specializing in marine biology, marine aquaculture, biotechnology, and ocean resource management. It is located on a 56-acre site at Makapu'u Point on the windward coast of O'ahu, Hawai'i. Learning, internship, and research opportunities for graduates and undergraduates abound in this hands-on learning environment.

Costs

For the 2011–12 academic year, tuition is $16,510 for most majors, while books, health insurance, and other expenses cost approximately $3190. Tuition for marine science majors is $19,400, and tuition for junior- or senior-year nursing majors is $24,070. The cost to live in on-campus residence halls or off-campus apartments is comparable; room and board are $12,230 for a double occupancy room. There is an additional $500 refundable security deposit required for residence halls and off-campus apartments.

Financial Aid

HPU offers most forms of federal financial aid, including student grant and loan programs, as well as loans for parents of dependent students. Over 60 percent of the University's students benefit from federal financial aid programs or a wide range of institutional scholarships. Students should complete the Free Application for Federal Student Aid (FAFSA) to be considered for federal aid programs. While aid can be awarded throughout the academic year, students should complete the application prior to the March 1 priority deadline to be considered for all available funding. Visit http://www.hpu.edu/financialaid for current financial aid and scholarship information.

Faculty

HPU faculty members are renowned for the personal interest they take in each of their students. HPU is proud to offer more than 500 full- and part-time faculty members with outstanding academic and business credentials from around the world, giving HPU students access to a world's worth of knowledge and experiences. A vast majority of HPU faculty members hold the highest degrees in their fields. The student-faculty ratio is 15:1, and the average class size is less than 25.

Student Government

HPU students can join one of the more than 70 student clubs; run for office in the Associated Students of Hawai'i Pacific University (ASHPU), the University's governing body; participate in Army or Air Force ROTC; write for the student newspaper, *Kalamalama*, edit the school's literary journal, *Hawai'i Pacific Review;* or join HPU's stage and pep band or international choral program.

A variety of on-campus activities and events are organized for students by the Student Life Office, including Movie on the Mall, Music on the Mall, intramural sports tournaments, and recreational activities. Annual events include Club Carnival, Welcome Week, Da Freakshow, Halloween Hoopla, and Pacific Bowl.

Admission Requirements

Hawai'i Pacific University seeks students who are motivated and show academic promise. The Admissions Office requires that applicants complete and forward the admission application and their high school transcripts. Transfer students should also submit college transcripts. SAT and/or ACT scores should be submitted if these scores are not posted in their transcripts. First-time freshmen are expected to have a minimum GPA of 2.5 (on a 4.0 scale) in college-preparatory courses. HPU recommends that students complete 4 years of English, 4 years of history or social science, 3 years of math, and 2 years of science. Transfer students with 24 or more postsecondary credits are required to have a GPA of 2.0 or above. For students with less than 24 credits, a combination of college and high school GPA is used.

The marine science and environmental science programs require a GPA of 3.0 or above and 3 years of science, including biology and chemistry (physics is recommended), as well as mathematics through trigonometry (calculus is recommended). Transfer students must demonstrate ability in science and math at the college level. Students not meeting the above criteria are encouraged to enroll at HPU without declaring a major to demonstrate the ability to do college-level work in science and math.

Application and Information

Candidates are notified of admission decisions on a rolling basis, usually within two weeks of receipt of application materials. Early entrance and deferred entrance are available.

For further information and for application materials, students should contact:

Office of Admissions
Hawai'i Pacific University
1164 Bishop Street, Suite 200
Honolulu, Hawai'i 96813
Phone: 808-544-0238
     866-CALL-HPU (toll-free in U.S. and Canada)
Fax: 808-544-1136
E-mail: admissions@hpu.edu
Web site: http://www.hpu.edu/petersonsundergraduate

HIGH POINT UNIVERSITY
HIGH POINT, NORTH CAROLINA

The University

High Point University (HPU) is a dynamic private university with historic ties to the United Methodist Church. At High Point, every student receives an extraordinary education in an inspiring environment with caring people. With 4,200 students, the University is large enough to guarantee high quality and diversity in programs and services yet small enough to enable community among students and faculty and staff members. HPU has a beautiful, 250-acre campus with state-of-the-art facilities in a small, caring environment. In a typical year, students come from forty-six states and fifty-one countries, making the campus a microcosm of the nation and the world, thereby creating an ideal learning environment.

The University fully recognizes its responsibility to provide the best liberal arts education possible, but faculty and staff members recognize that education, as often defined, is not sufficient. Therefore, the University intentionally seeks to provide a holistic education and develop character by encouraging personal responsibility and by inculcating values through curricular and cocurricular programs and services, including a required ethics course, the President's Seminar on Life Skills, and the University chapel, where services are offered each week. Although attendance is voluntary, chapel services are well attended each Wednesday.

In addition to the bachelor's degrees described below, the University offers four master's degrees: the Master of Business Administration (M.B.A.); the Master of Education (M.Ed.) in elementary education, educational leadership, and special education; the Master of Science (M.S.) in international management, management, and sport studies; and the Master of Arts (M.A.) in history, nonprofit management, and strategic communication.

Location

Together, High Point, Greensboro, and Winston-Salem form the Piedmont Triad of North Carolina, a metropolitan area of approximately 1.5 million people. More than 90,000 live in the city of High Point. Both Winston-Salem and Greensboro are within a half-hour drive from the campus, as is the Piedmont Triad International Airport (GSO). Both Raleigh and Charlotte are 1½ hours away, the Appalachian Mountains are 2 hours away, and the Atlantic Ocean and beaches are 3½ hours away.

The region is known nationally and internationally for the quality of its institutions of higher education. A multitude of schools are within a 60-mile radius: Duke University, Davidson College, the University of North Carolina at Chapel Hill, and Wake Forest University, along with twenty-eight other colleges and universities. Such an area is replete with athletic, cultural, recreational, and social activities for young adults.

Majors and Degrees

High Point University offers Bachelor of Arts degrees through the School of Art and Design, the Nido R. Qubein School of Communication, and the School of Education. Bachelor of Science degrees are offered through the Earl N. Phillips School of Business and the School of Health Sciences. The David R. Hayworth College of Arts and Sciences offers both Bachelor of Arts and Bachelor of Science degrees. These schools offer the following majors and concentrations:

The School of Art and Design offers programs in art education, graphic design and digital imaging, home furnishings, interior design, and studio art.

The Earl N. Phillips School of Business offers programs in accounting, business administration, business administration with a concentration in entrepreneurship, and international business.

The Nido R. Qubein School of Communication offers programs in electronic media production, game and interactive media design, journalism, media and popular culture studies, and strategic communication.

The School of Education offers programs in elementary education; secondary education (9–12 licensure) with concentrations in biology, comprehensive science, English, history, and mathematics; special education (K–12 licensure); and special subjects (K–12 licensure) with concentrations in art education, health/physical education, and Spanish.

The School of Health Sciences offers programs in athletic training and exercise science.

The David R. Hayworth College of Arts and Sciences offers programs in actuarial science; biochemistry; biology; chemistry; computer science; criminal justice; English with concentrations in literature and writing; history; human relations; international relations; mathematical economics; mathematics; modern foreign languages with concentrations in French and Francophone studies and Spanish; music with concentrations in instrumental studies, piano/organ, and voice; nonprofit leadership and management; philosophy; physics; political science; psychology; religion; sociology; and theater with concentrations in performance, technical, dramatic writing, and collaborative theater.

Academic Programs

The academic program includes sixty-eight majors administered through the David R. Hayworth College of Arts and Sciences, the Phillips School of Business, the Nido R. Qubein School of Communication, the Wilson School of Commerce, and the School of Education. In addition, the University allows students with well-defined objectives that cannot be satisfied within the regular curriculum to design their own individualized majors. An honors program recognizes and encourages creativity and academic achievement in top academic students.

The curriculum emphasizes the study of the liberal arts in the belief that there is no better way to encourage communication skills, critical thinking, and personal integrity, and that in the process of acquiring these skills, students become self-learners equipped to succeed in life and work.

Within the liberal arts framework, the University offers nine preprofessional programs: dentistry, engineering, law, medicine, ministry, pharmacy, physical therapy, physician assistant studies, and veterinary studies.

The curriculum prepares students to pursue graduate programs consistent with the majors listed above and professional programs beyond the baccalaureate degree in areas that include, but are not limited to, business, dentistry, law, medicine, ministry, pharmacy, physical therapy, physician assistant studies, and sports medicine.

Through the Student Career Intern Program, juniors and seniors at High Point University are able to explore career opportunities outside the classroom. The program enables a student to assume the responsibilities of a regular employee in a local or national business or agency before graduating from High Point, thereby enabling the student to evaluate a career choice prior to graduation.

Students who have completed Advanced Placement courses in high school and who have achieved a score of 4 or 5 on the Advanced Placement tests administered by the College Board may receive credit at High Point University. Applicants may also receive credit for university-parallel courses successfully completed prior to enrollment at High Point, including courses completed while in high school through dual-enrollment or international baccalaureate programs.

Off-Campus Programs

Students may choose to study abroad for a year, a semester, or a summer through the High Point University study-abroad program. The University's affiliation with international study programs administered by other institutions makes it possible for students to study in nearly twenty countries including Australia, England, Fiji, France, Japan, Russia, South Africa, and Spain. Subject to prior approval, transfer credit may be awarded for university-parallel work offered by institutions other than those with which the University has formal affiliation.

Students enrolled at High Point University may cross-register on the campus of any other member institution in the Greater Greensboro Consortium, which includes two state institutions and a women's college.

Academic Facilities

Smith Library, a fully electronically integrated library system, supports all undergraduate and graduate programs. The library contains more than 300,000 print volumes, including more than 50,000 electronic books, and more than 20,000 electronic journals. All electronic resources are accessible online by students and other patrons, both on and off campus.

The Learning Excellence Center, which is located in the library, provides tutoring and other programs designed to facilitate learning. Although over 95 percent of enrolled students own personal computers, more than 500 computers are available for student use in classrooms, laboratories, the library, the University Center, and other locations. A roaming profile enables students to save and access their personal documents from any campus computer, including their personal computers and those provided by the University. Computer laboratories in computer science and mathematics are equipped with Linux-based PCs connected to a Linux computing cluster.

Phillips Hall, opened in August 2007, houses a state-of-the-art School of Business designed after the Harvard School of Business. The Congdon Hall of Science provides science laboratories and modern equipment. The James H. and Jesse E. Millis Athletic and Convocation Center houses a state-of-the-art sports medicine center, along with facilities for physical education that include, but are not limited to, the Aerobic Center, an Olympic-size pool, racquetball courts, and tennis courts. The Charles E. and Pauline Lewis Hayworth Fine Arts Center includes the Pauline Theatre, the Sechrest Art Gallery, galleries for student exhibits, a laboratory for computer graphics, and studios for design, drawing, music, painting, photography, printmaking, and theater. Norton Hall, which was built on campus by the international furnishings industry, is a state-of-the-art facility that houses the Knabusch-Shoemaker International School of Furnishings and Design. The Nido R. Qubein School of Communication opened in fall 2009, with $5 million in television, radio, and video gaming studios. Another recently completed facility is the Plato S. Wilson School of Commerce, which includes a Wall Street–style ticker tape trading room for finance and investing classes, an entrepreneurship center, and many other modern amenities.

Costs

For 2011–12, High Point University's comprehensive fee (including tuition, room, board, and general fees) for full-time boarding students ranges from $37,800 to $41,750, depending upon type of boarding the student chooses.

Financial Aid

Students who require financial assistance should complete the Free Application for Federal Student Aid (FAFSA), which provides an estimate of how much the student and the parents/guardians of dependent students can contribute toward the cost of attending High Point University. The University's Office of Student Financial Services uses the results of the FAFSA to determine the types of assistance available to students. Scholarships, grants, loans, and college work-study are possible sources of support.

Presidential Fellowships, ranging from $9000 to $27,000 per year, are awarded on a competitive basis to academically talented entering freshmen through an application and interview process. The University awards up to 100 High Point fellowships and scholarships in amounts ranging from $2000 to $7000 to entering freshmen annually, also on a competitive basis.

Faculty

High Point University has a student-faculty ratio of 14:1 and an average class size of fewer than 20 students. More than 82 percent of faculty members have earned either the Ph.D. or another terminal degree. Full faculty members teach all classes, and one of the professors in each student's major is his or her adviser. High Point University does not use any graduate students or assistants to teach class. Faculty members routinely interact with students outside of class as well.

Student Government

High Point University intentionally seeks to involve students in campus life through student government; service on University-wide committees; and student activities, including sixteen NCAA Division I athletic teams, fourteen Greek organizations, and more than ninety other campus organizations. In addition, High Point University students annually provide more than 70,000 hours of voluntary service to the community of High Point.

Admission Requirements

Freshman applicants must be graduates of an accredited secondary school and must exhibit satisfactory performance in a college-preparatory curriculum of 18 units, distributed as follows: English, 4; foreign language, 2; mathematics, 3; history, 3; laboratory science, 3; and electives, 3. Freshman applicants must submit their scores on the SAT or the ACT. International applicants should submit both TOEFL and SAT or ACT scores. Campus visits and personal interviews are strongly recommended.

Application and Information

Application forms must be completed online by the student and submitted to the Office of Admissions, along with a nonrefundable $50 processing fee. Official transcripts (high school and college, where applicable) and a Counselor Report Form must be sent directly to the University by the appropriate school official. Students should request that a copy of their SAT, ACT, or TOEFL scores be sent to the Office of Admissions at High Point University by the testing agency. High Point University operates under a deadline admission plan, including early decision and early action. Because enrollment is limited by available residential spaces, early application is encouraged. All requests for application materials and information should be directed to:

Office of Undergraduate Admissions
High Point University
833 Montlieu Avenue
High Point, North Carolina 27262-3598
Phone: 336-841-9216
       800-345-6993 (toll-free)
E-mail: admiss@highpoint.edu
Web site: http://www.highpoint.edu

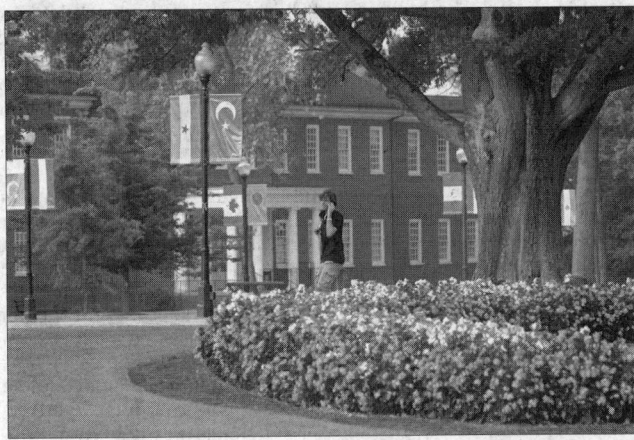

High Point University, which is located on a 250-acre campus, enrolls 4,200 students from forty-six states and fifty-one countries.

HILLSDALE COLLEGE
HILLSDALE, MICHIGAN

The College

Hillsdale College is a private, independent, nonsectarian institution of higher learning founded in 1844 by men and women who described themselves as "grateful to God for the inestimable blessings" resulting from civil and religious liberty and as "believing that the diffusion of learning is essential to the perpetuity of those blessings." The College has maintained institutional independence since its founding by refusing to accept aid from or control by federal authorities. Far-reaching private support from a national constituency has enabled Hillsdale to continue its trusteeship of the intellectual and spiritual inheritance derived from the Judeo-Christian faith and Greco-Roman culture.

The undergraduate enrollment for fall 2010 was 1,400, of whom 48 percent were men. The College draws students from forty-eight states and eight foreign countries. Approximately 40 percent of students are from Michigan. The entering freshman class in 2010 had an average high school grade point average of 3.75 and mean ACT (29) and SAT (1970) scores well above national averages. Hillsdale students are housed in dormitories, fraternity and sorority houses, and various off-campus dwellings. Single and double rooms are available on campus; there are no coed dormitories. Each College-owned residence hall is supervised by a resident director and resident advisers. All freshmen (except commuters) are required to live on campus; upper-class students seeking to live off campus must apply to the dean of men or dean of women for this privilege.

Hillsdale's Charger athletes compete in eleven intercollegiate NCAA Division II varsity sports as part of the Great Lakes Intercollegiate Athletic Conference (GLIAC). In the past 20 years, the College has produced 191 athletic and academic All-Americans, 25 conference champions, and seventeen teams that have finished tenth or better nationally. An active intramural program is also available. Four national fraternities, three national sororities, and more than 100 other social, academic, spiritual, and service organizations provide Hillsdale students with a diverse array of cocurricular opportunities. A resident drama troupe and dance company, a bagpipe and drum corps, a concert choir, and chamber chorale, a jazz program with big band and combos, instrumental chamber ensembles from string quartets to percussion ensemble, and a College-community orchestra and band constitute the College's performing arts organizations.

Special student services provided by the College include career planning and placement counseling, academic advising and tutoring, and a health service staffed by a physician and a resident nurse.

Location

Hillsdale College is located amidst the hills, dales, and lakes of south-central Michigan. The Indiana and Ohio turnpikes are each 30 minutes away, and the College is within close reach of such metropolitan areas as Detroit, Chicago, Cleveland, Toledo, Ft. Wayne, and Indianapolis. The town of Hillsdale is a county seat with a population of 10,000. Stores, churches, restaurants, and movie theaters are all within walking distance of the campus.

Majors and Degrees

Hillsdale awards Bachelor of Arts and Bachelor of Science degrees in accounting, art, biochemistry, biology, chemistry, classical studies, computational mathematics, economics, education, English, financial management, French, German, Greek, history, Latin, marketing/management, mathematics, music, philosophy, physical education, physics, political science, psychology, religion, Spanish, speech, and theater. Interdisciplinary majors in American studies, Christian studies, comparative literature, European studies, international studies in business and foreign language, political economy, and sociology and social thought are also available. Preprofessional programs are offered in allied health services (including optometry, physical therapy, nursing, and medical technology), dentistry, engineering, environmental sciences, forestry, law, medicine, osteopathy, theology, and veterinary medicine. Hillsdale also offers 2-2 and 3-2 cooperative programs in engineering.

Academic Programs

Hillsdale operates on a two-semester schedule, with the fall term beginning in late August and ending in mid-December and the spring term beginning in mid-January and ending in mid-May. Two 3-week summer sessions are also offered.

The College believes that a sound classical liberal arts education includes study in the humanities, natural sciences, and social sciences, and each student is required to complete a structured core of courses in these areas. All students declare a major by the end of the sophomore year. To graduate, students must complete a minimum 124 hours of course work and fulfill the requirements of at least one major field. It is not unusual for a student to complete two majors or a major and a minor. Each baccalaureate program is based on the completion of four years of study in the liberal arts. The B.A. program includes a foreign language proficiency requirement. The B.S. program requires additional studies in mathematics and the natural sciences.

The honors program enables exceptionally talented students interested in an interdisciplinary community of learning to develop their intellectual potential through an accelerated college core and honors seminars in the junior and senior years. Discussions, guest lectures, and travel opportunities contribute to the social cohesiveness of the group. All honors students complete a senior thesis on an interdisciplinary topic of their choosing.

The Center for Constructive Alternatives conducts four weeklong symposia during the academic year and is one of the largest college lecture series in America. These programs, dealing with themes ranging from historical to political, business, science, and the arts, are of major importance in the intellectual life of the College. Each brings to the campus distinguished scholars and public figures of national and international renown. All students are required to enroll in two full seminars for credit prior to graduation, one in the first two years and one in the final two years of the curriculum.

Off-Campus Programs

For thirty-five years, the Washington Hillsdale Internship Program (WHIP) has provided students the opportunity to participate in full-time, academically intensive internships in the nation's capital. The program has been significantly bolstered with the 2008 establishment of the Hillsdale College Allan P. Kirby, Jr. Center for Constitutional Studies and Citizenship in Washington, D.C. Past interns and fellows have been placed in locations as challenging and rewarding as the U.S. House of Representatives, the U.S. Senate, the White House, various think tanks including the Heritage Foundation, news and media outlets, national security agencies, lobbying firms, international trade and relations organizations, and private sector companies.

Through the College's affiliations with the Center for Medieval and Renaissance Studies and the Oxford Study Abroad Program, Hillsdale students are able to study abroad for a summer or a year at one of the more than thirty colleges of Oxford University. Hillsdale offers a summer business program in cooperation with Regent's College in London, England, and the opportunity to study subject areas ranging from ancient history to theoretical physics at the University of St. Andrews in St. Andrews, Scotland. Science students benefit from Hillsdale's 685-acre field research laboratory in northern Michigan, as well as from a marine biology program in the Florida Keys, internship opportunities with the Omaha Zoo, and a summer research program in South Africa. Foreign language students frequently study abroad in Argentina, France, Germany, and Spain. Qualified individual students who wish to study in another country for a semester or a year are assisted by their faculty adviser and the registrar in planning a program that enables them to gain academic credit as well as take full advantage of their experience.

Academic Facilities

The Hillsdale College Mossey Library is a three-floor facility with a collection of more than 440,000 volumes. In addition to the main study and research collections, the Library also contains a number of rare and special holdings, including the Ludwig von Mises, Russell Kirk,

Richardson Heritage, and Richard Weaver collections. Connected to other Michigan libraries through MelCat, and with college libraries nationwide via interlibrary loan, students have access to most any material necessary for on-campus research. Numerous individual study areas and group study rooms are available for students, as well as computer research terminals.

Lane and Kendall Halls at the front of campus serve as the primary academic facilities in the humanities and contain classroom space and faculty offices, as well as a special laboratory for experimental psychology. The Strosacker Science Center houses the departments of biology, chemistry, and physics. The Joseph H. Moss Family Laboratory Wing, completed in 2008, is a 17,000-square-foot addition that includes a microbiology/cell biology lab, anatomy/physiology lab with human cadaver access, conservation genetics lab, water lab, greenhouse, and organic/general chemistry labs. The 32,000-square-foot Herbert Henry Dow Science Building provides additional classrooms, research laboratories, animal rooms, and a computer lab. The Mary Randall Preschool is a circular laboratory school in which nursery school children are taught by students specializing in early childhood education and psychology. Experts in the field have called this building "a model for the nation." The Hillsdale Academy, a K–12 private model school, provides additional opportunities for classroom observation.

The Roche Sports Complex is a facility available to varsity athletes and the general student body alike. The building houses the 60,000-square-foot Jesse Philips Arena, which features a six-lane, 200-meter running track and basketball/volleyball court. The building also houses the John "Jack" McAvoy Natatorium for swimming and diving, an exercise physiology and sports medicine facility, three racquetball courts, extensive locker room space, and a weight/fitness room. Adjacent is the 7,000-seat capacity Frank "Muddy" Waters Stadium, which features an artificial surface football field; all-weather, Olympic-quality eight-lane running track; outdoor tennis courts; and fields for soccer, baseball, and women's softball.

The Sage Center for the Arts is home to the departments of art, theater, and speech. This 47,000-square-foot facility contains studios, classroom space, an exhibition gallery, a prop- and scene-construction shop, a sound studio, graphics lab, black box theatre, and the Markel Auditorium, a 353-seat performance hall (with orchestra pit). Completed in 2003, the 32,809-square-foot Howard Music Hall houses office, studio, classroom, rehearsal, and performance space for the John E. N. and Dede Howard Department of Music. Notable features include the McNamara Rehearsal Hall, Conrad Recital Hall, and studio space for percussion and jazz studies. Lower-level practice rooms are available to students during business hours without reservation.

Dedicated in January 2008, the 53,000-square-foot Grewcock Student Union is the center of student life. The two-story structure houses the cafeteria, bookstore, student mail center, offices for student activities and publications, a lounge with a 100-inch flat screen television, a formal lounge and conference room, AJ's Café, and a game area. The entire building is wireless, and any Hillsdale student can check out a laptop at the main desk. Couches around the massive two-story fireplace are popular study spots in the colder months.

Costs

Annual tuition for the 2011–12 academic year is $20,760, room is $4130, board is $4180, and mandatory fees are $540. Books, supplies, and personal expenses (including travel, recreation, and clothing) are estimated at $2800 per year.

Financial Aid

Financial aid at Hillsdale is available in many forms. Academic scholarships are awarded on a competitive basis, regardless of financial need, to students who rank in the top 10 percent of their high school class and have standardized test scores in the top 10 percent according to national test norms. The priority deadline for academic scholarship consideration is January 1. The application for admission also serves as the Hillsdale application for merit-based aid. Athletic scholarships are available on a competitive basis in men's baseball and football; men's and women's basketball, track, and cross-country; and women's swimming and volleyball. The departments of art and music also award a select number of scholarships based on strength of portfolio/audition. To apply for aid on the basis of financial need, students are required to file Hillsdale's Confidential Family Financial Statement (CFFS) in January or February of the year of prospective enrollment at Hillsdale. Grants and loans are available from the College. Students may defer payment of up to $500 per semester while working on campus.

Faculty

The faculty consists of 117 full-time members. No classes are taught by graduate students. The size and closeness of the College community enable personal attention and faculty mentorship inside the classroom and during office visits after class. Each student has a faculty adviser for core and major coursework who directs the program of study and provides academic and career counseling. Hillsdale's faculty considers teaching their first priority. Many faculty members also engage in research and scholarly writing, supported by summer and sabbatical leaves funded by the College, and are often invited to comment on the national scene in lecture programs and media outlets.

Student Government

Hillsdale's student government and campus organizations offer students special opportunities to develop leadership skills that enrich both their collegiate experience and lives after graduation. The governing organization of the student body is the Student Federation, which is composed of 18 elected representatives. This group funds student organizations, sponsors all-College entertainment, and acts upon matters of concern to the student community. The Men's Council and Women's Council serve as legislative and judicial bodies within their respective domains in cooperation with members of the administration. The Leadership Workshop, which works closely with the administration, faculty, and community organizations, provides an additional forum for students to cultivate and perfect their leadership skills.

Admission Requirements

Admission is a privilege extended to students who will benefit from, and contribute to, the academic, social, and spiritual environments of the College. Important determinants for admission are intellectual curiosity, ambition, leadership, and volunteerism. Accordingly, grade point average, test scores, class rank, strength of curriculum, extracurricular activities, interviews, self-evaluations, writing samples in the form of two essays, and recommendations are all reviewed carefully and are important in the evaluation process. Although some factors are necessarily more important than others, seldom is any single criterion, however important, decisive.

Transfer students must submit the standard application, including the high school record, SAT or ACT scores, transcripts from all colleges previously attended, and a transfer form from the dean of students of the most recent college attended. Applications by transfers are evaluated similarly to nontransfers.

Candidates for admission from other countries follow the regular entrance procedures. Students who come from a non-English-speaking country must demonstrate proficiency in English by satisfactory performance on the Test of English as a Foreign Language (TOEFL) or the Michigan Test of English Proficiency or at an ESL Center.

Application and Information

Students may apply to Hillsdale College any time after the completion of the junior year of high school. A formal application includes a completed application form accompanied by a nonrefundable fee of $35 (free if submitted online) and all required credentials. Application plans include Early Decision (November 15), Early Action (December 15), and Regular Decision (February 15). Hillsdale College has been distinguished since its founding in 1844 by voluntarily adhering to a nondiscriminatory policy regarding race, religion, sex, and national or ethnic origin—long before the government began regulating such matters.

All records and forms should be mailed to:

Admissions Office
Hillsdale College
Hillsdale, Michigan 49242-1298

Phone: 517-607-2327
Fax: 517-607-2223
E-mail: admissions@hillsdale.edu
Web site: http://www.hillsdale.edu

HOFSTRA UNIVERSITY
HEMPSTEAD, NEW YORK

The University

It's more than a degree. It's a superior education, access to exemplary resources and facilities, and a network of peers and mentors. At Hofstra University, students find their edge through career-enhancing, life-shaping experiences and possibilities.

Hofstra is a dynamic private institution where students can find their strengths and discover their futures. With extensive academic offerings, an outstanding faculty, and state-of-the-art facilities and technology, Hofstra's resources rival those of any major university in the nation. And with an average undergraduate class size of just 21 and a student-faculty ratio of 14:1, Hofstra students receive personal attention from faculty members who lead highly interactive classes while promoting critical thinking.

Hofstra University is included in the Princeton's Review's listings of Best 373 Colleges and Best Northeastern Colleges (2011), *U.S. News & World Report*'s America's Best Business Schools (2010), and the *Fiske Guide to Colleges* (2011). Hofstra is also ranked by *Forbes* magazine. Among private Long Island colleges, Hofstra is currently the only institution of academic excellence that grants the Phi Beta Kappa distinction, and it has the largest number of students going on to pursue graduate and professional courses of study. In addition, Hofstra North Shore–LIJ School of Medicine at Hofstra University will admit its first class in fall 2011.

At Hofstra, students choose from about 140 undergraduate and 150 graduate program options in liberal arts and sciences, business, engineering, communication, education, law, health and human services, and honors studies. Hofstra also offers more than 100 dual-degree programs, giving students the opportunity to earn both a graduate and undergraduate degree in less time than if each degree was pursued separately. More information about Hofstra's program options is available at http://hofstra.edu/academics or http://hofstra.edu/dualdegree.

Learning and growth takes place both inside and outside the classroom. Celebrating seventy-five years of academic excellence, Hofstra University hosts more than 500 cultural events each year, drawing together scholars, business leaders, authors, celebrities, health-care professionals, politicians, and journalists from around the world. Hofstra's cultural events foster a connection between course work and extracurricular interests, and facilitate personal, academic and professional growth among members of the University's student body. Students can choose from clubs, organizations, and intramural sports as diverse as the Geology Club, Danceworks, the Hofstra Organization of Latin Americans, and Quidditch.

Hofstra University also offers seventeen intercollegiate athletic programs that compete at the NCAA Division I level, comprising eight men's sports (baseball, basketball, cross-country, golf, lacrosse, soccer, tennis, and wrestling) and nine women's sports (basketball, cross-country, field hockey, golf, lacrosse, soccer, softball, tennis, and volleyball). Moreover, the University is home to more than 170 academic, media, multicultural, performance, preprofessional, religious, social, political, and sports clubs and organizations; and 20 active fraternity and sorority chapters.

Hofstra students are given the tools and resources needed to succeed in their future endeavors. Annual alumni surveys consistently show that a large percentage of graduates entering the workforce are employed within six months of receiving their diplomas. Many of the more than 119,000 Hofstra graduates have gone on to find personal success in many fields of endeavor. Outstanding alumni include award-winning film director and producer Francis Ford Coppola, best-selling author Nelson DeMille, and Chief of Vascular Surgery and Professor of Surgery Donna Mendes.

Location

A nationally recognized arboretum with an outdoor sculpture collection of about seventy-five pieces, the Hofstra campus is home to both ivy-covered classroom buildings and sleek, modern buildings. Hofstra University's 115 buildings include state-of-the-art teaching facilities, six theaters, a museum, newly renovated fitness center, and libraries containing 1.2 million print volumes and providing 24/7 electronic access to more than 95,000 journals and electronic books.

Hofstra's suburban campus is just 25 miles from New York City, giving students easy access to a metropolis that beckons with a world of cultural and internship opportunities. Students take advantage of the-aters, museums, concerts and professional sports, as well as the many beneficial internship opportunities the city offers. Broadway shows, the Metropolitan Museum of Art, Madison Square Garden, Chinatown and Little Italy, and Wall Street all are within easy reach.

Students can also explore Long Island, which offers world-class beaches and parks; the Hamptons; sport fishing and boating; Nassau Coliseum, home of the New York Islanders; and conveniently located malls.

Majors and Degrees

The Bachelor of Arts (B.A.) is awarded in African studies, American studies, anthropology, art history, Asian studies, audio/video/film, biology, chemistry, Chinese, Chinese studies, classics, comparative literature and languages, computer science, dance, drama, early childhood and childhood education (with dual major in another discipline), early childhood education (with dual major in another discipline), economics, elementary education (with dual major in another discipline), engineering science, English, English education, film studies and production, fine arts, foreign language education (French, German, Italian, Russian, Spanish), French, geography, geology, German, global studies, Hebrew, history, Ibero-American studies, Italian, Jewish studies, journalism, labor studies, Latin, Latin American and Caribbean studies, liberal arts, linguistics, mass media studies, math education (with a dual major in another discipline), mathematical economics, mathematics, music, philosophy, physics, political science, psychology, public relations, radio production, religion, Russian, science education (biology, chemistry, Earth science, physics), social studies education (with a dual major in another discipline), sociology, Spanish, speech communication and rhetorical studies, speech-language-hearing sciences, urban ecology, video/television, and women's studies.

The Bachelor of Business Administration (B.B.A.) is awarded in accounting, business, business education, entrepreneurship, finance, information technology, international business, legal studies in business, management, marketing, and supply chain management.

The Bachelor of Science (B.S.) is offered in applied physics, athletic training, biochemistry, biology, business economics, chemistry, community health, computer engineering, computer science, computer science and mathematics (dual degree), electrical engineering, environmental resources, exercise specialist studies, fine arts, forensic science, geology, health education, health science, industrial engineering, mathematical business economics, mathematics, mechanical engineering, music, physics, urban ecology, video/television, video/television and business, and video/television and film.

The Bachelor of Science in Education (B.S.Ed.) is offered with specializations in dance, fine arts, music, and physical education.

The Bachelor of Engineering (B.E.) is offered in engineering science with specializations in biomedical engineering and civil engineering.

The Bachelor of Fine Arts (B.F.A.) is awarded in theater arts with specializations in performance and production.

Combined degrees offered include Bachelor of Arts/Juris Doctor (B.A./J.D.) in engineering science/law, B.S./M.S. in physician assistant studies, B.S./M.S. and B.A./M.S. in computer science, B.S./M.D. and B.A./M.D. through the Hofstra North Shore–LIJ School of Medicine at Hofstra University, B.A./M.A. in sociology/applied social research and public policy, and various B.B.A./M.S. programs through the Frank G. Zarb School of Business.

Academic Programs

Requirements for graduation vary among schools and majors. A liberal arts core curriculum is an integral part of all areas of concentration. The University calendar is organized on a traditional semester system, including one January session and three summer sessions.

COLLEGE CLOSE-UPS

Hofstra offers innovative programs designed to meet the needs of its diverse student body. These include Honors College, Legal Education Accelerated Program (LEAP), Hofstra 4++4 Program, Living/Learning Communities, and First-Year Connections.

Hofstra's Honors College provides a rich academic and extracurricular experience for students who show both the potential and desire to excel. Honors students can elect to study in any of the University's undergraduate programs and are involved in all fields of advanced study, including premedicine, prelaw, engineering, business, communication and media arts, humanities, and social sciences.

The Legal Education Accelerated Program allows students to earn both a B.A. and a J.D. in just six years.

The Hofstra 4+4 Program allows students to earn both degrees (B.S.-B.A./M.D) in eight years through the new Hofstra North Shore–LIJ School of Medicine at Hofstra University.

In the Living/Learning Communities, the learning experience is not limited to the four walls of the classroom, or even to the borders of the campus. Here, students are exposed to environments that are intellectually stimulating, supportive, and conducive to building lasting friendships and a memorable first-year college experience.

First-Year Connections, an integrated academic and social program, helps first-year students connect with one another as well as all the resources provided and opportunities offered at the University. The program, which offers seminars and clusters, features small classes taught by distinguished faculty in areas of interest ranging from architecture to writing. These courses introduce students to the intellectual and social life of the University and satisfy the general education requirements for all majors.

Off-Campus Programs

Hofstra extends learning beyond the classroom through active internship programs and dynamic and varied study-abroad opportunities. The internship program takes advantage of the proximity of New York City, allowing students to gain on-the-job experience in areas such as finance, business, media, advertising, and entertainment. Through study-abroad programs in Europe, Asia, South America, and other locations, students can explore the world while earning college credits. More information is available at http://hofstra.edu/studyabroad.

Academic Facilities

Hofstra's students live and learn on a campus that is home to state-of-the-art facilities and resources. C. V. Starr Hall, home to the Frank G. Zarb School of Business, features the Martin B. Greenberg Trading Room, one of the most advanced academic trading rooms in the nation, with thirty-four Bloomberg Professional terminals and Internet access at every student seat. The School of Communication's Dempster Hall contains one of the largest noncommercial broadcast facilities in the Northeast, as well as a dynamic converged newsroom and multimedia classroom. Hagedorn Hall, where the School of Education, Health, and Human Services is located, provides a technology-rich learning environment, complete with interactive whiteboards, computer-driven instructor stations, and wireless communication.

The David S. Mack Sports and Exhibition Complex, a modern 93,000-square-foot facility, is home to the Hofstra Pride men's and women's basketball teams and wrestling team. It is also the site for commencements, exhibitions, trade shows, concerts, and other special events. Other recreational and athletic facilities include an indoor, Olympic-size swimming pool, modern fitness center, indoor sports and entertainment arena, and well-maintained athletic fields.

With twenty dining establishments and thirty-seven residence halls, students view Hofstra as their home away from home. Residential facilities accommodate more than 4,000 students in thirty-seven modern residence halls. Hofstra is 100 percent program-accessible to individuals with disabilities. Necessary services are provided for students with physical, learning, and/or psychological disabilities who meet the University's academic requirements for admission.

Hofstra's Joan and Donald E. Axinn Library contains more than 1.2 million print volumes and provides 24/7 electronic access to more than 49,000 full-text journals and 47,000 electronic books. There are special units for periodicals, reserve books, government documents, curriculum materials, special collections, and microfilm.

Costs

The annual cost of tuition and fees at Hofstra University for 2010–11 for a full-time undergraduate student was $31,800. The housing and dining plan was approximately $11,400. Books and supplies cost approximately $1000; personal expenses and transportation generally amount to $2822. For the full tuition and fees schedule, students should visit http://hofstra.edu/tuition.

Financial Aid

To help students achieve their educational goals, Hofstra University offers several financial-aid options. For 2010–11, Hofstra awarded more than $68.5 million in merit- and need-based financial aid. The average award for first-year students with financial need was $18,014, while the average financial-aid package for first-year students who had no financial need was $11,485. More than 1,000 first-year students received merit-based scholarships from Hofstra University, ranging from $1,000 to full-tuition scholarships. About 87 percent of all Hofstra students received some form of financial aid, including more than 94 percent of first-year students. For detailed information, students should visit http://hofstra.edu/FinancialAid.

Faculty

Hofstra's diverse student body of about 12,000 comes from forty-six U.S. states and territories and sixty-eight countries. Students are challenged and encouraged to debate, question, research, discuss, and think critically by faculty members who include Guggenheim and Fulbright scholars; Emmy Award–winners; prize-winning scientists; and leaders in business, education and the health sciences. Ninety-three percent of the full-time faculty members hold the highest degree in their fields. Most importantly, all classes are taught by faculty members, not graduate students, which allows for the optimal potential for a comprehensive and individualized learning experience.

Student Government

The Student Government Association is a student-run governing body that supervises and coordinates all student activities and serves as a liaison with the faculty and administration. The Student Government Association sends representatives to the committees of the University Senate. A judicial board has responsibility for promoting justice in the conduct of student affairs.

Admission Requirements

Hofstra is a competitive institution that seeks to enroll students who demonstrate academic ability, intellectual curiosity, and the motivation to be successful and contribute to the campus community. Careful consideration is given to a student's high school record, types of courses taken, SAT or ACT scores, letters of recommendation, extracurricular involvement, and the personal essay. The most competitive applicants will have followed a rigorous college preparatory curriculum within their high school and will have taken advantage of honors and advanced placement level courses where appropriate. The Office of Admission prefers to see a high school curriculum, which includes 4 years of English, 3 to 4 years of social studies, 2 to 3 years of foreign language, 3 years of mathematics, and 3 years of science. Prospective engineering majors need at least 4 years of mathematics, 1 year of chemistry, and 1 year of physics. Campus visits are strongly recommended. Hofstra accepts applications from first-year, transfer, and international students.

The University offers an early action plan for students whose first choice is Hofstra. There are two early action periods: when submitted by November 15, notification is made to the student by December 15; when submitted by December 15, notification is made to the student by January 15. Students applying for regular decision are considered on a rolling basis.

First-year applicants must submit an application, $70 application fee, high school transcript, SAT or ACT scores, essay, and letter of recommendation. Hofstra accepts applications via mail or online and participates in the Common Application; the online application fee is $50.

Application and Information

Hofstra University
Office of Undergraduate Admission
100 Hofstra University
Hempstead, New York 11549-1000
Phone: 516-463-6700
         800-HOFSTRA (toll-free)
Fax: 516-463-5100
E-mail: admission@hofstra.edu
Web site: http://www.hofstra.edu/admission

HOLLINS UNIVERSITY

ROANOKE, VIRGINIA

The University

Hollins University was founded in 1842 as Virginia's first chartered women's college. Today, Hollins is an independent arts and sciences university that enrolls approximately 1,024 students in its undergraduate programs for women and its coed graduate programs. Hollins is proud of its creative writing program, career internships, leadership opportunities, small class size, and study-abroad opportunities. Hollins prepares its students for career excellence in the social sciences, sciences, humanities, fine arts, and business. An 11:1 student-faculty ratio enables students to work closely with their professors both inside and outside the classroom. In addition to the Bachelor of Arts degree in twenty-seven major fields, Hollins awards a Bachelor of Science degree in four major fields, a B.A./B.F.A. degree in dance, a Master of Arts degree in children's literature, liberal studies, screenwriting and film studies, and teaching and a Master of Fine Arts degree in creative writing, children's literature, dance, playwriting, and screenwriting. In summer 2011, Hollins launched a postgraduate certificate program in children's book illustration. Hollins' coeducational graduate creative writing program has long been acknowledged as one of the best of its size in the country.

Hollins gives students the month of January to focus on an internship, innovative course work, senior thesis, independent study, or travel/study abroad.

The majority of Hollins students do at least one internship before graduation. Students have interned at the New York Stock Exchange, UBS Financial Services, Centers for Disease Control, ABC News, National Institute of Mental Health, Lincoln Center for the Performing Arts, the *London Times*, *Vanity Fair* magazine, and the Metropolitan Museum of Art, to name a few.

Through Hollins' innovative Batten Leadership Institute, undergraduates can earn a Certificate in Leadership Studies through a combination of classes, skills-building groups, seminars, and student-designed leadership projects. The 20-hour program gives students the opportunity to gain both practical and academic experience in leadership studies, serving as a perfect complement to any major field of study.

Situated on a quiet 475-acre campus in the Shenandoah Valley of the Blue Ridge Mountains, Hollins is ideal for the serious student looking to broaden her mind through a rigorous academic program. Students come to Hollins from forty-seven states and fourteen countries and bring with them cultural and ethnic diversity. Women returning to college can earn a bachelor's degree in the Horizon Program.

Because approximately 78 percent of Hollins women live on campus in dormitories, language houses, or University apartments, a large family of friends develops in the first year and replaces the need for sororities. There are twenty-eight clubs and organizations, including a multicultural club, Black Student Alliance, literary societies, and political, environmental, women's, and volunteer organizations. Many students volunteer in social service agencies locally and internationally, including a Hollins-directed Jamaica service project. The Wyndham Robertson Library features state-of-the-art technology, is a National Literary Landmark, and won the 2009 Excellence in Academic Libraries Award. The well-equipped athletic complex enables Hollins to compete and train its athletes effectively for NCAA Division III competition in basketball, golf, lacrosse, riding, soccer, swimming, tennis, and volleyball. Hollins' strong riding program offers top facilities, including stables where riders may board their horses. The academic program is enriched by guest lectures, dance and theater productions, and the annual Literary Festival. The Hollins Outdoor Program (HOP) provides outdoor adventure activities such as canoeing, hiking, rock climbing, and caving.

Location

Hollins is located on the outskirts of Roanoke, a cosmopolitan center with a population of approximately 250,000. Hollins is a 3½-hour drive from both Washington, D.C., and Richmond; 5 hours from Virginia Beach; and within easy driving distance of more than a dozen other colleges. The Roanoke Regional Airport is a 10-minute drive from the campus. The campus has been described as "achingly picturesque."

The Front Quadrangle is listed on the National Register of Historic Places. The Blue Ridge Mountains are minutes from campus and ideal for hiking the Appalachian Trail, camping, caving, and skiing.

Majors and Degrees

Hollins grants the Bachelor of Arts degree in art history, biology, business, chemistry, classical studies, communication studies, dance, economics, English and creative writing, environmental studies, film, French, gender and women's studies, history, interdisciplinary studies, international studies, mathematics, music, philosophy, physics, political science, psychology, religious studies, sociology, Spanish, studio art, and theater; the B.A./B.F.A. degree in dance; and the B.S. degree in biology, chemistry, mathematics, and psychology. Minors are offered in most major areas, and preprofessional programs are offered in education, law, medicine, and veterinary science. Students can earn certificates in leadership and arts management.

Academic Programs

Candidates for the Bachelor of Arts degree normally follow a four-year program. They are required to complete 128 credits of academic work and 16 January Short Term credits.

Candidates for the degree of Bachelor of Arts and Bachelor of Fine Arts in dance normally follow a four-year program. They are required to complete a minimum of 150 semester credits of academic work, 16 Short Term credits, and two physical education courses. Included in the 150 credits are 82 credits in dance and general education.

Candidates for the degree of Bachelor of Science normally follow a four-year program. They are required to complete a minimum of 140 semester credits of academic work, 16 Short Term credits, and two physical education courses. Included in the 140 credits are 60 credits in the major (biology, chemistry, mathematics, or psychology) and general education.

The University offers first-year seminars that focus on collaborative and active learning, critical thinking, creative problem solving, research, writing, and oral communication skills. Seminar instructors also serve as academic advisers who help students with both course selection and academic goal setting. Each seminar is limited to 15 students and also has an upper-class peer mentor who attends seminars, helps students with advising, and answers academic questions.

First-year students may enroll in an on-campus seminar, apply for a limited number of competitive local internships through Hollins' Career Center, or join a travel-study program during their first January Short Term. Students may spend subsequent Short Terms pursuing career internships, independent study, study-abroad experiences, or service projects. In Hollins' general education program, called Education through Skills and Perspectives, students choose from a wide variety of classes that reinforce the basics of a liberal arts education.

Students must choose a major by the end of their sophomore year and complete a minimum of 32 credits in the major field before graduation. Each first-year student must meet a writing requirement. Hollins grants 4 academic credits for Advanced Placement examination scores of 4 or 5 and in some cases for a score of 3. Hollins grants 8 academic credits for International Baccalaureate scores between 5 and 7 and up to 32 credits for an I.B. diploma with a score of 30 or higher.

Off-Campus Programs

For semester or full-year study, Hollins has its own programs in England and France and affiliated programs in Argentina, Germany, Ghana, Greece, Ireland, Italy, Japan, Mexico, South Africa, and Spain as well as with the School for Field Studies. About half of Hollins students have an international learning experience before graduation. Domestic exchange programs are possible with members of the six-college exchange.

Academic Facilities

The Wyndham Robertson Library's collections consist of more than a half-million titles, ranging from e-books to incunabula and from musical scores to manuscripts. Through a catalog shared with Roanoke College, students are offered access to the materials in the combined collections of both libraries. Access to a wide range of electronic databases enables students to locate articles and documents from more than 40,000 journals, magazines, newspapers, and other titles. Hollins houses a notable selection of children's books and the papers of former poet laureate William Jay Smith. The archives and special collections include books and manuscripts from many famous faculty members and alumni/alumnae, including R. H. W. Dillard, George Garrett, Eudora Welty, Margaret Wise Brown, Lee Smith, and Annie Dillard.

Extensive media facilities include a television studio and control room, a video editing suite, viewing and listening booths, and a screening room. The building has 40 public computers and wireless access, ample study seating, group study rooms, and many comfortable reading spaces.

Windows XP/Professional– and Macintosh-based computers are available in dedicated computer labs as well as various common areas around the university—many open 24 hours a day. Wireless access is abundant on campus.

The Dana Science Building houses accessible labs and research facilities for computerized recording and analysis of physiological and behavioral data, plant and animal tissue culture, animal learning laboratories, photomicroscopy, biochemistry and molecular biology, chromatography, spectrophotometry, electrochemistry, gas kinetics, centrifugation, and EEG and biofeedback equipment.

The Richard Wetherill Visual Arts Center houses the Eleanor D. Wilson Museum, which features the work of internationally renowned artists and emerging and regional artists.

Hollins also has dance studios, a career center, center for learning excellence, theater, and health and counseling center.

Costs

The 2011–12 costs are $30,220 for tuition and $10,670 for room and board, which included telephone, cable television, and computer connections for each student's room. The Student Government Association fee is $275, technology support fee is $290, and University green fee is $10. Other estimated costs include $1000 for books, $800 for transportation, and $1000 for other expenses.

Financial Aid

Financial aid is awarded on the basis of both academic merit and need. Eighty-one percent receive need-based aid in the form of grants, merit scholarships, low-interest loans, and campus jobs. The average financial aid package in 2010 was $22,803. The types of scholarships and grants available to undergraduates are Federal Pell Grants, Federal Supplemental Educational Opportunity Grants (FSEOG), state grants, University scholarships and grants, private scholarships and grants, academic merit scholarships, and aid for undergraduate students who are members of a minority group. Federal Perkins Loans, Federal PLUS loans, and Federal Stafford Student Loans are also available, as well as a tuition payment plan with Sallie Mae. A financial aid form should be filed with the financial aid office by February 15. Notification of awards is on a rolling basis.

Faculty

Faculty members are committed to teaching and are dedicated to their students. Although scholarly research and writing are emphasized, primary attention is placed on teaching. There are 71 full-time and 28 part-time faculty members, of whom 52 percent are women; 98 percent of the full-time faculty members hold the doctoral or corresponding terminal degree in their fields. A few courses are taught by graduate assistants.

Student Government

Each year, students sign the honor code, pledging not to lie, cheat, or steal. Hollins is thereby able to conduct daily operations with a great deal of trust. Final exams are freely scheduled and administered by students under the Independent Exam System. The campus judicial system is run by the students. Students who are elected to the Student Government Association have the authority to administer all student-related activities. Weekly Senate meetings are open to the entire campus. Students are represented on policymaking faculty committees and the Board of Trustees.

Admission Requirements

To be considered for admission, a student must have completed a minimum of 16 secondary school units in English, mathematics, science, social studies, and foreign language. All students must take the SAT or the ACT. In addition to standardized test scores, the Admissions Committee takes into account an applicant's secondary school record, class rank, essay, recommendation, and personal interview. Transfer students are accepted in both semesters. International applicants can submit TOEFL scores in place of the SAT or ACT.

At Hollins, the application process is very personal. The admissions counselors go to great lengths to ensure that Hollins and the applicant are a good match.

Application and Information

Hollins has a formal early decision plan. The early decision application deadline is December 1; the deadline is February 15 for regular admission. Notification of admission is on a rolling basis beginning December 15 for early decision candidates and late January for regular admission candidates. The application fee is $40. A $400 tuition deposit must be made by early January for early decision, May 1 for others. For more information, students should contact:

Office of Admissions
Hollins University
P.O. Box 9707
Roanoke, Virginia 24020
Phone: 540-362-6401
      800-456-9595 (toll-free)
E-mail: huadm@hollins.edu
Web site: http://www.hollins.edu
      http://www.facebook.com/HollinsUniversity?v=wall
      http://twitter.com/hollinsnews

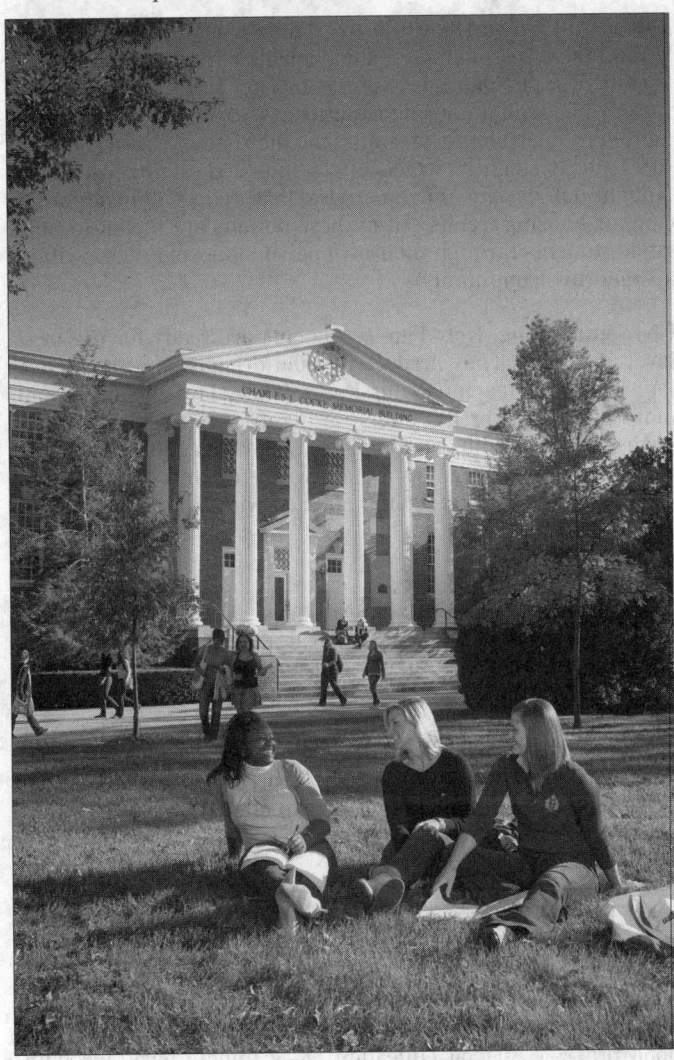

Students enjoying Hollins' historic Front Quadrangle.

HOLY FAMILY UNIVERSITY
PHILADELPHIA, PENNSYLVANIA

The University

Holy Family University is a fully accredited, Catholic, private, coeducational, four-year university located in Northeast Philadelphia's residential Torresdale neighborhood. Founded in 1954 by the Sisters of the Holy Family of Nazareth, Holy Family provides liberal arts and professional programs for more than 2,100 undergraduate students through day, evening, and summer sessions.

From the moment students arrive on campus, they are being prepared to make an impact. From classroom immersion and co-op experiences to service opportunities and Division II athletics, students learn and grow in an outcome-oriented environment that offers countless opportunities to get involved and engaged.

Holy Family University works to extend the learning experience beyond the classroom to create a holistic education that fosters a student's personal development. The University provides various residential housing experiences, including a traditional dormitory, apartment-style units, and the state-of-the-art Stevenson Lane Residence, which offers suite-style living with well thought-out design and amenities that reflect contemporary campus housing trends. All of these options are meant to help guide students through their own personal development within a supportive community.

Upon graduating, Holy Family students are ready for the next level of impact. They arrive with bold dreams, and they leave for careers in teaching, nursing, science, law, business, and more. The University offers a highly supportive learning environment that lifts and empowers students and values their aspirations. Holy Family is a place where dreams of every kind are honored, encouraged, and pursued with a passion.

Location

The University is based at its Northeast Philadelphia campus, which serves as home of the traditional undergraduate program. Located less than a mile from Bucks County, Holy Family offers the benefits of a big city in a quiet, park-like, suburban setting. The campus offers student housing for full-time undergraduates. With easy access to regional rail lines, city bus routes, and nearby expressways, students can experience all that Philadelphia has to offer.

Majors and Degrees

Holy Family offers undergraduate courses leading to the Bachelor of Arts (B.A.) and Bachelor of Science (B.S.) degrees. Majors include accounting, art, biochemistry, biology, biology-medical technology, communications, computer management information systems, criminal justice, education (early childhood pre K–4; special education PK–8; middle level 4–8 with concentrations in language arts and reading, mathematics, science, and social studies; secondary education with certifications in art, biology, English, history/social studies, and mathematics), English/literature, finance, fire science and public safety administration (transfers only), history, interdisciplinary humanities, international business, management-marketing, mathematics, nursing, psychobiology, psychology, psychology for business, radiologic science, religious studies, sociology, and sport marketing-management. Preprofessional programs are also available in art therapy, dentistry, law, medicine, optometry, physical therapy, podiatry, physician's assistant studies, and veterinary studies.

Academic Programs

Holy Family's curriculum stands within the mainstream of a 2,000-year-old Christian liberal arts tradition. The core curriculum of religious studies, philosophy, the humanities, and the social and natural sciences implements the objectives of the University in a general way. It also contributes to the formation of liberally educated students who find their education is functional in the twenty-first century. Students are encouraged to seek not merely information but also personal formation and enrichment.

In addition to the core curriculum, students take course work in their division concentrations within the School of Arts and Sciences, the School of Business Administration, the School of Education, the School of Nursing and Allied Health Professions, or the Division of Extended Learning. Interdisciplinary programs, specialized programs of study, and minors are also available.

Off-Campus Programs

Holy Family's cooperative education program is highly successful and nationally recognized. Co-ops and internships are designed to support classroom learning by enabling students to apply the concepts they've studied to actual job situations. These real-world lessons enhance students' skills and understanding and allow them to explore various work settings and careers, all while earning academic credit. Holy Family partners with more than 500 corporations, companies, government agencies, and nonprofit organizations throughout Greater Philadelphia, and the results are impressive. Students in the co-op program enjoy a 93 percent permanent placement rate, while the national average is just 76 percent.

Academic Facilities

The University Library houses more than 124,000 books, magazines, journals, DVDs, and videos to support the learning, teaching, and informational needs of the Holy Family community. The library offers print and online access to the full text of over 13,000 journals and periodicals, and over two dozen full-text databases are available on and off campus. In addition, the library has over 8,500 electronic books available from home or campus via NetLibrary and other interfaces.

The library's curriculum section contains elementary and secondary school textbooks, curriculum guides, instruction kits, and hundreds of children's books, both fiction and nonfiction. It also has a special English as a second language (ESL) collection for those who teach non-native speakers.

Computer laboratories are located in several facilities, including Holy Family Hall, the Education and Technology Center, the Campus Center, and the University Library. Wireless network access is also available throughout the campus buildings and residence halls.

In addition to general classrooms and laboratories, Holy Family has special facilities to enable students in certain majors to learn in environments that mirror those they will encounter in their professional lives. The Education and Technology Center houses five classrooms specially designed to model primary and secondary classroom instruction for the University's education students. These model classrooms allow children with certain disabilities, such as vision or hearing impairment, to be integrated fully into a regular classroom and provide Holy Family's Education graduates with valuable experience using adaptive technology in a classroom environment. The Nurse Education Building includes a nursing simulation and practice laboratory.

Costs

For 2010–11, tuition was $22,870, and room and board were $10,390. The University's general fee is $650 per year.

Financial Aid

Holy Family is committed to helping students and their families achieve the goal of a private university education. Holy Family maintains one of the lowest tuition rates among private colleges and universities in the region, and more than 85 percent of its students receive some form of financial aid. The University is committed to providing education to qualified students regardless of means and views financial assistance as a cooperative investment in a student's education.

In addition to state and federal programs, students can take advantage of a variety of Holy Family need- and merit-based scholarships and grants.

Faculty

Classes at Holy Family are usually no larger than 20 students, and many have as few as 7–10 students. A student-to-faculty ratio of 12:1 provides a smaller, more personal learning environment. Students know their professors, and those professors know them as well. Personalized, individual treatment is the norm: students are called on by name, receive answers to their questions, and most importantly, get additional help if they need it. This is not a college where hundreds of students crowd into an auditorium and silently take notes from a distant, faceless instructor. A Holy Family education is designed to be more—more personal, more welcoming, and more attuned to each student's success.

Student Government

Representatives to Holy Family's Student Government Association are elected by the student body for the following academic year and share responsibility for student life and activities. The Vice President for Student Services serves as an adviser to the Student Government Association and as the liaison between the students and the administration.

Admission Requirements

When it comes to potential students, Holy Family University is more interested in a student's quality of work and general promise and seriousness of purpose. While a student's academic record is considered, their interests, personal integrity, and desire to pursue a quality education are also important factors. Holy Family values diversity in all of its manifestations; neither religious affiliation nor ethnic characteristics influence the granting of admission.

Applicants are expected to have graduated from an accredited high school or equivalent; received acceptable scores on the SAT or ACT; and completed 4 units of English, 2 units of history, 3 units of mathematics, 2 units of modern foreign language, 2 units of science, and 3 electives.

Application and Information

For application forms, a catalog, or further information, students should contact:

Undergraduate Admissions Office
Holy Family University
9801 Frankford Avenue
Philadelphia, Pennsylvania 19114

Phone: 215-637-3050
Fax: 215-281-1022
E-mail: admissions@holyfamily.edu
Web site: http://www.holyfamily.edu
http://www.facebook.com/HolyFamilyUniversity
http://twitter.com/holyfamilyu

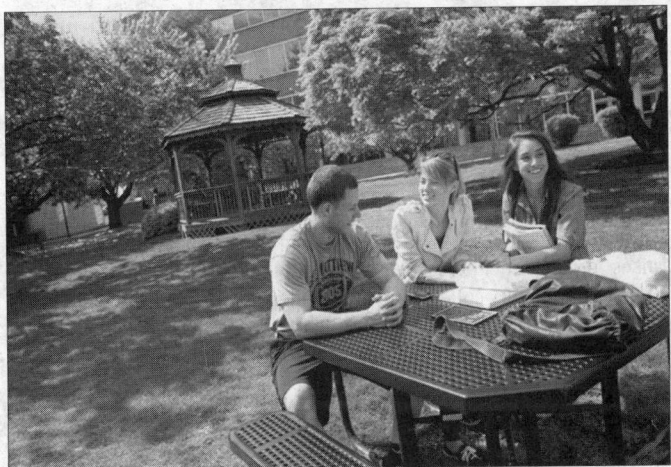

Holy Family's supportive scholarly community studies, works, and plays on a suburban-like campus just minutes from the vibrancy of Center City Philadelphia.

HOPE COLLEGE
HOLLAND, MICHIGAN

The College

The mission of Hope College is to educate students for lives of leadership and service in a global society through academic and co-curricular programs of recognized excellence in the liberal arts and in the context of the historic Christian faith.

Hope is regularly recognized for its distinctive blend of exceptional academics, diverse co-curricular programs, and vibrant yet unrestrictive Christian character. (www.hope.edu/admissions/christian/) Some institutions are recognized as academically excellent—Hope is one of them. Others for an integrated faith community—Hope is one of them. Hope is also among those with intentional opportunities to grow in leadership and service. Few institutions provide the blend of these three significant aspects like Hope College. It is this package—of exceptional academics, experiential learning, and an environment where faith is relevant but not prescriptive—which draws a certain student to be part of the Hope community.

What all Hope students have in common is the desire to grow, inside the classroom and beyond. Their commitment to fully develop their gifts is evident in the fact that Hope ranks in the top 5 percent of all liberal arts colleges in the number of students completing a Ph.D. The students' desire to serve manifests itself in the numbers who participate in service organizations, mission trips, and eventually enter service-oriented careers.

Government and foundation grants to individuals, to departments, and to the College demonstrate the quality of the institution. For example, in the spring 2010 semester, departments and faculty held seventy-one grants totaling more than $11 million.

Hope is nationally recognized for its collaborative learning opportunities and regularly is named to the *U.S. News & World Report* annual listing of the strongest schools in this area. Hope has one of the largest summer undergraduate research programs in the nation; each year, approximately 160 students participate in summer research at the College. In addition, the guide's 2010 edition includes Hope among the top 100 liberal arts colleges in the nation.

The *Fiske Guide to Colleges* 2010 includes Hope as one of the country's best and most interesting colleges and universities, and quotes one senior as observing that "Hope is a place where students are challenged to become better students, and more importantly, better people."

In 2009, *Mother Jones* magazine included Hope in its listing of ten "cool schools that will blow your mind, not your budget," citing the College as a best value for artists with a spiritual side.

The book *Colleges That Change Lives* cites Hope as one of forty life-changing colleges that are "outdoing the Ivies and the major universities in producing winners" and describes the College as a place that raises higher education's moral and intellectual levels.

Hope is among fifty colleges recommended by the Intercollegiate Studies Institute in its guide, noting that: "The students and faculty we spoke with confirm that the school walks its talk; Hope College is both academically serious and theologically earnest."

Hope is one of only ten church-related colleges and universities nationwide highlighted in the book *Putting Students First: How Colleges Develop Students Purposefully.*

Hope is the only private, four-year liberal arts college in the United States with national accreditation in art, dance, music, and theater.

In 2010, Hope enrolled 3,230 students from forty-two states and territories and thirty foreign countries.

Location

(www.hope.edu/pr/holland.html)

Hope is located in the vibrant community of Holland, Michigan. In recent years Holland has been recognized as the second happiest/healthiest city in America (Gallup-Healthways), one of the five safest cities *(Forbes)*, and an All-America City (National Civic League). Holland has long been known as a summer resort area, but it is also a fine spot for winter sports. Excellent relations exist between Holland and the College. Holland now has an area population of over 100,000.

Hope College's 77-acre wooded campus is in a residential area two blocks from Holland's central business district. The College is only a 30-minute drive from Grand Rapids and a 2½-hour drive from Chicago and Detroit. An 85-acre biological field station is located on the shores of Lake Michigan, 5 miles from the campus.

Majors and Degrees

(www.hope.edu/academic)

Hope's academic climate is rigorous without being harmfully competitive. There is a strong sense of cooperation and mutual respect and students regularly praise their faculty for the support they provide within the challenges they present. With over eighty majors, Hope offers a wider variety of career paths than most liberal arts colleges.

Hope College awards the Bachelor of Arts, Bachelor of Science, Bachelor of Music, and Bachelor of Science in Nursing degrees. Major programs include accounting (public accounting), ancient civilization, art** (studio art and art history concentrations), athletic training, biology*, chemistry* (biochemistry emphasis), communication, computer science, dance**, economics*, engineering (ABET-accredited biochemical, chemical, computer science, electrical, and mechanical emphases), engineering physics, engineering science, English** (literature and creative writing majors), French*, geology* (environmental emphasis), German*, history*, international studies, Japanese, kinesiology* (physical education, exercise science, and athletic training), Latin*, management, mathematics**, music** (instrumental education, vocal education, jazz studies emphasis, performance), nursing, philosophy, physics*, political science*, psychology, religion*, social work (CSWE approved), sociology* (criminal justice emphasis), Spanish*, special education (emotional impairments and learning disabilities endorsements), and theater*. Hope is fully accredited for certification in elementary, secondary, and special (emotionally impaired and learning disabilities endorsements) education. Preprofessional programs are offered in dance therapy, dentistry, law, library science, medicine, optometry, physical therapy, seminary, and veterinary medicine.

*Secondary teaching certification available; **secondary and/or elementary teaching certification available.

Academic Programs

(www.hope.edu/pr/hopedistinctions.html)

As a Phi Beta Kappa institution, Hope is widely respected as a liberal arts college that balances academic excellence with a deep concern for the quality of life of its students and alumni. Hope's commitment to the Christian faith provides an incentive for academic excellence and rigorous inquiry and a perspective on the wholeness and value of life. A core curriculum brings teachers and students together for the purpose of facilitating student growth in seven areas: communication skills, social adaptation, an understanding of American heritage and society, a respect for science and discovery, an awareness of other cultures, an understanding and appreciation of the arts, and an understanding of religion and its impact on society. To accomplish this, students select course work in the following disciplines: English, fine arts, foreign language, kinesiology, mathematics, natural science, philosophy, religion, and social science.

Off-Campus Programs

(www.hope.edu/admin/international/offcamp/intprograms.htm)

Hope College offers over 200 programs in more than seventy countries. Opportunities to integrate off-campus programs with nearly all academic programs are not only available but encouraged. Academic scholarships are applicable for off-campus programs.

International programs include Africa, Austria, China, France, Germany, Great Britain, India, Japan, Latin America, Russia, Spain, the Middle East, and the Netherlands. Hope also runs a summer study-abroad program in Vienna, Austria. Domestic programs include semesters in Philadelphia, Chicago, New York, and Washington, D.C.

Academic Facilities

(www.hope.edu/tour/)

Numerous additions have been made to campus facilities recently. The past decade has seen the addition of the $36-million Schaap Science/Nursing complex that contains the most modern laboratory equipment available. The physics laboratories include an electron particle accelerator. Students from many academic disciplines take advantage of state-of-the-art computer facilities. The theater, music, dance, and art departments are proud to offer excellent facilities as well. The DePree Art Center is a $1.3-million facility that contains a major art gallery, classrooms, and studios. The $11-million Martha Miller Center for communication and global studies and the $22-million Devos Field house were dedicated in fall 2005. Lubbers Hall, one of the College's most venerable academic buildings, underwent a $3-million renovation project during the summer of 2006. Major renovations to the Boeve Baseball Stadium and Wolters Softball Field were completed for the spring 2008 seasons, and the $5.3 million Van Andel Soccer Stadium was completed in fall 2009. Graves Hall, a centerpiece of the College's identity and early history, recently underwent a $5.7-million adaptive restoration. Current fund-raising is targeted toward a new music department facility and concert hall, new art gallery, and a new student center.

Costs

(www.hope.edu/admissions/finaid/cost.html)

Annual charges for the 2011–12 academic year are tuition, $26,860; room, $3780; board (twenty-one meals per week, reduced-cost meal plans are available), $4480; and activity fee, $160; for a total of $35,280. This is significantly less than colleges of similar academic caliber and reflects the College's commitment to make the Hope experience available to all who desire it.

Financial Aid

(www.hope.edu/admissions/finaid/)

Hope strives to balance a commitment to affordability with the desire to offer a world-class experience. The current capital campaign contains a significant focus on funds to provide financial assistance for deserving families. Aid includes academic and talent scholarships, grants, loans, and campus employment. The average need-based package for 2010 was $18,368. A complete description of required forms and deadlines is available on the Hope financial aid Web site (www.hope.edu/admin/finaid/). Also available are Hope's academic and talent scholarships which range from $2500 to $17,000 per year. Hope also sponsors National Merit Scholars with a $17,000-per-year tuition scholarship.

Faculty

The student-faculty ratio is 12:1. Hope's more than 300 faculty members play a pivotal role in the creation of Hope's dynamic environment. Their desire to touch individual lives, coupled with their love of teaching—in the classroom, the laboratory, the rehearsal hall, and private conversations—combine to create an atmosphere of mutual respect and collaboration.

The faculty members' focus on active scholarship and original research improves the quality of teaching. They remain up-to-date and productive in their fields of study and are thus better able to instill a love and enthusiasm for learning. Many conduct research programs in which students actively participate, sometimes as early as their freshman year. Faculty members also serve as academic advisers and frequently host student groups in their homes.

Student Activities

(www.hope.edu/student/life/groups.html)

The number and variety of clubs and activities at Hope reflects its identity as a "large, small school." The larger enrollment supports a wider range of offerings, yet Hope is small enough to enable easy participation. Activities range from intercollegiate athletics to Silent Praise, academic clubs to Habitat for Humanity, and Engineers Without Borders to traditional events like the Pull and the Dance Marathon. Hope has been recognized by the National Association of Campus Activities for both the range of activities and for the amount of student participation.

All programs and organizations are student-centered and intentionally seek to enhance the culture of the College, uphold the institutional mission, and inspire students.

Admission Requirements

(www.hope.edu/admissions/apply/)

Hope is interested in students who seek the rigors of a proven, demanding academic program; desire to grow through activities outside the classroom; and feel comfortable in an open, supportive, Christian campus community. Primary factors considered are the applicant's high school course selection, grades, rank, test scores, counselor's recommendation, essay, and involvement in extracurricular/leadership activities. A strong college-preparatory curriculum is essential.

The fall 2010 freshmen had a mean GPA of 3.72 (on a 4.0 scale), a middle 50 percent SAT score (critical reading and math) of 1060–1330, and a middle 50 percent ACT composite score of 23–29.

Campus visits are not required but are strongly recommended for interested students and their parents.

Application and Information

The first admission decisions are announced in mid-November. A traditional rolling admission process continues after mid-November until late spring for fall admission. Prospective freshmen are encouraged to submit applications during the first semester of their senior year in high school. Completed applications for admission must be on file by February 15 to ensure consideration for merit scholarships. A $300 enrollment deposit is requested by May 1.

To obtain additional information or complete an online registration form, prospective students should visit http://www.hope.edu/admissions/contact.

Hope College Admissions
69 East 10th Street
P.O. Box 9000
Holland, Michigan 49422-9000
Phone: 616-395-7850
        800-968-7850 (toll-free)
E-mail: admissions@hope.edu
Web site: http://www.hope.edu
        http://www.facebook.com/hopecollege
        http://twitter.com/#!/hopecollege
        http://www.youtube.com/hopecollege

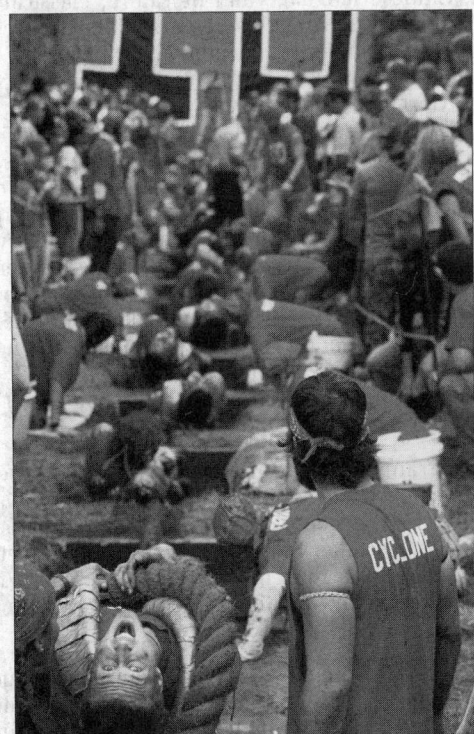

The Pull, an annual tug-of-war between freshmen and sophomores for the past 113 years, has been called "the most unique sporting event in the nation" by *Sports Illustrated*.

HUNTER COLLEGE OF THE CITY UNIVERSITY OF NEW YORK

NEW YORK, NEW YORK

www.hunter.cuny.edu

The College

In 1870, Thomas Hunter founded Hunter College to train young women to become school teachers. Their contributions helped make New York City's schools among the most highly regarded public school systems in the world. Today, Hunter College is a coeducational liberal arts college serving 21,000 undergraduate and graduate students of all racial, ethnic, and cultural backgrounds. Wide offerings in the liberal arts and sciences and three professional schools—education, health sciences, and social work—meet the highest academic standards. A distinguished faculty encourages intellectual and personal growth in each student.

Location

Hunter students study in the heart of Manhattan. Many of the world's finest museums, libraries, concert halls, cultural centers, and theaters are just a quick walk away.

Majors and Degrees

Hunter College offers bachelor's and master's degrees in the arts and sciences, education, health professions, nursing, and social work, along with several combined (B.A./M.A. or B.A./M.S.) degrees. The following programs of study are available: accounting, Africana and Puerto Rican/Latino studies, anthropology, archaeology, art history, biological sciences, chemistry, Chinese language and literature, classical studies, community health education, comparative literature, computer science, dance, economics, elementary education, environmental studies, English, English language arts, film, French, geography, German, Greek, Hebrew, history, honors curriculum, Italian, Jewish social studies, Latin, Latin American and Caribbean Studies, Latin and Greek, mathematics, media studies, medical laboratory sciences, music, nursing, nutrition and food science, philosophy, physics, political science, psychology, religion, Romance languages, Russian, secondary education, sociology, Spanish, statistics, studio art, theater, urban studies, and women's studies. Secondary education programs are for grades 7–12 unless otherwise noted and include biology, chemistry, Chinese, dance (pre-K–12), English, French, German, Hebrew, Italian, mathematics, music (pre-K–12, accelerated B.A./M.A. program only), physics, Russian, social studies, and Spanish.

Special programs in anthropology, biological sciences/environmental and occupational health sciences, biopharmacology, biotechnology, economics, English, history, mathematics, music, physics, sociology/social research, and statistics and applied mathematics lead to the combined bachelor's/master's degree, enabling highly qualified students to earn both degrees more quickly.

Hunter College also provides preprofessional advisement and preparation for advanced study in chiropractic, dentistry, engineering, law, medicine, optometry, osteopathy, pharmacy, podiatry, and veterinary medicine.

Academic Programs

Hunter instills a rich and informed sense of the possibilities of humanity in its students and expects them to carry their liberal arts education forward in their careers, their public responsibilities, and their personal lives.

The College trains its students in the sciences, the humanities, and a number of professional fields. As they strive to achieve their career goals, students are expected to perceive their chosen fields of study as only a part of a wider realm of knowledge. Undergraduate programs of study at Hunter consist of five parts, totaling 120 credits: a general education requirement, a pluralism and diversity requirement, a concentration of in-depth study (major), elective courses, and a minor.

Undergraduate students at Hunter who exhibit intellectual curiosity and exceptional ability may apply to the Thomas Hunter Scholars Program, an interdisciplinary program that individualizes study according to needs and interests and grants a Bachelor of Arts degree.

Students may earn sophomore standing (up to 30 credits) if they score well on the College-Level Examination Program (CLEP) subject tests, the Advanced Placement examinations of the College Board, and the Regents College Examination (RCE) Program of New York State.

Off-Campus Programs

Hunter College taps Manhattan to allow innumerable internships. Hosts have included Atlantic Records, CNN, the Council on Foreign Relations, DreamWorks SKG, Madison Square Garden, Metropolitan Museum of Art, New York City Council, Simon & Schuster, and many more. Interns perform curatorial and administrative work in museums, research and production work on TV news shows and newspapers, design work in commercial graphics, and booking, managing, and technical work in theaters.

Academic Facilities

The College is made up of five sites in Manhattan. The largest, a modern complex of buildings connected by skywalks at 68th Street and Lexington Avenue, sits above a convenient subway stop. This campus offers programs in the arts and sciences and in teacher education.

Downtown on East 25th Street, the Brookdale Campus houses the Division of the Schools of the Health Professions, which includes the Hunter-Bellevue School of Nursing, one of the nation's largest nursing programs, and the School of Health Sciences.

Uptown on East 79th Street, slated to soon be relocated to 116th Street, is the Hunter College School of Social Work, which was recently listed among the top ten schools of its kind in the nation by *U.S. News & World Report*.

On Manhattan's West Side, Hunter's Studio Art Building houses an 8,000-square-foot gallery and provides M.F.A. students with individual studios that are among the best in the city.

At East 94th Street, the Campus Schools house an elementary school and a high school for the intellectually gifted that are renowned, as is the College itself, for a long tradition of academic excellence.

All locations are minutes from Grand Central Terminal, Penn Station, and the New York/New Jersey Port Authority Bus Terminal, making Hunter easily accessible from Connecticut, Westchester, New Jersey, and Long Island.

The collections of the Hunter College libraries are housed in the Jacqueline Grennan Wexler Library and the Art Slide Library (located at the main campus), as well as at the branch libraries at the Brookdale Campus and the School of Social Work. The libraries hold over 750,000 volumes, 3,000 periodicals, a nonprint collection of more than 1 million microforms, and 250,000 art slides in addition to records, tapes, scores, music CDs, and videos. Recently, Hunter installed new computer, multimedia, and Internet labs and its first CD-ROM network. The CD-ROM network provides access to indexes, abstracts, and complete texts and multimedia resources, and Internet labs make the World Wide Web accessible.

Costs

Hunter College is affordable. In 2010–11, New York State residents enrolled as full-time, matriculated students paid $2415 per semester ($205 per credit part-time). Nonresidents enrolled as full-time, matriculated students paid $435 per credit. All students paid a Student Activity Fee ($84.50 per semester for full-time students and $54.45 per semester for part-time students) and a $15-per-semester Consolidated Fee.

Financial Aid

Hunter College participates in all state and federal financial aid programs. Financial aid is available to matriculated students in the form of grants, loans, and work-study. Grants provide funds that do not have to be repaid. Loans must be repaid in regular installments over a prescribed period of time. Work-study consists of part-time employment, either on campus or in an outside agency. More information is available from the Office of Financial Aid at 212-772-4820.

Entering freshmen whose high school records indicate a high level of academic achievement may apply to the Macaulay Honors College at Hunter College. This prestigious program offers a generous financial aid package, including a full academic scholarship, as well as extensive benefits, including a free room at the Hunter College Residence Hall for two years. In addition, Hunter College offers a wide array of other scholarships.

Faculty

Thanks to its location in the heart of New York City, Hunter College attracts a special kind of faculty member. Some are well-known scholars and researchers in their fields, such as biologists involved in advanced research on genetic structure. Others are professionals with active careers in the city, including well-known painters, sculptors, architects, and urban design experts. Hunter's faculty also includes environmental health scientists who work on occupational health and safety issues, nursing administrators who work in the country's leading hospitals, and film directors, theater critics, and musicians who are engaged in New York City's cultural milieu. Many members of the faculty are nationally renowned; they maintain Hunter's reputation for academic excellence through outstanding teaching and cutting-edge publications and by securing millions of dollars in annual grants for research.

Student Government

Several governing assemblies involve students in Hunter's governance. The College Senate, the legislative body of the College, includes faculty members, students, and administrators. Two Student Governments (undergraduate and graduate) also play essential roles in the life of the College. Students with voting power sit on faculty and administrative committees.

Admission Requirements

Candidates for freshman admission are considered based on the overall strength of their academic preparation, cumulative high school averages, and SAT or ACT scores. Freshman students who entered in fall 2010 had a high school academic grade point average of 88 and an SAT score of 1198 (math and verbal only). The College recommends 4 years of English, 4 years of social studies, 3 years of mathematics, 2 years of a foreign language, 2 years of laboratory sciences, and 1 year of performing or visual arts as the minimum academic preparation for success in college.

Students are considered transfer applicants if they have previously attended any college, university, and/or proprietary school since graduating from high school or secondary school. This applies whether or not the student is seeking transfer credit. Transfer students in fall 2010 had a cumulative grade point average of 3.07 with an average of 70.3 credits attempted. For more information, applicants should visit Hunter College's Web site.

Application and Information

Applicants are considered for fall (September) and spring (February) admission. Applications for the fall must be filed no later than September 15 and for spring, no later than February 1. All applications must be filed on the CUNY Web site at http://www.cuny.edu.

Welcome Center
Hunter College
695 Park Avenue, Room 100N
New York, New York 10065
Phone: 212-772-4490
E-mail: WelcomeCenter@hunter.cuny.edu
Web site: http://www.hunter.cuny.edu
http://on.fb.me/hunter_coll_cuny (Facebook)
http://www.flickr.com/photos/welcome_center

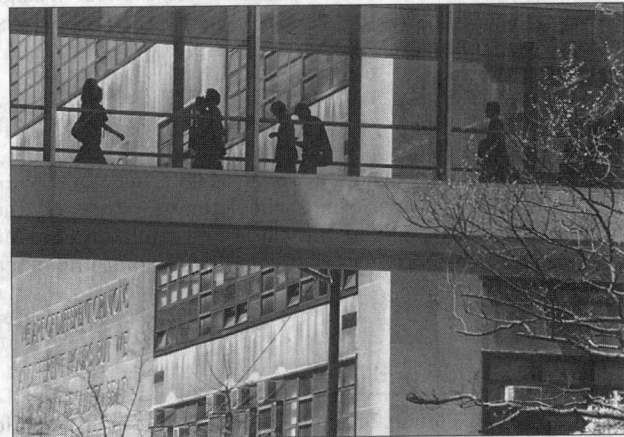

Students at Hunter College enjoy the convenience of skywalks that connect all four buildings at the 68th Street campus. Hunter's Upper East Side location provides easy access to some of New York's finest offerings; Central Park and the Metropolitan Museum of Art are just blocks away.

THE ILLINOIS INSTITUTE OF ART– CHICAGO

CHICAGO, ILLINOIS

A focused education from The Illinois Institute of Art–Chicago can help students turn their creative energy into a powerful tool that can make a difference in the world. Students are part of a collaborative and supportive community, where experienced instructors provide the guidance and skills needed to pursue a career in the creative economy.

The school's programs in the areas of design, media arts, fashion, and culinary give students the opportunity to learn by using professional-grade technology and build a portfolio of work to show potential employers after graduation.

The Illinois Institute of Art–Chicago is accredited by the Higher Learning Commission and is a member of the North Central Association, 230 South LaSalle Street, Suite 7-500, Chicago, Illinois, 60604-1413; phone: 800-621-7440; http://www.ncahlc.org.

The Illinois Institute of Art–Chicago is authorized by the Illinois Board of Higher Education, 431 East Adams, Second Floor, Springfield, Illinois 62701; phone: 217-782-2551; http://www.ibhe.state.il.us/default.htm.

The Associate of Applied Science degree program in culinary arts is accredited by the Accrediting Commission of the American Culinary Federation Education Foundation.

The interior design program leading to the Bachelor of Fine Arts degree is accredited by the Council for Interior Design Accreditation, 206 Grandville Avenue, Suite 350, Grand Rapids, Michigan 49503; http://www.accredit-id.org.

Location

The city of Chicago provides a backdrop like no other. With two locations downtown, the school offers students the opportunity to learn both in the classroom, and through the many events and experiences that come with being immersed in downtown Chicago.

Programs of Study and Degrees

No matter which course of study a student may choose, the professionals at The Illinois Institute of Art–Chicago will guide, support, and help each student as their talents evolve on their journey of personal and professional transformation. Students studying design learn to fine-tune their visual thinking and problem-solving skills, as they create everything from logos to TV ads. Programs in the area of media arts focus on utilizing technology to deliver information and entertainment, while students studying fashion learn to design clothes for the runway or run a retail shop. Culinary programs focus on the fundamental techniques while exposing students to a full menu of international cuisines and management techniques.

Bachelor's degree programs are offered in advertising, audio production, culinary management, digital filmmaking and video production, digital photography, fashion design, fashion marketing and management, game art and design, graphic design, hospitality management, illustration and design, interior design, and media arts and animation.

Associate degree programs are offered in culinary arts, fashion merchandising, graphic design, and hospitality management.

A certificate program is offered in professional baking and pastry.

The bachelor's degree programs in culinary management and interior design, as well as the associate degree programs in culinary arts and graphic design, are also available in an evening and weekend option format.

Academic Programs

The Illinois Institute of Art–Chicago operates on a year-round, four quarter system.

Academic Facilities

The Illinois Institute of Art–Chicago provides a learning environment with professional-grade technology applicable to each student's course of study. Students have the opportunity to build a portfolio of work that shows potential employers that they are trained to use the software, hardware, or equipment utilized within the industry. Depending upon the course of study, students are immersed in a creative environment—from classrooms to computer labs to studios—focused on relevant, hands-on education designed to prepare students for the real world.

Costs

Tuition cost varies by program. Prospective students should contact the school for current tuition costs. Other charges include a starting kit for all first-quarter students. Kits vary in price depending on the program of study.

Financial Aid

Financial aid is available for those who qualify. Students who require financial assistance should first complete and submit a Free Application for Federal Student Aid (FAFSA) and meet with a financial aid officer.

Faculty

Faculty members are experienced professionals who create a learning environment that is similar to the professional world students will face after graduation. Instructors are focused on

helping students develop the skills they need to transform their creative potential into marketable skills.

Admission Requirements

Applicants must provide proof of high school graduation or achievement of a General Educational Development (GED) certificate as a prerequisite for admission. In lieu of documenting high school graduation or a GED certificate, applicants may provide proof of attaining an associate degree or higher from an accredited institution. An official transcript indicating date of high school graduation, GED certificate (including test scores), or date of college graduation (including degree granted) is required as proof.

All individuals seeking admission to The Illinois Institute of Art–Chicago are interviewed in person or by phone by an assistant director of admissions, and each applicant must create an original essay of at least 150 words stating how an education at The Illinois Institute of Art–Chicago would help the student to achieve career goals. There is a $50 application fee.

For the most recent information regarding admission requirements, please refer to the current academic catalog.

Application and Information

To obtain an application, make arrangements for an interview, or tour the school, students should contact:

The Illinois Institute of Art–Chicago
350 North Orleans Street
Chicago, Illinois 60654-1593
Phone: 312-280-3500
        800-351-3450 (toll-free)
Fax: 312-280-8562
Web site: http://www.artinstitutes.edu/chicago

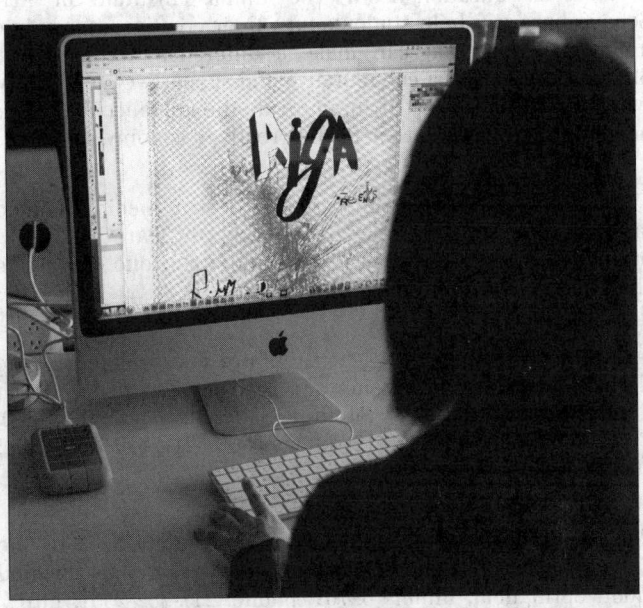

COLLEGE CLOSE-UPS

THE ILLINOIS INSTITUTE OF ART– SCHAUMBURG

SCHAUMBURG, ILLINOIS

A focused education from The Illinois Institute of Art–Schaumburg can help students turn their creative energy into a powerful tool that can make a difference in the world. Students are part of a collaborative and supportive community, where experienced instructors provide the guidance and skills needed to pursue a career in the creative economy.

The school's programs in the areas of design, media arts, and fashion give students the opportunity to learn by using professional-grade technology and build a portfolio of work to show potential employers after graduation.

The Illinois Institute of Art–Schaumburg is accredited by the Higher Learning Commission and is a member of the North Central Association, 230 South LaSalle Street, Suite 7-500, Chicago, Illinois 60604-1413; phone: 800-621-7440 (toll-free); http://www.ncahlc.org.

The Illinois Institute of Art–Schaumburg is authorized by the Illinois Board of Higher Education 431 East Adams, Second Floor, Springfield, Illinois 62701; phone: 217-782-2551; http://www.ibhe.state.il.us/default.htm.

The interior design program leading to the Bachelor of Fine Arts degree is accredited by the Council for Interior Design Accreditation, 206 Grandville Avenue, Suite 350, Grand Rapids, Michigan 49503; http://www.accredit-id.org.

Location

Located in suburban Chicago, in Schaumburg, the school provides easy access to the big city, while giving students a more suburban environment in which to live and learn.

Programs of Study and Degrees

No matter which course of study a student may choose, the professionals at The Illinois Institute of Art–Schaumburg will guide, support, and help each student as their talents evolve on their journey of personal and professional transformation. Students studying design learn to fine-tune their visual thinking and problem-solving skills, as they create everything from logos to TV ads. Programs in the area of media arts focus on utilizing technology to deliver information and entertainment, while students studying fashion learn to design clothes for the runway or run a retail shop.

Bachelor's degree programs are offered in advertising, audio production, digital filmmaking and video production, digital photography, fashion design, fashion marketing and management, game art and design, graphic design, hospitality management, interior design, media arts and animation, visual effects and motion graphics, and Web design and interactive media.

Associate degree programs are offered in graphic design and Web design and interactive media.

Diploma programs are offered in digital design, residential planning, and Web design.

The digital design, game art and design, graphic design, interior design, media arts and animation, residential planning, Web design, and Web design and interactive media programs are also available in an evening and weekend option format.

Academic Programs

The Illinois Institute of Art–Schaumburg operates on a year-round, four-quarter system.

Academic Facilities

The Illinois Institute of Art–Schaumburg provides a learning environment with professional-grade technology applicable to each student's course of study. Students have the opportunity to build a portfolio of work that shows potential employers that they are trained to use the software, hardware, or equipment utilized within the industry. Depending upon the course of study, students are immersed in a creative environment—from classrooms to computer labs to studios—focused on relevant, hands-on education designed to prepare students for the real world.

Costs

Tuition cost varies by program. Prospective students should contact the school for current tuition costs. Other charges include a starting kit for all first-quarter students. Kits vary in price depending on the program of study.

Financial Aid

Financial aid is available for those who qualify. Students who require financial assistance should first complete and submit a Free Application for Federal Student Aid (FAFSA) and meet with a financial aid officer.

Faculty

Faculty members are experienced professionals who create a learning environment that is similar to the professional world students will face after graduation. Instructors are focused on helping students develop the skills they need to transform their creative potential into marketable skills.

Admission Requirements

Applicants must provide proof of high school graduation or achievement of a General Educational Development (GED) certificate as a prerequisite for admission. In lieu of documenting high school graduation or a GED certificate, applicants may provide proof of attaining an associate degree or higher from an accredited institution. An official transcript indicating date of high school graduation, GED certificate (including test scores), or date of college graduation (including degree granted) is required as proof.

All individuals seeking admission to The Illinois Institute of Art–Schaumburg are interviewed in person or by phone by an assistant director of admissions, and each applicant must create an original essay of at least 150 words stating how an education at The Illinois Institute of Art–Schaumburg would help the student to achieve career goals. There is a $50 application fee.

For the most recent information regarding admission requirements, please refer to the current academic catalog.

Application and Information

To obtain an application, make arrangements for an interview, or tour the school, prospective students should contact:

The Illinois Institute of Art–Schaumburg
1000 North Plaza Drive, Suite 100
Schaumburg, Illinois 60173-4990
Phone: 847-619-3450
       800-314-3450 (toll-free)
Fax: 847-619-3064
Web site: http://www.artinstitutes.edu/schaumburg

The Art Institute of Atlanta; The Art Institute of Atlanta–Decatur[1]; The Art Institute of Austin[2]; The Art Institute of California–Hollywood; The Art Institute of California–Inland Empire; The Art Institute of California–Los Angeles; The Art Institute of California–Orange County; The Art Institute of California–Sacramento; The Art Institute of California–San Diego; The Art Institute of California–San Francisco; The Art Institute of California–Sunnyvale; The Art Institute of Charleston[1]; The Art Institute of Charlotte; The Art Institute of Colorado; The Art Institute of Dallas[3]; The Art Institute of Fort Lauderdale; The Art Institute of Fort Worth[3]; The Art Institute of Houston; The Art Institute of Houston–North[2]; The Art Institute of Indianapolis[4]; The Art Institute of Jacksonville[5]; The Art Institute of Las Vegas; The Art Institute of Michigan; The Art Institute of New York City; The Art Institute of Ohio–Cincinnati[6]; The Art Institute of Philadelphia; The Art Institute of Phoenix; The Art Institute of Pittsburgh; The Art Institute of Portland; The Art Institute of Raleigh–Durham; The Art Institute of Salt Lake City; The Art Institute of San Antonio[2];The Art Institute of Seattle; The Art Institute of Tampa[5]; The Art Institute of Tennessee–Nashville[1]; The Art Institute of Tucson; The Art Institute of Vancouver; The Art Institute of Virginia Beach[1,7]; The Art Institute of Washington[1,7]; The Art Institute of Washington–Northern Virginia[1,7]; The Art Institute of Wisconsin; The Art Institute of York–Pennsylvania; The Art Institutes International–Kansas City; The Art Institutes International Minnesota; The Illinois Institute of Art–Chicago; The Illinois Institute of Art–Schaumburg; The Illinois Institute of Art–Tinley Park; Miami International University of Art & Design; The New England Institute of Art.
[1]A branch of The Art Institute of Atlanta
[2]A branch of The Art Institute of Houston
[3]A campus of South University
[4]The Art Institute of Indianapolis is regulated by the Indiana Commission on Proprietary Education, 302 West Washington Street, Room E201, Indianapolis, Indiana 46204, AC-0080
[5]A branch of Miami International University of Art & Design
[6]The Art Institute of Ohio–Cincinnati, 8845 Governors Hill Drive, Suite 100, Cincinnati, Ohio 45249-3317, OH Reg. #04-01-1698B
[7]Certified by the State Council of Higher Education to operate in Virginia

THE ILLINOIS INSTITUTE OF ART–TINLEY PARK

TINLEY PARK, ILLINOIS

A focused education from The Illinois Institute of Art–Tinley Park can help students turn their creative energy into a powerful tool that can make a difference in the world. Students are part of a collaborative and supportive community, where experienced instructors provide the guidance and skills needed to pursue a career in the creative economy.

The school's programs in the areas of design, media arts, and fashion give students the opportunity to learn by using professional-grade technology and build a portfolio of work to show potential employers after graduation.

The Illinois Institute of Art–Tinley Park is an additional location of the Illinois Institute of Art–Chicago, which is accredited by the Higher Learning Commission and is a member of the North Central Association (NCA), 230 South LaSalle Street, Suite 7-500, Chicago, Illinois 60604-1413; phone: 800-621-7440; www.ncahlc.org.

The Illinois Institute of Art–Tinley Park is authorized by the Illinois Board of Higher Education, 431 East Adams, Second Floor, Springfield, Illinois 62701; phone: 217-782 -2551; www.ibhe.state.il.us/default.htm.

Location

Tinley Park is one of the fastest-growing Chicago suburbs and is close to the city's vast cultural and sports experiences. In 2009, *BusinessWeek* magazine listed Tinley Park as America's best place to raise children.

Programs of Study and Degrees

No matter which course of study a student may choose, the professionals at The Illinois Institute of Art–Tinley Park will guide, support, and help each student as their talents evolve on their journey of personal and professional transformation. Students studying design learn to fine-tune their visual thinking and problem-solving skills, as they create everything from logos to TV ads. Programs in the area of media arts focus on utilizing technology to deliver information and entertainment, while students studying fashion learn to market and merchandise clothing.

Bachelor's degree programs are offered in advertising, digital photography, fashion marketing and management, graphic design, interior design, and media arts and animation.

Associate degree programs are offered in fashion merchandising and graphic design.

Academic Programs

The Illinois Institute of Art–Tinley Park operates on a year-round, four quarter system.

Academic Facilities

The Illinois Institute of Art–Tinley Park provides a learning environment with professional-grade technology applicable to each student's course of study. Students have the opportunity to build a portfolio of work that shows potential employers that they are trained to use the software, hardware, or equipment utilized within the industry. Depending upon the course of study, students are immersed in a creative environment—from classrooms to computer labs to studios—focused on relevant, hands-on education designed to prepare students for the real world.

Costs

Tuition cost varies by program. Prospective students should contact the school for current tuition costs. Other charges include a starting kit for all first-quarter students. Kits vary in price depending on the program of study.

Financial Aid

Financial aid is available for those who qualify. Students who require financial assistance should first complete and submit a Free Application for Federal Student Aid (FAFSA) and meet with a financial aid officer.

Faculty

Faculty members are experienced professionals who create a learning environment that is similar to the professional world students will face after graduation. Instructors are focused on helping students develop the skills they need to transform their creative potential into marketable skills.

Admission Requirements

Applicants must provide proof of high school graduation or achievement of a General Educational Development (GED) certificate as a prerequisite for admission. In lieu of documenting high school graduation or a GED certificate, applicants may provide proof of attaining an associate degree or higher from an accredited institution. An official transcript indicating date of high school graduation, GED certificate (including test scores), or date of college graduation (including degree granted) is required as proof.

All individuals seeking admission to The Illinois Institute of Art–Tinley Park are interviewed in person or by phone by an assistant director of admissions, and each applicant must create an original essay of at least 150 words stating how an education at The Illinois Institute of Art–Tinley Park would help the student to achieve career goals. There is a $50 application fee.

For the most recent information regarding admission requirements, please refer to the current academic catalog.

Application and Information

To obtain an application, make arrangements for an interview, or tour the school, prospective students should contact:

The Illinois Institute of Art–Tinley Park
18670 Graphic Drive
Tinley Park, Illinois 60477
Phone: 708-781-4200
        800-342-3298 (toll-free)
Fax: 708-781-4201
Web site: http://www.artinstitutes.edu/tinleypark

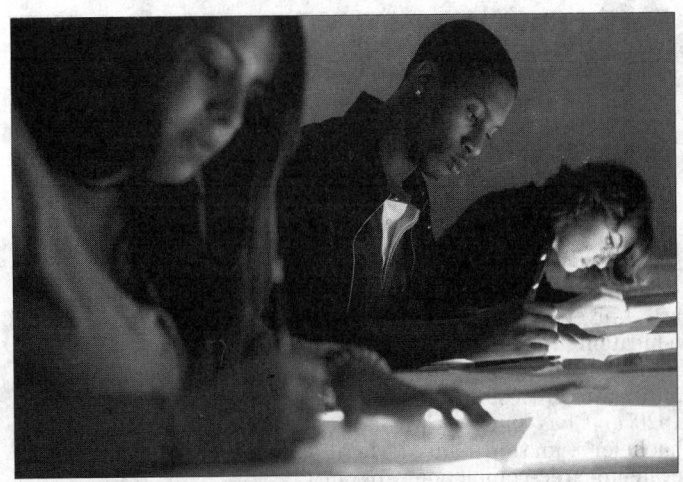

The Art Institute of Atlanta; The Art Institute of Atlanta–Decatur[1]; The Art Institute of Austin[2]; The Art Institute of California–Hollywood; The Art Institute of California–Inland Empire; The Art Institute of California–Los Angeles; The Art Institute of California–Orange County; The Art Institute of California–Sacramento; The Art Institute of California–San Diego; The Art Institute of California–San Francisco; The Art Institute of California–Sunnyvale; The Art Institute of Charleston[1]; The Art Institute of Charlotte; The Art Institute of Colorado; The Art Institute of Dallas[3]; The Art Institute of Fort Lauderdale; The Art Institute of Fort Worth[3]; The Art Institute of Houston; The Art Institute of Houston–North[2]; The Art Institute of Indianapolis[4]; The Art Institute of Jacksonville[5]; The Art Institute of Las Vegas; The Art Institute of Michigan; The Art Institute of New York City; The Art Institute of Ohio–Cincinnati[6]; The Art Institute of Philadelphia; The Art Institute of Phoenix; The Art Institute of Pittsburgh; The Art Institute of Portland; The Art Institute of Raleigh–Durham; The Art Institute of Salt Lake City; The Art Institute of San Antonio[2];The Art Institute of Seattle; The Art Institute of Tampa[5]; The Art Institute of Tennessee–Nashville[1]; The Art Institute of Tucson; The Art Institute of Vancouver; The Art Institute of Virginia Beach[1,7]; The Art Institute of Washington[1,7]; The Art Institute of Washington–Northern Virginia[1,7]; The Art Institute of Wisconsin; The Art Institute of York–Pennsylvania; The Art Institutes International–Kansas City; The Art Institutes International Minnesota; The Illinois Institute of Art–Chicago; The Illinois Institute of Art–Schaumburg; The Illinois Institute of Art–Tinley Park; Miami International University of Art & Design; The New England Institute of Art.

[1]A branch of The Art Institute of Atlanta
[2]A branch of The Art Institute of Houston
[3]A campus of South University
[4]The Art Institute of Indianapolis is regulated by the Indiana Commission on Proprietary Education, 302 West Washington Street, Room E201, Indianapolis, Indiana 46204, AC-0080
[5]A branch of Miami International University of Art & Design
[6]The Art Institute of Ohio–Cincinnati, 8845 Governors Hill Drive, Suite 100, Cincinnati, Ohio 45249-3317, OH Reg. #04-01-1698B
[7]Certified by the State Council of Higher Education to operate in Virginia

IMMACULATA UNIVERSITY
IMMACULATA, PENNSYLVANIA

The University

Immaculata University (IU), a comprehensive Catholic liberal arts university for students of all faiths, offers a high-quality education that is firmly grounded in values and tradition. Immaculata graduates are known for their skills and knowledge and for their desire to serve. The University was founded in 1920 and has since grown to enroll almost 4,000 students in bachelor's, master's, and doctoral degree programs and accelerated degree-completion programs.

Approximately 1,000 traditional-aged men and women attend the College of Undergraduate Studies, with 80 percent of them living in University-sponsored housing. The College of Lifelong Learning includes undergraduate programs that are open to adult men and women. Students represent seventeen states and twenty-seven countries, giving the campus both ethnic and geographic diversity. Resident students live in four residence halls containing double rooms. Both resident and nonresident students participate in more than sixty student clubs and organizations that represent interests in athletics, student government, academic disciplines, community action, music, dance, theater, and student publications.

Intercollegiate sports include women's basketball, cross-country, field hockey, golf, lacrosse, soccer, softball, tennis, track and field, and volleyball and men's baseball, basketball, cross-country, golf, lacrosse, soccer, tennis, and track and field. Immaculata competes in Division III athletics as part of the Colonial States Athletic Conference. A turf field, stadium, indoor batting cages, gymnasia, fitness room, and pool are available for student use and provide numerous opportunities for physical activities and wellness programs. The Student Association of Immaculata University provides the unity, enthusiasm, and leadership that are integral parts of the traditional undergraduate experience.

Immaculata University celebrates unique traditions as a part of the overall collegiate experience, such as Freshman Investiture, the academic capping of the newest members of the University community. Carol Night, one of Immaculata's best-loved traditions, involves students, faculty members, alumni, and families singing around the Christmas tree in the rotunda of Villa Maria Hall.

The main building, Villa Maria Hall, is of neo-Renaissance architecture in gray stone with a red tile roof. The other thirteen major campus buildings are also of gray stone with red tile roofs, unifying the aesthetic appearance of the campus.

Graduate degrees offered in the College of Graduate Studies include the Master of Arts in counseling psychology, cultural and linguistic diversity, educational leadership and administration, music therapy, nursing, nutrition education, and organization leadership. Doctoral degrees are offered in educational administration, clinical psychology, and school psychology. ACCEL, the accelerated degree-completion program, offers bachelor's degrees in financial management, human performance management, and information technology.

Location

Immaculata's 375-acre campus is located in historic Chester County, 20 miles west of Philadelphia and 10 miles south of Valley Forge. The area is primarily suburban, with numerous colleges and universities offering a wide range of cultural and social activities. Many places of interest in Philadelphia and Lancaster are easily reached by car, train, or bus. The campus is 15 minutes from the King of Prussia Mall, the second largest mall in the U.S. Southern New Jersey shore resorts and New York City are within 1½ hours by car, with Pocono Mountain ski resorts and Washington, D.C., only 2½ hours away by car or train. The University provides numerous opportunities for internships in the business, educational, and scientific communities throughout the area.

Majors and Degrees

The College of Undergraduate Studies at Immaculata offers the Bachelor of Arts, Bachelor of Music, Bachelor of Science, Associate of Arts, and Associate of Science degrees. Undergraduate major fields of study include accounting, allied health, biology, biology/psychology, business administration, chemistry, communication, criminology/sociology, education, English, exercise science, family and consumer sciences, fashion merchandising, finance, French, general science, history, information technology, international business/foreign language, marketing management, mathematics, mathematics/computer science, music, music education, music performance, music therapy, nursing, nutrition/dietetics, political science/international relations, prelaw, premedicine, pre–physical therapy, pre–veterinary medicine, psychology, sociology, sociology/social work, Spanish, Spanish/psychology, Spanish/social work, theology, and undecided. Allied health concentrations include: clinical laboratory science, diagnostic medical sonography, invasive cardiovascular technology, nuclear medicine technology, and surgical technology. IU also offers partnership programs with Thomas Jefferson University (TJU) in physical therapy, occupational therapy, bioscience technologies, and radiologic sciences. These programs allow students to seamlessly matriculate into TJU after three years of study at IU.

Academic Programs

Two factors are emphasized in the educational program at Immaculata: a comprehensive liberal arts background and a major field of concentration that prepares students to begin a career or to attend graduate school. The honors program offers an array of courses designed to give those who participate a special involvement in the learning process.

The Mary Bruder Center houses the offices for personal, career, and graduate study counseling and for educational and career testing. Workshops and seminars in resume writing, interviewing, career options, internship opportunities, and graduate fellowships are offered at regular intervals.

Off-Campus Programs

Both summer-abroad and junior-year-abroad programs combine travel with academic study to heighten the experience of students who seek these opportunities. Students can study in England and Ireland through IU and in other countries through the University's collaboration with Arcadia University.

Every undergraduate major department offers numerous internship opportunities for students in agencies, businesses, institutions, or corporations related to their study. Some majors, such as nutrition, fashion merchandising, and music therapy, require a multiweek internship for the degree to be granted.

Academic Facilities

The Gabriele Library houses 130,000 volumes and offers 714 periodical subscriptions. In addition to the computer center, students have access to networked computers in the library, an interactive language lab with a video screen, and a multifaceted science lab with computer-simulated experiments; they also have Internet/Intranet access from their residence halls. Well-equipped laboratories, art studios, media centers, and a 1,150-seat theater give students a variety of settings in which to pursue their interests.

State-of-the-art computer labs include the Campus Learning and Language Laboratory, the Sister Maria Socorro Studio Laboratory for Mathematics and Science, a new Biology Laboratory, and the Loyola Executive Technology Center. Classrooms and the library utilize wireless technology in the smart classrooms.

Costs

For 2011–12, tuition and fees are $28,850 and room and board are $11,460. An additional $1000 is estimated to cover books and personal spending. Immaculata offers a Fixed Tuition program. This guarantees the same tuition cost for four years for all full-time students entering the College of Undergraduate Studies. Immaculata is the only college in the Commonwealth of Pennsylvania to offer this program.

Financial Aid

Financial aid is available in the form of scholarships, grants, loans, and part-time campus employment through the resources of Immaculata, federal and state governments, and private endowments. Scholarships are awarded for academic excellence. Approximately 90 percent of the students receive some form of aid, and all students who demonstrate need are offered financial aid packages. The University requires that students submit the Free Application for Federal Student Aid (FAFSA) to be considered for financial aid. The University sends financial aid packages to accepted students as their files are completed by the end of February. The FAFSA reporting code is 003276.

Faculty

The faculty has more than 90 full-time and 200 part-time members, more than half of whom hold doctorates. Several members of the Immaculata faculty conduct research and present papers in various disciplines, both nationally and internationally. High-quality teaching is of the greatest importance to Immaculata's academic program. Full-time faculty members serve as academic counselors and activity moderators. The student-faculty ratio is 11:1.

Student Government

The Student Association of Immaculata University (SAIU) governs most aspects of student life for both resident and commuter students. The resident assistant program moderates residence life by holding open meetings to discuss safety issues and to set residence hall regulations. Students serve on the various University policymaking committees and handle all student activity funds.

Admission Requirements

In order to be considered for admission to the College of Undergraduate Studies, students must submit an official secondary school transcript indicating course selection for the senior year and SAT or ACT scores. The reporting code for the SAT is 2320, and the reporting code for the ACT is 3596. An essay and recommendations are required. The Admission Committee requires 14 or more course units, as follows: 4 units of English, 2 units of social science, 2 units of mathematics, 2 units of science (1 lab), and 2 consecutive years of the same foreign language. Most candidates exceed this curriculum. The mid-range GPA for the past two years was 3.2.

All admission credentials should be sent to the College of Undergraduate Studies. Students can apply online at the University's Web site, http://www.immaculata.edu/admissions. The application fee of $35 is waived for students who apply online or who visit the campus and complete an application during their visit. Students also have the option to apply through the Common Application, http://www.commonapp.org, which is free as well.

Application and Information

Applications are accepted from prospective freshman and transfer students on a rolling admissions basis, and decisions are made three to four weeks after an applicant's file is complete. The only exceptions are those students applying for nursing and the Thomas Jefferson University programs. The application deadline for Thomas Jefferson is December 15 and the priority deadline for nursing is January 17. All of the credentials required for admission must be received and the file completed by that date.

For further information, students should contact:

Rebecca H. Bowlby, Director of Admission
Immaculata University
P.O. Box 642
Immaculata, Pennsylvania 19345-0642
Phone: 610-647-4400 Ext. 3060
        877-42-TODAY (toll-free)
Fax: 610-640-0836
E-mail: admis@immaculata.edu
Web site: http://www.immaculata.edu

Fun on a fall day on the campus of Immaculata University.

IONA COLLEGE
NEW ROCHELLE, NEW YORK

The College

Iona College is a four-year, coed college in New Rochelle, a suburb of New York City. The 35-acre campus is located just 20 minutes by rail from the heart of Midtown Manhattan. A medium-size college, Iona offers more than forty majors and thirty minors in business and liberal arts. The most popular undergraduate majors are accounting, crimincal justice, finance, marketing, mass communication, and psychology. Iona was founded in 1940 by the Congregation of Christian Brothers and is a diverse community of learners and scholars dedicated to academic excellence in the tradition of the Christian Brothers and American Catholic higher education.

Iona's overall enrollment is 4,200 students, of whom 3,200 are traditional undergraduate students. The student body is talented and diverse, with students coming from thirty-five states. Thirty-three percent of the students are members of minority groups, and contribute to a college environment that values diversity.

More than seventy-five clubs and over 100 activities are available for student participation, including student government, Greek organizations, intramural sports, community service, a student-run newspaper, radio and TV stations, the yearbook, theater groups, a pipe band, ethnic-affinity groups, various honor societies, and music groups.

Iona offers twenty-one NCAA Division I athletic teams. Men's sports include baseball, basketball, cross-country, rowing, soccer, swimming and diving, track (indoor and outdoor), and water polo. Women's sports include basketball, cross-country, lacrosse, rowing, soccer, softball, swimming and diving, track (indoor and outdoor), and water polo.

The Office of Student Development organizes many activities for students to participate in each week, including trips to nearby New York City for theater, sports, and museums; on-campus movie nights; parties and dances; karaoke nights; wellness workshops; and other activities.

The College offers students four-year housing in five residence halls, with a sixth hall proposed for a 2012 fall opening. Sixty-seven percent of freshmen and over a third of the undergraduate population reside on campus. The residential experience includes living and learning environments, where students are housed together based on their academic and curricular interests. An off-campus housing office was recently established to work with nonresidential students and the local community. All students are offered a unique meal plan that enables them to dine at on- and off-campus locations. On-campus eateries include a food court, dining commons, Quiznos, and Starbucks café.

Location

Iona's campus is located in New Rochelle, New York, one of the oldest cities in the U.S. Founded in 1654, New Rochelle is a city of 70,000 on the shore of the Long Island Sound.

Majors and Degrees

Iona College offers Bachelor of Arts, Bachelor of Science, and Bachelor of Business Administration degrees through its School of Arts and Science and Hagan School of Business. Undergraduate majors include accounting, biochemistry, biology (general, pre-dental, pre–physical therapy, preprofessional, and premedicine), business administration, chemistry, computer science, criminal justice, economics, education (childhood and adolescence), English, environmental science, finance, foreign languages (French, Italian, and Spanish), history, information systems, interdisciplinary science, international business, international studies, management, marketing, mass communication (advertising, journalism, public relations, and television and video), mathematics, medical technology, philosophy, pre–physical therapy, physics, political science, psychology, religious studies, social work, sociology, speech communication studies, and speech/language pathology and audiology. Five-year combined bachelor's and master's degree programs are offered in computational/computer science, computer science, criminal justice, English, history, and psychology. A fast-track M.B.A. program is available to students after graduation.

There are also minors available in accounting, biology, business, chemistry, classical humanities, computer science, criminal justice, economics, English, film studies, finance, fine and performing arts, French, history, information systems, international business, Italian, management, marketing, mass communication, mathematics, peace and justice studies, philosophy, physics, political science, psychology, public policy, religious studies, sociology, Spanish, speech communication, sports and entertainment studies, women's studies, and writing. A number of programs offer a business minor in combination with a major or concentration.

An honors program is available for top students who desire additional enhancement to their academic program. Special courses, seminars, mentoring, advising, and off-campus opportunities are part of the honors students' curriculum.

Academic Programs

Many of Iona's programs are accredited by the highest specialized accrediting councils, including AACSB International–The Association to Advance Collegiate Schools of Business for the Hagan School of Business and the National Council for Accreditation of Teacher Education (NCATE) for the Department of Education. Mass communications (ACEJMC) is one of four accredited programs in the state of New York, and the Departments of Social Work (CSWE), Education, and Computer Science (ABET) boast the top accreditations available.

Off-Campus Programs

Iona College encourages students to broaden their educational experience through study and travel abroad. Iona sponsors summer, semester, and intersession programs in Australia, England, France, Ireland, Italy, and Spain. The College also offers a wide range of internships in most majors. In recent years, students have held internships at some of the best-known corporate names in New York City and the surrounding area.

Academic Facilities

To meet the demands of a new generation of students, Iona heavily invests in updating its campus and technology. The latest investment in campus infrastructure is the expansion and renovation of the main library. A new atrium and wing incorporate new study space; meeting rooms; classrooms with the latest technology, including Apple dual-boot iMacs; a digital archive room; and refurbished auditorium. The two campus libraries, Ryan Library and the Helen T. Arrigoni Library/ Technology Center, house extensive collections and offer computer access to collections worldwide. The on-site collections, including more than 261,000 volumes, 687 periodical titles, audiovisual materials, and microforms, have been developed to support Iona's curriculum and special interests.

As part of a multimillion-dollar capital campaign, a student union was added and the athletic center was expanded and updated. The Robert V. LaPenta Student Union features a bookstore, commons/lounge areas, a food court, a bistro, a state-of-the-art media center, and offices for student services and campus organizations. The Hynes Athletics Center includes a multipurpose arena, an Olympic-size swimming pool, a Nautilus center, training facilities, and coaching offices. It is the home to the Iona College Gaels Division I teams that compete in the Metro Atlantic Athletic Conference (MAAC). Featuring a state-of-the-art cardiovascular center, three multipurpose courts, a rowing tank, and an aerobics/dance studio, the Hynes Center also allows Iona's nonathletes to participate in an intramural program that includes many various sports. Classes in Pilates, yoga, salsa dancing, and more are also be offered by qualified instructors.

The Arts Center on North Avenue provides space for the study of art, dance, and theater and includes the Brother Kenneth Chapman Gallery.

The College was one of the first wireless campuses in the region and was recognized by the Intel Corporation as a "Most Unwired" campus. Students can access the Internet and other online tools from anywhere on campus. The College's thirty-six computing facilities are kept updated with the latest hardware and software.

Costs

For the 2010–11 academic year, tuition and fees were $26,850; room and board costs were $11,800.

Financial Aid

Financial aid is critical to a student's decision to attend any college, and Iona College is no exception. Iona uses a system of academic scholarships in combination with need-based financial aid to help students enroll. For the 2010–11 academic year, 94 percent of undergraduates received some financial aid, with the average aid award near $23,780. To apply for financial aid, students should file the Free Application for Federal Student Aid (FAFSA) and the Iona College Financial Aid Application forms by February 15.

Faculty

Iona College has approximately 170 full-time and 80 part-time faculty members; 92 percent possess a terminal degree in their field. Faculty members conduct research and write books and articles, but their primary responsibility is teaching undergraduate students. All classes are taught by faculty members—there are no teaching assistants.

The student-faculty ratio is 13:1. Faculty members are readily available to meet for individual conferences. In addition, because of the College's proximity to New York City, many faculty members include regular excursions to Manhattan as part of their classes and invite guest speakers to lecture about special topics.

Student Government

The Student Government Association (SGA) is a service organization that coordinates, supervises, and promotes student activities. The Office of Student Activities hosts hundreds of on- and off-campus events throughout the year.

Admission Requirements

Admission decisions at Iona are based on a wide range of criteria. Most important is an applicant's academic record, including the level of curriculum taken and grades earned. Also considered are SAT or ACT scores, grade trends, a writing sample, activities, and recommendations.

For the class entering in September 2010, the average grade point average was 3.4 (89 percent); middle 50 percent on the SAT ranged from 1080 to 1300. Slightly over 7,300 applications were submitted and about 4,300 (59 percent) of the applications were accepted and offered admission.

Application and Information

The Office of Admissions at Iona College works with each applicant on an individual basis. While the outcome of the admission decision may not be what every applicant hopes, Iona tries to ensure that each applicant is treated with courtesy and dignity. In order to be considered for admission, Iona requires students to submit an application (paper or online), a $50 application fee, an official transcript, SAT or ACT scores, a counselor recommendation, and an essay. Transfer students must also submit official transcripts from all colleges and universities previously attended.

The deadline for submitting applications for regular admission is February 15; for early action, it is December 1. Decisions are mailed by April 1 for regular admission and late December for early action. Deposits for all accepted students are due on May 1.

Campus visits are available on most weekdays that classes are in session and on selected Saturdays; appointments are recommended. A visit can be scheduled by calling the Campus Visit Center at 914-633-2622 or by e-mail at eenglish@iona.edu.

For more information, students should contact:

Office of Admissions
Iona College
715 North Avenue
New Rochelle, New York 10801
Phone: 914-633-2502
        800-231-IONA (toll-free)
Fax: 914-637-2778
E-mail: admissions@iona.edu
Web site: http://www.iona.edu
        http://www.twitter.com/ionacollege
        http://www.youtube.com/IonaCollegeVideos

Iona students take a break from classes out on the lawn in front of the Robert V. LaPenta Student Union.

JOHN CABOT UNIVERSITY

ROME, ITALY

The University

John Cabot University (JCU) was founded in 1972 and is the first overseas American university in Italy with regional accreditation by the Middle States Commission of Higher Education. JCU is a four-year liberal arts college following the American system of education with a distinctive European and international character. Located in the historic center of Rome, the University has unparalleled access to history, culture, and the active diplomatic and international communities associated with both the United Nations organizations and embassies to Italy and the Holy See. JCU's international setting, commitment to a serious liberal arts education, and unique relationship with leading multinational corporations, media, cultural, and other international organizations, provides degree-seeking students the academic training and opportunities to participate in exclusive internships and enter directly into demanding careers, or continue their studies at prestigious graduate programs.

The University has a diverse and unique student body, composed of American, Italian, and international degree-seeking students from more than fifty countries. This group is complemented by visiting American students from major universities across the United States. The visiting American students bring to Rome their own regional diversity which complements the European diversity at JCU resulting in a dynamic and engaging student body. JCU's commitment to creating a student community of both four-year degree and visiting students provides degree students with the friendly, close community of a small campus, with the active and energetic networks that come from studying with a larger pool of students from across the U.S.

The average class size is 15 students, and there are approximately 100 full- and part-time faculty members with advanced degrees from universities all over the world. Students work closely with professors and receive the individual attention needed to develop their academic talents and abilities. With a student-centered approach to both education and human relationships, the University offers an active learning environment while also teaching the essential ethical standards for responsibility and leadership in today's world. JCU graduates are accepted into a wide array of graduate programs in the U.S., U.K., and Italy such as Columbia University, Johns Hopkins University, London School of Economics, and Università Bocconi.

The University is licensed by the Delaware Department of Education to award its degrees and is authorized by the Italian Ministry of Research and Instruction to operate as an institution of American higher education in Rome. John Cabot University was accredited in 2003 by the Middle States Commission on Higher Education (http://www.msche.org). Since 2000, the University has also had a validation agreement with the University of Wales allowing students to simultaneously earn both the American B.A. and the British B.A. Honors degree for JCU majors in business administration, international affairs, marketing, and political science.

Location

John Cabot University is located in Rome, Italy, in the picturesque Trastevere neighborhood, just down the river from St. Peter's Basilica and the Vatican and a short walk from the Roman Forum. John Cabot University has two campuses within a 5-minute walk of each other and a residence dorm with 24/7 security, also a 5-minute walk away. The Frank J. Guarini Campus, a former convent, consists of a central main building of three floors and an adjacent wing connected by terraces and courtyards. The original separate chapel now serves as the student lounge. The property offers students a tranquil atmosphere in which to study and interact, while historic, bustling Rome is just a few steps away. Surrounded by the green gardens of the Accademia dei Lincei (the National Academy of Sciences, of which Galileo was an early member) and next door to the Villa Farnesina of Raphael's famous frescoes, the Guarini Campus is buttressed by the Aurelian Wall of the Roman Empire. The Guarini Campus is approached through the Porta Settimiana, which was built by Pope Alexander VI Borgia in 1498 and later restored by Pope Pius VI in 1798. John Cabot also has spacious classrooms in the Tiber Campus, which is along the

banks of the famous Tiber River. Both campuses are equipped with Wi-Fi and classrooms furnished with multimedia equipment. The JCU Frohing Library is one of the most impressive English language libraries in Rome. JCU's fine arts and art history classes often meet at famous monuments such as the Colosseum and the Forum, which are within easy reach of JCU. In effect, all of Rome is John Cabot University's campus, and students take advantage of JCU's urban setting, meeting with friends and faculty at local cafés and trattorias as well as in many of the piazzas that are hidden within the small streets of Rome's historic center.

Majors and Degrees

John Cabot University offers the Bachelor of Arts degree in thirteen majors: art history, business administration, classical studies, communications, economics and finance, English literature, history, humanistic studies, international affairs, international business, Italian studies, marketing, and political science. The University of Wales, in the United Kingdom, has validated JCU degrees in business administration, international affairs, marketing, and political science since 2000. As a result of this validation, students in these programs may simultaneously work toward both an American degree from John Cabot University and a European degree (validated Honors) from the University of Wales. Students may select minors in all of the major areas, as well as in computer science, creative writing, religion, philosophy, and psychology. John Cabot also offers the Associate of Arts degree in all major fields of study.

Each of these programs is designed to develop the characteristics of the individual student through a unique learning and living experience in a setting rich in history, culture, and geopolitical interaction. All majors are complemented by internship opportunities at the United Nations, museums, and international firms in Rome. JCU's Career Services Center offers support for students' preparation and transition into post-graduate activities. JCU's alumni network provides additional opportunities for graduates to continue their career development through international connections, valued in today's global world.

Academic Programs

Unlike most European university systems, the American system of higher education encourages experimentation and breadth, particularly during the first two years of the university experience. The curricula of the University's programs are, therefore, divided into two basic categories: the general distribution requirements of the first two years of study, which give the student a broad exposure to the basic disciplines of the liberal arts educational experience, and the specific, additional requirements of each degree awarded by the University.

The general distribution and other introductory courses equip the student to select an area of specialization as a degree candidate. Within each degree program, there are specific requirements that must be met by the student who wishes to earn a degree at John Cabot. These requirements include ten to twelve core courses deemed by faculty members to be essential to the discipline of the degree and comparable to the requirements for the same degree at recognized and accredited colleges and universities in the American system of higher education. In addition to the core requirements, other requisites include electives that support the core program and offer opportunities to take courses in other discipline areas of particular interest or need.

The academic year is divided into two semesters of fifteen weeks each, beginning in September and January (see the academic calendar for more details). In one semester, a student normally takes five courses, earning 15 credits in the semester and 30 credits in the year. A five-week summer session allows students to take one or two additional courses. To earn the Bachelor of Arts degree, a student must complete 120 credits (forty courses); to earn the Associate of Arts degree, a student must complete 60 credits (twenty courses).

Special programs include English language preparation for university study (ENLUS).

Off-Campus Programs

The Go Global program at JCU offers degree-seeking students the opportunity to study at universities in the United States as well as several international locations. This enriching opportunity contributes to educational growth and cultural awareness in general and helps prepare students for careers in international fields.

Academic Facilities

The Frohring Library, constructed in 1999, provides the latest in online access to academic journals and indexes and is the University center for research in support of the academic programs as well as a quiet place for study and pleasure reading. The computer laboratories contain desktop computers equipped with the latest software as well as high-speed printers and a full-color scanner. The Aula Magna Regina is the largest room in the University and serves as the theater for the drama club. The Aula Magna is also used for orientation, cultural and community events, concerts, and student activities.

Costs

Tuition for 2011–12 is $9900 or €6950 per semester and housing costs begin at $4600 per semester.

Financial Aid

U.S. citizens attending a college or university outside the United States are eligible to apply for the Federal Family Education Loans (FFEL), including the Stafford Student Loan and PLUS loans. The Free Application for Federal Student Aid (FAFSA) form must be completed to apply for a Stafford Student Loan. Current U.S. government legislation prohibits U.S. citizens enrolled in colleges or universities outside the United States from receiving Federal Pell Grants, Federal Supplemental Educational Opportunity Grants (FSEOG), Federal Perkins Loans, and Federal Work-Study Program funds, even though they may be eligible for such assistance. Academic scholarships are awarded each year based on merit and need. John Cabot University is proud to participate in the Secchia Family Foundation's Secchia Scholars program. The four types of Secchia Scholarships are the Norman R. Peterson Scholarship, the Order Sons of Italy in America Scholarships, the Secchia–De Vos Merit Scholarships and the Economic Club of Grand Rapids–Secchia Scholarship. Other institutional scholarships include the Presidential Scholarships, the John Cabot University Alumni Matching Scholarship, the Italian Merit Scholarships, the 100/100 Italian Maturità Scholarships, and the Maxwell Rabb Scholarship. A number of work-study assistantships are available for students who are interested in and capable of assisting the various administrative offices and academic departments of the University.

Faculty

The University has a distinguished faculty of approximately 100 part- and full-time professors from around the world who are actively engaged in research. In addition to teaching, faculty members take part in academic advising; planning and monitoring a student's progress through the academic program; and extracurricular activities, such as field trips, fund-raising events, and lectures and seminars.

Student Government

Student government at John Cabot University contributes significantly to the quality of student life. A Student Senate is elected each year to coordinate activities. During the year, the Student Government sponsors a number of programs, such as the International Student Government Conference, which brings together student leaders from Italy, Europe, and the Middle East. The Student Government works with a faculty adviser and staff adviser in planning social, cultural, intellectual, and sports activities to respond to students' interests and needs. Student Government also sponsors social events to raise funds for charitable activities.

Admission Requirements

Admission is selective. Successful applicants must have a scholastic record demonstrating a commitment to their studies and the ability to succeed at college-level work.

Each applicant is considered as an individual, and no single factor can guarantee acceptance to the University. The previous school's documentation of the applicant's academic ability, motivation, character, and contribution to school life is very important. This information should be reflected in the student's academic record and letters of recommendation. The University does not prescribe a fixed secondary school course of study but considers both the quality and breadth of the student's record. The University is open to all applicants without regard to race, national origin, religion, or gender. For applicants coming from the U.S. secondary school system, a standard college-preparatory program is expected. For applicants from other national systems, an essential requirement is successful completion of a secondary school program permitting university admission in the respective system. Students holding the Italian Diploma di Maturità, the International Baccalaureate, or other equivalent academic credentials may be granted advanced standing. Results of the SAT or the ACT are required for high school students graduating from an American secondary school. Applicants whose first language is not English or who did not attend a secondary school where classes were taught in English must demonstrate sufficient preparation in the English language. Standardized test scores, such as the Test of English as a Foreign Language (TOEFL) or the International English Language Testing System (IELTS), are useful in assessing a student's language capability. A minimum score of 550 on the TOEFL (213 on the computer-based exam or 85 on the Internet-based test), a minimum score of 6.5 on the IELTS, or an equivalent passing score on the John Cabot English Proficiency Test are accepted as evidence of sufficient preparation in the English language.

Application and Information

Admissions decisions are based on the review of official transcripts, results of standardized tests, the student's GPA, final examination results, a personal statement, and letters of recommendation from teachers or professors. Transfer students from another university must be in good academic standing. An application form completed in its entirety must be accompanied by two recent passport-size photographs and a nonrefundable application fee of $50 or €50. Students may complete the application online or use the printable application. The University deadline is June 1 for fall admission and November 15 for the spring semester. Candidates are urged to submit their application and supporting documents as early as possible.

Students may apply online or obtain an application by contacting:

Admissions Office
John Cabot University
Via della Lungara, 233
00165 Rome
Italy
Phone: 39-06-681-9121
Fax: 39-06-683-2088
E-mail: admissions@johncabot.edu
Web site: http://www.johncabot.edu
    http://on.fb.me/john_cabot_univ (Facebook)
    http://twitter.com/MyJCURome# (Twitter)
    http://bit.ly/johncabot_about_virtual_tour (Video)

U.S. Admissions Office
Karen Altieri, Manager
14100 Walsingham Road, Suite 36, #10
Largo, Florida 33774
Phone: 866-457-6160 (toll free)
E-mail: kaltieri@johncabot.edu

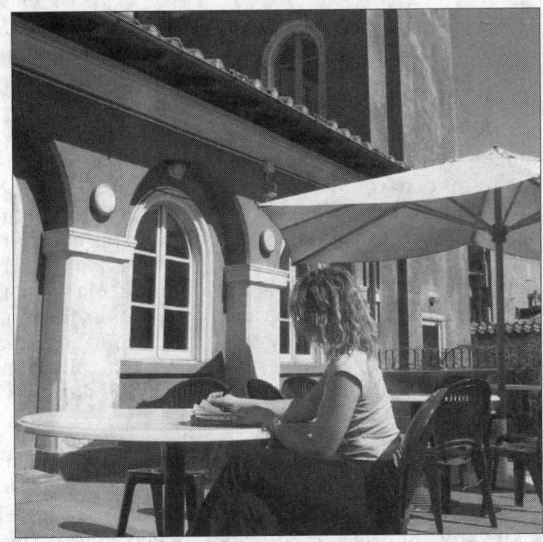
John Cabot University student on terrazzo.

JOHN CARROLL UNIVERSITY
UNIVERSITY HEIGHTS, OHIO

The University

In the Jesuit tradition of leadership, faith, and service, John Carroll University provides its students with a rigorous education, rooted in the liberal arts and focused on questions of moral and ethical value. The University wants its graduates to make a difference in their chosen careers and in bettering their communities. One of twenty-eight Jesuit colleges and universities in the United States, John Carroll offers degree programs at the undergraduate and graduate levels in fifty-four arts and sciences, business, and preprofessional fields.

John Carroll was founded in 1886 as St. Ignatius College. In 1923, its name was changed to Cleveland College briefly. Later it became John Carroll University, named after the first Catholic bishop of the United States. In 1934, the University moved from its original location on Cleveland's near west side to its current location in University Heights. Originally a men's college, the University and all its programs officially became coeducational in 1968.

In 2009–10, the enrollment was 3,600, with 3,100 students enrolled in full-time undergraduate programs and 500 in graduate programs. Students come from thirty-eight states, the Virgin Islands, Puerto Rico, and twenty other countries. The student body, including graduate students, is 46 percent men, 54 percent women, and 12 percent students of color. The University's eight residence halls house 1,860 students.

A well-rounded education includes learning and leadership activities outside the classroom. The University owns Thorn Acres, a 30-acre recreational facility used for fishing, canoeing, retreats, and student-group meetings. John Carroll offers more than 100 student organizations and clubs, as well as community volunteer service opportunities, men's and women's varsity and intramural sports, and academic honor societies. A natatorium, racquetball and tennis courts, two gymnasiums, and weight-training and fitness facilities are located in the Student Center. Office space is set aside for a host of student activities, including the newspaper, radio station, yearbook, Student Union, fraternities and sororities, and various other organizations. University Counseling Services provides free personal and psychological counseling, therapy, and testing. In addition, the Center for Career Services offers resources for students looking to choose a major or trying to land their first job.

Students at John Carroll, in the Jesuit spirit of "making a difference," take advantage of the numerous opportunities and programs offered to volunteer to help improve the local community as well as communities across the country and around the globe.

The Graduate School at John Carroll offers Master of Science degree programs in accountancy, biology, and mathematics; Master of Arts degree programs in biology, communications management, community counseling, education, English, history, humanities, integrated science, mathematics, nonprofit administration, and religious studies; the Master of Education; and Master of Business Administration degree programs. In addition, Economics America (the Cleveland Center for Economic Education), a nonprofit educational organization located on John Carroll's campus, provides advanced course work in economics for educators.

Location

Just 20 minutes from downtown Cleveland, John Carroll is located in the quiet, residential Heights neighborhood; it is surrounded by Shaker Heights, University Heights, and Cleveland Heights. The graceful walkways, rich landscape, and Gothic and contemporary architecture of the campus complement the surrounding community beautifully. The campus is easily accessible by bus, rapid transit, and car. Three shopping centers are within walking distance, so restaurants, theaters, banks, department stores, grocery stores, and specialty shops are all nearby. University Circle, 10 minutes from the campus, is the home of the Cleveland Symphony Orchestra; Cleveland Museums of Art, Natural History, and Health Education; and Garden Center of Greater Cleveland. Downtown Cleveland offers comedy clubs; world-class shopping; theater at the Cleveland Play House; the Warehouse District, an extensive entertainment district located near the Cuyahoga River; the Rock and Roll Hall of Fame; the Great Lakes Science Center; Progressive Field, home to the Cleveland Indians; Quicken Loans Arena, home to the Cleveland Cavaliers; and Cleveland Browns Stadium.

Majors and Degrees

There is a wide range of programs of study available to John Carroll University students. The School offers degree programs in over forty fields of study, including majors in the College of Arts and Sciences and the John M. and Mary Jo Boler School of Business. The University is expanding its undergraduate programs to meet new interests of students. This includes the Dolan Center for Science and Technology, which is home to several departments in the natural sciences.

In 2009, the University renamed its Department of Communication and Theatre Arts in memory of alumnus Tim Russert and established the Tim Russert Endowed Scholarship and a Meet the Press fellowship in partnership with NBC.

In terms of academics, JCU has consistently received high rankings from independent college profiling organizations. In 2009, JCU was named the seventh best among master's granting colleges and universities in the Midwest. The University's four-year graduation rates exceed U.S. and Ohio averages.

Information on all our academic programs can be found at http://www.jcu.edu/academics/.

Academic Programs

In keeping with the Jesuit tradition of liberal arts education, every undergraduate takes a core curriculum that includes a single-theme first-year seminar course, three courses in humanities, three in science and mathematics, three in philosophy, two in social sciences, two in religious studies, one in English composition and rhetoric, and one in speech communication. Therefore, all students enroll in the College of Arts and Sciences for their first two years. After the first two years, students select a major and are admitted to their respective degree programs.

To earn a degree, a student must complete a minimum of 128 credit hours with a grade point average of at least 2.0 (C) for all course work. The last 30 hours of instruction must be completed at John Carroll. Candidates for graduation must complete all the courses and proficiency requirements for the degree, and they must complete all the major requirements with an average of at least 2.0. All course work required for a declared minor or concentration must be completed with a GPA of at least 2.0.

The University operates on a semester calendar, with three 5-week summer sessions offered between academic years.

Off-Campus Programs

John Carroll offers many special educational opportunities, including programs in London, Vatican City, China, and Japan. The Center for Global Education works with students who hope to study abroad. Explore their Web site http://www.jcu.edu/global/ for more information.

John Carroll University is a member of the Northeast Ohio Commission on Higher Education and offers students the opportunity to take one course per semester at one of the other sixteen area universities while enrolled full-time at John Carroll. There is no additional charge for tuition; the only stipulation is that the course may not be offered at the home institution. Students often take courses in the performance-based arts or in specific engineering fields through this cross-registration program.

Academic Facilities

The Administration Building was built in 1935 and is John Carroll's oldest building. Along with administrative and faculty offices, Kulas Auditorium is located inside the Ad Building. A $7-million renovation of the Administration Building took place during the winter of 2002, when most of the spaces on the first two levels were renovated. During the renovation, a Student Service Center and an Einstein Bros. Bagel restaurant were incorporated into the basement level.

The Dolan Center for Science and Technology, a $66.4-million, 265,000-square-foot building, opened with a grand celebration on September 6, 2003. This facility houses the biology, chemistry, psychology, physics, mathematics, and computer science departments. With the Dolan Center, the University has advanced its science and mathematics curriculum, upgraded instructional technology, and expanded partnerships with area schools and employers. A number of years ago, a $6.8-million expansion of the Grasselli Library doubled the capacity of the building; it has also enhanced accessibility of electronic databases. The O'Malley Center for Communications and Language Arts features an electronic newsroom, computer-assisted and audio language laboratories, and a center for writing instruction. The Tim Russert Department of Communication and Theatre Arts features the Vincent Klein Television Studio, which recently received an over $500,000 facelift.

Costs

Tuition and fees are $31,710 for the 2011–12 academic year. Room and board are $9150. The average cost for books and supplies is $1200 per year.

Financial Aid

John Carroll works closely with families to lay out a reasonable financial plan to make private education at John Carroll an affordable opportunity. The financial aid process strikes a balance between scholarships and need-based assistance. Competitive merit awards that recognize significant academic, leadership, and service accomplishments are offered, but not at the expense of keeping John Carroll affordable for all students. Every year, students from across the economic spectrum enroll at John Carroll and go on to graduate.

In 2009–10, more than 80 percent of the student body received some type of need-based financial assistance. Merit-based scholarships are awarded to approximately half of the freshman class. Most students apply for need-based aid by completing the Free Application for Federal Student Aid (FAFSA). The financial aid application deadline is March 1.

For more information about JCU's scholarships and grants, please go to http://www.jcu.edu/aidjcu/.

Faculty

The majority of John Carroll's 240 faculty members teach undergraduate classes, although some teach graduate programs as well. Of the full-time faculty members, 94 percent hold doctorates or the appropriate terminal degree in their field, and 75.6 percent are tenured. The faculty's primary focus is teaching and scholarship. Counseling of students, research and publication, and community service are also important pursuits. John Carroll's faculty includes 8 resident Jesuit priests. The student-faculty ratio is 14:1.

Student Government

The John Carroll student body is self-governed, with the elected Student Union officers actively representing all students—undergraduate, graduate, full- and part-time, and day and evening—in all academic, social, religious, and disciplinary matters. Fifty-six men and women are elected to Student Union service for one-year terms.

Admission Requirements

Applications for admission from all serious candidates are welcome. John Carroll has a holistic review process for admission. Each applicant to the institution is reviewed individually, and all information is considered carefully to determine if the student will be able to succeed in the curriculum and what the student would contribute to the University community.

Admission criteria, in descending order of importance, are the quality of the high school curriculum, grade point average, extracurricular activities, test scores on either the SAT or ACT, the essay, and the recommendation of a high school counselor or teacher.

The deadline for applications to John Carroll is February 1. The priority scholarship deadline is December 1. Admission decisions are mailed to candidates approximately twice a month, starting in December. Please visit http://www.jcu.edu/admission/apply/ for more information.

Application and Information

John Carroll is a member of the Common Application group, and there is no fee to apply. John Carroll subscribes to the Candidates Reply Date of May 1. Accepted students who wish to reserve their place in the freshman class must submit their enrollment reservation form and $300 enrollment deposit by May 1 to ensure their place in the class. All deposits are refundable by written request up to the May 1 deadline.

To request more information, students are encouraged to contact:

Steve Vitatoe
Executive Director of Enrollment
John Carroll University
University Heights, Ohio 44118-4581

Phone: 888-335-6800
E-mail: admission@jcu.edu
Web site: http://www.jcu.edu/admission

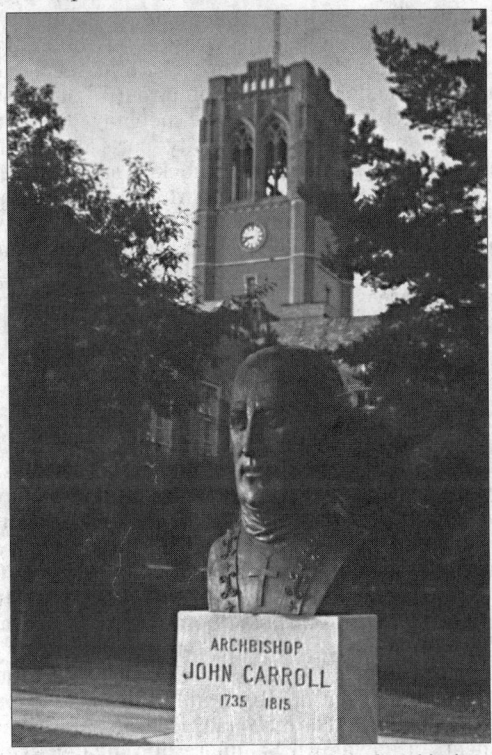

Grasselli Tower stands behind the bust of Archbishop John Carroll, the University's namesake, along the main quadrangle.

THE JOHNS HOPKINS UNIVERSITY
Krieger School of Arts and Sciences and Whiting School of Engineering
BALTIMORE, MARYLAND

The University

Privately endowed, the Johns Hopkins University (JHU) was founded in 1876 as the first American university committed to the idea that knowledge should be discovered, rather than merely transmitted. Daniel Coit Gilman, the first president of Johns Hopkins, stated that the object of the University was "not so much to impart knowledge as to whet the appetite, exhibit methods, develop powers, strengthen judgment, and invigorate the intellectual and moral forces." Today, Johns Hopkins continues to stress creative scholarship by providing research-oriented education for undergraduates. Students in all disciplines are encouraged to explore intellectual questions and discover new ideas within a supportive environment.

Johns Hopkins seeks diversity in its students, who come from all fifty states and from seventy-one other countries. Of the total undergraduate enrollment of approximately 5,000 students, about 47 percent are women and 53 percent are men. All out-of-town freshmen and sophomores must live in campus residence halls. In addition, University-owned housing, located directly across from the University on North Charles Street, is available for juniors and seniors. Upperclassmen may also live in private housing or in Greek housing. Johns Hopkins has thirteen fraternities and eight sororities in the Inter-Fraternity Council and the Panhellenic Council.

The Homewood campus is active and lively, with many different events such as films, concerts, seminars, and athletic games being offered each week. The Student Council runs a number of activities, including a popular Spring Fair each year. Men's varsity teams compete in twelve sports. In the fall, men's teams compete in cross-country, football, soccer, and water polo. In the winter, basketball, fencing, swimming, and wrestling are offered. The big sports season at Johns Hopkins is spring, with baseball, lacrosse, tennis, and track and field. The men's and women's lacrosse teams compete at the Division I level, and the men have won forty-four national championships. Women's varsity sports also include basketball, cross-country, fencing, field hockey, soccer, swimming, tennis, track and field, and volleyball. An extensive and popular intramural program is also available. The O'Connor Recreation Center contains basketball and volleyball courts, a running track, racquetball courts, a rock-climbing wall, a weight room, and fitness and aerobic areas. In addition to the athletic programs, there are over 360 student-run clubs that hold events throughout the year. From the performing arts to hobby-centered clubs, there are many options for students of all interests.

Location

Johns Hopkins University's Homewood campus is on 140 acres of lush greenery, bounded on all sides by residential areas. Johns Hopkins offers the best of both worlds—the tranquil seclusion of the campus plus the adjacent urban environment. Two museums are owned by the University: Homewood Museum, on campus, and Evergreen Museum & Library, located nearby on North Charles Street, both of which provide academic opportunities for students. The Baltimore Museum of Art is on the southwest corner of the campus. The Walters Art Museum, a 10-minute drive away, has a collection that spans civilization from Egypt to the nineteenth century, and many smaller museums, galleries, and outdoor showings feature local artists. The University is located just three miles from the heart of downtown Baltimore; the theater, symphony, and opera are 10 minutes away, as are Oriole Park at Camden Yards and M&T Bank Stadium. Weekend activities include visiting Baltimore's Inner Harbor, home to the National Aquarium and many other attractions; enjoying an ethnic festival by the water;

sailing on the Chesapeake Bay; and hiking around the Maryland countryside. Washington, D.C., is a 50-minute drive by car or a 1-hour train ride. Opportunities abound for on- and off-campus entertainment.

Majors and Degrees

Bachelor of Arts degrees are awarded in Africana studies, anthropology, archaeology, behavioral biology, biology, biophysics, chemistry, classics, cognitive science, earth and planetary sciences, East Asian studies, economics, English, film and media studies, French, German, global environmental change and sustainability, history, history of art, history of science and technology, interdisciplinary studies, international studies, Italian, Latin American studies, mathematics, natural sciences, Near Eastern studies, neuroscience, philosophy, physics, political science, psychology, public health studies, Romance languages, sociology, Spanish, and the Writing Seminars. A Bachelor of Arts degree in engineering is available for students who seek preparation for professional careers (such as law or business) with a technological orientation. The B.A. in engineering is awarded in applied mathematics and statistics, biomedical engineering, computer science, electrical engineering, general engineering, and geography. Bachelor of Science degrees are awarded in applied mathematics and statistics, biomedical engineering, chemical and biomolecular engineering, civil engineering, computer engineering, computer science, electrical engineering, environmental engineering, materials science and engineering, mechanical engineering, molecular and cellular biology, and physics.

Accelerated bachelor's/master's degree programs are offered in biology, biophysics, German, history, international studies, mathematics, neuroscience, policy studies, psychology, public health studies, and Spanish. Accelerated B.S./M.S.E. programs are offered in most engineering departments. A dual-degree program leading to a Bachelor of Arts or Bachelor of Science degree and a Bachelor of Music degree is available in cooperation with the University's Peabody Institute and Conservatory of Music.

Academic Programs

The departments in the Krieger School of Arts and Sciences and the Whiting School of Engineering comprise four general areas for undergraduate programs: engineering, humanities, natural sciences, and social sciences. If a student has special interests that fall outside the bounds of the departmental majors, an individual program can be devised, or a student may study independently with the guidance of a faculty member. Qualified students may complete their degree requirements in fewer than four years.

Johns Hopkins has an extremely flexible program. There are no required freshman courses. All students must fulfill distribution requirements as well as the requirements for their major; the distribution requirements include a writing element. In most majors, 120 credits are required for graduation. Johns Hopkins has a 4-1-4 calendar.

The University offers the Army ROTC program on campus and the Air Force ROTC program in cooperation with the University of Maryland College Park.

Off-Campus Programs

If qualified, a student may undertake a program for study abroad, normally during the junior year. Programs are offered at Johns Hopkins' international center in Bologna, Italy, as well as in Paris, France; Madrid, Spain; Berlin, Germany; and Latin America and through independent study-abroad programs with Johns Hopkins credit. Currently, there are more than 400 students studying abroad in over thirty countries. The University also participates in a cooperative program with other colleges in the Baltimore area. Undergraduates may take courses at the other divisions of Johns Hopkins University, including the Peabody Conservatory, the School of Nursing, the Bloomberg School of Public Health, the Nitze School of Advanced International Studies, the School of Education, the Carey Business School, and the School of Medicine.

Academic Facilities

The Milton S. Eisenhower Library on the Homewood campus is part of the University's Sheridan Libraries, which comprise the Milton S. Eisenhower Library, the John Work Garrett Library, the Albert D. Hutzler Undergraduate Reading Room, and the George Peabody Library. Together, these libraries provide one of the most comprehensive learning resources in the world, containing more than 3.5 million books, more than 55,000 print and electronic journals, more than 700,000 electronic books, more than 10,000 videos and DVDs, more than 216,000 maps, and significant rare books, manuscripts, and archival resources.

The Mattin Student Arts Center contains the Swirnow Theater, a dance studio, music practice rooms, film and digital labs, darkrooms, a café, art studios, and spaces for students to gather. Hodson Hall includes classrooms, a meeting room for the Board of Trustees, the archives of the Hodson Trust, and a 500-seat auditorium, in which every seat is wired to the Internet. Clark Hall houses a state-of-the-art research and teaching facility for biomedical engineering. Charles Commons, a 618-person residential complex and dining facility, also houses the University's two-story Barnes and Noble bookstore.

Wireless network coverage is available throughout most areas of the campus with the use of a supported wireless LAN card. Those living off campus can remotely access University systems and library resources. The Homewood Academic Computing Lab is open 24 hours a day, has more than 115 computers, and provides student consultants who can assist with problems that arise. The Brown Foundation Digital Media Center offers an environment where students can bring artistic inspiration to life using digital tools. It features twelve high-end computers that enable digital and audio composition and editing, animation, virtual painting, and 3-D modeling. All campus buildings are networked with each other and the other Johns Hopkins campuses.

Costs

Costs for 2010–11 were $40,680 for tuition, $12,510 for room and board, and $2200 for books and personal expenses. Travel expenses vary.

Financial Aid

Financial aid is based on demonstrated eligibility, as determined by the Free Application for Federal Student Aid (FAFSA) at the time of acceptance. Approximately 46 percent of students receive financial assistance. Students must reapply for financial aid each year with the FAFSA and the College Scholarship Service (CSS) Financial Aid PROFILE. Johns Hopkins offers several merit-based scholarships, including the Hodson Trust Scholarship. Johns Hopkins also offers Army ROTC scholarships worth up to full tuition. The Baltimore Scholars Program provides full-tuition scholarships to eligible Baltimore City public high school graduates. In addition, several scholarships and grants allow undergraduates to pursue research opportunities, even as freshmen.

Faculty

The University's intellectual reputation is based on the strength of its faculty, of whom 87 percent hold a doctorate. The student-faculty ratio is 12:1. The well-known professors at Johns Hopkins teach both undergraduate and graduate students, which means that students receive a great deal of personal attention both in and out of the classroom. Johns Hopkins has a large number of notable professors, including 45 American Academy of Arts and Sciences fellows, 3 National Medal of Science winners, 2 Presidential Medal of Freedom winners, and 7 MacArthur Fellows. Faculty members are always accessible to advise and assist students and to work with them on research projects.

Student Government

Johns Hopkins students enjoy the benefits of a well organized and far-reaching student government, which is led by a powerful Student Council. The council is composed of elected class representatives and officers, but it relies on the active participation of many students in its numerous committees, boards, and commissions. Through the Student Activities Commission, the University encourages initiative and independence by giving students full responsibility and control of funds for various clubs and organizations.

Admission Requirements

In choosing from a large number of applicants, the University selects those men and women who will benefit from a Johns Hopkins education, and who will add something to the campus community. A student's intellectual interests and accomplishments are of primary importance, and the Admissions Committee carefully examines each applicant's scholastic record, standardized test results, essays, and recommendations from secondary school officials and other sources about the student's character, intellectual curiosity, seriousness of purpose, and range of extracurricular involvement. The application essays are an important part of how the Admissions Committee learns more about students during the application review process. Two teacher recommendations are required. In addition, the SAT or the ACT with Writing Test is required. For students submitting SAT scores, Johns Hopkins recommends the submission of SAT Subject Tests, and if submitted, requests results from three tests. Students should consult the Web site for additional details on test requirements. Every year, the University enrolls a first-year class of approximately 1,275 men and women from all parts of the United States and a number of other countries. In addition, transfer students from other colleges and universities are admitted to the sophomore and junior classes. Advanced-standing credit is granted from college-level work completed at an accredited college or through the Advanced Placement and International Baccalaureate programs.

Application and Information

Johns Hopkins accepts the Common Application and the Universal College Application, both with a Johns Hopkins supplement. The application deadline is January 1. If applicants consider Johns Hopkins to be their first choice, they may apply under the Early Decision Plan. This requires that the application be filed by November 1. Notification is given by April 1 for regular decision students and by December 15 for those applying under the Early Decision Plan. Students wishing to enroll in the biomedical engineering (BME) program must indicate BME as their first choice of major on their application. Freshmen who are BME majors are admitted specifically as such.

Office of Undergraduate Admissions
The Johns Hopkins University
Mason Hall
3400 North Charles Street
Baltimore, Maryland 21218-2683

Phone: 410-516-8171
Fax: 410-516-6025
E-mail: gotojhu@jhu.edu
Internet: http://apply.jhu.edu

JOHNS HOPKINS UNIVERSITY
School of Nursing
BALTIMORE, MARYLAND

The University

Since its founding in 1876, Johns Hopkins University has been in the forefront of higher education. Originally established as an institution oriented toward graduate study and research, it is often called America's first true university. Today, Johns Hopkins' commitment to academic excellence continues in its nine academic divisions: Nursing, Medicine, Public Health, Arts and Sciences, Engineering, Education, Business, Advanced International Studies, and the Peabody Conservatory of Music. With a full-time enrollment of approximately 7,000 students, it is the smallest of the top-ranked universities in the United States and, by its own choice, remains small.

The School of Nursing was established in 1983 by Johns Hopkins University. By choosing to attend Johns Hopkins School of Nursing, students can become leaders in the nursing profession. Hopkins students enjoy the advantages of an education at an institution with a worldwide reputation and an outstanding network of alumni who are willing to serve as guides and mentors. Students at the School of Nursing are given the opportunity to participate in designing an educational program tailored to their individual needs. A rigorous academic curriculum, which includes a strong scientific orientation, gives students the background to understand the health-care decisions they are likely to make as professionals. Students learn in an atmosphere where excellence is expected, valued, and reinforced.

The School of Nursing is among the few schools in the country that emphasize baccalaureate-level research. Its graduates are prepared for professional practice through a process of study marked by clinical excellence, critical thinking, and intellectual curiosity.

In addition to the baccalaureate program, master's and doctoral programs and postdegree options are also offered. Recognized as a leader by peers, the School of Nursing was ranked first in the nation overall for graduate programs, along with two other schools, in the 2012 edition of *U.S. News & World Report*, compiled with input from deans, directors, and senior faculty members from nursing schools nationwide. The same publication also ranks the School first nationally in community/public health nursing, fifth in nursing service administration, and seventh in family nurse practitioner programs.

Location

Located on the East Baltimore Campus, the School of Nursing is one of the University's "four corners," the others being the School of Medicine, the School of Public Health, and the Johns Hopkins Hospital, all top-ranked nationally. The School of Nursing is only 10 minutes from the University's Homewood Campus, which is accessible to students via a free shuttle service.

Often referred to as the biggest small town in America, Baltimore has undergone one of the most successful transformations of any city in the country. Baltimore's famous Inner Harbor and the National Aquarium are focal points of this revitalization. The nation's capital is also less than an hour away by car or train.

Majors and Degrees

The School of Nursing offers an NLNAC-accredited upper-division program that leads to a Bachelor of Science degree with a major in nursing. A 13½-month accelerated option of study makes it possible for students who hold a bachelor's degree in another discipline to receive a bachelor's degree in nursing. Students who hold a bachelor's degree in another discipline are also eligible to apply to the Direct Entry Combined B.S. to M.S.N. option. In addition, students who do not hold a bachelor's degree may consider a traditional twenty-one-month program that leads the B.S. with a major nursing. Students may transfer to the School of Nursing after successful completion of the 60 semester hours of prerequisite course work

from any accredited college or university. Those students who hold a previous bachelor's degree may also consider the twenty-one-month option.

Students interested in pursuing the B.S. to M.S.N. option of study may select from a number of master's options, including clinical nurse specialist (in an area of interest, such as, but not limited to, forensic, geriatric, infectious disease, adult or pediatric health, or woman's health), nurse practitioner, public health, and, in collaboration with Shenandoah University Division of Nursing, a clinical nurse specialist in women's health and a certificate of completion in midwifery.

Academic Programs

The School of Nursing prepares students for professional nursing practice through an educational process that combines a strong academic curriculum with intensive clinical experience. The program is built on the University's commitment to research, teaching, patient service, and educational innovation and the consortium hospitals' commitment to excellence in clinical practice. The School's mission is to prepare its students academically and technologically for future challenges and to graduate professional nurses who can participate in all aspects of modern health care.

The upper-division courses in the baccalaureate nursing program are designed to meet the nursing needs of people in a complex and rapidly changing health-care system. The program is built on the liberal and general education prerequisites. The curriculum provides a balance among technologies, theories of nursing, and the caring functions of the nurse. High priority is placed on educating the nurse to practice in a variety of health-care settings, including overseas, as they exist today and in the future.

The School of Nursing is world known for the Community Outreach Program, which offers students opportunities to gain additional clinical experiences with underserved populations in East Baltimore. It is also the first school of nursing in the country to offer a Peace Corps Fellows Program. In addition, students can enroll in the Birth Companions Program—another opportunity to work with underserved populations.

The Army Reserve Officers' Training Corps (ROTC) is the principal source of commissioned officers for the Active Army, Army Reserve, and Army National Guard. All Army nurses are officers. Johns Hopkins University offers two- and three-year scholarships to students enrolled in Army ROTC, which is located on the Homewood Campus of Johns Hopkins University.

Academic Facilities

The William H. Welch Medical Library is the central resource library serving Johns Hopkins Medical Institutions. Students have free 24-hour-per-day access to the Welch Library Gateway, which leads users to local and remote bibliographic databases, full-text journals, and other resources available locally and on the Internet. In addition, the University's Milton S. Eisenhower Library, on the Homewood Campus, is available to School of Nursing students.

Computer laboratories located throughout the campus are equipped with a computer network and printers. Several classrooms and the auditorium have PC hookup and distance learning capabilities. Additional computer resources are available throughout the University.

Nursing practice and simulation labs are available to provide students with an opportunity to gain experience and confidence in performing a wide variety of nursing technologies. Students practice basic nursing technologies at numerous patient care stations designed to closely approximate hospital inpatient areas. Practice using actual medical equipment is an integral part of the laboratory experience, and patient simulators are provided to facilitate clinical skill mastery.

Clinical facilities throughout the Baltimore/Washington metropolitan area serve as clinical sites during student clinical rotations. These include the famed Johns Hopkins and its four affiliated hospitals, as well as a variety of other acute, research, long-term community, and specialty health-care institutions. Students also have opportunities to explore international clinical experiences in locations such as Haiti, Singapore, South Africa, Dubai, and Uganda, to name a few.

Costs

For the 2010–11 academic year, baccalaureate tuition was $33,168. Prospective students may visit www.nursing.jhu.edu/apply/finaid for more information.

Financial Aid

Johns Hopkins University School of Nursing attempts to provide financial assistance to all eligible accepted students. The School of Nursing will assist those students who qualify for need-based aid. Such assistance is usually in the form of loans, grants, scholarships, and work-study programs. While most of the financial aid received by students is based on financial need, many students also benefit from awards based on academic merit and achievement.

Faculty

The faculty members view professional nursing as a unique health service offering effective, humane, and competent care to individuals, families, groups, and communities. Nurses function in independent, interdependent, and dependent roles to promote and improve delivery of health care. With a low student-faculty ratio, faculty members view education as a process and as an enriching interaction in which both the teacher and learner must actively participate in an atmosphere of mutual trust.

Student Government

Each class within the School of Nursing has a government board and a president. There is also a Student Government Association (SGA), which includes all divisions of the entire University. Each class has representatives to the SGA, and anyone may attend the meetings. There are also a number of University and School of Nursing student organizations.

Admission Requirements

The School seeks individuals who will bring to the student body the qualities of scholarship, motivation, and commitment. The Admissions Committee is interested in each applicant as an individual and considers both academic potential and personal qualities. Therefore, academic records, test scores, recommendations, and a personal statement about goals and interests are all important. Interviews may be requested.

A complete application consists of an application form and nonrefundable $75 application fee; recommendations from 3 persons, 2 of whom must be instructors in current or recent courses and 1 from professional or volunteer experience; official college/university transcripts; an official high school transcript (unless the applicant has already completed a college degree or has been out of high school for over five years); and SAT or ACT scores, if they are not more than five years old and the student does not already hold a bachelor's degree. Applicants should have a GPA greater than 3.0 (on a 4.0 scale).

First-degree students are required to complete 60 semester hours of prerequisite course work essential for entry into the upper-division nursing curriculum. Courses may be completed at any accredited college or university and includes the natural sciences, humanities, social sciences, statistics, and electives. Students who possess a bachelor's degree must complete prerequisite course work in anatomy and physiology, microbiology, nutrition, human growth and development across the lifespan, and statistics. In addition, the School of Nursing has articulation agreements for direct transfer with the College of Notre Dame of Maryland; Dickinson College, Pennsylvania; Gettysburg College, Pennsylvania; Johns Hopkins University, Maryland; Juniata College, Pennsylvania; Loyola University of Maryland; Mount Holyoke College, Massachusetts; Mount St. Mary's University, Maryland; Randolph College, Virginia; St. Mary's College of Maryland; State University of New York at Geneseo; Virginia Tech, Virginia; Washington College, Maryland; Wittenberg University, Ohio; and Yeshiva University, New York.

International students must submit official test score reports of the Test of English as a Foreign Language (TOEFL) unless they have received a prior bachelor's degree in the U.S. or they have lived in the U.S. for more than five years. To be considered for admission, nonpermanent residents must establish their ability to finance their education in the U.S. International students must have their academic transcripts evaluated course-by-course by World Education Service (WES) or by the American Association of College Registrars and Admissions Officers (AACRAO). International registered nurses may have their transcripts evaluated course-by-course through the Commission on Graduates of Foreign Nursing Schools (CGFNS). Official results from WES, AACRAO, and CGFNS must be sent directly to Johns Hopkins University School of Nursing.

Johns Hopkins University is an affirmative action/equal opportunity institution.

Application and Information

All inquiries concerning the School of Nursing should be directed to:

Office of Admissions and Student Services
Johns Hopkins University
School of Nursing
525 North Wolfe Street
Student House 100
Baltimore, Maryland 21205-2110

Phone: 410-955-7548
Fax: 410-614-7086
E-mail: jhuson@son.jhmi.edu
Web site: http://www.nursing.jhu.edu
http://www.facebook.com/jhunursing
http://twitter.com/JHUNursing

Students engage the SimMan, a universal patient simulator.

JOHNSON & WALES UNIVERSITY

PROVIDENCE, RHODE ISLAND

The University

Johnson & Wales University (JWU), founded in 1914, is a nonprofit, private institution. A recognized leader in career education, the University offers accredited degrees to more than 17,000 graduate and undergraduate students, representing all fifty states and ninety-three countries. By integrating academics and professional skills, related work experiences, leadership opportunities, and career services, JWU prepares students who are seeking a competitive advantage in the global economy. More than 83,000 alumni from 140 countries pursue careers around the world. The University is committed to urban revitalization and thoughtful historic renovation. Through active civic participation and unique learning opportunities, JWU seeks to improve the quality of life in its campus communities in Providence, Rhode Island; North Miami, Florida; Denver, Colorado; and Charlotte, North Carolina.

JWU is a career-oriented institution offering programs that are geared to the success of a range of students. Most students are recent graduates of high school business, college-preparatory, and vocational/technical programs. The academic focus of the University is degree programs in business, culinary arts, education, hospitality, and technology. M.B.A. programs include global business leadership (with concentrations in accounting, financial management, international trade, organizational leadership, or marketing) and hospitality and tourism global business leadership (with concentrations in finance and marketing). M.A. programs in teaching (with or without certification) include business, food service, and special education. The Alan Shawn Feinstein Graduate School also offers the Certificate of Advanced Graduate Study (CAGS) in finance, human resources management, and hospitality. The University also offers a doctoral program in educational leadership.

Students are involved in a variety of extracurricular activities. Nearly 20 percent of the students at the University are members of national student organizations such as Business Professionals of America; DECA (Collegiate DECA), Future Business Leaders of America (Phi Beta Lambda); Family, Career, Community Leaders of America (FCCLA); National FFA; Junior Achievement; SkillsUSA; and Technology Association of America. The Office of Student Activities (OSA) and fraternities and sororities are among the many groups that schedule social functions throughout the academic year. Sports and fitness programs include aerobics, baseball, basketball, golf, ice hockey, sailing, soccer, tennis, volleyball, and wrestling.

The University maintains twenty-six residence halls throughout its four campuses. In addition, City View Towers, which is independently owned and operated, offers housing near the Charlotte campus for upperclassmen. Student services include academic counseling and testing, a tutorial center, and health services. JWU's Experiential Education and Career Services office provides extensive career planning and placement services.

Johnson & Wales University is accredited by the New England Association of Schools and Colleges Inc. (NEASC), through its Commission on Institutions of Higher Education.

Location

The location of each of the University's campuses enables students to take advantage of internship and part-time work activities offered by many nearby businesses, community groups, and government agencies. All of Johnson & Wales' city campuses retain a small-town feel and easy accessibility to students. The urban setting of the Providence campus provides students proximity to the city's many cultural and recreational facilities. The North Miami campus is a short trip from the sun and fun of Fort Lauderdale and the culture and diversity of Miami. The Denver campus offers students great opportunities as the nation's sixth-leading tourist destination and

Fortune magazine's "second best city in America to work and live." The Charlotte campus is located in a vibrant urban setting that combines commercial and residential life. More than 300 Fortune 500 companies have offices in Charlotte, which is known as the second-largest financial center in the U.S.

Majors and Degrees

The degree programs described in this section are for the 2011–12 academic year and are subject to change. Students may pursue concentrations related to their program of study to further tailor their degrees to their specific interests and career goals. They also have the opportunity to take concentrations through the School of Arts and Sciences.

Johnson & Wales University's Providence campus offers degree programs in accounting; baking and pastry arts; baking and pastry arts and food service management; business administration; business/information systems analysis; counseling psychology; creative advertising; criminal justice; culinary arts; culinary arts and food service management; culinary nutrition; electronics engineering; engineering design and configuration management; entrepreneurship; equine business management; equine business management/riding; fashion merchandising and retail marketing; finance; food service entrepreneurship; graphic design and digital media; hotel and lodging management; international business; international hotel and tourism management; management; management accounting; marketing; network engineering; restaurant, food, and beverage management; security management; software engineering; sports/entertainment/event management; strategic advertising; and travel, tourism, and hospitality management.

In its Adult & Continuing Education division, Johnson & Wales' Providence campus offers associate and bachelor's degrees in business, culinary arts, hospitality, and technology. JWU also offers diploma programs in baking and pastry arts and culinary arts; certificate programs are offered in criminal justice, finance, human resources management, management, and operations management.

The North Miami campus offers degree programs in baking and pastry arts; business administration; criminal justice; culinary arts; culinary arts and food service management; fashion merchandising and retail marketing; hotel and lodging management; management; marketing; pastry arts and food service management; restaurant, food, and beverage management; sports/entertainment/event management; and travel, tourism, and hospitality management.

The Denver campus offers degree programs in baking and pastry arts; baking and pastry arts and food service management; business administration; criminal justice; culinary arts; culinary arts and food service management; culinary nutrition; entrepreneurship; fashion merchandising and retail marketing; hotel and lodging management; international business; management; marketing; restaurant, food, and beverage management; security management; sports/entertainment/event management; and strategic advertising. Students can also earn degrees in culinary arts through the Adult & Continuing Education division.

The Charlotte campus offers degree programs in baking and pastry arts; baking and pastry arts and food service management; business administration; culinary arts; culinary arts and food service management; fashion merchandising and retail marketing; hotel and lodging management; management; management accounting; marketing; restaurant, food, and beverage management; and sports/entertainment/event management.

Academic Programs

Johnson & Wales University offers programs in business, culinary arts, hospitality, and technology within an academic structure of three 11-week terms.

Learning by doing is an important part of career training at JWU, and many programs include laboratory studies as well as formal internship requirements. Students get real-life work experience beginning their freshman year. Special advanced-placement programs are featured for high school seniors with exceptional skills in culinary arts or baking and pastry arts. In addition, JWU awards credit for certain courses based on the successful completion of Challenge, CLEP, or Portfolio Assessments. All degree candidates must successfully complete the required number of courses and/or quarter credit hours, as prescribed in the various curricula, with a minimum average of 2.0 or higher, depending on the program.

Off-Campus Programs

At Johnson & Wales students get hands-on learning experiences from the start, inside and outside the classroom. Many of the majors offer internships at University-owned facilities. The hotel-restaurant management program features an internship at the Johnson & Wales Inn, Radisson Airport Hotel, or Doubletree Hotel; all are full-service hotel complexes that are owned and/or operated by the University (the Radisson and Doubletree are corporate franchises). For all majors, optional selective career internships are available with cooperating businesses throughout the U.S. and worldwide, such as Marriott International, Compass Group NAD, Foxwoods Resort and Casino, and Putnam Investments. Most internships are one term in duration and carry 13.5 quarter hours of credit. International exchange and term-abroad programs are also offered.

Academic Facilities

The facilities of the Providence campus are located throughout the intimate state of Rhode Island and in nearby Massachusetts. The Downcity campus in Providence is home to the University's College of Business, The Hospitality College, and the School of Technology. A number of academic and residential facilities are located at this campus, as are several training facilities. The Harborside campus, also in Providence but located a short distance away from the Downcity campus, houses the University's College of Culinary Arts. This campus has five student residence halls as well as specialized classrooms and laboratories, production kitchens, bakeshops, dining rooms, a storeroom, and meat-cutting facilities. This campus is also home to the Alan Shawn Feinstein Graduate School, the School of Education, the University Recreation and Athletic Center, a student activities office, a bookstore, a gymnasium, a dining center, a snack bar, and an arcade.

JWU's North Miami campus is located in the heart of North Miami, between Miami and Fort Lauderdale. Facilities include academic classrooms, production/demonstration kitchens, a bakeshop, residence halls, and a specially designed conference center.

The Denver campus, located in the Park Hill neighborhood, combines old-world charm with the latest technological resources, including stately turn-of-the-century buildings and newer student centers in a quiet park landscape. The traditional residential campus is fully wired, with computers in every classroom and laboratory.

The Charlotte campus is located in the heart of Gateway Village in Uptown Charlotte. The academic center is home to a 200-seat auditorium, a production kitchen, state-of-the-art culinary laboratories, classrooms, seminar rooms, and computer labs.

Costs

Tuition at all campuses for 2011–12 is $23,955. Room and board plans range from $7710 to $11,541. There is also a general fee of $1152 charged to all students and an orientation fee of $300 for new students. Books and supplies are estimated at $800 to $900 per year, depending on the program.

Room and board fees vary at each campus. Students should consult the respective campus catalogs for further details.

Financial Aid

Johnson & Wales students are eligible to apply for a variety of financial aid programs, including the Federal Pell Grant, Federal Supplemental Educational Opportunity Grant, Federal Work-Study, and Federal Perkins Loan programs. They are also eligible for University-based student scholarship programs and state-supported grants and scholarships. In the past, approximately 91 percent of the University's entering students have received some sort of financial assistance. Students must submit the Free Application for Federal Student Aid (FAFSA) to the Federal Student Aid Processor to be considered for financial aid. Early application is strongly suggested for full consideration.

Faculty

The University's 492 full-time and 314 part-time faculty members (all campuses) are oriented toward instruction rather than research. Many are chosen for their professional experience in business, culinary arts, hospitality services, or technology. The student-faculty ratio is 28:1.

Student Government

Student Government Association (SGA) is the voice of students on campus and serves as the governing student organization on campus. Students are elected to major leadership positions in the spring, and senator positions are available to any interested student in the fall. SGA is responsible for allocating student funds, recognizing new organizations, and addressing student concerns on campus.

Admission Requirements

Johnson & Wales seeks students who are career-focused and have a true desire to succeed. Academic qualifications are important, but an applicant's motivation and interest in doing well are given special consideration. Graduation from high school or the equivalent credentials are required for admission. It is recommended that students applying for admission into the culinary arts and baking and pastry arts programs have some prior education or experience in food service. Although tests are not required for most programs, all applicants are encouraged to submit scores from the SAT or ACT. Students who wish to apply for the honors program must have either a score of at least 500 math and 500 critical reading on the SAT or a score of at least 21 math and 21 verbal on the ACT. High school juniors may apply for early admission under the Early Enrollment Program (EEP). Transfer students are required to submit official high school and college transcripts and to have a minimum GPA of 2.0. Credits to be transferred from other institutions are evaluated on the basis of their equivalent at Johnson & Wales.

Application and Information

Johnson & Wales does not require an application fee. After submitting the application, the student is responsible for requesting that appropriate transcripts be forwarded to JWU's Admissions Office. While there is no deadline, students are advised to apply as early as possible before the intended date of enrollment to ensure full consideration of their application. Applications are accepted for terms beginning in September, December, and March and for the summer sessions (for most programs).

Inquiries and applications should be addressed to:

Kenneth DiSaia
Senior Vice President of Enrollment Management
Johnson & Wales University
8 Abbott Park Place
Providence, Rhode Island 02903
Phone: 401-598-1000
      800-DIAL-JWU (toll-free)
Fax: 401-598-4901
E-mail: jwu@admissions.jwu.edu
Web site: http://www.jwu.edu
      http://www.facebook.com/jwuadmissions

JUNIATA COLLEGE
HUNTINGDON, PENNSYLVANIA

The College

Juniata College is an independent, coeducational college of liberal arts and sciences, founded in 1876 by members of the Church of the Brethren to prepare individuals "for the useful occupations of life." A prominent institution of higher education, Juniata enjoys national recognition on a major scale. Recent studies rank the College highly in the percentage of graduates that eventually earn doctoral degrees; one, in fact, ranked Juniata in the top 10 percent in the nation among all four-year private undergraduate institutions. Juniata's national reputation is strongest in several fields, including biology, chemistry, environmental science and education, health sciences, peace and conflict studies, and prelaw. The College is known for the personal attention it gives to students. Each student is assigned 2 faculty advisers, and the average student-faculty ratio is 13:1.

Juniata is a very strong community where student involvement is paramount. There are no fraternities or sororities, so the entire campus is involved in activities. School spirit and campus events are the heart and soul of the institution. Juniata's ninety-four clubs and organizations not only have a positive impact on the campus, but also on the community of Huntingdon and the surrounding area.

Location

Juniata is located in Huntingdon, a community of 10,000 people, in the scenic Allegheny Mountains of central Pennsylvania. It is 40 minutes from the cities of Altoona (population 65,000) and State College (population 55,000). The 110 acres on College Hill overlook the historic architecture of a classic river town. Juniata's campus also consists of a 365-acre field station and a 315-acre nature preserve. The surrounding area is suited for many outdoor activities, including swimming, fishing, hunting, rock climbing, and hiking. Raystown Lake, the largest recreational lake wholly in Pennsylvania, is 15 minutes from Juniata. Several major cities are within a short drive of the campus—3 hours to Pittsburgh, Baltimore, and Washington, D.C.; 4 hours to Philadelphia; and 5 hours to New York City. The nearest commercial airport is State College, the location of Penn State University. In addition, Huntingdon is on the main U.S. east-west railway line, with travel by train to East and West Coast cities available.

Majors and Degrees

Juniata awards B.A. and B.S. degrees in the arts, humanities, natural sciences, and social sciences. Rather than complete a traditional major, each Juniata student designs a Program of Emphasis (POE) tailored to the student's own goals and often crossing departmental lines. Working closely with 2 academic advisers, students select courses for either a designated or an individualized POE.

Current areas of study include accounting; anthropology; art (art history; museum studies, with an art history focus; and studio art); arts production; biochemistry; biology; chemistry; communication; communication and conflict resolution; computer science; digital media; earth and space science; English; entrepreneurship; environmental economics; environmental science; environmental studies; finance; geology; health professions (art therapy, audiology, biotechnology, chiropractic, cytotechnology, dentistry, genetic counseling, health administration, health communication, medical social work, medical technology, medicine, naturopathic medicine, nursing, occupational therapy, optometry, pharmacy, physical therapy, physician's assistant studies, podiatric medicine, public health, radiological sciences, and veterinary medicine); history; human resource management; information technology; international business; international politics; international studies; languages (French, German, Russian, and Spanish/Hispanic cultures); management; marketing; mathematics; peace and conflict studies; philosophy, politics, and economics; philosophy and religious studies; physics (engineering physics and physics); politics; pre-K–4 education; professional writing; psychology; religious studies; secondary education (biology, chemistry, earth and space science, English, French, general science, German, mathematics, physics, social studies, and Spanish); social work; sociology; theater performance; and wildlife conservation.

Secondary emphases are available in accounting, business, and economics; anthropology; biology; chemistry; communication and theater arts; computer programming; computer science; digital media; English; environmental studies; fine arts; French; German; history; information technology; international studies; mathematics; peace and conflict studies; philosophy; physics; politics; psychology; religious studies; Russian; Spanish; sociology; and women and gender studies.

Academic Programs

Designed to foster individual responsibility, Juniata's flexible and academically rigorous program allows for both acquisition of a broad range of knowledge and in-depth examination of a particular field. About a third of the students attending Juniata develop their own program through a flexible program of emphasis (POE).

Students must satisfactorily complete 120 semester credit hours before graduating. Writing, computer and bibliographical skills, and the transition to college are addressed in the freshman year. (Students can begin their blended academic-extracurricular explorations in one of the College's twenty-seven Inbound retreats that take place in the summer before freshman year.) Graduation requirements also include a two-course cultural analysis sequence, advanced communication/writing skills, quantitative studies, social sciences, humanities, international, fine arts, and natural sciences and an optional service learning component. In addition to these liberal arts topics, all students complete a 45–60 credit POE, and many choose to complete an integrative senior project to graduate with distinction.

Many students include independent study and independent research in their POEs. Although not required, over 90 percent of students participate in distinctive learning opportunities like internships, research with faculty, student teaching, and community service. The Juniata College Center for International Education provides excellent study-abroad opportunities that are taken advantage of by approximately 44 percent of the junior class. Experiences include summer, semester, and year-long opportunities.

Academic Facilities

Juniata's academic programs are complemented by up-to-date technology, labs, and bibliographic resources. In addition to the College's academic computer center, the campus has high-tech classroom/laboratory and computer labs devoted specifically to business, education, psychology, and world languages. The College supports the Juniata Center for Entrepreneurial Leadership (JCEL), a unique opportunity for students of all academic areas to develop their own businesses. JCEL provides students with a hands-on experience in every aspect of entrepreneurial endeavors. A human interaction lab offers students the opportunity to study communication and group interaction. In addition, the College has a distance learning and teleconferencing facility, multimedia classrooms, and a teaching and learning technology center (Solutions Center) for both student and faculty use. The Solutions Center was designed to give faculty members and students the resources for utilizing advanced technology in their course work and presentations. The William J. von Liebig Center for Science is a $20-million facility that provides state-of-the-art facilities for teaching and learning in chemistry and biology. The Brumbaugh Academic Center houses the business, communications, computer science, environmental sciences, information technology, mathematics, and physical sciences departments as well as a digital media studio. Good Hall and the College's Humanities Center are home to the social sciences and humanities. Many students in these disciplines take part in internships and undergraduate research as well as portfolio-building experiential endeavors such as art exhibition and curating museum exhibits.

For research projects, students in the natural sciences use laboratories equipped with sophisticated instrumentation typically reserved for graduate students. Juniata's Raystown Field Station serves as an ecology, zoology, and environmental science laboratory. The field station recently expanded facilities to allow students to live and learn at an on-site field laboratory. Juniata's Beeghly Library provides the

College with an online public-access catalog that is accessible campus-wide and an extensive CD-ROM network.

Costs

For 2010–11, the general fee was approximately $41,820, with tuition costs of $32,120, and room, board, and fee costs of $9700. Several special and occasional fees of $30–$300 for laboratory or studio use are also required.

Financial Aid

The Juniata College Office of Student Financial Planning is committed to building relationships with families striving to meet the long-term investment needs associated with quality education. Juniata succeeds by maximizing available assistance opportunities from Juniata programs as well as state and federal government programs in the form of grants, loans, and work-study initiatives. The College's commitment includes scholarship and loan programs. Juniata's Academic Scholarship Program offers aggressive scholarship programs designed to recognize and reward academic achievement. The College also offers fellowships that provide exceptional candidates with further enhanced experiential opportunities in the arts, environmental, peace studies, and study-abroad realms.

Juniata representatives work with each family, matching their individual circumstances to all applicable aid programs. For need-based aid, individual plans are developed using the Free Application for Federal Student Aid (FAFSA) as the basis for determining need. The results of the FAFSA needs analysis should reach Juniata by March 1.

Faculty

Juniata has 102 full-time and 47 part-time faculty members, of whom 94 percent hold a doctoral or terminal degree in their field. The student-faculty ratio is 13:1. Although faculty members engage in numerous scholarly pursuits and maintain professional ties to their academic fields, they consider teaching and advising their primary functions.

Student Government

Juniata seeks to provide an environment within which students can mature intellectually, socially, and personally in a manner consistent with academic programs. In campus life as well as in the classroom, many opportunities for growth and self-exploration exist. Students have a voice—and in most cases a vote—in all essential areas of campus governance.

Admission Requirements

Juniata seeks students who show strong academic promise, motivation, and maturity. The College seeks a wide geographic representation and a variety of cultural, social, and economic backgrounds. Selection is made without regard to race, sex, religion, creed, national origin, handicap, or the ability to afford a private college education. Careful consideration is given to the academic record, test results, and personal qualities of applicants. Applicants should have completed a minimum of sixteen college-preparatory courses in mathematics, social studies, world language, and laboratory science. International student candidates may be required to submit TOEFL scores. Interviews and campus visits are strongly recommended.

Transfer students who have completed A.A. or A.S. requirements in an approved collegiate transfer program at an accredited community or junior college may enter Juniata with junior-class standing and receive transfer credit for two years of course work. Students who transfer without a degree receive credit on a course-by-course basis. Students whose college has a formal transfer agreement with Juniata College should consult with their transfer coordinator to review requirements for that agreement. It is strongly recommended that transfer students have an interview.

Application and Information

Students may apply to Juniata after completion of their junior year in secondary school. A nonrefundable $30 fee must accompany the application (waived for students who visit campus or apply online). A complete secondary school transcript that indicates courses and grades (with a list of senior courses, if required) must be sent from the applicant's guidance office along with SAT or ACT scores or SAT Alternative Program, an essay, and a letter of recommendation. An on-campus interview is highly recommended but not required. Transfer students must complete the normal application requirements and submit an official transcript from each college previously attended.

Candidates for freshman admission can choose from three application deadlines: early decision, early action, and regular decision.

Early decision is designed for students who believe that Juniata College is their first choice. The early decision application deadline is December 1 of the student's senior year in secondary school, with notification no later than December 31. The student is asked to complete Juniata's institutional aid form in order to receive an early financial planning award. Students are required to submit a nonrefundable $400 matriculation deposit by February 25.

Early action allows students to apply and get a response earlier than regular decision while still adhering to the May 1 deposit deadline. The early action application deadline is January 1 of the student's senior year, with notification of a decision by January 31. Financial aid award packages are determined after the Free Application for Federal Student Aid (FAFSA) has been completed. (Juniata's FAFSA Code is 003279.) Students should fill out the FAFSA form as soon as possible after January 1 of their senior year in order to have it completed by the March 1 deadline.

The regular decision application deadline is March 15 of the student's senior year. Admissions decisions are made on a rolling basis. As with early action applicants, financial award packages are determined after the FAFSA has been completed. Students should fill out the FAFSA form as soon as possible after January 1 of their senior year in order to have it completed by the March 1 deadline.

Juniata accepts applications for transfer admission for either the spring or fall semesters. The application due date for fall applicants is June 1; the due date for spring applicants is December 1. It is to the student's benefit to submit all application materials before the due date. Juniata's transfer admission policy is rolling. In most cases, transfer students receive an admission decision within one month of receipt of all credentials. Necessary credentials include an essay, a statement of interest, a secondary school transcript, SAT or ACT scores, and college transcripts. Application forms and additional information may be obtained from Pamela Zilch at 877-JUNIATA (toll-free) or 814-641-3428.

Enrollment Center
Juniata College
1700 Moore Street
Huntingdon, Pennsylvania 16652
Phone: 814-641-3420
        877-JUNIATA (877-586-4282, toll-free)
Fax: 814-641-3100
E-mail: admissions@juniata.edu
Web site: http://www.juniata.edu/

On the campus of Juniata College.

KENDALL COLLEGE
CHICAGO, ILLINOIS

The College

For seventy-five years, Kendall College has offered engaging, specialized fields of study with a strong emphasis on immersive learning that is geared to a student's academic, personal, and professional success.

Whether choosing Kendall's acclaimed School of Culinary Arts, distinctive School of Hospitality Management, innovative School of Business, or well-established School of Education, students are encouraged to explore their talents, interests, and passions—and to discover a wealth of exciting opportunities.

Kendall's School of Culinary Arts has prepared outstanding culinary professionals for twenty-five years. Its bachelor's and associate degree programs are intensive, hands-on, and cutting-edge, utilizing twelve commercial-grade kitchens, an onsite fine-dining restaurant, and an equally well-regarded cafeteria. The programs are designed to help students successfully launch careers in the vast foodservice industry, equipped with superb culinary skills, and the equally critical business management and communication skills. Students intern locally, nationally, and internationally at top-notch hospitality and culinary venues. Kendall chef instructors possess formal culinary training and at least ten years of hands-on experience and expertise from all facets of the foodservice industry.

Kendall's School of Hospitality Management combines European customer-focused competencies with American management skills. The B.A. program offers a variety of concentrations: asset management, casino management, club management, meetings and events management, hotel and lodging management, restaurant and foodservice management, and sports and leisure management. Students intern locally, nationally, and internationally at leading hospitality and culinary venues.

Kendall's School of Business helps prepare graduates to succeed in today's global workforce by focusing on the service industries. The program offers a Bachelor of Arts in Business with seven concentration options: baking and pastry, food service management, management, personal chef and catering, professional cookery, psychology, and small business management. The curriculum is taught by an accomplished faculty of industry experts and uses situation-based challenges, actual case studies, management simulations, and integrative projects to produce employment-ready graduates.

The School of Education at Kendall offers a Bachelor of Arts degree in early childhood education, with optional Illinois Type 04 Teacher Certification preparation, as well as concentrations in childhood nutrition, English as a second language (ESL), infants and toddlers, and special education. Through continuing studies, additional licensure and licensure enhancement options are vailable to current teachers and those who already hold an undergraduate degree.

School of Education courses are offered in three convenient formats to support the needs of both full-time students and those choosing to work as they earn their degree. Formats include online, on campus, hybrid (a combination of online learning and campus instruction), or the option of mixing formats to suit a variety of schedules and learning preferences. All formats allow students to benefit from interaction with classmates and faculty in small class environments.

Kendall College is a member of the Laureate International Universities, a global network of more than fifty institutions of higher learning with more than 100 campuses in twenty-four countries. Through this partnership, students have broad access to study-abroad programs, internships, and professional opportunities in Asia, Australia, Europe, and Latin America.

Kendall College is accredited by the Higher Learning Commission and is a member of the North Central Association of Colleges and Schools (NCA), http://www.ncahlc.org, phone: 312-263-0456. The American Culinary Federation Education Foundation (ACFEFAC) has accredited the culinary arts associate program since 1988 and the baking and pastry associate program since 2008. The early childhood education program in the School of Education is approved by the Illinois State Board of Education for Type 04 Illinois Teacher Certification preparation (birth through grade 3).

Location

Kendall College's campus, located near the heart of downtown Chicago, prepares its graduates for exciting opportunities in the culinary, hospitality, and business industries. The school is minutes from some of the country's best restaurants, hotels, and companies, providing students prime access to internships and work experiences. The facility offers sweeping views of the Chicago skyline, access to newly developed areas on the Chicago River, and all the cultural and social benefits of the third-largest city in the United States. Kendall College's residence hall is Presidential Towers, located at 555 West Madison Avenue, just steps away from renowned museums, shopping, and entertainment.

Majors and Degrees

Kendall College awards Bachelor of Arts (B.A.) degrees in business, culinary arts, early childhood education, and hospitality management. The College also awards the Associate of Applied Science (A.A.S.) degree in baking and pastry, and culinary arts.

The culinary arts program offers certificates in baking and pastry, personal chef and catering, and professional cookery.

Academic Programs

Kendall College operates on a quarter system. The first quarter term extends from October to mid-December, the second term extends from January to March, and the third term extends from April to June. Summer sessions are offered from July to September.

Academic Facilities

The Chicago Riverworks campus provides wireless Internet access, computer labs, and two distance-learning videoconference facilities. Classrooms and study environments are designed to give students an effective setting in which to learn. There are student lounges, twelve commercial grade kitchens, an academic success center, parking spaces, and a number of nearby health clubs.

Costs

In 2010–11, full-time (12–19 credit hours/term) tuition in the School of Culinary Arts was $22,095 for three quarters.

Full-time tuition for the School of Hospitality Management was $19,608 for three quarters.

Full-time tuition in the School of Business was $13,545 for three quarters.

Full-time tuition in the School of Education was $250 per credit hour for in-classroom courses and $210 per credit hour for online courses.

Housing is located at Presidential Towers, located at 555 West Madison Avenue in Chicago. Students may lease double-occupancy one-bedroom apartments for $12,600 per twelve-month lease. Single-occupancy one-bedroom apartments are leased to students for $25,200 per twelve-month lease. Quad-occupancy two-bedroom apartments are leased to students for $10,200 per twelve-month lease.

Financial Aid

Kendall College administers federal, state, and institutional aid for undergraduates. The College works with each student to help file required applications leading to the awarding of financial aid. The College's goal is to assist students to receive all funding for which they are eligible. The financial aid packaging process ensures effective use of available funds, providing fair and equitable treatment of all applicants.

Faculty

The student-faculty ratio is approximately 19:1, providing students the benefit of small classes and the ability to engage one-on-one with the faculty and the material. Faculty members at Kendall College believe students work best when they are actively involved in making choices about their own learning.

Student Government

Kendall College's Student Government Federation (SGF) is the students' organization. It provides students with a leadership role, a voice within Kendall College, and access to improving the campus community. SGF represents the student body to various committees and boards within the College such as the Board of Trustees' Student Affairs Committee and the Faculty Senate. SGF also oversees all student clubs and organizations, along with program activities for students. SGF is elected at the beginning of the fall quarter with the term of service extending for three academic quarters.

Admission Requirements

Students who apply to Kendall College are evaluated on individual merit. Each applicant is evaluated on the basis of probable success at Kendall College. Cumulative grade point average(s) (GPAs), standardized test scores, personal statements, and admissions interviews are among the methods of evaluation. Special consideration is given to adult students who are returning to school. To determine official GPAs, the College must receive an official institution transcript directly from the institution or the organization housing the institution's records. Admissions interviews are required either via a face-to-face tour of the campus or on the phone to help determine the admission decision. An official high school transcript with graduation date and unweighted final GPA of at least 2.0 (on a 4.0 scale) are required for acceptance.

Students whose academic record does not meet Kendall admission standards in one or more admission categories (high school GPA, transfer GPA), but who demonstrate the potential for success at Kendall may be admitted with provisions.

Application and Information

Prospective students may obtain applications from the Office of Admissions or via the College's Web site at www.kendall.edu. Students may submit the admission application at any time. The Office of Admissions must be sent an official transcript.

For further information, students should contact:

Office of Admissions
Kendall College
900 N. North Branch Street
Chicago, Illinois 60642
Phone: 312-752-2020
        888-905-3632 (toll-free)
Fax: 312-752-2021
E-mail: admissions@kendall.edu
Web site: http://www.kendall.edu
      http://www.facebook.com/kendall.college
      http://twitter.com/kendallcollege

A view of Kendall College's Riverworks campus in Chicago.

KENT STATE UNIVERSITY

KENT, OHIO

The University

Kent State University has experienced tremendous growth since its founding in 1910. Today, Kent State is a multicampus network serving more than 38,000 students at eight locations throughout northeastern Ohio. The eight-campus network is anchored by a classic residential campus in Kent, Ohio. Throughout the network, students can pursue certificate, associate, bachelor's, master's, and doctoral degrees. The Kent Campus, serving more than 20,300 undergraduates and more than 5,400 graduates, offers 218 undergraduate study areas and numerous graduate degrees. Kent State's seven regional campuses are located in Ashtabula, Geauga (including the Twinsburg Center in Twinsburg, Ohio), Stark, Trumbull, and Tuscarawas counties, and the cities of Salem and East Liverpool.

As a residential campus, Kent State requires students to reside in one of the twenty-five residence halls until junior academic standing is achieved. Exceptions include commuting and nontraditional students. Students can easily walk to any of the more than 100 academic, residential, administrative, and recreational buildings. The University has an eighteen-hole golf course, a 291-acre airport, a two-rink indoor ice arena, three on-campus theaters, and a student recreation and wellness center. There are more than 200 student organizations, nineteen fraternities, nine sororities, and eighteen varsity sports. The Career Services Center provides career counseling and job placement assistance for students and alumni.

Location

Kent, Ohio, a city with a population of 28,000, is within easy traveling distance of the major metropolitan areas of northeastern Ohio. Within a 40-mile radius are concerts, cultural events, museums, nature preserves, recreational areas, and year-round sports.

Majors and Degrees

The College of Architecture and Environmental Design offers the Bachelor of Science and Master of Architecture degrees. The School of Interior Design offers a Bachelor of Arts in interior design.

The College of the Arts offers the Bachelor of Arts, Bachelor of Fine Arts, Bachelor of Music, and Bachelor of Science degrees. The college also offers multiple-degree programs. The academic divisions are the Schools of Art, Fashion Design and Merchandising, Music, and Theatre and Dance.

The College of Arts and Sciences awards Bachelor of Arts, Bachelor of Science, and Bachelor of General Studies degrees. Major fields of concentration are American Sign Language, American studies, anthropology, applied conflict management, applied mathematics, biology, biological chemistry, biology, biotechnology, botany, chemistry, classics, computer science, conservation, criminal justice studies, earth science, economics, English, French, French translation, geography, geology, German, German translation, history, international relations, Latin, Latin American studies, mathematics, medical technology, Pan-African studies, paralegal studies, philosophy, physics, political science, psychology, Russian, Russian translation, sociology, Soviet and East European studies, Spanish, Spanish translation, and zoology. Numerous interdisciplinary and preprofessional programs are available, including general studies, integrated life sciences, pre-dentistry, pre-engineering, prelaw, premedicine, pre-osteopathy, pre-pharmacy, and pre–veterinary medicine. Students may also design their own individualized major.

The College of Business Administration awards the Bachelor of Business Administration degree. Major fields of concentration are accounting, business management, computer information systems, economics, entrepreneurship, finance, managerial marketing, and marketing. Students can choose a minor in any of these programs as well as in health-care systems management and international business.

The College of Communication and Information offers the Bachelor of Arts, Bachelor of Fine Arts, and the Bachelor of Science degrees. Major fields of concentration are advertising, communication studies, electronic media, news, photo illustration, public relations, radio-television, visual communication design, and visual journalism.

The College of Education, Health, and Human Services offers the Bachelor of Science in Education, Bachelor of Arts, Bachelor of Science degrees, and Master of Arts degrees, with licensure programs available in adolescence/young adult education, early childhood education, intervention specialist studies (majors include deaf education, educational interpreter studies, gifted education, mild/moderate educational needs, and moderate/intensive educational needs), middle childhood education, multiage education, and career technical teacher education (vocational education). In addition, separate degree programs are offered in the Schools of Health Sciences; Foundations, Leadership, and Administration; Lifespan Development and Educational Sciences; and Teaching, Learning, and Curriculum Studies.

The College of Nursing awards the Bachelor of Science in Nursing degree. The four-year program includes clinical practicums in the Cleveland-Akron-Warren-Youngstown areas.

The College of Public Health offers a baccalaureate program called the Bachelor of Science in Public Health degree. This academic degree addresses the health of populations and communities through instruction, service, and community-based research. A Master of Public Health degree is also offered.

The College of Technology offers associate, bachelor's, and master's degree programs throughout Kent State's eight-campus system. Students can select from a number of specialized academic programs in aeronautics, industrial, electrical, manufacturing, or educational technologies. Construction management and air traffic control are two new undergraduate programs.

Academic Programs

Kent State's colleges and schools all maintain separate academic programs; completion of about 36 credits of liberal education course work (known as the Kent Core) is a University requirement for all students. The number of credit hours required for graduation varies but is generally 121 semester hours. Credits can be transferred from previous college work satisfactorily completed or earned through courses taken at one of Kent State's regional campuses. Credit by examination is available. Generally, to earn a degree, students must earn 30 semester hours in residence.

The Honors College provides opportunities for students and faculty members to develop and implement special learning experiences. It offers four-year programs of undergraduate study with concurrent enrollment in one of the University's degree-granting programs. In addition, the Honors College awards Advanced Placement and International Baccalaureate credit and specialized academic advising. Its Experimental and Integrative Studies Division offers nontraditional learning experiences for students and faculty members of the entire University community.

Support services are available for students needing assistance to ensure a successful college experience. The Academic Success

Center program offers tutoring, and Student Accessibility Services assists students with various physical disabilities and specific learning disabilities.

Army and Air Force ROTC programs are offered on campus.

Off-Campus Programs

Through the Office of International Affairs, Kent State offers students a variety of overseas academic programs that provide a balance of academic, linguistic, and cross-cultural experiences and learning opportunities. Credit is granted toward degrees.

Academic Facilities

The collections of the University libraries total more than 2.9 million bound volumes and 54,637 electronic and 3,180 print subscriptions. The Honors Center is a living-learning residential complex that houses undergraduate students as well as staff offices, a library-seminar room, a student computer facility, and an audiovisual center. The Center for Applied Conflict Management is an academic unit offering programs of study, research, and service activities that focus on the dynamics of change in human systems. The Instructional Television Service operates a closed-circuit, campuswide network and a production center for NETO, Inc., Channels 45 and 49, northeastern Ohio's public television stations. Audiovisual services support regularly scheduled classes with films and other educational materials. The Instructional Resources Center assists students in the production of educational media materials. The Language Laboratory provides tapes and other tools to assist students in foreign language studies. The Academic Testing Services Office offers test administration, test scoring, and research activities. The School of Fashion Design and Merchandising sponsors a working museum of fashion for students and the public. This school houses classrooms, labs, a library, and a collection of costumes donated from the Silverman-Rogers estate for hands-on study.

As a recognized leader in liquid crystal technology, Kent State's Glenn H. Brown Liquid Crystal Institute is the nation's only center devoted solely to liquid crystal research. With a recent grant from the National Science Foundation, Kent State became the home of Ohio's first Science and Technology Research Center for the Study of Advanced Liquid Crystalline Optical Materials.

Costs

Instructional and other fees for Ohio residents for 2010–11 were $9030 per year. For students residing outside Ohio, instructional and other fees were $16,990 per year. Although room rates vary, costs for board and a double room averaged $8376 per year. The average student spends $1320 per year for books and supplies and should budget extra money for personal needs and expenses. All fees and charges are subject to change.

Financial Aid

More than 80 percent of Kent State's freshmen receive assistance through scholarships, grants, loans, or employment opportunities. To be considered for financial aid awards, students must be admitted to the University and must submit the Free Application for Federal Student Aid (FAFSA) online. Ohio students should also check the Ohio College Opportunity Grant (OCOG) box on the FAFSA if they are interested in being considered. Students planning to attend the fall semester as freshmen should apply for financial aid online after January 1 and before March 1 of the same year. In order to meet the March 1 priority deadline, it is recommended that all financial aid forms be completed no later than February 1. Applications received after March 1 are considered, but sufficient funds to assist all late applicants may be lacking. Additional information is available from the Student Financial Aid Office at www.kent.edu/financialaid.

First-time freshmen and incoming transfer students from forty-nine states outside of Ohio are eligible for a $3980 University Award. For eligibility requirements, students should visit http://www.kent.edu/financialaid.

Kent State's Honors College awards merit scholarships to selected individuals who have the potential for superior scholarly and creative work at the University as determined by academic performance and creative artist competitions. For additional information, students should visit the Honors College Web site at http://www.kent.edu/honors.

The Student Financial Aid Office also administers numerous scholarships, including the Founder's Scholarship, the Trustee Scholarship, the Oscar Ritchie Memorial Scholarship, the President's Scholarship for out-of-state students, the President's Grant for out-of-state students who are children of alumni, and various departmental scholarships.

To be considered for freshman scholarships at the Kent Campus, students must complete an application for admission by January 15 for priority consideration. Scholarships range from $1000 to full tuition and fees. Freshmen applying after this date are considered for scholarships if funds are available.

Faculty

The University's commitment to scholarship and teaching excellence is enhanced by a full-time faculty of approximately 2,100 members. Some of the faculty members are research oriented, and others publish widely.

Student Government

Students have leadership opportunities through residence hall and Greek organizations and the Undergraduate Student Senate. The senate is responsible for allocating student activity fees to registered undergraduate organizations, appointing undergraduates to all University committees and to other positions, conducting elections, and polling student opinion. Two students serve on Kent State's Board of Trustees.

Admission Requirements

Kent State's freshman admission policy differs for students with varying degrees of preparation for college studies. The students most likely to be admitted and to succeed at the Kent campus are those who have graduated with at least 16 units of the recommended college-preparatory curriculum in high school, achieved a high school grade point average of 2.5 or higher, and acquired an ACT score of 21 or better (or a combined SAT critical reading and math score of 980 or better).

For freshmen, selective admission requirements apply to aeronautics flight technology, architecture, dance, education, fashion design and merchandising, interior design, music, nursing, sport administration, theater, and the six-year B.S./M.D. medical program with the Northeastern Ohio Universities College of Medicine (NEOUCOM). For transfer students, selective requirements apply to all of the preceding and to art and business. Students should refer to http://www.kent.edu/admissions for information.

Application and Information

Students are strongly encouraged to apply for admission online at www.kent.edu/admissions/apply. A $40 nonrefundable application fee is required. Application early in the senior year helps ensure priority consideration for fall registration, residence hall preference, and financial aid. Applications are processed on a rolling basis.

Nancy J. DellaVecchia
Director, Admissions Office
Kent State University
P.O. Box 5190
Kent, Ohio 44242-0001
Phone: 330-672-2444
        800-988-KENT (toll-free)
E-mail: kentadm@kent.edu
Web site: http://www.kent.edu
          http://www.kent.edu/admissions
          http://www.facebook.com/kentstate
          http://twitter.com/kentstateuniv

KETTERING UNIVERSITY

FLINT, MICHIGAN

The University

Founded in 1919, Kettering University is a private university specializing in technical degrees. The school enrolls about 2,000 undergraduate students and offers a 12:1 student-faculty ratio. Most classes have fewer than 20 students and are taught by Ph.D.-level professors, not teaching assistants. This combination of small class size and highly qualified teaching staff ensures students a much more personalized learning experience.

Kettering is a highly acclaimed university with the one of the country's most modern cooperative education and experiential learning programs. Whatever major is chosen, students alternate between study terms and full-time work terms. During study terms, students learn material in small, intense classes taught by University professors. During work terms, students work as paid professionals at corporations related to their studies and interests. Kettering students have done everything from testing ballistic systems for the U.S. government to reengineering crowd management at Disney World. Kettering has the only cooperative education and experiential learning program of its kind where students begin working as early as their freshman year. By graduation from Kettering, students have up to 2½ years of professional experience and an impressive resume. Traditionally, nearly all Kettering students graduate with job offers or grad school acceptances in hand.

Kettering University's cooperative education program pairs hands-on education with real-world experience—all undergraduate students alternate between on-campus study terms and full-time terms of cooperative employment with one of more than 550 corporate partners. This unique system of education prepares students to be technology innovators—professionals with cutting-edge skills who are ready to compete in tomorrow's business environment.

Kettering University is accredited by the North Central Association of Colleges and Schools, the Accreditation Board for Engineering and Technology (ABET), and the Association of Collegiate Business Schools and Programs (ACBSP). Kettering is also a member of the National Commission of Cooperative Education (NCCE) and the Association of Independent Technological Universities.

Besides being academically ahead of the game, Kettering students bring a wide range of skills and interests with them to campus. To make sure that students get a life along with an education, Kettering offers more than fifty student organizations, including thirteen fraternities and six sororities, an active student government, a state-of-the-art recreation and fitness facility, and very competitive intramural sports. Recreation facilities include athletic fields, tennis courts, and a recreation center with an Olympic-size, six-lane swimming pool; aerobic fitness rooms; a full line of Nautilus equipment; and basketball, tennis, and racquetball courts. A public golf course is adjacent to the campus.

Professional counseling, support services, and health-care services are available.

Kettering also offers Master of Science degree programs in engineering, engineering management, information technology, manufacturing management, manufacturing operations, and operations management, in addition to an M.B.A. program. To learn more about Kettering, visit the University's site on Facebook at http://www.facebook.com/KetteringAdmissions or on Twitter at http://www.twitter.com/KetteringU.

Location

Kettering University is located in Flint, Michigan, which is 60 miles west of Lake Huron and 60 miles north of Detroit. Flint has approximately 115,000 residents and a metropolitan area population of 450,000.

Flint is particularly proud of its Cultural Center, which is only 10 minutes from Kettering's campus. Built and endowed entirely by the gifts of private citizens, the Cultural Center includes the Alfred P. Sloan Museum, the Whiting Auditorium (home of the Flint Symphony and host to leading stage shows and entertainers), the Robert T. Longway Planetarium (Michigan's largest and best-equipped sky show facility), the Flint Institute of Arts, the F. A. Bower Theater, the Dort Institute of Music, Mott Community College, and the Flint Public Library. Nearby is the University of Michigan–Flint campus.

The area also offers numerous outdoor and indoor recreational opportunities. Within a few minutes' drive are downhill and cross-country skiing facilities, lakes for the entire range of water sports, a wide selection of good public golf courses, excellent indoor and outdoor skating rinks, and plentiful shopping facilities and restaurants

Majors and Degrees

Kettering University offers a 4½-year, professional, cooperative education program with Bachelor of Science degrees in applied mathematics, applied physics, biochemistry, bioinformatics, business administration, chemical engineering, chemistry, computer engineering, computer science, electrical engineering, engineering physics, industrial engineering, and mechanical engineering. Kettering also offers a Bachelor of Business Administration degree.

Kettering also offers a variety of dual-degree programs and enough minors, specialties, and concentrations to ensure that students' degrees are custom-fit to their interests and career goals. Examples include computer gaming, fuel cells and hybrid technology, system and data security, premed, and prelaw.

Academic Programs

Although each program at Kettering University has its own requirements, 160 credit hours are generally required for graduation. The program involves nine academic terms and nine work terms, two of which are focused on the capstone thesis project, which is a major work project assigned by the employer. Students alternate between eleven-week periods of academic study on the campus in Flint and twelve-week periods of related work experience with their corporate employer. The academic year consists of two 3-month academic terms on campus and two 3-month terms of paid work experience.

Academic Facilities

Kettering University offers some of the best facilities, labs, and educational resources in the world, and students start using them as early as their freshman year. The Crash Safety Center, for example, is the only one of its kind in the nation used in an undergraduate program. The University also offers labs in areas such as fuel-cell research, polymer optimization, machining, acoustics, and more.

Kettering is fully networked and allows 24-hour access to computer resources and the Internet from dorms and labs. A 445-student residence hall and an apartment complex are located on the campus for student housing. The library offers more than 94,000 cataloged volumes and 540 periodicals. And through online resources like Kettering Connect and Blackboard, students can always be in touch with professors and University staff members.

Costs

For 2010–11, tuition costs were $27,672 and room and board cost $6440.

Financial Aid

Kettering University wants to invest in its students, so it does what it takes to help finance education through scholarships, loans, and work-study opportunities. In fact, more than 92 percent of the students receive some sort of financial aid. Pair that with co-op earnings—between $40,000 and $65,000 over the course of the college career—and students are looking at one of the best values in education today. In addition, Kettering's Merit Scholarship program awards students with extremely generous scholarship packages.

Students should fill out the Free Application for Federal Student Aid (FAFSA) and request a copy of the analysis to be sent to Kettering University. The University works to create a financial aid package for based on those results.

Faculty

Kettering University's 144 full-time faculty members have teaching as their main responsibility. Most professors have industrial experience in addition to academic credentials and maintain contact with industry through consulting, sponsored research, and advising on student thesis projects. More than 80 percent of faculty members hold a doctorate. Because only half of the students are on campus at any one time, class sizes are small, and opportunities for enrichment and extra help are readily available.

Admission Requirements

Admission to Kettering University is competitive and based on scholastic achievement and extracurricular interests, activities, and achievements. Applicants are required to have earned the following: 3 years of English, 2 years algebra, 1 year of geometry, 1 semester of trigonometry, 2 years of lab science (1 must be physics or chemistry; both are recommended). Applicants must submit results of the SAT or ACT (Kettering's ACT code number is 1998 and the SAT code number is 1246).

Most Kettering University students are in the top 10 percent of their graduating class. Kettering University also welcomes students wishing to transfer from other colleges and universities. The transfer alternative is an excellent way to gain admission for students who do not enroll as freshmen.

Application and Information

There is more than one way to apply to Kettering. Students can apply online at http://www.admissions.kettering.edu or print an application and send it by mail. Students should call 800-955-4464 ext. 7865 for assistance.

Kettering officials review applications and let students know if they have been accepted. Although Kettering accepts and processes applications throughout the year, it is best to apply as early as possible. Once accepted, students receive information on programs and the professional co-op program, which are only available to admitted students. Students should complete the co-op registration (resume) online and pay a $300 tuition deposit (to be credited to the first-semester tuition). The deposit shows that a student is as serious about Kettering as Kettering is about the student and ensures a place in the entering class and eligibility to begin the co-op employment search process.

Admissions Office
Kettering University
1700 University Avenue
Flint, Michigan 48504
Phone: 810-762-7865
        800-955-4464 (toll-free in the United States and Canada)
E-mail: admissions@kettering.edu
Web site: http://www.admissions.kettering.edu
       http://www.facebook.com/KetteringAdmissions
       http://www.twitter.com/KetteringU

Kettering has the experts, the labs, and the programs that bring theory and practice together.

KEYSTONE COLLEGE
LA PLUME, PENNSYLVANIA

The College

Keystone College was founded in 1868 as Keystone Academy in La Plume, Pennsylvania. Initially opened as the only high school between Binghamton, New York, and Scranton, Pennsylvania, Keystone flourished as a secondary school for more than sixty-five years. Rechartered as Scranton-Keystone Junior College in 1934 and then Keystone Junior College in 1944, the College served as one of the premier two-year institutions in the Northeast until 1995. In this year the school was again renamed, as Keystone College, and began its tenure as an "ideal" four-year degree-granting college. Keystone College has a current enrollment of 1,700, including students from fourteen states and ten countries. Students can choose from over forty programs of study.

Keystone was recently ranked by *U.S. News and World Report* as one of the best regional baccalaureate colleges and also ranked in the top tier for highest proportion of classes under 20 students. Eighty percent of classes at Keystone College have fewer than 20 students, providing an individualized learning environment for all. These are just some of the reasons why Keystone has become one of the most popular colleges in the region.

Location

Located at the foot of the Endless Mountains in northeastern Pennsylvania, the 270-acre campus is both scenic and historic, with buildings dating back to 1870. Located 13 miles from Scranton, Pennsylvania, the campus offers easy access to major East Coast cities, including New York, Philadelphia, and Baltimore.

Majors and Degrees

The Bachelor of Arts degree is offered in communications and visual arts. The Bachelor of Science degree is offered in accounting; biology, with tracks in the medical professions; business (online or traditional); criminal justice, with a track in prelaw; early childhood education; elementary education, with a special education certification option; environmental biology; environmental resource management; forensic biology; information technology; organizational leadership; social sciences; psychology; sport and recreation management; teaching: art education; teaching: child and society; teaching: math education; and teaching: social studies education.

Postbaccalaureate certification is available in elementary education, early childhood education, teaching: art education (K–12), teaching: math education, and teaching: social studies education.

Associate of Applied Science degrees are offered in accounting, culinary arts, and information technology. The Associate in Fine Arts is offered in art. The Associate in Arts is offered in communications, environmental studies, forest/resource management, landscape architecture, liberal studies, liberal studies–education emphasis, and wildlife biology. The Associate in Science is offered in biology; business (online and traditional); criminal justice; early childhood education; health sciences with emphasis in medical technology, nursing/cytotechnology, occupational therapy/respiratory care, and radiotherapy/medical imaging/cardiac perfusion; and sport and recreation management. In addition, there are one-year programs in culinary arts, forestry technology, Microsoft Certified Systems Administrator, Microsoft Certified Systems Engineer, and pre–major studies (undeclared major).

Academic Programs

The College runs on a two-semester schedule (fall and spring) and has night, online, and weekend classes available. The number of credit hours required to earn a degree is dependent upon the field of study chosen, and students must have attained a minimum cumulative GPA of 2.0. Every student must complete a set of general core curriculum requirements as well as the courses specific to his or her major course of study. Depending on their course of study, students may be required to complete an internship or co-op before graduation.

Students have the opportunity to participate in both the Army and Navy ROTC programs in conjunction with other local participating institutions. There are opportunities for double majors as well as minors in various fields of study.

Academic Facilities

The Harry K. Miller Library is available on campus to all students. This facility offers standard print and online research opportunities. The Hibbard Campus Center is the setting for the student cafeteria, a full-service restaurant, The Chef's Table (a student-run restaurant), as well as a U.S. post office, a print shop, a student-run radio station (WKCV), and reception halls. The campus also boasts an art gallery, a celestial observatory, early childhood center, career development center, theater, and the Poinsard Greenhouse. Keystone College also serves as the home for the Urban Forestry Center, Willary Water Resource Center, and the Countryside Conservancy.

There are more than 120 computers available on campus for general student use, and both the Internet and campus network can be accessed from all residence halls and most buildings on campus.

Costs

Tuition and fees for Keystone College for the 2011–12 academic year are $19,920, while room and board costs are $9190. Books and general supplies average $1500 annually and vary according to major.

Financial Aid

The Financial Aid Office provides adequate funds and resources to meet the financial needs of students from all income categories. In fact, 90 percent of incoming freshmen receive financial aid. Scholarships are awarded based on merit, academic performance, and extracurricular involvement. Keystone College also participates in the following federally sponsored programs: Federal Perkins Loan, Federal Pell Grant, Federal Supplemental Educational Opportunity Grant (FSEOG), Federal PLUS Loan, and Federal Direct Student Loan. Keystone also offers College employment programs to students and alternative loans as well as state grants and Keystone grants. In order to be considered for financial aid, students must complete the Free Application for Federal Student Aid (FAFSA). Keystone's financial aid code is 003280.

Faculty

The student-faculty ratio is 10:1, and the average class size is 15 students. Counseling is available for academic, personal, and vocational issues. Keystone College is supported by strong interpersonal relationships among its students and faculty and staff members. All faculty members post regular office hours and are generally available outside of these hours.

Student Government

Student Senate is the central governing body of all student government organizations on the campus. It serves as the liaison between the student body and the College administration. Members of Student Senate are chosen by their peers and are responsible for improving and maintaining student life both on and off campus. Students may choose from more than twenty-five different clubs and organizations, including those with academic, service-oriented, and social interests.

Admission Requirements

Keystone accepts qualified students regardless of race, religion, handicap, or national origin, and admissions are on a rolling basis. Admission is based on prior academic performance and the ability of the applicant to profit from and contribute to the academic, interpersonal, and extracurricular life of the College. Keystone considers applicants who meet the following criteria: graduation from an approved secondary school or the equivalent (with official transcripts), satisfactory scores on the SAT or ACT, one teacher evaluation, essay, and evidence of potential for successful college achievement. All students are strongly encouraged to visit the campus for a personal interview with the admissions staff and a member of the faculty from the student's area of interest. Students applying to the art and teaching–art education programs are required to participate in a portfolio interview.

Transfer students in good academic and financial standing at their current institution are also encouraged to apply to Keystone. Transfer students should contact the Office of Admissions and may be required to submit high school transcripts or transcripts from each college attended or both.

Admissions decisions are made within two weeks from the day all required materials are received in the Office of Admissions.

Application and Information

Students wishing to be considered for admission must submit an application and a $30 processing fee, along with official high school transcripts, college transcripts (if applicable), a teacher evaluation, essay, and scores from either the SAT or ACT (submitted directly to the Office of Admissions; Keystone's CEEB code numbers are 2351 for the SAT, 3602 for the ACT).

Applications and any additional information about Keystone College may be obtained by contacting:

Office of Admissions
Keystone College
One College Green
P.O. Box 50
La Plume, Pennsylvania 18440
Phone: 570-945-8111
        800-824-2764 (toll-free), Option 1
E-mail: admissions@keystone.edu
Web site: http://www.keystone.edu

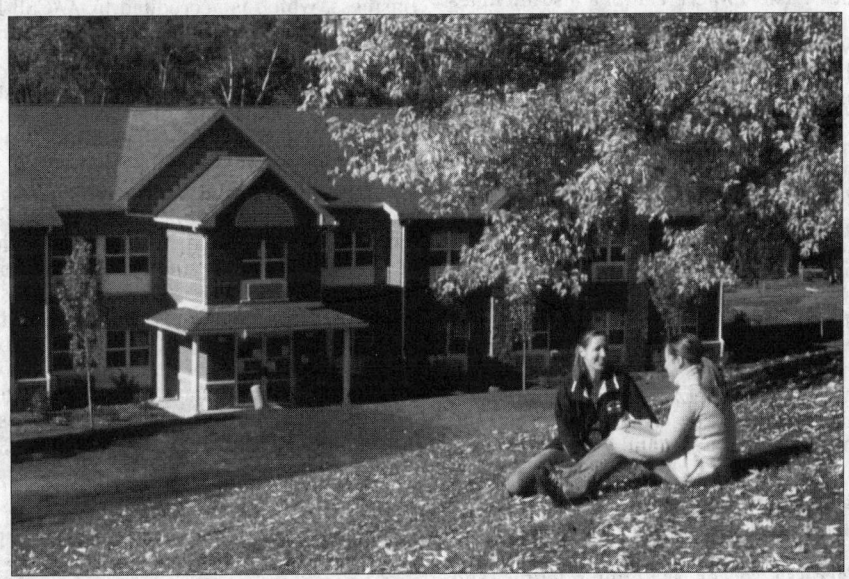

Students on the campus of Keystone College.

KING'S COLLEGE
WILKES-BARRE, PENNSYLVANIA

The College

King's College is an independent, coed, four-year Catholic college with 2,700 students. Founded in 1946 by the Holy Cross Fathers and Brothers from the University of Notre Dame, King's prepares students for a purposeful life, with an education that integrates the human values inherent in a broadly based liberal arts curriculum. The College encourages the religious, moral, personal, and social development of its students.

In addition to the undergraduate degrees, King's College offers a Master of Science (M.S.) degree in health-care administration, a Master of Education (M.Ed.) degree (with a concentration in reading or curriculum and development), and a five-year physician assistant studies program leading to a master's degree.

Academic advising begins before students enroll and continues with an innovative program of career development across the curriculum. King's Academic Skills Center includes a nationally certified tutoring program and a faculty-staffed writing center. More than 70 percent of students who attend King's graduate from the College, which is well above the national average, and 99 percent are employed or attend graduate school within six months of graduation.

The quaint urban campus comprises eight city blocks and features many buildings and centers that house King's numerous academic programs, including the Charles E. and Mary Parente Life Sciences Center, the Mulligan Physical Sciences Center, and the William G. McGowan School of Business. The 15-acre campus also includes Monarch Court; the Sheehy-Farmer Campus Center, which offers an art gallery, an outdoor waterfall and patio, a student restaurant, and marketplace dining; the J. Carroll McCormick Campus Ministry Center; and the William S. Scandlon Physical Education Center, which features a 3,200-seat basketball arena, wrestling facilities, racquetball and handball courts, an Olympic-size swimming pool, a wellness center, and a state-of-the-art sports medicine facility. The student health center is located in Hafey-Marian Hall, a modern six-story building housing classrooms and faculty offices, and a consulting physician is on call at all times. The six-story administration and science buildings form a unit that houses the College's newly renovated theater, the Susquehanna Room dining hall and coffee bar, administrative offices, science laboratories, and classrooms. Residence halls have cable television, Internet access, and 24-hour computer labs. Many of King's athletic teams train and compete just two miles from campus at the Robert L. Betzler Athletic Complex, a 33.5-acre athletic facility that includes McCarthy Stadium; a field house; and fields for baseball, softball, men's and women's soccer, football, and field hockey.

There are fifty student organizations that provide King's students with the opportunity to explore interests outside of the classroom. King's has 19 NCAA Division III teams including men's baseball, basketball, football, golf, lacrosse, soccer, swimming, tennis, and wrestling; women's basketball, field hockey, lacrosse, soccer, softball, swimming, tennis, and volleyball; and coed cross-country. The College offers cheerleading and ice hockey as club sports. Intramural sports include basketball, bowling, field hockey, flag football, racquetball, softball, street hockey, and volleyball. Other cocurricular activities include academic clubs in almost every department, the King's Players (theater), the nationally ranked debate team, Cantores Christi Regis (choir), Campus Ministry, the Experiencing the Arts Series, *The Crown* (student newspaper), the *Regis* (yearbook), and the *SCOP* (literary magazine).

Location

The King's campus is located in a residential area near downtown Wilkes-Barre, Pennsylvania, a city of approximately 50,000 on the banks of the Susquehanna River. A growing city, Wilkes-Barre has developed both economically and culturally, yet it has avoided many typical urban problems. The crime rate in the city is one of the lowest in the nation. Local events include the Cherry Blossom Festival, a national ice carving competition, and the Fine Arts Fiesta. Shopping malls, multiplex theaters, a brand new riverfront park, art galleries, and restaurants are nearby. Two blocks from King's is the F. M. Kirby Center, which has hosted national performances, music groups, traveling theater, and more. National recording acts regularly perform in nearby venues.

King's is a short drive from several ski resorts, state parks, and major lakes where students can participate in many seasonal outdoor activities. Students can also enjoy professional sports action including the New York Yankees' AAA baseball team, the Pocono International Raceway which hosts two NASCAR races each season, and the Pittsburgh Penguins' minor-league ice hockey team. The Mohegan Sun Arena is the host to many concerts and events, and is the site of the King's commencement. King's is close to major metropolitan areas including New York City and Philadelphia (each a 2½-hour drive); Washington, D.C. and the attractions of New England are within a 4-hour drive.

Majors and Degrees

King's awards the Master of Science, Master of Education, Bachelor of Arts, Bachelor of Science, Associate of Arts, and Associate of Science degrees. The College's thirty-five major programs are offered in the arts and sciences and the William G. McGowan School of Business, which is accredited by AACSB International—The Association to Advance Collegiate Schools of Business.

Arts and sciences include the humanities and social sciences division (computers and information systems, criminal justice, economics, English–literature, English–professional writing, French, history, mass communications, philosophy, political science, psychology, sociology, Spanish, theater, and theology); the education division, which recently received NCATE accreditation (preschool–grade 4, secondary certification, and special education); the science division (biology, chemistry, computer science, environmental science, environmental studies, general science, mathematics, and neuroscience); and the allied health division (clinical lab science, physician assistant studies, and athletics training education/sports medicine accredited by CAAHEP). Available majors in the William G. McGowan School of Business are accounting, business administration, finance, human resources management, international business, and marketing. King's offers preprofessional programs in chiropractic, dentistry, law, medicine, optometry, pharmacy, and veterinary science.

Academic Programs

The general education program at King's is recognized nationwide by its peers. King's is included in *Barron's Best Buys in College Education* and has been honored in sixteen consecutive issues of *U.S. News & World Report*'s *Best Colleges Guide.* The College was also recognized by the John Templeton Foundation Honor Roll for Character-Building Colleges, the Forbes/CCAP list of America's best colleges, and is one of sixteen institutions nationwide named to the Greater Expectations initiative. The core curriculum is recognized as a model curriculum. It incorporates traditional and new concepts in liberal arts education, develops competence in such areas as communications and problem solving, and measures students' progress throughout the program.

The honors program offers highly motivated students the challenge of learning in discussion-centered courses that explore distinctive subject matter with exciting and innovative approaches. Sixteen honor societies encourage students to excel in their chosen fields and recognize students for their academic distinction; members are honored each year at the All-College Honors Convocation. Science students receive hands-on lab training much earlier than students at other institutions and work together with faculty members on real-world research projects.

Off-Campus Programs

Experiential learning (via internships) is available in conjunction with almost every major. King's students have interned at CNN, the New York Stock Exchange, PricewaterhouseCoopers, the U.S. House of Representatives, U.S. Senators' offices, the U.S. Department of Energy, Walt Disney World, and Xerox Corporation, among other places. Every year, students are placed with local, regional, and national companies around the globe.

The International Internship Program and the study-abroad program are also options for King's students who work in a variety of professions. Many of King's students have studied on campuses throughout Europe, Thailand, China, and Australia.

Academic Facilities

King's facilities include the 51,000-square-foot, three-story D. Leonard Corgan Library, which contains several study rooms, a 100-seat auditorium, a 160,000-volume collection, and a computerized catalog, which students can access from their home or dorm. The library uses its affiliation with the Online Computer Library Center to provide students and faculty members with access to college and research libraries throughout the United States. The library provides full-text databases from every computer on campus. Students and faculty members have direct access to more than 1 million volumes through the local library cooperative (NEPBC).

King's features computer labs with more than 440 PCs; 24-hour labs in residence halls; e-mail accounts for all students; computerized library databases; multimedia classrooms with a variety of instructional aids; course discussions on electronic bulletin boards and chats via e-mail outside of the traditional classroom; a technology component of the core curriculum that requires all students to learn to access, process, and develop their own computer and information presentation skills; distance learning facilities for teleconferencing; satellite down-link capabilities in the 220-seat Burke Auditorium of the William G. McGowan School of Business; and cross-registration with area colleges that enables students to take courses complementary to their majors.

The $6.4-million Charles E. and Mary Parente Life Sciences Center, which contains a molecular biology laboratory and a genomics center, includes computer facilities, instrumentation rooms, a rooftop greenhouse, and environmental chambers. The $6-million Mulligan Physical Sciences Center includes modern research laboratories, computer facilities, and state-of-the-art instrumentation used for molecular identification.

Costs

For the 2010–11 academic year, tuition for full-time students was $25,644. Room and board totaled $10,642.

Financial Aid

King's assists all qualified students through its financial aid programs. Currently, more than 96 percent of King's students receive financial aid in the form of scholarships, grants, work-study, or loans. Aid is awarded on the basis of demonstrated financial need, the difference between the total cost of education and the expected family contribution.

In addition to financial aid programs, installment payment plans are available, offering students and/or their families the ability to make monthly payments throughout the academic year. Students who wish to be considered for financial aid must fill out the Free Application for Federal Student Aid (FAFSA) and the King's College Financial Aid Application. The preferred filing deadline for new freshmen is February 15. Forms are mailed to students accepted for admission but can be completed prior to acceptance.

Faculty

King's College has 125 full-time and 83 part-time faculty members. Eighty-one percent of the full-time faculty members have a Ph.D. or an equivalent terminal degree. Graduate assistants do not teach courses. The student-faculty ratio is 14:1.

Student Government

The student government coordinates and participates in numerous activities for both the student body and the surrounding community. It regularly holds open forums for students and senior administrators at the College, coordinates informal socials for the students with the College president, and makes presentations at each meeting of the Board of Directors. In addition, the student government sponsors events that foster awareness for social and justice issues and a celebration of cultural diversity. Community projects, which incorporate a strong service component, include CitySERVE, National Collegiate Alcohol Awareness Week, and fund-raisers for the United Way. The Association for Campus Events, a student-operated organization, also sponsors comedians, movies, and performers throughout the year.

Admission Requirements

King's encourages applications from qualified high school students and those who wish to transfer from another institution. To be considered for admission, students must be prepared to successfully pursue a program of study at the College, as evidenced by the quality of previous academic and extracurricular performance, the recommendation of school officials and character references, and the student's display of personal promise, maturity, and motivation. King's admits students of any race, sex, color, creed, or national or ethnic origin.

Admission decisions are made for both high school students and transfer students with the understanding that all current courses and examinations will be completed satisfactorily. Candidates should complete 4 years of mathematics (through trigonometry or precalculus). One year each of high school chemistry, biology, and physics is also strongly recommended.

The Office of Admission offers two methods for candidates to apply for admission: the SAT/ACT Traditional Choice and the Standardized Test Option/Essay Choice. Applicants are required to state their preference prior to the application review, and the decision is nonreversible. Students who select the SAT/ACT Traditional Choice must submit a completed application, official high school transcripts, SAT or ACT scores, guidance counselor recommendation, an essay, and the $30 application fee, which is waived if students apply online. Students who choose the Standardized Test Option/Essay Choice must submit a completed application, official high school transcripts, an official graded writing sample from either their junior or senior year—submitted and notarized by the high school guidance office, guidance counselor recommendation, an essay, and the $30 application fee, which is waived if students apply online.

Application and Information

Applicants should forward a completed application and the $30 fee to the Office of Admission or apply online at http://www.kings.edu in order to waive the application fee. Secondary and postsecondary (if applicable) transcripts must be sent. Admission decisions are not made until all credentials are received. King's subscribes to a rolling admission policy. Decisions are announced within two weeks from the date of application. Upon notification of acceptance, a $200 nonrefundable deposit is requested to reserve a place in the class. The deposit deadline is May 1 but may be extended upon request. To schedule an interview, obtain an application form, or for more information, students should contact:

Office of Admission
King's College
133 North River Street
Wilkes-Barre, Pennsylvania 18711
Phone: 570-208-5858
        888-KINGS-PA (toll-free)
E-mail: admissions@kings.edu
Web site: http://www.kings.edu
        http://www.facebook.com/kingscollegepa
        http://twitter.com/KingsCollege_PA

LAFAYETTE COLLEGE
EASTON, PENNSYLVANIA

The College

Classified as one of the nation's most academically competitive colleges, Lafayette focuses exclusively on undergraduates, offering a wide variety of academic choices in the humanities, social sciences, natural sciences, and engineering. The College is committed to providing the best education for men and women who possess the ability to benefit from the Lafayette experience, and the capacity to contribute to a vibrant campus community with no graduate programs and no graduate students.

The breadth and depth of Lafayette's curriculum are unusual and unexpected in a college of its size. One of just a few undergraduate colleges with fully accredited programs in engineering, Lafayette enrolls 2,400 students from more than forty U.S. states and territories, and more than 50 other countries. The College draws strength from the diversity of its students, who represent a wide range of interests, special talents, and aspirations.

Lafayette is a residential college where learning continues outside the classroom. Living in college housing is guaranteed and required for all four years. More than 95 percent of students live in College-owned residence halls, apartments, special-interest houses, fraternities, or sororities. An array of student organizations, cultural events, social opportunities, and varsity and intramural sports programs are available to all students.

Recent trends indicate that approximately two thirds of Lafayette graduates obtain a graduate or professional degree. A large and growing number obtain practical experience through employment, and then undertake full-time study for an advanced degree, often with an employer's financial support. Others continue academic pursuits on a part-time basis. A strong internship program with alumni and parent mentors helps pave the way to fulfilling careers for Lafayette graduates.

Location

Lafayette is located in a picturesque setting atop a hill overlooking the Delaware and Lehigh rivers and the progressive city of Easton, population 30,000, located 70 miles from New York City, and 60 miles from Philadelphia.

Easton, Allentown, and Bethlehem are the principal cities of the Lehigh Valley, Pennsylvania's third-largest metropolitan area, which has a population of about 800,000.

Shops, restaurants, and other business establishments that serve the needs of Lafayette students are located adjacent to the campus, and in nearby downtown Easton. Beyond Easton to the west and north are great ski slopes, top fishing rivers, and challenging hiking trails.

Majors and Degrees

Lafayette awards the Bachelor of Science (B.S.) degree in biochemistry, biology, chemical engineering, chemistry, civil engineering, computer science, electrical and computer engineering, geology, mathematics, mechanical engineering, neuroscience, physics, and psychology.

The Bachelor of Arts (A.B.) degree is awarded with the following majors: Africana studies; American studies; anthropology and sociology; art; Asian studies; biochemistry; biology;

chemistry; computer science; economics; engineering studies; English; film and media studies; French; geology; German; government and law; government and law and foreign language; history; international affairs; international economics and commerce; mathematics; mathematics-economics; music; philosophy; physics; policy studies; psychology; religion and politics; religious studies; Russian and East European studies; Spanish; and theater.

In addition, Lafayette offers a two-degree program leading to an A.B. in international studies and a B.S. in one of four engineering disciplines.

Academic Programs

Students are engaged, active learners taught to think critically and to connect ideas with students and faculty from different majors to solve real-world problems. They say that extensive course offerings, personal attention from faculty members, and a personal approach to learning are what make Lafayette special. The emphasis on small-group and team-based learning is part of an educational philosophy that places the highest value on giving students the greatest possible access to an exceptionally qualified and dedicated faculty—in the classroom, in research projects, and in social settings.

Interdisciplinary programs are offered in Africana studies; architectural studies; biotechnology/bioengineering; classical civilization; computational methods; environmental science; health and life science; health care and society; Jewish studies; Latin American and Caribbean studies; medieval, Renaissance, and early modern studies; Russian; women's and gender studies, and writing.

The Dean of the College's staff mentors students in their academic development, provides support for students interested in careers in law and the health professions, and works with students to pursue prestigious undergraduate and post-graduate fellowships and awards.

The academic year is divided into two semesters with a January interim session, where courses are offered on and off campus, including study overseas.

Off-Campus Programs

Lafayette recognizes that we live in an increasingly complex and interrelated global environment, and connecting the classroom to the world outside our walls is at the core of the College's mission. Off-campus study combines academic rigor with experiential learning through immersion in an international or culturally significant domestic setting.

Semester-long programs led by Lafayette professors are offered at Jacobs University Bremen; Saint Louis University in Madrid; Goldsmith's College at the University of London; and the University of Ghana. Lafayette students also choose from semester-long and yearlong programs, coordinated by affiliated institutions, in many countries.

During interim session, Lafayette faculty lead distinctive three-week courses around the world. Courses have been offered in Australia, China, East Africa, England, Guatemala,

Italy, Japan, New Zealand, Russia, Scandinavia, Spain, South Africa, Thailand, Turkey, and the West Indies, among many other locations.

Academic Facilities

With an endowment per student that ranks among the top 8 percent of private colleges and universities nationally, the College has invested more than $200 million in new academic, residential, and recreational facilities recently, including a science center, a center for psychology and neuroscience, a center for the visual arts, and a center for intramural and recreational sports. Improvements also include an expansion and transformation of the main library, a thorough modernization of the engineering complex, and new and renovated residence halls. An expansion of the downtown arts campus is under way to include new facilities for theater and for film and media studies.

Costs

The tuition for 2011–12 is $40,340. Additional costs include a standard room fee of $7580, board fee of $4782 (20 meals/week), activity/technology fee of $318, matriculation fee of $700 (for new students only), and an estimated $2000 for books, travel, and miscellaneous expenses.

Financial Aid

An education that is personal—featuring faculty time with students on-task in the classroom and in student-faculty research—and emphasizes teams of students learning together across different majors will always be more costly to deliver than the traditional large, lecture-based classes taught by graduate students at large public or private research universities.

Lafayette is committed to providing need-based scholarships and grants to meet the full need of every admitted student. In addition, the College provides the Marquis Scholarship, worth $20,000 per year to applicants whose grades, high school curriculum, SAT scores, and activity leadership put them in the top 10 percent of the pool of accepted students. Students with financial need above $20,000, who are awarded a Marquis Scholarship, will have their full need (minus a small loan and work opportunity) met with a grant.

In 2010–11, Lafayette provided $34 million in scholarship and need-based grant assistance to 50 percent of enrolled students. Detailed information regarding financial assistance is available from the Office of Student Financial Aid, Lafayette College, Easton, Pennsylvania 18042-1777 (phone: 610-330-5055).

Faculty

Lafayette is committed to reducing the student-to-faculty ratio from the current 10.6:1 to below 10:1. Ninety-nine percent of the College's 213 full-time faculty members hold the doctorate or other terminal degree in their field. All faculty members—full professors and heads of departments as well as junior faculty members—teach courses and serve as academic advisers to students. Many have earned wide recognition for their research and scholarship and won awards for superior teaching.

Admission Requirements

Lafayette seeks to enroll students who can benefit from and contribute to the Lafayette experience. To maintain a student body that reflects society and to enhance every student's educational experience, the College seeks to enroll students from diverse backgrounds—from different cultures and ethnicities, from different parts of the country and the world, and from across the socioeconomic spectrum. The Admissions Office selects students with a wide variety of academic and extracurricular interests and talents, using a holistic evaluation process that employs no formulas. The most important aspect of the College's evaluation of applicants' ability to succeed academically at Lafayette is a review of the quality of the courses taken in high school, grades in academic courses, and, when available, class rank.

Applicants are required to submit scores from either the SAT reasoning test or ACT (with writing). SAT subject test results are recommended but not required. Prospective math, science, or engineering majors are encouraged to take subject tests in mathematics and science.

A campus interview or regional interview with an alumni representative is strongly encouraged, especially for applicants seeking merit scholarships.

Application and Information

The application deadline is January 1. Applicants are notified about admission decisions on or about April 1. May 1 is the Common Candidates' Reply Date, by which admitted students must reply to the College's offer of admission.

Students who have decided that Lafayette is their first choice may request consideration of their applications under early decision. The deadline for early decision I applications is November 15, with notification by December 15.

Applicants who decide that Lafayette is their first choice after November 15 may submit an early decision II application until January 15 or convert a regular decision application to early decision II until February 1. Notification will be made within thirty days of a completed application.

To be considered for early decision admission, students must sign and submit the early decision plan agreement. Applicants admitted under early decision must withdraw their applications to other institutions.

Office of Admissions
Lafayette College
Easton, Pennsylvania 18042-1770
Phone: 610-330-5100
Web site: http://www.lafayette.edu

A view of Lafayette College's campus.

LAWRENCE TECHNOLOGICAL UNIVERSITY

SOUTHFIELD, MICHIGAN

The University

Lawrence Technological University is a premier private university offering over 100 undergraduate and graduate degrees in architecture and design, arts and sciences, engineering, and management. The University's Leadership Program, integrated into all bachelor's degrees, helps students gain critical thinking, teamwork, and communication skills. An honors program is available to highly qualified students, as well as Quest, which encourages students to explore their interests on a deeper level. Lawrence Tech is known for cutting-edge technology, small class sizes, and a commitment to theory and practice. The 102-acre campus features state-of-the-art learning facilities and many housing, recreation, and meal service options.

The University, including its graduate programs, is accredited by the Higher Learning Commission and is a member of the North Central Association of Colleges and Schools. Appropriate national professional agencies provide additional accreditation to various programs in architecture, interior architecture/design, imaging, administration and management, chemistry, and engineering.

Approximately 4,500 students attend Lawrence Tech; more than 500 live in on-campus housing. Women make up 28 percent of the student body, and twenty-eight states and forty-three countries are represented on campus.

Numerous fraternities, sororities, and social and professional organizations sponsor a variety of activities. Recreational facilities include the Don Ridler Field House, which features a fitness track, gymnasium, racquetball courts, game room, saunas, and a weight and conditioning room. Intramural sports leagues and tournaments in badminton, basketball, billiards, dodgeball, flag football, golf, racquetball, soccer, softball, table tennis, tennis, volleyball, and wallyball are active throughout the academic year. Club sports include mixed martial arts and the Blue Devil Bike Club. Lawrence Tech is expanding varsity sports to include men's ice hockey, soccer, and bowling, and women's volleyball, and is also joining the National Association of Intercollegiate Athletics.

Location

Southfield is a dynamic suburb that provides a pleasant balance between big-city entertainment opportunities and a quiet residential atmosphere. Lawrence Tech's campus is about a 30-minute drive north of downtown Detroit, which offers a rich variety of recreational and cultural activities.

Within a few miles of the campus, students can find many restaurants, parks, shopping areas, and recreational facilities. Research, manufacturing, scientific, and business enterprises are also nearby, aiding students in co-op and internship programs as well as those who work full- or part-time while attending classes. More than 200 Fortune 500 companies have headquarters or business operations in the Detroit metropolitan area.

Majors and Degrees

Most Lawrence Tech programs are available days or evenings; some are offered online and on weekends. Dual majors and customized degree programs are available. Preprofessional programs are offered in dentistry, law, and medicine. A postbaccalaureate certificate in premedical studies is also available.

The College of Architecture and Design offers bachelor's degrees in architecture, game art, graphic design, imaging–digital arts, industrial design, interior architecture, and transportation design. Certificates are available in animation and visual effects for film, building information modeling and computer visualization, and set design. Lawrence Tech enrolls more architectural stu-

dents than any other school in Michigan, and is one of the top 10 largest architecture schools in the nation.

The College of Arts and Sciences awards bachelor's degrees in chemical biology, chemistry, computer science (business software development, game software development, network software development, and scientific software development), English and communication arts, environmental chemistry, humanities, mathematics, mathematics and computer science, media communication, molecular and cell biology, physics, physics and computer science, and psychology (clinical psychology, industrial/organizational psychology, and premedical/biobehavioral psychology). Associate degrees are offered in chemical technology, general studies, and radio and television broadcasting. Minors offered are biology, business management, chemistry, computer science, economics, English, general sciences, history, mathematics, media communication, philosophy, physics, psychology, Spanish, technical and professional communication, and television and video production. Certificates can be earned in computer science, entrepreneurial strategy, film and production techniques, industrial/organizational psychology, technical and professional communication, and television and video production.

The College of Engineering offers bachelor's degrees in architectural engineering (combining bachelor's and master's programs), audio engineering technology, biomedical engineering, civil engineering, computer engineering, construction management, electrical engineering (biomedical instrumentation, embedded systems, electronics engineering, and electrical energy systems), engineering technology, industrial operations engineering, and mechanical engineering (alternative energy, automotive engineering, manufacturing engineering, mechanical system design, and thermal system design). The College offers evening associate programs in communications engineering technology, construction engineering technology, manufacturing engineering technology, and mechanical engineering technology. Also available are minors in aeronautical engineering and energy engineering, and certificates in alternative energy engineering technology, biochemical engineering, bioelectronics, biomechanics, electrical power systems, and embedded systems.

The College of Management awards bachelor's degrees in business management and information technology, as well as undergraduate and graduate certificates in health information technology management.

Academic Programs

Graduation from Lawrence Tech's undergraduate programs requires completion with an overall GPA of at least 2.0. Most disciplines combine a strong concentration in the major with a core curriculum of natural science, social science, humanities, and mathematics requirements.

Off-Campus Programs

Lawrence Tech students have the opportunity to participate in co-op programs, alternating semesters of classes and work. Internships are also available.

The University offers programs in Detroit, Lansing, Petoskey, and Traverse City, Michigan, and Toronto, Canada. Lawrence Tech also partners with universities in Asia, Europe, Mexico, and the Middle East.

Lawrence Tech's Detroit Studio and Innovation Center gives architecture students the opportunity to explore community-based architectural, urban design, and community development projects. Architecture students also regularly build homes for Habitat for Humanity.

The Global Engineering Program arranges for Lawrence Tech engineering students to work and study abroad and brings international engineering students to campus for further study.

Lawrence Tech also offers a study-abroad program, open to all students.

Academic Facilities

Lawrence Tech is Michigan's first wireless laptop campus and all undergraduates are provided high-end personal computers customized with specialized software—a unique benefit valued up to $15,000.

The library houses a wide selection of print and electronic materials, including numerous online databases and full-text periodical titles accessible on or off campus.

Lawrence Tech's modern facilities include architectural and design studios; senior project lab and studio space; fabrication labs; wind tunnel; wood, metal, and model shops; dedicated labs for constructing Baja- and Formula-style competition vehicles; physics, chemistry, biology, and tissue labs; structural testing center; alternative energy, mechanical, and electrical labs; thermal dynamics lab; graphics lab; clay modeling studio; and the DENSO Instructional Technology Lab.

Lawrence Tech also owns a nearby Frank Lloyd Wright–designed home that is used as a study center.

The A. Alfred Taubman Student Services Center consolidates all student support services—from admissions through career services—into a convenient one-stop center. This innovative 42,000-square-foot building utilizes energy-efficient and environmentally friendly features and technologies, serving as a living laboratory for students to study.

The Center for Innovative Materials Research is a state-of-the-art laboratory for the research, development, and testing of composite materials for defense and infrastructure applications. Students participate in related research projects as part of their academic programs.

The Automotive Engineering Institute provides students opportunities to conduct sponsored research on a unique 4 x 4 vehicle chassis dynamometer, which measures many areas of vehicle performance.

Costs

Tuition for all undergrads includes a laptop or tablet computer. The 2010–11 tuition for students majoring in arts and sciences and management was $740 per credit hour for freshmen and $786 per credit hour for sophomores. The tuition for juniors and seniors majoring in arts and sciences and management was $821 per credit hour. In architecture and design and engineering, tuition for freshmen and sophomores was $821 to $830 per credit hour; for juniors and seniors, it was $848 to $857 per credit hour.

A normal course load is 12–17 credit hours per semester. The undergraduate registration fee is $135 each semester. International students on temporary visas must have sufficient funds to pay for an entire year of tuition, room and board, and books at the time of first registration. Additional fees for specific labs and studio courses vary.

Financial Aid

Approximately 80 percent of full-time students receive financial assistance and the University awards over $43 million in scholarships, grants, loans, and work-study funds each academic year. Many privately funded scholarships are awarded to qualified students, based on need and/or scholastic performance. Part-time employment is available at the University for full-time students. Student loans are also available.

Faculty

Approximately 430 full- and part-time faculty members teach at Lawrence Tech. Many part-time faculty members hold full-time jobs in industry and bring their real-world perspective to the classroom. Almost 80 percent of the full-time faculty members hold a doctoral or terminal degree in their field. Faculty involvement is extensive in student chapters of professional associations that meet on campus. Many faculty members are active and/or registered professionals in their fields. Lawrence Tech's student-faculty ratio is 12:1. Most classes average 19 or fewer students, and less than 1 percent of the classes have more than 50.

Student Government

The Student Government sponsors and supports a variety of campus activities. More than sixty student clubs and organizations, including fraternities, sororities, honor societies, and student chapters of professional groups, are also active on campus.

Admission Requirements

Admissions decisions are based on a student's recalculated GPA, ACT/SAT scores, essay, and letters of recommendation. Strong emphasis is placed on grade trends as well as the strength of the curriculum and rigor of a student's senior schedule. A portfolio is required for transportation design, industrial design, and game art majors.

Application and Information

Programs start in August and January. An optional summer semester begins in May. Students must submit transcripts from all schools attended, along with a nonrefundable $30 application fee. To view a University catalog and obtain an application form, visit http://www.ltu.edu or contact:

Office of Admissions
Lawrence Technological University
21000 West Ten Mile Road
Southfield, Michigan 48075-1058

Phone: 248-204-3160 or 800-225-5588 (toll-free)
Fax: 248-204-2228
E-mail: admissions@ltu.edu
Web site: http://www.ltu.edu
     http://www.facebook.com/lawrencetech
     http://twitter.com/LawrenceTechU

Below Lawrence Tech's campus quadrangle are eighty-eight geothermal wells sunk 300 feet deep, which heat and cool the adjacent A. Alfred Taubman Student Services Center. *Lawrence Technological University Photo/Justin Munter.*

LEBANON VALLEY COLLEGE
ANNVILLE, PENNSYLVANIA

The College

Founded in 1866, Lebanon Valley College (LVC) was the first college east of the Alleghenies to offer higher education to both men and women. Now, 144 years later, the College remains a leader—enjoying the number two ranking on *U.S. News & World Report*'s Great Schools, Great Prices list, and for the seventeenth consecutive year, ranking among the top baccalaureate colleges in its category. A remarkable student body, an exceptional faculty, academic programs that stress experience-based education, and a groundbreaking merit-based scholarship program distinguish this private liberal arts college. Students who graduate in the top 30 percent of their high school class can receive an automatic LVC scholarship equivalent to one-quarter to one-half of the cost of tuition.

Lebanon Valley aims to educate its 1,600 students to become people of broad vision, capable of making informed decisions and prepared for a life of service to others. To that end, the College provides an education that imparts the knowledge, skills, and values necessary to live and work in a changing, diverse, and fragile world. Students obtain a solid foundation in a major of their choosing as well as wide exposure to a variety of disciplines and intellectual tools. In the process, they develop the desire and ability to think deeply, ask critical questions, solve complex problems, and communicate effectively, preparing themselves to be competitive and flexible in whatever career they pursue or challenge they encounter.

Lebanon Valley College professors strive to continue the College's proud tradition of inspired teaching with a dedication and commitment to community that has long been an LVC hallmark. A supportive intellectual community and a 13:1 student-faculty ratio ensure that students have direct access to the men and women who teach and guide them; relationships beyond the classroom are common.

One of the most significant aspects of teaching and learning at LVC is collaborative research. Each summer, dozens of LVC students work alongside their professors as funded research assistants, contributing to important discoveries while gaining invaluable skills and experiences. Many LVC students coauthor articles in scientific or other academic journals or present their work at professional conferences while they're still in college. This experiential learning supports independent student research, internships, and student-faculty research/scholarly work across all disciplines, and provides opportunities seldom found at the undergraduate level.

LVC's strong advising, straightforward requirements, and outstanding student support services mean that the majority of students are able to graduate in four years. If a student is not able to earn the LVC bachelor's degree in four years because of a course scheduling problem, the college will cover the costs of any additional course work the student needs.

LVC's fifty-three buildings provide for every aspect of college life. The College's twenty-eight student residences include four apartment-style halls. Academic buildings feature enhanced classrooms with the latest technology for teaching and learning. Two student centers, one of which is in the midst of a $13.3-million renovation, support community gatherings, group study, and extracurricular interests. Students enjoy a recreational sports center; a new varsity gymnasium; soccer, baseball, field hockey, and softball parks; and a state-of-the-art physical therapy facility. The baseball and soccer fields were each named National Collegiate Athletic Association (NCAA) field of the year in their respective categories, and the softball park has twice been recognized as regional field of the year.

LVC's Career Services staff helps students research careers and establish contacts with potential employers, and offers seminars on resume writing and interviewing skills. The Career Connections alumni database provides students direct access to successful alumni in their fields—men and women who have volunteered to mentor, advise, or otherwise assist LVC students or recent graduates. In an average year, approximately 80 percent of graduates who respond to an annual survey are employed, and approximately 26 percent are in graduate or professional school within six months of graduation.

Location

Annville is a small town of approximately 5,000 residents located near Pennsylvania Dutch country, just 10 minutes east of Hershey and within a 2- to 3-hour drive of Philadelphia, Baltimore, New York, and Washington, D.C. Nestled in a beautiful valley, the College is located on a 340-acre site. A wide variety of internship opportunities, potential employment options, cultural events, and other activities are available on campus and within the surrounding communities.

Majors and Degrees

The College confers five baccalaureate degrees. The Bachelor of Arts is available in art and art history, criminal justice, economics, English, French, German, historical communications, history, international studies, music, music business, philosophy, political science, religion, sociology, Spanish, and certain individualized majors.

The Bachelor of Science is available in accounting, actuarial science, biochemistry and molecular biology, biology, business administration, chemistry, computer science, cooperative engineering, cooperative forestry, digital communications, early childhood education, early childhood/special education, health-care management, health science, mathematics, music education, physics, psychobiology, psychology, and certain individualized majors.

The Bachelor of Science in Chemistry, Bachelor of Science in Medical Technology, and Bachelor of Music (with an emphasis in music recording technology) are also available.

Lebanon Valley offers master's degree programs in business, music education, and science education; a doctoral program in physical therapy; and preprofessional programs in dentistry, law, medicine, ministry, pharmacy, and veterinary medicine.

Academic Programs

Lebanon Valley has long been known for the strength of its academic programs and the achievement of its faculty members and alumni. The sciences are a particular strength, with well-equipped and up-to-date laboratories. For the past ten years, the National Science Foundation has recognized LVC among the top 15 percent of the nation's private, predominantly undergraduate institutions for producing the most Ph.D. students in biology, biochemistry, and chemistry.

Other particularly well-known and respected LVC programs include actuarial science (nearly 100 percent of graduates land high-paying jobs), physical therapy (which offers a six-year doctoral program), music (the music recording technology major is especially popular), business (which provides the fundamentals of accounting and business administration within a strong liberal arts context), and education (alumni of which are in high demand throughout the region).

Each student's academic program is complemented by a wide range of extracurricular activities. The College's more than eighty-five clubs, organizations, and other student-run initiatives mean ample opportunities for leadership. Many students choose to participate in community outreach, often by volunteering with children from surrounding communities. More than 25 percent of students play on one or more of LVC's Division III athletics teams, and many more play club or intramural sports. All students benefit from extensive campus programming that includes guest lectures, concerts, conferences, symposia, and a variety of cultural activities.

Off-Campus Programs

Students are encouraged to take advantage of numerous off-campus study opportunities offered by the College. Options abroad include programs in Argentina, Australia, England, France, Germany, Greece, Italy, the Netherlands, New Zealand, Northern Ireland, Spain, and Sweden. Internship-based programs in Washington, D.C., and Philadelphia are also popular options. A student's scholarship funding and financial aid can be transferred to any of the programs, making study abroad available to all students, regardless of their family's financial situation.

Internships are another important aspect of experience-based learning at LVC. With guidance from professors and help from professional counselors, students in every major find internship placements, gain professional experiences, and build confidence, all of which helps when it comes time to apply for a job.

Academic Facilities

While Lebanon Valley's tree-lined walkways and beautiful gardens recall campuses of yesteryear, the College teems with twenty-first-century technologies. The Bishop Library print collection contains more than 160,000 volumes, more than 28,000 electronic books and journals, and 100 online databases. More than 7,000 popular DVDs/videos and 6,500 music CDs are available to be checked out. The library, residence halls, smart classrooms, and administrative offices are all linked to the campus wireless network, maximizing the effectiveness and mobility of learning. Well-equipped, up-to-date laboratories provide students with the tools and technologies they need to conduct cutting-edge research—independently, or in partnership with faculty.

Costs

Annual tuition for the 2010–11 school year was $30,910. Room and board charges were $8365 and fees were $710.

Financial Aid

Committed to helping all families afford the first-rate education it offers, LVC has received national recognition for its generous and distinctive merit-based scholarship program, which rewards strong high school performance with automatic merit scholarships. Students who graduate in the top 30 percent of their high school class receive an automatic LVC scholarship equivalent to one-quarter to one-half the cost of tuition.

Need-based financial assistance is also available. In 2010–11, the College committed more than $22.5 million in merit- and need-based aid. Overall, 95 percent of LVC students receive some form of financial assistance from the College. Students and their families should complete Free Application for Federal Student Aid (FAFSA) and the LVC Financial Aid Institutional Data Form to determine eligibility. The priority deadline for filing for financial aid is March 1.

Faculty

The LVC faculty includes scientists, scholars, artists, and professionals in a wide range of fields, many of whom are respected contributors to their disciplines. LVC professors are dedicated to teaching and are drawn to the College for its close-knit community and for the opportunity to be actively involved in the students' educational growth. Most faculty members are involved in research, scholarship, and professional organizations and play an active role in helping students find internships and get started

with their own research. Of LVC's 99 professors, 86 percent have earned a Ph.D. or equivalent terminal degree. The College is committed to maintaining a low student-teacher ratio of 13:1 (FTE). The average class size is 20, and all courses are taught by professors, not graduate students.

Student Government

Lebanon Valley students participate in the College's governing system through Student Government and the Student Programming Board. Student Government fosters understanding, communication, and cooperation among students, faculty, and administration. The Student Government president meets every other week with LVC president Stephen MacDonald, ensuring that there is a clear line of communication between the student body and the administration. The Student Programming Board organizes off-campus trips and schedules comedians, musicians, and other on-campus entertainment.

Admission Requirements

The LVC admission process is selective, and the applicant's academic record is the most important factor in admission decisions. The College seeks students from a variety of backgrounds as well as those who display leadership abilities, a commitment to community involvement, and special talents or interests that might benefit or enrich the LVC community. Competitive applicants will have pursued a challenging high school course of study that includes at least 4 courses in English, 2 in foreign language, 3 in mathematics, 2 in science, and 1 in social studies. Additional course work in math and science is strongly recommended. More than 70 percent of recent incoming LVC students rank among the top 30 percent of their high school class. Submission of SAT or ACT scores is optional. Advanced standing is offered through CLEP and AP examinations.

Application and Information

To apply, students should submit a completed application, a $30 application fee, and official copies of their high school transcript. Although Lebanon Valley has a rolling admission process, students are encouraged to apply during the fall of their senior year. Personal visits to campus are encouraged.

For more information, applicants should contact:

William J. Brown Jr.
Dean of Enrollment
Lebanon Valley College
101 North College Avenue
Annville, Pennsylvania 17003-1400
Phone: 866-LVC-4ADM (866-582-423, toll-free)
Fax: 717-867-6026
E-mail: admission@lvc.edu
Web site: http://www.lvc.edu

LVC students gather for an afternoon class on the College's Academic Quad.

LE MOYNE COLLEGE
SYRACUSE, NEW YORK

The College

Le Moyne College is a four-year, coeducational Jesuit college of approximately 2,500 undergraduate students that uniquely balances a comprehensive liberal arts education with preparation for specific career paths or graduate study. Founded by the Society of Jesus in 1946, Le Moyne is the second youngest of the twenty-eight Jesuit colleges and universities in the United States. Its emphasis is on the education of the whole person and on the search for meaning and value as integral parts of an intellectual life. Le Moyne's personal approach to education is reflected in the quality of contact between students and faculty members. A wide range of student-directed activities, athletics, clubs, and service organizations complement the academic experience. Intramural sports are very popular with Le Moyne students; nearly 85 percent of the students participate. Le Moyne also has sixteen NCAA intercollegiate teams (eight for men and eight for women). Athletic facilities include a new soccer/lacrosse turf field, softball and baseball fields; tennis, basketball, and racquetball courts; a weight-training and fitness center; practice fields; and two gymnasiums. A recreation center houses an Olympic-size indoor swimming pool, jogging track, indoor tennis and volleyball courts, and additional basketball, racquetball, and fitness areas. Nearly 80 percent of students live in residence halls, apartments, and town houses on campus. The Residence Hall Councils and the Le Moyne Student Programming Board organize a variety of campus activities, including concerts, dances, a weekly film series, student talent programs, and special lectures as well as off-campus trips and skiing excursions. The College recently opened a plaza, which houses its bookstore, a café, and a pizzeria. The new Dolphin Den, which features a food court and a convenience store, has quickly become a popular space for students to meet, have a bite to eat, or just spend a quiet moment relaxing.

Location

Le Moyne's 160-acre, tree-lined campus is located in a residential setting 10 minutes from downtown Syracuse, the heart of New York State, whose metropolitan population is about 700,000. Syracuse is convenient to most major cities throughout the Northeast, New England, and Canada and offers a wide array of shopping centers and restaurants, many near Le Moyne. Syracuse offers year-round entertainment in the form of rock concerts at the Landmark Theatre, professional baseball and hockey, Bristol Omnitheatre, the Syracuse Symphony Orchestra, Syracuse Stage, Everson Museum of Art, and the Armory Square district downtown, which offers one-of-a-kind eateries, pubs, and coffeehouses in addition to a wide variety of social and cultural events. All are easily accessible via the excellent public transportation service, which schedules regular stops on Le Moyne's campus. Just a few miles outside the city are the rolling hills, picturesque lakes, and miles of open country for which central New York is renowned. An extensive network of state and county parks, recreational areas, and other facilities offer an abundance of recreational opportunities, including swimming, boating, hiking, downhill and cross-country skiing, snowboarding, and golf.

Majors and Degrees

Le Moyne College awards the Bachelor of Arts degree in biological sciences, communication (advertising, filmmaking, journalism, media studies, music, public relations, television/radio), computer science, criminology (human services, international affairs, law enforcement, research), economics, English (creative writing, literature), French, history, mathematics (actuarial science, pure mathematics, statistics), peace and global studies, philosophy, physics, political science, psychology, religious studies, sociology (anthropology, criminology and criminal justice, human services, research and theory), Spanish, and theater arts. The Bachelor of Science degree is awarded in biochemistry, biological sciences (health professions, molecular biology, neurobiology), chemistry, economics, environmental studies, general science, natural systems science, physics, psychology, and work and employment relations. The Bachelor of Science in business is awarded in accounting, applied management analysis, finance,

information systems, management and leadership, and marketing. A Bachelor of Science in Nursing is also offered.

Students may minor in business administration, Catholic studies, classical humanities, film, gender and women's studies, Irish literature, Italian, Latin, management information systems, music, urban and regional studies, or visual arts as well as most of the major fields of study offered. Preprofessional programs are offered in dentistry, law, medicine, occupational therapy, optometry, physical therapy, physician assistant studies, podiatry, and veterinary science. Students may prepare for teaching careers through certification programs in adolescent education, dual adolescent/special education, dual childhood/special education, middle childhood specialist studies, and TESOL.

Le Moyne College and the L. C. Smith College of Engineering and Computer Science at Syracuse University offer a dual-degree program in which students may earn a bachelor's degree from Le Moyne and a master's degree in engineering from Syracuse University in as few as five years. Concentrations include aerospace; chemical, electrical, and mechanical engineering; computer science; and other fields of engineering.

Formal accelerated 3-4 programs are offered in dentistry, optometry, and podiatry in cooperation with the State University of New York at Buffalo School of Dental Medicine, Pennsylvania College of Optometry at Salus University, and the New York College of Podiatric Medicine. Predental students may also participate in an early assurance program with the State University of New York at Buffalo School of Dental Medicine. Cooperative 3-2 dual-degree programs in engineering are available with Clarkson University, Manhattan College, and University of Detroit Mercy.

SUNY Upstate Medical University in Syracuse offers students pursuing careers in the health-related professions an accelerated 3-3 doctoral-level transfer program in physical therapy as well as two-year cooperative transfer programs in medical technology, and respiratory care. Premedical students at Le Moyne are also offered the opportunity to participate in a medical school early assurance program. An early assurance program for premedical students is also available through the State University of New York at Buffalo School of Medicine.

Academic Programs

While each major department has its own sequence requirements for the minimum 120 credit hours needed for the Le Moyne degree, the College is convinced that there is a fundamental intellectual discipline that should characterize the graduate of a superior liberal arts college. Le Moyne's core curriculum provides this foundation by including studies of English language and literature, philosophy, history, religious studies, natural sciences, and social sciences.

For exceptional students, Le Moyne offers an integral honors program that includes an interdisciplinary humanities sequence as well as departmental honors courses. Le Moyne also offers a part-time course of study during evening hours through its Center for Continuing Education.

Le Moyne students may enroll in Army and Air Force ROTC programs in conjunction with Syracuse University.

Off-Campus Programs

The study-abroad program allows qualified students to spend a semester or year in almost any country throughout the world. Le Moyne College has study-abroad programs or affiliations in China, Czech Republic, Dominican Republic, Germany, Italy, Spain, and the United Kingdom. Students can also use partner programs to study in locations such as Australia, Costa Rica, Egypt, France, Ireland, Japan, and South Africa. Le Moyne is a participant in the sixty-member New York State Visiting Student Program. As part of the mission of preparing future leaders, Le Moyne College places a strong emphasis on career preparation through internships and other forms of experiential education. Academic departments and the Office of Career Services both provide programs and services for students interested in interning part-time and full-time, both locally and in major cities such as New York and Washington, D.C. The Offices of Service Learning and the

Academic Deans are also involved in experiential education to promote learning outside the classroom. In the sciences, students take part in campus research with mentor faculty members. Others receive assistance in pursuing outstanding opportunities off campus in leading research laboratories and health-care settings. The College has maintained a long-standing relationship with the "Washington center" internship programs, where students from all majors complete full-time semester-long internships in Washington, D.C., with government, business, or major nonprofit organizations. Faculty members in the Political Science Department assist students interested in opportunities in Albany, New York State's seat of government, with either the New York State Senate or Assembly. Finally, the education programs at Le Moyne put students into school classrooms starting immediately as freshmen and continuing each year until graduation.

Academic Facilities

Le Moyne students benefit from an ongoing commitment to technological excellence. The College's thirty-five buildings are equipped with accounting, biology, chemistry, computer science, physics, psychology, and statistics laboratories. The W. Carroll Coyne Center for the Performing Arts houses generous production, performance, and classroom space; the latest light and sound technology; scene and costume shops; an aerobics and dance studio; and rehearsal rooms for instrumental and choral music. Academic facilities also include an extensively renovated color television studio; a radio/recording studio; a receiver-antenna satellite dish; transmission and scanning electron microscopes; a nuclear magnetic resonance spectrometer; a gas chromatograph/mass spectrophotometer; a 230,000-volume, open-stack library; and extensive on-site computer facilities. A fiber-optic network enables students to access the library system, the campus network, and the Internet from several computer labs around the campus or from their personal computers in their rooms. All classrooms are smart classrooms, with multimedia capabilities that expand and enrich the learning process. Le Moyne students have access to other libraries through the Central New York Library Resources Council, and the campus Academic Support Center is available to students for instructional support. In addition, Le Moyne is constructing a 48,000-square-foot addition to its existing science complex, scheduled to be completed for the beginning of the 2012 spring semester.

Costs

For 2011–12, Le Moyne's tuition is $27,390. Room and board charges are $10,890. Additional fees amount to approximately $990, and books and supplies cost approximately $700.

Financial Aid

Financial aid is offered to a large percentage of Le Moyne's students through scholarships, grants, loans, and work-study assignments. Le Moyne offers a generous program of merit-based academic and athletic scholarships as well as financial aid based on a student's need and academic promise. Federal funds are available through the Federal Pell Grant, Federal Work-Study, Federal Supplemental Educational Opportunity Grant, and Federal Perkins Loan programs. A student's eligibility for need-based financial aid is determined from both the Free Application for Federal Student Aid (FAFSA) and the Le Moyne Financial Aid Application Form. It is recommended that these forms be mailed by February 1.

Faculty

The Le Moyne full-time faculty numbers 158 men and women; 94 percent have earned the highest degree in their field. With an average class size of 22, a student-faculty ratio of 13:1, and private offices for all full-time faculty members, the College promotes a personal as well as an academic relationship between students and faculty members. All classroom instruction is done by faculty members, and they are happy to assist and encourage students who wish to pursue undergraduate research through tutorials or senior research projects. These projects are carried out in an atmosphere free of competition from graduate students for books, laboratories, or professors' time. Le Moyne emphasizes advising and academic counseling for students throughout their four years.

Student Government

The College encourages student leadership in all activities. Positions of leadership are open to students in all class years. Students are represented by a Student Senate and have formal representation through the senate on most College-wide committees involved in decision making and policy formation.

Admission Requirements

Le Moyne seeks qualified students who are well prepared for serious academic study. Secondary school preparation must have included at least 17 college-preparatory high school units, 4 of which must be in English, 4 in social studies, 3–4 in mathematics, 3–4 in foreign language, and 3–4 in science. It is also recommended that prospective science and mathematics majors complete 4 units of mathematics and science. The SAT or ACT is required and should be taken by December or January of the senior year in high school. Campus visits are strongly recommended, as the admission process is a personal one. As bases for selection, academic achievement and secondary school recommendations are of primary importance. SAT or ACT scores are important as they relate to the record of achievement and to recommendations. Out-of-state students are encouraged to apply.

Application and Information

The Admission Committee reviews applications and mails decisions on a rolling admission cycle beginning December 1. The priority deadline for applications is February 1; all students who wish to be considered for academic merit scholarships should have a completed application on file in the Office of Admission before this date. Transfer students are encouraged to apply before June 1 for the fall semester and December 1 for the spring semester. Orientation programs for incoming freshmen and transfer students take place in midsummer.

Dennis J. Nicholson
Dean of Admission
Le Moyne College
Syracuse, New York 13214-1399
Phone: 315-445-4300
        800-333-4733 (toll-free)
E-mail: admission@lemoyne.edu
Web site: http://www.lemoyne.edu

Grewen Hall, the oldest building on campus, overlooks Le Moyne's beautiful 160-acre campus.

LEWIS & CLARK COLLEGE
PORTLAND, OREGON

The College

Founded in 1867 in a small town south of Portland, Lewis & Clark College moved to its present location in Portland's southwest hills in 1942. The 137-acre campus is situated in a wooded residential area 6 miles from the center of the city and overlooks the lush Willamette Valley and Mount Hood in the distance.

The student body is known for its geographic diversity. In fall 2009, of the 1,977 undergraduates, 17 percent were from Oregon, and 83 percent came from forty-eight other states plus the District of Columbia and sixty-two countries. Approximately 67 percent live in housing on campus, most of which is coed (91 percent). There are no fraternities or sororities.

The College offers numerous cocurricular activities, including twelve music groups; nine media organizations; nine religious/spiritual life groups; seventeen international, cultural, and diversity groups; and more than fifty student organizations. Cultural events such as lectures, symposia, art exhibits, theater productions, concerts, recitals, and dance performances occur on a regular basis. Currently, there are nineteen NCAA Division III varsity athletic teams, nine club teams, and numerous intramural sports. Athletic facilities include three basketball courts, a competition-size swimming pool, a weight-training room, a stadium, a baseball/softball complex, and six tennis courts, three of which are covered by an airdome. The renowned College Outdoors Program offers adventures such as backpacking, rafting, skiing, snowshoeing, caving, winter camping, sea kayaking, and environmental service projects in Oregon's and Washington's nearby wilderness areas.

Location

Portland has long been known for its livability and its excellent transportation system. Public buses and a free College shuttle run from the Lewis & Clark campus to the center of Portland, 6 miles away. The metropolitan area (population 2 million) is bisected by the Willamette River. Mount Hood, offering skiing ten months per year, is 50 miles away, and Oregon's rugged coastline lies 90 miles to the west. The city has 10,447 acres of parks, thirty-three music associations, thirty-five theater and dance companies, more than ninety galleries and museums, and more than 1,000 restaurants. Professional sports teams compete in soccer, hockey, and NBA basketball.

Majors and Degrees

Lewis & Clark offers programs leading to the Bachelor of Arts degree. Academic majors include art (art history and studio art), biochemistry and molecular biology, biology, chemistry, communications, computer science, computer science and mathematics, East Asian studies, economics, English, environmental studies, foreign languages, French studies, German studies, Hispanic studies, history, international affairs, mathematics, music, philosophy, physics, political science, psychology, religious studies, sociology/anthropology, and theater. Students may also design a major or pursue a double major and numerous minors. Preprofessional programs are available in dentistry, education, law, and medicine.

Dual-degree (3-2 and 4-2) programs in engineering are offered in cooperation with Columbia University, Washington University (St. Louis), the University of Southern California, and Oregon Health and Science University. A 4-2 B.A./M.B.A. program is offered in cooperation with the University of Rochester's Simon Graduate School of Business Administration. A 4-1 B.A./M.A.T. program is offered through Lewis & Clark's Graduate School of Education and Counseling.

Academic Programs

The liberal arts curriculum offers sufficient structure to ensure depth and breadth of study, but it also incorporates a high degree of freedom in order to promote creative and critical thinking. In the four-year plan of study, approximately one third of a student's time is devoted to general education, one third to a major program, and one third to elective courses. Students are also encouraged to participate in departmental honors programs, undergraduate research, independent study, and internships.

The academic calendar consists of two 15-week semesters. A normal load is four 4-semester-hour academic courses, plus one or more activity courses. By graduation, a student is expected to have earned at least 128 semester hours—equivalent, roughly, to eight different classes a year. The fall semester begins early in September and ends before Christmas, and the spring semester begins in mid-January and ends in early May. There are also a limited number of courses offered during two summer sessions.

The community of scholars at Lewis & Clark College is dedicated to personal and academic excellence. Joining the Lewis & Clark community obligates each member to observe the principles of mutual respect, academic integrity, civil discourse, and responsible decision making.

Off-Campus Programs

Lewis & Clark offers nationally recognized international and off-campus study opportunities that have been in existence for more than forty-eight years. Approximately twenty-five different overseas study programs and three domestic programs are available annually. Usually, 20 to 24 students plus a faculty leader participate in each program. More than half of the College's graduates have taken advantage of these outstanding programs, often satisfying General Education or major requirements at the same time.

Overseas study may have either a general-culture focus or a specialized academic focus. On general-culture programs, students become immersed in the everyday life of the host country by living with local families, traveling, studying in classes and seminars, and working on independent projects. Programs with a more specific academic focus may include studying German language and literature in Munich; perfecting language skills in France, Ecuador, Russia, Japan, or China; or studying literature in England. Sites for overseas study programs from 2011 through 2014 are Australia, Brazil, Chile, China, Cuba, Dominican Republic, Ecuador, England, France, Germany, Ghana, Greece, India, Italy, Japan, Kenya/Tanzania, Morocco, New Zealand, Russia, Scotland, Senegal, and Spain. Domestic programs are available in the Arizona borderlands, New York, and Washington, D.C., for those interested in immigration, economics, political science, sociology, theater, or art. Students receive academic credit on all programs, both overseas and domestic.

Academic Facilities

The Aubrey R. Watzek Library (open 24 hours per day when school is in session) houses more than 300,000 volumes and includes electronic access to thousands of periodical titles. Its mission is to provide a solid core of materials designed to support the curriculum and the research needs of the Lewis & Clark community. The library offers individualized reference assistance in the use of both print and electronic resources. The library's Web site provides access to its catalog as well as to a full range of electronic databases and links to useful Internet resources. The library is a member of Summit, a consortium of thirty-six academic libraries that have a unified catalog that enables students to request and receive materials from member libraries within two days.

Music department facilities include Evans Auditorium, a 410-seat recital hall equipped with an orchestra pit and stage elevator; an extensive (more than 4,000) record, CD, and tape collection; twenty-two practice rooms; forty-three pianos, including several 6- and 7-foot concert grands and a 9-foot Steinway concert grand; two harpsichords; a Baroque organ; an electronic music studio with CD production capability; Zimbabwe marimbas; and an Indonesian gamelan orchestra. The 600-seat chapel houses an 85-rank Casavant organ.

The Fields Center for the Visual Arts is equipped with studio space for painting, drawing, ceramics, sculpture, design, and printmaking as well as a photography lab. The department also has a Visual Resources Collection of 50,000 slides and several thousand digital images representing artwork from a wide range of media, time periods, world regions, and cultures. The collection exists to support instruction in the art department as well as historical and cultural studies campuswide. The arts center contains gallery and classroom space as well. The humanities and social sciences also enjoy state-of-the-art classroom and lab facilities.

The natural sciences are housed in the Biology/Psychology, BoDine, and Olin Buildings, which are well equipped with modern instrumentation to support the College's emphasis on collaborative student-faculty research. These buildings contain numerous research laboratories and equipment, used by students in classes or research projects, in addition to teaching labs and classrooms. Among the notable facilities are a laboratory for the study of human-computer interactions, a scanning electron microscope, a modern greenhouse, an astronomical observatory with several telescopes, a molecular modeling laboratory equipped with high-speed computers, a laboratory for the study of parallel computing, a laboratory for studying the biomechanics of animal locomotion, and an astrophysics laboratory that is equipped to remotely operate and acquire data from a specialized telescope at Kitts Peak, Arizona. All labs are computerized for acquiring and analyzing data and are networked to allow sharing and acquisition of data remotely. Ecological investigations and studies of the environmental impacts of human activity can be conducted both on the College's heavily wooded campus and at the nearby Tryon Creek State Park.

Computer facilities include several computer laboratories in academic buildings that are for student use. More than 130 Macintosh, IBM, and compatible computers are available for student use, along with peripherals such as color scanners, color printers, digital cameras, and digital video editing. All residence halls have direct Internet access. Parts of the campus also have wireless network capability.

Costs

Tuition and fees for 2010–11 were $36,632. The room and board charge is $9566 for fourteen (flex) meals per week; other meal plans are also available. The estimate for books and personal expenses is $2040.

Financial Aid

In 2009–10, 72 percent of the College's students received some form of financial assistance. Institutional, state, and federal resources, including Federal Pell Grants, Federal Supplemental Educational Opportunity Grants, Federal Perkins Loans, and Federal Work-Study awards, may be part of an aid award. Other options include low-interest Federal Stafford Student Loans and opportunities to work on and off campus. To receive priority consideration for need-based financial aid, students must meet appropriate deadlines for admission and should submit the Free Application for Federal Student Aid (FAFSA) and the CSS/Financial Aid PROFILE application by February 15.

Merit-based awards are offered to exceptional students who are selected as Neely Scholars (up to five full-tuition scholarships), Trustee Scholars (up to ten half-tuition scholarships), Dean's Scholars (one-quarter tuition), and Leadership and Service Award recipients (one-quarter tuition). Students designated as National Merit finalists with Lewis & Clark officially named as their first choice receive $1000.

Faculty

The 139 full-time members of the faculty are committed to undergraduate teaching and advising and are also active in research, writing, and publishing. Involving students in the research process is of high priority. Ninety-six percent of the full-time faculty members hold a Ph.D. or the highest advanced degree in their discipline. The student-faculty ratio is 12:1. The average class size is 17, with 89 percent of classes having 29 or fewer students.

Student Government

The Associated Students of Lewis & Clark (ASLC) has a decentralized structure that encourages co-curricular participation by students and places a high priority on participation with faculty and staff in the process of enriching the academic environment. ASLC consists of a Student Senate, governing boards, and appointed students who serve on faculty constitutional, standing, and special committees. The 33 members of the Student Academic Affairs Board (SAAB) are appointed on a departmental basis to solicit, evaluate, and support undergraduate and faculty research, instruction, curriculum, and program enhancement. One quarter of the total ASLC budget of more than $400,000 is used by SAAB in support of undergraduate research grants and speakers.

Admission Requirements

Lewis & Clark College seeks first-year and transfer applicants who are committed to academic excellence and personal growth. Admission is competitive. Applications are carefully reviewed and examined for degree of academic preparation, ability to express ideas in essay form, participation in activities, citizenship and community service, and support given by the school through recommendations. Campus visits are encouraged. Interviews are available but not required. Recommended high school preparation includes 4 years of English, 4 years of history or social science, 4 years of mathematics, 3 years of laboratory science, 2 to 3 years of foreign language, and 1 year of fine arts. The SAT or ACT is required, unless the student is applying via the Portfolio Path.

Application and Information

First-year applicants should submit the Common Application (online or paper); the required Common Application Supplement; a personal essay; an official academic transcript, including senior grades from the first marking period; one recommendation from a counselor; and at least one reference from an academic teacher. The application fee is waived if the applicant uses the online Common Application. Application deadlines for the fall semester are November 1 for nonbinding early action (notification by January 1) and February 1 for regular decision (notification by April 1).

Transfer applicants are evaluated on a rolling basis. To ensure full consideration, the College strongly recommends that transfer students submit all credentials before the end of March.

The application deadline for first-year and transfer students for the spring semester is November 1 (notification within three weeks of file completion). The optional Portfolio Path admissions program provides an opportunity for applicants who have shown exceptional academic initiative to demonstrate the full extent of their pursuits by presenting a portfolio of their academic work. Under this plan, SAT or ACT scores are optional. See http://www.lclark.edu/college/offices/admissions/apply for more details regarding the Portfolio Path.

For more information about Lewis & Clark College or to arrange a visit, students should contact:

Office of Admissions
Lewis & Clark College
0615 Southwest Palatine Hill Road
Portland, Oregon 97219-7899
Phone: 503-768-7040
        800-444-4111 (toll-free)
Fax: 503-768-7055
E-mail: admissions@lclark.edu
Web site: http://www.lclark.edu

LIBERTY UNIVERSITY

LYNCHBURG, VIRGINIA

The University

Founded in 1971 by Dr. Jerry Falwell, Liberty University (LU) provides a Christian, comprehensive, coeducational environment committed to serious education at the undergraduate and graduate levels. The University is situated on a 6,500-acre campus with complete classroom, residence, study, leisure, and recreational facilities. Liberty University is approved by the State Council of Higher Education for Virginia and is accredited by the Commission on Colleges of the Southern Association of Colleges and Schools to award associate, bachelor's, master's, and doctoral degrees. There are more than 12,000 undergraduate and graduate students in the traditional resident program. The student body represents all fifty states and more than seventy countries.

Liberty's facilities include the 4,000-seat Earl H. Schilling Center; the 18,000-seat A. L. Williams Stadium (football); the 10,000-seat Vines Center (men's and women's basketball and volleyball and convocation services); the Matthes-Hopkins Track Complex, a superb outdoor-track facility; the Tolsma Indoor Track Center; Worthington Stadium, the baseball field; the LaHaye Ice Center; the state-of-the-art, 83,968-square-foot LaHaye Student Center that includes a lounge, five full-length basketball courts, cardio and weight rooms, a cafe, multipurpose rooms, an aerobic room, a 25-yard swimming pool, and two spas; the Williams Football Operations Center; and the Liberty Mountain Snowflex Centre—North America's only snowless ski slope.

Intercollegiate athletic competition is in NCAA Division I. Men compete in baseball, basketball, cross-country, football, golf, indoor track, soccer, tennis, and track and field. Women compete in basketball, cross-country, lacrosse, soccer, softball, tennis, track and field, and volleyball. Other sports programs at the club level include ice hockey, lacrosse, and volleyball for men and ice hockey and ice skating for women. Intramural competition is offered for both men and women in various sports, including Ultimate (Frisbee) and men's and women's flag football.

Residence halls include traditional-style hall housing, quad-living residences, and new apartment-style living within walking distance of main campus. These new apartments include full furnishings, a kitchen, laundry facilities, and the Campus East Clubhouse, which offers billiards, PlayStation, Xbox, satellite TV, a theater, a computer lounge, the Campus East Market, and a pool.

Liberty offers several majors in a wide variety of degrees on the graduate level, in addition to its undergraduate and associate degree programs. Teacher licensure is available at the graduate level in early childhood (NK–3), elementary (K–6), and secondary (7–12) education; administration/supervision; gifted education; reading; school counseling; and special education.

Through the Liberty Baptist Theological Seminary, the University offers many online and resident graduate degrees, includ-

ing a Master of Arts in Religion, Master of Religious Education, Master of Divinity, Master of Theology, and Doctor of Ministry.

Liberty University's School of Law opened in August 2004 and graduated its first class in May 2007. The American Bar Association (ABA) has fully accredited the Liberty University School of Law, which is housed in the University's Campus North facility. The school is equipped with multimedia technology and wireless Internet access, two seminar rooms, a mock trial courtroom, the Ehrhorn Law Library, a study center with 24-hour student access, law review offices, seven professional skills rooms, an administrative suite, a faculty suite, and an academic support suite.

For international students, Liberty offers the English Language Institute (ELI). English grammar, comprehension, and reading are taught for international students with little or no English skills. An English Language Institute certification is awarded upon completion of these programs.

Location

The University is located in the heart of Virginia in Lynchburg (population 68,000), with the scenic Blue Ridge Mountains as a backdrop. The city is more than 200 years old and is noted for its culture, beauty, and educational advantages. Nearby are such sites as Thomas Jefferson's Poplar Forest; Appomattox Court House; Natural Bridge; historic Lexington; Washington, D.C.; and other places of interest.

The city of Lynchburg offers a wide variety of activities for recreation and entertainment. Excellent sports facilities and programs, cultural events at the Lynchburg Fine Arts Center, beautiful lakes and streams, and many other local attractions enhance the lives of Lynchburg residents. Lynchburg also has more than 2,000 hotel rooms, numerous outlets and malls, and a number of restaurants that serve a wide variety of cuisines. Lynchburg is accessible by air, train, and bus.

Majors and Degrees

Liberty offers more than 229 programs of study—undergraduate and graduate courses, in residential and online formats. Visit www.liberty.edu/academics to view all of Liberty's academic programs.

The Teacher Licensure Option is available at the elementary (K–6), middle school (6–8), and secondary (7–12) levels in biology, business, computer science, English, history/social sciences, mathematics, and work and family studies and at the comprehensive (K–12) level in teaching English as a second language, health/physical education, music (choral or instrumental), and special education.

Academic Programs

In addition to all major requirements, students must complete general education courses in humanities, natural sciences and mathematics, social sciences, physical education, and religion.

Liberty is on the early semester calendar. During the summer, there are several one- and two-week intensive courses offered. Winter courses are also offered between semesters.

The University offers higher education degrees for the adult learner online. Liberty University Online also is accredited by the Commission on Colleges of the Southern Association of Colleges and Schools to award associate, bachelor's, master's, and doctoral degrees. For more information, students should call 800-424-9595 (toll-free) or visit the Web site at www.luonline.com.

Academic Facilities

The Arthur S. DeMoss Learning Center, the academic hub of the campus, is a 500,000-square-foot Jeffersonian-style building that encompasses many aspects of the University. All academic rooms are wired for Internet access, with large computer screens installed for interactive learning. This impressive facility is one of the largest academic buildings in central Virginia and houses the campus library, which currently contains 283,000 bound or microfilmed volumes. Students may find employment or volunteer their services in the University's 50,000-watt FM radio station or student-run radio and TV stations.

Costs

Tuition, room, board, and fees were $25,834 for 12 to 18 credit hours in 2011-12. Additional fees, such as lab fees, are required for specific classes and are listed in the class registration book. Automobiles are permitted if they are registered with the University.

Financial Aid

A variety of grants, scholarships, and on-campus jobs are available at Liberty. All federally funded student financial aid programs are available. Athletic, academic, merit, talent, National Merit, and other Liberty University assistance grants are also available for qualified candidates. Students are required to submit a Free Application for Federal Student Aid (FAFSA) to the U.S. Department of Education and include Liberty University's school code (010392) on that application. This form is the student's application for all financial aid. Approximately 95 percent of the student body received some type of aid last year.

Faculty

The University employs more than 2,000 full- and part-time faculty members. More than 70 percent of Liberty's full-time faculty members hold terminal degrees in their field.

Student Government

Students elect representatives to serve on the Student Senate. This group provides leadership recommendations and sugges-tions to the student development staff. Student Senate members also organize and direct activities and civic programs.

Admission Requirements

All applicants should be familiar with Liberty's philosophy and expectations before applying. Applicants to the A.A., B.A., and B.S. programs must be high school graduates and must submit an official copy of their high school transcript, indicating graduation date (or GED test scores, if applicable). Applicants must also submit either ACT or SAT scores, which are used for academic counseling and placement. High school transcripts and SAT/ACT requirements are waived if the student transfers at least 60 hours or holds an associate degree. Test scores are also waived if the applicant is 22 years of age or older. The applicant must demonstrate the ability to do college work. Three personal references may be requested if needed. Although interviews are not required, prospective students are encouraged to visit the campus. Four "College For A Weekend" events are available each year, giving prospective students an opportunity to participate in classes, attend social and athletic events, experience residence hall life, and interact with students and faculty members.

Application and Information

Admissions decisions are made on a rolling basis; however January 31 is the priority deadline for fall enrollment. Applicants are encouraged to complete the application process by January 1 to be considered for maximum scholarship opportunities. Applicants for the spring term should complete the process by November 1, although early October is preferred.

To learn more about Liberty University, students should contact:

Resident Admissions Office
Liberty University
1971 University Boulevard
Lynchburg, Virginia 24502

Phone: 800-543-5317 (toll-free)
Fax: 800-542-2311 (toll-free)
E-mail: admissions@liberty.edu
Web site: http://www.liberty.edu
http://www.libertyu.com

An aerial view of Liberty University.

LIM COLLEGE
NEW YORK, NEW YORK

The College

With its flagship location situated in a lovely town house in the center of the fashion capital of the world, LIM College has been a major force in fashion and business education for over seven decades. Its graduates can be found throughout all aspects of the industry, and its high standards of education have earned LIM College accreditation from the Middle States Association of Colleges and Schools.

LIM College is a highly personal school where students learn about the business of fashion, with an emphasis on academic and professional study. Lifelong friends are made at LIM College, as well as lifelong careers. Although most students come to the College directly from high school or transfer from other colleges, there are also those of nontraditional college age who enroll. Students come to LIM College from many parts of the country and the world. The current enrollment is approximately 1,500 undergraduates.

LIM College prides itself on its placement record. Prior to graduation, the Center for Career Development undertakes the important task of counseling each student with regard to her or his career. The office has had outstanding success in helping both four-year and two-year graduates obtain positions relevant to their studies. Over the last six years, more than 90 percent of graduates available for placement have been placed in positions related to their studies within six months of graduation.

The unique nature of LIM College's curriculum provides students with a foundation of core courses in liberal arts and business while offering diverse and intensive hands-on preparation in the fashion industry. This affords graduates the opportunity to accept executive training, merchandising, management, marketing, and communications positions in a wide variety of areas within the fashion and business worlds.

Support services are important at LIM College. In addition to academic and career advising, personal counseling is available. Because of the College's small size and the close relationships between students and staff members, any faculty member or administrator, including the president, is readily accessible to help and advise all students. LIM College's Advisory Board members, all successful fashion industry executives, may also serve as mentors to students, offering additional guidance and advice.

LIM College has a very dynamic student life. Active clubs include the Fashion Club, AMA, Student Life Activities Board, Student Council, and many more. There are also student publications including the *LIMLIGHT* yearbook and *Fashion Sense* magazine.

LIM College proudly opened a new residence hall in 2008. Located at 1760 Third Avenue, this state-of-the-art facility boasts a plethora of modern amenities. All rooms have private bathrooms, free wireless Internet access, free phone service, and 130 free cable channels. Rooms are also equipped with full refrigerators and 25-inch flat-screen televisions. The facility also contains a private gym, game room, computer lab, and three full-service kitchens.

LIM College's Open House Program offers students and their families the opportunity to tour the school's campus and learn not only of LIM College's unique academic programs, but also of the vast array of careers found in the fashion industry. The day also includes a special presentation on financial aid in either a group or individual setting. Current LIM College students assist in hosting the event and are available to answer questions.

Location

LIM College is situated in four buildings—on East 53rd, East 54th, and East 45th Streets; and on Fifth Avenue, one of the most fashionable locales in the world. A whole world of fashion is at the College's doorstep and includes such famous stores as Saks Fifth Avenue, Henri Bendel, Armani, and Ralph Lauren. New York City is the headquarters for the garment, cosmetics, advertising, publishing, and textile industries, all of which are essential to the fashion industry and are visited regularly by LIM College students. The College incorporates all of these resources into the curriculum. For example, the Fashion Magazines course includes trips to photography studios and modeling agencies as well as tours of magazine offices and advertising firms. New York City offers LIM College students an unparalleled learning experience.

Majors and Degrees

LIM College offers four-year programs in fashion merchandising, management, marketing, and visual merchandising, leading to a Bachelor of Business Administration (B.B.A.) or a Bachelor of Professional Studies (B.P.S.) degree, and a two-year program in fashion merchandising leading to the Associate in Applied Sciences (A.A.S.) degree. LIM College has recently added a Master of Business Administration (M.B.A.) to its curriculum in March 2009. The program features two exciting courses of study in either entrepreneurship or fashion management.

Academic Programs

LIM College offers a combination of classroom education and supervised practical fieldwork that has been designed to prepare students for executive training programs and other entry-level executive positions in various areas of the fashion industry. Classroom study is supplemented by unique courses such as Fashion Field Trip I & II, during which students take weekly field trips into the heart of the fashion industry, and Fashion Survey, which hosts guest lectures by luminaries from the fashion world.

Work experience is an integral part of a LIM College education. During the four-year bachelor's degree program, a student enters the fashion industry three times for internships. Each of the first two years of study contains a five-week, 3-credit work project. During Work Project I, freshmen are placed in full-time positions in order to learn the basics of retailing. Work Project II, sophomore year, allows qualified students to choose an internship in more specialized areas, such as cosmetics, magazines, designer showrooms, and fashion forecasting companies.

The third and most significant work experience is the Senior Co-op. Students spend one semester working full-time in the fashion industry in an area relevant to their career goals and ambitions. This is required for graduation from the bachelor's degree program. The responsibility, challenge, and fun of this semester prepare students for their next step—the business world. Over the last four years, 27 percent of LIM College students have converted their senior co-ops into full-time jobs after graduation.

Students who are applying to the associate degree program follow the first two years of the bachelor's degree program, including the required Work Projects.

To graduate, students must complete 127 credits for the bachelor's degree (130 for visual merchandising). Associate degree candidates must earn 68 credits. All students must maintain a grade point average of at least 2.0, and satisfactorily complete the cooperative work assignments.

LIM College accepts qualified students as transfers throughout the four years. The maximum number of credits that LIM will accept is 65. Transfer students must complete the last consecutive 46 credits at LIM College, including the Senior Co-op semester.

The College calendar runs on a traditional semester format, offering both fall and spring start dates. Also offered are summer and Saturday Fashion Lab programs for high school students. The specially selected courses, such as Fashion Buying and Fashion Magazines, blend academics with hands-on experience and are a great way to explore the fashion industry.

Off-Campus Programs

Study-abroad options are available, including study in locales such as Barcelona, Rome, Melbourne, London, and China.

Academic Facilities

The 5,000-square-foot Adrian G. Marcuse library contains 65,000 volumes and online books pertaining to fashion, management, marketing, and the liberal arts, as well as 125 professional and academic journals. The library has more than forty computer terminals that connect to the Internet and provide access to online databases through the library's subscriptions. DVDs and VHS cassettes useful for fashion-related studies are also at students' disposal. Personal computers are available for use in the library, lounges, and classrooms. The student-to-computer ratio is 4:1. The Math Center and Writing Centers offer one-on-one tutoring for all students.

LIM College's facility on Fifth Avenue is equipped with two fashion merchandising studios. There are also two new 1,100-square-foot visual merchandising studios, as well as a state-of-the-art Color and Materials Laboratory at the new location.

Costs

Tuition for the 2010–11 school year was $20,900 with additional mandatory fees of $575. Housing charges for the 2010–11 year were $15,875. Students who commute spend from $1200 to $2000 for transportation, depending on distance. The estimated cost of books and supplies are $1100. The personal expense allowance is $2000.

Financial Aid

LIM College believes that lack of funds should not keep students from attaining a degree; thus, admissions decisions and financial aid are totally separate, and a request for aid has no effect on admissions. About 83 percent of LIM College's students received some form of financial aid during the 2009–10 school year. Institutional scholarships, Federal Pell Grants, Federal Supplemental Educational Opportunity Grants, and New York State TAP grants are all available for eligible students. In addition, the College participates in the Federal Stafford Loan program for students and Federal PLUS Loan program for parents. The College also works with several private lenders to offer alternative education loans for students to supplement their federal loans. International students are eligible to apply for alternative loans with a credit-worthy U.S.-based co-signer. The Free Application for Federal Student Aid (FAFSA) should be filed by all applicants by March 1 for priority consideration. Aid is granted on the basis of financial need and scholarships are merit based, although some awards take need into consideration. Details of the financial aid programs are available on the LIM College Web site or are available directly from the Office of Student Financial Services.

LIM College features a Merit Scholarship Program for incoming freshmen and transfer students. These scholarship monies are awarded for academic achievement in high school or college.

Students can remain eligible for their scholarship throughout their stay at the College by maintaining a GPA of 3.0 or above. LIM College's nonprofit Fashion Education Foundation also administers a number of merit scholarships (both need and non-need based) other than direct institutional awards.

Faculty

LIM College prides itself on its faculty members. In the fall 2010 semester, 72 percent of the College's faculty had an advanced degree, including 100 percent of the faculty within the departments of Arts and Communications and Math, Finance, and Technology. All professional subject faculty members have wide business and professional experience and many, through their business contacts, bring guests to class to share in the lectures and discussions. The student-faculty ratio is 8:1 and the average class size is 19.

Each student is assigned an academic adviser. Work-study and career guidance is given to students by the Center for Career Development, with conferences held before, during, and after the cooperative work assignments and prior to permanent placement interviews. Students are always welcome to discuss career options at any other time as well.

Student Government

The Office of Student Life is the center of all student activities at LIM College. This department supports student government, approves other student organizations, and establishes operating budgets. One of LIM College's more popular clubs is the Fashion Club which plans an annual fashion show that recently hosted over 1,000 people. Another popular activity is the student-run *Fashion Sense* magazine. LIM College's Office of Student Life plans many other activities including diversity programming, philanthropic service, and new student orientation.

Admission Requirements

All undergraduate applicants are required to submit high school transcripts, SAT or ACT scores, two letters of recommendation, an essay, and the completed application with the application fee. Transfer students must also submit their college transcripts. The College will waive the standardized test requirement if the student has earned 30 credit hours. International students should have their transcripts evaluated by World Education Services and submit TOEFL, IETLS, or PTE test scores. It is also strongly suggested that all applicants create an activity sheet or resume highlighting their experience, with emphasis on business and fashion activities.

Application and Information

LIM College's Admissions Committee recognizes that many intangibles go into the making of a successful student, and it evaluates each applicant individually and holistically. The College uses a rolling admission policy. Applicants are informed of the admission decision within approximately four to six weeks after all admission requirements have been fulfilled. An application may be obtained from the LIM College Web site or by contacting the Admissions Office.

Kristina Gibson
Assistant Dean of Admissions
LIM College
12 East 53rd Street
New York, New York 10022-5268
Phone: 212-752-1530
    800-677-1323 (toll-free outside New York City)
Fax: 212-750-3432
E-mail: admissions@limcollege.edu
Web site: http://www.limcollege.edu
    http://www.facebook.com/LIMCollege
    http://twitter.com/LIMcollege

LIMESTONE COLLEGE

GAFFNEY, SOUTH CAROLINA

The College

Founded in 1845, Limestone is a fully accredited, private, coeducational liberal arts college. The College maintains a small student body and a well-qualified faculty in order to create an atmosphere in which each student develops intellectually, physically, and socially. The College endeavors to help students prepare for a satisfying, useful life through effective communication skills, responsible decision-making abilities, meaningful leisure-time activities, and lifelong aspirations. In addition to its programs on campus, Limestone offers several of its academic majors in an accelerated format called The Block Program at several locations throughout South Carolina. These programs are intended primarily for working adults. The College also has an impressive Virtual Campus Program on the Internet with many majors offered. The two programs were combined to compose the Extended Campus.

Extracurricular activities play a vital part in the development of all students at Limestone College. Among these activities are intercollegiate athletics in men's baseball, basketball, cross-country, golf, lacrosse, soccer, swimming, tennis, track and field, volleyball, and wrestling and in women's basketball, cross-country, golf, field hockey, lacrosse, soccer, softball, swimming, tennis, track and field, and volleyball. Students who are interested in music have the opportunity to participate in several instrumental and choral ensembles. A theater program is also available.

The 115-plus-acre Limestone campus is well laid out for pleasant college living. The classrooms, library, laboratories, auditorium, bookstore, post office, and administrative offices are housed in buildings that border the central and circular drives, making each easily accessible to the others. The back campus has a plaza of five dormitories, and a dining hall is located nearby. The Timken LYFE Center and Timken East, a physical education complex, offer a 1,500-seat basketball arena, an AAU-size swimming pool, steam room, sauna, Jacuzzi, dance studio, and auxiliary gyms. The Walt Griffin Physical Education Center, named for the current Limestone College president, offers three classrooms, nine offices, locker rooms, athletic training and education facilities, a state-of-the-art fitness center, and a wrestling practice facility. The College also has eight lighted tennis courts, a baseball field, a softball field, a soccer/lacrosse field, field hockey field, and several practice fields.

Location

Gaffney, a small city with a population of 15,000, provides an ideal setting for a college campus. Whereas the distractions associated with a large city are absent from daily life, the cultural programs and services offered in Charlotte, North Carolina, and Spartanburg and Greenville, South Carolina, are all within a 50-mile radius of the campus. All are connected to Gaffney by Interstate 85.

The climate is free from extreme heat or cold. The well-known resort areas of the Blue Ridge Mountains, the Great Smoky Mountains, and the beaches of the Atlantic Coast are accessible for weekend visits. In the immediate area, facilities are available for all water sports, horseback riding, golf, tennis, and skiing.

Majors and Degrees

Limestone College offers the Bachelor of Arts, Bachelor of Science, and Bachelor of Social Work degrees with majors in art (concentrations in studio art and graphic design); athletic training; biology; business administration (concentrations in accounting, computer science, e-business, economics, general business, human resource management, health care administration, management, and marketing); chemistry; computer science (concentrations in Internet management, management information systems, and programming); criminal justice; English; history; liberal studies; mathematics; music; physical education (concentrations in athletic training and strength/conditioning); preprofessional programs in law, medi-

cine, dentistry, chiropractic, veterinary medicine, nursing, pharmacy, and physical therapy; psychology; social work; sports management; and theater. Majors approved for South Carolina teacher certification are elementary education, English education, mathematics education, music education, physical education, and secondary education.

The Associate of Arts degree is offered with majors in business administration (concentrations in general business), computer science (majors in Internet management, management information systems, and programming), and liberal studies.

Academic Programs

The course of study leading to the B.A., B.S., B.S.W., or A.A. degree consists of four elements: requirements in communication and quantitative skills; a general liberal arts program, involving five different subject groups; courses in the major; and appropriate electives. The baccalaureate degree programs require the completion of a minimum of 123 semester hours. The associate degree programs require the completion of a minimum of 62 semester hours.

Advanced placement and credit are given for scores of 3 or higher on the Advanced Placement examinations of the College Board.

An Honors Program involving special courses, seminars, and lectures is available for exceptional students. Admission to this program is contingent upon outstanding high school grades and scores on the SAT of the College Board, the completion of a special application, and an interview. Almost 10 percent of all Limestone students are enrolled in this rigorous academic program.

A Program for Alternative Learning Styles (PALS) is available for qualified students with certified learning disabilities who might not otherwise succeed at the college level.

Academic Facilities

Limestone has outstanding computer facilities, including free e-mail accounts for all main campus students, residence hall high-speed Internet connections, and several well-equipped, state-of-the-art computer labs. There are also well-equipped science labs. The modern A. J. Eastwood Library houses approximately 112,976 volumes and is fully computerized, including student Internet access. Fullerton Auditorium, with a seating capacity of 975, is used for musical productions and is one of the finest such facilities in the state of South Carolina. The Limestone Center houses Limestone's theater department and the majority of the athletic offices. The intimate 150-seat theater has state-of-the-art lighting and sound, a self-contained workshop for set construction, and offices and classrooms. The athletic department portion of the building features a Hall of Fame room, a 75-person media room, and office suites for most team sports.

Costs

The direct cost for a student at Limestone College for the 2011–12 school year is $27,500; the tuition is $20,000, and room and board costs are $7500. In addition, the cost of books, supplies, laundry, travel, and personal expenses are estimated at $4000 per year.

Financial Aid

Limestone College, one of the least costly private colleges in South Carolina, endeavors to meet the financial need of any qualified student through scholarships, grants, loans, work-study opportunities, or a combination of these. Limestone offers merit scholarships to students with outstanding academic, leadership, or athletic abilities as well as to those who have exceptional talents in such areas as art, music, and theater.

More than 90 percent of Limestone College day students receive some type of financial aid. Because institutional financial aid is limited, students are urged to submit their applications for admission and financial aid as early as possible.

Faculty

Personal attention to students and high-quality instruction characterize the faculty at Limestone College. Nearly 82 percent of the faculty members hold Ph.D.'s or other terminal degrees in their fields. The student-faculty ratio is 12:1, and with 92 percent of classes being taught by full-time faculty and staff, students and instructors work closely together in both learning and counseling situations. Each student has an assigned faculty adviser for assistance in course selection and for personal counseling.

Student Government

The Student Government Association exemplifies the College's democratic tradition and the principles of honor and individual responsibility. It is every student's privilege to participate in the government of the learning community of which he or she is a member. The more highly organized activities, including student organizations and social events, are coordinated through the Student Government Association. The College also has a literary magazine and a yearbook.

Admission Requirements

Limestone College does not discriminate on the basis of race, color, creed, national origin, financial need, or physical handicap. Each candidate for admission is evaluated as an individual. The College recommends that applicants have the following high school preparation: English, 4 units; social science, 3 units; mathematics, 3 units; and science, 2 units.

Applicants must submit an official transcript of the secondary school record, scores on the SAT, and a nonrefundable $25 application fee. The application fee is waived if the student applies online at the College's Web site. Transfer applications are encouraged.

Application and Information

Completed application forms for admission and for financial aid should be sent to the Office of Admissions at Limestone College. It is recommended that applications be submitted by May 1. Any admission applications received after that date are considered on a space-available basis. The College practices a rolling admissions policy. As soon as the application, high school transcript, and test scores have been received, the applicant is notified of his or her status. Upon acceptance, a student is required to submit a $100 tuition deposit.

Vice President of Enrollment Services
Limestone College
1115 College Drive
Gaffney, South Carolina 29340-3799

Phone: 864-488-4554
Fax: 864-488-8206
E-mail: admiss@limestone.edu
Web site: http://www.limestone.edu
　　　　http://on.fb.me/limestone_coll (Facebook)
　　　　http://twitter.com/at_LimestoneCo (Twitter)

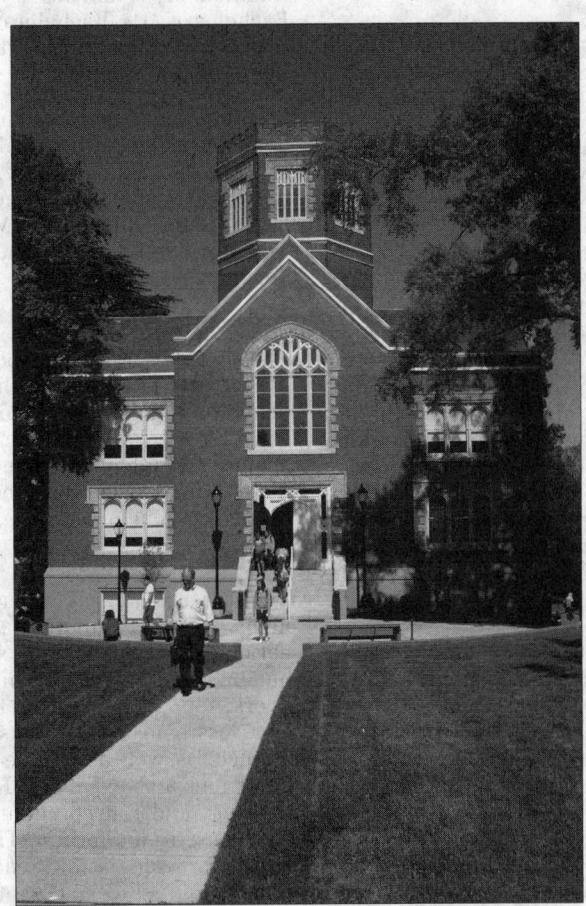

The Winnie Davis Hall of History, named in honor of the daughter of Jefferson Davis, was completed about 1904 and is listed on the National Register of Historic Places.

LINDENWOOD UNIVERSITY
ST. CHARLES, MISSOURI

LINDENWOOD

The University

An independent teaching university founded in 1827, Lindenwood is the oldest university west of the Missouri River. Lindenwood is a dynamic four-year liberal arts institution dedicated to excellence, delivering a high-quality education that leads to the development of the whole person and preparation for life and work after graduation, through more than 120 undergraduate and graduate degree programs.

Lindenwood University is a member of and/or accredited by the Higher Learning Commission of the North Central Association of Colleges and Schools, the Accreditation Council for Business Schools and Programs, the Council on Social Work Education, the Commission on Accreditation of Athletic Training Education, and the Missouri Department of Elementary and Secondary Education, and it is fully endorsed by the Society for Human Resource Management. Lindenwood is a member of the Teacher Education Accreditation Council and the Council for Higher Education Accreditation.

Lindenwood University is authorized to grant associate, bachelor's, master's, Education Specialist, and Doctor of Education degrees. Lindenwood is an independent, public-serving, liberal arts university that has a historical relationship with the Presbyterian Church and is committed to the values inherent in the Judeo-Christian tradition. Lindenwood welcomes students from all religious denominations.

The University's athletic teams compete in the Heart of America Athletic Conference and the National Association of Intercollegiate Athletics (NAIA). Although Lindenwood was accepted into the NCAA Division II in July 2010, Lindenwood will compete in the NCAA's Mid-America Intercollegiate Athletics Association starting in the 2012–13 season. Lindenwood's men and women athletes participate in forty-six sports programs. Over the last ten years, Lindenwood athletic teams have won more than forty national championships. On-campus athletic facilities consist of the Robert F. Hyland Performance Arena, the Harlen C. Hunter Stadium, the Lou Brock Sports Complex for baseball and softball, and an eight-lane all-weather running track. Students also participate in an assortment of intramural sports at the University's Fitness Center.

More than seventy student organizations and clubs, including the Lindenwood Student Government Association and the Student Senate, provide avenues for extended personal growth, leadership, and community service. The University radio station, 50,000-watt KCLC-FM, and LUTV, Lindenwood's HD television station, are staffed by students, as is the *Lindenwood Legacy* student newspaper.

Students wishing to live on campus may choose from residence halls, houses, and apartment-style living. Eight new residence halls have opened since 2000, and in 2010, Lindenwood acquired the former Days Inn in St. Charles for student housing. Sibley Hall, named in honor of founders Mary Easton and Major George C. Sibley, was built in 1856 to replace the original log cabin that served as the first University building. It is listed on the National Register of Historic Places and is now a women's residence hall. All residential buildings have easy access to University facilities.

Location

The 500-acre campus is located in St. Charles, Missouri, a city of about 55,000 people, situated 20 miles from downtown St. Louis. Resting on the banks of the Missouri River, just south of the Mississippi, St. Charles is the site of Missouri's first state capital. The area offers a wide range of opportunities for all types of interests and is particularly rich in state heritage and attractions associated with the history of America's westward expansion. Lindenwood's proximity to a major city allows students to enjoy theme parks, a delightful zoo, professional sporting events, Broadway plays and theater, performances of a world-renowned symphony orchestra, state parks, and lakes. St. Louis–Lambert International Airport is located just 5 miles from Lindenwood University on Interstate 70.

Majors and Degrees

With a foundation as solid as the campus' century-old linden trees, the academic programs of Lindenwood University have a tradition of excellence and innovation. Lindenwood awards Bachelor of Arts, Bachelor of Fine Arts, and Bachelor of Science degrees with majors in sixty-five subject areas—from accounting to unified sciences.

Preprofessional courses are offered in chiropractic science, dentistry, engineering, health, law, medicine, optometry, nursing, and veterinary science. In addition, programs in engineering are available in conjunction with Washington University in St. Louis, the University of Missouri–Columbia, the University of Missouri—St. Louis, and the Missouri University of Science and Technology in Rolla.

Academic Programs

The emphasis at Lindenwood University is on an individualized liberal arts education with career-oriented preparation. Students fulfill general education requirements, participate in the University's Work and Learn Program when qualified, and acquire an in-depth knowledge of at least one area of study as a major. Lindenwood requires the completion of 128 credit hours to earn a bachelor's degree.

Academic Facilities

The Margaret Leggat Butler Library houses volumes, microfilm items, and a computer lab and subscribes to hundreds of periodicals. Roemer Hall serves as the main administration building and has classrooms and faculty offices on the upper floors. Young Science Hall houses an auditorium, laboratories, and classrooms for natural science, mathematics, and computer science, as well as a state-of-the-art television studio. Newly renovated and expanded Harmon Hall houses the School of Business and Entrepreneurship with classrooms, offices, and the Dunseth Auditorium. The Lindenwood University Cultural Center provides a 750-seat auditorium, classrooms, meeting rooms, and offices. It is the site of theatrical productions, concerts, convocations, and lectures. In addition, the Spellmann Center houses a state-of-the-art cafeteria, Macintosh and PC computer labs, classrooms, conference rooms, networking and campus life offices, and career planning and placement services. The 132,000-square-foot J. Scheidegger Center for Fine and Performing Arts, completed in 2008, is home to Lindenwood's Theatre, Dance, and Music Departments, as well as the 1,200-seat Bezemes Family Theater, the 250-seat

Emerson Black Box Theater, the Boyle Family Gallery, and the Charter Communications LUTV HD Studio.

Costs

For the academic year 2010–11, tuition was $13,260. Students who chose to live on campus paid $6850 for room and board, plus $360 for communications service and $280 for a health and activity fee. There is a refundable $300 room deposit. Books and other supplies are extra.

Financial Aid

Financial aid is available to all qualified students. A student must submit the Free Application for Federal Student Aid (FAFSA). To qualify for the full amount of financial aid, students must submit their federal financial aid forms before April 1. As determined by the evaluation, a student's financial need may be met with a combination of federal, state, and institutional sources of aid. In addition, institutional awards are available in the areas of academics, leadership, athletics, drama, yearbook/newspaper, and music. Resident students may earn $2400 toward their expenses by working on campus.

Faculty

Lindenwood has 217 full-time faculty members, who serve as teachers, mentors, and advisers to their students. Faculty members advise students regarding majors and other matters to help them succeed academically.

Student Government

The Lindenwood Student Government Association (LSGA) is made up of representatives elected by the student body. LSGA has the responsibility of providing a balanced program of cultural, social, and recreational events and activities throughout the year.

Admission Requirements

To apply for admission, a student should submit a completed application form with a nonrefundable $30 application fee, a transcript of high school and/or college work, and ACT or SAT scores.

Applicants are evaluated on an individual basis, and admission is based on an analysis of the student's grade point average, ACT or SAT scores, extracurricular activities, recommendations, and personal qualifications. Students are admitted without regard to race, sex, or national origin.

Application and Information

Although admission to Lindenwood is on a rolling basis, students are encouraged to apply by April 15 for the fall semester and by December 1 for the spring semester. Notification of the admission decision is mailed soon after all required materials are received and evaluated by the Director of Undergraduate Admissions.

Applications for admission, financial aid, and scholarships and other information about Lindenwood University can be obtained by contacting:

Undergraduate Admissions
Lindenwood University
209 South Kingshighway
St. Charles, Missouri 63301-1695
Phone: 636-949-4949
Fax: 636-949-4989
Web site: http://www.lindenwood.edu
http://www.facebook.com/LUDayAdmissions

Student life at Lindenwood University.

LINFIELD COLLEGE
MCMINNVILLE, OREGON

Linfield
The Power of a Small College

The College

Linfield College (1858) is an independent, coeducational, residential, comprehensive liberal arts and sciences college dedicated to providing an educational environment conducive to learning and participation. There are 1,700 full-time students on the McMinnville campus. These students come primarily from the thirteen Western states (twenty-five states overall) but also from twenty-eight other countries. Students of color make up 17 percent of the student body, and 7 percent of students are international. Most students are between 18 and 22. Linfield is primarily residential, with seventeen residence halls, each accommodating between 10 and 100 residents. Each hall establishes its own calendar of social, educational, and recreational events throughout the year. Students who reside on campus eat their meals in the College dining hall. Houses and apartments are available for upper-division students. Social clubs, professional organizations, four sororities and four fraternities, service clubs, and almost forty other organizations play an important role in the daily life of a Linfield student. Linfield's winning athletics tradition fosters participation at all levels of competition. Women compete in intercollegiate basketball, cross-country, golf, lacrosse, soccer, softball, swimming, tennis, track and field, and volleyball. Men compete in intercollegiate baseball, basketball, cross-country, football, golf, soccer, swimming, tennis, and track and field. Water polo, Ultimate (Frisbee), and men's lacrosse are club sports. Linfield also has an extensive and active year-round intramural program.

Linfield hosts the Oregon Nobel Laureate Symposium. (There are only five such symposiums worldwide.) At each symposium, several Nobel laureates come to share their backgrounds and expertise within the context of a basic theme.

The Linfield–Good Samaritan School of Nursing, an academic unit of the College at its Portland campus, prepares students for careers in nursing and health sciences. This campus, at the Good Samaritan Hospital and Medical Center, has residence facilities, food service options, and a residence life program. In 2006, the Portland campus programs became open only to transfer admission.

Location

Located in McMinnville, 40 miles southwest of Portland, Linfield College is a leader in the cultural, educational, and recreational events of the fast-growing community of 35,000. Linfield is situated on 193 acres with most classrooms no more than a 10-minute walk from any of the twenty-four on-campus apartment buildings and residence halls. With most students living on campus, Linfield offers a welcoming and lively community.

Coffeehouses, cinemas, boutiques, a community theater, the Evergreen Air and Space Museum (including an IMAX theater), bowling alleys, and a wide variety of restaurants are within walking distance for Linfield students. The central Oregon coast is an hour to the west, and the outdoor activity areas of the Oregon Cascade Range, including year-round skiing at Mount Hood, are two hours to the east. Salem, the state capital of Oregon, is 25 miles to the southeast, and Eugene is 80 miles south. Rainfall in western Oregon averages 42 inches annually and the winter temperature averages 41°F.

Majors and Degrees

Linfield offers the Bachelor of Arts degree in communication arts, creative writing, electronic arts, English, Francophone African Studies, French studies, German, German studies, history, intercultural communication, Japanese, mass communication, music, philosophy, political science, religious studies, sociology, Spanish, studio art, and theater arts. The Bachelor of Arts or Bachelor of Science degree is offered in accounting, anthropology, applied physics, athletic training, biology, business, chemistry, computing science, economics, elementary education, environmental studies, exercise science, finance, general science, health education, health sciences: environmental and public health, health sciences: health administration, international business, mathematics, physical education, physics, and psychology. A Bachelor of Science in Nursing (B.S.N.) is also available. The College has programs to prepare students for advanced study in dentistry, law, and medicine. The education department offers a strong program of teacher certification at the secondary and elementary levels. A 3-2 engineering program is available in cooperation with Oregon State University, Washington State University, and the University of Southern California.

Academic Programs

The academic year is divided into two 15-week semesters (fall and spring) and an optional four-week winter term in January. The January Term offers regular departmental courses and off-campus and international study. Academic courses are assigned 1–5 semester credit hours each; 125 credits are required for a B.A. or a B.S. degree. Students divide their time equally among required general education courses, a major area of study, and elective subjects. The Linfield Curriculum courses, selected to provide a solid foundation in the liberal arts, require students to take 3 semester hours in each of the six modes of inquiry as well as one upper-division course in one of these areas. These modes of inquiry are as follows: the Vital Past; Ultimate Questions; Individuals, Systems, and Societies; the Natural World; Creative Studies; and Quantitative Reasoning. In addition, students are required to take a writing-intensive course, a course addressing global pluralisms, and a course dealing with United States pluralism. Individually designed majors are available with faculty approval. Students majoring in a foreign language spend an academic year in a country in which the language being studied is the native tongue.

The College offers courses in English with the English Language and Culture Program. These courses are designed to help international students whose native language is not English to achieve competence in academic and social English skills, so that they may work effectively in their undergraduate classes at Linfield.

Off-Campus Programs

Off-campus educational experiences include the Semester Abroad program, involving four months of study in Costa Rica, France, Austria, Japan, Norway, China, South Korea, Ireland, England, Ecuador, New Zealand, Senegal, Spain, and Australia. Transportation for the first round-trip is included in the cost of tuition, and most of these study programs cost the same as a semester on campus. January Term study-abroad programs for four weeks are also offered. Recent offerings included the Emergence of Modern Ghana (West Africa); Mainland Southeast Asia History (Cambodia, Vietnam, and China); American Expatriate Writers in Europe: The Lost Generation Tour (nine European cities); and Australia: From Colony to Asian Power.

Academic Facilities

Since 2000, the College has opened two residence halls, six apartment buildings, the James F. Miller Fine Arts Center, the Marshall Theatre and communication arts facility, the Vivian A. Bull Center for Music, and the Nicholson Library. The library covers 56,000 square feet and combines traditional collections of books and journals with the new and changing digital and electronic technology to provide access to the Web and Web-based designs. The studio theater has an audience seating capacity of up to 140 and includes space for set construction and design.

In 2011, Linfield is slated to reopen its former library to provide new classroom and office space for the departments of business, economics, English, and philosophy. This state-of-the-art facility, T. J. Day Hall, will also include the College's writing center and the Linfield Center for the Northwest (LCN). The LCN cultivates regionally relevant partnerships for training, research, service learning, and cultural or artistic exchanges. These opportunities promote student engagement in regional issues and produce real-world change. T. J. Day Hall will be Linfield's first LEED-certified Silver building, underscoring the College's commitment to sustainability and conservation.

Murdock and Graf Halls house the biology, chemistry, and physics departments and up-to-date laboratories and equipment. Other facilities include art galleries and studios, a 250-watt FM radio station, an experimental psychology lab, dance and music studios, a preschool, and a 425-seat auditorium that houses a three-manual, 48-rank Casavant pipe organ.

Linfield students benefit from a communications and technology network that includes phone service, voice mail, e-mail, and wireless Internet connections in each residence hall room. In addition, there is wireless access in the library and other academic areas of the campus.

The Health and Physical Education/Recreation Complex houses three gymnasiums; weight rooms; fitness laboratories with a hydrostatic weighing tank, a metabolic and pulmonary measuring system, and an electro-cardiovascular exercise ECG system; an eight-lane, 25-yard indoor pool; handball and racquetball courts; classrooms; offices; and a 28,000-square-foot field house.

Costs

For 2010–11, tuition and fees were $30,300 per two-semester year, board was $3860, and a double room was $4700. There was a $180 per-credit fee for on-campus January Term classes.

Financial Aid

Eligibility for most of Linfield's assistance programs is based on need as determined by a federally approved needs analysis processor. The only form required for need-based programs is the Free Application for Federal Student Aid (FAFSA). Linfield participates in the federal grant, loan, and work programs, and other forms of financial assistance on the basis of demonstrated need.

The College awards scholarships to full-time students based on scholastic achievement, independent of financial need. These academic scholarships vary from 20 to 75 percent of tuition. To be considered, students must have a minimum GPA of 3.4. A number of other criteria are used when determining scholarships. Linfield sponsors special scholarships for National Merit finalists. The College also sponsors an annual Competitive Scholarship Day in February each year. Participation is limited to high school seniors who meet particular academic requirements and apply by December 1. Each academic department offers prizes ranging from $10,000 to $16,000, divided over the student's four years at Linfield. Scholarships are also available to students from the departments of music, theater, and communication who demonstrate outstanding leadership and community service. Financial assistance for non-U.S. citizens is limited to partial-tuition scholarships and the opportunity to work part-time on campus.

Faculty

There are 114 full-time and 64 part-time faculty members, each of whom is committed to undergraduate teaching and scholarship. Ninety-five percent have doctoral or other terminal degrees within their field. The student-faculty ratio is 12:1, and faculty members serve as academic advisers. There are no teaching assistants.

Student Government

Students have a significant voice in establishing and changing College policies and regulations. The Student Senate, chosen through campus elections, is the focus of student opinion and debate. Students are represented on most College governing councils and committees with faculty members and trustees, and they are encouraged to express and implement their ideas on academic or extracurricular matters.

Admission Requirements

Admission to Linfield College is selective. Admission is granted to students who are likely to grow and succeed in a personal and challenging liberal arts environment. Each applicant is judged on individual merit, based on high school performance, a writing sample, recommendations from teachers and counselors, precollege standardized test results (ACT or SAT), and the depth and quality of an applicant's involvement in community and school activities. Linfield is a member of the Common Application Association.

International students whose education has been in a language other than English must submit certified English translations of their academic work. Proficiency in English is required, as demonstrated by an official TOEFL score report.

Application and Information

The early action deadline is November 15 (with notification by January 15) and the regular decision priority deadline is February 15 (with notification by April 1).

Interviews are not required, but students are encouraged to visit. Appointments should be made in advance and can be requested online at http://www.linfield.edu/stopby. The Linfield Web site provides students with information on student life, academic programs, and athletics. Interested students are encouraged to contact:

Director of Admission
Linfield College
McMinnville, Oregon 97128
Phone: 503-883-2213
       800-640-2287 (toll-free)
Fax: 503-883-2472
E-mail: admission@linfield.edu
Web site: http://www.linfield.edu
       http://www.facebook.com/LinfieldAmbassadors
       http://twitter.com/LCAmbassadors

LOYOLA MARYMOUNT UNIVERSITY
LOS ANGELES, CALIFORNIA

The University

Loyola Marymount University (LMU), situated on a picturesque campus, offers competitive students an education of high quality in a dynamic and supportive atmosphere. As successor to the oldest institution of learning in southern California, St. Vincent's College, the University is steeped in a tradition and history of dedication to academic excellence and the total development of its students. Although the emphasis is within the undergraduate program (full-time enrollment is approximately 5,600 and part-time enrollment is approximately 160), approximately 1,950 students pursue master's degrees in the fields of arts, arts in teaching, business administration, education, and science (including engineering). The Doctor of Education in educational leadership for social justice is offered by the School of Education. The School of Law, situated at a separate campus, has both day and evening divisions and offers the Juris Doctor degree. Law school enrollment is 1,320.

Over 60 percent of the undergraduate students live on campus and are able to choose accommodations in one of eleven residential halls or six apartment complexes. Students have access to a sports pavilion, one swimming pool, baseball and soccer fields, tennis and volleyball courts, and four indoor racquetball courts. The Fritz B. Burns Recreation Center includes three additional courts and a fitness center. LMU fields teams in twelve intercollegiate sports (baseball, basketball, cheer, crew, cross-country, golf, soccer, softball, swimming, tennis, women's volleyball, and water polo) and has club teams in lacrosse, rugby, men's volleyball, and more. Over 2,000 undergraduate students participate in the active intramural program, which includes coed sports. Student organizations include seven service organizations, the AM/FM radio station (KXLU), Chemistry Society, Black Student Union, Han Tao Chinese Cultural Club, MEChA, Business Law Society, Student-Athlete Advisory Committee, University choruses, fraternities and sororities, and various honor and service groups. LMU's Debate Team and Air Force ROTC detachment have received national recognition in their respective areas.

Location

LMU is ideally located on a 142-acre bluff that overlooks the southwest section of Los Angeles and the Pacific Ocean from Malibu to Santa Monica. The campus is close to the beach, and the University community enjoys a cool, clean coastal climate. LMU is near the metropolitan complex, but it has the benefits of the slower pace of its residential community, Westchester. Los Angeles International Airport is 10 minutes away, and nearby freeways provide easy access to the city and its cultural and recreational activities.

Majors and Degrees

Loyola Marymount University offers the B.A. in the fields of African American studies, animation, art history, Asian Pacific studies, biology, Chicano studies, classical civilizations, classics, communication studies, dance, economics, English, European studies, film and television production, French, Greek, history, humanities, Latin, liberal studies (elementary education), mathematics, music, philosophy, political science, production (film and television), psychology, recording arts, screenwriting, sociology, Spanish, studio arts, theater arts, theological studies, urban studies, and women's studies. The College of Business Administration offers the Bachelor of Science degree in accounting and applied information management systems and the Bachelor of Business Administration degree with majors in entrepreneurship, finance, management, and marketing. The College of Science and Engineering offers bachelor's degrees in applied mathematics, athletic training, biochemistry, biology, chemistry, computer science, engineering (civil, electrical, and mechanical), engineering physics, environmental science, mathematics, natural science, and physics. Areas of emphasis can include such fields as graphic arts and marine biology.

Academic Programs

While specific course requirements differ with each area of study, a common core with course work in the fields of American cultures, college writing, communication skills, creative and critical arts, history, literature, mathematics/science/technology, philosophy, social science, and theology provides the foundation for a well-rounded education for all LMU students. The interdepartmental honors program provides challenges for the exceptional student.

The academic calendar consists of two semesters and two 6-week optional summer sessions. The fall semester begins in late August and ends before Christmas. The spring semester usually begins in mid-January and ends in mid-May. Students may earn credit when receiving scores of 4 or 5 through Advanced Placement (AP) examinations.

Off-Campus Programs

Students who are interested in studying abroad have a choice of several University-sponsored programs. LMU offers programs in Africa, Australia, China, England, France, Germany, Greece, Honduras, Ireland, Italy, Japan, Mexico, New Zealand, the Philippines, South Korea, and Spain. The University also has numerous affiliated programs, including the Rome Center of Loyola University Chicago and the American Institute for Foreign Study. Courses may be conducted in English, the language of the country in which the student elects to study, or both. In addition, LMU offers internship programs through which students can earn practical training and sometimes even course credit. The programs range from student involvement in political campaigns to the counseling of underrepresented youths to professional work at film/TV studios.

Academic Facilities

The William H. Hannon Library is the newest and most sophisticated library facility in Los Angeles. The new, state-of-the-art 88,000-square-foot library is the cultural and intellectual hub of the Loyola Marymount University campus. Its three aboveground stories and two basement levels have space for more than 1 million volumes, and the more than 100 computer workstations, four classrooms, and dozens of group study rooms will facilitate all forms of learning. The Law School Library, located within the School of Law in downtown Los Angeles, contains more than 560,000 volumes and microforms and is a depository for government documents of the state of California and the United States. It also has complete holdings of all publications relating to California law. The communication arts complex houses the Louis B. Mayer Motion Picture Theatre, a full-size color-television studio, a motion-picture soundstage, and state-of-the-art industry equipment. Strub Theatre offers excellent theatrical facilities for the performing arts of drama and dance.

Costs

Tuition for the 2010–11 academic year was $34,730. The cost of room and board varies with options that students select—for example, a full- or partial-meal plan, an apartment on campus, or a residence hall. However, the average yearly cost is approximately $12,397. Students should expect to spend about $1620 for books and supplies and $2250 for additional miscellaneous expenses.

Financial Aid

Approximately 79 percent of the University's undergraduate students receive some type of financial assistance. The total amount of financial aid awarded to students for the 2009–10 academic year was $124 million. Students applying for aid must file the Free Application for Federal Student Aid (FAFSA). The CSS Financial Aid PROFILE is no longer required. All students are expected to apply for the Federal Pell Grant, and California residents must apply for the California grants. LMU offers both need-based aid and merit-based awards in amounts up to the full tuition Trustee Scholarship. The priority date for the financial aid application is February 1.

Faculty

LMU's faculty is dedicated to undergraduate teaching and is easily accessible to students. Ninety-nine percent of the faculty members hold a Ph.D. or terminal degree in their area of instruction; the average class size is 21.

Student Government

LMU believes that active student input is an essential part of the undergraduate years. Students sit on every University committee, including the Board of Trustees, with full voting rights. Students operate the campus recreation centers, manage the dormitories as resident advisers, and participate in over 160 clubs and organizations. Student actions have resulted in the development of such things as a campus farmer's market, outdoor concert series, club sports teams, social justice events, and community service programs.

Admission Requirements

Admission to LMU is selective, and a candidate is expected to present a strong record in college-preparatory courses. In determining an applicant's eligibility, the University gives careful consideration to the student's academic preparation, national test scores, letters of recommendation, extracurricular activities, and family relationships to the University. A personal interview is not required for admission. Prospective candidates are encouraged to visit the campus. LMU offers campus tours Monday through Saturday during the academic year and Monday through Friday during the summer.

Application and Information

Applicants must submit official transcripts from the last high school attended and from each college attended, arrange for SAT or ACT scores to be sent to the Office of Admission, submit a recommendation form from an official of the last school attended, and file the Common Application with the $60 nonrefundable fee. Applications are considered when all necessary documents have been received prior to the deadline of the semester for which application is made. The priority deadline for freshman applicants for the fall semester is November 1 for early action and January 15 for regular decision. Early action applicants receive a decision by December 20. The deadline for transfer applicants for the fall semester is March 15. Fall transfer applicants who apply by January 15 will receive early consideration for fall transfer. The priority deadline for spring semester admission is October 15 for both freshman and transfer applicants.

International students are welcome to apply to LMU and follow the same admission procedures as domestic students. International students must also demonstrate English proficiency by submitting TOEFL results with a minimum score of 80 or an IELTS exam of 6.5 overall bandwidth. LMU also offers conditional admission through ELS language centers. International students must also provide a statement of financial responsibility for all obligations covering the full period of time for which the student is making application. All records of previous academic training must be original or authentic copies with notarization and have notarized English translations.

For more information about Loyola Marymount University, prospective students should contact:

Matthew X. Fissinger
Director of Admission
Loyola Marymount University
1 LMU Drive, Suite 100
Los Angeles, California 90045

Phone: 310-338-2750
            800-LMU-INFO (toll-free)
Fax: 310-338-2797
E-mail: admissions@lmu.edu
Web site: http://www.lmu.edu/

Between classes at Loyola Marymount University.

LOYOLA UNIVERSITY MARYLAND

BALTIMORE, MARYLAND

The University

Loyola University Maryland is a private liberal arts school with the Catholic traditions of the Jesuits and the Sisters of Mercy. It is an educational community of students and faculty members cooperating for the intellectual, spiritual, and professional enrichment of all its members and for the improvement of the local community and society in general. The intellectual enterprise is a joint creation of the faculty members and the students. Loyola's current full-time undergraduate enrollment is 3,757 men and women; more than 80 percent of the student body lives on campus.

Loyola encourages cocurricular activities that contribute to the academic, social, and spiritual growth of the student. These include social and cultural organizations, Student Government activities, military science activities, national honor societies, and Division I athletic programs such as basketball, crew, cross-country, golf, lacrosse, soccer, swimming and diving, tennis, track, and volleyball. The majority of the student body participates in the wide variety of club and intramural sports offered.

In recent years, Loyola's campus has undergone significant expansion. Thirteen apartment complexes and four freshman residence halls provide Loyola students with on-campus housing. The Andrew White Student Center offers several dining choices, and spacious meeting and recreational space. The Student Center also provides facilities for athletics, the Communication Department, and the fine arts, including the McManus Theatre and the 4,000-seat Reitz Arena. The Center also has an art gallery, classrooms, black box theater and music, photography, and studio art labs. Loyola's recreational sports facility is the Fitness and Aquatic Center. This 110,000-square-foot athletic facility provides an indoor pool, basketball courts, squash courts, a climbing wall, fitness equipment, tracks, and outdoor playing fields. The Ridley Athletic Complex, completed in spring 2010, is a 6,000-seat grandstand stadium with locker rooms, a weight-training suite, an expertly staffed first aid suite, concession areas, and memorabilia for sale on-site.

Location

The Loyola campus is located in a lovely residential area of north Baltimore, 5 miles from the Inner Harbor area. This location offers the student the advantages of quiet residential living with the attractions of city life. The metropolitan area has a wide variety of theaters, museums, professional and intercollegiate sports events, and historical points of interest. Other colleges and universities in the vicinity help to expand the social calendar and academic life.

Majors and Degrees

Loyola offers programs in over forty majors. The Bachelor of Arts degree is awarded in art history, classical civilization, classics, communication, comparative cultures and literary studies, computer science, economics, elementary education, English, fine arts, French, German, global studies, history, philosophy, political science, psychology, sociology, speech pathology/audiology, theology, and writing. The Bachelor of Business Administration degree is awarded in accounting, business economics, finance, general business, information systems, international business, management, and marketing. The Bachelor of Science degree is awarded in biology, chemistry, computer science, engineering science, mathematical science, statistics, and physics.

Academic Programs

The curriculum at Loyola is divided into three parts: the core, the major, and electives. The core contains those courses that Loyola considers essential to the liberal arts curriculum. These courses, which are required of all students regardless of major, are completed throughout the four years. The core consists of a classical or modern language, English literature, writing, mathematics and natural science, social science, fine arts, history, philosophy, ethics, and theology. The major enables students to pursue in depth their specialized area of study. Electives give students the opportunity to broaden their intellectual and cultural background in areas of special interest. To prepare for graduate study, students may enroll in one of the five preprofessional programs: dental, law, medical, nursing, or veterinary.

An honors program and honors housing are available to outstanding students. The honors program stresses independent work by specially grouped students in many of the core courses. Honors housing provides an environment that is conducive to study and close social interaction.

Off-Campus Programs

Loyola University Maryland participates in a cooperative program with the College of Notre Dame of Maryland, Johns Hopkins University, Goucher College, Morgan State University, Towson University, the Peabody Conservatory of Music, and the Maryland College Institute of Art. Loyola students may cross-register at any of these area colleges and universities.

Students in good academic standing may pursue studies abroad through Loyola's programs in Accra, Ghana; Copenhagen, Denmark; Glasgow, Scotland; Leuven, Belgium; Bangkok, Thailand; Alcalá, Spain; Melbourne, Australia; Newcastle, England; Auckland, New Zealand; Beijing, China; Cork, Ireland; Rome, Italy; Paris, France; and San Salvador, El Salvador. Loyola has programs available in twenty-eight other countries in conjunction with other schools.

Academic Facilities

The Donnelly Science Center is undergoing an expansion and renovation, making it the largest academic building on the Evergreen campus. It features state-of-the-art laboratories for tomorrow's scientists and health-care professionals; and new classrooms and offices that give faculty members even more space for instruction and research.

The Sellinger School of Business and Management is Loyola's AACSB-accredited business school. Highlights of this school include experiential learning requirements, the Sellinger Scholars program, many student associations, and a brand new Student Experiential Learning Lab which features such things as a six-screen video display for breaking news and real-time market updates, and a scrolling price ticker. In addition, 90 percent of Sellinger classes are taught in Internet-linked, multimedia classrooms.

Costs

For 2011–12, tuition for all undergraduate students is $39,470 per year. Room for freshmen is $8850. Student fees are estimated at $1400.

Financial Aid

It is the intent of Loyola to assist qualified students who might not otherwise be able to provide for themselves an opportunity for higher education. Financial aid is awarded on academic ability and financial need. Seventy percent of the student body receive financial assistance in the forms of Loyola University Maryland scholarships, state scholarships, Federal Pell Grants, Federal Supplemental Educational Opportunity Grants, Federal Perkins Loans, and Federal Work-Study Program opportunities. To apply for financial assistance, students must submit the Free Application for Federal Student Aid and the Financial Aid PROFILE through the College Scholarship Service in Princeton, New Jersey. The financial aid application deadline is February 15.

Faculty

Loyola intends to maintain its faculty-student ratio of approximately 1:13 and an average class size of 25 students to ensure interest in the individual student. Of the 410 faculty members, 81 percent are full-time and 81 percent hold a doctoral or terminal degree in their field. No classes are taught by graduate students.

Student Government

The Student Government serves three chief functions, which make its existence not only valuable but also necessary. These functions are to represent the student body outside the University, to provide leadership within the student body, and to perform services, both social and academic, for the students. Responsibility for budgeting activities also rests with the Student Government. The president of the Student Government is a member of the College Academic Council.

Admission Requirements

Applicants for admission to Loyola University Maryland are evaluated according to their academic qualifications. The most important academic criteria include the secondary school record and recommendations from an academic source. Submission of SAT and ACT scores is optional for first-year applicants, excluding home-schooled students and NCAA athletic recruits. SAT and ACT scores will be reviewed as a core component, if submitted. Students who choose not to submit standardized test scores must submit an additional letter of recommendation or personal essay. The University welcomes applications from men and women of character, intelligence, and motivation, without discrimination on the grounds of race or religious belief.

Application and Information

Interested students seeking to enroll at Loyola may apply online using the Loyola Application or the Common Application. Each applicant must submit a counselor letter of recommendation, a teacher letter of recommendation, and a personal statement. Applicants for all forms of financial aid must submit the Financial Aid PROFILE of the College Scholarship Service and the Free Application for Federal Student Aid. A $50 application fee must accompany the application for admission.

For additional information, students are encouraged to contact:

Undergraduate Admission Office
Loyola University Maryland
4501 North Charles Street
Baltimore, Maryland 21210-2699
Phone: 410-617-5012
      800-221-9107 (toll-free)
Web site: http://www.loyola.edu
      http://www.facebook.com/LoyolaMarylandAdmission
      http://www.twitter.com/lumdadmission

Loyola's campus offers the freedom of a residential setting, yet it is only minutes from the resources of a major metropolitan area.

LUTHER COLLEGE
DECORAH, IOWA

The College

Luther College, which was founded in 1861, is a four-year residential liberal arts college of the Lutheran church (ELCA). The College, which was founded by Norwegian immigrants, is an academic community of faith and learning where students of promise from all beliefs and backgrounds have the freedom to learn, to express themselves, to perform, to compete, and to grow. The College, which is located in Decorah, Iowa, is home to 2,500 students from thirty-seven states and forty-four countries. Thirty-two percent of the students are from Iowa; 87 percent come from the four-state area of Iowa, Minnesota, Wisconsin, and Illinois. Each year, over 115 international students choose to study at Luther.

In keeping with its liberal arts tradition, the College requires students to develop a depth of knowledge in their chosen major and a breadth of knowledge through exposure to a wide range of subjects and intellectual approaches (general requirements). Learning at Luther is about engagement: faculty members who are passionate in their teaching and scholarship, students who are active and involved, and a College community characterized by personal attention, hands-on experiences, academic challenge, and community support. At Luther, all students become immersed in the liberal arts through the College's common year-long course for first-year students called Paideia. The course, which is uncommon in its approach, helps train students' minds and develop their research and writing skills as they explore human cultures and history. In addition, Luther offers a Phi Beta Kappa chapter and several departmental honor societies, evidence of the quality of teaching and learning on campus.

At Luther, students are encouraged to seek out connections between their lives in the classroom and their lives outside the classroom. The College provides a stimulating cultural and educational atmosphere by bringing distinguished public figures, theater groups, musicians, and educators to the campus. Cocurricular activities are an important part of college life. The College sponsors seven choirs, three orchestras, three bands, two jazz bands, and a full theater and dance program. Numerous student organizations and societies provide ample opportunities for student involvement in meaningful activities. As a community of faith, students can participate in daily chapel, weekly Sunday worship, outreach teams, and midweek Eucharist.

Nineteen intercollegiate sports are offered. Men may participate in ten sports: baseball, basketball, cross-country, football, golf, soccer, swimming, tennis, track and field, and wrestling. Women compete in nine intercollegiate sports: basketball, cross-country, golf, soccer, softball, swimming, tennis, track and field, and volleyball. Club sports include Ultimate (Frisbee), rugby, and women's lacrosse. Seventy percent of the student body is involved in an extensive intramural and recreational sports program. Available for recreational use and for the physical education program are twelve outdoor tennis courts, an eight-lane polyurethane 400-meter track, numerous cross-country running and ski trails, and 15 acres of intramural fields. The well-equipped field house contains a 25-yard indoor pool, three racquetball courts, four hardwood basketball courts, a wrestling complex, and a 3,000-seat gymnasium. A sports forum houses a six-lane, 200-meter indoor track; six indoor tennis courts; locker rooms; and athletic training facilities. The Legends Fitness for Life Center provides the latest fitness equipment and a 30-foot-high rock-climbing wall.

Location

The College is located in Decorah, a city of 8,100 people in the scenic bluff country of northeast Iowa. The Upper Iowa River, which runs through the campus, is designated as a National Scenic and Recreational River. Rich in Scandinavian heritage, Decorah is a popular recreation area, providing opportunities for canoeing, fishing, hunting, cross-country skiing, camping, hiking, cycling, and spelunking. Three airports are located within a 75-mile radius of Decorah: in Rochester, Minnesota; Waterloo, Iowa; and La Crosse, Wisconsin.

Majors and Degrees

Luther College grants the Bachelor of Arts (B.A.) degree and offers majors in accounting, Africana studies, anthropology, art, athletic training, biblical languages, biology, business (management), chemistry, classics, communication studies, computer science, economics, elementary education, English, environmental studies, French, German, health, history, management, management information systems, mathematics, mathematics/statistics, music, nursing, philosophy, physical education, physics, political science, psychology, religion, Russian studies, Scandinavian studies, secondary education, social work, sociology, Spanish, speech and theater, theater/dance, and women's and gender studies. Interdisciplinary programs are available in international management, international studies, museum studies, and music management. Preprofessional preparation is offered in dentistry, engineering, law, medicine, optometry, pharmacy, physical therapy, and veterinary medicine.

Academic Programs

Luther operates on a 4-1-4 academic calendar. The first semester runs from September to December, followed by a three-week January Term and the second semester, which runs from February to May. Two four-week summer sessions are offered in June and July. All students must complete at least thirty regular courses and two January-term courses in order to graduate from Luther. Each student must cover certain territory, including four common foundational courses: Paideia (two courses); foreign language (usually one or two courses); religion (two courses, one of which must be in biblical studies); and wellness (two 1-credit courses). In addition to a focused area of study (the major, which usually requires eight to ten courses), Luther requires all students to take courses in three general fields of inquiry: the natural world (two courses); human behavior (two courses); and human expression (two courses). Before graduating, students are required to bring together all they have learned in two culminating experiences: senior project (one course); and Paideia II (one course). Luther students will also develop the perspectives and skills they need in their lives as citizens and professionals equipped for distinguished service. Advanced placement and credit by examination are available. A qualified student may develop an interdisciplinary major with a faculty adviser.

Off-Campus Programs

Students may participate in off-campus programs during the fall and spring semesters, the January Term, and summer sessions. All of the programs carry academic credit. Luther participates in the Iowa General Assembly Legislative Intern Program during the spring semester of each year. Urban studies semesters may be arranged in conjunction with other colleges. The Washington Semester gives qualified juniors the opportunity to study at American University and work within one department of the federal government. Luther College also cosponsors a semester program in Washington, D.C., through the Lutheran College Washington Consortium. Students may elect to be exchange students at other colleges for one semester or a January Term.

Luther is an affiliate of the Institute of European Studies, which has centers in more than twenty European and Asian countries;

students studying at one of these centers receive credit in accordance with the provisions for transfer credit for study abroad under the Junior Year Abroad programs. A community studies program in Nottingham, England, is staffed by a Luther professor each year. In alternate years, a Luther professor directs on-site programs in Münster, Germany; Lillehammer, Norway; and Sliema, Malta. In addition, opportunities for study are available in a variety of settings, such as the Bahamas, China, Russia, Tanzania, and Norway.

Academic Facilities

The 1,000-acre campus includes the Preus Library, housing 350,000 volumes, 1,100 periodicals, and the College art collection. The library offers five online indexes and ten commercial online services and provides access to more than 480 other libraries. Modern, well-equipped laboratories in the Valders Hall of Science are supplemented by several other science-teaching facilities on campus: a planetarium, a greenhouse, an herbarium, a live-animal center, a human anatomy laboratory, a natural history museum, and a psychology sleep laboratory. Sampson Hoffland, a dynamic new 58,000-square-foot science and research center, was completed in fall 2008. The science facilities also include an extensive field study area and two electron microscopes. Within easy walking distance of the campus, the field study area offers an ideal setting for studies in aquatic biology, ecology, and field biology. Five ponds, two reestablished prairies, marshes, wooded areas, and agricultural lands are available for classwork and independent study. The College has fiber-based and wireless campus networks connecting a variety of PC and Macintosh computers (in several environments) to shared computing resources and to the Internet. More than 400 microcomputers and terminals are available for student use throughout the campus.

Luther College maintains radio station KWLC-AM, and the College's affiliate station, KLSE-FM, is part of the Minnesota Public Radio network. Luther also maintains the largest archaeological research center in Iowa. The Norwegian American Museum in Decorah, one of the finest ethnic museums in the country, provides an invaluable resource for museum and Scandinavian studies. The foreign language departments maintain a twenty-five-station electronic classroom, and the psychology department houses a twenty-station IBM interactive computer network.

The impressive F. W. Olin Building houses the economics and business, mathematics, and computer science departments. Among its technological wonders is the Luther Round Table Room, where students experience simultaneous decision making via a computer network.

The award-winning Jenson-Noble Hall of Music contains state-of-the-art computer facilities, a recording studio, and four pipe organs: 23-stop/34-rank and 42-stop/61-rank tracker organs for practice and performing and two Schlicker practice organs of 8 and 5 ranks, respectively. Jenson Hall of Music also contains 32,000 square feet of classrooms, studios, practice rooms, and rehearsal rooms for keyboard, vocal, and instrumental music. The Center for Faith and Life (CFL) houses a 42-stop/62-rank organ in the 1,600-seat auditorium for the performing arts. The CFL also houses the offices of the campus ministry, a 24-hour meditation chapel, a 200-seat recital hall, and one of four campus art galleries. The Center for the Arts serves as the home for theater, dance, and the arts.

Costs

For 2011–12, the comprehensive fee is $40,585, which includes tuition, facilities fees, room, board, subscription to student publications, and admission to College-supported concerts, lectures, and other events. A room telephone, cable TV, computer access from residence hall rooms, and a health-service program are also included. Private music lessons are $350 per semester. It is estimated that an additional $3000 is adequate for books, clothing, entertainment, and other personal expenses.

Financial Aid

More than 97 percent of all Luther students receive financial aid in the form of grants, such as the Federal Pell Grant; scholarships from Luther and other sources; loans; and jobs on campus. Luther awards Regent and Presidential Scholarships to those demonstrating superior academic achievement. The amount of aid given is determined by the College's analysis of the Free Application for Federal Student Aid (FAFSA). The priority deadline for a financial aid application is March 1. Students receive notification of financial aid awards after their acceptance for admission.

Faculty

There are 180 full-time faculty members; 94 percent hold a Ph.D., first professional, or other terminal degree. The student-faculty ratio is 12:1.

Student Government

Students share in the governance of the College and participate in social and cultural programming. They have full membership on most College committees, majority representation in the Community Assembly, and nonvoting representation on the Board of Regents.

Admission Requirements

Admission is selective. An applicant must be a graduate of an accredited high school and have completed at least 4 units of English, 3 units of mathematics, 3 units of social science, and 2 units of natural science. It is strongly recommended that the applicant have at least two years of a foreign language. Sixty-four percent of entering students rank in the top quarter of their high school class. Transfer students may enroll in either semester.

Application and Information

An application, SAT or ACT scores, an educator's reference, and a transcript of previous academic work are required for admission. On-campus interviews are recommended but not required. For more information about Luther, students should contact:

Admissions Office
Luther College
700 College Drive
Decorah, Iowa 52101-1042
Phone: 563-387-1287
      800-458-8437 (toll-free)
Fax: 563-387-2159
E-mail: admissions@luther.edu (admissions)
      finaid@luther.edu (financial aid)
      intladmissions@luther.edu (international)
Web site: http://admissions.luther.edu
      http://www.facebook.com/luthercollege1861
      http://twitter.com/luthercollege

Luther College's spacious 1,000-acre campus in the scenic bluff country of northeast Iowa.

LYNCHBURG COLLEGE

LYNCHBURG, VIRGINIA

The College

Lynchburg College is a fully accredited, coeducational, nonsectarian liberal arts college related to the Christian Church (Disciples of Christ). It offers undergraduate programs in the liberal arts, sciences, and professional disciplines (including business, communications, education, and nursing) and graduate programs in art, business, education, and nursing. A Doctorate of Physical Therapy program (http://www.lynchburg.edu/dpt) debuted in 2010. Lynchburg College (LC) is committed to the principle that every individual is of infinite worth, and it endeavors to provide a program of liberal education consistent with the needs of contemporary society. It draws its undergraduate student body of approximately 2,200 men and women from thirty-six states and fourteen countries. The College community is largely residential, with approximately 78 percent of the full-time undergraduate student body living on campus. Approximately 36 percent of the undergraduates are from out of state.

The 214-acre campus has long been considered one of the most beautiful in the South. Thirty-seven buildings of mostly Georgian Colonial design have the majestic Blue Ridge Mountains as a backdrop. The Claytor Nature Study Center (http://www.lynchburg.edu/claytor), a 470-acre farm in nearby Bedford County, is utilized for environmental and educational purposes as a learning laboratory to promote the property as a model of environmental management in cooperation with various organizations locally and nationally. The center is also home to the Belk Astronomical Observatory, one of the most publicly accessible dark sky observatories in Virginia, with a virtually unobstructed view of the night sky along the full horizon. The facility allows the College to conduct extensive stellar and planetary research.

A wide variety of activities are available in the Lynchburg College community: service and honor organizations, including the national Bonner Leader Program; more than 100 clubs and organizations; five fraternities; and six sororities as well as opportunities to participate in dramatic productions, student publications, religious activities, and musical performances. New Horizons provides adventure-based leadership and team-building opportunities for individuals and groups. Community service (http://www.lynchburg.edu/serve) is a distinguishing feature of the Lynchburg College students, staff, and faculty, who annually contribute more than 45,000 volunteer hours to the community through such projects as Habitat for Humanity, Camp Jaycees, Special Olympics, and other programs.

The varsity athletic program (http://athletics.lynchburg.edu) is diverse and includes twenty-one sports. The College participates in NCAA Division III and is a charter member of the Old Dominion Athletic Conference, which includes Bridgewater, Eastern Mennonite, Emory & Henry, Guilford, Hampden-Sydney, Hollins, Lynchburg, Randolph-Macon, Randolph, Roanoke, Sweet Briar, Virginia Wesleyan, and Washington and Lee. In addition, the College supports several club sports for men and women. The Turner Athletic Facility includes state-of-the-art exercise and fitness areas, a dance studio, and one of the top exercise physiology labs in Virginia.

Shellenberger Field is a state-of-the-art athletic facility with a brand new artificial turf field and eight-lane track. With a 3,000-spectator capacity including chair and bleacher seating and night lighting, it is a formidable venue for opponents who compete with the home team in men's and women's soccer, lacrosse, track and field, and field hockey. Intramural and club sports take advantage of this facility. Also included are Moon Field upgrades—a permanent softball outfield fence and new areas for the track and field events of javelin, hammer, shot put, and discus. The baseball field, Fox Field, was updated recently to include seating for up to 1,000 fans, batting cages, and a press box.

Location

Lynchburg College (http://www.lynchburg.edu) is located in central Virginia, 100 miles from Richmond, 180 miles southwest of Washington, D.C., and 50 miles east of Roanoke. Greater Lynchburg is a growing business and industrial center with a population of more than 240,000. The city is noted for its climate, culture, and historic landmarks. It is within an easy drive of the Blue Ridge Mountains, where many popular lakes and resorts are located. Air, bus, and railroad transportation place Lynchburg within easy reach of any urban center.

Majors and Degrees

Lynchburg College offers the Bachelor of Arts degree in the following fields: accounting, art (graphic design or studio art), business administration, communication studies (journalism or speech communication), economics (financial or general), English (literature or writing), French, history, international relations, management, marketing, music, philosophy, political science, religious studies, sociology (criminology or general), Spanish, sports management, and theater. The Bachelor of Science degree is offered in the following fields: athletic training, biology, biomedical science, chemistry, computer science, environmental science, exercise physiology, health and physical education, health promotion, human development and learning (elementary education or special education), mathematics, nursing, physics, and psychology. For more information, prospective students should visit http://www.lynchburg.edu/majors.

Preprofessional and professional courses are available for students who want preparation for careers in art therapy, dentistry, engineering, forestry and wildlife management, law, library science, medicine, ministry and ministry-related occupations, occupational therapy, optometry, pharmacy, physical therapy, and veterinary medicine.

Academic Programs

To be eligible for a degree, a student must complete at least 124 semester hours of college-level academic work. In addition, a degree candidate must have a grade point average of at least 2.0 on all work undertaken, plus an average of at least 2.0 or higher depending on the program on all work undertaken in the major field.

The curriculum at Lynchburg College is divided into two general areas; some additional hours are available for students to explore course work in free elective areas of their choice. The first of the two areas of study consists of General Education Requirements (GERs) selected from the broad disciplines of world literature, fine arts, philosophy, religious studies, mathematics, history, social science, laboratory science, foreign languages, and health and movement science. All students are exposed to each of these academic areas. The second of the two general areas is the major. The College offers thirty-eight majors, ranging from education and business to the sciences and the humanities, forty-five minors, as well as thirteen preprofessional programs. This curriculum offers students breadth (GERs) as well as depth (the major). Students may devote their free elective hours to a minor to further enhance their education.

Outstanding students may be selected to participate in the College's Westover Honors Program (http://www.lynchburg.edu/westoverhonors), the purpose of which is to attract, stimulate, challenge, and fulfill academically gifted students. The program offers a challenging curriculum that promotes intellectual curiosity and independent thinking and places strong emphasis on creative problem solving.

The College operates on an early semester calendar. The first semester begins in late August and ends before Christmas, and the second semester runs from mid-January to early May. An optional winter term abroad is also offered.

Lynchburg offers entry-level computer courses to all students. New students may bring a computer of their own or utilize one of the many available on campus. All students are assigned an e-mail account and have access to the Internet. In addition, all students are allowed to develop their own home pages on the World Wide Web, which they have access to through the computer resources provided by the College. All residence hall rooms are wired for network access and the Intranet, which serves the College community. Wireless Internet access is available in most areas of the campus.

Off-Campus Programs

Various agency and intercollegiate exchange programs are available. Students may engage in foreign-study programs and are encouraged to do so. In addition, any student who wishes to study abroad may do so as part of the College's study-abroad program (http://www.lynchburg.edu/studyabroad).

Internships, organized through the Academic and Career Services Office (http://www.lynchburg.edu/career), are available locally, nationally, and internationally. More than 1,000 internships are already established, and new sites are developed each year. In addition, Lynchburg College, Randolph College, and Sweet Briar College, as members of the Tri-College Consortium of Virginia, maintain cooperative relationships for sharing facilities and offerings.

Academic Facilities

The Hobbs Science Center provides an outstanding learning environment for students pursuing studies in biology, chemistry, physics, biomedical sciences, environmental science, psychology, mathematics, and computer science. In addition to state-of-the-art research labs, including a cadaver lab, students studying environmental science can utilize the online weather station, GIS and remote sensing software, and digitizer. This modern facility is also used during the summer by the Virginia Governor's School for Math and Science to provide programming for selected high school students. Extending over 470 acres, the Claytor Nature Study Center is a hands-on learning environment with natural woodlands, grasslands, two lakes, wetlands, and a mile-long stretch of the Big Otter River, and an 8,000-square-foot education/research facility.

Schewel Hall, Lynchburg College's new $12-million classroom and laboratory facility, houses the School of Business and Economics, the Communication Studies program, foreign languages, performing arts, and multiple venues for students to congregate and study. This 67,000-square-foot facility includes technology-based classrooms, computer laboratories, and specialized teaching-learning settings, including a model stock exchange room, a digital darkroom, and a multimedia development center with television and recording studios, and Sydnor Performance Hall, which seats 250.

The Daura Art Gallery (http://www.lynchburg.edu/daura) is the major repository of more than 1,000 works of the Catalan-American artist, Pierre Daura. The expansion of this facility makes the Daura Gallery the largest visual art exhibit center in the city of Lynchburg. Each year, it is the site for the Senior Art Show in which chosen student works are exhibited.

Lynchburg College's Claytor Nature Study Center provides an outdoor classroom and laboratory for hands-on, field-based environmental study and research. Located at the foot of the Blue Ridge Mountains in Bedford County, the Claytor Center offers two small lakes; woodlands; wetlands; grasslands; rare plants; conference, meeting, and retreat facilities; gardens; a primitive campground; and 3 miles of hiking trails. The Center was run as a farm from the late 1700s until the mid-1990s, when it was given to the college by A. Boyd Claytor III. The land is now managed for environmental conservation and restoration through agreements with the Virginia Outdoors Foundation and the USDA's Natural Resources Conservation Service. The A. Boyd Claytor III Education and Research Facility, a 7,700-square-foot multipurpose building, offers LC students and regional K–12 students and teachers an ideal location for learning with seminar, laboratory, classroom, conference, and retreat space.

The Belk Astronomical Observatory is a 700-square-foot facility that boasts an RC Optical Systems 20-inch (0.51 meter) Truss Ritchey-Chrétien telescope. The facility also includes a 384-square-foot observation deck equipped with twelve piers for mounting smaller telescopes. An observatory control room is equipped with instrumentation that will allow LC to pursue astronomical research in conjunction with other regional colleges and universities.

Costs

For resident students who entered in the 2010–11 session, total charges were $37,125; this includes $28,960 for tuition, $7220 for room and board, and $945 for student fees (http://www.lynchburg.edu/tuition).

Financial Aid

Lynchburg College administers a financial aid program of more than $20 million. These resources are awarded to students for meritorious achievement and/or for demonstrated need. Lynchburg College offers academic scholarships (http://www.lynchburg.edu/scholarships) that range from $3000 to $14,000 and are based on performance and accomplishments at the high school or community college level. These awards are renewable each year until the student graduates, as long as the recipient maintains a qualifying minimum academic average each year. Students are identified to receive these scholarships through the admission application; no separate application is necessary. Free early aid estimates are available for students. More than 96 percent of last year's entering class received academic and/or need-based financial aid. The average amount of aid received was $21,000.

To determine eligibility for need-based financial aid, the student should complete the Free Application for Federal Student Aid (FAFSA), which may be obtained at most high schools and at Lynchburg College. The FAFSA results determine the student's eligibility for federally funded grants and loans and other support such as work-study opportunities. In addition, students from Virginia are eligible to apply for the Virginia Tuition Assistance grant.

Faculty

The Lynchburg College faculty has 135 full-time members, 80 percent of whom hold the doctorate or terminal degree in their field. The student-faculty ratio is 12:1. While many faculty members are involved in research projects, it is a College policy that the faculty's top priorities must be in the classroom.

Student Government

The student government of Lynchburg College is regulated by agreements determined by the students, faculty, and administration. It is felt that the College should not be run by the faculty alone or by students alone, but through the cooperative interest of all. Campus government is vested in the Student Government Association, the Judicial Boards, the Campus Life Policies Committee, and the Office of the Dean of Student Development. The Student Government Association is also responsible for the Academic Honor Code, a prominent part of campus life.

Admission Requirements

A candidate for admission (www.lynchburg.edu/admissions) to Lynchburg College should be a graduate of an approved secondary school with a minimum of 16 academic units or the equivalent, as shown by examination. It is required that the academic work include major emphases in the areas of English, foreign language, social science, natural sciences, and mathematics. An applicant must demonstrate above-average academic ability in all areas of study, as admission is competitive. In support of the record, a student must present satisfactory scores on the ACT or SAT (critical reading and math scores are used to determine admission decisions and merit scholarship awards). It is recommended that all students have a personal interview and visit the campus beginning the spring semester of their junior year or during their senior year. Enrollment Office hours during the academic year are 9 to 5 Monday through Friday and 10 to noon on Saturday during the academic year.

Application and Information

Early decision admission applications (www.lynchburg.edu/apply) must be received by November 15; notification of acceptance is made by December 15. All other applications are processed on a rolling admissions basis. Applicants are notified of the status of their application usually within two to four weeks of the date their application file is completed.

For information, students should contact:

Sharon Walters-Bower, Director of Admissions
Lynchburg College
1501 Lakeside Drive
Lynchburg, Virginia 24501
Phone: 434-544-8300
       800-426-8101 (toll-free)
Fax: 434-544-8653
E-mail: admissions@lynchburg.edu
Web site: http://www.lynchburg.edu
      http://www.facebook.com/lynchburgcollege
      http://twitter.com/lynchburg
      http://www.youtube.com/lynchburgcollege

LYNDON STATE COLLEGE

LYNDONVILLE, VERMONT

The College

This small college shines a bright light. For the 1,400 students who come here from Vermont, New England, and around the world, Lyndon offers a hands-on, experiential education, nationally recognized professional programs, and an intimate, friendly atmosphere—all leading directly to rewarding careers or graduate study.

The hallmark of a Lyndon education is experience. The College offers hands-on learning opportunities alongside traditional lecture and discussion courses to give students a thorough and well-balanced career preparation. New students participate in the First-Year Experience, a one- or two-day field trip that serves as an introduction to their major. This gives them confidence that they are pursuing the right field of study and provides an opportunity to rub shoulders with faculty members and other students in their department early in their academic career.

Lyndon graduates are recruited on campus for careers at top corporations and organizations. There are 30 alumni (and counting) at ESPN. Lyndon grads are famously found everywhere there's weather, including Antarctica, the White House, the Olympics, and The Weather Channel. Graduates of Lyndon's Mountain Recreation Management program—the first program of its kind in the nation—are employed throughout the winter resort industry. The College's Music Business and Industry students may be backstage, working on concert tours for world-famous musicians.

Employers seek out Lyndon students because they experience applied theory by participating in fieldwork as early as their sophomore year. Some might be in a psychology/human services program that combines theoretical and clinical practice; others could travel to Africa with America's foremost polygamy scholar to assist with research; while others learn about bad weather on-site at Mount Washington, home of the most complex weather in the country and right down the road from campus. Lyndon's broadcast journalism students have a strong liberal arts foundation that helps them to contextualize and write the news on which they are reporting.

Lyndon students win prestigious national awards in their fields, such as Erica Kelleher, who was named *Ski Area Management* (SAM) magazine's Recruit of the Year. Lyndon's atmospheric sciences students regularly take first place in national weather forecasting competitions. The electronic journalism/television studies students routinely win national awards for their daily live news broadcasts—including a coveted Emmy award for the nation's best college newscast.

In academic disciplines such as mountain recreation management, Lyndon celebrates work and fun in equal measures. Alumni from the program designed and created Kingdom Trails, a 100-mile trail network consistently rated as one of the top 10 mountain bike systems in the country, located just 10 minutes from campus.

Campus events range from the intellectual to the physical, with abundant opportunities for learning and fun. Recent activities include concerts with local resident Neko Case and her band; visits from U.N. ambassadors; a lecture and arts series featuring master classes with luminaries such as U.S. Poet Laureate Ted Kooser; plays and first-run films in the on-campus theater; ice climbing up the frozen fountain; canoeing in the campus ponds and kayaking in neighboring rivers; skiing and snowboarding on nearby Burke Mountain and Jay Peak; NCAA Division III athletics; and traditional Vermont events such as Sugar on Snow.

Lyndon was established in 1911 as a one-room teacher-training college and has grown to a comprehensive four-year college. It still offers a strong education major but remains progressive in its development of new professional programs, such as criminal justice; exercise science and sports management; animation and illustration (B.F.A.); philosophy and film; music business and industry; a media major that integrates journalism with all media forms; and sustainability studies, the only undergraduate program of its kind in Vermont and one that reflects the Lyndon commitment to an evolving sustainable campus.

There are ten residence halls, including a new 132-unit, apartment-style hall for upperclassmen. Each residence hall room is equipped with Internet connections, cable TV connections, and telephone lines. Students who live on campus eat at the Stevens Dining Hall and the Hornet's Nest Snack Bar. All students are allowed to have vehicles on campus.

There are more than thirty active clubs and organizations including the campus radio station (91.5 FM The Impulse), the student newspaper *(The Critic)*, sports clubs, and numerous social and academic clubs. Intercollegiate sports include baseball, basketball, cross-country, lacrosse, soccer, softball, tennis, and volleyball. Intercollege competitive sports include hockey and rugby. Lyndon's intramural program attracts the majority of the student body. Lyndon has a theater which presents films and plays, and a 6,700-square-foot fitness center which is available to students and faculty and staff members. World-class outdoor recreational activities and sports facilities are available within minutes of the campus.

Location

The modern 174-acre campus is located in Lyndonville, Vermont, high on a hillside overlooking magnificent Burke Mountain in the heart of Vermont's scenic Northeast Kingdom, a *National Geographic*–designated geotourism area. It is located 1 mile west of Lyndonville and 9 miles north of St. Johnsbury and is easily accessible from all points by Interstate 91. Lyndon is a 3-hour drive from Boston and Springfield, Massachusetts, and 2 hours from Montreal.

Majors and Degrees

Lyndon State College offers bachelor's degrees in the following majors: accounting, animation/illustration (B.F.A.), arts management, atmospheric sciences/meteorology, business administration, computing, criminal justice, elementary education, electronic journalism arts/television studies, English, environmental science, exercise science, graphic design, human services, liberal studies, natural science, mathematics, mountain recreation management, music business and industry, new media, philosophy, physical education K–12, professional media communications, psychology, secondary education (English, mathematics, natural sciences, and social sciences), social sciences, sports management, and sustainability studies.

Associate degrees are offered in the areas of business administration, computing, electronic journalism arts/television studies, general studies, graphic design, human services, new media, professional media communications, special education, and visual arts.

Academic Programs

Lyndon operates on a two-semester calendar and a six-week summer-session schedule. To graduate with a bachelor's degree, a student must complete 122 semester hours of credit and meet College and program requirements. Sixty-two semester hours are required for an associate degree. Each student is tested for competence in writing and mathematics at entry to Lyndon; deficiencies must be made up in noncredit classes during the first two semesters. Lyndon has a general education distribution requirement of 42 semester hours.

For two-year programs, students are accepted into a concentration upon admission; for four-year programs, in the fourth semester. Academic departments advise and plan the student's core courses within the concentration. In bachelor's degree programs, most concentrations require at least 42 credits of junior- and senior-level course work. Lyndon requires that 30 of the last 39 hours toward any degree be spent in residence. Leaves of absence are granted to students in good academic standing.

Lyndon recognizes learning acquired from previous experience through an assessment course that documents nontraditional learning. The College offers fieldwork and practicums in most academic programs through the Cooperative Education Office.

Lyndon's Academic Support Center, Career Planning and Placement Office, Financial Aid Office, Student Life, and Health Services are just some of the entities that serve the needs and promote the well-being of students.

Off-Campus Programs

A key component of a Lyndon State education is the variety of opportunities for off-campus study for credit, on either a full-time or part-time basis. Students can apply professional theories and principles through practicums and internships in all majors.

Lyndon grants credit for study in other countries through an approved program such as the Experiment in International Living or the American Institute for Foreign Study. For students who prefer not to study abroad, but who would still enjoy experiencing another culture, Lyndon offers faculty- and staff-accompanied trips each semester to places such as Greece, Russia, Ecuador, England, China, and many other countries of personal and academic interest.

Academic Facilities

Lyndon State College is a modern campus; the oldest building was completed in 1964. The new Academic Center features state-of-the-art academic and computer classrooms and laboratories, including a fully equipped computer laboratory that is linked to the College's expanding computer information network.

The library maintains a collection of more than 110,000 circulating volumes as well as periodicals, audio and video materials, and microfiche collections.

The state-of-the-art meteorology laboratory, staffed by a technician, prepares weather information and forecast information that is broadcast over Vermont radio and television stations. Atmospheric science students also operate a 24-hour weather-reporting telephone line.

Operated daily by students, Lyndon TV/News 7 is a noncommercial, public-service television facility that provides local news and educational, cultural, and public-service programs. Radio station WWLR 91.5 FM, The Impulse, is staffed by student DJs.

Costs

The 2010–11 tuition for Vermont residents was $8232 per year; for nonresidents, it was $17,760. Room and board (twenty-one-meal plan) for one academic year were $8120. Required College fees, not including health and accident insurance, totaled $1144. Total expenses for a Vermont resident living on campus were $17,496; for a nonresident, $27,024. Miscellaneous expenses were estimated at $1100.

Financial Aid

Financial aid is available in the form of loans, grants, and campus employment under the Federal Work-Study Program. Approximately 85 percent of the student population receives some type of financial aid from institutional and outside sources. Approximately 35 percent of the students are employed by either the Federal Work-Study Program or the Lyndon dining hall.

Applicants for aid are required to complete the Free Application for Federal Student Aid (FAFSA). In addition to filing the FAFSA, transfer students are required to have a financial aid transcript completed by the financial aid officer of each college they attended. For a student to be considered an on-time applicant, the FAFSA should be filed in early February in order to reach the Lyndon's Financial Aid Office by the March 15 deadline.

Faculty

Lyndon's faculty consists of 155 members, 95 percent of whom hold the highest degree in their field from research institutions such as Harvard, Columbia, Yale, and USC. Many of Lyndon's professors have come to Lyndon to teach following prestigious careers at corporations and organizations such as CNN, National Public Radio, and Hewlett-Packard. Some are successful entrepreneurs, offering real world expertise to back up their classroom teaching.

Faculty members serve as academic advisers and mentors to students and student organizations. Student evaluation of teaching is a formal process and is used in personnel decisions.

Student Government

Students actively represent Lyndon on the Vermont State Colleges' Board of Trustees, in the Vermont State Colleges' Student Association, and on many campus committees. The Student Senate heads the student organizations.

Admission Requirements

Lyndon emphasizes academic success as reflected on high school or college transcripts, and social and academic potential as reflected in letters of recommendation. Lyndon seeks applicants whose academic record reveals maturity and motivation as well as a sense of responsibility and leadership.

Entrance requirements include 4 years of English and 2 to 3 years each of mathematics, science, and history. Foreign language is desired. International students seeking to attend Lyndon can find detailed information on the College's Web site. The SAT is required.

Students wishing to be considered for early action must apply by November 1. Admission decisions for first-year students are determined on the basis of the student's application, a copy of the secondary school transcript, one to three recommendations from secondary school guidance counselor(s) or teacher(s) that speak to the academic readiness and social preparedness of the applicant, and an interview either in person or by phone.

Applicants who have completed examinations taken through the College Board's Advanced Placement Program with a grade of 3 or higher are granted both advanced placement and course credit after evaluation by the Registrar's Office. Advanced standing is awarded for successful performance on the tests of the College-Level Examination Program. Lyndon grants up to 60 college credits for scores above the 40th percentile on the five general examinations in English composition, humanities, mathematics, natural science, and social science/history and for scores at or above the minimum score established by the College Board for a wide variety of subject examinations.

Admission requirements for transfer students are the same as those for freshman applicants, but an official transcript must also be obtained from each college-level institution that the applicant has attended. Transcripts are required even if no credit is being transferred from a particular institution. Transfer credit may be given at Lyndon for courses completed with the equivalent of a grade of C or better at accredited or officially approved institutions.

Lyndon may permit candidates to defer their enrollment for a period of two semesters.

Application and Information

A nonrefundable $40 fee (paper) or $25 (online) must accompany each application. First-year applicants who are unable to afford the application fee should complete the paper application and ask their guidance counselor to sign a College Board Fee Waiver, or print a copy of the NACAC Application Fee Waiver and ask their counselor to complete it. When these forms are ready, prospective students should mail them to Lyndon, along with their application, all transcripts of academic work completed, and their board scores.

For further information, students should contact:

Office of Admissions
Lyndon State College
P.O. Box 919
Lyndonville, Vermont 05851

Phone: 800-225-1998 (toll-free)
Fax: 802-626-6335
E-mail: admissions@lyndonstate.edu
Web site: http://www.lyndonstate.edu

Students on the set of Lyndon's award-winning News 7. Since 2004, the student-produced daily newscasts have garnered thirty-eight regional and national awards, including an Emmy for the nation's best college newscast.

LYNN UNIVERSITY

BOCA RATON, FLORIDA

The University

Founded in 1962, Lynn University is a thriving institution enrolling 2,081 students from forty-six states and eighty-two nations. The University's five colleges and two schools offer professional programs of study based upon a strong liberal arts foundation. The University has twenty-four undergraduate degrees with eight specializations, ten master's degrees with eighteen specializations, and a doctoral program in educational leadership with two specializations.

In addition to its renowned Conservatory of Music, the University comprises a School of Aeronautics and Colleges of Business and Management, Education, Hospitality Management, International Communication, and Liberal Education.

Signature qualities of Lynn University are its strong international character, with nearly a quarter of the student body from other nations; its relatively small size and a 17:1 student-to-faculty ratio that permit individualized attention; and its distinctive core curriculum, the Dialogues of Learning, which continues to garner national recognition.

The University is committed to providing the education, support, and environment that enable students to realize their full potential and prepare for future success. Lynn welcomes motivated students who want to become active participants in their education and who will thrive in a highly individualized learning environment. Lynn excels at educating students who have varying backgrounds and ability levels. Lynn's Institute for Achievement and Learning is an international pioneer in developing successful teaching and learning strategies for students with learning differences.

All first-year students are required to live on campus. In total, about 60 percent of Lynn's undergraduate students live in five residence halls. All residence halls include study and computer lounges, and a video game lounge is the latest addition to on-campus living.

Students enjoy using the University's two pools, athletic fields, a new tennis stadium, basketball courts, outdoor grills, and a fitness center. The Lynn Student Center houses the cafeteria, an auditorium, student activities offices, and a snack bar with flat screen TVs and pool tables.

Leadership and community service are hallmarks of the Lynn University experience. For example, during the January term, students participate in three days of fieldwork, completing a total of 12 hours of service with three community partners.

Lynn's student involvement program offers myriad ways to develop leadership talents and skills that give students an edge when entering the workplace. Lynn has more than thirty-five campus organizations and activities covering a variety of special interests, including student government, multicultural organizations, and Greek life.

The University's career center's comprehensive services include workshops, vocational and personality testing, a mentoring program, and career fairs. Alumni receive lifetime job placement assistance.

Every degree program requires that students complete at least one internship. Lynn students have gained internships at local television network affiliates, MTV-Latin America, the *Law and Order* TV show, the White House Office of Presidential Personnel, Merrill Lynch, SONY, the Department of Juvenile Justice, Bloomingdale's, and worldwide luxury resorts and entertainment properties including Disney World and the Boca Raton Resort and Club.

Lynn also has a top-ranked NCAA athletic program, which has earned nineteen national championships and twenty-six Sunshine Conference championships. The Fighting Knights intercollegiate athletic program includes men's and women's basketball, golf, soccer, and tennis; men's baseball; and women's softball and volleyball.

Location

Located in Boca Raton on Florida's southeastern coast, the Lynn campus is only 50 minutes from Miami, 30 minutes from West Palm Beach, and 30 minutes from Fort Lauderdale and is easily accessed from these cities' international airports. Because of its location in the heart of one of the world's leading business, sports, media, and hospitality industry centers, Lynn students benefit from a wide variety of internship as well as cultural and recreational opportunities. The safe,

beautiful 123-acre campus is in a residential area, 3 miles from the beach, 2 miles from Boca Raton's city center, and only a few minutes from first-class shopping and restaurants.

Majors and Degrees

The College of Liberal Education offers Bachelor of Arts (B.A.) and Bachelor of Science (B.S.) degrees in biology, criminal justice, English, human services, liberal arts, international relations, and psychology. Students may design a customized major with an adviser's guidance.

Lynn's Conservatory of Music awards the Bachelor of Music in composition and in music performance, with specializations in bass trombone, bassoon, cello, clarinet, double bass, flute, French horn, oboe, percussion, piano, trombone, trumpet, tuba, viola, and violin.

The College of Business and Management offers the B.S. in business administration, with specializations in aviation management, fashion management, finance, general management, and marketing.

The College of Hospitality Management offers a B.S. in hospitality management and in sports management. Specializations include resort and hotel management and vacation ownership/timeshare management.

The Eugene M. and Christine E. Lynn College of International Communication offers the B.A. or B.S. degree in advertising and public relations; communication, media, and politics; drama; film; graphic design; illustration/computer animation; multimedia journalism; photography; and radio, television, and Internet media.

The Donald E. and Helen L. Ross College of Education offers the B.S. in elementary education grades K–6, with specializations in exceptional student education, and pre-K/primary.

Academic Programs

Lynn University follows a semester calendar, with a four-week summer session. All classes are taught by faculty members. The University embraces students who have varying levels of academic abilities and learning styles along with a strong motivation to excel. Average class size is 17 students.

Lynn has an innovative and career-focused approach to liberal arts education that takes students beyond the traditional classroom. The curriculum challenges students to build increasing competencies not only in their chosen field of study, but in every area of life.

The nationally acclaimed Dialogues of Learning core curriculum is taught seminar-style to enhance students' critical thinking, reasoning, and communication skills by encouraging robust discussions of life's challenging topics and questions.

Lynn Degree 3.0 allows qualified students to graduate in three years. This select program provides priority class registration, a self-designed course of study, and special academic advising by the dean of the college in which the major is offered.

The three-week January term emphasizes experiential learning, and students can select a course outside of their major.

Students also benefit from an exceptionally strong academic advising program that pairs each incoming student with a faculty member in the student's chosen major field. The adviser becomes a mentor throughout the student's academic career and beyond. All faculty members are committed to great teaching and to challenging students to become active, intentional, and purposeful learners.

The honors program enables select students to test themselves academically and achieve special recognition for their efforts. Students have increased opportunities to participate in customized research and experiential learning, and to present their projects every year at state, regional, and national Collegiate Honors Council conferences. They also may publish their work in the Lynn scholarly journal, *The Scholar.*

The Institute for Achievement and Learning is an international model for higher education. Led by a nationally recognized learning specialist, the institute brings together an array of services and professionals that support students with many types of learning styles. It offers academic coaching, diagnostic testing and recommendations for students struggling academically, tutoring, group sessions to help reduce test-taking and learning-related anxiety, content-area tutoring and a distraction-reduced testing environment. Institute Fellows who are trained in a variety of teaching and learning methods teach specialized Dialogues of Learning classes. The institute also houses Lynn University's ADA Office.

Off-Campus Programs

All students are also strongly encouraged to complete study-abroad academic credits in their major, by either participating in a faculty-led short-term program during semester breaks, or studying abroad for a semester or a full academic year. Study-abroad destinations have included Australia, Bali, New Zealand, China, Hong Kong, Cambodia, Singapore, Thailand, South Africa, Morocco, Puerto Rico, Costa Rica, Argentina, Ireland, Scotland, England, Belgium, Luxembourg, Germany, Switzerland, Italy, France, Spain, and Portugal.

Academic Facilities

The majority of classroom buildings have interactive whiteboards and document projectors, the result of a recent million-dollar investment in upgrading campus technology. Computer labs are available in five buildings, and the campus is fully wireless.

The library includes a collection of approximately 95,000 books, journals, magazines, CDs, and music scores. It also has a large collection of DVDs and research databases with 76,000 e-journal titles (more are accessible through the library's Web site), more than 100,000 e-books, and 100 computer workstations.

Lynn has a fully equipped television studio and radio station, video editing and production facilities, a demonstration kitchen, and biology and chemistry laboratories. The School of Aeronautics, located at the nearby Boca Raton Airport, houses flight simulators and the University's fleet of Cessna 172 and Cirrus SR-20 aircraft. It offers a first-class flight academy.

Costs

Undergraduate tuition for the 2011–12 academic year is $30,200, with room and board fees beginning at $10,400, depending on meal plan and room type. Additional student fees vary depending on whether students live on or off campus. Books are purchased separately.

Financial Aid

Lynn is committed to making the University affordable for every student. Seventy-two percent of students receive some form of financial assistance and scholarships. The University's broad program of student financial aid includes scholarships, grants, work-study, and loans. Academic, athletic, and need-based scholarships are awarded. For complete information on the financial-aid process and available programs, along with financial aid and net price calculators, please visit the Cost and Aid section of the Lynn Web site at http://www.lynn.edu.

Faculty

Faculty members are thoroughly committed to teaching and are readily accessible to students. The University has a low student to faculty ratio of 17:1. Seventy percent of full-time faculty members hold doctoral degrees, and the vast majority bring real-world experience in their field—many in some of the world's most prestigious companies and industries—to the classroom. Lynn has Fulbright Scholars on its faculty, and professors are actively engaged in research.

Student Government

The Student Government Association represents all Lynn students. It provides a voice for representation and advocacy, and is a liaison amid the student body, faculty, staff, and administration, while promoting scholastic pride and ethical integrity.

Admission Requirements

Lynn encourages high school students to apply during the fall of their senior year and urges prospective students to visit the campus.

Lynn offers three ways to apply online: the Lynn application, Common Application, and Universal Application. Prospective students can also download, print, and mail or fax an application. All options can be found on the Admissions page of the University's Web site.

In addition to a completed application form, applicants must submit a personal statement or essay, nonrefundable $35 application fee, official transcripts from all schools attended, and official SAT or ACT scores. Students must also include a letter of recommendation from a school guidance counselor or teacher, commenting on the student's determination and motivation and academic performance.

Conservatory of Music students have additional application requirements, including an audition. Specific instructions can be found within the Admissions section of the University Web site.

International applicants for whom English is not a first language are required to submit results from the TOEFL/IELTS. Minimum scores required are 525 (paper-based), 197 (computer-based), or 71 (Internet-based) or IELTS score of 6.0. All transcripts of previous academic work must be accompanied by certified English translations. Additional requirements can be found in the Guide for International Students in the Admissions section of http://www.lynn.edu.

Transfer students who have completed a minimum of 12 academic college credits should submit an application form and official transcripts from the current college and all previous colleges attended, along with a recommendation from the dean of students at the candidate's current or last school attended. Transfer students with fewer than 12 credits must submit high school transcripts and ACT or SAT scores. Every effort is made to facilitate the transfer of credit from other institutions, and a credit evaluation is provided upon admission.

Application and Information

Lynn University evaluates applications on a rolling basis. For fall term admission, the priority deadline is March 1. The application fee is $35. For additional information or to arrange for an interview and tour of the campus, contact:

Office of Admission
Lynn University
3601 North Military Trail
Boca Raton, Florida 33431-5507
Phone: 561-237-7900
      800-888-5966 (toll-free)
Fax: 561-237-7100
E-mail: admission@lynn.edu
Web site: http://www.lynn.edu/admission
      http://www.facebook.com/lynnuniversity
      http://twitter.com/lynnuniversity

Lynn University's seven lakes are part of a 123-acre campus that's located only 3 miles from South Florida's beautiful beaches.

MANCHESTER COLLEGE
NORTH MANCHESTER, INDIANA

The College

At Manchester College, students find academics that matter. They find their place among students who are motivated to learn and faculty members with top degrees who know what it takes to succeed.

With a rich social life, students become part of the Manchester family that covers the globe. With lasting relationships, their college years will last a lifetime.

Manchester students learn how to give meaning to success. They get the most from their college experience so they can get the most out of life.

Tim Polakowski, a recent graduate from Illinois, now teaching English in South Korea as a Fulbright scholar, says he found success at Manchester College. "In high school, I knew I wanted to make a difference. Today, I feel that Manchester College has not only prepared me to make that difference, but also made a difference in me. The professors want you to succeed and the challenges in and out of the classroom prepare you for a life outside the norm. After a year studying in Spain, a semester south of the border, and working with on-campus groups like Habitat for Humanity, I'm more convinced than ever that Manchester was the right place for me."

The undergraduate enrollment for 2010–11 was 1,278. Most students are between the ages of 18 and 22. Students represent 22 states and 21 countries, and approximately 90 percent of the full-time students are from Indiana. Manchester is a college of the Church of the Brethren, and welcomes students of all faiths.

Manchester is a member of the National Collegiate Athletic Association Division III and offers ten men's and nine women's sports. The Physical Education and Recreation Center houses physical education classes, a fitness center, intercollegiate and intramural sports, and recreational activities. The College has a strong intramural program that involves more than 75 percent of its students.

Location

Located in the heart of Indiana's beautiful lake country, North Manchester is a thriving community of 6,000 people. It is within a half hour's drive of Indiana's second-largest city, Fort Wayne, and is only 3 hours from Chicago. Wide streets with large shade trees, graceful homes, and a beautiful park combine to provide a classic setting for college living.

Majors and Degrees

Manchester College grants Bachelor of Arts and Bachelor of Science degrees in more than fifty-five areas of study, including accounting, adapted physical education, art, athletic training, biochemistry, biology, biotechnology, business, chemistry, coaching, communication studies, computer science, criminal justice, early childhood education, economics, elementary education, engineering science, English, environmental studies, exercise science, finance, fitness and sport management, French, gender studies, gerontology, history, journalism, management, marketing, mathematics, media studies, medical technology, music, peace studies, philosophy, physical education, physics, political science, prelaw, premedicine, prenursing, prepharmacy, pre–occupational therapy, pre–physical therapy, psychology, religion, secondary education, social work, sociology, Spanish, and sports management. Individualized interdisciplinary majors can also be arranged to meet a student's particular goals.

Manchester offers master's degrees in teacher education and athletic training. The College has applied for accreditation to open a School of Pharmacy in 2012, which will award the Doctor of Pharmacy (Pharm.D.) degree to its graduates.

Academic Programs

The curriculum reflects a commitment to sound training in a specific area of study, the major and broad development of skills and understanding through the liberal arts and sciences. In addition, students may explore interests different from specific career or professional areas through elective courses. This combination prepares students for careers or graduate school immediately after graduation and equips them for the challenges and changes of the future.

Manchester College operates on a 4-1-4 calendar and offers online courses during two summer sessions. The College's innovative Fast Forward program allows students to complete a four-year degree in three years on campus and two summers online. Students save as much as $25,000 and enter graduate school or their careers a year earlier than their classmates.

Manchester's Triple Guarantee promises financial aid for all students, graduation within four years, and a job or enrollment in graduate school within six months of graduation. Find details at http://www.manchester.edu/tripleguarantee. Ninety-six percent of Manchester graduates are employed, in graduate school, or service work within six months of graduation.

Off-Campus Programs

Manchester College students may study abroad for a semester or year in ten countries: Philipps-Universität Marburg in Marburg/Lahn (Germany), the Institut International d'Études Françaises of the University of Strasbourg (France), the University of Nancy (France), the University of Barcelona (Spain), St. Mary's College in Cheltenham (England), Hokkai Gakuen University in Sapporo (Japan), the Dalian Institute of Foreign Languages in Dalian (People's Republic of China), the Athens Center (Greece), the Catholic University of Ecuador, Cochin (India), and Universidad Veracruzana (Mexico).

During January session, numerous classes are held off campus. In recent years, professors have taken classes to India, Kenya, England, Mexico, Russia, France, Jamaica, Ghana, Vietnam, Nicaragua, Haiti, Germany, Costa Rica, Cuba, and Hawaii as well as destinations in the continental United States.

Field experiences and internships are offered for credit in accounting, broadcasting, business, criminal justice, early childhood education, elementary education, forensic chemistry, gerontology, health sciences practicum, journalism, peace studies, physical education, political science, psychology, secondary education, and social work.

Academic Facilities

The $17-million Science Center, opened in 2005, provides extraordinary laboratories and fully wired classrooms. Students in astronomy use the 10-inch Newtonian reflector telescope in the Charles S. Morris Observatory.

The College Union, which was completely renovated in 2007, houses the Success Center, campus store, art gallery, dining facilities, and Oaks snack bar.

The Funderburg Library is a recently renovated three-story building that houses more than 170,000 books, 800 periodicals, and

4,500 audio recordings available for student use. Computer connections and interlibrary loan allow access to major library collections across the country.

Manchester has multiple large and small computer labs spread around campus—most are available around the clock and provide wireless access to the Internet. The Indiana state Internet connection, known as I-Light, provides high-speed bandwidth to students and ties directly to Internet2 and the major research colleges in the state. The College also provides no- to low-cost printing around campus. When they're not studying, residential students have access to the College's 119-channel cable TV system.

Costs

Tuition and fees for 2010–11 were $24,100 for full-time students. Room and board costs for the residence halls (double occupancy) were $8860. The total charges with fees were $33,780 for the academic year.

Financial Aid

Manchester offers extensive scholarship and grant assistance through institutional resources. Academic awards include Honors, Trustee, Presidential, and Dean's Scholarships. Special scholarships based on academic merit and interest are awarded in music and entrepreneurship. International students can receive scholarships based on academic accomplishments and financial need. Manchester awards significant need-based grants. In 2009–10, the average need-based financial aid package was $23,600.

All students receive some type of financial assistance, whether it is a scholarship, a grant, a loan, or campus employment. Questions about financial aid should be referred to the Office of Admissions.

Faculty

Nearly 90 percent of Manchester's 71 full-time faculty members hold the highest degree in their field, and 94 percent of all courses are taught by full-time faculty members. The primary emphasis of the faculty members is teaching, but many are actively engaged in research as well. Faculty members serve as academic advisers, with a specially trained group of faculty members acting as primary advisers for new students. The student-faculty ratio is 14:1.

Student Government

Students at Manchester assume responsibility for the governmental and judicial activities of the College. The Student Government Association provides a forum for discussion and investigation of community concerns and a channel for evaluating and solving community problems.

Each of the College's five residence halls elects a governing body, which is responsible for providing leadership.

The Manchester Activities Council organizes programming of student events. Students are offered a wide variety of leadership and participation opportunities as part of the College's student development program.

Admission Requirements

Manchester College seeks to enroll students whose scholastic record, test scores, and personality give promise of success in college. Graduation from an accredited high school or its equivalent is required.

The College recommends that students take 4 years of English, 3 years of laboratory science, 3 years of mathematics, 2 years of foreign language, and 2 years of social studies in high school. Students may take either the ACT or the SAT, and personal recommendations from a high school principal or guidance counselor are required.

For transfer students, transcripts of all previous college work are required.

Application and Information

Students may apply for admission prior to each term. Applications are accepted on a rolling basis. There is a nonrefundable $25 application fee. Online applications are free.

Interested students and their parents are encouraged to visit Manchester College and meet faculty members, coaches, and current students; sit in on classes; and take a campus tour. Arrangements can be made by writing or calling the Office of Admissions.

For application forms and further information, students may contact:

Office of Admissions
Manchester College
North Manchester, Indiana 46962-0365
Phone: 800-852-3648 (toll-free)
E-mail: admitinfo@manchester.edu
Web site: http://www.manchester.edu

Students on the campus of Manchester College.

MANHATTAN COLLEGE

RIVERDALE, NEW YORK

The College

With over 155 years of history as a Lasallian institution, Manhattan College maintains its fine reputation as an outstanding Catholic college, dedicated to educating students with strong moral values, a concern for the community, and a love of independent and critical thinking. Since its inception in 1853, Manhattan College has never wavered from its principal goal—to ensure that its students fulfill their potential and are well prepared to take their places as contributing members of society.

The College has an enrollment of 3,412 students, of whom 3,002 are undergraduates. Approximately 73 percent of Manhattan's students come from New York State; the remaining 27 percent represent thirty-nine other states and sixty other countries. Approximately 2,080 housing units are available, consisting of on-campus residence halls and off-campus apartments. Nearly 60 percent of undergraduates are resident students. Manhattan offers seventy extracurricular organizations and five student publications and fields twenty varsity and club sports teams. Of Manhattan's 40,000 active alumni, a large number are prominent leaders in business, government, education, the arts, the sciences, and engineering.

Location

The main campus of the College is located 10 miles north of midtown Manhattan in the suburban Riverdale section of the Bronx, about a mile from Westchester County. The area offers the calm and quiet of a residential, suburban setting as well as easy access to the many cultural and educational advantages of New York City. The College is easily accessible by subway, bus, or highway; three airports are also nearby.

Majors and Degrees

The liberal arts curriculum of the School of Arts provides programs that lead to a Bachelor of Arts or Bachelor of Science with majors in the humanities and the social sciences, including communication, economics, English, fine arts, French, government, history, labor relations, modern foreign languages, philosophy, psychology, religious studies, and sociology. Interdisciplinary majors include international studies, peace studies, and urban studies.

In the School of Science, programs lead to a Bachelor of Science or Bachelor of Arts with majors in biochemistry, biology, chemistry, computer science, mathematics, and physics. Premedical, predental, and pre–veterinary studies programs are also available.

The School of Engineering has a well-deserved reputation as one of the best small college engineering schools in the nation and offers programs leading to a Bachelor of Science in chemical, civil, computer, electrical, and mechanical engineering. The program is fully accredited by the Educational Accreditation Commission of ABET.

The School of Business, accredited by AACSB International, has programs leading to a Bachelor of Science in Business Administration with majors in accounting, computer information systems, economics, finance, global business studies, management, and marketing.

The School of Education offers a curriculum leading to a Bachelor of Arts in childhood education, childhood/special education (dual program), and adolescent education. The physical education curriculum leads to a Bachelor of Science in physical education and exercise science. The health education curriculum leads to a Bachelor of Science in allied health, with a concentration in health-care administration, health counseling, or scientific foundations. Curricula in radiological and health sciences lead to a Bachelor of Science in radiation therapy or nuclear medicine technology. All programs are approved by the New York State Education Department and accredited by the Teacher Education Accreditation Council (TEAC).

Academic Programs

The core curriculum shared by the School of Arts and the School of Science studies some of the vital works of humankind, explores new ideas, examines the meaning of scientific experimentation, and encourages a student to develop his or her thinking and leadership abilities. The major programs offer advanced work in specific humanistic and scientific disciplines and opportunities to work on research projects in collaboration with faculty scholars.

In the School of Engineering, all engineering students follow a common core curriculum during the first two years and choose a major at the beginning of the junior year. Each curriculum includes a generous selection of courses in basic sciences, the engineering sciences, humanistic studies, and mathematics.

The School of Business prepares students for positions of executive responsibility in business, government, and nonprofit organizations. The business curriculum is based on a strong commitment to liberal education and is well balanced between professional business courses, humanities, sciences, and social sciences. This is a reflection of the school's belief that executives should be broadly educated and should involve themselves, as well as their organizations, in efforts to solve social problems.

The School of Education prepares students for teaching, counseling, and health professions. Students complete the College's core curriculum in liberal arts and sciences and then complete a major in various programs in the school's three departments: Education, Physical Education and Exercise Science, and Radiological and Health Professions. All programs include internships/practicums in schools, hospitals, or other institutions. Graduates of the school's teacher-preparation programs receive New York State provisional teaching certification. The school also offers a five-year B.A./M.S. program in childhood/special education and special education.

Off-Campus Programs

Students in the liberal arts curricula who have demonstrated superior achievement in their first two years are encouraged to spend their junior year studying abroad. Manhattan College also offers summer study-abroad programs in many countries; arrangements can be made to study in a country of choice. Students in the School of Business may participate in the International Field Studies Seminar. As participants, they spend time in another country studying the effect of that environment on international firms. Career services and co-op education integrate classroom theory with the practical experience of a job in industry, business, the social services, the arts, or government. Portions of the education courses are conducted in New York City schools, so that student teachers may gain experience in urban education at an early stage.

Academic Facilities

There are more than forty scientific and engineering laboratories at Manhattan, including the Research and Learning Center, as well as a modern language laboratory and a computer information systems laboratory. Manhattan's newly built O'Malley Library is a state-of-the-art facility featuring modern accommodations for study and research. It is connected to the renovated and updated Cardinal Hayes Pavilion (formerly the Cardinal Hayes Library). The library combines Hayes' traditional neo-Georgian accents with strong contemporary lines. The five-story addition to the original building doubles the original square footage and connects the current library to the upper campus. Students and faculty members are able to enter directly from a brick walkway that starts at the Quadrangle.

Costs

For 2009–10, the tuition for Manhattan College was $25,150 per year plus program fees; first time undergraduate cost was $26,720. The cost of room and board for the year was $10,670.

Financial Aid

Manhattan grants or administers financial assistance in the form of tuition awards to students on the basis of need and/or ability. Need is evaluated by submitting the FAFSA. In addition to a merit scholarship fund, Manhattan offers endowed scholarships, special category scholarships and grants, student athletic grants, Federal Pell Grants, Federal Supplemental Educational Opportunity Grants, student loans, Federal Work-Study Program awards, and New York State financial assistance are also available to students who qualify. A total of 1,650 students receive financial aid from Manhattan College, and approximately 87 percent receive financial aid from government or private agencies.

Faculty

Manhattan's faculty has 201 full-time and 182 part-time teachers. The faculty-student ratio is approximately 1:12. Nearly 97 percent of the faculty members hold doctorates. The maximum teaching load on the undergraduate level is 9 credit hours per semester. Faculty members serve on the college senate, the council for faculty affairs, and numerous faculty and campus committees. In addition, they are available to students for informal guidance and counseling and also serve as official moderators of many campus organizations.

Student Government

The Manhattan Student Government is composed of students elected annually by their peers to fill posts outlined in the Student Government Constitution. The Student Government allocates funds to all student organizations. Members are also full voting members of the College Senate.

Admission Requirements

Manhattan has a long-standing policy of nondiscrimination. No applicant is refused admission because of race, color, religion, age, national origin, sex, or disability. All applicants must present an academic diploma from an accredited high school and must offer a minimum of 16 credits in academic subjects. Liberal arts candidates must be proficient in at least one foreign language. At the discretion of the Committee on Admissions, quantitative requirements may be modified for applicants with especially strong records who show promise of doing well in college. In the selection process, attention is given to scholastic ability, as indicated by grades and rank in class, as well as to standardized test scores and recommendations from teachers and counselors. All candidates must submit either SAT or ACT results. An interview with a member of the admission staff can be arranged but is not required. Applicants may submit scores on the General Educational Development test in lieu of a formal high school diploma; however, all such applicants must submit the results of the appropriate College Board tests. Manhattan College offers early acceptance for high school seniors, admission to advanced standing, advanced placement, and credit by examination. Junior college or other transfer students are welcome. Manhattan College requires applicants whose native language is not English to take the Test of English as a Foreign Language (TOEFL), the SAT, or ACT exam. The average SAT scores of entering freshmen in 2010 were 560 in mathematics and 540 in the verbal portion.

Application and Information

Application forms are furnished by the Admission Office on request and available on the Manhattan College Web site. The Common Application Form, which is available in many high school guidance offices and online, may also be used. After supplying the information required, students must send the application to the admission office at Manhattan College. The high school report, recommendation letters, and transcript must be submitted by the high school guidance counselor. This should be done after six terms of high school or right after the seventh term. There is a rolling admissions policy and a March 1 deadline for financial aid applications. A nonrefundable application fee of $60 is required.

William J. Bisset
Vice President for Enrollment Management
Manhattan College
Riverdale, New York 10471
Phone: 718-862-7200
       800-MC2-XCEL (toll-free)
E-mail: admit@manhattan.edu
Web site: http://www.manhattan.edu

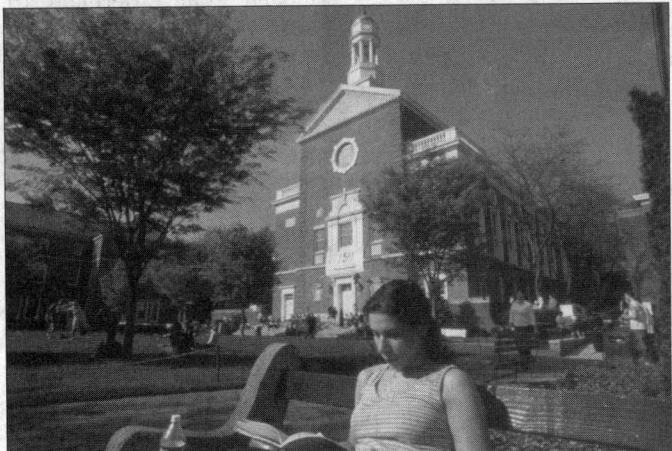

Students walking in the Quadrangle of the Manhattan College campus.

MANHATTANVILLE COLLEGE

PURCHASE, NEW YORK

The College

While the 100 beautiful acres that make up Manhattanville are located in a quiet suburban setting, the culture, entertainment, and excitement of New York City are only 30 miles away. The private coeducational college founded in 1841 draws its 1,700 students from fifty-three countries and thirty-six states. Manhattanville College has created a small global village. This richly diverse community embodies the College's mission: to educate students to be ethical and socially responsible leaders in a global community.

Learning is at the heart of Manhattanville, and the College's proximity to New York City creates a constant flow of opportunity that brings learning to life. Manhattanville students know how to have fun, but they also have a sense of purpose. The College's social conscience is informed by a commitment to serving the community. The Duchesne Center serves as the coordinator and catalyst for service learning, community outreach, culture, and leadership across the College campus and around the world. Last year, students participated in 33,000 hours of community service. Manhattanville students actively seek opportunities to serve humanitarian causes in the developing world.

Manhattanville's global perspective is enriched by its role as a Non-Governmental Organization of the United Nations. Select students have an opportunity to intern at the UN and to study with an ambassador. In addition, the College offers a Meet the Ambassadors Series on campus, where students attend lectures by leading ambassadors, followed by dinner at the home of the College's president.

Location

Manhattanville's campus lies in the heart of Westchester County, bordered on the east by Long Island Sound and on the west by the Hudson River. From the roof of Reid Castle, which serves as the campus's main hall, the skyline of Manhattan is visible. This proximity to the city that calls itself the "Capital of the World" is one of Manhattanville's many assets. The College provides free transportation to the city on Saturdays and to Manhattan-bound commuter trains during the week so students can take advantage of all New York City has to offer.

Majors and Degrees

http://www.Manhattanville.edu/AcademicMajors

Manhattanville College offers undergraduate degrees in more than fifty academic concentrations in the arts and sciences, including Bachelor of Arts (B.A.), Bachelor of Science (B.S.), Bachelor of Fine Arts (B.F.A.), and Bachelor of Music (B.Mus.) degrees; a self-designed major; a double major with teacher certification; and preparation for professional and graduate study (prelaw, premedical, pre–physical therapy, and pre–speech language pathology).

Students may choose from the following areas of study: African studies, American studies, art history, art (studio), Asian studies, biochemistry, biology, chemistry, classical civilizations, communications studies, computer science, creative writing, dance and theater, dance therapy, economics, education, English, environmental studies, film studies, finance, French, German, history, Holocaust and genocide studies, human resource management, international management, international studies, Irish studies, Italian, Latin American studies, legal studies, management, mathematics, museum studies, music, music education, music management, musical theater, music technology, neuroscience,

philosophy, physics, political science, prelaw, premedical, pre–physical therapy, pre–speech language pathology, psychology, self-designed major, social justice, sociology, Spanish, theater education, women's studies, world literature, and world religions.

Academic Programs

Manhattanville College offers full-time, part-time, and accelerated opportunities for study as well as dual-degree programs. The Manhattanville curriculum nurtures intellectual curiosity and independent thinking. Students and professors form close collaborative relationships beginning with the Preceptorial, an interdisciplinary survey of the liberal arts that is required of all freshmen.

The core of the Manhattanville curriculum is the Portfolio System, which provides for a level of flexibility that is unusual in traditional liberal arts education. Under the guidance of a faculty adviser, the student maps an academic and co-curricular program, establishing a major and minor from different branches of the liberal arts. The student may begin studies in the chosen field as early as the freshman year. Over the course of four years of study, the student assembles a portfolio consisting of study plans, evidence of academic proficiency in written critical analysis and qualitative research, annual evaluations, transcripts, and examples of the student's best work. A College-wide review board evaluates the portfolio. The ePortfolio system is used as a teaching and learning tool.

A special option for B.A. candidates is the Self-Designed Major. If a student's interests direct them beyond existing departmental majors, they may propose a program of study to the Board of Academic Standards. Manhattanville students also have the opportunity to earn academic credit for internships in New York City.

Manhattanville College offers college credit for A-level exams, International Baccalaureate, and Advanced Placement examinations.

Off-Campus Programs

Manhattanville offers more than 100 study-abroad opportunities through either direct exchange programs or study-abroad providers at various levels of language proficiency, including Argentina, Belgium (internship at the European Union), Chile, England, France, Germany, Ireland, Italy, Japan, South Africa, Mexico, and Spain, among others. There is also a world of over 450 domestic and international internship possibilities with leading groups such as Apple, Condé Nast, IBM, and MasterCard.

Academic Facilities

The Manhattanville Library capitalizes on the power of the Internet to connect students with information and analysis found in powerful subscription databases, electronic journals, and electronic books. Manhattanville is one of the first colleges in the U.S. to outsource a service that enables students to interact online with experienced reference librarians at any time of the day or night from anywhere in the world. The virtual research service, "Ask a Librarian 24/7," uses co-browsing to connect students with professional librarians who can answer questions about research and help students navigate the College's extensive array of subscription databases and other library resources. Manhattanville's teaching library, which supports the School of Education, ranks among the foremost undergraduate teaching libraries in the country. The Menendez Language Laboratory includes tapes and record libraries that provide materials for class instruction and individual practice in French, Spanish,

Russian, Italian, German, Chinese, Japanese, Hindi, Marathi, Modern Hebrew, and English as a second language. The College provides a writing clinic, a reading clinic, audiovisual facilities, and a bibliographic instruction program. The library building is open 24 hours a day, seven days a week through most of the fall and spring semesters, and it has computer labs, quiet study areas, group-study rooms, and a café where students and faculty members can meet informally.

Among the College's other academic facilities and resources are the art studio, science laboratories, the performing arts facilities, and student media facilities.

The College has state-of-the-art computers, computer labs, and campus networking for student use and instruction. In addition, advanced music technology systems offer performing arts students limitless opportunities for creativity.

Costs

For the 2010–11 academic year, tuition was $34,020 and the average room and board costs were $14,524.

Financial Aid

Manhattanville College offers both merit scholarships and need-based financial aid. Nearly 80 percent of students receive financial awards. The institutional form and the Free Application for Federal Student Aid (FAFSA) are required. The types of awards available are honors, merit, arts, and community service scholarships; Manhattanville grants and scholarships; Federal Perkins Loans; Federal Stafford Student Loans; Federal Pell Grants; Federal Supplemental Educational Opportunity Grants; Federal Work-Study Program awards; and Tuition Assistance Program awards.

For scholarship information and advice about financial aid eligibility, students should visit www.manhattanville.edu, click on Admissions, and then click on Financial Aid.

Faculty

Nearly 90 percent of faculty members have Ph.D. or terminal degrees in their fields. Many faculty members live on the campus. The Manhattanville curriculum nurtures intellectual curiosity and independent thinking. The student-faculty ratio of 12:1 promotes close and collaborative relationships between faculty members and students, aided by the structure of the curriculum and the Portfolio System, which fosters collaboration between student and faculty adviser. Faculty members, not teaching assistants, teach all Manhattanville classes, and 80 percent of the classes have 20 or fewer students.

Student Government

Students in large measure shape the quality of life on the Manhattanville campus. Elected representatives of the student body run the student government, which serves as a principal means of communication among the administration, faculty members, and students. Its board of directors is responsible for formulating policy on student life and for implementing this policy through various committees. Student government members also serve on the College's policymaking and ad hoc committees.

Admission Requirements

Manhattanville College admits candidates for undergraduate degrees if their academic records indicate a competence to engage in a challenging liberal arts curriculum. Admission to the College is selective, and the most important consideration is the student's secondary school performance. When weighing this aspect, the admissions committee evaluates the quality of the school, the strength of the student's program, and success in those studies. Next, the committee considers the various recommendations that are submitted on behalf of the student,

along with scores on required standardized tests or a graded writing sample (Manhattanville is a test-optional institution) and the student's personal statement. A campus interview is strongly recommended. Students who plan to specialize in music or dance and theater should come to Manhattanville for an audition or should secure permission to submit a DVD. Students who plan to apply for the B.F.A. degree program should present portfolios to the art department for evaluation. Students who plan to study dance and theater may audition for scholarships.

Application and Information

Applying is straightforward—submit the completed application; official high school transcript; letters of recommendation; a personal statement; and either SAT scores, ACT scores, or a graded writing sample. Transfer applicants should submit an official transcript and dean recommendation form from each school attended, a letter of recommendation, and a personal statement. Admission is rolling with a deadline of March 1. Early decision deadline is December 1. For details, students should visit http://mville.edu/UndergraduateAdmissions or contact the College via e-mail at admissions@mville.edu or by phone at 800-328-4553 (toll-free) or 914-323-5464.

The College subscribes to the Candidates Reply Date. Applications should be submitted as early in the senior year as possible. Candidates may apply online at www.manhattanville.edu.

Manhattanville College is committed to equality of educational opportunity, and is an equal opportunity employer. The College does not discriminate against current or prospective students and employees on the basis of race, color, sex, national and ethnic origin, religion, age, disability, or any other legally protected characteristic. This College policy is implemented in educational and admissions policies, scholarship and loan programs, athletic and other school-administered programs, and in employee-related programs.

For further information, students should contact:

Office of Undergraduate Admissions
Manhattanville College
2900 Purchase Street
Purchase, New York 10577
Phone: 914-323-5464
      800-32-VILLE (toll-free)
E-mail: admissions@mville.edu
Web site: http://www.manhattanville.edu
      http://www.facebook.com/Manhattanville
      http://www.twitter.com/mvillecollegeny

Reid Hall (The Castle) is the centerpiece of the Manhattanville College campus.

MANNES COLLEGE THE NEW SCHOOL FOR MUSIC

NEW YORK, NEW YORK

The College

Mannes College The New School for Music in New York City is one of the world's preeminent conservatories of classical music. The Mannes community is made up of students and a faculty of professional musicians from every corner of the world. Here, aspiring artists learn and play music with scholars, composers, conductors, and performing artists from some of the world's most revered orchestras, ensembles, and opera companies. Most of the more than 400 concerts produced by the School each year at its two concert halls or at venues throughout the New York metropolitan region feature Mannes students. With only 319 college students, Mannes provides an intimate, supportive atmosphere that allows for close and constructive relationships among students, faculty members, and administrators.

Part of The New School, a leading urban university, Mannes offers its own undergraduate academic curriculum focused on areas most pertinent to classical music. Students may choose to supplement this curriculum by taking courses at the other divisions of The New School. In addition, throughout their studies, students follow a program of instruction in the techniques of music. This program includes studies in ear training, sight singing, keyboard skills, theory, analysis, and dictation that are among the best in the world, all helping to train students to meet the unique challenges faced by musicians in the twenty-first century.

Graduate degrees offered include the Master of Music (M.M.), a two-year degree program offered in all orchestral instruments (violin, viola, cello, bass, flute, oboe, clarinet, bassoon, saxophone, horn, trumpet, trombone, tuba, harp, and percussion), piano, harpsichord, guitar, vocal accompaniment for pianists, voice, composition, conducting, and theory. Students receive private lessons in their major field and take performance classes (such as orchestra, opera, and chamber music), courses in the techniques of music, and chosen electives that focus on specialized topics of the student's interest.

Mannes also offers the Professional Studies Diploma (PSD), an advanced course of study designed to enhance performance or compositional skills. The PSD is generally pursued following a master's degree or the equivalent. Individual programs are designed in coordination with the associate/assistant dean. Orchestral instrument majors participate in the Mannes Orchestra, which performs at Lincoln Center and other major venues, during each semester of residency. Additionally, chamber music is a curricular component of some instrumental majors. All Mannes and some New School courses are available to qualified students; however, only graduate-level courses apply toward the Professional Studies Diploma.

Total enrollment is 319, 49 percent of whom are international students. There are 156 faculty members, and the student-teacher ratio is less than 2:1. The average class size is 10–12 students.

Through The New School, Mannes is proud to offer housing facilities that include apartment-style dormitory suites equipped with full kitchens, full bathrooms, air conditioning, Internet service, and other amenities. Residences available to Mannes students are located in Chelsea, Greenwich Village, Union Square, and lower Manhattan. All dormitories are equipped with a 24-hour security guard and resident advisers on every floor. All

incoming freshman are offered on-campus housing, but it is not a requirement for admission. The housing office offers assistance with off-campus housing.

Location

Mannes is located in Manhattan's Upper West Side, one of the finest residential areas of New York City. It is within walking distance of the Museum of Natural History and Lincoln Center for the Performing Arts (home to the New York Philharmonic, the Metropolitan Opera, and other world-renowned performing arts organizations). Mannes students benefit from and contribute to New York City's rich musical and cultural life.

Majors and Degrees

Undergraduate degrees offered include the Bachelor of Music (B.M.) in all orchestral instruments (bass, bassoon, cello, clarinet, flute, harp, horn, oboe, percussion, saxophone, trombone, trumpet, tuba, viola, and violin), composition, conducting, guitar, harpsichord, piano, theory, and voice. Students receive private lessons in their major field and take performance classes (such as chamber music, orchestra, or opera) and courses in the techniques of music and liberal arts, as well as electives.

A Bachelor of Science (B.S.) is offered in all majors by completing the Bachelor of Music curriculum and taking or transferring from another institution an additional 30 academic credits.

The Undergraduate Diploma (UDPL) is offered in all majors and is equivalent to the Bachelor of Music degree minus the liberal arts courses.

Academic Programs

Some outstanding performance opportunities include the Mannes Orchestra, led by David Hayes; the Mannes Opera Program, led by Joseph Colaneri; the Mannes Chorus; the Mannes Baroque Chamber Players; the Percussion Ensemble; NewMusicMannes; and numerous chamber music ensembles that perform year-round.

The Mannes Community Services Office employs students to perform in the widest range of New York settings, such as official receptions, galas, and public and private settings, and also encourages them to perform with many of New York's orchestras, choruses, and opera companies.

Mannes also offers concerto competitions for all performance majors, an audio recording facility, and career development advisement.

Academic Facilities

Degree candidates have access to the university's broad liberal arts curriculum, with offerings in the humanities, fine arts, and the social sciences. Mannes students share resources with The New School's other divisions, which include Parsons The New School for Design, Eugene Lang College The New School for Liberal Arts, The New School for General Studies, The New School for Drama, The New School for Social Research, Milano The New School for Management and Urban Policy, and The New School for Jazz and Contemporary Music.

Mannes' home is a Federal-style building on Manhattan's Upper West Side. The building houses classrooms, practice rooms, a state-of-the art computer lab, and the Harry Sherman Library, which offers access to more than 3 million books, 25,000 journals, a complete music and listening library, and study carrels. The New School also offers the facilities of the Bobst Library at

New York University through a consortium known as the Research Library Association of South Manhattan. The consortium's online catalog, Bobcat, is accessible over the Internet.

Mannes' two concert halls, seating 250 and 75 people, are the venues for hundreds of performances each year by students, faculty members, and artists-in-residence, as well as for master classes. The John Goldmark Practice Center, adjacent to Lincoln Center, provides additional practice rooms and an opera rehearsal room.

Costs

Tuition for the 2010–11 school year is as follows: for the B.M., B.S., M.M., and UDPL programs, $35,940; for the Professional Studies Diploma, $25,490; and for the ESL course work program, $4220. Fees total $2323 per academic year (university services $260, student health insurance $2053, Student Senate fee $10). Room and board costs approximately $15,260, depending upon a student's choice of specific meal plan and dormitory accommodations.

Financial Aid

Scholarships are available on the basis of merit and are determined at the time of the audition. Approximately 75 percent of Mannes students receive some form of scholarship. The average award ranges from 25 percent to 50 percent of tuition. In certain majors, opportunities exist for further assistance up to full tuition. Loans, grants, and work-study programs are available to students who fill out the Free Application for Federal Student Aid, the filing of which is required for U.S. citizens and permanent residents seeking financial aid of any type. A package of loans and information is sent along with the acceptance letter.

Faculty

Mannes is committed to providing broad and rigorous musical training in a friendly and supportive community that encourages artistic growth. The distinguished faculty includes some of New York City's most prominent musicians, including members of the Metropolitan Opera Orchestra and New York Philharmonic, as well as internationally known artists and ensembles. All students receive private lessons and participate in ensembles, and the 2:1 student-faculty ratio ensures personalized instruction and close interaction among, students, faculty and staff members, and administrators.

Admission Requirements

An application for admission to Mannes College The New School for Music consists of a completed Unified Application for Conservatory Admission–Mannes Edition (available online at http://www.unifiedapps.org), a $100 nonrefundable application fee, official high school or college academic transcripts for all schools attended (graduate degree applicants need only send college transcripts), and one letter of recommendation from a recent music teacher or an evaluation from a professional musician. International students must submit a recent TOEFL score. Mannes' school code is 2398. A minimum computer-based TOEFL score of 213 and a successful English test taken at the audition is required. A minimum computer-based TOEFL score of 250 is required for all graduate theory, composition, and conducting majors.

Audition requirements vary by field of study and program sought, outlines of which can be found in the Mannes College catalog. During the audition period, musicianship skills are tested for all degree and UDPL applicants. These tests in dictation, ear training, piano, and theory are required in order to complete the application for entrance to the undergraduate and master's degree programs. English language testing is required of applicants whose first language is not English.

Application and Information

The application deadline for the main March entrance auditions is December 1. The application deadline for the late auditions in May is April 1.For more information, students should contact:

Office of Admissions
Mannes College The New School for Music
150 West 85th Street
New York, New York 10024
Phone: 212-580-0210 Ext. 4862
      800-292-3040 (toll-free)
E-mail: mannesadmissions@newschool.edu
Web site: http://www.newschool.edu/mannes

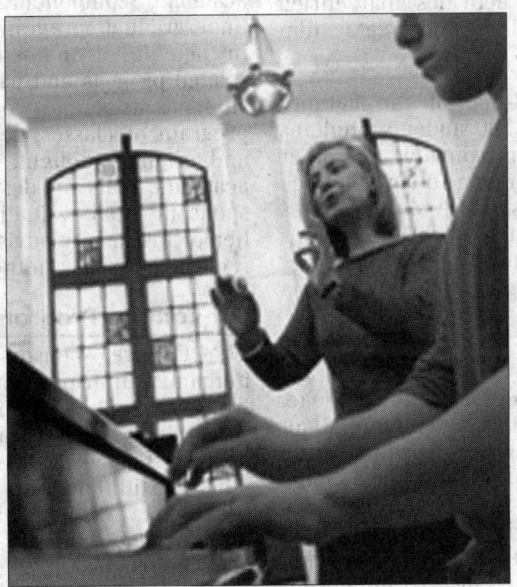

Mannes College The New School for Music.

MARLBORO COLLEGE
MARLBORO, VERMONT

Marlboro
College
Marlboro, Vermont

The College

Marlboro College, founded in 1946, is a small community of self-directed learners with a passion for intellectual engagement and a desire to create a course of study tailored to their own interests. Tucked away in the foothills of Vermont's Green Mountains, Marlboro offers a rigorous liberal arts curriculum through small classes and advanced one-to-one instruction, called tutorials. Marlboro's goal is to teach students to think clearly and learn independently, develop a command of concise and correct writing, and aspire to academic excellence, all while participating responsibly in a self-governing community. The College's 8:1 student-faculty ratio sparks dynamic exchanges between students and faculty members both in and out of the classroom and fosters a close-knit community in which asking questions is more important than knowing the right answers.

The fields and woodlands that make up its rural 350-acre campus include the original cluster of barns and other farm buildings that were converted by the first students and faculty members into classrooms and dormitories. The Outdoor Program offers instruction and equipment for backpacking, canoeing, cross-country skiing, kayaking, rock climbing, skating, and other sports that bring students in touch with the surrounding environment. The soccer team competes with other colleges, and more impromptu volleyball, basketball, softball, and Ultimate (Frisbee) compete as club teams. In addition, Marlboro's broomball (a game akin to hockey) tournament takes place each winter, with prizes for the winning teams and those with the best costumes. Campus committees organize many events both on and off campus, including concerts, lectures, poetry and fiction readings, art shows, and trips to Boston, Montreal, and New York for museum visits, shopping, and baseball games. Other activities that enrich campus life include parties, dances, plays, and weekly film screenings.

Marlboro is—and intends to remain—one of the nation's smallest liberal arts colleges, with some 300 students. Students come from nearly forty states and approximately six other countries. Transfer students—who make up one quarter of each incoming class—bring an important perspective to the campus community. More than 80 percent of all students live in campus housing, which consists of small dormitories (both single-sex and coed), several four-bedroom cottages, and a renovated country inn.

Location

The village of Marlboro, which is 2 miles from the College, consists of a post office, a town clerk's office, and an inn. About 1,200 residents live within the 36-square-mile township. During the summer, the village swells to accommodate the famous Marlboro Music Festival. The town of Brattleboro, 12 miles away, is a lively cultural and commercial center with bookstores, restaurants, coffee shops, a community food cooperative, and a movie theater. The College is 2 hours by car from Boston and 4 hours from New York City and Montreal.

Majors and Degrees

Marlboro confers the Bachelor of Arts and Bachelor of Science degrees in more than thirty areas of study, which can be combined in an endless number of ways. Students have the freedom to design their own majors, which allows them to make interdisciplinary connections and pursue individualized research. The College also offers Bachelor of Arts and Bachelor of Science degrees in international studies through its World Studies Program (WSP).

Areas of study offered at Marlboro include American studies, anthropology, art history, Asian studies, astronomy, biochemistry, biology, ceramics, chemistry, classics, computer science, cultural history, dance, development studies (in the WSP), economics, environmental studies, film/video studies, history, international studies, languages, literature, mathematics, music, painting, philosophy, photography, physics, political science, psychology, religion, sculpture, sociology, theater, visual arts, and writing.

Academic Programs

In the first two years, Marlboro students study broadly, discover new interests, and begin to see the connections that lead many to pursue interdisciplinary work. Each new student is paired with a faculty adviser and joins an advising group of sophomores, juniors, and seniors as well as freshmen. Students learn from each other at Marlboro in seminar-style classes.

Marlboro believes that clear writing both reflects and engenders clear thinking. The College, therefore, requires each new student to pass a Clear Writing Requirement within three semesters of enrolling at the College. Designated writing courses, faculty advisers, and student writing tutors all help new students meet the requirement.

Marlboro's Plan of Concentration, more than any other academic component, sets the College apart from other undergraduate programs. Undertaken by all Marlboro students in their junior and senior years, the plan is the collection of related projects and papers that form the final product of the student's academic work at Marlboro. It is an individualized program of classes, research, experiences, one-to-one study, and original thought, driven by the student's interests and academic goals and designed in close collaboration with faculty sponsors. Final evaluation of the student's plan is conducted by her or his faculty advisers and an outside examiner who is a recognized expert in the student's field.

Off-Campus Programs

The College sponsors multiple academic adventures and humanitarian trips each year, ranging from community service work in South Carolina and Costa Rica to interdisciplinary research in Cuba, China, Kenya, and Vietnam. Students working on their Plan of Concentration often travel abroad or attend other institutions for a period of time to augment their academic work. Marlboro faculty members may help plan these pursuits and frequently aid students in securing internships in academic fields.

The World Studies Program is a four-year program leading to a Bachelor of Arts or Bachelor of Science degree in international studies. The program involves intensive study on campus as well as a six- to eight-month internship abroad. In addition, WSP sponsors regular on-campus activities, which include a themed international dinner, music from around the world, and guest lectures and films related to current world issues.

Academic Facilities

Marlboro's academic facilities offer small classrooms and oversized faculty offices for students to meet in small groups and individually with their professors. Facilities are open 24 hours a day, supporting student research and creative explorations in a DNA lab, a state-of-the-art black-and-white/digital darkroom, a digital film-editing studio, two pottery studios, and an astronomical observatory. In the last five years, Marlboro's ongoing campus renewal project has doubled the size of the library and added a suite-style dorm. The new Rudolf and Irene Serkin Performing Arts Center has been added to offer more than 10,000 square feet for music, dance, and drama rehearsals and performances. In 2008, the campus added a new Total Health Center to provide additional space for medical and psychological counseling services and a fitness room.

Costs

Tuition and fees at Marlboro were $33,900 for the 2010–11 academic year. Room and board costs were $9420.

Financial Aid

More than 80 percent of all Marlboro students receive financial help. The College is committed to helping any student who qualifies for admission assemble the financial resources necessary to attend, and need is not a factor in the admission decision. Merit scholarships and grants are also available.

Faculty

Marlboro's 40 full-time faculty members are committed first and foremost to teaching. The lively exchange of ideas between teachers and students is the cornerstone of the Marlboro curriculum.

Student Government

All students and faculty and staff members are equal members of the College Town Meeting. Since the opening of the College in 1946, the community has come together every month to debate and decide budget initiatives, College policies, and other issues that affect daily life. A board of Selectpersons, elected by the College community, serves the College's interests and is responsible for drafting Town Meeting rules and regulations. Students serve with faculty and staff members on more than thirty College committees, including those that make faculty-hiring decisions. Other important committees include the social committee and the Community Court, which is responsible for enforcing campus regulations.

Admission Requirements

The Admissions Committee seeks students with intellectual promise; a high degree of motivation, self-discipline, personal stability, and social concern; and the ability and desire to contribute to the College community. All applicants are considered without regard to race, creed, sex, sexual orientation, gender identity or its expression, national or ethnic origin, age, or disability. Transfers, veterans, and older or returning students are encouraged to apply.

Like most colleges, Marlboro requires students to submit a variety of documentation, from high school transcripts to teacher recommendations. The Admissions Committee evaluates each applicant as a unique individual who possesses qualities that are not necessarily quantifiable.

A campus visit is strongly recommended for all applicants, and interviews are encouraged. Many campus interviews are conducted by faculty members in the applicant's area of interest. Marlboro does not use a formulaic approach in making admission decisions. Applicants are encouraged to demonstrate their particular strengths; the goal is a successful match between the student and the College.

Application and Information

New students and transfers are admitted for either the spring or the fall semester. Applicants for the fall semester have a choice of three admission plans. The early decision plan is for those students who have thoroughly researched Marlboro and for whom Marlboro is the first choice. Applicants should be aware that early decision is binding. The deadline for first-year students to submit application materials is November 15, and applicants are notified by December 15. Early action, a nonbinding plan, has a deadline of January 15. These applicants are notified of a decision on February 1. The regular admission deadline is March 1. The deadline for transfer students to submit applications materials for the fall semester is April 1, and for the spring semester it is November 15.

An application for admission must include a completed Common Application form and a Marlboro College Supplement Form with a "Why Marlboro" personal statement, a $50 fee, complete transcripts from all secondary schools and colleges, an analytical writing sample, and two letters of recommendation. SAT or ACT are not required, but will be taken into consideration if submitted by the prospective student. The Admissions Committee welcomes applications from home-schooled students. In lieu of a high school transcript, home-schooled students must submit a detailed description of their curriculum (including reading lists and academic study areas).

Office of Admissions
Marlboro College, 2582 South Road
Marlboro, Vermont 05344-0300
Phone: 802-257-4333
       800-343-0049 (toll-free)
Fax: 802-451-7555
E-mail: admissions@marlboro.edu
Web site: http://www.marlboro.edu

Marlboro College offers a rigorous liberal arts curriculum through small classes and advanced one-to-one instruction, called tutorials.

MARYMOUNT MANHATTAN COLLEGE

NEW YORK, NEW YORK

MarymountManhattan
a college of the liberal arts

The College

Marymount Manhattan College (MMC) is an urban, independent, coeducational, undergraduate liberal arts college. The mission of the College is to educate a socially and economically diverse population by fostering intellectual achievement and personal growth and by providing opportunities for career development. Inherent in this mission is the intent to develop an awareness of social, political, cultural, and ethical issues in the belief that this awareness will lead to concern for, participation in, and the improvement of society. To accomplish this mission, the College offers a strong program in the arts and sciences to students of all ages—as well as substantial preprofessional preparation. Central to these efforts is the particular attention given to the individual student. Marymount Manhattan College also seeks to be a resource and learning center for the metropolitan community.

The social and extracurricular life of the student body of approximately 2,000 students centers on more than forty clubs and organizations sponsored through the Office of Student Development and Activities, including the Global Citizens Society, Psychology Club, French Club, Philosophy Club, Science Society, Black and Latino Student Organization, the student newspaper and yearbook, WMMC Radio, Student Government Association, intramural sports, and other special interest organizations. Students attend musical events, and MMC's own off-Broadway theater, the only one on the Upper East Side of Manhattan, offers students an opportunity to participate in student productions.

The Office of Residence Life at Marymount Manhattan College is committed to providing residents with numerous opportunities and experiences that foster intellectual achievement and social and personal growth. Students are encouraged to become involved in the many activities that are sponsored by Residence Life and are assisted with assuming responsibility for their own lives and living environment. The College provides housing for approximately 800 students at various locations in Manhattan. The buildings offer suite-style, traditional dormitories, or apartment-style living, with classrooms, lounges, a laundry room, and rehearsal space. Additional off-campus facilities are obtained as needed.

The Office of Career Development and Internships serves the entire College community by providing an integrated program of academic and career counseling. The office helps students by offering internship opportunities and workshops in job placement, resume writing, and graduate school preparation. Other College services include personal and financial aid counseling and campus ministry.

Location

Marymount Manhattan College is centrally located on Manhattan's Upper East Side at 221 East 71st Street between Second and Third avenues. Within walking distance of the campus are the Frick, Metropolitan, Whitney, and Guggenheim museums; the Asian Society, French Institute, and National Audubon Society; Central Park; New York Hospital and Sloan-Kettering Research Center; and public libraries. All forms of public transportation are easily accessible. Within minutes of the College are shops, restaurants, and movie theaters. This location gives students the opportunity to take advantage of New York City's rich culture and to explore a variety of neighborhoods.

Majors and Degrees

Marymount Manhattan College offers programs leading to the Bachelor of Arts, Bachelor of Science, and Bachelor of Fine Arts degrees. Majors are offered in accounting, acting, art (concentrations in art history, graphic design, photography, and studio art), biology, business management, communication arts, dance, education, English, history, interdisciplinary studies, international studies, philosophy and religious studies, political science, psychology, sociology, speech-language pathology and audiology, and theater arts (B.A., B.S., and B.F.A. degrees). Minors offered are accounting, art history, arts management, Asian studies, biology, business management, chemistry, creative writing, drama therapy, economics, English and world literatures, environmental studies, forensic psychology, French, gender and sexuality studies, graphic design, Hispanic studies, history, industrial/organizational psychology, international studies, journalism, mathematics, media studies, music, musical theater, neuroscience, philosophy, photography, political economy, political science, promotional and professional communication, psychology, religious studies, sociology, social work, speech-language pathology and audiology, and theater.

Academic Programs

Marymount Manhattan College has designed its programs to enable students to meet the challenges of contemporary society. MMC is committed to the belief that a liberal arts education provides students with the ability and the flexibility to manage change and with broad understanding and the communication and problem-solving skills that are essential for success in any career and in life. To accomplish its goals, the College offers a liberal arts education, integrated with preprofessional training opportunities and individualized attention. The curricula are organized into five divisions: humanities, fine and performing arts, sciences, social sciences, and business management. Also offered are special-interest sequences that complement the student's major and minor, with added concentration in such areas as art history, creative writing, finance and investments, international business, marketing, photography, predentistry, prelaw, premedicine, pre–veterinary science, and social work. The College's small size provides students with an individually planned academic career, reflects students' academic needs and interests, and supports their career goals.

Candidates for the Bachelor of Arts, Bachelor of Science, and Bachelor of Fine Arts degrees must complete 120 credits. To qualify for a degree, a student must maintain an overall scholastic average of at least 2.0. Requirements for certificate programs vary.

The College recognizes various types of nontraditional credit, including credit for acceptable scores on the Advanced Placement (AP), International Baccalaureate (IB), College-Level Examination Program (CLEP), and New York State College Proficiency Examination (CPE) tests and credit for life experience.

MMC encourages its students to participate in internship programs in New York City that range from work at hospitals, financial institutions, magazines, publishing houses, and off-Broadway theaters to HBO and CBS.

Off-Campus Programs

The College's Academic Year Abroad offers an opportunity for students to broaden their educational experience and to gain cultural perspectives through study at other colleges in the Americas and overseas. Students may spend one or both semesters of their junior year in this program. MMC summer sessions and January intersessions also offer students opportunities in travel/study-abroad courses in Egypt, France, Great Britain, Greece, Eastern Europe, Ireland, Italy, Russia, and Spain.

Academic Facilities

The Thomas J. Shanahan Library at MMC is a library/learning center. It contains more than 100,000 volumes in open stacks and maintains an extensive periodical collection. The media center, on the main library floor, houses nonprint materials, microfiche, microfilm, filmstrips, slides, tapes, videotapes, DVDs, and records. Through the library's affiliation with the New York Metropolitan Reference and Research Library Agency, MMC faculty members and students have access to the materials of the member libraries. The library also participates in the Online Computer Library Center (OCLC), a computerized database of the holdings of some 4,000 libraries that is currently being used for cataloging and reference purposes.

The modern 250-seat Theresa Lang Theatre is equipped with an orchestra pit capable of accommodating 40 musicians. The theater has a special acoustical design, a sprung dance floor, a full technical balcony with equipment for lighting and sound, thirty-five counter-weighted-line sets in the fly system, dressing rooms with showers, and a scene shop. Students benefit from exposure to the numerous professional dance, opera, and theatrical groups that perform at the College.

Top-notch laboratory facilities strengthen education in two areas in which MMC has always excelled—science and communication arts.

MMC's science facilities in biology, chemistry, and physics underwent a total reconstruction valued at close to $1 million, thanks to the generosity of the Samuel Freeman Charitable Trust and the Ira De Camp Foundation. The Samuel Freeman Science Center opens many new doors of opportunity to students who are biology/premedicine majors or who are interested in pursuing careers in other science or health-related fields.

The College's Theresa Lang Center for Producing features the latest in digital computer technology and is one of the most advanced facilities of its kind in New York City. With digital multimedia capability, a decor inspired by top television postproduction houses, and access to the public library's B. Altman Advanced Learning Superblock, the center further enhances students' skills in traditional video and television production and allows them to develop, design, and evaluate cutting-edge multimedia projects. In conjunction with the Communication Arts Department, the College offers students the Media Library, where many videos and screening computers are available to students.

In fall 2009, the College opened the Commons, a two-tiered dining facility and student lounge. Students also have an outdoor dining option, since the Commons opens out onto the existing Lowerre Family Terrace, a 5,000-square-foot rooftop garden, complete with a stone water-wall, a deck, and Wi-Fi service, that connects the two main campus buildings.

Costs

For the 2010–11 academic year, full-time tuition and fees were $23,610. Room and board costs were $13,416 per year. For part-time students, tuition was $716 per credit. Additional fees are applicable for various laboratory and studio classes.

Financial Aid

The College administers a variety of financial aid programs, including scholarships sponsored by the College. Some of the awards are based on academic achievement; others are based on financial need. Students are also eligible for aid through a wide variety of state and federal programs. In addition, a number of jobs are available for students on campus, and the Offices of Financial Aid and Academic and Career Advisement can help students locate part-time off-campus jobs to help finance their education. More than 85 percent of MMC students receive some form of financial assistance. Therefore, limited finances alone need not prevent any student from attending the College. Priority consideration for merit- and need-based financial aid is November 15 for spring admission and March 15 for fall admission.

Faculty

Marymount Manhattan College's student-faculty ratio is 12:1. In addition to the staff of the advisement office, faculty members act as advisers to students. Full-time faculty members teach in all sessions and divisions (days, evenings, and some weekends). Part-time instructors, who are drawn from the wealth of experienced teaching professionals in New York City, supplement the full-time faculty.

Student Government

The Student Government Association responds to three areas of concern at MMC. The association primarily serves the needs of its constituents by managing the student government budget, planning and publicizing events, and establishing organizations that reflect the interests of the students. In addition, the association assists faculty and administrative groups and committees in their policy and procedural tasks and communicates the results of committee work to the student body. Finally, the Student Government Association provides special representatives for students' rights and freedoms through established and clearly defined channels of authority.

Admission Requirements

Marymount Manhattan College seeks candidates with qualities that indicate potential for success in higher education and the ability to contribute to the College community. Admission is based on a combination of factors: the student's academic program, including scholastic average; two recommendations (judicial form required for transfer students in lieu of one recommendation) from teachers, counselors, or employers; an essay; and SAT or ACT scores. TOEFL, IELTS, or PTE scores are required for international student applicants.

Each year the College enrolls an increasing number of transfer students. Transfer students may receive up to 90 credits for course work completed at a regionally accredited postsecondary institution with a grade of C- or better. Transcripts are evaluated on a course-by-course basis.

Application and Information

The admissions application must be received by March 15 (fall entry) and November 15 (spring entry) for priority consideration for MMC scholarships. Students may apply online. For application forms and for more information about Marymount Manhattan College, students should contact:

Office of Admissions
Marymount Manhattan College
221 East 71st Street
New York, New York 10021
Phone: 212-517-0430
      800-MARYMOUNT (toll-free)
Fax: 212-517-0448
E-mail: admissions@mmm.edu
Web site: http://www.mmm.edu
    http://on.fb.me/MarymountManhattanColl
      (Facebook)
    http://twitter.com/NYCMarymount (Twitter)

Marymount Manhattan College, in the heart of Manhattan.

MARYWOOD UNIVERSITY
SCRANTON, PENNSYLVANIA

The University

Marywood University is coeducational, comprehensive, residential, and Catholic. Founded in 1915 by the Sisters, Servants of the Immaculate Heart of Mary, the University serves men and women from a variety of backgrounds and religions. The University enrolls more than 3,400 students in an array of undergraduate and graduate programs. Motivated by a pioneering, progressive spirit, Marywood provides a framework for educational excellence that enables students to develop fully as persons and to master professional and leadership skills that are necessary for meeting human needs.

Students at Marywood have the opportunity to build on their academic interests and proactively shape their educational experience. Students' energy and intellectual curiosity guides their work, growth, and success. Marywood believes in the power of the individual and in the premise that education is the most empowering tool.

Marywood is fully accredited by the Commission on Higher Education of the Middle States Association of Colleges and Schools. Accreditations/approvals have been granted by Accreditation Review Committee on Education for the Physician Assistant, American Psychological Association, American Art Therapy Association, American Music Therapy Association, Commission on Accreditation for Dietetics Education, American Dietetic Association, Council on Academic Accreditation, American Speech-Language-Hearing Association, Association of Collegiate Business Schools and Programs, Commission on Accreditation of Athletic Training Education, Council for Accreditation of Counseling and Related Educational Programs, Council on Social Work Education, National Association of Schools of Art and Design, National Association of Schools of Music, National Council for Accreditation of Teacher Education, and National League for Nursing Accrediting Commission.

The athletic program for women and men at Marywood provides students with opportunities to play on competitive intercollegiate, club, and intramural teams. Students compete on an intercollegiate basis in baseball, basketball, cross-country, field hockey, lacrosse, soccer, softball, swimming/diving, tennis, and volleyball. Marywood is a member of NCAA Division III, the Colonial States Athletic Conference (CSAC), and the Eastern College Athletic Conference. Marywood's teams have been successful, winning titles in basketball, field hockey, lacrosse, soccer, softball, tennis, and volleyball. In addition, Marywood teams and individuals have participated in tournaments at the national level.

Prospective students can connect with Marywood online via Facebook (http://facebook.com/marywoodu), Twitter (http://twitter.com/marywoodu), and YouTube (http://youtube.com/marywoodu).

Location

Situated on a hilltop, Marywood's scenic 115-acre campus is part of an attractive residential area of the city of Scranton, in northeastern Pennsylvania. With a population of 78,000, Scranton is the fifth-largest city in Pennsylvania and is the county seat of Lackawanna County (the county population is approximately 213,000). Marywood is relatively close to many major cities of the Northeast; traveling by car, it is 1 hour to Binghamton; 2½ hours to New York and Philadelphia; 4 hours to Washington, D.C.; and 5½ hours to Boston. Several airlines serve the Wilkes-Barre/Scranton International Airport, which is 20 minutes from the campus. The Pocono Mountains, offering spectacular scenery and an abundance of outdoor recreational opportunities, including downhill skiing, are a short distance from the campus.

Majors and Degrees

Marywood University offers a variety of majors and minors at the undergraduate level. Individually designed majors, developed with faculty guidance, and double and interdisciplinary majors are also available. Several five-year bachelor's/master's degree programs are offered.

At the undergraduate level, Marywood University awards the Bachelor of Arts (B.A.), Bachelor of Architecture (B.Arch.), Bachelor of Business Administration (B.B.A.), Bachelor of Environmental Design in Architecture (B.E.D.A.), Bachelor of Fine Arts (B.F.A.), Bachelor of Music

(B.M.), Bachelor of Science (B.S.), Bachelor of Science in Nursing (B.S.N.), and Bachelor of Social Work (B.S.W.).

Marywood offers majors and minors in the following areas of study: accounting, ad hoc (self-designed), advertising and public relations, architecture and interior architecture/design, art (studio: ceramics, painting, sculpture; design: graphic design, illustration, photography), art education, art therapy, arts administration (art, music, theater), aviation management, biology, biotechnology, communication sciences and disorders (audiology, deaf studies, speech-language pathology), comprehensive social sciences (general, history, sociology), computer information and telecommunications systems, computer science (minor), criminal justice, dance/movement (minor), digital media and broadcast production (broadcast, corporate), early childhood special education, education (elementary, secondary), English, environmental science, family and consumer sciences education, financial planning, French, general science education, health and physical education (athletic training, education, physical activity), health services administration, history/political science, hospitality management, industrial/organizational psychology, international business, journalism, management, marketing, mathematics, medical technology/clinical laboratory science, multimedia (minor), music, music education, music therapy, nursing (preservice, post-RN), nutrition and dietetics (coordinated program, didactic program), performance, performing arts, philosophy, physician assistant studies, psychology, psychology/clinical practice, public administration, religious studies, retail business management, science, social sciences secondary education, social work, Spanish, special education/elementary education (dual certification), theater, and women's studies (minor).

Preprofessional programs are offered in chiropractic, communication sciences and disorders, dentistry, law, medicine, physician assistant studies, and veterinary medicine. A joint seven-year bachelor's/doctoral program in chiropractic involves three years of study on the Marywood campus and additional work at New York Chiropractic College, which is located in Seneca Falls, New York.

Marywood offers five-year bachelor's to master's degree programs in architecture, biotechnology, communication arts, criminal justice, financial information services, health services administration, physician assistant studies, and speech language pathology.

Academic Programs

Undergraduate degrees are offered in approximately sixty academic programs, including the arts, sciences, music, fine arts, social work, and nursing. All students are required to complete a core curriculum in the liberal arts in addition to the courses in their major. Opportunities for undergraduates abound through double majors, honors and independent-study programs, practicums, internships, and study abroad. Army and Air Force ROTC programs are available.

Off-Campus Programs

Study-abroad opportunities are available in countries such as Australia, Canada, England, France, Mexico, and Spain. Through Studio Art Centers International (SACI), art students may study in Florence, Italy.

Academic Facilities

In recent years, the University has made $100 million in improvements to the campus, including new athletic, residence hall, and dining facilities, and one of the finest studio arts facilities in the northeast. The Insalaco Center for Studio Arts features 60,000 square feet of fully equipped studios, labs, and classroom spaces for a broad variety of artistic disciplines. The O'Neill Center for Healthy Families gives students an opportunity to study and perform research in a first-rate human performance laboratory.

Costs

Tuition for full-time students (12–18 credits per semester) for the 2010–11 academic year was a flat fee of $26,000. There was also a general fee of $950 for full-time students. Costs for room and board for a full academic year are approximately $12,172, depending on which meal plan is selected and the desired room occupancy. Costs of books and supplies are estimated at $1000.

Financial Aid

Marywood offers a comprehensive program of financial aid to assist students in meeting educational costs. Eligibility for federal and state programs is based on demonstrated financial need, as determined by a federal eligibility formula that analyzes family income and assets. In addition, approximately $27 million in institutional aid is awarded annually to Marywood students. Applicants to Marywood are considered for all financial assistance programs for which they qualify. Candidates are required to submit the Free Application for Federal Student Aid (FAFSA) and the Marywood application form, preferably by February 15.

Faculty

Among faculty members at Marywood, 144 are full-time, and 84 percent of these hold the Ph.D. or the highest degree in their field. The student-faculty ratio is 13:1. Faculty members are evaluated on their teaching and on their scholarly and artistic activities.

Student Government

All matriculated students in the undergraduate school are members of the Student Government Association (SGA). The SGA operates with a number of committees, including the Student Council, the Resident Committee, and the Commuter Committee. The association plays a key role in establishing a positive campus environment.

Admission Requirements

Candidates for admission should demonstrate reasonable progress toward graduation in an accredited secondary school, have graduated from a secondary school, or offer evidence of an equivalent secondary education. Each candidate should show satisfactory academic preparation in 16 units of subject matter, including 4 units of English, 3 units of social studies, 2 units of mathematics, 1 unit of science with laboratory, and 6 additional units. Either SAT or ACT scores are required for those who wish to enter as freshmen.

In addition to fulfilling general admission requirements, candidates for admission to a degree program in architecture, art, education, music, nursing, pre–physician assistant studies, and speech language pathology must meet special standards established by the department. Prior to enrollment, music, theater, and art candidates are required to audition or to present an art portfolio.

For certain programs, candidates without the recommended distribution of units may be eligible for admission if their course work as a whole and the results of their tests offer evidence of a strong foundation for college work. Candidates who are deficient in required course work may complete the appropriate work during the summer or the first year in college.

A student who demonstrates satisfactory academic performance at another college may apply for admission as a transfer student. Academic courses presented for transfer should be equivalents of courses required by the programs of study at Marywood. Students should have earned a grade of C or higher in their course work; C– will not transfer. A student should expect to earn a minimum of 60 credits at Marywood University; ordinarily, at least one half of the credits required for a major must also be earned at Marywood.

International candidates are required to meet the academic standards for admission, demonstrate proficiency in the use of the English language, and submit documentation of having sufficient funds to cover educational and living expenses for the duration of study. To certify proficiency in the use of English, international applicants whose primary language is not English must submit scores from the Test of English as a Foreign Language (TOEFL).

Application and Information

Applications for admission are considered on a rolling basis; however, candidates are strongly encouraged to submit applications by March 1. Applications received after March 1 are considered on the basis of available space in particular programs. To be considered for admission, freshman applicants must submit to the Office of Admissions a completed application (paper or online), a nonrefundable $35 application fee (waived if applying online), an official high school transcript with an indication of class rank, an official report of scores from the SAT or ACT, and at least one letter of recommendation. Students can apply online at http://www.mymarywood.com/home/apply.html.

Transfer students must submit a completed application, a nonrefundable $35 application fee (waived if applying online), an official high school transcript, official academic transcript(s) reflecting all college course work for which the candidate has enrolled, and at least one letter of recommendation.

All submitted credentials become the property of Marywood and are not returnable to the applicant. Admission standards and policies are free of discrimination on grounds of race, color, national origin, sex, age, or disability.

For further information, interested students should contact:

Christian DiGregorio, Director
University Admissions
Marywood University
2300 Adams Avenue
Scranton, Pennsylvania 18509
Phone: 570-348-6234
        TO-MARYWOOD (866-279-9663, toll-free)
Fax: 570-961-4763
E-mail: yourfuture@marywood.edu
Web site: http://www.mymarywood.com
          http://www.facebook.com/marywoodu
          http://www.twitter.com/marywoodu
          http://www.youtube.com/marywoodu

The rotunda in the Liberal Arts Center on Marywood's campus.

MEMPHIS COLLEGE OF ART
MEMPHIS, TENNESSEE

The College

Memphis College of Art (MCA) is a professional center of art and design education dedicated to preparing individuals for lives of creating, problem solving, and critical thinking. Small by choice and purpose, MCA is a cultural wellspring of creativity that has been nurturing and educating artists of all levels since 1936. MCA offers state-of-the-art facilities, excellent faculty members, interdisciplinary programs, and cutting-edge exhibitions to the public and those students pursuing B.F.A., M.F.A., or M.A. in Art Education and M.A.T. degrees.

Rust Hall, the College's main building, is located within the 340-acre Overton Park in midtown Memphis. The Gibson Hall administration building, at the park's southeastern edge, houses faculty and staff offices including admissions, financial aid, business office, career services, and student affairs. Graduate programs, studios, classrooms, and labs are located in the new Nesin Graduate School in downtown Memphis. Daily shuttle service provides easy access to all three locations and to MCA's student housing. Student housing options include Fogelman and Metz Halls which offer apartment-style living spaces with full kitchen, private bedrooms, laundry, and shared studio space. Other campus houses offer a variety of choices and costs to fit any lifestyle.

Memphis College of Art is a private institution accredited by the Commission on Colleges of the Southern Association of Colleges and Schools and the National Association of Schools of Art and Design.

Location

The Memphis metropolitan area is home to over 1.1 million residents, and offers a rich history of blues, literature, the Mississippi River, and the national Civil Rights Museum. In this culture-soaked city, MCA has existed for seventy-five years as a veritable artist's colony where access to a professionally geared education is available to those whose passions burn brightest.

Majors and Degrees

Memphis College of Art offers concentrations and majors that lead to the Bachelor of Fine Arts (B.F.A.) degree along with programs of study that lead to a Master of Fine Arts (M.F.A.) degree and art education programs toward a Master of Art in Teaching (M.A.T.) and a Master of Art in Art Education (M.A.). Undergraduate areas of study are available in animation, digital cinema, digital media, drawing, graphic design, illustration, painting, photography, printmaking, sculpture, and sequential narrative.

Academic Programs

As a professional school of art and design, MCA offers degrees in visual arts at the undergraduate level. Within these degrees, students choose from an array of majors and concentrations that provide a variety of avenues to suit individual interests and needs. At the heart of the curriculum is a vigorous Foundations and Core program of studio practice and intellectual rigor driven by the Liberal Studies program.

With an emphasis on ideas, students cultivate critical thinking skills and essential perspectives on art and culture through MCA's Liberal Studies courses. The research, writing, and presentation skills necessary for a professional approach to art and design further the development of well-rounded artists.

Two 15-week semesters begin in August and January and three summer sessions are held from mid-May to July. A minimum of 120 credit hours are required to complete the bachelor's degree

Off-Campus Programs

Beginning with orientation, MCA offers many educational opportunities to support the academic endeavor. Internships; a consortium exchange program with four local colleges and forty-three national and international art colleges; yearly museum seminar trips to places such as Paris, Mexico City, or San Francisco; the Horn Island Summer Workshop; and the New York Studio Program are just some of the out-of-classroom experiences available to students.

Academic Facilities

The Memphis College of Art campus is unlike any other. MCA is nestled in a 340-acre virgin woodland park next door to the Brooks Museum of Art and the Memphis Zoo. The striking architecture of the main building, Rust Hall, offers a glimpse of the wonders created within. In addition to classrooms, studio space, and lecture halls, there are two galleries which host up to a dozen exhibitions a year and an extensive library of valuable resources; not to mention MCA's delicious—and affordable—cafe that serves up three hot meals a day to "starving" artists.

While MCA is proud of its small size, there's nothing small about the technology resources or facilities available to students. The G. Pillow Lewis Library has more than 17,000 volumes, 120 fine arts periodical subscriptions, and 200 periodical titles. Full-text databases are accessible through the Tennessee Electronic Library InfoTrac. MCA's Main Gallery hosts visiting artist– and juried exhibitions throughout the year, while the Lower Gallery is designated for student work. MCA's 4,400-square-foot shop has equipment for woodworking, metalworking, plastic molding, mat cutting, glass cutting, and stretcher and frame construction. MCA has large metal and clay sculpture studios, as well as separate foundry and welding areas for castings and metalwork. The clay studios have five wheels, a space for hand-building and glazing, a spray booth, and a semi-enclosed firing room with electric and gas kilns.

Printmaking, papermaking, and book arts studios provide easy interaction between these related media. Printmaking has two presses for stone and plate lithography, three etching presses, serigraphy equipment, and equipment for photo printmaking processes as well. Book arts includes three letterpresses and a bindery. The wet room is equipped with beaters, a 36-square-foot vacuum table, a hydraulic press, and a pulper.

There are four fully equipped digital labs with digital cameras, slide and transparency scanners, flatbed scanners, and high-resolution printers. A separate large-format printing lab provides for large-scale archival printing on a variety of media. Two sound and animation studios are available for animations and video work. Projectors, video cameras, and other equipment are available for loan to students through the digital media faculty.

Photo lab facilities include ten workstations equipped with Omega large-format enlargers and twelve workstations equipped with Beseler medium-format enlargers. A lighting studio houses strobe equipment, backgrounds, and medium- and large-format cameras. Digital SLR cameras, portable strobe- and hot-light sets, and backdrop stands are available for checkout. Also available are facilities for nonsilver alternative photo processes including digital negative printers and a large UV exposure unit.

Costs

Undergraduate tuition and fees are $25,050 for the 2011–12 school year. In addition to that, there are other student costs such as room and board, transportation, clothing, and books/art supplies. The following one-year budget estimates are based on higher-end resident housing and other miscellaneous costs. Some students may spend less than these estimates. Estimated total costs for attending MCA and living in campus housing or in an apartment for one year are $38,200 (based on the cost of Metz/Fogelman Halls and estimated living expenses). Estimated total costs for attending MCA and living at home for one year are $29,700.

Financial Aid

While many families may not be able to afford the full cost of attending MCA, the College does everything possible to help everyone who wants to pursue a degree. Ninety-five percent of students receive some type of financial assistance, with the vast majority (74 percent) using loan programs to help them reach their educational goals. MCA will help students apply for any federal, state, and institutional aid for which they may be eligible.

Faculty

MCA has 62 full- and part-time faculty members, selected for their studio experience, professional accomplishments, and teaching skills. MCA has a 10:1 student-faculty ratio and an average class size of 17.

Student Government

The Student Alliance (SA) at MCA is the formal representative of the student body. The SA works closely with the Office of Student Life through elected representatives. Students plan entertainment events, film series, and exhibitions in the student gallery space. Meetings of the elected representatives are held biweekly throughout the semester and these meetings are open to all students.

Admission Requirements

Application requirements include a completed application (available online at http://www.mca.edu/admissions), $25 application fee, high school or college transcripts, ACT or SAT scores (for freshmen applicants), and a portfolio of 10 to 20 pieces of artwork (submit digital images to portfolio@mca.edu). International applicants should submit a TOEFL or IELTS score in lieu of the ACT or SAT.

Application and Information

Applications are accepted on a rolling basis. Responses are sent approximately three weeks after the application process is completed. Students are considered for admission and institutional scholarships through the application process.

Additional information can be obtained by contacting:

Office of Admissions
Memphis College of Art
1930 Poplar Avenue
Memphis, Tennessee 38104
Phone: 901-272-5151
       800-727-1088 (toll-free)
E-mail: info@mca.edu
Web site: http://www.mca.edu
       http://www.mca.edu/aboutmcablogs
       http://twitter.com/memphisart

Memphis College of Art—a professional center of art and design education.

MENLO COLLEGE
ATHERTON, CALIFORNIA

The College

Menlo College, an independent, coeducational, nonsectarian institution, stands out among institutions of higher education in five exciting ways: programs, location, small size, sports, and alumni. Rather than offer a traditional set of majors as many institutions do, Menlo concentrates on providing excellent programs in business management with a strong foundation in the liberal arts. Menlo's location in the heart of the Silicon Valley allows the College to train tomorrow's leaders in an intimate, student-centered, academically challenging environment. The College is small enough to be a real community but large enough to support a wide array of intercollegiate sports, student organizations, and internship opportunities, giving students the confidence and breadth of experience to flourish after graduation. The College's distinguished alumni provide a strong base of support for graduates, which helps students make the transition from college to career with great success.

A Menlo education is a process that trains and cultivates leaders. This process begins with a broad-based liberal arts foundation in the humanities, mathematics, sciences, and social sciences. At the same time, students are also challenged to enrich and develop their writing, critical-thinking, and decision-making skills. Next, students enter rich major programs staffed with seasoned practitioners who are experts in their respective fields. The advantage is a cutting-edge curriculum that equips students to succeed. Menlo's superior business program is renowned throughout the world and has produced generations of dynamic and successful business, industrial, and civic leaders around the globe.

The learning process does not end in the classroom. Students are encouraged to participate in internships and study programs that bridge the gap between theory and practice. These opportunities range from Fortune 500 companies to innovative start-up enterprises, from San Francisco to South America, Asia, and Europe. Not only do participants gain hands-on experience, but also they grow personally as they encounter diverse peoples, cultures, and values.

As a whole, College-sponsored activities promote self-exploration and often lead to the discovery of hidden talents. Students can participate in a variety of clubs or organizations, ranging from the Alpha Chi National Honor Society and the Poetry, Art, and Music Society to the Menlo Oak Newspaper and the Outdoor Club. Leadership skills are cultivated through an activist student government and student life positions and special workshops that tackle pressing contemporary issues. In addition, Menlo's international exchange programs offer students opportunities to expand their horizons and bring global awareness to their futures.

This commitment to personal and intellectual growth, coupled with Menlo's ideal location in the heart of the Silicon Valley, draws students from all across the United States and around the world. The global village is a reality at Menlo, given the broad social, religious, cultural, and national makeup of the student body. The appreciation of different cultures that results becomes a tremendous advantage in the marketplace.

Menlo's warm, friendly atmosphere is enhanced by its residential status. Nearly two thirds of all students live in one of five residence halls. Nearby off-campus apartments (for students who are older than 21 or married) are also an option.

For those who enjoy the exhilaration of intercollegiate competition, Menlo offers men's baseball, basketball, cross-country, football, golf, soccer, and wrestling, and women's sports include basketball, cross-country, soccer, softball, volleyball, and wrestling. In addition, Menlo offers cheerleading as a coeducational sport. The College competes in the NAIA Pacific Conference. Intramural sports are also popular, and altogether almost 40 percent of students participate in sports.

To meet students' health needs, the College provides care via the Menlo Medical Clinic. Counseling services are offered by faculty and resident life staff members.

Whether in the classroom, in the laboratory, or on the playing field, Menlo College nurtures students by creating programs, activities, and services that foster individual success.

Location

Menlo College is located on the San Francisco peninsula in the town of Atherton, a residential community near the cities of Menlo Park and Palo Alto. Major freeways do not pass near the campus, nor is heavy industry nearby. The area ranks among the most attractive and exciting in the world, with numerous cultural resources and a temperate climate. San Francisco lies 30 miles to the north. Many other important educational centers are within an hour's drive of Menlo, making the area an exciting place in which to study and live. The campus is in the heart of Silicon Valley, where high-tech companies in the electronics, computer, aerospace, biotechnology, and pharmaceutical industries are literally transforming the world in which we live and work. Surrounding the San Francisco Bay Area is the great natural beauty of northern California, extending from the spectacular California coast to the majestic Sierra Nevada Mountains. Favorite spots such as Big Sur, Monterey Bay, Lake Tahoe, Napa Valley, and Yosemite National Park are just a few hours' drive from Menlo.

Majors and Degrees

Menlo College offers the following fields of study: accounting, entrepreneurship, finance, general business management, human resource management, international management, management information systems, marketing, marketing communication, media management, psychology, sports management, real estate, and an individually designed major where students can combine existing programs to create their own major.

Academic Programs

Menlo College operates on a semester calendar. To earn a bachelor's degree, students must complete 124 units of credit and maintain good academic standing.

Menlo's renowned Academic Success Center provides dynamic resources for increasing students' academic ability and morale. Included are innovative approaches to counseling and tutoring. The goal is to develop strong self-advocacy and to assist faculty members in meeting the needs of a varied student population using an assortment of individualized, small-group, and computer-based instruction. This method facilitates study and discussion of course material, tutoring, and test preparation.

Off-Campus Programs

The difference between obtaining an exciting professional position with opportunity for advancement and growth and settling for second best often comes down to experience. Internships enable students to apply theory to practice—to take classroom knowledge and test its relevancy. Through the Career Services Office and each academic department, qualified students are urged to participate in local, national, or international internships. Students spend one or more semesters working on or off campus in their fields of study obtaining academic credit and/or financial compensation and valuable insight. Menlo also has exchange agreements with Francisco de Vitoria University in Madrid, Spain; Peking University, in Beijing, China; Anáhuac University, in Mexico City; Universidad Adolfo Ibanez in Chile; Guangdong College of Business in Guangzhou, China; and with Kansai Gaidai University in Japan.

Academic Facilities

Bowman Library maintains a strong collection of books and periodicals, including electronic journals, books, and AV materials. The Bowman Library's Electronic Information Gateway provides access to general and specialized online research databases, including full-text periodicals and reference resources as well as high-speed access to the Internet and World Wide Web. The Bowman Library contains rooms for group study, viewing AV materials, and photocopying. In addition, wireless access to the campus network resources is available through the library's laptop computer checkout program.

The Resource for Online Services and Information Electronically (ROSIE) is Menlo College's electronic information gateway, providing access 24 hours a day, seven days a week through the Web from the library, dorms, and off-campus sites to the online catalog, electronic research databases, and reference assistance. For more information, students should visit http://www.menlo.edu/library. ROSIE also provides access to WOODIE, the online research-skills tutorial required of all students through the Menlo College General Education curriculum.

Menlo College's four computer labs provide students with access to state-of-the-art PC and Macintosh hardware, software, and networking capabilities. All computer-lab equipment is connected to the campus network as well as the Internet and World Wide Web. Classroom labs include both individual workstations and presentation facilities. The Open Access lab is open daily and is staffed by experienced monitors who are familiar with all lab equipment and applications and are able to provide students with the best possible technical and instructional services. With a 5:1 student-computer ratio, Menlo College offers students ample access to a wide range of computing resources for both classroom assignments and personal use.

Costs

Tuition and fees for 2010–11 were $33,150. Residence costs, including room and board, were $11,330.

Financial Aid

Menlo is noted for a strong program of merit and need-based aid. Approximately 80 percent of Menlo's students enroll with financial assistance, including Menlo scholarships, achievement awards, and on-campus employment as well as Federal Pell Grants, Federal Stafford Student Loans, State of California Grants, Federal PLUS loans, and others. Students transferring to Menlo are fully eligible to be considered for financial aid. Merit scholarships of up to $13,000 per year are available for both domestic and international students.

Faculty

Menlo's faculty members devote their full attention to teaching. The College faculty is composed of approximately 60 members, both full- and part-time. Guest lecturers from business, industry, and other professions add to the breadth of instruction. Faculty members are readily available to give students personal help and counseling. A student-teacher ratio of 15:1 allows for small classes and individual attention to students' progress.

Student Government

Students elect their own representatives to student government, which is responsible for legislative and executive decisions affecting student activities and the coordination of student affairs. At Menlo, students take the lead in shaping their education and the future of their College.

Admission Requirements

The Admissions Committee considers each candidate individually, through the assessment of academic achievement and personal qualities, talents, and interests. There is an early action plan for entering freshmen, and transfer students are welcome. Applicants are evaluated on the basis of their academic record, course of study, personal recommendations, school activities, essay, and scores on either the SAT or ACT. A personal visit is strongly recommended but not required. The College looks for freshmen with both breadth and depth of academic background in college preparatory subjects. Transfer students are evaluated on the strength of their college programs. Applicants are considered without regard to age, race, color, creed, gender, sexual orientation, national origin, marital status, disability, or any other characteristic protected by law.

Application and Information

Students may enter Menlo College at the opening of the fall or spring semester. Application deadlines are: early action deadline, December 1; priority deadline for freshmen, February 1 for fall and November 1 for spring; and priority deadline for transfers, April 1. For further information concerning admission, students should contact:

Office of Admissions
Menlo College
1000 El Camino Real
Atherton, California 94027-4301
Phone: 650-543-3753
        800-55-MENLO (toll-free)
Fax: 650-543-4496
E-mail: admissions@menlo.edu
Web site: http://www.menlo.edu

MEREDITH COLLEGE
RALEIGH, NORTH CAROLINA

The College

Meredith College, chartered in 1891, is today one of the largest independent private women's colleges in the United States. The College enrolls more than 2,100 undergraduate degree candidates, and the student-faculty ratio of 11:1 offers students individualized attention in all aspects of their experience at Meredith. With a focus on the liberal arts, students are encouraged in all areas from career preparation to personal development. Degree candidates choose from thirty-two majors and concentrations, including preprofessional studies.

The faculty is dedicated to teaching, advising, and challenging the students to meet their academic and personal goals. Undergraduate students pursue programs leading to Bachelor of Arts, Science, Music, and Social Work degrees; the College also offers Master of Business Administration, Master of Education, Master of Arts in Teaching, and Master of Science in nutrition degrees. College programs are accredited by the Southern Association of Colleges and Schools, the National Council for the Accreditation of Teacher Education, the Association to Advance Collegiate Schools of Business International (AACSB), the Council on Social Work Education, the Council for Interior Design Accreditation (formerly FIDER), and the National Association of Schools of Music. The College has an approved American Dietetic Association Plan V Program.

The College focuses heavily on leadership development for women. Students are encouraged to participate in a wide variety of campus activities, including performing groups, sports, publications, academic and personal interest clubs, and student government. More than 600 leadership positions are available for women to fill. Rich with diversity with students from thirty-five states and forty-two countries, Meredith celebrates its students' uniqueness and potential to return to their communities as active participants in whatever capacity that they choose. A member of NCAA Division III, Meredith fields intercollegiate teams in six sports: basketball, cross-country, softball, soccer, tennis, and volleyball. The College joined the USA South Athletic Conference in 2007.

Location

Meredith's beautiful 225-acre campus is on the western edge of Raleigh, North Carolina's capital city, and is adjacent to the booming Research Triangle area of Raleigh, Durham, and Chapel Hill. A total of eleven colleges and universities that serve approximately 108,000 students can be found here. Raleigh, a city of 350,000 people, is centrally located between the North Carolina coast and the mountain ranges of the western part of the state. Two interstates and the Raleigh-Durham International Airport (15 minutes from the campus) make Raleigh easily accessible.

Majors and Degrees

Meredith confers four baccalaureate degrees. A candidate for the Bachelor of Arts degree can select her major from art, biology, chemistry, communication, dance, economics, English, environmental studies, history, international studies, mathematics, music, political science, psychology, religion, sociology, Spanish, and theater. The Bachelor of Science degree is available in accounting, biology, business administration, chemistry, child development, computer information systems, computer science, exercise and sports science, family and consumer science, fashion merchandising and design, foods and nutrition, interior design, and mathematics. The Bachelor of Music degree candidate can major in music education or performance. The Bachelor of Social Work degree is available in social work. In addition, a student may work with the faculty to create a self-designed major.

Licensure programs taken in addition to a major are offered in birth to kindergarten (B–K), elementary (K–6), middle grades (6–9), secondary (9–12), and special subject areas (K–12).

Preprofessional preparation is available in dentistry, law, medicine, pharmacy, physical therapy, physician assistant studies, and veterinary medicine. Minors are offered in most major fields and in some other areas, such as communication, criminal justice, ethics, philosophy, and physical education. Concentrations are also available within most departments. A five-year dual-degree program with North Carolina State University is available in engineering.

Academic Programs

Meredith's academic program blends a strong liberal arts foundation with opportunities for career and preprofessional preparation. To achieve breadth in her education, each student must fulfill general education requirements in humanities and arts, social and behavioral sciences, mathematics and natural sciences, and health and physical education. By the end of her sophomore year, she declares a major and begins to study her chosen field in depth. She may round out her program by completing options such as a second major, a minor or a concentration, a teacher education program, an experiential learning component (an internship, co-op, or fieldwork), or a study-abroad program.

There are opportunities for advanced placement with credit for those who show by examination (AP, I.B., CLEP, and/or departmental examinations) that they have mastered the material for any college-level course. Each year approximately 45 entering students are invited to participate in the Honors Program. Nearly 30 entering students participate in the Teaching Fellows Program, which provides special seminars, mentors, honors classes, and cultural opportunities for the winners of the prestigious North Carolina Teaching Fellows Scholarship/Loan.

Off-Campus Programs

Through the Cooperating Raleigh Colleges consortium, students may take courses with typically no extra cost at North Carolina State and Shaw Universities and at Peace and St. Augustine's Colleges.

Women who are interested in expanding their international horizons can participate in either summer or academic-year intercultural programs in almost any country. Every summer, students and faculty members travel to England, Italy, and Switzerland for five or eleven weeks of study. It is possible to earn an entire semester of credit through this summer study at approximately the same price as a regular semester on campus in Raleigh. Meredith's newest study abroad program is a semester-long program in Sansepolcro, Italy. Those seeking a less traditional venue can work with the Office of Study Abroad to find a program appropriate to their academic or travel interests. Recent study abroad locations include Denmark, Iceland, Costa Rica, Kenya, and Morocco.

Students may take advantage of opportunities within the United States by completing a United Nations Semester at Drew University, a federal government semester through the Washington Semester program at American University, a semester at Marymount College in New York City, and a capital city semester in state government through Meredith's own program in Raleigh.

Academic Facilities

The Carlyle Campbell Library contains more than 190,000 volumes, 16,000 microforms, and over 3,000 newspaper and journal subscriptions with access to articles from more than 27,000 journals, magazines, and newspapers online. As part of its academic department facilities, the campus also houses a music library, art galleries, a research greenhouse, music practice rooms, a state-of-the-art language lab, an autism lab, computer labs, a child-care lab, an indoor swimming pool, lighted outdoor tennis courts, a putting green, a soccer field, and track. The campus is also cabled to provide network and e-mail access in classrooms, computer labs, and residence halls as well as wireless Internet access throughout much of the campus.

Costs

For 2010–11, tuition and fees were $26,200, and room and board were $7500.

Financial Aid

Meredith's financial aid program is designed to meet a high percentage of the analyzed need of the student. Approximately 65 percent of undergraduate students receive need-based assistance; when competitive scholarships and state entitlement grants are added, over 95 percent of Meredith students receive some form of financial assistance. The Free Application for Federal Student Aid (FAFSA) is used to determine eligibility for need-based federal, state, and institutional funds that include grants and scholarships, loans, and work-study. A freshman candidate may also file special application forms for the competitive scholarships that recognize students for superior academic ability and talent in art, music, or interior design. A North Carolina Teaching Fellow who is selected for Meredith's program may use her scholarship at the College and will have other gift assistance coordinated to match the stipend provided by the state.

Faculty

The College has 138 full-time faculty members. Ninety percent of the full-time faculty members have earned terminal degrees. The student-faculty ratio is 11:1, and the average class size is 17. Sixty-six percent of the full-time faculty members are women.

Student Government

Meredith has one of the oldest student government associations in the South and has an honor code that is a key ingredient of the Meredith community. All students assume primary responsibility for making and enforcing regulations; therefore, every student is a member of the Student Government Association (SGA). As members, students are encouraged to actively participate in branches of the SGA, such as the Association for Meredith Commuters, Elections Board, Honor Council, Residence Hall Board, Senate, Student Life, and Women in New Goal Settings.

Admission Requirements

Along with academic achievement, Meredith values individuality, integrity, and diversity. Each application is evaluated to determine how the student's academic preparation and ability match Meredith's requirements and challenges and to assess motivation, special talents, and commitment to learning. A freshman candidate is expected to have at least 16 units of academic credit earned in grades 9–12. Her program should include English (4 units), history/social studies (3 units), mathematics (3 units in algebra I, algebra II, and geometry or a higher level course), science (3 units), foreign language (2 units), and electives (1 unit from the academic subjects). Careful attention is given to an unweighted grade point average on the academic subjects and to class rank; test scores (SAT or ACT) are reviewed in relation to the high school record; recommendations from a school official and a teacher are also required. Applicants must also complete an essay of at least 250 words on a topic of their choice. An interview may be requested in some instances, and students are encouraged to visit for an admissions conference and campus tour.

For transfer admission from an accredited college or university, the student needs at least an overall C average in transferable courses, must be eligible to return to the last institution regularly attended, and must be recommended by college officials. If the student has fewer than 30 semester hours of transferable work, she must also meet Meredith's freshman admission requirements.

International students must also provide proof of English proficiency (if English is not their first language) via the TOEFL or IELTS exams. Results of national or external exams must be provided, along with original transcripts from any secondary and postsecondary institutions attended. If the student is receiving secondary instruction in English, they must also submit results from either the SAT or the ACT. Recommendations from a school counselor and academic teacher are also required, in addition to an essay.

International applicants are encouraged to meet the same 16 academic unit requirements as domestic applicants, as their curriculum allows.

Nontraditional age students are also welcome at Meredith College. Any prospective student of age 23 or older is encouraged to contact the Office of Admissions to learn about Meredith's conditional admissions program.

Application and Information

An application for admission should be sent to the Office of Admissions along with a nonrefundable $40 processing fee (or acceptable fee-waiver request). The student is responsible for requesting that her official high school transcript, SAT or ACT scores, and recommendations be sent to the Admissions Office. A transfer student must submit an official transcript from each postsecondary institution attended.

Meredith has two freshman admission plans: early decision and rolling admission. An early decision candidate must apply by October 30; this "first choice" plan means that if accepted under early decision, the student fully expects to enroll and will withdraw any other pending applications. The student is notified by November 15. A candidate under the rolling plan is encouraged to file early in the senior year, with February 15 as the recommended deadline. Notifications under this plan begin in mid-November. The candidates' reply dates are December 15 for early decision and May 1 for rolling admission candidates.

Transfer applicants are encouraged to apply by February 15. Notifications begin in late January, and May 1 is the candidates' reply date. For admission to the spring semester, a freshman or transfer student should apply by December 1.

For additional information and for planning a campus visit, students should visit http://www.meredith.edu/admissions or contact the College by e-mail at admissions@meredith.edu or by phone at 800-MEREDITH (toll-free).

Office of Admissions
Meredith College
3800 Hillsborough Street
Raleigh, North Carolina 27607-5298
Phone: 919-760-8581
       800-MEREDITH (toll-free)
Fax: 919-760-2348
E-mail: admissions@meredith.edu
Web site: http://www.meredith.edu
       http://www.facebook.com/MeredithAdmissions
       http://twitter.com/meredithcollege

Meredith College's beautiful 225-acre campus is located on the edge of North Carolina's capital city near urban activity and eleven other colleges and universities.

MESSIAH COLLEGE

GRANTHAM, PENNSYLVANIA

The College

Sharpening intellect, deepening faith, and inspiring action—since 1909, this has been Messiah College's goal for its students. Messiah College is an independent, nationally ranked, private Christian college with a socially, denominationally, and politically diverse undergraduate student body.

There are approximately 2,800 undergraduate students attending Messiah from thirty-seven U.S. states and thirty other countries. Nearly 8 percent of students are from underrepresented racial, ethnic, and cultural populations and 2.6 percent are international students. Messiah has a distinctive residential atmosphere and a strong sense of community; 88 percent of students live on campus.

Messiah College competes in twenty-two intercollegiate sports and maintains one of the most successful NCAA Division III athletics programs in the nation—gomessiah.com. Messiah athletic teams have garnered twelve national championships and regularly achieve national rankings and conference titles. Messiah athletes have been recognized as all-Americans and have featured in *Sports Illustrated, USA Today*, and on national network television. Several coaches have received national coaching awards.

Messiah students participate in more than sixty student groups and organizations, including theater and music groups, a campus newspaper, and a student-operated radio station. The College's Student Government Association (SGA) represents the student body and develops students' leadership skills.

Students have many opportunities to grow in faith and fellowship at Messiah College, including chapel and worship services, discipleship groups, ministry outreach teams, community service, mission trips, and a variety of other special programs. In April 2008, Messiah College was selected to host "The Compassion Forum," an unprecedented, nationally televised conversation with presidential candidates speaking on the integration of faith and public policy.

The College has been widely recognized for its commitment to service-learning and civic engagement, and teaches students to engage their Christian faith to build community, to serve as agents for peace and reconciliation, and to champion the rights of the poor and the dispossessed. In 2009, Messiah was named to the President's Higher Education Community Service Honor Roll, a distinction granted to only seven colleges in Pennsylvania. The College's service-learning program was nationally recognized by *U.S. News & World Report* as a 2010 "Program to Look For;" and in 2008, the College was awarded the Carnegie Foundation's prestigious Community Engagement Classification for curricular engagement and outreach and partnership. Opportunities for community engagement at Messiah include the College's Agapé Center for Service and Learning, Collaboratory for Strategic Partnerships and Applied Research, Harrisburg Institute, Philadelphia campus, Ernest L. Boyer Center, Center for Public Humanities, School of the Arts, and Oakes Museum.

The College offers both traditional residence halls and apartment-style residences on campus (http://www.messiah.edu/offices/residence_life/index.html). Staffed by trained, full-time professional Residence Directors, student Assistant Residence Directors, and Student Resident Assistants, these facilities provide an environment that fosters personal growth and responsibility as students experience living in an intentional Christian community.

All residence halls offer carpeting, air conditioning, cable television, Internet, and laundry facilities. Messiah does not have any fraternities or sororities at either the national or the local level.

The College operates a number of campus safety services for students (http://www.messiah.edu/offices/safety/department_services.html), such as an after-hours transport and accompaniment service; 24-hour emergency telephone alarm devices; a 24-hour, unarmed, professional security patrol; and student security patrols. In addition, all entrances to the residence halls are electronically operated. A crisis management and response team, emergency text-messaging system, and emergency evacuation plan are also in place on the campus.

Location

Messiah College, named a 2008 Green College by the National Association of Independent Colleges and Universities, is situated on 471 scenic wooded acres, just 12 miles from Harrisburg, Pennsylvania's capital. The College is approximately 2 hours from the major urban centers of Philadelphia, Baltimore, and Washington, D.C. There are many recreational and outdoor activities in the immediate vicinity, including the Yellow Breeches Creek, which flows through the campus, the nearby Susquehanna River, and the Appalachian Trail. The College also operates a satellite campus in Philadelphia in conjunction with Temple University.

Majors and Degrees

Messiah College awards Bachelor of Arts and Bachelor of Science degrees in more than fifty-five academic majors. It also offers six preprofessional programs and several graduate programs (http://www.messiah.edu/academics/graduate_studies/). Teacher certification is also available in many disciplines. Students must complete 123 units to graduate, except as noted in the requirements for selected majors. In addition to courses required by their major field, all students must complete core general educational requirements that include writing and oral communication, the arts and sciences, language and culture, Christian faith, social responsibility, and physical education. Students fulfill the remaining required units through elective courses.

Academic Programs

The College operates on a two-semester academic calendar, with a January term between the fall and spring terms. During January term, students take one intensive, three-week course of study with transcultural travel programs among the innovative courses offered during this term. A three-week May term immediately follows the spring term and is exclusively for cross-cultural studies.

Messiah's Internship Center (http://www.messiah.edu/external_programs/internship/index.html) is nationally recognized for excellence in training students for today's workforce. Messiah's Internship Center has been instrumental in the consistently high post-graduation placement rate of graduates.

Off-Campus Programs

Messiah offers study-abroad opportunities in more than 40 countries and is nationally ranked by the Institute of International Education among institutions sending students to study abroad. Qualified students may also participate in the Honors Program or design an individual major or an independent study program. Many students also participate in a variety of local, regional, and international service-learning programs and internships.

Academic Facilities

Messiah's outstanding academic facilities include Murray Library, a research library with more than 300,000 volumes (http://www.messiah.edu/murraylibrary); the Jordan Science Center, a state-of-the-art science facility providing technically advanced science laboratories and equipment as well as housing the College's Oakes Museum of Natural History that includes a unique treasury of large mammal, insect, seashell, and bird egg collections; Frey Hall, primarily an engineering, mathematics, and business building with engineering and physics labs, but also housing a variety of art studios; Climenhaga Fine Arts Center, complete with a 400-seat performance auditorium, a recital hall, and an art gallery; and Boyer Hall, a state-of-the-art academic facility that opened in 2003.

Students have access to hundreds of computers in general computer labs conveniently located across campus, as well as computers in department labs. All student rooms on campus are set up for both wired and wireless access to the campus network. In addition, wireless connections to the campus network are available in all major campus buildings and all academic halls.

Athletic and recreational facilities include the 90,000-square-foot Sollenberger Sports Center with an indoor track, wrestling and gymnastics areas, a natatorium including an eight-lane pool with separate diving well, racquetball and basketball courts, and exercise and fitness equipment; and the Starry Athletic Complex with a lighted artificial turf field for field hockey and lacrosse, lighted soccer stadium, eight-lane all-weather track, ten tennis courts, baseball and softball fields, and practice field space.

Costs

Messiah College is ranked third in its region in *U.S. News & World Report's* listing of "Great Schools at a Great Price." For the 2010–11 academic year, tuition was $26,680, room and board averaged $8240, and average basic fees were $800 (http://www.messiah.edu/admissions/financial_aid/).

Financial Aid

In 2006, the College announced an initiative to raise an additional $20 million in financial aid in five years. The percentage of first-year students receiving financial aid in the 2009–10 academic year was 100 percent. The average first-year student aid package for fall 2009 was $23,118 (http://www.messiah.edu/admissions/financial_aid/big_difference.html).

Faculty

Messiah College selects its educators for their Christian commitment as well as their proven teaching ability. They are practicing Christians who serve as role models for integrating a life of faith with intellectual pursuits. Every Messiah professor signs a statement of faith as an indication of his or her commitment to the mission of the College.

Messiah professors are also dedicated scholars and accomplished professionals, who have been educated at top universities all over the world. Eighty-one percent of the College's 170 full-time faculty members have earned the terminal degree in their field.

Messiah professors are often sought after by local, regional, and national journalists for their commentary, insight, and expertise. They are not only experts in their fields, but also accomplished scholars, who regularly author or publish many works.

All classes at Messiah College are taught by professors rather than teaching assistants. The student-to-faculty ratio at the College is 13:1.

Admission Requirements

Messiah seeks students with demonstrated academic promise who wish to share in the College's multidenominational, multicultural Christian community. Messiah encourages transfer, home-schooled, international, and minority students to apply. The College provides two methods for candidates to apply for admission: Standard Choice and Write Choice (http://www.messiah.edu/admissions/policies/).

Selective in its admission policy, the College considers academic achievement, extracurricular involvement, leadership skills, and Christian service. Thirty-four percent of the first year students in 2009–10 ranked in the top 10 percent of their high school class. Their average SAT composite score was 1145 and their average ACT score was 25. Within the past 12 years, Messiah has produced graduates who have distinguished themselves as Rhodes, Fulbright, Carnegie, and Truman scholars.

Application and Information

Messiah College operates on a rolling admission basis. The Admissions Office is open weekdays from 8 a.m. to 5 p.m. Appointments can be made Monday through Friday, and on some selected Saturdays by contacting the Visit Coordinator at 800-233-4220, by e-mail at visitmessiah@messiah.edu, online at http://www.messiah.edu/admissions/visit/visit_calendar.php, or via mobile app (http://www.messiah.edu/mobile/iMessiah/index.html). A two-week notice is suggested.

Office of Admissions
Box 3005
Messiah College
One College Avenue
Grantham, Pennsylvania 17027
Phone: 717-691-6000
      800-233-4220 (toll-free)
Fax: 717-691-2307
E-mail: admiss@messiah.edu
Web site: http://www.messiah.edu
     http://www.facebook.com/MessiahCollege
     http://twitter.com/messiahcollege

At Messiah College, Christian faith and intellect are intertwined, so students are equipped to see the world's realities in deeper ways and may bring a discerning spirit to all they do.

MIAMI INTERNATIONAL UNIVERSITY OF ART & DESIGN

MIAMI, FLORIDA

A focused education from Miami International University of Art & Design can help students turn their creative energy into a powerful tool that can make a difference in the world. Students are part of a collaborative and supportive community, where experienced instructors provide the guidance and skills needed to pursue a career in the creative economy.

The school's programs in the areas of design, media arts, and fashion give students the opportunity to learn by using professional-grade technology and build a portfolio of work to show potential employers after graduation.

Miami International University of Art & Design and its branch campuses, The Art Institute of Jacksonville and The Art Institute of Tampa, are accredited by the Commission on Colleges of the Southern Association of Colleges and Schools to award diplomas and associate, baccalaureate, and master's degrees. Contact the Commission on Colleges at 1866 Southern Lane, Decatur, Georgia 30033-4097 or call 404-679-4500 for questions about the accreditation of Miami International University of Art & Design.

Miami International University of Art & Design is licensed by the Commission for Independent Education, Florida Department of Education. Additional information regarding this institution may be obtained by contacting the commission at 325 West Gaines Street, Suite 1414, Tallahassee, Florida 32399-0400; phone: 888-224-6684 (toll-free).

The interior design program leading to the Bachelor of Fine Arts is accredited by the Council for Interior Design Accreditation, 206 Grandville Avenue, Suite 350, Grand Rapids, Michigan 49503; http://www.accredit-id.org.

Location

Miami is a culturally rich region that celebrates events year-round, including the African-American Heritage Festival, Haitian Heritage Week, the Viva Mexico Celebration, the Israel Independence Celebration, and Asian Cultural Week. The city is home to professional sports teams, and residents enjoy the sandy beaches, international cuisine, local clubs, the historic Art Deco District, Coral Gables, and Key Biscayne. The Florida Keys, Disney World, and the Bahamas are all just a short trip away.

Programs of Study and Degrees

No matter which course of study a student may choose, the professionals at Miami International University of Art & Design will guide, support, and help each student as their talents evolve on their journey of personal and professional transformation. Students studying design learn to fine-tune their visual thinking and problem-solving skills, as they create everything from logos to TV ads. Programs in the area of media arts focus on utilizing technology to deliver information and entertainment, while students studying fashion learn to design clothes for the runway or run a retail shop.

Bachelor's degree programs are available in advertising, audio production, computer animation, fashion design, fashion merchandising, film and digital production, graphic design, interior design, photography, visual and entertainment arts, visual effects and motion graphics, and Web design and interactive media.

Associate degrees are available in accessory design, fashion design, and fashion merchandising.

Master's degree programs are offered in design and media management, film, graphic design, interior design, and visual arts.

Academic Programs

Miami International University of Art & Design operates on a year-round, quarterly basis. Each quarter totals eleven weeks. Bachelor's degree programs are twelve quarters in length.

Academic Facilities

Miami International University of Art & Design provides a learning environment with professional-grade technology applicable to each student's course of study. Students have the opportunity to build a portfolio of work that shows potential employers that they are trained to use the software, hardware, or equipment utilized within the industry. Depending upon the course of study, students are immersed in a creative environment—from classrooms to computer labs to studios—focused on relevant, hands-on education designed to prepare students for the real world.

Costs

Tuition cost varies by program. Prospective students should contact the school for current tuition costs. Other charges include a starting kit for all first-quarter students. Kits vary in price, depending on the program of study.

Financial Aid

Financial aid is available for those who qualify. Students who require financial assistance should first complete and submit a Free Application for Federal Student Aid (FAFSA) and meet with a financial aid officer.

Faculty

Faculty members are experienced professionals who create a learning environment that is similar to the professional world students will face after graduation. Instructors are focused on

helping students develop the skills they need to transform their creative potential into marketable skills.

Admission Requirements

Applicants must provide proof of high school graduation or achievement of a General Educational Development (GED) certificate as a prerequisite for admission. In lieu of documenting high school graduation or a GED certificate, applicants may provide proof of attaining an associate degree or higher from an accredited institution. An official transcript indicating date of high school graduation, GED certificate (including test scores), or date of college graduation (including degree granted) is required as proof.

All individuals seeking admission to the school are interviewed in person or by phone by an assistant director of admissions, and each applicant must create an original essay of at least 150 words stating how an education at Miami International University of Art & Design would help the student to achieve career goals. There is a $50 application fee.

For the most recent information regarding admission requirements, please refer to the current academic catalog.

Application and Information

To obtain an application, arrange for an interview, or tour the school, prospective students should contact:

Miami International University of Art & Design
1501 Biscayne Boulevard, Suite 100
Miami, Florida 33132-1418
Phone: 305-428-5700
        800-225-9023 (toll-free)
Fax: 305-374-5933
Web site: http://www.artinstitutes.edu/miami

The Art Institute of Atlanta; The Art Institute of Atlanta–Decatur[1]; The Art Institute of Austin[2]; The Art Institute of California–Hollywood; The Art Institute of California–Inland Empire; The Art Institute of California–Los Angeles; The Art Institute of California–Orange County; The Art Institute of California–Sacramento; The Art Institute of California–San Diego; The Art Institute of California–San Francisco; The Art Institute of California–Sunnyvale; The Art Institute of Charleston[1]; The Art Institute of Charlotte; The Art Institute of Colorado; The Art Institute of Dallas[3]; The Art Institute of Fort Lauderdale; The Art Institute of Fort Worth[3]; The Art Institute of Houston; The Art Institute of Houston–North[2]; The Art Institute of Indianapolis[4]; The Art Institute of Jacksonville[5]; The Art Institute of Las Vegas; The Art Institute of Michigan; The Art Institute of New York City; The Art Institute of Ohio–Cincinnati[6]; The Art Institute of Philadelphia; The Art Institute of Phoenix; The Art Institute of Pittsburgh; The Art Institute of Portland; The Art Institute of Raleigh–Durham; The Art Institute of Salt Lake City; The Art Institute of San Antonio[2];The Art Institute of Seattle; The Art Institute of Tampa[5]; The Art Institute of Tennessee–Nashville[1]; The Art Institute of Tucson; The Art Institute of Vancouver; The Art Institute of Virginia Beach[1,7]; The Art Institute of Washington[1,7]; The Art Institute of Washington–Northern Virginia[1,7]; The Art Institute of Wisconsin; The Art Institute of York–Pennsylvania; The Art Institutes International–Kansas City; The Art Institutes International Minnesota; The Illinois Institute of Art–Chicago; The Illinois Institute of Art–Schaumburg; The Illinois Institute of Art–Tinley Park; Miami International University of Art & Design; The New England Institute of Art.

[1]A branch of The Art Institute of Atlanta
[2]A branch of The Art Institute of Houston
[3]A campus of South University
[4]The Art Institute of Indianapolis is regulated by the Indiana Commission on Proprietary Education, 302 West Washington Street, Room E201, Indianapolis, Indiana 46204, AC-0080
[5]A branch of Miami International University of Art & Design
[6]The Art Institute of Ohio–Cincinnati, 8845 Governors Hill Drive, Suite 100, Cincinnati, Ohio 45249-3317, OH Reg. #04-01-1698B
[7]Certified by the State Council of Higher Education to operate in Virginia

MICHIGAN TECHNOLOGICAL UNIVERSITY

HOUGHTON, MICHIGAN

Michigan Tech
Create the Future

The University

Michigan Technological University students create the future in engineering; forest resources; computing; technology; business; economics; natural, physical and environmental sciences; arts; humanities; and social sciences.

Approximately 7,000 students from all fifty states and more than eighty nations enjoy beautiful Upper Michigan while pursuing associate, bachelor's, master's, and Ph.D. degrees. Michigan Tech is ranked in the top tier of national universities, according to the *U.S. News & World Report*'s America's Best Colleges 2011. Tech is also rated highly for academics, career preparation, and quality of life in the Princeton Review's *Best 373 Colleges, 2011 Edition.* The University is also cited by the Princeton Review for its great athletic facilities and good town-gown relations, and Michigan Tech's excellent academics are reflected in student comments: the University "offers a real hands-on learning experience, not only in the classroom but in life." Students from many majors work together on real-world industry projects as part of the Enterprise program, from video games and nanosatellites to forest management and the EcoCAR challenge. Michigan Tech has one of the nation's largest programs in scientific and technical communication and has top-ten enrollments in environmental and mechanical engineering programs.

The latest improvements to the campus include Hillside Place, a new apartment complex for upperclassmen and, on the lakefront adjacent to campus, a new $25-million Great Lakes Research Center is being built, including aquatic laboratories, a hydraulics lab, coastal research instrumentation, boathouse, and offices and conference rooms in order to provide a home for interdisciplinary research and education related to the Great Lakes.

More than 57 percent of students are enrolled in the College of Engineering. The College of Sciences and Arts (CSA) accounts for 24.5 percent; Graduate School, 17.8 percent; the School of Business and Economics, 6.7 percent; the School of Technology, 5.2 percent; and the School of Forest Resources and Environmental Science, 4 percent. Overall enrollment has remained steady, and while students gain access to the latest theories, equipment, and scholarship, they work closely with faculty members who are acknowledged leaders in their fields.

Michigan Tech is accredited by the North Central Association of Colleges and Schools. Engineering programs are accredited by the Engineering Accreditation Commission of the Accreditation Board for Engineering and Technology (ABET), Inc.; technology programs are accredited by the Technology Accreditation Commission of ABET; and the surveying program is accredited by the Related Accreditation Commission of ABET. The forestry program is accredited by the Society of American Foresters, the chemistry program offers American Chemical Society–approved options, and the secondary teacher certification programs are approved by the Michigan Board of Education. The School of Business and Economics is accredited by AACSB International–The Association to Advance Collegiate Schools of Business. Only about 400 U.S. business programs have earned this distinction.

Residence halls are close to classrooms and well connected. They feature ultrafast Ethernet lines, and wireless zones abound across the campus. Residence halls also feature Finnish saunas, cable TV, lounges, and weight-lifting and laundry facilities. First-year students must live in the residence halls; they can choose from numerous meal plan and food options and eat at the cafeterias in Wadsworth, McNair, or Douglass Houghton Halls. Some cafeterias are open later, especially during exam weeks, and students can also eat, relax, and study at the Memorial Union Building (MUB), the center of campus life and home to many student organization offices and the bookstore. Guides to off-campus housing are available.

In athletics, the hockey Huskies have been national champions three times and compete in the Western Collegiate Hockey Association, which has produced more NCAA Division I National Champions than any other conference. Football, men's and women's basketball, tennis, cross-country, track, and women's soccer and volleyball teams compete in the Division II Great Lakes Intercollegiate Athletic Conference against teams from Michigan, Wisconsin, Ohio, Pennsylvania, Indiana, and Illinois. The men's and women's basketball teams have been rated number one in NCAA Division II, and the football team has hosted an NCAA Division II playoff game.

Most Michigan Tech students compete in intramural sports in everything from ultimate Frisbee and wrestling to water polo and floor hockey. Club sports include lacrosse, women's hockey, and paintball. The biggest game on campus, however, is broomball, where students slide around on ice and hit a large rubber ball using a broom. The Student Development Complex includes a health center, swimming and diving pools, two gyms (one with a running track), a rifle range, an ice arena, a weight room, and more. Little Huskies Child Development Center is located nearby.

Traditions include K-Day, which is an afternoon to enjoy McLain State Park on the shores of Lake Superior. The Parade of Nations is a celebration of the eighty nations of the world that have students, faculty, and staff members at Michigan Tech. At homecoming, students dress in their worst attire and parade through the campus in autos that barely run. During homecoming weekend, students enjoy a football game and other special activities. The biggest event is Winter Carnival, when massive snow statues emerge on campus and in the towns. Skits, queen competitions, first-class entertainment, ice hockey, and tourists everywhere make this a great experience. Before finals, students take a break for Spring Fling and celebrate with games, food booths, music, and more.

The student-run newspaper, the *Lode,* has won national and state awards, and the campus radio station, WMTU, is completely staffed by students.

Location

Michigan Tech is situated on the Keweenaw Waterway in the hills of Houghton, a friendly, safe environment. The area offers abundant opportunities for outdoor recreation, including the University's own ski hill; cross-country skiing, running, and biking trails; and golf course. A waterfront jogging and biking trail cuts through the campus. Houghton is about 4 hours' drive from Green Bay and Duluth, 7 hours from Minneapolis, and 10 hours from Detroit. The Houghton County Memorial Airport has daily flights to Chicago that connect to other major cities; bus service to Houghton is also available.

Majors and Degrees

The School of Technology awards Bachelor of Science degrees in computer network and system administration, construction management, electrical engineering technology, industrial technology, mechanical engineering technology, and surveying engineering.

The College of Engineering offers Bachelor of Science degrees in applied geophysics, biomedical engineering, chemical engineering, civil engineering, computer engineering, electrical engineering, engineering (mechanical design or manufacturing), environmental engineering, geological engineering, geology, materials science and engineering, and mechanical engineering.

The School of Business and Economics awards Bachelor of Science degrees in accounting, economics, finance, management, management information systems, marketing, and operations and systems management.

The School of Forest Resources and Environmental Science awards Bachelor of Science degrees in applied ecology and environmental sciences, forestry, and wildlife ecology and management.

The College of Sciences and Arts awards Bachelor of Science degrees in anthropology, applied physics, audio production and technology, biochemistry and molecular biology, bioinformatics, biological sciences, cheminformatics, chemistry, clinical laboratory science, communication and cultural studies, computer science, computer systems science, exercise science, health and physical education, mathematics, pharmaceutical chemistry, physics, preprofessional programs (medicine, dentistry, pharmacy, and law), psychology, scientific and technical communication, social sciences, software engineering, and theater and entertainment technology. The CSA awards the

Bachelor of Arts degree in communication and culture studies, liberal arts, scientific and technical communication, sound design, theater and electronic media performance, and theater and entertainment technology. The College of Sciences and Arts also awards a two-year associate degree in humanities.

The secondary education program offers certification in biology, business education, chemistry, computer science, earth science, economics, English, mathematics, physics, social studies, and technology and design.

Michigan Tech offers certificate programs in design engineering, industrial forestry, international business, media, mine environmental engineering, modern language and area study, and writing. An advanced certificate in modern language and area study and a graduate certificate in sustainability are also offered.

Michigan Tech's minors are aerospace studies, American studies, applied geophysics, art, astrophysics, biochemistry, biological sciences, chemistry, communication studies, computer science, diversity studies, earth sciences, ecology, economics, electronic materials, engineered wood products, enterprise, environmental studies, ethics and philosophy, geological engineering, historical studies, international modern languages (French, German, or Spanish), international studies, journalism, law and society, manufacturing, mathematical sciences, microbiology, military arts and science, mineral processing, mining, modern languages (French, German, or Spanish), municipal engineering, music, nanoscale science and engineering, pharmaceutical chemistry, physics, plant biotechnology, plant sciences, polymer science and engineering, product design, psychology, remote sensing, social and behavioral studies, state of Michigan secondary teacher certification (see options above), structural materials, technical theater, and theater arts.

Academic Programs

Michigan Tech operates on a fifteen-week fall and spring semester system with three options available for summer: two 7-week tracks and one 14-week track. Typically, it takes 130 credits to graduate, but that varies by department. Students must also complete general education requirements to help develop fundamental scholastic habits of careful reading, communication, critical reasoning, and balanced analysis and argument; the habit of applying multi-disciplinary perspectives in interpretation, analysis, and creative problem solving; respect for diversity; awareness of complex contexts of their study and their work; and knowledge of a broad range of topics and disciplines complementary to the major. Some graduate courses are open to undergraduates with faculty approval. The International Programs and Services Office helps international students adjust to life in Houghton. Nearly 1,000 students come from approximately eighty other nations to study at Michigan Tech. Students may also study abroad in one of thirty nations, improving their global perspective.

Off-Campus Programs

The Career Center works with more than 200 industries, businesses, and organizations to help students find co-op, internship, and summer employment opportunities. Job fairs are held on campus and in the region. Co-op assignments earn academic credits; internships do not. Students average seven job interviews before they graduate.

Academic Facilities

The J. R. Van Pelt and John and Ruanne Opie Library contains more than 800,000 volumes and regularly receives approximately 10,000 serials and periodicals. The library is a designated depository for official international, U.S. government, and Michigan state documents and for the U.S. Army Map Service. The archives maintain a collection of original materials concerning the history of the Keweenaw region, including the records of various copper-mining companies. The Rozsa Center for the Performing Arts is within walking distance of all residence halls and features nationally known lecturers, musicians, comedians, and theatrical performers as well as Michigan Tech's own productions. The A. E. Seaman Mineral Museum, the official "Mineralogical Museum of Michigan," is the home of one of the nation's premier collections of crystals, minerals, and ores. The collection contains more than 30,000 specimens, including the world's finest display from Michigan's copper- and iron-mining districts.

Costs

Tuition is $11,175 for Michigan residents and $23,685 for out-of-state students for an academic year; room and board are $8462. Computing and other fees total approximately $1200; books and supplies are approximately $1200.

Financial Aid

Currently, 89 percent of Michigan Tech's students receive financial aid, totaling more than $78 million annually. Four kinds of assistance are available to Michigan Tech students, including scholarships, which are awarded on the basis of student potential and, in some cases, financial need; grants, which are provided by the federal or state government or by Michigan Tech and do not need to be repaid; student loans, in which the interest charged is below regular interest rates (payment of the interest and principal on need-based loans does not begin until after students leave Michigan Tech); and part-time employment, which consists of on-campus student employment opportunities. The financial aid process begins with filing an application for admission. Students should apply for admission by January 15 of the year in which they plan to enroll.

Faculty

Most of the 464 faculty members possess terminal degrees. Ninety-five percent of undergraduate classes are taught by faculty members, and the student-faculty ratio is 12:1. Faculty members at Michigan Tech balance teaching and research and have long been known for their student guidance.

Student Government

Undergraduate Student Government and the Graduate Student Council are the two agencies of student involvement in University governance. Fraternities and sororities maintain a strong presence on campus, and there are more than 180 student organizations, including academic/professional, ethnic/cultural, service, religious, sporting, governmental, media, and honor societies. It is a great way for students to get involved and gain teamwork and leadership experience.

Admission Requirements

Michigan Tech has a selective admissions policy. The University admits only those applicants who give definite evidence that they are qualified through education, academic capability, aptitudes, interests, and character to complete the University's requirements. Once students are accepted for admission, every effort is made by the faculty and staff members to help students realize their potential.

Application and Information

Applications received by January 15 are given priority consideration for admission and merit-based scholarships. Undergraduate and graduate applications are free. First-year applicants are required to submit official ACT or SAT test scores. An information page must also be completed by a high school counselor or principal and sent to the admissions office with an official high school transcript. Transfer students must have official college transcripts sent directly to Michigan Tech. An official high school transcript and ACT/SAT scores may also be required. International students should contact the International Programs and Services office. Following acceptance, students receive a packet containing information regarding on-campus housing and various University deadlines.

Admissions Office
Michigan Technological University
1400 Townsend Drive
Houghton, Michigan 49931-1295
Phone: 888-688-1885 (toll-free)
Web site: http://admissions.mtu.edu

Overlooking the campus of Michigan Tech.

MIDAMERICA NAZARENE UNIVERSITY

OLATHE, KANSAS

The University

MidAmerica Nazarene University (MNU) is a comprehensive liberal arts university of approximately 1,700 students. MNU provides a personal environment where students gain broad-based knowledge and skills that can serve them professionally and personally throughout their lives.

Learning to live one's faith and having the chance to excel academically are integral aspects of the MNU experience. Revitalizing one's spirit, engaging in a premier academic experience, and building deep and lasting relationships are other important objectives at MNU.

The University offers forty undergraduate academic majors including degree-completion programs in management and human relations and public administration, a baccalaureate degree affiliation with European Nazarene College in Germany, and several graduate-level programs in nursing, education, business, and counseling. For more information on MNU's academic programs, visit http://www.mnu.edu.

MNU is accredited by the Commission on Institutions of Higher Education of the North Central Association of Colleges and Schools and is a member of the Council for Christian Colleges and Universities. The University also holds prestigious national accreditations in the School of Nursing and the School of Counseling and Education.

Residence halls at MNU are meant to provide more than a place for sleep and studies—they also provide an environment for personal growth. MNU believes that the learning that takes place outside the classroom is of equal value to that within the classroom. Each residence hall has a lobby or shared lobby where students can meet to study, watch television, or just hang out with friends. Each room is equipped for phone, cable television, and Internet service. Several of MNU's residence halls offer suite-style living options for up to six students.

There is always something happening at MNU. From spontaneous games of Frisbee on the University mall or hanging out with friends at the campus coffee shop, students enjoy a fun and active life through dozens of campuswide events. Special events include Spirit Week, Homecoming, Mock Rock, and Late Night Skates. With more than a dozen clubs and ministries, eight varsity sports teams, intramurals, an on-campus coffee bar, and more, there is always something to do on campus.

MNU is a member of the NAIA and the NCCAA. Scholarships are available in men's baseball and football; women's softball and volleyball; and men's and women's basketball, cheerleading, and soccer. Intramural sports include basketball, football, soccer, softball, table tennis, Ultimate (Frisbee), and volleyball. Detailed information about MNU's athletic programs can be found at http://www.mnusports.com.

Location

MidAmerica Nazarene University is located in Olathe, Kansas, a residential community of approximately 125,000 located 20 minutes from the heart of Kansas City, with all the cultural advantages of a major metropolitan area. Olathe offers a lifestyle of exceptional quality. The city's school district and health-care system are routinely recognized among the best in the nation. Outdoor recreation offers a variety of activities, including running, jogging, bicycling, fishing, boating, team sports, and just relaxing. The Olathe area is popular for hot-air ballooning and sailboarding. Olathe has two public lakes—Olathe Lake, with 172 acres of water surface, and Cedar Lake, with 45 acres. The proximity to downtown Kansas City provides internship opportunities in the areas of business, technology, and health care.

Majors and Degrees

Students can earn an Associate of Arts (A.A.) degree in general business, liberal arts, or music ministry.

The Bachelor of Arts (B.A.) degree is available in accounting, athletic training, the Bible and theology, biology, biology education, business administration, business education, chemistry, communication/business, computer, criminal justice, elementary education, English, English language arts education, forensic chemistry, graphic design, history, history and government education, international business, kinesiology, marketing, mass communication, mathematics, mathematics education, ministry, missions, music (applied pedagogy, music ministry, and music performance), music ministry, organizational leadership, physical education, psychology, secondary education, sociology, sports management, and youth and family ministry.

MNU also offers the Bachelor of Music Education (B.M.Ed.) degree and the Bachelor of Science in Nursing (B.S.N.) degree.

Academic Programs

Academics at MNU ignite the student's passion for learning. But MNU graduates will be prepared for more than just the workplace or graduate school; they will be also develop socially, spiritually, and intellectually, to lead a complete and dynamic life.

Through a 1-hour freshman seminar course, students are provided with an introduction to the traditions of MNU to help them adjust to the challenges of the higher educational experience. The general education program at MidAmerica Nazarene University exposes students to certain facts, ideas, and values in an attempt to awaken them to their potential and to assist them in developing ways of recognizing and expressing truth through the academic disciplines. A major provides a program of study that enables students to investigate a subject area in considerable depth. The University also offers several graduate programs in areas of nursing, counseling, education, and business.

Off-Campus Programs

MNU is a member of the Council for Christian Colleges and Universities (CCCU), a national association of more than 100 Christian colleges and universities of the liberal arts and sciences, which makes a number of off-campus learning opportunities available. Domestic programs are available in Washington, D.C.; Los Angeles; and Martha's Vineyard, Massachusetts. Students can also study abroad in China, Costa Rica, Egypt, Germany, Russia, and the United Kingdom.

Academic Facilities

The new 40,000-square-foot Bell Cultural Events Center features state-of-the-art practice, recital, and performance facilities for the fine arts division, as well as a black-box theater and 500-seat performance hall for music and drama productions. Osborne Hall houses the Division of Science and Mathematics, while Lunn Hall houses administrative offices. Dobson Hall contains an art studio and a graphic-design computer lab. The largest facility on campus, the 70,000-square-foot Cook Center, houses Bell Family Arena, two practice gyms, and the Sports Medicine and Athletics department offices. It is also home to MNU's Nursing and Health and Exercise Science departments. Metz Hall houses the Department of Behavioral Sciences, School of Business Administration, and School of Education and Counseling. One of several on-campus computer labs is also located in this facility. For a virtual tour of the MNU campus, visit http://www.mnu.edu/campus-virtual-tour.html.

Mabee Library and Learning Resource Center contains more than 481,000 volumes—360,000 in microforms and the balance in bound volumes. Mabee Library also houses a microcomputer laboratory for general use, the Ministry Resource Center, the Kresge Center, a multimedia room, the Teacher Education Resource Center, and the Marge Smith Archives. General science, educational media, business, computer science, reading and learning, and computation laboratories complement the class sessions and provide modern equipment.

Costs

For the 2010–11 academic year, the average total cost was $26,800. This includes block tuition of $19,250 (for 12–17 hours per semester) and all residential costs and meals (approximately $6750), as well as student fees.

Financial Aid

The perception that a private university isn't an affordable option is false—the truth is, any higher education requires a significant investment. But about 92 percent of students at MNU receive some form of financial aid. MNU scholarships are available and range between $1000 and full tuition per year. For all full undergraduates who enrolled in 2009–10, the average financial aid package—including grants, loans, and scholarships—totaled $19,539. Information and applications may be obtained from Student Financial Services at 913-971-3298 or https://www.mnu.edu/financial-aid-scholarships.html.

Faculty

MNU students receive personal attention from their instructors. It is not uncommon to find faculty members in residence hall rooms talking with students or even inviting students into their homes for Thanksgiving dinner. MNU faculty members have decades of real-world experience in many industries and fields.

Student Government

Associated Student Government exists to discover God's agenda as students serve God and the campus community. The government offers plenty of opportunities for students to get involved through many different campus activities and service-learning opportunities.

Admission Requirements

Prospective students should have graduated from an accredited high school and have completed the ACT or SAT exam. While the University does not require specific subjects for entrance, it does recommend that students complete 3 units of math, 4 units of English, 3 units of science, 3 units of social studies, and 1 unit of foreign language. Students over 18 who have not graduated from high school can submit GED scores.

Application and Information

Students must submit the completed application, the $25 nonrefundable application fee, official high school transcripts, ACT or SAT scores, a personal reference, and the housing, parent waiver, and health history forms provided by Admissions. International students must also submit TOEFL scores. The deadline for the fall semester is August 1; the spring semester deadline is December 15. For more information on how to apply to MNU, prospective students should visit https://www.mnu.edu/incoming-freshmen.html or contact:

MNU Admissions Team
MidAmerica Nazarene University
2030 East College Way
Olathe, Kansas 66062-1899

Phone: 913-971-3380
      800-800-8887 (toll-free)
E-mail: admissions@mnu.edu
Web site: http://www.mnu.edu
      http://on.fb.me/MNU_Admissions (Facebook)
      http://twitter.com/MNU_Admissions
      http://www.vimeo.com/choosemnu

MidAmerica Nazarene University offers over forty undergraduate and graduate degree programs in areas such as nursing, business, education, and counseling.

MILLERSVILLE UNIVERSITY OF PENNSYLVANIA

MILLERSVILLE, PENNSYLVANIA

Millersville University
SEIZE THE OPPORTUNITY

The University

Millersville University is the highest ranked public university in its class in Pennsylvania according to the *US News & World Report*. Millersville University offers a wide range of programs and a commitment to high-quality undergraduate instruction. Millersville's student body of approximately 8,300, including 7,200 undergraduates, is large enough for the University to offer a wide variety of programs. The University is small enough, however, to provide friendly service and individual attention. Students report that the relaxed, friendly campus atmosphere is one of the things they like best. The Millersville campus features a beautiful green and flowered landscape, a lake with resident swans, and clean, well-maintained facilities.

Millersville University was established more than 150 years ago, in 1855, as a normal school, the first one in Pennsylvania. It remained a teachers' college until 1962, when it was authorized to offer liberal arts degrees. It has been Millersville University of Pennsylvania since 1983.

The two reasons students most frequently cite for choosing Millersville are its excellent academic reputation and affordable tuition. The most popular majors are education, business administration, biology, psychology, English, and mathematics. Millersville's undergraduates are diverse; 1 in 8 students attends part-time, 14 percent are members of a racial/ethnic minority group, and 12 percent are more than 25 years old. Thirty-five percent of Millersville undergraduates are from Lancaster County, 60 percent from elsewhere in Pennsylvania, 5 percent from out of state, and 1 percent from other countries.

The University offers a wide range of intercollegiate varsity, intramural, and club sports; special interest clubs; fraternities and sororities; musical organizations; and publications. A broad program of cultural events is offered, with alcohol-free nightclubs particularly popular.

Thirty-five percent of undergraduates live in campus residence halls, with the rest commuting from home or living nearby. Coed dormitories and apartments are available for students. Freshmen and sophomores not commuting from home are required to live on campus. The possession, use, or sale of alcoholic beverages and illegal drugs is prohibited on the University campus. Smoking is prohibited in all academic and residential buildings on campus. Freshmen and sophomores living on campus are not permitted to have motor vehicles.

Special services provided for students include free tutoring, academic advisement, career planning and placement, personal counseling, health services, wellness activities, fee-for-service child care, and special facilities for commuters.

Location

Millersville, in the heart of Pennsylvania Dutch country, is 3 miles from Lancaster city, a growing metropolitan area. Lancaster County is an exceptionally friendly and beautiful area with a large number of stores, restaurants, theaters, parks, and tourist attractions. The campus is served by the area bus system, and Lancaster has train and air service.

Lancaster County is one of the fastest-growing counties in Pennsylvania and has one of the lowest unemployment rates in the state. The local economy is unusually sound and diverse. Sixty percent of Millersville graduates settle within the county.

Majors and Degrees

Millersville offers the Bachelor of Arts degree in anthropology, art, biology, chemistry, earth sciences, economics, English, French, geography, German, government and political affairs, history, international studies, mathematics, music, philosophy, physics, psychology, social work, sociology, and Spanish.

The Bachelor of Science degree is offered in biology, business administration, chemistry, communications and theater, computer science, earth sciences, geology, industrial technology, mathematics, meteorology, occupational safety and environmental health, oceanography, and physics.

The Bachelor of Science in Education degree with teaching certification is offered in art education, biology, chemistry, earth sciences, Pre-K–4 education, English, French, German, mathematics, middle level education, music education, physics, social studies, Spanish, and technology education.

The University also offers the Bachelor of Fine Arts degree in art, the Bachelor of Science in Nursing degree for RNs only, the Associate of Science degree in chemistry and in computer science, and the Associate of Technology degree in industrial technology.

Most majors offer several options that permit specialization, including accounting, finance, international business, management, and marketing in business. Students should refer to the Web site for a complete listing. More than thirty minors are offered along with 3-2 engineering programs for chemistry and physics majors. Special advisement is available for students interested in premedicine and prelaw.

Academic Programs

Millersville University places a strong emphasis on the liberal arts. Nearly half of the courses required for all its undergraduate degrees, including those with technical or professional majors, are in the liberal arts. This prepares students for a lifetime of learning and gives them a background in writing, speaking, analysis, and critical thinking across a broad range of subjects.

Millersville's baccalaureate degree programs have four common curricular elements: proficiency requirements in English composition and speech; the general education program, which constitutes about half the curriculum; the major field of study; and elective courses, if needed, to meet the minimum of 120 credits required for graduation. Within this framework, students have many choices in developing programs of study.

The general education program has requirements in writing, speaking, humanities, natural sciences and mathematics, social sciences, and interdisciplinary and/or multicultural study. There is also a health and physical education requirement.

Millersville offers a University Honors College, departmental honors programs, independent study, a pass/fail option, remedial courses, and special advisement to students who are undecided about a major.

The University operates on a 4-1-4 academic calendar with summer sessions.

Off-Campus Programs

An exchange agreement with Franklin and Marshall College allows Millersville students to take Franklin and Marshall courses not offered at Millersville. Cooperative education internships are available to students in most majors, and some majors offer or require specialized internships. Millersville has study-abroad programs in Australia, Chile, England, France, Germany, Ireland, Japan, Peru, Scotland, South Africa, and Spain. Qualified students who wish to study abroad elsewhere may do so through the University's cooperative arrangements with other colleges and universities.

Academic Facilities

Ganser Library houses more than 495,000 books and more than 558,000 other items and subscribes to more than 4,000 periodicals. Materials from other libraries are available through interlibrary loan. The library also houses computerized database-searching facilities, a curriculum center, a listening room, and archives.

Millersville's computing facilities support both PC and Macintosh platforms. There are 450 terminals and computers available in multiple computer labs across campus. On-campus access to the Internet is available for all faculty members and students. Wireless access is available in the library, the Student Center, and the cybercafé in Roddy Science Center.

Other University facilities include an extensive scientific instrumentation inventory, industry and technology laboratories, a variety of art studios and galleries, a large auditorium and a small theater, three gymnasiums, two swimming pools, radio and television production facilities, soundproof music practice modules, and a language laboratory.

Costs

Annual tuition and fees in 2010–11 were $7700 for Pennsylvania residents and $16,524 for out-of-state students. Annual room and board charges for 2010–11 were $8298. Students paid approximately $900 for books and incidentals.

Financial Aid

Approximately 82 percent of Millersville undergraduates receive financial aid through grants, scholarships, employment, and loans. Scholarships are available on the basis of academic performance. Federal Pell and Federal Supplemental Educational Opportunity grants and Pennsylvania Higher Education Assistance Agency (PHEAA) grants are awarded on the basis of need. Students may also qualify for Federal Perkins Loans and Federal Stafford Student Loans. On-campus and off-campus job opportunities are plentiful.

Students applying for a federal or state grant, Federal Work-Study, or a Federal Perkins Loan must complete the Free Application for Federal Student Aid. The forms are available from high school guidance offices, from the Financial Aid Office, or online at http://www.fafsa.ed.gov. Deadlines are given in the forms' instructions.

Faculty

Millersville University faculty members are dedicated to teaching and to offering individual attention. They take a personal interest in their students' lives and careers and are solely responsible for providing academic advisement. The University keeps a relatively low student-faculty ratio of 18:1 and an average class size of 25. No classes are taught by graduate assistants. Ninety-six percent of the 325 full-time faculty members hold a doctorate or the terminal degree in their field.

Student Government

Millersville University students participate in University governance through the Student Senate, faculty-student committees, and representation on the Faculty Senate, the Council of Trustees, and the Millersville Borough Council. The Student Senate works with faculty members and the administration on major University policies.

Admission Requirements

Millersville University admits approximately half its applicants. More than 80 percent of its full-time freshmen rank in the top 40 percent of their high school class. Academic records are the most important factor in admission decisions. Applicants must have successfully completed at least 4 years of high school English, 3 years of social studies, 3 years of mathematics (including a minimum of algebra I and II and geometry), and 3 years of science (2 units must be labs). In addition, 2 years of foreign language and 1 additional year each of math and science are strongly recommended.

Because an important part of the college experience is meeting people with backgrounds and interests different from one's own, Millersville University is committed to recruiting a diversified student body. SAT or ACT scores are required. Interviews, recommendations, and essays are not required. Out-of-state, international, and transfer applicants are welcome. Exceptional high school students may apply for early admission at the end of their junior year. Admitted applicants may request to defer their admission for one semester. Advanced standing is offered through CLEP and AP examinations.

Application and Information

To apply, students should submit a completed application along with a $50 processing fee and official copies of the high school record and SAT or ACT scores. The online application fee is $35. The University has a rolling admission policy, and students are encouraged to apply early (by mid-November) in their senior year for fall admission. Applicants are usually notified of a decision within a month after a completed application is received.

For application forms and additional information, students should contact:

Office of Admissions
Millersville University of Pennsylvania
P.O. Box 1002
Millersville, Pennsylvania 17551-0302
Phone: 717-872-3371
      800-MU-ADMIT (toll-free)
E-mail: admissions@millersville.edu
Web site: http://www.millersville.edu
     http://on.fb.me/MillersvilleU (Facebook)
     http://twitter.com/millersvilleu
     http://www.youtube.com/millersvilleu

Millersville University's campus includes shaded areas that invite students to study or relax with friends.

MILLIGAN COLLEGE
MILLIGAN COLLEGE, TENNESSEE

The College

Milligan College is a four-year private Christian liberal arts college in northeast Tennessee. From its beginning in 1866, Milligan College has integrated academic excellence with a Christian worldview, and its mission is to educate men and women as Christian servant-leaders. A comprehensive humanities program and a core curriculum are complemented by specialized training in more than twenty-five majors and several master's degrees. Christian perspectives are integrated throughout the curriculum and student life activities as students are prepared intellectually and spiritually to change lives and shape culture.

Milligan's student body of 1,000 comes from more than forty states and ten nations. Eighty percent of traditional students live on the campus in one of six residence halls. More than forty clubs and organizations provide opportunities to develop leadership skills. A wide variety of activities and campus events encourage social, cultural, and spiritual growth. Milligan College is affiliated with the Christian Churches/Churches of Christ, but the interdenominational student body is diverse.

All campus facilities are networked and most have wireless access. Every residence hall room and apartment features a high-speed data connection to the campus network and the Internet as well as telephone service, voice mail, and cable TV.

Milligan is well recognized as an NAIA athletic powerhouse with a highly competitive athletic program in twenty-three varsity sports. In the past ten years, Milligan has won more than fifty conference titles and made over fifty-seven national tournament appearances. Men's varsity teams include baseball, basketball, cross-country, golf, mountain biking, soccer, swimming, tennis, and indoor and outdoor track and field. Women's varsity teams include basketball, cheerleading, cross-country, dance, golf, mountain biking, soccer, softball, swimming, tennis, indoor and outdoor track and field, and volleyball.

Milligan is accredited by the Commission on Colleges of the Southern Association of Colleges and Schools (1866 Southern Lane, Decatur, Georgia 30033-4097; phone: 404-679-4501) to award bachelor's and master's degrees. Milligan offers a Master of Education degree, a Master of Science in Occupational Therapy degree, and a Master of Business Administration degree.

Milligan continues to be named among Southern colleges and universities in *U.S. News & World Report's* America's Best Colleges issue. More than 90 percent of its graduates are employed full-time, attending graduate school, or in voluntary service within six months after graduation, and more than 75 percent of premed students who take the MCAT are accepted to medical school.

Location

Milligan's picturesque 181-acre campus, which comprises more than twenty buildings of Colonial architecture, is located in the beautiful mountains of northeast Tennessee, just minutes from Johnson City and the dynamic Tri-Cities region. Students enjoy historical locations, theaters, parks, restaurants, and shops; explore the breathtaking Appalachian Mountains by hiking or camping in state parks near the campus; visit local lakes and rivers for outdoor recreation; or ski the nearby North Carolina slopes. Because Milligan believes leadership is about service, students are encouraged to be active in the local community. Many are employed in internships or part-time work in area businesses.

Majors and Degrees

The Bachelor of Science, Bachelor of Arts, and Bachelor of Science in Nursing degrees are offered. Undergraduate majors include accounting, applied finance and accounting, Bible (children's ministry, general studies, missions, pastoral ministry, youth ministry), biology, business administration (accounting, economics, general, health-care administration, international business, legal studies, management, marketing, sports management), chemistry, child and youth development, child life, communications (digital media studies, film studies, interpersonal and public communication, multimedia journalism, public relations), computer information systems, education (professional teacher licensure), English, fine arts (art, film studies, music, photography, theater arts), history, human performance and exercise science (exercise science, fitness and wellness, physical education, sports management), humanities, language arts, mathematics, music (performance, jazz studies), music education (licensure in vocal, instrumental), nursing, psychology (general, preprofessional), public leadership and service, sociology, and worship leadership.

Professional teacher licensure areas include early childhood, elementary education, K–12, middle grades, secondary, and special education. Preprofessional programs are available in dentistry, law, medicine, occupational therapy, optometry, pharmacy, and physical therapy. An accelerated program for adults is available in business administration and early childhood education.

Academic Programs

Milligan College offers students a liberal arts education taught from a perspective of God's activity with humanity. The College's strong core curriculum educates students toward the world in an open and constructive way. The candidate for the bachelor's degree must have completed a major and electives to total 128 semester hours of credit, with at least a 2.0 GPA. Core curriculum requirements include courses in humanities, the Bible, social sciences, ethnic studies, laboratory science, speech communication, mathematics, and health/fitness.

Realizing that not all college-level learning occurs in a college classroom, Prior Learning Assessment programs provide a method by which other modes of learning can be evaluated for college credit. The Advanced Placement (AP) program, the College-Level Examination Program (CLEP), Defense Activity for Non-Traditional Educational Support (DANTES) programs, and the International Baccalaureate (IB) program are available to all students interested in receiving college credit for studies or work experience already completed.

Milligan College operates on a semester system (semesters begin in August and January) with two 4-week summer sessions in June and July or one 8-week term. Also available are short-term classes during January term (one week before the onset of the spring semester) and May term (the weeks between the spring semester and the summer sessions).

Rising juniors are required to take a test covering general knowledge, and graduating seniors are required to take a test to demonstrate knowledge in their major field of study.

Off-Campus Programs

Students can go beyond geographical and cultural boundaries and earn up to 16 hours of credit with Milligan's Study Abroad Program or with the many off-campus learning opportunities sponsored by the Council for Christian Colleges & Universities. These include an American Studies Program in Washington, D.C.; Australia Studies Centre; China Studies Program; Contemporary Music Center near Martha's Vineyard; Latin American Studies Program in Costa Rica; Los Angeles Film Studies Center; Middle East Studies Program in Cairo; Oxford Summer Programme; Russian Studies Program; Scholars' Semester in Oxford; Summer Institute of Journalism in Washington, D.C.; and Uganda Studies Program.

Through an affiliation with the International Business Institute, business majors can earn college credit through an intensive ten-week summer program in Europe. Milligan also offers a three-week summer Humanities Tour in Europe, during which students explore the origins of Western civilization. In addition, internship opportunities offer students college credit and work experience in their field of interest.

Academic Facilities

Milligan College's library has extensive holdings and online access to other major libraries and databases. Special collections within the library contain materials on the history of the College, the Restoration Movement, and the local area. The library also participates in resource-sharing agreements with Emmanuel School of Religion and East Tennessee State University. A Writing and Study Skills Center offers access to resources, instruction, and tutoring for academic success. Television and radio production studios and an FM radio station provide on-site training for communication students. A darkroom and art gallery feature works by fine arts students. Standardized laboratory facilities, including a gross anatomy lab, are available for general and advanced work in the sciences.

Recent on-campus projects include a new state-of-the-art theater and convocation facility; a wellness center; renovation of the College's main classroom building and several other lecture halls and labs; the addition of a new education center, a new tennis complex, and a new physical plant facility; and a 30-acre land acquisition.

Costs

Tuition for 2010–11 was $22,660. Room and board were $5650. Additional fees were approximately $860. Typical annual miscellaneous costs (books, supplies, etc.) were approximately $1000. As a private institution, Milligan supplements student fees with income from endowments and gifts from alumni, friends, and churches in order to keep tuition below the national average of similar four-year private institutions.

Financial Aid

Approximately 96 percent of all students at Milligan College receive federal, state, institutional, and/or outside (such as from a church or private foundation) aid, including both academic scholarships and need-based grants. Each year, Milligan budgets more than $5 million in institutional scholarships, grants, and work-study opportunities. Financial assistance is allocated on the basis of need demonstrated by information supplied on the Free Application for Federal Student Aid (FAFSA), which should be completed by January 1 for priority consideration. Returning students must complete and submit a Milligan College Financial Aid Scholarship/Renewal Application. The Milligan College Office of Financial Aid begins mailing award letters between March 1 and March 15.

Faculty

More than 75 percent of Milligan's faculty members have earned the highest degree in their field from well-respected colleges and universities in the U.S. and abroad. Professors integrate biblical truths into their classes and are active leaders both on and off the campus. The low student-faculty ratio and small classes put the student at the center of attention and allow faculty members to cultivate special mentoring relationships with students. Professors serve as advisers to students from registration to graduation and are often instrumental in helping students find employment or gain admission to graduate school following graduation. Milligan's faculty members are mature and caring scholars who are committed to world-class scholarship, excellence in teaching, and their students.

Student Government

The Student Government Association (SGA) serves as the official representative voice of Milligan students and promotes academic, social, and spiritual activities for the campus community. SGA operates under a constitution approved and supported by the administration of the College, promotes well-ordered conduct among students, and enforces the regulations of the College. SGA leadership is provided by an executive council and representatives from throughout the campus. As a Christian college, Milligan adopts basic moral and social principles and expects students to serve Christ in an atmosphere of trust, encouragement, and respect for one another.

Admission Requirements

Character, ability, preparation, and seriousness of purpose are the qualities emphasized in considering applicants for acceptance to Milligan College. Overall excellence of performance in high school subjects as well as evidence of Christian commitment and academic potential provide the basis for admission to Milligan College. These qualities are evaluated by consideration of each applicant's academic record (based on transcripts), two personal references, ACT or SAT scores, and participation in extracurricular activities. Some majors, such as music and theater, may require auditions and interviews. All applicants should have a high school diploma or the equivalent and have completed a college-preparatory curriculum with course work in English, math, science, history and/or social sciences, foreign language, and some work in speech, music, or art in preparation for study in a liberal arts curriculum. Satisfactory scores on the ACT or SAT are required of all applicants to the freshman class. The average ACT score for the current first-year class is 23. Transfer students should have a grade point average of 2.5 or above and must follow the same application procedures as first-time students, with the addition of providing official transcripts of all previous college work. ACT or SAT scores and high school transcripts are not required for transfer students with at least 24 earned semester hours.

Application and Information

Applications are processed on a rolling basis, and early application is encouraged. Notification is also given on a rolling basis. An application packet, complete with detailed instructions and requirements, can be obtained from the Admissions Office.

For further information, students should contact:

Admissions Office
Milligan College
P.O. Box 210
Milligan College, Tennessee 37682
Phone: 423-461-8730
       800-262-8337 (toll-free)
Fax: 423-461-8982
E-mail: admissions@milligan.edu (general)
       visits@milligan.edu (visits)
Web site: http://www.milligan.edu

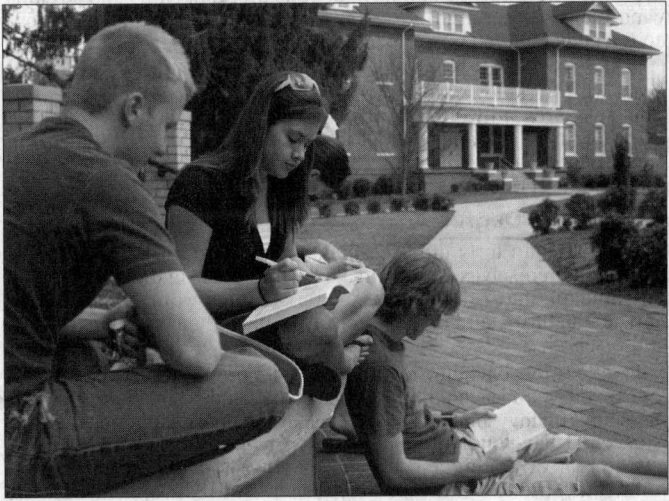

Milligan College is a Christian liberal arts college that unites humanities, sciences, and fine arts with a Christian worldview.

MILLS COLLEGE
OAKLAND, CALIFORNIA

MILLS

The College

For more than 150 years, Mills College has shaped women's lives. Offering a progressive liberal arts curriculum taught by nationally renowned faculty, Mills gives students the personal attention that leads to extraordinary learning. At Mills, students gain the ability to make their voices heard, the strength to risk bold visions, an eagerness to experiment, and a desire to change the world.

Nestled on 135 lush acres in the heart of the San Francisco Bay Area, Mills College is a hidden gem. The idyllic setting, combined with the College's community of forward-thinking individuals, makes Mills home to one of the most dynamic, creative liberal arts educations available to women today.

Historically a college for women only, Mills continues that proud tradition today at the undergraduate level. To provide enhanced professional opportunities for all students, Mills also offers renowned graduate programs that are open to both women and men. Ranked one of the top colleges in the West by *U.S. News & World Report*, Mills has also been named one of the greenest colleges in the nation by the Princeton Review.

Mills provides a collaborative, interactive learning environment that encourages intellectual exploration and self-discovery. The faculty of distinguished scholars and artists is dedicated to developing the strengths of every student, preparing them for lifelong intellectual, personal, and professional growth. With an impressive student-teacher ratio of 11:1, Mills women are assured of access to and support from these inspiring professors. The hallmark of a Mills education is the collaboration between students and faculty members that goes beyond the classroom and into innovative research.

Mills students also compete in seven intercollegiate sports—cross-country, rowing, soccer, swimming, tennis, track and field, and volleyball—as members of the National Collegiate Athletic Association (NCAA) Division III. Students may also participate in recreational activity courses for credit or take advantage of the on-campus fitness facilities and off-campus excursions.

Location

Located in the foothills of Oakland, California, Mills offers students access to the diverse metropolitan centers that make up the greater San Francisco Bay Area. Amid the rolling hills and the century-old eucalyptus trees of the Mills campus, students find a welcoming place to live and learn, with new friends and new ideas at every turn. The campus is heavily accented with Mediterranean-style buildings, many designed by architectural innovator Julia Morgan. Paths and streams wind their way through groves and meadows that pervade the 135-acre wooded campus.

Outside the campus gates, students have access to the dynamic Bay Area, with Berkeley, San Francisco, Napa, and Silicon Valley nearby. The close proximity allows Mills students to connect with centers of learning, business, and technology; pursue research and internship opportunities; and explore the Bay Area's many sources of cultural, social, and recreational enrichment.

Majors and Degrees

With more than forty different majors to choose from at Mills, students find themselves active, engaged participants in their own learning. Students have the chance to work directly with nationally renowned faculty members and get involved in their innovative work and research.

Mills offers the Bachelor of Arts (B.A.) degree in American studies; anthropology and sociology; art (history and studio); biochemistry and molecular biology; biology; biopsychology; business economics; chemistry; child development; computer science; dance; economics; English (creative writing and literature); environmental science; environmental studies; ethnic studies; French and Francophone studies; government; history; intermedia arts; international relations; Latin American studies; literary and cultural studies; mathematics; music; philosophy; political, legal, and economic analysis; psychology; public policy; sociology; Spanish and Spanish American studies; and women's,

gender, and sexuality studies. The major in child development meets the requirements for a state child development permit for teaching in preschool and day-care centers and provides a strong basis for graduate school and for many other careers. Special prelaw and premedical advising is available.

Mills offers the Bachelor of Science (B.S.) degree in biochemistry and molecular biology, biology, biopsychology, chemistry, environmental science, and mathematics. Mills also provides the first two years of courses leading to a Bachelor of Science in Nursing degree from Samuel Merritt University.

Students can also choose to create their own major, working with 3 faculty advisers to plan an individual program that draws courses from across the curriculum and creates an integrated and unique educational experience.

Mills offers seven unique programs that enable undergraduates with clear career goals in certain fields to streamline their college and graduate school programs. These degree programs are the 4+1 B.A./M.B.A. Business Administration Program, the 4+1 B.A./M.P.P. Public Policy Program, the 4+1 B.A./M.A. Infant Mental Health Program, the 4+1 B.A./M.A. Interdisciplinary Computer Science Program, the 4+1 B.A./M.A. Mathematics Program, the 3+2 B.A./B.S. Engineering Program, and the newest program, the 4+1 B.A./M.A./Credential Program in Teacher Education.

Academic Programs

To earn a Mills bachelor's degree, students complete 34 semester course credits (usually four courses each semester). Grading is traditional, and a pass-fail option is available outside the major.

The innovative general education program is guided by a thoughtfully constructed set of learning outcomes, instead of a list of required courses. Each student designs her own program with the guidance of her faculty adviser, tailoring it to the student's specific needs and interests. The program places the work a student does in her major in a larger context and ensures that she explores and appreciates realms of knowledge beyond her field. The general education requirements fall into three outcome categories: skills (written communication, quantitative and computational reasoning, and information literacy/information technology skills), perspectives (women and gender, and multicultural), and disciplinary experiences (creation and criticism in the arts, historical perspectives, natural sciences, and human institutions and behavior).

Career Services offers a comprehensive career counseling and coaching program to assist students in clarifying their goals. Workshops, individual counseling sessions, an extensive internship program, a strong alumnae network, and special opportunities to meet Bay Area business leaders and top professional women in every field all help students to focus their interests and plan career goals.

Off-Campus Programs

Mills has exchange or visiting programs with eleven American colleges and universities, including American, Barnard, Manhattanville, Mount Holyoke, Simmons, Spelman, Swarthmore, Wellesley, and Wheaton.

With programs in Europe, Africa, South America, Asia, and Australia—in nearly every country in the world—Mills encourages adventurous students with a minimum 3.0 GPA to study abroad. Students receiving financial aid may continue to do so while studying with an approved program. Mills also has exchange programs with universities in Hong Kong and South Korea.

Sophomores, juniors, and seniors may cross-register for one course per semester at the following schools: Berkeley City College; California College of the Arts; California State University, East Bay; Chabot College; City College of San Francisco; College of Alameda; College of Marin; Contra Costa College; Diablo Valley College; Graduate Theological Union; Holy Names University; Laney College; Merritt College; Napa Valley College; St. Mary's College of California; Skyline College; Sonoma State University; and University of California, Berkeley.

Academic Facilities

Mills' commitment to providing students with exceptional academic resources is underscored by the two environmentally friendly buildings on campus. Opened in fall 2009, the home of the Lorry I. Lokey Graduate School of Business hosts both undergraduate and graduate classes and achieved Leadership in Energy and Environmental Design (LEED) Gold certification. Students enjoy smart classrooms and lecture halls with the latest educational technology and light-filled community areas that encourage student collaboration. The Betty Irene Moore Natural Sciences Building provides students with a state-of-the-art learning environment that is also a model of green construction. The Platinum LEED-certified facility features high-tech classrooms, multiple teaching laboratories, and a research lab.

Newly renovated Littlefield Concert Hall reopened in 2009. The venue features an expanded stage area for larger performances and enhanced acoustic features for improved performing and recording quality. Nearby Lisser Hall contains a flexible proscenium stage as well as a small experimental theater.

The open-stack, computerized F. W. Olin Library provides students with access to more than 235,000 volumes in addition to more than 22,000 rare books and manuscripts. A Web-based catalog and more than 60 databases, including Academic Search, LexisNexis, PsycINFO, and Britannica Online are available 24 hours a day via the library's Web site.

The Mills College Art Museum houses the largest permanent collection of any liberal arts college on the West Coast and presents a changing array of innovative exhibitions. The highly regarded Children's School at Mills College provides hands-on experience for students preparing for careers in early childhood education.

Costs

In 2010–11, tuition was $36,428 and room and board were $11,644. Health insurance, a comprehensive fee covering such items as shuttle service, a discounted area bus pass, technology, and associated student fees totaled $3475 for resident and commuting students. Students should calculate the costs of travel, books, and personal expenses on an individual basis.

Financial Aid

Mills College is committed to ensuring that a Mills education is within reach for those who have the desire and the qualifications to attend. Financial aid options at Mills include grants and scholarships, loans, and student employment. Some are funded by Mills directly, and others are state and federal programs.

In fall 2010, more than 80 percent of undergraduates at the College received some type of financial assistance in the form of grants, scholarships, loans, or on-campus employment. Ninety-four percent of Mills students received some portion of their aid directly from Mills. Awards are based on need and academic merit. Scholarship amounts range from $1000 per year to full tuition. Mills makes a special effort to provide financial aid to all students who demonstrate need.

All first-year students and transfer candidates must file the Free Application for Federal Student Aid (FAFSA) and the Mills College Financial Aid Form to be considered for government aid and need-based Mills scholarship funds. The FAFSA is required for non-Mills aid, such as the Federal Pell Grant, and the Federal Supplemental Educational Opportunity Grant. California residents must also file the Cal Grant GPA Verification Form to be considered for a Cal Grant. More than 40 percent of Mills students have some of their determined need offset by such non-Mills awards.

Faculty

More than 60 percent of the Mills faculty members are women, enabling students to work with professional women mentors in every academic area. Faculty members are selected for their teaching ability and scholarly achievement; 88 percent of full-time faculty members hold the highest degrees in their fields. Nearly 30 percent of the full- and part-time faculty members are members of minority groups.

Student Government

An important goal of an education at Mills is to develop leadership skills, and participating in student government can be instrumental in furthering this goal. The Associated Students of Mills College (ASMC) is run by an executive board of 15 elected or appointed positions. Following a student-drafted Constitution, the board supports student organizations, student publications, campuswide events, and various student initiatives. From academic issues to social events to honor code concerns, the ASMC is the voice of the student body to the College administration.

Admission Requirements

Most first-year students admitted to Mills have a strong B average and have followed a full college-preparatory course in their secondary school, including 4 years of English, 3 to 4 years of mathematics, 2 to 4 years of foreign languages, 2 to 4 years of social sciences, and 2 to 4 years of a laboratory science. Additional course work in fine arts is given positive consideration, as is evidence of special talents or interests. Mills is interested in individuals, not statistical averages, so each application is carefully reviewed. Credit may be awarded for the College Board Advanced Placement tests and the International Baccalaureate program's higher level examinations.

Applications from transfers are welcome, as are those from students resuming their education or women who have delayed their entrance to college or who wish to continue work on their B.A. degrees. The SAT or ACT requirement is waived if 24 or more transferable semester hours are presented. For international applications, both the SAT and TOEFL are required. Applications should be accompanied by transcripts, letters of recommendation, SAT/ACT scores, and a writing sample. An interview, either on campus or with an alumna representative, is strongly recommended for all applicants. International students are required to interview if English is not their primary language.

Application and Information

For first-year students, fall admission application deadlines are November 15 for early action and February 1 for regular decision. All required materials are due by February 1.

For transfer students, fall admission application deadlines are March 1 for priority scholarship consideration and April 1 for regular decision.

The spring admission application deadline for both first-year and transfer students is November 1. Admission decisions are mailed on a rolling basis.

For more information, students should contact:

Office of Undergraduate Admission
Mills College
5000 MacArthur Boulevard
Oakland, California 94613
Phone: 510-430-2135
      800-87-MILLS (toll-free)
Fax: 510-430-3298
E-mail: admission@mills.edu
Web site: http://www.mills.edu
      http://www.facebook.com/millscollege (Facebook)
      http://twitter.com/millscollege (Twitter)
      http://youtube.com/millscollege (YouTube)

Mills women discover their best selves—and prepare to change the world.

MILWAUKEE SCHOOL OF ENGINEERING
MILWAUKEE, WISCONSIN

The University

Ambitious students who want personal and professional success find a home at Milwaukee School of Engineering (MSOE). For more than 108 years, top students have chosen a rigorous and collaborative education and the supportive guidance of expert faculty members who are dedicated to student success. The university is fully dedicated to every student who is willing to be challenged and work hard to become a better person as a successful MSOE graduate. The close-knit campus is nestled in a vibrant downtown Milwaukee neighborhood, and offers students an engaging learning and living environment.

Advancing beyond acquisition to the highly sophisticated application of knowledge is the foundation of MSOE's educational philosophy. This approach, which is the university's educational niche, produces graduates who are well-rounded, technologically experienced, and highly productive professionals and leaders. Graduates begin their careers as work-ready problem solvers and develop into leaders: creating new products, starting or heading companies, and working to better their communities.

For the past five years, MSOE's average graduate placement rate is 94 percent. The average starting salary for graduates is more than $52,500. Representatives from hundreds of firms from throughout the country, including Fortune 500 companies, visit MSOE during the academic year to interview graduating students for employment and discuss career opportunities. MSOE's long-standing ties with business, industry, and health care are represented by the Board of Regents, with more than 50 members, and the MSOE Corporation, with more than 200 members, who are elected from leaders in business and industry nationwide.

The student body of more than 2,600 men and women comes from throughout the United States and numerous countries. Since its founding, the university has encouraged the enrollment of students of any race, color, creed, or gender. Approximately half of the full-time students live in three high-rise residence halls.

MSOE's Counseling Services Office provides individual assistance for students with educational, personal, or vocational concerns. Free on-campus tutoring is provided by the Learning Resource Center.

The Student Life and Campus Center provides on-campus recreational activities. This facility houses student activity rooms, student organization offices, a TV viewing area, a marketplace eatery, and a game room. Additional recreation areas can be found in the residence halls. The Kern Center is a 210,000-square-foot health, wellness, fitness, and recreation facility that houses a 1,600-seat ice arena, a fitness center, a 1,200-seat basketball arena, a field house, a recreational running track, and a wrestling area.

More than seventy professional societies, fraternities, and other special-interest groups serve the campus. MSOE's students also participate in intramural sports programs. MSOE is a member of the National Collegiate Athletic Association (NCAA) Division III and the Northern Athletics Conference (NAC). The Athletic Department sponsors NCAA varsity teams in men's baseball, basketball, cross-country, golf, ice hockey, indoor and outdoor track and field, lacrosse, rowing, soccer, tennis, volleyball, and wrestling and women's basketball, cross-country, golf, indoor and outdoor track and field, soccer, softball, tennis, and volleyball that compete with teams from other private colleges and universities in the Midwest.

MSOE's newest attraction and home to the world's most comprehensive art collection dedicated to the evolution of human work opened in 2007. The Grohmann Museum welcomes visitors to three floors of galleries where the Eckhart G. Grohmann Collection "Man at Work" is housed. The collection comprises more than 800 paintings and sculptures from 1580 to the present, reflecting a variety of artistic styles and subjects that depict organized work from farming, mining, and trades to more unusual occupations such as seaweed gathering.

In addition to its eighteen undergraduate degree programs in the fields of engineering, building and infrastructure engineering, engineering technology, computers, business, nursing, and health-related areas, MSOE offers ten Master of Science degree programs: cardiovascular studies, civil engineering, engineering, engineering management (accelerated option available), marketing and export management, medical informatics (jointly offered with the Medical College of Wisconsin), new product management, perfusion, and structural engineering.

MSOE is a member of, and accredited by, the North Central Association of Colleges and Schools. Program-specific accrediting agencies are identified in the MSOE academic catalogs.

Location

The MSOE campus is located in the vibrant neighborhood of East Town in downtown Milwaukee. Nearby are the Bradley Center sports arena, the Frontier Airlines Center, the Marcus Center for the Performing Arts, the theater district, churches of most denominations, major hotels and office buildings, restaurants, and retail stores. Famous for its friendly atmosphere, Milwaukee offers students many opportunities for educational, cultural, and professional growth as well as ample employment opportunities. The metropolitan area has more than 15,000 acres of parks and river parkways and miles of bike trails. A few blocks east of the MSOE campus is Lake Michigan, which offers year-round natural beauty. MSOE also offers classes in other locations in Wisconsin for students who wish to pursue select programs in the evening on a part-time basis.

Majors and Degrees

Four-year programs are offered that lead to Bachelor of Science degrees in business management, construction management, engineering, and specific areas of engineering (architectural, biomedical, biomolecular, civil, computer, electrical, industrial, mechanical, and software), engineering technology—transfer programs only (electrical and mechanical), international business, management information systems, and nursing. A Bachelor of Science or Bachelor of Arts degree is offered in technical communication. A five-year, double-major option is available in a combination of business, construction management, engineering, and technical communication programs. An engineering/structural engineering dual degree (B.S./M.S. combination) also is available, as is a five-year freshman-to-master's degree in civil engineering. Study-abroad opportunities and many double majors also exist.

Academic Programs

MSOE guarantees that the classes needed to graduate in four years will be available for full-time undergraduate students who start and stay on track and meet academic requirements.

The degree programs at MSOE combine study in degree specialty courses with basic study in sciences, communication, mathematics, and humanities in a high-technology, applications-oriented atmosphere. Students who are admitted with advanced credit to a program leading to a bachelor's degree must complete at least 50 percent of the curriculum in residence at MSOE. MSOE operates on a quarter system. Students average between 16 and 19 credits per quarter, which represent a combination of lecture and laboratory courses. Undergraduate students average 600 hours of laboratory experience.

MSOE offers students the opportunity to participate in the Air Force Reserve Officer Training Corps (AFROTC) program, the Army ROTC program, or the Navy ROTC program.

Academic Facilities

The Fred Loock Engineering Center adjoins the Allen-Bradley Hall of Science, forming a prime technical education and applied research complex. Rosenberg Hall houses the Rader School of Business, technology-integrated classrooms, and the U.S. Export Service Center for Milwaukee.

The Walter Schroeder Library is a popular meeting place on campus and offers more than 60,000 volumes, with collections that represent the specialized curricula of the university. The library offers Web-based access to more than 90,000 e-journals, 30,000 e-books, hundreds of specialized databases, unique collections, government agencies, and other sources of information throughout the world.

All students participate in a Technology Package program that includes a notebook computer and affiliated services. A full range of software is available on these systems and via the local area network linked by a fiber-optic ring around the campus. Most areas also have wireless capability for laptop use. State-of-the-art architectural, biomolecular, computer, electrical, mechanical, industrial, nursing, science, and software laboratories complement the respective areas of study.

The Applied Technology Center™ (ATC) utilizes faculty and student expertise to solve technological problems confronting business and industry. The ATC is heavily involved in the transferring of new technologies into real business practice through the Rapid Prototyping Center (MSOE is the only university in the world to possess the five leading rapid prototyping technologies), the Fluid Power Institute™, the NanoEngineering Laboratory, the Photonics and Applied Optics Center, the Construction Science and Engineering Center, and the Center for BioMolecular Modeling.

There are more laboratories than classrooms at MSOE, many with industrial sponsorship from such companies as Johnson Controls, Harley-Davidson, Rockwell Automation/Allen-Bradley, Master Lock, Snap-on, General Electric, and Outboard Marine Corp. Undergraduates average an amazing 600 hours of laboratory experience.

Costs

For 2010–11, tuition was $29,520 per year plus $1140 for the Technology Package (notebook computer, software, insurance, maintenance, Internet access, and user services). The cost of room and board in the residence halls was approximately $7164 per year. Books and supplies average $400 per quarter but may be somewhat higher for the first quarter.

Financial Aid

Ninety-nine percent of full-time students receive financial aid. Qualified students are assisted by a comprehensive financial aid program, including MSOE and industry-supported scholarships, student loans, and part-time employment; Federal Perkins Loan, Federal Direct Loans, Federal Work-Study, Federal Direct PLUS Loans, Federal Pell Grant, and Federal Supplemental Educational Opportunity Grant Programs; and state-supported grant programs. Students can also visit MSOE's Web site for a financial aid estimate.

Faculty

MSOE faculty members engage and challenge students, with individual attention and practical perspectives gained from an average of seven years of professional employment experience in their area of expertise. They are at MSOE because they love to teach—there is no "publish or perish" tenure system. There are more than 200 men and women on the MSOE faculty (full-time and part-time). Many are registered professional engineers, architects, and/or nurses. They and their colleagues in nontechnical academic areas are active in related professional societies. The student-faculty ratio is 14:1. MSOE does not use teaching assistants.

Student Government

The MSOE Student Government Association (SGA) represents clubs and fraternities as well as residence halls and commuting students. SGA appoints representatives to the Campus Security and Disciplinary Hearing committees, the Executive Educational Council, and the Alumni Association's Board of Directors.

Admission Requirements

Each applicant to MSOE is reviewed individually on the basis of potential for success as determined by academic preparation. Admission may be gained by submitting an application for admission and the appropriate transcripts. High school students are encouraged to complete math through precalculus (including algebra and geometry), chemistry, biology (nursing), physics, and 4 years of English. All entering freshmen are also required to provide results from the ACT or the SAT.

Transfer opportunities exist into the junior year of the Bachelor of Science in business management, electrical engineering technology, mechanical engineering technology, management information systems, and technical communication programs with the appropriate associate degree or equivalent credits.

Application and Information

Classes start in September, November, March, and late May. Freshmen and transfer students may enter at the beginning of any quarter; however, entry in the fall quarter is recommended. An application for admission may be obtained by contacting the address below or by visiting MSOE's Web site. Applicants are encouraged to visit MSOE and have a preadmission counseling interview. Transfer students are required to submit transcripts from all prior institutions attended. An applicant's prior course work is reviewed to determine eligibility for admission. Required course work varies depending on the desired course of study.

Admission Office
Milwaukee School of Engineering
1025 North Broadway
Milwaukee, Wisconsin 53202-3109
Phone: 414-277-6763
     800-332-6763 (toll-free)
E-mail: explore@msoe.edu
Web site: http://www.msoe.edu
     http://www.facebook.com/milwaukeeschoolofengineer
     http://twitter.com/msoe

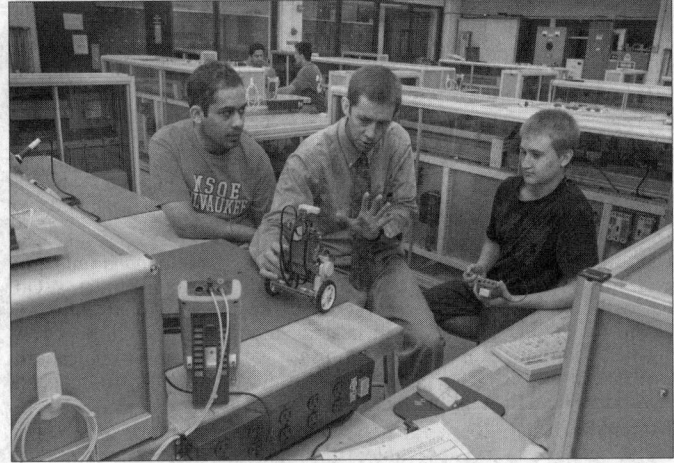

MSOE's undergraduate students average 600 hours of laboratory experience—just one more advantage to an MSOE education.

MISERICORDIA UNIVERSITY

DALLAS, PENNSYLVANIA

The University

Misericordia University is a high-quality liberal arts and professional studies institution rooted in a foundation of service to others and is committed to providing the challenging academics and personal attention students need to learn in order to succeed both professionally and personally. Founded by the Religious Sisters of Mercy in 1924, Misericordia offers undergraduate and graduate programs to resident and commuter students, as well as adult students. Current enrollment is more than 2,800 men and women.

Misericordia provides an academic atmosphere designed to stimulate critical thinking, independent judgment, and creativity, as well as encourage the development of curiosity, good study habits, and personal values. The University also cultivates a spirit of community service and a lifelong love of learning in its students through extracurricular activities, experiential learning, and challenging academic programs. In the National Survey of Student Engagement, Misericordia students say they are more involved in learning and have better relationships with faculty members and peers than students at other similar institutions. Misericordia is also recommended by the Princeton Review and the *Washington Monthly* magazine, and is ranked in the top tier of *U.S. News & World Report*'s America's Best Colleges 2010 in the Master's North category.

The University is fully accredited by the Middle States Association of Colleges and Schools. Its programs in nursing, social work, medical imaging, occupational therapy, physical therapy, and speech-language pathology are accredited by the National League for Nursing Accrediting Commission, the Council on Social Work Education, the Joint Review Committee on Education in Radiologic Technology, the American Occupational Therapy Association, the American Physical Therapy Association, and the American Speech-Language and Hearing Association, respectively. A new physician assistant studies program is pending accreditation.

Misericordia operates four residential facilities and eighteen townhouse units, with a total capacity for 850 students. A nearby home is reserved for upper-level students. Residents have a number of options, including single rooms and wellness housing. On average, students living in campus housing hold GPAs of more than 3.2. Each residence hall offers study rooms, laundry facilities, and recreational lounges. The new Metz Dining Hall is located in the Banks Student Life Center, which also houses the Cougar's Den coffeehouse, snack bar, and the newly renovated Student Union, which features big flat-screen televisions, and pool and foosball tables.

There are numerous campus activities for students. Besides Student Government, there are forty-one chartered student clubs and organizations. Cultural events, Campus Ministry, intramural and intercollegiate athletic programs for men and women, performing arts shows, art exhibits, and many other social activities complement and reinforce the academic experience. In keeping with the University's tradition of mercy, service, justice, and hospitality, students also have opportunities to develop leadership potential through service projects that benefit the surrounding communities. The University's Service Leadership Center engages students in the development of lifelong civic responsibility through academic course work.

Campus Ministry provides opportunities to participate in campus and community programs that promote social awareness in students. On spring break, students have served the needy in rural Appalachia, the storm-ravaged Gulf Coast, Texas, California, and the South Bronx. A six-week summer Cross-Cultural Ministry Experience in Guyana, South America, awaits selected participants; students have also volunteered abroad in Jamaica and Romania.

Personalized attention is the key to the support available in the Student Success Center. A psychologist, counselors, therapists, and peer counselors conduct workshops each semester on a variety of topics, including test anxiety, stress management, time management, and goal setting. Many services are free of charge to students and contacts are strictly confidential.

Misericordia was named a Best School for Standing by Grads in *Ki-*

plinger's Personal Finance magazine's December 2009 special edition, "The Best of Everything 2009." First-year students may join the Guaranteed Placement Program (GPP) through the Insalaco Center for Career Development. The GPP program includes academic standards; cocurricular activities, such as leadership and service projects; internships; resume development; and interviewing skills. If a student fulfills the program requirements and is not employed in his or her field or enrolled in graduate or professional school within six months of graduation, a paid internship is assured. The center also copresents the Choice Program, offering special guidance for students who haven't chosen a major. Opportunities for career exploration, cooperative education, and internships help students to develop the knowledge and skills they need to enter the working world.

Student Health Services occupies a convenient facility near campus housing. Health-care staff members provide first aid, assessment and treatment of common illnesses, and referrals for more serious health conditions. Health center activities are directed by a registered nurse with a master's degree in nursing administration, under the guidance of a physician. A nurse practitioner is also available. A self-care room offers reference materials and up-to-date information on personal health concerns. All services are confidential.

A rapidly evolving world and development of new technologies have increased the number of adults who seek higher education. Misericordia offers special bachelor's, master's, and doctoral programs for adults, including the Expressway Program, an accelerated bachelor's degree program; Women with Children, which provides housing and support services for single women with children; and evening, online, and weekend formats for people with families and full-time jobs.

At Misericordia University, students can earn master's and/or doctoral degrees by attending classes online, in the evening, and/or on weekends. The small-class format enhances critical thinking and decision-making skills and draws out a variety of viewpoints that help broaden the perspectives of the student. Master's degrees are available in education, nursing, occupational therapy, speech-language pathology, business administration, and organizational management. A doctoral program in physical therapy is available to students entering in a full-time and part-time format, and a doctoral program in occupational therapy is available for graduate students via part-time study, including online and in-class components.

Location

Located on a more than 124-acre campus in northeastern Pennsylvania, Misericordia University is the oldest institution of higher education in Luzerne County. Expansive lawns and thick stands of trees dominate the campus. It is 9 miles from the city of Wilkes-Barre. The area offers shopping centers, malls, cinemas, skiing, professional sporting events, and a variety of cultural activities. Pennsylvania's largest natural lake and two state parks are nearby, as are Pocono ski resorts. Metropolitan New York and Philadelphia are each within a 3-hour drive. Public and college-sponsored transportation serves the campus.

Majors and Degrees

Misericordia University awards the Bachelor of Arts (B.A.) degree in English, history, communications, government, liberal studies, and philosophy. The Bachelor of Science (B.S.) degree is awarded in accounting, biochemistry, biology, business administration, chemistry, clinical laboratory science, communications, computer science, diagnostic medial sonography, elementary education, health-care management, information technology, interdisciplinary studies, management, marketing, mathematics, math/computer science, medical imaging, professional studies, psychology, secondary education, special education, and sport management. A physician assistant studies program is pending accreditation and will welcome students in fall 2011. A Bachelor of Science in Nursing (B.S.N.) is awarded to nursing majors, and a Bachelor of Science in Social Work (B.S.W.) is awarded to social work majors. Specializations in accounting, early childhood education, prelaw, special education, and preprofessional occupations are also available. Certification programs include addictions counseling, child welfare services, diagnostic medical sonography, geriatric care management, gerontology, health-care informatics, and secondary education and may be taken in support of several degrees offered by Misericordia or as stand-alone programs.

The University offers five-year entry-level graduate majors in occupational therapy and speech-language pathology. Students graduate with a master's degree in speech-language pathology or occupational therapy and a bachelor's degree in health sciences. The physical therapy program is a 6½-year doctoral program. Students graduate with a bachelor's degree in one of several areas and a Doctor of Physical Therapy (D.P.T.) degree.

Academic Programs

Candidates for the B.A., B.S., B.S.N., or B.S.W. must fulfill a 48-credit liberal arts core curriculum in addition to the requirements of their chosen major to graduate. They must earn at least 36 credit hours in a chosen field. For regularly enrolled students, the average requirement for a baccalaureate degree is a total of 126 credits. Other options include minors, specializations, certifications, and electives.

Courses are offered on a semester basis, beginning in August and January and ending in December and May. Summer, weekend, and accelerated courses are also available.

Academic Facilities

The chemistry, physics, and biology departments all have modern, fully equipped research laboratories available to students in these fields of concentration. State-of-the-art equipment includes high-performance liquid chromatography (HPLC), a rotary evaporator, an infrared spectrophotometer, and gas chromatography. The University also houses an energized radiation laboratory for the medical imaging program. The new College of Health Sciences building provides classrooms and high-technology laboratories for the occupational therapy, physical therapy, speech-language pathology, and nursing programs in a facility completely devoted to these majors.

In addition to the four main computer labs, the Banks Student Life Center and Bevevino Library offer wireless Internet access. The University operates e-MU, a secure online portal where students can access e-mail, course schedules, group and chat functions, and student account and registration information from a single sign-on. The Communications Department features the area's only all-digital television control room and editing bays.

Mercy Hall, the original administrative building, underwent extensive renovations and offers multipurpose academic classrooms and facilities. Many key student service departments, including the registrar, student accounts, and financial aid are centralized in one area in Mercy Hall. Insalaco Hall, a new state-of-the-art classroom and conference building, provides a modern art gallery, café, computer labs, an ensemble room, fine arts classroom, music teaching and practice areas, and the Assistive Technology Research Institute.

The three-story Bevevino Library covers 37,500 square feet and houses stacks for 90,000 volumes. Materials include information and communication technology and a reference section that offers books, serials, and a variety of periodicals as well as reference search tools, CD-ROMs, and multiple online databases and microfilm. The Bevevino Library is a member of the Northeastern Pennsylvania Library Network, which provides users access to the 1.5-million-volume collections of participating libraries via its new virtual online catalog.

Costs

Tuition for 2010–11 was $23,750 per year. The general fee was $1240. Housing options include traditional rooms, suites, town houses, and wellness housing. The median room cost was $6000. All resident students must participate in a ten-, fourteen-, or nineteen- meal plan. In addition, town-house residents are eligible to choose a five-meal plan. The median board cost was $3595.

Financial Aid

All students applying for financial aid must complete the Free Application for Federal Student Aid (FAFSA) by May 1. This is used for Federal Pell Grants, Federal Supplemental Educational Opportunity Grants (FSEOG), subsidized and unsubsidized Federal Direct Student Loans, Federal Perkins Loans, nursing loans, and the Federal Work-Study Program. This application is also the basis upon which state and institutional aid is awarded. The University also offers a no-interest monthly payment plan. Many scholarships are available including $11.4 million in presidential scholarships based on academic ability and $2.3 million in McAuley Awards for students who have experience in leadership roles and volunteer service.

Faculty

There are 104 full-time faculty members. A student-faculty ratio of 13:1 results in students receiving a great deal of individual attention from a highly qualified faculty; 87 percent of the faculty members hold doctorates or other terminal degrees. Besides student academic advising, the faculty members also serve as advisers to clubs.

Student Government

An active student government organization serves as a liaison between the students and the faculty and staff members. The administration enables students to become involved by serving as student representatives on various University committees.

Admission Requirements

Misericordia University admits applicants based on their secondary school record, high school recommendation, extracurricular activities, and personal promise. The University requires SAT or ACT scores. Although a personal interview is highly recommended, it is not necessary for all majors. Misericordia offers both early decision and early admissions programs.

Transfer students with a cumulative average of at least 2.0 (4.0 scale) may be considered for admission and may receive advanced standing. Some majors require a 2.5 or higher cumulative average. Transfer students must submit official high school transcripts and a transcript of work completed at other colleges and universities.

Application and Information

Applicants must submit an official application form (available upon request), transcripts, and SAT or ACT scores. Applicants may also apply through the University's Web site. There is a nonrefundable application fee of $35, which is waived for students who visit the campus.

The University considers applications on a rolling basis. Usually, candidates are notified of the admission decision within three weeks of receipt of all required materials.

Office of Admissions
Misericordia University
301 Lake Street
Dallas, Pennsylvania 18612-1090
Phone: 570-674-6461
      866-262-6363 (toll free)
Fax: 570-675-2441
E-mail: admiss@misericordia.edu
Web site: http://admissions.misericordia.edu
      www.twitter.com/misericordiau

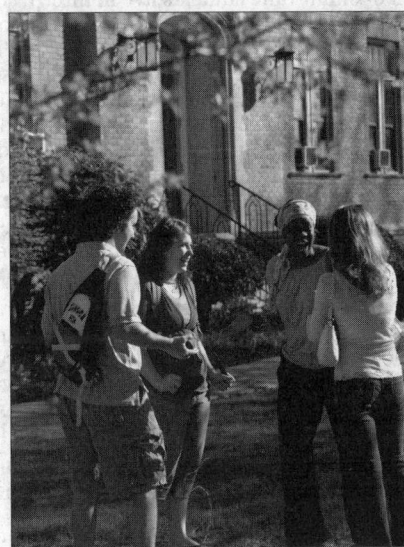

Students at Misericordia University pursue their studies with an emphasis on academic excellence, service leadership, and professional preparation.

MITCHELL COLLEGE
NEW LONDON, CONNECTICUT

The College

Mitchell is a private, coeducational four-year residential college. With 1,000 students and a 12:1 student-faculty ratio, the College provides a supportive student-centered learning environment that addresses the educational needs of all students, including those with learning disabilities. Mitchell is especially proud of its success in working with students who have yet to reach their full academic potential. To that end, the College maintains access for students with varied academic abilities who are highly motivated to succeed.

To help guide students, Mitchell College's mission is connected to five distinctive values: Character, Achievement, Respect, Engagement, and Self-Discovery (CARES). The CARES model provides a learning foundation that emphasizes character development, personal and social responsibility, respect for others, and community service. CARES is a comprehensive hands-on partnership that keeps students on course toward their goal of graduation and beyond.

Mitchell College's innovative PG year program, Thames Academy, continues to grow and strengthen. Launched in 2006, Thames Academy is a postgraduate/precollege program—a year of academic preparation for students between the end of their secondary school/high school education and the start of their college studies. As one of the country's foremost colleges in promoting student academic success, Mitchell provides a challenging education in a caring and supportive environment, focusing on student asset development, rather than deficit management.

Nearly all full-time students are of traditional college age, 18 to 22, and come from throughout the country and around the globe. Most students come from New England states, with about 60 percent from Connecticut, 30 percent from other New England states, and the remaining 10 percent from throughout United States and other countries. International students and representatives of multicultural groups make up approximately 32 percent of the student population. About 150 part-time students, many of whom are adult commuters, enhance the classroom experience.

Nearly 80 percent of full-time students live in three traditional residence halls, each housing 100 students. Each building has three floors with double rooms and common baths. The College also offers four historic Victorian and Colonial waterfront residence halls accommodating between 20 and 35 students each. One waterfront residence is dedicated to Thames Academy, the postgraduate/precollege transitional program. In addition to the traditional resident halls, Mitchell has themed, apartment-style living, accommodating 16 students. A new suite-style, 120-bed residence hall opened in fall 2008. Facilities include a fully equipped gymnasium, a new fitness center, new dining hall and café, athletic fields, a sailing dock, and indoor recreation areas.

Biking, communications, community service, choir, drama society, Hillel, music, the newspaper, the yearbook, skiing, multicultural affairs, psychology, radio, rugby, and environmental are among the clubs that bring together students with similar interests. Weekends are filled with guest comedians, bands, formal and casual dances, lectures, and organized trips to Boston and New York City.

The tradition of the scholar-athlete is strong at Mitchell. A member of the NCAA Division III, Mitchell College recently joined the New England Collegiate Conference. Other colleges in this conference include Wheelock College, Newbury College, Lesley University, Elms College, Bay Path College, Becker College, Southern Vermont College, and Daniel Webster College.

Mitchell College fields ten intercollegiate teams. Men play baseball, basketball, cross-country, golf, lacrosse, sailing, soccer, and tennis; women play basketball, cross-country, golf, sailing, soccer, softball, tennis, and volleyball. The College has a history of athletic excellence,

winning many national and New England championships. A full schedule of intramural sports is organized for students of all athletic experience and ability.

Location

New London, Connecticut, where Mitchell College makes its home, is a major center of activity in southeastern Connecticut, a region rich in historic significance. This small but sophisticated city, also home to Connecticut College and the U.S. Coast Guard Academy, is a maritime and resort center located midway between Boston and New York City on the main rail line.

The campus is situated in the city's most scenic residential section. Bordered by a long stretch of sandy beach, the campus consists of 68 acres of gently sloping hillside and forest. Places for shopping, banking, dining, and fun are within easy walking distance or can be accessed by buses that pass the College entrance. Major shopping malls, factory outlets, and fine and casual dining are minutes from the campus. The region is also home to major tourist attractions, such as the U.S.S. Nautilus and Submarine Museum, Mystic Marinelife Aquarium, Mystic Seaport, Olde Mystic Village, Ocean Beach Park, Stonington Vineyards, Foxwoods Resort and Casino, the Mohegan Sun Casino, and the Essex Steam Train.

Majors and Degrees

Baccalaureate degrees are offered in business administration, communication, criminal justice, early childhood education, environmental studies, homeland security, hospitality and tourism, human development and family studies, liberal and professional studies, psychology, and sport management. Associate degrees are offered in early childhood education, graphic design, and liberal arts.

Students undecided about their academic majors are enrolled in the Discovery Program, which is specially designed to provide special courses, additional advising, and services to explore their full potential and assistance in choosing a major.

Academic Programs

The academic calendar consists of two full semesters that run from September to December and from January to May. In addition to five summer sessions, Mitchell College also offers STEP, a five-week bridging program for incoming freshmen. Geared to 16–18-year-old rising high school juniors and seniors is STEP-UP, a summer two-week program. This program helps strengthen study skills while also increasing confidence and self-esteem.

All first-year freshman students participate in the First Year College. This comprehensive program is designed to ease the transition from high school to college and establish the foundation for academic success. Students are clustered into freshman interest groups based on a common interest in a theme of their choosing. Courses within the freshman college include expository writing, college writing and research, presentations, and information technology literacy. These courses are linked within a collaborative format consisting of a common theme, a team of instructors, and ability-based assessment.

If a student is having difficulty, it is recognized early. Mitchell grades at five, ten, and fifteen-week intervals. If a student is experiencing a problem, faculty members and the student's academic adviser work with the student to get back on course. Mitchell's Tutoring Center provides free, unlimited individualized tutoring by trained professionals (not peer tutors) in almost every academic discipline. It also offers assistance in improving writing, research, and computer skills as well as test and exam preparation and study skills development. Some of Mitchell's most successful students are regular users of the Tutoring Center, and they attribute much of their success to its programs.

Students with diagnosed learning disabilities may enroll in the College's nationally recognized Learning Resource Center, which provides instruction and support to complement a student's regular academic program. Each student is assigned two learning specialists to work one-on-one with the student and in small-group settings. The program is designed to teach the learning strategies a student needs to gain independence.

Off-Campus Programs

When not in class, Mitchell students gain the skills and experience they need to succeed in their careers and to make a difference in their communities. Nearly all academic programs require or encourage students to participate in volunteer opportunities, internships, or practical experiences as part of their curriculum.

Some of the opportunities include exploring the seacoast with a nationally recognized scientist, teaching at a local elementary school, partnering with a local police officer, helping to negotiate a bill through the state legislature, assisting with advertising campaigns, coaching developmentally challenged athletes and practicing the skills of injury prevention, and sparking the imagination of local school children through storytelling sessions.

Academic Facilities

Mitchell's unique 68-acre waterfront campus includes a 73,590-volume library, classroom buildings, and the Duques Academic Success Center. Located in the center of campus, the Duques Academic Success Center houses academic advising, the Career Center, the Learning Resource Center, tutoring, and classrooms.

Students have full use of Mitchell's state-of-the-art computing facilities with high-speed Internet access. The Mitchell College Library, dining hall, residence hall lounges, and most classrooms are equipped with wireless network and Internet access. Computer access is also available seven days a week in the library and computer labs. Campus computers are fully equipped for e-mail, scanning, network printing, and secure access to each student's individual network server storage. Students have access to extensive online information resources (including journal databases, music databases, and eBooks) via the library Web site. High-speed Internet is also available to each student living in the residence halls and most of the campus buildings have wireless Internet access. For those who do not own a computer, Mitchell offers a computer purchasing plan through Dell and additional service agreements through a local authorized Dell service provider.

Costs

Tuition, room and board, and fees for the 2010–11 year were $40,206. Additional annual miscellaneous expenses, including books, were estimated at $1500 per year. Students enrolled in the Learning Resource Center paid an additional $6800 per year.

Financial Aid

Mitchell annually awards more than $4 million in financial aid, both in need-based and merit-based scholarships and in grant programs designed to recognize academic and leadership abilities. Accepted students may qualify for grants and scholarships that do not need to be repaid. They include the Connecticut Independent College Student Grant Program, Federal Pell Grants, Federal Supplemental Educational Opportunity Grants, and Mitchell Scholarships. Self-help aid in the form of loans is also available. They include Federal Stafford Student Loans (subsidized and unsubsidized), Federal PLUS Loans, and Federal Perkins Loan programs. On-campus job opportunities are plentiful for students regardless of their financial aid status.

Mitchell Valued Potential (MVP) scholarships are awarded based on an individual student's ability to contribute to the College. They may be given to students who demonstrate potential in leadership, volunteerism, and involvement in school activities. Various payment plans are available.

Faculty

Thirty-four full-time and 58 part-time faculty members teach in Mitchell's classrooms. The student-faculty ratio is 12:1.

Student Government

The Student Government Association (SGA) is made up of officers and senators who represent the residents and commuters. It addresses issues with campus administration, organizes community projects, serves as the active voice for the student body, and sponsors at least one campuswide program each semester. The SGA also works in tandem with the Student Activities Office concerning club funding and overall programming.

Student involvement is not only encouraged but also expected of all Mitchell students. An active student leads to a well-rounded person. Students enhance their life with self-discipline skills, demonstrate selfless service, and become happier members of the College family through involvement in student activities, athletics, campus employment, and community service opportunities.

Admission Requirements

Each student is evaluated individually as soon as the completed application, along with the official transcript, is received. Admission is based on academic preparation, scholastic aptitude, personal character, and potential for academic success. Other important factors taken into consideration include the student's motivation, initiative, maturity, seriousness of purpose, and leadership potential. SAT or ACT test scores are optional. Campus visit and admissions interviews are required. Open houses and interview days are held in October, November, February, March, and April, and throughout the summer.

Application and Information

Mitchell uses a rolling admission policy. Students can expect to be notified of decisions within weeks of the College's receipt of completed applications and official transcripts sent directly from the students' high schools.

For more information, students should contact:

Kimberly S. Hodges
Director of Admissions
Mitchell College
437 Pequot Avenue
New London, Connecticut 06320-4498
Phone: 800-443-2811 (toll-free)
Fax: 860-444-1209
E-mail: admissions@mitchell.edu
Web site: http://www.mitchell.edu

Mitchell is known for its sense of community and commitment to students' academic success.

MOLLOY COLLEGE
ROCKVILLE CENTRE, NEW YORK

The College

In 1955, 44 students became part of an exciting new tradition in higher education on Long Island. As the first freshman class of Molloy College, located in Rockville Centre, New York, these young students made a commitment to academic excellence. So did the College, which had a distinguished faculty of 15 and a library containing 5,000 books.

Today, Molloy offers students a rich and multidimensional education experience. The Long Island school encourages critical thinking and creative exploration in a personal community setting. Molloy combines the strengths of academic excellence and leadership with personal, compassionate mentoring to bring out the best in every student.

For over fifty years, Molloy College has evolved to become a dynamic learning institution with outstanding faculty, advanced technology, and a wide range of academic programs. In addition, Molloy has expanded its reach, offering graduate level courses at its Suffolk Center in East Farmingdale, New York, along with a number of on-site opportunities at area hospitals and school districts.

Molloy College students possess the confidence needed to live and work in this fast-paced, ever-changing world. The College has expanded its global learning program, where students travel from Rockville Centre and study abroad in Belgium, India, Italy, France, Spain, Thailand, and Australia. By traveling from Long Island and immersing themselves in cultures in other parts of the world, students gain knowledge while learning acceptance and understanding.

Closer to home, Molloy College students make a difference in Rockville Centre as well as other nearby local communities. For example, as part of Molloy's tradition of service, students become involved in a number of service projects that include BoxTown, a program to raise social consciousness about the issue of homelessness.

Athletics and academics go hand-in-hand at Molloy College, where students are known for both their athletic and scholastic success. The Long Island school has a winning tradition in a number of NCAA Division II athletic programs, and in 2010 the women's softball team became one of only eight teams in the country to qualify for the College World Series.

Campus life in Rockville Centre, New York, is alive and vibrant, with more than forty student clubs and honor societies. Whether it is writing for a campus publication or serving as a student government representative, Molloy has something for each student.

In recent years, Molloy College has become a focal point for civic discourse with key community forums. Top regional, national, and international leaders (including former Secretary of State Colin Powell and *Newsweek International* editor Fareed Zakaria) have come to Rockville Centre to visit the College in order to address critical and timely issues.

The College launched two new initiatives recently to enhance students' experience. The Sustainability Institute at Molloy College is Long Island's first-ever venture combining environmental advocacy and sustainability education within an academic institution. Molloy also started its new Irish Studies Institute recently with a presentation from Bertie Ahern, the former prime minister of Ireland.

Through Molloy College's diversity of programs, personal attention from faculty, and commitment to improving both Long Island and the world, students develop an "I will" attitude that prepares them to enter the professional world—ready and able to make a difference.

Location

Located on a 30-acre campus in Rockville Centre, Long Island, Molloy College is close to metropolitan New York and all its diverse and rich resources. The College is easily accessible from all parts of Nassau, Suffolk, and Queens counties.

Majors and Degrees

Molloy College offers the A.A. degree in liberal arts; the A.A.S. degree in nuclear medicine technology, respiratory therapy, and cardiovascular technology; and B.A., B.S., B.F.A., or B.S.W. degrees in accounting, art, biology, business management, communication arts, computer information systems, computer science, criminal justice, English, environmental studies, history, interdisciplinary studies, international peace and justice studies, mathematics, modern languages, music, music therapy, nursing, philosophy, political science, psychology, social work, sociology, speech-language pathology/audiology, and theology. Teacher certification programs are available in childhood (1–6), adolescence (7–12), and special education. Dual certification is available for birth–grade 2/childhood 1–6.

Special advisement is offered for students interested in predental, prelaw, premedical, or pre–veterinary programs.

On the graduate level, Molloy College offers a Master of Science degree as well as post-master's certification in nursing and education. M.B.A. programs are available in business, accounting, and personal financial planning. A Master of Social Work is offered through Molloy's partnership with Fordham University. Molloy also offers graduate degrees in criminal justice, music therapy, and speech pathology. In 2010, the College launched its first doctoral program, a Ph.D. in nursing.

The internship program at the College offers students the opportunity for on-the-job experience along with the classroom exposure so essential to the completely educated person. Internships are available in all areas of study.

Academic Programs

Advanced Placement credit is granted for a score of 3 or better on the AP exam. CLEP and CPE credit is also given. Molloy has a 4-1-4 academic calendar.

Academic Facilities

The Molloy campus has several new additions. The College's first residence hall will open for the fall 2011 school year, and there is a also a brand new student center. Additionally, late in 2011 Molloy will debut a new 550-seat performing arts theater, which will serve the campus as well as the surrounding communities.

The James E. Tobin Library houses a collection of 110,000 volumes, along with hundreds of subscriptions to print journals and periodicals. Students and faculty members have access to the library's databases on campus and off campus as well as through the College's Web site. The library also houses a library instruction room, where librarians meet with professors and individual classes for instruction on the use of the databases and related research methods. The Tobin Library is a wireless facility. In the Media Center, over 3,000 DVDs and VHS tapes support the curriculum.

Students may use more than 300 computers located in nineteen labs and open space areas. The College has 100 percent wireless coverage for portable devices.

The Wilbur Arts Center features numerous art studios, music studios, a cable television studio, and the Lucille B. Hays Theatre.

Kellenberg Hall houses six science labs, a language lab, and the education resource center. The Casey Center houses two nursing labs, and the behavioral sciences research facility is located in Siena Hall.

Costs

For 2010–11, tuition and fees were $21,170. The cost for part-time students was $700 per credit.

Financial Aid

More than 85 percent of the student body of Molloy College is awarded financial aid in the form of scholarships, grants, loans, and Federal Work-Study Program employment. Financial aid awards are based on academic achievement and financial need. Completion of the Free Application for Federal Student Aid (FAFSA) is required. No-need scholarships and grants are also available.

Students who have attained a 95 percent or better high school average and a minimum combined score of 1280 on the SAT (composite math and verbal scores) are considered for the Molloy Scholars' Program, which awards full-tuition scholarships. Partial scholarships are available under Dominican, Community Service, and Fine Arts Scholarships. The Transfer Scholarship Program grants partial-tuition scholarships to students transferring into Molloy College with at least a 3.0 cumulative average. Athletic grants (Division II only) are awarded to full-time students based on athletic ability in a variety of sports. The Community Service Award is awarded to full-time freshmen demonstrating a commitment to their community and their school.

Faculty

The over 500 full-time and part-time faculty members at Molloy are dedicated as much to the students as to their respective fields. The 9:1 student-faculty ratio allows for small classes where students can receive the individual attention they deserve.

In addition to their teaching responsibilities, faculty members advise students in their fields to help them select courses that both satisfy major course requirements and lead to the attainment of career goals.

Student Government

Every member of the Molloy College student body belongs to the Molloy Student Association, whose elected leaders form the Molloy Student Government. This group of students provides the leadership necessary to keep extracurricular life at Molloy College alive, productive, and practical.

Admission Requirements

Recommended admission qualifications include graduation from a four-year public or private high school or equivalent (GED test) with a minimum of 18.5 units, including 4 in English, 4 in social studies, 3 in a foreign language, 3 in mathematics, and 3 in science. Nursing applicants must have taken courses in biology and chemistry. Mathematics applicants must have taken 4 units of math and 3 of science (including chemistry or physics).

Biology applicants must have credits in biology, chemistry, and physics and 4 units of math. A portfolio is required of art applicants, and music students must audition. Social work applicants must file a special application with the director of the social work program.

The admissions committee bases its selection of candidates on the secondary school record, SAT or ACT scores, class rank, and the school's recommendation. A particular talent or ability can be important. Character and personality, extracurricular participation, and alumni relationships are all considered. On-campus interviews are recommended but not required.

The St. Thomas Aquinas Program, which houses both HEOP and the Albertus Magnus Program, may be an option for students not normally eligible for admission.

Molloy College also offers an honors program for a select group of academically gifted students. The program is open to entering freshmen in all majors.

Application and Information

To apply to Molloy College, students should submit the following credentials to the Admissions Office: a completed application for admission, a nonrefundable $30 application fee, an official high school transcript or GED score report, official results of the SAT or ACT, and official college transcripts (transfer students only).

The College uses a rolling admission system. Students are advised of an admission decision within a few weeks after the application filing process is complete.

For further information, prospective students should contact:

Director of Admissions
Molloy College
1000 Hempstead Avenue
P.O. Box 5002
Rockville Centre, New York 11571-5002

Phone: 888-4-MOLLOY (toll-free)
Web site: http://www.molloy.edu

On the campus of Molloy College.

MONMOUTH UNIVERSITY
WEST LONG BRANCH, NEW JERSEY

The University

Monmouth University is a dynamic, first-tier, private university that empowers students to reach their full potential as leaders able to make significant contributions to their community and society. Through small classes, individual attention, and innovative faculty members, students are afforded a challenging learning environment on a campus that offers both classic beauty and the latest technology.

Monmouth University (MU) has a diverse student body comprised of more than 4,700 undergraduates and 1,700 graduate students. While many are from the Northeast, students come from more than half of the continental United States and from twenty-eight nations around the globe. For those choosing to participate in University housing, Monmouth offers traditional residence halls and garden-style apartments. Some beachfront campus housing, sponsored by the University, is also offered to students who meet certain requirements. Housing is guaranteed for first-year students.

When not attending class, students have an assortment of extracurricular activities to choose from, including special-interest groups, theater arts groups, sports intramurals, the African American Student Union, Hillel, and sororities and fraternities that engage in service work on behalf of both the University and the community. Beyond recreation, students can get involved with the Student Government Association, the campus newspaper *(The Outlook)*, the FM radio station (WMCX), the television station (Hawk TV), the yearbook *(Shadows)*, or the literary magazine *(Monmouth Review)*. The University has a myriad of events planned each year including art exhibits, concerts, lectures, and sightseeing trips that provide students with a shared experience outside the classroom.

The University is proud to host a successful NCAA Division I intercollegiate athletics program that includes nine men's teams (baseball, basketball, cross-country, football [FCS], golf, indoor track, outdoor track and field, soccer, and tennis) and eleven women's teams (basketball, bowling, cross-country, field hockey, golf, indoor track, lacrosse, outdoor track and field, soccer, softball, and tennis).

Being committed to an exceptional educational experience means having the facilities and services to provide state-of-the-art education and enrichment programs. The 153,200-square-foot Multipurpose Activity Center (MAC) provides just that. The MAC features a 4,100-seat arena with premium suites; a 200-meter, six-lane indoor track; locker rooms; a fitness center; educational and conference space; Champions' Hall; the University Store; and more. Boylan Gymnasium features an indoor pool, regulation-size basketball courts, a training room, and a fitness center. Also on campus are an outdoor tennis court; an all-weather track; and baseball, football, soccer, and softball fields.

Monmouth students are afforded special services, including the aptly named First Year at Monmouth Office designed to help incoming first-year students adapt to their new environment. The Center for Student Success offers academic advising and individual personal and career counseling, while Academic Skills Services provides personalized academic assistance including one-on-one tutoring. Employment counseling is available through Career Services.

Monmouth graduates, known for making their mark as leaders in their chosen fields, also make a lasting impact on their school and surrounding community during their time on campus. The student newspaper, *The Outlook*, was named most outstanding newspaper by the American Scholastic Press Association, while the Model United Nations Team received honorable mention at the 2010 National Model United Nations Conference. The Leon Hess Business School obtained Beta Gamma Sigma premier chapter status for a fourth year in a row, and the University's course in entrepreneurship was the recipient of the 2010 Innovative Entrepreneurship Course Award, a competition organized by the United States Association for Small Business and Entrepreneurship (USASBE). The Monmouth University Debate Hawks were named the 2010 Northeast region Policy Debate Program of the year by the Society Advocating More and Better Argumentation (SAMBA), and they helped start a debate team at nearby Asbury Park High School. Monmouth students reach their goals by engaging their advisers early and often, and MU seniors describe faculty members as significantly more available, helpful, and sympathetic than do students at comparable institutions.

Location

Part of a quality college experience is a location that is more than just a place, but a destination. Monmouth is a destination that offers something for everyone. The campus is in a residential area, a mile from the Atlantic Ocean and an hour from New York City and Philadelphia. While providing easy access to these locales, the University's secure 156-acre campus serves as a home base for students. Restaurants, shops, and theaters are within easy reach, and the PNC Bank Arts Center (an entertainment hub) is only a few miles away.

Monmouth is also close to many technology firms, financial institutions, and a business-industrial sector that provide both employment possibilities for graduates and opportunities for undergraduates to get experience through internships and the cooperative education program.

Majors and Degrees

Monmouth University offers thirty-three baccalaureate degree programs in six academic schools. While each program and course of study is unique, all schools share the University's commitment to providing the highest level of education through innovative techniques and personal attention. The Leon Hess Business School awards bachelor's degrees in business administration with concentrations in accounting, economics, finance, management, marketing, and real estate. The School of Education awards bachelor's degrees that allow students to earn certification as elementary teachers, as P–3 with teacher of students with disabilities endorsement, as secondary teachers, or with K–12 endorsement. The Wayne D. McMurray School of Humanities and Social Sciences awards bachelor's degrees in anthropology, art, communication, criminal justice, English, fine arts, foreign language, graphic design, history, history/political science, music, political science, psychology, and theater. A Spanish and international business bachelor's degree is awarded jointly through the Leon Hess Business School and the School of Humanities and Social Sciences. The School of Science awards bachelor's degrees in biology, chemistry, clinical laboratory sciences, computer science, marine and environmental biology and policy, mathematics, medical technology, and software engineering. The School of Social Work awards the Bachelor of Social Work degree. The Marjorie K. Unterberg School of Nursing and Health Studies awards the Bachelor of Science in health studies and the Bachelor of Science in Nursing, the latter of which is available to upper-division transfer students. A preprofessional advising program is available for students who intend to pursue careers in medicine, dentistry, or other health-care fields. Monmouth also offers the Five-Year Baccalaureate/Master's program, which enables students to earn both a bachelor's and a master's degree in five years, in business, computer science, criminal justice, education (select programs), English, history, political science/public policy, psychology/school counseling, social work, or software engineering.

Monmouth students can continue their studies with graduate degree programs in anthropology (new in 2011), business administration, computer science, corporate and public communication, criminal justice, Doctor of Nursing Practice (new in 2011), education, English, financial mathematics, health-care management, history, mental health counseling, nursing, psychological counseling, public policy, social work, or software engineering. There are also graduate certificate programs in numerous areas of interest.

Academic Programs

The curriculum at Monmouth is focused on creating the next generation of leaders, attuned to today's globally oriented, technological society yet grounded in the liberal arts. Under the general education curriculum, students in all degree programs acquire a breadth of knowledge beyond their major fields of study, including an appreciation of world culture. The University also emphasizes writing, speaking, and other interpersonal skills that are critical to personal and professional success. Monmouth equips every student with technological literacy and an experiential education—a real-world experience related to the student's academic major.

Beyond preparing students for successful careers in leadership roles, Monmouth University believes that a major goal of higher education is to help students develop values. These include a sense of citizenship and social responsibility that enables graduates to contribute actively to the democratic society in which they live. Academic programs at Monmouth prepare students to take the lead in an increasingly complex, multicultural world.

The Honors School at Monmouth University allows qualified students to participate in an educational environment that encourages and supports intellectual and personal excellence. Courses are clustered, with professors developing common themes and assignments. Honors classes are distinguished by in-depth coverage of material through discussion and writing, smaller class size, and a heightened student/faculty rapport. Extracurricular activities like cultural excursions to New York City are scheduled to reinforce the themes of the program.

Experiential education is available, enabling students to gain experience related to their majors while completing their studies. All education majors complete a semester of student teaching. The University also participates in the Washington Center, a partnership through which students may earn credit for experiential learning gained through internships and symposia in the nation's capital.

Genuine concern for the individual student characterizes the educational program. Professors conduct all courses and supervise all laboratories. Students benefit from direct interaction with professors recognized for their scholarly expertise.

Academic Facilities

Monmouth's fifty-four buildings provide a synthesis of historical architecture and modern aesthetics. The signature building is Woodrow Wilson Hall, a National Historic Landmark which houses both classrooms and administrative offices. The Jules L. Plangere Jr. Center for Communication and Instructional Technology provides state-of-the-art facilities for students.

The Monmouth University Library holds approximately 333,000 print and online monographs, 159 databases (including e-journals, videos, and e-books), and over 43,000 electronic and print journal subscriptions. Academic programs are amply supported by state-of-the-art computer hardware and software and classroom/laboratory facilities. The major components supporting Monmouth's academic programs include UNIX, Windows, and Apple server systems connected by a sophisticated campus Ethernet network spanning twenty-three buildings and encompassing more than 2,400 workstations campuswide. Workstations that are specifically dedicated to student use are distributed among forty-seven instructional and open-use laboratories and include PC and Apple workstations. Laptop plug-in ports and wireless connectivity are available throughout the campus. A campus communications network (HawkNet) connects all Monmouth University computing resources to the Internet. All students receive a computer account that provides them with e-mail and Internet access.

The Lauren K. Woods Theatre lets students experience all phases of the theater arts, from acting to lighting. Students maintain control of all aspects of a theatrical performance. The University supports communications facilities for radio and television, a student-run FM radio station, and studios for art and music majors.

Costs

For 2010–11, tuition and fees were approximately $26,356 per year. Room and board costs were approximately $9936 per year; actual costs are determined by the type of room and meal plan selected. Costs are subject to change for 2011–12.

Financial Aid

Monmouth believes that qualified students should not be denied an educational opportunity due to lack of financial resources. The financial aid staff counsels students and their families and assists them in obtaining the maximum financial aid to which they are entitled. In a cooperative effort, the University utilizes institutional, federal, and state resources and expects a reasonable family contribution toward the cost of attendance. In developing each student's award package, all resources available are utilized to address individual circumstances and provide equitable treatment for all applicants.

A wide range of University scholarships and grants are offered to the incoming class each year. These are available to all prospective full-time, first-year, and transfer students and are offered on the basis of academic performance and without regard to financial need. Eligibility for University scholarship and grant funding varies according to the quality of the student's previous academic record. Award amounts range from $3000 to $16,500. Scholarships and grants are renewed at the same amount for each year of the student's undergraduate career, provided the student maintains satisfactory levels of academic performance. Scholarship recipients are required to maintain a minimum 3.0 cumulative GPA; academic excellence grant recipients must maintain a minimum 2.5 cumulative GPA; and incentive grant recipients must maintain a minimum 2.0 cumulative GPA. The University also participates in all federal and state grant and loan programs. To establish eligibility for these programs and capitalize on the assistance available to them, students must complete the Free Application for Federal Student Aid (FAFSA) and are encouraged to do so as soon after January 1 as possible. Students and their families are invited to call 732-571-3463, send e-mail to finaid@monmouth.edu, or visit the Financial Aid Office for assistance.

Faculty

The University's professors are leaders in their fields and contribute through research, publishing, and consulting services to their respective academic areas. There are 253 full-time and 351 part-time faculty members. Approximately 85 percent of the full-time instructional faculty members have doctorates or terminal degrees in their fields. The average class size is 22, and the student-faculty ratio is 15:1. Professors often know each student by name, and faculty members are available to students for office consultation and extra help.

Student Government

Monmouth's Student Government Association (SGA) is an important and necessary voice in the University community; its views are recognized and respected. Six senators from each class, 2 commuter senators, 4 senators-at-large, and members who have been installed by the executive leadership express opinions and cast votes on University policy as it affects students. Senators meet with campus administrators and faculty members to present the opinions of the student body and take part in resolution-adopting events. The SGA also hosts a number of events annually, including Homecoming; Giving Trees; the Big Event/Day of Community Service; Springfest; the SGA Auction to benefit a local charity; and the Student Awards Ceremony. All students are strongly encouraged to participate in these activities. More information about SGA is available at http://www.monmouth.edu/sga.

Admission Requirements

Many factors are considered in an admission application. For freshman applicants, a committee evaluates the required high school transcripts and SAT or ACT scores. Counselor recommendations, a resume of activities including leadership positions held, and other information supporting the application are welcome. Campus tours and information sessions with admission counselors are available. Transfer students must submit official transcripts from all colleges attended. If transfer students have earned fewer than 24 transferable credits, they must fulfill freshman admission requirements as well.

Application and Information

Early action is a non-binding option for students with a strong desire to enroll at Monmouth. The early action application deadline is December 1 and the admission decision notification date is January 15. The application deadline for regular decision is March 1, with an admission decision notification date prior to April 1. Applications received after March 1 are considered on a space-available basis. Freshman housing is guaranteed for students who submit the required enrollment deposit, housing deposit, and housing contract by May 1. Students who submit their deposits and housing contract after May 1 will be placed on a housing wait list.

For further information, students should contact:

Office of Undergraduate Admission
Monmouth University
400 Cedar Avenue
West Long Branch, New Jersey 07764-1898
Phone: 732-571-3456
     800-543-9671 (toll-free)
Fax: 732-263-5166
E-mail: admission@monmouth.edu
Web site: http://www.monmouth.edu
     http://www.facebook.com/monmouthuniversity
     http://www.twitter.com/monmouthu

MONTCLAIR STATE UNIVERSITY

MONTCLAIR, NEW JERSEY

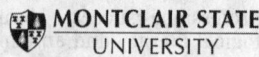

The University

For over 100 years, students have come to Montclair State University to fulfill their potential and reach for their dreams. Montclair State University is a four-year comprehensive public university that offers a broad range of educational and cultural opportunities. The second largest university in New Jersey, Montclair State is comprised of the College of the Arts, the College of Education and Human Services, the College of Humanities and Social Sciences, the College of Science and Mathematics, the School of Business, and the Graduate School. The University offers 250 undergraduate majors, minors, and concentrations, and graduate programs in 100 fields of study.

Montclair State has been designated a Center of Excellence in the fine and performing arts in New Jersey. It is accredited by the Middle States Association of Colleges and Schools, and its teacher education, administrative, and school service personnel programs are approved by the National Council for Accreditation of Teacher Education. The School of Business is also accredited by AACSB International—The Association to Advance Collegiate Schools of Business.

The total enrollment was 18,402 in fall 2010, 14,303 of whom were enrolled as undergraduates. The University is focused on the overall development and the well-being of its students. Believing that small class environments are more conducive to learning, the student-faculty ratio is 17:1, with professors interacting personally with their students to help further the learning process.

Residence halls—where almost 5,000 students will be living as of fall 2011—include traditional doubles, suite-style arrangements, and apartment communities. A beautiful 300-bed residence hall opened in 2010 and a new 2,000-bed residential-dining complex is scheduled to open in fall 2011, right next to the state-of-the-art Recreation Center. Montclair State University guarantees housing for all accepted students who want to live on campus and who submit a deposit by the deadline.

Special interest living communities enable residential students to live among people with whom they share interests. For example, the First Year Connections living community puts incoming freshmen together in a residence hall that has common areas where new students can meet and mingle. Whether it's the international living community—in a residence hall that has cooking facilities and is open all year to host international students—or living communities for arts students or students majoring in science and mathematics, Montclair State wants its students' residence experience to be enjoyable as they learn and build lifelong friendships.

The University's Center for Student Involvement provides clubs, organizations, activities, and events to meet the needs of all students, including intramural sports, Student Government Association, cultural organizations, religious organizations, service- and volunteer-based organizations, commuter association resources and services, diversity retreats, and Greek organizations.

With seventeen varsity sports for men and women, Montclair State University athletics has one of the most competitive programs around. To date, Montclair State has captured five NCAA Division III national championships and had over 260 of its athletes honored as all-Americans. Montclair State competes in the highest of Division III conferences, including the New Jersey Athletic Conference (NJAC), Eastern College Athletic Conference (ECAC), and the Skyline/Knickerbocker Conference.

Location

Montclair State is situated on a beautiful 246-acre suburban campus only 14 miles west of New York City. There are two New Jersey Transit train stations right on campus that provide easy access to Penn Station in New York City. This proximity to the city gives students the opportunity to take advantage of the unusually rich cultural, social, and educational environment of the metropolitan area, while Montclair's suburban setting offers a nice contrast to city life. Convenient access to all major New Jersey highways makes day trips to nearby mountain resorts and ocean beaches an easy option.

Majors and Degrees

Montclair State offers programs of study leading to the Bachelor of Arts degree in anthropology, broadcasting, child advocacy, classics, communication studies, dance education, economics, English, family and child studies, fashion studies, fine arts, French, general humanities, geography, history, Italian, jurisprudence, justice and families, justice studies, Latin, linguistics, music therapy, philosophy, political science, psychology, religious studies, sociology, Spanish, theater studies, and women's and gender studies. The Bachelor of Science degree is offered in aquatic and coastal studies, athletic training, biochemistry, biology, business administration, chemistry, computer science, geosciences, health education, information technology, mathematics, molecular biology, nutrition and food science, physical education, physics, and science informatics. The Bachelor of Fine Arts degree is awarded in animation and illustration, dance, filmmaking, fine arts, graphic design, industrial design, musical theater, and theater. The Bachelor of Music is awarded in music, and there is a five-year combined B.A./B.Mus. program. Additional dual-degree programs include combined bachelor/master's degree programs in education, combined B.S./M.S. degrees in aquatic and coastal sciences, biology, chemistry, and computer science, combined B.S./medical degrees with the University of Medicine and Dentistry of New Jersey and the New York institute of Technology School of Osteopathic Medicine, and a combined B.S./Pharm.D. with Rutgers University.

The Family and Child Studies major offers concentrations in child life specialist, early and middle childhood for elementary school certification K–5, and early childhood for preschool through third grade certification. In addition, teacher certification programs are offered in many of the subject areas mentioned for grades through 12.

Minors and interdisciplinary academic programs are available in many of the majors listed, as well as in areas such as African American studies; Arabic; Asian studies; archeology; cognitive science; criminal justice; environmental policy studies; gay, lesbian, bisexual, transgender, and queer studies; German; international studies; Jewish American studies; journalism; Latin American and Latino studies; microtonal music studies; paralegal studies; prelaw studies; public administration; Portuguese; Russian; Russian area studies, and urban studies. Part-time bachelor's degree programs are available.

The University offers robust career services and community-based learning programs that help students discover their aptitudes and uncover future career possibilities.

Academic Programs

Successful completion of a minimum of 120 semester hours is necessary for graduation. Course requirements include general education (34–58 semester hours), comprising communication, humanities and the arts, pure and applied sciences, social and behavioral sciences, a physical education requirement, a multicultural awareness requirement, and courses in the major field of study (32–82 semester hours).

The academic calendar is organized into two semesters (fall and spring) plus winter and summer session classes.

Off-Campus Programs

The Global Education Center at Montclair State organizes and administers a variety of study-abroad programs to destinations throughout the world. Exciting opportunities exist for students to study abroad internationally for a summer, semester, or year-long program.

Montclair State University students can study in more than fifty countries. Study abroad—whether a short-term, faculty-led program or a year-long exchange program—enables students to see the world, be personally enriched, become more culturally aware, and be immersed in a new language, all while earning academic credit and bolstering career possibilities.

Academic Facilities

University Hall is the largest and most sophisticated building in Montclair State University's history. It houses more than sixty instructional spaces for use by all of the University's colleges and schools, including one 200-seat and six 100-seat lecture halls, thirty-nine general classrooms, eleven specialized classrooms and laboratories, and a number of student study lounges and gathering spaces, including a Mission-style outdoor courtyard.

The south wing of University Hall provides a state-of-the-art home for the University's nationally recognized College of Education and Human Services, including the ADP Center for Teacher Preparation and Learning Technologies, the Center of Pedagogy, the Literacy Enrichment Center, the Institute for the Advancement of Philosophy for Children, and offices and conference rooms for the more than 150 faculty and staff members in the College of Education and Human Services.

The holdings of the Harry A. Sprague Library include more than 430,000 monographs as well as materials in diverse formats such as DVDs, CDs, videocassettes, audiocassettes, and microforms. The library subscribes to over 70 online index/abstract databases that give access to over 30,000 online journals and magazines available through computers in the library, and on and off campus. The University also subscribes to over 2,000 serials (magazines, journals, newspapers, annuals, and yearbooks) in print format. It serves as a depository for United States and New Jersey government publications that are available in print, microform, CD-ROM, and online formats.

Café Diem, a sleek and modern 4,300-square-foot Internet café at Sprague Library, offers food, beverages, and wireless access to the Internet for students and staff members. The Library and Café Diem are open 24/5 when classes are in session.

The state-of-the-art, 78,000-square-foot Student Recreation Center features a six-lane swimming pool; a two-court gymnasium with an elevated running track; two racquetball courts; fitness, strength, and cardio training areas; space for aerobics and other fitness activities; locker rooms; and a snack bar.

The completely renovated and vastly expanded Chapin Hall is the new home to the John J. Cali School of Music, the only university-based school of music in the state of New Jersey.

Costs

For the academic year 2010–11, full-time tuition and fees were approximately $10,000 for New Jersey residents and $18,300 for out-of-state students. Room and board charges for the school year average about $10,600 and vary depending on the assigned residence hall, type of room, and meal plan selected. Costs are subject to change.

Financial Aid

Four major types of financial aid programs are available at Montclair State: loans, grants, scholarships, and employment. Within each of these categories, funding may be available through federal, state, and/or institutional sources. State aid programs include Tuition Aid Grants, Educational Opportunity Fund Grants, Bloustein Distinguished Scholars, and state-funded scholarships and loans. Federal sources of aid include Federal Pell Grants, Federal Supplemental Educational Opportunity Grants, the Federal Work-Study Program, Federal Stafford Student Loans, Federal PLUS Program loans, and programs for veterans. Over 70 percent of undergraduates receive financial aid. Students should contact the Financial Aid Office regarding application materials and deadline dates.

Faculty

Faculty members teach both graduate and undergraduate courses, with few departments employing graduate assistants. Approximately 94 percent of the faculty members hold doctorates or the appropriate terminal degree in their disciplines. A student-faculty ratio of 17:1 permits considerable interaction between students and professors. All faculty members have posted office hours in order to provide students with assistance in course material and in planning a program of study. In addition, faculty members participate actively in student-oriented activities, serve as advisers to student clubs, and conduct extracurricular workshops and field trips.

Student Government

The Student Government Association (SGA), a parent corporation that includes within its structure various class organizations and services for the student body, is composed of all undergraduates. The substantial budget of the SGA allows for the development and financing of student activities and services. The Student Government Association Legislature acts as the final representative for the entire undergraduate student body and is composed of elected representatives from each class and major curriculum.

Admission Requirements

Montclair State is an Equal Opportunity/Affirmative Action institution and does not discriminate on the basis of sex, race, color, national origin, age, or physical handicap in providing access to its benefits and services, in compliance with relevant federal and state legislation.

Montclair State University considers a number of factors during the admission process. These factors include the rigor of high school curriculum, the overall grade point average (GPA), standardized test scores, and additional factors that contribute to successful degree attainment. These standards are subject to change depending on the demand for programs and the number of students that can be accommodated.

In preparation for the academic rigor of Montclair State University, students should have followed a challenging high school curriculum. Freshman applicants are required to have completed the following high school courses with satisfactory grades: 4 units of English, 3 units of math (in the algebra, geometry, algebra II sequence), 2 units of the same foreign language, 2 units of lab sciences, 2 units of social sciences, and 3 units of academic electives (which may include additional units of math, languages, sciences or social sciences).

Montclair State University reviews each application individually; however, when considering an applicant for freshman admission, certain minimum standards are followed. Strong candidates for admission generally meet the following criteria: a GPA of 3.0 or greater in the required curriculum, a combined SAT score of 1425 (math, critical reading, and writing), or ACT composite score of 20.

Application and Information

Applicants must submit a completed application form, a nonrefundable application fee, a copy of their official high school transcript, and copies of their SAT or ACT scores.

Early action deadline is November 15, with notification on December 15. The freshman priority application deadline is December 15. An admissions decision for students who have met this deadline will be mailed on February 1. Students who complete an application after December 15 will receive a decision on a rolling basis after February 1. All applications must be received by March 15.

To apply online, students should visit the University's Web site at http://www.montclair.edu.

Office of Undergraduate Admissions
Montclair State University
1 Normal Avenue
Montclair, New Jersey 07043
Phone: 973-655-4444
E-mail: undergraduate.admissions@montclair.edu
Web site: http://www.montclair.edu
http://www.facebook.com/MontclairStateUniversity
http://twitter.com/montclairstateu

Montclair State University has a beautiful suburban campus in Northern New Jersey and is just 14 miles from New York City.

MORNINGSIDE COLLEGE

SIOUX CITY, IOWA

The College

The Morningside College experience cultivates a passion for lifelong learning and a dedication to ethical leadership and civic responsibility. For more than 115 years, the goal of Morningside College has been to provide students with an education of the highest quality. Morningside is rooted in a strong church-related, liberal arts tradition, and its challenge is to prepare students to be flexible in thought, open in attitude, and confident in themselves.

Founded in 1894, Morningside College is a private, four-year, coeducational, liberal arts institution affiliated with the United Methodist Church. The College seeks both students and faculty members representing diverse social, cultural, ethnic, racial, and national backgrounds.

At the graduate level, Morningside confers a Master of Arts in Teaching, with professional educator or special education tracks.

Morningside College's 1,200 full-time undergraduate students are encouraged to participate in a wide variety of activities, including departmental, professional, and religious organizations; honor societies; and sororities and fraternities. A newspaper, literary magazine, and campus radio station are all student directed. These activities provide students with many opportunities to develop leadership, interpersonal, and social skills. Since nearly all activities on campus are student initiated and student directed, ample opportunities for leadership development exist. Music recitals and concerts, theater productions, and an academic and cultural arts and lecture series are held each semester. Intercollegiate athletics are available for men in baseball, basketball, cross-country, football, golf, soccer, swimming, tennis, track and field, and wrestling and for women in basketball, cross-country, golf, soccer, softball, swimming, tennis, track, and volleyball. A variety of intramural activities are available.

The Hindman-Hobbs Center includes a pool, saunas, racquetball courts, a weight room, basketball courts, a wrestling room, and a jogging track as well as classroom facilities and offices.

Location

Morningside College is located on a 68-acre campus in Sioux City, the fourth-largest city in Iowa. The campus is based in a residential section of the community, adjacent to a city park, swimming pool, and tennis courts and within 5 minutes of a major regional shopping mall and a new shopping center. The Sioux City metropolitan area offers a blend of urban shopping, commerce, and recreation in a scenic setting. Students find Morningside's Sioux City location to be advantageous in seeking internship opportunities and full- or part-time employment.

Majors and Degrees

The five undergraduate degrees conferred by Morningside College are the Bachelor of Arts, Bachelor of Science, Bachelor of Science in Nursing, Bachelor of Music, and Bachelor of Music Education. Career programs consist of accounting, advertising, art, biology, business administration, chemistry, computer science, corporate communications, elementary education, engineering physics, English, graphic arts, history, interdisciplinary studies, marketing, mass communications, mathematics,

music, nursing, philosophy, photography, political science, psychology, religious studies, Spanish, special education, and theater. Students choosing to teach in secondary school may be certified in most academic majors.

In cooperation with other institutions, Morningside offers preprofessional programs in dentistry, engineering, law, medical technology, medicine, the ministry, optometry, pharmacy, physical therapy, physician assistant studies, and veterinary medicine.

Academic Programs

Morningside operates on a two-semester system; sessions are held from late August to December and from January to early May. Evening classes are offered each semester. A three-week May Term and a six-week summer session are also available.

The Morningside College experience provides an education that develops the whole person through an emphasis on critical thinking, effective communication, cultural understanding, practical wisdom, spiritual discernment, and ethical action. By working with talented faculty members in a large number of majors, caring college staff members who provide numerous opportunities for valuable cocurricular experiences, and other exceptional and interesting students with whom they will form lifelong connections, Morningside students gain the knowledge, skills, and personal dispositions that will ensure their success.

Special opportunities include a voluntary Interdepartmental Honors Program, in which students meet weekly to discuss ideas that have shaped history from the ancient world into the future. Friday Is Writing Day, offered in a weekly discussion format, allows students and faculty members to read aloud and react to one another's writing.

Every entering full-time student is provided with a notebook computer that is used in classroom work. Student technology services include high-speed Internet connection, ports in all residence halls and classrooms, Web-accessible personal e-mail accounts, a digital library accessible day and night, specialized computer labs to support academic programs, and wireless network access points across campus.

Off-Campus Programs

Morningside students who qualify have the opportunity to take advantage of special programs for off-campus study. Programs are available for a semester or the entire school year. The College has agreements with schools in Italy, England, Japan, and Northern Ireland.

Students participate in exchange programs with the Consortium Institute of Management and Business Analysis (CIMBA) in Italy; Kansai Gaidai University in Japan; Queen's University, the University of Ulster, Belfast Metropolitan College, Stranmillis University College, and St. Mary's University College in Northern Ireland; and Edge Hill University and the Centre for Medieval and Renaissance Studies in England.

In addition, Morningside has opportunities for students to enroll for a semester at American University in Washington, D.C., to study the U.S. government in action. Students may also be nominated for a semester at Drew University in New Jersey to study the United Nations. Students who participate in these programs maintain their enrollment at Morningside College.

Academic Facilities

The Hickman-Johnson-Furrow Learning Center is the home of the library and the Academic Support Services Center. The library has more than 99,000 volumes, nearly 3,000 audio recordings and video materials, and nearly 440 current print periodical subscriptions. Online accessibility includes student/faculty access to more than 18,000 full-text journals. The library's Web-based, integrated online system allows seamless access to numerous subscription databases as well as other online catalogs and Web sites. The library building also houses the Spoonholder Café, classrooms, the Mass Communication Department, and a computer lab.

Charles City College Hall is listed individually on the National Register of Historic Places and houses classrooms and offices for the History and Political Science, Philosophy, Religious Studies, and Theatre Departments.

The Eugene C. Eppley Fine Arts Building is one of the finest music and art facilities in the Midwest. The auditorium seats 1,400 and is noted for its acoustical qualities and the majestic Sanford Memorial Organ. The MacCollin Classroom Building, adjoining the auditorium, houses offices, art studios, practice rooms, and classrooms for music and art students.

The Helen Levitt Art Gallery adjoins the Eppley Auditorium and is home to the Levitt art collection, which includes work by internationally famous artists.

Lewis Hall, the second-oldest building on campus, is the site of the Education, English, Modern Languages, and Nursing Departments as well as administrative offices and Student Services.

The Robert M. Lincoln Center houses the College's division of business administration and economics and contains a library, auditorium, a conference room, several classrooms, and the newly remodeled Center for Entrepreneurship Education.

The James and Sharon Walker Science Center, completely renovated in 2001, features up-to-date laboratories and classrooms and houses offices for the Natural Sciences and Mathematics Division.

Costs

Tuition and fees for 2010–11 were $22,980, and room and board were $7040. These figures do not include books and personal expenses.

Financial Aid

In 2009–10, more than $29 million was awarded in financial aid to Morningside students, with an average financial aid package of $23,385. The financial aid resources of federal, state, and College programs are available to Morningside students through a combination of scholarships, grants, loans, and work-study employment. Morningside values students who achieve both in and out of the classroom—people who are thinkers and doers. Morningside Celebration of Excellence Scholarships recognize academic excellence and outstanding service, and awards of up to $12,500 per year are renewable for four years. Morningside also values its ties with alumni and the United Methodist Church, and those awards are also renewable for four years.

Students are encouraged to submit the Free Application for Federal Student Aid (FAFSA) as early as possible. The College's code number is 001879. The annual priority deadline for need-based financial aid is March 1.

Faculty

Seventy-one percent of Morningside College's 77 full-time faculty members have earned the terminal degree in their chosen field. The College also employs 102 part-time instructors and has a 13:1 student-faculty ratio.

Student Government

Student government is directly responsible for regulation, supervision, and coordination of student campus activities. The president of the student body is a voting member of the Board of Directors, allowing for student input in decisions facing the Board.

Admission Requirements

Morningside College selects students for admission whose scholastic achievement and personal abilities provide a foundation for success at the college level. While the College seeks students who rank in the upper half of their graduating class, each application is considered on an individual basis. The student's academic record, class rank, and test scores are considered. Transfer students must have earned 24 transferable semester hours of a 2.25 or better cumulative GPA on previous college work to qualify for automatic admission. It is the policy and practice of Morningside College to not discriminate against persons on the basis of age, sex, religion, creed, race, color, national or ethnic origin, sexual orientation, or physical or mental disability.

Application and Information

Rolling admission allows for flexibility; however, prospective students are encouraged to apply as early as possible before the semester in which they wish to enroll. Transfer and international students are welcome. Catalogs, application forms, and financial aid forms are available from the Office of Admissions.

For further information, students should contact:

Office of Admissions
Morningside College
1501 Morningside Avenue
Sioux City, Iowa 51106
Phone: 712-274-5111
        800-831-0806 (toll-free)
E-mail: mscadm@morningside.edu
Web site: http://www.morningside.edu
        http://www.facebook.com/msideadmissions

Morningside College students enjoy small class sizes and one of the most attractive campuses in the Midwest.

MOUNT ALOYSIUS COLLEGE

CRESSON, PENNSYLVANIA

The College

Mount Aloysius College is a private, comprehensive, Catholic liberal arts college sponsored by the Sisters of Mercy. Established in 1853, the College today specializes in both undergraduate and graduate education. Since the founding of the College, more than 13,500 students have become proud Mount Aloysius College graduates. The College is committed to providing a small classroom size and a highly structured environment. Mount Aloysius College students come from the commonwealth of Pennsylvania, but many other states are represented on campus, including Connecticut, Delaware, Maine, Maryland, Missouri, New Jersey, New York, Vermont, Virginia, and West Virginia. Approximately 65 percent of the College's students are women. There are over 2,000 students enrolled (unduplicated headcount).

Mount Aloysius College is one of sixteen Mercy Colleges nationwide. As part of the Mercy College curriculum, students are encouraged to evaluate ethical issues and form a sound character consistent with traditional, Judeo-Christian values. Social growth is seen as a vital element of a complete liberal arts education, encompassing the important ability to relate closely to people.

The College recognizes that student activities play a distinctive role in the total campus educational program. There are approximately 100 organized clubs, groups, honor societies, and intramural sports programs, including a newspaper, residence hall associations, student government, cheerleading, dance team, scholarship-funded theater and choir programs, and a student activities planning board. Student activities include many social events, intramural sports programs, NCAA Division III athletic events, comedians, cultural and educational events, campus forums, and lectures by guest speakers.

Mount Aloysius College is a member of NCAA Division III. The following athletic programs are available to both women and men: basketball, cross-country, golf, soccer, and tennis. Men's baseball and women's softball and volleyball are also offered. Both intercollegiate and intramural athletes benefit from the Ray S. and Louise S. Walker Athletic Field Complex, which includes a softball field, one of the finest soccer fields in the area, and the Calandra-Smith baseball field.

Many buildings make up the 193-acre campus. The main building is a picturesque structure dating to 1897; it houses the admissions, financial aid, security, health, and academic offices, along with the Office of the President, classrooms, the nursing robotics center, and the Wolf-Kuhn art gallery. Cosgrave Center is the main hub on campus, serving as the Student Union. The building contains the dining hall, snack bar, bookstore, child-care center (part of the elementary education/early childhood program at the College), lounges, recreational rooms, student affairs offices, and meeting rooms. The College's Health and Physical Fitness Center is adjacent to Cosgrave Center. Its main athletic arena has a seating capacity of approximately 2,000 and serves as the home to all Mounties fans. The facility provides space for three basketball courts, three volleyball courts, a tennis court, a weight and exercise room equipped with a sauna, two locker rooms, office areas, changing rooms for sports officials, public restrooms, a lobby, and a vestibule. Ihmsen Halls are key housing facilities for residential students. Misciagna Residence is a state-of-the-art residence hall, providing twenty-five suites and private bathrooms. McAuley Hall features both double and single rooms. This hall houses a large multipurpose room as well as study lounges on each of its three floors. Alumni Hall, which was recently renovated to twenty-first century standards, is a historic, multipurpose room that is used for College drama, musicals, lectures, and many performing arts

events. The College operates twelve months per year and opens its facilities to the outside community as well.

The campus offers 100 percent wireless Internet access for laptops and PDAs. Wireless access points are installed in all buildings throughout the campus. In addition, several smart classrooms are located around campus.

Mount Aloysius is a comprehensive college that is fully accredited by the Middle States Association of Colleges and Schools and approved by the Pennsylvania Department of Education. All nursing programs and health studies programs are fully accredited by their professional accrediting bodies, including the National League for Nursing Accrediting Commission, the Commission on Accreditation in Physical Therapy Education, the American Association of Medical Assistants, and the Joint Commission on Accreditation for Programs of Surgical Technology.

In addition to its undergraduate programs, Mount Aloysius offers master's degrees in business administration, community counseling, criminal justice management in correctional administration, education, and psychology.

Location

Mount Aloysius College is located in the scenic southern Allegheny Mountains of west-central Pennsylvania, in the small town of Cresson, which is adjacent to U.S. Route 22. The College's setting is rural, with two midsized cities, Altoona and Johnstown, within a very short distance. The area has warm, beautiful summers; brisk, breathtaking autumns; invigorating, snowy winters; and cool, blooming springs. Facilities in the area are available for outdoor activities, including biking, golfing, swimming, horseback riding, waterskiing and water activities, hiking, spelunking, picnicking, and amusement and water parks.

Majors and Degrees

Mount Aloysius College awards bachelor's and associate degrees in the arts, sciences, and health studies fields in both career-oriented and traditional liberal arts programs. Baccalaureate degrees are available in accounting, behavioral and social science, biology and general science, business administration, which includes a fifth-year M.B.A. option, computer science, criminology, elementary/early childhood education and secondary education (with certifications), English, general science, history/political science, humanities, information technology, math/science, medical imaging, nursing (RN-B.S.N. program), nursing (2+2), occupational therapy (3-2), physical therapy (4-2), physician assistant studies (3-2), prelaw, psychology, sign language/interpreter education, and undecided/exploratory. Associate degrees are offered in applied technology, business administration, criminology, early childhood studies, general studies, legal studies, liberal arts, medical assistant studies, nursing, nursing (LPN to RN), physical therapist assistant studies, prenursing, radiography/medical imaging, sign language/deaf studies, and surgical technology.

Academic Programs

Whether preparing students for careers upon graduation or for graduate school, Mount Aloysius recognizes the importance of a broad and liberal education. Thus, in addition to receiving solid preparation for a chosen career, every student at the College receives a foundation in the arts, sciences, and humanities through an outstanding core curriculum. Strong emphasis is placed on the specialized courses within each program of study, and many academic programs combine classroom experience with internships and related training at area clinical sites, agencies, and institutions. In addition to its regular academic programs, Mount Aloysius offers independent and directed study with a commitment to service, which is a key ingredient in a Mercy education. The College has an excellent honors program and academic services area. The academic calendar has two traditional semesters and two or three optional summer sessions.

Off-Campus Programs

An important feature of many academic programs is off-campus training. The majority of the College's programs of study require credit-yielding practicums, through which students work and receive training at local and regional hospitals, public and private schools, or health or human service agencies. Students in all health programs participate in required on-the-job training during their time at the College.

Academic Facilities

In 1995, Mount Aloysius College opened both a new library and a new era, signifying greater access to information for the College community. This state-of-the-art facility is the campus hub for technology and studying. With a Buhl Electronic Classroom and more than 80,000 print and nonprint titles, the library is an impressive, 31,000-square-foot facility with ample seating space, four group-study rooms, a reading lounge, a law library and classroom, an unparalleled 18,000-volume ecumenical collection that was donated by Pastor Gerald Myers, and additional room for future expansion. This facility is completely automated, with an online catalog and access to remote libraries and the World Wide Web at more than thirty public workstations. Also located in the library is the Information Technology Center, home to fifteen multimedia computer workstations and some of the latest offerings in educational software.

Pierce Hall serves as the science center on campus and is a state-of-the-art, 31,000-square-foot facility that was completed in 1997 and houses all science laboratories, health science centers, and offices of faculty members in the health studies programs. Academic Hall is an impressive facility that is home to the College Honors Program. It also has classrooms, labs, seminar rooms, faculty offices, and electronic rooms. The College is proud of its bridge to the past and its progress in providing twenty-first-century buildings.

Costs

Annual tuition and fees for the 2011–12 academic year for full-time students were $17,930, and room and board were $8080.

Financial Aid

Mount Aloysius recognizes the expense involved in acquiring a liberal arts education and encourages all students to apply for all available aid. Through the Office of Financial Aid, the College assists students in applying for state and federal grants, loans, work-study awards, and College merit scholarships and grants. The College awards academic monies based on GPA and SAT or ACT scores; these awards are renewable over a four-year period and range from $1000 to $10,000 per year. Mount Aloysius College participates in all federal and state programs; 90 percent of the College's students receive some form of financial aid. *U.S. News & World Report* has ranked Mount Aloysius College as one of the best-priced private liberal arts colleges in the U.S.

Faculty

The Mount Aloysius faculty consists of approximately 60 full-time members, whose primary responsibility is teaching and advising students. Most full-time faculty members hold advanced or terminal degrees and are expected to maintain close instructional ties with students. Many professors hold national professional certificates in such disciplines as criminology, education, law, and nursing. The Mount Aloysius student-faculty ratio of 14:1 allows close contact between students and faculty members, providing personal attention in a highly structured environment—a key ingredient in the College's academic philosophy.

Student Government

The Student Government Association (SGA) represents students on all issues that concern the College. The SGA appoints student representatives to all student-oriented College committees. The College encourages active student participation in the general governance structure and in other matters concerning the development and implementation of policies on residential student life.

Admission Requirements

The College enrolls a freshman class of approximately 350 students, which amounts to a total class of 550 with transfer students. Admission is selective and is based on academic promise, as indicated by a student's secondary school performance and activities, standardized test scores, and special experience and talents. Applicants are required to have, or expect to earn, a diploma from an approved secondary school or a GED diploma. Submission of official transcripts and SAT or ACT scores is required. In addition to the general admission requirements, specific admission requirements exist for the health programs; students should visit the College's Web site (http://www.mtaloy.edu) for further information. Prospective students are highly encouraged to visit the scenic 193-acre campus. The College is open Monday to Friday from 8:30 to 5 and on select Saturdays.

Application and Information

To apply for admission to Mount Aloysius College, candidates are encouraged to submit their application and $30 application fee to the Office of Undergraduate and Graduate Admissions. In addition, students may apply online. For further information, students should contact:

Office of Undergraduate and Graduate Admissions
Mount Aloysius College
7373 Admiral Peary Highway
Cresson, Pennsylvania 16630
Phone: 814-886-6383
        888-823-2220 (toll-free)
Fax: 814-886-6441
E-mail: admissions@mtaloy.edu
Web site: http://www.mtaloy.edu

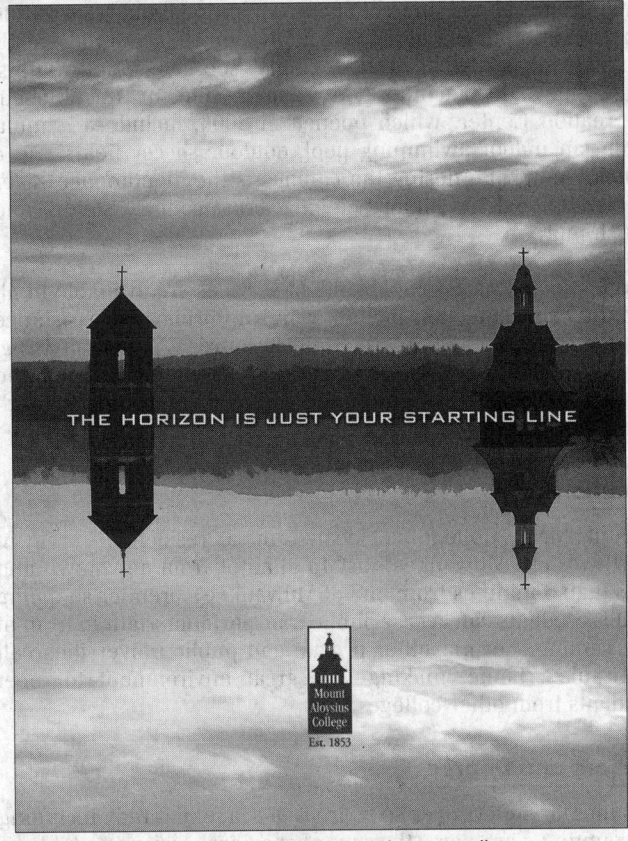

THE HORIZON IS JUST YOUR STARTING LINE

Mount Aloysius College Est. 1853

Student activities abound on the Mount Aloysius College campus.

MOUNT MARY COLLEGE

MILWAUKEE, WISCONSIN

The College

Mount Mary College, one of only fifty to sixty women's colleges in the nation, is home to nearly 1,900 undergraduate and graduate students. Located on a beautiful 80-acre wooded campus, only 15 minutes from downtown Milwaukee, students at Mount Mary are fully engaged in and outside of the classroom, learning not just the subject matter but also how to express opinions and develop leadership skills. Through exciting internships, club activities, community service, and campus ministry programs, students explore their interests and discover their skills. Special and professional interests are served by affiliates of national societies.

Caroline Hall, the student residence hall, provides accommodations for private occupancy and single and double suites. Over 90 percent of the rooms feature walk-in closets and over two thirds have private bathrooms. Every floor in Caroline Hall has newly renovated kitchens and lounge areas. All residence hall rooms have wireless computer access and are wired for cable television and telephone service. Mount Mary College sponsors many social activities including performances by comedians, holiday dances, and campus picnics.

Physical fitness and an interest in athletics are fostered through various activities, fitness programs, health and dance courses, and intramural and intercollegiate athletics. Mount Mary's Blue Angels are members of the NCAA Division III. The Blue Angels compete in basketball, cross-country, soccer, softball, tennis, and volleyball. Facilities on campus and in the Bloechl Recreation Center, which opened in 2006, include a gymnasium, an indoor swimming pool, outdoor soccer fields and a fitness center. Bordering the campus is the Menomonee River Parkway, ideal for biking, jogging, cross-country skiing, and much more.

Academic and professional student services are available to all Mount Mary students, including free tutoring and assistance with tests through the Academic Resource Center; advising, resume writing, and career planning through the Advising and Career Development Center; and personal counseling through the Counseling Center.

Location

Mount Mary College is located in a residential area in northwestern Milwaukee, just 15 minutes from downtown and less than 5 minutes from one of Milwaukee's premier shopping malls. Students can access public transportation right in front of the campus. Several other private and public universities call Milwaukee home, making it a great environment to meet students from other colleges.

Majors and Degrees

Mount Mary offers over sixty areas of academic study including accounting, art, art therapy, behavioral science, biology, business administration, chemistry, communication arts, diagnostic medical sonography, dietetics, education, English

(literature, professional writing, and education), fashion (apparel product development and merchandise management), graphic design, health sciences (preprofessional programs), history, interior design, international studies, justice, mathematics, nursing, occupational therapy, philosophy, psychology/behavioral science, public relations, radiologic technology, social work, Spanish, student designed, and theology. Columbia College of Nursing and Mount Mary College jointly offer a Bachelor of Science in Nursing (B.S.N.) degree. Special services for undeclared students help them find and focus on a major suited to their interests and talents.

In addition to undergraduate programs, Mount Mary also offers graduate programs in art therapy, business administration (M.B.A.), counseling (community, pastoral, and school), dietetics, education, English, and occupational therapy.

Academic Programs

Mount Mary's curriculum integrates leadership skills into each student's educational experience, developing leaders who take individual responsibility for social justice. The curriculum and co-curricular activities promote self-knowledge and competence, an entrepreneurial sense of vision, effective oral and written communication skills, and the ability to strengthen leadership in others. In their professions, churches, and communities, Mount Mary students model collaborative leadership, enabling them to work effectively both in leadership positions and as supportive team members.

Many academic programs at Mount Mary College offer internships, which allow students to relate theory to practice and interact with professionals while learning life skills. The process encourages students to reflect on the skills and knowledge they hope to gain and allows them to tailor their practical experience to the career goals they have set for the future. Many of the programs incorporate a work experience into the curriculum. Work experience includes student teaching, clinicals, fieldwork, practicum, and internships. Several majors also offer study abroad components allowing students to gain hands on experience in their major along with learning about another culture.

Off-Campus Programs

Mount Mary encourages its students to take advantage of a variety of study abroad opportunities. Accordingly, Mount Mary College has sponsored trips to a variety of countries including China, England, France, Guatemala, Ireland, Italy, Nicaragua, and Peru. In addition to these study-abroad programs, the College maintains affiliate relationships with numerous international colleges and universities, including the American College, Dublin, Ireland; the American Intercontinental University, London and Dubai; Nanzan College, Japan; Universidad Cathólica de Santa Maria (UCSM), Arequipa, Peru; and Notre Dame College, Kyoto, Japan.

The Office of International Studies also aids students in finding an accredited program that meets their individual needs.

Costs

For the 2010–11 academic year, undergraduate tuition was $21,668 for full-time students and $648 per credit for part-time students. Additional information about room and board and fees can be found online at http://www.mtmary.edu/tuition.htm. All costs are subject to change.

Financial Aid

The Financial Aid Office at Mount Mary College develops a financial package on an individual basis for qualified students. Upon acceptance, all students are automatically awarded an academic scholarship of up to $9000 per year. Additional scholarships are available. More than 95 percent of Mount Mary's full-time students receive some form of financial assistance. Students filing for financial aid should complete the Free Application for Federal Student Aid (FAFSA) online at http://www.fafsa.gov by March 1.

Faculty

Faculty members holding advanced degrees do all the teaching; no classes are taught by teaching assistants. In addition, every student is assigned a faculty advisor with whom they meet prior to registering each semester. With a total enrollment of nearly 1,900, Mount Mary offers a low faculty-to-student ratio with 12 to 20 students in most classes and no large lecture halls.

Student Government

Students are encouraged to participate in the governance of the College. Student Government makes recommendations about College policies and other matters of importance to students and serves as a liaison to the Mount Mary administration, faculty, and staff.

Admission Requirements

Candidates for admission are considered on the basis of academic preparation, scholarship, and evidence of the ability to do college work and benefit from it. Sixteen secondary school units are required; of these, 11 must be academic (3 in English, 2 in college-preparatory mathematics, 2 in science, 4 in history, language, or social science) and 4 in electives. Students must have achieved a minimum composite score of 18 on the ACT (870 on the SAT) and rank in the top 40 percent of their high school graduating class or have a minimum GPA of 2.5 (on a 4.0 scale). Students who do not meet the admission requirements are reviewed by an admission committee. International students must take the Test of English as a Foreign Language (TOEFL). Mount Mary does not discriminate against any individual for reasons of race, color, religion, age, national or ethnic origin, or disability. Mount Mary College is a women's college which accepts men into the undergraduate nursing program, postbaccalaureate certificate programs, and graduate programs.

Application and Information

Mount Mary has a rolling admission policy. Early acceptance is available, and Advanced Placement credits are honored. Interested students should submit an admission application, official high school transcripts, and ACT or SAT scores. After receiving their notification of acceptance, students wishing to enroll need to submit the $200 nonrefundable tuition deposit.

For further information, students should contact:

The Admission Office
Mount Mary College
2900 North Menomonee River Parkway
Milwaukee, Wisconsin 53222-4597

Phone: 414-256-1219
      800-321-6265 (toll-free)
Fax: 414-256-0180
E-mail: admiss@mtmary.edu
Web site: http://www.mtmary.edu
      http://www.facebook.com/mountmary?v=wall
      http://twitter.com/MountMary

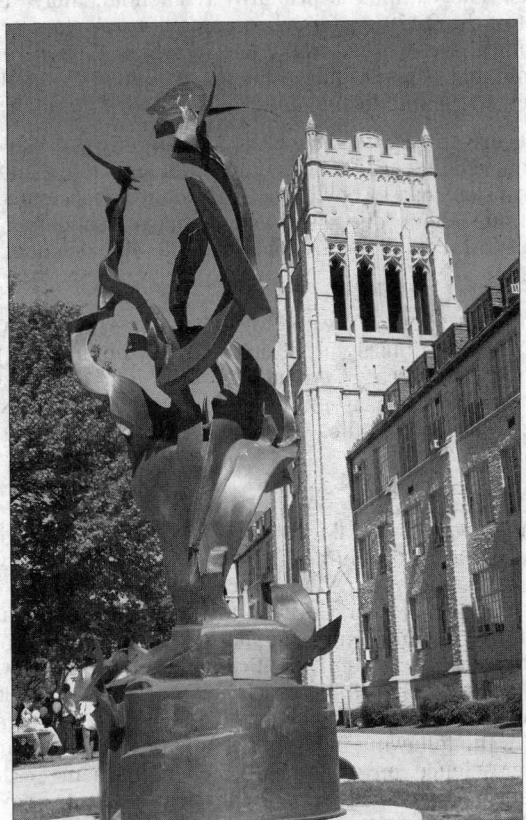

Mount Mary College is located on 80 acres in a convenient Milwaukee neighborhood. Students have a safe, secure environment in which to live and learn.

MUHLENBERG COLLEGE
ALLENTOWN, PENNSYLVANIA

The College

Founded in 1848, Muhlenberg College aims to develop independent critical thinkers who are intellectually agile, characterized by a zeal for reasoned and civil debate, knowledgeable about the achievements and traditions of diverse civilizations and cultures, able to express ideas with clarity and grace, committed to lifelong learning, equipped with ethical values, and prepared for lives of leadership and service.

Muhlenberg students achieve the College's goals by assuming strong individual responsibility for intense involvement in vigorous academic work and for personal involvement within the College community. The more than 100 student organizations provide outlets for the diversified cultural, athletic, religious, social, leadership, and service interests of the students. The campus is primarily residential; more than 90 percent of the 2,150 students live on campus. A close sense of community develops naturally, one in which their diversified academic and personal interests enable students to contribute positively to the intellectual and personal growth of their peers.

Students are aided by an active Career Planning and Placement Service in relating academic and personal knowledge and skills to appropriate career goals and in obtaining positions upon graduation. About one third of a typical graduating class proceeds immediately to graduate or professional school.

Location

Muhlenberg College is located in suburban west Allentown, an area made up primarily of attractive family homes and parks. The downtown area of Allentown, a city of approximately 104,000 people, is a 10-minute ride from the campus. The College is located 90 miles west of New York City and 60 miles north of Philadelphia.

Majors and Degrees

Muhlenberg offers the Bachelor of Arts (A.B.) degree in the following fields: accounting, American studies, anthropology, art, business, communication, dance, economics, English, film studies, finance, French, German, history, history/government, international studies, music, philosophy, philosophy/political thought, political economy, political science, psychology, religious studies, Russian studies, social science, sociology, Spanish, and theater arts. The Bachelor of Science (B.S.) degree is offered in the following fields: biochemistry, biology, chemistry, computer science, environmental science, mathematics, natural sciences, neuroscience, and physics. Students may also design their own major.

In addition, students may receive certification to teach at the elementary and secondary levels. Other opportunities include a 4-4 guaranteed-admission program with Drexel University College of Medicine; a 3-4 dental program with the University of Pennsylvania; a 3-3 B.S./Ph.D. program in physical therapy with Thomas Jefferson University; a 3-2½ B.S./M.S. program in occupational therapy with Thomas Jefferson University; a 3-2/4-2 combined program in engineering, offered in cooperation with Columbia University; and a 3-2 combined program in forestry, offered in cooperation with Duke University.

Academic Programs

The A.B. and B.S. programs emphasize breadth of study in the liberal arts as well as in-depth study of a particular academic major. All students must fulfill requirements in foreign culture, the humanities, social sciences, and natural sciences. Strong achievement on Advanced Placement examinations may enable a student to receive advanced placement, possibly with credit. Scores of 4 or 5 earn automatic credit. Scores of 3 are evaluated by the appropriate department.

Students work closely with academic advisers to formulate programs well suited to their individual interests, abilities, needs, and goals. Generally, students are expected to declare their major at the end of the freshman year; however, many students later change their academic major with no difficulty. A double major is possible, and several fields are available as minor programs. These minor fields are accounting, African American studies, anthropology, business, chemistry, computer science, economics, English, French, German, history, Jewish studies, mathematics, music, philosophy, physics, political science, public health, religion, sociology, Spanish, and women's studies. In addition, independent study and research are available. The College also enriches the freshman-year experience through more than thirty special-focus Freshman Seminars.

Off-Campus Programs

Study abroad is available through Muhlenberg's Semester-in-London Program, Netherlands Semester, or more than 150 affiliate agreements with international universities all over the world. In addition, the Lehigh Valley Association of Independent Colleges sponsors summer study-abroad options in England, France, Germany, Israel, and Spain. Credit for study-abroad programs sponsored by other institutions or by private agencies may also be transferred to Muhlenberg by special arrangement.

Students may participate in a variety of internships in local businesses, health-care facilities, schools, public agencies, theaters, broadcasting stations, and magazines. Government internships in Harrisburg, Pennsylvania, and Washington, D.C., and an Ethics and Public Affairs semester in Washington, D.C., are also available.

Students may enroll in courses offered at any of the five other member institutions of the Lehigh Valley Association of Independent Colleges: Lafayette College, Lehigh University, Cedar Crest College, DeSales University, and Moravian College.

Academic Facilities

Muhlenberg's library collection contains more than 200,000 volumes as well as numerous government documents, periodicals, and microforms. The $12-million Harry C. Trexler Library, a state-of-the-art library facility, opened in 1988. Students may also use library materials owned by the other institutions participating in the Lehigh Valley Association of Independent Colleges.

The Baker Center for the Arts was designed for Muhlenberg by the well-known architect Philip Johnson. It houses a modern theater complex, a recital hall, classrooms, art studios, and a fine arts gallery. The Trexler Performing Arts Pavilion opened in 2000 and provides dance performance and studio space, a new theater, a Black Box, and additional arts spaces.

Life science facilities include numerous laboratories, classrooms, two electron microscopes, a DNA sequencer, an isolation room used for growing and studying viruses, and a museum of natural history. Facilities supporting students in the physical sciences include equipment for optics, electronics, and atomic, nuclear, and solid-state physics. A new 40,000-square-foot addition to the science facilities opened in fall 2006. The College uses a UNIX/Windows computer system with Novell software.

Costs

The comprehensive tuition fee for the 2010–11 academic year was $38,380. The room and board fee averaged $8735. The total cost for a resident student was approximately $47,115.

Financial Aid

Muhlenberg College endeavors to make its educational opportunities available to all qualified students regardless of their financial circumstances. While most financial aid at Muhlenberg is based on financial need as demonstrated by the College Scholarship Service Financial Aid PROFILE, there is also significant merit aid available. Typically, about 70 percent of Muhlenberg's students qualify for and receive financial aid.

Faculty

The Muhlenberg faculty consists of 171 full-time and 120 part-time members. Ninety percent of full-time faculty members hold doctoral or terminal degrees. While many faculty members are distinguished for their scholarly research, teaching is the main emphasis of their work. Professors at all levels work closely with students both inside and outside of the classroom. Most department heads teach introductory courses.

Student Government

Muhlenberg students are expected to demonstrate a high level of responsibility with regard to their own governance and to participate extensively in internal decision-making and communication processes throughout the campus. These responsibilities are coordinated by the Student Council, which transacts all business pertaining to the student body. This organization is in charge of a student activities budget of more than $350,000. In addition, 2 students serve as representatives to the Board of Trustees, and students hold full voting privileges on many faculty committees.

Admission Requirements

The College selects students who give evidence of ability and scholastic achievement, seriousness of purpose, and the capacity to make constructive contributions to the College community. Approximately 70 percent of a typical freshman class ranked in the top fifth of their secondary school class. SAT scores for entering freshmen average approximately 610 verbal, 620 math, and 612 writing.

Submission of SAT or ACT scores is optional. An on-campus interview is strongly recommended for all applicants and required for students who choose not to submit standardized test scores.

Application and Information

Students who wish to be considered for admission should submit a completed application form as early as possible during their senior year of secondary school and no later than February 15. Candidates receive notice of admission decisions in late March. Early decision plans and transfer admission are possible.

For further information, interested students should contact:

Christopher Hooker-Haring
Dean of Admission and Financial Aid
Muhlenberg College
Allentown, Pennsylvania 18104-5586
Phone: 484-664-3200
E-mail: admissions@muhlenberg.edu
Web site: http://www.muhlenberg.edu

The Bell Tower of the Haas College Center stands as the focal point of the Muhlenberg College campus.

MUSKINGUM UNIVERSITY
NEW CONCORD, OHIO

The College

Since its founding in 1837, Muskingum has been a community of people learning from and with each other. Its mission is to offer high-quality academic programs in the liberal arts and sciences that educate the whole person intellectually, spiritually, socially, and physically. Muskingum's programs foster critical thinking, positive action, ethical sensitivity, and spiritual growth so that students may lead vocationally productive, personally satisfying, and socially responsible lives. Muskingum University is accredited by the North Central Association of Colleges and Schools and receives periodic reauthorization from the Ohio Board of Regents.

The University's proud heritage reaches back to the first half of the nineteenth century, when settlers were traveling westward over the newly completed National Road. During its first half-century, Muskingum adhered to the educational patterns of the classical college of the period. In 1877, Muskingum became associated with the Synod of Ohio of the United Presbyterian Church. Today, approximately 1,700 undergraduate students are enrolled at Muskingum; 90 percent of these students live on campus, representing twenty-eight states and fifteen other countries.

One of Muskingum's longest traditions is its affiliation with the Presbyterian Church. The Center for Church Life—a joint venture of Muskingum University, the Presbyterian Church Bicentennial Fund, and the Presbytery of Muskingum Valley— provides programs and services to support the ministries and missions of local congregations. On campus, the University Chaplain has created a multidimensional, unified campus ministry that allows students to worship and celebrate their faith.

While worship is important at Muskingum, students participate in other activities as well. More than ninety campus groups operate at the University, including varsity athletics, honor societies, music and religious organizations, and FM radio and cable TV stations. The residence halls are another center of student activity; living options range from traditional residence halls and sorority/fraternity houses to special program houses and College-owned apartments. Each residence hall provides lounges, computer labs, and television, kitchen, and laundry facilities.

Location

The village of New Concord, one of the many attractions along National Road, is a 1-hour drive from Columbus and a 2-hour drive from Pittsburgh and Cleveland. New Concord is surrounded by venues for boating, golfing, trail biking, skiing, hiking, camping, and rock climbing, all of which can be enjoyed in the town's temperate climate. New Concord is perhaps best known for its most famous resident—former astronaut and senator (and Muskingum alumnus) John Glenn, whose childhood home has become a museum.

Majors and Degrees

Bachelor's degrees are offered in the following areas: accounting, anthropology, art, biology, business, chemistry, Christian education, computer science, earth science, economics, early childhood education, engineering science, English, French, geology, German, health education, history, mathematics, middle childhood education, music, nursing, philosophy, physical education, physics, political science, psychology, religion, religion and philosophy, sociology, Spanish, special education, speech communication, and theater. Interdisciplinary majors include American studies, child and family studies, conservation science, criminal justice, environmental science, humanities, international affairs, international business, journalism, molecular biology, neuroscience, and public affairs. Students may also design their own interdisciplinary program. Preprofessional programs are available in Christian ministry, dentistry, engineering, law, medical technology, medicine, physical therapy, and veterinary medicine. Teacher licensure programs are available in the following areas: adolescent/young adult, art, early childhood, foreign language (French, German, or Spanish), middle childhood, music, physical education, and special education.

Academic Programs

Undergraduate programs combine solid classroom curricula with a level of field work and independent study that is rarely encountered in an undergraduate setting. The bachelor's degree requires completion of at least 124 credit hours with a minimum GPA of 2.0. The curriculum includes Liberal Arts Essentials, a series of courses that ensure the breadth that is inherent in a liberal arts education. This core requires 21–24 hours in core courses, including one English course, two writing courses, one speech course, one mathematics course, one art and humanities course, and one physical education course. Another 35–37 hours are completed in area requirements such as religious understanding, moral inquiry, Western civilization, foreign languages, social sciences, global studies, and other subjects. Students are also required to complete 15 credits in their major area of study, 12 of which must be completed at the College. Credit by examination allows students to earn credit for a course by passing a proficiency examination. A student earns credit for the course by scoring a C or better on the exam.

Off-Campus Programs

Selected students may spend one semester at American University in Washington, D.C., studying the American governmental system in action. Assignments may include the State Department, lobbying groups, or Capitol Hill. Students majoring in art may be able to spend their junior year studying at one of seventeen Art Institutes locations. Commercial art programs are available in the areas of fashion merchandising, industrial design technology, interior design, photography/multimedia, and visual communications. United Nations Semester is a program under which Muskingum students may apply for one semester of study at Drew University, during which time they take two courses involving on-site study at the United Nations headquarters in New York. International study provides the opportunity for sophomores, juniors, and seniors to study for one or two semesters at an international university in Asia, Canada, Europe, Latin America, or Puerto Rico.

Academic Facilities

The library contains 215,000 volumes, 574 print journals, and an extensive microfilm collection, plus access to more than 16,500 online journals, 17,000 electronic books, 1,200 electronic videos, and 110 research databases. The library is a member of the OPAL and OhioLINK consortia, thus giving students and faculty and staff members borrowing privileges at eighty-four academic libraries throughout the state. Brown Chapel serves as church, chapel, and auditorium for the University. Its main auditorium seats nearly 500, and the basement contains a lounge area, music practice rooms, and a small chapel. The John Glenn Physical Education Building houses two gymnasiums, a swimming pool, recreation and intramural equipment, and coaches' offices, while the Physical Education and Recreation Center holds a 2,800-seat gymnasium, four handball/racquetball courts, a baseball/softball hitting area, a weight room, and an athletic training room.

Costs

In the 2011–12 academic year, tuition is $10,500 per semester. Other costs per semester include a student activity fee of $118 and a technology fee of $187. Students living on campus could expect to pay $4270 per semester for room and board, as well as $66 for laundry services. Books and supplies, transportation, and other miscellaneous costs vary according to the student's specific needs.

Financial Aid

A small number of entering students receive the John Glenn Scholarship, a full-tuition award, while other students may receive academic scholarships ranging from $1000 to $12,000 per year. These awards are renewable with a GPA of 3.0 or higher. Other scholarships are available in the performing arts. These awards range from $500 to $2000 per year and are renewable with a satisfactory GPA. The College also offers Awards of Circumstance to students who meet the eligibility requirements. These awards range from $500 to $5000 per year. The limit on non-need assistance is $15,500 for recipients of Academic Scholarships unless the student has a sibling attending, then it is $16,500. Students may also be eligible for federal and state grants, and Federal PLUS loans.

Direct Stafford Loans are available to all students who are enrolled at least half-time. Federal Perkins Loans are available at an interest rate of 5 percent and are repayable after completion of studies. Federal PLUS loans are loans to parents of dependent students. The interest rate is 7.9 percent, and repayment begins within sixty days of disbursement. The University has a limited amount of funding available to be used as loan assistance to students. Repayment with 8 percent interest begins upon the student's departure from Muskingum.

Students may also borrow from other lenders. Campus job opportunities are available to students under the Federal Work-Study Program or the Muskingum Work Program. Most students are paid minimum wage and work 5–10 hours per week; students are limited to a total of 20 hours per week for all jobs combined.

Faculty

Of the more than 100 faculty members at the University, more than 90 percent hold a doctorate or the highest degree in their fields; 25 percent of them are full professors, while another 70 percent are associate and assistant professors. A student-faculty ratio of 16:1 allows for greater classroom participation.

Student Government

The Student Senate includes members elected from classes, social clubs, and residence areas. The Executive Board includes a president, vice president, secretary, and treasurer, all of whom are elected each spring, and four independent representatives. In addition, the sophomore, junior, and senior classes each elect a president, vice president, secretary, and treasurer. Student Senate meetings are held biweekly and are open to all members of the University community.

Admission Requirements

Prospective students must submit an application form, a Secondary School Report Form that has been completed and signed by a guidance counselor, official high school transcripts, official ACT or SAT scores, and, optionally, letters of recommendation, a personal written statement, and a recent photo. The admission decision is based on an evaluation of the student's overall background, including extracurricular activities, community service, and volunteerism. However, students who have completed a college-preparatory curriculum with a C+ average or better and scored 18 or higher on the ACT (860 or higher on the SAT) may be qualified for admission. The college-preparatory curriculum includes 4 years of English, 3 years of college-prep math, and at least 2 years each of laboratory science, social sciences, and foreign language.

Application and Information

Admission is made on a rolling basis, so prospective students may apply any time after the end of their senior year. After all application materials are received, the Admission Committee notifies the applicant of their decision within a few weeks. Interested students may request applications from:

Office of Admission
Muskingum University
163 Stormont Street
New Concord, Ohio 43762
Phone: 740-826-8137
       800-752-6082 (toll-free)
Fax: 740-826-8100
E-mail: adminfo@muskingum.edu
Web site: http://muskingum.edu/home/index.html
          http://on.fb.me/Muskingum_Univ (Facebook)

NAROPA UNIVERSITY
BOULDER, COLORADO

The College

A leader in contemplative education, Naropa University is a private, nonprofit, nonsectarian liberal arts institution that offers intellectually rigorous and personally transformative undergraduate and graduate programs. Naropa's unique learning approach joins the best of western and eastern approaches to higher education by balancing academic study, contemplative practice, and engagement in the world. As a result, Naropa students are better prepared to meet the world as it is and change it for the better.

Through contemplative practices such as sitting meditation, yoga, and t'ai-chi ch'uan, students develop mindfulness and are trained to acknowledge the direct experience of learning, moment by moment. This process brings precision, openness, and kindness to oneself and others; it teaches students how to integrate intellect and intuition; and it amplifies the confidence and desire to work for the benefit of others.

Naropa undergraduates are independent thinkers, intellectually curious, civic-minded, adventurous, spiritual, and caring. They come from forty-one states and territories and ten countries, representing a wide range of life experiences, backgrounds, and ages. Of the 1,063 degree-seeking students at Naropa University, 445 are undergraduate students.

Naropa University was founded thirty-seven years ago by Chögyam Trungpa Rinpoche, a Tibetan meditation master and scholar, who envisioned a liberal arts institution that would offer an educational experience that integrated knowledge of oneself with knowledge of the external world for a transformative learning path.

Accredited by the Higher Learning Commission and a member of the North Central Association of Colleges and Schools, Naropa University offers B.A. and B.F.A. degrees through its four-year undergraduate program as well as M.A., M.Div., and M.F.A. degrees through its graduate school.

Location

Naropa University is located at the base of the Rocky Mountain foothills in Boulder, Colorado, a city of 100,000 people that's known for its embrace of the environment, arts, technology, and health. For years Boulder has attracted intellectuals; artists; and seekers, people who are passionate about working for peace, fostering social justice, and exploring human spirituality.

Boulder has earned a well-deserved reputation for a great quality of life with a dynamic arts community, excellent music venues, and many cultural events. Hiking, skiing, and snowboarding enthusiasts have ample opportunity to pursue their sport and recreation activities. Boulder has bike paths all over town, and Boulder public transportation provides a frequent and comprehensive bus schedule throughout the day.

Naropa University has three campuses in Boulder, two of which serve undergraduate programs. The Arapahoe Campus is home to classrooms for most undergraduate classes, undergraduate advising, university administration, a performing arts center, a meditation hall, the Allen Ginsberg Library, a computer center, an art gallery, student lounges, the bookstore, and the Naropa Café. The Nalanda Campus, approximately 3½ miles from the Arapahoe Campus, is home to Naropa's performing and visual arts programs.

Majors and Degrees

Naropa University offers a B.F.A. in performance and ten B.A. degree programs: contemplative psychology, early childhood education, environmental studies, interdisciplinary studies, music, peace studies, religious studies, traditional Eastern arts, visual arts, and writing and literature.

The contemplative psychology major integrates Western psychology and Eastern approaches to healing mind and body. Students choose a concentration in psychological science, psychology of health and healing, somatic psychology, or transpersonal and humanistic psychology.

Nurturing the genuine and compassionate nature of teachers, the early childhood education major applies teaching methods drawn from Waldorf, Montessori, and Buddhist traditions. The major offers apprentice-style internships with master teachers from these traditions in a variety of contemplative preschool settings.

The environmental studies major is designed to empower students to develop the knowledge base and skill set needed to address complex environmental issues. The major emphasizes experiential learning, cutting-edge principles of sustainability, natural science, and active engagement with environmental issues.

Interdisciplinary studies invites students to design a unique major by selecting courses from two or three disciplines at Naropa. Recent examples of senior work include Documentary Poetics, The Embodied Teacher, and Shambhala Path of Hip-Hop Warriorship.

Naropa's music major gives students fundamental training in musicianship that includes harmonic analysis, ear training, rhythmic acuity, music theory, improvisation, composition, history, and multicultural perspectives.

The peace studies major offers an interdisciplinary and holistic approach to the study of peace and conflict that takes students into the community and brings the community into the classroom. Emphasis is placed on personal and social transformation, the needs of individuals, communities, and the global commons.

The major in religious studies emphasizes the role of contemplative practice in the world's great religions, especially Buddhism, and uses present traditions from perspectives sympathetic to the living religious communities themselves.

The traditional Eastern arts major is the only degree program of its kind in the country, combining the practice of sitting meditation with an in-depth study of the philosophy, history, and culture of a body-mind awareness discipline. Concentrations are offered in aikido, t'ai-chi ch'uan, and yoga teacher training.

The visual arts major includes studio electives in several painting media and calligraphic forms, sculpture, pottery, and photography. Required courses in drawing, the history of visual art, meditation and studio practice, studio foundations, and portfolio preparation form the foundation of the degree.

Writing and literature offers intensive training in the practice and study of writing through small writing workshops, literary studies courses, and exposure to a range of contemporary writing offered through the Summer Writing Program.

The B.F.A. in performance offers rigorous interdisciplinary training in dance, acting, and vocal work, combined with the rich experiential and intellectual traditions of contemplative education.

Academic Programs

Undergraduate students develop competencies in college-level academic studies and are exposed to a breadth of knowledge, practice, and experience necessary for success in their major and minor fields of study. Core course work is designed to help students think and read critically, write effectively, identify and understand multicultural issues, and cultivate awareness and compassion for others. Naropa's core requirements include the humanities, the arts, cultural and historical studies, diversity, world wisdom traditions, contemplative practice, body/mind practice, writing skills, and scientific inquiry. Students explore the meaning of effective citizenship through the integration of classroom learning and community engagement.

Upon completion of 30 semester credits, students may declare a major. Students must complete a total of 120 semester credits to earn an undergraduate degree.

Off-Campus Programs

Courses with a community-based learning component provide opportunities for students and faculty members to develop skills for participating in the public life of their communities. Through its emphasis on applied, experiential projects, community-based learning offers Naropa University faculty members and students innovative tools to forward the knowledge of their academic and artistic disciplines, augment student learning, and educate a citizenry to perform the public work of a democracy. AmeriCorps scholarship funds may also be available for Naropa students involved in community work.

Costs

Undergraduate tuition for the 2011–12 academic year is $26,200. The on-campus room and board costs vary depending on the options chosen, but are around $8500.

Financial Aid

Naropa University makes every attempt to assist students who do not have the financial resources to accomplish their educational objectives. Naropa offers institutional grants and scholarships as well as all types of federal student aid. Some financial aid for international students is also available. Approximately 67 percent of Naropa degree-seeking undergraduate students receive financial assistance in the form of scholarships, grants, assistantships, loans, and student employment.

Faculty

Naropa University faculty members are distinguished by a wealth of experience in the professional, artistic, and scholastic applications of their disciplines. They are mentors, people who are passionate about helping students write better, think more critically, and find their life purpose. Whether it's guiding students toward an interesting internship or advising a thesis, Naropa professors will inspire students to challenge themselves intellectually, professionally, and personally.

In addition to the outstanding core faculty, an international community of scholars and artists is consistently drawn to Naropa because of its strong vision and leadership in contemplative education. The average class size is 15, and Naropa's student-faculty ratio is 13:1.

Student Government

The Student Union of Naropa (SUN) consists of two active branches: United Naropa (UN) and Student Life Programming (SLP). Both groups share an overarching purpose: to represent the student voice, to empower student engagement, and to provide opportunities for student leadership.

United Naropa (UN) is comprised of students representing their academic departments with a focus on student action, connections, and communication among the departments, to ensure student input in decision making.

Student Life Programming (SLP) is a committee of students that organizes and supports student life beyond the classroom through planning various campus activities, overseeing the student lounges, and supervising student organizations. Both bodies of SUN have adopted a nonhierarchical structure for conducting their business.

Admission Requirements

Naropa University seeks students who have a strong appetite for learning and who enjoy experiential education in an academic setting. The Admissions Committee considers academic background, connection to Naropa's unique mission, and readiness to engage in contemplative, experiential college work when making admission decisions. A student's transcript, essays, interview, and letters of recommendation play important roles in the admissions process. SAT and ACT scores are optional.

Application and Information

A completed application for admission to Naropa University includes a $50 nonrefundable application fee, three essays, two letters of recommendation, official high school transcripts for first-year applicants (0 to 30 credits), and official transcripts from all previous college-level study. Many departments also require supplemental application materials. An interview, either in person or by telephone, is required for all programs, with the exception of writing and literature.

Prospective students are strongly encouraged to visit the University. The Office of Admissions hosts a preview weekend each semester, and guided campus tours are offered throughout the year.

The suggested deadline for receiving completed applications for the fall semester is January 15 and for the spring semester, October 15. Any applications received after the suggested deadline are reviewed on a space-available basis. For additional information, prospective students should contact:

Admissions Office
Naropa University
2130 Arapahoe Avenue
Boulder, Colorado 80302-6697
Phone: 303-546-3572
　　　　800-772-6951 (toll-free)
Fax: 303-546-3583
E-mail: admissions@naropa.edu
Web site: http://www.naropa.edu

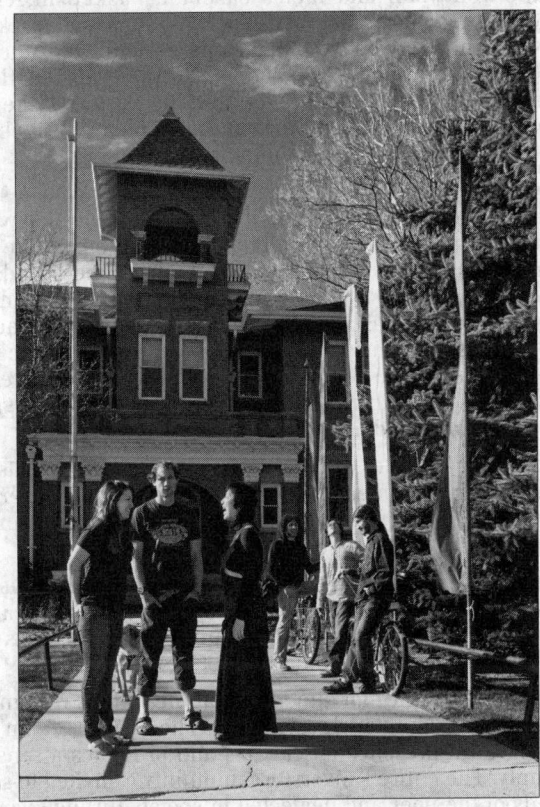

The Lincoln Building at Naropa University.

NEUMANN UNIVERSITY

ASTON, PENNSYLVANIA

The University

Neumann University (http://www.neumann.edu), a Catholic co-educational institution in the Franciscan tradition, recognizes the value of developing intellectual excellence, professional competence, and strong community life. As a university that balances the liberal arts with the professions, Neumann was founded to meet and expand the educational and professional horizons of men and women through instruction that is based on values, ethical behavior, and service to others. With the addition of the Living and Learning Center (multimedia-capable residences), Neumann University is able to serve a diverse geographic and demographic population.

Founded and sponsored by the Sisters of St. Francis of Philadelphia, the University is committed to a varied student body and welcomes students of all denominations. Current enrollment is 3,084.

The Life Center houses the Meagher Theatre, the Bruder Athletic Center, and the Crossroads Cafe dining facility. Intercollegiate sports include women's basketball, cross-country, field hockey, ice hockey, lacrosse, soccer, softball, tennis, track and field, and volleyball and men's baseball, basketball, cross-country, golf, ice hockey, lacrosse, soccer, tennis, and track and field. Neumann University competes as a member of the National Collegiate Athletic Association (NCAA) Division III, the Colonial States Athletic Conference, and the Eastern Collegiate Athletic Conference (ECAC). Intramural sports are available to all members of the campus community.

The Living and Learning Center is designed to provide a state-of-the-art residential experience, with a focus on education within a real-world living environment. Technologically smart, the center connects students to both faculty members and friends via the Internet, which is available in every suite and apartment. The system provides full access to campus resources and activities, as well as activities and resources worldwide. The center also houses a separate computer lab, a fitness center, a reflection room, various study rooms with warming kitchens for group study or meetings, and a laundry.

The University provides a full range of services to students, including career placement, which averages above 95 percent within six months of graduation; career and personal counseling; a tutoring program; and health services.

Neumann students are involved in a wide variety of campus and community activities. Major and special interest clubs are available for student participation. Clubs bring together students who share common interests and help foster new friendships.

At Neumann, the spiritual dimension of one's life is recognized as integral to total human development. The Ministry Team provides a pastoral presence on campus and promotes a sense of community. The entire University community is invited to serve the needs of the poor and neglected in society through various outreach programs, with special attention to the need for peace and justice in the world today.

Neumann is well positioned to respond to the academic and extracurricular needs of students who are of traditional or nontraditional age, commuters or residents, and full-time or part-time.

In addition to undergraduate programs, Neumann confers master's degrees in education, nursing, pastoral counseling, sport management, and strategic leadership as well as doctoral degrees in education (Ed.D.) and physical therapy (D.P.T.).

Location

Neumann, with a beautiful 63-acre suburban campus in Aston, Delaware County, Pennsylvania, is a short distance from Philadelphia; Wilmington, Delaware; southern New Jersey; and Maryland. It is easily accessible from major arteries such as I-95, Route 476, Route 1, and the Pennsylvania Turnpike.

Majors and Degrees

Neumann offers strong academic majors leading to a Bachelor of Arts degree or a Bachelor of Science degree in accounting, arts production and performance, athletic training, biology, business administration, communication and media arts, computer and information management, criminal justice, education, English, environmental studies, international business, liberal arts, marketing, nursing, political science, psychology, and sport management. The education programs lead to teacher certification in early elementary (PK–4), special education (PK–8) or secondary education. Preprofessional programs in law and medicine are also available. An accelerated evening program for adults leads to an Associate of Arts, Bachelor of Arts, or Bachelor of Science degree in liberal studies or professional studies.

Academic Programs

The academic program at Neumann University is composed of a core curriculum (required of all students), a major area of study (chosen by each student), and a wide range of elective offerings. Students may also choose a minor area of study. The University's broad base of liberal arts offerings prepares students for the intellectual and social challenges they will face in the employment marketplace and throughout their lives. The core is intended to provide basic knowledge of the liberal arts and sciences; develop verbal, written, and symbolic communication skills; and stimulate interest in a broad range of topics for the purpose of enhancing the individual's contributions to society, thereby enabling the individual to realize full human potential.

Classroom instruction is supplemented by cooperative education and internships, through which students can earn credit and gain experience by working in a job related to their career interest. Fieldwork and student teaching are required of all education majors. Clinical practice for the nursing major occurs in a variety of health-care facilities in the tristate area.

The honors program is an opportunity for academically talented students to explore imaginative and innovative perspectives on learning. It is also an opportunity to stimulate and motivate students to expand their knowledge and interest and to strive for greater excellence. Moreover, it is a reward for prior perseverance and dedication as well as an obligation to use skills and abilities in service to others. Admission to the honors program is by invitation.

Neumann University has transfer articulation agreements with numerous schools throughout the area.

Academic Facilities

The Child Development Center is a state-of-the-art, octagonal-shaped building, specifically designed to house an educational program for preschoolers. As a state-licensed day-care facility, it enrolls children of Neumann students, the faculty, and the community. The Child Development Center is part of the Division of

Education and Human Services. Students enrolled in education courses use the center for observation, practical experience, and student teaching.

The Academic Computing Center is located on the ground floor of the University. The computers are viewed as tools to support all fields of study and all students and faculty members. Neumann University has installed a wireless Local Area Network (LAN) that connects various computers and provides shared services such as printing, e-mail, and support for the instructional use of computers by providing for the sharing of files. Computers are available to all students, as is software related to various academic disciplines. Access to the Web and the Internet is available.

The Academic Resource Center is a service that enables students to meet Neumann's academic standards and successfully attain their personal educational goals. Free tutoring is provided to students in all core courses.

The University library contains a balanced collection of more than 75,000 volumes, 95,000 microfilm units, 2,000 videos, and 400 periodical subscriptions. Private study rooms and conference rooms are available for both student and faculty use. In addition to traditional media services support, a full-color video studio and a graphics production area are available. Serving as a comprehensive resource for students, other holdings include Neumann's online catalog system, FRANCIS, which is accessible via the Web. The library is a member of the Tri-State College Library Cooperative, the Consortium for Health Information and Library Services, SEPCHE, and the Online Computer Library Center, which provide additional convenient resources for students. The library subscribes to various online research services.

Costs

Tuition for full-time students (12 to 18 credits per semester) in 2010–11 was $22,256. Room and board were $10,162 (full meal plan).

Financial Aid

Typically, about 95 percent of Neumann undergraduate students receive some form of financial aid (scholarships, grants, and student loans).

Neumann offers a variety of renewable scholarships each year to entering full-time freshmen and transfer students. Interested applicants should contact the Office of Admissions and Financial Aid as soon as possible to determine eligibility.

In addition to Neumann scholarships, funds are available through the Federal Pell Grant, Federal Supplemental Educational Opportunity Grant, and Federal Work-Study Programs. Many states provide grant money to attend Neumann (non-Pennsylvania residents should check with their state's higher education agency for details). Veterans Administration benefits can be received by qualified veterans or their dependents. Federal Stafford Student Loans and Federal PLUS Program loans are available and can be applied for through Neumann's preferred lender or any participating bank. Neumann also offers institutional need-based grants. All students requesting financial aid must complete the Free Application for Federal Student Aid (FAFSA) each year to determine eligibility. In order to expedite processing, the FAFSA should be submitted by March 15 for the following school year. Financial aid funds are renewable annually based on need, as determined by the FAFSA results.

Faculty

Neumann students describe faculty members as sincere, hard working, determined, and energetic. Faculty members view themselves, first, as teachers and are proud partners in their students' journeys toward professional careers. Each student has a faculty adviser, who assists in arranging a program designed to meet the student's educational goals. Many faculty members serve as moderators of student clubs. The student-faculty ratio is 14:1.

Student Government

The Student Government Association (SGA) is the representative body for all students. Its function is to implement the aims and purposes of the University, foster cooperation in student relationships, assist the University in being responsive to the needs of the student body, and encourage personal responsibility for an intelligent system of student self-government. Through the Student Activities Board, social functions are planned throughout the year. Students serve on various University committees, including the Student Affairs Committee of the Board, Academic Advising Committee, Honors Program Committee, Registration/Orientation Task Force, and Student Judicial Board. For full-time students, a Student Government Association fee of $60 per semester is required.

Admission Requirements

Neumann has a rolling admission policy and accepts applications throughout the year. Applicants are considered on the basis of high school record, SAT or ACT scores, recommendations, class rank, and other indicators of potential to succeed in university-level studies. Applications for admission are reviewed without regard to sex, race, creed, color, national origin, age, sexual orientation, pregnancy, military status, religion, or disability. Applicants should be graduates of an accredited high school (or present equivalent credentials) and have a recommended curriculum of 16 units of high school course work, distributed as follows: 4 in English, 2 to 3 in science, 2 in mathematics, 2 in social studies, 2 in foreign language, and 4 in electives. Students intending to pursue a major in biology or clinical laboratory science must have at least 1 year of high school biology and chemistry, and high school physics is highly recommended.

Neumann participates in the Advanced Placement (AP) Program and the College-Level Examination Program (CLEP).

An interview and tour of the campus are highly recommended for all prospective students and parents. Visits can be arranged by contacting the Office of Admissions.

Application and Information

Applicants for freshman admission are requested to have SAT or ACT scores and high school transcripts sent to the Office of Admissions. A nonrefundable $35 application fee should accompany the completed application. A free application is available online at http://www.neumann.edu.

Neumann University welcomes applications from students who have attended or are currently attending either two-year or four-year regionally accredited institutions of higher learning.

For further information, students should contact:

Office of Admissions
Neumann University
One Neumann Drive
Aston, Pennsylvania 19014-1298
Phone: 610-558-5616
　　　　800-9NEUMANN (toll-free)
E-mail: neumann@neumann.edu
Web site: http://www.neumann.edu

NEW COLLEGE OF FLORIDA

SARASOTA, FLORIDA

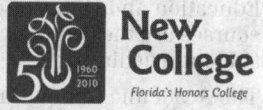

The College

New College of Florida offers serious students the opportunity to pursue rigorous academic study in an environment designed to promote depth in thinking, free exchange of ideas, and highly individualized interaction with faculty members.

Study is focused in the arts and sciences and is highly accelerated and independent. A recent study of the College's graduates found that 80 percent pursue graduate or professional study, gaining admission to Harvard, Yale, MIT, Brown, Georgetown, Berkeley, and other leading graduate programs. New College is competitive with other top schools in the nation when it comes to the percentage of graduates who go on to earn the Ph.D., especially in the sciences.

New College was founded as a private institution in 1960 with a devotion to the values implicit in a liberal arts education and a dedication to creating an innovative academic program where talented students and outstanding faculty members could come together and pursue learning through small classes, seminars, and individual tutorials to pursue advanced undergraduate research. Entry into Florida's public university system in 1975 served to strengthen and perpetuate the idealistic vision and academic mission of the College's founders. These qualities, as well as the College's national reputation, were enhanced further in 2001 when New College was designated as the official Honors College in the liberal arts and sciences for the Florida State University System. A public-private funding arrangement provides students at New College with a private honors college experience at a public college cost. As a result, the College is regularly featured in guidebooks as being among the nation's leading educational values and as one of the country's top small, public colleges.

New College's student population is 825, of whom approximately 60 percent are women. Approximately 20 percent of students are out-of-state or overseas residents. Through active recruitment of out-of-state students, the College plans to increase its percentage of non-Florida residents in the years ahead. First-year and second-year students must live on campus, but many continuing students choose to live on campus as well. In fact, five new, state-of-the-art residence halls opened at the start of the 2007–08 academic year, allowing New College to house nearly 80 percent of students on campus. The new residence halls include a variety of accommodation options to match student lifestyle interests and incorporate the latest in green building technology. Architecture for the new buildings complements existing campus living communities, such as the College's historic Pei Residence Halls, which were designed by the eminent architect I. M. Pei in the 1960s. The historic, 131-room Pei complex provides rooms with individual entrances, private baths, central air-conditioning, and various combinations of large picture windows, sliding glass doors, and/or balconies. Two other campus residence halls, Dort and Goldstein, provide apartment-style housing with four single rooms, two bathrooms, and a common living room and kitchenette in each unit. Dining facilities on campus include a campus dining hall with full meal plans available for both on- and off-campus students, a snack bar and deli, and the student-owned and -operated Four Winds Café. The College's Counseling and Wellness Center offers basic health care, personal counseling, and a variety of related services.

New College student life is informal. Activities are largely student initiated and include academic, artistic, religious, political, and recreational pursuits. The College's 110-acre bay front location on the Gulf of Mexico includes basketball, racquetball, tennis, and volleyball courts; a multipurpose soccer and athletic field; a running trail; a 25-meter swimming pool; and a comprehensive fitness center. Sailboats, kayaks, and canoes are also available for use by students and faculty members free of charge.

Learn more about New College of Florida by visiting its Web site, Facebook page, and YouTube channel (see Contact information).

Location

Situated along the coastline of the Gulf of Mexico in southwest Florida, New College serves as the northern gateway to Sarasota, a bustling city with more than 250,000 residents. Located 50 miles south of Tampa,

Sarasota is noted for its recreational, cultural, and artistic attractions, including beautiful white-sand beaches and an abundance of professional theater, art, and music venues. Notably, New College sits adjacent to the world-famous John and Mable Ringling Museum of Art, which offers students free entry to view its Baroque and Renaissance art collections.

The climate is semitropical, consisting of long, warm springs and autumns plus mild winters. Transportation from throughout the nation and within the city is readily accessible. Many major airlines serve Sarasota-Bradenton International Airport, which is adjacent to the College. Within the city, buses link the campus to downtown, shopping malls, parks, and beaches. While mass transit is available, bicycling is the favored means of transportation among students. The College's Office of Student Affairs offers group outings on a regular basis to the downtown Sarasota Farmers Market, grocery stores, and other venues around town.

Majors and Degrees

New College awards the Bachelor of Arts degree in liberal arts and sciences. Each of the College's more than thirty different areas of concentration (majors) is an individualized program of study that students design in consultation with, and with the approval of, faculty members. These include anthropology, applied mathematics, art, art history, biochemistry, biology, chemistry, Chinese language and culture, classics, economics, English, environmental studies, European studies, French language and literature, German language and literature, history, humanities, international and area studies, Latin American studies, literature, marine biology, mathematics, medieval and Renaissance studies, music, natural sciences, neurobiology, philosophy, physics, political science, psychology, public policy, religion, Russian language and literature, social sciences, sociology, Spanish language and literature, and urban studies. Partial areas of concentration include computational science, gender studies, and theater. Students may also pursue self-designed concentrations, with faculty permission. Premedical, prelaw, and pre-M.B.A. advising and guidelines are provided by faculty members and by the Center for Career Education and Off-Campus Studies.

Academic Programs

New College of Florida's academic program aims to encourage academic excellence, creativity, and personal initiative and to provide essential tools for lifelong intellectual, personal, and professional growth. The College's distinctive curriculum enables students, in close consultation with faculty members, to develop programs of seminars, tutorials, independent research, and off-campus experiences that meet each student's personal academic interests and goals.

At the end of each semester, rather than grades, students receive detailed narrative evaluations as well as satisfactory/unsatisfactory assessments of their work from individual faculty members. Graduation requirements include satisfactory completion of seven academic contracts (one per semester), three independent-study projects, a senior thesis, and an oral baccalaureate examination. In addition to the requirements for individual majors, students must complete eight courses within the liberal arts curriculum, with at least one course each in the humanities, social sciences, and natural sciences. Students must also meet basic mathematics and computer literacy requirements, and pass or be exempted from Florida's College-Level Academic Skills Test.

The College operates on a 4-1-4 calendar year. The College offers a January interterm when students undertake independent study projects, which they design and complete under faculty sponsorship.

Off-Campus Programs

Internships, fieldwork, and independent research away from the campus offer New College students the opportunity to gain new skills and evaluate career interests. New College believes that off-campus study can make a major contribution to an undergraduate education and facilitates such study through its flexible, individualized curriculum and special support services. New College is a member of the National

Student Exchange, which provides access to nearly 200 universities with programs in the U.S. and abroad (many with comparable tuition costs). Students may also participate in programs offered by independent providers, such as the School for International Training and AustraLearn, as well as international programs available through the Florida State University System and Center for Cross Cultural Studies. With faculty approval, students may pursue off-campus independent study or participate in programs including Living Routes, which offers nontraditional venues for study abroad.

Academic Facilities

New College's wireless-equipped Jane Bancroft Cook Library is befitting of one of the country's leading colleges for the liberal arts and has an open stack arrangement that allows free access to most materials. Administration, trustees, faculty members, and the New College Library Association have implemented an ambitious acquisition program to expand the current holdings of approximately 274,000 volumes. An expansion of the library's visual image collection is also in the works. In total, the library subscribes to more than 900 serial titles, including 700 magazines and journals and many state, national, and international newspapers. In addition, through computer networks and other cooperative programs, New College students and faculty members have access to hundreds of online databases and electronic journals and newspapers, as well as numerous online document delivery services. Through a comprehensive online interlibrary loan system, New College students have convenient access to holdings throughout the Florida State University System.

The Harry Sudakoff Conference Center on campus hosts visiting lecturers, meetings of campus and community organizations, and a wide range of special events. The Caples Fine Arts Complex includes the 264-seat Mildred Sainer Music and Arts Pavilion, which features student, local, and national performances; the Lota Mundy Music Building, which houses eight music practice rooms, plus the Benjamin and Barbara Slavin Electronic Music Studio; the Christianne Felsmann Fine Arts Building; the Betty Isermann Fine Arts Gallery and Studio; and a sculpture studio. Science facilities include the R. V. Heiser Natural Sciences Complex, which houses laboratories, classrooms, offices, a computer lab, two electron microscopes, and an auditorium, as well as the $2.5-million Rhoda and Jack Pritzker Marine Biology Research Center. The marine center, one of the leading marine research centers in southwest Florida, features state-of-the-art culture rooms, laboratories, and aquariums with water drawn from Sarasota Bay. Saltwater effluent from the tanks is cleaned by means of a wetland constructed in 2001 as part of a New College senior thesis project. In January 2010, the College broke ground on the new 35,000-square-foot, LEED-certified Academic Center, featuring 10 new classrooms, 45 faculty offices, an on-site café, and a central plaza. The new Academic Center is scheduled to open in 2011 and is expected to become a hub of student activity.

Costs

For the 2010–11 academic year, in-state tuition and fees at New College of Florida were $5347 and out-of-state tuition and fees were $27,598. Room and board costs were $8201.

Financial Aid

The actual cost of providing New College of Florida's highly individualized honors college experience is far greater than the state funding appropriated for support of the College. The New College Foundation secures independent funding to provide for the remaining costs. Part of the foundation's endowment produces income for scholarships.

Approximately 93 percent of New College students receive some form of financial assistance, including merit-based scholarships and need-based financial aid. To apply for financial aid, students should file the Free Application for Federal Student Aid (FAFSA). February 15 is the priority date for need-based financial aid. All first-time college students who complete applications by February 15 and who are admitted to New College are guaranteed merit scholarship funding. No additional scholarship application is necessary.

Faculty

Of New College's regular faculty members, 99 percent hold the highest degree awarded in their field of study, which in most cases is the doctorate. They have come to New College from the finest universities nationally and abroad, drawn to an environment that emphasizes excellence in teaching and fosters a close-knit community of scholars. Faculty members sponsor individual students in the formulation of their academic programs, gradually moving toward a form of

mentorship through which joint research is sometimes pursued. A 10:1 student-faculty ratio is a key factor in the College's individualized approach to education. At New College, all classes are taught by faculty, not by teaching assistants.

Student Government

Student input is a decisive factor in campus governance. Elected student representatives serve on the Board of Trustees and most major policymaking committees, and are voting participants in divisional and campuswide faculty meetings. The New College Student Alliance, the College's student government, has authority over funding for recreational events, social events, and student clubs and organizations on campus.

Admission Requirements

New College of Florida seeks highly capable students eager to take responsibility for their own education. The admissions staff reviews each candidate individually, assessing his or her potential for success within, and contribution to, the College's unique environment. Course selection, academic record, and writing ability are focal points of the committee's review. The majority of first-year students entering in fall 2010 ranked in the top 10 percent of their high school class. The middle 50 percent of SAT takers scored 1230–1390. The middle 50 percent of ACT takers scored 27–31.

All prospective students may apply for entrance to either the fall or the spring term. However, the College reserves the right to cancel the spring admission cycle if its enrollment goals have been met. Candidates must submit an admission application and fee/fee waiver, official transcript(s), SAT or ACT scores, and a letter of recommendation. A campus visit and demonstrated interest are recommended for all those with serious interest in applying.

Application and Information

Admissions application materials and descriptive literature are available through the New College Office of Admissions and Financial Aid. The College has two application deadlines for the fall class: February 15 (the priority deadline) and April 15. Notification of the admissions decision occurs by April 1 and April 25, respectively. A completed application and all supporting documents must be submitted to the Admissions Office before a candidate is considered for admission.

Inquiries and application requests should be directed to:

Kathleen M. Killion
Dean of Enrollment Services
New College of Florida
5800 Bay Shore Road
Sarasota, Florida 34243-2109

Phone: 941-487-5000
Fax: 941-487-5010
E-mail: admissions@ncf.edu
Web site: http://www.ncf.edu
http://www.facebook.com/newcollegeofflorida
http://www.youtube.com/user/NewCollegeofFL

College Hall, former home of circus magnate Charles Ringling, contributes to the picture-perfect setting for New College of Florida.

NEW ENGLAND COLLEGE
HENNIKER, NEW HAMPSHIRE

The College

New England College (NEC) is a place where students amaze themselves with what they learn and with what they can accomplish. A college that prepares students for the professional world, NEC also empowers its graduates with a broad knowledge base that results from a focus on the liberal arts and hands-on learning. In addition, students develop strong analytical and communication skills that are vital to success in any career. The College's current enrollment stands at 2,102 students (1,033 are undergraduates). The diverse student body, which represents thirty-three states and twenty-four other countries, enriches the College curriculum's multicultural focus and global perspective.

New England College prides itself on its commitment to each individual student and provides a strong support network to assist students with a variety of learning styles. The Pathways Center plays a key role in the academic and professional achievements of all students. It is an innovative combination of academic advising, study skills, and support services, as well as career planning and placement. The Pathways Center is an integral part of academic life at NEC; students begin honing their academic and professional skills, planning for their future, and building their resumes from the moment they arrive on campus. Thus, NEC graduates are extremely successful in finding employment upon graduation. As an example, education majors have enjoyed 100 percent job placement over the last twelve years.

The campus, which is nestled in the center of Henniker, a classic small New England town, consists of thirty-two buildings. Students take advantage of the many extracurricular activities available at NEC, ranging from outdoor recreation to theater productions and the student newspaper. There are over thirty clubs and organizations to choose from and thirteen Division III intercollegiate athletic teams in addition to numerous recreational sports club options. The campus offers 26 acres of playing fields, a fitness center with the latest exercise and strength-building equipment, a gymnasium, and an indoor field house for student athletic activities. The Lee Clement Ice Arena, home to the NEC Pilgrims, provides some of the best hockey games in the region. The College's new state-of-the-art outdoor artificial turf field is a great addition to the campus.

Location

New England College's location offers students the best of all worlds. Students have easy access to vibrant cities and the incomparable recreation and wilderness regions of New Hampshire. The College is located a short drive from the state capital, Concord, and about 30 minutes from the state's largest city, Manchester, and its airport. Portsmouth, Boston, and some of the best ocean beaches in New England can be reached in just 90 minutes. Alpine and Nordic skiing opportunities abound. Pats Peak, located only 3 miles from the campus, provides free skiing and snowboarding to all NEC students. The College's 225-acre campus offers excellent trails for cross-country skiing, mountain biking, and hiking. The Contoocook River flows through the center of the campus, spanned by the College's historic covered bridge, a popular subject for photographers, especially during autumn. Almost all NEC students reside on campus in the six residence halls located adjacent to classroom buildings and the student center.

Majors and Degrees

The College offers thirty-two majors and twenty-two minors—a remarkable number for a small college. Such variety permits students to consider a number of options before selecting a major, which is encouraged. Graduates of the undergraduate program are awarded the Bachelor of Arts or the Bachelor of Science, depending upon their major. A number of concentrations are offered within the majors, further permitting students to develop expertise based upon

their specific career goals. For instance, a student can major in art with a concentration in photography.

Majors available at NEC include accounting, art (4+1 M.S. program), art history, biological studies, biology, business administration, communication, comparative literature, computer information systems, creative writing, criminal justice, education: elementary or secondary, engineering (3+2 program with Clarkson University), English, environmental science, environmental studies, environmental sustainability, health sciences, history, kinesiology, mathematics, outdoor leadership, philosophy, physical education, political science, psychology, sociology, special education, sports and recreation management, and theater.

In addition, New England College offers a 3+3 program in conjunction with New York Law School that allows students to obtain their undergraduate and law degrees in six years. Other postgraduate opportunities include a 4+1 M.B.A. program with Union University in New York, and Bachelor of Science in Nursing (B.S.N.), Master of Physician Assistant, and Doctor of Pharmacy programs in conjunction with Massachusetts College of Pharmacy and Health Sciences.

Students may elect an individually designed major, combining elements from several majors, subject to faculty approval. Many students pursue internship options (required for 75 percent of majors) in a wide range of disciplines, including business, fine and performing arts, government, health care and human services, law, media and communications, professional sports, and many others. Recent internship sites have included National Public Radio, Disney World, the Verizon Wireless Center, the Army Corps of Engineers, the Manchester Monarchs, and Edge Sports. In addition, a joint venture between Edge Sports and the College has allowed students to manage the Edge Sports Magazine and Web site. This cross-curriculum project provides students with hands-on experience in the full production of these publications, from sales calls to marketing to layout and print.

Education majors have many opportunities to interact with children and adolescents, from the first year in their program to their capstone student-teaching experience.

Academic Programs

A comprehensive liberal arts college that also offers professional programs, NEC aims for its students to develop certain abilities: to think and communicate effectively, to understand the methods of the broad academic disciplines, to develop a strong sense of ethics, to respect other identities and cultures, and to develop a lifelong love of learning.

The First-Year Experience at NEC introduces students to college-level learning. It includes two writing courses, a computer technology course, seminars on what it means to be human and cultural diversity, a course in science, and a course in basic mathematics. The New England College curriculum is rooted in the belief that students learn best when actively involved with their subject matter; thus, NEC courses focus on learning by doing. Students may also apply to the honors program, where they can explore an academic discipline in more depth and graduate with either an honors certificate or honors diploma, depending on the tier in which the student enrolls. The academic year is divided into two main semesters, fall and spring. Additional sessions during January and the summer months offer students opportunities to take courses online or on campus. To graduate, students are required to complete a minimum of 120 credits as part of an approved program of study. CLEP and AP credits are accepted.

Off-Campus Programs

New England College encourages students to consider study-abroad options available to them via consortia agreements with a wide range of institutions located throughout the world. Students generally spend one semester when studying abroad, although some opt for a yearlong program. Some of the participating institutions are located in Australia, Canada, England, France, Japan, and South Africa. Students may also choose to participate in travel courses, which are generally offered during the January term. There are opportunities to participate in service leadership experiences in Nicaragua, the Dominican Republic, and other developing countries, as well as a trip to New Orleans, Louisiana to help with the devastation left by Hurricane Katrina. Travel courses as extensions of classroom experiences are also offered, most recently with a trip to Belize to study tropical marine biology and another to Greece to study that nation's cultural and political history.

NEC's membership in the New Hampshire College and University Consortium (NHCUC) enables NEC students to take courses at any of the NHCUC member institutions and apply these credits to their degree program at the College.

Academic Facilities

The College's Center for Educational Innovation (CEI) was opened in 2001. A state-of-the art facility, the CEI provides networked data ports, Internet access, videoconferencing, and the full range of electronic and broadcast media access that enables professors to enhance their teaching by connecting to today's global network of information. The Simon Center, at the heart of the NEC campus, serves as the student center for the College. The entire campus is wireless, enabling students to access the College's network and the Internet from laptop computers at any location on campus. The H. Raymond Danforth Library provides a comprehensive research facility in addition to housing the Academic Support Center, where students may receive comprehensive subject tutoring and organizational and time management skill training from professional tutors. The library holds more than 100,000 volumes as well as a new thirty-three-station computer laboratory with Internet access. The science building serves as the home of the science departments, although classes for many other disciplines are scheduled in this large facility. Also located in the science building is the newly renovated Mainstage Theatre, where a number of plays are presented each year by NEC's outstanding Theatre Department.

Costs

For the 2010–11 year, tuition and fees were $29,540. Room and board were $10,170 (double room with fifteen meals per week plan).

Financial Aid

New England College offers a wide range of scholarships and grants for incoming students, ranging from $1500 to $18,000. The majority of these awards are merit-based, taking into account the student's academic achievement or other talents and accomplishments, such as participation in the arts, community service, and student government. Some need-based grants are available as well and are awarded to students based upon information provided on the Free Application for Federal Student Aid (FAFSA), and the NEC financial aid application. All awards are renewable on an annual basis, depending upon the student's academic record and/or documented financial need.

Faculty

There are 68 full-time faculty members at New England College. Seventy-five percent hold terminal degrees in their fields. The NEC faculty is highly accomplished and active professionally, publishing books and articles, participating in national conferences, conducting scientific research, and creating works of art. The main focus of the NEC faculty members is teaching. They understand that students learn best by doing and so incorporate practical projects and activities into their course syllabi. The low student-teacher ratio (12:1) contributes to the friendly, highly personalized classroom experience. Students benefit from regular, personalized interaction with their professors, which helps them develop their knowledge and abilities beyond what they had ever thought possible.

Student Government

New England College's student government is actively involved in the academic, cultural, social, and organizational life of the institution. The Student Senate functions as a liaison between students and the NEC faculty, administration, alumni, and trustees. The Student Senate is responsible for its own budget, which funds numerous student-run clubs, organizations, social events, and recreational activities.

Admission Requirements

Freshman applicants must have received their high school diplomas (or equivalent) before attending New England College. A basic college-preparatory program is recommended, with course work in English, mathematics, science, social studies, and other academic electives. The Office of Admission takes into account the student's academic record, extracurricular activities and achievements, personal statement, and letters of recommendation, as well as the student's maturity and determination to succeed. Standardized tests (SAT or ACT) are not required, although most students submit scores. Students are encouraged to arrange an interview, conducted either in person or via telephone, with an admission counselor.

Application and Information

New England College has a rolling admission system; applications are reviewed as they become complete. All applicants must submit a completed application form, a $30 application fee, official high school transcripts covering at least the first marking period of the senior year, a personal essay, and two letters of recommendation from high school teachers or guidance counselors. Most students receive decisions within two weeks of their file's completion. Students are encouraged to apply early, as scholarship decisions are made shortly after admission, and they are considered for the full range of scholarship opportunities at the early part of the application cycle. Students whose native language is not English must submit TOEFL scores. Those students who do not meet TOEFL score minimums may participate in the English as a second language (ESL) program at NEC. Transfer students must also provide official college transcripts and a supporting letter from their college's dean of students.

Application forms may be obtained from the Office of Admission or at the New England College Web site. Students may submit their applications online. For further information, interested students should contact:

Office of Admission
New England College
98 Bridge Street
Henniker, New Hampshire 03242-3297

Phone: 800-521-7642 (toll-free)
Fax: 603-428-3155
E-mail: admission@nec.edu
Web site: http//www.nec.edu/undergrad_1
http://www.facebook.com/NECAdmission
http://www.youtube.com/necadmission

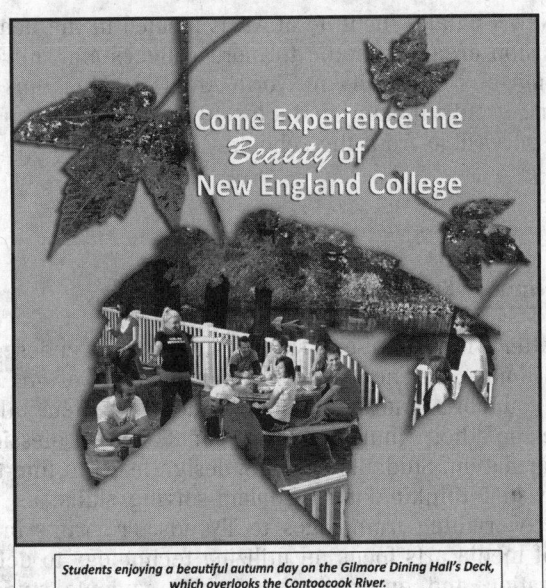

Come Experience the *Beauty* of New England College

Students enjoying a beautiful autumn day on the Gilmore Dining Hall's Deck, which overlooks the Contoocook River.

THE NEW ENGLAND INSTITUTE OF ART

BROOKLINE, MASSACHUSETTS

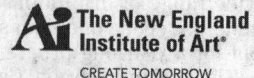

COLLEGE CLOSE-UPS

A focused education from The New England Institute of Art can help students turn their creative energy into a powerful tool that can make a difference in the world. Students are part of a collaborative and supportive community, where experienced instructors provide the guidance and skills needed to pursue a career in the creative economy.

The school's programs in the areas of design, media arts, and fashion give students the opportunity to learn by using professional-grade technology and build a portfolio of work to show potential employers after graduation.

The New England Institute of Art is accredited by the New England Association of Schools and Colleges (NEASC) through its Commission on Institutions of Higher Education (CIHE), 209 Burlington Road, Suite 201, Bedford, Massachusetts 01730-1433; phone: 781-271-0022.

The New England Institute of Art is authorized to award Associate in Science and Bachelor of Science degrees by the Commonwealth of Massachusetts, Massachusetts Department of Higher Education, One Ashburton Place, Room 1401, Boston, Massachusetts 02108-1696; phone: 617-994-6950.

Location

The New England Institute of Art is located in the heart of the Boston area, the home to more colleges and universities than any other city in North America. Museums and sporting events, theater, and a top 10 media market, are all easily accessible from the school.

Programs of Study and Degrees

No matter which course of study a student may choose, the professionals at The New England Institute of Art will guide, support, and help each student as their talents evolve on their journey of personal and professional transformation. Students studying design learn to fine-tune their visual thinking and problem-solving skills, as they create everything from logos to TV ads. Programs in the area of media arts focus on utilizing technology to deliver information and entertainment, while students studying fashion learn to market and merchandise clothing.

Bachelor's degree programs are offered in advertising, audio and media technology, digital filmmaking and video production, fashion and retail management, graphic design, interior design, media arts and animation, photography, sound and motion picture technical arts, and Web design and interactive media.

Associate degree programs are offered in audio production and photography.

Academic Programs

The New England Institute of Art operates on a year-round, four-quarter system.

Academic Facilities

The New England Institute of Art provides a learning environment with professional-grade technology applicable to each student's course of study. Students have the opportunity to build a portfolio of work that shows potential employers that they are trained to use the software, hardware, or equipment utilized within the industry. Depending upon the course of study, students are immersed in a creative environment—from classrooms to computer labs to studios—focused on relevant, hands-on education designed to prepare students for the real world.

Costs

Tuition cost varies by program. Prospective students should contact the school for current tuition costs. Other charges include a starting kit for all first-quarter students. Kits vary in price, depending on the program of study.

Financial Aid

Financial aid is available for those who qualify. Students who require financial assistance should first complete and submit a Free Application for Federal Student Aid (FAFSA) and meet with a financial aid officer.

Faculty

Faculty members are experienced professionals who create a learning environment that is similar to the professional world students will face after graduation. Instructors are focused on helping students develop the skills they need to transform their creative potential into marketable skills.

Admission Requirements

Applicants must provide proof of high school graduation or achievement of a General Educational Development (GED) certificate as a prerequisite for admission. In lieu of documenting high school graduation or a GED certificate, applicants may provide proof of attaining an associate degree or higher from an accredited institution. An official transcript indicating date of high school graduation, GED certificate (including test scores), or date of college graduation (including degree granted) is required as proof.

All individuals seeking admission to The New England Institute of Art are interviewed in person or by phone by an assistant director of admissions, and each applicant must create an original essay of at least 150 words stating how an education at The New England Institute of Art would help the student to achieve career goals. There is a $50 application fee.

For the most recent information regarding admission requirements, please refer to the current academic catalog.

Application and Information

To obtain an application, make arrangements for an interview, or tour the school, prospective students should contact:

The New England Institute of Art
10 Brookline Place West
Brookline, MA 02445-7295
Phone: 617-739-1700
        800-903-4425 (toll-free)
Fax: 617-582-4500
Web site: http://www.artinstitutes.edu/boston

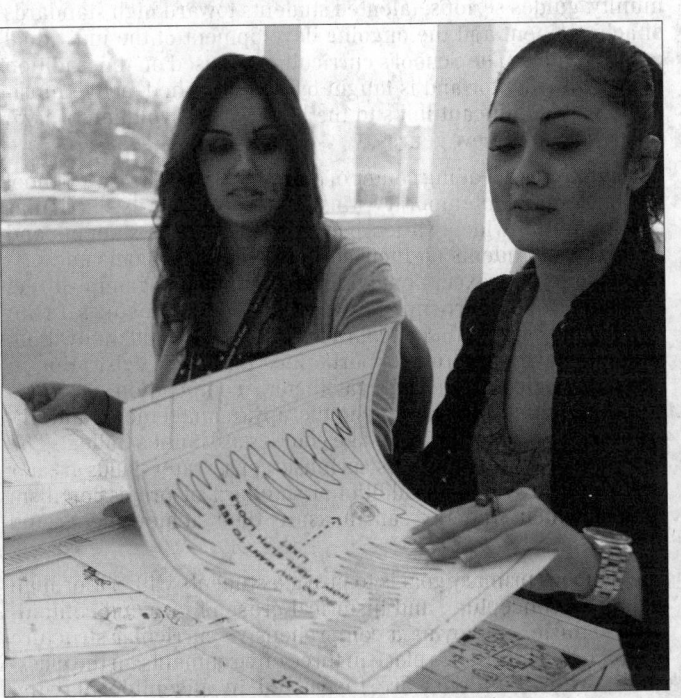

THE NEW SCHOOL FOR JAZZ AND CONTEMPORARY MUSIC

NEW YORK, NEW YORK

The School

Part of The New School, a leading university in New York City, The New School for Jazz and Contemporary Music offers a unique course of study in which a passionately engaged faculty of professional artists, drawn from New York's renowned jazz community, guides serious, talented students toward high standards of achievement and the ongoing development of the individual creative voice. The School's curriculum is based on the tradition of artist-as-mentor and is taught by accomplished, active musicians with significant links to the history and evolution of jazz, blues, pop, and new genres.

Recognized as a leading center of arts education, The New School for Jazz and Contemporary Music is known for its curricular depth and the widely varied backgrounds of both students and instructors. Students do their core work in classrooms and private studios with exceptional musician-educators, gaining direct exposure to modern music's traditions and practices in an intellectual context that encourages exploration and innovation. Students have numerous opportunities for cross-registration in classes ranging from classical theory, composition, counterpoint, and musicology to music therapy, management, and liberal arts. The opportunity to take courses at Mannes College The New School for Music, a classical music conservatory, adds greater depth and provides an additional standard of professionalism against which students can measure their achievements and progress.

The School's primary goal is to provide students with a thorough technical, conceptual, and historical grasp of jazz and contemporary music, employing a comprehensive curricular structure in which teaching takes place in three environments: in the classroom, where students are instructed in ensemble playing, instrumental music, music history, and related topics; in traditional, tutorial instrumental study, where students meet one-on-one with great jazz and classical performers who live, work, and teach in New York City; and in master classes. These scheduled lectures/performances/workshops have featured such artists as Jon Faddis, Jim Hall, Barry Harris, Lee Konitz, Wynton Marsalis, and Jimmy McGriff.

There are a variety of activities in which students can become involved at New School Jazz and throughout the university. Interested students may serve on most New School committees, including Student Life, Libraries, Diversity, Food Services, and the Student Advisory Council. Jazz students have opportunities for involvement on the Executive Committee, the Curriculum Committee, the Student Advisory Council, and in the Pan-African Cultural Organization. The New School is also home to a wide variety of student organizations and clubs. Students are encouraged to form new student groups by contacting the Office of Student Life.

All first-time freshmen are guaranteed dormitory housing for their first year. The New School maintains several residence halls as well as university-leased apartments, most located within six blocks of the Greenwich Village campus. Through the enthusiasm and creativity of the resident advisers, students are exposed to diverse programs that take advantage of the rich traditions of The New School and the cultural opportunities of New York City. For additional information, students should contact the Office of University Housing at universityhousing@newschool.edu or 212-229-5459 or visit the Web site at http://www.newschool.edu/studentaffairs/housing/.

Location

The New School is located in Greenwich Village, home to many of the city's fabled jazz nightclubs, such as the Village Vanguard, Blue Note, Smalls, and Jazz Standard. The area is also home to design and art studios, galleries, shops, and restaurants as well as avant-garde artists, musicians, and writers. World-famous performance venues such as Carnegie Hall and Lincoln Center are just a short subway ride away. With its rich cultural resources, international sophistication, and cutting-edge attitude, New York City is a vibrant environment that has inspired and challenged artists throughout its history.

Majors and Degrees

The New School for Jazz and Contemporary Music offers the Bachelor of Fine Arts (B.F.A.) for instrumentalists and for vocalists. A five-year combined Bachelor of Arts/Bachelor of Fine Arts (B.A./B.F.A.) program is also available in conjunction with Eugene Lang College The New School for Liberal Arts.

Academic Programs

The B.F.A. degree is granted upon completion of at least 134 credits and must include 90 credits of applied music, along with the required liberal studies and music history distribution. The B.A./B.F.A. degrees are granted upon completion of at least 90 credits of applied music, along with 90 credits of liberal arts, which includes the required Lang seminars and senior work and can also include music history or other liberal arts credits.

Student progress is monitored on the basis of entrance evaluations, ensemble work, student juries (normally in the second half of the sophomore year), successful completion of the core curriculum, and the normal accumulation of course credits. In addition to course work within The New School for Jazz and Contemporary Music, students take some classes at Mannes College. Once this foundation is acquired, students experiment with a large number of theory and performance electives to define personal goals.

Off-Campus Programs

The New School's proximity to several major jazz record labels and performance venues offers significant opportunities for students. Music industry internships, such as those at Blue Note Records, Verve Records, BMG Records, Jazz at Lincoln Center, the Blue Note Jazz Club, and the Knitting Factory, provide hands-on experience, develop networking skills, and create potential job opportunities.

Students appear weekly on stages and in clubs throughout the city and the greater metropolitan area. Performances include weekly professional sessions at the Fat Cat jazz club, and the Jazz Presents series showcasing faculty with alumni or current students. New School Jazz musicians have also appeared at a number of high-visibility venues, including Jazz at Lincoln Center's Dizzy's Club Coca-Cola, and performed live at radio stations WBGO and WBAI. Students have access to the Gig Office, which connects them to professional performance opportunities.

The New School for Jazz and Contemporary Music and Veneto Jazz offer a two-week workshop in Bassano del Grappa, Italy. The workshop is taught by 8 of the finest New York musicians and faculty members from The New School. Courses are divided into various levels and include master classes, theory, arranging, combos, and Big Band, and public performances take place in the city theaters. This workshop is part of the Veneto Jazz Festival, one of the most important European jazz festivals.

Academic Facilities

The New School for Jazz and Contemporary Music is located on the fifth and sixth floors of 55 West 13th Street, the university's primary building for technology services. The School's 20,000-square-foot, state-of-the-art facility was designed specifically to help young artists realize their goal of becoming effective music professionals. The facility offers administrative, classroom, practice, and rehearsal space, all constructed with attention to acoustics, soundproofing, and aesthetics. All classrooms are fully dedicated with Yamaha grand pianos, drum kits, amplifiers, vocal PA systems, and full-component stereo systems. Specialized instrumental practice and teaching rooms are offered, as well as a listening library and piano/MIDI labs.

Performance and recording needs are served in an intimate 120-seat performance space, with full capacity for professional sound, lighting, and recording. A second studio is used for recording and engineering. Both studios are connected to the university's server and Internet sites, with the possibility for both posted archival recordings and live streaming performance. Additional university performance facilities within a two-block radius of the Greenwich Village campus include a 170-seat performance auditorium and an excellent and acoustically balanced concert hall with an audience capacity of 500.

A library consortium links the libraries at The New School with those at New York University and Cooper Union, making library privileges available reciprocally to matriculated students. This constitutes a resource of more than 3 million volumes and includes the Avery Fisher Center for Music and Media, which provides access to the most up-to-date electronic media, records, tapes, video, and a library of music materials. In addition, New School students have access to a wealth of public library resources throughout the five boroughs of New York City, including the New York Public Library for the Performing Arts, which is located in Manhattan at Lincoln Center.

The Office of Academic Computing operates three general-access laboratories; each offers a wide variety of software, including word processing, spreadsheets, databases, e-mail, music notation, and graphics and statistical packages. Students using the centers are supported by a full-time staff and assisted by lab aides. Training seminars and documentation are available on supported software and hardware. The Knowledge Union is a state-of-the-art film, video, and multimedia production facility located on the eighth and ninth floors of 55 West 13th Street. Among its studios is a dedicated music lab where many New School Jazz music technology courses are held.

Costs

Tuition for all full-time (12–18 credits) students was $17,970 each semester for 2010–11 ($35,940 for the year). B.A./B.F.A. students paid $18,485 (12–21 credits) per term ($36,970 for the year). Fees totaled $150 per semester (university services $130, divisional fee $15, student senate fee $5), plus $1817 for student health insurance during the academic year. Although housing costs vary depending on accommodations and meal plan selected, room and board average about $15,260 per year.

Financial Aid

Students may receive a merit scholarship award, which is determined at the initial audition as part of the acceptance package. Students are encouraged to apply during Audition Period 1, as scholarships are available on a limited basis to students auditioning during Audition Period 2 (late auditions). Students are encouraged to file the FAFSA form (online at http://www.fafsa.ed.gov) to determine eligibility for federal grants and loans. Almost 75 percent of students receive some kind of financial aid, awarded on the basis of financial need and merit. The university's financial aid office is open year-round to assist students and their families with the task of meeting educational costs. For information on specific kinds of assistance, amounts of funding, loan repayment, and scholarships for students meeting certain criteria, students should contact the financial aid office at 212-229-8930 or financialaid@newschool.edu.

Faculty

The faculty members of The New School for Jazz and Contemporary Music are drawn from the top ranks of professional musicians in the New York area. This unique artist-as-faculty concept offers extraordinary resources for weekly classes, individual private lessons, special performance events, and master classes. The key to the success of the School lies in its use of experienced professionals to guide the intense involvement of students in the challenges of small-group playing. Students work with the creators, not just the interpreters, of jazz and its offshoots.

Admission Requirements

An applicant must submit the completed application, the nonrefundable $100 application fee, a personal statement, official high school/secondary school transcript or school records, and one letter of recommendation from a teacher, counselor, or professional who can comment on the applicant's qualifications for study at The New School for Jazz and Contemporary Music. International applicants should supply official English translations of all documents and credentials and scores from the TOEFL (minimum 550 on the paper-based exam is preferred).

A performance audition is required of all students. A prescreen tape or CD is required for all applicants on drums, guitar, and voice. Vocalists who pass the prescreen must audition live; drummers and guitarists may audition live or online, or submit an audition tape or CD. Live auditions are held in February, March, and April.

Prospective students and their parents are welcome to tour the facilities of The New School for Jazz and Contemporary Music. Tours are offered Tuesday, Wednesday, and Thursday at 3 p.m. while school is in session. Students also have the opportunity to observe one of the improvisation ensembles. Students interested in scheduling a tour should call the Jazz office at 212-229-5896 Ext. 4589 or schedule online at http://www.newschool.edu/jazz at least one week in advance.

Application and Information

Applications are available online at http://www.newschool.edu/jazz. The priority deadline for fall admission is January 1 (the latest application deadline is March 15); the priority deadline for spring is September 15 (the latest deadline is November 1). Applicants are notified by April 1 and November 15, respectively. For more information, students should contact:

Teri Lucas, Director of Admissions
The New School for Jazz and Contemporary Music
55 West 13th Street, 5th floor
New York, New York 10011
Phone: 212-229-5896 Ext. 4584
Fax: 212-229-8936
E-mail: jazzadm@newschool.edu
Web site: http://www.newschool.edu/jazz

NEW YORK SCHOOL OF INTERIOR DESIGN
NEW YORK, NEW YORK

New York
School
of Interior
Design
founded 1916

The School

The New York School of Interior Design (NYSID) is a nationally ranked, independent, nonprofit college accredited by National Association of Schools of Art and Design (NASAD). It was established in 1916 by architect Sherrill Whiton and chartered by the Board of Regents of the University of the State of New York in 1924. Throughout its history, the School has devoted all of its resources to a single field of study—interior design—and has played a significant role in the development of the interior design profession. Enrollment is approximately 800.

NYSID's curriculum is a reflection of the complex yet sophisticated profession of interior design. Courses stress the discipline's call to protect the health, safety, and welfare of the public while being functional and aesthetically pleasing. Today's students learn not only the colors and materials appropriate to residential interiors, but also how to design environmentally sound and accessible hospitals, offices, schools, restaurants, and more. Whether learning the importance of sustainability and historic preservation or the latest programs in computer-aided design, NYSID students obtain a wide range of skills and techniques taught by faculty members who work in the field. New York City is home to art and antique shops, museums, professional design studios, and showrooms that are all an exciting part of the college's "campus."

The atmosphere of the college is cosmopolitan, not only because of its excellent location but also because it attracts students from across the United States and abroad. International students make up approximately 13 percent of the student population. Many students also transfer from other colleges in order to obtain a more professional, career-directed education.

The School continues to maintain a close relationship with the interior design industry because of its select faculty and established reputation. This provides an excellent means for students to develop associations that offer opportunities to move into the profession after completing their degree program at NYSID.

In addition to the undergraduate programs in interior design listed below, NYSID also offers four graduate programs: a professional-level Master of Fine Arts (M.F.A.) degree in interior design, a post–professional-level M.F.A. degree in interior design, and Master of Professional Studies (M.P.S.) degrees in sustainable interior environments and interior lighting design.

Location

The New York School of Interior Design is located on Manhattan's Upper East Side, where a number of the major interior design studios are located. Many of the world's most important galleries, museums, and showrooms are close by, most within walking distance. The city is world-renowned for its architecture, cosmopolitan urban experience, cultural activities, and historic districts. The college can be reached easily by bus, car, subway, and train.

Majors and Degrees

The New York School of Interior Design offers four undergraduate programs in interior design: a four-year Bachelor of Fine Arts (B.F.A.) degree accredited by the Council for Interior Design Accreditation (CIDA), a two-year Associate in Applied Science (A.A.S.) degree, a 24-credit nondegree Basic Interior Design certificate, and a four-year Bachelor of Arts (B.A.) degree in the history of the interior and the decorative arts.

Academic Programs

The New York School of Interior Design is devoted exclusively to the design of the interior environment. The various academic programs make up an integrated curriculum covering interior design concepts; history of art, architecture, furniture, and interiors; technical and communication skills, materials and methods, and philosophy and theory; and professional design procedures and design problem solving.

The Basic Interior Design program consists of a 24-credit sequence of foundation courses in which all design students enroll. These courses provide a cultural, general, and professional introduction to the field of interior design. Although completion of the Basic Interior Design program may be the major goal for some, for most students it serves as the foundation for matriculation into the degree programs.

The A.A.S. degree program provides the minimum educational requirement to become a certified interior designer in New York State. The 66-credit program includes design, liberal arts, and professional courses.

The 132-credit Bachelor of Fine Arts degree program provides the education that, with practical experience, enables the graduate to take qualifying exams for interior design certification in many states and to join national and local professional associations. Studies focus on the development of a broad array of conceptual analysis, creative problem-solving, relevant cultural development, and technical skills. Students are required to take 32 credits of liberal arts courses in addition to 100 credits of professional design-related courses.

The 120-credit Bachelor of Arts in the history of the interior and the decorative arts program provides students with an undergraduate liberal arts degree in art history with a special focus on the interior environment and the objects it contains. Graduates of the program have the opportunity to apply to NYSID's professional-level graduate program with one year of advanced standing, allowing the student to complete the three-year program in just two years.

NYSID's curriculum is flexible and permits students to take courses on a full- or part-time basis during the day or evening and on weekends. The college maintains an active job placement service. Students may be placed in a wide variety of positions that reflect the full spectrum of job opportunities in the interior design profession.

Academic Facilities

The NYSID campus occupies two buildings on the Upper East Side as well as a new Graduate Center in the Gramercy Park area of Manhattan. The college has first-rate facilities with light-filled studios; a unique lighting laboratory; several computer facilities for computer-aided design (CAD); a large atelier for independent work furnished with drafting tables, computers, and a materials collection for use in projects; a lecture hall and seminar rooms; a well-stocked bookstore; and a handsome auditorium. The library's collection includes more than 16,000 books on design, architecture, and allied disciplines; over 100 periodical subscriptions; a product literature collection; and an electronic image database for the study of the history of interior design and the decorative arts.

Costs

Tuition for B.I.D., A.A.S., and B.F.A. programs for 2011–12 is $796 per credit, plus a $335 registration/technology/activities fee each semester. Typical expenses for the first year are projected to be $25,245 for tuition and $670 in registration fees. Students entering the B.A. program in fall 2011 will pay $11,960 per semester plus $335 in fees. NYSID room-only housing costs are approximately $15,600 for nine months.

Financial Aid

Financial assistance is available to students who are matriculated and in good academic standing. Both need- and merit-based scholarships are offered, and there are financial aid programs for both full- and part-time study. An applicant is considered for financial assistance upon completion of the Free Application for Federal

Student Aid (FAFSA). This single application will be reviewed to determine a student's eligibility for Federal Pell Grants, Federal Supplemental Educational Opportunity Grants, Federal Work-Study Program, NYSID scholarships, and New York State aid, if applicable.

Faculty

Since New York City is a world-class design center, many top designers, art historians, architects, and authorities on the decorative arts teach and lecture at the college. NYSID faculty work as practicing designers in addition to being educators, authors, and active members of professional design organizations, and as such, give NYSID students special insight into the practice of their chosen field. The student to faculty ratio at NYSID is 12:1.

Student Government

The Student Council of the New York School of Interior Design is the elected voice of the student body in academic, administrative, residential, and leisure matters at the college. It is the representative forum through which student concerns are brought to the attention of the administration. It also organizes and sponsors a number of social events throughout the academic year.

In addition, the college has an active student chapter of the American Society of Interior Designers (ASID). ASID organizes lectures, tours, workshops, and other events providing an inside view of the interior design industry. The Contract Club arranges visits to top commercial interior design firms providing the opportunity to see actual projects being designed, ask questions of senior designers, and tour professional working offices.

Admission Requirements

All applicants must submit an application, an application fee, an official secondary school transcript, SAT or ACT scores, and two letters of recommendation. Applicants to the A.A.S. and B.F.A. degree programs must meet the visual requirements by providing a portfolio as described in the catalog and Web site; transfer students must also submit college transcripts.

Additional application materials are required for international applicants. International applicants should contact the college's International Student Adviser for assistance in applying.

Application and Information

Admission decisions are made on a rolling basis. However, for processing purposes, it is recommended that the Admissions Office receive an application for fall admission by February 1. An application for spring admission should be received by October 1. Applicants are notified of the Admission Committee's decision by mail shortly after all required documents have been received and visual requirements fulfilled.

Inquiries and applications should be directed to:

The Office of Admissions
New York School of Interior Design
170 East 70th Street
New York, New York 10021-5110

Phone: 212-472-1500 Ext. 204
       800-33NYSID (toll-free)
Fax: 212-472-1867
E-mail: admissions@nysid.edu
Web site: http://www.nysid.edu
       http://www.facebook.com/nysidnyc
       http://twitter.com/NYSID

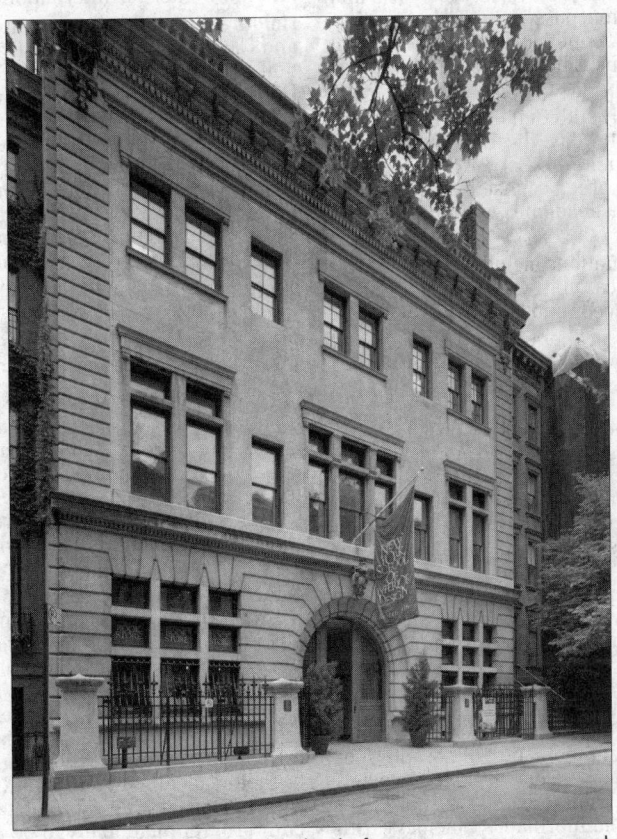

The campus of the New York School of Interior Design is centered on its building at 170 East 70th Street in the Upper East Side Historic District.

NIAGARA UNIVERSITY
NIAGARA UNIVERSITY, NEW YORK

NIAGARA UNIVERSITY
Education That Makes a Difference

The University

Niagara University (NU), founded in 1856, is a private, independent university rooted in a Catholic and Vincentian tradition. The suburban 160-acre campus combines the old and new; both ivy-covered buildings and modern architectural structures are among its thirty-three buildings. The University is easily accessible from every major city in the eastern and midwestern United States via the New York State Thruway, Buffalo International Airport, and rail and bus service.

There are more than 3,000 undergraduate and 950 graduate students enrolled at Niagara. A large percentage of these students take advantage of the more than eighty extracurricular and cocurricular activities offered. Volunteer work in the community is popular among the students and enhances community relations. Students work with numerous organizations, including Habitat for Humanity, Big Brothers/Big Sisters, and the Skating Association for the Blind and Handicapped.

University teams compete on the Division I level and are members of the NCAA, the Metro Atlantic Athletic Conference, Atlantic Hockey Conference, and College Hockey America Conference. Intercollegiate sports for men include baseball, basketball, cross-country, golf, ice hockey, soccer, swimming and diving, and tennis. Intercollegiate sports for women include basketball, cross-country, golf, ice hockey, lacrosse, soccer, softball, swimming and diving, tennis, and volleyball. Club sports include cheerleading, danceline, hockey, martial arts, rugby, and skiing. The Kiernan Center offers a variety of sports and recreational facilities, including a multipurpose gymnasium, a swimming and diving pool, an indoor track, racquetball courts, free-weight and Nautilus rooms, and aerobics rooms. There are several outdoor athletic fields and basketball and tennis courts.

Additional student services include the Health Center, which provides inpatient and outpatient care during the day; the Learning Center, which provides free tutoring services; and the Career Development Office, which offers professional and career counseling. Other services include counseling, orientation, academic planning, career planning, and job placement.

Niagara University's housing accommodations include five residence halls, a grouping of five small cottages, and a student apartment complex. Both coed and single-gender accommodations are available.

The University offers graduate studies in business, counseling, criminal justice, education, and interdisciplinary studies.

Location

Niagara University's picturesque 160-acre campus is located in the town of Lewiston, New York, 2 minutes off I-190 on Route 104. The campus is situated on Monteagle Ridge overlooking the lower Niagara River, which connects the two Great Lakes of Erie and Ontario. The University's suburban campus setting is just a few miles from the world-famous Niagara Falls, 20 minutes from Buffalo, which offers a variety of cultural events, sports, and entertainment opportunities, and just 90 minutes from Toronto, Canada's largest metropolitan area. In addition, the University is minutes away from the quaint village of Lewiston, New York, and the city of Niagara Falls, New York.

Majors and Degrees

The College of Arts and Sciences offers the Bachelor of Arts degree in chemistry, communication studies, English, French, history, international studies, liberal arts, life sciences, mathematics, philosophy, political science, psychology, religious studies, social sciences, sociology, and Spanish. The Bachelor of Science degree is awarded in biochemistry (with a concentration in bioinformatics), biology (with concentrations in bioinformatics and biotechnology), chemistry (with a concentration in computational chemistry), computer and information sciences, criminal justice and criminology, mathematics, nursing (completion program for students who are registered nurses), and social work. This division also offers the Bachelor of Fine Arts degree in theater studies (with concentrations in design technology, general theater, and performance). Preprofessional programs are offered in dentistry, law, medicine, pharmacy, veterinary medicine, and Army-ROTC. An Associate of Arts degree is available in general studies. In

addition, Niagara offers an environmental studies concentration to supplement a degree in biology, chemistry, or political science. Enrichment courses in fine arts and languages are also available.

In addition to the programs listed above NU offers a number of preprofessional partnerships. These include a 3+4 partnership in pharmacy with the State University of New York at Buffalo (SUNY), a 2+3 partnership in pharmacy with Lake Erie College of Osteopathic Medicine (LECOM), a 3+4 partnership in medicine with LECOM, and a 3+4 partnership in dentistry with SUNY at Buffalo. Qualified premedical Niagara students are eligible to apply for the early assurance program sponsored by the SUNY at Buffalo.

Niagara University's College of Business Administration is accredited by AACSB International—The Association to Advance Collegiate Schools of Business and offers a B.B.A. and a combination B.B.A./M.B.A. degree (five-year program) in accounting. This division offers B.S. degrees in economics, finance, management (with concentrations in human resources, international business, and supply chain management), and marketing. In addition, an A.A.S. degree can be earned in business.

Real-world learning occurs through internships, study abroad, and cooperative education programs as well as research being conducted in several business-focused campus centers. These centers include the Family Business Center, the Center for Supply Chain Management, and the Center for International Accounting.

Holding the highest accreditations possible in both the United States and Canada—the United States National Council for Teacher Education (NCATE) and Canada's Ontario College of Teachers—Niagara University's College of Education provides students with an option of earning dual certification to teach in both countries. The College of Education offers bachelor's degree programs leading to New York State initial certification in early childhood (birth–grade 6), childhood (grades 1–6), childhood and middle childhood (grades 1–9), middle childhood and adolescence (grades 5–12), adolescence (grades 7–12), certification for teaching students with disabilities (grades 1–6 childhood and grades 7–12 adolescence), and in Teaching English to Speakers of Other Languages (TESOL). All education majors pursue an academic concentration to establish expertise in one of the following subject areas: biology, business, chemistry, English, French, liberal arts, mathematics, social studies, and Spanish. Business education is offered only at grades 5–12. The academic concentration in liberal arts can only be pursued in the early childhood and childhood (birth–grade 6), and special education and childhood (grades 1–6). Most other states, and Puerto Rico, have reciprocity agreements with New York, meaning that an NU education would qualify education majors to teach in those states as well. In addition, the Canadian province of Ontario recognizes Niagara graduates as qualified for the Letter of Eligibility to teach in that province.

The College of Hospitality and Tourism Management provides a career-oriented curriculum leading to a B.S. degree in three specific areas: hotel and restaurant management (with concentrations in food and beverage management; luxury hospitality operations; and hotel planning, development, and operations), sport management (with concentrations in sport operations and revenue management), and tourism and recreation management (with concentrations in event and meeting management and tourism destination management). The College of Hospitality and Tourism Management offered the world's first bachelor's degree in tourism. NU's hotel and restaurant program, the second oldest in New York State, has the distinction of being the seventh program nationally to be accredited by the Accreditation Commission for Programs in Hospitality Administration by the Council of Hotel, Restaurant, and Institutional Education. The College introduces students to a comprehensive body of knowledge about the hotel, restaurant, tourism, and recreational areas and applies this knowledge to current industry challenges. The College requires that its students accumulate 800 hours of industry-related experience. These and other practical experiences offer NU students the knowledge necessary to advance in the field. Students work with industry leaders in classroom projects, join academic clubs and professional organizations, and participate in special trips to trade shows and conventions and specially designed study-abroad experiences, making NU a national leader in the area.

For students who are undecided about which major to choose, Niagara University offers an award-winning Academic Exploration Program (AEP). AEP provides a structured opportunity for students to participate in a thorough, organized process of selecting a major that meets their academic talents and career goals.

Academic Programs

Niagara University's curricula enable students to pursue their academic preferences and to complete courses that lead to proficiency in other academic areas. Courses that have been considered upper-division courses are available to all students. This provides students with the opportunity to avoid introductory and survey courses and permits motivated students to take advantage of more challenging courses early in their collegiate career. The honors program provides special academic opportunities that stimulate, encourage, and challenge participants. In addition, an accelerated three-year degree program is offered to qualified students.

Students pursuing a bachelor's degree must complete a total of 40 or 42 course units (120 or 126 hours) to meet graduation requirements. Niagara grants credit for successful scores on the Advanced Placement and College-Level Examination Program tests.

Internships, research, independent study, and cooperative education are available in many academic programs. An Army ROTC program is also offered.

The University operates on a two-semester plan (fall and spring). A comprehensive summer session offers a variety of courses.

NU is fully accredited by the Middle States Association of Colleges and Schools. Its programs in the respective areas are accredited by the National Council for Accreditation of Teacher Education, AACSB International–The Association to Advance Collegiate Schools of Business, and the Council on Social Work Education, and the chemistry department has the approval of the American Chemical Society. The travel, hotel, and restaurant administration program is accredited by the Commission for Programs in Hospitality Administration.

Off-Campus Programs

For those students who wish to study abroad, the University offers semester and summer programs in Chile, England, France, Mexico, Netherlands, Spain, Switzerland, Thailand, and many other countries. Upon request, programs may be offered in other countries. NU is also affiliated with Western New York Consortium. Through this program, students may take courses at other colleges and universities and apply the credits to Niagara's graduation requirements.

Academic Facilities

The University's open-stack library exceeds 200,000 books and has more than 21,000 periodical titles as well as reference databases accessible through the Web. The library is housed in a modern facility that includes seating for 500 people, including individual study carrels. The library is affiliated with the Online Computer Library Center (OCLC) network.

The Academic Complex, the home to the College of Education and the College of Business Administration (Bisgrove Hall), is a state-of-the-art learning facility. Dunleavy Hall, outstanding both educationally and architecturally, includes a computerized lecture hall and TV production rooms. The University's facilities also include the Computer Center; DePaul Hall of Science; St. Vincent's Hall; the Kiernan Center, NU's athletic and recreation center; the Elizabeth Ann Clune Center for Theatre; the Castellani Art Museum; Bailo Hall, which houses the Office of Admissions; and the Dwyer Arena, a dual-rink ice hockey complex.

Costs

Tuition for 2010–11 was $24,600. Room and board (with a choice of meal plans) cost an additional $10,650 per year. Fees were estimated at $1050 per year. Niagara estimates that an additional $2500 to $3050 per year is adequate for books, laundry, and other essentials, such as travel to and from home.

Financial Aid

Ninety-nine percent of the incoming students who enrolled at NU received a financial aid package averaging more than $21,000 per year. They receive assistance in the form of merit scholarships, loans, grants, or campus employment. Students seeking financial aid should file the Free Application for Federal Student Aid (FAFSA). New York State residents should also file a Tuition Assistance Program (TAP) application.

Faculty

Niagara University has a dedicated, accessible faculty who genuinely cares about the academic and personal growth of their students. Their commitment to teaching is their primary concern. A student-faculty ratio of 14:1 and an average class size of approximately 25 allow personal attention and classroom interaction.

Student Government

The Student Government represents all parts of the student body equally. It coordinates and legislates all student activities, serving as both liaison to and a participating member of the University. In addition, students serve on all major departmental committees and on the University Senate, which is the major advisory committee to the president and Board of Trustees.

Admission Requirements

The University welcomes men and women who have demonstrated aptitude and academic achievement at the high school level. Either SAT or ACT test scores are required. International students are required to submit the results of their TOEFL examination. Interviews are recommended. Transfer students are accepted in any semester. (Transfer credit is evaluated individually by the dean of each division.) Students who complete high school in less than four years are eligible for early admission. Students may also apply under an early action program. Economically and educationally disadvantaged students from New York State are eligible to apply for admission through the Higher Educational Opportunity Program (HEOP).

Application and Information

Niagara operates on a rolling admission basis and adheres to the College Board Candidates Reply Date. A visit to the campus is encouraged, and overnight accommodations in a residence hall are available through the Niagara Nights program.

Information on all aspects of the University can be obtained by contacting the Office of Admissions.

Harry Gong
Director of Admissions
Bailo Hall
Niagara University
Niagara University, New York 14109-2011
Phone: 716-286-8700
      800-462-2111 (toll-free)
Fax: 716-286-8710
E-mail: admissions@niagara.edu
Web site: http://www.niagara.edu
      http://www.facebook.com/niagarau
      http://twitter.com/niagarauniv

The main campus of Niagara University.

NORTHEASTERN UNIVERSITY
BOSTON, MASSACHUSETTS

The University

There is a certain energy about Northeastern. It comes from bright, ambitious students with a sense of purpose. In the classroom, in the workplace, in campus activities, and in the city of Boston—the ultimate college town—Northeastern students stimulate their minds, investigate career options, participate in community affairs, and graduate personally and professionally prepared for their future careers or for graduate school.

Northeastern is a leader in interdisciplinary and translational research; urban engagement; and the integration of classroom learning with real-world experience. We integrate rigorous classroom studies with experiential learning opportunities—anchored by the world's largest, most innovative cooperative education program—to prepare students for a lifetime of achievement. It is the Northeastern difference.

The current undergraduate enrollment of 15,005 is made up of students of all backgrounds, interests, and tastes, giving Northeastern its distinctive, urban style. This diversity shows in the range of available activities. Students can join a cultural club, participate in research, perform with the Silver Masque, go on a ski trip, play basketball, tutor local children, learn to ballroom dance, and much more. Students have many opportunities to make friends, try something new, become a leader, or simply have fun. Students can also find quiet corners of the campus that feel far from city streets where they can read or just relax, sprawled on a wooden bench under a shade tree; sip gourmet coffee from a nearby campus café; or listen to a midday jazz performance behind the Curry Student Center amid the art of Northeastern's sculpture park. The 73-acre campus is dynamic and welcoming, a beautiful stretch of leafy green in the heart of Boston. Its compact size lets students get to class on time or rush back for a forgotten book.

Location

Northeastern's residential campus lies in the heart of Boston, where the distinctive neighborhoods of the Back Bay, the South End, the Fenway, and Roxbury meet. In the past five years, Northeastern has built a host of new on-campus residence halls, more than doubling the amount of housing available to undergraduates. The newest residence halls offer apartment-style living with modern kitchens complete with dishwashers, disposals, and full-sized appliances; cable hookups; and data jacks. Many have amazing views of the Boston skyline.

The Back Bay area, known for its many cultural and educational institutions, is steps from Symphony Hall, the New England Conservatory of Music, the Museum of Fine Arts, and the Isabella Stewart Gardner Museum. The South End is home to elegant Victorian row houses, exciting arts, hidden gardens and some of the finest dining in Boston. The Fenway area, with its beautiful rose garden, bicycle and jogging paths, and Fenway Park (home of the Boston Red Sox), is just a few blocks away.

Majors and Degrees

Northeastern's academic programs are divided among eight colleges: the College of Arts, Media, and Design; the College of Business Administration; the College of Computer and Information Science; the College of Engineering; the Bouvé College of Health Sciences; the College of Professional Studies; the College of Science; and the College of Social Sciences and Humanities. Top-notch faculty members with a variety of research interests personally guide students through their studies.

The College of Arts, Media, and Design awards undergraduate degrees in architecture, art, cinema studies (combined major options only), communication studies, digital art, game design (combined major options only), graphic design, interactive media (combined major options only), journalism, music (concentrations in music history and analysis, music industry, and music technology), studio art (in collaboration with the School of the Museum of Fine Arts, Boston), and theater (including concentrations in performance and production).

The College of Business Administration offers two tracks: the Bachelor of Science in Business Administration (B.S.B.A.) and the Bachelor of Science in International Business (B.S.I.B.). The B.S.I.B. program includes language instruction and international study and work. The College offers concentrations in accounting, entrepreneurship and innovation, finance and insurance, management, management information systems, marketing, and supply chain management.

The College of Computer and Information Science awards degrees in computer science and information science and also offers combined majors, combining computer science with business, cognitive psychology, game design, mathematics, physics, biology, multimedia arts, music technology, or digital art.

The College of Engineering offers degrees in chemical, civil, computer, electrical, industrial, and mechanical engineering.

The Bouvé College of Health Sciences awards degrees in health sciences, nursing, pharmacy, and speech-language pathology and audiology. The college also offers a six-year Doctor of Pharmacy degree and a six-year program leading to a Master of Science in Physical Therapy.

The College of Professional Studies offers undergraduate and graduate degree programs in a wide range of disciplines, with an emphasis on global options. The college is also home to the School of Education.

The College of Science awards undergraduate degrees in applied physics, behavioral neuroscience, biochemistry, biology, biomedical physics, chemistry, environmental science, environmental studies, linguistics, mathematics, physics, and psychology.

The College of Social Sciences and Humanities awards undergraduate degrees in African American studies, American Sign Language, Asian studies, criminal justice, cultural anthropology, economics, English, history, human services, international affairs, Jewish studies (combined major options only), philosophy, political science, religious studies, sociology, and Spanish.

Academic Programs

At the heart of a Northeastern education lies award-winning professors and faculty mentors, rigorous and innovative curriculum, undergraduate research and global experiences that challenge and transform. Innovative programs encompass a wide range of majors, concentrations, and interdisciplinary studies along with honors, preprofessional, and study-abroad programs.

Northeastern's approach integrates academics with a variety of experiential learning opportunities including research, global experience, service learning, and the University's signature cooperative education program (co-op), enabling students to discover their path before they leave college.

Through the internationally known co-op program, after completing their freshman year, students alternate classroom learning with periods of full-time (usually paid) work or other types of practical learning related to their major or interests, earning their bachelor's degree in either four or five years. Graduates accumulate as many as eighteen months of professional experience, professional contacts, and the social confidence that gives them a significant edge in the job market over new graduates without experience. By working in varied jobs and settings, students learn what they like—and do not like—before committing to a permanent position. Many Northeastern students even go to work for a co-op employer after graduation. Co-op is an education in itself. Northeastern students graduate knowing what they only could have learned on the job: how to conduct themselves, what to wear, how to interpret a company's culture, how to get things done, and how to write a resume and interview successfully.

Co-op employers include some of the country's largest and most reputable companies, such as Pfizer, John Hancock, Fidelity Investments, General Electric, Massachusetts General Hospital, and the *Boston Globe*. Students also enjoy international placements for a semester or a year abroad; co-op employers recruit from Australia, Scotland, Italy, and Spain, among many other countries.

Experiential learning opportunities—including U.S. and international co-op, service-learning, research, and study abroad—are currently available in sixty-nine countries and 160 cities in the U.S. and around the world.

The University honors program gives students opportunities to participate in enriched educational experiences and offers opportunities that include honors sections of required academic courses, honors seminars, independent research, and study abroad. The University also offers Army, Naval Nursing, and Air Force ROTC. The Disability Resource Center provides many support services that enable students with disabilities to participate fully in the life of the University community.

Academic Facilities

Northeastern is home to thirty-seven research centers, including the Center for Labor Market Studies, the Barnett Institute of Chemical and Biological Analysis, the Center for High-rate Nanomanufacturing, the Institute on Race and Justice, and many others. Students have ample opportunities to work alongside their professors to aid and conduct research on a variety of topics as undergraduates.

The University libraries system comprises Snell Library, a 240,000 square foot central library on the Boston Campus, the School of Law Library (also on the Boston Campus) and a small supplemental collection at the Nahant Marine Science Center. Total non-law holdings for the academic year 2008 include 986,231 print volumes, 119,078 e-books, 2,399,716 microfilms, and 5,641 current serials subscriptions, with access to 31,031 electronic journals. In addition, Snell Library houses 23,273 audio, video, and computer software items, and 4,791 linear feet of archival material. The library is a selective depository of federal government publications and currently holds 158,623 printed government documents.

Northeastern University provides a broad range of academic and administrative computer resources available to students and faculty and staff members. Many computing resources are available, including Internet connections for all offices and University-owned residence halls, technology-assisted classrooms, computer labs, and the myNEU portal, which allows student to access many administrative and academic functions online. There is also extensive wireless network access, found in the library, Student Center, and many dorms.

Costs

For 2010–11, tuition was $36,360, and room and board were $12,310. Whether students choose to earn their undergraduate degree in four or five years (including experiential educational periods), tuition is charged only for the academic experience, not for the experiential educational periods.

Financial Aid

The University operates a substantial aid program designed to make attendance at Northeastern feasible for all qualified students. By coordinating the resources of the University and various public and private scholarship programs, the Office of Student Financial Services was recently able to provide more than $130 million in grant and scholarship assistance. About 80 percent of the freshman class received some form of financial aid. Northeastern participates in all federal aid programs. Financial aid is based on need and academic merit and may consist of grants, loans, work-study employment, or any combination of the three. To apply, students must file a Free Application for Federal Student Aid (FAFSA) and a CSS PROFILE form with the College Scholarship Service by the priority filing date of February 15.

Faculty

The University has 1,005 full-time faculty members with a wide variety of research and teaching interests and specialties and a staff of academic counselors in each college who work closely with students to assist them in developing programs suited to their interests and abilities. Each student is assigned both an academic and a co-op adviser. The co-op advisor aids in resume building and interview skills and tactics. In addition, the advisor aids in developing contacts with business and co-op employers as well as networking and eventual job searches.

Admission Requirements

Students may enter the University with advanced credit on the basis of test scores on Advanced Placement (AP) examinations, the College-Level Examination Program (CLEP), the International Baccalaureate (I.B.), or on successful completion of accredited college-level courses before enrollment at Northeastern. In addition to the application for admission, prospective freshmen must submit official high school transcript(s) (or official GED score reports), including their senior-year grades; official transcripts for any college-level course work taken while a secondary-school student; written recommendations from their secondary school guidance counselor and a teacher; and scores on the SAT (Northeastern's College Board code is 3667) or ACT, including the writing section. Please visit the University's Web site for additional admission details and transfer admissions requirements (www.northeastern.edu/admissions).

Application and Information

Admission to Northeastern is selective and competitive. For the 2010–11 academic year, the University received more than 43,000 applications for 2,800 places in the freshman class. Students who thrive in a challenging academic environment—and outside the classroom in activities like Northeastern's dynamic global experiential learning options—are best suited for a Northeastern education. Experiential learning will expand the student's initiative, adaptability, confidence, poise, and ability to work collaboratively, which are the foundations of leadership.

November 1 is the deadline for the early action admission program. Students who have carefully explored their college options and have decided that Northeastern is where they want to enroll may choose to apply under the early action program. The deadline for the regular admission program is January 15. If accepted for fall admission either through the early action program or the regular admission program, freshmen are required to send a tuition deposit by May 1 to secure a place in the class. For transfer students, the priority deadline for the fall is May 1. Admission decisions for transfer applicants are made on a space-available, rolling basis. November 1 is the deadline for January transfer admission for both freshman and transfer applicants and for international applicants for January admission. Admission decisions for spring applicants are made on a space-available, rolling basis. Northeastern offers a variety of visit options including information sessions and campus tours. For more information, or to register, visit www.northeastern.edu/admissions/visitcampus.

For more information, students should contact:

Office of Undergraduate Admissions
150 Richards Hall
Northeastern University
360 Huntington Avenue
Boston, Massachusetts 02115
Phone: 617-373-2200
E-mail: admissions@neu.edu
Web site: http://www.northeastern.edu/admissions

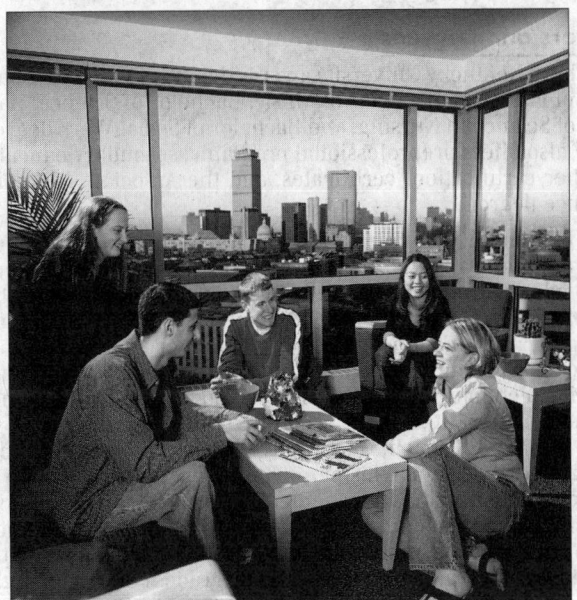

Northeastern University students in a West Village residence hall enjoy spectacular Boston vistas.

NORTHERN KENTUCKY UNIVERSITY

HIGHLAND HEIGHTS, KENTUCKY

ESTABLISHED 1968

The University

Northern Kentucky University (NKU) was founded in 1968 and is the newest of Kentucky's eight state universities. The atmosphere of the campus is futuristic, emphasizing a high-quality education by supporting the liberal arts. Major buildings are of modern, contemporary architectural design and are set on 300 acres of rolling countryside. NKU has an enrollment of approximately 15,000 students from forty-two states and ninety-two countries and is accredited by the Southern Association of Colleges and Schools. The Salmon P. Chase College of Law is accredited by both the American Bar Association and the Association of American Law Schools.

There are more than 200 student organizations. NKU competes in the NCAA Division II Great Lakes Valley Conference. Intercollegiate sports are offered for men and women in basketball, cheerleading, cross-country, golf, soccer, and tennis; for men in baseball; and for women in fast-pitch softball and volleyball. Intramural activities vary by semester, but include basketball, dodgeball, field hockey, flag football, ice hockey, racquetball, soccer, softball, Tae Kwan Do, volleyball, and many others. Students should visit the University's Web site for a complete listing at http://www.nku.edu/~camprec/index.htm.

Location

NKU is located in the largest metropolitan area of any state university in Kentucky. It is located at the junction of U.S. Highway 27 and Interstates 275 and 471 in Highland Heights, Kentucky, 8 miles southeast of Cincinnati, Ohio. NKU is only 60 miles from Dayton, 79 miles from Lexington, 93 miles from Louisville, and 114 miles from Indianapolis. While the immediate surroundings are suburban, NKU is part of the metropolitan area of greater Cincinnati.

Majors and Degrees

Northern Kentucky University awards the Bachelor of Arts, Bachelor of Fine Arts, Bachelor of Music, Bachelor of Science, Bachelor of Science in Nursing, and Bachelor of Social Work degrees. NKU also offers preprofessional programs, secondary education teacher certification, certificates, and the Associate of Applied Science degree.

The B.A. and B.S. degrees are offered in accounting, anthropology, athletic training, art (teaching), biological sciences, business administration, business education, business informatics, chemistry, chemistry/biology, computer education technology, computer information technology, computer science, criminal justice, early childhood education, economics, electronic engineering technology, electronic media and broadcasting, elementary education, English, entrepreneurship, environmental science, finance, French, geography, geology, German, graphic design, health science, history, industrial education, human resources, construction management, international studies, journalism, liberal studies, management, mechanical and manufacturing engineering, marketing, mathematics, media informatics, mental health–human services, middle grades education, organizational leadership, organizational systems technology, organizational systems technology management, philosophy, photography, physical education, physical education recreation, physics, political science, psychology, public relations, radio-TV, recreation-fitness, social studies (teaching), sociology, Spanish, special education, speech communication, sports business, and theater.

The B.F.A. degree is granted in art and in theater arts. The B.Mus. degree is offered in music. The B.S.N. degree is offered in the nursing major and the B.S.W. degree in the social work major.

Preprofessional programs are available in dentistry, engineering, forestry, human resources, law, medicine, optometry, pharmacy, physician assistant studies, physical therapy, veterinary medicine, and wildlife management. In addition, the University offers majors, minors, and areas of discipline for secondary education teacher certification.

The University also awards the A.A.S. degree in construction technology, criminal justice, human services, integrative studies, prebusiness studies, radiologic technology, and respiratory care.

Academic Programs

NKU operates on a semester calendar. To receive a bachelor's degree, students must complete a minimum of 120 credit hours. At least 60 credit hours are required for the associate degree.

The University offers a variety of career planning and placement, internship, independent study, work-study, and cooperative-education programs. There is also an Advising, Counseling, and Testing Center available. Other programs include an honors program, a program that allows for the dual enrollment of high school students, a program where students can combine their career interests in the liberal arts and engineering fields, and University 101, an orientation program for freshmen and transfer students.

NKU recognizes credit earned through the Advanced Placement (AP) Program and the general, subject, and institutional tests of specific College-Level Examination Program (CLEP). A maximum of 45 credit hours may be applied toward the bachelor's degree from the AP and CLEP examinations. The International Baccalaureate Program allows students to earn credit in science, mathematics, psychology, and languages.

Off-Campus Programs

A variety of study-abroad opportunities are available to NKU students through membership in several consortia, through NKU exchange agreements with international universities, and through independent NKU professor-led trips.

Study in Australia, Belize, England, Ghana, Hong Kong, India, Ireland, Jamaica, and Scotland is possible in a wide range of courses and programs available through NKU's membership in the Cooperative Center for Study Abroad (CCSA).

The Kentucky Institute for International Studies (KIIS) offers students academic language programs in Argentina, Austria, Brazil, China, Costa Rica, Czech Republic, Denmark, Ecuador, France, Germany, Greece, Italy, Japan, Mexico, Poland, Spain, Turkey, and Ukraine.

The NKU Office of International Programs has student and faculty exchanges with universities in Costa Rica, Denmark, France, Germany, Japan, Korea, Mexico, Russia, Scotland, and Spain.

Academic Facilities

Among the academic facilities at NKU are an anthropology museum, a biology museum, and an art gallery with rotating exhibits. NKU also has a new laser projection planetarium. NKU becomes only the seventh institution worldwide to boast such equipment, joining six major planetariums in cities such as Tokyo, Los Angeles, and London. Additionally, the University has nursing, respiratory care, and radiologic technology laboratories. In spring of 2008, NKU opened a 9000-seat arena called the Bank of Kentucky Center. NKU's brand-new Student Union, a student-centered facility, and focal point for campus programs and student organizations, was also completed in 2008. In the fall of 2011, NKU's Griffin Hall is scheduled to open. This building, the new home of the College of Informatics, is designed to help students interested in communication and media, computer science, information technology, or management information systems become the new generation of professionals who will build the region's information economy. The W. Frank Steely Library at NKU contains 311,155 book titles and maintains 1,729 paper periodical subscriptions (additional periodicals are available in electronic format). Computer laboratories offer students opportunities to learn and utilize a variety of software programs. The Computer Science Department and Criminal Justice Department have collaborated to offer students a computer forensics minor to teach students how to handle digital evidence and how to present such evidence in court.

Costs

Tuition and fees for 2010–11 were $7128 for Kentucky students $7128 and $13,896 for nonresidents. Other costs included $6500–$8000 for room and meals, about $850 for books and supplies, and $2773 for miscellaneous expenses.

Financial Aid

Last year, 80 percent of undergraduates received some form of financial assistance. To receive financial aid, applicants must complete the Free Application for Federal Student Aid (FAFSA). Academic, athletic, music-drama, and art scholarships and scholarships for members of minority groups are available at Northern Kentucky University.

The application deadline for all academic scholarships is January 15. There is no deadline for the University's financial aid application; however, students who wish to receive institutional aid must apply by March 1 for priority consideration. Applicants are notified of acceptance on a rolling basis.

Faculty

More than 82 percent of the faculty members at NKU hold a doctoral degree or the terminal degree in their field. Classes are small, with an average class size of 24 and a student-faculty ratio of 14:1. All classes are taught by faculty members; no classes are taught by graduate assistants.

Student Government

Student Government (SG) is the elected student assembly at Northern Kentucky University. It is the official student voice on campus and represents the student viewpoint on University committees. All SG meetings are open, and students are encouraged to attend.

Admission Requirements

Incoming freshmen must submit an application for admission; arrange for the official ACT, SAT, or COMPASS score report to be sent; and request that the high school send an official transcript. In order to be considered for regular admission, a student must meet precollege curriculum requirements for Kentucky and institutional admission standards. Out-of-state applicants must also meet the Kentucky precollege curriculum requirements.

Based on the review of official test results and the precollege curriculum, students are admitted into one of two categories: regular admission or admission with conditions. Students who have two or more deficiencies are encouraged to retake the ACT or SAT so an additional review can be completed. Students with two or more deficiencies may be asked to submit an essay, letters of recommendation, and an activities portfolio before an admission decision can be rendered. Some degree programs require that students meet additional criteria; students should refer to the current catalog for more information (http://www.nku.edu).

Application and Information

The $40 paper application fee may be waived for applicants with demonstrated need. The fall semester early action and scholarship deadline is January 15, assured consideration deadline is May 1, and the final deadline is August 1. The priority application deadline for the nursing program is January 31. The priority application deadline for the respiratory care program is February 15.

For more information, students should contact:

Office of Admissions
Northern Kentucky University
Highland Heights, Kentucky 41099
Phone: 859-572-5220
      800-637-9948 (toll-free)
E-mail: admitnku@nku.edu
Web site: http://admissions.nku.edu
      http://www.facebook.com/nkuedu
      http://twitter.com.nkuedu

Northern Kentucky University's modern campus is set in Highland Heights, just minutes from downtown Cincinnati.

NORWICH UNIVERSITY
NORTHFIELD, VERMONT

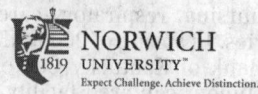

The University

Norwich University was established in 1819 as the first private military college in America. It was at Norwich that the idea of the citizen-soldier developed and eventually evolved into the Reserve Officer Training Corps (ROTC) program. Norwich was the first private college to offer civil engineering, and many University alumni were involved in the construction of the nation's continental railway system. In 1974, Norwich became one of the first military colleges to admit women into its Corps of Cadets, preceding the federal academies.

Norwich University offers a diverse blend of disciplines, teaching styles, and viewpoints. Students enrolled in the Corps of Cadets have a more disciplined, challenging, and structured path through college, while their civilian student classmates lead a more traditional collegiate lifestyle. However, both groups are coeducational and attend classes and participate in sports and other activities together.

In keeping with its mission, Norwich provides opportunities for all of its students to develop leadership skills with a strong commitment to community service. Both groups gain skills such as leadership, honor, and integrity, which are required to be successful in today's job market. These two diverse groups of students are very different and yet have much in common—they are Norwich.

Norwich University has an enrollment of 2,200 students from more than forty states and twenty countries. The University's minority enrollment is consistently higher (by percentage) than that of any other Vermont university or college.

The athletic facilities at Norwich are comparable to the best at any of New England's Division III universities. The main athletic complex, Andrews Hall, features a gymnasium, a modernized athletic training room, an equipment room, laundry facilities, five racquetball courts, and locker rooms. Kreitzberg Arena is a multipurpose facility with a seating capacity of 1,500 and a fully equipped weight room. It was here that the University's men's hockey team won the Division III National Championship in 2003. Plumley Armory has a huge gym as well as an indoor track, weight and aerobics rooms, a wrestling room, and an indoor swimming pool. Shapiro Field House has 50,000 square feet of floor space and includes a 200-meter indoor track, tennis courts, and a climbing wall. The 1,200-acre campus includes numerous playing fields for baseball, football, rugby, soccer, and softball. Norwich also has a paintball course, a rappel tower, an obstacle and confidence course.

Norwich has the only professional five-year Master of Architecture program in northern New England. The University also offers online graduate degrees in business administration, diplomacy, information security assurance, and justice administration.

Location

Norwich University is located in the heart of the Green Mountains of Vermont, right in the middle of ski country. Some of the nation's most popular resorts, such as Stowe, Sugarbush, and Killington, are located within an hour's drive. Vermont is world renowned as one of America's most beautiful states.

Nature's playground is just outside the dorm room—skiing, snowboarding, telemark skiing, cross-country skiing, snowshoeing, rock climbing, hiking, mountain biking, canoeing, kayaking, and more are available.

The University campus is located in the small town of Northfield, Vermont. Northfield is 10 miles south of the state capital of Montpelier and is 50 miles from Burlington, the largest city in Vermont. Both Montpelier and Burlington are cultural centers for the arts. Burlington International Airport is within an hour's drive. In addition, the cities of Boston and Montreal are only a 3-hour drive from the campus.

Majors and Degrees

Norwich offers students more than thirty academic majors from which to choose. The Bachelor of Arts degree is awarded in communications; criminal justice; English; history; international studies; peace, war, and diplomacy studies; political science; psychology; and Spanish. The Bachelor of Science degree is awarded in accounting, architecture, athletic training, biochemistry, biology, chemistry, civil/environmental engineering, communications, computer/electrical engineering, computer information systems, computer science, computer security and information assurance, economics, engineering management, environmental science, geology, international studies, management, mathematics, mechanical engineering, physical education, physics, sports medicine and health studies, strategic studies and defense analysis, and studies in war and peace. Teacher licensure, prelaw, premedical, and predental programs are also available.

Academic Programs

Norwich University is dedicated to the discovery, preservation, and dissemination of knowledge and the search for truth. Norwich is distinctive in that it maintains a strong emphasis on the development of leadership in both military and civilian pursuits and in providing for the educational needs of students. The University's mission is to foster in each student the growth of self-discipline, personal integrity, social responsibility, physical fitness, respect for law, and intellectual ability essential for full and effective participation in a free society.

For students enrolling in the Corps of Cadets, six semesters of Reserve Officer Training Corps are required. Norwich is considered the birthplace of ROTC; therefore, all four service branches can be found on campus. Prior to their junior year, cadets may elect to contract with their ROTC program and be considered upon graduation for a commission as officers in the Army, Navy, Air Force, or Marine Corps. Cadets not on an ROTC scholarship are not required to join the military.

Students typically take an average of five classes per semester. Each semester is sixteen weeks long, with holiday breaks at Thanksgiving, Christmas, and New Year's and in March during spring break. The academic year normally begins the last week in August and ends after the first week in May.

Academic Facilities

The academic facilities at Norwich are among the finest in New England. Completed in 1997, the math and science building was designed to keep classes small. Its labs hold no more than 16 students, and all of the classrooms are hardwired to allow for multimedia presentations. Students can find numerous computer labs across the campus, and the Kreitzberg Library offers students plenty of resources, space, and technology. Students may research Norwich's facilities on the University's Web site.

Costs

For 2010–11, tuition and fees were $14,369 per semester. The cost of room and board was $4979 per semester. Books and personal expenses averaged $1250 per semester. Cadets pay a uniform fee of $815 per semester in each of their first two years.

Financial Aid

Most families assume they cannot afford a private college education and fall victim to sticker shock, but a Norwich education can often be an affordable option for a family. Last year, 97 percent of Norwich students, with an average family income of $90,000, shared in more than $64 million of financial aid from all sources, including ROTC scholarships. This included an aggressive need-based financial aid program that enabled deserving students to secure a private education at Norwich.

Norwich awards many institutional scholarships based on academic merit. A student's high school GPA and ACT or SAT scores determine the level of scholarship. These scholarships may pay from $7000 to $18,000 of the student's tuition for four years. Students are required to maintain a specified GPA in order to renew the scholarship each year. Norwich also offers scholarships to students who attend the University's Future Leader Camp, participate in National Drill Team competitions, and who are in leadership positions in the Civil Air Patrol. Prospective students should contact an admissions counselor for more details about these scholarships.

Norwich also offers a large number of institutional grants based on financial need. A student must file the Free Application for Federal Student Aid (FAFSA) to be considered for these grants.

Students who bring a three- or four-year ROTC scholarship to Norwich are eligible for the General I. D. White Scholarship, which covers the cost of room and board. Students who are interested in applying for an ROTC scholarship should visit the individual ROTC detachment's Web page on the Norwich University Web site.

Faculty

The student-faculty ratio is 14:1. Faculty members are full-time instructors with advanced degrees; 80 percent hold a doctorate.

Small classes help promote a close relationship between faculty members and students. Students are assigned faculty advisers within each academic division.

Student Government

The Norwich University Corps of Cadets is a military organization made up of and led by cadets under the supervision of the Commandant of Cadets. Members of the Corps and student body preside over the University Honor Council. The University's honor code binds all Norwich students. Members of the Corps and student body also participate on the Student Affairs Committee, whose members include the Dean of Students, members of the faculty, and the Senior Vice President and Commandant of Cadets. This committee serves as the voice of the Norwich community and provides a channel of communication for change.

Admission Requirements

Admission to Norwich is based on a review of the applicant's academic record, personal essay, letters of recommendation, and extracurricular activities. Students at Norwich are heavily involved in community service and leadership development activities. Applicants should be able to demonstrate participation in activities both inside and outside of their high school.

Norwich is looking for students who want to become leaders, serve others, and give back to their communities. While the admissions office uses a rolling admissions system (meaning applications may be submitted at any time), there is a priority deadline of March 1. Students applying for admission or financial aid after March 1 are admitted on a space-available basis.

Application and Information

Students can visit the University's Web site or contact the University for more information.

Dean of Enrollment Management
Norwich University
27 I. D. White Avenue
Northfield, Vermont 05663

Phone: 800-468-6679 (toll-free)
Fax: 802-485-2032
E-mail: nuadm@norwich.edu
Web site: http://www.norwich.edu
　　　　　http://www.facebook.com/NorwichUniversity

A view of Norwich University's campus.

NOTRE DAME COLLEGE
SOUTH EUCLID, OHIO

The College

Notre Dame College (NDC) was established in 1922. A Catholic institution in the tradition of the Sisters of Notre Dame, the College educates a diverse population in the liberal arts for personal, professional, and global responsibility. The College believes that truly progressive education selectively blends traditional values with new ideas that represent real growth. Within the scope of a career-oriented liberal arts education, students can grow to meet the challenges of the present and the future. The College is accredited by the North Central Association of Colleges and Schools and is registered for the awarding of State Teachers' Licenses by the State of Ohio Department of Education.

A variety of clubs and activities enrich the educational experiences of the College's 2,120 students. The Campus Ministry program promotes the spiritual growth of the Notre Dame College community and facilitates community service, retreats, liturgy, and more. The Masquers promote talent in the performing arts and provide entertainment for the College community and general public. Campus publications include the *Notre Dame News* and *PIVOT*, the literary magazine. Faculty members and students schedule and coordinate lectures, plays, performances, and concerts. Most on-campus events are free, and students may purchase tickets at reduced rates for off-campus programs such as performances of the world-famous Cleveland Orchestra; the Cleveland Opera; and road shows of Broadway productions at the Palace Theatre, State Theatre, Ohio Theatre, and Cleveland Play House.

Notre Dame College is a member of the National Association of Intercollegiate Athletics (NAIA) and competes in the American Mideast Conference. Notre Dame College fields twenty-three athletic teams, including men's and women's intercollegiate basketball, bowling, cross-country, golf, soccer, swimming and diving, and track and field; men's baseball, football, tennis, water polo, and wrestling; and women's lacrosse, rowing, softball, and volleyball. In July 2009, NDC announced that its membership application for NCAA Division II had been approved. In the 2010–11 academic year NDC was a candidacy-year-two institution in the NCAA Division II membership process.

Location

The College is located in South Euclid, 25 minutes from downtown Cleveland and only 5 minutes from Legacy Village, Cleveland's lifestyle retail center. The area combines the excitement and cultural wealth of a major urban and educational center with the relaxed atmosphere of a suburban setting. University Circle in Cleveland, a 500-acre complex containing an unusual blend of cultural, educational, medical, religious, and social service institutions, is easily accessible from the College.

Situated on the shores of Lake Erie, Cleveland is the home of the Rock and Roll Hall of Fame and several professional sports teams. The Cleveland Metroparks offer a variety of activities and recreational opportunities. Snowy winters provide abundant opportunities for skiing and tobogganing, and popular ski areas are located a short distance from the city.

The beautiful 53-acre wooded campus provides the perfect setting for the Clara Fritzsche Library; the Administration Building, housing classrooms, labs, offices, and the Performing Arts Center; Connelly Center, the cafeteria and student center; the Keller Center, the recreational and fitness facility; and five residence halls, including two newer apartment-style facilities housing 288 upperclass students.

Majors and Degrees

The College awards the Bachelor of Arts degree in accounting (business administration); biology; chemistry; communication; education, including early childhood (pre-K–3), middle childhood (4–9), and young adult education and mild-moderate intervention specialist studies; English; graphic design; history/political science; information systems; international business; management; marketing; mathematics; psychology; public administration; sports management; studio art; and theology. The Bachelor of Science is awarded in biology, chemistry, and mathematics. A student can also design his or her own major that leads to a Bachelor of Arts or Bachelor of Science degree by combining two or three academic areas, such as graphic design, human resource management, and public relations.

Notre Dame College also offers a Bachelor of Science in Nursing program. An RN to B.S.N. completion program is also available.

A Master of Education (M.Ed.) degree, which is designed for classroom teachers, is offered, with concentrations available in special education, reading, and critical and creative thinking.

Teacher licensure is available in early childhood education, middle childhood education, adolescent/young adult education, and multiage for mild/moderate intervention specialist studies.

The Associate in Arts degree is awarded at the completion of two-year programs in business management, education paraprofessional studies, and pastoral ministry.

The Center for Pastoral Theology and Ministry grants a two-year catechetical diploma and the Bachelor of Arts degree.

Academic Programs

All students pursue a career-oriented liberal arts education. For the bachelor's degree, students must earn 128 semester hours of credit, with a minimum cumulative grade point average of 2.0. From 36 to 68 semester hours of credit are required in the major field of study.

Through a cooperative education program, students can earn a maximum of 6 credit hours for paid or volunteer work experience related to their academic field of study.

Advanced Placement credit is awarded to students who have demonstrated the ability to pursue course work beyond the level of entering freshmen, as indicated by their scores on the Advanced Placement (AP) or College-Level Examination Program (CLEP) tests of the College Board. College credit is given on the basis of a decision made jointly by the academic dean and the department involved.

Academic Facilities

The Clara Fritzsche Library, housing the modern Media Center, has a capacity for 100,000 volumes. As a member of Ohiolink, the College also has online access to members throughout the state, with access to more than 31 million library items and more than 90 research databases. The library also houses the smart classroom, a state-of-the-art classroom equipped with laptops for each student and two SmartBoards.

The Dwyer Learning Center consists of an electronic classroom, a student computer lab, a writing lab, a test proctoring room, and a tutoring room. The writing lab is staffed by English faculty members who provide professional writing assistance to students free of charge. The tutoring room is staffed with graduate assistants and upperclass peer tutors for one-on-one study skills and subject specific assistance.

The Academic Support Center for Students with Learning Differences (ASC) was designed to support students with disabilities such as Attention Deficit Disorder (ADD), Attention Deficit Hyperactivity Disorder (ADHD), dyslexia, Asperger's Syndrome, and SLD. In order to be accepted into the Learning Differences Program, students must meet the admission requirements of Notre Dame College. To participate in the Academic Support Center, students must submit documentation of a learning disability. Among its services, the ASC provides professional tutoring, advising, and lessons on adaptive equipment.

The multimedia lab for graphic design majors offers PC and Macintosh technology for advanced multimedia production capabilities.

The Center for Continuing and Professional Development offers course work for working adults on a variety of topics. The center offers seminars and short, flexibly scheduled courses for professionals throughout the year, along with certificate programs in athletic coaching, business intelligence, and intelligence for homeland security.

Costs

For the 2010–11 academic year, tuition charges were $23,080. Room and board costs were $7820 for double occupancy. Student fees were approximately $550.

Financial Aid

A comprehensive financial assistance program of more than $25 million assists nearly 93 percent of all full-time students. Students applying for aid must submit the Free Application for Federal Student Aid (FAFSA).

Faculty

The faculty has 62 full-time members and is augmented by highly qualified instructors in special areas. Faculty members hold advanced degrees from more than thirty universities in the United States, Canada, and Europe.

Student Government

The Undergraduate Student Government (USG) is the central coordinating group for all student organizations. In addition, students have representation on various College committees.

Admission Requirements

In fulfilling its mission, Notre Dame College seeks to attract students of diverse religious, racial, and economic backgrounds. Candidates for admission as first-time, full-time freshmen are reviewed on an individual basis, and decisions are based on a broad range of criteria. The most important consideration is the candidate's high school performance, as demonstrated by her/his overall grade average, class rank, grade trends, and level of courses completed. Aptitude for verbal and mathematical reasoning, as measured by performance on standardized tests, is also considered. In addition, counselor and teacher recommendations are reviewed.

Notre Dame College recommends that students complete at least 16 units of high school credit in academic subjects as a prerequisite for matriculation in the College. The distribution of these subject areas and the units are as follows: English, 4; mathematics, 3 (to include algebra I, geometry, and algebra II); science, 3 (with laboratory experience); social studies, 3; foreign language, 2 (from the same language); and fine arts, 1. Applicants should generally rank in the upper half of their high school graduating class and have a minimum average of C+. Either ACT or SAT scores are accepted.

Students wishing to transfer from other regionally accredited colleges and universities are admitted to advanced standing upon presentation of satisfactory evidence of scholarship and character.

Special consideration may be granted to an applicant whose academic preparation is not consistent with the requirements stated above.

Notre Dame College strongly recommends that prospective students schedule an appointment to visit the campus and talk with an admissions counselor.

Application and Information

The College maintains a rolling admission policy. Students should apply online at http://NotreDameCollege.edu or submit a completed application for undergraduate admission form, an official transcript of their high school record, and results of the ACT or SAT to:

Office of Admissions
Notre Dame College
4545 College Road
South Euclid, Ohio 44121

Phone: 216-373-5355
877-NDC-OHIO Ext. 5355 (toll-free)
Fax: 216-373-5278
E-mail: admissions@ndc.edu
Web site: http://NotreDameCollege.edu
http://www.facebook.com/NotreDameCollege
http://twitter.com/NotreDameOhio
http://www.youtube.com/notredamecollege

OBERLIN COLLEGE

OBERLIN, OHIO

The College

Oberlin College, which was founded in 1833, is an independent, coeducational liberal arts college dedicated to recruiting students from diverse backgrounds. Oberlin comprises two divisions: the College of Arts and Sciences, with roughly 2,200 students, and the Conservatory of Music, with about 600 students. Students in both divisions share one campus; they also share residence and dining halls as part of one academic community. Many students take courses in both divisions. Oberlin awards the Bachelor of Arts (B.A.) and the Bachelor of Music (B.Mus.) degrees. In Oberlin's distinctive double-degree program, students pursue the B.A. and the B.Mus. degrees in a unified, five-year program. Selected master's degrees are offered in the Conservatory.

Oberlin made interracial education central to its mission in 1835; by 1900, nearly half of all the black college graduates in the country—128 to be exact—had graduated from Oberlin. This core of Oberlin-educated men and women formed the first black professional class in the country. In 1837, Oberlin became the first consistently coeducational school in the United States. This legacy continues today in a strong sense of community—one that celebrates differences and recognizes them as opportunities for learning.

Today, Oberlin is a community of thinkers, scholars, scientists, musicians, athletes, activists, and artists—all of whom seek to make the world a better place. Students are united by a commitment to social justice and a willingness to confront social issues that many would prefer to ignore. As the *New York Times* noted in an article marking Oberlin's 150th anniversary, "In its century and a half, while Harvard worried about the classics and Yale about God, Oberlin worried about the state of America and the world beyond."

Recognizing that interaction with others of widely different backgrounds and experiences fosters the effective and concerned participation in the larger society so characteristic of Oberlin graduates, Oberlin is dedicated to recruiting a culturally, economically, geographically, and racially diverse group of students. Students from every walk of life and from around the world seek pathways of individual expression inside Oberlin's tight-knit community of learners, doers, and volunteers. More Oberlin graduates have gone on to earn Ph.D.'s than at any other American college. Its alumni, who include 3 Nobel laureates and 7 MacArthur "Genius" award recipients, are leaders in law, scientific and scholarly research, medicine, the arts, theology, communications, business, and government.

Oberlin has several distinctive academic programs. During the four-week Winter Term, students focus on career aspirations or explore new interests on or off campus. Past projects have taken students to every corner of the globe, from a geology department expedition to Java to a group of students working in a Russian orphanage. Oberlin's Experimental College, a student-run program, offers courses for limited academic credit taught by Oberlin students, townspeople, administrators, and faculty members. Oberlin's First Year Seminar Program is a series of small discussion-based seminars designed to hone students' writing and critical-thinking skills while establishing a context and direction for their personal development.

Oberlin offers a small-town atmosphere and is located not far from Cleveland. There is never a lack of something to do. More than 500 concerts and recitals take place on campus annually, from ticketed events like the Cleveland Orchestra to free student and faculty recitals. Each year, the Conservatory stages two operas, and the theater and dance programs present more than forty productions. Numerous lectures and readings feature guests prominent in a variety of disciplines. Roughly 200 student organizations exist, from the Bike Co-op to the Forensic Team. The College allows students to launch new clubs.

Location

Oberlin College is an integral part of the city of Oberlin, a town of about 8,300 residents located 35 miles southwest of Cleveland. The town is primarily residential, with tree-lined streets and fine old clapboard houses. The College is located in the center of town, close to the business district, and virtually everything a student needs is within walking or biking distance.

Majors and Degrees

Oberlin offers the Bachelor of Arts degree (awarded by the College of Arts and Sciences) and the Bachelor of Music degree (awarded by the Conservatory of Music). Oberlin also offers a distinctive double-degree program, a five-year course of study leading to the B.A. and B.Mus. degrees. Students wishing to enter the double-degree program must be accepted by both the College of Arts and Sciences and the Conservatory of Music.

The B.A. is awarded in African American studies; anthropology; archaeological studies; art (history, studio, and visual); biology; biochemistry; chemistry; cinema studies; classics (Greek, Latin, and classical civilization); comparative American studies; comparative literature; computer science; creative writing; dance; East Asian studies; economics; English; environmental studies; French; gender, sexuality, and feminist studies; geology; German language and literature; German studies; Hispanic studies; history; Jewish studies; Latin American studies; law and society; mathematics; music; neuroscience; philosophy; physics; politics; psychology; religion; Russian language, literature, and culture; Russian and East European studies; sociology; theater; and 3/2 engineering. In addition, many students pursue interdisciplinary individual majors as well as preprofessional studies in law and medicine.

The B.Mus. is awarded in composition, electronic and computer music, historical performance, jazz studies (performance or composition), music history, and performance (baroque cello/viola da gamba, baroque flute, baroque oboe, baroque violin, bassoon, clarinet, classical guitar, double bass, flute, harp, harpsichord, horn, lute, oboe, organ, percussion, piano, recorder, saxophone, trombone, trumpet, tuba, viola, violin, violoncello, and voice). A major in music theory is only offered as part of a double major.

The Conservatory of Music also offers combined five-year B.Mus. and M.Mus. degrees in opera theater and conducting as well as an M.Mus. in teaching and performance on historical instruments. A four-semester Artist Diploma is offered in certain performance departments.

Academic Programs

To receive the B.A. or the B.Mus. degree, students must complete a major; 9 credit hours in each of Oberlin's three divisions: humanities, natural sciences, and social sciences, as well as 9 hours in courses dealing with cultural diversity; and three Winter Term projects. Students must also demonstrate quantitative proficiency and writing proficiency. For the B.A., 112 credit hours are required for graduation; for the B.Mus., 124 hours are required. The recommended semester course load is 14 credit hours for students in the College of Arts and Sciences and 15 or 16 credit hours for students in the Conservatory of Music.

Academic Facilities

Oberlin's four libraries contain more than 2.4 million items, including 1.1 million catalogued volumes—an unusually large collection for a college of Oberlin's size. Other features include an online catalog, connections to several networks, access to numerous online and CD-ROM databases, and access to an additional 46 million volumes via OhioLINK. The College's Allen Memorial Art Museum is considered one of the top college or university art museums in the nation. Seventeenth-century Dutch and Flemish painting, European art of the late nineteenth and twentieth centuries, and contemporary art are especially well represented among the more than 14,000 objects spanning the range of art history in the museum. The one-of-a-kind art-rental program allows students to rent original works of art each semester for only $5, including works by such artists as Picasso, Rembrandt, and Toulouse-Lautrec.

The Conservatory of Music contains 153 practice rooms—all with windows—and has 207 Steinway pianos on campus. The Conservatory also has two concert halls, numerous instrument collections, state-of-the-art electronic music studios, and recording facilities. The Bertram and Judith Kohl Building, a state-of-the-art jazz studies facility opened in spring 2010. It is the result of what is believed to be the largest private gift in support of jazz education at a U.S. college and intends to be the first music facility in the world to achieve a Gold LEED rating.

Oberlin's Irvin E. Houck Computing Center provides more than 250 Macintosh and Dell computers for student use in several locations on campus. In all of the residence hall rooms, students have direct access to the Internet and the campus network from their personal computers. Computer accounts are automatically given to all students at no charge. The Paul and Edith Cooper International Learning Center is a state-of-the-art learning center specializing in foreign language education. The Cooper Center lab computers supports input and output in Arabic, Russian, German, Japanese, Chinese, Korean, Spanish, French, and Italian. A variety of technology—Skype, Audacity, and Second Life, for example—promotes interaction with people in distant parts of the world. The Social Science Data lab allows students and faculty to access a variety of economic, financial, and census data, from historical documents to the daily trading activity of the Kuala Lumpur Stock Exchange.

Oberlin's Science Center was designed to accommodate contemporary methods in science education. Everything is interconnected, promoting communication across disciplines and the collaborative research relationships for which Oberlin is so well known. The strength of Oberlin's science program and its supercomputer capability make Oberlin one of the leading undergraduate colleges in computational modeling. The Science Center complex is a testament to Oberlin's long-held belief that the best liberal arts education has a strong science component and that the best science education occurs in a liberal arts environment.

The Adam Joseph Lewis Center for Environmental Studies is the largest photovoltaic-run building among colleges and universities in the country. The Lewis Center is a living laboratory for the emerging field of ecological design and was named the most important green building constructed in the last thirty years by *Architect* magazine. The center is a classroom, a case study, and a stunning example of how environmental commitment, the latest technologies, and life-cycle thinking can come together to create living and working spaces that minimize the negative impact on the world. Oberlin has been invited to become the eighteenth city in the world to join the Clinton Climate Initiative along with cities such as London, Seoul, Stockholm, Sydney, and Toronto.

Costs

Tuition for the 2010–11 academic year was $41,234. Double-room and board fees were an additional $11,010. The student activity fee was $343.

Financial Aid

In an average year, Oberlin commits more than $53 million to financial aid. The Office of Financial Aid works to develop financial aid packages that meet the demonstrated financial need of all regularly admitted students who comply with the filing deadlines. The average aid package was $34,000, with 80 percent coming from grants. Canadian citizens are treated as U.S. citizens for financial aid purposes. Limited financial aid is also available for other international students.

To apply for assistance, students must submit the Financial Aid PROFILE of the College Scholarship Service and the Free Application for Federal Student Aid (FAFSA).

Faculty

Of Oberlin's 339 faculty members, 253 teach in the College of Arts and Sciences and 86 teach in the Conservatory of Music. They are eminently qualified for their positions, with more than 97 percent having earned doctoral or terminal degrees in their field, many from the world's finest graduate institutions. The student-faculty ratio is 11:1 in the College and 8:1 in the Conservatory.

Student Government

By serving on Oberlin's Student Senate and in other ways, Oberlin College students have the opportunity to influence College policy on academic and student-life issues. Student representatives sit on nearly every faculty committee, and allocation of the student activity fee is determined by a committee composed solely of students.

Admission Requirements

Admission to both the College of Arts and Sciences and the Conservatory of Music is highly selective. Candidates for admission must submit the results of the SAT or ACT with writing. The College also recommends that two SAT Subject Tests be taken. For the class of 2014, the median 50 percent of SAT scores were 660–740 critical reading, 640–720 math, and 650–740 writing. The median 50 percent of ACT scores was 28–32. Of those students who attend high schools that rank their students, 78 percent were in the top tenth of their high school class, and 96 percent were in the top fifth. For admission to the Conservatory of Music, the most important factor is the performance audition or, in the case of composition and electronic and computer music applicants, the compositions, tapes, and supporting materials submitted.

Application and Information

For more information, students should write to:

Office of Admissions, College of Arts and Sciences
Oberlin College
Oberlin, Ohio 44074

Phone: 440-775-8411
       800-622-OBIE (toll-free)
E-mail: college.admissions@oberlin.edu
       http://twitter.com/OberlinProspies
       http://admissions.oberlin.edu/facebook

Office of Admissions, Conservatory of Music
Oberlin College
Oberlin, Ohio 44074

Phone: 440-775-8413
E-mail: conservatory.admissions@oberlin.edu
Web site: http://www.oberlin.edu

Office of Financial Aid
Carnegie Building
Oberlin College
52 West Lorain Street
Oberlin, Ohio 44074

Phone: 440-775-8142
       800-693-3173 (toll-free)
E-mail: financial.aid@oberlin.edu

OHIO NORTHERN UNIVERSITY

ADA, OHIO

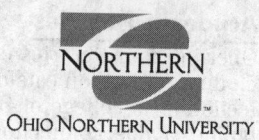

The University

Founded in 1871, Ohio Northern University (ONU) is a private, comprehensive university, comprising five colleges (Arts & Sciences, Business Administration, Engineering, Law, and Pharmacy) that blend liberal and professional education. Talented, motivated students engage in abundant activities in and out of the classroom and graduate with an education that provides one of the highest returns on investment in the nation.

Ohio Northern is a student-centered, service-oriented, values-based institution committed to a rigorous pursuit of academic inquiry and achievement. Education is a collaborative process, and students work side-by-side with accomplished faculty in a constant pursuit of new knowledge. The result is serious research, real collaboration, and meaningful learning experiences.

Students can choose from a variety of campus activities including nearly 200 student organizations; four national sororities and six national fraternities; fine arts, music, and theatrical events; and intramural and club sports. Residence hall living is an integral part of the educational program, contributing to a student's personal development. There are ten residence halls on campus as well as seven campus apartment complexes and an Affinity Housing complex.

A member of the NCAA Division III Ohio Athletic Conference, ONU has eleven men's teams (baseball, basketball, cross-country, football, golf, soccer, swimming and diving, tennis, indoor and outdoor track, and wrestling) and ten women's teams (basketball, cross-country, fast-pitch softball, golf, soccer, swimming and diving, tennis, indoor and outdoor track, and volleyball).

In addition to the undergraduate programs, ONU offers a Master's of Professional Practice in Accountancy (new for fall 2011), Juris Doctor, Doctor of Pharmacy (Pharm.D.), and Doctor of Pharmacy/Law.

Location

Ohio Northern University's campus is situated on 342 beautiful acres in the safe, friendly, rural village of Ada (population 5,500). Located in northwestern Ohio, ONU is easily accessible by major highways and conveniently located near major cities such as Columbus, Dayton, Toledo, and Fort Wayne, Indiana.

Majors and Degrees

Ohio Northern University offers the undergraduate degrees of Bachelor of Arts, Bachelor of Fine Arts, Bachelor of Music, Bachelor of Science, Bachelor of Science in Business Administration, Bachelor of Science in Civil Engineering, Bachelor of Science in Clinical Laboratory Science, Bachelor of Science in Computer Engineering, Bachelor of Science in Electrical Engineering, Bachelor of Science in Engineering Education (new for fall 2011), Bachelor of Science in Mechanical Engineering, and Bachelor of Science in Nursing.

Majors are offered in accounting, advertising design, applied mathematics, art education, athletic training, biochemistry, biology, chemistry, civil engineering, clinical laboratory science, communication studies, computer engineering, construction management, creative writing, criminal justice, early childhood education, electrical engineering, electronic media and broadcasting, engineering education, environmental and field biology, exercise physiology, finance, forensic biology, French, German, graphic design, health education, history, international business and economics, international theatre production, journalism, language arts education, literature, management, manufacturing technology, marketing, mathematical statistics, mathematics, mechanical engineering, middle childhood education, molecular biology, music, music education, musical theatre, nursing, performance, philosophy, physical education, physics, political science, professional writing, psychology, public relations, religion, social studies, sociology, Spanish, sport management, studio arts, technology education, theatre, and youth ministry.

Special preprofessional programs are available in art therapy, dentistry, law, medicine, occupational therapy, optometry, physical therapy, physician assisting, seminary, and veterinary medicine. Interdisciplinary degree programs are available in arts/engineering and arts–

business/pharmacy. Teacher licensure programs are offered at the early childhood, middle childhood, adolescent/young adult, and multiage levels within eighteen programs and two endorsement areas. Changes in programs of study are updated at http://www.onu.edu.

Academic Programs

The **Getty College of Arts & Sciences** creatively combines a traditional liberal arts education with cutting-edge preprofessional studies. The college offers more than fifty majors in sixteen academic departments, and students can earn a Bachelor of Arts, Bachelor of Fine Arts, Bachelor of Music, Bachelor of Science, Bachelor of Science in Clinical Laboratory Science, or Bachelor of Science in Nursing degree.

Students in the sciences have been honored by the Barry M. Goldwater Scholarship and Excellence in Education Foundation for six consecutive years. The college has also been recognized as one of the top 200 programs in the nation for creative students in *Creative Colleges: A Guide for Student Actors, Artists, Dancers, Musicians and Writers.*

Working closely with dedicated faculty members, students complete the general education requirements, delve deeply into advanced courses, and engage in research, internships, practicum experiences, study abroad, and more.

The **James F. Dicke College of Business Administration** focuses on creating ethical, entrepreneurial, and engaged business and civic leaders. The college offers a rigorous academic curriculum with signature programs in pharmaceutical business and forensic accounting. Internships are required by the college and are available year-round. There are international programs, including study abroad, work abroad, and study tours. An office of experiential learning supports students looking for these opportunities.

The course of study for the Bachelor of Science in Business Administration includes a four-year integrated general studies program and a four-year business core experience themed around business planning. To graduate, a student must satisfactorily complete a minimum of 122 semester hours of appropriate course work for the specific major(s) and maintain at least a 2.0 grade point average.

Personal attention and mentoring from faculty members, small intimate classes, and active student organizations combine with an emphasis on experiential learning, global awareness, and the entrepreneurial spirit. The college is listed in the top 111 business schools in the nation, with an A+ in teaching quality, by *Bloomberg BusinessWeek* and is accredited by the AACSB International—The Association to Advance Collegiate Schools of Business, making it one of the best business colleges in the world.

One of the top 50 undergraduate programs in the nation for the past four years (*U.S. News & World Report*), the **T.J. Smull College of Engineering** provides a premier undergraduate experience that inspires creativity and supports innovation. The college features five accredited, disciplinary majors in civil, computer, electrical, and mechanical engineering and computer science. Beginning in fall 2011, an additional engineering education degree will support the demand for high school math teachers with engineering degrees.

The courses for the first academic year are essentially the same for each degree program, offering students an easy track to move from one program to another if initially uncertain which disciplines they prefer to study. Students are required to maintain a minimum cumulative grade point average of 2.0 as well as a minimum cumulative grade point average of 2.0 for all engineering and computer science courses.

An optional five-year co-op program is available for students in each program, provided they maintain a minimum 2.5 GPA.

There is an emphasis on team projects, and students participate in various design competitions.

Many opportunities are available for valuable work experience through the co-op, internship, and Engineer-in-Residence programs, with an historically high job-placement rate for graduates.

For more than 125 years, the **Raabe College of Pharmacy** has offered distinctive, challenging, and comprehensive training for some of the nation's most talented pharmacists. This University signature program features a six-year Doctor of Pharmacy (Pharm.D.) degree accredited by the American Council on Pharmaceutical Education.

This program is direct-entry, admitting students immediately from high school into the college's professional program. This approach enables students to take pharmacy courses from the very first day. A rigorous curriculum utilizes an innovative modular format to organize learning around the human body systems and patient care implementation. Students complete a minimum of 216 semester hours and follow a prescribed curriculum and requirements, all while earning a grade of C or better in any course.

Cutting-edge clinical facilities include the Pharmacy Skills Center, where students access state-of-the-art compounding/counseling pods with portable OTC simulation stations. Students gain considerable experience through a strong undergraduate research program and may pursue minors or dual majors in other areas. Faculty members are teaching-focused but remain current in their research disciplines. Upon graduation, students are well schooled in every aspect of pharmacy and have a 100 percent placement rate.

Off-Campus Programs

Many majors may take part in study-abroad programs developed in consultation with faculty members. Field experiences and internships are available to most majors. Externships are required of all pharmacy majors and place students in retail and clinical experiences. Teacher licensure requires one semester of primary or secondary classroom teaching experience under the supervision of practicing teachers. Additional opportunities include computer science and mathematics co-op programs (professional practice), engineering co-op programs (professional practice, domestic and international), and an honors program. All off-campus learning experiences carry credit.

Academic Facilities

Among the nineteen modern academic buildings on campus, the newest is the Mathile Center for the Natural Sciences, which expands the science-learning environment. This 95,145-square-foot student-centered academic research and learning facility blends hands-on teaching excellence with advanced technology in a functional modern environment.

The College of Business Administration's Dicke Hall offers students a modern setting for high-tech classrooms, meeting rooms and a 150-seat lecture forum, as well as a real-time digital stock ticker.

ONU's Heterick Memorial Library and the Taggart Law Library provide information resources and services to support course offerings and foster independent study.

The Freed Center for the Performing Arts houses Communications and Theatre Arts classrooms and features a 550-seat theater/concert hall, a 120-seat studio theater, and television and radio production facilities. WONB-FM is the commercial-free voice of ONU.

Costs

Charges for the 2011–12 year are $42,171 for tuition, room, and board for the Colleges of Arts & Sciences and Business Administration, $44,409 for the College of Engineering, and $46,248 for the College of Pharmacy. These totals are based on tuition, double-occupancy room, a 19-meal-per-week plan, and a technology fee of $240 per year.

Financial Aid

Even with one of the highest returns on investment in the nation, ONU invests more than $50 million toward merit-based scholarships and need-based resources and makes every effort to ensure that no qualified applicant is denied admission because of inability to pay the total cost. To be considered, the student should submit the FAFSA to the University along with the admission application.

Faculty

More than 200 full-time faculty members bring extensive academic, work, travel, and life experience to their classrooms. Ohio Northern values excellence, innovation, technology, diversity, and its people. With an 11:1 student-faculty ratio, students get lots of personal attention from professors who are passionate about teaching and mentoring.

Student Government

The Student Senate provides self-government in many areas of student life and seeks to further ideals of character and service to the University. The Student Senate serves as the official representative group of the student body to the University administration and agencies in matters pertaining to the student body.

Admission Requirements

High school students applying for admission to the University should present an official transcript indicating at least 16 total units of study, including work in specific academic areas as indicated by each college. Applicants are also required to submit scores on the ACT and/or SAT. For scholarship purposes, the traditional sections of the ACT and the SAT are considered. An on-campus interview is also recommended.

Application and Information

A student's file is considered complete when it contains the application, $30 nonrefundable application fee (fee waived if student visits campus prior to application), official high school transcript, one letter of recommendation, personal statement, and ACT and/or SAT scores.

Early Action applications can be made to the Colleges of Arts & Sciences, Business Administration, and Engineering prior to December 1, while Regular Decision applications to these colleges can be made prior to February 1.

The College of Pharmacy's application deadline is November 1 for entering freshmen. A campus visit is strongly encouraged for consideration for admittance into this college.

Requests for catalogs, application forms, or additional information should be directed to:

Office of Admissions
Ohio Northern University
Ada, Ohio 45810

Phone: 888-408-4668 (toll-free)
Fax: 419-772-2821
E-mail: admissions-ug@onu.edu
Web site: http://www.onu.edu
         http://www.facebook.com/ohionorthern
         http://twitter.com/onuadmissions

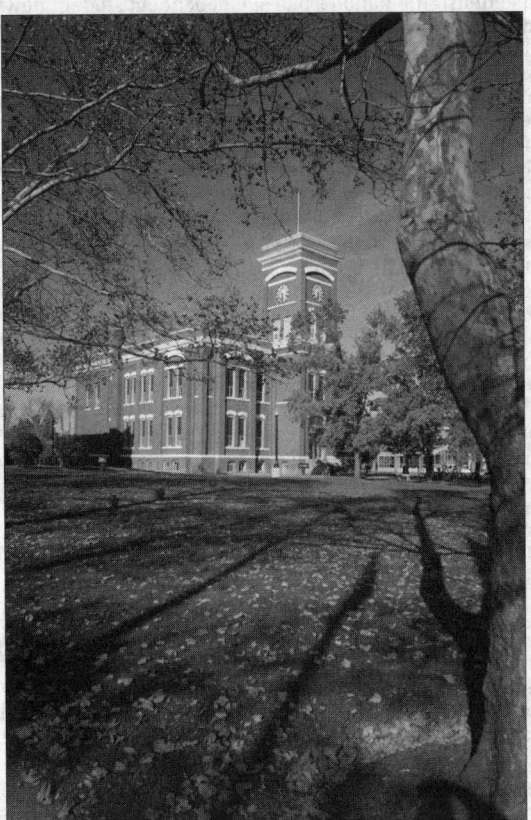

Hill Memorial and its clock tower are mainstays of the front of campus.

OHIO WESLEYAN UNIVERSITY
DELAWARE, OHIO

The University

A unique blend of liberal arts learning, preprofessional preparation, internships, research opportunities, study-travel, and study abroad sets Ohio Wesleyan University (OWU) apart. Founded by the United Methodist Church in 1842, the University is strongly committed to education for leadership and service, and to integrating theory and practice in a global context.

A selective residential institution, Ohio Wesleyan is home to approximately 1,850 undergraduates, with a nearly equal number of men and women. Students come to Ohio Wesleyan from forty-seven states and fifty-seven countries; most live on the attractive 200-acre campus. Housing options include six large residence halls, three newly remodeled residences specifically for seniors, several small living units (SLUs), and seven fraternity houses. The five sorority houses are non-residential.

Ohio Wesleyan has long been committed to education for a global society. The curriculum has an international perspective and OWU has one of the highest percentages of international students among undergraduate, liberal arts colleges in the United States.

One of the richest of OWU's cocurricular traditions is service. The University sends as many as ten mission teams throughout the world each year. Nearly the entire student body participates in at least one community service or philanthropic project each year. In 2009–10, students donated more than 45,000 hours to local, national, and international service and earned the President's Award for Excellence in General Community Service, one of only three colleges and universities in the country to be honored with this distinction.

Students publish the nation's oldest independent student newspaper. They also participate in cultural- and ethnic-interest groups such as the Student Union on Black Awareness (SUBA) and SANGAM and VIVA (which promote an understanding of the cultures of South Asia and Latin America, respectively), the College Republicans and College Democrats, and prelaw and premed clubs. Each year, students may enjoy more than 100 concerts, plays, dance programs, films, exhibits, and speakers. The Department of Theatre & Dance stages four major productions each year, while the Music Department sponsors four large performance groups and a variety of smaller ensembles.

OWU is home to twenty-three Division III varsity athletic teams, with women's golf a new addition in 2010–11. In 2009–10, the University was the runner-up for the North Coast Athletic Conference (NACA) All-Sports Trophy, after winning the trophy for three consecutive years prior and nine times overall. Ohio Wesleyan continues to lead the conference in team titles. In 2010, Ohio Wesleyan opened the Meek Aquatics and Recreation Center, which features a ten-lane pool, 1- and 3-meter diving boards, and a 13-foot-deep diving well. The entire building and pool is heated and cooled by ninety geothermal wells.

Intramural and club sports programs are extensive, and all students have access to racquet sports and weight-lifting facilities in the Branch Rickey Physical Education Center. Fitness equipment and health services are housed in the 7,000-square-foot Health and Wellness Center. Off-campus opportunities for backpacking, boating, camping, golf, skiing, and swimming are abundant.

Location

Delaware combines the small-town pace and maple-lined streets of the county seat (population 34,000) with easy access to the state capital, Columbus, the sixteenth-largest city in America. Twenty miles south of the campus, Columbus provides rich internship opportunities, international research centers, fine dining and shopping, and cultural events that complement those on campus.

Majors and Degrees

With ninety-three majors, sequences, and courses of study, Ohio Wesleyan offers the Bachelor of Arts in accounting; ancient, medieval, and Renaissance studies; astronomy; biological sciences (botany, genetics, microbiology, and zoology); chemistry; classics; computer science; economics (including accounting, international business, and management); education (elementary and secondary licensure in seventeen

areas); English literature and writing; fine arts; French; geography; geology; German; history; humanities; journalism; mathematics; music (applied or history/literature); philosophy; physical education; physics; planetary science; politics and government; psychology; religion; sociology/anthropology; Spanish; and theater and dance. Interdisciplinary majors include Black world studies, East Asian studies, environmental studies, international studies, Latin American studies, neuroscience, urban studies, and women's and gender studies. Preprofessional studies include prelaw, premedicine, pre-engineering, predentistry, pre–veterinary medicine, pre–public administration, preoptometry, pretheology, and pre–physical therapy. Students also may design majors in topical, period, or regional studies.

Two professional degrees are awarded: the Bachelor of Fine Arts in art history, arts education, and studio art, and the Bachelor of Music in music education and performance. Combined-degree (generally 3-2) programs are offered in engineering, medical technology, optometry, and physical therapy. Ohio Wesleyan is one of only thirteen colleges in the United States that has a 3-2 engineering program with the California Institute of Technology.

Academic Programs

Ohio Wesleyan provides opportunities for students to acquire not only depth in a major area but also knowledge about their cultural past through the insight provided by a broad liberal arts curriculum. At Ohio Wesleyan, education is placed in a context of values, and students are encouraged to develop the intellectual skills of effective communication, independent and logical thought, and creative problem solving. Students are required to demonstrate competence in English composition and a foreign language (often through placement testing) and to complete distributional study in the natural and social sciences, the humanities, and the arts. With few exceptions, the major requires the completion of eight to fifteen courses. Many students double major or take more than one minor in addition to their major, and self-designed majors are not uncommon. Thirty-four courses are required for graduation.

Advanced placement is available with or without credit. Under the four-year honors program, even first-year students have opportunities to work individually with faculty mentors on research, directed readings, or original creative work. Undergraduate students frequently present their research to prestigious societies such as the American Society for Microbiology, the American Microscopy Society, the American Chemical Society, the American Physical Society, the American Ornithologists' Union, and other nationally recognized organizations. Upperclass students also are encouraged to participate in independent study. One of the twenty-six scholastic honorary societies with chapters on campus, Ohio Wesleyan's chapter of Phi Beta Kappa is 104 years old.

Ohio Wesleyan places great emphasis on combining theory and practice within a global context, offering a robust array of study-abroad options. Students can arrange individual projects, but formal programs are offered in more than twenty countries.

To complement the University's international perspective, Ohio Wesleyan has instituted a program of competitive Theory-to-Practice grants that allow students to propose, create, and fund research experiences tied to their areas of interest, often in settings far beyond the campus. Recent students have studied in India, Austria, France, Costa Rica, Ecuador, Romania, Tanzania, South Africa, Canada, and England. In addition, a series of Sagan Fellows classes, related to Ohio Wesleyan's distinctive Sagan National Colloquium, offer intensive engaged learning experiences for small groups of students led by a faculty member designated as a Sagan Fellow.

Ohio Wesleyan offers the Economics Management Fellows program for talented first-year students with an interest in economics, economics management, or accounting. This program offers special classes and seminars, a generous book allowance, networking opportunities with alumni executives and others, and a study trip to New York to meet with business leaders and learn about careers in the financial sector.

Off-Campus Programs

Full-semester internships and apprenticeships, as well as programs of advanced research, are available to students. Many are approved by the Great Lakes Colleges Association, Inc. (GLCA), a highly regarded academic consortium of thirteen independent institutions. Programs are available at the Philadelphia Center, the GLCA New York Arts Program, and the Oak Ridge Science Semester. Other cooperative arrangements include the Newberry Library Program, Wesleyan in Washington, and the Drew University United Nations Semester. Students also conduct research locally at the U.S. Department of Agriculture (USDA) Laboratories in Delaware, the nearby Columbus Zoo, The Wilds, and several other sites. The Summer Science Research Program offers selected students the opportunity for an intensive, ten-week, one-to-one research experience with a faculty mentor. The program concludes with a symposium at which research results are presented to the entire campus.

Academic Facilities

The Beeghly Library houses more than 550,000 holdings, one of the largest collections in the country for a private university of Ohio Wesleyan's size. The library's federal documents depository is among the nation's oldest and largest, providing an additional 200,000 reference publications. Beeghly Library also offers the Online Computer Library Center's most advanced cataloging system. The collection is enhanced by OhioLINK and CONSORT membership. An Internet Café within the Beeghly Library provides students with a 24-hour study area.

The comprehensive academic computing system is accessible to students 24 hours per day, and all residence hall rooms are wired for campus network and global Internet access. The latest generation of wireless communication allows students to work online anywhere on the campus.

The Schimmel/Conrades Science Center includes a 145,000-square-foot, three-level building that houses state-of-the-art instrumentation, including a scanning electron microscope and scanning and transmission electron microscopes, all for undergraduate use. Located in the Science Center is the Hobson Science Library, which consolidates all of OWU's science holdings. The University has a state-of-the-art Geographic Information Systems Computer Laboratory.

The R.W. Corns Building houses the Woltemade Center for Economics, Business, and Entrepreneurship; the Department of Economics; the Sagan Academic Resource Center, which includes the Writing Resource Center, the Academic Skills Center, and the Quantitative Skills Center; and Information Systems.

Perkins Observatory features a 32-inch reflecting telescope and two smaller instruments, while an on-campus student observatory includes a 9.5-inch refracting telescope. Two University wilderness preserves cover a total of 100 acres. Other special facilities include the multistage Chappelear Drama Center; Sanborn Hall, home to the Music Department, Jemison Auditorium, and the Kinnison Music Library; and the 1,100-seat Gray Chapel, which houses the largest of only six Klais concert organs in the United States.

Costs

The general fee for 2010–11 was $45,674. This amount covers tuition and fees ($36,398) and room and board ($9276). Books and personal expenses average $1100. Nominal fees are charged for some studio art courses, off-campus study, private music lessons for students who are not majoring in music, and student teaching.

Financial Aid

OWU awards financial assistance to almost every entering freshman who demonstrates need. Aid packages include a combination of grants, loans, and employment. Federal and state aid are often part of an aid package. Nearly 70 percent of all undergraduates receive need-based financial assistance; another 25 percent are granted merit-based aid. More than three quarters of all aid is awarded in the form of grants and scholarships.

The University awards several merit scholarship programs, ranging from $5000 to full tuition. The school awarded more than 2,000 scholarships to new and prospective students for 2010–11. Private loan programs and flexible payment plans are available to all students, regardless of demonstrated financial need.

Faculty

The full-time faculty numbers 137, providing a student-faculty ratio of approximately 11:1. One hundred percent of the full-time tenure-track faculty members hold the highest degree in their fields. Although committed first to teaching and advising, most faculty members maintain active research programs and publish important articles and books; others are practicing artists who create and exhibit original works of art and theater.

Student Government

Students have a significant voice in the government of campus life. The Wesleyan Council on Student Affairs formulates basic policy. Students also sit on judicial boards, individual department student boards, and nine faculty committees. They are represented at all meetings of the Board of Trustees.

Admission Requirements

The admission process is competitive. Each student's application is individually reviewed. Although the applicant's academic record and strength of academic program are the most important factors, followed closely by teacher and counselor evaluations and SAT or ACT scores, many other aspects are considered, such as evidence of creativity, community service, and leadership. A minimum sixteen-course preparatory program is required. Four units of English and 3 each of mathematics, social studies, science, and foreign language are recommended, but variations of this program are considered. SAT Subject Tests are not required but may qualify students for advanced placement. Candidates for the Bachelor of Music degree must audition (tapes are accepted). Early action and transfer admission are offered. Campus interviews are strongly recommended but not required. For the 2009–10 school year, approximately 4,200 applications were received; 65 percent of the applicants gained admission.

Application and Information

Students are urged to complete the application as early as possible in the senior year, especially if they are applying for merit- or need-based financial aid. Once complete credentials (application, transcript, recommendations, and SAT or ACT scores) are received, decisions are made on a rolling basis after January 1. The student's response is required by May 1. The deadline for Early Action I application is November 30; the deadline for Early Action II application is January 15. Notification is given within four weeks after application is complete. After April 1, students are admitted on a space-available, rolling admission basis.

For further information, students should contact:

Office of Admission
Ohio Wesleyan University
Delaware, Ohio 43015
Phone: 740-368-3020
      800-922-8953 (toll-free)
Fax: 740-368-3314
E-mail: owuadmit@owu.edu
Web site: http://www.owu.edu
      http://www.facebook.com/OhioWesleyanUniversity
      http://twitter.com/ohiowesleyan

The Hamilton-Williams Campus Center is a magnificent meeting place for the campus community.

OLIVET NAZARENE UNIVERSITY
BOURBONNAIS, ILLINOIS

The University

Olivet Nazarene University (ONU) is a private, Christian liberal arts university with a strong emphasis on both academic excellence and Christ-centered living. ONU offers one of the finest liberal arts educations in the Midwest, world-class facilities for learning and entertainment, and an atmosphere that promotes fun, relationship building, and spiritual growth.

Olivet's high retention, graduation, and employment/placement rates demonstrate the University's commitment to students' success. The members of the faculty, staff, and administration are dedicated to teaching, encouraging, and mentoring each student as a whole person—academically, socially, and spiritually.

With 4,600 students (2,600 undergraduates), Olivet offers an ideal student population for a private institution, maintaining diversity without sacrificing personalized attention. Nearly half the student body comes from the Nazarene denomination, and the rest come from some thirty other denominations. Most U.S. states are represented, as are more than twenty countries.

The campus offers a championship-caliber athletics department (eighteen intercollegiate men's and women's sports in all, with men's and women's swimming to be added in fall 2012 and women's water polo to be added in fall 2014) and a large intramural sports program. Music and drama groups involve hundreds of students, and many clubs are organized for a wide variety of interests. Olivet students are also heavily involved in dozens of ministry groups and volunteer efforts, small-group Bible studies, and weekly student-led services.

The University recently completed a number of campus improvements, including construction of the 3,046-seat Betty and Kenneth Hawkins Centennial Chapel and the renovation of the lower level of Ludwig Center, the student union, to include a glass-enclosed gaming room featuring plasma TV screens, a convenience store, and new student leadership offices. In addition, the Department of Communication moved to a new, technologically advanced facility in Benner Library, which also houses some of the University's art programs, representing a partnership between the Departments of Communication and Art. Plans are under way for a new student life and recreation center slated to open in fall 2012.

The University is home to the Chicago Bears' summer training camp and Shine.FM, a 35,000-watt station ranked among the top stations in the nation and staffed by Olivet's broadcasting students.

In addition to its traditional undergraduate programs, Olivet offers eight degree-completion and continuing-studies programs, more than twenty master's degrees, and a Doctor of Education in ethical leadership. The School of Graduate and Continuing Studies strives to meet the needs of the ever-expanding number of adults returning to school. Adult degree-completion programs are designed to assist working adults so they can complete their degree requirements without an interruption to their employment. The school serves as a resource for adults striving to enhance their personal and professional lives in a constantly changing world.

In addition to the classes held on the main campus, the School of Graduate and Continuing Studies offers courses for students throughout the Chicago area. Numerous students gather with other working adults for classes in churches, schools, hospitals, and other convenient locations near their home or workplace.

Location

The main University campus is located just 50 miles south of Chicago's Loop in the historic village of Bourbonnais. The area includes malls, restaurants, entertainment, and natural recreation centered on the Kankakee River State Park system. Olivet students enjoy many activities nearby and often make the quick trip north for the limitless offerings of Chicago and its surroundings.

In addition to recreation, students find numerous opportunities for employment and internships in the area and among the vast professional resources of Chicago. Students, faculty members, and staff members also find themselves working side by side in local and regional ministry projects. Olivet students are recognized professionally and ministerially as a valuable commodity by area businesses, churches, and parachurch organizations.

Majors and Degrees

Olivet confers Bachelor of Arts (B.A.) and/or Bachelor of Science (B.S.) degrees in the following fields of study (includes all majors, minors, and concentrations): accounting, actuarial science, art, art (education), athletic training, biblical languages, biblical studies, biochemistry, biology, business administration, business administration systems, chemistry, Christian education, church music, children's ministry, coaching, commercial graphics, communication studies, computer engineering, computer science, corporate communication, criminal justice, dietetics, digital media: graphics, digital media: photography, drawing and illustration, early childhood education, earth and space science, economics and finance, electrical engineering, elementary education, engineering, English, English as a second language, English education, environmental science, exercise science, family and consumer sciences, family and consumer sciences education, fashion merchandising, film studies, finance, forensic chemistry, French, general science, general studies, geography, geological engineering, geology, Greek, health education, Hebrew, history, housing and environmental design, hospitality, information systems, information technology, intercultural studies, international business, international marketing, journalism, literature, management, marketing, mass communication, mathematics, mathematics education, mechanical engineering, media production, military affairs, military science, missions, music, music composition, music education, music performance, musical theater, nursing, painting, pastoral ministry, philosophy, philosophy and religion, physical education/health, physical science, political science, predental, prelaw, premedicine, preoptometry, prepharmacy, pre–physician's assistant, pre–physical therapy, preseminary, pre–veterinary science, psychology, public policy, public relations, radio, recreation and leisure studies, religion, religious studies, science education, secondary education, social science, social science education, social work, sociology, Spanish, Spanish education, sport management, television/video production, theater, writing, youth ministry, and zoology.

Academic Programs

Olivet seeks to offer an "Education with a Christian Purpose." The University believes that this commitment to Christ mandates nothing less than the highest-quality academic programs. Olivet's liberal arts curriculum requires that students complete 45 to 58 hours of general education courses. With the addition of major and minor programs of study, students must complete a minimum of 128 credit hours to obtain a bachelor's degree. Credit may be earned through AP and CLEP tests. Students may also participate in ROTC.

Olivet operates on a two-semester schedule, from August to May. Two summer sessions are also available.

Off-Campus Programs

Olivet students are encouraged to participate in the various off-campus study programs offered each semester. Sponsored programs include the Nazarene International Language Institute, the Institute for Family Studies (Focus on the Family), and the following Council for Christian Colleges and Universities programs: American Studies Program in Washington, D.C.; the Australian Studies Center; the China Studies Program; the Contemporary Music Center in Martha's Vineyard; the Los Angeles Film Studies Center; the Middle East Studies Program; the Russian Studies Program; the Scholar's Semester in Oxford; the Uganda Studies Program; and the Washington Journalism Center. Recognized programs include AuSable Institute, the International Business Institute, the Romanian Studies Program, and Tokyo Christian University. Costs are usually comparable to a semester at Olivet, and credit is given for these programs. In addition, some sources of financial aid are applicable.

Many Olivet students participate in numerous educational and missions-oriented short-term trips that are available during the Christmas, spring, and summer breaks.

Academic Facilities

Olivet's 250-acre campus offers leading-edge academic facilities. These include high-quality performance halls and athletic venues; excellent natural science, engineering, and nursing laboratories; smart classrooms; and an observatory. It is one of only a handful of small college campuses in the nation to have a planetarium, which was completely renovated in 2008 with the same technology used in Chicago's Adler Planetarium. Each department uses the top software in its field. More than a dozen campus computer labs are available for student use, and two network ports in each dorm room and the campuswide wireless network give students access to e-mail, the Internet, and classroom applications 24 hours a day.

Benner Library and Resource Center provides unlimited access to any material a student needs, either on-site or through the interlibrary loan system. Benner Library offers 175,000 books, 335,000 other items in various formats, 600 periodicals, 39,000 full-text electronic journals, and 70,000 electronic books and other electronic sources.

Costs

Tuition, based on 12 to 18 credit hours, is $26,750 for 2011–12. Room and board, based on double occupancy and a meal plan, are estimated to cost $6400 for the year. Additional fees will be $840 per year.

Financial Aid

Approximately 99 percent of traditional undergraduates receive a total of $35.4 million in federal and state grants and institutional scholarships.

Olivet's cost is below average for private colleges nationwide. The University also participates in all federal and state financial aid programs. The priority deadline for filing the Free Application for Federal Student Aid (FAFSA) is March 1. To apply for aid, students must fill out the FAFSA as well as Olivet's application for financial aid. The student must be an accepted applicant before a financial aid package can be created. Olivet offers a monthly installment plan in addition to the traditional three-payment plan. Olivet believes funding a student's education is a partnership between each family, Olivet, and the state and federal governments. The friendly staff is committed to making an Olivet education affordable to every young person.

Faculty

Olivet's more than 100 full-time faculty members are the key to excellence in and out of the classroom. Teaching is a ministry for these dedicated Christian individuals, and Olivet's student-faculty ratio gives them an opportunity to teach, mentor, and encourage students on a personal level. To that end, the faculty is heavily involved in campus life, whether sponsoring social organizations or participating in talent shows.

Student Government

The Associated Student Council is the student government organization on campus. Its executive council consists of a president, vice president of finance, vice president of spiritual life, vice president of social affairs, vice president of publicity, vice president of women's residential life, vice president of men's residential life, vice president of office management, the *GlimmerGlass* (student newspaper) editor, and the *Aurora* (yearbook) editor. They work alongside the University's administrative team to ensure the health and promotion of campus activities and organizations.

Admission Requirements

Admission to the University is moderately difficult. Students are considered for admission on the basis of their high school GPA and ACT or SAT scores. An ACT score is required for placement in courses. For international students, TOEFL results are an additional factor in the admission decision. Students with low test scores and GPAs may be admitted on a provisional basis. A campus visit and interview are strongly recommended for all prospective students.

Application and Information

Admission is on a rolling basis until the application deadline of May 1. An early decision is required for some scholarships. Students may apply via Olivet's home page online or in print. The application process includes the written (or electronic) application, high school transcripts, ACT or SAT scores, and a health form. An enrollment deposit is collected to prioritize both student housing and class registration.

For more information or to arrange a campus visit, students should contact:

Office of Admissions
Olivet Nazarene University
One University Avenue
Bourbonnais, Illinois 60914

Phone: 800-648-1463 (toll-free)
E-mail: admissions@olivet.edu
Web site: http://www.olivet.edu
     http://www.youtube.com/olivetnazareneu
     http://on.fb.me/OlivetNazareneUniversityClassof2016
     (Facebook)
     http://twitter.com/OlivetNazareneU
     http://www.flickr.com/photos/olivet/collections

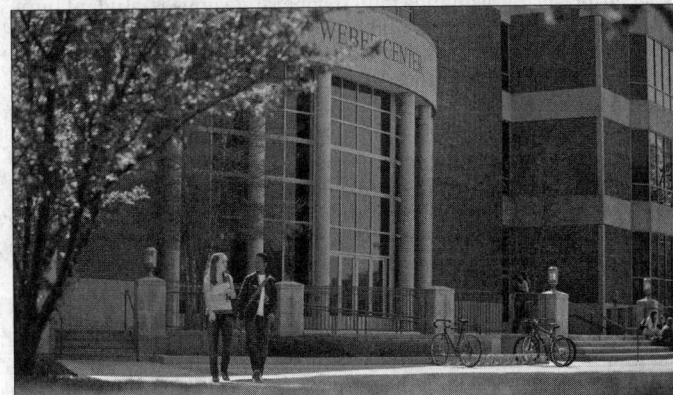

Olivet's 250-acre, parklike campus is just 50 minutes south of Chicago's Loop, with additional locations in Rolling Meadows, Illinois; the Greater Chicago area; and Hong Kong.

OREGON STATE UNIVERSITY

CORVALLIS, OREGON

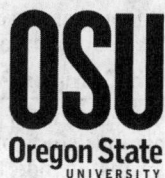

The University

Exceptional students, an outstanding faculty, and a challenging curriculum combine to make Oregon State University (OSU) a nationally and internationally recognized comprehensive university.

OSU has earned the Carnegie Foundation's "Very High Research Activity" designation for commitment to education and research. Widely recognized research programs add to the quality of teaching by bringing new knowledge into the classroom and by encouraging undergraduate students to work with faculty members on research projects in many fields. As a member of the non-tiered Oregon University System, OSU is the premier research university in the state of Oregon. In fact, OSU's economic impact to the state of Oregon exceeds $1.5 billion.

The University's 23,761 students come from all fifty states and more than ninety-one countries around the world to pursue a wide choice of undergraduate programs that prepare them for careers and leadership positions in science, engineering and computer-related fields, natural resources, government, teaching and social service, pharmacy, and other professions. Employers from across the nation recognize the value of an OSU degree, and more of them recruit at Oregon State University each year than at any other university in the state.

OSU is committed to offering students the resources they need to be successful in their education. In addition to utilizing Blackboard™ as an electronic tool to assist students with class materials, interactive topic conversations, and resources, OSU continues to innovate by systematically adding wireless networks to classrooms, libraries, and common areas on campus. Students also have access to one of the largest open-source software labs in the world, where new shareware is developed, housed, and distributed.

Students also benefit from more than 300 cocurricular activities on campus. These include student government, student media, theater and music, intramural and club sports, and numerous social, academic, cultural, and professional clubs and organizations. In addition, Dixon Recreation Center offers opportunities for swimming and diving, weight training, aerobic exercise, and the largest collegiate rock-climbing center in the Northwest. Two campus child-care facilities offer educationally oriented day-care programs for children of students and faculty and staff members.

OSU offers a wide range of housing and dining options, including special-program residence halls, cooperative houses, student family housing, and fraternity and sorority housing. Many apartments and houses are available within biking or walking distance of OSU for students who choose to live off campus. There are twenty-eight restaurants on campus.

Graduate degrees are offered through the Colleges of Agricultural Sciences, Business, Engineering, Forestry, Health and Human Sciences, Liberal Arts, and Science. Graduate and professional degrees are also offered through the Colleges of Oceanic and Atmospheric Sciences, Pharmacy, and Veterinary Medicine, and through the School of Education.

Location

The OSU main campus is in Corvallis, which is consistently ranked as one of the safest university communities on the West Coast. Farmers Insurance named Corvallis the Most Secure city in the U.S. for 2007 and 2008. With about 55,000 residents, Corvallis offers a friendly, university-oriented atmosphere. In fact, students rated OSU as the fifth-friendliest campus in the United States, according to CampusDirt.com. *Forbes* magazine also rated Corvallis as one of the top 5 smartest cities. Miles of bike lanes

and free city bus service make it easy for students to get around town. Within a couple hours of Corvallis are the Oregon Coast; the Cascade Mountains, with skiing, hiking, camping, and snowboarding; and Portland, Oregon's largest city. The OSU Cascades Campus in Bend, Oregon, represents a unique educational partnership involving four distinguished institutions, creating an innovative and collaborative university to serve the needs of central Oregon.

Majors and Degrees

Oregon State is a comprehensive university, with more than 200 academic programs. Undergraduate degrees are offered through the Colleges of Agricultural Sciences, Business, Education, Engineering, Forestry, Health and Human Sciences, Liberal Arts, and Science.

Students in any undergraduate major can strengthen their transcripts by earning an Honors Degree or an International Degree. Almost 600 top students are enrolled in the University Honors College, which offers a small-college atmosphere within the larger University. The University also offers twenty-eight preprofessional programs that prepare students for graduate programs and careers in fields such as health sciences, law, and education.

Academic Programs

All undergraduate students at Oregon State complete the Baccalaureate Core, which helps develop skills and knowledge in writing, critical thinking, cultural diversity, the arts, science, literature, lifelong fitness, and global awareness, ensuring that as graduates they will be well prepared for life as well as a career.

Many students take advantage of OSU's first-year experience program, called U-Engage, which offers opportunities for new students to interact with faculty members and other students throughout the year, thus easing the transition to college life. The year begins with a five-day CONNECT orientation that features Convocation (the official kickoff to the school year), small-group meetings between faculty members and students, a barbecue, outdoor movies, open houses, and more.

Undergraduate research is an important component of many academic programs, and more than 2,000 OSU undergraduates participate with faculty members and graduate students on research projects each year. One example is the Howard Hughes Medical Institute Summer Research Program, which funds undergraduate researchers to the tune of $1.9 million.

OSU has more majors, minors, and special programs than any other college in Oregon and offers a University Exploratory Studies Program for students who want to try various options before choosing a major field. Oregon State uses the quarter system for its academic year. Most majors require between 180 and 192 credit hours for a bachelor's degree.

The Academic Success Center helps OSU students deal with problems and develop the skills they need in college and beyond. The Center for Writing and Learning, the Math Learning Center, and departmental resource centers assist students in preparing for assignments in specific areas, while the African American, Hispanic American, Asian American, and Native American education offices, along with the Educational Opportunities Program, help mentor students throughout their college careers. University Counseling and Psychological Services offers learning resource materials and professional assistance to help students deal with problems, both in and out of the classroom. Career Services assists students in locating internships and in finding jobs when they graduate.

Off-Campus Programs

Through the International Degree, study-abroad, and international internship programs, OSU students can study, work, or conduct research almost anywhere in the world. Programs, which range from a term to a full year, are offered in Australia, Canada, China, Denmark, Ecuador, England, France, Germany, Hungary, Italy, Japan, Korea, Mexico, New Zealand, Norway, Russia, Spain, Thailand, Tunisia, and Vietnam.

OSU also participates in the National Student Exchange Program, allowing students to spend up to a year at one of more than 160 colleges and universities in the U.S. and its possessions, while paying in-state tuition and fees.

Academic Facilities

OSU's Valley Library is a state-of-the-art facility that offers modern electronic services including a wireless computer network, "Text a Librarian" service, and unique special collections as well as traditional library services to students and the community. The OSU library is the first academic library to be named Library of the Year by *Library Journal* (1999). Library holdings include more than 2.5 million books, periodicals, and government documents on paper or microform. A reciprocal agreement makes more than 5 million additional volumes in the Oregon University System available to OSU students and faculty members. OSU's special collections include the papers and memorabilia of Linus Pauling, the only winner of two unshared Nobel Prizes, and the Atomic Energy Collection. The Valley Library is an official depository for U.S. government and state of Oregon publications.

Students at OSU have access to more than 2,200 computers at labs around the campus, including some that are available 24 hours per day. In addition, all rooms in campus residence facilities are wired for high-speed access to the Internet, and wireless networks are located across the campus. Special research facilities include OSU's Mark O. Hatfield Marine Science Center, Oregon Nanoscience and Microtechnologies Institute (ONAMI), Center for Gene Research and Biotechnology, Forest Research Laboratory, Radiation Center, and Hinsdale Wave Research Lab.

Costs

In-state undergraduate tuition and fees are $7518 for the 2011–12 academic year, while nonresident charges are $21,294. The average cost for a residence hall double room and meal plan is $9444.

Financial Aid

OSU offers the full range of scholarships, grants, work-study, and loans from federal, state, and University sources, investing more than $130 million in student aid annually. Some form of financial assistance is received by 70 percent of the students at OSU and two thirds of nonresident students received scholarship and/or gift aid last year. To qualify, students must have applied for admission and must submit the Free Application for Federal Student Aid (FAFSA), listing OSU as one of their top six choices (Title IV code: 003210). Some students help meet educational expenses with one of the many part-time jobs available on or near the campus. For financial aid information, interested students should contact the Office of Financial Aid and Scholarships, 218 Kerr Administration Building, Corvallis, Oregon 97331 (phone: 541-737-2241, Web site: http://oregonstate.edu/financialaid).

Through the University Scholars Program, OSU offers a variety of scholarships and additional scholarship search assistance for new students who have strong academic records. University scholarships range from $1000 to $8000 annually for up to four years. In addition, many OSU colleges and departments offer scholarships to new students.

Faculty

Undergraduate education is a priority at OSU, and nationally prominent scholars and scientists regularly teach undergraduate courses at all levels. Students receive individual attention and the chance to know their professors both in and out of the classroom. Faculty members consistently receive awards for teaching and research, and many of them are nationally and internationally renowned. For example, Jane Lubchenco, marine biology professor, was chosen by President Obama to lead the National Oceanic and Atmospheric Administration (NOAA). Kelly Benoit-Bird was awarded the MacArthur Fellowship (a.k.a. The Genius Award) in 2010 for her innovative uses of sonar to track marine creatures. The more than $275 million in external research funds received annually by OSU faculty exceeds that of all other Oregon public universities combined.

Student Government

The Associated Students of Oregon State University (ASOSU) plays a major role in making policy and regulating activities for students and in governing the University through student participation on more than fifty University-wide committees. In recent years, ASOSU has become more involved with local, state, and national issues that affect the welfare of students.

Admission Requirements

A minimum 3.0 high school GPA (on a 4.0 scale) qualifies students for freshman admission to OSU when all subject requirements are met. Applicants for undergraduate admission are required to complete an Insight Resume, a written assessment designed to evaluate students' noncognitive attributes. These attributes include self-concept, realistic self-appraisal, handling the system, ability to set long-range goals, leadership, connections with a strong support person, community engagement, and nontraditional learning. High school subject requirements are 4 years of English, 3 years each of mathematics and social studies, and 2 years each of science and of the same foreign language. Students who do not meet the subject requirements may be considered for admission by earning a total score of at least 1410 on three SAT Subject Tests or by successfully completing course work to make up specific deficiencies. The alternatives must be completed by the time of high school graduation.

Transfer admission requires successful completion of at least 36 graded, transferable credits (24 semester credits) from accredited U.S. institutions, with a minimum GPA of 2.25. Grades of C- or better are required in college-level writing and mathematics. Students with less than 36 transferable credits are considered for admission on the basis of their high school records.

Application and Information

Applicants are required to complete OSU's online application, which can be found at the Web site. An *OSU Viewbook*, with information on specific academic programs, housing, financial aid, scholarships, and activities, is sent to students upon request.

Prospective students are encouraged to visit OSU to determine in person whether the University meets their needs. A visit, including a campus tour and an opportunity to talk to faculty members in the student's area of interest, can be arranged by calling the Office of Admissions.

To request more information, students should contact:

Office of Admissions
104 Kerr Administration Building
Oregon State University
Corvallis, Oregon 97331-2106
Phone: 800-291-4192 (toll-free)
Fax: 541-737-2482
E-mail: osuadmit@oregonstate.edu
Web site: http://oregonstate.edu/admissions

PACE UNIVERSITY
NEW YORK CITY AND WESTCHESTER, NEW YORK

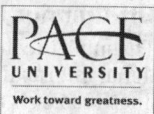

The University

Founded in 1906, Pace University is a leading private metropolitan university that offers an exceptional liberal arts education combined with superior career preparation, two strategic undergraduate New York locations, and robust scholarships and financial aid. The diverse student population of 7,900 undergraduates (4,900 in New York City and 3,000 in Westchester) is enrolled in more than 3,000 courses across 100-plus majors and combined degree programs. These are offered through five undergraduate schools and colleges: the Lubin School of Business, the Dyson College of Arts and Sciences, the Seidenberg School of Computer Science and Information Systems, the School of Education, and the Lienhard School of Nursing. Pace University offers career preparation through one of the largest internship programs in New York. Each year, over 1,200 students intern at more than 500 partner companies throughout metropolitan New York, Westchester County, and southern Connecticut.

Many student-led clubs and organizations are active on the campus, including the Pace Advertising Club, African Students Association, the Pace Press, the Student Government Association, and the Collegiate Italian American Organization. Pace also offers many campus activities, including student government associations, fraternities, sororities, two campus newspapers, two literary magazines, two yearbooks, and two campus broadcasting systems. Athletic facilities are available for students, and intercollegiate sports include baseball, basketball, cross-country, cheerleading, equestrian, football, golf, lacrosse, women's soccer, women's softball, swimming and diving, tennis, and track and field.

The student body is diverse, representing forty-eight states, five U.S. territories, and more than 100 countries.

Location

Pace University is a multicampus institution with campuses in both New York City and Westchester, New York. Both locations are within reach of cultural, business, and social resources and opportunities. The New York City campus is located in the heart of the Financial District in lower Manhattan, and within a short walking distance of Wall Street and the South Street Seaport. Lincoln Center, Broadway theaters, museums, and many world-famous attractions are minutes away by public transportation. Located 35 miles north of New York City, the Westchester campus offers a traditional college experience: state-of-the-art science and video production labs, competitive athletics, fraternities and sororities, and access to internship opportunities at many Fortune 500 companies. Both campuses are accessible by car and public transportation.

Students can take courses at either campus, and housing is available in both New York City and Westchester. Residence facilities feature Internet connectivity, voicemail, and cable TV access.

Majors and Degrees

The following programs are offered at both the New York City and Westchester campuses. The Bachelor of Business Administration (B.B.A.) is offered with majors in accounting–general, accounting–public, finance, information systems, international management, management (with concentrations in business, entrepreneurship, hospitality and tourism, and human resources), and marketing (with concentrations in advertising and integrated marketing communications and global marketing management). In addition, five-year combined B.B.A./M.B.A and B.B.A./M.S. programs in public accounting are available for qualified students. The Bachelor of Arts (B.A.) degree is granted in American studies, applied psychology and human relations, economics, environmental studies, film and screen studies, history, liberal studies, mathematics, modern languages and cultures, philosophy and religious studies, political science, and psychology. The Bachelor of Science (B.S.) degree is offered in biochemistry, biology, biology–preprofessional (occupational therapy, optometry, physical therapy, and podiatry), business economics, chemistry, clinical laboratory science, computer science, criminal justice, environmental science, information systems, information technology, mathematics, professional communication studies, professional computer studies, professional studies, professional technology studies, and technology systems.

Certain programs are available only on one campus. The B.S. program in forensic science; the B.B.A. programs in hospitality and tourism management, and management science major/ mathematics minor; the B.F.A. programs in acting, fine arts, and musical theater; and the B.A. programs in art history; communication science and disorders; communication studies; language, culture, and world trade; Latin American studies; sociology-anthropology; Spanish; teaching students with speech and language disabilities; theater arts; and women's and gender studies are offered only at the New York City campus. The B.A. programs in art, biological psychology, communications, communication arts and journalism, English, English and communications, education, personality and social psychology, and social science; and the B.S. programs in art, education, and nursing are available at the Westchester campus only.

Pace University offers two 5-year engineering programs in cooperation with Manhattan College and Rensselaer Polytechnic Institute. In one program, students attend Pace for three years and Manhattan College for two years, leading to a B.S. degree in science with a concentration in physics from Pace and a B.S. degree in electrical engineering from Manhattan. In the other program, students attend Pace for three years and either Manhattan College or Rensselaer for two years. Upon successful completion, students receive a B.S. degree in chemistry from Pace and either a Bachelor of Chemical Engineering (B.C.E.) in chemical engineering from Manhattan or a B.S. degree in engineering from Rensselaer.

Academic Programs

At Pace University, an innovative core curriculum allows students to develop critical thinking and communication skills by studying subject areas that are integrated around a theme. Students can choose from civic engagement and public values, critical writing, world traditions and cultures, and public speaking. Students also participate in community-based learning where they are given opportunities to practice their skills in real-life settings. Selective academic programs in the University are preparatory for professional training in dentistry, law, medicine, and veterinary science.

The Pforzheimer Honors College is a highly esteemed opportunity at Pace—a community of talented undergraduate scholars studying under the distinguished faculty of the University's five undergraduate schools and colleges. It is a place to excel and realize potential.

Pace University's internship program is nationally recognized and offers qualified students the opportunity to gain experience in their field of study while earning a four-year degree. Students can choose full-time, part-time, or summer positions working in an area directly related to their major course of study. *Businessweek* reported that Pace University is among the top 50 colleges in the nation whose graduates have the highest earning potential. Pace graduates reported earning $53,200 per year on average—comparable to the country's most selective Ivy League schools.

Academic Facilities

The Pace University Library is a comprehensive teaching library and student learning center, a virtual library that combines strong core collections with ubiquitous access to global Internet resources to support broad and diversified curricula. Reciprocal borrowing and access accords, traditional interlibrary loan services, and commercial document delivery options supplement the aggregate library. Pace offers Instructional Services librarians, a state-of-the-art electronic classroom, digital reference services, and multimedia applications. Pace's computer resource centers are linked to high-speed data networks and feature sophisticated hardware and software to facilitate active learning. Pace supports high-speed Internet and Internet2 access on every campus—residence facilities are wired, and most public areas are enabled for wireless connectivity. Full-motion videoconference facilities enable remote delivery of instruction between campus sites for synchronous learning applications.

Costs

For the 2010–11 academic year, undergraduate tuition was $32,656 per year for full-time study. The cost for an on-campus double-occupancy room and board was $12,000–$14,000, with different housing options available.

Financial Aid

Pace University strives to provide opportunities to students of diverse backgrounds and varied circumstances and is committed to offering financial aid to students to the fullest extent of its resources. University-sponsored scholarships are awarded to students on the basis of academic merit, service to the community, and financial need. The goal is to offer every student as much financial assistance as possible, based upon availability and need. Last year, Pace students received more than $260 million in aid. Pace's comprehensive student financial aid assistance program includes scholarships, grants, on-campus employment, student loans (federal and alternative plans), and tuition payment plans. Pace participates in all federal financial aid programs and the New York State Tuition Assistance Program (TAP) and honors awards from other states' incentive grant programs.

Students should submit the Free Application for Federal Student Aid (FAFSA) by February 15 for priority consideration for the fall semester. Further information about any financial aid programs can be obtained by contacting the Office of Financial Aid at any campus location.

Faculty

First and foremost, Pace University professors are dedicated teachers. All Pace classes are taught by professors. Students will never take a course taught by a teaching assistant. Faculty members also bring real-world experience and scholarship into the classroom through their work with outside companies and organizations and by leading cutting-edge research projects. Faculty members come from the best graduate and doctoral programs in the country. Professors—75 percent of whom hold Ph.D.'s—have earned degrees from the University of Pennsylvania, Harvard, Brown, Columbia, and Yale. Pace professors work closely with students to not only broaden their academic horizons, but to show how their work in the classroom is applicable to their future careers.

Admission Requirements

A minimum of 16 units from an accredited secondary school, or equivalent, are required. Academic subjects in high school should be distributed as follows: 4 units of English, 3–4 units of college-preparatory mathematics, 2 units of foreign language, 4 units of history/social science, 2 units of laboratory science, and 4–5 units of academic electives. It is recommended that students applying to the Lubin School of Business complete 4 units of preparatory mathematics. Applicants to the Lienhard School of Nursing should complete 3–4 units of science (2 of which should be laboratory science) and 3–4 units of college-preparatory mathematics. All applicants are required to take either the SAT or ACT examination and have results forwarded to the University. International students are required to take the TOEFL.

Application and Information

The freshman application deadline is February 15. Transfer applications are reviewed on a rolling basis. Requests for application forms and information for both the New York City and Westchester campuses should be addressed to:

Enrollment Information Center
Pace University
One Pace Plaza
New York, New York 10038
Phone: 800-874-7223 (toll-free)
E-mail: infoctr@pace.edu
Web site: http://www.pace.edu

PACIFIC UNIVERSITY
FOREST GROVE, OREGON

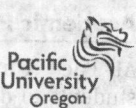
Pacific
University
Oregon

The University

Pacific University is a private, fully accredited four-year liberal arts university encompassing the undergraduate College of Arts and Sciences and nine graduate programs: seven in the health professions, an M.F.A. in writing, and one in teacher education. Founded in 1849 by Congregational pioneers, Pacific is still a frontier institution, proud of its tradition in liberal arts and sciences and innovative in its programs.

Pacific's 3,000 students come from all over the United States and twenty-eight countries, creating a diverse and dynamic student body. Students are taught by the University's full-time faculty members, each of whom is chosen for his or her distinctive devotion to teaching and an emphasis on individual mentoring.

The College of Arts and Sciences is noted for its exceptionally personalized approach to education that is grounded in a philosophy of service. It is recognized for outstanding programs in the natural sciences, education, business, psychology, world languages, and the humanities. Pacific's select group of graduate health profession programs includes the Pacific Northwest's only College of Optometry, as well as the School of Professional Psychology, School of Occupational Therapy, School of Physical Therapy, School of Dental Health Sciences, School of Pharmacy, and School of Physician's Assistant Studies. In addition, the College of Education offers undergraduate and master's-level programs leading to teacher licensure. Graduate programs in the college include the fifth-year M.A.T., M.A.T. Flex, M.Ed., and M.Ed. in visual function and learning (in conjunction with the optometry program).

The lively and vigorous campus springs from the college's residential nature. Freshmen and sophomores under 21 are required to live in one of the University's coed residence facilities. Students living on campus reside in one of five residence halls or Vandervelden Apartments. All on-campus rooms are connected to the campus computer network, which is linked to the Internet. Students who choose to live off campus may live in University-owned housing units or other nearby apartment complexes. Pacific is also the home of an active Greek system, including three fraternities and four sororities.

On campus, the University Center is a hub of activity, housing the dining commons, a new lounge, student government offices, Macintosh and PC lab facilities, the campus radio station, and the newspaper office. The Pacific Undergraduate Community Council (PUCC) provides funding to more than sixty student interest groups, ranging from the Outback program to the Hawaiian Club to the Politics and Law Forum. Pacific Outback provides a multitude of outdoor activities for interested students, such as kayaking, hiking, cross-country and downhill skiing trips, camping, and outings to Portland-area events.

In athletics, Pacific is a member of the NCAA Division III Northwest Conference. Men's intercollegiate sports are football, baseball, basketball, cross-country, golf, soccer, swimming, tennis, track and field, and wrestling. Women compete in basketball, cross-country, golf, lacrosse, soccer, softball, swimming, tennis, track and field, volleyball, and wrestling. Pacific athletes train and compete in the Stoller Center, which houses a gymnasium (with three basketball courts), a state-of-the-art fitness center, a versatile field house, three handball/racquetball courts, a dance studio, a wrestling room, and a complete sports medicine training facility.

Pacific and the city of Forest Grove have also partnered to build another outstanding athletic facility for the University and the community. This new facility features a 1,100-seat stadium with a nine-lane, 400-meter track and a FieldTurf soccer and lacrosse field; a brand-new Bond baseball field with a permanent grandstand; a new varsity softball field with permanent grandstand seating; and other new park amenities. The Lincoln Park Athletic Complex is one of the best outdoor facilities of any small college in the Northwest.

In addition to the Forest Grove campus, the University has a campus in Eugene, Oregon, serving the needs of the College of Education and another in Hillsboro, Oregon, serving the needs of the College of Health Professions, and it operates facilities in Portland that support the academic and clinical programs of the College of Optometry and the School of Professional Psychology.

Pacific offers seven graduate programs in the College of Health Professions: professional psychology (M.A. and Psy.D.), Doctor of Physical Therapy (D.P.T.), Master of Occupational Therapy (M.O.T.), dental health science (B.S. and M.S.), Doctor of Pharmacy, Doctor of Optometry, and a physician's assistant studies program (M.S.P.A.). Physical therapy students must have completed a bachelor's degree program with specific course work before applying to the program. The physician's assistant studies master's program is a twenty-eight-month consecutive program. Through the College of Optometry, students receive a degree (O.D.) with four years of graduate work. Optometry students can be admitted into the College of Optometry's four-year doctoral graduate program after completing three years of undergraduate prerequisite work.

Location

Situated in the northwest corner of Oregon between metropolitan Portland and the Pacific Ocean, the College of Arts and Sciences, College of Education, and College of Optometry are located in Forest Grove (population 18,000), about 35 minutes from the heart of Portland, a vibrant metropolitan area. The 55-acre, oak-covered campus is surrounded by green countryside and the foothills of the Coast Range Mountains, beyond which is the 300-mile stretch of Oregon coast. Opportunities abound in Oregon for hiking, skiing, camping, fishing, beachcombing, and bicycling. The climate is temperate throughout the year, with winter rainfall tapering off to a pleasant spring and sunny summer.

Majors and Degrees

Major programs leading to the B.A. or B.S. degree are offered through the College of Arts and Sciences in anthropology/sociology, applied science, art, bioinformatics, biology (with an emphasis in ecology and evolution or in molecular and cellular), business administration (with an emphasis in accounting, finance, management, or marketing), chemistry (with an emphasis in biological chemistry or chemical physics), computer science, coordinated studies in humanities, creative writing, economics, education and learning, environmental science (with an emphasis in biology or chemistry), exercise science (with an emphasis in human performance), French studies, German studies, history, international studies, Japanese studies, literature, mathematics, media arts and communications (with an emphasis in film production, film studies, integrated media, journalism, or video production), modern languages (with an emphasis in Chinese, French, German, Japanese, or Spanish), music (with an emphasis in education or performance), philosophy (with an emphasis in bioethics), social work, sociology, Spanish, and theater. A B.M. degree is offered in music. Secondary education certification is available in art, biology, English, French, German, health education (combined endorsement only), integrated science, Japanese, mathematics, music, reading (combined endorsement only), social studies (secondary education students only), and Spanish.

Academic Programs

Pacific provides an excellent education in the liberal arts and sciences. The core curriculum in the College of Arts and Sciences emphasizes writing, reasoning, and communication skills, with attention given to cross-cultural education and work in the natural sciences and the fine arts. All freshmen participate in a semester-long first-year seminar program designed to introduce students to college-level writing and research expectations. Pacific has a long tradition of ethical concern that is reflected in its undergraduate courses and its many opportunities for service both on campus and within the broader community. Pacific maintains small classes to ensure close contact among students and faculty members.

Special programs in the College of Arts and Sciences include the interdisciplinary Peace and Conflict Studies Program as well as minors in dance, disabilities studies, and feminist studies.

Basic requirements for the B.A. or B.S. degree are 120 semester hours of credit, completion of a major, and completion of the core requirements in the College of Arts and Sciences. The year is divided into two semesters, with a three-week winter term between the two semesters. Students typically take 15 credit hours during each semester and 3 credit hours during the winter term.

Pacific grants credit for both subject and general CLEP examinations. Each department or school at Pacific University determines whether or not a specific examination may substitute for a specific course. Students who score 4 or better on the Advanced Placement examinations of the College Board are given advanced placement and credit toward graduation. Pacific recognizes the International Baccalaureate program as providing college-level work. Six credit hours are awarded for each higher examination passed at a score of 5 or higher.

Off-Campus Programs

Pacific offers study-abroad programs in twelve different countries, as well as an agreement with the Oregon University System (OUS) giving Pacific students additional study-abroad sites. Foreign language and international studies majors are required to spend at least one semester studying abroad and may use financial aid toward their international study. Pacific also emphasizes internships, which are regularly arranged for students in business, communications, political science, psychology, sociology, and other fields. The internships, which may be arranged for periods lasting from fourteen weeks to an entire academic year, offer students the opportunity to become thoroughly acquainted with professional work and often lead to employment upon graduation.

Academic Facilities

The 55-acre Forest Grove campus contains buildings in a picturesque setting with green lawns and tall shade trees. Architecture at Pacific is a pleasant blend of the old and new. Representing the long history of Pacific University, Old College Hall was the first permanent structure; built in 1850, it contains museum galleries and historic exhibits. Recent construction includes five LEED certified buildings: the university library, Berglund Hall, Burlingham Hall, Gilbert Hall, and the Pacific University Health Professions Campus. Also included are a 90,000-square-foot Pacific Athletic Center and the Lincoln Park Athletic Complex. Historical Marsh Hall, which was originally constructed in 1893 and completely refurbished in 1977, holds classrooms, professors' offices, and administration facilities.

Wireless Internet can be accessed throughout the campus. Built in 2005, the new library houses superior technology, large study areas, and a collection of materials to support the curriculum and student and faculty research in a variety of formats, both traditional and electronic. While the library strives to build a strong core collection, it also participates in SUMMIT, a regional library consortium meeting the considerable research needs of Pacific's students and faculty members by allowing them access to the collections of sixty-two other northwest college and university libraries. Through computer technology, courier services, and interlibrary loans, students and faculty members can efficiently tap the research resources of the region and beyond.

Encompassing the Schools of Dental Health Science, Occupational Therapy, Pharmacy, Physical Therapy, Physician Assistant Studies, and Professional Psychology, Pacific University's College of Health Professions prepares its students through interdisciplinary activities to provide compassionate delivery of exemplary health care for a diverse population in a changing health-care environment. The Pacific University Health Professions Campus opened in fall 2006 and is located on a half-acre site on the Tuality Hospital Hillsboro campus. This location will also be the site of phase two, which will be built in the next five years.

Costs

Tuition and fees for the 2010–11 school year were $31,704. Room and board were $8524 for a double room and a University meal plan. Books and supplies were estimated at $1000. Total direct cost was $41,228. Pacific has consistently been named one of the best values west of the Mississippi by several national publications, including *U.S. News & World Report*.

Financial Aid

Financial assistance at Pacific is awarded on the basis of demonstrated need, academic merit, and talent. The Free Application for Federal Student Aid (FAFSA) is used in evaluating need. Prospective students are encouraged to apply for financial assistance by submitting the FAFSA to the federal processor as soon after January 1 as possible. Pacific provides financial assistance through grants, scholarships, loans, and part-time employment. Further information is available via e-mail at financialaid@pacificu.edu.

Faculty

Pacific's outstanding faculty members provide the foundation for the University's academic program. A student-faculty ratio of 13:1 allows for personal attention by the professors. Pacific's faculty is made up of 147 dedicated educators, of whom 96 percent hold terminal degrees in their field. As professionals, they uphold the University's standard of academic excellence and work closely with students. Pacific does not use graduate or teaching assistants; all faculty members teach their own courses.

Student Government

Participatory government at Pacific enables students to help shape the campus community in which they live and work. Students are encouraged to voice their opinions and to pursue new ideas that further not only personal growth but also the overall growth and development of the University. Pacific Undergraduate Community Council (PUCC), the official student government body, manages activity funds, reviews and supports student issues, and coordinates student participation within the system.

Admission Requirements

Pacific University is selective in considering new students. Primary consideration is given to a candidate's academic preparation and potential for successful study at the college level, as assessed by evaluating the student's transcripts of college-preparatory work, counselor and teacher recommendations, personal essay, SAT and/or ACT scores, and other student-submitted information. Transfer students must submit high school records and test scores if they have completed less than 30 semester hours, plus official transcripts from any institution previously attended.

Application and Information

Students may apply early and may be notified early through the modified rolling admissions plan. Pacific University is an exclusive member of the Common Application. The regular priority deadline for admission is February 1. For additional information, interested students should contact:

Office of Admissions
Pacific University
2043 College Way
Forest Grove, Oregon 97116

Phone: 503-352-2218
      800-677-6712 (toll-free)
E-mail: admissions@pacificu.edu
Web site: http://www.pacificu.edu
      http://www.facebook.com/pacificu

PARSONS THE NEW SCHOOL FOR DESIGN

NEW YORK, NEW YORK

THE NEW SCHOOL
A UNIVERSITY

The University

Parsons The New School for Design in New York City is one of the premier degree-granting colleges of art and design in the nation. A pioneer in art and design education since its founding in 1894, Parsons has cultivated outstanding artists, designers, scholars, businesspeople, and community leaders for more than a century. Today, when design thinking is increasingly being employed to solve complex global problems, Parsons is leading new approaches to art and design education.

Parsons comprises five schools—Art, Media, and Technology; Fashion; Constructed Environments; Art and Design History and Theory; and Design Strategies—and the programs within each span contemporary art and design practices. As part of The New School, a leading university in New York City, Parsons students also weave the liberal arts, social sciences, performance, management, and urban policy into a comprehensive education.

Parsons embraces curricular innovation, pioneering uses of technology, collaborative methods, and global perspectives on the future of design. Parsons graduates and faculty members appear on the short list of outstanding practitioners in every realm of art and design—creative, management, and scholarly. Responsive to societal needs and predictive of cultural trends, Parsons makes tangible, usable, and beautiful The New School's mission of bringing positive, innovative change to the world.

Approximately 4,100 undergraduate students and 490 graduate students are enrolled in Parsons The New School for Design. Nearly a third of all degree-seeking students are international, coming from sixty-eight countries. Some 2,000 continuing education students take individual courses or are enrolled in certificate programs. More than 700 children and young people attend weekend and summer precollege programs.

More than 1,100 students live in the university's residence halls in the Greenwich Village and Wall Street areas and take part in the social and educational programs and activities provided there. Through programming that addresses students' intellectual, artistic, and creative efforts, the residence life program fosters the development of the whole student. The University endeavors to provide comfortable and inclusive communities where students and staff members promote cultural awareness and academic success and develop new ideas and diverse experiences. For more information, students should contact the Office of University Housing at universityhousing@newschool.edu or call 212-229-5459 or visit the Web site at http://www.newschool.edu/studentaffairs/housing/.

Parsons and The New School are fully accredited by the Commission on Higher Education of the Middle States Association of Colleges and Schools. Its credits and degrees are recognized and accepted by other accredited colleges, universities, and professional schools throughout the United States. The New School, a privately supported institution, is chartered as a university by the Regents of the State of New York.

Location

Parsons' main campus is located downtown in Greenwich Village, a historic neighborhood with a style and atmosphere found nowhere else in New York City. The area is home to design and art studios, galleries, shops, and restaurants as well as avant-garde artists, musicians, and writers. With its rich cultural resources, international sophistication, and cutting-edge attitude, New York City is a vibrant environment that has inspired and challenged artists and designers throughout its history. Not surprisingly, Parsons faculty members use New York City as an urban design laboratory. The city offers more than eighty museums, such as the Metropolitan Museum of Art, the Museum of Modern Art, and Cooper-Hewitt, National Design Museum.

Majors and Degrees

Undergraduate degrees offered are an Associate in Applied Science (A.A.S.), a Bachelor of Business Administration (B.B.A.), a Bachelor of Fine Arts (B.F.A.), a Bachelor of Arts (B.A.), and a Bachelor of Science (B.S.). Students may also earn a Bachelor of Arts and a Bachelor of Fine Arts (B.A./B.F.A.) through a five-year, dual-degree program offered in conjunction with Eugene Lang College The New School for Liberal Arts, with classes and studios located conveniently on one campus.

Associate degrees are available in fashion marketing (available online and on campus), fashion studies, graphic design, and interior design. Bachelor's degrees are offered in architectural design, communication design, design and management, design and technology, environmental studies, fashion design, fine arts, illustration, integrated design, interior design, photography, product design, and urban design.

Academic Programs

The degree programs at Parsons are academically challenging, demanding, and, ultimately, professionally rewarding for emerging designers. On average, students register for 16 to 18 credits (six classes) per semester. Most students are in class for 20 to 30 hours per week and spend an equivalent amount of time in preparation. Studio critique sessions and critical studies seminars depend on thoughtful student input and discussion. All courses require active attendance and regular participation.

The A.A.S. degree requires 65 credits; the B.B.A. and B.F.A., 134 credits each; the B.S. and B.A. in Environmental Studies, 120 credits; and the B.A./B.F.A., 180 credits. The five-year B.A./B.F.A. program is offered in conjunction with Eugene Lang College The New School for Liberal Arts.

Off-Campus Programs

In 1920, Parsons School of Design, as it was known then, was the first art and design school in America to found a campus abroad. Today, the school offers its students the possibility to expand their horizons by studying at art and design schools around the world. During their junior year, bachelor's degree students may enroll for one or two semesters in another school in the United States or abroad. Several departments assist students in securing noncredit internships that provide valuable work experience and professional contacts. Current and past internships include Marc Jacobs, Polo-Ralph Lauren, HBO, MTV, the *New York Times, Rolling Stone* magazine, Marvel Comics, and the Museum of Modern Art.

Academic Facilities

Students at Parsons have access to extensive studio facilities and professionally staffed model, fabrication, and print shops, including rapid prototyping, photography, and imaging labs; and metalworking, jewelry, and woodworking facilities. Visit Parsons' individual program listings online to learn more. In addition to the facilities and services at specific academic programs, Parsons also offers resources for all students that provide optimal conditions for learning.

The Sheila C. Johnson Design Center is a new, award-winning campus center for Parsons that combines spaces for learning with galleries and meeting places at the intersection of Fifth Avenue and 13th Street. Features include the Anna-Maria and Stephen Kellen Gallery and Auditorium, and the Arnold and Sheila Aronson Galleries. The Center also provides a new home for the Anna-Maria and Stephen Kellen Archives, a significant collection of drawings, photographs, letters, and objects documenting twentieth-century design. An innovative and highly visible student critique area enables the public to observe the design dialogue that is central to a Parsons education.

The Angelo Donghia Materials Library and Study Center is composed of a library, a gallery, a computer lab, and a lecture hall. The library allows students and faculty members to review and check out state-of-the-art resources, putting the latest and most exclusive materials at their fingertips. Regular exhibitions at the gallery run by a full-time curator are open to the public, creating an open forum and dialogue with the larger interior design community.

Over the past several years, The New School has invested more than $30 million in a series of extensive labs. The Knowledge Union consists of state-of-the-art technology spread over four floors; the 600 networked workstations include all relevant platforms. Servers support work that ranges from traditional print output to online projects using webcasting and secure transaction technology. Specialty work—whether audio or video production, MIDI, recording, or physical computing installation—takes place in private studios spread across the campus. Portable production equipment, including digital still, video, and audio, is readily available. Digital projectors, surround sound, and active white boards feed into equipment racks that enable presentation of all media types.

The University Computing Center, on the third and fourth floors at 55 West 13th Street, is a central hub of technologies. Computers and hands-on classrooms support multimedia, Web design, and desktop publishing as well as word processing and research. The Fashion Computing Center at 560 Seventh Avenue provides computing support for the Parsons B.F.A. program in fashion design. It has more than forty UNIX, Macintosh, and Windows workstations and color and black-and-white printers. Software includes high-end graphic and three-dimensional modeling applications.

Costs

For 2010–11, full-time (12–19 credits) undergraduate students paid $19,255 or $18,485 in tuition, depending on their program of study, and approximately $290 in fees per semester plus $1817 for student health insurance. Although housing costs vary depending on accommodations and meal plan selected, room and board averaged about $15,260 per year. Additional fees may apply.

Financial Aid

Almost 75 percent of Parsons students receive some kind of financial aid, awarded on the basis of financial need and merit. The University's financial aid office is open year-round to assist students and their families with the task of meeting educational costs. For information on specific kinds of assistance, amounts of funding, loan repayment, and scholarships for students meeting certain criteria, prospective students should visit the Student Financial Services' Web site at http://www.newschool.edu/studentservices/financialaid/.

Faculty

More than 1,150 full- and part-time faculty members teach at Parsons. All of them are successful professionals in the design, art, and business fields. The student-faculty ratio is 9:1. Faculty members and visiting critics are principals in their own design firms, hold key positions in the art and design community, and

frequently have their work published. Parsons' strong ties to industry bring numerous guest lecturers and critics into forums and classrooms. Visiting critics have included Richard Meier, Donna Karan, Mayer Rus, Arthur Corwin, and Paula Scher.

Admission Requirements

Parsons seeks serious, responsible, and highly motivated applicants. Each applicant is reviewed individually with regard to experience, achievements, and potential for artistic growth. While Parsons recognizes the benefits of strong artistic preparation, some applicants are admitted based on their academic strengths more than their visual material. For B.F.A. applicants, a large part of the Admissions Committee's decision is based on portfolio evaluations and the Parsons Challenge, as well as academic achievement. For B.B.A., B.S., and B.A. applicants, academic achievement is weighted heavily along with the Parsons Challenge. The A.A.S. program is best suited to students who have had some prior college experience, are clear about their interests within the world of design, and are prepared for rapid immersion in a professional course of study.

All applicants must submit the completed application, the nonrefundable $50 application fee, and original copies of official high school and/or college transcripts. Bachelor's applicants who are residents of the United States must also submit SAT or ACT scores; international students must send in their TOEFL scores (minimum of 580 on the paper-based exam or 237 on the computerized exam). All applicants must submit the multipart Parsons Challenge exercise. A portfolio is required of all B.F.A. applicants (except those applying to study design and management). This must consist of eight to twelve pieces of work, including, but not limited to, drawings, paintings, photographs, digital media, or design. A personal interview is recommended for all applicants.

Application and Information

The admission and financial aid deadline for the fall semester is February 1, and the deadline for spring admission is October 15. The Admissions Committee reviews applications and sends students its decision a few weeks after all materials are received.

Admissions Office
Parsons The New School for Design
72 Fifth Avenue, Second Floor
New York, New York 10011

Phone: 212-229-8989
Fax: 212-229-8975
E-mail: thinkparsons@newschool.edu
Web site: http://www.newschool.edu/parsons

Part of the Parsons experience—taking part in critiquing student assignments.

PENN STATE ERIE, THE BEHREND COLLEGE

ERIE, PENNSYLVANIA

The College

Penn State Erie, The Behrend College, provides a comprehensive education in business, engineering, the humanities and social sciences, science, and nursing. Students benefit from the resources and opportunities of a major research university in a welcoming, student-centered learning environment. The College offers thirty-four bachelor's degree programs, six associate degree programs, and two graduate degree programs.

Among all public colleges and universities in Pennsylvania, Penn State Behrend ranks in the top five in student-to-faculty ratio, SAT scores, first-year student retention, and graduation rate. The College is the second largest institution in the Penn State system. Nearly 75 percent of students who start at Penn State Behrend and go on to graduate with Penn State degrees complete those degrees at the College.

More than 4,700 students attend classes in modern academic buildings and labs, and 1,650 students live on campus in traditional student housing, four-bedroom suites, and two-bedroom apartments. Beyond the classroom, Penn State Behrend students have the opportunity to learn and grow through involvement in more than 115 clubs and organizations.

A member of NCAA Division III and the Allegheny Mountain Collegiate Conference, Penn State Behrend fields twenty-two varsity sports: eleven teams for men (baseball, basketball, cross-country, golf, indoor track, soccer, swimming and diving, tennis, track and field, volleyball, and water polo) and eleven for women (basketball, cross-country, golf, indoor track, soccer, softball, swimming and diving, tennis, track and field, volleyball, and water polo). More than 65 percent of students participate in intramural sports.

Location

Penn State Behrend is conveniently located near Interstates 79, 86, and 90 in a suburb of Erie, Pennsylvania. Situated along Lake Erie's beautiful Presque Isle Bay, Erie is the fourth largest city in Pennsylvania, with a regional population of more than 280,000. The area has a variety of cultural, sports, and recreational resources, including Presque Isle State Park, the Commonwealth's most popular park, offering 7 miles of sandy beaches, boating, and trails for walking, jogging, biking, and more.

Activities in the Erie area include movie theaters, restaurants, museums, performing arts venues, and a zoo. A convention center in downtown Erie features Broadway plays and top-name performers in rock, classical, and country music. Erie is located within 2 hours of Buffalo, Cleveland, and Pittsburgh and is a comfortable 4-hour drive from Toronto.

Majors and Degrees

Penn State Behrend confers the Bachelor of Arts degree in communication, economics, English, general arts and sciences, history, political science, psychology, and science. The Bachelor of Fine Arts degree is offered in creative writing. The Bachelor of Science degree is offered in accounting; biology; business economics; business, liberal arts, and science; chemistry; computer engineering; computer science; electrical engineering; electrical and computer engineering technology; finance; interdisciplinary business with engineering studies; international business; management; management information systems; marketing; mathematics; mechanical engineering; mechanical engineering technology; physics; plastics engineering technology; psychol-

ogy; science; secondary education in mathematics teaching, and software engineering. An RN to B.S. program in nursing is also offered.

The Associate in Arts degree is awarded in one major—letters, arts, and sciences. The Associate in Science degree is offered in general business, and the Associate in Engineering degree is offered in electrical engineering technology, mechanical engineering technology, and plastics engineering technology. The College also offers an associate degree in nursing.

Academic Programs

Each bachelor's degree program requires completion of at least 46 credits in general education and at least 78 credits in the student's major field. Students must complete a minimum of 124 semester hours to earn a bachelor's degree; the exact number depends on the program. Associate degrees require a minimum of 60 semester hours. An honors program and the Schreyer Scholars Program are available to students who show exceptional promise. Several majors serve as excellent preparation for law or medical school. Special prelaw and premed advisers assist students in planning their programs. The College's Academic and Career Planning Center helps students who have not yet decided on an academic major to explore areas of study before selecting a specific program.

Penn State Behrend's Sam and Irene Black School of Business is the only business school in the Erie region accredited by AACSB International, the premier accrediting agency for schools of business worldwide. Students of the school enjoy unique learning opportunities made possible by a $20 million gift from the Black family of Erie.

The College's School of Engineering is the largest undergraduate-only engineering program in the country. The plastics engineering technology program is one of only four accredited plastics programs in the country. The school's ten engineering degrees are all accredited by the Accreditation Board for Engineering and Technology (ABET).

Faculty members in the College's School of Humanities and Social Sciences are regular recipients of university-wide teaching awards. The school's Bachelor of Fine Arts degree in creative writing is one of only a few such programs in the country. Students learn in a variety of advanced teaching environments, including state-of-the-art psychology and communications labs.

In the School of Science, the chemistry program is approved by the American Chemical Society and annually produces more ACS-certified graduates than other comparably-sized institutions. Introductory physics is taught using an innovative instructional method known as SCALE-UP, which stands for Student-Centered Activities for Large-Enrollment Undergraduate Programs. SCALE-UP uses an advanced lab environment without lectures to promote active, hands-on learning.

The College annually awards more than $250,000 in undergraduate research opportunities each year. Many students present their research at regional and national conferences, and others publish in refereed journals. This provides Penn State Behrend students with an advantage when looking for a job or applying to professional or graduate school. The Academic and Career Planning Center works closely with employers and each fall hosts recruiters on campus at its successful career fairs.

Academic Facilities

Penn State Behrend features a mix of contemporary and traditional buildings in a parklike setting. Among the most impressive facilities on campus is the $30-million Jack Burke Research and Economic Development Center, home to the College's colocated schools of engineering and business. The Burke Center features state-of-the-art teaching and research labs, including the largest academic plastics lab in the country. Another new addition to campus is Metzgar Admissions and Alumni Center, which serves as a convenient one-stop shop of services for prospective and current students. Knowledge Park, on the eastern edge of campus, gives companies housed there access to the College's strengths in applied research and technology transfer, while providing internship and job opportunities for students and graduates.

In addition to Penn State Behrend's library collection, students can draw on the resources of the entire Penn State University Libraries collection. The collection, one of the largest in the country, comprises more than 5 million cataloged items, 38,500 serial titles, and 2.5 million government documents. Computers connect students to major databases throughout the world.

Costs

Educational costs at Penn State Behrend vary depending on whether the student is a resident of Pennsylvania, whether enrollment is in the upper or lower division, and whether he or she lives off campus or in a residence hall. The 2010–11 tuition for Pennsylvania residents (lower division) was $12,412 for the academic year. For out-of-state students, the tuition was $18,990 for the academic year. On-campus rooms are a fixed cost, but board and all other costs are variable according to each student's spending habits. These variable costs are approximately $8370 for room and board, $1360 for books and supplies, and $1200 to $2400 for personal expenses, including clothing, laundry, travel, and miscellaneous items. Other costs are a nonrefundable $50 application fee, a nonrefundable $200 enrollment fee and general fee, and a $100 housing fee for students living in on-campus residences.

Financial Aid

More than 80 percent of students receive some form of aid, and students benefit from more than $1 million in annual Penn State Behrend scholarships. Awards are based on an analysis of the student's financial need. Students should file the Free Application for Federal Student Aid (FAFSA) by March 1 of their senior year of high school. Penn State's school code is 003329. The FAFSA and the application for admission are the only forms that first-year students need to complete to be considered for federal, state, and University aid. Aid includes federal grants, loans, and work-study awards. Pennsylvania Higher Education Assistance Agency Grants, and Penn State awards and scholarships.

Faculty

An engaged and engaging faculty is at the heart of the Penn State Behrend experience. More than 325 faculty members, almost all of whom have earned terminal degrees in their major fields, teach both undergraduate and graduate students. The student-to-faculty ratio is 17:1 and the average class size is 26. There are no graduate teaching assistants, and the use of part-time professors is limited. The faculty members are distinguished scholars and superb teachers. They are extensively involved in research and publishing, and they are caring people with a record of excellence in advising students. In the most recent survey of graduating Penn State Behrend seniors, 97 percent of the respondents rated the opportunities to interact with faculty as exceptional.

Student Government

The Student Government Association is the official representative of the student body of Penn State Behrend. In addition to representing students to the administration and faculty, the Student Government Association charters all student organizations and allocates funds to support and promote student activities.

Admission Requirements

As part of Penn State University, and in compliance with federal and state laws, Penn State Behrend is committed to the policy that all persons shall have equal access to admission without regard to race, religion, sex, national origin, ancestry, color, sexual orientation, handicap, age, or status as a disabled or Vietnam veteran. Each applicant is evaluated on the basis of his or her high school record and the results of the SAT or scores from the ACT.

Application and Information

Students interested in freshman admission to Penn State Behrend may obtain a Web application at www.admissions.psu.edu. Students who do not wish to file a Web application can obtain an admission application form from any Penn State campus or by writing to Penn State Behrend. Application forms are available in late summer. The recommended deadline for submitting an application is November 30. Applicants admitted to Penn State Behrend are notified approximately four to six weeks after the application and credentials are received. The student must make certain that the Educational Testing Service forwards the SAT scores to the Undergraduate Admissions Office, Pennsylvania State University, University Park, Pennsylvania 16802.

This description is available in alternative media upon request. For application forms, more information, or a campus visit, interested students should contact:

Office of Admissions
Penn State Erie, The Behrend College
4701 College Drive
Erie, Pennsylvania 16563-0105
Phone: 814-898-6100
    866-374-3378 (toll-free)
E-mail: behrend.admissions@psu.edu
Web site: www.behrend.psu.edu

Penn State Behrend was one of the first academic institutions in the country to bring its schools of business and engineering together under a single roof in the College's Jack Burke Research and Economic Development Center.

PHILADELPHIA UNIVERSITY
PHILADELPHIA, PENNSYLVANIA

The University

Founded in 1884, Philadelphia University is a private institution of higher learning for students with high motivation and academic ability. Philadelphia University is professionally oriented and offers undergraduate and graduate degree programs in the areas of architecture, business, design, engineering, fashion, general sciences, health sciences, and textile materials technology. The University's enrollment of approximately 2,500 undergraduates represents a diverse and talented group of students from thirty-eight states and forty-two countries. With an average class size of 18 and a 14:1 student-faculty ratio, students receive the personal attention so important to social and professional growth.

Through a unique blend of liberal and specialized education with an interdisciplinary focus, the University prepares students for today's complex, global workplace. Recognized as a premier professional university, Philadelphia University has established a phenomenal record of career success for its graduates. The University is committed to a technologically advanced approach to career planning, and students have full access to the Career Services Center's CareerLink, an Internet-based resume and job-listing management system that electronically stores resumes, job listings, and employer information. Students have access to job-search resources, including ReferenceUSA, a database of 1.5 million companies nationwide. Prospective employers gain access to students through the various career fairs and industry spotlights hosted by the center annually. The University's innovative academic programs that meet emerging needs in the marketplace, extensive networking with prospective employers (connecting students with 150 employers on campus and 1,200 employers electronically in recent years), and extensive career and professional development opportunities for students all add up to a ten-year average of nearly 90 percent placement rate within just a few months of graduation.

Philadelphia University believes the college experience of every student should extend well beyond the classroom. The Student Life Programs at Philadelphia University build bridges between the classroom and out-of-class experiences to create a dynamic learning community for students. Fifteen varsity teams compose the intercollegiate athletics program. Men participate in baseball, basketball, cross-country/track, golf, rowing, soccer, and tennis. Women's teams include basketball, cross-country/track, lacrosse, rowing, soccer, softball, tennis, and volleyball. An extensive intramural sports program is available to all students. Students are actively engaged in campus life, whether through one of the nationally ranked athletic teams, events sponsored by Student Government, a wide array of community service opportunities, an extensive intramural program, or participation in the more than thirty student clubs and organizations.

More than 1,200 students live on campus in residence halls, apartments, and townhouses. Professional and paraprofessional staff members live within each residential area to assist students with daily concerns and program activities to enhance residential living.

The University holds accreditation from the Middle States Association of Colleges and Schools, the National Architectural Accrediting Board (NAAB), Council for Interior Design Accreditation (CIDA), the American Chemical Society (ACS), Accreditation Review Commission on Education for the Physician Assistant (ARC-PA), National Association of Schools of Art and Design (NASAD), the Landscape Architecture Accreditation Board (LAAB), and the Engineering Accreditation Commission of the Accreditation Board for Engineering and Technology (ABET), Inc., as well as certification from the International College Reading and Learning Center Association.

Location

The University's sprawling, 100-acre campus is adjacent to Fairmount Park, the largest urban park system in the country. Students enjoy the best of both worlds—a beautiful campus with tree-lined walkways, spacious lawns, and classical architecture, and easy access to Philadelphia (just minutes away) for entertainment, cultural events, great night spots, and more than 300 years of American history.

Philadelphia also serves as a "living lab" where students frequently interact with area professionals for class projects, internships, and off-campus jobs.

Majors and Degrees

Philadelphia University offers the Bachelor of Science in more than thirty areas, including accounting, animation, architectural studies, architecture, biochemistry, biology, biopsychology, chemistry, construction management, digital design, engineering (with minor tracks in architectural, environmental, industrial, mechanical, and textile), environmental and conservation biology, environmental sustainability, fashion design, fashion industry management, fashion merchandising, finance, graphic design communication, health sciences, health sciences/occupational therapy (B.S./M.S.), industrial and systems engineering, industrial design, interior design, international business, landscape architecture, law and society, management, marketing, mechanical engineering, physician assistant studies, premedical studies, professional communication, psychology, psychology/occupational therapy (B.S./M.S.), public health, textile design, and textile materials technology.

The University also offers several five-year B.S./M.B.A. joint-degree programs and a five-year B.S./M.S. physician assistant studies program. The five-year architecture program leads to a Bachelor of Architecture (B.Arch.), and the five-year landscape architecture program leads to the Bachelor of Landscape Architecture (B.L.A.). For students wishing to keep their choices open, an undeclared option offers an introduction to college courses in preparation for entering a specific major in the sophomore year.

Academic Programs

Philadelphia University's commitment to quality professional education is realized in curricula that combine a solid foundation in liberal studies with career preparation. These curricula are designed to enhance students' ability and desire to learn; to ensure them an understanding of the ideas, traditions, and values of their own and other cultures; and to prepare them to apply the concepts and techniques of both general and specialized learning to their lives as citizens with productive careers. Degree requirements include successful completion of 121 to 138 credits (depending upon the major chosen), successful completion of both major and general education programs, and the satisfactory completion of at least 60 credits in residence at the University. All students have the option to participate in the University's Internship Program, through which they earn both academic credit and a salary.

As a rule, the University grants credit to students who obtain satisfactory grades in subject examinations developed by the Advanced Placement Program, the College-Level Examination

Program, and the Proficiency Examination Program. Students may, by invitation, participate in the honors program, which offers a number of courses expressly for honors students.

The University's academic calendar consists of two semesters and two summer sessions.

Off-Campus Programs

Internships are available, and the University's Internship Office has affiliations with a wide variety of organizations, such as L. L. Bean, Isdaner & Company, the Hillier Group, Citizens Bank, Burlington Industries, J. Crew, and Federated Department Stores.

Study abroad at Philadelphia University prepares students for successful participation and competition in an increasingly interdependent world and to perform with distinction in the international and multicultural contexts that are increasingly shaping professional life. Students at Philadelphia University may study abroad and receive credit for courses that apply directly to their challenging, professions-oriented curricula. Opportunities are available for fall, spring, and summer semesters. The University has its own programs in Rome and Milan, Italy, and affiliations with more than twenty-five programs all over the world and in most majors.

Academic Facilities

The University's newest building, the 72,000-square-foot Kanbar Campus Center, features an open design with walls of windows to optimize the spectacular natural setting. Also recently opened is the Gallagher Athletic, Recreation, and Convocation Center.

The Tuttleman Center at Philadelphia University, a 31,500-square-foot academic building, provides students and faculty members with access to the most sophisticated technologies for teaching and learning.

Many major labs and studios enable students to gain practical experience in engineering, design, textiles, apparel manufacturing, foreign languages, the sciences, computer technologies, and physician assistant studies. The University's Paul J. Gutman Library is a state-of-the-art information center. Through the contemporary information system, students can search the library's collections, as well as major indexes and full-text journals, from on or off campus. An international computer network links Philadelphia University to the resources of more than 14,000 libraries worldwide. With more than 400 study spaces and nine group study rooms, the library provides an ideal environment for reading and research. The Architecture and Design Center houses studio space, a photo lab, and computer-aided design labs. The Design Center at Philadelphia University houses an extensive collection of textile artifacts and hosts changing exhibits in its galleries.

General-purpose and departmental computing labs are updated using a multiyear migration strategy as changes in technology dictate. The labs are currently equipped with Pentium PCs and Macintoshes running at speeds from 1.0 to 1.8 MHz. The University operates a switched, 100-megabit network with building-to-building gigabit (1000-megabit) connections in high-traffic areas. The network provides students with access to the Internet, e-mail service, network storage (300 MB per student), digital library resources, online databases, and the Blackboard course management system.

Costs

The University's 2010–11 cost for regular tuition was $28,800. Room was $4698 and board was $4804.

Financial Aid

Philadelphia University's total financial aid program has amounted to more than $77 million annually. Approximately $30 million came from the University itself and the remainder from federal, state, and private sources. While 96 percent of the University's full-time day students receive direct institutional scholarship assistance, 98 percent receive some form of aid each year (e.g., other scholarships, loans, and job opportunities). Candidates for aid should complete the Free Application for Federal Student Aid by April 15. The University offers a wide range of institutional scholarships and grants to incoming students each year. Award amounts vary according to the quality of each student's academic record. The University's scholarship program is available to all prospective students (freshmen and transfer students). Scholarships are awarded regardless of financial need. Students and parents are strongly encouraged to call the admissions or financial aid offices for further information.

Faculty

Primarily a teaching institution, the University encourages close connections between the faculty and students. Classes intentionally are kept small, and faculty members make a practice of being available to students outside the classroom. Often, students can partner with faculty members to pursue joint research interests and gain career experience. The University's faculty is composed of a diverse group of professionals who not only hold strong academic credentials but also frequently possess impressive work experience. They are often sought out as consultants in their fields.

Student Government

The Student Government Association (SGA) is an independent, self-governing student group. In addition to the basic responsibility of protecting students' rights, SGA recommends students to University-wide committees, addresses student grievances, and sponsors campuswide events. The Campus Activities Board is the major programming organization on campus. Its primary responsibility is to provide a wide variety of cultural, scholastic, social, educational, and recreational programs.

Admission Requirements

The University evaluates applicants on the basis of their high school record (including GPA and quality of courses taken), scores on either the SAT or the ACT, essay, recommendation, and extracurricular activities. Normally, 15 units of secondary school preparation are required for admission. Three units of mathematics (including algebra II and geometry) are required for admission. Students who wish to enter a science curriculum are strongly encouraged to take 4 units of mathematics and 4 units of science. The University actively recruits qualified transfer students, who represent approximately one fifth of the incoming class each fall. The University also has a large international student population. These students must score at least 170 (computer-based) on the TOEFL in order to be considered for admission.

Application and Information

The University maintains a rolling admission plan. Applications are reviewed and decisions are made soon after an application, academic credentials, and standardized test scores are received. Students are encouraged to submit applications early in the senior year; applications received after March 1 are considered on a space-available basis. All applicants are encouraged to come to the campus for an interview with a member of the professional admission staff.

Greg Potts
Director of Admissions
Philadelphia University
4201 Henry Avenue
Philadelphia, Pennsylvania 19144
Phone: 215-951-2800
          800-951-7287 (toll-free)
Fax: 215-951-2907
E-mail: admissions@PhilaU.edu
Web site: http://www.PhilaU.edu

PITZER COLLEGE
CLAREMONT, CALIFORNIA

The College

Pitzer is a nationally recognized independent, residential liberal arts college. The College's emphasis on interdisciplinary studies, intercultural understanding, and social responsibility sets it apart from most other colleges in the country. The College believes students should take an active part in formulating their individualized plans of study, bringing a spirit of inquiry and adventure to the planning process. Because there are fewer required general education courses, Pitzer gives its students more freedom to choose the courses they want to take.

Pitzer offers the best of both worlds: membership in a small, close-knit academic community and access to the resources of a mid-size university through Pitzer's partnership with the Claremont Colleges. The Claremont Colleges are a consortium of five distinct undergraduate colleges (Pitzer, Claremont McKenna, Harvey Mudd, Pomona, and Scripps) and two graduate institutions (Claremont Graduate University and the Keck Institute for Applied Biological Sciences). Each college has its own personality, but all share major facilities, such as the library, bookstore, campus security, health services, counseling center, ethnic study centers, and chaplains' offices. The total enrollment of all of the colleges is nearly 6,300 students. Students at Pitzer may enroll in courses offered by the other colleges and may consult with professors on all of the adjoining campuses.

The College was founded in 1963. Today, Pitzer offers forty-three majors in the arts, humanities, sciences, and social sciences. Majors with the largest enrollments currently include anthropology, art, biology, economics, English, environmental studies, history, organizational studies, political studies, psychology, and sociology.

In 2010 the first-year class of 268 students represented twenty-seven different states and seven other countries. About 61 percent of the first-year students came from outside of California.

Pitzer has a deep commitment to welcoming members of underrepresented groups since its founding. In 2010, members of underrepresented groups made up approximately 34 percent of the entering class: 16 percent Chicano/Latino, 11 percent Asian American and Pacific Islander, and 7 percent African American.

Residential life plays a significant role in a student's educational experience. Each of Pitzer's residence halls establishes its own Hall Council to serve as a forum for addressing and meeting the needs of the community. Pitzer students have a long tradition of arranging their living communities based on common interests. All rooms are wired for Internet access, television, and phone service. Three new LEED-certified Gold residence halls opened in 2007.

Opportunities abound at Pitzer and the other Claremont Colleges. Students may participate in a wide variety of sports, clubs, community service programs, and social activities. Currently, more than 150 student organizations allow students to get involved in a wide variety of activities. Pitzer partners with Pomona College to field NCAA Division III teams in baseball, basketball, cross-country, football, golf, soccer, softball, swimming and diving, tennis, track and field, volleyball, and water polo. Club sports for men include crew, cycling, lacrosse, rugby, Ultimate (Frisbee), and volleyball. Club sports for women include crew, cycling, lacrosse, rugby, and Ultimate (Frisbee).

Location

Pitzer is located in the city of Claremont (population 35,000) at the base of the San Gabriel Mountains, about 35 miles east of Los Angeles and 78 miles west of Palm Springs. Pitzer is a short drive away from rock climbing at Joshua Tree National Park, ski resorts, the beaches of southern California, and the Getty, Norton Simon, and other Los Angeles County museums.

Majors and Degrees

Pitzer offers the Bachelor of Arts degree in Africana studies; American studies; anthropology; art; art history; Asian American studies; biochemistry; biology; biochemistry; black studies; chemistry; Chicano studies; classics; dance; economics; English and world literature; environmental analysis; gender and feminist studies; history; human biology; international and intercultural studies; linguistics; management engineering; mathematical economics; mathematics; media studies; modern language, literature, and cultures: Spanish; molecular biology; music; neuroscience; organismal biology; organizational studies; philosophy; physics; political economy; political studies; psychology; religious studies; science and management; science, technology, and society; sociology; Spanish; and theater.

Minors are available in Africana studies, anthropology, art, art history, Asian American studies, biology, black studies, classics, dance, economics, English/world literature, environmental analysis, gender and feminist studies, history, linguistics, mathematics, media studies, music, philosophy, science, technology and society, sociology, Spanish, and theater.

Academic Programs

To earn the Bachelor of Arts degree, students are required to complete thirty-two courses, about one third of which are in the major. Students work with faculty advisers to organize a curriculum that meets the educational objectives of the College: breadth of knowledge, understanding in depth, written expression, interdisciplinary and intercultural exploration, and social responsibility and the ethical implications of knowledge and action. Specific course requirements depend on the student's academic interests. Certain concentrations require a senior thesis.

The system of cross-registration at the Claremont Colleges provides Pitzer students with the opportunity to take advantage of the wide range of courses available at each of the other colleges. Advanced students may also enroll in certain courses at Claremont Graduate University with the instructor's approval.

The College observes a semester calendar; classes begin in early September and end in mid-May. There is a study break near the middle of each semester and another break between semesters from mid-December through mid-January.

Off-Campus Programs

Nearly 72 percent of students participate in study-abroad programs. Pitzer approves thirty-five international study options in Argentina, Australia, Botswana, Bulgaria, Canada, Chile, China, Costa Rica, Denmark, Ecuador, England, Finland, France, Germany, Ghana, Hong Kong, Hungary, Iceland, Ireland, Israel, Japan, Korea, Latvia, Mexico, Morocco, Nepal, Singapore, South Africa, Spain, Thailand, Turkey, and fourteen exchanges with U.S. institutions.

Academic Facilities

The central services of the Claremont Colleges include the Honnold-Mudd Library, which houses more than 2 million volumes and more than 6,000 serial subscriptions. Other shared facilities include theaters, music halls, music and dance studios, the Keck Joint Science Center (shared with Claremont McKenna and Scripps Colleges), and a wellness center that includes counseling and health services.

Specialized facilities at Pitzer include a newly renovated auditorium, a television studio, film editing suites, art galleries, social science laboratories, an arboretum, a reading library, and several computing facilities, including a 24-hour computer center.

Costs

Expenses for 2010–11 were as follows: tuition and fees, $41,130; room and board, $11,950; and books and personal expenses, $2000. Travel expenses vary. Costs are subject to change for 2011–12.

Financial Aid

Nearly 42 percent of Pitzer's students receive aid in the forms of grants, loans, and work-study. To apply for aid, students must complete the Free Application for Federal Student Aid (FAFSA) and the Financial Aid PROFILE. California residents should also apply for California state grants. Students must reapply for aid each spring.

Faculty

One hundred percent of Pitzer's faculty members hold a Ph.D. or the terminal degree in their fields. All courses are taught by the faculty members. The student-faculty ratio is 11:1. Faculty members are readily available for academic advising. Most faculty members are conversant with at least one other field of study in addition to the area of their degrees and may teach in more than one area.

Student Government

Pitzer's governmental structure is distinctive among American colleges. Instead of the traditional student government that restricts student participation to limited areas, students are represented on all standing committees of the College, including those that deal with the most vital and sensitive issues of the College community. Though it demands a serious time commitment from those who choose to participate, it offers interested students an active educational experience and the opportunity to make a genuine impact on the life of the College and its students, faculty, and staff.

Admission Requirements

Pitzer has developed a highly personalized admission process. Each applicant is considered on the basis of his or her own strengths. In general, the College seeks students who have performed well in high school, have shown a significant amount of involvement in activities outside of the classroom, are motivated to learn, and are interested in the opportunity to take an active role in planning their education in a liberal arts framework. The selection process is designed to help achieve a diverse and energetic class. Selection is based on high school transcripts, rigor of curriculum, recommendations, essays, extracurricular activities, and other special talents. Applicants are encouraged to visit the campus and arrange for an interview.

Application and Information

Pitzer College offers both early decision and regular decision for prospective applicants. Students interested in applying early must submit a completed application by November 15 and are notified late December. Interviews for early decision are required by December 1. Regular decision candidates must submit their applications for admission by January 1 and are notified by April 1. Interviews are not required but are highly recommended and should be completed by December 15. Applicants must supply an official transcript of grades, two teacher evaluations, one counselor or school official recommendation, and the application fee of $60 by the necessary deadline. Pitzer accepts the Common Application as the only application for admission for first-year students. When submitting the Common Application, students must complete a supplemental form, which is available on the Common Application Web site at http://www.commonapp.org. Pitzer College is test optional in the admission process. Students should contact the College for further details.

For additional information, students should contact:

Office of Admission
Pitzer College
1050 North Mills Avenue
Claremont, California 91711-6101
Phone: 909-621-8129
        800-PITZER1 (800-748-9371, toll-free)
Fax: 909-621-8770
E-mail: admission@pitzer.edu
Web site: http://www.pitzer.edu
        https://www.facebook.com/PitzerOfficeOfAdmission
        http://on.fb.me/Pitzer_Coll (("I'm Applying to
            Pitzer" Facebook page)
        http://twitter.com/pitzercollege

Students on the campus of Pitzer College.

POST UNIVERSITY
WATERBURY, CONNECTICUT

The University

Founded in 1890, Post University is a student-focused, career-driven university committed to providing students with the knowledge, personal skills, and experience required to be leaders in their chosen fields. Located in Waterbury, Connecticut, Post University is known for its quality academic programs, small classes, and competitive NCAA Division II athletics. In 2009, Post added a sprint football team. Its students come from the United States and abroad and are supported by faculty whose mission is to prepare students to compete and succeed in today's global workplace.

Post University attracts students from all races, cultures, geographies, and socio-economic backgrounds. This array of diverse viewpoints and experiences gives students many opportunities to learn about others and themselves.

Students enjoy all the benefits of a small, close-knit New England campus community, including the ability to form lifelong friendships with their peers; receive one-on-one attention from professors; and have regular interaction with other faculty members, students, and staff. They can also participate in a wide array of on-campus activities and have nearby access to two of the nation's most vibrant cities, New York and Boston. The smaller campus also means more opportunities to take on leadership roles within and beyond the classroom.

Approximately two thirds of Post University's students live on campus in one of six residence halls. The residence halls range from single rooms to suites consisting of private rooms around a shared living and eating facility. This is in addition to the campus's large dining room.

Post students participate in a year-round schedule of intercollegiate and intramural athletic activities. The Post University Eagles compete in the National Collegiate Athletic Association (NCAA) Division II and the Central Atlantic Collegiate Conference (CACC). Men's intercollegiate sports teams include baseball, basketball, cross-country, golf, soccer, swimming, and tennis. The Post University sprint football team competes against well-known institutions such as Army, Navy, Cornell, Princeton, and University of Pennsylvania in the Collegiate Sprint Football League. Women's teams include basketball, cross-country, lacrosse, soccer, softball, swimming, tennis, and volleyball. The University also sponsors active coeducational equestrian and international dressage teams. Intramural sports are diverse, ranging from softball and volleyball to basketball and flag football. Students enjoy the facilities of the Drubner Fitness Center, including a gymnasium, swimming pool, tennis and racquetball courts, and fitness and weight-training rooms.

Location

Post University offers students the best of both worlds. Located midway between New York City and Boston, Post University occupies a 58-acre hilltop residential campus in the suburbs of Waterbury, Connecticut. Post's campus and the surrounding community offer a safe, scenic, friendly, and convenient home for students. Its location in the heart of Connecticut provides convenient service from Amtrak's Northeast Corridor as well as airline service to Hartford.

Majors and Degrees

Students enrolled at Post University may earn an undergraduate degree in accounting, biology, business administration, child studies, computer information systems, criminal justice, environ-

mental sciences/studies, equine business management, finance, human services, legal studies, management, marketing, psychology, sociology, sport management, and early childhood education. In addition, Post University has a number of certificate programs that prepare students for the practice of specific specialties and which can be integrated into either an associate or baccalaureate degree.

Post University is accredited by the New England Association of Schools and Colleges, Inc. (NEASC) through its Commission on Institutions of Higher Education and is licensed by the Connecticut Department of Higher Education.

Academic Programs

For the bachelor's degree, students must complete a minimum of 120 credit hours. To receive an associate degree from Post, students must complete a minimum of 60 credit hours. The University has a two-semester calendar.

Off-Campus Programs

Post University offers students the opportunity to study abroad through a University-sponsored program and/or an approved study/internship-abroad program at another institution. The equine business management program offers a study-abroad option in the United Kingdom. Through these programs, students have an opportunity to broaden their perspectives and experiences. Courses taken abroad are accepted for degree credit at Post University.

To qualify for study abroad, a student must have a cumulative grade point average of 2.5 or better at the time of attendance.

Academic Facilities

Post University's campus offers wireless Internet access inside and outside. It includes a new computer lab; recently renovated dining hall; classrooms that are equipped with needed technology; and a gymnasium, pool and fitness center. Residence halls include single-room and suite options. The University also includes a Writing Center and a Tutoring Center that are available for student use at no additional charge. The University's library has more than 60,000 volumes, more than 400 periodical titles, and a growing media collection. As a government document depository, the library houses an extensive government publications collection. Post University also has reciprocal borrowing agreements with academic libraries throughout the state.

Costs

For 2011–12, full-time resident students pay a comprehensive fee of $34,650, covering tuition, room, and board. For commuting students, the comprehensive fee is $24,800 per year. Student services, technology, equine, laboratory fees, the $40 application fee, and an estimated $1000 to $1500 per year for books and supplies are not included in this total.

Financial Aid

Post University offers financial assistance through the Federal Work-Study, Federal Supplemental Educational Opportunity Grant, Federal Stafford Student Loan, and Federal Perkins Loan programs. Aid is awarded upon evidence of financial need, as determined by the Free Application for Federal Student Aid (FAFSA). In addition, the University has its own academic and athletic scholarship and grant programs, and participates in all applicable state programs. In order to apply for financial assistance, a student must apply for admission and be accepted to Post University, and then submit the FAFSA.

Faculty

Post University has 34 full-time and 235 part-time faculty members, who hold advanced degrees and bring relevant work experience in the fields they teach. All full-time faculty members serve as academic advisers and maintain weekly office hours for student consultation. The student-faculty ratio is 16:1, and students are never in classes with hundreds of students or taught by teaching assistants.

Student Government

Students play active roles in the day-to-day functioning of Post University. The students' official voice at the University is the Student Government Association (SGA), which expresses recommendations pertaining to student life, oversees the operations of each active student group, and decides on funding for each group. Students participate in a wide array of campus activities, programs, and athletics.

Admission Requirements

Post University welcomes applicants who are motivated to succeed academically and in their careers. Admission to Post University is based upon an evaluation of the candidate's qualifications and the recommendation of an admissions representative. All decisions are made without regard to race, creed, color, religion, national origin, handicap, or sexual orientation.

The applicant's academic experience, standardized test scores, personal qualities, recommendations, and individual characteristics are considered. Post University has a rolling admissions policy. The admissions committee makes a decision with respect to a candidate's admission to the University as soon as the candidate's file is complete. The minimum requirements to make an admissions decision include the submission of an application, official high school transcripts, and standardized test scores. International students are required to earn a minimum score of 500 on the paper-based version or 173 on the computer-based version of the TOEFL and adhere to the above requirements.

Campus visit appointments may be scheduled Monday through Thursday at 1; Friday at 11, 1, or 3; and Saturday at 11 or 1. Post periodically offers group information sessions, on-site and off-site open houses, and live Internet chats. To schedule a campus visit, students should call the Office of Admission at 800-345-2562 (toll-free) or send an e-mail message to admissions@Post.edu.

Post University welcomes transfer students and has a flexible credit transfer policy. Transfer candidates must have a minimum GPA of 2.0 and must provide transcripts from all other colleges and universities attended. Grades of C or higher may receive transfer credits. The maximum number of transfer credits allowed for bachelor's candidates is 90; the maximum for associate candidates is 30.

Students who have an associate degree from an accredited college or University may transfer all 60 credits toward a bachelor's degree in the same major.

Application and Information

To apply, students should submit the application form, the non-refundable $40 application fee, a recommendation, SAT or ACT scores, and high school or college transcripts. Online applications are available through the University's Web site at http://www.Post.edu.

For additional information, students should contact:

Office of Admissions
Post University
800 Country Club Road
P.O. Box 2540
Waterbury, Connecticut 06723-2540
Phone: 203-596-4520
        800-345-2562 (toll-free)
Fax: 203-756-5810
E-mail: admissions@Post.edu
Web site: http://www.Post.edu
        http://www.facebook.com/PostUniversity
        http://twitter.com/PostUniversity

Post University is a student-focused, career-driven institution committed to helping students develop the knowledge, personal skills, and experience they need to become leaders in their chosen fields.

PRATT INSTITUTE
BROOKLYN, NEW YORK

The Institute

Industrialist and philanthropist Charles Pratt founded Pratt Institute in 1887 to educate students for various professions on a non-degree level. As the educational preparation necessary for various professions expanded, Pratt Institute moved to offer baccalaureate degrees with its first granted in 1938 and its first graduate degree granted in 1950. Now, with twenty-seven undergraduate majors and concentrations, Pratt offers students a wide variety of programs in which to major or take elective courses.

With most programs in art, design, and architecture ranked among the top ten in the country, Pratt has been ranked among the top design schools in the U.S. by *Business Week*. Pratt has continued to add programs at all educational levels, including undergraduate programs in creative writing and critical and visual studies, undergraduate and graduate programs in art history and art education(teacher certification), and graduate programs in arts and cultural management, historic preservation, and design management.

Although the characteristics and educational requirements of the professions for which Pratt prepares people have changed over the course of a century, the Institute has succeeded in pursuing its abiding purpose—to blend theoretical learning with professional and humanistic development—and has kept its curricula current by hiring practicing professionals to teach. Standards are high, modeled after the professional world. Faculty members connect students with internships and eventually jobs after graduation. Industry projects provide students with real-world experience.

Pratt offers four-year bachelor's, two-year associate, and master's degrees. In educating more than five generations of students to be creative, technically skilled, and adaptable professionals as well as responsible citizens, Pratt has gained a national and international reputation that attracts undergraduate and graduate students from all U.S. states and eighty countries. Unlike the typical American college student, most students who choose Pratt are committed to their career objectives or at least to the study of art, design, architecture, or creative writing.

A short subway or bus ride from the museums, galleries, and design centers of both Manhattan and Brooklyn, Pratt Institute has twenty-five buildings of differing architectural styles spread about a 25-acre campus. Nineteen of the buildings house studios, classrooms, laboratories, administrative offices, auditoria, sports facilities, food services, and student centers. A new, green, LEED-certified Gold building houses student administrative services including admissions, digital arts programs, and various administrative offices. Six buildings are student residences, including the Stabile Hall freshman residence, which provides studio space on each floor. There are adequate parking facilities for residents and commuters. Student services include career planning and placement, health and counseling, and student development. More than sixty student organizations are available including fraternities and sororities, honorary societies, professional societies, and clubs.

Location

Pratt Institute, the country's premier college of art, design, writing, and architecture, is located in the Clinton Hill section of Brooklyn, just minutes from downtown Manhattan. Eighty-eight percent of Pratt's freshmen and over half of its undergraduates live on the school's beautifully landscaped 25-acre, tree-lined Brooklyn campus. The campus includes a contemporary sculpture garden (ranked among the top ten campus art collections by *Public Art Review*), an athletic center, residence halls, dining halls, outstanding studio facilities, and historic buildings. Students find a green oasis just minutes from the art capital of the world, Manhattan.

Majors and Degrees

Pratt Institute offers the Bachelor of Architecture, Bachelor of Fine Arts, Bachelor of Art, Bachelor of Industrial Design, Bachelor of Professional Studies, Bachelor of Science, Associate of Occupational Studies, and Associate of Applied Science degrees.

The Bachelor of Architecture degree program is a five-year, accredited program. For the Bachelor of Fine Arts degree, a candidate may choose to major in art and design education (teacher certification), art history, communications design (advertising, graphic design, illustration), digital arts (traditional and digital animation, interactive arts), fashion design, film/video, fine arts (ceramics, drawing, jewelry, painting, printmaking, sculpture), interior design, photography, or writing. The Bachelor of Arts is offered in critical and visual studies and art history. The Bachelor of Industrial Design is offered for students interested in car, product, and furniture design. In the Bachelor of Professional Studies degree program, the major is in construction management. Students seeking the Bachelor of Science degree can major in construction management.

The two-year Associate of Occupational Studies degree is offered in digital design and interactive media, graphic design, and illustration. The Associate of Applied Science is offered in painting/drawing and graphic design/illustration. The two-year Associate of Applied Science degree is transferable to a four-year program.

Students may also earn combined bachelor's/master's degrees. Programs include the B.F.A./M.S. in art and design education as well as art history.

Academic Programs

Educating artists and creative professionals to be responsible contributors to society has been the mission of Pratt Institute since it assembled its first group of students in 1887. Within the structure of that professional education, Pratt students are encouraged to acquire the diverse knowledge that is necessary for them to succeed in their chosen fields including sustainability. In addition to the professional studies, the curriculum in each of Pratt's schools includes a broad range of liberal arts courses. Students from all schools take these courses together and have the opportunity to examine the interrelationships of art, science, technology, and human need.

At the time of graduation, students in the associate degree programs have completed 67 credit hours of course work. In the bachelor's programs, credit-hour requirements range from 132 to 135 credits, depending on the particular program. For the Bachelor of Architecture degree, 170 credits are required.

Pratt's academic calendar consists of two semesters plus optional summer terms that allow students to choose alternative courses or various options usually not offered during the fall or spring semester. Two summer sessions are offered.

Off-Campus Programs

Pratt Institute offers credit for a wide variety of off-campus study programs. The Internship Program offers qualified students challenging on-the-job experience related to their major fields of interest; this extension of the classroom and laboratory into the professional world adds a practical dimension to periods of on-campus study.

International programs, available during all academic sessions, have included art and design offerings in the cities of Copenhagen and Rome and in the countries of England, France, Italy, and South Africa. Architecture programs have been held in Italy, Finland, and Japan. New programs are developed regularly in these and other countries. A semester-long program is offered in Rome each year.

Academic Facilities

Founded as the first free library in Brooklyn, the Pratt Institute Library now has more than 176,674 bound volumes, 84,604 art books, 237 print and online art and art history journals, a rare book collection, and subscriptions to journals online through JSTOR, EBSCO, and others. The library also has serial backfiles and other material, including government documents; 251,603 audiovisual materials; and 3,996 microforms and subscribes to 925 periodicals—the largest collection of any independent art school. With their ID cards, Pratt students also have access to numerous college libraries in the metropolitan area. The Multi-Media Center has been developed to facilitate and improve the educational communication process by providing materials in multimedia formats to support and enrich the Institute's curricula. These include slides, ¾-inch videotapes, 16-mm films, audiocassettes, and other formats appropriate for group use.

Extensive studio and state-of-the-art computer lab facilities are provided for all Pratt students. In the School of Art and Design, these include studio, shop, and technical facilities for work in all media, from the traditional to the most experimental. Gallery space, both on campus and at Pratt Manhattan, is extensive, showing the work of students, alumni, faculty members, staff members, and other well-known artists, architects, and designers. The Pratt Center for Community Development functions as a laboratory for the study of planning and advocacy issues in real-world situations including sustainable planning.

Costs

Tuition for the 2011–12 academic year is $37,500. Room charges are $6530 per academic year. A meal plan is available, and costs about $3680 for the year. The fees are approximately $1480. The estimated cost of books and supplies is $3000 per academic year. Students should allow an additional $1800 for transportation and personal expenses. For an updated list of tuition and fees, prospective students should visit http://www.pratt.edu/admissions/financing_your_education/costs_and_budgeting.

Financial Aid

Pratt Institute offers a large number of merit-based scholarships, need-based grants, loans, and awards based on academic achievement, talent, financial need, or all three. More than 75 percent of Pratt students receive financial assistance through one or more of these kinds of aid. Through funds from the federal and state governments, contributions from Pratt alumni, and industry scholarships, Pratt is able to maintain generous financial aid program in a time of escalating costs.

Faculty

The faculty at Pratt Institute is exceptional in that a large number of practicing professionals augment the regular full-time faculty. There are 124 full-time and 908 part-time faculty members; there are no graduate teaching assistants. In small classes and studios, students have easy access to professors whose natural environment is the design studio, the architectural office, or the industrial research department. Faculty members often connect students with internships and eventually jobs.

Student Government

The Student Government Association (SGA) maintains primary responsibility for all student interests and involvement at Pratt. The SGA structure includes the Executive Committee, Senate, Finance Committee, Buildings and Grounds Committee, Academic and Administrative Affairs Committee, and Program Board. Student representatives serve on the Board of Trustees and on its various committees. All undergraduate students are encouraged to become involved in the SGA, whose main functions are allocating and administering funds collected through the student activities fee, scheduling student activities, and representing the student viewpoint to the rest of the Pratt community.

Admission Requirements

Pratt Institute attracts and enrolls highly motivated and talented students from diverse backgrounds. Applications are welcome from all qualified students, regardless of age, sex, race, color, religion, national origin, or handicap. Admission standards at Pratt are high. One of the major components for admission consideration in art, design, or architecture is the evaluation of a student's art or writing portfolio, which must be submitted along with the other required documents.

All applicants must submit official transcripts and one letter of recommendation from a guidance counselor or teacher. Additional professional requirements are specific to each school or major. Instructions can be found at http://www.pratt.edu/apply. Prospective students should select their level (freshman or transfer) and international students should also read the international requirements. Most disciplines at Pratt require a portfolio.

The admission committee bases its decisions on careful reviews of all credentials submitted by applicants in relation to the requirements of the program to which students seek admission. The SAT or ACT and a strong college-preparatory background are required of all applicants for four-year programs. International students must submit TOEFL or IELTS scores or SAT scores, but not both. In certain cases, an extraordinary talent may offset a low grade or a test score.

Application and Information

Pratt has two admissions deadlines: November 1 for early action and January 5 for regular admissions. To receive full consideration, students must submit their applications by January 5 for anticipated entrance in the fall semester and by October 1 for anticipated entrance in the spring semester.

For more information about Pratt Institute, students should contact:

Office of Admissions
Pratt Institute
200 Willoughby Avenue
Brooklyn, New York 11205
Phone: 718-636-3514
          800-331-0834 (toll-free)
E-mail: admissions@pratt.edu
Web site: http://www.pratt.edu
          http://on.fb.me/pratt_admissions (Facebook)
          http://www.pratt.edu/request (Catalog request)

PRESBYTERIAN COLLEGE
CLINTON, SOUTH CAROLINA

PC
PRESBYTERIAN COLLEGE

The College

Founded in 1880, Presbyterian College (PC) is a fully accredited Carnegie I, private four-year college of liberal arts and sciences. The College is widely known for its excellent academic program and congenial, friendly atmosphere. Thirty states and ten countries are represented in the student body of 1,188 men and women. PC is associated with the Presbyterian Church USA, and approximately 30 percent of the students are members of the Presbyterian Church. The College welcomes students of all faiths.

Extracurricular activities are an extensive and vital part of the development of all students. There are intercollegiate athletic teams competing in NCAA Division I (FCS) for men in baseball, basketball, cheerleading, cross-country, football, golf, soccer, and tennis and for women in basketball, cheerleading, cross-country, golf, lacrosse, soccer, softball, tennis, and volleyball. An extensive intramural program provides exercise and entertainment in a variety of sports for both men and women. The Student Union Board provides a series of concerts, comedians, films, and special events. Students may also participate in a variety of fine arts, Greek, honorary, political, preprofessional, and religious organizations. More than 70 percent of PC students volunteer for community service. The College sponsors thirty-eight service projects, including tutoring, adult literacy, Big Brother/Big Sister, Habitat for Humanity, and Special Olympics.

The 240-acre campus has thirty major buildings of classical Jeffersonian architecture. These buildings are grouped around three plazas. Facilities include a 1,200-seat auditorium, a 342-seat recital hall, a science center with a new state-of-the-art $12-million biology addition, a library, an art gallery, a drama theater, eleven residence halls (including a newly constructed international house, an apartment complex, and a town-house development), six major classroom buildings, a dining hall, a health center, a student center, a gymnasium, a six-house fraternity court, and a 31-acre intramural park.

Students may keep automobiles on campus. Ninety-five percent of students live in a College residence hall. All single students are required to live on campus. Housing within the community is available for married students and some seniors. All residence halls are wired for Internet access, and some areas are wireless.

Location

Clinton, with a population of 10,000, is a college town located in the heart of the South Carolina Piedmont. Interstates 26 and 385 meet outside of Clinton and provide easy access from the metropolitan areas of Greenville, Spartanburg, and Columbia. It is a short drive from Clinton to the ski slopes of western North Carolina, the coast of South Carolina, and professional athletic events in Charlotte, North Carolina.

Majors and Degrees

Presbyterian College offers the Bachelor of Arts and the Bachelor of Science degrees, with majors in art, biology, business/accounting, business/management, chemistry, computer science, early childhood education, economics, English, fine arts (concentrations in art, drama/speech, and music), French, German, history, mathematics, medical physics, middle school education, modern foreign languages, music, music education, philosophy, physics, political science, psychology, religion, religion–Christian education, sacred music, social science, sociology, Spanish, special education, and theater arts.

Students may minor in African American studies, arts administration, athletic coaching, Chinese studies, Christian youth work, international studies, journalism, Latin American studies, media studies, physical education, prelaw studies, secondary education teacher certification, Southern studies, women's studies, and each of the major areas.

Preprofessional programs are offered in allied health sciences, Army ROTC, dentistry, law, medicine, ministry, pharmacy, physician's assistant studies, and veterinary medicine. The College offers dual-degree programs in engineering with Auburn, Clemson, and Vanderbilt Universities. A dual-degree program in forestry and environmental science is available with Duke University.

Academic Programs

All Presbyterian College students gain a comprehension of the liberal arts through a general education in English, fine arts, history, mathematics, modern foreign language, physical education, religion, science, and social science. To graduate, students must complete the required general education courses, fulfill the requirements of a major, attend forty cultural enrichment events, and pass 122 semester hours with a minimum cumulative average of 2.0. Students are also required to have an internship or intercultural experience, as well as a Capstone Research Experience.

The College operates on a semester system. The fall semester extends from late August to mid-December, and the spring semester runs from mid-January through early May. Classes meet Monday through Friday. An optional Maymester enables students to travel and study with other PC students and staff members. Two 5-week summer sessions are also offered.

Directed study, honors seminars, honors research, summer research, internships, and independent research are offered through academic departments.

Students may earn credit by submitting scores from the College Board's Advanced Placement subject examinations. CLEP credit is granted for successful scores on the subject exams only. Credit is awarded to students in an International Baccalaureate program who have earned grades of 5 or better on higher-level subject tests.

An Army ROTC program is available with generous scholarship opportunities.

Off-Campus Programs

Presbyterian College offers a variety of programs for students who are interested in spending a semester, summer, or academic year studying abroad. The College is associated with fifty programs in Australia, Austria, China, England, Finland, France, Honduras, Ireland, Italy, Japan, Korea, Mexico, the Netherlands, New Zealand, Scotland, Spain, and Wales. Students may also study for a semester in Washington, D.C. All credits that are earned through these programs count toward graduation from Presbyterian College. Other study-abroad programs may be developed by the student and his or her adviser to ensure credit toward graduation.

Special courses are available for students during PC's optional Maymester. These for-credit courses provide students with off-campus educational experiences in Africa and Australia and such areas as the Caribbean, Europe, the Galapagos Islands, and southwestern United States.

Students have the opportunity to participate in a summer program at Oxford University's Corpus Christi College in England. This three-week course includes study of two subjects in addition to travel and field trips in England.

Presbyterian College is affiliated with the Gulf Coast Research Laboratory and Duke University's marine research center. Students may enroll in marine science courses during the academic year or summer.

Academic Facilities

The new $12-million biology wing, which opened in 2008, supports the College's growing premed program and increases research opportunities. Harrington-Peachtree Hall, PC's mathematics and social science building, contains psychology labs, classrooms with state-of-the-art audiovisual technology, and a computer lab. The Harper Center houses an art gallery and flexible theater. Other academic facilities include Richardson Science Hall, Neville Hall for the humanities, and Jacobs Hall for economics and military science. Thomason Library contains 165,000 volumes, provides extensive reference sources, and features a media learning center. Computer facilities are available in all major academic buildings, with more than 100 computer terminals available for students. Through the College, all students may have free access to the Internet and a Web-based e-mail system. Wireless Internet is available as well.

Costs

For the 2010–11 school year, the cost of tuition was $27,580. Fees were $2600. Room and board, with the seventeen-meal plan, were $8670. The cost of books, supplies, travel, and personal expenses was estimated at an additional $2500 per year.

Financial Aid

Presbyterian College endeavors to meet the financial need of all accepted students through scholarships, grants, loans, work-study, or a combination of these. The College may award academic, athletic, leadership, and music grants-in-aid to students with superior talent or achievement. Approximately 90 percent of the students receive some financial assistance each year. The Free Application for Federal Student Aid (FAFSA) and an institutional form are required of all financial aid applicants. For priority consideration, all financial aid information should be submitted by March 1 of a student's senior year. For further information, students should contact the Financial Aid Office at the College.

Faculty

Presbyterian College has a full-time faculty of 84 members. Ninety-five percent of the faculty members hold doctoral or terminal degrees in their field. The student-faculty ratio is 13:1. Students and instructors work closely together in both learning and counseling situations. All faculty members teach lower-division and freshman classes as well as upper-division courses. No graduate students serve as instructors at PC. Each student has an assigned faculty adviser for assistance in course selection and personal counseling.

Student Government

All Presbyterian College students are encouraged to fully participate in campus government. The Student Senate is composed of an executive council, the class representatives, and the organizational representatives. The duly elected Student Senate regulates the affairs of the student body, oversees the Student Union Board and student publications, and approves Honor Council membership.

The Honor Council enforces the College's Honor Code. All students pledge to enforce the honor system and to not lie, steal, cheat, or plagiarize. The honor system fosters a great deal of trust among students and faculty members. Professors may give unsupervised exams; students may leave possessions unattended. Representatives from the student body serve on administrative, faculty, and trustee committees.

Admission Requirements

Presbyterian College normally requires for entrance the completion of a four-year high school course of study, including 4 units of English, 3 units of math, and 2 or more units each of foreign language, history, laboratory science, and social science. It is strongly suggested that students take as many honors, AP, and IB courses as available.

Admission is very selective. Once a student applies, the admissions committee carefully reviews the application, essay, high school transcript, recommendation from a high school official, and scores from the SAT or the ACT. The College admits students based on the applicant's academic and personal qualifications. An interview is not required, but interested students are encouraged to visit the campus. Presbyterian College strives to recruit a diverse student body. The College does not discriminate against applicants or students on the basis of handicap, national origin, race, religion, or sex.

Transfer students must submit a transfer application, an essay, college and high school transcripts, board scores, and clearance forms. To be considered for admission, a transfer student must have a minimum overall C average in college work.

Application and Information

The paper application fee is $40, and the online application fee is $25; both are nonrefundable. Application deadlines are as follows: Early decision (binding) candidates must apply by November 1, are notified by December 1, and must commit to PC by January 15 by submitting a nonrefundable $400 deposit; early action (nonbinding) candidates must apply by November 15, are notified by December 15, and must submit a nonrefundable $400 deposit by May 1; regular decision deadline is February 1 and notification is on March 15, with commitment by May 1 by submitting the $400 nonrefundable deposit.

Students may apply electronically at the College's Web site or through the Common Application Web site at https://www.commonapp.org.

For further information, students should contact:

Presbyterian College
503 South Broad Street
Clinton, South Carolina 29325
Phone: 864-833-8230
       800-960-7583 (toll-free)
Fax: 864-833-8195
E-mail: admissions@presby.edu
Web site: http://www.presby.edu

The fountain plaza behind Neville Hall at dusk.

PROVIDENCE COLLEGE
PROVIDENCE, RHODE ISLAND

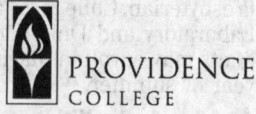

The College

Under the auspices of the Order of Preachers of the Province of St. Joseph, commonly known as the Dominicans, Providence College (PC) was established in 1917. Originally a college for men, it became co-educational in 1971. The College's full-time undergraduate enrollment is 3,850 students. Approximately 1,800 students live in nine residential halls and a suite-style residence facility, and an additional 900 upperclass students are housed in one of the five College apartment complexes. The remainder of the students live in apartments directly off campus or commute from home. At the graduate level, the College offers M.A., M.S., M.Ed., and M.B.A. degree programs.

The newly renovated Slavin Center, as the nucleus of student, social, cultural, and recreational activity, provides space for programs, informal social gatherings, and numerous facilities. It offers lounges; McPhail's Entertainment Facility; a dining facility; club offices; an ATM machine; a bookstore/gift shop; the Student Activities, Involvement, and Leadership Office (SAIL); and offices for the Student Congress, the Board of Programmers, student publications, and the Career Services Office.

The Concannon Fitness Center, a 23,000-square-foot, two-level, state-of-the-art facility, opened in September 2007. Emphasizing the College's commitment to health and fitness, the center offers eight types of cardiovascular machines, including eighteen treadmills, twelve cross-trainers, twelve arc-trainers, six upright bikes, and six recumbent bikes; all but six are equipped with cable TV. The center also offers fitness options, from selectorized strength pieces and cable motion pieces to numerous workout benches and free weights.

The Peterson Recreation Center is the site of intramural athletic activities on campus, which have one of the highest participation rates in the country. The center has five convertible basketball, tennis, and volleyball courts; a 220-yard track; three racquetball courts; a 25-meter pool; and an aerobics room. Providence College has a fine tradition of competition in intercollegiate athletics, and it continues to play an active role through its membership in the NCAA, Hockey East Conference, and the Big East Conference. Additional on-campus sports facilities include Alumni Hall, Schneider Arena, three large fields and recreational areas, and a new artificial-turf field for varsity, club, and intramural sports.

Location

The College is situated on a 105-acre campus in the city of Providence, Rhode Island. It has the advantages of an atmosphere that is far removed from the traffic and commerce of the metropolitan area but is also conveniently located near the many cultural attractions of a vibrant city that is not only the capital of a historic state but also the center of a variety of institutions of higher learning. Providence College has an established relationship with the Tony Award–winning Trinity Square Repertory Company, which is located in downtown Providence. Trinity provides special discount rates for students for the full spectrum of its programs. The Providence Performing Arts Center, which was originally a movie palace, has been restored to its former baroque splendor and now serves as the site of symphony concerts, opera, ballet, and road shows of Broadway musicals. In addition, the Dunkin' Donuts Center attracts well-known performers and rock groups, trade shows, and sports events. The center is also the home court of the Friars, PC's basketball team. A Providence College ID enables students to travel free on any RIPTA bus route throughout Rhode Island.

Majors and Degrees

Providence College offers bachelor's degrees in the School of Arts and Sciences, the School of Business, and the School of Professional Studies as detailed below.

School of Arts and Sciences: American studies, applied physics, art (studio), art history, biochemistry, biology, combined biology/optometry (3+4 program), chemistry, computer science, economics, business economics, quantitative economics, English: literature, English: creative writing, French, global studies, history, humanities, Italian, mathematics, music, music education (K–12), philosophy, political science, pre-engineering (3+2 program), psychology, public and community service studies, sociology, social science, Spanish, theater arts, theology, and women's studies.

School of Business: accountancy, finance, management, marketing, and a 4+1 M.B.A. program.

School of Professional Studies: health policy and management; social work; elementary/special education; and secondary education, with specializations in biology, chemistry, English, French, history, Italian, mathematics, physics, and Spanish.

Academic Programs

Providence College's motto consists of one word: "Veritas," the Latin word for truth. All teaching and learning at Providence begins with a belief in the truth—that faith and reason are compatible realities in the contemplation of truth, and that our greatest duty is to constantly seek it. All dimensions of the student experience are deeply rooted in the Dominican value of dynamic spirituality, with its concern for the whole person—mind and body, heart and soul—and respect for the gifts and uniqueness of every person. The College's programs are also designed to help students discover their particular aptitude and prepare them to undertake specialized studies leading to careers.

The rigorous core curriculum at Providence College, a values-centered examination of the traditional humanities curriculum, provides students of all majors with a well-balanced academic program. Through an in-depth immersion in the fundamental concepts and issues addressed by the social and natural sciences, literature, history, philosophy, mathematics, the fine arts, and theology, students learn to think critically and reason well. Demanding, exhilarating and memorable, the Development of Western Civilization program is the cornerstone of our core curriculum. It is one of the nation's most academically ambitious interdisciplinary programs which integrates the study of literature, history philosophy, theology, and the fine arts. Special academic programs are offered to enhance the educational experience and allow for a variety of interests, including double majors, individualized programs, nondepartmental courses, liberal arts honors, preprofessional medical and legal programs, the Early Identification Program (offered to Rhode Island residents in cooperation with Brown University Medical School), and Army ROTC.

The College participates in the Advanced Placement (AP) Program, which is administered by the College Board. Students who demonstrate superior performance (a score of 4 or 5) on any of the Advanced Placement examinations are considered for advanced-placement credit.

Providence College recognizes credit earned through the International Baccalaureate (I.B.), an internationally recognized curriculum and examination program. The College recognizes the Higher Level examinations when a score of 5, 6, or 7 has been achieved. Each examination that is successfully passed in the Higher Level of the I.B. program earns 3 credits.

Students who are granted AP or I.B. credit are still required to complete the College's full-time, eight-semester requirement.

PC operates on a two-semester calendar. Fall-semester classes begin in early September, and spring-semester classes begin in mid-January.

Off-Campus Programs

Providence College recognizes that a liberal arts education can be enriched through diverse intellectual and social experiences and encourages all of its students to study abroad. With a new Center for International Studies, there is renewed energy in the opportunities available for students to gain an international academic experience. Providence College is one of the few institutions to have study-abroad arrangements with both Oxford University and Cambridge University in England. Students may also study in Africa, Asia, Australia, New Zealand, Central and Latin America, Europe, and Russia. A few of the countries that are most popular among PC students are Spain, Italy, Ireland, and England. The Washington Semester is also an option for students, allowing them to enrich their education by spending one semester of academic study and experiential learning at American University in Washington, D.C.

Academic Facilities

The Phillips Memorial Library, which has received two national architectural awards for its design, is the center of intellectual activity at the College. PC's library is an electronic resource complete with radio-frequency technology, a wireless network, electronic classrooms, and the second-largest electronic database access in the state. The library has current holdings of 366,000 volumes in open stacks and seating accommodations for 750 students. Phillips Library also houses various faculty offices, reading and rare book rooms, archives, the Department of English, and the Office of Academic Services. The library is a member of the Consortium of Rhode Island Academic and Research Libraries, through which the resources of most of the libraries in the state are accessible to Providence College students. Located in Accinno Hall and Koffler Hall are the College's academic microcomputer laboratories, which serve the computer instruction and research needs of faculty members and students. The College's state-of-the-art science laboratories, computer workstations, and research facilities are located in the Albertus Magnus–Sowa–Hickey Science Complex. The Feinstein Academic Center is a newly renovated academic facility that is home to the Feinstein Institute for Public Service Program, the Liberal Arts Honors Program, and the Center for Teaching Excellence. The comprehensive new Smith Center for the Arts features a theater, a concert hall, a dance studio, a black-box theater, music practice rooms, and scenery and costume shops.

Costs

The total costs for the 2010–11 academic year were tuition, $38,610, and room and board, $11,780 (seven-day plan). Books, travel, and personal supplies were estimated to cost $800.

Financial Aid

Providence College's financial aid is distributed on the basis of demonstrated need and the student's ability to benefit from the educational opportunity the assistance offers. To apply for financial aid, candidates who are applying for Early Action must submit a College Scholarship Service PROFILE application by December 1 and the Free Application for Federal Student Aid (FAFSA) by February 1. Students applying for Regular Decision must submit both the College Scholarship Service PROFILE application and the FAFSA by February 1. Upon final determination of students' need, the Office of Financial Aid constructs aid packages consisting of work, loan, and grant assistance in accordance with federal regulations, the availability of funds, and institutional policy, as approved by the College's Financial Aid Advisory Committee. Sources of financial aid include Federal Work-Study Program awards, Federal Perkins Loans, Federal Pell Grants, Federal Supplemental Educational Opportunity Grants (FSEOG), Providence College grants-in-aid, Providence College Achievement Scholarships, and Merit Scholarships for highly qualified students.

Faculty

The faculty consists of 297 full-time professors and 96 special lecturers. The majority of PC instructors teach both undergraduate- and graduate-level courses; no graduate students or student assistants teach at either level. About 93 percent of the faculty members hold terminal degrees. Professors engage in advanced research, and frequently publish books and articles, but they are focused primarily on teaching and advising undergraduates; all students are assigned a faculty adviser in their major area. The student-faculty ratio is 11:1.

Student Government

The Student Congress represents the students in its emphasis upon lifestyles and student prerogatives. Its officers are elected annually by the entire student community, and representatives are elected by each class. The Student Congress has created the Providence College Bill of Rights, the most significant of its legislative actions. Student representatives are appointed annually by the Student Congress to all standing committees of the College. The Student Congress has primary responsibility for the allocation of $125,500 in student activity funds to support most student-run organizations.

Admission Requirements

The admission committee gives recognition to students with various talents, backgrounds, and geographic origins. Admission decisions are made without regard to race, color, sex, handicap, age, or national or ethnic origin. An estimate of the applicant's character and accomplishments by his or her college adviser in secondary school and an official transcript of the secondary school record should be sent to the College no later than November 1 for Early Action and January 15 for Regular Decision. The secondary school transcript should consist of courses of a substantially college-preparatory nature. Although individual cases may vary, the College highly recommends that a student complete 4 years of English; 4 of mathematics; 3 of one foreign language; 3 of science, with at least two laboratory courses; and 2 of social sciences. However, students who have been most competitive for admission in recent years have taken 4 years in all academic subject areas, taking advantage of honors or advanced-level courses that are available at their high school. Applicants are encouraged to submit letters of recommendation and evaluation from their secondary school teachers, especially from English teachers. Letters of recommendation from people who know the applicant personally and who have been involved in his or her scholastic development are most valuable.

Submission of standardized test scores is optional for students applying for admission. The academic review for admission at Providence College has always focused on each student's high school performance rather than standardized test results. This policy change allows each student to decide whether they wish to have their standardized test results considered as part of their application for admission. Students who choose not to submit SAT or ACT test scores are not penalized in the review for admission. Additional details about the test-optional policy can be found online at http://www.providence.edu/testoptionalpolicy.

Application and Information

As a member of the Common Application group, Providence College requires a completed Common Application as well as the Providence College Supplemental Form and an application fee of $55. The deadline for receiving freshman applications for the September term is November 1 for early action and January 15 for regular decision. The deadline for receiving freshman applications for the January term is December 1. The deadline for receiving transfer applications is April 1 for the fall term and December 1 for the spring term. Further information may be obtained by contacting:

Providence College
549 River Avenue
Providence, Rhode Island 02918-0001

Phone: 401-865-2535
      800-721-6444 (toll-free)
Fax: 401-865-2826
E-mail: pcadmiss@providence.edu
Web site: http://www.providence.edu

Harkins Hall, the administration building at Providence College.

PURCHASE COLLEGE,
STATE UNIVERSITY OF NEW YORK
PURCHASE, NEW YORK

The College

Enrolling just over 4,000 students, Purchase College is a selective public coeducational college that serves both residential and commuter students. A Purchase College education is founded upon a unique vision that combines the energy and excitement of professional training in the performing and the visual arts with the intellectual traditions and spirit of discovery of the sciences and the humanities. The College emphasizes creativity, individual accomplishment, openness, and exploration of the world. A student's education at Purchase College culminates in a senior project that serves as an excellent springboard to a career or advanced academic study.

Purchase students come from around the world, and nearly all of them share a love of imagination, originality, and new experiences. The mix of students in the liberal arts and sciences and the performing and visual arts contributes to a campus that is wide open to diversity in perspectives and ambitions. The intersection of the arts and liberal arts and sciences also fosters an appreciation of the contributions of both scholarly and artistic achievement to make a humane culture.

Founded in 1967, Purchase College has emerged and is increasingly recognized as a distinguished, imaginative, and dynamic institution for the study of the liberal arts and sciences and the visual and performing arts as well as for its service to the region and the state.

Purchase is primarily a full-time undergraduate institution, but as a public institution, Purchase College also promotes lifelong learning for students of all ages, backgrounds, and incomes through its School of Liberal Studies and Continuing Education, which offers a Bachelor of Arts in liberal studies as well as various credit and noncredit courses, certificate programs, and part-time degree programs.

In addition to its baccalaureate degrees, Purchase College also offers an M.F.A. in theater arts/stage design, visual arts, and dance and an M.A. in art history. The College also offers three postgraduate programs in music: Music Performance Certificate (one to two years of postbaccalaureate study), Master of Music, and Music Artist Diploma (one to two years of post-master's study).

Location

Built in the early 1970s on the 500-acre estate that was settled in 1734 by Judge Thomas Thomas, the Purchase campus combines the advantages of a semirural setting with proximity to the educational and cultural opportunities of Westchester County and New York City. As the only four-year public institution in Westchester, Purchase College is a cultural resource for the entire community. Approximately 250,000 people visit the campus each year to take advantage of its many programs and activities, including exhibits at the Neuberger Museum of Art, world-class performances at the Performing Arts Center, and public programs and lectures, such as the Royal and Shirley Durst Chair Lecture Series.

Majors and Degrees

Purchase College's liberal arts and sciences programs lead to Bachelor of Arts (B.A.) and Bachelor of Science (B.S.) degrees. The College offers a full range of disciplines in Humanities (art

history, cinema studies, creative writing, drama studies, history, journalism, language and culture, literature, and philosophy), Natural and Social Sciences (anthropology, biochemistry, biology, chemistry, economics, environmental studies, mathematics/computer science, political science, psychology, and sociology), and Film and Media Studies (cinema studies; media, society, and the arts; and new media). Students may also pursue arts management and premed or prelaw tracks. There are interdisciplinary programs in Asian studies, Latin American studies, lesbian and gay studies, and women's studies.

Purchase College offers professional conservatory training that leads to a Bachelor of Music degree; a Bachelor of Fine Arts (B.F.A.) degree in acting, dance, film, stage design/technology, or visual arts; and a B.A. in arts management or screen/playwriting.

Academic Programs

Purchase College operates on a semester calendar. Students typically take 16 credits per semester in order to fulfill the minimum requirement of 120 hours for a bachelor's degree as well as the SUNY-mandated general education requirements. Most liberal arts courses are 4 credits, as the College specializes in intensive study within the majors, and many courses include scheduled classwork in the arts, fieldwork, plenary sessions, and intensive tutorials.

Students in the liberal arts and sciences declare their major concentrations by the end of their sophomore year, electing intensive course work that builds toward their senior projects. The senior project represents a culmination of their four years at Purchase and can take the form of a research paper, presentation, or original expression of thought and research (e.g., a work of fiction, poetry, or art or a multimedia presentation). The curriculum in each major is organized to build on disciplinary expertise, research, and writing skills, starting with the freshman year and culminating in the senior project. Senior projects in natural sciences are often published or copublished with a faculty member.

The senior project is a solid foundation for graduate study, professional school, or a career. For many Purchase students, internships in agencies, businesses, and corporations are also an important part of their educational experience that often leads to full-time employment.

Purchase College has some of the few conservatory training programs for the arts within the State University of New York System. Much of this training is provided by instructors who are also practicing professionals. Proximity to New York City gives access to these professionals and their respective art worlds, establishing a valuable network of contacts for undergraduate students. Professional job placement begins at an early stage, with special assistance from the active career development office. For example, some students occasionally interrupt their study program to work with a professional dance company or with a professional filmmaker.

Academic Facilities

The College's extraordinary facilities include the first building in the United States designed exclusively for the study and performance of dance; a large science research center; The

Performing Arts Center and its five theaters; and the Neuberger Museum, which has an outstanding collection of modern American art. Both the center and the museum play central roles in the curriculum and the student experience. There is also an exceptionally well-equipped physical education building; an increasing number of multimedia and computer classrooms; and a 160,000-square-foot visual arts building.

Costs

For 2010–11, tuition for undergraduate in-state residents was $4970 for the academic year; it was $13,385 for out-of-state students. Room and board (dormitory double room and full meal plan) were about $10,000. Books and supplies were estimated at $2300. Costs are subject to change.

Financial Aid

Purchase College participates in all federal and state financial aid programs. All students who complete the Free Application for Federal Student Aid (FAFSA) receive some form of financial assistance, which may include low-interest student loans. It is strongly recommended that students file the FAFSA prior to April 1 in order to receive the maximum amount of financial aid for which they are eligible. Approximately 70 percent of all Purchase College undergraduates receive some type of financial assistance.

Scholarships based on merit only and scholarships based on both merit and need are available to qualified students.

Faculty

The Purchase College faculty is distinguished by depth of specialized knowledge as well as broad interdisciplinary interests, scholarly and professional activity, and dedication to undergraduate teaching. The liberal arts and sciences faculty includes prominent scholars in a variety of fields. More than 95 percent hold doctorates from prestigious schools, and several have won Guggenheim, Fulbright, NEH, and NEA awards, among others. The visual and performance arts faculty consists of leading teachers and practicing professionals in dance, film, music, theater, and visual arts.

Student Government

The Student Government Association, a campuswide organization, is made up of students elected by their peers. The organization is responsible for campus activities, sends representatives to faculty and administrative councils, and administers its own budget.

Admission Requirements

Applicants are considered by the Office of Admissions on an individual basis without regard to race, religion, geographic origin, or handicap. Major factors for admission consideration in the liberal arts and sciences programs are the high school and the academic records, including subjects studied, proficiency in English, test scores (SAT or ACT), and recommendations. All students write an application essay to demonstrate an appropriate fit with Purchase. The liberal arts program has become increasingly selective, and early application is encouraged. A rolling admission system is used, with selective deadlines in some programs.

In the visual and performing arts, students must demonstrate talent by means of an audition, interview, or portfolio review in addition to an assessment of their academic credentials. Because these programs are very competitive, early application is encouraged for both freshmen and transfers. Typically, auditions of conservatory candidates are completed by the end of March.

Application and Information

Students are urged to visit the campus for information sessions and open houses. For further information, students should contact:

Ms. Stephanie McCaine
Director of Admissions
Purchase College, State University of New York
735 Anderson Hill Road
Purchase, New York 10577-1400

Phone: 914-251-6300
Fax: 914-251-6314
E-mail: admission@purchase.edu
Web site: http://www.purchase.edu/admissions

A reason to cheer—graduation day at Purchase College.

QUEENS COLLEGE
OF THE CITY UNIVERSITY OF NEW YORK

FLUSHING, NEW YORK

The College

Queens College (QC), with more than 12,500 undergraduates, is one of the largest of the four-year colleges in the City University of New York (CUNY) system. The College opened its doors in 1937 with the goal of offering a first-rate education to talented people of all backgrounds and financial means. It enjoys a national reputation for its liberal arts and sciences and preprofessional programs. Students come from more than 150 different nations; the result is an unusually rich education that gives Queens College graduates a competitive edge in today's global society.

The 77-acre campus is lined with trees surrounding grassy open spaces and a traditional quad. Some of the original Spanish-style stucco and tile buildings from the early 1900s still stand, including Jefferson Hall, which houses the beautiful Welcome Center. Powdermaker Hall, the major classroom building, has state-of-the-art technology throughout, and the College's science labs recently underwent a $30-million renovation. The entire campus has Wi-Fi capability and students may relax and meet friends in the spacious Student Union and the College's many cafés, lounges, recreation, and dining areas.

With the opening of the College's first residence hall, The Summit, in August 2009, Queens College shed its commuter school identity. It now offers students the option of enjoying all the benefits of living on campus. The low-rise facility provides individually climate-controlled single- and double-room accommodations arranged in suites with shared kitchen and lounge areas. It also has its own exercise facility.

The administration remains dedicated to making its many commuter students feel that QC is their home away from home. The professionally staffed Child Development Center offers inexpensive child-care services to students with children. There are more than 100 clubs on campus, from the Accounting Honors Society and Alliance of Latin American Students to clubs for theater, fencing, environmental science, science fiction, and the fine arts. The only CUNY college that participates in Division II sports, Queens sponsors nineteen men's and women's teams and has some of the finest athletics facilities in the metropolitan area. Ongoing cultural events include readings by renowned authors such as Margaret Atwood, Toni Morrison, and Jonathan Franzen; concerts, theater, and dance performances by world-famous artists. QC is also home to the Godwin-Ternbach Museum, the only comprehensive museum in the borough of Queens, with art from antiquity to the present.

The College's centers and institutes serve students and the larger urban community by addressing society's most important challenges—such as cancer, AIDS, pollution, and racism—and exploring the heritages of the borough's many ethnic communities, including Asians, Greeks, Italians, and Jews.

Queens College has had a chapter of Phi Beta Kappa since 1950 (less than 10 percent of U.S. liberal arts colleges are members of Phi Beta Kappa, the nation's oldest and most respected undergraduate honors organization). In 1968, Queens College became a member of Sigma Xi, the national science honor society. The American Association of University Women includes Queens College in its list of approved colleges for membership.

Location

Queens College, located off Exit 24 of the Long Island Expressway, is in a residential area of Flushing and is easily accessible by public transportation. It is only 20 minutes from Manhattan, whose magnificent skyline overlooks the campus quad.

Majors and Degrees

The Bachelor of Arts degree is awarded in accounting, Africana studies, American studies, anthropology, art, art history, biology, Byzantine and modern Greek studies, chemistry, Chinese, communication arts and media, communication sciences and disorders, comparative literature, computer science, drama and theater, East Asian studies, economics, education (early childhood and elementary), English, environmental sciences, environmental studies, film studies, French, geology, German, Greek, Hebrew, history, home economics, Italian, Jew-

ish studies, labor studies, Latin, Latin American area studies, linguistics, mathematics, music, neuroscience, philosophy, physics, political science and government, psychology, Russian, sociology, Spanish, studio art, theater-dance, urban studies, and women's studies.

The Bachelor of Arts program in secondary school teaching includes the following subject areas: Africana studies, anthropology, biology, chemistry, economics, English, French, geology, German, history, Italian, Latin American area studies, mathematics, physics, political science and government, sociology, Spanish, and urban studies.

The College also awards the Bachelor of Arts in interdisciplinary studies; an individualized Bachelor of Arts program; the Bachelor of Business Administration; the Bachelor of Fine Arts in studio art; the Bachelor of Music in instrumental or vocal performance studies; and the Bachelor of Science in applied social science, computer science, environmental sciences, geology, graphic design, nutrition and exercise sciences, and physical education.

The Departments of Chemistry, Computer Science, Philosophy, Physics, and Political Science and the Aaron Copland School of Music offer qualified undergraduates the opportunity to take combined bachelor's and master's degree programs.

Pre-engineering students can take advantage of a 3-2 transfer program through the physics department that offers admission to Columbia University after three years at QC. Following two years at Columbia, students graduate with a B.A. in physics from Queens and an engineering B.A. from Columbia.

Special interdisciplinary programs include Africana studies, American studies, business and liberal arts, business administration, Byzantine and modern Greek studies, Honors in Mathematics and Natural Sciences, Honors in the Humanities, Honors in the Social Sciences, Irish studies, Italian American studies, journalism, Latin American and Latino studies, and religious studies. Special programs and advisement are also available in accounting, pre-engineering, prelaw, and the pre–health professions.

Academic Programs

Queens College awards bachelor's and master's degrees in the arts and humanities, education, mathematics and the natural sciences, and social sciences. Certificate programs provide additional training in specialties in education, library science, and psychology. QC also participates in doctoral programs overseen by CUNY's graduate center; many of these programs involve lab work or clinical studies conducted on the Flushing campus.

Honors programs are central to the College's tradition of value and excellence, enhancing education by providing opportunities for faculty mentorship, advanced research, or other individualized projects. These programs create a community of learners in which students enjoy small classes, while still having access to QC's many resources and diverse student body. The emphasis is on discussion and projects rather than lectures.

Queens College is the only CUNY institution in the borough participating in the Macaulay Honors College, which supports gifted students with full tuition, a free laptop, a $7500 grant over four years, and other benefits. A flagship program of the University, it provides an enhanced undergraduate education to academically gifted students. Since its inauguration in 2001, the Honors College has grown rapidly, drawing on the unique resources of CUNY and New York's cultural, scientific, government, and business communities to provide its students with a broad-based and challenging liberal arts education.

In addition, QC has its own multidisciplinary Freshman Honors Program and divisional honors programs in the humanities, math and natural sciences, and social sciences. Outstanding high school seniors may apply to become Queens College scholars. Prospective math teachers may qualify for scholarships and other incentives through QC's innovative math education program, TIME 2000. Business and Liberal Arts—designed for top-performing underclassmen regardless of their major—familiarizes students with basic business disciplines and offers internships sponsored by participating corporations.

The wide range of majors and interdisciplinary studies, combined with the award-winning Freshman Year Initiative program, encourages students to explore their interests and abilities to the fullest. In most cases, degree programs require the completion of 120 credits.

The Bachelor of Business Administration (B.B.A.) degree provides a solid business education that responds to the demand of employers for specific quantitative and technological skills. Students may choose from three majors: finance, international business, and actuarial studies. The B.B.A. also has an investments/chartered financial analyst track to prepare students for the CFA examination, the only such undergraduate program in New York.

Study-abroad opportunities range from relatively short summer and winter intersession courses to programs that last a semester or two. Exchange programs allow Queens College students to study for up to a year in Canada, France, Italy, or Japan, as well as other parts of the United States.

The Adult Collegiate Education program, offered to students 25 and older, includes the option of obtaining college credit for life achievement. The Weekend College allows busy students to pursue their degrees by taking classes on Saturdays and Sundays.

Academic Facilities

Among the many centers where research and creativity are joined in the pursuit of knowledge is the Kupferberg Center for the Visual and Performing Arts, which brings together the College's academic departments in the arts (music, drama, art, and media studies), and its museums (the Godwin-Ternbach, the Queens College Art Center, and the Louis Armstrong House Museum). The center's venues include the 2,200-seat Colden Auditorium; the Goldstein Theatre, designed especially for the staging of experimental student productions; and the Aaron Copland School of Music facility, which includes thirty-five practice rooms and the 491-seat LeFrak Concert Hall. The College is also home to the Gertz Center, which investigates communication disabilities and provides clinical experience for students of speech and hearing therapy.

Queens College administers the historic Louis Armstrong House Museum in Corona with its vast personal collection of Armstrong photographs, papers, recordings, and memorabilia that draws scholars and jazz fans from around the world. The Benjamin Rosenthal Library, with its soaring, light-filled atrium and art center, has more than 1 million print and electronic volumes.

Costs

For New York State residents, undergraduate tuition is $2415 per semester. For out-of-state and international students, undergraduate tuition is $435 per credit. In addition to tuition, there are various expenses each semester, such as student activity and technology fees.

Financial Aid

More than 50 percent of Queens College students receive need-based financial aid. The aid may include state and federal loans and grants, Tuition Assistance Program awards, Regents Scholarships, Federal Direct Student Loans, Federal Pell Grants, State Aid for Native Americans, and Federal Work-Study Program awards.

The Queens College Scholars Program offers a variety of merit-based scholarships to full-time freshmen, with awards of $2400 per year. Selection is competitive, and scholarships are awarded on the basis of the high school record, test scores (SAT and SAT Subject Tests), writing ability, letters of recommendation, and extracurricular activities. Scholarships are renewable with continued high academic achievement. Applicants who rank in or near the top 10 percent of their class and have a rigorous academic program, excellent grades, and minimum combined SAT (critical reading and math) scores of 1250 are encouraged to apply. The application deadline is December 1.

Faculty

The Queens College faculty consists of top scholars who are dedicated to teaching and research, and enjoy working in a diverse urban environment. Many are relatively new to campus; half were hired between 2002 and 2008. There are 636 full-time professors, almost 90 percent of whom have the terminal degree in their fields (not all fields offer doctorates); 65 percent have tenure. Many also teach in the doctoral programs at the CUNY Graduate Center. Faculty members have received numerous fellowships, awards, and research grants from such prestigious organizations as the National Science Foundation and the National Institutes of Health. In recent years, faculty members received two Guggenheim awards and two Fulbright grants. CUNY has recognized the excellence of the faculty by honoring 11 members with the title of Distinguished Professor in fields as diverse as chemistry, economics, English, history, and physics. Among the more widely known faculty members are scientist Steven Markowitz; historian Morris Rossabi; sociologist Stephen Steinberg; and poets Jeffrey Renard Allen, Nicole Cooley, and Kimiko Hahn.

Student Government

Through the Student Association, students at Queens run many services and activities that influence the daily operations of the College. Its elected officers and senators poll students regularly about relevant topics and sponsor such services as free legal advice, apartment and tutor referral, and voter registration. In addition, students constitute one third of the College's Academic Senate.

Admission Requirements

Queens College seeks to admit freshmen who have completed a strong college-preparatory program in high school with at least a B+ average. Admission is based on a variety of factors, including the applicant's high school grades, academic program, and SAT or ACT scores. Successful candidates have chosen a well-rounded program of study that includes academic course work in English (4 years), foreign language (3 years), math (3 years), lab science (2 years), and social studies (4 years).

The Search for Education, Elevation & Knowledge Program (SEEK) offers academic support, counseling, and financial assistance to motivated students who would not otherwise qualify for admission. The SEEK Program has its own admissions criteria, including financial need.

For earliest consideration, students should apply by January 1 for fall admission and by September 15 for spring admission.

Application and Information

The staff of the Undergraduate Office of Admissions is available to answer questions and give more information. To make an appointment for a tour or to meet with a counselor, students should contact:

Office of Admissions
Jefferson Hall
Queens College of the City University of New York
65-30 Kissena Boulevard
Flushing, New York 11367-1597
Phone: 718-997-5600
E-mail: admissions@qc.edu
Web site: http://www.qc.cuny.edu
http://on.fb.me/QueensColl_CUNY (Facebook)
http://twitter.com/QC_News
http://bit.ly/YouTube_CUNY-QC (YouTube)
http://bit.ly/itunes_CUNY-QC (iTunes)

A view of the Queens College quad, part of a 77-acre campus in New York City, where students from more than 150 nations receive a solid education for today's global society.

QUINNIPIAC UNIVERSITY

HAMDEN, CONNECTICUT

The University

Quinnipiac offers four-year and graduate-level degree programs leading to careers in health sciences, business, communications, natural sciences, education, liberal arts, and law. A curriculum that combines a career focus with a globally oriented liberal arts background prepares graduates for the future, whether they start their careers right after commencement or opt to pursue advanced study.

Quinnipiac is coeducational and nonsectarian and currently enrolls 5,859 full-time undergraduates, 1177 full-time graduate and law students, and 1130 part-time students in its undergraduate, graduate, professional, and continuing education programs. Twenty-five percent of the students are residents of Connecticut; the rest represent primarily the northeast corridor, in all a total of twenty-eight states and several countries. Quinnipiac is big enough to sustain a wide variety of people and programs but small enough to keep students from getting lost in the shuffle. Life on campus emphasizes students' personal, as well as academic, growth. The approximately eighty student organizations and extracurricular activities, including intramural and intercollegiate (NCAA Division I) athletics, give students a chance to exercise their talents, muscles, and leadership skills. The University has a student newspaper, TV station, and an FM radio station (WQAQ) and twenty-one intercollegiate teams in men's baseball, basketball, cross-country, ice hockey, lacrosse, soccer, and tennis, and in women's acrobatics and tumbling, basketball, cross-country, field hockey, golf, ice hockey, lacrosse, soccer, softball, tennis, track (indoor and outdoor), and volleyball. Teams compete in the Northeast Conference (NEC); men's and women's ice hockey teams are members in the ECAC.

The University has three distinct campus settings. The 250-acre Mount Carmel campus has fifty buildings including the Arnold Bernhard Library, academic facilities, an athletic and recreation center, and twenty-five residence halls of different styles, mainly for freshmen and sophomores, with traditional double and quad (4-person) rooms, suites, and multilevel suites with kitchens. About 95 percent of all freshmen and 75 percent of the total undergraduate population live in Quinnipiac housing. The nearby 250-acre York Hill campus includes the TD Bank Sports Center with twin 3,500-seat arenas for ice hockey and basketball; a new suite-style 1,800-bed residence halls for juniors and seniors; a lodge-like student center; spectacular views; and a multilevel parking garage for 2,000 vehicles. Seniors may also live in University-owned houses or apartments. Just 4 miles away is the 104-acre North Haven campus with state-of-the-art facilities for graduate and upper division offerings in several programs of the Schools of Health Sciences and Education. All four buildings in the facility have been acquired from Anthem Blue Cross and there are plans for phased expansion for additional graduate programs as well as a School of Medicine (proposed opening 2013–14).

The Athletic and Recreation Center includes a 24,000-square-foot recreation/fitness facility with a large free-weight room; an exercise machine center; aerobics studios; basketball, volleyball, and tennis courts; and a suspended indoor track. There are also lighted tennis courts, playing fields, and miles of scenic routes for running and biking.

Career Planning takes place in each of the schools with assistance from the deans' offices in health sciences, communications, education, business, and the college of arts and sciences. It begins with faculty advisement, along with career exploration, a strong focus on internships and clinical placements, exploration of various major and job fields, and exposure to prospective employers and job preparation. Approximately 30 percent of the undergraduate student population remains at Quinnipiac for their graduate degree in combined or direct entry majors, particularly in education, business, physical and occupational therapy, and physician assistant programs.

Graduate programs lead to the Master of Science degree in accounting, information technology systems, interactive communications, journalism, molecular and cell biology, organizational leadership, public relations, and teacher leadership; the Master of Health Science in medical lab sciences, cardiovascular perfusion, pathologist assistant studies, and physician assistant studies; and scheduled to begin soon,

a Doctor of Nursing Practice in adult and family nursing; the Master of Business Administration; the Master of Business Administration in Health Care Management, the Master of Business Administration–Chartered Financial Analyst, and the Master of Arts in Teaching. The Quinnipiac University School of Law offers full-time and part-time programs leading to a J.D. degree or J.D./M.B.A. degree in combination with the School of Business. Several of the graduate degree programs are offered online or in a hybrid format.

Location

Situated at the foot of Sleeping Giant Mountain in Hamden, Connecticut, Quinnipiac provides the best of the suburbs and the city. The University is only 8 miles from New Haven, 30 minutes from Hartford (the state capital), and less than 2 hours from New York City and Boston. Bordering the campus is the 1700-acre Sleeping Giant State Park, for walking and hiking. The free campus shuttle takes students to shopping and restaurants in nearby Hamden and North Haven, plus to New Haven, where they can visit the acclaimed Yale Center for British Art, attend a performance at the Schubert or Long Wharf Theater (which hosts productions by Quinnipiac's Theater Department), find great restaurants, and have easy access to Metro North and Amtrak at the New Haven train station.

Majors and Degrees

The School of Health Sciences grants bachelor's degrees in athletic training/sports medicine, biomedical science, diagnostic imaging, microbiology/molecular biology, nursing, occupational therapy (5½-year entry-level master's), physical therapy (6- or 7-year entry-level doctorate), and physician assistant studies (6-year freshman entry-level master's). Students who wish to prepare for entry into medical, dental, chiropractic, veterinary, or other medical schools work with a premed adviser and take classes that prepare them to sit for the various entrance exams.

The School of Business (accredited by AACSB International) offers bachelor's degree programs in accounting, advertising, biomedical marketing, entrepreneurship, finance, computer information systems, international business, management, and marketing. The school also offers a fast-track, five-year combined-degree program in which students may be awarded the B.S. degree in business and a graduate degree in accounting, business administration, or computer information systems (M.S. or M.B.A.).

The College of Arts and Sciences offers bachelor's degree programs in biochemistry, biology, chemistry, computer science, criminal justice, English, gerontology, history, interactive digital design, legal studies (paralegal), liberal studies, mathematics, political science, psychobiology, psychology, social services, sociology, Spanish, and theater. Students can also design their own majors. Students can also continue their study in graduate programs in business, law, journalism, or interactive communications.

The School of Communications offers undergraduate majors in communications/media studies; film, video, and interactive media; journalism; and public relations; and graduate programs in journalism, public relations, and interactive communications.

The School of Education's five-year program for undergraduates provides certification for teaching elementary and secondary grades through a B.A./Master of Arts in Teaching (M.A.T.) program (accredited by NCATE).

Academic Programs

All degree programs at Quinnipiac University are offered through one of the five academic schools. The academic year consists of two 15-week fall and spring semesters and two summer sessions. All baccalaureate candidates are required to complete the University Curriculum, which consists of up to 46 of the 120 semester hours of credit generally needed for graduation at the bachelor's degree level. The foundation of the University Curriculum is three university seminars, which focus on the broad theme of community: individual, national, and global in scope. The Writing Across the Curriculum initiative (WAC) stresses the improvement in writing skills in all subject areas.

The University honors program addresses the needs and interests of the most academically talented and committed students. Academically talented students are identified during the admission process and are invited to participate in the University honors program. Approximately 60 full-time freshmen enter the honors program each fall.

Advanced placement, credit, or both are given for appropriate scores on Advanced Placement tests and CLEP general and subject examinations as well as for scores of 4 or higher in the International Baccalaureate higher-level subjects.

Off-Campus Programs

Students can study abroad in a variety of countries. Most students choose a study-abroad option in their sophomore year. Students in any of the five undergraduate schools can also get hands-on experience in their field through off-campus internships. Academic credit is available for internships and affiliations, which are often part of degree requirements.

Academic Facilities

Academic life focuses on the Bernhard Library. This attractive facility provides individual carrels and small rooms for group study and is open 24/7 during the fall and spring semesters. A wireless network provides access to automated library systems and extensive Web-based resources.

Quinnipiac University was identified as one of the top ten most-wired campuses in the country by *PC Magazine* in January 2007. All incoming students must bring or purchase a University-recommended laptop. An information technology desk offers support to the laptop program.

The multimedia and video laboratories in the Ed McMahon Mass Communications Center each have the latest Mac workstations and software. The computer cluster in the Financial Technology Center at the School of Business is a high-tech, simulated trading floor providing students with the opportunity to access real-time financial data, conduct interactive trading simulations, and develop financial models in preparation for careers in finance.

The Lender School of Business has satellite capabilities and the Ed McMahon Mass Communications Center, and contains a state-of-the-art, fully digital, high-definition TV production studio; audio production, print journalism, and desktop publishing laboratories; and a news technology center.

The Graduate and Health Sciences Center on the North Haven campus provides state-of-the-art facilities for the health sciences programs in diagnostic imaging, nursing, occupational therapy, physical therapy, physician assistant studies, and radiologist assistant studies. In addition to a breathtaking location and expansive exterior and interior spaces, there are specialized facilities and equipment for the various health sciences disciplines, such as movement study/motion analysis and biomechanics labs; the ergonomics and assistive technology lab; a model adaptive apartment; orthopedics lab; several rehabilitative sciences labs; CT scan, MRI, radiography, ultrasound, and mammography facilities; and the latest clinical skills simulation labs for adults and pediatric/neonatal patients including an intensive care unit, physical diagnosis lab, physical exam suite, and health assessment labs, which duplicate care in an outpatient primary care setting.

Costs

The basic 2010–11 cost was $46,980, of which tuition and fees (12–16 credits per semester) were $34,250, and room and board averaged $12,730. Other expenses, estimated at $2000 per year, included books, laboratory, and course fees associated with specific courses, and personal travel expenses.

Financial Aid

Quinnipiac designs financial aid packages to include need-based grants and merit-based scholarships that do not have to be repaid, plus self-help financial aid programs such as federal and University-based work study, and loans. Students and families seeking need-based aid will file the College Scholarship Service's Financial Aid PROFILE plus the Free Application for Federal Student Aid (FAFSA) to determine need. Transfer students are eligible for the same need-based financial aid consideration as first-time freshmen.

Faculty

The faculty is characterized by its teaching competence and outstanding academic qualifications. Of the 308 full-time faculty members, 85 percent have earned a Ph.D. or the appropriate terminal degree in their field. The faculty also includes a number of part-time teachers who are practicing professionals and experts in their fields. Classes are taught by these scholars and professionals and not by student instructors, and a low student-faculty ratio promotes close associations among faculty members and students.

Student Government

The Student Government is the student legislative body of Quinnipiac. It represents student opinion, promotes student welfare, supervises student organizations, appropriates funds for student groups, and provides voting student representation on the Board of Trustees.

Admission Requirements

Quinnipiac seeks students from a broad range of backgrounds. On average, freshman students have a 3.4 GPA or better average in college preparatory courses (transfer students generally have a 2.5 GPA or better), rank in the top 25 percent of their high school class, and have an average combined score of 1120 on the SAT (critical reading plus math). Visits to the campus for either an interview, open house, group information session, or a campus tour are strongly encouraged. Transfer students are welcome to make an appointment to discuss requirements and the transfer of credit from previous institutions. Quinnipiac sponsors four open house programs during the year and several Saturday morning information sessions followed by a campus tour.

Application and Information

Quinnipiac generally receives between 15,000 and 17,000 applications for admission and admits about 60 percent, to enroll an incoming class of 1,700 freshmen and 200 transfer students. Quinnipiac has a rolling admission policy for its undergraduate programs and therefore recommends that freshman applicants submit their application materials starting early in the fall of their senior year and well before the deadline of February 1. Students applying to the physical therapy, nursing, and physician assistant studies programs should submit their applications by November 1. Applications begin to be reviewed as soon as they are complete, and the University begins notifying students of decisions in early January. For most programs, a completed application consists of a Quinnipiac application form; a transcript of completed high school courses, including grades for the first quarter of the senior year; a score report for either the SAT or ACT; a personal statement (250-word minimum essay); letter(s) of recommendation; and an application fee of $45. Quinnipiac is a member of the Common Application and recommends that applications be submitted online. Students placed on a waiting list are notified of any openings by June 1. When reviewing applications, the University uses the results of the critical reading and the mathematics sections of the SAT and/or the composite score on the ACT for admission and scholarship purposes. Transfer students must forward a transcript of college course work undertaken. Quinnipiac subscribes to the May 1 Candidates Reply Date Agreement. For information about full-time undergraduate study, students should contact:

Office of Undergraduate Admissions
Quinnipiac University
Hamden, Connecticut 06518-1940

Phone: 203-582-8600
      800-462-1944 (toll-free)
Fax: 203-582-8906
E-mail: admissions@quinnipiac.edu
Web site: http://www.quinnipiac.edu
     http://www.facebook.com/QuinnipiacUniversity
     http://twitter.com/QU_Admissions
     http://quadmissions.blogspot.com/
     http://www.youtube.com/quinnipiacuniversity
     http://www.quinnipiac.edu/rss.xml

For information regarding transfer and part-time study:

Office of Transfer and Part-time Admissions
Quinnipiac University
Hamden, Connecticut 06518-1940

Phone: 203-582-8612
Fax: 203-582-8906
E-mail: transferadmissions@quinnipiac.edu

RAMAPO COLLEGE OF NEW JERSEY

MAHWAH, NEW JERSEY

The College

Ramapo College of New Jersey is a comprehensive institution of higher education dedicated to the promotion of teaching and learning within a strong liberal arts–based curriculum, thus becoming known as New Jersey's public liberal arts college. Its curricular emphases include the liberal arts and sciences, social sciences, fine and performing arts, and professional programs, all within a residential and sustainable living and learning environment.

The College provides academic excellence through its four mission pillars: an interdisciplinary curriculum, international education, intercultural understanding, and experiential learning opportunities.

Ramapo College provides students with individual academic attention and social support within a caring, sensitive, and intellectually vigorous community. The College provides service and leadership opportunities for students and faculty through a combination of internships, field placements, community service, study abroad, and cooperative education. These opportunities allow students, faculty and staff to encounter the world beyond the campus.

In the 2010–11 academic year, over 6,000 students were enrolled. The average class size is 23 students, evidence of institutional commitment to teaching and learning. Ramapo College is committed to maintaining strength and opportunity through diversity of age, race, gender, sexual orientation, ethnicity, and economic background among faculty, staff, and students. The College is a selective institution committed to providing equal access to underrepresented populations. Barrier-free, the College maintains a continuing commitment to persons with disabilities.

Ramapo College provides a rich living and learning environment through more than 100 student organizations, Greek life, intramural sports, and Division III intercollegiate athletics. Housing is guaranteed for four years for incoming freshmen and offered to transfer students on a limited basis. A variety of dining options are available for residential and commuting students.

The College has consistently been recognized by third parties for its educational excellence. It is currently ranked as a Best Value College by *Kiplinger's Personal Finance*, a Best Northeastern College by the Princeton Review, and was fourth in the Best Regional Universities–North public category by *U.S. News & World Report*. Ramapo College is accredited by the Middle States Association of Colleges and Schools. The Anisfield School of Business is internationally accredited by the prestigious Association to Advance Collegiate Schools of Business (AACSB). Other accreditations include the Council on Social Work Education (CSWE), American Chemical Society (ACS), National League for Nursing Accrediting Commission (NLNAC), and Teacher Education Accreditation Council (TEAC).

Ramapo College also offers graduate programs including the Master of Science in Nursing, Master of Arts in Sustainability Studies, Master of Arts in Liberal Studies, Master of Arts in Educational Leadership, and Master of Science in Educational Technology.

Location

Ramapo College is located in suburban Mahwah, New Jersey. The campus is set on approximately 300 wooded acres with a stunning mountain backdrop. While these surroundings are tranquil, the campus is just 25 miles from the cultural and professional opportunities of New York City.

Majors and Degrees

Ramapo College offers programs of study leading to the Bachelor of Arts degree in American studies, Africana studies, communication arts, contemporary arts, economics, environmental studies, history, international business, international studies, law and society, literature, music, political science, psychology, social science, sociology, Spanish language studies, theater, and visual arts. The Bachelor of Science degree is awarded in accounting, allied health, biochemistry, bioinformatics, biology, biology/physical therapy track, biology/physician assistant track, business administration (including finance, management, and marketing), chemistry, clinical laboratory sciences, computer science, engineering physics, environmental science, information systems, integrated science studies, mathematics, and psychology. The Bachelor of Social Work and Bachelor of Science in Nursing degrees are also offered.

Ramapo also offers state-approved teacher education programs to train and certify elementary and secondary education teachers.

Academic Programs

Each course at Ramapo is offered through one of five academic schools: the Anisfield School of Business, American and International Studies, Contemporary Arts, Social Science and Human Services, and Theoretical and Applied Science. Each student is associated with one of these schools while at Ramapo. This association brings the student in contact with others who have the same or similar academic interests and provides the student with easy access to academic advisement and to the courses needed to satisfy degree requirements.

Academic Facilities

The campus features new and upgraded facilities that enhance all areas of campus life, including a library with electronic research facilities; a student life building with FM radio station, student offices, cafeteria, and entertainment and meeting rooms; housing for over 3,000 students; and modern academic buildings with 24-hour computer labs and the real-time Global Financial Market Trading Laboratory. The Angelica and Russ Berrie Center for Performing and Visual Arts offers Shakespearean and Broadway theaters, fine arts studios, art galleries, photography suite, and new music recording studio. The Bill Bradley Sports and Recreation Center features a 1,500-seat arena, fitness center, 25-meter pool, climbing wall, jogging track, and locker room facilities. Other key campus facilities include the Salameno Spirituality Center, established in 2009; the Marge Roukema Center for International Education and Entrepreneurship; and the Sharp Sustainability Center. Upcoming construction to create the Adler Center for Nursing Excellence is designed to add new, technologically advanced microbiology labs, classrooms, and student lounge and study areas.

Costs

Undergraduate tuition and tuition-related fees are calculated on a flat rate for full-time (12 or more credits) students. Full-time charges are calculated on a flat rate for 12–19 credits. The flat rate amount is based on 16 credits. If a full-time student takes more than 19 credits, the charges are calculated on the flat rate plus the per credit rate.

For the 2010–11 academic year, the costs per credit rate/semester flat rate were: $243.90/$5936.80 (in-state students); $487.80/$9839.20 (out-of-state students); and $365.85/$7888 (qualified Rockland County College graduates).

Financial Aid

Most financial aid is awarded on the basis of a student's financial need. To qualify for aid at Ramapo, students must complete the Free Application for Federal Student Aid (FAFSA). A student should apply for financial aid prior to March 1 to receive preferential consideration. Federal Perkins Loans, Federal Pell Grants, and Federal Work-Study Program funds are vital parts of the College financial aid program. New Jersey residents should also apply for a state-supported tuition-aid grant. In addition, Ramapo College offers scholarships for high-achieving incoming freshman students. Merit awards are offered for eight semesters as long as the student maintains the required grade point average. New student applicants are automatically considered for these scholarships provided they apply by December 15. Continuing students not receiving an initial scholarship award may apply for additional merit awards based on their academic achievement at the College through the Ramapo College Foundation.

Faculty

Ramapo College has 434 full- and part-time faculty members as of fall 2010, of whom 95 percent hold a doctoral or terminal degree. Faculty members have been recruited principally for their effectiveness as teachers of undergraduate students. Their graduate research training—from Ivy League institutions, from the great state universities of the nation, and from universities abroad—as well as their professional experience indicate that faculty members possess high quality and diverse experience in the subject matter of their courses. No courses at Ramapo College are taught by teaching assistants.

Student Government

There is an active student government elected each spring. The group meets on a weekly basis to discuss any issues that it feels affect the welfare of the student body. Executive officers of the student government meet regularly with the College president and other College administrators. Each year students elect a student trustee and student trustee alternate to serve on the Board of Trustees. A liaison is also elected to the College's Board of Governors. Members of the student government serve on various college-wide committees and are true representatives of the student body.

Ramapo College also has over 100 student organizations and twenty-six Greek organizations that are supported by the Office of Student Development. All students are encouraged to visit the club fairs held each semester to learn more and become involved.

Admission Requirements

High school seniors generally are expected to have completed a minimum of 18 academic units (although most have more), distributed as follows: 4 units of English, 3 units of social studies/history, 3 units of mathematics (including algebra, algebra II, and geometry), 3 units of science (including 3 of laboratory science), 2 units of a foreign language, and 3 units of academic electives. In addition, students applying from high school must take the SAT or the ACT and have their test scores sent to Ramapo.

The College hosts open house programs during the fall and spring that give students and their families the opportunity to learn about academic programs, admissions, and financial aid; to meet faculty and staff members and students; and to tour the campus. Students are encouraged to visit during these special events. Weekday tours of the campus are available as well and personal interviews are available during the Immediate Decision Days in the fall. Interested students should contact the Office of Admissions at 201-684-7300 or 7301, or visit http://www.ramapo.edu for further details about campus visits.

Application and Information

Applications for freshmen, international, EOF and transfer admission are available at www.ramapo.edu/admissions/apply.html. Paper applications are available if needed, but electronic submissions are preferred. Completed freshmen applications include a high school transcript, SAT or ACT scores, and a letter of recommendation.

Ramapo College practices a holistic review process. Each application is evaluated individually with emphasis placed on academic achievement in high school and standardized test scores. The College begins reviewing applications in September and offers rolling admission until March 1. Ramapo College offers a nonbinding immediate decision day for students meeting certain criteria. Please visit the College Web site or Facebook page for more information.

For a viewbook, application forms, and additional information, including current costs, students should contact:

Director of Admissions
Ramapo College of New Jersey
505 Ramapo Valley Road
Mahwah, New Jersey 07430

Phone: 201-684-7300 or 7301
E-mail: admissions@ramapo.edu
Web site: http://www.ramapo.edu
http://www.facebook.com/RamapoAdmissions

The Russ and Angelica Berrie Center for the Performing and Visual Arts on the campus of Ramapo College of New Jersey.

RANDOLPH COLLEGE
LYNCHBURG, VIRGINIA

The College

No two students are the same—each one is an original. That's the mindset at Randolph College. While DNA may be nature's starting point for individual development, what each student makes of themselves is subject to many different factors. And that's where Randolph College—a community of originals—can make a difference.

Academic excellence through the liberal arts and sciences and an emphasis on individual learning are Randolph's top priorities. Founded as Randolph-Macon Woman's College in 1891, it was the first women's college to be accredited by the Southern Association of Colleges and Schools and the first Southern women's college to be granted a Phi Beta Kappa charter. The College's enduring commitment to education has fostered strong programs in career development, experiential learning, and undergraduate research.

Randolph's current enrollment is about 525. Students come from more than forty states and thirty countries, choosing Randolph for its academic reputation, outstanding commitment to individual learning, and the warm, friendly community. There are six residence halls on the 100-acre campus, housing 90 percent of the students. The College's location near the Blue Ridge Mountains provides ample recreational opportunities, and proximity to neighboring colleges and major universities enhances the social and cocurricular life on and off campus. Most students are involved in at least one of the more than 40 clubs or organizations and activities, which include campus publications, an organic garden, WRRM radio, Chorale and Songshine, the Dance Group, political organizations, language clubs, theater, religious and volunteer organizations, and a nationally ranked riding program with its own world-class riding facility. The $6-million Student Center renovation, expected to be complete in 2013, will offer a two-level fitness center on the top floor; a 90-seat theater; the Skeller (a student grill); a wrap-around outside deck; an entertainment floor with pool tables, ping-pong, foosball, and other activities; a glass-enclosed studio for the student radio station, WWRM; and new student government and publications offices.

Intercollegiate sports for men include basketball, cross-country, lacrosse, riding, soccer, and tennis. Women's sports include basketball, cross-country, lacrosse, riding, soccer, softball, tennis, and volleyball. Courses are also offered in a variety of activities and sports, including aerobics, fencing, fitness walking, golf, kickboxing, weight training, and yoga.

The academic program is enhanced throughout the year by visiting speakers, performers, and artists. In recent years, these have included former Governor of Vermont and DNC Chairman Howard Dean; aquatic filmmaker and oceanographic explorer Fabien Cousteau; John Dau, a Lost Boy of Sudan known for his memoir and Sundance Film Festival award-winner *God Grew Tired of Us;* educator, poet, writer, and Civil Rights activist Nikki Giovanni; and Frances Mayes, alumna of the College and author of several works including *Under the Tuscan Sun.* In addition, the College sponsors numerous plays, awards, and exhibitions.

Location

Randolph College is situated on 100 wooded acres in the historic district of Lynchburg, Virginia, a suburban college town with small-town charm near the Blue Ridge Mountains. Shopping areas, movie theaters, restaurants, and coffee shops are convenient to the campus, and public transportation is readily available. Lynchburg is within easy driving distance of Washington, D.C., and Richmond, Virginia.

Majors and Degrees

Randolph College offers more than fifty majors, concentrations (minors), and programs of study leading to a Bachelor of Arts (B.A.), Bachelor of Science (B.S.), or Bachelor of Fine Arts (B.F.A.) degree. Majors are art (history, museum studies, and studio), biology, business, chemistry, classics, communication studies, curricular studies, dance, economics, engineering physics, English (creative writing and literature), environmental studies or science, French, global studies, health services, history, mathematics, music, philosophy, physical education and health with licensure, physics, physics education, political science, psychology, religious studies, sociology, Spanish, and theater. The double major is a popular option, and there is also the opportunity to develop a self-designed major such as comparative literature or mathematical biology. In addition, there is the education program, which offers courses that meet the requirements for primary and secondary education certification. Travel/study opportunities and visiting scholar programs augment the international curriculum.

Every student has the option of selecting up to two minors in addition to the major. Minors are offered in all of the major fields as well as the interdisciplinary areas of American culture, Asian studies, film studies, gender studies, global studies, human services, Renaissance studies, and sport and exercise studies. Students declare majors and concentrations in the spring of the sophomore year.

Randolph has 3-2 programs in engineering and nursing and preprofessional programs in law, medicine and veterinary studies, and teacher education.

Academic Programs

The academic program is structured to develop the student as a whole person. The curriculum is designed to ensure that students acquire a broad range of knowledge and depth in their chosen field while they are prepared for meaningful careers. Randolph College trains students to think critically and independently and speak and write effectively. The College's graduation requirement is 124 hours of credit with a quality point ratio of at least 2.0.

Students also use the Randolph Plan, an individualized, systematic plan that helps them define their personal, educational, and professional goals. Working with faculty and staff members, students move through a series of steps to identify the many courses, internships, study-abroad opportunities, and clubs and activities that constitute a coherent plan to meet their goals.

The College operates on a traditional semester system, with self-scheduled exams given before the December vacation and at the end of the second semester in May. Most classes meet either two or three times a week. Randolph College provides maximum opportunity for independent study and research.

The Writing Program includes formal evaluation of student writing skills in all courses at the end of every semester as well as writing-intensive sections across the curriculum. First-year students may be granted exemption from the English composition degree requirement on the basis of their entering record (usually Advanced Placement examination scores).

In a study conducted by the Higher Education Data Sharing (HEDS) Consortium, Randolph College ranks in the top 15 percent of institutions nationally in percentage of graduates who earned doctorates between 1997 and 2006. Over the same period, Randolph College ranked in the top 15 percent in biological sciences and the top 10 percent in humanities, notably English and foreign languages. Special advisers at the College counsel students who are preparing for medical, veterinary, or law school or other specialized graduate study. Research is encouraged in various areas of academic concentration, and in the senior year students may pursue honors work involving the presentation and defense of a thesis under the supervision of a faculty member. Class of 2010 graduates gained valuable experience through internships (46 percent), research (27 percent), volunteer service (50 percent), study abroad for a semester or academic year (26 percent), and employment during the summer (56 percent).

Off-Campus Programs

Internships provide an exciting opportunity for students to gain valuable work experience in area hospitals, veterinary clinics, schools, law firms, industries, courts, social service agencies, and radio and television stations. The College maintains a listing of nearly 1,000 internship opportunities through which students may earn up to 6 hours of credit toward their degree.

Many students choose to participate in study abroad, either through Randolph's flagship program, The World in Britain (affiliated with the University of Reading, England), or in other destinations around the globe on one of the College's affiliated programs or through another university sponsor. Recent study-abroad destinations include Australia, Belgium, Denmark, France, Ghana, Japan, Italy, Mexico, the Philippines, Russia, Scotland, and Spain.

Programs in this country include the Washington semester at American University and the Marine Biological Laboratory semester in environmental science. Randolph College participates in the Seven-College Exchange consortium in Virginia, along with Hampden-Sydney College, Hollins University, Mary Baldwin College, Randolph-Macon College, Sweet Briar College, and Washington and Lee University. The local Tri-College Consortium of Randolph College, Lynchburg College, and Sweet Briar College increases the number and diversity of courses open to students.

The College's spring semester American Culture Program offers an interdisciplinary immersion into the study of American culture both on campus and at key locations in Virginia and across the nation. The program capitalizes on the College's central location in historic Virginia as well as its own outstanding Maier Museum of Art's collection of American art. This one-semester program is open to students from Randolph College as well as to undergraduate students, both women and men, from other institutions.

The Susan F. Davenport Leadership Program is another unique opportunity at Randolph. It focuses on developing the skills and global perspectives students need to become leaders in the world today.

Academic Facilities

The recently renovated Lipscomb Library contains more than 200,000 volumes, as well as current magazine and journal titles with backfiles in microform and paper, extensive holdings in audiovisual formats, and domestic and foreign newspapers. Over 80,000 journal titles are available electronically. The Martin Science Building incorporates instrumentation, facilities for student-faculty research, and multimedia instructional centers. Equipment and resources readily available for hands-on student use include an FT-NMR, GC-MS, a seismograph, high-speed oscilloscopes and other instruments, exceptional herbarium and fossil collections, a greenhouse, and nature preserves. The Winfree Observatory houses a 14-inch pier-mounted telescope equipped with a computer-operated CCD camera for variable star research to support instruction in physics and astronomy. The Ethyl Science and Mathematics Resource Center in Martin offers a networked computer cluster with specific software for science and math applications and library, study, and lounge facilities.

The College's Maier Museum of Art houses an outstanding collection of nineteenth- and twentieth-century American paintings, while Presser Hall, the music building, has a concert auditorium, studios, and practice rooms. The Learning Resources Center and the Writing Lab offer academic support and tutorial services related to study skills, word processing, and the writing program.

Classroom equipment allows for appropriate technology integration into teaching and learning. The majority of classrooms on campus provide multimedia display capabilities, and several classrooms are equipped with student computer workstations for hands-on instruction in discipline-specific software and for general-purpose technology workshops. The campus also has a number of learning spaces equipped with special-purpose technology, including SMART Boards, computers-on-wheels for group collaboration, a small theater with computer/video display and surround sound, a media center/language lab where students can work on language drills and exercises as well as edit digital video, and a digital darkroom for high-end digital, still picture editing.

Macintosh and PC-compatible computers are provided in numerous labs on campus for student use 24 hours a day, seven days a week. Laser printers and scanners are also available in all computer labs. Web-based information resources allow students to view their student records, class schedules, and grades.

All computer labs and residence hall rooms have access to the Internet and to the College's extensive Web site. The Web site provides comprehensive information about the College and a variety of services to prospective students and their parents. Students enjoy the campus portal system and the College's 100 percent coverage for wireless connection to the network.

Costs

The 2010–11 comprehensive fee for room, board, and tuition was $38,739. The College recommends a budget of $2500 for books, supplies, fees, and personal expenses, excluding travel costs.

Financial Aid

Randolph College administers more than $15 million in aid each year through a comprehensive program of financial assistance, which includes academics-based scholarships, need-based grants, low-interest student loans, and campus employment. All students are encouraged to apply for financial aid, even those who assume that they are ineligible for assistance due to family income level. Academic scholarships, which range from $2000 per year to full tuition, are renewable for four years. The student's application for admission serves as the application for all academic scholarships. More than 95 percent of the College's students receive financial assistance of some kind. The average need-based financial aid package is $19,000. To apply for need-based aid, students are encouraged to submit the Free Application for Federal Student Aid (FAFSA) by February 1. International students are eligible for merit scholarships, which range from $2000 to $20,000 per year.

Admission Requirements

A minimum of 16 academic high school units is recommended and should be distributed as follows: 4 units of English, 3 units of mathematics, 3–4 units of a foreign language, 2 units of laboratory science, 2 units of social studies, and sufficient electives from these areas to make up the recommended total. Because of the flexible nature of the College's curriculum, favorable consideration may be given to students whose high school preparation departs from the recommendations outlined above. Each applicant must have maintained a strong academic record in college-preparatory courses and must submit scores on the SAT or ACT. Randolph College readily accepts the Common Application. An online application is available at http://www.randolphcollege.edu.

Application and Information

Each application for admission is evaluated when all necessary materials are received. Students are generally notified of a decision within three weeks of deadline dates or once all supporting credentials have been received. The application fee is $35. This fee may be waived in cases of hardship at the request of the student and the recommendation of their high school counselor. Randolph College also participates in the College Board test fee waiver program.

The deadline for submitting an application for early action is December 1 of a student's senior year. Students who apply by December 1 receive priority consideration for the Presidential Scholarship, a highly competitive full-tuition scholarship. The deadline for submitting an application for regular decision is February 15 of a student's senior year.

Accepted students must notify the College of their plans to enroll and submit the initial $300 enrollment deposit by May 1. The deposit is refundable if written notification is received by the Admissions Office prior to May 1.

For more information, students should contact:

Vice President for Enrollment Management
Randolph College
2500 Rivermont Avenue
Lynchburg, Virginia 24503
Phone: 434-947-8100
      800-745-7692 (toll-free)
E-mail: admissions@randolphcollege.edu
Web site: http://www.randolphcollege.edu
      http://www.facebook.com/randolphcollege
      http://twitter.com/randolphcollege

REED COLLEGE
PORTLAND, OREGON

The College

For its 1,447 students and 139 faculty members, Reed College is foremost an intellectual community. Since classes began in 1911, Reed has attracted students with a high degree of self-discipline and a genuine enthusiasm for academic work and intellectual challenge. Reed comprises a diverse student body; more than four fifths of Reed's students come from outside the Northwest, with 25 percent from the Northeast and 8 percent from outside the United States. A quarter of Reed's incoming students are members of historically underrepresented ethnic groups.

Campus social opportunities are open to all, with no closed clubs or organizations; there are no sororities or fraternities at Reed. Community life is full of activity and variety with more than seventy student organizations. Although there are competitive club sports at Reed, such as rugby, soccer, and Ultimate (Frisbee), there are no varsity athletic teams. Fitness and the development of lifelong skills take precedence over competition.

Location

Reed's 119-acre wooded campus is located in a quiet, residential section of southeast Portland. The nearby ocean and mountains of the Pacific Northwest provide a balance to the social and cultural offerings of the greater Portland metropolitan area.

Majors and Degrees

Reed awards the Bachelor of Arts degree in a wide variety of fields, based on work in traditional departments or in interdisciplinary combinations. Students may select from the following majors: American studies, anthropology, art, biochemistry and molecular biology, biology, chemistry, chemistry-physics, Chinese literature, Chinese studies, classics, classics-religion, dance-theater, economics, English literature, environmental studies, French literature, general literature, German literature, history, history-literature, international and comparative policy studies, linguistics, literature-theater, mathematics, mathematics-economics, mathematics-physics, music, philosophy, physics, political science, psychology, religion, Russian literature, sociology, Spanish literature, and theater.

Students may also design additional interdisciplinary majors. The approval of such special programs, which link two or more disciplines, is reviewed by the student's adviser and the departments concerned.

Reed offers several combined 3-2 programs, which allow the student to earn both a bachelor's degree from Reed and a professional degree from the cooperating institution. Science programs and institutions include engineering (California Institute of Technology, Columbia University, and Rensselaer Polytechnic Institute), computer science (University of Washington), and environmental sciences (Duke University). The College also has a combined program in fine arts (Pacific Northwest College of Art).

Academic Programs

Hallmarks of academic life at Reed include the small-group conference method of teaching and its reliance on active student participation, a de-emphasis of grades, a yearlong interdisciplinary humanities program, and an integrated academic program that balances the breadth of traditional course content and distribution requirements with flexibility in designing an in-depth senior thesis. The development of skills in preparation for a life of learning takes precedence over the mere memorization of facts. In addition to fulfilling the requirements for the major, taking the humanities course, and writing the senior thesis, students must satisfy a distributional requirement, consisting of two core classes

from each of the following academic groups: literature, philosophy, and the arts; history, social sciences, and psychology; the natural sciences; and math, foreign language, logic, and linguistics. Students must also take two classes from one other department outside their major course of study.

Off-Campus Programs

Reed participates in domestic exchange programs with Howard University in Washington, D.C.; Sarah Lawrence College in New York; and Sea Education Association in Massachusetts. In addition, Reed provides study-abroad opportunities for students in Germany (University of Munich, Tübingen University, Freie University), Russia (ACTR Russian Language, Middlebury School in Russia, National Theater Institute of Moscow, Smolny College at St. Petersburg University), Hungary (Budapest Semester in Mathematics), France (Université de Rennes II Haute Bretagne, Université de Paris), Spain (Hamilton College's Madrid Center, Middlebury School in Spain, University of Santiago de Compostela, University of Barcelona), Greece (College Year in Athens), Italy (Intercollegiate Centers for Classical Studies in Rome and Sicily, Florence Center of Syracuse University, Sarah Lawrence College Foreign Program in Florence), England (Sarah Lawrence College Foreign Programs in London Theater and at Wadham College at Oxford University, University of East Anglia, Sussex University, University of Nottingham), Ireland (Trinity College at the University of Dublin, University College Cork), Israel (Hebrew University), Egypt (American University in Cairo), Morocco (Al Akhawayn University), China (East China Normal University in Shanghai, Capital Normal University in Beijing, Fujian Normal University in Fuzhou), Costa Rica (Organization for Tropical Studies, University of Costa Rica), South Africa (Organization for Tropical Studies), Ecuador (Ecuador Program), and Argentina (University of Buenos Aires/FLASCO). Students may also arrange independent study plans in consultation with appropriate faculty members, the director for off-campus studies, and the registrar.

Academic Facilities

Students have access to Reed's substantial library collection (600,967 volumes, 2,700 periodicals, and 340,000 government documents) by searching the online catalog in the library or from any computer on the campus network. Through its participation in PORTALS (Portland Area Library System) and Summit, a union catalog of Oregon and Washington academic libraries, Reed provides online access to other library catalogs and databases. Students may borrow materials directly from academic libraries in the Portland area, and they have access to collections worldwide through interlibrary loan. In addition, the Reed library accommodates a first-rate art gallery, a language lab, and a music listening facility. The Reed library is open 18 hours most days and 24 hours a day during examinations.

Computer technology is highly developed at Reed and widely used for instruction, research, and communication by all members of the College community. A state-of-the-art campus network links all residence halls, classrooms, laboratories, offices, and the library to one another and to the global Internet. The Educational Technology Center houses more than 100 computers and a variety of other teaching and technology resources that are used by students and faculty and staff members. The science laboratories at Reed are among the best equipped of any undergraduate college in the United States. These include the A. A. Knowlton Laboratory of Physics, the Arthur F. Scott Laboratory of Chemistry, and the L. E. Griffin Memorial Biology Building, where a recent $10-million renovation includes improved student thesis space, a tiered-seating classroom, and new teaching labs. Reed's research nuclear reactor (the only such reactor in the country that is staffed primarily by undergraduates) and radiochemistry lab are actively used for student research, instruction, and training. For those interested in the arts, the campus houses studio art facilities that recently saw a $2-million expansion, performing arts facilities, twenty instrumental practice rooms, a computer music laboratory, a recording system, and an 800-seat auditorium. Other popular facilities include a radio station and a modern sports center. In fall 2008, Reed opened five new residence halls, which enable 75 percent of students to live on campus.

Costs

Tuition for 2010–11 was $40,940, and room and board were $10,650. The student body fee was $260, bringing the yearly total cost to approximately $51,850. The cost of books and incidental expenses averaged $2000.

Financial Aid

About half of the Reed student body receives financial assistance from the College. A full need-based financial aid program makes Reed accessible to students from a wide range of economic backgrounds. The College guarantees to meet the full demonstrated need of all continuing students in good academic standing who complete their financial aid applications on time. Reed's own funds are the primary source of grants to students. The College budgeted more than $23 million for this purpose in 2010–11. Reed also administers federal and state grants as well as federally subsidized loan programs. Campus employment and work-study programs are available. The size of a financial aid award is based solely upon analysis of the student's need. The average amount awarded to students receiving financial aid in 2010–11 was $34,196, which includes grants, loans, and work opportunities.

Faculty

All classes at Reed are taught by professors, about 90 percent of whom hold the highest degree in their field. The average class has 14 students. Reed students point to the opportunity to work closely with faculty members as one of the great benefits of a Reed education. Reed faculty members point to the opportunity to work with students who are serious scholars as one of the great benefits of teaching at Reed. Faculty members commit themselves primarily to teaching, with scholarly and scientific research furthering this primary goal; they view students as partners in learning, often serving as coauthors and coinvestigators on professional papers and research projects. This close association is due, in large part, to a 10:1 student-faculty ratio and the one-on-one relationship between thesis adviser (a professor) and student during the senior year.

Student Government

The Student Senate is the central body in student governance. The Senate consists of the student body president, vice president, and 8 student representatives, all elected by the students. Its two primary functions are to allocate student body funds and to represent student interests and concerns to the faculty, administration, and Board of Trustees. The Senate distributes approximately $40,000 each semester to the many student organizations on campus. As agreed under the community constitution, students participate fully in discussions and decisions on a wide variety of issues. The Student Committee on Academic Policy and Planning participates in debate about the curriculum at Reed; many other committees, from the Library Board to the Reactor Committee, have substantial student input. The Senate and student body president make all student appointments to such committees.

Admission Requirements

Reed welcomes applications from freshman and transfer candidates who are genuinely committed to the pursuit of a liberal arts education and a rigorous academic program. Those applicants are admitted who, in the view of the Admission Committee, are most likely to become successful members of and contribute significantly to the Reed community. The College is committed to maintaining a student body distinguished by its intellectual passion, yet diversified in its range of backgrounds, interests, and talents.

Admission decisions are based on many integrated factors, but academic accomplishments and talents are given the greatest weight in the selection process. A strong secondary school preparation, including honors and advanced courses where available, improves a student's chances for admission. Such a program usually includes 4 years of English and 3 to 4 years of mathematics (through precalculus), science, foreign language, and history or social studies. Given the wide variation in high school programs and quality, however, there are no fixed requirements for secondary school courses. Applicants are expected to have obtained a secondary school diploma prior to enrollment, although exceptions are occasionally made. There are no "cutoff points" for high school or college grades or for test scores.

Reed recognizes the qualities of character—in particular, motivation, intellectual curiosity, individual responsibility, and social consciousness—as important considerations in the selection process, beyond a demonstrated commitment to academic excellence. Thus, the Admission Committee looks for students whose accomplishments and interests in various fields of endeavor will contribute to the overall liveliness of the Reed community. Personal interviews, either on or off campus, are not a requirement in the admission process but are strongly recommended whenever possible. Applications for early decision should be submitted by November 15 (Option I) or December 20 (Option II), regular freshman admission by January 15, and transfer candidates by March 1.

Application and Information

The Office of Admission is open Monday through Friday from 8:30 a.m. until 5 p.m. (Pacific time) all year, except for major holidays. Students may apply online at http://www.reed.edu/apply/apply_reed.html. For further information or to arrange a campus tour, overnight stay, information session, or interview, students should contact:

Office of Admission
Reed College
3203 Southeast Woodstock Boulevard
Portland, Oregon 97202-8199
Phone: 503-777-7511
      800-547-4750 (toll-free)
Fax: 503-777-7553
E-mail: admission@reed.edu
Web site: http://www.reed.edu/

Typical fall day in front of Eliot Hall at Reed College.

THE RICHARD STOCKTON COLLEGE OF NEW JERSEY

POMONA, NEW JERSEY

The College

Stockton College is a nationally recognized, midsized public undergraduate and graduate college of the arts, sciences, and professional studies within the New Jersey system of higher education. Stockton has the look and feel of a private college, but is also one of the most affordable colleges in the state. With a clear focus on student engagement and commitment to student success, Stockton prepares future leaders for their communities, states, and nations.

Founded in 1969, the College was named for Richard Stockton, one of the New Jersey signers of the Declaration of Independence.

Stockton enrolls almost 8,000 students from New Jersey, the surrounding mid-Atlantic states, and many other countries, providing distinctive traditional educational programs and alternative educational experiences that extend learning beyond the classroom. Stockton's curriculum develops the students' analytic and creative capabilities and encourages individually planned courses of study that promote self-reliance, acceptance of change, and an educated response to change.

The College's parklike setting provides excellent opportunities for a wide range of outdoor recreational activities, including sailing, canoeing, hiking, jogging, and fishing. Students and faculty and staff members participate together in an extensive intramural and club sports program that includes aikido, crew, flag football, golf, ice hockey, soccer, softball, street hockey, swimming, volleyball, fencing, deep sea fishing, scuba, surfing, Ultimate (Frisbee), and weight training, to mention a few. At the intercollegiate level, Stockton fields NCAA Division III sports teams in men's baseball, basketball, lacrosse, and soccer; women's basketball, crew, field hockey, soccer, softball, tennis, and volleyball; and men's and women's cross-country and track and field. The multipurpose Sports Center has fitness facilities, racquetball courts, weight rooms, a gymnasium, and outdoor recreational facilities that include a field house, NCAA track, field-event venues, four playing fields for soccer, baseball, softball, and lacrosse; and six tennis courts.

The new 154,000-square-foot Campus Center, which opened in the spring of 2011, provides a focal point for the campus and a gathering point for students, faculty, staff, and visitors. Here, students can conduct College business with several departments—Admissions, the Registrar, Bursar, Bookstore, and Advising—in a single, convenient location. The center also houses student organization offices and most other student services are nearby. In addition, the center has a 255-seat theater; a main event room for performances and classes; and separate spaces for a food court, coffee shop, and game room, giving students plenty of space to meet and socialize.

Stockton students who participate in cocurricular activities can have their experiences documented through the College's student development program, ULTRA (Undergraduate Learning, Training, and Awareness), culminating in a cocurricular transcript issued to students.

The Residential Life Center provides a curricular/cocurricular facility within two student housing areas. With its large and small meeting rooms, convenience store, and computer lab, the center encourages activities and programs for both organized and informal student groups.

Lakeside Center, located in the garden apartment housing area, contains a convenience store, snack bar, outdoor concert area, computer lab, multipurpose room for large programs, and a small meeting room for student groups.

Stockton provides on-campus housing for over 3,000 students in traditional residence hall–style arrangements and apartment-style living. All complexes are completely furnished and air conditioned, with cable TV, telephone service, and Internet access (port-per-pillow) provided. Residence Life will assist students choosing to live off campus by providing a listing of suitable off-campus availabilities. Choices range from new townhouse complexes near campus to winter rentals in one of the local seashore towns.

The Richard Stockton College of New Jersey is accredited by the Commission on Higher Education of the Middle States Association of Colleges and Schools. In addition, the social work program is accredited by the Council on Social Work Education; the teacher education sequence is approved by the New Jersey Department of Education, the National Association of State Directors of Teacher Education and Certification, and the Teacher Education Accreditation Council; the nursing program is accredited by the New Jersey Board of Nursing and the Commission on Collegiate Nursing Education; the chemistry program (B.S.) is accredited by the American Chemical Society; the physical therapy program is accredited by the Commission on Accreditation in Physical Therapy Education (CAPTE) of the American Physical Therapy Association; the environmental health/public health program is accredited by the National Environmental Health Sciences and Protection Accreditation Council; the health administration/public health program is accredited by the Association of University Programs in Health Administration; and the occupational therapy program is accredited by the Accreditation Council for Occupational Therapy Education (ACOTE) of the American Occupational Therapy Association (AOTA).

Location

The Richard Stockton College of New Jersey is located on a stunning 2,000-acre campus in Pomona, New Jersey, nestled in the environmentally protected Pinelands National Reserve. The campus is just minutes west of Atlantic City and Jersey Shore beaches; an hour from Philadelphia and two hours from New York City. Courses are also offered online; at Stockton's Atlantic City campus, the Carnegie Library Center; and at the College's educational center in downtown Hammonton, New Jersey. Stockton also owns the historic Seaview Resort and two championship golf courses in Absecon, New Jersey, which allows the College to advance its educational mission, expand its hospitality and tourism management program, enhance the college experience for students, and preserve an iconic landmark in the region. Collaboration with the Noyes Museum of Art in Oceanville provides enriching exhibitions and educational programs through the only fine art venue in southern New Jersey.

A full schedule of concerts, art exhibitions, lectures, recreation, and sports on campus is complemented by the nearby Jersey Shore resort destinations as well as Stockton's own off-campus facilities. Within a 15-minute drive, students find shopping, dining, and cultural attractions, as well as the entertainment of Atlantic City.

Majors and Degrees

The Bachelor of Arts degree is offered in studies in the arts, applied physics, biology, business studies, chemistry, communication, computer science and information systems, criminal justice (forensic science), economics, education, environmental studies, geology, historical studies, languages and culture studies, liberal studies, literature, marine science, mathematics, philosophy and religion, political science, psychology, and sociology and anthropology.

A Bachelor of Fine Arts degree is offered in visual arts.

The Bachelor of Science degree is offered in applied physics, biochemistry/molecular biology, biology, business studies (accounting, finance, hospitality and tourism management, international business, management, marketing), chemistry, computational science, computer science and information systems, environmental science, geology, marine science, mathematics, nursing, psychology, public health, social work, and speech pathology and audiology.

Stockton's flexible curriculum allows students to prepare for professional careers, such as dentistry, law, medicine, pharmacy, and veterinary medicine, while pursuing a traditional major. The College also offers preprofessional preparation in occupational therapy, optometry, pharmacy, physical therapy, and podiatry, with the master's in occupational therapy and the doctorate in physical therapy completed at Stockton.

Stockton has accelerated seven-year dual-degree articulation agreements with the University of Medicine and Dentistry of New Jersey (Robert Wood Johnson Medical School, New Jersey Medical School, School of Osteopathic Medicine, New Jersey Dental School), the Pennsylvania College of Podiatric Medicine, the New York College of

Podiatric Medicine, the New York State College of Optometry, and Rutgers School of Pharmacy. Stockton also has an articulation program with Cornell University for veterinary medicine as well as five-year, dual-degree programs with New Jersey Institute of Technology (NJIT) and Rutgers University for students interested in engineering. Students participating in the engineering program earn a Bachelor of Science degree in chemistry, physics, or math from Stockton and a Bachelor of Science degree in engineering from NJIT or Rutgers. A dual degree in pharmacy allows students to graduate from Stockton with a Bachelor of Science degree in biochemistry/molecular biology and finish their Doctor of Pharmacy degree at the Ernest Mario School of Pharmacy at Rutgers University.

In addition to undergraduate degrees, Stockton offers the following graduate degrees: Doctor of Physical Therapy; Master of Arts degrees in criminal justice, Holocaust and genocide studies, education, educational leadership, and instructional technology; Master of Business Administration; and Master of Science degrees in communication disorders, computational science, nursing, occupational therapy, and social work; and a Professional Science Master's in environmental science. Certificate and endorsement programs are offered in bilingual/bicultural education, ESL (English as a second language), family nurse practitioner, forensic psychology, health professions prep, homeland security, learning disabilities teacher consultant studies, middle school endorsement, New Jersey standard supervisor endorsement, preschool–grade 3 endorsement, reading specialist, special education, and student assistance coordinator.

Academic Programs

To earn a baccalaureate degree at Stockton, a student must satisfactorily complete a minimum of 128 semester credits. Degree programs include a combination of general studies and program (major field) studies. The Bachelor of Arts student must earn 64 credits in general studies; the Bachelor of Science student must earn 48. General studies courses are broad cross-disciplinary courses designed to introduce students to all major areas of the curriculum and to the broadly applicable intellectual skills necessary for success in college. Students must select some courses from each major curricular area. The only required courses within general studies are the basic studies courses (up to three), but students may be exempt from these courses based on diagnostic testing. The Bachelor of Arts student must earn 64 credits in program studies; the Bachelor of Science student must earn 80. Program studies requirements are carefully structured and emphasize sequences of specific courses.

Stockton students have special opportunities to influence what and how they learn by participating in the major decisions that shape their academic lives. The opportunities of the preceptorial system enable students to work on a personalized basis with an assigned faculty-staff preceptor in planning and evaluating individual courses of study and in exploring various career alternatives. Stockton's academic programs emphasize curricular organization and methods of instruction that promote independent learning and research, cross-disciplinary study, problem solving, and decision making through analysis and synthesis.

Off-Campus Programs

Off-campus educational experiences for credit are a key feature of most degree programs at Stockton. Internships, research projects, and field studies extend the principles and methods learned beyond the classroom. Study abroad, Semester at Sea, and an honors program are also available.

The Washington Internship Program gives students the opportunity to gain professional work experience in the nation's capital. Stockton sends more students to the program than any other college or university outside the Washington, D.C., area.

Coordination of off-campus internship programs is provided by the academic divisional offices as well as Stockton's Regional Internship Center of Southern New Jersey; coordination of foreign study is provided by the coordinator of international education.

Academic Facilities

Stockton's award-winning academic complex serves as a living-learning center. Academic, recreational, and living spaces are mixed to promote interaction among students and faculty and staff members. The facilities, all constructed since 1971, include several large classroom/office buildings, a library, a lecture hall/auditorium, and the 550-seat Performing Arts Center.

The library contains more than 300,000 volumes, more than 2,600 periodical subscriptions, 280,000 government documents, more than 19,000 reels of microfilm, and about 68,000 other units of microtext. The media collection includes films, slides, videotapes, audiotapes, compact discs, and phonograph records. The library also houses a special collection on the New Jersey Pine Barrens and is a depository for federal, state, and Atlantic City documents.

Costs

Costs for the 2010–11 academic year, including flat-rate tuition and fees based on up to 40 credits per year, were $11,394 for in-state students and $17,304 for out-of-state students; on-campus housing and board were $10,380 (double-occupancy residence room and Ultimate 19 meal plan). Books, supplies, transportation, and personal items are extra. All costs are subject to change.

Financial Aid

Financial aid is available in the form of scholarships, grants, loans, and work-study. Need-based financial aid is awarded according to student and family need. Students seeking financial aid should file the Free Application for Federal Student Aid (FAFSA) by March 1. Merit-based aid is awarded to recognize academic excellence. Stockton offers aggressive and generous scholarship opportunities for academically talented freshmen and transfer students based on standardized test scores, grade point average, high school class rank, and college-level performance.

Faculty

Stockton's faculty members represent highly diverse academic, training, and social backgrounds, with 95 percent holding the terminal degree in their field. Faculty members work closely with students through small class sizes and individual research opportunities and share with students and staff members the initiative and responsibility for the College's social, recreational, athletic, and cultural programs and activities. This arrangement supports the exceptional rapport and learning relationships among students and faculty members.

Student Government

The RSCNJ Student Senate consists of 25 student members. The advisory council is made up of 1 faculty member and 2 staff members. Student senators hold office for one year, with elections held every spring. Among other duties, the Student Senate reviews and makes recommendations on budgets of funded student organizations and acts as the official representative of the student body.

Admission Requirements

Stockton operates on a rolling admission basis. For most freshman majors, the deadline for fall admission is May 1. Students should check the Web site for special program deadlines. Transfer student deadline for fall admission is June 1. Spring term (January) admission deadline for all students is December 1. Students may apply for admission to the fall or spring term and are notified of the admission decision as soon as their application file has been completed and reviewed. Freshman applicants must submit ACT and/or SAT scores. All students must submit official transcripts from all educational institutions attended. Admission is selective.

Stockton offers early acceptance programs for highly qualified high school students in their junior year. Armed Services veterans and those who have been away from formal education for some time are also invited to apply for admission. Stockton makes no distinction between part- and full-time students in offering admission.

Stockton offers special admission access to a limited number of New Jersey students from educationally and financially disadvantaged backgrounds. Students wishing to explore this opportunity should contact the Admissions Office.

Application and Information

For more information, prospective students should contact:

Dean of Enrollment Management
The Richard Stockton College of New Jersey
P.O. Box 195
Pomona, New Jersey 08240-0195
Phone: 609-652-4261
　　　　866-RSC-2885 (toll-free)
Fax: 609-626-5541
E-mail: admissions@stockton.edu
Web site: http://www.stockton.edu
　　　　http://www.facebook.com/richardstocktoncollege
　　　　http://twitter.com/RSCCollege

RICHMOND, THE AMERICAN INTERNATIONAL UNIVERSITY IN LONDON

LONDON, ENGLAND

The University

Richmond, The American International University in London, prepares men and women to serve with purpose and generosity in an interdependent and multicultural world. Richmond offers a strong academic program with many choices of fields of study, an exceptional faculty, superb campus life, and fellow students from all over the world. In the United States, Richmond is accredited by the Commission on Higher Education of the Middle States Association of Colleges and Schools, a regional accrediting body recognized by the U.S. Department of Education. Richmond is accredited in the United Kingdom by the Open University and holds related degree validation. The University's undergraduate and graduate degrees are designated by the United Kingdom's Department of Education and Employment. The University is a comprehensive American liberal arts and professional university. In addition to the undergraduate degree programs described below, Richmond offers Master of Arts degrees in art history and visual culture, and in international relations.

Freshmen and sophomores study and live at the Richmond campus, 7 miles from central London. Junior and senior years are spent at the Kensington campus in one of London's most beautiful residential and historic districts. As part of their four-year B.A. degree program, students may spend a semester or a year studying at one of the University's two international study centers in Florence and Rome, Italy. Richmond currently enrolls 1,000 students from more than 100 countries. Approximately 21 percent of the degree students are from Europe and the United Kingdom, 13 percent are from Asia, and 18 percent are from the Middle East. Fifteen percent of the student body represents the continent of Africa, and 3 percent are from South America. The remaining students are from North America. About 350 study-abroad students from various universities are enrolled for a semester or a year at Richmond.

Small classes, averaging 17 students, enable students to receive personal attention from professors in a supportive environment. The curriculum and academic advising system are structured to enable students to choose courses that provide broad knowledge, relevant skills, and an understanding of the world's many cultures and nations.

Richmond students supplement academic programs with activities that complement and balance the classroom experience. Many extracurricular and cocurricular programs are available to students, including student government, the Green Project, Model United Nations, Amnesty International, RTV (Richmond Television), and sports and business clubs.

Location

The Richmond Hill campus in the London suburb of Richmond offers a variety of entertainment, shopping, cultural, and recreational opportunities. Only yards from the University campus is Richmond Park, more than 2,200 acres of rolling hills and lush woodland, where one can ride horses, play tennis, jog, or simply relax. The journey from Richmond into Central London takes about 30 minutes.

The Kensington campus is located in the heart of London's Borough of Kensington, which has fine museums, libraries, theatres, concert halls, historic buildings, and well-known cultural and educational resources. The University takes full advantage of London's cultural and social resources through selected academic courses, work experience placements with

multinational corporations, and special visits to museums, art galleries, theatres, and concert halls.

Majors and Degrees

Richmond operates its academic program on the American system. The University offers the four-year Bachelor of Arts (B.A.) degree in twelve majors, with a further choice of nineteen minors. Majors offered by the University are art, design, and media; business administration (finance, international business, marketing); communications; economics; history; international journalism and media; international relations; political science; psychology; and sociology.

Academic Programs

In order to graduate with the dual-validated U.S. and U.K. degree [B.A./B.A. (Honors)], students must earn a minimum of 120 credits. Usually, this means taking a full load for four years, or eight semesters. Within these 120 credits, students must complete all course requirements for their majors. Students must also meet the University's Language Proficiency and General Education requirements. In addition, valuable work experience for credit is offered through the International Internship program. Recent placements have been at the International Herald Tribune, General Electric, The House of Commons, CNN, the United Nations, Lloyds Bank, the Museum of London, and Sony Music Corporation.

Credit is also awarded for Advanced Placement tests (6 credits for each subject grade of 3, 4, or 5); a grade of A, B, or C on the "A" Level exams is awarded 9 credits (6 for D or E). Credit is also awarded for the International Baccalaureate, the Baccalauréat de l'Enseignement du Second Degré (France), the Abitur/Reifzuegnis (Germany), the Diploma di Maturità (Italy), and the School Leaving Diploma (Denmark, Finland, Norway, and Sweden).

The fall semester begins in late August and ends in mid-December. The spring semester begins in mid-January and runs through mid-May. Two sessions of summer school run from mid-May to mid-June and mid-June to mid-July.

Off-Campus Programs

Students may complement their studies in London with a semester, year, or summer at one of two international study centers. The centers, each offering intensive study of the language and culture of the country, are in Florence and Rome, Italy. The Florence Study Center emphasizes studio and fine arts. The Rome Center offers study in the Italian language and culture, art history, economics, and political science.

Academic Facilities

Information technology is integrated into the curriculum in ways that are natural to the discipline under study. Supporting this are eight student computer laboratories with more than 140 current-specification computers, which connect to the Internet and are networked for student, faculty, and administrative use. Wireless network access is also available.

Richmond's libraries support the courses taught at each campus. Students may use either campus library. The libraries house over 90,000 items including books, DVDs, music CDs, company annual reports, and student theses. In addition, the libraries have subscriptions to a number of journal and magazine titles, along with a variety of national and international newspapers. Richmond students also have access to the many specialized libraries within the London area.

Costs

Tuition for the 2010–11 academic year was $27,000. Room and board were $13,100. Personal expenses, books and supplies, clothing, recreation, and travel costs also need to be factored in.

Financial Aid

Scholarships are awarded annually to students of high academic ability. Financial aid for U.S. citizens includes Federal Stafford Student Loans and Federal PLUS loans. All U.S. citizens must file the Free Application for Federal Student Aid (FAFSA) to qualify. Students should contact the admissions office for details regarding application procedures for scholarships and financial aid.

Faculty

The student-faculty ratio of 12:1 enables optimum interaction and individualized instructional assistance. The 98 faculty members (44 full-time, 54 part-time) have professional degrees from top European and American universities such as Harvard, the University of California (Berkeley), the University of Michigan, Cambridge, Oxford, the London School of Economics, the Royal College of Art, and the University of Bonn.

Student Government

The Richmond Student Union acts as a resource for all students, student organizations, and clubs to voice their opinions and ideas. The Student Union functions as a network between the student body and the administration. Using student ideas, it holds events and seeks to feature student talent while enhancing the overall University experience. The Student Union is ongoing in its development and thus offers possibilities for students to shape and change it. It is an organization directed by students for students and is structured to provide flexibility as well as the opportunity for all students to become involved.

Admission Requirements

Applicants are admitted on the basis of academic performance, references, intended major, and career interests. The required autobiographical essay is of paramount importance. Applicants to Richmond have usually completed a total of twelve years of primary and secondary school with a minimum grade of C+ (2.5 out of 4.0) in the American high school grading system, or its equivalent. British system students should have attained a minimum of five GCSE passes (grades of A, B, or C) in acceptable academic subjects, one of which must be mathematics or science. Equivalent qualifications gained under other educational systems are also considered for the purpose of admission.

Students must submit a completed application form, an essay, transcripts of all secondary and postsecondary school work, and one letter of recommendation. SAT or ACT scores are optional. The ATP code for Richmond is 0823L. The ACT code is 5244. Evidence of proficiency in the English language is required from students whose first language is not English or who did not attend English-speaking schools. Standardized test scores, such as the TOEFL or the ALIGU, or completion of recognized examinations, such as GCSE, Pitman, RSA, or lower Cambridge, are considered in assessing students' language capability.

Richmond admits students on a rolling basis, and applicants are encouraged to submit their application at the earliest opportunity. All documents in languages other than English must be accompanied by official translations. Applicants are usually notified of a decision within two to three weeks.

Application and Information

An application for admission and further information may be obtained by contacting the appropriate admissions office.

Applicants residing in the United States should contact:

Director of U.S. Admissions
U.S. Office of Admissions
Richmond, The American International University in
    London
343 Congress Street, Suite 3100
Boston, Massachusetts 02210-1214
Phone: 617-450-5617
Fax: 617-450-5601
E-mail: usadmissions@richmond.ac.uk
Web site: http://www.richmond.ac.uk

Applicants residing in all other countries should contact:

Director of Admissions
Office of Admissions
Richmond, The American International University in
    London
Queens Road, Richmond
Surrey TW10 6JP
England
Phone: 44-20-8332-9000
Fax: 44-20-8332-1596
E-mail: enroll@richmond.ac.uk
Web site: http://www.richmond.ac.uk

The Richmond Hill campus is situated near the River Thames in one of London's most attractive and secure areas. The impressive neo-Gothic structure was constructed in 1843.

RIDER UNIVERSITY
LAWRENCEVILLE AND PRINCETON, NEW JERSEY

The University

Founded in 1865, Rider University is an independent, coeducational, nonsectarian institution accredited by the Middle States Association of Colleges and Schools. Rider's business programs are accredited by AACSB International–The Association to Advance Collegiate Schools of Business, and its education programs are recognized by the National Council for the Accreditation of Teacher Education (NCATE). Westminster Choir College is accredited by the National Association of Schools of Music (NASM). Rider has campuses in Lawrenceville and Princeton, New Jersey.

Rider comprises four academic schools and colleges: the College of Business Administration; the College of Liberal Arts, Education, and Sciences; the College of Continuing Studies; and Westminster College of the Arts.

Ninety-six percent of Rider's faculty members hold a doctorate or other appropriate advanced degree. Primarily a teaching institution, Rider University selects instructors who are committed to imparting the knowledge and skills of a particular discipline. Full professors teach at all levels. There are no teaching assistants in the classrooms or laboratories.

Rider University's Lawrenceville campus is home to academic, recreational, and housing facilities. A state-of-the-art recreational facility features an indoor track, basketball courts, and exercise equipment. Approximately 65 percent of the 4,750 undergraduates live in University residence halls or in fraternities or sororities on the campus.

Rider participates in NCAA Division I in all of its intercollegiate sports. Women's sports are basketball, cross-country, field hockey, soccer, softball, swimming and diving, tennis, track and field, and volleyball. Men's sports are baseball, basketball, cross-country, golf, soccer, swimming and diving, tennis, track and field, and wrestling.

Preparation for career success goes beyond the classroom at Rider. The Office of Career Services enables students and alumni to increase career awareness through assessment, research, experiential learning, and the development of job-search competencies, resulting in informed decision making. Career Services encourages the ongoing documentation of acquired skills, experiences, achievements, and leadership development and is committed to building partnerships with students, alumni, faculty members, administrators, and employers.

Location

Rider University is located in New Jersey, with suburban campuses in Lawrenceville and Princeton. It is approximately 35 miles northeast of Philadelphia and 65 miles southwest of New York City. The location combines the advantages of accessibility to the cultural and recreational facilities of major urban areas and to the peaceful surroundings of a suburban community.

Westminster Choir College, a subsidiary of Westminster College of the Arts, is ideally located in picturesque Princeton, within walking distance of Princeton's Palmer Square, and is an outstanding atmosphere for living, performing, and learning.

All students have full access to the academic and recreational services available on both campuses.

Majors and Degrees

The College of Business Administration awards the Bachelor of Science in Business Administration (B.S.B.A.) degree in accounting, advertising, business administration, business economics, computer information systems, entrepreneurial studies, finance,

global supply chain management, human resource management, international business, management and leadership, and marketing.

The College of Liberal Arts, Education, and Sciences (CLAES) awards the Bachelor of Arts (B.A.) degree in elementary education and secondary education and the Bachelor of Science (B.S.) degree in business education.

The CLAES also awards the B.A. degree in American studies, communication, economics, English, French, German, global and multinational studies, graphic design, history, journalism, mathematics, philosophy, political science, psychology, public relations, radio and television, Russian, sociology, Spanish, and Web design and multimedia. It offers the B.S. degree in biochemistry, biology, behavioral neuroscience, chemistry, environmental science, geosciences, integrated sciences and math, and marine sciences.

The Westminster College of the Arts is composed of two divisions: Westminster Choir College and the School of Fine and Performing Arts. Westminster Choir College, located on the Princeton campus, awards the Bachelor of Music degrees in sacred music, music education, theory/composition, voice performance, piano, and organ performance.

Located on Rider's Lawrenceville campus, the School of Fine and Performing Arts currently offers a Bachelor of Arts in fine arts with tracks in music, theater, and art; a Bachelor of Arts in dance; a Bachelor of Arts in music; a Bachelor of Music in music theater; and the Bachelor of Arts in arts administration. Students accepted into these programs will live and study on the Lawrenceville campus.

Rider's postbaccalaureate premedical studies program is geared toward career changers who have not taken the undergraduate course prerequisites for admission to medical, dental, and veterinary schools.

Academic Programs

Rider University operates on the semester system. Each college requires a minimum of 120 semester hours of credit for graduation; the last 30 semester hours of credit must be earned at Rider University. The College of Business Administration requires that a student earn at least 45 semester hours, including the last 30, at Rider University.

The Baccalaureate Honors Program is available to students in all programs. Selection in Rider's honors program is competitive. The recommended criteria are a 1230 or higher SAT score (combined critical reading and math); applicants must have a minimum of 600 of each of the critical reading and math sections and a minimum score of 550 on the writing portion. Students submitting ACT scores should have a minimum score of 27, with a minimum score of 26 on the English and math components and a minimum score of 27 on the writing portion. All applicants must have a minimum 3.3 high school grade point average to qualify for this program.

Rider University recognizes the Advanced Placement (AP) Program and offers credit and placement for scores of 3, 4, or 5 on most AP tests. Credit is awarded for the College-Level Examination Program (CLEP) tests, provided that the minimum required score is obtained. The minimum score varies according to the specific area covered by the examination.

Off-Campus Programs

Rider University offers semester-long and academic-year programs at a variety of international sites through an extensive study-abroad program. Popular sites include Austria, Australia, England,

France, Greece, Italy, Ireland, Mexico, and Spain. Short-term, faculty-led study abroad programs are available in January and during the summer months. Summer study-abroad programs are also available in selected countries.

Academic Facilities

The Franklin F. Moore Library contains 481,958 volumes and 648,418 microforms, among many other resources. The library is automated with an integrated library system, sophisticated Web site, and other tools. To complement its on-campus holdings, the library offers 134 online databases for finding journal articles and other scholarly information. The Talbott Library on the Princeton campus houses 74,790 scores and music-related books and journals, and over 31,000 sound and video recordings. Talbott Library's Performance Collection comprises approximately 5,425 choral music titles in performance quantities. Special collections at Talbott include significant reference collections of choral octavos (more than 80,000 titles), organ music, hymnals, nineteenth-century American choral music, music education materials, and the Westminster Archives. In addition, the American Organ Archives of the Organ Historical Society are housed at Talbott Library.

The Office of Information Technology (OIT) is to ensure a pervasive, state-of-the-art, and well-utilized environment for the University. OIT is responsible for all university technology services including but not limited to computing, voice network, cable television, electronic classrooms, and instructional technology. There are two general access computer labs and computer kiosks for Internet access. Teaching computer labs are located on both campuses.

Other academic facilities include well-equipped laboratories for biochemistry, biology, biopsychology, chemistry, communications, environmental sciences, geology, physics, and psychology and performance facilities.

Costs

The total annual tuition charge for new students who began their studies in 2010–11 was $29,870, plus applicable mandatory fees. Room (standard double room) and board charges totaled $11,200 for the academic year.

Financial Aid

Rider University offers merit-based scholarships for qualified applicants. These scholarships are renewable for up to four years of study if the student maintains the minimum grade point average specified by the Scholarship Committee. Scholarships range from $7000 to $20,000 annually.

Other financial aid is based on demonstrated financial need. Students and their parents are required to file the Free Application for Federal Student Aid (FAFSA) prior to March 1 to be considered for financial assistance administered by Rider University. Students are eligible for consideration for Federal Pell Grants, Federal Supplemental Educational Opportunity Grants, Federal Work-Study Program awards, Federal Perkins Loans, New Jersey Tuition Aid Grants, New Jersey Distinguished Scholar Scholarships, Rider University grants, Trustee Scholarships, Alumni Scholarships, and other forms of institutional aid.

Faculty

There are 250 full-time and 372 part-time faculty members, 96 percent of whom hold a doctorate or terminal degree in their field. The same faculty members teach both graduate and undergraduate courses; graduate assistants do not teach classes at Rider University. The student-faculty ratio is approximately 13:1. Faculty members serve on student affairs committees and as faculty advisers to all student organizations.

Student Government

The active Student Government Association (SGA) sponsors concerts, lectures, plays, and other events. All social rules and regulations are made, enforced, and adjudicated by students. Each class, each residence hall, and many other student organizations are represented in the Student Government Association.

Admission Requirements

Students applying for admission to Rider University are expected to have completed a minimum of 16 acceptable college-preparatory units of study by the end of their senior year in high school. These 16 units must include 4 in English and 3 in mathematics, including algebra I, algebra II, and geometry. The other 9 units should be selected from traditional academic areas, including history, mathematics, science, social studies, foreign languages, and literature. Business or vocational courses completed in high school are not considered college-preparatory units. Students are required to submit official SAT or ACT results, a personal statement, and two letters of recommendation in support of their application. Most successful applicants rank in the upper half of their high school senior class.

Rider University seeks a diverse student body and encourages applications from students from varied ethnic, economic, and geographic backgrounds. Campus interviews are strongly recommended but not required for most candidates.

Application and Information

Rider University works on a rolling admissions basis, but it encourages applications for the fall semester to be submitted by January 15. Applications for the spring semester should be submitted by December 1. The application fee is $50. The early action option is available for fall applicants. Students interested in the early action option must submit all necessary documentation by November 15 and are notified of an admissions decision by December 15. Early action is a non-binding option. All other applicants are notified of the admission decision approximately three to four weeks after the completed application is received. Transfer applicants receive the same priority for admission, housing, and financial aid as freshman applicants. More information can be found at http://www.rider.edu/admissions and students can apply online at http://www.rider.edu/applynow.

Interested students are encouraged to contact:

Director of Undergraduate Admissions
Rider University
2083 Lawrenceville Road
Lawrenceville, New Jersey 08648-3099
Phone: 609-896-5042
     800-257-9026 (toll-free)
E-mail: admissions@rider.edu
Web site: http://www.rider.edu/admissions
    http://www.facebook.com/RiderUniversity?v=photos

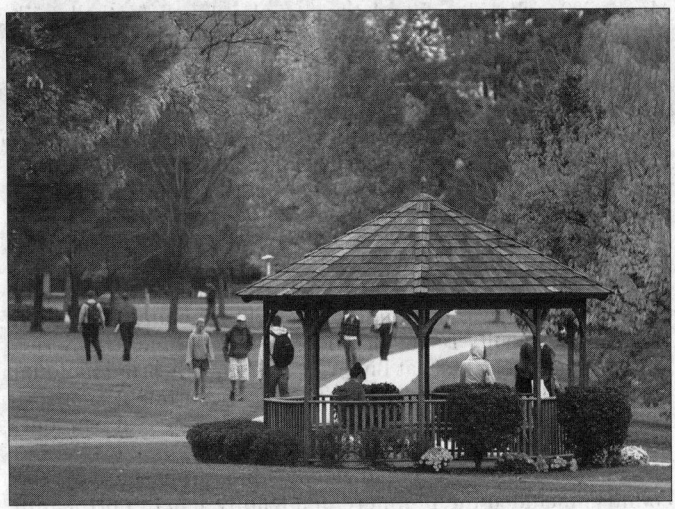

Rider students on the Lawrenceville campus.

RIPON COLLEGE

RIPON, WISCONSIN

The College

Together with the other members of its tightly knit learning community, Ripon students often feel as if they learn more deeply, live more fully, and achieve more success. There are more opportunities to be involved, lead, speak out, make a difference, and explore new interests than at many colleges many times its size. Through collaborative learning, group living, teamwork, and networking, students tap into the power of a community where all work together to ensure their success, at Ripon and beyond. The best residential liberal arts colleges strive to be true learning communities like Ripon. Ripon succeeds better than most, because the enrollment of just under 1,100 students is perfect for fostering connections inside and outside the classroom. Students flourish in this environment of mutual respect, where shared values are elevated and diverse ideas are valued. Students who are seeking academic challenge and want to benefit from an environment of personal attention and support should take a closer look at Ripon. In classes that average 20 students, professors are able to know the students and their strengths and capabilities extraordinarily well. They tailor course work to make sure students are always challenged to perform at the top of their game, yet they are always ready to provide extra support when needed. Faculty members collaborate with students on research projects, suggest independent-study topics, and connect them with internships and other active learning experiences.

A Ripon education can take graduates anywhere. A student could study psychology and play basketball and then become a seven-time Grammy winner like jazz singer Al Jarreau, '62; guide the space shuttle into orbit like Jeff Bantle, '80, a chief flight director with NASA; or become an international opera star like Gail Dobish, '76. A student could set records in medical science like neonatologist Dr. John Muraskas, '78, who is on record for saving the world's smallest premature baby, or cover world events like Richard Threlkeld, '59, former Moscow correspondent for CBS News, or a student might end up studying at Oxford University as a Rhodes Scholar like Zach Morris '02, who also found time to play touch football with former President Bill Clinton and spend an evening at Buckingham Palace with the Queen.

The list of student clubs and organizations is ever changing, reflecting students' ever-changing interests. A recent addition is FUERZA Alliance, designed to educate students about Latino cultures and to provide services to the Spanish-speaking community of Ripon.

Every day at Ripon is packed with a host of activities such as concerts (there are eight vocal and instrumental groups that perform regularly on campus, as well as many individual student and faculty recitals). The Caestecker Fine Arts Series and the Chamber Music at Ripon Series annually bring national performers to the campus. The Theatre Department sponsors two major productions annually, plus a series of student-directed one-act plays. The most recent Ripon Film Festival (an annual showcase for independent films from around the country) included the premiere of a feature-length horror film written, directed by, and starring a Ripon student.

Ripon's NCAA Division III intercollegiate teams compete in the Midwest Conference. Men's varsity sports include baseball, basketball, cross-country, cycling, football, golf, indoor and outdoor track and field, soccer, swimming and diving, and tennis. Women's varsity sports include basketball, cross-country, cycling, dance, golf, indoor and outdoor track and field, soccer, softball, swimming and diving, and tennis.

Location

Located on 250 tree-lined, rolling acres adjacent to downtown Ripon, the campus looks and feels like a college should. Ripon's twenty-six first-rate buildings are a striking combination of historic (ten campus structures listed on the National Register of Historic Places) and modern architecture.

Majors and Degrees

Majors include anthropology, art, art history, biology, business administration, chemistry, chemistry/biology, communication, computer science, economics, educational studies, English, environmental sciences, exercise science, foreign languages, French, German, global studies, history, Latin American area studies, mathematics, music, philosophy, physics, politics and government, psychobiology, psychology, religion, sociology/anthropology, Spanish, and theater. Programs are also available in leadership studies, sports medicine/athletic training, and women's studies.

Preprofessional programs include dentistry, journalism, law and government, library and information science, medicine, ministry, optometry, physical therapy, and veterinary medicine.

Dual-degree programs include allied health sciences/medical technology, engineering, forestry, and social welfare.

Certification programs include education certification, early childhood, elementary, elementary/middle school, secondary, secondary/middle, music K–12, and physical education K–12.

Academic Programs

Ripon's liberal arts curriculum is designed to introduce students to a wide variety of disciplines. About 40 percent of the students complete double or triple majors, whereas some create special self-designed majors. Excellent communications skills—written and oral—as well as critical-thinking and problem-solving skills are the hallmark of a Ripon education, regardless of major. In addition, the leadership studies program and the newly established ethical leadership program provide a strong foundation for leadership skills. An Army ROTC program is also available.

Off-Campus Programs

Ripon offers more than forty different off-campus programs of varying lengths to choose from, each one officially sanctioned by and affiliated with Ripon. Although most programs are connected with a major or minor program, all are open to every Ripon student, regardless of major.

U.S. programs include Chicago Urban Studies Semester, Fisk University–Ripon Exchange Program, Newberry Seminar in the Humanities, Oak Ridge Science Semester, Washington Semester, and Woods Hole Marine Biology.

International programs include Bonn, Germany, Program; Budapest Semester; Central European Studies Program in the Czech Republic; Costa Rica; Cross-Cultural Study Center in

Seville, Spain; Florence Program; France and Spain; Global Studies Program in Turkey; India Studies; Japan Study; London and Florence Program in the Arts; Madrid Program; Montpellier, France; Paris, France; Ripon and York St. John Exchange; Russia Program; Sea Education Association (marine biology abroad); Sea Semester at Woods Hole; Swansea Program; Tanzania; Toledo, Spain; and University of Wales in Bangor.

Academic Facilities

Constant additions and improvements, like a recent multimillion-dollar apartment-style residence hall, the renovation and classroom expansion of Todd Wehr Hall, and upgrades to upperclass residence halls, the library, the bookstore, dining facilities, and a coffee shop, maintain Ripon's ability to meet the needs of today and tomorrow. Technology services include high-speed Internet and e-mail, telephone, and video communication. Intranet and Internet services are accessible from systems located throughout the College. The campuswide network provides access from every room, and several wireless hot spots in key areas let students access the world without being tied down.

The library staff provides friendly, efficient circulation, reference, instruction, and interlibrary loan services that aid in research. The library also houses the College archives, a computer lab, and more than a dozen online databases. Library holdings include 164,000 volumes, 800 current periodicals, and microfilms.

The C. J. Rodman Center for the Arts is home to a theater with a state-of-the-art computerized lighting system, a recital hall with one of only fifty existing Bedient organs, an art gallery, and a sculpture garden.

The J. M. Storzer Center includes an Olympic-size pool, a first-class gymnasium, tennis and racquetball courts, a dance studio, training facilities, and a weight room. The outdoor playing fields and courts are among the best in their class. In addition, a large, modern exercise facility was recently added in the main student residence area.

Costs

Tuition is $28,414, room and board are $8270, and fees are $275, for a total cost of $36,959.

Financial Aid

Ripon has been consistently recognized as a best value by all of the national ranking organizations. More than 90 percent of Ripon students receive some form of merit-based scholarship and/or need-based grants and loans.

Ripon recognizes and rewards students' success in high school with its institutionally funded scholarships, based not only on academic merit but also on special achievements in other areas, such as the creative arts. The scholarships range from $1000 to full tuition. Ripon participates in all federal and state need-based financial aid programs. The financial aid counselors work individually with students and their families to investigate every possible financial resource for which they are eligible.

Faculty

Ripon has 57 full-time and 25 part-time faculty members. Ninety-seven percent of the full-time faculty members have Ph.D.'s.

Admission Requirements

Ripon enrolls students who are expected to contribute to and benefit from the academic and residential programs provided.

Ripon does not discriminate on the basis of gender, sexual orientation, race, color, age, religion, national or ethnic origin, or disability in the administration of its educational policies, admission practices, scholarship and loan programs, and athletic and other College-administered programs.

Application and Information

The faculty committee on academic standards establishes the criteria for admission. The school considers a variety of factors, including secondary school record, standardized test scores (SAT or ACT), recommendations, a written essay, and extracurricular or community service activities. Ripon's admission process reflects the personal attention students can expect to receive during their college careers, and applicants are encouraged to provide any additional information they consider helpful.

For further information, students should contact:

Steven M. Schuetz
Dean of Admission
Ripon College
300 Seward Street
P.O. Box 248
Ripon, Wisconsin 54971-0248
Phone: 800-947-4766 (toll-free)
E-mail: adminfo@ripon.edu
Web site: http://www.ripon.edu

Ripon College students and their families celebrate commencement on the lawn of Harwood Memorial Union.

RIVIER COLLEGE
NASHUA, NEW HAMPSHIRE

The College

Rivier College, a private Catholic college founded in 1933, has gained a reputation for academic excellence in more than forty programs. The College has adapted to changing needs by developing liberal arts/career-oriented programs designed to prepare graduates in many fields.

Rivier's School of Undergraduate Studies enrolls approximately 1,500 students, including 900 full-time day students. With a 15:1 student-faculty ratio, day students have plenty of opportunities to connect with faculty and become active members of the academic community.

Most full-time undergraduate day students are of traditional age: between 18 and 22 years old. Though the majority comes from New England, Rivier attracts students from states around the country, including Florida, California, and Delaware. International students represent countries in Africa, Asia, Europe, the Middle East, and South America. Students who live on campus reside in four modern residence halls. Most rooms are doubles, with some triples, quads, and singles available. Rivier also provides substance-free housing in Presentation Hall. The newest hall offers suite-style living, with several double and triple rooms sharing a kitchenette and common area. The Dion Center houses the dining room, the mail room, a campus store, student development offices, and meeting rooms. All students are permitted to have cars on the campus.

The Office of Student Development, the Student Government Association, and more than twenty-five student clubs and organizations provide a calendar of social, cultural, and recreational activities, including concerts, live entertainment, films, and sporting events. The College and student organizations frequently organize outings, including trips to Boston and New York. Students also enjoy a variety of performances by the Rivier Theater Company.

Rivier offers an orientation for new students to introduce them to the College's wide array of services. Academic advisers, staff at the Writing and Resource Center, and peer tutors help students meet their academic goals. The Health Services Center and Counseling Center ensure students' physical and emotional well-being. A full-time chaplain and Campus Ministry team coordinate spiritual activities and service opportunities, while a comprehensive career development service helps students prepare for employment after graduation.

Rivier offers a variety of team and individual sports, including NCAA Division III men's baseball, basketball, cross-country, lacrosse, soccer, and volleyball; and women's basketball, cross-country, field hockey, lacrosse, soccer, softball, and volleyball. The men's volleyball team has been nationally ranked every year since 2001. The Muldoon Health and Fitness Center is home to Rivier's varsity athletics and to many intramural sports and fitness activities, including volleyball, floor hockey, basketball, weight training, aerobics, self-defense, and more. The campus also has soccer and softball fields, as well as a beach volleyball court and cross-country trail. Student athletes and others can take advantage of an on-campus rehabilitation clinic offering free injury assessment, physical and occupational therapy, and athletic training.

Location

Nashua (population 87,000) is located in southern New Hampshire. The city of Boston lies within easy access 40 miles to the south. Local access to public transportation provides for easy travel to and from the campus. Recreational activities abound year-round at nearby lakes and ski areas, in the White Mountains to the north, and at the seacoast, just an hour's drive to the east.

Majors and Degrees

Rivier College awards Bachelor of Arts and Bachelor of Science degrees in the following areas of concentration: art (studio art, graphic design, and photography and digital media), biology (allied health and environmental science) and biology education, business, communications (advertising/public relations, journalism, photojournalism, scriptwriting, video production, and Web design/online publishing), criminal justice, education (early childhood/special education, elementary education/special education, and human development/interdisciplinary), English and English education, finance, history, human development, international studies, liberal studies, marketing, mathematics and mathematics education, modern languages (modern languages education and Spanish), nursing, political science, psychology, social studies education, and sociology. Five-year combined bachelor's/master's degree programs are available in business, English (teacher certification), and psychology. The College offers preprofessional programs in law, dentistry, medicine, and veterinary medicine. Associate degrees are offered in art, business management, early childhood education, liberal studies, and nursing.

Academic Programs

Rivier College takes special pride in its curriculum, which offers both professional studies and liberal arts to prepare students for a fast-changing, highly technological society. The broad-based curriculum focuses on preparing students for challenging and rewarding careers and furthering their personal growth. Core curriculum requirements vary slightly depending on the degree to be obtained, but generally include courses in English, mathematics and/or natural sciences, modern language and literature, philosophy, religious studies, social science, and Western civilization. No fewer than ten courses must be taken in the major field. Students may choose electives that suit their personal interests and professional goals. The bachelor's degree requires a minimum of 120 credits with a grade point average of at least 2.0. For the associate degree, the student must complete a minimum of 60 credits with a grade point average of at least 2.0.

All departments encourage qualified students to pursue internships in their field of study during their junior or senior year. Education specialists student teach in local schools. Nursing majors complete clinical rotations in health-care facilities throughout southern New Hampshire and northern Massachusetts. History, law, and political science majors may work in a law office, business, legal-assistance agency, or government agency. Sociology and psychology majors work with local social service agencies. English and communications majors work in public relations, broadcasting, or corporate communications positions. Art majors work in advertising or graphic design or at local galleries. Business majors work in marketing, management, and technology.

Honors awards include placement on the dean's list, membership in Kappa Gamma Pi, listing in *Who's Who Among Students in American Universities and Colleges*, listing in *The National Dean's List*, and degrees with honors. Academically talented students may also apply to the four-year honors program.

The college year is divided into two 15-week semesters, with first-semester examinations held before Christmas recess. Students usually take five courses each semester. Academic credit may be granted to incoming freshmen on the basis of scores on Advanced Placement tests and CLEP examinations. Students may also "challenge" courses and receive credit by special examination.

Off-Campus Programs

Through Rivier College's membership in the New Hampshire College and University Council, a sixteen-member consortium of senior and two-year colleges, Rivier students may register for courses at any of the member colleges and receive transfer credits.

Academic Facilities

Academic facilities include Memorial Hall, which houses fourteen classrooms, faculty offices, a lecture hall, a fully equipped digital imaging studio, a communications lab offering the most recent software and video/sound editing equipment, a behavioral science lab, the studio of community television station tv13 Nashua (WYCN), and art department facilities that include a gallery, a slide library, and studios. The Academic Computer Center features up to sixty-eight workstations with a full range of cutting-edge software and Internet/e-mail access. Regina Library houses more than 100,000 volumes and provides access to more than 3 million volumes in twelve area libraries, as well as online access to licensed databases in virtually every academic subject. The Writing and Resource Center offers assistance from professional writing consultants as well as student tutors. Other academic facilities include nursing and science laboratories; a physical assessment lab and nursing skills simulation lab, which provide nursing students with practical experience using blood pressure cuffs, ophthalmoscopes, IV pumps, patient simulators, and more; the McLean Center for Finance and Economics; the BAE Student Research Lab; a clinical psychology lab; electronic classrooms offering multimedia learning tools; and the Education Center, which houses an eight-classroom Early Childhood Center, observation rooms, and an educational resource center.

Costs

Tuition and fees for the academic year 2010–11 were $24,420; room and board, $9522; and books and supplies, approximately $700. Students should expect to pay a $100 activities fee and a $25 registration fee each semester.

Financial Aid

Financial aid is awarded on the basis of the financial need of the student and family. Approximately 98 percent of Rivier's full-time undergraduate students receive financial aid from the College or from government or private sources. Federal aid includes Federal Pell Grants, Federal Supplemental Educational Opportunity Grants, Federal Perkins Loans, Federal Stafford Student Loans, the Federal PLUS loan program, and the Federal Work-Study Program. To be considered for financial aid, a student must file the Free Application for Federal Student Aid (FAFSA) with the federal government as soon as possible after January 1 for the coming year. FAFSA results should be on file with the College Financial Aid Office prior to March 1 for the following academic year. Each applicant is assessed individually to determine the best combination of grant, work, scholarship, and loan amounts to meet the need of the student. The College awards more than $6 million in merit-based scholarships and grants annually, ranging in value from $1000 to full tuition. For more information, students should contact the Office of Financial Aid.

Faculty

The College employs 71 full-time faculty members. The full-time student–faculty ratio is 15:1. Part-time instructors in specialized areas are working professionals who bring current knowledge and expertise in their field to their classes. All classes are taught by faculty members, and department chairs serve as academic advisers to students in their major programs.

Student Government

Every full-time day student automatically becomes a member of the Student Government Association (SGA) upon registration and payment of the student activity fee. The main goals of the SGA are to stimulate active participation in all College functions, to establish and maintain effective channels of communication among members of the College community and the community at large, and to foster a mutual trust, encourage a spirit of cooperation, and initiate new endeavors. The SGA also supervises student clubs and organizations and oversees their finances. The SGA Executive Board serves as the channel of communication through which the views of the students on institutional policies reach the College administration.

Admission Requirements

Applicants for admission should ordinarily have completed, in an accredited high school, a minimum of 16 academic units, including 4 in English, 2 in a modern foreign language, 3 in mathematics, 2 in social science, 2 in science, and 3 in electives. The most successful candidates are in the upper half of their class, with at least a B average. Combined SAT scores average 1410–1500. A personal interview is strongly recommended but not required.

Rivier welcomes applications from qualified transfer candidates from accredited institutions, as well as applications from international students. Transfer students must forward transcripts of all previous college work and a high school transcript. International students must fulfill the requirements for general admission; they may also be required to submit Test of English as a Foreign Language (TOEFL) scores. Deferred admission may be granted to students who wish to postpone entrance for up to one year, provided they have not been enrolled full-time at another postsecondary institution.

Application and Information

Applications must be accompanied by a nonrefundable $25 application fee, SAT scores, one letter of recommendation, and a high school transcript. The School of Undergraduate Studies employs a system of rolling admission that allows qualified students to be admitted approximately one month after their application is completed. Transfers should apply by June 1 for fall admission and by December 1 for spring admission. Those applying for financial aid should observe the March 1 deadline. Interviews are arranged through the Admissions Office. Students may apply online at the College's Web site.

For an application or additional information, please contact:

Office of Undergraduate Admissions
Rivier College
420 South Main Street
Nashua, New Hampshire 03060
Phone: 603-897-8507
       800-44-RIVIER (toll-free)
Fax: 603-891-1799
E-mail: admissions@rivier.edu
Web site: http://www.rivier.edu

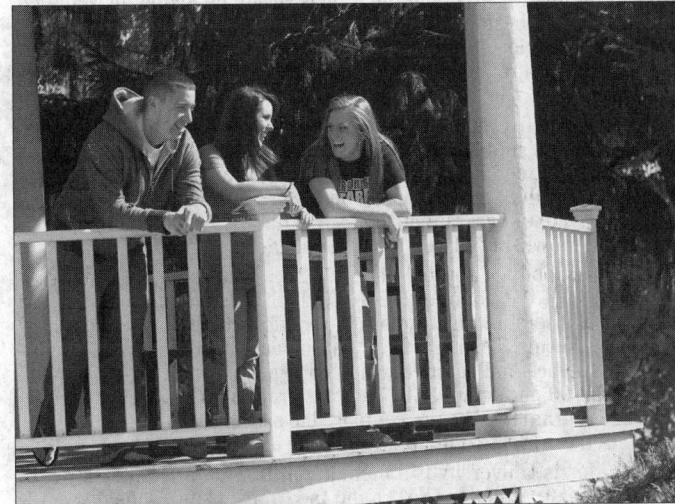

Students enjoy Rivier's great location in the heart of New England— approximately an hour's drive from Boston, the mountains, and the seacoast.

ROBERT MORRIS UNIVERSITY

CHICAGO, BENSENVILLE, DUPAGE, ELGIN, LAKE COUNTY, ORLAND PARK, PEORIA, SCHAUMBURG, AND SPRINGFIELD, ILLINOIS

The Experience University.
ROBERT MORRIS UNIVERSITY
ILLINOIS

The University

As an accredited, private, not-for-profit institution, Robert Morris University (RMU) grants associate, bachelor's, and master's degrees to more than 3,000 students each year. Its mission is to offer professional, career-focused education in a collegiate setting to diverse communities. Besides associate degrees in twelve different fields of study, RMU awards the Bachelor of Business Administration degree with concentrations in accounting, economics, health/fitness management, hospitality management, information systems management, and management; the Bachelor of Applied Science degree in graphic design; the Bachelor of Applied Science degree in computer studies; and the Bachelor of Professional Studies degree with concentrations in architectural technology, advanced culinary arts, applied health science, law office administration, organizational writing, and Web development. Master's degrees offered by RMU include the Master of Business Administration with concentrations in accounting, finance, human resource management, and management; the Master of Information; and the Master of Management with specializations in higher education administration and health-care administration. RMU is accredited by the Higher Learning Commission and is a member of the North Central Association of Colleges and Schools (230 South LaSalle Street, Suite 7-500, Chicago, Illinois 60604-1413; 312-263-0456; http://www.ncahigherlearningcommission.org).

The history of Robert Morris University dates back to the founding of the Moser School, one of the outstanding independent business schools in Chicago, in 1913. Robert Morris University also has origins in Illinois at the site of the former Carthage College. Here, Robert Morris University was chartered and offered associate degrees in both liberal and vocational arts from 1965 to 1974. With the acquisition of the Moser School in 1975, RMU expanded to include business and allied health programs. The University now provides students with a choice of nine locations: Chicago, Bensenville, DuPage, Elgin, Orland Park, Lake County, Peoria, Schaumburg, and Springfield, Illinois.

RMU offers programs in the School of Business Administration, the College of Nursing & Health Studies, the Institute of Technology & Media, the Institute of Culinary Arts, the Institute of Art & Design, the College of Liberal Arts, and the Morris Graduate School of Management. Each of these divisions uses the most modern computer technology. Acquisition of such technology is imperative to providing real-world educational experiences that are relevant to the evolving workplace.

RMU's unique five-quarter system is designed for continuous learning. It enables students to accelerate their education, completing a bachelor's degree in less than four years and an associate degree in eighteen months. In addition, Robert Morris University is the fifth-largest private undergraduate college in Illinois, and its tuition rate is among the lowest of Illinois' private colleges and universities.

The student body of approximately 7,727 is a cross-cultural mix representative of the communities served. Each student works with a team of advisers and instructors in an effort to achieve educational and career goals. The records of the University's students and graduates are the best indicators of what a prospective student can expect. More than 90 percent of RMU students graduate from the bachelor's degree program they begin, compared to significantly lower percentages at other private and public colleges and universities.

Robert Morris University is a member of the National Association of Intercollegiate Athletics (NAIA) and the Chicagoland Collegiate Athletic Conference (CCAC), Division II. RMU athletic teams compete in top-level facilities located near each campus. The University offers men's and women's basketball, club hockey, cross-country, golf, soccer, and swimming. It also offers men's baseball and women's bowling, dance, lacrosse, softball, tennis, and volleyball.

Housing options are available within a short distance of the main campus at Fornelli Hall and the University Center, which provide a wealth of amenities, shopping, entertainment, and events that bring the community together in apartment-style student living.

Location

Located in the heart of Chicago's bustling cultural and financial districts, the University's main campus is minutes from all that Chicago offers, including the Chicago Board of Trade, Art Institute, Field Museum, Merchandise Mart, lakefront, sports arenas, theaters, and all forms of public transportation. The Chicago campus is readily accessible from all parts of the city and suburbs by bus lines and trains. Parking is available in the immediate vicinity. Robert Morris University is across the street from the renowned Harold Washington Public Library.

The Bensenville campus opened to better serve the residents of western Cook and DuPage Counties and to meet the demands of employers in the area. The recently expanded Orland Park campus now includes a technology center with the latest computer facilities available to industry and education and is approximately 30 miles southwest of Chicago. It is accessible via public transportation and I-80 and I-55, which run parallel on the south and north ends of the campus, respectively. Orland Park is becoming a corporate center of the southwest Chicago suburbs, offering students opportunity for professional growth through internships and employment.

The DuPage campus opened on the border between Naperville and Aurora and serves students as well as employers along the East-West High Tech Corridor—the heart of rapid technological development and close to a wide range of employers. The RMU Institute of Culinary Arts started at the DuPage campus and grew so significantly so quickly, the program expanded to the main campus in downtown Chicago and Orland Park.

The Springfield campus represents the first step of the University's commitment to serve central Illinois. This campus has also expanded to a second building at the same location due to expansion of programs and increases in enrollment. The RMU presence in Illinois has further extended to a campus in Peoria, with a busy downtown location, and Waukegan, serving the northern region of Illinois. The most recent additions are the graduate studies center in Schaumburg and the undergraduate campus in Elgin.

All RMU campuses provide students with access to the unlimited variety of business services and enhance the students' understanding of the world of work, the employment process, and an appreciation for the attributes of each community.

Majors and Degrees

The Bachelor of Business Administration degree at Robert Morris University offers concentrations in accounting, economics, health/fitness management, hospitality management, information systems management, and management. The Bachelor of Applied Science degree in graphic design offers concentrations in graphic arts and digital video; the Bachelor of Professional Studies degree offers concentrations in architectural technology, advanced culinary arts, applied health sciences, Web development, organizational writing, and law office management; and the Bachelor of Applied Science degree in computer studies offers concentrations in systems integration and networking. The Associate of Applied Science degree is awarded in business administration, CADD (architectural/mechanical), computer networking, culinary arts, fitness and exercise, graphic design, interior space planning and design, medical assisting, nursing, paralegal studies, pharmacy technology, and surgical technology.

More than twenty-six transfer agreements have been established between RMU and community colleges, allowing students who have earned associate degrees at community colleges in the state of Illinois to complete their bachelor's degrees at RMU by transferring in as a junior.

Academic Programs

The University's academic calendar consists of five quarters, each of which is ten weeks long. The program of study is designed so that students can complete their course work and enter their careers in the shortest time possible.

By concentrating on the specialized subjects related to the student's chosen career field, the University's curricula provide students with the skills and knowledge necessary to enter the job market. Each major consists of courses prescribed by the University to lead to this objective. An associate degree requires at least 92 quarter hours of credit, with a minimum of 36 hours of credit in general education in the areas of communications, humanities, math and science, and social and behavioral science. A minimum of 52 quarter hours of credit are required in career courses, and the remaining hours are electives split between general education and career courses. A bachelor's degree requires a minimum of 188 quarter hours of credit.

Robert Morris University offers students the opportunity to gain experience in their majors and improve their skills through internships and externships. Internships offer many educational and professional benefits and provide students with the opportunity to earn academic credit for participating in a career-specific work experience.

Off-Campus Programs

Robert Morris University offers students the opportunity to study abroad in London, England; Florence, Italy; Hamburg, Germany; Paris, France; and Rome, Italy.

Academic Facilities

General-purpose classrooms are Internet and multimedia ready. Students have ample study, practice, and leisure space on campus. The Student Center at RMU's Chicago Campus has been recognized by *American School & University* as an outstanding design. Specialized laboratories are available for the systems integration, surgical technology, interior space planning and design, and culinary arts programs. The technology-based library has online capabilities that connect the University's various campuses. Students have access via the Internet to advanced research tools, sizable collections of reference and resource volumes, and periodical subscriptions.

Costs

Robert Morris University has one of the lowest tuition rates of any baccalaureate degree–granting private college in the state. Tuition for 2011–12 is $7200 per quarter. Book and supply costs vary by major from $400 to $600 per quarter. Housing and program fees are also applicable.

Financial Aid

Robert Morris University participates in the following federal and state financial aid programs: the Federal Pell Grant, Illinois Monetary Award (SSIG/IMA), Federal Supplemental Educational Opportunity Grant (FSEOG), Federal Stafford Student Loan, Federal Perkins Loan, Federal PLUS loan, and Federal Work-Study (FWS) Program. In addition, the University awards institutional grants on the basis of athletic, need, leadership, academic major, or a combination of these factors. All students must complete a financial planning interview with their admissions counselor, and all are urged to complete the Free Application for Federal Student Aid (FAFSA). Approximately 85 percent of the student body receives some financial assistance. In the 2010–11 academic year, the University awarded more than $22 million in institutional aid.

Faculty

The faculty members at Robert Morris University are selected on the basis of their academic credentials, career experiences in their field, and dedication to giving individual attention to every student. All faculty members possess a master's degree in their chosen field, and many possess a Ph.D. in their area of specialization. In addition to teaching courses, faculty members promote the progress of their students through the individualized academic, employment, and personal development counseling they provide.

Student Government

Robert Morris University has no formal student government. Student representatives serve on committees that make recommendations about campus issues. Student organizations and activities are available.

Admission Requirements

All graduates of accredited high schools or the equivalent (GED) are eligible for admission to the University. All candidates are encouraged to have a personal interview with an admissions representative and take a tour of the campus.

A variety of materials are considered for various applicants. Freshman applicants just graduating from high school must submit their high school record or GED score and test results from the ACT, SAT, Applied Education Skills Assessment (AESA), Advanced Placement, and SAT Subject Area tests.

Those enrolling as an adult must submit their high school record or GED score; test results from the ACT, SAT, AESA, College-Level Examination Program (CLEP), and DANTES; and evidence of a successful employment experience.

Transfer students must present a minimum of 12 transferable credit hours from an accredited institution and their academic records from any high schools and colleges previously attended.

International students must forward their official education records, the results from either the TOEFL or AESA, and an affidavit of financial support.

Homeschooled students must submit a complete transcript of all classes they have taken, curriculum documentation and its state certification, and results from any standardized exams they have taken.

Application and Information

Applications can be obtained by contacting the Admissions Office at any of the University's campuses. The completed application and the $50 nonrefundable application fee ($100 nonrefundable application fee for international students) should be sent to the Admissions Office. The University operates on a rolling admissions basis, and students can enroll during any of the five times offered during the year. For further information, prospective students should visit the Web site or contact:

Robert Morris University
Chicago–Main Campus
401 South State Street
Chicago, Illinois 60605

Phone: 800-762-5960 (toll-free)
Web site: http://www.robertmorris.edu

Robert Morris University
Bensenville Campus
1000 Tower Lane
Bensenville, Illinois 60106

Robert Morris University
DuPage Campus
905 Meridian Lake Drive
Aurora, Illinois 60504

Robert Morris University
1707 North Randall Road
Elgin, Illinois 60123

Robert Morris University
Orland Park Campus
82 Orland Square
Orland Park, Illinois 60462

Robert Morris University
Lake County Campus
1507 South Waukegan Road
Waukegan, Illinois 60085

Robert Morris University
Peoria Campus
211 Fulton Street
Peoria, Illinois 61602

Morris Graduate School of Management
A Division of Robert Morris University
Schaumburg Campus
1000 East Woodfield Road
Schaumburg, Illinois 60173

Robert Morris University
Springfield Campus
3101 Montvale Drive
Springfield, Illinois 62704

ROBERT MORRIS UNIVERSITY

MOON TOWNSHIP, PENNSYLVANIA

The University

A private university in Pittsburgh's suburban hills, Robert Morris University (RMU) is set on a 230-acre former estate that is a short drive from the cultural and commercial opportunities of a major city. Founded in 1921, RMU offers sixty undergraduate programs and twenty graduate programs, providing its 5,000 students academic excellence with a professional focus.

The University, which built its reputation in the business fields of accounting, finance, marketing, and management, has grown to include programs in communications, information systems, engineering, mathematics, science, education, social sciences, and nursing. RMU uses a Student Engagement Transcript to document internships, service-learning activities, study abroad, leadership roles, and other learning outside the classroom. This focus on engaged learning contributes to the 92 percent placement rate of graduates within six months of earning their degree.

RMU is a teaching-centered institution featuring small classes taught by professors and a student-faculty ratio of 15:1. The campus is growing, with a new business school building opening in fall 2011, a new media arts complex set to open the following year, and a new nursing simulation center in design stages. RMU will also open another apartment-style residence hall in fall 2011 to accommodate its growing student population.

Visiting international scholars and a variety of opportunities to study abroad—for a semester or just a few weeks—enrich students' global perspectives. Students can participate in any of nearly 100 clubs and organizations. The Student Life Office organizes dances, parties, movie screenings, comedy acts, health and wellness fairs, educational programs, and day trips. Business organizations, professional clubs, and honor societies provide students with career preparation opportunities.

The University's competitive athletics program fields twenty-three NCAA Division I teams, and the Colonials have won numerous titles and championships. Both football and basketball draw large crowds to Joe Walton Stadium and the Charles Sewall Center, allowing students to show their school spirit. The region's only Division I men's and women's ice hockey teams play at the RMU Island Sports Center, a 32-acre sports and recreation complex with two ice rinks, two multipurpose rinks, an indoor golf driving range, a miniature golf course, a pro shop, and a restaurant and banquet facility. Students can also participate in a number of club and intramural sports on campus.

Location

The 230-acre main campus is located in Moon Township, Pennsylvania, just 15 minutes from Pittsburgh International Airport and 17 miles from downtown Pittsburgh. The RMU Island Sports Center is 15 minutes from campus on Neville Island.

Majors and Degrees

Robert Morris University offers sixty undergraduate programs of study: accounting, actuarial science, advertising, biology, biomedical engineering, business, communication, computer information systems, corporate communications, economics, elementary education (early childhood, mid-level, and special education concentrations), engineering, English, environmental science, finance, graphic design, health services administration, history and government, hospitality and tourism management, industrial engineering, information sciences, intelligence systems, journalism, management, manufacturing engineering, marketing, mechanical engineering, media arts, nuclear medicine technology, nursing, organizational studies, photography, prelaw, premedicine, predentistry, pre–chiropractic studies, pre–osteopathic studies, pre–veterinary science, professional communications/information systems, public relations, psychology, secondary education (biology, business/computer/information technology, communication, English, mathematics, and social studies concentrations), social science, sociology, software development, software engineering, special education, sport management, sport psychology, theater, TV/video production, Web design, and Web development.

The University offers five-year integrated bachelor's/master's degree programs, medical school affiliation, cooperative education programs, and an honors program.

Academic Programs

Robert Morris is on a two-semester schedule with various summer sessions. A total of 126 credits are required for the bachelor's degree. Internship or co-op credits of 3 to 12 hours may be used toward degree requirements. The University participates in a cross-registration program with nine local colleges through the Pittsburgh Council on Higher Education consortium.

Academic Facilities

Learning resources include a traditional library with more than 137,000 bound volumes, 80 reference databases, and 600 periodical subscriptions.

The Academic Media Center, with full production facilities, provides students with opportunities to collaborate on projects in all areas of media, including television/video production, audio production, and photography.

State-of-the-art laboratory facilities support the engineering, mathematics, science, and nursing programs. Graphic and Web design students benefit from a cutting-edge design studio.

A new business school building with simulated stock trading floor, business library, and videoconferencing center is due to open in fall 2011 and a new media arts complex is planned to open in 2012. A new nursing simulation center is in the design stage.

Costs

Annual tuition for the 2010–11 year was a $20,940 flat rate, based on a 24- to 36-credit, two-semester schedule. Room and board fees were $10,660 based on double occupancy and a full meal plan.

Financial Aid

More than 90 percent of RMU undergraduates receive some sort of financial aid, including scholarships, grants, loans, and work-study programs. Both need-based and achievement-based awards are available. All applicants must complete the admissions application, the Free Application for Federal Student Aid, and the grant forms from their own state.

Faculty

The University has nearly 400 full- and part-time faculty members, 81 percent of whom hold terminal degrees. The student-faculty ratio is 15:1 and the average class size is 24. Students may take advantage of the expertise offered by the faculty in academic advisement and counseling, as well as counseling from the staff at the Center for Student Success.

Student Government

The Student Government Association represents all student organizations, including fraternities and sororities. Members participate in the planning of all social and cultural events on campus.

Admission Requirements

First-time freshmen must submit an application for admission with a $30 application fee (waived for online applicants), official high school transcripts or GED credential, and official SAT or ACT scores. Preference is given to applicants with a minimum 3.0 high school GPA and a combined SAT score of 1000 or a composite ACT score of 22.

Transfer students who have earned credits from another regionally accredited institution must submit transcripts from all postsecondary institutions attended and must have a minimum 2.0 GPA. Students with less than 30 college credits must also submit high school transcripts or GED credential.

Interviews are not required for admission except for students interested in the engineering, elementary education, and nursing programs. Students are encouraged to arrange for a campus visit with an enrollment manager.

Robert Morris University is committed to a policy of nondiscrimination on the basis of race, sex, color, religion, national origin, or handicap.

Application and Information

Students are encouraged to submit applications in the fall of their senior year of high school. Official transcripts and counselor recommendations should accompany the application; there is a $30 application processing fee that is waived for online applicants.

Robert Morris uses a rolling admission system; students are considered for acceptance as soon as all application materials have been received and evaluated.

For additional information and application materials, students should contact:

Kellie Laurenzi
Dean of Admissions
Robert Morris University
6001 University Boulevard
Moon Township, Pennsylvania 15108
Phone: 800-762-0097 (toll-free)
Web site: http://www.rmu.edu
　　　　http://www.facebook.com/rmunews
　　　　http://twitter.com/rmu
　　　　http://www.youtube.com/RMUNewsTube

Robert Morris University's Nicholson Center.

ROBERTS WESLEYAN COLLEGE

ROCHESTER, NEW YORK

The College

Roberts Wesleyan College (RWC) is characterized by its mission: scholarship, spiritual formation, and service. RWC was founded in 1866 as the first Free Methodist academic institution in North America. Since then, the institution has continually adapted its programs to meet the current academic, professional, and personal needs of its students. The integration of broad-based intellectual thought with the Judeo-Christian heritage continues to be the motivation for Roberts Wesleyan's existence. The College fosters wholesome principles by setting standards for student life, requiring regular chapel attendance, and maintaining a perspective rich in values within the classroom.

The current enrollment is 1,835: 1,313 women and 522 men. Although students come primarily from New York State, twenty-seven other states and nineteen other countries are represented. The majority of students are between 18 and 25 years of age, but there is a growing population of married and older students. The traditional undergraduate population is primarily residential, with approximately 65 percent of students living on campus.

RWC offers a broad selection of student activities. Student leaders work with the Associate Dean for Student Programming to plan numerous events each year, including social, cultural, and religious programs. The College's suburban Rochester location also allows students to take advantage of cultural and academic opportunities in the community. The College's intramural program complements the intercollegiate sports program. There are seven varsity sports for men: basketball, cross-country, golf, lacrosse, soccer, tennis, and track and field, and seven varsity sports for women: basketball, cross-country, lacrosse, soccer, tennis, track and field, and volleyball. Students may take advantage of the newly renovated Voller Athletic Center, which has a pool, four basketball courts, an indoor track, racquetball courts, a weight room, saunas, a student center, BT's Café, and a bookstore. Other College services available to students include the Career Services Office, academic advisement, counseling, and assistance from the Learning Center.

The College is a member of the Middle States Association of Colleges and Schools, the Association of Colleges and Universities of the State of New York, Rochester Area Colleges, the Association of Free Methodist Educational Institutions, the Council of Independent Colleges and Universities, and the Council for Christian Colleges & Universities. The programs in accounting, art, business, education, management, marketing, music, nursing, and social work are professionally accredited. The Art Department is accredited by the National Association of Schools of Art and Design. The Music Department is accredited by the National Association of Schools of Music. The Division of Nursing is accredited by the Commission on Collegiate Nursing Education. The Division of Social Work is accredited by the Council on Social Work Education. The Division of Business and Management is accredited by the International Assembly for Collegiate Business Education. The Division of Teacher Education is accredited by New York State Regents Accreditation of Teacher Education.

In addition to undergraduate programs, RWC offers the Master of Education, Master of Music in Education, Master of Science in Health Administration, Master of Science in Nursing Education, Master of Science in Nursing Leadership and Administration, Master of Science in School Counseling, Master of Science in School Psychology, Master of Science in Strategic Leadership, Master of Science in Strategic Marketing, and Master of Social Work degree programs. Northeastern Seminary at Roberts Wesleyan College offers the Master of Arts in Theological Studies, Master of Divinity, Master of Divinity/Master of Social Work (with RWC), and Doctor of Ministry degree programs.

Location

Roberts Wesleyan College is located 8 miles southwest of Rochester, New York, in the suburb of North Chili. Rochester, with a metropolitan-area population of more than 1 million, is a thriving cultural and corporate area. Eastman School of Music, the Rochester Philharmonic Orchestra, and several leading corporations, such as Eastman Kodak, Xerox, Paychex, Bausch & Lomb, and PAETEC are based there.

The College seeks a strong relationship with the community, and the resulting internships and opportunities for practical work are particularly advantageous for RWC students. Students and graduates benefit from the employment opportunities that result from Rochester's economy. Lake Ontario, Niagara Falls, Watkins Glen, Letchworth Park, and the Finger Lakes are all nearby.

Majors and Degrees

Baccalaureate degrees are offered in accounting and information management, adolescence education (biology, chemistry, English, mathematics, physics, social studies, and Spanish), art education, art–graphic design, art—studio art, art—time-based media, biblical studies, biochemistry, biology, biology with concentration in medical technology, business administration, chemistry, childhood education and special education (elementary education), communication, comprehensive science, comprehensive social studies, computer science, contemporary ministries, criminal justice, cross-disciplinary studies, early childhood education and special education, economic crime investigation, elementary education (childhood education and special education), engineering (with RIT, RPI, or Clarkson), English, forensic science, health administration, history, humanities, information systems management, international business, liberal arts, management and social entrepreneurship, marketing, mathematics, middle childhood education and special education, music, music education, music performance (instrument, piano, and voice), nursing, organizational management, pharmacy (with University at Buffalo), physical education, physics, psychology, religion/philosophy, secondary education (adolescence education), social work, Spanish, special education and childhood education (elementary education), and visual art education (art education).

A 3-2 program in engineering is offered in cooperation with Clarkson University, Rensselaer Polytechnic Institute (RPI), and Rochester Institute of Technology (RIT). The program leads to a B.S. in mathematics, chemistry, or physics from RWC and a B.S. in engineering from Clarkson, RPI, or RIT. A B.S./M.S. program is also available with RIT.

Secondary (grades 5–12) teaching certification may be earned in biology, chemistry, English, mathematics, physics, social studies, and Spanish. Preprofessional programs include dentistry, law, medicine, pharmacy, physical therapy, and veterinary medicine. Other areas of preparation include library science and medical technology.

Academic Programs

RWC endeavors to involve each student in learning experiences that promote commitment to Christian stewardship and service to society. Approximately 45 semester hours of core courses are required of each baccalaureate degree candidate. These liberal arts survey courses introduce four main fields of knowledge: biological science, physical science, and mathematics; history and the behavioral sciences; language, literature, and the fine arts; and biblical studies and philosophy. A minimum of 124 semester hours is required for graduation with a baccalaureate degree, including a minimum of 30 to 81 semester hours within the student's major discipline.

Many academic programs at Roberts Wesleyan include internships or practical work experiences. Independent study and cross-cultural study opportunities are also available. Students may receive credit through the Advanced Placement Program, the International Baccalaureate Program, or the College-Level Examination Program. The Learning Center provides assistance for students possessing exceptional skills or a deficiency in any area.

The College calendar consists of two 15-week semesters, September to December and January to May, and three sessions in the summer.

Off-Campus Programs

Various off-campus opportunities exist for which credit is awarded. These include the Appalachian Semester in Kentucky, Focus on the Family Institute in Colorado, Spanish language studies at the University of Murcia in Spain or the Instituto Espanol Murallas de Avila, EDUVenture in Irian Jaya, Jamaica Theological Seminary Semester, and a semester or full year of study at Richmond College in London,

England. Under the direction of an RWC professor, students may also participate in a short-term exchange study program with Osaka Christian College and Seminary in Osaka, Japan. There are also opportunities for off-campus experiences through the Council for Christian Colleges & Universities. These include the American Studies Program, Australia Studies Centre, China Studies Program, Contemporary Music Center, Latin American Studies Program, Los Angeles Film Studies Center, Middle East Studies Program, Programmes in Oxford, Uganda Studies Program, and Washington Journalism Center. The January Experience Program offers transcultural and enrichment courses in this country or abroad. In addition, through RWC's membership in the Rochester Area Colleges consortium, students may cross-register to take courses at other member institutions.

Academic Facilities

The 43,000-square-foot B. Thomas Golisano Library is a LEED-certified building with a geothermal heating and cooling system. The Golisano Library includes a 24-hour computer lab and study café, two smart classrooms for bibliographic instruction (including forty computer stations), two fireplaces for comfortable study areas, 375 student stations, and a graduate study room. The library holds 132,000 volumes (with room for 300,000), 1,100 periodicals, more than 100 online databases (most with full text, including JSTOR), Internet access, and 171,000 microforms, recordings, and filmstrips. Also included in the library are the Learning Center, the Historical Center, and Archives. Through its participation in the Rochester Regional Research Library Council, the library provides access to extensive interlibrary loan resources.

Well-equipped science laboratories, a lecture auditorium, and computer laboratories connected to the campus network are included in the Merlin G. Smith Science Center. The new Hastings Center for Academics houses the undergraduate divisions of business and teacher education. Other facilities include the music studios, practice rooms, and recital auditorium of Cox Hall; the newly renovated Carpenter Hall which includes classrooms and offices for the social science and social work divisions; the Cultural Life Center, which houses Shewan Recital Hall, Hale Auditorium, and Davison Art Gallery; the Rinker Community Service Center; and the soccer stadium and Mondo track. High-speed Internet connections for each student are available in all residence halls. The academic areas of campus are wireless.

Costs

Tuition for full-time study for the 2010–11 academic year was $23,460 but varies if a student's course load is fewer than 12 or more than 18 credit hours. There are additional fees for music and laboratory courses. Room and board was $8826; miscellaneous fees were $900. Book costs and personal expenses vary with individual needs.

Financial Aid

Roberts Wesleyan College offers a complete financial aid program, consisting of grants, scholarships, loans, and employment. Filing the Free Application for Federal Student Aid (FAFSA) is a prerequisite for determining eligibility for most financial aid programs. Sources of aid include Federal Pell Grants, Federal Supplemental Educational Opportunity Grants, Federal Perkins Loans, and Federal Stafford Student Loans; New York State Tuition Assistance Program awards; and institutional resources. Numerous on-campus employment opportunities are available. Institutional aid is also available in recognition of academic, athletic, artistic, and musical achievement. More than 97 percent of the student body receives financial aid each year. In 2007 RWC was ranked third in the Princeton Review's Top 10 Best Value Colleges. Currently, RWC is ranked as a 2011 top tier Northern master's university by *U.S. News & World Report* and listed by the Princeton Review as one of 2011's Best Northern Colleges. Roberts was also named to Kilpinger's 2010–11 listing of Best Value in Private Colleges.

Faculty

The primary concern of the faculty at RWC is to provide a high-quality educational experience. Sixty-eight percent of the professors hold the doctoral or terminal degree, and all are well respected within their specific discipline. The 100 full-time and 138 part-time faculty members are committed to Christian higher education and are genuinely interested in each student's development. A 14:1 student-faculty ratio allows for individualized attention, and most professors go beyond teaching and advising to participate in campus activities.

Student Government

All students belong to the Student Association and have the freedom to express their opinions to the staff, faculty, and administration. There are also elected senators and officers, under the direction of the Office of Student Services, who act as liaisons between the student body and administration in areas concerning academics and student activities.

Admission Requirements

Because the type of student a college enrolls significantly determines the personality of the institution, Roberts Wesleyan seeks students whose personal lives are characterized by honesty, integrity, and devotion to high moral and ethical standards. Admission consideration is given to applicants who rank in the upper third of their graduating class and have earned a minimum of 12 academic units of high school credit, with no fewer than 4 units in English, 2 units in algebra (or 1 in algebra and 1 in geometry), and 1 unit in biology, chemistry, or physics. Three years each of social studies, a foreign language, and science are strongly recommended. Further preparation in mathematics and science is required of applicants who wish to enter degree programs in nursing, mathematics, or science. Scores on the SAT or ACT and a formal recommendation are required. Special talents are considered an asset for applicants but are not required. An on-campus admission interview is strongly recommended. In admitting students, the College does not discriminate on the basis of race, age, color, sex, handicap, creed, or national or ethnic origin. Children of alumni and staff members are considered on the same basis as other applicants.

Transfer students have the same admission requirements as first-time students and must also have transcripts forwarded to the College from all institutions they have attended. Credit is usually accepted from regionally accredited institutions for any course in which a grade of C– or above has been earned if the course parallels a course given at RWC.

Application and Information

Applicants should submit an application form online, a completed recommendation form, SAT or ACT scores, and transcripts from all schools previously attended. Art students should prepare a portfolio for review by the art faculty, and music students should schedule an audition with the Music Department. Students are encouraged to submit an application prior to the February 1 priority deadline. Admission decisions are made on a rolling basis, and students are notified of the admission decision as soon as all of their credentials have been received and evaluated.

For more information and application forms, students should contact:

Office of Admissions
Roberts Wesleyan College
2301 Westside Drive
Rochester, New York 14624-1997
Phone: 585-594-6400
      800-777-4RWC (toll-free)
Fax: 585-594-6371
E-mail: admissions@roberts.edu
Web site: http://www.roberts.edu

The B. Thomas Golisano Library.

ROCHESTER INSTITUTE OF TECHNOLOGY

ROCHESTER, NEW YORK

R·I·T

The Institute

Rochester Institute of Technology (RIT) is one of the world's leading career-oriented, technological universities. RIT offers more than ninety undergraduate programs in areas such as engineering, computing, information technology, engineering technology, business, hospitality, science, art, design, photography, biomedical sciences, game design and development, and the liberal arts including psychology, advertising and public relations, and public policy. Students may choose from more than ninety different minors to develop personal and professional interests that complement their academic program. Experiential education is integrated into many programs through cooperative education, internships, study abroad, and undergraduate research. As home to the National Technical Institute for the Deaf (NTID), RIT is a leader in providing access services for deaf and hard-of-hearing students. RIT enrolls students from every state and more than ninety countries.

Close to 70 percent of RIT's approximately 11,300 full-time undergraduate students live on the campus in residence halls or campus apartments. The residence halls have eight special-interest houses where students with shared interests live and learn together.

Because RIT's student body is so diverse, there are many different activities, clubs, organizations, and sports in which students may participate. There are seventeen fraternities and twelve sororities, representing approximately 5 percent of the student population. A radio station and a biweekly student magazine allow those interested in media to gain experience on campus. A number of special interest clubs and career organizations are also available, and RIT offers twenty-three varsity sports, including Division I men's hockey. Recreational facilities include an ice rink, an aquatics center, a field house with an indoor track, and fitness facilities.

Location

The greater Rochester area has a population of about 745,000. Per-capita income is among the highest in the nation for metropolitan centers. The area's many internationally known industries employ a high proportion of scientists, technologists, and skilled workers. Rochester is the world center of photography, the largest producer of optical goods in the United States, and among the leaders in graphic arts and reproduction and in production of electronic equipment and precision instruments. Rochester's industries have always been closely associated with RIT's programs and progress.

Majors and Degrees

The College of Applied Science and Technology offers the Bachelor of Science in civil engineering technology, computer engineering technology, electrical engineering technology, electrical/mechanical engineering technology, manufacturing engineering technology, mechanical engineering technology, and telecommunications engineering technology. It also grants the Bachelor of Science in environmental sustainability, health and safety, hospitality and service management, nutrition management, packaging science, and safety technology. An undeclared option allowing freshmen to delay selecting a major for up to a year is available in the School of Engineering Technology.

The E. Philip Saunders College of Business offers the Bachelor of Science in accounting, finance, graphic media marketing, international business, management, management information systems, and marketing. An accelerated B.S./M.B.A. option is available, as is a minor in entrepreneurship. An undeclared option allowing freshmen to delay the selection of their major for up to one year is also available.

The B. Thomas Golisano College of Computing and Information Sciences offers the Bachelor of Science degree in applied networking and systems administration, computer science, game design and development, information technology, medical informatics, new media interactive development, and software engineering.

The Kate Gleason College of Engineering grants the Bachelor of Science in biomedical engineering, chemical engineering, computer engineering, electrical engineering, industrial and systems engineer-

ing, mechanical engineering, and microelectronic engineering. Degree options in aerospace, automotive, bioengineering, biomedical, energy and environment, ergonomics, information systems, manufacturing, and software engineering are also offered within the college. Accelerated B.S./M.S. options are available. The Engineering Exploration Program, which allows freshmen to delay the selection of their major for up to one year, is also available.

The College of Imaging Arts and Sciences offers the Bachelor of Fine Arts in advertising photography; ceramics and ceramic sculpture; digital cinema; film, video, and animation; fine art photography; fine arts studio, glass and glass sculpture; graphic design; illustration; industrial design; interior design; medical illustration; metals and jewelry design; new media design and imaging; photojournalism; 3D digital graphics; visual media; and woodworking and furniture design. The college also offers the Bachelor of Science in biomedical photographic communications, digital media, graphic media, imaging and photographic technology, and new media/publishing. An undeclared option allowing freshmen to delay the selection of their major for up to one year is also available in the School of Art, the School of Design, and the School for American Crafts.

The College of Liberal Arts confers the Bachelor of Science in advertising and public relations, criminal justice, economics, journalism, international studies, museum studies, philosophy, professional and technical communication, psychology, public policy, and urban and community studies. The Liberal Arts Exploration Program is designed to help undecided students formulate education and career plans.

The College of Science offers the Bachelor of Science in applied mathematics, applied statistics, biology, biochemistry, bioinformatics, biomedical sciences, biotechnology, chemistry, computational mathematics, diagnostic medical sonography (ultrasound), environmental chemistry, environmental science, imaging science, physician assistant studies, physics, and polymer chemistry. Special options are available in premedical studies (medicine, dentistry, veterinary medicine). Minors are available in astronomy, exercise science, imaging science, mathematics, physics, and statistics. Accelerated B.S./M.S. and B.S./M.B.A. programs are available. The General Science Exploration Program, which allows freshmen to delay the selection of their major for up to one year, is also available.

As home of the National Technical Institute for the Deaf, RIT is a leader in providing educational opportunities and access services for deaf and hard-of-hearing students. NTID awards associate degree programs and offers a prebaccalaureate studies program for the deaf and hard-of-hearing. The associate degree programs prepare students for immediate employment after graduation or transfer into one of RIT's bachelor's degree programs. The prebaccalaureate studies program prepares students, who may not qualify initially, for entry into a bachelor's degree program. Nearly 50 percent of the 1,300 deaf and hard-of-hearing students at RIT are enrolled directly into one of the bachelor's degree programs in the other seven colleges.

Academic Programs

Most students entering RIT enroll directly in the college and academic program of their choice; specialization is spread over the duration of their study. Options for undeclared students are available in several colleges and a University Studies program is available for students who wish to explore programs in two or more colleges. Approximately one third of the program of each professional curriculum consists of general education courses in the humanities, math and science, and social sciences. Students may choose from more than ninety different minors to develop personal and professional interests that complement their academic program. Double-major and accelerated dual-degree (combined bachelor's/masters) options are available. An honors program admits approximately 180 students each year. Air Force and Army ROTC programs are available on the campus. A Naval ROTC program is offered jointly with the University of Rochester.

Every academic program at RIT offers some form of experiential education opportunity. This takes many forms, including cooperative education, internships, study abroad, undergraduate research, and industry-sponsored project work. Notable among these programs is cooperative education (co-op). The College of Applied Science and Technology, the E. Philip Saunders College of Business, the B. Thomas Golisano College of Computing and Information Sciences, and the Kate Gleason College of Engineering all require co-op for undergraduate students. It is available on an optional basis in other RIT colleges. Co-op students alternate periods of full-time study with periods of full-time paid work experience in business and industry directly related to their field of study and career interests. Last year more than 3,500 students completed work assignments with nearly 1,900 employers, earning collectively in excess of $30 million.

Off-Campus Programs

RIT has three international branch campuses. The American College of Management and Technology is a branch campus in Croatia, offering an associate degree and a Bachelor of Science degree in hospitality and service management, a Master of Science degree in service management, and several certificate programs to serve the local tourism industries. The American University of Kosovo provides a career-oriented education that fosters the links between the university, industry, and government necessary to support the workforce development needs of Kosovo. RIT Dubai offers graduate and undergraduate programs for students from the Middle East, North Africa and Southeast Asia. RIT has a growing study-abroad program. Through affiliations with other institutions, RIT offers more than 150 study-abroad programs in twenty countries.

Academic Facilities

Excellent facilities add to the quality of academic life. Students have access to a laser-optics laboratory, an observatory, an animal-care facility, more than 100 color and black-and-white photography darkrooms, electronic prepress and publishing equipment, ceramic kilns, glass furnaces, a blacksmithing area, a student-operated restaurant, computer graphics and robotic labs, and some of the most up-to-date microelectronic, telecommunications, and computer engineering facilities in the U.S. Wallace Memorial Library is a true multimedia learning center. Its collections are exceptionally extensive in the areas of art and design, education for the deaf, photography, and printing.

RIT is a leader in academic computing, and students use state-of-the-art computer equipment regardless of their major. Central computer systems can be accessed via a high-speed data network connecting the library, academic facilities, residence hall rooms, and on-campus apartments. There are more than sixty locations campuswide, with wireless networking connectivity utilizing 802.11b technology. The RIT campus network is served by two OC3 connections, each operating at a data rate of 155 Mbps, and one T3 connection operating at 45 Mbps. RIT is among a select group of institutions with access to the Internet2 research network, a collaborative research and development effort led by more than 170 U.S. universities working in partnership with industry and government. Its goal is to develop a new family of advanced Internet applications and technologies.

Costs

For 2010–11, tuition for the normal academic year (three academic quarters) was $30,286. Students on the cooperative education plan pay tuition only for the quarters they are at RIT. Fees, including the activities and health fees, are $435 for the academic year. Room and board (twenty meals per week) cost $10,044.

Financial Aid

Approximately 77 percent of the full-time undergraduates receive some form of financial aid that includes RIT scholarships, alumni or industry-supported scholarships, and state and federal government grants. A variety of loans and part-time work positions are also available. The FAFSA must be submitted by March 1. Giving full recognition to scholarship apart from financial need, RIT awards a number of academic scholarships based on grades, test scores, and activities. Freshmen applying by February 1 and transfers applying as juniors by April 1 are considered for these scholarships.

Faculty

There are 798 full-time faculty members, 406 part-time faculty members, and an administrative and supporting staff of more than 1,800. Approximately 80 percent of the faculty members have earned a Ph.D. or the terminal degree in their field.

Student Government

The Student Government is the representative body for students. It works with RIT administration and faculty and staff members to communicate the needs and desires of the student body and to communicate the decisions of the administration to the students. Fraternity and sorority members, off-campus and hearing-impaired students, and students from minority groups elect special representative bodies. All full-time and part-time undergraduate and graduate students become members of the Student Government when they pay the student activities fee.

Admission Requirements

The general requirements for freshman entrance are a high school diploma (an equivalency diploma is considered), high school grades that give evidence of the ability to complete college work successfully, satisfactory scores on the SAT or ACT, and completion of prerequisite high school–level math and science courses indicated in the college catalog. An important factor for admission is the record of academic achievement in high school (or in another college in the case of transfer students). The results of standardized tests are supplementary. Students applying for programs in the fine and applied arts must submit a portfolio of original artwork.

Rochester Institute of Technology admits qualified men and women of any race, color, national or ethnic origin, religion, sexual orientation, gender identity, gender expression, or marital status. RIT does not discriminate on the basis of handicap in the recruitment or admission of students or in the operation of any of its programs or activities, as specified by federal laws and regulations.

Application and Information

An application, a nonrefundable processing fee of $50, official transcripts of all high school or college records, and SAT or ACT scores (for prospective freshmen) should be forwarded to RIT. Freshman applicants who provide all required materials for entry in the fall quarter by February 1 receive admission notification by March 15. Prospective freshmen who apply after February 1 and all transfer students are notified of the admission decision by mail on a rolling basis four to six weeks after their application is complete. RIT also offers an early decision plan; prospective freshmen must have their completed application and credentials on file in the Admissions Office by December 1 to receive notification by January 15.

For application forms, students should contact:

Director of Undergraduate Admissions
Rochester Institute of Technology
60 Lomb Memorial Drive
Rochester, New York 14623-5604

Phone: 585-475-6631
Fax: 585-475-7424
E-mail: admissions@rit.edu
Web site: http://www.rit.edu
http://www.facebook.com/RITfb
http://twitter.com/RITAdmissions

A view of the campus.

ROGER WILLIAMS UNIVERSITY

BRISTOL, RHODE ISLAND

The University

Roger Williams University (RWU) (http://thedock.rwu.edu/) is a 54-year-old independent, coeducational institution that provides a liberal arts education, as well as education for the professions. It has quickly established itself as a leader in higher education. A dynamic educational environment in which students live and learn to be global citizens, the University is committed to its mantra of "Learning to bridge the world."

With forty-one academic programs and a robust array of cocurricular activities available on its waterfront campus in historic Bristol, Rhode Island, RWU looks to a set of core values in fulfilling its mission to prepare students for life as twenty-first century citizen-scholars. Over the past decade the institution has achieved unprecedented academic and financial successes. In 2010, *U.S. News & World Report* named Roger Williams the eighth-ranked comprehensive college in the North, and the University has twice been recognized by the Princeton Review for its many sustainability efforts.

A mid-sized university comprising 3,634 full-time undergraduate students, personal attention is a guarantee at RWU. Professors teach all the courses, and with an average class size of 19, the student-to-faculty ratio is just 12:1. For students seeking additional academic support, the Center for Academic Development provides a multitude of tutoring, testing, and writing services.

All students take a common liberal arts curriculum to provide a solid foundation for their continued studies. The Career Center assists students in securing internships and job placement, as well as offering information sessions on resume writing and professional etiquette. At the time of commencement in 2008, 89 percent of RWU's graduating class had secured jobs or were accepted to graduate and professional schools for further study.

Students at Roger Williams are committed to community service as well as their education. All entering freshmen participate in an annual Community Connections day of service, during which teams led by upperclassmen and faculty and staff members extend a helping hand at local community organizations. Many students choose to continue volunteer service throughout their years at RWU, collaborating with the University's Feinstein Center for Service Learning and Community Outreach on projects with organizations such as Habitat for Humanity, local food banks, elder care facilities, local high schools, and others.

At RWU, students of diverse backgrounds from across the United States and fifty-five other countries come together for a community-oriented learning experience. Driven by a commitment to global citizenship, the University encourages all students to study abroad, whether it is for a year, semester, summer session or even a mini-mester.

On campus, students take part in programs at the Intercultural Center, home to international and multicultural student life, spiritual life, and LGBT initiatives. In fall 2009, RWU opened Global Heritage Hall, a new campus academic center that houses the Peggy and Marc Spiegel Center for Global and International Programs, as well as the Robert F. Stoico/FIRSTFED Global Languages Center and a series of heritage classrooms representing the myriad ethnic groups that both established and remain a strong presence in the local area.

Students can choose to live on or off campus in any of RWU's eight University residence halls (shuttle service is available to students who live in an off-campus residence). Residences range from traditional dorms to apartment-style suites. A new residence hall for upperclassmen, North Campus Hall, opened in the fall of 2009, combining living space, classroom and study space, a café, and a retail shop to create a modern living and learning community.

RWU students have access to more than eighty clubs and organizations and hundreds of events on campus every year. Students can join any of the University's intramural athletic teams, cheer on their twenty NCAA Division III varsity teams, debate current issues with professors and fellow students, listen to world-renowned speakers, attend concerts or plays at the Performing Arts Center, or run for Student Senate—the options go on and on.

The University is also committed to helping students maintain a healthy lifestyle. Many students stay fit at the state-of-the-art Campus Recreation Center, which includes a swimming pool, basketball and squash courts, weight lifting and cardio rooms, a Jacuzzi, and a sauna. The campus' waterfront location also provides ample opportunities for sailing and kayaking. Students also enjoy the locally grown, organic foods provided at RWU. The University's food service is consistently ranked in the top 5 percent nationwide, based on student satisfaction. Roger Williams University is accredited by the New England Association of Schools and Colleges.

Location

Roger Williams University is located in Bristol, Rhode Island, a seaside town that is home to antique stores, gourmet restaurants, ice cream shops, and spas. Providence, Rhode Island's capital and largest city, is just a 30-minute bus ride away and offers museums, coffee shops, the Providence Place Mall, live music, and more. Providence is also a regional transportation hub, with an international airport and bus and train stations. By travelling 30 minutes in the other direction, students can visit Newport, home of famous beaches, shopping, festivals, and open markets. Boston is also nearby, just an hour away.

Majors and Degrees

At the undergraduate level, RWU awards Bachelor of Science, Bachelor of Arts, and Bachelor of Fine Arts degrees. In addition, the University has several joint degree programs. Academic programs are offered through one college and five professional schools that combine a traditional liberal arts education with professional studies.

Professional programs are offered through the School of Architecture, Art and Historic Preservation, accredited by NAAB; the Gabelli School of Business, accredited by the prestigious AACSB International; the School of Engineering, Computing and Construction Management, accredited by ACCE, ABET, and EAC; and the School of Justice Studies.

Liberal arts majors are offered through the Feinstein College of Arts and Sciences and the School of Education. Continuing education opportunities are available through the School of Continuing Studies, and RWU is also home to Rhode Island's only law school, accredited by the ABA.

Academic Programs

Roger Williams employs a shared general education curriculum for all undergraduate students. The interdisciplinary program guarantees that all students, regardless of a major, receive a well-rounded education that combines a liberal arts background with a major academic area of interest. With forty-one different programs of study ranging from American studies and architecture to security assurance studies and theater, RWU offers a wide variety of choices for its students.

Off-Campus Programs

One of the University's core values is appreciation of global perspectives, and RWU encourages global exploration. All sophomores who maintain a 3.0 GPA receive a passport, free of charge, to encourage travel. Roger Williams has study-abroad opportunities on every continent but Antarctica. RWU's flagship programs are in Florence, Italy, and London, England, but RWU has forty-five affiliated programs in countries from Argentina to Vietnam and virtually everywhere in between.

The University also places an emphasis on internships, community service, and service learning. Career counselors work one-on-one with the students and alumni, providing career development guidance, assessment, employment-search skills, and placement assistance. Students who wish to be involved in volunteer service or service learning can contact the Feinstein Center for Service Learning and Community Engagement for on- and off-campus opportunities.

Academic Facilities

The University's 54,000-square-foot main library houses seating and quiet study and reading areas, computer databases, and an online catalog. The ground floor is also home to the Learning Commons, a dynamic space that encourages learning through collaboration by combining library resources and research assistance with the latest technology. And an online system allows students to take advantage of library resources and collections of four additional Rhode Island institutions.

The Marine and Natural Sciences Building houses the science and mathematics departments and features a wet lab with flowing seawater; research space; and modern physics, chemistry, and biology laboratories. RWU recently completed construction of a shellfish hatchery to further expand the University's work reseeding the oyster population in Mount Hope Bay.

The Engineering Building supports modern lab facilities equipped for computing, drafting, electronics, surveying, soil, fluid and materials mechanics, and digital and environmental systems.

The Performing Arts Center houses a dance studio, rehearsal rooms, and scene and costume shops as well as performance space, while the Fine Arts Building provides students with art and sculpting studios, an art gallery, and photography labs that support visual arts studies.

The award-winning School of Architecture, Art, and Historic Preservation Building includes design studios, review and seminar rooms, a library, a photography studio and darkroom, a model shop, computer labs, and an exhibition gallery.

The Gabelli School of Business (GSB) houses the Robert F. Stoico FIRSTFED Financial Services Center, a high-tech classroom/trading room featuring split computer screens for students. Also in GSB is the Center for Advanced Financial Education (CAFE), which provides hands-on training in securities analysis and portfolio management for students involved in the Student Investment Management Fund.

Costs

Tuition and fees for the 2010–11 year were $27,840 for 12–17 credit hours ($31,344 for architecture students). Room and board averaged $12,740.

Financial Aid

Students just shouldn't just look at the price of a Roger Williams education. There are many resources available to help finance their education, including need- and merit-based scholarships and educational loans. Because RWU is still growing, there are more opportunities to address each individual family's financial needs.

In the 2010–11 academic year, 88 percent of RWU's incoming students received financial aid through a combination of grants, scholarships, student loans, and on-campus jobs. The University's median freshman aid package is $20,807. The University awarded more than $30 million in financial assistance in the current year alone. As a private institution, RWU has greater ability than state schools to offer scholarships or tap endowment funds to help students.

The University requires the submission of the Free Application for Federal Student Aid (FAFSA) and the CSS/Financial Aid PROFILE. The Roger Williams University Title IV Federal Code Number is 003410. The FAFSA must be received at the federal processor no later than February 1 to be considered for maximum financial aid.

Prospective students can learn more about the true value of an RWU education at http://thedock.rwu.edu/scholarships-financial-aid/affordability.

Faculty

Renowned for their commitment to excellence in teaching, the Roger Williams University academic cadre features 625 faculty members, of whom 245 teach full time. Of the full-time faculty members, 38 percent have been with the University for more than ten years.

Student Government

The Student Government Association (SGA) represents the Roger Williams University student body. Elected by their peers, Student Senate members are responsible for the legislative and executive functions of the SGA and represent the entire student community to the faculty and administration.

Other leadership opportunities at Roger Williams include the Inter-Class Council, a group of peer-elected class representatives responsible for fostering school spirit, developing social programming opportunities for their respective classes, and representing their class to the Student Senate and University administration.

Admission Requirements

Roger Williams University seeks well-rounded, motivated students with a demonstrated capacity for academic achievement, and who also possess intellectual curiosity, strength of character, and a sense of social responsibility.

The admissions committee will evaluate an application based on a number of factors, including the rigor of a student's high school curriculum, their scholastic record, standardized test scores (SAT or ACT are accepted), writing ability, interests, community involvement, and talents. Transfer students are evaluated based on the same criteria, along with academic performance on the college level.

All students must submit an official application, letter(s) of recommendation, and official transcripts from all secondary and postsecondary schools attended to be considered for admission. RWU accepts applications for both early action and regular decision.

Application and Information

The deadline for early decision is November 1, and for regular decision, February 1. A nonrefundable fee of $50 must accompany the application. Application forms and admissions information may be obtained by contacting:

Office of Undergraduate Admission
Roger Williams University
One Old Ferry Road
Bristol, Rhode Island 02809-2921

Phone: 401-254-3500
      800-458-7144 Ext. 3500 (toll-free outside Rhode Island)
E-mail: admit@rwu.edu
Web site: http://www.rwu.edu
      http://www.facebook.com/rogerwilliamsuniversity
      http://twitter.com/myrwu

Roger Williams University is located on 140 scenic acres overlooking Mt. Hope Bay.

ROSEMONT COLLEGE
ROSEMONT, PENNSYLVANIA

The College

Founded in 1921, Rosemont College is an independent liberal arts institution in the Catholic tradition. Rosemont's reputation for academic excellence in an intimate setting is its hallmark. Rosemont College offers students an exceptional and comprehensive coeducational learning experience.

Rosemont College works to recognize and develop every student's unique talents. It believes that a student's educational experience should incorporate their goals, their strengths, and their efforts to make positive changes to the world. Students at Rosemont gain knowledge, develop critical skills, and grow as persons of character.

Rosemont is consistently highly ranked by *U.S. News & World Report*. It has been named to the John Templeton Foundation Honor Roll for Character-Building Colleges, a designation that recognizes colleges and universities that emphasize character building as an integral part of the college experience.

The nationally acclaimed, traditional Undergraduate College confers the Bachelor of Arts, the Bachelor of Fine Arts, and the Bachelor of Science degrees in twenty-four majors. Rosemont has approximately 7,000 living alumni, many of whom have been in the vanguard of expanding career and professional opportunities. They can be found in high-ranking positions in science and medicine, law, business, education, the social sciences, publishing, and the arts.

Building on its historic commitment to education, Rosemont also includes the Schools of Graduate Studies and Professional Studies, which are open to working people. The School of Professional Studies confers the Bachelor of Science and the Bachelor of Arts in three majors, while the School of Graduate Studies offers six graduate degrees, including Master of Arts in education and publishing programs, as well as a Master of Fine Arts degree in creative writing, a Master of Science in management, and a Master of Business Administration.

From the institution's early days through the present Cornelia Connelly, founder of the Society of the Holy Child Jesus, has been a driving force behind Rosemont's charge to educate students "to meet the wants of the age." Rosemont knows that students come to college with their eyes on their future. At Rosemont, their dreams are the starting point for an education that is truly their own. While at Rosemont, students will carve a unique path that leads from their dreams to the rest of their lives and all its rich possibilities.

Rosemont participates in NCAA Division III varsity teams for men's basketball, cross-country, golf, lacrosse, soccer, and tennis; and women's basketball, cross-country, lacrosse, soccer, softball, tennis, and volleyball.

Location

Rosemont's 56-acre campus is located in the town of Rosemont, a historic suburban community with many shops, movie theaters, restaurants, and bookstores. The city of Philadelphia is 11 miles east of Rosemont and just a 20-minute train ride from the campus. The College's proximity to Philadelphia provides students with a vast array of cultural and social opportunities, such as the Philadelphia Museum of Art, the Philadelphia Orchestra, the Pennsylvania Ballet, and various professional sports events, including Phillies, Flyers, and Eagles games. Within the Philadelphia area there are approximately eighty other colleges and universities. Rosemont is ideally located for recreational activities; it is only a short distance from both the Pocono Mountains and the New Jersey shore.

Majors and Degrees

Rosemont College awards the Bachelor of Arts, the Bachelor of Fine Arts, and the Bachelor of Science degrees. Majors are offered in accounting, biology, business, chemistry, communication, economics, education, English, English and communication, environmental studies, French, history, history of art, humanities, international business, philosophy, political science, psychology, religious studies, social science, sociology, Spanish, studio art and design, and women's studies. In addition, Rosemont offers ten preprofessional, certification, and dual-degree programs.

Academic Programs

To earn a Rosemont undergraduate degree, each candidate must complete 120 credits. In addition to the requirements of a major concentration, all students must complete general requirements. An internship, service-learning, or study-abroad experience is required prior to graduation. During their senior year, all students must successfully complete a comprehensive exam, exhibiting competency in their declared major.

Rosemont College offers dual-admission medical programs with the Drexel University College of Medicine and Temple University.

For students interested in a French and business major, Rosemont offers specialized courses in business French to prepare students for the examination of the Chambre de Commerce et d'Industrie de Paris. The Certificat Pratique de Français Commercial et Économique is awarded to students who successfully complete this exam.

Rosemont offers programs granting certification in the following teaching areas: art education, early childhood education/elementary education, elementary education, secondary education, and special education with a concentration in hearing impaired.

Off-Campus Programs

Through academic exchange programs that expand course offerings, students may take courses at neighboring Villanova University, Eastern University, Arcadia University, Cabrini College, Chestnut Hill College, Gwynedd-Mercy College, Holy Family College, Immaculata University, and Neumann College.

Rosemont students may participate in any of a variety of study-abroad programs. These programs give students the opportunity to combine travel with academic and cultural study. Students receive full credit at Rosemont for course work successfully completed on an approved program.

There are many opportunities for full-semester internships in various fields of study. Each candidate must be academically qualified and meet the approval of the appropriate faculty member. Fieldwork and practicum, as well as summer internships, are also available.

Academic Facilities

The Student Academic Support Center, located in the Brown Science Building, is the comprehensive source for academic assistance. The center offers a wide range of advising, experiential learning, and learning support services to enhance students' educational experiences at the College. All services are offered to all students at no cost.

The Gertrude Kistler Memorial Library creates a setting that is conducive to study and research. The library was the first academic building erected on the campus. It houses more than 159,000 volumes, approximately 563 current periodicals, and numerous electronic indexes and databases as well as access to the Internet. The library also houses a 10,000-volume collection of children's literature. The online catalog, the Rosemont Electronic Learning and Library System (TRELLIS), is the basic index to the library's collections. TRELLIS includes a number of computerized periodical indexes and encyclopedias and provides access to the Internet's World Wide Web.

The science building is composed of the Dorothy McKenna Brown Science Building and the McShain Performing Arts Center. The Brown Science Building provides laboratory facilities and lecture rooms for the natural sciences. State-of-the-art equipment includes a phase microscope with video camera and color TV monitor, physiographs, spectrophotometers, and an environment chamber. The building also houses two electronic classrooms equipped with the latest in Windows PC and Macintosh technology. Students have access to laser and full-color printers, and scanners, as well as numerous software resources for word processing, desktop publishing, indexing, and graphic arts. A mobile cart containing eleven wireless laptop computers is also housed in the Brown Science Building and is available for use throughout the building. The McShain Performing Arts Center is a 300-seat auditorium used for special forums, theatrical performances, and ceremonies.

The Global Curriculum Classroom located in Good Counsel Hall, houses a sympodium, an interactive smart computer/touch screen; integrated projector DVD/VCR; and sound system. A mobile cart equipped with twenty-four wireless laptop computers is also located in the Global Curriculum Classroom.

Costs

For 2010–11, tuition for full-time students was $26,500; room and board were $11,000.

Financial Aid

Many Rosemont students receive some form of financial aid. Financial aid includes scholarships, grants, loans, and work-study awards. Most financial packages are a combination of various forms of aid. To apply for aid, students should submit the Free Application for Federal Student Aid (FAFSA) by February 15.

Faculty

The faculty is one of Rosemont's most important assets. The faculty members are dedicated individuals who believe the student must be engaged to learn; therefore, all classes at Rosemont are small, which lends to the discussion or seminar format. Approximately 84 percent of the faculty members hold either the Ph.D. or the highest degree in their field.

Student Government

The student government at Rosemont coordinates the ongoing governing processes to be responsive to the needs and opinions of students, to stimulate change as needed, to provide a range of programs and activities, and to represent students to Rosemont College as a whole.

Admission Requirements

Rosemont College seeks to enroll men and women interested in the liberal arts and who have the capacity and the desire to pursue a rigorous academic program. A candidate for admission must present a satisfactory record of scholastic ability and personal integrity from an accredited high school as well as accept-

able scores on the SAT or ACT. Applicants' records are reviewed by the Admissions Committee. The student must have an official copy of their high school transcript sent to Rosemont's Office of Admissions. An applicant's secondary school preparation should include sixteen college-preparatory courses. For admission to the traditional college program, all applicants are advised to include in their high school program a minimum of 4 units of English, 2 units of foreign language, 2 units of social studies, 2 units of college-preparatory math, and 2 units of science, one of which must be a lab science. Applicants are expected to carry a full academic program during their senior year of high school.

Two recommendations are required in support of the student's application. The applicant should ask their guidance counselor or other adult who knows the student well (coach, mentor, etc.) and a teacher who has taught the student an academic subject to submit recommendations on their behalf and forward them to Rosemont's Office of Admissions. All applicants are required to submit results of the SAT. Students may also submit ACT scores. A personal interview with a member of the admissions staff is strongly recommended but not required as part of the application process. Students who are seriously considering Rosemont should visit the campus to enhance their understanding of the academic and social atmosphere. Arrangements can be made by calling the Office of Admissions or by clicking on the "visit Rosemont" link on the Rosemont Admissions Web site.

Application and Information

Applications are accepted on a rolling basis. Those interested in scholarships should apply no later than February 15. To arrange for an interview and a tour, or to receive additional information, students should contact:

Office of Admissions
Rosemont College
1400 Montgomery Avenue
Rosemont, Pennsylvania 19010-1699
Phone: 610-526-2966
      888-2ROSEMONT (toll-free)
E-mail: admissions@rosemont.edu
Web site: http://www.rosemont.edu

Rosemont College offers students academic excellence, character building, and a unique educational experience.

ROWAN UNIVERSITY
GLASSBORO, NEW JERSEY

The University

Founded in 1923, Rowan University has become a regional center for education, business, technology, and the arts and humanities. With state-of-the-art facilities, nationally ranked academic and athletic programs, and talented professors, Rowan offers an outstanding educational experience at an exceptional value. Currently, the University is home to more than 10,000 students in eighty-one majors, twenty-six minors, and forty-eight graduate programs across six academic colleges—Business, Communication, Education, Engineering, Fine and Performing Arts, and Liberal Arts and Sciences—and the College of Graduate & Continuing Education. Rowan's admission standards are competitive, attracting applicants from the top quarter of their high school classes. All courses are taught by professors without the aid of teaching assistants, and the average class size is 20.

The tree-lined Glassboro campus encompasses student residence halls, apartments, and townhouses; state-of-the-art classroom facilities; a student recreation center; theaters; galleries; and a planetarium. There are sixty-three computer labs and 120 technology-enhanced classrooms throughout the main campus and the Camden campus.

The University is in the midst of a $530-million program to expand the campus and further upgrade facilities, and has plans to create a West Campus on 600 acres nearby which it purchased recently. The anchor of the new tract is the South Jersey Technology Park at Rowan University, which will play a significant role in the economic development of the region.

Rowan University has announced intentions to partner with Cooper University Hospital to form Southern New Jersey's first four-year allopathic medical school. Cooper Medical School of Rowan University is in the process of building a $139-million, 200,000-square-foot facility that will provide medical education to approximately 400 students. The medical school expects its first class to begin study in the fall 2012 semester.

In addition, Rowan University and the town of Glassboro have partnered to create Rowan Boulevard, a roadway being constructed at the east end of campus to the historic downtown. The proposal includes construction of a mixed-use corridor lined with shops and restaurants on the street level, topped by apartments and offices. Key anchors for the project are an apartment complex for Rowan University students (opened in 2009), a Barnes & Noble college superstore (opened in 2010), and a Marriot Courtyard hotel and conference center (opening in 2011).

Rowan's eighteen varsity athletic teams compete in NCAA Division III, the New Jersey Athletic Conference, and the Eastern College Athletic Conference. More than 130 clubs, preprofessional organizations, honor societies, and fraternities and sororities foster a sense of community life.

Rowan University, established for teacher training and later known as Glassboro State College, made philanthropic history with the Rowan $100-million donation in 1992.

Location

The University is located on 200 acres in the historic southern New Jersey town of Glassboro, less than 30 minutes from Philadelphia, Pennsylvania, and less than an hour from the New Jersey shore. Because of the University's location halfway between New York and Washington, D.C., it was chosen as the site of the historic 1967 conference between President Johnson and Soviet Premier Kosygin. Facilities for all forms of surface and air transportation, including Philadelphia International Airport, are within minutes of the campus.

Just 20 minutes from the main campus, the Rowan University Camden Campus, in Camden, New Jersey, serves the urban community, with an emphasis on nontraditional students, in three degree programs plus English as a second language studies.

Majors and Degrees

The Bachelor of Arts degree is offered in accounting, advertising, Africana studies, American studies, art (general fine arts), communication studies, early childhood education, economics, education (K–12 subject matter in art, biology, chemistry, English, history, mathematics, music, physical science, physics, Spanish), elementary education, English, environmental studies, geography, health and exercise science (health promotion and fitness management, K–12 teacher certification), history, journalism, law and justice studies, liberal studies: humanities/social science, liberal studies: math/science, mathematics, music, political science, psychology, public relations, radio/TV/film, sociology, Spanish, theater, and writing arts. The Bachelor of Science degree is offered in accounting, athletic training, biochemistry, biological sciences, chemistry, computer science, engineering (chemical, civil and environmental, electrical and computer, mechanical), entrepreneurship, finance, human resource management, management, management information systems, marketing, mathematics, physical sciences, and physics. The Bachelor of Science in Nursing degree is also offered. The Bachelor of Fine Arts degree is offered in studio arts (ceramics, computer art, drawing and painting, graphic design, illustration, jewelry/metalry, photography, printmaking, puppetry, sculpture). The Bachelor of Music degree is offered in composition, jazz studies, music education, and performance.

Academic Programs

All degree programs include a general education requirement (approximately 60 semester hours) from the areas of communication, science and mathematics, social and behavioral sciences, humanities and languages, and fine arts. In addition, most academic majors have specific general education courses that students in that major must take. Each degree program includes individual major requirements and free electives. A minimum of 30 semester hours is required in a major program; many departments require more.

Students are encouraged to use free electives to establish a second major, minor, or concentration; strengthen their major program; pursue personal interests; or study abroad.

Internships are available in all majors, and some type of internship or academic field experience is required in most of them.

The University calendar is based on the two-semester system with a summer session.

Off-Campus Programs

Rowan University offers the opportunity to spend a semester or a year living and learning in a new country and culture through study abroad, with destinations to more than 200 programs in fifty nations in Africa, Asia, Australia, Europe, and South and Central America. Students can also earn work-study dollars while exploring careers and building credentials and experience through Off-Campus Work-Study.

Academic Facilities

In just the past decade, Rowan has added a number of new buildings that are notable for their modern architecture, bright open spaces, and state-of-the-art equipment. They include the Student Recreation Center, a full-service health club for students, faculty members, and alumni; the Campbell Library, which combines spacious new study areas with a rich collection of print and electronic resources for research; and Henry M. Rowan Hall, a $28-million engineering building with a technology spine and modular classrooms and laboratories. The $45-million, state-of-the-art Science

Hall, which opened in 2003, is home to the biological sciences, chemistry, and physics departments and features a fully equipped laser laboratory, a rooftop greenhouse and telescope, a planetarium, twenty-two research laboratories, and twenty-seven teaching laboratories. The recently opened Education Hall, home of the College of Education, features state-of-the-art technology, learning centers, classrooms, and office space. Rowan is also expanding its campus to accommodate the South Jersey Technology Park, a facility that will be shared by students, faculty members, and private industry.

Costs

In 2010–11, tuition and fees were $11,676 for New Jersey residents and $19,034 for out-of-state students, based on flat-rate tuition for full-time undergraduates taking 24 to 36 semester hours per year. Room and board costs for the year were $10,348, based on the double-residence room rate and a primary meal plan. All freshmen are required to live in residence halls, with guaranteed housing. Apartment-style housing is available on the campus for upperclass students in any one of the University-owned apartment complexes and town houses.

Financial Aid

Nearly 76 percent of all Rowan students receive some form of financial aid, such as grants, loans, or scholarships, from federal and state sources, alumni, friends of the University, and various other organizations. In 2010, Rowan awarded more than $110 million in total financial assistance to undergraduates. Students should submit a Free Application for Federal Student Aid (FAFSA) as soon as possible after January 1 and no later than March 15 to be evaluated for the earliest consideration.

Faculty

Rowan University has 1,041 faculty members (396 full-time). Faculty members' regularly scheduled office hours, participation in virtually all areas of campus governance and operations, and individual guidance and support for every student who needs them ensure a truly personal education. Part-time and adjunct faculty members, including business leaders, industry representatives, and practicing professionals, provide valuable links with the community and offer knowledge of practical experiences to Rowan students. The student-faculty ratio is 15:1, and all classes are taught by professors. There are no teaching assistants.

Student Government

The Student Government Association (SGA) is composed entirely of students chosen through campuswide elections. All students paying student activity fees are members of the SGA. Free legal advice, personal property insurance, and a tenants' association are some of the SGA's projects. The SGA oversees more than 130 chartered clubs on campus and sponsors intercollegiate athletics, social events, and service activities. The University administration wholly supports the concept of student rights and student participation in all areas of campus governance.

Admission Requirements

Rowan University carefully considers each application it receives and selects candidates who will be academically successful, contribute to student life on campus, and benefit most from the Rowan experience. Rowan's admission standards are competitive. The 2010 freshman class posted a mean SAT score of 1174 (math/critical reading combination), a top–20 percent class rank, and an average GPA of 3.5. The average transfer student GPA is 3.18.

Admission decisions are based on the strength and quality of the high school record, SAT or ACT scores, class rank, and letters of recommendation. An essay or interview is not required.

Applicants are expected to have completed a minimum of 16 college-preparatory units: 4 of English, 2 of laboratory science, 3 of college-preparatory mathematics (algebra I and II, geometry), 2 of social studies, and 5 of additional work in at least two of the following areas: English, social studies, languages, mathematics, and sciences. The College of Engineering seeks applicants with 3 units of laboratory science, including chemistry and physics, and 4 units of college-preparatory mathematics, including precalculus (calculus preferred).

Admission for transfer students is competitive and is based on college transcripts and available space in the desired major.

Application and Information

The University application, $65 application fee, high school and/or college transcript, and SAT or ACT scores should be forwarded to the Admissions Office. For September entrance, freshman and transfer applications are due March 1, with notification no later than April 15. The fall-enrollment deposit must be received by May 1. The application deadline for spring semester (January entrance) is November 1 for freshmen and transfers. Campus visits are highly recommended.

Prospective students should visit http://ru.rowan.edu. For additional information, students should contact:

Albert Betts
Director of Admissions
Rowan University
Glassboro, New Jersey 08028-1701
Phone: 856-256-4200
      877-RU-ROWAN (toll-free)
E-mail: admissions@rowan.edu
Web site: http://www.rowan.edu

Science Hall, Rowan's state-of-the-art science center, is one of the most advanced undergraduate research facilities at a public university on the East Coast.

RYERSON UNIVERSITY
TORONTO, CANADA

Everyone Makes a Mark

The University

Founded in 1948, Ryerson University is Canada's leader in providing a high standard of professionally relevant education that combines the traditional university focus on theory with a career-oriented emphasis on professional practice and application.

Ryerson offers undergraduate, master's, and Ph.D. programs. Undergraduate degree programs are offered through the University's five faculties: the Faculty of Arts; the Faculty of Engineering, Architecture, and Science; the Faculty of Community Services; the Ted Rogers School of Management; and the Faculty of Communications and Design. Known for attracting people with motivation, direction, and drive, Ryerson offers professionally targeted programs as well as contemporary arts and science degrees. Professional relevance is the essence of Ryerson, characterizing the people, curricula, and facilities that serve Ryerson's 28,000 undergraduate and graduate students. This special combination has earned Ryerson its reputation for excellence.

A vibrant and energetic campus community is characterized by on-campus residences, state-of-the-art athletic facilities, and numerous cultural, political, and recreational clubs. The University's location enables students to pursue their education in the financial, industrial, and cultural centre of Canada—the nation's largest city, Toronto.

Ryerson houses 840 students in three residences: Pitman Hall, O'Keefe House, and the International Living Learning Centre. Each residence has its own unique features and attributes. For more information, prospective students should visit http://www.ryerson.ca/housing.

Ryerson operates fourteen men's and women's varsity teams that continually qualify for postseason playoffs. Ryerson student athletes travel throughout Ontario, across Canada, and south to the United States to represent the University. Ryerson's intramural program is open to all students regardless of their skill level in sports and offers students the opportunity to meet people and get some exercise at the same time. More than twenty-five different leagues run throughout the academic year.

The Recreation and Athletics Centre (RAC) at Ryerson offers an extensive fitness centre with free weights and weight machines; a large cardio room with treadmills, elliptical trainers, stationary bicycles, recumbent bikes, and rowing machines; a three-lane, 160-yard, banked indoor running track; two sprung hardwood-floor dance studios; four international squash courts; six gymnasiums; a pool; spacious locker rooms with saunas; and helpful staff members. Athletic facilities are expected to be greatly enhanced with the scheduled 2011 opening of the $60-million Ryerson University Sports and Recreation Centre at Maple Leaf Gardens, a renovation to a historic Toronto landmark and sports treasure.

Location

Ryerson University is located right in the heart of downtown Toronto. Recognized internationally for its high quality of life, Toronto is a major cultural centre and Canada's hub for business and finance providing students with exciting learning opportunities. Ryerson's campus lies within walking distance of music, movies, theaters, and great food and shopping, and it is a short distance from professional sports complexes and international attractions. One of North America's cleanest, safest, and most ethnically diverse cities, Toronto offers many neighborhoods to explore, such as Chinatown, the Beaches, and the Danforth. Other attractions include Ontario Place, the Canadian National Exhibition (CNE), the Ontario Science Centre, and the Royal Ontario Museum (ROM).

Majors and Degrees

Ryerson offers the following undergraduate degrees: Bachelor of Arts, Bachelor of Applied Science, Bachelor of Architectural Science, Bachelor of Commerce, Bachelor of Design, Bachelor of Engineering, Bachelor of Fine Arts, Bachelor of Health Administration, Bachelor of Health Sciences, Bachelor of Interior Design, Bachelor of Journalism, Bachelor of Science, Bachelor of Science in Nursing, Bachelor of Social Work, Bachelor of Technology, and Bachelor of Urban and Regional Planning.

The full-time undergraduate programs available in Ryerson's five faculties are Faculty of Arts: arts and contemporary studies, criminal justice, English, geographic analysis, international economics and finance, politics and governance, psychology, sociology, and undeclared; Ted Rogers School of Management: business management (accounting, economics and management science, entrepreneurship, finance, global management, human resource management, law and business, marketing management), hospitality and tourism management, business technology management, and retail management; Faculty of Communications and Design: fashion (communication, design), graphic communications management, image arts (film studies, new media, photography studies), journalism, radio and television, and theater (performance acting, performance dance, performance production); Faculty of Community Services: child and youth care, early childhood education, midwifery, nursing, nutrition and food, occupational health and safety, public health and safety, social work, and urban and regional planning; and Faculty of Engineering, Architecture, and Science: architectural science, biology, chemistry, computer science, contemporary science, mathematics and its applications, medical physics, and undeclared, as well as several engineering programs (aerospace, biomedical, chemical, civil, computer, electrical, industrial, mechanical, and undeclared).

Academic Programs

Relevant curricula—a unique mix of professional, professionally related, and liberal studies course work—enable students to practice while they learn; students are well prepared with the skills necessary to enter their chosen career or profession upon graduation. In professional and professionally related courses, theory and practice are viewed as partners in the learning process. Lecture material is translated into practice through paid cooperative education and internship options, laboratory work, field trips, off-campus project work, and regular contact with business and industry. Liberal studies courses enhance the students' capacity to understand the social and cultural environment in which they will function, both as professionals and as educated citizens. With an education of this scope and rigor, graduates are uniquely adaptable to the challenges and opportunities in their professional fields.

Academic Facilities

Following a recent $210-million expansion that included the addition of six new buildings, Ryerson is continuing its plan to revitalize the University community. The student-centred campus is slated to be further transformed by a new state-of-the-art Student Learning Centre; the School of Image Arts, and Ryerson Gallery and Research Centre; and the Ryerson University Sports and Recreation Centre at Maple Leaf Gardens.

The Ryerson Library has more than 500,000 books and 2,000 print journal titles. More than $2 million is spent annually to support electronic resources which reflect the breadth of programs available at Ryerson; students can access these resources across campus and remotely. The Ronald D. Besse Information and Learning Commons combines the expertise of student services with new technologies to equip students with the academic skills needed to access and analyze information effectively. Assistance is available in a variety of forms, including research support, free workshops, and real-time chat support.

The Rogers Communications Centre (RCC) is the University's flagship building for studies in converging communications and interactive media, and is one of Canada's premier facilities for education in digital media communications. As an integral part of Ryerson University, the RCC houses and supports the Schools of Journalism and Radio and Television Arts.

Costs

Tuition for full-time international students for the 2010–11 academic year ranged from Can$17,498 to Can$18,665. The average cost for room and board was Can$10,000. Expenses vary according to the student's choice of board plan and housing facility.

Financial Aid

Various scholarships and bursaries and a dedicated series of financial-planning services are available. Every year, the University offers more than Can$10 million in scholarships, awards, and bursaries. International students can apply for an International Student Merit Scholarship after they have submitted an application for admission to Ryerson. The University has been authorized by the U.S. Department of Education to administer Federal Stafford Student Loans and the Federal PLUS Program.

Faculty

In addition to holding advanced degrees, many of Ryerson's professors are professionals who either are currently working in the industry or have worked in the industry in the past. They bring their expertise and up-to-date knowledge or even internship opportunities for students. Ryerson's relatively small class sizes enhance the learning process by maximizing student contact with faculty members.

Admission Requirements

To be eligible for admission to a Ryerson program, students must meet Ryerson's admission requirements from the jurisdiction or country from which the student is applying and hold the prerequisites for the specific program of interest. Individual programs may stipulate specific subject prerequisites for admission, including specific courses and minimum grades. Due to competition, candidates may be required to present averages/grades above the minimum. It is essential that the required subject prerequisites and grades for specific programs form part of an applicant's academic background, especially in the last two years of secondary and/or postsecondary studies. Programs may also stipulate nonacademic requirements for admission, such as a portfolio, an admission essay, an interview, or an audition. Students are strongly encouraged to check the requirements before applying to any programs at Ryerson. Applicants from a country where English is not the first language, or where English is an official language but not the first language, are required to present proof of English language proficiency at a satisfactory level.

Application and Information

Ryerson programs begin only in September of each year. Ryerson generally does not grant admission in the winter (January) or spring (May) terms. Application for admission should be made as early as possible.

All students must apply to Ryerson through the Ontario Universities' Application Centre (OUAC) at http://www.ouac.on.ca. Undergraduate Admissions and Recruitment must receive all officially certified academic transcripts that include promotion/graduation status. The date for guaranteed consideration for the fall 2011 semester for grades-plus-selective-admission programs (those that select students on the basis of grades plus auditions, interviews, portfolios, essays, etc.) is February 1 and March 1 for programs that select on the basis of grades.

Ryerson offers general walking tours of the campus, guided by current students representing a variety of the full-time undergraduate degree programs. These tours run Monday to Friday at 10 a.m. and 1 p.m. Visitors can register for campus tours online through the Undergraduate Admissions and Recruitment Web site.

Undergraduate Admissions and Recruitment
Ryerson University
350 Victoria Street
Toronto, Ontario M5B 2K3
Canada
Phone: 416-979-5036
Fax: 416-979-5067
E-mail: international@ryerson.ca
Web site: http://www.ryerson.ca/undergraduate/admission/
　　　　http://on.fb.me/RyersonU_Admissions (Facebook)
　　　　http://twitter.com/Ryerson_UAR (Twitter)

SACRED HEART UNIVERSITY
FAIRFIELD, CONNECTICUT

SACRED HEART UNIVERSITY

The University

Characterized by the personal attention it provides its students, Sacred Heart University (SHU) in Fairfield, Connecticut is an independent, comprehensive liberal arts university in the Catholic intellectual tradition. With more than forty-five academic programs for undergraduate, master's, and doctoral students in the arts, sciences, business, education, and health professions, Sacred Heart University is nationally recognized for its commitment to academic excellence, cutting-edge technology, championship Division I athletic teams, and award-winning community service program.

Fully accredited by the New England Association of Schools and Colleges (NEASC), SHU is the second-largest Catholic university in New England, and the first in America to be led and staffed by lay people. A vibrant residential university with 3,500 full-time undergraduates and more than 6,000 total undergraduate and graduate students, the University's academic programs are housed in its four distinctive colleges: the College of Arts and Sciences, AACSB-accredited John F. Welch College of Business, College of Education and Health Professions, and University College.

Exemplified by its mission and the Catholic intellectual tradition, Sacred Heart University is dedicated to the holistic development of its students through active, engaged learning that educates the whole person—mind, body, and spirit. Hands-on learning through research, internships, clinical placements, service learning, and study-abroad programs encourages students to apply their skills and knowledge outside the classroom, contributing to an exemplary 96 percent job and graduate school placement rate for graduating seniors.

With guaranteed housing for four years and over 90 percent of first-year students residing on campus, SHU provides a lively residential campus atmosphere with a rich student life program. There are over eighty student organizations, including popular performing arts groups (band, chorale, and theater arts), media groups, spirit groups, national Greek letter organizations, intramural and club sports, community service organizations, ministry groups, leadership programs, student governance groups, multicultural organizations, and academic honor societies. Cultural events abound on campus, including live entertainment and poetry nights at the Holy Grounds Café; the Student Affairs Lecture Series which brings renowned guest speakers to campus; and professional-quality theatrical, musical, and dance performances at the Edgerton Center for the Performing Arts. SHU's robust school spirit is embodied by the University's successful Division I intercollegiate athletics program. Among the largest Division I programs in the country, the Pioneers compete in thirty-one varsity sports, and students also participate in thirty club sports teams.

Location

Sacred Heart University's campus location offers the best of both worlds: a safe, suburban campus located on 69 acres in beautiful Fairfield, Connecticut and a central location between the urban centers of New York City (55 miles) and Boston, Massachusetts (150 miles). SHU students enjoy a multitude of social, recreational, and professional opportunities in Fairfield County. The area is rich in New England history and features miles of stunning coastline, beaches, nature preserves, sports stadiums, restaurants, entertainment, shopping, and cultural exhibits, all complemented by dozens of local, national, and multinational corporations and easy access to New York City via Metro-North Railroad.

Drawing on the rich resources in New England and the New York metropolitan area, students are immersed in enriching activities throughout the year, including group events such as Broadway shows in New York City and trips to historical Philadelphia and Washington, D.C. The University's shuttle system provides free service to the local transportation centers; popular downtown Fairfield; the nearby shopping mall, movie theaters, and other shopping and recreational attractions; and student-favorite spots such as the culturally rich city of New Haven and the beach during late spring and early fall.

Majors and Degrees

SHU offers bachelor's degrees within three colleges. The College of Arts and Sciences offers programs in biology (concentrations in ecology and conservation, molecular and cellular, neuroscience, and general biology), Catholic studies (minor), chemistry (concentrations in biochemistry and general chemistry), communication and technology studies, computer science/information technology (computer science track, information technology track, computer science gaming track, concentration in network security), criminal justice, English (concentrations in literature and writing), European studies (minor), fashion design (minor), French (minor), graphic design and visual arts, history, Irish studies (minor), Italian (minor), Latin American studies (minor), mathematics, media studies, Middle Eastern studies (minor), music (minor), philosophy, psychology, religious studies, social work, sociology, Spanish, and women's studies (minor), as well as preprofessional advising programs including predental studies, premedical studies, prelaw, preoptometry, preosteopathic studies, prephysician's assistant studies, prepharmacy, and pre–veterinary studies. Several five-year combined bachelor's and master's degree programs are offered in the college.

The AACSB-accredited John F. Welch College of Business offers programs in accounting, business administration (concentrations in business analysis, human resource management, international business, management, and marketing), business economics, finance, marketing (concentration in fashion marketing and merchandising), and sport management. The Welch College of Business also offers a five-year B.S./M.B.A. option with concentrations in accounting, finance, management, and marketing.

The College of Education and Health Professions includes elementary and secondary education certification programs. Many education students choose the five-year program in which students work toward earning Connecticut teacher certification while completing a Master of Arts in Teaching (M.A.T.) degree and interning at a local school district during the fifth year. Programs in the health sciences include athletic training, exercise science, health science (leadership track and preprofessional track), geriatric health and wellness (minor), nursing, and combined undergraduate/graduate programs in occupational therapy and physical therapy.

Academic Programs

Candidates for the bachelor's degree must complete a minimum of 120 credits. In addition to courses within the major field of study, the curriculum is made up of several components: the foundational core; the elective core; and SHU's innovative, nationally-recognized Common Core, "The Human Journey." The Common Core emphasizes collaborative, team-taught classes, capstone experiences, and out-of-the-classroom experiential learning.

Special academic programs include the Thomas More Honors Program and the Major in Success program, a comprehensive, individualized program to help undeclared students make informed decisions about a major and career path. Students in the John F. Welch College of Business participate in the Welch Experience, an integrated professional and academic program which includes experiential learning opportunities such as internships and study abroad, special mentoring programs, undergraduate research opportunities, targeted career development activities, access to business leaders, and the development of a state-of-the-art online portfolio for all students.

Off-Campus Programs

Fairfield County boasts the third-highest concentration of Fortune 500 companies in the U.S., world-class hospitals, nationally ranked elementary and secondary schools, and countless additional sites for students to intern and gain relevant work experience. SHU's Pioneer-Link internship and job database includes over 4,000 employers. Eighty percent of graduating seniors report participation in at least one internship, practicum, or field experience, which contributes to the University's 96 percent placement rate of graduating seniors in jobs and graduate school.

Study-abroad experiences are also a key component of the undergraduate experience. Students have the opportunity to study at SHU's own international campuses in Luxembourg and Ireland, and on programs led by University faculty in a number of countries each year. Other study-abroad opportunities are available through the University's membership in the College Consortium for International Studies.

Academic Facilities

Sacred Heart University is committed to anytime, anywhere learning, which is supported by the mobile computing program, a fully wireless campus, 24-hour computer labs with printing, a full program of group and one-on-one computer training, a help desk and IT call center, and easy digital equipment loans for students.

Other highlights of SHU's on-campus academic facilities are state-of-the-art laboratories dedicated to motion analysis, independent living, human performance, athletic training, acute care, ambulatory care, and clinical skills, which support SHU's health sciences programs; a model science classroom, educational technology laboratory, and the Book Ends literacy clinic, which offer education students exposure to stimulating teaching environments; and state-of-the art biology and chemistry laboratories in the newly-renovated science wing.

Cutting-edge studio and lab spaces for dedicated use by art and design students include an illustration studio, painting and drawing studio, graphic design studio, foundations studio, and fashion design studio.

The Ryan-Matura Library (under renovation to provide enhanced group study and gathering areas and a new café), contains 140,000 holdings including online and print books, periodicals, microforms, audio and video resources, course reserves, and an interlibrary loan program that allows students to access works from libraries worldwide.

Other SHU facilities include the 776-seat Edgerton Center for the Performing Arts; the Gallery of Contemporary Arts, which hosts student art and design exhibits; WHRT, the student-run radio station; and the William H. Pitt Health and Recreation Center, which houses the Sacred Heart University Sports Medicine and Rehabilitation Center.

Costs

Full-time undergraduate tuition and fees for 2010–11 were $31,440; room and board were an additional $12,340. Board only (for commuter students) ranged from $1050 to $3500, depending on the meal plan. The cost of books was estimated at $1000 per year.

Financial Aid

Financial aid is awarded on a first-come, first-served basis to admitted undergraduate students and may include loans and need-based aid (from University, federal, and state sources) and/or merit-based aid for academic and athletic achievement. Participation grants for select performing arts and community service programs are also awarded. Employment within the University is awarded under the terms of the Federal Work-Study Program. Completion of the College Scholarship Service PROFILE and the FAFSA are required in order to receive financial assistance.

Faculty

The University's student-faculty ratio is 13:1 and the average class size is 21 students. While research is important to the widely published faculty at SHU, the University's accessible, student-focused professors are committed to their primary role, teaching, allowing students across disciplines to benefit from forming close relationships with faculty members. Of the University's 579 faculty members, 95 percent have earned advanced degrees in their fields and over 85 percent teach undergraduate courses. The University does not employ teaching assistants, thus 100 percent of undergraduate courses are taught by faculty members. The student-faculty connection begins immediately, as each first-year student is assigned a faculty member as their academic adviser for course selection and registration. This relationship is a seamless one, as the academic adviser also serves as the student's professor in a select Core Curriculum course which meets weekly. Beyond their teaching, academic advising, and mentoring roles, faculty members serve as advisers to a variety of student clubs and organizations on campus; lead student service trips around the country and the world; serve as pre-fall program leaders for incoming first-year student groups; and participate in collaborative, co-curricular learning activities such as team-taught classes, capstone experiences, and cultural learning opportunities that extend beyond the customary classroom environment.

Student Government

Students play a major role in strategic planning and decision-making at SHU. Student government opportunities include the Executive Board, Student Government Senate, Class Boards, Council of Clubs and Organizations, and the Student Events Team.

Admission Requirements

Full-time students, both freshmen and transfer, may enroll in either the fall or spring semesters. Sacred Heart University believes in a personalized process in evaluating students for admission. The Admissions Office utilizes the Common Application and also requires high school transcripts (and college transcripts for transfer students) and a letter of recommendation. A campus visit and interview are strongly encouraged for applicants and are required for early decision candidates. Sacred Heart University will consider SAT or ACT scores if students elect to submit them; however standardized test scores are not required. Additional documentation is required for international applicants, and students who are not native English-speakers must submit TOEFL scores.

Application and Information

The Common Application is available online beginning August 1, 2011. The deadline for early decision applications is December 1. Regular admission is rolling with a January 15 priority deadline for financial assistance and housing. A campus visit is strongly encouraged and can be scheduled by calling 203-371-7881 or visiting http://www.sacredheart.edu/visitplanner.cfm.

For further admissions information, please contact:

Jamie P. Romeo
Associate Dean of Undergraduate Admissions
Sacred Heart University
5151 Park Avenue
Fairfield, Connecticut 06825

Phone: 203-371-7880
E-mail: enroll@sacredheart.edu
Web site: http://www.sacredheart.edu

The Campus Quad at Sacred Heart University.

SAINT ANSELM COLLEGE
MANCHESTER, NEW HAMPSHIRE

The College

Saint Anselm is a small liberal arts college of 2,000 undergraduates in the hills of southern New Hampshire, less than an hour north of Boston. Founded in 1889 by the Catholic Order of Saint Benedict, it maintains a strong sense of community that is characteristic of a Benedictine institution. The College has earned a national reputation for high academic standards. It prides itself on offering a challenging intellectual environment while encouraging the students' intellectual, social, spiritual, and physical development. Saint Anselm's extraordinary commitment to community engagement, evidenced by the involvement of students, faculty, and staff in projects that impact the local community and our world, has earned the College a new and special designation by the Carnegie Foundation for the Advancement of Teaching. Saint Anselm takes pride in being one of seventeen liberal arts colleges nationwide cited as an "institution of community engagement."

All Saint Anselm College students pursue specialized major courses of study in such areas as liberal arts, business, the sciences, nursing, and preprofessional preparation. A curriculum that emphasizes critical thinking, communication, research, and analysis skills leads to strong placement in graduate and professional schools. The College's primary goal, however, is to offer an educational experience that produces well-rounded graduates with a creative and open-minded spirit.

The beauty of Saint Anselm College's 400-acre campus changes with the seasons. Buildings surrounding the "quad" range from original ivy-covered brick to contemporary architecture, and the grounds include The New Hampshire Institute of Politics at Saint Anselm College and a church with an abbey. In addition to student housing, administration, and academic facilities, the campus includes a multipurpose activities center with a new fitness center; Davison Hall dining commons; Stoutenburgh Gymnasium, home of Saint Anselm varsity athletics; the Thomas F. Sullivan hockey arena; and Cushing Student Center, which houses academic and career counseling offices, student organizations, health services, and an academic resource center. A short drive away is a 100-acre tract used for retreats and environmental study and research.

Saint Anselm College has students from thirty-one states and eight countries, more than 88 percent of whom live on campus in traditional dormitories and modern apartments. The list of more than eighty clubs and organizations that match the students' diverse interests is constantly evolving and includes music, community service, theater, outdoor recreation, debating, prelaw, and premedicine, as well as a local chapter of the Knights of Columbus. Intercollegiate sports are offered for men in baseball, basketball, cross-country, football, golf, hockey, lacrosse, skiing, soccer, and tennis. For women, teams are organized in basketball, cross-country, field hockey, lacrosse, skiing, soccer, softball, tennis, and volleyball. There are nearly twenty club sports, including cheerleading, cycling, ice hockey, lacrosse, rugby, skating, and soccer.

Location

Less than an hour from Boston, Saint Anselm offers easy access to the cultural attractions of a large city, yet it is equally close to ski slopes, the Appalachian Trail, and the Atlantic coast. It has the feel of a rural campus, but is only minutes from downtown Manchester, the largest city in New Hampshire. In Manchester, students find excellent restaurants, galleries, shopping malls, and theaters as well as professional offices with internship and employment opportunities.

Majors and Degrees

Saint Anselm awards the Bachelor of Arts degree in the following academic programs and majors: accounting, biochemistry, biology, business, chemistry, classics, communication, computer science, computer science with business, computer science with mathematics, criminal justice, education (secondary and elementary), economics, English, environmental science, environmental politics and sustainability, financial economics, fine arts, French, history, international business, international relations, liberal studies in the great books, mathematics, mathematics with economics, natural science, nursing, peace and justice studies, philosophy, physics, politics, psychology, sociology, Spanish, and theology. It also offers a program leading to the Bachelor of Science in Nursing (B.S.N.) degree.

The College offers preprofessional programs in dentistry, law, medicine, and theology.

A 3-2 program in engineering is available in cooperation with the University of Notre Dame, Catholic University of America, Manhattan College, and the University of Massachusetts Lowell.

Academic Programs

Saint Anselm College provides students with a strong liberal arts background, including required courses in philosophy, theology, and foreign language. Students generally take ten to fifteen courses in their majors, while the liberal arts core courses and a wide range of electives make up the remainder of the forty courses required for graduation. Honors program participants distinguish themselves by taking additional courses in order to graduate with honors.

All Saint Anselm students participate in a nationally recognized humanities program, Portraits in Human Greatness, during their freshman and sophomore years. The program's interdisciplinary approach to Western culture integrates science, sociology, history, philosophy, and the arts. The heart of the program is its seminar component, which strengthens skills in reasoning, articulating ideas, and debating.

Saint Anselm College participates in the Advanced Placement Program of the College Board. Students who receive a score of 3 or better on the Advanced Placement examinations may obtain advanced placement and credit in the pertinent subject matter. Applicants who have completed examinations under the College-Level Examination Program may receive advanced placement and credit if the scores they receive are acceptable.

Off-Campus Programs

More than 40 percent of Saint Anselm students complete an internship related to their major field of study, usually during their junior or senior year. Internships help students apply theoretical knowledge, explore careers and graduate school choices, and improve employment prospects. Internships are arranged locally and in major cities such as Boston, New York, and Washington, D.C.

The College provides access to several approved semester-long study-abroad programs, and Saint Anselm faculty members often lead summer study trips abroad. The College has an archeological dig site in Umbria, Italy. Students of all academic majors can participate in fieldwork at the dig site. Service trips sponsored by the Office of Campus Ministry take place from Arizona to Maine as well as in Latin America.

Academic Facilities

Among the College's sixty buildings are facilities for classes, research, arts performances and exhibits, and campus events. Geisel Library holds 230,000 bound volumes and 68,000 microform titles and maintains a collection of 4,000 periodical titles and 1,700 video recordings, as well as CDs and audiotapes. Goulet Science Center has been expanded and renovated to meet the students' needs, and contains its own library. The 20,000-square-foot New Hampshire Institute of Politics is a center for civic education and engagement. It attracts diplomats, candidates, and political experts throughout the year and is in the national and international spotlight during presidential primary and election seasons. The Charles A. Dana Center houses a 700-seat theater and serves as the home of the humanities program. Poisson Computer Science Center contains more than 200 PCs and specially equipped classrooms and offices. Fine arts studios and a small theater are located in the Comiskey Center.

Costs

Tuition for the 2010–11 school year was $30,760, and room and board charges were $11,630. Books and other miscellaneous fees cost approximately $1850.

Financial Aid

Saint Anselm College offers financial aid through various federal and private programs. Assistance is awarded as a supplement to the reasonable financial sacrifice that the College expects will be made by the interested student and his or her parents. Eighty-eight percent of Saint Anselm's students receive some form of financial assistance to help defray the cost of their education. Financial aid packages consist of scholarships, grants, loans, and work opportunities. Merit awards (Presidential Scholarships) of up to $16,000 are awarded to outstanding students.

Two forms are required in applying for aid. The student must submit the CSS Financial Aid PROFILE and the Free Application for Federal Student Aid (FAFSA) to the College Scholarship Service by March 1.

Faculty

The College's faculty consists of full-time and part-time members. Ninety-six percent of the faculty members have earned doctorates or the appropriate terminal degrees in their fields. With a student-teacher ratio of 12:1, professors are extremely accessible. In addition to teaching, the faculty members serve as advisers to students in their departments. No classes are taught by graduate students or teaching assistants.

Student Government

Students participate in the affairs of the college in a variety of ways. Students are elected to positions as class officers and serve on the Student Senate and Campus Activities Board. They serve as student body representatives on the Board of Trustees and on administrative committees, including the college judiciary board, curriculum committee, and health committee. Saint Anselm encourages students to express their opinions and take active roles in shaping the life of their college and to be aware of their potential as active and engaged citizens to effect change in the world around them.

Admission Requirements

In selecting a freshman class, the admission committee considers each candidate personally and thoroughly, evaluating their high school record, letters of recommendation, and essay (part of the application). SAT/ACT test scores are optional for all academic majors except nursing. Of greatest importance is the student's high school transcript, in terms of both the quality of courses taken and the grades earned.

Transfer and international students are welcome to apply. The same general admission procedures are required, along with at least a C average in all transferable courses and, for international students, a satisfactory score on the TOEFL.

Application and Information

The Office of Admission is open from 8:30 to 4:30 on weekdays and is open for Saturday Visit programs in the fall. Please go to www.anselm.edu for a list of current visit programs. The College strongly recommends a campus visit and an interview in order to discover the many benefits of Saint Anselm.

Saint Anselm College is an exclusive user of the Common Application. Please go to www.comonapp.org to apply. Application deadlines are as follows: early action, November 15; nursing majors, November 15; and regular decision, February 15.

For more information, students should contact:

Office of Admission
Saint Anselm College
100 Saint Anselm Drive
Manchester, New Hampshire 03102
Phone: 603-641-7500
      888-426-7356 (toll-free)
E-mail: admission@anselm.edu
Web site: http://www.anselm.edu

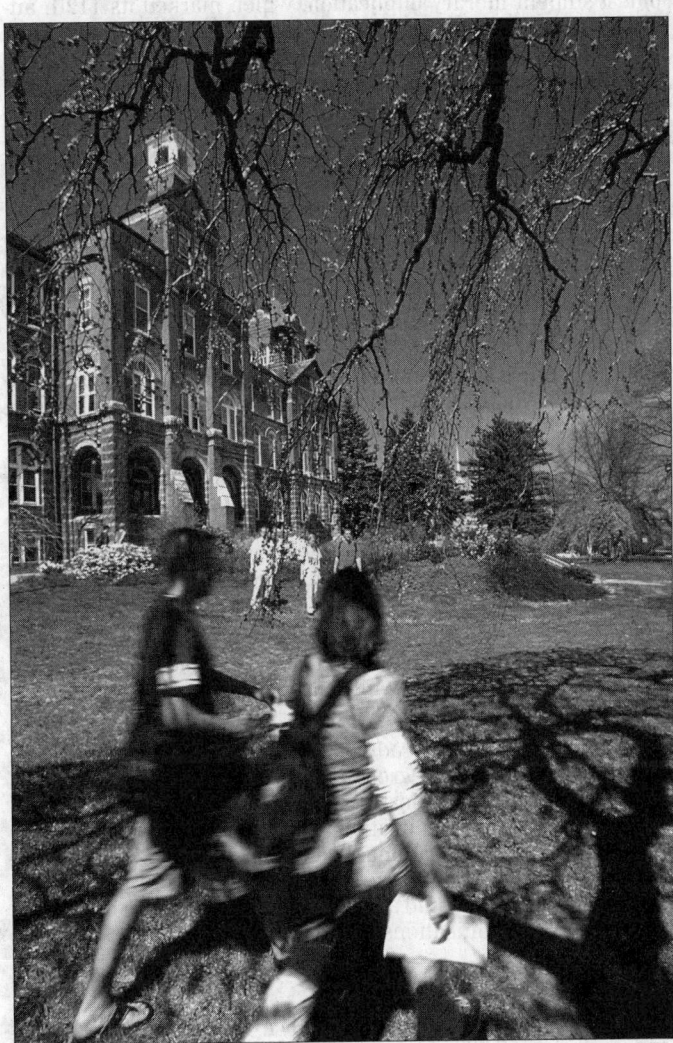

Saint Anselm College Alumni Hall.

ST. BONAVENTURE UNIVERSITY

ST. BONAVENTURE, NEW YORK

The University

St. Bonaventure University provides a values-based education with individual attention from professors, a beautiful residential setting, and a friendly, close-knit atmosphere. Of the 2,500 students enrolled, 2,000 are undergraduates. More than 74 percent of the undergraduates are full-time residents. Complementing St. Bonaventure's traditions are innovative degree programs, computerized career placement aids, comprehensive student life activities, and modern academic facilities. Among major campus events during the academic year are concerts and coffeehouse acts, indoor and outdoor recreational programs, current and classic film offerings, and dramatic and musical plays. Aspiring writers and broadcasters from all academic majors—Bonaventure has produced 5 Pulitzer Prize winners—find challenging and plentiful opportunities working with one of the four University media: WSBU-88.3 FM-The Buzz, the nationally ranked campus radio station; *The Bona Venture*, the award-winning weekly newspaper; *The Bonadieu*, the yearbook; and *The Laurel*, the nation's oldest student literary publication, which marked its 112th anniversary in 2011. Other organizations on campus include academic fraternities, academic honor societies, a variety of club and intramural sports, and arts organizations that include choral, instrumental, dance, and drama ensembles. The Thomas Merton Ministry Center is open 24 hours a day and aims to foster a community of friendship and mutual service. Many students take the opportunity to serve as Bona Buddies to area children or senior citizens; help with the national award–winning soup kitchen The Warming House; or volunteer in one of many service organizations, including SIFE and BonaResponds, one of the most active collegiate disaster relief organizations in the nation. Volunteer opportunities include immersion experiences and service opportunities with the poor, both in the U.S. and abroad.

St. Bonaventure University students enjoy two athletic facilities: the new $6.2-million Richter Center, which is open 24 hours a day, features three basketball courts, a running/walking track, racquetball/squash/wallyball courts, an aerobics room, a recreational area for roller hockey, a weight room, a cardiovascular fitness room, locker rooms, an equipment check-out, a reception area, and a climbing wall; and the Reilly Center, housing a 5,780-seat sports arena, swimming pool, and weight room. Also available are outdoor tennis and basketball courts and a nine-hole golf course. NCAA Division I athletics for men are baseball, basketball, cross-country, golf, soccer, swimming, and tennis. Division I competition for women includes basketball, cross-country, lacrosse, soccer, softball, swimming, and tennis. St. Bonaventure is a member of the Atlantic 10 conference.

In addition to its undergraduate programs, St. Bonaventure offers the Master of Arts degree in English and in Franciscan studies (summers only). A Master of Science in Education program includes adolescence education, counselor education, differentiated instruction, educational leadership, literacy, school building leader, and school district leader. A Master of Business Administration program and a Master of Arts program in integrated marketing communications are also offered.

Location

St. Bonaventure is located on Route 417 between Olean, a city of approximately 17,000 residents, and Allegany, a village with about 2,000 residents. Shops, restaurants, and movie theaters are all within walking distance. The campus is spread over 500 acres in a valley surrounded by the Allegheny Mountains. The free Bona Bus connects the campus with Olean and Allegany, carrying students to and from the area attractions. The region around St. Bonaventure provides a beautiful setting for many outdoor activities. Holiday Valley, a renowned ski resort, is just 20 miles away, and nearby Allegany State Park offers excellent facilities for swimming, boating, and hiking. St. Bonaventure is accessible by car, bus, and commercial air transportation, with Buffalo/Niagara International the nearest major airport.

Majors and Degrees

St. Bonaventure University grants the Bachelor of Arts degree with majors in art, art history, classical languages, English, gerontology, history, interdisciplinary studies, international studies, journalism and mass communication, modern languages (French and Spanish), music, philosophy, political science, psychology, sociology, theater, theology, and women's studies. The Bachelor of Science is granted with majors in biochemistry, bioinformatics, biology, chemistry, childhood studies, computer science, early childhood education, economics, elementary/special education (dual certification), environmental science, interdisciplinary studies, mathematics, physical education, physics, psychology, and sport studies. The Bachelor of Business Administration is granted with majors in accounting, finance, management sciences, and marketing. Popular five-year master's programs are also available in business, English, and integrated marketing communications, and dual-admission/combined-degree programs offer unique opportunities for students pursuing careers in medicine, dentistry, pharmacy, and physical therapy.

Academic Programs

Students in all majors begin their intellectual journey in Clare College, St. Bonaventure's nationally acclaimed core curriculum, which offers a values-based education grounded in the vision of St. Francis and St. Bonaventure.

A candidate for a bachelor's degree must complete at least 120 credit hours, with a cumulative index of 2.0 or better in the major field and the overall program. A pass/fail grade option, available to all upperclass students, may be elected for one course per semester, but not for courses in a student's major field.

Advanced credit is granted for grades of C or better on either the College Proficiency Examination or the College-Level Examination Program (CLEP) tests. Advanced placement is granted on the basis of scores obtained on the College Board's Advanced Placement (AP) examinations.

Men and women may also elect to participate in the University's Army ROTC program, MacArthur Award winner as best small unit in the nation in 1998.

Off-Campus Programs

Through St. Bonaventure's membership in the College Consortium for International Studies (CCIS), St. Bonaventure students have access to six continents. More than sixty semester-long international study programs, including St. Bonaventure–sponsored study in Italy, Spain, Ireland, and Australia, are available to students in good academic standing in their junior year. Faculty-directed, short-term opportunities include a three-week intersession in China, the Francis E. Kelly Oxford summer program, and a three-week travel study program to Mexico. For further information, students should contact the Office of International Studies. Fieldwork or internships are available in several major programs.

Academic Facilities

Friedsam Memorial Library houses more than 250,000 volumes and includes a trilevel resource center with a curriculum center, the University archives, and digital media and conferencing centers, as well as world-class special collections. An automated online card catalog greatly improves research capabilities.

The William F. Walsh Science Center opened in 2008 and doubled the space for science studies. The center houses state-of-the-art computer science, laboratory and classroom space, biology labs, organic and general chemistry labs, a Natural World lab, a 150-seat indoor amphitheater, and faculty offices integrated with lab space for better student-teacher accessibility. It is attached to historic De La Roche Hall, which received a major face-lift in 2008.

The John J. Murphy Professional Building provides the most up-to-date equipment for the School of Business and the School of Journalism and Mass Communication. The Bob Koop Broadcast Journalism Laboratory features a television studio with an anchor desk, digital and videotape editing bays, while a remote TV production studio allows for live broadcasting of athletic events. A fiber-optic network connects microcomputers in academic and administrative areas. There are seven labs for student use containing more than 100 Macintosh systems. St. Bonaventure students also have wireless Internet access across campus.

An annex to Plassmann Hall houses computer-adaptable education classrooms, seminar rooms, and offices for the education faculty. An observatory allows students access to three compact telescopes, two 8-inch Celestron telescopes, and one 11-inch Schmidt-Cassegrain telescope, along with a heated classroom.

The Regina A. Quick Center for the Arts provides acoustically designed classroom space for music courses and painting and drawing studios. The center also includes a musical instrument digital interface lab, a 325-seat theater, and an atrium that is often used for receptions and impromptu musical performances. The F. Donald Kenney Museum and Art Study Wing includes four climate-controlled galleries offering nationally acclaimed traveling exhibits, works from the University's permanent collections, and student exhibits.

Historic Hickey Dining Hall received a spectacular makeover in 2006, and a 5,500-square-foot coffee café and gourmet deli opened in spring 2007. Some residence halls were overhauled in 2006, while the new science center and a $2.2-million library addition opened in 2008. A new building for the School of Business is planned to be built this decade.

Costs

For 2010–11, the annual costs were $25,930 for tuition and $965 for fees. Room and meal plans averaged $9717 per year.

Financial Aid

Students who qualify for financial aid normally receive a package consisting of a combination of scholarships, grants, loans, and work-study awards. An average financial aid package for an incoming freshman is more than $22,000. Athletic grants-in-aid are available for men in baseball, basketball, golf, soccer, swimming, and tennis; and for women in basketball, lacrosse, soccer, softball, swimming, and tennis. Music scholarships are also available. Students must file the Free Application for Federal Student Aid (FAFSA) in order to be considered for financial assistance. For more complete details, a student should contact the director of financial aid at the University.

Faculty

Like the student body, the 155 full-time and 67 part-time faculty members at St. Bonaventure come from a wide range of geographic, ethnic, and religious backgrounds. The student-faculty ratio of 14:1 allows faculty members the time to help each student to understand different modes of thinking, develop as a person, and lay a foundation for lifelong learning. Eighty-four percent of the faculty members hold the terminal degree in their field. Friars, many of whom teach and live on campus, add to the unique atmosphere of St. Bonaventure.

Student Government

Life at St. Bonaventure is centered on the residence halls, and the foundation of student government begins in the dormitories with the Residence Hall Councils. The elected council members determine the norms by which the residents are guided in their daily lives. The Student Government, whose members are elected from the student body, serves as the general student-governing unit, and its members serve on every major University board and committee.

Admission Requirements

St. Bonaventure University welcomes applications for admission from all serious candidates from a variety of backgrounds. St. Bonaventure University provides equal opportunity without regard to race, creed, color, gender, age, national or ethnic origin, marital status, veteran status, or disability in admission, employment, and in all of its educational programs and activities. Applicants, who are welcome to apply online, must show evidence of academic achievement to be selected for admission. The criteria used in making admission decisions, in order of importance, are quality of the high school curriculum, grade point average in college-preparatory courses, ACT (preferred) or SAT scores, class rank, recommendations from high school teachers and counselors, and extracurricular activities.

Application and Information

For more information about St. Bonaventure University, prospective students should contact:

Office of Admissions
St. Bonaventure University
P.O. Box D
St. Bonaventure, New York 14778
Phone: 716-375-2400
　　　　 800-462-5050 (toll-free)
E-mail: admissions@sbu.edu
Web site: http://www.sbu.edu

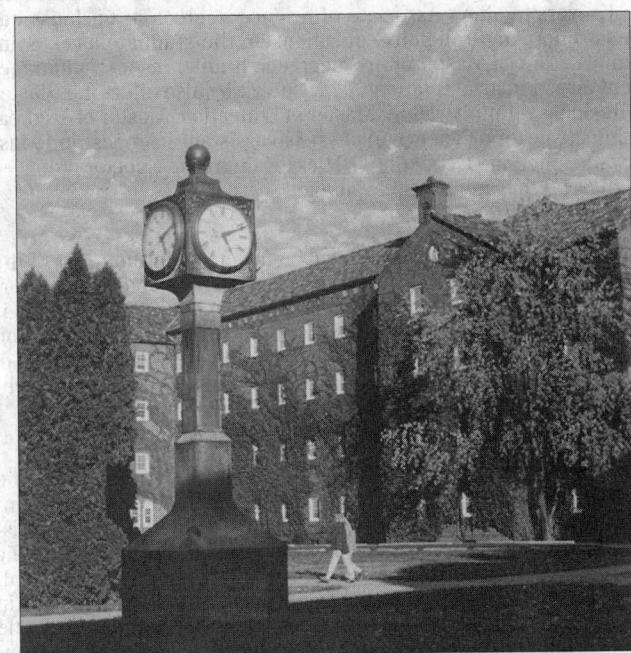

Built in 1928 and renovated in 1999, Devereux Hall is an example of the beautiful Florentine architecture found at St. Bonaventure University.

SAINT FRANCIS UNIVERSITY
LORETTO, PENNSYLVANIA

SAINT FRANCIS
UNIVERSITY
FOUNDED 1847

The University

Saint Francis University is a small, coeducational, liberal arts university. The University was founded in 1847 and conducted under the tradition of the Franciscan Friars of the Third Order Regular. The University is concerned with the development of each student for the world of today. For more than 150 years, the University's philosophy of education and student life has continued to emphasize two values: instruction of high quality and respect for the student as an individual. The University believes that a liberal arts education, encompassing a major field of study, is the soundest kind of preparation a student can have for a productive life. In recent years, Saint Francis University has garnered recognition for advances in study abroad and outreach in health care. Additionally, *U.S. News & World Report* has named Saint Francis as a Best Value institution. The University is accredited by the Middle States Association of Colleges and Schools. Departmental accreditations include the Accreditation Review Commission on Education for the Physician Assistant, Inc., Commission on Collegiate Nursing Education, Council on Social Work Education, and others. A complete list of accreditations may be found in the University catalog.

Students at Saint Francis University can find a number of outlets for their talents, interests, and abilities. Departmental clubs; volunteer organizations; social, business, and service fraternities; social sororities; and a service sorority are part of campus life. Athletics have played a major role in the University's history, and the athletics program offers twenty NCAA Division I sports for men and women as well as intramural sports. The newest sport to be added is women's bowling. All athletic teams compete in the Northeast Conference. The Student Activities Organization sponsors an impressive program of lectures, films, and concerts. The Southern Alleghenies Museum of Art, separately chartered, is located on the campus as well.

The full-time undergraduate enrollment is 704 men and 1,105 women; the University as a whole enrolls 2,449 students. Saint Francis University offers Associate of Science degrees in business administration, and religious education. On the graduate level, Saint Francis grants a Master of Arts degree in human resource management and industrial relations. The University also offers the Master of Business Administration, Master of Education, Master of Medical Science, Master of Science in physician assistant sciences, and Master of Science in Occupational Therapy degrees. A doctoral degree in physical therapy is also available.

Location

Saint Francis University is situated on 600 acres in the heart of the Allegheny Mountains. The campus is located in the borough of Loretto, which has a population of approximately 1,400. The campus is 6 miles from the county seat of Ebensburg, which has a population of 4,000. The cities of Johnstown and Altoona are within 25 miles of Loretto and have populations of 35,000 and 55,000, respectively. The University is a 90-minute drive east of Pittsburgh.

Majors and Degrees

Saint Francis University grants the Bachelor of Arts degree and offers majors in American studies, biology, computer science, engineering (3-2 program), English, English/communications, history, mathematics, philosophy, political science, psychology, public administration/government service, religious studies, and sociology. The Bachelor of Science degree is also granted, with majors in accounting, biology, chemistry, computer science, economics and finance, elementary education/special education, environmental engineering, environmental management (3-2 program), environmental studies (interdisciplinary), exercise physiology, management information systems, marketing, mathematics, medical technology, nursing, occupational therapy (five-year master's), phar-

macy (2+3 or 2+4), physical therapy (six-year doctoral degree), physician assistant science (five-year master's), podiatric science, psychology, public administration/government service, social work, and sociology.

Areas of preprofessional study include dentistry, engineering (3-2 program), law, medicine, optometry, podiatry, and veterinary medicine. Areas of concentration within majors include anthropology, biochemistry, bioinformatics, communications, computer science, criminal justice, environmental politics, environmental science, forensics, information and network security, international studies, management information systems, marine and environmental education specialties, marine biology, molecular biology, political communications, public management, public relations, software development, and Web application development. The University also grants secondary education certification in the areas of biology, chemistry, English, general science, mathematics, and social studies. A 3-2 cooperative program with Duke University in forestry and environmental management, a 3+4 accelerated program in primary care, a 2+3 accelerated program and a 3+3 program in pharmacy with Lake Erie College of Osteopathic Medicine, and a 3+4 accelerated program leading to the baccalaureate and Doctor of Dental Medicine degrees with Temple University are also offered.

It is possible for students to major in one area and minor in another or to have a double major. A self-designed major program is available as well. The University offers an honors program to challenge intellectually ambitious students from all disciplines. While pursuing their major field of study, students enroll in the full four-year curriculum, which allows in-depth, creative study in a variety of subject areas.

A continuing education program provides credit and noncredit courses on campus, online, and in the communities surrounding Loretto. The Office of Continuing Education offers Associate of Science degrees in business administration and religious education and Bachelor of Science degrees in accounting and management.

Academic Programs

The program of study leading to a bachelor's degree is usually completed in eight semesters. To qualify for graduation, a student must follow a program of study approved by the Office of the Provost that totals at least 128 credits distributed among liberal arts courses, major requirements, collateral requirements, and general electives. All students, regardless of major, are required to complete the University's general education program of 58 credits.

The academic calendar is divided into two semesters and three summer sessions.

Electronic capabilities at Saint Francis University enable students to access library holdings and communicate with professors, fellow students, and the world through the use of personal computers via e-mail and the Internet. Every classroom and residence hall room is wired for Internet access or can be accessed through the wireless network. The University has several classrooms equipped with state-of-the-art equipment that allows videoconferencing. All students receive a laptop computer as part of their tuition.

Off-Campus Programs

Students at Saint Francis University may, with permission of the University's administration, spend their junior year of study abroad or may earn credit for participation in summer programs conducted in Canada, France, Germany, Spain, and other countries by accredited American colleges and universities.

Students are encouraged to take advantage of the University's study abroad facility in Ambialet, France. The Semester in France program offers study for students within any major for the same tuition costs as studying on campus.

A number of departments offer students the opportunity for off-campus study. For some majors, such as nursing, occupational therapy, physical therapy, physician assistant science, education, medical technology, and social work, off-campus study is required; in all other majors, an internship is available as an elective. Such an internship can be a meaningful experience and can significantly enhance a student's career preparation.

Academic Facilities

The six-story Pasquerilla Library contains more than 150,000 volumes. Other features of the library are general study areas, seminar rooms, reading rooms, microfilm reading rooms, several multimedia classrooms, technologically equipped study rooms, and a collection of study items and educational materials for elementary and secondary education majors.

Scotus and Padua halls contain modern classroom facilities, language laboratories, two computer laboratories, a recording studio for radio and television, and lecture facilities (halls and an amphitheater). Sullivan Science Hall contains twelve well-equipped biology, chemistry, and physics laboratories; fully equipped electronic classrooms; a greenhouse for botanical research; an examining room for use in the physician assistant science program; and other facilities.

The recently completed DiSepio Institute for Rural Health and Wellness includes a human performance lab, a state-of-the-art fitness facility, conference space, and rehabilitation facilities. The focus of the Institute is delivering health and wellness programming and services to the campus community as well as the local population.

Costs

For 2010–11, tuition was $25,484, room and board were $9066, and technology program was $1050, for a total of $35,600.

Financial Aid

Approximately 90 percent of the Saint Francis University student body receives financial aid. In addition to participating in federal and state need-based student aid programs, Saint Francis University offers its own substantial grant program and a generous scholarship program that is based on SAT or ACT scores, high school average, and class rank. Academic awards range from $1000 to $16,000.

Faculty

Faculty members are chosen for their knowledge of subject matter, as well as for their ability to communicate. Of the teaching faculty at Saint Francis University, 80 percent hold a doctorate or the highest degree attainable in their specific field of expertise. No teaching assistants or graduate students teach classes at Saint Francis University.

Student Government

The Student Government Association's Steering Committee involves students who are interested in self-government. Students also serve on a number of committees in the Faculty Senate. The Student Government offices are located in the John F. Kennedy Student Center, which also houses a 600-seat auditorium, a campus bookstore and post office, a study lounge, and a café.

Admission Requirements

The admission committee considers applicants and renders decisions on the basis of the secondary school record, the recommendation of the secondary school principal or counselor, and the results of the SAT or ACT. Applicants to the School of Health Science should be aware of specified application requirements and deadlines. Applicants should have a minimum of 16 academic units and are strongly encouraged to visit the University campus for an admission interview and tour. Interviews and campus tours are available Monday through Friday throughout the year and select Saturday mornings while classes are in session.

Transfer students must submit a formal transfer application and a college clearance form in addition to official transcripts from each high school and college previously attended. Transfer students receive an advanced standing evaluation after an offer of admission has been made.

Saint Francis University, an equal opportunity/affirmative action employer, complies with applicable federal and state laws regarding nondiscrimination and affirmative action, including Title IX of the Educational Amendments of 1972, Titles VI and VII of the Civil Rights Act of 1964, and Section 504 of the Rehabilitation Act of 1973. Saint Francis University is committed to a policy of nondiscrimination and equal opportunity in employment, education programs and activities, and admissions that includes all persons regardless of race, gender, color, religion, national origin or ancestry, age, marital status, disability, or Vietnam-era veteran status. Inquiries or complaints may be addressed to the University's Director of Human Resources/Affirmative Action/Title IX Coordinator, Saint Francis University, Loretto, Pennsylvania 15940; telephone: 814-472-3264. For other University information, students should call 814-472-3000.

Application and Information

The University operates under a rolling admission policy. The application deadline for the physical therapy, occupational therapy, and physician assistant programs is January 15. For more information about Saint Francis University, students should contact:

Vice President for Enrollment Management
Saint Francis University
P.O. Box 600
Loretto, Pennsylvania 15940
Phone: 814-472-3100
            866-342-5738 (toll-free)
E-mail: admissions@francis.edu
Web site: http://www.francis.edu
               http://on.fb.me/StFrancis_PA (Facebook)
               http://twitter.com/SaintFrancisPA (Twitter)

Christian Hall.

ST. JOHN FISHER COLLEGE

ROCHESTER, NEW YORK

The College

Founded in 1948 by the Basilian fathers, St. John Fisher College is dedicated to serving the individual needs of its students. Originally a Catholic college for men, Fisher is now an independent, coeducational college with 58 percent women and 52 percent resident students. The College offers thirty-one undergraduate programs in business, the humanities, nursing, natural sciences, and social sciences, and is accredited by the Middle States Association of Colleges and Schools. The College also offers eleven master's programs and three doctoral programs leading to the Master of Business Administration, the Master of Science, the Master of Science in Education, the Doctor of Education, the Doctor of Nursing Practice, and the Doctor of Pharmacy.

Fisher's unique First-Year Program reaches beyond the transition to college to focus on developing responsible campus citizens with independent learning skills, who fully explore educational and career aspirations. The Learning Community Program gives first-year students the opportunity to take courses in clusters that focus on a central theme. Through this approach to learning, students and faculty members examine a complex topic from multiple perspectives and discover connections among various disciplines. Fisher's Learning Communities also enable students to learn cooperatively and develop close working relationships with other students and faculty members.

All of the residence halls have been renovated, giving all students access to the Internet and cable TV in their rooms. Keough Hall, the College's newest residence, opened in September 2005 and added more than 200 beds.

Fisher offers a full range of extracurricular activities designed to cater to the diverse interests of the 2,700 full-time and 200 part-time undergraduate students, over 700 master's students, and 400 doctoral students. Such activities include a student newspaper, a student TV club, a complete intramural program, and more than seventy student clubs and organizations. In addition, the Student Activities Board sponsors appearances by on-campus lecturers and entertainers.

Fisher is a member of NCAA Division III, ECAC, and the Empire 8. Men's intercollegiate sports are baseball, basketball, cross-country, football, golf, indoor and outdoor track, lacrosse, soccer, and tennis. Women's intercollegiate sports are basketball, cross-country, field hockey, golf, indoor and outdoor track, lacrosse, soccer, softball, tennis, and volleyball. Club sports include cross-country, ice hockey and men's and women's rugby. The Student Life Center, which is the hub of the athletic activities, includes courts for basketball, racquetball, squash, tennis, and volleyball; a sauna; a lounge; and a fitness area. Growney Stadium, complete with 2,100 bleacher seats and a press box, is equipped with an all-weather synthetic playing field to allow for all-season and nighttime play. Other on-campus athletics facilities include a nine-hole golf course, a softball field, a baseball complex, four outdoor tennis courts, and two grass practice fields. In summer 2011, a new track and field complex will open in time for fall sports. Each summer, Fisher is proud to host the Buffalo Bills training camp on campus.

Location

Located on 154 parklike acres, Fisher offers a balance of city activity and suburban tranquility. Just 10 minutes from the Fisher campus, Rochester, New York, the "World's Image Centre," offers many cultural attractions, including the Eastman Theater, the Rochester Philharmonic Orchestra, the International Museum of Photography at George Eastman House, the Rochester Museum and Science Center, the Memorial Art Gallery, and the Strasenburgh Planetarium. Home to a number of Fortune 500 companies, such as Eastman Kodak Company, Xerox Corporation, and Bausch and Lomb, the city of Rochester offers Fisher students opportunities for internships and employment after graduation.

Majors and Degrees

St. John Fisher College offers courses leading to the Bachelor of Arts and Bachelor of Science degrees. Undergraduate majors are offered in accounting, adolescence education, American studies, anthropology, applied information technology, biology, chemistry, childhood education, communication/journalism, computer science, corporate finance, economics, English, French, history, interdisciplinary studies, international studies, legal studies, management, mathematics, nursing, philosophy, physics, political science, psychology, religious studies, sociology, Spanish, special education, sport management, and statistics.

Fisher offers an RN to B.S. degree-completion program in nursing and a fast track to the B.S/M.S. in advanced practice nursing. The College also offers a cooperative engineering program with the University of Detroit, Clarkson University, Manhattan College, Columbia University, and the University at Buffalo, the State University of New York.

Academic Programs

The bachelor's degree is conferred upon those who complete a minimum of 120 semester hours of credit with a cumulative GPA of at least 2.0. Thirty hours of credit and half of the requirements for the major must be earned at St. John Fisher College. Graduates of Fisher's undergraduate accounting program or the M.B.A. with a concentration in accounting and 150 hours of credit are eligible to sit for the CPA exam in New York State.

Off-Campus Programs

Fisher offers a multitude of special programs that are designed to complement its academic programs. Students in various disciplines can take advantage of an internship program, Albany and Washington Semesters, and cross-registration with fourteen member colleges of the Rochester Area College Consortium. Study-abroad opportunities throughout the world are also available to students.

Academic Facilities

Over the last thirteen years, most of the academic and athletic facilities on campus have been upgraded and enhanced. Classrooms have been modernized and outfitted with state-of-the-art media facilities. Laboratory space has been upgraded with state-of-the-market educational technology. The Golisano Academic Gateway, complete with the Frontier Cyber Café and the learning resource center, opened in January 2001. The Ralph C. Wilson, Jr. Building opened in September 2003, expanding classroom capacity by 20 percent and providing additional faculty offices, seminar rooms, and meeting spaces.

The Campus Center opened in fall 2005 and serves as the hub and central gathering place of student activity on campus. This two-story facility supports general student gathering spaces, which include a performance space, recreational area, offices for student clubs and organizations, and the College Store (bookstore), all located on the first floor. The second floor of the Campus Center houses the Offices of the Dean of Students, Residential Life, Campus Life, and Campus Ministry, as well as additional student organization offices and meeting spaces.

The Charles J. Lavery Library meets the information needs of twenty-first-century students. A blend of traditional and electronic resources covering a broad range of subjects is available to the Fisher community. The library's print collection is supplemented by an extensive offering of online scholarly resources. Information resources include 232,838 volumes, 7,641 audiovisual items, and access to approximately 40,000 print and electronic periodical titles.

Professional librarians welcome students to the library reference desk during day and evening hours. There is also a 24/7 online-chat reference service. The librarians are information specialists committed to the academic success of all students. Individual research guidance is available by appointment. Librarians also teach classes in information literacy and subject-specific research to all levels of students.

Lavery Library is a member of the Rochester Regional Library Council, representing a regional collection of more than 3,400,000 titles. Interlibrary loan staff can obtain resources not owned by Lavery Library from regional, national, and international libraries.

Costs

Tuition for 2011–12 is $25,790. Room and board costs are $10,510 with a meal plan and a room in one of Fisher's residence halls, and fees are $470.

Financial Aid

Committed to helping students meet the cost of their education, Fisher works to assess each individual's financial need. Financial aid is provided through scholarships, grants, loans, and work-study arrangements and is awarded by Fisher, the state, and the federal government. In 2009–10, the average financial aid package for incoming Fisher students was nearly $20,000.

St. John Fisher College offers a generous academic scholarship program that is based on high school average, strength of curriculum, and SAT or ACT scores. Students eligible for academic scholarships are automatically notified by the Office of Freshman Admissions. Scholarship award amounts are $9500 to $12,500 per year. The College also offers an honors program and a science scholars program. The award in each of these programs is $3000, in addition to any academic scholarships for which the student qualifies.

Fifteen years ago, the College introduced the Service Scholars Program. This program is designed to recognize and reward high school seniors who demonstrate an ongoing interest in serving the needs of others through a commitment to community service. Scholarship awards equal one third of the total yearly cost of tuition, and room and board for four years. St. John Fisher College was recently named to the President's Higher Education Community Service Honor Roll for exemplary service efforts and service to disadvantaged youth.

In 1998, the College announced the creation of the Fannie and Sam Constantino First Generation Scholarship Program, designed to provide financial and academic assistance to high school students whose parents did not graduate from a postsecondary institution—much like the pioneer classes of St. John Fisher College. Recipients receive annual scholarships ranging from $5000 to one third of the total cost of Fisher's tuition, room, and board.

Faculty

Fisher's 209 full-time faculty members are dedicated to helping students, both in and out of the classroom, as they strive to achieve their goals. Eighty-five percent of full-time faculty members hold doctoral or terminal degrees. The student-teacher ratio of 13:1 offers a personal approach to education; 75 percent of all classes have fewer than 30 students. Fisher's Office of Academic Affairs and an outstanding faculty share responsibility for academic advising, helping students to explore the thirty-one majors that are available to them.

Student Government

Student leadership skills are developed through the Student Government Association, which is responsible for the social, cultural, and judicial areas of student life. Resident students elect a Resident Student Association, while commuting students elect a Commuter Council to represent them in planning special activities. The Student Activities Board is responsible for social activities and cultural events throughout the academic year.

Admission Requirements

Admission to St. John Fisher College is based primarily on the following: grade point average, strength of curriculum, scores on standardized tests (SAT/ACT); a personal statement, essay, or graded paper; extracurricular activities and/or work experience, and the counselor/teacher recommendation.

A candidate for admission to the freshman class must be a graduate of an approved secondary school and present a minimum of 16 units of college-preparatory course work in English, foreign languages, mathematics, and natural and social sciences. An applicant should present a secondary school average of 85 percent or above in these academic subjects.

Fisher welcomes qualified transfer students from two- and four-year colleges for both the fall and spring terms. To be considered for admission, transfer students must have a cumulative grade point average of 2.0 or better. If the student has obtained an A.A., A.S., or A.A.S. degree, 60 to 66 credit hours are transferred. All transfer applicants should consult the Undergraduate Bulletin for details.

The College has various special admission programs, including early decision, abbreviated procedures for veterans and other military personnel, and admission for part-time study.

The College offers the Arthur O. Eve Higher Education Opportunity Program (HEOP) for students who need special academic and financial assistance. The program provides academic support services, counseling, and financial aid for qualified students to help them achieve academic success.

Fisher grants college credit for satisfactory grades on the Advanced Placement test, the International Baccalaureate (I.B.) Program exams, and the College-Level Examination Program (CLEP). Only students who receive a 3 or higher in all AP subjects and a 4 or higher on the AP science and language exams are granted Advanced Placement credit. CLEP and I.B. scoring guidelines are available through the Office of Freshman Admissions. Credit is only granted for subject-specific CLEP exams. In addition, recognizing the college-level course work being completed at the high school level, St. John Fisher College will consider granting credit for any college course work in which a student earns a grade of "C" or better.

Application and Information

Applications are accepted on a rolling basis. Early-decision applications are due December 1. The admissions application deadline for merit scholarship consideration is January 15.

Although a personal interview is not required for admission, all applicants are encouraged to visit the College. Interviews and campus tours are available weekdays from 8:30 to 4:30 and on selected Saturdays throughout the academic year.

For additional information or an application, students should contact:

Office of Freshman Admissions
St. John Fisher College
3690 East Avenue
Rochester, New York 14618
Phone: 585-385-8064
   800-444-4640 (toll-free)
Fax: 585-385-8386
E-mail: admissions@sjfc.edu
Web site: http://www.sjfc.edu/admissions/freshman
   http://www.facebook.com/StJohnFisherCollege
   http://twitter.com/FisherNews
   http://www.youtube.com/user/StJohnFisherCollege

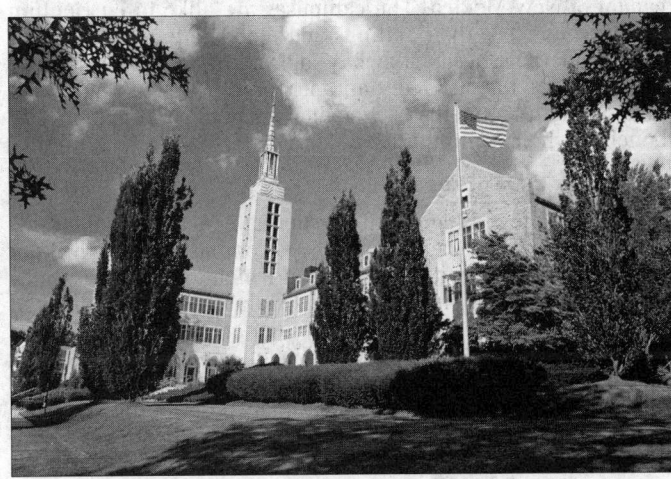

Kearney Hall, Fisher's main administration building.

ST. JOHN'S COLLEGE
ANNAPOLIS, MARYLAND, AND SANTA FE, NEW MEXICO

The College

St. John's College maintains two widely separated campuses, one in Annapolis, Maryland, and another in Santa Fe, New Mexico. Each has its own admissions and financial aid offices. A common curriculum, however, enables students and faculty members to move from one campus to the other. Both campuses are cohesive intellectual communities in which students are eagerly responsive to one another. Students also pursue interests in such activities as publications, dance, dramatics, photography, art, wilderness exploration, and sailing. The social climate is informal and lively, and students enjoy many celebrations each year. Facilities are available for almost any intramural sport; most students participate. There is a bookstore on each campus. In fall 2010, opening enrollment at the Annapolis campus was 217 women and 249 men, for a total of 466 students. The opening enrollment of 416 at the Santa Fe campus consisted of 168 women and 248 men.

The students on both campuses are outstanding, yet they fit no pattern. Though their backgrounds are varied geographically, academically, and otherwise, they are, most typically, young people who habitually read books and value good conversation. Their commitment to ideas and their enthusiasm for the St. John's program are well illustrated by the fact that about one fifth of them on each campus have transferred to St. John's as freshmen after a year or more of college elsewhere.

Location

St. John's is the third-oldest college in the United States. It has been located since 1696 in the Colonial seaport city of Annapolis, the capital of Maryland, 30 miles from Washington, D.C. In 1964, a second campus was opened at the foot of the mountains surrounding Santa Fe, a cultural center and the capital of New Mexico. The campuses are alike in curriculum and methods, but their settings and moods are as different as sailing on the Chesapeake Bay and skiing in the Sangre de Cristo Mountains, as Georgian and Spanish Colonial architecture. St. John's students participate in a number of activities of benefit to their communities at large.

Majors and Degrees

St. John's College is committed to liberal education in the most traditional and yet radical way. It accomplishes this through direct engagement with the books in which the greatest minds of Western civilization have expressed themselves and through translation, mathematical demonstration, musical analysis, and laboratory experimentation. Whether in Annapolis or in Santa Fe, all St. John's students follow the same course of study leading to the B.A. degree. One of the purposes of this program is to emphasize the unity of knowledge; thus, the faculty is not divided into departments and there are no majors.

Academic Programs

The academic program is a unified, cohesive whole; instruction takes the form of annual sequences of related seminars, tutorials, and laboratories, in each of which the books that form the core of the curriculum are the basis of study and discussion. To ensure that the intellectual life of the College extends beyond the classroom and that students bring a common frame of reference to the continuing discussion, this academic program is required of everyone, but no two students are expected to approach any subject in the same way or to reach the same conclusions about it. A central purpose of the St. John's program is to give students both the opportunity and the obligation to think for themselves. The books at the heart of the program serve to foster that thinking. They not only illuminate the enduring questions of human existence but also have great relevance to contemporary problems. They can change minds, move hearts, and touch spirits. They help all students to arrive independently at rational opinions and conclusions of their own. From this common curriculum, about 70 percent of the students go on to graduate and professional study in a wide range of fields.

There are two semesters a year. All classes are small discussion groups and range in size from between 12 and 16 students in tutorials to between 18 and 20 in seminars and laboratories. Final examinations are oral and individual. Students are not routinely informed of their grades. Instead, a student's tutors, as members of the faculty are called, evaluate the student's intellectual performance twice a year in his or her presence and with his or her help. St. John's students are participants in their own education. Annual essays and shorter papers, prepared by students without recourse to secondary sources, are based directly on the books of the program.

Seminars are devoted to reading works of the greatest minds and engaging in thoughtful discussion about them. The first-year seminar focuses on Greek authors; the second on the works of the Roman, medieval, and early Renaissance periods; the third on books of the seventeenth and eighteenth centuries; and the fourth on writings from the nineteenth and twentieth centuries. The seminar consists almost exclusively of student conversation. The aim of the discussions is to ascertain not how things were but how things are. Everyone's opinion must be heard and must also be supported by argument and evidence. The role of the tutors is not to give information or to produce the "right" interpretation; it is to guide the discussion, to aid in defining the issues, and to help the students to understand the authors, the issues, and themselves. If tutors do take a definite stand and enter the argument, they are expected to defend their positions just as students do. Reason is the only recognized authority.

Preceptorials replace seminars for seven weeks of the junior and senior years. In the preceptorial, students and tutors gather in groups of 8 or 9 to discuss, with more leisure than the pace and discipline of the seminar permit, books or topics of particular interest to them.

In the language tutorial, Greek is studied in the first two years and French in the last two. By translating works written in Greek and French into English and comparing those languages with each other as well as with English, the student gains an appreciation of all three and learns something of the nature of language in general.

The language of number and figure does not require a special aptitude. Rather, mathematics is an integral and necessary part of comprehending the world. The mathematics tutorial seeks to affect an understanding of the fundamental nature and intention of mathematics. Throughout the four years, the student is in contact not only with the pure science of mathematics but also with the foundations of mathematical physics and astronomy. The blackboard becomes an arena of logical struggle, which brings the imagination constantly into play.

The music tutorial aims at understanding music through study of musical theory and analysis of significant works. Students investigate rhythm, the diatonic system, ratios of musical intervals, melody, counterpoint, and harmony.

In the modern world, the liberal arts are practiced at their best and fullest in the laboratory. This practice puts into serious question the common distinction between the "natural sciences" and the "humanities." The laboratory is a part of the program in all years but the second. It weaves together the main themes of physics, biology, and chemistry with careful scrutiny of the interplay of hypothesis, theory, and observed fact.

On Friday evenings, the College community assembles for a formal lecture or concert by a tutor or visitor. It is the only time the students are lectured to. Afterward, interested students and faculty members engage the speaker or performer in questions and discussion.

Academic Facilities

The library on each campus—about 100,000 volumes in Annapolis, nearly 60,000 in Santa Fe—emphasizes material appropriate to the nature of the academic program, supplemented by a more general collection and by a variety of special collections. Recordings and representative periodicals and newspapers are included. Academic facilities on each campus also include the resources and equipment necessary for study and experimentation in physics, chemistry, and biology (including a planetarium in Annapolis); for audition and performance of music; for display and studio work in art, photography, and other crafts; and for drama productions.

Costs

For 2010–11, annual tuition and fees totaled $41,792. Room and board were $9984. Books and supplies ranged in cost from $250 to $300. Personal expenses depend on the student's habits and tastes.

Financial Aid

The criterion for financial assistance is need. On both campuses the application for financial aid is the CSS PROFILE, supplemented by the Free Application for Federal Student Aid (FAFSA). More than half of all St. John's students receive aid, usually in a combination of grants, loans, and employment. Federal Perkins Loans, Federal Pell Grants, Federal Supplemental Educational Opportunity Grants, Federal Work-Study Program employment, and College grants and jobs are available.

Faculty

The faculty-student ratio is 1:8 on each campus. Faculty members all hold the same rank. Their intellectual range and vitality come from teaching throughout the curriculum. This breadth and tension and the fact that St. John's is an intellectual community in which all teach and all learn are distinctive characteristics of the St. John's faculty.

Student Government

Inside the classroom and out, the dignity of the students as adults is respected. On both campuses, student government is part of the general College pattern. A Delegate Council and Student Committee on Instruction work with the faculty members and administrators on matters of mutual concern.

Admission Requirements

Criteria for admission to either campus are intellectual and academic, though any accomplishment showing initiative and drive may strengthen an application. The written application consists of a series of reflective essays. The academic record and recommendations are considered supplements to it. SAT or ACT scores are optional but may prove helpful. There are no minimums for grades or test scores; both may be made irrelevant by what the candidate writes. On each campus, applicants are judged on their own merits. Although interviews are not required except in special cases, interested students are urged to visit either campus for several days to sit in on seminars and tutorials.

Application and Information

Students may be admitted to either campus for the fall term or, if they are prepared to continue their studies through the following summer, in January on the Santa Fe campus. Application must be made to one campus or the other, not to both. Early application is advisable. Each campus seeks to complete its class by May 1. All applications for admission and financial aid are acted on as soon as they are complete, and the candidate is notified of the decision within two weeks.

St. John's is a member of the Common Application Group. For information about the academic program and the extracurricular life of the College, students should contact:

John Christensen
Director of Admissions
St. John's College
Annapolis, Maryland 21404

Phone: 800-727-9238 (toll-free)
E-mail: admissions@sjca.edu
Web site: http://www.stjohnscollege.edu

Larry Clendenin
Director of Admissions
St. John's College
Santa Fe, New Mexico 87501

Phone: 800-331-5232 (toll-free)
E-mail: admissions@sjcsf.edu
Web site: http://www.stjohnscollege.edu

St. John's College at Annapolis.

SAINT JOSEPH COLLEGE
WEST HARTFORD, CONNECTICUT

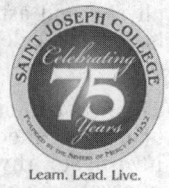

Learn. Lead. Live.

The College

Saint Joseph College is focused on helping students fulfill their potential by combining excellence in liberal arts with a career-focused, professional education for women. Since the College's founding in 1932, the vision of the Sisters of Mercy has continued to shape the way Saint Joseph College (SJC) has grown. SJC offers students the opportunity to study in competitive undergraduate and graduate degree programs, including the College's first doctoral program in pharmacy. With an emphasis on offering an academically rigorous education framed within a commitment to service in the community, Saint Joseph College is a place the student can quickly call home.

The core values of compassionate service, Catholic identity, commitment to women through academic excellence, and diversity are evident in the College's curriculum and daily life. Students from a multitude of faith traditions and backgrounds are empowered for success.

There are 1,062 undergraduates in The Women's Program. Faculty members and students emphasize leadership in academics, career, and community. Drawing on its Mercy heritage, the College is a community that promotes the growth of the whole person. This is accomplished in a caring environment that encourages strong ethical values, personal integrity, and a sense of responsibility to the needs of society. Women lead every organization on campus, from the Business Society and Student Government to honors societies. Students shine in artistic performances, as coordinators of community service projects, and on the athletic fields. Students also serve with faculty members and administrators on College-wide committees. In the field of athletics, the College's women compete in eight NCAA Division III sports: basketball, cross-country, lacrosse, softball, soccer, swimming/diving, tennis, and volleyball. The O'Connell Athletic Center features a six-lane pool, gymnasium, suspended jogging track, dance studio, fitness center, outdoor track, softball field, and tennis courts for all students' recreational purposes.

Saint Joseph College has a beautiful residential campus in the bustling town of West Hartford. Approximately 75 percent of the first-year students live on campus. Special student services include career planning, alumni mentoring, internship placement, counseling, health services, academic advisement, and campus ministry.

Saint Joseph College alumni have considerable impact on the welfare of their communities. They are leaders in many fields, including aerospace research, business, education, environmental science, law, medicine, and politics. Recent graduates enjoy successful careers in accounting, the arts, business, education, government, health care, human services, industry, the sciences, and nonprofit organizations.

Saint Joseph College is accredited by the New England Association of Schools and Colleges. Program accreditors include the American Chemical Society for chemistry, the Council on Social Work Education for social work, the American Dietetic Association for nutrition and dietetics, and the Commission on Collegiate Nursing Education for nursing.

Location

The College is located in suburban West Hartford, 4 miles from the state capitol and the city of Hartford's arts and entertainment district. Among the nearby attractions are the XL Center and Coliseum, Bushnell Performing Arts Center, where the latest Broadway musicals are performed, and the Wadsworth Atheneum, the oldest public art gallery in the United States. Hartford is a cosmopolitan city with diverse ethnic flavors. It is also the home of the Tony Award–winning Hartford Stage Company, the Hartford Symphony Orchestra, the Connecticut Opera Company, the Hartford Ballet, and the Dodge Music Center, which features indoor and outdoor concerts. West Hartford Center, just minutes from campus, offers an array of coffee bars, boutiques, restaurants, and a beautiful movie theater in the newly completed Blue Back Square.

Majors and Degrees

Saint Joseph College has always enjoyed a strong academic reputation based on a combination of liberal arts and career-focused, professional majors. The College awards the B.A. or B.S. in accounting, American studies, art history, biochemistry, biology, chemistry, child study, English, family studies, history, international studies, liberal studies, management, mathematics, nursing, nutrition and dietetics, philosophy, psychology, religious studies, social work, Spanish, special education, and women's studies. Preprofessional programs are offered in conjunction with an academic major and include prepharmacy, predentistry, prelaw, premedicine, pre–physical therapy, and pre–veterinary studies.

Teaching certification is offered in elementary education, secondary education, and special education.

Research, clinical, and work placements are important components of all academic programs.

Academic Programs

Each student must complete a minimum of 120 credits to obtain a baccalaureate degree, and 47 of those credits must be distributed among the general education/liberal arts courses at the College. Specifically, students must take courses in the humanities, social sciences, natural sciences, philosophy, religious studies, and physical education. An academic advisement counselor assists each student in planning her program of study.

Many unique facets to the academic programs offered increase students' propensity for success. An honors program and several dual degree programs are offered. The Center for Academic Excellence manages the College's award-winning Writing Portfolio Program, which enhances students' writing skills. The center also provides tutoring and other academic support services. An exciting component of most majors at Saint Joseph College is the internship. Students earn credit for internships at a variety of sites, including the state capitol, the Bushnell Performing Arts Center, Aetna, Legislative Office, the Connecticut Department of Economic Development, WVIT-TV, Connecticut Children's Medical Center, the Science Center of Connecticut, and numerous other businesses.

Off-Campus Programs

Students at Saint Joseph College may take courses at cooperating institutions through the Hartford Consortium for Higher Education. This is a special arrangement among five Hartford-area colleges—Saint Joseph College, Trinity College, University of Connecticut Greater Hartford Branch, Central Connecticut State University, and the University of Hartford—through which students are able to cross register for courses. No additional tuition is charged, and all credits are transferable.

Students at Saint Joseph College have countless opportunities for global study experiences through our many study abroad programs. Students are assisted by the Director of International Studies and Programs in planning for an international-study experience during a semester, winter recess, or even over spring break. Saint Joseph College also offers a specialized program in Guyana, South America, through the College's sister hospital. Students in the education and health science fields are encouraged to participate in this program for a work abroad experience during their junior or senior years.

Those students majoring in nursing, social work, and nutrition, and those in the graduate counseling program, may gain practical experience providing community-based, accessible health screenings and referrals; health and nutrition education; counseling services; and social work case management services at The Wellness Center on Church Street in Hartford. The College has also established a partnership with the Franciscan Center for Urban Ministry in order to reach out to its neighboring city and enhance the quality of life of its residents in need.

Academic Facilities

The Pope Pius XII Library has a collection of more than 134,000 volumes, including computer databases, periodicals, microforms, audiovisuals, a Sirsi online catalog, and OCLC interlibrary loans. A collection of materials used in elementary and secondary education is featured in the Curriculum Materials Center.

The College uses laboratory schools with several of its academic programs. The renowned School for Young Children, located one block from the campus, and its counterpart, the School for Young Children at Asylum Hill, in Hartford, are operating preschools that provide child study majors with training and experience. The College also recently opened a Charter School in Hartford to enhance the diversity of classroom experiences available to students while serving the community. The Gengras Center, located on the campus, is a special education school serving children and young adults (ages 4–21) from approximately fifty area cities and towns in Connecticut and Massachusetts. It provides for special education needs and also helps to prepare special education teachers.

The College's primary technology centers are located in McDonough Hall; Internet access is available throughout campus including many Wi-Fi hotspots. Additional facilities and services include a media center that provides production materials, expertise, and equipment for making and using a number of media instructional aids; science and nursing labs; and the Carol Autorino Center for the Arts and Humanities. The center includes Lynch Hall, which houses humanities, faculty offices, and classrooms; the Bruyette Athenaeum, featuring the 365-seat Hoffman Auditorium; the Saint Joseph College Art Gallery; a print study room; large lecture hall; reception room; and music practice rooms. The building also houses the College's archives.

Costs

The tuition and fees for full-time freshmen entering in 2011 are $30,310. Room and board cost is $11,205. The cost per credit for part-time students is $655.

Financial Aid

The goal of the Saint Joseph College Financial Aid Program is to place a high-quality, private education within the reach of as many qualified students as possible. This goal is achieved by offering need- and merit-based financial aid that includes a combination of grants, loans, and on-campus employment opportunities. More than 90 percent of full-time undergraduate students receive some form of financial assistance. Merit-based scholarship awards are available to all eligible first-year, transfer and international students.

Faculty

Saint Joseph College's faculty consists of 85 full-time faculty members and 4 librarians. Of the total faculty, 68.8 percent are women. Of the full-time faculty, 90 percent hold the highest possible degrees in their fields. Small classes benefit both students and professors. The student-faculty ratio is 11:1. The faculty and all members of the College community promote the welfare of students and help them attain the objectives set forth by the College's mission. Faculty members also serve as advisers to many extracurricular activities, including sports, campus ministry, and community service; direct students in independent study; involve students in scholarly research; and act as mentors before and after graduation.

Student Government

The Student Government Association works for effective communication among students, faculty members, and administrators. Students are encouraged to voice their opinions and concerns to the association for consideration and action. In addition, student representatives sit as voting members with faculty members and administrators on major College-wide committees. The Student Government Association encourages the development of leadership skills and provides funds annually for several of its members to attend leadership workshops and conferences.

Admission Requirements

Saint Joseph College seeks women who are anxious to accept the challenge of rigorous academic programs while pursuing the interests and careers that will help them achieve their goals. Applications are encouraged from interested students of every race, age, and religious affiliation. In accordance with Section 504 of the Rehabilitation Act of 1973, which prohibits discrimination on the basis of disability, and the Americans with Disabilities Act of 1990, Saint Joseph College is committed to the goal of achieving equal educational opportunities and full participation for people with disabilities in higher education.

Candidates for first-year admission should complete a four-year course of study in a regionally accredited secondary school or have equivalent homeschooling preparation. The program should include 16 academic units in college-preparatory courses distributed among the areas of English, mathematics, natural sciences, social studies, and foreign languages. Applicants are required to submit scores of the SAT or ACT tests. A personal interview is a highly recommended part of the admission procedure, since it offers a mutual opportunity for the student and Admissions Counselors to discuss educational and professional goals.

The Committee on Admissions operates on the principle that a student's ability, motivation, and maturity should be determined by a careful individual review of all the applicant's credentials, including the academic record, standardized test scores, written personal statement, and letter(s) of recommendation. Special consideration may be given to some applicants whose preparation varies from the recommended pattern but whose record gives evidence of genuine intellectual ability and interest. International students should contact the Office of Admissions for further information. Additional information is available online at http://www.sjc.edu/admissions.

Saint Joseph College admits qualified students for transfer in both fall and spring semesters.

Application and Information

The Committee on Admissions recommends that application for first-year admission be made in the first semester of the senior year in secondary school. All applications should be completed by April 1. A nonrefundable $50 fee must be sent with paper applications; the application fee is waived for students who apply online at http://www.sjc.edu/admissions. Students are encouraged to begin the financial aid process by completing the FAFSA form online at http://www.fafsa.ed.gov as soon as possible after January 1 of the year they are applying for admission. The priority deadline for completing the FAFSA is February 15. Students should complete the FAFSA using estimated income information if they or their families will not have completed their tax returns prior to February 15. Financial aid counselors are available to assist prospective students and families with the financial aid process.

Transfer applicants for the spring semester should apply by December 1; applicants for the fall semester, by June 1. Students applying to the nursing program should contact the College to learn about special deadlines. Transfer candidates who wish to apply for financial aid should complete or update the FAFSA online by November 15 if applying for the spring semester or by August 15 if applying for the fall semester.

For further information about admission to Saint Joseph College, students should contact:

Nancy D. Wunderly
Director of Admissions
Saint Joseph College
1678 Asylum Avenue
West Hartford, Connecticut 06117
Phone: 860-231-5216
        866-442-8752 (toll-free)
Fax: 860-231-5744
E-mail: admissions@sjc.edu
Web site: http://www.sjc.edu/admissions

ST. JOSEPH'S COLLEGE
BROOKLYN AND PATCHOGUE, NEW YORK

The College

Since 1916, St. Joseph's College has been inspiring students to transform their lives. A private coeducational institution with campuses in Brooklyn and Patchogue, Long Island, the College enrolls nearly 6,000 undergraduates and over 500 graduate students in its School of Arts and Sciences and School of Professional and Graduate Studies. St. Joseph's is regularly ranked as a top-tier comprehensive college in the North by *U.S. News & World Report*. In addition, St. Joseph's is the most affordable private college in the New York metropolitan area and Long Island.

St. Joseph's helps students turn aspirations into accomplishments. In addition to offering a liberal arts education of the highest quality, St. Joseph's offers students an unrivaled degree of personal attention, encouraging them to lead lives characterized by integrity, a commitment to upholding intellectual and spiritual values, social responsibility, and service to others.

St. Joseph's students immerse themselves in learning in ways that go far beyond the classroom, through independent projects, team-building assignments, internships, community service opportunities, and study-abroad programs designed to suit every schedule. Moreover, with just 15 students for every professor on campus, St. Joseph's students easily find mentors to guide them in everything from academics to focusing on future career and life goals.

Although most of St. Joseph's students commute at both campuses, the Brooklyn campus offers student housing through Educational Housing Services at the nearby St. George Residence. Each of the campuses offers a lively atmosphere enriched by social events, athletic competitions, and a Common Hour to encourage students to explore new possibilities for fun, leadership, and connections. On any given day at St. Joseph's, students might come to campus to hear a Pulitzer Prize–winning author, enjoy a jazz concert, join a community service effort, view an art exhibit, attend an athletic event, or engage in a political debate over dinner with other students and professors. Each campus supports over thirty student clubs and activities, including intercollegiate basketball; women's softball, swimming, tennis, and volleyball; men's baseball, tennis, and volleyball; and coed cross-country. The Long Island campus also offers men's soccer, and a coed equestrian team.

For undergraduates, St. Joseph's offers fast tracks to advanced degrees through special affiliated programs in accounting, podiatry, and computer science. The School of Professional and Graduate Studies at St. Joseph's College offers a wide range of graduate programs in education, human services, management, and nursing, including the Executive M.B.A., an M.B.A. in accounting, an M.B.A. in health care management, and the M.S. in nursing, to name a few.

Location

The Brooklyn campus is located in the Clinton Hill Historic District, a neighborhood where so many of New York's wealthiest citizens once lived that it was dubbed Brooklyn's "Gold Coast" in the 1920s. Today this area is home to several prestigious schools, including the Pratt Institute of Art and the Brooklyn Academy of Music, and serves as a hub of cultural and intellectual activity. This convenient location allows students to enjoy the freedom of a safe, well-landscaped campus easily accessible to New York City by car or public transportation.

St. Joseph's Long Island campus is located in the village of Patchogue on Great South Bay, about 50 miles from Manhattan and 60 miles from Montauk Point. Patchogue offers plenty to do, with fine harbors, shops, restaurants, athletic fields, and tennis courts right in the village. There are lovely parks nearby as well as museums, golf courses, hiking and ski trails, and beaches. Patchogue is easily accessible via Long Island Rail Road, bus service, or ferry. A major regional airport, McArthur Airport, is just minutes away.

Majors and Degrees

Through individual attention, interactive teaching, and intensive advising, St. Joseph's meets students where they are academically, then guides them through the essential next steps to help them stretch intellectually, personally, and professionally. St. Joseph's offers four-year programs leading to B.A. and B.S. degrees at both the Brooklyn and Patchogue campuses, with majors in accounting, business administration, biology, chemistry, child study, computer information systems, criminal justice, English, history, human relations, marketing, mathematics, recreation, psychology, social sciences: economics, sociology and political science, Spanish, and speech communication. Among these majors are a variety of minors and certificate programs from which students can choose.

No matter what major students choose, they can also earn additional certificates designed to help them delve deeper into specific interests and give them a head start when entering the workforce. Certificate programs include criminology/criminal justice; gerontology; information technology; leadership and supervision; management, marketing, advertising, and public relations; and religious studies.

For students interested in a fast track to an advanced degree after completing their undergraduate studies, St. Joseph's offers special affiliated programs. Through a partnership between St. Joseph's College and Polytechnic Institute of NYU, students at the Brooklyn campus can pursue a bachelor's degree in any field and a master's degree in computer science in a combined B.A./B.S. plus M.S. program. The Brooklyn campus also offers an accelerated biomedical program in cooperation with the New York College of Podiatric Medicine. This program allows students to receive a B.S. in biology and a doctorate in podiatric medicine within six years. Students at both the Brooklyn and Patchogue campuses can earn B.S./M.B.A. degrees in accounting within five years or can choose to pursue preprofessional programs in law, teaching, and numerous health fields, including dentistry, medicine, and optometry.

Those with nontraditional academic backgrounds or with professional training and experience can pursue degrees in community health, general studies, health administration, nursing, and organizational management through St. Joseph's School of Professional and Graduate Studies at either campus.

Academic Programs

The School of Arts and Sciences at each campus operates on the semester system, with additional courses offered in January and during the summer. St. Joseph's students take a core curriculum of 128 credits to graduate; a wide range of choices allows students to tailor their academic programs to their personal and professional needs. The College recognizes the Advanced Placement (AP) Program and offers credit and placement for scores of

3 or above on AP tests. In each case, the score is reviewed by the registrar and/or department chairperson to determine credit and placement.

The School of Professional and Graduate Studies on each campus offers flexible schedules, summer programs, and online courses to meet the needs of working students. Courses may meet for a semester or for six- or twelve-week sessions.

Academic Facilities

The Brooklyn campus is composed of eight buildings, including historic landmark buildings. Students majoring in the widely recognized child-study program use the Dillon Child Study Center, which is a laboratory preschool enrolling approximately 100 hundred students and a teaching and observation resource right on campus. McEntegart Hall, a modern five-level structure, houses the library, audiovisual resource center, curriculum library, archives, and computer labs. Other academic facilities include top-notch biology, chemistry, computer, physics, and psychology research laboratories. A state-of-the-art athletic complex is under construction on school grounds, with a scheduled completion date of 2012.

At the Long Island campus, students enjoy 28 acres of well-landscaped grounds and athletic fields. The main building houses administrative and faculty offices; laboratories for biology, chemistry, physics, and psychology; the computer center; art and music studios; the Local History Center; and the Office of Counseling. The library building houses a curriculum library, seminar rooms, administrative offices, and classrooms. This campus also features the John A. Danzi Recreation/Fitness Center, which includes a competition-sized swimming pool, fitness rooms, and a full-sized gym with an elevated track. The 33,000-square-foot Business and Technology Center allows St. Joseph's students to integrate technology into their studies. The Clare Rose Playhouse serves as a cultural center where students and local communities can explore theater production and performance.

A high-speed fiber-optic network connects all offices, institutional facilities, computer laboratories, and libraries on both the Brooklyn and Long Island campuses. Direct Internet access is available to all students and faculty and staff members through the College's server. The integrated online library system enables students to locate and check out books at either campus and provides links to online databases and other electronic information sources.

Costs

The 2010–11 annual full-time tuition rate for undergraduates was $17,000, or $555 per credit.

Financial Aid

St. Joseph's offers scholarships and grants-in-aid. Students who wish to apply for either form of assistance must file the Free Application for Federal Student Aid (FAFSA) and a state aid form. After a student has been accepted to the College and all financial aid forms are processed, the Financial Aid Office prepares aid packages that usually consist of federal, state, and College funds. St. Joseph's is fully approved for veterans. Campus work-study programs are also available.

Faculty

With nearly 500 faculty members who are widely respected scholars in their fields and a student-faculty ratio of 15:1, St. Joseph's students benefit from close professional and personal working relationships with their professors. Faculty members serve as academic advisers, are active on student affairs committees, and act as moderators in student organizations.

Admission Requirements

St. Joseph's College seeks a diverse student body and welcomes applications from high school students, transfer students, and those students who may have a nontraditional academic background. The College offers programs to serve all of these groups.

Students who wish to enter as freshmen are expected to have completed at least 18 units of college-preparatory work by the end of their senior year. This should include the following distribution: 4 years of English, 2 years of foreign language, 3 years of mathematics, 2 years of science, and 4 years of social studies. Applicants interested in accounting, allied health fields, biology, business administration, chemistry, or mathematics should have more extensive backgrounds in mathematics and science. In addition, the College requires the submission of official results from the critical reading and math sections of the SAT.

St. Joseph's College accepts a block transfer of credits from students holding an A.A. or A.S. degree in certain majors from an accredited junior or community college. All other transfers are considered on an individual basis.

Application and Information

Admission is offered on a rolling basis. Applications and supporting documents should be submitted online or to the appropriate school. The College reviews each application carefully and usually sends a decision one month after receiving all necessary credentials. For more information and an online application, students can access the Web site at http://www.sjcny.edu.

Brooklyn Campus:
Director of Admissions
St. Joseph's College
245 Clinton Avenue
Brooklyn, New York 11205
Phone: 718-940-5800

Long Island Campus:
Director of Admissions
St. Joseph's College
155 West Roe Boulevard
Patchogue, New York 11772

Phone: 631-687-4500
Web site: http://www.sjcny.edu
http://www.facebook.com/SJCNY
http://twitter.com/#!/SJCNY

Both campuses of St. Joseph's College provide up-to-date science, computer, and psychology laboratories.

SAINT JOSEPH'S UNIVERSITY

PHILADELPHIA, PENNSYLVANIA

The University

Saint Joseph's University is a nationally recognized, Catholic, Jesuit university. For more than 150 years, Saint Joseph's has advanced the professional and personal ambitions of men and women by providing a rigorous Jesuit education—one that demands high achievement, expands knowledge, deepens understanding, stresses effective reasoning and communication, develops moral and spiritual character, and imparts enduring pride. One of only 142 schools with a Phi Beta Kappa chapter and business school accreditation by AACSB International–The Association to Advance Collegiate Schools of Business, Saint Joseph's is the home of 4,600 full-time undergraduates and 4,200 part-time graduate, and doctoral students.

As a Jesuit university, Saint Joseph's believes each student realizes his or her fullest potential through challenging classroom study, hands-on learning opportunities, and a commitment to excellence in all endeavors. The University also reinforces the individual's lifelong engagement with the wider world. Graduates of Saint Joseph's attain success in their careers with the help of an extensive network of alumni who have become leading figures in business, law, medicine, education, the arts, technology, government, and public service.

A Saint Joseph's education encompasses all aspects of personal growth and development, reflecting the Ignatian credo of *cura personalis.* Guided by a faculty that is committed to both teaching and scholarship, students develop intellectually through an intense Jesuit liberal arts curriculum and advanced study in a chosen discipline. Students mature socially by participating in Saint Joseph's campus life, noted for its rich variety of activities, infectious enthusiasm, and mutual respect. Students grow ethically and spiritually by living their own values in the larger society beyond the campus.

Steeped in the Jesuit, Catholic tradition, Saint Joseph's provides a rigorous, intensive education that both disciplines and expands the mind. Students develop a lifelong desire to learn and grow while also acquiring the skills and knowledge necessary for success in their professional lives. At the core of this education is a general education requirement, which exposes students to primary fields of inquiry and the cultural values that shape their world. A Jesuit emphasis on engaged teaching and mentoring permeates the university. Faculty members at Saint Joseph's, many of whom are leading scholars in their disciplines, expect students to perform at the highest level and set demanding standards in the classroom.

Saint Joseph's is at the forefront of utilizing innovative technologies to enhance and promote learning. These technologies are widely integrated into the educational process both in class and beyond, where they are also used for individual and collaborative research projects. By mastering these tools and achieving technological fluency, Saint Joseph's students gain a valuable edge in their careers.

Saint Joseph's students engage enthusiastically in all facets of campus life—academic, social, athletic, ethical, and spiritual. Their active participation creates a vibrant, dynamic campus community, one that embraces a "not for spectators" attitude. In all their activities, students emphasize personal integrity as well as a respect and concern for others. This produces a mutually supportive, humane, and tolerant environment for individual success and service to others.

Location

Located on the edge of metropolitan Philadelphia, Saint Joseph's provides ready access to the vast career opportunities and cultural resources of America's sixth-largest city, while affording students a cohesive and intimate campus experience.

Because of its location, Saint Joseph's has close ties to the people, professional opportunities, and cultural life of Philadelphia. Students enjoy direct access to internships, cooperative education programs, and positions in virtually all careers, most of which have a major presence in the Philadelphia area. Saint Joseph's location also offers ample outlets for community involvement and service, and students can easily take advantage of Philadelphia's professional sports, entertainment, and cultural events.

Majors and Degrees

Saint Joseph's offers full-time baccalaureate degree programs in more than forty major fields of study and numerous specialty programs, which are administered by two separate colleges.

The College of Arts and Sciences awards the Bachelor of Arts degree in art education, Classics, economics, English, fine and performing arts, French, French studies, German, history, international relations, Italian, Latin, philosophy, political science, Spanish, and theology and the Bachelor of Science degree in actuarial science, biology, chemical biology, chemistry, computer science, criminal justice, education, environmental science, interdisciplinary health services, mathematics, physics, psychology, public administration, and sociology.

The Erivan K. Haub School of Business awards the Bachelor of Science degree in accounting, business intelligence, family business and entrepreneurship, finance, financial planning, food marketing, international business, international marketing, managing human capital, marketing, pharmaceutical marketing, risk and insurance, and sport marketing. A co-op program is available for all business majors.

Five-year B.S./M.S. programs are offered in education, international marketing, psychology, and writing studies. The University also offers special academic programs in aerospace studies (Air Force ROTC); Africana studies; allied health (bioscience technologies, nursing, occupational therapy, physical therapy (D.P.T.), and radiologic sciences); American studies, Asian studies, business ethics, European studies, faith-justice, gender, Latin American, medieval, Renaissance, and Russian and East Central European studies; writing studies; and teacher certification at the elementary and secondary levels. Preprofessional study is available in most major fields.

Academic Programs

At Saint Joseph's University, the aim of providing the student with the qualities of a liberally educated individual is pursued through a threefold plan encompassing 120 academic credits. The major concentration (30–45 credits) is intended to provide students with depth in a given field in order to prepare them for effective work in that field or graduate study. The general education program (60 credits) is intended to ensure that students have mastered basic skills necessary for further work, have been exposed to the main divisions of learning, and have been introduced to several new fields of study. Languages and literature, mathematics, natural sciences, history, social sciences, philosophy, and theology are among the areas of study included in the general education requirement. Free electives (15–30 credits) are intended to provide flexibility by encouraging students to pursue studies in areas they have found interesting, to test their interest in an unexplored area, or to deepen their knowledge in the major field.

A competitive honors program is available for qualified students, as are independent and interdisciplinary study options. Claver House provides a place for honors students to have meetings, take classes, study, and conduct research.

Off-Campus Programs

Saint Joseph's offers to an increasing number of students the opportunity to study abroad and directly sponsors programs each year in Europe, Africa, Asia, Australia, Latin America, and the UK. International study tours have been made to Africa, Australia, Brazil, Canada, Greece, Ireland, Italy, Japan, Scotland, and Spain.

Students may take advantage of an arrangement with the Washington Center for Internships and Academic Seminars, which allows for a one-semester internship in the nation's capital.

Fieldwork experiences are required in several majors, and the University's location provides for internship opportunities to support virtually all other disciplines. The Career Development Center has a full-time internship coordinator and provides opportunities for on-campus interviews. The Alumni Mentor Alliance matches students with alumni in their fields of interest to gain real-world perspectives.

Academic Facilities

The facilities at Saint Joseph's are a blend of the old and the new. Barbelin/Lonergan Hall is a fine example of collegiate Gothic architecture. Its spire carillon tower rises above the campus and is easily the most recognizable landmark at Saint Joseph's. Mandeville Hall, a modern international academic center, opened in 1998. Home of the Erivan K. Haub School of Business, Mandeville offers distance learning technology and unique learning environments. The Francis A. Drexel Library and the Campbell Collection in Food Marketing house a collection of approximately 352,500 volumes, 1,450 print journals, 7,500 full-text electronic journals, 2,700 online books, and 848,000 microforms. The University has begun construction of the Post Learning Commons and a new residence hall, scheduled to be completed in 2012.

Costs

Tuition for the 2010–11 academic year was $35,080. Room and board were $11,800. These costs do not include student fees associated with specific majors or residence halls.

Financial Aid

The majority of Saint Joseph's students receive merit and/or federal financial assistance. In the 2010–11 academic year, approximately 91 percent of the University's freshman class received assistance in the form of academic and athletic scholarships, grants, loans, and work-study funds, either singly or in combination.

Students are automatically considered for merit scholarships upon application to the University. Students who wish to be considered for federal financial assistance should submit the Free Application for Federal Student Aid (FAFSA). Residents from states other than Pennsylvania should file the FAFSA and the proper state grant application from the Education Assistance Agency of their resident state. The preferred deadline is February 15.

Faculty

Saint Joseph's possesses an esteemed research faculty that is committed to undergraduate teaching. A student-faculty ratio of 14:1 and an average class size of 24 offer excellent opportunities for student–faculty member exchange, both inside and outside the classroom. Approximately 98 percent of the full-time faculty members hold a doctorate or terminal degree in their field.

Student Government

The Office of Student Leadership and Activities is dedicated to enhancing the educational development of students by providing opportunities for involvement in cocurricular programs and services. These include leadership programs, student clubs and organizations, Greek life, event programming and planning, and the University Student Senate. Through innovative programming that complements academic and personal development, the University nurtures the mind, body, and spirit of each individual student while enhancing the Jesuit mission of the University.

The University Student Senate, the governing board for the student body, is dedicated to addressing student issues through advocacy and policy recommendations. The Senate consists of an executive board that includes the president, executive vice president, speaker of the Senate, vice president for financial affairs, vice president for student life, four elected representatives from each class, and five appointed at-large members. The Senate has four standing committees: Academic Affairs, Student Budget Allocations, Campus Life, and Administrative Services. Elections for the Senate take place in April. Freshman representatives are elected in September.

The Student Union Board, known as SUB, is a student-run organization that encourages the development of student leadership, responsibility, and social competency by planning and participating in campus programs. These activities are designed to enhance the educational, recreational, cultural, and social aspects of the collegiate experience. All registered undergraduate students are welcome to take part in the activities and to be a part of the standing committees that are responsible for the programming.

Admission Requirements

Candidates for admission to the freshman class must submit evidence of academic achievement in a college-preparatory program, which should emphasize study in English, mathematics, foreign languages (classical or modern), science, history, and social studies. Successful candidates have traditionally completed a secondary school background that included the following: English, 4 units; foreign languages, 2 units; history and social studies, 3 units; mathematics, 3 units (4 units for students interested in the natural sciences or math); and science, 2 units. Applicants are required to submit scores on the SAT or the ACT.

Application and Information

A completed application form may be submitted with the $60 application fee at any time after the student's junior year. Students are accepted to the University and merit scholarships are awarded within the context of a deadline admissions policy with an early action application deadline of November 15 and a regular decision deadline of February 1. Students should visit the admissions Web site at http://www.sju.edu/admissions for current admission information.

Office of Undergraduate Admissions
Saint Joseph's University
5600 City Avenue
Philadelphia, Pennsylvania 19131-1395
Phone: 610-660-1300
      888-BE-A-HAWK (232-4295) (toll-free)
Fax: 610-660-1314
E-mail: admit@sju.edu
Web site: http://www.sju.edu/admissions/
      http://www.facebook.com/sjuadmissions

Mandeville Hall, Saint Joseph's international academic center and home of the Haub School of Business.

ST. LAWRENCE UNIVERSITY

CANTON, NEW YORK

The University

St. Lawrence University invites students to learn new ways of seeing the world, voicing ideas, and connecting with others. Graduates have the tools with which to think clearly, express themselves persuasively, and step into the world community with an understanding of their responsibility to all people and to the planet.

Founded in 1856, St. Lawrence is the oldest continuously coeducational degree-granting institution of higher learning in New York State. Initially established as a theology school for the Universalist Church, it quickly evolved into the liberal arts college that it is today. St. Lawrence is a private, nonsectarian university of approximately 2,300 undergraduate men and women, with a small graduate program in education. St. Lawrence is known for its residential/academic First-Year Program, its international study opportunities and area studies programs, its students' strong interest in the environment and the outdoors, and its friendliness.

St. Lawrence students are self-starters. The self-designed major is popular, intramural sports leagues are always full, and more than 100 student organizations serve broad interests, from communication to community service and creativity to social action. The University routinely hosts well-known speakers, and concerts, plays, and films are regulars on the weekly events calendar.

St. Lawrence students have historically placed high value on athletic activity, and a large number participate in varsity, intramural, or club sports. The thirty-two varsity men's and women's teams compete at the Division III level of the NCAA, with the exception of men's and women's ice hockey, which compete in Division I. Recreational facilities include cross-country ski and running trails, indoor and outdoor tennis courts, an athletic complex with a gymnasium, two field houses, a 133-station fitness center, a three-story climbing wall, a pool, an ice rink, an equestrian center, a boathouse, a golf course, a nine-lane all-weather track, an artificial-turf field for lacrosse and field hockey, ten squash courts, and newly renovated performance fields for soccer, football, baseball, and softball.

Residential life is an important aspect of the St. Lawrence experience. The University's innovative and highly regarded First-Year Program creates communities where groups of approximately 30–35 first-year students live and learn together. In the upperclass years, students can choose from traditional dormitories, Greek chapter houses, and suites and theme cottages that focus on student interests such as low-impact living and community service. Seniors may also choose town houses. St. Lawrence sponsors a full range of student services, from counseling to career planning.

Location

St. Lawrence is situated on a 1,000-acre campus on the edge of the village of Canton, New York (population 6,400), the seat of St. Lawrence County. Canton, with its Victorian homes, tree-lined streets, village green, and small shops, is typical of college towns throughout the Northeast. Students and residents often mix in stores, at athletic events, and in community projects. Ottawa, Canada's capital, is 75 minutes to the north, while Lake Placid, one of America's hiking and skiing meccas, is 90 minutes to the southeast.

Majors and Degrees

St. Lawrence offers the Bachelor of Arts and Bachelor of Science degrees; students can choose from thirty-six majors and have the option of picking one of thirty-seven minors. Combined five-year programs with other institutions are in place in engineering and management, and specialized advising is offered in preparation for postgraduate work in dentistry, law, medicine, and veterinary medicine.

Academic Programs

St. Lawrence's foremost mission is to provide its students with a liberal arts education. Students complete requirements in six areas and concentrated work in a major field as well as demonstrating competence in writing. Close faculty-student interaction is a hallmark of a St. Lawrence education. Every semester, many students engage in independent or honors projects, often working with professors on joint research projects that lead to publication in leading scholarly journals. A senior project is required in most majors.

Off-Campus Programs

More than 50 percent of St. Lawrence students study in one of the University's international programs during their collegiate careers. St. Lawrence operates programs in Australia, Austria, Canada, China, Costa Rica, the Czech Republic, Denmark, England, France, India, Italy, Japan, Kenya, New Zealand, Spain, Thailand, and Trinidad and Tobago. In addition, the University's membership in the International Student Exchange Program permits students to directly enroll in universities in more than thirty-five additional countries. St. Lawrence also operates programs at two other campuses in the United States: Fisk University in Nashville, Tennessee, and American University in Washington, D.C. St. Lawrence also administers its own Adirondack Semester Program.

Academic Facilities

Owen D. Young Library and Launders Science Library contain more than half a million volumes as well as electronic resources and ample space for reading and research. Griffiths Arts Center is the home of the University's fine arts and performance and communication studies programs as well as two theaters and an art gallery in which selections from St. Lawrence's 7,000-piece collection are frequently shown. Facilities for the arts have undergone expansion into the building that was formerly the student center, and the Newell Center for Arts Technology opened in spring 2007. A unified science complex houses the Departments of Biology, Chemistry, Physics, Psychology, Geology, and Mathematics, Computer Science and Statistics and is connected via a covered hallway to the science library and computing center. The new 120,000-square-foot Johnson Hall of Science, the first gold LEED science building in New York State, opened in fall 2007. Richardson Hall, St. Lawrence's oldest building and on the National Register of Historic Places, is home to the English and religious studies departments. Other departments can be found in academic buildings clustered on one part of the campus, so classrooms are not a long walk apart.

Costs

The comprehensive fee for 2010–11 was $51,770, including tuition, fees, and average room and board. Students should allow approximately $1450 for books and personal expenses.

Financial Aid

St. Lawrence awards both merit scholarships and need-based financial aid. More than 80 percent of the University's students receive some form of financial assistance, including scholarships, grants, student loans, and campus jobs. St. Lawrence is committed to assisting as many students as possible and recognizes academic and personal achievement in making financial aid decisions. To apply for need-based financial aid, students must file the Free Application for Federal Student Aid (FAFSA) and the CSS Profile form between January 1 and February 1 and request that the results be sent directly to St. Lawrence.

Faculty

The 190 members of St. Lawrence's faculty are teachers and scholars. While teaching and advising are their primary responsibilities, they are also active researchers, artists, performers, and regular contributors in their academic disciplines. Faculty members teach all courses at St. Lawrence; no undergraduate courses are taught by graduate students. Active teaching assistants and tutoring programs, involving qualified upperclass students, are closely supervised by faculty members. The student-faculty ratio is about 12:1. Faculty members hold regular office hours, serve as academic advisers to students, and frequently take part in extracurricular activities on campus.

Student Government

The Thelomathesian Society, comprising all students on campus, is governed by a senate of elected representatives. The senate distributes funds in support of student activities and provides 2 student delegates to the University's Board of Trustees.

Admission Requirements

St. Lawrence seeks students who can be successful in a demanding academic program and who can contribute to the quality of life of the community. The University is committed to enrolling students who represent the widest possible diversity of economic, social, ethnic, and geographic backgrounds. Academic preparation and ability are the most important criteria, but demonstrated ability in the creative arts, athletics, or social service is also a measure of a student's potential to benefit St. Lawrence. Candidates may choose whether or not they submit standardized test scores (SAT or ACT). A campus visit is strongly encouraged, and interviews may be scheduled on campus or off campus in certain areas.

Although there is no set distribution of required high school courses, successful applicants typically show strong preparation in the humanities, the social sciences, mathematics, and the natural sciences. Honors, Advanced Placement, and International Baccalaureate courses are opportunities for applicants to demonstrate intellectual maturity and curiosity, qualities highly valued in the admission process.

Application and Information

St. Lawrence uses the Common Application, with the St. Lawrence Supplement, as its sole application form. The application is available on the University's Web site. The application processing fee is $60. Regular decision applications should be submitted by February 1, with notification by late March. Students who decide that St. Lawrence is their first choice may apply early decision. The priority deadline for early decision is November 1, but students may commit to early decision up until February 1. Students will generally be notified within one month of receipt of a completed application. Transfer candidates should submit applications no later than November 1 for the spring semester or March 1 for the fall semester.

To request an application or for more information, students should contact:

Office of Admissions and Financial Aid
St. Lawrence University
Canton, New York 13617
Phone: 315-229-5261
          800-285-1856 (toll-free)
E-mail: admissions@stlawu.edu
Web site: http://www.stlawu.edu
              http://www.facebook.com/SLU2016
              http://twitter.com/stlawu
              http://www.youtube.com/StLawrenceU

The St. Lawrence University Student Center.

SAINT LEO UNIVERSITY
SAINT LEO, FLORIDA

The University

Founded in 1889, Saint Leo University is now recognized as one of the nation's leading Catholic teaching universities and a school of international consequence. The main campus in Saint Leo, Florida, is home to the vibrant University College, serving the education needs of more than 1,850 traditional-age undergraduate students. The University also offers a variety of dynamic graduate programs, a weekend and evening program for working adults, and both undergraduate and graduate degree programs through seventeen education centers in seven states and through the Center for Online Learning, which houses the University's cutting-edge online degree programs.

The University College student body represents forty states and territories, as well as forty-two countries. International students make up 11 percent of the student population. Minority students represent 30 percent of the University College enrollment. Approximately 65 percent of traditional full-time students live in one of thirteen residence halls.

Students can participate in the nationally recognized honors program and the more than sixty different clubs and organizations on campus, including national fraternities and sororities. The Student Government Union and various campus organizations also sponsor movies, concerts, art exhibits, lectures, dances, and other special events throughout the academic year.

Saint Leo is a member of the Sunshine State Conference and competes in NCAA Division II intercollegiate athletics for men and women. Men's sports include baseball, basketball, cross-country, golf, lacrosse, soccer, swimming, and tennis. Women compete in basketball, cross-country, golf, lacrosse, soccer, softball, swimming, tennis, and volleyball. Cheerleading is offered as a club sport. Students can also participate in a wide variety of intramurals. Campus recreational facilities include lighted racquetball and tennis courts; soccer, baseball, and softball fields; a weight room/fitness center; and a heated outdoor Olympic-size swimming pool. The campus is bordered by a 154-acre lake and an eighteen-hole golf course.

Saint Leo is committed to giving its students an education that prepares them for the future. The goal of the University is to develop the whole person, both academically and personally, by providing a values-based education in the Benedictine tradition. In a recent satisfaction survey, 97 percent of respondents said they would recommend Saint Leo to a friend.

Saint Leo University is accredited by the Commission on Colleges of the Southern Association of Colleges and Schools to award the associate, bachelor's, and master's degrees. Saint Leo University's degree program in social work is accredited by the Commission on Accreditation of the Council on Social Work Education (B.S.W. level). The School of Business is accredited by the International Assembly for Collegiate Business Education (IACBE). The University's undergraduate sport business program is nationally approved by the Sport Management Program Review Council (SMPRC). Saint Leo University also has Teacher Education Programs approval by the State of Florida Department of Education.

In addition to associate and bachelor's degrees, Saint Leo University offers a Master of Business Administration (M.B.A.) degree, a Master of Education (M.Ed.) degree, a Master of Science (M.S.) degree in criminal justice, critical incident management, and instructional design, a Master of Arts (M.A.) degree in theology, a Master of Social Work (M.S.W.), and an education specialist degree.

Location

Saint Leo is located 35 minutes north of Tampa and 90 minutes west of Orlando. The lakeside campus occupies 186 acres of rolling hills and wooded grounds. The rural setting is conducive to academic success, but the University is located near enough to metropolitan areas to give the students the advantage of a wide variety of social and professional opportunities.

Majors and Degrees

Saint Leo University offers over forty traditional majors, preprofessional studies, specializations, endorsements, and programs. Degrees offered are the Bachelor of Arts, Bachelor of Science, and Bachelor of Social Work.

The School of Business offers degrees in accounting, business administration (specialization in international business), communication management, computer information systems, international hospitality and tourism management, management, marketing, and sport business. The School of Arts and Sciences offers majors in biology, English, environmental science, history, international studies, mathematics, medical technology, political science, psychology, religion, and sociology. The School of Education and Social Services offers majors in criminal justice, elementary education, middle grades education, and social work.

Preprofessional studies programs in chiropractic, dentistry, law, medicine, and veterinary science are also offered, including 4+4 medical school and 3+4 dental and chiropractic school programs.

Academic Programs

Saint Leo's LINK (Learning Interdisciplinary Knowledge) general education program ensures that all graduates have a solid grounding in theories, issues, and knowledge to prepare them for successful careers and graduate work. The program develops the skills that are the foundation of a liberal arts education and that today's employers demand. Students learn to communicate effectively; function at a high level, both alone and as a part of a team; develop a general knowledge base in many different areas; and analyze and solve problems effectively.

Students complete foundation courses of core requirements (writing, computer literacy, math, and wellness), Perspectives courses (liberal arts, fine arts, humanities, and physical, social, and behavioral sciences), and a senior capstone course that connects all prior course work in the major and leads to research and independent projects demonstrating mastery of the field.

Saint Leo has an academic skills program to assist first-year students in their adjustment to university life. Included in this program are freshman studies, tutoring, and advising. All first-year students at Saint Leo are assigned faculty advisers, who act as mentors from the first day that the student arrives on campus through the time when the student selects a major.

Students who demonstrate course mastery for any course listed in the catalog have the opportunity to receive up to 40 hours of credit through examination. Detailed information about credit by examination is available through the Registrar's Office.

Most students at Saint Leo earn the credits needed for their bachelor's degree through a four-year program of study. All major programs require a 2.0 minimum grade point average for graduation.

Off-Campus Programs

Saint Leo University is committed to helping students expand their horizons through study-abroad programs. Saint Leo University students have the opportunity to spend a semester studying in London, Madrid, Paris, Rome, Singapore, Australia, Ecuador, Germany, Greece, Ireland, Scotland, and various cities within the United Kingdom. Articulation agreements also afford study opportunities throughout Asia and the Pacific Rim. The University continues to add new programs and partnerships in order to provide students with a wide variety of educational and cultural experiences.

Students are also able to work with their professors and academic advisers to identify and pursue a wide variety of internship options, further enhancing the real-world experience component of their education.

Academic Facilities

The Cannon Memorial Library contains 102,212 volumes, and provides access to 120,320 e-books, 79,577 current periodical subscriptions (including 613 print and 78,964 e-journals), and 64 online databases. Also located in the library are the Hugh Culverhouse Computer Instruction Center classrooms, a student computer lab, and two VTT-equipped instruction/conference rooms.

Lab facilities include three teaching labs and one research lab for biology; two teaching labs, one research lab, and an instrumentation room for chemistry; and one physics lab. The state-of-the-art Donald R. Tapia School of Business building is scheduled to open in fall 2011. Most classrooms are located in Crawford Hall and Lewis Hall with additional classrooms in Saint Edward Hall, Saint Francis Hall, and the Bowman Activity Center.

All students are encouraged to utilize the University's Learning Resource Center (LRC). The LRC features study and meeting space for small groups as well as such technology as high-speed laser printers. Tutoring services are available to students and may be scheduled through the LRC.

The University's exciting new Student Community Center opened in late fall 2007; it includes substantial meeting space for groups of various sizes.

The University's campus is a mostly wireless environment. All students who reside in campus housing receive a state-of-the-art laptop computer. For students living off campus, laptops are available for use through the library.

Costs

For the 2011–12 school year, tuition is $18,200; freshman room and board costs are $9120, and mandatory fees are $670. Miscellaneous indirect costs for the year (such as books, personal living expenses, insurance, and travel) are estimated at $4255.

Financial Aid

Financial aid, both federally funded and awarded by the University, is available in the form of scholarships, grants, and loans. Financial aid is allocated on the basis of academic performance and need, as determined by the federal government from the financial information provided on the Free Application for Federal Student Aid (FAFSA). On-campus jobs are available for students, with priority given to students with demonstrated financial need. Ninety-seven percent of students receive some form of financial aid.

Faculty

At Saint Leo University, outstanding teaching and active learning go hand in hand. Caring and capable faculty members provide students with knowledge, guidance, academic support, and a broad range of learning opportunities both in and outside the classroom. Students enjoy small classes (average class size is 19) and develop close relationships with experienced, well-qualified professors. At Saint Leo, 88 percent of full-time instructional faculty members hold the terminal degree in their field.

Student Government

A significant contribution to the University comes from the activities initiated by the Student Government Union (SGU). The SGU is an annually elected body organized and conducted in accordance with democratic procedures. This organization strives to foster leadership and loyalty among the students, to formulate recommendations for student life, and to recognize all extracurricular activities.

Admission Requirements

All candidates for admission should be, or expect to be, graduates of secondary schools accredited by a regional or state accrediting agency. Applicants should show successful progress toward graduation with a minimum of 16 academic units of course work: 4 units of English, 3 units of mathematics (algebra I and II and geometry), 3 units of social studies, 2 units of science, and 4 units of electives, preferably to include 2 units of a foreign language. All domestic applicants are required to take the SAT or the ACT examination. A letter of recommendation from the student's guidance counselor is also required. Preferred candidates are students with a GPA of B or better and an average SAT combined score (critical reading and math) of 1030 or an average ACT score of 22. The records of students who do not meet these criteria are also reviewed by the Admission Committee and considered for the Learning Enhancement for Academic Progress (LEAP) program, a preparatory program that has a summer attendance component.

Once the applicant has submitted the application with the $35 application fee (fee is waived if application is submitted online), high school transcripts, test scores, and letter of recommendation, the file is reviewed and a decision is rendered. Notification is on a rolling basis and generally takes less than two weeks. The priority application deadline is March 1, but all applicants are encouraged to apply early.

Transfer and international students are also encouraged to apply. The same general admission procedures are required, along with at least a C average for all college work (for transfer students) and a score of at least 550 (paper-based test) or 78 (Internet-based test) on the TOEFL (for international students for whom English is not the primary language of instruction).

Campus visits and interviews are recommended but not required. The Office of Admission is open from Monday through Friday from 8 a.m. to 5 p.m. and on select Saturdays during the academic year from 9 a.m. to noon. Appointments are preferred. Campus tours are available Monday through Friday at 10 a.m. and 2 p.m., as well as at 10 a.m. on select Saturdays during the academic year. Summer tours are available Monday through Friday at 10 a.m. and 2 p.m. as well. The Office of Admission is closed on Sunday.

Application and Information

Additional information and application forms can be obtained by contacting the Office of Admission. Candidates may apply online at www.saintleo.edu/apply.

Scott Rhodes
Associate Vice President for Enrollment
Office of Admission—MC2008
Saint Leo University
P.O. Box 6665
Saint Leo, Florida 33574-6665
Phone: 352-588-8283
      800-334-5532 (toll-free)
Fax: 352-588-8257
E-mail: admission@saintleo.edu
Web site: http://www.saintleo.edu

The Saint Leo University campus.

ST. LOUIS COLLEGE OF PHARMACY

ST. LOUIS, MISSOURI

The College

Founded in 1864, St. Louis College of Pharmacy is one of the oldest and largest colleges of pharmacy in the nation and one of the very few that are not part of a larger university. Members of the first board of trustees included pharmacists, physicians, and business leaders, such as Henry Shaw, founder of the Missouri Botanical Garden, and John O'Fallon, nephew of explorer William Clark. St. Louis College of Pharmacy consistently graduates one of the top 20 largest classes of pharmacists in the nation. The College admits students directly from high school and integrates the liberal arts and sciences with a six-year professional curriculum leading to a Doctor of Pharmacy (Pharm.D.) degree.

The 1,215 students at the College are among the best prepared in Missouri. The average ACT score of the most recent freshman class, at 28, was the second highest in the state. The average class rank for incoming freshmen was in the top 15 percent, and the average high school grade point average was 3.88. Total enrollment for the 2010–11 academic year was 706 women and 509 men. Graduates have an enormous impact on the pharmacy profession and health of people nationwide. Nearly 3 out of 4 practicing pharmacists in the St. Louis region are graduates of St. Louis College of Pharmacy, providing current students with local mentors.

In addition to a well-rounded pharmaceutical curriculum, the College offers a full student-life experience with on-campus housing, more than fifty student organizations, and an athletic program for both intercollegiate and intramural sports. The College participates in nine NAIA sports: men's and women's cross-country, men's and women's basketball, men's and women's track and field, men's and women's tennis, and women's volleyball. An eight-story residence hall features suite- and efficiency-style units and is connected to a spacious dining facility that serves both fast-food and plate meals.

Location

Only a few miles from the Gateway Arch, St. Louis College of Pharmacy is located in the city's Central West End, surrounded by the nationally recognized medical community of Barnes-Jewish Hospital, Washington University School of Medicine, Siteman Cancer Center, and St. Louis Children's Hospital. The campus is one block from Forest Park, with its 1,300 acres of green space, tennis courts, ice-skating rink, golf course, and world-class museums, zoo, outdoor opera theater, and science center. Students at the College are near the cultural and entertainment scene of St. Louis on a safe, 5-acre campus within walking distance of public transportation.

Majors and Degrees

The College offers a six-year professional program leading to a Doctor of Pharmacy (Pharm.D.) degree.

Academic Programs

The Doctor of Pharmacy program includes intensive courses in biology, chemistry, mathematics, and physics, as well as electives in literature, humanities, and social and behavioral sciences. Introductory practice experiences throughout the curriculum give students the opportunity to apply their education and enable students to develop knowledge, communication skills, and professional values through interaction with other health-care practitioners and patients. The six-year Pharm.D. program is comprised of specialized didactic courses and includes a calendar year of clinical rotations.

Off-Campus Programs

Students have opportunities to participate in advanced practice experiences in twenty-six states at more than 600 community and hospital settings, including the U.S. Food and Drug Administration, Barnes-Jewish Hospital, Lindenwood Drug, Pfizer, Walgreens, St. Luke's Hospital, Copper Bend Pharmacy, Bristol-Myers Squibb, and the Banner Good Samaritan Medical Center.

Academic Facilities

The O. J. Cloughly Alumni Library, located in Jones Hall, houses a number of volumes covering the fields of pharmacy, allied sciences, and the liberal arts. The library also archives a variety of leading pharmaceutical and scientific periodicals, journals, bulletins, and reports. Jones Hall contains the majority of College classrooms, lecture halls, laboratories, and faculty and administrative offices. Whelpley Hall features a 300-seat auditorium in addition to small- and medium-sized classrooms.

Costs

For 2010–11, tuition and fees for students in years one and two were $22,400, years three through five were $24,600, and year six was $24,600. A notebook computer (issued to all new students) and lab fees are included in tuition costs. Room and board costs for the academic year were $8338 for first-year students and $7908 for students in their second year and above. Additional costs, including books, vary each year but average $675 per semester.

Financial Aid

Financial aid is awarded based on merit, need, and availability of funds. The College participates in all applicable federal and state financial aid programs. Scholarships, grants, loans, and student employment are offered to help qualified students pay for college expenses. Financial aid may be funded by the federal or state government, the College, benefactors and friends of the College, or other sponsoring organizations or agencies. Merit-based scholarships are offered to qualified students regardless of need. The percentage of students who receive financial aid is 94 percent. St. Louis College of Pharmacy offers $4.6 million in College-sponsored scholarships.

Students planning to attend the College in the fall semester should submit the Free Application for Federal Student Aid (FAFSA) along with signed copies of student and parent federal tax returns as early as possible during the previous spring semester. The College begins awarding financial aid in February and continues until all funds are exhausted. Further information on student financial aid may be obtained from the College's Financial Aid Office.

Faculty

The College's student-faculty ratio of 18:1 overall and 14:1 in the professional years ensures that learning is interactive and student focused. No classes are taught by graduate students. Of the 88 full-time faculty members, 92 percent hold a Ph.D. or the highest degree in their field. More than 200 pharmacists serve as adjunct instructors in the advanced practice experiences program.

Admission Requirements

All students applying for admission to St. Louis College of Pharmacy must present evidence of the satisfactory completion of a four-year course of study in, and graduation from, a high school approved by a recognized accrediting body. A high school transcript, including class standing, should be sent by the high school directly to the Director of Admissions. The high school course of study should include 4 units of English; 4 units of math, including algebra 1 and 2 and geometry; and at least 3 units of science, including biology/lab and chemistry lab. The College also requires that the SAT or ACT examination be completed.

Advanced credit may be earned through Advanced Placement examinations. Further details are available from the Office of Admissions.

Students transferring into St. Louis College of Pharmacy must submit transcripts of their college records and are required to have taken the PCAT. Transfer students must apply for admission through the Pharmacy College Application Service (PharmCAS) at http://www.pharmcas.org. Applications and admission materials sent to St. Louis College of Pharmacy will not be accepted—all materials for admission must be submitted directly to PharmCAS. For more information, students should visit the PharmCAS Web site.

Application and Information

Application deadlines can be found at http://www.stlcop.edu. The College offers an early decision selection process as well as a regular decision process for prospective students.

The application deadline for transfer students is March 1. However, the PharmCAS deadline for submission of all admission materials is February 1. Very few transfer students are accepted into the College, and as a result, admission is extremely competitive. Transfer students are only accepted into the third year of the six-year program.

For additional information or to apply, students should contact:

Registrar/Director of Admissions
St. Louis College of Pharmacy
4588 Parkview Place
St. Louis, Missouri 63110

Phone: 314-367-8700 Ext. 8313
       800-278-5267 (toll-free)
E-mail: pbryant@stlcop.edu
Web site: http://www.stlcop.edu
       http://www.facebook.com/STLCOP
       http://twitter.com/#!/STLCOPEUT

SAINT MARY'S COLLEGE

NOTRE DAME, INDIANA

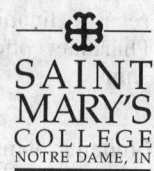

The College

She's a staff nurse in a Chicago neurology intensive care unit or a Peace Corps volunteer in Uganda. She's studied abroad in Rome or been a student teacher at Marquette School in South Bend. She's received a first place award in the North Central Sociological Association's National Student Competition or danced the entire night to help raise over $90,000 to benefit Riley's Children's Hospital. She's a woman using her talents to make a difference in our world—she's a Saint Mary's woman.

A Saint Mary's education will challenge students to reach beyond the ordinary and reach for new academic heights. Every area of study emphasizes the exceptional writing and critical thinking skills needed to become a confident leader, well-prepared for an ever-changing world. Saint Mary's offers professional programs such as accounting, education, nursing, social work, and communicative disorders. Nearly half of the students will complete a minimum of a semester-long study aboard experience in one of over thirty locations across the globe. There are established study-abroad programs in Italy, Ireland, Spain, and France; or students can seek a location a bit out of the ordinary like China, Honduras, or Argentina. And all Saint Mary's students complete a senior comprehensive, a graduate-quality project that is the capstone of their educational experience.

Founded by the Sisters of the Holy Cross in 1844, Saint Mary's is a nationally recognized Catholic college that empowers women by providing a strong liberal arts education foundation, leadership development, and attention to social responsibility.

With more than 1,555 students from forty-two states and seven countries, Saint Mary's brings together women from a wide range of geographical areas, social backgrounds, and educational experiences. International and diverse students comprise 14 percent of the student body.

Saint Mary's has a unique co-exchange program with the University of Notre Dame that encompasses both academics and extracurricular activities. Saint Mary's and Notre Dame's students can take courses and be part of the study-abroad programs at both institutions. Saint Mary's students can try out for Notre Dame's legendary marching band (10 percent of its members are Saint Mary's students); work for *The Observer*, the daily newspaper published jointed by Notre Dame/Saint Mary's; or gain broadcast experience on WVFI, the Notre Dame/Saint Mary's radio station or SMC-TV, Saint Mary's own TV station. In addition, dances, concerts, lectures, and social organizations open to students on both campuses create a fluid social life between Saint Mary's and Notre Dame.

One of the distinctive features of Saint Mary's is its campus life. There are over sixty clubs and organizations, eight varsity athletic teams, over twenty community service organizations, and numerous other opportunities to help develop leadership skills and abilities, with all these groups lead and organized by women. Most students choose to live on campus for a minimum of six semesters and many seniors opt to remain on campus their final year. Saint Mary's has five residence halls, each with its own distinctive character. Seniors may choose to live in Opus Hall, which offers apartment-style living on campus. Residence halls offer a full calendar of activities—from twice-yearly dances to coffee nights with the College President, intramural athletic events, and a full array of activities designed involve students in campus life. The College has a new student center, a dining hall, and a clubhouse for extracurricular activities. All residence halls have chapels, and the Church of Loretto, the main chapel, offers mass on a daily basis.

As an NCAA Division III school and a member of the Michigan Intercollegiate Athletic Association, Saint Mary's sponsors varsity teams in basketball, cross-country, golf, soccer, softball, swimming and diving, tennis, and volleyball. Club sports, cosponsored with Notre Dame, include equestrian, gymnastics, lacrosse, and figure ice skating. In addition, Saint Mary's offers many intramural sports.

The College's Angela Athletic Facility contains multipurpose courts for tennis, volleyball, and basketball; a training and fitness center; and racquetball courts. The campus has tennis courts and athletic fields for both soccer and softball.

Location

Saint Mary's 75-acre campus, set alongside the Saint Joseph River, has great natural beauty. The College is located just across the street from the University of Notre Dame, minutes north of the city of South Bend (with a population of more than 200,000), and only 90 miles from Chicago. Students from Saint Mary's and Notre Dame form a dynamic intercollegiate community. South Bend provides sites for internships and practicums and opportunities for volunteer service. One of the hallmarks of a Saint Mary's education is the way students use their God-given talents to enrich their community; annually, 75 percent of Saint Mary's students commit time to a variety of community service organizations.

Majors and Degrees

Saint Mary's College offers programs leading to the Bachelor of Arts, Bachelor of Science, Bachelor of Fine Arts, Bachelor of Business Administration, and Bachelor of Music degrees.

For a Bachelor of Arts degree, students may choose majors in art, biology, chemistry, communication studies, communicative disorders, economics, elementary education, English literature, English writing, French, history, humanistic studies, Italian, mathematics, music, philosophy, political science, psychology, religious studies, social work, sociology, Spanish, statistics and actuarial mathematics, and theater.

A Bachelor of Science degree may be obtained in biology (with concentrations in cellular/molecular biology, environmental biology, and general biology), chemistry, computational mathematics, mathematics, nursing, and statistics and actuarial mathematics.

The Bachelor of Music degree program, which is a member of the National Association of Schools of Music, offers concentrations in music education and music performance. For talented art students, Saint Mary's offers a Bachelor of Fine Arts degree with concentrations in several media.

The Bachelor of Business Administration degree program offers majors in accounting, business administration (with concentrations in accounting, finance, international business, management, and marketing), and management information systems.

Superior students who are candidates for either a Bachelor of Arts or a Bachelor of Science degree may design a program of study outside the traditional department structure, called a Student Designed Major.

For women interested in engineering fields, a five-year, dual-degree program offered in cooperation with the University of Notre Dame leads to a bachelor's degree from Saint Mary's College and a Bachelor of Science in Engineering degree from Notre Dame in aerospace, chemical, civil, computer, electrical, environmental, or mechanical engineering.

Saint Mary's education department, accredited by the National Council for Accreditation of Teacher Education, offers certification in elementary and secondary education. Secondary Education Certification is available in art, biology, business administration, chemistry, English literature, English writing, French, history, mathematics, music, music education, political science, psychology, sociology, and Spanish.

In addition, the College offers more than forty minors in a variety of fields, including American history, communicative disorders, information science, justice studies, Latin American studies, and women's studies.

Academic Programs

Graduation from Saint Mary's College requires successful completion of at least 128 semester hours of credit. Every student must also complete a comprehensive examination in her major, which may take the form of a thesis, a research or creative project, or a written or oral examination, depending on the discipline. All students must also demonstrate writing proficiency by satisfactorily completing a writing-intensive "W" course, usually in the first year, and an advanced portfolio of writings in the major discipline, usually in the senior year.

Off-Campus Programs

Through Saint Mary's international study programs, students can study with Irish students at the National University of Ireland Maynooth, just outside Dublin. They can absorb Italian art and culture on Saint Mary's campus in the center of Rome or experience South America through a full-immersion Spanish program in Argentina.

Saint Mary's students may also enroll in the Spanish language programs of the Center for Cross-Cultural Study in Seville, Spain, or in the French language and culture study in Dijon, France. An exchange program with the Australian University of Notre Dame based in Freemantle is also available, as is a program based in Pietermaritzburg, South Africa. A summer study program in China was recently added.

Saint Mary's students may study in other countries through a cooperative program with the University of Notre Dame.

A student majoring in political science has the opportunity to spend a semester at the American University in Washington, D.C. Saint Mary's also participates in student and faculty member exchange programs with the University of Notre Dame and members of the Northern Indiana Consortium for Education.

Academic Facilities

Students have abundant access to technology systems, software, and services. Residence halls are wired for network access, and secure wireless network access is available in most public areas on campus, including many classrooms in the new Spes Unica academic building. Computer labs for students are available in several campus buildings as well as computer "collaboratories," where students and faculty members can conduct online research in groups in classroom settings. Extensive support services are available to students and faculty and staff members for instructional, administrative, and network systems. Faculty members make significant use of information technology resources for teaching, research, and scholarship.

The modern Cushwa-Leighton Library houses an outstanding collection of more than 228,000 volumes, and it includes the Trumper Computer Center, the Instructional Technology Resource Center, the College archives, and a rare book room.

In addition to extensive biology, chemistry, and physics lab facilities, laboratories for psychology research and for foreign language study and practice are available to students. Art studios, music practice rooms, the O'Laughlin Auditorium, and Moreau's Little Theatre provide ample space for fine arts creation, practice, and performance. The new Spes Unica academic building opened in August 2008, providing students with state-of-the-art classrooms and gathering places.

The professionally staffed Early Childhood Development Center provides education and psychology majors with an unusual on-campus opportunity to work with young children. Other facilities include the Madeleva classroom building, Science Hall, Havican nursing facility, and Moreau Art Galleries.

Costs

Expenses for the 2010–11 academic year included tuition and fees, $31,020; room and board, $9480 (double occupancy); and miscellaneous expenses (books, transportation, and living costs), $2700.

Financial Aid

The College strives to make a Saint Mary's education available for every admitted student by offering eligible students financial aid packages that may include grants, scholarships, work-study, and loans. Competitive scholarships, awarded solely on academic merit, as well as grants determined by financial need are available. Last year, more than 90 percent of Saint Mary's students received more than $25 million in financial assistance, more than $19 million from the College alone.

All applicants for financial assistance must complete the College Board PROFILE and the Free Application for Federal Student Aid (FAFSA)

each year that they desire assistance. Applications for assistance must be received at the processing center by March 1 to be given priority consideration. For non–early decision candidates, decisions concerning financial aid are made in mid-March, as soon as possible after a student has been accepted and upon receipt of the College Board PROFILE and FAFSA forms.

Faculty

Saint Mary's has 134 full-time and 73 part-time faculty members. About 98 percent of full-time faculty members hold earned doctorates or other terminal degrees; of these, most teach first-year students as well as upper-division students. Faculty members work with students in all phases of college life, including academic counseling. All classes are taught by faculty members, not by teaching assistants.

Student Government

Students are active at every level of campus governance and share in community decision making. There are voting representatives on the president's two highest advisory boards, the Student Affairs Council and the Academic Affairs Council. A student is also a voting member of the College's Board of Trustees. The Student Government Association sponsors many extracurricular and cocurricular activities.

Admission Requirements

Applicants for admission to Saint Mary's College should be graduates of an accredited high school and have completed a four-year program of 16 or more academic units. These academic units must include four units of English, three units of college-preparatory mathematics, two units of the same foreign language, two units of social science, and two units of laboratory science. The remaining units should be completed in college-preparatory courses in the previously mentioned areas. An applicant's credentials should include an academic transcript showing current rank and senior-year subjects, a counselor/administrator recommendation, SAT or ACT scores (at least one test should include the writing exam), and an essay. There is no application fee for students who apply online at http://www.saintmarys.edu or by completing the Common Application.

Home-schooled students are encouraged to apply for admission and should contact the Office of Admission for specific details.

An interview with an admission officer is recommended. Saint Mary's encourages students to visit the campus. The Office of Admission can make arrangements for students who wish to attend classes or stay overnight.

Mature, well-qualified students who graduated from high school after three years and who wish to enter college immediately upon graduation may apply for early admission. Saint Mary's College also grants deferred admission upon request to candidates who are accepted in the normal application process.

Application and Information

Saint Mary's has two application and notification programs: Early Decision and modified rolling admission. Highly qualified students who have selected Saint Mary's as their first choice for admission may apply under the Early Decision program. The application deadline is November 15, and the notification date is December 15. Students who apply for modified rolling admission and whose application files are complete on or before December 1 are notified of the admission decision in mid-January. Candidates are encouraged to apply by early fall of their senior year. The priority application deadline for regular admission is February 15. Applications are accepted, however, as long as space is available.

Interested students are encouraged to contact:

Director of Admission
Saint Mary's College
Notre Dame, Indiana 46556-5001

Phone: 574-284-4587
        800-551-7621 (toll-free)
Fax: 574-284-4841
E-mail: admission@saintmarys.edu
Web site: http://www.saintmarys.edu

ST. MARY'S COLLEGE OF MARYLAND
The Public Honors College
ST. MARY'S CITY, MARYLAND

The College

St. Mary's College of Maryland (SMCM) is a public, state-supported, coeducational college dedicated to providing an excellent education in the liberal arts tradition. There are 1,978 full-time students, of whom 851 are men and 1,127 are women. Almost 85 percent of the students live on campus in dorms, suites, apartments, and town houses. Housing on campus is guaranteed for eight semesters for all full-time students.

In 1992, St. Mary's was designated the State of Maryland's Public Honors College in recognition of the academic excellence of its faculty and students. Every student participates in the intellectual and social life of the College. St. Mary's combines the educational and personal advantages of a small private college with the affordability of a public institution. Active learning and the development of critical thinking are encouraged in the discussion-oriented format made possible by modest class sizes. Student leadership in academic, cultural, and social spheres is aided by the community atmosphere, and opportunities are greater than at larger schools.

The campus covers 361 acres of riverfront, open space, and woodland. Among the waterfront facilities are a boathouse, river center, ocean kayaks, rowing shells, and a fleet of sailboats. Other facilities include a field house, lighted tennis courts, a baseball field, an outdoor track, and a stadium for field hockey, soccer, and lacrosse. The athletic facility includes an aquatic center with two indoor swimming pools including an Olympic-sized pool, a basketball stadium, a fitness center, an aerobic center, additional team rooms, and a rock-climbing wall. The College's teams compete in NCAA Division III and the Intercollegiate Sailing Association. Varsity sports for men are baseball, basketball, lacrosse, sailing, soccer, swimming, and tennis. For women, sports include basketball, field hockey, lacrosse, sailing, soccer, swimming, tennis, and volleyball. The College's sailing teams have earned national recognitions. Club sports available for both men and women include cross-country and track, equestrian, fencing, golf, rowing, rugby, sailing, soccer, and Ultimate (Frisbee).

The College is accredited by the Middle States Commission on Higher Education.

Location

St. Mary's College of Maryland is situated along the banks of the St. Mary's River. It is tidewater country, still inhabited by people who make their living from the land and water. Watermen harvest oysters and crabs from the St. Mary's, Potomac, and Patuxent rivers and the Chesapeake Bay; wild swans, ducks, and Canada geese winter in the creeks of St. Mary's County.

The Patuxent River Naval Air Station, the county's largest employer, is a naval aircraft testing facility, attracting over 100 contractors that sponsor internships for SMCM students. It is an environment that is alive, providing fresh air and space, conveniently located just 75 miles south of Washington, D.C.

Majors and Degrees

St. Mary's College offers the Bachelor of Arts degree in anthropology; art and art history; Asian studies; biochemistry; biology; chemistry; computer science; economics; engineering (dual degree program); English; history; international languages and cultures (Chinese, French, German, Latin American studies, Spanish, and courses in translation); mathematics; music; natural science; philosophy; physics; political science; psychology; public policy studies; religious studies; sociology; theater, film, and media studies; and student-designed majors.

Minors are available in African and African diaspora studies; anthropology; art history; art studio; Asian studies; biology; computer science; democracy studies; economics; educational studies; environmental studies; film and media studies; history; international languages and cultures (Chinese, French, German, Latin American studies, Spanish, and courses in translation); mathematics; museum studies; music; the neurosciences; philosophy; physics; political science; religious studies; sociology; theater studies; and women, gender, and sexuality studies.

Preprofessional sequences are offered in dentistry, law, medicine, and veterinary medicine.

St. Mary's also offers teaching certification through a one-year, full-time Master of Arts in Teaching program. This program requires participation in the county school system, aiding in the transition from theory to practice. Certificates can be obtained for grades 1 through 6 and middle school. Secondary education certificates for grades 7 through 12 are offered in English, math, social studies, biology, chemistry, physics, and modern languages. Certificate programs for K–12 in art, music, and theater, and an early childhood education certificate to supplement the elementary certificate are also offered. All certificate programs have been approved through the Maryland State Department of Education and may be eligible for reciprocity with other states.

Academic Programs

The undergraduate course of study at the College provides both diversity and depth, leading to a broad understanding of the humanities, arts, and sciences. All students must complete the core curriculum requirements in addition to the requirements for a major field of study.

The core curriculum requirements are designed to develop skills in critical thinking, information literacy, written communication and oral communication, as well as promote the capacity for integration and synthesis of knowledge across disciplines. The core curriculum begins with first-year students completing a seminar of unique topics in every discipline, designed by the faculty members. In addition, students will fulfill the experiential component of the core by completing an internship, taking a service-learning course, or studying abroad.

History, anthropology, and archaeology students can take advantage of the College's relationship with historic St. Mary's City, the fourth permanent English settlement in the New World and Maryland's first capital. Many experts consider this area to contain the most abundant and earliest undisturbed artifacts of any American seventeenth-century town.

St. Mary's College offers several courses in aquatic biology as an option within the biology major program. The College's location on the St. Mary's River, a tributary of the Potomac near the mouth of the Chesapeake Bay, is ideal for the study of estuarine ecology.

A strong music program provides advanced training in composition and piano performance and a jazz ensemble, percussion ensemble, choir, chamber vocal group, wind ensemble, and chamber orchestra for classical performances.

Independent study for credit is possible in every major, allowing students to investigate subjects not covered in normal course offerings. There is also an opportunity for students to design their own majors using components from several majors to create an interdisciplinary, individualized program of study.

Off-Campus Programs

Internship programs for academic credit are available for junior- and senior-level students. Within these semester-long internships, students find ways to explore their career and scholarly interests. In recent years, St. Mary's interns have worked in state and federal government offices and laboratories, in the news media, in museums and art galleries, in commercial organizations, and in positions abroad. In a number of cases, internships have led to either full-time employment after graduation or to graduate or professional study.

Opportunities to study abroad include: The Centre for Medieval and Renaissance Studies in Oxford, England; Fudan University in China; Heidelberg University in Germany, University of The Gambia in The Gambia; the Alba Program in Italy; Akita University in Japan; Lingnan University in Hong Kong; Payap University in Thailand; Université Michel de Montaigne and Sciences Po in France; Institute for Central American Development Studies in Costa Rica; the Buenos Aires Program in Argentina; George Washington University Partnership in Santiago, Chile; and other study-abroad programs are available for qualified St. Mary's students. St. Mary's also participates in the National Student Exchange Program with other colleges throughout the United States.

Academic Facilities

The College's laboratories are equipped for course work in anthropology, biology, chemistry, physics, psychology, and the neurosciences. There are also several smart classrooms and discipline-specific labs in Goodpaster, Kent, Montgomery, and Schaefer Halls. All of the computer labs have access to the library system, e-mail, the student portal, and the Internet. There is 24-hour access to College computers in Baltimore Hall and Lewis Quad. Upon enrollment, every student is given a network account that provides access to e-mail, the student portal, shared file systems, and other resources.

Students are encouraged but not required to own a computer, since they have access to computers in the College's general purpose and departmental computer labs. However, many students find it more convenient to own a computer so they can complete assignments in their rooms. Each residence hall room has high-speed Internet 1 and 2 access (ResNet). The College offers wireless access in all academic buildings of the campus for those with laptop computers.

The College library provides access to locally held resources and participates in a statewide consortium of academic libraries that supports intercampus borrowing (interlibrary loan) for books and access to more than 70 research databases. Students have access to a writing center, located in the library, which provides assistance in writing and researching papers.

The Media Services Department, through its editing lab and loans of video equipment, supports students pursuing multimedia and video projects. The College Archives house documents, photographs, and objects of significance to the history of the College and Southern Maryland.

The Montgomery Fine Arts Center includes facilities for practice and performance in music and theater and also houses the Boyden Gallery. Auerbach Auditorium, located in St. Mary's Hall, is also a popular venue for public lectures, concerts, and other events.

Costs

Annual costs for 2011–12 include tuition and fees of $14,445 for Maryland residents and $26,522 for nonresidents. The most typical residence hall rooms are available for $6140 per year, and the most typical cost for board is $4775 per year. Costs for books and supplies are estimated at $1000 per year. Semester charges for tuition, room, board, and other fees are payable at or prior to registration in the fall and in the spring.

Financial Aid

The Office of Financial Aid provides advice and assistance to students in need of financial aid and joins other College offices in awarding scholarships and loans and in offering part-time employment under the work-study program. Various scholarships are awarded to students on a merit basis, and other scholarships, loans, and grants for students are awarded on ability and need as determined by the federal government's Free Application for Federal Student Aid, which should be filed no later than March 1.

Faculty

Faculty appointments and promotions are made on the basis of commitment to undergraduate teaching, an interest in new approaches to education, and academic and scholarly achievement. The faculty members have experience in a wide range of activities, including government, business, research, environmental studies, civil rights, theater, musical performance, and writing. Since 1982, St. Mary's College has had 23 Fulbright Scholars on its faculty and staff. Ninety-nine percent of the regular full-time faculty members hold a doctorate or other terminal degree in their field.

A student-faculty ratio of 12:1, average class size of 16, the relatively small size of the College, and the informal atmosphere all encourage close and personal relationships between students and faculty members. Faculty members serve as academic advisers and provide much informal counseling and individual attention to students' academic and personal development outside of the formal structure.

Student Government

Student Government Association (SGA) is the center of many activities and sponsors a variety of social and cultural events, including campus movies, speakers, dances, concerts, and excursions to cultural centers such as Annapolis, Baltimore, and Washington, D.C. The SGA also sponsors over 100 student-run clubs and organizations. Opportunities exist for students to serve as voting members on several faculty committees.

Admission Requirements

The application deadline for freshman admissions is January 1. Strong high school preparation usually includes 4 units of English, 3 units of social science (including U.S. history), 3 units of laboratory science (exclusive of ninth-grade general courses in science), 3 units of mathematics, and 7 units of other academic electives. Upon entrance, the student should have obtained a high school diploma with a minimum of 22 units or should present evidence of equivalent achievement (e.g., a passing score on the high school equivalency examination administered by the student's state department of education). The applicant must present scores on the SAT and/or the ACT examination, which should be taken by the fall of the senior year. In addition, any student whose native language is not English must obtain a minimum score of 550 (paper-based) on the TOEFL. St. Mary's College is interested in evidence of talent and ability as demonstrated in a variety of ways by each student. While the most emphasis is placed on the student's academic record, SAT scores, essay, resume, and letters of recommendation are all considered in the admissions process.

Students enrolled in Advanced Placement courses may receive credit for scores of 4 or 5 on the examinations. In addition, St. Mary's may also award credit to students who receive a score of 5, 6, or 7 on the International Baccalaureate Higher Level examinations.

Transfer applicants with at least 24 semester hours of credit are evaluated on their college transcripts. Students who have earned fewer than 24 semester hours of credit must submit their high school records and SAT or ACT scores. Standardized test scores are required only for individuals who have graduated from high school within the past three years.

St. Mary's College of Maryland does not discriminate for reasons of age, citizenship, color, disability, gender/gender identity and expression, national origin, race, religion, sex, sexual orientation, or special disabled veteran and Vietnam-era veteran status in the admission of students. The College complies with the Title IX of the Education Amendments of 1972.

Application and Information

An application form, financial aid information, and other materials are available by contacting:

Office of Admissions
St. Mary's College of Maryland
18952 East Fisher Road
St. Mary's City, Maryland 20686
Phone: 240-895-5000
       800-492-7181 (toll-free)
Fax: 240-895-5001
E-mail: admissions@smcm.edu
Web site: http://www.smcm.edu/admissions

A bird's-eye view of St. Mary's College of Maryland.

SAINT MICHAEL'S COLLEGE
COLCHESTER, VERMONT

The College

The mindset at Saint Michael's College is that a college education should prepare students not only for a meaningful career, but for a meaningful life.

Students at St. Michael's start by building a strong liberal studies foundation, then dive deep into their majors. By the time they graduate, they've developed essential skills and knowledge that will help them achieve success in any field. And in the meantime, they've also been engaged in service (through the popular MOVE—Mobilization of Volunteer Efforts—program), in the great outdoors (with the College's ground-breaking Wilderness Program and Smuggs' ski pass), and with the close campus community in meaningful ways that educate the body, mind, and spirit.

Attitude is also an important part of the St. Michael's equation. Students and faculty are bright, engaged, and friendly, resulting in a close campus community located in a stunning Vermont setting. The College offers a perspective-changing exploration of the liberal arts anchored with a legacy of faith and service.

All of this underscores Saint Michael's successes. It is one of just 270 colleges and universities nationwide that hosts a prestigious Phi Beta Kappa chapter on campus. Recent graduates are Rhodes scholars, Pickering fellows, medical students, law students, dental students, medical researchers, pharmacists, new media specialists, sportswriters, nonprofit directors, and more. Alumni include a United States senator; one of the founders of MTV; and noted authors, scientists, investment bankers, social workers, teachers, professors, and scholars. No matter what career paths they choose, graduates of St. Michael's take with them a solid liberal arts foundation, a strong sense of self, and a desire to give back to their communities.

Students at Saint Michael's are actively involved with life on campus, taking on leadership roles, rallying support for worthy causes, and generally making things happen. Because everyone lives on campus (student housing is guaranteed for all four years), there's an strong sense of community. It's always easy to find someone ready for adventure, whether it's taking on a research project or rock climbing. Nearly one-third of St. Mike's students study abroad for a semester, a summer, or an academic year.

Location

Saint Michael's beautiful, safe, 440-acre campus is just 3 miles from Burlington, which is Vermont's largest city. Burlington is a vibrant college town that is home to 14,000 students who attend five other local colleges and universities. Downtown Burlington is a thriving business center that offers great opportunities for hands-on learning through internships. There are many shops, restaurants, and cafés; the Church Street Marketplace; and a lively local music scene, as well as an abundance of places to ski, skate, kayak, and bike. Students can qualify for St. Michael's special Smuggs' pass to take advantage of some of the best skiing in the East and the College's renowned Wilderness Program offers dozens of outdoor adventure opportunities. A cultural pass gives students unlimited access to fine arts performances at Burlington's famous Flynn Theater.

Burlington International Airport is only a 10-minute drive from the campus. In addition, an Amtrak station is in nearby Essex Junction and a Greyhound bus station is in Burlington; both are within a 15-minute drive of the campus.

Majors and Degrees

Saint Michael's College offers bachelor's degrees with a liberal arts foundation. The College has thirty-four majors in the following areas: accounting, American studies, art, biochemistry, biology, business administration, chemistry, classics, computer science, economics, elementary and secondary education, engineering, English, environmental science, French, gender/women's studies, history, information systems, journalism, mathematics, modern languages and literature, music, philosophy, physical science, physics, political science, psychology, religious studies, sociology, Spanish, and theater. In addition, advising programs for premedicine, prelaw, predentistry, and pre–veterinary studies are available, as well as thirty-seven minors, including interdisciplinary areas.

Dual-degree programs are available in engineering through Clarkson University (Potsdam, New York) and the University of Vermont (Burlington, Vermont); pharmacy through Albany College of Pharmacy's Burlington campus; and physical therapy through the University of Vermont. A 4+1 M.B.A. program is offered in conjunction with Clarkson University.

Academic Programs

Saint Michael's prepares its students for life after college with a dynamic liberal arts curriculum designed to foster intellectual curiosity and exploration, including a highly competitive honors program and many opportunities for self-directed study. The curriculum emphasizes a solid understanding of building blocks to a meaningful life as a well-rounded, thoughtful person: humanities, social sciences, religious studies, philosophy, natural sciences, mathematics, and fine arts. Students develop excellent communication skills through writing-intensive courses and foreign language requirements. The curriculum also addresses questions of ethics and responsible citizenship.

The Saint Michael's academic year includes two semesters and optional summer sessions. The College's focus is on undergraduate instruction and its small classes support this. Saint Michael's has a strong faculty-student research tradition. There are competitive opportunities for research for academic credit and with faculty throughout the academic year and during the summer.

Nowhere is Saint Michael's mission more evident than in its service-learning opportunities. Service learning is a credit-bearing, educational experience in which students in an academic course participate in a thoughtfully organized service activity that meets identified community needs. Students reflect on the service activities in ways that develop further understanding of course content, a broader appreciation of the discipline, and an enhanced sense of civic responsibility.

Off-Campus Programs

St. Michael's students can gain hands-on experience with internships related to their career goals and major. Internships are available both locally and in other selected areas around the U.S. and abroad. Sites have included scientific research laboratories, brokerage houses, hospitals, schools, newspapers, and accounting firms.

More than a third of St. Michael's students study abroad for a semester, a summer, or an academic year. Unique programs include study-abroad experiences at University of the Americas, Mexico; College of Ripon and York St. John, England; Kansai Gaidai University, Japan; and a Washington, D.C., semester program. In recent years, many students have studied abroad in locations such as Australia, Botswana, China, France, Ghana, Ireland, Italy, Nepal, Samoa, and Spain.

Academic Facilities

St. Michael's has a Main Campus and a North Campus. Main Campus is home to almost all academic administrative buildings;

North Campus, about a mile away, includes the art center, music center, and housing for upper-level students. The Jeremiah Durick Library holds 270,000 volumes, 150 research databases, access to articles from more than 57,000 online journals, and over 10,000 electronic books, maps, videos, and other items. Students have access to more than 120 computers connected to the College's campuswide information technology network. This network provides access to PC applications, including Microsoft Windows XP Professional, the Internet, e-mail, and the College library. Most campus areas have wireless Internet access.

Cheray Science Center has modern facilities for the study of biochemistry, biology, chemistry, environmental science, and physics.

Saint Edmund's Hall, an impressive academic complex, includes media labs, psychology labs, computer facilities, and language labs, in addition to traditional classroom and lecture hall space.

Costs

Tuition and residence fees for the 2010–11 academic year were $43,530. The residence fee includes housing and meals and is based on a standard double room and a standard meal plan. Housing options on campus include traditional residence halls, apartment-style housing, theme housing, and suite-style housing. Some science, journalism, language, and art courses require laboratory fees. Book, personal, and travel expenses vary according to course selection and individual needs.

Financial Aid

Approximately 90 percent of admitted students receive financial aid in the form of loans, grants, and work-study dollars. Students must file the FAFSA by February 15 for fall-semester enrollment.

Faculty

Saint Michael's faculty members are known not only for being experts in their fields but for sharing that expertise effectively with their students. Their doors are always open, too—it's not unusual for students to join professors for coffee or lunch, or to be invited to their homes for dinner. Faculty members are also visible and involved beyond the classroom—they can be seen at fundraisers and on the sidelines of athletic games. And chances are excellent that they'll know most of their students by name at the end of the first week of classes. Saint Michael's remarkable faculty includes 150 full-time professors, 94 percent of whom have the doctoral or terminal degree in their field. Many have been recipients of grants, awards, and honors in recent years. While undergraduate instruction is the focus of the College, faculty members remain active in their field through research and publication, often facilitated through sabbaticals.

Student Government

The Student Association (SA), an active and important part of campus life, is an elected body of students that authorizes and funds most other student activities and organizations. Representatives from the SA sit on many campuswide committees, including the Curriculum Committee and various committees of the Board of Trustees.

Admission Requirements

Successful applicants to Saint Michael's typically rank in the top 25 percent of their high school class and have a strong college-preparatory background. Students should have completed 16 units of courses in English, foreign language, mathematics, science, and social science. SAT or ACT scores are optional in the admission process. For reference, the average SAT score last year ranged between 1590 and 1890, and the average ACT score ranged between 25 and 26. In addition, students should submit a counselor recommendation and any teacher recommendations they choose. Transfer applicants must submit transcripts of all college work in addition to their final high school transcript.

Application and Information

Saint Michael's offers an Early Action admission program deadline of either November 1 or December 1, as well as a Regular Action deadline of February 1. The application deadline for transfer candidates is March 15. Students should consult the Web site for application deadlines and information. Candidates for the fall semester are notified of their admission decision on or before April 1. A limited number of students may be admitted to the spring semester and should have their applications in by November 1. The College adheres to the Candidates Reply Date of May 1 for the fall semester.

For further information, students should contact:

Office of Admission
Saint Michael's College
One Winooski Park, Box 7
Colchester, Vermont 05439

Phone: 800-762-8000 (toll-free)
Fax: 802-654-2906
E-mail: admission@smcvt.edu
Web site: http://www.smcvt.edu
http://www.facebook.com/SaintMichaelsCollege
http://twitter.com/SMCAdmissions

Students enjoy a sunny day on campus, with the Durick Library in the background.

ST. NORBERT COLLEGE

DE PERE, WISCONSIN

The College

A new state-of-the-art library, new apartment-style residence hall, new athletics facility, renovated student services center, new welcome center, new student union under construction, and plans to remodel science facilities—these are just a few of the exciting things happening at St. Norbert College. The riverfront campus is part of the thriving corporate, entertainment, educational, arts, and cultural environment of northeastern Wisconsin. Learning takes place in residence halls and classrooms, on campus, and, literally, around the world.

The St. Norbert learning community helps students become critical thinkers, strong writers, and able communicators, in a setting that encourages student-faculty collaborative research. The graduate-level work done by St. Norbert undergraduates, even as freshmen, is surprising and puts them ahead of their peers when heading to graduate school or the workforce.

St. Norbert seeks to challenge student viewpoints and encourage exploration of new or different ideas, in an environment where students from around the world come together in exploration of local and global perspectives.

Faculty members at St. Norbert are active researchers and creators who make ongoing contributions to their fields. They're also compassionate individuals who care not only about their students' grades, but also about their growth, making time for one-on-one conversations with students on a daily basis. Student success is their top priority, and they regularly give out their home phone numbers for easy student access.

St. Norbert College offers more than forty programs of study, including several preprofessional programs. Students can also design their own major, unique to their aspirations. Opportunities to study abroad abound, with more than seventy-five program sites in thirty-eight countries on six continents. There are also numerous service opportunities for students locally, nationally, and internationally.

Each St. Norbert student is paired with an adviser who helps ensure that the student is on track with classes and will graduate in four years. St. Norbert's innovative career services office provides service throughout the college years and beyond; the alumni career network can help students find their first job as well as their last one. When St. Norbert students are surveyed nine months after graduation, 95 percent of them are typically employed or attending graduate school.

Student life offers a blend of learning and fun. Students flourish within the academically challenging environment, but with more than sixty-five clubs and organizations on campus, there's no shortage of ways to become involved outside the classroom. The twenty Division III athletic teams produce conference champions, national champions, and more Academic All-Americans than any school in the Midwest Conference.

Students frequently comment on the sense of community and worldwide opportunities available at St. Norbert. They talk about the challenges of the classroom and the heartfelt rewards of the service opportunities. Graduates value the friendships with peers and faculty members that started at St. Norbert and may last a lifetime. Some students love the campus so much they refer to St. Norbert as their home.

Location

The St. Norbert campus, approximately 93 acres, is located on the banks of the Fox River in De Pere, Wisconsin, just minutes south of Green Bay, a metropolitan area of about 230,000 people and home to the world champion Green Bay Packers football team. Rich culture, arts, and entertainment are present in historic De Pere and the greater Green Bay area, recognized as one of the 100 best communities for young people by America's Promise Alliance. Located near the gateway to Door County, one of Wisconsin's favorite vacation spots, the campus is part of a vibrant eighteen-county region of 1.2 million people.

Majors and Degrees

St. Norbert offers programs leading to the Bachelor of Arts, Bachelor of Science, Bachelor of Music, and Bachelor of Business Administration degrees. Students also have the opportunity of applying their education at St. Norbert toward any of three master's degree programs: the Master of Science in Education, Master of Arts in Liberal Studies, and Master of Theological Studies.

St. Norbert College has partnered with several other institutions to further extend its offerings. Students can earn a nursing degree through a partnership with Bellin College in Green Bay; complete an engineering degree in four years through a partnership with Michigan Tech; or earn a master's degree in applied economics in just one additional year, rather than two, through a partnership with Marquette University.

Programs of study at St. Norbert include: accounting, American studies, anthropology, art–fine arts, art–graphic design, biology–biomedical, biology–organismal, business administration, chemistry, chemistry–biochemistry, classical studies, communication and media studies, computer science, computer science–business information systems, computer science–graphic design and implementation, economics, education, English, English–creative writing, environmental science, French, geography, geology, German, history, human services (social work), international business and language area studies, international studies, Japanese, leadership studies, mathematics, military science/ROTC, music, natural sciences, peace and justice, Philippine studies, philosophy, physics, political science, predental, pre-engineering, prelaw, premedical, prepharmacy, pre-veterinary, psychology, religious studies, religious studies–youth ministry, sociology, Spanish, teacher education, theater studies, and women's and gender studies.

Academic Programs

Degrees are awarded upon the successful completion of thirty-two courses (128 semester hours) that include an approved major sequence, course work in general education, and either an academic minor or electives. Academic majors can be started as early as the first semester of the freshman year. Early selection of a major is encouraged but not required in most majors. Students are not required to officially declare a major until the end of the sophomore year. The College offers a four-year graduation guarantee in all but two academic programs, and has the highest four-year graduation rate in Wisconsin.

The College's goal is to educate students broadly, regardless of major. Competence in writing and quantitative skills is required of all graduates. An honors program offers additional challenge in areas of general education to those of superior ability, and an honors degree is awarded to those who successfully complete the program.

Army ROTC is available and several St. Norbert students are recipients of full Army ROTC scholarships each year. Among the College's alumni are an impressive 11 Army generals who completed ROTC at St. Norbert.

Off-Campus Programs

St. Norbert students, regardless of major, can spend a summer, a semester, or a year abroad. The College has more than seventy-five study-abroad program sites in thirty-eight countries on six continents. Students completing liberal arts majors are encouraged to spend at least a semester abroad. An international study component is a part of majors in French, Spanish, and German, and both the international business program and the international studies major. All approved international study carries regular academic credit. St. Norbert scholarship assistance and other financial aid carry over to overseas study.

St. Norbert considers international experience vital to today's graduates and it is a key component of the college's educational mission. Study-abroad opportunities include a Third World science field trip; exchange programs in Australia, France, Japan, Germany, the Philippines, Spain, and Ukraine; student teaching in Europe, Africa, Australia, and Latin America; and other study sites throughout Europe,

South America, and Egypt. St. Norbert's international curriculum, taught by a faculty committed to global learning, prepares students to live in a global society. A Washington semester is also available through American University in Washington, D.C.

Additional service-learning opportunities are available throughout the year. Students can participate in the TRIPS (Turning Responsibility into Powerful Service) program in local, national, and international locations, or participate in a variety of other off-campus service opportunities.

Academic Facilities

A new $20-million state-of-the-art library opened in the fall of 2009. It houses more than 247,000 volumes, including books, journals and other serials, microforms, maps, and charts. More than 3,000 volumes are added to the collection each year. The 80,000-square-foot library features enhanced technology, flexible study and classroom spaces, and a welcome center with computers, media players, and a 24-hour computer study area.

The F. K. Bemis International Center provides students with opportunities to prepare for careers with greater international emphasis. Students from more than thirty countries attend St. Norbert College annually and 32 percent of each class studies abroad. The center also serves as a resource for K–12 schools and Wisconsin businesses for language instruction, translation, and interpretation.

The John Minahan Science Hall houses the science programs and thirty-eight laboratories. Planning is underway for renovation and expansion of this building to facilitate current and future research and education in the natural sciences.

Austin E. Cofrin Hall houses the business administration, computer science, mathematics, and economics programs. It also holds the campus' computing resources.

Thirteen residence halls provide the link between living and learning at St. Norbert. Some residence halls focus on community service or feature campus programs, such as the Women's Center in Sensenbrenner Hall or the honors program in Bergstrom Hall. A new apartment-style residence hall offers upperclassmen a transitional experience to living on their own. Many halls have chapels for students to reflect and pray.

A new outdoor athletics complex, Schneider Stadium, provides the practice and competition venue for football, soccer, and track and field.

Costs

For 2010–11, tuition and required fees for full-time students totaled $28,043. Room costs averaged $3700 per year, and the average meal plan for full-time students cost $3670 per year.

Financial Aid

Students share in more than $47 million of financial aid each year, including scholarships and grants, campus jobs, and educational loans. St. Norbert awards $22 million of its own scholarships and grants annually. There are both need-based and merit-based awards.

Wisconsin residents who show need can qualify for assistance provided by the state through the Wisconsin Tuition Grant Program. The College participates in the Federal Supplemental Educational Opportunity Grant, Federal Perkins Loan, and Federal Work-Study programs.

Need-based awards are made on the basis of the Free Application for Federal Student Aid (FAFSA; St. Norbert College's code is 003892) and the St. Norbert College institutional application for financial aid. Freshman applicants should submit these forms by March of their senior year of high school.

A multitude of work-study positions exists on campus, and students have paid internship opportunities on campus as well as in the community at Fortune 500 companies, hospitals, schools, or service organizations.

Faculty

The St. Norbert faculty is composed of 196 men and women, 135 of whom are full-time. At least 88 percent of the full-time faculty members hold the doctoral or other terminal degree in their field. The student-faculty ratio is approximately 14:1, and student success is a top priority of the faculty. They work closely with students in their major area of study, help students prepare for graduate school, write letters of recommendation, and work with those who seek independent study and research opportunities. Two-year research fellowships with faculty members are available to first-year students, who may ultimately have the opportunity to present their research findings collaboratively with faculty members at national conferences. Faculty members also work with Career Services in its professional practice program.

Student Government

The College's Student Government Association (SGA) is active on campus, with representation extending as far as the college's board of trustees. The president of the College and his cabinet respect the voice of the student body, and openly discuss issues that impact students and the college community. The SGA meets regularly and holds town-hall meetings for the campus community. Its goal is to serve as a representative governing body and to create an environment conducive to intellectual, spiritual, and personal growth throughout the campus community.

Admission Requirements

The College welcomes enrollment from a diverse group of students who are prepared academically and who will make a contribution to the St. Norbert living and learning community. Every completed application is considered carefully and students who are likely to succeed in this environment are accepted. In 2010, more than 87 percent of the freshman class ranked in the top half of their high school senior class, the average GPA was 3.5, and the average ACT composite score was 25. Students with superior scores and grades are invited to enroll in the honors program.

Application and Information

Because the College gives preference to students according to the date of admission and enrollment deposit, it benefits students to apply as early as possible in their senior year. Notification of the admission decision is made on a rolling basis beginning in late September. A $350 deposit is required to confirm enrollment. For more information about St. Norbert College, students should contact:

Executive Director of Enrollment
St. Norbert College
100 Grant Street
De Pere, Wisconsin 54115
Phone: 920-403-3005
        800-236-4878 (toll-free)
E-mail: admit@snc.edu
Web site: http://www.snc.edu
          http://www.snc.edu/go/socialmedia

The riverfront Campus Center is a favorite place for students to hang out, grab a bite to eat, study, work out, or relax on the St. Norbert campus.

ST. THOMAS AQUINAS COLLEGE
SPARKILL, NEW YORK

The College

St. Thomas Aquinas College (STAC) was founded in 1952 as a three-year teacher-training college with 30 students. Today, the College offers over 100 different majors, minors, specializations, and dual degree programs and has a total student body of 2,700 in all programs, on and off campus. Much growth and development has taken place over the College's history. The College offers a Master of Science in Education, with concentrations in literacy education, special education, and educational leadership as well as postgraduate certificate programs in literacy and special education. The College also offers a Master of Business Administration (M.B.A.) program with concentrations in finance, management, and marketing; and an online M.B.A. in general studies. St. Thomas offers a Master of Science in Teaching program for individuals without a background in teacher education who are seeking a career change. Certification is offered in childhood education, grades 1–6; childhood education and special education, grades 1–6; and adolescence education, grades 7–12. The College is home to New York University's Master in Social Work program.

The College's most dramatic growth has occurred to meet the challenges of the twenty-first century. Capital improvements continue to be made and new facilities added, so that the main campus now consists of twenty-four buildings on 48 acres. The suburban campus includes two residential complexes: Aquinas Village, which consists of self-contained townhouse units that house 300 students, and the McNelis Commons, which consists of townhouse residential units that house 375 students and a common dining hall and laundry building. Approximately 40 percent of the College's full-time student population resides on campus.

Extracurricular activities are provided through forty different organizations, including the Spartan Volunteers, a community service program; a student-run radio station (WSTK); the Laetare Players dramatic and musical club; and the student-edited campus newspaper and yearbook. The College has excellent sports facilities, and several of its athletic teams have competed in national championships. The College fields NCAA Division II teams in men's and women's cross-country, golf, indoor track and field, and tennis; women's basketball, lacrosse, soccer, and softball; and men's baseball, basketball, and soccer. There are a number of club sports including equestrian, ice hockey, cheerleading and dance, bowling, and ski and snowboarding, as well as intramural athletics.

The College has a campus ministry office, a health office, and residence life, career placement, and counseling services.

Location

The College is located in Sparkill, a hamlet in southern Rockland County, New York, 16 miles north of New York City and adjacent to Bergen County, New Jersey.

Majors and Degrees

St. Thomas Aquinas College's Business Administration division offers accounting (and accounting as a dual degree with an M.B.A. degree), business administration, finance, and marketing. Minors are offered in business administration, marketing, economics, human resource management, international business, and management information systems. Specializations are in management relations/industrial and organizational psychology.

The Humanities division offers degrees in art therapy, art and graphic design, communication arts, English, philosophy and religious studies, Romance languages, and Spanish. Minors include communication arts, journalism, performing arts, public relations, Spanish, art therapy, fine arts, religious studies, and writing.

The Natural Sciences and Mathematics division offers mathematics, computer and information sciences, biology, forensic science, medical technology, and natural sciences. There are specializations in biology, chemistry, and physics.

The Social Sciences division offers criminal justice, psychology, sports management, therapeutic recreation, social science, and history.

The Teacher Education division offers programs in grades 1–6 childhood education, the same plus special education, and grades 7–12 adolescence education, the latter offering certification in biology, English, history, mathematics, science and technology, natural science with either biology or chemistry, social sciences, and Spanish. In addition, there is a middle school extension that adds to either the elementary or secondary degree, enabling the student to certify for all middle school grades.

The College offers a five-year dual-degree program in mathematics/engineering with the George Washington University (GWU) or Manhattan College. Students study at St. Thomas for three years. After completion of their final two years at either GWU or Manhattan, they earn a B.S. in mathematics from STAC and a B.S. in engineering from one of the other two institutions. The College also offers several dual-degree options in biology: a dual degree in biology (B.S. from STAC) and biomedical engineering (M.S. from Polytechnic University), a dual degree in biology (B.S. from STAC) and physical therapy (D.P.T. from New York Medical College), a dual degree in biology (B.S. from STAC) and chiropractic (D.C. from New York Chiropractic College), and a dual degree in biology (B.S. from STAC) and podiatry (D.P.M. from New York College of Podiatric Medicine). There are several other strategic alliances, such as preferred admission to St. John's University School of Law in New York and a similar program with Barry University School of Law in Florida that includes scholarship funds. St. Thomas seeks out additional strategic opportunities for its undergraduate and graduate students on a regular basis; students should contact the College for information about new alliances.

Academic Programs

The College strives to develop students who are not only generally educated but also possess advanced knowledge in specialized areas, are prepared for further study, and have the background to undertake fulfilling careers. To earn a bachelor's degree, students must complete a total of 120 semester hours, including a minimum of 51 credits in a core curriculum; complete all requirements for the specific major; and complete the final 30 hours at St. Thomas. The College awards up to 30 credits for life experience and up to 30 credits for achievement on the College-Level Examination Program (CLEP). The College operates on a semester calendar (quarterly on the M.B.A. level). Students may enroll in classes in the fall, winter (a one-month session), spring, and summer (three separate sessions). Classes are scheduled during the day and evening, and students are permitted considerable academic flexibility in planning their programs.

Students can pursue independent study and internships, and many majors require a field practicum. The College maintains an active Center for Academic Excellence as a resource for enhancing academic performance, and students are encouraged to meet regularly with faculty advisers for academic guidance and career direction.

Several programs supplement the traditional academic areas. The College has a widely recognized program for college-age learning-disabled students, called the Pathways Program (at an additional cost). The College also participates in the New York State Higher Education Opportunity Program for economically and academically disadvantaged students and provides an Honors Program for exceptionally qualified students with a limited number of full-tuition-scholarships. The Honors Program includes summer study at Oxford University.

Off-Campus Programs

The College offers a campus interchange program involving three other fully accredited colleges (Barry University in Miami Shores, Florida; Dominican College of San Rafael in San Rafael, California; and Aquinas College in Grand Rapids, Michigan) through which a student may attend a semester at one of the participating colleges during the junior year. The College also offers a number of study-abroad opportunities for students throughout the entire year with as short a period as one week for a communication arts class in London.

The study-abroad program provides opportunities at colleges and universities in such places as Brazil, Canada, England, France, Hungary, Ireland, Italy, Morocco, and Spain. Several other locations are also available.

The College offers courses for an associate degree program at West Point for eligible students at the United States Military Academy.

Academic Facilities

The College's most dramatic growth occurred during the last decade as it modernized to meet the challenges of the twenty-first century. Costello Hall houses the science laboratories, technology theaters, and Azarian-McCullough Art Gallery. Spellman Hall houses a multiroom technology corridor with a state-of-the-art communication studio, and technology and language labs. Lougheed Library provides a variety of online research opportunities for students. Aquinas Hall houses athletic facilities and a new fitness center. Maguire Hall is home to classrooms, art studios, and the Sullivan Theater, and the newest building set to open in fall 2011 will house a variety of state-of-the-art classrooms as well as administrative offices. Additional meeting areas are provided in the Romano Student-Alumni Center and in the two residence complexes, McNelis Commons and Aquinas Village. There is an after hours club in the McNelis Commons dining hall for student activities and includes a wide-screen television.

Costs

For 2011–12, the tuition for full-time study (12 to 16 credits per semester) is $23,220. Room and board at the College Commons are $10,600. Certain studio, laboratory, and computer courses carry fees.

Financial Aid

In 2010–11, 80 percent of the student body received financial aid. The College is committed to providing competent but needy students with the resources necessary to continue their education. Students must submit the Free Application for Federal Student Aid each year. The College awards academic and merit scholarships from $5,000 up to full tuition scholarships and provides need-based aid from the College as well as athletic grants and all federal and New York State aid programs.

St. Thomas strives to partner with the student to make college education affordable. The College has one of the lowest private college tuition rates in New York State, and scholarships make it even more affordable. The College is also a member of the Yellow Ribbon program for veterans enabling a qualified veteran to study with a full tuition scholarship.

Faculty

The faculty has 70 full-time and 55 part-time members; 80 percent have terminal degrees. The student-faculty ratio is 17:1. All faculty members participate in the academic advising of students and serve on College committees. Many serve as advisers to extracurricular activities.

Student Government

The Student Government consists of elected members who officially represent the student body, are responsible for planning and implementing student-originated programs, and coordinate and oversee all extracurricular organizations. Through its various offices, students play a vital part in offering consultation on new policies, planning social and cultural events, managing student funds, and operating the judicial system. In addition, the All-College Forum, which is composed of elected students, faculty members, alumni, administrators, and trustees, meets regularly to discuss policies, procedures, long-range plans, and any problems affecting the College.

Admission Requirements

All applicants must have successfully completed an approved secondary school program or the equivalent, including 4 years in English, 3 years in mathematics, 3 years in science, 3 years of foreign language, and 4 years of social studies. Applicants whose high school background varies from the recommended pattern are considered if they demonstrate interest and ability. Freshman applicants must submit the application for admission, including an essay, high school transcripts, SAT or ACT scores, and their guidance counselor's recommendation. Transfer students must submit the application and official transcripts of all previous college work. An academic evaluation is prepared for every matriculant.

Application and Information

Candidates should submit completed application forms to the Admissions and Financial Aid Office and must request that their official transcripts be sent to the Admissions Office from their school. Students are notified of the admission decision on a rolling basis upon receipt of all the necessary credentials. The College is a member of the Common Application and students can find the link to apply on its Web site, http://www.stac.edu.

The College does not discriminate against students, faculty and staff members, and other beneficiaries on the basis of race, color, national origin, gender, age, sexual orientation, disability, marital status, genetic predisposition, carrier status, veteran status, or religious affiliation in admission to or in the provision of its programs and services. The Section 504 Coordinator, the Title IX Coordinator, and the Age Act Coordinator is the Executive Director of Human Resources, Marian Hall, 845-398-4038.

For more information or an application, students should contact:

Admissions and Financial Aid Office
St. Thomas Aquinas College
125 Route 340
Sparkill, New York 10976-1050
Phone: 800-999-STAC (toll-free)
Web site: http://www.stac.edu

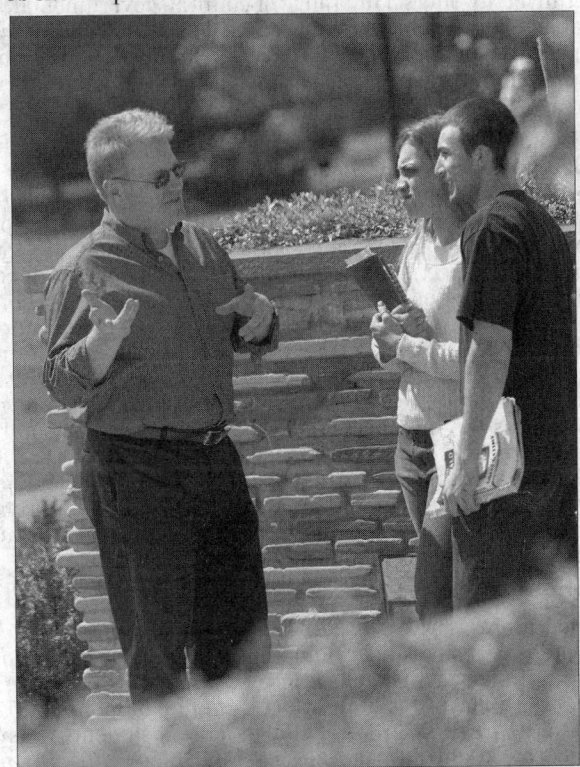

A view of the campus at St. Thomas Aquinas College.

ST. THOMAS UNIVERSITY

MIAMI, FLORIDA

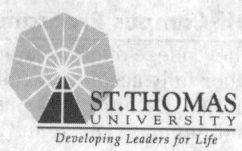

The University

Founded in 1961 by the Augustinian Order of Villanova, Pennsylvania, at the invitation of the late Most Reverend Coleman F. Carroll, the Archbishop of Miami, St. Thomas University has grown from an institution with an initial enrollment of 45 students to become one of Florida's most comprehensive Catholic coeducational universities, with more than 2,500 students in all programs of study. Founded originally as Biscayne College, the institution achieved university status in 1984 and changed its name to St. Thomas University. The University is sponsored by the Archdiocese of Miami and is accredited by the Southern Association of Colleges and Schools. At present, the undergraduate student population represents thirty-five states, the District of Columbia, Puerto Rico, the Virgin Islands, and sixty-five countries. Fifty-nine percent of the undergraduates are women; 20 percent of the undergraduates reside on campus.

The University is located in northwest Miami on a 140-acre campus with fifteen major buildings. The Student Center contains a student lounge, a bookstore, the rathskeller, and other facilities. Adjacent to the University's two dormitories are the dining hall and the University Inn.

Sports facilities include six tennis courts, a recreational swimming pool, two basketball courts, four baseball fields, and a soccer field. As a member of the NAIA, St. Thomas supports men's varsity teams in baseball, golf, soccer, and tennis; women's varsity teams in fast-pitch softball, golf, soccer, tennis, and volleyball; and men's and women's teams in basketball and cross-country.

The University offers a full range of cultural, governmental, and social activities, including publications and clubs. The Office of Campus Ministry provides liturgical celebrations in the University chapel and sponsors social justice and community service activities.

St. Thomas University offers a Master of Business Administration (M.B.A.); Master of International Business; Master of Science (M.S.) in educational administration, guidance and counseling, management, marriage and family therapy, mental health counseling, special education, and sports administration; Master of Accounting (M.Acc.); and Master of Arts (M.A.) degrees in communication arts and pastoral ministry. In addition, St. Thomas offers a Ph.D. in practical theology and an Ed.D. in educational leadership. The Ambassador Nicholas H. Morley Law Center was established in 1984 with a charter class of 160 students. St. Thomas University School of Law offers the Juris Doctor degree (J.D.) and is the only accredited Catholic law school south of Georgetown University's law school in Washington, D.C. The School of Law and the Graduate Studies Office offer four joint degree programs, including an M.B.A./J.D. in accounting and international business and an M.S./J.D. in marriage and family counseling and sports administration.

Location

Located midway between Fort Lauderdale and downtown Miami, the University is near numerous cultural and recreational facilities. In fact, St. Thomas is located approximately 1½ miles south of Pro Player Stadium, which is home to the Miami Dolphins. The area's subtropical climate allows students to enjoy the nearby Atlantic Ocean beaches and many other natural attractions, such as the Florida Keys, Everglades National Park, and state and county parks, throughout the year. A short drive from campus are Key Biscayne, Bal Harbor, Miami Beach, Fort Lauderdale, and other cities of Florida's Gold Coast. The city of Miami and surrounding Dade County, known as the "Gateway to South America," house an international banking and trade center and offer a truly cosmopolitan atmosphere.

Majors and Degrees

St. Thomas University awards the Bachelor of Arts (B.A.) or Bachelor of Business Administration (B.B.A.) degree through day and evening programs in twenty-eight major fields of study: accounting, biology, business management, communication arts, computer information systems, computer science, criminal justice, elementary education, English, environmental justice, finance, forensic science, global leadership, history, human services, international business, liberal studies, marketing, nursing (a 2+2 program with the University of Miami), pre-engineering (a 2+2 program with the Florida International University), political science, psychology, religious studies, secondary education (social studies), sports administration, and tourism and hospitality management. St. Thomas also offers a minor in environmental studies; preprofessional programs, which include dentistry, law, medicine, and veterinary studies; a joint B.A./J.D. program with the School of Law; and courses in French, humanities, Italian, philosophy, and South Florida regional studies.

Academic Programs

The University's academic calendar consists of two 15-week semesters, beginning in early September and in mid-January, along with two 6-week summer sessions.

To receive a bachelor's degree, students must complete at least 120 semester credits with a minimum grade point average of 2.0 overall and an average of at least 2.25 in their academic major; 30 of the last 36 semester credit hours must be earned and at least half of a student's academic major courses must be taken at St. Thomas University. All students must fulfill the general core education requirements of 42 semester credits, which include courses in English, humanities/foreign language, history, social science, mathematics/physical science, philosophy, and religious studies. An honors program is offered to qualified students to provide them with an interesting, stimulating, alternative way of fulfilling some or all of the University's general education requirements. The normal full-time academic load is 15 semester credit hours, but the load may range between 12 and 18 credit hours per semester. To graduate, all students must take an area of concentration or an academic major. A student may enter as an exploratory or undecided student but, with the assistance of a faculty adviser or a division chairperson, must declare his or her academic major by the second semester of the sophomore year.

Special academic features at the University include the Academic Support Center, Institute for Pastoral Ministries, summer school, and study abroad.

Off-Campus Programs

Internships are available in selected academic majors. A cooperative education program is also available. In addition, qualified students may participate in the Semester Abroad Program in Spain.

Academic Facilities

The 50,000-square-foot library houses a 145,000-volume book collection, 850 periodicals, a reference room, a technical processing area, a convocation hall that seats 600 people, four seminar rooms for small classes and group study, and a Media Center with two screening rooms, a video studio, and an audio-visual laboratory with individually wired carrels. Kennedy Hall, the University's main academic center, includes administrative offices, classrooms, science laboratories, the Academic Support Center, the chapel, and a computer lab.

Costs

Tuition for the 2010–11 academic year was $22,770 ($759 per undergraduate semester credit hour), and room and board costs were $8000 for a double room and $15,600 for a single room. Insurance, which is mandatory for all resident students, was estimated at $942 for the year. These costs do not include books, supplies, travel, and personal expenses and are subject to change.

Financial Aid

The University has established a financial aid program to assist as many students as possible. University scholarships and grants, along with federally funded scholarships, grants, loans, and work-study awards, are allocated in a financial aid package according to a student's financial need. Currently, about 90 percent of the University's students receive financial aid which encompasses need-based grants and institutional scholarships. To be eligible for any scholarship or financial aid program, an applicant should complete a Free Application for Federal Student Aid (FAFSA) with the Department of Education. The filing deadline for University financial aid funds is April 1. Applicants should indicate affirmatively on the FAFSA that their information may be forwarded from the U.S. Department of Education in order to be considered for any state grants for which they may be eligible. The application deadline for need-based state financial aid programs is April 1.

Florida applicants who have resided in Florida for the prior twelve consecutive months are eligible to be awarded a Florida Resident Access Grant to attend a private four-year college or university in Florida. The funds for the Florida Resident Grant Program are dependent upon yearly appropriations from the Florida legislature. These funds are outright grants and are not based on financial need.

Faculty

The St. Thomas University faculty is a teaching faculty that is dedicated to furthering the academic and personal growth of students. The undergraduate student-faculty ratio is 14:1. Faculty-student interaction is a hallmark of the University because classes are small and because members of the faculty are available outside the classroom. Faculty members also participate in the academic advisement program to give students individual academic guidance, and they serve as advisers to student clubs and organizations.

Student Government

The Undergraduate Student Government Association, of which all full-time undergraduates are members, provides students with the opportunity to become involved in representative government. This democratic body is governed by elected student officers who serve on the Administrative Council and by representatives from each class who compose the Student Assembly. The association also assists in planning a varied program of social and cultural activities. In addition, students are represented on key committees throughout the University community. The Resident Council, consisting of representatives from each of the four dormitories, voices the concerns of residential students and is involved in the planning and implementation of University policies regarding residential life.

Admission Requirements

St. Thomas University seeks academically prepared students who are eager to improve themselves intellectually, socially, and spiritually within the University community. The Admissions Committee evaluates applicants individually in light of personal accomplishments, motivation, and the academic major selected. The committee places primary emphasis on the secondary school record, SAT or ACT scores, class rank, a personal interview, a recommended 250- to 300-word personal essay, and a recommendation from a teacher or guidance counselor. The committee does not discriminate against applicants on the basis of race, sex, religion, or national origin; in fact, the University welcomes diversity. Applicants for most divisions must have earned 16 units from an accredited high school in a college-preparatory program that included 4 years of English, 2 years of mathematics, 2 years of social studies, 1 year of science, 1 year of a foreign language or computer elective, and six electives; applicants for the Division of Science must have earned 17 units, including 3 years of mathematics (including trigonometry) and 3 years of science, but they need have only four electives. All international applicants for either freshman or transfer entrance must also submit letters of financial guarantee.

The University offers deferred admission and dual enrollment. It also gives credit and advanced placement for scores of 3 or better on the Advanced Placement examinations of the College Board. Credit is also awarded for successful scores on both the general and subject tests of the College Board's College-Level Examination Program.

Transfer applicants should be in good academic standing with a GPA of at least 2.5 and not be on disciplinary or academic probation at their former college. The University grants junior-year status to any admitted transfer student graduating from a Florida community college with an Associate of Arts degree. Transfer applicants must submit official transcripts from each of their previous colleges.

Application and Information

To facilitate the admission and financial aid processes, students should submit applications during the fall or winter of their senior year in high school and have all supporting material forwarded directly to the University's Undergraduate Admissions Office. Application for entrance as a resident student for the fall semester should be filed by May 15; for entrance as a commuting student, by August 1. Application for the spring semester should be made by December 15. The University operates with a policy of rolling admissions; beginning December 15, applicants for the fall semester are notified of the admission decision within a three-week period provided that all appropriate information has been received. The University adheres to the College Board's Candidates Reply Date of May 1 and does not require a tuition deposit or a room reservation deposit until May 1 in order to allow students ample opportunity to select the college or university of their choice. Dormitory space, however, is limited and is assigned in the order that room reservation deposits are received.

For further information, students should contact:

St. Thomas University
Office of Admissions
Kennedy Hall
16401 Northwest 37th Avenue
Miami Gardens, Florida 33054
Phone: 305-628-6546
 800-367-9010 (toll-free outside Florida)
 800-367-9006 (toll-free in Florida)
Fax: 305-628-6591
E-mail: signup@stu.edu
Web site: http://www.stu.edu

SALISBURY UNIVERSITY
SALISBURY, MARYLAND

The University

A Maryland University of National Distinction, Salisbury University (SU) consistently ranks in the top 10 percent of public and private institutions in national guidebooks and magazines. A member of the University System of Maryland (USM), SU emphasizes undergraduate research, study abroad, professional internships, and community engagement as pillars of its academic programs.

A midsize university of 7,706 undergraduates and 388 full-time faculty members on a 182-acre campus, SU provides a private college feel with the opportunities and affordability of a public institution. This distinct combination is why 98 percent of recent graduates say they would recommend SU. The foundation of SU's success is the relationship between students and professors. Full professors serve as undergraduate advisers, and routinely lead students on trips and retreats, from exploring the Chesapeake Bay to touring Europe. Their professional concern for educating the whole student has had measurable results. According to the latest figures, SU has the fastest time-to-degree average and the highest four-year graduation rate of all comprehensive institutions in the USM. This success has not gone unnoticed. For the fourteenth consecutive year, SU is among *U.S. News & World Report*'s Top Public Universities in the North, one of the highest-placing public master's-level universities in Maryland. The Princeton Review's guides and *Kiplinger's Personal Finance* magazine, respectively, have named SU among the top 50 and top 100 best value public colleges in the nation.

Salisbury students come from twenty-seven states, the District of Columbia, and fifty-eight other countries. Some 60 percent are from Maryland's western shore (which contains the Metropolitan Baltimore-Washington corridor). Many of SU's 100-plus student organizations and clubs find a home in the Guerrieri University Center. An NCAA Division III member of intercollegiate athletics, SU has twenty-one varsity sports that compete in the Capital Athletic Conference and in the Atlantic Central Football Conference. Women's sports are basketball, cross-country, field hockey, lacrosse, soccer, softball, swimming, tennis, indoor and outdoor track and field, and volleyball. Men's sports are baseball, basketball, cross-country, football, lacrosse, soccer, swimming, tennis, and indoor and outdoor track and field. The Sea Gulls have won fourteen national championships, eight in men's lacrosse, five in field hockey, and one in women's lacrosse. One of the leading Division III programs, for the tenth time in school history, Salisbury athletics have been ranked in the top 25 of the national Directors' Cup standings. Nearly half of the student body participates in twenty-two intramural programs and fourteen additional sports clubs.

The University has three art galleries; supports film and distinguished lecture series and artist-in-residence programs; maintains WSCL/WSDL-FM (national public radio affiliates) and WXSU-FM (a student-run radio station); offers performing arts disciplines in music, theater, and dance; and serves as the home of the Salisbury Symphony Orchestra. Beyond the campus are Maryland's scenic Eastern Shore, the pleasures of Ocean City, Maryland (a nearby popular beach resort), and the activities of an energetic Outdoor Club. Faculty members lead trips abroad during spring break, and winter and summer terms.

Location

With a population of roughly 94,000, metropolitan Salisbury is the cultural and economic hub of Delmarva (containing portions of Delaware, Maryland, and Virginia), a historically and ecologically rich peninsula located between the Atlantic Ocean and Chesapeake Bay. The city is 30 minutes west of the white beaches of Assateague and Ocean City, Maryland; approximately 2 hours from Baltimore, Wilmington, Norfolk, and Washington, D.C.; and 4½ hours from New York City.

Majors and Degrees

Three undergraduate degrees are offered in addition to the Bachelor of Arts and Bachelor of Science: the Bachelor of Arts in Social Work (B.A.S.W.), the Bachelor of Science in Nursing (B.S.N.), and the Bachelor of Fine Arts (B.F.A.) in art. B.A. degrees are awarded in art, communication arts, conflict analysis and dispute resolution, economics, English, English for speakers of other languages, environmental studies, fine arts, French, history, interdisciplinary studies, international studies, music, philosophy, political science, psychology, sociology, Spanish, social work, and theater. Bachelor of Science degrees are awarded in accounting, athletic training, biology, business administration, chemistry, clinical laboratory science/medical technology, computer science, early childhood education, elementary education, exercise science, finance, geography and geosciences, health education, interdisciplinary studies, management, management information systems, marketing, mathematics, nursing, physical education, physics, and respiratory therapy.

The University also offers fourteen graduate programs.

Academic Programs

At Salisbury University, majors are designed to educate the whole student. No false distinctions are made between the liberal arts and the professions. While gaining a liberal education, for example, students in preprofessional programs prepare for careers in dentistry, law, medicine, optometry, pharmacy, physical therapy, podiatry, and veterinary science. Certification programs train educators for both elementary and secondary teaching. Dual-degree programs with the University of Maryland Eastern Shore (UMES) enable students to earn two bachelor's degrees in four years in biology/environmental marine science and social work/sociology. SU, UMES, and the University of Maryland College Park also collaborate on an electrical engineering degree. SU supports an Army Reserve Officers' Training Corps (ROTC) program on campus. Both the graduate and the undergraduate programs of SU's business school are accredited by The Association to Advance Collegiate Schools of Business and the Network of International Business Schools. Other national accreditations are in chemistry, education, allied health (respiratory therapy, exercise science, and athletic training programs), social work, clinical laboratory science (medical technology program), music, and nursing and through the Middle States Commission on Higher Education.

SU's fifty-six academic programs are administered through four schools: the Franklin P. Perdue School of Business, the Samuel W. and Marilyn C. Seidel School of Education and Professional Studies, the Charles R. and Martha N. Fulton School of Liberal Arts, and the Richard A. Henson School of Science and Technology. All four schools are endowed, a rarity among public institutions nationwide. These endowments have enriched the scholastic climate of the campus, providing expanded scholarships, resources, and opportunities.

University planning encourages interdisciplinary study. Students in all majors must take a minimum of nine courses in three disciplines: history, humanities and social sciences, and mathematical and natural sciences. Two courses are required in English composition and literature. All courses, from science to business to music, require written assignments in analysis/criticism, research, or creative writing.

SU's advising system has been praised by students in a Maryland Higher Education Commission survey as one of the best in the state. Exceptional orientation programs help freshmen make a successful transition to college. SU's New Student Seminars offer an orientation-in-the-wilderness experience, which won the Maryland Association for Higher Education Distinguished Program Award. Orientation options include cycling in Maine and canoeing in Canada.

Incoming students may earn credit through Advanced Placement and departmental challenge examinations and the College-Level Examination Program (CLEP) for nontraditional educational experiences. Internships have included work abroad, legislative service in Washington, D.C. and Annapolis, and media experience in fields from fine arts to television. Students who relish intellectual challenge are invited to join the honors program housed in the Thomas E. Bellavance Honors Center. Others present research at national and international conferences. SU is also the only university in Maryland to twice host the National Conference on Undergraduate Research. Study-abroad programs are popular. Education students teach in New Zealand, nursing students provide aid in Africa, and all students may enroll in new Salisbury Abroad programs in Ecuador, Estonia, China, and Spain for the same cost as tuition, room, and board in Maryland.

Academic Facilities

The SU campus is in the midst of an extensive transformation. Sea Gull Square, a new 600-bed residence hall and retail complex, is scheduled to open by fall 2011, the same time as a new home for the Perdue School of Business. Also under way are multimillion-dollar renovations for older residence halls, including the addition of geothermal heating and cooling systems. The campus' first parking garage opened in fall 2009. SU is pursuing the U.S. Green Building Council's LEED Gold certification for several current projects. New in 2008 was the University Fitness Center and SU's $65-million, 165,000-square-foot Teacher Education and Technology Center, lauded as a showcase facility for education in the mid-Atlantic region. The building, with its award-winning design, was the first new-construction project on Maryland's Eastern Shore to earn LEED Silver certification. With $5.3 million in new technology equipment, it features Smart classrooms and an Integrated Media Center with a 24-track audio recording studio, 15 editing suites, a cutting-edge digital exhibition gallery, a digital photography lab and one of the few campus-based high-definition digital video production studios in the nation.

Henson Science Hall, SU's $42-million science education and research building, is one of the largest in Maryland. Blackwell Library is the main research center on campus, with more than a quarter-million books and bound periodicals and computers with access to databases, such as FirstSearch. Fourteen computer labs are part of the campus network, providing students with various software applications, e-mail, and the Internet. Resident students have network connections in their rooms and all academic and administrative buildings offer wireless Internet access. Fulton Hall is home to the fine and performing arts, and the Center for Conflict Resolution engages students in mediation efforts at home and abroad. The only institution in the USM with an endowed theater program, SU boasts three theaters for performing arts, including the acoustically lauded Holloway Hall Auditorium. Off the main campus, the Edward H. Nabb Research Center for Delmarva History and Culture is a treasure trove of information for students and visitors. SU's Ward Museum of Wildfowl Art was named one of the "10 Great Places to See American Folk Art" by *USA Today*.

Costs

Maryland residents paid undergraduate tuition and fees of $6908 for the 2010–11 academic year. Tuition for out-of-state undergraduates was $15,404. Students living on campus paid about $8200 for room and board; the figure varies, depending on the residence hall and meal plan.

Financial Aid

Financial assistance is available to students through loans, grants, scholarships, and on- and off-campus employment. The University participates in the Federal Perkins Loan, Federal Pell Grant, Federal Supplemental Educational Opportunity Grant, and Federal Work-Study and Direct Loan Programs. Numerous other forms of financial aid on the state and local levels are based exclusively on demonstrated financial need. All students who wish to apply for financial assistance must complete the Free Application for Federal Student Aid (FAFSA) by February 15. Complete details are available through the University's Admissions and Financial Aid Offices.

The University's Work Experience Program provides on-campus jobs for students. They can work up to 20 hours a week and typically earn $1500 to $2000 per semester, in positions related to their academic interest or other areas. Non-need academic scholarships for incoming freshmen are awarded on the basis of high school performance and SAT scores, if provided. Applying for admission is the initial step in applying for these scholarships.

Faculty

Faculty members at Salisbury have won national teaching, research, and leadership awards. Ninety-six percent of the tenure-track faculty members, many of whom are National Endowment for the Humanities and Fulbright professors, have the Ph.D. or other highest degree in their field. Professors not only publish but also donate countless hours to community service, thus teaching by deed as well as word. The student-professor ratio is 17:1; smaller classes are not unusual.

Student Government

Shared governance is a hallmark of campus life, and students are actively involved in all its aspects. The Student Government Association (SGA) serves as a liaison between the faculty and administration. SGA officers serve on many University committees, both administrative and academic, including the President's Advisory Team. The all-student Appropriations Board budgets activity fees to clubs and organizations. Students are encouraged to participate in events, many sponsored by the Student Organization for Activity Planning.

Admission Requirements

The University seeks to admit outstanding students who bring diverse talents, experiences, and points of view to campus. Most successful candidates for admission have earned above-average high school grades in a strong academic program and a score above the national average on the SAT or ACT. The high school record, test scores, essay, and recommendations of the high school principal and guidance counselors are considered. Interviews are not required, but applicants are encouraged to discuss programs and procedures for housing and financial aid with the staff of the Admissions and Financial Aid Offices.

The University has an SAT/ACT optional admissions policy. Applicants who have earned a weighted GPA of 3.5 or higher on a 4.0 scale have the choice of submitting a standardized test score. The SAT or ACT is required for applicants with a weighted GPA below 3.5 or who wish to be considered for University scholarships.

Transfer students must have earned at least 24 semester hours at an accredited community college or four-year college or university and have a minimum 2.0 average (on a 4.0 scale). For transfer students who have attempted fewer than 24 hours at another institution, the University's admission policy for entering freshmen applies.

Application and Information

Applications are accepted beginning September 1 for the spring and fall semesters. Applications received by November 1 for the spring semester and by January 15 for the fall semester are given the fullest attention. The University reserves the right to close admissions when the projected enrollment is met. The application is available online at http://www.salisbury.edu/apply. For further information, students should contact:

Admissions Office
Salisbury University
1200 Camden Avenue
Salisbury, Maryland 21801-6862

Phone: 410-543-6161
      888-543-0148 (toll-free)
Fax: 410-546-6016
E-mail: admissions@salisbury.edu
Web site: http://www.salisbury.edu
      http://on.fb.me/SalisburyU (Facebook)
      http://twitter.com/salisburyu

Salisbury University's Holloway Hall.

SAMFORD UNIVERSITY
BIRMINGHAM, ALABAMA

The University

Samford University is a private, comprehensive liberal arts university with high academic standards. The University's well-prepared, accessible faculty members who take time to know and interact with students are responsible for its academic reputation. Samford, which has some 4,500 students, offers a wide range of extracurricular activities diverse enough to satisfy the social, cultural, physical, and spiritual needs of all of its students. A lively Greek system; an honors program; men's and women's intramural and varsity athletics, including seventeen NCAA Division I sports; music and drama groups; an award-winning debate program; and more than 100 other interest groups bond the students and faculty members into a community of friends and scholars. Students annually come from about forty-five states and more than thirty countries. A majority of undergraduate students live on campus, enhancing the sense of school spirit and involvement. Students enjoy modern recreational facilities, including a fitness/ wellness center, concert and recital halls, a theater, an indoor pool, racquetball and tennis courts, and an indoor track. Comfortable housing, including modern apartment-style units and fraternity/sorority residence facilities, is available.

Samford University is in the top tier of the 262 national institutions in the doctoral research university category, as published by *U.S. News & World Report;* was marked as "very competitive" by *Barron's Profiles of American Colleges;* and has been selected for *Peterson's Competitive Colleges.* Four Samford professors have been named Carnegie Professor of the Year for Alabama since 1994. Samford was ranked twenty-seventh among national universities by *Forbes* in a study conducted by the Center for College Affordability and Productivity. Its programs are also included in *The Templeton Guide: Colleges that Encourage Character Development.*

Special student services include an active Career Development Center, which offers guidance in career exploration as well as ample opportunities for placement interviews, and an Academic Success Center for first-year students. Externship programs provide work experience and business contacts and can also be an excellent source of financial assistance that complements the scholarship and federal aid programs available to students.

In addition to its extensive undergraduate program, Samford University grants the following graduate degrees: Doctor of Education in educational leadership, Doctor of Ministry, Doctor of Pharmacy, Doctor of Nursing Practice, Educational Specialist, Juris Doctor, Master of Accountancy, Master of Business Administration, Master of Comparative Law, Master of Divinity, Master of Science in Environmental Management, Master of Music, Master of Music Education, Master of Science in Education, Master of Science in Nursing, and Master of Theological Studies. Several joint graduate degree programs are also available.

Location

Samford's wooded 180-acre campus, with its Georgian architecture, is one of the most beautiful in the nation. Located in the picturesque, mountainous area of Shades Valley, the campus is less than 6 miles from the heart of Birmingham, Alabama's largest city and the state's industrial, business, and cultural center. Birmingham annually hosts the Regions Charity Classic Professional Golf Association Champions Tournament and other major sports events, and attracts national entertainment acts to its civic center, historic Alabama Theater, and Oak Mountain Outdoor Amphitheater. Gulf Coast beaches to the south and ski slopes to the north can be reached within 4½ hours by car. Alabama's abundant freshwater lakes and rivers are sites for enjoyable outings. The world's largest space and rocket museum, located in Huntsville, Alabama, is also only a short drive away. One of the South's largest shopping centers, the Riverchase Galleria, is only 7 miles from the campus. Samford students enjoy the best of two worlds: a suburban setting for study, contemplation, and social enjoyment and easy access to the varied offerings of a metropolitan area.

Majors and Degrees

Samford University offers an Associate of Science (A.S.) degree in the following concentrations: administrative/community services and natural/environmental sciences.

The Bachelor of Arts (B.A.) degree is attained through the following majors: classics, communication studies, English, English (with a concentration in film studies), family studies, family studies (with a concentration in child development), fine arts, fine arts (with a concentration in graphic design), French, German, Greek, history, interior design, journalism and mass communication (with concentrations in advertising, public relations, print, and electronic journalism), Latin, music, musical theater, philosophy, philosophy and religion, physics, political science, psychology, religion, religion (with a concentration in congregational studies), sociology, Spanish, and theater. The interdisciplinary concentrations offered in the Bachelor of Arts degree are Asian studies, international relations, language and world trade (with a specialty in French, German, Spanish, or world languages), Latin American studies, and public administration.

The University's evening degree program offers the Bachelor of Science in Interdisciplinary Studies (B.S.I.S.) degree in the following concentrations: administrative/community services, counseling foundations, manager and leadership development, and liberal studies.

The Bachelor of Music (B.M.) degree is offered in the following majors: church music, music, music education (instrumental, vocal, and choral), music theory/composition, musical theater, performance (instrumental, organ, piano, and voice), and performance with a pedagogy emphasis (piano).

Students can earn a Bachelor of Science (B.S.) degree through the following majors: athletic training, biochemistry, biology, biology (with an emphasis in marine science), chemistry, computer science, engineering and mathematics (dual degree), engineering and physics (dual degree), engineering physics, environmental science, exercise science, fine arts, fine arts (with a concentration in graphic design), fitness and health promotion, fitness and health promotion/nutrition and dietetics (dual major), geography, mathematics, music, nutrition and dietetics, physics, and sports medicine (premedicine). The interdisciplinary concentrations offered in the B.S. degree are biochemistry and environmental science/geographic information science.

The University offers the Bachelor of Science in Business Administration (B.S.B.A.) in accounting, economics, entrepreneurship, finance, management, and marketing (all with concentrations available in international business or social entrepreneurship).

The Bachelor of Science in Education (B.S.E.) is attained through the following majors: early childhood/special education/elementary/ collaborative teacher education, English/language arts education, history/social science education, physical education, physical education (with athletic training option), P–12 education, secondary education, and teacher education.

The University offers the Bachelor of Science in Nursing (B.S.N.) in the nursing major.

Various preprofessional programs are offered, including dentistry, engineering, law, medicine, optometry, pharmacy, and veterinary medicine.

The Degree with Honors is available to students whose academic achievement is remarkable.

Academic Programs

In order to graduate, students must complete a minimum of 128 semester credits with an average grade of C or better. Six courses make up the core curriculum: Cultural Perspectives I and II, Communication Arts I and II, Biblical Perspectives, and Concepts of Fitness and Health. The curriculum is designed to address ideas and issues that cross the usual disciplinary boundaries and to help students actively engage in learning rather than simply memorizing notes for an exam. The core is also designed to promote a global perspective, recognizing the influence and achievement of many cultures.

Students also complete several education courses to prepare them for work in a major field and/or to help them experience the sciences, the social sciences, the humanities, and the fine arts.

At least 40 credits must be earned in junior- and senior-level courses. At least 50 percent of credits must be earned at Samford. Between the end of the sophomore year and graduation, undergraduates (including transfer students) must pass a writing proficiency test.

The new University Fellows program is a highly selective, academically rigorous, honors program that includes a focus on great texts and a study abroad opportunity in the sophomore year.

Off-Campus Programs

The international studies program at Samford's Daniel House Study Centre in London, England, or a variety of other locations (Austria, Canada, China, Costa Rica, Ecuador, France, Germany, Greece, Italy, Japan, Mexico, Peru, Portugal, Russia, Spain, and Switzerland) offers opportunities to develop a broad worldview.

Academic Facilities

The Harwell Goodwin Davis Library furnishes the facilities and materials necessary for reference, research, and independent study. Its reading areas with individual carrels provide ideal working conditions for Samford students. The open-stack system allows students easy access to a collection of more than 1 million volumes of books, periodicals, microfilm and microfiche, records, and tape. The library annually adds 7,000 volumes and 2,600 government documents. The library's Multimedia Collection houses the Religious Education Curriculum Laboratory and provides audiovisual aids and hardware, computers, and computer software. A staff of professional librarians guides students in the use of the fully equipped library. The Alabama Baptist Historical Commission's collection of Baptist church records and other important historical materials is located in the library and maintained by the Special Collection Department. Historical documents are also preserved through an active microfilming program. The Samford library system includes the Lucille Stewart Beeson Law Library, which has more than 232,850 volumes; the Education Curriculum Laboratory; the Global Drug Information Center; the Global Center; and the Music Library, which has more than 8,000 CDs, records, scores, and audiocassettes. University library holdings are accessed through a state-of-the-art library system. Other libraries in the Birmingham area cooperate with Samford on a reciprocal basis.

Costs

The cost of attending Samford is significantly lower than that of many institutions of comparable size and commitment to quality. The basic charge for 2010–11—including tuition ($21,722), room, board, and fees—was about $29,390. The typical student spends about $750 per year for books and supplies.

Financial Aid

At Samford University, a student's educational costs are frequently offset by scholarship and other financial assistance programs, which annually total more than $20 million. The application for admission also serves as the application for merit-based scholarships. Students interested in need-based opportunities should complete the Free Application for Federal Student Aid (FAFSA) by the March 1 priority filing date. In addition, non-need-based scholarship awards, usually based on academic merit, range up to full tuition.

Faculty

Samford's faculty consists of 275 full-time and about 160 part-time members. All classes are taught by members of the faculty; the faculty-student ratio is 1:12 and the average class size is 22. Faculty members serve as academic advisers and also serve on many University committees.

Student Government

The Student Government Association (SGA) provides an excellent opportunity for students to participate in and influence governance. The SGA has autonomy in many programs, activities, and budgetary decisions; through the Student Senate, proposals related to improving campus life are sent to the University administration for consideration. The largest SGA organization is the Student Activities Council. Its committees provide a variety of activities, including concerts, lectures, dances, and outdoor recreation. The largest student-run activity is Step Sing, an annual variety show involving several hundred students that fills the 2,700-seat concert hall for three consecutive nights. Students are also involved in disciplining students who do not live up to University values. Alcohol is not permitted on campus.

Admission Requirements

Samford University seeks to enroll students capable of success in a challenging academic environment. Every applicant is evaluated individually on the basis of academic preparedness and potential, as well as personal fit with the mission and purpose of the University. The Admission Committee considers factors such as the strength of the high school curriculum, grade point average, standardized test scores, demonstrated leadership skills, and recommendations. The freshman class that entered in 2010 possessed an ACT composite middle 50 percent range of 22 to 29 with an average of 26; the SAT middle 50 percent range was 1010 to 1250. The average high school grade point average of the entering class was 3.61. These statistics continue to demonstrate the competitive environment of Samford. International students must also demonstrate proficiency on the Test of English as a Foreign Language (TOEFL). Transfer students should have completed at least 24 semester hours or 36 quarter hours and maintained at least a 2.5 cumulative grade point average. Early admission is available to high school juniors who present an outstanding academic record and the recommendations of their parents and principal. Credit can be earned through I.B. and Advanced Placement tests. One school recommendation and an essay are required of every applicant, and a campus visit is strongly recommended.

Application and Information

Applications are received and notifications processed on a monthly rolling basis beginning in October. Students may also apply online by visiting the University's Web site. Applications are accepted until the class is filled. December 1 is the deadline to apply to be eligible for all merit-based scholarships.

Application inquiries should be addressed to:

Jason E. Black
Dean of Admission
Samford University
800 Lakeshore Dr.
Birmingham, Alabama 35229
Phone: 205-726-3673
        800-888-7218 (toll-free)
Web site: http://admission.samford.edu

The Harwell G. Davis Library on the campus of Samford University.

SCHOOL OF THE ART INSTITUTE OF CHICAGO

CHICAGO, ILLINOIS

The School

Since its founding in 1866, the School of the Art Institute of Chicago (SAIC) has been providing a leading global vision for the education of artists, designers, and others who shape contemporary art practice. The School of the Art Institute of Chicago's primary purpose is to foster the conceptual and technical education of artists, designers, and scholars in a highly professional, studio-oriented, and academically rigorous environment, encouraging excellence, critical inquiry, and experimentation. SAIC was recognized as "the most influential art school in the nation" by a poll conducted by Columbia University and a panel of national art critics. *U.S. News & World Report* has consistently ranked SAIC's Master of Fine Arts program as number one of the top three in the nation.

SAIC's 2,483 undergraduate and 748 graduate students and a faculty of artists, designers, and scholars work in an environment that facilitates the exchange of ideas, the sharing of resources, and the critiquing and refining of technical abilities and conceptual concerns.

The School of the Art Institute of Chicago is distinguished from other art and design schools in the breadth and depth of its curriculum in both studio and academic areas, with more than 900 courses offered each semester. SAIC is committed to interdisciplinary exploration and the awareness that the boundaries between artistic fields are not always easily defined. Students are encouraged to experience the full range of studio practices and academic approaches; they do not declare a major but are free to design a path of study that best suits their creative development. A student may choose to do all their course work in one area of study or among multiple department areas. SAIC's credit/no-credit grading system encourages students to investigate, develop, or resolve a creative problem by exploring new approaches and to develop the self-motivation and discipline necessary for life as a practicing artist, designer, and scholar in the twenty-first century.

Liberal arts and art history are central to the life of the School of the Art Institute of Chicago and underscore one of SAIC's primary commitments: to enrich a strong studio program with a first-rate, nationally and regionally accredited liberal arts education. SAIC has one of the largest art history departments in the nation and is the only college in the country that offers a systematic series of courses on the history, theory, and philosophical bases of art criticism, taught by contemporary critics and scholars.

Students may live in one of two distinctive residence halls with loft-style rooms, each with their own bathroom, kitchen, voice mail, and Internet access. The residence halls have 24-hour security and controlled access as well as spacious, well-lit studios, lounge rooms with big screen TVs, computer labs, and laundry facilities. Students can immerse themselves in a community of fellow artists, live in the heart of Chicago's loop, and enjoy conveniences unavailable in most student apartments.

Students have access to a wide variety of unique resources, beginning with the premiere collection of SAIC's sister institution, the Art Institute of Chicago with its new Modern Wing, and the Ryerson & Burnham Libraries, the largest art and architecture research libraries in the country. The Gene Siskel Film Center, located in the same building as the 162 North State Street Residences, presents significant programs of world cinema and presentations by an international array of film and video artists. SAIC's Video Data Bank houses more than 1,600 titles and is the leading resource in the United States for videotapes by and about contemporary artists. The Poetry Center brings renowned poets and writers to Chicago to share their work with the public.

The School of the Art Institute of Chicago offers a broad spectrum of services to accommodate its diverse population, including an international student office, multicultural affairs office, health and counseling services, Disability and Learning Resource Center, an extensive program for academic advising, and a career development department.

The School of the Art Institute of Chicago is accredited by the Higher Learning Commission of the North Central Association of Colleges and Schools and by the National Association of Schools of Art and Design.

Location

The School of the Art Institute of Chicago is located in the heart of downtown Chicago, home to the nation's second-largest art scene that includes world-class museums, numerous galleries, alternative spaces, and organizations that support the arts. Chicago is a city of diverse neighborhoods, each with its own atmosphere, customs, and cuisine. Students have a wide variety of cultural and recreational resources from which to choose: ballet, opera, theater, orchestra halls, cinemas, libraries, architecture, blues and jazz clubs, parks, ethnic restaurants, a variety of world-class sports venues, and street festivals.

Chicago itself is a vital part of the campus, as a source of social and cultural activities and the stimulus for ideas and attitudes ultimately expressed through art. Peter Frank, art critic and curator says, "Of all American cities, Chicago has contributed the most solid and distinctive artwork and art thinking. The School of the Art Institute of Chicago is at the nucleus of this longstanding distinction."

The School of the Art Institute of Chicago is located across the street from an extraordinary space that rivals the quads of any other big-city college or university. Millennium Park is a twenty-first-century marvel, and SAIC, its faculty members, and students played a key role in its realization. One of the signature pieces of public art at the park, the Crown Fountain by Spanish artist Jaume Plensa, was created with the assistance of both SAIC students and faculty members, who collaborated with Plensa in producing the 1,000 video portraits that are screened continuously on the fountain's twin video towers. The park, with its unique mix of art, architecture, and nature, has become SAIC's quad.

Majors and Degrees

Students do not declare majors but are free to concentrate in one or any combination of the following areas: animation, architecture, art and technology, art education, art history, ceramics, designed objects, drawing, fashion design, fiber, filmmaking, interior architecture, new media, painting, performance, photography, print media, sculpture, sound, video, visual communication, visual and critical studies, and writing.

The Bachelor of Fine Arts (B.F.A.) degree in studio allows students to develop a particularized course of study in the visual arts. The openness of the curriculum allows for creative, idiosyncratic, and tailored programs, thereby emulating the very process of art making. Academic advising, provided by the Office of Student Affairs, helps students in determining their particular path of study. The School of the Art Institute of Chicago offers Illinois teacher certification (K–12) through its B.F.A. with an emphasis in art education, with a goal of graduating artists and teachers who are informed and engaged citizens, creators and critics of visual culture. The B.F.A. with an emphasis in art history, theory, and criticism emphasizes art history, theory, and criticism, while allowing students the ability to develop their own studio practice. The B.F.A. with an emphasis in writing offers a solid grounding in literary conventions, a practical exposure to form in fiction and poetry, and an enhanced ability to read and critique peers' work, while encouraging students to openly explore what "writing" is.

The Bachelor of Arts in visual and critical studies allows students to pursue in-depth academic study in the creative environment of an art school, sharing classes with students in the B.F.A. programs. Core courses provide students with diverse critical methods for exploring the cultural meanings of visual phenomena as they relate to social, economic, and material circumstances.

The Bachelor of Interior Architecture (B.I.A.) is intended for students interested in interdisciplinary study and a focus in contemporary, professional design practices, such as sustainability, embedded and emerging technologies, and designed objects.

Academic Programs

Completion of 132 hours is required for the B.F.A. and B.A. degrees; approximately two thirds is in studio areas and one third is in academic course work. All entering students who have completed fewer than 15 credit hours of college-level studio art must enroll in the First Year Experience. Students take liberal arts courses in the humanities, natural sciences, mathematics, and social sciences and are required to complete an art history requirement.

Off-Campus Arrangements

The off-campus study requirement is an opportunity for students to gain practical experience at the same time as they gain a broader sense of society and the world.

Students can choose from a wide variety of off-campus programs. The Mobility program allows students to attend partner schools within the United States and Canada and includes the New York Studio semester. SAIC also maintains semester exchange agreements with more than twenty schools in Europe, Asia, and South America. The Off-Campus Programs Office works closely with students to help them develop their individual programs. SAIC faculty members lead study trips during each summer and winter interim session to such destinations as Cuba, New York, Puerto Rico, Venice, and Vietnam.

SAIC is home to the largest and most successful arts-related cooperative education program in the country, providing employment opportunities throughout Chicago and worldwide with individual artists; museums; galleries; multimedia firms; film, video, and animation production houses; interior architecture firms; fashion designers; and community service organizations.

Academic Facilities

SAIC's campus encompasses six buildings in downtown Chicago. There are fully equipped studios for each area of concentration, and SAIC's policy allows 24-hour access to facilities.

The School of the Art Institute of Chicago is committed to new technologies and the integration of computer-based resources throughout the curriculum. Currently, more than sixty digital technology courses are taught each semester in nearly all departmental areas. An aggressive laptop program coupled with state-of-the-art facilities and accessible resources provides cutting-edge capability in every corner of SAIC. Facilities available to all students include general-access computer labs equipped with the latest-model Apple computers and high-end peripherals; a Service Bureau, providing professional digital output, including laser cutting and 3-D printing; a Media Center, offering a wide variety of equipment for student loan; wood and metal shops; and fabrication studios.

The John M. Flaxman Library's 120,000 items—books, magazines, movies, and special collections—support the entire SAIC curriculum in the arts, liberal arts, and sciences. Web-accessible resources include SAIC's own growing digital library, a traditional online library catalog, e-reserves, and a rich assortment of full-text licensed databases. The Joan Flasch Artists' Book Collection contains more than 3,000 artists' books along with a research collection of exhibition catalogs and other related material. The MacLean Visual Resource Center maintains a noncirculating collection of more than 500,000 slides.

Exhibition spaces include the acclaimed Sullivan Galleries offering 32,000 square feet of exhibition space—the only single contemporary exhibition site of its size in the Chicago Loop, and the Betty Rymer Gallery, which highlights work from departments and presents special exhibitions. In addition, Gallery X and the Lounge Gallery, sponsored by the Student Union Galleries, provide exhibition space for currently enrolled students.

Costs

Tuition for the 2011–12 academic year is $36,930 for full-time undergraduate students or $1231 per credit hour. Student housing for a double room is $10,100 for the academic year.

Financial Aid

The School of the Art Institute of Chicago makes every effort to assist students who need help in financing their education. Through an extensive financial aid program, a substantial amount of gift aid funding from private, institutional, state, and federal sources is distributed annually. In addition to scholarships and grants, SAIC grants merit scholarships and offers an extensive college work-study program. For the 2010–11 academic year, $21,000,000 in grant aid was awarded to undergraduate students, and 98 percent of the incoming class received some form of financial aid. To apply for financial aid, students should complete the FAFSA. To receive priority consideration, students should submit completed forms to the Financial Aid Office no later than March 1. All awards are made on a first-come, first-served basis to students in good standing who demonstrate need.

Faculty

Faculty members are selected for their skills, insight, and dedication as teachers and for their professional accomplishments as artists, designers, and scholars. There are currently more than 600 full- and part-time faculty members, among them NEA grant recipients, Louis Comfort Tiffany Foundation Fellowship recipients, and Rockefeller Foundation grant recipients. SAIC's faculty members have their work exhibited in museums, galleries, and festivals nationally and internationally. They publish books, plays, poetry, and criticism; organize and curate exhibitions; and design, build, and preserve buildings throughout the world. Each year, 100 or more well-known visiting artists, including poets, political activists, and visual artists, present workshops and provide individual student critiques through the Visiting Artists Program. Notable alumni include Claes Oldenburg, Ivan Albright, Georgia O'Keeffe, David Sedaris, Cynthia Rowley, and Vincente Minnelli.

Student Government

Student Government officers are elected each spring, and their mission is to promote student interests and concerns to the broader School community by serving on a variety of faculty and administrative staff committees. Student Government also provides funds for the more than forty student groups on campus. All students are encouraged to attend the weekly open Student Government meetings.

Admission Requirements

To be considered for the undergraduate program, applicants are required to submit SAIC's application or the Common Application; a nonrefundable application fee of $65 for domestic students ($85 for international students); a portfolio consisting of ten to fifteen examples of recent work, a minimum of 5 minutes of time-based work, or an "alternative" portfolio submission that demonstrates the applicant's creative intent; a statement of purpose; transcript(s) from high school(s) or an official copy of the high school equivalency certificate; transcripts from any college previously attended; and one letter of recommendation. Domestic applicants must submit either scores from the SAT or the ACT. Any transfer applicant who has successfully completed the School of the Art Institute of Chicago's English requirements and/or other liberal arts course work at another accredited college may be exempt from standardized test requirements for admission. All international undergraduate students who are not U.S. citizens or permanent residents or are nonnative English speakers are required to take either the TOEFL or the IELTS.

Application and Information

Prospective students are required to submit their applications electronically at http://www.saic.edu/ugapp. The applicant's portfolio and academic credentials are reviewed and evaluated by the Admissions Office. Students applying by the early application deadline of January 2 are eligible for priority housing and registration. Students who anticipate a need for financial assistance are urged to complete their applications for admission and financial aid by February 15 for the fall semester and November 15 for the spring semester in order to receive priority consideration. These dates are also priority deadlines for applicants who wish to be considered for the School of the Art Institute of Chicago's Merit Scholarship Program.

Admissions Office
School of the Art Institute of Chicago
36 South Wabash, Suite 1201
Chicago, Illinois 60603
Phone: 312-629-6100
         800-232-7242 (toll-free)
Fax: 312-629-6101
E-mail: ugadmiss@saic.edu
Web site: http://www.saic.edu/ug

SEATTLE PACIFIC UNIVERSITY

SEATTLE, WASHINGTON

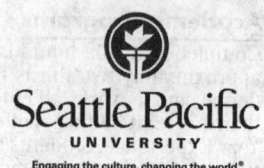

The University

With a long and distinguished history in Christian higher education, Seattle Pacific University (SPU) is positioned to engage the culture and influence the world for good. At a time when the legacy of the secularized modern university is under scrutiny, Seattle Pacific provides 4,000 students with a high-quality, comprehensive education grounded on the gospel of Jesus Christ. This combination of vital scholarship and thoughtful faith is a powerful one that brings about lasting change in the lives of graduates and in the people and communities they serve.

Founded in 1891, SPU has been named to the listing of America's Best Colleges by *U.S. News & World Report* and has been acknowledged as one of the country's character-building institutions. Located just minutes from downtown Seattle, the leading urban center in the Pacific Northwest, SPU is committed to engaging and serving in the modern city, cultivating a global consciousness, supporting the church, and addressing the crisis of meaning in modern culture. SPU believes these are some of the Christian university's most important contributions in this century.

SPU students come from forty-four states and twenty-seven countries, representing more than forty-seven different Christian denominations. More than half of Seattle Pacific's undergraduate students live on the campus in four residence halls and several apartment complexes. All residence facilities are wired to allow dedicated online connections to e-mail, the Internet, and the campus computer network.

Seattle Pacific University celebrates diversity and learning to live together in Christian community. In 2004, civil rights leader John Perkins and SPU President Philip Eaton founded the John Perkins Center on campus. The first of its kind in the nation, the Perkins Center helps SPU become a more diverse campus, practice reconciliation, build new relationships in the city, and bring about positive change in the world. The Ames Minority Leadership Scholarships support high school graduates who come from minority groups and have leadership potential. Prospective students from urban areas and diverse backgrounds annually visit the campus for Urban Youth Preview.

Seattle Pacific's intercollegiate athletic program fields NCAA Division II teams in men's and women's basketball, crew, cross-country, soccer, and track and field and women's gymnastics and volleyball. All students have access to twenty-two intramural sports as well as extramurals, special events, and health and fitness activities.

The University's unique leadership program encourages students to cultivate their individual talents through opportunities in student government, ministries, performing groups, publications, clubs, and organizations.

In addition to its bachelor's degrees, SPU awards M.A., M.B.A., M.Ed., M.F.A., M.S., M.A. (TESOL), M.S.N., Ed.D., and Ph.D. degrees.

Seattle Pacific University is accredited by the Washington State Board of Education, the Northwest Commission on Colleges and Universities, AACSB International–the Association to Advance Collegiate Schools of Business, the National Council for Accreditation of Teacher Education, the Washington State Board of Education for the preparation of elementary and secondary teachers, the Commission on Collegiate Nursing Education, the Washington State Nursing Care Quality Assurance Commission, the Accreditation Board for Engineering and Technology, the Commission on Accreditation/Approval for Dietetics Education of the American Dietetics Association, and the Commission on Accreditation for Marriage and Family Therapy Education. The doctoral degree program in clinical psychology is accredited by the American Psychological Association. SPU is approved by the American Council on Education, the Board of Regents of the State of New York, the Commission on Christian Education of the Free Methodist Church for preparation of ministers and missionaries, and the Department of Christian Education of the Free Methodist Church. SPU is a member of the Christian College Consortium, the Council for Chris-

tian Colleges and Universities, the American Association of Colleges for Teacher Education, and the National Association of Schools of Music.

Location

Seattle Pacific's beautiful 43-acre, tree-lined city campus lies in a residential area just 10 minutes from downtown Seattle, the business and cultural heart of the Pacific Northwest. A gateway to Canada and the Pacific Rim, Seattle offers easy access to a wide variety of outdoor recreation such as sailing, skiing, hiking, and camping. The city also offers world-class fine arts, including opera, theater, symphony, and ballet. Seattle Pacific takes advantage of its urban setting by providing hundreds of internship and service experiences in the city's hospitals, schools, businesses, and churches.

Majors and Degrees

An array of academic options in the arts, sciences, and professions allows Seattle Pacific students to specialize in one discipline while exploring many others. The University awards B.A. and B.S. degrees and offers sixty-one undergraduate majors.

The College of Arts and Sciences offers the following undergraduate majors: art; biochemistry; biology; biology education; biotechnology; chemistry; classics; communication; computational mathematics; computer engineering; computer science; electrical engineering; engineering and applied science; English; European studies (Europe, French, German, Latin, Russian, Spanish, and classics); exercise science; family and consumer sciences; fine and applied arts education; food and nutritional sciences; general studies; history; integrated studies; language arts education; Latin American studies (Spanish); mathematics; mathematics education; music; music education; philosophy; physical education; physics; political science; science education; social science education; sociology; textiles, clothing, and interiors; theater; and visual communication.

The School of Business and Economics offers undergraduate majors in accounting, business administration, and economics. The School of Education offers elementary certification with any major of the University, secondary certification with endorsements in most Washington state–approved areas, and a major in special education. The School of Health Sciences offers an undergraduate nursing degree. The School of Psychology, Family, and Community offers undergraduate majors in organizational behavior and psychology. The School of Theology offers majors in Christian theology, Christian scriptures, educational ministries, global and urban ministry, and youth ministry. Preprofessional programs are available in dentistry, law, medicine, optometry, pharmacy, physical therapy, and veterinary medicine.

Academic Programs

Seattle Pacific's academic disciplines set high standards for students. Undergraduate students are taught not by graduate assistants but by experienced professors who are recognized locally and nationally for the quality of their scholarship. Small class sizes mean students actively participate in their own education, gaining the confidence to achieve their goals. In addition, SPU's clear Christian commitment gives depth and perspective to classroom learning, balancing knowledge with values.

The Common Curriculum, which includes seven required courses spread out over four years, is at the heart of an undergraduate liberal arts education at Seattle Pacific. Very few comprehensive universities in an urban setting with an equal mix of residential and commuter students require participation in common learning over four years.

SPU students begin in the first quarter of their freshman year with University Seminar, a focused exploration of a special interdisciplinary topic. The fewer than 25 students enrolled in each course form a "cohort" and attend other freshman classes in the Common Curriculum together, with their University Seminar professor serving as their academic adviser during their first year. In their freshman, sophomore, and junior years, students participate in two parallel sequences of required courses that address key human questions from the perspective of various disciplines and the foundations of Christian faith.

Cumulative and developmental in nature, these classes are designed to support and enhance students' learning in the majors.

Off-Campus Programs

Seattle Pacific students have many opportunities to enhance their education with off-campus study. The Pacific Northwest itself provides a living laboratory for academic pursuits in all disciplines. SPU's own campuses on Whidbey Island and Blakely Island in Puget Sound are ideal for research and field study in areas such as marine biology and environmental science.

From summer 2010 to summer 2011, more than 125 students are slated to participate in SPU's faculty-led programs to Europe, South Africa, Belize, Galapagos, Vietnam, Japan, Rome, Korea, Russia, and China. Students can also choose to study with many other approved programs around the world. During quarter and summer breaks, students have the opportunity to join Seattle Pacific Reachout International (SPRINT) teams that travel to Camden, New Jersey, and countries such as China, Egypt, Russia, India, Rwanda, and Vietnam for a short-term mission experience.

Students may apply to take one or two quarters of study at one of the twelve other Christian College Consortium campuses, or they may enroll in programs sponsored by the Council for Christian Colleges and Universities, including American Studies in Washington, D.C.; Latin American Studies in Costa Rica; Film Studies in Los Angeles; Australian Studies Center in Sydney; Contemporary Music Center in Nashville, Tennessee; Middle East Studies in Cairo; China Studies; Oxford Program in Oxford, United Kingdom; Ugandan Studies; India Studies Program; or Journalism in Washington, D.C.

Academic Facilities

The University library provides book, journal, and media collections; databases; information services; instruction; technology; and space for study and research. Six librarians provide personal service and information literacy instruction for each subject area. The University library has approximately 200,000 volumes, and 1,300 journals (many online) and databases. SPU patrons may borrow materials from the thirty-six academic libraries in Washington and Oregon, which are part of the Orbis Cascade Alliance. The University Library has fourteen small rooms for study and meeting, a graduate student reading room, and a seminar and conference room. There are seventy networked computers in the library, and wireless access throughout the building. SPU's Center for Scholarship and Faculty Development is located in the library, and it includes Instructional Technology Services, which offers media production, satellite downlink, and duplication services.

Other educational facilities at SPU include a $24-million science facility for biology, chemistry, and related sciences. Otto Miller Hall, which houses computer science, electrical engineering, mathematics, and physics, has undergone a $5.4-million renovation. The University's flexible-forestage performing arts facility, E. E. Bach Theatre, is one of the city's finest, and the Royal Brougham Pavilion is one of the premier sports and recreation arenas in the Puget Sound area.

Costs

Tuition and fees for the 2010–11 academic year were $28,695; annual room and board were $8817 (based on 2 people in a room, full meal plan). Individualized meal plans are available. Book costs and personal expenses vary, depending on personal needs.

Financial Aid

Seattle Pacific expects to award nearly $77 million in scholarships and financial aid in 2011–12. Need-based financial aid is available in the form of scholarships, grants, loans, and employment. To be considered for maximum aid, students must submit the Free Application for Federal Student Aid (FAFSA) as soon as possible after January 1 and be admitted to the University by March 1. SPU participates in various federal aid programs, including the Federal Pell Grant, Federal Supplemental Educational Opportunity Grant, Federal Perkins Loan, Federal Work-Study Program, and Federal Stafford Student Loan. SPU also participates in the Federal Academic Competitiveness Grant, Federal SMART Grant, Federal TEACH Grant, Federal Parent PLUS Loan, Federal Graduate Student PLUS Loan, and Federal Nursing Student Loan.

Merit-based University scholarships are given annually to students who exhibit academic excellence and exemplify the ideals of the institution. Merit scholarships are available in amounts ranging from $1500 to full tuition. The Division of Fine Arts offers renewable scholarships (up to $3000) regardless of major. The Athletic Department awards scholarship aid to qualified athletes.

Faculty

The faculty at Seattle Pacific is composed of 211 full-time faculty members and 145 adjunct and other faculty members, who are committed to the highest academic standards. Eighty-five percent of SPU's full-time faculty members hold the Ph.D. or an equivalent terminal degree. Seattle Pacific professors are experts in their fields; they publish, speak, and conduct research throughout the world. Their first priority, however, is teaching. SPU faculty members also make themselves available to students outside the classroom and act as models of compassionate, educated Christians.

Student Government

All full-time students are members of the Associated Students of Seattle Pacific (ASSP). Each spring, students elect 5 ASSP executive officers, along with representatives to the ASSP Senate, the student governing body. ASSP provides services to students in the areas of campus activities, campus ministries, leadership development, and student publications.

Admission Requirements

Admission to Seattle Pacific is offered on the basis of academic credentials and personal qualifications. SPU selects those students who will benefit most from a Christian university education. Factors in the admission decision include high school or college grades, academic and personal recommendations, the application essays, and scores on the SAT or ACT. An applicant is also evaluated in terms of leadership potential, church and community activities, special talents, and personal responsibility. Prospective students are encouraged to visit the campus at any time.

Application and Information

Prospective students may visit the Seattle Pacific University Web site to apply online or request application materials. High school students should request these materials early in their senior year. While applications for autumn quarter are accepted until June 1, prospective students must be admitted by February 1 to be considered for scholarships and the best financial aid, housing, and course registration opportunities.

Applications are reviewed in the order they are received. Beginning December 1, decisions regarding admission are announced after all application materials have been received. If an interview is required, students are contacted by telephone.

Forms may be requested from:

Jobe Korb-Nice, Director of Undergraduate Admissions
Seattle Pacific University
3307 Third Avenue West, Suite 115
Seattle, Washington 98119-1922

Phone: 206-281-2021
         800-366-3344 (toll-free)
E-mail: admissions@spu.edu
Web site: http://www.spu.edu
        http://www.facebook.com/seattlepacific
        http://twitter.com/spubird

SPU's campus is located in a quiet residential neighborhood that's also just a few minutes from downtown Seattle.

SEATTLE UNIVERSITY
SEATTLE, WASHINGTON

The University

Seattle University (SU) provides an ideal environment for motivated students interested in self-reliance, awareness of different cultures, social justice, and the fulfillment that comes from making a difference in the world. Its location in the center of one of the nation's most diverse and progressive cities attracts a varied student body, faculty, and staff. Its urban setting promotes the development of leadership skills and independence and provides a variety of opportunities for students to apply what they learn through internships, clinical experiences, and volunteer work.

As a Jesuit institution, Seattle University is part of a network of twenty-eight colleges and universities and forty-six high schools across the United States noted for both academic strength and a commitment to social justice. Seattle U's core curriculum provides a rigorous liberal arts and sciences foundation designed to develop leadership skills, enhance global awareness, and enable graduates to serve others. In the Jesuit tradition, students are taught how to think, not what to think. Professional undergraduate offerings include highly respected Colleges of Business, Nursing, and Science and Engineering and career-oriented liberal arts programs such as communication, criminal justice, journalism, public affairs, and social work. The Albers School of Business and Economics and the University's Colleges of Education, Law, and Theology and Ministry offer graduate-level opportunities.

Seattle University is noted for its focus on the individual through small, faculty-taught classes and an engaging student life program. The result is graduates who enjoy successful and fulfilling lives. Seattle University is recognized as one of the leading institutions in the Pacific Northwest in producing Truman and Wilson scholars.

The Seattle University campus has undergone more than $200 million in recent improvements. Although its First Hill location is in the heart of the city, the 48-acre campus has been designated by the state as an official Backyard Wildlife Sanctuary for its distinctive landscaping and environmentally conscious practices.

Fall quarter 2010 had a freshman class of 1,055, with 58 percent coming from outside Washington State. The ethnic breakdown for the class was 52 percent white, 23 percent Asian American, and 18 percent African American, Latino, and American Indian. The 4,565 undergraduate students represent fifty-three states and territories and seventy-eight nations. International students make up approximately 10 percent of the student body.

Approximately 1,900 students in total and 92 percent of freshmen live on campus in four residence halls and an apartment complex. Students are required to live on campus for both their freshman and sophomore years unless they are able to commute from home.

Seattle University has more than 130 extracurricular clubs and organizations, including the Hui O Nani Hawaiian Club, Associated Students of African Descent, Outdoor Adventure and Recreation, Beta Alpha Psi (national accounting honorary), and other professional honoraries and clubs. SU Athletics (http://goseattleu.com/) is an NCAA Division I program and has seven varsity teams for men (baseball, basketball, cross-country, golf, soccer, swimming, tennis, and track) and nine for women (basketball, cross-country, golf, soccer, softball, swimming, tennis, track, and volleyball).

The Connolly Athletic Center serves as the major facility for varsity and intramural athletics and recreation. The center features two swimming pools, two full-size gymnasiums, and locker room saunas. A 6-acre complex provides fields for outdoor sports.

Seattle University receives the highest professional accreditation from the Accreditation Board for Engineering and Technology, AACSB International–The Association to Advance Collegiate Schools of Business, American Bar Association, American Chemical Society, Association of Theological Schools, Commission on Accreditation of Allied Health Education Programs, National Association of Schools of Public Affairs and Administration, National Council for Accreditation of Teacher Education, Commission on Collegiate Nursing Education, Council on Social Work Education, and Northwest Commission on Colleges and Universities.

Location

Nestled between two mountain ranges, containing three lakes, and situated along Puget Sound, Seattle is a magnificent setting for a university. The city pulses with music, art, and culture. Seattle is the Pacific Northwest's center for legal, medical, business, and high-tech industries, and Seattle University students supplement their studies through internships, research, volunteer projects, mentors, and meeting alumni in their fields.

Seattle's residents love the outdoors, and areas for skiing, hiking, backpacking, and climbing are within an hour of campus. Biking, walking, and jogging are also popular, with paths and trails throughout the city.

Seattle's sights and sounds, rich ethnic diversity, celebrated restaurants, eclectic entertainment, major-league athletics, theater, opera, and ballet are within walking distance, and are a central part of the Seattle University experience.

Majors and Degrees

Seattle University offers the following undergraduate degrees: Bachelor of Arts, Bachelor of Fine Arts, Bachelor of Music, Bachelor of Science, Bachelor of Science in Nursing, Bachelor of Social Work, Bachelor of Criminal Justice, Bachelor of Public Affairs, and the Bachelor of Arts in Business Administration.

The University offers programs in six major academic units. The Albers School of Business and Economics awards degrees in accounting, business administration, business economics, e-commerce/information systems, economics, finance, international business, international economic development, management, and marketing. The College of Arts and Sciences grants degrees in art history, Asian studies, communication studies, creative writing, criminal justice, cultural anthropology, drama, environmental studies, English, film studies, fine arts, French, history, international studies, journalism, liberal studies, military science/ROTC, philosophy, photography, political science, psychology, public affairs, social work, sociology, Spanish, sport and exercise science, strategic communication, string performance, theology/religious studies, visual art, and women studies. The College of Nursing offers a Bachelor of Science in Nursing degree. Matteo Ricci College awards degrees in humanities for leadership and humanities for teaching. The College of Science and Engineering offers degree programs in biochemistry, biology, chemistry, civil engineering, clinical laboratory science, computer engineering, computer science, diagnostic ultrasound, electrical engineering, environmental engineering, environmental science, general science, mathematics, mechanical engineering, and physics. Preprofessional programs include dentistry, law, medicine, optometry, and veterinary medicine.

Academic Programs

The Core Curriculum has several distinguishing characteristics in keeping with the Jesuit educational tradition: it provides an integrated freshman year; gives order and sequence to student learning; provides experience in the methods and content of the range of liberal arts, sciences, philosophy, and theology; calls for active learning in all classes, for practice in writing and thinking, and for an awareness of values; and it fosters a global perspective and a sense of social and personal responsibility.

Seattle University offers two honors program options for students seeking rigorous academic challenge. The University Honors Program is a small, humanities-focused learning community with a curriculum that examines the most significant texts and ideas of Western culture. The Core Honors Program involves seminar sections of nine required courses in English, history, philosophy, social science, and theology/religious studies; this option is particularly suited to students in professional degree programs, for whom participation in University Honors is less feasible due to specific major requirements and scheduling conflicts.

Seattle University operates on a quarter calendar. The fall quarter begins in mid-September; the winter quarter in early January; the spring quarter in late March; and the summer quarter in mid-June. Undergraduates typically take 15 credit hours per quarter for the fall, winter, and spring quarters.

Off-Campus Programs

Seattle University offers a diverse array of short- and long-term international study programs. Some are appropriate for any student interested in study of a particular culture or language, while others are designed to complement specific majors. Short-term programs include opportunities in Brazil, Costa Rica, France, India, Ireland, Italy, Japan, Korea, Mexico, South Africa, and Sweden. Long-term programs, which last an entire academic quarter or more, are available for Austria, Belize, China, Denmark, Ecuador, France, Ghana, Ireland, Japan, Mexico, and Spain. Students also have the opportunity to intern with non-governmental organizations in Asia, Africa, and Latin America through the unique International Development Internship Program (IDIP), which embodies the Jesuit emphasis on social justice and global awareness. Additional study-abroad programs in other nations, in conjunction with other colleges' overseas programs, are also offered. Arrangements are made through the Education Abroad Office.

Academic Facilities

Twelve academic buildings house classrooms, thirty-four instructional laboratories, twenty-five specialized laboratories, computer facilities, and other instructional equipment to support state-of-the-art instruction.

The newly renovated Lemieux Library and McGoldrick Learning Commons has nearly 300,000 volumes and 2,700 current serial subscriptions, 1,300 online databases, and microforms periodicals. Study carrels provide quiet study space while lounges accommodate study groups.

The Albers School of Business and Economics features classrooms designed to enhance student interaction and access to high-tech teaching equipment.

The College of Nursing's new 20,000-square-foot clinical performance laboratory is among the most technically advanced clinical laboratories in the country. It joins two clinical practice rooms and a suite of laboratories.

The Lee Center for the Arts is a showcase for theater and musical performances. This modern building seats 135 and includes a prop room, dressing room, costume shop, and professional lighting and sound booths that give students career-building technical skills.

The Chapel of St. Ignatius is Seattle University's spiritual center. This award-winning structure is recognized as a place of beauty, contemplation, and worship.

Costs

For academic year 2010–11, tuition was $30,825; room and meals were $9315. The estimate for books, fees, and personal expenses is $5353. Costs are subject to change.

Financial Aid

Seattle University awarded $37.3 million in its own financial aid to fall 2009 freshmen, including merit scholarships ranging from $7000 to $36,600. Ninety-two percent of freshmen received University aid. Students are required to apply for financial aid by February 1, as awards are made early each spring for the following fall quarter. Applications received after this deadline are evaluated in order received for any remaining aid. Students must submit the Free Application for Federal Student Aid (FAFSA) and be accepted for admission to be considered for financial assistance. Scholarships are awarded on the basis of academic achievement, extracurricular involvement, and community service.

Faculty

There are 708 faculty members, 91 percent of whom possess doctoral or terminal degrees. All classes are taught by faculty. With an average class size of 20 and a faculty-to-student ratio of 1:13, the primary responsibility of Seattle University professors is the success of their students. Faculty members are available to provide assistance outside of class, to help students with research, and to assist in arranging internships. Faculty advisers provide guidance, direction, and encouragement throughout a student's academic career. New students are assigned faculty advisers prior to registration according to their major.

Student Government

All undergraduates belong to the Associated Students of Seattle University (ASSU), the central student organization on campus. ASSU is organized around an elected president, an executive vice president, and an activities vice president. A 12-member representative council oversees every facet of the student body and is responsible for policymaking and providing a diverse activities program to meet the needs of Seattle University's student body. In addition, ASSU communicates student needs to the administration and faculty. ASSU oversees over 130 clubs and organizations.

Admission Requirements

Freshman applicants are required to have completed a college-preparatory program upon high school graduation, including 4 years of English, 3 years of social studies/history, 3 years of mathematics, 2 years of laboratory science, and 2 years of a foreign language. Applicants to the College of Science and Engineering must complete 4 units of college-preparatory mathematics for admission to any of its specific majors; laboratory chemistry and laboratory physics are prerequisites for engineering program consideration. Applicants to the nursing major must complete laboratory biology and chemistry to be considered for admission.

ACT or SAT scores, an official high school transcript, a counselor recommendation, a teacher recommendation, and an essay are also required for freshman admission consideration. The middle 50 percent of 2010 freshmen had GPAs between 3.4 and 3.9 on a 4.0 scale and ACT scores between 23 and 29 or SAT scores between 530 and 640 (critical reading), 530 and 640 (math), and 520 and 620 (writing).

College credit is awarded to those who have successfully completed Advanced Placement or International Baccalaureate examinations. Qualifying scores can be obtained by contacting the Office of the Registrar.

Application and Information

Seattle University is an exclusive member of the Common Application. A Seattle University Supplemental Application is also required. The application essay and the Supplemental Application's personal statement are carefully considered during application review.

Students can apply directly online at commonapp.org; the forms can also be downloaded from the Seattle University Web site at http://www.seattleu.edu. Hard copies can be requested from the Admissions Office.

High school students applying for early action consideration must apply by November 15 of their senior year. Those applying for regular admission consideration must apply by January 15. The priority application deadline for fall transfer applicants is March 1. Transfer students must submit official transcripts from all postsecondary institutions attended, regardless of whether course work was completed. Please note that applications will be accepted after these dates on a space available basis, but funds for financial aid may no longer be available.

Campus visits can be scheduled Monday through Friday and many Saturdays. Prospective students should contact Admissions for availability. With two weeks' notice, visitors can be scheduled to attend a class, meet with a faculty adviser, participate in a campus tour, and speak individually with an Admissions representative. For additional information students should contact:

Admissions Office
Seattle University
901 12th Avenue
Seattle, Washington 98122-1090
Phone: 206-296-2000
      800-426-7123 (toll-free)
E-mail: admissions@seattleu.edu
Web site: http://www.seattleu.edu
      http://www.facebook.com/seattleu (Facebook)
      http://twitter.com/seattleu (Twitter)

SETON HALL UNIVERSITY
SOUTH ORANGE, NEW JERSEY

The University

Seton Hall University has been preparing students to assume leadership roles for over 150 years. A Catholic university founded with the purpose of becoming "a home for the mind, the heart and the spirit," Seton Hall offers more than sixty majors and concentrations, as well as honors and leadership programs. With a 14:1 student-faculty ratio and an average class size of 23, Seton Hall offers all the advantages of a large university; however, with just 5,200 undergraduate students, the University also provides the personal attention of a small college. Seton Hall's mission of "preparing student leaders for a global society" is evident through its high academic standards, values-centered curriculum, and cutting-edge technology. Recently cited by the Intercollegiate Studies Institute's critically acclaimed college guide *Choosing the Right College* as "a Catholic university evolving from being a regional treasure to a national resource," Seton Hall was listed among 110 of the nation's top colleges.

The University comprises eight schools and colleges: the College of Arts and Sciences, the Stillman School of Business, the College of Education and Human Services, the College of Nursing, the Whitehead School of Diplomacy and International Relations, the Immaculate Conception Seminary School of Theology, and the School of Health and Medical Sciences, all on the South Orange campus. The School of Law is in nearby Newark.

Emphasizing Judeo-Christian intellectual traditions and values, the University was founded by Bishop James Roosevelt Bayley, the first Catholic bishop of Newark. Seton Hall was named after Bishop Bayley's aunt, St. Elizabeth Ann Seton, the founder of the first American community of the Sisters of Charity. Established as the first diocesan college in the United States in 1856 and organized into a University in 1950, Seton Hall continues to operate under the auspices of the Roman Catholic Diocese of Newark. As such, Seton Hall is both a Catholic university and a catholic university—meaning that the school fosters the values and traditions of the Catholic faith while also universally welcoming students of all denominations.

At Seton Hall, technology is integrated into the curriculum. Every undergraduate is issued a laptop computer with wireless connectivity to facilitate learning through technology both inside and outside the classroom. Seton Hall has integrated technology into course work by including the use of streaming video to increase learning, note-taking, and collaborative work online. The state-of-the-art laptop is upgraded after two years, and students who graduate in four years keep their laptops after graduation.

Seton Hall's on-campus recruiting events and career fairs help students find paid internships at companies like CNN, Prudential, AT&T, Pfizer, Johnson & Johnson, the United Nations, the FBI, ESPN, and the New Jersey Devils. More than 600 employers and alumni come to the campus each year to mentor and recruit students for internships and employment after graduation. In 2010, 463 internships were reported by undergraduate and graduate students. Stillman School of Business and College of Arts and Sciences interns earned more than $610,000 in 2010.

The relationships forged with these companies are so solid that more than 90 percent of the University's employers report that they would hire their Seton Hall interns after graduation if they had appropriate openings. Graduates of Seton Hall University join the ranks of the more than 70,000 alumni who work in leadership positions in business, industry, law, health care, and education nationally and internationally. Overall average starting salary for 2010 baccalaureate graduates was $46,000, with Seton Hall business and nursing students averaging $50,000, and diplomacy students almost $47,000. Students in the College of Education and College of Arts and Science averaged a starting salary of almost $37,000.

Unique opportunities with the School of Health and Medical Sciences allow students to enter dual-degree programs to earn advanced degrees in athletic training, physical therapy, occupational therapy, and physician assistant studies.

Six months after graduation, 70 percent of Seton Hall students have career-related employment.

Location

The suburban village of South Orange, New Jersey, is home to the University's 58-acre parklike campus. With the village center a short walk away, students find practically anything they need. Just beyond the border of the suburban residential community is New York City—the Big Apple—the capital of finance, fashion, art, theater, and international relations. Travel to New York is convenient via a midtown direct train from the village center. Just 14 miles away, New York City provides students with opportunities for cultural exploration and internships. Career opportunities also abound throughout northern New Jersey, which is the site of an extensive pharmaceutical, chemical, and financial center. Social, cultural, and recreational opportunities are available throughout the area, with the New Jersey Performing Arts Center, the Meadowlands sports complex, numerous state parks, and the beautiful New Jersey shore all close by.

Majors and Degrees

The College of Arts and Sciences offers the Bachelor of Arts (B.A.) in Africana and Diaspora studies, anthropology, art (art history, fine art, graphic design and advertising art, theater), Asian studies, athletic training, broadcasting and visual media, Catholic studies, classical studies, communication studies, creative writing, criminal justice, economics, English, environmental studies, French, history, Italian, journalism and public relations, liberal studies, Latin America and Latino/Latina studies, modern languages, music (music performance, music education), occupational therapy, philosophy, physical therapy, physician assistant studies, political science, psychology, religious studies, social and behavioral sciences, social work, sociology, Spanish, and theater studies and performance. It offers the Bachelor of Science (B.S.) in biochemistry, biology, chemistry, mathematics, and physics.

The College of Education and Human Services offers the B.S. in a unique integrated early childhood, elementary, and special education program and in secondary education.

The College of Nursing offers the Bachelor of Science in Nursing (B.S.N.).

The Stillman School of Business offers the B.S. in accounting, economics, finance, information technology management, management, marketing, and sport management. It also offers the B.A. in business administration with concentrations in arts and sciences, diplomacy, international studies, and occupational therapy.

The Whitehead School of Diplomacy and International Relations offers the B.S. in diplomacy and international relations.

Preprofessional programs are available in dentistry, law, medicine, optometry, seminary, and veterinary science. A dual-admission program with Seton Hall University School of Law is offered to qualified undergraduates. Engineering students participate in a five-year program (chemical, civil, computer, electrical, industrial, or mechanical) offered jointly with New Jersey Institute of Technology. Combination undergraduate and postgraduate programs in athletic training, occupational therapy, physical therapy, physician assistant studies, and speech-language pathology are also offered.

Academic Programs

The University uses a semester calendar. It also offers day, evening, and summer sessions.

Select students are invited to participate in the University Honors Program, which consists of four semester-long colloquia devoted to the history of civilization, from ancient through medieval and early modern cultures to contemporary civilization.

With the oldest college of nursing in New Jersey, Seton Hall provides nursing education that prepares its graduates for a variety of health-care settings. Clinical experience is provided in hospitals, public health agencies, schools, nursing homes, industrial organizations, and other community agencies. More than 97 percent of Seton Hall nursing students pass the national nursing exam. Graduates of Seton Hall hold leadership positions in nursing throughout the state.

Seton Hall's Stillman School of Business is accredited by AACSB International—The Association to Advance Collegiate Schools of Business, which puts it among the most rigorous business programs in the United States. Founded on a background of liberal arts courses, the Stillman School offers specialized programs in leadership studies, international business, and sport management.

The Whitehead School of Diplomacy and International Relations is the only school affiliated with the United Nations Association of the United States of America and offers a Bachelor of Science degree in international relations. This program emphasizes ethno political studies or world cultures and the development of management and leadership skills, as well as a high degree of competency in a second language. Requirements include study abroad and internships.

The University offers an Army ROTC program on campus.

Off-Campus Programs

Seton Hall offers study-abroad programs in more than forty countries including the Dominican Republic, England, France, Germany Japan, Korea, and the People's Republic of China. Seton Hall offers semester or yearlong exchange programs with colleges and universities in Austria, China, Germany, Ireland, Japan, Puerto Rico, South Korea, and the United Kingdom. Through the international student exchange program, students may study at any of the 101 universities in thirty-five countries for one academic year. Students have several opportunities for cooperative learning and internships in the metropolitan area. Many co-op positions are with Fortune 500 companies, while others are with leading government, cultural, charitable, and scientific organizations. A semester in Washington, D.C., is also available for students to obtain internships and to take classes at exchange universities.

Academic Facilities

At Seton Hall, there is an emphasis on the use of state-of-the-art technology and available facilities to aid in the overall development and college experience for all students. Seton Hall's award-winning Mobile Computing Program provides all incoming, full-time freshmen with a brand-new, fully loaded laptop. The Department of Information Technology also supports and maintains numerous public computer labs around campus. The Richie Regan Recreation Center serves the recreational and fitness needs of the Seton Hall community with cardio machines, an Olympic-sized pool, an indoor track, and six indoor basketball courts. The brand-new fitness center features a free-weight center, new cardiovascular equipment, plasma screen televisions, and wireless headsets to listen to the TVs.

The University's Walsh Library is a twenty-first-century research center with a computerized card catalog, four electronic multimedia rooms, ten CD-ROM information search and retrieval stations, 200 computer workstations for students, nearly 1 million holdings, and the University Gallery. The University Center houses most of Seton Hall's cultural, social, and recreational activities. The University Center is the hub of student activity and includes the Galleon Dining Room/food court, the Pirate's Cove (lounge and coffee house), Theatre-in-the-Round, an art gallery, a study lounge, and the student government office as well as a wide variety of student clubs and organizations. Services such as aptitude testing, career counseling, career services, health services, and personal counseling are also provided for all Seton Hall students. Fahy Hall contains classrooms and offices, a TV studio, two classroom amphitheaters, and language and journalism laboratories. McNulty Hall, renovated in October 2007, is a state-of-the-future science and technology center. The new center is home to more than thirty research and teaching laboratories, a confocal microscope laboratory, a computational chemistry laboratory, a radiochemistry laboratory, and a rooftop observatory and greenhouse. The Art Center (a registered National Historic landmark) houses an art gallery, studios, classrooms, and offices of the Department of Art and Music. The College of Nursing has multipurpose and audiovisual laboratories. Jubilee Hall, completed in 1997, contains state-of-the-art lecture halls, computer rooms, faculty offices, a 300-seat auditorium, conference rooms, and the University's new Trading Room, where students learn about stocks, bonds, and trading. There are also microcomputer laboratories in several locations on campus, and a large University-operated mainframe computer is located in the Computer Center. The University also has various centers and research institutes, including the Center for Catholic Studies, the G. K. Chesterton Institute, the Center for Jewish Christian Studies, and the 50-year-old Asia Center.

Costs

For the 2010–11 academic year, tuition and fees were $31,890 per year. This amount covered 36 credits and all fees, including a mobile-computing and orientation fee. The charge for room and board was $11,508.

Financial Aid

The University offers federal, state, and institutional aid. Most aid is based on need, but many scholarships are based on outstanding scholastic ability and achievement. Athletic grants are also available. Currently, about 91 percent of the students receive financial aid, with 86 percent receiving aid directly from Seton Hall. All applicants for aid are required to file the Free Application for Federal Student Aid (FAFSA) by March 1 for the fall semester and by October 1 for the spring semester.

Faculty

The University has 879 faculty members, and 88 percent of the full-time faculty members have doctoral degrees. The ratio of full-time students to full-time faculty members is 14:1. Faculty members serve as advisers to students in their respective departments.

Student Government

The Student Government Association consists of students who make up two legislative bodies that have the responsibility of representing their fellow students and providing programs of interest to the campus community. Students are elected to seats on the University Senate, which deals with all legislative matters pertinent to the University. In addition, the Resident Student Association represents the interests of resident students, and the Commuter Council represents the interests of commuter students.

Admission Requirements

Applicants are selected on their school achievement record, SAT or ACT scores, personal essay, and teacher and counselor recommendations. Students must graduate from an accredited high school or have passing scores on the GED test. Sixteen high school units are required: 4 in English, 3 in mathematics, 2 in social studies, 2 in a foreign language (taken consecutively), 1 in a laboratory science, and 4 in approved academic electives. Special admission policies exist for students who have been out of high school for an extended period. There is also a $55 application fee. The application fee may be waived for applicants with financial need.

Transfer applicants must have a minimum 2.5 grade point average and must be in good standing at the last institution attended. Applicants must submit transcripts from all colleges and universities attended. Credit is usually given for grades of 2.0 or higher in University-equivalent courses taken at approved institutions; a maximum of 100 semester hours of transferable credit are allowed toward a bachelor's degree.

Application and Information

The University offers a non-binding early action deadline of November 15. Those meeting the deadline will receive their admissions decision by December 30. The University also offers rolling admissions. The preferred application deadlines are March 1 for freshman and June 1 for transfers.

Office of Admissions
Seton Hall University
400 South Orange Avenue
South Orange, New Jersey 07079-2680
Phone: 800-THE-HALL (toll-free)
E-mail: thehall@shu.edu
Web site: http://www.shu.edu

SETON HILL UNIVERSITY
GREENSBURG, PENNSYLVANIA

The University

Seton Hill was founded by the Sisters of Charity in 1883 and chartered as a college by the commonwealth of Pennsylvania in 1918. In 2002, it became Seton Hill University.

Seton Hill, a coeducational liberal arts and sciences institution, is situated in the Laurel Highlands, an area of southwestern Pennsylvania known for its beautiful scenery and wealth of outdoor activities such as skiing, cycling, hiking, and white-water rafting. Recreational opportunities include on-campus lectures, theater productions, a fitness center, and aerobics classes, as well as University-sponsored trips to Pittsburgh for cultural and sports events. A new performing arts venue is in the works, and recently constructed are two new residence halls and a new recreation facility that includes new athletic fields.

Seton Hill has varsity teams for women in basketball, cross-country, equestrian competition, field hockey, golf, lacrosse, soccer, softball, tennis, track and field, and volleyball and for men in baseball, basketball, cross-country, equestrian competition, football, golf, lacrosse, soccer, tennis, track and field, and wrestling, as well as a variety of intramural teams.

At the graduate level, Seton Hill grants the Master of Arts degree in art therapy, elementary education, inclusive education (online), marriage and family therapy, special education, and writing popular fiction; a Master of Business Administration; and a Master of Science in physician assistant studies. Seton Hill has graduate certificate programs in entrepreneurship, genocide and holocaust studies (online), and writing popular fiction.

Location

Seton Hill University's beautiful 200-acre campus is located in Greensburg, Pennsylvania. As a private university, Seton Hill is able to maintain a safe, secure environment that allows students to concentrate on academics.

Seton Hill is easily accessible by car, train, or plane. Just 35 miles east of Pittsburgh, Greensburg enjoys all the advantages of a large city while maintaining a small-town atmosphere. The seat of Westmoreland County, Greensburg is home to the Westmoreland Museum of Art, the Westmoreland Symphony Orchestra, a large mall, several shopping centers, and a hospital.

Majors and Degrees

The University grants the Bachelor of Arts, Bachelor of Fine Arts, Bachelor of Science, Bachelor of Music, and Bachelor of Social Work degrees. Students choose from the following programs: accounting; art, including art and technology, art education, art history, art therapy, arts administration, fine arts studio–3D or 2D, graphic design, and studio art; biochemistry; biology; business, including entrepreneurial studies, human resources, information management, international organization, and marketing; chemistry; communication, including political communication; computer science; criminal justice; dietetics; education, including art; biology; business, computer, and information technology; chemistry; dual elementary/special; early childhood; elementary; English; family and consumer sciences; French; mathematics; music; social studies; Spanish; and special education; engineering (3+2); English, including creative writing, journalism/new media, and literature; family and consumer sciences, including child care administration and education; forensic science; history; hospitality and tourism; international studies; mathematics, including actuary science; medical technology; music, including music education, music therapy, performance, and sacred music; physicians assistant studies; political science; prelaw, preprofessional health; psychology; religious studies/theology; social work; sociology;

Spanish; sports management; and theater, including music theater, theater design and technology, theater arts, theater business, and theater performance.

The University offers osteopathic medicine through a (3+3 or 3+4) and pharmacy (3+3 or 3+4) cooperative program with Lake Erie College of Osteopathic Medicine.

The University also offers adult degree programs.

Academic Programs

Seton Hill offers five academic divisions, with the opportunity to self-design a major, all enhanced by the University's award-winning liberal arts core curriculum. Special programs are available for students who are undecided about their major.

The Seton Hill University Honors Program is available for students who have distinguished themselves academically in high school. It includes scholarship money as well as housing for qualified candidates.

Prior to graduation, all undergraduate students complete a portfolio, a four-year compilation of their academic, professional, and personal achievements at Seton Hill. Portfolios allow students to showcase their learning and assist them in documenting their accomplishments as they transition from students to practicing professionals.

Students hoping to one day own a business may be interested in Seton Hill University's E-Magnify, a center for entrepreneurs. The center is the first organization of its kind in the United States to offer courses in business ownership and entrepreneurial activities to students in any major.

Off-Campus Programs

Seton Hill University recognizes that important learning experiences occur in nonacademic settings. For this reason, the University offers a variety of internships, fieldwork experiences, and cooperative education opportunities. The Office of Career Development and University faculty members assist students in finding an off-campus placement where practical experience related to the major and valuable job contacts for the future may be gained.

In addition, students may opt to spend a semester or year studying abroad. Seton Hill also offers many travel-abroad opportunities during J-term and M-term semesters.

Academic Facilities

While all of Seton Hill's facilities feature modern technology, the University continues to add new classrooms, buildings, and centers that feature the very best in adaptable learning spaces that facilitate the incorporation of current interactive and assistive technologies into Seton Hill's teaching and learning environment. Seton Hill's new Technology Learning Commons includes the ultramodern MediaSphere and Inquiry Zone classroom/labs which include everything students need (from specially designed furniture to wall-sized monitors and SmartBoards) to create virtual worlds, teach online courses, or work on group projects with students or faculty members in other parts of the campus—or the globe. The new Performing Arts Center incorporates the very best design and technology into its performance venues, classrooms, technical areas, and studios—from Steinway pianos to the latest in lighting, sound, video, and acoustics. Seton Hill's twenty-one academic and residence facilities have been specifically designed to provide a seamless, supportive learning environment for students.

Costs

For full-time students, approximate costs for the 2010–11 academic year included tuition of $26,848, approximate room and board fees of $8810, and books and personal expenses amounting to approximately $1000 to $2000.

Financial Aid

Seton Hill's Financial Aid Office works with each student to develop an aid package from the wide variety of scholarships, grants, loans, and work-study programs available.

Seton Hill Presidential Scholarships are awarded to incoming freshman who have attained a cumulative high school grade point of average of a 3.3 or higher. SAT/ACT Seton Hill University Scholarships are awarded to students who achieve SAT scores of 900 or higher and ACT scores of 19 or higher. The SAT/ACT scholarship is to be added to the presidential scholarship amounts if the student meets both criteria. These scholarships are renewable for a total of 8 semesters as long as the student maintains a minimum cumulative GPA of 3.3 at the end of each academic year. Seton Hill provides eight full-tuition scholarships each year (two natural health sciences, two humanities, two social sciences, and two visual and performing arts). Honors Program Scholarships are available, if students have at least a 1200 on SAT's math and verbal or a 26 on the ACT composite score, and a cumulative high school GPA of a 3.5. Rising Star Scholarships are available to graduates from a Catholic high school. Division Scholarships are based on the student's academic excellence in their specific division of study. Selection for these scholarships is based on the SAT score and the student's GPA. In addition, Seton Hill offers Alumni and Sibling scholarships.

Faculty

With a student-faculty ratio of 15:1, Seton Hill faculty members can explore the needs of each student and offer individual attention. The low student-faculty ratio allows each student to become personally acquainted with the instructor. In addition, Seton Hill faculty members understand the importance of being accessible to their students.

The Seton Hill faculty consists of 70 full-time professors, 81 percent of whom have doctoral or terminal degrees.

Student Government

Through the Seton Hill Government Association, students participate in the government of the University and enjoy voting representation on a number of faculty committees. Each residence hall floor is represented by a senator, who acts as a liaison between the student senate and the student body. Participation in student government is a valuable experience that develops leadership skills and a working understanding of government.

In addition, the student government helps to sponsor numerous on-campus political, cultural, and social events. Off-campus activities include trips to Pittsburgh, New York City, and Washington, D.C.

Admission Requirements

Acceptance to the University is based on the successful completion of a college-preparatory curriculum in high school. Applicants should have completed at least 15 secondary school academic units. These units should include 4 units of English, 2 units of college-preparatory mathematics, 2 units of social science, 2 units of the same foreign language, 1 unit of laboratory science, and 4 academic electives.

Students who wish to transfer credits to Seton Hill from another college or university must present their transcripts for evaluation on a course-by-course basis. A transfer student will receive a credit evaluation upon admission to the University.

Application and Information

Seton Hill University has a rolling admissions policy. Decisions of the Admissions Committee are rendered shortly after all application materials have been submitted.

The first-time freshman applicant should submit a completed application form, a $35 nonrefundable application fee, an official secondary school transcript that includes the applicant's rank and cumulative grade point average, official score reports from either the SAT or ACT, an essay, and a recommendation form or letter from a guidance counselor or teacher.

Prospective students who do not have SAT or ACT scores may submit two graded written assignments from their junior or senior year for consideration.

For more information, students should contact:

Sherri Bett
Director of Admissions
One Seton Hill Drive
Box 991
Seton Hill University
Greensburg, Pennsylvania 15601

Phone: 800-826-6234 (toll-free)
Fax: 724-830-1294
E-mail: admit@setonhill.edu
Web site: http://www.setonhill.edu

The Administration Building is a picturesque focal point on the Seton Hill campus.

SHIPPENSBURG UNIVERSITY OF PENNSYLVANIA

SHIPPENSBURG, PENNSYLVANIA

SHIPPENSBURG UNIVERSITY

The University

Shippensburg University, founded in 1871, is a comprehensive public institution in south-central Pennsylvania enrolling more than 7,200 undergraduate students and approximately 1,200 graduate students. Of the undergraduates, 52 percent are women and 48 percent are men. The University comprises the College of Arts and Sciences, the College of Education and Human Services, the John L. Grove College of Business, and the School of Graduate Studies. There is also a School of Academic Programs and Services, which includes the Office of Undeclared Students.

Shippensburg University is a member of the Pennsylvania State System of Higher Education and is accredited by the Middle States Association of Colleges and Schools. The University's programs are also accredited by AACSB International (business); ABET, Inc. (computer science); the American Chemical Society; the Council on Social Work Education; the Council for the Accreditation of Counseling and Related Educational Programs; the International Association of Counseling Services; the Council for Exceptional Children; and the National Council for the Accreditation of Teachers. Shippensburg University is a member of the Council of Graduate Schools.

Graduate degrees conferred are the Master of Arts, Master of Business Administration, Master of Education, Master of Science, Master of Social Work, and Master of Public Administration. Programs are as follows: Master of Arts in applied history; Master of Science in administration of justice, biology, communication studies, computer science, counseling (college, community, mental health, student personnel), geoenvironmental studies, organizational development and leadership (business, communication, education, environmental management, higher education, historical management, individual and organizational development, public organizations, social structure and organization), and psychology; Master of Business Administration; Master of Public Administration; Master of Social Work; and Master of Education in counseling (elementary and secondary), curriculum and instruction (biology, early childhood education, elementary education, English, geography/earth science, history, mathematics, middle-level education, modern languages), reading, school administration, and special education (behavior disorders, comprehensive, learning disabilities, mental retardation). The School of Graduate Studies also offers post-master's degree curricula leading to various types of education certification, including supervisory certification, and is one of twenty-one national sites for a postgraduate academic training program in Reading Recovery.

More than 200 student clubs, organizations, and activity groups, resulting in nearly 600 leadership opportunities, are available. Organizations include academic clubs, community service groups, special interest organizations, media organizations, musical groups, performing arts troupes, and national or local fraternities and sororities.

Student activities are complemented by programs that bring nationally and internationally known figures to campus. The University's Luhrs Performing Arts Center has recently hosted CNN anchor Soledad O'Brien, world-renowned brain surgeon Ben Carson, singer Willie Nelson, and comedian Bill Engvall.

Each of the eight residence halls is equipped with lounges, exercise rooms, music practice rooms, study rooms, and computer connections to the online library catalog system. Each residence hall room has one cable television and two direct computer network connections. Most residence hall rooms are double occupancy; some single rooms are available. Seavers Complex houses six students in each unit. Student safety is emphasized through controlled access to the residence halls, trained supervisory personnel, and a keycard entry system. There is also an apartment-style student housing facility with one, two, or four bedrooms, living room, bathroom, and full kitchen.

The University offers a variety of athletic facilities for both intercollegiate and intramural sports. These include a 2,768-seat field house, an 8,000-seat stadium, a gymnasium, outdoor tennis courts, indoor and outdoor tracks, an indoor swimming pool, squash and handball courts, a rehabilitation center, and sand volleyball courts. The 62,000-square-foot student recreation center includes a cardio/strength area with thirty-nine cardiovascular machines with individual televisions, four multipurpose courts, a group fitness studio, and an elevated running track. The University is a member of the Pennsylvania State Athletic Conference and NCAA Division II. Men's intercollegiate sports include baseball, basketball, cross-country, football, soccer, swimming, track and field, and wrestling. Women's intercollegiate sports include basketball, cross-country, field hockey, lacrosse, soccer, softball, swimming, tennis, track and field, and volleyball. There are ten intramural sports, which include street hockey, and thirteen club sports, which include men's and women's rugby.

Etter Health Center is open from 7:30 a.m. to 11:30 p.m. and is equipped with modern examination, treatment, and emergency rooms. It has six beds for inpatient care and a self-care unit for minor health conditions. Chambersburg Hospital is only 20 minutes from campus.

Students have access to comprehensive counseling services on request in academic, career, psychological, social, personal growth, and religious areas. The Career Development Center offers career counseling, workshops in resume preparation, job interview techniques, and job search assistance.

Location

Shippensburg University is on 200 acres overlooking its namesake community, a borough of approximately 6,700 people in the Cumberland Valley. The University is about 40 minutes southwest of Harrisburg, 2 hours from both Baltimore and Washington, D.C., and 2½ hours from Philadelphia. The campus is within easy walking distance of the center of town.

Majors and Degrees

Undergraduate degrees conferred are the Bachelor of Arts (B.A.), Bachelor of Science (B.S.), Bachelor of Science in Business Administration (B.S.B.A.), Bachelor of Science in Education (B.S.Ed.), and Bachelor of Social Work (B.S.W.). The College of Arts and Sciences awards the B.A. degree in art (computer graphics); communication/journalism (electronic media, print media, public relations); English (writing); French; history (public history); human communication studies; interdisciplinary arts; political science; psychology; secondary certification (art, English, French, and Spanish); sociology; and Spanish. The B.S. degree is awarded in applied physics (nanofabrication); biology (biotechnology, ecology and environment, health professions, medical technology); chemistry (biochemistry, health professions, medical technology); computer science (computer graphics, embedded programming, related discipline, software engineering, systems programming); economics (business, mathematics, political science, public administration, social studies); geoenvironmental studies; geography (geographic information systems, human-environmental, land use); health-care administration; mathematics (applied, statistics); physics (nanofabrication); professional studies (technical management); public administration; and secondary education (biology, biology/environmental education, chemistry, mathematics). The B.S.Ed. degree is awarded in earth science, physics, social studies/economics, social studies/geography, social studies/history, and social studies/political science.

The John L. Grove College of Business awards the B.S.B.A. degree in accounting, finance (personal financial planning), information technology for business education, management (entrepreneurship, general, human resource, international), management information systems, marketing, and supply chain management (logistics).

The College of Education and Human Services awards the B.S. degree in criminal justice and exercise science; the B.S.W. degree in social work; and the B.S.Ed. degree in elementary education K–4, and mid-level education 4–8, (biology, chemistry, environmental education, mathematics, multicultural education/TESOL, sociology).

Preprofessional preparation is available for admission to schools of chiropractic, dentistry, engineering, forensic science, law, medicine, optometry, pharmacy, physical therapy, podiatry, and veterinary medicine.

Shippensburg University offers 2+2 transfer programs in the allied health fields of biotechnology, nursing, occupational therapy (2+3), P.A.C.E. Program (2+2, 3+3), and radiologic sciences.

Academic Programs

The University is on the semester system with a fall semester beginning in late August and a spring semester beginning in mid-January. Three terms, one of three weeks and two of five weeks, comprise the summer program. Online courses are offered during a four-week winter term.

The general education program, which comprises one half of the credits required for graduation, is the core of the undergraduate curriculum. It includes courses to develop competence in writing, speaking, mathematics, and historical perspectives. The program ensures exposure to logic and numbers; linguistic, literary, artistic, and cultural traditions; biological and physical sciences; political, economic, and geographic sciences; and social and behavioral sciences. Ample elective opportunities are available.

The University requires students to take one approved diversity course for a total of 3 credit hours.

Academic options include an honors program, independent study and research, internships, field experience (mandatory in such areas as teacher education, social work, and medical technology), the Marine Science Consortium Program at Wallops Island, a 3+2 engineering program, and Army ROTC.

Academic Facilities

The library and multimedia services unit helps students develop skills in information gathering, critical evaluation, and creating media presentations of research findings. It provides assistance in locating and delivering books and articles in the Lehman Library, the Luhrs Library Media Center, online databases, and from other libraries through interlibrary loan services. Students can receive online reference and research support, guidance in citing resources and avoiding plagiarism, and technology support .Digital cameras, digital camcorders, LCD projectors, laptops, and other equipment is available and can be checked out for student use.

Student instruction is supported by multiple computer systems for student e-mail and computer network connections to the Internet. Every student has e-mail, file storage, and home page accounts on the University's servers. Several hundred terminals or personal computers for student use are available in residence halls, the library, academic buildings, microcomputer labs, and the Computing Technologies Center. Students with their own computers also have access to the systems. All students can use the systems 24 hours a day and have unlimited computer time at no additional expense. Most buildings have wireless network capabilities and several have satellite capability for distance education. The University also has its own campus-wide information system available on and off campus.

Costs

For Pennsylvania residents, the cost per semester in 2010–11 included tuition of $2902; room and board, $3500; educational services fee, $290; technology fee, $116; student activities fee, $200; student union fee, $200; health services fee, $150; and recreation center fee, $170. Nonresidents paid tuition of $7255 per semester and a technology fee of $175; the remaining fees were the same. Maryland residents paid tuition of $6530.

Financial Aid

The University's extensive financial aid program helps students who deserve a college education but who cannot afford to pay the full cost themselves. Shippensburg offers a wide range of aid in the form of grants, scholarships, loans, and campus employment. Most aid is awarded as a package consisting of all types for which the applicant is qualified. Nearly 80 percent of undergraduates receive some form of financial assistance.

Faculty

The University has 427 full- and part-time faculty members. The undergraduate student-faculty ratio is 20:1. Nearly 90 percent of the full-time instructional faculty members hold a doctorate or other terminal degree in their field. Each student has a faculty adviser.

Student Government

Shippensburg's strong student organization, built around a Student Senate, standing committees, and an Activities Program Board, provides a highly diversified program of student activities. Students sit on many policymaking administration-faculty committees and administer their own budget for the Student Services, Inc.

Admission Requirements

Shippensburg University, in compliance with federal and state laws and University policy, is committed to human understanding and provides equal educational, employment, and economic opportunities for all people without regard to race, color, sex, age, creed, national origin, religion, veteran status, or disability. A student's potential for success is judged by the high school average, rank in class, aptitude test scores (SAT or ACT), and recommendations. The high school record is generally considered the most important factor. A college-preparatory program, consisting of 4 units of English, at least 3 units of math, 3 units in the sciences, 2 units of social studies, and 2 units in the same foreign language, is strongly recommended. A campus interview and visit are encouraged. Transfer students in good standing are welcome.

Application and Information

To be considered for admission, a student should submit an application with a $30 application fee online at http://www.ship.edu/admissions/apply. The high school transcript, recommendations, and aptitude test results should be sent by the high school. Transfer students must submit college transcripts. The Admissions Office operates on a rolling basis.

For application materials and additional information, students should contact:

Dean of Enrollment Services
Shippensburg University of Pennsylvania
1871 Old Main Drive
Shippensburg, Pennsylvania 17257
Phone: 717-477-1231
       800-822-8028 (toll-free)
Fax: 717-477-4016
E-mail: admiss@ship.edu
Web site: http://www.ship.edu

The 200-acre Shippensburg University campus is located 40 miles southwest of Harrisburg, Pennsylvania.

SHORTER UNIVERSITY
ROME, GEORGIA

The University

Since 1873, Shorter University has been combining academic excellence with a caring Christian commitment. The University was established through the generosity of a Baptist layman, Alfred Shorter, and the vision of his pastor. They led a group of northwestern Georgia Baptists in founding the school, which was originally named Cherokee Baptist Female College. The name was changed to Shorter Female College in 1878 and to Shorter College in 1923. The College became coeducational in 1951. On June 1, 2010, the College changed its name to Shorter University. Shorter's enrollment of 3,600 includes students in both traditional semester programs and innovative continuous programs for working adults. Approximately 1,500 of these students are located on the main campus in Rome, Georgia. Students come from all parts of the United States and from other countries around the world. Shorter University has an overall graduate school acceptance rate of 80 percent and an impressive 82 percent acceptance rate to medical colleges over the past twenty-one years. Shorter University is very committed to providing a high-quality education in an intentionally Christian atmosphere. Each year, the campus is visited by noted Christian leaders, scholars, and outstanding musical performers. The dean of the chapel and the campus minister work together to provide a wide range of opportunities for spiritual growth. The largest religious organization on campus is the Baptist Collegiate Ministries (BCM), which includes Christians of many denominations. Student publications include a newspaper, a yearbook, and a literary magazine. Highly skilled music and drama groups include the Shorter Chorale, the Shorter Chorus, the Shorter Theater Company, the Opera Workshop, and the Shorter Marching Band. The Shorter Chorale was selected to represent the United States in choral festivals held in Yugoslavia, France, and Austria and represented the University in St. Petersburg, Russia. The Chorale was also selected in 2008 to perform mass at the Vatican during a tour of Italy. Shorter has also been the home of numerous National Metropolitan Opera Audition winners and finalists. The University has three fraternities and three sororities as well as chapters of two national music fraternities and honor societies for majors in biology, communication, English, music, religion, and social sciences. Shorter University is a member of the Southern States Athletic Conference of the NAIA. The University also has a competitive cheerleading program and competes in the Mid-South Conference of the NAIA in football and track and field. Varsity teams compete in men's baseball, basketball, cross-country, football, golf, soccer, tennis, and track and field and in women's basketball, cheerleading, cross-country, fast-pitch softball, golf, soccer, tennis, track and field, and volleyball. Wrestling and men's and women's lacrosse are scheduled to be added in fall 2010.

Location

The University is situated on 150 acres atop Shorter Hill, in Rome, Georgia (area population 93,000). Rome is located just 65 miles northwest of Atlanta and 65 miles south of Chattanooga, Tennessee, and cultural opportunities abound. The city of Rome offers the Symphony Orchestra, Rome Little Theatre, Rome Area Council for the Arts events, popular concerts and attractions at The Forum, and the 334,859-volume modern city library. The University sponsors numerous events, including faculty, alumni, student, and guest musical recitals; four guest lecture series; recitals; drama and opera productions; art exhibits; and athletic events.

Majors and Degrees

Shorter University offers seven baccalaureate and five master's degrees: the Bachelor of Arts, the Bachelor of Science, the Bachelor of Science in Nursing, the Bachelor of Business Administration, the Bachelor of Science in Education, the Bachelor of Fine Arts, the Bachelor of Music, the Master of Education, the Master of Arts in Teaching, the Master of Arts, the Master of Accountancy, and the Master of Business Administration.

The Bachelor of Arts is offered in art, Christian studies, communication arts, English, English education, history and political science, international studies, liberal arts, music, psychology, sociology, and Spanish. The Bachelor of Science is offered in biology, chemistry, Christian studies, computer information systems, communication arts, criminal justice, ecology and field biology, general studies, history and political science, history education, mathematics, mathematics education, psychology, and sociology. The Bachelor of Business Administration is offered in accounting, accounting–M.Acc. bridge, business economics, management, marketing, management information systems, and sports management. The Bachelor of Science in Education is offered in early childhood education (K–4) and middle grades (4–8). Programs leading to certification in secondary school teaching are available in English, general science, history, and mathematics. Certification is also offered in music for grades K–12. The Bachelor of Fine Arts is offered in art, musical theater, and theater. The Bachelor of Music is offered in church music, music education, organ performance, piano pedagogy, piano performance, and voice performance. Preprofessional programs are available in allied health, dentistry, law, medicine, pharmacy, physical therapy, physician's assistant studies, and veterinary medicine. Courses are also available in French, German, health and physical education, and interdisciplinary studies.

Academic Programs

Shorter is accredited by the Southern Association of Colleges and Schools and the National Association of Schools of Music and strives to provide an academic environment of high quality. Teacher programs are approved by the Georgia Professional Standards Commission. Small classes (freshman lecture courses average 22 students) taught by dedicated and highly qualified professors (71 percent of freshman lecture courses are taught by full-time faculty members, 26 percent by full professors) ensure that each student receives an education that is both challenging and personally rewarding. For any degree, a candidate must have earned a minimum of 126 semester hours; some degrees require a greater number of hours. As part of the orientation program at the beginning of the fall semester, each new student is assigned to one of several small orientation groups that assist the student in adjusting to University life; the student is also assigned to an academic adviser, who assists in the selection and scheduling of courses. Early registration sessions are available in the summer. Freshman advisers are specially trained faculty and staff members. The academic calendar is divided into two semesters from September to May, with two "mini" sessions offered during the summer. On-campus evening classes are available in selected disciplines. Shorter offers an honors program that spans all four years and provides students with learning opportunities that are not generally available to undergraduates.

Off-Campus Programs

Shorter's School of Business and School of Education and Social Sciences offer the Professional Studies Programs, which are specifically designed for working adults, on campus and in Lawrenceville, Riverdale, and Marietta, Georgia. Majors are business, education, and human resources. Classes meet one evening or weekend per week, year-round, with a required weekly study group.

Shorter University offers several monthlong study-abroad programs immediately following the end of the second semester in May, including MAYTERM (in Europe), the Asia Program, and the Americas Program. Students earn 12 semester hours of credit through travel, study, and classroom experiences. Students are housed in student residences or college dormitories, and the cost of most meals is usually included. Shorter University faculty members accompany the students and teach the courses that are offered. MAYTERM is usually based at British American College London and includes visits to England and to one other European country. The Asia Program is generally based at Zhengzhou University in China or at Mahidol University in Thailand. The Americas Program includes two weeks in Ecuador and the Galapagos Islands and two weeks in another Central or South American country. Studies in other countries can be arranged on an individual basis through the Office of International Programs.

Academic Facilities

Livingston Library, which was dedicated in 1976 as a memorial to Ray Livingston, houses more than 213,297 books, 582 periodical subscriptions, 8,099 microform materials, 12,134 audio/video items, 38,312 e-books, and 7,000 e-journals. The library also contains conference rooms (for both individual and group study), projection rooms, a graphics preparation room, computer terminals, typewriters, and music listening facilities for student use. The Alice Allgood Cooper Fine Arts Building and the Randall H. Minor Fine Arts Building are connected to form an outstanding fine arts complex, providing up-to-date facilities for the departments of music, communication arts, and art. The Cooper Building contains classrooms, music faculty offices, the art department's drawing and painting studio, and Brookes Chapel, the meeting place for convocations, concerts, recitals, and lectures. A renovated home adjacent to the campus houses expanded art facilities. The Minor Building contains classrooms, twenty-five music practice rooms (with a baby grand piano in each), a choral rehearsal room, faculty offices, photography facilities, a theater, a desktop publishing lab, a radio studio, and an art gallery. Rome Hall was named in honor of the citizens of Rome in appreciation of their generous support of the University. It contains classrooms, science laboratories (including the Stergus Collection of Internal Organs, one of the most complete pathology collections in the United States), faculty offices, lounges, and the Robert T. Connor exhibit of some 150 African and North American animals and skins. Alumni Hall houses the educational materials center and faculty offices. The Winthrop-King Centre houses classrooms, offices for coaches, a basketball gym, a dance and aerobic studio, two racquetball courts, a fitness center, and an indoor jogging track. The Fitton Student Union contains the campus bookstore, a 24-hour study room, a 24-hour game room, and an indoor swimming pool. Two computer labs are available for general student use. Computer labs for business and communication arts are also available. Smaller computer labs are available for art, music, and recreation. All residence halls have computer and Internet access. The Robert H. Ledbetter College of Business is located adjacent to the main campus in a newly renovated facility that offers seven academic classrooms, three computer labs, faculty offices, and student lounges. The College of Nursing is located in the heart of Rome's medical community and provides state-of-the-art lab equipment, simulators, computer labs, and classroom facilities.

Costs

Tuition for the 2011–12 academic year is $17,500 and fees are $350. Room and board charges are $8600.

Financial Aid

Shorter University offers aid through each of the five federal programs: the Federal Pell Grant, Federal Supplemental Educational Opportunity Grant, Federal Work-Study Program, Federal Perkins Loan, and Federal Stafford Student Loan. Full-time students who are Georgia residents are eligible to receive the Georgia Tuition Equalization Grant and may be eligible to receive the HOPE Scholarship. Scholarships are offered for achievement in academics, music, art, theater, humanities, and athletics. Awards range from $500 to full tuition, room, and board. Academic scholarships are renewable each year, provided the student maintains at least the required grade point average. Special grants and scholarships are available to students who plan to enter church-related vocations or who are dependents of full-time employees of a Southern Baptist church, institution, or agency. Shorter University offers need-based aid to students with demonstrated financial need as determined by the Free Application for Federal Student Aid (FAFSA).

Faculty

The Shorter faculty is composed of 110 full-time, highly qualified professors, of whom 67 percent hold doctoral degrees. The University also employs 50 part-time faculty members. A favorable student-teacher ratio of 11:1 in traditional programs ensures that each student receives individual attention.

Student Government

One of Shorter's truly distinctive features is that students may participate in a wide variety of significant extracurricular activities, each of which affords a chance to develop social and leadership skills that prepare a student to win in a competitive world. The Student Government Association (SGA) is the official voice of the students. Through SGA's Executive Council, Senate, judicial boards, and special committees, students are directly involved in the life of the University.

Admission Requirements

Students are admitted into the freshman class based on their academic grade point average, SAT or ACT scores, and required essay. A review of the student's goals and their compatibility with the purpose of the University are also determining factors. The University requires 4 years of English, 4 years of mathematics (including 2 years of algebra), 3 years of history/social science, 3 years of science, and 2 units of foreign language. In addition to the general requirements for admission to the University, students majoring in music must meet the following requirements: each student must perform in an audition of approximately 10 minutes in his or her major medium, and each student must take a series of music placement tests. Students must successfully fulfill these requirements prior to the beginning of classes in August of their freshman year, since the music curriculum requires at least four years for completion. An audition is also required for students majoring in theater, and an art portfolio review is required for students majoring in art. High school students who have completed their junior year, have an outstanding academic record, and have completed the units outlined above may be considered for early admission. High school seniors entering their senior year may be admitted on a joint-enrollment basis. Such students should have above-average grades and SAT or ACT scores. Transfer and international students are also welcome to apply. For international students, a minimum paper-based TOEFL score of 500, Internet-based score of 61, or computer-based score of 173 is required. All international students must have their academic credentials evaluated by WES or another transcript evaluation service affiliated with the National Association of Credential Evaluation Services (NACES). For all transfer students, credit for college work below a C cannot be transferred. Homeschooled students should contact the Office of Admissions directly for requirements.

Application and Information

Shorter accepts students on a rolling basis. Campus visits are highly recommended through a personal campus tour or one of three Open Houses.

Director of Admissions
Shorter University
315 Shorter Avenue
Rome, Georgia 30165-4298
Phone: 706-233-7319
        800-868-6980 Ext. 7319 (toll-free)
Fax: 706-233-7224
E-mail: admissions@shorter.edu
Web site: http://www.shorter.edu

SIENA COLLEGE

LOUDONVILLE, NEW YORK

The College

Siena College is a four-year liberal arts college with a Franciscan and Catholic tradition. The College's 3,000 students pursue degrees in business, liberal arts, and the sciences. Siena's wide range of academic programs provides more than 1,200 combinations and the foundation for students' successful careers and lives after graduation.

Siena offers a welcoming, student-centered environment with an emphasis on community. The College integrates Franciscan values such as diversity, respect, and service into everyday life. Siena seeks to instill in students a desire to always seek better for themselves and others, and to measure success by personal growth and integrity, not just achievement.

Small classes and involved professors help students grow both academically and personally. Siena's faculty members, 90 percent of whom hold the highest degree in their fields, are committed first and foremost to teaching. The student-faculty ratio of 14:1 helps to develop interaction between students and faculty members, including research projects, which often lead to student presentations at national conferences and published, peer-reviewed articles.

Eighty-five percent of Siena's students live on campus in traditional residence hall rooms, suites, and townhouse units. More than sixty clubs and organizations provide something of interest for everyone. The College offers eighteen Division I intercollegiate sports, plus many club teams and intramurals.

The Franciscan Center for Service and Advocacy is the College's primary vehicle for service. From serving meals to the poor, teaching adults and teenagers how to read, or assisting at a homeless shelter, to mentoring a child as a big brother or sister, there are many opportunities for improving the world. In return, Siena students learn understanding, respect, and dignity.

Siena also provides numerous student support services, including counseling, tutoring, health services, peer counseling, and a career center.

Location

Siena's 174-acre campus is ideally located in Loudonville, New York, a residential community 2 miles north of Albany, the state capital. The Capital Region is also referred to as New York's Tech Valley, one of the country's foremost regions for innovation and technology.

Albany is a college town with a wide variety of educational and social activities off campus. The Times Union Center hosts performances by major concert artists and professional sporting events. Siena is close to a number of theaters, museums, shopping centers, and restaurants. The nearby Adirondacks, Berkshires, and Catskill Mountains provide numerous outdoor activities including hiking, skiing, and snowboarding. Boston, Montreal, and New York City are less than 3 hours away. The alumni network in the Capital Region is a strong one, supporting numerous Siena interns and hiring Siena graduates.

Majors and Degrees

The College offers bachelor's degrees in the following areas: accounting, actuarial studies, American studies, biochemistry, biology, chemistry, classics, computational science, computer science, economics, English, environmental studies, finance, French, history, marketing and management, mathematics, philosophy, physics, political science, psychology, religious studies, social work, sociology, and Spanish. In addition, the College offers thirty-eight minors and nine certificate programs. Siena College also offers an M.S. in accounting.

Academic Programs

A strong liberal arts core forms the basis for all of Siena's programs. The Core Curriculum, consisting of 42 credits from fourteen courses, provides every Siena student with a common, coherent educational experience. Through the core, students pursue courses in the traditional liberal arts and sciences. Core courses engage students in critical thinking and dialogue, stress effective communication, and introduce students to the perspectives and modes of knowing specific to the arts and sciences.

ROTC affiliation is available at Siena in a U.S. Army unit, and two partnership programs are available at nearby colleges.

Off-Campus Programs

Siena students are encouraged to study abroad. Programs directly affiliated with the College include Siena at Regent's College, London; the Siena in London Internship Experience; the Siena semester at the Centre d'Études Franco-Américain de Management in Lyon, France; and the Center for Cross-Cultural Studies in Seville, Spain. However, programs are available for all majors virtually anywhere in the world.

Locally, internships are available through government, business, and nonprofit organizations. More than 400 students work as interns at nearly 300 different organizations each year. Those organizations sometimes offer jobs to Siena student interns upon graduation.

Within six months of graduation, 96 present of Siena students have started either their career or graduate school. Siena graduates are hired because companies know and recognize the value of the College's education.

Academic Facilities

The Standish Library collection of more than 321,000 volumes consists of books, journals, microforms, compact discs, videocassettes, and a growing number of electronic information sources. More than 6,000 volumes are added annually, and 1,600 serial subscriptions are currently maintained, with electronic access to thousands of additional journals. Siena Hall, a high-technology teaching and learning center is also home to Siena's Hickey Financial Technology Center. The Hickey Center provides Siena's students the opportunity to trade stocks, bonds, cash, and currency in a virtual environment and provides students with access to leading sources of financial data.

All academic and residential buildings are interconnected with a high-speed Ethernet network connected via fiber optics. Every student residence space includes a connection point to access the College's network and the Internet. The network includes more than 2,500 ports. The computer facilities are accessible 24 hours a day, seven days a week. Numerous computers are available throughout the campus for student use.

Costs

Tuition at Siena remains on average $7000 lower than its top ten private competitors, allowing the College to provide a rigorous education at a moderate cost. In 2008, *Business Week* cited Siena College as having one of the biggest returns on investment. For 2010–11, tuition was $26,510 and room and board were $9930.

Financial Aid

More than 86 percent of students receive financial aid. Siena is committed to providing personal attention to every student's financial needs, recognizing that each situation is different. Aid packages are awarded in a layered approach, combining scholarships, grants, and loans.

Faculty

Siena's faculty members are committed to teaching. Student concerns and development are at the heart of the curriculum.

The student-faculty ratio of 14:1 helps to develop interaction with students, as does the fact that Siena professors teach labs. Students are assigned a faculty adviser to help in the planning of their course of study.

Student Government

The Student Senate oversees student involvement in academic and social life and interprets students' attitudes, opinions, and rights for the faculty and administration. It charters all student organizations and provides funds for many through fees collected by the College. The governing board is made up of officers and representatives of all four classes and of the commuting students.

Admission Requirements

Siena seeks bright, articulate people who will take advantage of the opportunities available at the College. The average SAT score of accepted freshman students is 1160. The high school curriculum, activities, recommendations, and campus visit all affect the final decision. Students seeking degrees in the science or business division should be well versed in mathematics. Those interested in American studies, English, history, or philosophy are likely to find a working knowledge of a foreign language very helpful.

Application and Information

The deadline for the submission of a regular application is March 1 of a student's senior year in high school. Decisions are sent starting in mid-March. Siena also offers an early decision and an early action program.

For more information, students should contact:

Admissions Office
Siena College
515 Loudon Road
Loudonville, New York 12211
Phone: 518-783-2423
      888-AT-SIENA (toll-free)
E-mail: admit@siena.edu
Web site: http://www.siena.edu

SIMMONS COLLEGE
BOSTON, MASSACHUSETTS

SIMMONS

The College

Decades before women gained the right to vote, Boston businessman John Simmons had a revolutionary idea: women should be able to earn independent livelihoods and lead meaningful lives. Simmons College was the result.

Founded in 1899, Simmons was the first college in the nation to offer women a liberal arts education integrated with professional preparation. Today, Simmons is known for providing transformative learning that links passion with lifelong purpose. The College provides a strong liberal arts education for undergraduate women that is integrated with career preparation, interdisciplinary study, and global perspectives. Simmons offers the many benefits of a small university: an innovative undergraduate women's college, renowned coeducational graduate programs and the world's first MBA program designed for women. Exceptional internship and research opportunities provide hands-on experience and career exposure. Yet it is the Simmons faculty that really makes the educational experience unique by challenging students to reach their full potential while providing individual support and mentoring. Furthermore, the Simmons community encourages dialogue, respect, and collaboration—making the Simmons experience as thoughtful as it is thought provoking.

Simmons's interdisciplinary approach offers great advantages: a broader education and view of the world; personalized plans of study; and a chance to develop a range of professional skills and strengths needed for graduate school and an increasingly competitive job market. This is reflected by the fact that over the past three years, more than 90 percent of Simmons graduates have secured employment or entered graduate school within one year of graduation. Every student explores a variety of subjects while gaining an in-depth theoretical and practical understanding of her major. First-year core courses emphasize critical thinking and writing skills, while integrating two or more subjects—ranging from sustainability and Buddhist studies to social justice and visual communication.

Students fulfill their independent learning requirement through internships, fieldwork, and research projects. In doing so, they develop skills, confidence, impressive resumes, and a network of professional contacts. Science students co-publish research with faculty in nationally recognized academic journals as undergraduate students. Many students spend one or more semesters interning for businesses and organizations, ranging from Boston Public Schools and *The Boston Globe* to the Museum of Fine Arts, Smash Advertising, and the World Affairs Council. In addition, Simmons's Longwood Medical Area partnerships provide outstanding clinical opportunities at Boston's world-renowned hospitals. On campus, students conduct research using state-of-the-art equipment in areas such as materials science, gene splicing, and computer modeling. Yet the most important aspect of Simmons's approach to hands-on learning is that professors frequently invite undergraduates to collaborate on professional research projects, articles, and presentations, as early as their freshman year.

Acquiring a global outlook is integral at Simmons—the institution strives to cross boundaries in order to create opportunities. This includes providing students with an understanding of languages, cultures, and international politics. Programs such as Africana studies, East Asian studies, international relations, and modern languages offer a direct route to cross-cultural immersion. Simmons encourages students to spend an entire semester or year abroad. Short-term international courses provide unique opportunities to study topics such as journalism in South Africa, music in Austria, or history and civilization in Japan. Students also make a collective investment in the community through service-learning projects administered by the award-winning Scott/Ross Center for Community Service. These opportunities range from education initiatives to physical therapy clinics in needy areas of Boston.

Approximately 90 percent of first-year Simmons undergraduates live in college housing two blocks from the main campus. The quintessential New England residence campus features nine brick residence halls and a private, landscaped quad, as well as Bartol Dining Hall, the state-of-the-art Holmes Sports Center, a student-run cafe, and the campus health center.

Students say that Simmons's location offers the best of both words—an intimate college experience in the heart of a vibrant and bustling city. Simmons's 1,969 undergraduates love the fact that they can easily access the city's rich social and cultural resources but also come home to a safe, friendly campus.

Location

Considered by many to be the best college town in the nation, Boston has more than fifty colleges and universities and approximately 250,000 students. The historic, tree-lined Simmons campus is located in Boston's eclectic Fenway neighborhood, which is alive with music and fine arts, medical care and research, action and activism, and the resounding cheers of baseball fans at legendary Fenway Park. From campus, it's a safe, easy stroll to other colleges and universities as well as shops, cafes, clubs, museums, movie theaters, parks, and public transportation. Students hop aboard the "T" (Boston's public transportation system) and head to destinations such as the Italian North End, Chinatown, Harvard Square, the boutiques of Newbury Street, the Harbor, and Boston's many other diverse neighborhoods.

Majors and Degrees

Simmons offers more than 40 majors and programs. Popular majors include psychology, nursing, biology, political science, and communications. Faculty advisors help each student create a plan that fulfills requirements and satisfies her personal and professional goals. A number of integrated degrees and accelerated programs allow students to go directly from an undergraduate program to earning a graduate degree in areas such as business, education, health care, liberal arts, physical therapy, and science information technology. Simmons also offers individually designed preprofessional programs for dentistry, law, medicine, and veterinary medicine. Simmons students typically declare a major by the end of their sophomore year, and nearly a third choose to double major.

Academic Programs

Simmons offers a strong foundation in the liberal arts that helps transform intellectual curiosity into meaningful life's work. A minimum of 128 semester hours is required for graduation. Students must demonstrate competence in math and foreign language, complete a core curriculum in the liberal arts and sciences (40 semester hours), complete the courses required for the selected major(s) (at least 28 semester hours for each major), fulfill an independent learning requirement (8 to 16 semester hours), and round out their program with appropriate electives. To complement the theoretical knowledge learned in the classroom, Simmons offers many experiential opportunities, including an outstanding honors program, an award-winning service-learning center, and an abundance of study-abroad options—from short travel courses to a full year abroad. The Dorothea Lynde Dix Scholars option is available for women who are 24 years or older seeking a first bachelor's degree, or anyone seeking a second bachelor's degree.

Off-Campus Programs

Simmons is a member of the Colleges of the Fenway consortium, which allows students to cross-register with neighboring colleges, including Emmanuel College, Massachusetts College of Art, Massachusetts College of Pharmacy and Allied Health Sciences, Wentworth Institute of Technology, and Wheelock College. A domestic exchange program allows juniors to spend a semester at Belmont University, Mills College, Spelman College, or Fisk University. Students interested in international study may elect to spend one semester or one year at an approved university exchange or participate in intensive study-abroad programs during the spring semester. There are more than twelve short-term study abroad programs, which bring students to another location abroad for three weeks, typically following the spring semester.

Qualified students, usually juniors, may also apply for the Washington Semester at American University in Washington, D.C. Other opportunities include Success Connection, a mentoring program that matches select seniors with highly successful Simmons alumnae, and the Barbara Lee Internship Fellows program, which places students in Massachusetts legislators' offices and policy advocacy groups for one semester.

Academic Facilities

The beautiful Simmons campus offers an attractive, practical mix of historic and modern architecture, including state-of-the-art facilities and conveniences. The Main College Building houses a dining area and coffee bar, lecture halls and classrooms, administrative and faculty offices, the bookstore, the Student Activities Center, art studios, music practice rooms, and the Trustman Art Gallery.

The Park Science Center offers technologically advanced learning environments, including faculty and student research facilities, fully equipped science laboratories, state-of-the art nursing simulation labs, environmental rooms, observation rooms for psychological testing, and food science kitchens.

One Palace Road, the home of Simmons's School of Social Work and Graduate School of Library and Information Science, features electronic classrooms and also houses the centers for academic support, counseling, media, and technology.

Lefavour Hall is home to the newly renovated Beatley Library, which offers a number of high-tech services, including a wireless network, laptop loans, sophisticated online library service, technology-equipped group study rooms, and the Writing Center. The Department of Communications is housed on the third floor, where Simmons Radio streams live every day, and students have access to iMac centers, scanners, printers, digital cameras, video equipment, and more.

The School of Management is the newest building on campus and the best physical example of Simmons's commitment to sustainability and green practices. The building was assessed by the U.S. Green Building Council and is LEED-certified Gold—the second-highest certification available. The Graduate School of Management and the Career Education Center are housed in this building.

Costs

Undergraduate tuition and fees for the 2010–11 academic year were $15,640 per semester; room and board charges were $6235 per semester. Total costs, not including books, supplies, and personal expenses, were $44,700.

Financial Aid

More than 80 percent of Simmons students receive some form of financial aid. Scholarships, grants, loans, and federal work-study are determined by the Free Application for Federal Student Aid (FAFSA). Simmons also awards academic merit scholarships, ranging from $5000 to $15,000 awards, renewable for four years.

Faculty

As a student-focused institution, Simmons offers a learning experience that is highly collaborative and personal. Professors include distinguished researchers, published authors, Fulbright scholars, health professionals, and community leaders. They advise numerous government, nonprofit, and corporate organizations in the United States and around the world, yet they passionately uphold their primary obligation to teach. Students say the small classes, intellectual focus, and welcoming environment contribute to their confidence and success. Of Simmons' 141 full-time undergraduate professors, two thirds are women. Nearly all of the liberal arts faculty members hold doctorates in their field. A 13:1 student-teacher ratio ensures that every student receives individual attention and reinforces the strong tie between students and professors.

Student Government

The Student Government Association (SGA) coordinates the policies and activities of various student organizations, allocates the student activities funds, and promotes the interests of the student body by working closely with the Simmons faculty and administration. Simmons fosters a student-centered environment and encourages each individual to actively participate in the College community in a way that is right for her. Simmons has more than fifty student organizations, clubs, and academic liaisons, including nine NCAA Division III varsity teams, honor societies, cultural organizations, volunteer programs, a literary magazine, and a campus newspaper. In addition, every academic department has a student liaison, who participates in department evaluations and helps promote educational and social activities for students and faculty and staff members.

Admission Requirements

There isn't one type of Simmons student, but there are common qualities. Simmons women are intellectually motivated, socially minded, career-oriented individuals who aspire to a future with purpose. With this in mind, the Simmons admission team reviews applications to see not only what applicants have accomplished, but also who they are and what kind of person they hope to become.

The admission team also evaluates high school performance, SAT or ACT scores, recommendations, and the application essay. If English is not the applicant's first language, the TOEFL, IELTS, or a comparable exam score is required. Additional English language proficiency exams are accepted on a case-by-case basis.

Simmons welcomes applications from prospective freshmen, transfer students, international students, and students who are beyond the traditional college age.

Although not required, an interview is highly recommended. This gives admission officers better perspective about an applicant's abilities, interests, and personality—and at the same time, allows the applicant to evaluate Simmons and decide if it's the right place for her.

Application and Information

Students may apply online, use the Common Application, or submit a print application, along with the $55 fee and all supporting credentials. The early action deadline (nonbinding) is December 1. The regular freshman application deadline is February 1. Transfer students are evaluated on a continual basis; the preferred filing date for applications for the fall semester is April 1. All students applying for the spring should submit their application by December 1.

Simmons encourages prospective students and their families to attend an admission event or request an individual visit. They are welcome to tour the campus, sit in on a class, talk to current students, and meet with a professor, department chair, or program director.

For further information, interested students should contact:

Office of Undergraduate Admission
Simmons College
300 The Fenway
Boston, Massachusetts 02115

Phone: 800-345-8468 (toll-free)
Fax: 617-521-3190
E-mail: ugadm@simmons.edu
Web site: http://www.simmons.edu
　　　　　http://www.facebook.com/SimmonsCollege
　　　　　http://twitter.simmons.edu

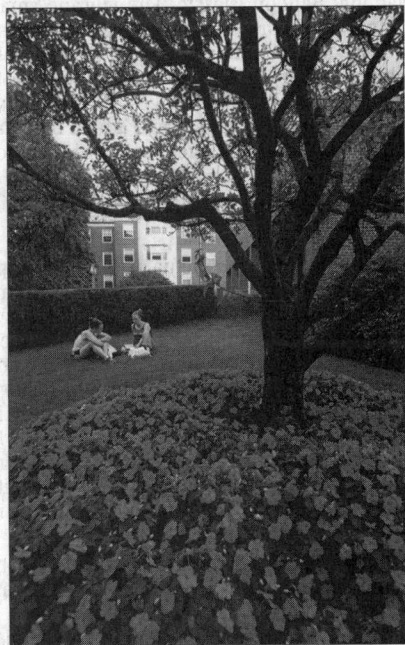

Simmons offers a private oasis in the heart of Boston—America's best college town.

SIMPSON COLLEGE
INDIANOLA, IOWA

The College

Founded in 1860, Simpson College is a private liberal arts college affiliated with the United Methodist Church. Simpson combines the best of a liberal arts education with outstanding career preparation and extracurricular programs. With a student to faculty ratio of 13:1, students have the opportunity to work closely with their professors. Simpson professors are as dedicated to their fields of study as they are to teaching—and it shows in the classroom. When this type of dedication and passion is combined with well-prepared and motivated students, the potential for success is virtually unlimited.

Extracurricular activities at Simpson are designed to supplement and reinforce the academic program and contribute toward a total learning experience. Activities range from an award-winning music program to nationally recognized NCAA Division III teams. Students may participate in student government, campus publications, religious life, music, theater, residence hall organizations, departmental clubs, and various other organizations. Simpson has seven Greek chapters on campus, including three national fraternities, one local fraternity, and three national sororities. Simpson competes in nineteen intercollegiate sports and has an extensive intramural program.

Simpson's beautiful tree-lined campus includes outstanding facilities that are continually enhanced and updated. Recent multimillion-dollar projects include the renovation and expansion of Blank Performing Arts Center (2011), renovation of athletic facilities (2010), and the scheduled addition of a stunning new student center (2012). The 4-4-1 academic calendar includes a May Term that provides students with unique learning opportunities in the classroom, internship settings, or while studying abroad. Simpson's 85-acre campus provides a setting that nurtures creativity, energy, and productivity.

Location

Simpson is located in Indianola, a residential community with a population of 14,400. Indianola is just 12 miles south of Des Moines, Iowa's capital city, with easy access to Interstates 35 and 80. The Des Moines International Airport is 20 minutes from campus. Indianola is host to nationally known events including the Des Moines Metropolitan Opera and the National Balloon Classic. The vibrant, small-town community has many choices for entertainment and recreation including Lake Ahquabi State Park, Summerset Trail, and unique restaurants and shops within walking distance of campus on the town square. Indianola's proximity to Des Moines gives students plenty of distinct advantages. Within minutes, students are right in the heart of some of the best entertainment and employment options Iowa and the Midwest have to offer.

Majors and Degrees

Simpson College grants Bachelor of Arts and Bachelor of Music degrees. Majors include accounting, actuarial science, applied philosophy, art education, art history, athletic training, biochemistry, biology, chemistry, computer information systems, computer science, criminal justice, economics, education (elementary and secondary), English, environmental science, exercise science, forensic science/biochemistry, French, German, graphic design, history, integrated marketing communication, interdisciplinary studies, international management, international relations, management, marketing, mathematics, multimedia journalism, music, music education, music performance, philosophy, physical education, physics, political science, psychology, religion, sociology, Spanish, sports administration, studio art, and theater arts.

Simpson also offers preprofessional programs in dentistry, engineering, law, medicine, optometry, pharmacy, physical therapy, theology/ministry, and veterinary medicine. Concentrations areas such as early childhood education and ethics are available, as well as many additional minors, including women's studies, social work, human resources management, Latin American studies, and coaching endorsements.

Academic Programs

Simpson College operates on a 4-4-1 academic calendar. The first semester starts in late August and ends in mid-December; the second semester starts in mid-January and ends in late April. A three-week session takes place during the month of May. During this period, students participate in a field experience/internship, study abroad, or take a course on campus with a hands-on focus.

The First Year Program is an extensive program of orientation, team-building, mentoring, community service, advising, and course work structured to help new students adapt to their first year of college. The program begins with summer orientation and continues throughout the academic year. College and Character, a national initiative of the John Templeton Foundation, named Simpson College one of the 60 colleges in the nation that offer students an exemplary program in their first year to develop moral character.

The academic component of the First-Year Program is the Simpson Colloquium, a joint classroom and advising concept that is unique among first-year programs. These courses are small in size—no more than 18 first-year students each—and all are taught by each student's faculty adviser.

With Simpson's curriculum, the courses students take delve deeper and focus more on projects that provide hands-on understanding of the subject matter. These courses allow students to work closely and build strong relationships with faculty members—just one of the hallmarks of a Simpson education. The curriculum encourages students to take advantage of Simpson's community partnerships, hold internships, study abroad, or conduct independent research. This curriculum was developed in response to research that indicates future employers are looking for effective communicators, innovators, and problem solvers. Simpson is on the forefront of providing the kind of experiential, liberal arts education college graduates need to succeed in their careers and achieve fulfillment in their lives.

Off-Campus Programs

Simpson provides many opportunities for studying abroad, with the choice of a semester-long program or a three-week May Term. Simpson's semester-long, faculty-led study-abroad programs include London, England; Schorndorf, Germany; Pathom, Thailand; Tahiti, French Polynesia; and Rosario, Argentina. Students also have the opportunity for semester study-abroad programs in France, Spain, Italy, Australia, and more locations.

Additionally, ten to fifteen travel courses are offered each May Term. Recent destinations include Africa, Central America, Great Britain, France, Greece, Ireland, New Zealand, the Galapagos Islands, Brazil, Argentina, and Scandinavia. May Term study abroad courses are led by Simpson faculty members and give students the opportunity to experience a different culture while gaining a stronger global perspective. Simpson has been recognized as one of the top 100 colleges in the nation for the highest percentage of students who study abroad—43 percent of Simpson students will travel abroad by the time they graduate.

The Capitol Hill Internship Program (CHIP) provides students with the opportunity to spend either the fall or spring semester in Washington, D.C. Past participants have had various experiences including interning for members of Congress, the Smithsonian Institution, the Republican National Committee, the Justice Department, CNN, the Australian Embassy, and FOX News. In addition, students participate in two seminars for course credit.

Academic Facilities

The Carver Science Center, named after Simpson's most distinguished alumnus George Washington Carver, provides state-of-the-art research facilities, computer labs, a cadaver lab, and classrooms.

Simpson has a wireless campus network with high-speed Internet access. There are numerous computer labs throughout campus where students can use standard office suite applications or specialized, discipline-specific applications.

The Henry H. and Thomas H. McNeill Hall houses classrooms for management, accounting, economics, and communication studies. In addition, the hall houses a seminar room and the Pioneer Hi-Bred International Conference Center.

The Amy Robertson Music Center houses the music department and contains the Sven and Mildred Lekberg Recital Hall, ten studios, twenty-two practice rooms, a music computer lab, and the band rehearsal room. The Salsbury Wing includes a choral rehearsal room, a classroom, and studios.

Dunn Library, a modern academic learning resource center, contains approximately 152,550 volumes, 296 current periodicals, 26,749 electronic journals, 2,985 DVDs and videotapes, 1,291 music CDs, and access to more than 7,480 e-books. Additional materials for research can be obtained through a national interlibrary loan network. The library also provides media equipment and services to classrooms and the entire campus. Hawley Academic Resource Center, which provides free academic support services to all students, is located within Dunn Library. The library is also home to the Iowa History Center.

The A. H. and Theo Blank Performing Arts Center is undergoing a multimillion-dollar expansion and renovation. The center accommodates Simpson's well-known programs in theater arts and opera and includes the magnificent 500-seat Pote Theatre, with both proscenium and hydraulically controlled thrust stages, a studio theater, the Barborka Gallery, technical facilities and shops, and classrooms.

Wallace Hall, named to the National Register of Historic Places in 1991, contains facilities for education, sociology, and applied social science.

Mary Berry Hall, renovated during the summer of 2008, houses the psychology department as well as faculty offices, six new labs, a control room for observation and data processing, and an animal care space. In addition, the building is home to humanities classrooms, a language lab, and the Farnham Art Gallery.

Costs

Tuition and fees for 2010–11 were $26,837; room charges were $3703; and board was $3936. These figures do not include books, music fees, or personal expenses.

Financial Aid

Simpson College seeks to make it financially possible for qualified students to experience the advantages of a Simpson education. Generous gifts from alumni, trustees, and friends of the College—in addition to state and federal student aid programs—make this opportunity possible. Simpson offers financial aid on both a need and non-need basis. Need is determined by filing the Free Application for Federal Student Aid.

Financial aid granted on a non-need basis includes generous academic scholarships (awarded on the basis of prior academic records) and talent scholarships (available in theater, music, and art). The talent scholarships are determined by audition/portfolio.

Also, specific scholarships such as the Great Ape Studies Scholarship, the United Methodist Service to Community Grant, the John C. Culver Fellowship, and the Wesley Service Scholarship can be obtained through application.

Faculty

Eighty-four percent of Simpson's 98 full-time faculty members have earned their terminal degrees. At Simpson, faculty members serve as academic advisers as well as teachers and often attend College plays, operas, and athletic events, reinforcing their sincere interest in the lives of the students.

Student Government

Each year students elect a president and vice president of the Student Government Association. In addition, students elect representatives to the Student Senate. The Student Senate appoints student members to all campus organizations in which students may hold membership. The senate also appoints 3 at-large students to attend plenary sessions of the Simpson College Board of Trustees.

Admission Requirements

Admission to Simpson College is selective and competitive. A strong academic record is essential. Applications are acted upon by an admissions committee, which is elected by the faculty and represents the five academic divisions of the College. These faculty members consider the college-preparatory courses taken and the grades received in those courses, rank in class, and standardized test scores (ACT and/or SAT), including test subscores, as well as a guidance counselor recommendation form.

Transfer applicants are accepted on the basis of successful completion of academic work at an accredited college or university. In addition, transfer applicants are required to submit official high school transcripts and ACT/SAT results.

Application and Information

Simpson's rolling admission policy allows flexibility; however, early application is recommended. Transfer and international students are welcome to apply. Students are strongly encouraged to visit the campus.

For additional information or to obtain application materials, students should contact:

Office of Admissions
Simpson College
701 North C Street
Indianola, Iowa 50125
Phone: 515-961-1624
        800-362-2454 Ext. 1624 (toll-free)
E-mail: admiss@simpson.edu
Web site: http://www.simpson.edu
        http://on.fb.me/Simpson_College (Facebook)
        http://twitter.com/simpsonnews
        http://www.youtube.com/simpsonweb

The George Washington Carver Science Center provides Simpson students with state-of-the-art labs and research facilities.

SKIDMORE COLLEGE
SARATOGA SPRINGS, NEW YORK

The College

Skidmore College is an independent liberal arts college of 2,400 men and women from fifty states and forty countries that prides itself on its creative approaches to just about everything. Hence, the College's core belief: "Creative thought matters." Founded by Lucy Skidmore Scribner as the Skidmore School of Arts in 1911, it became Skidmore College in 1922. In addition to being accredited by the Middle States Association of Colleges and Schools, the College has a chapter of Phi Beta Kappa and program accreditation with the Council on Social Work Education and the National Association of Schools of Art and Design.

Throughout its history, Skidmore has displayed a spirit of innovation and imagination in response to need and opportunity. In the 1960s the College built an entirely new campus; in 1971 it became coeducational; in 1983 it completely revised its curriculum, creating a comprehensive liberal studies program focused on interdisciplinarity (revised again in 2005 with the creation of the First-Year Experience program); and in 1993 it installed the Master of Arts in Liberal Studies program, primarily for adult learners. Skidmore has embraced change, seeing in it the opportunity to serve the needs and aspirations of its students. By expanding and refining its programs, the College has broadened its educational mission to respond to the opportunities and challenges of a global society.

Students enjoy a full schedule of intellectual, cultural, and social activities, such as lectures, visiting scholars in residence, art exhibits, concerts, and dance and theater performances. There are approximately 100 student organizations, including a weekly newspaper, a radio station, an Asian cultural association, an art and literary journal, and a student-volunteer network. There are no fraternities or sororities, which helps ensure an inclusive environment. A strong NCAA Division III intercollegiate sports program for men and women—nineteen teams in all—includes baseball, basketball, field hockey, golf, ice hockey, lacrosse, riding, rowing, soccer, softball, swimming and diving, tennis, and volleyball. Skidmore competes in, the Liberty League, which also includes Clarkson, Hamilton, Hobart and William Smith, Rensselaer Polytechnic Institute, St. Lawrence, Union, and Vassar. The College has a vigorous intramural program, club sports, and a growing health, fitness, and wellness program.

Skidmore's campus includes more than fifty buildings. The Williamson Sports and Recreation Complex has a pool and diving well, racquet-sport courts, basketball and volleyball courts, several intramural gyms, three dance studios, a weight room, a fitness center, and a human performance laboratory. Adjacent to the complex are Wachenheim Field, a small stadium with an artificial turf field for soccer, lacrosse, and intramurals, and a 400-meter all-weather track; dedicated softball and field hockey turf fields; and the lighted Wenger Tennis Courts. The Frances Young Tang Teaching Museum and Art Gallery, unique in its interdisciplinary approach, opened in 2000, and renovations to Case Center include a cyber café and an intercultural center.

Two major additions were made to the campus in 2006. The green Northwoods Apartments opened with 380 single-room units in ten new buildings. A new dining hall, Murray-Aikens, also opened, offering extensive vegetarian options, freshly made pasta, locally grown organic items, and a broad array of daily choices. The Arthur Zankel Music Center, an award-winning, state-of-the-art music building with a 600-seat auditorium, opened in 2010. Construction of new residence hall facilities is underway and is scheduled to be completed in 2013.

Location

Saratoga Springs, 30 miles north of Albany, New York's state capital, is perennially short-listed as one of the most interesting and vibrant small cities in the U.S. Famed for health, history, and horses—its mineral waters, Revolutionary War battlefield, and the nation's oldest thoroughbred racetrack—Saratoga is equally renowned as an arts and cultural destination. The Saratoga Performing Arts Center is summer home to the New York City Ballet, Philadelphia Orchestra, and Lake George Opera, and is a performing venue for top rock and jazz musicians. The city's downtown is just a 10-minute walk from Skidmore

and is brimming with galleries, clubs, museums, shops, coffeehouses, bistros, and restaurants. The city's location near the foothills of the Adirondack Mountains puts an abundance of outdoor recreational opportunities—major ski areas, state parks, large lakes, and mountainous regions of eastern New York, Vermont, and western Massachusetts—within an hour's drive. Boston, New York City, and Montreal are each approximately 180 miles from the campus.

Bus service is available from Saratoga Springs to New York City, Montreal, Boston, and other major cities. There are daily trains to and from New York City and Montreal. Rental cars are available at the Albany International Airport, which is served by major airlines. The College is located near Exit 15 of I-87 (the Northway).

Majors and Degrees

Skidmore College grants a Bachelor of Arts degree in the following liberal arts subjects: American studies, anthropology, Asian studies, biology, chemistry, classics, computer science, economics, English, environmental studies, foreign languages and literatures (French, German, and Spanish), French area studies, gender studies, geosciences, government, history, history of art, international affairs, mathematics, music, neuroscience, philosophy, physics, political economy, psychology, religious studies, and sociology. The Bachelor of Science degree is granted in areas of a more professional nature, including business, dance, education studies, exercise science, social work, studio art, and theater. There are more than twenty interdepartmental majors, economics–German and sociology–anthropology being just two examples. Self-determined majors, double majors, and minors are also available. In keeping with the College's creative spirit, more than half of Skidmore students choose a second major or minor.

Through partnerships with other institutions, Skidmore offers enhanced program/degree offerings in business, education, engineering, nursing, and physical and occupational therapy. These include: 4-1 M.B.A. programs with Clarkson University and Union Graduate, a 4+1 Master of Arts in Teaching program with Union College, 3-2 programs in engineering with Dartmouth College and Clarkson, a dual-degree engineering program with Rensselaer Polytechnic Institute, dual degree in liberal arts and sciences (Skidmore) and professional degree in physical therapy and occupational therapy (Sage Graduate School), and dual degree in liberal arts and sciences (Skidmore) and professional degree in nursing (New York University School of Nursing). Skidmore also has certification programs in teaching and social work and preprofessional programs in law and medicine.

Academic Programs

The Skidmore journey begins with the First-Year Experience which introduces students to the rigorous academic program and overall approach to learning and connects them with a faculty adviser/mentor. Talented but economically disadvantaged students who have been accepted into one of the Opportunity Programs (Higher Education Opportunity Program or Academic Opportunity Program) participate in a month-long summer program. A small percentage of students are accepted into Honors Forum on the basis of academic achievement and aspirations, leadership qualities, and civic commitment.

Generally, students choose a major by the end of sophomore year. In the interest of breadth, they are also expected to take one to two courses in both quantitative reasoning and expository writing, and at least one course in each of the following: lab science, social science, arts, humanities, and culture. There is plenty of academic support through Student Academic Services. In addition there are specific programs for prelaw and premed students. In their junior and senior years, students often add value to their courses of study through faculty-student collaborative research, internships, volunteerism and service learning, and off-campus study.

Off-Campus Programs

About 60 percent of Skidmore's students spend a semester or year off campus. In addition to Skidmore programs in China, England, France, and Spain, students can access 140 international programs through the college's approved programs structure, including programs in Africa, Asia, Europe, Latin America, and Australia. Students can also study at 200 other U.S. campuses, thanks to Skidmore's affiliation with National Student Exchange. All academic majors and minors can be accommodated and transfer credits are guaranteed for students studying on an approved program. Financial aid is transferable to most off-campus study programs.

The College also offers a Washington Semester (internship in conjunction with American University) and a semester at the Marine Biological Laboratory in Woods Hole, Massachusetts.

Arrangements for student internships (for academic credit) are made through Skidmore's academic departments or Office of Career Services. More than 50 percent of students are involved in volunteer work, much of it local. There are also up to fifty courses each semester with service-learning components.

Academic Facilities

Skidmore's 890-acre campus offers more than fifty buildings, designed and arranged to blend with the natural surroundings and to foster intellectual and social interaction. The newest building, the Arthur Zankel Music Center, features a spectacular 600-seat recital hall and a state-of-the-art recording studio. Skidmore's visual and performing arts space includes the Saisselin Art Building, with studios and the Schick Art Gallery, and Bernhard Theater, with a seating capacity of 350 and an experimental black box theater. The Tang Museum provides a focal point for cross-disciplinary study through the visual arts. The Dana Science Center offers state-of-the-art teaching and research space including centers for microscopy imaging and geographic information systems. Dana links the College's science departments to the Department of Mathematics and Computer Science in neighboring Harder Hall, which features a Linux lab with twenty-four workstations for advanced computer science projects.

Costs

In 2010–11 tuition was $40,350, required fees were $834, room was $6496, and board was $4490, for a total of $52,170.

Financial Aid

More than half of Skidmore's students receive some form of financial assistance. Aid is awarded on the basis of demonstrated financial need and is provided in the form of a student-aid package that usually includes a grant, campus job, and loan. Students interested in applying for admission are encouraged to do so regardless of their intention to seek financial aid. The FAFSA, a copy of the federal income tax form, and the CSS PROFILE must be filed each year. The application date is January 15 for entering freshmen. The College hosts an annual Filene Music Scholarship Competition to award four $40,000 ($10,000 per year) scholarships on the basis of musical ability without regard to financial need. Five $15,000 merit scholarships in math and science are also awarded annually. Other grants are available for superior math and science students. Detailed information concerning scholarships, grants, loans, and/or work awards can be obtained through the Office of Financial Aid.

Faculty

Skidmore College has 229 full-time teaching faculty members and 68 part-time members, including those with special appointments. Ninety-four percent of the liberal arts and sciences faculty members hold the doctoral degree or the highest degree in their field. The student-to-faculty ratio is about 9:1 and the average class size is 16. Although actively engaged in research and publication in their individual fields, the Skidmore faculty members regard teaching as their primary commitment. All students have faculty advisers who assist them in selecting courses and in designing individual academic programs.

Student Government

Students at Skidmore play an active role in College governance. Through the Student Government Association (SGA) and by membership on a number of major College committees, they participate in all phases of academic and social life. The SGA operates under the authority granted by the Board of Trustees and is dedicated to democratic self-government and responsible citizenship. Within the association, elected faculty members and student representatives serve on the All-College Council, the Academic Integrity Board, and the Social Integrity Board. Broad concerns of the SGA include educational policy, elections, social and student events, freshman orientation, student publications, and student clubs and organizations.

Admission Requirements

Those seeking admission to Skidmore's first-year class should complete a secondary school curriculum that includes at least 16 credits in college-preparatory courses. The Admissions Committee is also pleased to consider applications from qualified high school juniors who plan to accelerate and enter college early. Applicants typically have completed 4 years of English, 4 years of a foreign language, 4 years of mathematics, 4 years of social studies, and 3–4 years of laboratory science. Applicants must provide a secondary school transcript, standardized test scores (SAT I with writing or ACT with writing), letters of recommendation from two teachers of academic subjects, and a report from their guidance counselor. Skidmore recommends that applicants submit scores for three SAT II Subject Tests. The school also strongly recommends a campus visit and interview.

Through its participation in the Higher Education Opportunity Program (HEOP) Skidmore enrolls capable, energetic, and ambitious New York state residents who, because of their academic and financial situations, would not otherwise gain admission to the College under traditional requirements.

Application and Information

Applicants for admission must complete the Common Application—preferably online at www.commonapp.org—and submit it with a $65 fee or request a fee waiver from their adviser. All information should be postmarked by January 15. Applications from early decision candidates should be submitted by November 15 for the Round I early decision plan or by January 15 for the Round II early decision plan. Transfer candidates are urged to apply by April 1 for the next fall term and by November 15 for the next spring term. In addition to a high school transcript and standardized test scores, transfer candidates are required to submit, by the appropriate deadlines, an official transcript of all college-level work completed, recommendations from two professors, and a statement regarding personal and academic standing from the dean of students at the current college. International students are given special attention throughout the admissions process. Applicants whose first language is not English are encouraged to submit the results of the Test of English as a Foreign Language (TOEFL). There are a limited number of need-based financial aid awards available for outstanding international students.

Mary Lou W. Bates
Dean of Admissions and Financial Aid
Skidmore College
815 North Broadway
Saratoga Springs, New York 12866
Phone: 518-580-5570
        800-867-6007 (toll-free)
E-mail: admissions@skidmore.edu
Web site: http://www.skidmore.edu
          http://www.facebook.com/SkidmoreCollege
          http://twitter.com/skidmorecollege
          http://www.youtube.com/skidmorecollege

Autumn view of Skidmore's campus: Haupt Pond in the foreground, Case Center at left, and Scribner Library at right.

SMITH COLLEGE
NORTHAMPTON, MASSACHUSETTS

The College

Smith College was founded in 1871 as a liberal arts college for women and rapidly became one of the first such institutions to match the standards and facilities of the best colleges of the day. Today, with 2,750 undergraduates, Smith is the largest privately endowed college for women in the country. Graduate degrees (master's, Ph.D.) are offered in a number of departments and in the Smith College School for Social Work. Currently, forty-eight states and more than seventy countries are represented in the Smith student body. Approximately 60 percent of the students in each entering class were in the top 10 percent of their high school class; most chose Smith because of the excellence of its faculty and curriculum. Although most Smith students are between the ages of 18 and 22, Smith's Ada Comstock Scholars Program enables older women whose educations have been interrupted and who meet the College's admission standards to pursue an A.B. degree in part-time or full-time study.

Smith's house system is unusual and highly regarded. Each of the College's thirty-six houses is home to between 12 and 100 women. There are fifteen dining rooms that offer different menus, themes, and types of food. The house system stresses individual freedom, group autonomy, and mutual respect. Other residences, such as a cooperative house, a French house, and apartments, are also available. Smith offers a wide variety of extracurricular activities, ranging from service organizations to musical groups and from student publications to fourteen intercollegiate sports teams. The already varied cultural and social opportunities—lectures, workshops, dance and theatrical performances, art exhibits, concerts, and social events—are increased by participation in Five Colleges, Inc., a consortium that opens to Smith students classes and activities at Amherst, Hampshire, and Mount Holyoke colleges and at the University of Massachusetts. Smith's athletic facilities include two gymnasiums, five squash courts, a 75-foot six-lane swimming pool with 1- and 3-meter diving boards, a human performance laboratory, climbing wall, fitness center, and an indoor track and tennis facility, which houses four tennis courts and a 200-meter track. Outside are 30 acres of athletic fields, a 400-meter track, a 5,000-meter cross-country course, and twelve lighted tennis courts. Smith also has indoor and outdoor Olympic-size riding rings and a forty-two-unit stable.

Location

Northampton, a small cosmopolitan city with a population of more than 30,000, is in the Connecticut River valley of western Massachusetts. It is 93 miles west of Boston and 156 miles northeast of New York City. There are many shops and restaurants within walking distance of the campus and within the service area of a free Five College bus system. Buses run frequently to Boston and New York. Many students are involved in local organizations, and some intern in local city or county offices. Others participate on an extracurricular level in nonprofit agencies.

Majors and Degrees

Smith College awards the Bachelor of Arts (A.B.) degree. Areas of major concentration include Afro-American studies, American studies, anthropology, art, astronomy, biochemistry, biological sciences, chemistry, classical studies, classics, comparative literature, computer science, dance, East Asian languages and cultures, East Asian studies, economics, education and child study, engineering, English language and literature, film studies, environmental science and policy, French studies, geosciences, German studies, government, Greek, history, Italian language and literature, Italian studies, Jewish studies, Latin, Latin American and Latino/Latina studies, mathematics and statistics, medieval studies, music, neuroscience, philosophy, physics, Portuguese-Brazilian studies, psychology, religion,

Russian civilization, Russian literature, sociology, Spanish, theater, and women and gender studies. Interdepartmental majors and minors are offered in a variety of fields.

Academic Programs

The academic year is divided into two semesters, the first ending before winter recess. Noncredit Interterm courses are offered during January. Smith believes in the goals of a liberal arts education. With an open curriculum, students have flexibility to choose from more than 1,000 courses. The only requirement outside a student's field of concentration is one writing-intensive course. The normal course load consists of 16 credits in each of eight semesters, to total the 128 credits of academic work that are required. There are no specific distribution requirements, but 64 credits must be taken outside the major field of study. A student may also complete the requirements of two departmental majors or of one departmental major and another departmental minor. Concentrations in archives, biomathematical sciences, Buddhist studies, museum studies, and poetry offer students a way to organize intellectual and practical experiences around a focused area of interest. The Smith Centers for Engagement, Learning, and Leadership—the Global Studies Center; the Center for the Environment, Ecological Design, and Sustainability; the Center for Work and Life; and the Center for Community Collaborations—respond to emerging student and scholarly interests, provide contexts for internships and independent projects, and address real-world challenges.

Through credit earned on Advanced Placement or International Baccalaureate examinations and by summer study, some students may be able to accelerate and complete degree requirements in six or seven semesters. The Departmental Honors Program enables a student with a strong academic background to study a particular topic in depth or undertake research in the field of her major.

Off-Campus Programs

Smith students may take academic courses and participate in social and cultural activities at any of the institutions participating in the Five College consortium, described above. Smith students may also spend a year at another member institution of the Twelve College Exchange Program (Amherst, Bowdoin, Connecticut, Dartmouth, Mount Holyoke, Trinity, Vassar, Wellesley, Wesleyan, and Wheaton) or spend a year at Spelman College or Pomona College. Some students participate in the Jean Picker Semester-in-Washington Program in public policy, a fall internship program in Washington, D.C., sponsored by the College's Department of Government. The American Studies Program offers an internship at the Smithsonian Institution.

Smith offers Junior Year Abroad programs in Florence, Geneva, Hamburg, and Paris. Students may apply to affiliated programs in more than thirty other countries. Students eligible for financial aid are able to take that aid with them to any approved program.

Academic Facilities

The Smith College Libraries comprise the largest undergraduate library system of any liberal arts college in the country. The 1.4 million holdings are housed in the centrally located William Allan Neilson Library and in the libraries of the fine arts, performing arts, and science centers. The Neilson Library also houses a rare book room, the Nonprint Resource Center, the College archives, and the Sophia Smith Collection, a women's history archive. The Clark Science Center is a five-building complex that accommodates the nearly 30 percent of students who major in the sciences. The facilities include general laboratories, a molecular genetics facility, classrooms, a rooftop astronomy observatory, animal care facilities, scanning and transmission electron microscopes, an analytic ultracentrifuge, and a high-field nuclear magnetic resonance spectrometer. Ford Hall houses computer science, chemistry, biochemistry, molecular biology, and the Picker Engineering program. Academic computer facilities include networked Windows and Macintosh computers in public labs, classrooms, the libraries, and the foreign language center. All buildings and student residences are networked, and Internet access is available at no charge. There is wireless access in many buildings. Smith also has a digital design studio and several electronic classrooms. Bass Hall houses the psychology department, the scientific computing center, and Young Library, one of the largest undergraduate science libraries in the country. The Bass laboratories provide numerous facilities for research in neuroscience. The Mendenhall Center for the Performing Arts contains an experimental theater and a traditional theater, dance studios, and television and audio recording rooms. Sage Hall, the music building, includes an electronic music studio, a small recital hall, dozens of practice rooms, and a 750-seat concert hall. The Smith College Museum of Art houses one of the finest teaching collections in the country, and Hillyer Hall contains art studios as well as print-making, darkroom, and sculpture facilities. Smith's Center for Foreign Languages and Cultures maintains a multimedia laboratory and classroom housing a network of student workstations with integrated and interactive computer, audio, and video components.

Costs

Tuition for 2010–11 was $38,640. The room and board charge for regular student residences was $13,000. The activity fee was $258; books, supplies, and personal expenses were estimated at $2020.

Financial Aid

More than 70 percent of all Smith students receive some form of financial assistance from grants, loans, and/or campus jobs. Aid is awarded on the basis of need, as determined by the College. Each applicant must submit the Smith Aid Application (available on Smith's Web site), the Free Application for Federal Student Aid (FAFSA), the PROFILE form from the College Scholarship Service, and a copy of the current federal income tax return. Smith meets full demonstrated need for all admitted students who apply for aid by the published deadlines. The first portion of an aid award is an offer of a loan and campus employment; the remaining need is covered by grants from federal, state, and/or College funds. Merit-based aid is also available on a limited and highly competitive basis.

Faculty

The teaching of undergraduate women is the priority of the Smith faculty. There are approximately 290 faculty members; nearly all have earned doctoral degrees and are well-known in their professional fields. Close ties between undergraduates and their teachers are forged through small classes (70 percent have 20 or fewer students) and generous access to faculty members during and outside of regular office hours.

Student Government

Smith students assume much of the responsibility for their personal, social, and academic life at the College through the Student Government Association, which gives students representation on major college-policy committees.

Admission Requirements

Smith seeks students whose motivation, academic preparation, and diversity of interests will enable them to profit from and contribute to the varied possibilities of a liberal arts college. Smith is interested in the woman behind the numbers. As a highly competitive college, Smith gives primary consideration to the academic record of each candidate for admission. Strong high school programs have a basis of 4 years of English, at least 3 years in one foreign language or 2 years in each of two languages, 3 years of mathematics, 3 years of science, and 2 years of history. It is hoped that areas of special interest will have been pursued in depth. SAT or ACT scores are optional for U.S. citizens and U.S. permanent residents. Standardized tests (SAT, ACT, TOEFL or IELTS are required for international

citizens. SAT Subject Tests are optional for any applicant. An interview is strongly recommended. A first-choice early decision plan is available.

Applications are also welcomed from students who wish to transfer from other college-level institutions or who wish to enter the Visiting Students Program or the Ada Comstock Scholars Program.

Smith College is committed to maintaining a diverse community in an atmosphere of mutual respect and appreciation of differences. Smith College does not discriminate in its educational and employment policies on the bases of race, color, creed, religion, national/ethnic origin, sex, sexual orientation, or age or with regard to the bases outlined in the Veterans Readjustment Act and the Americans with Disabilities Act. Smith's admission policies and practices are guided by the same principle, concerning women applying to the undergraduate program and all applicants to the graduate programs.

Application and Information

A prospective first-year student interested in applying to Smith has three options: fall early decision, winter early decision, or regular decision. The fall early decision deadline is November 15, and applicants receive a decision on December 15. The deadline for winter early decision is January 2, and students receive a decision in late January. Regular decision applicants must complete the Common Application by January 15; all other parts of the application are due by February 1. These candidates receive their admission decision by April 1. The deadline for January transfer admission is November 15; students receive an admission decision in mid-December. The preferred deadline for September transfer admission is February 1, with notification in early April. Transfer applications are accepted until May 15, and decisions are made on a rolling basis. Application deadlines for the Visiting Student Programs are July 1 (for September admission) and November 15 (for January admission). Deadlines for the Ada Comstock Scholars Program are November 15 (for January admission) and February 1 (for September admission).

For more information about Smith College, students should contact:

Director of Admission
Smith College
Northampton, Massachusetts 01063
Phone: 413-585-2500
     800-383-3232 (toll-free)
Fax: 413-585-2527
E-mail: admission@smith.edu
Web site: http://www.smith.edu
    http://www.facebook.com/smithcollege
    http://twitter.com/smithcollege

Northampton combines small-town ambiance with big-city offerings.

SOUTHERN CONNECTICUT STATE UNIVERSITY

NEW HAVEN, CONNECTICUT

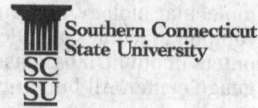

The University

The rich academic and social environment at Southern Connecticut State University encourages students to discover who they are, who they want to be, and how to realize their dreams. A public coeducational university founded in 1893, Southern offers 114 undergraduate and graduate programs. Fascinating internships, unique research opportunities, a challenging faculty, and a dynamic campus enrich every program. Southern is located in New Haven, the heart of "academic Connecticut."

Southern has five academic schools: Arts and Sciences, Business, Education, Health and Human Services, and Graduate Studies. Southern offers several programs, including the Honors College, for high-achieving students. The Honors College is a four-year alternative program featuring team-taught interdisciplinary courses, symposia, and requires students to complete an honors thesis or project in their senior year. The Office of Student Supportive Services offers tutorial support and coordinates special programs for veterans, international students, and students with learning, physical, and emotional/psychiatric disabilities.

The student body represents diverse ethnic and socioeconomic groups. Although most students reside in Connecticut, students from more than thirty states and more than forty countries also enroll at Southern. About 12,000 students attend Southern, including 9,000 undergraduates. More than a third of the 7,500 full-time undergraduates live on campus in ten residence halls and townhouses. Other students commute or reside in off-campus housing in the Southern neighborhood.

Competitive athletes and eager amateurs enjoy multifaceted intramural and intercollegiate sports programs at Southern. Intramural and club sports include coed three-on-three and five-on-five basketball, cheerleading, flag football, coed floor hockey, a golf tournament, ice hockey (men), karate, rugby (men and women), skiing and snowboarding, coed softball, ultimate Frisbee, coed soccer, a tennis tournament, Wiffle ball, and coed volleyball. A member of the National Collegiate Athletic Association (NCAA), the Eastern College Athletic Conference, and the Northeast-10 Conference, Southern offers student-athletes competitive opportunities in several intercollegiate sports. A university with a long tradition of athletic excellence, Southern is highly competitive among NCAA Division II colleges and universities, having earned ten NCAA team championships and seventy-one individual championships. Southern offers intercollegiate competition in men's baseball, basketball, cross-country, football, soccer, swimming, and track and field. Southern offers intercollegiate programs for women in basketball, cross-country, field hockey, gymnastics, lacrosse, soccer, softball, swimming, track and field, and volleyball. Outstanding facilities are available to all athletes in Moore Fieldhouse, Pelz Gymnasium, and the Jess Dow Field outdoor sports complex.

Location

New Haven, Connecticut, is a sophisticated city of 130,000 people that abuts picturesque Long Island Sound. Southern is located in the city's Westville section, near historic West Rock Park. Rich in tradition, New Haven is a classic college town; about 35,000 students attend its half-dozen fine universities and colleges. Only 75 miles from New York City and 3 hours from Boston, New Haven is an integral part of the economic, cultural, and social life of the Northeast. Students enjoy easy access to outstanding cultural opportunities, including movies, restaurants, clubs, concerts, seaside activities, sports, museums, and world-famous theater at the Yale Repertory, the Shubert, and Long Wharf.

Majors and Degrees

Southern offers the Bachelor of Arts (B.A.) and the Bachelor of Science (B.S.) degrees. The Bachelor of Arts degree is awarded in anthropology, art (art history and studio art), biology, chemistry (biochemistry), communication (communication disorders and media studies), earth science, economics, English, French, geography, German, history, Italian, journalism, liberal studies, mathematics, media studies, music, philosophy, physics, political science, psychology, sociology, Spanish, and theater.

The Bachelor of Science degree is awarded in anthropology (archeology, cultural, general, linguistics, and physical), art (ceramics, graphic design, jewelry making, painting, photography, printmaking, and sculpture), athletic training, biology, business (accounting, business economics, finance, international business, management, managing information systems, and marketing), chemistry and biochemistry, communication (creative message construction, interpersonal/relational, organizational communication, and video production), computer science (information systems), earth science (environmental, geology, and oceanography), exercise science (human performance and teacher education), geography, information and library science, journalism, mathematics, nursing, physics, political science, psychology (research), public health (environmental and health promotion), recreation and leisure (community, outdoor, and therapeutic), social work, and sociology.

The Bachelor of Science degree with teaching certification is offered in art education, early childhood education, and elementary education.

The Bachelor of Science degree with certification for secondary education is offered in biology, chemistry, earth science, English, exercise science, French, geography, German, history and social science, Italian, mathematics, physics, political science, Spanish, sociology, and special education.

Southern also offers preprofessional study in dentistry, engineering, law, medicine, and veterinary medicine.

Academic Programs

The University operates on a two-semester calendar. The fall semester usually begins the first week in September and ends in mid-December. The spring semester, which includes a one-week spring recess in March, typically begins the third week of January and ends in mid-May. Southern also offers several summer session programs and a three-week intersession program in January.

Southern maintains a strong commitment to the liberal arts and sciences as fundamental elements of a high-quality education. To ensure all students acquire the best education possible, Southern offers a strong yet flexible program that underscores the basics while encouraging individual choice. All baccalaureate degree candidates must complete a minimum of 122 hours of credit. Majors consist of at least 30 prescribed hours of credit in one specific, approved field. Degree candidates also must fulfill the all-university requirements, a common core of courses ranging from 41 to 54 credits in liberal studies. In addition, candidates for the B.A. degree must meet a foreign language requirement plus 28 credits of electives from areas of interest. Candidates for the B.S. degree must also satisfy the foreign language requirement and meet certain distribution requirements. Some professional B.S. degree programs enable students to develop a minor or a concentration in addition to the major with 12 credits in electives.

Off-Campus Programs

Southern's location in the heart of a major urban area enables the University to cultivate a growing list of meaningful regional internships. Aspiring social workers enjoy learning opportunities that extend beyond the classroom into New Haven's dynamic urban environment. Students in the B.S. nursing degree program acquire clinical experience at Yale–New Haven Hospital, the Hospital of Saint Raphael, and other sites that are linked by distance learning pro-

COLLEGE CLOSE-UPS

grams. Internships also are available for journalism students in city newsrooms and local TV stations. The University also offers internships at Long Wharf Theatre; ESPN Broadcasting; the Circle in the Square Theatre in New York City; MTV; Shearson Lehman Brothers, Inc.; and others.

Academic Facilities

A $260-million building program has transformed Southern campus life. The four-level, 125,000-square-foot Michael J. Adanti Student Center, which opened in 2006 and is a hub of campus life, includes a ballroom, movie theater, fitness center, an expansive bookstore, a food court, a TV lounge, and many meeting and conference rooms. Engleman Hall, the University's main academic building, was recently renovated and expanded to include state-of-the-art classrooms, departmental libraries, and conference rooms. A new wing has been added to the Hilton C. Buley Library. When renovations to the library are completed, it will double the size of the facility.

Southern supports more than ninety campus clubs and organizations, ranging from academic and career groups to religious, theatrical, and political clubs.

All on-campus housing includes high-speed Internet service via RES-NET. Other campus facilities include a satellite-equipped journalism lab; a modern television studio in the Ralph Earl Hall of Fine Arts; the John Lyman Center for the Performing Arts, a 1,650-seat theater for major productions; the Robert Kendall Drama Lab for experimental theater; the Center for the Environment; the Multicultural Center; the Communication Disorders Center; the Adaptive Technology Lab; and the Disability Resources Center.

Costs

Annual tuition and fees for 2010–11 for Connecticut residents are $8050. Tuition and fees for out-of-state residents are $18,415. On-campus room and board fees for the year are $9983. Student books, supplies, and personal expenses average about $2000 per year. All costs are subject to change. Prospective students should contact the Office of Financial Aid and Scholarships for current information.

Financial Aid

The Office of Financial Aid and Scholarships coordinates grants, scholarships, long-term low-interest loans, and part-time student employment for students and families who demonstrate financial need. The University offers the Federal Perkins Loan, the Federal Pell Grant, the Federal Supplemental Educational Opportunity Grant, the Federal Stafford Student Loan, the Federal PLUS loan, and the Federal Work-Study Program. Southern also provides alumni scholarships. Southern's tuition installment plan enables matriculated students to make monthly tuition payments throughout the academic year. More than 60 percent of Southern's undergraduates receive financial aid. Students who seek assistance must complete the Free Application for Federal Student Aid (FAFSA) and send it to the central processor for receipt by March 4, 2011. Prospective students can file the FAFSA form on paper or on the Web at http://www.fafsa.ed.gov.

Faculty

Like the University's student body, Southern's faculty members represent a broad spectrum of backgrounds, interests, and scholarly achievements. Southern's more than 700 faculty members share a deep commitment to teaching, writing, and research. Of the more than 400 full-time faculty members, about 85 percent hold a Ph.D. or terminal degree from major colleges and universities around the world. Many faculty members serve as academic advisers. In addition, the University offers counseling to help students with academic, personal, and career decisions.

Student Government

The Student Government Association is the voice of the undergraduate student body at Southern. The organization's 24 voting members meet regularly to discuss students' interests in a variety of areas, such as funding and academic policies. Student Government Association members also serve with administrators and faculty members on key University committees. Residential students govern themselves through their respective residence hall councils and the Inter-Residence Council.

Admission Requirements

Southern's selective admission policy considers each student as an individual, with particular consideration given to personal accomplishments and motivation. Southern seeks students with diverse cultural values and backgrounds; no applicant is accepted or rejected because of race, color, gender, sexual orientation, age, disability, religion, or national origin. Candidates must be high school graduates or hold an equivalency diploma. Their secondary school program should include at least 13 academic units of college-preparatory work, including 4 years of English, 3 years of mathematics (algebra 1, geometry, and algebra 2), 2 years of foreign language, 2 years of science (including 1 year of laboratory science), and 2 years of social sciences (including U.S. history). Other factors include the student's high school record, class rank (preferably in the upper 50 percent), and competitive SAT or ACT scores.

Application and Information

Candidates for admission should apply early in the fall of their high school senior year. The Admissions Office mails its first acceptance notice in early December. Early applicants have priority for housing and financial aid. Applicants must submit academic records, including a complete transcript of high school grades and class rank; an online admission application; a $50 nonrefundable fee; a written recommendation from a high school principal, teacher, or school guidance counselor; and a copy of the SAT or ACT score report. For additional information, students should contact the Admissions House, Southern Connecticut State University, 131 Farnham Avenue, New Haven, Connecticut 06515. Students are encouraged to apply online by visiting the University's Web site and clicking on Admissions. Students can find more information about the University on Facebook and on Twitter.

Paula Kennedy
Associate Director of Admissions
Admissions House
Southern Connecticut State University
131 Farnham Avenue
New Haven, Connecticut 06515-1355

Phone: 203-392-SCSU
       888-500-SCSU (toll-free)
Web site: http://www.SouthernCT.edu

Students walking over the footbridge in front of the Michael J. Adanti Student Center.

SOUTHERN NEW HAMPSHIRE UNIVERSITY

MANCHESTER, NEW HAMPSHIRE

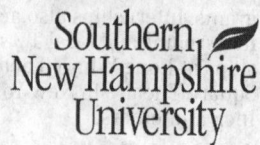

The University

At Southern New Hampshire University (SNHU), there are no limits to what students can achieve. Academic programs are created with the real world in mind, so students are prepared to launch successful careers when they graduate. Classes are taught by highly credentialed faculty who have professional experience and remain current in their fields. Academic and personal support is readily available, both inside and outside the classroom. If students need help, faculty and staff will rally around them quickly.

The University operates on the belief that college should change students' lives, not break the bank—a private university education should be affordable. That's why financial aid has been increased. Students with high school GPAs of 2.5 and higher can receive up to $18,000 in grants and scholarships. About 90 percent of the students receive some kind of financial aid.

The University has just over 2,000 traditional, full-time undergraduate day students, with a total enrollment in all divisions (day, evening, weekend, and online undergraduate and graduate students) of about 9,400. Programs are offered on campus, on location at the University's centers in New Hampshire and Maine, and online. SNHU offers undergraduate programs in business, culinary arts, education, hospitality, and liberal arts and graduate programs in business, community economic development, education, and hospitality.

SNHU is the first carbon-neutral school in New Hampshire. The wireless campus features a new academic center, a new dining hall (opened January 2010), new dorms and apartment buildings, a simulated stock trading room, multimedia classrooms, an auditorium, the museum-quality McIninch Art Gallery, virtual science labs, technology-ready buildings, a library with resources that can be accessed via the Internet, a fitness center that rivals members-only gyms, athletic fields, cooking labs, a bakery, and an award-winning, student-run restaurant.

Students can participate in one of the University's more than fifty student clubs or start new ones. Intercollegiate teams compete in Division II of the NCAA, the Eastern College Athletic Conference, and the Northeast-10 Conference. Sports include baseball, men's and women's basketball, cheerleading, men's and women's cross-country, golf, ice hockey, men's and women's lacrosse, men's and women's soccer, softball, men's and women's tennis, and volleyball. Intramural sports, including basketball, flag football, cricket, and volleyball, also are extremely popular. SNHU's powerful athletic teams dominate on the field—and in the classroom. The University's student-athletes earned honors from the NCAA and *USA Today* for high grades and 100 percent graduation rates.

Athletic facilities include an indoor, 25-meter, competition-size swimming pool; a racquetball court; an aerobic studio; cardiovascular equipment; four outdoor lighted tennis courts; a soccer/lacrosse turf field; baseball and softball fields; and two indoor gymnasiums with four basketball courts and areas for indoor soccer, indoor tennis, volleyball, and many other activities. The fitness center features 4,000 square feet of strength equipment and a 1,500-square-foot cardio deck.

The Wellness Center provides short-term health care, health education, and counseling services for students, and the buildings and facilities are accessible to the physically handicapped. A well-qualified student-services staff provides personal, career, and academic counseling; counselors are available on campus. Lifetime career services and counseling are available to all current students and to alumni.

Location

The University is ideally located, with easy access to downtown Manchester, New Hampshire's largest city and the most livable city in the East, according to *Money* magazine. It has also been named one of the top college towns in the country. Public transportation is available, and students may keep cars on campus. The mountains, beaches, and Boston are only an hour away. Morgan Quitno Press has repeatedly named New Hampshire the nation's most livable state.

Majors and Degrees

The University has three schools: the School of Arts and Sciences, the School of Business, and the School of Education. The University offers associate, bachelor's, master's, and doctoral degrees. Undergraduate programs provide students with a strong liberal arts foundation and the knowledge and skills they need to succeed in their careers.

The School of Arts and Sciences offers degrees in advertising (B.A. option); communication; community sociology; computer information technology (B.A. option); creative writing (three-year option available); English language and literature; environment, ethics, and public policy; game design and development (B.A. option); graphic design and media arts; history; justice studies (three-year option available); liberal arts; math; political science; psychology; psychology/child and adolescent development; forensic psychology; and public service. Students in any major within the School of Arts and Sciences may participate in the prelaw program.

The School of Business majors include accounting, accounting/finance, accounting/information systems, advertising (B.S. option), business administration, business studies, computer information technology (B.S. option), fashion merchandising, finance/economics, game design and development (B.S. option), hospitality business, international business, management advisory services, marketing, retailing, sport management, technical management, and the unique 3Year Honors Program in Business—the only three-year program of its kind in the country. Students save a full year of tuition by acquiring a bachelor's degree in just three years. Customized and outcomes-based, it is not a condensed four-year degree program and does not require night, weekend, or summer course work. The six-semester, 120-credit program features an interdisciplinary course of study and offers fifteen specializations. Students can start their careers earlier or use the fourth year to complete a master's degree.

The School of Education majors include child development, early childhood education, elementary education, English education, middle school math education, middle school science education, social studies education, and special education.

Other programs include associate degrees in baking and culinary arts and a bachelor's degree in culinary management.

An honors program, a prelaw program, and a pre-M.B.A. program are also available for students seeking additional challenges.

Academic Programs

At Southern New Hampshire University, undergraduate students receive a broad education in the liberal arts and intense practice in oral and written communication, coupled with the specific knowledge and skills they need to succeed in their chosen fields.

Recognizing that successful leaders must be able to view problems from a variety of perspectives, the University mandates that all students complete courses in writing, the fine arts, the social sciences, mathematics, science, and public speaking. First-year students must take SNHU 101, a critical-thinking seminar to help them make the transition to University life. Students also have the opportunity to take elective courses in whatever areas capture their curiosity and may elect to concentrate their electives to earn a minor. The University curriculum offers both structure and flexibility.

Off-Campus Programs

Southern New Hampshire University is adept at mixing academic theory with practical experience inside and outside the classroom. Half of the undergraduates participate in off-campus cooperative education experiences/internships, earning 3 to 12 academic credits. Such opportunities are based on a student's major and career goals and typically are taken during a student's junior or senior year. Students work with faculty members and the Career Development Office to find appropriate assignments. About 70 percent of those who complete co-ops/internships are offered positions by their employers.

The University has established relationships with a number of respected, high-profile employers who provide internship and job opportunities, including Fidelity Investments, Google, IBM, New York Life, Walt Disney World, LEGO Systems, the Boston Celtics, the Boston Red Sox, and Marriott International.

Students also work with real-world off-campus partners in their courses. For example, advertising students have created media campaigns for area businesses, marketing students have conducted market research for external groups, and education students assist local teachers in their classrooms. The University's graduates are in demand because businesses know they have been prepared to contribute both on the job and in their communities.

Opportunities for studying abroad are available at a number of partnering institutions in thirty-two countries around the world.

Academic Facilities

The main campus features a new academic center, a new dining hall, new dormitory and apartment buildings, state-of-the-art classrooms, wireless Internet access, auditoriums, technology labs, multimedia rooms, computer labs, a graphic arts lab, a student-run gourmet restaurant, a student-run bakery, a simulated stock trading room, a museum-quality art gallery, and more.

The Harry A. B. and Gertrude C. Shapiro Library features the Education Resource Center, networked computers, conference rooms, a career and placement resource center, and a growing collection of bound volumes, microfilm, microfiche, and ultrafiche; materials are available online as well. A recording studio, a listening room, and a closed-circuit television network that covers the entire campus are among the school's audiovisual assets.

Costs

Undergraduate tuition for the 2010–11 academic year was $26,112. Typical room and board charges were an additional $10,394. Students must pay $330 in student activity fees each year and should plan to budget funds for books, supplies, travel, and personal expenses.

All students are required to bring wireless laptop computers. Culinary arts students are required to purchase uniforms and knife sets.

Financial Aid

More than 90 percent of the University's students receive some form of financial aid, which may include need-based grants, academic and commuter scholarships, work-study funds, and loans. The average aid package has a value of more than $17,500 and includes a combination of scholarships, grants, loans, and employment sources.

The University participates in the Federal Work-Study Program, the Federal Perkins Loan Program, and the Federal Supplemental Educational Opportunity Grant Program. The school is also eligible under the Federal Stafford Student Loan Program and the Federal Pell Grant Program. Aid applicants must complete the Free Application for Federal Student Aid (FAFSA). The Office of Financial Aid can provide the appropriate forms, or students can go online to http://www.fafsa.ed.gov. Academic, athletic, and leadership scholarships are available for students who qualify.

Faculty

The University has more than 128 full-time faculty members and more than 200 part-time instructors. The student-faculty ratio is 15:1. Nearly 75 percent of the full-time faculty members hold Ph.D.'s or the equivalent in their areas of expertise.

The instructional programs blend theory with practice to stimulate students' professional development and personal growth. Faculty members bring extensive academic, work, travel, and life experiences to their classrooms. Although their primary goal is teaching, faculty members remain current in their disciplines. Outside the classroom, faculty members are management consultants, CPAs, analysts, small-business owners, economists, accountants, marketing professionals, entrepreneurs, innkeepers, chefs, world travelers, artists, poets, novelists, and much more.

Student Government

The Student Government Association is led by 25 students, including 5 officers, who represent all the students at the University. Its primary function is to represent the student body in campus affairs and to dispense student activity funds. One student is appointed to represent the student body on the Board of Trustees. Students are also appointed to most other standing committees, including the Financial Aid Advisory Committee, the Curriculum Advisory Committee, the Library Committee, and judiciary committees.

Admission Requirements

Applicants for admission are evaluated individually on the basis of academic credentials and personal characteristics. When reviewing applicants, primary emphasis is placed on a student's academic record, as demonstrated by the quality and level of college-preparatory course work and achievement attained. Most successful candidates admitted to SNHU present a program of study consisting of sixteen college-preparatory courses, including 4 years of English, 3 or more years of mathematics, 2 or more years of science, and 2 or more years of social science. Separate consideration is given to admission decisions for freshman, transfer, culinary arts, 3Year Honors Program, nontraditional, and international applicants. Students may apply online at http://www.snhu.edu or via the Common Application.

Application and Information

Applicants for undergraduate day programs must submit an application for admission, an up-to-date official high school transcript, a personal essay, and high school recommendations. Standardized test scores (SAT or ACT) are optional for most applicants. Candidates for the 3Year Honors Program need to submit test scores and are also required to have an interview. Transfer students must also submit official transcripts from all schools previously attended. International students whose native language is other than English must prove proficiency in the English language through the TOEFL examination. Admission decisions are based on the quality of academic performance, but a campus visit and interview are strongly recommended for all candidates. The University operates on a rolling admission basis, and applicants can expect a decision within one month of the receipt of their complete credentials. Applicants may also apply as Early Action candidates by submitting their application prior to November 15. SNHU is a member of the Common Application. There is a $40 application fee.

For more information about Southern New Hampshire University, students should contact:

Office of Undergraduate Admission
Southern New Hampshire University
2500 North River Road
Manchester, New Hampshire 03106-1045
Phone: 603-645-9611
       800-642-4968 (toll-free)
Fax: 603-645-9693
Web site: http://www.snhu.edu
       http://www.facebook.com/snhuadmission
       http://twitter.com/snhuadmission

Students on the campus of Southern New Hampshire University.

SOUTH UNIVERSITY

MONTGOMERY, ALABAMA

The University

Established in 1899, South University is a private academic institution dedicated to providing educational opportunities for the intellectual, social, and professional development of a diverse student population. To achieve this, the University offers focused and balanced curricula at the associate, bachelor's, and master's degree levels in the areas of business, criminal justice, healthcare management, health science, information technology, legal studies, medical assisting, nursing, RN to B.S.N. nursing degree completion, paralegal studies, physical therapist assisting, and psychology. In addition, the University offers a Master of Arts degree in professional counseling, a Master of Business Administration, and a Master of Business Administration in healthcare administration.

South University in Montgomery became part of South University in 1997 and has been part of the postsecondary education community in Alabama since 1887.

South University in Montgomery has a diverse student body enrolled in day, evening, weekend, and online classes. South University is designed to accommodate the range of needs of its student body. Students are primarily commuters who live within 50 miles of the city. They include men and women who have enrolled directly after completing high school, who have transferred from another college or university, or who have experience in the workforce and are pursuing an education that will prepare them to expand their current position or help them take a new professional direction.

South University in Montgomery is located in two buildings on a 3.75-acre campus. The facilities house computer, health science, and nursing labs; classrooms; a library; a student lounge; a bookstore; and faculty and administrative offices. Since most students live within driving distance of the campus, the campus does not currently offer or operate student housing. However, housing is planned in the near future. If housing is needed, prospective students should contact the Admissions Office.

South University is accredited by the Commission on Colleges of the Southern Association of Colleges and Schools (SACS, 1866 Southern Lane, Decatur, Georgia 30033-4097; 404-679-4501) to award associate, bachelor's, master's, and doctoral degrees. South University in Montgomery is authorized as an educational institution in the state of Alabama under Act No. 2004-282, Regular Session, Alabama Legislature, 2004, to conduct programs within the state of Alabama. The institution is also authorized by the State Approving Agency for the training of veterans under chapters 31, 34, and 35.

Certain programs offered at South University in Montgomery have earned programmatic accreditation. The Alabama Board of Nursing has authorized the Bachelor of Science in Nursing degree program to operate by the Alabama Board of Nursing. The nursing program is also accredited by the commission on Collegiate Nursing Education (CCNE), One DuPont Circle NW, Suite 530, Washington, D.C. 20036; phone: 202-887-6791; www.aacn.nche.edu. The Associate of Science degree program in medical assisting is accredited by the Commission on Accreditation of Allied Health Education Programs (CAAHEP, 1361 Park Street, Clearwater, Florida 33756; 727-210-2350) on recommendation of the Curriculum Review Board of the American Association of Medical Assistants Endowment (AAMAE). The Bachelor of Science in legal studies and Associate of Science in paralegal studies degree programs are approved by the American Bar Association (321 North Clark Street, Chicago, Illinois 60610; 312-988-5617). The Associate of Science in physical therapist assisting degree program is an expansion program accredited by the Commission on Accreditation in Physical Therapy Education of the American Physical Therapy Association (1111 North Fairfax Street, Alexandria, Virginia 22314; 703-684-2782).

Location

The campus is located on the rapidly growing east side of Alabama's capital city. As the state capital, Montgomery is a hub of government, banking, and law as well as a state center for culture and entertainment. Montgomery is situated in the middle of the southeastern U.S. and is less than a 3-hour drive from Atlanta and the Gulf of Mexico.

Majors and Degrees

South University in Montgomery awards the following two-year degrees: Associate of Science in business administration, Associate of Science in information technology, Associate of Science in medical assisting, Associate of Science in paralegal studies, and Associate of Science in physical therapist assisting.

The following four-year bachelor's degrees are awarded: Bachelor of Business Administration, Bachelor of Science in criminal justice, Bachelor of Science in healthcare management, Bachelor of Science in information technology, Bachelor of Science in legal studies, Bachelor of Science in health science, Bachelor of Science in Nursing, and Bachelor of Arts in psychology. A Bachelor of Science in Nursing completion program (RN to B.S.N.) for current registered nurses is also available.

Academic Programs

South University offers degree programs that are designed to meet the needs and objectives of students. Each curriculum combines didactic and practical educational experiences that provide students with the academic background needed to pursue the professions of their choice. In addition, faculty members strive to instill the value not only of education and professionalism but also of contribution and commitment to the advancement of community.

South University operates on a quarter academic calendar, and each University quarter comprises eleven weeks. Associate degree programs require a minimum of eight quarters to complete, and bachelor's degree programs require a minimum of twelve quarters for completion. Programs are offered on a year-round basis, providing students with the ability to work uninterrupted toward their degrees. More importantly, students have the opportunity to take classes on campus, online, or a combination of both through South University's unique Plus+ program. Combining campus and online classes provides students with maximum flexibility, allowing them to organize their college education around their work and/or family commitments.

Academic Facilities

The library has wireless technology throughout, comfortable seating, and quiet study space. The collection includes books, print and online periodicals, CDs, videos, and numerous online proprietary databases. Materials are housed in circulating, reference, and reserve collections and have been selected to support the academic programs. Also for student use, the library has a modern computer lab with ten workstations, each with Internet access, online database services, an office suite, tutorials, and class-support software.

Costs

For information about tuition and fees, prospective students should contact the South University Admissions Office.

Financial Aid

South University's Student Financial Services Office helps qualified students secure financial assistance to complete their studies. The University participates in several student aid programs. Forms of federal financial aid available to qualified students include the Federal Pell Grant Program, Federal Supplemental Educational Opportunity Grant (FSEOG) Program, Federal Work-Study Program, Federal Perkins Loan Program, Federal Stafford Student Loan Program (subsidized and unsubsidized), and Federal PLUS Loan Program. South University employs the Federal Methodology of Need Analysis, approved by the U.S. Department of Education, as a fair and equitable means of determining a family's ability to contribute to the student's educational expenses, as well as eligibility for other financial aid programs. Qualified students may apply for veterans' educational benefits. Students also are encouraged to investigate the availability of grants and scholarships through community resources.

Faculty

The South University in Montgomery faculty includes individuals of high academic distinction. Of the more than 40 instructors, 38 percent hold terminal degrees within their fields of expertise. In addition to teaching, faculty members strive to help students develop the requisites to appreciate knowledge and understand how experiences in the classroom and laboratory relate to professional performance in the workplace. The average student-faculty ratio per class is 13:1. Each student is assigned a faculty adviser, who oversees the student's progress and can answer questions about academic and career concerns. Students are encouraged to discuss program-related issues with and seek academic and career advice from their faculty advisers.

Admission Requirements

To be admitted to South University, prospective undergraduate students must be high school graduates or hold a GED certificate and submit an SAT or ACT score or a satisfactory score on the University-administered admissions examination. Transfer students must meet University-established criteria for acceptance as a transfer student.

All applicants must demonstrate English as a first language through submission of a diploma from a secondary school (or above) in which English is the official language of instruction. Applicants whose first language is not English must submit a Test of English as a Foreign Language (TOEFL) score. Applicants should contact the Admissions Office to determine other examinations/scores that are acceptable as an alternative to the TOEFL.

Applicants not meeting the entrance testing standards for general admission may be accepted under academic support admission.

Application and Information

Applicants must complete and submit an application form along with transcripts from high school and all colleges attended. Applicants must also complete all tests administered by the University or submit their SAT or ACT scores to the Registrar's Office. Applications are accepted on a rolling basis and should be made as far in advance as possible. Admissions officers are available weekdays, Saturdays, and by appointment. An appointment for an admissions interview or tour of the campus should be made in advance.

All international (nonimmigrant) applicants to South University must meet the same admissions standards as all other students. In addition, international applicants must have official educational records prepared in English, verify sufficient funds to cover the cost of the educational program, and meet certain other immigration-mandated criteria. South University in Montgomery is authorized under federal law to admit nonimmigrant students.

For additional information, prospective students should contact:

Anna Pearson
Director of Admissions
South University
5355 Vaughn Road
Montgomery, Alabama 36116-1120
Phone: 334-395-8800
      866-629-2962 (toll-free)
Fax: 334-395-8859
Web site: http://www.southuniversity.edu

South University in Montgomery, Alabama, has a diverse student body enrolled in day, evening, weekend, and online classes.

SOUTH UNIVERSITY

TAMPA, FLORIDA

SouthUniversity℠

The University

Established in 1899, South University is a private academic institution dedicated to providing educational opportunities for the intellectual, social, and professional development of a diverse student population.

The Tampa, Florida campus offers focused and balanced curricula at the associate and bachelor's degree levels in the areas of business administration, information technology, criminal justice, healthcare management, health science, nursing, RN to B.S.N. nursing degree completion, physical therapist assisting, and psychology. The University also offers a Master of Science in criminal justice, Master of Science in physician assistant studies, Master of Business Administration (M.B.A.), Master of Business Administration in healthcare administration, Master of Science in family nurse practitioner, Master of Science in adult health nurse practitioner, and Master of Science in nurse educator studies.

In addition, the Tampa campus offers students flexible scheduling with the choice of pursuing many of its courses on campus, online, or a combination of both through South University's unique Plus+ program. Combining campus and online classes provides students with maximum flexibility, allowing them to organize their college education around their work and/or family commitments.

The Tampa campus affords students the opportunity to learn in a modern facility based in a central location near Raymond James Stadium. Most students live within driving distance of the campus, but the Admissions Office does maintain information on various housing options should students relocate to the Tampa area for their education.

South University has a diverse student body enrolled in day, evening, and weekend classes. A sizeable portion of students have experience in the workforce and are pursuing an education that will prepare them to expand on their current career or take them in a new professional direction.

South University is accredited by the Commission on Colleges of the Southern Association of Colleges and Schools to award associate, bachelor's, master's, and doctoral degrees. The Commission on Colleges can be contacted at 1866 Southern Lane, Decatur, Georgia 30033; phone: 404-679-4500; for questions regarding the accreditation of South University. South University's Tampa campus is licensed to confer associate, bachelor's, and master's degrees through the Commission for Independent Education, Florida Department of Education, 325 West Gaines Street, Suite 1414, Tallahassee, Florida 32399; phone: 888-224-6684 (toll-free); Web site: http://www.fldoe.org/cie. The Tampa campus is approved for training veterans and other eligible individuals by the State of Florida Department of Veterans' Affairs, Division of Veterans' Benefits and Assistance, Bureau of State Approving for Veterans' Training.

Certain programs offered at South University in Tampa have earned programmatic accreditation. The physical therapist assisting program on the Tampa campus has been granted initial accreditation status by the Commission on Accreditation of Physical Therapy Education (CAPTE) of the American Physical Therapy Association, 1111 North Fairfax Street, Alexandria, Virginia 22314; phone: 703-684-2782. The Bachelor of Science in Nursing program at the Tampa campus is accredited by the Commission on Collegiate Nursing Education (CCNE), One DuPont Circle NW, Suite 530, Washington, D.C. 20036-1120; phone: 202-887-6791; Web site: http://www.aacn.nche.edu. The Bachelor of Science in Nursing program at South University is also authorized to operate by the Florida State Board of Nursing.

Location

Located on North Himes Avenue, South University's Tampa campus affords students the opportunity to enjoy all the culture and excitement a large city has to offer. Major league sporting events, major concerts, theater, world-renowned restaurants, and a cosmopolitan social scene are all within easy reach.

Majors and Degrees

South University in Tampa awards a two-year Associate of Science degree in information technology, criminal justice, and physical therapist assisting.

The following four-year bachelor's degrees are awarded: Bachelor of Business Administration, Bachelor of Science in information technology, Bachelor of Science in healthcare management, Bachelor of Science in health science, Bachelor of Science in Nursing, Bachelor of Science in Nursing completion program (RN to B.S.N.), and Bachelor of Arts in psychology.

Academic Programs

South University in Tampa offers degree programs that are designed to meet the needs and objectives of students. Some curricula combine didactic and practical educational experiences that provide students with the academic background needed to pursue the professions of their choice. In addition, faculty members strive to instill the value not only of education and professionalism but also of contribution and commitment to the advancement of community.

Each University quarter comprises eleven weeks. Associate degree programs require a minimum of eight quarters to complete, and bachelor's degree programs a minimum of twelve quarters to complete. Programs are offered on a year-round basis, providing students with the ability to work uninterrupted toward their degrees.

Academic Facilities

South University's Tampa campus provides ample classroom and student service areas and features several smart classrooms with audiovisual technology. The campus also contains a fully equipped medical lab, multiple computer labs featuring PC and Mac computers, and more. The library maintains a highly focused collection of resource materials, including current books, journals, and related materials. In addition, students have access to WebVoyager, an online catalog of holdings; the Internet; various bibliographic databases; and subject-specific software programs. Interlibrary loans are available through the Tampa Bay Library Consortium (TBLC), and OCLC, an organization serving 43,559 libraries in eighty-six countries and territories around the world.

Costs

Information about tuition and fees can be obtained by contacting the South University Admissions Office.

Financial Aid

South University's Office of Student Financial Services helps qualified students secure financial assistance to complete their studies. The University participates in several student aid programs. Forms of financial aid available to qualified students through federal resources include the Federal Pell Grant Program, Federal Supplemental Educational Opportunity Grant (FSEOG) Program, Federal Work-Study Program, Federal Perkins Loan Program, Federal Stafford Student Loan Program (subsidized and unsubsidized), and Federal PLUS Loan Program. South University employs the Federal Need Analysis Methodology, approved by the U.S. Department of Education, as a fair and equitable means of determining a family's ability to contribute to the student's educational expenses, as well as eligibility for other financial aid programs. Qualified students may also apply for the Florida State Assistance Grant (FSAG), Florida Bright Futures Scholarship Program, and veterans' educational benefits. Students also are encouraged to investigate the availability of grants and scholarships through community resources.

Faculty

The South University faculty includes individuals of high academic distinction. Of the more than 50 instructors on the campus, 46 percent hold terminal degrees in their fields of expertise. In addition to teaching, faculty members strive to help students develop the requisites to appreciate knowledge and understand how experiences in the classroom and laboratory relate to professional performance in the workplace. The average student-faculty ratio per class is 14:1. Each student is assigned a faculty adviser, who oversees the student's progress and can answer questions about academic and career concerns. Students are encouraged to discuss program-related issues with and seek academic and career advice from their faculty adviser.

Admission Requirements

To be admitted to South University, prospective students must be high school graduates or hold a GED certificate and submit SAT or ACT scores or achieve a satisfactory score on the University-administered admissions examination. Students who wish to transfer must meet the criteria established for acceptance as a transfer student.

All applicants to South University in Tampa must demonstrate English as a first language through submission of a diploma from a secondary school (or above) in which English is the official language of instruction. Applicants whose first language is not English must submit a Test of English as a Foreign Language (TOEFL) score. Applicants should contact the Admissions Office to determine other examinations/scores that are acceptable as an alternative to the TOEFL.

Application and Information

Applicants must complete and submit an application form, along with the general application fee, and official transcripts from all high schools and colleges attended. Applicants must also complete all tests administered by the University or submit their SAT or ACT scores to the Registrar's Office. Applications are accepted on a rolling basis and should be made as far in advance as possible.

All international (nonimmigrant) applicants to South University must meet the same admissions standards as all other students. In addition, international applicants must have official education records prepared in English, verify sufficient funds to cover the cost of the educational program, and meet certain other immigration-mandated criteria. South University in Tampa is authorized under federal law to admit nonimmigrant students.

Admissions officers are available weekdays, Saturdays, and by appointment. An appointment for an admissions interview or a tour of the campus should be made in advance. For additional information, all prospective students should contact:

Michele D'Alessio
Director of Admissions
South University
4401 North Himes Avenue, Suite 175
Tampa, Florida 33614-7095
Phone: 813-393-3800
          800-846-1472 (toll-free)
Fax: 813-393-3814
Web site: http://www.southuniversity.edu

South University offers students a flexible education and all the excitement and activities of Tampa, Florida.

SOUTH UNIVERSITY
WEST PALM BEACH, FLORIDA

The University

Established in 1899, South University is a private academic institution dedicated to providing educational opportunities for the intellectual, social, and professional development of a diverse student population. To achieve this, South University in West Palm Beach offers focused and balanced curricula at the associate and bachelor's degree levels in the areas of business, criminal justice, healthcare management, health science, legal studies, paralegal studies, information technology, nursing, RN to B.S.N. nursing degree completion, physical therapy assisting, and psychology. Other degree programs offered by the University include a Master of Arts degree in professional counseling; a Master of Business Administration (M.B.A.) and Master of Business Administration in healthcare administration, both in traditional and twelve-month accelerated programs; and a Master of Science in adult health nurse practitioner.

The West Palm Beach location of South University, established in 1974, strives to maintain small class sizes that permit students to receive more individualized instruction and interaction with faculty and staff members.

South University in West Palm Beach has a diverse student body enrolled in both day and evening classes. Students are primarily commuters who live within 50 miles of Palm Beach County. They include men and women who have enrolled directly after completing high school, who have transferred from another college or university, or who have experience in the workforce and are pursuing an education that will prepare them to grow in their current role or take a new professional direction.

In addition to classrooms and administrative offices, the campus includes a bookstore, student lounge, career services center, and ample parking. Since most students live within driving distance of the campus, the campus does not offer or operate student housing. If housing is needed, students should contact the Admissions Department.

South University is accredited by the Commission on Colleges of the Southern Association of Colleges and Schools to award associate, bachelor's, master's, and doctoral degrees. The Commission on Colleges can be contacted at 1866 Southern Lane, Decatur, Georgia 30033; phone: 404-679-4500; for questions regarding the accreditation of South University. South University's West Palm Beach campus is licensed to confer associate, bachelor's, and master's degrees by the Commission for Independent Education, Florida Department of Education, 325 West Gaines Street, Suite 1414, Tallahassee, Florida 32399; phone 888-224-6684; Web site: http://www.fldoe.org/cie. The campus is approved for training veterans and other eligible individuals by the State of Florida Department of Veterans' Affairs, Division of Veterans' Benefits and Assistance, Bureau of State Approving for Veterans' Training.

Certain programs offered at the campus have earned programmatic accreditation. The Associate of Science in physical therapist assisting degree program is accredited by the Commission on Accreditation in Physical Therapy Education of the American Physical Therapy Association, 1111 North Fairfax Street, Alexandria, Virginia 22314; phone: 703-684-2782. The Bachelor of Science in legal studies and Associate of Science in paralegal studies degree programs are approved by the

American Bar Association, 321 North Clark Street Court, Chicago, Illinois 60610; phone: 312-988-5617. The Bachelor of Science in Nursing program is accredited by the Commission on Collegiate Nursing Education (CCNE), One DuPont Circle, NW, Suite 530, Washington, D.C. 20036-1120; phone: 202-887-6791; Web site: http://www.aacn.nche.edu. The Bachelor of Science in Nursing program at South University is also authorized to operate by the Florida State Board of Nursing.

Location

South University West Palm Beach recently moved to a new 40,000-square-foot campus in the University Centre complex, located in Royal Palm Beach.

Majors and Degrees

The West Palm Beach campus of South University awards the following two-year degrees: Associate of Science in paralegal studies, and Associate of Science in physical therapist assisting.

The following four-year bachelor's degrees are awarded: Bachelor of Business Administration, Bachelor of Science in criminal justice, Bachelor of Science in information technology, Bachelor of Science in healthcare management, Bachelor of Science in health science, Bachelor of Science in legal studies, Bachelor of Science in Nursing, and Bachelor of Arts in psychology. A Bachelor of Science in Nursing completion program (RN to B.S.N.) for current registered nurses is also available.

Academic Programs

The West Palm Beach campus of South University offers degree programs that are designed to meet the needs and objectives of students. Each curriculum combines didactic and practical educational experiences that provide students with the academic background needed to pursue the professions of their choice. In addition, faculty members strive to instill the value not only of education and professionalism but also of contribution and commitment to the advancement of community.

Each University quarter comprises eleven weeks. Associate degree programs require a minimum of eight quarters to complete, and bachelor's degree programs require a minimum of twelve quarters for completion. Programs at the West Palm Beach campus are offered on a year-round basis, providing students with the ability to work uninterrupted toward their degrees.

Academic Facilities

In January 2010, South University West Palm Beach relocated to a new facility at University Centre in Royal Palm Beach, Florida, to better serve students and the broader Palm Beach County community. The facility features a hurricane-resistant infrastructure and includes several large labs, lecture halls, a library, and seminar rooms.

The West Palm Beach campus library houses a large collection that includes extensive law resources. Students may retrieve periodicals in paper or electronic form. Library-based computers provide access to several commercial online services, including Westlaw, the computerized legal research service; and the Southeastern Library Network (SOLINET). CD-ROM resources include the Grolier's Multimedia Encyclopedia and the EBSCO magazine full-text database. Internet access is available in the library.

Costs

For information on South University's tuition and fees, prospective students should contact the campus Admissions Office.

Financial Aid

South University's Office of Student Financial Services helps qualified students secure financial assistance to complete their studies. The University participates in several student aid programs. Forms of financial aid available to qualified students through federal resources include the Federal Pell Grant Program, Federal Supplemental Educational Opportunity Grant (FSEOG) Program, Federal Work-Study Program, Federal Perkins Loan Program, Federal Stafford Loan Program (subsidized and unsubsidized), and Federal PLUS Loan Program. Qualified students may also apply for the Florida State Assistance Grant (FSAG), Florida Bright Futures Scholarship Program, and veterans' educational benefits. Students also are encouraged to investigate the availability of grants and scholarships through community resources.

Faculty

The South University faculty includes individuals of high academic distinction. Of the more than 60 instructors on the West Palm Beach campus, 37 percent hold terminal degrees in their fields of expertise. In addition to teaching, faculty members strive to help students develop the requisites to appreciate knowledge and understand how experiences in the classroom and laboratory relate to professional performance in the workplace. The average student-faculty ratio is 16:1. Each student is assigned a faculty adviser, who oversees the student's progress and can answer questions about academic and career concerns. Students are encouraged to discuss program-related issues with and seek academic and career advice from their faculty advisers.

Admission Requirements

To be admitted to South University, prospective students must be high school graduates or hold a GED certificate and submit an SAT or ACT score or a satisfactory score on the University-administered admissions examination. Students who wish to transfer must meet the criteria established for acceptance as a transfer student.

All applicants to South University must demonstrate English as a first language through submission of a diploma from a secondary school (or above) in which English is the official language of instruction. Applicants whose first language is not English must submit a Test of English as a Foreign Language (TOEFL) score. Applicants should contact the Admissions Office to determine other examinations/scores that are acceptable as an alternative to the TOEFL.

Applicants not meeting the testing standards for general admission may be accepted under academic support admission. General admission to the University does not guarantee admission to the nursing program. To obtain specific entrance requirements for the nursing program, prospective students should contact the campus Admissions Office or visit the South University Web site.

Application and Information

Applicants must complete and submit an application form, along with the general application fee, and official transcripts from all high schools and colleges attended. Faxed documents are not considered official. Applicants must also complete all tests administered by the University or submit their SAT or ACT scores to the Registrar's Office. Applications are accepted on a rolling basis and should be made as far in advance as possible.

All international (nonimmigrant) applicants to South University's West Palm Beach campus must meet the same admissions standards as all other students. In addition, international applicants must have official education records prepared in English, verify sufficient funds to cover the cost of the educational program, and meet certain other immigration-mandated criteria. South University in West Palm Beach is authorized under federal law to admit nonimmigrant students.

Admissions officers are available weekdays, Saturdays, and weekends. An appointment for an admissions interview or tour of the campus should be made in advance. For additional information, all prospective students should contact:

Sabrina Mohammed
Director of Admissions
South University
University Centre
9801 Belvedere Road
Royal Palm Beach, Florida 33411
Phone: 561-273-6500
      866-629-2902 (toll-free)
Fax: 561-273-6420
Web site: http://www.southuniversity.edu

South University in West Palm Beach, Florida, relocated in 2010 to a new facility with classroom and lab space for its arts and sciences, business, health professions, and nursing programs.

SOUTH UNIVERSITY

SAVANNAH, GEORGIA

The University

South University is a private academic institution dedicated to providing educational opportunities for the intellectual, social, and professional development of a diverse student population. To achieve this, the Savannah campus offers focused and balanced curricula at the associate and bachelor's degree level including, but not limited to, the areas of business, medical assisting, nursing, RN to B.S.N. and RN to M.S.N. nursing degree completion, criminal justice, information technology, legal studies, and psychology. The University also offers master's degree programs in anesthesiology assistant studies, physician assistant studies, and healthcare administration. In addition, the campus offers a Master of Arts in professional counseling; a Master of Business Administration (M.B.A.) and Master of Business administration in healthcare administration, both in traditional and twelve-month accelerated programs; and a Doctor of Pharmacy degree through its School of Pharmacy—one of only three programs in the state of Georgia and the only one in the state that is currently available in an accelerated three-year format. South University is the first university or college in Savannah to offer a health professions doctoral degree program.

South University traces its heritage back to 1899 and today has grown into a multicampus system with locations in Columbia, South Carolina; Montgomery, Alabama; Novi, Michigan; Richmond and Virginia Beach, Virginia; Savannah, Georgia; and Tampa and West Palm Beach, Florida.

Students can also pursue degrees through a combination of on-campus and online classes as part of the University's unique Plus+ program, which provides maximum scheduling flexibility. This flexibility allows students to organize their college education around work and family commitments. For those who choose to take on-site courses, Savannah campus facilities and amenities include a bookstore, student lounges, a career services center, wireless Internet access, and ample parking in addition to classrooms and offices.

The cornerstone of the Savannah campus is the School of Pharmacy building, which joins the College of Business and College of Health Professions buildings. The University strives to maintain small class sizes that permit students to receive individualized instruction and interaction with faculty and staff members.

The Savannah campus of South University has a diverse student body enrolled in day, evening, and weekend classes. Undergraduate students are primarily commuters who live within 60 miles of the city. Graduate students come from all of the United States and as far away as California and Alaska. They include men and women who have enrolled directly after completing high school, who have transferred from another college or university, or who have experience in the workforce and are pursuing an education that will prepare them to grow in their current position or enable them to take a new professional direction. The University offers a school-sponsored housing option in conjunction with local apartment communities for students who are relocating to Savannah to pursue their degrees.

South University is accredited by the Commission on Colleges of the Southern Association of Colleges and Schools to award associate, bachelor's, master's, and doctoral degrees. The Commission on Colleges can be contacted at 1866 Southern Lane, Decatur, Georgia 30033; phone: 404-679-4500; for questions regarding the accreditation of South University. The Savannah campus is also authorized under the Georgia Non-public Postsecondary Educational Institutions Act of 1990 to confer those degrees. In addition, the campus is approved for training military veterans and other individuals by the State of Georgia Department of Veterans' Services, State Approving Agency, in Atlanta, Georgia.

Certain programs offered at the Savannah campus have earned programmatic accreditation. The South University Associate of Science degree in medical assisting is accredited by the Commission on Accreditation of Allied Health Education Programs (http://www.caahep.org) on recommendation of the Curriculum Review Board of the American Association of Medical Assistants Endowment (AAMEA). The Associate of Science in physical therapist assisting program is accredited by the Commission on Accreditation in Physical Therapy Education of the American Physical Therapy Association (CAPTE), 1111 North Fairfax Street, Alexandria, Virginia 22314; phone: 703-684-2782; e-mail: accreditation@apta.org; Web site: http://www.capteonline.org.

South University's Doctor of Pharmacy program is accredited by the Accreditation Council for Pharmacy Education, 20 North Clark Street, Suite 2500, Chicago, Illinois 60602-5109; phone: 312-664-3575; fax: 312-664-4652; Web site: http://www.acpeaccredit.org. The school is a member of the American Association of Colleges of Pharmacy (AACP).

The anesthesiologist assistant program has received accreditation from the Commission on Accreditation of Allied Health Educational Programs (CAAHEP) through its Accreditation Review Committee for Anesthesiologist Assistant Programs (ARC-AA). Contact ARC-AA in care of CAAHEP, 35 East Wacker Drive, Suite 1970, Chicago, Illinois 60601; 312-553-9355. The Master of Science in physician assistant studies program on the Savannah campus is accredited by the Accreditation Review Commission on Education for Physician Assistant Programs (ARC-PA), 1000 North Oak Avenue, Marshfield, Wisconsin 54449-5788; phone: 715-389-3785; or 12000 Findley Road, Suite 240, Johns Creek, Georgia 30097; phone: 770-476-1224; fax: 770-476-1738; Web site: http://www.arc-pa.org. This accreditation status qualifies graduating students to take the national certifying examination administered by the National Commission on Certification of Physician Assistants (NCCPA). The physician assistant studies program is a member of the Association of Physician Assistants Programs, the national organization representing physician assistant education programs. The Bachelor of Science in legal studies and Associate of Science in paralegal studies programs are approved by the American Bar Association, 321 North Clark Street, Chicago, Illinois 60610; phone: 312-988-5617.

Location

This campus, the largest among South University's locations, is located in the midtown section of historic Savannah, Georgia, minutes from downtown, cultural activities, and the beach. The buildings are situated on 9 acres of land and are easily accessible from any section of Savannah, the surrounding region, and coastal South Carolina.

Majors and Degrees

The Savannah campus of South University awards the following two-year degrees: Associate of Science in criminal justice, Associate of Science in business administration, Associate of Science in information technology, Associate of Science in medical assisting, Associate of Science in paralegal studies, and Associate of Science in physical therapist assisting.

Four-year degree programs include a Bachelor of Business Administration, Bachelor of Science in criminal justice, Bachelor of Science in healthcare management, Bachelor of Science in information technology, Bachelor of Science in legal studies, and Bachelor of Arts in psychology.

Academic Programs

The Savannah campus of South University offers degree programs that are designed to meet the needs and objectives of students. Each curriculum combines classroom and practical educational experiences that provide students with the academic background needed to pursue the professions of their choice. In addition, faculty members strive to instill the value not only of education and professionalism but also of contribution and commitment to the advancement of community.

South University operates on a quarter system, with each quarter comprising eleven weeks. Associate degree programs require a minimum of eight quarters to complete, and bachelor's degree programs require a minimum of twelve quarters for completion. Undergraduate programs are offered on a year-round basis, providing students with the ability to work uninterrupted toward their degrees.

Academic Facilities

The Savannah campus library has a large collection that includes an extensive law and health professions library. Students may retrieve periodicals in paper or electronic form. Library-based computers provide access to several commercial online services, including Westlaw, the computerized legal research service; GALILEO, the Georgia network of databases; and MEDLINE, for health sciences students. CD-ROM resources include the Encyclopedia Britannica, the Official Code of Georgia Annotated, ADAM, and the EBSCO magazine full-text database. Internet access is available on all computers throughout the campus, and the University offers wireless Internet access through an on-campus Wi-Fi network.

Costs

Tuition information is available by contacting the South University Admissions Department.

Financial Aid

South University's Student Financial Services Office helps qualified students secure financial assistance to complete their studies. The University participates in several student aid programs. Forms of financial aid available to qualified students through federal resources include the Federal Pell Grant Program, Federal Supplemental Educational Opportunity Grant (FSEOG) Program, Federal Work-Study Program, Federal Perkins Loan Program, Federal Stafford Loan Program (subsidized and unsubsidized), and Federal PLUS Loan Program. Qualified students may apply for the Georgia HOPE Scholarship, Georgia Tuition Equalization Grant, Georgia LEAP Grant Program, and veterans' educational benefits. Students are also encouraged to investigate the availability of grants and scholarships through community resources.

Faculty

The South University faculty includes individuals of high academic distinction. Of the more than 80 instructors on the Savannah campus, 40 percent hold terminal degrees. In addition to teaching, faculty members strive to help students develop the requisites to appreciate knowledge and understand how experiences in the classroom and laboratory relate to professional performance in the workplace. The average student-faculty ratio is 14:1. Each student is assigned a faculty adviser who oversees the student's progress and can answer questions about academic and career concerns. Students are encouraged to discuss program-related issues with and seek academic and career advice from their faculty advisers.

Admission Requirements

To be admitted to South University, prospective students must be high school graduates or hold a GED certificate and submit an appropriate SAT or ACT score (students should contact the Admissions Office) or a satisfactory score on the University-administered placement examination. Students who wish to transfer must meet the criteria established for acceptance as a transfer student.

All applicants to South University must demonstrate English proficiency. Students may furnish proof of English as a first language competency through submission of a diploma from a secondary school (or higher level) in which English is the official language of instruction. Applicants whose first language is not English must submit Test of English as a Foreign Language (TOEFL) scores. Applicants should contact the Admissions Office to determine other examinations/scores that are acceptable as an alternative to the TOEFL.

Applicants not meeting the testing standards for general admission may be accepted under academic support admission.

Application and Information

Applicants must complete an application form and submit it along with the general application fee as well as official transcripts from all high schools and colleges attended. Faxed documents are not considered official. Applicants must also complete all tests administered by the University or submit their SAT or ACT scores to the Registrar's Office. Applications are accepted on a rolling basis and should be made as far in advance as possible.

All international (nonimmigrant) applicants to South University must meet the same admissions standards as all other students. In addition, international applicants must have official educational records prepared in English, verify sufficient funds to cover the cost of the educational program, and meet certain other immigration-mandated criteria. South University in Savannah is authorized under federal law to admit nonimmigrant students.

Admissions officers are available weekdays, Saturdays, and by appointment. An appointment for an admissions interview or tour of the campus should be made in advance. For additional information, all prospective students should contact:

South University
709 Mall Boulevard
Savannah, Georgia 31406-4805
Phone: 912-201-8000
        866-629-2901 (toll-free)
Fax: 912-201-8070
Web site: http://www.southuniversity.edu

South University is located on the south side of historic Savannah, Georgia.

SOUTH UNIVERSITY

NOVI, MICHIGAN

South University℠

The University

Established in 1899, South University is a private academic institution dedicated to providing educational opportunities for the intellectual, social, and professional development of a diverse student population. The Novi, Michigan campus offers focused and balanced curricula at the bachelor's degree level in the areas of business administration, criminal justice, healthcare management, and psychology. Other degree programs offered at South University in Novi include a Master of Arts in professional counseling and a Master of Business Administration.

In addition, the Novi campus offers students flexible scheduling with the choice of pursuing many of its courses on campus, online, or a combination of both through South University's unique Plus+ program. Combining campus and online classes provides students with maximum flexibility, allowing them to organize their college education around their work and/or family commitments. Most students live within driving distance of the campus, but the Admissions Office does maintain information on various housing options should students relocate to the Novi area for their education.

South University has a diverse student body enrolled in day, evening, and weekend classes. A sizeable portion of students have experience in the workforce and are pursuing an education that will prepare them to expand on their current career or take them in a new professional direction.

South University is accredited by the Commission on Colleges, Southern Association of Colleges and Schools to award associate, bachelor's, master's, and doctoral degrees. For questions about the accreditation of South University, contact the Commission on Colleges at 1866 Southern Lane, Decatur, Georgia 30033-4097; phone: 404-679-4500.

South University in Novi is licensed under the laws of the Michigan Department of Energy, Labor, and Economic Growth to award bachelor's and master's degrees.

Location

South University's Novi campus occupies more than 30,000 square feet of a new building located at 41555 Twelve Mile Road in Novi, Michigan. The campus features spacious classrooms, a computer lab, nursing lab, health science lab, and physical therapy lab. The campus is located northwest of Detroit near the Ann Arbor area.

Majors and Degrees

South University in Novi awards the following four-year bachelor's degrees: Bachelor of Business Administration, Bachelor of Science in criminal justice, Bachelor of Science in healthcare management, and Bachelor of Arts in psychology.

Academic Programs

South University in Novi offers degree programs that are designed to meet the needs and objectives of students. Some curricula combine didactic and practical educational experiences that provide students with the academic background needed to pursue the professions of their choice. In addition, faculty members strive to instill the value not only of education and professionalism but also of contribution and commitment to the advancement of community.

Each University quarter comprises eleven weeks. Bachelor's degree programs require a minimum of twelve quarters to complete. Programs are offered on a year-round basis, providing students with the ability to work uninterrupted toward their degrees.

Academic Facilities

South University's Novi campus provides ample classroom and student service areas and features wireless technology, video conferencing equipment, smart classroom technology, and student computer labs.

The library at Novi is designed to provide comfortable seating and quiet study space. The library's collection includes print and online books, periodicals, journals, CDs, videos, newspapers and numerous databases.

Costs

Information about tuition and fees can be obtained by contacting the South University Admissions Office.

Financial Aid

South University's Office of Student Financial Services helps qualified students secure financial assistance to complete their studies. The University participates in several student aid programs. Forms of financial aid available to qualified students through federal resources include the Federal Pell Grant Program, Federal Supplemental Educational Opportunity Grant (FSEOG) Program, Federal Work-Study Program, Federal Perkins Loan Program, Federal Stafford Loan Program (subsidized and unsubsidized), and Federal PLUS Loan Program. South University employs the Federal Need Analysis Methodology, approved by the U.S. Department of Education, as a fair and equitable means of determining a family's ability to contribute to the student's educational expenses, as well as eligibility for other financial aid programs. Qualified students may apply for veterans' educational benefits. Students also are encouraged to investigate the availability of grants and scholarships through community resources.

Faculty

The South University faculty includes individuals of high academic distinction. In addition to teaching, faculty members strive to help students develop the requisites to appreciate knowledge and understand how experiences in the classroom and laboratory relate to professional performance in the workplace. The average student-faculty ratio is 14:1. Each student is assigned a faculty adviser who oversees the student's progress and can answer questions about academic and career concerns. Students are encouraged to discuss program-related issues with and seek academic and career advice from their faculty advisers.

Admission Requirements

To be admitted to South University, prospective students must be high school graduates or hold a GED certificate and submit SAT or ACT scores or a satisfactory score on the University-administered admissions examination. Students who wish to transfer must meet the criteria established for acceptance as a transfer student.

All applicants to South University in Novi must demonstrate English as a first language through submission of a diploma from a secondary school (or above) in which English is the official language of instruction. Applicants whose first language is not English must submit a Test of English as a Foreign Language (TOEFL) score. Applicants should contact the Admissions Office to determine other examinations/scores that are acceptable as an alternative to the TOEFL.

Applicants not meeting the testing standards for general admission may be accepted under academic support admission.

Application and Information

Applicants must complete and submit an application form, along with the general application fee, and official transcripts from all high schools and colleges attended. Faxed documents are not considered official. Applicants must also complete all tests administered by the University or submit their SAT or ACT scores to the Registrar's Office. Applications are accepted on a rolling basis and should be made as far in advance as possible.

All international (nonimmigrant) applicants to South University must meet the same admissions standards as all other students.

In addition, international applicants must have official education records prepared in English, verify sufficient funds to cover the cost of the educational program, and meet certain other immigration-mandated criteria. South University in Novi is authorized under federal law to admit nonimmigrant students.

Admissions officers are available weekdays, Saturdays, and weekends. An appointment for an admissions interview or tour of the campus should be made in advance. For additional information, all prospective students should contact:

Gary Malisos
Director of Admissions
South University
41555 Twelve Mile Road
Novi, Michigan 48377
Phone: 248-675-0200
          877-693-2085 (toll-free)
Fax: 248-675-0190
E-mail: gmalisos@southuniversity.edu
Web site: http://www.southuniversity.edu

South University–Novi is located in Novi, Michigan, a suburb of northwest Detroit, convenient to shopping, restaurants, and cultural and entertainment venues.

SOUTH UNIVERSITY

COLUMBIA, SOUTH CAROLINA

SouthUniversity℠

The University

Established in 1899, South University is a private academic institution dedicated to providing educational opportunities for the intellectual, social, and professional development of a diverse student population. The Columbia, South Carolina campus offers focused and balanced curricula at the associate and bachelor's degree levels in the areas of business, criminal justice, graphic design, healthcare management, health science, information technology, legal studies, nursing, RN to B.S.N. nursing degree completion, paralegal studies, and psychology. Other degree programs offered at South University in Columbia include a Master of Arts in professional counseling; a Master of Business Administration (M.B.A.) and a Master of Business Administration in healthcare administration, both in traditional and twelve-month accelerated programs; and a Doctor of Pharmacy (Pharm.D.).

In addition, the Columbia campus offers students flexible scheduling with the choice of pursuing many of its courses on campus, online, or a combination of both through South University's unique Plus+ program. Combining campus and online classes provides students with maximum flexibility, allowing them to organize their college education around their work and/or family commitments. Most students live within driving distance of the campus, but the Admissions Office does maintain information on various housing options should students relocate to the Columbia area for their education.

South University has a diverse student body enrolled in day, evening, and weekend classes. A sizeable portion of students have experience in the workforce and are pursuing an education that will prepare them to expand on their current career or take them in a new professional direction.

South University is accredited by the Commission on Colleges of the Southern Association of Colleges and Schools to award associate, bachelor's, master's, and doctoral degrees. For questions about the accreditation of South University, contact the Commission on Colleges at 1866 Southern Lane, Decatur, Georgia 30033-4097; phone: 404-679-4500.

South University in Columbia is licensed by the state of South Carolina to award associate, bachelor's, and master's degrees and certificates by the South Carolina Commission on Higher Education, 1333 Main Street, Suite 200, Columbia, South Carolina 29201; phone: 803-737-8860. The Columbia campus is also chartered by the state of South Carolina and approved by the South Carolina Commission on Higher Education (Veterans' Education Section) for the training of veterans and other eligible persons.

Certain programs offered at South University in Columbia have earned programmatic accreditation. South University's Doctor of Pharmacy program is accredited by the Accreditation Council for Pharmacy Education, 20 North Clark Street, Suite 2500, Chicago, Illinois 60602-5109; phone: 312-664-3575; fax: 312-664-4652; Web site: http://www.acpeaccredit.org. The school is a member of the American Association of Colleges of Pharmacy (AACP). The South University Associate of Science degree in medical assisting is accredited by the Commission on Accreditation of Allied Health Education Programs (http://www.caahep.org) upon the recommendation of the Medical Assisting

Education Review Board (MAERB) Commission on Accreditation of Allied Health Education Programs, 1361 Park Street, Clearwater, Florida 33756; phone: 727-210-2350. The South Carolina State Board of Nursing has granted South University approval to accept qualified applicants for admission into the nursing program.

The nursing programs are also accredited by the Commission on Collegiate Nursing Education (CCNE), One DuPont Circle NW, Suite 530, Washington, D.C. 20036; phone: 202-887-6791; www.aacn.nche.edu.

The Bachelor of Science in legal studies and Associate of Science in paralegal studies are both approved by the American Bar Association, 321 North Clark Street, Chicago, Illinois 60610; phone: 312-988-5617.

Location

South University's Columbia campus relocated to the Carolina Research Park in northeast Columbia in fall 2006. The campus features spacious classrooms, multiple computer labs, a fully equipped medical lab, and a student lounge. The campus is located just minutes from downtown in the Carolina Research Park off I-77 at Farrow Road and Park Lane.

The campus surroundings are highlighted by a natural wooded landscape and vast green space featuring a tranquil campus courtyard. Convenient to malls, shopping, and the growing northeast side of Columbia, the new campus location provides easier access to students from throughout the greater Columbia area.

Majors and Degrees

South University in Columbia awards the following two-year degrees: Associate of Science in business administration, Associate of Science in graphic design, Associate of Science in information technology, Associate of Science in medical assisting, and Associate of Science in paralegal studies.

The following four-year bachelor's degrees are awarded: Bachelor of Business Administration, Bachelor of Science in criminal justice, Bachelor of Science in graphic design, Bachelor of Science in healthcare management, Bachelor of Science in health science, Bachelor of Science in information technology, Bachelor of Science in legal studies, Bachelor of Science in Nursing, Bachelor of Science in Nursing (RN to B.S.N. degree completion program), and Bachelor of Arts in psychology.

Academic Programs

South University in Columbia offers degree programs that are designed to meet the needs and objectives of students. Some curricula combine didactic and practical educational experiences that provide students with the academic background needed to pursue the professions of their choice. In addition, faculty members strive to instill the value not only of education and professionalism but also of contribution and commitment to the advancement of community.

Each University quarter comprises eleven weeks. Associate degree programs require a minimum of eight quarters to complete, and bachelor's degree programs require a minimum of twelve quarters to complete. Programs are offered on a year-round basis, providing students with the ability to work uninterrupted toward their degrees.

Academic Facilities

South University's multimillion-dollar Columbia campus provides ample classroom and student service areas and features several smart classrooms with audiovisual technology. The campus also contains a tiered lecture hall with videoconferencing capability, a fully equipped medical lab, multiple computer labs featuring PC and Mac computers, and more.

The library houses a large collection that includes an extensive legal library. Students may retrieve periodicals in paper or electronic form. Students may also access several commercial online services, including Westlaw, the computerized legal research service; LIRN; SearchBank; Infotract; UMI ProQuest; and the Electronic Library. Internet access is available on all computers throughout the campus.

Costs

Information about tuition and fees can be obtained by contacting the South University Admissions Office.

Financial Aid

South University's Office of Student Financial Services helps qualified students secure financial assistance to complete their studies. The University participates in several student aid programs. Forms of financial aid available to qualified students through federal resources include the Federal Pell Grant Program, Federal Supplemental Educational Opportunity Grant (FSEOG) Program, Federal Work-Study Program, Federal Perkins Loan Program, Federal Stafford Student Loan Program (subsidized and unsubsidized), and Federal PLUS Loan Program. South University employs the Federal Need Analysis Methodology, approved by the U.S. Department of Education, as a fair and equitable means of determining a family's ability to contribute to the student's educational expenses, as well as eligibility for other financial aid programs. Qualified students may apply for the South Carolina HOPE Scholarship, LIFE Scholarship, and veterans' educational benefits. Students also are encouraged to investigate the availability of grants and scholarships through community resources.

Faculty

The South University faculty includes individuals of high academic distinction. Of the nearly 60 instructors on the campus, 46 percent hold terminal degrees in their fields of expertise. In addition to teaching, faculty members strive to help students develop the requisites to appreciate knowledge and understand how experiences in the classroom and laboratory relate to professional performance in the workplace. The average student-faculty ratio per class is 14:1. Each student is assigned a faculty adviser, who oversees the student's progress and can answer questions about academic and career concerns. Students are encouraged to discuss program-related issues with and seek academic and career advice from their faculty adviser.

Admission Requirements

To be admitted to South University, prospective students must be high school graduates or hold a GED certificate and submit SAT or ACT scores or achieve a satisfactory score on the University-administered admissions examination. Students who wish to transfer must meet the criteria established for acceptance as a transfer student.

All applicants to South University in Columbia must demonstrate English as a first language through submission of a diploma from a secondary school (or above) in which English is the official language of instruction. Applicants whose first language is not English must submit a Test of English as a Foreign Language (TOEFL) score. Applicants should contact the Admissions Office to determine other examinations/scores that are acceptable as an alternative to the TOEFL.

Application and Information

Applicants must complete and submit an application form, along with the general application fee, and official transcripts from all high schools and colleges attended. Applicants must also complete all tests administered by the University or submit their SAT or ACT scores to the Registrar's Office. Applications are accepted on a rolling basis and should be made as far in advance as possible.

All international (nonimmigrant) applicants to South University must meet the same admissions standards as all other students. In addition, international applicants must have official education records prepared in English, verify sufficient funds to cover the cost of the educational program, and meet certain other immigration-mandated criteria. South University in Columbia is authorized under federal law to admit nonimmigrant students.

Admissions officers are available weekdays, Saturdays, and by appointment. An appointment for an admissions interview or a tour of the campus should be made in advance. For additional information, all prospective students should contact:

Trisha Wade
Director of Admissions
South University
9 Science Court
Columbia, South Carolina 29203-6443
Phone: 803-799-9082
       866-629-3031 (toll-free)
Fax: 803-935-4382
E-mail: twade@southuniversity.edu
Web site: http://www.southuniversity.edu

South University is located on the fast-growing northeast side of Columbia, South Carolina.

SOUTH UNIVERSITY

RICHMOND, VIRGINIA

The University

South University is a private academic institution dedicated to providing educational opportunities for the intellectual, social, and professional development of a diverse student population. To achieve this, the Richmond campus offers focused and balanced curricula at the associate and bachelor's degree levels in the areas of business, criminal justice, health science, healthcare management, RN to B.S.N. nursing degree completion, legal studies, and psychology. In addition, the campus offers a Master of Arts in professional counseling and a Master of Business Administration (M.B.A.) program.

South University traces its heritage back to 1899 and today has grown into a multicampus system with locations in Columbia, South Carolina; Montgomery, Alabama; Novi, Michigan; Savannah, Georgia; Richmond and Virginia Beach, Virginia; and Tampa and West Palm Beach, Florida.

Students can also pursue degrees through a combination of on-campus and online classes as part of the University's unique Plus+ program, which provides maximum scheduling flexibility. This flexibility allows students to organize their college education around work and family commitments. For those who choose to take on-site courses, Richmond campus facilities and amenities include a bookstore, student lounge, wireless Internet access, and ample parking in addition to classrooms, labs, and offices.

The University strives to maintain small class sizes that permit students to receive individualized instruction and interaction with faculty and staff members.

The Richmond campus of South University has a diverse student body enrolled in day, evening, and weekend classes. Most students live within driving distance of the campus, but the Admissions Office does maintain information on various housing options should students relocate to the Richmond area for their education. The student body includes men and women who have enrolled directly after completing high school, who have transferred from another college or university, or who have experience in the workforce and are pursuing an education that will prepare them to grow in their current position or enable them to take a new professional direction.

South University is accredited by the Commission on Colleges of the Southern Association of Colleges and Schools to award associate, bachelor's, master's, and doctorate degrees. The Commission on Colleges can be contacted at 1866 Southern Lane, Decatur, Georgia 30033; phone: 404-679-4500; for questions regarding the accreditation of South University. South University's Richmond campus is certified to operate in Virginia by the State Council for Higher Education in Virginia, James Monroe Building, 101 North Fourteenth Street, Richmond, Virginia 23219; phone: 804-225-2600.

The Bachelor of Science in nursing program is accredited by the Commission on Collegiate Nursing Education (CCNE), One DuPont Circle NW, Suite 530, Washington, D.C. 20036-1120; phone: 202-887-6791; www.aacn.nche.edu. The Bachelor of Science in legal studies and Associate of Science in paralegal studies are approved by the American Bar Association, 321 North Clark Street, Chicago, Illinois 60610-4714; phone: 312-988-5671.

Location

South University Richmond is located in the West Broad Development in Glen Allen, Virginia, minutes from downtown Richmond and the area's cultural activities. The campus is situated in a vibrant and convenient community of mixed-use living space with shopping and restaurants within a short walk.

Majors and Degrees

The Richmond campus of South University offers a two-year Associate of Science in paralegal studies degree program.

Four-year degree programs include a Bachelor of Business Administration, Bachelor of Science in criminal justice, Bachelor of Science in health-care management, Bachelor of Science in health science, Bachelor of Science in Nursing, Bachelor of Science in legal studies, and Bachelor of Arts in psychology. A Bachelor of Science in Nursing completion program (RN to B.S.N.) for current registered nurses is also available.

Academic Programs

The Richmond campus of South University offers degree programs that are designed to meet the needs and objectives of students. Each curriculum combines classroom and practical educational experiences that provide students with the academic background needed to pursue the professions of their choice. In addition, faculty members strive to instill the value not only of education and professionalism but also of contribution and commitment to the advancement of community.

South University operates on a quarter system, with each quarter comprising eleven weeks. Associate degree programs require a minimum of eight quarters to complete, and bachelor's degree programs require a minimum of twelve quarters for completion. Undergraduate programs are offered on a year-round basis, providing students with the ability to work uninterrupted toward their degrees.

Academic Facilities

The Richmond campus library provides individual and group study areas, a computer lab, and a diversified collection of online, audiovisual, and printed materials. Professional librarians are available during all hours of operation to provide assistance in locating information and materials at South University libraries and at other libraries. The collections include books, magazines, audiovisual, and digital sources that support class assignments, tutorial needs, current events, and recreational reading. The computer lab offers Internet access, online databases with indexing and full text access to thousands of journals, tutorial programs, and an office suite of software programs. Internet access is available on all computers throughout the campus and the University offers wireless Internet access through an on-campus Wi-Fi network.

Costs

Tuition information is available by contacting the South University Admissions Department.

Financial Aid

South University's Student Financial Services Office helps qualified students secure financial assistance to complete their studies. The University participates in several student aid programs. Forms of financial aid available to qualified students through federal resources include the Federal Pell Grant Program, Federal Supplemental Educational Opportunity Grant (FSEOG) Program, Federal Work-Study Program, Federal Perkins Loan Program, Federal Stafford Loan Program (subsidized and unsubsidized), and Federal PLUS Loan Program. Students are also encouraged to investigate the availability of grants and scholarships through community resources.

Faculty

The South University faculty includes individuals of high academic distinction. In addition to teaching, faculty members strive to help students develop the requisites to appreciate knowledge and understand how experiences in the classroom and laboratory relate to professional performance in the workplace. The average student-faculty ratio is 14:1. Each student is assigned a faculty adviser who oversees the student's progress and can answer questions about academic and career concerns. Students are encouraged to discuss program-related issues with and seek academic and career advice from their faculty advisers.

Admission Requirements

To be admitted to South University, prospective students must be high school graduates or hold a GED certificate and submit an appropriate SAT or ACT score (students should contact the Admissions Office) or a satisfactory score on the University-administered placement examination. Students who wish to transfer must meet the criteria established for acceptance as a transfer student.

All applicants to South University must demonstrate English proficiency. Students may furnish proof of English as a first language competency through submission of a diploma from a secondary school (or higher level) in which English is the official language of instruction. Applicants whose first language is not English must submit Test of English as a Foreign Language (TOEFL) scores. Applicants should contact the Admissions Office to determine other examinations/scores that are acceptable as an alternative to the TOEFL.

Applicants not meeting the testing standards for general admission may be accepted under academic support admission.

Application and Information

Applicants must complete an application form and submit it along with the general application fee as well as official transcripts from all high schools and colleges attended. Faxed documents are not considered official. Applicants must also complete all tests administered by the University or submit their SAT or ACT scores to the Registrar's Office. Applications are accepted on a rolling basis and should be made as far in advance as possible.

All international (nonimmigrant) applicants to South University must meet the same admissions standards as all other students. In addition, international applicants must have official educational records prepared in English, verify sufficient funds to cover the cost of the educational program, and meet certain other immigration-mandated criteria. South University in Richmond is authorized under federal law to admit nonimmigrant students.

Admissions officers are available weekdays, Saturdays, and by appointment. An appointment for an admissions interview or tour of the campus should be made in advance. For additional information, all prospective students should contact:

Susan Miller
Director of Admissions
South University
2151 Old Brick Road
Glen Allen, Virginia 23060
Phone: 804-727-6800
          888-422-5076 (toll-free)
Fax: 804-727-6790
Web site: http://www.southuniversity.edu

South University at Richmond is located in Glen Allen, Virginia, at West Broad Village, a mixed-use area of residents, shopping, and restaurants.

SOUTH UNIVERSITY
VIRGINIA BEACH, VIRGINIA

SouthUniversity℠

The University

South University is a private academic institution dedicated to providing educational opportunities for the intellectual, social, and professional development of a diverse student population. To achieve this, the Virginia Beach campus offers focused and balanced curricula at the associate and bachelor's degree levels in the areas of business, criminal justice, health professions, healthcare management, health science, RN to B.S.N. nursing degree completion, legal studies, paralegal studies, and psychology. In addition, the campus offers a Master of Arts in Professional Counseling and a Master of Business Administration (M.B.A.) program.

South University traces its heritage back to 1899 and today has grown into a multicampus system with locations in Columbia, South Carolina; Montgomery, Alabama; Novi, Michigan; Savannah, Georgia; Richmond and Virginia Beach, Virginia; and Tampa and West Palm Beach, Florida.

Students can also pursue degrees through a combination of on-campus and online classes as part of the University's unique Plus+ program, which provides maximum scheduling flexibility. This flexibility allows students to organize their college education around work and family commitments. For those who choose to take on-site courses, Virginia Beach campus facilities and amenities include a bookstore, student lounge, wireless Internet access, and ample parking in addition to classrooms, labs and offices.

The University strives to maintain small class sizes that permit students to receive individualized instruction and interaction with faculty and staff members.

The Virginia Beach campus of South University has a diverse student body enrolled in day, evening, and weekend classes. Most students live within driving distance of the campus, but the Admissions Office does maintain information on various housing options should students relocate to the Virginia Beach area for their education. The student body includes men and women who have enrolled directly after completing high school, who have transferred from another college or university, or who have experience in the workforce and are pursuing an education that will prepare them to grow in their current position or enable them to take a new professional direction.

South University is accredited by the Commission on Colleges of the Southern Association of Colleges and Schools to award associate, bachelor's, master's, and doctorate degrees. The Commission on Colleges can be contacted at 1866 Southern Lane, Decatur, Georgia 30033; phone: 404-679-4500; for questions regarding the accreditation of South University. South University's Virginia Beach campus is certified to operate in Virginia by the State Council for Higher Education in Virginia, James Monroe Building, 101 North Fourteenth Street, Richmond, Virginia 23219; phone: 804-225-2600.

Location

The campus, located in the Convergence Center Business Park in Virginia Beach, is just minutes from shopping and outdoor and cultural activities.

Majors and Degrees

The Virginia Beach campus of South University awards two-year Associate of Science degrees in paralegal studies and criminal justice.

The following four-year bachelor's degrees are awarded: Bachelor of Business Administration, Bachelor of Science in criminal justice, Bachelor of Science in healthcare management, Bachelor of Science in health science, Bachelor of Science in legal studies, and Bachelor of Arts in psychology. A Bachelor of Science in Nursing completion program (RN to B.S.N.) for current registered nurses is also available.

Academic Programs

The Virginia Beach campus of South University offers degree programs that are designed to meet the needs and objectives of students. Each curriculum combines classroom and practical educational experiences that provide students with the academic background needed to pursue the professions of their choice. In addition, faculty members strive to instill the value not only of education and professionalism but also of contribution and commitment to the advancement of community.

South University operates on a quarter system, with each quarter comprising eleven weeks. Associate degree programs require a minimum of eight quarters to complete, and bachelor's degree programs require a minimum of twelve quarters for completion. Undergraduate programs are offered on a year-round basis, providing students with the ability to work uninterrupted toward their degrees.

Academic Facilities

The Virginia Beach campus library provides individual and group study areas, a computer lab, and a diversified collection of online, audiovisual, and printed materials. Professional librarians are available during all hours of operation to provide assistance in locating information and materials at South University libraries and at other libraries. The collections include books, magazines, audiovisual, and digital sources that support class assignments, tutorial needs, current events, and recreational reading. The computer lab offers Internet access, online databases with indexing and full text access to thousands of journals, tutorial programs, and an office suite of software programs. Internet access is available on all computers throughout the campus, and the University offers wireless Internet access through an on-campus Wi-Fi network.

Costs

Tuition information is available by contacting the South University Admissions Department.

Financial Aid

South University's Student Financial Services Office helps qualified students secure financial assistance to complete their studies. The University participates in several student aid programs. Forms of financial aid available to qualified students through federal resources include the Federal Pell Grant Program, Federal Supplemental Educational Opportunity Grant (FSEOG) Program, Federal Work-Study Program, Federal Perkins Loan Program, Federal Stafford Loan Program (subsidized and unsubsidized), and Federal PLUS Loan Program.

Students are also encouraged to investigate the availability of grants and scholarships through community resources.

Faculty

The South University faculty includes individuals of high academic distinction. In addition to teaching, faculty members strive to help students develop the requisites to appreciate knowledge and understand how experiences in the classroom and laboratory relate to professional performance in the workplace. The average student-faculty ratio is 14:1. Each student is assigned a faculty adviser who oversees the student's progress and can answer questions about academic and career concerns. Students are encouraged to discuss program-related issues with and seek academic and career advice from their faculty advisers.

Admission Requirements

To be admitted to South University, prospective students must be high school graduates or hold a GED certificate and submit an appropriate SAT or ACT score (students should contact the Admissions Office) or a satisfactory score on the University-administered placement examination. Students who wish to transfer must meet the criteria established for acceptance as a transfer student.

All applicants to South University must demonstrate English proficiency. Students may furnish proof of English as a first language competency through submission of a diploma from a secondary school (or higher level) in which English is the official language of instruction. Applicants whose first language is not English must submit Test of English as a Foreign Language (TOEFL) scores. Applicants should contact the Admissions Office to determine other examinations/scores that are acceptable as an alternative to the TOEFL.

Applicants not meeting the testing standards for general admission may be accepted under academic support admission.

Application and Information

Applicants must complete an application form and submit it along with the general application fee as well as official transcripts from all high schools and colleges attended. Faxed documents are not considered official. Applicants must also complete all tests administered by the University or submit their SAT or ACT scores to the Registrar's Office. Applications are accepted on a rolling basis and should be made as far in advance as possible.

All international (nonimmigrant) applicants to South University must meet the same admissions standards as all other students. In addition, international applicants must have official educational records prepared in English, verify sufficient funds to cover the cost of the educational program, and meet certain other immigration-mandated criteria. South University in Virginia Beach is authorized under federal law to admit nonimmigrant students.

Admissions officers are available weekdays, Saturdays, and by appointment. An appointment for an admissions interview or tour of the campus should be made in advance. For additional information, all prospective students should contact:

Richard Kriofsky
Director of Admissions
South University
301 Bendix Road
Virginia Beach, Virginia 23452
Phone: 757-493-6900
      877-206-1845 (toll-free)
Fax: 757-493-6990
Web site: http://www.southuniversity.edu

South University in Virginia Beach, Virginia, is conveniently located for day, evening, and weekend students.

SPRINGFIELD COLLEGE
SPRINGFIELD, MASSACHUSETTS

The College

Springfield College® graduates enter the workforce or advanced education with a competitive advantage—top-quality academic preparation and real-world experience.

Founded in 1885, Springfield College has an international reputation for educating leaders in health sciences, human and social services, sports and movement studies, education, business, and the arts and sciences. Accredited by the New England Association of Schools and Colleges, it is a private coeducational institution offering bachelor's, master's, and doctoral degree programs. It is designated by the YMCA of the U.S.A. as a premier leadership development center. Students perform fieldwork, internships, or service learning as early as their first year, gaining real-world experience while serving the community. It's a learning advantage based in the College's mission: education in spirit, mind, and body for leadership in service to others. The College has been named to the President's Higher Education Community Service Honor Roll, has received Carnegie Foundation Community Engagement Classification, and has won the Jostens/NADIIIAA Award of Merit for community service by student athletes. The Institute for International Sport named it one of the fifteen most influential educators through sport in America.

An ethnically diverse student body of 3,400 undergraduate and graduate students at the main campus comes from many U.S. states and abroad, with the majority from the Northeast.

Springfield College is a vibrant living and learning environment. The picturesque, 150-acre lakeside campus is technologically up-to-date. Several new and newly renovated state-of-the-art facilities blend with traditional campus architecture.

Ten campus residence halls provide guaranteed on-campus housing. Options include traditional residence halls and suite-style accommodations with private rooms for 2 to 4 students sharing a lounge, kitchen, and bathrooms. There are single-sex and coeducational residences. Seniors may elect to live off campus. The main student dining facility features a range of fresh food options. There are snack and other light-fare services around the campus, including a food court with a two-story atrium.

Enriching the undergraduate experience is a wide array of co-curricular activities, health and wellness programs, arts and cultural events, an extensive campus recreation program, and one of the largest athletics programs in the nation for a midsize college. There are more than 100 organizations and opportunities for involvement. More than 80 percent of undergraduates participate in some form of athletics, including varsity teams, intramurals, or club sports. There are men's and women's teams in basketball, cross-country, gymnastics, lacrosse, soccer, swimming, diving, tennis, track, and volleyball. Women's teams also include field hockey and softball, and there are additional men's teams in baseball, football, golf, and wrestling.

Location

On Lake Massasoit in the Pioneer Valley, Springfield College is located in Springfield, the fourth-largest city in Massachusetts. A wide range of social, cultural, and athletic activities enhance the valley, as well as twelve other colleges and universities. For example, Springfield Symphony Hall is the site of concerts, plays, musicals, and dance performances; the Springfield Civic Center is home to the American Hockey League's Springfield Falcons; and the Basketball Hall of Fame is an international attraction.

Nearby cities and towns offer many additional attractions. Northampton bustles with trendy shops, coffeehouses, galleries, theater productions, health food stores, nightclubs, and restaurants. The Berkshire Hills offer hiking, skiing, biking, and other outdoor activities. Boston lies 90 miles to the east, New York City is less than a 3-hour drive away, Vermont is 1 hour away, and Bradley International Airport is 20 miles south.

Majors and Degrees

Springfield College offers Bachelor of Science or Bachelor of Arts degrees in American studies, applied exercise science, art, art therapy, athletic training, biology, business administration, communications/sports journalism, communication disorders, computer and information sciences, computer graphics/digital arts, criminal justice, dance, early childhood education, elementary education, emergency medical services management, English, general studies, health science/general studies, health services administration, health education (health studies), history, mathematics, mathematics and computer technology, occupational therapy, physical education (movement and sport studies), physical therapy*, physician assistant studies**, psychology, recreation management, rehabilitation and disability studies, secondary education, sociology, sport management, sports biology, youth development, and undeclared major.*EnPlease check the XML tags for this paragraph.try-level six-and-a-half-year program culminating in a Doctor of Physical Therapy degree.**Entry-level five-year program culminating in a Master of Science degree.

Academic Programs

Consistent with Springfield College's humanics philosophy, undergraduate education is designed to promote an understanding of how the spirit, mind, and body work together in preparing students for a life of leadership in service to others.

The College has a two-semester academic calendar. To graduate, students must complete 120 credits, including required courses for the major field of study, electives, and required courses for all students (writing, computer applications, arts and humanities, analytical and natural sciences, social sciences, international/multicultural studies, social justice, and physical education). Students may also earn credit for successful completion of Advanced Placement (AP) high school courses, and through the DANTES subject standard test, and the College-Level Examination Program (CLEP) administered by the College Board.

Springfield College has agreements with several medical schools, which guarantee acceptance of its qualified students. In addition, many Springfield College programs allow undergraduates to take graduate-level courses.

There are campus chapters of the following honor societies: Beta Beta Beta (biology), Kappa Delta Pi (education), Phi Alpha (social work), Phi Epsilon Kappa (health, physical education, recreation, or safety), and Psi Chi (psychology).

Off-Campus Programs

For fieldwork, internships, and service learning, the College maintains relationships with businesses, not-for-profit organizations, public and private agencies, and schools. Sites have included the Basketball Hall of Fame, American Hockey League, the *Boston Globe*, YMCAs, American Heart Association, MassMutual, Children's Hospital, Hilton Head Crowne Plaza, Reebok Health and Fitness Center, Baystate Medical Center, parks and recreation departments, and many other venues.

Extensive study-abroad programs are available. Students may also enroll in courses at some of the other colleges in the Springfield area.

Academic Facilities

Technologically up-to-date, the campus has wireless zones, smart classrooms, computer labs, a videoconferencing facility, conference center, language laboratory, television studio, journalism lab, radio station, and more.

Science facilities include the recently renovated Schoo-Bemis Science Center, with state-of-the-art equipment; the new Athletic Training/Exercise Science Complex, cited as one of the most outstanding in the nation; and the Allied Health Sciences Center, with a human anatomy laboratory and sophisticated equipment for physical testing, analysis, and treatment. Herbert P. Blake Hall contains labs, testing, and treatment facilities. Locklin Hall contains a well-equipped rehabilitation, assessment, and counseling services center.

For arts studies and programs, the newly renovated Fuller Arts Center with Appleton Auditorium is the site of performances, and the Visual Arts Center contains studio work space and a public exhibition center.

The 52-acre East Campus comprises a forest ecosystem with camping facilities and lake shoreline. It is a training ground for students in several academic programs. The Springfield College Child Development Center is an exceptional fieldwork facility for students of education and psychology.

Babson Library, well known for its resources in physical education, psychology, education, health, and human services contains a rich collection of full-text print and digital materials. Library staff members assist with access to a full range of information sources.

Costs

For 2011–12, tuition and fees are $30,660 and room and board are $10,280.

Financial Aid

Students are encouraged to apply for grants, loans, and student employment. Springfield College financial aid is based on need and academic achievement. The College gives full consideration to students who submit the Free Application for Federal Student Aid and the Springfield College Financial Aid Application by March 15 for first-year students and May 1 for transfer students. Students not eligible for financial aid may be considered for campus employment.

Faculty

Most of the 342 faculty members hold doctorates or other terminal degrees. The student-teacher ratio is 13:1.

Student Government

The Student Government Association, managed by elected students, promotes students' interests and welfare. It guides and finances more than thirty student organizations, adopts policies affecting students, and is a liaison between students and the College administration.

Admission Requirements

Springfield College evaluates applicants on the basis of academic and personal factors. Applications for regular admission or early decision must be submitted to the Office of Undergraduate Admissions, and must include a completed application form, a high school transcript, one personal reference, and SAT I or ACT scores. Transfer students must also submit a transcript and a dean's report from each college attended.

Springfield College is interested in meeting each applicant and encourages candidates to visit the College and experience campus life. The College offers personal interviews, campus tours, and open-house programs and will also facilitate contact with alumni and current students.

Application and Information

Application due dates for the 2012–13 academic year are: undergraduate, April 1; transfer, August 1; athletic training and physical therapy applicants, December 1; and physician assistant studies and occupational therapy applicants, January 15.

Springfield College's Admissions Committee reviews applications upon receiving them. Application forms and information may be obtained from:

Office of Admissions
Springfield College
263 Alden Street
Springfield, Massachusetts 01109
Phone: 413-748-3136
       800-343-1257 (toll-free)
E-mail: admissions@spfldcol.edu
Web site: http://www.springfieldcollege.edu

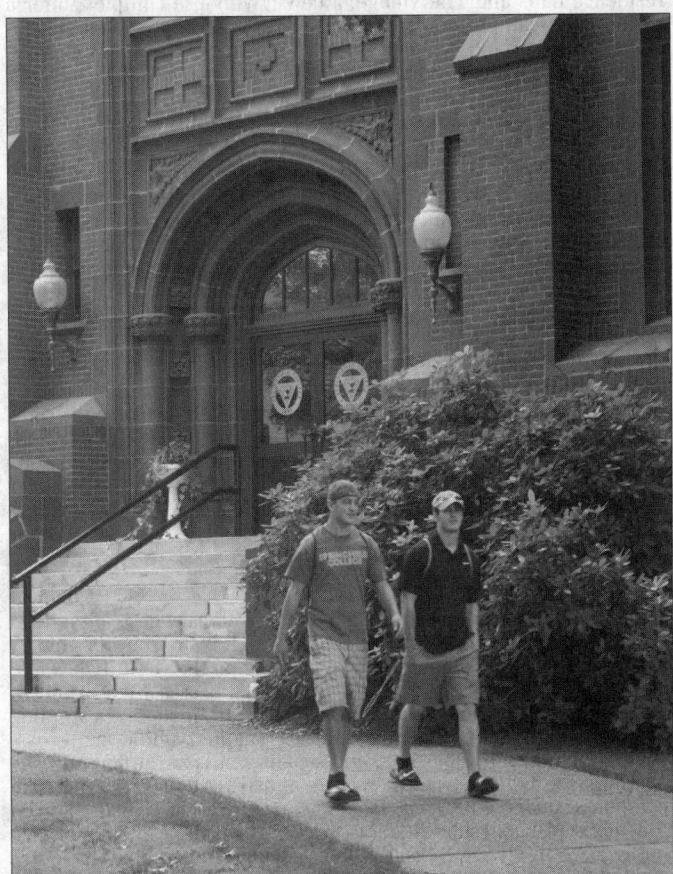

Students pass the Marsh Memorial building on Naismith Green at Springfield College.

STATE UNIVERSITY OF NEW YORK AT OSWEGO

OSWEGO, NEW YORK

The University

Founded in 1861, SUNY Oswego is well into its second century of meeting the needs of today's students. While proudly celebrating its sesquicentennial anniversary, Oswego is now a comprehensive college with an excellent academic reputation and commitment to teaching, learning, research, and service. As many as 3,386 men and 3,593 women are currently enrolled as full-time undergraduates. More than 110 liberal arts and career-oriented programs are offered through the College of Liberal Arts and Sciences, the School of Business, the School of Communication, Media, and the Arts, and through the School of Education. The School of Education is nationally accredited by the National Council for the Accreditation of Teacher Education (NCATE), and the School of Business is internationally accredited by AACSB–The Association to Advance Collegiate Schools of Business. Other individual programs within the College of Liberal Arts and Sciences and the School of Communication, Media, and the Arts are accredited by specific discipline-oriented accrediting organizations.

Located on 696 acres on the southern shore of Lake Ontario, the spacious tree-lined campus consists of forty-five buildings. Eleven residence halls and The Village, a new townhouse complex, offer a variety of on-campus housing opportunities to all degree-seeking students. More than 150 extracurricular organizations cover a wide range of social, academic, cultural, and intellectual interests. Theater, art, film, music, dance, and discussion events fill the campus cultural calendar. SUNY Oswego also offers a full slate of twenty-four NCAA Division III intercollegiate sports for men and women, along with a full complement of club sports and intramural athletics.

Oswego, a selective college, receives over 13,000 applications for some 2,000 freshman and transfer openings each fall. Accredited by the Middle States Association of Colleges and Schools, it has been recognized by a number of authoritative guides for its outstanding academic opportunities and high academic standards. In recent years, SUNY Oswego has been cited for excellence and selectivity in the Princeton Review's *Best Northeastern Colleges* and *U.S. News & World Report's Best Colleges Guide,* and honored as one of the top up-and-coming schools in *America's Best Colleges.*

Oswego is undergoing a comprehensive renewal project; recently completed projects, involving more than $400 million, include a $56-million campus and convocation center and a $35-million campus townhouse village for 350 students. Additional construction worth over $300 million is in process or in development. This includes investing $118 million in a new science complex and renovating several other academic buildings and residence halls.

Location

With a population of nearly 20,000, the city of Oswego is a modest-sized, friendly upstate New York community. It is the country's oldest freshwater port and one of the leading ports on the Great Lakes and St. Lawrence Seaway. The city and its surrounding area are well known for all kinds of summer and winter recreation, including camping, boating, sailing, fishing, tennis, golf, ice skating, alpine and cross-country skiing, snowboarding, and sledding. It is at the heart of the booming sports fishing industry, with a thriving tourism scene. The campus is conveniently located 35 miles northwest of Syracuse and 65 miles east of Rochester. Students traveling by rail or air may utilize bus service to Oswego through the Regional Transportation Center located adjacent to the Carousel Mall in Syracuse.

Majors and Degrees

SUNY Oswego awards the Bachelor of Arts (B.A.), Bachelor of Science (B.S.), and Bachelor of Fine Arts (B.F.A.) degrees.

Through the College of Liberal Arts and Sciences, students can earn a baccalaureate degree in American studies, anthropology, applied mathematics, applied mathematical economics, biochemistry, biology, chemistry, cinema and screen studies, cognitive science, computer science, creative writing, economics, English, French, geochemistry, geology, German, global and international studies, history, human development, information science, language and international trade,

linguistics, mathematics, meteorology, philosophy, philosophy-psychology, physics, political science, psychology, public justice, sociology, software engineering, Spanish, women's studies, and zoology.

The School of Business offers Bachelor of Science degree programs in accounting, business administration, finance, human resource management, management accounting, marketing, operations management and information systems, and risk management and insurance.

The School of Communication, Media, and the Arts offers baccalaureate degree programs in art, broadcasting and mass communication, communication, graphic design, journalism, music, public relations, and theater.

The School of Education offers Bachelor of Science degree programs in adolescence education, childhood education, teaching English to speakers of other languages (TESOL), technology education, technology management, vocational-teacher preparation, and wellness management.

In addition, three innovative five-year combined bachelor's and master's programs are available: a bachelor's degree in accounting with a master's in business administration, a bachelor's in psychology with an M.B.A., and a bachelor's in psychology with a master's in human computer interaction.

Cooperative programs include a 3+2 zoo technology program, resulting in a bachelor's degree in zoology at Oswego and an associate degree in zoo technology from Santa Fe Community College (Florida); 3+2 engineering programs leading to a bachelor's degree from Oswego in chemistry or physics and a B.S. in engineering from Case Western Reserve, Clarkson, or SUNY Binghamton; 2+2 programs leading to a B.S. in cardiovascular perfusion, medical imaging sciences, medical technology, radiation therapy, or respiratory care from SUNY Upstate Medical University in Syracuse; a 3+3 program leading to a B.S./D.P.T. in physical therapy from SUNY Upstate Medical University; and a 3+4 preoptometry program leading to a bachelor's in chemistry from Oswego and an O.D. in optometry from SUNY College of Optometry.

Academic Programs

Oswego offers students a broad range of courses in the liberal arts and in preprofessional and professional studies. In addition to core courses within a major, all students must satisfy general education requirements designed to strengthen basic writing and analytical proficiency, give students awareness of their cultural heritage, and provide a level of literacy in the social and behavioral sciences, natural sciences, and humanities. By completing these general education requirements during their first two years of study, Oswego students are able to select a major with a sense of confidence and purpose. However, students who are certain of their academic interest may begin working on their major program in their first year.

Before arriving on campus, students are assigned an adviser from either their major area or the college's Student Advisement Center. Advisers assist students who have not declared a major; help with academic, personal, and career concerns; and collaborate in scheduling courses needed for graduation. In addition, most students are matched with a first-year peer adviser, an older student, to help them face the challenges of their first year. The college has more than 500 undeclared students; many drawn by Oswego's reputation for helping learners find their way in education and life.

Students may consider applying for the college's Honors Program, which provides a challenging academic experience for high achievers regardless of major. Students also have the option of receiving credit through proficiency CLEP and Advanced Placement examinations.

Off-Campus Programs

Opportunities exist for students to broaden their knowledge of other countries by participating in one of forty different summer or semester overseas academic programs offered. Programs are available throughout the world, and costs are held as close as possible to the cost of an average semester on the Oswego campus. A newer option is short study-abroad quarter courses offering an intensive curriculum followed by a one-to-two-week experience in a foreign country. Through cooperative arrangements, Oswego also participates in semester programs in Albany and Washington.

Internships and other field experiences are available for students from all disciplines through the Experience-Based Education Office. Each year, more than 1,000 Oswego students participate in internships and career-awareness activities on the Oswego campus, in the local area, and throughout the Northeast, the country, and the world.

Academic Facilities

Penfield Library is a high-tech information center supporting the curriculum, teaching, and research of SUNY Oswego. The library houses a collection of over 475,000 bound volumes, including partial U.S. and New York State government documents depositories, and provides access to nearly 26,000 print and/or electronic journals, magazines, and newspapers. Through InterLibrary Loan, Penfield can provide additional materials from libraries all over the world. The library's listening area has more than 12,000 recordings, cassettes, and CDs. Additional facilities include the Lake Effect Café, an online catalog, a 24-hour study room with computers, study carrels, wireless Internet access, and computer labs with word processing.

Campuswide computer technology services support students in their classroom, residence, and Web activities. Students receive an account at the time of enrollment that can be activated online to access e-mail, the Web, and other Internet services. High-speed Internet service is available from all residence hall rooms via Ethernet and wireless networks. Wireless access is also available in most locations throughout the campus, including academic buildings, the Campus Center complex, Hewitt Union, Penfield Library, and all resident dining centers. Other services include technology training workshops, Internet troubleshooting via an active helpdesk, Web support for student clubs and organizations, free antivirus software and campuswide Gmail. The campus maintains hundreds of Macintosh and Windows-based computers in ten public-access labs. Students also have access to more than 500 computers and numerous Sun workstations in forty specialized departmental labs.

Adjacent to the campus, the college maintains Rice Creek Field Station, including the 26-acre Rice Pond and 350 acres of natural habitat. The facility has two lab/classrooms, a lecture room, and exhibit areas with an indoor viewing gallery, providing a unique vista of the creek and pond. College classes and community education programs are regularly held at the field station, which ranks among the five most extensively used facilities of its kind in the country.

Tyler Hall, Oswego's fine arts center, has two art galleries that feature annual traveling exhibitions, locally produced theme exhibitions, and the best work of students and faculty members. Tyler Hall's Waterman Theatre hosts student plays, musical performances, and productions by internationally renowned traveling artists.

The WRVO Stations, the college's 50,000-watt public radio outlet, provides outstanding on-campus internship opportunities. Communication Department facilities also include two new all-digital television studios, a modern radio lab, and two new journalism labs in Lanigan Hall. Student-run TV and radio stations and the college newspaper are located in the new Campus Center facilities.

Costs

Tuition for 2010–11 was $2485 per semester for New York State residents and $6690 per semester for nonresidents. Room and board charges were approximately $5800 per semester for entering students, depending on the meal plan selected, and additional fees totaled approximately $700 per semester. SUNY Oswego guarantees that a student's initial first-year costs for room and board will be frozen for up to four consecutive years. Although many activities on campus are free of charge, students need to budget for personal expenses.

Financial Aid

Need-based financial assistance consists of grants, loans, and part-time employment. Oswego offers approximately $75 million in aid to its student body annually. Students interested in financial aid must file a Free Application for Federal Student Aid (FAFSA). New York State residents also need to file an application for the state's Tuition Assistance Program. Priority is given to those applications on file by March 1 for the fall term and November 15 for the spring term.

Oswego offers a very generous merit scholarship program. Students receive over $2.5 million annually in merit scholarships and approximately 35 percent of the entering freshman class receives one. The average four-year renewable scholarship is more than $2300 per year.

For scholarship qualifications and details, students should visit http://www.oswego.edu/admissions/scholarships.

Faculty

Consisting of more than 300 full-time members, Oswego's faculty is dedicated to undergraduate students. With approximately 85 percent of them holding doctoral or other terminal degrees from many of the finest institutions in the country, students can be assured of the opportunity for an outstanding undergraduate education. The student-faculty ratio is approximately 18:1. While dedicated to teaching first and foremost, Oswego's faculty members are also actively engaged in research—often in partnership with undergraduate students—as well as publications and public service.

Student Government

Students at SUNY Oswego are represented by the Student Association, which has as its aim the efficient and intelligent governance of a democratic student body. The functions of the Student Association are divided among various committees that allocate funds to student organizations, intercollegiate and intramural athletics, the student newspaper, literary magazine, TV studios, and radio station, as well as various social, cultural, and intellectual activities on campus.

Admission Requirements

Admission to Oswego is competitive, with high school average, academic program, and standardized test scores being the most important criteria for applicants. Special talents such as artistic, musical, athletic, and creative writing skills are also considered. The Committee on Admissions accepts results on either the ACT or the SAT. Although not required, a campus admissions visit is encouraged.

Transfer students in good standing are encouraged to apply for admission. The average GPA for entering transfer students is 3.0.

Application and Information

Oswego accepts both The Common Application and the SUNY Application for admission. Both applications are available online at http://www.oswego.edu/apply or at high school guidance offices and college transfer offices. Oswego evaluates applications as they are completed and as space remains available. Applications completed by January 15 for the fall term or October 15 for the spring term are ensured equal consideration. Applications received after those dates are considered as space remains available.

Prospective students and their parents are encouraged to visit the campus to participate in a student-guided tour and speak with an admissions counselor. Visits can be scheduled online through the college's Web site (http://www.oswego.edu/visit). Interested candidates can also call the Office of Admissions in advance to schedule a visit. For further information, students should contact:

Office of Admissions
229 Sheldon Hall
SUNY Oswego
Oswego, New York 13126

Phone: 315-312-2250
Fax: 315-312-3260
E-mail: admiss@oswego.edu
Web site: http://www.oswego.edu

SUNY Oswego is located on 696 acres on the southern shore of Lake Ontario.

STATE UNIVERSITY OF NEW YORK COLLEGE OF ENVIRONMENTAL SCIENCE AND FORESTRY

SYRACUSE, NEW YORK

The College

Since it was founded in 1911 as the New York State College of Forestry, the SUNY College of Environmental Science and Forestry (ESF) has expanded both its role in education and its physical boundaries. The College has expanded its initial emphasis on forestry to include professional education in environmental science, landscape architecture, environmental studies, and engineering in addition to distinguished programs in the biological and physical sciences. Throughout its history, the College has focused on the environmental issues of the time in each of its three mission areas—instruction, research, and public service. The College is dedicated to educating future scientists and managers who, through specialized skills, will be able to use a holistic approach to solving the environmental and resource problems facing society.

A leader in its field, ESF is one of the doctoral degree–granting colleges in the State University of New York System. The College currently supports undergraduate and graduate degree programs in several disciplinary areas and in its broad program in environmental science. (Undergraduate programs are described in the Majors and Degrees section below.) Graduate programs lead to the Master of Science (M.S.), Master of Landscape Architecture (M.L.A.), Master of Professional Studies (M.P.S.), and Doctor of Philosophy (Ph.D.) degrees. ESF's research program has attracted a worldwide clientele, and support currently amounts to $14.5 million per year.

ESF's main campus is located on 12 acres adjacent to Syracuse University and the SUNY Upstate Medical University in an urban residential setting. There are 1,500 full-time and 300 part-time undergraduates enrolled (40 percent are women); the College's traditional affiliation with Syracuse University offers ESF students the opportunity for academic diversity and depth, as well as participation in cultural events, honorary societies, social fraternities and sororities, and professional and academic organizations.

ESF is celebrating its centennial anniversary throughout 2011 with special activities throughout the year. The highlight of the year will be in August with the opening of Centennial Hall, the College's first residence hall. Centennial Hall will be an environmentally friendly building that will house 452 ESF students in a combination of residence hall style rooms and student apartments. Go to http://www.esf.edu/welcome/campus/centennial.htm for more information.

Also under construction is the Gateway Building that will provide a new hub for campus activity and serve as a showcase for the College's sustainability efforts and an array of sustainable technologies. The building will use a high-tech combined-heat-and-power plant to generate more than enough energy for its own use and the excess will help provide power for other campus buildings.

Location

Syracuse, a metropolitan area of more than 730,000 people, is a leader in the manufacture of china, air-conditioning equipment, medical diagnostic equipment, drugs, automotive parts, and lighting equipment. It offers many cultural, recreational, and educational opportunities, including a symphony orchestra, museums, live theater, and historic points of interest. Syracuse is one of the few cities in the nation situated at the crossing point of two superhighways. The driving time to Syracuse from New York City, Philadelphia, Boston, Toronto, and Montreal is about 5 hours; from Buffalo and Albany, about 3 hours. The city is served by a modern international airport and major bus and rail lines.

Majors and Degrees

The SUNY College of Environmental Science and Forestry offers three undergraduate degrees: the Bachelor of Science (B.S.), the Bachelor of Landscape Architecture (B.L.A.), and the Associate in Applied Science (A.A.S.). The B.S. degree is awarded in aquatic and fisheries science, bioprocess engineering, biotechnology, chemistry, conservation biology, construction management, environmental biology, environmental resources engineering, environmental science, environmental studies, forest ecosystem science, forest health, forest resources

management, natural history and interpretation, natural resources management, paper engineering, paper science, wildlife science, and an undeclared option. A number of options and concentrations are offered within specific curricula. The B.L.A. degree, which requires an additional year of study, is awarded in landscape architecture. A.A.S. degrees are awarded in forest technology, land surveying technology, and a new program in environmental and natural resources conservation at The Ranger School campus in Wanakena, New York.

Academic Programs

Students at ESF all have opportunities for additional specialized study as well as research and field experience. The Department of Environmental and Forest Biology is the largest department on campus and encompasses seven different majors, including studies in biotechnology, conservation, wildlife, aquatic and fisheries science, forest health, and natural history and interpretation. With the exception of biotechnology students, biology students are required to complete a four-week period of summer field study, usually at ESF's Cranberry Lake Biological Station, after the junior year. Options for specialization within the chemistry program include biochemistry, environmental chemistry, and natural and synthetic polymer chemistry. Biology and chemistry students can also earn their secondary science teacher certification through Syracuse University.

The construction management program teaches management, analysis, and design of the construction process, with an emphasis on environmental and engineering issues.

Environmental resources engineering students learn skills in such areas as biological, environmental, and water resources engineering; mapping science; and geographic information systems. The closely related environmental science program also deals with engineering science, along with areas of focus in watershed science, health and the environment, earth and atmospheric systems science, environmental analysis, and renewable energy.

Bioprocess engineering students focus on the engineering, biology, and chemistry of ecologically sound industrial technologies and processes, giving students career opportunities in areas such as chemical engineering and bioengineering, pharmaceuticals, renewable energy, and environmental engineering. The forest resources management curriculum offers areas of focus in forest management, measurement, and policy, along with forest ecology and biology. The program also includes a minor in management in conjunction with Syracuse University. Natural resources management students can concentrate in either recreation or water resources management. Forest and natural resources management students are required to participate in a four-week period of summer field study, which is usually taken at ESF's Wanakena campus prior to the junior year.

Environmental studies offers specializations in environmental communication and culture, policy and management, and biological science applications. The landscape architecture program is a five-year bachelor's degree with options in site design, urban and regional planning, historic preservation, community and environmental design, and computer applications. During the first semester of the fifth year, the landscape architecture curriculum requires participation in off-campus independent study. Paper engineering students can study process and product design and environmental engineering applied to pulp, paper, and other related chemical industries, while paper science students focus on a variety of industry-related areas, including management and computer systems. In addition, ESF offers preparation for graduate study in dentistry, law, veterinary science, and medicine, and the College has a transfer articulation agreement with the College of Health Professions at nearby SUNY Upstate Medical University.

Academic Facilities

Specialized facilities and equipment include electron microscopes, plant-growth chambers, climate-controlled greenhouses, an animal environmental simulation chamber, a bioacoustical laboratory, a radioisotope laboratory, numerous computer labs, nuclear magnetic resonance spectrometers, gas chromatography apparatus, a mass spectrometer, ultracentrifuges, and X-ray and infrared spectropho-tometers. The photogrammetric and geodetic facilities of the environ-mental resources and forest engineering department are among the most extensive available in the United States. The paper science and engineering laboratory has a semicommercial paper mill with acces-sory equipment. The sustainable construction management and en-gineering faculty has a complete strength-of-materials laboratory, a pilot-scale plywood laboratory, and a machining laboratory. The land-scape architecture faculty has a one-of-a-kind environmental simu-lation laboratory with a visual simulator. The greenhouses and forest insectary are used to produce plant and insect materials for the class-room and laboratory. Extensive collections are available, including wood samples from all over the world, botanical materials, insects, birds, mammals, and fishes. The Theodore Roosevelt Wildlife Collec-tion contains more than 10,000 species of well-preserved vertebrate and invertebrate animals.

A complete renovation to the F. Franklin Moon Library was completed in 2007 with the addition of an Academic Success Center for tutorial support in mathematics and other SUNY ESF courses. A Writing Cen-ter is also located in Moon Library. Moon Library contains 106,000 cataloged items, and more than 1,800 journals and their correspond-ing indexes are currently received. The library also provides compre-hensive abstract and indexing services that are relevant to the Col-lege's programs. These facilities and services are supplemented by the collections of Syracuse University and the SUNY Upstate Medical University, both of which are within easy walking distance.

ESF's regional campuses in Tully, Warrensburg, Cranberry Lake, New-comb, and Wanakena, New York, have a great diversity of forest sites that are used as outdoor teaching laboratories and for intensive re-search. ESF also operates several field stations to support its instruc-tion, research, and public service programs.

Costs

Estimated costs for the 2011–12 academic year include resident tu-ition and fees of $5941 and out-of-state tuition and fees of $14,351. Room and board expenses are $14,032. Books, personal expenses, and travel are estimated at $2450.

Financial Aid

A wide variety of financial aid is available for ESF students, and more than 85 percent of the students receive some type of support. The forms of financial aid include merit- and need-based scholarships, grants, low-interest student loans, and student employment pro-grams. All students are encouraged to apply for financial aid by com-pleting the Free Application for Federal Student Aid (FAFSA).

Faculty

The members of the faculty at ESF are highly trained and are dedi-cated to the College's teaching, research, and public-service missions. There are 136 regular faculty members and 46 adjunct members. Many are nationally and internationally recognized for their expertise in specialized fields. Nearly all regular faculty members serve full-time, and most hold twelve-month appointments. Just over 80 percent are tenured, and more than half are full professors, of whom 93 per-cent have earned doctorates. There is no distinction between the un-dergraduate and graduate faculty. Faculty members teach at both lev-els, and no courses are taught by teaching assistants. Faculty members serve as advisers to students and student groups and encourage ex-cellence in scholarship and research. The student-faculty ratio is about 12:1.

Student Government

The College has a representative Undergraduate Student Association, and student representatives also participate in a counterpart associa-tion at Syracuse University. The ESF student government body orga-nizes and presents student social activities, and its representatives attend College administrative meetings, communicate students' con-cerns and ideas to the administration, and serve as a conduit of in-formation back to the student body. A formal set of student rules and regulations has been established. In addition, ESF students are obli-gated to abide by Syracuse University's general rules and regulations.

Admission Requirements

Students who are interested in the academic programs offered at ESF have four enrollment options: Early Action, Regular Freshman Entry, Guaranteed Transfer Admission, and Transfer Admission.

Outstanding high school seniors who have selected SUNY-ESF as a top choice may apply for Early Action, a nonbinding early application/ early notification program for fall-entry freshmen. Early Action allows students to apply to as many institutions as they wish and, if admitted, make their final college choice no later than May 1. Students filing an application for Early Action must meet the SUNY application filing deadline date of November 15 and have supporting credentials to SUNY-ESF by December 1. Students applying for Early Action are notified by January 1.

Regular Freshman Entry is for applicants who want to enroll imme-diately following high school. These candidates should demonstrate strong academic performance in a college-preparatory program, with emphasis on mathematics and science preparation. Students applying for Regular Freshmen Entry are notified by March 1. Freshman can-didates must apply to their intended programs of study.

Guaranteed Transfer Admission (GTA) candidates apply to ESF as high school seniors but are offered admission to either their sopho-more or junior year. Students who plan to attend another college prior to transferring to ESF select this option to ensure a place at ESF for their chosen entry date. This option may also be offered to students who do not meet the freshman admission criteria. Those who are accepted for Guaranteed Transfer Admission receive a letter of ac-ceptance for their sophomore or junior year of college, contingent upon the successful completion of all the prerequisite courses re-quired for the curriculum they have selected. The prerequisite courses are outlined and described in an enclosure with the student's accep-tance letter and can also be found on the College's Web site at http://www.esf.edu.

Students not applying or not accepted under these programs are con-sidered for admission to ESF on the basis of their previous college course work, overall academic aptitude, and interest in the College's programs. Consideration is given to both the quality and the appro-priateness of each student's prior academic experience. Students may spend one or two years at any accredited college of their choice. The College has developed Cooperative Transfer Programs with two-year colleges in New York, Connecticut, Massachusetts, New Jersey, and Pennsylvania. All admission acceptances are conditional upon satis-factory completion of course work in progress.

Application and Information

Students may apply for fall or spring admission. Admission decisions are made on a rolling basis until the class is filled. ESF accepts either the State University of New York Application form or the Common Application. Links to both applications can be found online at http://www.esf.edu/admissions/freshman/apply.htm. Requests for more in-formation should be directed to:

Office of Undergraduate Admissions
106 Bray Hall
State University of New York College of Environmental Science
    and Forestry
1 Forestry Drive
Syracuse, New York 13210-2779
Phone: 315-470-6600
Fax: 315-470-6933
E-mail: esfinfo@esf.edu
Web site: http://www.esf.edu
        http://www.facebook.com/sunyesf
        http://twitter.com/sunyesf/
        http://www.youtube.com/user/SUNYESFVIDEO

STATE UNIVERSITY OF NEW YORK INSTITUTE OF TECHNOLOGY

UTICA, NEW YORK

The College

The State University of New York Institute of Technology (SUNYIT) offers undergraduate degree programs in technology and professional studies. SUNYIT's broad curriculum embraces the humanities, communications, math, and science. Students enjoy close contact with faculty members in small classes, many with fewer than 20 students.

Founded in 1966, SUNYIT offers nineteen bachelor's degree programs for freshmen and undergraduate transfer students and thirteen graduate degrees, including the Master of Business Administration in technology management.

SUNYIT enrolled 2,300 undergraduate and 600 graduate students on both a full-time and part-time basis in fall 2010. The men-women ratio was approximately 1:1. International students comprise approximately 3 percent of the student body, representing over twenty nations, and 12.5 percent of students were members of minority groups.

SUNYIT students can receive services through the Campus Life, Career Services, Health and Wellness, and Counseling Center offices. Three residence halls provide on-campus housing for more than 800 students. In addition to providing a wide variety of intramural sports for students, SUNYIT has competitive intercollegiate teams in men's and women's basketball, bowling, cross-country, golf, lacrosse, soccer, swimming, and volleyball; men's baseball; and women's softball.

Location

SUNYIT is located in Marcy, New York, a few minutes from Utica. The city of Utica, which has a population of 60,000, is situated in the geographic center of New York State, approximately 220 miles from New York City and 190 miles from Buffalo on the New York State Thruway. Utica, a cultural and recreational center for this area of New York State, has a variety of recreational and educational opportunities. Museums, theaters, restaurants, and professional sports events are minutes away from campus by car or bus. As a natural gateway to the Adirondack Mountains, Utica provides residents with access to hiking, boating, skiing, and other outdoor activities. Served by bus, Amtrak, and airlines (airports in Syracuse and Albany), the Utica-Rome area is easily reached from locations throughout the eastern United States.

Majors and Degrees

SUNYIT awards the following baccalaureate degrees: Bachelor of Professional Studies (B.P.S.), Bachelor of Science (B.S.), Bachelor of Arts (B.A.), and Bachelor of Business Administration (B.B.A.). At the graduate level, the Master of Science (M.S.) and Master of Business Administration (M.B.A.) degrees are awarded.

Academic majors available to undergraduate students include accounting, applied mathematics, biology, business administration, civil engineering technology, communication and information design, computer and information science, computer engineering technology, computer information systems, electrical engineering, electrical engineering technology, health information management, health services management, industrial engineering technology, mechanical engineering technology, network and computer security, nursing, psychology, and sociology.

A number of options and concentrations within specific curricula are also available, as are minors in accounting; anthropology; communication and information design; computer information systems; computer science; criminal justice; finance;

health information management; health services management; human resources management; marketing; mathematics; nanotechnology; physics; psychology; quality engineering and system technology; science, technology, and society; sociology; and telecommunications.

Academic Programs

SUNYIT's academic year is divided into two semesters and runs from September through May. Summer sessions are also available.

Baccalaureate degree requirements vary from program to program but usually consist of a combination of specific major courses and liberal arts studies. Specializations and other options exist within the Departments of Business Management; Communication and Humanities; Computer Information Sciences; Engineering, Science, and Mathematics; Engineering Technologies; Nursing and Health Professions; and Social and Behavioral Sciences. Specializations are developed through the use of electives and individual advisement.

Off-Campus Programs

Internship and cooperative education experiences are integral to effective career planning and job search strategies. These experiences can influence career plans by providing an opportunity for occupational exploration, developing marketable career-related skills and characteristics, and establishing a network of contacts that can provide relevant and timely information critical to the career decision-making process. In addition, employers are increasingly using internships and cooperative education programs as training opportunities leading to full-time permanent employment. All students, regardless of major, are encouraged to consider gaining experience in their chosen field that complements classroom learning. For additional information, students should contact the academic department or the Office of Career Services.

Academic Facilities

SUNYIT's academic facilities are located on its large, scenic campus just north of the city of Utica, easily accessible by municipal bus service. The campus consists of four building complexes, a facilities building, and residence halls. Several new buildings are being constructed. The $13.8-million Student Center, which opened recently, has a dining area, office space and meeting rooms for student organizations and student services, and provides recreational opportunities. Scheduled to open in 2011 are the $23-million Oriskany Residence Hall that will provide on-campus housing for incoming freshmen and a $20-million field house that will host athletic events and large campus functions. Construction is slated to begin in 2011 on SUNYIT's $27-million technology complex that will be a hub of nanotechnology education and industry collaboration.

The Cayan Library, with 68,000 square feet of space, provides group and individual study rooms, and has an advanced computerized library instruction room.

Kunsela Hall contains administrative offices, classrooms, a bookstore, and laboratories for many technology programs. Donovan Hall houses classrooms, faculty offices, and laboratory facilities for other programs, including business, industrial engineering technology, mechanical engineering technology, communication and information design, nursing, and the arts and sciences. The Campus Center contains a cafeteria, gymnasium, recreational facilities, student services offices, a swimming pool, and meeting rooms for clubs, special activities, and a swimming pool.

Costs

Costs for the 2010–11 academic year included state resident tuition and fees of $6094. Out-of-state tuition and fees were $14,504. Room and board costs were $10,020; personal expenses, books, supplies, and travel cost approximately $3100. The total expenses were $19,214 for New York State residents and $27,624 for out-of-state students. Costs may be subject to change. Graduate student costs will vary; more information is available on the SUNYIT Web site.

Financial Aid

A wide variety of financial aid is available to students at SUNYIT. Academic scholarships are awarded for the entering fall class, and are based on merit, personal achievement, and other factors. Additional financial aid is awarded on the basis of need, as determined by an assessment of the Free Application for Federal Student Aid. At present, approximately 85 percent of the students receive financial assistance. The forms of financial aid available include Tuition Assistance Program awards (for New York State residents only), Federal Supplemental Educational Opportunity Grants, Federal Pell Grants, Federal Work-Study Program employment, Federal Perkins Loans, federal Nursing Student Loans, Federal Direct Student Loans, a variety of state-sponsored loans, and a broad range of private scholarships and grants. Students with a cumulative transfer GPA of 3.25 or better or a high school average of 90 are automatically considered for merit scholarships at the time of their application.

Faculty

SUNYIT faculty members come from all over the world and are committed to teaching, research, and service to the community. Among the faculty members are a Distinguished Service Professor, a Fulbright Scholar, and numerous recipients of the Chancellor's Award for Excellence in Teaching. More than 80 percent of SUNYIT's full-time faculty members have doctoral or terminal degrees. The faculty members are fully engaged in academic orientation and advisement, individualized instruction, cooperative faculty-student efforts in research projects, and concern for students as individuals. In the classroom, the average student-faculty ratio is 19:1.

Student Government

All full-time undergraduates are members of the SUNYIT Student Association. Its primary functions are to develop and monitor the student-activity-fee budget, to approve and oversee all student organizations, to debate issues of concern to students and take action as needed, and to develop programs of interest to all students. Student government consists of a 7-person executive committee and 11 senators. Students are encouraged to take an active role in the governance process, and many opportunities for involvement, in addition to those listed above, are available for interested students.

Admission Requirements

Generally, freshman applicants should carry a B/B+ average in a college-preparatory program and have achieved an SAT score in the 1000–1100 range (or approximately 22–24 composite ACT score). Admission is based on high school average, SAT or ACT scores, strength of course work, and other relevant information.

For transfer students, most programs require a minimum GPA of 2.5 for guaranteed admission; some programs require a higher GPA or additional application materials. Transfer students below a 2.5 GPA but above a 2.0 GPA may be admitted under special circumstances. Transfer students are required to furnish an official transcript from all previous colleges they attended.

Students with a cumulative GPA of at least 3.25 are automatically considered for merit scholarships; no separate application is required.

Application and Information

The deadline for all applications is August 1 for fall entry and December 1 for spring entry. Prospective students are encouraged to apply early as programs may close prior to application deadlines.

All applications are reviewed on an individual basis. All EOP applicants are also required to complete a supplemental application and are encouraged to apply for fall semester by December 1. The recommended application deadline for EOP and regular admission is February 15. However, applications received after that date will be considered on a rolling basis. Notification of admissions decisions begins on December 15.

SUNYIT participates in the SUNY Early Action program. Early action students must submit their application by November 1 and complete their application by November 15; applications are reviewed and students are notified of admission by December 15. Students admitted under early action are required to submit a deposit by May 1.

Students who wish to apply should apply online through the SUNYIT Web site. A copy of the State University of New York application booklet can also be obtained from a two-year college, a local high school, or the Admissions Office. Application forms for international students may also be obtained through the SUNYIT Web site or the Admissions Office.

SUNYIT adheres to the principle that all persons should have equal opportunity and access to its educational facilities without regard to race, creed, sex, or national origin.

Official transcripts from all previously attended high schools and colleges should be sent to the Director of Admissions. All communications and requests for additional information should also be directed to:

Director of Admissions
SUNY Institute of Technology
100 Seymour Road
Utica, New York 13502

Phone: 315-792-7500
      866-2SUNYIT (toll-free)
Fax: 315-792-7837
E-mail: admissions@sunyit.edu
Web site: http://www.sunyit.edu

SUNYIT student-athletes with the Wildcat mascot.

STATE UNIVERSITY OF NEW YORK MARITIME COLLEGE

FORT SCHUYLER, THROGGS NECK, NEW YORK

The College

Founded in 1874, the State University of New York Maritime College is the original, federally approved, commercial nautical institution in the United States. The primary mission of Maritime College is the preparation of men and women for a full spectrum of professional careers by providing high-quality undergraduate programs in international business, engineering, science, and technology, with particular emphasis on the marine industry. Most of the degree programs may be completed while concurrently preparing for the U.S. Merchant Marine officer's license as a third mate or third assistant engineer.

Maritime College graduates receive a well-rounded education that enables them to pursue career options in engineering or business, in private industry or government service, or at sea as civilian officers of merchant ships, research ships, and other U.S. vessels. In addition, while there is no military obligation, commissioning options exist for those seeking careers as officers in the U.S. Navy, Marine Corps, Coast Guard, or Air Force or in the National Oceanographic and Atmospheric Administration (NOAA). Maritime College is the only college that hosts a Naval ROTC program in the greater New York metropolitan area. The College has a consistent record of nearly 100 percent career placement upon graduation.

Maritime College fields twenty-one varsity sports and is nationally known for its sailing and crew teams.

Location

The scenic 56-acre campus is located at historic Fort Schuyler on the Throggs Neck peninsula, where the East River meets Long Island Sound. The College campus has a suburban setting yet is a short bus ride from midtown Manhattan. The peninsula offers panoramic views of the East River and Long Island Sound, with impressive sights of coastal Connecticut, the North Shore of Long Island, and the Manhattan skyline.

The College's extensive waterfront property allows berthing of its training ship, the *Empire State VI*. The waterfront activities center/boathouse is home to a fleet of 420s, Lasers, FJ's, and offshore racing yachts.

Majors and Degrees

The College offers Bachelor of Engineering (B.E.) degrees in electrical engineering, facilities engineering, marine engineering, mechanical engineering, and naval architecture. It offers Bachelor of Science (B.S.) degrees in general marine business and commerce (with a humanities concentration), international transportation and trade, marine environmental science (with a marine biology or oceanography and meteorology minor), marine operations, marine transportation, and maritime studies. With the exception of international transportation and trade and maritime studies, all degree programs may be combined with preparation for the professional license as a U.S. Merchant Marine officer through participation in Maritime's Regiment of Cadets. Students pursue the deck license option to qualify as a third mate, and the engine license option to qualify as a third assistant engineer.

The marine transportation program couples the nautical education and training required of a ship's deck officer with the

business administration academic core (liberal arts and sciences, accounting, economics, and marketing and management).

Graduates of this degree and license program are qualified to sail as third mates aboard oceangoing ships, on the Great Lakes, and on all types of inland and near-coastal vessels. In addition to careers at sea, the federal license enhances graduates' opportunities to find exciting positions in virtually all aspects of global transportation, from marine insurance to management of import/export industries and terminal operations. A related program, international transportation and trade, does offer license preparation. Also available is a major in general marine business and commerce, which includes deck license preparation and a humanities study area concentration. A B.S. in marine operations combines a deck or engine license with a technical background.

Maritime's Accreditation Board for Engineering and Technology (ABET)–accredited engineering programs include a marine engineering program, which provides graduates with a broad understanding of the energy and power industries and includes preparation for a third assistant engineer's license. The electrical, facilities, and mechanical engineering programs offer specialization within some of the areas covered by the marine engineering discipline, and students may pursue the license option or internship option. Naval architecture, offered with either a deck or engine license option or the intern option, is a challenging enterprise, demanding imagination and technical expertise in the design of seaborne structures from ultralarge tankers to high-speed recreational craft. Engine license candidates operate a live power plant aboard the training ship, while intern option students utilize an industrial co-op experience to gain the hands-on component for which Maritime graduates are renowned.

The marine environmental science program offers undergraduate study in the ocean and atmospheric sciences, with a strong emphasis on environmental chemistry, ecology, and environmental protection. Students choose a minor in either marine biology or meteorology and oceanography. Marine environmental science students may elect the deck license or intern options.

Maritime offers a two-year Associate in Applied Sciences (A.A.S.) degree program in marine technology/small-vessel operations (MTSVO) and is the only school in the country to offer an assistant engineer (limited oceans) associate degree. MTSVO qualifies graduates for a 200-ton U.S. Coast Guard mate's license, and the assistant engineer (limited oceans) program qualifies graduates to work as an officer in charge of an engineering watch or a designated duty engineer.

Academic Programs

The deck or engine license, issued by the Coast Guard qualifies graduates to sail on oceangoing vessels engaged in international commerce or coastal, Great Lakes, or inland waterway shipping. License candidates are required to be members of the Regiment of Cadets. This structured, military-style program emphasizes leadership, self-discipline, and individual responsibility. All programs include hands-on, professional experience, either during Summer Sea Terms aboard the *Empire State VI* or through industrial co-ops/internships.

The annual Summer Sea Term, which is an important part of Maritime College curricula, takes place abroad the 565-foot *Empire State VI*, the largest and best-equipped training ship in the United States. Summer Sea Term provides a leadership laboratory in which cadets assume responsibility for the operation of the ship under the supervision of licensed officers and staff. The *Empire State VI* visits at least three international ports throughout the course of the Sea Term. Recent ports of call include the Bahamas, England, France, Gibraltar, Greece, Iceland, and Italy.

Academic Facilities

Pre–Civil War Fort Schuyler houses the Stephen B. Luce Library with its more than 80,000 volumes and 375 periodical subscriptions, accessed through an online catalog. Full-text CD-ROM databases and online searches are also available. A $1.5-million Center for Simulation and Marine Operations is also housed in the fort. It contains two state-of-the-art full bridge simulators, a liquid cargo simulator, an electronic navigation simulator, ten Automatic Radar Plotting Aid (ARPA)–equipped radar simulators, and Global Maritime Distress and Safety System (GMDSS) simulators.

The Science and Engineering Building contains a marine diesel simulator; a ship model basin (towing tank); five computer classroom/laboratories; advanced electrical and mechanical engineering laboratories; and physics, chemistry, and meteorology laboratories.

Costs

For 2009–10, tuition for New York State residents was $4970. Maritime College has been designated as a regional maritime college, and students from Alabama, Connecticut, Delaware, Florida, Georgia, Louisiana, Maryland, Mississippi, New Jersey, North Carolina, Pennsylvania, Rhode Island, South Carolina, Virginia, and the District of Columbia paid a regional tuition rate of $6212 per year in 2009–10.

For students who are not residents of New York or any of the regional states, tuition was $11,740 per year in 2009–10. This rate also applied to international students.

Additional costs in the 2009–10 school year totaled approximately $17,000. This fee includes room and board, Summer Sea Term, uniform fees, and other costs.

Financial Aid

Maritime College students have access to several special forms of aid. Cadets who apply for and are selected for the federal Student Incentive Program receive $8000 per year for a maximum of four years. SIP participants agree to complete one of the license programs at the College and serve in the U.S. Naval Reserve (inactive duty, including the Merchant Marine Reserve). Full-tuition scholarships are also available through Navy ROTC. Four-year NROTC scholarship winners are also offered free room at the College, and the Maritime Academy Graduate Program (MARGRAD), a Coast Guard Commissioning Program, provides generous compensation to select Maritime College cadets beginning their sophomore year.

A variety of privately funded scholarships, including full-tuition Cadet Appointment Program (CAP) scholarships, are available to qualified students. Need-based aid—including Federal Pell Grants, grants, Federal Perkins Loans, Federal Stafford Student Loans, and Federal Work-Study awards—is available and requires the Free Application for Federal Student Aid (FAFSA).

New York State residents who are in great financial need and who have not been able to achieve up to their academic potential because of factors beyond their control may apply for assistance through the Educational Opportunity Program (EOP) when they apply for admission.

Faculty

Maritime College prides itself on an innovative, hands-on approach to instruction, directed by a dedicated faculty who are experts in their fields. The faculty members involved with license preparation course work have the appropriate United States Coast Guard licenses and professional credentials. Faculty members teaching in traditional academic disciplines possess appropriate credentials, with 35 holding the doctorate or other terminal degree in their field. Many faculty members, recognized as experts within the maritime industry, are involved with consulting work. A student-to-faculty ratio of 15:1 is maintained.

Student Government

The College has an active student government association. It oversees College-wide activities, over thirty clubs and organizations, and an intramural athletic program. Students are also represented on various faculty committees.

Admission Requirements

Admission is competitive and is based strictly on the applicant's abilities. Political nomination is not required. Decisions are based on strength of academic preparation, grades, SAT and/or ACT scores, outside activities and achievements, and trends in performance. Math, through at least intermediate algebra and trigonometry, and a year of either chemistry or physics are strongly recommended.

Application and Information

Applications (the SUNY Application for Admission and Maritime supplemental form) and additional information are available from the Office of Admissions. Prospective students are encouraged to schedule an interview and guided tour (arranged with the admissions office). Students may apply online through the College's Web page or through the Common Application. Two letters of recommendation and a 250-word essay are required in addition to a high school transcript, SAT or ACT scores, and a supplemental application.

Office of Admissions
State University of New York Maritime College
6 Pennyfield Avenue
Throggs Neck, New York 10465

Phone: 718-409-7221
E-mail: admissions@sunymaritime.edu
Web site: http://www.sunymaritime.edu

Maritime College—a degree and more!

STEPHEN F. AUSTIN STATE UNIVERSITY

NACOGDOCHES, TEXAS

The University

Ranked a Tier-1 Regional University by *U.S. News & World Report*, Stephen F. Austin State University (SFA) is a public four-year university located in the heart of Texas Forest Country, only a few hours' drive from Houston or Dallas. Established as a teachers' college that first held classes in 1923, the University today is perfectly sized. Enrolling nearly 13,000 students, SFA offers a wide variety of high-quality academic programs with the personalization one would expect to find at a private college.

SFA offers an array of strong undergraduate and graduate programs through its six colleges: Business, Education, Fine Arts, Forestry and Agriculture, Liberal and Applied Arts, and Sciences and Mathematics. Students can choose from eighty-three undergraduate majors, more than 120 study areas, and fifty graduate degrees, including three doctoral programs. SFA is accredited by the Commission on Colleges of the Southern Association of Colleges and Schools (1866 Southern Lane, Decatur, Georgia 30033-4097; phone: 404-679-4500) to award degrees at the bachelor's, master's, and doctoral levels.

Students study, live, and thrive on SFA's beautiful campus, with an impressive setting among towering pines that has led many groups to name it one of the most beautiful in the state. In fact, Kaplan Publishing has called SFA a "hidden treasure." The main campus encompasses 417 acres, part of the original homestead of Thomas J. Rusk, early Texas patriot and United States senator. In addition, SFA maintains a 728-acre agricultural research center that includes beef, poultry, and swine production and an equine center; an experimental forest; and a forestry field station on Lake Sam Rayburn.

Because living on campus is one of the best and most memorable experiences of one's college career, the campus offers numerous residence halls. Students who are younger than 21 with fewer than 60 semester hours live on campus and have the opportunity to enjoy the full college experience.

Recent progress at the University has been marked and continues at an unprecedented pace. Recently completed construction totals approximately $168 million, and additional improvements valued at more than $65 million are under way.

Two recently completed projects are highly popular with SFA students. The Baker Pattillo Student Center is a favorite meeting place and features a three-story atrium, food court, and movie theater. To recharge the body and spirit, students head to the Student Recreation Center where they enjoy the climbing wall, outdoor pool, lazy river, and many other amenities.

New student housing facilities also have opened in recent years, and construction of a new freshman residence hall is currently under way. Slated to open in fall 2011, the new four-story building will feature a 5,000-square-foot Freshman Success Center, where first-year students will have access to computers, tutoring, and other academic support services. To foster student interaction and campus involvement, group study rooms and other community spaces have been incorporated into the design.

Outside of class, students have numerous opportunities to make friends or develop leadership skills through SFA's thriving Greek community and more than 200 student organizations. The University competes in intercollegiate varsity sports including men's baseball, basketball, cross-country, football, golf, and track and field; and women's basketball, bowling, cross-country, golf, soccer, softball, tennis, track and field, and volleyball. With campus activities from movies to intramurals, there is always something to do.

Location

SFA is located in historic Nacogdoches. With a population of approximately 31,000, Nacogdoches offers the friendliness and hospitality of a small town with the conveniences of a city. A popular tourist destination, downtown Nacogdoches entices visitors with its charming brick streets and its many unique shops and dining opportunities. The city is steeped in history and offers a number of museums, including the Stone Fort Museum on the SFA campus. Recreational opportunities, including water skiing and fishing at Lake Nacogdoches, abound.

Nacogdoches is 140 miles from Houston; 180 miles from Dallas; 80 miles from Shreveport, Louisiana; and 260 miles from Austin.

Majors and Degrees

The University offers bachelor's degrees in accounting, agribusiness, agriculture development, agricultural machinery, general agriculture, animal science, applied arts and sciences, art, art history, biochemistry, biology, business economics, chemistry, child development and family living, communication (journalism, radio/television), communication disorders, communication studies, computer information systems, computer science, creative writing, criminal justice (corrections, law enforcement, legal assistant studies), dance, deaf and hard of hearing, economics, English, environmental science, family and consumer sciences, fashion merchandising, finance, foods and nutrition/dietetics, forestry (management, recreation, wildlife), French, general business, geography, geology, health science, history, horticulture, hospitality administration, information technology, interdisciplinary studies (teacher education), interior design, interior merchandising, international business, kinesiology, liberal studies, management, marketing, mathematics, music, nursing, orientation and mobility, philosophy, physics, political science, poultry science, psychology, public administration, rehabilitation services, social work, sociology, Spanish, spatial science, and theater.

Preprofessional programs include predentistry, pre-engineering, prelaw, premedicine, pre–occupational therapy, preoptometry, prepharmacy, pre–physical therapy, pre–physician's assistant studies, and pre–veterinary medicine.

The five most popular areas of undergraduate study at the University are interdisciplinary studies (teacher education), kinesiology, nursing, general business, and marketing. Other popular majors include psychology, biology, management, music, and art.

Academic Programs

At SFA, career preparation is a top priority. In addition to the academic education one should expect to receive in college, internships, hands-on study, and research opportunities are an important part of preparing students for rewarding careers and fulfilling lives. Through opportunities like these, SFA's students hone critical-thinking and communication skills and discover their calling, their world, and their future.

The Nelson Rusche College of Business awards 24 percent of the top ten bachelor's degrees at SFA through majors in general business, marketing, and management. The James I. Perkins College of Education is one of the largest, most comprehensive producers of Texas educators and routinely achieves one of the highest educator certification pass rates in the state. The College of Fine Arts has embraced increased societal globalization by developing international initiatives, including School of Music performance tours to England, Austria, and Italy; an academic exchange with the University of Tasmania in Australia; and School of Theatre academic exchanges with institutions in London, Barcelona, and Tallinn, Estonia. The Arthur Temple College of Forestry and Agriculture fulfills vital Texas needs through rural economic development and enhanced educational research opportunities with unique programs such as the Columbia Regional Geospatial Service Center, the National Center for Pharmaceutical Crops, and the Poultry Science Center. The College of Liberal and Applied Arts is the most diverse of SFA's colleges, providing opportunities to acquire both a knowledge base necessary for informed citizenship and the specific skills required for professional success. The Richard and Lucille Dewitt School of Nursing achieves one of the highest licensure pass rates and graduation/persistence rates in Texas. The College of Sciences and Mathematics is also home to the second-largest observatory in the Central Time Zone and the William W. Gibson Entomarium, one of the largest public insect collections in the state.

The School of Honors provides exceptional intellectual challenge and stimulation for academically talented students. All qualified students, regardless of their major, are eligible to apply for admission to the program, which offers scholarships, specialized classes, and access to laptop computers.

Off-Campus Programs

The Office of International Studies and Programs coordinates international enrollment and exchanges at SFA. Since the creation of the office, study groups have traveled to Austria, China, Costa Rica, England, Germany, Ireland, Italy, Mexico, Spain, and numerous other places. Students may choose to study abroad for a single semester or longer, depending on the number of credits desired and the availability of appropriate courses. SFA is a member of the International Student Exchange Program, which allows SFA students to study abroad at the University's regular cost for tuition and fees.

Academic Facilities

The University prides itself on providing students with exceptional classroom experiences. The Chemistry Building recently underwent a $7.35-million renovation, and two new academic buildings were added. The award-winning Department of Elementary Education prepares future teachers in its new home, the $30.8-million Early Childhood Research Center, which opened in 2009 and also houses the nationally accredited Early Childhood Lab and exemplary- rated University Charter School. The $13-million state-of-the-art Richard and Lucille DeWitt School of Nursing facility, which opened in 2010, features a 9,000-square-foot simulation laboratory that mimics a hospital setting and offers students access to the most technologically advanced training equipment available.

The Ralph W. Steen Library is one of the largest academic library facilities in the state. The library contains extensive electronic resources that are available to students both in-house and from remote locations. Three general-purpose student microlabs collectively house approximately 200 public-access workstations. Campus computing and instructional technology services are supported by three main offices and by laboratories and technology centers in various departments and colleges.

The library houses the award-winning Academic Assistance and Resource Center, which provides one-on-one peer tutoring and student-led study groups to improve intellectual development and ensure student success. It is the first learning center in the nation to achieve distinguished certification from the National Association for Developmental Education. The Texas Higher Education Coordinating Board has recognized the center's success and its contribution to higher education with a prestigious Star Award.

Costs

SFA is a tremendous value in education, in comparison with other state universities and with private institutions. Tuition and room-and-board fees are competitive with other Texas public universities. Annual tuition and fees for 2010–11 for full-time undergraduates was approximately $5732 for Texas residents, $6452 for border state residents, and $13,172 for out-of-state residents. Room and board rates averaged $7670 for the academic year.

Financial Aid

SFA awarded approximately $129.7 million in scholarships, grants, work-study, educational loans, waivers, and exemptions during 2009–10. Financial aid programs in which the University participates include the Federal Pell Grant, Federal Supplemental Educational Opportunity Grant, Texas Grant Program, Smart Grants, Federal Work-Study Program, Federal Perkins Loan, Federal Direct Loan Program, Federal Parent PLUS Loans, and Access Loan Program. More information is available at http://www.sfasu.edu/go/financial-aid.

SFA has hundreds of scholarships available to new and returning students. Scholarships are based on need, merit, or athletic and special skills. Selection criteria may include, but are not limited to, an applicant's academic record, degree goals, financial status, and performance on a standardized test. Prospective students can search scholarships at http://www.sfasu.edu/go/scholarships. The application deadline for most is February 1 for the fall semester. Included are scholarships offered by Office of Admissions, Office of Student Financial Assistance, Alumni Foundation, SFASU Foundation, Intercollegiate Athletics, and various academic departments and organizations. Scholarship amounts range from $100 to $8000.

Faculty

In the 2010–11 academic year, the full-time faculty numbered 524 members. With a student-faculty ratio of 19:1 and an average class size of 26, students receive personalized attention from their professors and instructors, of whom more than 80 percent hold the highest degrees in their field.

Student Government

The Student Government Association serves as the representative voice of the student body to the faculty and administration. Concerns and issues that are important to students can be made known through legislation passed by the SGA. A three-branch system, consisting of the executive, legislative, and judicial branches, is used.

Admission Requirements

Beginning in fall 2012, applicants for admission must meet the following high school class rank and minimum test scores: top 10 percent, no minimum score; 11–25 percent, 850 SAT/17 ACT; second quarter, 950 SAT/20 ACT; third quarter, 1100 SAT/24 ACT; fourth quarter, file review. First-time freshman applicants are required to have completed the Recommended High School Program or the Distinguished Achievement Program or demonstrate they have completed a high school curriculum more rigorous than what is required of the Minimum Graduation Plan.

Application and Information

All new undergraduate applicants for admission must complete the Texas Common Application and submit it with a $35 nonrefundable application fee. For additional information, prospective students should contact:

Office of Admissions
Stephen F. Austin State University
P.O. Box 13051, SFA Station
Nacogdoches, Texas 75962-3051

Phone: 936-468-2504
E-mail: admissions@sfasu.edu
Web site: http://TheLumberjackExperience.com
　　　　　http://www.facebook.com/sfasu

Vista Drive entrance at Stephen F. Austin State University.

STEVENSON UNIVERSITY

STEVENSON AND OWINGS MILLS, MARYLAND

The University

Stevenson University (SU), formerly Villa Julie College, is a coeducational, independent institution dedicated to providing its 3,400 undergraduate and graduate students with a career-focused liberal arts education. Individual attention from faculty members, extensive career preparation gained through real-world training, and two ideal locations just north of Baltimore, Maryland, in Stevenson and Owings Mills, make the University truly unique.

At SU, academic quality is viewed as a personalized education that fosters intellectual growth and prepares students to thrive in the working world after graduation. With a student-faculty ratio of 15:1, it is easy to understand why students often cite the congenial rapport with faculty members as one of the University's strong points.

Through Stevenson University's concept of Learning Beyond, students step outside of the classroom to take their learning to the next level. Experiential learning opportunities include study abroad, service learning, field placements, and independent research. In addition, through an approach known as Career Architecture[SM], each student develops a professional career plan based on their values, skills, and strengths.

Stevenson's graduates maintain a placement rate that tops 95 percent each year, with students acquiring jobs or going on to further their education within six months of graduation.

At SU, students enjoy more than forty-five clubs and organizations, multiple honor societies, and NCAA Division III athletics. The following sports are offered: men's and women's basketball, cross-country, golf, lacrosse, soccer, tennis, and volleyball; men's baseball and football; and women's field hockey and softball. Cheerleading, dance, and intramural sports are also extremely popular.

In addition to its undergraduate programs, the University offers the following master's degree programs: business and technology management, forensic science, forensic studies, and nursing.

Location

Stevenson University has two beautiful campuses in the heart of Maryland, in Stevenson and Owings Mills. SU students truly appreciate the beauty of a rural campus as well as the convenience and appeal of a more urban setting.

The original 60-acre Greenspring Campus is nestled among the rolling hills in Stevenson, Maryland. The Owings Mills Campus is a thriving center of student activity and offers both academic and residential facilities. Classes are held on both campuses, and the University provides a free shuttle service that runs between these locations.

Majors and Degrees

Stevenson University offers the following bachelor's degree programs: accounting; applied mathematics; biology; biotechnology; business administration; business communication; business information systems; chemistry; computer information systems; criminal justice; early childhood education: liberal arts and technology; elementary education: liberal arts and technology; English language and literature; fashion design; fashion merchandising; film, video, and theater; human services;

interdisciplinary studies; medical technology; middle school education; nursing; nursing: RN to B.S.; paralegal studies; psychology; public history; and visual communication design.

Stevenson's B.S. to M.S. degree programs give students the option of earning both a bachelor's and a master's degree in as few as five years. Graduate study begins in the spring semester of the junior year and runs concurrently with undergraduate work until the end of the spring semester of the senior year. All subsequent course work is at the graduate level.

Academic Programs

At SU, academic quality is regarded as a personalized curriculum that prepares students to enter the working world with the knowledge and skills that employers value. SU infuses the traditional liberal arts education with a distinct career focus. The University's goal is to prepare students for employment, graduate study, and productive involvement in today's world.

Academic Facilities

From recent enhancements to the Greenspring Campus to brand-new facilities at the Owings Mills Campus, the University provides modern facilities that serve the needs of all students.

The University's Greenspring Campus includes a 350-seat theater, multiple computer labs and classrooms, video and graphic studios, science laboratories, a student union, and athletic facilities. Each classroom and laboratory on the campus is capable of multimedia projection and computer-assisted learning.

Also at the Greenspring Campus is the Verizon Center for Excellence in Teaching and Learning. The center comprises classrooms equipped with technology that accommodates distance learning.

The Owings Mills Campus hosts the University's newest facilities, including an expansive student center and dining hall, a 10,000-square-foot community center, a newly renovated athletic complex with a new gymnasium, multiple classrooms and study spaces, a fitness center, and additional athletic fields. An athletic stadium is scheduled to open in 2011.

The Howard S. Brown School of Business and Leadership offers state-of-the-art technology housed in twelve traditional classrooms and seven seminar halls. The facility also includes two distance learning labs where students are able to interact with other learners worldwide, six computer labs utilizing the most up-to-date equipment, a student lounge, a law library, and a high-tech digital mock trial courtroom.

The University's library, located on the Greenspring Campus, has an extensive collection of more than 100,000 printed volumes, periodicals, videotapes and audiotapes, CDs, and microfilm and microfiche selections and an interlibrary loan consortium. In addition to the electronic databases it owns, the library has access to thousands of outside databases, such as LexisNexis Academic Universe, WESTLAW, Dialog, and Dow Jones News Retrieval.

Costs

Stevenson is among the most affordable universities in the state of Maryland. For the 2010–11 academic year, tuition and fees for full-time students were $22,090. Part-time tuition and fees were $521 per credit hour, plus a $75 registration and technology fee per semester. Room and board for the 2010–11 year were $10,826.

Financial Aid

Stevenson University offers financial assistance to qualified students in the form of grants, scholarships, loans, student employment, and a special payment plan. On average, approximately 90 percent of the University's students receive some form of financial assistance. The University has a generous scholarship program that grants awards based on academic merit. SU participates in all major federal aid programs as well as all Maryland state programs. Applicants are required to file the Free Application for Federal Student Aid (FAFSA). The priority deadline for filing is February 15.

Faculty

The faculty at Stevenson University is primarily a teaching faculty. The University's 15:1 student-teacher ratio demonstrates the institution's dedication to personalized education. A majority of the full-time faculty members have the doctoral or terminal degree offered in their field, and a significant number are widely published. In addition, many are concurrently employed as professional specialists in their fields.

Student Government

The Student Government Association (SGA) facilitates an environment that encourages students to express their thoughts and opinions concerning Stevenson University, its policies, and sponsored activities. The SGA serves as the principal governing body of all campus clubs and activities. In conjunction with the Office of Student Affairs, the SGA organizes an array of campuswide events that promote the social aspects of college life. Each student at Stevenson is welcome and encouraged to participate in all SGA functions.

Admission Requirements

Applications for admission to Stevenson University are reviewed on a rolling basis. In evaluating each applicant, the University considers the applicant's high school academic record, SAT or ACT scores, recommendations, writing sample, and any other special talents or personal interests. Admission to the University is determined without regard for race, color, sex, religion, national or ethnic origin, or handicap. SU complies with all applicable laws and federal regulations regarding discrimination and accessibility on the condition of handicap, age, veteran status, or otherwise.

Application and Information

Applications for admission to undergraduate programs should be received by March 1 for fall-semester entry and October 15 for spring-semester entry. Scholarship consideration adheres to earlier deadlines. Applications received after these dates are reviewed on a space-available basis. Students applying to the University as freshmen must submit official high school transcripts, standardized test scores, the Counselor Recommendation Form, typed responses to the essay questions listed on the application, and a $40 nonrefundable application fee. The application fee is waived for all students who apply online at www.stevenson.edu. Transfer students must submit official transcripts from all colleges or universities they have attended and should contact the Transfer Admissions Counselor to discuss additional credential requirements.

For further information and application forms, students should contact:

Admissions Office
Garrison Hall, Suite 200
Stevenson University
100 Campus Circle
Owings Mills, Maryland 21117-7804
Phone: 410-486-7001
      877-468-6852 (toll-free)
Fax: 443-352-4440
E-mail: admissions@stevenson.edu
Web site: http://www.stevenson.edu

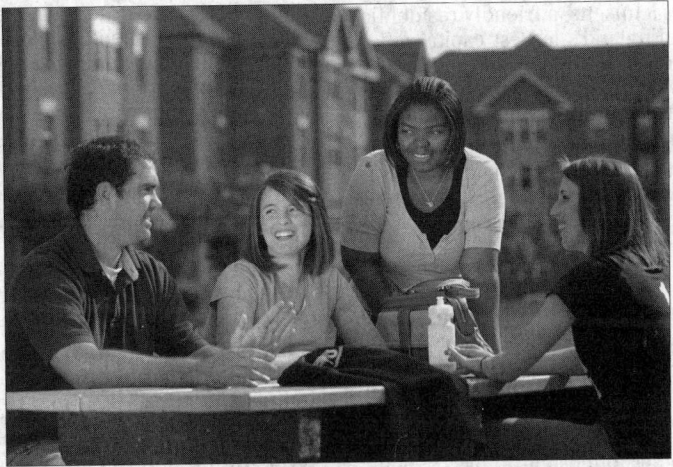

The residences at Stevenson University offer spacious apartments and suites with extensive amenities.

STONEHILL COLLEGE

EASTON, MASSACHUSETTS

The College

Stonehill College is a selective, coed Catholic college with a welcoming, academically challenging community of over 2,500 students on a beautiful, active campus located 22 miles south of Boston. Stonehill offers more than 80 diverse majors and minors in the liberal arts, sciences, and business to prepare students for a life of learning, leadership, and responsible citizenship. Nearly 80 percent of Stonehill students complete an internship, study abroad, practicum, or field experience by the time they graduate.

More than 80 percent of Stonehill students participate in at least one sport on campus. Stonehill competes in the Northeast-10 Conference, the largest NCAA Division II conference in the country, and offers twenty different varsity sports, including baseball, lacrosse, football, basketball, and soccer. The extensive intramural program offers two different levels of competition in basketball, dodgeball, field hockey, kickball, softball, and more. Club sports such as rugby and volleyball are yet another option, offering a spirited, fun experience without the demands of NCAA conference-sanctioned athletics.

Founded by the Congregation of Holy Cross in 1948, Stonehill's mission is "to educate the whole person so that each graduate thinks, acts, and leads with courage toward the creation of a more just and compassionate world." The idea of making the world a better place is part of the Catholic faith and an intrinsic element of the Stonehill experience. Each year, approximately 1,500 Stonehill students (more than 63 percent of the student body) participate in community service. Last year, Stonehill students provided more than 40,000 hours of service.

Stonehill consistently receives nationwide recognition as one of the country's top colleges. Recently, *U.S. News and World Report's* "America's Best Colleges" guide singled out Stonehill as a top up-and-coming school. The Princeton Review recently chose Stonehill as one of the best in the nation for career services, most accessible professors, intramural sports, study abroad, and more.

Location

Stonehill is located in Easton, Massachusetts, a friendly residential community nestled between New England's largest capital cities. Just 22 miles from Boston and 37 miles from Providence, it is perfectly situated for internships, service opportunities, job prospects, museums, professional sports games, cultural events, and more.

Whether the countless trees are in full bloom in the spring or the leaves are bursting into reds and golds in the fall, Stonehill is beautiful every season of the year. Encompassing 384 acres, Stonehill's New England college campus features traditional landscaping, ponds, wooded trails, and Georgian-style architecture.

Majors and Degrees

Students may receive Bachelor of Arts degrees in American studies, art history, Catholic studies, chemistry, communication, computer science, criminology, economics, education (early childhood/ elementary and secondary education minors), English, environmental studies, foreign languages, French, gender studies, graphic design, health-care administration, history, international studies, mathematics, multidisciplinary studies, philosophy, physics, political science, psychology, public administration, religious studies, sociology, Spanish, studio arts, and visual and performing arts (music and theater arts concentrations).

Bachelor of Science degrees are offered in biochemistry, biology, chemistry, computer science, mathematics, neuroscience, and physics. Bachelor of Science in Business Administration degrees are offered in accounting, finance, international business, management, and marketing. In addition, Stonehill College partners with the University of Notre Dame to offer a combination 3+2 program in engineering with concentrations in aeronautical, chemical, civil, computer, electrical, environmental geosciences, and mechanical engineering.

Preprofessional advising programs are offered in dentistry, education, law, medicine, veterinary science, and medical technology. Students interested in the field of education can receive early childhood, elementary, middle, and secondary school teacher certification. Students may pursue a double major as well as design their own major by combining various departmental courses into a comprehensive multidisciplinary program.

Academic Programs

The core of Stonehill's liberal arts curriculum is the Cornerstone Program, which leads students to examine themselves, society, culture, and the natural world through courses in ethics, sciences, language, and more.

Stonehill's students and alumni succeed because the entire college community collaborates to help them develop the knowledge, skills, and character to meet their professional goals and to live lives of purpose and integrity. Its graduates can be found around the world enrolled in top graduate programs, enjoying meaningful careers, and working to improve their communities.

Within one year of graduation, 97 percent of Stonehill graduates over the last five years were employed, volunteering, or in graduate school. Last year, 38 percent of graduating seniors were employed at organizations such as Goldman Sachs, the New England Patriots, and Brigham and Women's Hospital. Others joined or applied for year-long volunteer service programs such as the Peace Corps, Teach for America, AmeriCorps, and World Teach.

On average, Stonehill students graduate at a higher rate and in less time than students at many other colleges and universities. About 84 percent of Stonehill students graduate within four years. Stonehill's four-year graduation rate is much higher than at public institutions where the national average is five years.

Off-Campus Programs

At Stonehill, students are given experiential learning opportunities that allow them in-depth exploration of what they learn in the classroom and the opportunity to apply it in the real world. The National Survey of Student Engagement ranks Stonehill in the top 10 percent of colleges nationwide for its enriching educational experiences such as competitive internships, nationally ranked study-abroad opportunities, and cocurricular programs.

Students take part in interdisciplinary Learning Communities (LCs), which combine two academic courses from different disciplines with a team-taught seminar that explores an interrelated topic. Some LCs even incorporate travel to places like Ireland, Italy, the Florida Everglades, and the deserts of the Southwest.

In addition, Stonehill is among the top colleges for semester study-abroad programs. About 40 percent of Stonehill students study abroad before graduation in programs located in dozens of countries, including Argentina, Australia, China, Greece, Morocco, and South Africa.

Academic Facilities

Stonehill is dedicated to developing programs and projects that will continually improve quality of life for everyone on campus. Its multimillion dollar science center, opened in 2009, provides state-of-the-art facilities such as labs, observation rooms, research areas, and a café to faculty, staff, and students.

Kaplan's *Insiders Guide to the 320 Most Interesting Colleges* ranked Stonehill among the colleges with the "Best Freshman Housing." It's no wonder that more than 90 percent of Stonehill's students live on campus and very few leave on the weekends. In addition, all resident students are guaranteed housing for all four years. Students can choose from a variety of living options, including suites, townhouses, and double- and triple-occupancy rooms, and take advantage of amenities such as communal TV lounges, kitchen and laundry facilities, recreation rooms, pool tables, basketball courts, beach volleyball courts, and outdoor grills for barbeques.

Costs

For the 2010–11 academic year, Stonehill's costs were $32,620 for tuition and $12,610 for room and board.

Financial Aid

Stonehill is committed to helping each qualified student find the resources to make the dream of a Stonehill education become reality. Stonehill offers loans, grants, scholarships, employment programs, and tuition payment plans to help students become a part of the community here. In the 2010–11 academic year, Stonehill distributed $47.5 million in financial aid to a student body of 2,558. This year, 92 percent of full-time students received some form of aid. On average, students received $20,150 each in scholarships, grants, loans, and work-study. A wide range of competitive merit-based scholarships is also available to outstanding students who do not demonstrate a financial need.

To file for Stonehill scholarship and/or financial aid consideration, students should complete the online CSS PROFILE form at https://profileonline.collegeboard.com. Stonehill's CSS PROFILE code is 3770. In addition, students must file the Free Application for Federal Student Aid (FAFSA) online at http://www.fafsa.ed.gov to be considered for government funds. Stonehill's FAFSA code is 002217.

Faculty

With a student-faculty ratio of 13:1 and an average class size of 20, Stonehill sees individual attention as a key component of our academic programs. Stonehill's accomplished faculty champions its students throughout all four years and is dedicated to teaching and conducting publishable research with students to help with their integrated learning process. Students benefit from graduate-level access to high-tech equipment, attend professional academic conferences, and coauthor in-depth papers, while guided by faculty mentors. Stonehill students take advantage of collaborating one-on-one with their professors on a regular basis and they will always be taught by a faculty member, not a teaching assistant or graduate student.

Student Government

From enjoying on-campus activities to just hanging out with friends, students have plenty of opportunities for fun at Stonehill. The Student Government Association (SGA) is one of the country's most active—its programming won an award from the National Association of Campus Activities—so there's always something happening, from concerts and guest speakers to contests and game shows. More than seventy clubs and organizations are available, including the College's literary magazine *Rolling Stonehill*, the Ski/Snowboard Club, and the Neuroscience Society.

Stonehill also offers free transportation to Boston's public subway system, allowing easy access to the excitement of the city. And with Stonehill's unique Fun Fund, students can get up to $200 to pay for entertainment with friends, such as a show in New York City, a pottery class, or a Red Sox game.

Admission Requirements

Admission to Stonehill is selective. This year, more than 7,200 high school students applied for 675 first-year places to represent the Stonehill class of 2015. Stonehill actively seeks an academically strong and geographically, culturally, and ethnically diverse student body. In the admissions process, all information on each applicant is carefully considered, but academic performance and high school curriculum are given the greatest weight. The Admissions Committee evaluates the depth and strength of each applicant's course selection and the consistency of their grades. Competitive students should have completed a strong academic program from among their high school's most challenging offerings. Stonehill admission is test optional, but students may choose to submit scores from either the SAT or ACT. The Admissions Committee also evaluates extracurricular activities, work, volunteer and community activities, recommendations, and writing samples. Stonehill awards credit for strong scores on AP, CLEP, and higher-level International Baccalaureate exams.

Application and Information

Aspirants for Stonehill, as first-year, transfer, or international students may apply online at https://www.commonapp.org. The Common Application is also available in paper form at high school guidance offices.

Stonehill offers three admissions plans for first-year candidates: early decision (binding), early action (nonbinding), and regular decision. November 1 is the deadline for early acceptance and January 15 is the deadline for regular decision.

Dean of Admissions and Enrollment
Stonehill College
320 Washington Street
Easton, Massachusetts 02357-5610

Phone: 508-565-1373
Fax: 508-565-1545
E-mail: admissions@stonehill.edu
Web site: http://www.stonehill.edu
　　　　　http://stonehillcollegeadmissions.org/ (Admissions)

The MacPhaidin Library is a high-tech learning center, with fully networked seating areas for individual and collaborative study.

STRATFORD UNIVERSITY

FALLS CHURCH AND WOODBRIDGE, VIRGINIA

The University

Stratford University was founded in 1976 and has undergone constant changes as it has continued to expand and adapt to changing employer demands. Stratford is a small, private institution with a personalized approach to student needs. The Stratford community includes two campuses in northern Virginia just a short distance from Washington, D.C. and offers over thirty programs of study. The Stratford philosophy is to provide professional competencies that satisfy employer needs, utilizing a teaching method that accommodates a variety of different learning styles.

Stratford enrolls more than 2,000 students in its programs, offering small classes to ensure personal attention to each student. Stratford students represent a diverse population, from recent high school graduates to adult learners seeking to make a career change. The friendly and supportive environment at Stratford University ensures that students feel comfortable and well supported.

The University offers programs in technology, business, health sciences, hospitality, and culinary arts at both the undergraduate and graduate levels. The University is located in the heart of Fairfax County, Virginia, home of the Internet and numerous businesses that support the Internet, telecommunications, and information. User groups, national societies, and various technology councils provide networking avenues for Stratford students. Hospitality-related businesses abound in the Washington area, from world-class restaurants to boutique hotels; career opportunities are numerous. In addition, the business of government provides varied career paths for Stratford graduates.

The University provides a full array of career development and placement services. Students attend workshops on academic planning, resume writing, and effective interviewing skills. Career Services strives to help students make the contacts that lead to internships or permanent positions.

Stratford University partners with Collegiate Housing Services to offer comfortable and affordable dormitory-style apartments near both campuses. The typical housing configuration is a furnished, two-bedroom, two-bathroom apartment shared by up to 4 Stratford students of the same gender.

Location

Stratford University has two campuses in the greater Washington, D.C., region. Washington has much to offer. From politics to urban events, culture to recreation, the capital region is a great place to live, work, and study. Local sights include Mount Vernon, Old Town Alexandria, the White House, Capitol Hill, the Mall, and the Smithsonian Institute. Most of the sights are easily accessible by public transportation.

The prosperous D.C. job market is a draw for Stratford students. For both working students looking to upgrade skills and full-time students concerned with finding a job quickly after graduation, the region offers a wealth of jobs for graduates of all of Stratford's programs. As the nation's capital and a major tourist center, the metropolitan Washington area is a center for business, finance, industry, and entertainment.

Majors and Degrees

The School of Business Administration offers Associate of Applied Science (A.A.S.) and Bachelor of Science (B.S.) degrees in business administration. The School of Computer Information Systems offers A.A.S. degrees in digital design and in network management and security and four different B.S. degrees in information technology. The School of Culinary Arts and Hospitality confers A.A.S. degrees in advanced culinary arts, baking and pastry arts, and hotel and restaurant management; and a B.A. degree in hospitality management. The School of Health Sciences confers an A.A.S. degree in allied health with concentrations in medical assisting, clinical hemodialysis, phlebotomy technician, medical insurance billing and coding, and pharmacy technician. The School of Nursing offers the B.S. in Nursing degree. The business administration, hotel and restaurant management, and hospitality management programs are also offered online.

Academic Programs

Stratford University delivers competency-based educational programs that prepare individuals for employment in specific career areas. These competencies are employer centered. The curriculum in each program is designed to ensure that students have the required competencies demanded in their fields of endeavor. The instructional techniques at Stratford are student centered. At the beginning of each program, students are tested for both learning styles and learning modes, and instruction in all classes is individualized based on the results of this assessment. This dual emphasis results in student academic success, without lowering required employer-based standards. As a result, students who graduate enjoy a high placement rate.

The A.A.S. and the B.S. degree programs include core requirements, elective requirements, and general education arts and sciences requirements. The total requirement for the A.A.S. programs is 90 quarter credits. This normally takes approximately sixty weeks to complete. The total requirement for the B.S. degree programs is 180 quarter credits. The first 90 quarter credits are generally completed prior to beginning the 90 credits of junior- or senior-level courses. The B.S. programs take approximately 120 weeks to complete.

The diploma programs include core and elective requirements. The total requirement for these programs is 60 quarter credits, and they normally take fifty weeks to complete.

Students may receive transfer credit for courses transferred from accredited institutions. Also, certain training received from prior military schools, military service, or prior work experiences may be awarded as transfer credit. Stratford is approved for the training of veterans.

The course calendar is divided into five sessions, each of which is ten weeks in length. With start dates in January, March, May, August, and October, Stratford's flexible scheduling accommodates its busy students.

Academic Facilities

Stratford's libraries are located at the Falls Church and Woodbridge campuses, but all 2,400 titles are available online. In addition, the library subscribes to OCLC FirstSearch, ProQuest, Global Road Warrior, and EBSCOhost research database.

Both campuses have state-of-the-art facilities equipped with the latest technology and resources. All information systems classrooms are equipped with one computer for every student. Students may also access one of several computers for general use in the library/learning resource center. Culinary arts students at both campuses are trained in fully equipped professional kitchens.

Costs

Tuition is $370 per credit hour plus fees where applicable.

Financial Aid

Financial aid officers at Stratford are trained to guide students through the financial aid process to ensure that all available financial aid has been explored. Federal loans and grants (including PLUS, PELL, FSEOG, FWS) are applicable toward tuition at Stratford. The University is also approved for Veterans Association benefits, Vocational Rehabilitation benefits, and private institutional financing.

Stratford offers the Graduating High School Senior Scholarship Program and the Culinary Scholarship Programs. Stratford University also accepts private scholarships from foundations, service clubs, and other organizations.

Faculty

Stratford University's faculty members have been hand-chosen for their teaching ability, personality traits, and experience in their fields. The entire Stratford University staff works as a team to help students succeed.

Admission Requirements

Graduation from a secondary school or equivalent education as certified by the state department of education is normally required for admission.

Stratford is approved to offer I-20 certification for F1 visas for international students. Students for whom English is a second language are required to demonstrate English proficiency through a TOEFL or IELTS score.

Application and Information

Students must submit a completed application for admission and a $50 nonrefundable application fee. Applicants must also schedule an interview with admissions to complete the application process. Students may bring or have the registrar from their high school, college, or state GED office forward a copy of their transcripts to Stratford University. Student-issued copies of transcripts or diplomas can be submitted directly to the University.

Students interested in applying should contact:

Stratford University
7777 Leesburg Pike
Falls Church, Virginia 22043
Phone: 703-821-8570
      800-444-0804 (toll-free)
Fax: 703-734-5339

Stratford University
14349 Gideon Drive
Woodbridge, Virginia 22192
Phone: 703-897-1982
      888-546-1250 (toll-free)
Fax: 571-408-2499
E-mail: admissions@stratford.edu
Web site: http://www.stratford.edu

SUSQUEHANNA UNIVERSITY
SELINSGROVE, PENNSYLVANIA

The University

By nearly every indicator, Susquehanna University excels at preparing its graduates to achieve, lead, and serve in a diverse and interconnected world. Students benefit from more than fifty majors and minors encompassing a balance of liberal arts and professional studies programs, a devoted and passionate faculty, and state-of-the-art facilities that support intellectual and personal growth.

With more than 100 student organizations, twenty-three NCAA Division III varsity sports, and nationally recognized volunteer programs, students find opportunities to learn and grow well beyond the classroom.

A Susquehanna education is a proven advantage. Graduates consistently say their Susquehanna experiences have given them a competitive edge over other recent graduates entering the workplace. Ninety-four percent of students are employed full-time or enrolled in graduate school within six months of graduation—an exceptionally high percentage compared with other institutions.

Location

Students find themselves at home in the eclectic town of Selinsgrove, Pennsylvania, nestled between the banks of the Susquehanna River and the foothills of the Appalachian Mountains. Favorite activities include checking out the shops on Market Street; enjoying the local flavor of downtown restaurants; kayaking, floating, or tubing down the Susquehanna River; or hiking, caving, and camping in nearby state parks and forests.

Selinsgrove is a 3-hour drive from New York City, Philadelphia, Baltimore, and Washington, D.C. Pennsylvania's capital of Harrisburg is approximately 60 miles from the campus, and the Harrisburg International Airport is served by American, United, Delta, Northwest, US Airways, several commuter airlines, and major rental-car agencies. The Penn Valley Airport in Selinsgrove provides facilities for private and charter aircraft.

Majors and Degrees

Susquehanna students pursue a Bachelor of Arts, Bachelor of Music, or Bachelor of Science degree in the following areas: accounting, art history, biochemistry, biology, business administration (emphasis in entrepreneurship, finance, global management, information systems, or marketing), chemistry, communications (emphasis in broadcasting, communication studies, corporate communications, journalism, mass communications, public relations, or speech communications), computer science, creative writing, earth and environmental sciences, ecology, economics (emphasis in financial economics, general economics, global economy, or financial markets), education (certification in early childhood, elementary, or secondary), English, French, German, graphic design, history, information systems, international studies (emphasis in Asian studies, comparative cultural studies, developing world studies, diplomacy, European studies, international trade and development, or sustainable development), liberal studies, mathematics, music, music composition, music education, music performance, philosophy, physics, political science, psychology, religion, sociology, Spanish, studio art (emphasis in painting and drawing or photography), and theater (emphasis in performance, production, or design).

Preprofessional programs are offered in dentistry, law, medicine, ministry, teaching, and veterinary medicine and include one-on-one advising, related internships, and test preparation for the MCAT and LSAT. Cooperative programs in allied health are offered with Thomas Jefferson University in Philadelphia, in dentistry with Temple University School of Dental Medicine in Philadelphia, and in forestry and environmental management with Duke University in Durham, North Carolina.

Minors are available in almost every major area and in the following additional areas: actuarial science, advertising, anthropology, Asian studies, dance, diversity studies, film studies, Greek, healthcare studies, international business and foreign language, international relations, Jewish studies, legal studies, literature, music technology, music theory, publishing and editing, and women's studies.

Academic Programs

Susquehanna's Central Curriculum is a hybrid model of liberal arts and practical education that emphasizes critical-thinking skills and ethics, and teaches students to put those skills to work in today's world. Throughout their four years at Susquehanna, students develop intellectual skills through courses of their choosing that study the richness of thought, human interaction, human connections, and the natural world.

Susquehanna's campus community explores a university theme each academic year. The theme is intended to focus classroom discussion, lectures, artistic performances, and student activities around a central idea for in-depth exploration. Past themes include Life on the Fringes, Water, Religion in the Public Square, and What Does It Mean to Be Educated? Reflecting the theme, the Common Reading Program asks Susquehanna faculty, staff, and incoming students to read a related common text every summer.

Susquehanna houses the Arlin M. Adams Center for Law and Society as a complementary program to the Central Curriculum. The Adams Center explores the rich intersections between law and various other disciplines. It provides a forum and research opportunities for examining issues affecting human rights and social responsibility, involving science and technology, and requiring constitutional interpretation. The Adams Center provides several venues for student learning, including internships and field experiences, networking, professional seminars, independent study, research projects, enhanced library resources, symposia, dialogue series, and the *Justice for All?* radio program. Guest speakers for the Adams Center have included nationally known experts and a Supreme Court justice.

Off-Campus Programs

Susquehanna's Global Opportunities (GO) program, the only one of its kind in the nation, requires every student to have a cross-cultural experience away from campus, either in the United States or abroad. It might include a traditional semester study-abroad program (GO Long), a short-term faculty/staff-led program (GO Short), a self-designed experience proposed and accepted in advance, or service in a cross-cultural setting.

GO is flexible and affordable. Susquehanna currently offers thirty-six GO Long programs that cost approximately the same as, or less than, a semester on campus. GO Short programs are even more affordable, because they involve a shorter stay away from campus. Most forms of financial aid, including scholarships, are available during GO Long or GO Short experiences

About two thirds of Susquehanna's students participate in nationally recognized community service projects, with an annual average of more than 25,000 hours of community service delivered to the Susquehanna Valley and beyond.

Academic Facilities

Susquehanna's facilities include a rich mix of historic and new buildings. Two buildings are on the National Register of Historic Places and others, completed in recent years, have won architectural and design awards.

In fall 2010, a new science facility opened, which has transformed teaching and learning for all Susquehanna students. With a prominent spot on the 306-acre campus, the 75,000-square-foot science facility is the school's largest academic building. The facility houses Susquehanna's biology, chemistry, and earth and environmental sciences programs.

The new science building demonstrates Susquehanna's strong commitment to sustainability and environmental responsibility. The building meets the U.S. Green Building Council's LEED certification criteria. The investment benefits all students, because science education is a part of the Central Curriculum. The initiative will advance other programs at Susquehanna, with the current science building, Fisher Hall, being renovated to accommodate anticipated enrollment gains to 2,400 students. With the opening of the new science building, more than two thirds of Fisher Hall is available, offering a number of academic programs larger, more modern spaces.

Susquehanna's new science facility will complement the already outstanding academic facilities available to students. Apfelbaum Hall, completed in 1999, is home to the Sigmund Weis School of Business and the Department of Communications. Apfelbaum houses two television studios, multimedia classrooms, a presentation room, and numerous small-group study rooms. Bogar Hall, renovated in 2007, includes a language lab for students studying modern languages and the Writers Institute's Editing and Publishing Center. Cunningham Center for Music and Art, renovated and expanded in 2002, offers contemporary art and music teaching facilities and flexible practice and performance space, including Stretansky Concert Hall, a 320-seat venue designed to optimize choral and instrumental music. Weber Chapel Auditorium is home to a classic, 1,500-seat theater, with a revolving stage and recording studio for students studying music technology. Additional performance space for theater students is available in the Degenstein Center Theater, which houses a modern 450-seat proscenium teaching theater with a counterweight fly system and an intimate, black-box studio theater.

Every student takes full advantage of the Blough-Weis Library. The fully automated library offers more than 253,000 volumes, 32,000 microforms, 5,000 DVDs, 3,000 CDs, and subscriptions to more than 50,000 periodicals. Students and faculty members have online access from any computer connected to the Internet. The library also houses Susquehanna's Media Center and Tutorial Services.

Costs

Tuition and fees for 2011–12 are $35,860. Room and board costs were $9600. A student's personal expenses, including books, travel, and other costs, are estimated at $1600 to $1900 per year.

Financial Aid

Ninety-two percent of Susquehanna students receive some form of financial aid. All students are encouraged to apply for need-based financial aid by filing both the FAFSA and PROFILE forms. Every applicant for admission to Susquehanna also is considered for merit awards regardless of financial need. Renewable for four years, Susquehanna's merit scholarships are awarded based on a student's academic achievement, talent in a particular area of University interest, or community involvement. Susquehanna is a participant in the Tuition Exchange program for children of employees at participating institutions. The University also participates in the Yellow Ribbon Program for veterans of the wars in Iraq and Afghanistan.

Faculty

Susquehanna's faculty members serve as advisers and creative mentors to their students both in the classroom and beyond. Whether meeting one-on-one with a student for more in-depth instruction after class or making their homes available for barbecues, faculty members make themselves accessible to students in a variety of formal and informal settings. Professors who seek employment at Susquehanna value the opportunity to live and learn alongside their students. By graduation, many Susquehanna students have shared a stage with faculty members, whether through a recital or a national conference presentation.

Of Susquehanna's 128 full-time professors, 94 percent hold a doctorate or terminal degree in their field. The student-faculty ratio is 13:1.

Student Government

Susquehanna's Student Government Association is a self-governing organization providing representation of the student body in University affairs. The main function of the legislative body is the allocation of student activities fees to recognized clubs, student groups, campus projects, and University activities. Senators are elected each year and serve as student representatives to various offices and groups on campus.

Admission Requirements

Susquehanna's average accepted student earns a GPA of 3.25 in a competitive college-prep curriculum. For those students who choose to submit test scores, the midrange SAT score is 1010–1210, and the midrange ACT score is 23–27.

Susquehanna looks for exceptional students who are attracted by its academic challenges and extracurricular opportunities. Admission is competitive. The University considers what it can do for students and how students might contribute to Susquehanna. It assesses applications based on course selections, grades, and class rank as well as factors such as motivation, creativity, and leadership. Honors program students typically rank in the top 10 percent.

Students may choose to apply under the Write Option, which allows two graded, critical writing samples to serve as a substitute for SAT/ACT scores.

Susquehanna strongly encourages prospective students to visit the campus and interview with a member of the admissions staff. Counselors are happy to answer questions and explain programs firsthand. Students can see the facilities and perhaps meet with faculty members, coaches, and students. Susquehanna can usually arrange for class visits or overnight stays in residence halls.

Application and Information

Susquehanna accepts the Susquehanna Application as well as the Common Application and Universal Application, with no preference given to one over the other. All applications are free to file online.

Students applying to the Bachelor of Music degree program are required to audition. Students applying to major in graphic design or creative writing are required to submit a portfolio of their work.

Office of Admissions
Susquehanna University
514 University Avenue
Selinsgrove, Pennsylvania 17870-1164
Phone: 570-372-4260
        800-326-9672 (toll-free)
Fax: 570-372-2722
E-mail: suadmiss@susqu.edu
Web site: www.susqu.edu

Historic Seibert Hall at Susquehanna University.

SWEET BRIAR COLLEGE

SWEET BRIAR, VIRGINIA

The College

Deeply committed to the education of women since its founding in 1901, Sweet Briar College is consistently ranked as one of the top national liberal arts and sciences colleges in the country. Its excellent academic reputation, beautiful campus, and attention to the individual attract ambitious, intellectually self-confident women who want to excel. Students can expect their Sweet Briar experience to allow them to fulfill their promise as scholars and leaders, while enjoying the close-knit friendships and camaraderie that come with a personal, residential community.

A Sweet Briar education sets in motion the conviction that any goal is achievable. Small classes (averaging 12 students per class) and a student-faculty ratio of 7:1 ensure personal attention and academic interaction. Students work one-on-one with faculty members who are committed to each student's academic success. The College has a wide geographic, ethnic, and socioeconomic representation. About 700 women from more than forty states and nineteen countries are enrolled at Sweet Briar's Virginia campus; another 120 students are enrolled in Sweet Briar's coed Junior Year in France and Junior Year in Spain programs. Any student may have a car.

Students who derive the most from the Sweet Briar experience are those who participate in and contribute to community life, striking a good balance between academic work and the rest of life. They recognize that one of the advantages of the College is the unlimited opportunities for women to participate and assume leadership roles in many types of organizations and activities. More than fifty campus organizations are available, including honor societies, a literary journal, community service groups, a multicultural club, political groups, a student newspaper, drama and dance clubs, a radio station, and singing groups. Students plan and participate in an extensive array of concerts, films, and dance and theater productions as well as workshops and master classes by visiting scholars and performers. Recent visitors have included the writer Rebecca Skloot, environmental attorney Robert F. Kennedy Jr., columnist Christine Brennan, and country music singer Stephanie Quayle.

Twenty-one campus buildings, the work of renowned American architect Ralph Adams Cram, are on the National Register of Historic Places. In 2006, Sweet Briar opened a beautiful new studio arts facility. Sweet Briar is the only college in the United States with a residential artists' colony on its campus. Known as the Virginia Center for the Creative Arts, the colony is a working retreat for international writers, visual artists, and composers. In 2009, the College opened a 53,000-square-foot fitness and athletic center addition to the existing gymnasium, and a sixty-bed apartment-style residence facility for upper class students. The on-campus equestrian center, one of the largest and best college facilities in the country, attracts both competitive and recreational riders. Sweet Briar's equestrian program, both competitive and instructional, has consistently garnered national recognition. The 100-acre Rogers Riding Center has a 120-foot by 300-foot indoor arena with Perma-Flex footing, well-appointed stables for approximately 90 horses, several outdoor rings, numerous paddocks, and miles of hacking trails—all within walking distance of the main campus.

In 2009, Sweet Briar upgraded its computer network to a state-of-the-art wireless platform that allows high-speed Internet access from all academic and administrative buildings, as well as residence hall rooms. Connection to the campus network is also possible from most outdoor, student-used spaces.

In 2004, Sweet Briar launched two graduate degree programs: the Master of Arts in Teaching and the Master of Education. These programs are rooted in the teaching philosophy of differentiated curriculum and instruction. Sweet Briar also established a new degree program in engineering, only the second such undergraduate program at a women's college.

Varsity athletes compete in NCAA Division III field hockey, lacrosse, soccer, softball, swimming, tennis, and volleyball. Club sports include cross-country, fencing, and riding.

Location

Sweet Briar's 3,250-acre campus in the foothills of the Blue Ridge Mountains includes hiking, biking, and riding trails and two lakes that provide spectacular venues for outdoor recreational activities. The College is centrally located on the outskirts of Lynchburg, Virginia, southwest of Washington, D.C., and Charlottesville. Students also enjoy activities in nearby Roanoke and Richmond.

Majors and Degrees

Sweet Briar awards the Bachelor of Arts, Bachelor of Science, and Bachelor of Fine Arts degrees. The College offers thirty-four majors: anthropology, archaeology, art history, biochemistry and molecular biology, biology, business management, chemistry, classics, dance, economics, education, engineering and management, engineering science, English, English and creative writing, environmental science, environmental studies, French, German, German studies, government, history, international affairs, mathematics, modern languages and literatures, music, philosophy, physics, psychology, religion, sociology, Spanish, studio art, and theater.

Additional area studies, minors, and certificate programs include arts management, equine studies, engineering (3-2 dual degree), journalism, new media, and communications, Latin American studies, law and society, medieval and Renaissance studies, musical theater, prelaw, premed, pre–veterinary science, and statistics. Students may design an interdisciplinary major focused on a topic of special interest or may construct personalized majors.

Academic Programs

Sweet Briar's mission is to prepare women to be active, responsible members of a world community. Underscoring every one of the major fields of study is the idea that the best way to learn about the world is to experience it. The curriculum emphasizes hands-on learning, comprehensive understanding, analysis, reflection, creativity, and communication across disciplines. The academic programs are nationally celebrated. To add to this, the College recently adopted a strategic plan that includes emphasis on providing an education that is dynamic, sophisticated, connected, and entrepreneurial. Making the most effective use of Sweet Briar's unique campus as a "landscape for learning," the strategic plan aims at an educational experience that prepares students to engage with today's digital world, be ready to adapt to the dizzying rate of technological change, and encourage entrepreneurial thinking across disciplines.

The general education program has four components—English 104, skills requirements, experiences requirements, and knowledge areas requirements—that work together to ensure the development of strong communication and quantitative reasoning skills. Independent studies and seminars are included in most majors, with a culminating senior course or exercise required in most majors. Sweet Briar has a chapter of Phi Beta Kappa and was the first women's college to establish a chapter of the prelaw honorary society Phi Alpha Delta. It also has a four-year honors program that is nationally recognized for its innovative partnering of interdisciplinary academic and cocurricular programs. Honors students may take special tutorials and seminars as well as complete a yearlong research project culminating in an honors thesis on an original topic.

Sweet Briar's two-semester calendar allows students to participate in intensive courses, independent research projects, or internships on campus or throughout the world.

Off-Campus Programs

By the time they graduate, more than a third of Sweet Briar students have studied abroad. The Sweet Briar Junior Year in France, the first program in Paris for American students, is considered the most academically rigorous program available today. Students from 258 colleges and universities have participated in the coed program. The successful Junior Year in Spain is recognized as the premier program in Seville. The College has special relationships with the University of St. Andrews in Scotland, Heidelberg University in Germany, Doshisha Women's College in Japan, and the University of Urbino in Italy. In recent years, Sweet Briar students have also chosen the following destinations for study abroad: Australia, China, the Czech Republic, Denmark, Greece, Holland, Ireland, Jamaica, Korea, Mongolia, Morocco, New Zealand, and Thailand. Off-campus study may also include an Environmental Junior Year, the Washington Semester at American University, and summer programs at St. Anne's College in Oxford, England. In addition, summer programs are available in Australia; Central America, including Costa Rica; Münster, Germany; Rome and Urbino, Italy; Nepal; and Spain.

Sweet Briar participates in the Tri-College Consortium with Randolph College and Lynchburg College. In addition to taking courses at the other colleges, students can participate in combined social and cultural activities on those campuses.

Academic Facilities

Sweet Briar has the largest private undergraduate library collection in the state of Virginia, with resources of more than 240,000 volumes, 1,000 journal subscriptions, 430,000 microforms, 6,800 audiovisual materials, and special libraries in art, music, and the sciences. Some of the notable special holdings include Virginia Woolf, T. E. Lawrence, George Meredith, W. H. Auden, and a rare collection of twentieth-century Chinese works. Three computer labs with Macintosh and Windows/Intel Pentium computers are open free of charge 24 hours a day. The student-computer ratio is 6:1. A lab for Sweet Briar's new engineering department includes a 5-Kip-capacity Universal Test Machine; a United Tru-Blue Rockwell hardness tester; a set of gauged beams and test fixtures for mechanics experiments; eight new computers, each with NI ELVIS and Labview with Protoboards; and a well-equipped machine shop. Students studying science use state-of-the-art equipment that enhances faculty-student collaborative research. Biology equipment includes a scanning electron microscope with digital imaging system, equipment for plant and animal tissue culture, and DNA sequencing equipment. Chemistry students have access to two nuclear magnetic resonance spectrometers (NMR; 400 MHz and 60 MHz), an atomic absorption spectrometer (AAS), a diode array UV/Vis spectrometer, a Fourier-transform infrared spectrometer (FT-IR), a modular LASER laboratory, a gas chromatograph/mass spectrograph (GC/MS), a high-pressure liquid chromatograph (HPLC), and a differential scanning calorimeter (DSC). Physics equipment includes a scanning tunneling microscope, an X-ray crystallography system, a 10-inch-diameter reflecting telescope, and holographic instrumentation.

The environmental studies program occupies two sites. A renovated train station provides classroom and laboratory space equipped with a Rigaku Miniflex powder X-ray diffraction system for mineralogical analysis, a Rocklabs bench-top ring mill for grinding rock and soil samples, a drying oven and a high-temperature muffle furnace, and much more. An adjacent caboose car provides office space for faculty members. A water treatment plant was also converted to an environmental education/nature center and environmental lab; equipment includes water, soil, wastewater, and sediment sampling instrumentation, including N-Con composite samplers, macroinvertebrate samplers, and specialized water-collection devices.

The Babcock Fine Arts Center includes individual practice rooms, an electronic piano lab, dance studios, theaters, and Murchison Lane Auditorium for lectures and performing arts. Two former dairy barns were recently renovated for classroom and office space to house studio arts, including a ceramics and sculpture studio; four large studios for painting, drawing, and printmaking; and a photo studio and darkroom.

The Academic Resource Center (ARC) provides free of charge to all students academic support services that include assistance with papers and study strategies, a personalized time management system, stress management advice, tutoring information, and one-on-one peer mentoring. The ARC also provides support and learning strategies for students with diagnosed learning differences.

Costs

For 2010–11, tuition and fees were $30,195 and room and board totaled $10,780. Books and supplies were estimated at $1500 and personal expenses averaged $950.

Financial Aid

A family's financial circumstance does not limit a student's choices at Sweet Briar because of the College's generous financial aid program. More than 90 percent of enrolling students receive financial assistance from the College, including merit scholarships, need-based grants, loans, and work-study awards. Scholarships for international students are also available on a competitive basis.

Faculty

Sweet Briar's faculty members have been commended by numerous regional and national educational groups for their excellence in teaching. Faculty members are actively engaged in teaching, research, publication, and other forms of creative activity. More than 95 percent of full-time faculty members have a doctorate or the highest professional degree in his or her field. All classes are taught by a faculty member. About half of the faculty members are women.

Student Government

The Student Government Association (SGA) is founded upon a highly developed concept of honor and student ownership and involvement. The Honor System applies to all phases of academic and social life. Each entering student becomes a full member of the Student Government Association upon taking the Honor Pledge, which states that Sweet Briar women do not lie, cheat, steal, or violate the rights of others. Students participate in the governance of the College through the many offices and committee positions of the Student Government Association. SGA and its committees are largely responsible for the self-governance of the student body.

Admission Requirements

Sweet Briar seeks talented women who are adventurous, are enthusiastic about learning, and want to take an active part in their education. The Admissions Committee looks for qualities such as independent thinking, ethical principles, assertiveness, and an appreciation of diversity. Sweet Briar welcomes students of all economic, ethnic, geographic, religious, and social backgrounds.

Requirements normally include a minimum of 4 units in English, 3 in mathematics, 3 in social studies, 2 sequential years in a foreign language, and 3 units in science, as well as additional units in these subjects to total 16. Most candidates have 20 such academic units. Special attention is given to the difficulty of the applicant's curriculum and her academic achievement in the classroom; scores on the SAT or ACT are required. An interview at the College is strongly encouraged but not required. Candidates who are unable to visit the campus are invited to meet with staff members or to talk with alumnae in their hometowns.

Application and Information

Sweet Briar has dropped its early decision application program in favor of being responsive to all applicants. An application deadline of February 1 is maintained, but students are invited to apply for admission as early as September of their senior year. Sweet Briar will notify each student of acceptance within one month of the date her application becomes complete. Transfer applications for the fall semester are due by July 1. A completed application includes a transcript of the candidate's academic work, scores on the required test, recommendations from the guidance counselor and a teacher, and an essay written by the candidate. There is a $40 application fee, which may be waived at the request of the student's guidance counselor if it is deemed to be a financial burden. Sweet Briar also accepts the Common Application (a supplement is required). All materials should be sent to the admissions office at the address listed in this description. Information may be requested from the same office.

Dean of Admissions
Sweet Briar College
P.O. Box 1052
Sweet Briar, Virginia 24595
Phone: 434-381-6142
　　　 800-381-6142 (toll-free)
Fax: 434-381-6152
E-mail: admissions@sbc.edu
Web site: http://www.sbc.edu

SYRACUSE UNIVERSITY
SYRACUSE, NEW YORK

The University

Syracuse University (SU), which was founded in 1870, is an independent, privately endowed university with an international reputation. Students attend from all over the United States and from more than 100 other countries. There are about 17,300 students enrolled; 12,600 are undergraduates. Approximately 70 percent of the students live in University housing, which includes modern residence halls, apartments, and town houses. The 200-acre campus features a main grassy quadrangle surrounded by academic buildings, with residential facilities nearby. The campus is situated on a hill overlooking the downtown area of Syracuse. Social life is centered on the campus, and there are innumerable recreational, athletic, and academic activities. The 50,000-seat Carrier Dome is the site of concerts, sports events, and Commencement. All of campus is connected to the University's high-speed wired or wireless networks.

Location

The city of Syracuse (metropolitan-area population of 700,000) is the business, educational, and cultural hub of central New York. The city offers professional theater and opera, as well as visiting artists and performers. Highlights of the downtown area include the Everson Museum of Art, the Milton J. Rubenstein Museum of Science and Technology (MOST), the impressive Civic Center, and the Armory Square shopping area. Central New York has many lakes, parks, mountains, and outstanding recreational opportunities.

Majors and Degrees

Syracuse University awards B.A., B.S., B.Arch., B.I.D., B.Mus., and B.F.A. degrees.

The School of Architecture offers a five-year baccalaureate program leading to the first professional degree of B.Arch.

Departmental and interdisciplinary majors in the College of Arts and Sciences are African-American studies, American studies, anthropology, art, art history, biochemistry, biology, biophysical science, chemistry, classical civilization, classics (Greek and Latin), communication sciences and disorders, economics, English and textual studies, European literature, fine arts, French, geography, geology (Earth sciences), German, Greek, history, history of architecture, international relations, Italian, Latin, Latino–Latin American studies, linguistic studies, mathematics, Middle Eastern studies, modern foreign languages, music, music history and cultures, philosophy, physics, policy studies (public affairs), political philosophy, political science, psychology, religion, religion and society, Russian, Russian and Central European studies, sociology, Spanish, women's studies, and writing and rhetoric.

The College of Human Ecology majors include child and family studies, nutrition/dietetics, nutrition science, public health, social work, and sport management.

The School of Education offers majors in art education, elementary education (inclusive with special education), health and exercise science (including pre–physical therapy and 3+3 D.P.T.), music education, physical education, secondary education, selected studies in education, and special education (inclusive with elementary education and with early childhood education).

The L. C. Smith College of Engineering and Computer Science majors include aerospace, chemical, civil, computer, electrical, environmental, and mechanical engineering; bioengineering; and computer science.

The School of Information Studies offers a four-year bachelor's degree program in information management and technology.

The Martin J. Whitman School of Management majors include accounting, entrepreneurship and emerging enterprises, finance, management, marketing management, real estate, retail management, and supply chain management.

The S. I. Newhouse School of Public Communications majors are in the following areas: advertising, broadcast and digital journalism, graphic design, magazine, newspaper and online journalism, photography, public relations, and television/radio/film.

The College of Visual and Performing Arts majors are in the following areas: art and design, communication and rhetorical studies, drama, music, and transmedia. Art and design majors offered are ceramics, communications design, (includes advertising design), fashion design, fiber and textile arts, history of art, illustration, industrial and interaction design, interior design, jewelry and metalsmithing, painting, printmaking, and sculpture. Transmedia majors include art photography, art video, computer art, and film. Drama majors include theater design and technology, acting, musical theater, and stage management. Music majors include the Bandier Program for Music and the Entertainment Industries, music composition, music industry, performance organ, performance percussion, performance piano, performance strings, performance voice, and performance wind instruments. The Department of Communication and Rhetorical Studies offers a Bachelor of Science degree.

Academic Programs

The University operates on a two-semester calendar with two 6-week summer sessions. Students generally take five 3-credit-hour courses each semester. A minimum of 120 credit hours is required for graduation. Special programs include dual and combined enrollment, selected studies, internships, an honors program, ROTC, and preprofessional advising for students going on to study dentistry, law, medicine, or veterinary science.

Off-Campus Programs

The Syracuse University Abroad program operates centers in London, Madrid, Hong Kong, Beijing, Florence, Santiago (Chile), Strasbourg, and Istanbul. SU Abroad also offers opportunities through world partners in over thirty other countries, including Australia, Costa Rica, Ecuador, Egypt, India, Ireland, Japan, Korea, Poland, and Russia.

Academic Facilities

The academic buildings at Syracuse University span the century, with fifteen listed in the National Register of Historic Places and others representative of some of the most modern and technologically sophisticated architecture in the country. The Ernest Stevenson Bird Library houses approximately 3.1 million printed volumes, more than 16,000 online and print journals, and extensive collections of microforms, maps, images, music scores, sound recordings, video, rare books, and manuscripts. The University has computer facilities with laboratories and a data communications network that links computers to hundreds of terminals. The $107 million, 230,000-square-foot Life Sciences Complex combines research and teaching wings for biology, chemistry, and biochemistry. The Newhouse Communications Center has some of the finest facilities available for journalism and telecommunications. Slocum Hall, home to the School of Architecture, includes a new auditorium, gallery, and space for studio and research. The Center for Science and Technology is a state-of-the-art facility uniting research and academic programs in computer science and technology. It also houses the CASE Center for research in computer applications and software engineering. The new five-story addition to Link Hall, home of the L.C. Smith College of Engineering and Computer Science, features a three-story, high bay lab that houses a crane and space for civil engineering students to build and test structures. The high-tech Melvin A. Eggers Hall offers superior facilities for the University's social science programs. The new multimillion-dollar Whitman School of Management building provides students with access to the latest educational technologies and plenty of space for team meetings and work.

Costs

Tuition for 2010–11 was $34,970. The costs for housing and meals averaged $12,850, and fees were $1332. Books and supplies averaged $1308; travel expenses, $600; and personal expenses, $900. Therefore, the total cost of attendance was approximately $51,960.

Financial Aid

About 80 percent of all entering first-year and transfer students receive some form of financial aid. By filing the Free Application for Federal Student Aid (FAFSA) and the CSS Financial Aid PRO-FILE, students are automatically considered for all financial aid programs administered by Syracuse University, including federal financial aid, Syracuse University Grants, and Federal Work-Study Program awards. Merit-based scholarships are available to both first-year and transfer students, based on the information provided in the application for admission. Syracuse University evaluates candidates for admission without respect to financial need. Information on financial aid policies, procedures, and deadlines can be obtained from the Office of Financial Aid and Scholarship Programs.

Faculty

The majority of faculty members hold the highest degree in their professional field. There are over 900 full-time faculty members, including recognized experts in their fields who teach at both the graduate and undergraduate levels.

Student Government

The Syracuse University Student Association works to protect students' rights and offers services through its three branches—the executive, the legislative, and the judicial.

Admission Requirements

Syracuse University seeks a diverse student body from all social, cultural, and educational backgrounds. Each candidate is evaluated individually, based on the requirements of the college of the University to which he or she has applied. Emphasis is placed on students' high school performance, standardized test scores (SAT or ACT), an essay, recommendations, extracurricular activities and community service, and portfolios or auditions, when required. Special admission requirements and deadlines for some programs are described on the University's Web site and in the Undergraduate Application for Admission.

Syracuse University is an Equal Opportunity/Affirmative Action institution and does not discriminate on the basis of race, creed, color, gender, national origin, religion, marital status, age, disability, sexual orientation, or gender identity or expression.

Application and Information

Regular decision applicants for the fall semester should submit their completed application along with transcripts, standardized test scores, the essay, teacher recommendations, and the counselor evaluation by January 1 (postmarked deadline). Notification begins in mid-March. Completed applications for early decision applicants must be postmarked by November 15. Notification begins in mid-December.

Detailed information may be obtained by contacting:

Office of Admissions
100 Crouse-Hinds Hall
900 South Crouse Avenue
Syracuse University
Syracuse, New York 13244-2130
Phone: 315-443-3611
Web site: http://admissions.syr.edu

The historic buildings that make up the SU campus stand in testimony to the many years of distinction that are at the foundation of Syracuse University.

TEMPLE UNIVERSITY
PHILADELPHIA, PENNSYLVANIA

The University

Students who visit Temple University's Main Campus find they are quite impressed. Cutting-edge facilities and great faculty members create a dynamic academic environment that draws students from around the world. But what can transform a student's life at Temple happens outside the classroom as well. Temple is located in Philadelphia, a dynamic, world-class city with a diverse ethnic mix, a robust economy, and a thriving music and art scene. It is the perfect place to live and study. Two spectacular new academic buildings opened on Main Campus in January 2009—the Tyler School of Art and the Fox School of Business and Management's Alter Hall. More academic and residential buildings are scheduled to open in 2011 and 2012.

Students who prefer not to attend college in the city should take a look at the Ambler campus, Temple's 187-acre suburban home. Just about all undergraduate programs can be started there, and eighteen can be fully completed there. Ambler's $17-million Learning Center includes smart classrooms; fully integrated technology, including wireless access throughout the building; five computer lab/classrooms; a math, science, and writing center; a video editing lab; a café; and a 300-seat auditorium.

Temple's other local campus is the Health Sciences Center, where the College of Health Professions, Temple University Hospital, Temple University School of Medicine, and Temple Dental School are located.

Temple is in the city, but it has a large residential student population—about 12,000 students living on and around Main Campus. The calendar is crammed with theater, dance, and music performances. The Liacouras Center, Temple's 10,200-seat entertainment complex, hosts the University's NCAA Division I basketball games (free tickets for students!) as well as concerts. Great performers like Kanye West, Green Day, Maroon 5, John Mayer, Counting Crows, Rusted Root, Alicia Keys, and Bob Dylan have performed at the Liacouras Center. Temple has every type of student doing every type of activity. Beyond sports, students can join one of 100 or so clubs and organizations and take full advantage of the rich resources and recreation activities offered by Philadelphia and the surrounding area.

Location

Philadelphia has a lot more than juicy sandwiches and cream cheese. With more than 100 museums, 700 Zagat-rated restaurants, and the largest landscaped park in the country—Fairmount Park at 4,180 acres—Philly has a lot to offer. It is a walkable, manageable city that is just 1.5 miles from Temple's Main Campus. Just four stops on a quick subway ride and students are in Center City—or what most would call downtown. Shop, eat, play, or just chill. In addition, students can find a variety of internships in all fields in the Philadelphia area, and Temple has more than 100,000 alumni in the region who love to hire Temple students.

Majors and Degrees

The Tyler School of Art offers the Bachelor of Fine Arts with concentrations in ceramics/glass, fibers, graphic and interactive design, metals/jewelry/CAD-CAM, painting, photography, printmaking, and sculpture; the Bachelor of Arts in art history and visual studies; and the Bachelor of Science in art education. Tyler's Architecture Program confers the Bachelor of Science in architecture (preprofessional), architectural preservation, and facilities management.

The Fox School of Business and Management offers the Bachelor of Business Administration in accounting, actuarial science, business management, economics, entrepreneurship, finance, human resource management, international business administration, law and business, management information systems, marketing, real estate, and risk management and insurance.

The School of Communications and Theater offers the Bachelor of Arts in advertising; American culture and media arts; broadcasting, telecommunications, and mass media; communication studies; film and media arts; journalism; strategic and organizational communications; and theater.

The College of Education offers the Bachelor of Science in applied communications, career and technical education, elementary education, and secondary education.

The College of Engineering offers the Bachelor of Science in Engineering in civil engineering, electrical engineering, and mechanical engineering. The Bachelor of Science is offered in construction management technology and general engineering technology.

The College of Health Professions offers the Bachelor of Science in communication sciences; health information management; linguistics; nursing; public health; speech, language, and hearing; therapeutic recreation, and kinesiology.

The College of Liberal Arts offers the Bachelor of Arts in African American studies, American studies, anthropology, Asian studies, classics, criminal justice, economics, English, French, geography and urban studies, German, Hebrew, history, Italian, neuroscience (systems, behavior, and plasticity), philosophy, political science, psychology, religion, Russian, sociology, Spanish, and women's studies.

The Boyer College of Music and Dance offers the Bachelor of Music in composition, dance, jazz studies, music education, music history, music therapy, performance (specific instrument or voice), and theory; the Bachelor of Fine Arts is offered in dance.

The College of Science and Technology offers the Bachelor of Science in biochemistry, biology, biophysics, chemistry, computer science, environmental studies, geology, mathematical economics, mathematics, physics, neuroscience (cell and molecular), and prepharmacy.

The School of Social Administration offers the Bachelor of Social Work degree.

The School of Tourism and Hospitality Management offers the Bachelor of Science in sport and recreation management and in tourism and hospitality management.

In addition, Ambler College offers Bachelor of Science degree programs in horticulture and landscape architecture and in community and regional planning.

Academic Programs

Temple provides an excellent and affordable education, which not only prepares the student for the specific demands of a career, but also enhances an understanding of the world and the ability to continue learning throughout life.

All students are required to complete the General Education curriculum, a cross-section of courses that form the intellectual foundation of a Temple education, which includes a Philadelphia Experience theme. Many first-year students take advantage of Learning Communities—groups of 20 to 30 participants who pursue common studies under the direction of a faculty team. They spend a semester together, taking a few common courses, participating in faculty-led discussion groups, studying together, and taking field trips related to their studies.

University Studies is a home for the many students who have not declared a major and for students interested in graduate or professional programs in health fields. Academically qualified students may seek extra intellectual challenge through the honors program, taking about a quarter of their course work in the program's smaller, more demanding classes.

After graduation, students are well prepared for the job world. Temple's Career Center arranges cooperative education assignments, schedules on-campus interviews with employers and graduate schools, offers employment skills workshops, provides career and graduate school advisement, and maintains a network of thousands of successful Temple alumni.

Academic Facilities

With more than fifty computer labs and a 90 percent wireless campus, information is more accessible than ever. An exciting new addition to the Main Campus is the Teaching, Education, Collaboration, and Help (TECH) Center. With up to 700 computers (600 fixed workstations and up to 100 laptop loaners), the TECH Center is one of the largest of its kind in the nation; thirteen breakout rooms where students can work on group projects and practice presentations; six specialized labs within the primary center, including video editing, graphic design/CAD, music composition, language/interactive audio, quiet zone, and software development facility; a 24-hour computer help desk for students and faculty and staff members; a 4,260-square-foot Temple Welcome Center (run by the Admissions Office) to host visits to the University by prospective students and their families; and a Starbucks café.

Costs

Tuition and fees for the 2010–11 academic year were $12,424 for Pennsylvania residents and $22,252 for out-of-state residents (tuition rates can vary by major). Room and board for the academic year were about $9300.

Financial Aid

Scholarships, grants, loans, and work-study programs are available; 2 out of every 3 Temple students receive financial aid. Four-year academic merit scholarships for talented entering freshmen begin at $2500. Students need only apply for admission to be eligible for these scholarships. Applicants for need-based aid must file the Free Application for Federal Student Aid (FAFSA). Transfer students must file a financial aid transcript, even if they have received no aid from their previous school.

Faculty

At Temple, faculty members are valued not only for their ability to pursue knowledge, but also to share that knowledge with students. Full-time faculty members teach many introductory courses, and often act as academic advisers; from their first semester students can expect to have contact with the people at the forefront of their fields, winners of prestigious teaching and research awards such as the Lindback, the Golden Apple, the Sowell, the Fulbright, the Guggenheim, the Carnegie, and the National Endowment.

In 2007, Temple officially welcomed the largest group of new tenured and tenure-track faculty members in recent history. Faculty members were hired away from leading universities and research centers, including Princeton University, Brown University, the University of Wisconsin–Madison, the University of Maryland, Wellesley College, and the Cleveland Clinic. Nearly every college at Temple has been joined by at least one new presidential faculty recruit.

In addition to being superlative teachers and researchers, Temple faculty members are also known for their practical experience. For example, a marketing class may be led by a successful entrepreneur, or music lessons given by a member of the Philadelphia Orchestra. Marine biologists, newspaper editors, published authors, practicing architects, and health care professionals all bring their expertise to the classroom to enhance students' education.

Admission Requirements

For freshman admissions, high school grades (quality of courses, grade trends), standardized test scores, and other factors (the required essay, recommendations, extracurricular activities, work or leadership experience, and other personal circumstances) are considered. Temple uses a sliding scale rather than absolute cut-offs for GPA and test scores. SAT subject tests and personal interviews are not required. The deadline for freshman admission is March 1; however, students should apply in the fall of their senior year. Official copies of high school transcripts and standardized test scores must be sent directly to the admissions office. Counselor forms are not required. The deadline for spring admission is November 1.

Temple has rolling admissions. Freshman decisions begin in early fall, and letters are sent four to six weeks after that point. Temple's admissions process is holistic; every aspect of the student's academic history is considered. Typically, students with a B+ average or better in a strong, college-prep curriculum in grades 9–12 and in the top 30 percent of their graduating classes are accepted. The SAT is required with all three sections considered—admitted students average 500–600 on each section. If students opt to take the ACT, they must also complete the writing section.

Freshman students who apply are automatically considered for merit-based scholarships and honors. Recommendations are not required but are accepted and considered. There is no recommendation form. The best way to apply is online. The application fee is $50—most students apply online.

Temple University welcomes transfer applicants from both two-year and four-year colleges and universities around the country and the world. Transfer students comprise more than half of each entering class and are a vital part of the vibrant campus community. Applicants are considered transfer students if they will have attempted 15 or more college-level credits by the time they apply. If this is not the case, they should apply as freshman students. In making admissions decisions, careful consideration is given to the quality of a student's program and the number of credits earned and the grade point average achieved. A cumulative GPA of at least 2.5 (on a 4.0 scale) and academic progress is required for consideration, but is not a guarantee of admission. The following programs have higher minimum grade point average requirements: architecture, nursing, pharmacy, and film and media arts. For most programs, transfer students must complete the application process by June 1 for the fall semester or by November 1 for the spring semester. The fall semester transfer application deadline for music is March 1. The fall priority deadline for nursing is February 15. Transfer applicants must request that all high schools and colleges that they previously attended send official transcripts to the Office of Undergraduate Admissions at Temple University by these deadlines. SAT or ACT scores are not required if an applicant has earned at least 15 college-level credits.

Application and Information

A completed file should contain an application form accompanied by a nonrefundable application fee, a secondary school transcript (sent by the student's school), and SAT or ACT scores. The University has a rolling admission policy; applicants are notified of the admission decision as soon as possible after all credentials have been received and reviewed.

For additional information, students may contact:

Office of Undergraduate Admissions
Temple University (041-09)
Philadelphia, Pennsylvania 19122-6096
Phone: 215-204-7200
        888-340-2222 (toll-free)
E-mail: tuadm@temple.edu
Web site: http://www.temple.edu/undergrad
       http://www.facebook.com/templeu

TEXAS CHRISTIAN UNIVERSITY

FORT WORTH, TEXAS

The University

The mission of Texas Christian University (TCU) is to educate individuals to think and act as ethical leaders and responsible citizens in the global community, an idea that influences every area of the University.

Founded in 1873, TCU defied the American frontier status quo and offered an education grounded in values, innovation, and creativity. It was the first college in the Southwest to educate both men and women.

Today, TCU is a major teaching and research institution balanced by student-centered warmth typical of a smaller liberal arts college. The University rolls across some 269 picturesque tree-lined acres and within sixty buildings, from the traditional yellow-bricked neo-Georgians to a few angular ultramodern creations. Students find a diverse learning community offering over 100 undergraduate areas of study across seven colleges: business, communication, education, fine arts, health and human sciences, humanities and social sciences, and science and engineering. Approximately ninety percent of TCU's professors hold the highest degrees in their fields. It is also common to find qualified undergraduates assisting professors in the latest research activities.

TCU enrolls 7,853 full-time undergraduate men and women from nearly every state and over eighty countries. The University competes in the nation's top collegiate athletics tier, Division I-A, offering more than twenty sports. TCU is also a member of leading education organizations such as Phi Beta Kappa, Sigma Xi, and Mortar Board. Research-oriented Ph.D. programs are offered in chemistry, divinity, education, English, history, physics, and psychology. Facilities and services include twenty residence halls, each with telephone, cable, and high-speed Internet connections. Upperclassmen have the option of living in fully furnished apartments complete with full kitchens. Sophomores may live in fully furnished, newly built lofts. Other campus amenities include nine eateries—one being an all-you-can-eat buffet—a bistro in the library; a store; a post office; thirty-one tennis courts; and the University Recreation Center with five basketball courts, a climbing wall, six racquetball courts, an elevated running track, pool and game tables, video arcade, outdoor pool and patio, and a floor full of the latest in cardio-fitness equipment. Students publish an award-winning newspaper and magazine and operate a top Dallas–Fort Worth radio station featuring alternative music and campus sports coverage.

Location

Fort Worth is home to some of the finest museums in the Southwest, including the Kimbell Art Museum. In fact, its cultural district also includes Casa Mañana, the Amon Carter Museum, the Modern Art Museum of Fort Worth, and the Fort Worth Museum of Science and Natural History. Downtown, one finds the Texas Ballet Theater, the Fort Worth Opera, the Fort Worth Symphony, and the world-class Bass Performance Hall, called one of the top ten opera houses in the world by *Travel and Leisure* magazine.

While the TCU Horned Frogs are considered the home team of Fort Worth, other nearby sports teams include the Texas Rangers, Dallas Cowboys, Dallas Stars, and Dallas Mavericks. The Texas Motor Speedway, which features NASCAR auto racing, is located north of Fort Worth. Those looking for other entertainment will not be disappointed, either. The Fort Worth Zoo is 1 minute from the campus, and the world-famous Stockyards are just a bit farther. Six Flags Over Texas is only a short drive away, as is Hurricane Harbor.

Fort Worth is also home to some of America's greatest corporations, including Burlington Northern Santa Fe (BNSF), RadioShack, Bell Helicopter-Textron, American Airlines, Pier 1 Imports, and Lockheed Martin. Other companies that look to TCU for employees are Accenture, Intel, Frito-Lay, and Electronic Data Systems.

Majors and Degrees

Programs lead to bachelor's degrees in more than 100 major areas: actuarial science, allied-health professions (athletic training, pre–occupational therapy*, pre–physical therapy*, and pre–physician assistant studies*), anthropology, art (art education, art history, and studio, with concentrations in ceramics, painting, photography, and sculpture), art administration (minor), astronomy, ballet, ballet and modern dance, biochemistry, biology, British and colonial/postcolonial studies (minor), business (with concentrations in accounting, electronic business, finance, finance/real estate, entrepreneurial management, marketing, and supply and value chain management, all of which are available with an international emphasis), chemistry, child development, classical studies (minor), communication sciences and disorders (speech-language pathology and habilitation of the deaf), communication studies, computer information technology, computer science, coordinated program in dietetics, criminal justice, dietetics, economics, education (early childhood, exceptional children, middle school, secondary, all-level certification, and endorsement in English as a second language), energy technology and management (minor), engineering (electrical and mechanical), English, environmental earth resources, environmental science, fashion merchandising (fashion merchandising, merchandising and textiles), film-television-digital media (criticism, industry, and production), food management, foreign languages, French studies, general studies, geography, geology, graphic design, habilitation of the deaf, health and fitness, healthy aging (minor), history, interior design, international communications (emphasizing advertising/public relations and news), international economics, international relations, journalism (broadcast and news-editorial), Latino/Latina studies (minor), liberal studies, lighting (minor), mathematics, modern dance, modern languages and literature (majors in Spanish and French, and minors in German, Italian, and Japanese), movement science, music (church music, music education, music history, performance, piano pedagogy, and theory/composition), neuroscience, nursing, nutritional sciences, philosophy, physical education, physics, political science, pre–health professions (dentistry, medicine, optometry, pharmacy, and veterinary), prelaw, psychology, psychosocial kinesiology, ranch management, religion, Reserve Officers' Training Corps (ROTC; aerospace studies or military science), social work, sociology, Spanish (fluency and teaching) and Hispanic studies, speech-language pathology, sports broadcasting, sport psychology, strategic communication, theater (performance, production, and education), women's studies (minor), and writing. Programs that are indicated by an asterisk (*) begin at TCU and finish elsewhere.

Preprofessional programs are available in dentistry, law, and medicine. A certificate in ranch management is available; other certificate programs are offered by the Office of Extended Education.

Academic Programs

TCU specializes in a liberal arts and sciences education that strives to expose students to the world around them. Within the University core curriculum requirements, students have wide choices in the humanities, natural sciences, social sciences, fine arts, religion, and communication. Emphasis is placed on writing skills and critical and evaluative thinking. Freshmen are also given the opportunity to take part in Freshman Seminars, which are small classes taught by top professors.

The Center for Academic Services provides full-time advisers for students who choose to postpone the choice of a major. During the first four semesters of study, such students can satisfy University requirements while investigating potential majors. The Writing Center, also provided by the Center for Academic Services, is available to all students and faculty members who wish to refine or improve their writing skills. A full-time professional writing staff conducts individual consultation and group workshops.

Most TCU programs include internships, practicums, or other field experiences with organizations in the Dallas–Fort Worth area.

In addition, TCU's Honors College challenges students to pursue high intellectual goals. It joins interdisciplinary colloquiums and independent research with dedicated faculty members and motivated students in all fields of study.

Off-Campus Programs

Across the academic disciplines, TCU has a global perspective. Students can study abroad for a summer experience or a whole semester. Usually experiences will count toward a major or minor. Scholarships and financial aid that are awarded upon applying to the University may be used towards the cost of studying abroad. Other financial aid is also available. TCU's semester programs in London, Seville, and Florence offer classes at local universities and a variety of opportunities for immersion, cultural enrichment, and travel.

Academic Facilities

The library, open 24 hours a day during the school week, houses more than 2 million volumes, as well as an Internet collection that links students to hundreds of thousands of other periodicals and resources. It also has special collections in music, theology, government documents, and rare books. More than fifteen spacious computer labs are open to fit students' schedules, with a few open 24 hours a day. Of two concert halls, one is rated among the nation's best acoustically. The Neeley School of Business, geared toward e-business and entrepreneurship, is equipped with a trading room with stock market quote machines and newswire services, presentation rooms with videotape equipment, board rooms, a staffed computer resource center, and classrooms with a computer at every desk. Theater students enjoy the Walsh Center for Performing Arts, which includes the Pepsico Recital Hall, a theater, an all-Steinway piano wing, and two large rehearsal rooms.

Costs

For 2011–12, tuition and fees are $16,200 per semester, or $32,400 per academic year. Residence hall costs average $6450 per academic year. Board fees, which average $3960 per academic year, cover the cost of all meals in the primary, all-you-can-eat cafeteria. The board fee also includes a declining balance for other on-campus eateries, as well as many off-campus restaurants. Books and supplies average $1050 per year. The total annual cost for a resident student is $43,860.

Financial Aid

Approximately 78 percent of last year's freshman class received aid. Academic scholarships are based on the student's SAT or ACT scores, rank in class, and overall application. Awards range from $5500 to full tuition and include the Chancellor, Dean, Faculty, and TCU scholarships. National Merit Finalists who name TCU as their first choice receive a basic scholarship of $2000 and may be eligible for higher awards. Students with demonstrated financial need are eligible for federal-, state-, and University-funded awards, which include grants, loans, and work-study programs.

Faculty

The 532 full-time faculty members hold their highest degrees from more than 125 different institutions; 90 percent have the Ph.D. or other appropriate terminal degree. The University has kept classes comparatively small, with fewer than 4 percent of all classes having more than 50 students. Most instructors have an open-door policy for students, and all instructors post regular office hours. Some departments enlist part-time faculty members from the Dallas–Fort Worth professional community to augment their programs.

Student Government

The Student Government Association, composed of elected members, serves as the basis for student government. Its officers and programming council direct a varied program of entertainment, speakers, films, and social and cultural events. The House of Student Representatives makes many of its own policies within broad University guidelines. Residence halls form student councils to recommend policies and to provide activities for the hall. Students are voting members of all University-wide committees that recommend policy changes.

Admission Requirements

TCU evaluates applications by using broad criteria. Emphasis is placed on both test scores and on individual character. While academic credentials are most important, TCU also looks for talent, leadership potential, and personal determination to make a difference. Admitted students show above-average academic ability. Applicants are expected to have completed a college-preparatory curriculum during high school. A campus visit and interview are recommended before a decision is reached; admitted students are required to take part in an orientation session on campus before enrolling officially. Qualified students are admitted without regard to race, color, creed, age, sex, or ethnic or national origin, in accordance with Title IX and other government regulations.

Application and Information

Information about application deadlines and notification dates may be obtained from:

Raymond A. Brown
Dean of Admission
TCU Box 297013
Texas Christian University
3301 Bellaire Drive North
Fort Worth, Texas 76129
Phone: 817-257-7490
    800-TCU-FROG (828-3764; toll-free)
Fax: 817-257-7268
E-mail: frogmail@tcu.edu
Web site: http://www.tcu.edu

TCU graduates earn more than degrees that will improve their lives. They learn to change their world.

THOMAS MORE COLLEGE
CRESTVIEW HILLS, KENTUCKY

The College

Thomas More College features a very strong academic reputation, small class sizes, and an ongoing dedication to scholarly pursuits based on the foundation of a Catholic liberal arts curriculum. Located in Northern Kentucky, just minutes from Cincinnati, Ohio, the College provides vibrant on-campus residential life in close proximity to a major metropolitan area. The result is an outstanding location offering all of the activities and resources of a major city with a suburban setting. With small class sizes and engaged faculty dedicated to teaching, the academic experience is one of personal attention and a hands-on approach to learning that forms the basis of a Thomas More education.

The student population includes 1,900 undergraduates and graduates. There are 960 traditional undergraduates attending classes full-time, of whom 320 are resident students. The student body is drawn primarily from the states of Kentucky, Ohio, and Indiana, but many other states and a number of countries are also represented. In addition to its undergraduate programs, Thomas More College offers graduate programs in business administration (M.B.A.) teaching (M.A.T.) and is scheduled to launch a Master of Education (M.Ed.) program in the fall of 2011. Students who choose to live on campus reside in either a suite-style residence hall or one of three town-house-style residence halls. All residence halls offer comfortable, air-conditioned rooms; Internet and cable TV access; and free laundry facilities. The 27,000-square-foot Holbrook Student Center contains a spacious bookstore, computer and study lounges, campus life offices, a café, and a dance rehearsal studio.

The college experience is enhanced through participation in many academic, social, and sports organizations. Intercollegiate athletics are part of the Presidents' Athletic Conference governed by NCAA Division III. Thomas More College competes in men's baseball, basketball, cross-country, football, golf, soccer, and tennis and women's basketball, cross-country, fast-pitch softball, golf, soccer, tennis, and volleyball. Track and field was added as a club sport in 2009 and is slated to become a competitive sport in 2011. Intramural sports offered include, among others, coed flag football, basketball, cornhole, dodgeball, softball, and volleyball. Thomas More College was proud to open a new on-campus athletic complex in fall 2008 for football and soccer, in addition to the Connor Convocation Center which houses basketball and volleyball facilities, and the College's baseball and softball fields. Students can also enjoy beautiful facilities for swimming, tennis, racquetball, and basketball and a complete fitness area at the Five Seasons Sports Club, adjacent to the campus.

Location

Thomas More College is located in northern Kentucky, 10 minutes south of Cincinnati, Ohio. The campus is convenient to major highways, and the Greater Cincinnati/Northern Kentucky International Airport is just 10 minutes from the College. Thomas More's suburban setting provides a safe environment for students and numerous opportunities for employment and internships. All students are permitted to have cars on campus.

The College's location offers a wide array of cultural and sporting events. Local attractions include the Broadway Series, the Cincinnati Pops, the Cincinnati Zoo, the Newport Aquarium, the Riverbend Music Center, and the Cincinnati Reds and Bengals.

Numerous shopping areas and restaurants are also available, including the new Crestview Hills Town Center, located across the street from the College.

Majors and Degrees

Thomas More College offers bachelor's degrees in accounting, art, biology, business administration, chemistry, computer information systems, communications, criminal justice, economics, education, English, environmental science, forensic science, history, humanities, international studies, mathematics, medical technology, nursing, philosophy, physics, political science, psychology, Spanish, sports and entertainment marketing, sociology, speech and theater, and theology. Associate degrees are available in each of these content areas as well as art history, exercise science, French, pre–legal studies, and Web design.

Preprofessional programs are available in dentistry, engineering, law, medicine, occupational therapy, optometry, pharmacy, physical therapy, and veterinary science.

Academic Programs

To earn the Bachelor of Arts, Bachelor of Science, or Bachelor of Science in Nursing degree, a student must complete 128 credit hours, including 61 credit hours in liberal arts courses. The Associate of Arts degree requires the completion of 64 credit hours, including a liberal arts component. In addition to the traditional format, the College's TAP program offers associate, bachelor's, and master's degrees in business administration that are provided in an accelerated format for working adults.

The academic calendar for traditional students is composed of a fall and a spring semester and two summer sessions. The accelerated format includes classes year-round.

The Cooperative Education program enables students to gain hands-on professional experience in their field of interest. All students are eligible for this program after the completion of their freshman year. Cooperative Air Force and Army ROTC programs are available in conjunction with nearby universities. The nursing and sociology departments have excellent working relationships with nearby hospitals and social service agencies.

Off-Campus Programs

Nineteen area colleges, including Thomas More College, form the Greater Cincinnati Consortium of Colleges and Universities, through which all students at the local member colleges may take courses not available at their home institution. Thomas More encourages full-time students to take advantage of this opportunity for curriculum enrichment through cross-registration. In addition, students who wish to study abroad as part of their undergraduate education have a number of possibilities open to them.

Academic Facilities

The recently renovated library has a collection of more than 129,000 volumes of books, periodicals, and audiovisual materials; as a selective depository, it houses more than 8,400 volumes of U.S. government documents. In addition, the library's membership in the Southwest Ohio and Neighboring Libraries gives Thomas More students access to more than 15 million books and more than 75,000 periodicals held by seventy-five other libraries in the region.

Thomas More's computer facilities include computer classrooms and six labs for student use. Student computers are also available in some academic departments and in the library. All PCs are connected to a campuswide Novell network, with wireless access to e-mail, the Internet, and an on-campus Intranet server.

Students in the science programs receive hands-on experience through the use of the newly remodeled classrooms and labs and biology field station. These facilities allow students to participate in undergraduate research programs in such areas as immunology, forestry, environmental studies, astronomy, trace analysis, and synthesis. Research projects have been funded by the National Science Foundation and the National Institutes of Health.

Costs

The 2010–11 annual cost for Thomas More College was $24,000 for tuition and $6050 for room (double occupancy) and board. There was a differential fee of $30 per semester hour for all nursing courses. The Student Government fee was $60 per semester and the computer fee was $360 per semester for full-time students. The cost of books was estimated at $800 per year.

Financial Aid

Thomas More College is an excellent educational value offering a wide range of financial aid opportunities, assisting more than 90 percent of its full-time students in meeting college costs. Awards are determined on a rolling basis, with priority consideration given to applications filed by February 1. Financial aid awards are based on economic need, merit, scholastic achievement, and extracurricular activities. ROTC scholarships are also available. The filing of the Free Application for Federal Student Aid (FAFSA) and the Thomas More College Application for Financial Aid and Scholarship is required before any awards are determined. Other Thomas More College awards may require additional applications.

An extensive Federal Work-Study Program is in place, and there are excellent opportunities for outside employment in the immediate area.

Faculty

The faculty is committed to the ideals of a Catholic liberal arts education, with the main focus on teaching. The faculty has 135 members, including 71 who are full-time; 66 percent hold tenure and 69 percent hold doctoral or other terminal degrees. Faculty members serve as academic advisers to students in their disciplines. The student-faculty ratio is 16:1.

Student Government

The purpose of the Student Government Association is to serve as the official representative organization of the Thomas More

College student body; to serve as the liaison between the student body and the faculty, administration, and Board of Trustees; to promote student projects and activities and improve the quality of student life; to assist the Dean of Students in supervising student organizations and student activities on campus; to protect the rights of the individual; and to preserve the general welfare of the student body of Thomas More College.

Admission Requirements

The admission criteria are as follows: an applicant should have a high school grade point average (based on college-preparatory courses) of 85 percent or better (2.5 on 4.0 scale), and a minimum composite score of 20 on the ACT Assessment, with a minimum of 20 in English, or a minimum combined score of 1010 on the SAT, with a minimum of 480 on the verbal portion. If the applicant does not meet all the admission criteria, the file is forwarded to the Admissions Committee for individual consideration.

Transfer students with 24 or more semester hours of transferable credit and an overall grade point average of at least 2.0 on a 4.0 scale are automatically accepted. Transfer students with fewer than 24 transferable hours must meet the general admission criteria outlined above.

The applicant must provide a completed application with a nonrefundable $25 fee (waived for online applicants), high school transcripts, college transcripts (if applicable), and ACT or SAT score reports.

Application and Information

Thomas More College operates under a rolling admission policy, with a final application deadline of August 15. Admission decisions are usually made within two weeks of receiving all application materials. Students can apply online at the College's Web site. The $25 application fee is waived for online applications.

For further information or to schedule a campus visit, students should contact:

Billy Sarge
Assistant Director of Admissions and Director of
    Recruitment
Thomas More College
333 Thomas More Parkway
Crestview Hills, Kentucky 41017-3495
Phone: 859-344-3332
           800-825-4557 (toll-free)
E-mail: billy.sarge@thomasmore.edu
Web site: http://www.thomasmore.edu

Students on the Thomas More College campus.

TRANSYLVANIA UNIVERSITY
LEXINGTON, KENTUCKY

The University

Transylvania, a small, private, coeducational liberal arts college of approximately 1,100 students, consistently ranks among the best small colleges in the nation. With a rich history dating back to its founding in 1780, Transylvania (literally meaning "across the woods" in Latin) holds the distinction of being the sixteenth-oldest college in the nation and the first college founded west of the Allegheny Mountains. The University established the first schools of medicine and law in what was then the West and educated the doctors, lawyers, ministers, political leaders, and others who helped shape the young nation. Transylvania also founded the first college literary magazine in the West, *The Transylvanian*, still published by students today.

Transylvania continues as a pioneer in higher education, preparing future leaders in business, government, education, the sciences, and the arts. While the distinguished faculty engages in research and other scholarly activities, Transylvania's professors never lose sight of their primary role: teaching and influencing bright young minds. Over the past decade, Transylvania faculty members have won six Kentucky Professor of the Year awards. The excellence of Transylvania's faculty is evidenced by the common sight of professors working side-by-side with students in small classes. None of Transylvania's classes have more than 40 students and 72 percent of classes have 20 or fewer. Due in large part to these small classes and close collaborations with faculty members, a high percentage of graduates attend selective medical, law, and other graduate and professional programs.

Transylvania students are an active and involved group, enriching the lives of each of their peers through the vibrant and dynamic campus community. Students benefit from tremendous opportunities for learning outside the classroom and off campus, often choosing to participate in campus and community organizations. With over sixty active student organizations, Transylvania students find that their academic interests are broadened through their extracurricular involvement. Many students reach out to the Lexington community by pursuing research projects, internships, and volunteer activities that allow them to grow and learn in a broader context. Over two-thirds of Transylvania students also embrace the global community through study-abroad programs.

Location

Transylvania is located in Lexington, Kentucky, a city of 282,000 and a growing center of commerce, culture, research, and education. Known as the horse capital of the world, rolling green pastures of the famous Bluegrass region of central Kentucky surround the city. The area is home to over 30,000 college students, and Transylvania's park-like campus is just a 5-minute walk from a lively downtown, with easy access to diverse restaurants, shops, and entertainment. The proximity to downtown is an advantage for students who want convenient part-time jobs and internship opportunities in law offices, financial firms, hospitals, nonprofits, and other organizations. For students who need to travel long distances, Lexington is served by major airlines and is only 80 miles away from both Louisville and Cincinnati.

Majors and Degrees

The Bachelor of Arts degree is awarded in the following majors: accounting; anthropology; art history; art studio; biology; business administration (concentrations in finance, hospitality management, management, and marketing); chemistry (concentrations in chemistry and biochemistry); classics; computer science; drama; economics; education; educational studies; English; exercise science; French; German; history; mathematics; music; music technology; philosophy; physical education; physics; political science; psychology; religion; sociology; Spanish; and writing, rhetoric, and communication. Individually designed majors also may be arranged and students have the option to earn a double major. Minors are available in most majors and in classical studies, communication, environmental studies, German, hospitality management, international affairs, multicultural studies, and women's studies. Advising and undergraduate preparation are provided for preprofessional programs in dentistry, engineering, law, medicine, ministry, pharmacy, physical therapy, and veterinary medicine.

A cooperative program in engineering allows students to earn a B.A. in physics or math from Transylvania in three years and a B.S. in engineering from the University of Kentucky or Vanderbilt University in two years. A cooperative program in accounting allows students to earn a B.A. in accounting from Transylvania in four years and an M.S. in accounting from the University of Kentucky in one year; graduates qualify to take the CPA exam after the completion of the B.A.

Academic Programs

The academic year is based on a 4-4-1 academic calendar, with two 14-week terms (fall and winter) and a one-month May term. The fall term begins in early September and ends in mid-December. The winter term begins in mid-January and ends in late April. During the May term, students may participate in a variety of programs on or off campus. Students normally take four courses in each of the fall and winter terms and one course in the May term. Thirty-six courses are required to graduate. First-year students participate in a two-term program called Foundations of the Liberal Arts, which features small-group discussions with a faculty leader; lectures, films, concerts, and other presentations; and a tutorial program in basic communication, critical thinking, and study skills. Special study-skills clinics and workshops are offered on an optional basis. Students must complete requirements designed to ensure broad familiarity with the major areas of learning and human endeavor in the humanities and fine arts, social sciences, natural sciences and mathematics, logic, and languages.

Transylvania grants credit for scores of 4 or 5 on the Advanced Placement examinations of the College Board and at least 5 on the International Baccalaureate higher level exams. Detailed information may be obtained from the Office of the Registrar.

Off-Campus Programs

Experiencing diverse cultures through international study is a vital part of a Transylvania liberal arts education. Transylvania students are encouraged to study abroad for a summer, a semester, or during May Term. In recent years, Transylvania students have studied in fifty-two different countries. Scholarships are available for both semester-long and summer study abroad. Summer study programs, including those in Austria, Brazil, China, Costa Rica, Ecuador, France, Germany, Italy, Japan, Mexico, and Spain, are available through Transylvania's affiliation with the Kentucky Institute for International Studies. Transylvania also cooperates with the English-Speaking Union to offer advanced students scholarships for summer study at Cambridge and Oxford Universities. In addition to the study-abroad options offered, Transylvania provides several programs that allow students to get involved at the national, state, and local levels. Students may participate in seminars or internships in Washington, D.C., through the Washington Center and in the Canadian Parliamentary Internship Program in Ottawa. Internships with congressional offices, Kentucky state government, city government, and local firms are easily arranged. Participation in Reserve Officers' Training Corps (Air Force and Army ROTC) is offered in cooperation with the University of Kentucky. Alternative spring break options include service work outside Lexington. In recent years students have traveled to Florida, Illinois, Ohio, Michigan, Mississippi, Missouri, North Carolina, and Wisconsin for this activity. First-year students have the unique opportunity to spend the week immediately before Fall Orientation engaging in community service in Lexington through programs like Jump Start and the First Year Urban program.

Academic Facilities

Transylvania University's academic facilities pay homage to its rich historical design while staying technologically current. Students have access to wireless Internet in all of the academic buildings. Two Georgian-style buildings combine elegance with high-tech facilities to offer the latest advances in teaching and learning. The Cowgill Center for Business, Economics, and Education includes a multimedia classroom where professors from any discipline can use a large display screen to show the entire class information from one of the twenty-five networked computers. A specialized area for education majors includes a laboratory classroom for teacher training. The Lucille C. Little Theater, used for faculty- and student-directed productions and drama classes, is a technically innovative facility that includes computerized lighting and sound, flexible staging options, and movable seating. The Frances Carrick Thomas/J. Douglas Gay, Jr. Library offers sophisticated computerized databases, which are invaluable for research and can be accessed from any computer connected to Transylvania's server. The Mitchell Fine Arts Center provides music program facilities, including practice rooms, a recital hall, and an auditorium. It also houses the Career Development Center, which helps students explore career options, improve job search skills, arrange internships and part-time jobs, and apply to graduate schools and to professional positions. A fine arts technology lab can also be found in Mitchell. The Charles L. Shearer Art Building is dedicated to instructional space, student and faculty studios, and a student gallery. Other modern facilities include the newly renovated L. A. Brown Science Center, the Haupt Humanities Building, and the Clive M. Beck Athletic and Recreation Center, which includes a state-of-the-art fitness center. About 80 percent of all students, and 98 percent of first-year students, live on campus in seven residence halls—two for men, one for women, and four for men and women. These include traditional-style accommodations, apartment-style living for upperclass students, and suite-style rooms. All rooms are air-conditioned and offer access to Transylvania's free cable television and computer networks. Thomson Hall, a new suite-style hall, opened in 2008 and became only the second residence hall in the southeast to earn the EPA's Energy Star certification. Each residence hall has ample lounge and study space and easy access to computer labs and recreational facilities. The William T. Young Campus Center offers a competition-size indoor pool, a gymnasium, and other meeting and recreational facilities.

Costs

Transylvania charges an annual tuition that covers fall, winter, and May terms for a normal full-time schedule of courses. Additional special instruction fees are charged for certain designated courses such as applied music and May Term travel courses. For 2010–11, tuition and fees were $26,740 and room and board (double occupancy) were $8090.

Financial Aid

Transylvania is committed to providing financial aid to students and their families. Four types of financial assistance are available. Scholarships are based on academic performance, cocurricular involvement, and leadership. Grants, loans, and work-study are based on financial need. Over 90 percent of Transylvania students receive some form of financial assistance, and many receive more than one type of aid. Outstanding entering freshmen may qualify for one of twenty William T. Young Scholarships—each worth more than $100,000 over four years—that cover tuition and fees. Submission of Transylvania's Application for Admission and Scholarships by the appropriate deadline is all that is necessary to be considered for academic scholarships at Transylvania. Students who are interested in need-based aid must file the Free Application for Federal Student Aid (FAFSA).

Faculty

Transylvania's relatively small size and low student-faculty ratio of 12:1 allow for close, personal attention in teaching and advising. Ninety-seven percent of full-time faculty members hold a doctorate or the highest degree in their fields, and they have come to Transylvania from a variety of graduate and professional schools. Many faculty members are recognized for their scholarship and professional activities, but their central concern is teaching and advising students. Ninety-five percent of Transylvania's classes are taught by full-time faculty members.

Transylvania's commitment to outstanding teaching is also reflected in its nationally recognized Bingham Program for Excellence in Teaching, the first of its type in the nation to attract and retain gifted teachers through an external evaluation process and financial incentives.

Student Government

Students at Transylvania have a high degree of access to the administration and governing board of the University. The Student Government Association serves as a representative government, and students hold positions on standing committees of the faculty and the Board of Trustees.

Admission Requirements

Each applicant is considered individually on academic performance, SAT/ACT scores, extracurricular involvement, an essay, and recommendation letters. Applicants should present a college preparatory curriculum. Admission is also offered to transfer students, international students, and nontraditional students. Transylvania requires that international applicants score at least an 80 on the Internet-based TOEFL exam.

Transylvania enrolled 314 new students for the 2010–11 academic year. The middle 50 percent composite ACT score for the freshman class was 24 to 29. Nearly 50 percent were in the top 10 percent of their high school class.

Application and Information

Submission of a Transylvania Application for Admission and Scholarships or submission of the Common Application is all that is necessary to be considered for admission and most merit scholarships at Transylvania.

The early action deadline is December 1 for applicants who wish to learn of their admission by January 15 and who want to be considered for all Transylvania scholarships. February 1 is the regular admission and scholarships deadline for applicants who wish to be considered for all Transylvania scholarships except the William T. Young Scholarship. Applicants who apply after February 1 are considered on a space-available basis. The deadline for applications for the winter term, which begins in January, is December 1.

Students considering Transylvania are urged to visit the campus, and high school seniors are encouraged to stay overnight in a dorm with a student admissions ambassador.

Weekday visits may include a customized campus tour and opportunities to attend classes; talk with professors, coaches, students, and admissions and financial aid counselors; and enjoy meals on campus. Visits should be arranged through the Office of Admissions, preferably one to two weeks in advance. Preview days are held in the fall and spring, and special senior visit days are offered in the winter and spring for admitted students.

For more information and application materials, students should contact:

Office of Admissions
Transylvania University
300 North Broadway
Lexington, Kentucky 40508-1797
Phone: 859-233-8242
        800-872-6798 (toll-free)
E-mail: admissions@transy.edu
Web site: http://www.transy.edu
          http://www.facebook.com/transylvaniauniversity
          http://twitter.com/Transy

Small class sizes at Transylvania give professors and students the opportunity to work closely together, and many are directly involved in student research projects.

TRINE UNIVERSITY

ANGOLA, INDIANA

The University

Trine University is a private, independent, coeducational institution offering associate and baccalaureate degrees to students in more than thirty-five programs, including engineering, mathematics, science, computer science, business, education, communication, and criminal justice. Trine also offers a five-year combined Bachelor of Science and Master of Engineering program with majors in civil, mechanical, and biomedical engineering. Majors in entrepreneurship, informatics, and exercise science were recently introduced.

Since its founding in 1884, Trine has focused on providing an affordable, comprehensive, career-oriented, hands-on education. With a worldwide reputation for being job-ready, Trine graduates are in demand. In 2010, 90 percent of graduates were employed or enrolled in graduate school within six months of commencement.

Trine's current main campus undergraduate enrollment is more than 1,600. Over 1,000 students live on campus in one of sixteen residence halls, private villas, or fully furnished suite-style apartments—some of which overlook Trine's eighteen-hole championship golf course.

The University's 400-acre campus includes a $15.5-million University Center, which houses a dining hall, bookstore, fitness center, movie theater, post office, radio station, and the Center for Technology and Online Resources.

The University's inviting atmosphere complements the seriousness and determination with which Trine students pursue their academic goals. Students enjoy opportunities to develop friendships and to build leadership and teamwork skills through their participation in a range of campus organizations.

Trine has a reputation for academic rigor and success. Chemical engineering seniors have won the American Institute of Chemical Engineers (AIChE) national individual design competition two of the last four years and have produced the safest design each of the past four years. Mechanical engineering students can study in one of the top three cast metals programs in the country, as determined by the Foundry Education Foundation. In 2009, the American Society of Civil Engineers (ASCE) named Trine graduate Ben Groeneweg a New Face of Civil Engineering, an award presented to only 10 civil engineers nationally each year. Trine's Tau Alpha Omicron chapter of the American Criminal Justice Association (ACJA) annually wins regional and national awards for marksmanship, crime scene investigation, and physical agility.

Trine is a member of National Collegiate Athletic Association Division III and the Michigan Intercollegiate Athletic Association (MIAA), the nation's oldest athletic conference. Men's sports include baseball, basketball, cross-country, football, golf, lacrosse, soccer, tennis, track, and wrestling. Women's sports include basketball, cross-country, field hockey, golf, lacrosse, soccer, softball, tennis, track, and volleyball. Many students also play on intramural sports teams.

Trine's football team, the Thunder, is a three-time consecutive MIAA champion and advanced to round two of NCAA postseason play in both 2009 and 2010. Quarterback and 2010 graduate Eric Watt received the Gagliardi Trophy, the highest honor given to an NCAA Division III football player. Trine's softball, wrestling, and cross-country teams are also competitive at the national level.

The Keith Busse/Steel Dynamics Athletic and Recreation Center (ARC), which contains a 200-meter indoor track and training and practice facilities for other sports, opened in 2009 to develop Trine's track and field program year-round and to support tennis, additional sports, and intramurals.

The Fred Zollner Athletic Stadium opened in 2010 and serves the football, lacrosse, field hockey, and soccer programs. It has already welcomed a record number of fans to athletic events.

Student organizations include the student senate, honor societies, professional organizations, campus newspaper, FM radio station, drama club, music ensembles, pep and marching bands, Habitat for Humanity, and more. In addition, thirteen social fraternities and sororities provide on-campus opportunities for service and camaraderie for upperclassmen.

Trine is accredited by the Higher Learning Commission and is a member of the North Central Association of Colleges and Schools (http://www.ncahigherlearningcommission.org; phone: 312-263-0456). Trine's programs in chemical, civil, computer, electrical, and mechanical engineering are accredited by the Engineering Accreditation Commission of ABET (111 Market Place, Suite 1050, Baltimore, Maryland 21202-4012; phone: 410-347-7700). All teacher preparation programs are accredited by the National Council for Accreditation of Teacher Education and the Indiana Department of Education/Office of Licensing and Development. All B.S.B.A. programs in the Ketner School of Business are accredited by the Accreditation Council for Business Schools and Programs.

Location

Trine is in Angola, Indiana, the heart of northeast Indiana's scenic lake resort region, halfway between the metropolitan areas of Chicago, Illinois, and Cleveland, Ohio. Just a 45-minute drive from Fort Wayne, Indiana, Trine offers the safety and ease of a small-town environment, near some of the nation's most vital cities. Pokagon State Park provides year-round recreational opportunities for the community and is just 5 miles north of Trine's campus.

Majors and Degrees

The Allen School of Engineering and Technology awards Bachelor of Science degrees in chemical, civil, computer, electrical, and mechanical engineering; computer science; and design engineering technology. Minors are offered in aerospace, bioprocess, environmental, metallurgy, and robotics engineering.

Well-qualified high school graduates may be admitted directly into a five-year combined Bachelor of Science and Masters of Engineering program. Civil, mechanical, and biomedical engineers with the skills necessary to design complex systems are highly sought by industry professionals; therefore, the degree is practice-oriented with a heavy emphasis on design, as opposed to the research emphasis of a traditional Master of Science degree. Upon completion of this program, both the Bachelor of Science in civil, mechanical, or biomedical engineering and the Master of Engineering degree are awarded.

The Ketner School of Business awards Bachelor of Science in Business Administration degrees with majors in accounting, business administration, entrepreneurship, finance, golf management, management, marketing, and sport management. The school also awards a Bachelor of Science degree with a major in exercise science.

The Franks School of Education awards Bachelor of Science degrees in elementary, health and physical, mathematics, science, and social studies education.

The Jannen School of Arts and Sciences awards Bachelor of Arts degrees with majors in communication, general studies (prelegal, self-designated, and social studies), and psychology. The school also awards Bachelor of Science degrees with majors in biology, chemistry, criminal justice, forensic science, informatics, and mathematics. A premedical professional track is also available.

Academic Programs

Trine's engineering programs concentrate on providing a fundamental, application-oriented engineering education which includes extensive laboratory instruction. In addition to concentrated studies in a specialized area, students are required to complete courses in communication skills, socio-humanistic studies, and analysis and design.

The University's business programs include a broad range of practical experience to acquaint the student with the practices, procedures, and problems of the contemporary business professional. Guest lecturers frequently visit campus and students are given many experiential learning opportunities.

Off-Campus Programs

Co-op and internship opportunities are available and encouraged. Semesters of classroom study are alternated with professional work experience, which can help students gain a competitive edge in the job market and offset college expenses. The length of a co-op program depends upon the student's class status when entering the program. Work-study schedules require a minimum of three semesters on work assignments.

Academic Facilities

Fawick Hall of Engineering is home to the University's Chemical and Bioprocess, Civil and Environmental, Electrical and Computer, and Mechanical and Aerospace Engineering Departments, as well as the Engineering Technology Department. Trine students use sophisticated equipment such as a scanning electron microscope and rapid prototyping machines in their laboratories and design projects. Each computer lab has state-of-the-art software.

The Best Hall of Science contains classrooms, science laboratories; the Fairfield Lecture Room; the Department of Mathematics; the Department of Science; and the Department of Criminal Justice, Psychology, and Social Sciences.

Planned renovations to the Ketner School of Business and Franks School of Education include new infrastructure and technology, including a fiber-optic network, a wireless environment, and shared multimedia access to resources for teaching (SMART) classrooms. The new T. Furth Center for Performing Arts will preserve a landmark church while providing classrooms for choral and instrumental music and an auditorium for drama and music productions.

The University recently channeled over $2 million into campuswide technology upgrades. The Center for Technology and Online Resources houses a digital classroom, a "my office" area with multiple computers, and a global workspace with videoconferencing stations to facilitate learning.

More than 200 computers dedicated to student access are available in labs across campus. Every room in student residences is wired to the University network and the Internet, and residential common areas are fitted with wireless Internet access.

Costs

Tuition for the academic year (two semesters) in 2011–12 is $26,600 ($28,600 for engineering). Room and standard meal plan (nineteen meals per week) for the academic year costs $8800 (double occupancy).

Financial Aid

Financial aid may be awarded in the form of scholarships, grants, loans, or employment. Any of these aids or any combination may be necessary to supplement family and student resources to meet basic educational expenses. Trine requires the Free Application for Federal Student Aid (FAFSA) and recommends its submission by March 1.

Faculty

Trine has a full-time faculty of 82 members. Most have doctoral degrees and professional experience. The student-faculty ratio is 15:1.

Student Government

The student senate is organized for the purpose of providing funding for campus organizations to host events. Representatives elected from campus organizations form the senate, which also aids in formulating policies for these organizations.

Admission Requirements

Graduation from an approved high school or equivalent preparation is required for admission. Selection is made without regard to race, religion, or gender. The University requires applicants to take the ACT or SAT prior to approval for admission (writing sections are optional).

Admission requirements for engineering include 4 years of English, 1 year of chemistry, 1 year of physics, 1 year of social studies, 2 years of algebra, 1 year of geometry, and ½ year of trigonometry. All other applicants must have the following high school credits: 4 years of English, 3 years of mathematics, 3 years of science, and 3 years of social studies.

Graduates of preprofessional or college-parallel programs at approved community or junior colleges are eligible for transfer into Trine's baccalaureate programs. Qualified graduates of these programs may be granted junior standing upon transfer. In general, credit may be allowed in subjects that parallel Trine programs, provided the student earned a grade of C or better in the course.

Application and Information

Trine University's online application is available at http://www.trine.edu; there is no application fee. The University admits applicants on the basis of scholastic achievement and academic potential. Admission decisions are made on a rolling basis, without regard to race, religion, color, gender, sexual orientation, or age. Applicants are notified of their status within two weeks after their application, high school record, and test scores have been received. Transfer students must also submit an official copy of their college transcript(s).

Interested students and their parents are encouraged to visit the campus. Arrangements can be made by writing or calling the Office of Admission.

For additional information, students should call or write:

Office of Admission
Trine University
One University Avenue
Angola, Indiana 46703-1764
Phone: 260-665-4100
         800-347-4878 (toll-free within continental U.S.)
E-mail: admit@trine.edu
Web site: http://www.trine.edu
          http://www.facebook.com/trineadmissions
          http://www.youtube/trineuniversity
          http://www.trine.edu/blogs (student blogs)

TRINITY COLLEGE
HARTFORD, CONNECTICUT

Trinity College
HARTFORD CONNECTICUT

The College

Since its founding in 1823, Trinity has provided an undergraduate education of uncommon quality. Widely acknowledged as one of the top liberal arts colleges in the country, Trinity has been recognized by a panel of national education editors for its bold and innovative ideas to advance the cause of higher education and ensure greater access.

In its commitment to the rigorous pursuit of the liberal arts and to instruction that is personal and conversational, Trinity is an ideal college. At the same time, Trinity is in close touch with the world beyond its campus. In that respect and in terms of the outstanding opportunities Trinity's capital city location offers students, a Trinity education is indeed a real education.

While remaining faithful to the classic liberal arts tradition, Trinity offers a distinctive educational experience that prepares students for the challenges and opportunities of the twenty-first century. Building on its traditional strengths in the arts and humanities and exceptional offerings in science and engineering, Trinity engages students in a conversation with the world through its new Center for Urban and Global Studies, study-abroad programs, interdisciplinary programs, and innovative, rigorous programs that draw on the rich cultural, educational, and professional assets of Hartford. State-of-the-art electronic facilities support Trinity's advanced use of information technology in classrooms. The heart of a Trinity education, however, remains the personal encounter between professor and student, the intellectual partnership that discovers a world of ideas and ignites a passion for learning.

Trinity's students come from forty-seven states and forty-nine countries. The College believes that a diverse community makes learning flourish. Trinity's undergraduate enrollment of more than 2,200 students is about equally composed of men and women. More than 90 percent of undergraduates live on campus in College housing. Trinity is engaged in continuing campus revitalization programs that preserve its impressive Gothic buildings as it also develops a campus for the twenty-first century.

Trinity offers a rich array of extracurricular activities—films, plays, concerts, musical theater, sports, academic symposia, and visits by nationally and internationally known writers, speakers, and performers. Participation is an important word on campus, and Trinity students have abundant opportunities to lead and to be involved in numerous student clubs; special interest groups; theater, dance, and music groups; debate; academic programs; campus cinema; Trinity's radio station; and many student publications. With 19 acres of playing fields, Trinity also offers an extensive athletic program. About 40 percent of the student body participate on twenty-nine men's and women's varsity teams (Division III) and roster of intramural sports. The Ferris Athletic Center features a swimming pool, a fully equipped fitness center, crew tanks, eight international-size squash courts, basketball courts, and an indoor track.

Location

Situated on a beautiful 100-acre campus in the center of Hartford, the capital of Connecticut, Trinity offers the best of both worlds—a supportive and active campus community located in a city that provides students with myriad opportunities for internships, community service, and cultural exploration. Hartford's businesses, governmental agencies, cultural organizations, and nonprofit institutions offer Trinity students hundreds of opportunities to explore careers through the College's extensive internship program. Hartford has a number of cultural institutions, including the Wadsworth Atheneum (the oldest public art museum in the nation), Mark Twain House, Harriet Beecher Stowe Center,

Hartford Symphony, Hartford Stage, and a number of smaller theaters and clubs that provide a cultural stew of dance, theater, and music. The shopping districts of Hartford and surrounding suburbs are nearby. The impressive Connecticut coast is easily accessible, and Boston and New York are each about 2 hours from campus. Off campus, Trinity students have access to a field station in Ashford, Connecticut, dedicated to research in the natural sciences and a wide range of environmental educational endeavors.

Majors and Degrees

On the undergraduate level, the College offers a Bachelor of Arts degree and a Bachelor of Science degree. Trinity offers thirty-eight majors, including American studies; anthropology; art history; biochemistry; biology; chemistry; classical civilization; classics; computer science; economics; educational studies; engineering; English; environmental science; French; German studies; Hispanic studies; history; interdisciplinary computing; international studies; Italian studies; Jewish studies; language and culture studies (Arabic, Chinese, Hebrew, Japanese); mathematics; music; neuroscience; philosophy; physics; political science; student-designed interdisciplinary major; psychology; public policy and law; religion; sociology; studio arts; theater and dance; and women, gender, and sexuality. Trinity offers a five-year program in engineering and computer science, which leads to a bachelor's degree from Trinity and a master's degree from Rensselaer Polytechnic Institute through Rensselaer at Hartford.

Academic Programs

Featuring approximately 900 courses, Trinity's curriculum provides a framework within which students may explore the many dimensions of an undergraduate education. At the same time, the curriculum offers each student flexibility to experiment, to deepen old interests and develop new ones, and to acquire specialized training in a major field. Students must demonstrate proficiency in writing, mathematics, and a second language, and fulfill a five-part distribution requirement that consists of at least one course in each of the following categories: arts, humanities, natural sciences, numerical and symbolic reasoning, and social sciences. They must complete a writing intensive requirement and also take a first-year seminar and at least one course that focuses on global engagement.

Off-Campus Programs

More than 50 percent of Trinity students study abroad for a semester or a year at Trinity's Rome Campus, at one of six Trinity global learning sites, or in other approved study programs in more than forty countries on six continents. Trinity-sponsored global learning sites operate in Argentina, Austria, France, Spain, South Africa (Cape Town), and Trinidad. Through the theater and dance department, Trinity offers the Trinity/La MaMa Performing Arts Program in New York City, an extraordinary program that provides intensive study in theater, dance, and performance.

Academic Facilities

The Raether Library and Information Technology Center is home to the Raether and Watkinson Libraries, as well as the Computing Center. It is a place where students and faculty members come together for the serious work of scholarship, where researchers can pore over a book or conduct investigations through a wide selection of online databases. The Raether Library houses nearly 1 million print volumes and approximately 700,000 nonprint materials, including slides, microforms, sound recordings, and other materials in audiovisual and electronic formats. In addition, an online catalog linked with Wesleyan University and Connecticut College provides access to more than 2 million titles. The

Watkinson Library, with its impressive collection of rare books, manuscripts, and other unique resources, supports a broad range of research interests.

The campus is fully wired, with every student room connected to the College network and the Web. Public access computers are also available 24 hours a day in select facilities.

Costs

Costs for the 2010–11 academic year were $40,410 for tuition, $10,960 for room and board, and $2010 for fees.

Financial Aid

Each student admitted to Trinity who qualifies for aid receives a package that fully meets his or her calculated need. Students must file the Free Application for Federal Student Aid (FAFSA) as well as the Financial Aid PROFILE of the College Scholarship Service. Admissions applications are due by January 1; FAFSA and PRO-FILE applications are due by February 1. Students are notified of admission and aid decisions by the first week of April. Normally, need is met with a financial aid package that includes grant assistance, work-study, and federal student loans. Federal funds for which accepted students are eligible include Pell Grants, Federal Supplemental Educational Opportunity Grants (FSEOG), Perkins Loans, Stafford Loans, and PLUS Loans. The College administers a large student employment program, and most students who demonstrate need are granted an on-campus job as part of their financial aid package. The ratio of grant assistance to loans and work-study aid is sometimes affected by the academic strength of the student's record. Trinity continues to expand its aid budget to keep pace with the College's goal to increase the socioeconomic and ethnic diversity on campus. Forty percent of the students receive financial aid.

Faculty

The distinctive strength of a Trinity education has always been the close interaction between students and a faculty of devoted teacher-scholars. A student-faculty ratio of 10:1 enables supportive yet challenging educational experiences that establish a foundation for lifetime learning and enables students to pursue academic interests with passion. Students have numerous opportunities to collaborate with faculty members in conducting research; many students have made joint presentations at international, national, or local symposia or have published jointly prepared papers. All courses are taught by Trinity faculty members and not by graduate assistants.

Although the first calling of Trinity's professors is teaching, they are also active publishing scholars of national and international distinction. History professor Joan Hedrick, for example, won the Pulitzer Prize for her biography of Harriet Beecher Stowe. Other notable professors include Henry DePhillips, distinguished chemist and researcher on art restoration; Dan Lloyd, acclaimed philosopher and author of *Radiant Cool;* Lesley Farlow, accomplished dancer and choreographer; Samuel Kassow, distinguished historian; and Joseph Bronzino, an authority on biomedical engineering. Trinity professors pride themselves on their accessibility and keen interest in helping students.

Student Government

Trinity fosters the growth of future leaders by providing students with many opportunities to exercise and test their leadership skills. The Student Government Association (SGA), for example, provides students a strong voice in social, cultural, and—through membership on faculty committees—academic matters. Composed of elected class representatives, the SGA constantly seeks the expertise and insights of all interested students, and its committees offer enterprising students many chances to participate and to develop leadership skills.

Admission Requirements

Trinity seeks an ethnically and geographically diverse group of highly motivated students who have completed a rigorous course of study in secondary school and have demonstrated energy, talent, and leadership in a variety of extracurricular activities. Trinity has no specific GPA minimums or test-score cutoffs. The College is highly selective, and its candidates typically have an A–high school average. At least 16 academic units of college-preparatory course work are recommended, including a minimum of 4 years of English, 3 years of foreign language, 2 years of laboratory science, 2 years of algebra, 1 year of geometry, and 2 years of history. Last year, over 5,000 men and women from all over the nation and world applied for admission to the College, which enrolls an entering class of approximately 585 students. Transfer students with a 3.0 GPA in a strong course of study at another accredited college or university are considered for admission to the sophomore or junior classes.

Admissions officers review each application individually; decisions are based on each candidate's academic record (course of study and GPA), recommendations from secondary school teachers and counselors, test scores, personal strengths, talents, activities, and application and supplemental essays.

Application and Information

Students must submit completed applications to the Admissions Office. Application deadlines are November 15 for early decision I applicants (with notification by December 15), January 1 for early decision II applicants (with notification by February 15), and January 1 for regular decision applicants (with notification by April 1). Transfer applicants must submit applications by April 1 for admission in the following fall semester (with notification by early June) and by November 15 for admission in the following spring semester (with notification by early January). Prospective students may submit an electronic Common Application at http://www.commonapp.org.

Inquiries should be made to:

Larry Dow
Dean of Admissions and Financial Aid
Admissions Office
Trinity College
Hartford, Connecticut 06106-3100

Phone: 860-297-2180
Fax: 860-297-2287
E-mail: admissions.office@trincoll.edu
Web site: http://www.trincoll.edu/admissions
http://www.facebook.com/trincoll
http://www.youtube.com/trincoll#p/a/u/0/

The Long Walk at Trinity College. *(Photo by Bob Handelman)*

UNION COLLEGE
SCHENECTADY, NEW YORK

The College

Chartered by the state of New York in 1795, Union College is one of the nation's oldest and most distinguished liberal arts colleges. A four-year, independent residential college serving approximately 2,100 undergraduate men and women, Union is known for its academic rigor, flexible programs, and close-knit community.

True to its 200-year tradition of innovation, the Union curriculum offers a multitude of academic and intellectual options. There is an increasing emphasis on interdepartmental and interdisciplinary programs that blend liberal arts with science and technology in a way that encourages students to think creatively, ethically, and entrepreneurially. Approximately 60 percent of Union students major in the arts, humanities, and social sciences, and 40 percent major in the sciences and engineering.

Originally all-male, the College became coeducational in 1970; today, half of Union's students are women. The 2010–11 freshman class includes 16 percent students of color and 4 percent international students. Students come from forty-two countries and thirty-eight U.S. states and territories.

The international experience is a hallmark of a Union education, with more than 60 percent of students pursuing studies abroad. On campus, opportunities for leadership, discussion, and community abound in the Minerva system, offering residential, academic, and social programs. Every incoming student is assigned to one of seven Minerva Houses, which also involve faculty and staff.

There are about 100 student organizations, seventeen Greek organizations, and more than a dozen theme houses. Cultural events include concerts, theater, dance, film, and art exhibits at the Mandeville Gallery. On average, 86 percent of all students live in residence halls or college-owned houses, including traditional dorms, Minerva Houses, fraternity and sorority houses, townhouses, and College Park Hall, a renovated hotel. The Kenney Community Center connects students with Big Brothers Big Sisters, Habitat for Humanity, tutoring programs, and civic projects.

Union's comprehensive athletics program offers twenty-five varsity intercollegiate sports, organized intramurals, club sports, and recreational and fitness activities. Union is a member of the NCAA, Liberty League, and ECAC Hockey. Men's and women's ice hockey compete in NCAA Division I programs; other teams are Division III.

The Becker Career Center helps students with career planning, internships, and the graduate school and job search. Recent trends show that about a third of graduating seniors go directly to graduate or professional schools, and Union has earned an excellent reputation for placing graduates in medical, law, and business schools. Union's more than 22,000 alumni include U.S. President Chester A. Arthur (Class of 1848); Nobel Prize, National Book Award, and MacArthur "genius" award winners; Olympic medalists; and pioneers in business, engineering, entertainment, journalism, and medicine.

Location

Union is set on 100 acres in Schenectady, an historic city of 62,000 founded by the Dutch. Union became the first unified campus in America in 1813 with a distinctive design by noted French architect Joseph Jacques Ramée. Its centerpiece is the sixteen-sided Nott Memorial, a National Historic Landmark used for study, symposia, exhibits, and special events. Union is part of Upstate New York's picturesque Capital-Saratoga Region, with nearly 1 million residents. The region has a burgeoning high-tech industry and rich cultural heritage. A 15-minute drive from Albany International Airport, the College is 3 hours by car from New York City and Boston, 4 hours from Montreal, and close to East Coast ski slopes and the Adirondack Mountains.

Majors and Degrees

Union offers thirty-six majors; double majors; combined majors and minors; interdepartmental and multidisciplinary concentrations; and area, ethnic, and cultural studies programs. The self-designed Organizing Theme Major is for the student with intellectual curiosity in a particular topic involving multiple disciplines. Most students take three courses in each of the three 10-week terms that comprise Union's trimester system. The average introductory class has 19 students; the average upper-level class, 14.

Most of Union's newest majors, such as bioengineering, neuroscience, and religious studies, and minors such as computational methods, encourage learning at the intersection of the liberal arts and sciences. Among the courses that cross traditional disciplinary boundaries are The Illustrated Organism, a class for artists and scientists, and The New Wall of China, offered through the departments of Modern Languages and Literatures and Environmental Science, Policy, and Engineering. Union's Internal Education Foundation provides funding for special, innovative projects.

Union offers Bachelor of Arts (B.A.) and Bachelor of Science (B.S.) degrees. Students may declare up to two minors. Union also offers a leadership in medicine program with Albany Medical College and Union Graduate College; the law and public policy program with Albany Law School; and five-year bachelor's/M.B.A. or bachelor's/M.A.T. programs with Union Graduate College. The fourteen academic honor societies include Phi Beta Kappa, the first chapter established in New York (1817).

Academic Programs

Nearly every academic department requires students to complete some form of research in their subject area, and students have opportunities to work one-on-one with their professors. They often coauthor publications and present at conferences, such as the National Conference on Undergraduate Research (NCUR). Many participate in internships at businesses, hospitals, and social service organizations. The Steinmetz Symposium showcases the work of hundreds of student researchers through oral, dance, music, art, and poster sessions each spring.

The Campus Wide Computation Initiative, part of a National Science Foundation grant, helps students integrate computation into various fields of study. Through the Michael Rapaport ('59) Ethics Across the Curriculum initiative, faculty members from different departments offer courses that provide extensive training in everyday ethics. Writing Across the Curriculum requires all students to take five designated courses from at least two divisions and one Senior Writing Experience. The First-Year Preceptorial (FYP), a mandatory interdisciplinary course for first-year students, emphasizes critical reading and thinking skills, writing, speaking, and gender and cultural diversity. The Sophomore Research Seminar (SRS), also required, promotes research and writing skills.

Off-Campus Programs

More than 60 percent of all Union students go abroad. Most programs are led by Union faculty. Many programs combine elements of entrepreneurship, research, or community service. There are also opportunities for extended terms, formal exchanges, research trips, and independent study. Three-week mini-terms, for 1 credit, are offered during winter and summer in various U.S. cities and countries. Many students get involved in continuing hurricane relief efforts in New Orleans. The Civil Rights Public

History mini-term explores the American Civil Rights Movement in key cities and states. The newest mini-terms include Russia, Senegal, and Uruguay. Union's innovative Minerva Fellows program sends graduating seniors to developing countries to work with welfare and anti-poverty initiatives. All programs are central to Union's mission of educating engaged, ethical contributors to a global society.

Academic Facilities

Union's nearly 100 buildings include the F. W. Olin Center, which features interactive computerization capabilities that make the building adaptable for use by nearly every academic department. The Science and Engineering Center houses the Center for Bioengineering and Computational Biology. Here, students can use sophisticated research tools such as a nuclear magnetic resonance spectrometer, a Pelletron accelerator, a centrifuge, and a scanning electron microscope.

Schaffer Library has 600,000 volumes, 1,600 journals and 2 online databases that provide access to a quarter-million printed books, documents, and musical scores. Flanking the library are the Humanities and Social Sciences Buildings. The Arts Building, located in North Colonnade, includes the Burns Atrium, where work by students, faculty, and alumni is exhibited. The Taylor Music Center includes the Fred L. Emerson Auditorium, an all-Steinway performance and teaching space with state-of-the-art recording technology. The Yulman Theater is the College's major performance space.

The $22-million Peter Irving Wold Science and Engineering Center, scheduled to open in spring 2011, will provide a home for interdisciplinary studies across departments.

Costs

Union's comprehensive fee—which includes tuition, room, board, and mandatory fees—for the 2010–11 academic year was $52,329. Estimated cost for books and personal expenses is $1621.

Financial Aid

Union is committed to admitting an economically diverse student body and to meeting the full demonstrated need of all admitted students. The College offers $34 million annually in aid. The average Union need-based scholarship is $29,000; the average merit award is $10,000. The average financial aid package for the 2010–11 freshman class exceeded $29,000. Those families that are unable to pay full tuition and fees are typically covered by a financial aid package consisting of a grant, loan, and work opportunity. About half of all applicants apply for financial aid; more than 60 percent of all students receive financial assistance from the College.

Candidates for aid should complete the Free Application for Federal Student Aid (FAFSA) and the College Scholarship Service's PROFILE form and mail them directly to the appropriate agencies by February 1. For more information, visit http://www.union.edu/Admissions/index.php.

Faculty

Close student-faculty interaction and small classes are a hallmark of the Union experience. The close relationship between students and faculty motivates students to learn through inquiry and discourse. Excluding library staff, 96 percent of the faculty members hold the doctorate, first professional, or terminal degree. Class size is generally small, with a 10:1 student-faculty ratio. Many upper-level courses function as seminars.

Student Government

Students play an integral role in directing the present and future of Union. With full voting rights on the two councils that recommend changes to educational policy and student life, students are engaged and active leaders on campus. Students also participate in groups that advise the president on matters like budgetary planning and long-range needs. Each year, two students are elected to membership on the College's Board of Trustees. Opportunities for leadership also abound with the Minerva houses, theme houses, Kenney Community Center, and other clubs.

Admission Requirements

Approximately 5,000 applicants seek freshman class positions on an annual basis; more than 60 percent are in the top 10 percent of their secondary school class. In evaluating each application, admissions counselors look at the prospective student's grades, rigor of courses taken, class rank, teacher recommendations, and extracurricular involvement. Typically, 16 units of secondary school preparation are required for admission. These should include credits in certain fundamental subjects, such as English, a foreign language, mathematics, social studies, and science. It is strongly recommended that students visit Union for an admission interview and a student-guided tour. Alumni interviews may be requested online.

A student can choose not to submit his or her SAT or ACT scores for review, except for accelerated programs. Those interested in accelerated programs must submit the SAT and two SAT Subject Tests.

Application and Information

Early decision candidates have two options. The application deadline (including all supporting credentials) for Option I is November 15, with notification by December 15. Option II has a January 15 deadline (including all supporting credentials) and February 15 notification. Applications for regular decision admission must be filed by January 15, with decisions mailed by April 1.

Applications to the leadership in medicine program are due no later than December 15. Those for the law and public policy program must be filed no later than January 1. Those deferred under early decision and all regular applicants are given a final decision by April 1. Union adheres to the Candidates Reply Date of May 1.

Office of Admissions
Grant Hall
Union College
Schenectady, New York 12308
Phone: 518-388-6112
       888-843-6688 (toll-free)
Fax: 518-388-6986
E-mail: admissions@union.edu
Web site: http://www.union.edu
Web site: http://www.facebook.com/unioncollege
       http://twitter.com/unioncollegeny
       http://www.flickr.com/photos/union_college/sets/

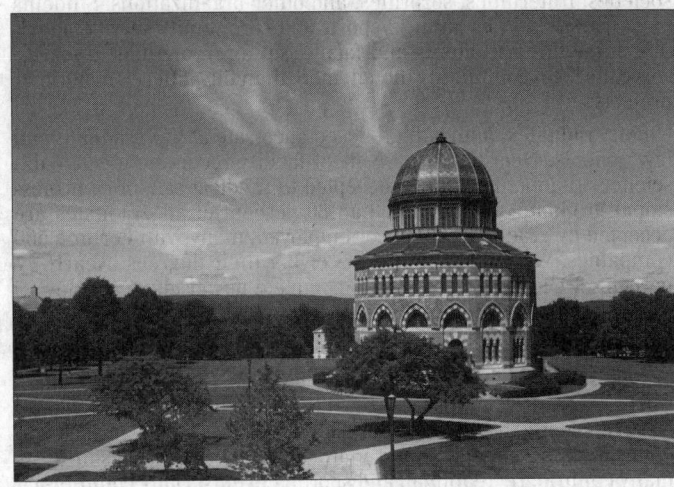

The sixteen-sided Nott Memorial is Union College's centerpiece.

UNION UNIVERSITY
JACKSON, TENNESSEE

The University

Union University believes that today's world is in need of great thinkers, a new generation of serious-minded intellects, who will engage the culture with the truths of Christian faith. That's why this private, four-year, liberal arts–based university is committed to readying this generation of change agents. Founded in 1823 and affiliated with the Tennessee Baptist Convention, Union critically and creatively builds upon the tradition of thought and inquiry, so carefully shaped by the great Christian scholars who have preceded them. Union is committed to its four core values of being excellence driven, Christ centered, people focused, and future directed.

Union has consistently received national recognition for academic excellence and value. *U.S. News & World Report* has ranked Union fifteenth among master's universities in the South. Union has been classified as a top tier institution every year since 1997. For two years in a row, Union is cited as one of only eighty-six schools nationally where the faculty has "an unusual commitment to undergraduate teaching." For a third consecutive year, Union was listed among sixty-eight schools to watch across the nation. Independent research by *America's 100 Best College Buys* ranks Union among the nation's best for combining academic quality and affordable price.

About 4,200 undergraduate and graduate students from forty states and thirty countries are represented in the student body.

On its Jackson campus, the University provides each resident student with a private bedroom within apartment-style complexes, most of which were built in 2008. The new units have four bedrooms with Internet connection, a kitchen, living room, washer/dryer unit, and two bathrooms.

A new student commons building features two fireplaces, TV and multi-purpose rooms, piano and band practice rooms, two kitchens, a gymnasium, a walking track, and outdoor grills and patios. The University coffeehouse is another favorite student destination for concerts, conversation, and study. Meals are served daily in the student dining hall as well as the Lexington Inn grill.

Union offers more than fifty major student-produced music and theater events each year. The University has sixty campus clubs, societies, fraternities, sororities, and other organizations. Students enjoy varsity and intramural sports and community service activities. In addition, students and faculty set aside one day a year to serve the local community though more than fifty different volunteer projects.

Union graduates enjoy a high acceptance rate at top graduate and law schools. Nearly 100 percent of faculty-recommended health science students have been accepted to medical school or professional graduate study. More than 80 percent of all graduates are accepted by graduate schools or employed, many with Fortune 500 companies, within a month of receiving their degrees. Nearly 77 percent of Union seniors plan to complete postgraduate work.

Location

The 290-acre campus is located in suburban Jackson, Tennessee, a growing community; the area's population is about 100,000. Jackson is located 80 miles east of Memphis and 120 miles west of Nashville along the I-40 corridor. Students find convenient access to entertainment, shopping, and many other services. Jackson hosts many cultural, recreational, and sporting events. Daily commercial flights are available at airports in Memphis and Nashville; limited commuter air service is available in Jackson.

Majors and Degrees

Undergraduate students can choose majors from among more than 100 programs of study.

The College of Arts and Sciences offers programs in advertising, applied linguistics, art (ceramics, digital media studies, drawing, graphic design, painting, sculpture, and photography), biology (cell biology, general zoology), broadcast journalism, chemical physics, chemistry, church music, computer information systems, computer science, conservation, criminal justice, digital media studies (art, communication arts, and computer science), engineering (electrical and mechanical), engineering physics, English (literature, creative writing), family studies, film studies, French (languages and culture or literature), history, honors studies, intercultural studies (global, regional), journalism, mathematics, media communications, medical technology, music, music education, music management, music marketing, music performance, music theory, physical science, physics, political science, psychology, public relations, social work, sociology, Spanish (languages and culture or literature), speech, sport ministry, teaching English as a second language, and theater.

The School of Theology and Missions offers programs in biblical studies, biblical studies languages, Christian ethics, Christian studies, church history, philosophy, sport management, theology, and youth ministry.

The McAfee School of Business Administration offers programs in accounting, business administration, economics, international business, management, and marketing.

The School of Education and Human Studies offers programs in learning foundations, elementary education, middle school education, special education, athletic training, physical education, physical education and health/teacher licensure, sport communication, sport management, sport marketing, sport ministry, sports medicine, exercise science and wellness, and teacher licensure for secondary areas.

The School of Nursing offers programs in nursing.

Preprofessional programs include chiropractics, cytotechnology, dental hygiene, dentistry, health information management, medicine, occupational therapy, optometry, pharmacy, physical therapy, physician assistant studies, podiatry, and veterinary medicine.

Academic Programs

Union University requires those seeking a bachelor's degree to complete 46 hours of general core curriculum, 18 to 21 hours of specific core curriculum, a minimum of 30 hours in the major academic program, and 18 hours in the minor academic program. The completion of the required 128 hours usually requires four years, with 32 hours per year.

For each undergraduate degree granted, at least 25 percent of the required semester hours must be earned through instruction at Union University. The last 56 semester hours of credit for a bachelor's degree must be earned at an accredited senior college.

The academic calendar is divided into fall (August to December) and spring (February to May) semesters, January term, and three summer terms. Evening accelerated courses are available each term.

Off-Campus Programs

Students from a variety of academic areas participate in internships with regional and national companies. Study abroad includes destinations such as Belgium, China, France, Italy, Jordan, Mexico, Oxford University, Poland, and Spain. Union students also have the opportunity to go on short-term mission Global Outreach trips to locations in the Africa, Asia, Central America, Europe, and the United States.

Academic Facilities

The new student commons and Providence Hall, a three-story pharmacy and nursing building, were recently completed. Other recent additions include eighteen residence life buildings, a conference and banquet facility, an athletic fieldhouse, and a 64,000-square-foot science building.

Union provides three large computer labs on the Jackson campus for student use, with full access to e-mail and the Internet. Each residential student has a port for the campus network and Internet access in their private bedroom. Wireless access is available in many areas. Additional computer labs are specialized for use by various departments.

The Emma Waters Summar Library houses open stacks of books for student use, as well as periodicals, microfilm and microfiche, archives, and electronic resources. Through its membership in cooperatives, there is easy access to the combined collections of more than 41,000 libraries worldwide. The Stephen Olford Center Library houses more than 32,000 volumes, including several unique collections. The R. C. Ryan Center for Biblical Studies Library is also available to students.

Pharmacy, science, and nursing students benefit from state-of-the-art laboratories and simulation environments. Communication students produce a daily live news program in the University's HD television studio.

Other academic amenities include top-quality lecture facilities; fine and performing arts practice rooms; theaters; broadcast studios; digital media labs; and biology, chemistry, physics, and engineering laboratories.

Costs

The cost for a typical student for the 2010–11 academic year was $21,700 in tuition (up to 16 hours per semester), $5870 for housing in an apartment-style residence hall, $1590 for meals (100 meals per semester), and $700 for the student services fee. These costs, excluding books, total $29,860 per academic year. Prices for housing and meals may vary slightly according to a student's preferences.

Financial Aid

More than 90 percent of Union students receive some financial aid based on need or merit. Union commits very competitive scholarships and grants to qualified students. The University helps connect students with other financial resources such as loans, student-work programs, privately funded scholarships, and a host of state and federal assistance programs.

Faculty

Union University invests in faculty members who are experts in their fields and committed to excellence in teaching, advising, and mentoring. *U.S. News & World Report* named Union one of only eighty-six schools nationally where faculty members have an unusual commitment to undergraduate teaching. The faculty members at Union put a priority on classroom teaching, but also join students in the pursuit of significant research, especially at the undergraduate level. Among full-time faculty members, more than 84 percent hold doctorates or the highest degree offered in their field of study. The student-faculty ratio is 12:1, and all classes are taught by faculty members.

Student Government

Union's Student Government Association functions through its executive, legislative, and judicial branches. Its elected officers and representatives serve as the official voice of the students in institutional affairs.

Admission Requirements

Applicants must graduate from an accredited high school with at least 20 units in the areas of English, foreign language, mathematics, social and natural sciences, and approved electives. In addition, students who qualify for unconditional admission must meet or exceed two of the following three admissions criteria: a 2.5 core GPA, a composite score of 22 on the ACT or 1020 (math and critical reading combined) on the SAT, and a ranking in the top 50 percent of their high school class. Union also actively admits home-schooled students. A state high school equivalency diploma is accepted in lieu of a high school diploma.

Transfer students who have completed at least 24 semester hours of transferable credit at an accredited college may also apply. Transfer students with less than 24 semester hours must meet freshman and transfer admission requirements. Transfer students must have at least a 2.3 cumulative GPA to qualify for unconditional admission.

Application and Information

Applicants must complete and return the Union University applications for undergraduate admission along with the $35 application fee. All official transcripts and results of either the ACT or SAT must be requested and mailed directly to the Office of Undergraduate Admissions. Applications are accepted and decisions rendered on a rolling basis.

For more information or to request an application, students should contact:

Office of Undergraduate Admissions
Union University
1050 Union University Drive
Jackson, Tennessee 38305-3697
Phone: 731-661-5100
   800-33-UNION (toll-free)
E-mail: info@uu.edu
Web site: http://www.uu.edu

The University is committed to its core values of being excellence driven, Christ centered, people focused, and future directed.

UNITED STATES AIR FORCE ACADEMY

COLORADO SPRINGS, COLORADO

The Academy

Established in 1954, the Air Force Academy prepares and motivates cadets for careers as Air Force officers. The Academy stresses character development, military training, and physical fitness as well as academics, emphasizing leadership in all areas.

The total enrollment is approximately 4,000; nearly 1,300 fourth-class (freshman) students enter each year. The composition of the student body mirrors that of the Air Force officer corps: about 22 percent women and 27 percent minorities. Students come from all fifty states and several other countries. Their common bond is the desire to be military officers. All cadets must live in on-campus dormitories and wear uniforms.

The Academy is accredited by the North Central Association of Colleges and Schools. Its engineering programs are approved by the Engineering Accreditation Commission of the Accreditation Board for Engineering and Technology, and its computer courses are approved by the Computing Sciences Accreditation Board. The chemistry and biochemistry majors fulfill the requirements of the Commission on Professional Training of the American Chemical Society.

All cadets must participate in intramural, club, or intercollegiate athletics every semester. The intramural sports include basketball, boxing (men's), cross-country, flag football, flickerball, mountain biking, racquetball, rugby (men's and women's), soccer, softball, team handball, tennis, Ultimate Frisbee, volleyball, and wallyball. The intercollegiate teams compete in Division I of the NCAA regionally and nationally. The men's teams include baseball, basketball, boxing, cheerleading, cross-country, diving, fencing, football, golf, gymnastics, hockey, indoor and outdoor track, lacrosse, rifle, soccer, swimming, tennis, water polo, and wrestling. The women's teams include basketball, cross-country, cheerleading, diving, fencing, gymnastics, indoor and outdoor track, rifle, soccer, swimming, tennis, and volleyball. Cadets may also choose from more than eighty extracurricular activities, which include professional organizations, mission support, competitive and recreational clubs, sports groups, and hobby clubs.

Qualified Academy graduates may enter flight training upon graduation, and approximately 75 percent of the students in each graduating class pursue graduate education at other institutions within ten years of their graduation. Each year, numerous Academy graduates receive graduate scholarships and fellowships, such as the Marshall, Rhodes, National Science Foundation, National Collegiate Athletic Association, and Guggenheim awards.

Location

The Academy campus sits in the foothills of the Rampart Range of the Rocky Mountains in a setting of natural beauty. Built on a mesa at 7,000 feet, it is one of Colorado's top tourist attractions. The Cadet Chapel, with its seventeen aluminum spires towering 150 feet into the air, highlights the contemporary architecture of the buildings in the cadet area. The space-age effect reflects the Academy's mission of preparing cadets to become officers and leaders in the Air Force of the future. The Academy borders the northern edge of Colorado Springs, which lies at the foot of the famous 14,100-foot Pikes Peak. Colorado

Springs has a metropolitan population of more than 500,000. Denver, the state's capital, has a population of almost 2.5 million in its greater metropolitan area and is located 55 miles north of the Academy. In addition to the social, sports, and cultural activities available in these cities, cadets enjoy skiing, hunting, horseback riding, white-water rafting, and other activities in the Colorado Rocky Mountains and nearby resorts.

Majors and Degrees

Graduates of the four-year service academy receive the Bachelor of Science (B.S.) degree and a commission as second lieutenants in the Air Force. The B.S. is granted in thirty-two majors: aeronautical engineering, astronautical engineering, basic sciences, behavioral sciences, biology, chemistry, civil engineering, computer engineering, computer science, economics, electrical engineering, English, environmental engineering, foreign area studies, general engineering, geospatial science, history, humanities, legal studies, management, mathematical sciences, mechanical engineering, meteorology, military strategic studies, operations research, physics, political science, social sciences, space operations, systems engineering, and systems engineering management. The Academy also offers minors in foreign languages and philosophy.

Academic Programs

A class enters the Academy during the last week in June or the first week in July. Incoming cadets undergo a strenuous 38-day summer training program that tests both their mental and physical abilities. Upperclass cadets conduct basic cadet training; commissioned officers serve as advisers. Basic cadets who complete this program are accepted into the Cadet Wing as fourth-class cadets. The academic year starts in early August and continues through May. During the first two years, cadets concentrate on core courses in engineering, humanities, science, and social science. During the last two years, they specialize in an academic major.

The required core courses prepare cadets for a broad scope of activity as Air Force officers. The core curriculum embraces courses in academic subjects, leadership and military training, and physical education and athletics. In addition, cadets complete the requirements for any of the thirty-two academic majors. To be eligible for graduation, cadets must also demonstrate an aptitude for commissioned service and leadership, demonstrate character consistent with professional military service, maintain a minimum cumulative grade point average and core grade point average of 2.0, and complete a minimum of 141 credit hours. The curriculum includes many elective courses.

All students must begin as freshmen; however, cadets who have taken some of the core course material prior to entry into the Academy may receive transfer or validation credit for this work. They may then substitute other courses for those granted transfer credit. Cadets who maintain the required grade point average may take advanced study classes.

The Academy aviation program familiarizes all cadets with operational activities of the Air Force. Optional courses provide instruction in soaring, parachuting, navigation, and basic flying. Those who take these courses may fulfill the requirements for Federal Aviation Administration pilot or glider certificates.

Cadets who qualify and are selected for pilot or navigator training may enter Air Education and Training Command flight programs following graduation from the Academy. Diversified summer programs in aviation and military training prepare cadets for officer responsibilities in the Air Force. Cadets may select their programs from several optional assignments at the Air Force Academy and other military installations.

Off-Campus Programs

Selected cadets may exchange visits with cadets from the Military Academy, Naval Academy, Coast Guard Academy, or one of fifteen international Air Force academies. The exchange program varies from one to two weeks for most of the international programs to a semester for the other U.S. service academies and the Canadian, Chilean, French, German, and Spanish Air Force academies, to name a few.

Academic Facilities

The Air Force Academy's excellent facilities support the academic, military, and athletics programs. Most classrooms accommodate small class sessions, averaging 17 students. Several classes and assemblies meet in larger lecture halls. Well-equipped laboratories supplement classroom instruction. Cadets conduct experiments using the aeronautics laboratory's wind tunnels, shock tubes, and rocket engines. A local network connects every dorm room, faculty and staff office, classroom, and laboratory at the Academy, and all entering cadets purchase notebook computers for academic and personal use. The Academy library, with more than 1.5 million volumes, supports all educational programs and maintains a collection of historical materials concerning aeronautics.

Costs

There are no tuition charges; the cost, including room, board, and medical and dental care, is borne entirely by the U.S. government. In addition, cadets receive a monthly salary to pay for supplies, clothing, and personal expenses. Careful management of the money covers obligations, with a small amount remaining for personal use.

Financial Aid

All cadets are on full scholarship at the Air Force Academy, as described above.

Faculty

The Academy's faculty is composed of Air Force officers and civilian professors. A few officers from other branches of the U.S. Armed Forces, those from allied nations, and distinguished civilian visiting professors supplement the faculty. There are no graduate student instructors. Faculty members must have a master's degree, and many have earned doctorates. Their educational backgrounds represent many outstanding colleges and universities in the United States, as well as some international institutions of higher education. Faculty members sponsor, coach, and referee extracurricular activities and athletics; adopt squadrons and attend their special events; and provide academic, career, and personal counseling.

Student Government

The Air Force Academy trains cadets for future leadership by allowing them to hold positions of responsibility in the Cadet Wing, the organization to which all cadets are assigned. The wing is under the operational supervision of first-class cadets (seniors). They hold cadet officer rank and command the wing and the subordinate units of groups, squadrons, flights, and elements. Through this organization, upperclass cadets are responsible for military training of the underclasses, the honor education and honor system, character development, and ethics and human relations programs.

Admission Requirements

Each year, young men and women who are U.S. citizens may be appointed from all states and territories of the nation. Citizens of other countries are admitted in limited numbers. Applicants must be at least 17 and not yet 23 years of age on July 1 of the year in which they desire to be admitted, be unmarried, have no dependents, and be of high moral character. They must be in good physical health.

Applicants must receive an official nomination. Members of Congress make the majority of the nominations for residents of their states and districts. Senators and representatives nominate young men and women who have excelled academically in high school, have demonstrated leadership potential through school activities, are physically fit, are respected by associates, and want to pursue military careers. Applicants need not know their member of Congress personally. Students may be eligible in nomination categories other than congressional. Students should ask high school counselors or Air Force Admissions Liaison Officers about other categories and apply for nominations in all categories for which they are eligible.

To enter the Academy upon graduation from high school, students should apply as soon as possible after January 31 of their junior year. If successful in receiving a nomination, they must take a physical fitness test, a medical exam, and either the SAT or the ACT.

Application and Information

High school juniors may obtain the application online at http://www.academyadmissions.com. Applicants should study the instructions and follow the proper application procedures. Air Force Admissions Liaison Officers, located in all states, assist students and counselors with the application and testing requirements.

HQ USAFA/RRS
2304 Cadet Drive, Suite 2300
USAF Academy, Colorado 80840-5025
Phone: 719-333-2520
      800-443-9266 (toll-free)
Web site: http://www.academyadmissions.com
      http://www.facebook.com/AcademyAdmissions

United States Air Force Academy Cadet Chapel.

UNITED STATES MERCHANT MARINE ACADEMY

KINGS POINT, NEW YORK

The Academy

The United States Merchant Marine Academy is a four-year, tuition-free federal service academy that was founded in 1943 to educate and train maritime shipping industry (merchant marine) officers, officers on active duty in the armed forces, and leaders in the maritime and intermodal transportation industry. It is an accredited, degree-granting college whose students are commissioned as Ensigns in the Navy Reserve upon graduation. The Academy is one of the world's foremost institutions in the field of maritime education and is operated under the Maritime Administration (MARAD) of the U.S. Department of Transportation.

There are approximately 975 men and women enrolled as midshipmen at the Academy. Their daily routine at Kings Point is very demanding. The academic day begins at 7:30 a.m. and concludes at 4 p.m. After classes, midshipmen are free to participate in recreational activities until dinnertime. After dinner, they are required to devote their time to study and academic preparation.

The extracurricular program is broad and varied. In addition to varsity athletics in twenty-five intercollegiate sports, the Academy has an extensive intramural program that permits all students to enjoy physical activity and competition.

The nonathletic activities are also wide ranging and abundant, falling into as many categories as there are individual interests. Publications and the Drill Team, Glee Club, Regimental Band, Scuba-Diving Club, Eagle Scout Association, International Relations Club, and Fencing Club are but a few of the pursuits available to the midshipmen. Regimental and class dances and informal mixers provide the midshipmen with an interesting social program.

Midshipmen are granted Liberty on weekends, Leave at Thanksgiving, Winter Holidays (December), spring trimester break, and annual leave in June-July after graduation and before the next academic term begins. Perhaps the most unusual and exciting part of the Academy curriculum is the Shipboard Training Program (Sea Year). Each midshipman, during three trimesters of the sophomore and junior years, serves 300–360 days at sea aboard commercially operated American-flag merchant ships. This exceptional work-study program takes the midshipmen to many parts of the world and provides them with practical experience on several different types of vessels. It can be said that the world is their campus during their three trimesters of sea service.

Location

The Academy is located on 80.5 acres of land at Kings Point, on the North Shore of Long Island. Kings Point is a suburban residential community only 20 miles east of midtown New York City, close to various cultural and recreational facilities.

Majors and Degrees

A graduate of the U.S. Merchant Marine Academy receives a Bachelor of Science degree, a merchant marine license as a third mate or third assistant engineer, and a commission as an Ensign in the U.S. Navy Reserve. Graduates may apply to the Army, Navy, Air Force, Marine Corps, Coast Guard, or National Oceanic and Atmospheric Administration (NOAA) to serve on active duty. Six major programs are offered: marine transportation for the preparation of deck officers; maritime operations and technology (a marine transportation program enhanced with marine engineering studies); marine engineering for students interested in becoming engineering officers; marine engineering systems, which, in addition to leading to a license as a third assistant engineer, is accredited by the Accreditation Board for Engineering and Technology (ABET) and includes a curriculum with greater depth in mathematics and a significant component of engineering design, as compared to the marine engineering curriculum; marine engineering and shipyard management, which is also accredited by ABET; and logistics and intermodal transportation, a marine transportation program focusing on logistics and intermodal systems management.

Academic Programs

During the first trimester of the plebe (or freshman) year, all students take a common program of mathematics, science, English, and professional courses. This background enables midshipmen to determine intelligently the area of their special interest. After the first trimester, midshipmen select their major and from then on concentrate on a program aligned with their career choice. The professional majors each consist of required core courses in technical and general education areas as well as selected electives. The option program consists of six courses for marine transportation and marine engineering majors, who have a choice of taking a series of related elective courses in a specific area of concentration or any individual elective course for which they qualify. These courses include such specialized fields as nuclear engineering, management science, computer science, chemistry, and naval architecture. By choosing to take the series of related courses, midshipmen can develop a proficiency in a subspecialty, supplementing their major field of study. Students in the marine engineering systems majors are not offered the choice of electives because of the required course load in their programs. General education courses make up about one third of each of the professional curriculums, and all midshipmen are required to take naval science courses prescribed by the Department of the Navy.

Thus, the Academy provides a balanced program of theoretical and practical study designed to provide the undergraduate with technical competence, leadership skills, and the well-rounded general education so essential for responsible citizenship in contemporary society.

Exemption credit may be awarded for college-level work completed at an accredited college if the course is equivalent to a course offered at the Academy.

Academic Facilities

With the exception of Wiley Hall, the former residence of Walter P. Chrysler and now an administration building, all the buildings of the Academy have been constructed since 1942. The Inter-Faith Chapel was dedicated in 1961, a three-story library was completed in 1968, and an indoor swimming pool and an engineering and science wing have been added since 1972. A modernization of all other academic buildings was completed in 1982. The Dean ('45) & Barbara White Admissions Center was dedicated in 2004. Upgrades to the dormitories and other facilities are currently under way.

Costs

Tuition, room and board, and medical and dental care are provided by the U.S. government. In addition, the government pays for books and the initial issue of uniforms. Each midshipman also receives $974.40 per month during periods when they are assigned aboard ship for training. Entering plebes are required to pay a little more than $2500 to cover the initial cost of a laptop computer as well as lab fees, equipment, and service, license, and activity fees. Upperclass members are also charged for service, license, and activity fees for the trimesters they are on campus (when they are not at sea).

Financial Aid

In effect, each midshipman receives a four-year scholarship from the U.S. government. Financial assistance is also available through the Federal Pell Grant Program, the Federal Stafford Student Loan Program, the Federal PLUS (parent loan) Program, the Federal Academic Competitiveness Grant, and the National Science and Mathematics Access to Retain Talent (SMART) Grant. A very limited number of need-based scholarships are also offered, and students may use outside scholarships to defray their costs.

Faculty

The Academy has 84 full-time faculty members and a student-faculty ratio of approximately 11:1. One third of the faculty members are licensed deck or engineering officers. Most hold advanced degrees in an academic discipline: 90 percent of the total faculty members hold master's degrees or higher; 50 percent have earned doctorates.

Student Government

The student body at the Academy is organized along military lines as a regiment, consisting of two battalions. Regimental life at the Academy is a form of student government and is an important part of the midshipman's total educational and leadership learning experience. The first classmen, or seniors, under the direction of the Commandant of Midshipmen, are responsible for exercising military command of the regiment and for administering the daily routine of the midshipmen. The military program is designed to develop leadership ability, self-discipline, and a sense of responsibility—attributes that are essential for effective citizenship as well as for a successful career as an officer.

Admission Requirements

Candidates for admission must be American citizens, be at least 17 years of age, must not have passed their twenty-fifth birthday by July 1 of the year of entry into the Academy, and be of good moral character. Candidates must be nominated by a U.S. representative or senator and must compete for vacancies allocated to their state in proportion to its representation in Congress. Candidates must achieve qualifying scores on the standard administration (timed) SAT or ACT. Candidates must have successfully completed chemistry or physics (including lab), as well as mathematics up to and including one semester of trigonometry or precalculus. Candidates' competitive standing is determined by their College Board score, their high school academic record and extracurricular participation, and their overall leadership potential. All candidates must meet the physical requirements for appointment as a midshipman in the Navy Reserve. Although not required, all applicants are strongly encouraged to perform a day or overnight visit to learn firsthand about midshipman life and academics. Visits are arranged through the Admissions Office when classes are in session, which is from mid-August to May.

Application and Information

Prospective candidates should write to the Admissions Office. They are sent detailed information on the nomination process, required tests, application procedures, and specific requirements. It is advisable to apply for a nomination during the late spring of the junior year in high school. The deadline for applications is March 1 of the year of desired entry.

Further information may be obtained by contacting:

Director of Admissions
U.S. Merchant Marine Academy
300 Steamboat Road
Kings Point, New York 11024-1699

Phone: 516-773-5391
        866-546-4778 (toll-free)
Fax: 516-773-5390
E-mail: admissions@usmma.edu
Web site: http://www.usmma.edu

An aerial view of the 80.5-acre "sea campus" of the U.S. Merchant Marine Academy at Kings Point, Long Island, on the shores of Long Island Sound.

UNIVERSITY AT BUFFALO, THE STATE UNIVERSITY OF NEW YORK

BUFFALO, NEW YORK

The University

The University at Buffalo (UB) is one of the nation's premier public research universities. With about 100 bachelor's degree programs (including combined degrees), 185 master's programs, and eighty-three doctoral degree programs, UB offers more academic choices than any other public university in New York and New England. In addition to twenty-seven departments in the College of Arts and Sciences, the University has the Schools of Architecture and Planning, Dental Medicine, Education, Engineering and Applied Sciences, Law, Management, Medicine and Biomedical Sciences, Nursing, Pharmacy and Pharmaceutical Sciences, Public Health and Health Professions, and Social Work, as well as the Roswell Park Cancer Institute Graduate Division.

Because the University at Buffalo is a research-intensive university, undergraduates study and work with faculty members who are leaders in their fields in academic and research facilities that support work at the most advanced levels of knowledge. Through the University's Center for Undergraduate Research and Creative Activities, Discovery Seminars, and Undergraduate Academies, UB undergraduates have the opportunity to collaborate with faculty members on groundbreaking research and creative projects. In fall 2010, UB's Honors College enrolled more than 300 freshmen with an average combined math and reading SAT score of 1382 and an average high school grade of 97.

As a large university with more than 29,000 students, including over 19,000 undergraduates, the University at Buffalo has a rich and varied student life. UB is home to a culturally diverse student body and ranks among the nation's leaders in international enrollment, with almost 5,000 students from 109 countries.

The University offers men's and women's sports programs at both the intramural and NCAA Division I levels; extensive recreational and entertainment facilities; more than 200 student organizations; the Distinguished Speaker Series, which has featured such guests as Al Gore, Stephen Colbert, Arnold Schwarzenegger, and His Holiness the Fourteenth Dalai Lama; and a busy calendar of festivals, concerts, films, and more.

UB's North Campus, the seat of most of the undergraduate academic programs, occupies 2 square miles in suburban Amherst. Its residence hall options include apartment-style living space on or adjacent to campus.

The South Campus, 3 miles away in a residential corner of Buffalo, is largely devoted to the health sciences and architecture. Buffalo's rapid transit line connects South Campus with the city center and the waterfront.

Recently, UB broadened its presence in Buffalo with a new Downtown Campus, home to the New York State Center for Excellence in Bioinformatics and Life Sciences, the Ross Eye Institute, and the Jacobs Executive Development Center. Additional expansion is planned in the near future.

Location

Buffalo is a Great Lakes city on an international border with a metropolitan area population of more than 1 million. It's a place of friendly neighborhoods with big-city activity for all tastes: professional sports teams; the Buffalo Philharmonic Orchestra; the renowned Albright-Knox Art Gallery; and a vibrant theater, dining, and club scene, all in a dramatic setting on Lake Erie and the Niagara River. The natural wonder of Niagara Falls is just a 20-minute drive from North Campus.

Majors and Degrees

The University is organized into one college and seven schools that serve undergraduates. The College of Arts and Sciences offers academic majors in African and African American studies, American studies, anthropology, art (studio art and fine arts), art history, Asian studies, bioinformatics and computational biology, biological sciences, chemistry, classics, communication, computational physics, dance, economics, English, environmental geosciences, film studies, geography, geological sciences, global gender studies, history, linguistics, mathematical physics, mathematics, mathematics/economics, media study,

medicinal chemistry, modern languages and literatures (French, German, Italian, and Spanish), music, music performance, music theater, philosophy, physics, political science, psychology, sociology, speech and hearing science, and theater. An interdisciplinary degree program in the social sciences is also offered, with concentrations in cognitive science, environmental studies, health and human services, international studies, legal studies, and urban and public policy studies.

The School of Architecture and Planning offers majors in architecture and environmental design.

The School of Engineering and Applied Sciences offers majors in computer science and engineering physics and in aerospace, biomedical, chemical, civil, computer, electrical, environmental, industrial, and mechanical engineering.

The School of Management offers a major in accounting and a major in business administration, with concentrations in financial analysis, human resources management, international business, management information systems, marketing, and operations and supply chain management.

The School of Medicine and Biomedical Sciences offers academic majors in biochemistry, biomedical sciences, biotechnology, medical technology, nuclear medicine technology, and pharmacology and toxicology. The School of Nursing offers an academic major in nursing.

The School of Pharmacy and Pharmaceutical Sciences offers an academic major in pharmaceutical sciences and a six-year Pharm.D. pharmacy program. The School of Public Health and Health Professions offers an academic major in exercise science and occupational therapy. Physical therapy is offered as a six-year doctorate; undergraduates major in exercise science.

The University has twenty-six combined-degree programs (B.A./M.A. and B.S./M.B.A., for example). Students whose objectives cannot be met through existing programs can formulate their own degree programs.

Academic Programs

Candidates for a baccalaureate degree are required to complete a minimum of 120 semester hours, 30 of which must be completed in residence, and earn a minimum grade point average of 2.0.

Students have great flexibility in planning their academic programs. All students must fulfill a University general education requirement. They must also complete an academic major, which is usually selected by the end of the sophomore year. Students also have ample opportunity for independent study under departmental or faculty auspices. Placement and credit are granted on the basis of Advanced Placement or College-Level Examination Program scores. The academic year has two semesters: one beginning in late August and the other in mid-January. An extensive summer session is also offered.

Off-Campus Programs

Many students take advantage of study-abroad programs. The University has exchange programs with sixty-five universities around the world. Programs include the full academic year or fall, spring, or summer sessions. Students may also take advantage of nearly 300 programs offered by other colleges in the SUNY system.

Academic Facilities

The University at Buffalo's academic library collections are the largest in the SUNY system; in addition to more than 3.6 million bound volumes, they include more than 30,000 serials and periodicals, 5.4 million microforms, 50,000 full-text electronic journals, almost 1 million full-text electronic books, specialized holdings including the world's largest collection of James Joyce manuscripts, and a renowned collection of twentieth-century poetry in manuscript. All library holdings are digitally cataloged and accessible from terminals and computers on and off campus. The University is among the first to have software that makes the entire SUNY library system—more than 18 million volumes—available to students. State-of-the-art computer workstations for student use are located at public sites in the University's libraries.

Costs

In 2010–11, tuition for New York state residents was $4970 and for out-of-state residents, $13,380. For all students, fees were $2166, and average room and board costs were $10,442. Students should expect additional expenses for books and supplies, transportation, and personal expenses. Costs are subject to change.

Financial Aid

The University participates in all New York state and federal financial aid programs, including the Tuition Assistance Program (available only to New York state residents) and the Federal Pell Grant, Federal Work-Study, Federal Direct Student Loan, and Federal Perkins Loan programs. The recommended deadline for completing the Free Application for Federal Student Aid is February 1 for fall semester entry. All inquiries concerning financial aid should be directed to the Office of Financial Aid in the Student Resource Center at 716-645-2450.

In fall 2010, UB awarded almost $4 million in merit scholarship support to incoming freshmen. UB's top incoming freshmen receive the Presidential Scholarship, which covers the full cost of attendance for all four years, and are invited to join the Honors College. Provost Scholarships range up to the full cost of tuition, depending on academic achievement, talent in the creative or performing arts, and the cost of attendance. The Daniel Acker Scholarship is for talented students who are traditionally underrepresented in higher education. Acker Scholars receive aid up to the full cost of tuition and participate in a comprehensive program of support services and activities. Athletic grants-in-aid are awarded to students recruited to participate in the University's NCAA Division I athletics program.

Faculty

The University's nationally renowned faculty includes winners of the National Medal of Science, the Nobel Prize, the Pulitzer Prize, and other awards. A large number have published books or scholarly articles. Many have held major national or international fellowships; conducted research funded by government agencies or national foundations; served as consultants to business, education, and government; or otherwise demonstrated professional expertise. More than 100 have won the SUNY Chancellor's Award for Excellence in Teaching, the largest number of recipients of any SUNY campus.

Student Government

All daytime undergraduate students are members of the Student Association and are entitled to participate in its activities. The Student Association is involved at every level of student life, from freshman orientation to commencement. Through membership on many University-wide policy committees, representatives of the association are given a legitimate, permanent voice in the policies and direction of the University.

Admission Requirements

Applicants are required to submit their high school transcript, the results of the ACT or SAT critical reading and math sections, and at least one recommendation from a high school counselor or teacher. Applicants should plan to take the SAT or ACT no later than November of their senior year. Application review and notification begins in early February and continues until the freshman class is filled. Most freshmen admitted to the University apply to the major of their choice during the sophomore year. However, architecture, accounting and business management, engineering and applied sciences, exercise science, nuclear medicine technology, nursing, and occupational therapy may offer departmental admission to freshman applicants.

Admission to programs in dance, music, music theatre, and theatre requires an audition.

Admission is competitive. Most successful students at the University have come with a strong level of academic preparation in basic academic areas. Among accepted freshmen in fall 2010, the mean high school average grade was 92 percent, 28 percent were in the top 10 percent of their high school class, and 49 percent scored 1200 or higher on the SAT (critical reading and math).

The University enrolls and provides specialized advisement and support to a limited number of freshmen who demonstrate academic potential through means other than quantitative measures. Creative talent, athletics, special academic achievement, demonstrated leadership, community service, and personal circumstances are examples of areas that the University may consider.

Transfer applicants must have completed a minimum of 12 semester hours at a regionally accredited college prior to application. Students with fewer than 24 semester hours are evaluated on the basis of their college and high school credentials in combination with standardized test score results. Admission of transfer students is based on the quality of previous academic performance and space availability. In order to receive consideration for transfer admission to UB, it is recommended that students present a strong record of college study, earning a minimum cumulative grade point average of 2.5 on a 4.0 scale. It should be noted, however, that requirements may vary depending on the academic program.

Admission to an academic department may occur concurrently with University admission if the applicant has fulfilled prerequisite requirements. These requirements include completed courses, but may also comprise essay, portfolio, exam, or audition requirements. Some departments have significantly higher GPA standards and early deadlines for application.

Application and Information

Students can apply online at http://www.suny.edu/student/apply_online.cfm or http://www.commonapp.org. Or they can visit http://www.admissions.buffalo.edu/apply for more information on applying to UB. For further information, please contact:

Office of Admissions
12 Capen Hall
University at Buffalo, the State University of New York
Buffalo, New York 14260-1660
Phone: 716-645-6900
        888-UB-ADMIT (toll-free)
E-mail: ubadmit@buffalo.edu
Web site: http://www.admissions.buffalo.edu
        http://on.fb.me/UB_admissions (Facebook)
        http://twitter.com/UBAdmissions (Twitter)

The University at Buffalo is one of the nation's premier public research universities and SUNY's largest and most comprehensive campus.

UNIVERSITY OF ADVANCING TECHNOLOGY

TEMPE, ARIZONA

The University

The University of Advancing Technology (UAT) is the technophile's college experience—a geek-friendly community uniquely suited to provide students passionate about technology an ideal place to live and grow. UAT offers students a well-rounded education in a non-traditional setting. Students who are seeking a strictly career-oriented technical college experience will not find it here. Because of UAT's dedication to both scholastic excellence and technological innovation, it stands apart in academia as an ideal destination for those who feel disenfranchised by conventional institutions of higher learning. For the student who is looking at the future of technology and wishes to become a vital part of it, UAT beckons.

As the twenty-first century unfolds, it is becoming more and more apparent how technology in all its manifestations profoundly alters how people work, live, play, and interact with each other. UAT students benefit from their fundamental understanding of both theoretical and applied aspects of technology. As technologists, UAT students see that there will always be newer and newer tools created to address mankind's emergent needs and desires. Changing the world through technology is inherent in UAT's mission. Current subjects of ongoing research and scholarship at UAT include robotics and embedded systems, technology forensics, network security, game development, and other areas of advanced technology.

UAT has always devoted all of its resources to creating a vital academic environment where students are challenged to achieve, explore new and traditional concepts, and practice what they learn in real-world situations. This combination of research, scholarship, and application creates technically adept graduates who are equally at home in academia and the working world and valued by both. UAT graduates thrive in the digital age and meet and surpass every expectation of their high-technology employers and peers. They enter the professional world with accredited associate and bachelor's degrees, and many return to pursue their master's degree.

When the University of Advancing Technology was founded in 1983 (as the CAD Institute), it was conceived as a small school for training engineers and architects in the completely new field of computer-aided engineering. Its original students came to the CAD Institute seeking professional development training and certifications. From this beginning as a technical school, the institution became involved with advances in computer graphics and unique approaches to technology education. In 1998, the school moved to its new urban campus in Tempe. In 2002, the school changed its name to University of Advancing Technology to reflect its current broad technology focus.

UAT's 1,000-plus students (from all fifty states and many other countries) still find plenty of time to participate in clubs and other activities that enhance UAT's ideal innovation environment, such as programming club, paintball, anime club, cold fusion users' group, fencing club, photography club, DC480 (network security), C++, and more. Special on-campus events include Academic Palooza, Tech Forum, game tournaments, LAN parties, Geek Week, live action games, Oktoberfest, Guitar Hero tournaments, and Thanksgiving dinner.

At any time, day or night, there are groups of students working on course work and projects, looking to create the next big thing. It is not uncommon to see students pulling all-nighters, exchanging ideas, and searching for solutions to perfect their creative innovations. There are also gatherings of students and instructors engaged in discussions of the latest technology developments and how they can make them better. UAT has an academic and social environment that integrates the contemporary and advancing principles of education and technology with its Synchronic Learning teaching model to create a unique collaborative educational environment.

UAT is accredited by the Higher Learning Commission and is a member of the North Central Association (http://www.ncahlc.org/). UAT also holds accreditations and certifications from such organizations as the Council for Higher Education Accreditation and the U.S. National Security Agency's Information Assurance Courseware Evaluation program. A complete listing of accreditations is available at http://www.uat.edu/accreditation.

Location

Located in sunny Tempe, Arizona, near the heart of downtown Phoenix, a booming urban center in the Sonoran desert, the University of Advancing Technology is 4 hours from the beaches of Mexico and 2 hours from snowboarding in Flagstaff. The campus is accessible from all parts of the Phoenix metropolitan region by public transportation, bicycle, or automobile. Students live on campus in Founder's Hall, the resident student complex, or off campus in nearby neighborhoods. The University is close to major freeways, bus lines, and Sky Harbor Airport, which is a major international airport that serves the entire Phoenix metropolitan area. Other local amenities include shopping, arts districts, and other attractions associated with a dynamic urban center.

Arizona is a land of incredible beauty, contrast, and opportunity. Tempe is located in the Valley of the Sun, which is surrounded by beautiful mountain ranges. Within a short drive are attractions like the Grand Canyon (4½ hours), a variety of lakes and rivers (30–90 minutes), the red rocks of Sedona (2 hours), and the exquisite Sonoran Desert, just outside of town. UAT is close to every desert sport imaginable—golf, mountain biking, hiking, swimming, rollerblading, and skateboarding.

Majors and Degrees

UAT offers Bachelor of Arts, Bachelor of Science, Associate of Arts, and Associate of Science degrees, on campus and online, in several advancing technology disciplines, including artificial life programming, advancing computer science, virtual modeling and design, game art and animation, game design, game programming, network security, robotics and embedded systems, and more. UAT offers Master of Science degrees in emerging technologies, information assurance, technology leadership, and more.

Academic Programs

The Bachelor of Arts and Bachelor of Science programs require a minimum of 120 semester credits, including 84 core credits, forty 300/400–level credits, and 36 general education credits. The Associate of Arts and Associate of Science programs require a minimum of 60 semester credits: 45 core credits, and 15 general education credits.

Academic Facilities

Students at UAT are immersed in a world of technology. From the miles of cables and walls of servers in the open-viewed server rooms to the vast array of industry technology in the NT lab, students who love technology feel right at home. The University is open 24/7 and deploys enough workstations for local system usage for all users. These workstations are purchased annually with a 33 percent cycle, which means one third of the workstations are new each year. When necessary the University deploys additional specialty workstations for specific uses, such as Xbox development workstations, 360 development workstations, and a 3-D printer that copies and builds three-dimensional models. The University offers students access to professional-level software applications that directly relate to the technology they're studying, at no additional charge.

As an institution, UAT is dedicated to planning, implementing, and sharing its research with others in technology and academia. The UAT research centers operate within the University to further knowledge creation, foster institutional and community awareness, and improve initiatives in their focal areas. In addition, each research center publishes works to the broader community through a variety of channels (technology journals, online journals, and conference papers). In 1992, the University founded its first research center, the Computer Reality Center. It performed research primarily for the computer graphics industry, with specific emphasis on the field of virtual reality. The center adopted the Hyperlearning model and developed UAT's current teaching model, Synchronic Learning. Synchronic Learning combines lecture, tutorial teaching, group recollection, student teachback, and discovery learning. Year-round classes are available both on campus and online, and students produce projects for a graduation portfolio to demonstrate an understanding of what they are learning.

Through research of learning and teaching methodologies, the Center for Learning Excellence develops and supports educational models that enable the University to build innovative and balanced learning experiences. Its main goal is to apply its research toward developing the UAT Faculty Certification Program. This program ensures baseline effective teaching preparation within UAT's learning model for all faculty members before they are assigned to the classroom. The center routinely assesses instruction at UAT in relation to student learning outcomes.

The Center for Institutional Research is the center for ongoing institutional research that accumulates, generates, maintains, communicates, and disseminates institutional information to support assessment and general awareness of student learning. The center also evaluates and reviews the efficacy of institutional policies.

The Center for Technology Studies conducts original research and produces works published in the broader community and furthers community understanding of technology disciplines, their applications, and their relevance in the global society. Within the center is the Center for Information Assurance, which produces knowledge solely within the information assurance disciplines at UAT: computer forensics and network security at the undergraduate level and information security at the graduate level.

Whenever and wherever possible, the campus and technology resources are open to allow students and professionals alike to participate collaboratively in this endeavor, whether as team members on a student project, speaking at Technology Forum, or submitting work to the University's *Journal of Advancing Technology*.

Costs

Undergraduate tuition for 2011–12 is $9700 per semester. Tuition for UAT-Online students is $5600 per semester. Housing costs are about $7300 per calendar year.

Financial Aid

Average aid per academic year for first-academic-year freshmen is $5038. The percentage of freshmen who receive aid is 76 percent. The percentage of freshmen who receive UAT academic scholarships is 21 percent. The average amount of scholarships received per freshman student per academic year is $1200.

Faculty

UAT's faculty comprises members who are thinkers, teachers, technological gurus, industry experts, and student mentors. They garner their skills, knowledge, and expertise from a range of experiences—from the classrooms of academe to the boardrooms of industry, from community meeting halls to international conferences. They are a group governed by their passion for technology, their students, and their own academic and professional growth. Sixty-four faculty members, distinguished by their academic abilities and accomplishments within their respective fields, serve as both instructors and mentors.

Student Government

The University-sanctioned student government was formed to give the student body at UAT a collective voice and set traditions within the University. University Student Government (USG) performs important roles in encouraging self-directed Student Life organizations, coordinating student community service activities, and providing a venue for feedback between students and staff members. Students are encouraged to participate in the Student Government, which holds monthly open meetings.

Admission Requirements

The University of Advancing Technology strives to admit undergraduate students who embody its passion for technology, are a cultural match to the University, demonstrate adequate academic achievement, and have a dedication to lifelong learning. All undergraduate applicants are evaluated based on these criteria: academic history and achievements; personal expression; desire to attend UAT; how they might fit with UAT's geek-friendly culture, passion, and aptitude for technology; and the supportiveness of the applicant's network of family, friends, and peers to achieve their educational goals (for UAT-Online applicants, employer support is also evaluated). All applicants are encouraged to submit high school transcripts, ACT and/or SAT scores, Advanced Placement scores, and college transcripts, so UAT's Admissions Office may thoroughly review the applicant's academic history.

In addition to the standard admission requirements, non-U.S. citizens applying for admission to the University of Advancing Technology must provide proof of English proficiency in one of the following ways: Test of English as a Foreign Language (TOEFL) with a score of 550 or higher on the paper-based test, 79 or higher on the Internet-based test, or 213 or higher on the computer-based test; successful completion of Level 108 from an ELS Center; ASPECT English Language Proficiency Level 5; or attendance for one year at a regionally accredited U.S. college or university and completion of English 101 (or equivalent) with grade C or better. Proof of English proficiency is not required if English is the applicant's native language. Official transcripts must be submitted with an English translation and be evaluated as a U.S. high school equivalent by Educational Credential Evaluators, Inc., P.O. Box 17499, Milwaukee, Wisconsin 53217-0499, U.S.A. (http://www.ece.org).

Application and Information

UAT has an admissions application that helps both the student and the admissions staff determine if the applicant and UAT are a good match. Students should complete and submit the application to the UAT Admissions Office prior to consideration. Students may apply online at http://www.uat.edu/admissions. To request an application, students should either e-mail admissions@uat.edu or call 877-UAT-GEEK (toll-free).

UAT Admissions
University of Advancing Technology
2625 West Baseline Road
Tempe, Arizona 85283-1056
Phone: 602-383-8228
       800-658-5744 (toll-free)
E-mail: admission@uat.edu
Web site: http://www.uat.edu
       http://www.facebook.com/GeekUniversity
       http://www.twitter.com/UATHappenings

UAT's unique technology-infused campus facilities have been designed to enhance collaborative learning and provide a rich campus life for students and faculty members.

UNIVERSITY OF ALASKA FAIRBANKS

FAIRBANKS, ALASKA

The University

Founded in 1917, the University of Alaska Fairbanks (UAF) provides education, research, and service in the Last Frontier. The Fairbanks campus, one of three in the statewide system of higher education, is the primary administrative and research center, with branches in Bethel, Dillingham, Kotzebue, and Nome, along with rural centers throughout the state.

The total UAF enrollment is close to 10,000 students. Eighty-five percent of the students are from Alaska. Fifteen percent are from other U.S. states and fifty-two foreign countries. There are eight residence halls on the Fairbanks campus, capable of lodging 1,020 occupants. The student apartment complex has furnished, two-bedroom units for 234 students with sophomore and upperclass standing. The Eileen Panigeo MacLean House has housing for 22 rural Alaska students. The University also manages 153 furnished apartments for students with families.

The main campus contains a core of academic buildings and residences, as well as miles of trails, two lakes, and a boreal forest research and recreational area. Most of the University's research institutes, including the noted Geophysical Institute and the International Arctic Research Center, are clustered on the campus's West Ridge, with incredible views of the Tanana Valley and Alaska Range. The University's Agricultural and Forestry Experiment Station is on campus, as are a Cooperative Fish and Wildlife Research Unit and various state and federal agencies and laboratories. The University awards graduate degrees in many of the same areas as the undergraduate studies, often in conjunction with one of its research institutes. The University has added or expanded several new buildings in the last five years, increasing research capabilities related to the biological sciences, cold-climate housing, and circumpolar studies. The North is a theme found in many other academic programs, including Alaska Native studies, anthropology, the arts, engineering, and the social sciences.

Intercollegiate athletics include men's and women's basketball, cross-country running and skiing, intercollegiate ice hockey (CCHA), and women's volleyball and swim teams. The University also has an outstanding rifle team which has produced several Olympic athletes, including a gold medalist, and has earned ten national championships. The Student Recreation Complex houses a variety of sports and physical activities facilities, including multipurpose areas for basketball, volleyball, badminton, tennis, calisthenics, dance, gymnastics, judo, and karate; a rifle and pistol range; courts for handball, racquetball, and squash; an elevated 200-meter, three-lane jogging track; a swimming pool; weight-training and modern fitness equipment areas; an ice arena for recreational skating and hockey; a special aerobics area; and a three-story climbing wall.

The student union, the William Ransom Wood Center, is the focus of various out-of-class activities for students and faculty members. The center houses meeting and exhibit rooms, lounges and television areas, the student government offices, campus information, a pub, bowling alley, games room, cafeteria, snack bar, and an espresso bar.

Location

The campus of the University of Alaska Fairbanks is situated on a ridge overlooking the valley of the Tanana River and the city of Fairbanks. Serving a population of more than 85,000 within the 7,561-square-mile North Star Borough, Fairbanks is a major trade center for outlying villages in Interior Alaska. The city is connected with the rest of the state and the lower forty-eight states by air and highway. Municipal bus service is available between downtown Fairbanks, the surrounding area, and the campus. Shuttle bus service is available around the UAF campus.

Fairbanks offers the sophistication of larger cities through such luxuries as first-run movies and fine restaurants, while maintaining the atmosphere of smaller, more personal towns. Denali National Park and Preserve and other vast wilderness areas are close at hand, and Anchorage is 350 miles south via the Parks Highway. Members of the Fairbanks community and the University join together in the Fairbanks Symphony, Arctic Chamber Orchestra, and in many other musical and theatrical enterprises.

Majors and Degrees

The University of Alaska Fairbanks awards occupational endorsements, certificates, and the A.A., A.S., A.A.S., B.A., B.A.S., B.B.A., B.E.M., B.F.A., B.M., B.S., and B.T. degrees in accounting; administrative assistant studies; airframe studies; Alaska Native studies; anthropology; applied accounting; applied business; applied physics; apprenticeship technology; art; arts and sciences; aviation maintenance technology; automotive technology; aviation technology; biological sciences; bookkeeping technician studies; business administration; chemistry; child development and family studies; civil engineering; communication; community health; computer science; culinary arts; diesel/heavy equipment; dental assisting; drafting technology; early childhood; earth science; economics; electrical engineering; elementary education; emergency services; English; entry-level welder studies; Eskimo (Inupiaq and Yup'ik); financial services representative studies; fisheries; food science and nutrition; film; foreign languages; general science; geography; geological engineering; geology; health-care reimbursement; health technology; high-latitude range management; history; human services; information technology specialist studies; instrumentation technology; interdisciplinary studies; Japanese studies; journalism; justice; law enforcement; linguistics; mathematics; mechanical engineering; medical assistant studies; medical office technologies; microcomputer support specialist studies; mining applications and technologies; mining engineering; music; Native language education; natural resources management (including forestry); Northern studies; nurse aide studies; paralegal studies; paramedic studies; petroleum engineering; philosophy; phlebotomy; physics; political science; power plant studies; power generation; process technology; professional piloting; psychology; renewable resources; rural development; rural human services; rural utilities business management; Russian studies; safety, health, and environmental awareness technology; social work; sociology; technology; theater; tribal management; veterinary science; welding and materials technology; and wildlife biology and conservation. Preprofessional advising is available in dentistry, law, library science, medicine, pharmacy, physical therapy, physician assistant studies, and veterinary medicine.

Academic Programs

The academic year is divided into two semesters; registration begins in early April for the fall semester and in November for the spring semester. Preregistration is available for returning students. In addition, there are three-week, six-week, and twelve-week summer sessions.

UAF requires all new students to participate in new student orientation in the fall and spring semesters. The University is organized into four colleges and four professional schools: the Colleges of Liberal Arts, Natural Science and Mathematics, Engineering and Mines, Rural and Community Development; and the Schools of Natural Resources and Agricultural Sciences, Education, Fisheries and Ocean Sciences, and Management. A minimum of 120 credits must be completed for the four-year baccalaureate degree programs.

Students who receive scores of 3 or higher on the College Board's Advanced Placement tests may be awarded credit by the University. Currently enrolled students may challenge courses for credit by successfully completing College-Level Examination Program (CLEP) examinations or by completing locally prepared examinations. Requests for advanced-placement credit and credit by examination are coordinated through the Office of Admissions and the registrar.

The honors program is designed for highly motivated undergraduate students who wish to acquire a superior understanding of the natural and social sciences, the arts, and the humanities. Prospective honors students need a minimum ACT plus writing composite score of 27 or a minimum combined SAT score of 1820, with an emphasis placed on high scores in English and mathematics.

Off-Campus Programs

The University maintains active exchange programs with various universities in Australia, Austria, Canada, Chile, China, Denmark, Finland, France, Germany, Iceland, Japan, Mexico, Norway, Russia, Sweden, Switzerland, and the United Kingdom. Membership in the University of the Arctic's north2north exchange program provides UAF students an extensive array of placement opportunities throughout the circumpolar North. UAF also offers a variety of study-abroad programs, including the Northwest Council on Study Abroad (NCSA), which provides study opportunities with UAF and other U.S. members in Argentina, Austria, England, France, Ghana, Greece, Ireland, Italy, Mexico, Morocco, New Zealand, and Spain. Additional study programs and internships are available worldwide through affiliates maintaining sites in locations such as Brazil, the Czech Republic, Fiji, Hong Kong, Hungary, India, Jordan, Malaysia, Peru, Poland, Singapore, South Africa, and Thailand, to name a few. UAF is also a member of the National Student Exchange, participating with more than 180 colleges and universities throughout the United States and U.S. territories and nine locations in Canada.

Academic Facilities

The Fine Arts Complex features a 480-seat theater, a 1,072-seat concert hall, FM public radio (KUAC) and educational-television (PBS) studios, an art gallery, and the Elmer E. Rasmuson Library. The library collection contains more than 1.1 million volumes, including the prestigious Alaska and Polar Regions Collection. Electronic catalogs provide access to collections in 11,000 libraries nationwide.

Students have free use of the University's academic computing facilities which are accessible from Windows and Macintosh computer labs and via remote access. Various schools and colleges have their own special-purpose computer labs.

The University of Alaska Museum of the North attracts nearly 100,000 visitors each year to Interior Alaska and is located on the UAF campus. The museum collects, preserves, and exhibits materials from Alaska and the North.

Costs

In 2011–12, tuition and fees are $2785 per semester for full-time (15 credits) students. Nonresident students pay an additional $5820 for 15 credits of tuition each semester. Generally, to qualify as a resident, students must show proof that they have been living in Alaska for two years. Residents of Alaska and cities having sister city agreements with any Alaska city are eligible for resident tuition rates. The approximate cost per semester for books and supplies is $1400. A double-occupancy residence hall room on campus costs $1805 per semester. Meal plans cost approximately $1655–$1975 per semester. All costs are subject to change.

Financial Aid

A large portion of financial aid is derived from the Alaska Supplemental Education Loan Program, which is available to all students attending UAF, regardless of residency. Three kinds of aid are available: grants and scholarships (which need not be repaid), loans, and part-time employment. Inquiries should be directed to the University's financial aid office or by e-mail to financialaid@uaf.edu.

Academic Merit and Human Achievement scholarships are one-year awards ranging from $2,500 to $15,000, granted by the Office of Admissions and the Registrar. Academic Merit scholarships are available to entering freshmen with a minimum 3.0 GPA and an SAT combined score of 1760 or an ACT plus writing composite score of 26. The Human Achievement scholarships are available to entering freshmen who demonstrate a strong commitment to community through service or other achievements. To apply, students should submit a scholarship application, an application for admission, a high school transcript, and test scores for review. Questions about this scholarship should be directed to the Office of Admissions and the Registrar. The deadline for University of Alaska and UAF-funded scholarships is February 15. Prospective students should check the Financial Aid Web site at www.uaf.edu/finaid for information about grants, loans, and other aid; and applicable due dates.

Faculty

Fifty-two percent of full-time faculty members and 32 percent of part-time faculty members hold doctoral, professional, or terminal degrees, and many are actively engaged in research. In keeping with University policy, faculty members provide academic counseling for students. The combination of a student-faculty ratio of 14:1 and easy access to instructors for help outside of class produces a maximum educational benefit for students.

Student Government

The Associated Students of the University of Alaska Fairbanks (ASUAF) protects students' rights through its various governmental functions and also offers educational, social, recreational, and service activities. The school newspaper, the *Sun Star*, is published weekly with the sponsorship of ASUAF, which also supports KSUA, the campus radio station; the international cinema and weekly movie series; and dances, concerts, and other entertainment. ASUAF publishes the results of its faculty evaluations and sends several student lobbyists to the Alaska state legislature in Juneau each spring. There is a student-member seat on the Board of Regents of the statewide university system.

Admission Requirements

For admission to a baccalaureate program, applicants must be high school graduates with a GPA of at least 2.5 in a 16-credit high school core curriculum; and a cumulative GPA of at least 3.0, or 2.5 plus an ACT plus writing score of 18 or SAT score of 1290 (including writing skills section). Transfer students must also have a minimum grade point average of 2.0 in all previous college work.

Applicants for a major in a scientific or technical field may be required to present a higher grade point average and to have completed specific background courses before being accepted into the major department. All entering freshmen are required to submit scores from the ACT plus writing or SAT examination prior to registration for placement in English and math courses.

Application and Information

The application deadlines are May 1 for the summer semester, June 15 for the fall semester, and November 1 for the spring semester. An application fee is required when the application is submitted. Applicants are notified of the admission decision once all application materials have been received. Students who desire campus housing should apply as early as possible; a deposit is required.

For further information, applicants should contact:

Office of Admissions and the Registrar
University of Alaska Fairbanks
P.O. Box 757480
Fairbanks, Alaska 99775-7480

Phone: 907-474-7500
      800-478-1823 (toll-free)
E-mail: admissions@uaf.edu
Web site: http://www.uaf.edu/admissions
      http://www.uaf.edu/admissions/parents
      https://uaonline.alaska.edu (to apply)

Constitution Park, located between the Rasmuson Library, Gruening Building, Constitution Hall, and Fine Arts Complex, is just one of the popular hangouts between classes.

UNIVERSITY OF COLORADO BOULDER

BOULDER, COLORADO

The University

The University of Colorado Boulder (CU-Boulder) is a dynamic community of scholars and learners situated on one of the most spectacular college campuses in the country. CU-Boulder is one of thirty-four U.S. public institutions belonging to the prestigious Association of American Universities (AAU) and the only member in the Rocky Mountain region. The university has a proud tradition of academic excellence, with four Nobel laureates and more than fifty members of prestigious academic societies. CU-Boulder was ranked the top green university in the nation in *Sierra* magazine's 2009 listing of greenest colleges, and was one of only three U.S. colleges and universities to receive a 2007 Presidential Award for General Community Service.

The campus offers more than 3,400 courses each year in approximately 150 areas of study. There are seventy-eight academic majors available at the bachelor's level, seventy at the master's level, and fifty-one at the doctoral level. Outstanding academic departments and programs include astrophysical and planetary sciences, biochemistry, biology, chemistry, engineering, English, entrepreneurial business, geography, integrative physiology, music, physics, and psychology. Talented undergraduate students may participate in honors programs, the Undergraduate Research Opportunities Program, and eleven residential academic programs or living and learning communities featuring small-class environments.

Total enrollment for fall 2009 at the Boulder campus was 30,196, including 25,408 undergraduate students. Students come from every state in the nation and about 100 countries. Approximately two thirds of the students come from Colorado. Many ethnic, religious, academic, and social backgrounds are represented, fostering the development of a multicultural community that enriches each student's educational experience.

Undergraduate students may apply to the following colleges and schools: Architecture and Planning, Arts and Sciences, Leeds School of Business, Engineering and Applied Science, Music, Journalism and Mass Communication, and Education. Students are admitted to Journalism and Mass Communication only after completing one or two years at CU-Boulder, with exceptions for highly qualified new freshmen. The School of Education accepts applications from students after they are enrolled in an approved degree program at CU-Boulder.

CU-Boulder offers a wide variety of campus activities. Students may participate in student government; clubs and organizations; intramural, club, and intercollegiate sports; and fraternities and sororities. An extensive calendar of cultural events is available.

Location

CU-Boulder is located in a scenic valley at the foot of the Rocky Mountains, 1 mile above sea level. With a population of approximately 100,000, Boulder is among the most dynamic, progressive, and attractive cities of its size in the United States. The Colorado state capital, Denver, is a 30-mile drive or bus ride (free for students) from Boulder. Boulder is surrounded by a greenbelt of more than 20,000 acres of open space. Much of the open space and nearby mountains are crisscrossed by an extensive system of hiking, biking, and riding trails. Many CU-Boulder students enjoy skiing, hiking, backpacking, rock climbing, white-water rafting, or mountain biking.

CU-Boulder is listed as one of the "most artistically successful campuses in the country" in *The Campus as a Work of Art* by Thomas Gaines. The 600-acre main campus, in the heart of Boulder, is distinguished by buildings featuring native sandstone walls and red-tiled roofs inspired by the rural Italian architectural style.

Majors and Degrees

CU-Boulder offers the following undergraduate majors: aerospace engineering; anthropology; applied mathematics; architectural engineering; art and art history–art history; art and art history–studio arts; Asian studies; astronomy; biochemistry; business-accounting; business-finance; business-management; business-marketing; business-operations and information management; chemical and biological engineering; chemical engineering; chemistry; Chinese; civil engineering; classics; communication; computer science; dance; ecology and evolutionary biology; economics; electrical and computer engineering; electrical engineering; engineering physics; English; environmental design–architecture; environmental design–design studies; environmental design–planning; environmental engineering; environmental studies; ethnic studies; film studies; French; geography; geology; Germanic studies; history; humanities; integrative physiology; international affairs; Italian; Japanese; journalism-advertising; journalism–broadcast news; journalism–broadcast production; journalism–media studies; journalism-news/editorial; linguistics; mathematics; mechanical engineering; molecular, cellular, and developmental biology; music; music–arts in music; music education; philosophy; physics; political science; psychology; religious studies; Russian studies; sociology; Spanish; speech, language, and hearing sciences; theater; and women's studies.

The following bachelor's degrees are offered: B.A., B.Envd., B.F.A., B.Mus., B.Mus.Ed., and B.S.

Concurrent bachelor's and master's degree programs are available in the following areas: applied mathematics, business (accounting, finance/accounting, operations and information management/accounting, operations and information management/telecommunications), classics, cognitive psychology, East Asian languages and civilizations (Chinese, Japanese), ecology and evolutionary biology, engineering physics/physics, film studies/art history, French, Germanic studies/German, integrative physiology, linguistics, mathematics, physics, religious studies, and in all engineering departments, including aerospace, architectural, chemical, civil, computer science, electrical, electrical and computer, environmental, and mechanical.

Academic Programs

The mission of the University of Colorado Boulder is to educate undergraduate and graduate students in the accumulated knowledge of humankind, discover new knowledge through research and creative work, and foster critical thought, artistic creativity, professional competence, and responsible citizenship. Depending on their degree program, students may be required to complete 120 or 128 (engineering) semester hours for graduation. CU-Boulder offers a very flexible curriculum. Students may graduate with more than one major and with two different degrees from different colleges. Minors also are offered in arts and sciences, business, and engineering. The College of Arts and Sciences and the College of Engineering and Applied Science offer a four-year graduation guarantee, providing specific requirements are met. Advising for preprofessional study in health sciences (e.g., medicine, dentistry, pharmacy) and law is available through the PreProfessional Advising Center. Students can receive information about course requirements, test deadlines, enrollment limitations, and discuss other concerns about professional study.

CU-Boulder operates on a two-semester academic calendar. The fall semester begins in late August, and the spring semester begins in early January. Summer Session lasts ten weeks; courses meeting for shorter periods (one to four, five, or eight weeks) are scheduled during the ten-week session.

Off-Campus Programs

CU-Boulder sponsors more than 270 study-abroad programs each year. Programs are offered on six continents in seventy countries, including Australia, Costa Rica, Denmark, Egypt, England, France, Germany, Hungary, Japan, Mexico, and the Russian Federation. About twenty-five percent of CU-Boulder students have studied abroad by the time they graduate.

Academic Facilities

The University library system consists of more than 3.9 million volumes, nearly 7 million titles on microform, more than 55,000 periodical subscriptions, and more than a million video, graphic, and audio titles. The libraries system includes a main library and five branch libraries: business, earth sciences, engineering, math-physics, and music. There is also a law library.

Other facilities and resources include a planetarium and observatory, a natural history museum, extensive computing resources, a state-of-the-art foreign language technology center, a concert hall, four indoor theaters, and one outdoor theater. The Integrated Teaching and Learning Laboratory and the Discovery Learning Center provide hands-on, real-world experience to engineering undergraduates.

Recent additions to the campus include the Center for Community, the home to twelve student-support offices, including the Office of International Education, Disability Services, Counseling and Psychological Services, and the Center for Multicultural Affairs, as well as a 900-seat street-market-style dining hall; a new humanities building, equipped with smart classrooms; a new visual arts facility; and the Alliance for Technology, Learning, and Society (ATLAS) Center. ATLAS was established in 1997 with the goal of integrating information technology with all disciplines, people, and communities.

Costs

Tuition rates vary by school and college. For 2010–11, annual expenses for Colorado residents who were undergraduate students in the College of Arts and Sciences totaled $21,052 ($8511 for tuition and fees, $10,792 for room and board, and an estimated $1749 for books and supplies). Nonresident tuition and fees were $29,100.

Financial Aid

More than half of Boulder undergraduate students receive some type of financial assistance, totaling more than $215 million in awards. Students receive aid in the form of grants, loans, work-study awards, and scholarships. Funding is provided from federal, state, University, and private sources. All students applying for need-based financial aid are required to submit the Free Application for Federal Student Aid (FAFSA). Application forms are available from high school and community college counselors, the CU-Boulder Office of Financial Aid, and online. The priority processing date is April 1. Students may apply for CU-Boulder scholarships online by March 1. For students applying for scholarships that have a financial need requirement, results of the FAFSA must be on file in the financial aid office on March 1. Students may also obtain loans directly from the Office of Financial Aid rather than from a private lender.

Faculty

Approximately 1,400 full-time instructional faculty members teach undergraduate and graduate courses. The faculty includes nationally and internationally recognized scholars with many academic honors and awards. Tom Cech, distinguished professor of chemistry and biochemistry, shared the 1989 Nobel Prize in chemistry with Sidney Altman of Yale University. Carl Wieman (also U.S. 2004 Professor of the Year) and Eric Cornell won the 2001 Nobel Prize in physics for their creation of a new state of matter, just above absolute zero. John Hall shared the 2005 Nobel Prize in physics with Theodor W. Hänsch of the Max Planck Institute for Quantum Optics and the Ludwig Maximilians University in Munich, Germany and Roy J. Glauber of Harvard University. Kristi Anseth, professor of chemical and biological engineering, is a national leader in the study of biomaterials and is considered by many to be the pioneer in the field of tissue engineering. Her work includes developing new techniques and materials that aid in the healing of bones and cartilage. Seven faculty members have received MacArthur Fellowships, known as the "genius grant," the most recent two being in linguistics (2002) and physics (2003).

Student Government

One of the most influential student governments in the nation, the University of Colorado Student Government (CUSG) administers an operating budget of $30 million. CUSG student leaders and volunteers, working with the University staff, make policy decisions concerning the operation of the University Memorial Center, Student Recreation Center, Wardenburg Health Center, cultural events, the campus radio station, and other programs. Student fees and student-generated revenue support all of these activities. The student government also takes an active role in advocating student concerns.

Admission Requirements

Many factors are considered by the University in making admission decisions. Previous academic achievement, the quality of courses taken, GPA, college entrance test scores, the trend in grades, the extent to which the applicant has completed the recommended high school curriculum, the two required personal essays, and letters of recommendation are all considered. About 25 percent of the freshman class typically ranks in the top 10 percent of their high school graduating class. In fall 2010, 56 percent of the freshmen were Colorado residents. The University seeks to enroll students from a wide range of ethnic, cultural, economic, geographic, and educational backgrounds. The application is available online, either as an interactive Web application or as a downloadable, printable PDF.

Application and Information

Beginning in August, students may submit an application for admission to the spring, summer, or fall term. Spring applicants are processed on a rolling basis. CU-Boulder begins notifying spring applicants about admission decisions in October. Decisions are made approximately four to six weeks after an application is complete. Full consideration is given to applications that are complete (including the application fee and all required credentials) by the October 1 spring deadline.

Freshman applications for summer and fall terms are processed as either early notification applications or as regular decision applications. Applicants who submit the online application and postmark all supporting credentials by the December 1 deadline are considered early notification applicants. Early notification applicants will be reviewed first and are notified of their initial decision on or before January 15. Early notification candidates may be offered admission, denied admission, or deferred to the regular decision process for further consideration. Applicants who are deferred to the regular decision applicant pool should submit mid-year senior grades and any new test scores and will be notified of a final admission decision on or before April 1. Applicants denied through early notification may not submit additional information and may not reapply under the regular decision process. Early notification applicants are not required to enroll at CU-Boulder if they are admitted. Admitted students who choose to attend must confirm their intent to enroll by May 1.

Freshman summer and fall applicants who do not complete their applications by the December 1 early notification deadline must submit the online application and postmark all supporting documents by the January 15 regular decision deadline. Regular decision applicants will be notified of their admission decision on or before April 1 and must, if they choose to attend, confirm their intent to enroll by May 1.

Summer and fall applications for transfer students are processed on a rolling basis, with full consideration given to transfer applications completed by the April 1 deadline.

For information and applications, students should contact:

Office of Admissions
University of Colorado Boulder
552 UCB
Boulder, Colorado 80309-0552
Phone: 303-492-6301
       303-492-5998 (TTY)
Web site: http://www.colorado.edu
      http://admissions.colorado.edu/undergraduate/apply
      http://on.fb.me/cuboulder (Facebook)
      http://twitter.com/mycuboulder (Twitter)

The University of Colorado Boulder is a major research and teaching university located in one of the most spectacular environments in the country, at the foot of the Rocky Mountains.

UNIVERSITY OF DENVER

DENVER, COLORADO

UNIVERSITY OF
DENVER

The University

Since its founding in 1864, the University of Denver (DU) has grown into one of the West's premier private universities, blending the friendliness and personal attention of a small college with the resources and intellectual diversity of an advanced research institution.

As the oldest private university in the Rocky Mountain region, the University is home not only to a top-ranked undergraduate program but also to a number of world-renowned research centers and professional programs, including the Josef Korbel School of International Studies, the Sturm College of Law, and the Daniels College of Business.

The 125-acre campus brings together 4,878 traditional undergraduate students and 6,301 graduate students from fifty states and seventy-four countries. In an environment that prizes innovation, cross-disciplinary exploration, and adventurous learning partnerships between students and faculty, DU students prepare to excel in their life's work and to confront today's great issues.

Whatever their backgrounds and majors, DU students are engaged and active, taking advantage of the region's many recreation and cultural opportunities—everything from world-class skiing and white-water rafting to award-winning professional theater and alternative music. On campus, students attend performances at the three-venue Newman Center for the Performing Arts and cheer for the seventeen varsity teams that compete in NCAA Division I at the Ritchie Center for Sports & Wellness.

The University of Denver is accredited by the North Central Association of Colleges and Schools. The Carnegie Foundation classifies the University of Denver as a Doctoral/Research University–Extensive.

Location

Located just 8 miles from bustling downtown Denver and mere minutes from the Rocky Mountain foothills, the University of Denver's tree-shaded campus is surrounded by pleasant urban neighborhoods offering coffee shops, retail stores, and diverse restaurants. The institution is located along a light rail line and major bus lines, providing access to the city's arts districts, shopping centers, sports arenas, and an extensive network of parks. DU students can ride all public transportation for free, using their University-supplied Eco-passes.

Majors and Degrees

The University of Denver offers twelve bachelor's degrees in over 100 programs of study, including the arts, business, computer science, engineering, humanities, international studies, mathematics, natural sciences, and social sciences. Students who are interested in preprofessional programs can choose from law, medical, dental, and veterinary programs that prepare them for professional study beyond their undergraduate degree.

In addition, the University offers 4+1 and 3+2 dual-degree programs that allow students to complete both a bachelor's and master's degree in five years or less. These dual-degree programs are offered in business, art history, international studies, public policy, and natural sciences, among others. Students in dual-degree programs maintain any financial aid and scholarships they have been awarded through their fifth year of study.

Academic Programs

Undergraduate programs at the University—which operates on the quarter system—emphasize experiential, active, and cross-disciplinary learning. All first-year undergraduate students are required to have laptop computers, which are used extensively in the classroom. DU students use their laptops as portable libraries and

laboratories, extending their educational reach well beyond the classroom walls. The entire campus provides wireless Internet access through a secure connection. This includes classrooms, social areas, and even the campus greens.

First-year students enroll in a first-year seminar. Generally limited to 15 students, these seminars focus on a topic that reflects the professor's research interests. The professor, who serves as a mentor throughout the student's first year, introduces the class to university-level work and inquiry, while also advising students on everything from time management to University procedures. The seminar is complemented by a two-quarter writing sequence that trains students to conduct research, construct arguments, and write persuasively for the academic setting. The University's emphasis on writing continues throughout the next three years, with upper-division writing-intensive classes across the disciplines. By the time they graduate, DU students have developed the communication skills that are essential for career success.

Undergraduate students also complete foundations courses in mathematics and computer science, the arts and humanities, natural sciences, and social sciences. DU's common curriculum ensures that students have a wide base of knowledge upon graduation.

Because the University believes in the value of hands-on learning, students are encouraged to collaborate with faculty members and peers on research projects and creative endeavors. Through the Partners in Scholarship (PinS) program, the University sponsors student work through grants that fund field studies, research trips, and special materials. At year's end, students share their research and findings at a special symposium for their peers.

Thanks to opportunities like these, the University's academic programs earn high marks from students. In the 2008 National Survey of Student Engagement, a study of student satisfaction at 774 colleges and universities nationwide, first-year students and seniors at DU ranked it significantly higher than other participating doctoral-extensive schools in their appraisal of their level of academic challenge, their involvement in active and collaborative learning, their interaction with faculty members, and their enriching educational experiences.

Off-Campus Programs

To groom students for the challenges of global citizenship, the University of Denver sponsors Cherrington Global Scholars, a for-credit program that aims to send every eligible junior and senior abroad for at least a quarter of study. The University believes so strongly in this opportunity to expand understanding and foster connections that it ensures that qualifying students pay no more for the experience than they would for a quarter spent on campus. The University budgets about $10 million each year in support of this outstanding program. Nearly 75 percent of all DU students participate in study-abroad programs, the third highest percentage in the nation.

Academic Facilities

In the last decade, the University has invested nearly $500 million in new buildings and learning centers to ensure that students can prepare for the challenges awaiting them after graduation. These include the Robert and Judi Newman Center for the Performing Arts, home to the University's celebrated Lamont School of Music and host to a performing arts series known for its adventurous offerings; the Daniels College of Business, which houses eleven case-style meeting rooms, nine seminar classrooms, and an Advanced Technology Center; the School of Hotel, Restaurant and Tourism Management, home to a full-production kitchen, a beverage-management center, a 120-person dining hall, a student-run coffee shop, and a student-faculty-staff commons; F. W. Olin Hall, which houses ten teaching labs, a greenhouse, and a full complement of classrooms and group study rooms; and the recently remodeled

Sturm Hall, complete with multimedia labs and smart-to-the-seat classrooms, which serves as the headquarters for the humanities and social sciences.

Other new facilities support the University's commitment to community living and wellness, such as the Nelson Residence Hall which features suites, common kitchens on each floor, a central courtyard, a grand dining hall, and an outdoor dining patio. The Ritchie Center for Sports and Wellness brings students and members of the Denver community together to work out, try new sports, and watch the Pioneer athletic teams. With a state-of-the-art fitness center, a natatorium, a field house, two ice arenas, a gymnastics venue, a lacrosse stadium, a newly remodeled soccer stadium, and a tennis pavilion, the Ritchie Center complex supports the active lifestyle that DU students value.

Nagel Residence Hall, which opened in August 2008, serves as a campus gathering place, welcoming students and faculty at its food court, providing numerous locations for group study sessions, and offering studio space for students wanting to explore their artistic side. In keeping with the University's far-reaching sustainability initiative, the green building is LEED certified, meaning it uses key resources more efficiently than conventional buildings.

The University recently completed construction on a spectacular new home for both the Morgridge College of Education and the Marsico Institute for Early Learning and Literacy. The influential institute serves as a regional and national hub for research and policy analysis on issues related to improving learning environments for young children.

The University is also home to the full-service Penrose Library whose special collections contain rare books and manuscripts as well as the Beck Archives of the Rocky Mountain Jewish Historical Society and the Carson-Brierly Dance Library.

Costs

For the 2010–11 academic year, tuition was $35,604, fees were estimated at $897, and on-campus room and board costs were $10,224—for a total cost of $46,725. Because the University of Denver is a private institution, costs are the same for in-state and out-of-state students.

Financial Aid

The University of Denver offers two types of financial assistance to students: need-based aid, which includes scholarships, grants, loans, and work-study based on financial need; and merit-based awards, which include scholarships based on merit or special talent. Each year, the financial aid office awards over $90 million in need- and merit-based assistance to undergraduate students. About 40 percent of full-time DU undergraduates demonstrate financial need and receive some form of need-based assistance.

To recognize achievement in the classroom, the sports arena, leadership, and in music, theater, and art, the University sponsors a number of merit-based scholarships—several of which cover full tuition. Although the requirements vary from scholarship to scholarship, most are renewable each year if the student maintains a specified minimum GPA. A complete listing of scholarships is posted at http://www.du.edu/finaid/.

Need-based financial aid is computed using a number of factors, including family income, assets, size, and the number of family members attending college at the same time. DU utilizes both the CSS Profile and the Free Application for Federal Student Aid (FAFSA) to determine need-based aid. Need-based awards generally combine scholarships, grants, loans, and work-study opportunities from a variety of federal, state, and institutional sources. The financial aid offer may also include any competitive scholarships the student has been awarded at the point of admission.

The priority deadline for applying for financial aid is March 1. Because financial aid funds are limited, students who complete their financial aid applications in a timely manner are more likely to maximize financial aid resources. Funding for certain awards may not be available as time passes. The student's financial aid package cannot be determined until he or she is officially admitted to DU.

For more information on applying for financial aid at DU, students should visit http://www.du.edu/finaid.

Faculty

DU professors teach 95 percent of undergraduate courses, ensuring that students work closely with the faculty members and that the intensity of the learning environment is maximized. The average class size is 21 students; 63 percent of undergraduate classes have fewer than 20 students and 96 percent of classes have fewer than 50 students.

Committed teachers, innovative researchers, and prolific publishers, University of Denver professors often include undergraduate students in their research projects and fieldwork. It is not uncommon for an undergraduate student to share publication credit with a professor or to participate in groundbreaking research with tangible benefits for humankind.

Student Government

At the University of Denver, the student population is represented by the Undergraduate Student Government (USG), whose elected representatives participate in the University's legislative process and communicate student issues to the administration. In addition, the USG oversees the allocation of the student activities fee and the licensing of DU's 100-plus student organizations.

The USG includes senators from each major, each geographic area (on-campus, off-campus), and each class (senior, junior, etc.). The USG Executive Board includes an adviser, graduate adviser, president, vice president, and a cabinet of members.

Admission Requirements

Admission to the University of Denver is selective. Students are evaluated individually on the basis of their academic record, test scores, essay, and recommendations.

In making its admission decisions, the University seeks to foster an academic community of geographically, ethnically, and economically diverse learners. The admission committee looks for students who are committed to integrity, innovation, inclusiveness, excellence, and community engagement.

Applicants are required to submit either the Common Application or the DU Pioneer Application, both of which are posted on the DU Web site. In addition, applicants are required to submit their high school transcripts, scores from either the SAT or ACT (DU uses the superscore system), an essay, and a high school counselor recommendation. Students may also submit a teacher recommendation, although it is not required.

Applicants are also strongly encouraged to participate in the Ammi Hyde Interview, a face-to-face 20-minute conversation with as many as 3 members of the University community. Interviews are conducted in over thirty major cities across the country in November and January and on campus throughout the year.

Application and Information

The University of Denver offers two application programs for first-year domestic students seeking fall-quarter admission. Early action (postmarked by November 1) is a nonbinding program leading to an admission decision in early January. Hyde Interviews for early action applicants are conducted in November. Regular decision (postmarked by January 15), also nonbinding, is the final admission deadline for fall-quarter consideration. Hyde Interviews for this option are conducted in January. Admission decisions are mailed in mid-March.

To learn more about the University of Denver, students should contact:

Office of Admission
University of Denver
2197 South University Boulevard
Denver, Colorado 80208-9401
Phone: 303-871-2036
        800-525-9495 (toll-free)
E-mail: admission@du.edu
Web site: http://www.du.edu/admission
          http://www.du.edu/apply/admission/index.html
          http://du.ctpprojects.com (videos)
          http://www.facebook.com/uofdenveradmission
          http://twitter.com/uofdenver

UNIVERSITY OF DUBUQUE
DUBUQUE, IOWA

The University

The University of Dubuque (UD) is a private, Presbyterian, professional university with a focus in the liberal arts, as well as a theological seminary located in Iowa's first city—Dubuque. The Key City is on the Mississippi River at the point where the borders of Wisconsin, Illinois, and Iowa meet. Founded in 1852, the University offers programs in the undergraduate and graduate college and in the graduate theological seminary. The University's mission of encouraging intellectual, moral, and spiritual development dates back to its founding.

Throughout its history, the University has been known as a place of educational opportunity. Even today, a large portion of its students are from first-generation or underrepresented populations. The University of Dubuque's welcoming interfaith community of approximately 1,600 students comes from across the country and around the globe.

Because students from many nations attend the University of Dubuque, UD offers students a cosmopolitan atmosphere. The school is convinced that students living in today's world are better prepared for life if they have a global perspective. American and international student interaction on campus, as well as the movement of faculty members and students across international boundaries, is essential for a meaningful education, human enrichment, and intercultural global awareness.

Location

The University of Dubuque's scenic 77-acre campus, located in eastern Iowa, is in the heart of the Midwest. Dubuque is a city for all seasons. From bluffs blazing with autumn oranges and reds to the river sparkling with summer's blues and greens, the area scenery is spectacular year-round. Dubuque, the oldest city in Iowa, is a dynamic community built along the majestic Mississippi River and surrounded by dramatic bluffs. The setting is ideal for outdoor enthusiasts, with four seasons of ample outlets for recreation, including hiking, biking, boating, skiing, camping, golfing, climbing, and caving.

Dubuque offers the amenities of a larger city with the security and comfort of a smaller town. A lively cultural scene includes the Grand Opera House, the Dubuque Symphony Orchestra, and the Dubuque Museum of Art. The National Mississippi River Museum and Aquarium and the National Farm Toy Museum provide glimpses of the area's past. The city's theater productions, boutiques, and restaurants are wonderful ways to take a study break.

Nearby are some of the Midwest's most interesting cities, an easy drive for a weekend road trip. Historic Galena offers quaint shops and period architecture, while vibrant Chicago is famous for its museums and night life. Madison, Milwaukee, and Minneapolis-St. Paul are only hours away.

Majors and Degrees

With nineteen undergraduate majors, the University prepares students for careers in a variety of fields. From future teachers to corporate leaders to aspiring pilots, the University of Dubuque helps students achieve their career goals. The University's education department has the most majors, and its future teachers graduate with twice as many field-experience hours as required by the state of Iowa.

The University' Nursing Program was reinstated in the fall 2004 semester. The program offers a Bachelor of Science in Nursing (B.S.N.) degree. Nursing began at University of Dubuque in 1976 and, until 1997, the program offered fully accredited RN-to-B.S.N., B.S.N., and M.S.N. nursing preparation. The University has been granted interim approval by the Iowa Board of Nursing and is accredited by the American Association of Colleges of Nursing.

Academic departments encourage internships as an experiential component to complement classroom learning. For example, environmental science majors take advantage of the natural classroom of the Mississippi River, where students study the interaction between people and the environment. Aviation majors complete internships at the Dubuque Regional Airport or major airlines in addition to flying state-of-the-art equipment from UD's Garlick Flight Operations Center.

Academic Programs

The University of Dubuque education aims at helping students develop patterns of scholarship that make them effective learners throughout life. UD students are nurtured in the virtues of scholarship: the desire for understanding different peoples and cultures, an interest in learning, the skills to use multiple resources to explore ideas and find answers for life's questions, an understanding of conceptual connections, and the ability to reason and communicate effectively. Each graduate develops depth of knowledge in a particular field of study based on an integration of this field, the liberal arts, and his or her values.

University of Dubuque students begin to understand their chosen field of study by experiencing how it relates to other areas of knowledge. The process of exploring a variety of interests and possibilities in course work and in University activities results in the choice of a major. Current trends indicate that today's graduates change jobs and/or careers several times during their lifetimes. Therefore, professional preparation is more than a narrow, vocationally oriented process through which students prepare for one specific job. Rather, it is the development of transferable skills and attributes that allow students to succeed in a changing job market.

In the University of Dubuque community, the arts foster intellectual, emotional, and spiritual development. In literature, the visual arts, dance, drama, and music, students not only find aesthetic pleasure but also learn about other people's ideas, beliefs, and experiences and come to deeper understandings of their own.

Because of the University's location near the Mississippi—one of the world's great river systems—students have an appreciation of environmental issues. Through academic endeavors involving formal and experiential learning, students develop an understanding of the basic processes that underpin various ecological communities and of the complex interaction of human activities on the environment. The University of Dubuque encourages individuals to integrate their knowledge of the environment into personal, ethical, and spiritual guidelines, which can be used to improve their lives, their communities, and society.

The Lester G. and Michael Lester Wendt Character Initiative, supported by a substantial endowment, integrates virtues and values such as truthfulness, honesty, fairness, and the Golden Rule across the curriculum and throughout the University.

The University's Learning Institute for Fulfillment and Engagement (LIFE) offers an accelerated baccalaureate degree program for adult learners. Geared to adult learners age 23 and over, the UD LIFE program is designed to offer a flexible format, allowing students to earn a bachelor's degree in as few as three years and a master's degree in as few as eighteen months. Offering classes on weekday evenings as well as online, the program helps adults balance their studies, career, and family life.

Off-Campus Programs

As a member of the Dubuque Tri-College Cooperative Effort, the University of Dubuque offers its students the opportunity to attend and receive credit for courses at Clarke College and Loras College, also in the city, thus providing access to the many different faculty members, professional societies, educational opportunities, and social activities of combined campuses of more than 3,500 students.

The University of Dubuque affirms the value of an international/intercultural experience and considers it to be an important component of any student's education. Overseas travel, exchanges, and study programs are available to help increase the global perspective of the students and to promote cross-cultural education.

Academic Facilities

The expanded and renovated University Science Center opened for classes in January 2007. With an additional 21,000 square feet of space, the University can devote the proper resources to its growing science programs. The new facility accommodates efficient laboratories, including state-of-the-art equipment and safety measures, bringing the science programs to the forefront of current teaching methods. Laboratory spaces include geology, zoology, general biology, cell/microbiology, science education, nursing, general chemistry, organic chemistry, geographic information systems (GIS), and five research labs to accommodate student-faculty collaborative research projects.

The Charles and Romana Myers Center, completed in September 2006, has added much-needed classroom and office space to the campus. Designed to be light, airy, and conducive to teaching and learning, the 44,000-square-foot facility houses classrooms, group study rooms, a seminar room, informal study nooks, and a 132-seat auditorium as well as administrative and faculty offices. The President's Office and the Wendt Center for Character Development are located in the building.

The Chlapaty Recreation and Wellness Center, which opened in October 2008, is an 87,000-square-foot facility enveloping the existing football stadium as well as additional construction looking west. Features include a 6,900-square-foot, two-level fitness center, including areas for cardiovascular workout and free weights/machines, as well as a room for activities such as pilates, yoga, etc.; a 200-meter, six-lane indoor track with synthetic flooring for fitness walking and performance; four multiuse courts nested in the center of the track for intramurals and indoor practices; a training room and examination rooms; home, visitor, officials, and faculty/staff locker rooms; a juice bar and lounge area; a 3,000-seat football stadium, including east side visitor seating for 1,000 and an expanded concessions area; and a lighted field, synthetic field turf surface, and new eight-lane outdoor track.

Costs

Tuition costs for the 2010–11 academic year were $21,000. Average room and board costs were $7370. These costs do not include books, supplies, personal expenses, and travel.

Financial Aid

Eighty-five percent of the University of Dubuque's students receive financial assistance through scholarships, awards and grants, loans, or work-study programs. The average financial assistance package for 2009–10 was $18,951. All levels of household incomes receive financial assistance.

To apply for financial assistance, applicants must submit a completed application package for admission to the University of Dubuque, file a FAFSA after January 1 and before April 1 (the priority deadline), and send or fax a copy of the completed FAFSA to the University of Dubuque Office of Student Financial Planning. Institutional, federal, state, and alternative loan programs are all available as forms of financial assistance.

Faculty

Seventy percent of University of Dubuque faculty members have earned a Ph.D. or other terminal degree. The student-faculty ratio is 15:1.

Student Government

The Student Government Association (SGA) represents the student body through general election of individual student representatives. The SGA sponsors four campus organizations, the University Program Council (UPC), the Spartan Spirit Club, *Under The Bell Tower* (student newspaper), and *The Key* (student yearbook). SGA provides student representatives for a number of key administrative committees.

Admission Requirements

An applicant for admission to the University of Dubuque undergraduate program is a graduate of a high school or equivalent (GED) and presents a minimum of 15 high school units, of which 10 are from academic fields (English, social studies, natural science, mathematics, foreign language). Either ACT or SAT scores are required. The admission committee looks at the application and transcript for indications of school achievement as well as aspiration, creativity, and adventurousness. Applicants to the University are usually active in cocurricular activities and these, as well as leadership qualities and character, are considered. An on-campus visit is encouraged. Two recommendations and an essay are requested and read with care.

Application and Information

First-year students are admitted to the University on a rolling basis. When the application and all supporting materials (e.g., transcripts and teacher and counselor recommendations) have been received, admission decisions are made by the admission committee and students are advised of the University's decision.

Transfer students who are enrolled or who were previously enrolled at another college or university may apply for transfer to the University of Dubuque. The University considers transfer applications for fall and spring semesters.

In addition to completing the application materials required for first-year applicants, transfer applicants must submit a complete official transcript for all college courses taken and grades received and a complete official transcript for all secondary school courses taken and grades received.

For further information, students should contact:

Office of Admission
University of Dubuque
2000 University Avenue
Dubuque, Iowa 52001
Phone: 563-589-3000
   800-722-5583 (toll-free)
E-mail: admssns@dbq.edu
Web site: http://www.dbq.edu

The University Science Center provides a handsome environment for exploration and discovery in an atmosphere conducive to today's interactive, interdisciplinary, hands-on learning styles.

THE UNIVERSITY OF FINDLAY

FINDLAY, OHIO

The University

The University of Findlay (UF) is a private coeducational institution with more than 3,900 full- and part-time students. Founded in 1882 by the Churches of God, General Conference, and the citizens of Findlay, it emphasizes preparation for careers and professions in an educational program that blends liberal arts and career education. Service is a priority at Findlay, with new students spending a half-day volunteering in the community before they even begin classes. In 2010, the University was named to the President's Higher Education Community Service Honor Roll for exemplary service efforts to America's communities for the second consecutive year.

Bachelor's degree programs are available in nearly sixty different majors. Master's degrees are offered in athletic training; business administration; education; environmental, safety, and health management; occupational therapy; physician assistant studies; and teaching English to speakers of other languages (TESOL) and bilingual education. A Doctor of Pharmacy (Pharm.D.) degree program graduated its first class in 2010, and a Doctor of Physical Therapy program is scheduled to graduate its first students in 2011.

The largest programs at Findlay are animal science/pre–veterinary medicine, equestrian studies, pharmacy, business administration, and education. Majors in the sciences and health professions include athletic training, chemistry, computer science, equestrian studies (English, Western, and equine business management), nuclear medicine, occupational therapy, physical therapy, and animal science/pre–veterinary medicine. Business degrees are founded in a comprehensive core program with eleven different majors.

Opportunities for internships and work-related experiences are available in most major fields.

Most of Findlay's students come from Ohio and the surrounding states of Michigan, Indiana, and Pennsylvania. More than thirty other states are also represented. UF also has a strong international-student population, with more than 370 international students from twenty-five countries and territories.

Resident students live in eight modern residence halls and several town-house-style apartments. Social life at Findlay centers on student organizations, fraternities, and sororities. Findlay has three officially recognized fraternities: Alpha Sigma Phi, Tau Kappa Epsilon, and Theta Chi; there are two sororities: Phi Sigma Sigma and Sigma Kappa. Organizations include department and special interest clubs, the newspaper, musical groups, a radio and TV station, Circle K, and Aristos Eklektos (honors).

Athletic programs are affiliated with NCAA Division II and the Great Lakes Intercollegiate Athletic Conference, with the exception of the equestrian teams, which have won national championships in the Intercollegiate Horse Show Association. Findlay offers twelve intercollegiate sports for men: baseball, basketball, cross-country, equestrian, football, golf, indoor track and field, outdoor track and field, soccer, swimming and diving, tennis, and wrestling. It has eleven varsity sports for women: basketball, cross-country, equestrian, golf, indoor track and field, outdoor track and field, soccer, softball, swimming and diving, tennis, and volleyball. Athletic scholarships are available.

Croy Physical Education Center has a 25-meter swimming pool, a gymnasium, offices, and classrooms. The Gardner Fitness Center is a state-of-the-art facility. The 130,000-square-foot Koehler Recreation and Fitness Complex, opened in 1999, contains the Malcolm Athletic Center, with a six-lane, NCAA-regulation track; sand pits for long jump; state-of-the-art timing system; wrestling room; four multipurpose courts; locker rooms; and offices for the athletic department. Also under the same roof are a cardio center, which serves an average of 500 patrons a day during the winter months, and a new student recreation center with basketball, volleyball, and tennis courts, a rock-climbing wall, a game room, and more.

Student services include career and placement counseling, the Cosiano Health Center, academic tutoring and personal counseling, and study skills assistance through the Academic Support Center.

Location

Findlay was voted the most livable micropolitan city in Ohio and scored among the top twelve in the United States. It is within easy driving distance of Toledo, Columbus, Detroit, and Fort Wayne. Interstate 75 and the Ohio Turnpike (Interstates 80 and 90) are major highways serving the area. Airports in Toledo, Columbus, and Detroit are convenient. The town of Findlay has more than 39,000 residents and is home to Marathon Oil Corporation and Cooper Tire and Rubber Company. The Findlay campus consists of more than 385 acres on several sites. A 152-acre campus-owned farm houses the pre–veterinary medicine and Western equestrian studies programs, including a 31,000-square-foot animal science center dedicated in 2009 with two 50-seat classrooms, a laboratory, a pharmacy, a student lounge, locker rooms, offices, instructional demonstration areas, holding pens, and other animal servicing areas. A second 32-acre facility houses the English riding program. Approximately 450 horses are stabled and trained at the equestrian facilities, which offer barns and indoor and outdoor riding arenas.

Many opportunities exist for students who want business-related and social service agency experience. The University has established strong relationships with the community, which supports athletic and cultural events on the campus. Besides the full program of on-campus activities, off-campus trips to cultural and entertainment events are scheduled. The city of Findlay, which has an excellent business climate, offers part-time job opportunities, volunteer service organizations, and the chance to be involved with the larger civic community. Findlay's campus is attractive, safe, comfortable, and friendly.

Majors and Degrees

The Bachelor of Arts (B.A.) degree is awarded in the following majors: adolescent/young adult/integrated English/language arts, adolescent/young adult/integrated social studies, art, art management, children's book illustration, criminal justice, digital media, English, English as an international language, graphic design, health communication, history, Japanese, journalism, law and the liberal arts, middle childhood/language arts/social studies, multiage/drama/theater, multiage/Japanese, multiage/Spanish, multiage/visual arts, organizational communication, philosophy/applied philosophy, political science, psychology, public relations, religious studies, social work, sociology, Spanish, studio art, teaching English to speakers of other languages, and theater. Minors are offered in numerous areas.

The Bachelor of Science (B.S.) degree is granted in accounting; adolescent/young adult/earth science; adolescent/young adult/integrated mathematics; adolescent/young adult/life science; animal science; biology (recommended for those interested in physician assistant or medical studies); business administration; business management; chemistry (recommended for those interested in medical studies); computer science; early childhood; economics; entrepreneurship; environmental, safety, and occupational health management; equestrian studies (English and Western emphases); equine business management; finance; forensic science; health education; health science (in preparation for occupational therapy or physical therapy); health studies; hospitality management; human resource management; international business; intervention specialist/mild to moderate disabilities; marketing; mathematics; medical technology; middle childhood/language arts/math; middle childhood/language arts/science; middle childhood/math/science; middle childhood/math/social studies; middle childhood/science/social studies; multiage/health education; multiage/physical education; nuclear medicine technology; operations and logistics; physical education; and strength and conditioning.

The Associate of Arts degree is available in accounting, computer science, criminal justice administration (corrections or law enforcement emphases), English as an international language, equestrian studies (English and Western riding), financial management, general social studies, human resource management, humanities, management information systems, massage therapy, nuclear medicine technology, personal training, religious studies, sales/retail management, and small business/entrepreneurship. Certificate programs are available in a variety of areas.

Academic Programs

Findlay operates on the semester system. Students must complete at least 124 semester hours with a minimum overall grade point average of 2.0 to earn a bachelor's degree. General education requirements and competency requirements in English, computer literacy, and speech must be fulfilled. The Gateway Program offers students the chance to develop those skills in writing, reading, and thinking needed for their success as college students. Study skills, time management, and academic advising are included. Students are selected for this program at the time of admission. The Honors Program provides additional challenge to those students who qualify on the basis of academic credentials. Study- and travel-abroad programs are offered by various departments. Credit and/or placement can be earned through Advanced Placement (AP) exams.

The Equestrian Program is a well-recognized program of its kind and serves approximately 280 students from throughout the United States and abroad. Majors in equine business management and in English and Western riding are offered. The instruction, both in the classroom and on horseback, makes use of the expertise of recognized national equestrian champions. The pre–veterinary medicine program, using the farm facilities, offers the advantages of hands-on experience with livestock and an internship program in a distinctive curriculum. Graduates of the pre–veterinary program have been accepted to all twenty-eight veterinary schools in the United States, and several internationally.

The Nuclear Medicine Institute provides the training necessary to qualify students for careers in nuclear medicine technology, a growing health-related career field.

Academic Facilities

The focal point of the Findlay campus is Old Main, which houses classrooms, faculty and administrative offices, the computer center, facilities for various student activities, and the Ritz Auditorium. Shafer Library is a member of a consortium that provides extensive resources to students. The Gardner Fine Arts Pavilion, dedicated in 1994, houses the Mazza Museum of International Art from Children's Books, the first and largest teaching museum in the world dedicated to literacy and children's book art. The University has numerous computer labs. In 2006, the University acquired and renovated a building at 300 Davis St., with its 62,000 square feet comprising the largest addition of academic space since the construction of Old Main. Other academic buildings include the Frost Science Center and the Egner Center for the Performing Arts, which houses a 200-seat theater.

Costs

Tuition for the 2010–11 academic year totaled $26,016 for most programs. Room and board cost $8810. The estimated cost for transportation, books, fees, and supplies was $2496. There are additional tuition charges for equestrian studies and pre–veterinary medicine.

Financial Aid

Assistance is based on need as well as scholastic achievement. In 2010–11, 80 percent of UF students received institutional financial aid from the University. The average need-based financial aid package for freshmen was $20,692 in fall 2010. Merit scholarships at UF range from $9000 to $14,000 a year. Notification of aid awards is made on a rolling basis. Work-study jobs are available. Scholarships for high-achieving students and student athletes are offered.

Faculty

The 15:1 student-faculty ratio results in small classes, with an average class size of 16 students. Professors know their students, and every student has a faculty adviser.

Student Government

The Student Government Association (SGA) and the Campus Program Board are involved in planning and implementing student activities. SGA provides leadership experience for students and enhances cooperation among faculty members, the administration, and students. A representative from SGA sits on the Board of Trustees. The Campus Program Board plans activities for recreation and cultural enrichment.

Admission Requirements

The University of Findlay considers each applicant on an individualized basis. The University accepts applications on a rolling basis, but it encourages students to complete applications by January 15, as the class fills rapidly. Application deadlines are August 1 for the fall semester and December 15 for the spring semester. Major factors associated with rendering a decision include GPA, standardized test scores, and strength of curriculum. Although it is not required, a campus admission visit is encouraged. Applicants to Findlay should have a college-preparatory high school background, including 4 years of English, 3 to 4 years of mathematics, 2 to 3 years of social studies, and 2 years of science. A foreign language is recommended but not required. Results of the ACT or SAT should be submitted with the application for admission. Transfer students must be eligible to return to the institution last attended and must submit transcripts of all college work. For students not meeting regular minimum admission requirements, Findlay has a Gateway Program, which provides skill building and academic support during the first semester of the freshman year. Findlay is an equal opportunity institution in admission and employment.

Application and Information

For application forms and other information, students may contact:

Office of Undergraduate Admissions
The University of Findlay
1000 North Main Street
Findlay, Ohio 45840
Phone: 419-434-4732
      800-548-0932 (toll-free)
E-mail: admissions@findlay.edu
Web site: http://www.findlay.edu
      http://on.fb.me/UFindlay (Facebook)

Old Main.

UNIVERSITY OF GREAT FALLS

GREAT FALLS, MONTANA

The University

The University of Great Falls is a private, Catholic liberal arts university sponsored by the Sisters of Providence within the jurisdiction of the Catholic Bishop of Great Falls–Billings. The University of Great Falls offers the Corps of Discovery, a distinctive, outside-of-the-classroom, personal-formation program. Students develop their leadership and team abilities through a variety of physical challenges, collaborative efforts, artistic endeavors, and spiritual and service activities.

The University's week-long orientation program and its Corps of Discovery freshman year experience are central to creating a learning community committed to student success, expressed in a commitment to liberal learning for living and making a living, which engages the whole person and the University community in the learning process.

The faculty and staff members of the University join with students in a cooperative and enthusiastic search for truth, meaning, and the analytical skills to resolve moral and ethical dilemmas. The low student-faculty ratio (12:1) equates to more individual attention and help with both academic and personal development. Although faculty members participate in applied research, the focus is on teaching. Because teaching students is the primary concern of faculty members, they combine traditional classroom instruction with education using multimedia computer technology and learning through internships, field experiences, and community service. Students may begin research in their freshman year.

The University was founded in 1932 by Bishop Edwin V. O'Hara to fill the need for an institution of higher education in Great Falls and the central Montana area. The present campus opened in 1960. Providence Tower, the main campus landmark, was constructed in 1964, and McLaughlin Memorial Center, a spacious physical education and recreation facility, was added in 1965. The campus consists of more than a dozen buildings, including Sullivan Hall, Emilie Hall, the DiRocco-Peressini Science Center, a theater/music building, an art building, Galerie Trinitas, Trinitas Chapel, and the library. The library, which was doubled in size in 1999, provides additional study room for students. The University of Great Falls has been accredited by the Northwest Association of Schools and Colleges since 1935.

The University's athletic programs include men's and women's basketball, cross-country, track, golf, soccer, and rodeo; men's wrestling; and women's softball and volleyball. Playing in the Frontier Conference, the Argonauts enhance the community's quality of life and offer student athletes opportunities to be a part of a highly competitive, nationally recognized program. Jason the Argonaut has been the school's mascot since the University of Great Falls started athletic programs in 1967. The chosen mascot stems from Greek mythology and the story of Jason and his band of courageous men, called the Argonauts, in their quest for the Golden Fleece.

Student-life activities abound in the University of Great Falls community. The Argo Café and lounge in the Student Center are a popular socializing and studying place that is central to the campus. The spacious campus offers a year-round setting for student-initiated activities. On a winter day, it is quite common to see students snowboarding on the large hill next to Emilie Hall. On fall and spring days, many students enjoy flag football, Ultimate (Frisbee), FOLF, and, of course, the seasonal water fights and slip 'n' slide. Students also have opportunities throughout the semester to participate in intramural sports, attend community events, and engage in a wide variety of outdoor recreation.

Location

The city of Great Falls is located in north-central Montana. Situated next to the five waterfalls of the Missouri River at an elevation of 3,300 feet, the city lies between the Rocky Mountains and Great Plains. The river, a historically significant waterway explored by the Lewis and Clark Expedition in 1805, provides abundant recreational opportunities such as boating, canoeing, and fishing its blue-ribbon trout waters. Great Falls is also home to the Lewis and Clark National Historic Trail Interpretive Center and the Charlie Russell Museum, which displays the treasured works of the famous Western artist Charles M. Russell. On the museum grounds, sit the Russell home and the artist's log studio. Great Falls exemplifies the Western heritage and ethos of the Big Sky Country of Montana.

Nestled near the Big Belt, Little Belt, and Highwood Mountain Ranges, Great Falls is centrally located in one of the nation's most scenic regions. For skiing enthusiasts, the Little Belt Mountains, an hour south of Great Falls, offer excellent downhill skiing at Showdown Ski Area and 17 miles of groomed cross-country trails at Silver Crest. In addition to skiing, the surrounding area provides extensive outdoor recreational activities, including biking, hiking, camping, technical rock climbing, white-water rafting, archaeological exploration, fishing, and hunting. About an hour west of the city lies the Rocky Mountain Front Range, which extends northward to one of the country's crown jewels, Glacier National Park. The majestic peaks of this area provide outdoor enthusiasts with hundreds of miles of trails and pristine lakes and streams. Four hours to the south of Great Falls is Yellowstone National Park, where abundant herds of bison and elk roam the vast spaces. Many other species of wildlife call Yellowstone home, including the reintroduced wolf.

The central location of Great Falls gives students the opportunity to explore numerous surrounding communities with local attractions and shops.

Majors and Degrees

The University of Great Falls offers forty undergraduate, eight graduate, and four distance learning degrees. Programs are designed for participative learning, supporting the liberal arts core and the preprofessional programs offered by the University.

Academic Programs

The University develops professional/career programs designed to meet society's present and future needs, as well as traditional academic degrees in appropriate fields. As part of the undergraduate core curriculum, students acquire fundamental skills and experiences that facilitate comprehension, information processing, and communication within particular disciplines. Beyond the learning required for their chosen majors, students embark on a path of self-discovery and learn to apply meaning to the world around them from historical, contemporary, and future perspectives.

Students experience deeper learning through the University's Integrated Learning Communities and a core curriculum built on a foundation of four questions: What does it mean to be human? What does it mean to participate in intellectual inquiry? What does it mean to make a living and to live as a productive human being? What does it mean to participate in the spiritual and religious dimensions of life? All students are required to complete courses in communications, composition, computer science, fine arts, history, literature, mathematics, natural science, social sciences, and theology and religion.

As part of the freshman experience, the University of Great Falls offers its Corps of Discovery program. Like the 1804 adventure lead by Captains William Clark and Meriwether Lewis, the Corps of Discovery at the University takes students on an extraordinary journey of adventure, discovery, and accomplishments. It is an opportunity for students to learn outside of the classroom while gaining the skills necessary to be successful academically and professionally. It is a life experience where lessons are learned from the desktop to the mountaintop.

The University of Great Falls serves students of all beliefs while offering a foundation for actively implementing spiritual values and a variety of religious teachings that are rooted in the Catholic tradition. Students are strongly encouraged to complement classroom learning with nonacademic learning in the areas of community service, wellness activities, and cultural arts.

Off-Campus Programs

The distance learning program provides instruction to students throughout the country and around the world, enabling them to complete three undergraduate degrees, three concentrations, three associate degrees, an Army paralegal degree, and three graduate degrees from their home or work. Students may choose, when necessary, to begin their lower-division course work at home and then move to the campus to complete their degree. Distance learning programs have been designed to enhance student/professor involvement and to increase communication between students within a class. Classes are small and use various platforms for different degree programs. The use of different technologies has allowed the University to become a recognized leader in delivering innovative models of education.

Academic Facilities

The University library provides informational resources for students and faculty and staff members. The collection contains more than 106,000 books and 400 journal subscriptions. Services include access to reference materials, interlibrary loan, and more than 50 online databases from InfoTrac, ProQuest, OCLC First Search, and LexisNexis. In addition, fax services, copiers, and workstations for the disabled are available for student use. Special collections include the McDonald Collection of Business Resources, the Bertsche Collection of Montana History, and the Korontzos Law Library. An audiovisual collection with DVDs, records, CDs, scores, and other media can be used in the library.

The main computer lab, which is centrally located in Sullivan Hall, houses more than forty personal computers, while other labs on campus house more than thirty-five additional personal computers. University students take advantage of the wireless Internet connection in the student center, Sullivan Hall, and the library. Students can access the Internet and e-mail through the University of Great Falls UGFNET from on-campus residence halls. The lab supports one of the most widely used Windows-based software suites, and peripheral equipment is always available.

The University offers student support services to help students achieve academic success. The Center for Academic Excellence serves first-generation students, students with limited income, and students with disabilities and is strongly committed to both their academic success and personal growth. To accomplish this goal, the center provides a wide range of services and activities to all eligible students, including academic support, personal counseling, minority student support, and support for students with disabilities. Tutoring, academic support, and personal counseling are also available in the Grandma Rice Retention Center.

The University collaborated with the Montana State University–Bozeman College of Nursing to establish a student health center. The center offers limited primary care to the University of Great Falls students and faculty and staff members. It is staffed by an advanced-practice registered nurse/family practitioner with prescriptive authority. The clinic focuses on treating acute illnesses as well as promoting wellness and education about at-risk behaviors.

The McLaughlin Memorial Center is a site used for health and physical education classes, as well as athletic competition. Facilities include a large gymnasium, a state-of-the-art wellness exercise center, a large conference room, and academic classrooms. The McLaughlin Memorial Center's state-of-the-art fitness and recreation area includes a juice bar, café, and comfortable fireside study and TV lounge areas for late night study sessions.

With seating for 357 people, the University Theater is used frequently by the campus and the community. Theater students produce one play per semester as part of their course requirement. Musicians, comedians, and local groups also perform regularly in the building.

Costs

Undergraduate tuition and fees for 2010–11 were $19,256. Room and board averaged $6600 for students living in University housing. Books and supplies were estimated at $900 for the year. The campus includes a variety of attractive and comfortable residence halls. First-year students reside in Providence Hall and Emile Hall. The University also has three apartment-style residences: Sikora Hall, Lincoln Hall, and Sister Rita Mudd Hall. The Villa apartments, nearby on 10th Avenue South, also offer upper-division student housing in an apartment-style setting.

Financial Aid

Approximately 95 percent of students at the University of Great Falls receive some form of financial assistance. The University offers more than $2.5 million annually in merit-based, athletic, and need-based Courage awards. Information on need-based financial assistance

programs is available from the Financial Aid Office. Scholarship information for new students is available from the Admissions Office. To be considered for financial aid, students should submit a Free Application for Federal Student Aid (FAFSA) form electronically at http://www.fafsa.ed.gov with the University of Great Falls' school code of 002527. To be considered for scholarships, students should submit an application for admission along with academic transcripts.

Faculty

The University of Great Falls has a student-faculty ratio of 12:1 and features faculty members who possess personal philosophies that are compatible with a Catholic learning environment. These experienced teachers, of whom 62 percent possess terminal degrees, are not only highly competent in their academic fields but also persons of integrity to whom students can look for example, inspiration, and information. Since a faculty member's influence is of paramount significance in education, an ability and willingness to mentor students about academic concerns and lifelong goals are traits that are expected of each teacher.

Student Government

The University's students are represented by the Associated Students of the University of Great Falls. The governing body is an elected Student Senate. The University student government was the first in Montana to eliminate the class structure in favor of giving greater representation to all students. One student is a full voting member of the Board of Trustees.

Admission Requirements

The University of Great Falls Admissions Office accepts applicants on a rolling basis. Students are strongly encouraged to submit their test scores from the ACT or the SAT. The scores from these tests are used in scholarship consideration, academic counseling, and course placement. The University also has an early admission program for students in high school. The University of Great Falls grants advanced standing credit for AP, I.B., CLEP, and ACE military programs.

Application and Information

The University of Great Falls is committed to a program of equal opportunity for education, employment, and participation in University activities without regard to race, color, gender, age, religion, marital status, physical handicap, national origin, or mental handicap. For additional information about the University of Great Falls, students are encouraged to create a personalized admissions page online (http://www.ugf.edu/tabid/318/Default.aspx.) Students may also contact an admission counselor through the Admissions Office.

Office of Admissions
University of Great Falls
1301 20th Street South
Great Falls, Montana 59405

Phone: 406-791-5202
       800-856-9544 (toll-free)
Fax: 406-791-5209
E-mail: enroll@ugf.edu
Web site: http://www.ugf.edu

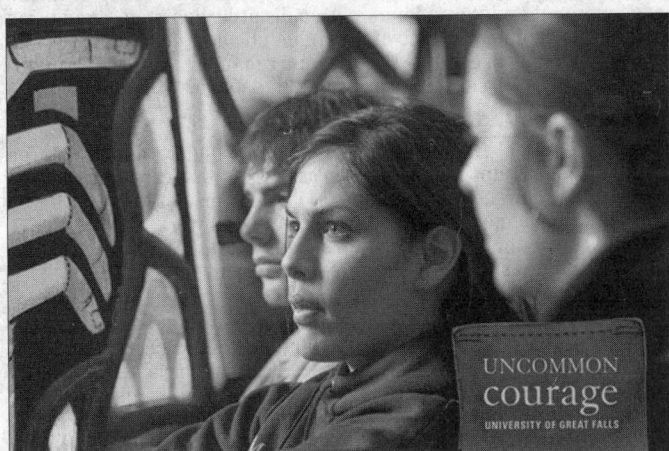

Why is courage our guiding light? Because the University of Great Falls was built on it.

UNIVERSITY OF GUELPH
GUELPH, ONTARIO, CANADA

The University

The University of Guelph is a high-quality, student-focused, residential college that is committed to innovative programs, dynamic student-faculty interaction, and an integration of learning and research. It offers a wide range of undergraduate and graduate programs in the arts, humanities, social sciences, engineering, and natural sciences. Building on these core disciplines, Guelph also has a strong commitment to interdisciplinary programs, to a selected range of professional and applied programs, and to agriculture and veterinary medicine as areas of special responsibility.

Established in 1964 when three century-old founding colleges joined with a new college of arts and science, the University of Guelph is a vital community of more than 18,000 students on a campus of historical and modern buildings and redbrick walkways. By Canadian standards, Guelph is of medium size, offering a wide range of academic programs while providing a safe, accommodating environment for learning. On-campus living is available for more than 5,200 students, with all new first-semester students guaranteed on-campus housing if they apply by the deadline.

Guelph features state-of-the-art athletic facilities that include a double arena with an Olympic-size ice surface, two pools, a field house and indoor track, aerobic and weight-training gymnasiums, six squash courts, and a climbing wall. Guelph offers thirty varsity sports teams and in recent years has fielded national and provincial championship football, hockey, track and field, and rugby teams.

Guelph ensures a personal approach to learning with a 1:20 faculty-student ratio in 63 percent of its classes. The success of the Center for New Students, which assists new students with the transition from secondary school to university, is reflected in Guelph's 90.5 percent student retention rate and a 96.6 percent graduate employment rate, both well above the Canadian national average.

The University of Guelph offers a Doctor of Veterinary Medicine degree as well as several diploma programs and more than eighty master's and doctoral degree programs. The graduate calendar is available on the Web at http://www.uoguelph.ca/GraduateStudies.

Location

The University of Guelph's main campus is located in the southwestern Ontario region the *New York Times* calls Canada's Technology Triangle, a locale known for its high-caliber educational institutions and innovative companies. This city of more than 118,000 features internationally recognized folk, jazz, and writers' festivals as well as a multipurpose performing arts center and a sports and entertainment center. Positioned within an hour's drive of Toronto, Canada's largest city, Guelph offers the comfort of small-community living with the excitement of an international metropolis at its doorstep. In addition to the main campus, the University of Guelph offers degrees in Toronto at the University of Guelph–Humber and regional campuses throughout Ontario in Alfred, Kemptville, and Ridgetown.

Majors and Degrees

The University of Guelph offers a number of undergraduate degree programs. Programs followed by an asterisk (*) indicate degrees that students can pursue in a traditional four-year or in a five-year co-op format. Co-ops offer students the opportunity to work in three to five different companies in paid work placements that result in one year of full-time work as a part of the degree experience.

The University of Guelph offers Bachelor of Arts degrees in anthropology; applied mathematics and statistics (co-op only); art history; classical studies; criminal justice and public policy; economics*; English; environmental governance; European studies; French studies; food, agriculture, and resource economics; geography; Hispanic studies; history; information systems and human behavior; international development; major to be determined; mathematical economics; mathematics; music; philosophy; political science; psychology*; sociology; statistics; studio art; and theater studies. In addition, a Bachelor of Arts and Sciences degree is available to students who excel in both arts/social sciences and sciences.

Bachelor of Applied Science degrees are available in applied human nutrition; child, youth, and family*; and adult development, families, and well-being*.

Bachelor of Commerce degrees are available in accounting, agricultural business*, hotel and food administration*, human resources management, management economics and finance*, marketing management*, public management*, real estate and housing*, tourism management, and undeclared (first year only).

Bachelor of Bio-Resource Management degrees are available in environmental management and equine management. Students in these programs begin their studies in the regional campuses and finish the final two years in Guelph.

The Bachelor of Computing degrees are available in computer science* and software engineering*.

Bachelor of Engineering degrees are available in biological engineering*, biomedical engineering*, computer engineering*, environmental engineering*, engineering systems and computing*, mechanical engineering*, water resources engineering*, and undeclared (first year only).

Bachelor of Science degrees are available in animal biology, applied mathematics and statistics*, biological and pharmaceutical chemistry, biomedical science, biochemistry*, biological science, biophysics*, chemical physics*, chemistry*, ecology, environmental biology, food science*, human kinetics, marine and freshwater biology, mathematics, microbiology*, molecular biology and genetics, nanoscience*, nutritional and nutraceutical sciences, physical science, physics*, plant science, psychology (brain and cognition), statistics, theoretical physics, toxicology*, wildlife biology, and zoology.

Bachelor of Science in Agriculture degrees are available in animal science; crop, horticulture, and turfgrass sciences; honors agriculture; and organic agriculture.

Bachelor of Science in Environmental Sciences degrees are available in earth and atmospheric science*, ecology*, environmental biology*, environmental economics and policy*, environmental geography*, and natural resources management*.

The University of Guelph also offers a Bachelor of Landscape Architecture degree and a Doctor of Veterinary Medicine degree.

University of Guelph–Humber programs include honors degrees in business administration (accounting, finance, not-for-profit enterprises, marketing, and small business management and entrepreneurship); applied science (early childhood services, family and community social services, justice studies, kinesiology, or psychology); and applied arts in media studies (journalism, public relations, digital communications, and image arts).

Academic Programs

The academic year is divided into three semesters: fall (September through December), winter (January through April), and summer (May through August), with the majority of students in attendance during the fall and winter semesters. Fall is the normal entry point for all semester one students. However, transfer students who apply by deadlines are considered for many programs at all entry points.

Four-year honors degrees require the completion of eight semesters. Three-year general degrees require the completion of six semesters. A typical full-time semester totals 2.5 credits.

Off-Campus Programs

An important part of Guelph's mission is to attract students from around the world and develop a global perspective in its students. The campus attracts more than 700 international students from over 100 countries, maintains fifty-six exchange programs with thirty countries, and offers six semester-abroad options. In addition, approximately 500 Guelph students study, research, or work each year in Africa, Australia, Europe, and South and Central America.

More than 2,000 students participate in co-op work semesters, making the co-op program at the University of Guelph one of the highest in co-op student enrollments among Ontario universities. Guelph also offers more than 100 distance degree credit courses to nearly 8,000 Open Learning course registrants.

Academic Facilities

Guelph's two libraries are linked with libraries at two other universities in the region, providing students with access to 7.5 million items through a new, state-of-the-art automated library system. Guelph's library holdings include Canada's largest collection of theater archives, extensive Scottish study materials, and one of the best collections of postcolonial African literature in Canada.

A 30-acre research park adjacent to the campus is home to a growing number of research-intensive industries. Industry and government trust Guelph's faculty members to meet their research needs, offering approximately Can$158.6 million annually for research that ranges from workplace efficiency to developing better approaches to food packaging and marketing to ensuring the availability of clean water.

All students receive free central computing accounts, which allow access to the University's integrated electronic services from on or off campus. These services include e-mail, access to the Internet, computer-assisted instruction, conferencing, course selection, and high-quality laser printing. All student residences are directly connected to the Internet via the campus high-speed network. Off-campus students have access to chargeable high-speed Internet providers.

The campus also features two art galleries; a sculpture park; two performance stages; a covered field house; a Can$144-million science complex; the Guelph Institute for the Environment; the Biodiversity Institute of Ontario, which is the world's first center for high-volume DNA barcoding; and the Can$70-million pathobiology/animal health laboratory. The 408-acre arboretum on the west side of the campus has nearly 5 miles of jogging trails and nature paths.

Costs

Full-time tuition for the 2010–11 academic year ranged from Can$2606 to Can$4236 per semester for Canadian residents and from Can$8461 to Can$11,074 per semester for international students. Mandatory fees totaled approximately Can$500 per semester, with slight variations according to each college. International students are obliged to purchase health-care coverage through the University. The cost for international students to attend Guelph for two semesters, including tuition and academic fees, health coverage, housing, clothing, food, and books, totaled between Can$28,890 and Can$34,116.

Financial Aid

The University of Guelph is committed to ensuring that a university education remains an attainable goal. In total, Can$14.3 million in annual student financial aid is given in the form of scholarships, awards, bursaries, and work-study opportunities. There are scholarships (ranging from Can$500 to Can$6000) and bursaries specifically designed for international students who are allowed to work on and off campus.

Faculty

The percentage of Guelph's 840 full-time professors who hold the Ph.D. degree or its equivalent is 99.9 percent, and all strive to bring the excitement and process of research into the learning environment. More than 100 professors have been recognized for excellence in teaching by external agencies, their peers, and students. No comparably sized university in the country has more 3M awards, Canada's most prestigious university teaching honor. Guelph has 19 Fellows of the Royal Society of Canada among its researchers.

Student Government

Students are involved at all levels of University government, from the residence council to the Senate and the Board of Governors. The Central Student Association (CSA), which represents all undergraduate students, oversees more than fifty student clubs that range from political to recreational. In addition, there are more than fifty academic and other student-government organizations located on campus. Students also have access to a number of service groups on campus, which range from the Ontario Public Interest Research Group to a community radio station and Habitat for Humanity.

Admission Requirements

Ontario applicants must present the Ontario Secondary School Diploma (OSSD), with a minimum of six 4U or 4M courses and specific subject requirements for the degree program desired. English 4U is required for all degree programs. For those outside Ontario, the secondary graduation certificate that would admit a student to a university in his or her home country is normally acceptable. Applicants must also satisfy the specific subject requirements for the program desired. Applicants who have completed the International Baccalaureate (I.B.) are granted credit for higher-level courses with grades of 5 or better. Applicants who have completed Advanced Placement (AP) exams with a minimum grade of 4 are eligible to receive University credit to a maximum of 2 credits, which is subject to the discretion of the appropriate faculty. United States applicants are required to have a minimum unweighted grade point average of 3.0 and a combined SAT score of at least 1100 (critical reading and math components) or an ACT score of at least 24. Applicants should include specific subject requirements at the highest secondary school level offered.

Interested students should call Admission Services or refer to its Web site at http://uoguelph.ca/admissions for application and deadline dates, detailed admission information, and downloadable application forms. Students interested in University of Guelph–Humber programs should contact Admission Services at http://www.guelphhumber.ca.

Application and Information

For additional information about admissions, academic programs, or University visits and tours, students should contact:

Admission Services
Office of Registrarial Services
Third Floor, University Centre
University of Guelph
Guelph, Ontario N1G 2W1
Canada

Phone: 519-821-2130 or 824-4120 Ext. 58721
Fax: 519-766-9481
E-mail: International inquiries: internat@registrar.uoguelph.ca
U.S. inquiries: usa@registrar.uoguelph.ca
Canadian inquiries: admission@registrar.uoguelph.ca
Web site: http://admission.uoguelph.ca
http://www.guelphhumber.ca

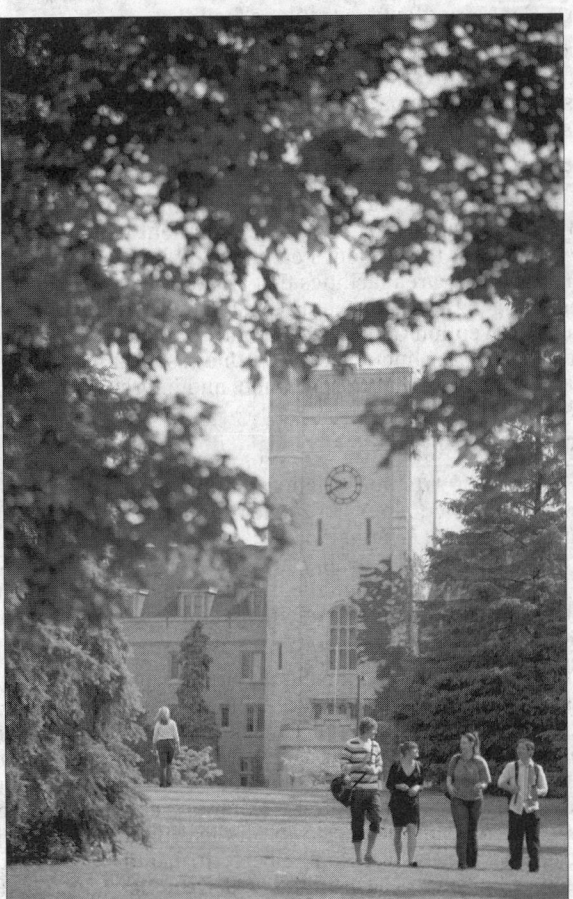

Students on the campus of the University of Guelph.

UNIVERSITY OF HARTFORD
WEST HARTFORD, CONNECTICUT

The University

The University of Hartford is a fully accredited, independent, nonsectarian institution. The University is composed of seven degree-granting schools and colleges: the College of Arts and Sciences; College of Engineering, Technology, and Architecture; College of Education, Nursing, and Health Professions; Hillyer College; the Barney School of Business; the Hartford Art School; and The Hartt School.

The current full-time undergraduate enrollment is more than 4,700 men and women. A wide range of interests, goals, and backgrounds is found among the students, who represent forty-six states and fifty-three countries. There are about 100 organized student groups, including clubs devoted to special interests or to political, professional, religious, or civic activities as well as service learning and community service activities and groups. Intercollegiate (NCAA Division I) and intramural athletics, student publications, and AM and FM radio stations provide further opportunities for extracurricular involvement. In addition, The Hartt School, the Hartford Art School, and the University Players present a variety of concerts, exhibitions, and theatrical productions each year. Recreational and fitness needs of the University community as well as intramural and intercollegiate sports are served by a well-equipped 130,000-square-foot Sports Center and outdoor athletic facilities.

More than 66 percent of all full-time undergraduates reside on campus. The University offers a wide array of types of residence halls, from traditional dormitory-style to fully equipped town house–style apartments.

Location

The University is located in the residential suburb of West Hartford. The area provides an environment conducive to the development of the student's cultural and intellectual pursuits. There are many area facilities that students can take advantage of including libraries, museums, theaters, the Hartford Civic Center and Convention Center, a symphony orchestra, several other colleges, modern shopping centers, fine restaurants, an international airport, surface transportation, and intercity highway systems.

Majors and Degrees

The College of Arts and Sciences offers majors in art history, biology, chemistry, chemistry-biology, cinema, communication, computer science, criminal justice, economics, English, foreign languages and cultures, history, international studies, Judaic studies, legal studies, mathematics, philosophy, physics, political economy, politics and government, psychology, rhetoric and professional writing, and sociology.

Within the College of Education, Nursing, and Health Professions, there are majors in early childhood education, elementary education, integrated special education/elementary education, secondary education with a concentration in English or mathematics, health sciences, nursing (for registered nurses only), radiologic technology, respiratory therapy, a combined B.S. in health science, and doctorate in physical therapy (B.S./D.P.T.) program, as well as a combined B.S. in health science and a Master of Science in Prosthetics and Orthotics (B.S./M.S.P.O.) program.

The Hartford Art School offers Bachelor of Fine Arts degrees in ceramics, design, drawing, illustration, media arts, painting, photography, printmaking, sculpture, and visual communication.

At the Hartt School, students can major in actor training, applied music (guitar, orchestral instrument, organ, piano, pre–cantorial studies, and voice), composition, dance (ballet pedagogy or performance emphases), jazz studies, music, music education, music history, music management, music production and technology, music theater, music theory, and performing arts management (interdisciplinary program offered in conjunction with the Barney School of Business). There are also 5-year double majors offered within the Hartt School.

Majors for the Bachelor of Science in Business Administration (B.S.B.A.) degree in the Barney School of Business are accounting, economics and finance, entrepreneurial studies, finance and insurance, management, and marketing.

Additional B.S. programs, offered by the College of Engineering, Technology, and Architecture include ABET-accredited programs in electrical, mechanical, civil, computer, and biomedical engineering as well as interdisciplinary B.S.E. options. The most popular B.S.E. options are acoustics and music (interdisciplinary program in conjunction with the Hartt School), biomedical engineering, and environmental engineering. Technology programs include the Bachelor of Science in architectural engineering technology, audio engineering technology, computer engineering technology, electronic engineering technology, and mechanical engineering technology as well as the Associate in Applied Science in electronic engineering technology (A.S.) and the Associate in Applied Science in computer engineering technology (A.S.).

Hillyer College offers the Associate of Arts and provides the general education course work required to complete most of the University's baccalaureate programs. Particular emphasis is placed on the development of academic skills through small classes and close faculty-student interaction.

University Studies offers the Bachelor of University Studies, a B.A. degree program created for the part-time adult student who typically has previous college experience and seeks to complete a baccalaureate degree. Also offered is a B.A. degree program in multimedia Web design and development for full-time undergraduates. Created for students who want to learn how to use and develop multimedia technologies that fit into today's wired world, this program combines courses across several disciplines where students create and use technology with user interaction in mind.

Academic Programs

The University of Hartford enjoys a national reputation for the breadth and depth of its academic programs. As highlighted above, more than seventy undergraduate majors are offered through seven schools and colleges. Students are encouraged to sample a variety of academic areas. Those who have special interests can develop interdisciplinary majors that combine courses from the different schools within the University. Academic advisers are assigned to all students to help guide them in curriculum choices, career exploration, and the transition to University life. In order to help students learn more about how different academic disciplines approach related problems, the All-University Curriculum was developed. Courses are often team taught from different fields of expertise, and topics are examined from the perspective of several academic disciplines. The University also has a special program to assist students who may be undecided about a major. A reading and writing center, where students on an individual basis are helped to increase their proficiency in writing, research, reading comprehension, and speed as well as study and test-taking skills, is available to the entire student body. Further help in math is given through the Math Tutoring Lab, which is staffed by full-time faculty members and math majors. Career Services provides vocational counseling and information on occupations, employers, testing, and graduate schools; serves as a reference and credential source; and provides an on-campus recruiting program for graduating students. University College addresses the needs of the part-time adult learner through courses, programs, and educational counseling. A trained counseling staff is available to assist part-time students in planning their education and resolving their special concerns and needs. Selected students are encouraged to participate in the Honors Program. Honors students have the opportunity to graduate with an Honors Degree.

Off-Campus Programs

Intercampus registration through the Hartford Consortium for Higher Education permits University of Hartford students to take certain courses at the School of the Hartford Ballet, Saint Joseph College, and Trinity College. Teaching majors in the College of Education, Nursing, and Health Professions have opportunities for field and/or clinical experiences where applicable. A central internship and cooperative education office is available to custom-tailor work experiences within many of the University's programs.

Academic Facilities

Seven schools and colleges are housed on the main campus. The Harry Jack Gray Center houses the William H. Mortensen Library; the Mildred P. Allen Memorial Library; the Museum of American Political Life; the Harry J. Gray Conference Center; the Joseloff Gallery; the University Bookstore; studios for architecture, art, radio, and television; and the Communication Department. The library has approximately 583,000 items, including books, musical scores, recordings, periodicals, journals, and microfilm units as well as the latest in computer technology, including high-speed and wireless Internet access. Extensive resources are also available through the Hartford Consortium for Higher Education, the Hartford Library, and the Inter-Library-Loan systems.

The new state-of-the-art Mort and Irma Handel Performing Arts Center, located 5 minutes from the main campus, is a 55,000-square-foot facility that houses five dance studios, four theater rehearsal studios, two black box theaters, a small dining facility, and faculty and staff offices. The Handel Performing Arts Center provides a rehearsal and performance environment for the Hartt School's dancers.

The Asylum Avenue campus is listed on the National Register of Historic Places. The 13-acre wooded campus contains beautiful examples of traditional ivy-covered Georgian architecture.

The University of Hartford Computer Center houses the central computer systems and operates a high-performance campus-wide network, which connects all student residential housing, all academic buildings on campus, and the University's remote locations. The University's network is connected via a high-speed telecommunication link to the Internet and the World Wide Web. The residential network gives each student resident his or her own high-speed Ethernet connection to the campus network and the Internet. The library is connected to the campus network and provides network access through computers in study carrels and study rooms and through wireless access. The online systems of the library include the online catalog for book, audio, and video collections; CD-ROM databases; and easy-to-use Web access for many of the library's online resources and electronic reserves. All of the University network resources may be accessed on campus in any University facility and off campus by using computers with network connectivity.

Public access computing labs, used by all students of the University, are provided at various locations around the campus. In addition, college-specific labs are available to students. All labs are equipped with microcomputers (both PCs and Macs) and are connected to the campus network and the Internet. Typical microcomputer software includes word processing, spreadsheet, database management, and graphics programs; programming languages; and Web browsers for accessing the Internet. Help is available from on-duty lab assistants. In addition to these computer labs, there are specialized computer facilities for instruction and learning. Wireless Internet access is available in all academic buildings, libraries, and dining facilities.

Costs

Tuition for incoming students was $28,582 for the 2010–11 academic year; student service fees, $1270; on-campus room costs, $7114; and board, $4998. A variety of on-campus housing accommodates 3,400 students.

Financial Aid

Financial aid for University of Hartford students totals approximately $98 million annually, including student loans. Scholarships, grants, loans, and work-study opportunities are provided through the federal government, private agencies, interested individuals, and University funds. University funds are disbursed based upon the college or school in which the student is enrolled, availability of funds, applicant pool, and competition for funds. More than 85 percent of all full-time undergraduate students receive some type of University assistance; the average out-of-pocket expense is $18,100 (estimate) per year. Partial-tuition scholarships are awarded to entering students who have demonstrated outstanding academic achievement or talent.

Faculty

There are 787 full-time and adjunct faculty members. The undergraduate and graduate faculties are essentially the same group, and 85 percent of the members hold the terminal degree in their field. Academic and personal advisory service is readily available. Each new student is assigned to a faculty adviser during summer orientation.

Student Government

The student governing body that represents all full-time students is the Student Government Association, through which students and faculty join in developing and coordinating the cocurricular activities of the University. Students are also represented on all major administrative committees, including the Board of Regents.

Admission Requirements

The Office of Admission considers the quality of the secondary school curriculum, academic performance in secondary school, ACT or SAT results, evidence of a desire to succeed, and leadership qualities shown by academic and extracurricular activities. Auditions, portfolios, and other tests are required of music and art applicants.

Application and Information

The University employs a rolling admission policy. For further information, students should visit the University on the Web at http://admission.hartford.edu or contact:

Office of Admission
University of Hartford
West Hartford, Connecticut 06117
Phone: 860-768-4296
       800-947-4303 (toll-free)
Fax: 860-768-4961
E-mail: admission@hartford.edu
Web site: http://admission.hartford.edu

UNIVERSITY OF HOUSTON

HOUSTON, TEXAS

The University

Founded in 1927, the University of Houston (UH) is the leading public research university in the vibrant international city of Houston. Each year, the University educates more than 37,000 students in more than 300 undergraduate and graduate academic programs, on campus and online. UH awards more than 6,500 degrees annually, and has nearly 200,000 alumni.

The University of Houston is the second most ethnically diverse major research university in the United States. Students come to UH from across the United States and more than 137 countries.

UH conducts research in each academic department, operating more than forty research centers and institutes on campus. Through these facilities, the University maintains creative partnerships with government and private industry. The research conducted breaks new ground in such vital areas as superconductivity, space commercialization, chemical engineering, economics, and education. The University's advanced professional programs include architecture, law, pharmacy, and optometry.

University of Houston public service and community activities, such as cultural offerings, clinical services, policy studies, and small-business initiatives, serve a diverse metropolitan population. Likewise, the resources of the Gulf Coast region complement and enrich the University's academic programs, providing students with professional expertise, practical experience, and career opportunities and allowing them to secure career-level jobs soon after graduation.

Location

In the midst of a bustling international city, the University of Houston's 667-acre campus is a lush, green oasis. Fountains and sculptures adorn the grounds, while manicured lawns and tree-filled parks offer breathing room. At the same time, the campus offers all the amenities and high-tech facilities required by modern university life; in the past few years, UH has made more than $220 million in campus improvements.

Majors and Degrees

Undergraduates at the University of Houston can choose from 120 majors and minors. At the graduate level, there are 139 master's, 54 doctoral, and three professional degree programs. Online study is possible through the University's Distance Education program, and noncredit courses can be taken through Continuing Education. Many of UH's academic programs rank among the nation's best.

Academic Programs

UH offers an undergraduate curriculum that provides students with a broad base in the liberal arts complemented by in-depth studies in disciplines of their choice, affording students a foundation for lifelong learning. UH enrolls a substantial number of National Merit Scholars each year, and the quality of UH students is further reflected in the growing enrollment in the Honors College.

The Honors College provides the advantages of a small community within the rich and diverse setting of a large, urban university. In addition to exclusive amenities and special privileges, Honors College students benefit from a dynamic learning environment and one-on-one mentoring from world-renowned faculty members. Through a challenging and well-balanced curriculum, its students learn both the skills they will need for professional success, and how and when to apply them.

Off-Campus Programs

The University is located in Houston, Texas, the nation's fourth-largest city and the energy capital of the world. UH students regularly test their skills through internships with national and international companies based in the city, and faculty members routinely partner with businesses and government agencies through research.

Academic Facilities

UH's world-class facilities include high-tech laboratories, modern classrooms, and nationally renowned facilities such as the Moores School of Music, the Athletics/Alumni Center and the LeRoy and Lucille Melcher Center for Public Broadcasting, which houses KUHT HoustonPBS, the nation's first educational television station; KUHF (88.7 FM), Houston's NPR station; the Center for Public Policy Polling; and television studio labs.

Costs

For Texas residents, the estimated annual tuition and fees are $8532, based on 15 credit hours taken per semester in fall and spring. Estimated room and board is $7886 for a total of $16,418. For nonresidents, estimated annual tuition and fees total $14,108 and room and board are estimated at $7886 for a total of $21,994.

These figures do not include laboratory fees, course fees, parking, and other such charges.

Financial Aid

The University of Houston believes that everyone deserves the opportunity to pursue an education. That's why it offers a wide array of financial aid packages such as grants, loans, and work-study programs, to help students invest in their future. However, funds are limited, and the financial aid process can take up to six weeks, so planning ahead is crucial.

Faculty

University of Houston faculty members are renowned scholars with real-world experience who work closely with each student. From the Tony Award to the Nobel Peace Prize and back to the classroom, UH faculty members make things happen on campus and around the world.

Student Government

The Student Government is the University's student government and official student representative organization. It works to improve the quality of education and campus life and participates in policymaking decisions. The association participates in student disciplinary cases and works to preserve student rights.

Admission Requirements

Freshman applicants whose admissions files are complete by December 1, 2011 and who rank in the top 20 percent of their high school class are automatically accepted. Those in the 21–50 percent range are admitted if they earn an SAT score of 1000 (critical reading and math) or an ACT composite of 21. An application after December 1 may not guarantee admission except to those students in the top 10 percent of their graduating class.

Students applying after December 1 or who attend schools that do not rank will be considered for admission under UH's individual/holistic review process, based on the following: first-generation college attendance; socioeconomic background; extent and rigor of the high school curriculum; special talents, abilities, or awards earned; family responsibilities; leadership activities; public service; and extracurricular activities.

Transfer applicants who have completed between 15 and 29 semester hours of college-level credit must have a 2.5 or higher cumulative grade point average; for those who have completed 30 or more semester hours, it is 2.0 or higher. All grades earned from college-level courses, including repeated courses, are used in computing the GPA. Those who have earned an Associate of Science or Associate of Arts degree from the last school they attended are eligible for admission. Official transcripts must be received from all previously attended institutions, and all colleges attended must be U.S. regionally accredited. Applicants who are not eligible to return immediately to the last institution attended will not be admitted.

International students seeking freshman enrollment must have completed the equivalent of twelve years or more of elementary and secondary schooling or graduated from an accredited high school in the U.S. Admission is based on earning at least a B average in all academic studies and a minimum score of 550 on the TOEFL paper exam or 79 on the Internet-based exam.

Transfer admission for international students (who have completed more than one year of full-time, university-level study overseas at a non-U.S. accredited institution) is based solely on the student's completed university record and TOEFL results. A minimum GPA of 2.5 (C+) is required. For those educational systems that do not have a higher or lower division (+ or -) in the grading scale, a cumulative grade of B is required. The minimal required TOEFL score is 550 on the paper exam or 79 on the Internet-based exam. The TOEFL requirement is not waived unless the student meets an exemption. International transfer students who have completed community college or university-level work at a U.S. institution must meet the admissions criteria for domestic transfer students.

Application and Information

Notifications of acceptance are based on a review of an applicant's complete file and continue on a rolling admission basis. An application fee of $50 is required. Students are urged to apply early. The freshman priority deadline for all semesters is December 1. Transfer students must apply by December 1 for the spring semester and May 1 for the summer and fall semesters.

Applicants should apply for admission using the Texas Common Application at http://www.applytexas.org and are reminded to select the University of Houston main campus as the receiving institution.

For additional information, students should visit http://www.uh.edu/admissions or contact:

Office of Admissions
Welcome Center
University of Houston
4400 University Drive
Houston, Texas 77204-2023
Phone: 713-743-1010
Web site: http://www.uh.edu/admissions
http://www.facebook.com/theuniversityofhouston
http://twitter.com/UH_Cougars

The University of Houston campus.

UNIVERSITY OF INDIANAPOLIS
INDIANAPOLIS, INDIANA

The University

The University of Indianapolis (UIndy) seeks to inspire excellence with a personal approach to education and a commitment to academic quality. Outstanding faculty members inspire students in small classes that allow individual attention, and students are encouraged to apply their knowledge to real-world situations through internships, active learning in the classroom, and community service. A private, residential, comprehensive university founded in 1902 and affiliated with the United Methodist Church, the University of Indianapolis welcomes students of many nations and faiths from around the world. Every year, more than 5,000 full-time and part-time students, both undergraduate and graduate, benefit from the University's commitment to offering outstanding academic programs in more than seventy major fields of study. The University of Indianapolis accepts qualified applicants for admission without regard to race, color, sex, sexual orientation, age, religion, creed, marital status, and ethnic or national origin.

Students indicate that they chose UIndy because of its challenging yet supportive atmosphere, relatively small size, and the advantages of its location in the distinctive Southside area of a thriving state capital city. As a result, there is a great sense of community and pride on the campus. The University helps students to determine and achieve their individual academic goals. UIndy has experienced much growth and has instituted many enhancements recently, including the renovation and addition to Esch Hall, which houses a new facility for the Communication Department, the expansion of the Schwitzer Student Center, and the addition of the Athletics and Recreation Center.

More than 2,900 full-time undergraduate students are enrolled. There are students from more than sixty countries and thirty-five states. Approximately 85 percent of freshmen live in on-campus housing. The warmth and sensitivity of the faculty, staff members, and students alike enable those who are a part of the campus to feel a strong sense of community.

In addition to the undergraduate division, the University also offers a graduate division, including the nationally recognized Krannert School of Physical Therapy. The University of Indianapolis offers twenty-two graduate programs and four doctoral programs, including those in the College of Health Sciences, which rank among the finest in the nation. The most popular programs in the undergraduate division include pre–physical therapy, business, athletic training, communication, nursing, education, premedical studies, psychology, and music.

Social life is organized through the Campus Program Board, Indianapolis Student Government, and Residence Hall Association, which are student organizations that plan weekly activities for all students. There are numerous social clubs and common-interest groups available for students who wish to become involved in extracurricular activities. There are six residence halls: five house both men and women, and one is only for women. Students must be admitted on a full-time basis in order to be assigned housing. NCAA Division II sports for men include baseball, basketball, cross-country, football, golf, soccer, swimming and diving, tennis, track and field (indoor and outdoor), and wrestling. NCAA Division II sports for women include basketball, cross-country, golf, soccer, softball, swimming and diving, tennis, track and field (indoor and outdoor), and volleyball. Intramural sports are offered for men and women in flag football, basketball, softball, soccer, volleyball, indoor soccer, Ultimate (Frisbee), and racquetball.

Location

The University is located in the University Heights neighborhood on the south side of Indianapolis, which is the nation's second-largest capital city. Indianapolis and the surrounding area constitute a metropolitan area of nearly 2 million people. The city offers numerous valuable internship and service-learning experiences as well as recreational and cultural opportunities for students. The campus is extremely accessible, just a few blocks from two major interstate highways (I-65 and I-465). Public transportation options in Indianapolis include IndyGo bus, Greyhound Lines, and Amtrak trains that arrive daily at historic Union Station, just 10 minutes from the campus. Indianapolis International Airport is about 15 minutes away.

Majors and Degrees

The undergraduate programs are offered through the College of Arts and Sciences, the School of Business, the School of Nursing, the School of Education, the College of Health Sciences, and the School of Psychological Sciences. The degrees awarded are the Associate in Arts, Associate in Science, Associate in Science in Nursing, Bachelor of Arts, Bachelor of Science, and Bachelor of Science in Nursing.

Baccalaureate and preprofessional fields of study include accounting (CMA/CPA), actuarial science, anthropology, archeology, art, athletic training, biology, business administration, chemistry, communication studies, computer engineering (dual degree), computer science, corporate communication, corrections, earth-space sciences, economics, electrical engineering (dual degree), electronic media, elementary education, English, entrepreneurship, environmental science, exercise science, experiential learning (concentrations in applied anthropology, applied history, and applied theater), finance, French, German, history, human biology, human communication, information systems, international business, international relations, journalism, law enforcement, management, marketing, mathematics, mechanical engineering (dual degree), medical technology, music, music performance, nursing, philosophy, physics, political science, pre–art therapy, predental studies, prelaw, premedical studies, pre–occupational therapy, pre–physical therapy, pretheology, pre–veterinary science, psychology, public relations, religion, respiratory therapy, secondary education, social work, sociology, Spanish, sports administration, sports information, sports marketing, studio art, theater, youth ministry, and visual communication design.

Teaching majors are offered in business education (all grades), chemistry, earth-space science, English, French, life science, mathematics, music (all grades), physical education (all grades), physics, social studies, Spanish, speech communication, theater, and visual arts (grades 5–12).

Associate degrees are awarded in business administration, chemistry, corrections, information systems, law enforcement, liberal arts, nursing, and physical therapist assistant studies.

Academic Programs

The University of Indianapolis provides a top-notch education that combines a liberal arts and career-oriented curriculum that graduates describe as life-changing. Students find a powerful combination of features designed to inspire them to excellence. Faculty and staff members take a personal interest in students and encourage them to explore their interests and apply what they learn, so they can excel when it comes time to make their place in the world.

Students can choose from more than seventy undergraduate academic programs. The goal of the liberal arts core classes is to provide learning above and beyond the student's major field, so students study topics and cultures that pique their interest in unexpected ways.

Students appreciate the curriculum because they don't have to wait to apply what they learn. At the University of Indianapolis, students have time—before they graduate—to practice what they learn. Most majors offer practical experiences, which give students an edge in the job market. The Indianapolis location is an excellent resource when it comes to finding internships, field experiences, service-learning opportunities, or part-time employment. Internships let students sample their future careers and gain some of the knowledge and experience they admire in their professors. The University offers a host of possibilities for virtually any major. The Office of Career Services helps students identify an appropriate major and arranges off-campus internships related to their field of study.

Off-Campus Programs

The University operates a fully owned branch campus in Athens, Greece, that offers students a unique exchange program. Located within walking distance of the storied Acropolis, the Plaka, Constitution Square, and other historic landmarks, the University of Indianapolis–Athens offers students the opportunity to explore and experience Greece both inside and outside the classroom. Currently, the Athens campus offers thirty-two undergraduate programs in the arts and sciences, business, and psychology. Short-term study trips, as well as full-semester study-abroad programs, are available to students through the Odyssey program. In addition, students at the main campus have many opportunities to travel to Athens on shorter trips during vacations or during the Spring Term in May. Other partnerships and extension sites for direct credit include Israel, Belize, and the People's Republic of China. Other off-campus study opportunities take place during the Spring Term, including assorted overseas travel options.

Academic Facilities

Krannert Memorial Library, which operates an online card catalog, houses more than 175,000 volumes, more than 1,000 periodicals, and more than 19,000 microfilm/microform/microfiche records. The library is home to a full media center. The communication department, with new state-of-the-art equipment for its radio station and television studio, is located in Esch Hall. Martin Hall contains outstanding resources for the Schools of Nursing, Physical Therapy, and Occupational Therapy and is connected to Lilly Science Hall, which recently underwent a major upgrade to all its science labs. Access to computers is available in all of the academic buildings and residence halls. Students have access to the campuswide information system from their rooms in the residence halls, and the whole campus is wireless. Ransburg Auditorium, with seating for nearly 800, is the setting for concerts, recitals, and theatrical productions. The Christel DeHaan Fine Arts Center features state-of-the-art music and art facilities, an art gallery, and a 450-seat, Viennese-style concert hall.

Costs

Direct costs for the 2011–12 academic year are $22,790 for tuition and $8270 for room and board. Indirect costs are estimated at $800 for books and supplies, an average of $630 for transportation, and $1370 to $1830 for miscellaneous and personal expenses.

Financial Aid

All applicants for admission are eligible to apply for financial aid. Indiana residents should file the Free Application for Federal Student Aid (FAFSA) by March 10 to qualify for State of Indiana financial aid programs. All students should file the FAFSA along with the University of Indianapolis Application for Financial Aid by March 10 for priority consideration. For the 2009–10 academic year, about 86 percent of the enrolled full-time students received financial aid with an average financial aid package of $18,127 for entering students.

Faculty

UIndy's student-faculty ratio is 14:1 and the average class size is 18. Graduate students do not teach any undergraduate classes.

Student Government

The Indianapolis Student Government (ISG) consists of students elected to leadership positions plus student representatives from each class, chosen for a one-year term in an annual student body election. ISG's main focus is to pass resolutions regarding student concerns.

Admission Requirements

Applicants for admission must be high school graduates or have a GED certificate and are expected to have taken a college-preparatory curriculum in high school. Applicants for regular admission should have completed a minimum of 4 years of English, 3 years of mathematics, 3 years of laboratory science, 2 years of social science (U.S. history, government, and economics), and 2 years of any foreign language. In addition, applicants for full-time admission without restrictions should rank in the upper half of their class and have average to above-average SAT or ACT scores. Essays are not required for admission. For immediate consideration, transfer applicants must have achieved a good overall record and have earned at least a C average in previous college or university work. An on-campus interview is recommended anytime after the junior year of high school. To apply for admission, the Application for Admission, official high school transcript, official college transcript (if applicable), and official SAT or ACT scores should be forwarded to the Office of Admissions.

Application and Information

All applications are reviewed on a rolling basis—an admission decision is made as soon as all documents are received, and notifications are mailed immediately thereafter. There is no deadline for applications, but high school seniors are encouraged to apply during the fall semester of their senior year. Scholarships are also awarded on a rolling basis. Admitted students are notified of scholarships they have been awarded shortly after they have been accepted.

Requests for appointments and information about the University should be directed to:

University of Indianapolis
1400 East Hanna Avenue
Indianapolis, Indiana 46227-3697
Phone: 317-STUDENT
      317-788-3216
      800-232-8634 (toll-free)
Fax: 317-788-3300
E-mail: admissions@uindy.edu
Web site: http://www.uindy.edu/
      http://www.facebook.com/uindy
      http://twitter.com/uindy
      http://www.youtube.com/uindytv

Smith Mall, the centerpiece of the University of Indianapolis campus, features a beautifully landscaped water garden canal.

UNIVERSITY OF MAINE

ORONO, MAINE

The University

Students who start at the University of Maine find that it's a springboard to anywhere, from work in Tanzania as a medical volunteer or on the Maine coast as a biomedical engineer. Students don't need to leave campus to find inspiration, however—the world comes to them. UMaine offers groundbreaking innovation, inspiring scholarship, and some of the most cutting-edge research anywhere.

UMaine provides far more than the academic experience. Students often comment that they're surprised by how much there is to do. The residence halls offer an abundance of opportunities for fun, camaraderie, service, and personal growth. The newly renovated Collins Center for the Arts brings national and international touring artists to campus and shows independent films. The School of Performing Arts has plays, readings, and musical performances planned, and Student Entertainment hosts national acts such as The Roots, O.A.R., Dropkick Murphys and The Decemberists. Students can get involved in more than 200 academic and social clubs and organizations, one of fifteen fraternities or seven sororities, Student Government, community service–oriented groups, intramural sports, and much more. There are free events planned on campus almost every evening, including game nights, first-run movies, live music, and karaoke. UMaine is the state's only Division I school, and athletic events, especially hockey, are a big part of student life.

Location

Orono is a classic college town, bounded by the Stillwater and Penobscot Rivers in the heart of Maine. The University of Maine is 10 minutes from the state's third-largest city, Bangor, and its international airport.

UMaine's 600-acre campus was designed by well-known landscape architect Frederick Law Olmsted, who also designed Central Park in New York City and the White House grounds in Washington, D.C. It's a traditional New England campus, with ivy-covered brick buildings, towering pines, and spectacular fall foliage.

Students take advantage of Maine's great outdoors whenever they can. There are 15 miles of walking, biking and cross-country skiing trails on the UMaine campus itself. Some of the best skiing in the East is located within an easy driving distance of campus, as are Bar Harbor, Acadia National Park, and Baxter State Park, the northern terminus of the Appalachian Trail.

Majors and Degrees

Founded in 1865, the University of Maine is the flagship campus of the UMaine System. As such, it offers the state's most comprehensive academic experience, with more than eighty-five majors and programs across five academic colleges: the College of Business, Public Policy, and Health; the College of Education and Human Development; the College of Engineering; the College of Liberal Arts and Sciences; and the College of Natural Sciences, Forestry, and Agriculture. In addition, the Explorations program is designed to help undecided students choose a suitable major from one of UMaine's colleges while making progress toward their degree. The Division of Lifelong Learning offers online classes and distance-learning opportunities for students who need a flexible class schedule.

Academic Programs

Students at the University of Maine benefit from a solid liberal arts foundation. They develop and refine the qualities needed to more fully engage with the world around them—critical thinking, curiosity, a sense of discovery, a broader perspective—no matter what discipline they choose.

UMaine's Honors College, one of the country's oldest honors programs, provides an in-depth, academically challenging curriculum for qualified students in any major.

UMaine is one of the National Science Foundation's top 100 public universities for research, with annual research expenditures of nearly $100 million, which provides exceptional opportunities for undergraduate research.

Off-Campus Programs

When UMaine students travel, they don't just go to Boston for the weekend. They go global, through study abroad, international volunteerism, and the worldwide research opportunities available to undergraduates. In recent semesters, UMaine students have traveled to China to learn more about the country's emerging financial markets, to Italy to explore Renaissance art history at the source, to Turkey to study film, and to Brazil to learn about a sensitive and diverse ecosystem from one of the world's leading conservation biologists (who just happens to be a UMaine professor).

Academic Facilities

In addition to state-of-the-art research and classroom facilities, the University of Maine is also home to the region's cultural hub, the Collins Center for the Arts, as well as several museums and galleries. The new, spa-like Student Recreation and Fitness Center is a campus hot spot and sports fans enjoy Alfond Arena and Alfond Stadium. Fogler Library, the state's largest library, houses approximately 1 million volumes, subscribes to over 4,000 periodicals and serial titles, and serves as a depository for over 2.2 million government documents. In addition, the library provides 24-hour access to countless online documents.

Undergraduates have access to campuswide wireless Internet and several computer clusters. In addition, students can take advantage of the newest and best technology through UMaine's Collaborative Media Lab.

Costs

The University of Maine System Board of Trustees adjusts costs annually. For the 2011–12 academic year, tuition is $279 per credit hour for undergraduate state residents, and $803 per credit hour for nonresident students. The average credit load for full-time students is 15 credit hours per semester or 30 credit hours for the academic year. Canadian and nonresident students who qualify for the New England Regional Program pay $419 per credit hour. Required University fees (about $2200 per year for a full-time student) include the Unified Fee, which provides a variety of health-care services and admission to cultural, recreational, and athletic events. Books and supplies have been estimated at $1000, and room and board at $9000 for the year. These costs are subject to change.

Financial Aid

The University requires all financial aid applicants to file the Free Application for Federal Student Aid (FAFSA) and encourages students to file online. The priority deadline to apply for aid is March 1. Awards usually consist of a combination of several types of aid, ranging from grants and scholarships to work-study jobs and student loans. In addition, students who apply through the early action admissions program (complete application submitted by December 15) will be considered for UMaine merit awards based on high school achievement as demonstrated by class rank and standardized test results (SAT and ACT).

Faculty

At the University of Maine, most undergraduate classes are taught by professors and many of those faculty members go on to become mentors and friends to their students. Students often work alongside some of the most renowned scholars and scientists in the world. And they're not just doing grunt work—they're heading into the woods with wildlife ecologists to study bear habitat, researching harassment with leading sociologists, and testing the strength of bridges with civil engineers.

Student Government

Student Government, Inc. is the independent, representative body for UMaine's undergraduate students. An elected president, vice president, and vice president of financial affairs direct and coordinate Student Government programs at the University of Maine. Student Government works closely with the Office of the Vice President for Student Affairs and appoints 200 student representatives to various University committees involved with the planning and implementation of residence hall programs, student discipline, athletics, and cultural activities on campus.

Admission Requirements

Admission to the University of Maine is a selective process. Successful applicants are those whose scholastic achievement, intellectual curiosity, and established study habits promise success in a comprehensive university environment. Strength of the high school curriculum, grades received, class rank, counselor recommendation, and SAT or ACT scores are the primary criteria for admission. Essays and information regarding school and community activities provide additional information that may help the admissions committee evaluate potential for success.

The University recognizes advanced work completed in secondary schools by means of Advanced Placement tests. In addition, students who demonstrate advanced knowledge may be exempted from certain courses and requirements if they pass examinations specially developed by the University's academic departments.

Application and Information

Applicants may submit either electronic or paper versions of the Common Application or the University of Maine System application. The University requires a supplement for the Common Application. Additional required documents for all applicants include official high school transcripts and counselor recommendations. Traditional-age applicants are required to submit scores from either the SAT or ACT.

The University of Maine has an early action deadline of December 15. Students whose complete applications are postmarked by December 15 are reviewed by the end of January. Early action candidates are given first consideration for the Honors College and merit scholarships awarded by the admissions office. Regular decision applicants are encouraged to submit their applications and all supporting documents by February 1 and are notified by rolling admission. Students applying for the spring semester are encouraged to submit applications by December 1. Applications after these dates are processed on a space-available basis. Applications and all supporting documents should be sent to UMS Processing, P.O. Box 412, Bangor, Maine 04402-0412.

Office of Admissions
5713 Chadbourne Hall
University of Maine
Orono, Maine 04469-5713

Phone: 207-581-1561
　　　　877-486-2364　(toll-free)
Fax: 207-581-1213
E-mail: um-admit@maine.edu
Web site: http://www.go.umaine.edu
　　　　http://www.facebook.com/UMaineAdmissions
　　　　http://twitter.com/GoUMaine

Fogler Library is located in the heart of the University of Maine campus.

UNIVERSITY OF MASSACHUSETTS BOSTON

BOSTON, MASSACHUSETTS

The University

Since 1964 the University of Massachusetts Boston (UMass Boston) has provided access to superior public education at a moderate cost, in the state's capital city of Boston. With more than 15,000 commuting students in its undergraduate, graduate, and continuing education programs, UMass Boston is the second-largest campus in the University of Massachusetts system. UMass Boston is a community of scholars who take pride in academic excellence, diversity, research, and service. The fabric of the school's academic research and scholarship is tightly woven into the public and community service needs of Boston and the modern metropolitan center.

The University's students represent an extraordinary range of backgrounds, talents, and interests. Many come straight from high school, while others transfer from two- and four-year colleges. Although the majority of students come from the Commonwealth of Massachusetts, many grew up in other states and countries and come from all levels of the economic, political, spiritual, and ethnic spectra.

UMass Boston has a vibrant student life. No matter what a student's social and intellectual interests, he or she can find activities to engage in. From student government to student literary endeavors; from a champion chess team to working with inner-city youth; from academically affiliated clubs and athletic opportunities to a unique course-credit-based leadership-development program, students are sure to find just the right activity to complement their own classroom experience.

The UMass Boston student body shares a strong motivation to succeed academically and to relate their classroom pursuits to career aspirations. The University Advising Center helps by providing comprehensive academic support, planning, and career advising services. A team of professional counselors provides personalized assistance for students to design their course of study, utilize tutorial and mentoring services, choose a major and career path, and develop interviewing, resume-writing, and job-search skills.

Location

From its beautifully landscaped peninsula on Boston Harbor, just south of downtown Boston, the University overlooks Dorchester Bay and the harbor islands. Its neighbors are the John F. Kennedy Presidential Library and the Massachusetts State Archives and Commonwealth Museum. It will soon share the site with the Edward M. Kennedy Center for the United States Senate as well.

With its entrance along a seaside promenade drive, just a half mile off Interstate Route 93, the campus is easily accessed by both public transportation and automobile. The Office of Undergraduate Admissions provides a number of free parking spaces for visitors in the campus's North Parking Lot. A free shuttle bus runs every few minutes for the half-mile ride between the Massachusetts Bay Transit Authority's (MBTA) JFK/UMass Red Line "T" stop and the front door of the school's Campus Center. Student MBTA discount "T" passes are available for frequent users.

Many students commute from their home communities, while others utilize the Office of Student Housing for free, personalized help with finding a rental property and/or roommates. The University wants all its students to be at home at UMass Boston.

Boston itself, with its worldwide standing as a cultural center and well-earned reputation as America's favorite college town, offers UMass Boston students a wealth of resources for exploration and entertainment. Everything from Fenway Park and the Bank of America Garden to Symphony Hall and the Museum of Fine Arts is easily accessible from UMass Boston.

Majors and Degrees

Five undergraduate colleges award bachelor's degrees: the College of Liberal Arts and the College of Science and Mathematics (with seventeen majors, ten minors and programs of study, and six certificate programs between them), the College of Management (with two majors and eleven concentrations), the College of Nursing and Health Sciences (with a B.S.N., an online RN-to-B.S.N., and an accelerated

B.S.N. program, as well as the B.S. in exercise and health sciences program), and the College of Public and Community Service (with four majors and two certificate programs). In addition, the College of Education and Human Development offers a non-licensure bachelor's degree in early education and care in inclusive settings (EECIS) and a program of study for those interested in teacher licensure at the undergraduate level. Also offered are premed and prelaw programs, along with programs for honors study, credit by examination, and advanced placement.

A joint arts or science bachelor's/master's degree program in business is available for high academic achievers, as is a bachelor's degree in liberal arts or science with a minor in management.

Academic Programs

The academic calendar runs from early September through the end of May. There is also a one-month optional winter session in January, and summer school sessions are available in June, July, and August. Matriculating students may choose to attend full- or part-time and may adjust their schedules from semester to semester. A minimum of 30 credits must be earned at UMass Boston as a residency requirement for graduation.

For the College of Liberal Arts and the College of Science and Mathematics, 120 credits are required to graduate. The general education curriculum comprises three elements: the distribution requirement, the core curriculum requirement, and the writing requirement. In addition, the requirements of the major must be fulfilled. The colleges offer both an honors program and an individual major option.

In the College of Management, the 120-credit undergraduate program leads to a B.S. degree in management or information technology. By fulfilling the general education, management, and elective course work requirements, students build a liberal arts foundation and receive the theoretical, technical, and functional training needed to succeed in the business world. An honors program is also offered.

The College of Nursing and Health Science's B.S. program in nursing requires 123 credits for graduation, including general education courses and 63 credits of intensive study in the principles and practices of nursing. The exercise and health sciences program prepares graduates for the technical aspects of a professional discipline and a solid foundation in liberal arts. Students may also elect to enter the honors program in nursing.

The College of Public and Community Service (CPCS) offers an innovative curriculum with strong emphasis on social justice. Students may draw upon a variety of supplemental learning options in pursuit of their degree, including classroom study, self-directed study, and project-based learning. The University's honors program is also open to CPCS students.

Off-Campus Programs

The National Student Exchange Program offers UMass Boston students the opportunity to study at one of more than seventy participating colleges and universities in forty states at a cost comparable to what they pay to attend UMass Boston. The study-abroad program is available for students with a 3.0 GPA or better who seek international travel and academic experiences as well as summer and winter session programs in other countries. UMass Boston also participates in the New England Regional Student Program and the Boston Five-College Exchange Program.

The cooperative education and internship programs place students in work assignments related directly to their fields of study so that they may apply what they learn in the classroom to practical work settings. Under the co-op program, students are placed in full-time, paid positions for six-month work periods. Under the internship program, students are placed on a part-time basis, usually 15 to 20 hours per week, during a semester or over the summer months. Some are paid internships; others are volunteer opportunities. Both co-op and internship placements combine relevant practical learning, valuable work experience, career awareness, resume enhancement, personal and professional growth, and, in many instances, opportunities for academic credit, good pay, and a permanent job after graduation.

Academic Facilities

The Joseph P. Healey Library holds a collection of more than 600,000 volumes, 85,000 electronic and print journals and newspapers, 60,000 electronic books, 100 databases, and more than 5,000 academic videos, DVDs, and films related to the campus's academic studies. The library's electronic resources are available on and off campus, 24/7 via library barcode (http://www.lib.umb.edu/node/1404). UMass Boston is an active member of the Boston Library Consortium, and is also a partner in nationwide resource-sharing networks of scholarly and study resources. These offer over 10 million book titles and a total of nearly 30 million volumes available via point-and-click. Students may obtain a library consortium card to check out books from any of the consortia libraries. Healey Library and the division of Information Technology also offer graduate students many services through the Commons at Healey. The Commons has a media center, media viewing room, the IT Service Desk, the Graduate Resource Center, and many other facilities in the building, including reference assistance from expert librarians who specialize in various fields.

The Information Technology Services Division (ITSD) provides seven-day-a-week access to general-use computer labs, including the Adaptive Computing Lab, Graduate Research Center, media and language labs, and a media viewing center, all located within the Healey Library Information Commons, which also houses the IT Service Desk. ITSD supports equipment from Dell, Sun, and Apple, and the Windows XP, Unix, Linux, and Apple operating systems. The campus has over ninety technology-enhanced classrooms and auditoria that are equipped with state-of-the-art audiovisual equipment and network connections. ITSD also provides wireless access in the Healey Library, the Campus Center, and other public spaces, as well as ensuring that a wide variety of information technology and data communications resources are available to students. The campus uses the Blackboard Vista learning management system in conjunction with the Wimba synchronous meeting tool. ITSD also provides support for a digital signage and Ethernet TV network and IP- and ISDN-based video-conferencing. The campus has a fiber-optic infrastructure with giga-bit backbone and 100 MB switched connectivity.

The Kennedy Presidential Library is linked to the University by a variety of educational programs, enabling students to conduct research utilizing the more than 28 million pages of documents, 6.5 million feet of film, and more than 100,000 still photographs in the library's archives. Next door, the Archives of the Commonwealth of Massachusetts are a rich depository, covering more than 5½ centuries of Massachusetts history.

The state-of-the-art Campus Center provides easy access to student services, dining services, and spectacular meeting spaces, along with computer terminals and wireless Internet access.

Costs

Tuition and fees for the fall 2010 semester were $5315.50 for Massachusetts residents studying full-time (12 or more credits) or $11,604 for out-of-state students. Students enrolling part-time were charged tuition according to the number of credits taken, with Massachusetts residents paying tuition at $71.50 per credit; out-of-state residents paid tuition of $406.50 per credit. Annual mandatory fees for in-state residents ranged up to $9137 and up to $13,179 for out-of-state students.

Financial Aid

Financial aid is based on need and/or merit. Applicants must complete the Free Application for Federal Student Aid (FAFSA), keeping in mind a priority deadline of March 1 for fall semester and November 1 for spring semester. Need-based aid is awarded to students who demonstrate financial need, as determined by federal methodology. Aid consists of grants, waivers, and merit scholarships as well as self-help in the form of loans and work-study employment. An on-time applicant is automatically considered for all financial aid programs administered by the University's Office of Financial Aid Services.

Faculty

UMass Boston is proud of its 964 distinguished faculty members, some 93 percent of whom have terminal degrees in their field. UMass Boston has a student-faculty ratio of about 15:1 and a small class size that averages but 26 students. The faculty's top priority is teaching and advising students, although they also conduct research, publish materials, and participate in grant activities and professional organizations. Faculty members maintain office hours for students and make themselves accessible as mentors. Faculty and academic issues are governed by the Faculty Council.

Student Government

The undergraduate Student Senate consists of elected members from the undergraduate colleges and programs, and it participates fully in matters related to the quality of student life and the allocation of the student activities trust fund. Students are also represented on numerous University- and college-based committees and councils that initiate major policy and procedural recommendations, forwarding those recommendations to governance bodies and the administration for enactment.

Admission Requirements

A freshman candidate for admission to the University should have earned a minimum of 16 academic units in high school that include 4 years of English, 3 years of mathematics, 3 years of science (including 2 with laboratory requirements), 2 years of social science (including 1 of U.S. history), 2 years of a single foreign language, and 2 years of electives in the arts or computer science (excluding vocational training). The student must also present satisfactory scores on either the SAT or ACT. The University looks for students with a strong academic background, as determined by a recalculated grade point average, and each candidate's academic program choices, motivation, achievement, and annual progress are closely scrutinized.

UMass Boston encourages qualified international students to apply for admission. A separate international application is required. The Test of English as a Foreign Language (TOEFL) is required of all students educated in a non-English language educational system.

Transfer students are considered based on a review of all college academic credentials. Several academic majors and programs have specific higher requirements for transfer students, but, in general, a minimum 2.5 GPA is required.

Participation in a campus visit and group informational session with an admissions counselor is strongly encouraged.

Application and Information

For information about the application process, deadlines, and informational materials, students should contact:

Enrollment Information Services
University of Massachusetts Boston
100 Morrissey Boulevard
Boston, Massachusetts 02125-3393

Phone: 617-287-6000
      617-287-6010 (TTY/TDD)
Fax: 617-287-6040
E-mail: enrollment.info@umb.edu
Web site: http://www.umb.edu
      http://on.fb.me/UMassBoston (Facebook)
      http://twitter.com/umassboston (Twitter)

UMass Boston students in conversation.

UNIVERSITY OF MASSACHUSETTS LOWELL

LOWELL, MASSACHUSETTS

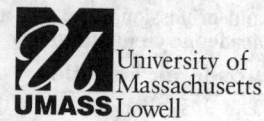

The University

Throughout its 100-year history, the University of Massachusetts (UMass) Lowell has excelled at providing innovative programs that meet both the needs of its students for a high-quality education and the needs of the region for skilled leadership. The University is part of the five-campus University of Massachusetts system and is comprised of six colleges: the College of Fine Arts, Humanities and Social Sciences, the College of Sciences, the Francis College of Engineering, the School of Health and Environment, the College of Management, and the Graduate School of Education.

Two types of learning communities help first-year students make the transition to college. In academic learning communities, groups of 20 or fewer students in three shared courses are assigned a senior faculty member/mentor to guide them through discussions around a shared academic interest. In living learning communities, residence hall assignments cluster students into suites and provide activities and discussions around a theme such as arts and culture, politics in the media, or science and technology.

The UMass Lowell education focuses on putting the lessons of the classroom into practice. Students have multiple opportunities for co-ops, internships, service learning activities and knowledge discovery through research, all of which give them hands-on experience in solving the issues of the real world. The real-world focus is also reflected in the interdisciplinary nature of many academic initiatives. In the Artbotics Project, for example, art and computer science students collaborated on the development of robots; and during the Urban Village Arts Series, design, English, and sound recording technology majors worked together to produce a CD of eight multimedia performances. Students graduate with the hands-on experience and practical problem-solving skills employers seek.

UMass Lowell offers dozens of programs that allow students to stay as little as one extra year to earn both bachelor's and master's degrees, giving them a competitive advantage as they enter the workplace. The undergraduate experience is enhanced by the diverse and international campus community and the extensive opportunities for studying abroad. UMass Lowell offers a robust honors program for those students who want to take academics to the next level, and the Centers for Learning, which offer a range of tutoring and other programs designed to help students succeed. The University maintains a student-faculty ratio of 14:1.

The University campus covers 100 acres on both sides of the Merrimack River and includes classroom and laboratory buildings, two libraries, a student center, two gymnasiums, three dining halls, a Center for the Performing Arts, two art galleries, and numerous residence halls. A campus recreation center provides additional social and recreational facilities. State-of-the-art laboratories include such special interest facilities as the six Sound Recording Technology Program studios, an interactive lab that enables nursing students to simulate medical emergencies, and a manufacturing lab where engineering and management students team up to produce microelectronic components.

UMass Lowell's 8,600 undergraduate students are ethnically, culturally, and economically diverse. Students are active in a wide variety of community service activities, including athletics-based programs for local high school students. These include the Adaptive Technology Program, in which students create modified devices for the disabled, and other community-based initiatives linked to academic programs. There are more than 120 campus organizations to choose from—academic, recreational, and special interest groups; the women's center; marching band; the student newspaper; an FM radio station; and the Off-Broadway Players, to name a few. A vibrant campus life includes rallying for the nationally ranked Division I River Hawks hockey team and taking part in an active recreational sports program. In conjunction with the six colleges, the Graduate School enrolls nearly 3,500 students in thirty-two master's degree and fifteen doctoral programs.

Location

The University is located in Lowell, a city of 110,000 that has gained national attention by successfully leveraging its history, ethnic diversity, and entrepreneurial spirit to create a vital urban center. The site of a National Historical Park that honors the city as the birthplace of the industrial revolution, Lowell is also home to an acclaimed professional theater company, annual Kerouac and folk festivals, and museums that include the Museum of American Textile History and the Whistler House Museum. Located 25 miles from the cultural and educational riches of Boston and Cambridge, Lowell is also within an hour of ocean beaches and the lakes and mountains of New Hampshire via major highways and regional train and bus service.

Majors and Degrees

Dual majors are permitted. Dual B.A./B.S. and an array of bachelor's to master's degree programs are available in liberal arts, science, and engineering fields. Predental and premedical programs are available.

The College of Fine Arts, Humanities, and Social Sciences offers baccalaureate programs in American studies, art, criminal justice, design, economics, English, environmental studies, history, liberal arts, modern languages, music business, music performance, music studies, philosophy, political science, psychology, sociology, and sound recording technology.

The College of Sciences offers baccalaureate programs in biological sciences; chemistry with an option in forensics science; computer science; environmental, earth, and atmospheric sciences (meteorology); mathematics; and physics.

The James B. Francis College of Engineering offers baccalaureate day programs in chemical, civil and environmental, electrical and computer, mechanical, and plastics engineering. Engineering programs are accredited by the Accreditation Board for Engineering and Technology, Inc. (ABET). Combined bachelor's/master's programs, internships, and co-op opportunities are available in the College of Engineering.

The School of Health and Environment offers baccalaureate day programs in clinical sciences, which is accredited by the National Accrediting Agency for Clinical Laboratory Sciences (NAACLS); community health education; environmental health; exercise physiology; medical technology; nursing, which is accredited by the National League for Nursing Accrediting Commission (NLNAC); and nutritional science.

The College of Management offers baccalaureate day programs, all of which are accredited by AACSB International—The Association to Advance Collegiate Schools of Business—in business administration (B.S.B.A.), with concentrations in accounting, entrepreneurship, finance, international business, management, management information systems, and marketing.

The University's Graduate School of Education offers widely respected master's and doctoral programs, as well as a range of Plus 1 initial certification courses.

The University's Division of Continuing Studies and Corporate Education offers evening programs through all six colleges. Through the College of Fine Arts, Humanities, and Social Sciences and the College of Sciences, baccalaureate programs in applied mathematics, criminal justice, information technology, and liberal arts are offered. Through the College of Engineering, associate and baccalaureate degrees are offered in civil engineering technology, electronic engineering technology, and mechanical engineering technology. Through the College of Management, an associate degree program in accounting and a baccalaureate degree program in business administration are available. Certificate programs are offered in accounting, computer-assisted manufacturing, computer engineering technology, data/telecommunications, electrooptics, environmental technology, graphic design and digital imagery, hazardous-waste management, Internet technology, land surveying, manufacturing technology, multimedia applications, nutrition, paralegal studies, plastics engineering technology, quality assurance, Spanish, technical writing, UNIX, wastewater treatment, water treatment, and Web site design and development.

Academic Programs

The University operates on a calendar of two semesters, a three-week intersession in January, and a summer term (with two sessions). Full-time undergraduates generally take five courses each semester. A minimum of 120 credits is required for baccalaureate degrees; the minimum credits required for professional degree programs are generally higher. A University general education requirement is imposed for all baccalaureate programs. Majors require 30–60 credits. Elective course options vary widely according to the degree program and major area. Professional degree program options and requirements follow specific accreditation guidelines. Maximum curricular freedom is permitted in B.A. programs. The academic climate is serious and competitive and requires self-motivation.

Academic Facilities

The University has two comprehensive libraries on campus that can also be accessed online. Most of the campus, including outside spaces, has wireless access. The University offers an opt-in emergency notification system and an online self-service system for registration, bill payment, and checking grades.

Costs

The annual costs for 2010–11 for full-time undergraduate residents of Massachusetts were $10,506 per year; for nonresidents of Massachusetts, they were $22,945 per year. Room and board charges were $9067 per year. Accident insurance is covered by fees; major medical insurance is optional. Books and supplies are estimated at $400 to $600, depending on the program. Quoted rates are subject to change.

Financial Aid

The University is committed to making higher education accessible to all qualified students. The University participates in federal and state programs, assisting students through grants-in-aid, loans, employment opportunities, and scholarships. The amount of an award is determined by need, as indicated by the Free Application for Federal Student Aid (FAFSA), which should be filed by March 1. The University awards a growing number of merit-based scholarships. In fiscal 2008, the campus awarded $100 million in financial aid and made offers to meet an average of 94 percent of each student's need.

Faculty

Faculty members are respected researchers who value their commitment to teaching and extend the learning experience beyond the classroom. The full-time resident faculty members number 420. The part-time day faculty members number 224. In addition, approximately 175 part-time faculty members are employed in continuing education programs. Most faculty members teach and conduct research in their disciplines. Graduate teaching assistants also hold part-time instructional positions, particularly as discussion section leaders and laboratory teaching assistants.

Student Government

The Student Government Association and the Residence Hall Association provide opportunities in student government at the all-campus level. Leadership opportunities are provided in residence halls and student organizations. Students also participate in the disciplinary system and in most University committees.

Admission Requirements

All undergraduate day applicants must have a high school diploma or a general equivalency diploma and satisfactory SAT scores. The incoming freshmen class for fall 2010 had an average GPA of 3.2 and the average SAT score was 1089. Students whose high school average is below the required minimum may be considered for admission if they present SAT verbal and mathematics scores that are higher than those specified for the admission of degree candidates by the college or program to which they wish to apply.

Transfer students are considered for fall- or spring-semester admissions. Transcripts of completed work must be on file prior to acceptance. Depending on the number of transfer credits and college GPA, transfer students who seek admission as matriculating day students may be asked to provide a high school record and SAT scores.

Application and Information

For day programs, the University practices rolling admissions, which means that applications are evaluated as soon as they are complete. Entering freshmen are admitted for the fall or spring semester. The preferred deadline for freshman applications is February 15 for the fall semester and December 1 for the spring semester. Applicants to the nursing program are encouraged to apply by the early action deadline of December 1. Otherwise the deadline for nursing applicants is February 1. The preferred deadline for transfer applications is August 15 for the fall semester and January 7 for the spring semester.

For application forms and further information, students should contact:

Office of Undergraduate Admissions
University of Massachusetts Lowell
883 Broadway Street
Suite 110
Lowell, Massachusetts 01854-5104

Phone: 978-934-3931
Web site: http://www.uml.edu
http://www.facebook.com/umlowell
http://www.twitter.com/umasslowell
http://www.youtube.com/user/umasslowell

The steps outside of Cumnock Hall are a popular gathering spot between classes.

The University of Massachusetts Lowell is an Equal Opportunity/Affirmative Action, Title IX employer.

UNIVERSITY OF MEMPHIS

MEMPHIS, TENNESSEE

The University

Located on a beautifully landscaped campus in the heart of one of the South's largest and most progressive cities, the University of Memphis (U of M) is the flagship institution of the Tennessee Board of Regents System. Since its beginning in 1912, the University of Memphis has matured into a major public, metropolitan university recognized regionally and nationally for its academic, research, and athletic programs. The University offers more than 254 areas of study from which to choose.

The University campus comprises 1,160 acres at eight sites. In addition to the main campus, the Park Avenue campus contains spacious living accommodations for married students, a research park, and outstanding varsity athletic training facilities. The University of Memphis also owns the Meeman Biological Field Station, a 623-acre tract used for biological and ecological studies. The Chucalissa Archaeological Museum in southwest Memphis is frequently used as a research and training facility in archaeology and anthropology.

The University of Memphis is an Equal Opportunity/Affirmative Action institution committed to the education of a diverse student body. It has a total enrollment of 22,421 students, including 17,510 undergraduates, from almost every state and many other countries. Approximately 57 percent of University of Memphis students are between the ages of 18 and 22, and members of minority groups account for 45 percent of the enrollment.

Location

The greater Memphis area has a population of approximately 1.1 million, which makes the city the eighteenth largest in the country. Centrally located on the Mississippi River, Memphis is an active hub for business, agriculture, and the transportation industry. The city has the Mid-South's largest medical center and offers many cultural and entertainment opportunities. Major museum exhibits, sporting events, concerts, art shows, lectures, and even barbecue contests take place throughout the year. The AAA baseball team, the Redbirds, and the NBA team, the Grizzlies, both make their homes in Memphis. With its many businesses, industries, and schools, Memphis provides students with employment opportunities in a variety of fields during and after their college careers.

Majors and Degrees

The College of Arts and Sciences offers undergraduate majors organized into three concentration groups: the humanities, the natural and mathematical sciences, and the social sciences. Three degree programs are offered: the Bachelor of Arts, the Bachelor of Science, and the Bachelor of Science in Chemistry. Majors include African and African American studies, anthropology, biology, chemistry, computer science, criminology and criminal justice, earth sciences, economics, English, foreign languages and literatures, history, international studies, mathematical sciences, philosophy, physics, political science, psychology, social work, and sociology. Minors are available in each of those areas—as well as interdisciplinary minors in aerospace studies, Asian studies, environmental studies, Judaic studies, legal thought and liberal studies, military science, naval science, nonprofit management studies, public administration, and women's studies.

The Fogelman College of Business & Economics offers programs of study leading to the Bachelor of Business Administration degree. Majors include accounting, business economics, finance, hospitality and resort management, international business, management, management information systems, marketing management, and logistics/supply chain management. The programs of the College of Business & Economics are fully accredited by AACSB International—The Association to Advance Collegiate Schools of Business.

The College of Communication and Fine Arts is made up of the Departments of Architecture, Art, Communication, Journalism, Theatre and Dance, and the Rudi E. Scheidt School of Music. Majors include architecture, art, art history, communication, interior design, journalism, music, music industry, and theater. The college offers

three undergraduate degrees: the Bachelor of Arts, the Bachelor of Fine Arts, and the Bachelor of Music.

The College of Education at the University of Memphis is among a select few institutions nationwide to meet, without a weakness, National Council for the Accreditation of Teacher Education standards. It is home to more nationally recognized educator programs than any other public university in Tennessee. In addition to teacher education, the college offers accredited degree programs in counseling, health and sport sciences, and leadership. College of Education faculty members serve the community through more than 1,000 days of direct service annually and a rigorous research agenda.

The Herff College of Engineering offers undergraduate programs in biomedical, civil, computer, electrical, and mechanical engineering and in engineering technology. High-ability students have the opportunity to work with faculty members on world-class research for global companies such as FedEx, for governmental organizations such as the U.S. Army Corp of Engineers, or for other premier organizations such as St. Jude Children's Research Hospital.

The University College offers two nontraditional degrees: the Bachelor of Liberal Studies and the Bachelor of Professional Studies, for students with experience, talents, and interests served through personally designed or multidisciplinary programs. Examples of programs that have been developed include alcohol and drug abuse services, biomedical illustration, commercial aviation, correctional administration, family and consumer studies, fire administration and fire prevention technology, health services administration, human services, merchandising (fashion and home furnishings), organizational leadership, law enforcement administration, paralegal studies, preschool and child-care administration, religion in society, and technology and management services.

The University of Memphis also offers specialized degree programs. The Loewenberg School of Nursing offers a Bachelor of Science in Nursing degree. The program is accredited by the National League for Nursing Accrediting Commission and the Commission on Collegiate Education in Nursing. Students benefit from exceptional learning opportunities at health-care agencies in the Memphis area, including ten major hospitals.

Preprofessional training is offered for students who intend to enter law school or a college of dentistry, medicine, nursing, optometry, pharmacy, physical therapy, or veterinary medicine. The University also offers Air Force, Army, and Navy ROTC programs.

The University of Memphis has joined forty-five Tennessee Board of Regents institutions in offering Regents Online Degree Programs. The U of M offers four degree programs: the Bachelor of Liberal Studies in interdisciplinary studies, the Bachelor of Professional Studies in information technology, the Bachelor of Professional Studies in organizational leadership, and the Bachelor of Professional Studies in international organizational leadership. These degree programs are entirely online and are transferable among the participating institutions.

Academic Programs

Freshmen who have not declared a major are advised through the Academic Counseling Center in preparation for formal enrollment in one of the degree-granting colleges. Those freshmen who have chosen a major are assigned to their degree-granting college immediately for academic advising. Each student initially selects courses from the General Education Program, which offers classes in the areas of communication skills, sciences, humanities, and social sciences, thereby ensuring the acquisition of breadth as well as depth of knowledge in various fields. In addition to meeting the requirements of the General Education Program, all students must meet the requirements for their specific degree, as established by the appropriate college or department. The University-wide Helen Hardin Honors Program, now in its thirty-eighth year, is available for academically talented students, and there is an active Emerging Leaders program.

The academic year begins in late August and is divided into two semesters and a summer session. The fall semester ends in mid-December, and the spring semester begins in mid-January. There are also courses offered during shorter sessions within the semesters.

Off-Campus Programs

Students at the University of Memphis have the opportunity to participate in study-abroad programs and the National Student Exchange program. These programs allow students to study in more than fifty other countries as well as in other locations within the continental United States. The University also offers credit and noncredit courses at various locations throughout west Tennessee.

Academic Facilities

The University Libraries of the University of Memphis comprises the Ned R. McWherter Library and three branch libraries: Communications Sciences, Mathematics, and Music. The McWherter Library has 360,000 square feet of space on four floors. The University Libraries' collections include more than 1.2 million bound volumes, 9 million manuscripts, 3.5 million microfilms and fiches, 586,682 government documents, and 12,966 CDs. The mission of the University Libraries is to provide access to and management of information services and resources to support teaching, learning, and research for U of M students, faculty, and staff. The library also serves the general public. It maintains a strong user-instruction program, which reached 7,580 students in 469 class sessions and sixty-five individual consultations last year. The learning commons extends throughout the McWherter Library, with a commons room on the first floor where the research and information services desk is located. All floors of the McWherter Library have wireless capabilities supporting the 168 public-use computers that give users access to all University-provided software applications. Laptop computers are available for 4-hour loan to students. The University Libraries is the regional federal depository library for the State of Tennessee and receives all publications, maps, and electronic data distributed by the government printing office. The library's Preservation and Special Collections Department has holdings on the history and culture of the South, the lower Mississippi River valley, the Mid-South region, Tennessee, the American Civil War, and African American history, including the Civil Rights Movement.

The Department of Theatre and Dance and the Rudi E. Scheidt School of Music, in their adjoining facilities, make an appreciable contribution to campus activities with live drama and concert series, films, and programming over WUMR, the student-staffed campus radio station.

Included among the many research facilities at the University of Memphis are the Benjamin L. Hooks Institute for Social Change, the Integrated Microscopy Center, the FedEx Center for Supply Chain Management, the Institute for Artificial Intelligence, the Ground Water Institute, and the Barbara K. Lipman Early Childhood School and Research Institute. The FedEx Institute of Technology, which opened in 2003, is a cutting-edge facility that brings together students, professors, researchers, and the global business community to formulate the ideas and products of tomorrow.

The state of Tennessee has designated five Centers of Excellence at the University: the Center for Applied Psychological Research, the Center for Research Initiatives and Strategies for the Communicatively Impaired, the Center for Research in Educational Policy, the Institute of Egyptian Art and Archaeology, and the Center for Earthquake Research and Information. In addition, the University houses twenty-five endowed Chairs of Excellence.

Costs

In 2010–11, in-state students paid a maintenance fee of $232 per hour for part-time study until they reached 12 hours ($2784), when the maintenance fee was lowered to $35 per hour for additional hours over 12. Out-of-state students paid a maintenance fee of $789 per hour for part-time study until they reached 12 hours ($9468), when the maintenance fee rate was reduced to $118 per hour for additional hours over 12. On-campus residence hall rates ranged from $3590 to $6710 for an academic year. All part-time students paid an additional program service fee of $78.50 per hour for part-time study until they reached six hours, when the program service fee was highest at $606.

Financial Aid

Financial assistance is provided through four basic sources: scholarships, grants, loans, and employment. Scholarships are offered through the Scholarship Office as well as through various academic, performance, and athletic departments. Residents of Tennessee may be eligible for the state's HOPE Scholarship. An application for admission is required to be considered for general and distinguished academic scholarship programs. Applicants for financial aid must submit the completed Free Application for Federal Student Aid (FAFSA) to the Financial Aid Office, which places the student under consideration for all financial aid programs. The priority deadline for filing the FAFSA is February 1. More than $200 million is awarded annually. The University operates two programs of student employment: the Federal Work-Study Program and a regular work program.

Faculty

The University of Memphis has 913 full-time faculty members. In addition, many adjunct professors are hired from the community to teach in their fields of expertise.

Student Government

The Student Government Association consists of officers, a senate, a cabinet, and a judiciary elected annually by the student body. Its goals are to present the opinions of the student body to the administration, to enact legislation beneficial to the students, and to promote a broad range of student activities.

Admission Requirements

The admission of entering freshmen is based on the transcript of a four-year course of study at an approved or accredited high school that includes prescribed units of English, mathematics, natural/physical sciences, U.S. history, social studies, foreign language, and visual/performing arts. The General Educational Development test and high school equivalency diploma are accepted when applicable. The admissions process is a competitive one and is based on a student's cumulative high school grade point average and ACT or SAT scores. The average ACT for the fall 2010 freshman class was 22, and the average GPA was 3.3. The admission of transfer students is based on the applicant's grade point average, academic standing at a former institution, and scores on the approved admission tests. Transfer students will often be required to provide a high school transcript.

Application and Information

Inquiries about admission and requests for information about any undergraduate college of the University should be addressed to the Office of Admissions. Applications and supporting credentials must be submitted to the Office of Admissions before the beginning of the intended term of entry. While the established application deadlines are July 1 for the fall semester, December 1 for the spring semester, and May 1 for the summer session, early application is strongly encouraged so applicants can be considered for scholarship opportunities and take advantage of early registration. A student must apply and be accepted by February 1 to be considered for academic merit scholarships. Additional scholarships may have earlier deadlines. Registration for fall classes occurs at New Student Orientation. Prospective students are encouraged to visit the University for a campus tour, which can be arranged by contacting the Office of Admissions.

Office of Admissions
Recruitment and Orientation Services
University of Memphis
101 John Wilder Tower
Memphis, Tennessee 38152-3520
Phone: 901-678-2169
        800-669-2678 (toll-free)
Web site: http://www.memphis.edu
         http://on.fb.me/UofMemphis (Facebook)
         http://www.twitter.com/uofmemphis

The McWherter Library.

UNIVERSITY OF NEW ENGLAND
BIDDEFORD AND PORTLAND, MAINE

The University

The University of New England (UNE) is an independent, coeducational, comprehensive university committed to academic excellence and the enhancement of the quality of life for the people, organizations, and communities it serves. The University fosters critical inquiry through a student-centered academic environment rich in research, scholarship, creative activity, and service while providing opportunities for acquiring and applying knowledge in selected clinical, professional, and community settings.

UNE's student body of 5,168 includes 2,124 full-time undergraduates, 568 part-time undergraduates, 855 doctor's degree–professional practice students, 1,330 full-time graduate students, and 291 part-time graduate students. Students are enrolled in a wide variety of academic programs in UNE's four colleges: the College of Arts and Sciences, the Westbrook College of Health Professions, the College of Pharmacy, and the College of Osteopathic Medicine (housing Maine's only medical school). At the undergraduate level students represent thirty-five different states and several other countries in over forty undergraduate degree programs.

UNE traces its history to 1831 with the founding of Westbrook College, one of Maine's oldest institutions of learning. Today's university represents the joining of three unique higher education institutions through the combining of St. Francis College and the New England College of Osteopathic Medicine in 1978 and Westbrook College in 1996.

The University has chosen as its primary fields of education business management, education, health sciences (both mental and physical), the humanities, the natural sciences, and social sciences. The University of New England's philosophy of education and student life places emphasis on the quality of instruction and the practical application of academic material.

Each program includes the opportunity for learning in a community-based setting. Internships, co-ops, clinicals, and student teaching add up to the practical experience that allows students at UNE to apply the skills learned in the classroom to real job situations.

The University of New England has two campuses. The Biddeford Campus is located on the southern coast of Maine, in Biddeford, 90 miles north of Boston and 20 miles south of Portland, Maine's largest city. UNE's Portland Campus is located in Portland, Maine. As both campuses are geographically placed in areas that afford a high-quality lifestyle, it is only natural that the University of New England consistently engages itself in providing its students with high-quality programming and high-quality education.

The University encourages students to become involved in activities, clubs, and sports. Popular interests include scuba diving, skiing, hiking, biking, varsity and intramural sports, swimming, community service programs, and photography. The University of New England offers a wide range of services on both campuses. Special features include a full health clinic, a dental hygiene clinic, career counseling, personal counseling, learning support services, and an extensive student leadership development program.

Student Support Services provides a wide-range of services to assist students with psychological and emotional health, academic support, educational and career planning, and equal opportunities during their academic experience. The Office of Career Services provides academic and career exploration assistance, assistance in applying to graduate schools, self-assessment and personal interest exploration, resume help, job listings, and job fairs. Learning Assistance Services, another department within Student Support Services, offers a comprehensive array of academic support, including placement testing, courses, workshops, tutoring, and individual consultations.

Both campuses offer a variety of cultural and social events. The Campus Center at the Biddeford Campus and the Finley Recreation Center on the Portland Campus provide a setting for many recreational and sports activities. The University of New England Athletic Department operates an NCAA Division III varsity athletics program. Varsity sports for men are basketball, cross-country, golf, lacrosse, soccer, and ice hockey. Varsity sports for women are basketball, cross-country, field hockey, lacrosse, soccer, softball, swimming, and volleyball. Intramural teams in basketball, floor hockey, softball, skiing, and volleyball are popular. The University also has a number of club sports teams.

On the Biddeford Campus, Decary Hall houses a cafeteria, classrooms, meeting rooms, and faculty and administrative offices. The Campus Center contains a fitness center, bookstore, gym, pool, student union, racquetball courts, an indoor track, a variety of multipurpose rooms, and administrative offices. The University maintains ten dormitories on campus. Marcil Hall houses a variety of classrooms, and faculty offices. The Harold Alfond Center for Health Sciences houses biology and chemistry labs as well as lecture halls, classrooms, a gross anatomy lab, and UNE's medical school facilities. The Marine Science Education and Research Center has classrooms, wet labs, aquaculture labs, and a marine mammal rehabilitation wing. There are three major recent additions to the Biddeford campus. The Pickus Center for Biomedical Research is a state-of-the-art facility; the Peter and Cecile Morgane Hall is a science center providing additional classrooms and laboratories for biology, chemistry, and physics; and the George and Barbara Bush Center houses the offices of UNE's president and provost and the ground-floor Windward Café with outdoor terraces and flexible areas for students to study, meet, and socialize.

On the University of New England's Portland Campus, there are two residence halls and the Alexander Hall Student Union, which houses the dining hall, bookstore, the Wing Lounge, and a variety of meeting rooms. The Finley Recreation Center has a gym and fitness facilities. Ludcke Auditorium, whose main structure was built in 1887, is home to concerts, plays, and a number of workshops and meetings. The new College of Pharmacy building welcomed the first professional pharmacy class in September of 2009.

Location

The University of New England's two campuses are located in the picturesque southern coastal beach communities of Maine. The 540-acre Biddeford Campus in Biddeford, home to the College of Arts and Sciences and the College of Osteopathic Medicine, is situated on a beautiful coastal site where the Saco River flows into the Atlantic Ocean and includes more than 4,000 feet of water frontage. Located 20 miles to the north is the Portland Campus, home to the Westbrook College of Health Professions and the College of Pharmacy. It is set on 41 acres in a quiet residential setting in Portland. Students at both campuses can enjoy the vibrant social life offered in nearby metropolitan Boston (located 90 miles to the south of Biddeford) or Portland and the dynamic outdoor recreational activities that have made Maine a prime tourist destination. Southern Maine is conveniently serviced by a number of airlines at the Portland International Jetport and by bus and train service with stations in Biddeford/Saco and Portland, making the University's campuses very accessible to all areas of the Northeastern United States and beyond.

Majors and Degrees

UNE offers highly competitive undergraduate and graduate programs in a variety of areas. On the undergraduate level, the University confers Bachelor of Arts and Bachelor of Science degrees.

Bachelor's degrees are offered in animal behavior, applied exercise science, aquaculture and aquarium science, art education, athletic training, biochemistry, biological sciences, business, chemistry, communications, dental hygiene, elementary education, English, environmental science, environmental studies, health sciences, history, liberal studies (including prelaw), marine biology, mathematics, medical biology (health and medical sciences tracks for predental, premedicine, and pre–veterinary studies), neuroscience, nursing, political science, psychology, psychology and social relations, sociology, secondary education (science, English, social sciences, mathematics) and sport management.

Individualized majors, various minors, the pre–physical therapy designation, an accelerated pre–physician assistant studies program, prepharmacy with a path to UNE's Pharm.D. program, and a secondary education certification (Teacher Certification Program) are also available at the undergraduate level.

Academic Programs

All undergraduate programs at UNE have a core curriculum as a common thread. Designed to provide a foundation in the liberal arts, the core reflects the values of the college and is designed to prepare students for living informed, thoughtful, and active lives in a complex and changing society. It provides an innovative common learning experience for all UNE undergraduates. It invites students to explore four college-wide themes: Environmental Awareness, Social and Global Awareness, Critical Thinking: Human Responses to Problems and Challenges, and Citizenship. Skills of communications, mathematics, and critical thinking are taught throughout the core.

A bachelor's degree is awarded upon successful completion of at least 120 credit hours and fulfillment of specific program and University requirements.

The University academic year consists of two semesters.

Off-Campus Programs

UNE is committed to supplementing the traditional learning process with practical applications. All students are encouraged to participate in cooperative education programs, field placements, and practicums. These experiences provide valuable learning situations and increase a student's exposure to job-related opportunities, and they are required for graduation by most majors. Students also have the opportunity to arrange a study-abroad experience. The Office of International Education promotes the goals of international cooperation and understanding through rigorous academic programs, overseas study opportunities, student-faculty research projects, and a host of special programs designed to address current issues in international relations and cultural studies.

Academic Facilities

On the Biddeford Campus, Decary Hall houses classrooms, laboratories, and faculty and administrative offices. The Jack Ketchum Library has been expanded to provide more library and classroom space as well as a media center and special event space. Marcil Hall houses classrooms, faculty offices, and the facility for the occupational therapy program. The Harold Alfond Center for Health Sciences houses labs and classrooms for the medical school, undergraduate health and life science programs, and graduate health programs. The Marine Science Education and Research Center is a $7.5-million facility featuring a marine mammal rehab center as well as classrooms, wet and dry laboratories, and research areas. The marine mammal rehabilitation center works primarily with seals, porpoise, and sea turtles. The Department of Creative and Fine Arts has moved to a new building which provides faculty offices and more studio space for drawing, painting, printmaking, sculpting, and photography. The new Peter and Ceceile Morgane Hall houses biology and chemistry laboratories, undergraduate classrooms, and faculty office space. Two other new facilities have opened recently: the Pickus Center for Biomedical Research, and the George and Barbara Bush Center.

On the University's Portland Campus, Ludcke Auditorium is used for a variety of academic programs. Coleman Dental Hygiene Building houses classroom, clinic, and faculty space. The Blewett Science Center, home of UNE nursing programs, consists of science labs and classrooms. The University created a Performance Enhancement and Evaluation Center (PEEC) that is an entire center devoted to learning and assessment of patient evaluation skills. The equipment includes two METI Human Patient Simulators and two Laerdal SimMan simulators. Proctor Hall is also a classroom building and is home to the Proctor Learning and Career Center. Josephine S. Abplanalp Library houses study space and computer terminals, along with an outstanding collection of books and periodicals and the Maine Women Writers Collection. The University of New England libraries have over 150,000 volumes and print journals, over 22,000 print and electronic full-text journal titles, and 6,000 electronic books. The new building for the College of Pharmacy opened in the summer of 2009.

Costs

The costs per academic year for 2011–12 are tuition, $29,432; room and board, $11,866; and fees, $1071.

Financial Aid

In 2010–11, approximately 99.1 percent of all full-time students received some form of financial assistance. The average package was $25,268. Financial award packages include scholarships, grants, loans, and employment. The University of New England has an extensive scholarship program that is based on academic performance. These scholarships can range from $3000 to $18,000.

Faculty

The men and women who teach at the University of New England are an experienced group of people with more than 85 percent having earned the highest degree in their fields, and they bring to the University varied backgrounds as teachers and practitioners of their disciplines. They are highly competent, demanding, concerned, accessible, and willing to give individual attention to students. Most important, they have come to the University for many of the same reasons that prompt their students to attend. The match between what the faculty has to offer and what the students need and expect is the key to the rare educational environment at the University of New England.

Student Government

The Student Senate is a vital part of the student life at both campuses of the University of New England. The student government has its own operating budget, which is derived from the student fees. The organization covers student services and public relations.

Admission Requirements

The University welcomes applications from students who are seriously pursuing an education of high quality. Candidates can file their admission application after the completion of their junior year of high school. All applicants are considered on an individual basis.

Students applying for admission are expected to submit a completed application, a $40 nonrefundable application fee, transcripts of all academic work (high school and college), and scores on either the ACT or SAT. Students who do not use English as their primary language must submit TOEFL scores. Students applying for admission should have completed a curriculum that includes English, mathematics, science, and social sciences. International students must also complete the International Student Supplemental Application. Applicants who are considering majors in the life or health sciences should show strength and preparation in mathematics and science. All prospective students are strongly encouraged to visit the campuses of the University of New England for an information session and tour. Information sessions and tours are held weekdays from 10 a.m. to 4 p.m. An appointment should be requested by letter, telephone, or via the Web site at https://www.une.edu/admissions/visit/visit.asp.

Application and Information

The undergraduate freshman admission application deadline is February 15; applications received after that date are reviewed on a space-available basis. There is a December 1 priority application deadline with a December 31 notification date. Applications for the spring term are accepted through December 15.

For application information, students should contact:

Office of Admissions
University Campus
University of New England
Hills Beach Road
Biddeford, Maine 04005
Phone: 207-283-0171
      800-477-4863 Ext. 2297 (toll-free)
Fax: 207-602-5900
E-mail: admissions@une.edu
Web site: http://www.une.edu/

UNIVERSITY OF NEW HAMPSHIRE

DURHAM, NEW HAMPSHIRE

The University

The University of New Hampshire (UNH) is a rising star among American research universities, a community of exceptional faculty members and talented and energetic students from forty-four states and twenty-six countries. The University has a sizeable undergraduate population of approximately 12,500 but still feels cozy and intimate. This is due in part to a campus layout that is manageable and beautiful—with college greens, water, and a pleasing mix of classic and modern buildings that gradually give way to 2,600 acres of woods, fields, and farms. It is also due to the school's traditions of strong student-faculty interaction and active student culture. As one student put it, "It's easy to meet people and get involved in campus activities here. You need to have some initiative, but student leaders, residence hall staff, and others also seek you out."

The University offers students a variety of housing options, including halls of 100 to 600 students and two on-campus apartment complexes. Themed housing, such as honors, first-year experience, or international, is offered by dorm or floor. Holloway Commons, a spectacular dining and conference facility with seating for 850 and an after-hours café, opened in 2003, and Southeast Residential Community (SERC) Buildings A & B, 326- and 227-bed residence halls, opened in 2006. Parsons Hall, a chemistry teaching and research facility, underwent a $50-million renovation in 2009.

The Memorial Union Building (MUB) is the University's community center. Housed in the MUB are two movie theaters, the UNH Copy Center, the UNH Bookstore, the Ticket Office, specific lounge/study space for both nontraditional and graduate students, and Granite Square Station, the undergraduate mail center. Computing and Information Services provides a computer cluster and a help desk with walk-in service. The MUB Food Court offers expanded dining options, and food service is also available in the Coffee Office. The Student Senate Office; Office of Multicultural Student Affairs; WUNH-radio; *The New Hampshire,* the student newspaper; and nearly 160 other student organizations originate in the MUB. Students at the University can participate in a rich cultural life. Numerous lectures, films, concerts, exhibitions, meet-the-artist receptions, master classes, dance performances, and theatrical productions are offered throughout the year. The UNH Celebrity Series, the Art Gallery, and the Departments of Music, Theater and Dance, and Art and Art History bring artists of international stature to campus. Most events are free for students.

Many opportunities for athletics and recreation, regardless of skill or ability, are offered through Campus Recreation. The Hamel Student Recreation Center is available to all full-time matriculating students. The center offers participants two multipurpose courts, a group exercise studio, a club/martial art studio, an 8,000-square-foot fitness center with more than 100 exercise stations, three basketball/volleyball courts, an indoor track, a lounge, several classrooms, locker rooms, towel and lock service at the equipment room, and saunas. Campus Recreation offers a variety of activities designed to make it easier to reach personal fitness goals and have fun. Participants may take part in one of the many group exercise classes, such as step aerobics, cycling, or cardio kickboxing. Other opportunities include Pilates, yoga, tai chi, a climbing wall, racquetball, personal training, or massage therapy. Noncredit courses are also offered, including CPR and first aid. The intramural sports program consists of more than twenty different sports and activities offered to

men's, women's, and co-rec teams. Campus Recreation forms and assists special interest groups or sport club teams to reflect the varied recreation and cultural preferences of campus community members. Some clubs are intensely competitive, requiring a daily commitment to workouts and conditioning. They compete either on an inter-collegiate basis with New England teams or sponsor University tournaments. Other clubs meet on a casual come-when-you-can basis. In addition, Campus Recreation offers ice skating, manages a large outdoor recreation facility with its own sailing and canoe center, runs a children's camp (Camp Wildcat) in the summer, and supports the men's and women's sport club crew boat house. UNH also has twenty different men's and women's Division I sports teams, including football, which is Division I-AA.

Location

Nestled in New Hampshire's seacoast region, the town of Durham is an outdoor-lover's dream, with ocean, ski and hiking mountains, and charming working-port cities nearby. Popular road trips for students include Boston (about an hour), Portsmouth (about 20 minutes), and the White Mountains (about an hour). With a nonstudent population of 8,000, Durham is a classic college town that caters to the student clientele. Durham's Main Street includes restaurants, coffeehouses, a bookstore, pizza shops, and other student hangouts.

Majors and Degrees

The University of New Hampshire comprises seven colleges and schools: College of Liberal Arts, College of Engineering and Physical Sciences, College of Health and Human Services, College of Life Sciences and Agriculture, Whittemore School of Business and Economics, Thompson School of Applied Science (which offers two-year associate degree programs), and the University of New Hampshire at Manchester, the University's urban campus. The University offers more than 100 majors through these fully accredited academic divisions. New Hampshire enjoys a strong reputation in a wide range of academic fields, with biology, business administration, English, communication, engineering, environmental studies, history, hospitality management, kinesiology, marine and animal sciences, performing arts, political science, and psychology among those topping the list. The business school offers several options under the business administration major that include accounting, entrepreneurial venture creation, information systems, international business and economics, management, and a student-designed track.

Academic Programs

The Discovery Program, which encompasses the University's general education requirements, provides students with a broad foundation in the liberal arts and an introduction to the methods of inquiry needed for academic success. All students must complete ten courses which include writing skills; quantitative reasoning; biological and physical sciences; historical perspectives; world cultures; fine and performing arts; social science; humanities; and environment, technology, and society. A senior year Capstone Experience as well as inquiry courses allow students to reflect on their education and synthesize knowledge and skills gained from the Discovery Program. Depending on their academic program, students may begin course work in their major as early as their first year.

A major research university, UNH prides itself on producing students who have had meaningful research experiences with a world-class faculty. Programs such as the Undergraduate Research Opportunities Program and International Research Opportunities Program provide research grants each year for undergraduates to work closely with faculty members, on campus or abroad, on original projects. Over 900 students participated in the Undergraduate Research Conference in 2010. Students majoring in a wide range of subjects can access a wealth of research centers and facilities, some on the campus itself, others in surrounding towns. As New Hampshire's major public institution, the University is involved in a wide range of outreach programs with state and industry groups. These partnerships provide abundant opportunities for students interested in internships.

Academic Facilities

The Dimond Library is the state's only public university research library. The library offers three grand reading rooms, seating for 1,200 students, and state-of-the-art technology, including wireless and Internet. The Parker Adaptive Technology Room provides an array of technological options for patrons who have learning, mobility, or vision disabilities. Through ResNet, students who live on-campus have high-speed Internet access to UNH library resources, class software and information, e-mail, and other services. The Environmental Technology Building is a multidisciplinary science and engineering research facility with a focus on environmental technology development. Most of the University's cultural events take place in the Paul Creative Arts Center, which houses two theaters, dressing rooms, a well-equipped scene shop, a costume shop, a green room, storage facilities, classrooms, and the faculty and staff offices. New Hampshire Hall contains the Newman Dance Studio and a smaller stage studio.

Costs

The 2010–11 tuition and fees for undergraduate in-state students were $13,672. For out-of-state students, tuition and fees were $27,642. Room (double) and board (unlimited meal plan) cost $9052.

Financial Aid

Approximately 60 percent of students receive some form of need-based financial assistance from UNH. University scholarships ranging from $1000 to $10,000 are awarded automatically to qualified first-year students who apply for admission. Amounts are subject to change. Other scholarships are awarded by individual academic departments. The average financial aid package, including gift, loan, and employment assistance, was $12,602 for New Hampshire residents and $17,207 for nonresidents. The University participates in the Federal Pell Grant program, the Federal Supplemental Educational Opportunity Grant program, the Federal Perkins Loan program, the Federal Work-Study Program, and the Federal Stafford Student Loan program. Students are required to submit the Free Application for Federal Student Aid (FAFSA) by March 1.

Faculty

The University of New Hampshire has 621 full-time and 387 part-time faculty members, of whom 84 percent hold doctoral degrees and 11 percent hold master's degrees. The student-faculty ratio is 18:1. The UNH faculty includes winners of the Pulitzer Prize, Guggenheim awards, and many other prestigious awards and honors, while the University ranks among the top campuses in the nation in the percentage of faculty members who have won Fulbright scholarships. This research productivity has a powerful effect on students, who can share the experience of discovery.

Student Government

The Student Senate comprises a governing body of student officers and senators. They are the voice of the student body, representing student opinion to members of the faculty, staff, and administration as well as the University community and the state legislature. The Senate believes that all students have the right to participate in University decisions and policy making. Committees of the Senate include areas in academics, residential life, commuters, health and human services, judicial affairs, and community change. They also approve and monitor the rates and uses of all mandatory student fees.

Admission Requirements

Admission to a bachelor's degree program is based upon successful completion of a strong secondary school program of college-preparatory course work. Primary consideration is given to the academic record, as demonstrated by the quality of the candidate's secondary school course selection and achievement. Consideration is also given to the student's recommendation, personal essay, additional information, character, initiative, leadership, special talents, and SAT or ACT with writing component results. Most successful candidates present at least 4 years of English and mathematics and 3 or more years of laboratory science, social science, and foreign language. Recommended mathematics preparation includes the equivalent of algebra I, geometry, algebra II, and trigonometry or advanced math. Students who plan to specialize in health, physical sciences, life sciences, engineering, or mathematics should present at least 4 years of mathematics, including trigonometry as well as laboratory course work in chemistry and/or physics. Students pursuing business-related studies should also have completed 4 years of mathematics, including trigonometry.

All candidates for admission to bachelor's degree programs are required to submit SAT or ACT scores with writing component results. SAT Subject Tests are not required. A foreign language SAT Subject Test may satisfy the foreign language requirement of the Bachelor of Arts degree programs. Required scores vary by test. International students whose primary language is not English must submit TOEFL or IELTS results. The recommended minimum TOEFL score is 213 (computer-based) or 550 (paper-based) or 80 (Internet-based). The minimum IELTS score is 6.5.

Candidates applying for programs in the Department of Music must make arrangements with the department chairperson for an audition (603-862-2404).

Application and Information

High school students who seek fall-semester admission may apply anytime after the start of the senior year and before the February 1 regular decision deadline. Admission notifications are provided on a continuous basis through April 15. Admitted first-year students have until May 1 to confirm their intent to enroll at the University. The review of candidates begins with the receipt of all required application materials. The Early Action (EA) Program allows candidates to receive a response by mid-January of their senior year; EA candidates must submit admission applications by November 15. In some cases, the Admission Committee requests senior mid-year grade reports in order to make a final admission decision. All positive admission decisions made prior to the completion of a candidate's course work in progress are considered provisional and are subject to the verification of satisfactory senior-year achievement when final high school transcripts are reviewed.

Office of Admissions
University of New Hampshire
3 Garrison Avenue
Durham, New Hampshire 03824-3501
Phone: 603-862-1360
Fax: 603-862-0077
Web site: http://www.unh.edu/admissions
http://www.facebook.com/universityofnewhampshire

UNIVERSITY OF NEW HAVEN
WEST HAVEN, CONNECTICUT

The University

The University of New Haven's (UNH) mission is to prepare career-ready graduates for meaningful roles in today's global economy and to nurture the pursuit of lifelong learning. Founded in 1920, the University of New Haven is a private, independent institution focused on combining professional education with liberal arts and sciences. UNH is committed to educational innovation, continuous improvement in career and professional education, and support of scholarship and professional development. UNH became a four-year college in 1958. Moving to its present location in West Haven in 1960, UNH rapidly expanded its programs, facilities, and faculty, attracting a student body that now stands at almost 6,000—including the current enrollment of 3,079 full-time day students among its undergraduates.

The University is fully accredited by the New England Association of Schools and Colleges (NEASC). Individual programs, departments, and schools hold various forms of national professional accreditation. Four of the University of New Haven's bachelor's degree programs—chemical, civil, electrical, and mechanical engineering—are fully accredited by the Engineering Accreditation Commission of the Accreditation Board for Engineering and Technology, Inc. (EAC/ABET). The computer science program is fully accredited by the Computing Accreditation Commission of the Accreditation Board for Engineering and Technology, Inc. (CAC/ABET).

Despite a broad academic program, UNH is small enough to accommodate individualized educational needs. Programs evolve and adapt to meet changing career interests as well as the requirements of business, industry, and professional fields. Small classes foster close student-faculty relationships. Accelerated weekend and evening programs in business and convenient evening hours provide access for part-time students in engineering, computers, public safety, and the arts and sciences.

The main campus is in West Haven, Connecticut, on a hillside close to Long Island Sound. UNH also operates a satellite branch, the Southeastern Center in New London, Connecticut. Main campus administrative and classroom buildings support the University's four academic colleges: the College of Arts and Sciences, the College of Business, the Tagliatela College of Engineering, and the Henry C. Lee College of Criminal Justice and Forensic Sciences. Following the addition of the Graduate School in 1969, New Haven College was designated a university. Twenty-nine master's degree programs attract full- and part-time graduate students, while nearly 100 associate and bachelor's degree programs are available to entering freshmen and transfer students in a great variety of academic disciplines. In 2007, UNH established University College to oversee the graduate school admissions process as well as its evening, accelerated, cohort, and executive degree programs.

Other main campus buildings include the Marvin K. Peterson Library, Echlin Hall, the Bayer Hall admissions building, the Campus Bookstore, new residence halls and apartments, and Bartels Hall, the campus center, which houses dining facilities and student activities. The Charger Gymnasium and athletic fields are located on the North Campus, just two short blocks from Maxcy Hall, the main administration building. The David

A. Beckerman Recreational Center, a state-of-the-art athletic facility for the benefit of all students, opened in fall 2007.

The University of New Haven has one of the most respected and successful NCAA Division II athletics programs in the country, with Charger teams combining to make over 120 post-season tournament appearances. In fall 2008, UNH joined the Northeast-10, one of the most prestigious and celebrated conferences in the nation. UNH and its student athletes have won numerous conference, regional, and national awards, both athletically and academically. The University offers seventeen varsity sports: men's baseball, basketball, cross-country, football, soccer, indoor and outdoor track and field, and volleyball; and women's basketball, cross-country, lacrosse, soccer, softball, tennis, indoor and outdoor track and field, and volleyball. In fall 2009, football made its highly anticipated return, playing its first varsity season since 2003.

Approximately two thirds of the full-time undergraduate day students live on campus in the fourteen residence halls. More than eighty clubs and organizations are open to students. Included are student chapters of professional societies, religious organizations, social groups, special-interest clubs, student councils, cultural groups, and fraternities and sororities.

Location

West Haven is contiguous to New Haven. There are theaters that attract star performers from the entertainment world, a deepwater harbor and beaches, fine restaurants, museums, and galleries in the area. Numerous social and cultural programs are presented by the many colleges and universities in the area. New Haven is served by a local airport and major railroads, and its location at the junction of two interstate highways places the University of New Haven within easy driving distance of New York, Boston, Cape Cod, and the ski areas of New England.

Majors and Degrees

The College of Arts and Sciences offers a Bachelor of Arts degree in art, chemistry, communication, English, global studies, graphic design, history, interior design, liberal studies, mathematics, music, music and sound recording, music industry, political science, and psychology; and a Bachelor of Science degree in biology, biotechnology, dental hygiene, environmental science, marine biology, mathematics, music and sound recording, and nutrition and dietetics.

The College of Business offers the Bachelor of Science degree in accounting, finance, hospitality and tourism management, management, management of sport industries, and marketing. In addition, the College of Business has launched a fast-track study program for the fall 2011 semester, allowing academically strong students the opportunity to earn a Bachelor of Science degree in business and a Master of Business Administration (M.B.A.) in just four years.

The Tagliatela College of Engineering offers a Bachelor of Science degree in chemical engineering, chemistry, civil engineering, computer engineering, computer science, electrical engineering, general engineering, information technology, mechanical engineering, sustainability studies, and system engineering. The Tagliatela College of Engineering also offers a new certificate program in biomedical engineering.

The Henry C. Lee College of Criminal Justice and Forensic Sciences offers a Bachelor of Science degree in criminal justice, fire protection engineering, fire science, forensic science, and legal studies.

Academic Programs

The University of New Haven offers a broad range of programs in both liberal arts and professional areas. Experiential learning is emphasized, and there are diverse and numerous opportunities for career-oriented internships, cooperative education, independent study, and industrial projects. Certain types of professional experience are required in a number of degree programs. The Center for Learning Resources offers a tutoring service open to all students.

The undergraduate division operates on a 4-1-4 calendar. Credit is given for successful scores on the CLEP and Advanced Placement examinations. A University honors program provides outstanding study opportunities in most undergraduate disciplines. The residence requirement for all degrees is 30 credit hours.

UNH believes that all students pursuing a bachelor's degree should develop a common set of skills; the University's goal is to prepare all graduates for the complex lives they will lead in a changing world. This can best be done through the University Core Curriculum, which consists of a minimum of 40 credit hours in six basic competencies.

Academic Facilities

The Marvin K. Peterson Library contains more than 400,000 volumes in hard copy and provides access to about 20,000 electronic books and 20,000 e-journals from the library Web site and Voyager online catalog. Databases are available on a wide variety of subjects, with a focus on business, criminal justice/forensic science, engineering, and psychology, as well as general arts and sciences. Through interlibrary loan services, the University community has access to the holdings of more than 8,650 libraries.

Communication majors participate in workshops along with studying sound, film, and television production and radio broadcasting techniques in well-equipped radio/television studios and laboratories. The Tagliatela College of Engineering has modern laboratories and equipment to support its programs. The College of Arts and Sciences maintains art studios, state-of-the-art recording studios, music practice rooms, and science, psychology, and language labs. Hands-on instruction and demonstrations are available in kitchen facilities for students in the hospitality and tourism and the nutrition and dietetics programs. Dental hygiene students gain experience in the Dental Hygiene Clinic.

There are more than a dozen computer labs for student use and teaching on campus. One of these is devoted to forensic computing instruction for the Henry C. Lee College of Criminal Justice and Forensic Sciences.

Costs

Full-time undergraduate tuition for the 2011–12 academic year, including all fees, is $31,750; room and board cost $13,300.

Financial Aid

UNH offers a comprehensive financial aid program that includes University resources as well as state, federal, and private-aid programs. Approximately 82 percent of full-time undergraduate students receive some form of assistance. Students receive federal aid through the Federal Pell Grant, Federal Supplemental Educational Opportunity Grant, Federal Work-Study, Federal Perkins Loan, Federal Direct Student Loan, and Federal Direct PLUS loan programs. The University also administers programs sponsored by the state of Connecticut for Connecticut residents attending the University. Some students also qualify for financial aid from other states and from private companies, organizations, and foundations.

Faculty

It is a long-standing University policy that the faculty members teach a mix of undergraduate and graduate courses in order to preserve academic quality at all levels. Faculty members are selected and promoted primarily on the basis of teaching effectiveness, professional qualifications and performance, and contributions to the academic community. No classes are taught by teaching assistants. Some faculty members hold administrative positions and continue to teach. There are 207 full-time and 400 part-time faculty members, making the student-faculty ratio 16:1. The majority of full-time faculty members (more than 90 percent) hold terminal degrees in their disciplines.

Student Government

The Undergraduate Student Government Association supervises annual expenditures by undergraduate clubs and organizations, directs liaison committees, supports student publications and the student-operated FM radio station, and schedules cultural and social events. Student representatives are elected annually to the University's Board of Governors.

Admission Requirements

To be eligible for admission, one must be a high school graduate or present evidence of equivalent preparation. Scores from the SAT or the ACT are required. The admission decision is based on the student's overall high school record, SAT or ACT results, letter(s) of recommendation, and a 250–300-word personal essay.

Prospective students are encouraged to visit the campus for an information session and tour. To arrange a campus visit, please go to: www.newhaven.edu/visitus. Out-of-state residents are considered for admission on the same basis as state residents.

Application and Information

To apply to the University of New Haven, a student must submit the completed application form, a nonrefundable $25 fee for electronic submission ($75 for paper submission), official records of all academic work completed, SAT or ACT results, a letter of recommendation, and a personal essay. International students are required to demonstrate proficiency in English as well as provide documentation of financial support. The University of New Haven does not discriminate on the basis of age, color, sex, religion, race, sexual orientation, national origin, or disability in admission or treatment of students, in administration or distribution of financial aid, or in recruitment or treatment of employees. The University is authorized under federal law to enroll nonimmigrant alien students who meet the University's academic and English proficiency standards. The admissions office employs a rolling admissions system with the opportunity to apply for early action.

Undergraduate Admissions
University of New Haven
300 Boston Post Road
West Haven, Connecticut 06516
Phone: 203-932-7319
      800-DIAL-UNH (342-5864) Ext. 7319 (toll-free)
E-mail: adminfo@newhaven.edu
Web site: http://www.newhaven.edu

UNIVERSITY OF NEW ORLEANS
NEW ORLEANS, LOUISIANA

The University

The University of New Orleans (UNO) is part of the rich cultural tapestry of its hometown, which is one of the most extraordinary cities in the world. Established in 1958 to bring publicly supported higher education to the New Orleans area, UNO is fully accredited by the Commission on Colleges of the Southern Association of Colleges and Schools. With an enrollment of nearly 12,000 students (approximately 9,000 undergraduates and 3,000 graduate students) in fall 2010, UNO offers both undergraduate and graduate degrees through the doctoral level.

UNO derives its strength from its urban setting and strives to enhance the economic, social, and cultural amenities of New Orleans through its numerous research projects, outreach programs, and special cooperative agreements. The University of New Orleans attracts students from all fifty states (approximately 12 percent) and 102 countries; a majority of the students are Louisiana residents (approximately 88 percent). The diverse student population (42 percent of students are members of ethnic minorities) provides an excellent opportunity for personal growth and understanding.

For students who are interested in on-campus housing, UNO offers two unique styles of living. Privateer Place overlooks beautiful Lake Pontchartrain and includes a swimming pool and Jacuzzi. Privateer Place contains seventy-two 2-person unfurnished efficiency apartments, 216 furnished two-bedroom apartments, and sixty furnished four-bedroom apartments. In fall 2007, UNO opened a new $38.5-million residence hall complex (Pontchartrain Hall), composed of two 4-story buildings totaling about 220,000 square feet. The facility includes 236 suite-style units that can accommodate 749 students, as well as TV and recreation rooms, study lounges, laundry facilities, and a convenience store. All complexes have disability-accessible rooms available.

Campus dining facilities are conveniently located near all on-campus housing facilities and heavily populated student areas, with various hours of operation. Other student services include six on-campus computer labs that provide free Internet access, a learning resource center that offers additional tutoring services, student counseling services, an on-campus medical office and pharmacy, student legal counseling, and religious centers.

UNO has more than 125 active student organizations on campus, including academic, professional, Greek, social, political, and religious organizations. UNO's newest addition is the University pep band, the UNO Blue Zoo, which performs at athletic and other University-related events. *Bayou* is UNO's annual national literary magazine that collects submissions from writers worldwide. UNO's student newspaper, *Driftwood,* is published weekly, and *Ellipsis,* a literary magazine, is published annually.

As a Division I independent (in transition to NCAA Division II) member of the National Collegiate Athletic Association (NCAA), UNO fields men's teams in basketball, baseball, and tennis and women's teams in basketball, volleyball, and tennis. UNO students can also participate in many recreational and intramural sports. Students have access to a new 85,000-square-foot Recreation and Fitness Center, which features a 12,000-square-foot cardiovascular, circuit, and free-weight-training room; an indoor track; a lap pool; racquetball courts; an outdoor sundeck; a juice bar; and a social lounge. UNO also offers a variety of Intercollegiate Club Sports like football (2010 national champions, conference champions, and regional champions; member of the Midwest Conference), rugby, soccer, sailing, cricket, karate, and hockey. Recreational sports have intramural activities for individuals and groups throughout the year.

Location

The University's 195-acre main campus is set in one of the most beautiful residential areas on the south shore of Lake Pontchartrain, only minutes from the fun and excitement of downtown New Orleans and the French Quarter. New Orleans is a cosmopolitan city, known for its great Southern hospitality and its unique tourist attractions. Renowned for Creole and Cajun cuisine, Mardi Gras, and jazz music festivals, New Orleans culture offers a unique environment for students to grow, both socially and academically. Whether exploring the art galleries of the Warehouse District or strolling down stately St. Charles Avenue, New Orleans has something for everyone, and the University of New Orleans is a part of it all.

Many of UNO's hotel, restaurant, and tourism administration majors find internships in the city's best hotels and restaurants. Film students have the opportunity to work at the Nims Center film studio complex as New Orleans becomes the "Hollywood South." Naval architecture students have access to the nation's largest undergraduate program in naval architecture and marine engineering as well as to the UNO–Avondale Maritime Center. As New Orleans continues to attract computer technology–based businesses to what has been called "the Silicon Bayou," the UNO Research and Technology Park continues to expand, producing more than 8,000 new jobs. Computer science majors are able to network with potential employers in one of the fastest-growing computer technology markets in the country.

Majors and Degrees

Bachelor of Science degrees are offered in accounting; biological sciences; chemistry; civil and environmental engineering; computer science; earth and environmental science; electrical engineering; entrepreneurship; finance; general business administration; hotel, restaurant, and tourism administration; management; marketing; mathematics; mechanical engineering; naval architecture and marine engineering; physics; psychology; transportation studies; urban studies and planning; and preprofessional programs in dentistry, medicine (with biology, chemistry, and psychology tracks), nursing, pharmacy, physical therapy studies, and veterinary medicine.

Bachelor of Arts degrees are offered in anthropology; early childhood education; elementary education; English; English education; film, theater, and communication arts; fine arts–history; fine arts–studio (with options that include digital media, painting, photography, and sculpture); French; geography; history; international studies; mathematics education; music (with options such as instrumental, jazz studies, theory and composition, and vocal); music education; philosophy; political science; secondary education; social science education; sociology; Spanish; and women's studies.

A four-year Bachelor of Interdisciplinary Studies degree program is available for students who wish to design individual curricula. Credit programs in paralegal studies, medical coding, and medical transcripts are also offered. Additional interdisciplinary minors are offered in interdisciplinary studies in African studies, Asian studies, entrepreneurship, environmental studies, Latin American and Caribbean studies, medical coding, Native American studies, paralegal studies, and print journalism.

Academic Programs

Most baccalaureate degree programs require a minimum of 120 semester hours with a minimum grade point average of 2.0 (C) in all work attempted in the college major. Also, all students must successfully complete an approved course demonstrating computer literacy. Other course requirements vary according to program. Programs leading to degrees with honors are offered in most academic majors. Credit for selected courses may be earned either through advanced-standing exams administered by the academic departments or through the College Board's Advanced Placement and College-Level Examination Program tests. College credit may also be gained for certain armed services and other nonacademic training.

The academic year is composed of sixteen-week fall and spring semesters and three summer sessions.

Off-Campus Programs

The University of New Orleans Division of International Education coordinates international study programs in Austria, Costa Rica, the Czech Republic, Ecuador, France, Greece, Honduras, and Italy. UNO's partnership with the University of Innsbruck, Austria, affords students an opportunity to participate in the largest international summer school of any American university in Europe. UNO offers college-credit exchange programs in Brazil and Canada. Students may also attend another school within the continental United States via the National Student Exchange (NSE) for one semester or one year.

UNO offers several off-campus facilities throughout the metropolitan New Orleans area, demonstrating UNO's commitment to community outreach. Off-campus locations offer both credit and noncredit courses, with hours varying from sunrise to evening and weekend classes.

Academic Facilities

The Earl K. Long Library's 1.5-million-volume collection includes approximately 12,000 journals, of which 3,800 are current subscriptions. Microform holdings include microfilm, microcard, and microfiche formats; microtext readers and reader-printers are also available. Other facilities include individual study carrels, a music listening room, computer terminals connected to the Computer Research Center, a Kurzweil reader for the visually impaired, and photocopy services. The Office of Educational Support Services includes a media resources center, which provides important media aids for the instructional staff in classroom presentations, and Television Resources, which coordinates a closed-circuit cable system and TV production studio. WWNO, the first public radio station in Louisiana, is located on the UNO campus.

All enrolled students and faculty and staff members receive a LAN and e-mail account. The University's computer network provides connections to approximately 5,000 locations campuswide as well as wireless connections throughout the campus. High-speed ResNet service is available to students living in Privateer Place, and a free dial-up Internet modem pool provides access for all off-campus enrolled students and faculty and staff members.

The UNO Lee Circle Center for the Arts includes the Ogden Museum, which houses the largest collection of Southern art in the world. The center also houses the National D-Day Museum, which includes the world's largest collection of World War II color film. The 70,000-square-foot Nims Center, located 20 minutes from the main campus, houses a professional-quality sound stage, including a 10,000-square-foot studio for University film projects. The Nims Center is also available for professional film projects.

Costs

In 2010–11, combined undergraduate fees for full-time students for the fall and spring semesters were $4759 for Louisiana residents and $14,347 for nonresidents; summer session fees for full-time students were $1315 for Louisiana residents and $3704 for nonresidents. Residence hall and board fees totaled approximately $4500 (double occupancy) for the fall and spring semesters. Costs of books and supplies total approximately $1000 per year. Additional charges include a $50 application fee, a $10 registration fee, field service and laboratory fees (usually $10 to $35) for some courses, an $80 car registration fee (includes parking pass), and a $30 late application fee. All fees are subject to change and can be confirmed by calling the Office of Admissions.

Financial Aid

The Office of Student Financial Aid develops financial aid packages to assist students with their educational expenses. This package is usually a combination of grants, loans, student employment, and/or scholarships, which, along with family contribution, help to finance the student's education. To be eligible for most federal financial aid programs, students must enroll for at least 6 credit hours (half-time) in an eligible program (one that leads to a degree or certificate).

More than three quarters of all freshmen in fall 2010 who showed financial need and took at least 6 credit hours were offered some form of financial aid. The priority date for the financial aid application is May 1. All applications postmarked on or before January 15 are considered for UNO's numerous academic scholarships, including those of international students. The University of New Orleans also offers scholarships in jazz studies; classical music; fine arts; film, theater, and communication arts; and creative writing. These scholarships require either an audition or the submission of a portfolio or manuscript along with the scholarship application.

Faculty

UNO has 525 full-time and 175 part-time faculty members, most of whom participate in both graduate and undergraduate instruction and research activity. Graduate students serve as teaching assistants in laboratory courses under the close supervision of the faculty. Approximately 80 percent of the faculty members hold doctorates. Most full-time faculty members devote themselves exclusively to University-related pursuits and are integrally involved in student affairs through counseling, teaching, research, and social activities. The student-faculty ratio is 19:1.

Student Government

Every student enrolled at UNO is a member of the Student Government (SG). SG offers students a way to create effective change, express opinions and concerns, and utilize resources to enhance their educational experiences. Some of the programs SG currently offers and/or sponsors are Student Legal Services, the Academic Travel Fund, 24-hour study hall during finals week, UNO pep band (the Blue Zoo), the Mechanical Engineering Mini Baja Competition, UNO Jazz Night at the University Center, musical excursions, the UNO student literary magazine (Ellipsis), recreation and intramural sports, cheerleaders, and the Privateer dance team.

Admission Requirements

Students seeking admission to the University of New Orleans should submit their application as early as possible in their senior year. Admission requirements for Louisiana residents and nonresidents for fall 2011 include the completion of the Board of Regents core curriculum (in years): English (4), mathematics (3), science (3), social studies (3), foreign language (2), fine arts (1), mathematics/science elective (1), and computer science (½). Residents must also have either a high school cumulative GPA of at least 2.5 or an ACT composite score of at least 23 (1060 SAT) or rank in the top 25 percent of their high school graduating class, and students must not require more than one developmental/remedial course. Out-of-state students who do not meet the GPA, test score, and rank requirements must have a minimum ACT composite score of 26 (SAT 1170) for automatic admission.

Transfer requirements include the completion of 18 semester hours of nondevelopmental work, a minimum 2.25 cumulative GPA, and completion of all developmental course work before transferring. Students with fewer than 18 semester hours must meet both freshman and transfer requirements.

Application and Information

The University of New Orleans has a rolling admissions policy. The application fee is $50. Priority deadlines for application are as follows: July 1 for the fall semester, November 15 for the spring semester, and May 1 for the summer semester. Deadlines for international students are June 1, October 1, and March 1, respectively.

Office of Admissions
103 Administration Building
University of New Orleans
2000 Lakeshore Drive
New Orleans, Louisiana 70148
Phone: 504-280-6595
      800-256-5-UNO (toll-free)
Fax: 504-280-5522
Web site: http://www.uno.edu

THE UNIVERSITY OF NORTH CAROLINA WILMINGTON
WILMINGTON, NORTH CAROLINA

The University

The University of North Carolina Wilmington (UNCW), a public, comprehensive university, combines a small-college commitment to excellence in teaching with a research university's opportunities for student involvement in significant faculty scholarship. The University provides a personal learning environment that integrates teaching and mentoring with research and service, and promotes cultural diversity, community engagement, and individual growth and development. The school is named among 20011's "Best in the Southeast" by The Princeton Review for the seventh consecutive year, and it was one of the top three Best Values in North Carolina according to *Kiplinger's* in 2011. *Forbes'* 2010 list of "America's Best College Buys" ranks UNCW at number 17 in the nation. UNCW offers fifty-two majors, thirty-six graduate degree programs and two doctoral degrees. The University is accredited by the Commission on Colleges of the Southern Association of Colleges and Schools and is one of the seventeen constituent institutions that comprise the public university system in the state of North Carolina.

UNCW enrolls 13,000 students in seventy-three baccalaureate degree concentrations and thirty-six graduate degree programs. Of the nearly 2,000 freshman students, approximately three fourths surveyed said the school was their first choice. Moreover, the University has the third-highest freshman SAT (critical reading and math only) average (1170), the fourth-highest freshman retention rate (85.4 percent), and the third-highest six-year graduation rate (67.1 percent) in the UNC system. With an average GPA of 3.8, incoming students already have demonstrated their motivation and ability to succeed in an academic setting.

At UNCW, students as well as faculty and staff members take full advantage of the university's closeness to the coast and its connections to the community. The internationally respected biology and marine biology programs have created promising research and development opportunities in the biotechnology, pharmacology, and mariculture fields. The Watson School of Education works closely with more than 100 area schools and agencies to improve the quality of public schools in the region. The School of Nursing has settled into a new, high-tech building equipped with patient simulation labs that replicate clinic, hospital, and home healthcare settings. The labs prepare students with extensive training prior to their placement in a wide range of clinical-practice experiences.

Campus life is a vibrant part of the UNCW experience. Students can live in one of twelve residential campus communities, with numerous options among residence halls, suites, and apartment buildings. Students enjoy a variety of cutting-edge cuisines at the University's fifteen dining locations. Students may participate in more than 200 student organizations, including political, academic, professional, sports, service, ethnic, religious, and student media groups. As a member of NCAA Division I, UNCW fields nineteen varsity teams, including men's and women's basketball, golf, soccer, track and field, cross country, swimming and diving, and tennis; women's softball and volleyball; and men's baseball.

Several facilities serve as hubs for the entire campus community. The Fisher Student Center and the Fisher University Union include a two-story bookstore, a 360-seat movie theater, offices for student organizations, student lounges, a large game room, an art exhibition gallery and display spaces, a convenience store, and dining areas. Nearby, Randall Library's technology resource and assistance centers connect students, faculty, and staff to extensive collections of information, both on campus and in the world at large. The Campus Commons features a lake with lighted fountains, a network of sidewalks, a clock tower, and an open-air amphitheater. Monthly exhibitions of paintings, sculptures, and graphic arts are held in a variety of spaces on campus, including Claude Howell Gallery, Randall Library, Cultural Arts Building, Warwick Center, and the Ann Flack Boseman Gallery.

The Department of Campus Recreation offers numerous activities to support students' health and well-being. The University is adding a new wing to the Student Recreation Center, which will double its size. The facility currently includes multipurpose courts, a group exercise room, climbing wall, an elevated, multilane walking and jogging track, and a large selection of elliptical trainers, stair climbers, treadmills, weight machines, and more. Other facilities include the Gazebo Complex, which features four tennis courts, three basketball courts, two volleyball courts, and a softball field; and a natatorium with an eight-lane swimming pool and an adjacent diving tank.

Location

The campus occupies 660 acres in the southeastern part of North Carolina, midway between the Cape Fear River and the Atlantic Ocean. The city of Wilmington is situated on the east bank of the Cape Fear River, about 15 miles from Carolina Beach and 10 miles from Wrightsville Beach. Several main highways lead into the city, and a nearby airport (ILM) provides easy access from the city to other destinations.

Wilmington combines historical beauty and modern convenience. Visitors can visit many art galleries, museums, and historical landmarks; enjoy an evening of theater, music, and nightlife; or visit the city's many shops and restaurants. Ocean breezes and the nearness of the Gulf Stream give Wilmington a delightful year-round climate. Nature lovers can go biking, hiking, or bird watching in one of Wilmington's parks or play golf on one of the city's six courses. Wilmington's proximity to the river and the ocean makes it an ideal haven for water lovers, whether they prefer taking a riverboat cruise or spending the day surfing and swimming at the beach.

Majors and Degrees

Bachelor of Arts degree programs are available in: anthropology, art history, athletic training, biology, chemistry, communication studies, criminal justice, economics, education of young children, elementary education, English, environmental studies, film studies, French, geography, geology, German studies, history, mathematics, middle grades education, music, parks and recreation management, philosophy and religion, physical education and health, physics, political science, psychology, sociology, Spanish, special education, studio art, theater, and therapeutic recreation.

Bachelor of Science degrees are available in biology, business administration, chemistry, clinical research, computer science, environmental science, geology, marine biology, mathematics, nursing, physics, and statistics. Also available are a Bachelor of Fine Arts degree in creative writing and a Bachelor of Social Work. Bachelor of Music degrees are available in music education and music performance.

Academic Programs

To earn a bachelor's degree, students must complete a minimum of 124 semester hours with a minimum GPA of 2.0. All students must complete a minimum of 45 semester hours in general education courses that include 6 hours in composition courses; 2 hours in physical education; 12–18 hours in humanities courses (including at least 3 hours each in literature, history, philosophy, and language courses; 3–9 hours in fine arts courses; 10–16 hours in natural science and mathematics courses, with at least 7 hours (including at least one laboratory science course) in the life and physical sciences and at least 3 hours in mathematics; 6–12 hours in social and behavioral sciences; and up to 6 hours in interdisciplinary courses. Some requirements may be satisfied by passing Advanced Placement, IB, or CLEP examinations.

The academic year consists of three semesters. The fall semester begins in late August and ends in early December. Following a winter break, the spring semester extends from early January to early May. The summer semester begins in mid-May and ends in mid-July.

Off-Campus Programs

Academic areas across campus sponsor study-abroad programs that are designed to strengthen relationships between the University and the international community, including international students and institutions in other countries. For example, the Cameron School of Business offers an International Master of Business Administration (I.M.B.A.), the Watson School of Education conducts programs in Belize, and the School of Nursing partners with a rural health clinic in

Peru. Many of the University's study-abroad programs are coordinated by the Office of International Programs. These may last a few weeks, a semester, or an entire academic year; several occur during the summer. The University has developed more than 500 programs in over fifty countries, including Argentina, Ghana, Israel, Thailand, Italy, and China.

The University also coordinates travel experiences that include more than study, such as internships that may consist of a combination of course work and/or supervised work experience in a government agency, profit or nonprofit agency, or company. Students and recent graduates may work abroad as family caretakers or English-language teachers, either in exchange for room and board or for a salary. Volunteer opportunities in other countries may involve health-care, agriculture, community development, language training, youth camps, or house-building projects.

Academic Facilities

The William Madison Randall Library holds more than 2.1 million items, including more than 1 million books, journals, and government documents; more than 65,000 multimedia items, and a vast microform collection. In addition, the library provides extensive indexes and full texts for thousands of journals and books, including NC LIVE, Lexis-Nexis, Science Direct, and JSTOR. The library's specialized collections include the Rare Book Collection and the Southeastern North Carolina Collection, devoted to publications about or written by residents of the Lower Cape Fear region. In addition, the library is a selective depository for United States government publications and a full depository for North Carolina documents.

Costs

In 2010–11, full-time undergraduate tuition and fees cost a total of $5582 per year for in-state residents and $16,464 for non-residents. Students living on campus can also expect to spend $7608 per academic year on room and board, $985 on books and supplies, $1452 on transportation, $673 on health insurance if not covered under another policy, and $500 on miscellaneous costs. Room, board, and transportation costs for commuters vary. Students enrolled part-time pay according to the number of credit hours earned each semester; costs range from $677.36 to $2329.39 for in-state students and $2064.74 to $6491.51 for non-residents.

Financial Aid

In order to be considered for the maximum amount of financial assistance, prospective students should submit the Free Application for Federal Student Aid (FAFSA) as early as possible, but definitely by March 1. In an average year, the University awards nearly $80 million to assist students. Most of this aid is need-based, but a number of merit-based scholarships are available for the most outstanding students.

The University offers several scholarships—including scholarships specifically for incoming freshmen and students enrolled in specific programs—that have been generously donated in honor of individuals or organizations. Award amounts and eligibility criteria vary, but most of these scholarships are renewable as long as the student is enrolled in a degree program and continues to meet the eligibility requirements. For students with exceptional financial need, the University developed the S.O.A.R program designed to help eligible participants reduce student loan debt. The Federal Pell Grant Program and the Federal Supplemental Educational Opportunity Grant (FSEOG) Program along with several North Carolina State programs also help offset the cost of attendance for low-income families. Some programs are limited to in-state students only.

Several federal loan programs are available for students who require additional assistance. Loan amount limits are established by the federal government. Some students also participate in federal work-study, which awards money to students who work up to 20 hours per week on campus.

Faculty

The University seeks to attract and maintain a faculty of outstanding individuals who are capable of contributing to the enrichment of its diverse and comprehensive instructional and research programs. Of the nearly 900-strong faculty, almost 86 percent hold terminal degrees and over 60 percent are tenured. Faculty members come from all geographic regions of the United States and several foreign countries, bringing a rich variety of educational experiences, training, and scholarship.

Student Government

The Student Government Association is devoted to the best interest of the University and committed to upholding a high standard of morals and conduct. Student activity fees support the Student Government Association in its objectives and activities. The student body president and class representatives are elected by the student body, and the president appoints an executive board, which includes a chief of staff, treasurer, and secretary.

Admission Requirements

All prospective students must meet the following minimum course requirements for enrollment: 6 course units in language (including 4 units in English grammar, composition, and literature, and 2 units of the same foreign language); 4 units of mathematics (one for which algebra II is a prerequisite); 3 units in science (including at least 1 unit in biology, 1 unit in the physical sciences, and one laboratory course); and 2 units in social science (including 1 unit in United States history).

Prospective students are required to submit the following materials: a completed application for admission, official transcripts from all high schools attended, answer to the essay question on the application, official SAT or ACT with writing scores, and a $60 application fee. When reviewing a freshman application, the admissions committee looks carefully at the applicant's academic achievements including difficulty of course work, writing, grade point average, standardized test scores, and extracurricular activities. Students admitted to the University had a mean SAT combined math and critical reading score of 1196 and/or an ACT composite average of 25. UNCW requires the writing portion of the ACT.

Application and Information

Students applying for early action should have their applications postmarked November 1 or earlier and are notified on or around January 20. Regular decision applications must be postmarked by February 1; students are notified of the University's decision on or around April 1.

Transfer applicants may apply for fall or summer session. Applications must be postmarked by March 1. Decision letters are mailed on a rolling basis.

To request application materials or receive additional information, interested students may contact:

Office of Admissions
University of North Carolina Wilmington
601 South College Road
Wilmington, North Carolina 28403-5904

Phone: 910-962-3243
Fax: 910-962-3038
E-mail: admissions@uncw.edu
Web site: http://www.uncw.edu/

The Fisher Student Center.

UNIVERSITY OF OREGON
EUGENE, OREGON

COLLEGE CLOSE-UPS

The University

At the University of Oregon (UO), students are part of a community dedicated to making a difference in the world. Whether changing a community, a law, or one person's mind, UO gives students the inspiration and resources needed to succeed. Potential students interested in joining the UO's virtual community are invited to visit both the University's admissions Web site at http://admissions.uoregon.edu and Facebook page at http://www.facebook.com/UOAdmissions.

Many of UO's academic programs are internationally recognized for academic excellence. The architecture, sustainable design, chemistry, economics, English, psychology, molecular biology, biochemistry, physics, neuroscience, special education, entrepreneurship, and sports business programs all rank among the top 10 in the U.S. Programs in comparative literature, finance, historic preservation, and mathematics rank in the top 20 in the U.S.

With a student-teacher ratio of 20:1 and an average class size of 21, students find it easy to connect with faculty members and peers. Students have access to all the resources of a major research university, with 263 comprehensive academic programs (including new programs in cinema studies, African studies, Latin American studies, and queer studies) and more than 250 student organizations.

Set in a 295-acre arboretum, the University of Oregon is aesthetically and environmentally green. Academic programs and student activities bring students to the forests, mountains, and rivers of Oregon's wilderness areas. The world's first green chemistry-teaching methods were developed by UO students and faculty. The Lillis Business Complex was the first certified-green business school facility in the United States. Students have access to nationally recognized programs in sustainable business, architecture, and technology. UO's campus recycling program is a national award-winner, and the University recently signed an agreement to eliminate its carbon footprint.

Students learn to see the world differently at UO, attending classes alongside peers from all fifty states, two U.S. territories, and eighty-six countries, and learning from faculty members of diverse religious, cultural, and ethnic heritages. Global degree options include twenty-eight languages, as well as international, ethnic, religious, African, Asian, Latin American, Judaic, and Russian and East European studies. The UO offers 165 study programs in ninety-five countries, giving students the opportunity to experience the history, arts, social institutions, customs, and beliefs of new cultures, all while earning credit toward their degree. The IE3 Global Internships Program offers students professional experience through internships worldwide. More information can be found at http://studyabroad.uoregon.edu.

With seventeen NCAA Division I teams, as well as forty-two club sports, students have a variety of sports to play and teams to cheer for. The excitement begins in the fall, when students root for the Ducks' football team at Autzen Stadium. In winter, the men's and women's basketball teams thrill the crowds at the state-of-the-art Matthew Knight Arena. In the spring, UO track stars compete at the world-famous Hayward Field, often the site for NCAA championships and U.S. Olympic team trials in track and field. Additional information regarding UO athletic programs is available at http://www.goducks.com.

Location

The UO is located in the center of Eugene (population 345,880), a classic college town that's small enough to bike across but large enough to offer diverse art, music, and social venues. The Hult Center for Performing Arts and the Grammy-wininng Oregon Bach Festival lure a variety of acclaimed musical acts each year. *Rolling Stone* magazine included Eugene in its list of top 10 College Towns that Rock.

The city of Eugene embraces the outdoors, with more than 100 city parks, 250 miles of bicycle trails, rock climbing areas, and beautiful public gardens, all within the city limits. Getting to Eugene is easy; the city is served by several major airlines and is on the main north-south Amtrak artery connecting Seattle and San Diego. More information is available at http://admissions.uoregon.edu/original.

Majors and Degrees

A complete list of undergraduate academic majors, minors, certificates, and preparatory programs is located at http://admissions. uoregon.edu/majors.

The School of Architecture and Allied Arts offers programs in architecture; art; art history; ceramics; community arts; digital arts; fibers; historic preservation; interior architecture; landscape architecture; material and product studies; metalsmithing and jewelry; multimedia; nonprofit administration; painting; photography; planning, public policy, and management; printmaking; product design; and sculpture.

The College of Arts and Sciences offers programs in African studies; anthropology; Asian studies; biochemistry; biology; chemistry; Chinese; cinema studies; classics; clinical laboratory science–medical technology*; comparative literature; computer and information science; computer information technology; dentistry*; East Asian studies; economics; engineering*; English; environmental science; environmental studies; ethnic studies; European studies; folklore; forensic science*; French; general science; general social science; geography; geological sciences; German; German studies; Greek; health sciences*; history; humanities; human physiology; independent study; international studies; Italian; Japanese; Judaic studies; Latin; Latin American studies; law*; linguistics; marine biology; mathematics; mathematics and computer science; medicine*; medieval studies; nursing*; occupational therapy*; optometry*; peace studies; pharmacy*; philosophy; physical therapy*; physician assistant studies*; physics; podiatry*; political science; psychology; queer studies; religious studies; Romance languages; Russian and East European studies; Scandinavian; second-language acquisition and teaching; social work*; sociology; Southeast Asian studies; Spanish; theater arts; veterinary medicine*; women's and gender studies; and writing, speaking, and critical reasoning.

The Charles H. Lundquist College of Business offers programs in accounting; business administration with concentrations in entrepreneurship, finance, information systems and operations management, marketing, and sports business; and global management.

The College of Education offers programs in communication disorders and sciences, educational foundations, family and human services, special education, and teacher education.*

The School of Journalism and Communication offers programs in communication studies, journalism, journalism: advertising, journalism: communication studies, and journalism: public relations.

The School of Music and Dance offers programs in dance, music, music composition, music education, music: jazz studies, and music performance.

An * denotes preparatory programs.

Academic Programs

The UO operates on a quarter system, and students spend about one third of their education on each of three areas: the general education requirements, major requirements, and elective credit. General education requirements include courses in the natural sciences, social sciences, humanities, and multicultural course work.

Freshman Interest Groups (FIGs) bring together a small group of first-year students interested in the same academic area in three related interdisciplinary courses. Freshman Seminars are small-group discussion courses taught by some of the UO's most outstanding faculty members. These academically rigorous programs provide a helpful transition to college-level work. Details are available at http://firstyear.uoregon.edu. The Professional Distinctions Program gives students a competitive edge in the job market by complementing course work with a practical area of concentration. Skills are built through career workshops, internships, and other professional experiences. Learn more at http://uodistinctions.uoregon.edu.

The Robert D. Clark Honors College (CHC) offers the academic rigor of an outstanding small liberal arts college with the resources of a major research university. High-achieving students prepare for participation and leadership in society, and come to understand the role of knowledge in their lives as global citizens. CHC classes are limited to 19 or fewer students and complement any UO major. The CHC application process is competitive, with an average of more than 1,500 applications for the 200 openings each year. Additional information about CHC can be found at http://honors.uoregon.edu.

Upon acceptance, qualified students will be invited to join the College Scholars program, which provides access to specialized courses, internship opportunities, and special scholarships. Faculty members help students develop their plans to achieve department honors or professional distinctions upon graduation. More details are available at http://csch.uoregon.edu.

Off-Campus Programs

The Career Center offers off-campus internships in fields related to students' academic majors or extracurricular interests. Both paid and volunteer internships are widely available. The IE3 Global Internships Program provides academic credit while students gain career experience through overseas internships. Additional information can be found at http://career.uoregon.edu and http://ie3global.ous.edu.

Pine Mountain Observatory, near Bend, Oregon, offers study options in physics and astronomy. Students can participate in the annual Archaeology Field School in central Oregon's Northern Great Basin. The Oregon Institute of Marine Biology on the Pacific coast offers access to deep sea, coastal watershed, and estuary habitat. More details are available at http://admissions.uoregon.edu/beyondeugene.

Cooperatively run by students, the top-ranked Outdoor Program takes students beyond the campus to Oregon's great outdoors. Activities available include snowboarding, skiing, rock climbing, hiking, surfing, white-water rafting, and kayaking. Interested students can visit http://outdoorprogram.uoregon.edu for more information.

Academic Facilities

The University of Oregon Libraries, an Association of Research Libraries member, houses the second-largest research collection in the Northwest, including 3 million volumes and 75,000 journal subscriptions, both print and electronic. More information can be found at http://libweb.uoregon.edu.

Three campus museums are valuable resources in the sciences and visual arts. The Jordan Schnitzer Museum of Art offers exhibitions of classical and contemporary art. The Museum of Natural and Cultural History features Native American artifacts, archaeological finds, and historically and scientifically significant items. Students appear in music, dance, and theater performances in newly refurbished facilities, including proscenium and black box performance spaces. Films, lectures, and cultural events are an everyday part of campus life. Additional details regarding arts and culture at UO are available at http://www.uoregon.edu/arts-and-culture.

Science facilities are among the best in the nation. Cutting-edge equipment is housed in the underground Lokey Laboratories, designed to minimize vibrations and stray electric fields. The UO is a pioneer in integrative science, and the new Lewis Integrative Science Building encourages interdisciplinary research and studies in areas such as nanotechnology, neuroscience, and solar energy. More information can be found at http://isci.uoregon.edu. Wireless Internet access is available in all buildings, and computer labs are available in the library, residence halls, and academic facilities across campus.

Costs

Resident undergraduate tuition and fees for the 2010–11 academic year were $8190. Room and board in on-campus residence halls cost $9144 per academic year for double occupancy. Books and supplies were estimated at $1050 and personal expenses $2412. The total was $20,796.

Nonresident undergraduate tuition and fees for the 2010–11 academic year were $25,830. Room and board in on-campus residence halls cost $9144 per academic year for double occupancy. Books and supplies were estimated at $1050 and personal expenses $2412. The total cost for nonresidents was $38,436. Additional cost details are available at http://financialaid.uoregon.edu/cost_of_attendance.

Financial Aid

The UO makes a concerted effort to enable students to attend, regardless of family income. Financial aid in the form of grants, loans, and employment is available to qualifying students. The majority of students receive scholarships and financial aid that are awarded through the federal government, the University, and academic departments.

To apply for financial aid, students must file the Free Application for Federal Student Aid (FAFSA) in early February. The UO's federal school code is 003223.

Incoming freshmen will be considered automatically for Dean's scholarships, Staton scholarships, Laurel scholarships, and general University scholarships by completing the UO admission application by January 15. Presidential scholarships and Diversity Excellence scholarships require separate applications due January 15.

Dean's scholarships are awarded to academically successful entering freshmen and range from $1000 to $7000 per year. Staton scholarships in the amount of $5600 are awarded to incoming Oregon students with extraordinary financial need, and are renewable for up to four years. General University and Laurel scholarships range from $1000 to $3000 per year. Presidential scholarships, awarded each year to Oregon's brightest incoming freshmen, amount to $8000 per year, and are renewable for up to four years. Diversity Excellence Scholarships (DES) are tuition-based, and awards range from partial- to full-tuition as well as fee waivers.

Western Undergraduate Exchange (WUE) offers selected freshmen from certain Western states to study at the University of Oregon for 150 percent of UO resident tuition.

More information regarding financial aid and scholarships can be found at http://financialaid.uoregon.edu.

Faculty

UO faculty members are recognized for their outstanding teaching skills and renowned for their original research.

Student Government

The Associated Students of the University of Oregon (ASUO) offers more than 250 student organizations, including cultural organizations, fraternities and sororities, student government, campus ministries, political groups, performing arts groups, international student clubs, and honor societies. The UO Student Vote Coalition led the nation in registering student voters in each of the past three presidential elections. The UO also ranks eleventh in the nation for current Peace Corps volunteers. Additional details regarding the ASUO are available at http://asuo.uoregon.edu.

Admission Requirements

The early notification deadline for fall 2012 admission is November 1, 2011. The standard admission deadline for fall 2012 is January 15, 2012. To be eligible for freshman admission, an applicant must have a high school GPA of at least 3.0 on a 4.0 scale, be a graduate of a standard or accredited high school, submit SAT or ACT scores, and complete an application essay.

The UO requires the following college-preparatory courses: 4 years of English in preparatory composition and literature; 3 years of mathematics, including 1 year of algebra and 2 additional years of college-preparatory mathematics; 3 years of science in such areas as biology, chemistry, or physics; and 3 years of social science that could include 1 year of U.S. history, 1 year of global studies such as world history or geography, and one elective. Two years of the same second language in high school or two college terms of the same second language are also required.

Other factors considered for admission include the strength of high school course work, grade trend, class rank, essay, and senior-year course load. Academic potential and special talents also are considered. Additional admissions information is available at http://admissions.uoregon.edu/freshmen.

Application and Information

To apply, candidates should submit a completed application for admission, transcripts, SAT or ACT scores, essay, and a nonrefundable $50 application fee to the Office of Admissions.

For information and an application, students should contact:

Office of Admissions
1217 University of Oregon
Eugene, Oregon 97403-1217

Phone: 541-346-3201
      800-BE-A-DUCK (toll-free)
Web site: http://admissions.uoregon.edu
      http://admissions.uoregon.edu/virtualtour
      http://www.facebook.com/UOAdmissions
      http://twitter.com/BeAnOregonDuck

UNIVERSITY OF PITTSBURGH AT BRADFORD

BRADFORD, PENNSYLVANIA

The University

The University of Pittsburgh at Bradford (Pitt-Bradford) can take students beyond—beyond the classroom by offering internships and research opportunities; beyond the degree by providing a robust Career Services Office and an informal alumni network; beyond 9 to 5 by offering an active student life, a friendly residence-life environment, excellent athletic and cultural facilities, and a wide range of recreational opportunities; beyond place by exposing students to the world and offering many study-abroad opportunities; and beyond students' expectations by giving them a college experience that can transform them.

At Pitt-Bradford, students live and learn on a safe, intimate campus, where they receive individual and personalized attention from committed professors who work at their side. In addition, students earn a degree from the University of Pittsburgh, which commands respect around the world.

Students can work out in a state-of-the-art fitness center or swim in the six-lane swimming pool in the Sport and Fitness Center. The building also houses facilities for intercollegiate and intramural athletic events.

The Frame-Westerberg Commons offers students a place to eat, gather, and participate in campus life. The building houses the dining hall, where students can help themselves to a wide assortment of meals; a bookstore, which features an after-hours convenience store; offices for many student clubs and organizations; and areas to read or relax.

There are more than forty clubs and organizations, varying from the campus radio station and newspaper to academic clubs, honor societies, and fraternities and sororities. Pitt-Bradford competes in Division III of the NCAA and fields seven men's teams in baseball, basketball, cross-country, golf, soccer, swimming, and tennis and seven women's teams in basketball, cross-country, soccer, softball, swimming, tennis, and volleyball.

Location

Pitt-Bradford encompasses 317 acres in the foothills of the Allegheny Mountains, only steps from the Allegheny National Forest. Pitt-Bradford also is a short drive from larger cities such as Buffalo, New York (80 miles north); Pittsburgh (160 miles southeast); and Erie, Pennsylvania (90 miles west). Pitt-Bradford can also be reached easily by car and plane.

At Pitt-Bradford, students have many opportunities to participate in cocurricular opportunities in the region, including cross-country and downhill skiing, snowboarding, snowshoeing, ice skating, biking, fishing, hiking, and hunting.

Majors and Degrees

Students may pursue four-year degrees in accounting, applied mathematics, athletic training, biology, biology education 7–12, broadcast communications, business education K–12, business management, chemistry, chemistry education 7–12, computer information systems and technology, criminal justice, economics, elementary education, English, English education 7–12, entrepreneurship, environmental studies, environmental education K–12, health and physical education, history/political science, hospitality management, human relations, interdisciplinary arts, mathematics education 7–12, nursing, physical sciences, psychology, public relations, radiological science, social sciences, social studies education 7–12, sociology, sport and recreation management, sports medicine, and writing.

Pitt-Bradford also offers associate degrees in engineering science, information systems, liberal studies, nursing (RN), and petroleum technology.

Students may also study engineering for up to two years at Pitt-Bradford and then complete a program at the Oakland campus in bioengineering, chemical and petroleum engineering, civil and environmental engineering, electrical and computer engineering, industrial engineering, materials science and engineering, or mechanical engineering.

Pitt-Bradford also provides programs offered in conjunction with the University of Pittsburgh School of Dental Medicine and the Pennsylvania College of Optometry. Students begin their studies at Pitt-Bradford and, after three years, transfer to the appropriate graduate school to complete four more years of study.

Pitt-Bradford also offers the first two years of study leading to the doctorate in pharmacy. Students must complete the program at the Oakland campus, where admission is competitive. The Pittsburgh School of Pharmacy preadmits some qualified high school seniors, pending completion of the first two years of the preprofessional program at Pitt-Bradford.

The University also has an agreement with Lake Erie College of Osteopathic Medicine (LECOM), which allows qualifying students to continue their education in medicine at LECOM after their third year at Pitt-Bradford. Students who have successfully completed their first year of medical school classes at LECOM will receive their bachelor's degree from Pitt-Bradford. They will then continue at LECOM to finish their medical studies.

Academic Programs

The academic programs stress critical-thinking and communication skills and encourage hands-on learning through field experience, internships, and faculty-student collaboration on research. A Pitt-Bradford bachelor's degree requires 120–128 credit hours (requirements differ slightly among programs). Students need to complete between 60 and 70 credit hours to earn an associate degree.

The accounting major prepares students for the workplace, which has a growing need for accountants. The major also prepares students to earn a master's degree in either professional accountancy or business administration.

The biology program prepares students for careers in health-related professions, education, and research; technical positions in governmental agencies; and careers with food, pharmaceutical, chemical, and biotechnology companies. Most students interested in medicine, dentistry, optometry, pharmacy, osteopathy, physical therapy, occupational therapy, podiatry, chiropractic medicine, veterinary medicine, preclinical dietetics and nutrition, and a variety of careers in health and rehabilitation sciences are biology majors.

Students who choose to major in broadcast communications, English, public relations, or writing are able to work on the award-winning student newspaper, *The Source;* broadcast over the college radio station, WDRQ; and publish original works in the award-winning student literary magazine, *Baily's Beads.* Students also have access to an all-digital television studio and two digital radio facilities.

The business management program places a strong emphasis on teaching practical applications; courses often focus on cases taken from real business situations. Students may concentrate in accounting, finance, international business, or management information systems.

In the criminal justice program, students are able to intern with local and regional police departments, county court and probation offices, and a federal prison. New, state-of-the-art crime-scene investigatory tools enable students to "work a crime scene" using many of the same tools as professional law enforcement agents. In 2008, the University opened a Crime Scene Investigation (CSI) House, which enables students to process simulated crime scenes and collect "evidence" just like the pros.

An education major prepares a student for a career as a teacher in a world of rapid political, economic, scientific, and cultural change. The Education Department seeks to graduate students who have general knowledge and specific content knowledge, as well as sound theory and practice.

Students who graduate from the hospitality management program are prepared to work in a large hotel or resort, in a convention bureau or center, in the areas of event or banquet management, or on a cruise ship. As part of the program, students complete 800 hours of field work at such places as the ski resort in nearby Ellicottville, New York, and Glendorn, a luxurious mountain resort in Bradford.

The nursing program at Pitt-Bradford offers an Associate of Science degree that can be completed in two years and a Bachelor of Science in Nursing degree that requires two additional years. Students may commence this program upon completion of the associate degree.

In psychology, students gain knowledge in the scientific and theoretical aspects of psychology as well as the application of this knowledge. The major prepares students for graduate work in psychology and related disciplines and for employment in social service agencies, mental health centers, industries, and not-for-profit and governmental agencies.

Students may relocate to another University of Pittsburgh campus to complete academic programs not offered at Pitt-Bradford, but they may earn no more than 70 credits before transferring. All students in the arts and sciences may relocate, provided they are in good standing. Engineering students may relocate if they maintain a grade point average of at least 2.5.

Academic Facilities

In addition to the T. Edward and Tullah Hanley Library on campus, Pitt-Bradford students have online access to the entire University of Pittsburgh library system.

Blaisdell Hall, the fine arts and communication arts building, houses the art, communication arts, theater, and music programs and features state-of-the-art equipment. Students can find a computer-graphics lab, two art studios, a music/theater rehearsal hall, and a radio and television studio. The building also houses a multipurpose theater and serves as the cultural center for the region by housing plays, concerts, lectures, and other arts-related events.

Fisher Hall houses the science programs, such as biology, chemistry, engineering, petroleum technology, and physics. The science labs, which were updated during the summer of 2010, are filled with up-to-date scientific equipment, enabling students to perform a variety of experiments. The building also has two computer-aided learning centers and, on the roof, a campus greenhouse.

In Swarts Hall, students take courses in business, education, sociology, anthropology, psychology, history/political science, languages, English, writing, and criminal justice. The building also houses a new nursing suite and multimedia classrooms that can turn a typical class into an audio and visual experience.

There is more to the Sport and Fitness Center than sports. The building also houses the athletic training, sports medicine, and sport and recreation management programs. The building houses a human performance lab and an athletic training room.

In the Ceramic Studio, students get their hands dirty—literally. In the building, students will find sixteen motorized pottery wheels, a manual kick wheel, a work table, and a kiln to help them take slabs of clay and create art.

Costs

For 2010–11, tuition for full-time students was $5643 per fifteen-week term for Pennsylvania residents and $10,543 for out-of-state students. Nursing tuition was $7228 per term for Pennsylvania residents and $13,445 for out-of-state students. Room and board expenses were $3825 per term. Other costs include an activity fee of $85 per term, a health fee of $50 per term, and a computer fee of $175 per term. Books and supplies cost approximately $500 per term.

Financial Aid

Pitt-Bradford believes that the cost of a college education should not be a deterrent to any student regardless of family financial circumstances. A variety of grants, scholarships, loans, and work-study opportunities are administered through the Financial Aid Office. All aid applicants must submit the Free Application for Federal Student Aid (FAFSA) by March 1 to receive priority consideration. Pennsylvania residents who complete the FAFSA by March 1 are also eligible for Pennsylvania Higher Education Assistance Agency (PHEAA) grants. Students who live outside of Pennsylvania should contact their state agency to learn more about the prerequisites for grants.

The University awards merit-based scholarships upon entry to those who demonstrate exceptional academic achievement. The University ROTC program is another possible source of financial aid. The University encourages veterans to contact the VA about educational benefits.

To learn more about financial assistance, students should contact the Financial Aid Office or visit the financial aid Web site at http://www.upb.pitt.edu/financialaid.aspx.

Faculty

Pitt-Bradford's 78 full-time faculty members hold doctorates and master's degrees from some of the most prestigious universities in the nation, including Cornell, Harvard, Stanford, and the University of Pittsburgh. Teaching is the primary activity of the faculty, and personal attention is emphasized in the classroom. Faculty members welcome the chance to meet with their students and know them by name. The student-faculty ratio is 18:1.

Student Government

Because Pitt-Bradford is a personalized campus, opportunities for leadership abound. Many students become campus leaders as early as their sophomore year. Regardless of students' background or interests, most find many places to become involved at Pitt-Bradford.

The Student Activities Council schedules comedy performances, lectures, art exhibits, movies, and trips to such places as Toronto, Canada; Niagara Falls, New York; Cooperstown, New York; and New York City.

Admission Requirements

In reviewing applications, the Admissions Committee considers three primary factors in evaluating an applicant's ability to succeed in college work: the high school record, the results of standardized tests (SAT or ACT), and the high school's recommendations. In addition, personal qualifications, extracurricular activities, and potential to contribute to the college community may be taken into consideration.

Application and Information

Pitt-Bradford has a rolling admissions program, and students may apply at any time. All candidates are notified as soon as action is taken on their application.

Candidates for admission should complete and return the application with a nonrefundable $45 fee. Students must also submit an official copy of their high school record and scores from either the SAT or ACT. In addition to fulfilling the above requirements, transfer applicants must submit all official college transcripts and must have a minimum cumulative grade point average of 2.0.

The Office of Admissions welcomes campus visits by students and their families; such visits help students arrive at a final decision about Pitt-Bradford. Interviews and tours are scheduled Monday through Friday, 9 a.m. to 3 p.m., and on selected Saturdays. Arrangements for these visits can be made by contacting the Office of Admissions or by going online to http://www.upb.pitt.edu/visit.aspx.

For application forms, catalogs, and further information, students should contact:

Office of Admissions
University of Pittsburgh at Bradford
300 Campus Drive
Bradford, Pennsylvania 16701-2898
Phone: 814-362-7555
      800-872-1787 (toll-free)
Web site: http://www.upb.pitt.edu
      http://www.facebook.com/PittBradford

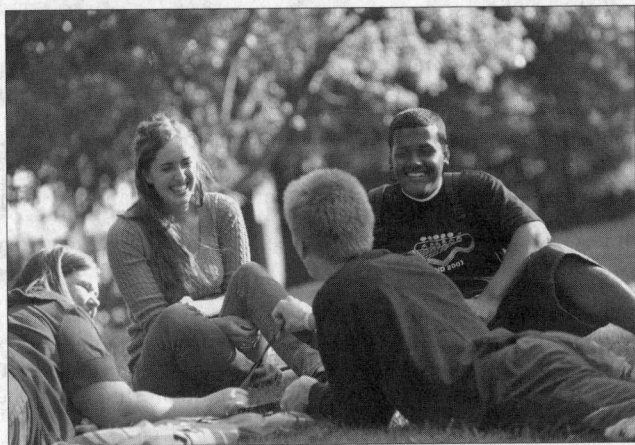

Students on the campus of the University of Pittsburgh at Bradford.

UNIVERSITY OF PITTSBURGH AT JOHNSTOWN

JOHNSTOWN, PENNSYLVANIA

University of Pittsburgh at Johnstown

The University

Founded in 1927 as one of the first regional campuses of a major university in the United States, the University of Pittsburgh at Johnstown (Pitt-Johnstown) is a four-year, degree-granting, fully accredited, coeducational, residential undergraduate college of the University of Pittsburgh. With 3,000 well-qualified students and a suburban campus of striking beauty, Pitt-Johnstown combines the strong academic reputation and outstanding resources of a major research university with the personal appeal of a smaller college.

There are thirty-six campus buildings, including a library, student union, sports center, performing arts center, and chapel, in addition to a 40-acre nature preserve and outdoor recreation areas. The college has six different styles of housing, including residence halls, small-group lodges, apartments, and the Living/Learning Center. A brand-new state-of-the-art health and wellness complex features workout equipment, an elevated track, climbing wall, courts, and an aquatic center.

In addition to the undergraduate degrees listed in the Majors and Degrees section, the University also offers postbaccalaureate nondegree teaching certificates.

Location

Located in a suburb of Johnstown, a city of 25,000 only 70 miles east of Pittsburgh, the spacious 655-acre campus is the third largest in Pennsylvania and is recognized as one of the most attractive in the Eastern states. The University's facilities blend easily with the rustic wooded setting, creating a campus of distinctive natural beauty. Shops, entertainment, and cultural activities are conveniently available, and the city is in the heart of Pennsylvania ski country.

Majors and Degrees

Pitt-Johnstown offers the Bachelor of Arts (B.A.) degree in business (accounting, economics, finance, marketing, and management), communication, creative writing, economics, English literature, environmental studies, geography, history, humanities, journalism, professional writing, secondary education (several social science strands, communication, and English), social sciences, sociology, and theater arts. The Bachelor of Science (B.S.) degree is awarded in biology, chemistry, civil engineering technology, computer engineering technology, computer science, ecology, electrical engineering technology, elementary education, geology, mathematics, mechanical engineering technology, natural sciences, nursing, psychology, and secondary education (biology, chemistry, earth and space science, general science, mathematics, and physics).

An Associate of Science (A.S.) degree is available in respiratory care and surgical technology.

Dual teaching certification and dual education degree programs are offered. A cooperative program with a local hospital allows students to combine a B.S. in biology with a certificate in medical technology. A certificate in international studies can be earned in conjunction with any major.

With the assistance of academic advisers, Pitt-Johnstown students can construct interdisciplinary majors, double majors, and self-designed majors. They can also develop their specific fields of study with preprofessional preparation for advanced study in such areas as dental medicine, law, medicine, optometry, physical therapy, and veterinary medicine.

Academic Programs

Pitt-Johnstown seeks to provide contemporary, innovative academic programs that combine the practical concerns of career orientation with the spirit of inquiry and the traditional goals of higher education. Practical experience of all types is encouraged, including campus activities, community service, media work, and research projects. A seminar series introduces freshmen to rigorous intellectual work through small-group elective seminars. Students who show extra potential receive special advising, registration privileges, and scholarships through the President's Scholars Program. Students may complete preliminary requirements for upper-division programs that require relocation to the Pittsburgh campus, including requirements for programs in pharmacy and other health-related areas. In some programs, guaranteed admission is offered to qualified students.

Off-Campus Programs

The University of Pittsburgh at Johnstown takes pride in offering international programming options to students. As part of the University Center for International Studies (UCIS), the International Services Office promotes exposure to different cultures, languages, and more by having undergraduates earn credits at institutions throughout the world. Students may also consider pursuing one of several international studies certificates. These certificate programs enable students to become specialized in a particular area of the world or a global theme.

Academic Facilities

In addition to the numerous volumes housed in the Pitt-Johnstown library, students have online request and retrieval access to the extensive collections contained in the University Libraries system, including electronic journals and electronic books. The college maintains computer classrooms and laboratories equipped with more than 300 computers, including Windows-based PC's, Macintosh computers, and powerful UNIX-based workstations. All classrooms are wired for Internet access, and all computers at Pitt-Johnstown are connected to the Internet, allowing students access to information from around the world and to a large suite of software shared with the University's other campuses. In addition to microcomputer facilities, which include both UNIX and VMS time-sharing systems, Pitt-Johnstown supports off-campus access to the network. To ensure compatibility with the latest technology, computers are replaced on a four-year cycle.

Costs

For full-time students in arts and sciences and education programs, 2010–11 tuition was $5643 per fifteen-week term for Pennsylvania residents and $10,543 for nonresidents. For full-time students in engineering programs, tuition was $6053 per fifteen-week term for Pennsylvania residents and $11,536 for nonresidents. Room and board expenses were approximately $4000 per term, depending on housing style and meal plan. Other costs included activities and facilities fees of $181 per term and a computing service fee of $175 per term. A $10 fee was charged for each physical education course. Books and supplies were estimated at $450 each term. All costs are subject to change.

Financial Aid

Nearly 88 percent of all Pitt-Johnstown students receive some form of financial assistance. In addition to the Pennsylvania Higher Education Assistance Agency (PHEAA) state grant, the Federal Pell Grant, and the Federal Stafford Student Loan, a variety of loans, grants, scholarships, and student-employment positions are awarded through the University. Applicants for all types of financial aid must submit the Free Application for Federal Student Aid (FAFSA) by April 1 prior to the academic year for which assistance is requested.

Faculty

Holding degrees from more than 100 distinguished American and international universities, the 133 full-time members of the Johnstown faculty represent a broad diversity in background and experience. Personally committed to undergraduate teaching, each faculty member is actively involved in a full range of intellectual activities as well as student advising, curriculum development, and the extracurricular and cultural life of the University community. Classes at Pitt-Johnstown are small, and opportunities for faculty-student interaction outside of the classroom are plentiful. Personalized instruction is emphasized. Full-time faculty members teach almost all courses. The student-faculty ratio is 20:1, and the typical class size is 25–30.

Student Government

The Student Senate plays a significant role in building cooperation among all members of the University community. It deals with matters affecting the entire student body and formally represents students in relations with the administration, faculty, and other nonstudent groups. The Programming Board, an administrative branch of the senate, schedules diversified entertainment.

Admission Requirements

All applicants for full-time study must have completed, or be in the process of completing, at least 15 units of work in an accredited secondary school. In addition, candidates must take either the SAT or the ACT. Writing sections of the entrance exams are considered for placement in freshman composition courses. Admission decisions are made after careful study of each applicant's high school record, performance on college entrance examinations, high school recommendations, and personal qualifications. Interviews are not required; however, applicants are encouraged to arrange a visit to the campus by phoning or writing the Office of Admissions.

Application requirements for transfer students include high school and college transcripts. Transfer students should have a minimum quality point average of 2.0.

High school graduates and transfer students must file an application, with a $45 fee, on forms provided by the school.

Application and Information

The candidate is notified as soon as action is taken on the application.

For more information about University of Pittsburgh at Johnstown, students should contact:

Office of Admissions
157 Blackington Hall
University of Pittsburgh at Johnstown
Johnstown, Pennsylvania 15904
Phone: 814-269-7050
      800-765-4875 (toll-free)
Web site: http://www.pitt-johnstown.pitt.edu

UNIVERSITY OF PUGET SOUND

TACOMA, WASHINGTON

The College

Founded in 1888, University of Puget Sound is an independent college committed to the liberal arts and sciences, superb teaching, and the recognition of each student as an individual. A nationally acclaimed teaching faculty, well-planned facilities, and a limited enrollment ensure excellence in education.

Puget Sound, the only national liberal arts college in western Washington, is one of only two independent colleges in Washington State to be granted a chapter by Phi Beta Kappa. A record number of Puget Sound graduates have received undergraduate and postgraduate honors, including Rhodes, National Science Foundation, Fulbright, Rotary, Watson, Phi Kappa Phi, Truman, Goldwater, Hertz, and National Endowment for the Humanities fellowships and scholarships. Equally impressive, among national colleges and universities with fewer than 5,000 undergraduate students, Puget Sound is in the top five for number of alumni currently serving as Peace Corps volunteers worldwide.

Puget Sound enrolls 2,600 students, with more than 75 percent coming from outside Washington State. In addition, forty-seven states and fourteen other countries are represented in the student body. Puget Sound is a 24-hour-a-day, seven-day-a-week residential community. Special theme houses and halls are available for students with common interests. The neighboring residential community provides many facilities for those who wish to live off campus. Athletic facilities include Memorial Fieldhouse and Pamplin Fitness Center, Wallace Pool, Peyton Field at Baker Stadium, an indoor climbing wall, and numerous varsity and intramural athletic fields.

Students find that participating in activities sponsored by the student government is an excellent way to learn outside the classroom and improve leadership abilities. Athletics include twenty-three varsity teams, various club teams, and numerous intramural teams. In addition, students are involved in a variety of clubs and associations, such as forensics, theater, music, radio station (Puget Sound's radio station received an award from MTV for best college radio station in the nation), art and literary magazine, weekly newspaper, yearbook, Student Senate, religious groups, a variety of faculty and trustee committees, Black Student Union, Hui-O-Hawaii, Earth Activists, B-GLAD (Bisexuals, Gays, Lesbians, and Allies for Diversity), Asian Pacific American Student Union, Community for Hispanic Awareness, and Habitat for Humanity. Seventy-five percent of students participate in community service activities, one of the highest participation rates in the country.

Graduate degrees offered include the Master of Occupational Therapy, Doctor of Physical Therapy, Master of Arts in Teaching, and Master of Education.

Location

The campus is located in a residential neighborhood in the historic North End of Tacoma. Thirty-five miles south of Seattle and easily accessible from Interstate 5, Tacoma is a dynamic city of 200,000 people. It was recently ranked by *Money* magazine as one of the most livable medium-sized cities in the country. The college occupies thirty-nine buildings on a 97-acre campus. The architecture is Tudor Gothic, with its distinctive red-brick pattern arches and porticoes. Located close to the shores of Puget Sound and a short distance from ski slopes and the Pacific Ocean, the college is also a hub for much of Tacoma's cultural life. Tacoma also features Point Defiance Zoo and Aquarium, many parks, museums, a new convention center, and hospitals.

Majors and Degrees

Puget Sound offers more than forty-five majors leading to the Bachelor of Arts, Bachelor of Science, and Bachelor of Music degrees. Academic programs are art, Asian studies (interdisciplinary emphasis), biochemistry, biology, business, chemistry, classics, communication, comparative sociology, computer science, computer science in business, economics, English, exercise science, foreign languages and literature (majors in French, German, international affairs, and Spanish; course offerings in Chinese, Greek, Japanese, and Latin), geology, history, international political economy, mathematics, molecular and cellular biology, music, natural science, philosophy, physics, politics and government, psychology, religion, and theater arts. Minors are offered in Latin American studies, African-American studies, environmental policy and decision making, gender studies, neuroscience, and many other areas. The introduction of a special interdisciplinary major allows exceptional students the opportunity to pursue a degree in a recognized interdisciplinary or emergent field.

Puget Sound offers a dual-degree program in engineering, leading to a joint Bachelor of Arts/Bachelor of Science degree in engineering. Students in this program complete prerequisites in chemistry, mathematics/computer science, and physics, then transfer to an accredited engineering school for course work in chemical, civil, electrical, environmental, mechanical, or petroleum engineering, among others. Affiliated schools are Washington University in St. Louis, Columbia University, Duke University, and the University of Southern California.

Academic Programs

Academic rigor, freedom to take courses from across the curriculum, and opportunities for interdisciplinary study characterize the academic experience. At the heart of the academic program is the core curriculum—eight course groupings around which major and elective studies are arranged over a four-year period. The emphasis throughout a student's undergraduate education is on the acquisition of intellectual skills: the ability to express oneself clearly, both orally and in writing; the ability to reason quantitatively; and the ability to think logically, critically, and independently. By mastering the literature and techniques of a specific academic major, the student learns to cultivate the unique power of his or her own mind and to respond vigorously, but humanely, to important social, moral, and intellectual challenges.

A particularly well-designed curriculum for the freshman year and a model program of academic advising and career counseling enable each student to develop his or her own skills and interests in preparation for a lifetime of creative work and leisure. Puget Sound's highly successful and award-winning student orientation process—Prelude, Passages and Perspectives—is a nine-day program that allows new students to become involved in writing and thinking seminars, academic workshops, community service, and a three-day excursion to the nearby Olympic Peninsula.

The academic year is divided into two semesters, beginning in late August and mid-January, and a thirteen-week summer session (two miniterms). A normal academic load is 4 units (typically four courses) per semester. Each unit of credit is equivalent to 6 quarter hours or 4 semester hours. Thirty-two units are required for graduation.

Off-Campus Programs

Puget Sound offers an outstanding selection of international opportunities for its students and operates or offers programs in more than fifty countries, including Australia, England, Scotland, Spain,

France, Germany, Italy, Austria, China, Japan, Taiwan, Argentina, and Chile, among others. The Pacific Rim/Asia Study-Travel Program offers students an intense year of study and travel in six to eight Asian countries.

Puget Sound's location in one of the fastest-growing regions of the country places its internship program at the forefront of national liberal arts colleges. In fact, Tacoma was named the number one midsized city in the nation for entrepreneurship by *Entrepreneur* magazine. Opportunities for student research abound, as students may apply for summer research grants in the sciences, social sciences, humanities, and the arts.

Academic Facilities

Collins Memorial Library contains more than 550,000 volumes of books and periodicals plus a sizable collection of federal and Washington State government publications, maps, microforms, videotapes, cassettes, compact discs, and other media materials. These resources are strengthened through participation in the Orbis Cascade Alliance, a consortium of twenty-seven public and private institutions of higher education in Oregon and Washington, with combined holdings of more than 22 million volumes. Other major academic facilities include Thompson Science Complex, Kittredge Art Gallery, Schneebeck Concert Hall, Norton Clapp Theatre, Gordon D. Alcorn Arboretum, Lowry Wyatt Hall, and Slater Museum of Natural History. Harned Hall, a 51,000-square-foot addition to the newly remodeled Thompson Science Complex, opened in 2006. The new Center for Health Sciences is scheduled to open in the fall of 2011.

Puget Sound, as a natural resource, provides students of environmental science and marine biology with a superb outdoor laboratory. A working relationship with Point Defiance Zoo and Aquarium, just minutes north of the campus, offers teaching and research opportunities in marine and biological sciences. Equipment and facilities in the Thompson Science Complex include a modern greenhouse; an observatory; an aquarium with a tidal cycle; a state-of-the-art genetics laboratory; a scanning electron microscope and a transmission electron microscope; ultraviolet, visible, fluorescence, infrared, and nuclear magnetic resonance spectrophotometric equipment; and a seismograph. Students also have access to human cadavers as learning tools. Special facilities are available for students of occupational and physical therapy, education, counseling, foreign languages, and psychology. The music building has twenty-two individual practice rooms.

Wireless Internet access is available throughout campus. In addition, students have access to computer labs and state-of-the-art video editing facilities.

Costs

Tuition and required student fees were $37,030 and $360, respectively, for the 2010–11 academic year. Room and board were $9650. It is estimated that an additional $3300 per year is adequate for books, laundry, and other essentials, including travel to and from home.

Financial Aid

More than 90 percent of Puget Sound students receive financial aid in one or a combination of the following forms: scholarships, grants, low-interest loans, and part-time employment. Most financial aid is awarded on the basis of demonstrated financial need, as determined through analysis of the Free Application for Federal Student Aid (FAFSA). In addition, the college's Financial Aid Office administers scholarships based on academic merit that range from $4000 to $17,000 per year. In 2010–11, the middle 50 percent of Puget Sound's financial aid packages for first-year students were between $19,000 and $35,000, including need-based aid. For continuing students (sophomores, juniors, and seniors), the range was between $20,000 and $38,000. Typically, loans make up less than 25 percent of these awards. Many other talent awards are available in the arts, selected academic areas, forensics, and leadership.

Faculty

Members of the faculty work closely with individual students both in the classroom and in student-originated research projects within and across the disciplines. Ninety-three percent of the faculty members teach full-time; 98 percent of tenured faculty members hold a Ph.D. or an equivalent terminal degree. In agreement with Ted Taranovski, Professor Emeritus of History, faculty members feel that the University of Puget Sound is "an institution geared to human beings—small enough to give one a sense of community and yet large enough to provide an excellent academic curriculum; it is not an impersonal machine where people become cogs." In recent years, professors at Puget Sound have been recognized for their academic and teaching achievements through awards and distinctions, including the Graves Award in the Humanities and fellowships from various organizations, including the National Endowment for the Humanities, the American Council of Learned Societies, and the Danforth Foundation. In the last four years, three Puget Sound professors have been named Washington State Professor of the Year by the Carnegie Foundation for the Advancement of Teaching. Puget Sound has received more of these awards than any other college or university in the state.

Admission Requirements

Each applicant to the University of Puget Sound is considered individually and is admitted on the basis of his or her qualifications and achievements. In considering applicants for freshman admission, the Admission Committee evaluates the following: high school course selection, high school grade point average, rank in graduating class (if available), SAT or ACT scores, a counselor's and an academic teacher's recommendations, an essay, a recommended interview, and extracurricular activities. College credit is awarded to students who have earned scores of 4 or higher on Advanced Placement examinations. Credit for a score of 3 is available for selected examinations only. Credit is also available for a score of 5, 6, or 7 on the International Baccalaureate higher-level examinations.

Application and Information

Prospective freshmen may apply for admission anytime after the beginning of the senior year in high school using the *Common Application* for freshmen. Admission decisions are generally mailed on or before April 1. The application deadline is January 15. Students who have decided that Puget Sound is their first-choice college may choose one of two early decision plans. Early Decision I has a November 15 application deadline, with admission and tentative financial aid notification by December 15. Early Decision II has a January 2 application deadline, with admission and tentative financial aid notification by February 15. Transfer students are admitted in both semesters. Students applying for transfer admission should submit the *Common Application* for transfers.

For more information about Puget Sound or for application materials, students should contact:

Office of Admission
University of Puget Sound
1500 North Warner Street, #1062
Tacoma, Washington 98416-1062
Phone: 253-879-3211
　　　　800-396-7191 (toll-free)
E-mail: admission@pugetsound.edu
Web site: http://www.pugetsound.edu

UNIVERSITY OF REDLANDS

REDLANDS, CALIFORNIA

The University

The University of Redlands has, for more than 100 years, offered its select student body a tradition of superior liberal arts education. While students may select from a variety of programs that prepare them for professional or graduate school, the heart and foundation of Redlands is in liberal studies. Its outstanding faculty, educated in the world's finest colleges and universities, provides students with extraordinary opportunities for learning and growth through excellent teaching and close, informal interaction. Intense intellectual activity is balanced by opportunities for quiet reflection, fun, and recreation.

The University College of Arts and Sciences enrolls more than 2,300 students. Sixty percent of the freshman class comes from California and the remainder from forty-two other states and ten countries. In addition to a strong academic program in the liberal arts, the sciences, preprofessional programs, and the arts, many extracurricular programs are available to the student, including debate, music, drama, dance, and athletics. Internships are available for students in many academic programs. The School of Music and the Department of Theatre Arts provide a rich selection of cultural events throughout the year. Prominent speakers are invited to the campus each year to give major addresses and participate in classes and public discussion groups, and many social functions are organized by the Student Life Office and individual residence halls. Additional social opportunities are provided for interested students by local nonresidential fraternities and sororities. The student services center provides assistance in the areas of career and personal counseling and academic support.

Seventy percent of the students live on campus in residence halls that offer a variety of accommodations, including single gender, coed by separate wings, and coed by alternate suites.

The University of Redlands is one of a select number of schools that have a chapter of Phi Beta Kappa, the nation's oldest and most prestigious academic honor society. In addition, 6 Redlands students have been awarded Fulbright awards within the past two years.

The University of Redlands offers master's programs in the fields of business, communicative disorders, education, geographic information systems, and music. The School of Education offers a Doctorate in Leadership for Educational Justice Ed.D. program.

Location

The University is located in the city of Redlands within the San Bernardino Valley. Overlooking the 160-acre campus are the two highest mountains in southern California, Mt. San Gorgonio and Mt. San Bernardino, each more than 10,000 feet high. Redlands has a population of 70,000 and is situated at an elevation of 1,500 feet. Metropolitan Los Angeles to the west and Palm Springs to the east are both about an hour's drive away by freeway.

Majors and Degrees

The B.A. degree is offered in the academic areas of art history, Asian studies, biology, business administration, communicative disorders, creative writing, economics, English literature, environmental studies, French, German, government, history, international relations, music, philosophy, psychology, race and ethnic studies, religion, sociology/anthropology, Spanish, studio art, theater arts, and women's and gender studies. The B.S. degree is offered in accounting, biology, business administration, chemistry, economics, environmental management, environmental science, mathematics, and physics. The professional degree of Bachelor of Music (B.M.) is offered by the School of Music. Primary and secondary credentials are granted by the School of Education.

Strong interdisciplinary programs in Latin American studies, prelaw, and premedicine are also available.

Academic Programs

Academic majors are offered in the spirit of a liberal arts program, with emphasis on developing the whole student. In addition to the standard academic program, international-study programs, independent study, and an honors program are offered to provide greater diversity.

A liberal arts education, by definition, is an exposure to a wide variety of academic disciplines. Typically, such exposure carries no underlying theme but is distributed among broad categories such as the humanities, arts, social sciences, and natural sciences. The University of Redlands has never considered itself typical and, as a result, has developed an unusual approach to the implementation of its liberal arts philosophy by restructuring the general education requirements to provide a contemporary curriculum. This common experience emphasizes competence in writing, computing, problem solving, and creative skills, all of which are fundamental to a lifetime of learning and career development. In addition, the requirements include a first-year seminar that integrates the academic program and close personal relationships between students and faculty members. The overriding emphasis of this innovative curriculum is on a thorough investigation of human values as they affect the individual and society. An examination of the worth of the individual, respect for nature and life, free inquiry, and the understanding of other cultures are a few of the topics covered through various courses. The University hopes that this experience will broaden each student's understanding and better equip them to deal with today's dynamic society.

The Johnston Center for Integrative Studies provides a nontraditional approach for a select group of highly motivated students. Johnston Center students are exempted from most of the academic structure of Redlands and instead negotiate their entire course of study with a faculty/peer committee. Drawing from the Redlands curriculum as well as from courses created each semester by the Johnston community, each student proposes an individually designed general studies program and an area of concentration. Course performance is evaluated in a narrative format rather than with letter grades. These students live in the Johnston Center Complex, a living/learning community that includes student rooms, faculty offices, classrooms, and space for weekly community meetings. Students who are enrolled in the Johnston Center are expected to contribute to the life of the center's community.

The academic calendar divides the school year into a 4-4-1 plan, providing a fall semester, a spring semester, and a May term. The four classes taken in the fall semester are completed prior to the third Friday in December. The spring semester begins in January and runs through April. The four-week May term offers students the chance to pursue one subject in depth. Extensive off-campus opportunities, including internships, international study, and on-campus independent study, are available.

Academic Facilities

The institution has facilities with a mix of Greek, Spanish, and modern California architecture. The newly renovated ground floor of the Armacost Library includes rooms for collaboration and learning, the Fletcher Jones Computing Center, a student study area, the Bulldog café, and an Internet lounge. Other facilities include the Stauffer Complex for Science, Mathematics, and Environmental Studies; and a brand-new Center for the Arts, featuring the Glen Wallichs Theatre, Frederick Loewe Performance Hall, and an art gallery. The library houses 400,000 publications and online databases such as Dialog, ABI/INFORM, PsychLIT, ERIC, Wilson Indexes, and the Music Index. These facilities and surrounding common spaces also have access to a wireless network.

Costs

Tuition for 2011–12 is $37,002, and room and board costs are $11,206.

Financial Aid

Recognizing that many worthy and capable students find it impossible to obtain a college education without financial assistance, the University has established a program of aid. Most aid is need-based, but no-need scholarships based on academic achievement in high school and/or college are available. Presidential Scholarships are also available, based on grades and test scores, as are Achievement Awards. Talent Awards, ranging from $500 to $8000 each, are available in art, creative writing, music, and theater.

Students seeking financial assistance should inquire through the Office of Admissions when applying for admission. The Free Application for Federal Student Aid (FAFSA) should be submitted by March 2. FAFSA forms received after this date are evaluated subject to the availability of funding. Forms may be obtained most conveniently from high school counselors' offices and college financial aid offices, as well as online at http://www.fafsa.gov.

Faculty

The highly qualified full-time faculty numbers 167 men and women, 90 percent of whom hold doctorates or other terminal degrees in their field. The wide variety of academic backgrounds represented in the faculty provides students with an excellent opportunity to live and work in an atmosphere of intellectual inquiry. Academic advising is handled by faculty members, and all students are assigned an adviser in the area of their major interest.

Student Government

Authority and responsibility for student government is delegated to the Associated Students of the University by the president and the faculty to make possible genuine participation by students in the governance of the University. The organization is composed of all students in the college, and its officers are chosen by the student body. More than sixty positions of representation are open to students on faculty, administrative, trustee, and alumni committees. Among other activities and responsibilities, the student government finances and operates a student-union complex, on-campus shuttle, information center, vending program, convocation series, Internet radio station, and weekly newspaper.

Admission Requirements

Graduation from an accredited high school or the equivalent is necessary for admission. No set pattern of courses in high school is required, but applicants should have had 4 years of work in English and should have completed an academic program strongly emphasizing such studies as foreign language, science, mathematics (including algebra II), and social science. An average grade of at least B should have been maintained in the high school program. Applicants are requested to submit the results of the SAT I or the ACT. The writing portion is used for placement in English classes. SAT Subject Tests are not required. Standardized test scores are not required of transfers who bring at least 24 transferable units to the University.

Transfer students should have maintained a minimum 2.8 grade point average and may transfer up to 66 units of credit from a community college. There is a 30-unit residence requirement for transfers from other four-year institutions.

Application and Information

Applications are processed on a rolling basis. Those wishing to be considered for an academic or merit scholarship should apply by November 15. Those applying for need-based financial aid should apply by January 15. Transfer applicants should apply by March 1. Applications made after this date are considered on a space-available basis.

Further inquiries should be addressed to:

Office of Admissions
University of Redlands
P.O. Box 3080
Redlands, California 92373-0999

Phone: 800-455-5064 (toll-free)
Fax: 909-335-4089
E-mail: admissions@redlands.edu
Web site: http://www.redlands.edu

The University of Redlands stands out brilliantly against the majestic San Bernardino Mountains.

UNIVERSITY OF RHODE ISLAND
KINGSTON, RHODE ISLAND

The University

As a land-grant college since its founding in 1892, the University of Rhode Island provides its students with an outstanding education and prepares them for responsible citizenship. The University also fosters significant research and takes its expertise to the community through a variety of extension and outreach programs. The current undergraduate enrollment is about 13,000 men and women. The center of the spacious country campus is a quadrangle of handsome, old granite buildings surrounded by other, newer academic buildings, student residence halls, and fraternity and sorority houses. On the plain below Kingston Hill are gymnasiums, athletic fields, tennis courts, a freshwater pond, agricultural fields, greenhouses, and a large convocation center. There are twenty-one residence halls on campus, offering a variety of living accommodations, including several new residence halls and apartment buildings for upperclass students. A variety of dining centers and meal plans are offered to all students. There are approximately 1,000 fraternity and sorority members living in nationally affiliated houses that are privately owned by alumni corporations. Some students commute from home, and other students commute from houses or apartments in the local and surrounding beach communities. Approximately 50 percent of the undergraduate students come from outside Rhode Island.

Lectures, art programs, music and dance concerts, film programs, and theater presentations are available. An extensive program of intercollegiate and intramural athletics is offered and is sufficiently varied to provide an opportunity for every student to participate. The Mackal Field House, Tootell Physical Education Center and the Keaney Gymnasium provide excellent facilities, including three pools, four gymnasiums, weight-training rooms, a dance studio, and a modern athletic training room. The Mackal Field House provides gymnasium space for a variety of recreational uses as well as an indoor track. In addition to a football stadium, there are twelve tennis courts, two softball diamonds, a baseball field, a lighted lacrosse/soccer field, a hockey field, and numerous practice fields for recreation and competition. The 8,000-seat Ryan Center houses the men's and women's basketball programs in addition to concerts and other large events. The Boss Ice Arena houses the club hockey teams and is also available for student skating. A sailing pavilion and rowing facility are located near campus. The Memorial Union Building houses a wide variety of educational, social, cultural, and recreational services, including lounges, study rooms, a radio station, the campus newspaper, a game room, dining facilities, a bookstore, a coffee shop, a restaurant, a ballroom, and a special events room.

Location

The University's 1,200-acre campus is located in the historic village of Kingston, 30 miles south of Providence. Bus transportation is available from the campus to most locations in the area, including Wakefield, where the nearest shopping facilities are located. The Kingston Amtrak train station is 1 mile from campus, and the T. F. Green Airport in Warwick, Rhode Island, is only 25 miles from campus. The campus is 6 miles from the ocean, and weekend ski trips to the mountains are easily managed in the winter season.

Majors and Degrees

The College of Arts and Sciences offers the Bachelor of Arts, Bachelor of Science, Bachelor of Fine Arts, and Bachelor of Music degrees. The Bachelor of Arts degree is offered in African and African American studies, anthropology, art history, art studio, chemistry, Chinese, classical studies, communication studies, comparative literature, computer science, economics, English, film media, French, German, history, Italian, journalism, Latin American studies, mathematics, music, music history, philosophy, physics, political science, psychology, public relations, sociology, Spanish, women's studies, and writing and rhetoric. The Bachelor of Science degree is available in applied sociology, chemistry, chemistry and chemical oceanography, computer science, economics, mathematics, physics, and physics and physical oceanography. The Bachelor of Fine Arts degree is offered in art and theater, and the Bachelor of Music degree is available in music education and music theory, performance, and composition.

The College of Business Administration offers the Bachelor of Science degree in accounting, entrepreneurial management, finance, general business administration, global business management, marketing, and supply chain management. Business degree programs are accredited by the Association to Advance Collegiate Schools of Business. A five-year International Business Program is also offered.

The College of Engineering offers the Bachelor of Science degree in biomedical, chemical, chemical and ocean, civil, computer, electrical, industrial, mechanical, and ocean engineering. A five-year International Engineering Program is also offered, as is an Engineering/M.B.A. Program. Engineering degree programs are accredited by the Accreditation Board for Engineering and Technology, Inc.

The College of the Environment and Life Sciences offers the Bachelor of Science degree in animal science and technology, aquaculture and fishery technology, biological sciences, biology, clinical laboratory science, environmental economics and management, environmental horticulture and turfgrass management, environmental science and management, geology and geological oceanography, geosciences, marine affairs, marine biology, microbiology, nutrition and dietetics, resource economics and commerce, and wildlife and conservation biology. The Bachelor of Landscape Architecture degree is awarded in landscape architecture and is accredited by the American Society of Landscape Architects.

The College of Human Science and Services offers the Bachelor of Science degree in communicative disorders, early childhood education, elementary and secondary education, human development and family studies, kinesiology, textile marketing, and textiles, fashion merchandising, and design.

The College of Nursing offers the Bachelor of Science degree in nursing, which is approved by the Commission on Collegiate Nursing Education and the Rhode Island Board of Nurse Registration and Nursing Education.

The College of Pharmacy offers a Bachelor of Science in Pharmaceutical Sciences. The College also offers a six-year Doctor of Pharmacy degree, which is accredited by the American Council on Pharmaceutical Education.

Preprofessional preparation is available in dentistry, law, medicine, physical therapy, and veterinary studies.

Academic Programs

All programs of study aim for a balance of the natural and social sciences, the humanities, and professional subjects. All freshmen who enter the University to earn a bachelor's degree are first enrolled in University College; its advising program helps students choose a concentration and appropriate courses. A student must meet the curricular requirements of the college in which the degree is to be earned. As a general rule, 120 credits are required for a Bachelor of Arts degree and 130 for a Bachelor of Science degree, including the specified general education requirements. The University of Rhode Island operates on a two-semester calendar, with semesters beginning in September and January. Two 5-week summer sessions are also available. Credit is granted to students who have passed a College Board Advanced Placement examination with a grade of 3 or better. In addition, credit may be given for satisfactory scores on departmental proficiency examinations or College-Level Examination Program (CLEP) subject examinations and for the International Baccalaureate Program exam (IB Higher Level Tests). The University Honors Program offers academically talented students opportunities to broaden their intellectual development and to strengthen their preparation in their major fields of study.

Off-Campus Programs

The Office of Internships and Experiential Education offers internships for academic credit, including one-semester and one-year programs. Additionally, the University has exchange agreements with universities in England, France, Germany, Japan, and Spain. Other off-campus study and exchange programs are also available.

Academic Facilities

The University library has more than 1 million bound volumes and 1.5 million titles available electronically. Active research programs are carried on in all seven colleges. The Graduate School of Oceanography, located on the Narragansett Bay Campus, provides undergraduates with a living research lab for science-related courses. The University houses a large collection of American historic textiles, a center for robotics research, a planetarium, the Watson House Museum, a Confucius Institute, two animal science farms, and the state Crime Lab for forensic study.

Costs

The comprehensive cost for 2010–11 was estimated at $38,568 for out-of-state students and $20,166 for Rhode Islanders. This covers tuition, fees, and room and board. Books, travel, and personal expenses are not included in these figures. Laboratory fees are extra. The University participates in the cooperative plan of the New England Board of Higher Education, whereby students from other New England states are able to enroll in certain degree programs that are not offered in their own states and pay reduced tuition.

Financial Aid

To be considered for financial aid at the University, students must submit the Free Application for Federal Student Aid (FAFSA). Although there is no deadline for applying, priority is given to applications received by March 1. Most students receive notification of admission decisions on or about April 1. Merit scholarships are available to incoming freshmen with superior academic credentials. Consideration for these scholarships is given to freshmen who apply by the December 1 early action deadline. For 2010–11, 75 percent of new students who completed applications were awarded some form of aid. In addition, students have opportunities for employment through work-study programs that use federal, state, and institutional funds.

Faculty

The faculty consists of 817 full-time equivalent members, or 1 professor for every 16.5 students. Approximately 88 percent of the full-time faculty members hold doctoral degrees. Faculty members serve both the graduate and undergraduate populations and have wide-ranging interests and responsibilities. In addition to teaching and research, they serve as student advisers.

Student Government

The Student Senate is a legislative body that represents the students to the administration and faculty and supervises extracurricular activities. It also distributes the activities funds among the various student organizations through its funding committee. Individual residence halls form their own governments. The Interfraternity Council supervises fraternity affairs, and the Panhellenic Association governs sorority life. The Commuter Association provides social activities and other assistance for commuter students.

Admission Requirements

Admission to the University is competitive. Applicants are given individual consideration, but it is expected that all candidates have completed at least 18 units of college-preparatory work; specific unit requirements vary for each of the seven colleges of the University. Academic achievement in a challenging high school program receives the strongest consideration in the review of an applicant's credentials. An audition is required for the Bachelor of Music degree. All freshman candidates must submit a high school transcript and scores on the SAT or the ACT examination, which should be taken no later than January 1 of the senior year. International students for whom English is not the primary language must take the Test of English as a Foreign Language (TOEFL). Scores on equivalency examinations may be presented by applicants who have not been able to complete formal high school studies. Transfer students may enter in either semester (although some degree programs admit students only in the fall semester) and must submit transcripts of all previous work at both the high school and college levels. Early admission is available to high school juniors with superior records.

Students are selected primarily on the basis of academic competence and without regard to age, race, religion, color, sex, creed, national origin, disability, or sexual orientation.

Application and Information

Visits to the campus are encouraged. Information sessions and tours are scheduled daily during the week and on many Saturdays throughout the year. Students should visit the Admission Web site (http://www.uri.edu/admission) for details about these sessions as well as open house programs and directions to the campus. Admission representatives attend college fairs in Rhode Island and throughout the Northeast during the academic year.

Students are encouraged to submit applications early in their final year of high school, as the University subscribes to a rolling admission policy and reviews applications as they become complete. The early action deadline is December 1, and students receive notification by January 31. The regular deadline for fall term freshman applications is February 1, and the deadline for transfer applications is May 1. Most decisions are reported in March. The closing date for spring-term applications is November 1. Applications are available online. Requests for information should be directed to:

Office of Admission
University of Rhode Island
14 Upper College Road
Kingston, Rhode Island 02881

Phone: 401-874-7000
E-mail: admission@uri.edu
Web site: http://www.uri.edu/admission

UNIVERSITY OF ROCHESTER
ROCHESTER, NEW YORK

The University

Founded in 1850, Rochester is one of the leading private universities in the country, one of sixty-two members of the prestigious Association of American Universities, and one of eight national private research institutions in the premier University Athletic Association. Including the Eastman School of Music, the University has a full-time enrollment of 5,193 undergraduates and 3,175 graduate students. Rochester's personal scale and the breadth of its research and academic programs permit both attention to the individual and unusual flexibility in planning undergraduate studies.

Along with the distinctive Rochester Curriculum to help make the most of the undergraduate years, students in the College of Arts, Sciences, and Engineering (the College) also have access to resources at the Eastman School of Music, the William E. Simon Graduate School of Business Administration, the Margaret Warner Graduate School of Education and Human Development, the School of Medicine and Dentistry, and the School of Nursing. Special opportunities include the Take Five program, which allows selected undergraduates a tuition-free fifth year or semester of academic study; Rochester Early Medical Scholars (REMS), an eight-year combined B.A. or B.S./M.D. program; Rochester Early Business Scholars (REBS), a six-year combined B.A. or B.S./M.B.A program; Graduate Engineering at Rochester (GEAR), a 3-2 B.S./M.S. program; Guaranteed Rochester Accelerated Degree in Education (GRADE), a five-year B.A. or B.S./M.S. program; study abroad; Quest courses, first-year classes designed to allow collaborative research between faculty and students; seven certificate programs; Senior Scholars Program; and employment opportunities that include a national summer jobs program and paid internships.

Set on a bend in the Genesee River, the River Campus is home to almost all undergraduates who live in a variety of residence halls, fraternity houses, and special-interest housing. Most of the campus is built in a consistent neoclassical architecture, yet all academic buildings are wireless, and all residence halls are wired for the Internet and cable television. Facilities include Wilson Commons, the student union; the multipurpose Goergen Athletic Center; and a new research facility, the Goergen Hall of Biomedical Engineering and Optics.

Rochester students participate in more than 240 organizations, including twenty-three varsity teams, thirty-six intramural and club sports, eighteen fraternities and thirteen sororities, performing arts groups, musical ensembles, WRUR radio, URTV, and campus publications.

Location

With Lake Ontario on its northern border, the scenic Finger Lakes to the south, and more than a million people, Rochester is rated among the most livable cities in the United States. Cultural and recreational opportunities include museums, parks, orchestras, planetarium, theater companies, and professional sports teams.

Majors and Degrees

The University offers a Bachelor of Arts program through the College, with majors in African and African-American studies; American Sign Language; anthropology; archaeology, technology, and historical structures; art history; astronomy; bioethics; biology; brain and cognitive sciences; business; chemistry; classics; comparative literature; computer science; economics; English; environmental studies; epidemiology; film and media studies; financial economics; French; geological sciences; German; health, behavior and society; health policy; history; interdepartmental studies; international relations; Japanese; linguistics; mathematics; mathematics/statistics; music; philosophy; physics; political science; psychology; religion; Russian; Russian studies; Spanish; statistics; studio arts; and women's studies.

Bachelor of Science programs are offered in the College, with majors in applied mathematics; biological sciences (biochemistry, cell and developmental biology, ecology and evolutionary biology, microbiology, molecular genetics, or neuroscience); brain and cognitive sciences; chemistry; environmental science; geological sciences; geomechanics; physics; and physics and astronomy.

The College also offers certificate programs in actuarial studies, Asian studies, biophysics, biotechnology, literary translation studies, mathematical modeling in political science and economics, medphysics, and Polish and Central European studies.

The Hajim School of Engineering and Applied Sciences—part of the College—offers Bachelor of Science programs in biomedical, chemical, computer science; electrical and computer, and mechanical engineering; geomechanics; optics; and engineering and applied science, an interdepartmental program with specializations in a variety of areas. A B.A. program in engineering science is also offered.

In addition to the College's Bachelor of Arts in Music, a Bachelor of Music degree is offered through the Eastman School, with majors in applied music, composition, jazz studies and contemporary media, music education, musical arts, and music theory. Students may pursue a double-degree in Eastman and the College.

A Bachelor of Science degree is offered through the School of Nursing for those who already have their RN certification.

Additional opportunities include 3-2 or guaranteed 4-2 admissions programs offered through the William E. Simon Graduate School of Business Administration, in which students earn both a B.A. or B.S. from the College and an M.B.A. from the Simon School; 3-2 B.S./M.S. programs in biological sciences—biomedical engineering, chemical engineering, electrical and computer engineering, mechanical engineering, neuroscience, and optics; a program leading to a B.A. or B.S. and a master's in public health; and a guaranteed admission program leading to a B.A. or B.S. in an undergraduate major and an M.S. from the Margaret Warner Graduate School of Education and Human Development. Transfer students can pursue a 3-2 program that combines a B.A. and a B.S. in an engineering concentration.

Academic Programs

The University's calendar includes two regular semesters. The distinctive Rochester Curriculum allows students to select their major from one of the three branches of learning (the humanities, the natural sciences, and the social sciences). In each of the two branches outside their major, students choose a cluster of three courses that allows them to dig deeply in an area that particularly interests them. For most students, there are no other distribution requirements, except choosing one of seventy freshman writing classes.

The Take Five program lets selected students take a tuition-free fifth year or semester in order to pursue their varied interests.

The Quest program offers first-year students the advantages of small classes, student/teacher collaboration, and original research. Quest courses teach students how to learn, as undergraduates and beyond.

Students may arrange independent study courses or pursue research in all departments. Those whose interests may not be fully realized through a traditional major, double major, or major/minor, may work with faculty advisers to design an interdepartmental concentration.

Undergraduates from any academic discipline may devote their senior year to a self-designed creative project in the form of scholarly research, a scientific experiment, or a literary or artistic work through the Senior Scholars Program.

Undergraduates enrolled in the College may take private instruction at the Eastman School of Music. A double-degree program leading to the Bachelor of Music degree from Eastman and a bachelor's degree from the College is also available.

The Rochester Early Medical Scholars program is an eight-year B.A. or B.S./M.D. program for exceptionally talented undergraduates. Students enrolled in this program enter the University of Rochester with assurance of admission to the University's medical school upon successful completion of their undergraduate degree program.

The Graduate Engineering at Rochester (GEAR) program provides selected students with an assurance of admission into one of seven engineering master's programs at the Hajim School of Engineering and Applied Sciences: biomedical engineering, chemical engineering, computer science, electrical and computer engineering, material science, mechanical engineering, or optics. GEAR students receive a 50 percent tuition award in their fifth year of study in the form of a teaching assistantship.

The University's research centers include the Frederick Douglass Institute for African and African-American Studies, the Susan B. Anthony Institute for Gender and Women's Studies, the Center for Future Health, the Center for Judaic Studies, the W. Allen Wallis Institute of Political Economy, the Center for Visual Science, the Sign Language Research Center, the Skalny Center for Polish and Central European Studies, the Center for Optics Manufacturing, the Laboratory of Laser Energetics, the Center for Electronic Imaging Systems, and the Center for Biomedical Ultrasound, and many others in the School of Medicine and Dentistry and Strong Medicine.

Off-Campus Programs

Full-year and semester-long study-abroad opportunities and special summer and winter trips are offered through seventy different study-abroad programs. Semester and full-year destinations include Argentina, Australia, Austria, Belgium, Chile, China, Czech Republic, Egypt, England, France, Germany, Ghana, Hungary, Ireland, Israel, Italy, Japan, Jordan, Mexico, Netherlands, New Zealand, Peru, Poland, Russia, Senegal, Spain, Sweden, and Taiwan. International internships are offered in Berlin, Bonn, Brussels, London, Madrid, and Paris.

Academic Facilities

As one of the smallest of the 151 American universities classified by the Carnegie Foundation for the Advancement of Teaching as offering an extensive range of doctoral programs, Rochester offers an environment that combines the vast learning resources of a national university with the intensive personalized attention of a private college. Research opportunities for undergraduates are available in every field. Major research facilities include a comprehensive Medical Center; an extensive on-campus computer system; direct access to the CYBER 205 Supercomputer in Princeton, New Jersey; fifteen electron microscopes; a 12-trillion watt, 24-beam laser fusion laboratory; and a 3-million-volume library system, including the Eastman School's Sibley Music Library, the largest collection of any music school in the Western Hemisphere. The University is widely known as the nation's premier institution for the study of optics and is home to the Omega, the world's most powerful ultraviolet laser.

Costs

In 2010–11, tuition and fees cost $40,282; room and board averaged $11,640; and books, transportation, and other expenses averaged $2808. Part-time study is offered on a per-course basis.

Financial Aid

The University offers a strong program of financial assistance, including academic merit scholarships, grants, loans, tuition payment plans, and part-time jobs. Applicants should submit the CSS PROFILE application and the Free Application for Federal Student Aid (FAFSA). Special awards include full-tuition Renaissance Scholarships, Bausch & Lomb Honorary Science Scholarships, Frederick Douglass and Susan B. Anthony Scholarships, George Eastman Young Leaders Scholarships, Xerox Scholarships for Innovation and Information Technology, International Baccalaureate Scholarships, Seventh Generation Scholarships, FIRST Scholarships, National Merit Scholarships, National Achievement Scholarships, Urban League Scholarships, AHORA Scholarships, and other merit-based awards. In 2009, the University joined the Yellow Ribbon program and created the Rochester Pledge Scholarship, guaranteeing coverage of full tuition and mandatory fees for qualified U.S. Armed Forces veterans who enroll in undergraduate studies at the College or the Eastman School of Music. The University also awards room and board grants to selected Naval ROTC scholars and Phi Theta Kappa Scholarships for transfer students. Special applications are not required for merit scholarship consideration.

Faculty

Students work closely with a faculty of internationally renowned scholars, all of whom engage both in advanced research and in teaching at the undergraduate level. The University's faculty is held in high regard by colleagues at sister institutions, and many of its departments are widely recognized as among the best in the country.

Student Government

All undergraduates are members of the Students' Association, which has an annually elected president and a student Senate; there is also a Judicial Council, whose members are appointed by the Senate. The Students' Association in the College strives to coordinate student activities; protect academic freedom; improve students' cultural, social, and physical welfare; develop educational standards and facilities; and provide a forum for the expression of student views and interests.

Admission Requirements

The University of Rochester seeks to admit students who will take advantage of its resources, be strongly motivated to do their best, and contribute to the life of the University community. An applicant's character, extracurricular activities, job experience, academic accomplishments, and career goals are considered. More than three quarters of last year's enrolled students ranked in the top tenth of their secondary school classes. The middle 50 percent of admitted freshmen scored between 600 and 690 on the SAT critical reading exam and 630 and 730 on the SAT math and between 29 and 32 on the ACT.

The recommended application filing date for freshman applicants is January 1 for fall admission and October 1 for spring admission. An early decision plan is available. Transfer students can enter in the fall and spring semesters. Transfer applications are due by June 1 for fall enrollment and October 1 for spring. The University accepts the Common Application and the Universal College Application. An electronic online application is available on the University's Web site. Applicants for freshman admission are required to submit scores from either the SAT or ACT. SAT Subject Test results are reviewed but are not required. An interview is recommended. Candidates for admission from lower-income groups are encouraged to investigate the Higher Education Opportunity Program (New York State residents only), for supportive services and financial aid.

The University of Rochester provides equal opportunity in admissions and student aid regardless of sex, age, race, color, creed, disability, sexual orientation, and national or ethnic origin and complies with all applicable nondiscrimination laws. Questions on compliance should be directed to the particular school or department and/or to the University's Intercessor at University of Rochester, P.O. Box 270039, Rochester, New York 14627-0039; phone: 585-275-9125.

Application and Information

To obtain application forms and further information on admission and financial aid, students should contact:

Dean of Admissions and Financial Aid
University of Rochester
P.O. Box 270251
Rochester, New York 14627-0251
Phone: 585-275-3221
        888-822-2256 (toll-free)
Web site: http://www.enrollment.rochester.edu/admissions
          http://www.facebook.com/University.of.Rochester
          http://twitter.com/uradmissions

Director of Admissions
Eastman School of Music
26 Gibbs Street
Rochester, New York 14604
Phone: 585-274-1060
        800-388-9695 (toll-free)
Web site: http://www.rochester.edu/eastman

Rush Rhees Library on the University of Rochester's Eastman Quadrangle.

UNIVERSITY OF SAN DIEGO

SAN DIEGO, CALIFORNIA

The University

Known for its commitment to Catholic tradition and the liberal arts, the University of San Diego (USD) has created academic programs providing students with the skills necessary to grow and advance personally and professionally. Beyond the traditional arts, sciences, and humanities, USD has developed exceptional programs in business, engineering, marine science, international relations, and the health sciences. With a holistic philosophy, USD seeks to foster competence, international and cultural sensitivity, professional responsibility, and a spirit of compassionate service in each student.

The students who share in the life at USD and contribute to its growth are a diverse group representing all fifty states and more than sixty countries. There are currently 5,388 undergraduates out of a total University enrollment of 8,201 students. Ninety-five percent of USD's freshman students and 46 percent of upperclassmen reside on the campus, many in recently constructed facilities. The residence halls consist of traditional dormitories, suites, and apartment-style buildings. Several meal plans are available to accommodate different schedules and tastes in food.

A friendly campus atmosphere, the opportunity for close interaction between faculty members and students, and small classes that facilitate personal attention and faculty accessibility characterize the educational environment at the University of San Diego. Numerous campus activities are available to students, including social and cultural events, special-interest groups and clubs, and intercollegiate and intramural sports. The Office of Campus Recreation complements the academic experience at the University by offering students many opportunities to use their leisure time constructively and enjoyably. The Shiley Theatre is the center of many cultural activities on campus, including concerts, lectures, plays, and recitals. There are also more than eighty student-controlled clubs and organizations, including nationally affiliated fraternities and sororities, national honor societies, and service organizations.

Location

The 180-acre campus sits on a mesa commanding inspiring views of the Pacific Ocean, Mission Bay, and San Diego harbor. Located on the southern tip of California, San Diego offers a wide variety of recreational, business, science, art, and cultural activities. With an average daily temperature of 66 degrees in February and 78 degrees in August, the area is perfect for biking, jogging, tennis, softball, and all aquatic sports. In addition, San Diego is noted for its outstanding zoo, museums, Spanish missions, Sea World, and major sports teams. The proximity to Mexico provides an excellent opportunity for gaining firsthand insights into Mexican culture. The city of San Diego also offers educational advantages to students in the fields of social services, education, environmental and marine science, art, music, and archaeology. The San Diego International Airport, downtown, Mission Bay, and the Aquatic Center are just a few minutes from the campus.

Majors and Degrees

The University confers the Bachelor of Arts, Bachelor of Science, Bachelor of Business Administration, and Bachelor of Accountancy degrees. Undergraduate major programs are offered in accountancy, anthropology, art history, biology, biochemistry, business administration (with minors in accounting, finance, information technology management, international business, law and ethics, management, marketing, real estate, and supply chain management), business economics, chemistry, communication studies, computer science, economics, electrical engineering, English, environmental studies, ethnic studies, French, history, interdisciplinary humanities, industrial and systems engineering, international relations, liberal studies, marine science, mathematics, mechanical engineering, music, philosophy, physics, political science, psychology, sociology, Spanish, theater arts, theology and religious studies, and visual arts.

Minors are available in most major areas of study and in architecture, Asian studies, Catholic studies, environmental studies, gender studies, German, Italian, leadership studies, and peace and justice studies.

Advanced degree and teaching credential programs are available in bilingual/cross-cultural studies, counselor education, educational administration, elementary and secondary education, pupil personnel services, and special education.

Academic Programs

The Freshman Preceptorial program begins each USD student's academic career with a combination of advising, orientation, and an introduction to college-level scholarship. The preceptor, a faculty member in the student's intended area of study has frequent contact with each advisee and continues advising throughout the student's general education program. Once the student declares a major, the responsibility of advising shifts to a department faculty member, who provides guidance about specialized and professional study. Several programs, such as those in marine science and international relations, combine multiple disciplines, and special advisers are assigned to these areas. All of USD's programs are built solidly on the liberal arts, developing critical thinking skills through an emphasis on fundamental disciplines, written and oral communication, and an understanding of the past. USD gives special attention to the exploration of human and spiritual values, the interrelations of knowledge, and the development of a cross-cultural and international perspective.

The University operates on a 4-1-4 academic calendar. Normally, the student is in residence for eight semesters and completes approximately forty-four courses, completing a minimum of 124 units.

The honors program at the University gives promising students the opportunity for both independent academic research and intensive exchange of ideas with other honors students. Selection of students to the program is made primarily on the basis of past academic achievement. The program is competitive in its selection process and offers preceptorial and seminar course work.

College credit may be granted for Advanced Placement courses taken in secondary schools when the classes are completed with scores of 3, 4, or 5 on the appropriate Advanced Placement tests given by the College Board. Certain subjects require a score of 4 or 5 in order to receive college credit.

A number of subject examinations of the College-Level Examination Program (CLEP) have been approved by the University faculty, and in certain specified areas students may qualify for college credit by satisfactory performance on the CLEP tests.

Off-Campus Programs

University of San Diego undergraduate students can live and study in many countries, including Australia, Austria, Costa Rica, England, France, Germany, Ireland, Italy, Japan, Mexico, Scotland, Spain, or the West Indies, while earning credit at USD.

USD conducts a five-week summer session in Guadalajara, Mexico, in cooperation with several other American universities. The summer's experiences include concerts, lectures, and planned tours and excursions.

Academic Facilities

Named Alcalá Park after the Spanish university city of Alcalá de Henares, the campus is built in the style of the sixteenth-century Spanish Renaissance. Several important academic buildings have been constructed in recent years.

Opened in 2004, the 150,000-square-foot Donald Shiley Center for Science and Technology contains seventy-three state-of-the-art laboratory facilities for biology, biochemistry, chemistry, physics, environmental studies, and marine science. In addition, the center features aquariums, an astronomy deck, and a greenhouse.

Through the Joan Kroc Institute for Peace and Justice, the students and faculty members of the University of San Diego have stepped into an active role in the worldwide quest for human dignity and hope. A new School of Peace Studies has been established. The school is a magnet for political leaders and distinguished academics. Students may participate in both undergraduate and graduate programs of study.

Most recently, work was completed on the School of Leadership and Education Sciences building. The 80,000-square-foot facility is home to several undergraduate and graduate programs. In addition to classrooms and offices, the building offers observation rooms, demonstration classrooms, and labs.

The Student Life Pavilion (SLP) and the University Center form the hub of student life. Student organization offices, lounges, and a variety of dining options are located in these adjoining buildings. Tu Mercado, a full-service market, which also offers a deli, coffee bar, and gelato shop, is in the SLP. Pavilion Dining within the SLP houses the majority of campus eateries and has won several awards. A gathering place for students, the SLP is also home to the United Front Multicultural Center and USD Radio.

Camino Hall is home to Shiley Theatre and holds offices of the Fine Arts Department, soundproof practice rooms for music students, and foreign language laboratories. Founders Hall includes Founders Chapel and the Founders Art Gallery, which features exhibits by both professional and student artists.

Costs

Tuition for the 2011–12 academic year is $38,150. Estimated residence costs, including room and board, average $11,870 per year, depending on accommodations. Personal expenses, including books, are estimated at $3000.

Financial Aid

In order to be considered for need-based financial assistance, students must complete the Free Application for Federal Student Aid (FAFSA). During the 2011–12 academic year, more than 70 percent of undergraduate students received some form of financial assistance. Financial assistance can be in the form of loans, grants, scholarships, and student employment. The University offers academic, athletic, and leadership scholarships that are not dependent on financial need.

Faculty

The University of San Diego has a faculty of 393 full-time members and 450 part-time members. More than 97 percent of the faculty members hold earned doctorates or the terminal degree, and all are committed to teaching as their primary responsibility. Only faculty members teach classes, and the members of the undergraduate and graduate faculty are the same. The undergraduate student-faculty ratio of 13:1 fosters small classes, personal instruction, and individual attention, as well as faculty involvement in academic advising and University activities.

Student Government

The officers of USD's Associated Students and the class senators, who together make up the central representative group of the undergraduate students, are responsible for overseeing campus activities and the distribution of student funds.

Admission Requirements

Admission is based upon evidence of the applicant's ability to achieve success—academically, socially, and personally—at the University of San Diego. The admissions process is highly selective. Decisions are based on the following items: the student's high school record, SAT or ACT with writing scores, a letter of academic recommendation, and an essay. The Admission Committee also considers the student's level of commitment to community service, leadership skills, and special talents.

Applicants are expected to present a well-balanced secondary school program comprising at least four academic subjects each year. Both the content of the program and the quality of the student's performance are considered.

Transfer students are considered for admission after the successful completion of 24 semester units of academic course work at an accredited college or university, with a GPA of 3.0 or better.

The University welcomes international students who can demonstrate an ability to undertake college work with success in the United States. TOEFL scores are required for admission. SAT scores are required if the student wishes to be considered for merit scholarships. Although need-based financial aid is not available to international students, they are considered for merit scholarships.

Students are selected without regard to race, religion, handicap, or national or ethnic origin.

Application and Information

Application for admission is made through the Admissions Office. Forms should be completed and filed, together with a transcript of credits, as early as possible and no later than January 15 for freshmen and March 1 for transfers. Freshman applicants can also be considered for early action admission. The early action deadline is November 15. USD only accepts the Common Application. Upon receipt of all necessary materials, each application is reviewed. Candidates are notified of acceptance by April 15. USD observes the Candidates Reply Date of May 1 and requires accepted applicants to notify the University of their intentions by that date.

Arrangements for an admission information session and a campus tour may be made through the Admissions Office. For additional information about the University of San Diego, students should contact:

Office of Undergraduate Admissions
University of San Diego
5998 Alcalá Park
San Diego, California 92110
Phone: 619-260-4506
        800-248-4873 (toll-free)
Fax: 619-260-6836
E-mail: admissions@sandiego.edu
Web site: http://www.sandiego.edu

The University of San Diego is committed to academic excellence, creating a diverse and inclusive community, and preparing leaders dedicated to ethical conduct and compassionate service.

UNIVERSITY OF SAN FRANCISCO

SAN FRANCISCO, CALIFORNIA

The University

From its beginnings as a one-room schoolhouse, founded in 1855 by the Jesuits, the University of San Francisco (USF) has developed into one of the premier Jesuit Catholic universities on the West Coast. Throughout its history, USF has been committed to preparing students to improve the world in which they live. With more than 9,000 undergraduate and graduate students, the University has remained faithful to the Jesuit tradition and has maintained its small class size and low student-faculty ratio. Its programs in the arts, the sciences, business, education, nursing, and law foster a love of learning grounded by the challenge to serve society. The University's foundation encompasses academic excellence; the Jesuit, Catholic learning tradition; a multicultural, diverse community; and a global perspective that begins in San Francisco, which offers unparalleled opportunities for internships, service, and connections.

USF is one of the most diverse university campuses in the United States. Living and learning with a student body that consists of students from forty-seven states and seventy-five other countries is a unique opportunity. All new incoming freshman and sophomore students under the age of 21 are required to live on the campus, unless living with their parents. More than 90 percent of the incoming freshmen and 55 percent of all undergraduates live on-campus.

The University offers five on-campus residence halls, two on-campus apartment-style residences, and one off-campus traditional residence hall. Gillson and Hayes-Healy house freshmen, while Phelan and Lone Mountain are for sophomores and upper-division students. Fromm Hall is the only all-female residence hall. Located just twelve blocks from the USF campus, Pedro Arrupe Hall is the off-campus traditional residence hall offered to upper-division students. Loyola Village is a student residential community that features apartment-style living for students who are 21 or over or in their junior year. Most rooms in residence halls are doubles, with some single rooms available for upper-division students. Each residence hall has laundry facilities, study/computer rooms, television lounges, and 24-hour front desks.

On the campus, students have access to various University facilities. The Koret Health and Recreation Center is an exciting complex that provides facilities for exercise, racquetball, court games, weight training, personal training, and various aquatic activities in an Olympic-size pool. Tai Chi, yoga, hip-hop, and spinning are just some of the classes offered at Koret. Outdoor adventures include horseback riding, sailing, and sea kayaking. Intramural and club sports are offered in the fall and spring semesters and include basketball, boxing, flag football, fencing, karate, lacrosse, rugby, and co-ed volleyball. Special aquatic sports include a Masters swim team and a water polo club. NCAA Division I sports include baseball, basketball, cross-country, golf, soccer, tennis, track and field, and women's volleyball.

Dining facilities are located all over campus and are within walking distance of the residence halls and classrooms. Located on the main campus, The Market Café offers a food court experience with a variety of choices, including global, vegan, homestyle classics, and vegetarian options. Other dining options include Outtakes Café, Outtahere Café, Crossroads Café, Club Ed in the School of Education, and Kendrick Café at the Law School.

Undergraduates keep busy by participating in nearly eighty on-campus, student-run associations, fraternities and sororities, honor societies, and clubs, such as the USF Rugby Club and Los Locos, a club that supports USF athletics. Among these clubs are the oldest continuously performing theater group west of the Mississippi River, an award-winning FM radio station, an award-winning weekly newspaper, and a literary magazine.

For students interested in giving back to the community, the Office of Service-Learning and Community Action forms a partnership between the local community and USF. Students may participate in community service activities that include preparing meals for the homeless, tutoring underprivileged children, habitat restoration, and annual events such as AIDS Walk San Francisco.

Location

The University of San Francisco is located on a stunning 58-acre campus in a residential neighborhood just minutes from downtown San Francisco, the Financial District, Fisherman's Wharf, and the Pacific Ocean. The hilltop campus, renowned for its beautiful landscaping, borders the 1,000-acre Golden Gate Park and offers spectacular panoramic views of the city. The dynamic city of San Francisco keeps students entertained with concerts, the ballet, opera, museum exhibits, theater, and sporting events. Because of the diversity and geographical compactness of San Francisco, students find research facilities, opportunities for community involvement, and employment experiences that cannot be matched by most cities.

Majors and Degrees

The College of Arts and Sciences offers both B.A. and B.S. degrees. Majors include advertising, architecture and community design, art history/art management, biology, chemistry, communication studies, comparative literature and culture, computer science, design, economics, economics B.A.-M.A. (five-year program), education (dual-degree in teacher preparation), English, environmental science, environmental studies, exercise and sports science, fine arts, French studies, history, international and development economics B.A.-M.A. (five-year program), Japanese studies, Latin American studies, mathematics, media studies, performing arts and social justice, philosophy, physics, physics/engineering, politics, psychology, sociology, Spanish, theology/religious studies, undeclared arts, and undeclared science. The School of Business and Professional Studies offers Bachelor of Business Administration degrees in accounting, business administration, entrepreneurship, finance, hospitality industry management, international business, and marketing with a concentration in multicultural marketing, as well as a 3+1 bachelor's degree in business administration and advanced global entrepreneurship management. The School of Nursing offers a four-year Bachelor of Science in Nursing for qualified high school graduates and for second-baccalaureate candidates.

USF has sixty minors and offers unique programs that enhance the learning experience at USF. Special programs include astronomy; African and African-American studies; Asia Pacific studies B.A.-M.A. (five-year program); Catholic studies and social thought; ethnic studies; film studies; honors program in the humanities; intensive English program; journalism; Judaic studies; Latino/a and Chicano/a Studies; Middle Eastern studies; neuroscience; 4+3 dual degrees in law, military science, premedical, and other pre-professional health studies; public relations; Saint Ignatius Institute program; a five-year dual-degree teacher preparation program that results in teacher certification at the elementary or secondary level; and the School of Business honors cohort program.

Academic Programs

The University of San Francisco is committed to providing students with the essentials of a well-rounded education. A baccalaureate degree is issued upon the successful completion of a 128-unit curriculum. The curriculum consists of 44 units of core courses chosen from six specified categories in addition to 80–85 units that are divided among departmental major requirements and electives. An honors program is available for selected superior students seeking a strong academic challenge. The academic year is based on the two-semester system, with a summer session and a winter intersession also available.

In an effort to encourage high school students to move rapidly into the study of subjects now customarily reserved for colleges, the University of San Francisco honors advanced placement credits, as certified by the College Board's Advanced Placement Program tests and the International Baccalaureate program. The University also cooperates with the College-Level Examination Program (CLEP). Students intending to earn such credit must take the CLEP examinations prior to registering at the University for their freshman courses.

The USF Pre-Professional Health Committee serves to guide and recommend students to medical and dental professional health schools as well as to schools for pharmacy, optometry, veterinary medicine, and podiatry. A student may complete the premedical or other pre–health science requirements as part of, or in addition to, the requirements of an academic major. The Pre-Professional Health Committee assists students with the application process, develops a professional file for each student, collects and mails recommendations to professional schools, conducts interviews in preparation for application, and endorses approved candidates via a committee letter of recommendation sent to all professional schools selected by the student.

The St. Ignatius Institute has an integrated core curriculum based on the great books of Western civilization and an emphasis upon the great works of Christianity. Any undergraduate student at the University, regardless of major, may take courses through the Institute to meet general education requirements. The University also offers Army ROTC. ROTC scholarships are available for qualified applicants and continuing students.

Off-Campus Programs

The University of San Francisco's Center for Global Education has numerous study-abroad programs available to students with junior standing and a cumulative minimum GPA of 3.0. Exchanges with Jesuit universities include locations in Japan, Mexico, China, Spain, Philippines, El Salvador, and Chile. USF's St. Ignatius Institute program includes an exchange with Oxford University in England. Affiliations with other Jesuit universities make travel to other countries possible, e.g., Gonzaga University's study-abroad program in Florence, Italy, and Loyola University of Chicago's program in Rome. USF is also an associate member of the Institute of European and Asian Studies, which offers programs in Durham and London, England; Paris, Dijon, and Nantes, France; Berlin and Freiburg, Germany; Vienna, Austria; Madrid and Salamanca, Spain; Milan, Italy; Tokyo and Nagoya, Japan; Moscow, Russia; Adelaide and Canberra, Australia; Beijing, China; and Singapore. Numerous other study-abroad opportunities are also available. USF assists students in selecting a location, applying to programs, making financial arrangements, registering for academic credit, securing a passport and visa, and making travel plans.

Academic Facilities

University of San Francisco students have access to Gleeson Library's more than 1.8 million holdings and Harney Science Center, which houses the Computer Center, Applied Math Laboratory, the Institute of Chemical Biology, and the Physics Research Laboratories. Cowell Hall, the base for nursing classes and the Nursing Skills Laboratory, also includes the Instructional Media Center. Students also have access to Phelan Hall, the home of KUSF, the University's FM radio station, and *The Foghorn*, the official campus newspaper. Malloy Hall, headquarters for the School of Business and Professional Studies, houses an additional computer laboratory and special seminar rooms. Kalmanovitz Hall, the new home for humanities and social sciences, features state-of-the-art classrooms, a rooftop sculpture garden, and seventeen laboratories for language, writing, media, and psychology.

Costs

Tuition for the 2010–11 school year was $36,380. Room and board were $11,990 for the academic year. Books, travel, and other expenses are about $5100 per year.

Financial Aid

A wide variety of scholarships, grants, loans, and work-study programs are available at the University. Domestic students who wish to be considered for financial aid must submit the Free Application for Federal Student Aid (FAFSA) by February 1. More than two thirds of all USF students receive some type of financial aid. There are also many on- and off-campus jobs available.

The University Scholars Program is available to new domestic freshmen applicants who have an exceptional cumulative GPA, SAT combined score, or ACT composite score. Scholars are awarded a non-need-based scholarship that pays a significant percentage of the cost of tuition for four years of undergraduate study. To remain eligible, University Scholars are expected to maintain a minimum GPA of 3.25. Eligible students are identified during the admission process and must apply under early action by the November 15 deadline.

Faculty

The University has 763 full- and part-time faculty members; 92 percent of them hold doctoral or terminal degrees in the field they teach.

The University of San Francisco fosters a close relationship between students and faculty members. This is reflected in the small size of classes, the low student-faculty ratio, and the faculty members' availability for advising. Classes are not taught by student teachers or teachers' assistants.

Student Government

All undergraduates are members of the Associated Students of the University of San Francisco (ASUSF). ASUSF is the official representative body of undergraduate students at USF. The ASUSF government has three functions: to represent the official student viewpoint, to recommend policies, and to fund activities and services. ASUSF consists of three branches: the executive branch, the Student Senate, and the Student Court. The Senate comprises an executive board and student senators.

Admission Requirements

The University seeks students who are sincerely interested in pursuing a well-rounded education. The admission process is selective, and each application is reviewed individually. To enhance the quality and diversity of its student body, the University of San Francisco encourages men and women of all races, nationalities, and religious beliefs to apply. Eligibility is based on high school course work and GPA, the application essay, an academic and personal recommendation, and satisfactory test scores. Domestic applicants are required to submit SAT or ACT test scores with writing. International applicants are required to submit TOEFL or IELTS test scores; however, if an international applicant submits sufficient SAT or ACT test scores, the TOEFL or IELTS may be waived.

Application and Information

A completed application includes the application form, the application fee, a personal essay, all academic transcripts, standardized test scores, and up to two letters of recommendation. For the fall semester, the application deadlines are November 15 for early action and January 15 for regular action.

Inquiries should be addressed to:

Office of Admission
University of San Francisco
2130 Fulton Street
San Francisco, California 94117-1080
Phone: 415-422-6563
       800-CALL-USF (toll-free outside California)
Fax: 415-422-2217
E-mail: admission@usfca.edu
Web site: http://www.usfca.edu
      http://www.facebook.com/University.of.San.Francisco
      http://twitter.com/USFCA
      http://www.youtube.com/usfcalifornia

St. Ignatius Church, where freshman convocation and all graduation ceremonies are performed by each college.

UNIVERSITY OF SOUTHERN MAINE

PORTLAND, MAINE

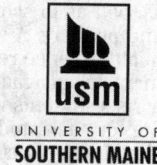

The University

Since its founding in 1878 as the Western Maine Normal School, the University of Southern Maine (USM) has evolved into a selective, comprehensive, regional, residential public university. USM undergraduates learn from exceptional professors who give personal attention to students. The average class size at USM is 22 students. Students can enjoy the friendly atmosphere of a small residential New England college campus combined with many opportunities typically available only at large, national, urban universities.

The University of Southern Maine offers students a unique blend of academic and residential life opportunities on two campuses only 8 miles apart in Portland and Gorham. USM's third campus, Lewiston-Auburn College, serves the educational needs for this growing region of the state. The Portland and Gorham campuses enjoy full classroom facilities, library services, athletic facilities, and student centers. The Portland campus is the site of the Southworth Planetarium, which is ranked among the top ten small planetariums in the United States. On the Gorham campus there are seven residence halls, cross-country running trails, an art gallery, a campus center, a theater, and a concert hall. The sports complex features an Olympic-size ice arena and a field house that features a six-lane, 200-meter track; four tennis courts; basketball courts; and baseball and softball practice areas. The diverse student body of 4,700 full-time undergraduates representing students from thirty-five states and thirty-seven countries includes accomplished artists, musicians, writers, actors, and numerous All-American athletes. Approximately 1,500 students reside in University-owned housing.

The athletic program is a vital part of the USM community and the greater Portland area. In addition to a full intramural program, USM currently fields intercollegiate athletic teams (NCAA Division III) for men in baseball, basketball, cross-country, ice hockey, indoor and outdoor track, lacrosse, soccer, tennis, and wrestling, and for women in basketball, cross-country, field hockey, ice hockey, indoor and outdoor track, lacrosse, soccer, softball, tennis, and volleyball. Cheerleading and golf are coeducational offerings.

USM offers master's degrees in the areas of abilities and disabilities education, adult education, American and New England studies, applied medical science, biology, business administration (M.B.A.), community planning and development, computer science, counselor education, creative writing, educational leadership, educational psychology, health policy and management, leadership studies, literacy education, music, nursing, occupational therapy, professional educator, public policy and management, school psychology, social work, special education, statistics, and teacher education. Doctoral degrees are offered in law, public policy and management, and school psychology. The School of Education and Human Development also offers a postbaccalaureate fifth-year program leading to either elementary or secondary teacher certification.

Location

USM's location in southern Maine is an ideal place to be a college student. Students have access to a rich array of social, cultural, and athletic activities in Portland, as well as the endless opportunities provided by proximity to the Atlantic Ocean, mountains, lakes, and woods. Therefore, it is no surprise that Portland is continuously recognized as one of the best cities in the country for outdoor recreation. The coast of Maine, one of the most spectacular scenic regions in the country, offers many fine beaches for relaxing and islands for exploring, while nearby mountains and forests offer skiing and hiking. The city of Portland is a haven for the nearly 35,000 college students from the twelve colleges and universities that are within an hour's drive of USM.

Majors and Degrees

USM offers sixty-four bachelor's degrees, twenty-six master's degrees, and three doctoral degrees through its College of Science, Technology, and Health; College of Arts, Humanities, and Social Sciences; College of Management and Human Service; Lewiston-Auburn College; and School of Law.

Undergraduate majors include accounting, applied technical leadership, art (including B.F.A. and art education), arts and humanities, athletic training, biochemistry, biology, chemistry, communication, computer science, criminology, economics, electrical engineering, elementary education, K–8 (with dual certifications in special education or English as a second language), English, environmental planning and policy, environmental science, exercise physiology, finance, French, geography-anthropology, geosciences, health fitness, health sciences, history, industrial technology, leadership and organizational studies, linguistics, management, marketing, mathematics (including secondary education), mechanical engineering, media studies, music, music education, music performance, musical theater, natural and applied sciences, nursing, philosophy, physics, political sciences, psychology, radiation therapy (only for transfers with related associate's degrees), recreation and leisure studies, social and behavioral science, social work, sociology, sport management, theater, and women and gender studies. Self-designed majors include classical humanities, classical languages, foreign languages, French studies, general science, German studies, Hispanic studies, international studies, Russian studies, and social science.

Academic Programs

USM's educational programs are designed to meet the needs of a changing society. The USM Core is a coherent, integrative, and rigorous liberal education that enables graduates to be world-minded, intentional, lifelong learners. The USM Core engages the academic community in learning experiences that both illuminate and transcend the perspectives of various disciplines. It systematically fosters the values and dispositions, knowledge, and skills that prepare students for successful citizenship in a complex and dynamic world. The USM Core enables students to demonstrate informed understandings of interrelationships between human cultures and the natural world; engage in analytical, contextual, and integrative thinking about complex issues; demonstrate effective communication using multiple forms of expression; engage in critical reflection upon and informed action in their roles as participants in multiple communities; and engage in ethical action and contribute to the social and environmental welfare of local and global communities.

The honors program provides an enriched undergraduate education to students who are outstanding in their ability, curiosity, creativity, and motivation. Approximately 40 students are admitted to the honors program each year. Students work closely with faculty members in a series of small seminar-type courses. Later, honors students participate in an advanced seminar and undertake a major independent research project under the direction of a faculty member. All honors program work stresses independent learning, original thinking, and the development of skills in research, writing, and oral expression. Speakers, seminars, discussion groups, artistic presentations, and social events are scheduled regularly at Honors House.

The Russell Scholars Program, an innovative living and learning community, features collaborative teaching and learning, interdisciplinary courses, and a residential component. It includes a mentoring program, community service projects, and internships. In addition to the traditional and self-designed majors that are currently offered, motivated students may choose to design an academic program that is specifically suited to their personal career goals. In conjunction with a faculty committee, students have self-designed majors in many areas, including organizational behavior, public relations, and medical technology.

Off-Campus Programs

USM offers study-abroad programs in cooperation with institutions in Austria, Canada, China, England, France, Ireland, Italy, Japan, the Netherlands, Russia, and Scotland. USM also participates in the National Student Exchange. USM programs range from long to short term, and offer a variety of options and themes for study including baseball and American society, criminology in Sweden, and Dominican Republic health outreach program.

Academic Facilities

USM comprises more than 140 acres in Gorham, Portland, and Lewiston. The campus facilities include seventy-eight buildings with more than 130 classrooms and ninety-five laboratories. The library's collection includes more than a million books, documents, journals, and microforms. Full reference, circulation, and interlibrary loan services are available at each location. An online catalog provides access to and remote borrowing from all University of Maine System libraries. Access to the Internet and other computerized indexes and databases is available at workstations in the library and remotely to authorized users. Special collections include the Jean Byers Sampson Center for Diversity in Maine and the renowned Osher Map Library. USM has a variety of computer resources available for student use. Networked microcomputers are available on the Portland, Gorham, and Lewiston-Auburn campuses. Internet access and e-mail services are available from any of the networked computers. Students who own computers can connect from their residence hall rooms. The computer science department offers UNIX on Digital/Compaq Alpha systems and Windows NT. Specialized Windows NT labs are also available for students in electrical engineering, environmental science and policy, geography, and geosciences. Music and foreign language departments have specialized Macintosh labs. Student microlab centers, staffed by student assistants, have been established on all three campuses. The labs have Windows- and Macintosh-compatible computers with many general-purpose and course-specific software packages, including software for work processing, spreadsheets, mathematics/statistics, and databases.

Costs

Expenses for the 2010–11 academic year were $242 per credit hour for in-state tuition and $654 per credit hour for out-of-state tuition. Room and board averaged $9394. USM also participates in the New England Regional Program, which allows reduced tuition for some out-of-state New England students. Tuition and fees are set annually.

Financial Aid

Lack of funds should not deter students from applying for admission to USM. During 2010–11, more than $84 million was awarded to students through various financial aid programs, including grants, loans, and employment opportunities. More than 8,800 students received an average of $13,500 in financial aid. USM also helped more than 8,500 students borrow more than $60 million in low-interest loans from commercial banks. The average loan was $7058. The Office of Student Financial Aid is available to help students explore funding sources outside USM. All students must complete the Free Application for Federal Student Aid (FAFSA). These forms are available from most high school guidance offices. For priority consideration, students are encouraged to apply by February 15.

Faculty

USM's dedicated faculty members represent a wide range of knowledge and expertise. They include Fulbright Fellows and authors of national note in every academic discipline. In the last ten years, more than 100 faculty members—all with doctoral degrees or the most advanced degrees appropriate to their disciplines—have been recruited from major institutions throughout the country. Faculty members are teachers who can communicate the excitement of learning and the joy of discovery to their students. USM does not employ graduate teaching assistants for undergraduate classes; labs and discussion groups are taught by faculty members themselves. The student-faculty ratio is approximately 15:1. Average class size is 22 students.

Student Government

A 21-member Senate, elected by undergraduates, is the principal governing body for student life. Students having problems in any aspect of University life have recourse through the Senate and the Student Grievance Committee.

Admission Requirements

Admission to USM is competitive and based primarily on the applicant's academic background, rigor of the high school program, and grades achieved. USM also considers SAT or ACT scores, individual talents, and activities. Evaluations of transfer students emphasize their most recent college grades. USM recognizes that prospective students may come from differing academic backgrounds, some far removed from high school; therefore, USM has established different admission categories to accommodate the needs of various students. The admission staff members can arrange tours of the campuses, provide information about academic programs, and discuss admission requirements. Music and musical theater programs require an audition.

Application and Information

To apply to USM, students should submit a completed University of Maine System Application, an online application, or the Common Application and a nonrefundable fee of $40. The application asks for details of their academic, extracurricular, and personal background and an essay on their interest in USM and the degree program to which they are applying. Admission is on a rolling basis. Priority deadlines for admission are February 15 for the fall semester and December 1 for the spring semester. For more information, students should contact:

Office of Undergraduate Admission
University of Southern Maine
P.O. Box 9300
Portland, Maine 04104-9300
Phone: 207-780-5670
       207-780-5646 (TTY)
Fax: 207-780-5640
E-mail: usmadm@usm.maine.edu
Web site: http://www.usm.maine.edu
      http://www.facebook.com/USouthernMaine
      http://twitter.com/USouthernMaine

THE UNIVERSITY OF THE ARTS
Visual Arts, Design, Film, Music, Dance, Theater
PHILADELPHIA, PENNSYLVANIA

The University

The University of the Arts (UArts) is located in the heart of Philadelphia's vibrant professional arts community. For over 135 years, UArts has been a leader in educating artists, performers, and creative individuals in a wide range of disciplines. More than 2,300 students from forty states and thirty countries are enrolled in the undergraduate and graduate programs in the visual and performing arts, film and design. Comprising the College of Art, Media, and Design (CAMD) and the College of Performing Arts (CPA), the University offers intensive concentration within a major field as well as creative challenges in multidisciplinary exploration. CAMD is one of the country's leading art colleges, with nationally renowned design, fine arts, crafts, and film programs. CPA features outstanding programs in dance, music, and theater arts.

The University sponsors a variety of activities and regular gallery and museum trips to New York City and Washington, D.C. One fourth of the students live in University housing, which provides coed apartment-style accommodations with complete kitchen and bath facilities and laundry rooms on the premises. Resident advisers live on each floor, and there is 24-hour security. Out-of-town freshmen are guaranteed housing if their contracts are received by May 1. The University also assists students in finding off-campus residences. Dining services are offered in several facilities across the campus and are available to all students.

The graduate programs of the University of the Arts offer an impressive combination of strengths: exceptionally accomplished faculty members, a remarkably individualized and interactive learning environment, access to outstanding facilities and resources, specialized studios, and programs of study that are both highly focused and highly flexible. UArts offers graduate degrees in art education; book arts/printmaking; ceramics, painting and sculpture; industrial design; jazz studies; museum communication; museum education; museum exhibition, planning and design; music education; and teaching visual arts. A postbaccalaureate certificate in crafts is also offered.

Location

The University's campus spans the vibrant Avenue of the Arts from South Street to Walnut Street and is the cultural hub of Center City Philadelphia. Next door to the University's historic Hamilton Hall is the city's magnificent Kimmel Center for the Performing Arts; in adjacent blocks are the famous Academy of Music, Wilma Theater, Suzanne Roberts Theater, and the University's historic Merriam Theater, which books touring Broadway shows for the public and hosts UArts student performances. The area also has excellent museums (Philadelphia Museum of Art and Barnes Museum), galleries, music and dance facilities, superb restaurants, and retail stores. Of historic importance, but also modern and sophisticated, the city is both one of the nation's major metropolitan centers and a series of small, close-knit neighborhoods with beautiful tree-lined squares. Fairmount Park, one of the country's largest public park systems, provides facilities for sports activities and picnicking. Statistics show that UArts is one of the safest campuses in the city.

Majors and Degrees

The College of Art, Media, and Design confers degrees in four areas: film (the B.F.A. in animation, film and video, and writing for film and television), visual arts (the B.F.A. in crafts, illustration, multidisciplinary fine arts, painting/drawing, photography, printmaking, and sculpture), design (the B.F.A. in graphic design, interactive design, and motion design); and the B.S. in industrial design. The college also offers a certificate program in art education and a concentration in art therapy. The School of Music confers the B.M. in composition, instrumental performance (with a jazz/contemporary focus), and vocal performance. A four-year diploma in music is also available. The School of Dance offers the B.F.A. in ballet, dance education, jazz dance, and modern dance. The School of Theater Arts offers the B.F.A. in acting; musical theater; theater design and technology; and directing, playwriting, and production. A two-year certificate is available in dance and music.

Academic Programs

Students are attracted to the University of the Arts because of its dynamic, creative atmosphere. Whether majoring in dance, sculpture, graphic design, or multimedia, they enjoy interacting and collaborating with their talented peers in other disciplines. Students are encouraged, to the extent that their busy schedules allow, to take elective courses outside their chosen major, and many participate in collaborative projects with students from a range of other programs. All students take 42 credits in liberal arts, which gives them vital exposure to humanities, social science, and science and provides them with the historical and theoretical framework of their major field.

The freshman year in the visual art and design programs in the College of Art, Media, and Design is devoted to the Foundation Program; its focus is exploratory, allowing students to investigate various disciplines before deciding on a specific major. Students are assigned to small sections, each with a team of 3 instructors. In the fall, students take two-dimensional design, three-dimensional design, and drawing; in the spring, they may substitute a Time and Motion course for one of these. General program requirements vary from department to department. At the end of the freshman year, students select a major in animation, crafts, graphic design, illustration, painting/drawing, photography, printmaking/book arts, or sculpture, and they may add a concentration in art education or art therapy. In the B.F.A. programs in interactive design and motion design, students learn the integration of image, sound, text, and interactivity into works that tell stories, with opportunities to study areas including game design.

In the film programs (animation, film and video, and writing for film and television), freshmen may choose to enter directly into a core studies program that focuses on the sensory bases of moving-image art, cinematic art, and storytelling. Through their senior year, they develop their knowledge and experience in areas including documentary video, narrative video, and screenwriting. Students produce portfolio-quality work, as well as to collaborate, as well as to combine different application areas. Film students take courses in film history, history of television, video production, and cinema arts. Internships in professional settings provide students with real-life experience in the field. Writing for film and television students learn to create feature-length screenplays, episodic television series, and movies for television.

A minimum of 123 credits is required for graduation, including 18 credits in the Foundation Program (or core studies for film students), 42 credits in the major, 42 credits in liberal arts, 15 credits in electives (9 credits of which must be taken in a department other than the major), and 6 credits in other areas outside the major. Students may request credit by exam in liberal arts subjects and by portfolio exam in studio art subjects.

In the College of Performing Arts, the School of Music program stresses individualized training, with a performance emphasis. Students undergo intensive training in theory and musicianship. Private lessons are supplemented by master classes and ensemble work. In the School of Dance, two years of ballet, modern, and jazz dance are required before students choose a major in the junior year. Electives include improvisation, repertory, partnering, Spanish dance, ethnic dance, character, and mime. In the Ira Brind School of Theater Arts, students can choose one of three majors. Acting majors focus on developing a strong rehearsal and performance process through a wide range of acting, speech, and movement techniques. Musical theater majors train in a similar foundation technique while strengthening their skills in music and dance. Directing, playwriting, and production majors study a range of disciplines, such as stage management, directing, playwriting, dramaturgy, production and arts administration, and mask and stage combat, preparing for careers or graduate study in these or related fields. The design and technology major explores the full spectrum of theatrical design and technical production.

In the College of Performing Arts, a minimum of 126 to 130 credits is required for graduation, 42 of which must be in liberal arts. Participation in the 17-credit MATPREP Program enables students to complete bachelor's and master's degrees in teaching music in five years.

The University has close working relationships, including internships, with professional theater, dance, and music groups in Philadelphia and elsewhere. Students are also encouraged to seek professional roles.

Academic Facilities

The University facilities are composed of numerous buildings along Philadelphia's dynamic Avenue of the Arts, with studios, classrooms, galleries, theaters, lounges, cafes, dormitories, performance spaces, and administrative offices. Terra Hall provides seventeen floors of studios, computer labs, classrooms, state-of-the-art performing spaces, and TV and video production and recording studios. All design departments provide individual workstations for seniors and exhibition spaces that feature student and faculty work throughout the year. The University also maintains several public galleries, where students may exhibit their work along with curator-managed exhibitions of the work of distinguished guest artists. These include the Rosenwald-Wolf Gallery, the Arronson and Solmssen Court Galleries, and the Mednick Gallery. Student performances are held in the University's formal theaters, such as the 1,800-seat Merriam Theater—one of the city's most historic venues, the 239-seat state-of-the-art Caplan Center for the Performing Arts recital hall and black box theater, the 200-seat dance theater, the Gershman Hall black box theater, the Arts Bank main theater and cabaret theater, and in the many informal spaces on campus.

The campus has a multifunctional telephone system and campuswide wired and wireless Internet access. Academic computing resources include more than twenty labs on Macintosh and PC platforms that are used for special applications, such as animation, digital imaging, 3-D modeling, multimedia, music, CAD, Web page design, and more, as well as some for word processing and general purposes. A number of smart classrooms enable faculty members to use computer applications and Internet access in their presentations; smart studios allow students to function as they would in the professional world, with a computer in the studio or office.

Students work in a large number and variety of specialized facilities—both high tech and more traditional technology—throughout the campus that support the learning of their craft. Among these are the typography lab, the Borowsky Center for Publication Arts, digital video editing suites, photo/film/animation labs and darkrooms, a scanner lab, an SGI lab, a bronze foundry and plaster workshop, and crafts studios and workshops for ceramics, metals, wood, glassblowing, papermaking, and fibers. The performing arts facilities include a recording studio; music technology (MIDI) studios; editing suites; music studios and practice rooms; computer labs; dance and movement studios, with barres, mirrors, and resilient floors; and acting studios.

Library facilities include Albert M. Greenfield Library, which contains an extensive collection of books, journals, photographs, and videotapes devoted to the arts; a Picture Resource File; Special Collections, with special strengths in book arts and textiles; a slide library with a collection of more than 140,000 slides of art works and historical images; and a music library with manuscripts, journals, scores, and listening and viewing facilities. Holdings include books and periodicals, music scores, mounted pictures, slides, music recorded in LP and CD formats, videocassettes, videodiscs, and multimedia formats.

Costs

Tuition for the 2011–12 academic year is $33,500. Accommodations in 3- or 4-person apartment-style dormitory units start at $8100. The nineteen-meal-per-week board plan is $4200.

Financial Aid

Last year, UArts provided $9 million in scholarships and grants to new students, alone. About one third went to those demonstrating financial need; the balance was awarded in talent- or merit-based scholarships. Overall, UArts students receive more than $40 million in scholarships, grants, loans, and part-time employment each year. Typically,

83 percent of the students enrolled on a full-time basis are eligible for some type of need-based aid. All students should apply using the FAFSA as early as possible after January 1. Financial need is defined as the difference between the cost of education and the family's federally calculated contribution to those costs, called the expected family contribution (EFC). Where need exists, UArts assists in meeting costs within its available resources.

The University funds Presidential scholarships, Promising Young Artist Awards, and artist grants based on artistic potential and academic achievement. Financial aid is also available on the applicant's demonstrated financial need. Applicants must submit the Free Application for Federal Student Aid (FAFSA). March 1 is the suggested filing date. The University administers the following federal, campus-based student assistance programs: Federal Perkins Loans, Federal Work-Study, and Federal Supplemental Educational Opportunity Grants. Applicants who wish to be considered for scholarships should complete applications for admission and financial aid prior to March 31. Families from many different income levels can qualify for some type of financial assistance. In addition, the University's location in a large, active city provides students with diverse opportunities for part-time employment.

Faculty

Faculty members are practicing professionals who are deeply committed to the development of their students and highly engaged in that process. As active participants in the arts, they have successfully achieved recognition in their specific fields of study. This real-world experience gives them the knowledge and understanding so vital in the training of young, emerging artists, not just professionally but also in terms of personal growth. The faculty consists of 477 full- and part-time members; the majority hold advanced degrees. The faculty-student ratio is about 1:9.

Student Government

Student Council serves as the voice of the students within the University. It also supports a variety of student organizations, including a community service organization, a student-run gallery, and many others.

Admission Requirements

In addition to submitting a portfolio or auditioning, applicants should submit their high school transcript, SAT or ACT scores, one letter of recommendation, and a personal statement of purpose.

The placement of transfer students is made after an evaluation of their portfolio or audition and a determination of their approved credits. Transfer students may be given advanced standing.

International applicants are required to submit scores on the Test of English as a Foreign Language (TOEFL); a minimum score of 550 on the paper-based TOEFL or 213 on the computer-based TOEFL is required. Early entrance and deferred entrance are possible.

Application and Information

The University of the Arts follows a system of rolling admission. All students are notified within two weeks of the receipt of all required materials. Students are encouraged to submit applications by March 15 for fall admission and December 1 for spring admission. For additional information, students should contact:

Office of Admission
University of the Arts
320 South Broad Street
Philadelphia, Pennsylvania 19102
Phone: 215-717-6030
        800-616-ARTS (toll-free)
Fax: 215-717-6045
Web site: http://www.uarts.edu

UNIVERSITY OF THE CUMBERLANDS

WILLIAMSBURG, KENTUCKY

The University

Founded in 1889, Cumberland College became University of the Cumberlands on July 1, 2005, reflecting the diversity and excellence of options offered in high-quality education. The University is committed to providing a superior education within an exceptional Christian atmosphere at an affordable cost. Recognition by *U.S. News & World Report* in its list of America's Best Colleges and by the John Templeton Foundation as a member of its Honor Roll of Character Building Colleges signals that a University of the Cumberlands (UC) education is an exceptional value. Emphasizing the growth of the individual student, the University strives to instill in students the desire to be agents of change in the world and to use knowledge for the benefit of others as well as themselves.

UC is one of the few institutions where all students complete a leadership program. All students participate in community service as a component of this program.

University of the Cumberlands is a four-year, coed, liberal arts institution for higher education that offers a broad curriculum with more than thirty-five programs of undergraduate study, including eight preprofessional programs for professional and health science careers. Graduates enjoy a high acceptance rate to graduate and professional schools, particularly in science, business, and education. In fact, within five years of graduation, 66 percent of UC's alumni have completed or are pursuing a graduate or professional degree.

Graduate studies at University of the Cumberlands offer individual graduate courses as well as a Master of Arts in Teaching and a Master of Arts in Education degree programs with certification or concentration in various areas. Other master's programs include business administration (M.B.A.), professional counseling, physician assistant studies (M.P.A.S.), and Christian studies. Doctoral programs include educational leadership and clinical psychology.

One of the largest private institutions in the state of Kentucky, UC serves a diverse body of more than 1,800 undergraduate students from forty states and thirty countries. Primarily a residential campus, UC provides on-campus housing for about 75 percent of its students in the University's ten residence halls. A director, assisted by student staff members, supervises each hall.

Extracurricular activities abound. More than forty clubs and organizations provide students with a wide variety of activities, including a debate team, theater, musical performance groups, academic societies, an FM radio station, a student newspaper, student government, Baptist Campus Ministries, Appalachian Ministries, Mountain Outreach, Patriot Adventure Club, departmental clubs, and intramural sports.

University of the Cumberlands participates in intercollegiate competition. UC is a member of the NAIA Division I Mid-South Conference and offers opportunities in women's basketball, cross-country, golf, soccer, softball, swimming, tennis, track and field, volleyball, and wrestling; men's baseball, basketball, cross-country, football, golf, soccer, swimming, tennis, track and field, and wrestling; and coed cheerleading. The O. Wayne Rollins Convocation/Physical Education Center houses a 2,700-seat athletic arena, the Dinah Taylor Aquatic Center, an indoor batting cage, a weight room, an indoor walking/jogging track, locker rooms, an intramural gymnasium, athletic training facilities, athletic offices, and classrooms.

The James H. Taylor II Stadium complex, which seats 2,400, includes a football field; an eight-lane, 400-meter all-weather track and field; the Patriot Pavilion; and a football practice field.

The Doyle Buhl Stadium and James Keelty Field are the home of Patriot baseball, with dugouts and locker rooms.

UC also has separate golf, soccer, softball, tennis, and wrestling facilities.

Location

One of the state's oldest cities, Williamsburg is located in southern Kentucky, 185 miles south of Cincinnati, Ohio, and 70 miles north of Knoxville, Tennessee. Williamsburg is known for its beautiful homes and the hospitality of its people. The University of the Cumberlands campus is situated on three hills above the town and, about 1 mile from exit 11, is easily accessed from Interstate 75. UC has a well-kept campus that blends stately old buildings with new ones and has a panoramic view of the surrounding mountains and the Cumberland River Valley, an area known throughout the country for its lovely waterfalls, forests, and lakes. Famed Cumberland Falls State Resort Park is just 20 minutes from campus.

Majors and Degrees

University of the Cumberlands is accredited by the Commission on Colleges of the Southern Association of Colleges and Schools to award baccalaureate, master's, and doctoral degrees. It is approved by the Kentucky State Department of Education for teacher education and certification. Inquiries concerning the accreditation status of the University may be directed to the Commission on Colleges at 1866 Southern Lane, Decatur, Georgia 30033-4097 or by calling 404-676-4500.

Major fields of study are accounting, art, biology, business administration, chemistry, church music, communication arts, education, English, exercise and sport science, fitness and sport management, health, history, human services, journalism and public relations, management information systems, mathematics, music, philosophy, physics, political science, psychology, religion, Spanish, special education, and theater arts.

Minor fields can be chosen from the major fields or in biblical languages or French.

Preprofessional and special curricula are offered in military science, predentistry, pre-engineering, prelaw, premedicine, preoptometry, prepharmacy, pre–physical therapy, pre–physician assistant studies, pre–veterinary medicine, and religious vocations.

Academic Programs

University of the Cumberlands seeks to provide academic specialization within a broad framework of a liberal arts education. To supplement the in-depth knowledge acquired within each major, 37 semester hours of general studies from the areas of Christian faith and values, cultural and aesthetic values, the English language, humanities, leadership and community service, natural and mathematical sciences, physical education, and social sciences are required. Students must earn at least 128 semester hours to graduate with a bachelor's degree.

The academic year begins in late August, with the first semester ending in mid-December. The second semester runs from early January to early May. Two 4-week undergraduate summer sessions and two 4-week graduate summer sessions are also offered. Orientation, preregistration, and academic advising by faculty members begin in the summer preceding entrance.

Students may receive credit for successful scores on the Advanced Placement examinations of the College Board, the College-Level Examination Program (CLEP), and special departmental tests. Through the honors program, highly qualified students have the opportunity to undertake advanced independent study.

Students benefit from such special services as free tutorial assistance and those offered by the Career Services Center, the Center for Leadership Studies, and the Academic Resource Center.

Academic Facilities

The University of the Cumberlands campus contains thirty-five buildings reflecting antebellum architectural style. The new Correll Science Complex features state-of-the-art biology, chemistry, and physics labs providing graduate-level research opportunities.

The McGaw Music Building contains individual rehearsal and studio areas as well as a recital hall. The Norma Perkins Hagan Memorial Library houses more than 150,500 book titles, 1,630 periodical subscriptions, and 715,878 microform titles. Sophisticated computer equipment provides access to an additional 20 million or more items from many of the nation's outstanding libraries. The instructional media center includes a children's library, a computerized language lab, and a listening library.

Other special academic features include a computer center, an art gallery, a word processing center for English composition, a theater, a 600-seat chapel, four large lecture halls, and the Distance Learning Laboratory.

Recent additions to the campus include the state-of-the-art Hutton School of Business, a 27,000-square-foot addition to the Science Building, and a new women's residence hall.

Costs

For 2011–12, the basic academic year expenses are $18,000 for tuition and fees and $6826 for room and board, for a total of $24,826. There are no additional fees for out-of-state students. The average cost for books and supplies is approximately $500 per semester.

Financial Aid

University of the Cumberlands sponsors a large financial aid program that coordinates monies from federal, state, private, and University sources. Ninety-five percent of UC students share more than $29 million in aid.

To apply for financial aid, it is necessary to complete the Free Application for Federal Student Aid (FAFSA). For further information about financial aid opportunities, students should contact the Director of Financial Planning at 800-343-1609 (toll free). Applications made by March 1 are given priority for the fall semester.

Numerous scholarships and grants are available.

Faculty

There are 101 full-time and 18 part-time faculty members who are respected scholars and whose primary responsibility is to teach. Graduate assistants do not teach courses. The student-faculty ratio is 13:1, enabling students to receive ample attention and assistance from professors. Faculty members also serve as advisers to help students in planning their academic programs.

Admission Requirements

In compliance with federal law, including provisions of Title IX of the Educational Amendments of 1972 and Section 504 of the Rehabilitation Act of 1973, University of the Cumberlands does not illegally discriminate on the basis of race, sex, color, national or ethnic origin, age, disability, or military service in its administration of education policies, programs, or activities; admissions policies; or employment. Under federal law, the University reserves the right to discriminate on the basis of sex in its undergraduate admissions programs. Further, the University reserves the right to deny admission to any applicant whose academic preparation, character, or personal conduct is determined to be inconsistent with the purpose and objectives of the University. Where possible, the University will seek to reasonably accommodate a student's disability. However, the University's obligation to reasonably accommodate a student's disability ends where the accommodation would pose an undue hardship on the University or where the accommodation in question would fundamentally alter the academic program. Inquiries or complaints should be directed to the Vice President for Academic Affairs.

The purpose of the admission process is to identify applicants who are likely to succeed academically at University of the Cumberlands and at the same time contribute positively to the campus community. The process considers such factors as high school records (including courses taken, grade trends, and rank in class), college records (if transferring from another institution), scores on the ACT or SAT, extracurricular activities and honors, and personal conduct.

Campus tours are available on weekdays by appointment and on selected Saturdays. Prospective students can take a tour of the beautiful campus; talk with students, professors, and coaches; spend the night in the residence halls; attend an athletic or extracurricular event; and get answers to their questions during a session with an admissions counselor.

Application and Information

Applicants may apply online at http://www.ucumberlands.edu or may contact the Office of Admissions for an application form. Return the completed form to the University, along with the appropriate application fee, official transcripts of all high school and college work, and a copy of ACT or SAT scores. Each student is notified regarding official admission within ten working days after the application procedure has been completed.

Students accepted for admission must submit the required enrollment deposit.

Additional information can be obtained at:

Office of Admissions
University of the Cumberlands
Williamsburg, Kentucky 40769

Phone: 606-539-4241
    800-343-1609 (toll-free)
E-mail: admiss@ucumberlands.edu
Web site: http://www.ucumberlands.edu
    http://twitter.com/UCumberlands
    http://www.youtube.com/UCumberlandsTV

Students on the campus of University of the Cumberlands.

UNIVERSITY OF THE SCIENCES

PHILADELPHIA, PENNSYLVANIA

The University

University of the Sciences was founded in 1821 as the Philadelphia College of Pharmacy, America's first college of pharmacy. University of the Sciences is located on a 35-acre campus in the academic section of historic Philadelphia known as University City. Besides University of the Sciences, the University of Pennsylvania and Drexel University also call University City home. The University currently enrolls more than 2,600 undergraduate students in twenty-seven majors and over 300 students in twenty-one graduate programs. The campus consists of twenty-two buildings. The University offers a wide variety of cocurricular activities that include intercollegiate and intramural athletics; literary publications; social, professional, religious, and honors organizations; and musical and drama groups. University of the Sciences competes athletically at the NCAA Division II level and is a member of the Central Atlantic Collegiate Conference.

Location

The University's location in the University City section of Philadelphia offers considerable advantage and appeal. It not only offers a wide variety of educational opportunities, it also is a culturally, architecturally, and socially diverse community that caters to the local college student population. The University of the Sciences is also actively involved with a number of local community organizations that are designed to foster improvement, development, and unity in the University City community. The Philadelphia metropolitan area is the home of more than forty other colleges and universities. University of the Sciences students realize that Philadelphia and its immediate region provide abundant off-campus clinical and scientific opportunities, which are required in a number of programs. Within a short 10-minute trolley ride to the Center City area are the vast cultural, historical, and shopping attractions of the sixth-largest city in the United States.

Majors and Degrees

University of the Sciences includes four undergraduate colleges: Philadelphia College of Pharmacy, which offers programs in pharmacy, pharmaceutical sciences, and pharmacology and toxicology; Samson College of Health Sciences, which offers programs in exercise science and wellness management, health science, medical technology, occupational therapy, physical therapy, and physician assistant studies; Misher College of Arts and Sciences, which offers majors in biochemistry, biology, chemistry, environmental science, humanities and science, microbiology, pharmaceutical chemistry, physics, and psychology; and the newest college, Mayes College of Healthcare Business and Policy, which offers a number of graduate programs as well as a bachelor's degree in pharmaceutical and health-care business. Students with strong academic interests in multiple areas may pursue double degrees, including two B.S. degrees or one B.S. degree and one entry-level professional degree.

Academic Programs

Three majors are offered in Philadelphia College of Pharmacy: a six-year Doctor of Pharmacy (Pharm.D.) program and four-year B.S. degree programs in pharmacology and toxicology and in pharmaceutical sciences. In the Doctor of Pharmacy program, students are guaranteed a seat in the professional phase (years 3–6) as long as the preprofessional phase (years 1–2) is successfully completed and an acceptable academic record is maintained. The pharmacy program at the University is recognized worldwide and prepares students for the increasingly clinical nature of pharmacy practice.

Pharmacology and toxicology, pharmaceutical sciences, and pharmaceutical and health-care business are unique B.S. degree programs that provide excellent career opportunities and address specific manpower needs within the pharmaceutical and health-care industries. Many graduates pursue postgraduate study as well as enter careers in research, manufacturing, and business.

Six programs of study are available in Samson College of Health Sciences: exercise science and wellness management, health science, medical technology, occupational therapy, physical therapy, and physician assistant studies. Both physical therapy and occupational therapy programs are direct-entry, integrated undergraduate/professional degree programs that lead to the Doctor of Physical Therapy (D.P.T.) and Doctor of Occupational Therapy (Dr.O.T.), respectively. The physical therapy program was one of America's first programs to receive approval to offer the six-year, direct-entry D.P.T. In both the physical therapy and occupational therapy programs, students are admitted as first-year students and are guaranteed a professional-phase seat, provided an acceptable academic record is maintained. In the newest major in Samson College of Health Sciences, the B.S. degree in exercise science and wellness management, students learn about healthy lifestyles and living as well as how sports and leisure activities improve community well-being.

The physician assistant studies program at University of the Sciences is a five-year program that leads to the Bachelor of Science and Master of Science degrees in health science and is in partnership with the Philadelphia College of Osteopathic Medicine (PCOM). Students enrolled in the physician assistant studies program complete their preprofessional component (years 1–3) in the natural sciences, social sciences, and humanities at University of the Sciences. The professional component of the program (years 4–5) is completed at PCOM. A four-year B.S. degree in health science for students who want to focus on general health care and community service is also available.

Medical technology students at University of the Sciences receive an excellent three-year academic foundation in preparation for their fourth year, which is spent in a clinical setting at an approved hospital school of medical technology.

Nine different four-year Bachelor of Science degree programs are offered in the Misher College of Arts and Sciences. They include biochemistry, biology, chemistry, environmental science, humanities and science, microbiology, physics, pharmaceutical chemistry, and psychology. Psychology students may elect to remain at the University for an additional year and qualify for the M.S. in health psychology program. Misher College of Arts and Sciences combines the expertise of an outstanding group of scientists, researchers, and educators with academic facilities that are not often found at an institution the size of University of the Sciences. This combination creates an academic atmosphere of especially high quality. Misher College also offers a popular advisory track in forensic science, which can stand alone as a minor. A forensic science certificate can be earned when paired with a major in biology, biochemistry, chemistry, environmental science, medical technology, microbiology, or pharmaceutical chemistry.

The newest major in Misher College of Arts and Sciences is the B.S. in humanities and science. This major provides a unique combination of scientific and humanistic study, which is particularly attractive to students who want to pursue medical, dental, or veterinary studies.

The University of the Sciences' strong tradition of excellence prepares graduates to enter postbaccalaureate degrees in medicine, dentistry, veterinary medicine, and other health professions. Traditionally, premed students choose to major in chemistry, biochemistry, biology, microbiology, pharmacology and toxicology, or psychology. The curricula in these and most of the other programs include the basic courses required for admission to medical school. Beginning with the first year, premed students receive individualized counseling by the preprofessional adviser and their faculty adviser in selecting courses to meet their career goals. Premed students may also elect to take advantage of the University's agreements with Philadelphia College of Osteopathic Medicine or The Commonwealth Medical Colllege, which reserve a number of seats each year for University of the Sciences students.

Students may enroll at University of the Sciences in the Misher preprofessional program, and through a special orientation program, be introduced to the various academic disciplines and career opportunities available to them. Misher preprofessional students formally declare a major during the spring semester of the first year and choose from premedical, predental, preveterinarian, and pre-health professional specializations.

Academic Facilities

Classes and laboratory course work are conducted in ten academic buildings on the University of the Sciences' campus, while the remaining buildings serve as residence halls or support-service facilities. University of the Sciences houses more than 100 scientific laboratories and many computer terminals for student use. The Joseph W. England Library contains more than 84,000 volumes and 8,400 periodicals in addition to numerous electronic information programs.

Costs

Tuition for the 2010–11 academic year was $29,290; room and board were $12,034. Costs are subject to change.

Financial Aid

Types and sources of aid include Federal Perkins Loans; Health Professions Student Loans; Federal Work-Study Program; USciences Merit Awards; Athletic Grants; University need-based grants, deferred tuition payment plans; federal student loans; and scholarships received from states, municipalities, and service clubs or other organizations. All applicants who seek financial assistance must complete the Free Application for Federal Student Aid (FAFSA). The University's merit scholarship and grant program provides awards for both first-year and transfer candidates.

Faculty

There are 161 full-time faculty members. Of these, more than 100 have doctoral degrees. All full-time faculty members teach undergraduates, and many also teach graduate students and conduct research. Graduate assistants do not teach but serve as laboratory aides.

Student Government

Student government is composed of representatives from all undergraduate classes and class officers. It takes an active part in governance through participation in faculty and administrative committees and sponsors a number of campus activities and functions.

Admission Requirements

University of the Sciences seeks students whose aptitudes and achievements are in the areas of science, mathematics, and humanities. Sixteen total high school credits are required and must include English (4 credits), mathematics (3 credits, including algebra I and II and plane geometry), and science (3 credits of laboratory science, including at least two of the following: biology, chemistry, and physics). Physical science, IPS, general science, or similar courses do not fulfill the laboratory science requirement. Class rank, if provided by the applicant's high school, and grade point average are also considered in the admission decision process. Candidates are required to submit the results of their SAT and/or ACT examinations. Supplemental testing or an interview may be requested to clarify a specific aspect of a candidate's record. For students whose first language is not English, the Test of English as a Foreign Language (TOEFL) is suggested. Applications for transfer are welcome, although the number of seats available each year is less than that for first-year students, since all students admitted to University of the Sciences are admitted for the entire program length. Advanced standing may be achieved through the College Board's Advanced Placement Program, the International Baccalaureate Program, or earned college credit.

University of the Sciences does not discriminate in the administration of its educational policies, admission policies, scholarship and loan programs, or athletic and other University-administered programs on the basis of sex, age, handicap, race, creed, color, or national origin. All students are entitled to all of the rights, privileges, programs, and activities generally accorded or made available to students at the University. This institutional policy complies with the requirements of Title IX of the Education Amendments of 1972 (45 CRF 86), Section 504 of the Rehabilitation Act of 1973, and other applicable statutes and regulations.

Application and Information

An Admission Application may be obtained by calling the Admission Office. Applicants may submit an online application at http://www.usciences.edu/applying. Each paper application must be accompanied by a nonrefundable $45 application fee. However, there is no fee for an online application. University of the Sciences is also a member of the Common Application. First-year applications for admission are considered until the entering class roster has been completed. University of the Sciences follows a rolling admission policy, and applicants are notified of the admission decision after the University has received all required data. Students accepted into any of the programs have until May 1 to submit a nonrefundable enrollment reservation deposit of $300 for non-pharmacy candidates and $500 for pharmacy candidates to hold a place in the class. Applicants accepted after May 1 have two weeks to submit a tuition deposit.

Applicants for transfer to the professional programs should submit completed applications no later than the following dates: physical therapy (December 1), pharmacy (December 1), occupational therapy (March 1), and physician assistant studies (March 15). All transfer applications are reviewed on a rolling basis except for physical therapy and pharmacy, which are reviewed during the spring semester.

Executive Director of Admission and Enrollment Services
University of the Sciences in Philadelphia
600 South 43rd Street
Philadelphia, Pennsylvania 19104-4495
Phone: 215-596-8810
       888-996-8747 (toll-free)
Fax: 215-596-8821
E-mail: admit@usciences.edu
Web site: http://www.usciences.edu

It all begins at University of the Sciences, where students embark on a challenging learning experience; where they get the education and training to be successful science and health-care professionals; and where they go on to become pharmacists, occupational therapists, biologists, doctors, or health-policy specialists—just to name a few. USciences: where health care and science converge.

UNIVERSITY OF THE WEST

ROSEMEAD, CALIFORNIA

The University

University of the West (UWest) is a Buddhist-founded campus open to students of all backgrounds who are interested in gaining cultural competency as well as a solid undergraduate or advanced education in religious studies, business administration, psychology, or languages. UWest is accredited by the Western Association of Schools and Colleges (WASC).

Founded in 1991 by Buddhist Venerable Master Hsing Yun, who is one of the earliest promoters of Humanistic Buddhism, University of the West's stated goals are to deliver an education informed by Buddhist wisdom and values as well as to serve as a bridge between East and West.

UWest welcomes students of all beliefs and backgrounds. Outside the well-known Buddhist studies programs, Buddhist knowledge is available to students of all programs on a voluntary basis through workshops and other campus activities.

Students and faculty members come together as a community of scholars to participate in an ongoing dialogue to advance knowledge, address societal and cultural issues, and promote education and understanding across cultures. At UWest, creativity, service, and leadership are fostered together with tolerance, ethical commitment, and social consciousness.

A range of activities that enhance learning and physical and mental well-being, such as yoga, martial arts, music, meditation, and travel, are available to students outside of the classroom.

The Student Recreation Center is equipped with fitness and weight-training equipment, table tennis, billiards, and a student lounge with a kitchen. The two residential halls each have a 24-hour study room, a multipurpose student lounge on each floor, and a laundry facility. Each room is furnished and has its own air-conditioning unit, private bathroom, telephone, and high-speed Internet access. Recreational facilities include a swimming pool, a spa, and exercise and game rooms.

UWest is a member of NAFSA: Association of International Educators and the American Association of Collegiate Registrars and Admissions Officers.

Location

UWest is located in the city of Rosemead in Los Angeles County. It occupies 10 acres of beautifully landscaped grounds and has modern, well-equipped facilities. The campus sits on a hillside overlooking the verdant Whittier Narrows nature preserve with an unobstructed view of the San Gabriel Mountain range and the Puente Hills range. UWest is about 10 minutes by car from downtown Los Angeles, which a Harvard scholar called "the most complex Buddhist city in the world."

Majors and Degrees

Undergraduate programs at UWest include accounting, computer information systems, international business, marketing, psychology, general education, and English as a second language.

Graduate programs offered at the University are the Executive Master of Business Administration (E.M.B.A.); Master of Business Administration (M.B.A.) with concentrations in com-

puter information systems, finance, international business, or nonprofit management and organization; Master of Arts (M.A.) in psychology with concentrations in multicultural counseling generalist (marriage and family therapist track) or Buddhist psychology (marriage and family therapist track); M.A. in religious studies with concentrations in Buddhist studies or comparative religious studies; and the Master of Divinity (M.Div.) in Buddhist chaplaincy.

UWest also offers an advanced degree program for the Doctor of Religious Studies (Ph.D.) with specializations in Buddhist studies or comparative religious studies.

Academic Programs

The business administration program offers deep perspectives on Eastern and Western business theory and practice. Students are educated in small, interactive classes with an average faculty-student ratio of 1:8.

The Department of Religious Studies' programs in Buddhist studies and comparative religious studies offer students the unique opportunity to study religion in a setting that is informed by Buddhist wisdom and values, and dedicated to furthering religious and cultural understanding between East and West, and among religions in general. All Buddhist traditions are covered, and students can choose to study any of the Buddhist canonical languages, i.e., Canonical Chinese, Pali, Sanskrit, or Tibetan. The library contains one of the best American collections of writing from all the major Buddhist traditions, including the largest set of Dunhuang Cave manuscript reproductions in the U.S.

UWest's undergraduate major in psychology prepares students as competitive graduate school candidates in the particular fields of research psychology, applied counseling psychology, clinical psychology, school psychology, Buddhist psychology, and social work. The M.A. in psychology with a concentration in multicultural counseling generalist (marriage and family therapist track) and the M.A. in psychology with a concentration in Buddhist psychology (marriage and family therapist track) prepares students to pass California's rigorous Marriage and Family Therapist licensure exam.

All of the bachelor's programs require the completion of a minimum of 120 semester units.

The ESL program provides a variety of instructional formats to improve students' command of the English language and familiarize them with American life and culture, including a residential English program and the Program in American Cultural Education (PACE), which provides short-term immersive experiences in the classroom, combined with travel and cultural experiences in the Los Angeles region.

Academic Facilities

The library provides access to the University's collection as well as Internet access to several major databases including LexisNexis, ProQuest, and JSTOR.

Three research centers are located on campus. The Center for the Study of Minority and Small Business helps the Department of Business Administration reach out to minority-owned and small businesses and provides resources and support so students at UWest are exposed to and become familiar with business realities and the existing business environment.

The Institute of Chinese Buddhist Studies develops interdisciplinary research, teaching, and other scholarly activities relating to Chinese Buddhism.

The Digital Sanskrit Buddhist Canon is a joint research project by the University of the West and the Nagarjuna Institute of Exact Methods (NIEM) in Nepal for translating the vast corpus of Sanskrit Buddhist texts.

Costs

Undergraduate tuition for the 2010–11 academic year was $325 per unit for courses in the business administration and psychology programs. Graduate tuition is $340 per unit for the business administration program, $350 per unit for psychology, $340 per unit in the Buddhist chaplain program, and $335 for religious studies.

Room and board with meal plan are $4692 for single occupancy, $3145 for double occupancy, and $2440 for quadruple occupancy. Further details of costs and fees are available at http://www.uwest.edu under Admissions/Admissions Procedures/Tuition and Fees.

Financial Aid

Financial aid is available in the form of federal and state aid, a work-study program, private scholarships, and grants (both need- and merit-based). UWest offers full- and half-tuition fellowships, scholarships for room and board, and the UWest Scholarship of $2000 per academic year. The International Buddhist Education Foundation scholarship provides 50 students in the religious studies program with scholarships of $2000 to $4000 depending on academic level. UWest also offers private scholarships ranging from $500 to $2000 per semester.

Faculty

Among full-time faculty members, 82 percent have doctoral degrees. Adjunct faculty members are required to have a minimum of a master's degree and at least ten years of experience working in the fields relevant to the subjects they teach. UWest has 70 faculty members.

Student Government

The UWest Student Association acts as a liaison between the University and the students to provide services and programs that enhance the quality of education by extending the learning environment beyond the classroom into the extracurricular lives of UWest students. It also provides a forum for student expression and interests. All students who are enrolled at the University are included as members of the Student Association.

Admission Requirements

Applicants are required to supply accurate and complete information on the application for admission form and to submit official transcripts from each school or college attended. Other application requirements and documentation can be found on the University's Web site. Student selection is based on academic achievement and potential, irrespective of ethnicity, gender, disability, or religion. A minimum GPA of 2.0 is required of undergraduate applicants. Graduate applicants must have a minimum GPA of 2.5. Undergraduate applicants must submit one letter of recommendation with their application. An essay is not required for undergraduates. Graduate applicants must submit a 500-word essay and three letters of recommendation as part of their application. International students must meet the minimum TOEFL or IELTS requirement as published in the UWest catalog.

Application and Information

Application deadlines for domestic applicants are June 1 for fall, September 2 for spring, and April 2 for summer. There is a $50 nonrefundable application fee for domestic applicants and a $100 nonrefundable application fee for international applicants ($50 for all ESL applicants). Application-fee waivers are available to undergraduate students through the Enrollment Office.

Ms. Jason Kosareff
Enrollment Counselor
University of the West
1409 North Walnut Grove Avenue
Rosemead, California 91770

Phone: 855-GO-UWEST
Fax: 626-571-1413
E-mail: info@uwest.edu
Web site: http://www.uwest.edu

A panoramic view of UWest's campus.

UNIVERSITY OF TULSA

TULSA, OKLAHOMA

The University

The University of Tulsa (TU) is a four-year, private, liberal arts university featuring highly personalized study in engineering, natural sciences, business, health professions, the humanities, and fine and performing arts. TU features three undergraduate colleges—the Henry Kendall College of Arts and Sciences, the Collins College of Business, and the College of Engineering and Natural Sciences. On the graduate level, the University offers the Graduate School and College of Law.

The University is fully accredited by the North Central Association of Colleges and Universities and is an NCAA Division I participant in Conference USA. TU maintains an affiliation with the Presbyterian Church (USA).

A customizable array of majors, minors, concentrations within majors, and certificate programs allows undergraduates to assemble a personalized education, which can include a self-designed major. TU's low 11:1 student-faculty ratio, average class size of 19, and emphasis on individual attention anchor an educational culture where students are rigorously challenged and comprehensively supported.

Long regarded for its programs in accounting; petroleum, mechanical, and chemical engineering; English; environmental law; MIS; and psychology, TU is also emerging as a leader in computer science and information security. TU was the first institution selected by the National Science Foundation for the Federal Cyber Service Initiative.

The University's 34-acre sports and recreation complex features a student fitness facility, competition-grade tennis complex, NCAA soccer and softball fields, multiuse recreational fields, and an NCAA track and field. TU offers ample extracurricular opportunities through 160 campus-based organizations, including intramural sports, special interest clubs, preprofessional organizations, fraternities and sororities, and campus ministry groups. Residence life offers a variety of living arrangements, including traditional residence halls, suite-style halls, premium-grade student apartments, and special living communities.

Fall 2009 enrollment was 4,187, with 3,084 undergraduates and 1,103 graduate and law students and a 55:45 ratio of men to women. International and multicultural students made up 30 percent of the student population, with sixty-two countries represented.

Based on academic reputation and other factors, *U.S. News & World Report* ranks TU eighty-eighth among doctoral/research universities in the U.S.

Location

The University of Tulsa features a residential campus in midtown Tulsa, Oklahoma. Tulsa's prominent industries include energy, telecommunications and data, finance, medicine, aerospace, transportation, and education—all of which present rich internship opportunities for students and employment opportunities for graduates. *Newsweek* has named Tulsa one of ten "New Frontier" technology cities, *Southern Living* magazine named Tulsa one of its five favorite Southern cities and RelocateAmerica lists Tulsa among its top 10 best places to live. Tulsa has more than 400,000 residents and features cultural assets including the Performing Arts Center, ballet, theater, symphony, opera, two nationally renowned museums, and cultural festivals such as Jazzfest, Mayfest, and Oktoberfest. Professional sports in Tulsa include baseball, basketball, golf, hockey, arena football, and horse racing. The extensive River Parks development, 3 miles from the campus, has facilities for outdoor activities, jogging and bicycle trails, and an outdoor floating amphitheater.

Majors and Degrees

The Henry Kendall College of Arts and Sciences grants the Bachelor of Arts, Bachelor of Fine Arts, Bachelor of Music, Bachelor of Music Education, or Bachelor of Science degrees in anthropology, art, art history, arts management, communication, deaf education, economics, education, English, environmental policy, film studies, French, German, history, music, music education, musical theater, organizational studies, philosophy, political science, psychology, religion, Russian studies, sociology, Spanish, speech/language pathology, and theater. Students can create their own designated area of concentration

with the approval of the dean of the college. Teacher certification at the elementary and secondary levels is available through the college. Available minors include classics, creative writing, dance, early childhood intervention, film scoring, Greek, Latin, and Russian.

The Collins College of Business awards the Bachelor of Science in athletic training, business administration (majors in accounting, economics, finance, management, management information systems, and marketing), energy management, exercise and sports science, (with tracks available in physical education and preprofessional tracks for physical therapy and physician's assistant), international business and language (with emphases in Chinese, French, German, Russian, and Spanish), and nursing. The college offers minors in accounting, advertising, business administration, coaching, finance, international business studies, management information systems, and marketing communication. Management majors may choose concentrations in business law, entrepreneurship and family business management, and human resource management. Marketing majors may choose an emphasis in integrated marketing communication. The college is home to several specialized centers, including the Energy Management Program, Family Owned Business Institute, the Genave King Rogers Center for Business Law, and the Williams Risk Management Center.

The College of Engineering and Natural Sciences offers the Bachelor of Science degree in applied mathematics, biochemistry, biogeosciences, biology, chemical engineering, chemistry, computer science, electrical engineering, engineering physics, geology (options in environmental science and geophysics), information technology, mathematics, mechanical engineering, petroleum engineering, and physics. The college also offers a B.A. in chemistry, earth and environmental science, and geology. The college features state-of-the-art research facilities, including the Center for Information Security and the Williams Communications Fiber Optic Networking Laboratory. From 1995 to 2010, 46 TU engineering students received the prestigious Barry M. Goldwater Scholarship, the nation's premier award for undergraduate students in engineering, math, or science, while 31 students received National Science Fellowships.

Academic Programs

A TU education links a broad, humanities-based core curriculum and a highly flexible group of majors, minors, concentrations, and certificate programs. With so many program options and high-level faculty support, TU students can receive an education that is well-rounded, in-depth, and uniquely personalized. Candidates for graduation must complete at least 124 semester hours of course work, with more hours required of engineering and business administration majors.

The University offers a number of special academic programs. The Honors Program engages students in intensive multidisciplinary work and in specialized study culminating in a major research or creative project during the senior year. The Tulsa Undergraduate Research Challenge program (TURC) combines advanced research, scholarship, and community service. The Federal Cyber Service Initiative (Cyber Corps) prepares students for advanced federal careers in computer security. TU's Office of Research and Sponsored Programs funds five Interdisciplinary Institutes to research alternative energy; individual differences determined by biochemical and psychological factors; bioinformatics and computational biology; nanotechnology; and trauma, abuse, and neglect. Other special programs include internships, study abroad, and Air Force ROTC.

Qualified students may receive advanced standing or credit for scores on the tests of the Advanced Placement and College-Level Examination programs. Students who complete the International Baccalaureate diploma with a score of 28 or above receive at least 30 college credits, the equivalent of one year in college.

The University of Tulsa operates on a semester calendar. The fall term begins in late August, the spring term in early January, and the summer session in mid-May.

Off-Campus Programs

TU students can choose from several study-abroad options, including summer, semester, and yearlong programs. TU has direct international exchange partnerships with universities in Austria, Finland, France, Germany, England, Scotland, Singapore, Spain, and Switzerland, and is part of the ISEP Exchange Program Network. TU also offers a wide selection of international study options through consortia and study-abroad affiliate programs. All approved study-abroad programs allow students to choose courses in various disciplines, and with their college's approval, apply those courses towards their majors or other graduation requirements. Federal financial aid and scholarships are portable with TU's study-abroad programs.

The city of Tulsa and TU have agreed to a public-private partnership whereby TU manages the city's Gilcrease Museum, home to the world's most comprehensive collection of art and artifacts of the American West. The partnership provides strategic opportunities for the museum and unparalleled opportunities for academic research of the museum's extensive holdings.

Academic Facilities

McFarlin Library and Mabee Legal Information Center house about 4 million items, including subscriptions to scholarly and popular journals. The Mabee Legal Information Center has almost 408,000 total volumes. McFarlin holdings include more than 900,000 print volumes, over 120,000 electronic book titles, and over 40,000 electronic periodicals. McFarlin's Department of Special Collections is internationally recognized, particularly for holdings in Native American history and nineteenth- and twentieth-century Irish, English, and American literature. McFarlin is home to the papers of Nobel Laureate V. S. Naipaul. McFarlin is also developing a specialization in World War I literature, correspondence, and artifacts. Special Collections rare book holdings currently number about 130,000 volumes.

Keplinger Hall is the $15-million home to the College of Engineering and Natural Sciences. Equipment here includes a comprehensive multi-million-dollar telecommunications networking laboratory developed with Williams Communications and other industry partners. Construction began in 2010 on Rayzor Hall, the future home to the electrical engineering and computer science departments.

The TU Center for Information Security is developing defenses against cyberterrorist attacks and information warfare and supports the University's National Security Agency (NSA)–accredited certificate program in information assurance, a curriculum that integrates information security with computer law and policy issues. TU is designated a Center of Excellence in Information Assurance by the NSA and is one of the original six institutions selected by the National Science Foundation for the Federal Cyber Service Initiative (Cyber Corps).

The Mary K. Chapman Center for Communicative Disorders links the University to the community with its clinical facility and its curricula in education of the deaf and speech/language pathology. The Tulsa Center for the Study of Women's Literature offers concentrated studies in women's literature and in feminist literary critical theory. TU's engineering students can participate in research projects through ten consortia funded by the petroleum industry. The Family-Owned Business Institute provides for the development and dissemination of information relevant to the succession and stability of the family business. The TU Innovation Institute combines research and interdisciplinary programs in innovation, product development, and entrepreneurship.

The Genave King Rogers Center for Business Law supports the business law specialization within the management major. The Williams Risk Management Center in the Collins College of Business, an advanced learning environment, combines the latest in trading floor technology and advanced study in risk-management theories and techniques. Chapman Theatre is the home of TU's symphony orchestra, concert band, wind ensemble, jazz workshop, modern choir, theater, and opera productions. The Roxana Rozsa and Robert Eugene Lorton Performance Center, due to open in fall 2011, is designed to be TU's showcase facility for the musical and performing arts. The Donald W. Reynolds Center serves as the campus arena and convocation center. This $28-million facility is the site for student concerts, several intercollegiate athletic programs, and the state's only accredited academic program in athletic/sports medicine; it also has facilities for strength training and video editing. Collins Hall, which houses administrative, alumni, and admission offices, opened in 2007. Other facilities include the Allen Chapman Activity Center, which features student organization offices, the Great Hall for lectures and entertainment, a food court, and the University bookstore.

Costs

For 2010–11, the typical cost for students living on campus was $37,703, including $28,060 for tuition, $9018 for room and board, and fees of $625. Expenses for books average about $1200 per year.

Financial Aid

In 2009, 86 percent of undergraduates received some form of financial aid (including grants, scholarships, work-study, and loans). Academic, athletic, and performance scholarships are available, as well as federally funded grants, loans, and Federal Work-Study awards. The University of Tulsa participates in the National Merit program and offers full-tuition, room, and board scholarships for selected National Merit Finalists. University Scholarships are also awarded to qualified students. Performance scholarships are available in music, theater, and athletics. Applicants for aid should submit the Free Application for Federal Student Aid (FAFSA) and the TU Financial Aid Application by March 1 for priority consideration.

Faculty

The University has 309 full-time faculty members, with 96 percent having earned the highest degree in their field of study. The faculty is primarily a teaching faculty, although most of its members are also involved in funded research or publishing activities. Many faculty members serve as student advisers and work collaboratively with students in and outside the classroom. The faculty includes a number of distinguished scholars, with 30 endowed chairs, 2 visiting endowed chairs, 3 endowed professorships, 2 fellows, and 9 Wellspring chairs.

Student Government

All full-time students are members of the Student Association, which consists of legislative, executive, and judicial branches. Regular elections are held for representatives from each college, who appropriate nearly $500,000 annually for student organizations and special events. The executive cabinet's main function is to schedule speakers, artists, and events on campus that are sponsored by the Student Association.

Admission Requirements

TU seeks students who demonstrate intellectual promise in a challenging curriculum and are committed to the liberal education reflected in the University's mission. TU uses an individualized and holistic approach in evaluating candidates for admission.

Performance in high school college-preparatory subjects and scores on the SAT or ACT are the primary criteria considered in the admission evaluation. Academic and extracurricular achievement, school records, and personal qualities are also carefully considered. The counselor recommendation and information about the applicants' extracurricular activities and job experience are also considered. Campus visits and interviews are highly recommended but not required.

The recommended high school curriculum consists of four years of English and math, three years of science and social science, and a solid foundation in a foreign language and computer science. In addition, students are encouraged to take an active part in their school and community or hone special talents that demonstrate traits such as leadership, initiative, maturity, and creativity.

Application and Information

Students are encouraged to complete an application for admission and scholarships by the priority date of February 1. The admission process is rolling, and applicants are reviewed and notified as their admission files are completed. The reply date for students is May 1. An application, accompanied by a six-semester secondary school transcript, ACT or SAT scores, and a guidance counselor's recommendation are required when applying for admission. Completed applications should be sent to the Office of Admission. For additional information, students should view the online tour (http://www.utulsa.edu/virtualtour), or contact:

John C. Corso
Associate Vice President for Enrollment and Student Services
University of Tulsa
800 South Tucker Drive
Tulsa, Oklahoma 74104-3189
Phone: 918-631-2307 (in Tulsa)
      800-331-3050 (toll-free)
Fax: 918-631-5003
E-mail: admission@utulsa.edu
Web site: http://www.utulsa.edu/admission

UNIVERSITY OF WINDSOR
WINDSOR, ONTARIO, CANADA

University of Windsor
thinking forward

The University

The University of Windsor offers a very broad range of programs—its 16,000 full- and part-time students are enrolled in some 150 bachelor's, master's, and doctoral degree programs. Academic disciplines range from humanities and liberal arts to science. Professional studies are offered in business, engineering, education, law, computer science, creative writing, kinesiology, nursing, social work, clinical psychology, music, dramatic art, and visual arts.

The University has an impressive commitment to research in a richly diverse community, with a special focus on automotive-, environmental-, and social justice–oriented interdisciplinary research. It is also firmly committed to providing increased opportunities for students to participate in research at the undergraduate level.

Community and business partnerships have helped to establish research institutions at the University of Windsor that are unmatched in Canada. The University's Great Lakes Institute for Environmental Research is the world's leading institution in large lakes research, attracting top students from around the world.

The University of Windsor is Canada's most international campus—10 percent of its population comes from eighty countries outside of Canada. This sharing of international experiences helps prepare Windsor graduates for the global workforce.

The University began as Assumption College in 1857, affiliated with the University of Western Ontario. In 1954, it was admitted to full membership in the National Conference of Canadian Universities and Colleges, the University Articulation Board of Ontario, and the Association of the British Commonwealth. The University became the University of Windsor in 1963, and, a year later, it became a member of the International Association of Universities. In recent years, the University has spent millions of dollars in new buildings, classroom upgrades, and lab renovations, including a new residence hall and facilities for health education, dramatic arts, and a medical education building. The Centre for Engineering Innovation is also in the process of being built.

Today, the campus offers more than 150 undergraduate and graduate programs across nine faculties for 16,000 full- and part-time students. It offers nine cooperative education programs for approximately 1,100 students. Most come from the Ontario region, but some come from other regions of Canada; 10 percent of students are international students. More than 95 percent of graduates find employment within six months.

The University operates several residences on or adjacent to the campus, offering many accommodation choices from traditional residence rooms to suite-style accommodations. All residences are coed, with some single-gender floors. Most rooms are double rooms, but some single-occupancy spaces are available throughout the residence halls. Each residence hall includes wireless Internet, laundry rooms, common lounge areas for watching TV or relaxing, vending machines, kitchen areas, and other amenities. Residence life staff members are available at each residence hall to assist students. A variety of meal plans are available for students, allowing them to eat at one of the University's dining facilities or off campus at partnering restaurants.

Location

The tree-lined campus of the University of Windsor is in the midst of Windsor, Ontario. Windsor is Canada's southernmost city and is located just across the river from Detroit. The city is bordered by Lake Erie, Lake St. Clair, and the Detroit River. Its temperate climate makes it ideal for recreational activities, such as biking, golfing, hiking, and swimming, and it makes it possible to enjoy such outdoor attractions as Dieppe Gardens, Jackson Park, and the Odette Sculpture Park. Windsor also offers restaurants, shopping venues, museums, and galleries as well as performances in dance, music, and theatre.

Majors and Degrees

Students may earn a Bachelor of Arts degree in anthropology, art history, classical civilization, communication studies, criminology, developmental psychology, diaspora studies, drama, drama and communication studies, drama in education and community, economics, English language and literature, English literature and creative writing, family and social relations, forensics, French studies, history, international relations and development studies, labour studies, liberal and professional studies, modern languages (German, Italian, Spanish), modern languages and second language education, music, philosophy, political science, psychology, social justice, sociology, sociology and criminology, visual arts, visual arts and art history, visual arts and communication studies, or women's studies.

Bachelor of Commerce degrees are available in business administration, business administration co-op, business and computer science, business and computer science co-op, and business and economics.

Bachelor of Computer Science degrees are available, including computer science, computer science co-op, computer science (honours applied computing) which is also available with co-op, and computer science and education.

The Bachelor of Education is available as a consecutive program. It is also available in concurrent programs that include the Bachelor of Arts/Bachelor of Education/Early Childhood Education Diploma; Bachelor of Arts-French/Bachelor of Education; Bachelor of Math/Bachelor of Education; Bachelor of Science (chemistry or biological sciences)/Bachelor of Education; and Bachelor of Computer Science/Bachelor of Education.

Bachelor's degrees in engineering can be obtained in civil, electrical, environmental, industrial, industrial (with a minor in business administration), mechanical, mechanical (automotive option), mechanical (environmental option), and mechanical (materials option).

Bachelor of Fine Arts degrees are available in acting and in visual arts.

Bachelor of Mathematics degrees are available in mathematics, general mathematics, mathematics and statistics, and mathematics and computer science.

The Bachelor of Music, Bachelor of Music Therapy, and Bachelor of Arts in Music are available.

Bachelor of Science degrees are offered in behavior, cognition, and neuroscience; biochemistry; biochemistry and biotechnology; biology; biology and biotechnology; chemistry; chemistry and physics; computer information systems (co-op); computer science with software engineering specialization (co-op); environmental science; general science; and physics (physics and high technology, medical physics) (co-op).

The Bachelor of Social Work degree is available in social work, social work and diaspora studies, and social work and women's studies.

Other degrees offered include a Bachelor of Arts and Science; Bachelor of Environmental Studies; Bachelor of Forensic Science; Bachelor of Human Kinetics; Bachelor of Laws; combined Bachelor of Laws and Doctor of Jurisprudence; and Bachelor of Nursing.

There are also many programs in Science and in Arts and Social Sciences that combine two or more majors.

Academic Programs

During each regular academic year, the fall term runs from early September to early December, and the winter term runs from early January to mid-April. In addition, the University schedules courses during a summer term, which includes Intersession (May–June) and Summer Session (July–August), each of which is approximately six weeks in duration. Some courses run from May through August (twelve weeks). Bachelor's degrees typically require the completion of thirty courses, including ten to sixteen courses within the major program of study; six to eight courses in arts, languages, sciences, or social sciences; and ten to twelve courses in any area within or outside the major program of study. Honours programs of study require the completion of forty courses.

Academic Facilities

The Leddy Library, the main campus library for the University, has a collection that consists of more than 3 million items, including electronic resource holdings of more than 23,000 digital journal titles and several hundred thousand digital monographs and data sets. The University of Windsor campus offers wireless Internet and also has more than 350 hard-wired computer workstations that provide access to library resources and the Internet and run Microsoft, Adobe, SPSS, and other programs.

The Academic Writing Centre provides writing assistance to University students through individualized writing programs, small group workshops, and classroom presentations. The Computer Literacy Skills (CLS) program provides all members of the University community with the tools necessary to gain the confidence and experience to effectively use campus computer systems and productivity software. This is achieved through both e-learning and instructor-led workshops. Academic resource centers are available for mathematics and statistics and chemistry and physics.

Costs

For 2010–11, annual full-time tuition (in Canadian dollars) ranged from $5910 to $8130 for Canadian students and $16,396 to $20,811 for international students, depending on the program of study. Residence fees were $4692 to $5221 per year for a double room or $5669 to $6320 per year for a single room. These rates included activity fees, wireless Internet, refrigerator rental, cable TV, and laundry and telephone fees. Meal plans cost an additional $3514 to $4094 per year, depending on the meal plan selected. Books and other materials typically cost approximately $800 to $1000 per year.

Financial Aid

U.S./Mexico Entrance Scholarships: For newly admitted students with U.S./Mexican citizenship or permanent resident status, an entrance scholarship is available. A renewable scholarship (for up to eight terms) valued at $3000 per term is offered to engineering, education, and nursing students. A renewable scholarship of $1500 per term is offered to students in other programs of study (except for law). The renewability of each subsequent semester's scholarship instalment is contingent upon the student's successful completion of the previous term—a cumulative GPA of 11.0 (A-) is required.

Entrance Scholarships: Outstanding Scholars Awards of $12,000 to $16,000 (over four years) are given to students entering the University directly from high school who demonstrate and maintain outstanding academic achievement. The candidate must be entering one of the selected academic programs supported by the Outstanding Scholars Award.

In-Course Scholarships and Awards: The University of Windsor also offers a variety of awards for students in their second, third, and fourth years of study through In-Course Scholarships and Awards.

For further information, students should visit the Scholarship and Bursary section of the University's Web site.

Faculty

There are approximately 524 faculty members at the University, with a fairly equal number of full, associate, and assistant professors and many lecturers. The ratio of men to women faculty members is approximately 3:2. Faculty members are from around the world and have won numerous awards, earning national and international acclaim.

Student Government

The University of Windsor Student Alliance (UWSA) represents all full-time undergraduate students who pay fees to the organization on a semester basis and are considered members of the organization. The UWSA strives to enhance student life through advocacy, representation, and services, such as the used book store and the student health and dental plan. It works to ensure that all qualified students are able to obtain a university education, regardless of their financial situation. The UWSA also provides students with an element of campus life outside of the classroom. Events are organized on and off campus, and students can participate through clubs, committees, and all aspects of the community.

Admission Requirements

Admission is competitive for many of the University's programs. Direct entry is available to most programs within the Faculty of Arts and Social Sciences, although some require specific grade 12 U prerequisites. Auditions are required in acting and music programs. Programs within the Faculties of Science, Engineering, Human Kinetics, and Nursing and the Odette School of Business Administration require prerequisite courses at the grade 12 U level and fulfillment of minimum average requirements in these prerequisite courses. Admission to the University requires a GPA of at least 70 percent (some programs require 75 to 80 percent); specific departments may require completion of certain high school courses in English, math, and sciences for admission. Applicants from the United States must submit ACT or SAT test scores with their applications; other international students must submit certification in compliance with their country's requirements. Application requirements vary depending on the program of study.

Application and Information

Applications must be submitted online through the Ontario Universities' Application Centre (OUAC), 170 Research Lane, Guelph, Ontario N1G 5E2; http://www.ouac.on.ca.

For more information, students should contact:

Office of Liaison and Student Recruitment
University of Windsor
401 Sunset Avenue
Windsor, Ontario N9B 3P4
Canada
Phone: 519-973-7014
      800-864-2860 (toll-free in Canada and the U.S.)
Fax: 519-561-1428
Web site: http://www.uwindsor.ca
      http://www.facebook.com/#!/UWindsor

UNIVERSITY OF WYOMING

LARAMIE, WYOMING

The University

Being a student at the University of Wyoming (UW) means more than just a quality education; it's also an opportunity for adventure. The University of Wyoming is a welcoming community of 13,000 students, offering the benefits of a larger university, such as awesome research opportunities and NCAA Division I-A athletics, while still having the individual feel of a small school with reasonable class sizes and individual attention.

The University of Wyoming, a public land-grant institution founded in 1886, is a reflection of the global community it serves. It provides an environment for success and endless outdoor activities and challenges.

The research done by the professors and students of the University of Wyoming pushes the boundaries of modern science and technology and has resulted in UW's classification as a Carnegie Doctoral/Research University–Extensive.

It is this academic ambition that has allowed UW to provide high-quality undergraduate and graduate education, research, and service since its inception.

Wyoming, unique among the fifty states, has only one university. UW enjoys tremendous support from within its state as well as from an alumni network that spans the globe. Students from all fifty states of the United States and over eighty other countries attend UW classes in Laramie and at outreach sites around the state. The variety of students at UW enriches the educational experience for all by fostering a multicultural environment that encourages sharing and learning about those with different heritages and cultural backgrounds. It is this dialogue that continues to promote respect and appreciation for diversity.

UW offers bachelor's degree programs in six undergraduate colleges: the Colleges of Agriculture and Natural Resources, Arts and Sciences, Business, Education, Engineering and Applied Science, and Health Sciences. Undergraduate education is a high priority at UW. The average class size is 30 students, and the student-to-faculty ratio is 14:1. UW also offers graduate and professional programs, including the Doctor of Pharmacy and the Juris Doctor.

There are more than 200 recognized campus clubs and organizations, including fifteen national fraternities and sororities, honor and professional societies, political and religious organizations, and special interest groups. Students also have the opportunity to participate in more than sixty different intramural and club sports. UW is a Division I member of the NCAA and competes in the Mountain West Conference in seventeen men's and women's sports. Campus recreational facilities include the Wyoming Union, which includes the UW bookstore, eating establishments, student computers, study areas, and a variety of services and resources for students. Additional facilities on campus include Half Acre Gym, an indoor climbing wall, an eighteen-hole golf course, tennis and racquetball courts, weight rooms, two swimming pools, rifle and archery ranges, indoor and outdoor tracks, softball and baseball fields, and a hockey rink.

UW houses 2,400 students in six residence halls, and freshmen are required to live on campus during their first year. While primarily coed, the residence halls offer a number of unique living environments, including quiet/study floors, special interest floors, honors floors, single-sex floors, and other academic living environments. UW also offers a variety of different Freshman Interest Groups, or FIGS, which are learning communities that offer common living areas and clustered classes to students with similar academic areas of interest.

Location

UW's 785-acre campus is located at the foot of the Rocky Mountains in Laramie, a scenic town of 30,000 people in southeastern Wyoming. No matter the time of year, UW students can be found outdoors. Many enjoy the easy access to Alpine and Nordic skiing, snowboarding, snowmobiling, hiking, backpacking, camping, hunting, fishing, rock climbing, and mountain biking. Laramie—with its blue skies, clean air, and 320 days of sunshine a year—is a friendly and supportive university town, conveniently located 45 miles west of Wyoming's capital, Cheyenne, and only 130 miles northwest of Denver, Colorado.

Majors and Degrees

UW offers more than eighty undergraduate programs within its six colleges, leading to B.A., B.S., B.F.A., and B.S.N. degrees.

The College of Agriculture and Natural Resources offers undergraduate majors in agricultural business (with options in agribusiness management, farm and ranch management, and international agriculture), agricultural communications, agroecology, animal and veterinary sciences (with options in animal biology, business, communication, meat science and food technology, pre–veterinary science, production, and range livestock), family and consumer science (with options in child development, dietetics, family and community services, human nutrition and food, premedicine, and textiles and merchandising), microbiology, molecular biology, and rangeland ecology and watershed management.

The College of Arts and Sciences offers undergraduate majors in American Indian studies, American studies, anthropology, art, astronomy/astrophysics, biology, botany, chemistry, communication, criminal justice, English, earth system science, French, geography, geology, geology and earth science, German, history, humanities/fine arts, international studies, journalism, management, mathematical sciences, mathematics, microbiology, music (with options in education, performance, and theory and composition), philosophy, physics, political science, psychology, Russian, social science, sociology, Spanish, statistics, theater and dance, wildlife and fisheries biology and management, women's studies, and zoology and physiology as well as the option of a self-designed major.

The College of Business offers undergraduate majors in accounting, business administration, business economics, economics, finance, management, and marketing.

The College of Education offers undergraduate majors in elementary education (options in creative arts, international educational studies, American cultural diversity, environmental studies, interdisciplinary early childhood, or individual and society), and secondary education (options in agriculture education, art, English, industrial technology, mathematics, modern languages, sciences, and social studies).

The College of Engineering and Applied Science offers undergraduate majors in architectural engineering (with structural systems or mechanical systems options), chemical engineering (with biomaterials and polymers, biomedical engineering, biotechnology, chemistry, environmental engineering, international, or mathematics options), civil engineering (with environmental, geotechnical, international, structural, transportation, or water resources options), computer engineering (with an international option), computer science (with business or international options), electrical engineering (with bioengineering, computer, or international options), mechanical engineering (with aerodynamics, energy systems, international, manufacturing and design, or materials and solid mechanics options), and petroleum engineering (with an international option).

The College of Health Sciences offers majors in dental hygiene, kinesiology and health promotion (with an athletic coaching option), nursing, pharmacy, physical education teaching, social work, dental hygiene, and speech-language and hearing sciences.

UW offers preprofessional programs in dentistry, law, medicine, nursing, occupational therapy, optometry, pharmacy, physical therapy, and veterinary medicine.

The School of Environment and Natural Resources also offers interdisciplinary studies that can be combined with course work in seven other fields of study, including the humanities, physical sciences, and social sciences.

Two interdisciplinary degrees are offered at UW. Energy resource science offers a diverse curriculum that combines engineering, science, business, law, and natural resources content to build a fundamental understanding of interaction and trade-offs between energy, environment, policy, and the economy. Earth system science, on the other hand, provides an integrated approach to issues of global environmental change. Students must choose one of the options of anthropology, atmospheric science, biology, botany, geography, geology and geophysics, secondary education, or soil science.

Academic Programs

The UW academic calendar consists of two semesters and a complete summer session. Depending on their degree program, students are required to complete 120 to 164 credit hours for graduation. Undergraduate programs for most majors can be completed in four years. Students may choose to double major within the same college, or they may pursue majors in two separate colleges for a cross-college major. Minors are also available in many areas. All students are required to complete the University Studies Program, which is a core curriculum that assists students in developing their knowledge of oral and written communication, mathematics, science, diversity, global awareness, government, and culture.

The University Honors Program provides academically ambitious undergraduates innovative and intellectual learning opportunities. Award-winning faculty members, unique and challenging course work, and senior research projects are the hallmarks of this program.

Off-Campus Programs

UW has over 700 international students and close to 100 international researchers/scholars during any given academic year. This diverse community represents some ninety countries. The International Students and Scholars Office provides support to this population through an extensive orientation program, the Friendship Families program, and the International Student Association, which arranges International Education Week and the weekly International Coffee Hour, along with other activities.

International Programs coordinates the National Student Exchange (NSE), which is a domestic student exchange consortium of more than 180 colleges and universities throughout the U.S. In addition, NSE host sites are available in Canada, Puerto Rico, the Virgin Islands, and Guam. Membership in the NSE provides UW students with access to thousands of unique academic programs, classes, and faculty members on host campuses for either a semester or an academic year.

The UW Outreach School extends the university learning experience to Wyoming and the nation through credit and noncredit programs, University of Wyoming Television, Wyoming Public Radio, and the UW/Casper College Center. Credit programs are delivered via Internet/Web-based instruction, compressed video, audio teleconferencing, flexible enrollment (correspondence study), and on-site instruction. Select programs are offered, and degree availability may be limited.

Academic Facilities

The University Libraries' collections number nearly 1.5 million volumes and offer links to a variety of library service collections. William Robertson Coe Library is the flagship library, housing the learning commons and materials from all academic disciplines outside of geology and law. Coe Library houses a media collection of DVDs, CDs, and microformats, as well as a collection of music and film. Other library facilities include a geology library (Learning Resource Center), a plant research center (Rocky Mountain Herbarium Library), and a compact shelving facility (Library Annex) which houses the majority of UW Libraries' bound periodicals and government documents. Additional on-campus collections are housed in the American Heritage Center and the George W. Hopper Law Library. An off-campus branch library is located at the National Park Service Research Center in Jackson, Wyoming. UW Libraries participate in the Colorado Alliance of Research Libraries and in Region Four of the National Network of Libraries of Medicine. In addition, UW Libraries' research launch point (http://www-lib.uwyo.edu) provides high-speed access to UW's online library catalog and over 400 databases.

Costs

UW tuition and fees for full-time undergraduates in the 2011–12 academic year are $4112 for Wyoming residents and $12,842 for nonresidents (based on an average class load of 15 credit hours). Room and board (double occupancy, unlimited meal plan) costs are $8732. Estimated expenses include $1200 for books and supplies, $889 for travel costs, and $2200 for personal expenses.

Financial Aid

Nearly 90 percent of all UW students receive financial assistance. More than $85 million is available in the form of scholarships, loans, grants, and work-study opportunities. The Free Application for Federal Student Aid (FAFSA) is required for need-based assistance (loans, grants, work-study) and for many scholarships. The priority deadline for FAFSA is March 1. Most scholarships at UW are based on academic merit. UW participates in the Western Undergraduate Exchange (WUE) program. The Rocky Mountain Scholars Award is available to nonresident students.

Faculty

More than 700 professors from the world's most respected colleges and universities have come to teach at UW. Recognized nationally and internationally as experts, 86 percent of faculty members hold the highest degree in their field. UW professors are deeply committed to the success of their students. Only a small number of undergraduate courses are taught by graduate assistants, and many of the most distinguished and accomplished professors at UW teach first-year courses. UW maintains a low student-faculty ratio (14:1), which allows for individualized attention, instruction, and academic advising, as well as the inclusion of undergraduates in cutting-edge research projects.

Student Government

The Associated Students of the University of Wyoming (ASUW) is composed all students at UW. ASUW serves as the voice of the students, and its legislation impacts many aspects of student life. The ASUW Senate acts as a liaison between the student body and the administration as well as the UW Board of Trustees and local and state governments. The student body president also sits as an *ex officio* member of the UW Board of Trustees. UW encourages all students to actively participate in ASUW.

Admission Requirements

To ensure admission, high school graduates and new first-year students with fewer than 30 transferable college credit hours should have a cumulative high school GPA of 3.0 or above. Students should have a composite ACT score of 20 or greater or an SAT critical reading/math score of 960 or greater. In addition, all students should complete 4 units of English, 3 units of mathematics, 3 units of science (including a physical science), and 3 units of cultural context courses (behavioral or social sciences, visual arts, performing arts, humanities, or foreign languages). A limited number of students who are unable to qualify for assured admission may be admitted with conditions if they have a minimum 2.5 GPA or a 2.25 GPA with a composite ACT score of at least 20 or an SAT critical reading/math score of at least 960. Freshman students admitted with conditions will be required to take part in Synergy, a national award-winning mentoring and support program that assists in the transition to college and increases the academic success rate for participants. Transfer students with 30 or more transferable semester credit hours must have a minimum cumulative college GPA of 2.0.

Application and Information

Students must submit a completed UW Application for Admission, official high school or college transcripts, ACT or SAT scores, and a $40 nonrefundable application fee. Students may apply and pay the application fee online at http://www.uwyo.edu/apply. UW strongly encourages all prospective students and their parents to visit the campus.

Admissions Office
Department 3435
University of Wyoming
1000 East University Avenue
Laramie, Wyoming 82071-3435
Phone: 307-766-5160
  800-DIAL-WYO (342-5996; toll-free)
E-mail: why-wyo@uwyo.edu
Web site: http://www.uwyo.edu

UTICA COLLEGE
UTICA, NEW YORK

The College

A private, independent college founded in 1946, Utica College (UC) is known for its excellent academic programs, outstanding faculty members, personal attention, and diverse student population. The hallmarks of Utica College's academic programs are the integration of liberal and professional studies and a strong emphasis on internships, research, and other experiential learning opportunities, but UC is best known for the close, personal relationship students have with both faculty and staff members. Approximately 3,600 undergraduate and graduate students attend UC, including men and women from a wide variety of socioeconomic and cultural backgrounds as well as older students, veterans, and students with disabilities. While most students come from New York, New England, and the Middle Atlantic States, students are drawn to UC from all parts of the United States, and there is a growing international student population.

Academic programs of note include accounting, construction management, economic crime investigation, education, geoscience, journalism, management, nursing, occupational therapy, physical therapy, psychology–child life, risk management and insurance, and public relations. Utica College also offers a robust study-abroad program as well as an honors program.

Utica College is located on a modern, 128-acre campus on the southwestern edge of Utica, New York. Its facilities include a recently completed science and technology complex comprised of state-of-the-art learning and research facilities for health professions and justice studies, the Frank E. Gannett Memorial Library, a fully equipped high-definition television studio and convergence media center, the Ralph F. Strebel Student Center, seven residence halls, an athletic center, a 1,200-seat stadium, and numerous athletic fields.

Half of UC's students live on campus in residence halls that feature a variety of housing options, modern amenities, and lounges for studying or relaxing with friends. Freshmen primarily live in North and South Halls, which offer mostly double-occupancy rooms. Campus dining services provide a wide variety of options, including American and international cuisines, vegetarian meals, a large salad bar, and lighter fare such as burgers and pizza. Students enjoy a range of dining venues, from the main dining commons in Strebel Student Center to a student-run coffeehouse, convenient cafés in the Library and academic buildings, and a Subway sandwich shop on campus.

Whether students live on or off campus, they can take advantage of more than eighty student organizations, focusing on community service, music, theater, and politics as well as fraternities, sororities, and major-related clubs that provide opportunities for students to organize career-related events. Students can write for the student newspaper, work at the College's radio station, submit entries for the literary magazine, or work on the yearbook. Students also have the opportunity to enjoy lectures, concerts, poetry readings, art exhibits, plays, and nationally recognized speakers.

Utica College offers twenty-five NCAA Division III varsity sports, including men's baseball, basketball, cross-country, football, ice hockey, lacrosse, soccer, swimming and diving, tennis, and track and field; women's basketball, cross-country, field hockey, ice hockey, lacrosse, soccer, softball, swimming and diving, tennis, track and field, volleyball, and water polo; and coed golf. UC also offers club sports and a wide variety of intramural opportunities. Utica College is a member of the Empire 8 Athletic Conference, the Eastern College Athletic Conference, and the New York State Women's Collegiate Athletic Association. Nearly a third of all UC students participate in at least one Division III intercollegiate sport, and more than 45 percent are active in intramural or nonvarsity club sports.

Athletic facilities include the 1,200-seat multisport Gaetano Stadium with a state-of-the-art field turf synthetic grass playing surface; the Clark Athletic Center, which contains a large gymnasium, racquetball courts, a swimming pool, saunas, a recently renovated 6,400-square-foot free-weight room and fully equipped fitness facility, and numerous outdoor fields and courts. Ice hockey games are played at the downtown Utica Memorial Auditorium, which features pro-style hockey locker rooms and training facilities.

Graduate degrees are available in business administration, criminal justice administration, cybersecurity–intelligence and forensics, economic crime management, education, health-care administration, liberal studies, occupational therapy, and physical therapy.

Location

The city of Utica is located in the heart of the historic Mohawk Valley in the center of New York State. Just 90 miles west of Albany and 50 miles east of Syracuse, Utica has a thriving arts community, beautiful parks, and expanding shopping centers featuring national retailers. There are numerous recreational facilities, including a municipal ski slope and an excellent golf course less than a mile from the Utica College campus. Other nearby recreational opportunities include tennis, swimming, boating, fishing, hiking, and camping.

Majors and Degrees

Utica College offers undergraduate degree programs in accounting, biochemistry, biology, business economics, chemistry, communication arts, computer science, construction management, criminal justice, criminal justice–economic crime investigation, cybersecurity and information assurance, economics, English, foreign language, geoscience, gerontology, government and politics, health studies, health studies–human behavior, health studies–management, history, international studies, journalism studies, liberal studies, management, mathematics, nursing, occupational therapy, philosophy, physical therapy, physics, psychology, psychology–child life, public relations, public relations/journalism studies, risk management and insurance, sociology and anthropology, and therapeutic recreation.

Students interested in the occupational therapy or physical therapy major earn a bachelor's degree in health studies with direct entry into UC's graduate programs, as long as academic requirements are met. Utica College offers a master's degree in occupational therapy and a doctorate in physical therapy (D.P.T.).

Students may minor in anthropology, chemistry, communication arts, computer science, creative writing, economics, English language, film studies, French, gender studies, geoscience, gerontology, government, history, human rights advocacy, literature, management, mathematics, philosophy, psychology, recreation leadership, sociology, Spanish, theater, and writing.

Preprofessional programs include dentistry, law, medicine, optometry, podiatry, and veterinary medicine. Special programs are available in teacher education, gerontology, engineering, and joint health professions.

Academic Programs

Students may choose from thirty-seven undergraduate majors and twenty-seven minors in a wide variety of fields as well as accelerated programs, independent study, cooperative education, field placements, and internships. Utica College also offers a rapidly growing education program; students wishing to pursue a career in teaching choose either a liberal arts major (to teach elementary education) or a major in their intended field (to teach at the secondary level).

For those students who are undecided, the Academic Support Services Center provides academic advising and career counseling, and Career Services offers students opportunities to explore career options.

To earn a bachelor's degree, students must complete a minimum of 120 to 128 credits, satisfy major and major-related requirements, and complete any special program requirements. In addition, all Utica College students, regardless of their major, must complete a liberal arts core program as part of the degree requirements.

Utica College's ground programs operate on a semester system, with the fall term beginning in late August and ending shortly before Christmas, and the spring term beginning in late January and ending in early May. Summer and winter sessions offer students opportunities to accelerate their studies or take classes for which they have no time during the regular academic year.

First-year seminar offers freshmen and transfer students opportunities to earn academic credit while learning how to make the transition to college. Utica College offers the Higher Education Opportunity Program (HEOP), the Collegiate Science and Technology Entry Program (CSTEP), and a Summer Institute, which serves as an academic bridge between high school and college.

Off-Campus Programs

UC's Study Abroad program gives students opportunities to widen their global perspectives through exchange programs with universities in Spain, Italy, Poland, Finland, Hungary, Peru, Scotland, and Wales, as well as American College in Dublin, Ireland. UC students are also eligible to participate in Syracuse University's Division of International Programs Abroad in Madrid, Strasbourg, Florence, London, and Hong Kong. Special study-abroad opportunities include the College's annual forensic anthropology field school in Albania as well as learning experiences in London, Mexico, the Dominican Republic, and elsewhere.

Students are encouraged to complete internships and field placements to gain professional experience with businesses and organizations while they are earning college credit. Utica College's cooperative education program allows students to earn money while gaining professional experience.

Academic Facilities

The Frank E. Gannett Memorial Library includes a collection of some 200,000 volumes, 1,200 serial subscriptions, hundreds of online journals, and a microform collection of more than 60,000 journals, newspapers, and books. Located on the lower level of the library are the Media Center, computer labs, the Edith Langley Barrett Fine Art Gallery, and a large concourse—the site of special events, such as musical recitals, receptions, and guest lectures.

Classes, laboratories, and faculty offices are located in the main academic complex and within UC's new science and technology complex. F. Eugene Romano Hall, phase one of the new science and technology complex, opened in summer 2007 and provides state-of-the-art classroom, laboratory, and clinical space, as well as learning technology for students in the health sciences. The second phase, Utica College's innovative Economic Crime and Justice Studies building, opened in November 2008 and provides an appropriate platform for cutting-edge research and advanced learning at both the undergraduate and graduate levels.

Named in honor of one of UC's most celebrated faculty members, Professor Emeritus of Public Relations Raymond Simon, UC's state-of-the-art high-definition broadcast facility provides a hands-on learning environment for the next generation of media professionals.

Utica College maintains eight academic computer laboratories with both IBM-compatible and Macintosh computers, including two portable wireless laptop laboratories. Students have additional Internet access in the Pioneer Café and in all student residence hall rooms. Other resources include the Academic Support Services Center, the Math/Science Center, and the Writing Center.

Costs

For 2010–11, tuition was $28,100; room and board costs were $11,290. Student activity and technology fees totaled $520. Books and supplies average $1028 per year.

Financial Aid

The College has been recognized as a best buy in education and works to control costs and keep its education affordable. The average financial aid package for 2009–10 freshmen was $28,000. About two thirds of that aid came from grants and a third from loans and/or jobs. More than 90 percent of the freshmen received a financial aid package. At the same time, UC awarded numerous merit scholarships to students with outstanding grades and test scores.

Almost every federal and state financial aid program is available through Utica College. Students apply for institutional and governmental financial aid by filing the Free Application for Federal Student Aid (FAFSA) by February 15. UC offers three different deferred-payment programs that spread payments over the academic year.

Faculty

Utica College's faculty is diverse, energetic, accomplished, and devoted to their students. The vast majority have earned their Ph.D. or other terminal degree, and while many are involved in research, the primary focus of faculty members is teaching. The typical class size is 20 students, the student-faculty ratio is 15:1, and all faculty members are involved in assisting students with their academic planning.

Student Government

One of Utica College's strongest traditions is student participation in the College's governance structure. Students may serve on a number of student governing bodies, and students also serve on all standing committees of the College.

Admission Requirements

Utica College admits students who can best benefit from the educational opportunities the College offers. The Admission Committee gives each application individual attention, and the potential for a student's success at UC is measured primarily by an evaluation of past academic performance, scholastic ability, and personal characteristics. Freshman applicants must have completed 16 academic units, including 4 years of English. Students should follow a college-preparatory program, including 3 units of mathematics, 3 units of science, 2 units of foreign language, and 3 units of social studies.

Application and Information

Students may apply for fall, spring, or summer admission. Materials required include a completed Utica College application form, official high school or college transcripts, and a $40 application fee. Utica College prefers, but does not require, SAT or ACT scores, with the exception of the programs listed below. A personal interview for all applications is strongly suggested.

Occupational therapy, physical therapy, nursing, and joint health professions program applicants must submit SAT or ACT scores, a preferred letter of clinical recommendation if applicable, and a personal statement. International students must complete the international student application form. The application fee is waived for students who apply to HEOP or CSTEP; however, SAT or ACT scores are required to be considered for either program.

The College conducts a rolling admissions program; however certain programs do have application deadlines. For students applying to the occupational therapy or physical therapy programs, the joint health professions program, or for academic achievement awards, the application deadline is January 15. For students applying to the nursing program, the preferred application deadline is February 1. The application deadline for the HEOP program is January 15. Students should note that a tuition deposit of $200 is required by April 1 to secure a place in the HEOP program.

Additional admissions information can be found online at http://www.utica.edu/admissions.

Inquiries should be sent to:

Director of Enrollment Management
Utica College
1600 Burrstone Road
Utica, New York 13502-4892
Phone: 315-792-3006
        800-782-8884 (toll-free)
E-mail: admiss@utica.edu
Web site: http://www.utica.edu
          http://www.facebook.com/UticaCollegeAdmissions
          http://twitter.com/uticacollege

The Addison Miller White Hall Plaza.

VERMONT TECHNICAL COLLEGE

RANDOLPH CENTER, VERMONT

The College

Founded in 1866, Vermont Technical College's (VTC) main campus is situated on a hilltop in Randolph Center, Vermont, in the heart of the Green Mountains. The College also has campuses in Williston, Bennington, and Brattleboro, Vermont—plus a network of extended nursing campuses statewide. Vermont Technical College is the only technical college in the Vermont State Colleges system. Most of the 1,650 students enrolled come from Vermont and the other New England states.

Through its bachelor's, associate, and certificate programs, the College provides students with a broad-based, practical education. As a result, Vermont Tech graduates are prepared to work effectively in a variety of positions that support the activities of engineers, scientists, members of the medical profession, and other professionals. Degrees offered in such allied health fields as nursing, dental hygiene, and respiratory therapy prepare students to assume medical positions operating on the frontline of patient care.

There are twenty-two major buildings on the 544-acre main campus, including a Student Health and Physical Education (SHAPE) facility with a double-court gymnasium; a six-lane indoor pool; two racquetball courts; a brand-new, state-of-the-art fitness center; and a wireless café/lounge. The four residence halls can house up to 600 students, and additional housing is available at the College's Williston campus, just minutes from Burlington, Vermont. Every student room has connections for direct access to the campuswide computer network, telephone service, and cable TV lines.

Campus life at Vermont Tech includes sports, recreation, social events, and community service-learning opportunities. The Student Life Office arranges weekly activities and social events and provides students with support and counseling. There are many student clubs, from the student-run radio station WVTC-FM to student chapters of professional organizations. There is also an on-campus ski hill, where students can snowboard and ski after classes conclude for the day.

Students enthusiastically participate in the College's varsity and intramural sports clubs. Fall varsity sports include men's baseball and men's and women's cross-country, golf, and soccer. In the winter, the men's and women's basketball teams take the court. In the spring, the women's softball, men's baseball, and golf teams swing into action for their "second season." Varsity athletic programs are well-supported and on the rise at Vermont Tech.

Vermont Tech maintains national affiliations with the National Association of Intercollegiate Athletics (NAIA) and the United States Collegiate Athletic Association (USCAA), thereby offering its athletes two opportunities for postseason national championship competition. Vermont Tech athletes compete in the Sunrise Conference (NAIA) and the Yankee Small College Conference (YSCC). The College has a rich history of athletic success, with many conference championships in various sports to its credit. In 2007, the women's soccer team won the YSCC championship, and the men's baseball coach, Chuck Bradley, was named YSCC Coach of the Year. Both the men's and women's basketball teams achieved top-ten USCAA national ranking during the 2005–06 and 2006–07 seasons.

The College is accredited by the New England Association of Schools and Colleges. In addition, the following degree programs are accredited by the Technology Accreditation Commission of the Accreditation Board for Engineering and Technology, Inc. (TAC of ABET): architectural and building engineering technology, architectural engineering technology, civil and environmental engineering technology, computer engineering technology, electrical engineering technology, electromechanical engineering technology, and mechanical engineering technology. The veterinary technology program is accredited by the American Veterinary Medical Association

as a program for educating veterinary technicians. Practical nursing programs are approved by the Vermont Board of Nursing and accredited by the National League for Nursing Accrediting Commission (NLNAC). The associate degree program in nursing is approved by the Vermont Board of Nursing. The dental hygiene program is accredited by the American Dental Association Commission on Dental Accreditation (CODA), and the respiratory therapy program is accredited by the Committee on Accreditation of Respiratory Care Programs (CoARC).

Location

Vermont Tech's location is rural but far from isolated—exit 4 of Interstate 89 is just 1 mile away. For day-to-day needs, the nearby village of Randolph offers a variety of shops and restaurants as well as a movie theater, a bowling alley, and the Chandler Music Hall. For special shopping and events, Burlington and Montpelier, Vermont, and Hanover, New Hampshire, are within an hour's drive. Boston and Montreal are just 3 hours away. There is convenient bus service from Randolph, and Amtrak's Vermonter stops in Randolph twice daily.

Vermont Tech also maintains a satellite campus in Williston, Vermont, just minutes from downtown Burlington. Nearly 400 students from northwestern Vermont take advantage of Williston's bachelor's, associate, and certificate programs.

Students enjoy the variety of recreational activities available to them in Vermont. Some of the top ski resorts in the East are less than an hour from the campus. Students can also hike on the Appalachian Trail, canoe on numerous lakes and rivers, camp in the Green Mountain National Forest, and bike on the miles of country roads.

Majors and Degrees

Vermont Technical College offers a Bachelor of Science degree in architectural engineering technology, business technology and management, computer engineering technology, construction management, dental hygiene, diversified agriculture, electromechanical engineering technology, equine studies, information technology, software engineering, and sustainable design and technology.

Vermont Tech offers four programs leading to the Associate in Engineering degree: civil and environmental engineering technology, computer engineering technology, electrical engineering technology, and mechanical engineering technology.

Programs leading to the Associate in Applied Science degree include agribusiness management technology, architectural and building engineering technology, automotive technology, business technology and management, construction management, dairy farm management technology, diesel power technology, fire science, general engineering technology, landscape development and ornamental horticulture, and veterinary technology.

Programs leading to the Associate in Science degree include dental hygiene, information technology, nursing, respiratory therapy, and software engineering. The nursing programs (certificate and associate degree) offered by Vermont Tech are located at eleven different sites throughout Vermont, including Bennington, Brattleboro, and Williston, as well as on the College's main campus in Randolph Center.

Academic Programs

Whether preparing for an associate or a bachelor's degree, Vermont Tech students receive a rigorous broad-based education centered on a core curriculum that includes both technical and general education electives. The number of credits required for graduation ranges from 65 to 72 for the associate degree and from 130 to 139 for the bachelor's degree, depending on the program. Honors courses are offered in all engineering technology programs. Most degree programs also offer project courses, in which students work as teams on real-world applications in their fields of study.

Academic Facilities

Vermont Tech students learn in modern laboratories with state-of-the-art equipment. Hartness Library is the on-campus library, serving about 3,000 on-campus, extended-campus, and distance education students of Vermont Tech and the Community College of Vermont. Open more than 80 hours per week during the academic year, Hartness houses an extensive collection of material and offers professional staff assistance with library research and information literacy skills. A library Web site (http://www.vctclib.org) gives access to thousands of full-text periodicals and reference databases. Students can request books 24 hours per day.

Facilities housed in the major academic buildings include four computer-aided drafting and design labs (one 13-station, one 19-station, and two 21-station); four 21-station general academic computing labs; an 8-station electrical/electronics lab; recently renovated mechanical labs that include computer numerically controlled equipment and computer-aided manufacturing software; state-of-the-art veterinary technology facilities, including a 12-station lab area, a radiography suite and darkroom, and a surgery suite; a biotechnology lab with instrumentation typical of the most modern research labs; a nursing lab with a dedicated computer room and nursing station; two civil engineering labs; architectural drafting studios; a campuswide microcomputer network with Internet access; four instrumented electronics labs; and a fully equipped automotive technology center with the latest in computerized diagnostics. Facilities at the College's Williston campus include an 8,400-square-foot dental hygiene clinic that features twenty-two dental operatories, four radiographic units, a dedicated classroom, faculty offices, and a patient reception area.

Agriculture students gain practical experience at the College's dairy facility, where a main free-stall barn houses a milking herd of 80 registered Holsteins. Students have the opportunity to participate in all aspects of the farm's management. Veterinary technology students work with several species of domestic animals in the livestock facility on the farm. Conant Hall houses most of the College's academic support services. Students visit the support services offices to sign up for tutoring, meet with counselors to discuss personal or academic issues, or visit the career/transfer center to update their resumes and explore career options and internship opportunities. Disabilities Services, where students with a disability can find out about classroom accommodations or assistive technology, is also located in Conant Hall, as is the College's Learning Center. At the Learning Center, students may take advantage of drop-in and scheduled tutoring, supplemental instruction, study groups, and review sessions; the General Education Department's Writing and Communication Center is on the same floor and provides students with help in reading, writing, oral presentations, study skills, and assistive-technology training.

Costs

Tuition for 2010–11 was $10,248 per year for Vermont residents and $19,584 for out-of-state students. The yearly room rate was $4836, and the annual meal plan was $3284. Other required annual fees totaled $756. An additional $1407 health insurance fee was required of students not covered by another medical plan. New students were assessed a $214 orientation fee. Many of Vermont Tech's programs are available at reduced tuition to New England students through the New England Regional Student Program, sponsored by the New England Board of Higher Education.

Financial Aid

About 80 percent of Vermont Tech students receive financial aid from federal, state, and campus-based sources. There are a growing number of institutional scholarships available, including the Vermont Technical College Scholars Program, as well as work-study opportunities. Prospective students seeking aid must file the Free Application for Federal Student Aid (FAFSA). Some state agencies may require additional information. Students are urged to apply for financial aid by the March 1 priority deadline so awards can be announced by May. However, applications are reviewed on a rolling basis after March 1 until available funds are exhausted. The Vermont Tech Web site provides more financial aid information.

Faculty

The College's excellence in instruction is a direct result of the quality of the faculty at Vermont Tech. More than 140 full- and part-time faculty members bring a special blend of industrial experience and teaching expertise to the College. Almost all have advanced degrees. Students are assured of individual attention as a result of the 11:1 student-faculty ratio.

Admission Requirements

Each applicant receives individual consideration for admission based on receipt and review of the official secondary school transcript, letters of recommendation, proof of high school graduation or a high school equivalency diploma, and SAT scores. A personal interview is strongly recommended for all applicants. Because of the technical nature of the curriculum, applicants should have a strong math and science aptitude.

Application and Information

Vermont Technical College follows a rolling admission policy, but timely application is recommended. Applicants are notified of their status within two weeks of receipt of their completed application and supporting documents. For more information on Vermont Technical College, students should contact:

Office of Admissions
Vermont Technical College
P.O. Box 500
Randolph Center, Vermont 05061
Phone: 802-728-1000
       800-442-VTC-1 (admissions, toll-free)
Fax: 802-728-1390
E-mail: admissions@vtc.edu
Web site: http://www.vtc.edu

The high-tech campus of Vermont Technical College is situated in a scenic New England village in the heart of Vermont.

VILLANOVA UNIVERSITY
VILLANOVA, PENNSYLVANIA

The University

Founded in 1842 by the Order of Saint Augustine (pronounced ah-GUST-in), Villanova University is the oldest and largest Catholic university in Pennsylvania and welcomes students of all faiths. The Augustinian values of *veritas, unitas, caritas* (translated as truth, unity, and love) guide academic and social life at the University, which tends to attract students who are interested in volunteerism, social justice, and the common good. Villanovans annually provide more than 200,000 hours of service to the local, regional, and global community.

Villanova offers more than forty-five rigorous academic programs through the College of Liberal Arts and Sciences, the Villanova School of Business, the College of Engineering, and the College of Nursing. Undergraduate full-time enrollment is 6,394; total University enrollment is 10,482. There are more than 265 student organizations and chapters of thirty-six national honor societies, including Phi Beta Kappa and Phi Kappa Phi.

Located just 12 miles west of Philadelphia, Villanova's picturesque campus has sixty-five buildings, including twenty-six residence halls. Award-winning dining services are available in three residence dining halls and sixteen à la carte eateries, all with a variety of culinary options. Students also have ready access to several athletic and fitness facilities on campus; the newest is the Davis Center for Athletics, with state-of-the-art cardio machines, weight equipment, and free weights. Group exercise classes, including yoga and Pilates, also are regularly held. Nearly 20 percent of the student body enjoys varsity or club athletics, and thirteen intramural sports attract approximately 3,000 student participants annually.

To facilitate the transition to college life, first-year students are encouraged to join a themed Learning Community. Community members live in the same residence halls, take their year-long Augustine and Culture Seminar together, and participate in cocurricular activities. These typically include lectures, plays, themed dinners, and cultural trips. Through Learning Communities, students form deeper, often lifelong, relationships with their classmates and professors and become more fully engaged in their studies.

Location

Villanova students reap all the benefits of living within the beautiful and tranquil Philadelphia Main Line suburbs. Yet because of the University's convenient proximity to the city of Philadelphia, students also have endless opportunities to complement campus life with cultural, recreational, and social activities found only in a vibrant, major metropolitan area. Whether it's visiting world-class art and science museums, touring historic sites, sampling the impressive restaurant scene, browsing through countless stores and shops, or cheering on local professional sports teams, there is something for everyone to enjoy.

Majors and Degrees

Villanova's College of Liberal Arts and Sciences grants the Bachelor of Arts degree in Arab and Islamic studies, art history, classical studies*, communication*, criminal justice*, cultural studies, economics, English, environmental studies, French and Francophone studies, gender and women's studies, geography, global interdisciplinary studies, history, honors, humanities, human services, Italian, Latin American studies, liberal arts*, philosophy, political science*, psychology*, secondary education*, sociology, Spanish studies*, and theology and religious studies*. The college grants the Bachelor of Science degree in astronomy and astrophysics, biochemistry, biology*, chemistry*, comprehensive science, computer science*, environmental science, honors, mathematical sciences*, mathematical sciences/applied statistics*, and physics*. (* denotes programs that offer accelerated bachelor's/master's degrees.)

The college also offers interdisciplinary concentrations in Africana studies, Augustine in dialogue with faith and culture, cognitive science, East Asian studies, elementary education (in conjunction with Rosemont College), ethics, Irish studies, peace and justice, Russian area studies, teacher certification, and writing and rhetoric.

Villanova School of Business offers the Bachelor of Science degree in accountancy and the Bachelor of Business Administration in economics, finance, management, management information systems, and marketing. The School of business also offers an international business co-major and minors in business law and corporate governance, entrepreneurship, international business, and real estate.

Through the College of Engineering, Villanova grants the Bachelor of Science degree (with accelerated bachelor's/master's degree options also available) in chemical engineering, civil engineering, computer engineering, electrical engineering, and mechanical engineering.

Villanova offers the Bachelor of Science in Nursing degree through the College of Nursing. Villanova also offers the following Health Science Affiliation programs: Drexel University College of Medicine, Doctor of Medicine; University of Pennsylvania School of Dental Medicine, Doctor of Dental Medicine; Salus University/Pennsylvania College of Optometry, Doctor of Optometry; and Jefferson College of Health Professions of Thomas Jefferson University, Doctor of Physical Therapy, Master of Science in Occupational Therapy, bioscience technologies, and radiologic technologies.

An honors concentration is available to students in all four colleges.

Academic Programs

The College of Liberal Arts and Sciences provides a wide array of degree programs, concentrations, and majors, along with interdisciplinary majors in the humanities, international studies, comprehensive science, and environmental science. Villanova is one of the few institutions in the country that offers an undergraduate program in astronomy and astrophysics, and one of only eighteen Catholic colleges or universities in the nation to have a chapter of Phi Beta Kappa, the prestigious liberal arts honor society.

The Villanova School of Business (VSB), one of the top-ranked business schools in the nation, offers majors in accounting, economics, finance, management, management information systems, and marketing. The school also offers a business honors degree, an international business co-major, and minors in entrepreneurship, real estate, and business law and corporate governance. VSB is home to the Applied Finance Lab, which provides access to many of the real-time technologies available to Wall Street traders. Nearly half of the students participate in international academic, internship, and volunteer experiences.

The College of Engineering, ranked among the best engineering programs in the nation, offers degree programs in chemical engineering, civil and environmental engineering, computer engineering, electrical engineering, and mechanical engineering. The college is home to three research units: the Center for Advanced Communications, the Center for Nonlinear Dynamics and Control, and the Center for the Advancement of Sustainability in Engineering. The Villanova Center for Engineering Education and Research houses state-of-the-art instructional and research labs and the 10,000-square-foot Structural Engineering Teaching and Research Laboratory offers additional engineering-related facilities.

The College of Nursing is a tangible expression of Villanova's mission, tradition, and commitment to human service and seeks to educate nurses within the framework of Christian beliefs and values and the heritage of the Order of St. Augustine. Students can work with community members in need, while completing their rigorous course work. The college is housed in Driscoll Hall, which features a 200-seat auditorium and a 200-seat lecture hall; future-oriented clinical simulation labs for health assessment, adult health, maternal/child health, anesthesia, and critical care; simulation labs for standardized patient observation and testing; a center for nursing research and scholarship; places for prayer and reflection; space for global health studies and international student activities; and areas for student, faculty, and alumni events and social interaction.

Naval and Marine Reserve Officers Training Corps (ROTC) programs are available on campus. Villanova has had an NROTC program for more than fifty years; the program is structured to complement a normal college lifestyle. Midshipmen are encouraged to participate fully in their academic programs as well as in extracurricular activities.

Off-Campus Programs

Villanova has a rich study-abroad program. Each year, approximately 750 students take advantage of study-abroad programs in nearly forty nations, including Ireland, Switzerland, Peru, England, France, Germany, Italy, China, Chile, Russia, Poland, Thailand, Spain, Australia, Rwanda, the West Indies, Madagascar, and Samoa.

Academic Facilities

Villanova's state-of-the-art classrooms and labs are in keeping with the University's position as a leading institution of higher learning and are complemented with a vast array of learning and career resources. Falvey Memorial Library contains more than 1,000,000 items and offers access to a number of databases. The Office of Learning Support Services assists students with learning disabilities, neurologically-based disorders, and chronic illnesses. The Villanova Career Center helps students develop professional skills and learn about career options. Ninety-seven percent of recent Villanova graduates are employed full-time or enrolled in graduate school within six months of degree completion. Approximately 4,000 jobs are posted on Villanova's job boards each year, and the median starting salary for graduates is $51,000. Over 400 student internships are posted on campus annually, offering valuable professional development and the possibility of full-time employment.

Technology is widely available. Each incoming student receives a new laptop computer (upgraded at the end of sophomore year) and all residence halls are connected to the campus network. Students can participate in learning experiences across campus; receive curricular advising services; and access tests, Webcasts, and library reserves online. Through Villanova's student portal, they can keep track of deadlines, class schedules, and financial aid information. Villanova's technology also provides easy access to meal plans, parking registration, laundry reservations, voting processes, ride sharing/carpooling, and basketball ticket lotteries. Students and parents can also sign up for the University's emergency notification system.

Costs

For the 2010–11 academic year, the average tuition was $39,085 and room and board were $10,620.

Financial Aid

For the 2010–11 freshman class, 93 percent of those who applied for need-based aid were eligible to receive some type of assistance, and 77 percent of those eligible received Villanova Grants. The average grant award was $21,322. The average assistance package for students with demonstrated need (combining grants, scholarships, loans, and student employment) was $29,348.

Villanova offers a Presidential Scholarship program, which seeks to attract academic, civic, and cultural leaders who represent diverse intellectual, social, racial or economic backgrounds, including those from families in which few or no members have attended college. These scholarships are renewable for a total of eight consecutive semesters, based on academic performance at Villanova.

Faculty

Villanova has 586 full-time faculty members; nearly 90 percent of them hold doctoral degrees. The student-to-faculty ratio is 12:1 and the average class size is 22.

Student Government

Empowering the Villanova student body since 1925, the Student Government Association (SGA) has three branches (administrative, community, and student relations) and twelve committees. The SGA provides opportunities for student leaders to serve the Villanova community as liaisons, representatives, and student senators.

Admission Requirements

Admission to Villanova is competitive. In addition to attracting academically talented, well-rounded students, Villanova seeks applicants who have a compassionate mindset and a desire to transform the world and make it a better place.

Villanova is a Common Application member institution. Prospective students are also required to complete the Villanova Supplement for Undergraduate Admission and submit an official high school transcript and Common Application School Report. Applicants must have their standardized test scores (SAT or ACT) reported directly by the College Board or ACT.

In the Villanova admissions process, high school performance is an extremely important selectivity factor. Each student's high school record, GPA, and class rank, along with each student's demonstration of character and personal abilities, are carefully considered. Extracurricular and volunteer activities are helpful to applicants in this regard. Another important factor is the personal essay. Since interviews are not part of the admission process, a well-crafted essay is essential for prospective students to explain who they are and why they should be selected to become Villanovans. (A recommendation from the secondary school counselor is also carefully considered.)

Prospective students who are not from the U.S. are warmly welcomed to apply for admission to Villanova. Applicants who are non-native English speakers must take the TOEFL or IELTS evaluations and have scores reported directly from the College Board. The International Student Services Office supports enrolled international students in areas including immigration rights and responsibilities; educational, social, and personal counseling; cultural adjustment issues; and campus and community activities.

Transferring to Villanova is possible, but selective. Students applying to transfer to Villanova must complete a transfer application and submit official transcripts from each postsecondary school attended and a completed Dean of Students Transfer Evaluation form.

Application and Information

The deadline for early action and Health Affiliation program applications is November 1; regular decision deadline is January 7.

Villanova Office of University Admission
800 Lancaster Avenue
Villanova, Pennsylvania 19085-1672

Phone: 610-519-4000
Fax: 610-519-6450
E-mail: gotovu@villanova.edu
Web site: http://www.villanova.edu
         http://on.fb.me/Villanova_Univ

St. Thomas of Villanova Church.

VIRGINIA MILITARY INSTITUTE

LEXINGTON, VIRGINIA

The Institute

The Virginia Military Institute (VMI) is the nation's oldest state-supported military college, founded in 1839 in Lexington, Virginia, and located at the southern end of the Shenandoah Valley. VMI offers qualified young men and women a demanding combination of academic study and rigorous military training that exists nowhere else, and grants B.A. and B.S. degrees in fourteen disciplines within the general fields of engineering, science, and liberal arts. The Institute's emphasis on qualities of honor, integrity, and responsibility contributes to its unique educational philosophy. Professional leadership training is provided to all cadets through the Reserve Officers' Training Corps (ROTC) programs, maintained at VMI by the Department of Defense. Cadets may pursue commissions in the U.S. Army, Air Force, Navy, or Marine Corps.

In every field of endeavor, whether it is leadership in business, industry, public service, education, the professions, or careers in the military, success comes early to a high number of VMI graduates. In an independent survey of college graduates seeking employment, armed forces commission, or admission to graduate or professional school following graduation, 95 percent of VMI graduates met their goal by the following October.

VMI's breadth is diverse. The curricula for the selected major begin in the first year. More than 25 percent of cadets major in civil, electrical, or mechanical engineering, and more than 50 percent of cadets major in liberal arts fields. The two most popular fields are international studies and economics/business.

The academic excellence of VMI and its stature among institutions of higher education are highlighted by the fact that *U.S. News & World Report* has named VMI among the nation's top three public liberal arts colleges for nine years in a row. Its engineering programs remain in the top tier of best undergraduate accredited programs at schools offering only bachelor's or master's degrees.

VMI's alumni support is unparalleled in many ways, especially in their financial support.

VMI alumni include Nobel Peace Prize winner George C. Marshall, 11 Rhodes scholars, and 39 college presidents. VMI alumni have distinguished themselves in every American conflict since the Mexican War, and they include 7 Medal of Honor recipients and 265 general and flag officers. More than 1,500 alumni have served in war zones and in support of operations in the war on terror since 2001.

After nearly 160 years of preparing young men for distinguished leadership roles, VMI made the transition to being coeducational in 1997, successfully assimilating women in the Corps of Cadets. The Institute graduated its first women cadets in May 1999.

Today, 1,569 young men and women in the VMI Corps of Cadets represent forty-four states and eleven other countries. More than 100 cadets study abroad each year, one third compete in intercollegiate athletics, and all have significant leadership opportunities.

All cadets reside in Barracks, at the centerpiece of the VMI Post. The original structure was built in 1850 and is a National Historic Landmark. An additional wing was added in 1949. A third section of the Barracks, which includes a bookstore, visitor center, and food court, was completed in 2009. All cadet rooms are equipped for computer technology.

VMI cadets uphold an honor system as old as the Institute. An oath of honor is taken by each cadet, "not to lie, cheat, or steal, nor tolerate those who do," and the oath is practiced in daily life. As it is basic to cadet life, it is ingrained and builds strong character. Honor is at the cornerstone of every cadet's lifelong commitment to integrity, duty, self-discipline, and self-reliance.

One of the oldest VMI traditions is the orientation and instruction provided to new cadets by older cadets. Regardless of background or prior training, every cadet in the first year at VMI is a Rat, and each is a Brother Rat to the other. They live under the Rat System until Break Out in late winter, and their bonds formed by this experience last a lifetime.

VMI places great emphasis on physical fitness and training programs, whether cadets participate in athletics, ROTC training, or physical education programs. VMI offers sixteen intercollegiate athletics programs at the NCAA Division I level and supports numerous club sports and intramural activities. The VMI "Keydet" Club is one of the oldest and most productive athletic foundations in the country, raising more than $1 million annually for athletic scholarships and grants-in-aid to 185 cadets in all sixteen sports. Athletic grounds and facilities are within easy access to the Post.

VMI is a member of the Big South conference.

Location

Lexington is in Rockbridge County, Virginia, an area rich in history and natural beauty. VMI adjoins the campus of Washington and Lee University, the nation's ninth-oldest institution of higher learning. Both colleges are within walking distance to historic downtown Lexington, a popular tourist destination. Interstate Highways 81 and 64 intersect only minutes from VMI, north of Lexington's downtown area. U.S. Highways 11 (north-south) and 60 (east-west), the area's crossroads for two centuries, intersect in downtown Lexington. Air service to VMI is available from Roanoke Regional Airport, less than an hour's drive from Lexington.

Majors and Degrees

VMI offers the baccalaureate degree in fourteen curricula. The B.S. is awarded in chemistry, civil engineering, computer science, electrical engineering, mechanical engineering, and physics. The B.A. is conferred in economics and business, English, history, international studies, modern languages, and psychology. A B.S. or B.A. can be earned in biology and applied mathematics. A course of study leading to a B.S. or B.A. is chosen upon entering VMI, but a transfer from one major field of study to another is permitted.

Academic Programs

VMI's demanding academic program reflects established needs and emerging trends of an ever-changing, global society. A newly funded undergraduate research initiative extends through summer, affording cadets and faculty members financial incentives and continuous support for a wide range of investigative projects. The Institute's international programs include faculty and student exchanges with more than a dozen international academies and universities, seven international internships, and numerous study-abroad programs each semester and during the summer.

VMI is accredited by the Southern Association of Colleges and Schools and is a member of American Council on Education, the Association of American Colleges, the College Entrance Examination Board, and the Association of Virginia Colleges. VMI's engineering and computer science programs are ABET-accredited; the chemistry program is accredited by ACS; and the economic/business curriculum is accredited by AACSB International.

Academic Facilities

The VMI Post covers 134 acres, of which 12 acres are designated a National Historic District. VMI's academic facilities, Superintendent's quarters, library, alumni hall, and other administrative buildings, along with Barracks, encircle a 12-acre parade ground used for marching drills, weekly parades, training exercises, and social gatherings. The physics department has X-ray and nuclear physics laboratories and operates both an observatory and planetarium. The George C. Marshall Research Museum and the VMI Museum are located on Post.

Costs

Charges at VMI are based on a cadet's classification as a Virginia or out-of-state resident. Total charges cover most direct expenses, including tuition, room, board (twenty-one meals per week), fees, uniforms, laundry, routine medical care, and barber services. Total costs for 2010–11 were $19,660 for Virginia residents and $37,652 for nonresidents. (Books and transportation are additional.) ROTC pay and allowances to qualified cadets total up to $10,000 over four years, and should be considered in net costs at VMI.

Financial Aid

Although aid is generally awarded on the basis of financial need, numerous scholarships are awarded for academic and athletic excellence and as room and board supplements to ROTC scholarship recipients. Students interested in financial assistance should write to VMI's Director of Financial Aid.

Faculty

All VMI faculty members teach in the classroom, and 97 percent of full-time faculty members hold doctoral or terminal degrees. The cadet-faculty ratio is 12:1, permitting a close, mentor relationship between a cadet and instructor. Faculty research is conducted in partnership with cadets. ROTC instructors are experienced military officers and make an outstanding contribution to cadet leadership training.

Student Government

VMI has two systems of student government. The regimental system oversees cadet accountability for conduct, appearance, military training, and all ceremonial functions. The regiment of the Corps is divided into two battalions of four companies each, plus a band company.

Although Institute regulations govern the discipline of cadets, a large measure of supervision resides in each of the four closely knit classes within the Corps. The class system administers the Corps' standards and the privileges accorded each class and governs with the regimental system to oversee cadet appearance and conduct.

Representatives to the Honor Court are elected from the Corps, by the Corps, to enforce the rules of the honor system and prosecute Honor Court cases.

Admission Requirements

Applicants must be unmarried, 16 to 22 years of age (a one-year age waiver may be granted for an applicant who has served in active duty in the armed forces or in certain other circumstances), physically fit for enrollment in ROTC, and graduated from an accredited secondary school with 16 or more academic units. Recommended course credits include 4 English, 3 social studies, 3 laboratory sciences, 3 foreign language, 3 mathematics (including 2 years of algebra and 1 of geometry), and 2 electives. The average GPA of incoming freshmen is approximately 3.3. Other qualifications include rank in the upper 50 percent of the senior class (significance of rank depends on class size and other factors), above-average scores on SAT or ACT, and satisfactory character recommendations. Extracurricular activities are viewed as favorable indicators of leadership and character traits. Transfer students are accepted, but two years of residency at VMI are required. Admissions standards are applied without regard to gender, race, nationality, or religion, and all factors are weighed in the final determination of the applicant's qualifications.

Application and Information

An application may be submitted anytime between September 1 and February 1 of the senior year in high school and should be accompanied by a nonrefundable $40 application fee, a transcript of the school record for grade 9 through the last completed semester, and SAT or ACT scores. Visits to the Institute are highly recommended. Open House visits are held throughout the academic year.

Interested students should contact:

Director of Admissions
Virginia Military Institute
Lexington, Virginia 24450
Phone: 540-464-7211
      800-767-4207 (toll-free)
Fax: 540-464-7746
E-mail: admissions@vmi.edu
Web site: http://www.vmi.edu

VMI Barracks, a National Historic Landmark and home to the VMI Corps of Cadets.

WALSH UNIVERSITY

NORTH CANTON, OHIO

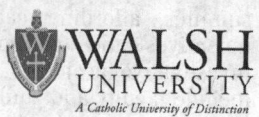

The University

Walsh University is a fully accredited, liberal arts and sciences Catholic university in North Canton, Ohio, offering fifty-five majors, seven graduate programs, and an accelerated-degree program for working adults. With 2,963 students and a 15:1 student-faculty ratio, the University offers a very friendly, supportive, and safe campus and a unique broad-based curriculum with close student-faculty interaction. Most residence halls and academic buildings on Walsh's 136-acre campus are new or have been renovated within the last several years, providing state-of-the-art facilities for students. Walsh also offers generous financial aid packages to 95 percent of full-time students.

Active and involved in campus and community life, more than 60 percent of Walsh students participate in extracurricular programs. Students also have the opportunity to participate in a variety of intramural sports. Walsh also offers seventeen intercollegiate sports including football, baseball, soccer, and volleyball. Walsh is currently Division II in the NAIA league, but has been accepted into the NCAA Division II membership process and expects to have full standing in that division by 2013.

Walsh University welcomes students from around the world of all faiths and backgrounds. The University currently has students from numerous countries and looks forward to continued growth.

Walsh University was founded in 1960 by the Brothers of Christian Instruction and is accredited by the North Central Association/Higher Learning Commission, National League for Nursing Accrediting Commission, Ohio Department of Education, Ohio Board of Counseling and Social Work, American Physical Therapy Association, the Commission on Accreditation in Physical Therapy Education, Council for Accreditation of Counseling and Related Educational Programs, and the National Council for Accreditation of Teacher Education. Walsh is a member of the Ohio College Association, the National Association of Independent Colleges and Universities, and the Association of Catholic Colleges and Universities.

In addition to its undergraduate degree programs, Walsh offers seven graduate degree programs that include an accelerated M.B.A., a Master of Science in Nursing, Master of Arts in Counseling and Human Development, Master of Arts in Education (M.A.Ed.), Master of Arts in Theology, Doctor of Nursing Practice (D.N.P.), and a Doctor of Physical Therapy.

Location

Walsh University has a beautiful, tree-lined campus located just 3 miles east of I-77 in North Canton, a safe, pleasant residential suburban community. Canton, which is about 5 miles south of the Walsh campus, is a city of 84,000 that offers a wide array of cultural, recreational, and athletic activities. Home of the Professional Football Hall of Fame, the President McKinley National Memorial, and the National First Ladies Library, the city also hosts a symphony orchestra, an art museum, and a civic opera, theater guild, and ballet. A number of major companies are headquartered in Stark County, including the Hoover Company, the Timken Company, and Diebold, Inc.

Majors and Degrees

Bachelor of Arts and Bachelor of Science degrees are offered in the following majors: accounting (general and specialized CPA tracks), bioinformatics, biology, chemistry, clinical laboratory science, communication, comprehensive science, computer science, corporate communication, criminal justice–sociology, education (early childhood, middle childhood, adolescence to young adulthood, integrated language arts, integrated mathematics teacher licensure, integrated science teacher licensure, integrated social studies teacher, intervention specialist, life science/biology teacher licensure, life science/biology and chemistry teacher licensure, multiage physical education, and physical education), English, family studies–sociology, finance, French, general business, general studies, global business, history, international relations, Latin American business, management, management information systems, marketing, mathematics, museum studies, nursing, philosophy/theology, physical education, political science, psychology, psychology–community/clinical, research methods and data analysis–sociology, and Spanish.

Walsh offers preprofessional programs in dentistry, law, medicine, natural resources, optometry, physical therapy, podiatry, and veterinary science. Each is developed within the context of a regular academic major. Walsh's physical therapy graduates have the option to continue their studies by entering Walsh's newly accredited Doctor of Physical Therapy degree program. Students enrolled in the University's B.A./M.A. program can earn a bachelor's degree in behavioral science and a master's degree in counseling and human development in 5½ years. An affiliation with Case Western Reserve University's (CWRU) program in dentistry leads to a B.S. from Walsh and ultimately a D.D.S. from CWRU.

In addition, Walsh offers the Associate of Arts degree in accounting, finance, human services, liberal arts, management, and marketing.

Academic Programs

The student's academic program comprises courses within the liberal arts, a major field of study, and elective courses. Major course work, constituting one fourth or more of a student's program of studies, is designed to help students prepare for their careers. Forty percent of a student's program of studies is within the liberal arts. Elective courses, which constitute the remaining portion of a student's program of studies, enable students to develop personal interests, take more courses within their major field, or enroll in additional core courses. The University encourages students to give careful thought to selecting a program of study and a major. While many students select double majors as a way to improve their career opportunities, the design of individual programs requires consultation with a faculty adviser and a division chair. To earn a bachelor's degree, students must successfully complete 130 semester hours.

Designed for the academically gifted, the honors program offers challenges that lead students to achieve academic excellence. Honors students take advantage of such offerings as special seminars, independent studies, internships, and research projects.

The University's School for Professional Studies Program is for working adults who have earned college credits and who wish to earn their bachelor's degree in an accelerated format. Classes are scheduled on nights and weekends to accommodate busy schedules.

Academic Facilities

The Walsh Library contains 141,000 volumes, 270 current periodical subscriptions on paper, and 41,071 electronically. Databases bring many full-text articles immediately for download or print, and information technology systems enable online requests for physical delivery of material, often via rapid courier. Library staff members give introductory lectures on research techniques. The library has a quiet study room, a snack lounge, and a mini-theater. All library resources are available via the Internet.

Faculty

Walsh University fosters close working relationships between faculty members and students. Beyond classroom teaching, faculty members serve as student counselors and tutors and take on roles as advisers for student organizations. The Walsh faculty is composed of full-time, part-time, and adjunct members. The student-faculty ratio is 15:1. The majority of full-time faculty members hold Ph.D.'s or terminal degrees in their respective fields.

Student Government

Walsh University Student Government provides capable, responsible student governance. Through its executive, legislative, and judicial branches, it fosters student involvement in the governance of the University, serves as a forum for student opinion, and functions as a liaison between students, faculty and staff members, and the administration. Along with the Student Affairs staff, it plans student activities and community projects.

Costs

Tuition for the 2010–11 academic year was $21,380. Tuition, fees, and room and board charges total approximately $30,640 per year and vary by residence hall. Books and personal expenses cost an estimated $700–$900 for the year. The University reserves the right to change the cost structure without notice.

Financial Aid

Walsh is dedicated to providing outstanding liberal arts education at an affordable price. The primary purpose of Walsh University's financial aid program is to assist deserving students who cannot otherwise meet the costs of a college education. Financial aid takes the form of scholarships, work-study awards, grants, or loans, depending upon the resources available. The University offers a number of scholarships in amounts from $1500 to full tuition, in addition to institutional need-based grants. The Alumni Association offers scholarships as well. State and federal grants and loans are available to students along with the University's work-study program that provides work compatible with a student's academic schedule. Financial aid is awarded for one year and is renewable in subsequent years if the student shows a continuing need and maintains an appropriate academic record.

Applicants for admission may apply for financial aid by submitting the Free Application for Federal Student Aid (FAFSA) and the University's financial aid form. To allow for timely notification of financial awards, the University recommends that the FAFSA be mailed by March 15 in order to receive full analysis by May 1. Prospective students may obtain a FAFSA from their high school guidance counselor or from the University's financial aid office. The Walsh financial aid form is available from the financial aid and admissions offices of the University.

Admission Requirements

Every student seeking admission to Walsh University is reviewed individually to assess the student's ability to meet the rigors of the University's curriculum. The composition of high school classes, grades achieved, class rank, and standardized test scores are all taken into consideration before an admission decision is rendered. Essays and interviews are highly recommended but not required.

Walsh grants credit for college-level work completed in high school and for credits earned through the College Level Examination Program. Qualified high school juniors and seniors may enroll for college credit under the University's postsecondary enrollment program. The University seeks a diverse student body.

Application and Information

Early application is recommended. Walsh University operates under a rolling admissions policy. The completed admission application, $25 application fee, ACT or SAT scores, and a high school transcript are required for a student's application to be considered for admission. Transfer students must also submit transcripts from all colleges and universities attended.

Interested students are encouraged to contact:

Brett Freshour
Dean of Enrollment Management
Walsh University
2020 East Maple Street NW
North Canton, Ohio 44720-3336
Phone: 330-492-7172
       800-362-9846 (toll-free)
Fax: 330-490-7165
E-mail: admissions@walsh.edu
Web site: http://www.walsh.edu
       http://www.facebook.com/walshu
       http://www.twitter.com/walshuniversity
       http://www.youtube.com/ohiowalshuniversity

On the campus of Walsh University.

WEBB INSTITUTE
GLEN COVE, NEW YORK

The Institute

Webb Institute was founded in 1889 to provide an opportunity for worthy young students to obtain an education in the "art and science of designing ships and their propulsion systems." The Institute has followed this basic objective to the present, and its graduates are active throughout the United States in the ship design, ship construction, yacht design, and marine operations industries and in appropriate government offices.

The 26-acre campus is the former estate of Herbert L. Pratt and is located on Long Island Sound. Because of the Institute's small size and intensive academic program, varsity sports are limited. However, Webb participates in intercollegiate basketball, cross-country, sailing, soccer, tennis, and volleyball, for which ample facilities are provided. The campus has a gymnasium, tennis courts, playing fields, and a beach. Golf and swimming facilities are available nearby.

Webb Institute maintains an enrollment that ranges from 70 to 90 students, all of whom live on campus. Webb students must be U.S. citizens or permanent residents with a green card.

Location

Glen Cove is a city of more than 25,000 residents and is located on Long Island's North Shore, which is nearly an hour from New York City. Convenient train service from Glen Cove to New York brings the variety of cultural, educational, and recreational activities available in the city within easy reach of Webb students.

Majors and Degrees

Webb Institute offers an engineering program in ship design, which involves both naval architecture and marine engineering. The undergraduate degree awarded is the Bachelor of Science in naval architecture and marine engineering.

Academic Programs

The engineering program in ship design consists of fundamental foundation courses in mathematics, science, and engineering sciences, capped by extensive professional design courses. A coherent program in humanities supplements the technical program to round out undergraduate education.

In addition, students have a two-month, cooperative job experience each year in the U.S. marine and maritime industry. During this period, freshmen work as helper mechanics in shipyards, sophomores obtain seagoing experience aboard ship, and juniors and seniors work as engineering assistants in design and technical offices of various marine firms. This important part of the program provides excellent articulation of the educational and career experiences. Innovative engineering ideas are encouraged in the thesis

required during the last year. The program is fully accredited. Graduates are well equipped to pursue postgraduate studies.

Semesters run from late August to mid-December and from late February to late June. January and February are winter work periods, and the period from late June to late August is designated for vacation.

Academic Facilities

Full laboratory support is provided for chemistry, physics, metallurgy, and various engineering courses. A ship-model testing tank is available for ship and boat hull studies. Computer facilities are provided on campus. The Livingston Library contains extensive holdings in naval architecture, marine engineering, and general engineering, as well as collections in literature, arts, social sciences, and music.

Costs

All students admitted to Webb are accepted on a tuition- and fee-free basis (full scholarship). Room and board costs were approximately $12,000 in 2010–11. Nearly $800 per year is required for books and supplies. A $150 room deposit fee is payable on entry and refunded, less any breakage costs, on departure. The Student Organization requires a $100 deposit on entry, also refundable on departure.

Financial Aid

As stated, a full scholarship that covers tuition and fees is awarded to all accepted candidates. The winter work co-op in industry provides income for students that significantly assists in covering other expenses. Supplementary aid opportunities are available through the Federal Pell Grant, Federal Stafford Student Loans, and in-house grant programs. Students requiring financial assistance must submit the Free Application for Federal Student Aid (FAFSA) after March 31 but not later than July 1 of the year of entry.

Faculty

Webb Institute has a highly qualified faculty. Many members possess engineering licenses and engage in sponsored research programs, consult for commercial firms, and research and write technical papers. Classes are limited to 25 students, and the student-faculty ratio is 8:1. Each student is assigned a faculty adviser, and consultation with individual faculty members is encouraged.

Student Government

The Student Organization is highly active in student administrative, social, and educational affairs. It is supplemented by an Honor Council and honor system. Together, these entities provide students with a high degree of responsibility for ordering and conducting student life.

Admission Requirements

Admission to Webb is highly competitive. The qualifying requirements for admission are graduation from high school with a B+ (87) or better average in 16 credits of basic high school subjects. Admission selections are based on high school standing (generally in the upper 10 percent) and scores on the College Board's SAT and Subject Tests in Mathematics (Level 1 or 2), and Physics or Chemistry. The final selection follows a personal interview conducted at Webb or at a location convenient to the applicant. The entering class is usually restricted to 25 freshmen.

All application papers must be submitted by February 15, and all required College Board tests must be taken before that date. Advanced placement is not given in any of the course offerings. Campus visits by interested students are strongly recommended; prior appointments must be made. An early decision plan is available for qualified candidates.

Webb Institute does not discriminate in admission in the areas of gender, race, or religion. Academic qualities and career motivation are the only criteria.

Application and Information

For a catalog and application forms, students may contact:

Office of Admissions
Webb Institute
Glen Cove, New York 11542
Phone: 516-671-2213
E-mail: admissions@webb-institute.edu
Web site: http://www.webb-institute.edu

The academic facilities of Webb Institute are located on Long Island Sound in the former residence of Herbert L. Pratt.

WELLS COLLEGE

AURORA, NEW YORK

The College

Wells College is consistently ranked among the nation's top liberal arts colleges that offer high-quality education at an affordable price and has one of the most beautiful campuses in the United States. The College was established in 1868 by Henry Wells, who also founded the Wells Fargo and American Express companies.

At Wells, professors are dedicated to teaching, and because of the intimate nature of the campus community (the student body is 600), they get to know their students as individuals in and outside the classroom. Students frequently collaborate with their professors on original research and creative projects. At most other schools, these opportunities are only available to graduate students. Because faculty members at Wells know their students so well, they are especially effective advisers and mentors. Students have a competitive edge entering careers and top graduate and professional schools.

Another aspect of the Wells tradition is hands-on learning. In addition to dynamic classroom teaching, Wells students have a variety of other experiential opportunities: internships, service, study abroad, and off-campus study. Professors encourage students to apply theory in practical settings and to discover what they want to do in life through involvement.

Wells currently fields intercollegiate teams at the NCAA Division III level in men's and women's cross-country, field hockey, men's and women's lacrosse, men's and women's soccer, softball, men's and women's swimming, men's and women's basketball, men's and women's golf, men's and women's volleyball, and women's tennis. There are also a number of intramural opportunities, including basketball, soccer, swimming, skiing, tennis, and volleyball. Athletic facilities include indoor and outdoor tennis courts, a gymnasium, a newly renovated fitness center, a nine-hole golf course, and a campus boathouse and dock used in teaching sailing, canoeing, and lifeguarding.

Wells has a full range of active student organizations, including a literary magazine and newspaper, music and drama groups, environmental and political organizations, and abundant opportunities for community service, among others. A busy calendar of cultural events, symposia, and lectures enhances the academic and social life of the College.

Location

Wells is located in the village of Aurora on the eastern shore of Cayuga Lake—part of New York's scenic Finger Lakes region. The area is well known for its high concentration of prestigious colleges and universities, including Cornell University, Ithaca College, Hobart and William Smith Colleges, Colgate University, Hamilton College, and Syracuse University. Aurora is 25 miles from Ithaca and 60 miles from both Rochester and Syracuse. Students have abundant opportunities for outdoor recreation and sports, including sailing, swimming, horseback riding, skiing, and hiking.

Majors and Degrees

Wells offers majors and concentrations in African American studies, American cultures, American studies, anthropology/cross-cultural sociology, art history, biochemistry and molecular biology, biology, chemistry, computer science, creative writing, economics, English, environmental policies and values, environmental studies, ethics and philosophy, French, government and politics, historical and comparative studies, history, human nature and values, international studies, literature, management, mathematics, performing arts, physics, psychology, public affairs, religion, sociology, Spanish, studio art, theater and dance, visual arts, and women's studies. Students also have the option of a self-designed major. In addition, they can choose minors from a list of more than thirty programs.

Wells has also added an innovative Center for Business & Entrepreneurship, founded upon the tradition of liberal arts: learning that emphasizes critical thinking and problem-solving. The role of the center is to help students build the skills and develop the discernment to know how and where they most want to serve society. As such, the center will offer students the opportunity to explore growing fields like arts administration, green businesses, not-for-profit organizations, and hospitality.

The College has preprofessional programs in dentistry, education, engineering, law, medicine, teaching, and veterinary medicine. Wells has a cross-registration agreement with nearby Ithaca College, Cayuga Community College, and Cornell University and affiliations with Cornell's engineering school.

Wells awards the Bachelor of Arts degree and has a number of programs through which students can earn their bachelor's degree at Wells and a graduate or professional degree from an affiliated university. Participating schools are Clarkson University, Columbia University, Cornell University (engineering), and the University of Rochester (business, community health, and education).

Academic Programs

All Wells students benefit from an academic environment similar to honors programs available to only a small number of students at other schools. The College has a tradition of preparing students for leadership in their chosen fields, and the breadth of knowledge they gain and the range of life experiences they encounter enable them to achieve their career goals and establish a foundation for a rich and fulfilling life.

All students entering Wells to pursue a four-year course of study leading to a bachelor's degree are required to take the First-Year Experience (WLLS 101) and the New Student Experience (WLLS 111). Distribution requirements are a foreign language (two courses or exemption by exam), formal reasoning (one course), arts and humanities (three courses), natural and social sciences (three courses), and physical education (four courses). Team sports and dance technique can partially satisfy requirements.

Approximately sixteen courses must be taken in the student's major, and at least six must be taken at Wells. Eighteen credit hours must be taken at the 300 level or above. A senior project or thesis and a comprehensive evaluation are required for graduation.

A student must successfully complete 120 semester hours (60 of which must be taken at Wells and through affiliated programs, such as study abroad) to be recommended by the faculty for a degree. To learn more about the academic program and requirements for transfer students, prospective students should visit the Wells College Web site.

Off-Campus Programs

Students can spend January term, a semester, or even a year in another college or university abroad or in the United States. Typically, Wells students choose to study off campus for a semester during the junior year, but many different possibilities are available depending on a student's academic program and interests.

The College offers affiliated study-abroad experiences in Denmark, the Dominican Republic, France, Germany, Great Britain, Ireland, Italy, Japan, Mexico, Senegal, Spain, and Sweden. Currently, the three most popular programs are study abroad in Florence, Italy; Paris, France; and Seville, Spain. These off-campus study experiences are flexible as well as financially and academically accessible. After at least one semester at Wells, a student's financial aid applies to one semester of off-campus study.

Wells provides off-campus study options in the United States through its affiliations with American University, serving a wide range of academic and internship interests in Washington, D.C.; the Salt

Center, offering documentary field studies in Portland, Maine; and the Public Leadership Education Network (PLEN), providing leadership development through seminars and internships in Washington, D.C. As part of the PLEN affiliation, students can spend a semester studying at the London School of Economics and Political Science and hold an internship in the British government. Through the School for Field Studies, Wells offers semester-long study-abroad experiences in Africa, Australia, the Caribbean, and other locations. The College also offers credit-bearing courses during the January term that take students to a single destination in the U.S. or abroad for intensive study that requires travel in a region or country with a faculty member.

Academic Facilities

From the contemporary elegance of Weld House to the nineteenth-century Glen Park mansion, the former home of College founder Henry Wells, the residence halls encompass enough variety to satisfy every taste. Students eat their meals together in the majestic Tudor-style dining hall in Main Building.

The Louis Jefferson Long Library has received numerous awards for its architectural design. Facilities include an online computer center, individual study carrels, seminar and group-study rooms, and an art gallery. There are department libraries in art, economics, English, mathematics, music, philosophy, and the sciences located across the campus.

The Barler Hall of Music houses a recital hall with superb acoustics, vocal and instrumental practice rooms, a music library, and a listening laboratory. Facilities for printmaking, painting, ceramics, sculpture, and photography are located in the Campbell Arts Building. The Cleveland Hall of Languages contains state-of-the-art equipment for learning foreign languages. Stratton Science Hall, completed in 2007, houses state-of-the-art laboratories for chemistry, biology, environmental science, and physics as well as a computer laboratory. Morgan Hall houses the Book Arts Center and the Wells College Press. Macmillan Hall has classrooms, faculty and administrative offices, several computer laboratories, and department libraries. The east wing of Macmillan contains the Margaret Phipps Auditorium, a theater facility used for teaching, concerts, lectures, and dramatic productions.

Costs

Wells has a long-term commitment to providing talented students with access to the best education, which requires offering excellence at an affordable price. Wells is ranked among the best liberal arts colleges in the nation, yet the cost of a Wells education is considerably less than the tuition charged by comparable schools.

The cost of a Wells education for the 2010–11 academic year was $30,680 for tuition, $11,000 for room and board, and $1500 for fees.

Financial Aid

Approximately 90 percent of Wells students receive financial aid packaged in the form of grants, scholarships, loans, and work-study opportunities. The College works closely with students and their families to design a financial aid package that meets their needs and their budgets.

Award determinations are made on a rolling basis following acceptance. College financial aid is complex; however, Wells College's well-informed financial aid and admissions professionals are always pleased to answer questions and discuss methods of financing higher education with prospective students.

Applicants are considered for merit aid that is based largely on academic achievements and leadership abilities.

Faculty

At Wells, learning takes place in small, seminar-style classes where students are partners with faculty members in the learning process. Starting immediately in their first semester, students take classes with scholars who are recognized experts in their fields, not teaching assistants.

Nearly all Wells professors hold terminal degrees in their areas of expertise. They have been educated at the world's leading research universities, including Harvard, Yale, Columbia, Cornell, Brown, and Stanford. What students discover in Wells' classes is the importance of exploring ideas with others.

Wells is student centered, and academic programs focus on collaborative learning and teaching that meets the needs of students' different learning styles. As one would expect at a nationally recognized liberal arts college, professors are also engaged in research and a full range of scholarly activities. Their books are published by leading academic presses, their articles appear in top journals, and they are a presence at national and international conferences. Due to close faculty-student interaction, students have numerous opportunities to collaborate with faculty members on research, publications, and presentations.

Student Government

The student body is self-governing through the Collegiate Association. The three main governing bodies of the association are the Student-Faculty Administration Board, the Collegiate Council, and the Community Court. Students serve on faculty committees that make decisions concerning administrative and curricular matters.

Leadership development is an inherent part of the Wells experience, and students are encouraged to take an active role in student government and in the life of the campus community.

Admission Requirements

Wells admits students on the basis of the strength of their academic preparation. A student is expected to possess intellectual curiosity, motivation, and maturity to profit from the experience. In all cases, the College seeks students who have followed a solid college-preparatory program throughout high school.

Wells seeks students from varied backgrounds with diverse interests and talents in order to promote a stimulating learning community. Every admissions decision is made on an individual basis.

Wells students share an enthusiasm for academic pursuits and a serious intent to use their education in the future to enhance both their lives and the communities in which they choose to live.

Application and Information

Applications should be received early in the senior year of high school and not later than March 1 of the year in which entrance is desired. Applications from early decision and early action candidates must be received by December 15.

Transfer applications are reviewed on a rolling basis. Transfer students are eligible for merit scholarships and financial aid.

A campus visit is highly recommended for prospective students. For more information about Wells College or to schedule a campus visit, students should contact:

Admissions Office
Wells College
Aurora, New York 13026

Phone: 800-952-9355 (toll-free)
E-mail: admissions@wells.edu
Web site: http://www.wells.edu
　　　　　http://www.facebook.com/wellscollege

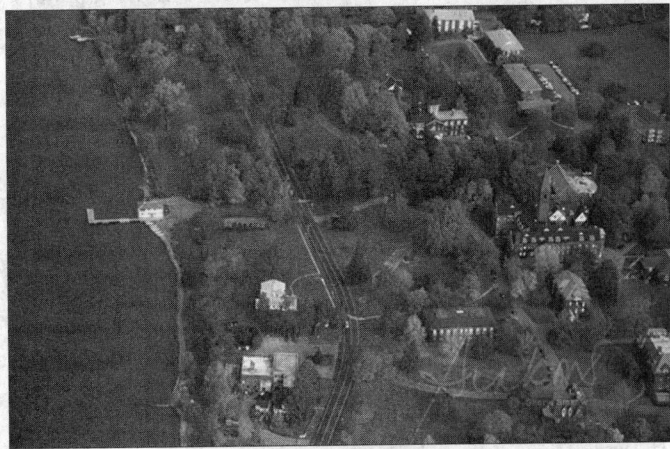

Wells College campus and Cayuga Lake.

WENTWORTH INSTITUTE OF TECHNOLOGY

BOSTON, MASSACHUSETTS

The Institute

Wentworth Institute of Technology was founded in 1904 to provide education in the mechanical arts. Today, Wentworth has a current undergraduate day enrollment of approximately 3,800 men and women (3,400 full-time). The education acquired at Wentworth enables graduates to assume creative and responsible careers in business and industry. Wentworth is located on a 35-acre campus on Huntington Avenue in Boston.

Wentworth provides dormitory and suite-style residence halls on campus for men and women. Students in the residence halls are on a full meal plan. Upperclass students have the option of living in on-campus apartments and students residing in the apartments may prepare their own meals. A cafeteria, snack bar, and convenience store are available for those wishing to purchase their meals.

Career counseling and placement assistance are available to all alumni and to students who have completed at least one semester of study at the Institute. While many graduates of Wentworth are employed in the Boston area, alumni have secured positions throughout the United States and abroad.

Location

Boston is the educational center of New England. It is a city of charm, tradition, and elegance—a major center of art, science, music, history, medicine, and education. Wentworth is situated near the heart of Boston and is surrounded by institutions that provide the cultural advantages for which the city is famous. The Museum of Fine Arts, with its store of art treasures, is diagonally across the street, and admission is free to any student with a Wentworth ID card. Symphony Hall is just a few blocks away. The Harvard Medical School, the New England Conservatory of Music, Emmanuel College, Simmons College, Massachusetts College of Pharmacy and Health Sciences, Massachusetts College of Art and Design, Roxbury Community College, and Northeastern University are among the many educational institutions within a few blocks of the campus.

Majors and Degrees

Degree programs are offered in the fields of architecture, computer science, construction management, design, engineering, engineering technology, and management. Master's degree programs are awarded in architecture and construction management. Bachelor's degrees are awarded in the following majors: the Bachelor of Architecture and the Bachelor of Science in biomedical engineering, civil engineering technology, computer engineering technology, computer network and information systems, computer science, construction management, electromechanical engineering (optional concentration in biomedical systems engineering), electrical engineering, electronic engineering technology, engineering interdisciplinary, facilities planning and management, industrial design, interior design, management (optional concentrations in communication, project leadership, and technology management), mechanical engineering, and mechanical engineering technology. Baccalaureate degrees in architecture and interior design are designated as first professional degrees. Completion of a Wentworth baccalaureate degree usually requires four years (five years for the electromechanical engineering degree).

Academic Programs

At Wentworth, college-level study in technological fundamentals and principles is combined with appropriate laboratory, field,

and studio experience. Students apply theory to practical problems, and they acquire skills and techniques by using, operating, and controlling equipment and instruments that are particular to their area of specialization. In addition, study in the social sciences and humanities provides a balanced understanding of the world in which graduates work. Wentworth's programs of study are more practical than theoretical in approach, and the Institute's academic requirements demand extensive time and effort.

During the first two years of study in a degree program at Wentworth, students lay the foundation for more advanced study in the third and fourth (and fifth, where applicable) years. While nearly all majors allow continuous study from the freshman through the senior year, the architecture major requires a petition for acceptance to the baccalaureate program during the sophomore year.

All bachelor's degree programs are conducted as cooperative (co-op) education programs: upon entering their third year, students alternate semesters of academic study at Wentworth with semester-long periods of employment in industry. Two semesters of co-op employment are required; one additional (summer) semester of co-op is optional. Both students and the companies that hire them are enthusiastic about the co-op program and agree that it is a mutually valuable experience.

Off-Campus Programs

Students have the option to study abroad in Wentworth's established programs in Germany and Ireland. As part of various programs and classes, Wentworth students have also traveled to many destinations, such as Nicaragua, the United Kingdom, Italy, Austria, the Czech Republic, Russia, and throughout Scandinavia.

Wentworth's membership in the Colleges of the Fenway (COF) gives students the intimacy of a small college community and the resources of a major university. The COF consortium members are Emmanuel College, Massachusetts College of Art and Design, Massachusetts College of Pharmacy and Health Sciences, Simmons College, Wentworth Institute of Technology, and Wheelock College. The consortium offers the benefits of cross-registration and access to social events, intramural teams, dance and theater troupes, a chorus and orchestra, professional activities, libraries, and campus facilities at five other colleges within walking distance of one another. The COF's Global Education Opportunities Center provides access to exchange programs and overseas institutions as well as cross-registration for faculty-led travel courses.

Academic Facilities

Wentworth's twenty-seven buildings house classrooms, laboratories, studios, administrative offices, and other facilities. Beatty Hall houses the Alumni Library, computer center, classrooms, dining areas, and office space. State-of-the-art laboratories, such as the Richard H. Lufkin Technology Center and the Davis Center for Advanced Graphics and Interactive Learning, are situated throughout the campus.

Costs

For 2011–12, tuition is $24,000, books and supplies are approximately $1000, and the average room and board are about $11,300 (this figure varies according to accommodation). Tuition includes a brand new laptop that is outfitted with the complete suite of software used in the student's academic program.

Financial Aid

Scholarships are available to students who demonstrate need and academic promise. Merit-based scholarships are also available. Wentworth also provides federal and state financial assistance, such as Federal Pell and Federal Supplemental Educational Opportunity Grants, Federal Perkins Loans, Federal Work-Study Program awards, Gilbert Matching Grants, and Massachusetts No-Interest Loans, to students with financial need in accordance with federal and state guidelines.

Wentworth participates in the Federal Direct Lending program. As a result, students are eligible to borrow under the Federal Direct Stafford Student Loan program and parents may borrow under the Federal Direct PLUS program. Individuals participating in these programs borrow money directly from the federal government rather than through lending institutions.

In addition to these need-based programs, Wentworth also participates in the MEFA loan program sponsored by the Massachusetts Educational Financing Authority. Wentworth offers several payment options through payment plans and alternative loan financing.

To apply for financial aid, new students should complete the Free Application for Federal Student Aid (FAFSA) by March 1. Applications received after this date are considered as funds allow.

Faculty

Wentworth's faculty includes 146 full-time and 123 part-time members. The primary responsibility of every faculty member is teaching. Although professors may engage in some research and related work, student development remains the central mission of Wentworth's faculty. Upon entering Wentworth, every student is assigned a faculty adviser.

Student Government

Wentworth's Student Government performs an essential function as the official representative of the student body. Its purposes are to receive and express student opinion, to advance the best interests of the student body with the administration and faculty and with other institutions and associations, to support all extracurricular activities of the student body, and to serve as a bond between the student body and the faculty to foster cooperation and understanding. The Student Government is made up of elected representatives from each class section and the officers elected by the student body at large. The Student Government sponsors social functions and student organizations and serves as an advocate for student concerns.

Admission Requirements

Applicants must be graduates of secondary schools (or have passed the GED test) and must meet specific entrance requirements. All programs require four years of English, a laboratory science, and mathematics through algebra II in a college-preparatory program. Both the electromechanical engineering and the computer science programs require a background in precalculus or trigonometry. All programs require the submission of SAT or ACT scores. International students and transfers are welcome.

Application and Information

Students are admitted to Wentworth for September and January enrollment. Notification of admission is made on a rolling basis. The preferred method for applying is online at http://www. wit.edu/apply. The online application fee is $50. An application form, the application fee, transcripts from the secondary school and any colleges previously attended, SAT or ACT scores, a personal statement, and a letter of recommendation should be sent to:

Admissions Office
Wentworth Institute of Technology
550 Huntington Avenue
Boston, Massachusetts 02115
Phone: 617-989-4000
       800-556-0610 (toll-free)
Fax: 617-989-4010
E-mail: admissions@wit.edu
Web site: http://www.wit.edu
      http://twitter.com/WITadmissions

Wentworth Hall.

WESLEYAN COLLEGE

MACON, GEORGIA

The College

Wesleyan College, chartered in 1836, has the distinction of being the world's first college chartered to grant degrees to women. Today, Wesleyan is still dedicated to the education of women and is regarded as one of the nation's finest liberal arts colleges. According to the seventh annual report of the National Survey of Student Engagement (NSSE), Wesleyan outperformed the top 10 percent of colleges and universities in all five categories studied: active and collaborative learning, enriching educational experiences, level of academic challenge, student-faculty interaction, and supportive campus environment.

Wesleyan is a four-year liberal arts college affiliated with the United Methodist Church. Enrollment is limited to fewer than 1,000 students, primarily to support a learner-based curriculum that limits classes to no more than 20 students and to provide opportunities for meaningful participation in the life of the College community. Wesleyan's student body has been cited as among the nation's most diverse. Students from across the U.S. and almost twenty other countries value a rigorous academic program renowned for its high quality. A student-faculty ratio of 10:1 ensures that each student is more than just a grade or a number. The acceptance rate of Wesleyan students into medical, law, business, and other graduate programs is exemplary.

Beyond the academic, Wesleyan offers a thriving residence life program, NCAA Division III athletics, a championship IHSA equestrian program, and meaningful opportunities for community involvement and leadership. The College's beautiful 200-acre wooded campus, along with thirty historically significant buildings, is listed in the National Register of Historic Places as the Wesleyan College Historic District. Beautiful, white-columned Georgian-style buildings surround a classic quadrangle that plays host to many College events. Some residence halls offer single rooms and suites. On-campus apartment-style living is available for upperclass women. Approximately 90 percent of the students reside on campus.

An equestrian center, athletic complex (with fitness center, tennis courts, track, and lighted softball and soccer fields), gymnasium with a heated pool, lake with a jogging trail, and a recently renovated arboretum complete the campus offerings.

Most of the extracurricular activities of Wesleyan's students are coordinated through Activity Councils. The Campus Activities Board plans concert-dance weekends, events with nearby colleges, international fashion shows, holiday trips, and special dinners. The Student Recreation Council coordinates competitive activities in basketball, fencing, golf, soccer, softball, swimming, among others. Wesleyan is a member of the National Collegiate Athletic Association (NCAA) Division III. There are intercollegiate basketball, cross-country, soccer, softball, tennis, volleyball, and IHSA equestrian teams. The Council on Religious Concerns encourages religious life on campus and sponsors activities that involve students with community life. Students volunteer at local institutions such as the Georgia Industrial Children's Home, Macon Outreach, the Methodist Children's Home, and neighborhood schools and churches. They also participate in interest clubs, student publications, performing arts groups, honor societies, and professional fraternities. A number of College traditions are perpetuated by spirited but friendly competition among the four classes.

Location

Wesleyan is located in a suburb of the beautiful, historic city of Macon, Georgia, the third-largest city in the state. Macon is the cultural, educational, medical, and economic leader of middle Georgia and is located about an hour's drive south of Atlanta. The city of Macon offers varied entertainment and many cultural opportunities, including the Georgia Music and Sports Halls of Fame. Visits by nationally and internationally acclaimed speakers and a series of popular and classical concerts are held on the Wesleyan campus each year, as are special events associated with Macon's renowned Cherry Blossom Festival.

Majors and Degrees

Wesleyan offers undergraduate degrees in twenty-nine majors and twenty-six minors; self-designed majors and interdisciplinary

programs; and eight preprofessional programs: dental, engineering, allied health services, law, medicine, pharmacy, seminary, and veterinary medicine. The Master of Education and an accelerated Executive Master of Business Administration programs enroll both men and women. Wesleyan also offers a dual-degree program in engineering with the Georgia Institute of Technology in Atlanta; Auburn University in Auburn, Alabama; and Mercer University in Macon.

The Bachelor of Arts (A.B.) is offered in accounting, advertising and marketing communication, art history, biology, business administration, chemistry, computer information systems, communication, economics, education (early childhood), educational studies, English, environmental studies, French, history, human services (family services or management concentration), international business, international relations, mathematics, music (performance emphasis—piano, organ, and voice), neuroscience, philosophy, political science, psychology, religious studies, Spanish, studio art, theater, and women's studies. In addition to these majors, the following academic concentrations are offered as minors: accounting, art history, biology, business management, chemistry, communication, economics, educational studies, environmental studies, English, finance, French, history, mathematics, music, neuroscience, philosophy, photography, physics, political science, psychology, religious studies, Spanish, studio art, technology in business administration, theater, and women's studies. Self-designed interdisciplinary majors are also available.

Students may elect to pursue their academic or professional interests through a double major, a major in combination with a minor program of studies, an interdisciplinary major, or an independently developed program of studies.

Wesleyan's dual-degree program in engineering is offered in cooperation with Georgia Institute of Technology, Auburn University, and Mercer University. Three years of study at Wesleyan and two years of study at Georgia Tech, Auburn, or Mercer lead to an A.B. degree from Wesleyan and a B.S. degree from the other institution. Wesleyan's traditional undergraduate programs for women are complemented by a growing number of day, evening, and certificate programs for non-traditional students seeking a flexible schedule.

Academic Programs

The College's goal is to prepare students for a lifetime of learning. Each major program contains general education requirements for breadth of learning and major field requirements for career and/or graduate school preparation. Degree programs require completion of 120 semester hours with a cumulative average of C (2.0) or better.

Wesleyan provides a challenging academic environment coupled with individualized attention. Each student is assisted by a faculty adviser, a preprofessional or career adviser, and a peer counselor in the selection of academic and internship experiences that lead to intellectual and career fulfillment. All classes are offered in a seminar style, with an emphasis on interactive or participatory learning. Each student has a research or internship experience.

Each entering full-time student is able to utilize information technology toward the enhancement of learning and career preparation is central to the academic program. The networked campus is connected to the Internet, which gives each student access to a world of information from her residence hall. Many common academic areas offer wireless Internet access.

Credit by examination and exemption from required courses are possible with acceptable scores on the Advanced Placement (AP), International Baccalaureate (I.B.), Cambridge International Examinations (CIE), and College-Level Examination Program (CLEP) tests or acceptable grades in high school–college joint enrollment courses. Students may also exempt courses by taking departmental examinations. Thirty semester hours of credit is the maximum a student can receive by exemption through AP, I.B., CIE, CLEP, or departmental exams.

The College operates on an early semester plan. First-semester classes begin in late August and end in early December. The second semester begins in earlyJanuary and ends with graduation in early May. Wesleyan offers an optional May term and summer school sessions.

Off-Campus Programs

Through Wesleyan's International Study Abroad and Exchange Program, students can study abroad for one full year, one semester, a May term, or a summer session. Through cooperative agreements with the Institute for the International Education of Students (IES), National Student Exchange (NSE), and Business Education Initiative (BEI) students may study abroad in Argentina, Australia, Austria, China, France, Germany, Great Britain, Japan, Russia, Spain, and other countries. In addition, Wesleyan has direct exchange agreements with Sookmyung Women's University (South Korea), Osaka University (Japan), Ewha Women's University (South Korea), Ulyanovsk State University (Russia), and various schools in Northern Ireland.

Off-campus opportunities are available through the internship program, which places students with area businesses, community agencies, health organizations, arts groups, and the media. Summer internships can be arranged in other locations. Academic credit for off-campus experiences varies.

Academic Facilities

Willet Memorial Library offers a variety of print and electronic resources to support student research and the College's curriculum. The core collection includes more than 143,000 volumes plus subscriptions to 615 periodicals. There are 33,438 items in microform and 4,267 tapes and records. Through the library's participation in GALILEO, students have access to more than 150 bibliographic and full-text databases. The library has informal study areas, individual carrels, seminar rooms, and two smart classrooms. The Georgia Room houses 4,500 rare volumes and treasures of Americana.

The Porter Fine Arts Building serves as a cultural center for the campus and community. It houses the music and theater departments, and, in addition to classrooms, offices, and studios, it contains two art galleries and a studio theater. Its Porter Auditorium has a seating capacity of 1,200 and contains one of the largest pipe organs in the Southeast. Tate Hall contains classrooms for the Humanities and Social and Behavioral Sciences divisions. Taylor Hall houses the Education, Business, and Psychology divisions and offers new classroom spaces. The art department is located in a 10,000-square-foot building designed exclusively for teaching the studio arts.

The new Munroe Science Center, opened in 2007, is a state-of-the-art science facility that serves the increasing number of Wesleyan students enrolled and majoring in biology and chemistry. It also addresses the great need throughout the nation for women skilled in medicine, scientific research, and mathematics. Through its eleven teaching laboratories and nine research laboratories, the new facility encourages faculty/student collaboration on research projects, contains interactive laboratories for specific experimentation, and offers individualized instruction in an environmentally efficient and safe setting. State-of-the-art laboratories include cell biology, ecology, physiology, immunology, and instrumental analysis labs as well as general biology, physics, and chemistry labs. Although teaching laboratories serve as classrooms, a small seminar room and two technologically advanced classrooms also are used for instruction. Specialty science spaces include an astronomy observation deck, a greenhouse, a vivarium, an environmental room, and a community learning center.

Costs

Tuition for 2011–12 is $18,500. Room and board cost $8200. Students should also keep in mind the additional cost of books, supplies, travel, and personal expenses.

Financial Aid

Students seeking financial assistance are required to submit the Free Application for Federal Student Aid (FAFSA). Any student who demonstrates financial need is qualified for some type of assistance.

Wesleyan offers scholarships to incoming first-year students on the basis of academic ability, leadership, or special talents. Transfer scholarships are available based on cumulative grade point average and hours earned. Minimum requirements are a 3.0 GPA and 30 semester hours or 45 quarter hours.

Wesleyan participates in the Federal Perkins Loan, Federal Pell Grant, Federal Supplemental Educational Opportunity Grant, Federal Work-Study, and Federal Family Education Loan programs. Any Georgia resident who wishes to attend a private college in the state and has at least a B average may apply for the Georgia Tuition Equalization Grant and HOPE Grant. Georgia Student Incentive Grants are also available, as are certain loans, other scholarships, and part-time employment. Approximately 85 percent of students receive financial assistance.

Faculty

The academic program at Wesleyan is guided by an exceptionally able, dedicated, and caring faculty. There are 50 full-time faculty members; 99 percent have earned doctoral or terminal degrees. The student-faculty ratio is 10:1. No courses are ever taught by graduate assistants. Faculty members serve as academic advisers and help students plan their academic program. Many professors participate in extracurricular activities with students on campus.

Student Government

Wesleyan's Student Government Association (SGA) represents the student body. Students elect representatives to serve on Senate, which is the legislative body. SGA emphasizes responsibility and order; supports an active liberal arts environment; and contributes to cocurricular life at the College, development of leadership, and responsible citizenship, all in conjunction with Student Affairs. The College also offers more than forty student clubs and organizations.

Admission Requirements

Applicants to Wesleyan must submit a completed application with a $30 application fee (fee is waived for online applications), official academic transcripts, official SAT or ACT scores, an evaluation written by a teacher, a recommendation from a guidance counselor or principal, and an essay. The completion of a minimum of 16 academic course units in a secondary school is required. Wesleyan feels that a campus visit is extremely beneficial, and visitors can be full participants in campus activities. An interview is strongly recommended. Applications from transfer and international students are welcome. Credit for work below a grade of C cannot be transferred, and a minimum score of 80 (Internet-based test), 550 (paper-based), or 213 (computer-based) on the Test of English as Foreign Language (TOEFL) or an International English Language Testing System (IELTS) score of 6.0 with no subscore below 5.0 is required of international students. Wesleyan accepts qualified students without regard to race, religion, national or ethnic origin, age, sexual orientation, or disability.

Application and Information

Admission to Wesleyan is selective. For additional information, students should contact:

Wesleyan College Admission
4760 Forsyth Road
Macon, Georgia 31210
Phone: 478-757-5206
      800-447-6610 (toll-free)
E-mail: admission@wesleyancollege.edu
Web site: http://www.wesleyancollege.edu
      http://on.fb.me/Wesleyan_Coll_adm (Facebook)

Wesleyan has the distinction of being the world's first college chartered to grant degrees to women.

WESLEY COLLEGE

DOVER, DELAWARE

The College

Wesley College, the oldest private college in Delaware, is a fully accredited, coeducational, comprehensive liberal arts institution.

Nestled in a quiet, historic residential community, Wesley College is affiliated with the United Methodist Church, with an enrollment of more than 2,300 full- and part-time students, mostly representing the mid-Atlantic region. The average class size is 17 students, and the student-faculty ratio, 17:1.

The Wesley residence community is made up of seven buildings. Each building has special characteristics that make it unique. The facilities, including two apartment-style and suite-style housing facilities, are all air conditioned, and all rooms offer Internet access. The purpose of the Residence Program is to enhance the academic mission of Wesley by providing educational and social experiences outside the classroom to help develop contributing members of society.

Each building has a Resident Director and assistant. Student staff members are selected and trained and live on each floor to provide additional resources to their peers. The living arrangement in each hall enables students to get to know one another well and to develop close-knit relationships. Students come from all over the United States and overseas, providing the opportunity to meet and live with people from diverse backgrounds.

Wesley is a member of NCAA Division III intercollegiate athletics and the Capital Athletic Conference. Men have teams in baseball, basketball, cross-country running, football, golf, lacrosse, soccer, tennis, and track and field. Women compete in basketball, cheerleading, cross-country running, field hockey, golf, lacrosse, soccer, softball, tennis, track and field, and volleyball. A well-organized intramural program offers a wide variety of athletic competitions, including, but not limited to, basketball, flag football, soccer, and volleyball. In addition, the College offers a men's club ice hockey program.

In addition to its undergraduate degrees, Wesley College awards the Master of Business Administration (M.B.A.); Master of Science (M.S.) in environmental science; Master of Education (M.Ed.) in curriculum and instruction; Master of Arts (M.A.) in curriculum and instruction; Master of Arts in Teaching (M.A.T), initial certificate; and the Master of Science in Nursing (M.S.N.) degrees.

Location

Dover is the capital of the country's first state and has approximately 35,000 residents. New York City, Baltimore, Philadelphia, and Washington, D.C., are within a 2- to 3-hour drive of the campus. The College is located within Dover's major residential community, with stores and banks within easy walking distance and malls a short commute away.

Seafood is a specialty in Dover because of the city's proximity to the Delaware and Chesapeake Bays and to the Atlantic Ocean. Delaware Transit Corporation (DART) provides bus service throughout the city of Dover. Daily bus service is available to and from the campus. In addition, Delaware's famous beaches are also within easy driving distance of the campus.

Many students become involved in local activities, including volunteer work at private and public agencies. On-campus volunteer activities include a unique partnership between a state-funded elementary and secondary charter school (Campus Community Schools) and the College. Many students are employed in community businesses through the cooperative education program at Wesley. Others work in part-time jobs to earn extra money. Many local residents also attend Wesley on a part-time basis and enjoy full use of the College's facilities.

Majors and Degrees

Bachelor of Arts and Bachelor of Science degrees are awarded in accounting, American studies, biological chemistry, biology, business administration, education (K–8), English, environmental studies, history, international studies, kinesiology: exercise science, kinesiology: sports management, legal studies, liberal studies, mathematics, media arts, medical technology, nursing, physical education (K–12), political science, and psychology.

Academic Programs

The comprehensive academic calendar year consists of two semesters and a double summer session. Winter sessions are available in England and France, offering unique opportunities for travel and study.

Bachelor's degree candidates begin with the foundation core curriculum, which emphasizes an overarching theme of the individual in a global community. Interdisciplinary threads bind the core curriculum and the major programs into a purposeful design. These threads are critical thinking, communication across disciplines, technological literacy, multicultural awareness, aesthetic appreciation, and ethical sensibility. The core provides a distinctive undergraduate experience for students, establishes coherent links between the curricular and cocurricular programs, and provides community service options beyond the College campus.

Academic Facilities

The Robert H. Parker Library provides for both individual and group study in its several large reading rooms and smaller study areas. It contains a book collection and extensive video collection to support the academic program. The library houses the Office of Academic Support Services, the Writing Center, the Office of Information Systems, faculty offices, classrooms, and a computer lab. Students also have access to the Dover Public Library and Delaware State University Library.

Costs

For 2010–11, Wesley's tuition and fees were $20,580 per year. Room and board costs ranged from $9550 to $13,300 per year. Books and supplies cost about $2000 per year.

Financial Aid

Financial aid is available in the form of endowed scholarships, federal scholarships, grants, work-study programs, and loans. Approximately 90 percent of Wesley students receive financial aid. Wesley uses the Free Application for Federal Student Aid (FAFSA). Students and their families are urged to complete and send their FAFSA as early as possible. Financial aid awards must be confirmed by the student within fifteen days of notification.

Wesley College provides numerous academic scholarships to its top undergraduate students. Applications for these awards are not required. Interested seniors should contact the Office of Admissions.

Faculty

Wesley College emphasizes teaching. More than 80 percent of faculty members hold a doctoral or other terminal degree in their subject area and attend workshops and conferences to keep abreast of current activities in their fields. Most faculty members serve as academic advisers to students. All have regularly scheduled office hours and are available for student conferences on a regular basis.

Student Government

Student leadership develops through various aspects of College governance. Student representatives work in close cooperation with faculty members and administrators.

Admission Requirements

Many factors are considered in the selection of a Wesley student. The most important are the applicant's secondary school courses and grades, along with the required SAT or ACT scores. On-campus interviews are strongly recommended. Secondary school recommendations are also important. International students should submit their applications for admission by February 1 for the following fall semester. Admission decisions are made without regard to race, religion, color, age, gender, handicap, or national origin. Applicants should have 16 secondary school units in English, social studies, laboratory science, mathematics, and electives.

Students, parents, and counselors are welcome to contact the Office of Admissions for information and assistance.

Wesley College reserves the right to change some or all rates, policies, or courses when necessary, without prior notice.

Application and Information

Secondary school records should be attached to the Wesley College application form. Copies of official school records may also be submitted via fax.

To schedule an admissions interview and campus tour, students should call the Office of Admissions. A College prospectus, application form, and financial aid information are available by contacting:

Arthur T. Jacobs Sr.
Director of Admissions
Wesley College
120 North State Street
Dover, Delaware 19901
Phone: 302-736-2400
       800-937-5398 Ext. 2400 (toll-free)
Fax: 302-736-2382
E-mail: admissions@wesley.edu
Web site: http://www.wesley.edu

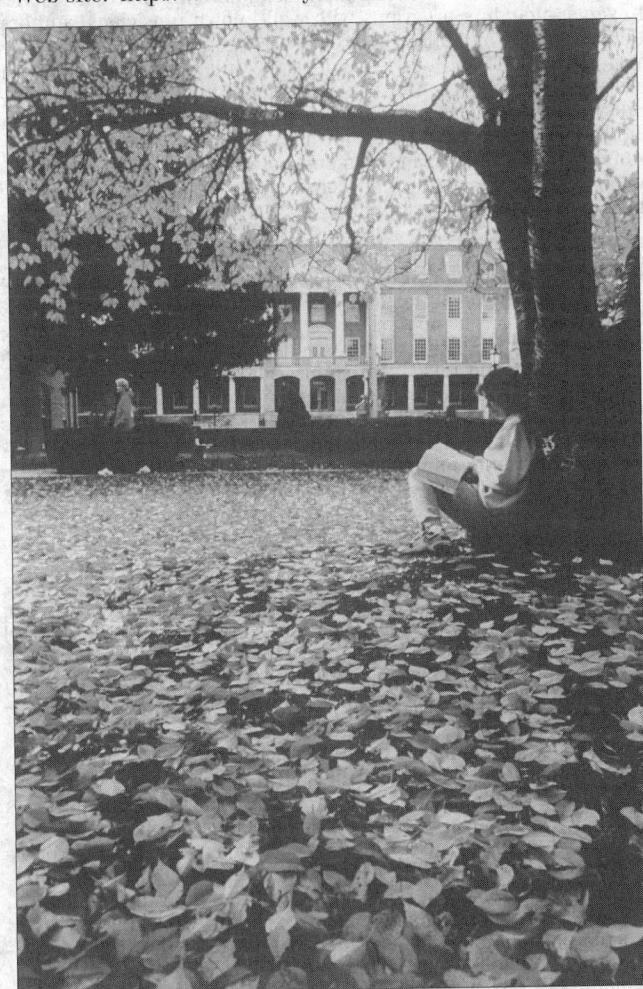

A student relaxes in the beautiful surroundings of Wesley College.

WEST CHESTER UNIVERSITY OF PENNSYLVANIA
WEST CHESTER, PENNSYLVANIA

The University

West Chester University of Pennsylvania (WCU) is the second largest of the fourteen institutions in the Pennsylvania State System of Higher Education and the fourth-largest university in the Philadelphia metropolitan area. Officially founded in 1871, the University traces its heritage to the West Chester Academy, which existed from 1812 to 1869. The University's 402-acre campus has well-maintained facilities, including nine residence halls and two garden-style apartment complexes, plus a new performing arts center. In keeping with West Chester's rich heritage, the University's Quadrangle buildings, part of the original campus, are on the National Register of Historic Places.

While the University attracts the majority of its students from Pennsylvania, New Jersey, and Delaware, it also enrolls many students from other areas across the United States and from more than fifty countries. The undergraduate enrollment includes approximately 11,920 women and men.

Each year, the University community schedules an impressive series of events, including programs with well-known musicians, authors, political figures, and others. More than 210 campus groups in music, theater, athletics, and other activities, as well as clubs, fraternities, sororities, service organizations, and honor societies, provide students with the opportunity to participate in a full range of programs. The University offers twenty-four intercollegiate sports and twenty-four club sports for men and women. In addition to the facilities in the health and physical education complex, the University has a field house and a gymnasium for varsity sports.

Location

The University is located in West Chester, a community in southeastern Pennsylvania that is strategically located at the center of the mid-Atlantic corridor. The seat of Chester County government for more than two centuries, West Chester retains much of its historical charm in its buildings and unspoiled countryside, yet it offers the twenty-first-century advantages of a town in the heart of a thriving suburban area. West Chester is just 25 miles west of Philadelphia and 17 miles north of Wilmington, Delaware, putting the libraries, museums, cultural resources, entertainment, and historical sites of both cities within easy reach. It is also only 2 hours from New York City and 3 hours from Washington, D.C.

Majors and Degrees

The Bachelor of Arts is offered in American studies, anthropology, art, biology, communication studies, communicative disorders, English, French, geography–geographic analysis, geography–urban/regional planning, German, history, Latin, liberal studies, literature, mathematics, philosophy, political science, political science–international relations, political science–applied public policy, psychology, Russian, sociology, Spanish, theater arts, and women's studies.

The Bachelor of Science is offered in accounting, athletic training, biochemistry, biology, biology–cell and molecular biology, biology–ecology, biology–medical technology, biology–microbiology, business management, chemistry, chemistry–biology (premed), computer science, criminal justice, economics, exercise science, finance, forensic and toxicological chemistry, geoscience–earth systems, geoscience–environmental, geosciences–geology, health and physical education, health science–general, health science–respiratory care, liberal studies–science and mathematics, liberal studies–professional studies, marketing, mathematics, nutrition and dietetics, pharmaceutical product development, physics, physics–engineering, public health–environmental, and public health–health promotion.

The Bachelor of Science in Nursing, the Bachelor of Fine Arts (studio arts), the Bachelor of Music (music education, performance, theory and composition, studies in an outside field), and the Bachelor of Social Work degrees are also offered.

The Bachelor of Science in Education degree is offered in biology, chemistry, communication–media, communication–speech, communication–theatre emphasis, early childhood education, earth-space science–astronomy, earth-space science–geology, elementary education, English, mathematics, physics, and special education.

Paraprofessional studies are available in medicine. Also available are early admission assurance programs with Drexel School of Medicine, Pennsylvania State University College of Medicine, Temple University School of Medicine, Temple University School of Dentistry, and Arcadia University Physician Assistant Program. In cooperation with Pennsylvania State University, West Chester University offers a 3-2 dual-degree program combining liberal arts, physics, and engineering. A similar, dual degree cooperative physics/engineering program is available through affiliation with the School of Engineering and Textiles of Philadelphia University. As a member of the State System of Higher Education (PASSHE), special admission opportunities for scholarships to the Widener School of Law–Harrisburg Campus are also available.

Teacher certification programs are available in biology, chemistry, communications, early childhood education, elementary education, English, French, general science, German, health and physical education, Latin, mathematics, music education, physics, Russian, secondary education, social studies, Spanish, and special education. Certificates are also available in adapted physical education, athletic training, biology–medical technology, education for sustainability, and Russian studies.

Interdisciplinary areas of study include computer security certificate, ethnic studies, Honors College, Latin American studies, and Russian studies. Minors are available in most majors and in several interdisciplinary areas. The University also offers ROTC programs with cross-enrollment agreement with Widener University for Army ROTC and with St. Joseph's University for Air Force ROTC.

Academic Programs

West Chester University is a comprehensive institution now in its second century. The University comprises the College of Arts and Sciences, the College of Business and Public Affairs, the College of Education, the College of Health Sciences, and the College of Visual and Performing Arts. It operates on a two-semester basis; summer sessions are available.

An honors program is available to qualified students for both upper and lower division study; internships and field experiences, self-designed majors, and independent study are also offered. A variety of credit-by-examination programs are available.

Off-Campus Programs

Through the Study Abroad Program, students may spend one or more semesters in countries such as England, Italy, France, Australia, Spain, and Ireland. West Chester also sponsors a number of annual courses that include study abroad during spring, summer, and winter breaks.

West Chester University participates in the National Student Exchange Program, in which students spend up to a year at any one of more than 170 member schools across the United States, broadening their cultural and academic horizons. Automatic transfer of credit is arranged.

Academic Facilities

There are two libraries on campus: the Francis Harvey Green Library and the Presser Music Library. Library collections include more than 1,790,000 print and electronic volumes; 2,300 print journals; 934,000 microforms; 46,000 sound recordings; 9,600 films, videos, and DVDs; 3,500 maps; and Internet access to more than 150 databases; and the full-text from more than 48,000 journals. Unique digital collections include University graduate and undergraduate catalogs, 1874 to date; title pages and autographs from the Philips Autograph Library; the letters of General Anthony Wayne; and historic postcards. Services include free interlibrary loan, electronic and print reserves, more than ninety public computer workstations, twenty laptops for use in the library, and a Starbucks coffee shop.

The University's extensive computer facilities include more than 750 PC and Macintosh workstations that are available to students in more than forty computer labs. Many of the buildings and exteriors are wireless zones and Internet access is available in residence halls and computer labs. The University has Braille printers, translators, and speech synthesizers for its visually impaired students. Students can use the computing facilities 16 hours a day.

The Merion Science Center, with modern multimedia lecture halls, extensive laboratories, and study areas where students can work together, connects to the Schmucker Science Center, which houses a fully equipped observatory and planetarium. The Center's extensive laboratories have a variety of advanced instruments such as a single-side band microscope—the world's second—as well as field inversion electrophoresis equipment for DNA analysis, and equipment for RFLP, PCR and DNA sequencing. The GIS computer lab has a first-order community base station and mobile GPS units to support coursework in geography, marketing and other subjects. Undergraduates have hands-on access to this equipment, as well as automated spectrophotometers, electron analytical equipment, atomic absorption spectrometers, and a variety of chromatographs, including gas chromatograph–mass spectrometers.

The campus includes a 100-acre natural area for environmental studies; speech and hearing and reading clinics; two theaters; music facilities with practice, rehearsal, and listening rooms; a large, health and physical education complex that houses a gymnasium and a natatorium with two pool areas and a diving well; dance studios; research laboratories; physical therapy rooms; saunas; and a health resource center.

West Chester University is committed to providing barrier-free facilities for persons with impaired mobility.

Costs

West Chester University provides a high-quality education at an affordable cost. Full-time undergraduate students who are legal residents of Pennsylvania paid $5804 for annual tuition for 12 to 18 semester hours in 2010–11. For more than 18 semester hours or fewer than 12, the cost was $242 per semester hour. Out-of-state students paid $14,510 per year for 12 to 18 semester hours and $605 per semester hour for more than 18 or fewer than 12. Room and board were $7372 per year for on-campus residents in University-owned residence halls. Student fees were $1486 per year, plus a technology fee of $232 for in-state students and $350 for out-of-state students. Tuition is determined by the state.

Financial Aid

The financial aid available to students includes work-study programs, grants, loans, special awards, and scholarships. A limited number of merit scholarships are awarded based on the student's academic standing and accomplishments in high school. Students who qualify are invited to apply. About 70 percent of all full-time undergraduate students receive some form of aid.

Faculty

West Chester University has a faculty of approximately 700 members. The majority hold doctoral degrees, and many are engaged in research and serve as consultants in their field of expertise. The student-faculty ratio is 18:1.

Student Government

The Student Governmental Association represents all students on the West Chester campus. In addition, the Residence Hall Association represents resident students, and the Off Campus and Commuter Association represents commuting students.

Admission Requirements

Applicants to West Chester University are evaluated on the basis of scholarship, character, and potential for achievement. The requirements for freshman admission consideration include graduation from an approved secondary school or a General Educational Development (GED) certificate from an approved agency; satisfactory scores on either the SAT, ACT, or TOEFL (for international applicants); and completion of a personal statement. Transfer applicants must have a minimum cumulative grade point average of 2.0 for admissions consideration. Certain academic programs may require an interview or specific course prerequisites. The University does have several other admissions options such as early admission and special admissions programs, including ACT 101. Based on the scores received on Advanced Placement (AP) tests and subject examinations administered through the College-Level Examination Program (CLEP), students may receive advanced placement or credit.

Application and Information

Students are admitted for the fall or spring semester. Freshman applicants for the fall semester are urged to begin the application procedure at the start of their senior year in high school. Transfers should begin the process beginning in January for the fall semester. Applicants for the spring semester should apply by November 1. International students must apply by March 1 for the fall semester and September 1 for the spring semester. The University operates on a modified rolling admission policy; applicants with the strongest qualifications are given priority, and their applications are processed expeditiously. Students are encouraged to visit WCU's campus. To arrange a visit or to attend an information session, students may call the Office of Admissions. For updated information or directions, students should visit the University's Web site.

For additional information and required forms, students may contact:

Office of Admissions
Emil J. Messikomer Hall
West Chester University of Pennsylvania
100 West Rosedale Avenue
West Chester, Pennsylvania 19383

Phone: 610-436-3411
   877-315-2165 (toll-free)
E-mail: ugadmiss@wcupa.edu
Web site: http://www.wcupa.edu
   http://www.facebook.com/WCUPA
   http://twitter.com/WCUofPA
   http://www.youtube.com/user/WCUofPA

A view of the west side of the Quadrangle at West Chester University.

WESTERN CONNECTICUT STATE UNIVERSITY

DANBURY, CONNECTICUT

The University

Founded in 1903, Western Connecticut State University (West-Conn) is dedicated to providing both a high-quality university education and a memorable campus experience at an affordable cost. With programs in the arts and sciences, business, and professional studies, WestConn takes pride in providing an outstanding education to more than 4,500 full-time undergraduates and nearly 2,000 graduate or part-time students.

WestConn offers excellent educational programs through five academic units: the Ancell School of Business, the School of Arts and Sciences, the School of Professional Studies, the School of Visual and Performing Arts, and the Division of Graduate Studies and External Programs. The most popular majors include communication, theater arts, education, business, justice and law administration, music, and nursing.

In addition to the University's full menu of undergraduate degrees, the Ancell School of Business offers the Master of Business Administration, Master of Health Administration, and Master of Science in justice administration. The School of Arts and Sciences offers the Master of Arts in biological and environmental sciences, earth and planetary sciences, English, history, and mathematics; the Master of Fine Arts is offered in professional writing. The School of Professional Studies offers the Master of Science in counselor education, elementary education, nursing, and secondary education; also offered is WestConn's Doctor of Education (Ed.D.) in instructional leadership. Prelaw and pre–health professions programs also are available. West-Conn's newly formed School of Visual and Performing Arts offers the Master of Fine Arts in visual arts and the Master of Music Education.

The University also is rich with a number of learning and social activities beyond the classroom. Students run academic and fraternal organizations, publish an award-winning newspaper and yearbook, and run a radio station. They stage theater and musical productions, participate in cooperative education and internship programs, and administer their own campus government association.

The University provides services for learning-disabled students, study abroad, a University Scholars program, precollegiate and access initiatives, international student services, and community service learning opportunities. A variety of NCAA Division III men's and women's sports are represented on campus, and students enjoy intramural sports and a premier recreation center that includes a swimming pool, an indoor track, and weight-lifting machines. The campus also features a child-care center, a counseling center, a health services office, a career development center, and campus ministries.

WestConn is accredited by the New England Association of Schools and Colleges; the Board of Governors for Higher Education, State of Connecticut; the Connecticut State Department of Education; the American Chemical Society; the Commission on Collegiate Nursing Education; the Council on Social Work Education (baccalaureate level); the Council for Accreditation of Counseling and Related Educational Programs; and the National Association of Schools of Music.

Location

WestConn offers two campuses in Danbury, in the heart of western Connecticut, as well as a satellite campus in Waterbury.

Danbury is a major city in Fairfield County in the foothills of the Berkshire Mountains, just 65 miles north of Manhattan and 50 miles west of Hartford.

In Danbury, the Midtown campus is a 34-acre, fifteen-building campus with an interesting mix of old and new architecture, and it offers easy access to downtown entertainment, restaurants, and shopping. The 364-acre Westside campus is ideal for hikers and nature buffs who want to discover its woodland wonders while enjoying state-of-the-art facilities. The WestConn-at-Waterbury campus offers a convenient location closer to the center of the state, with the same level of excellent service.

Majors and Degrees

The Ancell School of Business offers the Bachelor of Business Administration in accounting, finance, management, management information systems, and marketing, as well as the Bachelor of Science in justice and law administration.

The School of Arts and Sciences offers the Associate in Science, Bachelor of Arts, and Bachelor of Science degrees. The Associate in Science is offered in liberal arts. The Bachelor of Arts is offered in American studies, anthropology/sociology, biology, chemistry, communication, computer science, earth and planetary sciences–astronomy, economics, English, English–professional writing, history, mathematics, political science, psychology, social sciences, and Spanish. The Bachelor of Science is offered in medical technology and meteorology.

The School of Professional Studies offers the Bachelor of Arts and Bachelor of Science degrees. The Bachelor of Arts is offered in social work. The Bachelor of Science is offered in elementary education, health education, health promotion studies, nursing, and secondary education.

The School of Visual and Performing Arts offers the Bachelor of Arts, Bachelor of Science, and Bachelor of Music degrees. The Bachelor of Arts is offered in art, music, and theater arts. The Bachelor of Science is offered in music education, and the Bachelor of Music is offered with options in classical: voice or instrument or in jazz studies. Auditions are required for entrance into any of the music degree options.

Academic Programs

The University has developed a diverse mix of programs that are designed to inspire students. From the enlightening category of the arts to specialized fields of education, the emphasis is on the individual student's learning experience.

Special offerings at WestConn include the nation's first program in computer information security management and the only licensed meteorology program in Connecticut.

Academic Facilities

A number of facilities contribute to academic life on campus. The newly renovated and expanded library holds more than 200,000 volumes and over 400,000 bound periodicals, microforms, government documents, music scores, electronic resources, and audiovisual items. WestConn's extraordinary Science Building opened in 2005 to great acclaim for its ecology-friendly green design and cutting-edge lab and classroom equipment. Students are also encouraged to make use of West-Conn's exceptional computer laboratory facilities and are invited to hone their craft in superior theater and musical facilities. Along with the rest of the greater Danbury community, they benefit from the offerings of the WestConn International Center;

German Studies Center; Institute for Holistic Health Studies; Meteorological Studies and Weather Center; Jane Goodall Center for Excellence in Environmental Studies; Center for Collaboration; Center for Business Research; Center for Excellence in Learning and Teaching; Center for Excellence in the Study of Culture and Values; Center for Galactic Astronomy; Center for Graphics Research; Center for Professional Development; Center for Technology, Research, and Productivity; Westside Nature Preserve; and Westside Observatory and Planetarium.

Costs

As part of the Connecticut State System of Higher Education, WestConn provides a high-quality private university education at an exceptionally reasonable public school cost. It is estimated that a full-time, in-state undergraduate student who lives and has meals on campus paid approximately $18,000 for 2010–11. This estimate of annual costs includes tuition, fees, and room and board. Books, laboratory fees, health insurance, and personal expenses were not included in the estimate.

WestConn participates in the New England Regional Student Program of the New England Board of Higher Education. This program offers residents of other New England states the opportunity to enroll at WestConn at Connecticut resident tuition rates, plus an additional fee, in programs that are not available in their home states. Details about the regional program can be obtained by contacting the Office of University Admissions.

Financial Aid

Any student who is matriculated at WestConn and registering for at least 6 credits per semester may apply for student aid, which includes federal, state, and institutional funding. Students must complete the Free Application for Federal Student Aid (FAFSA) and be sure to list WestConn's school code of 001380 in the college release section. If the student's file is selected for verification, appropriate signed copies of federal income tax returns must be submitted. Academic scholarships are available to students with superior academic credentials. Students with demonstrated financial need also have the opportunity to participate in work-study programs. For more information, students should contact the Financial Aid Office at 203-837-8580 or wcsufinancialaid@wcsu.edu.

Faculty

Nationally respected, WestConn's faculty members and administrators are continually cited for scholarly achievement. The faculty-student ratio is 1:15.6, and nearly 90 percent of the University's full-time faculty members have doctoral, terminal, or first professional degrees.

Admission Requirements

WestConn welcomes applications from all qualified individuals. Admission to the four undergraduate schools is competitive. University admissions criteria include grade point average, types of courses taken, extracurricular activities, and standardized test results. Applications are reviewed by admissions professionals. If an applicant feels that individual circumstances warrant special consideration, a personal letter explaining those circumstances may be submitted with the application.

Academic preparation is the most important factor in determining admission. Freshman candidates for admission must have a high school diploma from an accredited secondary school or an equivalency diploma. General Educational Development (GED) test scores must be converted into a State of Connecticut Equivalency Diploma.

WestConn applicants should present evidence of successful completion of the following academic units in high school with a cumulative grade average of B- (80) or higher: 4 years of English, including writing skills and literature; 3 years of mathematics, including algebra I, geometry, and algebra II; 2 years of social sciences, including U.S. history; 2 years of laboratory sciences; and 2 to 3 years of a single foreign language (3 years are recommended). Academic course work in computer science, visual arts, theater, music, or dance may be substituted for one of the areas above. Those applicants who do not meet these guidelines may be considered under the Educational Achievement and Access Program. For more information about the program, students should contact the Office of University Admissions.

For specific information about transfer student admission, early admission, freshman entrance with advanced standing, special transfer arrangements for associate degree recipients, guest student admission, readmit admission, fresh-start admission, and international student admission, students should contact the Office of University Admissions.

Interviews are not required, but candidates are encouraged to attend an information session before they enroll. These sessions provide information about the University and the admissions process and provide an important opportunity to assess how the University can help students meet their long-term educational goals. They also afford students the opportunity to meet with professors, other potential students, and current students. Student-guided tours are available. While on tour, students are able to visit the library, the residence halls, science and computer laboratories, the student center, and the recreation center. For information about appointments and campus visits, students should call the Office of University Admissions.

Application and Information

WestConn seeks to enroll students who will benefit from and contribute to the University. Rolling admissions for the fall semester begin December 1, with class spaces filled on a first-come basis. Rolling admissions for the spring semester begin October 1, with class spaces filled on a first-come basis. To apply, students should obtain an application from the Office of University Admissions or from a secondary school or community college guidance office. WestConn welcomes transfer and international student applications.

For application forms and more information, students should contact:

Office of University Admissions
Western Connecticut State University
181 White Street
Danbury, Connecticut 06810
Phone: 203-837-9000
877-837-WCSU (toll-free)
E-mail: admissions@wcsu.edu
Web site: http://www.wcsu.edu
http://www.facebook.com/WestConn
http://twitter.com/westconn/

A view of the Western Connecticut State University Midtown campus.

WESTERN MICHIGAN UNIVERSITY
KALAMAZOO, MICHIGAN

WESTERN MICHIGAN
UNIVERSITY

The University

Western Michigan University (WMU) is one of the country's top public universities and enjoys global recognition for its outstanding programs in many fields. WMU is also home to the Lee Honors College, which has been in continuous operation longer than almost any other honors program in the nation. The college adds to the University's dynamic academic climate by providing small seminar classes, opportunities for research alongside faculty members, and the chance to explore new horizons through independent study.

Western Michigan University is focused on preparing its graduates for the competitive world of work as well as graduate and professional school. WMU is one of fewer than 100 public universities in the United States to have a chapter of Phi Beta Kappa, the nation's premier honor society. In addition, *U.S. News & World Report* has ranked WMU among America's top-100 public universities for the past twelve years.

With more than 25,000 students, WMU is a large, complex university offering a broad range of programs at both the undergraduate and graduate levels. Yet it maintains a comfortable student-faculty ratio, has 30 or fewer students in two thirds of all undergraduate classes, and is one of the most affordable of Michigan's fifteen public universities, ranking tenth from the top in tuition and required fees.

Founded in 1903, WMU has seven degree-granting colleges: Arts and Sciences, Aviation, the Haworth College of Business, Education and Human Development, Engineering and Applied Sciences, Fine Arts, and Health and Human Services. The Lee Honors College challenges academically talented undergraduates while the Graduate College assists students pursuing advanced degrees. WMU offers 239 academic programs, 140 of them at the undergraduate level. The University has a vibrant graduate component that includes sixty-nine master's and twenty-nine doctoral degree programs, so it attracts faculty members who have distinguished themselves internationally through their research.

WMU focuses on enhancing its out-of-class opportunities by providing internship opportunities and engaging students in research and service. In addition, the Haenicke Institute for Global Education provides access to study-abroad programs all over the world and supports international students coming to study at WMU.

The University is home to a diverse student body that represents nearly every state in the nation and ninety-four other countries. Minority students are well represented and make up 16 percent of the student population. The main-campus enrollment of more than 23,000 students includes about 5,000 who live in twenty campus residence halls that offer a variety of living arrangements and supportive programming.

There are more than 300 registered student organizations, including a wide range of Greek, academic honorary, and professional organizations. WMU offers nationally recognized arts programs, a lively cultural calendar, scores of wellness programs, and intramural and club sports. The University also fields sixteen NCAA Division I-A Mid-American Conference and Central Collegiate Hockey Association sports teams, six for men and ten for women.

Location

WMU is located in Kalamazoo, an ideal college town of more than 72,000, situated just 40 miles from scenic Lake Michigan. Local residents have always supported WMU's growth and now the University is southwest Michigan's second-largest employer. Kalamazoo and the broader region encompass numerous prosperous businesses, industries, and Fortune 500 companies, including Haworth, Kellogg, Stryker, and Whirlpool. Many of these firms offer internships to WMU students.

Southwest Michigan is composed of gently rolling hills, small recreational lakes, and dense woodlands. The area embraces all four seasons with relatively cool, sunny summers and moderate winters. Fall is a particularly beautiful time to enjoy hiking or riding a bike on the Kal-Haven trail connecting Kalamazoo to the Lake Michigan resort town of South Haven. Other outdoor recreation abounds, from downhill skiing to nearly every imaginable water sport.

There's plenty to do in Kalamazoo on weekends. It's not unusual to find faculty members rubbing elbows with students at annual events like the Taste of Kalamazoo or Blues Festival and summer Art Hops or Mixers on the Mall.

The city also offers a wide array of lively entertainment, including sports such as professional baseball, hockey, and women's football; music, from jazz to heavy metal; brew pubs, intimate coffee houses, and comedy clubs; and dining, from fast food and family fare to international and gourmet cuisine.

Majors and Degrees

WMU provides a range of academic majors to meet nearly every student's needs. The College of Arts and Sciences offers undergraduate degrees in Africana studies; anthropology; biochemistry; biology; biomedical sciences; business-oriented chemistry; chemistry; communication studies; community and regional planning; criminal justice; earth science; economics; English; environmental studies; film, video, and media studies; French; gender and women's studies; geochemistry; geography; geology; geophysics; German; global and international studies; history; hydrogeology; interpersonal communication; journalism; Latin; mathematics; organizational communication; philosophy; physics; political science; psychology; public history; public relations; religion (comparative); sociology; Spanish; statistics; student-planned major; telecommunications and information management (joint program); tourism and travel; and preprofessional programs (dentistry, law, medicine).

The College of Aviation offers programs in aviation flight science, aviation maintenance technology, and aviation science and administration.

The Haworth College of Business offers programs in accountancy, advertising and promotion, computer information systems, economics, electronic business design, finance, food and consumer package goods marketing, general business, human resource management, integrated supply management, management, marketing, personal financial planning, sales and business marketing, and telecommunications and information management (joint program).

The College of Education and Human Development offers programs in early childhood professional education; elementary education with emphases on language arts, mathematics, science, and social studies; and special education, physical education, and school health education at all levels. Secondary-only majors include biology, business, chemistry, earth science, English, family and consumer sciences, French, geography, German, history, industrial technology (vocational and nonvocational), Latin, marketing, mathematics, occupational education studies, physics, political science, social studies, Spanish, and technology and design. Nonteaching programs include athletic training, child and family development, community health education, dietetics, exercise science, family studies, food service administration, interior design, recreation, and textile and apparel studies.

The College of Engineering and Applied Sciences offers programs in aeronautical engineering, chemical engineering, civil engineering, computer engineering, computer science, construction engineering, electrical engineering, engineering design technology, engineering management technology, graphic and printing science, industrial and entrepreneurial engineering, manufacturing engineering, manufacturing engineering technology, mechanical engineering, paper engineering, and paper science.

The College of Fine Arts offers programs in art, art education, art history, dance, graphic design, music, music composition, music education, music performance (instrumental, jazz studies, keyboard, and voice concentrations), music theater performance, music therapy, and theater (arts management, design and technical production, performance, stage management, and theater studies concentrations).

The College of Health and Human Services offers programs in interdisciplinary health services, nursing (tracks for non–RNs and those already licensed as RNs), occupational therapy, social work, and speech pathology and audiology.

Academic Programs

WMU is committed to student academic success, beginning with First-Year Experience programs to assist new freshmen in transitioning to college. The Center for Academic Success programs helps students improve reading, writing, and study skills as well as obtain tutors. Many offices and programs are dedicated to meeting the needs of such special populations as transfer students, students who have aged out of foster care, and military veterans. Military Times ranks WMU fifteenth on its list of best schools for military veterans.

A comprehensive general education program provides the foundation for all of WMU's programs. Advisers help students explore their program options and plan their individual courses of study. Student academic success is recognized through University, college, and department awards, honor societies, and merit-based scholarships. The Western Edge graduation compact offers students a rapid path to degree completion, merit-based retention scholarship, and four-year freeze on room and board rates.

Off-Campus Programs

WMU has seven regional sites and a full complement of online courses. It actively assists students seeking internships in their chosen fields of study, and maintains partnerships with organizations around the world to provide training, research, and study-abroad opportunities for graduate and undergraduate students.

Academic Facilities

The University provides computer labs across the campus and network access to the Internet as well as to 70,000 libraries worldwide. Specialized labs support the work of students in engineering, graphic arts, and many other fields. An apartment complex for upperclassmen is due to open in fall 2011, and new construction is continuously transforming the campus. Students have access to acclaimed fine arts performance spaces, world-class aviation facilities, a leading-edge building for the College of Health and Human Services, and an innovative College of Engineering and Applied Sciences building that is located in a thriving business and research park. WMU builds in a sustainable way and has earned wide recognition for its numerous green initiatives.

Costs

A college education may be one of the best investments a person can make, as it never depreciates over time. During their lifetime, WMU's graduates can expect to earn nearly twice that of someone with a high school diploma. The University's tuition and fees are consistently among the lowest in Michigan. For 2010–11, resident tuition and fees cost $9006, while room and board cost $7895. Books, supplies, and personal and travel expenses vary based on individual factors.

Financial Aid

The University annually awards more than $229 million in financial assistance to undergraduate students. Students who are qualified for need-based aid usually receive assistance through a combination of gift-aid (grants and scholarships), self-help (student loans), and employment (work-study).

A variety of merit scholarships are available to students who achieve academic success in high school. A combination of awards can be sufficient to cover nearly all direct costs of attending WMU. Most merit awards are renewable by enrolling full-time and earning a minimum 3.0 cumulative grade point average while at WMU. The two most recognized awards are the Medallion Scholarship, valued at $50,000 over four years, and the Dean's Scholarship, which is either $6000 or $3000 and is based on how well students do in the Medallion Scholarship competition.

There are also scholarships for students who have earned associate degrees from state and regional community colleges and who have earned high grade point averages while completing degrees.

Faculty

WMU's commitment to academic excellence means that its professors have a passion for teaching and many of its 917 full-time and 524 part-time faculty members conduct research. It also means that full-time faculty members teach most courses and those having tenure often teach freshman-level courses. In addition, hundreds of these scholars have academic or research experience outside of the United States, bringing a global perspective into the classroom.

Student Government

Governance structures include the Western Student Association and its Student Senate and the Residence Hall Association. Each provides students with a wide variety of opportunities for leadership.

Admission Requirements

For potential freshmen, doing well in a solid academic curriculum in high school is the greatest preparation and predictor for success in college. The major factors WMU considers in its admission decision are high school grade point average and ACT or SAT scores (optional writing test recommended), number and rigor of college preparatory courses completed, and trends of grades. WMU strongly recommends that students complete a rigorous college prep curriculum that minimally includes 4 years of English; 3 years of mathematics, Algebra I and higher (fourth year preferred); 3 years of social sciences; 2 years of science (at least two of biology, chemistry, or physics); and 2 years of foreign language.

Beginning in 2011, students graduating from a Michigan high school are expected to meet the requirements of the Michigan Merit Curriculum (see http://www.michigan.gov/highschool for complete information). Before enrolling at WMU, admission personnel will request and review prospective students' final high school grades to confirm their admission. A transcript verifying high school graduation or an official GED score report is required for all freshman applicants.

Transfer students must have an official college transcript sent from each institution attended. Applicants with at least a 2.0 (C) grade point average (as computed by WMU) in transferable course credits will be considered for admission. Courses completed as well as the trend of most recent grades will also be taken into account. Those who have earned fewer than 26 semester hours (39 quarter/term hours) of academic credit at the time of their application must also submit either an official GED score report or an official high school transcript and, if they graduated from high school in the last two years, ACT or SAT scores.

Application and Information

For an application or more information, students should contact:

Office of Admissions
Western Michigan University
1903 West Michigan Avenue
Kalamazoo, Michigan 49008-5211

Phone: 269-387-2000
Web site: http://www.wmich.edu/admissions
http://www.facebook.com/wmich
http://twitter.com/wmunews

The impressive high-tech home to WMU's College of Health and Human Services was the first higher education building in the nation recognized for sustainability with a LEED-EB Gold designation.

WESTERN WASHINGTON UNIVERSITY
BELLINGHAM, WASHINGTON

The University

A special mix of academic excellence, active learning, personal attention to students, a residential environment, respect for diversity, and beautiful surroundings consistently earns Western Washington University national recognition. For the past fourteen years, *U.S. News & World Report* rankings have included Western as the top public master's-granting university in the Northwest. *Forbes* magazine ranks Western thirty-third nationally among 100 Best Buy Colleges and Universities, *Kiplinger's Personal Finance* magazine places Western fifty-fourth among the nation's 100 Best Values for Public Colleges, and *Time* magazine rates Bellingham as one of the most active cities in the U.S.

Western Washington University (WWU) is organized into seven undergraduate units—the College of Business and Economics, the College of Fine and Performing Arts, Fairhaven College of Interdisciplinary Studies, the College of Humanities and Social Sciences, Huxley College of the Environment, the College of Sciences and Technology, and Woodring College of Education—and the Graduate School. Undergraduates take advantage of unique opportunities to engage in research and showcase their work regionally and nationally, experiences frequently reserved for graduate students at larger institutions and not available at smaller colleges.

The University enrolls around 14,600 students; 94 percent are undergraduates and 55 percent are women. The new student body includes 2,700 freshmen, 800 transfers, and 200 graduate students. The freshman retention rate of 85 percent and graduation rate of 70 percent places Western in the top tier of public master's-granting institutions.

Students are not required to live on campus, but housing is guaranteed to new students. Living on campus allows students to extend learning beyond the classroom, develop leadership skills, and gain a deeper understanding of the university beyond academics. The residence halls vary in size, vintage, style of architecture, and living options, but all are within a 10-minute walk to the center of campus, and offer a rich and unique residential experience. Ninety percent of freshman and 40 percent of all Western students choose to live on campus. A large percentage of students living off campus reside within 20 minutes of campus, making Western an exceptional residential community.

Location

A coastal city of 75,000, Bellingham lies 90 miles north of Seattle and 55 miles south of Vancouver, British Columbia, Canada. The University's proximity to two major cities provides easy access for national and international visiting artists, scholars, and touring groups. Puget Sound and the San Juan Islands lie directly to the west; Mount Baker and the North Cascades Mountain Range are an hour to the east. Bellingham offers a vibrant urban community with a natural setting, providing outstanding entertainment and recreation opportunities. With mountains, glaciers, rivers, saltwater, and many other natural habitats nearby, Western's location is ideal for fieldwork and outdoor research. The campus overlooks Bellingham Bay and includes spectacular views of the snow-capped Canadian Coast range and the San Juan Islands.

Majors and Degrees

Western's undergraduate programs lead to the Bachelor of Arts, Bachelor of Arts in Education, Bachelor of Fine Arts, Bachelor of Music, and Bachelor of Science degrees. Majors available are accounting; accounting/computer science; American cultural studies; anthropology*, with concentrations in archaeology, biocultural, biology, or social studies; art*; art–design; art history; art studio; behavioral neuroscience; biochemistry; biology*; biology/anthropology; cellular and molecular biology; business administration; Canadian-American studies; chemistry*; communication; communication sciences and disorders; community health; computer science; dance (choreography or performance); early childhood education; East Asian studies; economics*; ecology; electronics engineering technology; elementary education; elementary education and special education (dual endorsement); English* (creative writing or literature); environmental

education; environmental science; environmental studies/economics; environmental studies/journalism; environmental planning and policy; evolution and organismal biology; finance; financial economics; emergency planning and hazards mitigation; French*; general studies; geography*; geology; German*; history*; humanities*; human resource management; human services; industrial design; industrial technology (CAD/CAM or vehicle design); international business; Japanese*; journalism; kinesiology; language, literacy and cultural studies; linguistics; management; management information systems; manufacturing engineering technology; manufacturing and supply-chain management; marine biology; marketing; mathematics*; mathematics–applied; mathematics/computer science; music*; music composition; music history and literature; music performance; operations management; philosophy; physical education and health*; physics and astronomy*; plastics engineering technology; plastics engineering technology–vehicle engineering; political science; political science and social studies; politics/philosophy/economics; psychology*; recreation; secondary education; sociology*; sociology/social studies; Spanish*; special education; teaching English to speakers of other languages (TESOL); and theater arts*. Preprofessional programs are offered in dental, engineering, law, medicine, nursing, pharmacy, and physical therapy. Minors are offered in many of these areas as well.

*Related teaching endorsements available.

Additionally, Fairhaven College of Interdisciplinary Studies, a small college within Western, provides students the distinctive opportunity to design an academic program reflective of individual interests and goals. The Fairhaven experience is characterized by interactive and experiential learning, a focus on global issues and social justice, collaboration with faculty and other students, and access to all of the offerings of the University at large.

Academic Programs

Western's curriculum includes breadth in the liberal arts and sciences as well as professional programs in education, business, and the arts, and a selected number of small graduate programs.

The University offers multiple options for integrating new students into a vibrant learning community. Viking Launch is an opportunity for interested new freshmen to begin studies a week before fall quarter officially begins, through enrollment in an interactive seminar taught by some of the University's best professors. The honors program and a variety of distinguished scholar programs provide academic opportunities for students seeking an added challenge.

First-Year Experience (FYE) courses provide first-year students with a small-group experience. First-Year Interest Groups (FIG) offer freshmen a unique learning community during their first quarter on campus. A group of twenty-five students enroll in three courses together—one small seminar and two larger general education courses. In support of the University's goal to infuse leadership development throughout the curriculum, the Karen W. Morse Institute for Leadership offers a variety of courses for students and workshops for faculty, and sponsors speakers and events focusing on leadership.

Off-Campus Programs

Most students enrich their education through internships, international study, fieldwork, service learning, and other hands-on experiences. WWU works closely with many community and governmental agencies and businesses to develop internship and service-learning opportunities. The Center for International Studies promotes and develops a broad array of study-abroad programs, specifically those that give students a chance to broaden their global perspectives, gain foreign-language fluency, engage in service learning and volunteer opportunities, and acquire global citizenship skills. In addition to quarter- or semester-long programs, Western offers faculty-led short-term travel opportunities each quarter in a variety of disciplines and countries around the world.

Academic Facilities

The main campus and its 85 buildings occupy 215 acres along Sehome Hill, overlooking Bellingham Bay and downtown Bellingham.

Two of the facilities, the state-of-the-art Wade King Recreation Center and the Academic Instructional Center, are LEED certified. Western Libraries, consisting of both the main library and a branch music library in the Performing Arts Center, house more than 1.4 million volumes of books, periodicals, government documents, sound recordings, and videos, among other items. The collection includes unique intellectual and cultural heritage materials covering the history of the University and the geographical area, as well as special collections in support of the University's curricula. Students have access to online periodical databases and other resources, many with full-text access. WWU's collection is supplemented by resources from the Orbis Cascade Alliance, a consortium of thirty-four academic libraries. In addition to the WWU network and WWU wireless network, students can use more than twenty general computer labs, numerous departmental labs with scanners and printers, residence hall computer labs, and the Student Technology Center (STC).

Costs

In 2010–11, tuition and fees for Washington residents and nonresidents were $6975 and $17,321, respectively. Room and board averaged $8419; books and supplies averaged $1000.

Financial Aid

Western is committed to helping reduce the cost of attendance for students who cannot afford full tuition, on-campus housing and meals, books, and related expenses. Students who submit the Free Application for Federal Student Aid (FAFSA) are considered for need-based aid in the form of grants, tuition waivers, work-study employment, and loans. Western's financial aid priority date is February 15; no additional institutional financial aid application is required. More than 60 percent of students at WWU receive some sort of financial aid. The Scholarship Center (www.finaid.wwu.edu/scholarships) offers information on a wide variety of opportunities, such as merit-based, diversity, area high school, and academic department scholarships. About 15 percent of Western's entering freshman class is awarded scholarships based upon information provided in the application for admission.

Faculty

Distinguished faculty members teach more than 98 percent of the classes at Western. There are 623 full-time-equivalent faculty members, with 87 percent holding the highest degree in their fields. The student-faculty ratio is 23:1; in addition, 74 percent of class sections have 30 or fewer students and 4 percent of classes have 75 or more students.

Student Government

Through an active student government and more than 250 clubs, a campuswide leadership program, academic departments, campus jobs, and unlimited involvement in the Bellingham community and beyond, Western students have opportunities to develop qualities such as initiative, a strong work ethic, analytical skills, communication skills, and the ability to work in teams. Concerts, art shows, dance performances, theater, and improvisation offer countless opportunities to showcase talent. And the Western Vikings recently placed sixth nationally among 310 NCAA Division II schools in the Sports Director's Cup all-sports standings.

Whether the preference is to take the lead or to work behind the scenes, Western students are involved, making a difference, developing skills that will last a lifetime, and having fun.

Admission Requirements

Admission is competitive. Factors considered include the level and difficulty of courses, grade trends, leadership, school and community involvement, special talents, multicultural experience, and strength of character; personal hardship or circumstances are also considered. The applicant's high school curriculum should include a minimum of 4 years of English; 3 years of math; 3 years of social studies; 2 years of science; 2 years of a foreign language; and 1 semester or trimester in fine or performing arts. Most students go above and beyond the minimum course requirements; 50 percent enter with college credit earned in AP, I.B., or other college-credit options.

Application and Information

Freshman application deadlines for fall, winter, and spring quarters are January 31, October 1, and January 15, respectively. Transfer and postbaccalaureate application deadlines are the same, with the exception of the fall quarter deadline, which is April 1.

Office of Admissions
Western Washington University
516 High Street
Bellingham, Washington 98225-9009

Phone: 360-650-3440
Web site: http://admissions.wwu.edu

Western Washington University's campus is nestled between Mount Baker's peak and the waters of Bellingham Bay.

WESTMINSTER COLLEGE

SALT LAKE CITY, UTAH

The College

Westminster College offers students a unique learning environment, a vibrant community, and a track record of success. Enrolling approximately 3,000 students, Westminster College is the only private, comprehensive liberal arts college in Utah. Students are encouraged to take advantage of a dynamic urban setting with unparalleled access to an ecological wonderland which the College uses as an extension of its classrooms through internships, field work, undergraduate research, and an impressive outdoor recreation program. The learning environment is led by faculty members who love to teach. Deeply committed to each student's success, Westminster College is a challenging and supportive community of learners.

Westminster offers a full range of activities on campus: fifty clubs, health and wellness programming, plays, concerts, lectures, and the like. The College also enjoys the benefits of a diverse and vibrant city that serves as a center of state government, banking, and high technology—all of which students experience through internships, a campus concierge, and classes that expose students to the Salt Lake City's resources, challenges, and opportunities. In addition, Westminster is located near the Rocky Mountains and provides an outdoor recreation program that can get students to excellent ski resorts within 20 minutes or the solitude of forests or the wonders of national parks.

The College has been recognized by *U.S. News & World Report,* the Princeton Review, and Kaplan/*Newsweek.* Its goal is to add value to each student's experience at Westminster. After graduation, some students have gone to work at firms such as Goldman Sachs, General Electric, American Express, and Hewlett-Packard; others have continued their education at schools such as Columbia, Georgetown, Berkeley, and the University of London.

Westminster is tucked into the quaint and eclectic Sugar House neighborhood of Salt Lake City and provides a welcome academic haven. Distinguished by old-growth trees, a small creek, and a graceful blend of old and new architecture, the urban College campus still provides plenty of green space in the midst of the city. The College's on-campus housing, which accommodates 500 students, includes new apartment-style suites featuring entertainment systems and cooking facilities. Off-campus rental housing is readily available in the neighborhood.

The current enrollment is approximately 3,000. Undergraduates make up 75 percent of the student body, with graduate students making up 25 percent. Students come to Westminster from thirty-seven states and twenty-four countries. The average undergraduate student age is 24, and the undergraduate ratio of men to women is 41:59.

Westminster offers intercollegiate basketball, cross-country, golf, lacrosse, and soccer for men; basketball, cross-country, golf, soccer, and volleyball for women; and men's and women's ski and snowboard teams. Most teams compete in the Frontier Conference (NAIA).

Student services include academic advising, career planning and placement, internships, personal counseling, tutoring, and testing.

Residential students are required to participate in a meal plan. Daily selections include a burger bar, a pizza station, a Mexican buffet, a fruit and salad bar, and daily specials.

Location

In 2007, *Outside* magazine gave Salt Lake kudos for its progressive thinking, and described it as "a near-perfect location for avid outdoor adventures." In 2010 *Forbes* ranked SLC first for job growth.

Downtown Salt Lake is 10 minutes from campus by bus, car, or bicycle. The city offers internship and employment opportunities, cultural resources, clubs and restaurants, professional sports, and shopping. A metropolitan area of 1.3 million people, Salt Lake is rated as one of the ten most fun places to live, was home of the 2002 Winter Olympics, and offers easy access to the Sundance Film Festival.

A new campus concierge program facilitates student access to cultural events, recreational and entertainment options, student discounts, and volunteer opportunities. Salt Lake and the surrounding areas have four distinct seasons, with limited amounts of rain and snow in the valley and moderate temperatures. However, the Wasatch Mountains that border the Salt Lake Valley on the east are famous for the "greatest snow on earth." With approximately 500 inches of annual snowfall, these mountains are ideal for winter sports enthusiasts as well as for those who enjoy summer hiking, biking, and camping. Ten excellent ski and snowboard resorts lie within an hour's drive of the campus, and sixteen national parks and recreational areas are within a day's drive or less. Golf, backpacking, mountain biking, kayaking, wakeboarding, mountain climbing, canyoneering, spelunking, and rafting are all within easy reach of the campus.

Majors and Degrees

Westminster College offers more than seventy academic programs. Bachelor of Arts and Bachelor of Science degrees are awarded in accounting, art, arts administration, aviation–flight operations, aviation–management, biology, chemistry, communication, computer information systems, computer science, economics, economics prelaw, elementary education, English, environmental studies, finance, financial services, fine arts, history, international business, justice studies, management, marketing, mathematics, neuroscience, nursing, philosophy, physics, political studies, psychology, social sciences, sociology, Spanish and Latin American studies, special education, and theater. Preprofessional programs include predental, prelaw, and premedical courses. Other academic programs include Chinese, engineering 3–2, and honors. In addition to the above majors, the College offers minors in many of those program areas and minors only subjects ranging from anthropology to paleontology.

Academic Programs

Westminster encourages students to think for themselves, draw conclusions ... and change their minds. Through engaging college-wide learning goals, students experiment with ideas, raise questions, and critically examine alternatives. That philosophy is just one reason that Westminster offers a unique environment for learning. Others include its commitment to students and their learning; its emphasis on an active and engaged style of learning; a campus that is warm, welcoming, and active; and graduates who have mastered the skills that employers want and society needs. By integrating a liberal arts foundation with professional education, Westminster exhibits features of both a liberal arts college and a comprehensive university.

Courses are designed to involve students in active, experiential, cross-disciplinary, and collaborative learning. Each student must complete at least 124 semester hours for a bachelor's degree. While approximately 40 hours consist of liberal arts, students are also exposed to practical, career-oriented experiences. Credit is awarded for successful scores on AP and CLEP examinations. The College has a 4-4-1 calendar, consisting of two 15-week semesters followed by a one-month May term, as well as a summer session. May Term is Westminster's intensive semester: a month of offbeat and inspiring classes, laid-back trips around Utah, and adventures outside the U.S. After a year of hitting the books, May Term is a unique experience taking students outside the classroom and leading them to discoveries about themselves and the world. Students who attend full-time during fall and spring semesters earn free May-term tuition.

Student may also enroll in Reserve Officer Training Corps programs through cooperative agreements with a nearby University.

Off-Campus Programs

Westminster students may participate in travel/study trips (for credit) during May term and the summer session. Students can also make individual arrangements for international study by advisement from the College's International Studies Chair and the Career Resource Center and through a cooperative agreement with the Foreign Study Office at the University of Utah.

Students are encouraged to participate in service-learning activities through the Center for Civic Engagement, to take advantage of internships and other opportunities offered by the Career Resource Center, and to consider integrating campus work-study opportunities with their traditional academic activities.

Westminster is also a member of the Utah Asian Studies Consortium, which promotes connections between faculty members and students in Utah and businesses and schools in Asia, offering May-term trips, internships, semester study-abroad programs, and other opportunities in several Asian countries.

Academic Facilities

Classes are never more than a 5-minute walk away on the pristine, tree-filled 27-acre campus. The Emma Eccles Jones Conservatory of Music and Theatre illustrates the careful blend of architecture. The Gore School of Business, Aviation, and Entrepreneurship, one of the most technologically advanced business education facilities in the nation, integrates innovative, new laboratories and state-of-the-art classroom facilities with the Center for Financial Analysis, offering real-time access to world market data, a behavioral simulation lab, and a flight simulation and testing center.

The Flight Operations Center, which includes a state-of-the-art hangar, flight simulators, and thirteen new aircraft, is located at Salt Lake International Airport. The Dolores Doré Eccles Health, Wellness, and Athletic Center includes a lap pool, exercise facilities, and a climbing wall and houses the School of Nursing and Health Sciences. A new Science Center is scheduled to open in fall 2010. The building, which will meet the exacting environmental standards of the United States Green Building Council, is designed to encourage interaction between various scientific disciplines and allow students to work with state-of-the-art equipment as part of their classroom activity and Westminster's undergraduate research program. Current facilities include major classroom buildings, multiple computer and presentation classrooms, a unique bi-level athletic field/parking garage structure, an award-winning library, a ceramics studio, and a nursing laboratory.

All students have Internet access and e-mail accounts, using a high-speed gigabit network. A secure student Web portal consolidates online e-mail, course, and registration services. Network connections abound in all classrooms and every residence-hall room and library seat. Eighty percent of classrooms are set up for multimedia presentations. Technical support is available seven days a week.

Costs

Tuition and fees for 2010–11 were $25,980 for the academic year for a full-time student (12 to 16 semester credit hours). This figure includes costs for the fall semester, spring semester, and May term. Room and board costs were $7274 for the same period. Books and supplies were estimated at $1000 per year.

Financial Aid

For 2010–11, more than 98 percent of freshmen at Westminster received some form of financial aid, averaging $22,607. Aid programs include need-based institutional grants and need-based federal aid programs, such as grants, loans, and employment (Federal Work-Study Program). The Free Application for Federal Student Aid (FAFSA) is the only form required for new students seeking financial aid. Students wishing to apply for federal aid programs should plan to submit applications by early April. Merit-based scholarships are available to incoming freshmen and transfer students as well as to continuing students through a generous endowment and institutional aid programs. Every full-time student is automatically considered for the College's merit-based scholarships, based on their GPA from previous academic course work. Scholarships are also offered for music, theater, athletics, and extracurricular achievements.

Faculty

Full-time faculty members number 130. The student-faculty ratio is 11:1. All faculty members teach; no full-time research faculty positions exist and no graduate students teach. Many full-time faculty members are actively involved as advisers and sponsors of campus-based student activities. Approximately 94 percent of the faculty members hold a Ph.D. or the highest degree available in their fields.

Student Government

The official student governing body is the Associated Students of Westminster College (ASWC), which sponsors all student activities and organizations and provides funding and authorization for them. The ASWC is made up of three branches: the executive cabinet, the legislative assembly, and the judiciary branch. The branches function in a similar fashion to the federal government system. The president of the ASWC is considered the primary spokesperson for the student body and has access to all senior administrators of the College.

Admission Requirements

Westminster College seeks students who will thrive in its classrooms and bring vibrancy to the campus. Each application is reviewed individually; the College takes into consideration individual talents and character; quality of academic preparation, which includes both difficulty of course work and grades; extracurricular activities; recommendations, and ACT or SAT scores. Westminster admits students whose academic records indicate that they possess the skills and maturity necessary for success in college work. Students are admitted without discrimination as to race, color, religion, gender, gender identification, sexual orientation, age, national or ethnic origin, disability, or a person's status as a veteran. Although the College does not require a specific pattern of school subjects, it does strongly recommend a solid college preparatory high school academic program.

Transfer students must have earned at least a 2.5 cumulative GPA in previous college work. In addition to all other admissions criteria, international students must have at least a 3.0 GPA in non-U.S. high school or college work and a Test of English as a Foreign Language (TOEFL) score of at least 550 (or equivalent).

Application and Information

To apply for admission, a student must submit an application, an application fee, and official transcripts of previous high school and/or college class work. Freshman applicants must submit ACT or SAT scores. Applicants are notified of their status within two weeks of receipt of all required materials. Westminster operates on a rolling admissions basis, so it is best to send applications in as soon as possible. To preserve the faculty-student ratio, classes are limited. Westminster reserves the right to close the class earlier than the dates specified if enrollment goals are met before those dates. New applicants are accepted for the start of all sessions. For applications and additional information, students should contact:

Office of Admissions
Westminster College
1840 South 1300 East
Salt Lake City, Utah 84105
Phone: 801-832-2200
      800-748-4753 (toll-free)
Web site: http://www.westminstercollege.edu

Westminster College offers high-quality education in one of the unique learning environments in the country.

WESTMONT COLLEGE

SANTA BARBARA, CALIFORNIA

The College

Westmont College is a nationally ranked Christian liberal arts college in the evangelical tradition that remains focused on undergraduate education. One of the country's most dynamic interdenominational Christian colleges, Westmont combines a world-class education with an unbeatable coastal Southern California location to prepare students for fulfilling lives of leadership and service.

Residence life, athletics, off-campus programs, and opportunities for local and international outreach contribute to balanced personal and spiritual development. Alumni enter a wide variety of professions and vocations and pursue professional-, master's-, and doctoral-level programs at the world's finest research universities, including UCLA, Stanford, Harvard, Yale, Princeton, the University of Chicago, Cambridge, and many others. Westmont's 1,200 students come from a majority of states and many countries throughout the world, with the highest percentage from California. Approximately 60 percent are women, 25 percent are students of color, and 2 percent are international students. Approximately 80 percent of the students live in the five residence halls on campus or the apartment complex off campus.

As a member of the National Association of Intercollegiate Athletics and the Golden State Athletic Conference, Westmont provides intercollegiate sports competition for men and women in basketball, cross-country, soccer (NAIA champions), tennis, and track and field; men in baseball, club polo, club rugby, club soccer, and club volleyball; and women in volleyball and club polo. The intramural program also offers a wide variety of activities.

There are numerous clubs and organizations, including a student newspaper, literary magazine, yearbook, radio station, choral and music ensembles, multicultural club organizations, political organizations, theater productions, community service organizations, and Christian service, mission, and outreach programs. The Ruth Kerr Memorial Student Center (1983) houses the main campus dining facilities. An integral component of the Westmont experience is the Chapel Program, which students are required to attend three days a week. Chapel provides speakers and programs to inspire and challenge students to continue growing in their relationship with Christ.

Location

Ruth Kerr, president of the Kerr Manufacturing Company, was one of the founders of Westmont College. She was instrumental in opening the first campus in Los Angeles in 1937 and in moving the College to Santa Barbara in 1945. Westmont is located on a 111-acre campus, rich with trees, in Montecito, an estate area of Santa Barbara between the Pacific Ocean and the Santa Ynez Mountains. Students enjoy the beach and mountain trails year-round. Santa Barbara has a wealth of history and culture, and theaters, libraries, community concerts, and other civic offerings are just minutes from the campus.

Majors and Degrees

Westmont awards Bachelor of Arts (B.A.) and Bachelor of Science (B.S.) degrees in twenty-six majors, including alternative major, art, biology, chemistry, communication studies, computer science, economics and business, education, engineering physics, English, English and modern languages, French, history, kinesiology and physical education, mathematics, music, philosophy, physics, political science, psychology, religious studies, social science, sociology and anthropology, Spanish, and theater arts. A teacher-preparation program, approved by the California Commission for Teacher Preparation and Licensing, enables students to qualify for either the single-subject or the multiple-subject credential. Preprofessional programs include athletic training, dentistry, engineering, law, medicine, ministry and missionary studies, pharmacy, physical therapy, and veterinary studies. A 3-2 program combining liberal arts and engineering is offered in cooperation with Stanford University; the University of Southern California; the University of California, Santa Barbara; Boston University; Washington University (St. Louis); and other institutions having accredited schools of engineering.

Academic Programs

Westmont offers majors, minors, and concentrations in dozens of exciting fields and disciplines, such as dance, European studies, neuroscience, and theater arts. All majors and programs of study feature thought-provoking and inspiring ways to integrate belief, thought, and action and to come to a deeper, more accurate understanding of the world. Westmont's commitment to academic freedom is clear, not only in courses that demand students' best critical thinking, but also through a wide range of opportunities and organizations that explore the world of ideas. Students consider issues of science and religion through the Pascal Society and attend lectures in the humanities sponsored by the Erasmus Society. As an exclusively undergraduate college, Westmont has a deep understanding of the ideas and issues that absorb students. From its faculty and staff members to its alumni, Westmont is committed to helping students grow through their questions toward an ever-deeper faith.

Off-Campus Programs

Off-campus programs include the Europe Semester, which is offered each fall and provides the broadest geographical scope, with extended stays in Athens, Florence, Jerusalem, London, Paris, and Rome. The England Semester, offered every other year, combines travel and residential study in the British Isles for literature students. Westmont in Istanbul allows students to live in Constantinople, a city that is of the past and of the future. The Mediterranean Semester places students in Europe (France) and the Middle East (Israel/Palestine, Jordan, and Syria) and promotes cultural immersion and exploration. Students attending the Westmont in Mexico Semester gain skills for cross-cultural living, experience incarnational ministry, and improve their Spanish language abilities. Semesters in France and Spain offer French and Spanish majors the opportunity to study these languages in their home countries, as does the Latin American Studies Program, which combines the study of Spanish culture and language in Belize, Chile, Costa Rica, and Honduras. Similar programs are offered at Jerusalem University College in Israel; Daystar University in Nairobi, Kenya; the Middle East Studies Program at the American University in Cairo, Egypt; and in the Russian Studies Program in Moscow, Nizhni Novgorod, and St. Petersburg (through Westmont's membership in the Council for Christian Colleges & Universities). Participants in the International Business Institute program visit the major economic and political capitals of Europe and Asia. The Westmont Economics/Business Program in Asia introduces students to the diverse economic growth in the Pacific Rim. The East Asia Program addresses contemporary world issues in China, Japan, and Taiwan. An additional summer program in Asia offers students an opportunity to study life and culture in Sri Lanka. Domestic off-campus programs include the San Francisco Urban Program, which studies modern American urban society and offers internships; the Washington Semester, highlighting national political processes and incorporating internships; a semester at Bethune-Cookman, a historically black college in Florida; the Consortium Visitor Program, enabling students to study at any of the Christian College Consortium's twelve other member colleges; and other programs sponsored by the Council for Christian Colleges and Universities.

Academic Facilities

New buildings consist of the Adams Center for the Visual Arts, with a museum, studios, offices, and classrooms; Winter Hall for Science and Mathematics; and the newly renovated observatory, all of which may be viewed at http://www.westmont.edu/buildings. The trilevel Roger John Voskuyl Library, named for Westmont's third president, provides resources and services to support the research and information needs of faculty, staff, students, and the surrounding community. The library collections include 237,000 books, media items, music scores, and microforms as well as 300 print periodical titles and 105 online databases with access to 12,000 online periodicals. The Westmont College Archives collection is comprised of items relating to its history from 1940 to the present and that of its predecessors—Western Bible College and the Bible Missionary Institute. The Westmont community has access to additional resources through the Gold Coast Library Network, Camino, and interlibrary loan services. Westmont's computing network consists of both wired and wireless components. Students receive Google Apps accounts through Westmont, providing e-mail, calendaring, document sharing, and 4 GB storage per student. Although well over 90 percent of Westmont students bring their own computers, the College provides a general access computer lab on the main floor of the library. Westmont's Learning Commons is also housed in the library and brings together library, technology, and other campus services in an environment designed to foster collaborative and creative work, as well as social interaction. The learning spaces in the library are designed for different types of learning styles, including quiet areas, conference rooms, group-study rooms, individual study stations, and more. Voskuyl Library is also home to other Westmont departments providing student support services: Academic Advising, Disability Services, Internship Programs, and the Office of Life Planning, the Writer's Corner, and the Information Technology offices. Porter Theatre contains state-of-the-art equipment for dramatic productions and concerts. The newly renovated George Carroll Observatory contains a 24-inch search-grade reflector telescope, the most powerful one between San Francisco and Los Angeles. The Mericos H. Whittier Science Building and Winter Hall for Science and Mathematics house the College's science program and equipment, including an ultracentrifuge, a liquid scintillation counter, physiographic units and other equipment for advanced physiological studies, low-pressure liquid chromatography equipment, sophisticated environmental instrumentation, atomic absorption spectrophotometers, Fourier-transform NMR spectrometers, infrared and ultraviolet-visible spectrophotometers, gas and high-performance liquid chromatographs, and gamma-ray spectrometers.

Costs
Tuition and fees for 20011–12 are $35,650, and room and board for the academic year are $11,340. The cost of books and personal expenses is estimated at $3000.

Financial Aid
Westmont has a strong financial aid program, so no student should hesitate to apply for lack of financial resources. Eighty-five percent of Westmont's students receive some form of financial assistance; $22 million in total financial aid was awarded for 2010–11. Westmont offers Monroe full-tuition scholarships, which are available only to first-year applicants who apply via the early action (nonbinding) process. A select group of these applicants are invited to the campus to participate in a formal competition process. Students should contact the Office of Admission for further details. Other awards include the President's, Provost's, and Dean's Scholarships, which ranged from $10,000 to $14,000 in 2010–11. These merit scholarships are awarded to students who have demonstrated impressive academic achievement. Westmont also gives awards to students who demonstrate strength in art, music, theater arts, dance, cultural diversity, and athletics. After submitting the Free Application for Federal Student Aid (FAFSA), students may be eligible for generous state grants, aid from federal programs, institutional grants, loans, and work-study programs.

Faculty
One of the highest priorities at Westmont is the attraction and retention of outstanding Christian teachers and scholars. The College's professors are dedicated to the integration of faith and learning, while also being actively involved in the lives of students. There are 90 full-time and 52 part-time faculty members. The student-faculty ratio is 12:1; the average class size is 18. Eighty-nine percent of tenure-track faculty members hold a terminal degree. Westmont's faculty members are committed to teaching at the undergraduate level, and they have additional advising responsibilities with either incoming first-year students or students in their major. A director of first-year programs is responsible for the advising and orientation of new students. Although teaching is their primary scholarly activity, many faculty members engage in research, write books, and publish articles in leading journals and periodicals.

Student Government
The Westmont College Student Association (WCSA) is an entirely self-governing body. Students elect their own WCSA representatives, who are then responsible for organizing social, cultural, and educational activities. They actively participate in and are voting members on almost all faculty committees, while also allocating the student budget to various clubs and organizations. Westmont Student Ministries, another student-managed organization, is responsible for organizing on- and off-campus ministries and mission opportunities.

Admission Requirements
Westmont selects candidates for admission from those prospective students who produce evidence that they are prepared for the academic stimulation and spiritual vitality that are central to the character of Westmont. For example, students should place a high priority on undergraduate education, and living and learning in a classic liberal arts environment should be valued. Applicants must have a clear understanding of the Christian mission of the College as well as an explicit desire to benefit from being in this environment. In addition, applicants should possess the strong moral character, values, personal integrity, and social concern that would be in accord with the Westmont community. All applicants must submit one academic letter of recommendation, official high school or college transcripts, and official SAT or ACT scores. A pastoral/character reference is optional. An interview is strongly encouraged. For transfer students from an accredited two- or four-year college or university or a Bible college or university that is accredited by the American Association of Bible Colleges, the evaluation is based on achievement in solid, transferable course work; an assessment of the personal areas covered by the application (as stated above); and the quality of the written responses. High school records must be submitted if the applicant has completed fewer than 24 college-level credits at the time of application.

Application and Information
Entrance to Westmont is possible at the beginning of either the fall or spring semester. Westmont offers an early action plan. High school seniors interested in applying for early action must submit the application by November 1; notifications are mailed on December 20. The priority deadline for regular decision is February 10 for first-year applicants and March 1 for transfers; notifications are mailed on a rolling basis. Applications should be submitted online via Common Application with an application fee of $25. The Office of Admission encourages applicants to complete the application process as early as possible. Visitors are welcome at any time. Campus visitors can stay overnight in the residence halls, attend classes and chapel, speak with professors or coaches, have a music audition, share a portfolio with the art department, and have meals with Westmont students. Several Preview Day events are planned each semester. Westmont desires to enroll a well-rounded and balanced first-year class. A goal of Westmont is to create a dynamic as well as culturally and traditionally diverse community of learners who bring with them a variety of attributes, accomplishments, backgrounds, and interests. For further information regarding admissions, students should contact:

Office of Admission
Westmont College
955 La Paz Road
Santa Barbara, California 93108

Phone: 800-777-9011 (toll-free)
Fax: 805-565-6234
E-mail: admissions@westmont.edu
Web site: http://www.westmont.edu/
http://www.facebook.com/westmont
http://twitter.com/westmontnews

Nestled in the beautiful hills of Santa Barbara, California, Westmont is home to 1,200 undergraduate scholars, all seeking to engage the academy, church, and world.

WHEATON COLLEGE

WHEATON, ILLINOIS

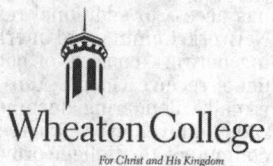

The College

Ranked by *U.S. News & World Report* as one of the nation's top liberal arts colleges, Wheaton College attracts exceptional students from all fifty states and more than thirty countries. An interdenominational Christian liberal arts college, Wheaton takes the pursuit of faith and learning seriously. In addition to upholding an academically rigorous curriculum, Wheaton is committed to being a community that fearlessly pursues God's truth; invests in developing whole, well-rounded students; and prepares its graduates to lead lives that make a difference in the world.

Wheaton College's 150-year history demonstrates the benefits of stable leadership in private Christian higher education—it has had only 7 presidents since it was founded in 1860. Interdenominational and international in constituency, the student body consists of approximately 2,400 undergraduates (including 200 students in the Conservatory of Music). Approximately 80 percent of the undergraduate students come from outside Illinois.

Wheaton has been faithful to its original precepts, and its legacy is shown in the lives of its graduates. Many distinguished schools currently enroll Wheaton graduates in the dramatic arts, education, law, medicine, music, philosophy, science, and sociology. These include Notre Dame, Princeton, SMU, Yale, and the Universities of Chicago and Missouri–Kansas City; several of the Big Ten music schools; and the A.R.T./MXAT Institute for Advanced Theater Training at Harvard. Alumni also excel in a wealth of endeavors around the world, with many holding positions in business and finance, government and foreign service, teaching, ministry, law, medicine, and the arts. Wheaton graduates actively contribute to their communities and churches, and no matter what position they hold, they strive to make a difference in the world around them.

Wheaton offers a rich, life-changing education, with graduates trained for life, not just jobs. Students are taught to think, reason, and express themselves effectively. They should be able to attain knowledge and measure it against the truth of God's word, and understand the importance of service and the value of a faith that acts. Developing strong, life-long relationships—with classmates, professors, and Jesus Christ—is a priority. Graduates are well-positioned for whatever they want to pursue and prepared to face the challenges of life. The Wheaton experience is distinctive and living and learning at Wheaton is extraordinary.

Location

Wheaton's 80-acre campus is located in a residential suburb (population 50,000) 25 miles west of Chicago, and the educational and cultural features of the Chicago metropolitan area are easily accessible by train and regularly visited by students.

Majors and Degrees

Wheaton grants the Bachelor of Arts and Bachelor of Science degrees and, through the Wheaton Conservatory of Music, the Bachelor of Music and Bachelor of Music Education degrees.

The following majors are available in the arts and sciences: ancient languages, anthropology, applied health science, archaeology, art, biblical and theological studies, biology, business/economics, chemistry, Christian education and ministry, communication, computer science, economics, education, English, environmental studies, geology, history, interdisciplinary studies, international relations, mathematics, modern languages (French, German, and Spanish), music, philosophy, physics, political science, psychology, and sociology. Also, 3-2 programs are offered in engineering and nursing, as is a five-year cooperative engineering program with Illinois Institute of Technology and other engineering schools.

The Wheaton Conservatory of Music offers a full range of professional music majors, including composition, education, history/ literature, performance, music with elective studies in an outside field, and music with an emphasis in a music-related field (such as media/film music, pedagogy, conducting, and collaborative piano). Students seeking these professional music degrees are accepted directly into the program by audition.

An on-campus program in military science leads to a commission in the U.S. Army at graduation. In addition to the majors offered, Wheaton has programs leading to teacher certification and to athletic training certification as well as programs preparing students for careers in business, health professions, law, and ministry.

Academic Programs

Wheaton is a distinctively Christian college where faculty members and students work together, both inside and outside the classroom, to apply Christian principles and values to the needs and problems of the individual and society. The vigorous search for knowledge and wisdom in any area of human activity is based on the belief that all truth is God's truth.

The academic curriculum combines with artistic, athletic, religious, service, and social activities to achieve a lively interaction of Christian faith, learning, and living. Because of the College's strong commitment to developing effective servant/leaders for the church and society worldwide, there is a particularly strong integration of faith and learning in all degree programs.

The major field is selected during the second semester of general education courses taken to meet competency and area requirements. Students must demonstrate competence (either by examination or by taking prescribed courses) in foreign language, mathematics, speech, and writing. All students must complete area requirements in applied health science, art, biblical studies, history, literature, music, natural science, philosophy, and social science. A student may be granted advanced placement or college credit on the basis of examination (SAT Subject Tests or AP). The number of credits granted and the level of placement are determined by the registrar and the chair of the department in which the course is taught.

Wheaton offers ten natural science majors—applied health science, biology, chemistry, computer science, environmental studies, geology, liberal arts engineering, liberal arts nursing, mathematics, and physics—in six academic departments. The Wheaton faculty members engage the study of science authoritatively, enthusiastically, and creatively in the classrooms and laboratories and beyond the campus. They are creative and offer more than two dozen general education courses in the natural sciences as well as the majors listed above. The programming includes the use of state-of-the-art technologies and techniques on the main Wheaton campus, cutting edge geological and biological studies in a large science station in the scientifically rich area of the Black Hills of South Dakota, and marine biology studies in Belize. In 2010, Wheaton's science departments will move into a new $80-million science and mathematics facility with expanded teaching labs and research equipment.

Off-Campus Programs

Wheaton offers a variety of off-campus opportunities to enhance students' programs of study. The Wheaton Passage program is a popular camp experience available to new students at the College's Honey Rock Camp in northern Wisconsin. Another program, Human Needs and Global Resources (HNGR), combines classroom study with a six-month, field-based, service-learning internship in the Global South. A similar program in urban studies, Wheaton in Chicago, focuses on urban issues in U.S. cities and includes a semester living in College-owned housing in urban Chicago.

Other special summer programs for credit include field study at the Wheaton College Science Station in the Black Hills of South Dakota;

working with youth at Honey Rock Camp; interdisciplinary study in East Asia; the study of English literature in England; language study in France, Germany, and Spain; the Wheaton in the Holy Lands program, involving biblical and archaeological studies; the Arts in London program, which includes course work in music, theater, and art; and an international study program based in England and the Netherlands, offering courses in economics, political science, and psychology.

Wheaton is a member of the Council of Christian Colleges and Universities, based in Washington, D.C. The council's activities increase students' learning opportunities by bringing special programs to campus and by providing off-campus study. Off-campus programs include American Studies in Washington, D.C.; the Washington Journalism Center in Washington, D.C.; the Los Angeles Film Studies Center; the Contemporary Music Center in Martha's Vineyard; Latin American Studies in Costa Rica; Middle East Studies in Cairo; the Australia Studies Center; China Studies Program; the Scholar's Semester in Oxford; Russia Studies Program; and Uganda Studies Program. Wheaton has also recently affiliated with the International Sustainable Development Studies Institute in Thailand. In addition, Wheaton's membership in the Christian College Consortium allows students a semester of study at one of the other twelve consortium colleges.

Cooperative programs in social science are available at American and Drew universities, and students may participate in a European seminar conducted by Gordon College.

Academic Facilities

A new $80-million science and mathematics facility is under construction and scheduled to open in fall 2010. The 128,000-square-feet of space will include eight teaching labs and research space designed to promote collaborative teacher-student research.

In 2009, an $11 million renovation of Adams Hall added art gallery and studio space. Edman Chapel, often the venue for concerts by world-class musicians, has undergone a $9 million renovation that added rehearsal space, including a large rehearsal room named for alum John Nelson, conductor of Ensemble Orchestral de Paris.

In 2008, Wheaton's Memorial Student Center reopened after an extensive renovation to house the J. Dennis Hastert Center for Economics, Government, and Public Policy. The facility provides classroom, research, and public discussion space geared toward the study of economics, politics, and values in business, government, and ministry. Other recent additions to campus facilities include the Todd Beamer Student Center (2004); the Wade Center (2001), which houses the books and papers of seven British authors, including C. S. Lewis and J. R. R. Tolkien; and the Sports and Recreation Complex (2000).

Costs

Tuition for the 2009–10 year was $26,520; room and board for the year were $7770.

Financial Aid

Realizing that a private college education is costly, Wheaton is committed to providing the necessary need-based financial aid so students can attend. Last year Wheaton awarded over $17 million in grants and scholarships and over $5.7 million in loans.

The average need-based aid package for freshmen is about $17,085 and some merit aid is also available. The Career Development Center helps students to secure part-time jobs, as well as future employment.

Faculty

Over 90 percent of Wheaton's 194 full-time faculty members hold earned doctorates, and more than one third graduated from the top twenty-five graduate schools as designated in *U.S. News & World Report*. The professors' primary commitment as educators and advisers is enriched by their considerable research, publishing, and artistic performance activities. In addition, the professors are active Christians who strive to show how a profound commitment to the truthfulness of God's word structures a vision of all of life, including intellectual life. They are dedicated to honoring a Christian perspective and to modeling Christ's love to their students.

All undergraduate courses are taught by faculty members.

To ensure a rich range of perspectives and expertise, every department at Wheaton has at least 3 full-time professors, and most have 5 to 10. The student-faculty ratio is 12:1.

Student Government

Student Government ensures a student voice in institutional affairs and provides a wide range of opportunities to develop leadership abilities. Student Government's 2009–10 vision is "To be excellent stewards of the influence we have been given while staying committed to each other and to the college."

Besides Student Government, there are over thirty academic, cultural, social justice, and entertainment student groups on campus. In addition, the Office of Christian Outreach provides opportunities for student ministry through student-run mission trips and ministries in urban and suburban Chicago.

Admission Requirements

Wheaton is a selective college that seeks to enroll students who evidence a vital Christian experience, high moral character, personal integrity, social concern, strong academic ability and motivation, and the desire to pursue Christian higher education as defined in the aims and objectives of the College. These qualities are evaluated by consideration of each applicant's academic record, autobiographical essays, test scores, recommendations, optional interview, and participation in extracurricular activities. For students applying to the Conservatory of Music, strong consideration is given to the evaluation of the required audition.

Applicants must have a high school diploma or the equivalent and, at the time of graduation, should have completed a college-preparatory curriculum with a minimum of 18 acceptable units.

Satisfactory scores on the SAT or on the ACT examination are required of all applicants to the freshman class. The middle 50 percent range of scores for those admitted is 27–31 (ACT) and 1220–1400 (SAT composite math and verbal scores).

Application and Information

An application packet, complete with detailed instructions and requirements, can be obtained from the Admissions Office or online. For early action (nonbinding), students seeking admission in the fall term should apply to either the College of Arts and Sciences or the Conservatory of Music by November 1. The regular action deadline is January 10; the transfer application deadline is March 1. An admissions counselor can provide more information about Wheaton in general or the application process in particular.

Further information is available from:

Admissions Office
Wheaton College
501 College Avenue
Wheaton, Illinois 60187
Phone: 630-752-5005
   800-222-2419 (toll-free)
E-mail: admissions@wheaton.edu
Web site: http://www.wheaton.edu

WHITMAN COLLEGE
WALLA WALLA, WASHINGTON

The College

Challenging its students to excel in sciences, humanities, art, and social sciences, Whitman College is one of the nation's leading liberal arts colleges. It combines the educational prestige of the best liberal arts colleges of the East with the outdoor values and vitality of the Pacific Northwest. Since 1882, men and women have chosen this private, independent college because of its commitment to undergraduate education. With just 1,450 students and an average class size of 15, Whitman encourages its students to be active participants in their own education. In 1913, the College led the nation by requiring all students to successfully complete a comprehensive oral examination in their major field of study upon graduation. The installation of a chapter of Phi Beta Kappa in 1919 marked the general recognition of the high quality of Whitman's curriculum and the standards of teaching and learning that distinguish the College. Nearly 60 percent of Whitman graduates enroll in a graduate program of some type within five years of earning their undergraduate degree.

Current enrollment includes students from forty-five states and thirty countries. As a residential college, Whitman has approximately 70 percent of its students living on campus. A variety of residence hall living options are available, including coeducational housing, apartment-style living, eleven special-interest houses, four fraternity houses, and an all-women's residence hall that houses, among others, the members of three national sororities. First-year students and sophomores are required to live on campus.

Whitman has an extremely active student body. They participate in more than 130 interest groups, clubs, and organizations, ranking first in the country in parliamentary debate in 2011. The highly acclaimed theater department produces eight to ten shows during the academic year, while the music department supports more than two dozen different musical groups on campus. The College fields fourteen varsity teams (seven for men and seven for women) and offers twelve club sports and sixteen intramural activities. The Whitman club cycling team has won the national championship three times in the past six years.

Location

Whitman is located in Walla Walla, a historic community of 30,000 nestled in the foothills of the Blue Mountains of southeastern Washington. The Walla Walla Valley has four distinct seasons and enjoys 300 days of sunshine a year. With rich natural terrain at its doorstep, outdoor activities abound. These include cross-country and downhill skiing, backpacking, hiking, kayaking, rafting, and rock climbing. Whitman imports a wide array of cultural activities to the campus, including concerts, art exhibits, environmental forums, internationally renowned speakers and performers, and cinema arts films. Students also perform with the community symphony, browse in the area's seventeen art galleries, and act in the community theater.

Majors and Degrees

Whitman College confers the Bachelor of Arts (B.A.) degree, with departmental majors in anthropology; art (history, studio, and visual culture studies); Asian studies; biochemistry, biophysics, and molecular biology (BBMB); biology; chemistry; classics; economics; English; foreign languages and literatures (French, German studies, or Spanish); gender studies; geology; history; Latin American studies; mathematics; music; philosophy; physics; politics; psychology; religion; rhetoric and film studies; sociology; and theater. Combined or interdepartmental major study programs are offered in Asian studies, astronomy-geology, biology-geology, chemistry-geology, economics-mathematics, environmental studies (emphasis in biology, chemistry, economics, geology, physics, politics, or sociology), geology-physics, mathematics-physics, and physics-astronomy. Minor study options are available in each of the departmental programs as well as Chinese, computer science, Japanese, Latin American and Caribbean literature, sports studies/recreation and athletics, and world literature. Students with special interests may develop combined or interdepartmental major programs, subject to faculty approval. Whitman offers outstanding cooperative programs in engineering with Caltech,

Columbia, Duke, the University of Washington, and Washington University in St. Louis; in environmental management or forestry with Duke; in law with Columbia School of Law; in education with the University of Puget Sound and Whitworth College; and in computer science or oceanography with the University of Washington.

Academic Programs

Whitman's primary goal is to provide an atmosphere in which students can learn how to learn. At the heart of Whitman's academic curriculum is the general studies program. Through this program, students develop skills such as intellectual reasoning, critical analysis of major works, effective writing, solid understanding of humanity's cultural and historic roots, valid bases for judgment of values, and confident abilities to ask tough questions and lead others. The required general studies program consists of a first-year Encounters course and certain distribution requirements. Encounters is a two-semester course, organized around a variable theme, examining encounters between peoples and cultures and the formation and transformation of dominant and competing worldviews. To satisfy distribution requirements, students must complete at least 6 semester credits in fine arts, humanities, science, and social sciences; take two courses dealing with alternative voices; and take at least one course in quantitative analysis. Every candidate for a bachelor's degree must complete at least 124 credits in appropriate course work with acceptable grades and a senior assessment. Honors programs are available for qualified students. Whitman helps fund student research and internships, and approximately 125 students present professional-level research at the Annual Whitman Undergraduate Conference. Scores of 4 and 5 on the College Board's Advanced Placement tests are accepted for credit (the economics, English, and history departments accept only a score of 5). Whitman observes a two-semester calendar with a weeklong break for Thanksgiving, a month off over the winter holiday, and two weeks for spring break.

Off-Campus Programs

Whitman is noted for its strong study-abroad and domestic off-campus study programs. Each year, nearly half of the junior class studies abroad. There are 180 different programs available, spanning six of the seven continents (excluding Antarctica). In addition to academic course work, many students pursue internships and research opportunities. The College is formally affiliated with the Institute for the International Education of Students, which has programs in Australia, Austria, China, England, France, Germany, and Italy. The school for field studies has opportunities in Australia, the Caribbean, Costa Rica, Kenya, and Mexico. Students may also study at the Universities of East Anglia and York in England; St. Andrews University in Scotland; Doshisha University in Kyoto, Japan; and the University of Otago in Dunedin, New Zealand, and at programs in Argentina, Botswana, China, Costa Rica, Egypt, Greece, India, Ireland, Italy, Japan, Mexico, Spain, Sri Lanka, and Taiwan. Each year, 4 Whitman graduates are selected to teach English to university students in Kunming or Xi'an in the People's Republic of China. The College offers urban-semester study and internships in Chicago, Philadelphia, and Washington, D.C. Students may participate in one of more than 300 science research internships available through the College. A signature program of the College is Semester in the West, a semester-long, interdisciplinary traveling field-study program that investigates a myriad of issues throughout the intermountain West.

Academic Facilities

To enhance Whitman's learning environment, students have access to exceptional facilities and technological and cultural resources. Penrose Memorial Library, open 24/7, houses more than 350,000 volumes, 550,000 government documents, and 2,000 subscriptions. In addition, the ORBIS Cascade Alliance provides access to approximately 3.5 million volumes that can be delivered to Whitman in less than 72 hours. Reid Campus Center, a $13-million, 51,000-square-foot campus building, features a ballroom, a cyber lounge, coffeehouse performance space, and flexible dining and meeting facilities. Olin Hall of Humanities and Fine Arts features an audiovisual center, extensive art studios, a foreign language learning lab, and the Donald Sheehan Art Gallery. A newer addition to Olin now houses the computing equipment and is the center for the campuswide fiber-optic network. The student-computer ratio on campus is 5:1. Maxey Hall, which houses the social sciences, includes a natural history and anthropology museum, a 350-seat auditorium, and animal demonstration labs. The Hall of Science houses a sophisticated physics lecture/demonstration hall and laboratory, expanded chemistry work stations, the Clise Planetarium, and support facilities for two electron microscopes. It also contains laboratories for botany, ecology, vertebrate biology, physiology and developmental biology, and biochemistry and genetics; preparation and display cases for the herbarium and the preserved animal collections; a seismograph; and large, well-equipped student research laboratories. Some of the newest features include organic chemistry and geology labs, computer stations, and new greenhouse spaces. The 105,000-square-foot Hall of Science has a wireless network for Internet access, more student-faculty research labs, and enhanced classroom space. The total cost of the project was $17 million. Off campus, Whitman operates an observatory as well as the Johnston Wilderness Center—a 27-acre mountain property serving as an environmental studies field station. The Hall of Music houses an acoustically perfect performance hall and twenty-seven practice rooms that are open 24 hours a day. The theater department in Harper Joy Theater consists of two main stages. Cordiner Hall is a 1,500-seat auditorium featuring a 3,000-pipe Holtkamp organ. The Fouts Center for the Arts, a state-of-the-art, 38,000-square-foot visual arts facility, opened in fall 2008.

Costs

Tuition and fees for 2010–11 were $38,450. Room and board cost $9720. The estimated cost of books, supplies, and incidentals is $1400. Associated student body fees are $320.

Financial Aid

Financial aid offers are usually a combination of scholarships, student employment opportunities, and low-interest loans. In 2010–11, Whitman provided more than $21 million in scholarships. Forty-seven percent of Whitman students qualified for need-based aid. Roughly 50 percent of the students are employed on campus. Whitman also has an extensive achievement scholarship program that rewards students who have demonstrated excellence in academics. Merit scholarships range from $6000 to $12,000 and are renewable for four years, given academic eligibility. Special awards are also available for students who demonstrate exceptional talent in art, music, debate, theater, and leadership. To apply for financial aid, students must submit the Free Application for Federal Student Aid (FAFSA) and the CSS PROFILE. Early decision candidates should apply for financial aid by January 1; regular decision and transfer candidates must apply by February 1. Spring-semester candidates need to complete their forms no later than December 1.

Faculty

Whitman College's faculty is composed of men and women selected, retained, and promoted for their demonstrated effectiveness as teachers as well as for leadership within their chosen fields. Ninety-eight percent of the faculty members hold a doctoral degree or terminal degree in their field, and all serve as academic advisers. The student-faculty ratio is 9:1. Recognized nationally for faculty accessibility, Whitman offers personal attention outside the classroom, setting it apart from peer institutions. At Whitman, students collaborate with professors on research projects, compete with them on athletic fields, serve with them on College committees, and dine with them in their homes. In the past five years, Whitman faculty members have distinguished themselves by receiving awards, honors, and fellowships from the National Institute of Mental Health, National Endowment for the Humanities, Battelle Research Institute, Washington State Arts Commission, Burlington Northern Foundation, Department of Health and Human Services, and Department of Energy.

Student Government

The College encourages its students to participate and take leadership roles in self-governing campus organizations. The largest of these organizations is the Associated Students of Whitman College (ASWC), in which every student is a member. ASWC acts through an elected student congress and executive council and is responsible for the *Whitman Pioneer* (a weekly student newspaper), choral contest, Renaissance Faire, campus radio station KWCW (90.5 FM), and a multitude of all-campus concerts, speakers, films, and social events.

Admission Requirements

Whitman is a highly selective college that seeks academic excellence and diversity within its student body. Competition for admission is keen; about 70 percent of entering first-year students ranked in the top 10 percent of their high school class. Ninety-three percent were in the top quarter. The Admission Committee looks for evidence of demonstrated intellectual achievement, motivation, creativity, responsibility, and maturity. The middle 50 percent of the class of 2014 scored in the following ranges on the SAT: 630–730 critical reasoning, 610–700 math, and 620–710 reading. The minimum TOEFL scores for international students are 85 on the Internet-based test and 560 on the paper test. The following pattern of high school subjects is highly recommended: 4 years of English, mathematics, science, and history or social sciences; at least 2 years of a foreign language; and 1 year of an art elective. Students who have decided early in their senior year that Whitman is their first-choice school are encouraged to apply for admission through early decision.

Application and Information

The application deadlines and notification dates for admission to Whitman are as follows: early decision candidates apply by November 15 or January 1 and receive notification of admission by December 20 or February 1; regular decision applicants for the fall semester apply by January 15, and letters are postmarked by April 1; transfer students apply by March 1 and receive notification by April 15; and spring-semester candidates apply by November 15 and receive notification by December 15. First-year candidates are required to submit the following credentials: the Common Application (for selective colleges), including the School Report Form; secondary school transcript; one teacher recommendation; and an application fee of $50. Whitman also requires test scores (SAT or ACT) and a Personal Supplement (Whitman's own analytical writing requirement). International applicants must also submit a TOEFL score. For more information, students should contact:

Office of Admission
Whitman College
345 Boyer Avenue
Walla Walla, Washington 99362-2046
Phone: 509-527-5176
        877-462-9448 (toll-free)
Fax: 509-527-4967
E-mail: admission@whitman.edu
Web site: http://www.whitman.edu

Students on the Whitman College campus.

WILKES UNIVERSITY
WILKES-BARRE, PENNSYLVANIA

The University

Sitting in that first class at Wilkes University, students may notice something a little unexpected: professors and instructors genuinely interested in students' thoughts and aspirations.

A crucial part of personal engagement is hands-on learning. All Wilkes students can take advantage of numerous opportunities to get real-world experience in their field of interest, from starting a business to conducting research to actually using high-tech instruments that even graduate students at other institutions rarely touch.

Located at the foothills of the Pocono Mountains, along the shore of the Susquehanna River and within walking distance of downtown Wilkes-Barre, Pennsylvania, Wilkes University is a private, comprehensive institution with more than 2,300 undergraduate students.

The University is structured into the College of Arts, Humanities, and Social Sciences; the College of Science and Engineering; the Nesbitt College of Pharmacy and Nursing; the Sidhu School of Business and Leadership; the School of Education; and University College (for undecided students). Wilkes offers a broad range of bachelor's and master's degree programs in the humanities, social and natural sciences, engineering, business administration, nursing, and education as well as the Doctor of Pharmacy, Doctor of Education, and Doctor of Nursing Practice degrees.

The Wilkes campus features a parklike quadrangle surrounded by modern classroom buildings and historic nineteenth-century mansions that have been restored as student residences and academic buildings. Campus facilities include a sports and conference center, an outdoor athletic complex and field house, a science classroom building, a modern academic classroom/office building, a performing arts center, an indoor recreation center, and a student center with a food court, café, entertainment rooms, post office, and ballroom.

Programs are designed to prepare students with a well-rounded liberal arts foundation that cultivates independent thinking and gives students the credentials necessary for entrance into graduate and professional schools and professional life. Academic advising integrated with career planning is stressed, and hands-on experiences are provided in laboratory, internship, and cooperative education settings. Free tutorial services are available to all students as well.

The University is accredited by the Middle States Association of Colleges and Schools and has specialized accreditation in the sciences, engineering, nursing, education, and business. More than 97 percent of students are employed or attending graduate/professional school within one year of receiving their degrees.

First-year students enrolling prior to May 1 are guaranteed housing. Campus housing is available for all four years. Architecturally, residence halls vary from modern, multifloor buildings to mansions listed on the National Register of Historic Places. Medical and dental care, department stores, specialty shops, and other services are available within three blocks of campus. A large number of nearby houses of religious worship welcome students' participation.

At Wilkes University, student activities complement academic life. Intercollegiate athletics encompass sixteen Division III sports, and an active and varied intramural program is offered. Nearly seventy clubs and organizations recognize student achievement and provide opportunities for leadership development, professional growth, and community service. The student-run Programming Board schedules movies and performances by comedians, musicians, and other entertainers, while other organizations sponsor dinner dances, block parties, and special events. The professionally run Student Development Office organizes various activities based on leadership, adventure, or cultural themes, as well as coordinates a unique e-mentor program designed to assist freshmen with the transition to college life. Wilkes students are active community volunteers, participating in numerous local and national service projects each year.

Master's degrees are awarded in business administration, creative writing, education, electrical engineering, engineering management, mechanical engineering, mathematics, and nursing. The University also offers terminal degrees in the fields of creative writing (M.F.A.), education (Ed.D.), nursing practice (D.N.P.), and pharmacy (Pharm.D.). In addition, Wilkes is the first school in Pennsylvania to offer a dual Doctor of Pharmacy and Master of Business Administration degree.

Location

The Luzerne County seat, Wilkes-Barre is a medium-sized city of 50,000 in the midst of a metropolitan area of 400,000. A wide range of recreational facilities are minutes away, including PNC Field (home of the Scranton/Wilkes-Barre Yankees Triple A baseball team); the Mohegan Sun Arena, which serves as home for the Wilkes-Barre/Scranton Penguins hockey team; the Pocono Mountain ski resorts; numerous golf courses; state parks; outdoor tennis courts; and Pocono Downs harness racing.

The University is located in the historical district, between the entertainment and residential sections of the city. The entertainment district begins at the F. M. Kirby Center of Performing Arts, featuring symphony, ballet, theatrical, and musical performances, and encompasses the Wilkes University/King's College Barnes and Noble bookstore and café, a fourteen-screen movie complex, a nightclub, and numerous shops and restaurants. Other area cultural offerings include art galleries, ethnic and community festivals, and numerous libraries and museums. The city is also approximately 2 hours from the cultural resources of both New York City and Philadelphia.

Wilkes-Barre is in proximity to the intersection of Interstates 80, 81, and 476 and within 3 to 6 hours of other major cities, such as Washington, D.C.; Baltimore; and Boston. The Wilkes-Barre/Scranton International Airport enables travelers to arrive at most domestic destinations via one-stop or nonstop flights.

Majors and Degrees

Wilkes University offers Bachelor of Arts, Bachelor of Business Administration, Bachelor of Science, and Bachelor of Fine Arts degrees. Majors include accounting; applied and engineering sciences; biochemistry; biology; business administration (concentrations in economics, finance, international business, management, and marketing); chemistry; clinical laboratory sciences; communications (concentrations in journalism, organizational communications, public relations, rhetoric and public communications, and telecommunications); computer information systems; computer science; criminology; earth and environmental sciences; electrical engineering; elementary, secondary, and special education (all with certification); engineering management; English (concentrations in literature and creative writing); entrepreneurship; environmental engineering; history; integrative media; international studies; mathematics; mechanical engineering; musical theater; nursing; philosophy; political science; psychology; sociology; Spanish; and theater arts.

The premedical and prelaw preparation programs are particularly strong. In addition to the University's prepharmacy program, other preprofessional programs are available in dentistry, optometry, podiatry, and veterinary science. The University offers affiliated programs in medicine with the Philadelphia College of Osteopathic Medicine and The Commonwealth Medical College; in optometry with the Pennsylvania College of Optometry and the State University of New York (SUNY) College of Optometry; in podiatry with Temple University School of Podiatric Medicine; in occupational therapy with Temple University; in physical therapy with Drexel University, Temple University, and Widener University; in medical technology/clinical laboratory sciences with Robert Packer Hospital; and in psychology with Widener University.

Academic Programs

Through a rigorous curriculum that emphasizes hands-on experience and training, Wilkes helps students to prepare in all majors to adapt to a technologically and socially evolving world. To graduate, students are required to complete a core curriculum and must complete from 120 to 136 credits, depending upon their major field. Graduates demonstrate mastery of the fundamental intellectual skills as well as the essential concepts and techniques of their field. Wilkes also teaches students responsibility and independence by expecting and encouraging active participation in the classroom and laboratory.

The University operates on a dual-semester calendar, with optional summer sessions and a January intersession. Advanced Placement test credits, College Level Examination Program (CLEP) credits, and International Baccalaureate (I.B.) credits are accepted.

Off-Campus Programs

An extensive cooperative education program is available to all students, with credit applicable in most major fields. Many government offices and private businesses in northeastern Pennsylvania, as well as in New York City, Philadelphia, Harrisburg, and Washington, D.C., employ Wilkes students. The study-abroad adviser works with interested students, placing them in the situation best suited to their academic pursuits. Most recently, students have attended programs in Austria, England, the Dominican Republic, France, Germany, Italy, and Spain.

Academic Facilities

The Eugene S. Farley Library has more than 220,000 volumes of books and bound journals, 857 current print journal and newspaper subscriptions, hundreds of database searches, and 800,000 microforms. Complete laboratory facilities are available for biology, chemistry, earth and environmental sciences, engineering, nursing, pharmacy, and psychology. Student-produced programming is broadcast from WCLH-FM, the University's 2,000-watt radio station, and transmitted from a professional-quality television studio via a local cable provider. Technology-enhanced classrooms contain Intel-based Apple computers for student use. The Sordoni Art Gallery is professionally equipped and staffed and produces exhibits each year by regionally, nationally, and internationally known artists. The Dorothy Dickson Darte Center for the Performing Arts contains a fully equipped 500-seat main theater and a 45-seat black box theater presentation of plays, concerts, ballet, and other performances and lectures. Adjoining the center are studios, practice and rehearsal rooms, and faculty offices for the Department of Performing Arts. Breiseth Hall accommodates extensive computer facilities, psychology research laboratories, an integrative media lab, and modern classrooms with the latest audiovisual equipment. The University also operates a state-of-the-art distance learning facility that allows global conferencing and study using Internet and videoconferencing technology.

Costs

For the 2010–11 academic year, tuition and fees were $27,178 per year, and room and board were $11,400. Books cost approximately $900 per year.

Financial Aid

Financial aid is available to those students who demonstrate quality academic ability and/or financial need, as verified by the Free Application for Federal Student Aid (FAFSA). Merit-based and need-based aid is available from Wilkes University for qualified students. Scholarships ranging from $6000 to $13,000 per year are available to students solely on the basis of academic ability. Approximately 96 percent of the student body receive some type of financial assistance, including scholarships, grants, loans, and work-study awards.

Faculty

Wilkes University has a nationally recruited full-time faculty of 149 members, approximately 90 percent of whom have earned Ph.D.'s or terminal degrees in their chosen field. Faculty evaluation criteria emphasize teaching excellence and effective advising, while recognizing continued scholarly activities. The student-faculty ratio is 15:1.

Student Government

An active student government provides a structure for student participation in University governance and student discipline. The Inter-Residence Hall Council and Commuter Council coordinate extracurricular activities for on-campus and commuter students.

Admission Requirements

Admission to Wilkes University is traditional. SAT or ACT scores are required. In cases where a student has taken the examination more than once, scores from the highest testing in each category are used in the evaluation process. Applicants for the freshman class should either have completed or be in the process of completing a college-preparatory course of study, including 3 to 4 years of mathematics, social studies, science, and English. Additional courses should be elected in academic subjects according to individual interests. Acceptable electives include foreign language and computing, among others. Students who have not followed this pattern may still qualify for admission if there is other strong evidence of preparation for college work. Letters of recommendation are not required but may be submitted. Students intending to pursue a major in pharmacy or pharmaceutical science or a major in the College of Pharmacy and Nursing should have completed algebra I and II, geometry, and trigonometry prior to enrollment. Students intending to major in nursing should have completed courses in biology and chemistry. An audition is required for all prospective musical theater and theater arts students. Transfer students must submit a transcript from every college previously attended. All students are admitted to the University and not to specific departments, with the exception of the professional Nesbitt College of Pharmacy and Nursing and the Department of Performing Arts. Students individually receive academic advisement at the time of registration and throughout their enrollment.

Wilkes University is an Equal Opportunity/Affirmative Action institution. No applicant shall be denied admission to the University because of race, color, gender, religion, national or ethnic origin, sexual orientation, or handicap.

Application and Information

Applications for admission should be completed early in the senior year of secondary school and sent to the Admissions Office. Applications are reviewed after all of the student's credentials have been received. The review of applications begins on September 15, and notification of the University's decision reaches the student two to four weeks after the application file is complete. The priority deadline for all applications is March 1; applications for the Guaranteed Seat Pharmacy Program must be received by February 1. Other health science programs may have additional deadlines; students should contact the Admissions Office for more information.

Admissions Office
Wilkes University
84 West South Street
Wilkes-Barre, Pennsylvania 18766

Phone: 570-408-4400
800-945-5378 Ext. 4400 (toll-free)
Web site: http://www.wilkes.edu

WILLIAM PATERSON UNIVERSITY OF NEW JERSEY

WAYNE, NEW JERSEY

The University

William Paterson University offers a supportive and challenging environment that encourages students to push themselves, gain confidence, and understand that remarkable things are within their reach. A public institution located in suburban Wayne, New Jersey, it serves 11,361 full- and part-time students through five colleges: College of the Arts and Communication, Cotsakos College of Business, College of Education, College of Humanities and Social Sciences, and College of Science and Health.

The University is accredited by the Middle States Commission on Higher Education. Students can choose from 250 undergraduate and graduate academic programs on a beautiful campus with the facilities and equipment students need to succeed. Located on a 370-acre hilly, wooded site, William Paterson borders on High Mountain Preserve, which is nearly 1,200 acres of wetlands and woodlands, the campus is just three miles from Paterson's historic Great Falls and only 20 miles from the rich cultural, artistic, and commercial life of New York City.

William Paterson's small classes are taught by professors who are experts in their fields. Students enjoy individualized attention from faculty mentors who are committed to helping them develop strengths and uncover new ones. Financial aid is available to qualified students.

William Paterson offers students an active campus experience. Twenty-four percent of undergraduates reside on campus in ten residence halls or apartment-style facilities, which accommodate 2,600 students. Portions of the residence halls are dedicated to dynamic learning communities, as well as substance-free living.

Social, cultural, and recreational activities complement the academic programs. Cultural events take place throughout the year, featuring both William Paterson's own talent as well as renowned professional artists. Among events are concerts presenting jazz, classical, and contemporary music; theater productions; gallery exhibits; and the University's Distinguished Lecturer Series. The recently renovated University Commons complex, including the redesigned John Victor Machuga Student Center, is the heart of the campus. This state-of-the-art campus center provides students with an exquisite setting for a vast array of social and extracurricular activities, dining venues, and student support services. There are more than seventy-five clubs and organizations to develop diverse activities for the entire student body. William Paterson has twenty-five social fraternities and sororities, and twenty-four honor societies. Students staff the campus radio station (WPSC) and the television station (WPC-TV), which develops a number of widely distributed television programs for local and statewide cable networks. The Recreation Center serves as the focal point for physical recreation. The 4,000-seat facility accommodates badminton, basketball, indoor tennis, volleyball, and racquetball courts, an exercise room, saunas, and Jacuzzis. The University has thirteen intercollegiate sports teams, five for men and seven for women, including successful NCAA teams in men's baseball and women's softball. In 2002, the Pioneers won the coed cheerleading and dance team national championship. In addition, bowling, rugby, horseback riding, and ice hockey are organized as club sports. The University has a competition-size indoor pool, outdoor tennis courts, and a lighted athletics field complex.

Guided by the University's mission to provide lifelong learning, the Center for Continuing and Professional Education brings the University to students and students to the University. From noncredit courses to corporate training and advanced computer skills training, the center offers today's working adults professional development and flexible scheduling.

Majors and Degrees

William Paterson University grants five undergraduate degrees—the B.A., B.S., B.F.A., B.M., and B.S.N.—and offers degree programs through its five colleges: Arts and Communication; the Cotsakos College of Business, which in 2005 became one of 15 percent of schools internationally to achieve prestigious accreditation from AACSB International (The Association to Advance Collegiate Schools of Business); Education; Humanities and Social Sciences; and Science and Health.

The Bachelor of Arts degree is awarded in Africana–world studies; anthropology; art; art history; Asian studies; communication; communication disorders; early childhood education; earth science; economics; elementary education; English; French and Francophone studies; geography; history; Latin American and Latino studies; liberal studies; mathematics; music; philosophy; political science; psychology; secondary education; sociology; Spanish; and women's and gender studies. The Bachelor of Science degree is conferred in accounting; applied chemistry; applied health; athletic training; biology; biotechnology; business administration; computer science; environmental science; exercise science; mathematics; physical education; professional sales; and public health. The Bachelor of Fine Arts degree, the Bachelor of Music degree, and the Bachelor of Science in Nursing are also offered. Urban studies, a cross-disciplinary minor, is part of the curriculum, as well. In addition, the Cotsakos College of Business allows students to experience several noteworthy offerings, including the Financial Learning Center, one of the few, advanced, simulated electronic trading rooms found in an academic environment, and the Russ Berrie Institute for Professional Sales, which advances professional sales for both students and business professionals.

Certification is available in early childhood, elementary, secondary, and special education. Preprofessional programs in engineering, law, medicine (dentistry, optometry, podiatry, and veterinary science), pharmacy, physical therapy, and speech-language pathology are arranged at the request of students. Students who have completed the premedical program in the College of Science and Health are consistently accepted by American medical schools.

Academic Programs

Students must complete a minimum of 120 credits to earn a baccalaureate degree. Degree programs include a 31- to 40-credit University core curriculum requirement, 30–60 credits in a major, and 20–40 credits in elective courses. (In specialized degree programs, such as the B.F.A., the B.M., and the B.S.N., University core curriculum and major course requirements may differ.) Students uncertain of which career path to follow may take advantage of advisement and counseling programs. In addition, the core curriculum requirements enable students to take up to 40 credits before declaring a major, so that they can acquire a basic understanding of all major fields of knowledge before having to choose a specific area. Diagnostic testing and career seminars, provided by the Career Development Office, also ensure that students receive the guidance necessary to make wise course selections and career decisions.

William Paterson offers a variety of special programs. Its Honors College is designed for those ambitious and well-qualified students who want to add a challenging dimension to their majors. Currently, there are ten program tracks—biopsychology, cognitive science, humanities, independent study, life science and environmental ethics, management, marketing, music, performing and literary arts, and social sciences.

Students who successfully complete Advanced Placement tests and/or College-Level Examination Program tests may receive credit for acceptable scores. Credit may also be awarded for military training and experience. William Paterson University operates on a two-semester and a one-summer-session system.

Off-Campus Programs

William Paterson offers a special opportunity for off-campus study. Semester Abroad, a 15-credit program, is open to sophomores and juniors who wish to study for a semester at selected institutions in Australia, Denmark, Great Britain, Greece, Israel, Spain, and other countries around the world.

Academic Facilities

William Paterson's facilities are easily accessible, promote interaction among students, and encourage participation by all students in the various academic, cultural, and recreational programs. The University's David and Lorraine Cheng Library contains a collection of more than 360,000 volumes, more than 17,000 audiovisual items, and access to over 23,000 electronic and print periodicals and journals. Special-collections rooms, media services, group studies, carrels, and computer labs provide space for a variety of student uses, and an extensive collection of online journals and resources is accessible campuswide from the library Web site. Supporting William Paterson's varied cultural and artistic offerings are the Power Arts Center, a 42,600-square-foot facility accommodating an array of studio arts, such as design, photography, sculpture, ceramics, printmaking, woodworking, and painting; the Ben Shahn Center for Visual Arts, which contains art galleries, studios, and classrooms; and the Shea Center for Performing Arts, which has a 922-seat theater as well as band, choral, and orchestra practice rooms and classrooms.

Hobart Hall, a state-of-the-art communication facility, is designed to educate communication majors with the most contemporary communication technologies, including teleconferences. The facility houses two broadcast-quality TV studios, a multipurpose computer lab, a film studio, an FCC-licensed FM radio station, an uplink and four downlink satellite dishes, audio and video digital nonlinear editing systems, a cable system linking nearly all of the buildings on campus, and a computerized telephone system for voice and data transmission. In addition, William Paterson has created fiber-optic links throughout the campus. The Atrium, a two-story academic building, contains a writing center, multimedia language lab, tutorial center, and computing support facilities.

Among the other academic resources are extensive computer facilities, a filmmaking laboratory, a professionally equipped television production truck, a child-care center, a nursing instructional center, a language lab, and a speech and hearing clinic. William Paterson University has dual accreditation from the American Speech-Language-Hearing Association for its speech and hearing clinic and its undergraduate and graduate programs in communication disorders. The $85-million Science Building addition and renovation provides students with new, comprehensive research facilities designed to encourage an interactive learning environment. The University has also installed the largest array of solar panels in the nation.

Costs

Annual tuition (including fees) for the 2010–11 academic year was $11,238 for full-time (12 credits or more) students who are New Jersey residents and $18,262 for full-time nonresident students. Room and board cost approximately $10,380 per year. Total annual costs for a student living on campus were $21,618 for New Jersey residents and $28,642 for out-of-state students. These amounts are subject to change by the University's Board of Trustees.

Financial Aid

Financial aid is available through a number of federal and state grant, loan, scholarship, and work-study programs. To apply for need-based aid, students must file the Free Application for Federal Student Aid (FAFSA) with the United States Department of Education by the priority date of April 1.

Both the University and the Alumni Association award a number of competitive scholarships, based solely on academic merit, to entering freshmen. They are the Scholarships for Academic Excellence, Educational Enrichment Scholarships, Trustee and Presidential Scholarships, and New Jersey's Outstanding Scholars Recruitment Program. Academic Achievement Scholarships are awarded only on a competitive basis to continuing students. Each year, more than 1,000 scholarships are awarded, which total more than $23 million.

Faculty

William Paterson's 380 full-time and 664 part-time faculty members bring to the classroom a valuable blend of accomplished scholarship and practical, applied experience. Faculty members assist students with curriculum and career planning, which engenders open, personal communication between the students and faculty.

Through a formal reciprocal exchange relationship with various institutions worldwide, and through the Fulbright Scholarship Program, William Paterson University often receives visiting international scholars. The University's faculty members have won more than thirty-six Fulbright awards, one of the most prestigious academic distinctions in the world.

Student Government

The Student Government Association (SGA), of which all full-time and part-time students are automatically members, has become an influential voice in University decision making. Elected officers and various committees convey students' perspectives to the administration and advance their causes. The SGA is also responsible for chartering campus organizations and allocating student activity fees.

Admission Requirements

Admission is competitive. Admissions decisions for entering freshmen are based on a complete review of the students' academic record (course of study, grades, and rank) as well as the results of the SAT or ACT. Applicants are considered eligible if they have taken a minimum of 16 Carnegie units and have demonstrated strong academic ability. The students' secondary school record must show the following courses: English, 4 years (composition and literature); mathematics, 3 years (algebra I and II and geometry); laboratory science, 2 years (biology, chemistry, or physics); social science, 2 years (American history, world history, or political science); and additional college-preparatory subjects, 5 units (advanced mathematics, literature, foreign language, or social sciences). In addition, students selecting a major in art or music (except musical studies) must submit a portfolio for review by the Art Department or must audition for the Music Department.

Transfer students must present at least 12 college-level credits with a minimum 2.0 GPA; science and nursing majors must have a minimum 2.5 GPA; and teacher certification program applicants must have a minimum 2.75 GPA. Applicants with fewer than 12 college credits must submit a high school transcript. There are some limitations on the number of credits accepted; for example, a maximum of 70 credits from a two-year institution or 90 credits from a four-year college or university. Application review is completed only upon receipt of official transcripts from high schools and especially colleges and universities. Unofficial transcripts or transcripts sent by students will not be used for admissions.

Application and Information

Application forms and transcripts from candidates for freshman status must be received by June 1 for fall admission and December 1 for spring admission. Transfer students, readmitted students, and students seeking a second bachelor's degree must submit their materials by June 1 and December 1 for fall and spring entry, respectively. However, the University closes the application process earlier when the number of new and continuing students strains its ability to provide effective programs and services. A $50 application fee is required. Applications are reviewed on a rolling basis. Campus tours are available during the fall and spring semesters on weekdays by appointment when classes are in session.

Office of Admissions
William Paterson University of New Jersey
Wayne, New Jersey 07470

Phone: 973-720-2125
E-mail: admissions@wpunj.edu
Web site: http://www.wpunj.edu
http://apps.facebook.com/williampaterson
http://twitter.com/wpunj_admission

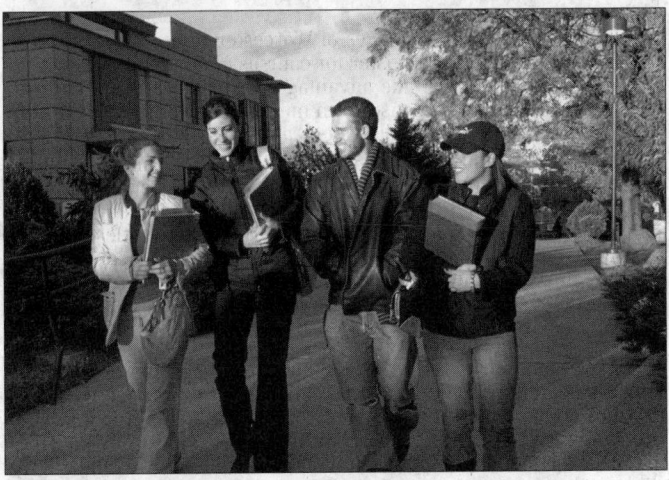

William Paterson University's hilltop suburban campus offers an environment where students may develop both intellectually and socially.

WORCESTER POLYTECHNIC INSTITUTE

WORCESTER, MASSACHUSETTS

The University

Worcester Polytechnic Institute (WPI) believes in the power of its students to make an impact. They may want to be on the first Mars mission, find alternative energy sources, or work on cancer research. To prepare them for leadership and achievement after college, students do much more than study science and technology in the classroom and lab. They complete projects on campus and around the globe where they connect what they have learned in the classroom with pressing real-life challenges, from human health and the environment to business and engineering as well as the arts and humanities. Students grow personally, professionally, and intellectually as they discover how to apply their talents and turn ideas into tangible solutions.

WPI's aim is to educate students broadly so they can achieve greatly. Though WPI has a more than a 145-year history, the curriculum, like its students, is both innovative and practical. Small classes, a flexible curriculum, and one-on-one interaction with professors at the top of their field make learning at WPI an experience unlike any other.

WPI has been widely recognized for its academic program. WPI was the only technological university out of sixteen national Leadership Institutions selected by the Association of American Colleges and Universities to serve as models of outstanding practices in liberal education. WPI is consistently ranked among the top national universities by *U.S. News & World Report*. In the National Survey of Student Engagement, WPI ranked number one for student-faculty interactions, which is a measure of the quality and quantity of time faculty members spend with undergraduates.

More than thirty areas of study in engineering, science, business management, and the liberal arts allow many academic options, from molecular biology to music. Exciting new interdisciplinary programs are driven by real-world demand, such as interactive media and game development, robotics engineering, and environmental studies and engineering. The school also offers preprofessional programs and a five-year B.S./M.S. program.

With so many offerings, it is not surprising that more than 40 percent of students change their major at least once. At WPI, a comprehensive academic advising program and a wide array of academic support services help students make the right choices and reach their goals.

WPI students have received some of the nation's highest academic honors: the prestigious Marshall Scholarship, the NIH–Oxford/Cambridge Biomedical Research Scholarship, the Fulbright Scholarship, the Goldwater Scholarship, the Rotary Ambassadorial Scholarship, and the Society of Women Engineers Award. In addition, 2 students were recently named to the *USA Today* All-USA College Academic Team.

WPI is a member of the Colleges of Worcester Consortium, through which WPI students may register for courses at other colleges within the consortium and may take advantage of a wide range of cultural programming offered by consortium members. A consortium shuttle provides free transportation between campuses.

WPI has twenty varsity (NCAA Division III) athletics teams and thirty-four club and intramural sports. WPI won the Worcester Cup for four of the last six years for the highest overall winning percentage in all sports in Worcester County. There are thirteen fraternities and five sororities, more than fifteen music or theater ensembles, and dozens of academic clubs, international organizations, religious groups, and other organizations. There are more than 200 student clubs and activities.

Location

With its beautiful architecture, grassy quad, and ivy-covered walls, WPI has a traditional New England campus. Students stop and chat with their friends and professors on tree-lined paths, play pool between classes at the Campus Center, or get a coffee with friends. They study in the sun by the fountain in Reunion Plaza, go cosmic bowling, stop and smell the roses in the formal English garden behind Higgins House, or see a student play at the Little Theatre.

Home to twelve other colleges and universities and more than 35,000 college students, Worcester is a great college town. Late-night diners, clubs, museums, concert venues, and theaters are right down the hill from WPI in Worcester's vibrant downtown. Boston is less than an hour away by commuter rail, and there are great skiing and snowboarding at nearby Wachusett Mountain. Worcester is centrally located, with easy access to Providence, New York City, the Berkshires, the White Mountains, and Cape Cod.

Majors and Degrees

WPI offers the Bachelor of Science and the Bachelor of Arts degrees. Degree programs are offered in a wide variety of engineering and science: disciplines: actuarial mathematics, aerospace engineering, biochemistry, biology and biotechnology, biomedical engineering, chemical engineering, chemistry, civil engineering, computer science, electrical and computer engineering, environmental engineering, environmental science, fire protection engineering, industrial engineering, interactive media and game development, mathematical sciences, mechanical engineering, physics, and robotics engineering.

In addition, there are programs in the areas of business and liberal arts: business/management; economics; environmental and sustainability studies; history; humanities and arts; international studies; literature; management engineering; management information systems; music; philosophy and religion; professional writing; psychology/psychological science; society, technology, and policy; system dynamics; and theater.

Four new interdisciplinary majors have been added to the curriculum: interactive media and game development, environmental engineering, bioinformatics and computational biology, and robotics engineering, which is the first undergraduate program in robotics in the nation. WPI offers several preprofessional programs, including dentistry, law, medicine, and veterinary medicine. Students may also design their own majors by combining courses offered in various WPI departments. Undergraduates who wish to continue their studies toward a master's degree at WPI may enroll in a combined, continuous B.S./M.S. program.

Academic Programs

Students take the equivalent of three courses (as either traditional courses or project work) during each of four 7-week terms (two in the fall and two in the spring). At WPI, learning is about more than just theories and ideas. Students learn how to put ideas into practice through the project-enriched curriculum. WPI undergraduates complete two projects before graduation: one directly related to their major and one working with a team of students to solve a problem at the intersection of society and technology—helping to bring electricity to remote villages in Thailand or studying the bioethics of cloning, for example. Students gain valuable professional skills, a talent for team work, and the confidence to dive right in no matter what the challenge.

WPI's academic program encourages collaboration, not competition. Students work closely together in project-oriented classes. Learning how to work in teams prepares students to achieve results and become leaders in life after college, no matter what path they take.

Top-tier employers seek out WPI graduates for their real-world experience and ability to work collaboratively. With a placement rate of more than 90 percent, students are recruited by leading organizations such as Pfizer, General Electric, Fidelity Investments, and IBM. Each year, WPI graduates are accepted at many prestigious graduate schools, including MIT, Yale, Princeton, Johns Hopkins, and Tufts University Medical School.

WPI graduates' starting salaries are higher than those of many other college graduates, according to the National Association of Colleges and Employers. In addition, WPI was recently recognized by the Boston Globe for having the third highest average starting salaries in New England and the twelfth highest of all universities in the nation.

Off-Campus Programs

WPI has sent more engineering and science students abroad than any other university as part of its hands-on, project-enriched curriculum.

About half of WPI students complete projects outside the United States and two-thirds do projects off campus. With WPI's Global Perspective Program, students experience the challenge of solving real-world problems with their fellow students and immerse themselves in another culture. Students complete projects on campus or at any of the more than twenty-five project centers located on five continents around the globe, including Thailand, Australia, South Africa, Costa Rica, and the U.S. Recent project sponsors include NASA Johnson Space Center, Johnson & Johnson, Morgan Stanley, Environmental Protection Agency, and UNESCO. Through their seven-week project experience, students learn valuable professional skills, including communication, teamwork, and problem solving.

Academic Facilities

Among the many teaching, research, and project facilities available to undergraduates at WPI are a 71,000-square-foot campus center and a new Life Sciences and Bioengineering Center at Gateway Park, which is a state-of-the-art 130,000-square-foot facility at the life sciences-based campus that houses research in regenerative medicine, molecular nanotechnology, biosensors, plant systems, tissue engineering, and untethered health care. An $11-million renovation created the new undergraduate Life Sciences Laboratory Center, which opened in 2009. The center has become WPI's main facility for undergraduate teaching and research in biology and biotechnology, biomedical engineering, chemistry and biochemistry, and chemical engineering. WPI's other state-of-the-art research facilities include two atomic-force microscopes, medical imaging laboratories, a fire science laboratory, a new team-based chemistry lab, a laser holography lab, a computer music lab, a satellite navigation lab, thirty multimedia classrooms and lecture halls, and a research library with thousands of electronic journals, books, databases, and nearly 300,000 volumes.

The university also has an exceptional computer and networking infrastructure. The facilities include nearly 600 computers in open-access, 24/7 labs; powerful UNIX workstations; a Web-based student information system; a high-speed data network that reaches every building and residence hall; and extensive roaming wireless access.

In addition to these existing facilities, a state-of-the-art apartment-style residence hall, with over 200 beds, opened in fall 2008. The building features recreation and fitness space, technology suites on the each floor, meeting rooms on the ground floor for group projects, and wireless access.

WPI is scheduled to open a brand-new sports and recreation center in 2012. Plans include a four-court gymnasium, indoor jogging track, 14,000 square feet of fitness space, racquetball and squash courts, competition pool, workout studios, and rowing tanks.

Costs

For 2010–11, full-time tuition was $38,140. Room and board charges were $11,540.

Financial Aid

For families with established financial need, aid, including financial aid packages, on-campus jobs, and loan programs, is available. In addition, all applicants are considered for merit scholarships. More information is available from WPI's Office of Financial Aid (http://www.wpi.edu/+finaid).

Faculty

Besides being passionate about teaching, WPI's 396 full- and part-time faculty members are committed researchers and scholars with world-class credentials. They are leading contributors to the fields of bioengineering, cryptography, energy, fuel cells, information technology, and more. Thirteen members of the current faculty are Fulbright Scholars, and more than 50 are fellows of top national and international societies. Since 1994, 17 WPI professors have won the National Science Foundation's CAREER Award, which is its most prestigious award for young faculty members. WPI has a 14:1 student-faculty ratio. According to *U.S. News & World Report,* faculty resources, which include salary, class size, and student-faculty ratio, rank thirtieth among national universities.

Student Government

Through the Student Government Association, the Interfraternity Council, the Panhellenic Association, and the International Student Council, students self-govern and develop their own social programs. WPI prides itself on being a caring community that respects the contributions of individuals, appreciates the diversity of the student body, and emphasizes the importance of cooperation and teamwork.

Admission Requirements

Applicants for admission must have completed 4 years of English, 4 years of mathematics (including precalculus), and 2 years of lab science. Admission requirements include a school transcript, SAT or ACT scores or alternative materials through WPI's Flex Path, recommendations from a science or math teacher and a counselor, and a personal essay. For international students whose first language is not English, a TOEFL or IELTS score is required.

The university has high standards for applicants but also looks for more than just outstanding academic performance. WPI takes care to admit students who will likely thrive at the university. They tend to be creative and curious; like to work in teams to get things done; are comfortable making their own decisions and setting their own courses; love math and science but feel just as passionate about literature, music, movies, and the arts; prefer to be leaders, not followers; and are ready to make a positive impact on the world around them.

Students are encouraged to visit the WPI campus to learn more about the university, see its facilities, and hear firsthand about the WPI experience from students and faculty members. WPI is open most school holidays and offers a wide range of options for tours, group information sessions, open houses, personal interviews, and Saturday visits. Details and schedules may be obtained from the Admissions Office Web site.

The deadline for early action round 1 is November 10, with notification by December 20. The deadline for early action round 2 is January 1, with notification by February 10. The regular decision deadline is February 1, with notification by April 1. For transfer admissions, the priority deadline is April 15; students are notified of admission decisions on a rolling basis.

Application and Information

To schedule a visit or request more information, students should contact:

Office of Admissions
Bartlett Center
Worcester Polytechnic Institute
100 Institute Road
Worcester, Massachusetts 01609-2280

Phone: 508-831-5286
Fax: 508-831-5875
E-mail: admissions@wpi.edu
Web site: http://admissions.wpi.edu
http://www.facebook.com/WPIAdmissions
http://twitter.com/WPIAdmissions

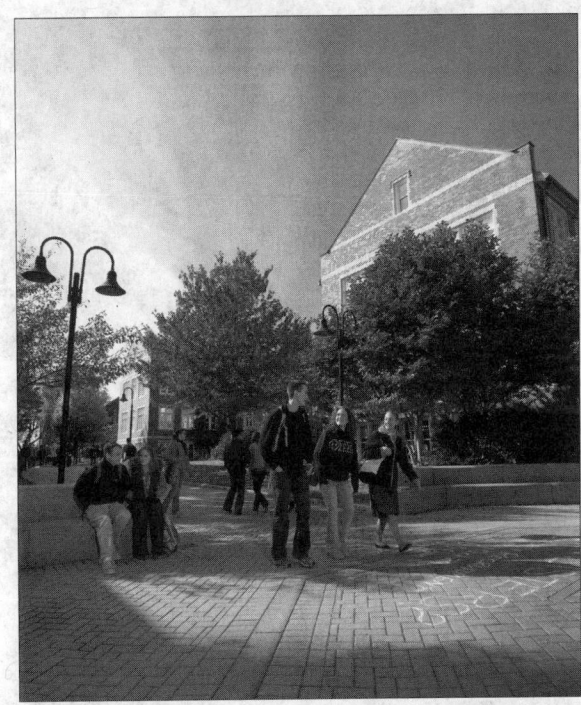

A view of the campus at Worcester Polytechnic Institute.

Indexes

Majors

ACCOUNTING

Abilene Christian U (TX)
Adams State Coll (CO)
Adelphi U (NY)
AIB Coll of Business (IA)
Alabama Ag and Mech U (AL)
Alabama State U (AL)
Albany State U (GA)
Albertus Magnus Coll (CT)
Albright Coll (PA)
Alcorn State U (MS)
Alderson-Broaddus Coll (WV)
Alfred U (NY)
Alma Coll (MI)
Alvernia U (PA)
Amberton U (TX)
American U (DC)
Anderson U (IN)
Andrews U (MI)
Angelo State U (TX)
Appalachian State U (NC)
Aquinas Coll (MI)
Arcadia U (PA)
Arizona State U (AZ)
Arkansas State U (AR)
Arkansas Tech U (AR)
Asbury U (KY)
Ashland U (OH)
Assumption Coll (MA)
Athabasca U (AB, Canada)
Athens State U (AL)
Atlantic Union Coll (MA)
Auburn U (AL)
Auburn U Montgomery (AL)
Augsburg Coll (MN)
Augustana Coll (IL)
Augustana Coll (SD)
Averett U (VA)
Avila U (MO)
Azusa Pacific U (CA)
Baker Coll of Auburn Hills (MI)
Baker Coll of Owosso (MI)
Baker U (KS)
Baldwin-Wallace Coll (OH)
Ball State U (IN)
Barry U (FL)
Barton Coll (NC)
Belhaven U (MS)
Bellarmine U (KY)
Belmont Abbey Coll (NC)
Belmont U (TN)
Bemidji State U (MN)
Benedictine Coll (KS)
Benedictine U (IL)
Bentley U (MA)
Berry Coll (GA)
Bethany Coll (KS)
Bethany Coll (WV)
Bethel Coll (IN)
Bethune-Cookman U (FL)
Biola U (CA)
Birmingham-Southern Coll (AL)
Blackburn Coll (IL)
Bloomfield Coll (NJ)
Bloomsburg U of Pennsylvania (PA)
Bluefield Coll (VA)
Bluefield State Coll (WV)
Bluffton U (OH)
Bob Jones U (SC)
Boise State U (ID)
Boston Coll (MA)
Boston U (MA)
Bowie State U (MD)
Bowling Green State U (OH)
Brenau U (GA)
Brewton-Parker Coll (GA)
Briar Cliff U (IA)
Bridgewater State U (MA)
Brock U (ON, Canada)
Brown Mackie Coll–Tucson (AZ)
Bryant U (RI)
Bucknell U (PA)
Buena Vista U (IA)
Butler U (IN)
Cabrini Coll (PA)
California Baptist U (CA)
California State U, Chico (CA)
California State U, Dominguez Hills (CA)
California State U, Fullerton (CA)
California State U, Long Beach (CA)

California State U, Northridge (CA)
California State U, San Bernardino (CA)
California State U, San Marcos (CA)
Calumet Coll of Saint Joseph (IN)
Calvin Coll (MI)
Cameron U (OK)
Campbellsville U (KY)
Canisius Coll (NY)
Capital U (OH)
Carlow U (PA)
Carroll U (WI)
Carson-Newman Coll (TN)
Case Western Reserve U (OH)
Castleton State Coll (VT)
The Catholic U of America (DC)
Cedar Crest Coll (PA)
Cedarville U (OH)
Centenary Coll (NJ)
Central Coll (IA)
Central Connecticut State U (CT)
Central Michigan U (MI)
Central Pennsylvania Coll (PA)
Central State U (OH)
Champlain Coll (VT)
Chapman U (CA)
Chatham U (PA)
Chestnut Hill Coll (PA)
Christian Brothers U (TN)
Christopher Newport U (VA)
Claremont McKenna Coll (CA)
Clarion U of Pennsylvania (PA)
Clark Atlanta U (GA)
Clarke U (IA)
Clayton State U (GA)
Clearwater Christian Coll (FL)
Cleary U (MI)
Clemson U (SC)
Cleveland State U (OH)
Coastal Carolina U (SC)
Coll of Charleston (SC)
Coll of Mount St. Joseph (OH)
The Coll of New Jersey (NJ)
Coll of Saint Benedict (MN)
Coll of St. Joseph (VT)
The Coll of Saint Rose (NY)
The Coll of St. Scholastica (MN)
Coll of Staten Island of the City U of New York (NY)
Coll of the Holy Cross (MA)
Coll of the Ozarks (MO)
The Coll of William and Mary (VA)
Colorado State U (CO)
Columbia Coll (MO)
Columbia Coll (SC)
Columbus State U (GA)
Concordia Coll (MN)
Concordia Coll–New York (NY)
Concordia U (QC, Canada)
Concordia U Chicago (IL)
Concordia U, St. Paul (MN)
Concordia U Wisconsin (WI)
Concord U (WV)
Corban U (OR)
Creighton U (NE)
Culver-Stockton Coll (MO)
Cumberland U (TN)
Dakota State U (SD)
Dakota Wesleyan U (SD)
Dallas Baptist U (TX)
Davenport U, Grand Rapids (MI)
Defiance Coll (OH)
Delaware State U (DE)
Delta State U (MS)
DePaul U (IL)
DEREE - The American Coll of Greece (Greece)
DeSales U (PA)
Dickinson State U (ND)
Dillard U (LA)
Dixie State Coll of Utah (UT)
Doane Coll (NE)
Dominican Coll (NY)
Dominican U (IL)
Dordt Coll (IA)
Dowling Coll (NY)
Drake U (IA)
Drury U (MO)
Duquesne U (PA)
East Central U (OK)
Eastern Illinois U (IL)

Eastern Michigan U (MI)
Eastern New Mexico U (NM)
Eastern Washington U (WA)
East Tennessee State U (TN)
ECPI Coll of Technology, Virginia Beach (VA)
Edgewood Coll (WI)
Elizabeth City State U (NC)
Elizabethtown Coll (PA)
Elmhurst Coll (IL)
Elmira Coll (NY)
Elon U (NC)
Emory & Henry Coll (VA)
Emporia State U (KS)
Endicott Coll (MA)
Everest U, Lakeland (FL)
Everest U, Tampa (FL)
Everest U, Tampa (FL)
Fairfield U (CT)
Fairleigh Dickinson U, Coll at Florham (NJ)
Fairleigh Dickinson U, Metropolitan Campus (NJ)
Fairmont State U (WV)
Faulkner U (AL)
Fayetteville State U (NC)
Felician Coll (NJ)
Ferris State U (MI)
Ferrum Coll (VA)
Fitchburg State U (MA)
Flagler Coll (FL)
Florida Ag and Mech U (FL)
Florida Atlantic U (FL)
Florida Gulf Coast U (FL)
Florida Inst of Technology (FL)
Florida Intl U (FL)
Florida National Coll (FL)
Florida Southern Coll (FL)
Florida State U (FL)
Fort Lewis Coll (CO)
Francis Marion U (SC)
Franklin Coll (IN)
Franklin Pierce U (NH)
Franklin U (OH)
Freed-Hardeman U (TN)
Friends U (KS)
Furman U (SC)
Gallaudet U (DC)
Gannon U (PA)
Gardner-Webb U (NC)
Geneva Coll (PA)
George Fox U (OR)
Georgetown Coll (KY)
Georgetown U (DC)
Georgia Coll & State U (GA)
Georgian Court U (NJ)
Georgia Southern U (GA)
Georgia State U (GA)
Gettysburg Coll (PA)
Goldey-Beacom Coll (DE)
Gordon Coll (MA)
Governors State U (IL)
Grace Bible Coll (MI)
Grace Coll (IN)
Graceland U (IA)
Grand Canyon U (AZ)
Grand Valley State U (MI)
Grand View U (IA)
Greensboro Coll (NC)
Greenville Coll (IL)
Grove City Coll (PA)
Guilford Coll (NC)
Hamline U (MN)
Hannibal-LaGrange U (MO)
Harding U (AR)
Hardin-Simmons U (TX)
Harrison Coll, Indianapolis (IN)
Harrison Coll, Lafayette (IN)
Harrison Coll, Muncie (IN)
Hartwick Coll (NY)
Hawai`i Pacific U (HI)
HEC Montreal (QC, Canada)
Hendrix Coll (AR)
Hillsdale Coll (MI)
Hofstra U (NY)
Holy Family U (PA)
Hope Coll (MI)
Hunter Coll of the City U of New York (NY)
Huntingdon Coll (AL)
Huntington U (IN)

Husson U (ME)
Huston-Tillotson U (TX)
Idaho State U (ID)
Illinois Coll (IL)
Illinois State U (IL)
Illinois Wesleyan U (IL)
Immaculata U (PA)
Indiana State U (IN)
Indiana Tech (IN)
Indiana U of Pennsylvania (PA)
Indiana U–Purdue U Fort Wayne (IN)
Indiana Wesleyan U (IN)
Inter American U of Puerto Rico, Bayamón Campus (PR)
Inter American U of Puerto Rico, Guayama Campus (PR)
Inter American U of Puerto Rico, Metropolitan Campus (PR)
Inter American U of Puerto Rico, Ponce Campus (PR)
Inter American U of Puerto Rico, San Germán Campus (PR)
Iowa State U of Science and Technology (IA)
Iowa Wesleyan Coll (IA)
Ithaca Coll (NY)
Jacksonville State U (AL)
James Madison U (VA)
Jamestown Coll (ND)
John Brown U (AR)
John Carroll U (OH)
Johnson & Wales U (RI)
Johnson & Wales U - Charlotte Campus (NC)
Johnson State Coll (VT)
Juniata Coll (PA)
Kansas State U (KS)
Kean U (NJ)
Kennesaw State U (GA)
Kent State U (OH)
Kentucky Wesleyan Coll (KY)
Keuka Coll (NY)
Keystone Coll (PA)
King Coll (TN)
King's Coll (PA)
Kutztown U of Pennsylvania (PA)
Kuyper Coll (MI)
LaGrange Coll (GA)
Lakehead U (ON, Canada)
Lake Superior State U (MI)
Lamar U (TX)
La Roche Coll (PA)
La Salle U (PA)
Lasell Coll (MA)
Lebanon Valley Coll (PA)
Lee U (TN)
Lehigh U (PA)
Lehman Coll of the City U of New York (NY)
Le Moyne Coll (NY)
LeTourneau U (TX)
Lewis U (IL)
Liberty U (VA)
Limestone Coll (SC)
Lincoln Memorial U (TN)
Lincoln U (MO)
Lindenwood U (MO)
Linfield Coll (OR)
Lipscomb U (TN)
Lock Haven U of Pennsylvania (PA)
Long Island U, Brentwood Campus (NY)
Long Island U, Brooklyn Campus (NY)
Long Island U, C.W. Post Campus (NY)
Longwood U (VA)
Loras Coll (IA)
Louisiana Coll (LA)
Louisiana State U and Ag and Mech Coll (LA)
Louisiana State U in Shreveport (LA)
Lourdes Coll (OH)
Loyola Marymount U (CA)
Loyola U Chicago (IL)
Loyola U Maryland (MD)
Loyola U New Orleans (LA)
Lubbock Christian U (TX)
Luther Coll (IA)

Lycoming Coll (PA)
Lynchburg Coll (VA)
Lyndon State Coll (VT)
Lyon Coll (AR)
MacMurray Coll (IL)
Madonna U (MI)
Malone U (OH)
Manchester Coll (IN)
Manhattan Coll (NY)
Mansfield U of Pennsylvania (PA)
Maranatha Baptist Bible Coll (WI)
Marian U (WI)
Marietta Coll (OH)
Marist Coll (NY)
Marquette U (WI)
Marshall U (WV)
Mars Hill Coll (NC)
Maryville U of Saint Louis (MO)
Marywood U (PA)
Massachusetts Coll of Liberal Arts (MA)
The Master's Coll and Sem (CA)
McKendree U (IL)
McMurry U (TX)
Medaille Coll (NY)
Medgar Evers Coll of the City U of New York (NY)
Menlo Coll (CA)
Merrimack Coll (MA)
Mesa State Coll (CO)
Messiah Coll (PA)
Metropolitan State U (MN)
Miami U (OH)
Michigan State U (MI)
MidAmerica Nazarene U (KS)
Middle Tennessee State U (TN)
Midway Coll (KY)
Midwestern State U (TX)
Milligan Coll (TN)
Millikin U (IL)
Millsaps Coll (MS)
Minnesota School of Business–Blaine (MN)
Minnesota State U Mankato (MN)
Minnesota State U Moorhead (MN)
Minot State U (ND)
Misericordia U (PA)
Mississippi State U (MS)
Mississippi U for Women (MS)
Mississippi Valley State U (MS)
Missouri Baptist U (MO)
Missouri State U (MO)
Molloy Coll (NY)
Monmouth Coll (IL)
Montana State U Billings (MT)
Moravian Coll (PA)
Morehead State U (KY)
Morningside Coll (IA)
Mountain State U (WV)
Mount Allison U (NB, Canada)
Mount Aloysius Coll (PA)
Mount Marty Coll (SD)
Mount Mercy U (IA)
Mount Saint Mary Coll (NY)
Mount St. Mary's Coll (CA)
Mount St. Mary's U (MD)
Mount Vernon Nazarene U (OH)
Muhlenberg Coll (PA)
Murray State U (KY)
National U (CA)
Nazareth Coll of Rochester (NY)
Nebraska Wesleyan U (NE)
Neumann U (PA)
Newbury Coll (MA)
New England Coll (NH)
Newman U (KS)
New Mexico Highlands U (NM)
New Mexico State U (NM)
New York Inst of Technology (NY)
New York U (NY)
Niagara U (NY)
North Carolina Ag and Tech State U (NC)
North Carolina State U (NC)
North Central Coll (IL)
North Dakota State U (ND)
Northeastern Illinois U (IL)
Northeastern State U (OK)
Northeastern U (MA)
Northern Arizona U (AZ)
Northern Illinois U (IL)

Northern Kentucky U (KY)
Northern Michigan U (MI)
Northern State U (SD)
North Georgia Coll & State U (GA)
North Greenville U (SC)
Northwest Christian U (OR)
Northwestern Coll (IA)
Northwestern Coll (MN)
Northwestern Oklahoma State U (OK)
Northwestern State U of Louisiana (LA)
Northwest Missouri State U (MO)
Northwest Nazarene U (ID)
Northwest U (WA)
Nova Southeastern U (FL)
Nyack Coll (NY)
Oglethorpe U (GA)
The Ohio State U (OH)
Ohio U (OH)
Ohio Valley U (WV)
Ohio Wesleyan U (OH)
Oklahoma Christian U (OK)
Oklahoma City U (OK)
Oklahoma Panhandle State U (OK)
Oklahoma State U (OK)
Oklahoma Wesleyan U (OK)
Old Dominion U (VA)
Oregon State U (OR)
Ouachita Baptist U (AR)
Our Lady of the Lake U of San Antonio (TX)
Pace U (NY)
Pacific U (OR)
Paine Coll (GA)
Palm Beach Atlantic U (FL)
Peirce Coll (PA)
Penn State Abington (PA)
Penn State Altoona (PA)
Penn State Beaver (PA)
Penn State Berks (PA)
Penn State Brandywine (PA)
Penn State DuBois (PA)
Penn State Erie, The Behrend Coll (PA)
Penn State Fayette, The Eberly Campus (PA)
Penn State Greater Allegheny (PA)
Penn State Hazleton (PA)
Penn State Lehigh Valley (PA)
Penn State Mont Alto (PA)
Penn State New Kensington (PA)
Penn State Schuylkill (PA)
Penn State Shenango (PA)
Penn State U Park (PA)
Penn State Wilkes-Barre (PA)
Penn State Worthington Scranton (PA)
Penn State York (PA)
Pennsylvania Coll of Technology (PA)
Pepperdine U, Malibu (CA)
Philadelphia U (PA)
Pittsburg State U (KS)
Point Park U (PA)
Portland State U (OR)
Prairie View A&M U (TX)
Providence Coll (RI)
Purdue U (IN)
Purdue U Calumet (IN)
Queens Coll of the City U of New York (NY)
Quincy U (IL)
Quinnipiac U (CT)
Radford U (VA)
Ramapo Coll of New Jersey (NJ)
Randolph-Macon Coll (VA)
Regis U (CO)
Reinhardt U (GA)
Rhode Island Coll (RI)
Rider U (NJ)
Robert Morris U (PA)
Rockford Coll (IL)
Roosevelt U (IL)
Rosemont Coll (PA)
Rutgers, The State U of New Jersey, Camden (NJ)
Rutgers, The State U of New Jersey, Newark (NJ)
Rutgers, The State U of New Jersey, New Brunswick (NJ)
Sacred Heart U (CT)
Sage Coll of Albany (NY)
Saginaw Valley State U (MI)
St. Ambrose U (IA)
Saint Anselm Coll (NH)
St. Bonaventure U (NY)
St. Catherine U (MN)
St. Edward's U (TX)
Saint Francis U (PA)

St. Francis Xavier U (NS, Canada)
St. John Fisher Coll (NY)
Saint John's U (MN)
St. John's U (NY)
Saint Joseph Coll (CT)
Saint Joseph's Coll (IN)
St. Joseph's Coll, Long Island Campus (NY)
St. Joseph's Coll, New York (NY)
Saint Joseph's Coll of Maine (ME)
Saint Joseph's U (PA)
Saint Leo U (FL)
Saint Louis U (MO)
Saint Martin's U (WA)
Saint Mary-of-the-Woods Coll (IN)
Saint Mary's Coll (IN)
Saint Mary's Coll of California (CA)
Saint Mary's U of Minnesota (MN)
Saint Michael's Coll (VT)
St. Norbert Coll (WI)
St. Thomas Aquinas Coll (NY)
St. Thomas U (FL)
Saint Xavier U (IL)
Salem State U (MA)
Salisbury U (MD)
Salve Regina U (RI)
Samford U (AL)
Sam Houston State U (TX)
San Diego State U (CA)
San Francisco State U (CA)
San Jose State U (CA)
Santa Clara U (CA)
Savannah State U (GA)
Schreiner U (TX)
Scripps Coll (CA)
Seattle Pacific U (WA)
Seton Hill U (PA)
Shepherd U (WV)
Shippensburg U of Pennsylvania (PA)
Shorter U (GA)
Siena Coll (NY)
Siena Heights U (MI)
Silver Lake Coll (WI)
Simpson Coll (IA)
Simpson U (CA)
Slippery Rock U of Pennsylvania (PA)
Southeastern Louisiana U (LA)
Southeastern Oklahoma State U (OK)
Southeastern U (FL)
Southeast Missouri State U (MO)
Southern Arkansas U–Magnolia (AR)
Southern California Inst of Technology (CA)
Southern Connecticut State U (CT)
Southern Illinois U Carbondale (IL)
Southern Illinois U Edwardsville (IL)
Southern Methodist U (TX)
Southern Nazarene U (OK)
Southern Oregon U (OR)
Southern Polytechnic State U (GA)
Southern Utah U (UT)
Southern Wesleyan U (SC)
Southwestern Adventist U (TX)
Southwestern Assemblies of God U (TX)
Southwestern Coll (KS)
Spalding U (KY)
Spring Arbor U (MI)
Spring Hill Coll (AL)
State U of New York at Binghamton (NY)
State U of New York at Fredonia (NY)
State U of New York at New Paltz (NY)
State U of New York at Oswego (NY)
State U of New York at Plattsburgh (NY)
State U of New York Coll at Geneseo (NY)
State U of New York Coll at Old Westbury (NY)
State U of New York Coll at Oneonta (NY)
Stephen F. Austin State U (TX)
Stephens Coll (MO)
Stetson U (FL)
Stevenson U (MD)
Stonehill Coll (MA)
Strayer U - Akron Campus (OH)
Strayer U - Alexandria Campus (VA)
Strayer U - Allentown Campus (PA)
Strayer U - Anne Arundel Campus (MD)
Strayer U - Arlington Campus (VA)

Strayer U - Augusta Campus (GA)
Strayer U - Baymeadows Campus (FL)
Strayer U - Birmingham Campus (AL)
Strayer U - Brickell Campus (FL)
Strayer U - Cedar Hill Campus (TX)
Strayer U - Center City Campus (PA)
Strayer U - Chamblee Campus (GA)
Strayer U - Charleston Campus (SC)
Strayer U - Cherry Hill Campus (NJ)
Strayer U - Chesapeake Campus (VA)
Strayer U - Chesterfield Campus (VA)
Strayer U - Christiana Campus (DE)
Strayer U - Cincinnati Campus (OH)
Strayer U - Cobb County Campus (GA)
Strayer U - Columbia Campus (SC)
Strayer U - Columbus Campus (GA)
Strayer U - Columbus Campus (OH)
Strayer U - Coral Springs Campus (FL)
Strayer U - Cranberry Woods Campus (PA)
Strayer U - Delaware County Campus (PA)
Strayer U - Doral Campus (FL)
Strayer U - Douglasville Campus (GA)
Strayer U - Fairborn Campus (OH)
Strayer U - Fairview Park Campus (OH)
Strayer U - Florence Campus (KY)
Strayer U - Fort Lauderdale Campus (FL)
Strayer U - Fredericksburg Campus (VA)
Strayer U - Greensboro Campus (NC)
Strayer U - Greenville Campus (SC)
Strayer U - Henrico Campus (VA)
Strayer U - Huntersville Campus (NC)
Strayer U - Huntsville Campus (AL)
Strayer U - Irving Campus (TX)
Strayer U - Jackson Campus (MS)
Strayer U - Katy Campus (TX)
Strayer U - King of Prussia Campus (PA)
Strayer U - Knoxville Campus (TN)
Strayer U - Lawrenceville Campus (NJ)
Strayer U - Lexington Campus (KY)
Strayer U - Lithonia Campus (GA)
Strayer U - Little Rock Campus (AR)
Strayer U - Loudoun Campus (VA)
Strayer U - Louisville Campus (KY)
Strayer U - Lower Bucks County Campus (PA)
Strayer U - Maitland Campus (FL)
Strayer U - Manassas Campus (VA)
Strayer U - Mason Campus (OH)
Strayer U - Metairie Campus (LA)
Strayer U - Milwaukee Campus (WI)
Strayer U - Miramar Campus (FL)
Strayer U - Morrow Campus (GA)
Strayer U - Nashville Campus (TN)
Strayer U - Newport News Campus (VA)
Strayer U - North Austin Campus (TX)
Strayer U - North Charlotte Campus (NC)
Strayer U - North Indianapolis Campus (IN)
Strayer U - North Raleigh Campus (NC)
Strayer U - Northwest Houston Campus (TX)
Strayer U - Orlando East Campus (FL)
Strayer U - Owings Mills Campus (MD)
Strayer U - Palm Beach Gardens Campus (FL)
Strayer U - Penn Center West Campus (PA)
Strayer U - Piscataway Campus (NJ)
Strayer U - Plano Campus (TX)
Strayer U - Prince George's Campus (MD)
Strayer U - Rockville Campus (MD)
Strayer U - Roswell Campus (GA)
Strayer U - RTP Campus (NC)
Strayer U - Salt Lake Campus (UT)
Strayer U - Sand Lake Campus (FL)
Strayer U - Savannah Campus (GA)

Strayer U - Shelby Oaks Campus (TN)
Strayer U - South Charlotte Campus (NC)
Strayer U - South Raleigh Campus (NC)
Strayer U - Takoma Park Campus (DC)
Strayer U - Tampa East Campus (FL)
Strayer U - Tampa Westshore Campus (FL)
Strayer U - Teays Valley Campus (WV)
Strayer U - Thousand Oaks Campus (TN)
Strayer U - Virginia Beach Campus (VA)
Strayer U - Washington Campus (DC)
Strayer U - White Marsh Campus (MD)
Strayer U - Willingboro Campus (NJ)
Strayer U - Woodbridge Campus (VA)
Suffolk U (MA)
Sul Ross State U (TX)
Susquehanna U (PA)
Syracuse U (NY)
Tabor Coll (KS)
Talladega Coll (AL)
Tarleton State U (TX)
Taylor U (IN)
Temple U (PA)
Tennessee Technological U (TN)
Tennessee Wesleyan Coll (TN)
Texas A&M Intl U (TX)
Texas A&M U (TX)
Texas A&M U–Corpus Christi (TX)
Texas A&M U–Kingsville (TX)
Texas Christian U (TX)
Texas Lutheran U (TX)
Texas Southern U (TX)
Texas State U–San Marcos (TX)
Texas Tech U (TX)
Texas Wesleyan U (TX)
Texas Woman's U (TX)
Thiel Coll (PA)
Thomas Edison State Coll (NJ)
Thomas More Coll (KY)
Thomas U (GA)
Tiffin U (OH)
Towson U (MD)
Transylvania U (KY)
Trevecca Nazarene U (TN)
Trine U (IN)
Trinity U (TX)
Troy U (AL)
Truman State U (MO)
Tulane U (LA)
Tuskegee U (AL)
Union Coll (KY)
Union Coll (NE)
Union U (TN)
United States Intl U (Kenya)
Université de Sherbrooke (QC, Canada)
Université du Québec en Outaouais (QC, Canada)
U at Buffalo, the State U of New York (NY)
The U of Alabama (AL)
The U of Alabama at Birmingham (AL)
The U of Alabama in Huntsville (AL)
U of Alaska Fairbanks (AK)
U of Arkansas (AR)
U of Arkansas at Pine Bluff (AR)
U of Baltimore (MD)
U of Bridgeport (CT)
The U of British Columbia (BC, Canada)
The U of British Columbia–Okanagan (BC, Canada)
U of Central Florida (FL)
U of Charleston (WV)
U of Cincinnati (OH)
U of Colorado Boulder (CO)
U of Dayton (OH)
U of Delaware (DE)
U of Denver (CO)
U of Dubuque (IA)
U of Evansville (IN)
The U of Findlay (OH)
U of Florida (FL)
U of Georgia (GA)
U of Hartford (CT)
U of Hawaii at Manoa (HI)
U of Hawaii–West Oahu (HI)
U of Houston (TX)

U of Houston–Clear Lake (TX)
U of Houston–Downtown (TX)
U of Houston–Victoria (TX)
U of Idaho (ID)
U of Illinois at Chicago (IL)
U of Illinois at Springfield (IL)
U of Indianapolis (IN)
The U of Iowa (IA)
The U of Kansas (KS)
U of La Verne (CA)
U of Lethbridge (AB, Canada)
U of Louisiana at Lafayette (LA)
U of Louisiana at Monroe (LA)
U of Louisville (KY)
U of Maine at Augusta (ME)
U of Maine at Presque Isle (ME)
U of Manitoba (MB, Canada)
U of Mary Hardin-Baylor (TX)
U of Maryland, Coll Park (MD)
U of Maryland U Coll (MD)
U of Massachusetts Amherst (MA)
U of Massachusetts Dartmouth (MA)
U of Memphis (TN)
U of Miami (FL)
U of Michigan–Dearborn (MI)
U of Michigan–Flint (MI)
U of Minnesota, Crookston (MN)
U of Minnesota, Duluth (MN)
U of Minnesota, Twin Cities Campus (MN)
U of Mississippi (MS)
U of Missouri (MO)
U of Missouri–St. Louis (MO)
U of Mobile (AL)
U of Montevallo (AL)
U of Mount Union (OH)
U of Nebraska at Omaha (NE)
U of Nebraska–Lincoln (NE)
U of Nevada, Las Vegas (NV)
U of Nevada, Reno (NV)
U of New Brunswick Fredericton (NB, Canada)
U of New Brunswick Saint John (NB, Canada)
U of New Haven (CT)
The U of North Carolina at Asheville (NC)
The U of North Carolina at Charlotte (NC)
The U of North Carolina at Greensboro (NC)
The U of North Carolina at Pembroke (NC)
The U of North Carolina Wilmington (NC)
U of North Dakota (ND)
U of Northern Iowa (IA)
U of North Florida (FL)
U of North Texas (TX)
U of Notre Dame (IN)
U of Oklahoma (OK)
U of Oregon (OR)
U of Ottawa (ON, Canada)
U of Pennsylvania (PA)
U of Pittsburgh (PA)
U of Pittsburgh at Bradford (PA)
U of Pittsburgh at Greensburg (PA)
U of Pittsburgh at Johnstown (PA)
U of Portland (OR)
U of Puerto Rico at Humacao (PR)
U of Redlands (CA)
U of Regina (SK, Canada)
U of Rhode Island (RI)
U of Richmond (VA)
U of Rio Grande (OH)
U of St. Francis (IL)
U of Saint Mary (KS)
U of St. Thomas (MN)
U of St. Thomas (TX)
U of San Diego (CA)
U of San Francisco (CA)
U of Saskatchewan (SK, Canada)
The U of Scranton (PA)
U of Sioux Falls (SD)
U of South Alabama (AL)
U of South Carolina (SC)
The U of South Dakota (SD)
U of Southern California (CA)
U of Southern Indiana (IN)
U of Southern Maine (ME)
U of Southern Mississippi (MS)
U of South Florida (FL)
The U of Tampa (FL)
The U of Tennessee (TN)
The U of Tennessee at Martin (TN)
The U of Texas at Arlington (TX)
The U of Texas at Austin (TX)
The U of Texas at Dallas (TX)
The U of Texas at San Antonio (TX)
The U of Texas at Tyler (TX)

The U of Texas of the Permian Basin (TX)
The U of Texas–Pan American (TX)
U of the Cumberlands (KY)
U of the Incarnate Word (TX)
U of the Ozarks (AR)
U of the Southwest (NM)
U of the Virgin Islands (VI)
The U of Toledo (OH)
U of Tulsa (OK)
U of Utah (UT)
U of Washington (WA)
U of Washington, Bothell (WA)
U of Waterloo (ON, Canada)
The U of Western Ontario (ON, Canada)
U of West Florida (FL)
U of West Georgia (GA)
U of Wisconsin–Eau Claire (WI)
U of Wisconsin–Green Bay (WI)
U of Wisconsin–La Crosse (WI)
U of Wisconsin–Madison (WI)
U of Wisconsin–Parkside (WI)
U of Wisconsin–Platteville (WI)
U of Wisconsin–River Falls (WI)
U of Wisconsin–Stevens Point (WI)
U of Wisconsin–Superior (WI)
U of Wisconsin–Whitewater (WI)
U of Wyoming (WY)
Upper Iowa U (IA)
Ursuline Coll (OH)
Utah State U (UT)
Utah Valley U (UT)
Valdosta State U (GA)
Valparaiso U (IN)
Villanova U (PA)
Virginia Commonwealth U (VA)
Virginia Polytechnic Inst and State U (VA)
Virginia State U (VA)
Viterbo U (WI)
Wagner Coll (NY)
Wake Forest U (NC)
Walden U (MN)
Walla Walla U (WA)
Walsh U (OH)
Wartburg Coll (IA)
Washburn U (KS)
Washington & Jefferson Coll (PA)
Washington and Lee U (VA)
Washington State U (WA)
Washington U in St. Louis (MO)
Waynesburg U (PA)
Wayne State U (MI)
Webber Intl U (FL)
Weber State U (UT)
Webster U (MO)
West Chester U of Pennsylvania (PA)
Western Carolina U (NC)
Western Connecticut State U (CT)
Western Illinois U (IL)
Western Intl U (AZ)
Western Kentucky U (KY)
Western Michigan U (MI)
Western New England U (MA)
Western State Coll of Colorado (CO)
West Liberty U (WV)
Westminster Coll (MO)
Westminster Coll (UT)
West Virginia U (WV)
Wheeling Jesuit U (WV)
Wichita State U (KS)
Widener U (PA)
Wilkes U (PA)
William Jewell Coll (MO)
William Paterson U of New Jersey (NJ)
Wilmington Coll (OH)
Wilmington U (DE)
Wingate U (NC)
Winona State U (MN)
Wofford Coll (SC)
Woodbury U (CA)
Wright State U (OH)
Xavier U (OH)
Xavier U of Louisiana (LA)
York Coll of Pennsylvania (PA)
York Coll of the City U of New York (NY)
Youngstown State U (OH)

ACCOUNTING AND BUSINESS/ MANAGEMENT
Bethel U (TN)
Chestnut Hill Coll (PA)
Florida Ag and Mech U (FL)

Florida Inst of Technology (FL)
Illinois State U (IL)
Intl Business Coll, Fort Wayne (IN)
Keystone Coll (PA)
Maranatha Baptist Bible Coll (WI)
Menlo Coll (CA)
Mitchell Coll (CT)
Presbyterian Coll (SC)
Rocky Mountain Coll (MT)
Santa Clara U (CA)
Sierra Nevada Coll (NV)
Tabor Coll (KS)
The U of Western Ontario (ON, Canada)
Walla Walla U (WA)
Washington and Lee U (VA)
Western State Coll of Colorado (CO)
Young Harris Coll (GA)

ACCOUNTING AND COMPUTER SCIENCE
California State U, Chico (CA)
Goldey-Beacom Coll (DE)
Husson U (ME)
San Jose State U (CA)

ACCOUNTING AND FINANCE
Bethel U (MN)
Boise State U (ID)
Clarkson U (NY)
DEREE - The American Coll of Greece (Greece)
Drake U (IA)
Ferris State U (MI)
Lourdes Coll (OH)
Northern Michigan U (MI)
Saint Francis U (PA)
Salem State U (MA)
U of North Dakota (ND)
U of Waterloo (ON, Canada)
The U of Western Ontario (ON, Canada)
Western State Coll of Colorado (CO)

ACCOUNTING RELATED
Bentley U (MA)
Brigham Young U (UT)
Central Michigan U (MI)
Duquesne U (PA)
Franklin U (OH)
Keystone Coll (PA)
Maryville U of Saint Louis (MO)
McDaniel Coll (MD)
North Dakota State U (ND)
Northern Michigan U (MI)
Rocky Mountain Coll (MT)
Saint Mary-of-the-Woods Coll (IN)
Saint Mary's Coll of California (CA)
State U of New York at Oswego (NY)

ACCOUNTING TECHNOLOGY AND BOOKKEEPING
Bryant U (RI)
Canisius Coll (NY)
Ferris State U (MI)
ITT Tech Inst, Indianapolis (IN)
ITT Tech Inst, Cordova (TN)
Lewis-Clark State Coll (ID)
Rowan U (NJ)
St. Edward's U (TX)
U of Hawaii at Manoa (HI)

ACOUSTICS
American U (DC)

ACTING
Arcadia U (PA)
Bard Coll (NY)
Barry U (FL)
Bennington Coll (VT)
Boston U (MA)
Brigham Young U (UT)
California State U, Long Beach (CA)
Central Michigan U (MI)
Chapman U (CA)
Coker Coll (SC)
Columbia Coll Chicago (IL)
DePaul U (IL)
Drake U (IA)
Florida State U (FL)
Greensboro Coll (NC)
Hofstra U (NY)
Illinois Wesleyan U (IL)
Ithaca Coll (NY)
Johnson State Coll (VT)

Kean U (NJ)
Keene State Coll (NH)
Kent State U (OH)
Lindenwood U (MO)
Long Island U, C.W. Post Campus (NY)
Michigan State U (MI)
Northwest Missouri State U (MO)
Ohio U (OH)
Old Dominion U (VA)
Pace U (NY)
Penn State Abington (PA)
Penn State Altoona (PA)
Penn State Beaver (PA)
Penn State Berks (PA)
Penn State Brandywine (PA)
Penn State DuBois (PA)
Penn State Erie, The Behrend Coll (PA)
Penn State Fayette, The Eberly Campus (PA)
Penn State Greater Allegheny (PA)
Penn State Hazleton (PA)
Penn State Lehigh Valley (PA)
Penn State Mont Alto (PA)
Penn State New Kensington (PA)
Penn State Schuylkill (PA)
Penn State Shenango (PA)
Penn State U Park (PA)
Penn State Wilkes-Barre (PA)
Penn State Worthington Scranton (PA)
Penn State York (PA)
Roosevelt U (IL)
Salem State U (MA)
Sarah Lawrence Coll (NY)
Seton Hill U (PA)
Shenandoah U (VA)
Slippery Rock U of Pennsylvania (PA)
Suffolk U (MA)
Temple U (PA)
Texas Tech U (TX)
Trinity U (TX)
U of Hartford (CT)
U of Maryland, Baltimore County (MD)
U of Miami (FL)
U of Northern Iowa (IA)
U of Regina (SK, Canada)
U of Southern California (CA)
The U of the Arts (PA)
Virginia Intermont Coll (VA)
Webster U (MO)
Western Michigan U (MI)
Wright State U (OH)

ACTUARIAL SCIENCE
Appalachian State U (NC)
Arcadia U (PA)
Ball State U (IN)
Bellarmine U (KY)
Bob Jones U (SC)
Brigham Young U (UT)
Bryant U (RI)
Butler U (IN)
Carroll U (WI)
Central Coll (IA)
Central Michigan U (MI)
Concordia U (QC, Canada)
Concordia U Wisconsin (WI)
Dakota Wesleyan U (SD)
Drake U (IA)
Eastern Michigan U (MI)
Elmhurst Coll (IL)
Georgia State U (GA)
Indiana U Northwest (IN)
Indiana U South Bend (IN)
Lebanon Valley Coll (PA)
Maryville U of Saint Louis (MO)
The Master's Coll and Sem (CA)
New Jersey Inst of Technology (NJ)
North Central Coll (IL)
Northwestern Coll (IA)
The Ohio State U (OH)
Ohio U (OH)
Penn State Abington (PA)
Penn State Altoona (PA)
Penn State Beaver (PA)
Penn State Berks (PA)
Penn State Brandywine (PA)
Penn State DuBois (PA)
Penn State Erie, The Behrend Coll (PA)
Penn State Fayette, The Eberly Campus (PA)
Penn State Greater Allegheny (PA)
Penn State Hazleton (PA)

Penn State Lehigh Valley (PA)
Penn State Mont Alto (PA)
Penn State New Kensington (PA)
Penn State Schuylkill (PA)
Penn State Shenango (PA)
Penn State U Park (PA)
Penn State Wilkes-Barre (PA)
Penn State Worthington Scranton (PA)
Penn State York (PA)
Pittsburg State U (KS)
Purdue U (IN)
Queens Coll of the City U of New York (NY)
Quinnipiac U (CT)
Rider U (NJ)
Robert Morris U (PA)
Roosevelt U (IL)
St. John's U (NY)
Saint Joseph's U (PA)
Siena Coll (NY)
Simon Fraser U (BC, Canada)
Simpson Coll (IA)
Slippery Rock U of Pennsylvania (PA)
Spring Arbor U (MI)
State U of New York at Binghamton (NY)
Temple U (PA)
Texas Christian U (TX)
Thiel Coll (PA)
The U of Iowa (IA)
U of Manitoba (MB, Canada)
U of Michigan–Flint (MI)
U of Minnesota, Duluth (MN)
U of Minnesota, Twin Cities Campus (MN)
U of Nebraska–Lincoln (NE)
U of Pennsylvania (PA)
U of Regina (SK, Canada)
U of St. Thomas (MN)
The U of Texas at Dallas (TX)
The U of Texas at San Antonio (TX)
U of Waterloo (ON, Canada)
The U of Western Ontario (ON, Canada)
U of Wisconsin–Madison (WI)
Valparaiso U (IN)
Worcester Polytechnic Inst (MA)

ADMINISTRATIVE ASSISTANT AND SECRETARIAL SCIENCE
Baker Coll of Muskegon (MI)
Baker Coll of Owosso (MI)
Campbellsville U (KY)
Inter American U of Puerto Rico, Bayamón Campus (PR)
Lamar U (TX)
Lewis-Clark State Coll (ID)
Lincoln Christian U (IL)
Maranatha Baptist Bible Coll (WI)
North Carolina Ag and Tech State U (NC)
Northwest Missouri State U (MO)
Sul Ross State U (TX)
Tabor Coll (KS)
U of Puerto Rico at Humacao (PR)
Valdosta State U (GA)

ADULT AND CONTINUING EDUCATION
Atlantic Union Coll (MA)
Auburn U (AL)
Brock U (ON, Canada)
Dakota Wesleyan U (SD)
Eastern Washington U (WA)
Fisher Coll (MA)
Free Will Baptist Bible Coll (TN)
Laurentian U (ON, Canada)
Louisiana Coll (LA)
Louisiana State U and Ag and Mech Coll (LA)
Mars Hill Coll (NC)
San Diego Christian Coll (CA)
Tabor Coll (KS)
U of Georgia (GA)
U of Minnesota, Twin Cities Campus (MN)
U of Nevada, Las Vegas (NV)
U of New Brunswick Fredericton (NB, Canada)
U of Regina (SK, Canada)
U of San Francisco (CA)
The U of Toledo (OH)

ADULT AND CONTINUING EDUCATION ADMINISTRATION
Concordia Coll–New York (NY)

Marshall U (WV)
Penn State Abington (PA)
Penn State Altoona (PA)
Penn State Beaver (PA)
Penn State Berks (PA)
Penn State Brandywine (PA)
Penn State DuBois (PA)
Penn State Erie, The Behrend Coll (PA)
Penn State Fayette, The Eberly Campus (PA)
Penn State Greater Allegheny (PA)
Penn State Hazleton (PA)
Penn State Lehigh Valley (PA)
Penn State Mont Alto (PA)
Penn State New Kensington (PA)
Penn State Schuylkill (PA)
Penn State Shenango (PA)
Penn State U Park (PA)
Penn State Wilkes-Barre (PA)
Penn State Worthington Scranton (PA)
Penn State York (PA)

ADULT DEVELOPMENT AND AGING
Arizona State U (AZ)
Madonna U (MI)
St. Thomas U (NB, Canada)
York Coll of the City U of New York (NY)

ADULT HEALTH NURSING
Concordia Coll–New York (NY)
Humboldt State U (CA)
Pennsylvania Coll of Technology (PA)
U of Sioux Falls (SD)
Worcester State U (MA)

ADVERTISING
Adams State Coll (CO)
Appalachian State U (NC)
Art Center Coll of Design (CA)
The Art Inst of Ohio–Cincinnati (OH)
Barry U (FL)
Belmont U (TN)
Boise State U (ID)
Brigham Young U (UT)
California State U, Fullerton (CA)
Central Michigan U (MI)
Columbia Coll Chicago (IL)
Drake U (IA)
Drury U (MO)
Fashion Inst of Technology (NY)
Ferris State U (MI)
Florida Southern Coll (FL)
Fontbonne U (MO)
Franklin Pierce U (NH)
Gannon U (PA)
Grand Valley State U (MI)
Harding U (AR)
Hawai`i Pacific U (HI)
The Illinois Inst of Art–Tinley Park (IL)
Intl Acad of Design & Technology (FL)
Iowa State U of Science and Technology (IA)
Johnson & Wales U (RI)
Kent State U (OH)
Lindenwood U (MO)
Louisiana Coll (LA)
Loyola U Chicago (IL)
Marist Coll (NY)
Marquette U (WI)
Metropolitan State U (MN)
Michigan State U (MI)
Minneapolis Coll of Art and Design (MN)
Morningside Coll (IA)
Murray State U (KY)
New York Inst of Technology (NY)
Northeastern State U (OK)
Northern Arizona U (AZ)
Northwest Missouri State U (MO)
Oklahoma Christian U (OK)
Oklahoma City U (OK)
Pace U (NY)
Penn State Abington (PA)
Penn State Altoona (PA)
Penn State Beaver (PA)
Penn State Berks (PA)
Penn State Brandywine (PA)
Penn State DuBois (PA)
Penn State Erie, The Behrend Coll (PA)

INDEXES

INDEXES

Penn State Fayette, The Eberly
Campus (PA)
Penn State Greater Allegheny (PA)
Penn State Hazleton (PA)
Penn State Lehigh Valley (PA)
Penn State Mont Alto (PA)
Penn State New Kensington (PA)
Penn State Schuylkill (PA)
Penn State Shenango (PA)
Penn State U Park (PA)
Penn State Wilkes-Barre (PA)
Penn State Worthington Scranton
(PA)
Penn State York (PA)
Purdue U (IN)
South Dakota State U (SD)
Southeast Missouri State U (MO)
Stephen F. Austin State U (TX)
Texas A&M U (TX)
Texas State U–San Marcos (TX)
U of Arkansas (AR)
U of Central Missouri (MO)
U of Delaware (DE)
U of Georgia (GA)
U of Maine (ME)
U of Minnesota, Crookston (MN)
U of Minnesota, Twin Cities
Campus (MN)
U of Saskatchewan (SK, Canada)
U of Wisconsin–River Falls (WI)
U of Wyoming (WY)
Vermont Tech Coll (VT)

**AGRICULTURAL AND DOMESTIC
ANIMAL SERVICES RELATED**
Sterling Coll (VT)
Tarleton State U (TX)

**AGRICULTURAL AND
EXTENSION EDUCATION**
North Carolina State U (NC)
Northwestern Oklahoma State U
(OK)
Penn State Abington (PA)
Penn State Altoona (PA)
Penn State Beaver (PA)
Penn State Berks (PA)
Penn State Brandywine (PA)
Penn State DuBois (PA)
Penn State Erie, The Behrend Coll
(PA)
Penn State Fayette, The Eberly
Campus (PA)
Penn State Greater Allegheny (PA)
Penn State Hazleton (PA)
Penn State Lehigh Valley (PA)
Penn State Mont Alto (PA)
Penn State New Kensington (PA)
Penn State Schuylkill (PA)
Penn State Shenango (PA)
Penn State Wilkes-Barre (PA)
Penn State Worthington Scranton
(PA)
Penn State York (PA)
Purdue U (IN)
U of Georgia (GA)

**AGRICULTURAL AND FOOD
PRODUCTS PROCESSING**
Kansas State U (KS)
Texas A&M U (TX)
The U of British Columbia (BC,
Canada)
U of Florida (FL)
U of Nebraska–Lincoln (NE)
Washington State U (WA)

**AGRICULTURAL AND
HORTICULTURAL PLANT
BREEDING**
Delaware State U (DE)
Sterling Coll (VT)

**AGRICULTURAL ANIMAL
BREEDING**
U of Nevada, Reno (NV)

**AGRICULTURAL BUSINESS AND
MANAGEMENT**
Alcorn State U (MS)
Arizona State U (AZ)
Brigham Young U (UT)
California State Polytechnic U,
Pomona (CA)
California State U, Chico (CA)
Clemson U (SC)
Cornell U (NY)

Delaware State U (DE)
Dickinson State U (ND)
Florida Southern Coll (FL)
Fort Lewis Coll (CO)
Freed-Hardeman U (TN)
Hardin-Simmons U (TX)
Iowa State U of Science and
Technology (IA)
Kansas State U (KS)
Lincoln U (MO)
Louisiana State U and Ag and Mech
Coll (LA)
Lubbock Christian U (TX)
Michigan State U (MI)
Montana State U (MT)
North Carolina Ag and Tech State U
(NC)
The Ohio State U (OH)
Oklahoma Panhandle State U (OK)
Oklahoma State U (OK)
Oregon State U (OR)
Rocky Mountain Coll (MT)
Southern Arkansas U–Magnolia
(AR)
Sul Ross State U (TX)
Tennessee Technological U (TN)
Texas A&M U (TX)
Texas A&M U–Kingsville (TX)
Texas Tech U (TX)
Tuskegee U (AL)
U of Central Missouri (MO)
U of Delaware (DE)
U of Guelph (ON, Canada)
U of Hawaii at Hilo (HI)
U of Idaho (ID)
U of Louisiana at Monroe (LA)
U of Minnesota, Twin Cities
Campus (MN)
U of Missouri (MO)
U of Nebraska–Lincoln (NE)
The U of Tennessee at Martin (TN)
U of Wisconsin–Platteville (WI)
U of Wisconsin–River Falls (WI)
Upper Iowa U (IA)
Utah State U (UT)
Washington State U (WA)
Wilmington Coll (OH)

**AGRICULTURAL BUSINESS AND
MANAGEMENT RELATED**
Delaware State U (DE)
Penn State New Kensington (PA)
Purdue U (IN)
U of California, Davis (CA)
U of Minnesota, Twin Cities
Campus (MN)
The U of Tennessee (TN)
Utah State U (UT)

**AGRICULTURAL BUSINESS
TECHNOLOGY**
U of Minnesota, Crookston (MN)
Washington State U (WA)

**AGRICULTURAL
COMMUNICATION/JOURNALISM**
Auburn U (AL)
Kansas State U (KS)
North Dakota State U (ND)
The Ohio State U (OH)
Oklahoma State U (OK)
Purdue U (IN)
South Dakota State U (SD)
Texas A&M U (TX)
Texas Tech U (TX)
U of Georgia (GA)
U of Idaho (ID)
U of Nebraska–Lincoln (NE)
U of Wisconsin–Madison (WI)
U of Wyoming (WY)
Washington State U (WA)

AGRICULTURAL ECONOMICS
Alabama Ag and Mech U (AL)
Alcorn State U (MS)
Auburn U (AL)
Brigham Young U (UT)
Clemson U (SC)
Colorado State U (CO)
Cornell U (NY)
Kansas State U (KS)
Michigan State U (MI)
Mississippi State U (MS)
North Carolina Ag and Tech State U
(NC)
North Dakota State U (ND)
Northwest Missouri State U (MO)
The Ohio State U (OH)

Oklahoma State U (OK)
Oregon State U (OR)
Purdue U (IN)
South Dakota State U (SD)
Southern Illinois U Carbondale (IL)
Tarleton State U (TX)
Texas A&M U (TX)
Texas Tech U (TX)
The U of Arizona (AZ)
U of Arkansas at Pine Bluff (AR)
U of Central Missouri (MO)
U of Delaware (DE)
U of Florida (FL)
U of Georgia (GA)
U of Guelph (ON, Canada)
U of Idaho (ID)
U of Maine (ME)
U of Manitoba (MB, Canada)
U of Maryland, Coll Park (MD)
U of Massachusetts Amherst (MA)
U of Minnesota, Twin Cities
Campus (MN)
U of Missouri (MO)
U of Nebraska–Lincoln (NE)
U of Nevada, Reno (NV)
U of Saskatchewan (SK, Canada)
U of Wisconsin–Madison (WI)
U of Wisconsin–River Falls (WI)
Utah State U (UT)
Virginia Polytechnic Inst and State
U (VA)
Washington State U (WA)
West Virginia U (WV)

AGRICULTURAL ENGINEERING
Auburn U (AL)
California Polytechnic State U, San
Luis Obispo (CA)
Clemson U (SC)
Cornell U (NY)
Dordt Coll (IA)
Florida Ag and Mech U (FL)
Iowa State U of Science and
Technology (IA)
Kansas State U (KS)
Michigan State U (MI)
Missouri U of Science and
Technology (MO)
New Mexico State U (NM)
North Carolina Ag and Tech State U
(NC)
North Carolina State U (NC)
North Dakota State U (ND)
The Ohio State U (OH)
Oklahoma State U (OK)
Penn State Abington (PA)
Penn State Beaver (PA)
Penn State Brandywine (PA)
Penn State DuBois (PA)
Penn State Erie, The Behrend Coll
(PA)
Penn State Fayette, The Eberly
Campus (PA)
Penn State Greater Allegheny (PA)
Penn State Hazleton (PA)
Penn State Lehigh Valley (PA)
Penn State Mont Alto (PA)
Penn State New Kensington (PA)
Penn State Schuylkill (PA)
Penn State Shenango (PA)
Penn State U Park (PA)
Penn State Wilkes-Barre (PA)
Penn State Worthington Scranton
(PA)
Penn State York (PA)
Purdue U (IN)
Rutgers, The State U of New
Jersey, New Brunswick (NJ)
South Dakota State U (SD)
State U of New York Coll of
Environmental Science and
Forestry (NY)
Tennessee Technological U (TN)
Texas A&M U (TX)
The U of Arizona (AZ)
U of Arkansas (AR)
U of California, Los Angeles (CA)
U of California, Santa Cruz (CA)
U of Delaware (DE)
U of Florida (FL)
U of Georgia (GA)
U of Hawaii at Manoa (HI)
U of Idaho (ID)
U of Maine (ME)
U of Manitoba (MB, Canada)
U of Maryland, Coll Park (MD)
U of Minnesota, Twin Cities
Campus (MN)

Oklahoma State U (OK)
Oregon State U (OR)
Purdue U (IN)
South Dakota State U (SD)
Southern Illinois U Carbondale (IL)
Tarleton State U (TX)
Texas A&M U (TX)
Texas Tech U (TX)
The U of Arizona (AZ)
U of Arkansas at Pine Bluff (AR)
U of Central Missouri (MO)
U of Delaware (DE)
U of Florida (FL)
U of Georgia (GA)
U of Guelph (ON, Canada)
U of Idaho (ID)
U of Maine (ME)
U of Manitoba (MB, Canada)
U of Maryland, Coll Park (MD)
U of Massachusetts Amherst (MA)
U of Minnesota, Twin Cities
Campus (MN)
U of Missouri (MO)
U of Nebraska–Lincoln (NE)
U of Nevada, Reno (NV)
U of Saskatchewan (SK, Canada)
U of Wisconsin–Madison (WI)
U of Wisconsin–River Falls (WI)
Utah State U (UT)
Virginia Polytechnic Inst and State
U (VA)
Washington State U (WA)
West Virginia U (WV)

U of Nebraska–Lincoln (NE)
U of Saskatchewan (SK, Canada)
The U of Tennessee (TN)
U of Wisconsin–Madison (WI)
U of Wisconsin–River Falls (WI)
Utah State U (UT)
Walla Walla U (WA)

**AGRICULTURAL/FARM
SUPPLIES RETAILING AND
WHOLESALING**
Texas A&M U (TX)

**AGRICULTURAL
MECHANIZATION**
California Polytechnic State U, San
Luis Obispo (CA)
Clemson U (SC)
Iowa State U of Science and
Technology (IA)
Kansas State U (KS)
Montana State U (MT)
North Carolina Ag and Tech State U
(NC)
North Carolina State U (NC)
North Dakota State U (ND)
Penn State Abington (PA)
Penn State Altoona (PA)
Penn State Beaver (PA)
Penn State Berks (PA)
Penn State Brandywine (PA)
Penn State DuBois (PA)
Penn State Erie, The Behrend Coll
(PA)
Penn State Fayette, The Eberly
Campus (PA)
Penn State Greater Allegheny (PA)
Penn State Hazleton (PA)
Penn State Lehigh Valley (PA)
Penn State Mont Alto (PA)
Penn State New Kensington (PA)
Penn State Schuylkill (PA)
Penn State Shenango (PA)
Penn State U Park (PA)
Penn State Wilkes-Barre (PA)
Penn State Worthington Scranton
(PA)
Penn State York (PA)
Purdue U (IN)
South Dakota State U (SD)
Stephen F. Austin State U (TX)
U of Idaho (ID)
U of Minnesota, Crookston (MN)
U of Missouri (MO)
U of Nebraska–Lincoln (NE)
U of Wisconsin–River Falls (WI)
Washington State U (WA)

**AGRICULTURAL
MECHANIZATION RELATED**
U of Minnesota, Twin Cities
Campus (MN)

**AGRICULTURAL POWER
MACHINERY OPERATION**
U of Minnesota, Crookston (MN)

AGRICULTURAL PRODUCTION
Stephen F. Austin State U (TX)
Texas A&M U (TX)

**AGRICULTURAL PRODUCTION
RELATED**
Tarleton State U (TX)

**AGRICULTURAL PUBLIC
SERVICES RELATED**
Oklahoma State U (OK)

**AGRICULTURAL TEACHER
EDUCATION**
Arkansas State U (AR)
Auburn U (AL)
California Polytechnic State U, San
Luis Obispo (CA)
California State Polytechnic U,
Pomona (CA)
California State U, Chico (CA)
Clemson U (SC)
Coll of the Ozarks (MO)
Colorado State U (CO)
Cornell U (NY)
Delaware State U (DE)
Dordt Coll (IA)
Eastern New Mexico U (NM)
Iowa State U of Science and
Technology (IA)

Kansas State U (KS)
Louisiana State U and Ag and Mech
Coll (LA)
Mississippi State U (MS)
Missouri State U (MO)
Montana State U (MT)
New Mexico State U (NM)
North Carolina Ag and Tech State U
(NC)
North Carolina State U (NC)
North Dakota State U (ND)
Northwest Missouri State U (MO)
The Ohio State U (OH)
Oklahoma Panhandle State U (OK)
Oklahoma State U (OK)
Penn State U Park (PA)
Purdue U (IN)
South Dakota State U (SD)
Southern Arkansas U–Magnolia
(AR)
State U of New York at Oswego
(NY)
Tarleton State U (TX)
Tennessee Technological U (TN)
The U of Arizona (AZ)
U of Arkansas (AR)
U of Arkansas at Pine Bluff (AR)
U of Delaware (DE)
U of Florida (FL)
U of Georgia (GA)
U of Idaho (ID)
U of Minnesota, Crookston (MN)
U of Minnesota, Twin Cities
Campus (MN)
U of Missouri (MO)
U of Nebraska–Lincoln (NE)
U of Nevada, Reno (NV)
The U of Tennessee (TN)
The U of Tennessee at Martin (TN)
U of Wisconsin–Madison (WI)
U of Wisconsin–Platteville (WI)
U of Wisconsin–River Falls (WI)
U of Wyoming (WY)
Utah State U (UT)
Washington State U (WA)
West Virginia U (WV)
Wilmington Coll (OH)

AGRICULTURE
Alcorn State U (MS)
American U of Beirut (Lebanon)
Auburn U (AL)
Austin Peay State U (TN)
Berea Coll (KY)
California State U, Stanislaus (CA)
Cameron U (OK)
Cornell U (NY)
Delaware State U (DE)
Dordt Coll (IA)
Ferrum Coll (VA)
Florida Ag and Mech U (FL)
Hampshire Coll (MA)
Illinois State U (IL)
Iowa State U of Science and
Technology (IA)
Lincoln U (MO)
Lubbock Christian U (TX)
Mississippi State U (MS)
Missouri State U (MO)
Montana State U (MT)
Murray State U (KY)
New Mexico State U (NM)
North Carolina Ag and Tech State U
(NC)
North Carolina State U (NC)
North Dakota State U (ND)
Northwestern Oklahoma State U
(OK)
Northwest Missouri State U (MO)
Oregon State U (OR)
Penn State Abington (PA)
Penn State Altoona (PA)
Penn State Beaver (PA)
Penn State Berks (PA)
Penn State Brandywine (PA)
Penn State DuBois (PA)
Penn State Erie, The Behrend Coll
(PA)
Penn State Fayette, The Eberly
Campus (PA)
Penn State Greater Allegheny (PA)
Penn State Hazleton (PA)
Penn State Lehigh Valley (PA)
Penn State Mont Alto (PA)
Penn State New Kensington (PA)
Penn State Schuylkill (PA)
Penn State Shenango (PA)
Penn State U Park (PA)

Penn State Wilkes-Barre (PA)
Penn State Worthington Scranton (PA)
Penn State York (PA)
Prairie View A&M U (TX)
Purdue U (IN)
Rutgers, The State U of New Jersey, New Brunswick (NJ)
Sam Houston State U (TX)
South Dakota State U (SD)
Southeast Missouri State U (MO)
Southern Arkansas U–Magnolia (AR)
Southern Illinois U Carbondale (IL)
Stephen F. Austin State U (TX)
Sterling Coll (VT)
Texas A&M U (TX)
Texas A&M U–Kingsville (TX)
Texas State U–San Marcos (TX)
Texas Tech U (TX)
Truman State U (MO)
Tuskegee U (AL)
U of Arkansas at Pine Bluff (AR)
The U of British Columbia (BC, Canada)
U of Delaware (DE)
U of Georgia (GA)
U of Guelph (ON, Canada)
U of Hawaii at Hilo (HI)
U of Lethbridge (AB, Canada)
U of Louisiana at Lafayette (LA)
U of Manitoba (MB, Canada)
U of Maryland, Coll Park (MD)
U of Minnesota, Twin Cities Campus (MN)
U of Missouri (MO)
U of Nebraska–Lincoln (NE)
The U of Tennessee at Martin (TN)
U of Vermont (VT)
U of Wisconsin–River Falls (WI)
Utah State U (UT)
Virginia State U (VA)
Washington State U (WA)
Western Illinois U (IL)
Western Kentucky U (KY)
Wilmington Coll (OH)

AGRICULTURE AND AGRICULTURE OPERATIONS RELATED
Coll of the Atlantic (ME)
Michigan State U (MI)
Tarleton State U (TX)
U of California, Davis (CA)
U of Minnesota, Twin Cities Campus (MN)

AGROECOLOGY AND SUSTAINABLE AGRICULTURE
The Evergreen State Coll (WA)
U of Minnesota, Crookston (MN)
U of New Hampshire (NH)
U of Wyoming (WY)

AGRONOMY AND CROP SCIENCE
Auburn U (AL)
California Polytechnic State U, San Luis Obispo (CA)
California State U, Chico (CA)
Coll of the Ozarks (MO)
Colorado State U (CO)
Delaware State U (DE)
Hardin-Simmons U (TX)
Iowa State U of Science and Technology (IA)
Kansas State U (KS)
Mississippi State U (MS)
Missouri State U (MO)
New Mexico State U (NM)
North Carolina State U (NC)
Northwest Missouri State U (MO)
The Ohio State U (OH)
Oklahoma Panhandle State U (OK)
Oregon State U (OR)
Penn State Abington (PA)
Penn State Altoona (PA)
Penn State Beaver (PA)
Penn State Berks (PA)
Penn State Brandywine (PA)
Penn State DuBois (PA)
Penn State Erie, The Behrend Coll (PA)
Penn State Fayette, The Eberly Campus (PA)
Penn State Greater Allegheny (PA)
Penn State Hazleton (PA)
Penn State Mont Alto (PA)
Penn State New Kensington (PA)

Penn State Shenango (PA)
Penn State Wilkes-Barre (PA)
Penn State Worthington Scranton (PA)
Penn State York (PA)
Purdue U (IN)
South Dakota State U (SD)
Tarleton State U (TX)
Tennessee Technological U (TN)
Texas A&M U (TX)
Texas A&M U–Kingsville (TX)
Texas Tech U (TX)
Tuskegee U (AL)
U of Arkansas (AR)
U of Delaware (DE)
U of Guelph (ON, Canada)
U of Manitoba (MB, Canada)
U of Minnesota, Crookston (MN)
U of Minnesota, Twin Cities Campus (MN)
U of Nebraska–Lincoln (NE)
U of Saskatchewan (SK, Canada)
The U of Tennessee at Martin (TN)
U of Vermont (VT)
U of Wisconsin–Madison (WI)
U of Wisconsin–Platteville (WI)
U of Wisconsin–River Falls (WI)
Utah State U (UT)
Virginia Polytechnic Inst and State U (VA)
Washington State U (WA)

AIRCRAFT POWERPLANT TECHNOLOGY
Embry-Riddle Aeronautical U–Daytona (FL)
Embry-Riddle Aeronautical U–Worldwide (FL)
Thomas Edison State Coll (NJ)

AIR FORCE ROTC/AIR SCIENCE
La Salle U (PA)
The U of Iowa (IA)
U of Washington (WA)
Weber State U (UT)

AIRFRAME MECHANICS AND AIRCRAFT MAINTENANCE TECHNOLOGY
Kansas State U (KS)
LeTourneau U (TX)
Purdue U (IN)
Southeastern Oklahoma State U (OK)
Thomas Edison State Coll (NJ)
Vaughn Coll of Aeronautics and Technology (NY)
Wilmington U (DE)

AIRLINE PILOT AND FLIGHT CREW
Auburn U (AL)
Bridgewater State U (MA)
Delaware State U (DE)
Delta State U (MS)
Eastern Michigan U (MI)
Embry-Riddle Aeronautical U–Daytona (FL)
Embry-Riddle Aeronautical U–Prescott (AZ)
Indiana State U (IN)
Inter American U of Puerto Rico, Bayamón Campus (PR)
Kansas State U (KS)
LeTourneau U (TX)
Quincy U (IL)
Rocky Mountain Coll (MT)
Saint Louis U (MO)
Southeastern Oklahoma State U (OK)
Southern Illinois U Carbondale (IL)
U of Dubuque (IA)
U of Louisiana at Monroe (LA)
U of Minnesota, Crookston (MN)
U of North Dakota (ND)
Utah Valley U (UT)
Western Michigan U (MI)
Westminster Coll (UT)

AIR TRAFFIC CONTROL
Arizona State U (AZ)
Daniel Webster Coll (NH)
Embry-Riddle Aeronautical U–Daytona (FL)
Embry-Riddle Aeronautical U–Prescott (AZ)
Inter American U of Puerto Rico, Bayamón Campus (PR)
LeTourneau U (TX)

Thomas Edison State Coll (NJ)
U of North Dakota (ND)

AIR TRANSPORTATION RELATED
Florida Inst of Technology (FL)
Thomas Edison State Coll (NJ)
U of North Dakota (ND)

ALGEBRA AND NUMBER THEORY
U of New Brunswick Saint John (NB, Canada)

ALLIED HEALTH AND MEDICAL ASSISTING SERVICES RELATED
Cedarville U (OH)
Coll of Saint Elizabeth (NJ)
Jones Coll, Jacksonville (FL)
Ramapo Coll of New Jersey (NJ)
Widener U (PA)

ALLIED HEALTH DIAGNOSTIC, INTERVENTION, AND TREATMENT PROFESSIONS RELATED
California Baptist U (CA)
Fairleigh Dickinson U, Coll at Florham (NJ)
Fairleigh Dickinson U, Metropolitan Campus (NJ)
Georgian Court U (NJ)
Hofstra U (NY)
Immaculata U (PA)
Lewis U (IL)
Millersville U of Pennsylvania (PA)
Northern Michigan U (MI)
Rutgers, The State U of New Jersey, Newark (NJ)
Tennessee Wesleyan Coll (TN)
Thomas Edison State Coll (NJ)
The U of Toledo (OH)

ALTERNATIVE AND COMPLEMENTARY MEDICINE RELATED
Johnson State Coll (VT)

AMERICAN GOVERNMENT AND POLITICS
American Jewish U (CA)
Bard Coll (NY)
Bennington Coll (VT)
Bridgewater State U (MA)
Claremont McKenna Coll (CA)
Gallaudet U (DC)
The Master's Coll and Sem (CA)
Misericordia U (PA)
Oklahoma Christian U (OK)
Southern Nazarene U (OK)
Suffolk U (MA)
United States Military Acad (NY)
The U of Akron (OH)
Wayland Baptist U (TX)
Western Michigan U (MI)

AMERICAN HISTORY
Bard Coll (NY)
Bennington Coll (VT)
The Coll of Saint Rose (NY)
Gettysburg Coll (PA)
Keene State Coll (NH)
Morningside Coll (IA)
Salem State U (MA)
Sarah Lawrence Coll (NY)
Suffolk U (MA)
United States Military Acad (NY)
The U of Montana Western (MT)
U of Regina (SK, Canada)
The U of Western Ontario (ON, Canada)

AMERICAN INDIAN/NATIVE AMERICAN STUDIES
Arizona State U (AZ)
Bemidji State U (MN)
Colgate U (NY)
Concordia U (QC, Canada)
Creighton U (NE)
Dartmouth Coll (NH)
East Central U (OK)
The Evergreen State Coll (WA)
Fort Lewis Coll (CO)
Hampshire Coll (MA)
Humboldt State U (CA)
Laurentian U (ON, Canada)
Michigan State U (MI)
Northeastern State U (OK)

Northern Arizona U (AZ)
Northland Coll (WI)
Portland State U (OR)
St. Thomas U (NB, Canada)
San Diego State U (CA)
San Francisco State U (CA)
Sonoma State U (CA)
Stanford U (CA)
Trent U (ON, Canada)
U of Alaska Fairbanks (AK)
U of California, Berkeley (CA)
U of California, Davis (CA)
U of California, Los Angeles (CA)
U of Hawaii at Manoa (HI)
The U of Iowa (IA)
U of Lethbridge (AB, Canada)
U of Minnesota, Duluth (MN)
U of Minnesota, Twin Cities Campus (MN)
The U of North Carolina at Pembroke (NC)
U of North Dakota (ND)
U of Oklahoma (OK)
U of Ottawa (ON, Canada)
U of Regina (SK, Canada)
U of Saskatchewan (SK, Canada)
U of Science and Arts of Oklahoma (OK)
The U of South Dakota (SD)
U of Washington (WA)
The U of Western Ontario (ON, Canada)
U of Wisconsin–Eau Claire (WI)
U of Wisconsin–Green Bay (WI)
U of Wyoming (WY)

AMERICAN LITERATURE
Bard Coll (NY)
Bennington Coll (VT)
Castleton State Coll (VT)
Middlebury Coll (VT)
Saint Joseph's Coll of Maine (ME)
St. Lawrence U (NY)
Sarah Lawrence Coll (NY)
U of California, Los Angeles (CA)
Washington U in St. Louis (MO)
Wheeling Jesuit U (WV)

AMERICAN NATIVE/NATIVE AMERICAN EDUCATION
The Coll of St. Scholastica (MN)
Northeastern State U (OK)
U of Lethbridge (AB, Canada)
U of Regina (SK, Canada)

AMERICAN NATIVE/NATIVE AMERICAN LANGUAGES
Bemidji State U (MN)
U of Hawaii at Manoa (HI)
U of Regina (SK, Canada)

AMERICAN SIGN LANGUAGE (ASL)
Augustana Coll (SD)
Bethel Coll (IN)
Gardner-Webb U (NC)
Maryville Coll (TN)
Northeastern U (MA)
St. Catherine U (MN)
U of Houston (TX)
U of Rochester (NY)
Utah Valley U (UT)

AMERICAN STUDIES
Albion Coll (MI)
Albright Coll (PA)
American U (DC)
Amherst Coll (MA)
Arizona State U (AZ)
Ashland U (OH)
Atlantic Union Coll (MA)
Bard Coll (NY)
Bard Coll at Simon's Rock (MA)
Barnard Coll (NY)
Bates Coll (ME)
Bennington Coll (VT)
Boston U (MA)
Bowling Green State U (OH)
Brandeis U (MA)
Brown U (RI)
Cabrini Coll (PA)
California State U, Chico (CA)
California State U, Fullerton (CA)
California State U, Long Beach (CA)
California State U, San Bernardino (CA)
Carleton Coll (MN)
Case Western Reserve U (OH)
Cedarville U (OH)

Christopher Newport U (VA)
Claflin U (SC)
Claremont McKenna Coll (CA)
Clarkson U (NY)
Colby Coll (ME)
Coll of Saint Elizabeth (NJ)
The Coll of Saint Rose (NY)
Coll of Staten Island of the City U of New York (NY)
The Coll of William and Mary (VA)
Columbia Coll (MO)
Columbia U, School of General Studies (NY)
Connecticut Coll (CT)
Cornell U (NY)
Creighton U (NE)
Cumberland U (TN)
DePaul U (IL)
Dickinson Coll (PA)
Dominican Coll (NY)
Dominican U (IL)
Eckerd Coll (FL)
Elmhurst Coll (IL)
Elmira Coll (NY)
Emmanuel Coll (MA)
Erskine Coll (SC)
Fairfield U (CT)
Franklin & Marshall Coll (PA)
Franklin Coll (IN)
Franklin Pierce U (NH)
Georgetown Coll (KY)
Georgetown U (DC)
Gettysburg Coll (PA)
Goucher Coll (MD)
Hamilton Coll (NY)
Hampshire Coll (MA)
Hawai'i Pacific U (HI)
Hendrix Coll (AR)
Hillsdale Coll (MI)
Hobart and William Smith Colls (NY)
Hofstra U (NY)
Idaho State U (ID)
Illinois Wesleyan U (IL)
Indiana U Bloomington (IN)
Kansas State U (KS)
Keene State Coll (NH)
Kent State U (OH)
Kenyon Coll (OH)
King Coll (TN)
Knox Coll (IL)
Lafayette Coll (PA)
Lake Forest Coll (IL)
Lebanon Valley Coll (PA)
Lehigh U (PA)
Lehman Coll of the City U of New York (NY)
Lesley U (MA)
Lindenwood U (MO)
Lindsey Wilson Coll (KY)
Lipscomb U (TN)
Long Island U, C.W. Post Campus (NY)
Lycoming Coll (PA)
Manhattanville Coll (NY)
Marist Coll (NY)
Marlboro Coll (VT)
Mary Baldwin Coll (VA)
Miami U (OH)
Michigan State U (MI)
Middlebury Coll (VT)
Mills Coll (CA)
Montana State U (MT)
Montreat Coll, Montreat (NC)
Mount Allison U (NB, Canada)
Mount Ida Coll (MA)
Mount St. Mary's Coll (CA)
Muhlenberg Coll (PA)
Nazareth Coll of Rochester (NY)
Nova Southeastern U (FL)
Oglethorpe U (GA)
Oklahoma City U (OK)
Oklahoma State U (OK)
Pace U (NY)
Penn State Abington (PA)
Penn State Berks (PA)
Penn State Brandywine (PA)
Penn State Erie, The Behrend Coll (PA)
Penn State Harrisburg (PA)
Penn State Lehigh Valley (PA)
Penn State Schuylkill (PA)
Penn State Worthington Scranton (PA)
Penn State York (PA)
Pitzer Coll (CA)
Pomona Coll (CA)
Providence Coll (RI)
Purdue U (IN)
Queens Coll of the City U of New York (NY)

Ramapo Coll of New Jersey (NJ)
Reed Coll (OR)
Rider U (NJ)
Rutgers, The State U of New Jersey, Newark (NJ)
Rutgers, The State U of New Jersey, New Brunswick (NJ)
Saint Francis U (PA)
St. John Fisher Coll (NY)
Saint Joseph Coll (CT)
Saint Louis U (MO)
Saint Mary's Coll of California (CA)
Saint Michael's Coll (VT)
St. Olaf Coll (MN)
Salve Regina U (RI)
San Francisco State U (CA)
San Jose State U (CA)
Sarah Lawrence Coll (NY)
Scripps Coll (CA)
Sewanee: The U of the South (TN)
Shenandoah U (VA)
Siena Coll (NY)
Skidmore Coll (NY)
Smith Coll (MA)
Sonoma State U (CA)
Southern Nazarene U (OK)
Springfield Coll (MA)
Stanford U (CA)
State U of New York at Fredonia (NY)
State U of New York at Oswego (NY)
State U of New York Coll at Geneseo (NY)
State U of New York Coll at Old Westbury (NY)
Stetson U (FL)
Stonehill Coll (MA)
Stony Brook U, State U of New York (NY)
Syracuse U (NY)
Temple U (PA)
Tennessee Wesleyan Coll (TN)
Texas A&M U (TX)
Texas State U–San Marcos (TX)
Towson U (MD)
Trinity Coll (CT)
Tufts U (MA)
Tulane U (LA)
Union Coll (NY)
U at Buffalo, the State U of New York (NY)
The U of Alabama (AL)
U of Arkansas (AR)
U of California, Berkeley (CA)
U of California, Davis (CA)
U of California, Santa Cruz (CA)
U of Dayton (OH)
U of Florida (FL)
U of Hawaii at Manoa (HI)
U of Idaho (ID)
The U of Iowa (IA)
The U of Kansas (KS)
U of Maryland, Baltimore County (MD)
U of Maryland, Coll Park (MD)
U of Mary Washington (VA)
U of Massachusetts Boston (MA)
U of Miami (FL)
U of Michigan (MI)
U of Michigan–Dearborn (MI)
U of Minnesota, Twin Cities Campus (MN)
U of Mount Union (OH)
U of New England (ME)
The U of North Carolina at Chapel Hill (NC)
The U of North Carolina at Pembroke (NC)
U of Notre Dame (IN)
U of Pennsylvania (PA)
U of Pittsburgh at Greensburg (PA)
U of Richmond (VA)
U of Rio Grande (OH)
U of Southern California (CA)
U of Southern Mississippi (MS)
U of South Florida (FL)
The U of Texas at Austin (TX)
The U of Texas at Dallas (TX)
The U of Texas at San Antonio (TX)
The U of Texas–Pan American (TX)
The U of Toledo (OH)
U of Washington, Bothell (WA)
The U of Western Ontario (ON, Canada)
U of Wyoming (WY)
Utah State U (UT)
Valparaiso U (IN)

Vanderbilt U (TN)
Vassar Coll (NY)
Virginia Wesleyan Coll (VA)
Washington Coll (MD)
Washington U in St. Louis (MO)
Wayne State U (MI)
Webster U (MO)
Wellesley Coll (MA)
Wells Coll (NY)
Wesleyan Coll (GA)
Wesleyan U (CT)
West Chester U of Pennsylvania (PA)
Western Connecticut State U (CT)
Wheaton Coll (MA)
Wheelock Coll (MA)
Wilfrid Laurier U (ON, Canada)
Willamette U (OR)
Williams Coll (MA)
Wittenberg U (OH)
Yale U (CT)
Youngstown State U (OH)

ANALYTICAL CHEMISTRY
The U of Western Ontario (ON, Canada)
West Chester U of Pennsylvania (PA)

ANATOMY
Andrews U (MI)
Minnesota State U Mankato (MN)
Tulane U (LA)
U of Saskatchewan (SK, Canada)
The U of Western Ontario (ON, Canada)

ANCIENT/CLASSICAL GREEK
Amherst Coll (MA)
Augustana Coll (IL)
Bard Coll (NY)
Barnard Coll (NY)
Boston Coll (MA)
Boston U (MA)
Brigham Young U (UT)
Brock U (ON, Canada)
Bryn Mawr Coll (PA)
California State U, Long Beach (CA)
Carleton Coll (MN)
Creighton U (NE)
Dartmouth Coll (NH)
DePauw U (IN)
Duquesne U (PA)
Franklin & Marshall Coll (PA)
Gettysburg Coll (PA)
Hampden-Sydney Coll (VA)
Hobart and William Smith Colls (NY)
Hunter Coll of the City U of New York (NY)
Indiana U Bloomington (IN)
Kenyon Coll (OH)
Lawrence U (WI)
Loyola U Chicago (IL)
Loyola U New Orleans (LA)
Monmouth Coll (IL)
Mount Allison U (NB, Canada)
Mount Holyoke Coll (MA)
Multnomah U (OR)
Ohio U (OH)
Randolph Coll (VA)
Randolph-Macon Coll (VA)
Rice U (TX)
Rockford Coll (IL)
Rutgers, The State U of New Jersey, New Brunswick (NJ)
St. Olaf Coll (MN)
Samford U (AL)
Santa Clara U (CA)
Smith Coll (MA)
Stanford U (CA)
Swarthmore Coll (PA)
U of California, Berkeley (CA)
U of California, Los Angeles (CA)
U of Georgia (GA)
The U of Iowa (IA)
U of Miami (FL)
U of Michigan (MI)
U of Minnesota, Twin Cities Campus (MN)
U of Nebraska–Lincoln (NE)
U of New Hampshire (NH)
U of Notre Dame (IN)
U of Richmond (VA)
U of St. Thomas (MN)
The U of Scranton (PA)
The U of Texas at Austin (TX)
U of Vermont (VT)
U of Washington (WA)

The U of Western Ontario (ON, Canada)
Vassar Coll (NY)
Wake Forest U (NC)
Washington U in St. Louis (MO)
Wellesley Coll (MA)
Wheaton Coll (MA)
Yale U (CT)

ANCIENT NEAR EASTERN AND BIBLICAL LANGUAGES
Belmont U (TN)
Carson-Newman Coll (TN)
Concordia U (CA)
Concordia U Chicago (IL)
Concordia U Wisconsin (WI)
Geneva Coll (PA)
Lipscomb U (TN)
Luther Coll (IA)
The Master's Coll and Sem (CA)
Mid-Continent U (KY)
Northwest Nazarene U (ID)
Northwest U (WA)
Union U (TN)
Walla Walla U (WA)

ANCIENT STUDIES
Bates Coll (ME)
Boston U (MA)
Bowdoin Coll (ME)
Columbia U, School of General Studies (NY)
Concordia U (QC, Canada)
Lehigh U (PA)
Missouri State U (MO)
Mount Holyoke Coll (MA)
Ohio Wesleyan U (OH)
Rockford Coll (IL)
St. Olaf Coll (MN)
Santa Clara U (CA)
Stanford U (CA)
The U of Iowa (IA)
The U of Kansas (KS)
U of Maryland, Baltimore County (MD)
U of Miami (FL)
U of Michigan (MI)
U of Minnesota, Twin Cities Campus (MN)
U of Nebraska–Lincoln (NE)
The U of Texas at Austin (TX)
Washington U in St. Louis (MO)
Wheaton Coll (MA)

ANIMAL BEHAVIOR AND ETHOLOGY
Bucknell U (PA)
Canisius Coll (NY)
Carroll U (WI)
Franklin & Marshall Coll (PA)
Hampshire Coll (MA)
Northern Arizona U (AZ)

ANIMAL GENETICS
Dartmouth Coll (NH)
Jacksonville State U (AL)
Ohio Wesleyan U (OH)
Rutgers, The State U of New Jersey, New Brunswick (NJ)
Sarah Lawrence Coll (NY)
The U of British Columbia (BC, Canada)
U of Manitoba (MB, Canada)
Worcester Polytechnic Inst (MA)

ANIMAL HEALTH
Sul Ross State U (TX)
U of Georgia (GA)

ANIMAL/LIVESTOCK HUSBANDRY AND PRODUCTION
Angelo State U (TX)
Dordt Coll (IA)
Purdue U (IN)
Rutgers, The State U of New Jersey, New Brunswick (NJ)
Tarleton State U (TX)
Texas A&M U (TX)
The U of British Columbia (BC, Canada)
U of Minnesota, Twin Cities Campus (MN)

ANIMAL NUTRITION
U of Georgia (GA)

ANIMAL PHYSIOLOGY
Minnesota State U Mankato (MN)

Rutgers, The State U of New Jersey, New Brunswick (NJ)
Sonoma State U (CA)
Texas State U–San Marcos (TX)
The U of Akron (OH)
U of Minnesota, Twin Cities Campus (MN)
U of New Brunswick Fredericton (NB, Canada)
Utah State U (UT)

ANIMAL SCIENCES
Abilene Christian U (TX)
Alabama Ag and Mech U (AL)
Angelo State U (TX)
Arkansas State U (AR)
Auburn U (AL)
Berry Coll (GA)
California Polytechnic State U, San Luis Obispo (CA)
California State Polytechnic U, Pomona (CA)
California State U, Chico (CA)
Clemson U (SC)
Coll of the Ozarks (MO)
Colorado State U (CO)
Cornell U (NY)
Delaware State U (DE)
Dordt Coll (IA)
Hardin-Simmons U (TX)
Iowa State U of Science and Technology (IA)
Kansas State U (KS)
Louisiana State U and Ag and Mech Coll (LA)
Lubbock Christian U (TX)
Michigan State U (MI)
Middle Tennessee State U (TN)
Mississippi State U (MS)
Missouri State U (MO)
Montana State U (MT)
New Mexico State U (NM)
North Carolina Ag and Tech State U (NC)
North Carolina State U (NC)
North Dakota State U (ND)
Northwest Missouri State U (MO)
The Ohio State U (OH)
Oklahoma Panhandle State U (OK)
Oklahoma State U (OK)
Oregon State U (OR)
Penn State Abington (PA)
Penn State Altoona (PA)
Penn State Beaver (PA)
Penn State Berks (PA)
Penn State Brandywine (PA)
Penn State DuBois (PA)
Penn State Erie, The Behrend Coll (PA)
Penn State Fayette, The Eberly Campus (PA)
Penn State Greater Allegheny (PA)
Penn State Hazleton (PA)
Penn State Lehigh Valley (PA)
Penn State Mont Alto (PA)
Penn State New Kensington (PA)
Penn State Schuylkill (PA)
Penn State Shenango (PA)
Penn State U Park (PA)
Penn State Wilkes-Barre (PA)
Penn State Worthington Scranton (PA)
Penn State York (PA)
Purdue U (IN)
Rutgers, The State U of New Jersey, New Brunswick (NJ)
South Dakota State U (SD)
Southeast Missouri State U (MO)
Southern Illinois U Carbondale (IL)
Stephen F. Austin State U (TX)
Sul Ross State U (TX)
Tarleton State U (TX)
Tennessee Technological U (TN)
Texas A&M U (TX)
Texas A&M U–Kingsville (TX)
Texas State U–San Marcos (TX)
Texas Tech U (TX)
Tuskegee U (AL)
U of Arkansas (AR)
The U of British Columbia (BC, Canada)
U of California, Davis (CA)
U of Delaware (DE)
U of Denver (CO)
The U of Findlay (OH)
U of Florida (FL)
U of Guelph (ON, Canada)
U of Hawaii at Hilo (HI)

U of Hawaii at Manoa (HI)
U of Idaho (ID)
U of Maine (ME)
U of Manitoba (MB, Canada)
U of Maryland, Coll Park (MD)
U of Massachusetts Amherst (MA)
U of Minnesota, Crookston (MN)
U of Minnesota, Twin Cities Campus (MN)
U of Missouri (MO)
U of Nebraska–Lincoln (NE)
U of Nevada, Reno (NV)
U of New Hampshire (NH)
U of Rhode Island (RI)
U of Saskatchewan (SK, Canada)
The U of Tennessee (TN)
The U of Tennessee at Martin (TN)
U of Vermont (VT)
U of Wisconsin–Madison (WI)
U of Wisconsin–Platteville (WI)
U of Wisconsin–River Falls (WI)
U of Wyoming (WY)
Utah State U (UT)
Virginia Polytechnic Inst and State U (VA)
Washington State U (WA)
West Virginia U (WV)

ANIMAL SCIENCES RELATED
North Carolina Ag and Tech State U (NC)
Penn State Abington (PA)
Penn State Beaver (PA)
Penn State Brandywine (PA)
Penn State DuBois (PA)
Penn State Erie, The Behrend Coll (PA)
Penn State Fayette, The Eberly Campus (PA)
Penn State Greater Allegheny (PA)
Penn State Hazleton (PA)
Penn State Lehigh Valley (PA)
Penn State Mont Alto (PA)
Penn State New Kensington (PA)
Penn State Schuylkill (PA)
Penn State Shenango (PA)
Penn State Wilkes-Barre (PA)
Penn State Worthington Scranton (PA)
Penn State York (PA)
Purdue U (IN)
U of California, Davis (CA)

ANIMATION, INTERACTIVE TECHNOLOGY, VIDEO GRAPHICS AND SPECIAL EFFECTS
American U (DC)
Art Center Coll of Design (CA)
The Art Inst of Ohio–Cincinnati (OH)
The Art Inst of Seattle (WA)
The Art Inst of York–Pennsylvania (PA)
Bennington Coll (VT)
Brigham Young U (UT)
California Coll of the Arts (CA)
Champlain Coll (VT)
The Cleveland Inst of Art (OH)
Cogswell Polytechnical Coll (CA)
Coll for Creative Studies (MI)
Coll of the Atlantic (ME)
Concordia U (QC, Canada)
Davenport U, Grand Rapids (MI)
DePaul U (IL)
DigiPen Inst of Technology (WA)
Eastern Michigan U (MI)
East Tennessee State U (TN)
Emily Carr U of Art + Design (BC, Canada)
Fashion Inst of Technology (NY)
Ferris State U (MI)
Huntington U (IN)
The Illinois Inst of Art–Tinley Park (IL)
Intl Acad of Design & Technology (FL)
Kent State U at Tuscarawas (OH)
Loyola Marymount U (CA)
Massachusetts Coll of Art and Design (MA)
Montclair State U (NJ)
Mount Ida Coll (MA)
Nevada State Coll at Henderson (NV)
New Jersey Inst of Technology (NJ)
Northeastern U (MA)
Northwestern Coll (MN)
Pacific Northwest Coll of Art (OR)

Texas A&M U–Kingsville (TX)
Tufts U (MA)
U of Cincinnati (OH)
U of Colorado Boulder (CO)
The U of Kansas (KS)
U of Miami (FL)
U of Nebraska–Lincoln (NE)
U of Oklahoma (OK)
The U of Texas at Austin (TX)
U of Wyoming (WY)

ARCHITECTURAL ENGINEERING TECHNOLOGY
Bluefield State Coll (WV)
Delaware State U (DE)
Fitchburg State U (MA)
Indiana State U (IN)
Indiana U–Purdue U Indianapolis (IN)
Keene State Coll (NH)
New England Inst of Technology (RI)
Northern Kentucky U (KY)
Purdue U (IN)
Purdue U North Central (IN)
Southern Polytechnic State U (GA)
Texas Tech U (TX)
U of Hartford (CT)
U of Southern Mississippi (MS)
Vermont Tech Coll (VT)
Washington U in St. Louis (MO)

ARCHITECTURAL HISTORY AND CRITICISM
Brown U (RI)
Carnegie Mellon U (PA)
Case Western Reserve U (OH)
Columbia U, School of General Studies (NY)
Cornell U (NY)
DePaul U (IL)
Lehigh U (PA)
Sarah Lawrence Coll (NY)
Savannah Coll of Art and Design (GA)
The U of Kansas (KS)
U of San Diego (CA)
U of Virginia (VA)

ARCHITECTURAL TECHNOLOGY
Carnegie Mellon U (PA)
New York City Coll of Technology of the City U of New York (NY)
U of Maine at Augusta (ME)
Washington U in St. Louis (MO)
Western Kentucky U (KY)

ARCHITECTURE
American U of Beirut (Lebanon)
Andrews U (MI)
Arizona State U (AZ)
Auburn U (AL)
Ball State U (IN)
Barnard Coll (NY)
Bennington Coll (VT)
Boston Architectural Coll (MA)
California Coll of the Arts (CA)
California Polytechnic State U, San Luis Obispo (CA)
California State Polytechnic U, Pomona (CA)
Carnegie Mellon U (PA)
The Catholic U of America (DC)
City Coll of the City U of New York (NY)
Clemson U (SC)
Columbia U, School of General Studies (NY)
Connecticut Coll (CT)
Cooper Union for the Advancement of Science and Art (NY)
Cornell Coll (IA)
Cornell U (NY)
Drury U (MO)
Florida Ag and Mech U (FL)
Florida Atlantic U (FL)
Georgia Inst of Technology (GA)
Hampshire Coll (MA)
Hobart and William Smith Colls (NY)
Illinois Inst of Technology (IL)
Inter American U of Puerto Rico, San Germán Campus (PR)
Iowa State U of Science and Technology (IA)
Ithaca Coll (NY)
Keene State Coll (NH)
Kent State U (OH)
Lawrence Technological U (MI)
Lebanese American U (Lebanon)

Lehigh U (PA)
Louisiana State U and Ag and Mech Coll (LA)
Marywood U (PA)
Massachusetts Coll of Art and Design (MA)
Massachusetts Inst of Technology (MA)
Miami U (OH)
Mississippi State U (MS)
New Jersey Inst of Technology (NJ)
North Carolina State U (NC)
Northeastern U (MA)
The Ohio State U (OH)
Oklahoma State U (OK)
Parsons The New School for Design (NY)
Penn State U Park (PA)
Philadelphia U (PA)
Polytechnic U of Puerto Rico (PR)
Portland State U (OR)
Prairie View A&M U (TX)
Pratt Inst (NY)
Princeton U (NJ)
Rensselaer Polytechnic Inst (NY)
Rice U (TX)
Savannah Coll of Art and Design (GA)
Smith Coll (MA)
South Dakota State U (SD)
Southern Illinois U Carbondale (IL)
Southern Polytechnic State U (GA)
Syracuse U (NY)
Temple U (PA)
Texas A&M U (TX)
Texas Tech U (TX)
Tulane U (LA)
Tuskegee U (AL)
U at Buffalo, the State U of New York (NY)
The U of Arizona (AZ)
U of Arkansas (AR)
U of California, Berkeley (CA)
U of California, Los Angeles (CA)
U of Central Florida (FL)
U of Cincinnati (OH)
U of Houston (TX)
U of Idaho (ID)
The U of Kansas (KS)
U of Louisiana at Lafayette (LA)
U of Manitoba (MB, Canada)
U of Maryland, Coll Park (MD)
U of Memphis (TN)
U of Miami (FL)
U of Michigan (MI)
U of Minnesota, Twin Cities Campus (MN)
U of Nebraska–Lincoln (NE)
U of Nevada, Las Vegas (NV)
The U of North Carolina at Charlotte (NC)
U of Notre Dame (IN)
U of Oklahoma (OK)
U of Oregon (OR)
U of Pennsylvania (PA)
U of San Francisco (CA)
U of Southern California (CA)
The U of Tennessee (TN)
The U of Texas at Arlington (TX)
The U of Texas at Austin (TX)
The U of Texas at San Antonio (TX)
U of the District of Columbia (DC)
U of Utah (UT)
U of Virginia (VA)
U of Washington (WA)
U of Waterloo (ON, Canada)
Virginia Polytechnic Inst and State U (VA)
Washington State U (WA)
Washington U in St. Louis (MO)
Wellesley Coll (MA)
Wentworth Inst of Technology (MA)
Woodbury U (CA)
Yale U (CT)

ARCHITECTURE RELATED
Carnegie Mellon U (PA)
Case Western Reserve U (OH)
Coll of the Holy Cross (MA)
Georgia Inst of Technology (GA)
Lipscomb U (TN)
Mount Holyoke Coll (MA)
New York Inst of Technology (NY)
Northern Michigan U (MI)
U of Cincinnati (OH)
U of Illinois at Chicago (IL)
U of Louisiana at Lafayette (LA)
U of Minnesota, Twin Cities Campus (MN)

U of Utah (UT)
Washington U in St. Louis (MO)

AREA STUDIES RELATED
Appalachian State U (NC)
Boston U (MA)
Bridgewater State U (MA)
Claremont McKenna Coll (CA)
Eastern Michigan U (MI)
Gannon U (PA)
Gettysburg Coll (PA)
Hofstra U (NY)
Illinois Wesleyan U (IL)
Kent State U (OH)
Lake Forest Coll (IL)
Lycoming Coll (PA)
Northeastern State U (OK)
Prescott Coll (AZ)
Ramapo Coll of New Jersey (NJ)
U of Alaska Fairbanks (AK)
U of California, Los Angeles (CA)
U of California, Santa Barbara (CA)
U of Michigan–Dearborn (MI)
U of Minnesota, Twin Cities Campus (MN)
U of Pittsburgh (PA)
U of Virginia (VA)
Utah State U (UT)
Virginia Commonwealth U (VA)
Washington U in St. Louis (MO)

ARMY ROTC/MILITARY SCIENCE
Jacksonville State U (AL)
La Salle U (PA)
Longwood U (VA)
Minnesota State U Mankato (MN)
The U of Iowa (IA)
U of Minnesota, Twin Cities Campus (MN)
U of Washington (WA)

ART
Alabama State U (AL)
Albany State U (GA)
Alberta Coll of Art & Design (AB, Canada)
Albertus Magnus Coll (CT)
Albion Coll (MI)
Albright Coll (PA)
Alfred U (NY)
Allegheny Coll (PA)
Alma Coll (MI)
Alverno Coll (WI)
American U (DC)
Amherst Coll (MA)
Anderson U (SC)
Andrews U (MI)
Angelo State U (TX)
Anna Maria Coll (MA)
Appalachian State U (NC)
Aquinas Coll (MI)
Arcadia U (PA)
Arizona State U (AZ)
Arkansas State U (AR)
Arkansas Tech U (AR)
Armstrong Atlantic State U (GA)
Art Center Coll of Design (CA)
Athens State U (AL)
Atlantic Union Coll (MA)
Auburn U Montgomery (AL)
Augsburg Coll (MN)
Augustana Coll (IL)
Augustana Coll (SD)
Austin Coll (TX)
Austin Peay State U (TN)
Averett U (VA)
Avila U (MO)
Baldwin-Wallace Coll (OH)
Ball State U (IN)
Bard Coll (NY)
Bates Coll (ME)
Belhaven U (MS)
Belmont U (TN)
Bemidji State U (MN)
Benedictine Coll (KS)
Berea Coll (KY)
Berry Coll (GA)
Bethany Coll (WV)
Bethany Lutheran Coll (MN)
Bethel Coll (IN)
Bethel U (MN)
Birmingham-Southern Coll (AL)
Blackburn Coll (IL)
Bluefield Coll (VA)
Bluffton U (OH)
Bob Jones U (SC)
Boise State U (ID)
Bowdoin Coll (ME)
Bowie State U (MD)
Bowling Green State U (OH)

Briar Cliff U (IA)
Brock U (ON, Canada)
Brown U (RI)
Bryn Mawr Coll (PA)
Bucknell U (PA)
Buena Vista U (IA)
California Baptist U (CA)
California Coll of the Arts (CA)
California State Polytechnic U, Pomona (CA)
California State U, Bakersfield (CA)
California State U, Chico (CA)
California State U, Dominguez Hills (CA)
California State U, Fullerton (CA)
California State U, Long Beach (CA)
California State U, Los Angeles (CA)
California State U, Monterey Bay (CA)
California State U, Northridge (CA)
California State U, San Bernardino (CA)
California State U, Stanislaus (CA)
Calvin Coll (MI)
Cameron U (OK)
Campbellsville U (KY)
Capital U (OH)
Carnegie Mellon U (PA)
Carroll U (WI)
Carson-Newman Coll (TN)
Castleton State Coll (VT)
The Catholic U of America (DC)
Cedar Crest Coll (PA)
Centenary Coll of Louisiana (LA)
Central Coll (IA)
Central Connecticut State U (CT)
Central Michigan U (MI)
Central State U (OH)
Centre Coll (KY)
Chapman U (CA)
City Coll of the City U of New York (NY)
Claflin U (SC)
Claremont McKenna Coll (CA)
Clarion U of Pennsylvania (PA)
Clark Atlanta U (GA)
Clarke U (IA)
Cleveland State U (OH)
Colby Coll (ME)
Colgate U (NY)
Coll of Mount St. Joseph (OH)
The Coll of New Jersey (NJ)
Coll of Saint Benedict (MN)
Coll of Saint Elizabeth (NJ)
Coll of Saint Mary (NE)
The Coll of St. Scholastica (MN)
Coll of the Atlantic (ME)
Coll of the Ozarks (MO)
The Coll of William and Mary (VA)
Columbia Coll (MO)
Columbia Coll Chicago (IL)
Concordia Coll (MN)
Concordia Coll–New York (NY)
Concordia U (CA)
Concordia U Chicago (IL)
Concordia U Wisconsin (WI)
Connecticut Coll (CT)
Corcoran Coll of Art and Design (DC)
Cornell Coll (IA)
Creighton U (NE)
Culver-Stockton Coll (MO)
Dallas Baptist U (TX)
Davidson Coll (NC)
Delaware State U (DE)
Denison U (OH)
DePaul U (IL)
Dickinson State U (ND)
Dillard U (LA)
Doane Coll (NE)
Dominican U of California (CA)
Drake U (IA)
Drew U (NJ)
Earlham Coll (IN)
East Central U (OK)
Eastern Illinois U (IL)
Eastern Michigan U (MI)
Eastern New Mexico U (NM)
Eastern Oregon U (OR)
East Tennessee State U (TN)
Edgewood Coll (WI)
Edinboro U of Pennsylvania (PA)
Elmhurst Coll (IL)
Elmira Coll (NY)
Elon U (NC)
Emmanuel Coll (MA)
Emory & Henry Coll (VA)
Emporia State U (KS)
Erskine Coll (SC)
Evangel U (MO)

The Evergreen State Coll (WA)
Fairfield U (CT)
Fayetteville State U (NC)
Felician Coll (NJ)
Ferrum Coll (VA)
Florida Atlantic U (FL)
Florida Gulf Coast U (FL)
Florida Intl U (FL)
Florida Southern Coll (FL)
Fontbonne U (MO)
Fort Lewis Coll (CO)
Framingham State U (MA)
Francis Marion U (SC)
Franklin Pierce U (NH)
Freed-Hardeman U (TN)
Friends U (KS)
Furman U (SC)
Gardner-Webb U (NC)
George Fox U (OR)
Georgia Coll & State U (GA)
Georgian Court U (NJ)
Georgia Southern U (GA)
Georgia State U (GA)
Gettysburg Coll (PA)
Gordon Coll (MA)
Goucher Coll (MD)
Governors State U (IL)
Graceland U (IA)
Grand View U (IA)
Greensboro Coll (NC)
Greenville Coll (IL)
Grinnell Coll (IA)
Guilford Coll (NC)
Hannibal-LaGrange U (MO)
Hanover Coll (IN)
Hartwick Coll (NY)
Haverford Coll (PA)
Hendrix Coll (AR)
Hillsdale Coll (MI)
Hobart and William Smith Colls (NY)
Hollins U (VA)
Holy Cross Coll (IN)
Holy Family U (PA)
Houghton Coll (NY)
Humboldt State U (CA)
Hunter Coll of the City U of New York (NY)
Huntington U (IN)
Idaho State U (ID)
Illinois Coll (IL)
Illinois State U (IL)
Illinois Wesleyan U (IL)
Indiana State U (IN)
Indiana U Bloomington (IN)
Indiana U East (IN)
Indiana U Kokomo (IN)
Indiana U Northwest (IN)
Indiana U of Pennsylvania (PA)
Indiana U South Bend (IN)
Indiana U Southeast (IN)
Indiana Wesleyan U (IN)
Inter American U of Puerto Rico, San Germán Campus (PR)
Iowa State U of Science and Technology (IA)
Iowa Wesleyan Coll (IA)
Ithaca Coll (NY)
Jacksonville State U (AL)
James Madison U (VA)
Jamestown Coll (ND)
Johnson State Coll (VT)
Judson Coll (AL)
Kalamazoo Coll (MI)
Kansas State U (KS)
Kean U (NJ)
Kennesaw State U (GA)
Kenyon Coll (OH)
Keystone Coll (PA)
Knox Coll (IL)
Kutztown U of Pennsylvania (PA)
Lafayette Coll (PA)
Lake Forest Coll (IL)
Lakehead U (ON, Canada)
Lamar U (TX)
Lebanon Valley Coll (PA)
Lehigh U (PA)
Lehman Coll of the City U of New York (NY)
Lesley U (MA)
Lewis & Clark Coll (OR)
Lewis U (IL)
Lincoln Memorial U (TN)
Lindenwood U (MO)
Linfield Coll (OR)
Lock Haven U of Pennsylvania (PA)
Long Island U, Brooklyn Campus (NY)
Longwood U (VA)
Louisiana Coll (LA)
Louisiana State U in Shreveport (LA)

Lourdes Coll (OH)
Loyola U Maryland (MD)
Loyola U New Orleans (LA)
Lubbock Christian U (TX)
Luther Coll (IA)
Lycoming Coll (PA)
Lynchburg Coll (VA)
Lyon Coll (AR)
Macalester Coll (MN)
MacMurray Coll (IL)
Manchester Coll (IN)
Mansfield U of Pennsylvania (PA)
Marietta Coll (OH)
Marist Coll (NY)
Marlboro Coll (VT)
Marshall U (WV)
Mars Hill Coll (NC)
Mary Baldwin Coll (VA)
Maryland Inst Coll of Art (MD)
Marylhurst U (OR)
Massachusetts Coll of Liberal Arts (MA)
McDaniel Coll (MD)
McKendree U (IL)
Mercer U (GA)
Mesa State Coll (CO)
Miami U (OH)
Michigan State U (MI)
Middle Tennessee State U (TN)
Midwestern State U (TX)
Millersville U of Pennsylvania (PA)
Mills Coll (CA)
Minnesota State U Mankato (MN)
Minnesota State U Moorhead (MN)
Minot State U (ND)
Mississippi Valley State U (MS)
Missouri Southern State U (MO)
Missouri State U (MO)
Molloy Coll (NY)
Monmouth Coll (IL)
Monmouth U (NJ)
Montana State U (MT)
Montana State U Billings (MT)
Moravian Coll (PA)
Morehouse Coll (GA)
Mount Mercy U (IA)
Mount Olive Coll (NC)
Mount St. Mary's Coll (CA)
Mount St. Mary's U (MD)
Mount Vernon Nazarene U (OH)
Muhlenberg Coll (PA)
Nazareth Coll of Rochester (NY)
Nebraska Wesleyan U (NE)
Newberry Coll (SC)
New England Coll (NH)
New Jersey City U (NJ)
Newman U (KS)
New Mexico Highlands U (NM)
Nicholls State U (LA)
North Carolina Ag and Tech State U (NC)
North Central Coll (IL)
North Dakota State U (ND)
Northeastern Illinois U (IL)
Northeastern State U (OK)
Northeastern U (MA)
Northern Illinois U (IL)
Northern State U (SD)
North Georgia Coll & State U (GA)
Northland Coll (WI)
Northwestern Coll (IA)
Northwest Nazarene U (ID)
Notre Dame de Namur U (CA)
Oberlin Coll (OH)
Oglethorpe U (GA)
The Ohio State U (OH)
Ohio U (OH)
Oklahoma Christian U (OK)
Oklahoma Panhandle State U (OK)
Oklahoma State U (OK)
Old Dominion U (VA)
Oregon State U (OR)
Otis Coll of Art and Design (CA)
Our Lady of the Lake U of San Antonio (TX)
Pace U (NY)
Pacific Lutheran U (WA)
Pacific U (OR)
Paier Coll of Art, Inc. (CT)
Parsons The New School for Design (NY)
Penn State Abington (PA)
Penn State Altoona (PA)
Penn State Beaver (PA)
Penn State Berks (PA)
Penn State Brandywine (PA)
Penn State DuBois (PA)

Penn State Erie, The Behrend Coll (PA)
Penn State Fayette, The Eberly Campus (PA)
Penn State Greater Allegheny (PA)
Penn State Hazleton (PA)
Penn State Lehigh Valley (PA)
Penn State Mont Alto (PA)
Penn State New Kensington (PA)
Penn State Schuylkill (PA)
Penn State Shenango (PA)
Penn State U Park (PA)
Penn State Wilkes-Barre (PA)
Penn State Worthington Scranton (PA)
Penn State York (PA)
Pepperdine U, Malibu (CA)
Piedmont Coll (GA)
Pikeville Coll (KY)
Pittsburg State U (KS)
Pitzer Coll (CA)
Pomona Coll (CA)
Portland State U (OR)
Pratt Inst (NY)
Presbyterian Coll (SC)
Prescott Coll (AZ)
Purchase Coll, State U of New York (NY)
Purdue U (IN)
Radford U (VA)
Randolph Coll (VA)
Reed Coll (OR)
Reinhardt U (GA)
Rhodes Coll (TN)
Rice U (TX)
Rider U (NJ)
Ripon Coll (WI)
Rivier Coll (NH)
Roanoke Coll (VA)
Rocky Mountain Coll (MT)
Rollins Coll (FL)
Rowan U (NJ)
Rutgers, The State U of New Jersey, Camden (NJ)
Rutgers, The State U of New Jersey, Newark (NJ)
Rutgers, The State U of New Jersey, New Brunswick (NJ)
Saginaw Valley State U (MI)
St. Ambrose U (IA)
St. Andrews Presbyterian Coll (NC)
St. Catherine U (MN)
St. Edward's U (TX)
Saint John's U (MN)
St. Lawrence U (NY)
Saint Mary-of-the-Woods Coll (IN)
Saint Mary's Coll (IN)
Saint Mary's Coll of California (CA)
St. Mary's Coll of Maryland (MD)
Saint Michael's Coll (VT)
St. Norbert Coll (WI)
St. Olaf Coll (MN)
St. Thomas Aquinas Coll (NY)
Saint Xavier U (IL)
Salem State U (MA)
Salisbury U (MD)
Samford U (AL)
Sam Houston State U (TX)
San Diego State U (CA)
San Francisco State U (CA)
San Jose State U (CA)
Sarah Lawrence Coll (NY)
School of the Museum of Fine Arts, Boston (MA)
Scripps Coll (CA)
Seattle Pacific U (WA)
Sewanee: The U of the South (TN)
Shepherd U (WV)
Shippensburg U of Pennsylvania (PA)
Shorter U (GA)
Siena Heights U (MI)
Sierra Nevada Coll (NV)
Silver Lake Coll (WI)
Simmons Coll (MA)
Simon Fraser U (BC, Canada)
Simpson Coll (IA)
Skidmore Coll (NY)
Slippery Rock U of Pennsylvania (PA)
Smith Coll (MA)
Sonoma State U (CA)
Southeastern Louisiana U (LA)
Southeastern Oklahoma State U (OK)
Southeast Missouri State U (MO)
Southern Adventist U (TN)

Southern Arkansas U–Magnolia (AR)
Southern Illinois U Carbondale (IL)
Southern Illinois U Edwardsville (IL)
Southern Oregon U (OR)
Southern Utah U (UT)
Spelman Coll (GA)
Spring Arbor U (MI)
Springfield Coll (MA)
Stanford U (CA)
State U of New York at Binghamton (NY)
State U of New York at Fredonia (NY)
State U of New York at New Paltz (NY)
State U of New York at Oswego (NY)
State U of New York at Plattsburgh (NY)
State U of New York Coll at Old Westbury (NY)
State U of New York Coll at Oneonta (NY)
State U of New York Coll at Potsdam (NY)
State U of New York Empire State Coll (NY)
Stephen F. Austin State U (TX)
Stetson U (FL)
Suffolk U (MA)
Sul Ross State U (TX)
Tarleton State U (TX)
Taylor U (IN)
Temple U (PA)
Tennessee Technological U (TN)
Texas A&M U–Corpus Christi (TX)
Texas Lutheran U (TX)
Texas State U–San Marcos (TX)
Texas Tech U (TX)
Texas Wesleyan U (TX)
Texas Woman's U (TX)
Thiel Coll (PA)
Thomas Edison State Coll (NJ)
Tiffin U (OH)
Towson U (MD)
Transylvania U (KY)
Trinity Coll (CT)
Trinity U (TX)
Troy U (AL)
Truman State U (MO)
Tulane U (LA)
Union U (TN)
Université du Québec en Outaouais (QC, Canada)
U at Buffalo, the State U of New York (NY)
The U of Alabama at Birmingham (AL)
The U of Alabama in Huntsville (AL)
U of Alaska Fairbanks (AK)
U of Arkansas (AR)
U of Arkansas at Pine Bluff (AR)
U of Arkansas–Fort Smith (AR)
U of California, Berkeley (CA)
U of California, Los Angeles (CA)
U of California, Santa Cruz (CA)
U of Central Florida (FL)
U of Charleston (WV)
U of Cincinnati (OH)
U of Dallas (TX)
U of Delaware (DE)
U of Denver (CO)
U of Evansville (IN)
The U of Findlay (OH)
U of Georgia (GA)
U of Hawaii at Hilo (HI)
U of Hawaii at Manoa (HI)
U of Houston (TX)
U of Idaho (ID)
U of Indianapolis (IN)
The U of Iowa (IA)
U of La Verne (CA)
U of Louisiana at Lafayette (LA)
U of Maine (ME)
U of Maine at Farmington (ME)
U of Maine at Presque Isle (ME)
U of Manitoba (MB, Canada)
U of Mary Hardin-Baylor (TX)
U of Massachusetts Boston (MA)
U of Memphis (TN)
U of Miami (FL)
U of Michigan (MI)
U of Minnesota, Duluth (MN)
U of Minnesota, Twin Cities Campus (MN)
U of Missouri (MO)
U of Mobile (AL)

The U of Montana Western (MT)
U of Montevallo (AL)
U of Nebraska at Omaha (NE)
U of Nevada, Las Vegas (NV)
U of Nevada, Reno (NV)
U of New Hampshire (NH)
The U of North Carolina at Asheville (NC)
The U of North Carolina at Charlotte (NC)
The U of North Carolina at Greensboro (NC)
U of North Dakota (ND)
U of Northern Iowa (IA)
U of North Florida (FL)
U of North Texas (TX)
U of Oregon (OR)
U of Puget Sound (WA)
U of Rhode Island (RI)
U of Rio Grande (OH)
U of Saint Mary (KS)
U of San Diego (CA)
U of San Francisco (CA)
U of Science and Arts of Oklahoma (OK)
U of Sioux Falls (SD)
U of South Alabama (AL)
U of Southern Indiana (IN)
U of Southern Maine (ME)
U of South Florida (FL)
The U of Tampa (FL)
The U of Tennessee at Chattanooga (TN)
The U of Texas at Arlington (TX)
The U of Texas at Austin (TX)
The U of Texas at San Antonio (TX)
The U of Texas at Tyler (TX)
The U of Texas of the Permian Basin (TX)
The U of Texas–Pan American (TX)
U of the District of Columbia (DC)
U of the Incarnate Word (TX)
U of the Pacific (CA)
The U of Toledo (OH)
U of Utah (UT)
U of Virginia (VA)
U of Washington (WA)
U of Washington, Bothell (WA)
The U of Western Ontario (ON, Canada)
U of West Florida (FL)
U of West Georgia (GA)
U of Wisconsin–Eau Claire (WI)
U of Wisconsin–Green Bay (WI)
U of Wisconsin–La Crosse (WI)
U of Wisconsin–Madison (WI)
U of Wisconsin–Parkside (WI)
U of Wisconsin–Platteville (WI)
U of Wisconsin–River Falls (WI)
U of Wisconsin–Whitewater (WI)
U of Wyoming (WY)
Upper Iowa U (IA)
Utah State U (UT)
Valdosta State U (GA)
Valparaiso U (IN)
Vanderbilt U (TN)
Virginia Intermont Coll (VA)
Virginia Polytechnic Inst and State U (VA)
Virginia Wesleyan Coll (VA)
Viterbo U (WI)
Wabash Coll (IN)
Wagner Coll (NY)
Walla Walla U (WA)
Wartburg Coll (IA)
Washburn U (KS)
Washington & Jefferson Coll (PA)
Washington Coll (MD)
Washington U in St. Louis (MO)
Watkins Coll of Art, Design, & Film (TN)
Wayland Baptist U (TX)
Waynesburg U (PA)
Wayne State Coll (NE)
Wayne State U (MI)
Weber State U (UT)
Webster U (MO)
Wells Coll (NY)
Wesleyan U (CT)
West Chester U of Pennsylvania (PA)
Western Carolina U (NC)
Western Connecticut State U (CT)
Western Illinois U (IL)
Western Michigan U (MI)
Western Oregon U (OR)
Western State Coll of Colorado (CO)

Westfield State U (MA)
Westminster Coll (UT)
Westmont Coll (CA)
West Virginia U (WV)
Wheaton Coll (IL)
Whitman Coll (WA)
Wichita State U (KS)
Willamette U (OR)
William Jewell Coll (MO)
William Paterson U of New Jersey (NJ)
Wingate U (NC)
Winona State U (MN)
Winthrop U (SC)
Wittenberg U (OH)
Wright State U (OH)
Xavier U (OH)
Xavier U of Louisiana (LA)
Yale U (CT)
York Coll of the City U of New York (NY)
Youngstown State U (OH)

ART HISTORY, CRITICISM AND CONSERVATION

Adams State Coll (CO)
Adelphi U (NY)
Albertus Magnus Coll (CT)
Allegheny Coll (PA)
American U (DC)
American U of Beirut (Lebanon)
The American U of Paris (France)
Aquinas Coll (MI)
Arcadia U (PA)
Augsburg Coll (MN)
Augustana Coll (IL)
Baker U (KS)
Baldwin-Wallace Coll (OH)
Bard Coll (NY)
Bard Coll at Simon's Rock (MA)
Barnard Coll (NY)
Beloit Coll (WI)
Bennington Coll (VT)
Birmingham-Southern Coll (AL)
Bloomsburg U of Pennsylvania (PA)
Boise State U (ID)
Boston Coll (MA)
Bowdoin Coll (ME)
Bowling Green State U (OH)
Brandeis U (MA)
Bridgewater State U (MA)
Brown U (RI)
Bryn Mawr Coll (PA)
Bucknell U (PA)
California State U, Chico (CA)
California State U, Dominguez Hills (CA)
California State U, Fullerton (CA)
California State U, Long Beach (CA)
California State U, San Bernardino (CA)
Calvin Coll (MI)
Canisius Coll (NY)
Carleton Coll (MN)
Case Western Reserve U (OH)
The Catholic U of America (DC)
Centre Coll (KY)
Chapman U (CA)
Chatham U (PA)
City Coll of the City U of New York (NY)
Claremont McKenna Coll (CA)
Clarke U (IA)
Clark U (MA)
Colby Coll (ME)
Colgate U (NY)
Coll of Charleston (SC)
Coll of the Holy Cross (MA)
The Coll of William and Mary (VA)
The Coll of Wooster (OH)
The Colorado Coll (CO)
Colorado State U (CO)
Columbia U, School of General Studies (NY)
Concordia U (QC, Canada)
Connecticut Coll (CT)
Cornell Coll (IA)
Cornell U (NY)
Dartmouth Coll (NH)
Denison U (OH)
DePaul U (IL)
DePauw U (IN)
DEREE - The American Coll of Greece (Greece)
Dominican U (IL)
Dominican U of California (CA)
Drake U (IA)
Drew U (NJ)

Drury U (MO)
Duquesne U (PA)
Eastern Michigan U (MI)
Eastern Washington U (WA)
Elizabethtown Coll (PA)
Elon U (NC)
Eugene Lang Coll The New School for Liberal Arts (NY)
Fairfield U (CT)
Ferris State U (MI)
Florida Intl U (FL)
Florida Southern Coll (FL)
Florida State U (FL)
Franklin & Marshall Coll (PA)
Franklin Coll Switzerland (Switzerland)
Furman U (SC)
Gallaudet U (DC)
Georgetown U (DC)
Gettysburg Coll (PA)
Governors State U (IL)
Grand Valley State U (MI)
Hamilton Coll (NY)
Hamline U (MN)
Hampshire Coll (MA)
Hanover Coll (IN)
Hartwick Coll (NY)
Harvard U (MA)
Haverford Coll (PA)
Hobart and William Smith Colls (NY)
Hofstra U (NY)
Hollins U (VA)
Holy Cross Coll (IN)
Hope Coll (MI)
Humboldt State U (CA)
Hunter Coll of the City U of New York (NY)
Indiana U Bloomington (IN)
Indiana U–Purdue U Indianapolis (IN)
Inter American U of Puerto Rico, San Germán Campus (PR)
Ithaca Coll (NY)
James Madison U (VA)
John Carroll U (OH)
The Johns Hopkins U (MD)
Juniata Coll (PA)
Kalamazoo Coll (MI)
Kean U (NJ)
Kent State U (OH)
Kenyon Coll (OH)
Knox Coll (IL)
Lafayette Coll (PA)
Lake Forest Coll (IL)
La Salle U (PA)
Lawrence U (WI)
Lehigh U (PA)
Lehman Coll of the City U of New York (NY)
Lindenwood U (MO)
Long Island U, C.W. Post Campus (NY)
Longwood U (VA)
Lourdes Coll (OH)
Loyola Marymount U (CA)
Loyola U Chicago (IL)
Lycoming Coll (PA)
MacMurray Coll (IL)
Madonna U (MI)
Manhattanville Coll (NY)
Marist Coll (NY)
Marlboro Coll (VT)
Mars Hill Coll (NC)
Maryland Inst Coll of Art (MD)
Maryville Coll (TN)
Massachusetts Coll of Art and Design (MA)
McDaniel Coll (MD)
Messiah Coll (PA)
Miami U (OH)
Michigan State U (MI)
Middlebury Coll (VT)
Millsaps Coll (MS)
Mills Coll (CA)
Minnesota State U Mankato (MN)
Missouri State U (MO)
Moravian Coll (PA)
Mount Allison U (NB, Canada)
Mount Holyoke Coll (MA)
Nazareth Coll of Rochester (NY)
New Coll of Florida (FL)
New England Coll (NH)
North Carolina State U (NC)
North Central Coll (IL)
Northern Arizona U (AZ)
Northern Illinois U (IL)
Northern Michigan U (MI)
Oberlin Coll (OH)
Oglethorpe U (GA)
The Ohio State U (OH)

Ohio U (OH)
Ohio Wesleyan U (OH)
Oklahoma City U (OK)
Old Dominion U (VA)
Pace U (NY)
Penn State Abington (PA)
Penn State Altoona (PA)
Penn State Beaver (PA)
Penn State Berks (PA)
Penn State Brandywine (PA)
Penn State DuBois (PA)
Penn State Erie, The Behrend Coll (PA)
Penn State Fayette, The Eberly Campus (PA)
Penn State Greater Allegheny (PA)
Penn State Hazleton (PA)
Penn State Lehigh Valley (PA)
Penn State Mont Alto (PA)
Penn State New Kensington (PA)
Penn State Schuylkill (PA)
Penn State Shenango (PA)
Penn State U Park (PA)
Penn State Wilkes-Barre (PA)
Penn State Worthington Scranton (PA)
Penn State York (PA)
Pepperdine U, Malibu (CA)
Pitzer Coll (CA)
Pomona Coll (CA)
Portland State U (OR)
Pratt Inst (NY)
Presbyterian Coll (SC)
Princeton U (NJ)
Principia Coll (IL)
Providence Coll (RI)
Purchase Coll, State U of New York (NY)
Purdue U (IN)
Queens Coll of the City U of New York (NY)
Randolph Coll (VA)
Randolph-Macon Coll (VA)
Rhode Island Coll (RI)
Rhodes Coll (TN)
Rice U (TX)
Roanoke Coll (VA)
Rockford Coll (IL)
Rollins Coll (FL)
Rosemont Coll (PA)
Rutgers, The State U of New Jersey, New Brunswick (NJ)
St. Bonaventure U (NY)
St. Catherine U (MN)
Saint Joseph Coll (CT)
St. Lawrence U (NY)
Saint Louis U (MO)
Saint Mary's Coll of California (CA)
St. Olaf Coll (MN)
Salem State U (MA)
Salve Regina U (RI)
San Diego State U (CA)
San Jose State U (CA)
Santa Clara U (CA)
Sarah Lawrence Coll (NY)
Savannah Coll of Art and Design (GA)
Scripps Coll (CA)
Seton Hill U (PA)
Sewanee: The U of the South (TN)
Siena Heights U (MI)
Skidmore Coll (NY)
Smith Coll (MA)
Sonoma State U (CA)
Southern Connecticut State U (CT)
Southern Methodist U (TX)
Stanford U (CA)
State U of New York at Binghamton (NY)
State U of New York at Fredonia (NY)
State U of New York at New Paltz (NY)
State U of New York at Plattsburgh (NY)
State U of New York Coll at Geneseo (NY)
State U of New York Coll at Oneonta (NY)
State U of New York Coll at Potsdam (NY)
Stephen F. Austin State U (TX)
Stonehill Coll (MA)
Stony Brook U, State U of New York (NY)
Suffolk U (MA)
Susquehanna U (PA)
Swarthmore Coll (PA)
Sweet Briar Coll (VA)
Syracuse U (NY)

Temple U (PA)
Texas Christian U (TX)
Texas Tech U (TX)
Towson U (MD)
Transylvania U (KY)
Trinity Coll (CT)
Trinity U (TX)
Truman State U (MO)
Tufts U (MA)
Tulane U (LA)
U at Buffalo, the State U of New York (NY)
The U of Akron (OH)
The U of Alabama (AL)
The U of Arizona (AZ)
The U of British Columbia (BC, Canada)
The U of British Columbia–Okanagan (BC, Canada)
U of California, Berkeley (CA)
U of California, Davis (CA)
U of California, Irvine (CA)
U of California, Los Angeles (CA)
U of California, Santa Barbara (CA)
U of California, Santa Cruz (CA)
U of Cincinnati (OH)
U of Colorado Boulder (CO)
U of Dallas (TX)
U of Dayton (OH)
U of Delaware (DE)
U of Denver (CO)
U of Evansville (IN)
U of Georgia (GA)
U of Guelph (ON, Canada)
U of Hartford (CT)
U of Illinois at Chicago (IL)
The U of Iowa (IA)
The U of Kansas (KS)
U of La Verne (CA)
U of Lethbridge (AB, Canada)
U of Louisville (KY)
U of Maine (ME)
U of Manitoba (MB, Canada)
U of Maryland, Coll Park (MD)
U of Mary Washington (VA)
U of Massachusetts Amherst (MA)
U of Massachusetts Dartmouth (MA)
U of Memphis (TN)
U of Miami (FL)
U of Michigan (MI)
U of Michigan–Dearborn (MI)
U of Minnesota, Duluth (MN)
U of Minnesota, Twin Cities Campus (MN)
U of Mississippi (MS)
U of Missouri (MO)
U of Missouri–St. Louis (MO)
U of Nebraska at Omaha (NE)
U of Nebraska–Lincoln (NE)
U of Nevada, Las Vegas (NV)
U of Nevada, Reno (NV)
The U of North Carolina at Chapel Hill (NC)
The U of North Carolina at Charlotte (NC)
The U of North Carolina Wilmington (NC)
U of Northern Iowa (IA)
U of North Texas (TX)
U of Notre Dame (IN)
U of Oklahoma (OK)
U of Oregon (OR)
U of Ottawa (ON, Canada)
U of Pennsylvania (PA)
U of Pittsburgh (PA)
U of Redlands (CA)
U of Regina (SK, Canada)
U of Rhode Island (RI)
U of Richmond (VA)
U of Rochester (NY)
U of St. Thomas (MN)
U of San Diego (CA)
U of San Francisco (CA)
U of Saskatchewan (SK, Canada)
U of South Carolina (SC)
U of Southern California (CA)
U of South Florida (FL)
The U of Tennessee (TN)
The U of Texas at Arlington (TX)
The U of Texas at Austin (TX)
The U of Texas at San Antonio (TX)
U of the Incarnate Word (TX)
U of the Pacific (CA)
The U of Toledo (OH)
U of Tulsa (OK)
U of Utah (UT)
U of Vermont (VT)
U of Washington (WA)
U of Waterloo (ON, Canada)

The U of Western Ontario (ON, Canada)
U of West Florida (FL)
U of Wisconsin–Madison (WI)
U of Wisconsin–Superior (WI)
U of Wisconsin–Whitewater (WI)
Ursuline Coll (OH)
Vanderbilt U (TN)
Vassar Coll (NY)
Villanova U (PA)
Virginia Commonwealth U (VA)
Wake Forest U (NC)
Washburn U (KS)
Washington and Lee U (VA)
Washington U in St. Louis (MO)
Wayne State U (MI)
Webster U (MO)
Wellesley Coll (MA)
Wells Coll (NY)
Wesleyan Coll (GA)
Wesleyan U (CT)
Western Kentucky U (KY)
Western Michigan U (MI)
West Virginia U (WV)
Wheaton Coll (MA)
Whitman Coll (WA)
Wichita State U (KS)
Willamette U (OR)
William Paterson U of New Jersey (NJ)
Williams Coll (MA)
Winthrop U (SC)
Wofford Coll (SC)
Wright State U (OH)
Yale U (CT)
York Coll of the City U of New York (NY)
Youngstown State U (OH)

ARTIFICIAL INTELLIGENCE
Worcester Polytechnic Inst (MA)

ARTS, ENTERTAINMENT, AND MEDIA MANAGEMENT
St. Edward's U (TX)
Shenandoah U (VA)
U of Wisconsin–Green Bay (WI)

ARTS, ENTERTAINMENT, AND MEDIA MANAGEMENT RELATED
Trevecca Nazarene U (TN)

ART TEACHER EDUCATION
Abilene Christian U (TX)
Adams State Coll (CO)
Adelphi U (NY)
Albright Coll (PA)
Alfred U (NY)
Alma Coll (MI)
Alverno Coll (WI)
Anderson U (SC)
Andrews U (MI)
Anna Maria Coll (MA)
Appalachian State U (NC)
Arcadia U (PA)
Arkansas Tech U (AR)
Armstrong Atlantic State U (GA)
Asbury U (KY)
Ashland U (OH)
Assumption Coll (MA)
Augsburg Coll (MN)
Augustana Coll (IL)
Augustana Coll (SD)
Averett U (VA)
Baker U (KS)
Barton Coll (NC)
Belmont U (TN)
Beloit Coll (WI)
Bemidji State U (MN)
Berea Coll (KY)
Bethany Coll (KS)
Bethel U (MN)
Birmingham-Southern Coll (AL)
Blackburn Coll (IL)
Bob Jones U (SC)
Boise State U (ID)
Boston U (MA)
Bowling Green State U (OH)
Brenau U (GA)
Bridgewater Coll (VA)
Bridgewater State U (MA)
Buena Vista U (IA)
California State U, Chico (CA)
California State U, Long Beach (CA)
Calumet Coll of Saint Joseph (IN)
Calvin Coll (MI)
Campbellsville U (KY)
Capital U (OH)
Carlow U (PA)

Carroll U (WI)
Carson-Newman Coll (TN)
Case Western Reserve U (OH)
Central Connecticut State U (CT)
Central Michigan U (MI)
City Coll of the City U of New York (NY)
Claflin U (SC)
Clarke U (IA)
Coker Coll (SC)
Coll for Creative Studies (MI)
Coll of Mount St. Joseph (OH)
The Coll of New Jersey (NJ)
The Coll of Saint Rose (NY)
Coll of the Ozarks (MO)
Colorado State U (CO)
Columbus State U (GA)
Concordia Coll (MN)
Concordia U (QC, Canada)
Concordia U Chicago (IL)
Concordia U, St. Paul (MN)
Concordia U Wisconsin (WI)
Concord U (WV)
Corcoran Coll of Art and Design (DC)
Culver-Stockton Coll (MO)
Dakota Wesleyan U (SD)
Defiance Coll (OH)
Delaware State U (DE)
DePaul U (IL)
Dickinson State U (ND)
Dowling Coll (NY)
Eastern Michigan U (MI)
Eastern Washington U (WA)
Edgewood Coll (WI)
Elizabeth City State U (NC)
Elmhurst Coll (IL)
Elmira Coll (NY)
Escuela de Artes Plasticas de Puerto Rico (PR)
Evangel U (MO)
Fairmont State U (WV)
Fayetteville State U (NC)
Ferris State U (MI)
Flagler Coll (FL)
Florida Ag and Mech U (FL)
Florida Intl U (FL)
Florida Southern Coll (FL)
Fontbonne U (MO)
Francis Marion U (SC)
Franklin Pierce U (NH)
Freed-Hardeman U (TN)
Friends U (KS)
Gallaudet U (DC)
Georgia State U (GA)
Goddard Coll (VT)
Grace Coll (IN)
Graceland U (IA)
Grand Valley State U (MI)
Greensboro Coll (NC)
Hannibal-LaGrange U (MO)
Harding U (AR)
Hardin-Simmons U (TX)
Hofstra U (NY)
Hope Coll (MI)
Humboldt State U (CA)
Huntington U (IN)
Indiana State U (IN)
Indiana U Bloomington (IN)
Indiana U–Purdue U Fort Wayne (IN)
Indiana U–Purdue U Indianapolis (IN)
Indiana Wesleyan U (IN)
Inter American U of Puerto Rico, San Germán Campus (PR)
Iowa Wesleyan Coll (IA)
Ithaca Coll (NY)
Johnson State Coll (VT)
Kennesaw State U (GA)
Kent State U (OH)
Kentucky Wesleyan Coll (KY)
Keystone Coll (PA)
Lamar U (TX)
Lawrence U (WI)
Lehman Coll of the City U of New York (NY)
Lincoln Memorial U (TN)
Lincoln U (MO)
Lindenwood U (MO)
Lindsey Wilson Coll (KY)
Lipscomb U (TN)
Long Island U, Brooklyn Campus (NY)
Long Island U, C.W. Post Campus (NY)
Longwood U (VA)
Loras Coll (IA)
Louisiana Coll (LA)
Louisiana State U in Shreveport (LA)

Penn State New Kensington (PA)
Penn State Schuylkill (PA)
Penn State Shenango (PA)
Penn State U Park (PA)
Penn State Wilkes-Barre (PA)
Penn State Worthington Scranton (PA)
Penn State York (PA)
Purdue U (IN)
Rutgers, The State U of New Jersey, New Brunswick (NJ)
Saint Louis U (MO)
San Francisco State U (CA)
San Jose State U (CA)
State U of New York at Oswego (NY)
State U of New York Coll at Oneonta (NY)
State U of New York Maritime Coll (NY)
Stony Brook U, State U of New York (NY)
Texas A&M U (TX)
United States Air Force Acad (CO)
The U of Arizona (AZ)
The U of British Columbia (BC, Canada)
U of California, Berkeley (CA)
U of California, Davis (CA)
U of Guelph (ON, Canada)
The U of Kansas (KS)
U of Louisiana at Monroe (LA)
U of Louisville (KY)
U of Miami (FL)
U of Michigan (MI)
U of Missouri (MO)
U of Nebraska–Lincoln (NE)
The U of North Carolina at Asheville (NC)
U of North Dakota (ND)
U of South Alabama (AL)
U of Utah (UT)
U of Washington (WA)
U of Waterloo (ON, Canada)
U of Wisconsin–Madison (WI)
Valparaiso U (IN)
Western Connecticut State U (CT)

ATMOSPHERIC SCIENCES AND METEOROLOGY RELATED
Purdue U (IN)
U of California, Los Angeles (CA)
U of the Incarnate Word (TX)

ATOMIC/MOLECULAR PHYSICS
Harvard U (MA)
San Diego State U (CA)
U of Waterloo (ON, Canada)

AUDIOLOGY
Biola U (CA)
California State U, Long Beach (CA)
Cleveland State U (OH)
Indiana U–Purdue U Fort Wayne (IN)
Purdue U (IN)
Stephen F. Austin State U (TX)
U of Colorado Boulder (CO)
U of Montevallo (AL)
U of Northern Colorado (CO)
U of Oklahoma Health Sciences Center (OK)
The U of Western Ontario (ON, Canada)

AUDIOLOGY AND SPEECH-LANGUAGE PATHOLOGY
Adelphi U (NY)
Andrews U (MI)
Arkansas State U (AR)
Auburn U (AL)
Augustana Coll (SD)
Ball State U (IN)
Bloomsburg U of Pennsylvania (PA)
Boston U (MA)
California State U, Long Beach (CA)
Calvin Coll (MI)
Clarion U of Pennsylvania (PA)
The Coll of Saint Rose (NY)
Delta State U (MS)
Eastern New Mexico U (NM)
East Stroudsburg U of Pennsylvania (PA)
Elmhurst Coll (IL)
Elmira Coll (NY)
Fontbonne U (MO)
Governors State U (IL)
Hardin-Simmons U (TX)

Hofstra U (NY)
Hunter Coll of the City U of New York (NY)
Idaho State U (ID)
Illinois State U (IL)
Indiana State U (IN)
Indiana U Bloomington (IN)
Indiana U of Pennsylvania (PA)
Ithaca Coll (NY)
Kent State U (OH)
Lamar U (TX)
La Salle U (PA)
Lehman Coll of the City U of New York (NY)
Louisiana State U and Ag and Mech Coll (LA)
Louisiana State U in Shreveport (LA)
Marquette U (WI)
Marywood U (PA)
Michigan State U (MI)
Minnesota State U Mankato (MN)
Minnesota State U Moorhead (MN)
Missouri State U (MO)
Molloy Coll (NY)
Murray State U (KY)
Nazareth Coll of Rochester (NY)
New York U (NY)
Nicholls State U (LA)
Northeastern State U (OK)
Northeastern U (MA)
The Ohio State U (OH)
Ohio U (OH)
Old Dominion U (VA)
Our Lady of the Lake U of San Antonio (TX)
Purdue U (IN)
The Richard Stockton Coll of New Jersey (NJ)
St. John's U (NY)
Saint Louis U (MO)
Southeastern Louisiana U (LA)
Southern Connecticut State U (CT)
Southern Illinois U Edwardsville (IL)
State U of New York at Fredonia (NY)
State U of New York at Plattsburgh (NY)
Stephen F. Austin State U (TX)
Syracuse U (NY)
Temple U (PA)
Texas A&M U–Kingsville (TX)
Texas State U–San Marcos (TX)
Texas Woman's U (TX)
Thiel Coll (PA)
U at Buffalo, the State U of New York (NY)
The U of Alabama (AL)
U of Arkansas (AR)
U of Central Florida (FL)
U of Florida (FL)
U of Hawaii at Manoa (HI)
The U of Iowa (IA)
U of Louisiana at Lafayette (LA)
U of Louisiana at Monroe (LA)
U of Minnesota, Twin Cities Campus (MN)
U of Mississippi (MS)
The U of North Carolina at Greensboro (NC)
U of North Texas (TX)
U of Oklahoma Health Sciences Center (OK)
U of Pittsburgh (PA)
U of Redlands (CA)
U of South Alabama (AL)
U of Southern Mississippi (MS)
U of South Florida (FL)
The U of Texas at Dallas (TX)
The U of Texas–Pan American (TX)
U of the District of Columbia (DC)
U of the Pacific (CA)
The U of Toledo (OH)
U of Tulsa (OK)
U of Utah (UT)
U of Virginia (VA)
U of Washington (WA)
The U of Western Ontario (ON, Canada)
U of Wisconsin–Madison (WI)
U of Wisconsin–Stevens Point (WI)
U of Wyoming (WY)
Utah State U (UT)
Washington State U (WA)
West Chester U of Pennsylvania (PA)
Western Michigan U (MI)

West Virginia U (WV)
Wichita State U (KS)

AUDIOVISUAL COMMUNICATIONS TECHNOLOGIES RELATED
Greenville Coll (IL)
Webster U (MO)

AUDITING
Carlow U (PA)

AUSTRALIAN/OCEANIC/PACIFIC LANGUAGES
U of Hawaii–West Oahu (HI)

AUTOBODY/COLLISION AND REPAIR TECHNOLOGY
Lewis-Clark State Coll (ID)
Pennsylvania Coll of Technology (PA)

AUTOMOBILE/AUTOMOTIVE MECHANICS TECHNOLOGY
Lewis-Clark State Coll (ID)
Walla Walla U (WA)

AUTOMOTIVE ENGINEERING TECHNOLOGY
Central Michigan U (MI)
Ferris State U (MI)
Indiana State U (IN)
Minnesota State U Mankato (MN)
Pennsylvania Coll of Technology (PA)
Southern Illinois U Carbondale (IL)
Weber State U (UT)

AVIATION/AIRWAY MANAGEMENT
Auburn U (AL)
Averett U (VA)
Baker Coll of Muskegon (MI)
Bridgewater State U (MA)
California State U, Los Angeles (CA)
Delaware State U (DE)
Dixie State Coll of Utah (UT)
Dowling Coll (NY)
Eastern Michigan U (MI)
Eastern New Mexico U (NM)
Embry-Riddle Aeronautical U–Daytona (FL)
Embry-Riddle Aeronautical U–Worldwide (FL)
Fairmont State U (WV)
Florida Inst of Technology (FL)
Indiana State U (IN)
Inter American U of Puerto Rico, Bayamón Campus (PR)
Kent State U (OH)
Lewis U (IL)
Marywood U (PA)
Minnesota State U Mankato (MN)
Mountain State U (WV)
The Ohio State U (OH)
Ohio U (OH)
Purdue U (IN)
Quincy U (IL)
Rocky Mountain Coll (MT)
Saint Louis U (MO)
Salem State U (MA)
South Dakota State U (SD)
Southeastern Oklahoma State U (OK)
Southern Illinois U Carbondale (IL)
Tarleton State U (TX)
Texas Southern U (TX)
U of Dubuque (IA)
U of Nebraska at Omaha (NE)
U of North Dakota (ND)
U of North Texas (TX)
The U of Western Ontario (ON, Canada)
Vaughn Coll of Aeronautics and Technology (NY)
Western Michigan U (MI)
Westminster Coll (UT)
Wilmington U (DE)
Winona State U (MN)

AVIONICS MAINTENANCE TECHNOLOGY
Averett U (VA)
Fairmont State U (WV)
LeTourneau U (TX)
Pennsylvania Coll of Technology (PA)

Purdue U (IN)
Southern Illinois U Carbondale (IL)
Vaughn Coll of Aeronautics and Technology (NY)
Western Michigan U (MI)
Wilmington U (DE)

AYURVEDIC MEDICINE
Maharishi U of Management (IA)

BAKING AND PASTRY ARTS
Johnson & Wales U (CO)
Johnson & Wales U (FL)
Johnson & Wales U (RI)
Johnson & Wales U - Charlotte Campus (NC)
The Restaurant School at Walnut Hill Coll (PA)

BALLET
Brigham Young U (UT)
Friends U (KS)
Indiana U Bloomington (IN)
Texas Christian U (TX)
U of Utah (UT)

BANKING AND FINANCIAL SUPPORT SERVICES
Buena Vista U (IA)
Delaware State U (DE)
Husson U (ME)
National U (CA)
Providence Coll (RI)
Sam Houston State U (TX)
Texas Southern U (TX)
U of Nebraska at Omaha (NE)
U of Nebraska–Lincoln (NE)
U of North Florida (FL)
U of North Texas (TX)
The U of Texas at Arlington (TX)
U of the Incarnate Word (TX)
West Liberty U (WV)

BEHAVIORAL SCIENCES
Andrews U (MI)
Athens State U (AL)
Augsburg Coll (MN)
Bemidji State U (MN)
Brown U (RI)
California Baptist U (CA)
California State U, Dominguez Hills (CA)
Carnegie Mellon U (PA)
Coll of St. Joseph (VT)
Columbia Coll (SC)
Concordia Coll–New York (NY)
Concordia U (CA)
Dakota Wesleyan U (SD)
Drew U (NJ)
Evangel U (MO)
Freed-Hardeman U (TN)
George Fox U (OR)
Goddard Coll (VT)
Granite State Coll (NH)
Indiana U Kokomo (IN)
Inter American U of Puerto Rico, San Germán Campus (PR)
The Johns Hopkins U (MD)
Laurentian U (ON, Canada)
Loyola U Chicago (IL)
Marlboro Coll (VT)
Mars Hill Coll (NC)
Minnesota State U Mankato (MN)
Missouri Baptist U (MO)
National U (CA)
Northeastern U (MA)
Northern Michigan U (MI)
Oklahoma Wesleyan U (OK)
Point Park U (PA)
Purdue U (IN)
Purdue U North Central (IN)
San Jose State U (CA)
Tennessee Wesleyan Coll (TN)
Texas Wesleyan U (TX)
Trevecca Nazarene U (TN)
Tufts U (MA)
United States Air Force Acad (CO)
U of Houston–Clear Lake (TX)
The U of Kansas (KS)
U of La Verne (CA)
U of Maine at Fort Kent (ME)
U of Maine at Presque Isle (ME)
U of Missouri (MO)
U of North Texas (TX)
U of Wisconsin–Green Bay (WI)
Utah Valley U (UT)
Walsh U (OH)
Western Intl U (AZ)

Widener U (PA)
William Paterson U of New Jersey (NJ)
Wilmington U (DE)
York Coll of Pennsylvania (PA)

BIBLICAL STUDIES
Abilene Christian U (TX)
Amridge U (AL)
Anderson U (IN)
Andrews U (MI)
Appalachian Bible Coll (WV)
Arlington Baptist Coll (TX)
Asbury U (KY)
Atlanta Christian Coll (GA)
Azusa Pacific U (CA)
Baptist Bible Coll of Pennsylvania (PA)
The Baptist Coll of Florida (FL)
Barclay Coll (KS)
Belhaven U (MS)
Belmont U (TN)
Bethany Bible Coll (NB, Canada)
Bethel Coll (IN)
Bethel U (MN)
Beulah Heights U (GA)
Biola U (CA)
Bluefield Coll (VA)
Blue Mountain Coll (MS)
Bob Jones U (SC)
Boston Baptist Coll (MA)
Bryan Coll (TN)
California Baptist U (CA)
Calvary Bible Coll and Theological Sem (MO)
Calvin Coll (MI)
Campbellsville U (KY)
Carolina Christian Coll (NC)
Carson-Newman Coll (TN)
Cedarville U (OH)
Cincinnati Christian U (OH)
Clear Creek Baptist Bible Coll (KY)
Clearwater Christian Coll (FL)
Columbia Bible Coll (BC, Canada)
Corban U (OR)
Covenant Coll (GA)
Crandall U (NB, Canada)
Crossroads Bible Coll (IN)
Dallas Baptist U (TX)
East Texas Baptist U (TX)
Emmaus Bible Coll (IA)
Evangel U (MO)
Faith Baptist Bible Coll and Theological Sem (IA)
Faulkner U (AL)
Florida Coll (FL)
Freed-Hardeman U (TN)
Free Will Baptist Bible Coll (TN)
Gardner-Webb U (NC)
Geneva Coll (PA)
George Fox U (OR)
Grace Bible Coll (MI)
Grace Coll (IN)
Grand Canyon U (AZ)
Great Lakes Christian Coll (MI)
Hannibal-LaGrange U (MO)
Harding U (AR)
Hardin-Simmons U (TX)
Heritage Christian U (AL)
Houghton Coll (NY)
Huntington U (IN)
Indiana Wesleyan U (IN)
John Brown U (AR)
Johnson Bible Coll (TN)
King Coll (TN)
Kuyper Coll (MI)
Lee U (TN)
LeTourneau U (TX)
Lincoln Christian U (IL)
Lipscomb U (TN)
Lubbock Christian U (TX)
Malone U (OH)
Maple Springs Baptist Bible Coll and Sem (MD)
Maranatha Baptist Bible Coll (WI)
Marlboro Coll (VT)
The Master's Coll and Sem (CA)
Master's Coll and Sem (ON, Canada)
Messiah Coll (PA)
MidAmerica Nazarene U (KS)
Mid-Atlantic Christian U (NC)
Mid-Continent U (KY)
Milligan Coll (TN)
Montreat Coll, Montreat (NC)
Mount Vernon Nazarene U (OH)
Multnomah U (OR)
New Hope Christian Coll (OR)

North Greenville U (SC)
Northwest Christian U (OR)
Northwestern Coll (MN)
Northwest Nazarene U (ID)
Northwest U (WA)
Nyack Coll (NY)
Ohio Valley U (WV)
Oklahoma Christian U (OK)
Ouachita Baptist U (AR)
Palm Beach Atlantic U (FL)
Philadelphia Biblical U (PA)
St. Louis Christian Coll (MO)
San Diego Christian Coll (CA)
Simpson U (CA)
Southeastern Bible Coll (AL)
Southwestern Assemblies of God U (TX)
Spring Arbor U (MI)
Tabor Coll (KS)
Taylor U (IN)
Union U (TN)
Universidad Teologica del Caribe (PR)
U of Evansville (IN)
U of Mary Hardin-Baylor (TX)
The U of Western Ontario (ON, Canada)
Wheaton Coll (IL)
William Jessup U (CA)

BILINGUAL AND MULTILINGUAL EDUCATION
Belmont U (TN)
Boise State U (ID)
Boston U (MA)
Calvin Coll (MI)
Goddard Coll (VT)
Long Island U, Brooklyn Campus (NY)
Loyola U Chicago (IL)
Midwestern State U (TX)
Nevada State Coll at Henderson (NV)
Northeastern Illinois U (IL)
Prescott Coll (AZ)
Southwestern Assemblies of God U (TX)
State U of New York Coll at Old Westbury (NY)
Texas A&M Intl U (TX)
Texas A&M U–Corpus Christi (TX)
Texas Christian U (TX)
Texas Wesleyan U (TX)
U of Delaware (DE)
The U of Findlay (OH)
U of Maine at Fort Kent (ME)
U of Nebraska at Omaha (NE)
U of Regina (SK, Canada)
U of San Francisco (CA)
U of the Southwest (NM)
U of Washington (WA)
Washington State U (WA)
Weber State U (UT)
Western Illinois U (IL)
York Coll of the City U of New York (NY)

BIOCHEMISTRY
Abilene Christian U (TX)
Adams State Coll (CO)
Adelphi U (NY)
Albright Coll (PA)
Allegheny Coll (PA)
Alma Coll (MI)
Alvernia U (PA)
American U (DC)
Anderson U (IN)
Andrews U (MI)
Angelo State U (TX)
Arizona State U (AZ)
Asbury U (KY)
Auburn U (AL)
Augustana Coll (IL)
Augustana Coll (SD)
Austin Coll (TX)
Azusa Pacific U (CA)
Barnard Coll (NY)
Bates Coll (ME)
Belmont U (TN)
Beloit Coll (WI)
Benedictine Coll (KS)
Berry Coll (GA)
Biola U (CA)
Boston Coll (MA)
Bowdoin Coll (ME)
Brandeis U (MA)
Bridgewater State U (MA)
Brock U (ON, Canada)
Brown U (RI)
Bucknell U (PA)

California Polytechnic State U, San Luis Obispo (CA)
California State U, Chico (CA)
California State U, Dominguez Hills (CA)
California State U, Fullerton (CA)
California State U, Long Beach (CA)
California State U, Los Angeles (CA)
California State U, Northridge (CA)
California State U, San Bernardino (CA)
California State U, San Marcos (CA)
Calvin Coll (MI)
Canisius Coll (NY)
Capital U (OH)
Carroll U (WI)
Case Western Reserve U (OH)
The Catholic U of America (DC)
Cedar Crest Coll (PA)
Central Connecticut State U (CT)
Central Michigan U (MI)
Centre Coll (KY)
Chapman U (CA)
Chatham U (PA)
Chestnut Hill Coll (PA)
Christian Brothers U (TN)
City Coll of the City U of New York (NY)
Claflin U (SC)
Claremont McKenna Coll (CA)
Clarke U (IA)
Clark U (MA)
Clemson U (SC)
Coastal Carolina U (SC)
Colby Coll (ME)
Colgate U (NY)
Coll of Mount St. Joseph (OH)
Coll of Saint Benedict (MN)
Coll of Saint Elizabeth (NJ)
The Coll of Saint Rose (NY)
The Coll of St. Scholastica (MN)
Coll of Staten Island of the City U of New York (NY)
The Coll of Wooster (OH)
The Colorado Coll (CO)
Colorado State U (CO)
Columbia U, School of General Studies (NY)
Connecticut Coll (CT)
Cornell Coll (IA)
Dakota Wesleyan U (SD)
Dartmouth Coll (NH)
Denison U (OH)
DePauw U (IN)
DeSales U (PA)
Dickinson Coll (PA)
Doane Coll (NE)
Dominican U (IL)
Drake U (IA)
Drew U (NJ)
Duquesne U (PA)
Earlham Coll (IN)
Eastern Michigan U (MI)
Eastern New Mexico U (NM)
Eastern Oregon U (OR)
East Stroudsburg U of Pennsylvania (PA)
Eckerd Coll (FL)
Elizabethtown Coll (PA)
Elmira Coll (NY)
Emmanuel Coll (MA)
Fairfield U (CT)
Fairleigh Dickinson U, Coll at Florham (NJ)
Fairleigh Dickinson U, Metropolitan Campus (NJ)
Ferris State U (MI)
Florida Inst of Technology (FL)
Florida State U (FL)
Fort Lewis Coll (CO)
Franklin & Marshall Coll (PA)
Freed-Hardeman U (TN)
Furman U (SC)
Geneva Coll (PA)
Georgetown U (DC)
Georgian Court U (NJ)
Georgia Inst of Technology (GA)
Gettysburg Coll (PA)
Grinnell Coll (IA)
Grove City Coll (PA)
Hamilton Coll (NY)
Hamline U (MN)
Hampden-Sydney Coll (VA)
Harding U (AR)
Hartwick Coll (NY)
Harvard U (MA)
Haverford Coll (PA)
Hobart and William Smith Colls (NY)
Hofstra U (NY)
Holy Family U (PA)

Hood Coll (MD)
Houghton Coll (NY)
Humboldt State U (CA)
Huntingdon Coll (AL)
Idaho State U (ID)
Illinois Inst of Technology (IL)
Illinois State U (IL)
Indiana U Bloomington (IN)
Indiana U of Pennsylvania (PA)
Indiana U South Bend (IN)
Indiana Wesleyan U (IN)
Inter American U of Puerto Rico, Bayamón Campus (PR)
Iowa State U of Science and Technology (IA)
Ithaca Coll (NY)
Jamestown Coll (ND)
John Brown U (AR)
Juniata Coll (PA)
Kansas State U (KS)
Kennesaw State U (GA)
Kenyon Coll (OH)
Kettering U (MI)
Keuka Coll (NY)
King Coll (TN)
Knox Coll (IL)
Kutztown U of Pennsylvania (PA)
Lafayette Coll (PA)
LaGrange Coll (GA)
Lake Forest Coll (IL)
La Salle U (PA)
Laurentian U (ON, Canada)
Lawrence Technological U (MI)
Lawrence U (WI)
Lee U (TN)
Lehigh U (PA)
Lehman Coll of the City U of New York (NY)
Le Moyne Coll (NY)
Lewis U (IL)
Lipscomb U (TN)
Loras Coll (IA)
Louisiana State U and Ag and Mech Coll (LA)
Loyola Marymount U (CA)
Loyola U Chicago (IL)
Lyon Coll (AR)
Madonna U (MI)
Manchester Coll (IN)
Manhattan Coll (NY)
Manhattanville Coll (NY)
Mansfield U of Pennsylvania (PA)
Marietta Coll (OH)
Marist Coll (NY)
Marlboro Coll (VT)
Maryville Coll (TN)
Maryville U of Saint Louis (MO)
McDaniel Coll (MD)
McMurry U (TX)
Mercer U (GA)
Merrimack Coll (MA)
Messiah Coll (PA)
Miami U (OH)
Michigan State U (MI)
Middlebury Coll (VT)
Millsaps Coll (MS)
Mills Coll (CA)
Minnesota State U Mankato (MN)
Misericordia U (PA)
Mississippi State U (MS)
Missouri Southern State U (MO)
Monmouth Coll (IL)
Montclair State U (NJ)
Moravian Coll (PA)
Mount Allison U (NB, Canada)
Mount Holyoke Coll (MA)
Mount St. Mary's Coll (CA)
Mount St. Mary's U (MD)
Muhlenberg Coll (PA)
Nazareth Coll of Rochester (NY)
Nebraska Wesleyan U (NE)
New Coll of Florida (FL)
Newman U (KS)
New Mexico State U (NM)
New York U (NY)
Niagara U (NY)
North Carolina State U (NC)
North Central Coll (IL)
Northeastern U (MA)
Northern Michigan U (MI)
Northwestern Coll (MN)
Northwest Nazarene U (ID)
Notre Dame de Namur U (CA)
Oberlin Coll (OH)
The Ohio State U (OH)
Oklahoma Christian U (OK)
Oklahoma City U (OK)
Oklahoma State U (OK)
Old Dominion U (VA)
Pace U (NY)

Penn State Abington (PA)
Penn State Altoona (PA)
Penn State Beaver (PA)
Penn State Berks (PA)
Penn State Brandywine (PA)
Penn State DuBois (PA)
Penn State Erie, The Behrend Coll (PA)
Penn State Fayette, The Eberly Campus (PA)
Penn State Greater Allegheny (PA)
Penn State Hazleton (PA)
Penn State Lehigh Valley (PA)
Penn State Mont Alto (PA)
Penn State New Kensington (PA)
Penn State Schuylkill (PA)
Penn State Shenango (PA)
Penn State U Park (PA)
Penn State Wilkes-Barre (PA)
Penn State Worthington Scranton (PA)
Penn State York (PA)
Philadelphia U (PA)
Pittsburg State U (KS)
Pitzer Coll (CA)
Pomona Coll (CA)
Portland State U (OR)
Providence Coll (RI)
Purchase Coll, State U of New York (NY)
Purdue U (IN)
Quinnipiac U (CT)
Ramapo Coll of New Jersey (NJ)
Reed Coll (OR)
Regis Coll (MA)
Regis U (CO)
Rhodes Coll (TN)
Rice U (TX)
The Richard Stockton Coll of New Jersey (NJ)
Rider U (NJ)
Ripon Coll (WI)
Roanoke Coll (VA)
Rockford Coll (IL)
Rockhurst U (MO)
Rollins Coll (FL)
Rose-Hulman Inst of Technology (IN)
Rosemont Coll (PA)
Rowan U (NJ)
Russell Sage Coll (NY)
Rutgers, The State U of New Jersey, New Brunswick (NJ)
Saginaw Valley State U (MI)
St. Bonaventure U (NY)
St. Catherine U (MN)
St. Edward's U (TX)
Saint John's U (MN)
Saint Joseph Coll (CT)
Saint Joseph's Coll (IN)
Saint Joseph's U (PA)
St. Lawrence U (NY)
Saint Louis U (MO)
Saint Mary's Coll of California (CA)
St. Mary's Coll of Maryland (MD)
Saint Mary's U of Minnesota (MN)
Saint Michael's Coll (VT)
Salem State U (MA)
Samford U (AL)
San Francisco State U (CA)
San Jose State U (CA)
Santa Clara U (CA)
Schreiner U (TX)
Scripps Coll (CA)
Seattle Pacific U (WA)
Seton Hill U (PA)
Siena Coll (NY)
Simon Fraser U (BC, Canada)
Simpson Coll (IA)
Slippery Rock U of Pennsylvania (PA)
Smith Coll (MA)
South Dakota State U (SD)
Southern Adventist U (TN)
Southern Methodist U (TX)
Southern Nazarene U (OK)
Southern Oregon U (OR)
Southwestern Coll (KS)
Spelman Coll (GA)
Spring Arbor U (MI)
Spring Hill Coll (AL)
State U of New York at Binghamton (NY)
State U of New York at Fredonia (NY)
State U of New York at Plattsburgh (NY)
State U of New York Coll at Geneseo (NY)

State U of New York Coll at Old Westbury (NY)
State U of New York Coll at Oneonta (NY)
State U of New York Coll at Potsdam (NY)
State U of New York Coll of Environmental Science and Forestry (NY)
Stephen F. Austin State U (TX)
Stetson U (FL)
Stonehill Coll (MA)
Stony Brook U, State U of New York (NY)
Suffolk U (MA)
Susquehanna U (PA)
Swarthmore Coll (PA)
Syracuse U (NY)
Tabor Coll (KS)
Temple U (PA)
Tennessee Technological U (TN)
Texas A&M U (TX)
Texas Christian U (TX)
Texas State U–San Marcos (TX)
Texas Tech U (TX)
Texas Wesleyan U (TX)
Texas Woman's U (TX)
Trent U (ON, Canada)
Trinity Coll (CT)
Trinity U (TX)
Tulane U (LA)
Union Coll (NE)
Union Coll (NY)
United States Air Force Acad (CO)
Université de Sherbrooke (QC, Canada)
U at Buffalo, the State U of New York (NY)
The U of Akron (OH)
The U of Arizona (AZ)
The U of British Columbia (BC, Canada)
The U of British Columbia–Okanagan (BC, Canada)
U of California, Los Angeles (CA)
U of California, Santa Barbara (CA)
U of California, Santa Cruz (CA)
U of Cincinnati (OH)
U of Colorado at Colorado Springs (CO)
U of Colorado Boulder (CO)
U of Dallas (TX)
U of Dayton (OH)
U of Delaware (DE)
U of Denver (CO)
U of Evansville (IN)
U of Georgia (GA)
U of Guelph (ON, Canada)
U of Houston (TX)
U of Idaho (ID)
U of Illinois at Chicago (IL)
The U of Iowa (IA)
The U of Kansas (KS)
U of Lethbridge (AB, Canada)
U of Maine (ME)
U of Maryland, Coll Park (MD)
U of Massachusetts Boston (MA)
U of Miami (FL)
U of Michigan (MI)
U of Michigan–Dearborn (MI)
U of Michigan–Flint (MI)
U of Minnesota, Duluth (MN)
U of Minnesota, Twin Cities Campus (MN)
U of Missouri (MO)
U of Missouri–St. Louis (MO)
U of Mount Union (OH)
U of Nebraska–Lincoln (NE)
U of Nevada, Las Vegas (NV)
U of Nevada, Reno (NV)
U of New Brunswick Fredericton (NB, Canada)
U of New England (ME)
The U of North Carolina at Greensboro (NC)
U of Northern Iowa (IA)
U of North Texas (TX)
U of Notre Dame (IN)
U of Oklahoma (OK)
U of Oregon (OR)
U of Ottawa (ON, Canada)
U of Pennsylvania (PA)
U of Puget Sound (WA)
U of Regina (SK, Canada)
U of Rochester (NY)
U of St. Thomas (MN)
U of St. Thomas (TX)
U of San Diego (CA)
U of Saskatchewan (SK, Canada)
U of Southern California (CA)

INDEXES

The U of Tampa (FL)
The U of Tennessee (TN)
The U of Texas at Arlington (TX)
The U of Texas at Austin (TX)
The U of Texas at Dallas (TX)
U of the Incarnate Word (TX)
U of the Pacific (CA)
U of the Sciences in Philadelphia (PA)
U of Tulsa (OK)
U of Vermont (VT)
U of Washington (WA)
U of Waterloo (ON, Canada)
The U of Western Ontario (ON, Canada)
U of Wisconsin–La Crosse (WI)
U of Wisconsin–Madison (WI)
U of Wisconsin–River Falls (WI)
U of Wisconsin–Stevens Point (WI)
Valparaiso U (IN)
Vassar Coll (NY)
Villanova U (PA)
Virginia Polytechnic Inst and State U (VA)
Viterbo U (WI)
Walla Walla U (WA)
Wartburg Coll (IA)
Washburn U (KS)
Washington Adventist U (MD)
Washington & Jefferson Coll (PA)
Washington and Lee U (VA)
Washington State U (WA)
Washington U in St. Louis (MO)
Wellesley Coll (MA)
Wells Coll (NY)
Wesleyan U (CT)
West Chester U of Pennsylvania (PA)
Western Kentucky U (KY)
Western Michigan U (MI)
Western State Coll of Colorado (CO)
Westminster Coll (MO)
Wheaton Coll (MA)
Whitman Coll (WA)
Widener U (PA)
Wilkes (PA)
William Jewell Coll (MO)
Winona State U (MN)
Worcester Polytechnic Inst (MA)
Xavier U of Louisiana (LA)

BIOCHEMISTRY AND MOLECULAR BIOLOGY

Bellarmine U (KY)
Boston U (MA)
California Baptist U (CA)
California State U, Long Beach (CA)
Culver-Stockton Coll (MO)
Florida Southern Coll (FL)
Harding U (AR)
Hardin-Simmons U (TX)
Harvard U (MA)
Hendrix Coll (AR)
Illinois Inst of Technology (IL)
Indiana U Bloomington (IN)
Lebanon Valley Coll (PA)
Lewis & Clark Coll (OR)
Liberty U (VA)
Marquette U (WI)
Michigan State U (MI)
Minnesota State U Moorhead (MN)
Nebraska Wesleyan U (NE)
North Dakota State U (ND)
Oregon State U (OR)
Purdue U (IN)
Simmons Coll (MA)
The U of British Columbia (BC, Canada)
U of California, Irvine (CA)
U of Maryland, Baltimore County (MD)
U of Massachusetts Amherst (MA)
U of New Hampshire (NH)
U of Regina (SK, Canada)
U of Waterloo (ON, Canada)
The U of Western Ontario (ON, Canada)
Whitman Coll (WA)
Wittenberg U (OH)

BIOCHEMISTRY, BIOPHYSICS AND MOLECULAR BIOLOGY RELATED

Amherst Coll (MA)
Blackburn Coll (IL)
Purdue U (IN)
Rensselaer Polytechnic Inst (NY)

Sweet Briar Coll (VA)
Towson U (MD)
U of California, Santa Barbara (CA)
U of Waterloo (ON, Canada)

BIOENGINEERING AND BIOMEDICAL ENGINEERING

Alfred U (NY)
Arizona State U (AZ)
Boston U (MA)
Brown U (RI)
Bucknell U (PA)
California Polytechnic State U, San Luis Obispo (CA)
California State U, Long Beach (CA)
Carnegie Mellon U (PA)
Case Western Reserve U (OH)
City Coll of the City U of New York (NY)
Clemson U (SC)
The Coll of New Jersey (NJ)
Colorado School of Mines (CO)
Delaware State U (DE)
Florida Gulf Coast U (FL)
Florida Intl U (FL)
Gannon U (PA)
Georgia Inst of Technology (GA)
Hofstra U (NY)
Illinois Inst of Technology (IL)
Indiana Tech (IN)
Indiana U–Purdue U Indianapolis (IN)
The Johns Hopkins U (MD)
Lawrence Technological U (MI)
Lehigh U (PA)
LeTourneau U (TX)
Louisiana State U and Ag and Mech Coll (LA)
Marquette U (WI)
Massachusetts Inst of Technology (MA)
Michigan State U (MI)
Milwaukee School of Eng (WI)
Mississippi State U (MS)
New Jersey Inst of Technology (NJ)
North Carolina Ag and Tech State U (NC)
North Carolina State U (NC)
Oregon State U (OR)
Penn State Abington (PA)
Penn State Altoona (PA)
Penn State Beaver (PA)
Penn State Berks (PA)
Penn State Brandywine (PA)
Penn State DuBois (PA)
Penn State Erie, The Behrend Coll (PA)
Penn State Fayette, The Eberly Campus (PA)
Penn State Greater Allegheny (PA)
Penn State Hazleton (PA)
Penn State Lehigh Valley (PA)
Penn State Mont Alto (PA)
Penn State New Kensington (PA)
Penn State Schuylkill (PA)
Penn State Shenango (PA)
Penn State U Park (PA)
Penn State Wilkes-Barre (PA)
Penn State Worthington Scranton (PA)
Penn State York (PA)
Purdue U (IN)
Rensselaer Polytechnic Inst (NY)
Rice U (TX)
Rose-Hulman Inst of Technology (IN)
Rutgers, The State U of New Jersey, New Brunswick (NJ)
Saint Louis U (MO)
Santa Clara U (CA)
Stanford U (CA)
State U of New York at Binghamton (NY)
State U of New York Coll of Environmental Science and Forestry (NY)
Stony Brook U, State U of New York (NY)
Syracuse U (NY)
Temple U (PA)
Texas A&M U (TX)
Trinity Coll (CT)
Tulane U (LA)
Union Coll (NY)
U at Buffalo, the State U of New York (NY)
The U of Akron (OH)

The U of Alabama at Birmingham (AL)
The U of British Columbia (BC, Canada)
U of California, Berkeley (CA)
U of California, Davis (CA)
U of California, Irvine (CA)
U of California, Merced (CA)
U of California, Santa Cruz (CA)
U of Cincinnati (OH)
U of Guelph (ON, Canada)
U of Houston (TX)
U of Idaho (ID)
U of Illinois at Chicago (IL)
The U of Iowa (IA)
U of Louisville (KY)
U of Massachusetts Dartmouth (MA)
U of Memphis (TN)
U of Miami (FL)
U of Michigan (MI)
U of Nebraska–Lincoln (NE)
U of Ottawa (ON, Canada)
U of Pennsylvania (PA)
U of Pittsburgh (PA)
U of Rhode Island (RI)
U of Rochester (NY)
U of South Carolina (SC)
U of Southern California (CA)
The U of Texas at Austin (TX)
The U of Texas at Dallas (TX)
U of the Pacific (CA)
The U of Toledo (OH)
U of Utah (UT)
U of Virginia (VA)
U of Wisconsin–Madison (WI)
Vanderbilt U (TN)
Virginia Commonwealth U (VA)
Walla Walla U (WA)
Washington State U (WA)
Washington U in St. Louis (MO)
Wayne State U (MI)
Wentworth Inst of Technology (MA)
Western New England U (MA)
Wichita State U (KS)
Widener U (PA)
Worcester Polytechnic Inst (MA)
Wright State U (OH)
Yale U (CT)

BIOETHICS/MEDICAL ETHICS

American Jewish U (CA)
William Jewell Coll (MO)

BIOINFORMATICS

Canisius Coll (NY)
Chatham U (PA)
Claflin U (SC)
The Coll of Saint Rose (NY)
Davenport U, Grand Rapids (MI)
Gannon U (PA)
Indiana U Bloomington (IN)
Iowa State U of Science and Technology (IA)
Lakehead U (ON, Canada)
Loyola U Chicago (IL)
New Jersey Inst of Technology (NJ)
Polytechnic Inst of NYU (NY)
Portland State U (OR)
Purdue U (IN)
Ramapo Coll of New Jersey (NJ)
Rensselaer Polytechnic Inst (NY)
St. Bonaventure U (NY)
St. Edward's U (TX)
U at Buffalo, the State U of New York (NY)
U of California, Irvine (CA)
U of California, Santa Cruz (CA)
U of Denver (CO)
U of Maryland, Baltimore County (MD)
U of Nebraska at Omaha (NE)
U of Northern Iowa (IA)
U of Pennsylvania (PA)
U of Pittsburgh (PA)
U of St. Thomas (TX)
U of Saskatchewan (SK, Canada)
U of the Sciences in Philadelphia (PA)
U of Waterloo (ON, Canada)
The U of Western Ontario (ON, Canada)
Virginia Commonwealth U (VA)
Webster U (MO)
Wheaton Coll (MA)

BIOLOGICAL AND BIOMEDICAL SCIENCES RELATED

Alderson-Broaddus Coll (WV)
Arizona State U (AZ)
Bethel U (MN)
Boston U (MA)
Central Michigan U (MI)
The Coll of Saint Rose (NY)
Cornell U (NY)
Dakota State U (SD)
Delaware State U (DE)
The Evergreen State Coll (WA)
Grand Valley State U (MI)
Guilford Coll (NC)
Holy Names U (CA)
Indiana U Bloomington (IN)
Indiana U–Purdue U Indianapolis (IN)
Inter American U of Puerto Rico, Bayamón Campus (PR)
Kent State U (OH)
King Coll (TN)
Logan U–Coll of Chiropractic (MO)
Louisiana State U in Shreveport (LA)
Lynchburg Coll (VA)
Messiah Coll (PA)
Nevada State Coll at Henderson (NV)
Our Lady of the Lake Coll (LA)
Our Lady of the Lake U of San Antonio (TX)
Penn State Abington (PA)
Penn State Altoona (PA)
Penn State Beaver (PA)
Penn State Berks (PA)
Penn State Brandywine (PA)
Penn State DuBois (PA)
Penn State Erie, The Behrend Coll (PA)
Penn State Fayette, The Eberly Campus (PA)
Penn State Greater Allegheny (PA)
Penn State Hazleton (PA)
Penn State Lehigh Valley (PA)
Penn State Mont Alto (PA)
Penn State New Kensington (PA)
Penn State Schuylkill (PA)
Penn State Shenango (PA)
Penn State U Park (PA)
Penn State Wilkes-Barre (PA)
Penn State Worthington Scranton (PA)
Penn State York (PA)
Rutgers, The State U of New Jersey, Newark (NJ)
Sage Coll of Albany (NY)
Saint Mary's Coll of California (CA)
San Jose State U (CA)
Syracuse U (NY)
Texas Wesleyan U (TX)
Trevecca Nazarene U (TN)
Union Coll (NY)
U of Louisiana at Lafayette (LA)
U of Michigan (MI)
U of Minnesota, Twin Cities Campus (MN)
U of New Hampshire (NH)
U of North Dakota (ND)
U of Ottawa (ON, Canada)
U of Rochester (NY)
U of Wisconsin–Parkside (WI)
Ursuline Coll (OH)
Utah State U (UT)
Washington U in St. Louis (MO)
Western State Coll of Colorado (CO)

BIOLOGICAL AND PHYSICAL SCIENCES

Alfred U (NY)
Allegheny Coll (PA)
Alma Coll (MI)
Alvernia U (PA)
American U (DC)
Angelo State U (TX)
Athabasca U (AB, Canada)
Augsburg Coll (MN)
Averett U (VA)
Baldwin-Wallace Coll (OH)
Belmont U (TN)
Bemidji State U (MN)
Bennington Coll (VT)
Bluefield State Coll (WV)
Brevard Coll (NC)
Brock U (ON, Canada)
Buena Vista U (IA)
Calvin Coll (MI)

Castleton State Coll (VT)
Clarion U of Pennsylvania (PA)
Coll of Saint Benedict (MN)
Coll of the Atlantic (ME)
Covenant Coll (GA)
Dakota Wesleyan U (SD)
Delta State U (MS)
DePaul U (IL)
Dowling Coll (NY)
Eastern Michigan U (MI)
East Stroudsburg U of Pennsylvania (PA)
The Evergreen State Coll (WA)
Fairleigh Dickinson U, Metropolitan Campus (NJ)
Freed-Hardeman U (TN)
Gettysburg Coll (PA)
Grand Valley State U (MI)
Houghton Coll (NY)
Huntington U (IN)
Indiana U Kokomo (IN)
Indiana U of Pennsylvania (PA)
Indiana U–Purdue U Indianapolis (IN)
Iowa Wesleyan Coll (IA)
John Brown U (AR)
John Carroll U (OH)
The Johns Hopkins U (MD)
Keene State Coll (NH)
Keystone Coll (PA)
King Coll (TN)
King's Coll (PA)
Kutztown U of Pennsylvania (PA)
Lakehead U (ON, Canada)
Lee U (TN)
Le Moyne Coll (NY)
Lock Haven U of Pennsylvania (PA)
Louisiana State U in Shreveport (LA)
Lyndon State Coll (VT)
Mansfield U of Pennsylvania (PA)
Mars Hill Coll (NC)
Maryville U of Saint Louis (MO)
The Master's Coll and Sem (CA)
Michigan State U (MI)
Middle Tennessee State U (TN)
Minnesota State U Mankato (MN)
Mississippi State U (MS)
Mount Allison U (NB, Canada)
Mount Vernon Nazarene U (OH)
North Central Coll (IL)
Northwest Missouri State U (MO)
Oklahoma City U (OK)
Oklahoma Panhandle State U (OK)
Oklahoma Wesleyan U (OK)
Palmer Coll of Chiropractic (IA)
Penn State Abington (PA)
Penn State Altoona (PA)
Penn State Beaver (PA)
Penn State Berks (PA)
Penn State Brandywine (PA)
Penn State DuBois (PA)
Penn State Erie, The Behrend Coll (PA)
Penn State Fayette, The Eberly Campus (PA)
Penn State Greater Allegheny (PA)
Penn State Hazleton (PA)
Penn State Lehigh Valley (PA)
Penn State Mont Alto (PA)
Penn State New Kensington (PA)
Penn State Schuylkill (PA)
Penn State Shenango (PA)
Penn State U Park (PA)
Penn State Wilkes-Barre (PA)
Penn State Worthington Scranton (PA)
Penn State York (PA)
Portland State U (OR)
Purdue U (IN)
Quinnipiac U (CT)
Ramapo Coll of New Jersey (NJ)
Rockford Coll (IL)
Saint Anselm Coll (NH)
St. Francis Xavier U (NS, Canada)
Saint John's U (MN)
St. Mary's Coll of Maryland (MD)
St. Norbert Coll (WI)
Saint Xavier U (IL)
Sam Houston State U (TX)
San Francisco State U (CA)
Sarah Lawrence Coll (NY)
Scripps Coll (CA)
Sierra Nevada Coll (NV)
Simon Fraser U (BC, Canada)
Southern Arkansas U–Magnolia (AR)
Spalding U (KY)

U of Indianapolis (IN)
The U of Iowa (IA)
The U of Kansas (KS)
U of La Verne (CA)
U of Lethbridge (AB, Canada)
U of Louisiana at Lafayette (LA)
U of Louisiana at Monroe (LA)
U of Louisville (KY)
U of Maine (ME)
U of Maine at Augusta (ME)
U of Maine at Farmington (ME)
U of Maine at Fort Kent (ME)
U of Maine at Presque Isle (ME)
U of Manitoba (MB, Canada)
U of Mary Hardin-Baylor (TX)
U of Maryland, Baltimore County (MD)
U of Maryland, Coll Park (MD)
U of Mary Washington (VA)
U of Massachusetts Amherst (MA)
U of Massachusetts Boston (MA)
U of Massachusetts Dartmouth (MA)
U of Massachusetts Lowell (MA)
U of Memphis (TN)
U of Miami (FL)
U of Michigan (MI)
U of Michigan–Dearborn (MI)
U of Michigan–Flint (MI)
U of Minnesota, Crookston (MN)
U of Minnesota, Duluth (MN)
U of Minnesota, Twin Cities Campus (MN)
U of Mississippi (MS)
U of Missouri (MO)
U of Missouri–St. Louis (MO)
U of Mobile (AL)
The U of Montana Western (MT)
U of Montevallo (AL)
U of Mount Union (OH)
U of Nebraska at Omaha (NE)
U of Nebraska–Lincoln (NE)
U of Nevada, Las Vegas (NV)
U of Nevada, Reno (NV)
U of New Brunswick Fredericton (NB, Canada)
U of New Brunswick Saint John (NB, Canada)
U of New England (ME)
U of New Hampshire (NH)
U of New Haven (CT)
The U of North Carolina at Asheville (NC)
The U of North Carolina at Chapel Hill (NC)
The U of North Carolina at Charlotte (NC)
The U of North Carolina at Greensboro (NC)
The U of North Carolina at Pembroke (NC)
The U of North Carolina Wilmington (NC)
U of North Dakota (ND)
U of Northern Colorado (CO)
U of Northern Iowa (IA)
U of North Florida (FL)
U of North Texas (TX)
U of Notre Dame (IN)
U of Oregon (OR)
U of Ottawa (ON, Canada)
U of Pennsylvania (PA)
U of Pittsburgh (PA)
U of Pittsburgh at Bradford (PA)
U of Pittsburgh at Greensburg (PA)
U of Pittsburgh at Johnstown (PA)
U of Portland (OR)
U of Puerto Rico at Humacao (PR)
U of Puget Sound (WA)
U of Redlands (CA)
U of Regina (SK, Canada)
U of Rhode Island (RI)
U of Richmond (VA)
U of Rio Grande (OH)
U of Rochester (NY)
U of St. Francis (IL)
U of Saint Mary (KS)
U of St. Thomas (MN)
U of St. Thomas (TX)
U of San Diego (CA)
U of San Francisco (CA)
U of Saskatchewan (SK, Canada)
U of Science and Arts of Oklahoma (OK)
The U of Scranton (PA)
U of Sioux Falls (SD)
U of South Alabama (AL)
U of South Carolina (SC)
U of South Carolina Aiken (SC)
U of South Carolina Beaufort (SC)
U of South Carolina Upstate (SC)

U of Southern California (CA)
U of Southern Indiana (IN)
U of Southern Maine (ME)
U of Southern Mississippi (MS)
U of South Florida (FL)
The U of Tampa (FL)
The U of Tennessee (TN)
The U of Tennessee at Chattanooga (TN)
The U of Tennessee at Martin (TN)
The U of Texas at Arlington (TX)
The U of Texas at Austin (TX)
The U of Texas at Dallas (TX)
The U of Texas at San Antonio (TX)
The U of Texas at Tyler (TX)
The U of Texas of the Permian Basin (TX)
The U of Texas–Pan American (TX)
U of the Cumberlands (KY)
U of the District of Columbia (DC)
U of the Incarnate Word (TX)
U of the Ozarks (AR)
U of the Pacific (CA)
U of the Sciences in Philadelphia (PA)
U of the Southwest (NM)
U of the Virgin Islands (VI)
The U of Toledo (OH)
U of Tulsa (OK)
U of Utah (UT)
U of Vermont (VT)
U of Virginia (VA)
U of Washington (WA)
U of Washington, Bothell (WA)
U of Waterloo (ON, Canada)
The U of Western Ontario (ON, Canada)
U of West Florida (FL)
U of West Georgia (GA)
U of Wisconsin–Eau Claire (WI)
U of Wisconsin–Green Bay (WI)
U of Wisconsin–La Crosse (WI)
U of Wisconsin–Madison (WI)
U of Wisconsin–Platteville (WI)
U of Wisconsin–River Falls (WI)
U of Wisconsin–Stevens Point (WI)
U of Wisconsin–Superior (WI)
U of Wisconsin–Whitewater (WI)
U of Wyoming (WY)
Upper Iowa U (IA)
Ursuline Coll (OH)
Utah State U (UT)
Utah Valley U (UT)
Valdosta State U (GA)
Valparaiso U (IN)
Vanderbilt U (TN)
Vassar Coll (NY)
Victory U (TN)
Villanova U (PA)
Virginia Commonwealth U (VA)
Virginia Intermont U (VA)
Virginia Military Inst (VA)
Virginia Polytechnic Inst and State U (VA)
Virginia State U (VA)
Virginia Wesleyan Coll (VA)
Viterbo U (WI)
Wabash Coll (IN)
Wagner Coll (NY)
Wake Forest U (NC)
Walla Walla U (WA)
Walsh U (OH)
Wartburg Coll (IA)
Washburn U (KS)
Washington Adventist U (MD)
Washington & Jefferson Coll (PA)
Washington and Lee U (VA)
Washington Coll (MD)
Washington State U (WA)
Washington U in St. Louis (MO)
Wayland Baptist U (TX)
Waynesburg U (PA)
Wayne State Coll (NE)
Wayne State U (MI)
Webster U (MO)
Wellesley Coll (MA)
Wells Coll (NY)
Wesleyan Coll (GA)
Wesleyan U (CT)
West Chester U of Pennsylvania (PA)
Western Carolina U (NC)
Western Connecticut State U (CT)
Western Illinois U (IL)
Western Kentucky U (KY)
Western Michigan U (MI)
Western New England U (MA)
Western Oregon U (OR)
Western State Coll of Colorado (CO)
Westfield State U (MA)

West Liberty U (WV)
Westminster Coll (MO)
Westminster Coll (UT)
Westmont Coll (CA)
West Virginia U (WV)
Wheaton Coll (IL)
Wheaton Coll (MA)
Wheeling Jesuit U (WV)
Whitman Coll (WA)
Wichita State U (KS)
Widener U (PA)
Wilfrid Laurier U (ON, Canada)
Wilkes U (PA)
Willamette U (OR)
William Jewell Coll (MO)
William Paterson U of New Jersey (NJ)
Williams Coll (MA)
Wilmington Coll (OH)
Wingate U (NC)
Winona State U (MN)
Winthrop U (SC)
Wittenberg U (OH)
Wofford Coll (SC)
Worcester Polytechnic Inst (MA)
Worcester State U (MA)
Wright State U (OH)
Xavier U (OH)
Xavier U of Louisiana (LA)
Yale U (CT)
York Coll of Pennsylvania (PA)
York Coll of the City U of New York (NY)
Young Harris Coll (GA)
Youngstown State U (OH)

BIOLOGY/BIOTECHNOLOGY LABORATORY TECHNICIAN

Cleveland State U (OH)
Delaware State U (DE)
Gannon U (PA)
Niagara U (NY)
Penn State Abington (PA)
Penn State Altoona (PA)
Penn State Beaver (PA)
Penn State Berks (PA)
Penn State Brandywine (PA)
Penn State DuBois (PA)
Penn State Erie, The Behrend Coll (PA)
Penn State Fayette, The Eberly Campus (PA)
Penn State Greater Allegheny (PA)
Penn State Hazleton (PA)
Penn State Lehigh Valley (PA)
Penn State Mont Alto (PA)
Penn State New Kensington (PA)
Penn State Schuylkill (PA)
Penn State Shenango (PA)
Penn State U Park (PA)
Penn State Wilkes-Barre (PA)
Penn State Worthington Scranton (PA)
Penn State York (PA)
Point Park U (PA)
Purdue U Calumet (IN)
State U of New York at Fredonia (NY)
State U of New York Coll at Oneonta (NY)
Stevenson U (MD)
U of Delaware (DE)
U of New Haven (CT)
Washburn U (KS)
Worcester Polytechnic Inst (MA)
York Coll of the City U of New York (NY)

BIOLOGY TEACHER EDUCATION

Abilene Christian U (TX)
Adams State Coll (CO)
Alma Coll (MI)
Alvernia U (PA)
Anderson U (IN)
Appalachian State U (NC)
Arkansas State U (AR)
Arkansas Tech U (AR)
Assumption Coll (MA)
Augustana Coll (IL)
Averett U (VA)
Bethany Coll (KS)
Bethel U (MN)
Bethune-Cookman U (FL)
Biola U (CA)
Blackburn Coll (IL)
Bluefield Coll (VA)
Blue Mountain Coll (MS)
Brewton-Parker Coll (GA)
Bridgewater Coll (VA)
Bridgewater State U (MA)

Bryan Coll (TN)
Buena Vista U (IA)
Cabrini Coll (PA)
California State U, Chico (CA)
California State U, Long Beach (CA)
Calvin Coll (MI)
Campbellsville U (KY)
Carroll U (WI)
Cedarville U (OH)
Central Michigan U (MI)
Christian Brothers U (TN)
City Coll of the City U of New York (NY)
Clearwater Christian Coll (FL)
Coker Coll (SC)
The Coll of New Jersey (NJ)
The Coll of Saint Rose (NY)
Coll of the Ozarks (MO)
Colorado State U (CO)
Concordia Coll (MN)
Concordia U Chicago (IL)
Concordia U, St. Paul (MN)
Corban U (OR)
Culver-Stockton Coll (MO)
Cumberland U (TN)
Dakota State U (SD)
Dakota Wesleyan U (SD)
Daytona State Coll (FL)
Delaware State U (DE)
Dixie State Coll of Utah (UT)
Dominican Coll (NY)
Dordt Coll (IA)
Dowling Coll (NY)
Eastern Michigan U (MI)
Eastern Washington U (WA)
East Texas Baptist U (TX)
Edgewood Coll (WI)
Elizabeth City State U (NC)
Elmhurst Coll (IL)
Elmira Coll (NY)
Evangel U (MO)
Fayetteville State U (NC)
Ferris State U (MI)
Fitchburg State U (MA)
Florida Inst of Technology (FL)
Fort Lewis Coll (CO)
Franklin Coll (IN)
Freed-Hardeman U (TN)
Free Will Baptist Bible Coll (TN)
Grace Coll (IN)
Grand Canyon U (AZ)
Grand Valley State U (MI)
Greensboro Coll (NC)
Greenville Coll (IL)
Harding U (AR)
Hofstra U (NY)
Hope Coll (MI)
Hunter Coll of the City U of New York (NY)
Huntington U (IN)
Husson U (ME)
Indiana U Bloomington (IN)
Indiana U–Purdue U Fort Wayne (IN)
Indiana U South Bend (IN)
Indiana Wesleyan U (IN)
Indian River State Coll (FL)
Inter American U of Puerto Rico, Metropolitan Campus (PR)
Inter American U of Puerto Rico, Ponce Campus (PR)
Inter American U of Puerto Rico, San Germán Campus (PR)
Iowa Wesleyan Coll (IA)
Ithaca Coll (NY)
Jamestown Coll (ND)
Johnson State Coll (VT)
Juniata Coll (PA)
Keene State Coll (NH)
Kennesaw State U (GA)
Kentucky Wesleyan Coll (KY)
Keuka Coll (NY)
King Coll (TN)
Le Moyne Coll (NY)
Liberty U (VA)
Limestone Coll (SC)
Lincoln Memorial U (TN)
Lincoln U (MO)
Lindenwood U (MO)
Lindsey Wilson Coll (KY)
Lipscomb U (TN)
Long Island U, C.W. Post Campus (NY)
Louisiana State U in Shreveport (LA)
Lubbock Christian U (TX)
Manchester Coll (IN)
Manhattanville Coll (NY)
Mansfield U of Pennsylvania (PA)
Maranatha Baptist Bible Coll (WI)
Marian U (WI)

Marist Coll (NY)
Maryville Coll (TN)
Marywood U (PA)
Mayville State U (ND)
McKendree U (IL)
McMurry U (TX)
Merrimack Coll (MA)
Messiah Coll (PA)
Metropolitan State U (MN)
Miami Dade Coll (FL)
Miami U (OH)
Michigan State U (MI)
MidAmerica Nazarene U (KS)
Millersville U of Pennsylvania (PA)
Millikin U (IL)
Minnesota State U Moorhead (MN)
Minot State U (ND)
Misericordia U (PA)
Missouri State U (MO)
Molloy Coll (NY)
Montana State U Billings (MT)
Moravian Coll (PA)
Morningside Coll (IA)
Morris Coll (SC)
Mount Vernon Nazarene U (OH)
Nazareth Coll of Rochester (NY)
Nevada State Coll at Henderson (NV)
New York Inst of Technology (NY)
Niagara U (NY)
North Dakota State U (ND)
Northeastern State U (OK)
Northern Arizona U (AZ)
Northern Michigan U (MI)
Northland Coll (WI)
Northwestern Coll (IA)
Northwestern State U of Louisiana (LA)
Northwest Missouri State U (MO)
Northwest Nazarene U (ID)
Northwest U (WA)
Ohio Wesleyan U (OH)
Pace U (NY)
Paine Coll (GA)
Palm Beach Atlantic U (FL)
Pittsburg State U (KS)
Point Park U (PA)
Prescott Coll (AZ)
Rhode Island Coll (RI)
Rivier Coll (NH)
Rocky Mountain Coll (MT)
Rust Coll (MS)
Sacred Heart U (CT)
Saginaw Valley State U (MI)
St. Ambrose U (IA)
St. Catherine U (MN)
St. Edward's U (TX)
Saint Francis U (PA)
St. John Fisher Coll (NY)
St. John's U (NY)
St. Joseph's Coll, Long Island Campus (NY)
St. Joseph's Coll, New York (NY)
Saint Joseph's Coll of Maine (ME)
Saint Mary's U of Minnesota (MN)
St. Petersburg Coll (FL)
Saint Xavier U (IL)
Salve Regina U (RI)
Schreiner U (TX)
Seton Hill U (PA)
Southeastern Louisiana U (LA)
Southeastern U (FL)
Spring Arbor U (MI)
State U of New York at New Paltz (NY)
State U of New York at Plattsburgh (NY)
State U of New York Coll at Old Westbury (NY)
State U of New York Coll at Oneonta (NY)
State U of New York Coll at Potsdam (NY)
State U of New York Coll of Environmental Science and Forestry (NY)
Tabor Coll (KS)
Talladega Coll (AL)
Texas A&M Intl U (TX)
Texas Wesleyan U (TX)
Trevecca Nazarene U (TN)
Union Coll (NE)
The U of Arizona (AZ)
U of Arkansas–Fort Smith (AR)
U of Charleston (WV)
U of Delaware (DE)
U of Dubuque (IA)
U of Evansville (IN)
U of Illinois at Chicago (IL)
The U of Iowa (IA)

INDEXES

INDEXES

DeVry U, Pomona (CA)
DeVry U, Westminster (CO)
DeVry U, Miramar (FL)
DeVry U, Orlando (FL)
DeVry U, Decatur (GA)
DeVry U, Chicago (IL)
DeVry U, Kansas City (MO)
DeVry U, Fort Washington (PA)
DeVry U, Houston (TX)
DeVry U, Irving (TX)
DeVry U, Arlington (VA)
DeVry U, Federal Way (WA)
Drake U (IA)
Earlham Coll (IN)
Eastern Michigan U (MI)
Eastern Oregon U (OR)
East Texas Baptist U (TX)
Edgewood Coll (WI)
Florida State U (FL)
Framingham State U (MA)
Franklin Coll (IN)
Franklin U (OH)
Free Will Baptist Bible Coll (TN)
Georgia Coll & State U (GA)
Grace Coll (IN)
Grand Valley State U (MI)
Hawai`i Pacific U (HI)
HEC Montreal (QC, Canada)
Hillsdale Free Will Baptist Coll (OK)
Hofstra U (NY)
Hollins U (VA)
Huntingdon Coll (AL)
Idaho State U (ID)
Indiana U Bloomington (IN)
Indiana U East (IN)
Indiana U Kokomo (IN)
Indiana U Northwest (IN)
Indiana U of Pennsylvania (PA)
Indiana–Purdue U Indianapolis (IN)
Indiana U South Bend (IN)
Indiana U Southeast (IN)
Iowa Wesleyan Coll (IA)
Ithaca Coll (NY)
The Johns Hopkins U (MD)
Johnson State Coll (VT)
Judson Coll (AL)
Juniata Coll (PA)
Kansas State U (KS)
Kendall Coll (IL)
Kentucky State U (KY)
Keystone Coll (PA)
Lewis U (IL)
Liberty U (VA)
Limestone Coll (SC)
Linfield Coll (OR)
Loras Coll (IA)
Lourdes Coll (OH)
Loyola U Maryland (MD)
Manchester Coll (IN)
Maryville Coll (TN)
Maryville U of Saint Louis (MO)
Massachusetts Inst of Technology (MA)
McMurry U (TX)
Medgar Evers Coll of the City U of New York (NY)
Mercer U (GA)
Mesa State Coll (CO)
Midway Coll (KY)
Midwestern State U (TX)
Milwaukee School of Eng (WI)
Mississippi U for Women (MS)
Missouri Southern State U (MO)
Missouri State U (MO)
Montana State U (MT)
Montana State U Billings (MT)
Montana Tech of The U of Montana (MT)
Morehead State U (KY)
Mount Allison U (NB, Canada)
Mount Mercy U (IA)
Mount St. Mary's U (MD)
Mount Vernon Nazarene U (OH)
Murray State U (KY)
New England Inst of Technology (RI)
New Mexico State U (NM)
Niagara U (NY)
Northeastern Illinois U (IL)
Northeastern U (MA)
Northern Illinois U (IL)
Northern Kentucky U (KY)
Northern Michigan U (MI)
The Ohio State U at Lima (OH)
The Ohio State U at Marion (OH)
The Ohio State U–Mansfield Campus (OH)

The Ohio State U–Newark Campus (OH)
Ohio Valley U (WV)
Oklahoma Christian U (OK)
Oklahoma City U (OK)
Pace U (NY)
Penn State Abington (PA)
Penn State Altoona (PA)
Penn State Berks (PA)
Penn State Lehigh Valley (PA)
Penn State Schuylkill (PA)
Purdue U (IN)
Randolph Coll (VA)
Regis Coll (MA)
Reinhardt U (GA)
Rhode Island Coll (RI)
Roosevelt U (IL)
Saginaw Valley State U (MI)
St. Ambrose U (IA)
Saint Anselm Coll (NH)
Saint Joseph's Coll (IN)
Saint Leo U (FL)
Saint Mary's Coll of California (CA)
St. Thomas U (FL)
Saint Xavier U (IL)
Sam Houston State U (TX)
Savannah State U (GA)
Schreiner U (TX)
Skidmore Coll (NY)
Southern Arkansas U–Magnolia (AR)
Southern Methodist U (TX)
Southern Wesleyan U (SC)
Spalding U (KY)
Stephen F. Austin State U (TX)
Suffolk U (MA)
Sweet Briar Coll (VA)
Tarleton State U (TX)
Texas A&M U–Kingsville (TX)
Texas Tech U (TX)
Transylvania U (KY)
Trinity Coll of Florida (FL)
Troy U (AL)
TUI U (CA)
The U of Arizona (AZ)
U of Arkansas (AR)
The U of British Columbia (BC, Canada)
U of Central Florida (FL)
U of Denver (CO)
U of Georgia (GA)
U of Hawaii at Manoa (HI)
U of Houston–Clear Lake (TX)
U of Houston–Downtown (TX)
The U of Kansas (KS)
U of Maine (ME)
U of Mary Hardin-Baylor (TX)
U of Maryland, Coll Park (MD)
U of Massachusetts Dartmouth (MA)
U of Minnesota, Twin Cities Campus (MN)
U of Missouri–St. Louis (MO)
U of Nebraska at Omaha (NE)
U of Nevada, Reno (NV)
U of North Texas (TX)
U of Notre Dame (IN)
U of Oregon (OR)
U of Pittsburgh (PA)
U of Redlands (CA)
U of Regina (SK, Canada)
U of Rhode Island (RI)
U of San Francisco (CA)
U of Science and Arts of Oklahoma (OK)
U of South Alabama (AL)
The U of South Dakota (SD)
U of Southern Indiana (IN)
The U of Tennessee (TN)
The U of Texas at Austin (TX)
The U of Texas at Dallas (TX)
The U of Texas at San Antonio (TX)
U of the Cumberlands (KY)
The U of Toledo (OH)
U of Tulsa (OK)
U of Utah (UT)
U of Virginia (VA)
U of Washington (WA)
The U of Western Ontario (ON, Canada)
U of West Florida (FL)
U of Wisconsin–Whitewater (WI)
Utah State U (UT)
Virginia Commonwealth U (VA)
Wake Forest U (NC)
Washburn U (KS)
Washington & Jefferson Coll (PA)

Washington State U (WA)
Washington U in St. Louis (MO)
Webber Intl U (FL)
Webster U (MO)
West Chester U of Pennsylvania (PA)
Western Intl U (AZ)
Western Michigan U (MI)
Western New England U (MA)
Western Oregon U (OR)
Westmont Coll (CA)
Wright State U (OH)
Youngstown State U (OH)

BUSINESS/CORPORATE COMMUNICATIONS

Amridge U (AL)
Aquinas Coll (MI)
Augustana Coll (SD)
Bentley U (MA)
Brock U (ON, Canada)
Calvin Coll (MI)
Chestnut Hill Coll (PA)
Cleary U (MI)
Concordia U Chicago (IL)
Duquesne U (PA)
Elon U (NC)
Hawai`i Pacific U (HI)
Holy Names U (CA)
Jones Intl U (CO)
Lycoming Coll (PA)
Marietta Coll (OH)
MidAmerica Nazarene U (KS)
Morningside Coll (IA)
North Dakota State U (ND)
Penn State Abington (PA)
Purdue U (IN)
Rockhurst U (MO)
Saint Leo U (FL)
Southwestern Coll (KS)
Stevenson U (MD)
The U of Findlay (OH)
U of Rio Grande (OH)
U of St. Thomas (MN)
The U of Western Ontario (ON, Canada)
Western Intl U (AZ)

BUSINESS FAMILY AND CONSUMER SCIENCES/HUMAN SCIENCES

Brigham Young U (UT)
The Ohio State U (OH)
Purdue U (IN)
U of Houston (TX)
Virginia Polytechnic Inst and State U (VA)

BUSINESS, MANAGEMENT, AND MARKETING RELATED

Adelphi U (NY)
Arizona State U (AZ)
Athens State U (AL)
Benedictine U (IL)
Bentley U (MA)
Bridgewater State U (MA)
California State U, Dominguez Hills (CA)
California State U, Stanislaus (CA)
Claflin U (SC)
Clemson U (SC)
Concordia Coll–New York (NY)
Corban U (OR)
The Evergreen State Coll (WA)
Franklin Coll Switzerland (Switzerland)
Greenville Coll (IL)
Inter American U of Puerto Rico, Bayamón Campus (PR)
Loyola U Chicago (IL)
Messiah Coll (PA)
Missouri U of Science and Technology (MO)
Mount Vernon Nazarene U (OH)
Nebraska Wesleyan U (NE)
New Jersey Inst of Technology (NJ)
New York U (NY)
Old Dominion U (VA)
Point Park U (PA)
Presentation Coll (SD)
Purdue U (IN)
Purdue U North Central (IN)
Sacred Heart U (CT)
Saint Mary's U of Minnesota (MN)
Seton Hill U (PA)
Sierra Nevada Coll (NV)
Skidmore Coll (NY)
Southeastern U (FL)

Southern California Inst of Technology (CA)
State U of New York at Plattsburgh (NY)
State U of New York Maritime Coll (NY)
Syracuse U (NY)
Texas Wesleyan U (TX)
Trevecca Nazarene U (TN)
Troy U (AL)
U of Louisiana at Lafayette (LA)
U of Minnesota, Crookston (MN)
The U of Toledo (OH)
The U of Western Ontario (ON, Canada)
U of Wisconsin–Stout (WI)
Walla Walla U (WA)
Wentworth Inst of Technology (MA)
Western State Coll of Colorado (CO)
Young Harris Coll (GA)

BUSINESS/MANAGERIAL ECONOMICS

Alabama Ag and Mech U (AL)
Allegheny Coll (PA)
Anderson U (IN)
Andrews U (MI)
Arcadia U (PA)
Arkansas State U (AR)
Auburn U (AL)
Auburn U Montgomery (AL)
Augsburg Coll (MN)
Ball State U (IN)
Bard Coll (NY)
Belmont U (TN)
Beloit Coll (WI)
Benedictine U (IL)
Bentley U (MA)
Bethany Coll (KS)
Bethany Coll (WV)
Boise State U (ID)
Boston Coll (MA)
Brock U (ON, Canada)
Buena Vista U (IA)
California Inst of Technology (CA)
California State U, Fullerton (CA)
California State U, Long Beach (CA)
California State U, San Bernardino (CA)
Campbellsville U (KY)
Canisius Coll (NY)
Capital U (OH)
Carnegie Mellon U (PA)
Carson-Newman Coll (TN)
Chapman U (CA)
Chatham U (PA)
Christopher Newport U (VA)
Clarion U of Pennsylvania (PA)
Clark Atlanta U (GA)
Cleveland State U (OH)
Coastal Carolina U (SC)
Coll of the Ozarks (MO)
The Coll of Wooster (OH)
Dallas Baptist U (TX)
Delaware State U (DE)
DePaul U (IL)
Duquesne U (PA)
Eastern Michigan U (MI)
Eastern Washington U (WA)
East Tennessee State U (TN)
Elizabethtown Coll (PA)
Elmira Coll (NY)
Emmanuel Coll (MA)
Fort Lewis Coll (CO)
Freed-Hardeman U (TN)
Georgia Coll & State U (GA)
Georgia Inst of Technology (GA)
Georgia Southern U (GA)
Georgia State U (GA)
Grand Valley State U (MI)
Greensboro Coll (NC)
Grove City Coll (PA)
Hampden-Sydney Coll (VA)
HEC Montreal (QC, Canada)
Hofstra U (NY)
Hope Coll (MI)
Huntington U (IN)
Illinois Coll (IL)
Indiana U–Purdue U Fort Wayne (IN)
Inter American U of Puerto Rico, Bayamón Campus (PR)
Inter American U of Puerto Rico, Metropolitan Campus (PR)
Inter American U of Puerto Rico, San Germán Campus (PR)
Ithaca Coll (NY)

James Madison U (VA)
Jamestown Coll (ND)
Kalamazoo Coll (MI)
Kennesaw State U (GA)
Kent State U (OH)
Lafayette Coll (PA)
Lake Forest Coll (IL)
Lake Superior State U (MI)
La Salle U (PA)
Lehigh U (PA)
Lewis U (IL)
Limestone Coll (SC)
Lincoln Memorial U (TN)
Lincoln U (MO)
Lipscomb U (TN)
Longwood U (VA)
Louisiana State U and Ag and Mech Coll (LA)
Louisiana State U in Shreveport (LA)
Loyola U Chicago (IL)
Loyola U New Orleans (LA)
Marquette U (WI)
Marshall U (WV)
Mars Hill Coll (NC)
Messiah Coll (PA)
Miami U (OH)
Middle Tennessee State U (TN)
Midwestern State U (TX)
Mills Coll (CA)
Mississippi State U (MS)
Montana State U Billings (MT)
Morehead State U (KY)
Mount Allison U (NB, Canada)
New York U (NY)
Niagara U (NY)
North Carolina State U (NC)
Northern Arizona U (AZ)
Northern Kentucky U (KY)
Northern State U (SD)
Northwest Missouri State U (MO)
Oglethorpe U (GA)
Ohio U (OH)
Ohio Wesleyan U (OH)
Oklahoma City U (OK)
Oklahoma State U (OK)
Old Dominion U (VA)
Penn State Abington (PA)
Penn State Altoona (PA)
Penn State Beaver (PA)
Penn State Berks (PA)
Penn State Brandywine (PA)
Penn State DuBois (PA)
Penn State Erie, The Behrend Coll (PA)
Penn State Fayette, The Eberly Campus (PA)
Penn State Greater Allegheny (PA)
Penn State Hazleton (PA)
Penn State Lehigh Valley (PA)
Penn State Mont Alto (PA)
Penn State New Kensington (PA)
Penn State Schuylkill (PA)
Penn State Shenango (PA)
Penn State Wilkes-Barre (PA)
Penn State Worthington Scranton (PA)
Penn State York (PA)
Presbyterian Coll (SC)
Purdue U (IN)
Quinnipiac U (CT)
Randolph-Macon Coll (VA)
Rhode Island Coll (RI)
Rider U (NJ)
Sacred Heart U (CT)
Saginaw Valley State U (MI)
Saint Anselm Coll (NH)
Saint Louis U (MO)
Samford U (AL)
Sam Houston State U (TX)
Shorter U (GA)
Sonoma State U (CA)
Southern Connecticut State U (CT)
Southern Illinois U Carbondale (IL)
Southern Illinois U Edwardsville (IL)
State U of New York at Plattsburgh (NY)
State U of New York Coll at Oneonta (NY)
State U of New York Coll at Potsdam (NY)
Stephen F. Austin State U (TX)
Stetson U (FL)
Texas A&M Intl U (TX)
Texas State U–San Marcos (TX)
Texas Wesleyan U (TX)
Union U (TN)
The U of Alabama (AL)

The U of Alabama at Birmingham (AL)
U of Arkansas (AR)
U of California, Irvine (CA)
U of California, Los Angeles (CA)
U of California, Santa Cruz (CA)
U of Central Florida (FL)
U of Dayton (OH)
U of Delaware (DE)
U of Denver (CO)
U of Evansville (IN)
U of Georgia (GA)
U of Hawaii at Manoa (HI)
U of Idaho (ID)
U of Indianapolis (IN)
The U of Iowa (IA)
U of Lethbridge (AB, Canada)
U of Louisiana at Lafayette (LA)
U of Louisville (KY)
U of Maine at Farmington (ME)
U of Manitoba (MB, Canada)
U of Memphis (TN)
U of Miami (FL)
U of Mississippi (MS)
U of Missouri (MO)
U of Nebraska at Omaha (NE)
U of Nebraska–Lincoln (NE)
U of Nevada, Reno (NV)
U of New Brunswick Fredericton (NB, Canada)
U of New Haven (CT)
The U of North Carolina at Charlotte (NC)
The U of North Carolina at Greensboro (NC)
The U of North Carolina Wilmington (NC)
U of North Dakota (ND)
U of North Florida (FL)
U of North Texas (TX)
U of Oklahoma (OK)
U of Pittsburgh at Johnstown (PA)
U of Rochester (NY)
U of San Diego (CA)
U of Saskatchewan (SK, Canada)
U of South Carolina (SC)
U of Southern Mississippi (MS)
U of South Florida (FL)
The U of Tennessee (TN)
The U of Tennessee at Martin (TN)
The U of Texas at Arlington (TX)
The U of Texas at San Antonio (TX)
The U of Texas of the Permian Basin (TX)
U of the Incarnate Word (TX)
The U of Toledo (OH)
The U of Western Ontario (ON, Canada)
U of West Florida (FL)
U of West Georgia (GA)
U of Wisconsin–Platteville (WI)
U of Wisconsin–Superior (WI)
U of Wisconsin–Whitewater (WI)
U of Wyoming (WY)
Valdosta State U (GA)
Villanova U (PA)
Virginia Commonwealth U (VA)
Virginia Polytechnic Inst and State U (VA)
Virginia State U (VA)
Washburn U (KS)
Washington U in St. Louis (MO)
Weber State U (UT)
West Chester U of Pennsylvania (PA)
Western Illinois U (IL)
Western Kentucky U (KY)
Western State Coll of Colorado (CO)
West Liberty U (WV)
Westminster Coll (UT)
Westmont Coll (CA)
West Virginia U (WV)
Wheaton Coll (IL)
Widener U (PA)
William Jewell Coll (MO)
William Paterson U of New Jersey (NJ)
Wilmington Coll (OH)
Winona State U (MN)
Wofford Coll (SC)
Wright State U (OH)
Xavier U (OH)
Youngstown State U (OH)

BUSINESS OPERATIONS SUPPORT AND SECRETARIAL SERVICES RELATED
Delaware State U (DE)
U of Georgia (GA)

BUSINESS STATISTICS
Alabama Ag and Mech U (AL)
Cleveland State U (OH)
Ferris State U (MI)
HEC Montreal (QC, Canada)
Purdue U (IN)
Southern Oregon U (OR)
Southwest U (LA)
U of Central Missouri (MO)
U of Denver (CO)

BUSINESS TEACHER EDUCATION
Adams State Coll (CO)
Alabama State U (AL)
Alfred U (NY)
Appalachian State U (NC)
Arkansas State U (AR)
Arkansas Tech U (AR)
Armstrong Atlantic State U (GA)
Auburn U (AL)
Ball State U (IN)
Belmont U (TN)
Bethany Coll (KS)
Bethel Coll (IN)
Bethel U (MN)
Bethune-Cookman U (FL)
Bluefield Coll (VA)
Bowling Green State U (OH)
Buena Vista U (IA)
California State U, Dominguez Hills (CA)
Calumet Coll of Saint Joseph (IN)
Campbellsville U (KY)
Carson-Newman Coll (TN)
Central Michigan U (MI)
Colorado State U (CO)
Concordia Coll (MN)
Concordia U Wisconsin (WI)
Concord U (WV)
Corban U (OR)
Dakota State U (SD)
Dakota Wesleyan U (SD)
Delaware State U (DE)
Dickinson State U (ND)
Doane Coll (NE)
Dordt Coll (IA)
Dowling Coll (NY)
Eastern Michigan U (MI)
Eastern New Mexico U (NM)
Eastern Washington U (WA)
Edgewood Coll (WI)
Emmanuel Coll (GA)
Evangel U (MO)
Fairmont State U (WV)
Fayetteville State U (NC)
Ferris State U (MI)
Florida Ag and Mech U (FL)
Friends U (KS)
Grace Coll (IN)
Hannibal-LaGrange U (MO)
Hardin-Simmons U (TX)
Hofstra U (NY)
Huntington U (IN)
Illinois State U (IL)
Immaculata U (PA)
Indiana State U (IN)
Jarvis Christian Coll (TX)
John Brown U (AR)
Kent State U (OH)
La Salle U (PA)
Lee U (TN)
Lehman Coll of the City U of New York (NY)
Liberty U (VA)
Lincoln U (MO)
Lindenwood U (MO)
Louisiana Coll (LA)
Louisiana State U and Ag and Mech Coll (LA)
Maranatha Baptist Bible Coll (WI)
McKendree U (IL)
MidAmerica Nazarene U (KS)
Middle Tennessee State U (TN)
Minot State U (ND)
Mississippi State U (MS)
Missouri Baptist U (MO)
Missouri State U (MO)
Morehead State U (KY)
Mount Vernon Nazarene U (OH)
Nazareth Coll of Rochester (NY)
New York Inst of Technology (NY)
Niagara U (NY)
Nicholls State U (LA)
North Carolina Ag and Tech State U (NC)
Northern Kentucky U (KY)
Northwestern Coll (IA)

Northwestern State U of Louisiana (LA)
Northwest Missouri State U (MO)
Ohio Wesleyan U (OH)
Oklahoma Panhandle State U (OK)
Oklahoma Wesleyan U (OK)
Purdue U (IN)
Rider U (NJ)
Robert Morris U (PA)
Rust Coll (MS)
St. Ambrose U (IA)
Saint Mary's Coll (IN)
St. Petersburg Coll (FL)
Schreiner U (TX)
Southeast Missouri State U (MO)
Southern Arkansas U–Magnolia (AR)
Southern Utah U (UT)
Southwestern Coll (KS)
Tabor Coll (KS)
Temple U (PA)
Texas Christian U (TX)
Texas Wesleyan U (TX)
Thomas More Coll (KY)
Trevecca Nazarene U (TN)
Union Coll (NE)
Union U (TN)
U of Arkansas at Pine Bluff (AR)
The U of British Columbia (BC, Canada)
U of Central Missouri (MO)
The U of Findlay (OH)
U of Indianapolis (IN)
U of Lethbridge (AB, Canada)
U of Maine at Fort Kent (ME)
U of Minnesota, Twin Cities Campus (MN)
U of Missouri (MO)
U of Missouri–St. Louis (MO)
The U of Montana Western (MT)
U of Nebraska–Lincoln (NE)
U of Nevada, Reno (NV)
U of New Brunswick Fredericton (NB, Canada)
U of North Dakota (ND)
U of Northern Iowa (IA)
U of Regina (SK, Canada)
U of Rio Grande (OH)
U of Southern Indiana (IN)
U of Southern Mississippi (MS)
The U of Tennessee at Martin (TN)
The U of Toledo (OH)
U of West Georgia (GA)
U of Wisconsin–Superior (WI)
U of Wisconsin–Whitewater (WI)
Upper Iowa U (IA)
Utah State U (UT)
Utah Valley U (UT)
Valdosta State U (GA)
Victory U (TN)
Virginia Intermont Coll (VA)
Virginia State U (VA)
Viterbo U (WI)
Walla Walla U (WA)
Wayland Baptist U (TX)
Wayne State Coll (NE)
Weber State U (UT)
Western Kentucky U (KY)
Western Michigan U (MI)
Wilmington Coll (OH)
Winona State U (MN)
Wright State U (OH)
Youngstown State U (OH)

CAD/CADD DRAFTING/DESIGN TECHNOLOGY
Cameron U (OK)
Eastern Michigan U (MI)
Murray State U (KY)

CANADIAN GOVERNMENT AND POLITICS
The U of British Columbia (BC, Canada)

CANADIAN HISTORY
U of Regina (SK, Canada)

CANADIAN STUDIES
Acadia U (NS, Canada)
Athabasca U (AB, Canada)
Brock U (ON, Canada)
Franklin Coll (IN)
Mount Allison U (NB, Canada)
St. Francis Xavier U (NS, Canada)
St. Lawrence U (NY)
Simon Fraser U (BC, Canada)

State U of New York at Plattsburgh (NY)
Trent U (ON, Canada)
The U of British Columbia (BC, Canada)
U of Lethbridge (AB, Canada)
U of Manitoba (MB, Canada)
U of New Brunswick Fredericton (NB, Canada)
U of Ottawa (ON, Canada)
U of Regina (SK, Canada)
U of Vermont (VT)
U of Washington (WA)
U of Waterloo (ON, Canada)
The U of Western Ontario (ON, Canada)
Wilfrid Laurier U (ON, Canada)

CARDIOVASCULAR TECHNOLOGY
Medical U of South Carolina (SC)
Pennsylvania Coll of Technology (PA)

CARIBBEAN STUDIES
Columbia U, School of General Studies (NY)
Hofstra U (NY)

CASINO MANAGEMENT
Central Michigan U (MI)

CELL AND MOLECULAR BIOLOGY
Adams State Coll (CO)
Bennington Coll (VT)
Bridgewater State U (MA)
Bucknell U (PA)
Cedarville U (OH)
Concordia U (QC, Canada)
Connecticut Coll (CT)
Florida State U (FL)
Fort Lewis Coll (CO)
Grand Valley State U (MI)
Harvard U (MA)
Missouri State U (MO)
Northwest Nazarene U (ID)
Ohio U (OH)
Pittsburg State U (KS)
Purdue U (IN)
Salem State U (MA)
State U of New York at Binghamton (NY)
Texas A&M U (TX)
Texas Tech U (TX)
U of California, Berkeley (CA)
U of California, Los Angeles (CA)
U of Colorado Boulder (CO)
U of Michigan (MI)
U of Saskatchewan (SK, Canada)
The U of Tennessee at Martin (TN)

CELL BIOLOGY AND ANATOMICAL SCIENCES RELATED
Purdue U (IN)
Rutgers, The State U of New Jersey, New Brunswick (NJ)
Tulane U (LA)
Washington & Jefferson Coll (PA)
Yale U (CT)

CELL BIOLOGY AND ANATOMY
Huntingdon Coll (AL)
Purdue U (IN)
The U of Western Ontario (ON, Canada)
Western State Coll of Colorado (CO)

CELL BIOLOGY AND HISTOLOGY
Beloit Coll (WI)
California State U, Dominguez Hills (CA)
California State U, Long Beach (CA)
California State U, San Marcos (CA)
Colby Coll (ME)
The Coll of Saint Rose (NY)
Humboldt State U (CA)
Juniata Coll (PA)
Mansfield U of Pennsylvania (PA)
Marlboro Coll (VT)
Montana State U (MT)
Northeastern State U (OK)
Purdue U (IN)
Rutgers, The State U of New Jersey, New Brunswick (NJ)
San Francisco State U (CA)
Sonoma State U (CA)
Tulane U (LA)

The U of Arizona (AZ)
The U of British Columbia (BC, Canada)
U of California, Davis (CA)
U of California, Irvine (CA)
U of California, Santa Barbara (CA)
U of California, Santa Cruz (CA)
U of Georgia (GA)
U of Maine (ME)
U of Minnesota, Duluth (MN)
U of Minnesota, Twin Cities Campus (MN)
U of Utah (UT)
U of Washington (WA)
William Jewell Coll (MO)
Worcester Polytechnic Inst (MA)

CELL PHYSIOLOGY
Purdue U (IN)

CELTIC LANGUAGES
U of California, Berkeley (CA)

CERAMIC ARTS AND CERAMICS
Adams State Coll (CO)
Alberta Coll of Art & Design (AB, Canada)
Alfred U (NY)
Aquinas Coll (MI)
Arcadia U (PA)
Bard Coll at Simon's Rock (MA)
Bennington Coll (VT)
Bethany Coll (KS)
Brigham Young U (UT)
California Coll of the Arts (CA)
California State U, Long Beach (CA)
The Cleveland Inst of Art (OH)
Coll of the Atlantic (ME)
Columbia Coll (MO)
Concordia U (QC, Canada)
Concord U (WV)
Emily Carr U of Art + Design (BC, Canada)
Franklin Pierce U (NH)
Hofstra U (NY)
Indiana Wesleyan U (IN)
Inter American U of Puerto Rico, San Germán Campus (PR)
Kent State U (OH)
Maine Coll of Art (ME)
Marlboro Coll (VT)
Maryland Inst Coll of Art (MD)
Marywood U (PA)
Massachusetts Coll of Art and Design (MA)
Minnesota State U Mankato (MN)
Minnesota State U Moorhead (MN)
Northern Arizona U (AZ)
Northern Michigan U (MI)
Northwest Nazarene U (ID)
Ohio U (OH)
Pittsburg State U (KS)
Pratt Inst (NY)
Providence Coll (RI)
Rutgers, The State U of New Jersey, New Brunswick (NJ)
Salve Regina U (RI)
School of the Museum of Fine Arts, Boston (MA)
Seton Hill U (PA)
State U of New York at New Paltz (NY)
Temple U (PA)
Texas Christian U (TX)
U of Dallas (TX)
U of Hartford (CT)
The U of Iowa (IA)
The U of Kansas (KS)
U of Massachusetts Dartmouth (MA)
U of Miami (FL)
U of Michigan (MI)
U of Oregon (OR)
U of Regina (SK, Canada)
U of the District of Columbia (DC)
U of Washington (WA)
Virginia Intermont Coll (VA)
Washington U in St. Louis (MO)
Western State Coll of Colorado (CO)

CERAMIC SCIENCES AND ENGINEERING
Alfred U (NY)
Clemson U (SC)
Missouri U of Science and Technology (MO)
Rutgers, The State U of New Jersey, New Brunswick (NJ)
U of Washington (WA)

CHEMICAL AND BIOMOLECULAR ENGINEERING

Massachusetts Inst of Technology (MA)
Milwaukee School of Eng (WI)
Purdue U (IN)

CHEMICAL ENGINEERING

American U of Beirut (Lebanon)
Arizona State U (AZ)
Auburn U (AL)
Brown U (RI)
Bucknell U (PA)
California Inst of Technology (CA)
California State Polytechnic U, Pomona (CA)
California State U, Long Beach (CA)
Calvin Coll (MI)
Carnegie Mellon U (PA)
Case Western Reserve U (OH)
Christian Brothers U (TN)
City Coll of the City U of New York (NY)
Clarkson U (NY)
Clemson U (SC)
Cleveland State U (OH)
Colorado School of Mines (CO)
Colorado State U (CO)
Cooper Union for the Advancement of Science and Art (NY)
Cornell U (NY)
Elon U (NC)
Florida Ag and Mech U (FL)
Florida Inst of Technology (FL)
Gannon U (PA)
Georgia Inst of Technology (GA)
Illinois Inst of Technology (IL)
Iowa State U of Science and Technology (IA)
The Johns Hopkins U (MD)
Kansas State U (KS)
Kettering U (MI)
Lafayette Coll (PA)
Lakehead U (ON, Canada)
Lamar U (TX)
Lehigh U (PA)
Louisiana State U and Ag and Mech Coll (LA)
Manhattan Coll (NY)
Massachusetts Inst of Technology (MA)
Miami U (OH)
Michigan State U (MI)
Mississippi State U (MS)
Missouri U of Science and Technology (MO)
Montana State U (MT)
New Jersey Inst of Technology (NJ)
New Mexico Inst of Mining and Technology (NM)
New Mexico State U (NM)
North Carolina Ag and Tech State U (NC)
North Carolina State U (NC)
Northeastern U (MA)
The Ohio State U (OH)
Ohio U (OH)
Oklahoma State U (OK)
Oregon State U (OR)
Penn State Abington (PA)
Penn State Altoona (PA)
Penn State Beaver (PA)
Penn State Berks (PA)
Penn State Brandywine (PA)
Penn State DuBois (PA)
Penn State Erie, The Behrend Coll (PA)
Penn State Fayette, The Eberly Campus (PA)
Penn State Greater Allegheny (PA)
Penn State Hazleton (PA)
Penn State Lehigh Valley (PA)
Penn State Mont Alto (PA)
Penn State New Kensington (PA)
Penn State Schuylkill (PA)
Penn State Shenango (PA)
Penn State U Park (PA)
Penn State Wilkes-Barre (PA)
Penn State Worthington Scranton (PA)
Penn State York (PA)
Polytechnic U of Puerto Rico (PR)
Prairie View A&M U (TX)
Princeton U (NJ)
Purdue U (IN)
Rensselaer Polytechnic Inst (NY)
Rice U (TX)

Rose-Hulman Inst of Technology (IN)
Rowan U (NJ)
Rutgers, The State U of New Jersey, New Brunswick (NJ)
San Jose State U (CA)
South Dakota School of Mines and Technology (SD)
Stanford U (CA)
State U of New York Coll of Environmental Science and Forestry (NY)
Syracuse U (NY)
Tennessee Technological U (TN)
Texas A&M U (TX)
Texas Tech U (TX)
Thiel Coll (PA)
Trine U (IN)
Tufts U (MA)
Tulane U (LA)
Tuskegee U (AL)
United States Military Acad (NY)
Université de Sherbrooke (QC, Canada)
U at Buffalo, the State U of New York (NY)
The U of Akron (OH)
The U of Alabama (AL)
The U of Alabama in Huntsville (AL)
The U of Arizona (AZ)
U of Arkansas (AR)
The U of British Columbia (BC, Canada)
U of California, Berkeley (CA)
U of California, Davis (CA)
U of California, Irvine (CA)
U of California, Los Angeles (CA)
U of California, Santa Barbara (CA)
U of Cincinnati (OH)
U of Colorado Boulder (CO)
U of Dayton (OH)
U of Delaware (DE)
U of Florida (FL)
U of Georgia (GA)
U of Guelph (ON, Canada)
U of Houston (TX)
U of Idaho (ID)
U of Illinois at Chicago (IL)
The U of Iowa (IA)
The U of Kansas (KS)
U of Louisiana at Lafayette (LA)
U of Louisville (KY)
U of Maine (ME)
U of Maryland, Baltimore County (MD)
U of Maryland, Coll Park (MD)
U of Massachusetts Amherst (MA)
U of Massachusetts Lowell (MA)
U of Michigan (MI)
U of Minnesota, Duluth (MN)
U of Minnesota, Twin Cities Campus (MN)
U of Mississippi (MS)
U of Missouri (MO)
U of Nebraska–Lincoln (NE)
U of Nevada, Reno (NV)
U of New Brunswick Fredericton (NB, Canada)
U of New Hampshire (NH)
U of New Haven (CT)
U of North Dakota (ND)
U of Notre Dame (IN)
U of Oklahoma (OK)
U of Ottawa (ON, Canada)
U of Pennsylvania (PA)
U of Pittsburgh (PA)
U of Rhode Island (RI)
U of Rochester (NY)
U of Saskatchewan (SK, Canada)
U of South Alabama (AL)
U of South Carolina (SC)
U of Southern California (CA)
U of South Florida (FL)
The U of Tennessee (TN)
The U of Tennessee at Chattanooga (TN)
The U of Texas at Austin (TX)
The U of Toledo (OH)
U of Tulsa (OK)
U of Utah (UT)
U of Virginia (VA)
U of Washington (WA)
U of Waterloo (ON, Canada)
The U of Western Ontario (ON, Canada)
U of Wisconsin–Madison (WI)
U of Wyoming (WY)
Vanderbilt U (TN)

Villanova U (PA)
Virginia Commonwealth U (VA)
Virginia Polytechnic Inst and State U (VA)
Washington and Lee U (VA)
Washington State U (WA)
Washington U in St. Louis (MO)
Wayne State U (MI)
Western Michigan U (MI)
West Virginia U (WV)
Widener U (PA)
Winona State U (MN)
Worcester Polytechnic Inst (MA)
Xavier U (OH)
Yale U (CT)
Youngstown State U (OH)

CHEMICAL ENGINEERING RELATED

Purdue U (IN)

CHEMICAL ENGINEERING TECHNOLOGY

Purdue U (IN)

CHEMICAL PHYSICS

Adams State Coll (CO)
Augustana Coll (SD)
Bowdoin Coll (ME)
Carnegie Mellon U (PA)
Hamilton Coll (NY)
Hendrix Coll (AR)
Lewis U (IL)
Maryville Coll (TN)
Michigan State U (MI)
Saginaw Valley State U (MI)
Simon Fraser U (BC, Canada)
Swarthmore Coll (PA)
U of Waterloo (ON, Canada)

CHEMICAL TECHNOLOGY

Inter American U of Puerto Rico, Bayamón Campus (PR)
Inter American U of Puerto Rico, Guayama Campus (PR)
U of Regina (SK, Canada)

CHEMISTRY

Abilene Christian U (TX)
Acadia U (NS, Canada)
Adams State Coll (CO)
Adelphi U (NY)
Alabama Ag and Mech U (AL)
Alabama State U (AL)
Albany State U (GA)
Albertus Magnus Coll (CT)
Albion Coll (MI)
Albright Coll (PA)
Alcorn State U (MS)
Alderson-Broaddus Coll (WV)
Alfred U (NY)
Allegheny Coll (PA)
Alma Coll (MI)
Alvernia U (PA)
Alverno Coll (WI)
American U (DC)
American U of Beirut (Lebanon)
Amherst Coll (MA)
Anderson U (IN)
Andrews U (MI)
Angelo State U (TX)
Appalachian State U (NC)
Aquinas Coll (MI)
Arcadia U (PA)
Arizona State U (AZ)
Arkansas State U (AR)
Arkansas Tech U (AR)
Armstrong Atlantic State U (GA)
Asbury U (KY)
Ashland U (OH)
Assumption Coll (MA)
Athens State U (AL)
Auburn U (AL)
Augsburg Coll (MN)
Augustana Coll (IL)
Augustana Coll (SD)
Austin Coll (TX)
Austin Peay State U (TN)
Averett U (VA)
Azusa Pacific U (CA)
Baker U (KS)
Baldwin-Wallace Coll (OH)
Ball State U (IN)
Bard Coll (NY)
Bard Coll at Simon's Rock (MA)
Barnard Coll (NY)
Barry U (FL)
Barton Coll (NC)

Bates Coll (ME)
Belhaven U (MS)
Bellarmine U (KY)
Belmont U (TN)
Beloit Coll (WI)
Bemidji State U (MN)
Benedictine Coll (KS)
Benedictine U (IL)
Bennington Coll (VT)
Berea Coll (KY)
Berry Coll (GA)
Bethany Coll (KS)
Bethany Coll (WV)
Bethany Lutheran Coll (MN)
Bethel Coll (IN)
Bethel U (MN)
Bethel U (TN)
Bethune-Cookman U (FL)
Biola U (CA)
Birmingham-Southern Coll (AL)
Blackburn Coll (IL)
Bloomfield Coll (NJ)
Bloomsburg U of Pennsylvania (PA)
Bluefield Coll (VA)
Bluffton U (OH)
Bob Jones U (SC)
Boise State U (ID)
Boston Coll (MA)
Boston U (MA)
Bowdoin Coll (ME)
Bowling Green State U (OH)
Brandeis U (MA)
Briar Cliff U (IA)
Bridgewater Coll (VA)
Bridgewater State U (MA)
Brock U (ON, Canada)
Brown U (RI)
Bryn Mawr Coll (PA)
Bucknell U (PA)
Buena Vista U (IA)
Butler U (IN)
Cabrini Coll (PA)
California Baptist U (CA)
California Inst of Technology (CA)
California Polytechnic State U, San Luis Obispo (CA)
California State Polytechnic U, Pomona (CA)
California State U, Bakersfield (CA)
California State U, Chico (CA)
California State U, Dominguez Hills (CA)
California State U, Fullerton (CA)
California State U, Long Beach (CA)
California State U, Los Angeles (CA)
California State U, Northridge (CA)
California State U, San Bernardino (CA)
California State U, San Marcos (CA)
California State U, Stanislaus (CA)
Calvin Coll (MI)
Cameron U (OK)
Campbellsville U (KY)
Canisius Coll (NY)
Capital U (OH)
Carleton Coll (MN)
Carlow U (PA)
Carnegie Mellon U (PA)
Carroll U (WI)
Carson-Newman Coll (TN)
Case Western Reserve U (OH)
The Catholic U of America (DC)
Cedar Crest Coll (PA)
Cedarville U (OH)
Centenary Coll of Louisiana (LA)
Central Coll (IA)
Central Connecticut State U (CT)
Central Michigan U (MI)
Central State U (OH)
Centre Coll (KY)
Chapman U (CA)
Chatham U (PA)
Chestnut Hill Coll (PA)
Christian Brothers U (TN)
Christopher Newport U (VA)
The Citadel, The Military Coll of South Carolina (SC)
City Coll of the City U of New York (NY)
Claflin U (SC)
Claremont McKenna Coll (CA)
Clarion U of Pennsylvania (PA)
Clark Atlanta U (GA)
Clarke U (IA)
Clarkson U (NY)
Clark U (MA)
Clayton State U (GA)

Clemson U (SC)
Cleveland State U (OH)
Coastal Carolina U (SC)
Coker Coll (SC)
Colby Coll (ME)
Colgate U (NY)
Coll of Charleston (SC)
Coll of Mount St. Joseph (OH)
The Coll of New Jersey (NJ)
Coll of Saint Benedict (MN)
Coll of Saint Elizabeth (NJ)
Coll of Saint Mary (NE)
The Coll of Saint Rose (NY)
The Coll of St. Scholastica (MN)
Coll of Staten Island of the City U of New York (NY)
Coll of the Holy Cross (MA)
Coll of the Ozarks (MO)
The Coll of William and Mary (VA)
The Coll of Wooster (OH)
The Colorado Coll (CO)
Colorado School of Mines (CO)
Colorado State U (CO)
Columbia Coll (MO)
Columbia Coll (SC)
Columbia U, School of General Studies (NY)
Columbus State U (GA)
Concordia Coll (MN)
Concordia U (CA)
Concordia U (QC, Canada)
Concordia U Chicago (IL)
Concord U (WV)
Connecticut Coll (CT)
Coppin State U (MD)
Cornell Coll (IA)
Cornell U (NY)
Covenant Coll (GA)
Creighton U (NE)
Dalton State Coll (GA)
Dartmouth Coll (NH)
Davidson Coll (NC)
Delaware State U (DE)
Delta State U (MS)
Denison U (OH)
DePaul U (IL)
DePauw U (IN)
DeSales U (PA)
Dickinson Coll (PA)
Dickinson State U (ND)
Dillard U (LA)
Doane Coll (NE)
Dominican U (IL)
Dominican U of California (CA)
Dordt Coll (IA)
Dowling Coll (NY)
Drake U (IA)
Drew U (NJ)
Drury U (MO)
Duquesne U (PA)
Earlham Coll (IN)
East Central U (OK)
Eastern Illinois U (IL)
Eastern Michigan U (MI)
Eastern New Mexico U (NM)
Eastern Oregon U (OR)
Eastern Washington U (WA)
East Stroudsburg U of Pennsylvania (PA)
East Tennessee State U (TN)
East Texas Baptist U (TX)
Eckerd Coll (FL)
Edgewood Coll (WI)
Edinboro U of Pennsylvania (PA)
Elizabeth City State U (NC)
Elizabethtown Coll (PA)
Elmhurst Coll (IL)
Elmira Coll (NY)
Elon U (NC)
Emmanuel Coll (MA)
Emory & Henry Coll (VA)
Emporia State U (KS)
Erskine Coll (SC)
Evangel U (MO)
Fairfield U (CT)
Fairleigh Dickinson U, Coll at Florham (NJ)
Fairleigh Dickinson U, Metropolitan Campus (NJ)
Fairmont State U (WV)
Fayetteville State U (NC)
Ferris State U (MI)
Ferrum Coll (VA)
Florida Ag and Mech U (FL)
Florida Atlantic U (FL)
Florida Gulf Coast U (FL)
Florida Inst of Technology (FL)
Florida Intl U (FL)

INDEXES

Texas Woman's U (TX)
Thiel Coll (PA)
Thomas More Coll (KY)
Towson U (MD)
Transylvania U (KY)
Trent U (ON, Canada)
Trevecca Nazarene U (TN)
Trine U (IN)
Trinity Coll (CT)
Trinity U (TX)
Troy U (AL)
Truman State U (MO)
Tufts U (MA)
Tulane U (LA)
Tuskegee U (AL)
Union Coll (KY)
Union Coll (NE)
Union Coll (NY)
Union U (TN)
United States Air Force Acad (CO)
United States Military Acad (NY)
United States Naval Acad (MD)
Université de Sherbrooke (QC, Canada)
U at Buffalo, the State U of New York (NY)
The U of Akron (OH)
The U of Alabama (AL)
The U of Alabama at Birmingham (AL)
The U of Alabama in Huntsville (AL)
U of Alaska Fairbanks (AK)
The U of Arizona (AZ)
U of Arkansas (AR)
U of Arkansas at Pine Bluff (AR)
U of Arkansas–Fort Smith (AR)
The U of British Columbia (BC, Canada)
The U of British Columbia–Okanagan (BC, Canada)
U of California, Berkeley (CA)
U of California, Davis (CA)
U of California, Irvine (CA)
U of California, Los Angeles (CA)
U of California, Merced (CA)
U of California, Santa Barbara (CA)
U of California, Santa Cruz (CA)
U of Central Florida (FL)
U of Central Missouri (MO)
U of Charleston (WV)
U of Cincinnati (OH)
U of Colorado at Colorado Springs (CO)
U of Colorado Boulder (CO)
U of Colorado Denver (CO)
U of Dallas (TX)
U of Dayton (OH)
U of Delaware (DE)
U of Denver (CO)
U of Evansville (IN)
The U of Findlay (OH)
U of Florida (FL)
U of Georgia (GA)
U of Guelph (ON, Canada)
U of Hartford (CT)
U of Hawaii at Hilo (HI)
U of Hawaii at Manoa (HI)
U of Houston (TX)
U of Houston–Clear Lake (TX)
U of Houston–Downtown (TX)
U of Idaho (ID)
U of Illinois at Chicago (IL)
U of Illinois at Springfield (IL)
The U of Iowa (IA)
The U of Kansas (KS)
U of La Verne (CA)
U of Lethbridge (AB, Canada)
U of Louisiana at Lafayette (LA)
U of Louisiana at Monroe (LA)
U of Louisville (KY)
U of Maine (ME)
U of Manitoba (MB, Canada)
U of Mary Hardin-Baylor (TX)
U of Maryland, Baltimore County (MD)
U of Maryland, Coll Park (MD)
U of Mary Washington (VA)
U of Massachusetts Amherst (MA)
U of Massachusetts Boston (MA)
U of Massachusetts Dartmouth (MA)
U of Massachusetts Lowell (MA)
U of Memphis (TN)
U of Miami (FL)
U of Michigan (MI)
U of Michigan–Dearborn (MI)
U of Michigan–Flint (MI)
U of Minnesota, Duluth (MN)

U of Minnesota, Twin Cities Campus (MN)
U of Mississippi (MS)
U of Missouri (MO)
U of Missouri–St. Louis (MO)
U of Montevallo (AL)
U of Mount Union (OH)
U of Nebraska at Omaha (NE)
U of Nebraska–Lincoln (NE)
U of Nevada, Las Vegas (NV)
U of Nevada, Reno (NV)
U of New Brunswick Fredericton (NB, Canada)
U of New Brunswick Saint John (NB, Canada)
U of New England (ME)
U of New Hampshire (NH)
U of New Haven (CT)
The U of North Carolina at Asheville (NC)
The U of North Carolina at Chapel Hill (NC)
The U of North Carolina at Charlotte (NC)
The U of North Carolina at Greensboro (NC)
The U of North Carolina at Pembroke (NC)
The U of North Carolina Wilmington (NC)
U of North Dakota (ND)
U of Northern Colorado (CO)
U of Northern Iowa (IA)
U of North Florida (FL)
U of North Texas (TX)
U of Notre Dame (IN)
U of Oklahoma (OK)
U of Oregon (OR)
U of Ottawa (ON, Canada)
U of Pennsylvania (PA)
U of Pittsburgh (PA)
U of Pittsburgh at Bradford (PA)
U of Pittsburgh at Greensburg (PA)
U of Pittsburgh at Johnstown (PA)
U of Portland (OR)
U of Puerto Rico at Humacao (PR)
U of Puget Sound (WA)
U of Redlands (CA)
U of Regina (SK, Canada)
U of Rhode Island (RI)
U of Richmond (VA)
U of Rio Grande (OH)
U of Rochester (NY)
U of Saint Mary (KS)
U of St. Thomas (MN)
U of St. Thomas (TX)
U of San Diego (CA)
U of San Francisco (CA)
U of Saskatchewan (SK, Canada)
U of Science and Arts of Oklahoma (OK)
The U of Scranton (PA)
U of Sioux Falls (SD)
U of South Alabama (AL)
U of South Carolina (SC)
U of South Carolina Aiken (SC)
U of South Carolina Upstate (SC)
The U of South Dakota (SD)
U of Southern California (CA)
U of Southern Indiana (IN)
U of Southern Maine (ME)
U of Southern Mississippi (MS)
U of South Florida (FL)
The U of Tampa (FL)
The U of Tennessee (TN)
The U of Tennessee at Chattanooga (TN)
The U of Tennessee at Martin (TN)
The U of Texas at Arlington (TX)
The U of Texas at Austin (TX)
The U of Texas at Dallas (TX)
The U of Texas at San Antonio (TX)
The U of Texas at Tyler (TX)
The U of Texas of the Permian Basin (TX)
The U of Texas–Pan American (TX)
U of the Cumberlands (KY)
U of the District of Columbia (DC)
U of the Incarnate Word (TX)
U of the Ozarks (AR)
U of the Pacific (CA)
U of the Sciences in Philadelphia (PA)
U of the Virgin Islands (VI)
The U of Toledo (OH)
U of Tulsa (OK)
U of Utah (UT)
U of Vermont (VT)

U of Virginia (VA)
U of Washington (WA)
U of Waterloo (ON, Canada)
The U of Western Ontario (ON, Canada)
U of West Florida (FL)
U of West Georgia (GA)
U of Wisconsin–Eau Claire (WI)
U of Wisconsin–Green Bay (WI)
U of Wisconsin–La Crosse (WI)
U of Wisconsin–Madison (WI)
U of Wisconsin–Parkside (WI)
U of Wisconsin–River Falls (WI)
U of Wisconsin–Stevens Point (WI)
U of Wisconsin–Superior (WI)
U of Wisconsin–Whitewater (WI)
U of Wyoming (WY)
Upper Iowa U (IA)
Utah State U (UT)
Utah Valley U (UT)
Valdosta State U (GA)
Valparaiso U (IN)
Vanderbilt U (TN)
Vassar Coll (NY)
Villanova U (PA)
Virginia Commonwealth U (VA)
Virginia Military Inst (VA)
Virginia Polytechnic Inst and State U (VA)
Virginia State U (VA)
Virginia Wesleyan Coll (VA)
Viterbo U (WI)
Wabash Coll (IN)
Wagner Coll (NY)
Wake Forest U (NC)
Walla Walla U (WA)
Walsh U (OH)
Wartburg Coll (IA)
Washburn U (KS)
Washington Adventist U (MD)
Washington & Jefferson Coll (PA)
Washington and Lee U (VA)
Washington Coll (MD)
Washington State U (WA)
Washington U in St. Louis (MO)
Wayland Baptist U (TX)
Waynesburg U (PA)
Wayne State Coll (NE)
Wayne State U (MI)
Weber State U (UT)
Wellesley Coll (MA)
Wells Coll (NY)
Wesleyan Coll (GA)
Wesleyan U (CT)
West Chester U of Pennsylvania (PA)
Western Carolina U (NC)
Western Connecticut State U (CT)
Western Illinois U (IL)
Western Kentucky U (KY)
Western Michigan U (MI)
Western New England U (MA)
Western Oregon U (OR)
Western State Coll of Colorado (CO)
Westfield State U (MA)
West Liberty U (WV)
Westminster Coll (MO)
Westminster Coll (UT)
Westmont Coll (CA)
West Virginia U (WV)
Wheaton Coll (IL)
Wheaton Coll (MA)
Wheeling Jesuit U (WV)
Whitman Coll (WA)
Wichita State U (KS)
Widener U (PA)
Wilfrid Laurier U (ON, Canada)
Wilkes U (PA)
Willamette U (OR)
William Jewell Coll (MO)
Williams Coll (MA)
Wilmington Coll (OH)
Wingate U (NC)
Winona State U (MN)
Winthrop U (SC)
Wittenberg U (OH)
Wofford Coll (SC)
Worcester Polytechnic Inst (MA)
Worcester State U (MA)
Wright State U (OH)
Xavier U (OH)
Xavier U of Louisiana (LA)
Yale U (CT)
York Coll of Pennsylvania (PA)
York Coll of the City U of New York (NY)
Youngstown State U (OH)

CHEMISTRY RELATED

Boston U (MA)
Bowling Green State U (OH)
Bridgewater State U (MA)
California State U, Chico (CA)
Carnegie Mellon U (PA)
Coll of Charleston (SC)
Connecticut U (CT)
Dartmouth Coll (NH)
Delaware State U (DE)
Duquesne U (PA)
Edinboro U of Pennsylvania (PA)
Florida Inst of Technology (FL)
Florida State U (FL)
Keene State Coll (NH)
Lawrence Technological U (MI)
Loyola U New Orleans (LA)
Mount Olive Coll (NC)
Northern Arizona U (AZ)
Northern Michigan U (MI)
Northland Coll (WI)
Purdue U (IN)
Saginaw Valley State U (MI)
Saint Anselm Coll (NH)
St. Edward's U (TX)
Saint Mary's Coll of California (CA)
Sam Houston State U (TX)
Stony Brook U, State U of New York (NY)
Taylor U (IN)
Texas Wesleyan U (TX)
Towson U (MD)
U at Buffalo, the State U of New York (NY)
U of California, Berkeley (CA)
U of California, Santa Barbara (CA)
U of Denver (CO)
U of Georgia (GA)
U of Houston–Downtown (TX)
U of Northern Iowa (IA)
U of Notre Dame (IN)
The U of Scranton (PA)
U of Southern Mississippi (MS)
U of the Pacific (CA)
U of Wisconsin–Eau Claire (WI)
U of Wisconsin–Madison (WI)
U of Wisconsin–Whitewater (WI)
Washington & Jefferson Coll (PA)
Washington U in St. Louis (MO)
Wayne State U (MI)
Western Illinois U (IL)
Western Michigan U (MI)
Western State Coll of Colorado (CO)
Whitman Coll (WA)

CHEMISTRY TEACHER EDUCATION

Adams State Coll (CO)
Alma Coll (MI)
Alvernia U (PA)
Anderson U (IN)
Appalachian State U (NC)
Arkansas State U (AR)
Assumption Coll (MA)
Augustana Coll (IL)
Averett U (VA)
Bethany Coll (KS)
Bethel U (MN)
Bethune-Cookman U (FL)
Bluefield Coll (VA)
Boston U (MA)
Bridgewater Coll (VA)
Buena Vista U (IA)
Cabrini Coll (PA)
California State U, Chico (CA)
Calvin Coll (MI)
Cameron U (OK)
Campbellsville U (KY)
Carroll U (WI)
Cedarville U (OH)
Central Michigan U (MI)
Christian Brothers U (TN)
City Coll of the City U of New York (NY)
Coker Coll (SC)
The Coll of New Jersey (NJ)
The Coll of Saint Rose (NY)
Coll of the Ozarks (MO)
Colorado State U (CO)
Concordia Coll (MN)
Concordia U Chicago (IL)
Concordia U, St. Paul (MN)
Delaware State U (DE)
Dordt Coll (IA)
Dowling Coll (NY)
Eastern Michigan U (MI)
Eastern Washington U (WA)

East Texas Baptist U (TX)
Edgewood Coll (WI)
Elizabeth City State U (NC)
Elmhurst Coll (IL)
Elmira Coll (NY)
Evangel U (MO)
Ferris State U (MI)
Florida Inst of Technology (FL)
Fort Lewis Coll (CO)
Franklin Coll (IN)
Grand Canyon U (AZ)
Grand Valley State U (MI)
Greenville Coll (IL)
Hofstra U (NY)
Hope Coll (MI)
Huntingdon Coll (AL)
Huntington U (IN)
Husson U (ME)
Indiana U Bloomington (IN)
Indiana U–Purdue U Fort Wayne (IN)
Indiana U South Bend (IN)
Indiana U Southeast (IN)
Indiana Wesleyan U (IN)
Inter American U of Puerto Rico, Metropolitan Campus (PR)
Inter American U of Puerto Rico, San Germán Campus (PR)
Iowa Wesleyan Coll (IA)
Ithaca Coll (NY)
Jamestown Coll (ND)
Juniata Coll (PA)
Keene State Coll (NH)
Kent State U (OH)
Kentucky Wesleyan Coll (KY)
King Coll (TN)
Le Moyne Coll (NY)
Lincoln Memorial U (TN)
Lincoln U (PA)
Lindenwood U (MO)
Lipscomb U (TN)
Long Island U, Brooklyn Campus (NY)
Long Island U, C.W. Post Campus (NY)
Louisiana State U in Shreveport (LA)
Lubbock Christian U (TX)
Manchester Coll (IN)
Manhattanville Coll (NY)
Mansfield U of Pennsylvania (PA)
Marist Coll (NY)
Marquette U (WI)
Maryville Coll (TN)
Mayville State U (ND)
McMurry U (TX)
Merrimack Coll (MA)
Messiah Coll (PA)
Miami Dade Coll (FL)
Miami U (OH)
Michigan State U (MI)
Millersville U of Pennsylvania (PA)
Millikin U (IL)
Minnesota State U Moorhead (MN)
Minot State U (ND)
Misericordia U (PA)
Missouri State U (MO)
Montana State U Billings (MT)
Moravian Coll (PA)
Morningside Coll (IA)
Mount Marty Coll (SD)
Mount Vernon Nazarene U (OH)
Nazareth Coll of Rochester (NY)
New York Inst of Technology (NY)
Niagara U (NY)
North Dakota State U (ND)
Northeastern State U (OK)
Northern Arizona U (AZ)
Northern Michigan U (MI)
Northland Coll (WI)
Northwest Missouri State U (MO)
Northwest Nazarene U (ID)
Ohio Wesleyan U (OH)
Pace U (NY)
Pittsburg State U (KS)
Purdue U (IN)
Rhode Island Coll (RI)
Sacred Heart U (CT)
Saginaw Valley State U (MI)
St. Ambrose U (IA)
St. Catherine U (MN)
St. Edward's U (TX)
Saint Francis U (PA)
St. John Fisher Coll (NY)
St. Joseph's Coll, Long Island Campus (NY)
St. Joseph's Coll, New York (NY)
Saint Joseph's Coll of Maine (ME)

Saint Mary's U of Minnesota (MN)
Schreiner U (TX)
Seton Hill U (PA)
Southeastern Louisiana U (LA)
Spring Arbor U (MI)
State U of New York at New Paltz (NY)
State U of New York at Plattsburgh (NY)
State U of New York Coll at Old Westbury (NY)
State U of New York Coll at Oneonta (NY)
State U of New York Coll at Potsdam (NY)
State U of New York Coll of Environmental Science and Forestry (NY)
Syracuse U (NY)
Tabor Coll (KS)
Talladega Coll (AL)
Transylvania U (KY)
Trevecca Nazarene U (TN)
Union Coll (NE)
The U of Arizona (AZ)
U of Arkansas–Fort Smith (AR)
U of Delaware (DE)
U of Evansville (IN)
U of Illinois at Chicago (IL)
The U of Iowa (IA)
U of Louisiana at Lafayette (LA)
U of Louisiana at Monroe (LA)
U of Maine (ME)
U of Mary Hardin-Baylor (TX)
U of Michigan–Dearborn (MI)
U of Missouri (MO)
U of Missouri–St. Louis (MO)
U of Nebraska–Lincoln (NE)
The U of North Carolina at Charlotte (NC)
The U of North Carolina Wilmington (NC)
U of Pittsburgh at Johnstown (PA)
U of Regina (SK, Canada)
U of St. Thomas (MN)
The U of Tennessee at Martin (TN)
U of Waterloo (ON, Canada)
U of Wisconsin–River Falls (WI)
U of Wisconsin–Superior (WI)
Utah State U (UT)
Utah Valley U (UT)
Valparaiso U (IN)
Viterbo U (WI)
Washington State U (WA)
Washington U in St. Louis (MO)
Waynesburg U (PA)
Wayne State Coll (NE)
Weber State U (UT)
Western Michigan U (MI)
Western State Coll of Colorado (CO)
Wheeling Jesuit U (WV)
Widener U (PA)
William Jewell Coll (MO)
Winona State U (MN)
Xavier U (OH)
Xavier U of Louisiana (LA)

CHILD-CARE AND SUPPORT SERVICES MANAGEMENT

Brigham Young U (UT)
Chestnut Hill Coll (PA)
Ferris State U (MI)
Messiah Coll (PA)
National-Louis U (IL)
Rust Coll (MS)
Saint Mary-of-the-Woods Coll (IN)
Seton Hill U (PA)
Siena Heights U (MI)
Thomas Edison State Coll (NJ)
U of Minnesota, Twin Cities Campus (MN)
Walden U (MN)
Wheelock Coll (MA)

CHILD-CARE PROVISION

Brigham Young U (UT)
Walden U (MN)
Wayne State Coll (NE)

CHILD DEVELOPMENT

Albertus Magnus Coll (CT)
Alcorn State U (MS)
Appalachian State U (NC)
Ashland U (OH)
Atlanta Christian Coll (GA)
Auburn U (AL)
Bennington Coll (VT)
Brigham Young U (UT)
California State U, Long Beach (CA)
California State U, Los Angeles (CA)

California State U, Northridge (CA)
Carson-Newman Coll (TN)
Central Michigan U (MI)
Coll of the Ozarks (MO)
Concordia U, St. Paul (MN)
Delaware State U (DE)
Eastern Washington U (WA)
East Tennessee State U (TN)
Florida State U (FL)
Freed-Hardeman U (TN)
Gallaudet U (DC)
Goddard Coll (VT)
Goodwin Coll (CT)
Hannibal-LaGrange U (MO)
Harding U (AR)
Humboldt State U (CA)
Kansas State U (KS)
Kuyper Coll (MI)
Lesley U (MA)
Lewis-Clark State Coll (ID)
Lincoln Christian U (IL)
Madonna U (MI)
Michigan State U (MI)
Milligan Coll (TN)
Minnesota State U Mankato (MN)
Missouri Baptist U (MO)
Mount Ida Coll (MA)
National U (CA)
North Carolina Ag and Tech State U (NC)
Nova Southeastern U (FL)
Ohio U (OH)
Oklahoma Christian U (OK)
Pacific Oaks Coll (CA)
Pittsburg State U (KS)
Portland State U (OR)
Quinnipiac U (CT)
Saint Joseph Coll (CT)
St. Joseph's Coll, Long Island Campus (NY)
St. Joseph's Coll, New York (NY)
San Diego State U (CA)
Seton Hill U (PA)
Springfield Coll (MA)
State U of New York Coll at Oneonta (NY)
Tennessee Technological U (TN)
Texas Southern U (TX)
Texas Tech U (TX)
Texas Woman's U (TX)
Towson U (MD)
Tufts U (MA)
Union Inst & U (OH)
The U of Akron (OH)
U of Alaska Fairbanks (AK)
U of Georgia (GA)
U of Guelph (ON, Canada)
U of La Verne (CA)
U of Maine (ME)
U of Manitoba (MB, Canada)
U of Nevada, Reno (NV)
The U of North Carolina at Charlotte (NC)
The U of North Carolina at Greensboro (NC)
U of Saint Mary (KS)
The U of Tennessee at Martin (TN)
The U of Texas at Arlington (TX)
U of the Incarnate Word (TX)
The U of Western Ontario (ON, Canada)
Vanderbilt U (TN)
Walden U (MN)
Western Michigan U (MI)
West Virginia U (WV)
Wheelock Coll (MA)
Youngstown State U (OH)

CHINESE

Bard Coll (NY)
Bates Coll (ME)
Bennington Coll (VT)
Boston U (MA)
California State U, Long Beach (CA)
California State U, Los Angeles (CA)
Calvin Coll (MI)
Carnegie Mellon U (PA)
Claremont McKenna Coll (CA)
Colgate U (NY)
Coll of the Holy Cross (MA)
Concordia Coll (MN)
Connecticut Coll (CT)
Dartmouth Coll (NH)
DePaul U (IL)
Georgetown U (DC)
Grinnell Coll (IA)
Hamilton Coll (NY)
Hobart and William Smith Colls (NY)
Hofstra U (NY)

Hunter Coll of the City U of New York (NY)
Lawrence U (WI)
Macalester Coll (MN)
Michigan State U (MI)
Middlebury Coll (VT)
New Coll of Florida (FL)
The Ohio State U (OH)
Pacific Lutheran U (WA)
Pacific U (OR)
Penn State U Park (PA)
Pomona Coll (CA)
Portland State U (OR)
Queens Coll of the City U of New York (NY)
Reed Coll (OR)
Rutgers, The State U of New Jersey, New Brunswick (NJ)
San Francisco State U (CA)
San Jose State U (CA)
Scripps Coll (CA)
Stanford U (CA)
Swarthmore Coll (PA)
Trinity Coll (CT)
Trinity U (TX)
Tufts U (MA)
United States Military Acad (NY)
The U of British Columbia (BC, Canada)
U of California, Berkeley (CA)
U of California, Davis (CA)
U of California, Los Angeles (CA)
U of California, Santa Barbara (CA)
U of Colorado Boulder (CO)
U of Georgia (GA)
U of Hawaii at Manoa (HI)
U of Houston (TX)
The U of Iowa (IA)
U of Maryland, Coll Park (MD)
U of Massachusetts Amherst (MA)
U of Minnesota, Twin Cities Campus (MN)
U of Notre Dame (IN)
U of Oklahoma (OK)
U of Oregon (OR)
U of Pittsburgh (PA)
U of Puget Sound (WA)
U of Regina (SK, Canada)
U of Richmond (VA)
U of Utah (UT)
U of Vermont (VT)
U of Washington (WA)
U of Wisconsin–Madison (WI)
Vassar Coll (NY)
Wake Forest U (NC)
Washington U in St. Louis (MO)
Wellesley Coll (MA)
Williams Coll (MA)
Wofford Coll (SC)
Yale U (CT)

CHINESE STUDIES

The Coll of William and Mary (VA)
Drew U (NJ)
Pacific Lutheran U (WA)
Sarah Lawrence Coll (NY)
U of California, Irvine (CA)
U of North Dakota (ND)
U of the West (CA)

CHIROPRACTIC ASSISTANT

Hawai'i Pacific U (HI)

CHRISTIAN STUDIES

Alderson-Broaddus Coll (WV)
Anderson U (SC)
Bethany Coll (KS)
Bethel Coll (IN)
Bethel U (TN)
Bluefield Coll (VA)
Bryan Coll (TN)
California Baptist U (CA)
The Coll of St. Scholastica (MN)
Concordia U Wisconsin (WI)
Crossroads Bible Coll (IN)
Dallas Baptist U (TX)
Friends U (KS)
Gordon Coll (MA)
Grand Canyon U (AZ)
Hardin-Simmons U (TX)
Hillsdale Coll (MI)
Inter American U of Puerto Rico, Guayama Campus (PR)
Inter American U of Puerto Rico, Metropolitan Campus (PR)
Iowa Wesleyan Coll (IA)
Lindenwood U (MO)
Loyola U New Orleans (LA)
McMurry U (TX)
Mercer U (GA)

Missouri Baptist U (MO)
Ouachita Baptist U (AR)
Roanoke Coll (VA)
Sacred Heart U (CT)
Simpson U (CA)
Stonehill Coll (MA)
Tennessee Wesleyan Coll (TN)
Truett-McConnell Coll (GA)
U of Mary Hardin-Baylor (TX)
Ursuline Coll (OH)
Wayland Baptist U (TX)

CINEMATOGRAPHY AND FILM/VIDEO PRODUCTION

American U (DC)
Art Center Coll of Design (CA)
The Art Inst of Ohio–Cincinnati (OH)
The Art Inst of Seattle (WA)
Bard Coll (NY)
Bennington Coll (VT)
Biola U (CA)
Bob Jones U (SC)
Brigham Young U (UT)
California Inst of the Arts (CA)
California State U, Long Beach (CA)
California State U, Northridge (CA)
Chapman U (CA)
City Coll of the City U of New York (NY)
Cleveland State U (OH)
Collins Coll (AZ)
Columbia Coll Chicago (IL)
Concordia U (QC, Canada)
DePaul U (IL)
Eastern New Mexico U (NM)
Eastern Washington U (WA)
Emily Carr U of Art + Design (BC, Canada)
The Evergreen State Coll (WA)
Fairleigh Dickinson U, Coll at Florham (NJ)
Fitchburg State U (MA)
Five Towns Coll (NY)
George Fox U (OR)
Grand Canyon U (AZ)
Hawai`i Pacific U (HI)
Hunter Coll of the City U of New York (NY)
Ithaca Coll (NY)
John Brown U (AR)
Keene State Coll (NH)
Long Island U, C.W. Post Campus (NY)
Loyola Marymount U (CA)
Maharishi U of Management (IA)
Massachusetts Coll of Art and Design (MA)
Miami Dade Coll (FL)
Middlebury Coll (VT)
Minneapolis Coll of Art and Design (MN)
Montana State U (MT)
Montclair State U (NJ)
New Mexico Highlands U (NM)
New Mexico State U (NM)
New York U (NY)
Northern Michigan U (MI)
Ohio U (OH)
Oklahoma City U (OK)
Pacific Union Coll (CA)
Palm Beach Atlantic U (FL)
Point Park U (PA)
Pratt Inst (NY)
Purchase Coll, State U of New York (NY)
Quinnipiac U (CT)
Regent U (VA)
Sarah Lawrence Coll (NY)
Savannah Coll of Art and Design (GA)
School of the Museum of Fine Arts, Boston (MA)
School of Visual Arts (NY)
Southern Adventist U (TN)
Southern Illinois U Carbondale (IL)
State U of New York at Binghamton (NY)
Syracuse U (NY)
U of Advancing Technology (AZ)
U of Central Florida (FL)
U of Illinois at Chicago (IL)
The U of Iowa (IA)
U of Miami (FL)
U of North Carolina School of the Arts (NC)
The U of North Carolina Wilmington (NC)
U of Oregon (OR)
U of Regina (SK, Canada)
U of Rhode Island (RI)

U of Southern California (CA)
The U of the Arts (PA)
Virginia Commonwealth U (VA)
Wayne State U (MI)
Webster U (MO)

CITY/URBAN, COMMUNITY AND REGIONAL PLANNING

Alabama Ag and Mech U (AL)
Appalachian State U (NC)
Arizona State U (AZ)
Ball State U (IN)
Bridgewater State U (MA)
California Polytechnic State U, San Luis Obispo (CA)
California State Polytechnic U, Pomona (CA)
California State U, Chico (CA)
Concordia U (QC, Canada)
Cornell U (NY)
Eastern Washington U (WA)
Florida Atlantic U (FL)
Indiana U of Pennsylvania (PA)
Iowa State U of Science and Technology (IA)
Mansfield U of Pennsylvania (PA)
Massachusetts Inst of Technology (MA)
Miami U (OH)
Michigan State U (MI)
Minnesota State U Mankato (MN)
Missouri State U (MO)
Portland State U (OR)
Savannah Coll of Art and Design (GA)
State U of New York Coll of Environmental Science and Forestry (NY)
Stony Brook U, State U of New York (NY)
Temple U (PA)
Texas A&M U (TX)
Texas State U–San Marcos (TX)
The U of Akron (OH)
The U of Arizona (AZ)
U of California, Davis (CA)
U of Cincinnati (OH)
U of Nevada, Las Vegas (NV)
U of New Hampshire (NH)
U of San Francisco (CA)
U of Saskatchewan (SK, Canada)
U of Virginia (VA)
U of Washington (WA)
U of Waterloo (ON, Canada)
The U of Western Ontario (ON, Canada)
Western Michigan U (MI)
Westfield State U (MA)

CIVIL ENGINEERING

Alabama Ag and Mech U (AL)
American U of Beirut (Lebanon)
Arizona State U (AZ)
Arkansas State U (AR)
Auburn U (AL)
Boise State U (ID)
Brown U (RI)
Bucknell U (PA)
California Baptist U (CA)
California Polytechnic State U, San Luis Obispo (CA)
California State Polytechnic U, Pomona (CA)
California State U, Chico (CA)
California State U, Fullerton (CA)
California State U, Long Beach (CA)
California State U, Los Angeles (CA)
California State U, Northridge (CA)
Calvin Coll (MI)
Carnegie Mellon U (PA)
Case Western Reserve U (OH)
The Catholic U of America (DC)
Central Connecticut State U (CT)
Christian Brothers U (TN)
The Citadel, The Military Coll of South Carolina (SC)
City Coll of the City U of New York (NY)
Clarkson U (NY)
Clemson U (SC)
Cleveland State U (OH)
The Coll of New Jersey (NJ)
Colorado State U (CO)
Concordia U (QC, Canada)
Cooper Union for the Advancement of Science and Art (NY)
Cornell U (NY)
Delaware State U (DE)
Dordt Coll (IA)
Florida Ag and Mech U (FL)

Florida Atlantic U (FL)
Florida Gulf Coast U (FL)
Florida Inst of Technology (FL)
Florida Intl U (FL)
George Fox U (OR)
Georgia Inst of Technology (GA)
Georgia Southern U (GA)
Hofstra U (NY)
Idaho State U (ID)
Illinois Inst of Technology (IL)
Indiana U–Purdue U Fort Wayne (IN)
Iowa State U of Science and Technology (IA)
The Johns Hopkins U (MD)
Kansas State U (KS)
Lafayette Coll (PA)
Lakehead U (ON, Canada)
Lamar U (TX)
Lawrence Technological U (MI)
Lebanese American U (Lebanon)
Lehigh U (PA)
Louisiana State U and Ag and Mech Coll (LA)
Loyola Marymount U (CA)
Manhattan Coll (NY)
Marquette U (WI)
Massachusetts Inst of Technology (MA)
Merrimack Coll (MA)
Michigan State U (MI)
Milwaukee School of Eng (WI)
Minnesota State U Mankato (MN)
Mississippi State U (MS)
Missouri U of Science and Technology (MO)
Montana State U (MT)
New Jersey Inst of Technology (NJ)
New Mexico Inst of Mining and Technology (NM)
New Mexico State U (NM)
North Carolina Ag and Tech State U (NC)
North Carolina State U (NC)
North Dakota State U (ND)
Northeastern U (MA)
Northern Arizona U (AZ)
The Ohio State U (OH)
Ohio U (OH)
Oklahoma State U (OK)
Old Dominion U (VA)
Oregon State U (OR)
Penn State Abington (PA)
Penn State Altoona (PA)
Penn State Beaver (PA)
Penn State Berks (PA)
Penn State Brandywine (PA)
Penn State DuBois (PA)
Penn State Erie, The Behrend Coll (PA)
Penn State Fayette, The Eberly Campus (PA)
Penn State Greater Allegheny (PA)
Penn State Harrisburg (PA)
Penn State Hazleton (PA)
Penn State Lehigh Valley (PA)
Penn State Mont Alto (PA)
Penn State New Kensington (PA)
Penn State Schuylkill (PA)
Penn State Shenango (PA)
Penn State U Park (PA)
Penn State Wilkes-Barre (PA)
Penn State Worthington Scranton (PA)
Penn State York (PA)
Polytechnic Inst of NYU (NY)
Polytechnic U of Puerto Rico (PR)
Portland State U (OR)
Prairie View A&M U (TX)
Princeton U (NJ)
Purdue U (IN)
Purdue U Calumet (IN)
Rensselaer Polytechnic Inst (NY)
Rice U (TX)
Rose-Hulman Inst of Technology (IN)
Rowan U (NJ)
Rutgers, The State U of New Jersey, New Brunswick (NJ)
Saint Louis U (MO)
Saint Martin's U (WA)
San Diego State U (CA)
San Francisco State U (CA)
San Jose State U (CA)
Santa Clara U (CA)
South Dakota School of Mines and Technology (SD)
South Dakota State U (SD)

Southern Illinois U Carbondale (IL)
Southern Illinois U Edwardsville (IL)
Southern Methodist U (TX)
Southern Polytechnic State U (GA)
Stanford U (CA)
Syracuse U (NY)
Temple U (PA)
Tennessee Technological U (TN)
Texas A&M U (TX)
Texas A&M U–Kingsville (TX)
Texas Tech U (TX)
Trine U (IN)
Tufts U (MA)
United States Air Force Acad (CO)
United States Coast Guard Acad (CT)
United States Military Acad (NY)
Université de Sherbrooke (QC, Canada)
U at Buffalo, the State U of New York (NY)
The U of Akron (OH)
The U of Alabama (AL)
The U of Alabama at Birmingham (AL)
The U of Alabama in Huntsville (AL)
U of Alaska Fairbanks (AK)
The U of Arizona (AZ)
U of Arkansas (AR)
The U of British Columbia (BC, Canada)
The U of British Columbia–Okanagan (BC, Canada)
U of California, Berkeley (CA)
U of California, Davis (CA)
U of California, Irvine (CA)
U of California, Los Angeles (CA)
U of Central Florida (FL)
U of Cincinnati (OH)
U of Colorado Boulder (CO)
U of Colorado Denver (CO)
U of Dayton (OH)
U of Delaware (DE)
U of Evansville (IN)
U of Florida (FL)
U of Hartford (CT)
U of Hawaii at Manoa (HI)
U of Houston (TX)
U of Idaho (ID)
U of Illinois at Chicago (IL)
The U of Iowa (IA)
The U of Kansas (KS)
U of Louisiana at Lafayette (LA)
U of Louisville (KY)
U of Maine (ME)
U of Manitoba (MB, Canada)
U of Maryland, Coll Park (MD)
U of Massachusetts Amherst (MA)
U of Massachusetts Dartmouth (MA)
U of Massachusetts Lowell (MA)
U of Memphis (TN)
U of Miami (FL)
U of Michigan (MI)
U of Minnesota, Duluth (MN)
U of Minnesota, Twin Cities Campus (MN)
U of Mississippi (MS)
U of Missouri (MO)
U of Missouri–St. Louis (MO)
U of Mount Union (OH)
U of Nebraska–Lincoln (NE)
U of Nevada, Las Vegas (NV)
U of Nevada, Reno (NV)
U of New Brunswick Fredericton (NB, Canada)
U of New Hampshire (NH)
U of New Haven (CT)
The U of North Carolina at Charlotte (NC)
U of North Dakota (ND)
U of North Florida (FL)
U of Oklahoma (OK)
U of Ottawa (ON, Canada)
U of Pittsburgh (PA)
U of Portland (OR)
U of Rhode Island (RI)
U of Saskatchewan (SK, Canada)
U of South Alabama (AL)
U of South Carolina (SC)
U of Southern California (CA)
U of South Florida (FL)
The U of Tennessee (TN)
The U of Tennessee at Chattanooga (TN)
The U of Texas at Arlington (TX)
The U of Texas at Austin (TX)
The U of Texas at San Antonio (TX)

The U of Texas at Tyler (TX)
U of the District of Columbia (DC)
U of the Pacific (CA)
The U of Toledo (OH)
U of Utah (UT)
U of Vermont (VT)
U of Virginia (VA)
U of Washington (WA)
U of Waterloo (ON, Canada)
The U of Western Ontario (ON, Canada)
U of Wisconsin–Madison (WI)
U of Wisconsin–Platteville (WI)
U of Wyoming (WY)
Utah State U (UT)
Valparaiso U (IN)
Vanderbilt U (TN)
Villanova U (PA)
Virginia Military Inst (VA)
Virginia Polytechnic Inst and State U (VA)
Walla Walla U (WA)
Washington State U (WA)
Wayne State U (MI)
Western Kentucky U (KY)
Western Michigan U (MI)
West Virginia U (WV)
Widener U (PA)
Worcester Polytechnic Inst (MA)
Youngstown State U (OH)

CIVIL ENGINEERING RELATED
California Polytechnic State U, San Luis Obispo (CA)
Carnegie Mellon U (PA)
Embry-Riddle Aeronautical U–Daytona (FL)
Oregon State U (OR)
Purdue U (IN)

CIVIL ENGINEERING TECHNOLOGY
Alabama Ag and Mech U (AL)
Bluefield State Coll (WV)
Central Connecticut State U (CT)
Delaware State U (DE)
Fairleigh Dickinson U, Metropolitan Campus (NJ)
Fairmont State U (WV)
Florida Ag and Mech U (FL)
Georgia Southern U (GA)
Lakehead U (ON, Canada)
Lincoln U (MO)
Murray State U (KY)
Pennsylvania Coll of Technology (PA)
Point Park U (PA)
Purdue U (IN)
Savannah State U (GA)
Southern Polytechnic State U (GA)
Temple U (PA)
Texas Southern U (TX)
Thomas Edison State Coll (NJ)
United States Military Acad (NY)
U of Houston–Downtown (TX)
The U of North Carolina at Charlotte (NC)
U of North Texas (TX)
U of Pittsburgh at Johnstown (PA)
The U of Toledo (OH)
Wentworth Inst of Technology (MA)
Youngstown State U (OH)

CLASSICAL, ANCIENT MEDITERRANEAN AND NEAR EASTERN STUDIES AND ARCHAEOLOGY
Bowdoin Coll (ME)
Creighton U (NE)
Hampshire Coll (MA)
Lycoming Coll (PA)
Michigan State U (MI)
Purdue U (IN)
Syracuse U (NY)
U of California, Berkeley (CA)
U of California, Davis (CA)
U of California, Irvine (CA)
U of California, Los Angeles (CA)
U of Illinois at Chicago (IL)
U of Michigan (MI)
U of Ottawa (ON, Canada)
U of Southern California (CA)
Vanderbilt U (TN)

CLASSICS AND CLASSICAL LANGUAGES
Acadia U (NS, Canada)

Amherst Coll (MA)
Asbury U (KY)
Assumption Coll (MA)
Augustana Coll (IL)
Augustana Coll (SD)
Austin Coll (TX)
Ball State U (IN)
Barnard Coll (NY)
Beloit Coll (WI)
Boston Coll (MA)
Boston U (MA)
Bowdoin Coll (ME)
Bowling Green State U (OH)
Brandeis U (MA)
Brown U (RI)
Bryn Mawr Coll (PA)
Bucknell U (PA)
Calvin Coll (MI)
Carleton Coll (MN)
Case Western Reserve U (OH)
The Catholic U of America (DC)
Centre Coll (KY)
Christendom Coll (VA)
Christopher Newport U (VA)
Claremont McKenna Coll (CA)
Clark U (MA)
Colby Coll (ME)
Colgate U (NY)
Coll of Charleston (SC)
Coll of Saint Benedict (MN)
Coll of the Holy Cross (MA)
The Coll of William and Mary (VA)
The Coll of Wooster (OH)
The Colorado Coll (CO)
Columbia U, School of General Studies (NY)
Concordia Coll (MN)
Concordia U (QC, Canada)
Connecticut Coll (CT)
Cornell Coll (IA)
Cornell U (NY)
Dartmouth Coll (NH)
Davidson Coll (NC)
Denison U (OH)
DePauw U (IN)
Dickinson Coll (PA)
Drew U (NJ)
Duquesne U (PA)
Earlham Coll (IN)
Elmira Coll (NY)
The Evergreen State Coll (WA)
Franklin & Marshall Coll (PA)
Furman U (SC)
Georgetown U (DC)
Gettysburg Coll (PA)
Grand Valley State U (MI)
Grinnell Coll (IA)
Hamilton Coll (NY)
Hampden-Sydney Coll (VA)
Hanover Coll (IN)
Harvard U (MA)
Haverford Coll (PA)
Hellenic Coll (MA)
Hendrix Coll (AR)
Hillsdale Coll (MI)
Hobart and William Smith Colls (NY)
Hofstra U (NY)
Hollins U (VA)
Hope Coll (MI)
Hunter Coll of the City U of New York (NY)
Illinois Wesleyan U (IL)
Indiana U Bloomington (IN)
John Carroll U (OH)
The Johns Hopkins U (MD)
Kalamazoo Coll (MI)
Kent State U (OH)
Kenyon Coll (OH)
Knox Coll (IL)
La Salle U (PA)
Laurentian U (ON, Canada)
Lawrence U (WI)
Lehigh U (PA)
Lehman Coll of the City U of New York (NY)
Loyola U Chicago (IL)
Loyola U Maryland (MD)
Loyola U New Orleans (LA)
Luther Coll (IA)
Macalester Coll (MN)
Manhattan Coll (NY)
Manhattanville Coll (NY)
Marlboro Coll (VT)
Marquette U (WI)
Mercer U (GA)
Miami U (OH)
Middlebury Coll (VT)
Millsaps Coll (MS)

Monmouth Coll (IL)
Montclair State U (NJ)
Moravian Coll (PA)
Mount Allison U (NB, Canada)
Mount Holyoke Coll (MA)
New York U (NY)
North Central Coll (IL)
North Dakota State U (ND)
Oberlin Coll (OH)
The Ohio State U (OH)
Ohio U (OH)
Ohio Wesleyan U (OH)
Pacific Lutheran U (WA)
Penn State Abington (PA)
Penn State Altoona (PA)
Penn State Beaver (PA)
Penn State Berks (PA)
Penn State Brandywine (PA)
Penn State DuBois (PA)
Penn State Erie, The Behrend Coll (PA)
Penn State Fayette, The Eberly Campus (PA)
Penn State Greater Allegheny (PA)
Penn State Hazleton (PA)
Penn State Lehigh Valley (PA)
Penn State Mont Alto (PA)
Penn State New Kensington (PA)
Penn State Schuylkill (PA)
Penn State Shenango (PA)
Penn State U Park (PA)
Penn State Wilkes-Barre (PA)
Penn State Worthington Scranton (PA)
Penn State York (PA)
Pitzer Coll (CA)
Pomona Coll (CA)
Princeton U (NJ)
Randolph Coll (VA)
Randolph-Macon Coll (VA)
Reed Coll (OR)
Rhodes Coll (TN)
Rice U (TX)
Rockford Coll (IL)
Rollins Coll (FL)
Rutgers, The State U of New Jersey, Newark (NJ)
Rutgers, The State U of New Jersey, New Brunswick (NJ)
Saint Anselm Coll (NH)
St. Bonaventure U (NY)
St. Francis Xavier U (NS, Canada)
Saint John's U (MN)
Saint Joseph's Coll of Maine (ME)
Saint Louis U (MO)
Saint Michael's Coll (VT)
St. Olaf Coll (MN)
Samford U (AL)
San Diego State U (CA)
San Francisco State U (CA)
Santa Clara U (CA)
Sarah Lawrence Coll (NY)
Scripps Coll (CA)
Seattle Pacific U (WA)
Sewanee: The U of the South (TN)
Siena Coll (NY)
Skidmore Coll (NY)
Smith Coll (MA)
Southern Illinois U Carbondale (IL)
Stanford U (CA)
State U of New York at Binghamton (NY)
Swarthmore Coll (PA)
Sweet Briar Coll (VA)
Syracuse U (NY)
Temple U (PA)
Texas A&M U (TX)
Texas Tech U (TX)
Transylvania U (KY)
Trent U (ON, Canada)
Trinity Coll (CT)
Trinity U (TX)
Truman State U (MO)
Tufts U (MA)
Tulane U (LA)
Union Coll (NY)
U at Buffalo, the State U of New York (NY)
The U of Akron (OH)
U of Arkansas (AR)
The U of British Columbia (BC, Canada)
U of California, Berkeley (CA)
U of California, Irvine (CA)
U of California, Santa Barbara (CA)
U of California, Santa Cruz (CA)
U of Colorado Boulder (CO)
U of Dallas (TX)

U of Evansville (IN)
U of Florida (FL)
U of Georgia (GA)
U of Guelph (ON, Canada)
U of Hawaii at Manoa (HI)
U of Illinois at Chicago (IL)
The U of Iowa (IA)
The U of Kansas (KS)
U of Maine (ME)
U of Manitoba (MB, Canada)
U of Maryland, Coll Park (MD)
U of Mary Washington (VA)
U of Massachusetts Amherst (MA)
U of Massachusetts Boston (MA)
U of Miami (FL)
U of Michigan (MI)
U of Minnesota, Twin Cities Campus (MN)
U of Missouri (MO)
U of Nebraska–Lincoln (NE)
U of New Brunswick Fredericton (NB, Canada)
U of New Brunswick Saint John (NB, Canada)
U of New Hampshire (NH)
The U of North Carolina at Asheville (NC)
The U of North Carolina at Chapel Hill (NC)
The U of North Carolina at Greensboro (NC)
U of North Dakota (ND)
U of Notre Dame (IN)
U of Oklahoma (OK)
U of Oregon (OR)
U of Ottawa (ON, Canada)
U of Pennsylvania (PA)
U of Pittsburgh (PA)
U of Puget Sound (WA)
U of Regina (SK, Canada)
U of Rhode Island (RI)
U of Rochester (NY)
U of St. Thomas (MN)
U of South Carolina (SC)
U of Southern California (CA)
U of Southern Maine (ME)
U of South Florida (FL)
The U of Tennessee (TN)
The U of Texas at Austin (TX)
The U of Texas at San Antonio (TX)
U of the Pacific (CA)
The U of Toledo (OH)
U of Utah (UT)
U of Vermont (VT)
U of Virginia (VA)
U of Washington (WA)
U of Waterloo (ON, Canada)
The U of Western Ontario (ON, Canada)
U of Wisconsin–Madison (WI)
Valparaiso U (IN)
Vanderbilt U (TN)
Vassar Coll (NY)
Villanova U (PA)
Virginia Wesleyan Coll (VA)
Wabash Coll (IN)
Wake Forest U (NC)
Washington and Lee U (VA)
Washington U in St. Louis (MO)
Wayne State U (MI)
Wellesley Coll (MA)
Wesleyan U (CT)
Wheaton Coll (MA)
Whitman Coll (WA)
Wilfrid Laurier U (ON, Canada)
Willamette U (OR)
Williams Coll (MA)
Wright State U (OH)
Xavier U (OH)
Yale U (CT)

CLASSICS AND CLASSICAL LANGUAGES RELATED

Austin Coll (TX)
Bryn Mawr Coll (PA)
California State U, Long Beach (CA)
Canisius Coll (NY)
Columbia U, School of General Studies (NY)
Concordia Coll (MN)
Eckerd Coll (FL)
Lawrence U (WI)
Marquette U (WI)
New Coll of Florida (FL)
Ohio U (OH)
Rutgers, The State U of New Jersey, Newark (NJ)
Saint Louis U (MO)
Tulane U (LA)
U of California, Los Angeles (CA)

U of St. Thomas (MN)
Wheaton Coll (IL)
Xavier U (OH)

CLINICAL CHILD PSYCHOLOGY

St. John's U (NY)

CLINICAL LABORATORY SCIENCE/MEDICAL TECHNOLOGY

Abilene Christian U (TX)
Albany Coll of Pharmacy and Health Sciences (NY)
American U of Beirut (Lebanon)
Anderson U (IN)
Andrews U (MI)
Angelo State U (TX)
Arizona State U (AZ)
Arkansas State U (AR)
Arkansas Tech U (AR)
Armstrong Atlantic State U (GA)
Atlantic Union Coll (MA)
Auburn U (AL)
Augustana Coll (SD)
Austin Peay State U (TN)
Averett U (VA)
Ball State U (IN)
Barry U (FL)
Bellarmine U (KY)
Belmont U (TN)
Bemidji State U (MN)
Benedictine U (IL)
Bethune-Cookman U (FL)
Blackburn Coll (IL)
Blue Mountain Coll (MS)
Boise State U (ID)
Boston U (MA)
Bowling Green State U (OH)
Brigham Young U (UT)
California State U, Chico (CA)
California State U, Dominguez Hills (CA)
Cameron U (OK)
Campbellsville U (KY)
Carroll U (WI)
Carson-Newman Coll (TN)
The Catholic U of America (DC)
Cedarville U (OH)
Central Michigan U (MI)
Clarion U of Pennsylvania (PA)
Coker Coll (SC)
Coll of Saint Elizabeth (NJ)
Coll of Saint Mary (NE)
The Coll of Saint Rose (NY)
Coll of Staten Island of the City U of New York (NY)
Concord U (WV)
Defiance Coll (OH)
DePaul U (IL)
DeVry U, Phoenix (AZ)
Dordt Coll (IA)
East Central U (OK)
Eastern Illinois U (IL)
Eastern Michigan U (MI)
Eastern New Mexico U (NM)
East Stroudsburg U of Pennsylvania (PA)
Elmhurst Coll (IL)
Elmira Coll (NY)
Elon U (NC)
Emory & Henry Coll (VA)
Evangel U (MO)
Fairleigh Dickinson U, Coll at Florham (NJ)
Fairleigh Dickinson U, Metropolitan Campus (NJ)
Ferris State U (MI)
Florida Gulf Coast U (FL)
Gannon U (PA)
Georgia Health Sciences U (GA)
Georgian Court U (NJ)
Graceland U (IA)
Grand Valley State U (MI)
Greensboro Coll (NC)
Hartwick Coll (NY)
Holy Family U (PA)
Houghton Coll (NY)
Idaho State U (ID)
Illinois Coll (IL)
Illinois State U (IL)
Indiana State U (IN)
Indiana U Bloomington (IN)
Indiana U Kokomo (IN)
Indiana U of Pennsylvania (PA)
Indiana U–Purdue U Fort Wayne (IN)
Indiana U–Purdue U Indianapolis (IN)
Indiana U South Bend (IN)

Indiana U Southeast (IN)
Indiana Wesleyan U (IN)
Inter American U of Puerto Rico, Metropolitan Campus (PR)
Inter American U of Puerto Rico, San Germán Campus (PR)
Jamestown Coll (ND)
Kansas State U (KS)
Kean U (NJ)
Kent State U (OH)
Kentucky Wesleyan Coll (KY)
Keuka Coll (NY)
King Coll (TN)
King's Coll (PA)
Kutztown U of Pennsylvania (PA)
Lake Superior State U (MI)
Lamar U (TX)
Lebanon Valley Coll (PA)
Lee U (TN)
Lincoln Memorial U (TN)
Lincoln U (MO)
Long Island U, Brooklyn Campus (NY)
Long Island U, C.W. Post Campus (NY)
Longwood U (VA)
Loras Coll (IA)
Louisiana Coll (LA)
Loyola U Chicago (IL)
Madonna U (MI)
Malone U (OH)
Manchester Coll (IN)
Mansfield U of Pennsylvania (PA)
Marist Coll (NY)
Marquette U (WI)
Marshall U (WV)
Mary Baldwin Coll (VA)
Maryville U of Saint Louis (MO)
Marywood U (PA)
Mayville State U (ND)
McKendree U (IL)
Miami U (OH)
Michigan State U (MI)
Midwestern State U (TX)
Minnesota State U Mankato (MN)
Minnesota State U Moorhead (MN)
Minot State U (ND)
Misericordia U (PA)
Mississippi State U (MS)
Missouri Southern State U (MO)
Missouri State U (MO)
Monmouth U (NJ)
Moravian Coll (PA)
Morningside Coll (IA)
Mount Marty Coll (SD)
Mount Mercy U (IA)
Mount Saint Mary Coll (NY)
Mount Vernon Nazarene U (OH)
North Dakota State U (ND)
Northeastern State U (OK)
Northern Illinois U (IL)
Northern Michigan U (MI)
Northern State U (SD)
Northwestern Coll (IA)
Northwest Missouri State U (MO)
Oklahoma Christian U (OK)
Oklahoma Panhandle State U (OK)
Old Dominion U (VA)
Oregon State U (OR)
Our Lady of the Lake Coll (LA)
Prairie View A&M U (TX)
Purdue U (IN)
Purdue U Calumet (IN)
Quincy U (IL)
Ramapo Coll of New Jersey (NJ)
Rhode Island Coll (RI)
Rockhurst U (MO)
Rutgers, The State U of New Jersey, Camden (NJ)
Rutgers, The State U of New Jersey, Newark (NJ)
Rutgers, The State U of New Jersey, New Brunswick (NJ)
Sage Coll of Albany (NY)
Saginaw Valley State U (MI)
St. Catherine U (MN)
St. Edward's U (TX)
Saint Francis U (PA)
St. John's U (NY)
Saint Joseph's Coll (IN)
Saint Leo U (FL)
Saint Louis U (MO)
Saint Mary-of-the-Woods Coll (IN)
Saint Mary's U of Minnesota (MN)
St. Thomas Aquinas Coll (NY)
Salem State U (MA)
Salisbury U (MD)
Salve Regina U (RI)
Santa Fe Coll (FL)
Seton Hill U (PA)

South Dakota State U (SD)
Southeast Missouri State U (MO)
Southern Adventist U (TN)
Southern Arkansas U–Magnolia (AR)
Southern Wesleyan U (SC)
Southwestern Adventist U (TX)
State U of New York at Fredonia (NY)
State U of New York at Plattsburgh (NY)
State U of New York Upstate Medical U (NY)
Stony Brook U, State U of New York (NY)
Tarleton State U (TX)
Texas A&M U–Corpus Christi (TX)
Texas Southern U (TX)
Texas State U–San Marcos (TX)
Texas Woman's U (TX)
Thiel Coll (PA)
Thomas Edison State Coll (NJ)
Thomas More Coll (KY)
Trevecca Nazarene U (TN)
Tuskegee U (AL)
Union Coll (NE)
Union U (TN)
U at Buffalo, the State U of New York (NY)
The U of Alabama at Birmingham (AL)
The U of Arizona (AZ)
U of Arkansas for Medical Sciences (AR)
U of Bridgeport (CT)
U of Central Florida (FL)
U of Central Missouri (MO)
U of Cincinnati (OH)
U of Delaware (DE)
U of Evansville (IN)
The U of Findlay (OH)
U of Hartford (CT)
U of Hawaii at Manoa (HI)
U of Idaho (ID)
U of Illinois at Springfield (IL)
U of Indianapolis (IN)
The U of Iowa (IA)
The U of Kansas (KS)
U of Louisiana at Monroe (LA)
U of Maine (ME)
U of Mary Hardin-Baylor (TX)
U of Massachusetts Dartmouth (MA)
U of Michigan–Flint (MI)
U of Minnesota, Twin Cities Campus (MN)
U of Mississippi (MS)
U of Mount Union (OH)
U of Nevada, Las Vegas (NV)
U of New England (ME)
U of New Hampshire (NH)
The U of North Carolina at Chapel Hill (NC)
The U of North Carolina at Charlotte (NC)
The U of North Carolina at Greensboro (NC)
U of North Dakota (ND)
U of North Texas (TX)
U of Rhode Island (RI)
U of Rio Grande (OH)
U of St. Francis (IL)
U of Scranton (PA)
U of Sioux Falls (SD)
U of South Alabama (AL)
U of Southern Mississippi (MS)
U of South Florida (FL)
The U of Tennessee (TN)
The U of Texas at Arlington (TX)
The U of Texas at Austin (TX)
The U of Texas at San Antonio (TX)
The U of Texas at Tyler (TX)
The U of Texas–Pan American (TX)
The U of Texas Southwestern Medical Center at Dallas (TX)
U of the District of Columbia (DC)
U of the Sciences in Philadelphia (PA)
The U of Toledo (OH)
U of Utah (UT)
U of Vermont (VT)
U of Washington (WA)
U of West Florida (FL)
U of Wisconsin–La Crosse (WI)
U of Wisconsin–Stevens Point (WI)
Utah State U (UT)
Virginia Commonwealth U (VA)
Wake Forest U (NC)
Walla Walla U (WA)
Wartburg Coll (IA)
Wayne State U (MI)

Western Carolina U (NC)
Western Connecticut State U (CT)
Western Illinois U (IL)
Western Kentucky U (KY)
West Liberty U (WV)
West Virginia U (WV)
Wichita State U (KS)
Wilkes U (PA)
William Jewell Coll (MO)
Winona State U (MN)
Wright State U (OH)
Xavier U (OH)
York Coll of Pennsylvania (PA)
York Coll of the City U of New York (NY)
Youngstown State U (OH)

CLINICAL/MEDICAL LABORATORY ASSISTANT

Edinboro U of Pennsylvania (PA)
Saint Louis U (MO)

CLINICAL/MEDICAL LABORATORY SCIENCE AND ALLIED PROFESSIONS RELATED

Allen Coll (IA)
Auburn U (AL)
Bloomfield Coll (NJ)
Hunter Coll of the City U of New York (NY)
Mississippi State U (MS)
Roosevelt U (IL)
Saint Louis U (MO)
U of Massachusetts Lowell (MA)

CLINICAL/MEDICAL LABORATORY TECHNOLOGY

Auburn U (AL)
Barry U (FL)
Delaware State U (DE)
Edinboro U of Pennsylvania (PA)
Holy Family U (PA)
Indiana U–Purdue U Fort Wayne (IN)
Long Island U, C.W. Post Campus (NY)
Longwood U (VA)
Northern State U (SD)
Our Lady of the Lake Coll (LA)
Penn State DuBois (PA)
St. Thomas Aquinas Coll (NY)
Sonoma State U (CA)
Tabor Coll (KS)
The U of British Columbia (BC, Canada)
U of Science and Arts of Oklahoma (OK)
Viterbo U (WI)
Washburn U (KS)
Winona State U (MN)
York Coll of the City U of New York (NY)

CLINICAL/MEDICAL SOCIAL WORK

New Mexico Highlands U (NM)
U of St. Thomas (MN)

CLINICAL NUTRITION

Loyola U Chicago (IL)
Messiah Coll (PA)
U of North Dakota (ND)

CLINICAL PSYCHOLOGY

Averett U (VA)
Biola U (CA)
Husson U (ME)
Keene State Coll (NH)
Lakehead U (ON, Canada)
Lamar U (TX)
Mansfield U of Pennsylvania (PA)
Moravian Coll (PA)
Simon Fraser U (BC, Canada)
The U of British Columbia (BC, Canada)
U of Michigan–Flint (MI)
U of New Brunswick Fredericton (NB, Canada)
Western State Coll of Colorado (CO)

COGNITIVE PSYCHOLOGY AND PSYCHOLINGUISTICS

Averett U (VA)
Brown U (RI)
California State U, Stanislaus (CA)
Dartmouth Coll (NH)
Free Will Baptist Bible Coll (TN)
The Johns Hopkins U (MD)
Lawrence U (WI)

State U of New York at Fredonia (NY)
State U of New York at New Paltz (NY)
Truman State U (MO)
The U of Arizona (AZ)
The U of British Columbia (BC, Canada)
U of Cincinnati (OH)
U of Georgia (GA)
U of Houston (TX)
The U of Kansas (KS)
U of Maine (ME)
U of Massachusetts Amherst (MA)
U of Minnesota, Twin Cities Campus (MN)
U of Oklahoma Health Sciences Center (OK)
U of Oregon (OR)
U of Redlands (CA)
U of Rhode Island (RI)
The U of South Dakota (SD)
The U of Texas at Austin (TX)
The U of Toledo (OH)
U of Vermont (VT)
The U of Western Ontario (ON, Canada)
U of Wisconsin–Eau Claire (WI)
U of Wisconsin–River Falls (WI)
U of Wisconsin–Stevens Point (WI)
Wayne State U (MI)
Western Carolina U (NC)
Western Illinois U (IL)
Western Kentucky U (KY)
Wichita State U (KS)
Winthrop U (SC)
Worcester State U (MA)
Xavier U of Louisiana (LA)

COMMUNICATIONS TECHNOLOGIES AND SUPPORT SERVICES RELATED

Alverno Coll (WI)
Chestnut Hill Coll (PA)
Framingham State U (MA)
Indiana U Bloomington (IN)
Lesley U (MA)
Lewis U (IL)
Saint Mary-of-the-Woods Coll (IN)
Salve Regina U (RI)
The U of Scranton (PA)

COMMUNICATIONS TECHNOLOGY

Cedarville U (OH)
Eastern Michigan U (MI)
East Stroudsburg U of Pennsylvania (PA)
Inter American U of Puerto Rico, Bayamón Campus (PR)
Lawrence Technological U (MI)
Michigan State U (MI)
Sacred Heart U (CT)
Saint Mary-of-the-Woods Coll (IN)
Salve Regina U (RI)
Southern Adventist U (TN)
Suffolk U (MA)
York Coll of the City U of New York (NY)

COMMUNITY HEALTH AND PREVENTIVE MEDICINE

Bowling Green State U (OH)
Florida Gulf Coast U (FL)
Governors State U (IL)
Hofstra U (NY)
Indiana U Bloomington (IN)
Minnesota State U Moorhead (MN)
Portland State U (OR)
Texas A&M U–Kingsville (TX)
Tufts U (MA)
U of Florida (FL)
U of Wisconsin–Eau Claire (WI)
U of Wisconsin–La Crosse (WI)
Western Kentucky U (KY)

COMMUNITY HEALTH SERVICES COUNSELING

Delaware State U (DE)
Eastern Washington U (WA)
Indiana State U (IN)
Indiana U–Purdue U Fort Wayne (IN)
James Madison U (VA)
Johnson C. Smith U (NC)
Longwood U (VA)
Marian U (WI)
Michigan State U (MI)
Minnesota State U Moorhead (MN)

Morris Coll (SC)
Northeastern Illinois U (IL)
Northern Illinois U (IL)
Northern Michigan U (MI)
Ohio U (OH)
Prairie View A&M U (TX)
Texas A&M U (TX)
The U of Kansas (KS)
U of Massachusetts Lowell (MA)
U of Nebraska at Omaha (NE)
U of Northern Iowa (IA)
U of Pennsylvania (PA)
U of the Cumberlands (KY)
U of West Florida (FL)
Western Connecticut State U (CT)
Worcester State U (MA)
Youngstown State U (OH)

COMMUNITY ORGANIZATION AND ADVOCACY

Alverno Coll (WI)
Bemidji State U (MN)
Bryant U (RI)
Central Michigan U (MI)
Cleveland State U (OH)
DePaul U (IL)
Emory & Henry Coll (VA)
Goddard Coll (VT)
Indiana Wesleyan U (IN)
Lewis U (IL)
Mercer U (GA)
New Mexico State U (NM)
New York U (NY)
Northern State U (SD)
Northland Coll (WI)
Prescott Coll (AZ)
Providence Coll (RI)
Roosevelt U (IL)
Saint Martin's U (WA)
Siena Heights U (MI)
Southern Arkansas U–Magnolia (AR)
State U of New York Empire State Coll (NY)
Thomas Edison State Coll (NJ)
U of Alaska Fairbanks (AK)
U of Baltimore (MD)
U of Delaware (DE)
U of Hartford (CT)
U of Massachusetts Boston (MA)
U of Saint Mary (KS)
The U of Toledo (OH)

COMMUNITY PSYCHOLOGY

Clayton State U (GA)
Goddard Coll (VT)
Montana State U Billings (MT)
New York Inst of Technology (NY)
Rogers State U (OK)
U of Miami (FL)
U of Minnesota, Crookston (MN)
U of Saint Mary (KS)
U of Washington, Bothell (WA)
Wilfrid Laurier U (ON, Canada)

COMPARATIVE LITERATURE

The American U of Paris (France)
Arcadia U (PA)
Bard Coll (NY)
Barnard Coll (NY)
Barry U (FL)
Beloit Coll (WI)
Blackburn Coll (IL)
Boston U (MA)
Brandeis U (MA)
Brock U (ON, Canada)
Brown U (RI)
Bryn Mawr Coll (PA)
California State U, Fullerton (CA)
California State U, Long Beach (CA)
Carson-Newman Coll (TN)
Case Western Reserve U (OH)
Castleton State Coll (VT)
Christendom Coll (VA)
Christopher Newport U (VA)
City Coll of the City U of New York (NY)
Clark U (MA)
Coll of the Atlantic (ME)
Coll of the Holy Cross (MA)
Coll of the Humanities and Sciences, Harrison Middleton U (AZ)
The Coll of Wooster (OH)
The Colorado Coll (CO)
Columbia U, School of General Studies (NY)
Cornell U (NY)
Dartmouth Coll (NH)
Earlham Coll (IN)

Eckerd Coll (FL)
Eugene Lang Coll The New School for Liberal Arts (NY)
Franklin Coll Switzerland (Switzerland)
Franklin Pierce U (NH)
Georgetown U (DC)
Gettysburg Coll (PA)
Graceland U (IA)
Grove City Coll (PA)
Hamilton Coll (NY)
Harvard U (MA)
Haverford Coll (PA)
Hillsdale Coll (MI)
Hobart and William Smith Colls (NY)
Hofstra U (NY)
Houghton Coll (NY)
Hunter Coll of the City U of New York (NY)
Indiana U Bloomington (IN)
Inter American U of Puerto Rico, San Germán Campus (PR)
John Carroll U (OH)
The Johns Hopkins U (MD)
Johnson State Coll (VT)
Lake Superior State U (MI)
Lycoming Coll (PA)
Manchester Coll (IN)
Marlboro Coll (VT)
Mills Coll (CA)
Minnesota State U Mankato (MN)
Mount Allison U (NB, Canada)
New Coll of Florida (FL)
New England Coll (NH)
New York U (NY)
Northwest U (WA)
Oberlin Coll (OH)
The Ohio State U (OH)
Ohio Wesleyan U (OH)
Pacific U (OR)
Penn State Abington (PA)
Penn State Altoona (PA)
Penn State Beaver (PA)
Penn State Berks (PA)
Penn State Brandywine (PA)
Penn State DuBois (PA)
Penn State Erie, The Behrend Coll (PA)
Penn State Fayette, The Eberly Campus (PA)
Penn State Greater Allegheny (PA)
Penn State Hazleton (PA)
Penn State Lehigh Valley (PA)
Penn State Mont Alto (PA)
Penn State New Kensington (PA)
Penn State Schuylkill (PA)
Penn State Shenango (PA)
Penn State U Park (PA)
Penn State Wilkes-Barre (PA)
Penn State Worthington Scranton (PA)
Penn State York (PA)
Princeton U (NJ)
Purchase Coll, State U of New York (NY)
Purdue U (IN)
Queens Coll of the City U of New York (NY)
Quinnipiac U (CT)
Ramapo Coll of New Jersey (NJ)
Reed Coll (OR)
Rockford Coll (IL)
Rutgers, The State U of New Jersey, New Brunswick (NJ)
St. Catherine U (MN)
Saint Francis U (PA)
Saint Mary's Coll of California (CA)
San Diego State U (CA)
San Francisco State U (CA)
Sarah Lawrence Coll (NY)
Sewanee: The U of the South (TN)
Shimer Coll (IL)
Smith Coll (MA)
Sonoma State U (CA)
Stanford U (CA)
State U of New York at Binghamton (NY)
State U of New York Coll at Geneseo (NY)
State U of New York Coll at Old Westbury (NY)
Stony Brook U, State U of New York (NY)
Swarthmore Coll (PA)
Trent U (ON, Canada)
Trinity Coll (CT)
United States Military Acad (NY)
U of Baltimore (MD)
U of California, Berkeley (CA)
U of California, Davis (CA)

U of California, Irvine (CA)
U of California, Los Angeles (CA)
U of California, Merced (CA)
U of California, Santa Barbara (CA)
U of California, Santa Cruz (CA)
U of Delaware (DE)
U of Georgia (GA)
The U of Iowa (IA)
U of La Verne (CA)
U of Massachusetts Amherst (MA)
U of Michigan (MI)
U of Minnesota, Twin Cities Campus (MN)
U of Nevada, Las Vegas (NV)
U of New Brunswick Fredericton (NB, Canada)
The U of North Carolina at Chapel Hill (NC)
U of Oregon (OR)
U of Pennsylvania (PA)
U of Pittsburgh at Greensburg (PA)
U of Pittsburgh at Johnstown (PA)
U of Redlands (CA)
U of Rochester (NY)
U of Saskatchewan (SK, Canada)
U of South Carolina (SC)
U of Southern California (CA)
The U of Texas at Dallas (TX)
The U of Toledo (OH)
U of Utah (UT)
U of Virginia (VA)
U of Washington (WA)
The U of Western Ontario (ON, Canada)
U of Wisconsin–Madison (WI)
Washington U in St. Louis (MO)
Wellesley Coll (MA)
Willamette U (OR)
William Paterson U of New Jersey (NJ)
Williams Coll (MA)
Yale U (CT)

COMPUTATIONAL BIOLOGY

Case Western Reserve U (OH)
Purdue U (IN)

COMPUTATIONAL MATHEMATICS

Arizona State U (AZ)
Asbury U (KY)
California Inst of Technology (CA)
Carnegie Mellon U (PA)
Coll of Saint Benedict (MN)
Embry-Riddle Aeronautical U–Daytona (FL)
Indiana U–Purdue U Fort Wayne (IN)
Marist Coll (NY)
Marquette U (WI)
Michigan State U (MI)
Saint John's U (MN)
Siena Coll (NY)
U of California, Davis (CA)
U of California, Los Angeles (CA)
U of Puerto Rico at Humacao (PR)
U of Southern California (CA)
U of Waterloo (ON, Canada)

COMPUTATIONAL SCIENCE

Purdue U (IN)

COMPUTER AND INFORMATION SCIENCES

Adelphi U (NY)
Alabama Ag and Mech U (AL)
Albany State U (GA)
Alcorn State U (MS)
Alverno Coll (WI)
Amberton U (TX)
American Public U System (WV)
American U (DC)
American U in Bulgaria (Bulgaria)
The American U of Paris (France)
Andrews U (MI)
Angelo State U (TX)
Anna Maria Coll (MA)
Aquinas Coll (MI)
Arcadia U (PA)
Arizona State U (AZ)
Arkansas State U (AR)
Arkansas Tech U (AR)
Assumption Coll (MA)
Athabasca U (AB, Canada)
Auburn U (AL)
Austin Peay State U (TN)
Avila U (MO)
Baker Coll of Muskegon (MI)
Ball State U (IN)

Barnard Coll (NY)
Barton Coll (NC)
Bellarmine U (KY)
Bennington Coll (VT)
Bentley U (MA)
Berea Coll (KY)
Bethel U (MN)
Bloomfield Coll (NJ)
Bluefield State Coll (WV)
Bob Jones U (SC)
Boise State U (ID)
Boston Coll (MA)
Bowie State U (MD)
Bowling Green State U (OH)
Brewton-Parker Coll (GA)
Bryant U (RI)
Bucknell U (PA)
Butler U (IN)
California State U, Los Angeles (CA)
California State U, San Bernardino (CA)
California State U, Stanislaus (CA)
Cameron U (OK)
Carroll U (WI)
Castleton State Coll (VT)
The Catholic U of America (DC)
Cedar Crest Coll (PA)
Central Connecticut State U (CT)
Central State U (OH)
Champlain Coll (VT)
Chapman U (CA)
Chatham U (PA)
Chestnut Hill Coll (PA)
Christopher Newport U (VA)
The Citadel, The Military Coll of South Carolina (SC)
Clarion U of Pennsylvania (PA)
Clark Atlanta U (GA)
Clarke U (IA)
Clemson U (SC)
Cleveland State U (OH)
Coastal Carolina U (SC)
Coll of Charleston (SC)
Coll of Mount St. Joseph (OH)
The Coll of New Jersey (NJ)
Coll of Saint Elizabeth (NJ)
Coll of Saint Mary (NE)
The Coll of Saint Rose (NY)
The Coll of St. Scholastica (MN)
The Coll of William and Mary (VA)
Colorado State U (CO)
Columbia Coll (MO)
Columbus State U (GA)
Concordia Coll (MN)
Concordia U Chicago (IL)
Cornell U (NY)
Covenant Coll (GA)
Dakota State U (SD)
Dallas Baptist U (TX)
Delaware State U (DE)
DEREE - The American Coll of Greece (Greece)
Dickinson Coll (PA)
Dixie State Coll of Utah (UT)
Doane Coll (NE)
Dominican Coll (NY)
Dowling Coll (NY)
Drury U (MO)
Earlham Coll (IN)
East Central U (OK)
Eastern Michigan U (MI)
Eastern New Mexico U (NM)
Eastern Oregon U (OR)
Eastern Washington U (WA)
East Stroudsburg U of Pennsylvania (PA)
East Tennessee State U (TN)
ECPI Coll of Technology, Virginia Beach (VA)
Edgewood Coll (WI)
Edinboro U of Pennsylvania (PA)
Elizabethtown Coll (PA)
Elon U (NC)
Emmanuel Coll (GA)
Emmaus Bible Coll (IA)
Emporia State U (KS)
Fairfield U (CT)
Fairleigh Dickinson U, Coll at Florham (NJ)
Felician Coll (NJ)
Fisher Coll (MA)
Fitchburg State U (MA)
Florida Ag and Mech U (FL)
Florida Atlantic U (FL)
Florida Gulf Coast U (FL)
Florida Intl U (FL)
Fort Lewis Coll (CO)
Framingham State U (MA)
Francis Marion U (SC)
Franklin Coll (IN)

Franklin U (OH)
Freed-Hardeman U (TN)
Friends U (KS)
Gallaudet U (DC)
Gannon U (PA)
Gardner-Webb U (NC)
Geneva Coll (PA)
George Fox U (OR)
Georgetown Coll (KY)
Georgia Coll & State U (GA)
Georgia Inst of Technology (GA)
Georgia Southern U (GA)
Georgia State U (GA)
Goldey-Beacom Coll (DE)
Grace Bible Coll (MI)
Grand Valley State U (MI)
Greenville Coll (IL)
Grove City Coll (PA)
Guilford Coll (NC)
Hamilton Coll (NY)
Hannibal-LaGrange U (MO)
Harrisburg U of Science and
    Technology (PA)
Hartwick Coll (NY)
Hawai'i Pacific U (HI)
Herzing U (GA)
Herzing U, Madison (WI)
Holy Family U (PA)
Hope Coll (MI)
Huston-Tillotson U (TX)
Idaho State U (ID)
Illinois Inst of Technology (IL)
Indiana State U (IN)
Indiana U Bloomington (IN)
Indiana U Kokomo (IN)
Indiana U Northwest (IN)
Indiana U of Pennsylvania (PA)
Indiana U–Purdue U Indianapolis
    (IN)
Indiana U South Bend (IN)
Indiana U Southeast (IN)
Indiana Wesleyan U (IN)
Inter American U of Puerto Rico,
    Metropolitan Campus (PR)
Iowa Wesleyan Coll (IA)
Ithaca Coll (NY)
Jacksonville State U (AL)
James Madison U (VA)
John Jay Coll of Criminal Justice of
    the City U of New York (NY)
The Johns Hopkins U (MD)
Johnson C. Smith U (NC)
Jones Coll, Jacksonville (FL)
Juniata Coll (PA)
Kansas State U (KS)
Kean U (NJ)
Keene State Coll (NH)
Kennesaw State U (GA)
Kentucky State U (KY)
Kentucky Wesleyan Coll (KY)
King's Coll (PA)
Knox Coll (IL)
Kuyper Coll (MI)
LaGrange Coll (GA)
Lane Coll (TN)
La Roche Coll (PA)
La Salle U (PA)
Lehman Coll of the City U of New
    York (NY)
Le Moyne Coll (NY)
Lewis-Clark State Coll (ID)
Liberty U (VA)
Lincoln Memorial U (TN)
Lindenwood U (MO)
Lock Haven U of Pennsylvania (PA)
Long Island U, Brooklyn Campus
    (NY)
Long Island U, C.W. Post Campus
    (NY)
Loyola Marymount U (CA)
Loyola U Chicago (IL)
Loyola U Maryland (MD)
Lubbock Christian U (TX)
Mansfield U of Pennsylvania (PA)
Marist Coll (NY)
Marquette U (WI)
Marshall U (WV)
Mars Hill Coll (NC)
Maryville Coll (TN)
Massachusetts Coll of Liberal Arts
    (MA)
The Master's Coll and Sem (CA)
Mayville State U (ND)
McDaniel Coll (MD)
McMurry U (TX)
Mesa State Coll (CO)
Miami U (OH)
Michigan State U (MI)

Midway Coll (KY)
Midwestern State U (TX)
Millersville U of Pennsylvania (PA)
Milligan Coll (TN)
Minnesota State U Moorhead (MN)
Misericordia U (PA)
Mississippi State U (MS)
Missouri Baptist U (MO)
Missouri Southern State U (MO)
Monmouth U (NJ)
Montreat Coll, Montreat (NC)
Morehead State U (KY)
Morehouse Coll (GA)
Mount St. Mary's U (MD)
Mount Vernon Nazarene U (OH)
Murray State U (KY)
Neumann U (PA)
Neumont U (UT)
New England Coll (NH)
New England Inst of Technology
    (RI)
New Jersey City U (NJ)
New Jersey Inst of Technology (NJ)
New Mexico Highlands U (NM)
New Mexico State U (NM)
New York Inst of Technology (NY)
New York U (NY)
Northeastern Illinois U (IL)
Northeastern U (MA)
Northern Arizona U (AZ)
Northern Kentucky U (KY)
Northern Michigan U (MI)
North Georgia Coll & State U (GA)
Northwest Missouri State U (MO)
Notre Dame de Namur U (CA)
Nova Southeastern U (FL)
The Ohio State U (OH)
Ohio U (OH)
Oklahoma Panhandle State U (OK)
Oklahoma State U (OK)
Old Dominion U (VA)
Oregon State U (OR)
Penn State Abington (PA)
Penn State Altoona (PA)
Penn State Beaver (PA)
Penn State Berks (PA)
Penn State Brandywine (PA)
Penn State DuBois (PA)
Penn State Erie, The Behrend Coll
    (PA)
Penn State Fayette, The Eberly
    Campus (PA)
Penn State Greater Allegheny (PA)
Penn State Harrisburg (PA)
Penn State Hazleton (PA)
Penn State Lehigh Valley (PA)
Penn State Mont Alto (PA)
Penn State New Kensington (PA)
Penn State Schuylkill (PA)
Penn State Shenango (PA)
Penn State U Park (PA)
Penn State Wilkes-Barre (PA)
Penn State Worthington Scranton
    (PA)
Penn State York (PA)
Philadelphia U (PA)
Pikeville Coll (KY)
Portland State U (OR)
Prairie View A&M U (TX)
Principia Coll (IL)
Purdue U (IN)
Purdue U Calumet (IN)
Ramapo Coll of New Jersey (NJ)
Rhode Island Coll (RI)
Rice U (TX)
Rider U (NJ)
Rollins Coll (FL)
Rowan U (NJ)
Rutgers, The State U of New
    Jersey, Camden (NJ)
Rutgers, The State U of New
    Jersey, Newark (NJ)
Sacred Heart U (CT)
Saginaw Valley State U (MI)
St. Bonaventure U (NY)
St. Catherine U (MN)
St. Edward's U (TX)
St. Francis Xavier U (NS, Canada)
St. John's U (NY)
Saint Joseph's Coll (IN)
Saint Joseph's U (PA)
Saint Leo U (FL)
Saint Louis U (MO)
Saint Mary-of-the-Woods Coll (IN)
St. Mary's Coll of Maryland (MD)
St. Norbert Coll (WI)
Saint Xavier U (IL)

Salem State U (MA)
Salisbury U (MD)
Sam Houston State U (TX)
Shepherd U (WV)
Shippensburg U of Pennsylvania
    (PA)
Shorter U (GA)
Siena Coll (NY)
Siena Heights U (MI)
Sierra Nevada Coll (NV)
Simmons Coll (MA)
Simpson Coll (IA)
Skidmore Coll (NY)
Skyline Coll (VA)
South Dakota State U (SD)
Southeastern Oklahoma State U
    (OK)
Southeast Missouri State U (MO)
Southern Arkansas U–Magnolia
    (AR)
Southern Nazarene U (OK)
Southern Wesleyan U (SC)
Springfield Coll (MA)
Spring Hill Coll (AL)
State U of New York at Binghamton
    (NY)
State U of New York at New Paltz
    (NY)
State U of New York at Plattsburgh
    (NY)
State U of New York Coll at Old
    Westbury (NY)
State U of New York Coll at
    Potsdam (NY)
Stephen F. Austin State U (TX)
Stetson U (FL)
Stevenson U (MD)
Suffolk U (MA)
Swarthmore Coll (PA)
Syracuse U (NY)
Tarleton State U (TX)
Taylor U (IN)
Temple U (PA)
Tennessee Wesleyan Coll (TN)
Texas A&M U–Kingsville (TX)
Texas Christian U (TX)
Texas Southern U (TX)
Texas State U–San Marcos (TX)
Texas Tech U (TX)
Texas Wesleyan U (TX)
Texas Woman's U (TX)
Tiffin U (OH)
Towson U (MD)
Transylvania U (KY)
Trinity U (TX)
Troy U (AL)
Truman State U (MO)
Tulane U (LA)
Union Coll (NY)
United States Military Acad (NY)
United States Naval Acad (MD)
The U of Alabama (AL)
The U of Alabama at Birmingham
    (AL)
The U of Alabama in Huntsville (AL)
U of Alaska Fairbanks (AK)
The U of Arizona (AZ)
U of Arkansas (AR)
U of Arkansas–Fort Smith (AR)
U of Baltimore (MD)
U of California, Irvine (CA)
U of California, Los Angeles (CA)
U of Central Florida (FL)
U of Central Missouri (MO)
U of Cincinnati (OH)
U of Colorado at Colorado Springs
    (CO)
U of Colorado Denver (CO)
U of Delaware (DE)
U of Dubuque (IA)
U of Florida (FL)
U of Guelph (ON, Canada)
U of Hartford (CT)
U of Hawaii at Manoa (HI)
U of Houston (TX)
U of Houston–Clear Lake (TX)
U of Houston–Downtown (TX)
The U of Kansas (KS)
U of Louisiana at Lafayette (LA)
U of Maine at Augusta (ME)
U of Mary Hardin-Baylor (TX)
U of Maryland, Coll Park (MD)
U of Maryland U Coll (MD)
U of Mary Washington (VA)
U of Massachusetts Boston (MA)
U of Massachusetts Dartmouth
    (MA)
U of Michigan (MI)

U of Michigan–Dearborn (MI)
U of Michigan–Flint (MI)
U of Minnesota, Duluth (MN)
U of Mississippi (MS)
U of Missouri (MO)
U of Missouri–St. Louis (MO)
U of Mobile (AL)
U of Nebraska–Lincoln (NE)
U of Nevada, Reno (NV)
U of New Hampshire (NH)
U of New Haven (CT)
U of North Dakota (ND)
U of North Florida (FL)
U of North Texas (TX)
U of Notre Dame (IN)
U of Oregon (OR)
U of Ottawa (ON, Canada)
U of Pittsburgh at Greensburg (PA)
U of Rhode Island (RI)
U of Saint Mary (KS)
U of St. Thomas (MN)
U of San Francisco (CA)
U of Science and Arts of Oklahoma
    (OK)
U of Sioux Falls (SD)
U of South Alabama (AL)
U of South Carolina (SC)
U of South Carolina Beaufort (SC)
U of South Carolina Upstate (SC)
The U of South Dakota (SD)
U of Southern California (CA)
U of Southern Indiana (IN)
U of Southern Mississippi (MS)
U of South Florida (FL)
The U of Tampa (FL)
The U of Texas at Austin (TX)
The U of Texas at Dallas (TX)
The U of Texas at Tyler (TX)
The U of Texas of the Permian
    Basin (TX)
The U of Texas–Pan American (TX)
U of Vermont (VT)
U of Virginia (VA)
U of Washington (WA)
U of Washington, Bothell (WA)
The U of Western Ontario (ON,
    Canada)
U of West Florida (FL)
U of West Georgia (GA)
U of Wisconsin–Eau Claire (WI)
U of Wisconsin–La Crosse (WI)
U of Wisconsin–Madison (WI)
U of Wisconsin–River Falls (WI)
U of Wisconsin–Stevens Point (WI)
U of Wisconsin–Superior (WI)
U of Wisconsin–Whitewater (WI)
Utah State U (UT)
Valdosta State U (GA)
Vassar Coll (NY)
Virginia Commonwealth U (VA)
Virginia Polytechnic Inst and State
    U (VA)
Viterbo U (WI)
Wake Forest U (NC)
Walden U (MN)
Wartburg Coll (IA)
Washburn U (KS)
Washington State U (WA)
Washington U in St. Louis (MO)
Waynesburg U (PA)
Wayne State Coll (NE)
Wayne State U (MI)
Webber Intl U (FL)
Webster U (MO)
Wentworth Inst of Technology (MA)
West Chester U of Pennsylvania
    (PA)
Western Illinois U (IL)
Western Kentucky U (KY)
Western Michigan U (MI)
Westminster Coll (UT)
Wheeling Jesuit U (WV)
Wichita State U (KS)
Widener U (PA)
Wilkes U (PA)
Winona State U (MN)
Worcester Polytechnic Inst (MA)
Worcester State U (MA)
Wright State U (OH)
Xavier U of Louisiana (LA)
Yale U (CT)

**COMPUTER AND INFORMATION
SCIENCES AND SUPPORT
SERVICES RELATED**

Arizona State U (AZ)
Bloomsburg U of Pennsylvania (PA)
Cabrini Coll (PA)

California State U, Chico (CA)
California State U, Los Angeles
    (CA)
Coll of Staten Island of the City U of
    New York (NY)
Columbia Coll (SC)
Columbia Coll Chicago (IL)
DePaul U (IL)
The Evergreen State Coll (WA)
Ferris State U (MI)
Hofstra U (NY)
Husson U (ME)
Indiana Tech (IN)
Indiana U East (IN)
Indiana U–Purdue U Indianapolis
    (IN)
Inter American U of Puerto Rico,
    Bayamón Campus (PR)
Inter American U of Puerto Rico,
    Guayama Campus (PR)
John Jay Coll of Criminal Justice of
    the City U of New York (NY)
Keene State Coll (NH)
Lehigh U (PA)
Limestone Coll (SC)
Long Island U, C.W. Post Campus
    (NY)
Mayville State U (ND)
Missouri U of Science and
    Technology (MO)
Mountain State U (WV)
New Jersey Inst of Technology (NJ)
New York U (NY)
Purdue U (IN)
Purdue U Calumet (IN)
Purdue U North Central (IN)
Southern Adventist U (TN)
Taylor U (IN)
Tiffin U (OH)
U of Evansville (IN)
U of Maryland U Coll (MD)
U of Michigan–Flint (MI)
U of Mount Union (OH)
U of Northern Iowa (IA)
U of Notre Dame (IN)
U of Pittsburgh (PA)
The U of Scranton (PA)
U of Washington, Bothell (WA)
Utah State U (UT)
Walden U (MN)
Washington U in St. Louis (MO)

**COMPUTER AND INFORMATION
SCIENCES RELATED**

California State U, Dominguez Hills
    (CA)
California State U, Monterey Bay
    (CA)
Carnegie Mellon U (PA)
Coll of Charleston (SC)
The Colorado Coll (CO)
Columbia U, School of General
    Studies (NY)
Dakota Wesleyan U (SD)
Eastern Illinois U (IL)
Limestone Coll (SC)
Maryville Coll (TN)
Missouri State U (MO)
Neumont U (UT)
New Jersey Inst of Technology (NJ)
Taylor U (IN)
Université de Sherbrooke (QC,
    Canada)
U of California, Irvine (CA)
U of Wisconsin–Stout (WI)
Wagner Coll (NY)
Walden U (MN)
West Virginia U (WV)
Wilfrid Laurier U (ON, Canada)

**COMPUTER AND INFORMATION
SYSTEMS SECURITY**

American Public U System (WV)
Champlain Coll (VT)
Dakota State U (SD)
Davenport U, Grand Rapids (MI)
DePaul U (IL)
East Stroudsburg U of Pennsylvania
    (PA)
ECPI Coll of Technology, Virginia
    Beach (VA)
Emporia State U (KS)
Goldey-Beacom Coll (DE)
Indiana Tech (IN)
ITT Tech Inst, Bessemer (AL)
ITT Tech Inst, Madison (AL)
ITT Tech Inst, Mobile (AL)
ITT Tech Inst, Phoenix (AZ)

COMPUTER HARDWARE TECHNOLOGY

Purdue U (IN)
Temple U (PA)

COMPUTER/INFORMATION TECHNOLOGY SERVICES ADMINISTRATION RELATED

Anna Maria Coll (MA)
Champlain Coll (VT)
Chestnut Hill Coll (PA)
Concordia U, St. Paul (MN)
Dordt Coll (IA)
Endicott Coll (MA)
Florida State Coll at Jacksonville (FL)
Friends U (KS)
Holy Names U (CA)
Kent State U at Trumbull (OH)
Limestone Coll (SC)
Marywood U (PA)
Missouri State U (MO)
Point Park U (PA)
Robert Morris U (PA)
Saint Mary's U of Minnesota (MN)
St. Petersburg Coll (FL)
Southern Methodist U (TX)
State U of New York Coll of Technology at Alfred (NY)
State U of New York Coll of Technology at Delhi (NY)
U of Maryland, Baltimore County (MD)
U of Maryland U Coll (MD)
Washington U in St. Louis (MO)

COMPUTER INSTALLATION AND REPAIR TECHNOLOGY

Inter American U of Puerto Rico, Bayamón Campus (PR)

COMPUTER PROGRAMMING

Andrews U (MI)
Arcadia U (PA)
Baker Coll of Owosso (MI)
Belmont U (TN)
Bloomfield Coll (NJ)
Brock U (ON, Canada)
Clemson U (SC)
The Coll of Saint Rose (NY)
DePaul U (IL)
Dordt Coll (IA)
ECPI Coll of Technology, Virginia Beach (VA)
Everest U, Lakeland (FL)
Everest U, Tampa (FL)
Franklin Pierce U (NH)
Gannon U (PA)
Hardin-Simmons U (TX)
Inter American U of Puerto Rico, Bayamón Campus (PR)
Inter American U of Puerto Rico, San Germán Campus (PR)
Intl Business Coll, Fort Wayne (IN)
Kent State U (OH)
Lamar U (TX)
La Salle U (PA)
Limestone Coll (SC)
Marist Coll (NY)
Minnesota State U Mankato (MN)
Morningside Coll (IA)
Neumont U (UT)
Pennsylvania Coll of Technology (PA)
Purdue U (IN)
Saint Francis U (PA)
Union Coll (KY)
Université de Sherbrooke (QC, Canada)
U of Advancing Technology (AZ)
U of Michigan–Dearborn (MI)
U of Mount Union (OH)
The U of Toledo (OH)
The U of Western Ontario (ON, Canada)
Walla Walla U (WA)
Winona State U (MN)
Youngstown State U (OH)

COMPUTER PROGRAMMING RELATED

Neumont U (UT)
Purdue U (IN)

COMPUTER PROGRAMMING (SPECIFIC APPLICATIONS)

DePaul U (IL)

Kent State U (OH)
Neumont U (UT)
Purdue U (IN)
Southern Polytechnic State U (GA)
U of Washington, Bothell (WA)

COMPUTER PROGRAMMING (VENDOR/PRODUCT CERTIFICATION)

Marist Coll (NY)
Neumont U (UT)
Purdue U (IN)

COMPUTER SCIENCE

Abilene Christian U (TX)
Acadia U (NS, Canada)
Adams State Coll (CO)
Alabama State U (AL)
Albion Coll (MI)
Albright Coll (PA)
Alderson-Broaddus Coll (WV)
Allegheny Coll (PA)
Alma Coll (MI)
American Coll of Thessaloniki (Greece)
American U (DC)
American U of Beirut (Lebanon)
Amherst Coll (MA)
Anderson U (IN)
Andrews U (MI)
Appalachian State U (NC)
Arcadia U (PA)
Arizona State U (AZ)
Armstrong Atlantic State U (GA)
Ashland U (OH)
Athens State U (AL)
Augsburg Coll (MN)
Augustana Coll (IL)
Augustana Coll (SD)
Austin Coll (TX)
Azusa Pacific U (CA)
Baker Coll of Muskegon (MI)
Baker Coll of Owosso (MI)
Baker U (KS)
Baldwin-Wallace Coll (OH)
Bard Coll (NY)
Bard Coll at Simon's Rock (MA)
Barry U (FL)
Belmont U (TN)
Beloit Coll (WI)
Bemidji State U (MN)
Benedictine Coll (KS)
Benedictine U (IL)
Bennington Coll (VT)
Berry Coll (GA)
Bethany Coll (WV)
Bethune-Cookman U (FL)
Biola U (CA)
Birmingham-Southern Coll (AL)
Blackburn Coll (IL)
Bloomsburg U of Pennsylvania (PA)
Bluffton U (OH)
Bob Jones U (SC)
Boise State U (ID)
Boston Coll (MA)
Boston U (MA)
Bowdoin Coll (ME)
Brandeis U (MA)
Bridgewater Coll (VA)
Bridgewater State U (MA)
Brock U (ON, Canada)
Brown U (RI)
Bryan Coll (TN)
Buena Vista U (IA)
California Inst of Technology (CA)
California Polytechnic State U, San Luis Obispo (CA)
California State Polytechnic U, Pomona (CA)
California State U, Bakersfield (CA)
California State U, Chico (CA)
California State U, Dominguez Hills (CA)
California State U, Fullerton (CA)
California State U, Long Beach (CA)
California State U, Los Angeles (CA)
California State U, Northridge (CA)
California State U, San Bernardino (CA)
California State U, San Marcos (CA)
California State U, Stanislaus (CA)
Calumet Coll of Saint Joseph (IN)
Calvin Coll (MI)
Cameron U (OK)
Canisius Coll (NY)
Capital U (OH)
Carleton Coll (MN)

Carnegie Mellon U (PA)
Carson-Newman Coll (TN)
Case Western Reserve U (OH)
The Catholic U of America (DC)
Cedarville U (OH)
Central Coll (IA)
Central Michigan U (MI)
Central Pennsylvania Coll (PA)
Central State U (OH)
Centre Coll (KY)
Chapman U (CA)
Christian Brothers U (TN)
Christopher Newport U (VA)
City Coll of the City U of New York (NY)
Claflin U (SC)
Claremont McKenna Coll (CA)
Clark Atlanta U (GA)
Clarkson U (NY)
Clark U (MA)
Clayton State U (GA)
Clemson U (SC)
Coker Coll (SC)
Colby Coll (ME)
Coll of Saint Benedict (MN)
Coll of Saint Elizabeth (NJ)
Coll of the Holy Cross (MA)
Coll of the Ozarks (MO)
The Coll of Wooster (OH)
Columbia U (MO)
Columbia U, School of General Studies (NY)
Concordia Coll (MN)
Concordia U (QC, Canada)
Concordia U Wisconsin (WI)
Concord U (WV)
Connecticut Coll (CT)
Coppin State U (MD)
Cornell Coll (IA)
Cornell U (NY)
Creighton U (NE)
Dallas Baptist U (TX)
Daniel Webster Coll (NH)
Dartmouth Coll (NH)
Delaware State U (DE)
Denison U (OH)
DePaul U (IL)
DePauw U (IN)
DeSales U (PA)
Dickinson State U (ND)
Dillard U (LA)
Doane Coll (NE)
Dominican U (IL)
Dordt Coll (IA)
Dowling Coll (NY)
Drake U (IA)
Drew U (NJ)
Drury U (MO)
Duquesne U (PA)
Eastern Michigan U (MI)
Eckerd Coll (FL)
Elizabeth City State U (NC)
Elmhurst Coll (IL)
Elon U (NC)
Embry-Riddle Aeronautical U–Daytona (FL)
Embry-Riddle Aeronautical U–Prescott (AZ)
Emory & Henry Coll (VA)
Endicott Coll (MA)
Evangel U (MO)
Everest U, Lakeland (FL)
Fairleigh Dickinson U, Metropolitan Campus (NJ)
Fairmont State U (WV)
Fayetteville State U (NC)
Felician Coll (NJ)
Fitchburg State U (MA)
Florida Inst of Technology (FL)
Florida Southern Coll (FL)
Fontbonne U (MO)
Fort Lewis Coll (CO)
Franklin Coll (IN)
Franklin Pierce U (NH)
Franklin U (OH)
Freed-Hardeman U (TN)
Furman U (SC)
Gardner-Webb U (NC)
Georgetown Coll (KY)
Georgetown U (DC)
Georgia State U (GA)
Gettysburg Coll (PA)
Gordon Coll (MA)
Goucher Coll (MD)
Governors State U (IL)
Graceland U (IA)
Grand View U (IA)
Grinnell Coll (IA)

Hampden-Sydney Coll (VA)
Hampshire Coll (MA)
Hanover Coll (IN)
Harding U (AR)
Hartwick Coll (NY)
Harvard U (MA)
Harvey Mudd Coll (CA)
Haverford Coll (PA)
Hawai`i Pacific U (HI)
Hendrix Coll (AR)
Hillsdale Coll (MI)
Hobart and William Smith Colls (NY)
Hofstra U (NY)
Hood Coll (MD)
Houghton Coll (NY)
Humboldt State U (CA)
Hunter Coll of the City U of New York (NY)
Huntington U (IN)
Huston-Tillotson U (TX)
Illinois Coll (IL)
Illinois Inst of Technology (IL)
Illinois State U (IL)
Illinois Wesleyan U (IL)
Indiana Tech (IN)
Indiana U–Purdue U Fort Wayne (IN)
Inter American U of Puerto Rico, Bayamón Campus (PR)
Inter American U of Puerto Rico, Metropolitan Campus (PR)
Inter American U of Puerto Rico, Ponce Campus (PR)
Inter American U of Puerto Rico, San Germán Campus (PR)
Iowa Wesleyan Coll (IA)
Ithaca Coll (NY)
Jamestown Coll (ND)
John Carroll U (OH)
Kalamazoo Coll (MI)
Kent State U (OH)
Kentucky Wesleyan Coll (KY)
Kettering U (MI)
King Coll (TN)
King's Coll (PA)
The King's U Coll (AB, Canada)
Lafayette Coll (PA)
Lake Forest Coll (IL)
Lakehead U (ON, Canada)
Lake Superior State U (MI)
Lamar U (TX)
La Roche Coll (PA)
La Salle U (PA)
Laurentian U (ON, Canada)
Lawrence Technological U (MI)
Lawrence U (WI)
Lebanese American U (Lebanon)
Lebanon Valley Coll (PA)
Lehigh U (PA)
Lehman Coll of the City U of New York (NY)
LeTourneau U (TX)
Lewis & Clark Coll (OR)
Lewis-Clark State Coll (ID)
Lewis U (IL)
Limestone Coll (SC)
Lindenwood U (MO)
Linfield Coll (OR)
Lipscomb U (TN)
Lock Haven U of Pennsylvania (PA)
Long Island U, Brooklyn Campus (NY)
Long Island U, C.W. Post Campus (NY)
Longwood U (VA)
Loras Coll (IA)
Louisiana State U and Ag and Mech Coll (LA)
Louisiana State U in Shreveport (LA)
Luther Coll (IA)
Lynchburg Coll (VA)
Lyon Coll (AR)
Macalester Coll (MN)
Madonna U (MI)
Maharishi U of Management (IA)
Malone U (OH)
Manchester Coll (IN)
Manhattan Coll (NY)
Manhattanville Coll (NY)
Mansfield U of Pennsylvania (PA)
Marietta Coll (OH)
Marist Coll (NY)
Marlboro Coll (VT)
Mars Hill Coll (NC)
Maryville Coll (TN)
Massachusetts Coll of Liberal Arts (MA)

Massachusetts Inst of Technology (MA)
McKendree U (IL)
Mercer U (GA)
Merrimack Coll (MA)
Messiah Coll (PA)
Metropolitan State U (MN)
MidAmerica Nazarene U (KS)
Middlebury Coll (VT)
Middle Tennessee State U (TN)
Milligan Coll (TN)
Millsaps Coll (MS)
Mills Coll (CA)
Minnesota State U Moorhead (MN)
Minot State U (ND)
Mississippi Valley State U (MS)
Missouri State U (MO)
Missouri U of Science and Technology (MO)
Molloy Coll (NY)
Monmouth Coll (IL)
Montana State U (MT)
Montana Tech of The U of Montana (MT)
Montclair State U (NJ)
Moravian Coll (PA)
Mountain State U (WV)
Mount Allison U (NB, Canada)
Mount Holyoke Coll (MA)
Mount Marty Coll (SD)
Mount Vernon Nazarene U (OH)
National U (CA)
Nebraska Wesleyan U (NE)
Neumont U (UT)
Newbury Coll (MA)
New England Inst of Technology (RI)
New Mexico Inst of Mining and Technology (NM)
Niagara U (NY)
North Carolina Ag and Tech State U (NC)
North Carolina State U (NC)
North Dakota State U (ND)
Northeastern Illinois U (IL)
Northeastern State U (OK)
Northeastern U (MA)
Northern Arizona U (AZ)
Northern Illinois U (IL)
Northwestern Coll (IA)
Northwestern U (IL)
Northwestern Oklahoma State U (OK)
Northwest Nazarene U (ID)
Nova Southeastern U (FL)
Oberlin Coll (OH)
The Ohio State U (OH)
Ohio U (OH)
Ohio Wesleyan U (OH)
Oklahoma Christian U (OK)
Oklahoma City U (OK)
Ouachita Baptist U (AR)
Pace U (NY)
Pacific Lutheran U (WA)
Pacific States U (CA)
Pacific Union Coll (CA)
Pacific U (OR)
Palm Beach Atlantic U (FL)
Penn State Erie, The Behrend Coll (PA)
Pepperdine U, Malibu (CA)
Philadelphia U (PA)
Piedmont Coll (GA)
Polytechnic Inst of NYU (NY)
Polytechnic U of Puerto Rico (PR)
Pomona Coll (CA)
Portland State U (OR)
Prairie View A&M U (TX)
Presbyterian Coll (SC)
Providence Coll (RI)
Purdue U (IN)
Queens Coll of the City U of New York (NY)
Quincy U (IL)
Quinnipiac U (CT)
Radford U (VA)
Randolph-Macon Coll (VA)
Regis U (CO)
Rensselaer Polytechnic Inst (NY)
Rhodes Coll (TN)
Ripon Coll (WI)
Roanoke Coll (VA)
Rockford Coll (IL)
Rocky Mountain Coll (MT)
Roosevelt U (IL)
Rose-Hulman Inst of Technology (IN)
Rust Coll (MS)

ITT Tech Inst, Rancho Cordova (CA)
ITT Tech Inst, Sylmar (CA)
ITT Tech Inst, Lake Mary (FL)
ITT Tech Inst, Fort Wayne (IN)
ITT Tech Inst (MD)
ITT Tech Inst (NE)
ITT Tech Inst (OR)
ITT Tech Inst, Cordova (TN)
ITT Tech Inst, Knoxville (TN)
ITT Tech Inst, Nashville (TN)
Kansas State U (KS)
Kean U (NJ)
Montana Tech of The U of Montana (MT)
Northern Michigan U (MI)
Northwestern Oklahoma State U (OK)
Ohio U (OH)
Our Lady of the Lake U of San Antonio (TX)
Pennsylvania Coll of Technology (PA)
Purdue U (IN)
Regis U (CO)
Roosevelt U (IL)
St. Ambrose U (IA)
The U of Akron (OH)
The U of Findlay (OH)
U of Minnesota, Twin Cities Campus (MN)
The U of North Carolina at Greensboro (NC)
U of Pennsylvania (PA)
U of the Incarnate Word (TX)
U of Wisconsin–Stout (WI)
Walden U (MN)
Weber State U (UT)
Wentworth Inst of Technology (MA)
Western Illinois U (IL)
Western State Coll of Colorado (CO)

COMPUTER TEACHER EDUCATION
Alma Coll (MI)
Alvernia U (PA)
Bridgewater Coll (VA)
Bryan Coll (TN)
Buena Vista U (IA)
Colorado State U (CO)
Concordia U Chicago (IL)
Dakota State U (SD)
Dordt Coll (IA)
Duquesne U (PA)
Eastern Michigan U (MI)
Edgewood Coll (WI)
Hardin-Simmons U (TX)
Keene State Coll (NH)
Liberty U (VA)
Long Island U, Brooklyn Campus (NY)
Lubbock Christian U (TX)
McMurry U (TX)
Michigan State U (MI)
Southeastern Louisiana U (LA)
Texas A&M U–Corpus Christi (TX)
Texas Christian U (TX)
Union Coll (NE)
U of the Cumberlands (KY)
U of Wisconsin–River Falls (WI)
Wright State U (OH)

COMPUTER TECHNOLOGY/ COMPUTER SYSTEMS TECHNOLOGY
Bob Jones U (SC)
Central Michigan U (MI)
Colorado State U (CO)
Florida Atlantic U (FL)
Prairie View A&M U (TX)
Purdue U (IN)
Rensselaer Polytechnic Inst (NY)
Wayne State U (MI)

CONDUCTING
Bard Coll (NY)
Chapman U (CA)
Mannes Coll The New School for Music (NY)

CONSERVATION BIOLOGY
Arizona State U (AZ)
Boston U (MA)
Florida Inst of Technology (FL)
Philadelphia U (PA)
Prescott Coll (AZ)
Sterling Coll (VT)

U of Idaho (ID)
U of Louisiana at Lafayette (LA)
The U of Western Ontario (ON, Canada)
U of Wisconsin–Madison (WI)

CONSTRUCTION ENGINEERING
American U of Beirut (Lebanon)
California State U, Long Beach (CA)
Concordia U (QC, Canada)
John Brown U (AR)
Marquette U (WI)
National U (CA)
North Carolina State U (NC)
North Dakota State U (ND)
Oregon State U (OR)
Purdue U (IN)
Southern Polytechnic State U (GA)
State U of New York Coll of Environmental Science and Forestry (NY)
Texas Tech U (TX)
The U of Alabama (AL)
U of Nebraska–Lincoln (NE)
U of Nevada, Las Vegas (NV)
U of New Brunswick Fredericton (NB, Canada)
U of Southern California (CA)

CONSTRUCTION ENGINEERING TECHNOLOGY
Bemidji State U (MN)
Bowling Green State U (OH)
California State Polytechnic U, Pomona (CA)
California State U, Chico (CA)
California State U, Long Beach (CA)
Central Michigan U (MI)
Colorado State U (CO)
Fairleigh Dickinson U, Metropolitan Campus (NJ)
Fitchburg State U (MA)
Florida Ag and Mech U (FL)
Florida Inst of Technology (FL)
Florida Intl U (FL)
Georgia Southern U (GA)
Indiana U–Purdue U Fort Wayne (IN)
John Brown U (AR)
Kansas State U (KS)
Mesa State Coll (CO)
Michigan State U (MI)
Montana State U (MT)
Northern Michigan U (MI)
Oklahoma State U (OK)
Pittsburg State U (KS)
Prairie View A&M U (TX)
Purdue U (IN)
San Diego State U (CA)
South Dakota State U (SD)
Southern Illinois U Edwardsville (IL)
Southern Utah U (UT)
State U of New York Coll of Technology at Alfred (NY)
Texas A&M U (TX)
Texas State U–San Marcos (TX)
Thomas Edison State Coll (NJ)
Tuskegee U (AL)
The U of Akron (OH)
U of Florida (FL)
U of Houston (TX)
U of Louisiana at Monroe (LA)
U of Maine (ME)
U of Nebraska–Lincoln (NE)
U of Nevada, Reno (NV)
U of North Florida (FL)
U of North Texas (TX)
The U of Toledo (OH)
U of Wisconsin–Stout (WI)
Wayne State U (MI)
Western Carolina U (NC)
Western Kentucky U (KY)

CONSTRUCTION MANAGEMENT
Appalachian State U (NC)
Arizona State U (AZ)
California Baptist U (CA)
California State U, Northridge (CA)
Central Connecticut State U (CT)
Clemson U (SC)
Colorado State U (CO)
Eastern Michigan U (MI)
Ferris State U (MI)
Illinois State U (IL)
ITT Tech Inst, Bessemer (AL)
ITT Tech Inst, Madison (AL)
ITT Tech Inst, Mobile (AL)
ITT Tech Inst, Phoenix (AZ)

ITT Tech Inst, Tempe (AZ)
ITT Tech Inst, Tucson (AZ)
ITT Tech Inst, Anaheim (CA)
ITT Tech Inst, Clovis (CA)
ITT Tech Inst, Concord (CA)
ITT Tech Inst, Corona (CA)
ITT Tech Inst, Lathrop (CA)
ITT Tech Inst, Oxnard (CA)
ITT Tech Inst, Rancho Cordova (CA)
ITT Tech Inst, San Bernardino (CA)
ITT Tech Inst, San Diego (CA)
ITT Tech Inst, San Dimas (CA)
ITT Tech Inst, Sylmar (CA)
ITT Tech Inst, Torrance (CA)
ITT Tech Inst, Thornton (CO)
ITT Tech Inst, Fort Lauderdale (FL)
ITT Tech Inst, Fort Myers (FL)
ITT Tech Inst, Jacksonville (FL)
ITT Tech Inst, Lake Mary (FL)
ITT Tech Inst, Miami (FL)
ITT Tech Inst, Pinellas Park (FL)
ITT Tech Inst, Tallahassee (FL)
ITT Tech Inst, Tampa (FL)
ITT Tech Inst, Atlanta (GA)
ITT Tech Inst, Duluth (GA)
ITT Tech Inst, Kennesaw (GA)
ITT Tech Inst (ID)
ITT Tech Inst, Burr Ridge (IL)
ITT Tech Inst, Mount Prospect (IL)
ITT Tech Inst, Orland Park (IL)
ITT Tech Inst, Fort Wayne (IN)
ITT Tech Inst, Indianapolis (IN)
ITT Tech Inst, Merrillville (IN)
ITT Tech Inst, Newburgh (IN)
ITT Tech Inst, South Bend (IN)
ITT Tech Inst, Cedar Rapids (IA)
ITT Tech Inst, Clive (IA)
ITT Tech Inst, Lexington (KY)
ITT Tech Inst, Louisville (KY)
ITT Tech Inst, St. Rose (LA)
ITT Tech Inst (MD)
ITT Tech Inst, Swartz Creek (MI)
ITT Tech Inst, Troy (MI)
ITT Tech Inst, Wyoming (MI)
ITT Tech Inst (MS)
ITT Tech Inst, Arnold (MO)
ITT Tech Inst, Earth City (MO)
ITT Tech Inst, Kansas City (MO)
ITT Tech Inst, Springfield (MO)
ITT Tech Inst (NE)
ITT Tech Inst (NV)
ITT Tech Inst (NM)
ITT Tech Inst, Charlotte (NC)
ITT Tech Inst, Charlotte (NC)
ITT Tech Inst, High Point (NC)
ITT Tech Inst, Morrisville (NC)
ITT Tech Inst, Akron (OH)
ITT Tech Inst, Dayton (OH)
ITT Tech Inst, Hilliard (OH)
ITT Tech Inst, Maumee (OH)
ITT Tech Inst, Norwood (OH)
ITT Tech Inst, Strongsville (OH)
ITT Tech Inst, Warrensville Heights (OH)
ITT Tech Inst, Youngstown (OH)
ITT Tech Inst, Oklahoma City (OK)
ITT Tech Inst, Tulsa (OK)
ITT Tech Inst (OR)
ITT Tech Inst, Columbia (SC)
ITT Tech Inst, Greenville (SC)
ITT Tech Inst, Chattanooga (TN)
ITT Tech Inst, Cordova (TN)
ITT Tech Inst, Johnson City (TN)
ITT Tech Inst, Knoxville (TN)
ITT Tech Inst, Nashville (TN)
ITT Tech Inst, Arlington (TX)
ITT Tech Inst, Austin (TX)
ITT Tech Inst, DeSoto (TX)
ITT Tech Inst, Houston (TX)
ITT Tech Inst, Houston (TX)
ITT Tech Inst, Richardson (TX)
ITT Tech Inst, San Antonio (TX)
ITT Tech Inst, Webster (TX)
ITT Tech Inst (UT)
ITT Tech Inst, Chantilly (VA)
ITT Tech Inst, Norfolk (VA)
ITT Tech Inst, Richmond (VA)
ITT Tech Inst, Salem (VA)
ITT Tech Inst, Springfield (VA)
ITT Tech Inst, Everett (WA)
ITT Tech Inst, Seattle (WA)
ITT Tech Inst, Spokane Valley (WA)
ITT Tech Inst, Green Bay (WI)
ITT Tech Inst, Greenfield (WI)
ITT Tech Inst, Madison (WI)
John Brown U (AR)

Lawrence Technological U (MI)
Louisiana State U and Ag and Mech Coll (LA)
Michigan State U (MI)
Milwaukee School of Eng (WI)
Mississippi State U (MS)
Missouri State U (MO)
North Dakota State U (ND)
Northern Arizona U (AZ)
Northern Kentucky U (KY)
The Ohio State U (OH)
Pittsburg State U (KS)
Purdue U (IN)
Southern Alberta Inst of Technology (AB, Canada)
Southern Polytechnic State U (GA)
State U of New York Coll of Environmental Science and Forestry (NY)
U of Denver (CO)
U of Northern Iowa (IA)
U of Oklahoma (OK)
The U of Texas at Tyler (TX)
U of Washington (WA)
Vermont Tech Coll (VT)
Virginia Polytechnic Inst and State U (VA)
Washington State U (WA)
Wentworth Inst of Technology (MA)
Western Carolina U (NC)
Western Illinois U (IL)

CONSTRUCTION TRADES
Purdue U (IN)

CONSTRUCTION TRADES RELATED
John Brown U (AR)
Purdue U (IN)

CONSUMER ECONOMICS
Delaware State U (DE)
South Dakota State U (SD)
The U of Arizona (AZ)
U of Delaware (DE)
U of Georgia (GA)
The U of Tennessee (TN)
U of Utah (UT)
U of Wisconsin–Madison (WI)

CONSUMER MERCHANDISING/ RETAILING MANAGEMENT
The Art Inst of York–Pennsylvania (PA)
Belmont U (TN)
Fontbonne U (MO)
Governors State U (IL)
HEC Montreal (QC, Canada)
Madonna U (MI)
Newbury Coll (MA)
Oregon State U (OR)
Purdue U (IN)
San Francisco State U (CA)
Simmons Coll (MA)
U of Memphis (TN)
U of Nebraska–Lincoln (NE)
Winona State U (MN)

CONSUMER SERVICES AND ADVOCACY
Carson-Newman Coll (TN)
Purdue U (IN)
State U of New York Coll at Oneonta (NY)
U of Wisconsin–Madison (WI)

COOKING AND RELATED CULINARY ARTS
Kendall Coll (IL)

CORRECTIONS
Adams State Coll (CO)
Asbury U (KY)
Coker Coll (SC)
Coll of the Ozarks (MO)
Jacksonville State U (AL)
Lake Superior State U (MI)
Lamar U (TX)
Lewis-Clark State Coll (ID)
Minnesota State U Mankato (MN)
Oklahoma City U (OK)
Saint Louis U (MO)
Saint Mary's U of Minnesota (MN)
Southeast Missouri State U (MO)
Spring Arbor U (MI)
Stephen F. Austin State U (TX)
Texas State U–San Marcos (TX)

Tiffin U (OH)
Tulane U (LA)
U of Arkansas at Pine Bluff (AR)
U of Minnesota, Crookston (MN)
U of Pittsburgh (PA)
Washburn U (KS)
Western Oregon U (OR)
Winona State U (MN)

CORRECTIONS AND CRIMINAL JUSTICE RELATED
Albany State U (GA)
Averett U (VA)
Bethune-Cookman U (FL)
Bob Jones U (SC)
Coker Coll (SC)
Corban U (OR)
Delaware State U (DE)
DeVry U, Pomona (CA)
DeVry U, Miramar (FL)
DeVry U, Orlando (FL)
DeVry U, Chicago (IL)
DeVry U, Kansas City (MO)
DeVry U, Houston (TX)
DeVry U, Federal Way (WA)
Emporia State U (KS)
Florida Inst of Technology (FL)
Harding U (AR)
Indiana Tech (IN)
La Roche Coll (PA)
Limestone Coll (SC)
Russell Sage Coll (NY)
Sam Houston State U (TX)
Savannah State U (GA)
The U of Alabama at Birmingham (AL)
U of Alaska Fairbanks (AK)
U of Michigan–Flint (MI)

COSTUME DESIGN
Greensboro Coll (NC)
Shenandoah U (VA)

COUNSELING PSYCHOLOGY
Atlanta Christian Coll (GA)
Bob Jones U (SC)
Coker Coll (SC)
Crown Coll (MN)
Eastern Washington U (WA)
Emmanuel Coll (MA)
Fort Lewis Coll (CO)
Grace Coll (IN)
Great Lakes Christian Coll (MI)
Jamestown Coll (ND)
Johnson & Wales U (RI)
Lesley U (MA)
Mid-Continent U (KY)
Midwestern State U (TX)
Morningside Coll (IA)
Newman U (KS)
Oak Hills Christian Coll (MN)
Paine Coll (GA)
Pittsburg State U (KS)
Saint Xavier U (IL)
San Diego Christian Coll (CA)
Santa Clara U (CA)
Southwestern Assemblies of God U (TX)
U of the Cumberlands (KY)
Washington Adventist U (MD)
Wayne State Coll (NE)

COUNSELOR EDUCATION/ SCHOOL COUNSELING AND GUIDANCE
Amberton U (TX)
Belmont U (TN)
Buena Vista U (IA)
Clemson U (SC)
East Central U (OK)
Eastern New Mexico U (NM)
Edinboro U of Pennsylvania (PA)
Florida Gulf Coast U (FL)
Goddard Coll (VT)
John Brown U (AR)
Kutztown U of Pennsylvania (PA)
Lamar U (TX)
Marshall U (WV)
Midwestern State U (TX)
Tarleton State U (TX)
Texas A&M U–Corpus Christi (TX)
Université de Sherbrooke (QC, Canada)
The U of British Columbia (BC, Canada)
U of Hawaii at Manoa (HI)
U of New Brunswick Fredericton (NB, Canada)

The U of North Carolina at
  Pembroke (NC)
The U of South Dakota (SD)
U of Wisconsin–River Falls (WI)
Wichita State U (KS)
Wright State U (OH)

COURT REPORTING
AIB Coll of Business (IA)

CRAFTS, FOLK ART AND ARTISANRY
Bridgewater State U (MA)
Brigham Young U (UT)
The Cleveland Inst of Art (OH)
Coll for Creative Studies (MI)
Indiana U–Purdue U Fort Wayne
  (IN)
Kent State U (OH)
Kutztown U of Pennsylvania (PA)
Maine Coll of Art (ME)
The U of the Arts (PA)
Virginia Commonwealth U (VA)

CREATIVE WRITING
Adams State Coll (CO)
Alderson-Broaddus Coll (WV)
Allegheny Coll (PA)
Arcadia U (PA)
Arkansas Tech U (AR)
Asbury U (KY)
Ashland U (OH)
Augustana Coll (IL)
Baldwin-Wallace Coll (OH)
Bard Coll (NY)
Bard Coll at Simon's Rock (MA)
Belhaven U (MS)
Beloit Coll (WI)
Bennington Coll (VT)
Biola U (CA)
Bluffton U (OH)
Bob Jones U (SC)
Bowie State U (MD)
Bowling Green State U (OH)
Brandeis U (MA)
Briar Cliff U (IA)
Bridgewater State U (MA)
Brown U (RI)
Bucknell U (PA)
Butler U (IN)
California Coll of the Arts (CA)
California State U, Long Beach (CA)
California State U, San Bernardino
  (CA)
Canisius Coll (NY)
Capital U (OH)
Carlow U (PA)
Carnegie Mellon U (PA)
Carroll U (WI)
Carson-Newman Coll (TN)
Central Michigan U (MI)
Champlain Coll (VT)
Chapman U (CA)
Chatham U (PA)
City Coll of the City U of New York
  (NY)
Colby Coll (ME)
Coll of the Atlantic (ME)
The Colorado Coll (CO)
Colorado State U (CO)
Columbia Coll Chicago (IL)
Columbia U, School of General
  Studies (NY)
Concordia U (QC, Canada)
Corban U (OR)
Cornell Coll (IA)
Dartmouth Coll (NH)
Denison U (OH)
Dominican U of California (CA)
Eastern Michigan U (MI)
Eckerd Coll (FL)
Emily Carr U of Art + Design (BC,
  Canada)
Emory & Henry Coll (VA)
Fairleigh Dickinson U, Coll at
  Florham (NJ)
Florida State U (FL)
Franklin & Marshall Coll (PA)
Franklin Coll Switzerland
  (Switzerland)
Franklin Pierce U (NH)
Gettysburg Coll (PA)
Goddard Coll (VT)
Hamilton Coll (NY)
Hamline U (MN)
Hampshire Coll (MA)
Hofstra U (NY)
Houghton Coll (NY)
Indiana Wesleyan U (IN)
Ithaca Coll (NY)

The Johns Hopkins U (MD)
Johnson State Coll (VT)
Knox Coll (IL)
Lehman Coll of the City U of New
  York (NY)
Lewis-Clark State Coll (ID)
Linfield Coll (OR)
Loras Coll (IA)
Loyola U Maryland (MD)
Lycoming Coll (PA)
Marlboro Coll (VT)
Massachusetts Coll of Liberal Arts
  (MA)
Massachusetts Inst of Technology
  (MA)
McMurry U (TX)
Mills Coll (CA)
Minnesota State U Mankato (MN)
Minnesota State U Moorhead (MN)
Moravian Coll (PA)
Morehead State U (KY)
New England Coll (NH)
North Central Coll (IL)
Northern Michigan U (MI)
Oberlin Coll (OH)
Ohio U (OH)
Ohio Wesleyan U (OH)
Oklahoma Christian U (OK)
Pacific U (OR)
Pittsburg State U (KS)
Pratt Inst (NY)
Purchase Coll, State U of New York
  (NY)
Purdue U (IN)
Randolph Coll (VA)
Rocky Mountain Coll (MT)
St. Catherine U (MN)
Saint Joseph's Coll (IN)
St. Lawrence U (NY)
Saint Mary's Coll (IN)
San Francisco State U (CA)
Sarah Lawrence Coll (NY)
Savannah Coll of Art and Design
  (GA)
Seton Hill U (PA)
Siena Heights U (MI)
Sierra Nevada Coll (NV)
Slippery Rock U of Pennsylvania
  (PA)
Southern Methodist U (TX)
Southern Vermont Coll (VT)
Southwestern Coll (KS)
Spalding U (KY)
State U of New York at Binghamton
  (NY)
State U of New York at Oswego
  (NY)
Stephen F. Austin State U (TX)
Stephens Coll (MO)
Suffolk U (MA)
Susquehanna U (PA)
Sweet Briar Coll (VA)
Texas Christian U (TX)
Trinity Coll (CT)
Truman State U (MO)
The U of Arizona (AZ)
The U of British Columbia (BC,
  Canada)
The U of British Columbia–
  Okanagan (BC, Canada)
U of Cincinnati (OH)
U of Denver (CO)
U of Evansville (IN)
The U of Findlay (OH)
U of Houston (TX)
U of Idaho (ID)
U of Maine at Farmington (ME)
U of Miami (FL)
U of Michigan (MI)
U of Mount Union (OH)
U of Nebraska at Omaha (NE)
The U of North Carolina Wilmington
  (NC)
U of Pittsburgh (PA)
U of Pittsburgh at Bradford (PA)
U of Pittsburgh at Greensburg (PA)
U of Pittsburgh at Johnstown (PA)
U of Redlands (CA)
U of St. Thomas (MN)
U of Southern California (CA)
Valparaiso U (IN)
Virginia Intermont Coll (VA)
Washington U in St. Louis (MO)
Waynesburg U (PA)
Wells Coll (NY)
Western Michigan U (MI)
Western New England U (MA)
Western State Coll of Colorado (CO)
Wheeling Jesuit U (WV)
Wofford Coll (SC)

CRIMINALISTICS AND CRIMINAL SCIENCE
Florida Gulf Coast U (FL)
Indiana Tech (IN)
Inter American U of Puerto Rico,
  Ponce Campus (PR)
Saint Leo U (FL)
Southern Wesleyan U (SC)

CRIMINAL JUSTICE/LAW ENFORCEMENT ADMINISTRATION
Abilene Christian U (TX)
Adams State Coll (CO)
Adelphi U (NY)
Albertus Magnus Coll (CT)
Alfred U (NY)
Alvernia U (PA)
American Public U System (WV)
Anderson U (IN)
Anderson U (SC)
Anna Maria Coll (MA)
Arcadia U (PA)
Arizona State U (AZ)
Ashworth Coll (GA)
Athens State U (AL)
Austin Peay State U (TN)
Averett U (VA)
Barton Coll (NC)
Bemidji State U (MN)
Bethel U (TN)
Blackburn Coll (IL)
Bluefield Coll (VA)
Bob Jones U (SC)
Boise State U (ID)
Bowie State U (MD)
Brevard Coll (NC)
Briar Cliff U (IA)
Brookline Coll, Phoenix (AZ)
Brown Mackie Coll–Albuquerque
  (NM)
Brown Mackie Coll–Boise (ID)
Brown Mackie Coll–Fort Wayne (IN)
Brown Mackie Coll–Greenville (SC)
Brown Mackie Coll–Indianapolis (IN)
Brown Mackie Coll–Louisville (KY)
Brown Mackie Coll–Merrillville (IN)
Brown Mackie Coll–Michigan City
  (IN)
Brown Mackie Coll–Northern
  Kentucky (KY)
Brown Mackie Coll–Phoenix (AZ)
Brown Mackie Coll–St. Louis (MO)
Brown Mackie Coll–South Bend (IN)
Brown Mackie Coll–Tucson (AZ)
Brown Mackie Coll–Tulsa (OK)
Bryant & Stratton Coll (WI)
Bryant & Stratton Coll - Wauwatosa
  Campus (WI)
California Baptist U (CA)
California State U, Bakersfield (CA)
California State U, Long Beach (CA)
California State U, San Bernardino
  (CA)
California State U, Stanislaus (CA)
Calumet Coll of Saint Joseph (IN)
Campbellsville U (KY)
Canisius Coll (NY)
Castleton State Coll (VT)
Cedarville U (OH)
Champlain Coll (VT)
Chestnut Hill Coll (PA)
The Citadel, The Military Coll of
  South Carolina (SC)
Claflin U (SC)
Coker Coll (SC)
The Coll of New Jersey (NJ)
Coll of St. Joseph (VT)
The Coll of Saint Rose (NY)
Columbia Coll (MO)
Concordia U Wisconsin (WI)
Coppin State U (MD)
Culver-Stockton Coll (MO)
Cumberland U (TN)
Curry Coll (MA)
Dallas Baptist U (TX)
Dalton State Coll (GA)
Delaware State U (DE)
Dordt Coll (IA)
Drury U (MO)
East Central U (OK)
East Tennessee State U (TN)
East Texas Baptist U (TX)
ECPI Coll of Technology, Virginia
  Beach (VA)
Elmira Coll (NY)
Evangel U (MO)
Everest U, Tampa (FL)

Everest U, Tampa (FL)
Fairleigh Dickinson U, Metropolitan
  Campus (NJ)
Faulkner U (AL)
Fayetteville State U (NC)
Felician Coll (NJ)
Ferris State U (MI)
Florida National Coll (FL)
Franklin Pierce U (NH)
Georgia Coll & State U (GA)
Governors State U (IL)
Graceland U (IA)
Grand Valley State U (MI)
Grand View U (IA)
Granite State Coll (NH)
Greenville Coll (IL)
Hannibal-LaGrange U (MO)
Hawai'i Pacific U (HI)
Holy Family U (PA)
Indiana Tech (IN)
Indiana U–Purdue U Fort Wayne
  (IN)
Inter American U of Puerto Rico,
  Guayama Campus (PR)
ITT Tech Inst, Bessemer (AL)
ITT Tech Inst, Madison (AL)
ITT Tech Inst, Mobile (AL)
ITT Tech Inst, Phoenix (AZ)
ITT Tech Inst, Tempe (AZ)
ITT Tech Inst, Tucson (AZ)
ITT Tech Inst (AR)
ITT Tech Inst, Anaheim (CA)
ITT Tech Inst, Clovis (CA)
ITT Tech Inst, Concord (CA)
ITT Tech Inst, Corona (CA)
ITT Tech Inst, Lathrop (CA)
ITT Tech Inst, Oxnard (CA)
ITT Tech Inst, Rancho Cordova (CA)
ITT Tech Inst, San Bernardino (CA)
ITT Tech Inst, San Diego (CA)
ITT Tech Inst, San Dimas (CA)
ITT Tech Inst, Sylmar (CA)
ITT Tech Inst, Torrance (CA)
ITT Tech Inst, Thornton (CO)
ITT Tech Inst, Fort Lauderdale (FL)
ITT Tech Inst, Fort Myers (FL)
ITT Tech Inst, Jacksonville (FL)
ITT Tech Inst, Lake Mary (FL)
ITT Tech Inst, Miami (FL)
ITT Tech Inst, Tallahassee (FL)
ITT Tech Inst, Tampa (FL)
ITT Tech Inst, Atlanta (GA)
ITT Tech Inst, Duluth (GA)
ITT Tech Inst, Kennesaw (GA)
ITT Tech Inst (ID)
ITT Tech Inst, Burr Ridge (IL)
ITT Tech Inst, Mount Prospect (IL)
ITT Tech Inst, Orland Park (IL)
ITT Tech Inst, Fort Wayne (IN)
ITT Tech Inst, Indianapolis (IN)
ITT Tech Inst, Merrillville (IN)
ITT Tech Inst, Newburgh (IN)
ITT Tech Inst, South Bend (IN)
ITT Tech Inst, Cedar Rapids (IA)
ITT Tech Inst, Clive (IA)
ITT Tech Inst, Lexington (KY)
ITT Tech Inst, Louisville (KY)
ITT Tech Inst, St. Rose (LA)
ITT Tech Inst, Canton (MI)
ITT Tech Inst, Swartz Creek (MI)
ITT Tech Inst, Troy (MI)
ITT Tech Inst, Wyoming (MI)
ITT Tech Inst (MN)
ITT Tech Inst (MS)
ITT Tech Inst, Arnold (MO)
ITT Tech Inst, Earth City (MO)
ITT Tech Inst, Kansas City (MO)
ITT Tech Inst, Springfield (MO)
ITT Tech Inst (NV)
ITT Tech Inst (NM)
ITT Tech Inst, Charlotte (NC)
ITT Tech Inst, Charlotte (NC)
ITT Tech Inst, High Point (NC)
ITT Tech Inst, Morrisville (NC)
ITT Tech Inst, Akron (OH)
ITT Tech Inst, Dayton (OH)
ITT Tech Inst, Hilliard (OH)
ITT Tech Inst, Maumee (OH)
ITT Tech Inst, Norwood (OH)
ITT Tech Inst, Strongsville (OH)
ITT Tech Inst, Warrensville Heights
  (OH)
ITT Tech Inst, Youngstown (OH)
ITT Tech Inst, Oklahoma City (OK)
ITT Tech Inst, Tulsa (OK)
ITT Tech Inst (OR)
ITT Tech Inst, Columbia (SC)
ITT Tech Inst, Greenville (SC)
ITT Tech Inst, Chattanooga (TN)
ITT Tech Inst, Cordova (TN)

ITT Tech Inst, Knoxville (TN)
ITT Tech Inst, Nashville (TN)
ITT Tech Inst (UT)
ITT Tech Inst, Chantilly (VA)
ITT Tech Inst, Norfolk (VA)
ITT Tech Inst, Richmond (VA)
ITT Tech Inst, Salem (VA)
ITT Tech Inst, Springfield (VA)
ITT Tech Inst, Everett (WA)
ITT Tech Inst, Seattle (WA)
ITT Tech Inst, Spokane Valley (WA)
ITT Tech Inst, Green Bay (WI)
ITT Tech Inst, Greenfield (WI)
ITT Tech Inst, Madison (WI)
Jacksonville State U (AL)
John Jay Coll of Criminal Justice of
  the City U of New York (NY)
Johnson & Wales U (CO)
Johnson & Wales U (FL)
Johnson & Wales U (RI)
Judson Coll (AL)
Kean U (NJ)
Keuka Coll (NY)
Keystone Coll (PA)
LA Coll Intl (CA)
Lake Superior State U (MI)
Lamar U (TX)
Liberty U (VA)
Limestone Coll (SC)
Lincoln Memorial U (TN)
Lincoln U (MO)
Lindsey Wilson Coll (KY)
Lock Haven U of Pennsylvania (PA)
Longwood U (VA)
Lubbock Christian U (TX)
MacMurray Coll (IL)
Mansfield U of Pennsylvania (PA)
Marist Coll (NY)
Mars Hill Coll (NC)
McKendree U (IL)
Merrimack Coll (MA)
Michigan State U (MI)
MidAmerica Nazarene U (KS)
Middle Tennessee State U (TN)
Midwestern State U (TX)
Mississippi Valley State U (MS)
Missouri Southern State U (MO)
Mitchell Coll (CT)
Moravian Coll (PA)
Morris Coll (SC)
Mount Aloysius Coll (PA)
Mount Ida Coll (MA)
Mount Mercy U (IA)
Mount Olive Coll (NC)
Mount Vernon Nazarene U (OH)
National U (CA)
Nevada State Coll at Henderson
  (NV)
New England Coll (NH)
New England Inst of Technology
  (RI)
Newman U (KS)
New York Inst of Technology (NY)
Niagara U (NY)
Northeastern State U (OK)
Northwest Nazarene U (ID)
Ohio U–Zanesville (OH)
Oklahoma City U (OK)
Pace U (NY)
Penn Foster Coll (AZ)
Penn State Abington (PA)
Penn State Altoona (PA)
Penn State Beaver (PA)
Penn State Berks (PA)
Penn State Brandywine (PA)
Penn State DuBois (PA)
Penn State Erie, The Behrend Coll
  (PA)
Penn State Fayette, The Eberly
  Campus (PA)
Penn State Greater Allegheny (PA)
Penn State Hazleton (PA)
Penn State Lehigh Valley (PA)
Penn State Mont Alto (PA)
Penn State New Kensington (PA)
Penn State Schuylkill (PA)
Penn State Shenango (PA)
Penn State U Park (PA)
Penn State Wilkes-Barre (PA)
Penn State Worthington Scranton
  (PA)
Penn State York (PA)
Piedmont Coll (GA)
Point Park U (PA)
Portland State U (OR)
Radford U (VA)
Regent U (VA)
Regis U (CO)
Rogers State U (OK)

Rutgers, The State U of New Jersey, New Brunswick (NJ)
Sacred Heart U (CT)
Saint Francis U (PA)
St. John's U (NY)
St. Joseph's Coll, Long Island Campus (NY)
St. Joseph's Coll, New York (NY)
Saint Martin's U (WA)
Saint Mary's U of Minnesota (MN)
St. Thomas Aquinas Coll (NY)
St. Thomas U (FL)
Salem State U (MA)
Salve Regina U (RI)
San Diego State U (CA)
San Francisco State U (CA)
Shenandoah U (VA)
Simpson Coll (IA)
Sonoma State U (CA)
Southeastern U (FL)
Southern Illinois U Carbondale (IL)
Southern Vermont Coll (VT)
Southwest U (LA)
Springfield Coll (MA)
State U of New York at Fredonia (NY)
State U of New York at Oswego (NY)
State U of New York Coll at Potsdam (NY)
Strayer U - Alexandria Campus (VA)
Strayer U - Allentown Campus (PA)
Strayer U - Arlington Campus (VA)
Strayer U - Augusta Campus (GA)
Strayer U - Baymeadows Campus (FL)
Strayer U - Birmingham Campus (AL)
Strayer U - Brickell Campus (FL)
Strayer U - Cedar Hill Campus (TX)
Strayer U - Center City Campus (PA)
Strayer U - Chamblee Campus (GA)
Strayer U - Charleston Campus (SC)
Strayer U - Chesapeake Campus (VA)
Strayer U - Chesterfield Campus (VA)
Strayer U - Christiana Campus (DE)
Strayer U - Cobb County Campus (GA)
Strayer U - Columbia Campus (SC)
Strayer U - Columbus Campus (GA)
Strayer U - Coral Springs Campus (FL)
Strayer U - Cranberry Woods Campus (PA)
Strayer U - Delaware County Campus (PA)
Strayer U - Doral Campus (FL)
Strayer U - Douglasville Campus (GA)
Strayer U - Florence Campus (KY)
Strayer U - Fort Lauderdale Campus (FL)
Strayer U - Fredericksburg Campus (VA)
Strayer U - Greensboro Campus (NC)
Strayer U - Greenville Campus (SC)
Strayer U - Henrico Campus (VA)
Strayer U - Huntersville Campus (NC)
Strayer U - Huntsville Campus (AL)
Strayer U - Irving Campus (TX)
Strayer U - Jackson Campus (MS)
Strayer U - Katy Campus (TX)
Strayer U - King of Prussia Campus (PA)
Strayer U - Knoxville Campus (TN)
Strayer U - Lexington Campus (KY)
Strayer U - Lithonia Campus (GA)
Strayer U - Little Rock Campus (AR)
Strayer U - Loudoun Campus (VA)
Strayer U - Louisville Campus (KY)
Strayer U - Lower Bucks County Campus (PA)
Strayer U - Maitland Campus (FL)
Strayer U - Manassas Campus (VA)
Strayer U - Metairie Campus (LA)
Strayer U - Milwaukee Campus (WI)
Strayer U - Miramar Campus (FL)
Strayer U - Morrow Campus (GA)
Strayer U - Nashville Campus (TN)
Strayer U - Newport News Campus (VA)

Strayer U - North Austin Campus (TX)
Strayer U - North Charlotte Campus (NC)
Strayer U - North Indianapolis Campus (IN)
Strayer U - North Raleigh Campus (NC)
Strayer U - Northwest Houston Campus (TX)
Strayer U - Orlando East Campus (FL)
Strayer U - Palm Beach Gardens Campus (FL)
Strayer U - Penn Center West Campus (PA)
Strayer U - Plano Campus (TX)
Strayer U - Roswell Campus (GA)
Strayer U - RTP Campus (NC)
Strayer U - Salt Lake Campus (UT)
Strayer U - Sand Lake Campus (FL)
Strayer U - Savannah Campus (GA)
Strayer U - Shelby Oaks Campus (TN)
Strayer U - South Charlotte Campus (NC)
Strayer U - South Raleigh Campus (NC)
Strayer U - Takoma Park Campus (DC)
Strayer U - Tampa East Campus (FL)
Strayer U - Tampa Westshore Campus (FL)
Strayer U - Teays Valley Campus (WV)
Strayer U - Thousand Oaks Campus (TN)
Strayer U - Virginia Beach Campus (VA)
Strayer U - Washington Campus (DC)
Strayer U - Woodbridge Campus (VA)
Suffolk U (MA)
Sul Ross State U (TX)
Texas A&M U–Corpus Christi (TX)
Texas Southern U (TX)
Thomas Edison State Coll (NJ)
Thomas U (GA)
Tiffin U (OH)
Trevecca Nazarene U (TN)
Trine U (IN)
Union Coll (KY)
Union Inst & U (OH)
The U of Arizona (AZ)
U of Arkansas–Fort Smith (AR)
U of Baltimore (MD)
U of Central Missouri (MO)
U of Colorado at Colorado Springs (CO)
U of Colorado Denver (CO)
U of Dayton (OH)
U of Delaware (DE)
U of Dubuque (IA)
The U of Findlay (OH)
U of Guelph (ON, Canada)
U of Hawaii–West Oahu (HI)
U of Louisville (KY)
U of Maine at Augusta (ME)
U of Maine at Presque Isle (ME)
U of Mary Hardin-Baylor (TX)
U of Massachusetts Lowell (MA)
U of Memphis (TN)
U of Minnesota, Crookston (MN)
U of Nevada, Las Vegas (NV)
U of New Brunswick Saint John (NB, Canada)
U of New Haven (CT)
U of Oklahoma (OK)
U of Pittsburgh at Bradford (PA)
U of Pittsburgh at Greensburg (PA)
U of Regina (SK, Canada)
U of St. Francis (IL)
U of South Alabama (AL)
U of South Carolina (SC)
U of South Carolina Upstate (SC)
The U of South Dakota (SD)
The U of Tennessee at Chattanooga (TN)
The U of Tennessee at Martin (TN)
The U of Texas–Pan American (TX)
U of Washington (WA)
U of Wisconsin–Parkside (WI)
U of Wisconsin–Platteville (WI)
Utah Valley U (UT)
Villanova U (PA)
Virginia Commonwealth U (VA)

Virginia Intermont Coll (VA)
Walden U (MN)
Washburn U (KS)
Washington State U (WA)
Wayland Baptist U (TX)
Waynesburg U (PA)
Western Illinois U (IL)
Western Intl U (AZ)
Western Oregon U (OR)
West Liberty U (WV)
Widener U (PA)
Wilmington Coll (OH)
Wilmington U (DE)
Winona State U (MN)
York Coll of Pennsylvania (PA)

CRIMINAL JUSTICE/POLICE SCIENCE
American U (DC)
Athabasca U (AB, Canada)
Bemidji State U (MN)
Drury U (MO)
Fairmont State U (WV)
Ferris State U (MI)
Husson U (ME)
Jacksonville State U (AL)
Kent State U at Tuscarawas (OH)
Lake Superior State U (MI)
Lamar U (TX)
Louisiana Coll (LA)
MacMurray Coll (IL)
Marian U (WI)
Metropolitan State U (MN)
Middle Tennessee State U (TN)
Minnesota State U Mankato (MN)
Newbury Coll (MA)
Northern State U (SD)
Northwestern Oklahoma State U (OK)
Oklahoma City U (OK)
Rowan U (NJ)
Stephen F. Austin State U (TX)
Texas State U–San Marcos (TX)
U of Hartford (CT)
U of Pittsburgh at Greensburg (PA)
U of Regina (SK, Canada)
U of the Virgin Islands (VI)
U of Wisconsin–Superior (WI)
Walden U (MN)
Washburn U (KS)
Western Connecticut State U (CT)
Western Oregon U (OR)
Winona State U (MN)

CRIMINAL JUSTICE/SAFETY
Alabama State U (AL)
Albany State U (GA)
Alcorn State U (MS)
American U (DC)
Amridge U (AL)
Andrew Jackson U (AL)
Angelo State U (TX)
Anna Maria Coll (MA)
Appalachian State U (NC)
Arizona State U (AZ)
Auburn U Montgomery (AL)
Augsburg Coll (MN)
Baldwin-Wallace Coll (OH)
Ball State U (IN)
Bellarmine U (KY)
Bethany Coll (KS)
Bethel Coll (IN)
Bloomsburg U of Pennsylvania (PA)
Bluefield State Coll (WV)
Bluffton U (OH)
Bowling Green State U (OH)
Bridgewater State U (MA)
Buena Vista U (IA)
California State U, Chico (CA)
California State U, Dominguez Hills (CA)
California State U, Fullerton (CA)
California State U, Los Angeles (CA)
Central Pennsylvania Coll (PA)
Central State U (OH)
Champlain Coll (VT)
Clark Atlanta U (GA)
Clayton State U (GA)
Columbia Southern U (AL)
Columbus State U (GA)
Concordia U, St. Paul (MN)
Dakota Wesleyan U (SD)
Delta State U (MS)
DeSales U (PA)
Dominican Coll (NY)
Eastern New Mexico U (NM)

Edgewood Coll (WI)
Edinboro U of Pennsylvania (PA)
Elizabeth City State U (NC)
Endicott Coll (MA)
Everest U, Lakeland (FL)
Ferrum Coll (VA)
Fitchburg State U (MA)
Florida Ag and Mech U (FL)
Florida Atlantic U (FL)
Florida Gulf Coast U (FL)
Florida Intl U (FL)
Friends U (KS)
Gannon U (PA)
Georgian Court U (NJ)
Georgia Southern U (GA)
Georgia State U (GA)
Grace Coll (IN)
Grand Canyon U (AZ)
Granite State Coll (NH)
Greensboro Coll (NC)
Guilford Coll (NC)
Hamline U (MN)
Harding U (AR)
Hardin-Simmons U (TX)
Harrison Coll, Indianapolis (IN)
Harrison Coll, Muncie (IN)
Holy Family U (PA)
Husson U (ME)
Huston-Tillotson U (TX)
Illinois State U (IL)
Immaculata U (PA)
Indiana U Bloomington (IN)
Indiana U East (IN)
Indiana U Kokomo (IN)
Indiana U Northwest (IN)
Indiana U–Purdue U Indianapolis (IN)
Indiana U South Bend (IN)
Indiana U Southeast (IN)
Indiana Wesleyan U (IN)
Indian River State Coll (FL)
Inter American U of Puerto Rico, Metropolitan Campus (PR)
Inter American U of Puerto Rico, Ponce Campus (PR)
Iowa Wesleyan Coll (IA)
Jamestown Coll (ND)
Kennesaw State U (GA)
Kent State U at Trumbull (OH)
Kentucky State U (KY)
Kentucky Wesleyan Coll (KY)
King's Coll (PA)
Kutztown U of Pennsylvania (PA)
Lane Coll (TN)
La Roche Coll (PA)
La Salle U (PA)
Lasell Coll (MA)
Lewis U (IL)
Limestone Coll (SC)
Lindenwood U (MO)
Long Island U, Brentwood Campus (NY)
Long Island U, C.W. Post Campus (NY)
Loras Coll (IA)
Louisiana State U in Shreveport (LA)
Lourdes Coll (OH)
Loyola U Chicago (IL)
Lubbock Christian U (TX)
Lynn U (FL)
Madonna U (MI)
Marshall U (WV)
Marymount U (VA)
Marywood U (PA)
Medaille Coll (NY)
Mercer U (GA)
Mesa State Coll (CO)
Messiah Coll (PA)
Metropolitan State U (MN)
Michigan State U (MI)
Minnesota State U Moorhead (MN)
Minot State U (ND)
Missouri Baptist U (MO)
Mitchell Coll (CT)
Molloy Coll (NY)
Monmouth U (NJ)
Montana State U Billings (MT)
Mountain State U (WV)
Mount Marty Coll (SD)
Mount Vernon Nazarene U (OH)
Murray State U (KY)
Neumann U (PA)
New Jersey City U (NJ)
New Mexico Highlands U (NM)
New Mexico State U (NM)
North Carolina Ag and Tech State U (NC)

North Dakota State U (ND)
Northeastern Illinois U (IL)
Northeastern U (MA)
Northern Kentucky U (KY)
Northern Michigan U (MI)
North Georgia Coll & State U (GA)
Northwestern Coll (MN)
Northwestern State U of Louisiana (LA)
Nova Southeastern U (FL)
Nyack Coll (NY)
Penn State Abington (PA)
Penn State Altoona (PA)
Penn State Erie, The Behrend Coll (PA)
Penn State Fayette, The Eberly Campus (PA)
Penn State Harrisburg (PA)
Penn State Schuylkill (PA)
Penn State Wilkes-Barre (PA)
Pikeville Coll (KY)
Point Park U (PA)
Potomac State Coll of West Virginia (WV)
Prairie View A&M U (TX)
Quincy U (IL)
Quinnipiac U (CT)
Rhode Island Coll (RI)
Roanoke Coll (VA)
Roosevelt U (IL)
Rosemont Coll (PA)
Rutgers, The State U of New Jersey, Camden (NJ)
Rutgers, The State U of New Jersey, Newark (NJ)
Saginaw Valley State U (MI)
St. Ambrose U (IA)
Saint Anselm Coll (NH)
St. Edward's U (TX)
Saint Joseph's Coll (IN)
Saint Joseph's Coll of Maine (ME)
Saint Leo U (FL)
Saint Louis U (MO)
Saint Xavier U (IL)
Sam Houston State U (TX)
San Diego State U (CA)
San Jose State U (CA)
Seton Hill U (PA)
Shippensburg U of Pennsylvania (PA)
Siena Heights U (MI)
Southeastern Louisiana U (LA)
Southeastern Oklahoma State U (OK)
Southern Arkansas U–Magnolia (AR)
Southern Illinois U Edwardsville (IL)
Southwestern Assemblies of God U (TX)
State U of New York at Plattsburgh (NY)
State U of New York Coll at Oneonta (NY)
State U of New York Coll at Potsdam (NY)
Tarleton State U (TX)
Temple U (PA)
Texas A&M Intl U (TX)
Texas Christian U (TX)
Texas State U–San Marcos (TX)
Texas Wesleyan U (TX)
Texas Woman's U (TX)
Thiel Coll (PA)
Thomas Edison State Coll (NJ)
Thomas More Coll (KY)
Troy U (AL)
Truman State U (MO)
The U of Akron (OH)
The U of Alabama (AL)
U of Arkansas (AR)
U of Bridgeport (CT)
U of Central Florida (FL)
U of Cincinnati (OH)
U of Evansville (IN)
U of Georgia (GA)
U of Houston–Downtown (TX)
U of Houston–Victoria (TX)
U of Illinois at Chicago (IL)
U of Illinois at Springfield (IL)
U of Louisiana at Lafayette (LA)
U of Louisiana at Monroe (LA)
U of Maryland U Coll (MD)
U of Massachusetts Boston (MA)
U of Michigan–Dearborn (MI)
U of Mount Union (OH)
U of Nebraska at Omaha (NE)
The U of North Carolina at Charlotte (NC)

INDEXES

The U of North Carolina at
Pembroke (NC)
The U of North Carolina Wilmington
(NC)
U of North Dakota (ND)
U of Northern Colorado (CO)
U of North Florida (FL)
U of North Texas (TX)
U of Portland (OR)
U of Regina (SK, Canada)
U of Richmond (VA)
The U of Scranton (PA)
U of Southern Indiana (IN)
U of Southern Mississippi (MS)
The U of Texas at Arlington (TX)
The U of Texas at San Antonio (TX)
The U of Texas at Tyler (TX)
The U of Texas of the Permian
Basin (TX)
U of the Cumberlands (KY)
U of the Southwest (NM)
The U of Toledo (OH)
U of West Florida (FL)
U of Wisconsin–Eau Claire (WI)
U of Wisconsin–Superior (WI)
U of Wyoming (WY)
Valdosta State U (GA)
Virginia State U (VA)
Virginia Wesleyan Coll (VA)
Viterbo U (WI)
Walden U (MN)
Wayne State Coll (NE)
Wayne State U (MI)
West Chester U of Pennsylvania
(PA)
Western Carolina U (NC)
Western Michigan U (MI)
Western New England U (MA)
Westfield State U (MA)
Westminster Coll (UT)
Wichita State U (KS)
Wilfrid Laurier U (ON, Canada)
Wilkes U (PA)
Worcester State U (MA)
Xavier U (OH)
Youngstown State U (OH)

CRIMINOLOGY
Adams State Coll (CO)
Albright Coll (PA)
Alderson-Broaddus Coll (WV)
Arcadia U (PA)
Arkansas State U (AR)
Auburn U (AL)
Barry U (FL)
Biola U (CA)
Butler U (IN)
Cabrini Coll (PA)
Cameron U (OK)
Capital U (OH)
Castleton State Coll (VT)
Cedar Crest Coll (PA)
Centenary Coll (NJ)
Central Connecticut State U (CT)
Cleveland State U (OH)
Coker Coll (SC)
Coll of Mount St. Joseph (OH)
Delaware State U (DE)
Dominican U (IL)
Drury U (MO)
Eastern Michigan U (MI)
Eastern Washington U (WA)
Elizabethtown Coll (PA)
Elmhurst Coll (IL)
Emmanuel Coll (MA)
Fairleigh Dickinson U, Coll at
Florham (NJ)
Florida Southern Coll (FL)
Florida State U (FL)
Husson U (ME)
Indiana State U (IN)
Indiana U of Pennsylvania (PA)
John Jay Coll of Criminal Justice of
the City U of New York (NY)
Johnson C. Smith U (NC)
Lebanon Valley Coll (PA)
Le Moyne Coll (NY)
Lindenwood U (MO)
Loyola U New Orleans (LA)
Lycoming Coll (PA)
Lynchburg Coll (VA)
Marquette U (WI)
Mary Baldwin Coll (VA)
Marymount U (VA)
Maryville U of Saint Louis (MO)
Mississippi State U (MS)
Missouri State U (MO)
Mount St. Mary's U (MD)
Niagara U (NY)
North Carolina State U (NC)

Northern Arizona U (AZ)
The Ohio State U (OH)
Ohio U (OH)
Ohio U–Chillicothe (OH)
Old Dominion U (VA)
Paine Coll (GA)
Regis U (CO)
The Richard Stockton Coll of New
Jersey (NJ)
Rivier Coll (NH)
Sage Coll of Albany (NY)
Saint Anselm Coll (NH)
St. Edward's U (TX)
Saint Francis U (PA)
St. John's U (NY)
Saint Joseph's U (PA)
St. Thomas U (NB, Canada)
Simon Fraser U (BC, Canada)
Slippery Rock U of Pennsylvania
(PA)
Southern Oregon U (OR)
Southern Wesleyan U (SC)
State U of New York Coll at Old
Westbury (NY)
Stonehill Coll (MA)
Suffolk U (MA)
Texas A&M U–Kingsville (TX)
Thomas U (GA)
U of California, Irvine (CA)
U of Denver (CO)
U of Florida (FL)
U of Houston–Clear Lake (TX)
U of La Verne (CA)
U of Maryland, Coll Park (MD)
U of Massachusetts Dartmouth (MA)
U of Memphis (TN)
U of Miami (FL)
U of Minnesota, Duluth (MN)
U of Minnesota, Twin Cities Campus
(MN)
U of Missouri–St. Louis (MO)
U of Mount Union (OH)
U of Nevada, Reno (NV)
U of New Hampshire (NH)
U of Northern Iowa (IA)
U of Ottawa (ON, Canada)
U of Saint Mary (KS)
U of St. Thomas (MN)
U of Southern Maine (ME)
The U of Tampa (FL)
The U of Texas at Dallas (TX)
The U of Texas of the Permian
Basin (TX)
The U of Western Ontario (ON,
Canada)
U of West Georgia (GA)
Upper Iowa U (IA)
Valparaiso U (IN)
Virginia Wesleyan Coll (VA)
Walden U (MN)
Western State Coll of Colorado (CO)
Wheeling Jesuit U (WV)
Wright State U (OH)

**CRISIS/EMERGENCY/DISASTER
MANAGEMENT**
American Public U System (WV)
Arkansas Tech U (AR)
Walden U (MN)

CROP PRODUCTION
North Dakota State U (ND)
U of Minnesota, Crookston (MN)
U of Minnesota, Twin Cities Campus
(MN)
Washington State U (WA)

CULINARY ARTS
Coll of the Ozarks (MO)
Johnson & Wales U (CO)
Johnson & Wales U (FL)
Johnson & Wales U (RI)
Johnson & Wales U - Charlotte
Campus (NC)
Kendall Coll (IL)
Mountain State U (WV)
Newbury Coll (MA)
Nicholls State U (LA)
The Restaurant School at Walnut
Hill Coll (PA)
U of Nevada, Las Vegas (NV)

CULINARY ARTS RELATED
Johnson & Wales U (CO)
Johnson & Wales U (FL)
Johnson & Wales U (RI)
Mississippi U for Women (MS)
Newbury Coll (MA)
U of Cincinnati (OH)
U of Nevada, Las Vegas (NV)

**CULTURAL RESOURCE
MANAGEMENT AND POLICY
ANALYSIS**
California State U, Dominguez Hills
(CA)
U of Waterloo (ON, Canada)

**CULTURAL STUDIES/CRITICAL
THEORY AND ANALYSIS**
Goddard Coll (VT)
The U of Tampa (FL)
Western Kentucky U (KY)

**CURRICULUM AND
INSTRUCTION**
Albertus Magnus Coll (CT)
Calvin Coll (MI)
Eastern Washington U (WA)
Franklin Pierce U (NH)
Free Will Baptist Bible Coll (TN)
Midwestern State U (TX)
Minnesota State U Moorhead (MN)
Northwest Missouri State U (MO)
Pittsburg State U (KS)
Prescott Coll (AZ)
Randolph Coll (VA)
Tarleton State U (TX)
U of Cincinnati (OH)
U of Minnesota, Twin Cities Campus
(MN)
U of Regina (SK, Canada)
The U of South Dakota (SD)
Utah State U (UT)
Walden U (MN)
Wichita State U (KS)
Wright State U (OH)

**CUSTOMER SERVICE
MANAGEMENT**
U of Wisconsin–Stout (WI)

**CYBER/COMPUTER FORENSICS
AND COUNTERTERRORISM**
U of Maryland U Coll (MD)

**CYBER/ELECTRONIC
OPERATIONS AND WARFARE**
U of Maryland U Coll (MD)

**CYTOGENETICS/GENETICS/
CLINICAL GENETICS
TECHNOLOGY**
Northern Michigan U (MI)
Saint Mary's U of Minnesota (MN)

CYTOTECHNOLOGY
Albany Coll of Pharmacy and Health
Sciences (NY)
Barry U (FL)
The Coll of Saint Rose (NY)
Edgewood Coll (WI)
Elmhurst Coll (IL)
Illinois Coll (IL)
Indiana U Bloomington (IN)
Indiana U–Purdue U Indianapolis
(IN)
Indiana U South Bend (IN)
Indiana U Southeast (IN)
Long Island U, Brooklyn Campus
(NY)
Long Island U, C.W. Post Campus
(NY)
Marian U (WI)
Marshall U (WV)
Massachusetts Coll of Liberal Arts
(MA)
Saint Louis U (MO)
Saint Mary's U of Minnesota (MN)
Slippery Rock U of Pennsylvania
(PA)
State U of New York at Plattsburgh
(NY)
Stony Brook U, State U of New York
(NY)
Thiel Coll (PA)
U of Arkansas for Medical Sciences
(AR)
The U of Kansas (KS)
U of North Dakota (ND)
U of North Texas (TX)
Winona State U (MN)

CZECH
The U of Texas at Austin (TX)

**DAIRY HUSBANDRY AND
PRODUCTION**
U of Vermont (VT)

DAIRY SCIENCE
California Polytechnic State U, San
Luis Obispo (CA)
Eastern New Mexico U (NM)
Iowa State U of Science and
Technology (IA)
South Dakota State U (SD)
Texas A&M U (TX)
U of Georgia (GA)
U of Minnesota, Twin Cities Campus
(MN)
U of New Hampshire (NH)
U of Wisconsin–Madison (WI)
U of Wisconsin–River Falls (WI)
Utah State U (UT)
Virginia Polytechnic Inst and State U
(VA)

DANCE
Adelphi U (NY)
Alma Coll (MI)
Amherst Coll (MA)
Anderson U (IN)
Appalachian State U (NC)
Arizona State U (AZ)
Ball State U (IN)
Bard Coll (NY)
Bard Coll at Simon's Rock (MA)
Barnard Coll (NY)
Belhaven U (MS)
Bennington Coll (VT)
Birmingham-Southern Coll (AL)
Brenau U (GA)
Butler U (IN)
California Inst of the Arts (CA)
California State U, Fullerton (CA)
California State U, Long Beach (CA)
California State U, Los Angeles (CA)
Cedar Crest Coll (PA)
Chapman U (CA)
Claremont McKenna Coll (CA)
The Colorado Coll (CO)
Colorado State U (CO)
Columbia Coll (SC)
Columbia Coll Chicago (IL)
Columbia U, School of General
Studies (NY)
Concordia U (QC, Canada)
Connecticut Coll (CT)
Cornell U (NY)
Denison U (OH)
DEREE - The American Coll of
Greece (Greece)
DeSales U (PA)
Dickinson Coll (PA)
Dominican U of California (CA)
Eastern Michigan U (MI)
Elon U (NC)
Eugene Lang Coll The New School
for Liberal Arts (NY)
Florida State U (FL)
Franklin & Marshall Coll (PA)
Georgian Court U (NJ)
Goucher Coll (MD)
Grand Canyon U (AZ)
Grand Valley State U (MI)
Hamilton Coll (NY)
Hampshire Coll (MA)
Hobart and William Smith Colls (NY)
Hofstra U (NY)
Hollins U (VA)
Hope Coll (MI)
Hunter Coll of the City U of New
York (NY)
Indiana U Bloomington (IN)
Ithaca Coll (NY)
Johnson State Coll (VT)
The Juilliard School (NY)
Keene State Coll (NH)
Kennesaw State U (GA)
Kent State U (OH)
Kenyon Coll (OH)
Lamar U (TX)
La Roche Coll (PA)
Lehman Coll of the City U of New
York (NY)
Lindenwood U (MO)
Long Island U, Brooklyn Campus
(NY)
Long Island U, C.W. Post Campus
(NY)
Loyola Marymount U (CA)
Manhattanville Coll (NY)
Marlboro Coll (VT)
Middlebury Coll (VT)
Mills Coll (CA)
Missouri State U (MO)
Montclair State U (NJ)
Mount Holyoke Coll (MA)
Muhlenberg Coll (PA)

New Mexico State U (NM)
New York U (NY)
Nova Southeastern U (FL)
Oberlin Coll (OH)
The Ohio State U (OH)
Ohio U (OH)
Oklahoma City U (OK)
Palm Beach Atlantic U (FL)
Pitzer Coll (CA)
Point Park U (PA)
Pomona Coll (CA)
Prescott Coll (AZ)
Purchase Coll, State U of New York
(NY)
Radford U (VA)
Randolph Coll (VA)
Reed Coll (OR)
Rhode Island Coll (RI)
Rutgers, The State U of New Jersey,
New Brunswick (NJ)
Saint Mary's Coll of California (CA)
St. Olaf Coll (MN)
Sam Houston State U (TX)
San Diego State U (CA)
San Francisco State U (CA)
San Jose State U (CA)
Sarah Lawrence Coll (NY)
Scripps Coll (CA)
Seton Hill U (PA)
Shenandoah U (VA)
Simon Fraser U (BC, Canada)
Skidmore Coll (NY)
Slippery Rock U of Pennsylvania
(PA)
Smith Coll (MA)
Southern Methodist U (TX)
Southern Utah U (UT)
Springfield Coll (MA)
State U of New York at Fredonia
(NY)
State U of New York Coll at Potsdam
(NY)
Stephen F. Austin State U (TX)
Stephens Coll (MO)
Swarthmore Coll (PA)
Sweet Briar Coll (VA)
Temple U (PA)
Texas State U–San Marcos (TX)
Texas Tech U (TX)
Texas Woman's U (TX)
Towson U (MD)
Trinity Coll (CT)
Tulane U (LA)
U at Buffalo, the State U of New
York (NY)
The U of Akron (OH)
The U of Alabama (AL)
The U of Arizona (AZ)
U of California, Berkeley (CA)
U of California, Irvine (CA)
U of California, Santa Barbara (CA)
U of Cincinnati (OH)
U of Colorado Boulder (CO)
U of Florida (FL)
U of Georgia (GA)
U of Hartford (CT)
U of Hawaii at Manoa (HI)
U of Houston (TX)
U of Idaho (ID)
The U of Iowa (IA)
The U of Kansas (KS)
U of Maryland, Baltimore County
(MD)
U of Maryland, Coll Park (MD)
U of Massachusetts Amherst (MA)
U of Michigan (MI)
U of Minnesota, Twin Cities Campus
(MN)
U of Nebraska–Lincoln (NE)
U of Nevada, Las Vegas (NV)
The U of North Carolina at Charlotte
(NC)
The U of North Carolina at
Greensboro (NC)
U of North Carolina School of the
Arts (NC)
U of North Texas (TX)
U of Oklahoma (OK)
U of Oregon (OR)
U of Richmond (VA)
U of South Carolina (SC)
U of Southern Mississippi (MS)
U of South Florida (FL)
The U of Texas at Austin (TX)
The U of Texas–Pan American (TX)
The U of the Arts (PA)
U of Utah (UT)
U of Washington (WA)
U of Wisconsin–Madison (WI)
U of Wisconsin–Stevens Point (WI)

Utah State U (UT)
Utah Valley U (UT)
Valdosta State U (GA)
Virginia Commonwealth U (VA)
Washington U in St. Louis (MO)
Wayne State U (MI)
Weber State U (UT)
Webster U (MO)
Wells Coll (NY)
Wesleyan U (CT)
West Chester U of Pennsylvania (PA)
Western Kentucky U (KY)
Western Michigan U (MI)
Western Oregon U (OR)
Westmont Coll (CA)
Wheaton Coll (MA)
Winthrop U (SC)
Wright State U (OH)

DANCE RELATED

Anderson U (IN)
Brigham Young U (UT)
California State U, Long Beach (CA)
Coker Coll (SC)
Sarah Lawrence Coll (NY)
Utah Valley U (UT)
Western Michigan U (MI)

DANCE THERAPY

Columbia Coll Chicago (IL)
Prescott Coll (AZ)

DATA MODELING/ WAREHOUSING AND DATABASE ADMINISTRATION

National U (CA)
Neumont U (UT)
Purdue U (IN)

DATA PROCESSING AND DATA PROCESSING TECHNOLOGY

Arkansas State U (AR)
Bemidji State U (MN)
The Coll of Saint Rose (NY)
Delaware State U (DE)
Midway Coll (KY)
Pace U (NY)
Stephen F. Austin State U (TX)
U of Advancing Technology (AZ)
U of Arkansas (AR)
U of Miami (FL)
U of New Brunswick Fredericton (NB, Canada)
U of Southern Indiana (IN)
U of Southern Mississippi (MS)
U of Washington (WA)
Utah Valley U (UT)

DEAF STUDIES

California State U, Northridge (CA)

DEMOGRAPHY AND POPULATION

The U of Western Ontario (ON, Canada)

DENTAL ASSISTING

Delaware State U (DE)

DENTAL HYGIENE

Armstrong Atlantic State U (GA)
Clayton State U (GA)
Dixie State Coll of Utah (UT)
Eastern Washington U (WA)
East Tennessee State U (TN)
Ferris State U (MI)
Georgia Health Sciences U (GA)
Idaho State U (ID)
Indiana U Bloomington (IN)
Indiana U South Bend (IN)
Lewis U (IL)
Metropolitan State U (MN)
Midwestern State U (TX)
Minnesota State U Mankato (MN)
Mount Ida Coll (MA)
New York U (NY)
Northern Arizona U (AZ)
The Ohio State U (OH)
The Ohio State U at Lima (OH)
Old Dominion U (VA)
Pennsylvania Coll of Technology (PA)
St. Petersburg Coll (FL)
Southern Illinois U Carbondale (IL)
Texas Woman's U (TX)
Thomas Edison State Coll (NJ)

U of Arkansas for Medical Sciences (AR)
U of Bridgeport (CT)
The U of British Columbia (BC, Canada)
U of Hawaii at Manoa (HI)
U of Louisiana at Lafayette (LA)
U of Louisiana at Monroe (LA)
U of Louisville (KY)
U of Maine at Augusta (ME)
U of Manitoba (MB, Canada)
U of Michigan (MI)
U of Minnesota, Twin Cities Campus (MN)
U of New England (ME)
U of New Haven (CT)
The U of North Carolina at Chapel Hill (NC)
U of Oklahoma Health Sciences Center (OK)
U of Pittsburgh (PA)
The U of South Dakota (SD)
U of Southern California (CA)
U of Southern Indiana (IN)
U of Washington (WA)
U of Wyoming (WY)
Utah Valley U (UT)
Vermont Tech Coll (VT)
Virginia Commonwealth U (VA)
Western Kentucky U (KY)
West Liberty U (WV)
West Virginia U (WV)
Wichita State U (KS)

DENTAL SERVICES AND ALLIED PROFESSIONS RELATED

Clayton State U (GA)
Delaware State U (DE)
Indiana U–Purdue U Indianapolis (IN)
U of Minnesota, Twin Cities Campus (MN)

DESIGN AND APPLIED ARTS RELATED

Alverno Coll (WI)
Arizona State U (AZ)
Art Center Coll of Design (CA)
Athabasca U (AB, Canada)
Azusa Pacific U (CA)
Bemidji State U (MN)
California Coll of the Arts (CA)
Columbia U, School of General Studies (NY)
Concordia U (QC, Canada)
Ferris State U (MI)
Florida Ag and Mech U (FL)
Franklin Pierce U (NH)
Hampshire Coll (MA)
Harding U (AR)
Hofstra U (NY)
Inter American U of Puerto Rico, San Germán Campus (PR)
Lamar U (TX)
Mansfield U of Pennsylvania (PA)
Maryland Inst Coll of Art (MD)
McMurry U (TX)
Midwestern State U (TX)
Minnesota State U Mankato (MN)
New York Inst of Technology (NY)
Otis Coll of Art and Design (CA)
Paier Coll of Art, Inc. (CT)
Parsons The New School for Design (NY)
Penn State Altoona (PA)
Penn State Berks (PA)
Penn State U Park (PA)
Point Park U (PA)
Portland State U (OR)
Pratt Inst (NY)
Purdue U (IN)
Reinhardt U (GA)
Salem State U (MA)
Savannah Coll of Art and Design (GA)
School of the Museum of Fine Arts, Boston (MA)
School of Visual Arts (NY)
Schreiner U (TX)
Sewanee: The U of the South (TN)
Shawnee State U (OH)
State U of New York at Fredonia (NY)
Taylor U (IN)
U of California, Los Angeles (CA)
U of Dayton (OH)
U of Illinois at Chicago (IL)

U of Massachusetts Dartmouth (MA)
U of Oregon (OR)
The U of Toledo (OH)
U of Wisconsin–Stout (WI)
Washburn U (KS)
Washington U in St. Louis (MO)
William Paterson U of New Jersey (NJ)
Winona State U (MN)

DESIGN AND VISUAL COMMUNICATIONS

Alberta Coll of Art & Design (AB, Canada)
Albright Coll (PA)
Alma Coll (MI)
American U (DC)
The American U in Dubai (United Arab Emirates)
Anderson U (IN)
The Art Inst of Ohio–Cincinnati (OH)
Auburn U (AL)
Bennington Coll (VT)
Bethel Coll (IN)
Bowling Green State U (OH)
California Coll of the Arts (CA)
California Inst of the Arts (CA)
California State U, Chico (CA)
Central Connecticut State U (CT)
Champlain Coll (VT)
Coll of Mount St. Joseph (OH)
Collins Coll (AZ)
Columbia Coll Chicago (IL)
Creative Center (NE)
Drury U (MO)
Emily Carr U of Art + Design (BC, Canada)
Endicott Coll (MA)
Escuela de Artes Plasticas de Puerto Rico (PR)
Ferris State U (MI)
Franklin Coll Switzerland (Switzerland)
Holy Cross Coll (IN)
Iowa State U of Science and Technology (IA)
Iowa Wesleyan Coll (IA)
Kean U (NJ)
La Roche Coll (PA)
Lawrence Technological U (MI)
Lehigh U (PA)
Lewis U (IL)
Liberty U (VA)
Linfield Coll (OR)
Loyola U Chicago (IL)
Lubbock Christian U (TX)
Madonna U (MI)
Missouri State U (MO)
New Mexico Highlands U (NM)
New York City Coll of Technology of the City U of New York (NY)
North Carolina State U (NC)
Northeastern State U (OK)
Northern Arizona U (AZ)
The Ohio State U (OH)
Pacific Northwest Coll of Art (OR)
Paier Coll of Art, Inc. (CT)
Parsons The New School for Design (NY)
Purdue U (IN)
Radford U (VA)
Rensselaer Polytechnic Inst (NY)
Robert Morris U (PA)
Saginaw Valley State U (MI)
St. Ambrose U (IA)
Saint Mary-of-the-Woods Coll (IN)
San Francisco State U (CA)
Savannah Coll of Art and Design (GA)
Seattle Pacific U (WA)
Southern Illinois U Carbondale (IL)
Spring Arbor U (MI)
Texas Tech U (TX)
Université du Québec en Outaouais (QC, Canada)
U of Advancing Technology (AZ)
U of Cincinnati (OH)
U of Evansville (IN)
U of Hartford (CT)
The U of Kansas (KS)
U of Massachusetts Dartmouth (MA)
U of Miami (FL)
U of Michigan–Flint (MI)
U of Minnesota, Twin Cities Campus (MN)
U of Notre Dame (IN)

The U of Tennessee at Martin (TN)
The U of Texas at Austin (TX)
U of Wisconsin–Green Bay (WI)
U of Wisconsin–Stevens Point (WI)
Utah Valley U (UT)
Viterbo U (WI)
Washington U in St. Louis (MO)
Watkins Coll of Art, Design, & Film (TN)
Weber State U (UT)
West Virginia U (WV)

DESKTOP PUBLISHING AND DIGITAL IMAGING DESIGN

California Baptist U (CA)
Purdue U (IN)
Texas State U–San Marcos (TX)

DEVELOPMENTAL AND CHILD PSYCHOLOGY

Antioch U Midwest (OH)
Belmont U (TN)
Bridgewater State U (MA)
California State U, Bakersfield (CA)
California State U, San Bernardino (CA)
Carson-Newman Coll (TN)
Castleton State Coll (VT)
Eastern Washington U (WA)
Emmanuel Coll (MA)
Fitchburg State U (MA)
Humboldt State U (CA)
Keene State Coll (NH)
Liberty U (VA)
Longwood U (VA)
Marlboro Coll (VT)
Maryville Coll (TN)
Metropolitan State U (MN)
Mills Coll (CA)
Minnesota State U Mankato (MN)
Mount St. Mary's Coll (CA)
Northeastern State U (OK)
Northern Michigan U (MI)
Purdue U (IN)
Quinnipiac U (CT)
St. Joseph's Coll, Long Island Campus (NY)
St. Joseph's Coll, New York (NY)
Sarah Lawrence Coll (NY)
Savannah State U (GA)
Sonoma State U (CA)
Spelman Coll (GA)
Suffolk U (MA)
Texas Christian U (TX)
Tufts U (MA)
The U of British Columbia (BC, Canada)
U of California, Santa Cruz (CA)
U of Delaware (DE)
The U of Kansas (KS)
U of Minnesota, Twin Cities Campus (MN)
U of New Brunswick Fredericton (NB, Canada)
The U of Texas at Dallas (TX)
U of the District of Columbia (DC)
The U of Toledo (OH)
U of Wisconsin–Green Bay (WI)
Vanderbilt U (TN)
Wilfrid Laurier U (ON, Canada)

DEVELOPMENTAL BIOLOGY AND EMBRYOLOGY

Purdue U (IN)

DEVELOPMENT ECONOMICS AND INTERNATIONAL DEVELOPMENT

Brown U (RI)
Calvin Coll (MI)
Clark U (MA)
Georgia Southern U (GA)
John Brown U (AR)
Penn State Altoona (PA)
Penn State Berks (PA)
Prescott Coll (AZ)
Taylor U (IN)
U of California, Los Angeles (CA)
U of New Brunswick Saint John (NB, Canada)
U of Ottawa (ON, Canada)
U of Vermont (VT)

DIAGNOSTIC MEDICAL SONOGRAPHY AND ULTRASOUND TECHNOLOGY

Baptist Coll of Health Sciences (TN)

The U of Tennessee at Martin (TN)
Benedictine U (IL)
Georgia Health Sciences U (GA)
Lewis U (IL)
Misericordia U (PA)
Mountain State U (WV)
Newman U (KS)
State U of New York Downstate Medical Center (NY)
U of Arkansas for Medical Sciences (AR)
U of Missouri (MO)
Washburn U (KS)
Weber State U (UT)

DIESEL MECHANICS TECHNOLOGY

Lewis-Clark State Coll (ID)

DIETETICS

Abilene Christian U (TX)
Acadia U (NS, Canada)
Andrews U (MI)
Appalachian State U (NC)
Ashland U (OH)
Ball State U (IN)
Bastyr U (WA)
Bowling Green State U (OH)
California Polytechnic State U, San Luis Obispo (CA)
California State Polytechnic U, Pomona (CA)
California State U, Chico (CA)
California State U, Long Beach (CA)
California State U, Los Angeles (CA)
California State U, San Bernardino (CA)
Carson-Newman Coll (TN)
Case Western Reserve U (OH)
Central Michigan U (MI)
Coll of Saint Elizabeth (NJ)
Coll of the Ozarks (MO)
Delaware State U (DE)
Dominican U (IL)
Eastern Michigan U (MI)
Florida Intl U (FL)
Fontbonne U (MO)
Georgia State U (GA)
Harding U (AR)
Idaho State U (ID)
Immaculata U (PA)
Iowa State U of Science and Technology (IA)
Jacksonville State U (AL)
Kansas State U (KS)
Keene State Coll (NH)
Lamar U (TX)
Lehman Coll of the City U of New York (NY)
Life U (GA)
Lipscomb U (TN)
Mansfield U of Pennsylvania (PA)
Marshall U (WV)
Marywood U (PA)
Miami U (OH)
Michigan State U (MI)
Minnesota State U Mankato (MN)
Missouri State U (MO)
Nicholls State U (LA)
North Dakota State U (ND)
Northern Illinois U (IL)
Northwest Missouri State U (MO)
The Ohio State U (OH)
Ohio U (OH)
Ouachita Baptist U (AR)
Purdue U (IN)
St. Catherine U (MN)
San Diego State U (CA)
San Francisco State U (CA)
San Jose State U (CA)
Seton Hill U (PA)
Simmons Coll (MA)
State U of New York Coll at Oneonta (NY)
Tennessee Technological U (TN)
Texas Christian U (TX)
Texas Southern U (TX)
Texas Tech U (TX)
Texas Woman's U (TX)
Tuskegee U (AL)
The U of Alabama (AL)
The U of British Columbia (BC, Canada)
U of Central Missouri (MO)
U of Cincinnati (OH)
U of Dayton (OH)
U of Delaware (DE)
U of Georgia (GA)

INDEXES

INDEXES

Wayne State U (MI)
Weber State U (UT)
Webster U (MO)
Wellesley Coll (MA)
Wells Coll (NY)
Wesleyan U (CT)
West Chester U of Pennsylvania (PA)
Western Carolina U (NC)
Western Connecticut State U (CT)
Western Illinois U (IL)
Western Kentucky U (KY)
Western Oregon U (OR)
Western State Coll of Colorado (CO)
Westfield State U (MA)
Westminster Coll (UT)
Westmont Coll (CA)
West Virginia U (WV)
Wheaton Coll (MA)
Whitman Coll (WA)
Wichita State U (KS)
Wilkes U (PA)
Willamette U (OR)
William Jewell Coll (MO)
William Paterson U of New Jersey (NJ)
Williams Coll (MA)
Wilmington Coll (OH)
Winona State U (MN)
Winthrop U (SC)
Wittenberg U (OH)
Wofford Coll (SC)
Wright State U (OH)
Yale U (CT)
York Coll of Pennsylvania (PA)
York Coll of the City U of New York (NY)
Young Harris Coll (GA)
Youngstown State U (OH)

DRAMATIC/THEATER ARTS AND STAGECRAFT RELATED
Adams State Coll (CO)
Baldwin-Wallace Coll (OH)
Brigham Young U (UT)
California State U, Chico (CA)
Coastal Carolina U (SC)
DePaul U (IL)
Drake U (IA)
Fayetteville State U (NC)
Grand Canyon U (AZ)
Indiana U South Bend (IN)
Lehigh U (PA)
Lindenwood U (MO)
Nebraska Wesleyan U (NE)
North Central Coll (IL)
North Greenville U (SC)
Palm Beach Atlantic U (FL)
Pepperdine U, Malibu (CA)
Purdue U (IN)
Seton Hill U (PA)
Southern Illinois U Carbondale (IL)
Southwestern Coll (KS)
U at Buffalo, the State U of New York (NY)
U of Lethbridge (AB, Canada)
U of Miami (FL)
U of Michigan–Flint (MI)
U of Nevada, Las Vegas (NV)
U of Northern Colorado (CO)
U of Regina (SK, Canada)
Webster U (MO)
Western Kentucky U (KY)
Western Michigan U (MI)

DRAWING
Adams State Coll (CO)
Alberta Coll of Art & Design (AB, Canada)
Aquinas Coll (MI)
Arcadia U (PA)
Bard Coll at Simon's Rock (MA)
Bennington Coll (VT)
Bethany Coll (KS)
Biola U (CA)
Birmingham-Southern Coll (AL)
Boise State U (ID)
Brigham Young U (UT)
California Coll of the Arts (CA)
California State U, Long Beach (CA)
Carson-Newman Coll (TN)
The Cleveland Inst of Art (OH)
Coll of the Atlantic (ME)
Colorado State U (CO)
Columbus State U (GA)
Drake U (IA)
Emily Carr U of Art + Design (BC, Canada)
Ferris State U (MI)
Georgia State U (GA)

Governors State U (IL)
Grace Coll (IN)
Indiana U–Purdue U Fort Wayne (IN)
Inter American U of Puerto Rico, San Germán Campus (PR)
Lewis U (IL)
Lindenwood U (MO)
Longwood U (VA)
Lyme Acad Coll of Fine Arts (CT)
Marlboro Coll (VT)
Maryland Inst Coll of Art (MD)
Minneapolis Coll of Art and Design (MN)
Minnesota State U Mankato (MN)
Mount Allison U (NB, Canada)
New England Coll (NH)
Northern Michigan U (MI)
Otis Coll of Art and Design (CA)
Paier Coll of Art, Inc. (CT)
Portland State U (OR)
Pratt Inst (NY)
Providence Coll (RI)
Rutgers, The State U of New Jersey, New Brunswick (NJ)
Sarah Lawrence Coll (NY)
Savannah Coll of Art and Design (GA)
School of the Museum of Fine Arts, Boston (MA)
School of Visual Arts (NY)
Seton Hill U (PA)
Sewanee: The U of the South (TN)
Sonoma State U (CA)
State U of New York at Fredonia (NY)
U of Hartford (CT)
The U of Iowa (IA)
U of Michigan (MI)
U of Missouri–St. Louis (MO)
U of Regina (SK, Canada)
U of San Francisco (CA)
The U of Toledo (OH)
Virginia Intermont Coll (VA)
Washington U in St. Louis (MO)
Winona State U (MN)

DUTCH/FLEMISH
U of California, Berkeley (CA)

EARLY CHILDHOOD EDUCATION
Adams State Coll (CO)
Alabama State U (AL)
Albany State U (GA)
Alma Coll (MI)
Alvernia U (PA)
Anderson U (SC)
Anna Maria Coll (MA)
Antioch U Midwest (OH)
Arcadia U (PA)
Arizona State U (AZ)
Arkansas State U (AR)
Arkansas Tech U (AR)
Arlington Baptist Coll (TX)
Ashworth Coll (GA)
Atlanta Christian Coll (GA)
Auburn U (AL)
Baldwin-Wallace Coll (OH)
Bennington Coll (VT)
Berry Coll (GA)
Bethel Coll (IN)
Bloomsburg U of Pennsylvania (PA)
Bob Jones U (SC)
Boston U (MA)
Brewton-Parker Coll (GA)
Bridgewater State U (MA)
Brigham Young U (UT)
Bucknell U (PA)
Butler U (IN)
California Baptist U (CA)
California State U, Chico (CA)
California State U, Dominguez Hills (CA)
California State U, Fullerton (CA)
California State U, Los Angeles (CA)
California State U, Stanislaus (CA)
Cameron U (OK)
Canisius Coll (NY)
Capital U (OH)
Carlow U (PA)
Carroll U (WI)
The Catholic U of America (DC)
Cedarville U (OH)
Central Michigan U (MI)
Central State U (OH)
Champlain Coll (VT)
Chatham U (PA)
Chestnut Hill Coll (PA)
Christian Brothers U (TN)

City Coll of the City U of New York (NY)
Claflin U (SC)
Clark Atlanta U (GA)
Clemson U (SC)
Cleveland State U (OH)
Coastal Carolina U (SC)
Coker Coll (SC)
Coll of Central Florida (FL)
Coll of Charleston (SC)
Coll of Mount St. Joseph (OH)
The Coll of New Jersey (NJ)
Coll of Saint Mary (NE)
Coll of the Ozarks (MO)
Colorado State U (CO)
Columbia Coll (SC)
Columbia Coll Chicago (IL)
Columbus State U (GA)
Concordia Coll–New York (NY)
Concordia U Chicago (IL)
Concordia U, St. Paul (MN)
Coppin State U (MD)
Crown Coll (MN)
Delaware State U (DE)
DePaul U (IL)
Dowling Coll (NY)
Duquesne U (PA)
East Central U (OK)
Eastern New Mexico U (NM)
Eastern Washington U (WA)
East Stroudsburg U of Pennsylvania (PA)
Edgewood Coll (WI)
Elizabethtown Coll (PA)
Endicott Coll (MA)
Evangel U (MO)
Fayetteville State U (NC)
Felician Coll (NJ)
Fitchburg State U (MA)
Florida Ag and Mech U (FL)
Florida Atlantic U (FL)
Florida Gulf Coast U (FL)
Florida Intl U (FL)
Florida State Coll at Jacksonville (FL)
Florida State U (FL)
Fort Lewis Coll (CO)
Francis Marion U (SC)
Free Will Baptist Bible Coll (TN)
Gannon U (PA)
Georgia Coll & State U (GA)
Georgia State U (GA)
Governors State U (IL)
Grace Bible Coll (MI)
Granite State Coll (NH)
Greensboro Coll (NC)
Greenville Coll (IL)
Hannibal-LaGrange U (MO)
Harding U (AR)
Hardin-Simmons U (TX)
Hillsdale Coll (MI)
Hofstra U (NY)
Holy Family U (PA)
Hood Coll (MD)
Idaho State U (ID)
Illinois Coll (IL)
Illinois State U (IL)
Indiana U Bloomington (IN)
Indiana U Kokomo (IN)
Indiana U of Pennsylvania (PA)
Indiana U–Purdue U Indianapolis (IN)
Inter American U of Puerto Rico, San Germán Campus (PR)
Iowa Wesleyan Coll (IA)
John Brown U (AR)
Juniata Coll (PA)
Keene State Coll (NH)
Kendall Coll (IL)
Kennesaw State U (GA)
Kent State U at Tuscarawas (OH)
Keystone Coll (PA)
King's Coll (PA)
Kutztown U of Pennsylvania (PA)
LaGrange Coll (GA)
Lake Superior State U (MI)
Lasell Coll (MA)
Lebanon Valley Coll (PA)
Lindenwood U (MO)
Louisiana State U and Ag and Mech Coll (LA)
Lourdes Coll (OH)
Loyola U Chicago (IL)
Lubbock Christian U (TX)
Lyon Coll (AR)
Madonna U (MI)
Malone U (OH)
Maranatha Baptist Bible Coll (WI)
Marian U (WI)
Marywood U (PA)

Mayville State U (ND)
McMurry U (TX)
Messiah Coll (PA)
Miami U (OH)
Michigan State U (MI)
Midwestern State U (TX)
Millersville U of Pennsylvania (PA)
Milligan Coll (TN)
Millikin U (IL)
Minnesota State U Moorhead (MN)
Misericordia U (PA)
Missouri State U (MO)
Mitchell Coll (CT)
Morehead State U (KY)
Morris Coll (SC)
Mount Aloysius Coll (PA)
Mount Ida Coll (MA)
Mount Olive Coll (NC)
Mount Saint Mary Coll (NY)
Mount Vernon Nazarene U (OH)
Murray State U (KY)
Naropa U (CO)
National-Louis U (IL)
Newman U (KS)
New Mexico State U (NM)
New York U (NY)
Nicholls State U (LA)
Northeastern Illinois U (IL)
Northeastern State U (OK)
Northern Arizona U (AZ)
Northern Illinois U (IL)
North Georgia Coll & State U (GA)
North Greenville U (SC)
Northwestern Coll (MN)
Northwestern Oklahoma State U (OK)
Northwestern State U of Louisiana (LA)
Nyack Coll (NY)
The Ohio State U at Lima (OH)
The Ohio State U at Marion (OH)
The Ohio State U–Mansfield Campus (OH)
The Ohio State U–Newark Campus (OH)
Ohio U (OH)
Ohio U–Chillicothe (OH)
Ohio Wesleyan U (OH)
Oklahoma Christian U (OK)
Ouachita Baptist U (AR)
Pacific Union Coll (CA)
Pittsburg State U (KS)
Point Park U (PA)
Presbyterian Coll (SC)
Prescott Coll (AZ)
Purdue U (IN)
Purdue U North Central (IN)
Reinhardt U (GA)
Rhode Island Coll (RI)
Ripon Coll (WI)
Rivier Coll (NH)
Roosevelt U (IL)
Rowan U (NJ)
St. Ambrose U (IA)
Salem State U (MA)
Salisbury U (MD)
Salve Regina U (RI)
San Francisco State U (CA)
San Jose State U (CA)
Sarah Lawrence Coll (NY)
Schreiner U (TX)
Shawnee State U (OH)
Shippensburg U of Pennsylvania (PA)
Silver Lake Coll (WI)
Simmons Coll (MA)
South Dakota State U (SD)
Southeastern Louisiana U (LA)
Southeast Missouri State U (MO)
Southern Arkansas U–Magnolia (AR)
Southern Connecticut State U (CT)
Southern Illinois U Carbondale (IL)
Southern Illinois U Edwardsville (IL)
Southern Nazarene U (OK)
Southern Wesleyan U (SC)
Southwestern Coll (KS)
Springfield Coll (MA)
Spring Hill Coll (AL)
State U of New York Coll at Geneseo (NY)
State U of New York Coll at Old Westbury (NY)
Stephens Coll (MO)
Stonehill Coll (MA)
Tennessee Wesleyan Coll (TN)
Texas Christian U (TX)
Thomas U (GA)
Towson U (MD)
Trevecca Nazarene U (TN)

Trinity Lutheran Coll (WA)
Troy U (AL)
Truett-McConnell Coll (GA)
The U of Alabama (AL)
The U of Alabama at Birmingham (AL)
U of Arkansas (AR)
U of Arkansas–Fort Smith (AR)
U of Central Florida (FL)
U of Hartford (CT)
U of Hawaii–West Oahu (HI)
The U of Kansas (KS)
U of Maine at Farmington (ME)
U of Michigan–Dearborn (MI)
U of Michigan–Flint (MI)
U of Minnesota, Crookston (MN)
U of Missouri (MO)
U of Missouri–St. Louis (MO)
U of Mobile (AL)
The U of Montana Western (MT)
U of Mount Union (OH)
The U of North Carolina at Chapel Hill (NC)
The U of North Carolina at Greensboro (NC)
U of North Dakota (ND)
U of North Florida (FL)
U of Oklahoma (OK)
U of Regina (SK, Canada)
U of Science and Arts of Oklahoma (OK)
The U of Scranton (PA)
U of South Alabama (AL)
U of South Carolina Aiken (SC)
U of South Carolina Beaufort (SC)
U of Southern Indiana (IN)
U of South Florida (FL)
The U of Tennessee at Chattanooga (TN)
U of the Virgin Islands (VI)
U of Tulsa (OK)
U of Vermont (VT)
U of West Florida (FL)
U of Wisconsin–Stevens Point (WI)
U of Wisconsin–Stout (WI)
U of Wisconsin–Whitewater (WI)
Ursuline Coll (OH)
Utah Valley U (UT)
Valdosta State U (GA)
Vanderbilt U (TN)
Virginia Intermont Coll (VA)
Walsh U (OH)
Washington State U (WA)
Wayland Baptist U (TX)
Wayne State Coll (NE)
Wesleyan Coll (GA)
West Chester U of Pennsylvania (PA)
Western Kentucky U (KY)
Western Michigan U (MI)
Wheeling Jesuit U (WV)
Wheelock Coll (MA)
Widener U (PA)
Wilmington U (DE)
Worcester State U (MA)
Wright State U (OH)
Xavier U (OH)
Xavier U of Louisiana (LA)
York Coll of Pennsylvania (PA)
Youngstown State U (OH)

EARTH SCIENCE EDUCATION
Calvin Coll (MI)
Central Michigan U (MI)
Florida Inst of Technology (FL)
Minnesota State U Moorhead (MN)
Purdue U (IN)
The U of Montana Western (MT)
U of Wisconsin–Madison (WI)

EAST ASIAN LANGUAGES
Arizona State U (AZ)
Eckerd Coll (FL)
Grinnell Coll (IA)
Indiana U Bloomington (IN)
Michigan State U (MI)
Smith Coll (MA)
The U of Kansas (KS)
U of Pennsylvania (PA)
U of Puget Sound (WA)
U of Southern California (CA)
The U of Texas at Austin (TX)
Washington and Lee U (VA)

EAST ASIAN LANGUAGES RELATED
Claremont McKenna Coll (CA)
Columbia U, School of General Studies (NY)
Dartmouth Coll (NH)

INDEXES

Mercer U (GA)
Merrimack Coll (MA)
Messiah Coll (PA)
Metropolitan State U (MN)
Miami U (OH)
Michigan State U (MI)
Middlebury Coll (VT)
Middle Tennessee State U (TN)
Midwestern State U (TX)
Millersville U of Pennsylvania (PA)
Millsaps Coll (MS)
Mills Coll (CA)
Minnesota State U Mankato (MN)
Minnesota State U Moorhead (MN)
Minot State U (ND)
Mississippi State U (MS)
Missouri State U (MO)
Missouri U of Science and
　Technology (MO)
Monmouth Coll (IL)
Montana State U (MT)
Montclair State U (NJ)
Moravian Coll (PA)
Morehouse Coll (GA)
Mount Allison U (NB, Canada)
Mount Holyoke Coll (MA)
Mount St. Mary's U (MD)
Muhlenberg Coll (PA)
Murray State U (KY)
National U (CA)
Nazareth Coll of Rochester (NY)
Nebraska Wesleyan U (NE)
Nevada State Coll at Henderson
　(NV)
New Coll of Florida (FL)
New Jersey City U (NJ)
New Mexico State U (NM)
New York Inst of Technology (NY)
New York U (NY)
Niagara U (NY)
North Carolina Ag and Tech State U
　(NC)
North Central Coll (IL)
North Dakota State U (ND)
Northeastern Illinois U (IL)
Northeastern U (MA)
Northern Arizona U (AZ)
Northern Illinois U (IL)
Northern Michigan U (MI)
Northern State U (SD)
Northwestern Coll (IA)
Northwest Missouri State U (MO)
Oberlin Coll (OH)
Oglethorpe U (GA)
The Ohio State U (OH)
Ohio U (OH)
Ohio Wesleyan U (OH)
Oklahoma State U (OK)
Old Dominion U (VA)
Oregon State U (OR)
Pace U (NY)
Pacific Lutheran U (WA)
Pacific U (OR)
Penn State Abington (PA)
Penn State Altoona (PA)
Penn State Beaver (PA)
Penn State Berks (PA)
Penn State Brandywine (PA)
Penn State DuBois (PA)
Penn State Erie, The Behrend Coll
　(PA)
Penn State Fayette, The Eberly
　Campus (PA)
Penn State Greater Allegheny (PA)
Penn State Hazleton (PA)
Penn State Lehigh Valley (PA)
Penn State Mont Alto (PA)
Penn State New Kensington (PA)
Penn State Schuylkill (PA)
Penn State Shenango (PA)
Penn State U Park (PA)
Penn State Wilkes-Barre (PA)
Penn State Worthington Scranton
　(PA)
Penn State York (PA)
Pepperdine U, Malibu (CA)
Pittsburg State U (KS)
Pitzer Coll (CA)
Point Park U (PA)
Pomona Coll (CA)
Portland State U (OR)
Presbyterian Coll (SC)
Princeton U (NJ)
Principia Coll (IL)
Providence Coll (RI)
Purchase Coll, State U of New York
　(NY)
Purdue U (IN)
Purdue U Calumet (IN)

Queens Coll of the City U of New
　York (NY)
Quinnipiac U (CT)
Radford U (VA)
Ramapo Coll of New Jersey (NJ)
Randolph Coll (VA)
Randolph-Macon Coll (VA)
Reed Coll (OR)
Regis U (CO)
Rensselaer Polytechnic Inst (NY)
Rhode Island Coll (RI)
Rhodes Coll (TN)
Rice U (TX)
The Richard Stockton Coll of New
　Jersey (NJ)
Rider U (NJ)
Ripon Coll (WI)
Roanoke Coll (VA)
Robert Morris U (PA)
Rockford Coll (IL)
Rockhurst U (MO)
Rollins Coll (FL)
Roosevelt U (IL)
Rose-Hulman Inst of Technology
　(IN)
Rosemont Coll (PA)
Rowan U (NJ)
Rutgers, The State U of New Jersey,
　Camden (NJ)
Rutgers, The State U of New Jersey,
　Newark (NJ)
Rutgers, The State U of New Jersey,
　New Brunswick (NJ)
Saginaw Valley State U (MI)
St. Ambrose U (IA)
Saint Anselm Coll (NH)
St. Catherine U (MN)
St. Edward's U (TX)
Saint Francis U (PA)
St. Francis Xavier U (NS, Canada)
St. John Fisher Coll (NY)
Saint John's U (MN)
St. John's U (NY)
Saint Joseph's Coll (IN)
Saint Joseph's U (PA)
St. Lawrence U (NY)
Saint Martin's U (WA)
Saint Mary's Coll (IN)
Saint Mary's Coll of California (CA)
St. Mary's Coll of Maryland (MD)
Saint Michael's Coll (VT)
St. Norbert Coll (WI)
St. Olaf Coll (MN)
St. Thomas U (FL)
St. Thomas U (NB, Canada)
Salem State U (MA)
Salisbury U (MD)
San Diego State U (CA)
San Francisco State U (CA)
San Jose State U (CA)
Santa Clara U (CA)
Sarah Lawrence Coll (NY)
Scripps Coll (CA)
Seattle Pacific U (WA)
Seton Hill U (PA)
Sewanee: The U of the South (TN)
Shepherd U (WV)
Shippensburg U of Pennsylvania
　(PA)
Shorter U (GA)
Siena Coll (NY)
Simmons Coll (MA)
Simon Fraser U (BC, Canada)
Simpson Coll (IA)
Skidmore Coll (NY)
Slippery Rock U of Pennsylvania
　(PA)
Smith Coll (MA)
Sonoma State U (CA)
South Dakota State U (SD)
Southeast Missouri State U (MO)
Southern Connecticut State U (CT)
Southern Illinois U Carbondale (IL)
Southern Illinois U Edwardsville (IL)
Southern Methodist U (TX)
Southern Oregon U (OR)
Southern Utah U (UT)
Spelman Coll (GA)
Stanford U (CA)
State U of New York at Binghamton
　(NY)
State U of New York at Fredonia
　(NY)
State U of New York at New Paltz
　(NY)
State U of New York at Oswego
　(NY)
State U of New York at Plattsburgh
　(NY)

State U of New York Coll at
　Geneseo (NY)
State U of New York Coll at Oneonta
　(NY)
State U of New York Coll at Potsdam
　(NY)
State U of New York Empire State
　Coll (NY)
Stephen F. Austin State U (TX)
Stetson U (FL)
Stonehill Coll (MA)
Stony Brook U, State U of New York
　(NY)
Strayer U - Akron Campus (OH)
Strayer U - Alexandria Campus (VA)
Strayer U - Allentown Campus (PA)
Strayer U - Anne Arundel Campus
　(MD)
Strayer U - Arlington Campus (VA)
Strayer U - Augusta Campus (GA)
Strayer U - Baymeadows Campus
　(FL)
Strayer U - Birmingham Campus
　(AL)
Strayer U - Brickell Campus (FL)
Strayer U - Cedar Hill Campus (TX)
Strayer U - Center City Campus
　(PA)
Strayer U - Chamblee Campus (GA)
Strayer U - Charleston Campus (SC)
Strayer U - Chesapeake Campus
　(VA)
Strayer U - Chesterfield Campus
　(VA)
Strayer U - Christiana Campus (DE)
Strayer U - Cincinnati Campus (OH)
Strayer U - Cobb County Campus
　(GA)
Strayer U - Columbia Campus (SC)
Strayer U - Columbus Campus (GA)
Strayer U - Columbus Campus (OH)
Strayer U - Coral Springs Campus
　(FL)
Strayer U - Cranberry Woods
　Campus (PA)
Strayer U - Delaware County
　Campus (PA)
Strayer U - Doral Campus (FL)
Strayer U - Douglasville Campus
　(GA)
Strayer U - Fairborn Campus (OH)
Strayer U - Fairview Park Campus
　(OH)
Strayer U - Florence Campus (KY)
Strayer U - Fort Lauderdale Campus
　(FL)
Strayer U - Fredericksburg Campus
　(VA)
Strayer U - Greensboro Campus
　(NC)
Strayer U - Greenville Campus (SC)
Strayer U - Henrico Campus (VA)
Strayer U - Huntersville Campus
　(NC)
Strayer U - Huntsville Campus (AL)
Strayer U - Irving Campus (TX)
Strayer U - Katy Campus (TX)
Strayer U - King of Prussia Campus
　(PA)
Strayer U - Knoxville Campus (TN)
Strayer U - Lexington Campus (KY)
Strayer U - Lithonia Campus (GA)
Strayer U - Loudoun Campus (VA)
Strayer U - Louisville Campus (KY)
Strayer U - Lower Bucks County
　Campus (PA)
Strayer U - Maitland Campus (FL)
Strayer U - Manassas Campus (VA)
Strayer U - Mason Campus (OH)
Strayer U - Metairie Campus (LA)
Strayer U - Milwaukee Campus (WI)
Strayer U - Miramar Campus (FL)
Strayer U - Morrow Campus (GA)
Strayer U - Nashville Campus (TN)
Strayer U - Newport News Campus
　(VA)
Strayer U - North Austin Campus
　(TX)
Strayer U - North Charlotte Campus
　(NC)
Strayer U - North Indianapolis
　Campus (IN)
Strayer U - North Raleigh Campus
　(NC)
Strayer U - Northwest Houston
　Campus (TX)
Strayer U - Orlando East Campus
　(FL)
Strayer U - Owings Mills Campus
　(MD)

Strayer U - Palm Beach Gardens
　Campus (FL)
Strayer U - Penn Center West
　Campus (PA)
Strayer U - Plano Campus (TX)
Strayer U - Prince George's Campus
　(MD)
Strayer U - Rockville Campus (MD)
Strayer U - Roswell Campus (GA)
Strayer U - RTP Campus (NC)
Strayer U - Salt Lake Campus (UT)
Strayer U - Sand Lake Campus (FL)
Strayer U - Savannah Campus (GA)
Strayer U - Shelby Oaks Campus
　(TN)
Strayer U - South Charlotte Campus
　(NC)
Strayer U - South Raleigh Campus
　(NC)
Strayer U - Takoma Park Campus
　(DC)
Strayer U - Tampa East Campus
　(FL)
Strayer U - Tampa Westshore
　Campus (FL)
Strayer U - Teays Valley Campus
　(WV)
Strayer U - Thousand Oaks Campus
　(TN)
Strayer U - Virginia Beach Campus
　(VA)
Strayer U - Washington Campus
　(DC)
Strayer U - White Marsh Campus
　(MD)
Strayer U - Woodbridge Campus
　(VA)
Suffolk U (MA)
Susquehanna U (PA)
Swarthmore Coll (PA)
Sweet Briar Coll (VA)
Syracuse U (NY)
Talladega Coll (AL)
Tarleton State U (TX)
Taylor U (IN)
Temple U (PA)
Tennessee Technological U (TN)
Texas A&M U (TX)
Texas A&M U–Corpus Christi (TX)
Texas Christian U (TX)
Texas Lutheran U (TX)
Texas Southern U (TX)
Texas State U–San Marcos (TX)
Texas Tech U (TX)
Thomas Edison State Coll (NJ)
Thomas More Coll (KY)
Towson U (MD)
Transylvania U (KY)
Trent U (ON, Canada)
Trinity Coll (CT)
Trinity U (TX)
Truman State U (MO)
Tufts U (MA)
Tulane U (LA)
Tuskegee U (AL)
Union Coll (NY)
Union U (TN)
United States Air Force Acad (CO)
United States Military Acad (NY)
United States Naval Acad (MD)
U at Buffalo, the State U of New
　York (NY)
The U of Akron (OH)
U of Alaska Fairbanks (AK)
The U of Arizona (AZ)
U of Arkansas (AR)
U of Baltimore (MD)
The U of British Columbia (BC,
　Canada)
The U of British Columbia–
　Okanagan (BC, Canada)
U of California, Berkeley (CA)
U of California, Davis (CA)
U of California, Irvine (CA)
U of California, Los Angeles (CA)
U of California, Merced (CA)
U of California, Santa Barbara (CA)
U of California, Santa Cruz (CA)
U of Central Florida (FL)
U of Central Missouri (MO)
U of Cincinnati (OH)
U of Colorado at Colorado Springs
　(CO)
U of Colorado Boulder (CO)
U of Colorado Denver (CO)
U of Dallas (TX)
U of Dayton (OH)
U of Delaware (DE)
U of Denver (CO)
U of Evansville (IN)

The U of Findlay (OH)
U of Florida (FL)
U of Georgia (GA)
U of Guelph (ON, Canada)
U of Hartford (CT)
U of Hawaii at Hilo (HI)
U of Hawaii at Manoa (HI)
U of Hawaii–West Oahu (HI)
U of Houston (TX)
U of Idaho (ID)
U of Illinois at Chicago (IL)
U of Illinois at Springfield (IL)
The U of Iowa (IA)
The U of Kansas (KS)
U of La Verne (CA)
U of Lethbridge (AB, Canada)
U of Louisville (KY)
U of Maine (ME)
U of Manitoba (MB, Canada)
U of Mary Hardin-Baylor (TX)
U of Maryland, Baltimore County
　(MD)
U of Maryland, Coll Park (MD)
U of Mary Washington (VA)
U of Massachusetts Amherst (MA)
U of Massachusetts Boston (MA)
U of Massachusetts Dartmouth (MA)
U of Massachusetts Lowell (MA)
U of Memphis (TN)
U of Miami (FL)
U of Michigan (MI)
U of Michigan–Dearborn (MI)
U of Michigan–Flint (MI)
U of Minnesota, Duluth (MN)
U of Minnesota, Twin Cities Campus
　(MN)
U of Mississippi (MS)
U of Missouri (MO)
U of Missouri–St. Louis (MO)
U of Mount Union (OH)
U of Nebraska at Omaha (NE)
U of Nebraska–Lincoln (NE)
U of Nevada, Las Vegas (NV)
U of New Brunswick Fredericton
　(NB, Canada)
U of New Brunswick Saint John (NB,
　Canada)
U of New Hampshire (NH)
The U of North Carolina at Asheville
　(NC)
The U of North Carolina at Chapel
　Hill (NC)
The U of North Carolina at Charlotte
　(NC)
The U of North Carolina at
　Greensboro (NC)
The U of North Carolina Wilmington
　(NC)
U of Northern Colorado (CO)
U of Northern Iowa (IA)
U of North Florida (FL)
U of North Texas (TX)
U of Notre Dame (IN)
U of Oklahoma (OK)
U of Oregon (OR)
U of Ottawa (ON, Canada)
U of Pennsylvania (PA)
U of Pittsburgh (PA)
U of Pittsburgh at Bradford (PA)
U of Pittsburgh at Johnstown (PA)
U of Portland (OR)
U of Puget Sound (WA)
U of Redlands (CA)
U of Regina (SK, Canada)
U of Rhode Island (RI)
U of Richmond (VA)
U of Rio Grande (OH)
U of Rochester (NY)
U of St. Thomas (MN)
U of San Diego (CA)
U of San Francisco (CA)
U of Saskatchewan (SK, Canada)
U of Science and Arts of Oklahoma
　(OK)
The U of Scranton (PA)
U of South Carolina (SC)
The U of South Dakota (SD)
U of Southern California (CA)
U of Southern Indiana (IN)
U of Southern Maine (ME)
U of South Florida (FL)
The U of Tampa (FL)
The U of Tennessee (TN)
The U of Tennessee at Chattanooga
　(TN)
The U of Tennessee at Martin (TN)
The U of Texas at Arlington (TX)
The U of Texas at Austin (TX)
The U of Texas at Dallas (TX)
The U of Texas at Tyler (TX)

INDEXES

Wells Coll (NY)
Westfield State U (MA)
West Liberty U (WV)
Westmont Coll (CA)
Wheeling Jesuit U (WV)
Wichita State U (KS)
Wilfrid Laurier U (ON, Canada)
Wilkes U (PA)
William Jessup U (CA)
William Paterson U of New Jersey (NJ)
Wilmington Coll (OH)
Winona State U (MN)
Wittenberg U (OH)
Xavier U (OH)
Xavier U of Louisiana (LA)
Youngstown State U (OH)

EDUCATIONAL ADMINISTRATION AND SUPERVISION RELATED

Kendall Coll (IL)
Purdue U (IN)
The U of Montana Western (MT)

EDUCATIONAL ASSESSMENT, EVALUATION, AND RESEARCH RELATED

Penn State Altoona (PA)
Penn State Berks (PA)
Penn State U Park (PA)
Purdue U (IN)

EDUCATIONAL ASSESSMENT, TESTING, AND MEASUREMENT

Purdue U (IN)

EDUCATIONAL EVALUATION AND RESEARCH

Purdue U (IN)

EDUCATIONAL, INSTRUCTIONAL, AND CURRICULUM SUPERVISION

Kutztown U of Pennsylvania (PA)
Prescott Coll (AZ)
Purdue U (IN)
U of Wisconsin–River Falls (WI)
Wright State U (OH)

EDUCATIONAL/INSTRUCTIONAL TECHNOLOGY

California State U, Chico (CA)
Cameron U (OK)
Eastern Washington U (WA)
Ithaca Coll (NY)
Jacksonville State U (AL)
Kutztown U of Pennsylvania (PA)
Midwestern State U (TX)
Minnesota State U Moorhead (MN)
Purdue U (IN)
U of Maine (ME)
The U of Toledo (OH)
Western Illinois U (IL)
Western Oregon U (OR)
Widener U (PA)

EDUCATIONAL LEADERSHIP AND ADMINISTRATION

Cleveland State U (OH)
DePaul U (IL)
Eastern Washington U (WA)
Edinboro U of Pennsylvania (PA)
Free Will Baptist Bible Coll (TN)
Kendall Coll (IL)
Lamar U (TX)
Midwestern State U (TX)
Prescott Coll (AZ)
Purdue U (IN)
Tarleton State U (TX)
The U of British Columbia (BC, Canada)
U of Cincinnati (OH)
U of Minnesota, Crookston (MN)
U of Regina (SK, Canada)
U of San Francisco (CA)
U of the Incarnate Word (TX)
U of Wisconsin–Superior (WI)
Wright State U (OH)

EDUCATIONAL PSYCHOLOGY

DePaul U (IL)
Edinboro U of Pennsylvania (PA)
Jacksonville State U (AL)
Mississippi State U (MS)
Purdue U (IN)
Shenandoah U (VA)
U of Georgia (GA)
U of Pittsburgh (PA)

U of Regina (SK, Canada)

EDUCATIONAL STATISTICS AND RESEARCH METHODS

Bucknell U (PA)
Purdue U (IN)

EDUCATIONAL SYSTEM ADMINISTRATION AND SUPERINTENDENCY

Dordt Coll (IA)
Purdue U (IN)

EDUCATION (MULTIPLE LEVELS)

Adams State Coll (CO)
Augustana Coll (SD)
Averett U (VA)
Baptist Bible Coll of Pennsylvania (PA)
Biola U (CA)
Birmingham-Southern Coll (AL)
Bowling Green State U (OH)
Canisius Coll (NY)
Central State U (OH)
Chestnut Hill Coll (PA)
Coll of Coastal Georgia (GA)
Coll of Saint Elizabeth (NJ)
Coll of Saint Mary (NE)
The Coll of St. Scholastica (MN)
Concordia U Chicago (IL)
Concordia U Wisconsin (WI)
Crandall U (NB, Canada)
Crossroads Bible Coll (IN)
Dakota Wesleyan U (SD)
DePaul U (IL)
Dickinson State U (ND)
Dominican U (IL)
Dordt Coll (IA)
Dowling Coll (NY)
Eastern Oregon U (OR)
Eastern Washington U (WA)
Edinboro U of Pennsylvania (PA)
Felician Coll (NJ)
Gannon U (PA)
Gardner-Webb U (NC)
Goddard Coll (VT)
Hamline U (MN)
Harding U (AR)
Hillsdale Coll (MI)
Hofstra U (NY)
Illinois Coll (IL)
Indiana U Bloomington (IN)
Indiana Wesleyan U (IN)
Ithaca Coll (NY)
John Carroll U (OH)
Juniata Coll (PA)
Keystone Coll (PA)
Lake Superior State U (MI)
Liberty U (VA)
Lindenwood U (MO)
Lubbock Christian U (TX)
Manchester Coll (IN)
Manhattan Coll (NY)
Martin Luther Coll (MN)
McKendree U (IL)
Merrimack Coll (MA)
Mount Saint Mary Coll (NY)
New England Coll (NH)
Northland Coll (WI)
Northwest Christian U (OR)
Northwestern Coll (IA)
Nyack Coll (NY)
Ohio Wesleyan U (OH)
Purdue U (IN)
Quincy U (IL)
Rhode Island Coll (RI)
The Richard Stockton Coll of New Jersey (NJ)
St. Ambrose U (IA)
Saint Louis U (MO)
Saint Mary-of-the-Woods Coll (IN)
Samford U (AL)
San Diego Christian Coll (CA)
Shawnee State U (OH)
Tabor Coll (KS) .
Tarleton State U (TX)
Tennessee Wesleyan Coll (TN)
Texas Lutheran U (TX)
Troy U (AL)
U of Louisville (KY)
U of Maine (ME)
U of Maine at Fort Kent (ME)
U of Memphis (TN)
The U of Montana Western (MT)
U of Nebraska–Lincoln (NE)
U of Rio Grande (OH)
U of St. Thomas (MN)
The U of Tennessee at Martin (TN)
U of Washington (WA)

Utah State U (UT)
Virginia Wesleyan Coll (VA)
Wake Forest U (NC)
Walla Walla U (WA)
Washington State U (WA)
Washington U in St. Louis (MO)
Wayland Baptist U (TX)
Western Kentucky U (KY)
William Jewell Coll (MO)
Wright State U (OH)

EDUCATION POLICY ANALYSIS

Purdue U (IN)

EDUCATION RELATED

Albany State U (GA)
Arizona State U (AZ)
Bowling Green State U (OH)
Brigham Young U (UT)
Cedarville U (OH)
Central State U (OH)
Concordia Coll (MN)
Concordia U, St. Paul (MN)
Delaware State U (DE)
DePaul U (IL)
Eastern Oregon U (OR)
Edgewood Coll (WI)
The Evergreen State Coll (WA)
Grace Coll (IN)
Indiana U Bloomington (IN)
Kendall Coll (IL)
Lindsey Wilson Coll (KY)
Mercer U (GA)
Midwestern State U (TX)
Mitchell Coll (CT)
Mount Holyoke Coll (MA)
Northland Coll (WI)
Northwest Missouri State U (MO)
Northwest Nazarene U (ID)
Point Park U (PA)
Prescott Coll (AZ)
Purdue U (IN)
Saginaw Valley State U (MI)
St. Petersburg Coll (FL)
Southern Adventist U (TN)
State U of New York Coll at Potsdam (NY)
Sterling Coll (VT)
Swarthmore Coll (PA)
Syracuse U (NY)
Towson U (MD)
U of Lethbridge (AB, Canada)
U of Minnesota, Twin Cities Campus (MN)
U of Waterloo (ON, Canada)
Wayne State U (MI)
Wright State U (OH)

EDUCATION (SPECIFIC LEVELS AND METHODS) RELATED

Anderson U (SC)
Boston U (MA)
Brigham Young U (UT)
Colorado State U (CO)
Columbia Coll Chicago (IL)
Concordia Coll–New York (NY)
Delaware State U (DE)
Immaculata U (PA)
Inter American U of Puerto Rico, Metropolitan Campus (PR)
John Brown U (AR)
Kendall Coll (IL)
Lynchburg Coll (VA)
Prescott Coll (AZ)
Purdue U (IN)
Rowan U (NJ)
The U of Toledo (OH)
Washington U in St. Louis (MO)
Wright State U (OH)
Xavier U (OH)

EDUCATION (SPECIFIC SUBJECT AREAS) RELATED

Appalachian State U (NC)
Averett U (VA)
Avila U (MO)
Bowling Green State U (OH)
Brigham Young U (UT)
Central Michigan U (MI)
The Coll of Saint Rose (NY)
Columbia Coll Chicago (IL)
Eastern Michigan U (MI)
Gardner-Webb U (NC)
Graceland U (IA)
Hope Coll (MI)
Indiana U Bloomington (IN)
Juniata Coll (PA)
Madonna U (MI)
Marquette U (WI)

Marywood U (PA)
Minot State U (ND)
Mississippi State U (MS)
Missouri State U (MO)
Murray State U (KY)
Northern Arizona U (AZ)
Northern Michigan U (MI)
Old Dominion U (VA)
Point Park U (PA)
Prescott Coll (AZ)
Purdue U (IN)
Regent U (VA)
St. Edward's U (TX)
Southwestern Coll (KS)
State U of New York Coll at Potsdam (NY)
Syracuse U (NY)
Taylor U (IN)
Thomas More Coll (KY)
The U of Akron (OH)
The U of Arizona (AZ)
U of Lethbridge (AB, Canada)
U of Louisiana at Lafayette (LA)
U of Louisiana at Monroe (LA)
U of Michigan–Flint (MI)
U of Nebraska–Lincoln (NE)
U of Nevada, Reno (NV)
U of New Hampshire (NH)
The U of North Carolina Wilmington (NC)
U of Ottawa (ON, Canada)
U of Regina (SK, Canada)
U of St. Thomas (MN)
U of the Cumberlands (KY)
The U of Toledo (OH)
U of Wisconsin–Eau Claire (WI)
U of Wisconsin–Stout (WI)
Utah State U (UT)
Wayne State U (NE)
Wright State U (OH)

ELECTRICAL AND ELECTRONIC ENGINEERING TECHNOLOGIES RELATED

Embry-Riddle Aeronautical U–Daytona (FL)
Grove City Coll (PA)
North Carolina Ag and Tech State U (NC)
Penn State Berks (PA)
Pennsylvania Coll of Technology (PA)
Point Park U (PA)
Purdue U (IN)
Southern Illinois U Carbondale (IL)
Vaughn Coll of Aeronautics and Technology (NY)
Virginia State U (VA)
Wayne State U (MI)

ELECTRICAL AND ELECTRONICS ENGINEERING

Alabama Ag and Mech U (AL)
Alfred U (NY)
American U of Beirut (Lebanon)
Arizona State U (AZ)
Arkansas State U (AR)
Arkansas Tech U (AR)
Auburn U (AL)
Bloomsburg U of Pennsylvania (PA)
Bob Jones U (SC)
Boise State U (ID)
Boston U (MA)
Brown U (RI)
Bucknell U (PA)
California Baptist U (CA)
California Inst of Technology (CA)
California Polytechnic State U, San Luis Obispo (CA)
California State Polytechnic U, Pomona (CA)
California State U, Chico (CA)
California State U, Fullerton (CA)
California State U, Long Beach (CA)
California State U, Los Angeles (CA)
California State U, Northridge (CA)
Calvin Coll (MI)
Carnegie Mellon U (PA)
Case Western Reserve U (OH)
The Catholic U of America (DC)
Cedarville U (OH)
Central Connecticut State U (CT)
Central Michigan U (MI)
Christian Brothers U (TN)
The Citadel, The Military Coll of South Carolina (SC)
City Coll of the City U of New York (NY)
Clarkson U (NY)

Clemson U (SC)
Cleveland State U (OH)
The Coll of New Jersey (NJ)
Colorado State U (CO)
Concordia U (QC, Canada)
Cooper Union for the Advancement of Science and Art (NY)
Cornell U (NY)
Delaware State U (DE)
Dominican U (IL)
Dordt Coll (IA)
Eastern Washington U (WA)
Embry-Riddle Aeronautical U–Daytona (FL)
Embry-Riddle Aeronautical U–Prescott (AZ)
Fairfield U (CT)
Fairleigh Dickinson U, Metropolitan Campus (NJ)
Florida Ag and Mech U (FL)
Florida Atlantic U (FL)
Florida Inst of Technology (FL)
Florida Intl U (FL)
Franklin W. Olin Coll of Eng (MA)
Gannon U (PA)
George Fox U (OR)
Georgia Inst of Technology (GA)
Georgia Southern U (GA)
Grove City Coll (PA)
Harding U (AR)
Hofstra U (NY)
Idaho State U (ID)
Illinois Inst of Technology (IL)
Indiana Tech (IN)
Indiana U–Purdue U Fort Wayne (IN)
Indiana U–Purdue U Indianapolis (IN)
Inter American U of Puerto Rico, Bayamón Campus (PR)
Inter American U of Puerto Rico, Ponce Campus (PR)
Iowa State U of Science and Technology (IA)
John Brown U (AR)
The Johns Hopkins U (MD)
Johnson & Wales U (RI)
Kansas State U (KS)
Kettering U (MI)
Lafayette Coll (PA)
Lakehead U (ON, Canada)
Lake Superior State U (MI)
Lamar U (TX)
Lawrence Technological U (MI)
Lebanese American U (Lebanon)
Lehigh U (PA)
LeTourneau U (TX)
Louisiana State U and Ag and Mech Coll (LA)
Loyola Marymount U (CA)
Loyola U Maryland (MD)
Manhattan Coll (NY)
Marquette U (WI)
Massachusetts Inst of Technology (MA)
Merrimack Coll (MA)
Miami U (OH)
Michigan State U (MI)
Milwaukee School of Eng (WI)
Minnesota State U Mankato (MN)
Mississippi State U (MS)
Missouri U of Science and Technology (MO)
Montana State U (MT)
Montana Tech of The U of Montana (MT)
New England Inst of Technology (RI)
New Jersey Inst of Technology (NJ)
New Mexico Highlands U (NM)
New Mexico Inst of Mining and Technology (NM)
New Mexico State U (NM)
New York Inst of Technology (NY)
North Carolina Ag and Tech State U (NC)
North Carolina State U (NC)
North Dakota State U (ND)
Northeastern U (MA)
Northern Arizona U (AZ)
Northern Illinois U (IL)
The Ohio State U (OH)
Ohio U (OH)
Oklahoma Christian U (OK)
Oklahoma State U (OK)
Old Dominion U (VA)
Oregon State U (OR)
Penn State Abington (PA)
Penn State Altoona (PA)
Penn State Beaver (PA)

Penn State Berks (PA)
Penn State Brandywine (PA)
Penn State DuBois (PA)
Penn State Erie, The Behrend Coll (PA)
Penn State Fayette, The Eberly Campus (PA)
Penn State Greater Allegheny (PA)
Penn State Harrisburg (PA)
Penn State Hazleton (PA)
Penn State Lehigh Valley (PA)
Penn State Mont Alto (PA)
Penn State New Kensington (PA)
Penn State Schuylkill (PA)
Penn State Shenango (PA)
Penn State U Park (PA)
Penn State Wilkes-Barre (PA)
Penn State Worthington Scranton (PA)
Penn State York (PA)
Polytechnic Inst of NYU (NY)
Polytechnic U of Puerto Rico (PR)
Portland State U (OR)
Prairie View A&M U (TX)
Princeton U (NJ)
Purdue U (IN)
Purdue U Calumet (IN)
Rensselaer Polytechnic Inst (NY)
Rice U (TX)
Rose-Hulman Inst of Technology (IN)
Rowan U (NJ)
Rutgers, The State U of New Jersey, New Brunswick (NJ)
Saginaw Valley State U (MI)
Saint Louis U (MO)
San Diego State U (CA)
San Francisco State U (CA)
San Jose State U (CA)
Santa Clara U (CA)
Seattle Pacific U (WA)
South Dakota School of Mines and Technology (SD)
South Dakota State U (SD)
Southern California Inst of Technology (CA)
Southern Illinois U Carbondale (IL)
Southern Illinois U Edwardsville (IL)
Southern Methodist U (TX)
Southern Polytechnic State U (GA)
Stanford U (CA)
State U of New York at Binghamton (NY)
State U of New York at New Paltz (NY)
State U of New York Maritime Coll (NY)
Stony Brook U, State U of New York (NY)
Suffolk U (MA)
Syracuse U (NY)
Temple U (PA)
Tennessee Technological U (TN)
Texas A&M U (TX)
Texas A&M U–Kingsville (TX)
Texas Christian U (TX)
Texas State U–San Marcos (TX)
Texas Tech U (TX)
Trine U (IN)
Trinity Coll (CT)
Tufts U (MA)
Tulane U (LA)
Tuskegee U (AL)
Union Coll (NY)
United States Air Force Acad (CO)
United States Coast Guard Acad (CT)
United States Military Acad (NY)
United States Naval Acad (MD)
Université de Sherbrooke (QC, Canada)
U at Buffalo, the State U of New York (NY)
The U of Akron (OH)
The U of Alabama (AL)
The U of Alabama at Birmingham (AL)
The U of Alabama in Huntsville (AL)
U of Alaska Fairbanks (AK)
The U of Arizona (AZ)
U of Arkansas (AR)
The U of British Columbia (BC, Canada)
The U of British Columbia–Okanagan (BC, Canada)
U of California, Berkeley (CA)
U of California, Davis (CA)
U of California, Irvine (CA)

U of California, Los Angeles (CA)
U of California, Santa Barbara (CA)
U of California, Santa Cruz (CA)
U of Central Florida (FL)
U of Cincinnati (OH)
U of Colorado at Colorado Springs (CO)
U of Colorado Boulder (CO)
U of Colorado Denver (CO)
U of Dayton (OH)
U of Delaware (DE)
U of Denver (CO)
U of Evansville (IN)
U of Florida (FL)
U of Hartford (CT)
U of Hawaii at Manoa (HI)
U of Houston (TX)
U of Idaho (ID)
U of Illinois at Chicago (IL)
The U of Iowa (IA)
The U of Kansas (KS)
U of Louisiana at Lafayette (LA)
U of Louisville (KY)
U of Maine (ME)
U of Manitoba (MB, Canada)
U of Maryland, Coll Park (MD)
U of Massachusetts Amherst (MA)
U of Massachusetts Dartmouth (MA)
U of Massachusetts Lowell (MA)
U of Memphis (TN)
U of Miami (FL)
U of Michigan (MI)
U of Michigan–Dearborn (MI)
U of Minnesota, Duluth (MN)
U of Minnesota, Twin Cities Campus (MN)
U of Mississippi (MS)
U of Missouri (MO)
U of Missouri–St. Louis (MO)
U of Nebraska–Lincoln (NE)
U of Nevada, Las Vegas (NV)
U of Nevada, Reno (NV)
U of New Brunswick Fredericton (NB, Canada)
U of New Hampshire (NH)
U of New Haven (CT)
The U of North Carolina at Charlotte (NC)
U of North Florida (FL)
U of North Texas (TX)
U of Notre Dame (IN)
U of Oklahoma (OK)
U of Ottawa (ON, Canada)
U of Pennsylvania (PA)
U of Pittsburgh (PA)
U of Portland (OR)
U of Regina (SK, Canada)
U of Rhode Island (RI)
U of Rochester (NY)
U of St. Thomas (MN)
U of San Diego (CA)
U of Saskatchewan (SK, Canada)
The U of Scranton (PA)
U of South Alabama (AL)
U of South Carolina (SC)
U of Southern California (CA)
U of Southern Maine (ME)
U of South Florida (FL)
The U of Tennessee (TN)
The U of Tennessee at Chattanooga (TN)
The U of Texas at Arlington (TX)
The U of Texas at Austin (TX)
The U of Texas at Dallas (TX)
The U of Texas at San Antonio (TX)
The U of Texas at Tyler (TX)
The U of Texas–Pan American (TX)
U of the District of Columbia (DC)
U of the Pacific (CA)
The U of Toledo (OH)
U of Tulsa (OK)
U of Utah (UT)
U of Vermont (VT)
U of Virginia (VA)
U of Washington (WA)
U of Washington, Bothell (WA)
U of Waterloo (ON, Canada)
The U of Western Ontario (ON, Canada)
U of West Florida (FL)
U of Wisconsin–Madison (WI)
U of Wisconsin–Platteville (WI)
U of Wyoming (WY)
Utah State U (UT)
Valparaiso U (IN)
Vanderbilt U (TN)
Villanova U (PA)

Virginia Commonwealth U (VA)
Virginia Military Inst (VA)
Virginia Polytechnic Inst and State U (VA)
Walla Walla U (WA)
Washington State U (WA)
Washington U in St. Louis (MO)
Wayne State U (MI)
Wentworth Inst of Technology (MA)
Western Carolina U (NC)
Western Kentucky U (KY)
Western Michigan U (MI)
Western New England U (MA)
West Virginia U (WV)
Wichita State U (KS)
Widener U (PA)
Wilkes U (PA)
Worcester Polytechnic Inst (MA)
Wright State U (OH)
Yale U (CT)
York Coll of Pennsylvania (PA)
Youngstown State U (OH)

ELECTRICAL, ELECTRONIC AND COMMUNICATIONS ENGINEERING TECHNOLOGY

Arizona State U (AZ)
Baker Coll of Owosso (MI)
Bluefield State Coll (WV)
Bowling Green State U (OH)
California State Polytechnic U, Pomona (CA)
California State U, Long Beach (CA)
Cameron U (OK)
Central Michigan U (MI)
Cleveland State U (OH)
Delaware State U (DE)
DeVry Coll of New York (NY)
DeVry U, Phoenix (AZ)
DeVry U, Pomona (CA)
DeVry U, Westminster (CO)
DeVry U, Miramar (FL)
DeVry U, Orlando (FL)
DeVry U, Decatur (GA)
DeVry U, Chicago (IL)
DeVry U, Kansas City (MO)
DeVry U, North Brunswick (NJ)
DeVry U, Columbus (OH)
DeVry U, Fort Washington (PA)
DeVry U, Houston (TX)
DeVry U, Irving (TX)
DeVry U, Arlington (VA)
DeVry U, Federal Way (WA)
DeVry U Online (IL)
Eastern Michigan U (MI)
ECPI Coll of Technology, Virginia Beach (VA)
Fairleigh Dickinson U, Metropolitan Campus (NJ)
Fairmont State U (WV)
Ferris State U (MI)
Fitchburg State U (MA)
Florida Ag and Mech U (FL)
Georgia Southern U (GA)
Hamilton Tech Coll (IA)
Herzing U (GA)
Herzing U, Madison (WI)
Indiana State U (IN)
Indiana U–Purdue U Fort Wayne (IN)
Indiana U–Purdue U Indianapolis (IN)
Inter American U of Puerto Rico, Bayamón Campus (PR)
Inter American U of Puerto Rico, San Germán Campus (PR)
ITT Tech Inst, Bessemer (AL)
ITT Tech Inst, Madison (AL)
ITT Tech Inst, Mobile (AL)
ITT Tech Inst, Phoenix (AZ)
ITT Tech Inst, Tempe (AZ)
ITT Tech Inst, Tucson (AZ)
ITT Tech Inst (AR)
ITT Tech Inst, Anaheim (CA)
ITT Tech Inst, Clovis (CA)
ITT Tech Inst, Concord (CA)
ITT Tech Inst, Corona (CA)
ITT Tech Inst, Lathrop (CA)
ITT Tech Inst, Oxnard (CA)
ITT Tech Inst, Rancho Cordova (CA)
ITT Tech Inst, San Bernardino (CA)
ITT Tech Inst, San Diego (CA)
ITT Tech Inst, San Dimas (CA)
ITT Tech Inst, Sylmar (CA)
ITT Tech Inst, Torrance (CA)
ITT Tech Inst, Thornton (CO)
ITT Tech Inst, Fort Lauderdale (FL)

ITT Tech Inst, Fort Myers (FL)
ITT Tech Inst, Jacksonville (FL)
ITT Tech Inst, Lake Mary (FL)
ITT Tech Inst, Miami (FL)
ITT Tech Inst, Tallahassee (FL)
ITT Tech Inst, Tampa (FL)
ITT Tech Inst, Atlanta (GA)
ITT Tech Inst, Duluth (GA)
ITT Tech Inst, Kennesaw (GA)
ITT Tech Inst (ID)
ITT Tech Inst, Burr Ridge (IL)
ITT Tech Inst, Mount Prospect (IL)
ITT Tech Inst, Orland Park (IL)
ITT Tech Inst, Fort Wayne (IN)
ITT Tech Inst, Indianapolis (IN)
ITT Tech Inst, Merrillville (IN)
ITT Tech Inst, South Bend (IN)
ITT Tech Inst, Clive (IA)
ITT Tech Inst, Lexington (KY)
ITT Tech Inst, Louisville (KY)
ITT Tech Inst, St. Rose (LA)
ITT Tech Inst (MD)
ITT Tech Inst, Norwood (MA)
ITT Tech Inst, Woburn (MA)
ITT Tech Inst, Canton (MI)
ITT Tech Inst, Swartz Creek (MI)
ITT Tech Inst, Troy (MI)
ITT Tech Inst, Wyoming (MI)
ITT Tech Inst (MN)
ITT Tech Inst (MS)
ITT Tech Inst, Arnold (MO)
ITT Tech Inst, Earth City (MO)
ITT Tech Inst, Kansas City (MO)
ITT Tech Inst, Springfield (MO)
ITT Tech Inst (NE)
ITT Tech Inst (NV)
ITT Tech Inst (NM)
ITT Tech Inst, Charlotte (NC)
ITT Tech Inst, Charlotte (NC)
ITT Tech Inst, High Point (NC)
ITT Tech Inst, Morrisville (NC)
ITT Tech Inst, Akron (OH)
ITT Tech Inst, Hilliard (OH)
ITT Tech Inst, Maumee (OH)
ITT Tech Inst, Norwood (OH)
ITT Tech Inst, Strongsville (OH)
ITT Tech Inst, Warrensville Heights (OH)
ITT Tech Inst, Youngstown (OH)
ITT Tech Inst, Oklahoma City (OK)
ITT Tech Inst, Tulsa (OK)
ITT Tech Inst (OR)
ITT Tech Inst, Greenville (SC)
ITT Tech Inst, Chattanooga (TN)
ITT Tech Inst, Cordova (TN)
ITT Tech Inst, Johnson City (TN)
ITT Tech Inst, Knoxville (TN)
ITT Tech Inst, Nashville (TN)
ITT Tech Inst, Arlington (TX)
ITT Tech Inst, Austin (TX)
ITT Tech Inst, DeSoto (TX)
ITT Tech Inst, Houston (TX)
ITT Tech Inst, Houston (TX)
ITT Tech Inst, Richardson (TX)
ITT Tech Inst, San Antonio (TX)
ITT Tech Inst, Webster (TX)
ITT Tech Inst (UT)
ITT Tech Inst, Chantilly (VA)
ITT Tech Inst, Norfolk (VA)
ITT Tech Inst, Richmond (VA)
ITT Tech Inst, Salem (VA)
ITT Tech Inst, Springfield (VA)
ITT Tech Inst, Everett (WA)
ITT Tech Inst, Seattle (WA)
ITT Tech Inst, Spokane Valley (WA)
ITT Tech Inst, Green Bay (WI)
ITT Tech Inst, Greenfield (WI)
ITT Tech Inst, Madison (WI)
Jacksonville State U (AL)
Kansas State U (KS)
Kent State U at Tuscarawas (OH)
Lakehead U (ON, Canada)
Lake Superior State U (MI)
LeTourneau U (TX)
Miami Dade Coll (FL)
Milwaukee School of Eng (WI)
Minnesota State U Mankato (MN)
Morehead State U (KY)
New England Inst of Technology (RI)
New York Inst of Technology (NY)
Northern Kentucky U (KY)
Northwestern State U of Louisiana (LA)
Oklahoma State U (OK)
Penn State Erie, The Behrend Coll (PA)
Pittsburg State U (KS)

Prairie View A&M U (TX)
Purdue U (IN)
Purdue U Calumet (IN)
Savannah State U (GA)
South Dakota State U (SD)
Southern Polytechnic State U (GA)
Southern Utah U (UT)
Texas A&M U (TX)
Texas A&M U–Corpus Christi (TX)
Texas Tech U (TX)
Thomas Edison State Coll (NJ)
Troy U (AL)
The U of Akron (OH)
U of Central Missouri (MO)
U of Cincinnati (OH)
U of Dayton (OH)
U of Hartford (CT)
U of Houston (TX)
U of Maine (ME)
U of Massachusetts Lowell (MA)
U of Memphis (TN)
U of New Hampshire (NH)
U of New Hampshire at Manchester (NH)
The U of North Carolina at Charlotte (NC)
U of North Texas (TX)
U of Pittsburgh at Johnstown (PA)
U of Regina (SK, Canada)
U of Southern Mississippi (MS)
The U of Toledo (OH)
Vaughn Coll of Aeronautics and Technology (NY)
Vermont Tech Coll (VT)
Wayne State U (MI)
Wentworth Inst of Technology (MA)
Western Carolina U (NC)
World Coll (VA)
Youngstown State U (OH)

ELECTRICAL, ELECTRONICS AND COMMUNICATIONS ENGINEERING RELATED

Marquette U (WI)

ELECTRICAL/ELECTRONICS EQUIPMENT INSTALLATION AND REPAIR

Lewis-Clark State Coll (ID)

ELECTRICAL/ELECTRONICS MAINTENANCE AND REPAIR TECHNOLOGY RELATED

Pennsylvania Coll of Technology (PA)

ELECTROMECHANICAL ENGINEERING

Wentworth Inst of Technology (MA)

ELECTROMECHANICAL TECHNOLOGY

Bowling Green State U (OH)
John Brown U (AR)
Murray State U (KY)
Purdue U Calumet (IN)
State U of New York Coll of Technology at Alfred (NY)
Temple U (PA)
U of Northern Iowa (IA)
The U of Toledo (OH)
Vermont Tech Coll (VT)
Wayne State U (MI)

ELEMENTARY AND MIDDLE SCHOOL ADMINISTRATION/ PRINCIPALSHIP

Berea Coll (KY)
Piedmont Coll (GA)
Purdue U (IN)
U of Cincinnati (OH)

ELEMENTARY EDUCATION

Abilene Christian U (TX)
Acadia U (NS, Canada)
Alabama Ag and Mech U (AL)
Alabama State U (AL)
Albion Coll (MI)
Albright Coll (PA)
Alcorn State U (MS)
Alderson-Broaddus Coll (WV)
Alfred U (NY)
Alma Coll (MI)
Alvernia U (PA)
Alverno Coll (WI)
American U (DC)

INDEXES

ENGINEERING ACOUSTICS
Purdue U (IN)

ENGINEERING CHEMISTRY
Purdue U (IN)

ENGINEERING DESIGN
Purdue U (IN)

ENGINEERING FIELDS RELATED
Purdue U (IN)

ENGINEERING/INDUSTRIAL MANAGEMENT
California State U, Chico (CA)
California State U, Long Beach (CA)
Claremont McKenna Coll (CA)
Clarkson U (NY)
Clemson U (SC)
Eastern Michigan U (MI)
Fort Lewis Coll (CO)
Illinois Inst of Technology (IL)
John Brown U (AR)
Lake Superior State U (MI)
Lawrence Technological U (MI)
Massachusetts Maritime Acad (MA)
Miami U (OH)
Middle Tennessee State U (TN)
Missouri State U (MO)
Missouri U of Science and Technology (MO)
Morehead State U (KY)
Purdue U (IN)
Saginaw Valley State U (MI)
South Dakota State U (SD)
Sweet Briar Coll (VA)
United States Merchant Marine Acad (NY)
United States Military Acad (NY)
U of Illinois at Chicago (IL)
U of Michigan–Flint (MI)
U of Portland (OR)
The U of Tennessee at Chattanooga (TN)
U of the Incarnate Word (TX)
U of the Pacific (CA)
U of Vermont (VT)
Western Michigan U (MI)
Wichita State U (KS)
Widener U (PA)
Wilkes U (PA)
Worcester Polytechnic Inst (MA)

ENGINEERING MECHANICS
Clemson U (SC)
Dordt Coll (IA)
Fairfield U (CT)
The Johns Hopkins U (MD)
Lehigh U (PA)
Lipscomb U (TN)
Purdue U (IN)
United States Air Force Acad (CO)
U of Wisconsin–Madison (WI)
Virginia Polytechnic Inst and State U (VA)
Western Illinois U (IL)
Worcester Polytechnic Inst (MA)

ENGINEERING PHYSICS/ APPLIED PHYSICS
Adams State Coll (CO)
Arkansas Tech U (AR)
Augustana Coll (IL)
Augustana Coll (SD)
Bemidji State U (MN)
Brown U (RI)
Carroll U (WI)
Case Western Reserve U (OH)
Christian Brothers U (TN)
Colorado School of Mines (CO)
Colorado State U (CO)
Cornell U (NY)
Dartmouth Coll (NH)
Delaware State U (DE)
Eastern Michigan U (MI)
Embry-Riddle Aeronautical U–Daytona (FL)
Fairfield U (CT)
Fort Lewis Coll (CO)
John Carroll U (OH)
Juniata Coll (PA)
Kettering U (MI)
Lehigh U (PA)
Loras Coll (IA)
Miami U (OH)
Morningside Coll (IA)
Murray State U (KY)
New Mexico State U (NM)

North Carolina Ag and Tech State U (NC)
Northern Arizona U (AZ)
Northwest Nazarene U (ID)
The Ohio State U (OH)
Oregon State U (OR)
Providence Coll (RI)
Purdue U (IN)
Randolph Coll (VA)
Rensselaer Polytechnic Inst (NY)
Rose-Hulman Inst of Technology (IN)
St. Ambrose U (IA)
Saint Louis U (MO)
Saint Mary's U of Minnesota (MN)
Samford U (AL)
Santa Clara U (CA)
South Dakota State U (SD)
Southeast Missouri State U (MO)
Tarleton State U (TX)
Taylor U (IN)
Thiel Coll (PA)
Tufts U (MA)
U at Buffalo, the State U of New York (NY)
The U of Arizona (AZ)
The U of British Columbia (BC, Canada)
U of California, Berkeley (CA)
U of Colorado Boulder (CO)
U of Illinois at Chicago (IL)
The U of Kansas (KS)
U of Maine (ME)
U of Massachusetts Boston (MA)
U of Michigan (MI)
U of Nebraska at Omaha (NE)
U of Nevada, Reno (NV)
U of Northern Iowa (IA)
U of Oklahoma (OK)
U of Pittsburgh (PA)
U of Saskatchewan (SK, Canada)
The U of Tennessee (TN)
U of the Pacific (CA)
The U of Toledo (OH)
U of Tulsa (OK)
U of Wisconsin–Madison (WI)
Washington and Lee U (VA)
Westmont Coll (CA)
Worcester Polytechnic Inst (MA)
Wright State U (OH)
Yale U (CT)

ENGINEERING RELATED
Alfred U (NY)
Anderson U (SC)
Arizona State U (AZ)
Auburn U (AL)
Boston U (MA)
California State U, Chico (CA)
California State U, Long Beach (CA)
Carnegie Mellon U (PA)
Claremont McKenna Coll (CA)
Eastern Illinois U (IL)
Gettysburg Coll (PA)
Hawai`i Pacific U (HI)
Indiana Tech (IN)
Indiana U–Purdue U Indianapolis (IN)
Iowa State U of Science and Technology (IA)
Kentucky Wesleyan Coll (KY)
Lipscomb U (TN)
Loras Coll (IA)
Maryville U of Saint Louis (MO)
McNally Smith Coll of Music (MN)
Milwaukee School of Eng (WI)
Mississippi State U (MS)
Northern Michigan U (MI)
Ohio Wesleyan U (OH)
Penn State Altoona (PA)
Penn State Berks (PA)
Penn State U Park (PA)
Principia Coll (IL)
Purdue U (IN)
Rose-Hulman Inst of Technology (IN)
State U of New York at Oswego (NY)
Texas Wesleyan U (TX)
Transylvania U (KY)
Tufts U (MA)
The U of Alabama in Huntsville (AL)
The U of Arizona (AZ)
U of California, Davis (CA)
U of Maryland, Coll Park (MD)
U of Michigan–Dearborn (MI)
U of Pennsylvania (PA)
U of the Cumberlands (KY)
U of Waterloo (ON, Canada)
Waynesburg U (PA)

Wentworth Inst of Technology (MA)
Wheaton Coll (IL)
Worcester Polytechnic Inst (MA)
Wright State U (OH)
York Coll of Pennsylvania (PA)

ENGINEERING-RELATED TECHNOLOGIES
Purdue U (IN)
United States Merchant Marine Acad (NY)

ENGINEERING SCIENCE
Abilene Christian U (TX)
Belmont U (TN)
Benedictine U (IL)
Bethel U (MN)
Bob Jones U (SC)
California Polytechnic State U, San Luis Obispo (CA)
California State U, Fullerton (CA)
Claremont McKenna Coll (CA)
The Coll of New Jersey (NJ)
Colorado State U (CO)
Hofstra U (NY)
Iowa State U of Science and Technology (IA)
Lamar U (TX)
Lipscomb U (TN)
New Jersey Inst of Technology (NJ)
Ohio Wesleyan U (OH)
Penn State Abington (PA)
Penn State Altoona (PA)
Penn State Beaver (PA)
Penn State Berks (PA)
Penn State Brandywine (PA)
Penn State DuBois (PA)
Penn State Erie, The Behrend Coll (PA)
Penn State Fayette, The Eberly Campus (PA)
Penn State Greater Allegheny (PA)
Penn State Hazleton (PA)
Penn State Lehigh Valley (PA)
Penn State Mont Alto (PA)
Penn State New Kensington (PA)
Penn State Schuylkill (PA)
Penn State Shenango (PA)
Penn State U Park (PA)
Penn State Wilkes-Barre (PA)
Penn State Worthington Scranton (PA)
Penn State York (PA)
Purdue U (IN)
Rensselaer Polytechnic Inst (NY)
Rutgers, The State U of New Jersey, New Brunswick (NJ)
St. Thomas Aquinas Coll (NY)
Simon Fraser U (BC, Canada)
Smith Coll (MA)
Sonoma State U (CA)
State U of New York Coll at Oneonta (NY)
Sweet Briar Coll (VA)
Trinity U (TX)
Tufts U (MA)
Tulane U (LA)
United States Air Force Acad (CO)
U of California, Berkeley (CA)
U of Manitoba (MB, Canada)
U of Miami (FL)
U of Michigan (MI)
U of Michigan–Flint (MI)
U of Portland (OR)
U of Rochester (NY)
U of South Carolina (SC)
The U of Tennessee (TN)
The U of Western Ontario (ON, Canada)
Vanderbilt U (TN)
Wartburg Coll (IA)
Wright State U (OH)
Yale U (CT)

ENGINEERING TECHNOLOGIES AND ENGINEERING RELATED
Arkansas State U (AR)
Ball State U (IN)
Bowling Green State U (OH)
Cameron U (OK)
Eastern Washington U (WA)
Elizabeth City State U (NC)
New Jersey Inst of Technology (NJ)
North Carolina Ag and Tech State U (NC)
Northwest Missouri State U (MO)
Old Dominion U (VA)
Pennsylvania Coll of Technology (PA)

Purdue U (IN)
Rogers State U (OK)
Shawnee State U (OH)
Silver Lake Coll (WI)
Thomas Edison State Coll (NJ)
United States Military Acad (NY)
The U of British Columbia (BC, Canada)
U of Hartford (CT)
U of Minnesota, Twin Cities Campus (MN)
The U of North Carolina at Charlotte (NC)

ENGINEERING TECHNOLOGY
Austin Peay State U (TN)
Berry Coll (GA)
California State Polytechnic U, Pomona (CA)
California State U, Long Beach (CA)
Dordt Coll (IA)
Eastern New Mexico U (NM)
East Tennessee State U (TN)
ECPI Coll of Technology, Virginia Beach (VA)
Fairmont State U (WV)
Lawrence Technological U (MI)
LeTourneau U (TX)
Miami U (OH)
Middle Tennessee State U (TN)
Midwestern State U (TX)
New Jersey Inst of Technology (NJ)
Northern Illinois U (IL)
Pittsburg State U (KS)
Purdue U (IN)
Southeastern Louisiana U (LA)
Southeast Missouri State U (MO)
Southern Illinois U Carbondale (IL)
Southern Polytechnic State U (GA)
Temple U (PA)
Texas A&M U (TX)
Texas A&M U–Corpus Christi (TX)
Texas State U–San Marcos (TX)
Texas Tech U (TX)
Tuskegee U (AL)
U of Hartford (CT)
U of Maine (ME)
U of Memphis (TN)
U of Pittsburgh at Johnstown (PA)
U of South Carolina Upstate (SC)
The U of Texas at Tyler (TX)
U of West Florida (FL)
U of Wisconsin–River Falls (WI)
U of Wisconsin–Stout (WI)
Walla Walla U (WA)
Western Carolina U (NC)
Youngstown State U (OH)

ENGLISH
Abilene Christian U (TX)
Acadia U (NS, Canada)
Adams State Coll (CO)
Adelphi U (NY)
Alabama Ag and Mech U (AL)
Alabama State U (AL)
Albany State U (GA)
Albertus Magnus Coll (CT)
Albion Coll (MI)
Albright Coll (PA)
Alcorn State U (MS)
Alderson-Broaddus Coll (WV)
Alfred U (NY)
Allegheny Coll (PA)
Alma Coll (MI)
Alvernia U (PA)
Alverno Coll (WI)
American Public U System (WV)
American U (DC)
American U of Beirut (Lebanon)
Amherst Coll (MA)
Anderson U (IN)
Anderson U (SC)
Andrews U (MI)
Angelo State U (TX)
Anna Maria Coll (MA)
Appalachian State U (NC)
Aquinas Coll (MI)
Aquinas Coll (TN)
Arcadia U (PA)
Arizona State U (AZ)
Arkansas State U (AR)
Arkansas Tech U (AR)
Armstrong Atlantic State U (GA)
Asbury U (KY)
Ashland U (OH)
Assumption Coll (MA)
Athabasca U (AB, Canada)
Athens State U (AL)
Atlanta Christian Coll (GA)
Auburn U (AL)

Auburn U Montgomery (AL)
Augsburg Coll (MN)
Augustana Coll (IL)
Augustana Coll (SD)
Austin Coll (TX)
Austin Peay State U (TN)
Averett U (VA)
Avila U (MO)
Azusa Pacific U (CA)
Baker U (KS)
Baldwin-Wallace Coll (OH)
Ball State U (IN)
Bard Coll (NY)
Barnard Coll (NY)
Barry U (FL)
Barton Coll (NC)
Bates Coll (ME)
Belhaven U (MS)
Bellarmine U (KY)
Belmont Abbey Coll (NC)
Belmont U (TN)
Beloit Coll (WI)
Bemidji State U (MN)
Benedictine Coll (KS)
Benedictine U (IL)
Bennington Coll (VT)
Berea Coll (KY)
Berry Coll (GA)
Bethany Coll (KS)
Bethany Coll (WV)
Bethany Lutheran Coll (MN)
Bethel Coll (IN)
Bethel U (MN)
Bethel U (TN)
Bethune-Cookman U (FL)
Biola U (CA)
Birmingham-Southern Coll (AL)
Blackburn Coll (IL)
Bloomfield Coll (NJ)
Bloomsburg U of Pennsylvania (PA)
Bluefield Coll (VA)
Blue Mountain Coll (MS)
Bluffton U (OH)
Bob Jones U (SC)
Boise State U (ID)
Boston Coll (MA)
Boston U (MA)
Bowdoin Coll (ME)
Bowie State U (MD)
Bowling Green State U (OH)
Brandeis U (MA)
Brenau U (GA)
Brevard Coll (NC)
Brewton-Parker Coll (GA)
Briar Cliff U (IA)
Bridgewater Coll (VA)
Bridgewater State U (MA)
Brock U (ON, Canada)
Brown U (RI)
Bryan Coll (TN)
Bryant U (RI)
Bryn Athyn Coll of the New Church (PA)
Bryn Mawr Coll (PA)
Bucknell U (PA)
Buena Vista U (IA)
Butler U (IN)
Cabrini Coll (PA)
California Baptist U (CA)
California Inst of Technology (CA)
California Polytechnic State U, San Luis Obispo (CA)
California State Polytechnic U, Pomona (CA)
California State U, Bakersfield (CA)
California State U, Chico (CA)
California State U, Dominguez Hills (CA)
California State U, Fullerton (CA)
California State U, Long Beach (CA)
California State U, Los Angeles (CA)
California State U, Northridge (CA)
California State U, San Bernardino (CA)
California State U, San Marcos (CA)
California State U, Stanislaus (CA)
Calumet Coll of Saint Joseph (IN)
Calvin Coll (MI)
Cameron U (OK)
Campbellsville U (KY)
Canisius Coll (NY)
Capital U (OH)
Carleton Coll (MN)
Carlow U (PA)
Carnegie Mellon U (PA)
Carroll U (WI)
Carson-Newman Coll (TN)
Case Western Reserve U (OH)
The Catholic U of America (DC)
Cedar Crest Coll (PA)

Penn State Erie, The Behrend Coll (PA)
Penn State Fayette, The Eberly Campus (PA)
Penn State Greater Allegheny (PA)
Penn State Harrisburg (PA)
Penn State Hazleton (PA)
Penn State Lehigh Valley (PA)
Penn State Mont Alto (PA)
Penn State New Kensington (PA)
Penn State Schuylkill (PA)
Penn State Shenango (PA)
Penn State U Park (PA)
Penn State Wilkes-Barre (PA)
Penn State Worthington Scranton (PA)
Penn State York (PA)
Pepperdine U, Malibu (CA)
Piedmont Coll (GA)
Pikeville Coll (KY)
Pittsburg State U (KS)
Pitzer Coll (CA)
Point Park U (PA)
Pomona Coll (CA)
Portland State U (OR)
Prairie View A&M U (TX)
Presbyterian Coll (SC)
Prescott Coll (AZ)
Princeton U (NJ)
Principia Coll (IL)
Providence Coll (RI)
Purdue U (IN)
Purdue U Calumet (IN)
Purdue U North Central (IN)
Queens Coll of the City U of New York (NY)
Quincy U (IL)
Quinnipiac U (CT)
Radford U (VA)
Randolph Coll (VA)
Randolph-Macon Coll (VA)
Reed Coll (OR)
Regent U (VA)
Regis Coll (MA)
Regis U (CO)
Reinhardt U (GA)
Rhode Island Coll (RI)
Rhodes Coll (TN)
Rice U (TX)
The Richard Stockton Coll of New Jersey (NJ)
Rider U (NJ)
Ripon Coll (WI)
Rivier Coll (NH)
Roanoke Coll (VA)
Robert Morris U (PA)
Rockford Coll (IL)
Rockhurst U (MO)
Rocky Mountain Coll (MT)
Rollins Coll (FL)
Roosevelt U (IL)
Rosemont Coll (PA)
Rowan U (NJ)
Russell Sage Coll (NY)
Rust Coll (MS)
Rutgers, The State U of New Jersey, Camden (NJ)
Rutgers, The State U of New Jersey, Newark (NJ)
Rutgers, The State U of New Jersey, New Brunswick (NJ)
Sacred Heart U (CT)
Saginaw Valley State U (MI)
St. Ambrose U (IA)
St. Andrews Presbyterian Coll (NC)
St. Bonaventure U (NY)
St. Catherine U (MN)
St. Edward's U (TX)
Saint Francis U (PA)
St. Francis Xavier U (NS, Canada)
St. John Fisher Coll (NY)
Saint John's U (MN)
St. John's U (NY)
Saint Joseph Coll (CT)
Saint Joseph's Coll (IN)
St. Joseph's Coll, Long Island Campus (NY)
St. Joseph's Coll, New York (NY)
Saint Joseph's Coll of Maine (ME)
Saint Joseph's U (PA)
St. Lawrence U (NY)
Saint Leo U (FL)
Saint Louis U (MO)
Saint Martin's U (WA)
Saint Mary-of-the-Woods Coll (IN)
Saint Mary's Coll (IN)
Saint Mary's Coll of California (CA)
St. Mary's Coll of Maryland (MD)
Saint Mary's U of Minnesota (MN)

Saint Michael's Coll (VT)
St. Norbert Coll (WI)
St. Olaf Coll (MN)
St. Thomas Aquinas Coll (NY)
St. Thomas U (FL)
St. Thomas U (NB, Canada)
Saint Xavier U (IL)
Salem State U (MA)
Salisbury U (MD)
Salve Regina U (RI)
Samford U (AL)
Sam Houston State U (TX)
San Diego Christian Coll (CA)
San Diego State U (CA)
San Francisco State U (CA)
San Jose State U (CA)
Santa Clara U (CA)
Sarah Lawrence Coll (NY)
Savannah State U (GA)
Schreiner U (TX)
Scripps Coll (CA)
Seattle Pacific U (WA)
Seton Hill U (PA)
Sewanee: The U of the South (TN)
Shawnee State U (OH)
Shenandoah U (VA)
Shepherd U (WV)
Shippensburg U of Pennsylvania (PA)
Shorter U (GA)
Siena Coll (NY)
Siena Heights U (MI)
Sierra Nevada Coll (NV)
Silver Lake Coll (WI)
Simmons Coll (MA)
Simon Fraser U (BC, Canada)
Simpson Coll (IA)
Simpson U (CA)
Skidmore Coll (NY)
Slippery Rock U of Pennsylvania (PA)
Smith Coll (MA)
Sonoma State U (CA)
South Dakota State U (SD)
Southeastern Baptist Theological Sem (NC)
Southeastern Louisiana U (LA)
Southeastern Oklahoma State U (OK)
Southeastern U (FL)
Southeast Missouri State U (MO)
Southern Adventist U (TN)
Southern Arkansas U–Magnolia (AR)
Southern Connecticut State U (CT)
Southern Illinois U Carbondale (IL)
Southern Illinois U Edwardsville (IL)
Southern Methodist U (TX)
Southern Nazarene U (OK)
Southern Oregon U (OR)
Southern Utah U (UT)
Southern Vermont Coll (VT)
Southern Wesleyan U (SC)
Southwestern Adventist U (TX)
Southwestern Assemblies of God U (TX)
Southwestern Coll (KS)
Spelman Coll (GA)
Spring Arbor U (MI)
Springfield Coll (MA)
Spring Hill Coll (AL)
Stanford U (CA)
State U of New York at Binghamton (NY)
State U of New York at Fredonia (NY)
State U of New York at New Paltz (NY)
State U of New York at Oswego (NY)
State U of New York at Plattsburgh (NY)
State U of New York Coll at Geneseo (NY)
State U of New York Coll at Oneonta (NY)
State U of New York Coll at Potsdam (NY)
Stephen F. Austin State U (TX)
Stephens Coll (MO)
Stetson U (FL)
Stevenson U (MD)
Stonehill Coll (MA)
Stony Brook U, State U of New York (NY)
Suffolk U (MA)
Sul Ross State U (TX)
Susquehanna U (PA)
Swarthmore Coll (PA)
Sweet Briar Coll (VA)

Tabor Coll (KS)
Talladega Coll (AL)
Tarleton State U (TX)
Taylor U (IN)
Temple U (PA)
Tennessee Technological U (TN)
Tennessee Wesleyan Coll (TN)
Texas A&M Intl U (TX)
Texas A&M U (TX)
Texas A&M U–Corpus Christi (TX)
Texas A&M U–Kingsville (TX)
Texas Christian U (TX)
Texas Lutheran U (TX)
Texas Southern U (TX)
Texas State U–San Marcos (TX)
Texas Tech U (TX)
Texas Wesleyan U (TX)
Texas Woman's U (TX)
Thiel Coll (PA)
Thomas Edison State Coll (NJ)
Thomas More Coll (KY)
Thomas U (GA)
Tiffin U (OH)
Towson U (MD)
Transylvania U (KY)
Trent U (ON, Canada)
Trevecca Nazarene U (TN)
Trinity Coll (CT)
Trinity U (TX)
Troy U (AL)
Truett-McConnell Coll (GA)
Truman State U (MO)
Tufts U (MA)
Tulane U (LA)
Tuskegee U (AL)
Union Coll (KY)
Union Coll (NE)
Union Coll (NY)
Union U (TN)
United States Air Force Acad (CO)
United States Naval Acad (MD)
Université de Sherbrooke (QC, Canada)
U at Buffalo, the State U of New York (NY)
The U of Akron (OH)
The U of Alabama (AL)
The U of Alabama at Birmingham (AL)
The U of Alabama in Huntsville (AL)
U of Alaska Fairbanks (AK)
U of Alaska Southeast (AK)
The U of Arizona (AZ)
U of Arkansas (AR)
U of Arkansas at Pine Bluff (AR)
U of Arkansas–Fort Smith (AR)
U of Baltimore (MD)
U of Bridgeport (CT)
The U of British Columbia (BC, Canada)
The U of British Columbia–Okanagan (BC, Canada)
U of California, Berkeley (CA)
U of California, Davis (CA)
U of California, Irvine (CA)
U of California, Los Angeles (CA)
U of California, Santa Barbara (CA)
U of Central Florida (FL)
U of Central Missouri (MO)
U of Charleston (WV)
U of Cincinnati (OH)
U of Colorado at Colorado Springs (CO)
U of Colorado Boulder (CO)
U of Colorado Denver (CO)
U of Dallas (TX)
U of Dayton (OH)
U of Delaware (DE)
U of Denver (CO)
U of Dubuque (IA)
U of Evansville (IN)
The U of Findlay (OH)
U of Florida (FL)
U of Georgia (GA)
U of Guelph (ON, Canada)
U of Hartford (CT)
U of Hawaii at Hilo (HI)
U of Hawaii at Manoa (HI)
U of Hawaii–West Oahu (HI)
U of Houston (TX)
U of Houston–Clear Lake (TX)
U of Houston–Downtown (TX)
U of Houston–Victoria (TX)
U of Idaho (ID)
U of Illinois at Chicago (IL)
U of Illinois at Springfield (IL)
U of Indianapolis (IN)
The U of Iowa (IA)
The U of Kansas (KS)
U of La Verne (CA)

U of Lethbridge (AB, Canada)
U of Louisiana at Lafayette (LA)
U of Louisiana at Monroe (LA)
U of Louisville (KY)
U of Maine (ME)
U of Maine at Farmington (ME)
U of Maine at Fort Kent (ME)
U of Maine at Presque Isle (ME)
U of Manitoba (MB, Canada)
U of Mary Hardin-Baylor (TX)
U of Maryland, Baltimore County (MD)
U of Maryland, Coll Park (MD)
U of Maryland U Coll (MD)
U of Mary Washington (VA)
U of Massachusetts Amherst (MA)
U of Massachusetts Boston (MA)
U of Massachusetts Dartmouth (MA)
U of Massachusetts Lowell (MA)
U of Memphis (TN)
U of Miami (FL)
U of Michigan (MI)
U of Michigan–Dearborn (MI)
U of Michigan–Flint (MI)
U of Minnesota, Duluth (MN)
U of Minnesota, Twin Cities Campus (MN)
U of Mississippi (MS)
U of Missouri (MO)
U of Missouri–St. Louis (MO)
U of Mobile (AL)
The U of Montana Western (MT)
U of Montevallo (AL)
U of Mount Union (OH)
U of Nebraska at Omaha (NE)
U of Nebraska–Lincoln (NE)
U of Nevada, Las Vegas (NV)
U of Nevada, Reno (NV)
U of New Brunswick Fredericton (NB, Canada)
U of New Brunswick Saint John (NB, Canada)
U of New England (ME)
U of New Hampshire (NH)
U of New Hampshire at Manchester (NH)
U of New Haven (CT)
The U of North Carolina at Asheville (NC)
The U of North Carolina at Chapel Hill (NC)
The U of North Carolina at Charlotte (NC)
The U of North Carolina at Greensboro (NC)
The U of North Carolina at Pembroke (NC)
The U of North Carolina Wilmington (NC)
U of North Dakota (ND)
U of Northern Colorado (CO)
U of Northern Iowa (IA)
U of North Florida (FL)
U of North Texas (TX)
U of Notre Dame (IN)
U of Oklahoma (OK)
U of Oregon (OR)
U of Ottawa (ON, Canada)
U of Pennsylvania (PA)
U of Pittsburgh at Bradford (PA)
U of Pittsburgh at Greensburg (PA)
U of Pittsburgh at Johnstown (PA)
U of Portland (OR)
U of Puget Sound (WA)
U of Redlands (CA)
U of Regina (SK, Canada)
U of Rhode Island (RI)
U of Richmond (VA)
U of Rio Grande (OH)
U of Rochester (NY)
U of St. Francis (IL)
U of Saint Mary (KS)
U of St. Thomas (MN)
U of St. Thomas (TX)
U of San Diego (CA)
U of San Francisco (CA)
U of Saskatchewan (SK, Canada)
U of Science and Arts of Oklahoma (OK)
The U of Scranton (PA)
U of Sioux Falls (SD)
U of South Alabama (AL)
U of South Carolina (SC)
U of South Carolina Aiken (SC)
U of South Carolina Beaufort (SC)
U of South Carolina Upstate (SC)
The U of South Dakota (SD)
The U of Southern California (CA)
U of Southern Indiana (IN)
U of Southern Maine (ME)

U of Southern Mississippi (MS)
U of South Florida (FL)
The U of Tampa (FL)
The U of Tennessee (TN)
The U of Tennessee at Chattanooga (TN)
The U of Tennessee at Martin (TN)
The U of Texas at Arlington (TX)
The U of Texas at Austin (TX)
The U of Texas at San Antonio (TX)
The U of Texas at Tyler (TX)
The U of Texas of the Permian Basin (TX)
The U of Texas–Pan American (TX)
U of the Cumberlands (KY)
U of the Incarnate Word (TX)
U of the Ozarks (AR)
U of the Pacific (CA)
U of the Southwest (NM)
U of the Virgin Islands (VI)
U of the West (CA)
The U of Toledo (OH)
U of Tulsa (OK)
U of Utah (UT)
U of Vermont (VT)
U of Virginia (VA)
U of Washington (WA)
U of Waterloo (ON, Canada)
The U of Western Ontario (ON, Canada)
U of West Florida (FL)
U of West Georgia (GA)
U of Wisconsin–Eau Claire (WI)
U of Wisconsin–Green Bay (WI)
U of Wisconsin–La Crosse (WI)
U of Wisconsin–Madison (WI)
U of Wisconsin–Parkside (WI)
U of Wisconsin–Platteville (WI)
U of Wisconsin–River Falls (WI)
U of Wisconsin–Stevens Point (WI)
U of Wisconsin–Superior (WI)
U of Wisconsin–Whitewater (WI)
U of Wyoming (WY)
Upper Iowa U (IA)
Ursuline Coll (OH)
Utah State U (UT)
Utah Valley U (UT)
Valdosta State U (GA)
Valparaiso U (IN)
Vanderbilt U (TN)
Vassar Coll (NY)
Victory U (TN)
Villanova U (PA)
Virginia Commonwealth U (VA)
Virginia Intermont Coll (VA)
Virginia Military Inst (VA)
Virginia Polytechnic Inst and State U (VA)
Virginia State U (VA)
Virginia Wesleyan Coll (VA)
Viterbo U (WI)
Wabash Coll (IN)
Wagner Coll (NY)
Wake Forest U (NC)
Walla Walla U (WA)
Walsh U (OH)
Wartburg Coll (IA)
Washburn U (KS)
Washington Adventist U (MD)
Washington & Jefferson Coll (PA)
Washington and Lee U (VA)
Washington Coll (MD)
Washington State U (WA)
Washington U in St. Louis (MO)
Wayland Baptist U (TX)
Waynesburg U (PA)
Wayne State Coll (NE)
Wayne State U (MI)
Weber State U (UT)
Webster U (MO)
Wellesley Coll (MA)
Wells Coll (NY)
Wesleyan Coll (GA)
Wesleyan U (CT)
West Chester U of Pennsylvania (PA)
Western Carolina U (NC)
Western Connecticut State U (CT)
Western Illinois U (IL)
Western Kentucky U (KY)
Western Michigan U (MI)
Western New England U (MA)
Western Oregon U (OR)
Western State Coll of Colorado (CO)
Westfield State U (MA)
West Liberty U (WV)
Westminster Coll (MO)
Westminster Coll (UT)
Westmont Coll (CA)
West Virginia U (WV)

INDEXES

Wheaton Coll (IL)
Wheaton Coll (MA)
Wheeling Jesuit U (WV)
Whitman Coll (WA)
Wichita State U (KS)
Widener U (PA)
Wilfrid Laurier U (ON, Canada)
Wilkes U (PA)
Willamette U (OR)
William Jessup U (CA)
William Jewell Coll (MO)
William Paterson U of New Jersey (NJ)
Williams Coll (MA)
Wilmington Coll (OH)
Wingate U (NC)
Winona State U (MN)
Winthrop U (SC)
Wittenberg U (OH)
Wofford Coll (SC)
Worcester State U (MA)
Wright State U (OH)
Xavier U (OH)
Xavier U of Louisiana (LA)
Yale U (CT)
York Coll of Pennsylvania (PA)
York Coll of the City U of New York (NY)
Young Harris Coll (GA)
Youngstown State U (OH)

ENGLISH AS A SECOND/ FOREIGN LANGUAGE (TEACHING)

American U (DC)
Bethel U (MN)
Bridgewater Coll (VA)
Brigham Young U (UT)
Brock U (ON, Canada)
Calvin Coll (MI)
The Catholic U of America (DC)
Concordia U (QC, Canada)
Concordia U, St. Paul (MN)
Concordia U Wisconsin (WI)
Crown Coll (MN)
Doane Coll (NE)
Eastern Washington U (WA)
Gardner-Webb U (NC)
Grand Canyon U (AZ)
Hawai'i Pacific U (HI)
Houghton Coll (NY)
Indiana Wesleyan U (IN)
Inter American U of Puerto Rico, Guayama Campus (PR)
Inter American U of Puerto Rico, Metropolitan Campus (PR)
Inter American U of Puerto Rico, Ponce Campus (PR)
Inter American U of Puerto Rico, San Germán Campus (PR)
Lebanese American U (Lebanon)
Le Moyne Coll (NY)
Liberty U (VA)
Lipscomb U (TN)
Maryville Coll (TN)
Multnomah U (OR)
Niagara U (NY)
Northwestern Coll (MN)
Northwest U (WA)
Nyack Coll (NY)
Oklahoma Christian U (OK)
Oklahoma Wesleyan U (OK)
Queens Coll of the City U of New York (NY)
Salisbury U (MD)
Stony Brook U, State U of New York (NY)
Tarleton State U (TX)
Texas Wesleyan U (TX)
Union U (TN)
The U of British Columbia (BC, Canada)
U of Cincinnati (OH)
U of Delaware (DE)
The U of Findlay (OH)
U of Minnesota, Twin Cities Campus (MN)
U of New Brunswick Fredericton (NB, Canada)
U of New Brunswick Saint John (NB, Canada)
U of Northern Iowa (IA)
U of Puerto Rico at Humacao (PR)
U of Washington (WA)
U of Wisconsin–River Falls (WI)
Washington State U (WA)
Wichita State U (KS)
Winona State U (MN)

Wright State U (OH)

ENGLISH/FRENCH AS A SECOND/FOREIGN LANGUAGE (TEACHING) RELATED

U of Ottawa (ON, Canada)

ENGLISH LANGUAGE AND LITERATURE RELATED

Burlington Coll (VT)
Columbia Coll (SC)
Columbia U, School of General Studies (NY)
Concordia Coll (MN)
Concordia Coll–New York (NY)
Dakota State U (SD)
Doane Coll (NE)
Emmanuel Coll (MA)
Ferris State U (MI)
Fort Lewis Coll (CO)
Harvard U (MA)
Hofstra U (NY)
Milligan Coll (TN)
Moravian Coll (PA)
Patrick Henry Coll (VA)
Purdue U (IN)
Saint Leo U (FL)
Saint Mary-of-the-Woods Coll (IN)
Saint Mary's Coll of California (CA)
Sarah Lawrence Coll (NY)
Skidmore Coll (NY)
State U of New York at Binghamton (NY)
Thiel Coll (PA)
U of Maine at Augusta (ME)
U of Michigan (MI)
U of Nevada, Reno (NV)
U of Pennsylvania (PA)
The U of Western Ontario (ON, Canada)
Viterbo U (WI)
Washington U in St. Louis (MO)
Webster U (MO)
Western Kentucky U (KY)

ENGLISH/LANGUAGE ARTS TEACHER EDUCATION

Abilene Christian U (TX)
Adams State Coll (CO)
Alma Coll (MI)
Alvernia U (PA)
Alverno Coll (WI)
Anderson U (IN)
Anderson U (SC)
Anna Maria Coll (MA)
Appalachian State U (NC)
Aquinas Coll (MI)
Arkansas State U (AR)
Arkansas Tech U (AR)
Arlington Baptist Coll (TX)
Assumption Coll (MA)
Auburn U (AL)
Augustana Coll (IL)
Averett U (VA)
The Baptist Coll of Florida (FL)
Barry U (FL)
Bethany Coll (KS)
Bethel Coll (IN)
Bethel U (MN)
Bethune-Cookman U (FL)
Blackburn Coll (IL)
Bluefield Coll (VA)
Blue Mountain Coll (MS)
Bob Jones U (SC)
Boston U (MA)
Brewton-Parker Coll (GA)
Bridgewater Coll (VA)
Bridgewater State U (MA)
Bryan Coll (TN)
Buena Vista U (IA)
Cabrini Coll (PA)
California State U, Chico (CA)
California State U, Long Beach (CA)
Calumet Coll of Saint Joseph (IN)
Cameron U (OK)
Campbellsville U (KY)
Capital U (OH)
Carroll U (WI)
The Catholic U of America (DC)
Cedarville U (OH)
Central Michigan U (MI)
Christian Brothers U (TN)
Claflin U (SC)
Clearwater Christian Coll (FL)
Coker Coll (SC)
The Coll of New Jersey (NJ)
The Coll of Saint Rose (NY)
Coll of the Ozarks (MO)

Colorado State U (CO)
Columbus State U (GA)
Concordia Coll (MN)
Concordia U Chicago (IL)
Corban U (OR)
Covenant Coll (GA)
Crown Coll (MN)
Culver-Stockton Coll (MO)
Dakota State U (SD)
Dakota Wesleyan U (SD)
Delaware State U (DE)
Delta State U (MS)
Dixie State Coll of Utah (UT)
Dominican Coll (NY)
Dowling Coll (NY)
Duquesne U (PA)
Eastern Michigan U (MI)
Eastern Washington U (WA)
East Texas Baptist U (TX)
Edgewood Coll (WI)
Elizabeth City State U (NC)
Elmhurst Coll (IL)
Elmira Coll (NY)
Emmanuel Coll (GA)
Faith Baptist Bible Coll and Theological Sem (IA)
Fayetteville State U (NC)
Ferris State U (MI)
Fitchburg State U (MA)
Florida Ag and Mech U (FL)
Florida Atlantic U (FL)
Fort Lewis Coll (CO)
Franklin Coll (IN)
Freed-Hardeman U (TN)
Free Will Baptist Bible Coll (TN)
Friends U (KS)
Gardner-Webb U (NC)
Goddard Coll (VT)
Grace Coll (IN)
Grand Canyon U (AZ)
Grand Valley State U (MI)
Greensboro Coll (NC)
Greenville Coll (IL)
Hannibal-LaGrange U (MO)
Harding U (AR)
Hardin-Simmons U (TX)
Hofstra U (NY)
Hope Coll (MI)
Huntingdon Coll (AL)
Huntington U (IN)
Indiana U Bloomington (IN)
Indiana U Northwest (IN)
Indiana U–Purdue U Fort Wayne (IN)
Indiana U–Purdue U Indianapolis (IN)
Indiana U South Bend (IN)
Indiana U Southeast (IN)
Indiana Wesleyan U (IN)
Inter American U of Puerto Rico, San Germán Campus (PR)
Iowa Wesleyan Coll (IA)
Ithaca Coll (NY)
Jamestown Coll (ND)
Johnson State Coll (VT)
Judson Coll (AL)
Juniata Coll (PA)
Keene State Coll (NH)
Kennesaw State U (GA)
Kent State U (OH)
Kentucky Wesleyan Coll (KY)
Keuka Coll (NY)
King Coll (TN)
La Roche Coll (PA)
Le Moyne Coll (NY)
Lewis-Clark State Coll (ID)
Liberty U (VA)
Limestone Coll (SC)
Lincoln U (MO)
Lipscomb U (TN)
Long Island U, Brooklyn Campus (NY)
Long Island U, C.W. Post Campus (NY)
Louisiana State U in Shreveport (LA)
Malone U (OH)
Manchester Coll (IN)
Manhattanville Coll (NY)
Mansfield U of Pennsylvania (PA)
Maranatha Baptist Bible Coll (WI)
Marian U (WI)
Marist Coll (NY)
Marquette U (WI)
Maryville Coll (TN)
Marywood U (PA)
Mayville State U (ND)
McKendree U (IL)

McMurry U (TX)
Medaille Coll (NY)
Merrimack Coll (MA)
Messiah Coll (PA)
Metropolitan State U (MN)
Miami U (OH)
MidAmerica Nazarene U (KS)
Midwestern State U (TX)
Millersville U of Pennsylvania (PA)
Millikin U (IL)
Minnesota State U Moorhead (MN)
Minot State U (ND)
Misericordia U (PA)
Mississippi Valley State U (MS)
Missouri State U (MO)
Molloy Coll (NY)
Montana State U Billings (MT)
Morningside Coll (IA)
Morris Coll (SC)
Mount Marty Coll (SD)
Mount Vernon Nazarene U (OH)
Nazareth Coll of Rochester (NY)
Nebraska Wesleyan U (NE)
Nevada State Coll at Henderson (NV)
Nicholls State U (LA)
North Carolina State U (NC)
North Dakota State U (ND)
Northeastern State U (OK)
Northern Arizona U (AZ)
Northern Michigan U (MI)
North Greenville U (SC)
Northwestern Coll (MN)
Northwestern Oklahoma State U (OK)
Northwestern State U of Louisiana (LA)
Northwest Missouri State U (MO)
Northwest Nazarene U (ID)
Northwest U (WA)
Nyack Coll (NY)
Oklahoma Christian U (OK)
Pace U (NY)
Paine Coll (GA)
Palm Beach Atlantic U (FL)
Philadelphia Biblical U (PA)
Pittsburg State U (KS)
Point Park U (PA)
Prescott Coll (AZ)
Reinhardt U (GA)
Rhode Island Coll (RI)
Rivier Coll (NH)
Rocky Mountain Coll (MT)
Rust Coll (MS)
Sacred Heart U (CT)
Saginaw Valley State U (MI)
St. Ambrose U (IA)
St. Catherine U (MN)
Saint Francis U (PA)
St. John Fisher Coll (NY)
St. John's U (NY)
St. Joseph's Coll, Long Island Campus (NY)
St. Joseph's Coll, New York (NY)
Saint Joseph's Coll of Maine (ME)
Saint Joseph's U (PA)
Saint Mary's U of Minnesota (MN)
Saint Xavier U (IL)
Salve Regina U (RI)
Samford U (AL)
Schreiner U (TX)
Seattle Pacific U (WA)
Seton Hill U (PA)
Simpson U (CA)
Southeastern Louisiana U (LA)
Southeastern Oklahoma State U (OK)
Southeastern U (FL)
Southeast Missouri State U (MO)
Southern Adventist U (TN)
Southern Nazarene U (OK)
Southern Wesleyan U (SC)
Southwestern Assemblies of God U (TX)
Southwestern Coll (KS)
Spring Arbor U (MI)
State U of New York at New Paltz (NY)
State U of New York at Plattsburgh (NY)
State U of New York Coll at Oneonta (NY)
Syracuse U (NY)
Tabor Coll (KS)
Talladega Coll (AL)
Taylor U (IN)
Temple U (PA)
Texas A&M Intl U (TX)

Texas Christian U (TX)
Texas Wesleyan U (TX)
Tiffin U (OH)
Trevecca Nazarene U (TN)
Union Coll (NE)
The U of Akron (OH)
The U of Arizona (AZ)
U of Arkansas–Fort Smith (AR)
U of Central Florida (FL)
U of Delaware (DE)
U of Dubuque (IA)
U of Evansville (IN)
U of Georgia (GA)
U of Idaho (ID)
U of Illinois at Chicago (IL)
U of Indianapolis (IN)
U of Lethbridge (AB, Canada)
U of Louisiana at Monroe (LA)
U of Maine (ME)
U of Maine at Farmington (ME)
U of Maine at Fort Kent (ME)
U of Mary Hardin-Baylor (TX)
U of Maryland, Coll Park (MD)
U of Michigan–Flint (MI)
U of Minnesota, Twin Cities Campus (MN)
U of Mississippi (MS)
U of Missouri–St. Louis (MO)
The U of Montana Western (MT)
U of Nebraska–Lincoln (NE)
U of Nevada, Reno (NV)
The U of North Carolina at Charlotte (NC)
The U of North Carolina at Greensboro (NC)
The U of North Carolina at Pembroke (NC)
The U of North Carolina Wilmington (NC)
U of Oklahoma (OK)
U of Pittsburgh at Johnstown (PA)
U of Regina (SK, Canada)
U of Rio Grande (OH)
U of St. Francis (IL)
U of St. Thomas (MN)
The U of South Dakota (SD)
U of South Florida (FL)
The U of Tennessee at Chattanooga (TN)
The U of Tennessee at Martin (TN)
The U of Toledo (OH)
U of Vermont (VT)
U of West Florida (FL)
U of Wisconsin–River Falls (WI)
U of Wisconsin–Superior (WI)
Ursuline Coll (OH)
Utah Valley U (UT)
Valparaiso U (IN)
Victory U (TN)
Virginia Intermont Coll (VA)
Viterbo U (WI)
Washington Adventist U (MD)
Washington State U (WA)
Washington U in St. Louis (MO)
Wayland Baptist U (TX)
Waynesburg U (PA)
Wayne State Coll (NE)
Wayne State U (MI)
Weber State U (UT)
Western Carolina U (NC)
Western Michigan U (MI)
Western State Coll of Colorado (CO)
Westmont Coll (CA)
Wheeling Jesuit U (WV)
Widener U (PA)
William Jewell Coll (MO)
Wingate U (NC)
Winona State U (MN)
York Coll of Pennsylvania (PA)
Youngstown State U (OH)

ENGLISH LITERATURE (BRITISH AND COMMONWEALTH)

American U of Beirut (Lebanon)
Bard Coll (NY)
Bennington Coll (VT)
Concordia U (QC, Canada)
Ferris State U (MI)
Gannon U (PA)
Hofstra U (NY)
Hunter Coll of the City U of New York (NY)
Indiana U–Purdue U Fort Wayne (IN)
Marian U (WI)
New York U (NY)
Pace U (NY)

St. Lawrence U (NY)
Saint Mary's Coll (IN)
Sarah Lawrence Coll (NY)
Syracuse U (NY)
U of Pittsburgh (PA)
Washington U in St. Louis (MO)
Wheeling Jesuit U (WV)

ENTOMOLOGY
Cornell U (NY)
Iowa State U of Science and
    Technology (IA)
Michigan State U (MI)
The Ohio State U (OH)
Oklahoma State U (OK)
Purdue U (IN)
State U of New York Coll of
    Environmental Science and
    Forestry (NY)
Texas A&M U (TX)
U of California, Davis (CA)
U of Delaware (DE)
U of Florida (FL)
U of Georgia (GA)
U of Manitoba (MB, Canada)
U of Minnesota, Twin Cities Campus
    (MN)
U of Nebraska–Lincoln (NE)
U of New Brunswick Fredericton
    (NB, Canada)
U of New Hampshire (NH)
U of Wisconsin–Madison (WI)
Utah State U (UT)

ENTREPRENEURIAL AND SMALL BUSINESS RELATED
Crown Coll (MN)
Fairleigh Dickinson U, Coll at
    Florham (NJ)
Fairleigh Dickinson U, Metropolitan
    Campus (NJ)
Fashion Inst of Technology (NY)
Florida State U (FL)
Kendall Coll (IL)
Loyola U Chicago (IL)
Purdue U (IN)
Stetson U (FL)

ENTREPRENEURSHIP
The American U of Paris (France)
Anderson U (IN)
Avila U (MO)
Ball State U (IN)
Belmont U (TN)
Brigham Young U (UT)
Bryant U (RI)
Buena Vista U (IA)
California State U, Dominguez Hills
    (CA)
California State U, Fullerton (CA)
Canisius Coll (NY)
Central Michigan U (MI)
Clarkson U (NY)
Cleary U (MI)
Coll of the Atlantic (ME)
Crown Coll (MN)
Duquesne U (PA)
Eastern Michigan U (MI)
Ferris State U (MI)
Gannon U (PA)
George Fox U (OR)
Grove City Coll (PA)
Hampshire Coll (MA)
Hawai`i Pacific U (HI)
HEC Montreal (QC, Canada)
Hofstra U (NY)
Indiana Wesleyan U (IN)
Inter American U of Puerto Rico,
    Bayamón Campus (PR)
Inter American U of Puerto Rico,
    Metropolitan Campus (PR)
Inter American U of Puerto Rico,
    San Germán Campus (PR)
Iowa State U of Science and
    Technology (IA)
Johnson & Wales U (CO)
Johnson & Wales U (RI)
Juniata Coll (PA)
Kendall Coll (IL)
Lasell Coll (MA)
Lindenwood U (MO)
Marquette U (WI)
Mars Hill Coll (NC)
Menlo Coll (CA)
Messiah Coll (PA)
Millikin U (IL)
Missouri State U (MO)
National U (CA)
Northeastern State U (OK)
Northeastern U (MA)

Northern Kentucky U (KY)
Northern Michigan U (MI)
Oklahoma State U (OK)
Pace U (NY)
Purdue U (IN)
Quinnipiac U (CT)
Reinhardt U (GA)
Rider U (NJ)
Rowan U (NJ)
St. Edward's U (TX)
Saint Louis U (MO)
Saint Mary's U of Minnesota (MN)
Salem State U (MA)
Samford U (AL)
Seton Hill U (PA)
Sierra Nevada Coll (NV)
South Dakota State U (SD)
Southern Polytechnic State U (GA)
Southern Vermont Coll (VT)
Southwestern Coll (KS)
State U of New York at Binghamton
    (NY)
State U of New York at Plattsburgh
    (NY)
Stetson U (FL)
Suffolk U (MA)
Syracuse U (NY)
Temple U (PA)
Thomas Edison State Coll (NJ)
Trine U (IN)
Union Coll (NE)
The U of British Columbia–
    Okanagan (BC, Canada)
U of Hartford (CT)
U of Illinois at Chicago (IL)
U of Indianapolis (IN)
U of Miami (FL)
U of Minnesota, Crookston (MN)
U of Nevada, Las Vegas (NV)
U of Nevada, Reno (NV)
The U of North Carolina at
    Pembroke (NC)
U of North Dakota (ND)
U of Ottawa (ON, Canada)
U of Pittsburgh at Bradford (PA)
U of St. Thomas (MN)
The U of Scranton (PA)
U of Southern Indiana (IN)
The U of Tampa (FL)
The U of Texas at San Antonio (TX)
The U of Toledo (OH)
U of Utah (UT)
U of Vermont (VT)
The U of Western Ontario (ON,
    Canada)
Washington State U (WA)
Washington U in St. Louis (MO)
Western Carolina U (NC)
Western Kentucky U (KY)
Western State Coll of Colorado (CO)
Wichita State U (KS)
Wilkes U (PA)
Xavier U (OH)
York Coll of Pennsylvania (PA)

ENVIRONMENTAL BIOLOGY
American U (DC)
Arcadia U (PA)
Averett U (VA)
Barnard Coll (NY)
Beloit Coll (WI)
Bennington Coll (VT)
Bethel Coll (IN)
Blackburn Coll (IL)
Boston U (MA)
Bridgewater State U (MA)
California State Polytechnic U,
    Pomona (CA)
Cedar Crest Coll (PA)
Cedarville U (OH)
Colgate U (NY)
Coll of the Atlantic (ME)
Columbia U, School of General
    Studies (NY)
East Stroudsburg U of Pennsylvania
    (PA)
Elizabethtown Coll (PA)
Ferris State U (MI)
Fitchburg State U (MA)
Fort Lewis Coll (CO)
Franklin Pierce U (NH)
Friends U (KS)
Grace Coll (IN)
Greenville Coll (IL)
Houghton Coll (NY)
Humboldt State U (CA)
Inter American U of Puerto Rico,
    Bayamón Campus (PR)
Iowa Wesleyan Coll (IA)
Jacksonville State U (AL)

Keystone Coll (PA)
Lakehead U (ON, Canada)
Lindenwood U (MO)
Manchester U (IN)
Marlboro Coll (VT)
The Master's Coll and Sem (CA)
McDaniel Coll (MD)
Michigan State U (MI)
Midway Coll (KY)
Minnesota State U Mankato (MN)
Monmouth U (NJ)
Northwestern Coll (IA)
Pacific Union Coll (CA)
Philadelphia U (PA)
Pittsburg State U (KS)
Prescott Coll (AZ)
Purdue U (IN)
St. Lawrence U (NY)
Saint Mary's U of Minnesota (MN)
Salem State U (MA)
Southern Nazarene U (OK)
State U of New York Coll of
    Environmental Science and
    Forestry (NY)
Sterling Coll (VT)
Suffolk U (MA)
Texas A&M U (TX)
Tulane U (LA)
The U of British Columbia (BC,
    Canada)
U of Charleston (WV)
U of Dayton (OH)
U of Dubuque (IA)
U of Guelph (ON, Canada)
U of La Verne (CA)
U of Mount Union (OH)
U of New Brunswick Saint John (NB,
    Canada)
U of Pittsburgh at Johnstown (PA)
U of Regina (SK, Canada)
U of Saskatchewan (SK, Canada)
The U of Tennessee at Martin (TN)
Western State Coll of Colorado (CO)
Westfield State U (MA)
Wingate U (NC)
Winona State U (MN)

ENVIRONMENTAL CHEMISTRY
Purdue U (IN)

ENVIRONMENTAL CONTROL TECHNOLOGIES RELATED
Delaware State U (DE)
Inter American U of Puerto Rico,
    Bayamón Campus (PR)
New York Inst of Technology (NY)
Purdue U (IN)
Thomas Edison State Coll (NJ)

ENVIRONMENTAL DESIGN/ ARCHITECTURE
Art Center Coll of Design (CA)
Auburn U (AL)
Ball State U (IN)
Bennington Coll (VT)
Boston Architectural Coll (MA)
Bowling Green State U (OH)
Coll of the Atlantic (ME)
Cornell U (NY)
Kent State U (OH)
Lawrence Technological U (MI)
Montana State U (MT)
North Carolina State U (NC)
North Dakota State U (ND)
Otis Coll of Art and Design (CA)
Prescott Coll (AZ)
Purdue U (IN)
Rutgers, The State U of New Jersey,
    New Brunswick (NJ)
State U of New York Coll of
    Environmental Science and
    Forestry (NY)
Texas A&M U (TX)
Texas Tech U (TX)
U at Buffalo, the State U of New
    York (NY)
U of Colorado Boulder (CO)
U of Houston (TX)
U of Manitoba (MB, Canada)
U of Massachusetts Amherst (MA)
U of Memphis (TN)
U of Minnesota, Twin Cities Campus
    (MN)
U of Oklahoma (OK)
U of Pennsylvania (PA)

ENVIRONMENTAL EDUCATION
Coll of the Atlantic (ME)
Johnson State Coll (VT)

Nevada State Coll at Henderson
    (NV)
Purdue U (IN)
Sonoma State U (CA)
State U of New York Coll of
    Environmental Science and
    Forestry (NY)
U of Minnesota, Crookston (MN)

ENVIRONMENTAL ENGINEERING TECHNOLOGY
California State U, Long Beach (CA)
City Coll of the City U of New York
    (NY)
Ferris State U (MI)
Lake Superior State U (MI)
Middle Tennessee State U (TN)
North Carolina State U (NC)
Purdue U (IN)
Shawnee State U (OH)
Temple U (PA)
United States Military Acad (NY)
The U of British Columbia (BC,
    Canada)
U of Delaware (DE)
U of Guelph (ON, Canada)
U of Wisconsin–Whitewater (WI)

ENVIRONMENTAL/ ENVIRONMENTAL HEALTH ENGINEERING
Arizona State U (AZ)
California Inst of Technology (CA)
California Polytechnic State U, San
    Luis Obispo (CA)
Carnegie Mellon U (PA)
Central State U (OH)
Christian Brothers U (TN)
Clarkson U (NY)
Colorado School of Mines (CO)
Colorado State U (CO)
Cornell U (NY)
Florida Gulf Coast U (FL)
Florida Intl U (FL)
Gannon U (PA)
Georgia Inst of Technology (GA)
Hofstra U (NY)
Humboldt State U (CA)
The Johns Hopkins U (MD)
Lafayette Coll (PA)
Lehigh U (PA)
Louisiana State U and Ag and Mech
    Coll (LA)
Manhattan Coll (NY)
Marquette U (WI)
Massachusetts Inst of Technology
    (MA)
Massachusetts Maritime Acad (MA)
Missouri U of Science and
    Technology (MO)
Montana Tech of The U of Montana
    (MT)
New Jersey Inst of Technology (NJ)
New Mexico Inst of Mining and
    Technology (NM)
North Carolina State U (NC)
Northeastern State U (OK)
Northern Arizona U (AZ)
Old Dominion U (VA)
Oregon State U (OR)
Penn State Abington (PA)
Penn State Altoona (PA)
Penn State Beaver (PA)
Penn State Berks (PA)
Penn State Brandywine (PA)
Penn State DuBois (PA)
Penn State Erie, The Behrend Coll
    (PA)
Penn State Fayette, The Eberly
    Campus (PA)
Penn State Greater Allegheny (PA)
Penn State Harrisburg (PA)
Penn State Hazleton (PA)
Penn State Lehigh Valley (PA)
Penn State Mont Alto (PA)
Penn State New Kensington (PA)
Penn State Schuylkill (PA)
Penn State Shenango (PA)
Penn State U Park (PA)
Penn State Wilkes-Barre (PA)
Penn State Worthington Scranton
    (PA)
Penn State York (PA)
Polytechnic U of Puerto Rico (PR)
Rensselaer Polytechnic Inst (NY)
Rice U (TX)
San Diego State U (CA)
South Dakota School of Mines and
    Technology (SD)

Southern Methodist U (TX)
Stanford U (CA)
State U of New York Coll of
    Environmental Science and
    Forestry (NY)
Suffolk U (MA)
Syracuse U (NY)
Taylor U (IN)
Texas Tech U (TX)
Tufts U (MA)
Tulane U (LA)
United States Air Force Acad (CO)
United States Military Acad (NY)
U at Buffalo, the State U of New
    York (NY)
U of California, Berkeley (CA)
U of California, Irvine (CA)
U of California, Merced (CA)
U of Central Florida (FL)
U of Cincinnati (OH)
U of Colorado Boulder (CO)
U of Delaware (DE)
U of Florida (FL)
U of Georgia (GA)
U of Idaho (ID)
U of Miami (FL)
U of Nevada, Reno (NV)
U of New Hampshire (NH)
U of North Dakota (ND)
U of Notre Dame (IN)
U of Oklahoma (OK)
U of Pennsylvania (PA)
U of Regina (SK, Canada)
U of Saskatchewan (SK, Canada)
U of Southern California (CA)
U of Vermont (VT)
U of Waterloo (ON, Canada)
The U of Western Ontario (ON,
    Canada)
U of Wisconsin–Platteville (WI)
Utah State U (UT)
Wilkes U (PA)
Worcester Polytechnic Inst (MA)
Yale U (CT)

ENVIRONMENTAL HEALTH
American U of Beirut (Lebanon)
Boise State U (ID)
Bowling Green State U (OH)
California State U, Northridge (CA)
Colorado State U (CO)
Drury U (MO)
East Central U (OK)
East Tennessee State U (TN)
Illinois State U (IL)
Indiana U of Pennsylvania (PA)
Iowa Wesleyan Coll (IA)
New Mexico State U (NM)
Ohio U (OH)
Purdue U (IN)
Salisbury U (MD)
Texas Southern U (TX)
U of Georgia (GA)
U of Massachusetts Lowell (MA)
The U of North Carolina at Chapel
    Hill (NC)
U of Regina (SK, Canada)
U of Southern Maine (ME)
U of Washington (WA)
U of Wisconsin–Eau Claire (WI)
Western Carolina U (NC)
Western Kentucky U (KY)
Wright State U (OH)
York Coll of the City U of New York
    (NY)

ENVIRONMENTAL PSYCHOLOGY
Embry-Riddle Aeronautical U–
    Daytona (FL)
Purdue U (IN)

ENVIRONMENTAL SCIENCE
Abilene Christian U (TX)
Albright Coll (PA)
Alderson-Broaddus Coll (WV)
Allegheny Coll (PA)
Alverno Coll (WI)
Anna Maria Coll (MA)
Appalachian State U (NC)
Assumption Coll (MA)
Auburn U (AL)
Averett U (VA)
Barnard Coll (NY)
Bellarmine U (KY)
Benedictine U (IL)
Bennington Coll (VT)
Berry Coll (GA)
Bethel U (MN)
Bethune-Cookman U (FL)
Blackburn Coll (IL)

Briar Cliff U (IA)
Bridgewater Coll (VA)
Brigham Young U (UT)
Brown U (RI)
Bryant U (RI)
Buena Vista U (IA)
California State U, Long Beach (CA)
California State U, Monterey Bay (CA)
Canisius Coll (NY)
Capital U (OH)
Carroll U (WI)
Cedarville U (OH)
Central Michigan U (MI)
Chatham U (PA)
Chestnut Hill Coll (PA)
Claflin U (SC)
Clarkson U (NY)
Cleveland State U (OH)
Colby Coll (ME)
The Colorado Coll (CO)
Columbia Coll (MO)
Columbia U, School of General Studies (NY)
Concordia U (QC, Canada)
Concordia U Chicago (IL)
Concord U (WV)
Delaware State U (DE)
DePaul U (IL)
DEREE - The American Coll of Greece (Greece)
Dickinson Coll (PA)
Dominican U (IL)
Drake U (IA)
Drury U (MO)
Duquesne U (PA)
Earlham Coll (IN)
Eastern New Mexico U (NM)
Eastern Washington U (WA)
Endicott Coll (MA)
The Evergreen State Coll (WA)
Fairleigh Dickinson U, Metropolitan Campus (NJ)
Florida Ag and Mech U (FL)
Florida Inst of Technology (FL)
Franklin & Marshall Coll (PA)
Gannon U (PA)
Gardner-Webb U (NC)
Gettysburg Coll (PA)
Hardin-Simmons U (TX)
Hartwick Coll (NY)
Hawai`i Pacific U (HI)
Hood Coll (MD)
Humboldt State U (CA)
Hunter Coll of the City U of New York (NY)
Idaho State U (ID)
Indiana U Bloomington (IN)
Indiana–Purdue U Indianapolis (IN)
Inter American U of Puerto Rico, Metropolitan Campus (PR)
Inter American U of Puerto Rico, Ponce Campus (PR)
Inter American U of Puerto Rico, San Germán Campus (PR)
John Brown U (AR)
The Johns Hopkins U (MD)
Juniata Coll (PA)
Kean U (NJ)
Keuka Coll (NY)
King's Coll (PA)
Kutztown U of Pennsylvania (PA)
Lewis U (IL)
Lincoln U (MO)
Lindenwood U (MO)
Long Island U, C.W. Post Campus (NY)
Louisiana State U and Ag and Mech Coll (LA)
Lourdes Coll (OH)
Loyola U Chicago (IL)
Lynchburg Coll (VA)
Madonna U (MI)
Marietta Coll (OH)
Marshall U (WV)
Marylhurst U (OR)
Maryville U of Saint Louis (MO)
Marywood U (PA)
Massachusetts Coll of Liberal Arts (MA)
Massachusetts Maritime Acad (MA)
McDaniel Coll (MD)
Mercer U (GA)
Mesa State Coll (CO)
Messiah Coll (PA)
Miami U (OH)
Michigan State U (MI)

Midwestern State U (TX)
Mills Coll (CA)
Monmouth Coll (IL)
Montana State U (MT)
Muhlenberg Coll (PA)
National U (CA)
Nazareth Coll of Rochester (NY)
Nevada State Coll at Henderson (NV)
New England Coll (NH)
New Mexico State U (NM)
North Carolina State U (NC)
Northeastern State U (OK)
Northern Arizona U (AZ)
Northern Kentucky U (KY)
Northern Michigan U (MI)
Northwest U (WA)
The Ohio State U (OH)
Oklahoma State U (OK)
Oregon State U (OR)
Pace U (NY)
Paine Coll (GA)
Piedmont Coll (GA)
Pitzer Coll (CA)
Point Park U (PA)
Prescott Coll (AZ)
Queens Coll of the City U of New York (NY)
Ramapo Coll of New Jersey (NJ)
Randolph Coll (VA)
Rensselaer Polytechnic Inst (NY)
Roanoke Coll (VA)
Rocky Mountain Coll (MT)
St. Bonaventure U (NY)
Saint Francis U (PA)
Saint Joseph's Coll of Maine (ME)
Saint Louis U (MO)
Saint Michael's Coll (VT)
St. Norbert Coll (WI)
Salisbury U (MD)
Samford U (AL)
Sam Houston State U (TX)
Santa Clara U (CA)
Scripps Coll (CA)
Siena Heights U (MI)
Sierra Nevada Coll (NV)
Simmons Coll (MA)
Simon Fraser U (BC, Canada)
Simpson Coll (IA)
Southeast Missouri State U (MO)
Southern Methodist U (TX)
Stephen F. Austin State U (TX)
Stetson U (FL)
Suffolk U (MA)
Sweet Briar Coll (VA)
Taylor U (IN)
Temple U (PA)
Texas A&M U (TX)
Texas A&M U–Corpus Christi (TX)
Texas Christian U (TX)
Texas State U–San Marcos (TX)
Thomas Edison State Coll (NJ)
Thomas More Coll (KY)
Trinity Coll (CT)
Troy U (AL)
United States Military Acad (NY)
The U of Alabama (AL)
U of Arkansas (AR)
U of California, Berkeley (CA)
U of California, Los Angeles (CA)
U of Charleston (WV)
U of Denver (CO)
U of Dubuque (IA)
U of Evansville (IN)
U of Florida (FL)
U of Hawaii at Manoa (HI)
U of Houston (TX)
U of Houston–Clear Lake (TX)
U of Idaho (ID)
U of Illinois at Chicago (IL)
U of Lethbridge (AB, Canada)
U of Maine (ME)
U of Maryland, Baltimore County (MD)
U of Maryland, Coll Park (MD)
U of Massachusetts Amherst (MA)
U of Michigan–Dearborn (MI)
U of Michigan–Flint (MI)
U of Mobile (AL)
U of Mount Union (OH)
U of Nebraska at Omaha (NE)
U of New England (ME)
U of New Hampshire (NH)
The U of North Carolina at Chapel Hill (NC)
The U of North Carolina at Pembroke (NC)

The U of North Carolina Wilmington (NC)
U of Northern Iowa (IA)
U of Notre Dame (IN)
U of Oklahoma (OK)
U of Oregon (OR)
U of Ottawa (ON, Canada)
U of Rochester (NY)
U of St. Francis (IL)
U of St. Thomas (TX)
U of San Francisco (CA)
U of Saskatchewan (SK, Canada)
U of South Carolina (SC)
U of South Florida (FL)
The U of Tennessee at Chattanooga (TN)
The U of Texas at Arlington (TX)
The U of Texas at San Antonio (TX)
The U of Texas of the Permian Basin (TX)
U of the Incarnate Word (TX)
U of the Sciences in Philadelphia (PA)
U of Utah (UT)
U of Vermont (VT)
U of Virginia (VA)
U of Washington, Bothell (WA)
U of Waterloo (ON, Canada)
The U of Western Ontario (ON, Canada)
U of West Florida (FL)
U of West Georgia (GA)
U of Wisconsin–Green Bay (WI)
U of Wisconsin–River Falls (WI)
Upper Iowa U (IA)
Valdosta State U (GA)
Valparaiso U (IN)
Vassar Coll (NY)
Villanova U (PA)
Virginia Intermont Coll (VA)
Walla Walla U (WA)
Washington State U (WA)
Wayland Baptist U (TX)
Wayne State U (MI)
Wesleyan Coll (GA)
Western Carolina U (NC)
Westminster Coll (MO)
Wheaton Coll (MA)
Wheeling Jesuit U (WV)
Willamette U (OR)
Youngstown State U (OH)

ENVIRONMENTAL STUDIES

Acadia U (NS, Canada)
Adelphi U (NY)
Albion Coll (MI)
Alfred U (NY)
Allegheny Coll (PA)
American Public U System (WV)
American U (DC)
Amherst Coll (MA)
Appalachian State U (NC)
Ashland U (OH)
Augustana Coll (IL)
Austin Peay State U (TN)
Bard Coll (NY)
Bard Coll at Simon's Rock (MA)
Barton Coll (NC)
Bates Coll (ME)
Bellarmine U (KY)
Beloit Coll (WI)
Bemidji State U (MN)
Bennington Coll (VT)
Bethany Coll (WV)
Bethel U (MN)
Birmingham-Southern Coll (AL)
Boise State U (ID)
Bowdoin Coll (ME)
Brandeis U (MA)
Brevard Coll (NC)
Brown U (RI)
Bucknell U (PA)
California State U, San Bernardino (CA)
Calvin Coll (MI)
Canisius Coll (NY)
Carleton Coll (MN)
Case Western Reserve U (OH)
Castleton State Coll (VT)
Central Coll (IA)
Central Michigan U (MI)
Chatham U (PA)
Christopher Newport U (VA)
City Coll of the City U of New York (NY)
Claremont McKenna Coll (CA)
Clarion U of Pennsylvania (PA)
Cleveland State U (OH)

Colby Coll (ME)
Colgate U (NY)
Coll of Saint Benedict (MN)
Coll of the Atlantic (ME)
Coll of the Holy Cross (MA)
The Coll of William and Mary (VA)
The Colorado Coll (CO)
Columbia Southern U (AL)
Concordia Coll (MN)
Concordia U Wisconsin (WI)
Connecticut Coll (CT)
Cornell Coll (IA)
Creighton U (NE)
Curry Coll (MA)
Dartmouth Coll (NH)
Davidson Coll (NC)
Denison U (OH)
DePaul U (IL)
DePauw U (IN)
Dickinson Coll (PA)
Dickinson State U (ND)
Doane Coll (NE)
Dordt Coll (IA)
Drake U (IA)
Drury U (MO)
Earlham Coll (IN)
Eckerd Coll (FL)
Edinboro U of Pennsylvania (PA)
Elmhurst Coll (IL)
Elmira Coll (NY)
Elon U (NC)
Emmanuel Coll (MA)
Emory & Henry Coll (VA)
Endicott Coll (MA)
Eugene Lang Coll The New School for Liberal Arts (NY)
The Evergreen State Coll (WA)
Ferrum Coll (VA)
Florida Intl U (FL)
Florida Southern Coll (FL)
Fort Lewis Coll (CO)
Framingham State U (MA)
Franklin & Marshall Coll (PA)
Franklin Coll Switzerland (Switzerland)
Franklin Pierce U (NH)
Furman U (SC)
Georgetown U (DC)
Georgia Coll & State U (GA)
Gettysburg Coll (PA)
Goddard Coll (VT)
Goucher Coll (MD)
Guilford Coll (NC)
Hamilton Coll (NY)
Hamline U (MN)
Hampshire Coll (MA)
Harvard U (MA)
Hawai`i Pacific U (HI)
Hendrix Coll (AR)
Hobart and William Smith Colls (NY)
Hofstra U (NY)
Hollins U (VA)
Humboldt State U (CA)
Illinois Coll (IL)
Illinois Wesleyan U (IL)
Immaculata U (PA)
Indiana U Bloomington (IN)
Inter American U of Puerto Rico, Metropolitan Campus (PR)
Inter American U of Puerto Rico, San Germán Campus (PR)
Iowa State U of Science and Technology (IA)
Ithaca Coll (NY)
John Brown U (AR)
John Carroll U (OH)
The Johns Hopkins U (MD)
Johnson State Coll (VT)
Juniata Coll (PA)
Keene State Coll (NH)
Keystone Coll (PA)
King's Coll (PA)
The King's U Coll (AB, Canada)
Knox Coll (IL)
Lake Forest Coll (IL)
Lakehead U (ON, Canada)
Lake Superior State U (MI)
Lamar U (TX)
La Salle U (PA)
Lasell Coll (MA)
Lawrence U (WI)
Lehigh U (PA)
Le Moyne Coll (NY)
Lesley U (MA)
Lewis & Clark Coll (OR)
Lincoln Memorial U (TN)
Linfield Coll (OR)
Lipscomb U (TN)

Long Island U, C.W. Post Campus (NY)
Longwood U (VA)
Louisiana State U in Shreveport (LA)
Luther Coll (IA)
Lynchburg Coll (VA)
Macalester Coll (MN)
Maharishi U of Management (IA)
Manchester Coll (IN)
Mansfield U of Pennsylvania (PA)
Marietta Coll (OH)
Marist Coll (NY)
Marlboro Coll (VT)
Maryville Coll (TN)
Maryville U of Saint Louis (MO)
Massachusetts Coll of Liberal Arts (MA)
Massachusetts Maritime Acad (MA)
McDaniel Coll (MD)
Mercer U (GA)
Merrimack Coll (MA)
Messiah Coll (PA)
Miami U (OH)
Michigan State U (MI)
Middlebury Coll (VT)
Mills Coll (CA)
Minnesota State U Mankato (MN)
Mitchell Coll (CT)
Molloy Coll (NY)
Montana State U Billings (MT)
Montreat Coll, Montreat (NC)
Moravian Coll (PA)
Mount Allison U (NB, Canada)
Mount Holyoke Coll (MA)
Mount Olive Coll (NC)
Mount St. Mary's U (MD)
Naropa U (CO)
Neumann U (PA)
New Coll of Florida (FL)
New England Coll (NH)
New Mexico Highlands U (NM)
New Mexico Inst of Mining and Technology (NM)
Northeastern Illinois U (IL)
Northeastern U (MA)
Northern Arizona U (AZ)
Northern State U (SD)
Northland Coll (WI)
Nova Southeastern U (FL)
Oberlin Coll (OH)
Ohio Wesleyan U (OH)
Pace U (NY)
Pacific Lutheran U (WA)
Pacific U (OR)
Penn State Altoona (PA)
Penn State U Park (PA)
Piedmont Coll (GA)
Pomona Coll (CA)
Portland State U (OR)
Prescott Coll (AZ)
Principia Coll (IL)
Purchase Coll, State U of New York (NY)
Queens Coll of the City U of New York (NY)
Ramapo Coll of New Jersey (NJ)
Randolph Coll (VA)
Randolph-Macon Coll (VA)
Reed Coll (OR)
Regis U (CO)
The Richard Stockton Coll of New Jersey (NJ)
Rider U (NJ)
Ripon Coll (WI)
Robert Morris U (PA)
Rocky Mountain Coll (MT)
Rollins Coll (FL)
Rosemont Coll (PA)
Rowan U (NJ)
Rutgers, The State U of New Jersey, Newark (NJ)
Rutgers, The State U of New Jersey, New Brunswick (NJ)
Saint Anselm Coll (NH)
St. Edward's U (TX)
Saint Francis U (PA)
St. Francis Xavier U (NS, Canada)
Saint John's U (MN)
St. John's U (NY)
Saint Joseph's Coll of Maine (ME)
Saint Joseph's U (PA)
St. Lawrence U (NY)
Saint Leo U (FL)
Saint Michael's Coll (VT)
St. Olaf Coll (MN)
St. Thomas U (FL)
St. Thomas U (NB, Canada)

San Diego State U (CA)
San Francisco State U (CA)
San Jose State U (CA)
Santa Clara U (CA)
Sarah Lawrence Coll (NY)
Sewanee: The U of the South (TN)
Shenandoah U (VA)
Shepherd U (WV)
Shippensburg U of Pennsylvania (PA)
Shorter U (GA)
Siena Coll (NY)
Skidmore Coll (NY)
Smith Coll (MA)
Sonoma State U (CA)
South Dakota State U (SD)
Southern Methodist U (TX)
Southern Oregon U (OR)
Southern Vermont Coll (VT)
Spelman Coll (GA)
Stanford U (CA)
State U of New York at Binghamton (NY)
State U of New York at Fredonia (NY)
State U of New York at Plattsburgh (NY)
State U of New York Coll at Oneonta (NY)
State U of New York Coll at Potsdam (NY)
State U of New York Coll of Environmental Science and Forestry (NY)
Sterling Coll (VT)
Stonehill Coll (MA)
Stony Brook U, State U of New York (NY)
Sul Ross State U (TX)
Sweet Briar Coll (VA)
Tabor Coll (KS)
Tarleton State U (TX)
Temple U (PA)
Tennessee Wesleyan Coll (TN)
Texas A&M U (TX)
Texas A&M U–Corpus Christi (TX)
Thiel Coll (PA)
Thomas Edison State Coll (NJ)
Trent U (ON, Canada)
Trine U (IN)
Tufts U (MA)
Tulane U (LA)
Tuskegee U (AL)
United States Military Acad (NY)
Université de Sherbrooke (QC, Canada)
U of Alaska Southeast (AK)
The U of Arizona (AZ)
The U of British Columbia (BC, Canada)
The U of British Columbia–Okanagan (BC, Canada)
U of California, Berkeley (CA)
U of California, Davis (CA)
U of California, Irvine (CA)
U of California, Santa Barbara (CA)
U of California, Santa Cruz (CA)
U of Cincinnati (OH)
U of Colorado Boulder (CO)
U of Dayton (OH)
U of Delaware (DE)
U of Dubuque (IA)
U of Evansville (IN)
The U of Findlay (OH)
U of Georgia (GA)
U of Guelph (ON, Canada)
U of Indianapolis (IN)
The U of Iowa (IA)
The U of Kansas (KS)
U of Maine at Farmington (ME)
U of Maine at Fort Kent (ME)
U of Maine at Presque Isle (ME)
U of Manitoba (MB, Canada)
U of Maryland, Baltimore County (MD)
U of Maryland U Coll (MD)
U of Michigan (MI)
U of Michigan–Dearborn (MI)
U of Minnesota, Duluth (MN)
U of Minnesota, Twin Cities Campus (MN)
U of Missouri (MO)
The U of Montana Western (MT)
U of Nebraska–Lincoln (NE)
U of Nevada, Las Vegas (NV)
U of New England (ME)
The U of North Carolina at Asheville (NC)
The U of North Carolina at Chapel Hill (NC)

The U of North Carolina Wilmington (NC)
U of North Dakota (ND)
U of Oklahoma (OK)
U of Oregon (OR)
U of Ottawa (ON, Canada)
U of Pennsylvania (PA)
U of Pittsburgh at Bradford (PA)
U of Pittsburgh at Johnstown (PA)
U of Portland (OR)
U of Redlands (CA)
U of Rhode Island (RI)
U of Richmond (VA)
U of Rochester (NY)
U of St. Thomas (TX)
U of San Diego (CA)
U of San Francisco (CA)
U of Southern California (CA)
U of Southern Maine (ME)
The U of Tampa (FL)
The U of Tennessee at Martin (TN)
The U of Texas of the Permian Basin (TX)
U of the District of Columbia (DC)
U of the Ozarks (AR)
U of the Pacific (CA)
The U of Toledo (OH)
U of Tulsa (OK)
U of Utah (UT)
U of Vermont (VT)
U of Washington (WA)
U of Washington, Bothell (WA)
U of Waterloo (ON, Canada)
The U of Western Ontario (ON, Canada)
U of West Georgia (GA)
U of Wisconsin–Green Bay (WI)
U of Wisconsin–River Falls (WI)
U of Wyoming (WY)
Vassar Coll (NY)
Villanova U (PA)
Virginia Commonwealth U (VA)
Virginia Polytechnic Inst and State U (VA)
Virginia Wesleyan Coll (VA)
Walla Walla U (WA)
Washington & Jefferson Coll (PA)
Washington and Lee U (VA)
Washington Coll (MD)
Washington U in St. Louis (MO)
Waynesburg U (PA)
Wellesley Coll (MA)
Wells Coll (NY)
Wesleyan U (CT)
Western Michigan U (MI)
Western State Coll of Colorado (CO)
Westminster Coll (MO)
Westminster Coll (UT)
Wheaton Coll (IL)
Wheeling Jesuit U (WV)
Widener U (PA)
Wilfrid Laurier U (ON, Canada)
William Paterson U of New Jersey (NJ)
Williams Coll (MA)
Wofford Coll (SC)
Worcester Polytechnic Inst (MA)
Yale U (CT)

ENVIRONMENTAL TOXICOLOGY
Clarkson U (NY)
U of California, Davis (CA)
U of Guelph (ON, Canada)

EPIDEMIOLOGY
U of Rochester (NY)

EQUESTRIAN STUDIES
Asbury U (KY)
Averett U (VA)
Centenary Coll (NJ)
Colorado State U (CO)
Houghton Coll (NY)
Johnson & Wales U (RI)
Judson U (AL)
Midway Coll (KY)
Mount Ida Coll (MA)
North Dakota State U (ND)
Rocky Mountain Coll (MT)
Rutgers, The State U of New Jersey, New Brunswick (NJ)
Saint Mary-of-the-Woods Coll (IN)
Stephens Coll (MO)
Sul Ross State U (TX)
The U of Findlay (OH)
U of Wisconsin–River Falls (WI)
Virginia Intermont Coll (VA)

ETHICS
Bridgewater State U (MA)

Carnegie Mellon U (PA)
Drake U (IA)
U of Michigan–Flint (MI)
U of Ottawa (ON, Canada)
U of Southern California (CA)
U of Washington, Bothell (WA)
The U of Western Ontario (ON, Canada)

ETHNIC, CULTURAL MINORITY, GENDER, AND GROUP STUDIES RELATED
Arizona State U (AZ)
Bard Coll at Simon's Rock (MA)
Boston U (MA)
Bowling Green State U (OH)
Burlington Coll (VT)
California Polytechnic State U, San Luis Obispo (CA)
California State Polytechnic U, Pomona (CA)
California State U, Chico (CA)
California State U, Stanislaus (CA)
Carnegie Mellon U (PA)
Claremont McKenna Coll (CA)
The Colorado Coll (CO)
Columbia U, School of General Studies (NY)
Connecticut Coll (CT)
Cornell U (NY)
Dakota Wesleyan U (SD)
Eugene Lang Coll The New School for Liberal Arts (NY)
The Evergreen State Coll (WA)
Grinnell Coll (IA)
Hampshire Coll (MA)
Hawai`i Pacific U (HI)
Indiana U Bloomington (IN)
Laurentian U (ON, Canada)
Lawrence U (WI)
Marlboro Coll (VT)
Metropolitan State U (MN)
Mills Coll (CA)
Mount Holyoke Coll (MA)
Oregon State U (OR)
Prescott Coll (AZ)
Saint Michael's Coll (VT)
Santa Clara U (CA)
Savannah State U (GA)
Skidmore Coll (NY)
Southern Adventist U (TN)
Stonehill Coll (MA)
U of California, Berkeley (CA)
U of Colorado at Colorado Springs (CO)
U of Colorado Boulder (CO)
U of Denver (CO)
U of Hawaii at Manoa (HI)
U of Illinois at Chicago (IL)
U of Nebraska–Lincoln (NE)
U of New Brunswick Saint John (NB, Canada)
U of Pittsburgh (PA)
U of Regina (SK, Canada)
U of Southern California (CA)
The U of Texas at Dallas (TX)
The U of Western Ontario (ON, Canada)
Washington State U (WA)
Washington U in St. Louis (MO)
Wellesley Coll (MA)
Westfield State U (MA)
Whitman Coll (WA)
Wichita State U (KS)
Williams Coll (MA)
Yale U (CT)

ETHNIC STUDIES
Bowling Green State U (OH)
Colorado State U (CO)
Goddard Coll (VT)
Minnesota State U Moorhead (MN)
St. Olaf Coll (MN)
U of San Diego (CA)
The U of Texas at Austin (TX)

EUROPEAN HISTORY
Bard Coll (NY)
Bennington Coll (VT)
Gettysburg Coll (PA)
Keene State Coll (NH)
Salem State U (MA)
Sarah Lawrence Coll (NY)
Suffolk U (MA)
U of Regina (SK, Canada)

EUROPEAN STUDIES
American U in Bulgaria (Bulgaria)
The American U of Paris (France)

Amherst Coll (MA)
Bard Coll (NY)
Bard Coll at Simon's Rock (MA)
Belmont U (TN)
Beloit Coll (WI)
Bennington Coll (VT)
Brandeis U (MA)
California State U, Fullerton (CA)
Canisius Coll (NY)
Carnegie Mellon U (PA)
Carroll U (WI)
Central Michigan U (MI)
Claremont McKenna Coll (CA)
Emory & Henry Coll (VA)
Fort Lewis Coll (CO)
Georgetown Coll (KY)
Gettysburg Coll (PA)
Hampshire Coll (MA)
Hillsdale Coll (MI)
Hobart and William Smith Colls (NY)
Loyola Marymount U (CA)
Marlboro Coll (VT)
Middlebury Coll (VT)
Millsaps Coll (MS)
Mount Holyoke Coll (MA)
New Coll of Florida (FL)
New York U (NY)
Ohio U (OH)
Portland State U (OR)
Sacred Heart U (CT)
St. John's Coll (MD)
Saint Joseph's U (PA)
Saint Mary's Coll of California (CA)
San Diego State U (CA)
Sarah Lawrence Coll (NY)
Scripps Coll (CA)
Seattle Pacific U (WA)
Sewanee: The U of the South (TN)
Stony Brook U, State U of New York (NY)
Texas State U–San Marcos (TX)
Trinity U (TX)
United States Military Acad (NY)
The U of British Columbia (BC, Canada)
U of California, Irvine (CA)
U of California, Los Angeles (CA)
U of Guelph (ON, Canada)
The U of Kansas (KS)
U of Minnesota, Twin Cities Campus (MN)
U of Missouri (MO)
U of New Hampshire (NH)
The U of North Carolina at Chapel Hill (NC)
U of Richmond (VA)
U of South Carolina (SC)
The U of Texas at Austin (TX)
The U of Toledo (OH)
U of Vermont (VT)
U of Washington (WA)
Vanderbilt U (TN)
Washington U in St. Louis (MO)

EUROPEAN STUDIES (WESTERN)
Claremont McKenna Coll (CA)
Illinois Wesleyan U (IL)
U of Nebraska–Lincoln (NE)
Vanderbilt U (TN)

EVOLUTIONARY BIOLOGY
Bennington Coll (VT)
Case Western Reserve U (OH)
Coll of the Atlantic (ME)
Columbia U, School of General Studies (NY)
Dartmouth Coll (NH)
Harvard U (MA)
Northern Arizona U (AZ)
Rice U (TX)
Rutgers, The State U of New Jersey, New Brunswick (NJ)
Tulane U (LA)
Yale U (CT)

EXECUTIVE ASSISTANT/ EXECUTIVE SECRETARY
Inter American U of Puerto Rico, Bayamón Campus (PR)

EXERCISE PHYSIOLOGY
Baldwin-Wallace Coll (OH)
Biola U (CA)
The Coll of St. Scholastica (MN)
Concordia U Wisconsin (WI)
Fitchburg State U (MA)
Grand Canyon U (AZ)
Lynchburg Coll (VA)
Saint Francis U (PA)

U at Buffalo, the State U of New York (NY)
U of California, Davis (CA)
U of Florida (FL)
U of Massachusetts Amherst (MA)
West Virginia U (WV)

EXPERIMENTAL PSYCHOLOGY
Keene State Coll (NH)
Longwood U (VA)
Marlboro Coll (VT)
Moravian Coll (PA)
Northern Michigan U (MI)
Paine Coll (GA)
Tiffin U (OH)
Tufts U (MA)
The U of British Columbia (BC, Canada)
U of South Carolina (SC)
The U of Toledo (OH)
Wilfrid Laurier U (ON, Canada)

FACILITIES PLANNING AND MANAGEMENT
Eastern Michigan U (MI)
Fitchburg State U (MA)
Missouri State U (MO)
New York City Coll of Technology of the City U of New York (NY)

FAMILY AND COMMUNITY SERVICES
Alderson-Broaddus Coll (WV)
Andrews U (MI)
Curry Coll (MA)
Harding U (AR)
Iowa State U of Science and Technology (IA)
John Brown U (AR)
Keystone Coll (PA)
Lubbock Christian U (TX)
Messiah Coll (PA)
Michigan State U (MI)
Oklahoma Christian U (OK)
Our Lady of the Lake U of San Antonio (TX)
Prairie View A&M U (TX)
Southern Utah U (UT)
Stevenson U (MD)
Texas Tech U (TX)
Union U (TN)
U of California, Santa Cruz (CA)
U of Delaware (DE)
U of Florida (FL)
U of Maryland, Coll Park (MD)
U of Miami (FL)
U of Minnesota, Twin Cities Campus (MN)
U of Northern Iowa (IA)
U of Wisconsin–Madison (WI)
Youngstown State U (OH)

FAMILY AND CONSUMER ECONOMICS RELATED
Alabama Ag and Mech U (AL)
Andrews U (MI)
Ashland U (OH)
Bob Jones U (SC)
Bowling Green State U (OH)
Brigham Young U (UT)
Carson-Newman Coll (TN)
Fairmont State U (WV)
Iowa State U of Science and Technology (IA)
Louisiana Coll (LA)
Minnesota State U Mankato (MN)
The U of Akron (OH)
U of Delaware (DE)
U of Hawaii at Manoa (HI)
U of Minnesota, Twin Cities Campus (MN)
U of Missouri (MO)
U of Nebraska–Lincoln (NE)
U of Northern Iowa (IA)
U of Wisconsin–Stevens Point (WI)
Utah State U (UT)
Virginia State U (VA)

FAMILY AND CONSUMER SCIENCES/HOME ECONOMICS TEACHER EDUCATION
Appalachian State U (NC)
Ashland U (OH)
Bluffton U (OH)
Bridgewater Coll (VA)
Carson-Newman Coll (TN)
Central Michigan U (MI)
Colorado State U (CO)
Fairmont State U (WV)

INDEXES

Penn State U Park (PA)
Penn State Wilkes-Barre (PA)
Penn State Worthington Scranton (PA)
Penn State York (PA)
Pitzer Coll (CA)
Pomona Coll (CA)
Purchase Coll, State U of New York (NY)
Queens Coll of the City U of New York (NY)
Quinnipiac U (CT)
Rhode Island Coll (RI)
Rutgers, The State U of New Jersey, New Brunswick (NJ)
San Francisco State U (CA)
Sarah Lawrence Coll (NY)
Savannah Coll of Art and Design (GA)
School of the Museum of Fine Arts, Boston (MA)
School of Visual Arts (NY)
Simon Fraser U (BC, Canada)
Smith Coll (MA)
Southeastern U (FL)
Southern Methodist U (TX)
Southwestern Coll (KS)
Stanford U (CA)
State U of New York at Fredonia (NY)
Stephens Coll (MO)
Stevenson U (MD)
Suffolk U (MA)
Temple U (PA)
U at Buffalo, the State U of New York (NY)
The U of British Columbia (BC, Canada)
U of California, Berkeley (CA)
U of California, Davis (CA)
U of California, Irvine (CA)
U of California, Los Angeles (CA)
U of California, Santa Barbara (CA)
U of California, Santa Cruz (CA)
U of Colorado Boulder (CO)
U of Georgia (GA)
U of Hartford (CT)
The U of Iowa (IA)
The U of Kansas (KS)
U of Manitoba (MB, Canada)
U of Michigan (MI)
U of Minnesota, Twin Cities Campus (MN)
U of Nebraska–Lincoln (NE)
U of Nevada, Las Vegas (NV)
U of North Carolina School of the Arts (NC)
U of Oklahoma (OK)
U of Pennsylvania (PA)
U of Pittsburgh (PA)
U of Regina (SK, Canada)
U of Richmond (VA)
U of Rochester (NY)
U of Southern California (CA)
The U of Tampa (FL)
The U of Toledo (OH)
U of Tulsa (OK)
U of Utah (UT)
U of Vermont (VT)
U of Waterloo (ON, Canada)
The U of Western Ontario (ON, Canada)
Vanderbilt U (TN)
Vassar Coll (NY)
Washington U in St. Louis (MO)
Watkins Coll of Art, Design, & Film (TN)
Wayne State U (MI)
Webster U (MO)
Wellesley Coll (MA)
Wesleyan U (CT)
Whitman Coll (WA)
Wilfrid Laurier U (ON, Canada)
Wright State U (OH)
Yale U (CT)

FILM/VIDEO AND PHOTOGRAPHIC ARTS RELATED
Arizona State U (AZ)
Art Center Coll of Design (CA)
Birmingham-Southern Coll (AL)
Brigham Young U (UT)
Chatham U (PA)
Coll of the Atlantic (ME)
Columbus Coll of Art & Design (OH)
DeSales U (PA)
Fairfield U (CT)
Five Towns Coll (NY)
Hampshire Coll (MA)
Hollins U (VA)

La Roche Coll (PA)
Maryland Inst Coll of Art (MD)
Northern Michigan U (MI)
Nossi Coll of Art (TN)
Pratt Inst (NY)
Ringling Coll of Art and Design (FL)
Rocky Mountain Coll of Art + Design (CO)
School of the Museum of Fine Arts, Boston (MA)
School of Visual Arts (NY)
Scripps Coll (CA)
Spring Arbor U (MI)
Stevenson U (MD)
Swarthmore Coll (PA)
Trevecca Nazarene U (TN)
U of Illinois at Chicago (IL)
U of Minnesota, Twin Cities Campus (MN)
U of Regina (SK, Canada)
U of Southern California (CA)
The U of the Arts (PA)
Wellesley Coll (MA)
Western Michigan U (MI)
Woodbury U (CA)

FINANCE
Abilene Christian U (TX)
Adams State Coll (CO)
Adelphi U (NY)
Alabama Ag and Mech U (AL)
Alabama State U (AL)
Albertus Magnus Coll (CT)
Albright Coll (PA)
Alfred U (NY)
American U (DC)
The American U of Paris (France)
Anderson U (IN)
Angelo State U (TX)
Appalachian State U (NC)
Aquinas Coll (TN)
Arcadia U (PA)
Arizona State U (AZ)
Arkansas State U (AR)
Ashland U (OH)
Auburn U (AL)
Auburn U Montgomery (AL)
Augsburg Coll (MN)
Averett U (VA)
Avila U (MO)
Baldwin-Wallace Coll (OH)
Ball State U (IN)
Barry U (FL)
Bellarmine U (KY)
Belmont U (TN)
Benedictine U (IL)
Bentley U (MA)
Berry Coll (GA)
Bethany Coll (KS)
Bob Jones U (SC)
Boise State U (ID)
Boston Coll (MA)
Boston U (MA)
Bowling Green State U (OH)
Bridgewater State U (MA)
Brock U (ON, Canada)
Bryant U (RI)
Butler U (IN)
Cabrini Coll (PA)
California State U, Bakersfield (CA)
California State U, Chico (CA)
California State U, Dominguez Hills (CA)
California State U, Fullerton (CA)
California State U, Long Beach (CA)
California State U, Northridge (CA)
California State U, San Bernardino (CA)
Canisius Coll (NY)
Carroll U (WI)
Castleton State Coll (VT)
The Catholic U of America (DC)
Cedarville U (OH)
Centenary Coll (NJ)
Central Connecticut State U (CT)
Central Michigan U (MI)
Christopher Newport U (VA)
Clarion U of Pennsylvania (PA)
Cleary U (MI)
Clemson U (SC)
Cleveland State U (OH)
Coastal Carolina U (SC)
The Coll of St. Scholastica (MN)
The Coll of William and Mary (VA)
Colorado State U (CO)
Columbia Coll (MO)
Columbus State U (GA)
Concordia U (QC, Canada)
Concordia U, St. Paul (MN)
Corban U (OR)

Creighton U (NE)
Culver-Stockton Coll (MO)
Dakota State U (SD)
Dallas Baptist U (TX)
Davenport U, Grand Rapids (MI)
Delaware State U (DE)
Delta State U (MS)
DePaul U (IL)
DEREE - The American Coll of Greece (Greece)
DeSales U (PA)
Dickinson State U (ND)
Dominican Coll (NY)
Dowling Coll (NY)
Drake U (IA)
Drury U (MO)
Duquesne U (PA)
East Central U (OK)
Eastern Illinois U (IL)
Eastern Michigan U (MI)
Eastern Washington U (WA)
East Tennessee State U (TN)
Elmhurst Coll (IL)
Emporia State U (KS)
Fairfield U (CT)
Fairleigh Dickinson U, Coll at Florham (NJ)
Fairleigh Dickinson U, Metropolitan Campus (NJ)
Fairmont State U (WV)
Fayetteville State U (NC)
Ferris State U (MI)
Fitchburg State U (MA)
Florida Atlantic U (FL)
Florida Gulf Coast U (FL)
Florida Intl U (FL)
Florida Southern Coll (FL)
Florida State U (FL)
Fort Lewis Coll (CO)
Francis Marion U (SC)
Franklin Pierce U (NH)
Franklin U (OH)
Freed-Hardeman U (TN)
Friends U (KS)
Gannon U (PA)
Gardner-Webb U (NC)
George Fox U (OR)
Georgetown U (DC)
Georgia Southern U (GA)
Georgia State U (GA)
Goldey-Beacom Coll (DE)
Governors State U (IL)
Grace Coll (IN)
Grand Valley State U (MI)
Grove City Coll (PA)
Hamline U (MN)
Harding U (AR)
Hardin-Simmons U (TX)
Hawai`i Pacific U (HI)
HEC Montreal (QC, Canada)
Hillsdale Coll (MI)
Hofstra U (NY)
Husson U (ME)
Idaho State U (ID)
Illinois Coll (IL)
Illinois State U (IL)
Immaculata U (PA)
Indiana State U (IN)
Indiana U of Pennsylvania (PA)
Indiana U–Purdue U Fort Wayne (IN)
Indiana Wesleyan U (IN)
Inter American U of Puerto Rico, Bayamón Campus (PR)
Inter American U of Puerto Rico, Metropolitan Campus (PR)
Inter American U of Puerto Rico, Ponce Campus (PR)
Inter American U of Puerto Rico, San Germán Campus (PR)
Iowa State U of Science and Technology (IA)
Ithaca Coll (NY)
Jacksonville State U (AL)
James Madison U (VA)
John Carroll U (OH)
Johnson & Wales U (RI)
Juniata Coll (PA)
Kansas State U (KS)
Kean U (NJ)
Kennesaw State U (GA)
Kent State U (OH)
King Coll (TN)
King's Coll (PA)
Kutztown U of Pennsylvania (PA)
Lake Forest Coll (IL)
Lakehead U (ON, Canada)
Lake Superior State U (MI)
Lamar U (TX)
La Roche Coll (PA)

La Salle U (PA)
Lasell Coll (MA)
Lehigh U (PA)
Le Moyne Coll (NY)
LeTourneau U (TX)
Lewis U (IL)
Lincoln Memorial U (TN)
Lindenwood U (MO)
Linfield Coll (OR)
Long Island U, Brooklyn Campus (NY)
Long Island U, C.W. Post Campus (NY)
Longwood U (VA)
Loras Coll (IA)
Louisiana Coll (LA)
Louisiana State U and Ag and Mech Coll (LA)
Louisiana State U in Shreveport (LA)
Loyola U Chicago (IL)
Loyola U Maryland (MD)
Loyola U New Orleans (LA)
Lubbock Christian U (TX)
Lycoming Coll (PA)
MacMurray Coll (IL)
Manchester Coll (IN)
Manhattan Coll (NY)
Manhattanville Coll (NY)
Marian U (WI)
Marietta Coll (OH)
Marquette U (WI)
Marshall U (WV)
Mars Hill Coll (NC)
The Master's Coll and Sem (CA)
McKendree U (IL)
McMurry U (TX)
Menlo Coll (CA)
Merrimack Coll (MA)
Metropolitan State U (MN)
Miami U (OH)
Michigan State U (MI)
Middle Tennessee State U (TN)
Midwestern State U (TX)
Millikin U (IL)
Minnesota State U Mankato (MN)
Minnesota State U Moorhead (MN)
Minot State U (ND)
Mississippi State U (MS)
Missouri State U (MO)
Montana State U Billings (MT)
Morehead State U (KY)
Mount Vernon Nazarene U (OH)
Murray State U (KY)
National U (CA)
Newbury Coll (MA)
New England Coll (NH)
New Mexico Highlands U (NM)
New Mexico State U (NM)
New York Inst of Technology (NY)
New York U (NY)
Nicholls State U (LA)
North Carolina Ag and Tech State U (NC)
North Central Coll (IL)
North Dakota State U (ND)
Northeastern Illinois U (IL)
Northeastern State U (OK)
Northeastern U (MA)
Northern Arizona U (AZ)
Northern Illinois U (IL)
Northern Kentucky U (KY)
Northern Michigan U (MI)
Northern State U (SD)
North Georgia Coll & State U (GA)
Northwestern Coll (MN)
Northwest Missouri State U (MO)
Northwest Nazarene U (ID)
Nova Southeastern U (FL)
The Ohio State U (OH)
Ohio U (OH)
Oklahoma Christian U (OK)
Oklahoma City U (OK)
Oklahoma State U (OK)
Old Dominion U (VA)
Oregon State U (OR)
Our Lady of the Lake U of San Antonio (TX)
Pace U (NY)
Pacific U (OR)
Palm Beach Atlantic U (FL)
Penn State Abington (PA)
Penn State Altoona (PA)
Penn State Beaver (PA)
Penn State Berks (PA)
Penn State Brandywine (PA)
Penn State DuBois (PA)
Penn State Erie, The Behrend Coll (PA)
Penn State Fayette, The Eberly Campus (PA)

Penn State Greater Allegheny (PA)
Penn State Harrisburg (PA)
Penn State Hazleton (PA)
Penn State Lehigh Valley (PA)
Penn State Mont Alto (PA)
Penn State New Kensington (PA)
Penn State Schuylkill (PA)
Penn State Shenango (PA)
Penn State U Park (PA)
Penn State Wilkes-Barre (PA)
Penn State Worthington Scranton (PA)
Penn State York (PA)
Philadelphia U (PA)
Pittsburg State U (KS)
Polytechnic U of Puerto Rico (PR)
Portland State U (OR)
Prairie View A&M U (TX)
Providence Coll (RI)
Queens Coll of the City U of New York (NY)
Quincy U (IL)
Quinnipiac U (CT)
Radford U (VA)
Regis U (CO)
Rhode Island Coll (RI)
Rider U (NJ)
Rivier Coll (NH)
Robert Morris U (PA)
Rockford Coll (IL)
Roosevelt U (IL)
Rowan U (NJ)
Rutgers, The State U of New Jersey, Camden (NJ)
Rutgers, The State U of New Jersey, Newark (NJ)
Rutgers, The State U of New Jersey, New Brunswick (NJ)
Sacred Heart U (CT)
Saginaw Valley State U (MI)
St. Ambrose U (IA)
Saint Anselm Coll (NH)
St. Bonaventure U (NY)
St. Edward's U (TX)
Saint Francis U (PA)
St. John Fisher Coll (NY)
St. John's U (NY)
Saint Joseph's Coll of Maine (ME)
Saint Joseph's U (PA)
Saint Louis U (MO)
Saint Martin's U (WA)
St. Thomas Aquinas Coll (NY)
St. Thomas U (FL)
Salem State U (MA)
Salisbury U (MD)
Salve Regina U (RI)
Samford U (AL)
Sam Houston State U (TX)
San Diego State U (CA)
San Francisco State U (CA)
San Jose State U (CA)
Santa Clara U (CA)
Schreiner U (TX)
Shippensburg U of Pennsylvania (PA)
Siena Coll (NY)
Sierra Nevada Coll (NV)
Simmons Coll (MA)
Slippery Rock U of Pennsylvania (PA)
Southeastern Louisiana U (LA)
Southeastern Oklahoma State U (OK)
Southeastern U (FL)
Southeast Missouri State U (MO)
Southern Adventist U (TN)
Southern Connecticut State U (CT)
Southern Illinois U Carbondale (IL)
Southern Methodist U (TX)
Southern Nazarene U (OK)
Southwestern Coll (KS)
Spring Arbor U (MI)
Spring Hill Coll (AL)
State U of New York at Binghamton (NY)
State U of New York at Fredonia (NY)
State U of New York at New Paltz (NY)
State U of New York at Oswego (NY)
State U of New York at Plattsburgh (NY)
State U of New York Coll at Old Westbury (NY)
Stephen F. Austin State U (TX)
Stetson U (FL)
Stonehill Coll (MA)
Suffolk U (MA)
Syracuse U (NY)

INDEXES

INDEXES

San Jose State U (CA)
Simmons Coll (MA)
Texas A&M U (TX)
Texas Tech U (TX)
Tuskegee U (AL)
U of Arkansas (AR)
The U of British Columbia (BC, Canada)
U of California, Davis (CA)
U of Delaware (DE)
U of Florida (FL)
U of Georgia (GA)
U of Guelph (ON, Canada)
U of Idaho (ID)
U of Maine (ME)
U of Manitoba (MB, Canada)
U of Maryland, Coll Park (MD)
U of Massachusetts Amherst (MA)
U of Minnesota, Twin Cities Campus (MN)
U of Missouri (MO)
U of Nebraska–Lincoln (NE)
U of Saskatchewan (SK, Canada)
The U of Tennessee (TN)
U of the District of Columbia (DC)
U of Wisconsin–Madison (WI)
U of Wisconsin–River Falls (WI)
Virginia Polytechnic Inst and State U (VA)
Washington State U (WA)

FOOD SCIENCE AND TECHNOLOGY RELATED

North Dakota State U (ND)
The U of British Columbia (BC, Canada)

FOOD SERVICE AND DINING ROOM MANAGEMENT

Johnson & Wales U (CO)
Johnson & Wales U (FL)
Johnson & Wales U - Charlotte Campus (NC)

FOOD SERVICE SYSTEMS ADMINISTRATION

Central Michigan U (MI)
Dominican U (IL)
Iowa State U of Science and Technology (IA)
Johnson & Wales U (RI)
Lipscomb U (TN)
Northwest Missouri State U (MO)
Ohio U (OH)
State U of New York Coll at Oneonta (NY)
The U of North Carolina at Greensboro (NC)
U of Wisconsin–Stout (WI)
Western Michigan U (MI)

FOODS, NUTRITION, AND WELLNESS

Acadia U (NS, Canada)
Alcorn State U (MS)
Andrews U (MI)
Arizona State U (AZ)
Ashland U (OH)
Auburn U (AL)
Bastyr U (WA)
Bluffton U (OH)
Bob Jones U (SC)
Bowling Green State U (OH)
Bridgewater Coll (VA)
California State U, Los Angeles (CA)
California State U, San Bernardino (CA)
Carson-Newman Coll (TN)
Cedar Crest Coll (PA)
Coll of the Ozarks (MO)
Delaware State U (DE)
Dominican U (IL)
Georgia Southern U (GA)
Goddard Coll (VT)
Hunter Coll of the City U of New York (NY)
Indiana State U (IN)
Indiana U of Pennsylvania (PA)
Iowa State U of Science and Technology (IA)
Ithaca Coll (NY)
Jacksonville State U (AL)
James Madison U (VA)
Kent State U (OH)
Lehman Coll of the City U of New York (NY)

Lincoln U (MO)
Madonna U (MI)
The Master's Coll and Sem (CA)
Middle Tennessee State U (TN)
Minnesota State U Mankato (MN)
Montclair State U (NJ)
Murray State U (KY)
New Mexico State U (NM)
New York U (NY)
North Carolina Ag and Tech State U (NC)
Northeastern State U (OK)
Northern Illinois U (IL)
The Ohio State U (OH)
Ohio U (OH)
Oklahoma State U (OK)
Pepperdine U, Malibu (CA)
Prairie View A&M U (TX)
Purdue U (IN)
Radford U (VA)
St. Catherine U (MN)
St. Francis Xavier U (NS, Canada)
Saint Louis U (MO)
Seattle Pacific U (WA)
South Dakota State U (SD)
Southern Illinois U Carbondale (IL)
State U of New York at Plattsburgh (NY)
Stephen F. Austin State U (TX)
Syracuse U (NY)
Tennessee Technological U (TN)
Texas A&M U (TX)
Texas State U–San Marcos (TX)
Texas Tech U (TX)
Texas Woman's U (TX)
Trevecca Nazarene U (TN)
Tuskegee U (AL)
U of Arkansas (AR)
The U of British Columbia (BC, Canada)
U of Dayton (OH)
U of Delaware (DE)
U of Georgia (GA)
U of Idaho (ID)
U of Maine (ME)
U of Manitoba (MB, Canada)
U of Maryland, Coll Park (MD)
U of Minnesota, Twin Cities Campus (MN)
U of Missouri (MO)
U of Nebraska–Lincoln (NE)
U of Nevada, Reno (NV)
The U of North Carolina at Chapel Hill (NC)
U of Northern Iowa (IA)
U of Ottawa (ON, Canada)
U of Rhode Island (RI)
The U of Tennessee (TN)
The U of Texas at Austin (TX)
The U of Western Ontario (ON, Canada)
Virginia Polytechnic Inst and State U (VA)
Washington State U (WA)
Wayne State U (MI)
Youngstown State U (OH)

FOOD TECHNOLOGY AND PROCESSING

Brigham Young U (UT)
Iowa State U of Science and Technology (IA)

FOREIGN LANGUAGES AND LITERATURES

Arkansas State U (AR)
Arkansas Tech U (AR)
Assumption Coll (MA)
Auburn U (AL)
Auburn U Montgomery (AL)
Augustana Coll (SD)
Austin Peay State U (TN)
Bennington Coll (VT)
Boston U (MA)
California Polytechnic State U, San Luis Obispo (CA)
California State U, Monterey Bay (CA)
Cameron U (OK)
Carnegie Mellon U (PA)
The Citadel, The Military Coll of South Carolina (SC)
Colorado State U (CO)
Covenant Coll (GA)
Delta State U (MS)
Duquesne U (PA)
Eastern Illinois U (IL)
East Tennessee State U (TN)

Elmira Coll (NY)
Elon U (NC)
Emporia State U (KS)
Eugene Lang Coll The New School for Liberal Arts (NY)
Framingham State U (MA)
Francis Marion U (SC)
Gannon U (PA)
Gordon Coll (MA)
Grace Coll (IN)
Hamilton Coll (NY)
James Madison U (VA)
Juniata Coll (PA)
Kansas State U (KS)
Knox Coll (IL)
Lewis & Clark Coll (OR)
Long Island U, Brooklyn Campus (NY)
Long Island U, C.W. Post Campus (NY)
Loyola U New Orleans (LA)
Lycoming Coll (PA)
Manchester Coll (IN)
Marshall U (WV)
Massachusetts Inst of Technology (MA)
Middle Tennessee State U (TN)
Minnesota State U Moorhead (MN)
Mississippi State U (MS)
Monmouth U (NJ)
Montana State U (MT)
New Mexico State U (NM)
New York U (NY)
Northern Arizona U (AZ)
Old Dominion U (VA)
Pace U (NY)
Penn State Berks (PA)
Penn State Lehigh Valley (PA)
Pitzer Coll (CA)
Presbyterian Coll (SC)
Principia Coll (IL)
Purdue U (IN)
Purdue U Calumet (IN)
Radford U (VA)
The Richard Stockton Coll of New Jersey (NJ)
Rutgers, The State U of New Jersey, New Brunswick (NJ)
St. Lawrence U (NY)
Saint Louis U (MO)
St. Mary's Coll of Maryland (MD)
Samford U (AL)
Sarah Lawrence Coll (NY)
Scripps Coll (CA)
Southern Adventist U (TN)
Southern Illinois U Edwardsville (IL)
State U of New York Coll at Old Westbury (NY)
Stonehill Coll (MA)
Suffolk U (MA)
Sweet Briar Coll (VA)
Syracuse U (NY)
Texas A&M U (TX)
Thomas Edison State Coll (NJ)
Troy U (AL)
Tulane U (LA)
Union Coll (NY)
Union U (TN)
The U of Alabama (AL)
The U of Alabama at Birmingham (AL)
The U of Alabama in Huntsville (AL)
U of Alaska Fairbanks (AK)
U of California, Santa Cruz (CA)
U of Central Florida (FL)
U of Delaware (DE)
U of Hartford (CT)
U of Idaho (ID)
U of Louisiana at Lafayette (LA)
U of Maine (ME)
U of Maryland, Baltimore County (MD)
U of Mary Washington (VA)
U of Massachusetts Lowell (MA)
U of Memphis (TN)
U of Minnesota, Twin Cities Campus (MN)
U of Montevallo (AL)
U of Nebraska at Omaha (NE)
U of North Dakota (ND)
U of Northern Colorado (CO)
U of Northern Iowa (IA)
U of Ottawa (ON, Canada)
U of Puget Sound (WA)
U of Rochester (NY)
The U of Scranton (PA)
U of South Alabama (AL)
U of South Carolina Beaufort (SC)

U of Southern Mississippi (MS)
The U of Tennessee at Chattanooga (TN)
The U of Texas at Arlington (TX)
The U of Texas at Tyler (TX)
U of Wisconsin–River Falls (WI)
Virginia Commonwealth U (VA)
Washington Coll (MD)
Washington State U (WA)
Wayne State Coll (NE)
Wayne State U (MI)
West Virginia U (WV)
Wichita State U (KS)
Widener U (PA)
Wright State U (OH)
Youngstown State U (OH)

FOREIGN LANGUAGES RELATED

Arizona State U (AZ)
Augustana Coll (SD)
Bennington Coll (VT)
The Evergreen State Coll (WA)
Georgia Southern U (GA)
Hood Coll (MD)
Indiana State U (IN)
Indiana U of Pennsylvania (PA)
Kennesaw State U (GA)
New York U (NY)
Purchase Coll, State U of New York (NY)
Saint Mary's Coll of California (CA)
Southern Illinois U Carbondale (IL)
State U of New York at Binghamton (NY)
U of Alaska Fairbanks (AK)
U of California, Berkeley (CA)
U of California, Los Angeles (CA)
U of Lethbridge (AB, Canada)
U of Michigan–Flint (MI)
U of Northern Iowa (IA)
U of St. Thomas (MN)
U of West Georgia (GA)
Winona State U (MN)
Yale U (CT)

FOREIGN LANGUAGE TEACHER EDUCATION

Arkansas State U (AR)
Arkansas Tech U (AR)
Auburn U (AL)
Boston U (MA)
Bowling Green State U (OH)
Cameron U (OK)
Carroll U (WI)
Concordia Coll (MN)
Dowling Coll (NY)
Eastern Michigan U (MI)
Elmira Coll (NY)
Gannon U (PA)
Gardner-Webb U (NC)
Grand Valley State U (MI)
Greensboro Coll (NC)
Hofstra U (NY)
Kent State U (OH)
Long Island U, C.W. Post Campus (NY)
Manchester Coll (IN)
Miami U (OH)
Moravian Coll (PA)
Nazareth Coll of Rochester (NY)
New York U (NY)
Ohio Wesleyan U (OH)
Penn State Abington (PA)
Penn State Altoona (PA)
Penn State Beaver (PA)
Penn State Berks (PA)
Penn State Brandywine (PA)
Penn State DuBois (PA)
Penn State Erie, The Behrend Coll (PA)
Penn State Fayette, The Eberly Campus (PA)
Penn State Greater Allegheny (PA)
Penn State Mont Alto (PA)
Penn State Shenango (PA)
Penn State U Park (PA)
Penn State Worthington Scranton (PA)
Penn State York (PA)
Rhode Island Coll (RI)
Saint Francis U (PA)
Saint Joseph's U (PA)
Seton Hill U (PA)
Southeast Missouri State U (MO)
State U of New York at New Paltz (NY)

State U of New York Coll at Old Westbury (NY)
Temple U (PA)
Texas Wesleyan U (TX)
The U of Arizona (AZ)
U of Central Florida (FL)
U of Delaware (DE)
U of Georgia (GA)
U of Maine (ME)
U of Maryland, Coll Park (MD)
U of Nebraska–Lincoln (NE)
U of Nevada, Reno (NV)
U of Northern Iowa (IA)
U of Oklahoma (OK)
U of St. Thomas (MN)
The U of South Dakota (SD)
U of South Florida (FL)
The U of Tennessee at Chattanooga (TN)
U of Vermont (VT)
U of West Florida (FL)
Valparaiso U (IN)
Virginia Wesleyan Coll (VA)
Washington State U (WA)
Wayne State Coll (NE)
Wheeling Jesuit U (WV)
William Jewell Coll (MO)
Youngstown State U (OH)

FORENSIC CHEMISTRY

Delaware State U (DE)
Slippery Rock U of Pennsylvania (PA)
U of Rhode Island (RI)

FORENSIC PSYCHOLOGY

The Coll of Saint Rose (NY)
Florida Inst of Technology (FL)
John Jay Coll of Criminal Justice of the City U of New York (NY)
St. Ambrose U (IA)
Tiffin U (OH)
Walla Walla U (WA)
Western State Coll of Colorado (CO)

FORENSIC SCIENCE AND TECHNOLOGY

Albany State U (GA)
Alvernia U (PA)
Anna Maria Coll (MA)
Arkansas State U (AR)
Bethany Coll (KS)
Bluefield Coll (VA)
Cedar Crest Coll (PA)
Cedarville U (OH)
Champlain Coll (VT)
Chatham U (PA)
Chestnut Hill Coll (PA)
The Coll of Saint Rose (NY)
Columbia Coll (MO)
Defiance Coll (OH)
Delaware State U (DE)
Eastern New Mexico U (NM)
Emmanuel Coll (MA)
Fayetteville State U (NC)
Friends U (KS)
Hofstra U (NY)
Indiana U–Purdue U Indianapolis (IN)
Inter American U of Puerto Rico, Bayamón Campus (PR)
Jacksonville State U (AL)
John Jay Coll of Criminal Justice of the City U of New York (NY)
Keystone Coll (PA)
King Coll (TN)
Lewis U (IL)
Long Island U, C.W. Post Campus (NY)
Loyola U Chicago (IL)
Madonna U (MI)
Marian U (WI)
Mountain State U (WV)
Mount Ida Coll (MA)
Mount Marty Coll (SD)
Mount Olive Coll (NC)
Newman U (KS)
New Mexico Highlands U (NM)
Northwest Nazarene U (ID)
Pace U (NY)
Penn State Altoona (PA)
Penn State Berks (PA)
Penn State U Park (PA)
Point Park U (PA)
Russell Sage Coll (NY)
St. Andrews Presbyterian Coll (NC)
St. Edward's U (TX)

Saint Francis U (PA)
Seton Hill U (PA)
Simpson Coll (IA)
Southern Wesleyan U (SC)
Texas A&M U (TX)
Thomas More Coll (KY)
Tiffin U (OH)
Towson U (MD)
Trine U (IN)
U of Baltimore (MD)
U of Central Florida (FL)
The U of Findlay (OH)
U of Mississippi (MS)
U of Nebraska–Lincoln (NE)
U of New Haven (CT)
U of North Dakota (ND)
The U of Tampa (FL)
Utah Valley U (UT)
Virginia Commonwealth U (VA)
Washburn U (KS)
Waynesburg U (PA)
Western Carolina U (NC)
West Virginia U (WV)
Wichita State U (KS)
York Coll of Pennsylvania (PA)
Youngstown State U (OH)

FOREST ENGINEERING
Oregon State U (OR)
State U of New York Coll of Environmental Science and Forestry (NY)
U of Maine (ME)
U of New Brunswick Fredericton (NB, Canada)
U of Washington (WA)

FOREST/FOREST RESOURCES MANAGEMENT
Clemson U (SC)
Elizabethtown Coll (PA)
Lakehead U (ON, Canada)
Louisiana State U and Ag and Mech Coll (LA)
North Carolina State U (NC)
Oregon State U (OR)
State U of New York Coll of Environmental Science and Forestry (NY)
Stephen F. Austin State U (TX)
Texas A&M U (TX)
The U of British Columbia (BC, Canada)
U of California, Berkeley (CA)
U of Idaho (ID)
U of Washington (WA)
West Virginia U (WV)

FORESTRY
Albright Coll (PA)
California Polytechnic State U, San Luis Obispo (CA)
Coll of Saint Benedict (MN)
Delaware State U (DE)
Georgia Southern U (GA)
Humboldt State U (CA)
Iowa State U of Science and Technology (IA)
Iowa Wesleyan Coll (IA)
Lakehead U (ON, Canada)
Michigan State U (MI)
Mississippi State U (MS)
New Mexico Highlands U (NM)
The Ohio State U (OH)
Oklahoma State U (OK)
Purdue U (IN)
Saint John's U (MN)
Sewanee: The U of the South (TN)
Southern Illinois U Carbondale (IL)
State U of New York Coll of Environmental Science and Forestry (NY)
Stephen F. Austin State U (TX)
Texas A&M U (TX)
The U of British Columbia (BC, Canada)
U of California, Berkeley (CA)
U of Florida (FL)
U of Georgia (GA)
U of Maine (ME)
U of Massachusetts Amherst (MA)
U of Minnesota, Twin Cities Campus (MN)
U of Missouri (MO)
U of Nevada, Reno (NV)
U of New Brunswick Fredericton (NB, Canada)
U of New Hampshire (NH)
The U of Tennessee (TN)
U of the District of Columbia (DC)

U of Vermont (VT)
U of Washington (WA)
U of Wisconsin–Stevens Point (WI)
Utah State U (UT)
Virginia Polytechnic Inst and State U (VA)

FORESTRY RELATED
Sterling Coll (VT)
U of Minnesota, Twin Cities Campus (MN)
Utah State U (UT)

FOREST SCIENCES AND BIOLOGY
Auburn U (AL)
Colorado State U (CO)
Northern Arizona U (AZ)
Penn State Abington (PA)
Penn State Altoona (PA)
Penn State Beaver (PA)
Penn State Berks (PA)
Penn State Brandywine (PA)
Penn State DuBois (PA)
Penn State Erie, The Behrend Coll (PA)
Penn State Fayette, The Eberly Campus (PA)
Penn State Greater Allegheny (PA)
Penn State Hazleton (PA)
Penn State Lehigh Valley (PA)
Penn State Mont Alto (PA)
Penn State New Kensington (PA)
Penn State Schuylkill (PA)
Penn State Shenango (PA)
Penn State U Park (PA)
Penn State Wilkes-Barre (PA)
Penn State Worthington Scranton (PA)
Penn State York (PA)
State U of New York Coll of Environmental Science and Forestry (NY)
U of Idaho (ID)
U of Washington (WA)
U of Wisconsin–Madison (WI)

FOREST TECHNOLOGY
Penn State Abington (PA)
Penn State Altoona (PA)
Penn State Beaver (PA)
Penn State Berks (PA)
Penn State Brandywine (PA)
Penn State DuBois (PA)
Penn State Erie, The Behrend Coll (PA)
Penn State Fayette, The Eberly Campus (PA)
Penn State Greater Allegheny (PA)
Penn State Hazleton (PA)
Penn State Lehigh Valley (PA)
Penn State Mont Alto (PA)
Penn State New Kensington (PA)
Penn State Schuylkill (PA)
Penn State Shenango (PA)
Penn State U Park (PA)
Penn State Wilkes-Barre (PA)
Penn State Worthington Scranton (PA)
Penn State York (PA)

FRANCHISING
St. Catherine U (MN)

FRENCH
Acadia U (NS, Canada)
Adelphi U (NY)
Albion Coll (MI)
Albright Coll (PA)
Alfred U (NY)
Allegheny Coll (PA)
Alma Coll (MI)
American U (DC)
The American U of Paris (France)
Amherst Coll (MA)
Anderson U (IN)
Andrews U (MI)
Angelo State U (TX)
Appalachian State U (NC)
Aquinas Coll (MI)
Arcadia U (PA)
Arizona State U (AZ)
Asbury U (KY)
Ashland U (OH)
Assumption Coll (MA)
Athabasca U (AB, Canada)
Auburn U (AL)
Augsburg Coll (MN)
Augustana Coll (IL)
Augustana Coll (SD)

Austin Coll (TX)
Baker U (KS)
Baldwin-Wallace Coll (OH)
Ball State U (IN)
Bard Coll (NY)
Bard Coll at Simon's Rock (MA)
Barnard Coll (NY)
Barry U (FL)
Bates Coll (ME)
Beloit Coll (WI)
Benedictine Coll (KS)
Bennington Coll (VT)
Berea Coll (KY)
Berry Coll (GA)
Birmingham-Southern Coll (AL)
Boise State U (ID)
Boston Coll (MA)
Boston U (MA)
Bowdoin Coll (ME)
Bowling Green State U (OH)
Brandeis U (MA)
Bridgewater Coll (VA)
Brock U (ON, Canada)
Brown U (RI)
Bryn Mawr Coll (PA)
Bucknell U (PA)
Butler U (IN)
Cabrini Coll (PA)
California State U, Chico (CA)
California State U, Fullerton (CA)
California State U, Long Beach (CA)
California State U, Los Angeles (CA)
California State U, Northridge (CA)
California State U, San Bernardino (CA)
California State U, Stanislaus (CA)
Calvin Coll (MI)
Canisius Coll (NY)
Capital U (OH)
Carleton Coll (MN)
Carnegie Mellon U (PA)
Carson-Newman Coll (TN)
Case Western Reserve U (OH)
The Catholic U of America (DC)
Centenary Coll of Louisiana (LA)
Central Coll (IA)
Central Connecticut State U (CT)
Central Michigan U (MI)
Centre Coll (KY)
Chapman U (CA)
Chatham U (PA)
Chestnut Hill Coll (PA)
Christopher Newport U (VA)
City Coll of the City U of New York (NY)
Claremont McKenna Coll (CA)
Clarion U of Pennsylvania (PA)
Clark Atlanta U (GA)
Clark U (MA)
Cleveland State U (OH)
Coker Coll (SC)
Colby Coll (ME)
Colgate U (NY)
Coll of Charleston (SC)
Coll of Saint Benedict (MN)
Coll of the Holy Cross (MA)
The Coll of William and Mary (VA)
The Coll of Wooster (OH)
The Colorado Coll (CO)
Colorado State U (CO)
Columbia Coll (SC)
Columbia U, School of General Studies (NY)
Columbus State U (GA)
Concordia Coll (MN)
Concordia U (QC, Canada)
Connecticut Coll (CT)
Cornell Coll (IA)
Cornell U (NY)
Creighton U (NE)
Dartmouth Coll (NH)
Davidson Coll (NC)
Delaware State U (DE)
Denison U (OH)
DePaul U (IL)
DePauw U (IN)
Dickinson Coll (PA)
Doane Coll (NE)
Dominican U (IL)
Drew U (NJ)
Drury U (MO)
Earlham Coll (IN)
Eastern Michigan U (MI)
Eastern Washington U (WA)
East Stroudsburg U of Pennsylvania (PA)
Eckerd Coll (FL)
Edgewood Coll (WI)
Elizabethtown Coll (PA)
Elmhurst Coll (IL)

Elmira Coll (NY)
Elon U (NC)
Emory & Henry Coll (VA)
Erskine Coll (SC)
Fairfield U (CT)
Fairleigh Dickinson U, Coll at Florham (NJ)
Fairleigh Dickinson U, Metropolitan Campus (NJ)
Fairmont State U (WV)
Florida Ag and Mech U (FL)
Florida Atlantic U (FL)
Florida Intl U (FL)
Francis Marion U (SC)
Franklin & Marshall Coll (PA)
Franklin Coll (IN)
Furman U (SC)
Gallaudet U (DC)
Gardner-Webb U (NC)
Georgetown Coll (KY)
Georgetown U (DC)
Georgia Coll & State U (GA)
Georgia Southern U (GA)
Georgia State U (GA)
Gettysburg Coll (PA)
Gordon Coll (MA)
Goucher Coll (MD)
Grace Coll (IN)
Grand Valley State U (MI)
Greensboro Coll (NC)
Grinnell Coll (IA)
Grove City Coll (PA)
Guilford Coll (NC)
Hamilton Coll (NY)
Hamline U (MN)
Hampden-Sydney Coll (VA)
Hanover Coll (IN)
Harding U (AR)
Hartwick Coll (NY)
Haverford Coll (PA)
Hendrix Coll (AR)
Hillsdale Coll (MI)
Hobart and William Smith Colls (NY)
Hofstra U (NY)
Hollins U (VA)
Holy Family U (PA)
Hood Coll (MD)
Hope Coll (MI)
Humboldt State U (CA)
Hunter Coll of the City U of New York (NY)
Idaho State U (ID)
Illinois Coll (IL)
Illinois State U (IL)
Illinois Wesleyan U (IL)
Immaculata U (PA)
Indiana U Bloomington (IN)
Indiana U Northwest (IN)
Indiana U of Pennsylvania (PA)
Indiana U–Purdue U Fort Wayne (IN)
Indiana U–Purdue U Indianapolis (IN)
Indiana U South Bend (IN)
Indiana U Southeast (IN)
Iowa State U of Science and Technology (IA)
Ithaca Coll (NY)
Jacksonville State U (AL)
Jamestown Coll (ND)
John Carroll U (OH)
Johnson C. Smith U (NC)
Juniata Coll (PA)
Kalamazoo Coll (MI)
Keene State Coll (NH)
Kent State U (OH)
Kenyon Coll (OH)
King Coll (TN)
King's Coll (PA)
Knox Coll (IL)
Kutztown U of Pennsylvania (PA)
Lafayette Coll (PA)
Lake Forest Coll (IL)
Lakehead U (ON, Canada)
Lamar U (TX)
Lane Coll (TN)
La Salle U (PA)
Laurentian U (ON, Canada)
Lawrence U (WI)
Lebanon Valley Coll (PA)
Lee U (TN)
Lehigh U (PA)
Lehman Coll of the City U of New York (NY)
Le Moyne Coll (NY)
Lewis & Clark Coll (OR)
Lindenwood U (MO)
Linfield Coll (OR)
Lipscomb U (TN)

Lock Haven U of Pennsylvania (PA)
Long Island U, C.W. Post Campus (NY)
Longwood U (VA)
Loras Coll (IA)
Louisiana Coll (LA)
Louisiana State U and Ag and Mech Coll (LA)
Louisiana State U in Shreveport (LA)
Loyola Marymount U (CA)
Loyola U Chicago (IL)
Loyola U Maryland (MD)
Loyola U New Orleans (LA)
Luther Coll (IA)
Lycoming Coll (PA)
Lynchburg Coll (VA)
Macalester Coll (MN)
Manchester Coll (IN)
Manhattan Coll (NY)
Manhattanville Coll (NY)
Marist Coll (NY)
Marlboro Coll (VT)
Marquette U (WI)
Mary Baldwin Coll (VA)
Marywood U (PA)
McDaniel Coll (MD)
Mercer U (GA)
Merrimack Coll (MA)
Messiah Coll (PA)
Miami U (OH)
Michigan State U (MI)
Middlebury Coll (VT)
Millersville U of Pennsylvania (PA)
Millsaps Coll (MS)
Mills Coll (CA)
Minnesota State U Mankato (MN)
Minot State U (ND)
Missouri Southern State U (MO)
Missouri State U (MO)
Molloy Coll (NY)
Monmouth Coll (IL)
Montclair State U (NJ)
Moravian Coll (PA)
Morehead State U (KY)
Morehouse Coll (GA)
Mount Allison U (NB, Canada)
Mount Holyoke Coll (MA)
Mount St. Mary's Coll (CA)
Mount St. Mary's U (MD)
Muhlenberg Coll (PA)
Murray State U (KY)
Nazareth Coll of Rochester (NY)
Nebraska Wesleyan U (NE)
New Coll of Florida (FL)
New York U (NY)
Niagara U (NY)
North Carolina Ag and Tech State U (NC)
North Carolina State U (NC)
North Central Coll (IL)
North Dakota State U (ND)
Northeastern Illinois U (IL)
Northern Arizona U (AZ)
Northern Illinois U (IL)
Northern Kentucky U (KY)
Northern Michigan U (MI)
Northern State U (SD)
North Georgia Coll & State U (GA)
Oberlin Coll (OH)
Oglethorpe U (GA)
The Ohio State U (OH)
Ohio U (OH)
Ohio Wesleyan U (OH)
Oklahoma City U (OK)
Oklahoma State U (OK)
Oregon State U (OR)
Ouachita Baptist U (AR)
Pacific Lutheran U (WA)
Pacific U (OR)
Penn State Abington (PA)
Penn State Altoona (PA)
Penn State Beaver (PA)
Penn State Berks (PA)
Penn State Brandywine (PA)
Penn State DuBois (PA)
Penn State Erie, The Behrend Coll (PA)
Penn State Fayette, The Eberly Campus (PA)
Penn State Greater Allegheny (PA)
Penn State Hazleton (PA)
Penn State Lehigh Valley (PA)
Penn State Mont Alto (PA)
Penn State New Kensington (PA)
Penn State Schuylkill (PA)
Penn State Shenango (PA)
Penn State U Park (PA)
Penn State Wilkes-Barre (PA)
Penn State Worthington Scranton (PA)

INDEXES

GAME AND INTERACTIVE MEDIA DESIGN

The Cleveland Inst of Art (OH)
Dakota State U (SD)
DigiPen Inst of Technology (WA)
Franklin U (OH)
Indiana Wesleyan U (IN)
ITT Tech Inst, Bessemer (AL)
ITT Tech Inst, Tempe (AZ)
ITT Tech Inst, Tucson (AZ)
ITT Tech Inst (AR)
ITT Tech Inst, Anaheim (CA)
ITT Tech Inst, Lathrop (CA)
ITT Tech Inst, Oxnard (CA)
ITT Tech Inst, Rancho Cordova (CA)
ITT Tech Inst, San Bernardino (CA)
ITT Tech Inst, San Diego (CA)
ITT Tech Inst, San Dimas (CA)
ITT Tech Inst, Sylmar (CA)
ITT Tech Inst, Torrance (CA)
ITT Tech Inst, Lake Mary (FL)
ITT Tech Inst, Tampa (FL)
ITT Tech Inst, Duluth (GA)
ITT Tech Inst, Kennesaw (GA)
ITT Tech Inst (ID)
ITT Tech Inst, Fort Wayne (IN)
ITT Tech Inst, Indianapolis (IN)
ITT Tech Inst, Newburgh (IN)
ITT Tech Inst, Louisville (KY)
ITT Tech Inst, St. Rose (LA)
ITT Tech Inst (MD)
ITT Tech Inst, Norwood (MA)
ITT Tech Inst, Woburn (MA)
ITT Tech Inst, Canton (MI)
ITT Tech Inst, Swartz Creek (MI)
ITT Tech Inst, Troy (MI)
ITT Tech Inst, Wyoming (MI)
ITT Tech Inst (MN)
ITT Tech Inst, Earth City (MO)
ITT Tech Inst (NE)
ITT Tech Inst (NV)
ITT Tech Inst (OR)
ITT Tech Inst, Greenville (SC)
ITT Tech Inst, Cordova (TN)
ITT Tech Inst, Knoxville (TN)
ITT Tech Inst, Nashville (TN)
ITT Tech Inst (UT)
ITT Tech Inst, Norfolk (VA)
ITT Tech Inst, Richmond (VA)
ITT Tech Inst, Springfield (VA)
ITT Tech Inst, Everett (WA)
ITT Tech Inst, Seattle (WA)
ITT Tech Inst, Spokane Valley (WA)
ITT Tech Inst, Green Bay (WI)
ITT Tech Inst, Greenfield (WI)
Marist Coll (NY)
Shawnee State U (OH)
Southwestern Coll (KS)
U of California, Irvine (CA)
The U of Texas at Dallas (TX)

GAY/LESBIAN STUDIES

Bennington Coll (VT)
Cornell U (NY)
Hampshire Coll (MA)
Mills Coll (CA)
Sarah Lawrence Coll (NY)
Trinity Coll (CT)
The U of Western Ontario (ON, Canada)

GENERAL STUDIES

Albertus Magnus Coll (CT)
Alfred U (NY)
American Public U System (WV)
Anderson U (IN)
Angelo State U (TX)
Anna Maria Coll (MA)
Antioch U Midwest (OH)
Aquinas Coll (MI)
Arkansas State U (AR)
Arkansas Tech U (AR)
Athabasca U (AB, Canada)
Austin Peay State U (TN)
Ball State U (IN)
Bluefield State Coll (WV)
Bob Jones U (SC)
Brenau U (GA)
Brewton-Parker Coll (GA)
Calumet Coll of Saint Joseph (IN)
The Catholic U of America (DC)
Central Coll (IA)
Clearwater Christian Coll (FL)
Coll of Mount St. Joseph (OH)
Columbia Coll (MO)
Concordia U, St. Paul (MN)
Concordia U Wisconsin (WI)
Crown Coll (MN)
Dallas Baptist U (TX)

Daniel Webster Coll (NH)
Daniel Webster Coll–Portsmouth Campus (NH)
DePaul U (IL)
Dordt Coll (IA)
Drury U (MO)
East Central U (OK)
Eastern New Mexico U (NM)
East Tennessee State U (TN)
Emporia State U (KS)
Fairfield U (CT)
Fairleigh Dickinson U, Coll at Florham (NJ)
Fairleigh Dickinson U, Metropolitan Campus (NJ)
Florida Gulf Coast U (FL)
Florida Inst of Technology (FL)
Fort Lewis Coll (CO)
Georgia Southern U (GA)
Grand Canyon U (AZ)
Harding U (AR)
Idaho State U (ID)
Illinois State U (IL)
Indiana U Bloomington (IN)
Indiana U East (IN)
Indiana U Kokomo (IN)
Indiana U Northwest (IN)
Indiana U of Pennsylvania (PA)
Indiana U–Purdue U Fort Wayne (IN)
Indiana U–Purdue U Indianapolis (IN)
Indiana U South Bend (IN)
Indiana U Southeast (IN)
Indiana Wesleyan U (IN)
John Brown U (AR)
Kent State U (OH)
Kent State U at Geauga (OH)
Kent State U at Stark (OH)
Kent State U at Trumbull (OH)
Kutztown U of Pennsylvania (PA)
LaGrange Coll (GA)
Lakehead U (ON, Canada)
La Roche Coll (PA)
La Salle U (PA)
Lincoln Christian U (IL)
Lindenwood U (MO)
Lipscomb U (TN)
Louisiana State U and Ag and Mech Coll (LA)
Louisiana State U in Shreveport (LA)
Loyola U Chicago (IL)
Loyola U New Orleans (LA)
Madonna U (MI)
Marist Coll (NY)
Marshall U (WV)
Mayville State U (ND)
Mid-Continent U (KY)
Minot State U (ND)
Misericordia U (PA)
Montana Tech of The U of Montana (MT)
Morehead State U (KY)
Morehouse Coll (GA)
Mount Marty Coll (SD)
Murray State U (KY)
National U (CA)
New Coll of Florida (FL)
New Mexico Inst of Mining and Technology (NM)
New Mexico State U (NM)
Nicholls State U (LA)
Northcentral U (AZ)
Northeastern State U (OK)
Northern Arizona U (AZ)
North Georgia Coll & State U (GA)
Northwestern Oklahoma State U (OK)
Northwestern State U of Louisiana (LA)
Northwest U (WA)
Nova Southeastern U (FL)
Ohio Wesleyan U (OH)
Oklahoma State U (OK)
Pace U (NY)
Palm Beach Atlantic U (FL)
Pittsburg State U (KS)
Point Park U (PA)
Providence Coll (RI)
Rider U (NJ)
Saginaw Valley State U (MI)
St. John's Coll (NM)
St. Joseph's Coll, New York (NY)
Saint Louis U (MO)
Salem State U (MA)
Samford U (AL)
Seattle Pacific U (WA)
Seton Hill U (PA)
Shawnee State U (OH)
Shepherd U (WV)

Shimer Coll (IL)
Shippensburg U of Pennsylvania (PA)
Shorter U (GA)
Siena Heights U (MI)
Simon Fraser U (BC, Canada)
Southeastern Louisiana U (LA)
Southeastern Oklahoma State U (OK)
Southeast Missouri State U (MO)
Southern Arkansas U–Magnolia (AR)
Southern Methodist U (TX)
Southwestern Coll (KS)
Springfield Coll (MA)
Spring Hill Coll (AL)
Temple U (PA)
Texas Christian U (TX)
Texas Southern U (TX)
Texas State U–San Marcos (TX)
Texas Tech U (TX)
Texas Woman's U (TX)
Tiffin U (OH)
Trinity Coll of Florida (FL)
U of Alaska Fairbanks (AK)
U of Alaska Southeast (AK)
U of Bridgeport (CT)
The U of British Columbia–Okanagan (BC, Canada)
U of Charleston (WV)
U of Dayton (OH)
U of Hartford (CT)
U of Idaho (ID)
U of Louisiana at Lafayette (LA)
U of Louisiana at Monroe (LA)
U of Maine at Farmington (ME)
U of Mary Hardin-Baylor (TX)
U of Maryland U Coll (MD)
U of Massachusetts Amherst (MA)
U of Memphis (TN)
U of Miami (FL)
U of Michigan (MI)
U of Michigan–Dearborn (MI)
U of Missouri (MO)
U of Mobile (AL)
U of Nevada, Reno (NV)
U of New Haven (CT)
U of North Dakota (ND)
U of North Texas (TX)
U of St. Thomas (TX)
U of South Florida (FL)
The U of Tennessee at Martin (TN)
The U of Texas at Arlington (TX)
The U of Texas at Tyler (TX)
The U of Texas–Pan American (TX)
U of the Cumberlands (KY)
U of the Ozarks (AR)
U of the Southwest (NM)
U of the West (CA)
The U of Toledo (OH)
U of Utah (UT)
U of Washington (WA)
U of Wisconsin–Stevens Point (WI)
Victory U (TN)
Virginia Intermont Coll (VA)
Western Illinois U (IL)
Western Kentucky U (KY)
West Virginia U (WV)
Wichita State U (KS)
Widener U (PA)
Youngstown State U (OH)

GENETICS

Cedar Crest Coll (PA)
Clemson U (SC)
Iowa State U of Science and Technology (IA)
New Mexico State U (NM)
North Carolina State U (NC)
Ohio Wesleyan U (OH)
U of California, Davis (CA)
U of California, Irvine (CA)
U of Georgia (GA)
U of New Hampshire (NH)
The U of Western Ontario (ON, Canada)
U of Wisconsin–Madison (WI)
Washington State U (WA)

GEOCHEMISTRY

Bowdoin Coll (ME)
Bridgewater State U (MA)
Brown U (RI)
California Inst of Technology (CA)
The Coll of Saint Rose (NY)
Grand Valley State U (MI)
Northern Arizona U (AZ)
State U of New York at Fredonia (NY)

State U of New York at New Paltz (NY)
State U of New York at Oswego (NY)
State U of New York Coll at Geneseo (NY)
U of Maine at Farmington (ME)
U of New Brunswick Fredericton (NB, Canada)
U of Waterloo (ON, Canada)
Western Michigan U (MI)

GEOGRAPHIC INFORMATION SCIENCE AND CARTOGRAPHY

Brigham Young U (UT)
Central Michigan U (MI)
East Central U (OK)
Kennesaw State U (GA)
Northern Arizona U (AZ)
Northern Michigan U (MI)
Salem State U (MA)
Samford U (AL)
State U of New York at Binghamton (NY)
State U of New York Coll at Oneonta (NY)
Stephen F. Austin State U (TX)
Texas A&M U (TX)
Texas A&M U–Corpus Christi (TX)
Texas State U–San Marcos (TX)
The U of Akron (OH)
U of Lethbridge (AB, Canada)
U of Oklahoma (OK)
U of Ottawa (ON, Canada)
The U of Texas at Dallas (TX)
U of Wisconsin–Madison (WI)
U of Wisconsin–Platteville (WI)
Western Kentucky U (KY)
Western Michigan U (MI)

GEOGRAPHY

Adams State Coll (CO)
Appalachian State U (NC)
Aquinas Coll (MI)
Arizona State U (AZ)
Arkansas State U (AR)
Auburn U (AL)
Augustana Coll (IL)
Ball State U (IN)
Bard Coll at Simon's Rock (MA)
Bemidji State U (MN)
Bloomsburg U of Pennsylvania (PA)
Boston U (MA)
Bowling Green State U (OH)
Bridgewater State U (MA)
Brock U (ON, Canada)
Bucknell U (PA)
California State Polytechnic U, Pomona (CA)
California State U, Chico (CA)
California State U, Dominguez Hills (CA)
California State U, Fullerton (CA)
California State U, Long Beach (CA)
California State U, Los Angeles (CA)
California State U, Northridge (CA)
California State U, San Bernardino (CA)
California State U, Stanislaus (CA)
Calvin Coll (MI)
Central Connecticut State U (CT)
Central Michigan U (MI)
Central State U (OH)
City Coll of the City U of New York (NY)
Clark U (MA)
Colgate U (NY)
Concordia U (QC, Canada)
Concordia U Chicago (IL)
Concord U (WV)
Dartmouth Coll (NH)
DePaul U (IL)
Dickinson State U (ND)
Eastern Illinois U (IL)
Eastern Michigan U (MI)
Eastern Washington U (WA)
East Stroudsburg U of Pennsylvania (PA)
East Tennessee State U (TN)
Edinboro U of Pennsylvania (PA)
Elmhurst Coll (IL)
Emory & Henry Coll (VA)
Fayetteville State U (NC)
Fitchburg State U (MA)
Florida Ag and Mech U (FL)
Florida Atlantic U (FL)
Florida Intl U (FL)
Florida State U (FL)
Framingham State U (MA)
Francis Marion U (SC)

Georgia Coll & State U (GA)
Georgia Southern U (GA)
Georgia State U (GA)
Grand Valley State U (MI)
Harrisburg U of Science and Technology (PA)
Hofstra U (NY)
Humboldt State U (CA)
Hunter Coll of the City U of New York (NY)
Illinois State U (IL)
Indiana State U (IN)
Indiana U Bloomington (IN)
Indiana U of Pennsylvania (PA)
Indiana U–Purdue U Indianapolis (IN)
Indiana U Southeast (IN)
Jacksonville State U (AL)
James Madison U (VA)
The Johns Hopkins U (MD)
Kansas State U (KS)
Keene State Coll (NH)
Kennesaw State U (GA)
Kent State U (OH)
Kutztown U of Pennsylvania (PA)
Lakehead U (ON, Canada)
Laurentian U (ON, Canada)
Lehman Coll of the City U of New York (NY)
Long Island U, C.W. Post Campus (NY)
Longwood U (VA)
Louisiana State U and Ag and Mech Coll (LA)
Louisiana State U in Shreveport (LA)
Macalester Coll (MN)
Mansfield U of Pennsylvania (PA)
Marshall U (WV)
Miami U (OH)
Michigan State U (MI)
Middlebury Coll (VT)
Millersville U of Pennsylvania (PA)
Minnesota State U Mankato (MN)
Missouri State U (MO)
Montclair State U (NJ)
Morehead State U (KY)
Mount Allison U (NB, Canada)
Mount Holyoke Coll (MA)
New Mexico State U (NM)
Northeastern Illinois U (IL)
Northeastern State U (OK)
Northern Arizona U (AZ)
Northern Illinois U (IL)
Northern Kentucky U (KY)
Northern Michigan U (MI)
Northwest Missouri State U (MO)
The Ohio State U (OH)
Ohio U (OH)
Ohio Wesleyan U (OH)
Oklahoma State U (OK)
Old Dominion U (VA)
Oregon State U (OR)
Penn State Abington (PA)
Penn State Altoona (PA)
Penn State Beaver (PA)
Penn State Berks (PA)
Penn State Brandywine (PA)
Penn State DuBois (PA)
Penn State Erie, The Behrend Coll (PA)
Penn State Fayette, The Eberly Campus (PA)
Penn State Greater Allegheny (PA)
Penn State Hazleton (PA)
Penn State Lehigh Valley (PA)
Penn State Mont Alto (PA)
Penn State New Kensington (PA)
Penn State Schuylkill (PA)
Penn State Shenango (PA)
Penn State U Park (PA)
Penn State Wilkes-Barre (PA)
Penn State Worthington Scranton (PA)
Penn State York (PA)
Pittsburg State U (KS)
Portland State U (OR)
Radford U (VA)
Rhode Island Coll (RI)
Rowan U (NJ)
Rutgers, The State U of New Jersey, New Brunswick (NJ)
Salem State U (MA)
Salisbury U (MD)
Samford U (AL)
Sam Houston State U (TX)
San Diego State U (CA)
San Francisco State U (CA)
San Jose State U (CA)
Shippensburg U of Pennsylvania (PA)

Penn State New Kensington (PA)
Penn State Schuylkill (PA)
Penn State Shenango (PA)
Penn State U Park (PA)
Penn State Wilkes-Barre (PA)
Penn State Worthington Scranton (PA)
Penn State York (PA)
Pepperdine U, Malibu (CA)
Pomona Coll (CA)
Portland State U (OR)
Presbyterian Coll (SC)
Princeton U (NJ)
Principia Coll (IL)
Queens Coll of the City U of New York (NY)
Randolph-Macon Coll (VA)
Reed Coll (OR)
Rhodes Coll (TN)
Rice U (TX)
Rider U (NJ)
Ripon Coll (WI)
Rosemont Coll (PA)
Rutgers, The State U of New Jersey, Camden (NJ)
Rutgers, The State U of New Jersey, Newark (NJ)
Rutgers, The State U of New Jersey, New Brunswick (NJ)
St. Ambrose U (IA)
Saint John's U (MN)
Saint Joseph's U (PA)
St. Lawrence U (NY)
Saint Louis U (MO)
Saint Mary's Coll of California (CA)
St. Norbert Coll (WI)
St. Olaf Coll (MN)
Samford U (AL)
San Diego State U (CA)
San Francisco State U (CA)
San Jose State U (CA)
Santa Clara U (CA)
Sarah Lawrence Coll (NY)
Scripps Coll (CA)
Sewanee: The U of the South (TN)
Simpson Coll (IA)
Skidmore Coll (NY)
Smith Coll (MA)
South Dakota State U (SD)
Southeast Missouri State U (MO)
Southern Connecticut State U (CT)
Southern Illinois U Carbondale (IL)
Southern Methodist U (TX)
Southern Oregon U (OR)
Southern Utah U (UT)
Stanford U (CA)
State U of New York at Binghamton (NY)
State U of New York at New Paltz (NY)
State U of New York at Oswego (NY)
Stetson U (FL)
Stony Brook U, State U of New York (NY)
Suffolk U (MA)
Susquehanna U (PA)
Swarthmore Coll (PA)
Sweet Briar Coll (VA)
Syracuse U (NY)
Temple U (PA)
Tennessee Technological U (TN)
Texas A&M U (TX)
Texas Christian U (TX)
Texas State U–San Marcos (TX)
Texas Tech U (TX)
Transylvania U (KY)
Trent U (ON, Canada)
Trinity Coll (CT)
Trinity U (TX)
Truman State U (MO)
Tufts U (MA)
Tulane U (LA)
Union Coll (NE)
Union Coll (NY)
United States Military Acad (NY)
U at Buffalo, the State U of New York (NY)
The U of Arizona (AZ)
U of Arkansas (AR)
The U of British Columbia (BC, Canada)
U of California, Berkeley (CA)
U of California, Davis (CA)
U of California, Los Angeles (CA)
U of California, Santa Barbara (CA)
U of California, Santa Cruz (CA)
U of Central Missouri (MO)

U of Cincinnati (OH)
U of Dallas (TX)
U of Dayton (OH)
U of Delaware (DE)
U of Denver (CO)
U of Evansville (IN)
U of Florida (FL)
U of Georgia (GA)
U of Hawaii at Manoa (HI)
U of Houston (TX)
U of Indianapolis (IN)
The U of Iowa (IA)
U of Lethbridge (AB, Canada)
U of Maine (ME)
U of Manitoba (MB, Canada)
U of Maryland, Coll Park (MD)
U of Miami (FL)
U of Michigan (MI)
U of Minnesota, Twin Cities Campus (MN)
U of Mississippi (MS)
U of Missouri (MO)
U of Missouri–St. Louis (MO)
U of Mount Union (OH)
U of Nebraska at Omaha (NE)
U of Nebraska–Lincoln (NE)
U of Nevada, Las Vegas (NV)
U of Nevada, Reno (NV)
U of New Brunswick Fredericton (NB, Canada)
U of New Brunswick Saint John (NB, Canada)
U of New Hampshire (NH)
The U of North Carolina at Asheville (NC)
The U of North Carolina at Chapel Hill (NC)
The U of North Carolina at Charlotte (NC)
The U of North Carolina at Greensboro (NC)
The U of North Carolina Wilmington (NC)
U of North Dakota (ND)
U of Northern Colorado (CO)
U of Northern Iowa (IA)
U of North Texas (TX)
U of Notre Dame (IN)
U of Oklahoma (OK)
U of Oregon (OR)
U of Ottawa (ON, Canada)
U of Pennsylvania (PA)
U of Pittsburgh (PA)
U of Puget Sound (WA)
U of Redlands (CA)
U of Regina (SK, Canada)
U of Rhode Island (RI)
U of Rochester (NY)
U of St. Thomas (MN)
U of Saskatchewan (SK, Canada)
The U of Scranton (PA)
U of South Carolina (SC)
The U of South Dakota (SD)
U of Southern Indiana (IN)
U of South Florida (FL)
The U of Tennessee (TN)
The U of Texas at Arlington (TX)
The U of Texas at Austin (TX)
The U of Toledo (OH)
U of Tulsa (OK)
U of Utah (UT)
U of Virginia (VA)
U of Washington (WA)
U of Waterloo (ON, Canada)
The U of Western Ontario (ON, Canada)
U of West Georgia (GA)
U of Wisconsin–La Crosse (WI)
U of Wisconsin–Platteville (WI)
U of Wisconsin–River Falls (WI)
U of Wisconsin–Stevens Point (WI)
U of Wisconsin–Whitewater (WI)
U of Wyoming (WY)
Utah State U (UT)
Valparaiso U (IN)
Vanderbilt U (TN)
Vassar Coll (NY)
Virginia Polytechnic Inst and State U (VA)
Virginia Wesleyan Coll (VA)
Wabash Coll (IN)
Wake Forest U (NC)
Walla Walla U (WA)
Wartburg Coll (IA)
Washburn U (KS)
Washington & Jefferson Coll (PA)
Washington and Lee U (VA)

Washington Coll (MD)
Washington U in St. Louis (MO)
Wayne State U (MI)
Weber State U (UT)
Webster U (MO)
Wellesley Coll (MA)
Wesleyan U (CT)
West Chester U of Pennsylvania (PA)
Western Carolina U (NC)
Western Kentucky U (KY)
Western Michigan U (MI)
Western Oregon U (OR)
Wheaton Coll (IL)
Wheaton Coll (MA)
Whitman Coll (WA)
Willamette U (OR)
Williams Coll (MA)
Wittenberg U (OH)
Wofford Coll (SC)
Wright State U (OH)
Xavier U (OH)
Yale U (CT)
Youngstown State U (OH)

GERMANIC LANGUAGES

Bennington Coll (VT)
Eastern Michigan U (MI)
Grand Valley State U (MI)
Indiana U Bloomington (IN)
New Coll of Florida (FL)
U of Colorado Boulder (CO)
The U of Kansas (KS)
U of Massachusetts Amherst (MA)
The U of Texas at San Antonio (TX)
U of Wisconsin–Eau Claire (WI)
U of Wisconsin–Green Bay (WI)
U of Wisconsin–Madison (WI)
Washington U in St. Louis (MO)

GERMANIC LANGUAGES RELATED

Calvin Coll (MI)
Columbia U, School of General Studies (NY)

GERMAN LANGUAGE TEACHER EDUCATION

Alma Coll (MI)
Auburn U (AL)
Augustana U (SD)
California State U, Chico (CA)
Calvin Coll (MI)
The Catholic U of America (DC)
Central Michigan U (MI)
Colorado State U (CO)
Concordia Coll (MN)
Concordia U Wisconsin (WI)
Delaware State U (DE)
Eastern Michigan U (MI)
Elmhurst Coll (IL)
Grand Valley State U (MI)
Hofstra U (NY)
Hope Coll (MI)
Hunter Coll of the City U of New York (NY)
Indiana U Bloomington (IN)
Indiana U–Purdue U Fort Wayne (IN)
Indiana U–Purdue U Indianapolis (IN)
Ithaca Coll (NY)
Juniata Coll (PA)
Marquette U (WI)
Messiah Coll (PA)
Miami U (OH)
Michigan State U (MI)
Millersville U of Pennsylvania (PA)
Minot State U (ND)
Missouri State U (MO)
Moravian Coll (PA)
Northern Arizona U (AZ)
Ohio U (OH)
Ohio Wesleyan U (OH)
St. Ambrose U (IA)
State U of New York at New Paltz (NY)
The U of Arizona (AZ)
U of Evansville (IN)
U of Illinois at Chicago (IL)
The U of Iowa (IA)
U of Lethbridge (AB, Canada)
U of Louisiana at Lafayette (LA)
U of Minnesota, Duluth (MN)
U of Missouri–St. Louis (MO)
U of Nebraska–Lincoln (NE)
The U of North Carolina at Charlotte (NC)

The U of North Carolina at Greensboro (NC)
The U of South Dakota (SD)
The U of Tennessee at Martin (TN)
The U of Toledo (OH)
U of Wisconsin–River Falls (WI)
Valparaiso U (IN)
Washington U in St. Louis (MO)
Weber State U (UT)
Western Michigan U (MI)

GERMAN STUDIES

American U (DC)
Bard Coll (NY)
Bard Coll at Simon's Rock (MA)
Barnard Coll (NY)
Brock U (ON, Canada)
Brown U (RI)
Case Western Reserve U (OH)
Central Coll (IA)
Claremont McKenna Coll (CA)
Coll of the Holy Cross (MA)
The Coll of Wooster (OH)
Connecticut Coll (CT)
Cornell U (NY)
Franklin & Marshall Coll (PA)
Georgetown U (KY)
Hamilton Coll (NY)
Ithaca Coll (NY)
Kutztown U of Pennsylvania (PA)
Manhattanville Coll (NY)
Moravian Coll (PA)
Mount Holyoke Coll (MA)
North Carolina State U (NC)
Northern Michigan U (MI)
Smith Coll (MA)
Stanford U (CA)
Suffolk U (MA)
Swarthmore Coll (PA)
Sweet Briar Coll (VA)
U of California, Irvine (CA)
U of Illinois at Chicago (IL)
U of Minnesota, Duluth (MN)
U of Richmond (VA)
The U of Western Ontario (ON, Canada)
Wellesley Coll (MA)
Wheaton Coll (MA)

GERONTOLOGY

Alfred U (NY)
Alma Coll (MI)
Barton Coll (NC)
Bethune-Cookman U (FL)
Bowling Green State U (OH)
California State U, Chico (CA)
Case Western Reserve U (OH)
Dowling Coll (NY)
Indiana U Kokomo (IN)
Ithaca Coll (NY)
John Carroll U (OH)
Lakehead U (ON, Canada)
Lindenwood U (MO)
Madonna U (MI)
Miami U (OH)
Minnesota State U Moorhead (MN)
Missouri State U (MO)
Mount St. Mary's Coll (CA)
Quinnipiac U (CT)
St. Bonaventure U (NY)
St. Thomas U (NB, Canada)
San Diego State U (CA)
State U of New York at Fredonia (NY)
State U of New York Coll at Oneonta (NY)
Thomas Edison State Coll (NJ)
Towson U (MD)
U of Arkansas at Pine Bluff (AR)
U of Guelph (ON, Canada)
U of Maryland U Coll (MD)
U of Nebraska at Omaha (NE)
U of Nevada, Las Vegas (NV)
U of Northern Iowa (IA)
U of North Texas (TX)
U of Regina (SK, Canada)
The U of Scranton (PA)
U of Southern California (CA)
U of South Florida (FL)
Weber State U (UT)
Wichita State U (KS)
York Coll of the City U of New York (NY)
Youngstown State U (OH)

GOLF COURSE OPERATION AND GROUNDS MANAGEMENT

Ferris State U (MI)

GRAPHIC AND PRINTING EQUIPMENT OPERATION/PRODUCTION

Fairmont State U (WV)
Ferris State U (MI)
Georgia Southern U (GA)
Lewis-Clark State Coll (ID)
Western Illinois U (IL)

GRAPHIC COMMUNICATIONS

Arizona State U (AZ)
California Polytechnic State U, San Luis Obispo (CA)
Carroll U (WI)
Clemson U (SC)
Eastern Washington U (WA)
Grand View U (IA)
Illinois State U (IL)
Lynn U (FL)
Southern Nazarene U (OK)
U of New Brunswick Saint John (NB, Canada)
U of North Dakota (ND)
U of Northern Iowa (IA)
Walla Walla U (WA)

GRAPHIC COMMUNICATIONS RELATED

U of Maryland U Coll (MD)
U of the District of Columbia (DC)

GRAPHIC DESIGN

Abilene Christian U (TX)
Adams State Coll (CO)
Alberta Coll of Art & Design (AB, Canada)
Albertus Magnus Coll (CT)
Alma Coll (MI)
American U (DC)
American U of Beirut (Lebanon)
Anna Maria Coll (MA)
Appalachian State U (NC)
Arizona State U (AZ)
Art Center Coll of Design (CA)
The Art Inst of Boston at Lesley U (MA)
The Art Inst of Seattle (WA)
The Art Inst of York–Pennsylvania (PA)
Auburn U (AL)
Augustana Coll (IL)
Belhaven U (MS)
Boston U (MA)
Briar Cliff U (IA)
Bridgewater State U (MA)
Brigham Young U (UT)
Cabrini Coll (PA)
California Baptist U (CA)
California State Polytechnic U, Pomona (CA)
California State U, Chico (CA)
California State U, Dominguez Hills (CA)
California State U, Long Beach (CA)
Cedarville U (OH)
Centenary Coll (NJ)
Central Michigan U (MI)
Champlain Coll (VT)
Chapman U (CA)
City Coll of the City U of New York (NY)
The Cleveland Inst of Art (OH)
Coastal Carolina U (SC)
Coker Coll (SC)
Coll for Creative Studies (MI)
Coll of Mount St. Joseph (OH)
Collins Coll (AZ)
Colorado State U (CO)
Columbia Coll (MO)
Concordia U Wisconsin (WI)
Concord U (WV)
Corcoran Coll of Art and Design (DC)
Creighton U (NE)
Curry Coll (MA)
Dominican U of California (CA)
Dordt Coll (IA)
Dowling Coll (NY)
Drake U (IA)
Eastern Washington U (WA)
East Stroudsburg U of Pennsylvania (PA)
Edgewood Coll (WI)
Elizabeth City State U (NC)
Emmanuel Coll (MA)
Fashion Inst of Technology (NY)
Ferris State U (MI)
Fitchburg State U (MA)

Flagler Coll (FL)
Florida Ag and Mech U (FL)
Florida Southern Coll (FL)
Florida State U (FL)
Georgia Southern U (GA)
Grace Coll (IN)
Grand View U (IA)
Harding U (AR)
Hardin-Simmons U (TX)
Huntington U (IN)
The Illinois Inst of Art–Tinley Park (IL)
Indiana U–Purdue U Fort Wayne (IN)
Intl Acad of Design & Technology (FL)
Intl Business Coll, Fort Wayne (IN)
Iowa State U of Science and Technology (IA)
ITT Tech Inst (UT)
John Brown U (AR)
Lasell Coll (MA)
Lebanese American U (Lebanon)
Limestone Coll (SC)
Madonna U (MI)
Maine Coll of Art (ME)
Mansfield U of Pennsylvania (PA)
Marietta Coll (OH)
Mars Hill Coll (NC)
Maryland Inst Coll of Art (MD)
Marymount U (VA)
Maryville U of Saint Louis (MO)
Marywood U (PA)
Mesa State Coll (CO)
MidAmerica Nazarene U (KS)
Montclair State U (NJ)
Moravian Coll (PA)
Morningside Coll (IA)
Mountain State U (WV)
Mount Ida Coll (MA)
Mount Mercy U (IA)
Mount Vernon Nazarene U (OH)
Newbury Coll (MA)
North Carolina Ag and Tech State U (NC)
North Carolina State U (NC)
North Central Coll (IL)
Northeastern U (MA)
Northern Michigan U (MI)
Northwestern Coll (IA)
Northwestern Coll (MN)
Northwest Nazarene U (ID)
Nossi Coll of Art (TN)
Ohio U (OH)
Ouachita Baptist U (AR)
Pacific Northwest Coll of Art (OR)
Pacific Union Coll (CA)
Paier Coll of Art, Inc. (CT)
Palm Beach Atlantic U (FL)
Penn State Abington (PA)
Penn State Altoona (PA)
Penn State Beaver (PA)
Penn State Berks (PA)
Penn State Brandywine (PA)
Penn State DuBois (PA)
Penn State Erie, The Behrend Coll (PA)
Penn State Fayette, The Eberly Campus (PA)
Penn State Greater Allegheny (PA)
Penn State Hazleton (PA)
Penn State Lehigh Valley (PA)
Penn State Mont Alto (PA)
Penn State New Kensington (PA)
Penn State Schuylkill (PA)
Penn State Shenango (PA)
Penn State U Park (PA)
Penn State Wilkes-Barre (PA)
Penn State Worthington Scranton (PA)
Penn State York (PA)
Pennsylvania Coll of Art & Design (PA)
Philadelphia U (PA)
Portland State U (OR)
Pratt Inst (NY)
Queens Coll of the City U of New York (NY)
Quincy U (IL)
Rider U (NJ)
Ringling Coll of Art and Design (FL)
Rivier Coll (NH)
Rocky Mountain Coll of Art + Design (CO)
Sacred Heart U (CT)
Sage Coll of Albany (NY)
St. Ambrose U (IA)
St. Edward's U (TX)
St. John's U (NY)

Saint Mary's U of Minnesota (MN)
Salve Regina U (RI)
Samford U (AL)
San Diego State U (CA)
San Jose State U (CA)
Savannah Coll of Art and Design (GA)
School of the Museum of Fine Arts, Boston (MA)
School of Visual Arts (NY)
Schreiner U (TX)
Simpson Coll (IA)
South Dakota State U (SD)
Southern Adventist U (TN)
Spring Arbor U (MI)
Spring Hill Coll (AL)
Stephens Coll (MO)
Stonehill Coll (MA)
Susquehanna U (PA)
Temple U (PA)
Texas State U–San Marcos (TX)
Union Coll (NE)
The U of Akron (OH)
U of Arkansas–Fort Smith (AR)
U of Bridgeport (CT)
U of Denver (CO)
U of Florida (FL)
U of Hartford (CT)
U of Illinois at Chicago (IL)
The U of Kansas (KS)
U of Miami (FL)
U of Michigan (MI)
U of Minnesota, Duluth (MN)
U of Missouri–St. Louis (MO)
U of North Dakota (ND)
U of Rio Grande (OH)
U of San Francisco (CA)
The U of Tampa (FL)
The U of Tennessee at Martin (TN)
The U of the Arts (PA)
U of the Incarnate Word (TX)
Ursuline Coll (OH)
Villa Maria Coll of Buffalo (NY)
Virginia Commonwealth U (VA)
Viterbo U (WI)
Walla Walla U (WA)
Washington U in St. Louis (MO)
Waynesburg U (PA)
Wayne State Coll (NE)
Western Michigan U (MI)
Western State Coll of Colorado (CO)
Wichita State U (KS)
York Coll of Pennsylvania (PA)
Youngstown State U (OH)

GREENHOUSE MANAGEMENT
U of Minnesota, Crookston (MN)

HEALTH AND MEDICAL ADMINISTRATIVE SERVICES RELATED
Clayton State U (GA)
Concordia Coll–New York (NY)
Kent State U (OH)
Missouri Southern State U (MO)
Mount Mercy U (IA)
National-Louis U (IL)
Pennsylvania Coll of Technology (PA)
U of Baltimore (MD)
U of Minnesota, Crookston (MN)
U of Minnesota, Duluth (MN)
Ursuline Coll (OH)
Western Michigan U (MI)

HEALTH AND PHYSICAL EDUCATION/FITNESS
Abilene Christian U (TX)
American U (DC)
Angelo State U (TX)
Arkansas State U (AR)
Asbury U (KY)
Austin Peay State U (TN)
Averett U (VA)
Baker U (KS)
Baldwin-Wallace Coll (OH)
Belmont U (TN)
Berea Coll (KY)
Bethel Coll (IN)
Bethel U (MN)
Bethel U (TN)
Biola U (CA)
Blackburn Coll (IL)
Blue Mountain Coll (MS)
Bluffton U (OH)
Bob Jones U (SC)
Bridgewater Coll (VA)
Bryan Coll (TN)

California Polytechnic State U, San Luis Obispo (CA)
California State Polytechnic U, Pomona (CA)
California State U, Chico (CA)
California State U, Dominguez Hills (CA)
California State U, Fullerton (CA)
California State U, Monterey Bay (CA)
Cameron U (OK)
Canisius Coll (NY)
Capital U (OH)
Carroll U (WI)
Castleton State Coll (VT)
Cedarville U (OH)
Central Michigan U (MI)
Claflin U (SC)
Coll of the Ozarks (MO)
Concordia Coll (MN)
Concordia U (CA)
Concordia U Wisconsin (WI)
Delaware State U (DE)
DePaul U (IL)
Doane Coll (NE)
Dordt Coll (IA)
East Central U (OK)
Eastern Michigan U (MI)
Eastern Washington U (WA)
East Tennessee State U (TN)
East Texas Baptist U (TX)
Elmhurst Coll (IL)
Emory & Henry Coll (VA)
Evangel U (MO)
Ferrum Coll (VA)
Freed-Hardeman U (TN)
Free Will Baptist Bible Coll (TN)
Friends U (KS)
Gardner-Webb U (NC)
George Fox U (OR)
Georgia Southern U (GA)
Greensboro Coll (NC)
Guilford Coll (NC)
Hanover Coll (IN)
Hardin-Simmons U (TX)
Houghton Coll (NY)
Indiana U of Pennsylvania (PA)
Iowa State U of Science and Technology (IA)
Iowa Wesleyan Coll (IA)
Ithaca Coll (NY)
Jacksonville State U (AL)
James Madison U (VA)
Jarvis Christian Coll (TX)
John Brown U (AR)
Johnson State Coll (VT)
Keene State Coll (NH)
Liberty U (VA)
Lincoln Memorial U (TN)
Linfield Coll (OR)
Loras Coll (IA)
Lubbock Christian U (TX)
Luther Coll (IA)
Lynchburg Coll (VA)
Lyndon State Coll (VT)
Maryville Coll (TN)
Marywood U (PA)
The Master's Coll and Sem (CA)
Mayville State U (ND)
Miami U (OH)
Middle Tennessee State U (TN)
Milligan Coll (TN)
Minnesota State U Moorhead (MN)
Mississippi U for Women (MS)
Monmouth Coll (IL)
Monmouth U (NJ)
Montana State U Billings (MT)
Morehead State U (KY)
Morehouse Coll (GA)
Mount Vernon Nazarene U (OH)
New England Coll (NH)
Northern Illinois U (IL)
Northern Michigan U (MI)
Northwestern Coll (MN)
Northwestern State U of Louisiana (LA)
Northwest Nazarene U (ID)
The Ohio State U (OH)
Ohio U (OH)
Oklahoma Panhandle State U (OK)
Oregon State U (OR)
Prairie View A&M U (TX)
Quincy U (IL)
Randolph Coll (VA)
Roanoke Coll (VA)
Rocky Mountain Coll (MT)
Rowan U (NJ)
St. Ambrose U (IA)
St. Catherine U (MN)
Saint Joseph's Coll (IN)

Saint Mary's Coll of California (CA)
Salem State U (MA)
Samford U (AL)
San Diego State U (CA)
San Jose State U (CA)
Shawnee State U (OH)
Slippery Rock U of Pennsylvania (PA)
South Dakota State U (SD)
Southeast Missouri State U (MO)
Southern Wesleyan U (SC)
Spring Arbor U (MI)
Stephen F. Austin State U (TX)
Tabor Coll (KS)
Tennessee Wesleyan Coll (TN)
Texas A&M Intl U (TX)
Texas A&M U (TX)
Texas A&M U–Kingsville (TX)
Texas Christian U (TX)
Texas Southern U (TX)
Texas State U–San Marcos (TX)
Texas Tech U (TX)
Texas Wesleyan U (TX)
Texas Woman's U (TX)
U of Arkansas (AR)
U of Delaware (DE)
The U of Kansas (KS)
U of Louisville (KY)
U of Massachusetts Boston (MA)
U of Mobile (AL)
U of Montevallo (AL)
U of Nebraska at Omaha (NE)
U of Nebraska–Lincoln (NE)
The U of North Carolina at Chapel Hill (NC)
The U of North Carolina at Charlotte (NC)
The U of North Carolina at Pembroke (NC)
The U of North Carolina Wilmington (NC)
U of Northern Iowa (IA)
U of North Texas (TX)
U of Ottawa (ON, Canada)
U of Regina (SK, Canada)
U of Rio Grande (OH)
U of St. Thomas (MN)
U of San Francisco (CA)
U of Science and Arts of Oklahoma (OK)
U of Southern Mississippi (MS)
The U of Tampa (FL)
The U of Tennessee at Martin (TN)
The U of Texas at Austin (TX)
The U of Texas at San Antonio (TX)
The U of Texas at Tyler (TX)
The U of Texas–Pan American (TX)
U of the Cumberlands (KY)
U of Utah (UT)
U of West Florida (FL)
U of Wisconsin–La Crosse (WI)
U of Wisconsin–Stevens Point (WI)
U of Wisconsin–Superior (WI)
Utah Valley U (UT)
Valparaiso U (IN)
Virginia Intermont Coll (VA)
Walla Walla U (WA)
Walsh U (OH)
Washington Adventist U (MD)
Weber State U (UT)
Wesleyan U (CT)
West Chester U of Pennsylvania (PA)
Wichita State U (KS)
Wingate U (NC)
Wright State U (OH)
Youngstown State U (OH)

HEALTH AND PHYSICAL EDUCATION RELATED
Adelphi U (NY)
Arizona State U (AZ)
Averett U (VA)
Avila U (MO)
Bethany Coll (KS)
Bloomsburg U of Pennsylvania (PA)
Bowling Green State U (OH)
Brewton-Parker Coll (GA)
Bridgewater State U (MA)
California State U, Long Beach (CA)
Coker Coll (SC)
Concordia Coll (MN)
Concordia U Wisconsin (WI)
Cornell Coll (IA)
East Stroudsburg U of Pennsylvania (PA)
Edinboro U of Pennsylvania (PA)
Greensboro Coll (NC)
Ithaca Coll (NY)

John Brown U (AR)
Limestone Coll (SC)
Lock Haven U of Pennsylvania (PA)
Mayville State U (ND)
Midwestern State U (TX)
Missouri Southern State U (MO)
Naropa U (CO)
North Greenville U (SC)
Pittsburg State U (KS)
Regis Coll (MA)
Reinhardt U (GA)
Rocky Mountain Coll (MT)
Saint Mary's Coll of California (CA)
South Dakota State U (SD)
Southern Nazarene U (OK)
Texas Lutheran U (TX)
Towson U (MD)
The U of Iowa (IA)
U of New England (ME)
U of Utah (UT)
U of Wisconsin–Superior (WI)
Valdosta State U (GA)
Virginia Intermont Coll (VA)
Wayne State Coll (NE)

HEALTH AND WELLNESS
Antioch U Midwest (OH)
Indiana Wesleyan U (IN)
Texas Tech U (TX)
Trevecca Nazarene U (TN)
U of Houston (TX)

HEALTH COMMUNICATION
Grand Valley State U (MI)
Juniata Coll (PA)
North Dakota State U (ND)
U of Houston (TX)
Walden U (MN)

HEALTH/HEALTH-CARE ADMINISTRATION
Adams State Coll (CO)
Appalachian State U (NC)
Arcadia U (PA)
Auburn U (AL)
Augustana Coll (SD)
Baker Coll of Auburn Hills (MI)
Baker Coll of Owosso (MI)
Baker Coll of Port Huron (MI)
Baldwin-Wallace Coll (OH)
Baptist Coll of Health Sciences (TN)
Belhaven U (MS)
Belmont U (TN)
Benedictine U (IL)
Bowling Green State U (OH)
Brandeis U (MA)
Brock U (ON, Canada)
Brown Mackie Coll–Albuquerque (NM)
Brown Mackie Coll–Boise (ID)
Brown Mackie Coll–Greenville (SC)
Brown Mackie Coll–Louisville (KY)
Brown Mackie Coll–Merrillville (IN)
Brown Mackie Coll–Miami (FL)
Brown Mackie Coll–Michigan City (IN)
Brown Mackie Coll–Northern Kentucky (KY)
Brown Mackie Coll–St. Louis (MO)
Brown Mackie Coll–South Bend (IN)
Brown Mackie Coll–Tucson (AZ)
California Baptist U (CA)
California State U, Dominguez Hills (CA)
California State U, Long Beach (CA)
California State U, San Bernardino (CA)
Calumet Coll of Saint Joseph (IN)
Central Michigan U (MI)
Chestnut Hill Coll (PA)
Clayton State U (GA)
Cleary U (MI)
CollAmerica–Flagstaff (AZ)
Columbia Southern U (AL)
Concordia U Wisconsin (WI)
Corban U (OR)
Creighton U (NE)
Dallas Baptist U (TX)
Davenport U, Grand Rapids (MI)
Dillard U (LA)
Dominican Coll (NY)
Eastern Michigan U (MI)
Eastern Washington U (WA)
ECPI Coll of Technology, Virginia Beach (VA)
Ferris State U (MI)
Florida Ag and Mech U (FL)
Florida Atlantic U (FL)
Florida Inst of Technology (FL)
Florida Intl U (FL)

INDEXES

Franklin U (OH)
Friends U (KS)
Goldey-Beacom Coll (DE)
Governors State U (IL)
Grand Canyon U (AZ)
Granite State Coll (NH)
Harding U (AR)
Harrison Coll, Indianapolis (IN)
Harrison Coll, Muncie (IN)
Husson U (ME)
Idaho State U (ID)
Immaculata U (PA)
Indiana U–Purdue U Fort Wayne (IN)
Indiana U–Purdue U Indianapolis (IN)
Indian River State Coll (FL)
Ithaca Coll (NY)
James Madison U (VA)
Jefferson Coll of Health Sciences (VA)
LA Coll Intl (CA)
Lebanon Valley Coll (PA)
Lee U (TN)
Lehman Coll of the City U of New York (NY)
Lewis U (IL)
Limestone Coll (SC)
Lindenwood U (MO)
Lourdes Coll (OH)
Loyola U Chicago (IL)
Madonna U (MI)
Marian U (WI)
Mary Baldwin Coll (VA)
Marywood U (PA)
Mercy Coll of Health Sciences (IA)
Mercy Coll of Northwest Ohio (OH)
Midway Coll (KY)
Minnesota School of Business–Blaine (MN)
Minnesota State U Moorhead (MN)
Misericordia U (PA)
Montana State U Billings (MT)
Mount Mercy U (IA)
Mount St. Mary's Coll (CA)
Newbury Coll (MA)
New England Coll (NH)
Northeastern State U (OK)
The Ohio State U at Lima (OH)
Ohio U (OH)
Oregon State U (OR)
Our Lady of the Lake Coll (LA)
Peirce Coll (PA)
Penn State Abington (PA)
Penn State Altoona (PA)
Penn State Beaver (PA)
Penn State Berks (PA)
Penn State Brandywine (PA)
Penn State DuBois (PA)
Penn State Erie, The Behrend Coll (PA)
Penn State Fayette, The Eberly Campus (PA)
Penn State Greater Allegheny (PA)
Penn State Hazleton (PA)
Penn State Lehigh Valley (PA)
Penn State Mont Alto (PA)
Penn State New Kensington (PA)
Penn State Schuylkill (PA)
Penn State Shenango (PA)
Penn State U Park (PA)
Penn State Wilkes-Barre (PA)
Penn State Worthington Scranton (PA)
Penn State York (PA)
Providence Coll (RI)
St. John's U (NY)
St. Joseph's Coll, Long Island Campus (NY)
St. Joseph's Coll, New York (NY)
Saint Leo U (FL)
St. Thomas U (FL)
San Jose State U (CA)
Santa Fe Coll (FL)
Shippensburg U of Pennsylvania (PA)
Simpson U (CA)
Southern Adventist U (TN)
Southern Illinois U Carbondale (IL)
Southern Vermont Coll (VT)
Southwestern Adventist U (TX)
Spring Arbor U (MI)
Springfield Coll (MA)
State U of New York at Fredonia (NY)
Stonehill Coll (MA)
Texas Southern U (TX)
Texas State U–San Marcos (TX)

Towson U (MD)
TUI U (CA)
The U of Arizona (AZ)
U of Central Florida (FL)
U of Evansville (IN)
U of Hawaii–West Oahu (HI)
U of Houston–Clear Lake (TX)
U of La Verne (CA)
U of Michigan–Dearborn (MI)
U of Michigan–Flint (MI)
U of Minnesota, Crookston (MN)
U of Nevada, Las Vegas (NV)
U of New England (ME)
U of New Hampshire (NH)
The U of North Carolina at Chapel Hill (NC)
U of North Florida (FL)
U of Pennsylvania (PA)
U of Rhode Island (RI)
U of St. Francis (IL)
The U of Scranton (PA)
U of Southern Indiana (IN)
U of Wisconsin–Eau Claire (WI)
Upper Iowa U (IA)
Ursuline Coll (OH)
Walden U (MN)
Washington Adventist U (MD)
Washington U in St. Louis (MO)
Waynesburg U (PA)
Weber State U (UT)
West Chester U of Pennsylvania (PA)
Western Carolina U (NC)
Western Illinois U (IL)
Western Kentucky U (KY)
Wichita State U (KS)

HEALTH INFORMATION/MEDICAL RECORDS ADMINISTRATION
Alabama State U (AL)
Arkansas Tech U (AR)
Baker Coll of Auburn Hills (MI)
The Coll of St. Scholastica (MN)
Coppin State U (MD)
Dakota State U (SD)
Davenport U, Grand Rapids (MI)
Duquesne U (PA)
East Central U (OK)
Fairleigh Dickinson U, Metropolitan Campus (NJ)
Ferris State U (MI)
Florida Ag and Mech U (FL)
Georgia Health Sciences U (GA)
Georgian Court U (NJ)
Illinois State U (IL)
Indiana U Bloomington (IN)
Indiana U East (IN)
Indiana U–Purdue U Indianapolis (IN)
Indiana U South Bend (IN)
Indiana U Southeast (IN)
Kean U (NJ)
Long Island U, C.W. Post Campus (NY)
The Ohio State U (OH)
Pennsylvania Coll of Technology (PA)
Regis U (CO)
Saint Louis U (MO)
Stephens Coll (MO)
Temple U (PA)
Texas Southern U (TX)
Texas State U–San Marcos (TX)
The U of Alabama at Birmingham (AL)
U of Central Florida (FL)
U of Cincinnati (OH)
U of Illinois at Chicago (IL)
The U of Kansas (KS)
U of Louisiana at Lafayette (LA)
U of Pittsburgh (PA)
The U of Toledo (OH)
Western Carolina U (NC)

HEALTH INFORMATION/MEDICAL RECORDS TECHNOLOGY
Franklin U (OH)
Resurrection U (IL)
St. John's U (NY)
U of Arkansas for Medical Sciences (AR)
Walden U (MN)

HEALTH/MEDICAL PHYSICS
Bloomsburg U of Pennsylvania (PA)

California State U, Dominguez Hills (CA)
California State U, Northridge (CA)
Oregon State U (OR)
U of Nevada, Las Vegas (NV)

HEALTH/MEDICAL PREPARATORY PROGRAMS RELATED
Abilene Christian U (TX)
Allegheny Coll (PA)
Asbury U (KY)
Avila U (MO)
Benedictine U (IL)
Bloomsburg U of Pennsylvania (PA)
Bob Jones U (SC)
Cedarville U (OH)
Cleveland State U (OH)
Cumberland U (TN)
Duquesne U (PA)
Gannon U (PA)
Guilford Coll (NC)
Ithaca Coll (NY)
Juniata Coll (PA)
Lee U (TN)
Le Moyne Coll (NY)
Lipscomb U (TN)
Lock Haven U of Pennsylvania (PA)
Lubbock Christian U (TX)
Madonna U (MI)
Maryville U of Saint Louis (MO)
Mercer U (GA)
Northern Illinois U (IL)
Northern Michigan U (MI)
Pittsburg State U (KS)
Southern Nazarene U (OK)
State U of New York at Binghamton (NY)
The U of Akron (OH)
U of Minnesota, Twin Cities Campus (MN)
U of Missouri (MO)
U of Nevada, Reno (NV)
U of Regina (SK, Canada)
U of South Alabama (AL)
U of Waterloo (ON, Canada)
Virginia Intermont Coll (VA)

HEALTH/MEDICAL PSYCHOLOGY
Bridgewater State U (MA)
Jefferson Coll of Health Sciences (VA)
U of the Sciences in Philadelphia (PA)

HEALTH OCCUPATIONS TEACHER EDUCATION
Midwestern State U (TX)
New York Inst of Technology (NY)
Northwest U (WA)
U of Maine at Farmington (ME)

HEALTH PROFESSIONS RELATED
Alderson-Broaddus Coll (WV)
Alma Coll (MI)
Arizona State U (AZ)
Armstrong Atlantic State U (GA)
Athens State U (AL)
Azusa Pacific U (CA)
Baldwin-Wallace Coll (OH)
Bastyr U (WA)
Boise State U (ID)
Boston U (MA)
Bowling Green State U (OH)
Brock U (ON, Canada)
California State U, Long Beach (CA)
California State U, Los Angeles (CA)
California State U, San Bernardino (CA)
Castleton State Coll (VT)
Clemson U (SC)
Cleveland State U (OH)
Concordia Coll–New York (NY)
Corban U (OR)
DeSales U (PA)
East Tennessee State U (TN)
Elizabethtown Coll (PA)
The Evergreen State Coll (WA)
Fairmont State U (WV)
Florida Atlantic U (FL)
Gannon U (PA)
Georgetown U (DC)
Gettysburg Coll (PA)
Grand Canyon U (AZ)

Inter American U of Puerto Rico, San Germán Campus (PR)
Johnson State Coll (VT)
King Coll (TN)
King's Coll (PA)
Lamar U (TX)
Lock Haven U of Pennsylvania (PA)
Long Island U, Brooklyn Campus (NY)
Long Island U, C.W. Post Campus (NY)
Longwood U (VA)
Manchester Coll (IN)
Marquette U (WI)
Maryville U of Saint Louis (MO)
Milligan Coll (TN)
Minnesota State U Mankato (MN)
Misericordia U (PA)
Missouri Southern State U (MO)
Mount Olive Coll (NC)
New Jersey City U (NJ)
Newman U (KS)
Northeastern State U (OK)
Northeastern U (MA)
Northern Illinois U (IL)
The Ohio State U (OH)
Old Dominion U (VA)
Pacific U (OR)
Pennsylvania Coll of Technology (PA)
Point Park U (PA)
Purdue U (IN)
Randolph Coll (VA)
St. Joseph's Coll, Long Island Campus (NY)
St. Joseph's Coll, New York (NY)
Saint Joseph's U (PA)
San Francisco State U (CA)
Sonoma State U (CA)
Southeastern Louisiana U (LA)
Stony Brook U, State U of New York (NY)
Syracuse U (NY)
Tennessee Wesleyan Coll (TN)
Texas A&M U–Corpus Christi (TX)
Texas Christian U (TX)
Thomas Edison State Coll (NJ)
Towson U (MD)
The U of Alabama (AL)
The U of Alabama at Birmingham (AL)
U of Arkansas (AR)
U of Bridgeport (CT)
The U of British Columbia–Okanagan (BC, Canada)
U of California, Santa Cruz (CA)
U of Charleston (WV)
U of Cincinnati (OH)
U of Colorado at Colorado Springs (CO)
U of Hartford (CT)
U of Louisiana at Monroe (LA)
U of Maryland, Baltimore County (MD)
U of Nevada, Reno (NV)
U of New Brunswick Saint John (NB, Canada)
U of New England (ME)
The U of North Carolina Wilmington (NC)
U of Northern Iowa (IA)
U of Pennsylvania (PA)
U of Pittsburgh (PA)
U of St. Thomas (MN)
U of Southern Maine (ME)
The U of Tennessee at Martin (TN)
The U of Texas at Tyler (TX)
U of Waterloo (ON, Canada)
The U of Western Ontario (ON, Canada)
U of Wisconsin–Parkside (WI)
U of Wisconsin–Stevens Point (WI)
Walden U (MN)
Walla Walla U (WA)
Washington U in St. Louis (MO)
Wayne State U (MI)
West Liberty U (WV)
Wichita State U (KS)
Wilfrid Laurier U (ON, Canada)
William Paterson U of New Jersey (NJ)
Winona State U (MN)
Worcester State U (MA)
Youngstown State U (OH)

HEALTH SERVICES ADMINISTRATION
Brown Mackie Coll–Phoenix (AZ)

Brown Mackie Coll–Tulsa (OK)
Chapman U (CA)
East Stroudsburg U of Pennsylvania (PA)
Florida National Coll (FL)
Freed-Hardeman U (TN)
Indiana U Northwest (IN)
Indiana U–Purdue U Fort Wayne (IN)
Indiana U–Purdue U Indianapolis (IN)
Indiana U South Bend (IN)
Inter American U of Puerto Rico, Ponce Campus (PR)
Prescott Coll (AZ)
Robert Morris U (PA)
Saint Louis U (MO)
St. Petersburg Coll (FL)
Slippery Rock U of Pennsylvania (PA)
Ursuline Coll (OH)

HEALTH SERVICES/ALLIED HEALTH/HEALTH SCIENCES
Albany Coll of Pharmacy and Health Sciences (NY)
Alderson-Broaddus Coll (WV)
Anna Maria Coll (MA)
Baptist Coll of Health Sciences (TN)
Boston U (MA)
Brenau U (GA)
Brevard Coll (NC)
California Baptist U (CA)
California State U, Chico (CA)
California State U, Dominguez Hills (CA)
California State U, Fullerton (CA)
California State U, Northridge (CA)
The Coll of St. Scholastica (MN)
Coll of the Ozarks (MO)
Columbus State U (GA)
Corban U (OR)
Drury U (MO)
Ferrum Coll (VA)
Florida Ag and Mech U (FL)
Florida Atlantic U (FL)
Florida Gulf Coast U (FL)
Friends U (KS)
Goodwin Coll (CT)
Graceland U (IA)
Greensboro Coll (NC)
Hendrix Coll (AR)
Hofstra U (NY)
Idaho State U (ID)
Kent State U (OH)
Lebanon Valley Coll (PA)
Liberty U (VA)
Marywood U (PA)
Merrimack Coll (MA)
Miami Dade Coll (FL)
Monmouth U (NJ)
Montclair State U (NJ)
Mountain State U (WV)
National U (CA)
Nicholls State U (LA)
Northern Kentucky U (KY)
Nova Southeastern U (FL)
Sacred Heart U (CT)
Saginaw Valley State U (MI)
Saint Joseph's U (PA)
San Diego State U (CA)
San Jose State U (CA)
Spalding U (KY)
Stephen F. Austin State U (TX)
Stetson U (FL)
Texas A&M U (TX)
Texas A&M U–Kingsville (TX)
Texas State U–San Marcos (TX)
Texas Tech U (TX)
Texas Woman's U (TX)
Thomas Edison State Coll (NJ)
TUI U (CA)
U of Central Florida (FL)
U of Florida (FL)
U of Hartford (CT)
U of Miami (FL)
U of Michigan–Flint (MI)
U of Minnesota, Crookston (MN)
U of North Florida (FL)
U of North Texas (TX)
U of Ottawa (ON, Canada)
U of Southern Mississippi (MS)
The U of Texas at San Antonio (TX)
The U of Texas–Pan American (TX)
U of the Sciences in Philadelphia (PA)
U of Utah (UT)

The U of Western Ontario (ON, Canada)
U of West Florida (FL)
Ursuline Coll (OH)
Victory U (TN)
Washburn U (KS)
Washington U in St. Louis (MO)
Western Kentucky U (KY)
Westminster Coll (UT)
Wheaton Coll (IL)
Wheeling Jesuit U (WV)
Widener U (PA)

HEALTH TEACHER EDUCATION
Alma Coll (MI)
Appalachian State U (NC)
Armstrong Atlantic State U (GA)
Ashland U (OH)
Auburn U (AL)
Augsburg Coll (MN)
Austin Peay State U (TN)
Averett U (VA)
Ball State U (IN)
Belmont U (TN)
Bemidji State U (MN)
Bethel U (MN)
Bluefield Coll (VA)
Bridgewater State U (MA)
California State U, Chico (CA)
California State U, San Bernardino (CA)
Campbellsville U (KY)
Capital U (OH)
Carroll U (WI)
Cedarville U (OH)
Central Michigan U (MI)
Concordia Coll (MN)
Concordia U, St. Paul (MN)
Concord U (WV)
Curry Coll (MA)
Defiance Coll (OH)
Delaware State U (DE)
DePaul U (IL)
Eastern Illinois U (IL)
Eastern Oregon U (OR)
Eastern Washington U (WA)
East Stroudsburg U of Pennsylvania (PA)
Elon U (NC)
Fayetteville State U (NC)
Freed-Hardeman U (TN)
Gardner-Webb U (NC)
Georgia Coll & State U (GA)
Graceland U (IA)
Grand Valley State U (MI)
Harding U (AR)
Hofstra U (NY)
Houghton Coll (NY)
Hunter Coll of the City U of New York (NY)
Idaho State U (ID)
Illinois State U (IL)
Indiana U Bloomington (IN)
Indiana U Southeast (IN)
Inter American U of Puerto Rico, San Germán Campus (PR)
Iowa State U of Science and Technology (IA)
Iowa Wesleyan Coll (IA)
Ithaca Coll (NY)
Jacksonville State U (AL)
John Brown U (AR)
Johnson C. Smith U (NC)
Kent State U (OH)
Lamar U (TX)
Lee U (TN)
Lehman Coll of the City U of New York (NY)
Liberty U (VA)
Lincoln Memorial U (TN)
Long Island U, C.W. Post Campus (NY)
Longwood U (VA)
Louisiana Coll (LA)
Malone U (OH)
Manchester Coll (IN)
Maryville Coll (TN)
Mayville State U (ND)
Miami U (OH)
Michigan State U (MI)
Middle Tennessee State U (TN)
Minnesota State U Mankato (MN)
Minnesota State U Moorhead (MN)
Missouri Baptist U (MO)
Montana State U Billings (MT)
Montclair State U (NJ)
Morehead State U (KY)
Mount Vernon Nazarene U (OH)
Murray State U (KY)
New Mexico Highlands U (NM)

North Dakota State U (ND)
Northeastern State U (OK)
Northern Arizona U (AZ)
Northern Illinois U (IL)
Northern Michigan U (MI)
Northern State U (SD)
Northwestern Oklahoma State U (OK)
Ohio Wesleyan U (OH)
Portland State U (OR)
Rhode Island Coll (RI)
Rocky Mountain Coll (MT)
St. Ambrose U (IA)
Salisbury U (MD)
Simpson Coll (IA)
Southern Illinois U Carbondale (IL)
Southern Illinois U Edwardsville (IL)
Southern Oregon U (OR)
Springfield Coll (MA)
State U of New York at Oswego (NY)
Tabor Coll (KS)
Tennessee Technological U (TN)
Texas A&M U–Corpus Christi (TX)
TUI U (CA)
Union Coll (KY)
The U of Alabama at Birmingham (AL)
The U of Arizona (AZ)
U of Charleston (WV)
U of Cincinnati (OH)
U of Dayton (OH)
U of Delaware (DE)
U of Georgia (GA)
U of Maine (ME)
U of Maine at Farmington (ME)
U of Maine at Presque Isle (ME)
U of Maryland, Coll Park (MD)
U of Minnesota, Duluth (MN)
U of Minnesota, Twin Cities Campus (MN)
U of Mount Union (OH)
U of Nevada, Las Vegas (NV)
U of Nevada, Reno (NV)
U of New Brunswick Fredericton (NB, Canada)
U of Northern Iowa (IA)
U of Regina (SK, Canada)
U of Rio Grande (OH)
U of St. Thomas (MN)
The U of South Dakota (SD)
U of the Cumberlands (KY)
U of the District of Columbia (DC)
The U of Toledo (OH)
U of Wisconsin–La Crosse (WI)
Utah State U (UT)
Utah Valley U (UT)
Virginia Commonwealth U (VA)
Washington State U (WA)
Wayne State U (MI)
Western Connecticut State U (CT)
Western Illinois U (IL)
Western Michigan U (MI)
West Liberty U (WV)
William Paterson U of New Jersey (NJ)
Wilmington Coll (OH)
Winona State U (MN)
York Coll of the City U of New York (NY)
Youngstown State U (OH)

HEALTH UNIT MANAGEMENT/ WARD SUPERVISION
Southern Illinois U Carbondale (IL)

HEATING, AIR CONDITIONING, VENTILATION AND REFRIGERATION MAINTENANCE TECHNOLOGY
Lewis-Clark State Coll (ID)

HEAVY EQUIPMENT MAINTENANCE TECHNOLOGY
Ferris State U (MI)
Pittsburg State U (KS)

HEBREW
Bard Coll (NY)
Brandeis U (MA)
Brigham Young U (UT)
Columbia U, School of General Studies (NY)
Concordia U Wisconsin (WI)
Dartmouth Coll (NH)
Hofstra U (NY)
Hunter Coll of the City U of New York (NY)

Lehman Coll of the City U of New York (NY)
Multnomah U (OR)
New York U (NY)
The Ohio State U (OH)
Queens Coll of the City U of New York (NY)
State U of New York at Binghamton (NY)
Temple U (PA)
U of California, Los Angeles (CA)
U of Cincinnati (OH)
U of Michigan (MI)
U of Minnesota, Twin Cities Campus (MN)
The U of Texas at Austin (TX)
U of Utah (UT)
U of Wisconsin–Madison (WI)
Washington U in St. Louis (MO)

HERBALISM
Bastyr U (WA)

HISPANIC-AMERICAN, PUERTO RICAN, AND MEXICAN-AMERICAN/CHICANO STUDIES
Arizona State U (AZ)
Boston Coll (MA)
Brown U (RI)
California State U, Dominguez Hills (CA)
California State U, Fullerton (CA)
California State U, Long Beach (CA)
California State U, Los Angeles (CA)
California State U, Northridge (CA)
Cedar Crest Coll (PA)
Claremont McKenna Coll (CA)
The Colorado Coll (CO)
Columbia U, School of General Studies (NY)
Connecticut Coll (CT)
Dartmouth Coll (NH)
Fort Lewis Coll (CO)
Gettysburg Coll (PA)
Hofstra U (NY)
Hunter Coll of the City U of New York (NY)
Lewis & Clark Coll (OR)
Loyola Marymount U (CA)
Mills Coll (CA)
Our Lady of the Lake U of San Antonio (TX)
Pitzer Coll (CA)
Pomona Coll (CA)
Rutgers, The State U of New Jersey, Newark (NJ)
Rutgers, The State U of New Jersey, New Brunswick (NJ)
San Diego State U (CA)
San Francisco State U (CA)
Scripps Coll (CA)
Sonoma State U (CA)
Southern Methodist U (TX)
Stanford U (CA)
State U of New York Coll at Oneonta (NY)
Sul Ross State U (TX)
Trent U (ON, Canada)
Tulane U (LA)
The U of Arizona (AZ)
U of California, Berkeley (CA)
U of California, Davis (CA)
U of California, Irvine (CA)
U of California, Los Angeles (CA)
U of California, Santa Barbara (CA)
U of California, Santa Cruz (CA)
U of Michigan (MI)
U of Minnesota, Twin Cities Campus (MN)
U of Northern Colorado (CO)
U of Southern California (CA)
U of Southern Maine (ME)
The U of Texas at San Antonio (TX)
The U of Texas–Pan American (TX)
U of Washington (WA)
Wheaton Coll (MA)

HISPANIC AND LATIN AMERICAN LANGUAGES
Hamilton Coll (NY)

HISTORIC PRESERVATION AND CONSERVATION
Coll of Charleston (SC)
Delaware State U (DE)
Saint Mary's Coll of California (CA)
Salve Regina U (RI)
Savannah Coll of Art and Design (GA)

Southeast Missouri State U (MO)
U of Mary Washington (VA)
Ursuline Coll (OH)

HISTORY
Abilene Christian U (TX)
Acadia U (NS, Canada)
Adams State Coll (CO)
Adelphi U (NY)
Alabama State U (AL)
Albany State U (GA)
Albertus Magnus Coll (CT)
Albion U (MI)
Albright Coll (PA)
Alcorn State U (MS)
Alderson-Broaddus Coll (WV)
Alfred U (NY)
Allegheny Coll (PA)
Alma Coll (MI)
Alvernia U (PA)
Alverno Coll (WI)
American Public U System (WV)
American U (DC)
American U in Bulgaria (Bulgaria)
American U of Beirut (Lebanon)
The American U of Paris (France)
Amherst Coll (MA)
Anderson U (IN)
Anderson U (SC)
Andrews U (MI)
Angelo State U (TX)
Anna Maria Coll (MA)
Appalachian State U (NC)
Aquinas Coll (MI)
Aquinas Coll (TN)
Arcadia U (PA)
Arizona State U (AZ)
Arkansas State U (AR)
Arkansas Tech U (AR)
Armstrong Atlantic State U (GA)
Asbury U (KY)
Ashland U (OH)
Assumption Coll (MA)
Athabasca U (AB, Canada)
Athens State U (AL)
Auburn U (AL)
Auburn U Montgomery (AL)
Augsburg Coll (MN)
Augustana Coll (IL)
Augustana Coll (SD)
Austin Coll (TX)
Austin Peay State U (TN)
Averett U (VA)
Avila U (MO)
Azusa Pacific U (CA)
Baker U (KS)
Baldwin-Wallace Coll (OH)
Ball State U (IN)
Bard Coll (NY)
Barnard Coll (NY)
Barry U (FL)
Barton Coll (NC)
Bates Coll (ME)
Belhaven U (MS)
Bellarmine U (KY)
Belmont Abbey Coll (NC)
Belmont U (TN)
Beloit Coll (WI)
Bemidji State U (MN)
Benedictine Coll (KS)
Benedictine U (IL)
Bennington Coll (VT)
Bentley U (MA)
Berea Coll (KY)
Berry Coll (GA)
Bethany Coll (KS)
Bethany Coll (WV)
Bethany Lutheran Coll (MN)
Bethel Coll (IN)
Bethel U (MN)
Bethel U (TN)
Biola U (CA)
Birmingham-Southern Coll (AL)
Blackburn Coll (IL)
Bloomfield Coll (NJ)
Bloomsburg U of Pennsylvania (PA)
Bluefield Coll (VA)
Blue Mountain Coll (MS)
Bluffton U (OH)
Bob Jones U (SC)
Boise State U (ID)
Boston Coll (MA)
Boston U (MA)
Bowdoin Coll (ME)
Bowie State U (MD)
Bowling Green State U (OH)
Brandeis U (MA)
Brenau U (GA)
Brevard Coll (NC)
Brewton-Parker Coll (GA)

Briar Cliff U (IA)
Bridgewater Coll (VA)
Bridgewater State U (MA)
Brock U (ON, Canada)
Brown U (RI)
Bryan Coll (TN)
Bryant U (RI)
Bryn Athyn Coll of the New Church (PA)
Bryn Mawr Coll (PA)
Bucknell U (PA)
Buena Vista U (IA)
Butler U (IN)
Cabrini Coll (PA)
California Baptist U (CA)
California Inst of Technology (CA)
California Polytechnic State U, San Luis Obispo (CA)
California State Polytechnic U, Pomona (CA)
California State U, Bakersfield (CA)
California State U, Chico (CA)
California State U, Dominguez Hills (CA)
California State U, Fullerton (CA)
California State U, Long Beach (CA)
California State U, Los Angeles (CA)
California State U, Northridge (CA)
California State U, San Bernardino (CA)
California State U, San Marcos (CA)
California State U, Stanislaus (CA)
Calvin Coll (MI)
Cameron U (OK)
Campbellsville U (KY)
Canisius Coll (NY)
Capital U (OH)
Carleton Coll (MN)
Carlow U (PA)
Carroll U (WI)
Carson-Newman Coll (TN)
Case Western Reserve U (OH)
Castleton State Coll (VT)
The Catholic U of America (DC)
Cedar Crest Coll (PA)
Cedarville U (OH)
Centenary Coll (NJ)
Centenary Coll of Louisiana (LA)
Central Coll (IA)
Central Connecticut State U (CT)
Central Michigan U (MI)
Central State U (OH)
Centre Coll (KY)
Chapman U (CA)
Chatham U (PA)
Chestnut Hill Coll (PA)
Christendom Coll (VA)
Christian Brothers U (TN)
Christopher Newport U (VA)
The Citadel, The Military Coll of South Carolina (SC)
City Coll of the City U of New York (NY)
Claflin U (SC)
Claremont McKenna Coll (CA)
Clarion U of Pennsylvania (PA)
Clark Atlanta U (GA)
Clarke U (IA)
Clarkson U (NY)
Clark U (MA)
Clayton State U (GA)
Clearwater Christian Coll (FL)
Clemson U (SC)
Cleveland State U (OH)
Coastal Carolina U (SC)
Coker Coll (SC)
Colby Coll (ME)
Colgate U (NY)
Coll of Charleston (SC)
Coll of Mount St. Joseph (OH)
The Coll of New Jersey (NJ)
Coll of Saint Benedict (MN)
Coll of Saint Elizabeth (NJ)
Coll of St. Joseph (VT)
The Coll of Saint Rose (NY)
The Coll of St. Scholastica (MN)
Coll of Staten Island of the City of New York (NY)
Coll of the Holy Cross (MA)
Coll of the Ozarks (MO)
The Coll of William and Mary (VA)
The Coll of Wooster (OH)
The Colorado Coll (CO)
Colorado State U (CO)
Columbia Coll (MO)
Columbia Coll (SC)
Columbia U, School of General Studies (NY)
Columbus State U (GA)
Concordia Coll (MN)

Concordia Coll–New York (NY)
Concordia U (CA)
Concordia U (QC, Canada)
Concordia U Chicago (IL)
Concordia U, St. Paul (MN)
Concordia U Wisconsin (WI)
Concord U (WV)
Connecticut Coll (CT)
Coppin State U (MD)
Corban U (OR)
Cornell Coll (IA)
Cornell U (NY)
Covenant Coll (GA)
Crandall U (NB, Canada)
Creighton U (NE)
Crown Coll (MN)
Culver-Stockton Coll (MO)
Cumberland U (TN)
Curry Coll (MA)
Dakota Wesleyan U (SD)
Dallas Baptist U (TX)
Dalton State Coll (GA)
Dartmouth Coll (NH)
Davidson Coll (NC)
Defiance Coll (OH)
Delaware State U (DE)
Delta State U (MS)
Denison U (OH)
DePaul U (IL)
DePauw U (IN)
DEREE - The American Coll of
  Greece (Greece)
DeSales U (PA)
Dickinson Coll (PA)
Dickinson State U (ND)
Dillard U (LA)
Doane Coll (NE)
Dominican Coll (NY)
Dominican U (IL)
Dominican U of California (CA)
Dordt Coll (IA)
Dowling Coll (NY)
Drake U (IA)
Drew U (NJ)
Drury U (MO)
Duquesne U (PA)
Earlham Coll (IN)
East Central U (OK)
Eastern Illinois U (IL)
Eastern Michigan U (MI)
Eastern New Mexico U (NM)
Eastern Oregon U (OR)
Eastern Washington U (WA)
East Stroudsburg U of Pennsylvania
  (PA)
East Tennessee State U (TN)
East Texas Baptist U (TX)
Eckerd Coll (FL)
Edgewood Coll (WI)
Edinboro U of Pennsylvania (PA)
Elizabeth City State U (NC)
Elizabethtown Coll (PA)
Elmhurst Coll (IL)
Elmira Coll (NY)
Elon U (NC)
Emmanuel Coll (MA)
Emory & Henry Coll (VA)
Emporia State U (KS)
Endicott Coll (MA)
Erskine Coll (SC)
Eugene Lang Coll The New School
  for Liberal Arts (NY)
Evangel U (MO)
Fairfield U (CT)
Fairleigh Dickinson U, Coll at
  Florham (NJ)
Fairleigh Dickinson U, Metropolitan
  Campus (NJ)
Fairmont State U (WV)
Faulkner U (AL)
Fayetteville State U (NC)
Felician Coll (NJ)
Ferris State U (MI)
Ferrum Coll (VA)
Fitchburg State U (MA)
Flagler Coll (FL)
Florida Ag and Mech U (FL)
Florida Atlantic U (FL)
Florida Gulf Coast U (FL)
Florida Intl U (FL)
Florida Southern Coll (FL)
Florida State U (FL)
Fontbonne U (MO)
Fort Lewis Coll (CO)
Framingham State U (MA)
Francis Marion U (SC)
Franklin & Marshall Coll (PA)
Franklin Coll (IN)

Franklin Coll Switzerland
  (Switzerland)
Franklin Pierce U (NH)
Freed-Hardeman U (TN)
Free Will Baptist Bible Coll (TN)
Friends U (KS)
Furman U (SC)
Gannon U (PA)
Gardner-Webb U (NC)
Geneva Coll (PA)
George Fox U (OR)
Georgetown Coll (KY)
Georgetown U (DC)
Georgia Coll & State U (GA)
Georgian Court U (NJ)
Georgia Southern U (GA)
Georgia State U (GA)
Gettysburg Coll (PA)
Gordon Coll (MA)
Goucher Coll (MD)
Grace Coll (IN)
Graceland U (IA)
Grand Canyon U (AZ)
Grand Valley State U (MI)
Grand View U (IA)
Great Lakes Christian Coll (MI)
Greensboro Coll (NC)
Greenville Coll (IL)
Grinnell Coll (IA)
Grove City Coll (PA)
Guilford Coll (NC)
Hamilton Coll (NY)
Hamline U (MN)
Hampden-Sydney Coll (VA)
Hampshire Coll (MA)
Hannibal-LaGrange U (MO)
Hanover Coll (IN)
Harding U (AR)
Hardin-Simmons U (TX)
Hartwick Coll (NY)
Harvard U (MA)
Haverford Coll (PA)
Hawai'i Pacific U (HI)
Hendrix Coll (AR)
Hillsdale Coll (MI)
Hobart and William Smith Colls (NY)
Hofstra U (NY)
Hollins U (VA)
Holy Cross Coll (IN)
Holy Family U (PA)
Holy Names U (CA)
Hood Coll (MD)
Hope Coll (MI)
Houghton Coll (NY)
Humboldt State U (CA)
Hunter Coll of the City U of New
  York (NY)
Huntingdon Coll (AL)
Huntington U (IN)
Huston-Tillotson U (TX)
Idaho State U (ID)
Illinois Coll (IL)
Illinois State U (IL)
Illinois Wesleyan U (IL)
Immaculata U (PA)
Indiana State U (IN)
Indiana U Bloomington (IN)
Indiana U Northwest (IN)
Indiana U of Pennsylvania (PA)
Indiana U–Purdue U Fort Wayne
  (IN)
Indiana U–Purdue U Indianapolis
  (IN)
Indiana U South Bend (IN)
Indiana U Southeast (IN)
Indiana Wesleyan U (IN)
Inter American U of Puerto Rico,
  Metropolitan Campus (PR)
Iowa State U of Science and
  Technology (IA)
Iowa Wesleyan Coll (IA)
Ithaca Coll (NY)
Jacksonville State U (AL)
James Madison U (VA)
Jamestown Coll (ND)
Jarvis Christian Coll (TX)
John Brown U (AR)
John Carroll U (OH)
The Johns Hopkins U (MD)
Johnson C. Smith U (NC)
Johnson State Coll (VT)
Judson Coll (AL)
Juniata Coll (PA)
Kalamazoo Coll (MI)
Kansas State U (KS)
Kean U (NJ)
Keene State Coll (NH)
Kennesaw State U (GA)

Kent State U (OH)
Kent State U at Stark (OH)
Kentucky Wesleyan Coll (KY)
Kenyon Coll (OH)
Keuka Coll (NY)
King Coll (TN)
King's Coll (PA)
The King's U Coll (AB, Canada)
Knox Coll (IL)
Kutztown U of Pennsylvania (PA)
Lafayette Coll (PA)
LaGrange Coll (GA)
Lake Forest Coll (IL)
Lakehead U (ON, Canada)
Lake Superior State U (MI)
Lamar U (TX)
Lane Coll (TN)
La Roche Coll (PA)
La Salle U (PA)
Lasell Coll (MA)
Laurentian U (ON, Canada)
Lawrence U (WI)
Lebanese American U (Lebanon)
Lebanon Valley Coll (PA)
Lee U (TN)
Lehigh U (PA)
Lehman Coll of the City U of New
  York (NY)
Le Moyne Coll (NY)
LeTourneau U (TX)
Lewis & Clark Coll (OR)
Lewis U (IL)
Liberty U (VA)
Limestone Coll (SC)
Lincoln Memorial U (TN)
Lincoln U (MO)
Lindenwood U (MO)
Lindsey Wilson Coll (KY)
Linfield Coll (OR)
Lipscomb U (TN)
Lock Haven U of Pennsylvania (PA)
Long Island U, Brooklyn Campus
  (NY)
Long Island U, C.W. Post Campus
  (NY)
Longwood U (VA)
Loras Coll (IA)
Louisiana Coll (LA)
Louisiana State U and Ag and Mech
  Coll (LA)
Louisiana State U in Shreveport
  (LA)
Lourdes Coll (OH)
Loyola Marymount U (CA)
Loyola U Chicago (IL)
Loyola U Maryland (MD)
Loyola U New Orleans (LA)
Lubbock Christian U (TX)
Luther Coll (IA)
Lycoming Coll (PA)
Lynchburg Coll (VA)
Lyon Coll (AR)
Macalester Coll (MN)
MacMurray Coll (IL)
Madonna U (MI)
Malone U (OH)
Manchester Coll (IN)
Manhattan Coll (NY)
Manhattanville Coll (NY)
Mansfield U of Pennsylvania (PA)
Marian U (WI)
Marietta Coll (OH)
Marist Coll (NY)
Marlboro Coll (VT)
Marquette U (WI)
Marshall U (WV)
Mars Hill Coll (NC)
Mary Baldwin Coll (VA)
Marymount U (VA)
Maryville Coll (TN)
Maryville U of Saint Louis (MO)
Marywood U (PA)
Massachusetts Coll of Liberal Arts
  (MA)
Massachusetts Inst of Technology
  (MA)
The Master's Coll and Sem (CA)
McDaniel Coll (MD)
McKendree U (IL)
McMurry U (TX)
Mercer U (GA)
Merrimack Coll (MA)
Mesa State Coll (CO)
Messiah Coll (PA)
Metropolitan State U (MN)
Miami U (OH)
Michigan State U (MI)
MidAmerica Nazarene U (KS)

Middlebury Coll (VT)
Middle Tennessee State U (TN)
Midwestern State U (TX)
Millersville U of Pennsylvania (PA)
Milligan Coll (TN)
Millikin U (IL)
Millsaps Coll (MS)
Mills Coll (CA)
Minnesota State U Mankato (MN)
Minnesota State U Moorhead (MN)
Minot State U (ND)
Misericordia U (PA)
Mississippi State U (MS)
Mississippi U for Women (MS)
Mississippi Valley State U (MS)
Missouri Baptist U (MO)
Missouri Southern State U (MO)
Missouri State U (MO)
Missouri U of Science and
  Technology (MO)
Molloy Coll (NY)
Monmouth Coll (IL)
Monmouth U (NJ)
Montana State U (MT)
Montana State U Billings (MT)
Montclair State U (NJ)
Montreat Coll, Montreat (NC)
Moravian Coll (PA)
Morehead State U (KY)
Morehouse Coll (GA)
Morningside Coll (IA)
Morris Coll (SC)
Mount Allison U (NB, Canada)
Mount Holyoke Coll (MA)
Mount Marty Coll (SD)
Mount Mercy U (IA)
Mount Olive Coll (NC)
Mount Saint Mary Coll (NY)
Mount St. Mary's Coll (CA)
Mount St. Mary's U (MD)
Mount Vernon Nazarene U (OH)
Muhlenberg Coll (PA)
Multnomah U (OR)
Murray State U (KY)
National U (CA)
Nazareth Coll of Rochester (NY)
Nebraska Wesleyan U (NE)
Nevada State Coll at Henderson
  (NV)
Newberry Coll (SC)
New Coll of Florida (FL)
New England Coll (NH)
New Jersey City U (NJ)
New Jersey Inst of Technology (NJ)
Newman U (KS)
New Mexico Highlands U (NM)
New Mexico State U (NM)
New York U (NY)
Niagara U (NY)
Nicholls State U (LA)
North Carolina Ag and Tech State U
  (NC)
North Carolina State U (NC)
North Central Coll (IL)
North Dakota State U (ND)
Northeastern Illinois U (IL)
Northeastern State U (OK)
Northeastern U (MA)
Northern Arizona U (AZ)
Northern Illinois U (IL)
Northern Kentucky U (KY)
Northern Michigan U (MI)
Northern State U (SD)
North Georgia Coll & State U (GA)
Northwest Christian U (OR)
Northwestern Coll (IA)
Northwestern Coll (MN)
Northwestern Oklahoma State U
  (OK)
Northwestern State U of Louisiana
  (LA)
Northwest Missouri State U (MO)
Northwest Nazarene U (ID)
Northwest U (WA)
Notre Dame de Namur U (CA)
Nova Southeastern U (FL)
Nyack Coll (NY)
Oberlin Coll (OH)
Oglethorpe U (GA)
The Ohio State U (OH)
The Ohio State U at Lima (OH)
The Ohio State U at Marion (OH)
The Ohio State U–Mansfield
  Campus (OH)
The Ohio State U–Newark Campus
  (OH)
Ohio U (OH)
Ohio U–Chillicothe (OH)

Ohio Valley U (WV)
Ohio Wesleyan U (OH)
Oklahoma Christian U (OK)
Oklahoma City U (OK)
Oklahoma Panhandle State U (OK)
Oklahoma State U (OK)
Oklahoma Wesleyan U (OK)
Old Dominion U (VA)
Ouachita Baptist U (AR)
Our Lady of the Lake U of San
  Antonio (TX)
Pace U (NY)
Pacific Lutheran U (WA)
Pacific Union Coll (CA)
Pacific U (OR)
Paine Coll (GA)
Palm Beach Atlantic U (FL)
Patrick Henry Coll (VA)
Penn State Abington (PA)
Penn State Altoona (PA)
Penn State Beaver (PA)
Penn State Berks (PA)
Penn State Brandywine (PA)
Penn State DuBois (PA)
Penn State Erie, The Behrend Coll
  (PA)
Penn State Fayette, The Eberly
  Campus (PA)
Penn State Greater Allegheny (PA)
Penn State Hazleton (PA)
Penn State Lehigh Valley (PA)
Penn State Mont Alto (PA)
Penn State New Kensington (PA)
Penn State Schuylkill (PA)
Penn State Shenango (PA)
Penn State U Park (PA)
Penn State Wilkes-Barre (PA)
Penn State Worthington Scranton
  (PA)
Penn State York (PA)
Pepperdine U, Malibu (CA)
Piedmont Coll (GA)
Pikeville Coll (KY)
Pittsburg State U (KS)
Pitzer Coll (CA)
Point Park U (PA)
Pomona Coll (CA)
Portland State U (OR)
Prairie View A&M U (TX)
Presbyterian Coll (SC)
Prescott Coll (AZ)
Princeton U (NJ)
Principia Coll (IL)
Providence Coll (RI)
Purchase Coll, State U of New York
  (NY)
Purdue U (IN)
Purdue U Calumet (IN)
Queens Coll of the City U of New
  York (NY)
Quincy U (IL)
Quinnipiac U (CT)
Radford U (VA)
Ramapo Coll of New Jersey (NJ)
Randolph Coll (VA)
Randolph-Macon Coll (VA)
Reed Coll (OR)
Regent U (VA)
Regis Coll (MA)
Regis U (CO)
Reinhardt U (GA)
Rhode Island Coll (RI)
Rhodes Coll (TN)
Rice U (TX)
The Richard Stockton Coll of New
  Jersey (NJ)
Rider U (NJ)
Ripon Coll (WI)
Rivier Coll (NH)
Roanoke Coll (VA)
Rockford Coll (IL)
Rockhurst U (MO)
Rocky Mountain Coll (MT)
Rollins Coll (FL)
Roosevelt U (IL)
Rosemont Coll (PA)
Rowan U (NJ)
Russell Sage Coll (NY)
Rutgers, The State U of New
  Jersey, Camden (NJ)
Rutgers, The State U of New
  Jersey, Newark (NJ)
Rutgers, The State U of New
  Jersey, New Brunswick (NJ)
Sacred Heart U (CT)
Saginaw Valley State U (MI)
St. Ambrose U (IA)
Saint Anselm Coll (NH)

INDEXES

The Catholic U of America (DC)
Central Michigan U (MI)
Christian Brothers U (TN)
Coker Coll (SC)
The Coll of New Jersey (NJ)
Coll of the Ozarks (MO)
Concordia U Chicago (IL)
Concordia U Wisconsin (WI)
Covenant Coll (GA)
Culver-Stockton Coll (MO)
Cumberland U (TN)
Dakota Wesleyan U (SD)
Dominican Coll (NY)
Dordt Coll (IA)
Eastern Michigan U (MI)
East Texas Baptist U (TX)
Elizabeth City State U (NC)
Elmhurst Coll (IL)
Elmira Coll (NY)
Evangel U (MO)
Ferris State U (MI)
Fitchburg State U (MA)
Free Will Baptist Bible Coll (TN)
Friends U (KS)
Gardner-Webb U (NC)
Grand Valley State U (MI)
Greenville Coll (IL)
Hannibal-LaGrange U (MO)
Hardin-Simmons U (TX)
Hope Coll (MI)
Huntingdon Coll (AL)
Indiana U–Purdue U Fort Wayne (IN)
Inter American U of Puerto Rico, Metropolitan Campus (PR)
Inter American U of Puerto Rico, San Germán Campus (PR)
Iowa Wesleyan Coll (IA)
Ithaca Coll (NY)
Jamestown Coll (ND)
Johnson State Coll (VT)
Keene State Coll (NH)
King Coll (TN)
Lee U (TN)
Liberty U (VA)
Lincoln Memorial U (TN)
Lindenwood U (MO)
Lipscomb U (TN)
Lubbock Christian U (TX)
Manchester Coll (IN)
Maranatha Baptist Bible Coll (WI)
Marquette U (WI)
Maryville Coll (TN)
Mayville State U (ND)
McKendree U (IL)
McMurry U (TX)
Merrimack Coll (MA)
Michigan State U (MI)
MidAmerica Nazarene U (KS)
Millersville U of Pennsylvania (PA)
Minot State U (ND)
Misericordia U (PA)
Missouri State U (MO)
Montana State U Billings (MT)
Moravian Coll (PA)
Morningside Coll (IA)
Mount Marty Coll (SD)
Mount Vernon Nazarene U (OH)
Nazareth Coll of Rochester (NY)
Nevada State Coll at Henderson (NV)
North Dakota State U (ND)
Northern Arizona U (AZ)
Northern Michigan U (MI)
Northland Coll (WI)
Northwest Nazarene U (ID)
Ohio Wesleyan U (OH)
Paine Coll (GA)
Palm Beach Atlantic U (FL)
Prescott Coll (AZ)
Rhode Island Coll (RI)
Rocky Mountain Coll (MT)
Sacred Heart U (CT)
Saginaw Valley State U (MI)
St. Ambrose U (IA)
St. Edward's U (TX)
Saint Francis U (PA)
St. John Fisher Coll (NY)
Saint Joseph's Coll of Maine (ME)
Saint Xavier U (IL)
Salve Regina U (RI)
Samford U (AL)
Schreiner U (TX)
Spring Arbor U (MI)
State U of New York at New Paltz (NY)
Tabor Coll (KS)
Talladega Coll (AL)

Texas A&M Intl U (TX)
Texas A&M U–Corpus Christi (TX)
Texas Christian U (TX)
Texas Lutheran U (TX)
Texas Wesleyan U (TX)
Tiffin U (OH)
Trevecca Nazarene U (TN)
Union Coll (NE)
The U of Arizona (AZ)
U of Arkansas–Fort Smith (AR)
U of Delaware (DE)
U of Illinois at Chicago (IL)
The U of Iowa (IA)
U of Maine (ME)
U of Michigan–Flint (MI)
The U of Montana Western (MT)
The U of North Carolina at Charlotte (NC)
U of Pittsburgh at Johnstown (PA)
U of Rio Grande (OH)
The U of South Dakota (SD)
The U of Tennessee at Martin (TN)
U of Wisconsin–River Falls (WI)
U of Wisconsin–Superior (WI)
Valparaiso U (IN)
Victory U (TN)
Virginia Intermont Coll (VA)
Wartburg Coll (IA)
Washington State U (WA)
Washington U in St. Louis (MO)
Wayne State Coll (NE)
Weber State U (UT)
Western Michigan U (MI)
Western State Coll of Colorado (CO)
Wheeling Jesuit U (WV)
Widener U (PA)
Xavier U of Louisiana (LA)

HOLOCAUST AND RELATED STUDIES
Keene State Coll (NH)

HOME FURNISHINGS AND EQUIPMENT INSTALLATION
Brigham Young U (UT)

HOMELAND SECURITY
American Public U System (WV)
Dakota Wesleyan U (SD)
Embry-Riddle Aeronautical U–Daytona (FL)
Saint Leo U (FL)
Tulane U (LA)

HOMELAND SECURITY, LAW ENFORCEMENT, FIREFIGHTING AND PROTECTIVE SERVICES RELATED
Clayton State U (GA)
Eastern Michigan U (MI)
Embry-Riddle Aeronautical U–Daytona (FL)
Florida State Coll at Jacksonville (FL)
Lewis U (IL)
Madonna U (MI)
Marian U (WI)
Massachusetts Maritime Acad (MA)
Miami Dade Coll (FL)
Midway Coll (KY)
North Dakota State U (ND)
Northwestern Oklahoma State U (OK)
Penn State Altoona (PA)
Penn State Berks (PA)
Penn State U Park (PA)
Point Park U (PA)
St. Ambrose U (IA)
St. Petersburg Coll (FL)
Savannah State U (GA)
Thomas Edison State Coll (NJ)
Tiffin U (OH)
Virginia Commonwealth U (VA)
Washburn U (KS)
Western Illinois U (IL)

HOMELAND SECURITY RELATED
U of Maryland U Coll (MD)

HORSE HUSBANDRY/EQUINE SCIENCE AND MANAGEMENT
Bethany Coll (WV)
Johnson & Wales U (RI)
Midway Coll (KY)
Oklahoma Panhandle State U (OK)

Stephens Coll (MO)
Tiffin U (OH)
U of Minnesota, Crookston (MN)
Vermont Tech Coll (VT)

HORTICULTURAL SCIENCE
Auburn U (AL)
California Polytechnic State U, San Luis Obispo (CA)
Clemson U (SC)
Coll of the Ozarks (MO)
Colorado State U (CO)
Ferrum Coll (VA)
Florida Southern Coll (FL)
Iowa State U of Science and Technology (IA)
Kansas State U (KS)
Michigan State U (MI)
Mississippi State U (MS)
Missouri State U (MO)
Montana State U (MT)
New Mexico State U (NM)
North Carolina State U (NC)
North Dakota State U (ND)
Northwest Missouri State U (MO)
Oklahoma State U (OK)
Oregon State U (OR)
Penn State Abington (PA)
Penn State Altoona (PA)
Penn State Beaver (PA)
Penn State Berks (PA)
Penn State Brandywine (PA)
Penn State DuBois (PA)
Penn State Erie, The Behrend Coll (PA)
Penn State Fayette, The Eberly Campus (PA)
Penn State Greater Allegheny (PA)
Penn State Hazleton (PA)
Penn State Lehigh Valley (PA)
Penn State Mont Alto (PA)
Penn State New Kensington (PA)
Penn State Schuylkill (PA)
Penn State Shenango (PA)
Penn State U Park (PA)
Penn State Wilkes-Barre (PA)
Penn State Worthington Scranton (PA)
Penn State York (PA)
Purdue U (IN)
Southeast Missouri State U (MO)
Stephen F. Austin State U (TX)
Tarleton State U (TX)
Temple U (PA)
Tennessee Technological U (TN)
Texas A&M U (TX)
The U of British Columbia (BC, Canada)
U of Cincinnati (OH)
U of Delaware (DE)
U of Florida (FL)
U of Guelph (ON, Canada)
U of Hawaii at Hilo (HI)
U of Idaho (ID)
U of Minnesota, Crookston (MN)
U of Minnesota, Twin Cities Campus (MN)
U of Nebraska–Lincoln (NE)
U of New Hampshire (NH)
U of Saskatchewan (SK, Canada)
U of Vermont (VT)
U of Wisconsin–Madison (WI)
U of Wisconsin–River Falls (WI)
Utah State U (UT)
Virginia Polytechnic Inst and State U (VA)
Washington State U (WA)

HOSPITAL AND HEALTH-CARE FACILITIES ADMINISTRATION
Avila U (MO)
Carlow U (PA)
Carson-Newman Coll (TN)
Clayton State U (GA)
Concordia Coll (MN)
ECPI Coll of Technology, Virginia Beach (VA)
Ithaca Coll (NY)
Long Island U, C.W. Post Campus (NY)
Newman U (KS)
New York City Coll of Technology of the City U of New York (NY)
St. Joseph's Coll, Long Island Campus (NY)
St. Joseph's Coll, New York (NY)
Saint Joseph's U (PA)
Saint Louis U (MO)

Thomas Edison State Coll (NJ)
The U of Alabama (AL)
The U of South Dakota (SD)
The U of Toledo (OH)
Ursuline Coll (OH)
Youngstown State U (OH)

HOSPITALITY ADMINISTRATION
American Public U System (WV)
Appalachian State U (NC)
Arkansas Tech U (AR)
Boston U (MA)
California State Polytechnic U, Pomona (CA)
Central Michigan U (MI)
Coll of Charleston (SC)
Coll of the Ozarks (MO)
Concord U (WV)
Delaware State U (DE)
Delta State U (MS)
DePaul U (IL)
Eastern Michigan U (MI)
East Stroudsburg U of Pennsylvania (PA)
Endicott Coll (MA)
Fairleigh Dickinson U, Coll at Florham (NJ)
Fairleigh Dickinson U, Metropolitan Campus (NJ)
Ferris State U (MI)
Fisher Coll (MA)
Florida Atlantic U (FL)
Florida Intl U (FL)
Florida State U (FL)
Georgia State U (GA)
Grand Valley State U (MI)
Husson U (ME)
Indiana U of Pennsylvania (PA)
Indiana U–Purdue U Fort Wayne (IN)
James Madison U (VA)
Johnson & Wales U (CO)
Johnson & Wales U (FL)
Johnson & Wales U (RI)
Johnson State Coll (VT)
Kendall Coll (IL)
Lasell Coll (MA)
Lebanese American U (Lebanon)
Lewis-Clark State Coll (ID)
Lewis U (IL)
Lexington Coll (IL)
Madonna U (MI)
Marywood U (PA)
Metropolitan State U (MN)
Michigan State U (MI)
Missouri State U (MO)
National U (CA)
New Mexico State U (NM)
New York City Coll of Technology of the City U of New York (NY)
North Dakota State U (ND)
Northern Arizona U (AZ)
Northern Michigan U (MI)
Northwestern State U of Louisiana (LA)
The Ohio State U (OH)
The Ohio State U at Lima (OH)
Oklahoma State U (OK)
The Richard Stockton Coll of New Jersey (NJ)
Robert Morris U (PA)
Roosevelt U (IL)
Rutgers, The State U of New Jersey, Camden (NJ)
St. John's U (NY)
Saint Leo U (FL)
Salem State U (MA)
San Diego State U (CA)
San Francisco State U (CA)
San Jose State U (CA)
Seton Hill U (PA)
Stephen F. Austin State U (TX)
Stratford U, Falls Church (VA)
Temple U (PA)
Thomas Edison State Coll (NJ)
Tiffin U (OH)
Trine U (IN)
TUI U (CA)
Tuskegee U (AL)
U of Central Florida (FL)
U of Cincinnati (OH)
U of Denver (CO)
U of Louisiana at Lafayette (LA)
U of Massachusetts Amherst (MA)
U of Memphis (TN)
U of Minnesota, Crookston (MN)
U of Nebraska–Lincoln (NE)
U of Nevada, Las Vegas (NV)

U of Nevada, Reno (NV)
U of New Brunswick Saint John (NB, Canada)
U of New Hampshire (NH)
U of New Haven (CT)
The U of North Carolina at Greensboro (NC)
U of North Texas (TX)
U of Pittsburgh at Bradford (PA)
U of South Carolina (SC)
U of South Carolina Beaufort (SC)
U of West Florida (FL)
U of Wisconsin–Stout (WI)
Utah Valley U (UT)
Virginia State U (VA)
Washington State U (WA)
Webber Intl U (FL)
Western Carolina U (NC)
Western Kentucky U (KY)
Youngstown State U (OH)

HOSPITALITY ADMINISTRATION RELATED
Auburn U (AL)
California State U, Dominguez Hills (CA)
California State U, Fullerton (CA)
Delaware State U (DE)
DEREE - The American Coll of Greece (Greece)
Kendall Coll (IL)
Kent State U (OH)
Lynn U (FL)
Mitchell Coll (CT)
Niagara U (NY)
Penn State Abington (PA)
Penn State Altoona (PA)
Penn State Beaver (PA)
Penn State Berks (PA)
Penn State Brandywine (PA)
Penn State DuBois (PA)
Penn State Erie, The Behrend Coll (PA)
Penn State Fayette, The Eberly Campus (PA)
Penn State Greater Allegheny (PA)
Penn State Hazleton (PA)
Penn State Lehigh Valley (PA)
Penn State Mont Alto (PA)
Penn State New Kensington (PA)
Penn State Schuylkill (PA)
Penn State Shenango (PA)
Penn State U Park (PA)
Penn State Wilkes-Barre (PA)
Penn State Worthington Scranton (PA)
Penn State York (PA)
Southern Illinois U Carbondale (IL)
U of Central Florida (FL)
U of Louisiana at Lafayette (LA)
U of Nevada, Las Vegas (NV)
U of Southern Mississippi (MS)
Widener U (PA)

HOSPITALITY AND RECREATION MARKETING
Ferris State U (MI)
Kendall Coll (IL)
Tuskegee U (AL)
U of Delaware (DE)

HOTEL/MOTEL ADMINISTRATION
Ashland U (OH)
Auburn U (AL)
Bethune-Cookman U (FL)
California State U, Long Beach (CA)
Central Michigan U (MI)
Concord U (WV)
Cornell U (NY)
Ferris State U (MI)
Georgia Southern U (GA)
Grand Valley State U (MI)
Harrison Coll, Indianapolis (IN)
Inter American U of Puerto Rico, Ponce Campus (PR)
Iowa State U of Science and Technology (IA)
Johnson & Wales U (CO)
Johnson & Wales U (FL)
Johnson & Wales U (RI)
Johnson & Wales U - Charlotte Campus (NC)
Kansas State U (KS)
Kendall Coll (IL)
Keuka Coll (NY)
Mount Ida Coll (MA)
Newbury Coll (MA)

U at Buffalo, the State U of New York (NY)
U of Baltimore (MD)
U of Bridgeport (CT)
U of California, Irvine (CA)
U of California, Santa Cruz (CA)
U of Cincinnati (OH)
U of Dayton (OH)
U of Guelph (ON, Canada)
U of Hartford (CT)
U of Houston (TX)
U of Illinois at Chicago (IL)
The U of Iowa (IA)
U of Mary Hardin-Baylor (TX)
U of Maryland, Baltimore County (MD)
U of Maryland, Coll Park (MD)
U of Maryland U Coll (MD)
U of Massachusetts Lowell (MA)
U of Miami (FL)
U of Michigan–Flint (MI)
U of Nebraska at Omaha (NE)
U of New Brunswick Fredericton (NB, Canada)
U of New Haven (CT)
The U of North Carolina at Chapel Hill (NC)
U of North Texas (TX)
U of Oklahoma (OK)
U of Pittsburgh (PA)
U of San Francisco (CA)
The U of Scranton (PA)
U of South Carolina (SC)
U of South Carolina Upstate (SC)
U of South Florida (FL)
The U of Texas of the Permian Basin (TX)
U of the District of Columbia (DC)
U of the Pacific (CA)
The U of Toledo (OH)
U of Tulsa (OK)
U of Vermont (VT)
U of Washington (WA)
U of Washington, Bothell (WA)
The U of Western Ontario (ON, Canada)
U of Wisconsin–Green Bay (WI)
U of Wisconsin–River Falls (WI)
U of Wisconsin–Superior (WI)
Utah State U (UT)
Utah Valley U (UT)
Valdosta State U (GA)
Virginia Commonwealth U (VA)
Virginia Polytechnic Inst and State U (VA)
Washington Adventist U (MD)
Washington U in St. Louis (MO)
Wayne State Coll (NE)
Wayne State U (MI)
Westfield State U (MA)
West Liberty U (WV)
Wheeling Jesuit U (WV)
Widener U (PA)
Wilkes U (PA)
Winona State U (MN)
Woodbury U (CA)
Worcester Polytechnic Inst (MA)
York Coll of the City U of New York (NY)

INFORMATION TECHNOLOGY

Abilene Christian U (TX)
American Public U System (WV)
Arkansas Tech U (AR)
Armstrong Atlantic State U (GA)
Bluefield Coll (VA)
Bluffton U (OH)
Bob Jones U (SC)
Brigham Young U (UT)
Bryant U (RI)
Cabrini Coll (PA)
California State U, Chico (CA)
California State U, Dominguez Hills (CA)
California State U, Fullerton (CA)
California State U, Los Angeles (CA)
Cameron U (OK)
Carnegie Mellon U (PA)
Central Michigan U (MI)
Clayton State U (GA)
Coll of the Ozarks (MO)
Collins Coll (AZ)
Columbia Southern U (AL)
Columbus State U (GA)
Cornell U (NY)
Curry Coll (MA)

Daniel Webster Coll–Portsmouth Campus (NH)
DePaul U (IL)
DEREE - The American Coll of Greece (Greece)
Fairleigh Dickinson U, Metropolitan Campus (NJ)
Ferris State U (MI)
Florida Ag and Mech U (FL)
Florida Intl U (FL)
Franklin U (OH)
Furman U (SC)
Harding U (AR)
Houghton Coll (NY)
Humboldt State U (CA)
Illinois Inst of Technology (IL)
Illinois State U (IL)
Indiana State U (IN)
Indiana U Bloomington (IN)
Indiana U East (IN)
Indiana U Kokomo (IN)
Indiana U Northwest (IN)
Indiana U–Purdue U Indianapolis (IN)
Indiana U South Bend (IN)
Indiana U Southeast (IN)
Jamestown Coll (ND)
Johnson C. Smith U (NC)
Juniata Coll (PA)
Kentucky State U (KY)
Keystone Coll (PA)
Kutztown U of Pennsylvania (PA)
La Roche Coll (PA)
Lawrence Technological U (MI)
Lindenwood U (MO)
Lipscomb U (TN)
Long Island U, C.W. Post Campus (NY)
Loyola U Chicago (IL)
Marian U (WI)
Marist Coll (NY)
Marquette U (WI)
Merrimack Coll (MA)
Minnesota School of Business–Blaine (MN)
Minnesota State U Moorhead (MN)
Misericordia U (PA)
Montclair State U (NJ)
Mount Aloysius Coll (PA)
Mount Marty Coll (SD)
Mount Saint Mary Coll (NY)
National U (CA)
Nazareth Coll of Rochester (NY)
Neumont U (UT)
Newbury Coll (MA)
New England Inst of Technology (RI)
New Jersey Inst of Technology (NJ)
New Mexico Inst of Mining and Technology (NM)
New Mexico State U (NM)
Northern Kentucky U (KY)
Ohio U–Chillicothe (OH)
Point Park U (PA)
Regent U (VA)
Rensselaer Polytechnic Inst (NY)
Rivier Coll (NH)
Robert Morris U Illinois (IL)
Sacred Heart U (CT)
St. John Fisher Coll (NY)
San Diego State U (CA)
San Jose State U (CA)
Slippery Rock U of Pennsylvania (PA)
Southern Polytechnic State U (GA)
Stephen F. Austin State U (TX)
Stratford U, Falls Church (VA)
Temple U (PA)
Texas Christian U (TX)
Thomas More Coll (KY)
Tiffin U (OH)
Trevecca Nazarene U (TN)
TUI U (CA)
United States Intl U (Kenya)
United States Military Acad (NY)
Université de Sherbrooke (QC, Canada)
The U of British Columbia–Okanagan (BC, Canada)
U of Central Florida (FL)
U of Cincinnati (OH)
U of Denver (CO)
U of Houston–Clear Lake (TX)
U of Massachusetts Boston (MA)
U of New Hampshire (NH)
The U of North Carolina at Pembroke (NC)
U of Rio Grande (OH)

U of St. Francis (IL)
U of Saint Mary (KS)
U of South Florida (FL)
U of Tulsa (OK)
The U of Western Ontario (ON, Canada)
U of West Florida (FL)
U of Wisconsin–Stevens Point (WI)
U of Wisconsin–Whitewater (WI)
Vermont Tech Coll (VT)
Virginia State U (VA)
Walden U (MN)
Washington & Jefferson Coll (PA)
Western Kentucky U (KY)
Wilmington U (DE)
Youngstown State U (OH)

INFORMATION TECHNOLOGY PROJECT MANAGEMENT

American Public U System (WV)
ITT Tech Inst, Oxnard (CA)
ITT Tech Inst, Orland Park (IL)
ITT Tech Inst (MD)
ITT Tech Inst, Swartz Creek (MI)
ITT Tech Inst, Wyoming (MI)
ITT Tech Inst, Arnold (MO)
ITT Tech Inst, Knoxville (TN)
ITT Tech Inst, Norfolk (VA)
ITT Tech Inst, Green Bay (WI)
ITT Tech Inst, Greenfield (WI)
Pace U (NY)

INORGANIC CHEMISTRY

The U of Western Ontario (ON, Canada)

INSTITUTIONAL FOOD WORKERS

Immaculata U (PA)
Kendall Coll (IL)

INSTRUMENTATION TECHNOLOGY

Northern Michigan U (MI)

INSURANCE

Appalachian State U (NC)
Delta State U (MS)
Gannon U (PA)
Georgia State U (GA)
Idaho State U (ID)
Illinois State U (IL)
Illinois Wesleyan U (IL)
Indiana State U (IN)
Mississippi State U (MS)
Missouri State U (MO)
Northern Michigan U (MI)
The Ohio State U (OH)
St. John's U (NY)
Saint Joseph's U (PA)
Southern Methodist U (TX)
Temple U (PA)
U of Florida (FL)
U of Georgia (GA)
U of Hartford (CT)
U of Houston–Downtown (TX)
U of Louisiana at Lafayette (LA)
U of Louisiana at Monroe (LA)
U of Minnesota, Twin Cities Campus (MN)
U of Mississippi (MS)
U of Nebraska–Lincoln (NE)
U of North Texas (TX)
U of Pennsylvania (PA)
U of South Carolina (SC)
U of Wisconsin–La Crosse (WI)
U of Wisconsin–Madison (WI)

INTERCULTURAL/ MULTICULTURAL AND DIVERSITY STUDIES

Biola U (CA)
California Baptist U (CA)
Calvary Bible Coll and Theological Sem (MO)
Columbia Bible Coll (BC, Canada)
Concordia U (QC, Canada)
Evangel U (MO)
The Evergreen State Coll (WA)
Goddard Coll (VT)
Indiana Wesleyan U (IN)
Macalester Coll (MN)
Northwest U (WA)
St. Catherine U (MN)
Trinity Lutheran Coll (WA)
U of the Incarnate Word (TX)

Western Oregon U (OR)
Wilfrid Laurier U (ON, Canada)

INTERDISCIPLINARY STUDIES

Albright Coll (PA)
Alfred U (NY)
Amberton U (TX)
Amherst Coll (MA)
Angelo State U (TX)
Augsburg Coll (MN)
Austin Peay State U (TN)
Bard Coll (NY)
Bard Coll at Simon's Rock (MA)
Barnard Coll (NY)
Beloit Coll (WI)
Bentley U (MA)
Bethany Coll (WV)
Birmingham-Southern Coll (AL)
Blackburn Coll (IL)
Bluefield Coll (VA)
Boise State U (ID)
Boston Coll (MA)
Boston U (MA)
Bowdoin Coll (ME)
Brock U (ON, Canada)
Bryn Athyn Coll of the New Church (PA)
Bucknell U (PA)
Burlington Coll (VT)
California Baptist U (CA)
California State U, Bakersfield (CA)
California State U, Long Beach (CA)
California State U, Los Angeles (CA)
California State U, San Bernardino (CA)
Calvin Coll (MI)
Carleton Coll (MN)
Carson-Newman Coll (TN)
Cedarville U (OH)
Centenary Coll of Louisiana (LA)
Central Coll (IA)
Christopher Newport U (VA)
Clark U (MA)
Colby Coll (ME)
Coll of the Atlantic (ME)
The Coll of William and Mary (VA)
The Coll of Wooster (OH)
Columbia Coll Chicago (IL)
Connecticut Coll (CT)
Corban U (OR)
Cornell Coll (IA)
Crandall U (NB, Canada)
Dallas Baptist U (TX)
Delta State U (MS)
DePauw U (IN)
Earlham Coll (IN)
Eckerd Coll (FL)
Elmhurst Coll (IL)
Elmira Coll (NY)
Emmanuel Coll (MA)
Emory & Henry Coll (VA)
Eugene Lang Coll The New School for Liberal Arts (NY)
Fairleigh Dickinson U, Metropolitan Campus (NJ)
Florida Inst of Technology (FL)
Franklin U (OH)
Freed-Hardeman U (TN)
Geneva Coll (PA)
George Fox U (OR)
Georgetown U (DC)
Gettysburg Coll (PA)
Goddard Coll (VT)
Goucher Coll (MD)
Greensboro Coll (NC)
Grinnell Coll (IA)
Guilford Coll (NC)
Hamilton Coll (NY)
Harrisburg U of Science and Technology (PA)
Hendrix Coll (AR)
Hillsdale Coll (MI)
Hillsdale Free Will Baptist Coll (OK)
Hollins U (VA)
Huston-Tillotson U (TX)
Illinois Coll (IL)
Iowa State U of Science and Technology (IA)
Ithaca Coll (NY)
John Brown U (AR)
John Carroll U (OH)
The Johns Hopkins U (MD)
Jones Coll, Jacksonville (FL)
Judson Coll (AL)
Kalamazoo Coll (MI)
Kentucky Wesleyan Coll (KY)
Keuka Coll (NY)
King Coll (TN)

The King's Coll (NY)
Kuyper Coll (MI)
Lake Superior State U (MI)
Lamar U (TX)
Lane Coll (TN)
Lasell Coll (MA)
Lee U (TN)
Lehman Coll of the City U of New York (NY)
LeTourneau U (TX)
Lewis-Clark State Coll (ID)
Liberty U (VA)
Long Island U, Brooklyn Campus (NY)
Long Island U, C.W. Post Campus (NY)
Louisiana Coll (LA)
Loyola U Maryland (MD)
Marist Coll (NY)
Marlboro Coll (VT)
Mars Hill Coll (NC)
Martin Luther Coll (MN)
Massachusetts Coll of Liberal Arts (MA)
Middle Tennessee State U (TN)
Midwestern State U (TX)
Mills Coll (CA)
Minneapolis Coll of Art and Design (MN)
Molloy Coll (NY)
Mount Allison U (NB, Canada)
Mount Saint Mary Coll (NY)
National U (CA)
Nebraska Wesleyan U (NE)
Newbury Coll (MA)
North Dakota State U (ND)
North Greenville U (SC)
Northwest U (WA)
Nyack Coll (NY)
Oberlin Coll (OH)
Oglethorpe U (GA)
Pepperdine U, Malibu (CA)
Piedmont Coll (GA)
Pittsburg State U (KS)
Pomona Coll (CA)
Prairie View A&M U (TX)
Rhodes Coll (TN)
Ripon Coll (WI)
Rocky Mountain Coll (MT)
Russell Sage Coll (NY)
Rutgers, The State U of New Jersey, New Brunswick (NJ)
St. Andrews Presbyterian Coll (NC)
St. John's Coll (MD)
Saint Joseph's Coll of Maine (ME)
Saint Mary's Coll (IN)
Saint Mary's Coll of California (CA)
St. Thomas U (NB, Canada)
San Diego Christian Coll (CA)
Sarah Lawrence Coll (NY)
Seattle Pacific U (WA)
Sierra Nevada Coll (NV)
Simpson Coll (IA)
Smith Coll (MA)
Sonoma State U (CA)
South Dakota School of Mines and Technology (SD)
Southern Oregon U (OR)
Southwestern Coll (KS)
Stanford U (CA)
State U of New York at Fredonia (NY)
State U of New York Coll at Oneonta (NY)
State U of New York Empire State Coll (NY)
Stephens Coll (MO)
Stevenson U (MD)
Suffolk U (MA)
Sweet Briar Coll (VA)
Tarleton State U (TX)
Tennessee Technological U (TN)
Tennessee Wesleyan Coll (TN)
Texas A&M U–Corpus Christi (TX)
Texas Woman's U (TX)
Towson U (MD)
Trent U (ON, Canada)
Trinity Coll (CT)
United States Air Force Acad (CO)
Université de Sherbrooke (QC, Canada)
The U of Alabama (AL)
U of Baltimore (MD)
U of Bridgeport (CT)
The U of British Columbia (BC, Canada)
U of California, Santa Barbara (CA)
U of Central Florida (FL)

INDEXES

Aquinas Coll (MI)
Ashland U (OH)
Augsburg Coll (MN)
Augustana Coll (SD)
Austin Coll (TX)
Azusa Pacific U (CA)
Bard Coll (NY)
Barry U (FL)
Beloit Coll (WI)
Benedictine U (IL)
Bennington Coll (VT)
Berry Coll (GA)
Bethany Coll (WV)
Bethel U (MN)
Bethune-Cookman U (FL)
Bob Jones U (SC)
Boston U (MA)
Bowling Green State U (OH)
Bridgewater Coll (VA)
Bridgewater State U (MA)
Brown U (RI)
Bryant U (RI)
Bucknell U (PA)
Butler U (IN)
California State U, Chico (CA)
California State U, Long Beach (CA)
California State U, Monterey Bay (CA)
Calvin Coll (MI)
Canisius Coll (NY)
Capital U (OH)
Carleton Coll (MN)
Carroll U (WI)
Case Western Reserve U (OH)
Cedarville U (OH)
Centenary Coll (NJ)
Central Michigan U (MI)
Centre Coll (KY)
Chatham U (PA)
City Coll of the City U of New York (NY)
Claremont McKenna Coll (CA)
Clark U (MA)
Cleveland State U (OH)
Colby Coll (ME)
Colgate U (NY)
The Coll of New Jersey (NJ)
Coll of Staten Island of the City U of New York (NY)
The Coll of William and Mary (VA)
The Coll of Wooster (OH)
Concordia Coll–New York (NY)
Connecticut Coll (CT)
Cornell Coll (IA)
Creighton U (NE)
Denison U (OH)
DePaul U (IL)
Dickinson Coll (PA)
Drake U (IA)
Drury U (MO)
Duquesne U (PA)
Eastern Michigan U (MI)
Eastern Washington U (WA)
East Tennessee State U (TN)
Eckerd Coll (FL)
Edgewood Coll (WI)
Elmira Coll (NY)
Embry-Riddle Aeronautical U–Prescott (AZ)
Emory & Henry Coll (VA)
Fairfield U (CT)
Fairleigh Dickinson U, Metropolitan Campus (NJ)
Ferrum Coll (VA)
Florida Intl U (FL)
Florida State U (FL)
Francis Marion U (SC)
Franklin Coll Switzerland (Switzerland)
Georgetown U (DC)
Georgia Inst of Technology (GA)
Georgia Southern U (GA)
Gettysburg Coll (PA)
Gordon Coll (MA)
Goucher Coll (MD)
Graceland U (IA)
Grand Valley State U (MI)
Guilford Coll (NC)
Hamilton Coll (NY)
Hampden-Sydney Coll (VA)
Hampshire Coll (MA)
Hawai'i Pacific U (HI)
Hendrix Coll (AR)
Hillsdale Coll (MI)
Hobart and William Smith Colls (NY)
Hollins U (VA)
Holy Names U (CA)
Houghton Coll (NY)
Idaho State U (ID)
Illinois Coll (IL)

Illinois Wesleyan U (IL)
Immaculata U (PA)
Indiana U Bloomington (IN)
Indiana U of Pennsylvania (PA)
Indiana U–Purdue U Indianapolis (IN)
Indiana U Southeast (IN)
Indiana Wesleyan U (IN)
Iowa State U of Science and Technology (IA)
James Madison U (VA)
John Brown U (AR)
John Carroll U (OH)
The Johns Hopkins U (MD)
Juniata Coll (PA)
Kennesaw State U (GA)
Kent State U (OH)
Kenyon Coll (OH)
Knox Coll (IL)
Lafayette Coll (PA)
Lake Forest Coll (IL)
La Roche Coll (PA)
Lawrence U (WI)
Lebanese American U (Lebanon)
Lee U (TN)
Lehigh U (PA)
Lewis & Clark Coll (OR)
Lindenwood U (MO)
Lock Haven U of Pennsylvania (PA)
Long Island U, C.W. Post Campus (NY)
Longwood U (VA)
Loras Coll (IA)
Loyola U Chicago (IL)
Lynchburg Coll (VA)
Lynn U (FL)
Manhattan Coll (NY)
Manhattanville Coll (NY)
Mansfield U of Pennsylvania (PA)
Marlboro Coll (VT)
Marshall U (WV)
Mars Hill Coll (NC)
Mary Baldwin Coll (VA)
Maryville Coll (TN)
McKendree U (IL)
Mercer U (GA)
Miami U (OH)
Michigan State U (MI)
Middlebury Coll (VT)
Middle Tennessee State U (TN)
Mills Coll (CA)
Minnesota State U Mankato (MN)
Missouri Southern State U (MO)
Morehouse Coll (GA)
Morningside Coll (IA)
Mount Allison U (NB, Canada)
Mount Holyoke Coll (MA)
Mount Mercy U (IA)
Mount St. Mary's U (MD)
Muhlenberg Coll (PA)
Murray State U (KY)
Nazareth Coll of Rochester (NY)
New York U (NY)
Niagara U (NY)
Northeastern U (MA)
Northern Arizona U (AZ)
Northern Kentucky U (KY)
Northern Michigan U (MI)
North Georgia Coll & State U (GA)
Northwest Nazarene U (ID)
Nova Southeastern U (FL)
Oglethorpe U (GA)
The Ohio State U (OH)
Ohio U (OH)
Ohio Wesleyan U (OH)
Old Dominion U (VA)
Oregon State U (OR)
Pacific U (OR)
Penn State Abington (PA)
Penn State Altoona (PA)
Penn State Beaver (PA)
Penn State Berks (PA)
Penn State Brandywine (PA)
Penn State DuBois (PA)
Penn State Erie, The Behrend Coll (PA)
Penn State Fayette, The Eberly Campus (PA)
Penn State Greater Allegheny (PA)
Penn State Hazleton (PA)
Penn State Lehigh Valley (PA)
Penn State Mont Alto (PA)
Penn State New Kensington (PA)
Penn State Schuylkill (PA)
Penn State Shenango (PA)
Penn State U Park (PA)
Penn State Wilkes-Barre (PA)
Penn State Worthington Scranton (PA)
Penn State York (PA)

Pepperdine U, Malibu (CA)
Point Park U (PA)
Pomona Coll (CA)
Portland State U (OR)
Quinnipiac U (CT)
Reed Coll (OR)
Regis Coll (MA)
Rhodes Coll (TN)
Rider U (NJ)
Roanoke Coll (VA)
Rockhurst U (MO)
Rollins Coll (FL)
Roosevelt U (IL)
Saginaw Valley State U (MI)
Saint Anselm Coll (NH)
St. Catherine U (MN)
Saint Francis U (PA)
St. John Fisher Coll (NY)
Saint Joseph's Coll (IN)
Saint Joseph's U (PA)
Saint Leo U (FL)
Saint Louis U (MO)
Saint Mary's Coll of California (CA)
St. Norbert Coll (WI)
Saint Xavier U (IL)
Samford U (AL)
San Diego State U (CA)
San Francisco State U (CA)
Sarah Lawrence Coll (NY)
Seton Hill U (PA)
Sewanee: The U of the South (TN)
Shawnee State U (OH)
Simmons Coll (MA)
Simpson Coll (IA)
Skidmore Coll (NY)
Sonoma State U (CA)
Southern Methodist U (TX)
Southern Nazarene U (OK)
Southern Oregon U (OR)
Southern Polytechnic State U (GA)
Southwestern Adventist U (TX)
Spring Hill Coll (AL)
Stanford U (CA)
State U of New York at Binghamton (NY)
State U of New York at New Paltz (NY)
State U of New York at Oswego (NY)
State U of New York Coll at Geneseo (NY)
State U of New York Coll at Oneonta (NY)
Stetson U (FL)
Stonehill Coll (MA)
Suffolk U (MA)
Susquehanna U (PA)
Sweet Briar Coll (VA)
Syracuse U (NY)
Taylor U (IN)
Temple U (PA)
Texas Christian U (TX)
Texas State U–San Marcos (TX)
Texas Wesleyan U (TX)
Tiffin U (OH)
Towson U (MD)
Trent U (ON, Canada)
Trinity Coll (CT)
Tufts U (MA)
Tulane U (LA)
Union Coll (NE)
United States Intl U (Kenya)
United States Military Acad (NY)
The U of Akron (OH)
The U of Alabama (AL)
U of Arkansas (AR)
U of Bridgeport (CT)
The U of British Columbia (BC, Canada)
The U of British Columbia–Okanagan (BC, Canada)
U of California, Davis (CA)
U of Cincinnati (OH)
U of Dayton (OH)
U of Delaware (DE)
U of Denver (CO)
U of Evansville (IN)
U of Georgia (GA)
U of Hartford (CT)
U of Idaho (ID)
U of Indianapolis (IN)
U of La Verne (CA)
U of Maine (ME)
U of Maine at Presque Isle (ME)
U of Mary Washington (VA)
U of Memphis (TN)
U of Miami (FL)
U of Minnesota, Duluth (MN)
U of Minnesota, Twin Cities Campus (MN)

U of Mississippi (MS)
U of Mount Union (OH)
U of Nebraska–Lincoln (NE)
U of Nevada, Reno (NV)
U of New Brunswick Fredericton (NB, Canada)
U of New Brunswick Saint John (NB, Canada)
U of Ottawa (ON, Canada)
U of Pennsylvania (PA)
U of Redlands (CA)
U of Richmond (VA)
U of Rochester (NY)
U of St. Thomas (MN)
U of St. Thomas (TX)
U of San Diego (CA)
The U of Scranton (PA)
U of South Carolina (SC)
U of Southern California (CA)
U of Southern Indiana (IN)
U of Southern Maine (ME)
U of Southern Mississippi (MS)
U of South Florida (FL)
The U of Tennessee at Martin (TN)
U of the Incarnate Word (TX)
U of the Pacific (CA)
The U of Toledo (OH)
U of Virginia (VA)
U of Washington (WA)
U of Waterloo (ON, Canada)
The U of Western Ontario (ON, Canada)
U of West Florida (FL)
U of West Georgia (GA)
U of Wisconsin–Parkside (WI)
U of Wisconsin–Platteville (WI)
U of Wisconsin–Stevens Point (WI)
U of Wisconsin–Superior (WI)
U of Wisconsin–Whitewater (WI)
Valparaiso U (IN)
Vassar Coll (NY)
Virginia Military Inst (VA)
Virginia Polytechnic Inst and State U (VA)
Virginia Wesleyan Coll (VA)
Wagner Coll (NY)
Walsh U (OH)
Wartburg Coll (IA)
Washington Coll (MD)
Washington U in St. Louis (MO)
Webster U (MO)
Wellesley Coll (MA)
Wells Coll (NY)
Wesleyan Coll (GA)
Western Kentucky U (KY)
Western Oregon U (OR)
Westminster Coll (MO)
Wheaton Coll (IL)
Wheaton Coll (MA)
Widener U (PA)
Wilkes U (PA)
William Jewell Coll (MO)
Wittenberg U (OH)
Wofford Coll (SC)
Wright State U (OH)
Xavier U (OH)
York Coll of Pennsylvania (PA)

INVESTMENTS AND SECURITIES
Johnson & Wales U (RI)
U of Nebraska at Omaha (NE)
U of Nebraska–Lincoln (NE)
U of North Dakota (ND)

IRANIAN LANGUAGES
U of Maryland, Coll Park (MD)
The U of Texas at Austin (TX)
U of Utah (UT)

IRISH STUDIES
Sacred Heart U (CT)

ISLAMIC STUDIES
Boston Coll (MA)
DePaul U (IL)
The Ohio State U (OH)
Swarthmore Coll (PA)
U of Minnesota, Twin Cities Campus (MN)
The U of Texas at Austin (TX)
The U of Western Ontario (ON, Canada)
Washington U in St. Louis (MO)
Wellesley Coll (MA)

ITALIAN
Arizona State U (AZ)
Assumption Coll (MA)
Bard Coll (NY)
Barnard Coll (NY)

Bennington Coll (VT)
Boston Coll (MA)
Boston U (MA)
Brock U (ON, Canada)
Brown U (RI)
Bryn Mawr Coll (PA)
California State U, Long Beach (CA)
Central Connecticut State U (CT)
Claremont McKenna Coll (CA)
Coll of the Holy Cross (MA)
The Colorado Coll (CO)
Columbia U, School of General Studies (NY)
Concordia U (QC, Canada)
Connecticut Coll (CT)
Cornell U (NY)
Dartmouth Coll (NH)
DePaul U (IL)
Dominican U (IL)
Fairfield U (CT)
Georgetown U (DC)
Gettysburg Coll (PA)
Haverford Coll (PA)
Hofstra U (NY)
Hunter Coll of the City U of New York (NY)
Indiana U Bloomington (IN)
Ithaca Coll (NY)
The Johns Hopkins U (MD)
La Salle U (PA)
Laurentian U (ON, Canada)
Lehman Coll of the City U of New York (NY)
Long Island U, C.W. Post Campus (NY)
Loyola U Chicago (IL)
Marlboro Coll (VT)
Middlebury Coll (VT)
Montclair State U (NJ)
Mount Holyoke Coll (MA)
Nazareth Coll of Rochester (NY)
New York U (NY)
The Ohio State U (OH)
Penn State Abington (PA)
Penn State Altoona (PA)
Penn State Beaver (PA)
Penn State Berks (PA)
Penn State Brandywine (PA)
Penn State DuBois (PA)
Penn State Erie, The Behrend Coll (PA)
Penn State Fayette, The Eberly Campus (PA)
Penn State Greater Allegheny (PA)
Penn State Hazleton (PA)
Penn State Lehigh Valley (PA)
Penn State Mont Alto (PA)
Penn State New Kensington (PA)
Penn State Schuylkill (PA)
Penn State Shenango (PA)
Penn State U Park (PA)
Penn State Wilkes-Barre (PA)
Penn State Worthington Scranton (PA)
Penn State York (PA)
Providence Coll (RI)
Queens Coll of the City U of New York (NY)
Rosemont Coll (PA)
Rutgers, The State U of New Jersey, Newark (NJ)
Rutgers, The State U of New Jersey, New Brunswick (NJ)
St. John's U (NY)
Saint Joseph's U (PA)
Saint Mary's Coll (IN)
Saint Mary's Coll of California (CA)
San Francisco State U (CA)
Santa Clara U (CA)
Sarah Lawrence Coll (NY)
Scripps Coll (CA)
Smith Coll (MA)
Southern Connecticut State U (CT)
Stanford U (CA)
State U of New York at Binghamton (NY)
Stony Brook U, State U of New York (NY)
Syracuse U (NY)
Temple U (PA)
Trinity Coll (CT)
Tulane U (LA)
U at Buffalo, the State U of New York (NY)
The U of Arizona (AZ)
The U of British Columbia (BC, Canada)
U of California, Berkeley (CA)
U of California, Davis (CA)
U of California, Los Angeles (CA)

U of California, Santa Barbara (CA)
U of Colorado Boulder (CO)
U of Delaware (DE)
U of Denver (CO)
U of Georgia (GA)
U of Houston (TX)
U of Illinois at Chicago (IL)
The U of Iowa (IA)
U of Maryland, Coll Park (MD)
U of Massachusetts Amherst (MA)
U of Massachusetts Boston (MA)
U of Michigan (MI)
U of Minnesota, Twin Cities Campus (MN)
U of Notre Dame (IN)
U of Oklahoma (OK)
U of Oregon (OR)
U of Ottawa (ON, Canada)
U of Pennsylvania (PA)
U of Pittsburgh (PA)
U of Rhode Island (RI)
The U of Scranton (PA)
U of Southern California (CA)
U of South Florida (FL)
The U of Tennessee (TN)
The U of Texas at Austin (TX)
U of Virginia (VA)
U of Washington (WA)
U of Wisconsin–Madison (WI)
Vassar Coll (NY)
Villanova U (PA)
Washington U in St. Louis (MO)
Wellesley Coll (MA)
Wesleyan U (CT)
Yale U (CT)
York Coll of the City U of New York (NY)
Youngstown State U (OH)

ITALIAN STUDIES
Arcadia U (PA)
Assumption Coll (MA)
Boston U (MA)
Brock U (ON, Canada)
Brown U (RI)
Coll of the Holy Cross (MA)
The Colorado Coll (CO)
Columbia U, School of General Studies (NY)
Dickinson Coll (PA)
Franklin Coll Switzerland (Switzerland)
Miami U (OH)
Scripps Coll (CA)
Southern Methodist U (TX)
Sweet Briar Coll (VA)
Tulane U (LA)
U of California, Santa Cruz (CA)
U of Richmond (VA)
U of Vermont (VT)
Wellesley Coll (MA)
Wheaton Coll (MA)

JAPANESE
Aquinas Coll (MI)
Ball State U (IN)
Bates Coll (ME)
Bennington Coll (VT)
Boston U (MA)
California State U, Fullerton (CA)
California State U, Long Beach (CA)
California State U, Los Angeles (CA)
Calvin Coll (MI)
Carnegie Mellon U (PA)
Claremont McKenna Coll (CA)
Colgate U (NY)
Connecticut Coll (CT)
Dartmouth Coll (NH)
Eastern Michigan U (MI)
Elizabethtown Coll (PA)
Georgetown U (DC)
Gettysburg Coll (PA)
Hobart and William Smith Colls (NY)
Lawrence U (WI)
Linfield Coll (OR)
Macalester Coll (MN)
Michigan State U (MI)
Middlebury Coll (VT)
North Central Coll (IL)
The Ohio State U (OH)
Pacific U (OR)
Penn State Abington (PA)
Penn State Altoona (PA)
Penn State Beaver (PA)
Penn State Berks (PA)
Penn State Brandywine (PA)
Penn State DuBois (PA)

Penn State Erie, The Behrend Coll (PA)
Penn State Fayette, The Eberly Campus (PA)
Penn State Greater Allegheny (PA)
Penn State Hazleton (PA)
Penn State Lehigh Valley (PA)
Penn State Mont Alto (PA)
Penn State New Kensington (PA)
Penn State Schuylkill (PA)
Penn State Shenango (PA)
Penn State U Park (PA)
Penn State Wilkes-Barre (PA)
Penn State Worthington Scranton (PA)
Penn State York (PA)
Pomona Coll (CA)
Portland State U (OR)
San Diego State U (CA)
San Francisco State U (CA)
San Jose State U (CA)
Sarah Lawrence Coll (NY)
Scripps Coll (CA)
Stanford U (CA)
Swarthmore Coll (PA)
Trinity Coll (CT)
U of Alaska Fairbanks (AK)
U of California, Berkeley (CA)
U of California, Davis (CA)
U of California, Irvine (CA)
U of California, Los Angeles (CA)
U of California, Santa Barbara (CA)
U of Colorado Boulder (CO)
The U of Findlay (OH)
U of Georgia (GA)
U of Hawaii at Hilo (HI)
U of Hawaii at Manoa (HI)
The U of Iowa (IA)
U of Maryland, Coll Park (MD)
U of Massachusetts Amherst (MA)
U of Minnesota, Twin Cities Campus (MN)
U of Mount Union (OH)
The U of North Carolina at Charlotte (NC)
U of Notre Dame (IN)
U of Oregon (OR)
U of Pittsburgh (PA)
U of Puget Sound (WA)
U of Regina (SK, Canada)
U of Rochester (NY)
U of St. Thomas (MN)
U of the Pacific (CA)
U of Utah (UT)
U of Vermont (VT)
U of Washington (WA)
The U of Western Ontario (ON, Canada)
U of Wisconsin–Madison (WI)
Vassar Coll (NY)
Wake Forest U (NC)
Washington U in St. Louis (MO)
Wellesley Coll (MA)
Williams Coll (MA)
Yale U (CT)

JAPANESE STUDIES
Case Western Reserve U (OH)
Claremont McKenna Coll (CA)
Earlham Coll (IN)
Gettysburg Coll (PA)
Hope Coll (MI)
U of San Francisco (CA)
Willamette U (OR)

JAZZ/JAZZ STUDIES
Bard Coll (NY)
Bennington Coll (VT)
Bowling Green State U (OH)
Brigham Young U (UT)
Capital U (OH)
Central State U (OH)
City Coll of the City U of New York (NY)
Concordia U (QC, Canada)
DePaul U (IL)
Drake U (IA)
Five Towns Coll (NY)
Florida Ag and Mech U (FL)
Florida State U (FL)
Hofstra U (NY)
Hope Coll (MI)
Ithaca Coll (NY)
Johnson State Coll (VT)
Lamar U (TX)
Limestone Coll (SC)
Long Island U, Brooklyn Campus (NY)

Loyola U New Orleans (LA)
Michigan State U (MI)
New England Conservatory of Music (MA)
The New School for Jazz and Contemporary Music (NY)
North Central Coll (IL)
Oberlin Coll (OH)
The Ohio State U (OH)
Peabody Conservatory of The Johns Hopkins U (MD)
Roosevelt U (IL)
Rutgers, The State U of New Jersey, New Brunswick (NJ)
St. Francis Xavier U (NS, Canada)
Sarah Lawrence Coll (NY)
Shenandoah U (VA)
Temple U (PA)
Texas State U–San Marcos (TX)
The U of Akron (OH)
U of Hartford (CT)
The U of Iowa (IA)
U of Miami (FL)
U of Michigan (MI)
U of Minnesota, Duluth (MN)
U of Nevada, Las Vegas (NV)
The U of North Carolina at Greensboro (NC)
U of North Florida (FL)
U of North Texas (TX)
U of Oregon (OR)
U of Rochester (NY)
U of Southern California (CA)
The U of Texas at Austin (TX)
Webster U (MO)
Western Michigan U (MI)
William Paterson U of New Jersey (NJ)

JEWISH/JUDAIC STUDIES
American Jewish U (CA)
American U (DC)
Arizona State U (AZ)
Bard Coll (NY)
Barnard Coll (NY)
Bennington Coll (VT)
Brown U (RI)
California State U, Chico (CA)
California State U, Northridge (CA)
City Coll of the City U of New York (NY)
Clark U (MA)
Concordia U (QC, Canada)
DePaul U (IL)
Dickinson Coll (PA)
Eugene Lang Coll The New School for Liberal Arts (NY)
Florida Atlantic U (FL)
Hebrew Coll (MA)
Hofstra U (NY)
Hunter Coll of the City U of New York (NY)
Indiana U Bloomington (IN)
Lehman Coll of the City U of New York (NY)
Northeastern U (MA)
Oberlin Coll (OH)
The Ohio State U (OH)
Penn State Abington (PA)
Penn State Altoona (PA)
Penn State Beaver (PA)
Penn State Berks (PA)
Penn State Brandywine (PA)
Penn State DuBois (PA)
Penn State Erie, The Behrend Coll (PA)
Penn State Fayette, The Eberly Campus (PA)
Penn State Greater Allegheny (PA)
Penn State Hazleton (PA)
Penn State Lehigh Valley (PA)
Penn State Mont Alto (PA)
Penn State New Kensington (PA)
Penn State Schuylkill (PA)
Penn State Shenango (PA)
Penn State U Park (PA)
Penn State Wilkes-Barre (PA)
Penn State Worthington Scranton (PA)
Penn State York (PA)
Queens Coll of the City U of New York (NY)
Rutgers, The State U of New Jersey, New Brunswick (NJ)
San Diego State U (CA)
San Francisco State U (CA)
Scripps Coll (CA)

State U of New York at Binghamton (NY)
Temple U (PA)
Trinity Coll (CT)
Tufts U (MA)
Tulane U (LA)
The U of Arizona (AZ)
U of California, Los Angeles (CA)
U of Florida (FL)
U of Hartford (CT)
U of Manitoba (MB, Canada)
U of Maryland, Coll Park (MD)
U of Massachusetts Amherst (MA)
U of Miami (FL)
U of Michigan (MI)
U of Minnesota, Twin Cities Campus (MN)
U of Oklahoma (OK)
U of Oregon (OR)
U of Pennsylvania (PA)
U of Southern California (CA)
The U of Texas at Austin (TX)
U of Washington (WA)
The U of Western Ontario (ON, Canada)
U of Wisconsin–Madison (WI)
Vanderbilt U (TN)
Vassar Coll (NY)
Washington U in St. Louis (MO)
Wellesley Coll (MA)
Yale U (CT)

JOURNALISM
Abilene Christian U (TX)
Allegheny Coll (PA)
American U (DC)
American U in Bulgaria (Bulgaria)
Andrews U (MI)
Angelo State U (TX)
Appalachian State U (NC)
Arkansas State U (AR)
Arkansas Tech U (AR)
Asbury U (KY)
Ashland U (OH)
Auburn U (AL)
Augustana Coll (SD)
Averett U (VA)
Ball State U (IN)
Barry U (FL)
Belmont U (TN)
Bemidji State U (MN)
Bennington Coll (VT)
Bethel U (MN)
Biola U (CA)
Boston U (MA)
Bowling Green State U (OH)
Brigham Young U (UT)
Butler U (IN)
California Baptist U (CA)
California Polytechnic State U, San Luis Obispo (CA)
California State U, Chico (CA)
California State U, Dominguez Hills (CA)
California State U, Fullerton (CA)
California State U, Long Beach (CA)
California State U, Northridge (CA)
Campbellsville U (KY)
Canisius Coll (NY)
Carroll U (WI)
Carson-Newman Coll (TN)
Castleton State Coll (VT)
Cedarville U (OH)
Central Connecticut State U (CT)
Central Michigan U (MI)
Central State U (OH)
Chatham U (PA)
Cincinnati Christian U (OH)
The Coll of St. Scholastica (MN)
Coll of the Ozarks (MO)
Colorado State U (CO)
Columbia Coll Chicago (IL)
Concordia U (QC, Canada)
Concordia U Chicago (IL)
Corban U (OR)
Creighton U (NE)
Curry Coll (MA)
Delaware State U (DE)
Delta State U (MS)
DePaul U (IL)
Doane Coll (NE)
Dominican U (IL)
Dordt Coll (IA)
Drake U (IA)
Duquesne U (PA)
Eastern Illinois U (IL)
Eastern Michigan U (MI)
Eastern Washington U (WA)

Edinboro U of Pennsylvania (PA)
Elon U (NC)
Florida Ag and Mech U (FL)
Florida Southern Coll (FL)
Franklin Coll (IN)
Franklin Pierce U (NH)
Gannon U (PA)
Gardner-Webb U (NC)
George Fox U (OR)
Georgia Coll & State U (GA)
Georgia Southern U (GA)
Georgia State U (GA)
Gettysburg Coll (PA)
Grace Coll (IN)
Grand Valley State U (MI)
Grand View U (IA)
Hawai`i Pacific U (HI)
Hofstra U (NY)
Humboldt State U (CA)
Huntington U (IN)
Illinois Inst of Technology (IL)
Illinois State U (IL)
Indiana U Bloomington (IN)
Indiana U of Pennsylvania (PA)
Indiana U–Purdue U Indianapolis (IN)
Indiana U Southeast (IN)
Indiana Wesleyan U (IN)
Inter American U of Puerto Rico, Ponce Campus (PR)
Iowa State U of Science and Technology (IA)
Ithaca Coll (NY)
John Brown U (AR)
Johnson State Coll (VT)
Kansas State U (KS)
Keene State Coll (NH)
Kent State U (OH)
Keystone Coll (PA)
Lamar U (TX)
La Salle U (PA)
Lasell Coll (MA)
Lebanese American U (Lebanon)
Lehigh U (PA)
Lewis U (IL)
Liberty U (VA)
Lincoln U (MO)
Lindenwood U (MO)
Lipscomb U (TN)
Lock Haven U of Pennsylvania (PA)
Long Island U, Brooklyn Campus (NY)
Long Island U, C.W. Post Campus (NY)
Longwood U (VA)
Loras Coll (IA)
Louisiana Coll (LA)
Loyola U Chicago (IL)
Lyndon State Coll (VT)
Madonna U (MI)
Mansfield U of Pennsylvania (PA)
Marietta Coll (OH)
Marist Coll (NY)
Marquette U (WI)
Marshall U (WV)
Massachusetts Coll of Liberal Arts (MA)
Mercer U (GA)
Messiah Coll (PA)
Miami U (OH)
Michigan State U (MI)
Minnesota State U Mankato (MN)
Missouri State U (MO)
Mount Mercy U (IA)
Mount Vernon Nazarene U (OH)
Multnomah U (OR)
Murray State U (KY)
New England Coll (NH)
New Mexico State U (NM)
New York U (NY)
North Central Coll (IL)
Northeastern State U (OK)
Northeastern U (MA)
Northern Arizona U (AZ)
Northern Illinois U (IL)
Northern Kentucky U (KY)
Northwestern Coll (IA)
Northwestern Coll (MN)
Northwest Missouri State U (MO)
The Ohio State U (OH)
Ohio U (OH)
Ohio Wesleyan U (OH)
Oklahoma Christian U (OK)
Oklahoma City U (OK)
Oklahoma State U (OK)
Pacific U (OR)
Paine Coll (GA)
Palm Beach Atlantic U (FL)

Patrick Henry Coll (VA)
Penn State Abington (PA)
Penn State Altoona (PA)
Penn State Beaver (PA)
Penn State Berks (PA)
Penn State Brandywine (PA)
Penn State DuBois (PA)
Penn State Erie, The Behrend Coll (PA)
Penn State Fayette, The Eberly Campus (PA)
Penn State Greater Allegheny (PA)
Penn State Hazleton (PA)
Penn State Lehigh Valley (PA)
Penn State Mont Alto (PA)
Penn State New Kensington (PA)
Penn State Schuylkill (PA)
Penn State Shenango (PA)
Penn State U Park (PA)
Penn State Wilkes-Barre (PA)
Penn State Worthington Scranton (PA)
Penn State York (PA)
Pepperdine U, Malibu (CA)
Pittsburg State U (KS)
Point Park U (PA)
Purchase Coll, State U of New York (NY)
Quinnipiac U (CT)
Radford U (VA)
Rider U (NJ)
Roosevelt U (IL)
Rowan U (NJ)
Rust Coll (MS)
Rutgers, The State U of New Jersey, Newark (NJ)
Rutgers, The State U of New Jersey, New Brunswick (NJ)
St. Ambrose U (IA)
St. Bonaventure U (NY)
St. Catherine U (MN)
Saint Francis U (PA)
St. John's U (NY)
Saint Joseph's Coll of Maine (ME)
Saint Mary-of-the-Woods Coll (IN)
Saint Mary's U of Minnesota (MN)
Saint Michael's Coll (VT)
St. Thomas Aquinas Coll (NY)
St. Thomas U (NB, Canada)
Salem State U (MA)
Samford U (AL)
San Diego State U (CA)
San Francisco State U (CA)
San Jose State U (CA)
Savannah State U (GA)
Seton Hill U (PA)
Shippensburg U of Pennsylvania (PA)
Slippery Rock U of Pennsylvania (PA)
South Dakota State U (SD)
Southeastern U (FL)
Southern Adventist U (TN)
Southern Arkansas U–Magnolia (AR)
Southern Connecticut State U (CT)
Southern Illinois U Carbondale (IL)
Southern Methodist U (TX)
Southwestern Adventist U (TX)
Southwestern Coll (KS)
Spring Hill Coll (AL)
State U of New York at New Paltz (NY)
State U of New York at Oswego (NY)
State U of New York at Plattsburgh (NY)
Stephen F. Austin State U (TX)
Stony Brook U, State U of New York (NY)
Suffolk U (MA)
Syracuse U (NY)
Tabor Coll (KS)
Talladega Coll (AL)
Temple U (PA)
Tennessee Technological U (TN)
Texas Christian U (TX)
Texas Southern U (TX)
Texas State U–San Marcos (TX)
Texas Tech U (TX)
Texas Wesleyan U (TX)
Thomas Edison State Coll (NJ)
Tiffin U (OH)
Trevecca Nazarene U (TN)
Troy U (AL)
Union Coll (NE)
Union U (TN)
United States Intl U (Kenya)
The U of Alabama (AL)
U of Alaska Fairbanks (AK)

The U of Arizona (AZ)
U of Arkansas (AR)
U of Baltimore (MD)
U of Bridgeport (CT)
U of California, Irvine (CA)
U of Central Florida (FL)
U of Central Missouri (MO)
U of Cincinnati (OH)
U of Colorado Boulder (CO)
U of Dayton (OH)
U of Delaware (DE)
U of Denver (CO)
The U of Findlay (OH)
U of Florida (FL)
U of Georgia (GA)
U of Hawaii at Manoa (HI)
U of Houston (TX)
U of Idaho (ID)
The U of Iowa (IA)
The U of Kansas (KS)
U of La Verne (CA)
U of Maine (ME)
U of Maryland, Coll Park (MD)
U of Massachusetts Amherst (MA)
U of Memphis (TN)
U of Miami (FL)
U of Michigan–Flint (MI)
U of Minnesota, Twin Cities Campus (MN)
U of Mississippi (MS)
U of Missouri (MO)
U of Nebraska at Omaha (NE)
U of Nevada, Reno (NV)
U of Northern Colorado (CO)
U of North Texas (TX)
U of Oklahoma (OK)
U of Oregon (OR)
U of Ottawa (ON, Canada)
U of Pittsburgh at Greensburg (PA)
U of Pittsburgh at Johnstown (PA)
U of Portland (OR)
U of Regina (SK, Canada)
U of Rhode Island (RI)
U of Richmond (VA)
U of St. Thomas (MN)
U of South Carolina (SC)
U of Southern California (CA)
U of Southern Indiana (IN)
U of Southern Mississippi (MS)
The U of Tennessee (TN)
The U of Texas at Arlington (TX)
The U of Texas at Austin (TX)
The U of Texas at Tyler (TX)
The U of Texas–Pan American (TX)
U of the Cumberlands (KY)
U of the Incarnate Word (TX)
The U of Toledo (OH)
U of West Georgia (GA)
U of Wisconsin–Eau Claire (WI)
U of Wisconsin–Madison (WI)
U of Wisconsin–River Falls (WI)
U of Wisconsin–Superior (WI)
U of Wisconsin–Whitewater (WI)
U of Wyoming (WY)
Utah State U (UT)
Valparaiso U (IN)
Walla Walla U (WA)
Wartburg Coll (IA)
Washington Adventist U (MD)
Washington and Lee U (VA)
Washington State U (WA)
Waynesburg U (PA)
Wayne State U (MI)
Weber State U (UT)
Webster U (MO)
Western Illinois U (IL)
Western Kentucky U (KY)
Western Michigan U (MI)
Western New England U (MA)
West Virginia U (WV)
Wilfrid Laurier U (ON, Canada)
Winona State U (MN)
Youngstown State U (OH)

JOURNALISM RELATED

Arizona State U (AZ)
Benedictine U (IL)
Bob Jones U (SC)
Boston U (MA)
California State U, Long Beach (CA)
Central Michigan U (MI)
Champlain Coll (VT)
Columbia Coll (SC)
Kent State U (OH)
Kentucky State U (KY)
Oklahoma State U (OK)
Roosevelt U (IL)
Simpson Coll (IA)
Southern Adventist U (TN)
Southern Nazarene U (OK)

The U of Akron (OH)
U of Nebraska–Lincoln (NE)
U of Oregon (OR)
U of St. Thomas (MN)
The U of Western Ontario (ON, Canada)

KEYBOARD INSTRUMENTS

Abilene Christian U (TX)
Acadia U (NS, Canada)
Andrews U (MI)
Anna Maria Coll (MA)
Baldwin-Wallace Coll (OH)
Baptist Bible Coll of Pennsylvania (PA)
Bard Coll (NY)
Barry U (FL)
Belmont U (TN)
Bennington Coll (VT)
Birmingham-Southern Coll (AL)
Bob Jones U (SC)
Brigham Young U (UT)
Butler U (IN)
California Baptist U (CA)
California State U, Chico (CA)
Calvary Bible Coll and Theological Sem (MO)
Campbellsville U (KY)
Capital U (OH)
Carnegie Mellon U (PA)
Carson-Newman Coll (TN)
The Catholic U of America (DC)
Chapman U (CA)
Cincinnati Christian U (OH)
Coker Coll (SC)
The Colburn School Conservatory of Music (CA)
Columbia Coll (SC)
Dallas Baptist U (TX)
Dordt Coll (IA)
Drake U (IA)
East Texas Baptist U (TX)
Florida State U (FL)
Furman U (SC)
Grand Canyon U (AZ)
Hardin-Simmons U (TX)
Hillsdale Free Will Baptist Coll (OK)
Hope Coll (MI)
Houghton Coll (NY)
Illinois Wesleyan U (IL)
Indiana U–Purdue U Fort Wayne (IN)
Inter American U of Puerto Rico, San Germán Campus (PR)
Ithaca Coll (NY)
Kent State U (OH)
Lamar U (TX)
Lawrence U (WI)
Lee U (TN)
Lincoln Christian U (IL)
Lipscomb U (TN)
Louisiana Coll (LA)
Mannes Coll The New School for Music (NY)
Maryville Coll (TN)
The Master's Coll and Sem (CA)
McMurry U (TX)
Millikin U (IL)
Minnesota State U Mankato (MN)
Minnesota State U Moorhead (MN)
Mount Allison U (NB, Canada)
Newberry Coll (SC)
New England Conservatory of Music (MA)
The New School for Jazz and Contemporary Music (NY)
Northwestern Coll (MN)
Nyack Coll (NY)
Oberlin Coll (OH)
The Ohio State U (OH)
Ohio U (OH)
Oklahoma City U (OK)
Ouachita Baptist U (AR)
Palm Beach Atlantic U (FL)
Peabody Conservatory of The Johns Hopkins U (MD)
Rider U (NJ)
Roosevelt U (IL)
Samford U (AL)
San Francisco Conservatory of Music (CA)
Sarah Lawrence Coll (NY)
Shenandoah U (VA)
Shorter U (GA)
Southeastern U (FL)
Southern Methodist U (TX)
Spring Arbor U (MI)
State U of New York at Fredonia (NY)

State U of New York at New Paltz (NY)
Stetson U (FL)
Texas Christian U (TX)
Union U (TN)
The U of British Columbia (BC, Canada)
U of Cincinnati (OH)
U of Delaware (DE)
The U of Iowa (IA)
The U of Kansas (KS)
U of Miami (FL)
U of Nebraska at Omaha (NE)
U of Redlands (CA)
U of Southern California (CA)
The U of Tennessee at Martin (TN)
U of the Pacific (CA)
U of Tulsa (OK)
U of Washington (WA)
The U of Western Ontario (ON, Canada)
Valparaiso U (IN)
Walla Walla U (WA)
Weber State U (UT)
Western Michigan U (MI)
Willamette U (OR)
Xavier U of Louisiana (LA)

KINDERGARTEN/PRESCHOOL EDUCATION

Alabama Ag and Mech U (AL)
Albright Coll (PA)
Alma Coll (MI)
Alvernia U (PA)
Anna Maria Coll (MA)
Appalachian State U (NC)
Arcadia U (PA)
Armstrong Atlantic State U (GA)
Ashland U (OH)
Athens State U (AL)
Atlantic Union Coll (MA)
Augsburg Coll (MN)
Ball State U (IN)
Barry U (FL)
Bluefield Coll (VA)
Bluffton U (OH)
Boise State U (ID)
Boston Coll (MA)
Bowie State U (MD)
Bowling Green State U (OH)
Bucknell U (PA)
Butler U (IN)
Cabrini Coll (PA)
California Polytechnic State U, San Luis Obispo (CA)
Carson-Newman Coll (TN)
Champlain Coll (VT)
Cincinnati Christian U (OH)
Clarion U of Pennsylvania (PA)
The Coll of Saint Rose (NY)
Columbia Bible Coll (BC, Canada)
Columbia Coll Chicago (IL)
Concordia U (QC, Canada)
Concordia U Wisconsin (WI)
Concord U (WV)
Curry Coll (MA)
Dallas Baptist U (TX)
Delaware State U (DE)
Eastern Illinois U (IL)
Edinboro U of Pennsylvania (PA)
Elizabeth City State U (NC)
Elmhurst Coll (IL)
Erskine Coll (SC)
Evangel U (MO)
Faulkner U (AL)
Florida Ag and Mech U (FL)
Fontbonne U (MO)
Furman U (SC)
Georgia State U (GA)
Governors State U (IL)
Greensboro Coll (NC)
Grove City Coll (PA)
Hillsdale Coll (MI)
Holy Family U (PA)
Humboldt State U (CA)
Hunter Coll of the City U of New York (NY)
Inter American U of Puerto Rico, Guayama Campus (PR)
Inter American U of Puerto Rico, Metropolitan Campus (PR)
Inter American U of Puerto Rico, Ponce Campus (PR)
Inter American U of Puerto Rico, San Germán Campus (PR)
Jacksonville State U (AL)
Jarvis Christian Coll (TX)
John Brown U (AR)
John Carroll U (OH)
Kean U (NJ)

Kendall Coll (IL)
Kent State U (OH)
King Coll (TN)
Kutztown U of Pennsylvania (PA)
Lamar U (TX)
Lasell Coll (MA)
Lesley U (MA)
Lincoln Christian U (IL)
Lincoln Memorial U (TN)
Lock Haven U of Pennsylvania (PA)
Long Island U, C.W. Post Campus (NY)
Longwood U (VA)
Loras Coll (IA)
Louisiana Coll (LA)
Mansfield U of Pennsylvania (PA)
Marshall U (WV)
Mars Hill Coll (NC)
Martin Luther Coll (MN)
Metropolitan State U (MN)
Michigan State U (MI)
Middle Tennessee State U (TN)
Minnesota State U Mankato (MN)
Minnesota State U Moorhead (MN)
Mississippi Valley State U (MS)
Missouri Baptist U (MO)
Mount Vernon Nazarene U (OH)
Neumann U (PA)
Newberry Coll (SC)
New Jersey City U (NJ)
New Mexico Highlands U (NM)
North Carolina Ag and Tech State U (NC)
Northeastern Illinois U (IL)
Northern Illinois U (IL)
Northern Kentucky U (KY)
Northwestern Oklahoma State U (OK)
Nova Southeastern U (FL)
Ohio Wesleyan U (OH)
Oklahoma Christian U (OK)
Oklahoma City U (OK)
Our Lady of the Lake U of San Antonio (TX)
Pacific Oaks Coll (CA)
Pacific U (OR)
Philadelphia Biblical U (PA)
Piedmont Coll (GA)
Prescott Coll (AZ)
St. Catherine U (MN)
Saint Mary-of-the-Woods Coll (IN)
St. Thomas Aquinas Coll (NY)
Saint Xavier U (IL)
Sarah Lawrence Coll (NY)
Siena Heights U (MI)
Silver Lake Coll (WI)
Southeastern Oklahoma State U (OK)
Southern Wesleyan U (SC)
State U of New York at Fredonia (NY)
State U of New York Coll at Oneonta (NY)
Stephens Coll (MO)
Susquehanna U (PA)
Tabor Coll (KS)
Tennessee Technological U (TN)
Texas A&M Intl U (TX)
Texas A&M U–Corpus Christi (TX)
Thomas U (GA)
Tufts U (MA)
Union U (TN)
Université de Sherbrooke (QC, Canada)
Université du Québec en Outaouais (QC, Canada)
The U of Arizona (AZ)
U of Arkansas (AR)
U of Arkansas at Pine Bluff (AR)
The U of British Columbia (BC, Canada)
U of Cincinnati (OH)
U of Dayton (OH)
U of Delaware (DE)
U of Georgia (GA)
U of Manitoba (MB, Canada)
U of Mary Hardin-Baylor (TX)
U of Maryland, Coll Park (MD)
U of Minnesota, Crookston (MN)
U of Minnesota, Duluth (MN)
U of Minnesota, Twin Cities Campus (MN)
U of Missouri (MO)
U of Nevada, Las Vegas (NV)
U of New Brunswick Fredericton (NB, Canada)
The U of North Carolina at Charlotte (NC)
The U of North Carolina at Pembroke (NC)

INDEXES

Purdue U (IN)
State U of New York Coll of Environmental Science and Forestry (NY)
Temple U (PA)
Texas A&M U (TX)
Texas Tech U (TX)
The U of Arizona (AZ)
U of Arkansas (AR)
The U of British Columbia (BC, Canada)
U of California, Berkeley (CA)
U of California, Davis (CA)
U of Florida (FL)
U of Georgia (GA)
U of Guelph (ON, Canada)
U of Idaho (ID)
U of Maryland, Coll Park (MD)
U of Massachusetts Amherst (MA)
U of Minnesota, Twin Cities Campus (MN)
U of Nebraska–Lincoln (NE)
U of Nevada, Las Vegas (NV)
U of Oregon (OR)
U of Rhode Island (RI)
U of Washington (WA)
U of Wisconsin–Madison (WI)
Utah State U (UT)
Virginia Polytechnic Inst and State U (VA)
Washington State U (WA)
West Virginia U (WV)

LANDSCAPING AND GROUNDSKEEPING

Andrews U (MI)
Florida Ag and Mech U (FL)
Florida Southern Coll (FL)
Mississippi State U (MS)
Oklahoma State U (OK)
Penn State Abington (PA)
Penn State Altoona (PA)
Penn State Beaver (PA)
Penn State Berks (PA)
Penn State Brandywine (PA)
Penn State DuBois (PA)
Penn State Erie, The Behrend Coll (PA)
Penn State Fayette, The Eberly Campus (PA)
Penn State Greater Allegheny (PA)
Penn State Hazleton (PA)
Penn State Lehigh Valley (PA)
Penn State Mont Alto (PA)
Penn State New Kensington (PA)
Penn State Schuylkill (PA)
Penn State Shenango (PA)
Penn State U Park (PA)
Penn State Wilkes-Barre (PA)
Penn State Worthington Scranton (PA)
Penn State York (PA)
South Dakota State U (SD)
Tennessee Technological U (TN)
U of Maine (ME)
U of Minnesota, Crookston (MN)
U of Nebraska–Lincoln (NE)

LAND USE PLANNING AND MANAGEMENT

California State U, Bakersfield (CA)
Central Michigan U (MI)
Montana State U (MT)
State U of New York Coll of Environmental Science and Forestry (NY)
U of Saskatchewan (SK, Canada)
The U of Western Ontario (ON, Canada)
U of Wisconsin–Platteville (WI)
U of Wisconsin–River Falls (WI)

LANGUAGE INTERPRETATION AND TRANSLATION

Bard Coll (NY)
Brigham Young U (UT)
Concordia U (QC, Canada)
Laurentian U (ON, Canada)
Southern Nazarene U (OK)
Université du Québec en Outaouais (QC, Canada)
U of Ottawa (ON, Canada)

LASER AND OPTICAL ENGINEERING

Delaware State U (DE)

LATIN

Acadia U (NS, Canada)

Amherst Coll (MA)
Augustana Coll (IL)
Austin Coll (TX)
Ball State U (IN)
Bard Coll (NY)
Barnard Coll (NY)
Boston Coll (MA)
Boston U (MA)
Bowling Green State U (OH)
Bryn Mawr Coll (PA)
Butler U (IN)
Calvin Coll (MI)
Carleton Coll (MN)
The Catholic U of America (DC)
Claremont McKenna Coll (CA)
Colgate U (NY)
The Coll of Wooster (OH)
Concordia Coll (MN)
Cornell Coll (IA)
Creighton U (NE)
Dartmouth Coll (NH)
DePauw U (IN)
Duquesne U (PA)
Franklin & Marshall Coll (PA)
Furman U (SC)
Gettysburg Coll (PA)
Hampden-Sydney Coll (VA)
Haverford Coll (PA)
Hobart and William Smith Colls (NY)
Hofstra U (NY)
Hunter Coll of the City U of New York (NY)
John Carroll U (OH)
Kent State U (OH)
Kenyon Coll (OH)
Lawrence U (WI)
Lehman Coll of the City U of New York (NY)
Louisiana State U and Ag and Mech Coll (LA)
Loyola U Chicago (IL)
Marlboro Coll (VT)
Mercer U (GA)
Missouri State U (MO)
Monmouth Coll (IL)
Montclair State U (NJ)
Mount Allison U (NB, Canada)
Mount Holyoke Coll (MA)
Oberlin Coll (OH)
Ohio U (OH)
Queens Coll of the City U of New York (NY)
Randolph Coll (VA)
Randolph-Macon Coll (VA)
Rhodes Coll (TN)
Rice U (TX)
Rockford Coll (IL)
Rutgers, The State U of New Jersey, New Brunswick (NJ)
Saint Joseph's U (PA)
Saint Mary's Coll of California (CA)
St. Olaf Coll (MN)
Samford U (AL)
Santa Clara U (CA)
Sarah Lawrence Coll (NY)
Sewanee: The U of the South (TN)
Smith Coll (MA)
Stanford U (CA)
State U of New York at Binghamton (NY)
Swarthmore Coll (PA)
Tufts U (MA)
Tulane U (LA)
The U of British Columbia (BC, Canada)
U of California, Berkeley (CA)
U of California, Irvine (CA)
U of Delaware (DE)
U of Georgia (GA)
The U of Iowa (IA)
U of Maine (ME)
U of Manitoba (MB, Canada)
U of Miami (FL)
U of Michigan (MI)
U of Minnesota, Twin Cities Campus (MN)
U of Missouri (MO)
U of Nebraska–Lincoln (NE)
U of New Brunswick Fredericton (NB, Canada)
U of New Hampshire (NH)
U of Ottawa (ON, Canada)
U of Richmond (VA)
U of St. Thomas (MN)
The U of Scranton (PA)
The U of Texas at Austin (TX)
U of Vermont (VT)
U of Washington (WA)
The U of Western Ontario (ON, Canada)

U of Wisconsin–Madison (WI)
Vassar Coll (NY)
Virginia Wesleyan Coll (VA)
Wabash Coll (IN)
Wake Forest U (NC)
Washington U in St. Louis (MO)
Wellesley Coll (MA)
West Chester U of Pennsylvania (PA)
Western Michigan U (MI)
Wheaton Coll (MA)
Wichita State U (KS)
Wright State U (OH)
Yale U (CT)

LATIN AMERICAN AND CARIBBEAN STUDIES

Burlington Coll (VT)
Coll of Charleston (SC)
Mount Holyoke Coll (MA)
Rollins Coll (FL)
Union Coll (NY)
U of Michigan (MI)
U of Wisconsin–Madison (WI)

LATIN AMERICAN STUDIES

Adelphi U (NY)
Albright Coll (PA)
American U (DC)
Assumption Coll (MA)
Bard Coll (NY)
Bard Coll at Simon's Rock (MA)
Barnard Coll (NY)
Beloit Coll (WI)
Bennington Coll (VT)
Blackburn Coll (IL)
Boston U (MA)
Bowdoin Coll (ME)
Brandeis U (MA)
Brown U (RI)
Bucknell U (PA)
California State U, Chico (CA)
California State U, Fullerton (CA)
California State U, Los Angeles (CA)
California State U, Northridge (CA)
Carleton Coll (MN)
Carnegie Mellon U (PA)
City Coll of the City U of New York (NY)
Claremont McKenna Coll (CA)
Colby Coll (ME)
Colgate U (NY)
The Coll of William and Mary (VA)
Columbia U, School of General Studies (NY)
Connecticut Coll (CT)
Cornell Coll (IA)
Dartmouth Coll (NH)
Denison U (OH)
DePaul U (IL)
Dickinson Coll (PA)
Earlham Coll (IN)
Flagler Coll (FL)
Fort Lewis Coll (CO)
Gettysburg Coll (PA)
Hamline U (MN)
Hampshire Coll (MA)
Haverford Coll (PA)
Hobart and William Smith Colls (NY)
Hofstra U (NY)
Hood Coll (MD)
Hunter Coll of the City U of New York (NY)
Illinois Wesleyan U (IL)
The Johns Hopkins U (MD)
Kent State U (OH)
Lake Forest Coll (IL)
Lehman Coll of the City U of New York (NY)
Macalester Coll (MN)
Marlboro Coll (VT)
Miami U (OH)
Middlebury Coll (VT)
Millsaps Coll (MS)
New Coll of Florida (FL)
New York U (NY)
Oberlin Coll (OH)
Ohio U (OH)
Ohio Wesleyan U (OH)
Pace U (NY)
Penn State Abington (PA)
Penn State Altoona (PA)
Penn State Beaver (PA)
Penn State Berks (PA)
Penn State Brandywine (PA)
Penn State DuBois (PA)
Penn State Erie, The Behrend Coll (PA)
Penn State Fayette, The Eberly Campus (PA)

Penn State Greater Allegheny (PA)
Penn State Hazleton (PA)
Penn State Lehigh Valley (PA)
Penn State Mont Alto (PA)
Penn State New Kensington (PA)
Penn State Schuylkill (PA)
Penn State Shenango (PA)
Penn State U Park (PA)
Penn State Wilkes-Barre (PA)
Penn State Worthington Scranton (PA)
Penn State York (PA)
Pomona Coll (CA)
Portland State U (OR)
Queens Coll of the City U of New York (NY)
Rhode Island Coll (RI)
Rice U (TX)
Ripon Coll (WI)
Rutgers, The State U of New Jersey, New Brunswick (NJ)
St. Edward's U (TX)
Saint Mary's Coll of California (CA)
St. Olaf Coll (MN)
Samford U (AL)
San Diego State U (CA)
Sarah Lawrence Coll (NY)
Scripps Coll (CA)
Seattle Pacific U (WA)
Skidmore Coll (NY)
Smith Coll (MA)
Southern Methodist U (TX)
State U of New York at Binghamton (NY)
State U of New York at New Paltz (NY)
State U of New York at Plattsburgh (NY)
Syracuse U (NY)
Temple U (PA)
Texas Tech U (TX)
Trinity U (TX)
Tulane U (LA)
United States Military Acad (NY)
The U of Alabama (AL)
The U of Arizona (AZ)
The U of British Columbia (BC, Canada)
U of California, Berkeley (CA)
U of California, Los Angeles (CA)
U of California, Santa Cruz (CA)
U of Delaware (DE)
U of Denver (CO)
U of Georgia (GA)
U of Idaho (ID)
U of Illinois at Chicago (IL)
The U of Iowa (IA)
The U of Kansas (KS)
U of Miami (FL)
U of Minnesota, Twin Cities Campus (MN)
U of Missouri (MO)
U of Nebraska at Omaha (NE)
U of Nebraska–Lincoln (NE)
The U of North Carolina at Chapel Hill (NC)
The U of North Carolina at Charlotte (NC)
U of Oregon (OR)
U of Pennsylvania (PA)
U of Richmond (VA)
U of San Francisco (CA)
U of South Carolina (SC)
The U of Texas at Austin (TX)
The U of Toledo (OH)
U of Utah (UT)
U of Vermont (VT)
U of Washington (WA)
The U of Western Ontario (ON, Canada)
U of Wisconsin–Eau Claire (WI)
Vanderbilt U (TN)
Vassar Coll (NY)
Washington Coll (MD)
Washington U in St. Louis (MO)
Wellesley Coll (MA)
Wesleyan U (CT)
Westminster Coll (UT)
Willamette U (OR)
Yale U (CT)

LATIN TEACHER EDUCATION

Assumption Coll (MA)
Boston U (MA)
Brigham Young U (UT)
Concordia Coll (MN)
Duquesne U (PA)
Indiana U Bloomington (IN)
Kent State U (OH)
Marquette U (WI)

Miami U (OH)
Missouri State U (MO)
Ohio Wesleyan U (OH)
Western Michigan U (MI)

LAY MINISTRY

Southeastern Bible Coll (AL)
Trevecca Nazarene U (TN)

LEGAL ADMINISTRATIVE ASSISTANT/SECRETARY

Clayton State U (GA)
Intl Business Coll, Fort Wayne (IN)
Lewis-Clark State Coll (ID)
U of Cincinnati (OH)

LEGAL ASSISTANT/PARALEGAL

Anna Maria Coll (MA)
Boston U (MA)
California State U, Chico (CA)
Calumet Coll of Saint Joseph (IN)
Champlain Coll (VT)
Clayton State U (GA)
Coll of Mount St. Joseph (OH)
Coll of Saint Mary (NE)
Concordia U Wisconsin (WI)
Davenport U, Grand Rapids (MI)
East Central U (OK)
Eastern Michigan U (MI)
Everest U, Tampa (FL)
Faulkner U (AL)
Florida Gulf Coast U (FL)
Gannon U (PA)
Grand Valley State U (MI)
Husson U (ME)
Intl Business Coll, Fort Wayne (IN)
Jones Coll, Jacksonville (FL)
Lake Superior State U (MI)
Lewis-Clark State Coll (ID)
Lewis U (IL)
Madonna U (MI)
Marymount U (VA)
Maryville U of Saint Louis (MO)
Minnesota School of Business–Blaine (MN)
Minnesota State U Moorhead (MN)
Mississippi U for Women (MS)
Morehead State U (KY)
New York City Coll of Technology of the City U of New York (NY)
Nova Southeastern U (FL)
Peirce Coll (PA)
Pennsylvania Coll of Technology (PA)
Quinnipiac U (CT)
Roosevelt U (IL)
Saint Mary-of-the-Woods Coll (IN)
St. Petersburg Coll (FL)
Southern Illinois U Carbondale (IL)
Stephen F. Austin State U (TX)
Stevens Inst of Business & Arts (MO)
Stevenson U (MD)
Suffolk U (MA)
Texas Woman's U (TX)
Thomas Edison State Coll (NJ)
U of Central Florida (FL)
U of Cincinnati (OH)
U of Evansville (IN)
U of Hartford (CT)
U of Houston–Clear Lake (TX)
U of La Verne (CA)
U of Southern Mississippi (MS)
The U of Tennessee at Chattanooga (TN)
U of West Florida (FL)
Ursuline Coll (OH)
Valdosta State U (GA)
Winona State U (MN)

LEGAL PROFESSIONS AND STUDIES RELATED

Ball State U (IN)
Central Pennsylvania Coll (PA)
Hamline U (MN)
Loyola U Chicago (IL)
Maryville U of Saint Louis (MO)
Missouri Southern State U (MO)
Montclair State U (NJ)
New Jersey Inst of Technology (NJ)
Ramapo Coll of New Jersey (NJ)
Skidmore Coll (NY)
Temple U (PA)
Texas Wesleyan U (TX)
Tulane U (LA)
U of Illinois at Springfield (IL)
U of Nebraska–Lincoln (NE)
U of Pennsylvania (PA)

U of Tulsa (OK)

LEGAL STUDIES

Adams State Coll (CO)
American Public U System (WV)
American U (DC)
Amherst Coll (MA)
Anna Maria Coll (MA)
Brenau U (GA)
Bridgewater State U (MA)
Brown Mackie Coll–Albuquerque (NM)
Brown Mackie Coll–Boise (ID)
Brown Mackie Coll–Fort Wayne (IN)
Brown Mackie Coll–Greenville (SC)
Brown Mackie Coll–Indianapolis (IN)
Brown Mackie Coll–Louisville (KY)
Brown Mackie Coll–Merrillville (IN)
Brown Mackie Coll–Michigan City (IN)
Brown Mackie Coll–Phoenix (AZ)
Brown Mackie Coll–St. Louis (MO)
Brown Mackie Coll–South Bend (IN)
Brown Mackie Coll–Tucson (AZ)
Brown Mackie Coll–Tulsa (OK)
Burlington Coll (VT)
California State U, Chico (CA)
Central Michigan U (MI)
Christopher Newport U (VA)
Claremont McKenna Coll (CA)
The Coll of Saint Rose (NY)
Coll of the Atlantic (ME)
DeSales U (PA)
Dickinson Coll (PA)
Florida National Coll (FL)
Goldey-Beacom Coll (DE)
Hampshire Coll (MA)
Harding U (AR)
Hood Coll (MD)
James Madison U (VA)
John Jay Coll of Criminal Justice of the City U of New York (NY)
Lake Superior State U (MI)
Lasell Coll (MA)
Laurentian U (ON, Canada)
Lipscomb U (TN)
Manhattanville Coll (NY)
Minnesota State U Moorhead (MN)
Montclair State U (NJ)
Mountain State U (WV)
National U (CA)
Newbury Coll (MA)
Northwest U (WA)
Oberlin Coll (OH)
Point Park U (PA)
Quinnipiac U (CT)
Sage Coll of Albany (NY)
St. John's U (NY)
Saint Joseph's U (PA)
Saint Louis U (MO)
Scripps Coll (CA)
State U of New York at Fredonia (NY)
Stevenson U (MD)
Suffolk U (MA)
Tiffin U (OH)
United States Air Force Acad (CO)
Université de Sherbrooke (QC, Canada)
U of Baltimore (MD)
U of California, Berkeley (CA)
U of California, Santa Barbara (CA)
U of California, Santa Cruz (CA)
U of Hartford (CT)
U of Maryland U Coll (MD)
U of Massachusetts Amherst (MA)
U of Miami (FL)
U of New Brunswick Fredericton (NB, Canada)
U of New Haven (CT)
U of Pittsburgh (PA)
The U of Western Ontario (ON, Canada)
U of Wisconsin–Madison (WI)
U of Wisconsin–Superior (WI)
Virginia Intermont Coll (VA)
Walden U (MN)
Washburn U (KS)
Webster U (MO)
Western Intl U (AZ)
Western New England U (MA)
Wilmington U (DE)
Winona State U (MN)

LIBERAL ARTS AND SCIENCES AND HUMANITIES RELATED

Anna Maria Coll (MA)

Auburn U (AL)
Barton Coll (NC)
Belhaven U (MS)
Bennington Coll (VT)
Brigham Young U (UT)
Bryan Coll (TN)
California Polytechnic State U, San Luis Obispo (CA)
California State U, Dominguez Hills (CA)
Carnegie Mellon U (PA)
Clarkson U (NY)
The Colorado Coll (CO)
Crown Coll (MN)
Fairfield U (CT)
Florida Atlantic U (FL)
Georgia Coll & State U (GA)
Goddard Coll (VT)
Hampshire Coll (MA)
The Johns Hopkins U (MD)
Loyola U New Orleans (LA)
Malone U (OH)
Marshall U (WV)
Marymount Coll, Palos Verdes, California (CA)
Mitchell Coll (CT)
Mount Aloysius Coll (PA)
North Carolina State U (NC)
Ohio U (OH)
Ohio U–Chillicothe (OH)
Oklahoma Panhandle State U (OK)
Purdue U (IN)
Sacred Heart U (CT)
Saint Anselm Coll (NH)
St. John's Coll (NM)
Saint Louis U (MO)
Saint Mary's Coll of California (CA)
Salem State U (MA)
Sarah Lawrence Coll (NY)
Shimer Coll (IL)
Southern Methodist U (TX)
State U of New York Maritime Coll (NY)
Tulane U (LA)
The U of Akron (OH)
U of California, Los Angeles (CA)
U of California, Santa Barbara (CA)
U of Louisville (KY)
U of Mary Washington (VA)
U of Massachusetts Amherst (MA)
U of Minnesota, Twin Cities Campus (MN)
U of Oklahoma (OK)
U of Rhode Island (RI)
U of South Alabama (AL)
U of Wisconsin–River Falls (WI)
U of Wisconsin–Whitewater (WI)
Valdosta State U (GA)
Vassar Coll (NY)
Walsh U (OH)
Wayland Baptist U (TX)
Western Illinois U (IL)
Wichita State U (KS)

LIBERAL ARTS AND SCIENCES/ LIBERAL STUDIES

Abilene Christian U (TX)
Adams State Coll (CO)
Alcorn State U (MS)
Alderson-Broaddus Coll (WV)
Alma Coll (MI)
Alvernia U (PA)
Alverno Coll (WI)
American Jewish U (CA)
American U (DC)
Amridge U (AL)
Angelo State U (TX)
Anna Maria Coll (MA)
Antioch U Midwest (OH)
Appalachian State U (NC)
Aquinas Coll (MI)
Aquinas Coll (TN)
Arcadia U (PA)
Arizona State U (AZ)
Armstrong Atlantic State U (GA)
Ashland U (OH)
Athabasca U (AB, Canada)
Auburn U Montgomery (AL)
Augsburg Coll (MN)
Augustana Coll (IL)
Augustana Coll (SD)
Azusa Pacific U (CA)
Ball State U (IN)
Barry U (FL)
Beacon Coll (FL)
Bellarmine U (KY)
Bemidji State U (MN)
Benedictine Coll (KS)

Bennington Coll (VT)
Bentley U (MA)
Bethany Lutheran Coll (MN)
Bethel Coll (IN)
Bethune-Cookman U (FL)
Biola U (CA)
Bluefield Coll (VA)
Boise State U (ID)
Bowling Green State U (OH)
Brenau U (GA)
Bridgewater Coll (VA)
Brigham Young U (UT)
Brock U (ON, Canada)
Bryan Coll (TN)
Butler U (IN)
Cabrini Coll (PA)
California Baptist U (CA)
California Polytechnic State U, San Luis Obispo (CA)
California State Polytechnic U, Pomona (CA)
California State U, Bakersfield (CA)
California State U, Chico (CA)
California State U, Dominguez Hills (CA)
California State U, Fullerton (CA)
California State U, Long Beach (CA)
California State U, Los Angeles (CA)
California State U, Monterey Bay (CA)
California State U, Northridge (CA)
California State U, San Bernardino (CA)
California State U, San Marcos (CA)
California State U, Stanislaus (CA)
Calumet Coll of Saint Joseph (IN)
Cambridge Coll (MA)
Canisius Coll (NY)
Carlow U (PA)
Carnegie Mellon U (PA)
Carson-Newman Coll (TN)
The Catholic U of America (DC)
Cedar Crest Coll (PA)
Central Michigan U (MI)
Chapman U (CA)
Chestnut Hill Coll (PA)
Christian Brothers U (TN)
Clarion U of Pennsylvania (PA)
Clarkson U (NY)
Clayton State U (GA)
Cleveland State U (OH)
Coastal Carolina U (SC)
Coll of Mount St. Joseph (OH)
Coll of Saint Benedict (MN)
Coll of St. Joseph (VT)
Coll of Staten Island of the City U of New York (NY)
Coll of the Atlantic (ME)
Colorado State U (CO)
Columbia Coll (SC)
Columbia Coll Chicago (IL)
Columbus State U (GA)
Concordia Coll–New York (NY)
Concordia U (CA)
Concordia U Wisconsin (WI)
Coppin State U (MD)
Corban U (OR)
Cornell Coll (IA)
Cornell U (NY)
Culver-Stockton Coll (MO)
Cumberland U (TN)
Dakota State U (SD)
Dakota Wesleyan U (SD)
Dallas Baptist U (TX)
Defiance Coll (OH)
DEREE - The American Coll of Greece (Greece)
DeSales U (PA)
DeVry U, Pomona (CA)
DeVry U, Westminster (CO)
DeVry U, Miramar (FL)
DeVry U, Chicago (IL)
DeVry U, Kansas City (MO)
DeVry U, Houston (TX)
DeVry U, Irving (TX)
DeVry U, Federal Way (WA)
Dickinson State U (ND)
Dominican U (IL)
Dominican U of California (CA)
Dowling Coll (NY)
Duquesne U (PA)
Eastern Illinois U (IL)
Eastern New Mexico U (NM)
Eastern Oregon U (OR)
East Stroudsburg U of Pennsylvania (PA)
East Tennessee State U (TN)

Elmira Coll (NY)
Emmanuel Coll (MA)
Endicott Coll (MA)
Eugene Lang Coll The New School for Liberal Arts (NY)
The Evergreen State Coll (WA)
Faulkner U (AL)
Felician Coll (NJ)
Ferrum Coll (VA)
Fitchburg State U (MA)
Flagler Coll (FL)
Florida Atlantic U (FL)
Florida Coll (FL)
Florida Gulf Coast U (FL)
Florida Intl U (FL)
Fontbonne U (MO)
Fort Lewis Coll (CO)
Framingham State U (MA)
Francis Marion U (SC)
Franklin Pierce U (NH)
Freed-Hardeman U (TN)
Friends U (KS)
Gannon U (PA)
Georgetown Coll (KY)
Georgetown U (DC)
Gettysburg Coll (PA)
Governors State U (IL)
Graceland U (IA)
Grand Valley State U (MI)
Grand View U (IA)
Granite State Coll (NH)
Greenville Coll (IL)
Hannibal-LaGrange U (MO)
Harvard U (MA)
Hillsdale Free Will Baptist Coll (OK)
Hofstra U (NY)
Holy Cross Coll (IN)
Holy Family U (PA)
Holy Names U (CA)
Houghton Coll (NY)
Humboldt State U (CA)
Husson U (ME)
Illinois Coll (IL)
Illinois Inst of Technology (IL)
Illinois Wesleyan U (IL)
Immaculata U (PA)
Indiana State U (IN)
Indiana U Bloomington (IN)
Iowa State U of Science and Technology (IA)
Iowa Wesleyan Coll (IA)
Ithaca Coll (NY)
James Madison U (VA)
The Johns Hopkins U (MD)
Johnson C. Smith U (NC)
Johnson State Coll (VT)
Juniata Coll (PA)
Kent State U (OH)
Kent State U at Tuscarawas (OH)
Kentucky State U (KY)
Keuka Coll (NY)
Lakehead U (ON, Canada)
Lamar U (TX)
La Roche Coll (PA)
Lasell Coll (MA)
Laurentian U (ON, Canada)
Lesley U (MA)
Lewis U (IL)
Limestone Coll (SC)
Lincoln Memorial U (TN)
Lincoln U (MO)
Lindenwood U (MO)
Lock Haven U of Pennsylvania (PA)
Long Island U, Brooklyn Campus (NY)
Long Island U, C.W. Post Campus (NY)
Longwood U (VA)
Louisiana Coll (LA)
Louisiana State U and Ag and Mech Coll (LA)
Loyola Marymount U (CA)
Lubbock Christian U (TX)
Lynn U (FL)
MacMurray Coll (IL)
Manchester Coll (IN)
Manhattan Coll (NY)
Mansfield U of Pennsylvania (PA)
Marian U (WI)
Marietta Coll (OH)
Mars Hill Coll (NC)
Marymount Coll, Palos Verdes, California (CA)
Marymount U (VA)
Maryville U of Saint Louis (MO)
Massachusetts Coll of Liberal Arts (MA)

Massachusetts Inst of Technology (MA)
The Master's Coll and Sem (CA)
Medaille Coll (NY)
Mercer U (GA)
Merrimack Coll (MA)
Mesa State Coll (CO)
Metropolitan State U (MN)
Miami U (OH)
Middlebury Coll (VT)
Middle Tennessee State U (TN)
Midway Coll (KY)
Midwestern State U (TX)
Misericordia U (PA)
Mississippi State U (MS)
Mississippi U for Women (MS)
Mitchell Coll (CT)
Monmouth Coll (IL)
Montana State U (MT)
Montana State U Billings (MT)
Montana Tech of The U of Montana (MT)
Morris Coll (SC)
Mount Allison U (NB, Canada)
Mount Aloysius Coll (PA)
Mount Ida Coll (MA)
Mount Marty Coll (SD)
Mount St. Mary's Coll (CA)
Murray State U (KY)
National-Louis U (IL)
Neumann U (PA)
New Coll of Florida (FL)
Newman U (KS)
New Mexico Highlands U (NM)
New Saint Andrews Coll (ID)
The New School for General Studies (NY)
New York City Coll of Technology of the City U of New York (NY)
New York U (NY)
Niagara U (NY)
North Carolina Ag and Tech State U (NC)
North Carolina State U (NC)
North Central Coll (IL)
Northeastern Illinois U (IL)
Northern Arizona U (AZ)
Northern Illinois U (IL)
Northern Kentucky U (KY)
Northern Michigan U (MI)
North Greenville U (SC)
Northwestern State U of Louisiana (LA)
Northwest Nazarene U (ID)
Notre Dame de Namur U (CA)
Ohio Valley U (WV)
Oklahoma Christian U (OK)
Oklahoma City U (OK)
Oklahoma State U (OK)
Oregon State U (OR)
Our Lady of the Lake U of San Antonio (TX)
Pacific U (OR)
Patrick Henry Coll (VA)
Penn State Abington (PA)
Penn State Altoona (PA)
Penn State Beaver (PA)
Penn State Berks (PA)
Penn State Brandywine (PA)
Penn State DuBois (PA)
Penn State Erie, The Behrend Coll (PA)
Penn State Fayette, The Eberly Campus (PA)
Penn State Greater Allegheny (PA)
Penn State Lehigh Valley (PA)
Penn State Mont Alto (PA)
Penn State New Kensington (PA)
Penn State Schuylkill (PA)
Penn State Shenango (PA)
Penn State U Park (PA)
Penn State Wilkes-Barre (PA)
Penn State Worthington Scranton (PA)
Penn State York (PA)
Pepperdine U, Malibu (CA)
Point Park U (PA)
Polytechnic Inst of NYU (NY)
Pomona Coll (CA)
Portland State U (OR)
Prescott Coll (AZ)
Providence Coll (RI)
Purchase Coll, State U of New York (NY)
Purdue U North Central (IN)
Quincy U (IL)
Quinnipiac U (CT)
Ramapo Coll of New Jersey (NJ)

INDEXES

MATERIALS ENGINEERING

MATERIALS SCIENCE

MATERNAL AND CHILD HEALTH

MATHEMATICAL BIOLOGY

MATHEMATICAL STATISTICS AND PROBABILITY

MATHEMATICS

Our Lady of the Lake U of San Antonio (TX)
Pace U (NY)
Pacific Lutheran U (WA)
Pacific Union Coll (CA)
Pacific U (OR)
Paine Coll (GA)
Palm Beach Atlantic U (FL)
Penn State Abington (PA)
Penn State Altoona (PA)
Penn State Beaver (PA)
Penn State Berks (PA)
Penn State Brandywine (PA)
Penn State DuBois (PA)
Penn State Erie, The Behrend Coll (PA)
Penn State Fayette, The Eberly Campus (PA)
Penn State Greater Allegheny (PA)
Penn State Hazleton (PA)
Penn State Lehigh Valley (PA)
Penn State Mont Alto (PA)
Penn State New Kensington (PA)
Penn State Schuylkill (PA)
Penn State Shenango (PA)
Penn State U Park (PA)
Penn State Wilkes-Barre (PA)
Penn State Worthington Scranton (PA)
Penn State York (PA)
Pepperdine U, Malibu (CA)
Piedmont Coll (GA)
Pikeville Coll (KY)
Pittsburg State U (KS)
Pitzer Coll (CA)
Polytechnic Inst of NYU (NY)
Pomona Coll (CA)
Portland State U (OR)
Prairie View A&M U (TX)
Presbyterian Coll (SC)
Princeton U (NJ)
Principia Coll (IL)
Providence Coll (RI)
Purchase Coll, State U of New York (NY)
Purdue U (IN)
Purdue U Calumet (IN)
Queens Coll of the City U of New York (NY)
Quincy U (IL)
Quinnipiac U (CT)
Radford U (VA)
Ramapo Coll of New Jersey (NJ)
Randolph Coll (VA)
Randolph-Macon Coll (VA)
Reed Coll (OR)
Regent U (VA)
Regis U (CO)
Reinhardt U (GA)
Rensselaer Polytechnic Inst (NY)
Rhode Island Coll (RI)
Rhodes Coll (TN)
Rice U (TX)
The Richard Stockton Coll of New Jersey (NJ)
Rider U (NJ)
Ripon Coll (WI)
Rivier Coll (NH)
Roanoke Coll (VA)
Rockford Coll (IL)
Rockhurst U (MO)
Rocky Mountain Coll (MT)
Rollins Coll (FL)
Roosevelt U (IL)
Rose-Hulman Inst of Technology (IN)
Rosemont Coll (PA)
Rowan U (NJ)
Russell Sage Coll (NY)
Rust Coll (MS)
Rutgers, The State U of New Jersey, Camden (NJ)
Rutgers, The State U of New Jersey, Newark (NJ)
Rutgers, The State U of New Jersey, New Brunswick (NJ)
Sacred Heart U (CT)
Saginaw Valley State U (MI)
St. Ambrose U (IA)
Saint Anselm Coll (NH)
St. Bonaventure U (NY)
St. Catherine U (MN)
St. Edward's U (TX)
Saint Francis U (PA)
St. Francis Xavier U (NS, Canada)
St. John Fisher Coll (NY)
Saint John's U (MN)
St. John's U (NY)
Saint Joseph Coll (CT)
Saint Joseph's Coll (IN)

St. Joseph's Coll, Long Island Campus (NY)
St. Joseph's Coll, New York (NY)
Saint Joseph's Coll of Maine (ME)
Saint Joseph's U (PA)
St. Lawrence U (NY)
Saint Leo U (FL)
Saint Louis U (MO)
Saint Martin's U (WA)
Saint Mary-of-the-Woods Coll (IN)
Saint Mary's Coll (IN)
Saint Mary's Coll of California (CA)
St. Mary's Coll of Maryland (MD)
Saint Mary's U of Minnesota (MN)
Saint Michael's Coll (VT)
St. Norbert Coll (WI)
St. Olaf Coll (MN)
St. Thomas Aquinas Coll (NY)
St. Thomas U (FL)
St. Thomas U (NB, Canada)
Saint Xavier U (IL)
Salem State U (MA)
Salisbury U (MD)
Salve Regina U (RI)
Samford U (AL)
Sam Houston State U (TX)
San Diego Christian Coll (CA)
San Diego State U (CA)
San Francisco State U (CA)
San Jose State U (CA)
Santa Clara U (CA)
Sarah Lawrence Coll (NY)
Savannah State U (GA)
Schreiner U (TX)
Scripps Coll (CA)
Seattle Pacific U (WA)
Seton Hill U (PA)
Sewanee: The U of the South (TN)
Shawnee State U (OH)
Shenandoah U (VA)
Shepherd U (WV)
Shippensburg U of Pennsylvania (PA)
Shorter U (GA)
Siena Coll (NY)
Siena Heights U (MI)
Silver Lake Coll (WI)
Simmons Coll (MA)
Simon Fraser U (BC, Canada)
Simpson Coll (IA)
Simpson U (CA)
Skidmore Coll (NY)
Slippery Rock U of Pennsylvania (PA)
Smith Coll (MA)
Sonoma State U (CA)
South Dakota School of Mines and Technology (SD)
South Dakota State U (SD)
Southeastern Louisiana U (LA)
Southeastern Oklahoma State U (OK)
Southeastern U (FL)
Southeast Missouri State U (MO)
Southern Adventist U (TN)
Southern Arkansas U–Magnolia (AR)
Southern Connecticut State U (CT)
Southern Illinois U Carbondale (IL)
Southern Illinois U Edwardsville (IL)
Southern Methodist U (TX)
Southern Nazarene U (OK)
Southern Oregon U (OR)
Southern Polytechnic State U (GA)
Southern Utah U (UT)
Southern Wesleyan U (SC)
Southwestern Adventist U (TX)
Southwestern Coll (KS)
Spelman Coll (GA)
Spring Arbor U (MI)
Springfield Coll (MA)
Spring Hill Coll (AL)
Stanford U (CA)
State U of New York at Binghamton (NY)
State U of New York at Fredonia (NY)
State U of New York at New Paltz (NY)
State U of New York at Oswego (NY)
State U of New York at Plattsburgh (NY)
State U of New York Coll at Geneseo (NY)
State U of New York Coll at Old Westbury (NY)
State U of New York Coll at Oneonta (NY)

State U of New York Coll at Potsdam (NY)
State U of New York Empire State Coll (NY)
Stephen F. Austin State U (TX)
Stetson U (FL)
Stonehill Coll (MA)
Stony Brook U, State U of New York (NY)
Suffolk U (MA)
Sul Ross State U (TX)
Susquehanna U (PA)
Swarthmore Coll (PA)
Sweet Briar Coll (VA)
Syracuse U (NY)
Tabor Coll (KS)
Talladega Coll (AL)
Tarleton State U (TX)
Taylor U (IN)
Temple U (PA)
Tennessee Technological U (TN)
Tennessee Wesleyan Coll (TN)
Texas A&M Intl U (TX)
Texas A&M U (TX)
Texas A&M U–Corpus Christi (TX)
Texas A&M U–Kingsville (TX)
Texas Christian U (TX)
Texas Lutheran U (TX)
Texas Southern U (TX)
Texas State U–San Marcos (TX)
Texas Tech U (TX)
Texas Wesleyan U (TX)
Texas Woman's U (TX)
Thiel Coll (PA)
Thomas Edison State Coll (NJ)
Thomas More Coll (KY)
Towson U (MD)
Transylvania U (KY)
Trent U (ON, Canada)
Trevecca Nazarene U (TN)
Trine U (IN)
Trinity Coll (CT)
Trinity U (TX)
Troy U (AL)
Truman State U (MO)
Tufts U (MA)
Tulane U (LA)
Tuskegee U (AL)
Union Coll (KY)
Union Coll (NE)
Union Coll (NY)
Union U (TN)
United States Air Force Acad (CO)
United States Military Acad (NY)
United States Naval Acad (MD)
Université de Sherbrooke (QC, Canada)
U at Buffalo, the State U of New York (NY)
The U of Akron (OH)
The U of Alabama (AL)
The U of Alabama at Birmingham (AL)
The U of Alabama in Huntsville (AL)
U of Alaska Fairbanks (AK)
U of Alaska Southeast (AK)
The U of Arizona (AZ)
U of Arkansas (AR)
U of Arkansas at Pine Bluff (AR)
U of Arkansas–Fort Smith (AR)
U of Bridgeport (CT)
The U of British Columbia (BC, Canada)
The U of British Columbia–Okanagan (BC, Canada)
U of California, Berkeley (CA)
U of California, Davis (CA)
U of California, Irvine (CA)
U of California, Los Angeles (CA)
U of California, Santa Barbara (CA)
U of California, Santa Cruz (CA)
U of Central Florida (FL)
U of Central Missouri (MO)
U of Cincinnati (OH)
U of Colorado at Colorado Springs (CO)
U of Colorado Boulder (CO)
U of Colorado Denver (CO)
U of Dallas (TX)
U of Dayton (OH)
U of Delaware (DE)
U of Denver (CO)
U of Dubuque (IA)
U of Evansville (IN)
The U of Findlay (OH)
U of Florida (FL)
U of Georgia (GA)
U of Guelph (ON, Canada)
U of Hartford (CT)
U of Hawaii at Hilo (HI)

U of Hawaii at Manoa (HI)
U of Houston (TX)
U of Houston–Clear Lake (TX)
U of Houston–Downtown (TX)
U of Houston–Victoria (TX)
U of Idaho (ID)
U of Illinois at Chicago (IL)
U of Illinois at Springfield (IL)
U of Indianapolis (IN)
The U of Iowa (IA)
The U of Kansas (KS)
U of La Verne (CA)
U of Lethbridge (AB, Canada)
U of Louisiana at Lafayette (LA)
U of Louisiana at Monroe (LA)
U of Louisville (KY)
U of Maine (ME)
U of Maine at Farmington (ME)
U of Manitoba (MB, Canada)
U of Mary Hardin-Baylor (TX)
U of Maryland, Baltimore County (MD)
U of Maryland, Coll Park (MD)
U of Mary Washington (VA)
U of Massachusetts Amherst (MA)
U of Massachusetts Boston (MA)
U of Massachusetts Dartmouth (MA)
U of Massachusetts Lowell (MA)
U of Memphis (TN)
U of Miami (FL)
U of Michigan (MI)
U of Michigan–Dearborn (MI)
U of Michigan–Flint (MI)
U of Minnesota, Duluth (MN)
U of Minnesota, Twin Cities Campus (MN)
U of Mississippi (MS)
U of Missouri (MO)
U of Missouri–St. Louis (MO)
U of Mobile (AL)
The U of Montana Western (MT)
U of Montevallo (AL)
U of Mount Union (OH)
U of Nebraska at Omaha (NE)
U of Nebraska–Lincoln (NE)
U of Nevada, Las Vegas (NV)
U of Nevada, Reno (NV)
U of New Brunswick Fredericton (NB, Canada)
U of New Brunswick Saint John (NB, Canada)
U of New England (ME)
U of New Hampshire (NH)
U of New Haven (CT)
The U of North Carolina at Asheville (NC)
The U of North Carolina at Chapel Hill (NC)
The U of North Carolina at Charlotte (NC)
The U of North Carolina at Greensboro (NC)
The U of North Carolina at Pembroke (NC)
The U of North Carolina Wilmington (NC)
U of North Dakota (ND)
U of Northern Colorado (CO)
U of Northern Iowa (IA)
U of North Florida (FL)
U of North Texas (TX)
U of Notre Dame (IN)
U of Oklahoma (OK)
U of Oregon (OR)
U of Ottawa (ON, Canada)
U of Pennsylvania (PA)
U of Pittsburgh (PA)
U of Pittsburgh at Johnstown (PA)
U of Portland (OR)
U of Puget Sound (WA)
U of Redlands (CA)
U of Regina (SK, Canada)
U of Rhode Island (RI)
U of Richmond (VA)
U of Rio Grande (OH)
U of Rochester (NY)
U of St. Francis (IL)
U of Saint Mary (KS)
U of St. Thomas (MN)
U of St. Thomas (TX)
U of San Diego (CA)
U of San Francisco (CA)
U of Saskatchewan (SK, Canada)
U of Science and Arts of Oklahoma (OK)
The U of Scranton (PA)
U of Sioux Falls (SD)
U of South Carolina (SC)
U of South Carolina Upstate (SC)
The U of South Dakota (SD)

U of Southern California (CA)
U of Southern Indiana (IN)
U of Southern Maine (ME)
U of Southern Mississippi (MS)
U of South Florida (FL)
The U of Tampa (FL)
The U of Tennessee (TN)
The U of Tennessee at Chattanooga (TN)
The U of Tennessee at Martin (TN)
The U of Texas at Arlington (TX)
The U of Texas at Austin (TX)
The U of Texas at Dallas (TX)
The U of Texas at San Antonio (TX)
The U of Texas at Tyler (TX)
The U of Texas of the Permian Basin (TX)
The U of Texas–Pan American (TX)
U of the Cumberlands (KY)
U of the District of Columbia (DC)
U of the Incarnate Word (TX)
U of the Ozarks (AR)
U of the Pacific (CA)
U of the Virgin Islands (VI)
The U of Toledo (OH)
U of Tulsa (OK)
U of Utah (UT)
U of Vermont (VT)
U of Virginia (VA)
U of Washington (WA)
U of Waterloo (ON, Canada)
The U of Western Ontario (ON, Canada)
U of West Florida (FL)
U of West Georgia (GA)
U of Wisconsin–Eau Claire (WI)
U of Wisconsin–Green Bay (WI)
U of Wisconsin–La Crosse (WI)
U of Wisconsin–Madison (WI)
U of Wisconsin–Parkside (WI)
U of Wisconsin–Platteville (WI)
U of Wisconsin–River Falls (WI)
U of Wisconsin–Stevens Point (WI)
U of Wisconsin–Superior (WI)
U of Wisconsin–Whitewater (WI)
U of Wyoming (WY)
Upper Iowa U (IA)
Ursuline Coll (OH)
Utah State U (UT)
Utah Valley U (UT)
Valdosta State U (GA)
Valparaiso U (IN)
Vanderbilt U (TN)
Vassar Coll (NY)
Villanova U (PA)
Virginia Commonwealth U (VA)
Virginia Military Inst (VA)
Virginia Polytechnic Inst and State U (VA)
Virginia State U (VA)
Virginia Wesleyan Coll (VA)
Viterbo U (WI)
Wabash Coll (IN)
Wagner Coll (NY)
Wake Forest U (NC)
Walla Walla U (WA)
Walsh U (OH)
Wartburg Coll (IA)
Washburn U (KS)
Washington Adventist U (MD)
Washington & Jefferson Coll (PA)
Washington and Lee U (VA)
Washington Coll (MD)
Washington State U (WA)
Washington U in St. Louis (MO)
Wayland Baptist U (TX)
Waynesburg U (PA)
Wayne State Coll (NE)
Wayne State U (MI)
Weber State U (UT)
Webster U (MO)
Wellesley Coll (MA)
Wells Coll (NY)
Wesleyan Coll (GA)
Wesleyan U (CT)
West Chester U of Pennsylvania (PA)
Western Carolina U (NC)
Western Connecticut State U (CT)
Western Illinois U (IL)
Western Kentucky U (KY)
Western Michigan U (MI)
Western New England U (MA)
Western Oregon U (OR)
Western State Coll of Colorado (CO)
Westfield State U (MA)
West Liberty U (WV)
Westminster Coll (MO)
Westminster Coll (UT)
Westmont Coll (CA)

INDEXES

West Virginia U (WV)
Wheaton Coll (IL)
Wheaton Coll (MA)
Wheeling Jesuit U (WV)
Whitman Coll (WA)
Wichita State U (KS)
Widener U (PA)
Wilfrid Laurier U (ON, Canada)
Wilkes U (PA)
Willamette U (OR)
William Jewell Coll (MO)
William Paterson U of New Jersey (NJ)
Williams Coll (MA)
Wilmington Coll (OH)
Wingate U (NC)
Winona State U (MN)
Winthrop U (SC)
Wittenberg U (OH)
Wofford Coll (SC)
Worcester Polytechnic Inst (MA)
Worcester State U (MA)
Wright State U (OH)
Xavier U (OH)
Xavier U of Louisiana (LA)
Yale U (CT)
York Coll of Pennsylvania (PA)
York Coll of the City U of New York (NY)
Youngstown State U (OH)

MATHEMATICS AND COMPUTER SCIENCE

Anderson U (IN)
Bennington Coll (VT)
Boston U (MA)
Bowdoin Coll (ME)
Brown U (RI)
Bryan Coll (TN)
Central Coll (IA)
Central Michigan U (MI)
Chestnut Hill Coll (PA)
The Colorado Coll (CO)
Delaware State U (DE)
DePaul U (IL)
Drew U (NJ)
Eastern Illinois U (IL)
Florida Southern Coll (FL)
Friends U (KS)
Hampden-Sydney Coll (VA)
Hofstra U (NY)
Immaculata U (PA)
Indiana U–Purdue U Fort Wayne (IN)
Ithaca Coll (NY)
Lake Superior State U (MI)
Lawrence Technological U (MI)
Lawrence U (WI)
Long Island U, C.W. Post Campus (NY)
Loyola U Chicago (IL)
Manchester Coll (IN)
Massachusetts Inst of Technology (MA)
Mount Allison U (NB, Canada)
Paine Coll (GA)
Piedmont Coll (GA)
Saint Francis U (PA)
St. Joseph's Coll, Long Island Campus (NY)
St. Joseph's Coll, New York (NY)
St. Lawrence U (NY)
Saint Mary's Coll (IN)
Saint Mary's Coll of California (CA)
Saint Mary's U of Minnesota (MN)
Salem State U (MA)
Santa Clara U (CA)
Southern Oregon U (OR)
Springfield Coll (MA)
Stanford U (CA)
Tabor Coll (KS)
Temple U (PA)
U of Illinois at Chicago (IL)
U of Oregon (OR)
U of Regina (SK, Canada)
U of St. Francis (IL)
The U of Tampa (FL)
The U of Texas at Austin (TX)
U of Waterloo (ON, Canada)
Washington U in St. Louis (MO)
Whitman Coll (WA)
Yale U (CT)

MATHEMATICS AND STATISTICS

Dakota State U (SD)
Luther Coll (IA)

MATHEMATICS AND STATISTICS RELATED

The American U of Paris (France)
Anderson U (IN)
Carnegie Mellon U (PA)
Columbia U, School of General Studies (NY)
Delaware State U (DE)
The Evergreen State Coll (WA)
Hofstra U (NY)
Indiana U of Pennsylvania (PA)
Lycoming Coll (PA)
New York U (NY)
Ohio U (OH)
Oregon State U (OR)
Purchase Coll, State U of New York (NY)
St. Joseph's Coll, Long Island Campus (NY)
St. Joseph's Coll, New York (NY)
Saint Mary's Coll of California (CA)
Seattle Pacific U (WA)
Taylor U (IN)
Tulane U (LA)
The U of British Columbia–Okanagan (BC, Canada)
U of New Hampshire (NH)
The U of North Carolina at Charlotte (NC)
U of Pittsburgh (PA)
U of Regina (SK, Canada)
U of Rochester (NY)
The U of Scranton (PA)
U of South Alabama (AL)
Western State Coll of Colorado (CO)

MATHEMATICS RELATED

California Baptist U (CA)
Hillsdale Coll (MI)
Reinhardt U (GA)
Seton Hill U (PA)
Sweet Briar Coll (VA)
United States Military Acad (NY)
U of California, Los Angeles (CA)
U of Miami (FL)
U of Pittsburgh (PA)
U of Waterloo (ON, Canada)
Wheelock Coll (MA)

MATHEMATICS TEACHER EDUCATION

Abilene Christian U (TX)
Adams State Coll (CO)
Alma Coll (MI)
Alvernia U (PA)
Anderson U (IN)
Anderson U (SC)
Appalachian State U (NC)
Arkansas State U (AR)
Arkansas Tech U (AR)
Assumption Coll (MA)
Auburn U (AL)
Augustana Coll (IL)
Averett U (VA)
Baptist Bible Coll of Pennsylvania (PA)
Berry Coll (GA)
Bethany Coll (KS)
Bethel Coll (IN)
Bethel U (MN)
Biola U (CA)
Blackburn Coll (IL)
Bluefield Coll (VA)
Blue Mountain Coll (MS)
Bob Jones U (SC)
Boston U (MA)
Bowie State U (MD)
Bridgewater Coll (VA)
Brock U (ON, Canada)
Bryan Coll (TN)
Buena Vista U (IA)
Cabrini Coll (PA)
California State U, Chico (CA)
California State U, Long Beach (CA)
Calvin Coll (MI)
Cameron U (OK)
Campbellsville U (KY)
Capital U (OH)
Carroll U (WI)
Castleton State Coll (VT)
Cedarville U (OH)
Central Michigan U (MI)
Chipola Coll (FL)
Christian Brothers U (TN)
City Coll of the City U of New York (NY)
Claflin U (SC)
Clearwater Christian Coll (FL)
Clemson U (SC)
Coker Coll (SC)
The Coll of New Jersey (NJ)
The Coll of Saint Rose (NY)
Coll of the Ozarks (MO)
Colorado State U (CO)
Columbus State U (GA)
Concordia Coll (MN)
Concordia U Chicago (IL)
Concordia U, St. Paul (MN)
Corban U (OR)
Covenant Coll (GA)
Culver-Stockton Coll (MO)
Cumberland U (TN)
Dakota State U (SD)
Dakota Wesleyan U (SD)
Daytona State Coll (FL)
Delaware State U (DE)
Delta State U (MS)
Dominican U (NY)
Dowling Coll (NY)
Duquesne U (PA)
Eastern Michigan U (MI)
Eastern Washington U (WA)
East Texas Baptist U (TX)
Edgewood Coll (WI)
Elizabeth City State U (NC)
Elmhurst Coll (IL)
Elmira Coll (NY)
Emmanuel Coll (GA)
Fayetteville State U (NC)
Felician Coll (NJ)
Ferris State U (MI)
Fitchburg State U (MA)
Florida Ag and Mech U (FL)
Florida Atlantic U (FL)
Florida Inst of Technology (FL)
Franklin Coll (IN)
Freed-Hardeman U (TN)
Friends U (KS)
Gardner-Webb U (NC)
Geneva Coll (PA)
Grace Coll (IN)
Grand Canyon U (AZ)
Grand Valley State U (MI)
Greensboro Coll (NC)
Greenville Coll (IL)
Hannibal-LaGrange U (MO)
Harding U (AR)
Hardin-Simmons U (TX)
Hawai'i Pacific U (HI)
Hofstra U (NY)
Hope Coll (MI)
Hunter Coll of the City U of New York (NY)
Huntingdon Coll (AL)
Huntington U (IN)
Indiana U Bloomington (IN)
Indiana U Northwest (IN)
Indiana U–Purdue U Fort Wayne (IN)
Indiana U South Bend (IN)
Indiana U Southeast (IN)
Indiana Wesleyan U (IN)
Indian River State Coll (FL)
Inter American U of Puerto Rico, Metropolitan Campus (PR)
Inter American U of Puerto Rico, San Germán Campus (PR)
Iowa Wesleyan Coll (IA)
Ithaca Coll (NY)
Jamestown Coll (ND)
John Brown U (AR)
Johnson C. Smith U (NC)
Johnson State Coll (VT)
Judson Coll (AL)
Juniata Coll (PA)
Keene State Coll (NH)
Kennesaw State U (GA)
Kentucky Wesleyan Coll (KY)
Keuka Coll (NY)
Keystone Coll (PA)
King Coll (TN)
Le Moyne Coll (NY)
Lewis-Clark State Coll (ID)
Liberty U (VA)
Limestone Coll (SC)
Lincoln Memorial U (TN)
Lincoln U (MO)
Lindenwood U (MO)
Lindsey Wilson Coll (KY)
Lipscomb U (TN)
Long Island U, Brooklyn Campus (NY)
Long Island U, C.W. Post Campus (NY)
Louisiana State U in Shreveport (LA)
Loyola U Chicago (IL)
Lyndon State Coll (VT)
Madonna U (MI)
Manchester Coll (IN)
Manhattanville Coll (NY)
Mansfield U of Pennsylvania (PA)
Maranatha Baptist Bible Coll (WI)
Marist Coll (NY)
Marquette U (WI)
Maryville Coll (TN)
Marywood U (PA)
Mayville State U (ND)
McKendree U (IL)
McMurry U (TX)
Medaille Coll (NY)
Merrimack Coll (MA)
Messiah Coll (PA)
Metropolitan State U (MN)
Miami Dade Coll (FL)
Miami U (OH)
Michigan State U (MI)
MidAmerica Nazarene U (KS)
Midwestern State U (TX)
Millersville U of Pennsylvania (PA)
Millikin U (IL)
Minnesota State U Moorhead (MN)
Minot State U (ND)
Misericordia U (PA)
Mississippi Valley State U (MS)
Missouri State U (MO)
Molloy Coll (NY)
Montana State U Billings (MT)
Moravian Coll (PA)
Morningside Coll (IA)
Morris Coll (SC)
Mount Marty Coll (SD)
Mount Vernon Nazarene U (OH)
Nazareth Coll of Rochester (NY)
Nevada State Coll at Henderson (NV)
New York Inst of Technology (NY)
New York U (NY)
Niagara U (NY)
Nicholls State U (LA)
North Carolina State U (NC)
North Dakota State U (ND)
Northeastern State U (OK)
Northern Arizona U (AZ)
Northern Michigan U (MI)
North Greenville U (SC)
Northland Coll (WI)
Northwestern Coll (MN)
Northwestern Oklahoma State U (OK)
Northwestern State U of Louisiana (LA)
Northwest Missouri State U (MO)
Northwest Nazarene U (ID)
Northwest U (WA)
Nyack Coll (NY)
Ohio Valley U (WV)
Ohio Wesleyan U (OH)
Oklahoma Christian U (OK)
Pace U (NY)
Paine Coll (GA)
Palm Beach Atlantic U (FL)
Pepperdine U, Malibu (CA)
Philadelphia Biblical U (PA)
Pittsburg State U (KS)
Point Park U (PA)
Prescott Coll (AZ)
Regis Coll (MA)
Rhode Island Coll (RI)
Rivier Coll (NH)
Rocky Mountain Coll (MT)
Rust Coll (MS)
Sacred Heart U (CT)
St. Ambrose U (IA)
St. Catherine U (MN)
St. Edward's U (TX)
Saint Francis U (PA)
St. John Fisher Coll (NY)
St. John's U (NY)
St. Joseph's Coll, Long Island Campus (NY)
St. Joseph's Coll, New York (NY)
Saint Joseph's Coll of Maine (ME)
Saint Joseph's U (PA)
Saint Mary's U of Minnesota (MN)
St. Petersburg Coll (FL)
Saint Xavier U (IL)
Salve Regina U (RI)
Schreiner U (TX)
Seattle Pacific U (WA)
Seton Hill U (PA)
Shawnee State U (OH)
Shorter U (GA)
Simpson U (CA)
Southeastern Louisiana U (LA)
Southeastern Oklahoma State U (OK)
Southeastern U (FL)
Southeast Missouri State U (MO)
Southern Nazarene U (OK)
Southern Wesleyan U (SC)
Southwestern Coll (KS)
Spring Arbor U (MI)
State U of New York at New Paltz (NY)
State U of New York Coll at Old Westbury (NY)
State U of New York Coll at Oneonta (NY)
State U of New York Coll at Potsdam (NY)
Syracuse U (NY)
Tabor Coll (KS)
Talladega Coll (AL)
Taylor U (IN)
Temple U (PA)
Texas A&M Intl U (TX)
Texas A&M U–Corpus Christi (TX)
Texas Christian U (TX)
Texas Lutheran U (TX)
Texas Wesleyan U (TX)
Trevecca Nazarene U (TN)
Trine U (IN)
Union Coll (NE)
The U of Akron (OH)
The U of Arizona (AZ)
U of Arkansas–Fort Smith (AR)
U of Central Florida (FL)
U of Cincinnati (OH)
U of Delaware (DE)
U of Evansville (IN)
U of Georgia (GA)
U of Illinois at Chicago (IL)
U of Indianapolis (IN)
The U of Iowa (IA)
U of Lethbridge (AB, Canada)
U of Louisiana at Monroe (LA)
U of Maine (ME)
U of Maine at Farmington (ME)
U of Maine at Fort Kent (ME)
U of Mary Hardin-Baylor (TX)
U of Maryland, Coll Park (MD)
U of Michigan–Dearborn (MI)
U of Michigan–Flint (MI)
U of Minnesota, Duluth (MN)
U of Mississippi (MS)
U of Missouri (MO)
U of Missouri–St. Louis (MO)
The U of Montana Western (MT)
U of Nebraska–Lincoln (NE)
U of Nevada, Reno (NV)
U of New Hampshire (NH)
The U of North Carolina at Charlotte (NC)
The U of North Carolina at Greensboro (NC)
The U of North Carolina at Pembroke (NC)
The U of North Carolina Wilmington (NC)
U of Northern Iowa (IA)
U of North Florida (FL)
U of Oklahoma (OK)
U of Pittsburgh at Johnstown (PA)
U of Regina (SK, Canada)
U of Rio Grande (OH)
U of St. Francis (IL)
U of St. Thomas (MN)
The U of South Dakota (SD)
U of South Florida (FL)
The U of Tennessee at Chattanooga (TN)
The U of Tennessee at Martin (TN)
The U of Toledo (OH)
U of Tulsa (OK)
U of Vermont (VT)
U of Waterloo (ON, Canada)
U of West Florida (FL)
U of Wisconsin–River Falls (WI)
U of Wisconsin–Superior (WI)
Ursuline Coll (OH)
Utah State U (UT)
Utah Valley U (UT)
Valparaiso U (IN)
Viterbo U (WI)
Walsh U (OH)
Wartburg Coll (IA)
Washington Adventist U (MD)
Washington State U (WA)

Washington U in St. Louis (MO)
Waynesburg U (PA)
Wayne State Coll (NE)
Wayne State U (MI)
Western Carolina U (NC)
Western Michigan U (MI)
Western State Coll of Colorado (CO)
Westmont Coll (CA)
Wheeling Jesuit U (WV)
Widener U (PA)
Wingate U (NC)
Winona State U (MN)
York Coll of Pennsylvania (PA)
Youngstown State U (OH)

MECHANICAL DRAFTING AND CAD/CADD

Eastern Michigan U (MI)
Indiana U–Purdue U Indianapolis (IN)
Purdue U (IN)
Purdue U Calumet (IN)

MECHANICAL ENGINEERING

Alabama Ag and Mech U (AL)
Alfred U (NY)
American U of Beirut (Lebanon)
Andrews U (MI)
Arizona State U (AZ)
Arkansas State U (AR)
Arkansas Tech U (AR)
Auburn U (AL)
Baker Coll of Flint (MI)
Boston U (MA)
Brown U (RI)
Bucknell U (PA)
California Baptist U (CA)
California Inst of Technology (CA)
California Polytechnic State U, San Luis Obispo (CA)
California State Polytechnic U, Pomona (CA)
California State U, Chico (CA)
California State U, Fullerton (CA)
California State U, Long Beach (CA)
California State U, Los Angeles (CA)
California State U, Northridge (CA)
Calvin Coll (MI)
Carnegie Mellon U (PA)
Case Western Reserve U (OH)
The Catholic U of America (DC)
Cedarville U (OH)
Central Michigan U (MI)
Christian Brothers U (TN)
City Coll of the City U of New York (NY)
Clarkson U (NY)
Clemson U (SC)
Cleveland State U (OH)
The Coll of New Jersey (NJ)
Colorado State U (CO)
Concordia U (QC, Canada)
Cooper Union for the Advancement of Science and Art (NY)
Cornell U (NY)
Delaware State U (DE)
Dordt Coll (IA)
Eastern Washington U (WA)
Embry-Riddle Aeronautical U–Daytona (FL)
Embry-Riddle Aeronautical U–Prescott (AZ)
Fairfield U (CT)
Florida Ag and Mech U (FL)
Florida Atlantic U (FL)
Florida Inst of Technology (FL)
Florida Intl U (FL)
Franklin W. Olin Coll of Eng (MA)
Gannon U (PA)
George Fox U (OR)
Georgia Inst of Technology (GA)
Georgia Southern U (GA)
Grove City Coll (PA)
Harding U (AR)
Hofstra U (NY)
Idaho State U (ID)
Illinois Inst of Technology (IL)
Indiana Tech (IN)
Indiana U East (IN)
Indiana U–Purdue U Fort Wayne (IN)
Indiana U–Purdue U Indianapolis (IN)
Inter American U of Puerto Rico, Bayamón Campus (PR)
Iowa State U of Science and Technology (IA)
John Brown U (AR)
The Johns Hopkins U (MD)
Kansas State U (KS)

Kettering U (MI)
Lafayette Coll (PA)
Lakehead U (ON, Canada)
Lake Superior State U (MI)
Lamar U (TX)
Lawrence Technological U (MI)
Lebanese American U (Lebanon)
Lehigh U (PA)
LeTourneau U (TX)
Lipscomb U (TN)
Louisiana State U and Ag and Mech Coll (LA)
Loyola Marymount U (CA)
Manhattan Coll (NY)
Marquette U (WI)
Massachusetts Inst of Technology (MA)
Miami U (OH)
Michigan State U (MI)
Milwaukee School of Eng (WI)
Minnesota State U Mankato (MN)
Mississippi State U (MS)
Missouri U of Science and Technology (MO)
Montana State U (MT)
New England Inst of Technology (RI)
New Jersey Inst of Technology (NJ)
New Mexico Inst of Mining and Technology (NM)
New Mexico State U (NM)
New York Inst of Technology (NY)
North Carolina Ag and Tech State U (NC)
North Carolina State U (NC)
North Dakota State U (ND)
Northeastern U (MA)
Northern Arizona U (AZ)
Northern Illinois U (IL)
The Ohio State U (OH)
Ohio U (OH)
Oklahoma Christian U (OK)
Oklahoma State U (OK)
Old Dominion U (VA)
Oregon State U (OR)
Penn State Abington (PA)
Penn State Altoona (PA)
Penn State Beaver (PA)
Penn State Berks (PA)
Penn State Brandywine (PA)
Penn State DuBois (PA)
Penn State Erie, The Behrend Coll (PA)
Penn State Fayette, The Eberly Campus (PA)
Penn State Greater Allegheny (PA)
Penn State Harrisburg (PA)
Penn State Hazleton (PA)
Penn State Lehigh Valley (PA)
Penn State Mont Alto (PA)
Penn State New Kensington (PA)
Penn State Schuylkill (PA)
Penn State Shenango (PA)
Penn State U Park (PA)
Penn State Wilkes-Barre (PA)
Penn State Worthington Scranton (PA)
Penn State York (PA)
Polytechnic Inst of NYU (NY)
Polytechnic U of Puerto Rico (PR)
Portland State U (OR)
Prairie View A&M U (TX)
Princeton U (NJ)
Purdue U (IN)
Purdue U Calumet (IN)
Purdue U North Central (IN)
Rensselaer Polytechnic Inst (NY)
Rice U (TX)
Rose-Hulman Inst of Technology (IN)
Rowan U (NJ)
Rutgers, The State U of New Jersey, New Brunswick (NJ)
Saginaw Valley State U (MI)
Saint Louis U (MO)
Saint Martin's U (WA)
San Diego State U (CA)
San Francisco State U (CA)
San Jose State U (CA)
Santa Clara U (CA)
South Dakota School of Mines and Technology (SD)
South Dakota State U (SD)
Southern Illinois U Carbondale (IL)
Southern Illinois U Edwardsville (IL)
Southern Methodist U (TX)
Southern Polytechnic State U (GA)
Stanford U (CA)
State U of New York at Binghamton (NY)

State U of New York Maritime Coll (NY)
Stony Brook U, State U of New York (NY)
Syracuse U (NY)
Temple U (PA)
Tennessee Technological U (TN)
Texas A&M U (TX)
Texas A&M U–Corpus Christi (TX)
Texas A&M U–Kingsville (TX)
Texas Christian U (TX)
Texas Tech U (TX)
Trine U (IN)
Trinity Coll (CT)
Tufts U (MA)
Tuskegee U (AL)
Union Coll (NY)
United States Air Force Acad (CO)
United States Coast Guard Acad (CT)
United States Military Acad (NY)
United States Naval Acad (MD)
Université de Sherbrooke (QC, Canada)
U at Buffalo, the State U of New York (NY)
The U of Akron (OH)
The U of Alabama (AL)
The U of Alabama at Birmingham (AL)
The U of Alabama in Huntsville (AL)
U of Alaska Fairbanks (AK)
The U of Arizona (AZ)
U of Arkansas (AR)
The U of British Columbia (BC, Canada)
The U of British Columbia–Okanagan (BC, Canada)
U of California, Berkeley (CA)
U of California, Davis (CA)
U of California, Irvine (CA)
U of California, Los Angeles (CA)
U of California, Merced (CA)
U of California, Santa Barbara (CA)
U of Central Florida (FL)
U of Cincinnati (OH)
U of Colorado at Colorado Springs (CO)
U of Colorado Boulder (CO)
U of Colorado Denver (CO)
U of Dayton (OH)
U of Delaware (DE)
U of Denver (CO)
U of Evansville (IN)
U of Florida (FL)
U of Hartford (CT)
U of Hawaii at Manoa (HI)
U of Houston (TX)
U of Idaho (ID)
U of Illinois at Chicago (IL)
U of Indianapolis (IN)
The U of Iowa (IA)
The U of Kansas (KS)
U of Louisiana at Lafayette (LA)
U of Louisville (KY)
U of Maine (ME)
U of Manitoba (MB, Canada)
U of Maryland, Baltimore County (MD)
U of Maryland, Coll Park (MD)
U of Massachusetts Amherst (MA)
U of Massachusetts Dartmouth (MA)
U of Massachusetts Lowell (MA)
U of Memphis (TN)
U of Miami (FL)
U of Michigan (MI)
U of Michigan–Dearborn (MI)
U of Michigan–Flint (MI)
U of Minnesota, Twin Cities Campus (MN)
U of Mississippi (MS)
U of Missouri (MO)
U of Missouri–St. Louis (MO)
U of Mount Union (OH)
U of Nebraska–Lincoln (NE)
U of Nevada, Las Vegas (NV)
U of Nevada, Reno (NV)
U of New Brunswick Fredericton (NB, Canada)
U of New Hampshire (NH)
U of New Haven (CT)
The U of North Carolina at Charlotte (NC)
U of North Dakota (ND)
U of North Florida (FL)
U of North Texas (TX)
U of Notre Dame (IN)
U of Oklahoma (OK)
U of Ottawa (ON, Canada)
U of Pennsylvania (PA)

U of Pittsburgh (PA)
U of Portland (OR)
U of Rhode Island (RI)
U of Rochester (NY)
U of St. Thomas (MN)
U of San Diego (CA)
U of Saskatchewan (SK, Canada)
U of South Alabama (AL)
U of South Carolina (SC)
U of Southern California (CA)
U of South Florida (FL)
The U of Tennessee (TN)
The U of Tennessee at Chattanooga (TN)
The U of Texas at Arlington (TX)
The U of Texas at Austin (TX)
The U of Texas at Dallas (TX)
The U of Texas at San Antonio (TX)
The U of Texas at Tyler (TX)
The U of Texas of the Permian Basin (TX)
The U of Texas–Pan American (TX)
U of the District of Columbia (DC)
U of the Pacific (CA)
The U of Toledo (OH)
U of Tulsa (OK)
U of Utah (UT)
U of Vermont (VT)
U of Virginia (VA)
U of Washington (WA)
U of Waterloo (ON, Canada)
The U of Western Ontario (ON, Canada)
U of Wisconsin–Madison (WI)
U of Wisconsin–Platteville (WI)
U of Wyoming (WY)
Utah State U (UT)
Valparaiso U (IN)
Vanderbilt U (TN)
Villanova U (PA)
Virginia Commonwealth U (VA)
Virginia Military Inst (VA)
Virginia Polytechnic Inst and State U (VA)
Walla Walla U (WA)
Washington State U (WA)
Washington U in St. Louis (MO)
Wayne State U (MI)
Wentworth Inst of Technology (MA)
Western Kentucky U (KY)
Western Michigan U (MI)
Western New England U (MA)
West Virginia U (WV)
Wichita State U (KS)
Widener U (PA)
Wilkes U (PA)
Winona State U (MN)
Worcester Polytechnic Inst (MA)
Wright State U (OH)
Yale U (CT)
York Coll of Pennsylvania (PA)
Youngstown State U (OH)

MECHANICAL ENGINEERING/ MECHANICAL TECHNOLOGY

Alabama Ag and Mech U (AL)
Arizona State U (AZ)
Bluefield State Coll (WV)
Boise State U (ID)
California State U, Long Beach (CA)
Central Connecticut State U (CT)
Central Michigan U (MI)
Delaware State U (DE)
Eastern Michigan U (MI)
Eastern Washington U (WA)
Fairleigh Dickinson U, Metropolitan Campus (NJ)
Fairmont State U (WV)
Ferris State U (MI)
Georgia Southern U (GA)
Indiana U–Purdue U Fort Wayne (IN)
Kent State U at Tuscarawas (OH)
Lakehead U (ON, Canada)
Lake Superior State U (MI)
LeTourneau U (TX)
Mesa State Coll (CO)
Midwestern State U (TX)
Milwaukee School of Eng (WI)
Montana State U (MT)
Nicholls State U (LA)
Northern Michigan U (MI)
Oklahoma State U (OK)
Penn State Erie, The Behrend Coll (PA)
Pennsylvania Coll of Technology (PA)
Pittsburg State U (KS)
Point Park U (PA)
Southern Polytechnic State U (GA)

State U of New York Coll of Technology at Alfred (NY)
Texas A&M U–Corpus Christi (TX)
Texas Tech U (TX)
Thomas Edison State Coll (NJ)
United States Military Acad (NY)
The U of Akron (OH)
The U of British Columbia (BC, Canada)
U of Dayton (OH)
U of Hartford (CT)
U of Houston (TX)
U of Maine (ME)
U of New Hampshire (NH)
U of New Hampshire at Manchester (NH)
The U of North Carolina at Charlotte (NC)
U of North Texas (TX)
U of Pittsburgh at Johnstown (PA)
U of Rio Grande (OH)
U of the District of Columbia (DC)
The U of Toledo (OH)
Virginia State U (VA)
Wayne State U (MI)
Wentworth Inst of Technology (MA)
Youngstown State U (OH)

MECHANICAL ENGINEERING TECHNOLOGIES RELATED

Cleveland State U (OH)
Delaware State U (DE)
Grove City Coll (PA)
Indiana State U (IN)
Indiana U–Purdue U Indianapolis (IN)
New York Inst of Technology (NY)
Pennsylvania Coll of Technology (PA)
Purdue U (IN)
Purdue U North Central (IN)
U of Hartford (CT)
U of Massachusetts Lowell (MA)
Vaughn Coll of Aeronautics and Technology (NY)

MECHANICS AND REPAIR

Lewis-Clark State Coll (ID)

MEDICAL ADMINISTRATIVE ASSISTANT AND MEDICAL SECRETARY

Baker Coll of Auburn Hills (MI)

MEDICAL ANTHROPOLOGY

Creighton U (NE)

MEDICAL/CLINICAL ASSISTANT

Intl Business Coll, Fort Wayne (IN)

MEDICAL/HEALTH MANAGEMENT AND CLINICAL ASSISTANT

Davenport U, Grand Rapids (MI)
Lewis-Clark State Coll (ID)

MEDICAL ILLUSTRATION

Arcadia U (PA)
The Cleveland Inst of Art (OH)
Iowa State U of Science and Technology (IA)

MEDICAL INFORMATICS

Montana Tech of The U of Montana (MT)
Montclair State U (NJ)
U of Waterloo (ON, Canada)
Walden U (MN)

MEDICAL MICROBIOLOGY AND BACTERIOLOGY

Adams State Coll (CO)
Auburn U (AL)
Bowling Green State U (OH)
California Polytechnic State U, San Luis Obispo (CA)
Humboldt State U (CA)
Indiana U Bloomington (IN)
Inter American U of Puerto Rico, Bayamón Campus (PR)
Inter American U of Puerto Rico, San Germán Campus (PR)
Minnesota State U Mankato (MN)
Mississippi State U (MS)
Mississippi U for Women (MS)
Montana State U (MT)
New Mexico State U (NM)
Ohio Wesleyan U (OH)
Penn State Abington (PA)

INDEXES

Indiana Wesleyan U (IN)
Iowa Wesleyan Coll (IA)
Ithaca Coll (NY)
Jacksonville State U (AL)
Johnson Bible Coll (TN)
Johnson State Coll (VT)
Kennesaw State U (GA)
Kent State U (OH)
Kent State U at Stark (OH)
Kentucky Wesleyan Coll (KY)
Keystone Coll (PA)
King Coll (TN)
Kutztown U of Pennsylvania (PA)
Lake Superior State U (MI)
Lee U (TN)
Le Moyne Coll (NY)
Lesley U (MA)
Lincoln U (MO)
Lindenwood U (MO)
Lindsey Wilson Coll (KY)
Lourdes Coll (OH)
Lubbock Christian U (TX)
Malone U (OH)
Manchester Coll (IN)
Manhattan Coll (NY)
Marian U (WI)
Mars Hill Coll (NC)
Maryville U of Saint Louis (MO)
The Master's Coll and Sem (CA)
McKendree U (IL)
McMurry U (TX)
Medaille Coll (NY)
Mercer U (GA)
Merrimack Coll (MA)
Miami U (OH)
Michigan State U (MI)
MidAmerica Nazarene U (KS)
Midway Coll (KY)
Millersville U of Pennsylvania (PA)
Minnesota State U Moorhead (MN)
Misericordia U (PA)
Missouri Baptist U (MO)
Missouri State U (MO)
Morehead State U (KY)
Mount Mercy U (IA)
Mount Olive Coll (NC)
Mount Vernon Nazarene U (OH)
Murray State U (KY)
Nebraska Wesleyan U (NE)
Newberry Coll (SC)
Nicholls State U (LA)
North Carolina State U (NC)
Northern Kentucky U (KY)
North Georgia Coll & State U (GA)
Northwestern State U of Louisiana (LA)
Northwest Missouri State U (MO)
Nova Southeastern U (FL)
The Ohio State U (OH)
The Ohio State U at Lima (OH)
The Ohio State U at Marion (OH)
The Ohio State U–Mansfield Campus (OH)
The Ohio State U–Newark Campus (OH)
Ohio Wesleyan U (OH)
Ouachita Baptist U (AR)
Paine Coll (GA)
Piedmont Coll (GA)
Pikeville Coll (KY)
Presbyterian Coll (SC)
Reinhardt U (GA)
Sacred Heart U (CT)
Saint Leo U (FL)
Saint Louis U (MO)
Salem State U (MA)
Schreiner U (TX)
Shippensburg U of Pennsylvania (PA)
Shorter U (GA)
Southeastern Louisiana U (LA)
Southeast Missouri State U (MO)
Southern Arkansas U–Magnolia (AR)
State U of New York Coll at Old Westbury (NY)
State U of New York Coll at Oneonta (NY)
Stevenson U (MD)
Tabor Coll (KS)
Tarleton State U (TX)
Texas Lutheran U (TX)
Thomas U (GA)
Transylvania U (KY)
Union Coll (KY)
The U of Akron (OH)
U of Arkansas–Fort Smith (AR)
U of Central Missouri (MO)

U of Cincinnati (OH)
U of Florida (FL)
U of Georgia (GA)
The U of Kansas (KS)
U of Mary Hardin-Baylor (TX)
U of Minnesota, Duluth (MN)
U of Missouri (MO)
U of Mount Union (OH)
The U of North Carolina at Chapel Hill (NC)
The U of North Carolina at Charlotte (NC)
The U of North Carolina at Greensboro (NC)
The U of North Carolina at Pembroke (NC)
The U of North Carolina Wilmington (NC)
U of North Dakota (ND)
U of Northern Iowa (IA)
U of North Florida (FL)
U of Regina (SK, Canada)
U of St. Thomas (MN)
U of Sioux Falls (SD)
U of South Carolina (SC)
U of South Carolina Aiken (SC)
U of South Carolina Upstate (SC)
The U of Tennessee at Chattanooga (TN)
U of the Cumberlands (KY)
U of the Ozarks (AR)
U of Vermont (VT)
The U of Western Ontario (ON, Canada)
U of West Florida (FL)
U of West Georgia (GA)
U of Wisconsin–Platteville (WI)
Ursuline Coll (OH)
Valdosta State U (GA)
Valparaiso U (IN)
Victory U (TN)
Virginia Wesleyan Coll (VA)
Walsh U (OH)
Washington U in St. Louis (MO)
Wayland Baptist U (TX)
Wayne State Coll (NE)
West Chester U of Pennsylvania (PA)
Western Carolina U (NC)
Western Kentucky U (KY)
Westminster Coll (MO)
Wheeling Jesuit U (WV)
William Jewell Coll (MO)
Wingate U (NC)
Winona State U (MN)
Wright State U (OH)
Xavier U (OH)
Xavier U of Louisiana (LA)
Youngstown State U (OH)

MILITARY APPLIED SCIENCES RELATED

United States Military Acad (NY)

MILITARY HISTORY

American Public U System (WV)
Rogers State U (OK)

MILITARY STUDIES

Hawai`i Pacific U (HI)
Pacific Lutheran U (WA)
United States Air Force Acad (CO)

MILITARY TECHNOLOGIES AND APPLIED SCIENCES RELATED

American Public U System (WV)

MINING AND MINERAL ENGINEERING

Colorado School of Mines (CO)
Laurentian U (ON, Canada)
Missouri U of Science and Technology (MO)
Montana Tech of The U of Montana (MT)
New Mexico Inst of Mining and Technology (NM)
Penn State Abington (PA)
Penn State Altoona (PA)
Penn State Beaver (PA)
Penn State Berks (PA)
Penn State Brandywine (PA)
Penn State DuBois (PA)
Penn State Erie, The Behrend Coll (PA)
Penn State Fayette, The Eberly Campus (PA)
Penn State Greater Allegheny (PA)

Penn State Hazleton (PA)
Penn State Lehigh Valley (PA)
Penn State Mont Alto (PA)
Penn State New Kensington (PA)
Penn State Schuylkill (PA)
Penn State Shenango (PA)
Penn State U Park (PA)
Penn State Wilkes-Barre (PA)
Penn State Worthington Scranton (PA)
Penn State York (PA)
South Dakota School of Mines and Technology (SD)
Southern Illinois U Carbondale (IL)
U of Alaska Fairbanks (AK)
The U of Arizona (AZ)
The U of British Columbia (BC, Canada)
U of Minnesota, Twin Cities Campus (MN)
U of Nevada, Reno (NV)
U of Utah (UT)
Virginia Polytechnic Inst and State U (VA)
West Virginia U (WV)

MINING TECHNOLOGY

Bluefield State Coll (WV)

MISSIONARY STUDIES AND MISSIOLOGY

Abilene Christian U (TX)
Asbury U (KY)
Baptist Bible Coll of Pennsylvania (PA)
Bethel Coll (IN)
Biola U (CA)
Bob Jones U (SC)
California Baptist U (CA)
Calvary Bible Coll and Theological Sem (MO)
Cedarville U (OH)
Columbia Bible Coll (BC, Canada)
Concordia U, St. Paul (MN)
Concordia U Wisconsin (WI)
Corban U (OR)
Crown Coll (MN)
Dordt Coll (IA)
East Texas Baptist U (TX)
Emmaus Bible Coll (IA)
Faith Baptist Bible Coll and Theological Sem (IA)
Freed-Hardeman U (TN)
Free Will Baptist Bible Coll (TN)
Gardner-Webb U (NC)
Grace Bible Coll (MI)
Hannibal-LaGrange U (MO)
Harding U (AR)
Hardin-Simmons U (TX)
Hillsdale Free Will Baptist Coll (OK)
Huntington U (IN)
Indiana Wesleyan U (IN)
Kuyper Coll (MI)
LeTourneau U (TX)
Lincoln Christian U (IL)
Lipscomb U (TN)
Lubbock Christian U (TX)
Maranatha Baptist Bible Coll (WI)
MidAmerica Nazarene U (KS)
Mid-Atlantic Christian U (NC)
Mid-Continent U (KY)
Mount Vernon Nazarene U (OH)
Multnomah U (OR)
New Hope Christian Coll (OR)
North Greenville U (SC)
Northwestern Coll (MN)
Northwest Nazarene U (ID)
Northwest U (WA)
Nyack Coll (NY)
Oklahoma Christian U (OK)
Ouachita Baptist U (AR)
Palm Beach Atlantic U (FL)
Simpson U (CA)
Southeastern Baptist Theological Sem (NC)
Southeastern U (FL)
Southern Nazarene U (OK)
Spring Arbor U (MI)
Trevecca Nazarene U (TN)
Trinity Coll of Florida (FL)
William Jessup U (CA)

MODELING, VIRTUAL ENVIRONMENTS AND SIMULATION

DigiPen Inst of Technology (WA)
U of Colorado at Colorado Springs (CO)

MODERN GREEK

Belmont U (TN)
Boston U (MA)
Butler U (IN)
Calvin Coll (MI)
Colgate U (NY)
Concordia U Wisconsin (WI)
Cornell Coll (IA)
Furman U (SC)
Haverford Coll (PA)
John Carroll U (OH)
Lehman Coll of the City U of New York (NY)
Marlboro Coll (VT)
Oberlin Coll (OH)
The Ohio State U (OH)
Rhodes Coll (TN)
Saint Louis U (MO)
Saint Mary's Coll of California (CA)
Sewanee: The U of the South (TN)
Trent U (ON, Canada)
Tufts U (MA)
Tulane U (LA)
U of Manitoba (MB, Canada)
U of Michigan (MI)
U of New Brunswick Fredericton (NB, Canada)
Wabash Coll (IN)
Wright State U (OH)

MODERN LANGUAGES

Albion Coll (MI)
Alma Coll (MI)
Beloit Coll (WI)
Bemidji State U (MN)
Claremont McKenna Coll (CA)
Clark U (MA)
Clemson U (SC)
The Coll of William and Mary (VA)
Cornell Coll (IA)
Dallas Baptist U (TX)
Franklin Coll Switzerland (Switzerland)
Gettysburg Coll (PA)
Grove City Coll (PA)
Kenyon Coll (OH)
King Coll (TN)
La Salle U (PA)
Laurentian U (ON, Canada)
Lee U (TN)
Long Island U, Brooklyn Campus (NY)
Longwood U (VA)
Louisiana Coll (LA)
Marlboro Coll (VT)
Middlebury Coll (VT)
Minnesota State U Mankato (MN)
Mount Allison U (NB, Canada)
Nazareth Coll of Rochester (NY)
Pacific U (OR)
Pomona Coll (CA)
Presbyterian Coll (SC)
Purchase Coll, State U of New York (NY)
Rivier Coll (NH)
St. Bonaventure U (NY)
Saint Francis U (PA)
St. Francis Xavier U (NS, Canada)
St. Lawrence U (NY)
Saint Mary's Coll of California (CA)
Saint Michael's Coll (VT)
St. Thomas Aquinas Coll (NY)
Sarah Lawrence Coll (NY)
Suffolk U (MA)
Trent U (ON, Canada)
Trinity U (CT)
U of Louisiana at Lafayette (LA)
U of Maine (ME)
U of New Brunswick Fredericton (NB, Canada)
U of Ottawa (ON, Canada)
U of Southern Maine (ME)
The U of Western Ontario (ON, Canada)
Virginia Military Inst (VA)
Walla Walla U (WA)
Walsh U (OH)
Washington U in St. Louis (MO)
Westmont Coll (CA)
Widener U (PA)
Wilmington Coll (OH)
Wright State U (OH)

MOLECULAR BIOCHEMISTRY

Clarkson U (NY)
Polytechnic Inst of NYU (NY)
Simon Fraser U (BC, Canada)
U of California, Davis (CA)
U of Richmond (VA)

MOLECULAR BIOLOGY

Alverno Coll (WI)
Arizona State U (AZ)
Assumption Coll (MA)
Auburn U (AL)
Beloit Coll (WI)
Blackburn Coll (IL)
Boston U (MA)
Brown U (RI)
California State U, San Marcos (CA)
Central Connecticut State U (CT)
Centre Coll (KY)
Chestnut Hill Coll (PA)
Clarion U of Pennsylvania (PA)
Clark U (MA)
Colby Coll (ME)
Colgate U (NY)
The Coll of Wooster (OH)
Connecticut Coll (CT)
Dartmouth Coll (NH)
Florida Inst of Technology (FL)
Gettysburg Coll (PA)
Grove City Coll (PA)
Humboldt State U (CA)
Juniata Coll (PA)
Kenyon Coll (OH)
Lakehead U (ON, Canada)
Lawrence Technological U (MI)
Lehigh U (PA)
Marlboro Coll (VT)
Messiah Coll (PA)
Michigan State U (MI)
Middlebury Coll (VT)
Millikin U (IL)
Montclair State U (NJ)
Pitzer Coll (CA)
Pomona Coll (CA)
Princeton U (NJ)
Rollins Coll (FL)
Rutgers, The State U of New Jersey, New Brunswick (NJ)
San Francisco State U (CA)
San Jose State U (CA)
Sarah Lawrence Coll (NY)
Scripps Coll (CA)
Simon Fraser U (BC, Canada)
Stetson U (FL)
Tulane U (LA)
The U of British Columbia–Okanagan (BC, Canada)
U of California, Santa Barbara (CA)
U of California, Santa Cruz (CA)
U of Denver (CO)
U of Guelph (ON, Canada)
U of Idaho (ID)
The U of Kansas (KS)
U of Maine (ME)
U of Michigan–Flint (MI)
U of Minnesota, Duluth (MN)
U of New Brunswick Fredericton (NB, Canada)
U of Pittsburgh (PA)
U of Puget Sound (WA)
The U of Texas at Dallas (TX)
U of Vermont (VT)
U of Washington (WA)
U of Wisconsin–Eau Claire (WI)
U of Wisconsin–Madison (WI)
U of Wisconsin–Parkside (WI)
U of Wyoming (WY)
Vanderbilt U (TN)
Wayland Baptist U (TX)
Wells Coll (NY)
Wesleyan U (CT)
Western New England U (MA)
Whitman Coll (WA)
William Jewell Coll (MO)
Worcester Polytechnic Inst (MA)
Yale U (CT)

MOLECULAR GENETICS

Michigan State U (MI)
The Ohio State U (OH)
Texas A&M U (TX)
U of Guelph (ON, Canada)
U of Rochester (NY)
U of Vermont (VT)
Washington State U (WA)

MONTESSORI TEACHER EDUCATION

Oklahoma City U (OK)
Siena Heights U (MI)
Xavier U (OH)

MOVEMENT THERAPY AND MOVEMENT EDUCATION

Brock U (ON, Canada)
Pacific Lutheran U (WA)

Texas Christian U (TX)
U of Vermont (VT)

MULTICULTURAL EDUCATION
Carnegie Mellon U (PA)
Fort Lewis Coll (CO)
Goddard Coll (VT)
Indiana Wesleyan U (IN)

MULTI/INTERDISCIPLINARY STUDIES RELATED
Abilene Christian U (TX)
Adams State Coll (CO)
Adelphi U (NY)
Albright Coll (PA)
Allegheny Coll (PA)
Anderson U (IN)
Angelo State U (TX)
Anna Maria Coll (MA)
Arcadia U (PA)
Arizona State U (AZ)
Arkansas State U (AR)
Arkansas Tech U (AR)
Austin Coll (TX)
Baldwin-Wallace Coll (OH)
Bates Coll (ME)
Bellarmine U (KY)
Bentley U (MA)
Berea Coll (KY)
Berry Coll (GA)
Bethel U (MN)
Bethel U (TN)
Bloomfield Coll (NJ)
Bluffton U (OH)
Boston U (MA)
Bowling Green State U (OH)
Brandeis U (MA)
Brevard Coll (NC)
Bucknell U (PA)
Buena Vista U (IA)
California Polytechnic State U, San Luis Obispo (CA)
California State U, Chico (CA)
California State U, Dominguez Hills (CA)
California State U, Long Beach (CA)
California State U, Los Angeles (CA)
California State U, Monterey Bay (CA)
California State U, Stanislaus (CA)
Cameron U (OK)
Capital U (OH)
Central Connecticut State U (CT)
Clarkson U (NY)
Cleveland State U (OH)
The Coll of New Jersey (NJ)
Coll of Saint Benedict (MN)
Coll of Saint Elizabeth (NJ)
The Coll of Saint Rose (NY)
The Coll of William and Mary (VA)
The Coll of Wooster (OH)
The Colorado Coll (CO)
Columbia Coll Chicago (IL)
Cornell Coll (IA)
Cornell U (NY)
Covenant Coll (GA)
Dallas Baptist U (TX)
Dartmouth Coll (NH)
Davidson Coll (NC)
Delta State U (MS)
DePauw U (IN)
Dixie State Coll of Utah (UT)
Earlham Coll (IN)
East Central U (OK)
Eastern Illinois U (IL)
Eastern Michigan U (MI)
Eastern New Mexico U (NM)
Eastern Oregon U (OR)
Eastern Washington U (WA)
East Tennessee State U (TN)
East Texas Baptist U (TX)
Edgewood Coll (WI)
Embry-Riddle Aeronautical U–Daytona (FL)
Embry-Riddle Aeronautical U–Prescott (AZ)
Emporia State U (KS)
The Evergreen State Coll (WA)
Florida Inst of Technology (FL)
Florida Southern Coll (FL)
Franklin & Marshall Coll (PA)
Franklin U (OH)
Gannon U (PA)
Georgetown Coll (KY)
Georgetown U (DC)
Georgia Inst of Technology (GA)
Georgian Court U (NJ)

Georgia State U (GA)
Goucher Coll (MD)
Grace Bible Coll (MI)
Grand Canyon U (AZ)
Granite State Coll (NH)
Greenville Coll (IL)
Hamline U (MN)
Hampshire Coll (MA)
Hood Coll (MD)
Hope Coll (MI)
Humboldt State U (CA)
Illinois Wesleyan U (IL)
Immaculata U (PA)
Indiana U Bloomington (IN)
Indiana U–Purdue U Indianapolis (IN)
Indiana U Southeast (IN)
Iowa State U of Science and Technology (IA)
Ithaca Coll (NY)
John Brown U (AR)
Juniata Coll (PA)
Keene State Coll (NH)
Kennesaw State U (GA)
Kent State U (OH)
Kentucky Wesleyan Coll (KY)
Knox Coll (IL)
Lane Coll (TN)
Lasell Coll (MA)
Lebanon Valley Coll (PA)
Lewis-Clark State Coll (ID)
Lewis U (IL)
Liberty U (VA)
Long Island U, Brooklyn Campus (NY)
Lourdes Coll (OH)
Loyola Marymount U (CA)
Luther Coll (IA)
Lycoming Coll (PA)
Manchester Coll (IN)
Marian U (WI)
Marquette U (WI)
Marylhurst U (OR)
Maryville Coll (TN)
Marywood U (PA)
McDaniel Coll (MD)
McMurry U (TX)
Mercer U (GA)
Messiah Coll (PA)
Metropolitan State U (MN)
Mid-Continent U (KY)
Middle Tennessee State U (TN)
Midway Coll (KY)
Millikin U (IL)
Millsaps Coll (MS)
Minnesota State U Moorhead (MN)
Mississippi State U (MS)
Mississippi U for Women (MS)
Missouri Baptist U (MO)
Monmouth U (NJ)
Montana State U Billings (MT)
Montclair State U (NJ)
Morningside Coll (IA)
Mountain State U (WV)
Mount Holyoke Coll (MA)
Mount Mercy U (IA)
Mount St. Mary's U (MD)
Naropa U (CO)
National-Louis U (IL)
Nevada State Coll at Henderson (NV)
Newman U (KS)
New York Inst of Technology (NY)
North Central Coll (IL)
Northeastern State U (OK)
Northern Arizona U (AZ)
Northern Illinois U (IL)
Northwest Christian U (OR)
Northwestern Coll (MN)
Northwestern Oklahoma State U (OK)
Northwestern State U of Louisiana (LA)
Northwest Missouri State U (MO)
Ohio Wesleyan U (OH)
Old Dominion U (VA)
Pace U (NY)
Palm Beach Atlantic U (FL)
Penn State Erie, The Behrend Coll (PA)
Penn State Harrisburg (PA)
Pikeville Coll (KY)
Point Park U (PA)
Prairie View A&M U (TX)
Prescott Coll (AZ)
Princeton U (NJ)
Queens Coll of the City U of New York (NY)

Radford U (VA)
Regis Coll (MA)
Rice U (TX)
The Richard Stockton Coll of New Jersey (NJ)
Robert Morris U (PA)
Robert Morris U Illinois (IL)
Rocky Mountain Coll (MT)
Rogers State U (OK)
Rollins Coll (FL)
Rowan U (NJ)
Rutgers, The State U of New Jersey, Camden (NJ)
Rutgers, The State U of New Jersey, Newark (NJ)
Sage Coll of Albany (NY)
St. Ambrose U (IA)
Saint Anselm Coll (NH)
Saint John's U (MN)
Saint Mary's Coll of California (CA)
St. Mary's Coll of Maryland (MD)
Sam Houston State U (TX)
San Diego Christian Coll (CA)
San Diego State U (CA)
San Francisco State U (CA)
San Jose State U (CA)
Scripps Coll (CA)
Shippensburg U of Pennsylvania (PA)
Simmons Coll (MA)
Sonoma State U (CA)
South Dakota State U (SD)
Southeastern Oklahoma State U (OK)
Southeast Missouri State U (MO)
Southern Arkansas U–Magnolia (AR)
Southern Illinois U Carbondale (IL)
Southern Methodist U (TX)
State U of New York at Binghamton (NY)
State U of New York Coll at Potsdam (NY)
Stephen F. Austin State U (TX)
Sterling Coll (VT)
Stevenson U (MD)
Stonehill Coll (MA)
Stony Brook U, State U of New York (NY)
Syracuse U (NY)
Tarleton State U (TX)
Temple U (PA)
Tennessee Wesleyan Coll (TN)
Texas A&M U (TX)
Texas A&M U–Kingsville (TX)
Texas Southern U (TX)
Texas State U–San Marcos (TX)
Texas Tech U (TX)
Texas Wesleyan U (TX)
Texas Woman's U (TX)
Thomas Edison State Coll (NJ)
Thomas More Coll (KY)
Truett-McConnell Coll (GA)
Truman State U (MO)
Tulane U (LA)
U at Buffalo, the State U of New York (NY)
The U of Akron (OH)
U of Alaska Fairbanks (AK)
U of Alaska Southeast (AK)
The U of Arizona (AZ)
U of Arkansas–Fort Smith (AR)
U of California, Berkeley (CA)
U of California, Davis (CA)
U of California, Irvine (CA)
U of California, Los Angeles (CA)
U of California, Santa Barbara (CA)
U of Cincinnati (OH)
U of Colorado at Colorado Springs (CO)
U of Colorado Denver (CO)
U of Denver (CO)
U of Evansville (IN)
U of Florida (FL)
U of Houston (TX)
U of Houston–Clear Lake (TX)
U of Houston–Downtown (TX)
U of Houston–Victoria (TX)
U of Idaho (ID)
U of Lethbridge (AB, Canada)
U of Maryland, Baltimore County (MD)
U of Maryland, Coll Park (MD)
U of Maryland U Coll (MD)
U of Mary Washington (VA)
U of Massachusetts Amherst (MA)
U of Massachusetts Boston (MA)

U of Massachusetts Dartmouth (MA)
U of Memphis (TN)
U of Michigan (MI)
U of Michigan–Dearborn (MI)
U of Michigan–Flint (MI)
U of Minnesota, Crookston (MN)
U of Minnesota, Twin Cities Campus (MN)
U of Mobile (AL)
U of Nebraska at Omaha (NE)
U of New Hampshire (NH)
The U of North Carolina at Pembroke (NC)
U of North Dakota (ND)
U of Northern Colorado (CO)
U of North Texas (TX)
U of Oregon (OR)
U of Pittsburgh (PA)
U of Richmond (VA)
U of St. Francis (IL)
U of Saint Mary (KS)
U of St. Thomas (MN)
The U of South Dakota (SD)
U of Southern California (CA)
U of South Florida (FL)
The U of Tennessee (TN)
The U of Texas at Arlington (TX)
The U of Texas at Austin (TX)
The U of Texas at Tyler (TX)
The U of Texas of the Permian Basin (TX)
The U of Texas–Pan American (TX)
The U of Toledo (OH)
U of Virginia (VA)
U of Washington, Bothell (WA)
U of Waterloo (ON, Canada)
The U of Western Ontario (ON, Canada)
U of Wisconsin–Green Bay (WI)
U of Wisconsin–River Falls (WI)
U of Wisconsin–Stevens Point (WI)
U of Wisconsin–Stout (WI)
U of Wisconsin–Superior (WI)
U of Wyoming (WY)
Utah State U (UT)
Utah Valley U (UT)
Valparaiso U (IN)
Vanderbilt U (TN)
Vassar Coll (NY)
Villanova U (PA)
Virginia Commonwealth U (VA)
Virginia Intermont Coll (VA)
Virginia Wesleyan Coll (VA)
Viterbo U (WI)
Walden U (MN)
Washington & Jefferson Coll (PA)
Washington and Lee U (VA)
Washington Coll (MD)
Washington State U (WA)
Washington U in St. Louis (MO)
Wayne State U (MI)
Western Kentucky U (KY)
Western Michigan U (MI)
Wheaton Coll (IL)
Wichita State U (KS)
Wilkes U (PA)
Xavier U (OH)
Yale U (CT)

MUSEUM STUDIES
Beloit Coll (WI)
Centenary Coll of Louisiana (LA)
Coll of the Atlantic (ME)
Juniata Coll (PA)
Randolph Coll (VA)
The U of Iowa (IA)
Walsh U (OH)

MUSIC
Abilene Christian U (TX)
Acadia U (NS, Canada)
Adams State Coll (CO)
Adelphi U (NY)
Alabama State U (AL)
Albany State U (GA)
Albion Coll (MI)
Albright Coll (PA)
Alderson-Broaddus Coll (WV)
Allegheny Coll (PA)
Alma Coll (MI)
Alverno Coll (WI)
American U (DC)
Amherst Coll (MA)
Anderson U (SC)
Andrews U (MI)
Angelo State U (TX)

Anna Maria Coll (MA)
Aquinas Coll (MI)
Arizona State U (AZ)
Arkansas State U (AR)
Arkansas Tech U (AR)
Arlington Baptist Coll (TX)
Armstrong Atlantic State U (GA)
Asbury U (KY)
Ashland U (OH)
Assumption Coll (MA)
Atlanta Christian Coll (GA)
Auburn U (AL)
Augsburg Coll (MN)
Augustana Coll (IL)
Augustana Coll (SD)
Austin Coll (TX)
Austin Peay State U (TN)
Averett U (VA)
Avila U (MO)
Azusa Pacific U (CA)
Baker U (KS)
Baldwin-Wallace Coll (OH)
Ball State U (IN)
Baptist Bible Coll of Pennsylvania (PA)
Bard Coll (NY)
Bard Coll at Simon's Rock (MA)
Barnard Coll (NY)
Bates Coll (ME)
Belhaven U (MS)
Bellarmine U (KY)
Belmont U (TN)
Beloit Coll (WI)
Bemidji State U (MN)
Benedictine Coll (KS)
Benedictine U (IL)
Bennington Coll (VT)
Berea Coll (KY)
Berry Coll (GA)
Bethany Bible Coll (NB, Canada)
Bethany Coll (KS)
Bethany Coll (WV)
Bethany Lutheran Coll (MN)
Bethel Coll (IN)
Bethel U (MN)
Bethel U (TN)
Biola U (CA)
Birmingham-Southern Coll (AL)
Blackburn Coll (IL)
Bloomsburg U of Pennsylvania (PA)
Bluefield Coll (VA)
Blue Mountain Coll (MS)
Bluffton U (OH)
Boise State U (ID)
Boston Coll (MA)
Boston U (MA)
Bowdoin Coll (ME)
Bowling Green State U (OH)
Brandeis U (MA)
Brenau U (GA)
Brevard Coll (NC)
Briar Cliff U (IA)
Bridgewater State U (MA)
Brock U (ON, Canada)
Brown U (RI)
Bryan Coll (TN)
Bryn Mawr Coll (PA)
Bucknell U (PA)
Butler U (IN)
California Baptist U (CA)
California Polytechnic State U, San Luis Obispo (CA)
California State Polytechnic U, Pomona (CA)
California State U, Bakersfield (CA)
California State U, Chico (CA)
California State U, Dominguez Hills (CA)
California State U, Fullerton (CA)
California State U, Long Beach (CA)
California State U, Los Angeles (CA)
California State U, Monterey Bay (CA)
California State U, Northridge (CA)
California State U, San Bernardino (CA)
California State U, Stanislaus (CA)
Calvin Coll (MI)
Cameron U (OK)
Campbellsville U (KY)
Canisius Coll (NY)
Capital U (OH)
Carleton Coll (MN)
Carroll U (WI)
Carson-Newman Coll (TN)
Case Western Reserve U (OH)
Castleton State Coll (VT)

Freed-Hardeman U (TN)
Free Will Baptist Bible Coll (TN)
Friends U (KS)
Furman U (SC)
Gardner-Webb U (NC)
Geneva Coll (PA)
George Fox U (OR)
Georgetown U (KY)
Georgia Coll & State U (GA)
Georgia Southern U (GA)
Gettysburg Coll (PA)
Gordon Coll (MA)
Graceland U (IA)
Grand Valley State U (MI)
Greensboro Coll (NC)
Greenville Coll (IL)
Grove City Coll (PA)
Hamline U (MN)
Hannibal-LaGrange U (MO)
Harding U (AR)
Hardin-Simmons U (TX)
Hartwick Coll (NY)
Hofstra U (NY)
Hope Coll (MI)
Houghton Coll (NY)
Humboldt State U (CA)
Huntingdon Coll (AL)
Huntington U (IN)
Idaho State U (ID)
Illinois State U (IL)
Illinois Wesleyan U (IL)
Immaculata U (PA)
Indiana U Bloomington (IN)
Indiana U–Purdue U Fort Wayne (IN)
Indiana U South Bend (IN)
Indiana Wesleyan U (IN)
Inter American U of Puerto Rico, San Germán Campus (PR)
Iowa State U of Science and Technology (IA)
Iowa Wesleyan Coll (IA)
Ithaca Coll (NY)
Jacksonville State U (AL)
Jamestown Coll (ND)
Jarvis Christian Coll (TX)
John Brown U (AR)
Johnson State Coll (VT)
Judson Coll (AL)
Kansas State U (KS)
Kean U (NJ)
Keene State Coll (NH)
Kennesaw State U (GA)
Kent State U (OH)
Lamar U (TX)
Lawrence U (WI)
Lebanon Valley Coll (PA)
Lee U (TN)
Liberty U (VA)
Limestone Coll (SC)
Lincoln U (MO)
Lindenwood U (MO)
Lipscomb U (TN)
Long Island U, Brooklyn Campus (NY)
Long Island U, C.W. Post Campus (NY)
Longwood U (VA)
Louisiana Coll (LA)
Louisiana State U and Ag and Mech Coll (LA)
Loyola U New Orleans (LA)
Lubbock Christian U (TX)
Malone U (OH)
Manchester Coll (IN)
Manhattanville Coll (NY)
Mansfield U of Pennsylvania (PA)
Maranatha Baptist Bible Coll (WI)
Marian U (WI)
Marietta Coll (OH)
Mars Hill Coll (NC)
Maryville Coll (TN)
Marywood U (PA)
The Master's Coll and Sem (CA)
McKendree U (IL)
Mercer U (GA)
Messiah Coll (PA)
Miami U (OH)
Michigan State U (MI)
MidAmerica Nazarene U (KS)
Midwestern State U (TX)
Millersville U of Pennsylvania (PA)
Milligan Coll (TN)
Millikin U (IL)
Minnesota State U Mankato (MN)
Minnesota State U Moorhead (MN)
Minot State U (ND)
Mississippi State U (MS)

Mississippi Valley State U (MS)
Missouri Baptist U (MO)
Missouri State U (MO)
Montana State U (MT)
Montana State U Billings (MT)
Moravian Coll (PA)
Morningside Coll (IA)
Mount Marty Coll (SD)
Mount Mercy U (IA)
Mount Vernon Nazarene U (OH)
Nazareth Coll of Rochester (NY)
Nebraska Wesleyan U (NE)
Newberry Coll (SC)
New Jersey City U (NJ)
New Mexico State U (NM)
New York U (NY)
Nicholls State U (LA)
North Carolina Ag and Tech State U (NC)
North Central Coll (IL)
North Dakota State U (ND)
Northeastern State U (OK)
Northern Arizona U (AZ)
Northern Illinois U (IL)
Northern Michigan U (MI)
Northern State U (SD)
North Georgia Coll & State U (GA)
North Greenville U (SC)
Northwestern Coll (IA)
Northwestern Coll (MN)
Northwestern Oklahoma State U (OK)
Northwestern State U of Louisiana (LA)
Northwest Missouri State U (MO)
Northwest Nazarene U (ID)
Northwest U (WA)
Nyack Coll (NY)
Oberlin Coll (OH)
The Ohio State U (OH)
Ohio Wesleyan U (OH)
Oklahoma Christian U (OK)
Oklahoma City U (OK)
Oklahoma State U (OK)
Ouachita Baptist U (AR)
Pacific Lutheran U (WA)
Pacific U (OR)
Palm Beach Atlantic U (FL)
Peabody Conservatory of The Johns Hopkins U (MD)
Penn State U Park (PA)
Pepperdine U, Malibu (CA)
Pittsburg State U (KS)
Presbyterian Coll (SC)
Providence Coll (RI)
Queens Coll of the City U of New York (NY)
Quincy U (IL)
Rhode Island Coll (RI)
Rider U (NJ)
Ripon Coll (WI)
Rocky Mountain Coll (MT)
Roosevelt U (IL)
Rutgers, The State U of New Jersey, New Brunswick (NJ)
Saginaw Valley State U (MI)
St. Ambrose U (IA)
St. Catherine U (MN)
Saint Mary-of-the-Woods Coll (IN)
Saint Mary's Coll (IN)
Saint Mary's U of Minnesota (MN)
St. Norbert Coll (WI)
St. Olaf Coll (MN)
Saint Xavier U (IL)
Salve Regina U (RI)
Samford U (AL)
San Diego Christian Coll (CA)
San Diego State U (CA)
Schreiner U (TX)
Seton Hill U (PA)
Shenandoah U (VA)
Shorter U (GA)
Silver Lake Coll (WI)
Simpson Coll (IA)
Simpson U (CA)
Sonoma State U (CA)
South Dakota State U (SD)
Southeastern Louisiana U (LA)
Southeastern Oklahoma State U (OK)
Southeastern U (FL)
Southeast Missouri State U (MO)
Southern Adventist U (TN)
Southern Arkansas U–Magnolia (AR)
Southern Methodist U (TX)
Southern Nazarene U (OK)
Southern Utah U (UT)

Southern Wesleyan U (SC)
Southwestern Assemblies of God U (TX)
Southwestern Coll (KS)
Spring Arbor U (MI)
State U of New York at Fredonia (NY)
State U of New York Coll at Potsdam (NY)
Stetson U (FL)
Susquehanna U (PA)
Syracuse U (NY)
Tabor Coll (KS)
Talladega Coll (AL)
Tarleton State U (TX)
Taylor U (IN)
Temple U (PA)
Tennessee Technological U (TN)
Texas A&M U–Corpus Christi (TX)
Texas Christian U (TX)
Texas Lutheran U (TX)
Texas Wesleyan U (TX)
Towson U (MD)
Transylvania U (KY)
Trevecca Nazarene U (TN)
Union Coll (NE)
Union U (TN)
The U of Akron (OH)
The U of Alabama (AL)
The U of Arizona (AZ)
The U of British Columbia (BC, Canada)
U of Central Florida (FL)
U of Central Missouri (MO)
U of Charleston (WV)
U of Cincinnati (OH)
U of Colorado Boulder (CO)
U of Dayton (OH)
U of Delaware (DE)
U of Evansville (IN)
U of Florida (FL)
U of Georgia (GA)
U of Hartford (CT)
U of Idaho (ID)
U of Indianapolis (IN)
The U of Iowa (IA)
The U of Kansas (KS)
U of Lethbridge (AB, Canada)
U of Louisiana at Lafayette (LA)
U of Louisiana at Monroe (LA)
U of Louisville (KY)
U of Maine (ME)
U of Mary Hardin-Baylor (TX)
U of Maryland, Coll Park (MD)
U of Miami (FL)
U of Michigan (MI)
U of Michigan–Flint (MI)
U of Minnesota, Duluth (MN)
U of Minnesota, Twin Cities Campus (MN)
U of Missouri (MO)
U of Missouri–St. Louis (MO)
The U of Montana Western (MT)
U of Mount Union (OH)
U of Nebraska at Omaha (NE)
U of Nebraska–Lincoln (NE)
U of Nevada, Reno (NV)
U of New Brunswick Fredericton (NB, Canada)
The U of North Carolina at Charlotte (NC)
The U of North Carolina at Greensboro (NC)
The U of North Carolina at Pembroke (NC)
The U of North Carolina Wilmington (NC)
U of North Dakota (ND)
U of Northern Colorado (CO)
U of Northern Iowa (IA)
U of North Florida (FL)
U of Oklahoma (OK)
U of Oregon (OR)
U of Portland (OR)
U of Puget Sound (WA)
U of Redlands (CA)
U of Regina (SK, Canada)
U of Rhode Island (RI)
U of Rio Grande (OH)
U of Rochester (NY)
U of St. Francis (IL)
U of St. Thomas (MN)
U of St. Thomas (TX)
U of Saskatchewan (SK, Canada)
U of Sioux Falls (SD)
U of South Carolina (SC)
U of South Carolina Aiken (SC)

The U of South Dakota (SD)
U of Southern California (CA)
U of Southern Maine (ME)
U of Southern Mississippi (MS)
U of South Florida (FL)
The U of Tampa (FL)
The U of Tennessee at Chattanooga (TN)
The U of Tennessee at Martin (TN)
U of the Cumberlands (KY)
U of the District of Columbia (DC)
U of the Incarnate Word (TX)
U of the Pacific (CA)
U of the Virgin Islands (VI)
The U of Toledo (OH)
U of Tulsa (OK)
U of Vermont (VT)
U of Washington (WA)
U of West Florida (FL)
U of West Georgia (GA)
U of Wisconsin–Green Bay (WI)
U of Wisconsin–Madison (WI)
U of Wisconsin–River Falls (WI)
U of Wisconsin–Stevens Point (WI)
U of Wisconsin–Superior (WI)
U of Wisconsin–Whitewater (WI)
U of Wyoming (WY)
Utah State U (UT)
Utah Valley U (UT)
Valdosta State U (GA)
Valparaiso U (IN)
Vanderbilt U (TN)
VanderCook Coll of Music (IL)
Viterbo U (WI)
Walla Walla U (WA)
Wartburg Coll (IA)
Washburn U (KS)
Washington Adventist U (MD)
Washington State U (WA)
Wayland Baptist U (TX)
Wayne State Coll (NE)
Weber State U (UT)
Webster U (MO)
Western Carolina U (NC)
Western Connecticut State U (CT)
Western Michigan U (MI)
Western State Coll of Colorado (CO)
West Liberty U (WV)
Wheaton Coll (IL)
Wichita State U (KS)
William Jewell Coll (MO)
William Paterson U of New Jersey (NJ)
Wilmington Coll (OH)
Wingate U (NC)
Winona State U (MN)
Winthrop U (SC)
Wright State U (OH)
Xavier U (OH)
Xavier U of Louisiana (LA)
York Coll of Pennsylvania (PA)
Youngstown State U (OH)

MUSIC TECHNOLOGY
Bethune-Cookman U (FL)
Shenandoah U (VA)
Stetson U (FL)
Transylvania U (KY)
Trevecca Nazarene U (TN)
U of Michigan (MI)
The U of Texas at Austin (TX)

MUSIC THEORY AND COMPOSITION
Adams State Coll (CO)
American U (DC)
Arizona State U (AZ)
Augustana Coll (IL)
Baldwin-Wallace Coll (OH)
Bard Coll (NY)
Bard Coll at Simon's Rock (MA)
Bennington Coll (VT)
Biola U (CA)
Birmingham-Southern Coll (AL)
Boston U (MA)
Bowling Green State U (OH)
Bucknell U (PA)
Butler U (IN)
California Baptist U (CA)
California Inst of the Arts (CA)
California State U, Chico (CA)
California State U, Long Beach (CA)
Calvin Coll (MI)
Capital U (OH)
Carnegie Mellon U (PA)
Carson-Newman Coll (TN)
The Catholic U of America (DC)

Cedarville U (OH)
Central Michigan U (MI)
Chapman U (CA)
Christopher Newport U (VA)
City Coll of the City U of New York (NY)
The Coll of Wooster (OH)
Colorado State U (CO)
Concordia Coll (MN)
Concordia U (QC, Canada)
Concordia U Chicago (IL)
Dallas Baptist U (TX)
DePaul U (IL)
DePauw U (IN)
Drury U (MO)
Florida State U (FL)
Gardner-Webb U (NC)
Georgia Southern U (GA)
Hardin-Simmons U (TX)
Hofstra U (NY)
Hope Coll (MI)
Houghton Coll (NY)
Illinois Wesleyan U (IL)
Indiana Wesleyan U (IN)
Ithaca Coll (NY)
Keene State Coll (NH)
Lawrence U (WI)
Linfield Coll (OR)
Lipscomb U (TN)
Long Island U, Brooklyn Campus (NY)
Loyola U New Orleans (LA)
Manchester Coll (IN)
Mannes Coll The New School for Music (NY)
Marylhurst U (OR)
Maryville Coll (TN)
McNally Smith Coll of Music (MN)
Michigan State U (MI)
Moravian Coll (PA)
New England Conservatory of Music (MA)
The New School for Jazz and Contemporary Music (NY)
Northwestern Coll (MN)
Northwest Nazarene U (ID)
Nyack Coll (NY)
Oberlin Coll (OH)
The Ohio State U (OH)
Ohio U (OH)
Oklahoma City U (OK)
Ouachita Baptist U (AR)
Palm Beach Atlantic U (FL)
Randolph Coll (VA)
Rice U (TX)
Rider U (NJ)
Roosevelt U (IL)
Rowan U (NJ)
St. Olaf Coll (MN)
Samford U (AL)
San Francisco Conservatory of Music (CA)
Sarah Lawrence Coll (NY)
Shenandoah U (VA)
Southern Adventist U (TN)
State U of New York Coll at Potsdam (NY)
Stetson U (FL)
Susquehanna U (PA)
Syracuse U (NY)
Temple U (PA)
Texas Christian U (TX)
Texas Tech U (TX)
Trinity U (TX)
Tulane U (LA)
The U of British Columbia (BC, Canada)
U of Central Missouri (MO)
U of Cincinnati (OH)
U of Delaware (DE)
U of Georgia (GA)
U of Idaho (ID)
The U of Kansas (KS)
U of Mary Hardin-Baylor (TX)
U of Miami (FL)
U of Michigan (MI)
U of Nebraska at Omaha (NE)
U of Nevada, Las Vegas (NV)
The U of North Carolina at Greensboro (NC)
U of Northern Iowa (IA)
U of North Texas (TX)
U of Oregon (OR)
U of Redlands (CA)
U of Regina (SK, Canada)
U of Rhode Island (RI)
U of Rochester (NY)
U of Southern California (CA)

The U of Texas at Austin (TX)
The U of Texas at San Antonio (TX)
The U of the Arts (PA)
U of the Pacific (CA)
U of Tulsa (OK)
U of Washington (WA)
The U of Western Ontario (ON, Canada)
U of West Georgia (GA)
Valparaiso U (IN)
Vanderbilt U (TN)
Wartburg Coll (IA)
Washington State U (WA)
Washington U in St. Louis (MO)
Webster U (MO)
Western Connecticut State U (CT)
Western Michigan U (MI)
Wheaton Coll (IL)
Whitman Coll (WA)
Willamette U (OR)
William Jewell Coll (MO)
Youngstown State U (OH)

MUSIC THERAPY
Alverno Coll (WI)
Anna Maria Coll (MA)
Appalachian State U (NC)
Arizona State U (AZ)
Augsburg Coll (MN)
Baldwin-Wallace Coll (OH)
The Coll of Wooster (OH)
Colorado State U (CO)
Concordia U Wisconsin (WI)
Duquesne U (PA)
Eastern Michigan U (MI)
Elizabethtown Coll (PA)
Florida State U (FL)
Georgia Coll & State U (GA)
Immaculata U (PA)
Indiana U–Purdue U Fort Wayne (IN)
Loyola U New Orleans (LA)
Lubbock Christian U (TX)
Marylhurst U (OR)
Maryville U of Saint Louis (MO)
Marywood U (PA)
Molloy Coll (NY)
Montclair State U (NJ)
Nazareth Coll of Rochester (NY)
Saint Mary-of-the-Woods Coll (IN)
Sam Houston State U (TX)
Seattle Pacific U (WA)
Seton Hill U (PA)
Shenandoah U (VA)
Slippery Rock U of Pennsylvania (PA)
Southern Methodist U (TX)
State U of New York at Fredonia (NY)
State U of New York at New Paltz (NY)
Temple U (PA)
Texas Woman's U (TX)
U of Dayton (OH)
U of Evansville (IN)
U of Georgia (GA)
The U of Iowa (IA)
The U of Kansas (KS)
U of Louisville (KY)
U of Miami (FL)
U of Minnesota, Twin Cities Campus (MN)
U of North Dakota (ND)
U of the Incarnate Word (TX)
U of the Pacific (CA)
Utah State U (UT)
Wartburg Coll (IA)
Western Michigan U (MI)
Wilfrid Laurier U (ON, Canada)

NATURAL RESOURCE ECONOMICS
Baldwin-Wallace Coll (OH)
Colorado State U (CO)
Michigan State U (MI)
U of New Hampshire (NH)

NATURAL RESOURCE RECREATION AND TOURISM
U of Idaho (ID)

NATURAL RESOURCES AND CONSERVATION RELATED
California Polytechnic State U, San Luis Obispo (CA)
Lakehead U (ON, Canada)
Mount Mercy U (IA)
Northwest Missouri State U (MO)
Penn State Abington (PA)

Penn State Altoona (PA)
Penn State Berks (PA)
Penn State Brandywine (PA)
Penn State DuBois (PA)
Penn State Erie, The Behrend Coll (PA)
Penn State Fayette, The Eberly Campus (PA)
Penn State Greater Allegheny (PA)
Penn State Hazleton (PA)
Penn State Lehigh Valley (PA)
Penn State Mont Alto (PA)
Penn State New Kensington (PA)
Penn State Schuylkill (PA)
Penn State Shenango (PA)
Penn State U Park (PA)
Penn State Wilkes-Barre (PA)
Penn State Worthington Scranton (PA)
Penn State York (PA)
Sterling Coll (VT)
Texas A&M U–Kingsville (TX)
U of Alaska Fairbanks (AK)
The U of British Columbia (BC, Canada)
U of California, Davis (CA)
U of Louisiana at Lafayette (LA)
U of New Hampshire (NH)
U of Wisconsin–Stevens Point (WI)
Utah State U (UT)

NATURAL RESOURCES/ CONSERVATION
Ball State U (IN)
Carroll U (WI)
Central Michigan U (MI)
Clemson U (SC)
Colorado State U (CO)
Cornell U (NY)
The Evergreen State Coll (WA)
Grand Valley State U (MI)
Humboldt State U (CA)
Kent State U (OH)
Manchester Coll (IN)
Marist Coll (NY)
Marlboro Coll (VT)
Montana State U (MT)
Mount Vernon Nazarene U (OH)
New Jersey Inst of Technology (NJ)
North Carolina State U (NC)
Northern Michigan U (MI)
Northland Coll (WI)
Oregon State U (OR)
Penn State Abington (PA)
Penn State Altoona (PA)
Penn State Beaver (PA)
Penn State Berks (PA)
Penn State Brandywine (PA)
Penn State DuBois (PA)
Penn State Erie, The Behrend Coll (PA)
Penn State Fayette, The Eberly Campus (PA)
Penn State Greater Allegheny (PA)
Penn State Hazleton (PA)
Penn State Lehigh Valley (PA)
Penn State Mont Alto (PA)
Penn State New Kensington (PA)
Penn State Schuylkill (PA)
Penn State Shenango (PA)
Penn State U Park (PA)
Penn State Wilkes-Barre (PA)
Penn State Worthington Scranton (PA)
Penn State York (PA)
Prescott Coll (AZ)
Purdue U (IN)
Rutgers, The State U of New Jersey, New Brunswick (NJ)
Southeastern Oklahoma State U (OK)
State U of New York at Plattsburgh (NY)
State U of New York Coll at Potsdam (NY)
State U of New York Coll of Environmental Science and Forestry (NY)
Sterling Coll (VT)
Stony Brook U, State U of New York (NY)
Suffolk U (MA)
Texas A&M U (TX)
Texas Tech U (TX)
U of Alaska Southeast (AK)
The U of British Columbia (BC, Canada)
U of California, Berkeley (CA)
U of California, Davis (CA)

U of Georgia (GA)
U of Louisiana at Lafayette (LA)
U of Maryland, Coll Park (MD)
U of Massachusetts Amherst (MA)
U of Michigan–Flint (MI)
U of Minnesota, Crookston (MN)
U of Minnesota, Twin Cities Campus (MN)
U of Missouri (MO)
U of Nebraska–Lincoln (NE)
U of Nevada, Reno (NV)
U of New Hampshire (NH)
U of Vermont (VT)
U of Wisconsin–River Falls (WI)
U of Wisconsin–Stevens Point (WI)
Upper Iowa U (IA)
Washington State U (WA)
Washington U in St. Louis (MO)
Winona State U (MN)

NATURAL RESOURCES/ CONSERVATION RELATED
Arizona State U (AZ)
Prescott Coll (AZ)
Sierra Nevada Coll (NV)
Sterling Coll (VT)

NATURAL RESOURCES LAW ENFORCEMENT AND PROTECTIVE SERVICES
U of Minnesota, Crookston (MN)

NATURAL RESOURCES MANAGEMENT AND POLICY
Albright Coll (PA)
Angelo State U (TX)
Bowling Green State U (OH)
California State U, Chico (CA)
Carnegie Mellon U (PA)
Clark U (MA)
Colorado State U (CO)
Delaware State U (DE)
Dominican U of California (CA)
Humboldt State U (CA)
Iowa State U of Science and Technology (IA)
Johnson State Coll (VT)
Louisiana State U and Ag and Mech Coll (LA)
New Mexico Highlands U (NM)
North Carolina State U (NC)
North Dakota State U (ND)
Oregon State U (OR)
Prescott Coll (AZ)
Roanoke Coll (VA)
Sewanee: The U of the South (TN)
South Dakota State U (SD)
State U of New York Coll of Environmental Science and Forestry (NY)
Sterling Coll (VT)
Texas A&M U (TX)
Tuskegee U (AL)
The U of British Columbia (BC, Canada)
U of California, Berkeley (CA)
U of Delaware (DE)
U of Guelph (ON, Canada)
U of Hawaii at Manoa (HI)
U of Idaho (ID)
U of La Verne (CA)
U of Maine (ME)
U of Miami (FL)
U of Minnesota, Crookston (MN)
U of Minnesota, Twin Cities Campus (MN)
U of Nebraska–Lincoln (NE)
U of Nevada, Reno (NV)
U of Rhode Island (RI)
The U of Tennessee at Martin (TN)
U of Washington (WA)
U of Wisconsin–Stevens Point (WI)
Western Carolina U (NC)
Wichita State U (KS)
Xavier U (OH)

NATURAL RESOURCES MANAGEMENT AND POLICY RELATED
Delaware State U (DE)
Great Basin Coll (NV)
Humboldt State U (CA)
Keystone Coll (PA)
Massachusetts Maritime Acad (MA)
Moravian Coll (PA)
Prescott Coll (AZ)
Rutgers, The State U of New Jersey, New Brunswick (NJ)
St. Petersburg Coll (FL)

Sterling Coll (VT)
The U of British Columbia (BC, Canada)
U of Minnesota, Twin Cities Campus (MN)
U of Saskatchewan (SK, Canada)
The U of Tennessee at Martin (TN)

NATURAL SCIENCES
Alderson-Broaddus Coll (WV)
Arcadia U (PA)
Atlantic Union Coll (MA)
Augsburg Coll (MN)
Azusa Pacific U (CA)
Bemidji State U (MN)
Benedictine Coll (KS)
Blue Mountain Coll (MS)
California State U, Dominguez Hills (CA)
California State U, Los Angeles (CA)
California State U, San Bernardino (CA)
Calvin Coll (MI)
Case Western Reserve U (OH)
Castleton State Coll (VT)
Central Coll (IA)
Christian Brothers U (TN)
Colgate U (NY)
Coll of Mount St. Joseph (OH)
Coll of Saint Benedict (MN)
Coll of Saint Mary (NE)
The Coll of St. Scholastica (MN)
Coll of the Atlantic (ME)
Coll of the Humanities and Sciences, Harrison Middleton U (AZ)
Colorado State U (CO)
Concordia Coll (MN)
Concordia U Chicago (IL)
Dallas Baptist U (TX)
Defiance Coll (OH)
Doane Coll (NE)
Dordt Coll (IA)
Edgewood Coll (WI)
The Evergreen State Coll (WA)
Felician Coll (NJ)
Georgian Court U (NJ)
Houghton Coll (NY)
Humboldt State U (CA)
Indiana U East (IN)
Inter American U of Puerto Rico, San Germán Campus (PR)
Iowa Wesleyan Coll (IA)
The Johns Hopkins U (MD)
Johnson C. Smith U (NC)
Juniata Coll (PA)
Kansas State U (KS)
Lakehead U (ON, Canada)
Lee U (TN)
Lesley U (MA)
LeTourneau U (TX)
Lewis-Clark State Coll (ID)
Longwood U (VA)
Loyola Marymount U (CA)
Madonna U (MI)
Marlboro Coll (VT)
The Master's Coll and Sem (CA)
Minnesota State U Mankato (MN)
Mount Allison U (NB, Canada)
Mount Saint Mary Coll (NY)
Muhlenberg Coll (PA)
New Coll of Florida (FL)
Oklahoma Wesleyan U (OK)
Oregon State U (OR)
Our Lady of the Lake U of San Antonio (TX)
Pacific Union Coll (CA)
Pepperdine U, Malibu (CA)
Saint John's U (MN)
St. Thomas Aquinas Coll (NY)
San Jose State U (CA)
Sarah Lawrence Coll (NY)
Shimer Coll (IL)
Shorter U (GA)
Siena Heights U (MI)
Spelman Coll (GA)
State U of New York Coll at Geneseo (NY)
Tabor Coll (KS)
Taylor U (IN)
Thomas Edison State Coll (NJ)
Trent U (ON, Canada)
U of Alaska Fairbanks (AK)
U of Hawaii at Hilo (HI)
U of La Verne (CA)
U of Maine (ME)
U of Nebraska at Omaha (NE)
U of Pennsylvania (PA)
U of Pittsburgh at Greensburg (PA)
U of Pittsburgh at Johnstown (PA)

U of Puget Sound (WA)
U of Science and Arts of Oklahoma (OK)
The U of Toledo (OH)
U of Wisconsin–River Falls (WI)
U of Wisconsin–Stevens Point (WI)
Virginia Wesleyan Coll (VA)
Viterbo U (WI)
Washington U in St. Louis (MO)
Western Oregon U (OR)
Winona State U (MN)
Xavier U (OH)

NAVAL ARCHITECTURE AND MARINE ENGINEERING
Massachusetts Maritime Acad (MA)
State U of New York Maritime Coll (NY)
United States Coast Guard Acad (CT)
United States Merchant Marine Acad (NY)
United States Naval Acad (MD)
U of Michigan (MI)
U of Minnesota, Twin Cities Campus (MN)
U of Wisconsin–Madison (WI)

NAVY/MARINE CORPS ROTC/ NAVAL SCIENCE
State U of New York Maritime Coll (NY)
U of Washington (WA)

NEAR AND MIDDLE EASTERN STUDIES
American Public U System (WV)
Bard Coll (NY)
Brandeis U (MA)
Brown U (RI)
Claremont McKenna Coll (CA)
Columbia U, School of General Studies (NY)
Cornell U (NY)
Dartmouth Coll (NH)
Dickinson Coll (PA)
Emory & Henry Coll (VA)
Hampshire Coll (MA)
Harvard U (MA)
Hood Coll (MD)
The Johns Hopkins U (MD)
New York U (NY)
Oberlin Coll (OH)
Portland State U (OR)
Princeton U (NJ)
Rutgers, The State U of New Jersey, New Brunswick (NJ)
Sacred Heart U (CT)
Sarah Lawrence Coll (NY)
Scripps Coll (CA)
Smith Coll (MA)
Syracuse U (NY)
Texas State U–San Marcos (TX)
United States Military Acad (NY)
The U of Arizona (AZ)
U of California, Berkeley (CA)
U of California, Santa Barbara (CA)
U of Massachusetts Amherst (MA)
U of Michigan (MI)
U of Minnesota, Twin Cities Campus (MN)
U of Richmond (VA)
The U of Texas at Austin (TX)
The U of Toledo (OH)
U of Utah (UT)
U of Washington (WA)
Washington U in St. Louis (MO)
Wellesley Coll (MA)

NETWORK AND SYSTEM ADMINISTRATION
Champlain Coll (VT)
Dordt Coll (IA)
Simmons Coll (MA)

NEUROBIOLOGY AND ANATOMY
Andrews U (MI)
Georgetown U (DC)
Harvard U (MA)
New Coll of Florida (FL)
St. Lawrence U (NY)
U of California, Davis (CA)

NEUROSCIENCE
Allegheny Coll (PA)
Amherst Coll (MA)
Augustana Coll (IL)
Baldwin-Wallace Coll (OH)
Bard Coll (NY)

INDEXES

Barnard Coll (NY)
Bates Coll (ME)
Boston U (MA)
Bowdoin Coll (ME)
Bowling Green State U (OH)
Brandeis U (MA)
Brock U (ON, Canada)
Brown U (RI)
Bucknell U (PA)
Carnegie Mellon U (PA)
Cedar Crest Coll (PA)
Centenary Coll of Louisiana (LA)
Central Michigan U (MI)
Claremont McKenna Coll (CA)
Clark U (MA)
Colby Coll (ME)
Colgate U (NY)
The Coll of William and Mary (VA)
The Coll of Wooster (OH)
The Colorado Coll (CO)
Columbia U, School of General
  Studies (NY)
Concordia U (QC, Canada)
Connecticut Coll (CT)
Dickinson Coll (PA)
Dominican U (IL)
Drake U (IA)
Drew U (NJ)
Earlham Coll (IN)
Emmanuel Coll (MA)
Franklin & Marshall Coll (PA)
Furman U (SC)
Hamilton Coll (NY)
Hampshire Coll (MA)
Haverford Coll (PA)
Indiana U Bloomington (IN)
John Carroll U (OH)
The Johns Hopkins U (MD)
Kenyon Coll (OH)
King Coll (TN)
King's Coll (PA)
Knox Coll (IL)
Lake Forest Coll (IL)
Lawrence U (WI)
Lehigh U (PA)
Loyola U Chicago (IL)
Macalester Coll (MN)
Massachusetts Inst of Technology
  (MA)
Middlebury Coll (VT)
Mount Holyoke Coll (MA)
Muhlenberg Coll (PA)
New York U (NY)
Northeastern U (MA)
Northwest Nazarene U (ID)
Oberlin Coll (OH)
Ohio U (OH)
Ohio Wesleyan U (OH)
Pitzer Coll (CA)
Pomona Coll (CA)
Regis U (CO)
Rice U (TX)
St. Lawrence U (NY)
Scripps Coll (CA)
Skidmore Coll (NY)
Smith Coll (MA)
Stonehill Coll (MA)
Temple U (PA)
Texas Christian U (TX)
Thiel Coll (PA)
Trinity Coll (CT)
Trinity U (TX)
Tulane U (LA)
Union Coll (NY)
The U of Alabama at Birmingham
  (AL)
U of California, Irvine (CA)
U of California, Los Angeles (CA)
U of California, Santa Cruz (CA)
U of Cincinnati (OH)
U of Delaware (DE)
U of Evansville (IN)
U of Illinois at Chicago (IL)
U of Lethbridge (AB, Canada)
U of Miami (FL)
U of Michigan (MI)
U of Minnesota, Twin Cities
  Campus (MN)
U of Mount Union (OH)
U of New Hampshire (NH)
U of Pennsylvania (PA)
U of Pittsburgh (PA)
U of Rochester (NY)
The U of Scranton (PA)
U of Southern California (CA)
The U of Texas at Dallas (TX)
Vanderbilt U (TN)
Washington and Lee U (VA)

Washington State U (WA)
Washington U in St. Louis (MO)
Wellesley Coll (MA)
Westminster Coll (UT)
Westmont Coll (CA)

NONPROFIT MANAGEMENT
Arizona State U (AZ)
Austin Peay State U (TN)
Concordia U Chicago (IL)
Franklin U (OH)
Friends U (KS)
Gettysburg Coll (PA)
Grace Coll (IN)
Hawai`i Pacific U (HI)
Huntington U (IN)
Pace U (NY)
Southern Adventist U (TN)
Southern Vermont Coll (VT)
Tiffin U (OH)
Trevecca Nazarene U (TN)
U of Baltimore (MD)
U of Guelph (ON, Canada)
U of South Carolina Upstate (SC)

NORWEGIAN
Brigham Young U (UT)
Pacific Lutheran U (WA)
St. Olaf Coll (MN)

NUCLEAR ENGINEERING
Georgia Inst of Technology (GA)
Idaho State U (ID)
Kansas State U (KS)
Massachusetts Inst of Technology
  (MA)
Missouri U of Science and
  Technology (MO)
North Carolina State U (NC)
Oregon State U (OR)
Penn State Abington (PA)
Penn State Altoona (PA)
Penn State Beaver (PA)
Penn State Berks (PA)
Penn State Brandywine (PA)
Penn State DuBois (PA)
Penn State Erie, The Behrend Coll
  (PA)
Penn State Fayette, The Eberly
  Campus (PA)
Penn State Greater Allegheny (PA)
Penn State Hazleton (PA)
Penn State Lehigh Valley (PA)
Penn State Mont Alto (PA)
Penn State New Kensington (PA)
Penn State Schuylkill (PA)
Penn State Shenango (PA)
Penn State U Park (PA)
Penn State Wilkes-Barre (PA)
Penn State Worthington Scranton
  (PA)
Penn State York (PA)
Purdue U (IN)
Rensselaer Polytechnic Inst (NY)
Texas A&M U (TX)
United States Military Acad (NY)
The U of Arizona (AZ)
U of California, Berkeley (CA)
U of Florida (FL)
U of Michigan (MI)
The U of Tennessee (TN)
U of Wisconsin–Madison (WI)
Worcester Polytechnic Inst (MA)

**NUCLEAR ENGINEERING
TECHNOLOGY**
Thomas Edison State Coll (NJ)
United States Merchant Marine
  Acad (NY)
United States Military Acad (NY)

**NUCLEAR MEDICAL
TECHNOLOGY**
Allen Coll (IA)
Baptist Coll of Health Sciences (TN)
Barry U (FL)
Benedictine U (IL)
Cedar Crest Coll (PA)
Ferris State U (MI)
Georgia Health Sciences U (GA)
Indiana U Bloomington (IN)
Indiana U East (IN)
Indiana U of Pennsylvania (PA)
Indiana U–Purdue U Indianapolis
  (IN)
Indiana U South Bend (IN)
Indiana U Southeast (IN)
Lewis U (IL)

Long Island U, Brooklyn Campus
  (NY)
Long Island U, C.W. Post Campus
  (NY)
Loras Coll (IA)
Manhattan Coll (NY)
North Central Coll (IL)
Old Dominion U (VA)
Robert Morris U (PA)
Roosevelt U (IL)
Saint Louis U (MO)
Saint Mary's U of Minnesota (MN)
Salem State U (MA)
Thomas Edison State Coll (NJ)
U at Buffalo, the State U of New
  York (NY)
The U of Alabama at Birmingham
  (AL)
U of Arkansas for Medical Sciences
  (AR)
U of Cincinnati (OH)
The U of Findlay (OH)
The U of Iowa (IA)
U of Missouri (MO)
U of Nevada, Las Vegas (NV)
U of Oklahoma Health Sciences
  Center (OK)
U of St. Francis (IL)
U of the Incarnate Word (TX)
U of Vermont (VT)
U of Wisconsin–La Crosse (WI)
Weber State U (UT)
Wheeling Jesuit U (WV)
York Coll of Pennsylvania (PA)

**NUCLEAR/NUCLEAR POWER
TECHNOLOGY**
U of North Texas (TX)

NURSING ADMINISTRATION
Clarkson Coll (NE)
Clayton State U (GA)
Huntington U (IN)
Midwestern State U (TX)
Nebraska Wesleyan U (NE)
Nova Southeastern U (FL)
Seattle Pacific U (WA)
U of San Francisco (CA)
The U of Western Ontario (ON,
  Canada)
Wheeling Jesuit U (WV)

NURSING PRACTICE
Brenau U (GA)
Concordia Coll–New York (NY)
Florida National Coll (FL)
Misericordia U (PA)
Rowan U (NJ)
Stratford U, Falls Church (VA)

NURSING SCIENCE
Brock U (ON, Canada)
Cedar Crest Coll (PA)
Clarkson Coll (NE)
Coll of Saint Elizabeth (NJ)
Columbia Coll (PR)
Holy Family U (NJ)
Holy Names U (CA)
Kean U (NJ)
Kent State U at Geauga (OH)
Kent State U at Trumbull (OH)
Midway Coll (KY)
Millersville U of Pennsylvania (PA)
Missouri Baptist U (MO)
Monmouth U (NJ)
National U (CA)
New Jersey City U (NJ)
New Jersey Inst of Technology (NJ)
North Carolina Ag and Tech State U
  (NC)
The Ohio State U (OH)
Rowan U (NJ)
St. Francis Xavier U (NS, Canada)
Southern Adventist U (TN)
State U of New York Upstate
  Medical U (NY)
Trinity Coll of Nursing and Health
  Sciences (IL)
U of California, Irvine (CA)
U of Delaware (DE)
U of Illinois at Chicago (IL)
U of New Hampshire at Manchester
  (NH)
U of Pittsburgh at Johnstown (PA)
Wayne State U (MI)
Wichita State U (KS)
Xavier U (OH)

NUTRITION SCIENCES
Auburn U (AL)
Boston U (MA)
California State U, Los Angeles
  (CA)
Case Western Reserve U (OH)
Coll of Saint Benedict (MN)
Concordia Coll (MN)
Cornell U (NY)
Elmhurst Coll (IL)
Goddard Coll (VT)
Huntington Coll of Health Sciences
  (TN)
Johnson & Wales U (CO)
Johnson & Wales U (RI)
La Salle U (PA)
Lebanese American U (Lebanon)
Louisiana State U and Ag and Mech
  Coll (LA)
Messiah Coll (PA)
Michigan State U (MI)
New York Inst of Technology (NY)
North Carolina State U (NC)
Russell Sage Coll (NY)
Rutgers, The State U of New
  Jersey, New Brunswick (NJ)
Saint John's U (MN)
Saint Joseph Coll (CT)
Southern Illinois U Carbondale (IL)
Texas Woman's U (TX)
The U of Arizona (AZ)
U of California, Berkeley (CA)
U of California, Davis (CA)
U of Delaware (DE)
U of Guelph (ON, Canada)
U of Hawaii at Manoa (HI)
U of Illinois at Chicago (IL)
U of Massachusetts Amherst (MA)
U of Massachusetts Lowell (MA)
U of Minnesota, Twin Cities
  Campus (MN)
U of Nevada, Las Vegas (NV)
U of New Hampshire (NH)
The U of North Carolina at
  Greensboro (NC)
U of Northern Colorado (CO)
U of Saskatchewan (SK, Canada)
U of Southern Indiana (IN)
U of the District of Columbia (DC)
U of the Incarnate Word (TX)
U of Vermont (VT)
U of Wisconsin–Madison (WI)

**OCCUPATIONAL HEALTH AND
INDUSTRIAL HYGIENE**
Grand Valley State U (MI)
Montana Tech of The U of Montana
  (MT)
North Carolina Ag and Tech State U
  (NC)
Ohio U (OH)

**OCCUPATIONAL SAFETY AND
HEALTH TECHNOLOGY**
Columbia Southern U (AL)
Embry-Riddle Aeronautical U–
  Daytona (FL)
Fairmont State U (WV)
Grand Valley State U (MI)
Indiana State U (IN)
Indiana U of Pennsylvania (PA)
Indiana U Southeast (IN)
Jacksonville State U (AL)
Keene State Coll (NH)
Marshall U (WV)
Millersville U of Pennsylvania (PA)
Murray State U (KY)
National U (CA)
Slippery Rock U of Pennsylvania
  (PA)
Southeastern Louisiana U (LA)
Southeastern Oklahoma State U
  (OK)
U of Central Missouri (MO)
U of Houston–Downtown (TX)
U of New Haven (CT)
U of North Dakota (ND)
U of Regina (SK, Canada)
U of Wisconsin–Whitewater (WI)

OCCUPATIONAL THERAPY
Alabama State U (AL)
Baker Coll of Flint (MI)
Boston U (MA)
Brenau U (GA)
Calvin Coll (MI)
Coll of Saint Benedict (MN)
Concordia U Wisconsin (WI)

Dominican Coll (NY)
Dominican U of California (CA)
Drury U (MO)
Duquesne U (PA)
Eastern Michigan U (MI)
Eastern Washington U (WA)
Elizabethtown Coll (PA)
Elmhurst Coll (IL)
Grand Valley State U (MI)
Hawai`i Pacific U (HI)
Husson U (ME)
Illinois Coll (IL)
Ithaca Coll (NY)
Keuka Coll (NY)
Long Island U, Brooklyn Campus
  (NY)
McKendree U (IL)
Nazareth Coll of Rochester (NY)
Nevada State Coll at Henderson
  (NV)
New York Inst of Technology (NY)
Penn State Mont Alto (PA)
Quinnipiac U (CT)
Sacred Heart U (CT)
St. Catherine U (MN)
Saint Francis U (PA)
Saint John's U (MN)
San Jose State U (CA)
Spalding U (KY)
Springfield Coll (MA)
State U of New York Downstate
  Medical Center (NY)
Stephens Coll (MO)
Stony Brook U, State U of New York
  (NY)
Towson U (MD)
Tuskegee U (AL)
U at Buffalo, the State U of New
  York (NY)
The U of Findlay (OH)
The U of Kansas (KS)
U of Manitoba (MB, Canada)
U of Minnesota, Twin Cities
  Campus (MN)
U of Missouri (MO)
U of New England (ME)
U of New Hampshire (NH)
U of Ottawa (ON, Canada)
U of Pittsburgh (PA)
The U of South Dakota (SD)
U of Southern California (CA)
U of Southern Indiana (IN)
U of the Sciences in Philadelphia
  (PA)
U of Utah (UT)
U of Washington (WA)
The U of Western Ontario (ON,
  Canada)
Wartburg Coll (IA)
Western Michigan U (MI)
Worcester State U (MA)
Xavier U (OH)
York Coll of the City U of New York
  (NY)
Young Harris Coll (GA)

OCEAN ENGINEERING
California State U, Long Beach (CA)
Florida Atlantic U (FL)
Florida Inst of Technology (FL)
Texas A&M U (TX)
United States Naval Acad (MD)
U of Rhode Island (RI)
Virginia Polytechnic Inst and State
  U (VA)

**OCEANOGRAPHY (CHEMICAL
AND PHYSICAL)**
Central Michigan U (MI)
Coll of the Atlantic (ME)
Elizabeth City State U (NC)
Florida Inst of Technology (FL)
Hawai`i Pacific U (HI)
Humboldt State U (CA)
Kutztown U of Pennsylvania (PA)
Lamar U (TX)
Louisiana State U and Ag and Mech
  Coll (LA)
Millersville U of Pennsylvania (PA)
North Carolina State U (NC)
Rider U (NJ)
United States Coast Guard Acad
  (CT)
United States Naval Acad (MD)
The U of British Columbia (BC,
  Canada)
U of Miami (FL)
U of Michigan (MI)

U of South Carolina (SC)
U of Washington (WA)
U of West Florida (FL)

OFFICE MANAGEMENT
Adams State Coll (CO)
Ball State U (IN)
Bob Jones U (SC)
Clayton State U (GA)
East Central U (OK)
Eastern Michigan U (MI)
Indiana State U (IN)
Indiana U of Pennsylvania (PA)
Inter American U of Puerto Rico, Guayama Campus (PR)
Inter American U of Puerto Rico, Metropolitan Campus (PR)
Inter American U of Puerto Rico, Ponce Campus (PR)
Inter American U of Puerto Rico, San Germán Campus (PR)
Loyola U Chicago (IL)
Maranatha Baptist Bible Coll (WI)
Middle Tennessee State U (TN)
Mississippi Valley State U (MS)
Mount Vernon Nazarene U (OH)
Murray State U (KY)
Southeast Missouri State U (MO)
Tabor Coll (KS)
Tarleton State U (TX)
U of Central Missouri (MO)
U of South Carolina (SC)
U of Southern Indiana (IN)
Weber State U (UT)

OPERATIONS MANAGEMENT
Arizona State U (AZ)
Auburn U (AL)
Ball State U (IN)
Bethany Coll (KS)
Boise State U (ID)
Boston Coll (MA)
Boston U (MA)
California State U, Chico (CA)
California State U, Dominguez Hills (CA)
California State U, Long Beach (CA)
Central Michigan U (MI)
Concordia U (QC, Canada)
Dalton State Coll (GA)
Eastern Washington U (WA)
Edinboro U of Pennsylvania (PA)
Ferris State U (MI)
Fort Lewis Coll (CO)
Franklin U (OH)
Indiana U–Purdue U Fort Wayne (IN)
Indiana–Purdue U Indianapolis (IN)
Iowa State U of Science and Technology (IA)
Kent State U (OH)
Le Moyne Coll (NY)
Loyola U Chicago (IL)
Marian U (WI)
Metropolitan State U (MN)
Miami U (OH)
Minnesota State U Moorhead (MN)
Missouri Baptist U (MO)
National U (CA)
Northeastern State U (OK)
Northern Illinois U (IL)
The Ohio State U (OH)
Purdue U (IN)
Purdue U North Central (IN)
Saginaw Valley State U (MI)
Tennessee Technological U (TN)
Texas Southern U (TX)
Thomas Edison State Coll (NJ)
Trine U (IN)
The U of Akron (OH)
U of Cincinnati (OH)
U of Delaware (DE)
U of Houston (TX)
U of Idaho (ID)
U of Indianapolis (IN)
U of Massachusetts Dartmouth (MA)
U of Michigan–Flint (MI)
U of Minnesota, Crookston (MN)
U of Minnesota, Twin Cities Campus (MN)
The U of North Carolina at Asheville (NC)
The U of North Carolina at Charlotte (NC)
U of North Dakota (ND)
U of North Texas (TX)
U of Pennsylvania (PA)
U of St. Thomas (MN)
U of Saskatchewan (SK, Canada)

The U of Scranton (PA)
U of Southern Indiana (IN)
The U of Texas at San Antonio (TX)
The U of Toledo (OH)
U of Utah (UT)
U of Wisconsin–Madison (WI)
U of Wisconsin–Stout (WI)
U of Wisconsin–Whitewater (WI)
Utah State U (UT)
Utah Valley U (UT)
Washington State U (WA)
Washington U in St. Louis (MO)
Wentworth Inst of Technology (MA)
Widener U (PA)

OPERATIONS RESEARCH
California State U, Fullerton (CA)
Carnegie Mellon U (PA)
Cornell U (NY)
Long Island U, Brooklyn Campus (NY)
New York U (NY)
Princeton U (NJ)
Southern Methodist U (TX)
United States Air Force Acad (CO)
United States Coast Guard Acad (CT)
United States Military Acad (NY)
United States Naval Acad (MD)
U of California, Berkeley (CA)
U of New Brunswick Fredericton (NB, Canada)
U of Waterloo (ON, Canada)

OPHTHALMIC AND OPTOMETRIC SUPPORT SERVICES AND ALLIED PROFESSIONS RELATED
Saint Joseph's Coll of Maine (ME)
Tennessee Wesleyan Coll (TN)

OPHTHALMIC LABORATORY TECHNOLOGY
Abilene Christian U (TX)
U of Ottawa (ON, Canada)

OPHTHALMIC TECHNOLOGY
U of Arkansas for Medical Sciences (AR)

OPTICAL SCIENCES
Saginaw Valley State U (MI)
The U of Arizona (AZ)
U of Rochester (NY)

OPTOMETRIC TECHNICIAN
Indiana U Bloomington (IN)
Texas A&M U–Corpus Christi (TX)

ORGANIC CHEMISTRY
Concordia U (QC, Canada)
Sarah Lawrence Coll (NY)
The U of Western Ontario (ON, Canada)

ORGANIZATIONAL BEHAVIOR
Anderson U (IN)
Anderson U (SC)
Athabasca U (AB, Canada)
Benedictine U (IL)
Bluffton U (OH)
Boston U (MA)
Brown U (RI)
Calvary Bible Coll and Theological Sem (MO)
Carroll U (WI)
Claflin U (SC)
Coll of Mount St. Joseph (OH)
The Coll of St. Scholastica (MN)
Denison U (OH)
DePaul U (IL)
Greenville Coll (IL)
Indian River State Coll (FL)
John Brown U (AR)
Lewis U (IL)
Loyola U Chicago (IL)
Manhattan Coll (NY)
Miami U (OH)
Mid-Atlantic Christian U (NC)
Mid-Continent U (KY)
Midway Coll (KY)
National U (CA)
Northern Kentucky U (KY)
Palm Beach Atlantic U (FL)
Penn State Abington (PA)
Penn State Altoona (PA)
Penn State Beaver (PA)
Penn State Berks (PA)
Penn State Brandywine (PA)
Penn State DuBois (PA)

Penn State Erie, The Behrend Coll (PA)
Penn State Fayette, The Eberly Campus (PA)
Penn State Greater Allegheny (PA)
Penn State Harrisburg (PA)
Penn State Hazleton (PA)
Penn State Lehigh Valley (PA)
Penn State Mont Alto (PA)
Penn State New Kensington (PA)
Penn State Schuylkill (PA)
Penn State Shenango (PA)
Penn State U Park (PA)
Penn State Wilkes-Barre (PA)
Penn State Worthington Scranton (PA)
Penn State York (PA)
Pitzer Coll (CA)
Regent U (VA)
Rider U (NJ)
Robert Morris U (PA)
Roosevelt U (IL)
St. Ambrose U (IA)
Saint Louis U (MO)
Santa Clara U (CA)
Scripps Coll (CA)
Simpson U (CA)
Temple U (PA)
United States Military Acad (NY)
U of Cincinnati (OH)
U of Michigan (MI)
U of Mobile (AL)
U of North Texas (TX)
U of Oklahoma (OK)
U of St. Francis (IL)
U of San Francisco (CA)
U of the Incarnate Word (TX)
The U of Toledo (OH)
U of Tulsa (OK)
The U of Western Ontario (ON, Canada)
Wayne State U (MI)
Woodbury U (CA)

ORGANIZATIONAL COMMUNICATION
Aquinas Coll (MI)
Assumption Coll (MA)
Brigham Young U (UT)
Buena Vista U (IA)
California State U, Chico (CA)
Calvin Coll (MI)
Capital U (OH)
Cedarville U (OH)
Central Michigan U (MI)
Cleveland State U (OH)
Concordia Coll (MN)
Emmanuel Coll (GA)
Franklin U (OH)
George Fox U (OR)
Indiana U–Purdue U Fort Wayne (IN)
Lindenwood U (MO)
Lipscomb U (TN)
Lubbock Christian U (TX)
Marian U (WI)
Marist Coll (NY)
Marylhurst U (OR)
McKendree U (IL)
Missouri State U (MO)
Montana State U Billings (MT)
Murray State U (KY)
North Central Coll (IL)
Northwest Missouri State U (MO)
Northwest U (WA)
Ohio U (OH)
Pace U (NY)
Palm Beach Atlantic U (FL)
Roosevelt U (IL)
Saint Louis U (MO)
Shorter U (GA)
Southeastern U (FL)
Southeast Missouri State U (MO)
Suffolk U (MA)
Tabor Coll (KS)
Temple U (PA)
Trevecca Nazarene U (TN)
The U of Akron (OH)
U of Idaho (ID)
U of Mount Union (OH)
U of Northern Iowa (IA)
Viterbo U (WI)
Walden U (MN)
Washington State U (WA)
Western Kentucky U (KY)
Western Michigan U (MI)
Xavier U (OH)

ORGANIZATIONAL LEADERSHIP
Atlanta Christian Coll (GA)

Brenau U (GA)
Carroll U (WI)
Columbia Southern U (AL)
Indiana Wesleyan U (IN)
LaGrange Coll (GA)
Lincoln Christian U (IL)
Marquette U (WI)
Our Lady of the Lake U of San Antonio (TX)
St. Thomas U (FL)
Southwest U (LA)
Spring Hill Coll (AL)
Union Inst & U (OH)
U of Evansville (IN)
U of Houston (TX)
Western Kentucky U (KY)
Wheeling Jesuit U (WV)

ORNAMENTAL HORTICULTURE
California Polytechnic State U, San Luis Obispo (CA)
Iowa State U of Science and Technology (IA)
Tarleton State U (TX)
Texas A&M U (TX)
U of Delaware (DE)
U of Florida (FL)
The U of Tennessee (TN)
U of the District of Columbia (DC)
U of Wisconsin–Platteville (WI)

ORTHOPTICS
St. Catherine U (MN)

ORTHOTICS/PROSTHETICS
St. Petersburg Coll (FL)
U of Washington (WA)

OUTDOOR EDUCATION
Huntington U (IN)
Sierra Nevada Coll (NV)
Young Harris Coll (GA)

PACIFIC AREA/PACIFIC RIM STUDIES
Claremont McKenna Coll (CA)
Hawai`i Pacific U (HI)
U of Hawaii–West Oahu (HI)

PAINTING
Adams State Coll (CO)
Alberta Coll of Art & Design (AB, Canada)
Aquinas Coll (MI)
Arcadia U (PA)
Art Center Coll of Design (CA)
Bennington Coll (VT)
Bethany Coll (KS)
Biola U (CA)
Birmingham-Southern Coll (AL)
Boston U (MA)
Brigham Young U (UT)
California Coll of the Arts (CA)
California State U, Long Beach (CA)
The Cleveland Inst of Art (OH)
Colorado State U (CO)
Columbia Coll (MO)
Concordia U (QC, Canada)
Drake U (IA)
Emily Carr U of Art + Design (BC, Canada)
Escuela de Artes Plasticas de Puerto Rico (PR)
Ferris State U (MI)
Harding U (AR)
Hofstra U (NY)
Indiana U–Purdue U Fort Wayne (IN)
Indiana Wesleyan U (IN)
Inter American U of Puerto Rico, San Germán Campus (PR)
Lewis U (IL)
Lyme Acad Coll of Fine Arts (CT)
Maine Coll of Art (ME)
Maryland Inst Coll of Art (MD)
Marywood U (PA)
Massachusetts Coll of Art and Design (MA)
Minneapolis Coll of Art and Design (MN)
Northern Arizona U (AZ)
Northern Michigan U (MI)
Northwest Nazarene U (ID)
Ohio U (OH)
Pacific Northwest Coll of Art (OR)
Paier Coll of Art, Inc. (CT)
Pittsburg State U (KS)
Pratt Inst (NY)
Providence Coll (RI)

Ringling Coll of Art and Design (FL)
Rocky Mountain Coll of Art + Design (CO)
Rutgers, The State U of New Jersey, New Brunswick (NJ)
Salem State U (MA)
Salve Regina U (RI)
Sarah Lawrence Coll (NY)
Savannah Coll of Art and Design (GA)
School of the Museum of Fine Arts, Boston (MA)
School of Visual Arts (NY)
Seton Hill U (PA)
State U of New York at New Paltz (NY)
Temple U (PA)
Texas Christian U (TX)
U of Dallas (TX)
U of Hartford (CT)
U of Houston (TX)
U of Illinois at Chicago (IL)
The U of Iowa (IA)
The U of Kansas (KS)
U of Massachusetts Dartmouth (MA)
U of Miami (FL)
U of Missouri–St. Louis (MO)
U of Oregon (OR)
U of Regina (SK, Canada)
U of San Francisco (CA)
The U of the Arts (PA)
U of Washington (WA)
Virginia Commonwealth U (VA)
Virginia Intermont Coll (VA)
Washington U in St. Louis (MO)
Western State Coll of Colorado (CO)

PALEONTOLOGY
Northern Arizona U (AZ)

PAPER SCIENCE AND ENGINEERING
U of Wisconsin–Stevens Point (WI)

PARKS, RECREATION AND LEISURE
Alabama State U (AL)
Alcorn State U (MS)
Arizona State U (AZ)
Ashland U (OH)
Belmont U (TN)
Bemidji State U (MN)
Bethune-Cookman U (FL)
Biola U (CA)
Bluffton U (OH)
Boston U (MA)
Bowling Green State U (OH)
Brevard Coll (NC)
Bridgewater State U (MA)
Brock U (ON, Canada)
California Polytechnic State U, San Luis Obispo (CA)
California State U, Chico (CA)
California State U, Long Beach (CA)
California State U, Northridge (CA)
Calvin Coll (MI)
Campbellsville U (KY)
Carson-Newman Coll (TN)
Central Michigan U (MI)
Central State U (OH)
Concordia U (QC, Canada)
Cumberland U (TN)
Dordt Coll (IA)
Eastern Washington U (WA)
Elon U (NC)
Emporia State U (KS)
Evangel U (MO)
Ferrum Coll (VA)
Fort Lewis Coll (CO)
Georgia Coll & State U (GA)
Georgia Southern U (GA)
Gordon Coll (MA)
Graceland U (IA)
Grand Canyon U (AZ)
Greenville Coll (IL)
Houghton Coll (NY)
Humboldt State U (CA)
Huntington U (IN)
Indiana U Bloomington (IN)
Ithaca Coll (NY)
Jacksonville State U (AL)
Johnson State Coll (VT)
Kutztown U of Pennsylvania (PA)
Lakehead U (ON, Canada)
Lake Superior State U (MI)
Limestone Coll (SC)
Lindenwood U (MO)
Lindsey Wilson Coll (KY)
Lock Haven U of Pennsylvania (PA)

INDEXES

Stony Brook U, State U of New York (NY)
The U of British Columbia (BC, Canada)
U of California, Santa Barbara (CA)
U of Ottawa (ON, Canada)
U of Saskatchewan (SK, Canada)
The U of Western Ontario (ON, Canada)

PHARMACOLOGY AND TOXICOLOGY
U at Buffalo, the State U of New York (NY)
U of the Sciences in Philadelphia (PA)
The U of Western Ontario (ON, Canada)
U of Wisconsin–Madison (WI)

PHARMACY
Butler U (IN)
Drake U (IA)
Lipscomb U (TN)
Long Island U, Brooklyn Campus (NY)
Manchester Coll (IN)
Northeastern U (MA)
The Ohio State U (OH)
Purdue U (IN)
Rutgers, The State U of New Jersey, New Brunswick (NJ)
St. John's U (NY)
St. Louis Coll of Pharmacy (MO)
South Dakota State U (SD)
The U of British Columbia (BC, Canada)
The U of Iowa (IA)
The U of Kansas (KS)
U of Louisiana at Monroe (LA)
U of Manitoba (MB, Canada)
U of Minnesota, Twin Cities Campus (MN)
U of Saskatchewan (SK, Canada)
U of the Pacific (CA)
U of the Sciences in Philadelphia (PA)
The U of Toledo (OH)
U of Utah (UT)
U of Washington (WA)

PHARMACY ADMINISTRATION AND PHARMACY POLICY AND REGULATORY AFFAIRS
DeSales U (PA)
Drake U (IA)
U of Michigan (MI)

PHARMACY, PHARMACEUTICAL SCIENCES, AND ADMINISTRATION RELATED
Albany Coll of Pharmacy and Health Sciences (NY)
Duquesne U (PA)
North Dakota State U (ND)
U at Buffalo, the State U of New York (NY)
U of California, Irvine (CA)
The U of North Carolina at Chapel Hill (NC)
U of the Sciences in Philadelphia (PA)
The U of Toledo (OH)
Wilkes U (PA)

PHILOSOPHY
Acadia U (NS, Canada)
Adelphi U (NY)
Albertus Magnus Coll (CT)
Albion Coll (MI)
Albright Coll (PA)
Alfred U (NY)
Allegheny Coll (PA)
Alma Coll (MI)
Alvernia U (PA)
Alverno Coll (WI)
American Public U System (WV)
American U (DC)
American U of Beirut (Lebanon)
Amherst Coll (MA)
Anderson U (IN)
Anna Maria Coll (MA)
Appalachian State U (NC)
Aquinas Coll (MI)
Arcadia U (PA)
Arizona State U (AZ)
Arkansas State U (AR)
Asbury U (KY)
Ashland U (OH)

Assumption Coll (MA)
Auburn U (AL)
Augsburg Coll (MN)
Augustana Coll (IL)
Augustana Coll (SD)
Austin Coll (TX)
Austin Peay State U (TN)
Azusa Pacific U (CA)
Baker U (KS)
Baldwin-Wallace Coll (OH)
Ball State U (IN)
Bard Coll (NY)
Bard Coll at Simon's Rock (MA)
Barnard Coll (NY)
Barry U (FL)
Bates Coll (ME)
Belhaven U (MS)
Bellarmine U (KY)
Belmont U (TN)
Beloit Coll (WI)
Bemidji State U (MN)
Benedictine Coll (KS)
Benedictine U (IL)
Bennington Coll (VT)
Bentley U (MA)
Berea Coll (KY)
Bethany Coll (KS)
Bethel Coll (IN)
Bethel U (MN)
Biola U (CA)
Birmingham-Southern Coll (AL)
Bloomfield Coll (NJ)
Bloomsburg U of Pennsylvania (PA)
Boise State U (ID)
Boston Coll (MA)
Boston U (MA)
Bowdoin Coll (ME)
Bowling Green State U (OH)
Brandeis U (MA)
Bridgewater State U (MA)
Brock U (ON, Canada)
Brown U (RI)
Bryn Mawr Coll (PA)
Bucknell U (PA)
Butler U (IN)
Cabrini Coll (PA)
California Baptist U (CA)
California Inst of Technology (CA)
California Polytechnic State U, San Luis Obispo (CA)
California State Polytechnic U, Pomona (CA)
California State U, Bakersfield (CA)
California State U, Chico (CA)
California State U, Dominguez Hills (CA)
California State U, Fullerton (CA)
California State U, Long Beach (CA)
California State U, Los Angeles (CA)
California State U, Northridge (CA)
California State U, San Bernardino (CA)
California State U, Stanislaus (CA)
Calvin Coll (MI)
Canisius Coll (NY)
Capital U (OH)
Carleton Coll (MN)
Carlow U (PA)
Carnegie Mellon U (PA)
Carson-Newman U (TN)
Case Western Reserve U (OH)
Castleton State Coll (VT)
The Catholic U of America (DC)
Cedarville U (OH)
Centenary Coll of Louisiana (LA)
Central U (IA)
Central Connecticut State U (CT)
Central Michigan U (MI)
Centre Coll (KY)
Chapman U (CA)
Christendom Coll (VA)
Christian Brothers U (TN)
Christopher Newport U (VA)
City Coll of the City U of New York (NY)
Claremont McKenna Coll (CA)
Clarion U of Pennsylvania (PA)
Clark Atlanta U (GA)
Clarke U (IA)
Clark U (MA)
Clemson U (SC)
Cleveland State U (OH)
Coastal Carolina U (SC)
Colby Coll (ME)
Colgate U (NY)
Coll of Charleston (SC)
The Coll of New Jersey (NJ)
Coll of Saint Benedict (MN)
Coll of Saint Elizabeth (NJ)
The Coll of Saint Rose (NY)

Coll of Staten Island of the City U of New York (NY)
Coll of the Atlantic (ME)
Coll of the Holy Cross (MA)
The Coll of William and Mary (VA)
The Coll of Wooster (OH)
The Colorado Coll (CO)
Colorado State U (CO)
Columbia U, School of General Studies (NY)
Concordia Coll (MN)
Concordia Coll–New York (NY)
Concordia U (QC, Canada)
Concordia U Chicago (IL)
Connecticut Coll (CT)
Cornell Coll (IA)
Cornell U (NY)
Covenant Coll (GA)
Creighton U (NE)
Curry Coll (MA)
Dakota Wesleyan U (SD)
Dallas Baptist U (TX)
Dartmouth Coll (NH)
Davidson Coll (NC)
Delaware State U (DE)
Denison U (OH)
DePaul U (IL)
DePauw U (IN)
DEREE - The American Coll of Greece (Greece)
DeSales U (PA)
Dickinson Coll (PA)
Divine Word Coll (IA)
Doane Coll (NE)
Dominican U (IL)
Dordt Coll (IA)
Dowling Coll (NY)
Drake U (IA)
Drew U (NJ)
Drury U (MO)
Duquesne U (PA)
Earlham Coll (IN)
Eastern Illinois U (IL)
Eastern Michigan U (MI)
Eastern Washington U (WA)
East Stroudsburg U of Pennsylvania (PA)
East Tennessee State U (TN)
Eckerd Coll (FL)
Edinboro U of Pennsylvania (PA)
Elizabethtown Coll (PA)
Elmhurst Coll (IL)
Elmira Coll (NY)
Elon U (NC)
Emory & Henry Coll (VA)
Erskine Coll (SC)
Eugene Lang Coll The New School for Liberal Arts (NY)
Fairfield U (CT)
Fairleigh Dickinson U, Coll at Florham (NJ)
Fairleigh Dickinson U, Metropolitan Campus (NJ)
Felician Coll (NJ)
Ferrum Coll (VA)
Flagler Coll (FL)
Florida Atlantic U (FL)
Florida Gulf Coast U (FL)
Florida Intl U (FL)
Florida Southern Coll (FL)
Florida State U (FL)
Fort Lewis Coll (CO)
Franklin & Marshall Coll (PA)
Franklin Coll (IN)
Freed-Hardeman U (TN)
Furman U (SC)
Gallaudet U (DC)
Gannon U (PA)
Geneva Coll (PA)
George Fox U (OR)
Georgetown Coll (KY)
Georgetown U (DC)
Georgia Coll & State U (GA)
Georgia Southern U (GA)
Georgia State U (GA)
Gettysburg Coll (PA)
Gordon Coll (MA)
Goucher Coll (MD)
Grand Valley State U (MI)
Greenville Coll (IL)
Grinnell Coll (IA)
Grove City Coll (PA)
Guilford Coll (NC)
Hamilton Coll (NY)
Hamline U (MN)
Hampden-Sydney Coll (VA)
Hampshire Coll (MA)
Hanover Coll (IN)
Hardin-Simmons U (TX)
Hartwick Coll (NY)

Harvard U (MA)
Haverford Coll (PA)
Hendrix Coll (AR)
Hillsdale Coll (MI)
Hobart and William Smith Colls (NY)
Hofstra U (NY)
Hollins U (VA)
Holy Apostles Coll and Sem (CT)
Holy Names U (CA)
Hood Coll (MD)
Hope Coll (MI)
Houghton Coll (NY)
Humboldt State U (CA)
Hunter Coll of the City U of New York (NY)
Huntington U (IN)
Idaho State U (ID)
Illinois Coll (IL)
Illinois State U (IL)
Illinois Wesleyan U (IL)
Indiana State U (IN)
Indiana U Bloomington (IN)
Indiana U Northwest (IN)
Indiana U of Pennsylvania (PA)
Indiana U–Purdue U Fort Wayne (IN)
Indiana U–Purdue U Indianapolis (IN)
Indiana U South Bend (IN)
Indiana U Southeast (IN)
Indiana Wesleyan U (IN)
Iowa State U of Science and Technology (IA)
Ithaca Coll (NY)
John Carroll U (OH)
The Johns Hopkins U (MD)
Juniata Coll (PA)
Kalamazoo Coll (MI)
Kansas State U (KS)
Kennesaw State U (GA)
Kent State U (OH)
Kenyon Coll (OH)
King's Coll (PA)
The King's U Coll (AB, Canada)
Knox Coll (IL)
Kutztown U of Pennsylvania (PA)
Lafayette Coll (PA)
Lake Forest Coll (IL)
Lakehead U (ON, Canada)
La Salle U (PA)
Laurentian U (ON, Canada)
Lawrence U (WI)
Lebanese American U (Lebanon)
Lebanon Valley Coll (PA)
Lehigh U (PA)
Lehman Coll of the City U of New York (NY)
Le Moyne Coll (NY)
Lewis & Clark Coll (OR)
Lewis U (IL)
Liberty U (VA)
Lincoln Christian U (IL)
Lindenwood U (MO)
Linfield Coll (OR)
Lipscomb U (TN)
Lock Haven U of Pennsylvania (PA)
Long Island U, Brooklyn Campus (NY)
Long Island U, C.W. Post Campus (NY)
Loras Coll (IA)
Louisiana Coll (LA)
Louisiana State U and Ag and Mech Coll (LA)
Loyola Marymount U (CA)
Loyola U Chicago (IL)
Loyola U Maryland (MD)
Loyola U New Orleans (LA)
Luther Coll (IA)
Lycoming Coll (PA)
Lynchburg Coll (VA)
Macalester Coll (MN)
MacMurray Coll (IL)
Madonna U (MI)
Malone U (OH)
Manchester Coll (IN)
Manhattan Coll (NY)
Manhattanville Coll (NY)
Mansfield U of Pennsylvania (PA)
Marietta Coll (OH)
Marist Coll (NY)
Marlboro Coll (VT)
Marquette U (WI)
Mary Baldwin Coll (VA)
Marymount U (VA)
Maryville Coll (TN)
Massachusetts Coll of Liberal Arts (MA)
Massachusetts Inst of Technology (MA)

McDaniel Coll (MD)
McKendree U (IL)
Mercer U (GA)
Merrimack Coll (MA)
Messiah Coll (PA)
Metropolitan State U (MN)
Miami U (OH)
Michigan State U (MI)
Middlebury Coll (VT)
Middle Tennessee State U (TN)
Millersville U of Pennsylvania (PA)
Millikin U (IL)
Millsaps Coll (MS)
Mills Coll (CA)
Minnesota State U Mankato (MN)
Minnesota State U Moorhead (MN)
Misericordia U (PA)
Mississippi State U (MS)
Missouri State U (MO)
Missouri U of Science and Technology (MO)
Molloy Coll (NY)
Monmouth Coll (IL)
Montana State U (MT)
Montclair State U (NJ)
Moravian Coll (PA)
Morehead State U (KY)
Morehouse Coll (GA)
Morningside Coll (IA)
Mount Allison U (NB, Canada)
Mount Holyoke Coll (MA)
Mount Mercy U (IA)
Mount St. Mary's Coll (CA)
Mount St. Mary's U (MD)
Mount Vernon Nazarene U (OH)
Muhlenberg Coll (PA)
Murray State U (KY)
Nazareth Coll of Rochester (NY)
Nebraska Wesleyan U (NE)
Newberry Coll (SC)
New Coll of Florida (FL)
New England Coll (NH)
New Jersey City U (NJ)
Newman U (KS)
New Mexico State U (NM)
New York U (NY)
Niagara U (NY)
North Carolina State U (NC)
North Central Coll (IL)
North Dakota State U (ND)
Northeastern Illinois U (IL)
Northeastern U (MA)
Northern Arizona U (AZ)
Northern Illinois U (IL)
Northern Kentucky U (KY)
Northern Michigan U (MI)
Northwestern Coll (IA)
Northwest Missouri State U (MO)
Northwest Nazarene U (ID)
Northwest U (WA)
Notre Dame de Namur U (CA)
Nova Southeastern U (FL)
Nyack Coll (NY)
Oberlin Coll (OH)
Oglethorpe U (GA)
The Ohio State U (OH)
Ohio U (OH)
Ohio Wesleyan U (OH)
Oklahoma City U (OK)
Oklahoma State U (OK)
Old Dominion U (VA)
Oregon State U (OR)
Ouachita Baptist U (AR)
Our Lady of the Lake U of San Antonio (TX)
Pacific Lutheran U (WA)
Pacific U (OR)
Paine Coll (GA)
Palm Beach Atlantic U (FL)
Penn State Abington (PA)
Penn State Altoona (PA)
Penn State Beaver (PA)
Penn State Berks (PA)
Penn State Brandywine (PA)
Penn State DuBois (PA)
Penn State Erie, The Behrend Coll (PA)
Penn State Fayette, The Eberly Campus (PA)
Penn State Greater Allegheny (PA)
Penn State Hazleton (PA)
Penn State Lehigh Valley (PA)
Penn State Mont Alto (PA)
Penn State New Kensington (PA)
Penn State Schuylkill (PA)
Penn State Shenango (PA)
Penn State U Park (PA)
Penn State Wilkes-Barre (PA)
Penn State Worthington Scranton (PA)

Penn State York (PA)
Pepperdine U, Malibu (CA)
Piedmont Coll (GA)
Pitzer Coll (CA)
Pomona Coll (CA)
Portland State U (OR)
Presbyterian Coll (SC)
Princeton U (NJ)
Principia Coll (IL)
Providence Coll (RI)
Purchase Coll, State U of New York (NY)
Purdue U (IN)
Purdue U Calumet (IN)
Queens Coll of the City U of New York (NY)
Randolph Coll (VA)
Randolph-Macon Coll (VA)
Reed Coll (OR)
Regis U (CO)
Rensselaer Polytechnic Inst (NY)
Rhode Island Coll (RI)
Rhodes Coll (TN)
Rice U (TX)
Rider U (NJ)
Ripon Coll (WI)
Roanoke Coll (VA)
Rockford Coll (IL)
Rockhurst U (MO)
Rocky Mountain Coll (MT)
Rollins Coll (FL)
Roosevelt U (IL)
Rosemont Coll (PA)
Rutgers, The State U of New Jersey, Camden (NJ)
Rutgers, The State U of New Jersey, Newark (NJ)
Rutgers, The State U of New Jersey, New Brunswick (NJ)
Sacred Heart Major Sem (MI)
Sacred Heart U (CT)
St. Ambrose U (IA)
Saint Anselm Coll (NH)
St. Bonaventure U (NY)
St. Catherine U (MN)
St. Charles Borromeo Sem, Overbrook (PA)
St. Edward's U (TX)
Saint Francis U (PA)
St. Francis Xavier U (NS, Canada)
St. Gregory the Great Sem (NE)
St. John Fisher Coll (NY)
Saint John's U (MN)
St. John's U (NY)
Saint Joseph Coll (CT)
Saint Joseph's Coll (IN)
Saint Joseph's Coll of Maine (ME)
Saint Joseph's U (PA)
St. Lawrence U (NY)
Saint Louis U (MO)
Saint Mary's Coll (IN)
Saint Mary's Coll of California (CA)
St. Mary's Coll of Maryland (MD)
Saint Mary's U of Minnesota (MN)
Saint Michael's Coll (VT)
St. Norbert Coll (WI)
St. Olaf Coll (MN)
St. Thomas Aquinas Coll (NY)
St. Thomas U (NB, Canada)
Saint Xavier U (IL)
Salisbury U (MD)
Salve Regina U (RI)
Samford U (AL)
Sam Houston State U (TX)
San Diego State U (CA)
San Francisco State U (CA)
San Jose State U (CA)
Santa Clara U (CA)
Sarah Lawrence Coll (NY)
Scripps Coll (CA)
Seattle Pacific U (WA)
Sewanee: The U of the South (TN)
Siena Coll (NY)
Siena Heights U (MI)
Simmons Coll (MA)
Simon Fraser U (BC, Canada)
Simpson Coll (IA)
Skidmore Coll (NY)
Slippery Rock U of Pennsylvania (PA)
Smith Coll (MA)
Sonoma State U (CA)
Southeast Missouri State U (MO)
Southern Connecticut State U (CT)
Southern Illinois U Carbondale (IL)
Southern Illinois U Edwardsville (IL)
Southern Methodist U (TX)
Southern Nazarene U (OK)

Spelman Coll (GA)
Spring Arbor U (MI)
Spring Hill Coll (AL)
Stanford U (CA)
State U of New York at Binghamton (NY)
State U of New York at Fredonia (NY)
State U of New York at New Paltz (NY)
State U of New York at Oswego (NY)
State U of New York at Plattsburgh (NY)
State U of New York Coll at Geneseo (NY)
State U of New York Coll at Old Westbury (NY)
State U of New York Coll at Oneonta (NY)
State U of New York Coll at Potsdam (NY)
Stephen F. Austin State U (TX)
Stetson U (FL)
Stonehill Coll (MA)
Stony Brook U, State U of New York (NY)
Suffolk U (MA)
Susquehanna U (PA)
Swarthmore Coll (PA)
Sweet Briar Coll (VA)
Syracuse U (NY)
Tabor Coll (KS)
Taylor U (IN)
Temple U (PA)
Texas A&M U (TX)
Texas Christian U (TX)
Texas Lutheran U (TX)
Texas State U–San Marcos (TX)
Texas Tech U (TX)
Thiel Coll (PA)
Thomas Edison State Coll (NJ)
Thomas More Coll (KY)
Towson U (MD)
Transylvania U (KY)
Trent U (ON, Canada)
Trinity Coll (CT)
Trinity U (TX)
Tufts U (MA)
Tulane U (LA)
Union Coll (NY)
Union U (TN)
Université de Sherbrooke (QC, Canada)
U at Buffalo, the State U of New York (NY)
The U of Akron (OH)
The U of Alabama (AL)
The U of Alabama at Birmingham (AL)
The U of Alabama in Huntsville (AL)
U of Alaska Fairbanks (AK)
The U of Arizona (AZ)
U of Arkansas (AR)
The U of British Columbia (BC, Canada)
The U of British Columbia–Okanagan (BC, Canada)
U of California, Berkeley (CA)
U of California, Davis (CA)
U of California, Irvine (CA)
U of California, Los Angeles (CA)
U of California, Santa Barbara (CA)
U of California, Santa Cruz (CA)
U of Central Florida (FL)
U of Cincinnati (OH)
U of Colorado at Colorado Springs (CO)
U of Colorado Boulder (CO)
U of Colorado Denver (CO)
U of Dallas (TX)
U of Dayton (OH)
U of Delaware (DE)
U of Denver (CO)
U of Dubuque (IA)
U of Evansville (IN)
The U of Findlay (OH)
U of Florida (FL)
U of Georgia (GA)
U of Guelph (ON, Canada)
U of Hartford (CT)
U of Hawaii at Hilo (HI)
U of Hawaii at Manoa (HI)
U of Hawaii–West Oahu (HI)
U of Houston (TX)
U of Houston–Downtown (TX)
U of Idaho (ID)
U of Illinois at Chicago (IL)

U of Illinois at Springfield (IL)
U of Indianapolis (IN)
The U of Iowa (IA)
The U of Kansas (KS)
U of La Verne (CA)
U of Lethbridge (AB, Canada)
U of Louisiana at Lafayette (LA)
U of Louisville (KY)
U of Maine (ME)
U of Manitoba (MB, Canada)
U of Maryland, Baltimore County (MD)
U of Maryland, Coll Park (MD)
U of Mary Washington (VA)
U of Massachusetts Amherst (MA)
U of Massachusetts Boston (MA)
U of Massachusetts Dartmouth (MA)
U of Massachusetts Lowell (MA)
U of Memphis (TN)
U of Miami (FL)
U of Michigan (MI)
U of Michigan–Dearborn (MI)
U of Michigan–Flint (MI)
U of Minnesota, Duluth (MN)
U of Minnesota, Twin Cities Campus (MN)
U of Mississippi (MS)
U of Missouri (MO)
U of Missouri–St. Louis (MO)
U of Mount Union (OH)
U of Nebraska at Omaha (NE)
U of Nebraska–Lincoln (NE)
U of Nevada, Las Vegas (NV)
U of Nevada, Reno (NV)
U of New Brunswick Fredericton (NB, Canada)
U of New Brunswick Saint John (NB, Canada)
U of New Hampshire (NH)
The U of North Carolina at Asheville (NC)
The U of North Carolina at Chapel Hill (NC)
The U of North Carolina at Charlotte (NC)
The U of North Carolina at Greensboro (NC)
U of North Dakota (ND)
U of Northern Colorado (CO)
U of Northern Iowa (IA)
U of North Florida (FL)
U of North Texas (TX)
U of Notre Dame (IN)
U of Oklahoma (OK)
U of Oregon (OR)
U of Ottawa (ON, Canada)
U of Pennsylvania (PA)
U of Pittsburgh (PA)
U of Portland (OR)
U of Puget Sound (WA)
U of Redlands (CA)
U of Regina (SK, Canada)
U of Rhode Island (RI)
U of Richmond (VA)
U of Rochester (NY)
U of St. Thomas (MN)
U of St. Thomas (TX)
U of San Diego (CA)
U of San Francisco (CA)
U of Saskatchewan (SK, Canada)
The U of Scranton (PA)
U of Sioux Falls (SD)
U of South Alabama (AL)
U of South Carolina (SC)
The U of South Dakota (SD)
U of Southern California (CA)
U of Southern Indiana (IN)
U of Southern Maine (ME)
U of Southern Mississippi (MS)
U of South Florida (FL)
The U of Tampa (FL)
The U of Tennessee (TN)
The U of Tennessee at Martin (TN)
The U of Texas at Arlington (TX)
The U of Texas at Austin (TX)
The U of Texas at San Antonio (TX)
The U of Texas–Pan American (TX)
U of the Incarnate Word (TX)
U of the Ozarks (AR)
U of the Pacific (CA)
U of the West (CA)
The U of Toledo (OH)
U of Tulsa (OK)
U of Utah (UT)
U of Vermont (VT)
U of Virginia (VA)
U of Washington (WA)

U of Waterloo (ON, Canada)
The U of Western Ontario (ON, Canada)
U of West Florida (FL)
U of West Georgia (GA)
U of Wisconsin–Eau Claire (WI)
U of Wisconsin–Green Bay (WI)
U of Wisconsin–La Crosse (WI)
U of Wisconsin–Madison (WI)
U of Wisconsin–Parkside (WI)
U of Wisconsin–Platteville (WI)
U of Wisconsin–Stevens Point (WI)
U of Wyoming (WY)
Ursuline Coll (OH)
Utah State U (UT)
Utah Valley U (UT)
Valdosta State U (GA)
Valparaiso U (IN)
Vanderbilt U (TN)
Vassar Coll (NY)
Villanova U (PA)
Virginia Commonwealth U (VA)
Virginia Polytechnic Inst and State U (VA)
Virginia Wesleyan Coll (VA)
Wabash Coll (IN)
Wagner Coll (NY)
Wake Forest U (NC)
Walla Walla U (WA)
Walsh U (OH)
Wartburg Coll (IA)
Washburn U (KS)
Washington & Jefferson Coll (PA)
Washington and Lee U (VA)
Washington Coll (MD)
Washington State U (WA)
Washington U in St. Louis (MO)
Wayne State U (MI)
Webster U (MO)
Wellesley Coll (MA)
Wells Coll (NY)
Wesleyan Coll (GA)
Wesleyan U (CT)
West Chester U of Pennsylvania (PA)
Western Carolina U (NC)
Western Illinois U (IL)
Western Michigan U (MI)
Western New England U (MA)
Western Oregon U (OR)
Westminster Coll (MO)
Westminster Coll (UT)
Westmont Coll (CA)
West Virginia U (WV)
Wheaton Coll (IL)
Wheaton Coll (MA)
Wheeling Jesuit U (WV)
Whitman Coll (WA)
Wichita State U (KS)
Wilfrid Laurier U (ON, Canada)
Wilkes U (PA)
Willamette U (OR)
William Jewell Coll (MO)
William Paterson U of New Jersey (NJ)
Williams Coll (MA)
Wilmington Coll (OH)
Wingate U (NC)
Wittenberg U (OH)
Wofford Coll (SC)
Worcester Polytechnic Inst (MA)
Wright State U (OH)
Xavier U (OH)
Xavier U of Louisiana (LA)
Yale U (CT)
York Coll of Pennsylvania (PA)
York Coll of the City U of New York (NY)
Youngstown State U (OH)

PHILOSOPHY AND RELIGIOUS STUDIES

Bethune-Cookman U (FL)
Concordia Coll–New York (NY)
Dakota Wesleyan U (SD)
LaGrange Coll (GA)
Montreat Coll, Montreat (NC)
Pace U (NY)
St. Andrews Presbyterian Coll (NC)
Southwestern Coll (KS)

PHILOSOPHY AND RELIGIOUS STUDIES RELATED

Alderson-Broaddus Coll (WV)
Arizona State U (AZ)
Barton Coll (NC)
Berry Coll (GA)
Bethune-Cookman U (FL)

Bowling Green State U (OH)
Bridgewater Coll (VA)
Buena Vista U (IA)
Claflin U (SC)
Claremont McKenna Coll (CA)
Coll of the Humanities and Sciences, Harrison Middleton U (AZ)
Coll of the Ozarks (MO)
Columbia Coll (MO)
Covenant Coll (GA)
The Evergreen State Coll (WA)
Florida Ag and Mech U (FL)
Friends U (KS)
Graceland U (IA)
Hendrix Coll (AR)
Holy Names U (CA)
Iowa Wesleyan Coll (IA)
James Madison U (VA)
John Brown U (AR)
Juniata Coll (PA)
Kean U (NJ)
Lyon Coll (AR)
Marquette U (WI)
Mary Baldwin Coll (VA)
Millsaps Coll (MS)
Ouachita Baptist U (AR)
Quincy U (IL)
Radford U (VA)
The Richard Stockton Coll of New Jersey (NJ)
Rocky Mountain Coll (MT)
Rowan U (NJ)
Saint Joseph's Coll (IN)
Samford U (AL)
San Francisco State U (CA)
Sarah Lawrence Coll (NY)
Southwestern Coll (KS)
State U of New York at Oswego (NY)
Syracuse U (NY)
Union U (TN)
U of Maine at Farmington (ME)
U of Mary Washington (VA)
The U of North Carolina at Pembroke (NC)
The U of North Carolina Wilmington (NC)
U of Notre Dame (IN)
The U of Tennessee at Chattanooga (TN)
U of the Ozarks (AR)
Viterbo U (WI)
Washington U in St. Louis (MO)
Wheaton Coll (MA)

PHILOSOPHY RELATED

Claremont McKenna Coll (CA)
Lewis U (IL)
Marlboro Coll (VT)
Marquette U (WI)
U of Massachusetts Boston (MA)
U of Pennsylvania (PA)
U of Regina (SK, Canada)
Wheeling Jesuit U (WV)

PHOTOGRAPHIC AND FILM/ VIDEO TECHNOLOGY

Kent State U (OH)
St. John's U (NY)
Towson U (MD)
Villa Maria Coll of Buffalo (NY)

PHOTOGRAPHY

Adams State Coll (CO)
Alberta Coll of Art & Design (AB, Canada)
Albertus Magnus Coll (CT)
Aquinas Coll (MI)
Arcadia U (PA)
Art Center Coll of Design (CA)
The Art Inst of Boston at Lesley U (MA)
The Art Inst of Seattle (WA)
Bard Coll (NY)
Bard Coll at Simon's Rock (MA)
Barry U (FL)
Bennington Coll (VT)
Bridgewater State U (MA)
Burlington Coll (VT)
California Coll of the Arts (CA)
California Inst of the Arts (CA)
California State U, Long Beach (CA)
Carroll U (WI)
Carson-Newman Coll (TN)
Chatham U (PA)
The Cleveland Inst of Art (OH)
Coker Coll (SC)

Coll for Creative Studies (MI)
Colorado State U (CO)
Columbia Coll (MO)
Columbia Coll Chicago (IL)
Concordia U (QC, Canada)
Concordia U Wisconsin (WI)
Corcoran Coll of Art and Design (DC)
Dominican U (IL)
Emily Carr U of Art + Design (BC, Canada)
Ferris State U (MI)
Fitchburg State U (MA)
Gallaudet U (DC)
Governors State U (IL)
Grand Valley State U (MI)
Hofstra U (NY)
Indiana U–Purdue U Fort Wayne (IN)
Indiana Wesleyan U (IN)
Inter American U of Puerto Rico, San Germán Campus (PR)
Intl Acad of Design & Technology (FL)
Ithaca Coll (NY)
John Brown U (AR)
Long Island U, C.W. Post Campus (NY)
Maine Coll of Art (ME)
Marlboro Coll (VT)
Maryland Inst Coll of Art (MD)
Marywood U (PA)
Massachusetts Coll of Art and Design (MA)
Minneapolis Coll of Art and Design (MN)
Morningside Coll (IA)
Mount Allison U (NB, Canada)
New England Coll (NH)
New York U (NY)
Northeastern State U (OK)
Northern Arizona U (AZ)
Northern Michigan U (MI)
Ohio U (OH)
Otis Coll of Art and Design (CA)
Pacific Northwest Coll of Art (OR)
Pacific Union Coll (CA)
Paier Coll of Art, Inc. (CT)
Parsons The New School for Design (NY)
Pennsylvania Coll of Art & Design (PA)
Point Park U (PA)
Pratt Inst (NY)
Prescott Coll (AZ)
Purchase Coll, State U of New York (NY)
Ringling Coll of Art and Design (FL)
Rivier Coll (NH)
Rutgers, The State U of New Jersey, New Brunswick (NJ)
Sage Coll of Albany (NY)
St. Edward's U (TX)
St. John's U (NY)
Salem State U (MA)
Salve Regina U (RI)
Sam Houston State U (TX)
Sarah Lawrence Coll (NY)
Savannah Coll of Art and Design (GA)
School of the Museum of Fine Arts, Boston (MA)
School of Visual Arts (NY)
Southern Adventist U (TN)
State U of New York at New Paltz (NY)
Syracuse U (NY)
Temple U (PA)
Texas Christian U (TX)
Texas State U–San Marcos (TX)
Thomas Edison State Coll (NJ)
The U of Akron (OH)
U of Central Florida (FL)
U of Central Missouri (MO)
U of Dayton (OH)
U of Hartford (CT)
U of Houston (TX)
U of Illinois at Chicago (IL)
The U of Iowa (IA)
U of La Verne (CA)
U of Massachusetts Dartmouth (MA)
U of Miami (FL)
U of Missouri–St. Louis (MO)
U of Oregon (OR)
The U of the Arts (PA)
U of Washington (WA)
Virginia Commonwealth U (VA)
Virginia Intermont Coll (VA)
Washington U in St. Louis (MO)

Watkins Coll of Art, Design, & Film (TN)
Weber State U (UT)
Webster U (MO)
Western State Coll of Colorado (CO)
Youngstown State U (OH)

PHOTOJOURNALISM

Central Michigan U (MI)
Corcoran Coll of Art and Design (DC)
Hawai`i Pacific U (HI)
Ohio U (OH)
Pittsburg State U (KS)
Point Park U (PA)
St. John's U (NY)
Sierra Nevada Coll (NV)
U of Miami (FL)
U of Missouri (MO)
Walla Walla U (WA)
Western Kentucky U (KY)

PHYSICAL AND BIOLOGICAL ANTHROPOLOGY

The U of Western Ontario (ON, Canada)

PHYSICAL CHEMISTRY

Rice U (TX)
The U of Western Ontario (ON, Canada)

PHYSICAL EDUCATION TEACHING AND COACHING

Abilene Christian U (TX)
Adams State Coll (CO)
Adelphi U (NY)
Alabama Ag and Mech U (AL)
Alabama State U (AL)
Albany State U (GA)
Albion Coll (MI)
Alderson-Broaddus Coll (WV)
Alma Coll (MI)
Anderson U (IN)
Anderson U (SC)
Appalachian State U (NC)
Aquinas Coll (MI)
Arkansas State U (AR)
Arkansas Tech U (AR)
Armstrong Atlantic State U (GA)
Asbury U (KY)
Ashland U (OH)
Athens State U (AL)
Auburn U (AL)
Augsburg Coll (MN)
Augustana Coll (SD)
Averett U (VA)
Azusa Pacific U (CA)
Ball State U (IN)
Baptist Bible Coll of Pennsylvania (PA)
Barry U (FL)
Barton Coll (NC)
Belmont U (TN)
Bemidji State U (MN)
Benedictine Coll (KS)
Berry Coll (GA)
Bethany Coll (KS)
Bethany Coll (WV)
Bethel Coll (IN)
Bethel U (MN)
Bethune-Cookman U (FL)
Biola U (CA)
Blackburn Coll (IL)
Bluefield Coll (VA)
Blue Mountain Coll (MS)
Boise State U (ID)
Boston U (MA)
Bowling Green State U (OH)
Brewton-Parker Coll (GA)
Briar Cliff U (IA)
Bridgewater Coll (VA)
Bridgewater State U (MA)
Brock U (ON, Canada)
Bryan Coll (TN)
Buena Vista U (IA)
California Baptist U (CA)
California State U, Bakersfield (CA)
California State U, Chico (CA)
California State U, Long Beach (CA)
California State U, San Bernardino (CA)
California State U, Stanislaus (CA)
Calvin Coll (MI)
Cameron U (OK)
Campbellsville U (KY)
Canisius Coll (NY)
Capital U (OH)
Carroll U (WI)

Carson-Newman Coll (TN)
Castleton State Coll (VT)
Cedarville U (OH)
Central Connecticut State U (CT)
Central Michigan U (MI)
The Citadel, The Military Coll of South Carolina (SC)
Clarke U (IA)
Clearwater Christian Coll (FL)
Cleveland State U (OH)
Coastal Carolina U (SC)
Coker Coll (SC)
Coll of Charleston (SC)
The Coll of New Jersey (NJ)
Coll of the Ozarks (MO)
Columbus State U (GA)
Concordia Coll (MN)
Concordia U Chicago (IL)
Concordia U, St. Paul (MN)
Concordia U Wisconsin (WI)
Concord U (WV)
Corban U (OR)
Cornell Coll (IA)
Crown Coll (MN)
Culver-Stockton Coll (MO)
Cumberland U (TN)
Dakota State U (SD)
Dakota Wesleyan U (SD)
Dallas Baptist U (TX)
Defiance Coll (OH)
Delaware State U (DE)
Delta State U (MS)
Denison U (OH)
DePaul U (IL)
DePauw U (IN)
Dickinson State U (ND)
Doane Coll (NE)
Dordt Coll (IA)
Dowling Coll (NY)
Drury U (MO)
East Central U (OK)
Eastern Michigan U (MI)
Eastern New Mexico U (NM)
East Stroudsburg U of Pennsylvania (PA)
East Texas Baptist U (TX)
Elizabeth City State U (NC)
Elmhurst Coll (IL)
Elon U (NC)
Endicott Coll (MA)
Erskine Coll (SC)
Evangel U (MO)
Fairmont State U (WV)
Faulkner U (AL)
Fayetteville State U (NC)
Florida Ag and Mech U (FL)
Florida Intl U (FL)
Florida Southern Coll (FL)
Fort Lewis Coll (CO)
Franklin Coll (IN)
Freed-Hardeman U (TN)
Free Will Baptist Bible Coll (TN)
Friends U (KS)
Gallaudet U (DC)
Gardner-Webb U (NC)
Georgia Coll & State U (GA)
Georgia Southern U (GA)
Gettysburg Coll (PA)
Graceland U (IA)
Grand Canyon U (AZ)
Grand Valley State U (MI)
Grand View U (IA)
Greensboro Coll (NC)
Greenville Coll (IL)
Hamline U (MN)
Hannibal-LaGrange U (MO)
Hardin-Simmons U (TX)
Hillsdale Coll (MI)
Hofstra U (NY)
Hope Coll (MI)
Houghton Coll (NY)
Humboldt State U (CA)
Hunter Coll of the City U of New York (NY)
Huntingdon Coll (AL)
Huntington U (IN)
Husson U (ME)
Huston-Tillotson U (TX)
Idaho State U (ID)
Illinois Coll (IL)
Illinois State U (IL)
Indiana State U (IN)
Indiana Tech (IN)
Indiana U Bloomington (IN)
Indiana U–Purdue U Indianapolis (IN)
Indiana Wesleyan U (IN)
Inter American U of Puerto Rico, Guayama Campus (PR)

Inter American U of Puerto Rico, Metropolitan Campus (PR)
Inter American U of Puerto Rico, San Germán Campus (PR)
Iowa Wesleyan Coll (IA)
Ithaca Coll (NY)
Jacksonville State U (AL)
Jamestown Coll (ND)
Jarvis Christian Coll (TX)
John Carroll U (OH)
Johnson C. Smith U (NC)
Johnson State Coll (VT)
Kean U (NJ)
Keene State Coll (NH)
Kennesaw State U (GA)
Kent State U (OH)
Kentucky State U (KY)
Kentucky Wesleyan Coll (KY)
Lakehead U (ON, Canada)
Lamar U (TX)
Lane Coll (TN)
Laurentian U (ON, Canada)
Lee U (TN)
LeTourneau U (TX)
Lewis-Clark State Coll (ID)
Lewis U (IL)
Liberty U (VA)
Limestone Coll (SC)
Lincoln Memorial U (TN)
Lincoln U (MO)
Lindenwood U (MO)
Lindsey Wilson Coll (KY)
Lipscomb U (TN)
Lock Haven U of Pennsylvania (PA)
Long Island U, Brooklyn Campus (NY)
Long Island U, C.W. Post Campus (NY)
Longwood U (VA)
Loras Coll (IA)
Louisiana Coll (LA)
Louisiana State U and Ag and Mech Coll (LA)
Louisiana State U in Shreveport (LA)
Lubbock Christian U (TX)
Lyndon State Coll (VT)
MacMurray Coll (IL)
Malone U (OH)
Manchester Coll (IN)
Manhattan Coll (NY)
Maranatha Baptist Bible Coll (WI)
Marshall U (WV)
Mars Hill Coll (NC)
Maryville Coll (TN)
The Master's Coll and Sem (CA)
Mayville State U (ND)
McKendree U (IL)
McMurry U (TX)
Messiah Coll (PA)
Miami U (OH)
Michigan State U (MI)
MidAmerica Nazarene U (KS)
Millikin U (IL)
Minnesota State U Mankato (MN)
Minnesota State U Moorhead (MN)
Minot State U (ND)
Mississippi State U (MS)
Mississippi Valley State U (MS)
Missouri Baptist U (MO)
Missouri State U (MO)
Monmouth Coll (IL)
Montana State U Billings (MT)
Montclair State U (NJ)
Morehead State U (KY)
Mount Vernon Nazarene U (OH)
Nebraska Wesleyan U (NE)
Newberry Coll (SC)
New England Coll (NH)
New Mexico Highlands U (NM)
New Mexico State U (NM)
Nicholls State U (LA)
North Central Coll (IL)
North Dakota State U (ND)
Northeastern Illinois U (IL)
Northeastern State U (OK)
Northern Arizona U (AZ)
Northern Illinois U (IL)
Northern Kentucky U (KY)
Northern Michigan U (MI)
Northern State U (SD)
North Georgia Coll & State U (GA)
Northwestern Coll (IA)
Northwestern Coll (MN)
Northwestern Oklahoma State U (OK)
Northwestern State U of Louisiana (LA)
Northwest Missouri State U (MO)
Northwest Nazarene U (ID)
The Ohio State U (OH)

Ohio U (OH)
Ohio Valley U (WV)
Ohio Wesleyan U (OH)
Oklahoma Christian U (OK)
Oklahoma City U (OK)
Oklahoma State U (OK)
Oklahoma Wesleyan U (OK)
Old Dominion U (VA)
Ouachita Baptist U (AR)
Pacific Union Coll (CA)
Palm Beach Atlantic U (FL)
Pepperdine U, Malibu (CA)
Philadelphia Biblical U (PA)
Pittsburg State U (KS)
Prescott Coll (AZ)
Purdue U (IN)
Queens Coll of the City U of New York (NY)
Quincy U (IL)
Radford U (VA)
Reinhardt U (GA)
Rhode Island Coll (RI)
Ripon Coll (WI)
Roanoke Coll (VA)
Rockford Coll (IL)
Rocky Mountain Coll (MT)
Rowan U (NJ)
Sage Coll of Albany (NY)
Saginaw Valley State U (MI)
St. Ambrose U (IA)
St. Andrews Presbyterian Coll (NC)
St. Bonaventure U (NY)
St. Catherine U (MN)
St. Edward's U (TX)
St. Francis Xavier U (NS, Canada)
Saint Joseph's Coll (IN)
Saint Joseph's Coll of Maine (ME)
Salem State U (MA)
Salisbury U (MD)
Samford U (AL)
San Diego Christian Coll (CA)
San Francisco State U (CA)
Schreiner U (TX)
Shenandoah U (VA)
Simpson Coll (IA)
Slippery Rock U of Pennsylvania (PA)
Sonoma State U (CA)
Southeastern Louisiana U (LA)
Southeastern Oklahoma State U (OK)
Southeast Missouri State U (MO)
Southern Adventist U (TN)
Southern Arkansas U–Magnolia (AR)
Southern Illinois U Carbondale (IL)
Southern Illinois U Edwardsville (IL)
Southern Nazarene U (OK)
Southern Oregon U (OR)
Southern Utah U (UT)
Southern Wesleyan U (SC)
Southwestern Coll (KS)
Spring Arbor U (MI)
Springfield Coll (MA)
State U of New York at Plattsburgh (NY)
State U of New York Coll at Potsdam (NY)
Sul Ross State U (TX)
Syracuse U (NY)
Tabor Coll (KS)
Tarleton State U (TX)
Taylor U (IN)
Tennessee Technological U (TN)
Texas A&M Intl U (TX)
Texas A&M U–Corpus Christi (TX)
Texas Christian U (TX)
Texas Lutheran U (TX)
Texas Wesleyan U (TX)
Towson U (MD)
Transylvania U (KY)
Trevecca Nazarene U (TN)
Trine U (IN)
Union Coll (KY)
Union Coll (NE)
Union U (TN)
Université de Sherbrooke (QC, Canada)
The U of Akron (OH)
The U of Alabama (AL)
The U of Alabama at Birmingham (AL)
The U of Arizona (AZ)
U of Arkansas at Pine Bluff (AR)
U of Central Florida (FL)
U of Central Missouri (MO)
U of Delaware (DE)
U of Dubuque (IA)
U of Evansville (IN)
The U of Findlay (OH)

U of Georgia (GA)
U of Idaho (ID)
U of Indianapolis (IN)
The U of Kansas (KS)
U of Lethbridge (AB, Canada)
U of Louisiana at Lafayette (LA)
U of Louisiana at Monroe (LA)
U of Maine (ME)
U of Maine at Presque Isle (ME)
U of Manitoba (MB, Canada)
U of Mary Hardin-Baylor (TX)
U of Maryland, Coll Park (MD)
U of Memphis (TN)
U of Michigan (MI)
U of Minnesota, Duluth (MN)
U of Minnesota, Twin Cities Campus (MN)
U of Missouri–St. Louis (MO)
The U of Montana Western (MT)
U of Mount Union (OH)
U of Nevada, Las Vegas (NV)
U of Nevada, Reno (NV)
U of New Brunswick Fredericton (NB, Canada)
The U of North Carolina at Greensboro (NC)
The U of North Carolina at Pembroke (NC)
The U of North Carolina Wilmington (NC)
U of North Dakota (ND)
U of Northern Iowa (IA)
U of North Florida (FL)
U of Pittsburgh (PA)
U of Pittsburgh at Bradford (PA)
U of Regina (SK, Canada)
U of Rio Grande (OH)
U of St. Thomas (MN)
U of San Francisco (CA)
U of Saskatchewan (SK, Canada)
U of South Alabama (AL)
U of South Carolina (SC)
U of South Carolina Upstate (SC)
The U of South Dakota (SD)
U of Southern Indiana (IN)
U of Southern Mississippi (MS)
U of South Florida (FL)
U of the Cumberlands (KY)
U of the District of Columbia (DC)
U of the Incarnate Word (TX)
U of the Ozarks (AR)
U of the Southwest (NM)
The U of Toledo (OH)
U of Vermont (VT)
U of West Georgia (GA)
U of Wisconsin–River Falls (WI)
U of Wisconsin–Stevens Point (WI)
U of Wisconsin–Superior (WI)
U of Wisconsin–Whitewater (WI)
U of Wyoming (WY)
Upper Iowa U (IA)
Utah State U (UT)
Utah Valley U (UT)
Valdosta State U (GA)
Valparaiso U (IN)
Virginia Intermont Coll (VA)
Virginia State U (VA)
Walla Walla U (WA)
Walsh U (OH)
Wartburg Coll (IA)
Washburn U (KS)
Washington State U (WA)
Wayland Baptist U (TX)
Wayne State Coll (NE)
Wayne State U (MI)
Weber State U (UT)
Western Carolina U (NC)
Western Illinois U (IL)
Western Michigan U (MI)
Western State Coll of Colorado (CO)
West Liberty U (WV)
Westminster Coll (MO)
Westmont Coll (CA)
West Virginia U (WV)
Wichita State U (KS)
Wilfrid Laurier U (ON, Canada)
William Jewell Coll (MO)
William Paterson U of New Jersey (NJ)
Wilmington Coll (OH)
Winona State U (MN)
Winthrop U (SC)
Wright State U (OH)
Xavier U of Louisiana (LA)
York Coll of the City U of New York (NY)
Youngstown State U (OH)

PHYSICAL FITNESS TECHNICIAN
Trevecca Nazarene U (TN)

PHYSICAL SCIENCES
Arkansas Tech U (AR)
Auburn U Montgomery (AL)
Bemidji State U (MN)
Bennington Coll (VT)
Biola U (CA)
Brock U (ON, Canada)
California State U, Stanislaus (CA)
Calvin Coll (MI)
Christian Brothers U (TN)
Colgate U (NY)
Colorado State U (CO)
Concordia U Chicago (IL)
Dakota State U (SD)
Defiance Coll (OH)
Doane Coll (NE)
East Stroudsburg U of Pennsylvania (PA)
Emporia State U (KS)
The Evergreen State Coll (WA)
Florida Inst of Technology (FL)
Freed-Hardeman U (TN)
Graceland U (IA)
Hampshire Coll (MA)
Juniata Coll (PA)
Kansas State U (KS)
Keene State Coll (NH)
Linfield Coll (OR)
Long Island U, Brooklyn Campus (NY)
Loras Coll (IA)
Lyndon State Coll (VT)
The Master's Coll and Sem (CA)
Mesa State Coll (CO)
Michigan State U (MI)
Midwestern State U (TX)
Minnesota State U Mankato (MN)
Minot State U (ND)
Mississippi U for Women (MS)
Montana Tech of The U of Montana (MT)
Mount Vernon Nazarene U (OH)
Muhlenberg Coll (PA)
New Mexico Inst of Mining and Technology (NM)
Northern Arizona U (AZ)
Penn State Erie, The Behrend Coll (PA)
Ripon Coll (WI)
Rowan U (NJ)
St. Francis Xavier U (NS, Canada)
St. John's U (NY)
Saint Michael's Coll (VT)
San Diego State U (CA)
San Francisco State U (CA)
Southern Nazarene U (OK)
Southern Utah U (UT)
Suffolk U (MA)
Texas A&M Intl U (TX)
Trent U (ON, Canada)
Trine U (IN)
Troy U (AL)
United States Military Acad (NY)
United States Naval Acad (MD)
U of California, Berkeley (CA)
U of Dayton (OH)
U of Guelph (ON, Canada)
U of Houston–Clear Lake (TX)
U of Maryland, Coll Park (MD)
U of Minnesota, Twin Cities Campus (MN)
U of North Dakota (ND)
U of Ottawa (ON, Canada)
U of Pittsburgh (PA)
U of Pittsburgh at Bradford (PA)
U of Rio Grande (OH)
U of Southern California (CA)
U of the Pacific (CA)
The U of Toledo (OH)
U of Utah (UT)
U of Wisconsin–River Falls (WI)
U of Wisconsin–Superior (WI)
U of Wyoming (WY)
Villanova U (PA)
Washington State U (WA)
Wesleyan Coll (GA)
Western Kentucky U (KY)
Westfield State U (MA)
William Paterson U of New Jersey (NJ)
Winona State U (MN)
Worcester State U (MA)

PHYSICAL SCIENCES RELATED
Bowling Green State U (OH)

Cedar Crest Coll (PA)
Central Connecticut State U (CT)
The Coll of St. Scholastica (MN)
Covenant Coll (GA)
Eastern Michigan U (MI)
John Brown U (AR)
Morehouse Coll (GA)
Northern Arizona U (AZ)
Stony Brook U, State U of New York (NY)
Union Coll (NY)
The U of Alabama in Huntsville (AL)
U of California, Davis (CA)
U of Mary Washington (VA)
U of Massachusetts Lowell (MA)
The U of North Carolina at Chapel Hill (NC)
U of the Ozarks (AR)
U of Utah (UT)
U of Wisconsin–Eau Claire (WI)
Wayne State U (MI)
Worcester Polytechnic Inst (MA)
Xavier U (OH)

PHYSICAL SCIENCE TECHNOLOGIES RELATED
Delaware State U (DE)
Missouri State U (MO)

PHYSICAL THERAPY
Andrews U (MI)
Armstrong Atlantic State U (GA)
Bellarmine U (KY)
Biola U (CA)
Boston U (MA)
Coll of Saint Benedict (MN)
Concordia U (QC, Canada)
Concordia U Wisconsin (WI)
Duquesne U (PA)
Elmhurst Coll (IL)
Grand Valley State U (MI)
Hawai`i Pacific U (HI)
Husson U (ME)
Indiana U–Purdue U Indianapolis (IN)
Indiana U Southeast (IN)
Ithaca Coll (NY)
Keystone Coll (PA)
Long Island U, Brooklyn Campus (NY)
Loyola U Chicago (IL)
Maryville U of Saint Louis (MO)
Mount Saint Mary Coll (NY)
Mount Vernon Nazarene U (OH)
Nazareth Coll of Rochester (NY)
New York Inst of Technology (NY)
Northeastern U (MA)
Northern Illinois U (IL)
Northwest Nazarene U (ID)
Oklahoma Wesleyan U (OK)
Quinnipiac U (CT)
Sacred Heart U (CT)
Saint Francis U (PA)
Saint John's U (MN)
Saint Mary's U of Minnesota (MN)
Simmons Coll (MA)
Springfield Coll (MA)
State U of New York Coll of Environmental Science and Forestry (NY)
State U of New York Downstate Medical Center (NY)
Stony Brook U, State U of New York (NY)
Tarleton State U (TX)
The U of Findlay (OH)
U of Hartford (CT)
U of Manitoba (MB, Canada)
U of Minnesota, Twin Cities Campus (MN)
U of North Dakota (ND)
U of Ottawa (ON, Canada)
The U of South Dakota (SD)
The U of Tennessee at Chattanooga (TN)
U of the Sciences in Philadelphia (PA)
The U of Toledo (OH)
U of Utah (UT)
U of Washington (WA)
The U of Western Ontario (ON, Canada)
Wichita State U (KS)
Winona State U (MN)
Young Harris Coll (GA)

PHYSICAL THERAPY TECHNOLOGY
U of Cincinnati (OH)

PHYSICIAN ASSISTANT
Augsburg Coll (MN)
Bethel U (TN)
Brenau U (GA)
Butler U (IN)
City Coll of the City U of New York (NY)
Cleveland State U (OH)
Duquesne U (PA)
Elmhurst Coll (IL)
Gannon U (PA)
Grand Valley State U (MI)
Hofstra U (NY)
Long Island U, Brooklyn Campus (NY)
New York Inst of Technology (NY)
Pennsylvania Coll of Technology (PA)
Philadelphia U (PA)
Quinnipiac U (CT)
Saint Francis U (PA)
St. John's U (NY)
Saint Joseph's Coll of Maine (ME)
Seton Hill U (PA)
Southern Illinois U Carbondale (IL)
Springfield Coll (MA)
State U of New York Downstate Medical Center (NY)
Union Coll (NE)
The U of South Dakota (SD)
The U of Texas–Pan American (TX)
U of Washington (WA)
U of Wisconsin–Parkside (WI)
Wagner Coll (NY)
Wake Forest U (NC)
Wichita State U (KS)
York Coll of the City U of New York (NY)

PHYSICS
Abilene Christian U (TX)
Acadia U (NS, Canada)
Adams State Coll (CO)
Adelphi U (NY)
Alabama Ag and Mech U (AL)
Albion Coll (MI)
Albright Coll (PA)
Alfred U (NY)
Allegheny Coll (PA)
Alma Coll (MI)
American U (DC)
American U of Beirut (Lebanon)
Amherst Coll (MA)
Anderson U (IN)
Andrews U (MI)
Angelo State U (TX)
Appalachian State U (NC)
Aquinas Coll (MI)
Arizona State U (AZ)
Arkansas State U (AR)
Armstrong Atlantic State U (GA)
Ashland U (OH)
Athens State U (AL)
Auburn U (AL)
Augsburg Coll (MN)
Augustana Coll (IL)
Augustana Coll (SD)
Austin Coll (TX)
Austin Peay State U (TN)
Azusa Pacific U (CA)
Baker U (KS)
Baldwin-Wallace Coll (OH)
Ball State U (IN)
Bard Coll (NY)
Bard Coll at Simon's Rock (MA)
Barnard Coll (NY)
Bates Coll (ME)
Bellarmine U (KY)
Belmont U (TN)
Beloit Coll (WI)
Bemidji State U (MN)
Benedictine Coll (KS)
Benedictine U (IL)
Bennington Coll (VT)
Berea Coll (KY)
Berry Coll (GA)
Bethel U (MN)
Biola U (CA)
Birmingham-Southern Coll (AL)
Bloomsburg U of Pennsylvania (PA)
Bluffton U (OH)
Bob Jones U (SC)
Boise State U (ID)
Boston Coll (MA)

Boston U (MA)
Bowdoin Coll (ME)
Bowling Green State U (OH)
Brandeis U (MA)
Bridgewater Coll (VA)
Bridgewater State U (MA)
Brock U (ON, Canada)
Brown U (RI)
Bryn Mawr Coll (PA)
Bucknell U (PA)
Buena Vista U (IA)
Butler U (IN)
California Inst of Technology (CA)
California Polytechnic State U, San Luis Obispo (CA)
California State Polytechnic U, Pomona (CA)
California State U, Bakersfield (CA)
California State U, Chico (CA)
California State U, Dominguez Hills (CA)
California State U, Fullerton (CA)
California State U, Long Beach (CA)
California State U, Los Angeles (CA)
California State U, Northridge (CA)
California State U, San Bernardino (CA)
California State U, Stanislaus (CA)
Calvin Coll (MI)
Cameron U (OK)
Canisius Coll (NY)
Carleton Coll (MN)
Carnegie Mellon U (PA)
Carroll U (WI)
Carson-Newman Coll (TN)
The Catholic U of America (DC)
Cedarville U (OH)
Central Coll (IA)
Central Connecticut State U (CT)
Central Michigan U (MI)
Centre Coll (KY)
Chatham U (PA)
Christian Brothers U (TN)
Christopher Newport U (VA)
The Citadel, The Military Coll of South Carolina (SC)
City Coll of the City U of New York (NY)
Claremont McKenna Coll (CA)
Clarion U of Pennsylvania (PA)
Clark Atlanta U (GA)
Clarkson U (NY)
Clark U (MA)
Clemson U (SC)
Cleveland State U (OH)
Coastal Carolina U (SC)
Colby Coll (ME)
Colgate U (NY)
Coll of Charleston (SC)
The Coll of New Jersey (NJ)
Coll of Saint Benedict (MN)
Coll of Staten Island of the City U of New York (NY)
Coll of the Holy Cross (MA)
The Coll of William and Mary (VA)
The Coll of Wooster (OH)
The Colorado Coll (CO)
Colorado State U (CO)
Columbia U, School of General Studies (NY)
Concordia Coll (MN)
Concordia U (QC, Canada)
Cornell Coll (IA)
Cornell U (NY)
Covenant Coll (GA)
Creighton U (NE)
Curry Coll (MA)
Dartmouth Coll (NH)
Davidson Coll (NC)
Delaware State U (DE)
Denison U (OH)
DePaul U (IL)
DePauw U (IN)
Dickinson Coll (PA)
Dillard U (LA)
Doane Coll (NE)
Dordt Coll (IA)
Drake U (IA)
Drew U (NJ)
Drury U (MO)
Duquesne U (PA)
Earlham Coll (IN)
East Central U (OK)
Eastern Illinois U (IL)
Eastern Michigan U (MI)
Eastern Washington U (WA)

East Stroudsburg U of Pennsylvania (PA)
East Tennessee State U (TN)
Eckerd Coll (FL)
Edinboro U of Pennsylvania (PA)
Elizabeth City State U (NC)
Elizabethtown Coll (PA)
Elmhurst Coll (IL)
Elon U (NC)
Emory & Henry Coll (VA)
Emporia State U (KS)
Erskine Coll (SC)
Fairfield U (CT)
Fairleigh Dickinson U, Metropolitan Campus (NJ)
Florida Ag and Mech U (FL)
Florida Atlantic U (FL)
Florida Inst of Technology (FL)
Florida Intl U (FL)
Florida State U (FL)
Francis Marion U (SC)
Franklin & Marshall Coll (PA)
Furman U (SC)
Geneva Coll (PA)
Georgetown Coll (KY)
Georgetown U (DC)
Georgia Coll & State U (GA)
Georgia Inst of Technology (GA)
Georgian Court U (NJ)
Georgia Southern U (GA)
Georgia State U (GA)
Gettysburg Coll (PA)
Gordon Coll (MA)
Goucher Coll (MD)
Grand Valley State U (MI)
Greenville Coll (IL)
Grinnell Coll (IA)
Grove City Coll (PA)
Guilford Coll (NC)
Hamilton Coll (NY)
Hamline U (MN)
Hampden-Sydney Coll (VA)
Hampshire Coll (MA)
Hanover Coll (IN)
Harding U (AR)
Hardin-Simmons U (TX)
Hartwick Coll (NY)
Harvard U (MA)
Harvey Mudd Coll (CA)
Haverford Coll (PA)
Hendrix Coll (AR)
Hillsdale Coll (MI)
Hobart and William Smith Colls (NY)
Hofstra U (NY)
Hollins U (VA)
Hope Coll (MI)
Houghton Coll (NY)
Humboldt State U (CA)
Hunter Coll of the City U of New York (NY)
Huntington U (IN)
Idaho State U (ID)
Illinois Coll (IL)
Illinois Inst of Technology (IL)
Illinois State U (IL)
Illinois Wesleyan U (IL)
Indiana U Bloomington (IN)
Indiana U of Pennsylvania (PA)
Indiana U–Purdue U Fort Wayne (IN)
Indiana U–Purdue U Indianapolis (IN)
Indiana U South Bend (IN)
Iowa State U of Science and Technology (IA)
Ithaca Coll (NY)
Jacksonville State U (AL)
James Madison U (VA)
John Carroll U (OH)
The Johns Hopkins U (MD)
Juniata Coll (PA)
Kalamazoo Coll (MI)
Kansas State U (KS)
Kent State U (OH)
Kentucky Wesleyan Coll (KY)
Kenyon Coll (OH)
Kettering U (MI)
King Coll (TN)
Knox Coll (IL)
Kutztown U of Pennsylvania (PA)
Lafayette Coll (PA)
Lake Forest Coll (IL)
Lakehead U (ON, Canada)
Lamar U (TX)
Lane Coll (TN)
Laurentian U (ON, Canada)
Lawrence Technological U (MI)
Lawrence U (WI)
Lebanon Valley Coll (PA)
Lehigh U (PA)

Lehman Coll of the City U of New York (NY)
Le Moyne Coll (NY)
Lewis & Clark Coll (OR)
Lewis U (IL)
Lincoln U (MO)
Linfield Coll (OR)
Lipscomb U (TN)
Lock Haven U of Pennsylvania (PA)
Long Island U, Brooklyn Campus (NY)
Long Island U, C.W. Post Campus (NY)
Longwood U (VA)
Loras Coll (IA)
Louisiana Coll (LA)
Louisiana State U and Ag and Mech Coll (LA)
Louisiana State U in Shreveport (LA)
Loyola Marymount U (CA)
Loyola U Chicago (IL)
Loyola U Maryland (MD)
Loyola U New Orleans (LA)
Luther Coll (IA)
Lycoming Coll (PA)
Lynchburg Coll (VA)
Macalester Coll (MN)
Manchester Coll (IN)
Manhattan Coll (NY)
Manhattanville Coll (NY)
Mansfield U of Pennsylvania (PA)
Marietta Coll (OH)
Marlboro Coll (VT)
Marquette U (WI)
Marshall U (WV)
Mary Baldwin Coll (VA)
Massachusetts Coll of Liberal Arts (MA)
Massachusetts Inst of Technology (MA)
McDaniel Coll (MD)
McMurry U (TX)
Mercer U (GA)
Merrimack Coll (MA)
Messiah Coll (PA)
Miami U (OH)
Michigan State U (MI)
Middlebury Coll (VT)
Middle Tennessee State U (TN)
Midwestern State U (TX)
Millersville U of Pennsylvania (PA)
Millikin U (IL)
Millsaps Coll (MS)
Minnesota State U Mankato (MN)
Minnesota State U Moorhead (MN)
Minot State U (ND)
Mississippi State U (MS)
Missouri Southern State U (MO)
Missouri State U (MO)
Missouri U of Science and Technology (MO)
Monmouth Coll (IL)
Montana State U (MT)
Montclair State U (NJ)
Moravian Coll (PA)
Morehead State U (KY)
Morehouse Coll (GA)
Morningside Coll (IA)
Mount Allison U (NB, Canada)
Mount Holyoke Coll (MA)
Mount Vernon Nazarene U (OH)
Muhlenberg Coll (PA)
Murray State U (KY)
Nebraska Wesleyan U (NE)
New Coll of Florida (FL)
New Jersey City U (NJ)
New Jersey Inst of Technology (NJ)
New Mexico Highlands U (NM)
New Mexico Inst of Mining and Technology (NM)
New Mexico State U (NM)
New York Inst of Technology (NY)
New York U (NY)
North Carolina Ag and Tech State U (NC)
North Carolina State U (NC)
North Central Coll (IL)
North Dakota State U (ND)
Northeastern Illinois U (IL)
Northeastern U (MA)
Northern Arizona U (AZ)
Northern Illinois U (IL)
Northern Kentucky U (KY)
Northern Michigan U (MI)
North Georgia Coll & State U (GA)
Northwest Missouri State U (MO)
Northwest Nazarene U (ID)
Oberlin Coll (OH)
Oglethorpe U (GA)
The Ohio State U (OH)

Ohio U (OH)
Ohio Wesleyan U (OH)
Oklahoma City U (OK)
Oklahoma State U (OK)
Old Dominion U (VA)
Oregon State U (OR)
Ouachita Baptist U (AR)
Pacific Lutheran U (WA)
Pacific Union Coll (CA)
Pacific U (OR)
Penn State Abington (PA)
Penn State Altoona (PA)
Penn State Beaver (PA)
Penn State Berks (PA)
Penn State Brandywine (PA)
Penn State DuBois (PA)
Penn State Erie, The Behrend Coll (PA)
Penn State Fayette, The Eberly Campus (PA)
Penn State Greater Allegheny (PA)
Penn State Hazleton (PA)
Penn State Lehigh Valley (PA)
Penn State Mont Alto (PA)
Penn State New Kensington (PA)
Penn State Schuylkill (PA)
Penn State Shenango (PA)
Penn State U Park (PA)
Penn State Wilkes-Barre (PA)
Penn State Worthington Scranton (PA)
Penn State York (PA)
Piedmont Coll (GA)
Pittsburg State U (KS)
Pitzer Coll (CA)
Polytechnic Inst of NYU (NY)
Pomona Coll (CA)
Portland State U (OR)
Prairie View A&M U (TX)
Presbyterian Coll (SC)
Princeton U (NJ)
Principia Coll (IL)
Purchase Coll, State U of New York (NY)
Purdue U (IN)
Purdue U Calumet (IN)
Queens Coll of the City U of New York (NY)
Radford U (VA)
Ramapo Coll of New Jersey (NJ)
Randolph Coll (VA)
Randolph-Macon Coll (VA)
Reed Coll (OR)
Rensselaer Polytechnic Inst (NY)
Rhode Island Coll (RI)
Rhodes Coll (TN)
Rice U (TX)
The Richard Stockton Coll of New Jersey (NJ)
Rider U (NJ)
Roanoke Coll (VA)
Rockhurst U (MO)
Rollins Coll (FL)
Rose-Hulman Inst of Technology (IN)
Rowan U (NJ)
Rutgers, The State U of New Jersey, Camden (NJ)
Rutgers, The State U of New Jersey, Newark (NJ)
Rutgers, The State U of New Jersey, New Brunswick (NJ)
Saginaw Valley State U (MI)
St. Ambrose U (IA)
Saint Anselm Coll (NH)
St. Bonaventure U (NY)
St. Catherine U (MN)
St. Francis Xavier U (NS, Canada)
St. John Fisher Coll (NY)
Saint John's U (MN)
St. John's U (NY)
Saint Joseph's U (PA)
St. Lawrence U (NY)
Saint Louis U (MO)
Saint Mary's Coll of California (CA)
St. Mary's Coll of Maryland (MD)
Saint Michael's Coll (VT)
St. Norbert Coll (WI)
St. Olaf Coll (MN)
Salisbury U (MD)
Samford U (AL)
Sam Houston State U (TX)
San Diego State U (CA)
San Francisco State U (CA)
San Jose State U (CA)
Santa Clara U (CA)
Sarah Lawrence Coll (NY)
Scripps Coll (CA)
Seattle Pacific U (WA)
Sewanee: The U of the South (TN)

Shippensburg U of Pennsylvania (PA)
Siena Coll (NY)
Simmons Coll (MA)
Simon Fraser U (BC, Canada)
Simpson Coll (IA)
Skidmore Coll (NY)
Slippery Rock U of Pennsylvania (PA)
Smith Coll (MA)
Sonoma State U (CA)
South Dakota School of Mines and Technology (SD)
South Dakota State U (SD)
Southeastern Louisiana U (LA)
Southeast Missouri State U (MO)
Southern Adventist U (TN)
Southern Arkansas U–Magnolia (AR)
Southern Connecticut State U (CT)
Southern Illinois U Carbondale (IL)
Southern Illinois U Edwardsville (IL)
Southern Methodist U (TX)
Southern Nazarene U (OK)
Southern Oregon U (OR)
Southern Polytechnic State U (GA)
Spelman Coll (GA)
Spring Arbor U (MI)
Stanford U (CA)
State U of New York at Binghamton (NY)
State U of New York at Fredonia (NY)
State U of New York at New Paltz (NY)
State U of New York at Oswego (NY)
State U of New York at Plattsburgh (NY)
State U of New York Coll at Geneseo (NY)
State U of New York Coll at Oneonta (NY)
State U of New York Coll at Potsdam (NY)
Stephen F. Austin State U (TX)
Stetson U (FL)
Stonehill Coll (MA)
Stony Brook U, State U of New York (NY)
Suffolk U (MA)
Susquehanna U (PA)
Swarthmore Coll (PA)
Sweet Briar Coll (VA)
Syracuse U (NY)
Tarleton State U (TX)
Taylor U (IN)
Temple U (PA)
Tennessee Technological U (TN)
Texas A&M U (TX)
Texas A&M U–Kingsville (TX)
Texas Christian U (TX)
Texas Lutheran U (TX)
Texas Southern U (TX)
Texas State U–San Marcos (TX)
Texas Tech U (TX)
Thiel Coll (PA)
Thomas More Coll (KY)
Towson U (MD)
Transylvania U (KY)
Trent U (ON, Canada)
Trevecca Nazarene U (TN)
Trinity Coll (CT)
Trinity U (TX)
Truman State U (MO)
Tufts U (MA)
Tulane U (LA)
Tuskegee U (AL)
Union Coll (NE)
Union Coll (NY)
Union U (TN)
United States Air Force Acad (CO)
United States Military Acad (NY)
United States Naval Acad (MD)
Université de Sherbrooke (QC, Canada)
U at Buffalo, the State U of New York (NY)
The U of Akron (OH)
The U of Alabama (AL)
The U of Alabama at Birmingham (AL)
The U of Alabama in Huntsville (AL)
U of Alaska Fairbanks (AK)
The U of Arizona (AZ)
U of Arkansas (AR)
U of Arkansas at Pine Bluff (AR)
The U of British Columbia (BC, Canada)

The U of British Columbia–Okanagan (BC, Canada)
U of California, Berkeley (CA)
U of California, Davis (CA)
U of California, Irvine (CA)
U of California, Los Angeles (CA)
U of California, Merced (CA)
U of California, Santa Barbara (CA)
U of California, Santa Cruz (CA)
U of Central Florida (FL)
U of Central Missouri (MO)
U of Cincinnati (OH)
U of Colorado at Colorado Springs (CO)
U of Colorado Boulder (CO)
U of Colorado Denver (CO)
U of Dallas (TX)
U of Dayton (OH)
U of Delaware (DE)
U of Denver (CO)
U of Evansville (IN)
U of Florida (FL)
U of Georgia (GA)
U of Guelph (ON, Canada)
U of Hartford (CT)
U of Hawaii at Hilo (HI)
U of Hawaii at Manoa (HI)
U of Houston (TX)
U of Houston–Clear Lake (TX)
U of Idaho (ID)
U of Illinois at Chicago (IL)
U of Indianapolis (IN)
The U of Iowa (IA)
The U of Kansas (KS)
U of La Verne (CA)
U of Lethbridge (AB, Canada)
U of Louisiana at Lafayette (LA)
U of Louisville (KY)
U of Maine (ME)
U of Manitoba (MB, Canada)
U of Maryland, Baltimore County (MD)
U of Maryland, Coll Park (MD)
U of Mary Washington (VA)
U of Massachusetts Amherst (MA)
U of Massachusetts Boston (MA)
U of Massachusetts Dartmouth (MA)
U of Massachusetts Lowell (MA)
U of Memphis (TN)
U of Miami (FL)
U of Michigan (MI)
U of Michigan–Dearborn (MI)
U of Michigan–Flint (MI)
U of Minnesota, Duluth (MN)
U of Minnesota, Twin Cities Campus (MN)
U of Mississippi (MS)
U of Missouri (MO)
U of Missouri–St. Louis (MO)
U of Mount Union (OH)
U of Nebraska at Omaha (NE)
U of Nebraska–Lincoln (NE)
U of Nevada, Las Vegas (NV)
U of Nevada, Reno (NV)
U of New Brunswick Fredericton (NB, Canada)
U of New Brunswick Saint John (NB, Canada)
U of New Hampshire (NH)
The U of North Carolina at Asheville (NC)
The U of North Carolina at Chapel Hill (NC)
The U of North Carolina at Charlotte (NC)
The U of North Carolina at Greensboro (NC)
The U of North Carolina at Pembroke (NC)
The U of North Carolina Wilmington (NC)
U of North Dakota (ND)
U of Northern Colorado (CO)
U of North Florida (FL)
U of North Texas (TX)
U of Notre Dame (IN)
U of Oklahoma (OK)
U of Oregon (OR)
U of Ottawa (ON, Canada)
U of Pennsylvania (PA)
U of Pittsburgh (PA)
U of Portland (OR)
U of Puerto Rico at Humacao (PR)
U of Puget Sound (WA)
U of Redlands (CA)
U of Regina (SK, Canada)
U of Rhode Island (RI)
U of Richmond (VA)
U of Rochester (NY)
U of St. Thomas (MN)

U of San Diego (CA)
U of San Francisco (CA)
U of Saskatchewan (SK, Canada)
U of Science and Arts of Oklahoma (OK)
The U of Scranton (PA)
U of South Alabama (AL)
U of South Carolina (SC)
The U of South Dakota (SD)
U of Southern California (CA)
U of Southern Maine (ME)
U of Southern Mississippi (MS)
U of South Florida (FL)
The U of Tennessee (TN)
The U of Tennessee at Chattanooga (TN)
The U of Texas at Arlington (TX)
The U of Texas at Austin (TX)
The U of Texas at Dallas (TX)
The U of Texas at San Antonio (TX)
The U of Texas–Pan American (TX)
U of the Cumberlands (KY)
U of the District of Columbia (DC)
U of the Pacific (CA)
U of the Sciences in Philadelphia (PA)
The U of Toledo (OH)
U of Tulsa (OK)
U of Utah (UT)
U of Vermont (VT)
U of Virginia (VA)
U of Washington (WA)
U of Waterloo (ON, Canada)
The U of Western Ontario (ON, Canada)
U of West Florida (FL)
U of Wisconsin–Eau Claire (WI)
U of Wisconsin–La Crosse (WI)
U of Wisconsin–Madison (WI)
U of Wisconsin–Parkside (WI)
U of Wisconsin–River Falls (WI)
U of Wisconsin–Stevens Point (WI)
U of Wisconsin–Whitewater (WI)
U of Wyoming (WY)
Utah State U (UT)
Utah Valley U (UT)
Valdosta State U (GA)
Valparaiso U (IN)
Vanderbilt U (TN)
Vassar Coll (NY)
Villanova U (PA)
Virginia Commonwealth U (VA)
Virginia Military Inst (VA)
Virginia Polytechnic Inst and State U (VA)
Virginia State U (VA)
Wabash Coll (IN)
Wagner Coll (NY)
Wake Forest U (NC)
Walla Walla U (WA)
Wartburg Coll (IA)
Washburn U (KS)
Washington & Jefferson Coll (PA)
Washington and Lee U (VA)
Washington Coll (MD)
Washington State U (WA)
Washington U in St. Louis (MO)
Wayne State U (MI)
Weber State U (UT)
Wellesley Coll (MA)
Wells Coll (NY)
Wesleyan U (CT)
West Chester U of Pennsylvania (PA)
Western Illinois U (IL)
Western Kentucky U (KY)
Western Michigan U (MI)
Western State Coll of Colorado (CO)
Westminster Coll (MO)
Westminster Coll (UT)
Westmont Coll (CA)
West Virginia U (WV)
Wheaton Coll (IL)
Wheaton Coll (MA)
Wheeling Jesuit U (WV)
Whitman Coll (WA)
Wichita State U (KS)
Widener U (PA)
Wilfrid Laurier U (ON, Canada)
Willamette U (OR)
William Jewell Coll (MO)
Williams Coll (MA)
Winona State U (MN)
Wittenberg U (OH)
Wofford Coll (SC)
Worcester Polytechnic Inst (MA)
Wright State U (OH)

Xavier U (OH)
Xavier U of Louisiana (LA)
Yale U (CT)
York Coll of the City U of New York (NY)
Youngstown State U (OH)

PHYSICS RELATED

Angelo State U (TX)
Arcadia U (PA)
Bridgewater Coll (VA)
Bridgewater State U (MA)
Brigham Young U (UT)
California State U, Chico (CA)
Carson-Newman Coll (TN)
Coll of Saint Benedict (MN)
The Coll of Wooster (OH)
Delaware State U (DE)
Embry-Riddle Aeronautical U–Daytona (FL)
Embry-Riddle Aeronautical U–Prescott (AZ)
Florida Inst of Technology (FL)
Fort Lewis Coll (CO)
Hampden-Sydney Coll (VA)
Indiana U of Pennsylvania (PA)
Lawrence Technological U (MI)
Linfield Coll (OR)
Morehouse Coll (GA)
New Jersey Inst of Technology (NJ)
Pittsburg State U (KS)
Presbyterian Coll (SC)
Rensselaer Polytechnic Inst (NY)
Rutgers, The State U of New Jersey, Newark (NJ)
Saint John's U (MN)
Southern Arkansas U–Magnolia (AR)
Spring Arbor U (MI)
Trevecca Nazarene U (TN)
U of Alaska Fairbanks (AK)
U of California, Davis (CA)
U of Nevada, Las Vegas (NV)
U of Northern Iowa (IA)
U of North Texas (TX)
U of Notre Dame (IN)
U of Regina (SK, Canada)
U of Rhode Island (RI)
U of Rochester (NY)
The U of Western Ontario (ON, Canada)
Whitman Coll (WA)

PHYSICS TEACHER EDUCATION

Alma Coll (MI)
Anderson U (IN)
Appalachian State U (NC)
Arkansas State U (AR)
Auburn U (AL)
Bethel U (MN)
Bridgewater Coll (VA)
Buena Vista U (IA)
Cedarville U (OH)
Central Michigan U (MI)
Christian Brothers U (TN)
City Coll of the City U of New York (NY)
The Coll of New Jersey (NJ)
Colorado State U (CO)
Concordia Coll (MN)
Delaware State U (DE)
Eastern Michigan U (MI)
Eastern Washington U (WA)
Elmhurst Coll (IL)
Florida Inst of Technology (FL)
Grand Valley State U (MI)
Greenville Coll (IL)
Hofstra U (NY)
Hope Coll (MI)
Husson U (ME)
Indiana U Bloomington (IN)
Indiana U–Purdue U Fort Wayne (IN)
Indiana U South Bend (IN)
Iowa Wesleyan Coll (IA)
Ithaca Coll (NY)
Juniata Coll (PA)
King Coll (TN)
Le Moyne Coll (NY)
Lincoln U (MO)
Lipscomb U (TN)
Louisiana State U in Shreveport (LA)
Manchester Coll (IN)
Mansfield U of Pennsylvania (PA)
Marquette U (WI)
Maryville Coll (TN)
Messiah Coll (PA)

Miami Dade Coll (FL)
Miami U (OH)
Michigan State U (MI)
Millersville U of Pennsylvania (PA)
Minnesota State U Moorhead (MN)
Minot State U (ND)
Missouri State U (MO)
Moravian Coll (PA)
Morningside Coll (IA)
Mount Vernon Nazarene U (OH)
New York Inst of Technology (NY)
North Dakota State U (ND)
Northeastern State U (OK)
Northern Arizona U (AZ)
Northern Michigan U (MI)
Northwest Missouri State U (MO)
Ohio Wesleyan U (OH)
Pittsburg State U (KS)
Queens Coll of the City U of New York (NY)
Rhode Island Coll (RI)
Saginaw Valley State U (MI)
St. Ambrose U (IA)
St. John Fisher Coll (NY)
St. John's U (NY)
Saint Mary's U of Minnesota (MN)
Southeastern Louisiana U (LA)
State U of New York at New Paltz (NY)
State U of New York Coll at Oneonta (NY)
State U of New York Coll at Potsdam (NY)
Syracuse U (NY)
Trevecca Nazarene U (TN)
Union Coll (NE)
The U of Arizona (AZ)
U of Central Missouri (MO)
U of Delaware (DE)
U of Evansville (IN)
U of Illinois at Chicago (IL)
U of Louisiana at Lafayette (LA)
U of Maryland, Baltimore County (MD)
U of Michigan–Flint (MI)
U of Missouri (MO)
U of Missouri–St. Louis (MO)
U of Nebraska–Lincoln (NE)
U of Regina (SK, Canada)
U of Rio Grande (OH)
U of St. Thomas (MN)
The U of South Dakota (SD)
U of Waterloo (ON, Canada)
U of West Georgia (GA)
U of Wisconsin–River Falls (WI)
Utah State U (UT)
Valparaiso U (IN)
Washington State U (WA)
Washington U in St. Louis (MO)
Weber State U (UT)
Western Michigan U (MI)
Wheeling Jesuit U (WV)
William Jewell Coll (MO)
Winona State U (MN)
Xavier U (OH)

PHYSIOLOGICAL PSYCHOLOGY/ PSYCHOBIOLOGY

Albright Coll (PA)
Arcadia U (PA)
Averett U (VA)
Carnegie Mellon U (PA)
Centre Coll (KY)
Claremont McKenna Coll (CA)
Florida Atlantic U (FL)
Holy Family U (PA)
Holy Names U (CA)
Houghton Coll (NY)
The Johns Hopkins U (MD)
Lebanon Valley Coll (PA)
Mills Coll (CA)
Mount Allison U (NB, Canada)
Northwest Missouri State U (MO)
Oberlin Coll (OH)
Pace U (NY)
Quinnipiac U (CT)
Ripon Coll (WI)
Saint Mary's Coll of California (CA)
Simmons Coll (MA)
Southern Adventist U (TN)
State U of New York at Binghamton (NY)
Swarthmore Coll (PA)
U of California, Los Angeles (CA)
U of Colorado Denver (CO)
U of New Brunswick Fredericton (NB, Canada)
U of New England (ME)

U of St. Thomas (TX)
The U of Western Ontario (ON, Canada)
Vassar Coll (NY)
Washington Coll (MD)
Wheaton Coll (MA)

PHYSIOLOGY

Brigham Young U (UT)
California State U, Long Beach (CA)
Marquette U (WI)
Michigan State U (MI)
Northern Arizona U (AZ)
Northern Michigan U (MI)
Oklahoma State U (OK)
San Jose State U (CA)
Southern Illinois U Carbondale (IL)
The U of British Columbia (BC, Canada)
U of California, Los Angeles (CA)
U of California, Santa Barbara (CA)
U of Colorado Boulder (CO)
U of Oregon (OR)
U of Ottawa (ON, Canada)
U of Saskatchewan (SK, Canada)
The U of Western Ontario (ON, Canada)
U of Wyoming (WY)

PLANETARY ASTRONOMY AND SCIENCE

California Inst of Technology (CA)
Florida Inst of Technology (FL)
U of Waterloo (ON, Canada)
The U of Western Ontario (ON, Canada)

PLANT MOLECULAR BIOLOGY

Pittsburg State U (KS)

PLANT NURSERY MANAGEMENT

Colorado State U (CO)

PLANT PATHOLOGY/ PHYTOPATHOLOGY

Michigan State U (MI)
New Mexico State U (NM)
State U of New York Coll of Environmental Science and Forestry (NY)
U of Wisconsin–Madison (WI)

PLANT PHYSIOLOGY

Pittsburg State U (KS)
State U of New York Coll of Environmental Science and Forestry (NY)

PLANT PROTECTION AND INTEGRATED PEST MANAGEMENT

California State Polytechnic U, Pomona (CA)
Iowa State U of Science and Technology (IA)
Penn State U Park (PA)
State U of New York Coll of Environmental Science and Forestry (NY)
U of Delaware (DE)
U of Hawaii at Manoa (HI)
U of Minnesota, Twin Cities Campus (MN)
U of Nebraska–Lincoln (NE)
Washington State U (WA)

PLANT SCIENCES

Arkansas State U (AR)
Auburn U (AL)
Cornell U (NY)
Lakehead U (ON, Canada)
Louisiana State U and Ag and Mech Coll (LA)
Lubbock Christian U (TX)
Middle Tennessee State U (TN)
Montana State U (MT)
The Ohio State U (OH)
Rutgers, The State U of New Jersey, New Brunswick (NJ)
Southeast Missouri State U (MO)
Southern Illinois U Carbondale (IL)
State U of New York Coll of Environmental Science and Forestry (NY)
Tuskegee U (AL)
U of California, Santa Cruz (CA)
U of Florida (FL)

U of Louisiana at Lafayette (LA)
U of Maine (ME)
U of Maryland, Coll Park (MD)
U of Massachusetts Amherst (MA)
U of Minnesota, Crookston (MN)
U of Minnesota, Twin Cities Campus (MN)
U of Missouri (MO)
U of Rhode Island (RI)
The U of Tennessee (TN)
U of Vermont (VT)
The U of Western Ontario (ON, Canada)
Utah State U (UT)
Washington State U (WA)

PLANT SCIENCES RELATED

Auburn U (AL)
Sterling Coll (VT)
U of Hawaii at Manoa (HI)
Utah State U (UT)
West Virginia U (WV)

PLASTICS AND POLYMER ENGINEERING TECHNOLOGY

Eastern Michigan U (MI)
Ferris State U (MI)
Pennsylvania Coll of Technology (PA)
Pittsburg State U (KS)
Shawnee State U (OH)

PLAYWRITING AND SCREENWRITING

Bard Coll (NY)
Bennington Coll (VT)
Brigham Young U (UT)
Chapman U (CA)
Columbia Coll Chicago (IL)
Concordia U (QC, Canada)
DePaul U (IL)
Loyola Marymount U (CA)
Metropolitan State U (MN)
Ohio U (OH)
Palm Beach Atlantic U (FL)
Point Park U (PA)
Purchase Coll, State U of New York (NY)
Sarah Lawrence Coll (NY)
Slippery Rock U of Pennsylvania (PA)
U of Southern California (CA)

POLISH

U of Illinois at Chicago (IL)
U of Michigan (MI)
U of Pittsburgh (PA)
U of Wisconsin–Madison (WI)

POLITICAL COMMUNICATION

Cedarville U (OH)
Nebraska Wesleyan U (NE)
Suffolk U (MA)
Wheeling Jesuit U (WV)

POLITICAL ECONOMY

The Evergreen State Coll (WA)

POLITICAL SCIENCE AND GOVERNMENT

Abilene Christian U (TX)
Acadia U (NS, Canada)
Adelphi U (NY)
Alabama Ag and Mech U (AL)
Alabama State U (AL)
Albany State U (GA)
Albertus Magnus Coll (CT)
Albion Coll (MI)
Albright Coll (PA)
Alcorn State U (MS)
Alderson-Broaddus Coll (WV)
Alfred U (NY)
Allegheny Coll (PA)
Alma Coll (MI)
Alvernia U (PA)
Alverno Coll (WI)
American Jewish U (CA)
American Public U System (WV)
American U (DC)
American U of Beirut (Lebanon)
Amherst Coll (MA)
Anderson U (IN)
Andrews U (MI)
Angelo State U (TX)
Anna Maria Coll (MA)
Appalachian State U (NC)
Aquinas Coll (MI)
Arcadia U (PA)

Piedmont Coll (GA)
Pittsburg State U (KS)
Pitzer Coll (CA)
Point Park U (PA)
Pomona Coll (CA)
Portland State U (OR)
Prairie View A&M U (TX)
Presbyterian Coll (SC)
Princeton U (NJ)
Principia Coll (IL)
Providence Coll (RI)
Purchase Coll, State U of New York (NY)
Purdue U (IN)
Purdue U Calumet (IN)
Queens Coll of the City U of New York (NY)
Quincy U (IL)
Quinnipiac U (CT)
Radford U (VA)
Ramapo Coll of New Jersey (NJ)
Randolph Coll (VA)
Randolph-Macon Coll (VA)
Reed Coll (OR)
Regis Coll (MA)
Regis U (CO)
Rhode Island Coll (RI)
Rhodes Coll (TN)
Rice U (TX)
The Richard Stockton Coll of New Jersey (NJ)
Rider U (NJ)
Ripon Coll (WI)
Rivier Coll (NH)
Roanoke Coll (VA)
Rockford Coll (IL)
Rockhurst U (MO)
Rocky Mountain Coll (MT)
Rollins Coll (FL)
Roosevelt U (IL)
Rosemont Coll (PA)
Rowan U (NJ)
Russell Sage Coll (NY)
Rust Coll (MS)
Rutgers, The State U of New Jersey, Camden (NJ)
Rutgers, The State U of New Jersey, Newark (NJ)
Rutgers, The State U of New Jersey, New Brunswick (NJ)
Saginaw Valley State U (MI)
St. Ambrose U (IA)
Saint Anselm Coll (NH)
St. Bonaventure U (NY)
St. Catherine U (MN)
St. Edward's U (TX)
Saint Francis U (PA)
St. Francis Xavier U (NS, Canada)
St. John Fisher Coll (NY)
Saint John's U (MN)
St. John's U (NY)
Saint Joseph's Coll (IN)
Saint Joseph's Coll of Maine (ME)
Saint Joseph's U (PA)
St. Lawrence U (NY)
Saint Leo U (FL)
Saint Louis U (MO)
Saint Martin's U (WA)
Saint Mary's Coll (IN)
Saint Mary's Coll of California (CA)
St. Mary's Coll of Maryland (MD)
Saint Michael's Coll (VT)
St. Norbert Coll (WI)
St. Olaf Coll (MN)
St. Thomas U (FL)
St. Thomas U (NB, Canada)
Saint Xavier U (IL)
Salem State U (MA)
Salisbury U (MD)
Salve Regina U (RI)
Samford U (AL)
Sam Houston State U (TX)
San Diego State U (CA)
San Francisco State U (CA)
San Jose State U (CA)
Santa Clara U (CA)
Sarah Lawrence Coll (NY)
Savannah State U (GA)
Schreiner U (TX)
Scripps Coll (CA)
Seattle Pacific U (WA)
Seton Hill U (PA)
Sewanee: The U of the South (TN)
Shenandoah U (VA)
Shepherd U (WV)
Shippensburg U of Pennsylvania (PA)
Siena Coll (NY)

Simmons Coll (MA)
Simon Fraser U (BC, Canada)
Simpson Coll (IA)
Skidmore Coll (NY)
Slippery Rock U of Pennsylvania (PA)
Smith Coll (MA)
Sonoma State U (CA)
South Dakota State U (SD)
Southeastern Louisiana U (LA)
Southeastern Oklahoma State U (OK)
Southeast Missouri State U (MO)
Southern Arkansas U–Magnolia (AR)
Southern Connecticut State U (CT)
Southern Illinois U Carbondale (IL)
Southern Illinois U Edwardsville (IL)
Southern Methodist U (TX)
Southern Oregon U (OR)
Southern Polytechnic State U (GA)
Southern Utah U (UT)
Spelman Coll (GA)
Spring Arbor U (MI)
Spring Hill Coll (AL)
Stanford U (CA)
State U of New York at Binghamton (NY)
State U of New York at Fredonia (NY)
State U of New York at New Paltz (NY)
State U of New York at Oswego (NY)
State U of New York at Plattsburgh (NY)
State U of New York Coll at Geneseo (NY)
State U of New York Coll at Oneonta (NY)
State U of New York Coll at Potsdam (NY)
Stephen F. Austin State U (TX)
Stetson U (FL)
Stonehill Coll (MA)
Stony Brook U, State U of New York (NY)
Suffolk U (MA)
Sul Ross State U (TX)
Susquehanna U (PA)
Swarthmore Coll (PA)
Sweet Briar Coll (VA)
Syracuse U (NY)
Tarleton State U (TX)
Taylor U (IN)
Temple U (PA)
Tennessee Technological U (TN)
Texas A&M Intl U (TX)
Texas A&M U (TX)
Texas A&M U–Corpus Christi (TX)
Texas A&M U–Kingsville (TX)
Texas Christian U (TX)
Texas Lutheran U (TX)
Texas Southern U (TX)
Texas State U–San Marcos (TX)
Texas Tech U (TX)
Texas Wesleyan U (TX)
Texas Woman's U (TX)
Thiel Coll (PA)
Thomas Edison State Coll (NJ)
Thomas More Coll (KY)
Thomas U (GA)
Towson U (MD)
Transylvania U (KY)
Trent U (ON, Canada)
Trinity Coll (CT)
Trinity U (TX)
Troy U (AL)
Truman State U (MO)
Tufts U (MA)
Tulane U (LA)
Tuskegee U (AL)
Union Coll (NY)
Union U (TN)
United States Air Force Acad (CO)
United States Coast Guard Acad (CT)
United States Military Acad (NY)
United States Naval Acad (MD)
U at Buffalo, the State U of New York (NY)
The U of Alabama (AL)
The U of Alabama at Birmingham (AL)
The U of Alabama in Huntsville (AL)
U of Alaska Fairbanks (AK)
The U of Arizona (AZ)
U of Arkansas (AR)

U of Arkansas at Pine Bluff (AR)
U of Baltimore (MD)
The U of British Columbia (BC, Canada)
The U of British Columbia–Okanagan (BC, Canada)
U of California, Berkeley (CA)
U of California, Davis (CA)
U of California, Irvine (CA)
U of California, Los Angeles (CA)
U of California, Merced (CA)
U of California, Santa Barbara (CA)
U of California, Santa Cruz (CA)
U of Central Florida (FL)
U of Central Missouri (MO)
U of Charleston (WV)
U of Cincinnati (OH)
U of Colorado at Colorado Springs (CO)
U of Colorado Boulder (CO)
U of Colorado Denver (CO)
U of Dallas (TX)
U of Dayton (OH)
U of Delaware (DE)
U of Denver (CO)
U of Evansville (IN)
The U of Findlay (OH)
U of Florida (FL)
U of Georgia (GA)
U of Guelph (ON, Canada)
U of Hartford (CT)
U of Hawaii at Hilo (HI)
U of Hawaii at Manoa (HI)
U of Hawaii–West Oahu (HI)
U of Houston (TX)
U of Houston–Clear Lake (TX)
U of Houston–Downtown (TX)
U of Idaho (ID)
U of Illinois at Chicago (IL)
U of Illinois at Springfield (IL)
U of Indianapolis (IN)
The U of Iowa (IA)
The U of Kansas (KS)
U of La Verne (CA)
U of Lethbridge (AB, Canada)
U of Louisiana at Lafayette (LA)
U of Louisiana at Monroe (LA)
U of Louisville (KY)
U of Maine (ME)
U of Maine at Farmington (ME)
U of Maine at Presque Isle (ME)
U of Manitoba (MB, Canada)
U of Mary Hardin-Baylor (TX)
U of Maryland, Baltimore County (MD)
U of Maryland, Coll Park (MD)
U of Maryland U Coll (MD)
U of Mary Washington (VA)
U of Massachusetts Amherst (MA)
U of Massachusetts Boston (MA)
U of Massachusetts Dartmouth (MA)
U of Massachusetts Lowell (MA)
U of Memphis (TN)
U of Miami (FL)
U of Michigan (MI)
U of Michigan–Dearborn (MI)
U of Michigan–Flint (MI)
U of Minnesota, Duluth (MN)
U of Minnesota, Twin Cities Campus (MN)
U of Mississippi (MS)
U of Missouri (MO)
U of Missouri–St. Louis (MO)
U of Mobile (AL)
U of Montevallo (AL)
U of Mount Union (OH)
U of Nebraska at Omaha (NE)
U of Nebraska–Lincoln (NE)
U of Nevada, Las Vegas (NV)
U of Nevada, Reno (NV)
U of New Brunswick Fredericton (NB, Canada)
U of New Brunswick Saint John (NB, Canada)
U of New England (ME)
U of New Hampshire (NH)
U of New Haven (CT)
The U of North Carolina at Asheville (NC)
The U of North Carolina at Chapel Hill (NC)
The U of North Carolina at Charlotte (NC)
The U of North Carolina at Greensboro (NC)
The U of North Carolina at Pembroke (NC)

The U of North Carolina Wilmington (NC)
U of North Dakota (ND)
U of Northern Colorado (CO)
U of Northern Iowa (IA)
U of North Florida (FL)
U of North Texas (TX)
U of Notre Dame (IN)
U of Oklahoma (OK)
U of Oregon (OR)
U of Ottawa (ON, Canada)
U of Pennsylvania (PA)
U of Pittsburgh (PA)
U of Pittsburgh at Bradford (PA)
U of Pittsburgh at Greensburg (PA)
U of Pittsburgh at Johnstown (PA)
U of Portland (OR)
U of Puget Sound (WA)
U of Redlands (CA)
U of Regina (SK, Canada)
U of Rhode Island (RI)
U of Richmond (VA)
U of Rio Grande (OH)
U of Rochester (NY)
U of St. Francis (IL)
U of Saint Mary (KS)
U of St. Thomas (MN)
U of St. Thomas (TX)
U of San Diego (CA)
U of San Francisco (CA)
U of Saskatchewan (SK, Canada)
U of Science and Arts of Oklahoma (OK)
The U of Scranton (PA)
U of Sioux Falls (SD)
U of South Alabama (AL)
U of South Carolina (SC)
U of South Carolina Aiken (SC)
U of South Carolina Upstate (SC)
The U of South Dakota (SD)
U of Southern California (CA)
U of Southern Indiana (IN)
U of Southern Maine (ME)
U of Southern Mississippi (MS)
U of South Florida (FL)
The U of Tampa (FL)
The U of Tennessee (TN)
The U of Tennessee at Chattanooga (TN)
The U of Tennessee at Martin (TN)
The U of Texas at Arlington (TX)
The U of Texas at Austin (TX)
The U of Texas at Dallas (TX)
The U of Texas at San Antonio (TX)
The U of Texas at Tyler (TX)
The U of Texas of the Permian Basin (TX)
The U of Texas–Pan American (TX)
U of the Cumberlands (KY)
U of the District of Columbia (DC)
U of the Incarnate Word (TX)
U of the Ozarks (AR)
U of the Pacific (CA)
The U of Toledo (OH)
U of Tulsa (OK)
U of Utah (UT)
U of Vermont (VT)
U of Virginia (VA)
U of Washington (WA)
U of Waterloo (ON, Canada)
The U of Western Ontario (ON, Canada)
U of West Florida (FL)
U of West Georgia (GA)
U of Wisconsin–Eau Claire (WI)
U of Wisconsin–Green Bay (WI)
U of Wisconsin–La Crosse (WI)
U of Wisconsin–Madison (WI)
U of Wisconsin–Parkside (WI)
U of Wisconsin–Platteville (WI)
U of Wisconsin–River Falls (WI)
U of Wisconsin–Stevens Point (WI)
U of Wisconsin–Superior (WI)
U of Wisconsin–Whitewater (WI)
U of Wyoming (WY)
Utah State U (UT)
Utah Valley U (UT)
Valdosta State U (GA)
Valparaiso U (IN)
Vanderbilt U (TN)
Vassar Coll (NY)
Villanova U (PA)
Virginia Commonwealth U (VA)
Virginia Polytechnic Inst and State U (VA)
Virginia State U (VA)
Virginia Wesleyan Coll (VA)
Wabash Coll (IN)

Wagner Coll (NY)
Wake Forest U (NC)
Walsh U (OH)
Wartburg Coll (IA)
Washburn U (KS)
Washington Adventist U (MD)
Washington & Jefferson Coll (PA)
Washington and Lee U (VA)
Washington Coll (MD)
Washington State U (WA)
Washington U in St. Louis (MO)
Wayne State Coll (NE)
Wayne State U (MI)
Weber State U (UT)
Webster U (MO)
Wellesley Coll (MA)
Wells Coll (NY)
Wesleyan Coll (GA)
Wesleyan U (CT)
West Chester U of Pennsylvania (PA)
Western Carolina U (NC)
Western Connecticut State U (CT)
Western Illinois U (IL)
Western Kentucky U (KY)
Western Michigan U (MI)
Western New England U (MA)
Western Oregon U (OR)
Western State Coll of Colorado (CO)
Westfield State U (MA)
West Liberty U (WV)
Westminster Coll (MO)
Westminster Coll (UT)
Westmont Coll (CA)
West Virginia U (WV)
Wheaton Coll (IL)
Wheaton Coll (MA)
Wheeling Jesuit U (WV)
Whitman Coll (WA)
Wichita State U (KS)
Widener U (PA)
Wilfrid Laurier U (ON, Canada)
Wilkes U (PA)
Willamette U (OR)
William Jessup U (CA)
William Jewell Coll (MO)
William Paterson U of New Jersey (NJ)
Williams Coll (MA)
Wilmington Coll (OH)
Winona State U (MN)
Winthrop U (SC)
Wittenberg U (OH)
Wofford Coll (SC)
Woodbury U (CA)
Wright State U (OH)
Xavier U (OH)
Xavier U of Louisiana (LA)
Yale U (CT)
York Coll of Pennsylvania (PA)
York Coll of the City U of New York (NY)
Young Harris Coll (GA)
Youngstown State U (OH)

POLITICAL SCIENCE AND GOVERNMENT RELATED

American Jewish U (CA)
American U in Bulgaria (Bulgaria)
Brandeis U (MA)
Buena Vista U (IA)
Capital U (OH)
Claflin U (SC)
Claremont McKenna Coll (CA)
Columbia U, School of General Studies (NY)
Delaware State U (DE)
Georgetown Coll (KY)
Lebanese American U (Lebanon)
Muhlenberg Coll (PA)
Regis Coll (MA)
Sacred Heart U (CT)
Saint Mary's Coll of California (CA)
Saint Mary's Coll of Minnesota (MN)
Southern Vermont Coll (VT)
Trevecca Nazarene U (TN)
U of California, Davis (CA)
U of Hartford (CT)
U of Northern Iowa (IA)
Virginia Intermont Coll (VA)
Western Michigan U (MI)
Whitman Coll (WA)

POLYMER CHEMISTRY

Clemson U (SC)
Georgia Inst of Technology (GA)
Pittsburg State U (KS)

State U of New York Coll of Environmental Science and Forestry (NY)
The U of Akron (OH)
U of Wisconsin–Stevens Point (WI)
Winona State U (MN)

POLYMER/PLASTICS ENGINEERING
Case Western Reserve U (OH)
Penn State Erie, The Behrend Coll (PA)
The U of Akron (OH)
U of Massachusetts Lowell (MA)
U of Southern California (CA)
U of Wisconsin–Stout (WI)
Winona State U (MN)

PORTUGUESE
Florida Intl U (FL)
Georgetown U (DC)
Indiana U Bloomington (IN)
Marlboro Coll (VT)
The Ohio State U (OH)
Rutgers, The State U of New Jersey, New Brunswick (NJ)
Smith Coll (MA)
Tulane U (LA)
United States Military Acad (NY)
U of California, Los Angeles (CA)
U of California, Santa Barbara (CA)
U of Florida (FL)
The U of Iowa (IA)
U of Massachusetts Amherst (MA)
U of Massachusetts Dartmouth (MA)
The U of Texas at Austin (TX)
U of Wisconsin–Madison (WI)
Yale U (CT)

POULTRY SCIENCE
Auburn U (AL)
Delaware State U (DE)
Mississippi State U (MS)
North Carolina State U (NC)
Stephen F. Austin State U (TX)
Texas A&M U (TX)
Tuskegee U (AL)
U of Arkansas (AR)
U of Georgia (GA)
U of Wisconsin–Madison (WI)
Virginia Polytechnic Inst and State U (VA)

PRE-CHIROPRACTIC
Millikin U (IL)

PRE-DENTISTRY STUDIES
Abilene Christian U (TX)
Acadia U (NS, Canada)
Albertus Magnus Coll (CT)
Allegheny Coll (PA)
Alma Coll (MI)
American U (DC)
Anderson U (IN)
Arcadia U (PA)
Ashland U (OH)
Atlantic Union Coll (MA)
Auburn U (AL)
Augsburg Coll (MN)
Augustana Coll (SD)
Baldwin-Wallace Coll (OH)
Ball State U (IN)
Barry U (FL)
Belmont Abbey Coll (NC)
Beloit Coll (WI)
Bethany Coll (WV)
Birmingham-Southern Coll (AL)
Blackburn Coll (IL)
Boise State U (ID)
Boston U (MA)
California State U, Chico (CA)
Calvin Coll (MI)
Campbellsville U (KY)
Carroll U (WI)
Cedar Crest Coll (PA)
Cedarville U (OH)
Centenary Coll of Louisiana (LA)
Chapman U (CA)
City Coll of the City U of New York (NY)
Clark U (MA)
Coll of Saint Benedict (MN)
Concordia Coll (MN)
Concordia U Chicago (IL)
Cumberland U (TN)
Defiance Coll (OH)
Dickinson State U (ND)
Dominican U (IL)
Dordt Coll (IA)
Drake U (IA)

Drury U (MO)
Elmhurst Coll (IL)
Elmira Coll (NY)
Emory & Henry Coll (VA)
Evangel U (MO)
Florida Southern Coll (FL)
Franklin Pierce U (NH)
Furman U (SC)
Gardner-Webb U (NC)
Georgia Southern U (GA)
Gettysburg Coll (PA)
Graceland U (IA)
Grand Valley State U (MI)
Grove City Coll (PA)
Hamline U (MN)
Hillsdale Coll (MI)
Hobart and William Smith Colls (NY)
Hofstra U (NY)
Houghton Coll (NY)
Illinois Coll (IL)
Indiana U–Purdue U Fort Wayne (IN)
Indiana Wesleyan U (IN)
Iowa State U of Science and Technology (IA)
Iowa Wesleyan Coll (IA)
John Carroll U (OH)
Juniata Coll (PA)
Kent State U (OH)
Kentucky Wesleyan Coll (KY)
Keuka Coll (NY)
King's Coll (PA)
Lake Superior State U (MI)
Lamar U (TX)
La Salle U (PA)
Lawrence U (WI)
Lehigh U (PA)
Le Moyne Coll (NY)
LeTourneau U (TX)
Limestone Coll (SC)
Lindenwood U (MO)
Lindsey Wilson Coll (KY)
Lipscomb U (TN)
Lock Haven U of Pennsylvania (PA)
Longwood U (VA)
Loyola U New Orleans (LA)
MacMurray Coll (IL)
Manchester Coll (IN)
Marquette U (WI)
Maryville U of Saint Louis (MO)
Mayville State U (ND)
McKendree U (IL)
Mercer U (GA)
Midwestern State U (TX)
Millikin U (IL)
Minnesota State U Mankato (MN)
Molloy Coll (NY)
Mount Allison U (NB, Canada)
Mount Mercy U (IA)
Mount Vernon Nazarene U (OH)
Nazareth Coll of Rochester (NY)
Newman U (KS)
Niagara U (NY)
North Central Coll (IL)
Northern Michigan U (MI)
Northern State U (SD)
North Georgia Coll & State U (GA)
Northwestern Oklahoma State U (OK)
Northwest Nazarene U (ID)
Notre Dame de Namur U (CA)
Oglethorpe U (GA)
The Ohio State U (OH)
Ohio Wesleyan U (OH)
Oklahoma City U (OK)
Oklahoma Wesleyan U (OK)
Ouachita Baptist U (AR)
Pacific U (OR)
Pepperdine U, Malibu (CA)
Pittsburg State U (KS)
Purdue U Calumet (IN)
Quinnipiac U (CT)
Regis U (CO)
Rhode Island Coll (RI)
Ripon Coll (WI)
Rivier Coll (NH)
Rockford Coll (IL)
Rutgers, The State U of New Jersey, New Brunswick (NJ)
Sacred Heart U (CT)
Saint Anselm Coll (NH)
St. Catherine U (MN)
Saint Francis U (PA)
St. Francis Xavier U (NS, Canada)
Saint John's U (MN)
Saint Mary-of-the-Woods Coll (IN)
Saint Michael's Coll (VT)
St. Thomas U (FL)
Sarah Lawrence Coll (NY)
Simpson Coll (IA)

Sonoma State U (CA)
Spring Hill Coll (AL)
State U of New York at Oswego (NY)
State U of New York at Geneseo (NY)
State U of New York Coll at Oneonta (NY)
State U of New York Coll of Environmental Science and Forestry (NY)
Stetson U (FL)
Sul Ross State U (TX)
Susquehanna U (PA)
Tabor Coll (KS)
Tarleton State U (TX)
Tennessee Technological U (TN)
Texas A&M U–Corpus Christi (TX)
Texas Wesleyan U (TX)
Thiel Coll (PA)
Trinity U (TX)
Union U (TN)
U of Bridgeport (CT)
U of Central Missouri (MO)
U of Cincinnati (OH)
U of Dallas (TX)
U of Dayton (OH)
U of Evansville (IN)
U of Hartford (CT)
U of Illinois at Chicago (IL)
U of Indianapolis (IN)
The U of Iowa (IA)
U of Manitoba (MB, Canada)
U of Maryland, Coll Park (MD)
U of Massachusetts Amherst (MA)
U of Minnesota, Duluth (MN)
U of Minnesota, Twin Cities Campus (MN)
U of Nebraska–Lincoln (NE)
U of New Brunswick Fredericton (NB, Canada)
U of New England (ME)
U of Pittsburgh at Johnstown (PA)
U of Portland (OR)
U of Regina (SK, Canada)
U of Rio Grande (OH)
U of St. Francis (IL)
U of San Francisco (CA)
U of Sioux Falls (SD)
The U of Tennessee (TN)
The U of Tennessee at Martin (TN)
The U of Toledo (OH)
U of Wisconsin–Parkside (WI)
U of Wisconsin–River Falls (WI)
Upper Iowa U (IA)
Utah State U (UT)
Virginia Wesleyan Coll (VA)
Wagner Coll (NY)
Walla Walla U (WA)
Walsh U (OH)
Washburn U (KS)
Washington Adventist U (MD)
Washington Coll (MD)
Washington U in St. Louis (MO)
Waynesburg U (PA)
Wells Coll (NY)
West Liberty U (WV)
Westmont Coll (CA)
Widener U (PA)
William Paterson U of New Jersey (NJ)
Wilmington Coll (OH)
Winona State U (MN)
Wofford Coll (SC)
Young Harris Coll (GA)
Youngstown State U (OH)

PRE-ENGINEERING
Asbury U (KY)
Azusa Pacific U (CA)
Baldwin-Wallace Coll (OH)
Bethel U (TN)
Delaware State U (DE)
Drake U (IA)
Faulkner U (AL)
Houghton Coll (NY)
Le Moyne U (NY)
Midwestern State U (TX)
Northwest Nazarene U (ID)
Ouachita Baptist U (AR)
Pittsburg State U (KS)
Saint Joseph's Coll of Maine (ME)
Scripps Coll (CA)
Simpson Coll (IA)
Slippery Rock U of Pennsylvania (PA)
Spring Hill Coll (AL)
Wagner Coll (NY)
Waynesburg U (PA)
Wheeling Jesuit U (WV)

PRE-LAW STUDIES
Abilene Christian U (TX)
Acadia U (NS, Canada)
Albertus Magnus Coll (CT)
Albion Coll (MI)
Albright Coll (PA)
Allegheny Coll (PA)
Alma Coll (MI)
Alvernia U (PA)
American U (DC)
Anderson U (IN)
Andrews U (MI)
Aquinas Coll (MI)
Arcadia U (PA)
Ashland U (OH)
Atlantic Union Coll (MA)
Auburn U (AL)
Augsburg Coll (MN)
Augustana Coll (SD)
Azusa Pacific U (CA)
Bard Coll (NY)
Barry U (FL)
Belmont Abbey Coll (NC)
Beloit Coll (WI)
Bemidji State U (MN)
Bennington Coll (VT)
Bethany Coll (WV)
Bethel Coll (IN)
Biola U (CA)
Birmingham-Southern Coll (AL)
Blackburn Coll (IL)
Bowling Green State U (OH)
California State U, Dominguez Hills (CA)
Calumet Coll of Saint Joseph (IN)
Calvin Coll (MI)
Campbellsville U (KY)
Cedar Crest Coll (PA)
Cedarville U (OH)
Centenary Coll of Louisiana (LA)
Champlain Coll (VT)
Christopher Newport U (VA)
City Coll of the City U of New York (NY)
Claremont McKenna Coll (CA)
Clark U (MA)
Clearwater Christian Coll (FL)
Coll of Saint Benedict (MN)
Concordia Coll (MN)
Concordia Coll–New York (NY)
Concordia U Chicago (IL)
Concordia U Wisconsin (WI)
Corban U (OR)
Creighton U (NE)
Crown Coll (MN)
Cumberland U (TN)
Curry Coll (MA)
Defiance Coll (OH)
Dickinson State U (ND)
Dominican Coll (NY)
Dominican U (IL)
Dordt Coll (IA)
Drake U (IA)
Drury U (MO)
Elmhurst Coll (IL)
Elmira Coll (NY)
Emmanuel Coll (GA)
Emory & Henry Coll (VA)
Evangel U (MO)
Faulkner U (AL)
Florida Inst of Technology (FL)
Fontbonne U (MO)
Francis Marion U (SC)
Franklin Pierce U (NH)
Furman U (SC)
Gannon U (PA)
Gardner-Webb U (NC)
Gettysburg Coll (PA)
Grand View U (IA)
Grove City Coll (PA)
Hamline U (MN)
Hannibal-LaGrange U (MO)
Hartwick Coll (NY)
Haverford Coll (PA)
Hawai`i Pacific U (HI)
Hobart and William Smith Colls (NY)
Hofstra U (NY)
Houghton Coll (NY)
Huntington U (IN)
Illinois Coll (IL)
Indiana Wesleyan U (IN)
Iowa State U of Science and Technology (IA)
Iowa Wesleyan Coll (IA)
Ithaca Coll (NY)
John Carroll U (OH)
Juniata Coll (PA)
Kentucky Wesleyan Coll (KY)
Keuka Coll (NY)
Keystone Coll (PA)

King Coll (TN)
King's Coll (PA)
Lakehead U (ON, Canada)
Lake Superior State U (MI)
Lawrence U (WI)
Le Moyne Coll (NY)
LeTourneau U (TX)
Limestone Coll (SC)
Lincoln Memorial U (TN)
Lindenwood U (MO)
Lindsey Wilson Coll (KY)
Lipscomb U (TN)
Longwood U (VA)
Louisiana Coll (LA)
Lubbock Christian U (TX)
MacMurray Coll (IL)
Manchester Coll (IN)
Mansfield U of Pennsylvania (PA)
Marlboro Coll (VT)
Marquette U (WI)
Mars Hill Coll (NC)
Massachusetts Coll of Liberal Arts (MA)
The Master's Coll and Sem (CA)
Mayville State U (ND)
McKendree U (IL)
Michigan State U (MI)
Midwestern State U (TX)
Millikin U (IL)
Minnesota State U Mankato (MN)
Molloy Coll (NY)
Mount Allison U (NB, Canada)
Mount Mercy U (IA)
Mount Vernon Nazarene U (OH)
National U (CA)
Nazareth Coll of Rochester (NY)
Newbury Coll (MA)
New England Coll (NH)
Newman U (KS)
Niagara U (NY)
North Central Coll (IL)
Northern Arizona U (AZ)
Northern Michigan U (MI)
Northern State U (SD)
Northwestern Oklahoma State U (OK)
Northwest Nazarene U (ID)
Notre Dame de Namur U (CA)
Nova Southeastern U (FL)
Oglethorpe U (GA)
Ohio Wesleyan U (OH)
Oklahoma Christian U (OK)
Oklahoma City U (OK)
Oklahoma Wesleyan U (OK)
Ouachita Baptist U (AR)
Pacific Lutheran U (WA)
Palm Beach Atlantic U (FL)
Pepperdine U, Malibu (CA)
Pittsburg State U (KS)
Purdue U Calumet (IN)
Quinnipiac U (CT)
Regis U (CO)
Rensselaer Polytechnic Inst (NY)
Rhode Island Coll (RI)
Ripon Coll (WI)
Rivier Coll (NH)
Rockford Coll (IL)
Rutgers, The State U of New Jersey, New Brunswick (NJ)
Saint Anselm Coll (NH)
St. Catherine U (MN)
Saint Francis U (PA)
St. Francis Xavier U (NS, Canada)
Saint John's U (MN)
St. Joseph's Coll, Long Island Campus (NY)
St. Joseph's Coll, New York (NY)
Saint Mary-of-the-Woods Coll (IN)
Saint Michael's Coll (VT)
St. Thomas U (FL)
Sarah Lawrence Coll (NY)
Seattle Pacific U (WA)
Seton Hill U (PA)
Siena Heights U (MI)
Simpson Coll (IA)
Smith Coll (MA)
Sonoma State U (CA)
Southern Oregon U (OR)
Southern Vermont Coll (VT)
State U of New York at Binghamton (NY)
State U of New York at Fredonia (NY)
State U of New York at New Paltz (NY)
State U of New York at Oswego (NY)
State U of New York Coll at Geneseo (NY)

State U of New York Coll at Oneonta (NY)
State U of New York Coll of Environmental Science and Forestry (NY)
Stephens Coll (MO)
Stetson U (FL)
Suffolk U (MA)
Sul Ross State U (TX)
Susquehanna U (PA)
Tabor Coll (KS)
Talladega Coll (AL)
Tennessee Technological U (TN)
Texas A&M U–Corpus Christi (TX)
Texas Wesleyan U (TX)
Thiel Coll (PA)
Trine U (IN)
Trinity U (TX)
Union U (TN)
United States Military Acad (NY)
U of Bridgeport (CT)
U of California, Santa Barbara (CA)
U of California, Santa Cruz (CA)
U of Cincinnati (OH)
U of Dallas (TX)
U of Dayton (OH)
The U of Findlay (OH)
U of Indianapolis (IN)
The U of Iowa (IA)
U of Louisiana at Lafayette (LA)
U of Manitoba (MB, Canada)
U of Maryland, Coll Park (MD)
U of Minnesota, Twin Cities Campus (MN)
U of New Brunswick Fredericton (NB, Canada)
U of Pittsburgh at Greensburg (PA)
U of Pittsburgh at Johnstown (PA)
U of Portland (OR)
U of Regina (SK, Canada)
U of Rio Grande (OH)
U of St. Francis (IL)
U of Sioux Falls (SD)
The U of Toledo (OH)
U of Wisconsin–River Falls (WI)
U of Wisconsin–Superior (WI)
Utah State U (UT)
Victory U (TN)
Virginia Intermont Coll (VA)
Wabash Coll (IN)
Wagner Coll (NY)
Walla Walla U (WA)
Washburn U (KS)
Washington Adventist U (MD)
Washington Coll (MD)
Wayland Baptist U (TX)
Waynesburg U (PA)
Webber Intl U (FL)
Wells Coll (NY)
Western State Coll of Colorado (CO)
West Liberty U (WV)
Westminster Coll (MO)
Westmont Coll (CA)
William Paterson U of New Jersey (NJ)
Wilmington Coll (OH)
Wingate U (NC)
Winona State U (MN)
Wofford Coll (SC)
Xavier U of Louisiana (LA)
Young Harris Coll (GA)
Youngstown State U (OH)

PREMEDICAL STUDIES
Abilene Christian U (TX)
Acadia U (NS, Canada)
Albertus Magnus Coll (CT)
Albion Coll (MI)
Allegheny Coll (PA)
Alma Coll (MI)
Alvernia U (PA)
American U (DC)
Anderson U (IN)
Andrews U (MI)
Arcadia U (PA)
Ashland U (OH)
Atlantic Union Coll (MA)
Auburn U (AL)
Augsburg Coll (MN)
Augustana Coll (IL)
Augustana Coll (SD)
Averett U (VA)
Baldwin-Wallace Coll (OH)
Ball State U (IN)
Bard Coll (NY)
Bard Coll at Simon's Rock (MA)
Barry U (FL)

Belmont Abbey Coll (NC)
Beloit Coll (WI)
Bemidji State U (MN)
Bennington Coll (VT)
Bethany Coll (WV)
Bethel Coll (IN)
Birmingham-Southern Coll (AL)
Blackburn Coll (IL)
Bluffton U (OH)
Bob Jones U (SC)
Boise State U (ID)
California State U, Chico (CA)
Calvin Coll (MI)
Campbellsville U (KY)
Carroll U (WI)
Cedar Crest Coll (PA)
Cedarville U (OH)
Centenary Coll of Louisiana (LA)
Chapman U (CA)
City Coll of the City U of New York (NY)
Claremont McKenna Coll (CA)
Clark U (MA)
Clearwater Christian Coll (FL)
Coll of Saint Benedict (MN)
Coll of the Holy Cross (MA)
Concordia Coll (MN)
Concordia U Chicago (IL)
Concord U (WV)
Cumberland U (TN)
Defiance Coll (OH)
Dickinson State U (ND)
Dominican U (IL)
Dordt Coll (IA)
Drake U (IA)
Drury U (MO)
Earlham Coll (IN)
Elmhurst Coll (IL)
Elmira Coll (NY)
Emory & Henry Coll (VA)
Evangel U (MO)
Florida Southern Coll (FL)
Franklin Pierce U (NH)
Furman U (SC)
Gannon U (PA)
Gardner-Webb U (NC)
Georgia Southern U (GA)
Gettysburg Coll (PA)
Graceland U (IA)
Grand Valley State U (MI)
Grove City Coll (PA)
Hamline U (MN)
Hartwick Coll (NY)
Haverford Coll (PA)
Hawai`i Pacific U (HI)
Hillsdale Coll (MI)
Hobart and William Smith Colls (NY)
Hofstra U (NY)
Houghton Coll (NY)
Huntington U (IN)
Illinois Coll (IL)
Immaculata U (PA)
Indiana U–Purdue U Fort Wayne (IN)
Indiana Wesleyan U (IN)
Inter American U of Puerto Rico, Bayamón Campus (PR)
Iowa State U of Science and Technology (IA)
Iowa Wesleyan Coll (IA)
Ithaca Coll (NY)
John Carroll U (OH)
Johnson State Coll (VT)
Juniata Coll (PA)
Kent State U (OH)
Kentucky Wesleyan Coll (KY)
Keuka Coll (NY)
Keystone Coll (PA)
King Coll (TN)
King's Coll (PA)
La Salle U (PA)
Lawrence U (WI)
Lehigh U (PA)
Le Moyne Coll (NY)
LeTourneau U (TX)
Limestone Coll (SC)
Lincoln Memorial U (TN)
Lindenwood U (MO)
Lindsey Wilson Coll (KY)
Lipscomb U (TN)
Lock Haven U of Pennsylvania (PA)
Longwood U (VA)
Loyola U New Orleans (LA)
MacMurray Coll (IL)
Marlboro Coll (VT)
Marquette U (WI)
Mars Hill Coll (NC)
Maryville U of Saint Louis (MO)

Massachusetts Coll of Liberal Arts (MA)
The Master's Coll and Sem (CA)
Mayville State U (ND)
McKendree U (IL)
Mercer U (GA)
Mercy Coll of Health Sciences (IA)
Michigan State U (MI)
Midwestern State U (TX)
Millikin U (IL)
Minnesota State U Mankato (MN)
Molloy Coll (NY)
Mount Allison U (NB, Canada)
Mount Mercy U (IA)
Mount Vernon Nazarene U (OH)
Nazareth Coll of Rochester (NY)
Newman U (KS)
New York Inst of Technology (NY)
Niagara U (NY)
North Central Coll (IL)
Northern Michigan U (MI)
Northern State U (SD)
North Georgia Coll & State U (GA)
Northwestern Oklahoma State U (OK)
Northwest Nazarene U (ID)
Notre Dame de Namur U (CA)
Nova Southeastern U (FL)
Oglethorpe U (GA)
Ohio Wesleyan U (OH)
Oklahoma City U (OK)
Oklahoma Wesleyan U (OK)
Ouachita Baptist U (AR)
Pacific Lutheran U (WA)
Pacific U (OR)
Penn State Abington (PA)
Penn State Altoona (PA)
Penn State Beaver (PA)
Penn State Berks (PA)
Penn State Brandywine (PA)
Penn State DuBois (PA)
Penn State Erie, The Behrend Coll (PA)
Penn State Fayette, The Eberly Campus (PA)
Penn State Greater Allegheny (PA)
Penn State Hazleton (PA)
Penn State Lehigh Valley (PA)
Penn State Mont Alto (PA)
Penn State New Kensington (PA)
Penn State Schuylkill (PA)
Penn State Shenango (PA)
Penn State U Park (PA)
Penn State Wilkes-Barre (PA)
Penn State Worthington Scranton (PA)
Penn State York (PA)
Pepperdine U, Malibu (CA)
Philadelphia U (PA)
Pittsburg State U (KS)
Pomona Coll (CA)
Purdue U Calumet (IN)
Quinnipiac U (CT)
Regis U (CO)
Rensselaer Polytechnic Inst (NY)
Rhode Island Coll (RI)
Ripon Coll (WI)
Rivier Coll (NH)
Rockford Coll (IL)
Rutgers, The State U of New Jersey, New Brunswick (NJ)
Sacred Heart U (CT)
St. Andrews Presbyterian Coll (NC)
Saint Anselm Coll (NH)
St. Catherine U (MN)
Saint Francis U (PA)
St. Francis Xavier U (NS, Canada)
Saint John's U (MN)
Saint Mary-of-the-Woods Coll (IN)
Saint Michael's Coll (VT)
St. Thomas Aquinas Coll (NY)
St. Thomas U (FL)
Samford U (AL)
Sarah Lawrence Coll (NY)
Simpson Coll (IA)
Slippery Rock U of Pennsylvania (PA)
Smith Coll (MA)
Sonoma State U (CA)
Southeastern U (FL)
Southern Oregon U (OR)
Southern Wesleyan U (SC)
Spring Hill Coll (AL)
State U of New York at Binghamton (NY)
State U of New York at Fredonia (NY)

State U of New York at Oswego (NY)
State U of New York Coll at Geneseo (NY)
State U of New York Coll at Oneonta (NY)
State U of New York Coll of Environmental Science and Forestry (NY)
Stetson U (FL)
Sul Ross State U (TX)
Susquehanna U (PA)
Tabor Coll (KS)
Tarleton State U (TX)
Tennessee Technological U (TN)
Texas A&M U–Corpus Christi (TX)
Texas Lutheran U (TX)
Texas Wesleyan U (TX)
Thiel Coll (PA)
Trine U (IN)
Trinity U (TX)
Union U (TN)
Université de Sherbrooke (QC, Canada)
U of Arkansas (AR)
U of Bridgeport (CT)
U of California, Santa Cruz (CA)
U of Central Missouri (MO)
U of Cincinnati (OH)
U of Dallas (TX)
U of Dayton (OH)
U of Evansville (IN)
The U of Findlay (OH)
U of Hartford (CT)
U of Indianapolis (IN)
The U of Iowa (IA)
U of Maine (ME)
U of Manitoba (MB, Canada)
U of Massachusetts Amherst (MA)
U of Minnesota, Duluth (MN)
U of Minnesota, Twin Cities Campus (MN)
U of Nebraska–Lincoln (NE)
U of Nevada, Reno (NV)
U of New Brunswick Fredericton (NB, Canada)
U of New England (ME)
U of Notre Dame (IN)
U of Pittsburgh at Johnstown (PA)
U of Portland (OR)
U of Regina (SK, Canada)
U of Rio Grande (OH)
U of St. Francis (IL)
U of San Francisco (CA)
U of Sioux Falls (SD)
The U of Tennessee (TN)
The U of Tennessee at Martin (TN)
The U of Toledo (OH)
U of Wisconsin–Madison (WI)
U of Wisconsin–Parkside (WI)
U of Wisconsin–River Falls (WI)
Upper Iowa U (IA)
Utah State U (UT)
Virginia Intermont Coll (VA)
Virginia Wesleyan Coll (VA)
Wabash Coll (IN)
Wagner Coll (NY)
Walla Walla U (WA)
Walsh U (OH)
Washburn U (KS)
Washington Adventist U (MD)
Washington Coll (MD)
Washington State U (WA)
Washington U in St. Louis (MO)
Waynesburg U (PA)
Wells Coll (NY)
West Chester U of Pennsylvania (PA)
West Liberty U (WV)
Westmont Coll (CA)
Wheeling Jesuit U (WV)
Widener U (PA)
William Paterson U of New Jersey (NJ)
Wilmington Coll (OH)
Wingate U (NC)
Winona State U (MN)
Wofford Coll (SC)
Xavier U of Louisiana (LA)
Young Harris Coll (GA)
Youngstown State U (OH)

PRENURSING STUDIES
Allegheny Coll (PA)
American U (DC)
Brigham Young U (UT)
California State U, Fullerton (CA)
Cleveland State U (OH)

Delaware State U (DE)
Dordt Coll (IA)
Gettysburg Coll (PA)
Humboldt State U (CA)
Juniata Coll (PA)
Limestone Coll (SC)
Lindenwood U (MO)
Lipscomb U (TN)
McMurry U (TX)
Oklahoma City U (OK)
Ouachita Baptist U (AR)
San Diego State U (CA)
State U of New York Coll at Geneseo (NY)
Tennessee Wesleyan Coll (TN)
Wright State U (OH)

PRE-OCCUPATIONAL THERAPY
Millikin U (IL)

PRE-OPTOMETRY
Lehigh U (PA)
Le Moyne Coll (NY)
Millikin U (IL)
Simpson Coll (IA)
U of Evansville (IN)
Young Harris Coll (GA)

PRE-PHARMACY STUDIES
Abilene Christian U (TX)
Allegheny Coll (PA)
American U (DC)
Ashland U (OH)
Auburn U (AL)
Baldwin-Wallace Coll (OH)
Barry U (FL)
Belmont Abbey Coll (NC)
Benedictine U (IL)
Bethel U (TN)
Carroll U (WI)
Coll of Saint Benedict (MN)
Cumberland U (TN)
Dordt Coll (IA)
Drury U (MO)
Elmhurst Coll (IL)
Gardner-Webb U (NC)
Georgia Southern U (GA)
Gettysburg Coll (PA)
Houghton Coll (NY)
Iowa Wesleyan Coll (IA)
Juniata Coll (PA)
King Coll (TN)
King's Coll (PA)
Le Moyne Coll (NY)
Limestone Coll (SC)
Lindsey Wilson Coll (KY)
Lipscomb U (TN)
Long Island U, C.W. Post Campus (NY)
Longwood U (VA)
Madonna U (MI)
Mayville State U (ND)
Midwestern State U (TX)
Millikin U (IL)
Mount Allison U (NB, Canada)
Mount Vernon Nazarene U (OH)
Northern Michigan U (MI)
Northwest Nazarene U (ID)
Oklahoma City U (OK)
Ouachita Baptist U (AR)
Pittsburg State U (KS)
Saint John's U (MN)
Saint Joseph's Coll of Maine (ME)
Saint Mary-of-the-Woods Coll (IN)
Simpson Coll (IA)
Slippery Rock U of Pennsylvania (PA)
Tabor Coll (KS)
Tarleton State U (TX)
Texas Southern U (TX)
Union U (TN)
U of Central Missouri (MO)
U of Charleston (WV)
U of Cincinnati (OH)
U of Evansville (IN)
The U of Iowa (IA)
U of Minnesota, Duluth (MN)
U of Minnesota, Twin Cities Campus (MN)
U of Nebraska–Lincoln (NE)
U of Regina (SK, Canada)
U of St. Francis (IL)
The U of Tennessee (TN)
The U of Tennessee at Martin (TN)
U of Wisconsin–Parkside (WI)
U of Wisconsin–River Falls (WI)
Washburn U (KS)
Washington U in St. Louis (MO)

ITT Tech Inst, Norfolk (VA)
ITT Tech Inst, Richmond (VA)
ITT Tech Inst, Springfield (VA)
ITT Tech Inst, Everett (WA)
ITT Tech Inst, Seattle (WA)
ITT Tech Inst, Spokane Valley (WA)
ITT Tech Inst, Green Bay (WI)
ITT Tech Inst, Greenfield (WI)
ITT Tech Inst, Madison (WI)

PSYCHIATRIC/MENTAL HEALTH SERVICES TECHNOLOGY

Indiana U–Purdue U Fort Wayne (IN)
Northern Kentucky U (KY)

PSYCHOLOGY

Abilene Christian U (TX)
Acadia U (NS, Canada)
Adams State Coll (CO)
Adelphi U (NY)
Alabama Ag and Mech U (AL)
Alabama State U (AL)
Albany State U (GA)
Albertus Magnus Coll (CT)
Albion Coll (MI)
Albright Coll (PA)
Alcorn State U (MS)
Alderson-Broaddus Coll (WV)
Alfred U (NY)
Allegheny Coll (PA)
Alma Coll (MI)
Alvernia U (PA)
Alverno Coll (WI)
American Jewish U (CA)
American Public U System (WV)
American U (DC)
American U of Beirut (Lebanon)
The American U of Paris (France)
Amherst Coll (MA)
Anderson U (IN)
Anderson U (SC)
Andrews U (MI)
Angelo State U (TX)
Anna Maria Coll (MA)
Appalachian State U (NC)
Aquinas Coll (MI)
Arcadia U (PA)
Arizona State U (AZ)
Arkansas State U (AR)
Arkansas Tech U (AR)
Armstrong Atlantic State U (GA)
Asbury U (KY)
Ashland U (OH)
Assumption Coll (MA)
Athabasca U (AB, Canada)
Athens State U (AL)
Atlanta Christian Coll (GA)
Atlantic Union Coll (MA)
Auburn U (AL)
Auburn U Montgomery (AL)
Augsburg Coll (MN)
Augustana Coll (IL)
Augustana Coll (SD)
Austin Coll (TX)
Austin Peay State U (TN)
Averett U (VA)
Avila U (MO)
Azusa Pacific U (CA)
Baker U (KS)
Baldwin-Wallace Coll (OH)
Ball State U (IN)
Baptist Bible Coll of Pennsylvania (PA)
Barclay Coll (KS)
Bard Coll (NY)
Bard Coll at Simon's Rock (MA)
Barnard Coll (NY)
Barry U (FL)
Barton Coll (NC)
Bastyr U (WA)
Bates Coll (ME)
Belhaven U (MS)
Bellarmine U (KY)
Belmont Abbey Coll (NC)
Belmont U (TN)
Beloit Coll (WI)
Bemidji State U (MN)
Benedictine Coll (KS)
Benedictine U (IL)
Bennington Coll (VT)
Berea Coll (KY)
Berry Coll (GA)
Bethany Coll (KS)
Bethany Coll (WV)
Bethel Coll (IN)
Bethel U (MN)
Bethel U (TN)

Bethune-Cookman U (FL)
Biola U (CA)
Birmingham-Southern Coll (AL)
Blackburn Coll (IL)
Bloomfield Coll (NJ)
Bloomsburg U of Pennsylvania (PA)
Bluefield Coll (VA)
Blue Mountain Coll (MS)
Bluffton U (OH)
Boise State U (ID)
Boston Coll (MA)
Boston U (MA)
Bowdoin Coll (ME)
Bowie State U (MD)
Bowling Green State U (OH)
Brandeis U (MA)
Brenau U (GA)
Brevard Coll (NC)
Brewton-Parker Coll (GA)
Briar Cliff U (IA)
Bridgewater Coll (VA)
Bridgewater State U (MA)
Brock U (ON, Canada)
Brown U (RI)
Bryan Coll (TN)
Bryant U (RI)
Bryn Mawr Coll (PA)
Bucknell U (PA)
Buena Vista U (IA)
Burlington Coll (VT)
Butler U (IN)
Cabrini Coll (PA)
California Baptist U (CA)
California Polytechnic State U, San Luis Obispo (CA)
California State Polytechnic U, Pomona (CA)
California State U, Bakersfield (CA)
California State U, Chico (CA)
California State U, Dominguez Hills (CA)
California State U, Fullerton (CA)
California State U, Long Beach (CA)
California State U, Los Angeles (CA)
California State U, Monterey Bay (CA)
California State U, Northridge (CA)
California State U, San Bernardino (CA)
California State U, San Marcos (CA)
California State U, Stanislaus (CA)
Calumet Coll of Saint Joseph (IN)
Calvin Coll (MI)
Cambridge Coll (MA)
Cameron U (OK)
Campbellsville U (KY)
Canisius Coll (NY)
Capital U (OH)
Carleton Coll (MN)
Carlos Albizu U, Miami Campus (FL)
Carlow U (PA)
Carnegie Mellon U (PA)
Carroll U (WI)
Carson-Newman Coll (TN)
Case Western Reserve U (OH)
Castleton State Coll (VT)
The Catholic U of America (DC)
Cedar Crest Coll (PA)
Cedarville U (OH)
Centenary Coll (NJ)
Centenary Coll of Louisiana (LA)
Central Coll (IA)
Central Connecticut State U (CT)
Central Michigan U (MI)
Central State U (OH)
Centre Coll (KY)
Chapman U (CA)
Chatham U (PA)
Chestnut Hill Coll (PA)
Christian Brothers U (TN)
Christopher Newport U (VA)
Cincinnati Christian U (OH)
The Citadel, The Military Coll of South Carolina (SC)
City Coll of the City U of New York (NY)
Claremont McKenna Coll (CA)
Clarion U of Pennsylvania (PA)
Clark Atlanta U (GA)
Clarke U (IA)
Clarkson U (NY)
Clark U (MA)
Clearwater Christian Coll (FL)
Clemson U (SC)
Cleveland State U (OH)
Coastal Carolina U (SC)

Coker Coll (SC)
Colby Coll (ME)
Colgate U (NY)
Coll of Charleston (SC)
Coll of Coastal Georgia (GA)
Coll of Mount St. Joseph (OH)
The Coll of New Jersey (NJ)
Coll of Saint Benedict (MN)
Coll of Saint Elizabeth (NJ)
Coll of St. Joseph (VT)
Coll of Saint Mary (NE)
The Coll of Saint Rose (NY)
The Coll of St. Scholastica (MN)
Coll of Staten Island of the City U of New York (NY)
Coll of the Atlantic (ME)
Coll of the Holy Cross (MA)
Coll of the Ozarks (MO)
The Coll of William and Mary (VA)
The Coll of Wooster (OH)
The Colorado Coll (CO)
Colorado State U (CO)
Columbia Coll (MO)
Columbia Coll (SC)
Columbia Southern U (AL)
Columbia U, School of General Studies (NY)
Columbus State U (GA)
Concordia Coll (MN)
Concordia Coll–New York (NY)
Concordia U (CA)
Concordia U (QC, Canada)
Concordia U Chicago (IL)
Concordia U, St. Paul (MN)
Concordia U Wisconsin (WI)
Concord U (WV)
Connecticut Coll (CT)
Coppin State U (MD)
Corban U (OR)
Cornell Coll (IA)
Cornell U (NY)
Covenant Coll (GA)
Crandall U (NB, Canada)
Creighton U (NE)
Crown Coll (MN)
Culver-Stockton Coll (MO)
Cumberland U (TN)
Curry Coll (MA)
Dakota Wesleyan U (SD)
Dallas Baptist U (TX)
Dartmouth Coll (NH)
Davidson Coll (NC)
Defiance Coll (OH)
Delaware State U (DE)
Delta State U (MS)
Denison U (OH)
DePaul U (IL)
DePauw U (IN)
DEREE - The American Coll of Greece (Greece)
DeSales U (PA)
Dickinson Coll (PA)
Dickinson State U (ND)
Dillard U (LA)
Doane Coll (NE)
Dominican Coll (NY)
Dominican U (IL)
Dominican U of California (CA)
Dordt Coll (IA)
Dowling Coll (NY)
Drake U (IA)
Drew U (NJ)
Drury U (MO)
Duquesne U (PA)
Earlham Coll (IN)
East Central U (OK)
Eastern Illinois U (IL)
Eastern Michigan U (MI)
Eastern New Mexico U (NM)
Eastern Oregon U (OR)
Eastern Washington U (WA)
East Stroudsburg U of Pennsylvania (PA)
East Tennessee State U (TN)
East Texas Baptist U (TX)
Eckerd Coll (FL)
Edgewood Coll (WI)
Edinboro U of Pennsylvania (PA)
Elizabeth City State U (NC)
Elizabethtown Coll (PA)
Elmhurst Coll (IL)
Elmira Coll (NY)
Elon U (NC)
Emmanuel Coll (GA)
Emmanuel Coll (MA)
Emory & Henry Coll (VA)
Emporia State U (KS)
Endicott Coll (MA)

Erskine Coll (SC)
Eugene Lang Coll The New School for Liberal Arts (NY)
Evangel U (MO)
Fairfield U (CT)
Fairleigh Dickinson U, Coll at Florham (NJ)
Fairleigh Dickinson U, Metropolitan Campus (NJ)
Fairmont State U (WV)
Faulkner U (AL)
Fayetteville State U (NC)
Felician Coll (NJ)
Ferris State U (MI)
Ferrum Coll (VA)
Fitchburg State U (MA)
Flagler Coll (FL)
Florida Ag and Mech U (FL)
Florida Atlantic U (FL)
Florida Gulf Coast U (FL)
Florida Inst of Technology (FL)
Florida Intl U (FL)
Florida Southern Coll (FL)
Florida State U (FL)
Fontbonne U (MO)
Fort Lewis Coll (CO)
Framingham State U (MA)
Francis Marion U (SC)
Franklin & Marshall Coll (PA)
Franklin Coll (IN)
Franklin Pierce U (NH)
Freed-Hardeman U (TN)
Friends U (KS)
Furman U (SC)
Gallaudet U (DC)
Gannon U (PA)
Gardner-Webb U (NC)
Geneva Coll (PA)
George Fox U (OR)
Georgetown Coll (KY)
Georgetown U (DC)
Georgia Coll & State U (GA)
Georgian Court U (NJ)
Georgia Southern U (GA)
Georgia State U (GA)
Gettysburg Coll (PA)
Goldey-Beacom Coll (DE)
Gordon Coll (MA)
Goucher Coll (MD)
Governors State U (IL)
Grace Coll (IN)
Graceland U (IA)
Grand Canyon U (AZ)
Grand Valley State U (MI)
Grand View U (IA)
Greensboro Coll (NC)
Greenville Coll (IL)
Grinnell Coll (IA)
Grove City Coll (PA)
Guilford Coll (NC)
Hamilton Coll (NY)
Hamline U (MN)
Hampden-Sydney Coll (VA)
Hampshire Coll (MA)
Hannibal-LaGrange U (MO)
Hanover Coll (IN)
Harding U (AR)
Hardin-Simmons U (TX)
Hartwick Coll (NY)
Harvard U (MA)
Haverford Coll (PA)
Hawai`i Pacific U (HI)
Hendrix Coll (AR)
Hillsdale Coll (MI)
Hillsdale Free Will Baptist Coll (OK)
Hobart and William Smith Colls (NY)
Hofstra U (NY)
Hollins U (VA)
Holy Cross Coll (IN)
Holy Family U (PA)
Holy Names U (CA)
Hood Coll (MD)
Hope Coll (MI)
Houghton Coll (NY)
Humboldt State U (CA)
Hunter Coll of the City U of New York (NY)
Huntingdon Coll (AL)
Huntington U (IN)
Husson U (ME)
Huston-Tillotson U (TX)
Idaho State U (ID)
Illinois Coll (IL)
Illinois Inst of Technology (IL)
Illinois State U (IL)
Illinois Wesleyan U (IL)
Immaculata U (PA)
Indiana State U (IN)

Indiana Tech (IN)
Indiana U Bloomington (IN)
Indiana U East (IN)
Indiana U Kokomo (IN)
Indiana U Northwest (IN)
Indiana U of Pennsylvania (PA)
Indiana U–Purdue U Fort Wayne (IN)
Indiana U–Purdue U Indianapolis (IN)
Indiana U South Bend (IN)
Indiana U Southeast (IN)
Indiana Wesleyan U (IN)
Inter American U of Puerto Rico, Metropolitan Campus (PR)
Inter American U of Puerto Rico, San Germán Campus (PR)
Iowa State U of Science and Technology (IA)
Iowa Wesleyan Coll (IA)
Ithaca Coll (NY)
Jacksonville State U (AL)
James Madison U (VA)
Jamestown Coll (ND)
John Brown U (AR)
John Carroll U (OH)
The Johns Hopkins U (MD)
Johnson C. Smith U (NC)
Johnson State Coll (VT)
Judson Coll (AL)
Juniata Coll (PA)
Kalamazoo Coll (MI)
Kansas State U (KS)
Kean U (NJ)
Keene State Coll (NH)
Kennesaw State U (GA)
Kent State U (OH)
Kent State U at Stark (OH)
Kentucky State U (KY)
Kentucky Wesleyan Coll (KY)
Kenyon Coll (OH)
Keuka Coll (NY)
Keystone Coll (PA)
King Coll (TN)
King's Coll (PA)
The King's U Coll (AB, Canada)
Knox Coll (IL)
Kutztown U of Pennsylvania (PA)
Lafayette Coll (PA)
LaGrange Coll (GA)
Lake Forest Coll (IL)
Lakehead U (ON, Canada)
Lake Superior State U (MI)
Lamar U (TX)
La Roche Coll (PA)
La Salle U (PA)
Lasell Coll (MA)
Laurentian U (ON, Canada)
Lawrence Technological U (MI)
Lawrence U (WI)
Lebanese American U (Lebanon)
Lebanon Valley Coll (PA)
Lee U (TN)
Lehigh U (PA)
Lehman Coll of the City U of New York (NY)
Le Moyne Coll (NY)
LeTourneau U (TX)
Lewis & Clark Coll (OR)
Lewis-Clark State Coll (ID)
Lewis U (IL)
Liberty U (VA)
Life U (GA)
Limestone Coll (SC)
Lincoln Christian U (IL)
Lincoln Memorial U (TN)
Lincoln U (MO)
Lindenwood U (MO)
Lindsey Wilson Coll (KY)
Linfield Coll (OR)
Lipscomb U (TN)
Lock Haven U of Pennsylvania (PA)
Long Island U, Brooklyn Campus (NY)
Long Island U, C.W. Post Campus (NY)
Longwood U (VA)
Loras Coll (IA)
Louisiana Coll (LA)
Louisiana State U and Ag and Mech Coll (LA)
Louisiana State U in Shreveport (LA)
Lourdes Coll (OH)
Loyola Marymount U (CA)
Loyola U Chicago (IL)
Loyola U Maryland (MD)
Loyola U New Orleans (LA)

St. Joseph's Coll, New York (NY)
Santa Clara U (CA)
Slippery Rock U of Pennsylvania (PA)
Southern Connecticut State U (CT)
State U of New York Coll at Old Westbury (NY)
Tufts U (MA)
TUI U (CA)
U of Lethbridge (AB, Canada)
U of Massachusetts Amherst (MA)
U of Rochester (NY)
U of Southern Mississippi (MS)
The U of Tampa (FL)
The U of Texas at Austin (TX)
U of Washington (WA)
West Chester U of Pennsylvania (PA)
Westminster Coll (UT)
William Paterson U of New Jersey (NJ)
Winona State U (MN)

PUBLIC HEALTH/COMMUNITY NURSING

Capital U (OH)
Northern Illinois U (IL)
The U of Western Ontario (ON, Canada)
Walla Walla U (WA)
Wright State U (OH)

PUBLIC HEALTH EDUCATION AND PROMOTION

Appalachian State U (NC)
California State U, Long Beach (CA)
Central Michigan U (MI)
Coastal Carolina U (SC)
Eastern Washington U (WA)
Georgia Southern U (GA)
Inter American U of Puerto Rico, Ponce Campus (PR)
Ithaca Coll (NY)
Laurentian U (ON, Canada)
Liberty U (VA)
Louisiana State U in Shreveport (LA)
Lynchburg Coll (VA)
Malone U (OH)
Marymount U (VA)
New Mexico State U (NM)
Oklahoma State U (OK)
Prescott Coll (AZ)
Simmons Coll (MA)
Southeastern Louisiana U (LA)
Temple U (PA)
Thomas Edison State Coll (NJ)
U of Georgia (GA)
The U of Iowa (IA)
U of Michigan–Flint (MI)
The U of North Carolina at Charlotte (NC)
The U of North Carolina at Greensboro (NC)
The U of North Carolina Wilmington (NC)
U of St. Thomas (MN)
U of Southern California (CA)
The U of Texas at Austin (TX)
The U of Toledo (OH)
U of Utah (UT)
U of Wisconsin–La Crosse (WI)
Walla Walla U (WA)

PUBLIC HEALTH RELATED

Hampshire Coll (MA)
Indiana U Bloomington (IN)
Indiana U–Purdue U Indianapolis (IN)
The Richard Stockton Coll of New Jersey (NJ)
U of California, Berkeley (CA)
U of California, Irvine (CA)
U of Maryland, Coll Park (MD)
U of South Carolina (SC)
Utah State U (UT)

PUBLIC POLICY ANALYSIS

Albion Coll (MI)
Anna Maria Coll (MA)
Arizona State U (AZ)
Bentley U (MA)
Brigham Young U (UT)
Carnegie Mellon U (PA)
Chatham U (PA)
Coll of the Atlantic (ME)
The Coll of William and Mary (VA)
Cornell U (NY)
Dakota Wesleyan U (SD)
DePaul U (IL)

Dickinson Coll (PA)
Georgia Inst of Technology (GA)
Georgia State U (GA)
Hamilton Coll (NY)
Hampshire Coll (MA)
Hobart and William Smith Colls (NY)
Indiana U–Purdue U Fort Wayne (IN)
Indiana Wesleyan U (IN)
Massachusetts Coll of Liberal Arts (MA)
Michigan State U (MI)
Mills Coll (CA)
New Coll of Florida (FL)
Northern Arizona U (AZ)
Penn State Harrisburg (PA)
Pomona Coll (CA)
Princeton U (NJ)
Regent U (VA)
Rice U (TX)
Sage Coll of Albany (NY)
St. Mary's Coll of Maryland (MD)
Sarah Lawrence Coll (NY)
Scripps Coll (CA)
Southeastern U (FL)
Southern Methodist U (TX)
Stanford U (CA)
Suffolk U (MA)
Trevecca Nazarene U (TN)
Trinity Coll (CT)
U of Charleston (WV)
U of Denver (CO)
U of Michigan (MI)
The U of North Carolina at Chapel Hill (NC)
U of Pennsylvania (PA)
U of Regina (SK, Canada)
U of Rhode Island (RI)
U of Southern California (CA)
The U of Texas at Dallas (TX)
The U of Toledo (OH)
U of Wisconsin–Whitewater (WI)
Vanderbilt U (TN)
Virginia Polytechnic Inst and State U (VA)
Wagner Coll (NY)
Walden U (MN)
Washington State U (WA)
Wells Coll (NY)

PUBLIC POLICY ANALYSIS RELATED

Carlow U (PA)

PUBLIC RELATIONS, ADVERTISING, AND APPLIED COMMUNICATION

Butler U (IN)
California State U, Dominguez Hills (CA)
Houghton Coll (NY)
Lasell Coll (MA)
Massachusetts Coll of Liberal Arts (MA)
Simpson Coll (IA)

PUBLIC RELATIONS, ADVERTISING, AND APPLIED COMMUNICATION RELATED

Abilene Christian U (TX)
Belmont U (TN)
Brigham Young U (UT)
Buena Vista U (IA)
Carroll U (WI)
Champlain Coll (VT)
The Coll of St. Scholastica (MN)
Columbia Coll (MO)
DePaul U (IL)
Duquesne U (PA)
Grace Coll (IN)
Hardin-Simmons U (TX)
John Brown U (AR)
Keystone Coll (PA)
Marietta Coll (OH)
Marywood U (PA)
Northern Michigan U (MI)
Oklahoma State U (OK)
Saint Mary's U of Minnesota (MN)
Shorter U (GA)
Spring Arbor U (MI)
Spring Hill Coll (AL)
State U of New York at Plattsburgh (NY)
Syracuse U (NY)
Temple U (PA)
The U of Tampa (FL)
U of Vermont (VT)
U of Wisconsin–River Falls (WI)
Virginia State U (VA)

Washington State U (WA)
Western Michigan U (MI)

PUBLIC RELATIONS/IMAGE MANAGEMENT

American U (DC)
Andrews U (MI)
Appalachian State U (NC)
Auburn U (AL)
Avila U (MO)
Baldwin-Wallace Coll (OH)
Barry U (FL)
Biola U (CA)
Bob Jones U (SC)
Boston U (MA)
Bowie State U (MD)
Bowling Green State U (OH)
California Baptist U (CA)
California State U, Chico (CA)
California State U, Fullerton (CA)
California State U, Long Beach (CA)
Capital U (OH)
Carroll U (WI)
Castleton State Coll (VT)
Central Michigan U (MI)
Champlain Coll (VT)
Chapman U (CA)
Cleveland State U (OH)
Coll of the Ozarks (MO)
Colorado State U (CO)
Columbia Coll Chicago (IL)
Curry Coll (MA)
Delaware State U (DE)
Drake U (IA)
Drury U (MO)
Duquesne U (PA)
Eastern Michigan U (MI)
Ferris State U (MI)
Florida Ag and Mech U (FL)
Florida Southern Coll (FL)
Franklin U (OH)
Freed-Hardeman U (TN)
Georgia Southern U (GA)
Greenville Coll (IL)
Harding U (AR)
Hawai`i Pacific U (HI)
Hofstra U (NY)
Huntington U (IN)
Illinois State U (IL)
Indiana Wesleyan U (IN)
Inter American U of Puerto Rico, Ponce Campus (PR)
Ithaca Coll (NY)
John Brown U (AR)
Johnson & Wales U (RI)
Kent State U (OH)
La Salle U (PA)
Lasell Coll (MA)
Lee U (TN)
Lewis U (IL)
Lipscomb U (TN)
Long Island U, C.W. Post Campus (NY)
Loras Coll (IA)
Mansfield U of Pennsylvania (PA)
Marist Coll (NY)
Marquette U (WI)
The Master's Coll and Sem (CA)
McKendree U (IL)
Miami U (OH)
Michigan State U (MI)
MidAmerica Nazarene U (KS)
Middle Tennessee State U (TN)
Minnesota State U Mankato (MN)
Monmouth U (IL)
Montana State U Billings (MT)
Mount Mercy U (IA)
Mount Saint Mary Coll (NY)
Mount Vernon Nazarene U (OH)
Murray State U (KY)
New England Coll (NH)
North Dakota State U (ND)
Northeastern State U (OK)
Northern Arizona U (AZ)
Northern Kentucky U (KY)
Northern Michigan U (MI)
Northwestern Coll (IA)
Northwestern Coll (MN)
Northwest Missouri State U (MO)
Ohio U–Zanesville (OH)
Oklahoma Christian U (OK)
Oklahoma City U (OK)
Paine Coll (GA)
Pepperdine U, Malibu (CA)
Point Park U (PA)
Purdue U Calumet (IN)
Quinnipiac U (CT)
Rider U (NJ)
Roosevelt U (IL)
Rowan U (NJ)

St. Ambrose U (IA)
Saint Francis U (PA)
St. John's U (NY)
Saint Joseph's Coll of Maine (ME)
Salem State U (MA)
San Diego State U (CA)
San Jose State U (CA)
Simmons Coll (MA)
Slippery Rock U of Pennsylvania (PA)
Southern Adventist U (TN)
Southern Methodist U (TX)
State U of New York at New Paltz (NY)
State U of New York at Oswego (NY)
Stephens Coll (MO)
Suffolk U (MA)
Temple U (PA)
Texas State U–San Marcos (TX)
Texas Tech U (TX)
Tiffin U (OH)
Union Coll (NE)
Union U (TN)
The U of Akron (OH)
The U of Alabama (AL)
U of Central Missouri (MO)
U of Dayton (OH)
U of Delaware (DE)
The U of Findlay (OH)
U of Florida (FL)
U of Georgia (GA)
U of Idaho (ID)
U of Louisiana at Lafayette (LA)
U of Miami (FL)
U of Northern Iowa (IA)
U of Oregon (OR)
U of Ottawa (ON, Canada)
U of Pittsburgh at Bradford (PA)
U of Rhode Island (RI)
U of Rio Grande (OH)
U of South Carolina (SC)
U of Southern California (CA)
The U of Tennessee (TN)
The U of Texas at Arlington (TX)
The U of Texas at Austin (TX)
U of Wisconsin–River Falls (WI)
Ursuline Coll (OH)
Walden U (MN)
Walla Walla U (WA)
Wartburg Coll (IA)
Washington State U (WA)
Wayne State U (MI)
Weber State U (UT)
Webster U (MO)
Western Kentucky U (KY)
Western New England U (MA)
Winona State U (MN)
Xavier U (OH)
York Coll of Pennsylvania (PA)

PUBLISHING

California State U, Chico (CA)
Graceland U (IA)
Minnesota State U Moorhead (MN)
Saint Mary's U of Minnesota (MN)
U of Missouri (MO)

PURCHASING, PROCUREMENT/ACQUISITIONS AND CONTRACTS MANAGEMENT

Arizona State U (AZ)
Central Michigan U (MI)
Saint Joseph's U (PA)
U of Houston–Downtown (TX)
U of the District of Columbia (DC)

QUALITY CONTROL AND SAFETY TECHNOLOGIES RELATED

Madonna U (MI)

QUALITY CONTROL TECHNOLOGY

Bowling Green State U (OH)
California State U, Dominguez Hills (CA)
California State U, Long Beach (CA)
Ferris State U (MI)
San Jose State U (CA)
Winona State U (MN)

RADIATION BIOLOGY

Suffolk U (MA)

RADIATION PROTECTION/HEALTH PHYSICS TECHNOLOGY

Indiana U Bloomington (IN)
Indiana U East (IN)

Indiana U–Purdue U Indianapolis (IN)
Indiana U South Bend (IN)
Indiana U Southeast (IN)
Lewis U (IL)
Thomas Edison State Coll (NJ)

RADIO AND TELEVISION

American U (DC)
Appalachian State U (NC)
Arkansas State U (AR)
Auburn U (AL)
Ball State U (IN)
Barry U (FL)
Belmont U (TN)
Bemidji State U (MN)
Biola U (CA)
Bob Jones U (SC)
Boston U (MA)
Butler U (IN)
California State U, Fullerton (CA)
California State U, Long Beach (CA)
California State U, Los Angeles (CA)
California State U, Monterey Bay (CA)
Castleton State Coll (VT)
Cedarville U (OH)
Colorado State U (CO)
Columbia Coll Chicago (IL)
Curry Coll (MA)
Delaware State U (DE)
Drake U (IA)
Evangel U (MO)
Franklin Pierce U (NH)
Freed-Hardeman U (TN)
Georgia Southern U (GA)
Grand Valley State U (MI)
Grand View U (IA)
Hardin-Simmons U (TX)
Hofstra U (NY)
Ithaca Coll (NY)
John Brown U (AR)
Kent State U (OH)
Lamar U (TX)
La Salle U (PA)
Lasell Coll (MA)
Lebanese American U (Lebanon)
Lewis U (IL)
Loyola Marymount U (CA)
Lyndon State Coll (VT)
Marietta Coll (OH)
Marist Coll (NY)
The Master's Coll and Sem (CA)
Messiah Coll (PA)
Michigan State U (MI)
Minot State U (ND)
Murray State U (KY)
New York Inst of Technology (NY)
North Central Coll (IL)
Northern Arizona U (AZ)
Northwestern Coll (MN)
Northwest Missouri State U (MO)
Ohio U (OH)
Oklahoma Christian U (OK)
Oklahoma City U (OK)
Pacific U (OR)
Pittsburg State U (KS)
Rider U (NJ)
Rowan U (NJ)
Sacred Heart U (CT)
St. Ambrose U (IA)
San Diego State U (CA)
San Francisco State U (CA)
San Jose State U (CA)
Southeastern U (FL)
Southern Illinois U Carbondale (IL)
Southwestern Coll (KS)
State U of New York at Fredonia (NY)
State U of New York at Plattsburgh (NY)
Stephen F. Austin State U (TX)
Stephens Coll (MO)
Syracuse U (NY)
Temple U (PA)
Texas Christian U (TX)
Texas Southern U (TX)
Texas State U–San Marcos (TX)
Texas Tech U (TX)
Texas Wesleyan U (TX)
Trevecca Nazarene U (TN)
Troy U (AL)
Union U (TN)
The U of Akron (OH)
The U of Alabama (AL)
The U of Arizona (AZ)
U of Central Florida (FL)
U of Central Missouri (MO)
U of Cincinnati (OH)
U of Dayton (OH)

U of Florida (FL)
U of Miami (FL)
U of Missouri (MO)
U of Montevallo (AL)
U of North Texas (TX)
U of Pittsburgh at Bradford (PA)
U of Sioux Falls (SD)
U of Southern California (CA)
U of Southern Indiana (IN)
U of Southern Mississippi (MS)
The U of Texas at Arlington (TX)
The U of Texas at Austin (TX)
U of the Incarnate Word (TX)
The U of Western Ontario (ON, Canada)
U of Wisconsin–River Falls (WI)
U of Wisconsin–Superior (WI)
Walla Walla U (WA)
Wartburg Coll (IA)
Waynesburg U (PA)
Wayne State U (MI)
Weber State U (UT)
Webster U (MO)
Western Illinois U (IL)
Western Kentucky U (KY)
Winona State U (MN)
Xavier U (OH)
Youngstown State U (OH)

RADIO AND TELEVISION BROADCASTING TECHNOLOGY
Alabama Ag and Mech U (AL)
Asbury U (KY)
The Coll of Saint Rose (NY)
Coll of the Ozarks (MO)
Ferris State U (MI)
Gannon U (PA)
Gardner-Webb U (NC)
New England Inst of Technology (RI)
New York U (NY)
Northwest Nazarene U (ID)
Point Park U (PA)
Rowan U (NJ)
Suffolk U (MA)
Trevecca Nazarene U (TN)
U of Georgia (GA)
Worcester State U (MA)

RADIOLOGIC TECHNOLOGY/ SCIENCE
Alderson-Broaddus Coll (WV)
Austin Peay State U (TN)
Averett U (VA)
Baptist Coll of Health Sciences (TN)
Bluefield State Coll (WV)
Champlain Coll (VT)
Clarion U of Pennsylvania (PA)
Coll of St. Joseph (VT)
Friends U (KS)
Holy Family U (PA)
Indiana U Bloomington (IN)
Indiana U Kokomo (IN)
Indiana U Northwest (IN)
Indiana U South Bend (IN)
Indiana U Southeast (IN)
Inter American U of Puerto Rico, Ponce Campus (PR)
Jamestown Coll (ND)
Kent State U (OH)
Manhattan Coll (NY)
Marian U (WI)
Marshall U (WV)
Mesa State Coll (CO)
Missouri State U (MO)
North Dakota State U (ND)
Northern Michigan U (MI)
Northwestern State U of Louisiana (LA)
The Ohio State U (OH)
Presentation Coll (SD)
Quinnipiac U (CT)
St. John's U (NY)
State U of New York Upstate Medical U (NY)
U of Arkansas–Fort Smith (AR)
U of Charleston (WV)
U of Louisiana at Monroe (LA)
U of Missouri (MO)
U of Oklahoma Health Sciences Center (OK)
U of Pittsburgh at Bradford (PA)
U of St. Francis (IL)
U of South Alabama (AL)
Virginia Commonwealth U (VA)
Widener U (PA)

RADIO, TELEVISION, AND DIGITAL COMMUNICATION RELATED
Brigham Young U (UT)
Central Michigan U (MI)
Clark Atlanta U (GA)
Drake U (IA)
Drury U (MO)
Hofstra U (NY)
John Brown U (AR)
Keystone Coll (PA)
Madonna U (MI)
Marist Coll (NY)
Marquette U (WI)
Mitchell Coll (CT)
Neumann U (PA)
North Dakota State U (ND)
Rogers State U (OK)
Sacred Heart U (CT)
San Francisco State U (CA)
Spring Hill Coll (AL)
The U of Akron (OH)
Washington State U (WA)
Western Carolina U (NC)

RANGE SCIENCE AND MANAGEMENT
Colorado State U (CO)
Humboldt State U (CA)
Montana State U (MT)
New Mexico State U (NM)
North Dakota State U (ND)
Oregon State U (OR)
South Dakota State U (SD)
Sul Ross State U (TX)
Tarleton State U (TX)
Texas A&M U (TX)
U of Idaho (ID)
U of Nebraska–Lincoln (NE)
U of Wyoming (WY)
Utah State U (UT)

READING TEACHER EDUCATION
Aquinas Coll (MI)
Boise State U (ID)
Clarion U of Pennsylvania (PA)
Concordia U Chicago (IL)
Dordt Coll (IA)
East Central U (OK)
Eastern Michigan U (MI)
Eastern Washington U (WA)
Edinboro U of Pennsylvania (PA)
Grand Valley State U (MI)
Harding U (AR)
Hardin-Simmons U (TX)
Iowa Wesleyan Coll (IA)
Kutztown U of Pennsylvania (PA)
Longwood U (VA)
Lyndon State Coll (VT)
Michigan State U (MI)
Midwestern State U (TX)
St. Joseph's Coll, Long Island Campus (NY)
St. Joseph's Coll, New York (NY)
State U of New York Coll at Oneonta (NY)
Texas A&M Intl U (TX)
Texas A&M U–Corpus Christi (TX)
Texas Wesleyan U (TX)
The U of British Columbia (BC, Canada)
U of Central Missouri (MO)
U of Cincinnati (OH)
The U of North Carolina at Pembroke (NC)
U of Northern Iowa (IA)
U of Wisconsin–River Falls (WI)
U of Wisconsin–Superior (WI)
Upper Iowa U (IA)
Washington State U (WA)
Wheelock Coll (MA)
Wingate U (NC)
Winona State U (MN)
Wright State U (OH)

REAL ESTATE
Angelo State U (TX)
Arizona State U (AZ)
California State U, Dominguez Hills (CA)
Central Michigan U (MI)
Clarion U of Pennsylvania (PA)
Colorado State U (CO)
DePaul U (IL)
Florida Atlantic U (FL)
Florida Intl U (FL)
Georgia State U (GA)
La Roche Coll (PA)

Marquette U (WI)
Marylhurst U (OR)
Menlo Coll (CA)
Minnesota State U Mankato (MN)
Mississippi State U (MS)
New Mexico State U (NM)
New York U (NY)
The Ohio State U (OH)
Portland State U (OR)
San Diego State U (CA)
Southern Methodist U (TX)
Syracuse U (NY)
Temple U (PA)
Texas Christian U (TX)
Thomas Edison State Coll (NJ)
The U of British Columbia (BC, Canada)
U of Central Florida (FL)
U of Cincinnati (OH)
U of Denver (CO)
U of Georgia (GA)
U of Guelph (ON, Canada)
U of Miami (FL)
U of Missouri (MO)
U of Nebraska at Omaha (NE)
U of Nevada, Las Vegas (NV)
U of Northern Iowa (IA)
U of North Texas (TX)
U of Pennsylvania (PA)
U of St. Thomas (MN)
U of San Diego (CA)
U of South Carolina (SC)
The U of Texas at Arlington (TX)
U of West Georgia (GA)
U of Wisconsin–Madison (WI)
U of Wisconsin–Stout (WI)
Virginia Commonwealth U (VA)
Washington State U (WA)

RECORDING ARTS TECHNOLOGY
American U (DC)
The Art Inst of Seattle (WA)
Butler U (IN)
Cogswell Polytechnical Coll (CA)
Columbia Coll Chicago (IL)
Five Towns Coll (NY)
Greenville Coll (IL)
Indiana U Bloomington (IN)
Intl Acad of Design & Technology (FL)
Ithaca Coll (NY)
Lebanon Valley Coll (PA)
Loyola Marymount U (CA)
Malone U (OH)
New England Inst of Technology (RI)
Peabody Conservatory of The Johns Hopkins U (MD)
Savannah Coll of Art and Design (GA)
State U of New York at Fredonia (NY)
Texas Southern U (TX)
Texas State U–San Marcos (TX)
U of Hartford (CT)
York Coll of Pennsylvania (PA)

REGIONAL STUDIES
The Colorado Coll (CO)
Columbia U, School of General Studies (NY)
Houghton Coll (NY)
Mercer U (GA)
Prescott Coll (AZ)
United States Military Acad (NY)
Washington U in St. Louis (MO)

REGISTERED NURSING, NURSING ADMINISTRATION, NURSING RESEARCH AND CLINICAL NURSING RELATED
American Public U System (WV)
Anna Maria Coll (MA)
Cleveland State U (OH)
St. Joseph's Coll, Long Island Campus (NY)
St. Joseph's Coll, New York (NY)

REGISTERED NURSING/ REGISTERED NURSE
Abilene Christian U (TX)
Adams State Coll (CO)
Adelphi U (NY)
Albany State U (GA)
Alcorn State U (MS)
Alderson-Broaddus Coll (WV)

Allen Coll (IA)
Alvernia U (PA)
Alverno Coll (WI)
American U of Beirut (Lebanon)
Anderson U (IN)
Andrews U (MI)
Angelo State U (TX)
Anna Maria Coll (MA)
Appalachian State U (NC)
Aquinas Coll (TN)
Arizona State U (AZ)
Arkansas State U (AR)
Arkansas Tech U (AR)
Armstrong Atlantic State U (GA)
Athabasca U (AB, Canada)
Atlantic Union Coll (MA)
Auburn U (AL)
Auburn U Montgomery (AL)
Augsburg Coll (MN)
Augustana Coll (SD)
Austin Peay State U (TN)
Azusa Pacific U (CA)
Baker U (KS)
Ball State U (IN)
Baptist Coll of Health Sciences (TN)
Barry U (FL)
Barton Coll (NC)
Bellarmine U (KY)
Belmont U (TN)
Bemidji State U (MN)
Benedictine U (IL)
Berea Coll (KY)
Berry Coll (GA)
Bethel Coll (IN)
Bethel U (MN)
Bethel U (TN)
Bethune-Cookman U (FL)
Biola U (CA)
Bloomfield Coll (NJ)
Bloomsburg U of Pennsylvania (PA)
Bob Jones U (SC)
Boise State U (ID)
Boston Coll (MA)
Bowie State U (MD)
Bowling Green State U (OH)
Briar Cliff U (IA)
Brookline Coll, Phoenix (AZ)
California Baptist U (CA)
California State U, Bakersfield (CA)
California State U, Chico (CA)
California State U, Dominguez Hills (CA)
California State U, Fullerton (CA)
California State U, Long Beach (CA)
California State U, Los Angeles (CA)
California State U, Northridge (CA)
California State U, San Bernardino (CA)
California State U, Stanislaus (CA)
Calvin Coll (MI)
Capital U (OH)
Carlow U (PA)
Carson-Newman Coll (TN)
Case Western Reserve U (OH)
Castleton State Coll (VT)
The Catholic U of America (DC)
Cedarville U (OH)
Central Connecticut State U (CT)
Chamberlain Coll of Nursing (AZ)
Chamberlain Coll of Nursing (FL)
Chamberlain Coll of Nursing, Addison (IL)
Chamberlain Coll of Nursing, Chicago (IL)
Chamberlain Coll of Nursing (MO)
Chamberlain Coll of Nursing (OH)
Chamberlain Coll of Nursing (VA)
Chatham U (PA)
Chipola Coll (FL)
Clarion U of Pennsylvania (PA)
Clarke U (IA)
Clarkson Coll (NE)
Clayton State U (GA)
Clemson U (SC)
Cleveland State U (OH)
Coll of Coastal Georgia (GA)
Coll of Mount St. Joseph (OH)
The Coll of New Jersey (NJ)
Coll of Saint Benedict (MN)
Coll of Saint Mary (NE)
The Coll of St. Scholastica (MN)
Coll of Staten Island of the City U of New York (NY)
Coll of the Ozarks (MO)
Columbia Centro Universitario (PR)
Columbia Coll of Nursing (WI)
Columbus State U (GA)

Concordia Coll (MN)
Concordia U (CA)
Concordia U Wisconsin (WI)
Coppin State U (MD)
Creighton U (NE)
Crown Coll (MN)
Culver-Stockton Coll (MO)
Cumberland U (TN)
Curry Coll (MA)
Dakota Wesleyan U (SD)
Davenport U, Grand Rapids (MI)
Defiance Coll (OH)
Delaware State U (DE)
Delta State U (MS)
DePaul U (IL)
DeSales U (PA)
Dickinson State U (ND)
Dillard U (LA)
Dixie State Coll of Utah (UT)
Dominican Coll (NY)
Dominican U of California (CA)
Dordt Coll (IA)
Duquesne U (PA)
East Central U (OK)
Eastern Illinois U (IL)
Eastern Michigan U (MI)
Eastern New Mexico U (NM)
Eastern Washington U (WA)
East Stroudsburg U of Pennsylvania (PA)
East Tennessee State U (TN)
East Texas Baptist U (TX)
ECPI Coll of Technology, Virginia Beach (VA)
Edgewood Coll (WI)
Edinboro U of Pennsylvania (PA)
Elmhurst Coll (IL)
Elmira Coll (NY)
Emporia State U (KS)
Endicott Coll (MA)
Fairfield U (CT)
Fairleigh Dickinson U, Metropolitan Campus (NJ)
Fairmont State U (WV)
Fayetteville State U (NC)
Felician Coll (NJ)
Ferris State U (MI)
Fitchburg State U (MA)
Florida Ag and Mech U (FL)
Florida Atlantic U (FL)
Florida Intl U (FL)
Florida Southern Coll (FL)
Florida State Coll at Jacksonville (FL)
Framingham State U (MA)
Francis Marion U (SC)
Gannon U (PA)
Gardner-Webb U (NC)
George Fox U (OR)
Georgetown U (DC)
Georgia Coll & State U (GA)
Georgia Health Sciences U (GA)
Georgian Court U (NJ)
Georgia Southern U (GA)
Georgia State U (GA)
Goldfarb School of Nursing at Barnes-Jewish Coll (MO)
Goodwin Coll (CT)
Governors State U (IL)
Graceland U (IA)
Grand Valley State U (MI)
Grand View U (IA)
Great Basin Coll (NV)
Hannibal-LaGrange U (MO)
Harding U (AR)
Hardin-Simmons U (TX)
Hartwick Coll (NY)
Hawai'i Pacific U (HI)
Holy Names U (CA)
Hope Coll (MI)
Humboldt State U (CA)
Hunter Coll of the City U of New York (NY)
Husson U (ME)
Idaho State U (ID)
Illinois State U (IL)
Illinois Wesleyan U (IL)
Immaculata U (PA)
Indiana State U (IN)
Indiana U Bloomington (IN)
Indiana U East (IN)
Indiana U Kokomo (IN)
Indiana U Northwest (IN)
Indiana U of Pennsylvania (PA)
Indiana U–Purdue U Fort Wayne (IN)
Indiana U–Purdue U Indianapolis (IN)

INDEXES

Penn State Beaver (PA)
Penn State Berks (PA)
Penn State Brandywine (PA)
Penn State DuBois (PA)
Penn State Erie, The Behrend Coll (PA)
Penn State Fayette, The Eberly Campus (PA)
Penn State Greater Allegheny (PA)
Penn State Hazleton (PA)
Penn State Lehigh Valley (PA)
Penn State Mont Alto (PA)
Penn State New Kensington (PA)
Penn State Schuylkill (PA)
Penn State Shenango (PA) .
Penn State U Park (PA)
Penn State Wilkes-Barre (PA)
Penn State Worthington Scranton (PA)
Penn State York (PA)
Southern Illinois U Carbondale (IL)
Springfield Coll (MA)
Stephen F. Austin State U (TX)
Thomas U (GA)
Troy U (AL)
U of Maine at Farmington (ME)
U of Manitoba (MB, Canada)
U of Massachusetts Lowell (MA)
U of North Texas (TX)
The U of Texas–Pan American (TX)
U of Waterloo (ON, Canada)
The U of Western Ontario (ON, Canada)

REHABILITATION SCIENCE
Arkansas Tech U (AR)
U of North Dakota (ND)
U of Pittsburgh (PA)
U of the Incarnate Word (TX)

RELIGIOUS EDUCATION
Andrews U (MI)
Asbury U (KY)
Ashland U (OH)
Baptist Bible Coll of Pennsylvania (PA)
Barclay Coll (KS)
Bethany Bible Coll (NB, Canada)
Biola U (CA)
Bob Jones U (SC)
Bryan Coll (TN)
Calvary Bible Coll and Theological Sem (MO)
Campbellsville U (KY)
Cedarville U (OH)
Cincinnati Christian U (OH)
Coll of Mount St. Joseph (OH)
Coll of Saint Benedict (MN)
Columbia Coll (SC)
Concordia U (CA)
Concordia U Chicago (IL)
Concordia U, St. Paul (MN)
Corban U (OR)
Crossroads Bible Coll (IN)
Crown Coll (MN)
Dallas Baptist U (TX)
Defiance Coll (OH)
East Texas Baptist U (TX)
Edgewood Coll (WI)
Faith Baptist Bible Coll and Theological Sem (IA)
Florida Southern Coll (FL)
Free Will Baptist Bible Coll (TN)
Gardner-Webb U (NC)
Great Lakes Christian Coll (MI)
Hannibal-LaGrange U (MO)
Harding U (AR)
Hebrew Coll (MA)
Hillsdale Free Will Baptist Coll (OK)
Holy Family U (PA)
Houghton Coll (NY)
Huntingdon Coll (AL)
Indiana Wesleyan U (IN)
John Carroll U (OH)
Kuyper Coll (MI)
La Salle U (PA)
Lee U (TN)
Lincoln Christian U (IL)
Lindsey Wilson Coll (KY)
Louisiana Coll (LA)
Loyola U Chicago (IL)
Loyola U New Orleans (LA)
Malone U (OH)
The Master's Coll and Sem (CA)
Master's Coll and Sem (ON, Canada)
Messiah Coll (PA)

Mid-Continent U (KY)
Missouri Baptist U (MO)
Morris Coll (SC)
Mount Vernon Nazarene U (OH)
Multnomah U (OR)
New Hope Christian Coll (OR)
Northwestern Coll (IA)
Northwest Nazarene U (ID)
Northwest U (WA)
Nyack Coll (NY)
Oak Hills Christian Coll (MN)
Oklahoma Christian U (OK)
Oklahoma City U (OK)
Pepperdine U, Malibu (CA)
Saint John's U (MN)
St. Louis Christian Coll (MO)
Saint Mary's U of Minnesota (MN)
Seattle Pacific U (WA)
Simpson U (CA)
Southern Adventist U (TN)
Southern Nazarene U (OK)
Taylor U (IN)
Texas Wesleyan U (TX)
Thiel Coll (PA)
Union Coll (NE)
Universidad Teologica del Caribe (PR)
U of Dayton (OH)
U of the Cumberlands (KY)
Washington Adventist U (MD)
Wayland Baptist U (TX)
Wheaton Coll (IL)

RELIGIOUS/SACRED MUSIC
Anderson U (IN)
Anderson U (SC)
Aquinas Coll (MI)
Asbury U (KY)
Baptist Bible Coll of Pennsylvania (PA)
Barclay Coll (KS)
Belmont U (TN)
Bethany Lutheran Coll (MN)
Bethel U (MN)
Bethel U (TN)
Bluefield Coll (VA)
Blue Mountain Coll (MS)
Calvary Bible Coll and Theological Sem (MO)
Calvin Coll (MI)
Campbellsville U (KY)
Cedarville U (OH)
Cincinnati Christian U (OH)
Clarke U (IA)
Clearwater Christian Coll (FL)
Coll of the Ozarks (MO)
Concordia Coll–New York (NY)
Concordia U Chicago (IL)
Concordia U, St. Paul (MN)
Concordia U Wisconsin (WI)
Corban U (OR)
Crown Coll (MN)
Dallas Baptist U (TX)
Drake U (IA)
East Texas Baptist U (TX)
Emmanuel Coll (GA)
Evangel U (MO)
Faith Baptist Bible Coll and Theological Sem (IA)
Free Will Baptist Bible Coll (TN)
Furman U (SC)
Gardner-Webb U (NC)
Great Lakes Christian Coll (MI)
Hannibal-LaGrange U (MO)
Hardin-Simmons U (TX)
Hebrew Coll (MA)
Hillsdale Free Will Baptist Coll (OK)
Huntington U (IN)
Indiana Wesleyan U (IN)
John Brown U (AR)
Johnson Bible Coll (TN)
Kuyper Coll (MI)
Lee U (TN)
Liberty U (VA)
Lincoln Christian U (IL)
Lincoln U (MO)
Louisiana Coll (LA)
Madonna U (MI)
Malone U (OH)
Maranatha Baptist Bible Coll (WI)
The Master's Coll and Sem (CA)
Missouri Baptist U (MO)
Moravian Coll (PA)
Mount Vernon Nazarene U (OH)
Multnomah U (OR)
Newberry Coll (SC)
New Hope Christian Coll (OR)
North Greenville U (SC)

Northwest Nazarene U (ID)
Northwest U (WA)
Nyack Coll (NY)
Oklahoma City U (OK)
Ouachita Baptist U (AR)
Presbyterian Coll (SC)
Rider U (NJ)
St. Louis Christian Coll (MO)
Saint Mary's U of Minnesota (MN)
St. Olaf Coll (MN)
Samford U (AL)
San Diego Christian Coll (CA)
Seton Hill U (PA)
Shorter U (GA)
Southeastern U (FL)
Southern Nazarene U (OK)
Southern Wesleyan U (SC)
Southwestern Assemblies of God U (TX)
Texas Christian U (TX)
Trevecca Nazarene U (TN)
Trinity Lutheran Coll (WA)
Union U (TN)
U of Hartford (CT)
U of Mary Hardin-Baylor (TX)
U of Mobile (AL)
Valparaiso U (IN)
Wartburg Coll (IA)
Wayland Baptist U (TX)
William Jewell Coll (MO)

RELIGIOUS STUDIES
Albertus Magnus Coll (CT)
Albion Coll (MI)
Albright Coll (PA)
Allegheny Coll (PA)
Alma Coll (MI)
Alvernia U (PA)
Alverno Coll (WI)
American Public U System (WV)
Amherst Coll (MA)
Anderson U (IN)
Anderson U (SC)
Andrews U (MI)
Appalachian State U (NC)
Aquinas Coll (MI)
Arizona State U (AZ)
Arlington Baptist Coll (TX)
Ashland U (OH)
Athens State U (AL)
Atlantic Union Coll (MA)
Augsburg Coll (MN)
Augustana Coll (IL)
Augustana Coll (SD)
Austin Coll (TX)
Averett U (VA)
Avila U (MO)
Azusa Pacific U (CA)
Baker U (KS)
Baldwin-Wallace Coll (OH)
Ball State U (IN)
Bard Coll (NY)
Barnard Coll (NY)
Bates Coll (ME)
Beloit Coll (WI)
Bemidji State U (MN)
Benedictine Coll (KS)
Berea Coll (KY)
Bethany Bible Coll (NB, Canada)
Bethany Coll (KS)
Bethany Coll (WV)
Bethany Lutheran Coll (MN)
Biola U (CA)
Birmingham-Southern Coll (AL)
Bloomfield Coll (NJ)
Bluefield Coll (VA)
Bluffton U (OH)
Boston U (MA)
Bowdoin Coll (ME)
Brevard Coll (NC)
Brewton-Parker Coll (GA)
Brown U (RI)
Bryn Mawr Coll (PA)
Bucknell U (PA)
Butler U (IN)
Cabrini Coll (PA)
California State U, Bakersfield (CA)
California State U, Fullerton (CA)
California State U, Long Beach (CA)
California State U, Northridge (CA)
Calumet Coll of Saint Joseph (IN)
Calvin Coll (MI)
Campbellsville U (KY)
Canisius Coll (NY)
Capital U (OH)
Carleton Coll (MN)
Carroll U (WI)
Carson-Newman Coll (TN)

Case Western Reserve U (OH)
The Catholic U of America (DC)
Centenary Coll of Louisiana (LA)
Central Coll (IA)
Central Michigan U (MI)
Centre Coll (KY)
Chapman U (CA)
Christian Brothers U (TN)
Claremont McKenna Coll (CA)
Clark Atlanta U (GA)
Clarke U (IA)
Cleveland State U (OH)
Colby Coll (ME)
Colgate U (NY)
Coll of Charleston (SC)
Coll of Mount St. Joseph (OH)
The Coll of Saint Rose (NY)
The Coll of St. Scholastica (MN)
Coll of the Holy Cross (MA)
The Coll of William and Mary (VA)
The Coll of Wooster (OH)
The Colorado Coll (CO)
Columbia Bible Coll (BC, Canada)
Columbia Coll (SC)
Columbia U, School of General Studies (NY)
Concordia Coll (MN)
Concordia Coll–New York (NY)
Concordia U (CA)
Concordia U (QC, Canada)
Concordia U Chicago (IL)
Concordia U Wisconsin (WI)
Connecticut Coll (CT)
Corban U (OR)
Cornell Coll (IA)
Cornell U (NY)
Crandall U (NB, Canada)
Culver-Stockton Coll (MO)
Dartmouth Coll (NH)
Davidson Coll (NC)
Defiance Coll (OH)
Denison U (OH)
DePaul U (IL)
DePauw U (IN)
Dickinson Coll (PA)
Doane Coll (NE)
Dominican U of California (CA)
Dordt Coll (IA)
Drake U (IA)
Drew U (NJ)
Drury U (MO)
Earlham Coll (IN)
Eastern New Mexico U (NM)
East Texas Baptist U (TX)
Eckerd Coll (FL)
Edgewood Coll (WI)
Elizabethtown Coll (PA)
Elmira Coll (NY)
Elon U (NC)
Emmanuel Coll (MA)
Emory & Henry Coll (VA)
Erskine Coll (SC)
Eugene Lang Coll The New School for Liberal Arts (NY)
Fairfield U (CT)
Faulkner U (AL)
Felician Coll (NJ)
Ferrum Coll (VA)
Florida Intl U (FL)
Florida Southern Coll (FL)
Fontbonne U (MO)
Franklin & Marshall Coll (PA)
Franklin Coll (IN)
Furman U (SC)
Gardner-Webb U (NC)
George Fox U (OR)
Georgetown Coll (KY)
Georgian Court U (NJ)
Georgia State U (GA)
Gettysburg Coll (PA)
Goucher Coll (MD)
Graceland U (IA)
Grand Canyon U (AZ)
Grand View U (IA)
Greensboro Coll (NC)
Greenville Coll (IL)
Grinnell Coll (IA)
Grove City Coll (PA)
Guilford Coll (NC)
Hamilton Coll (NY)
Hamline U (MN)
Hampden-Sydney Coll (VA)
Hampshire Coll (MA)
Hartwick Coll (NY)
Harvard U (MA)
Haverford Coll (PA)
Hellenic Coll (MA)
Hendrix Coll (AR)

Hillsdale Coll (MI)
Hobart and William Smith Colls (NY)
Hofstra U (NY)
Hollins U (VA)
Holy Apostles Coll and Sem (CT)
Holy Family U (PA)
Holy Names U (CA)
Hood Coll (MD)
Hope Coll (MI)
Houghton Coll (NY)
Humboldt State U (CA)
Hunter Coll of the City U of New York (NY)
Huntingdon Coll (AL)
Huntington U (IN)
Illinois Coll (IL)
Illinois Wesleyan U (IL)
Indiana U Bloomington (IN)
Indiana U of Pennsylvania (PA)
Indiana U–Purdue U Indianapolis (IN)
Iowa State U of Science and Technology (IA)
Jamestown Coll (ND)
Jarvis Christian Coll (TX)
John Brown U (AR)
John Carroll U (OH)
Judson Coll (AL)
Juniata Coll (PA)
Kalamazoo Coll (MI)
Kenyon Coll (OH)
King Coll (TN)
Lafayette Coll (PA)
LaGrange Coll (GA)
Lake Forest Coll (IL)
Lane Coll (TN)
La Roche Coll (PA)
La Salle U (PA)
Laurentian U (ON, Canada)
Lawrence U (WI)
Lebanon Valley Coll (PA)
Lehigh U (PA)
Le Moyne Coll (NY)
LeTourneau U (TX)
Lewis & Clark Coll (OR)
Lewis U (IL)
Liberty U (VA)
Lindenwood U (MO)
Linfield Coll (OR)
Loras Coll (IA)
Lourdes Coll (OH)
Loyola U Maryland (MD)
Loyola U New Orleans (LA)
Luther Coll (IA)
Lycoming Coll (PA)
Lynchburg Coll (VA)
Macalester Coll (MN)
MacMurray Coll (IL)
Madonna U (MI)
Manchester Coll (IN)
Manhattan Coll (NY)
Manhattanville Coll (NY)
Marian U (WI)
Marlboro Coll (VT)
Mars Hill Coll (NC)
Mary Baldwin Coll (VA)
Marylhurst U (OR)
Marymount U (VA)
Maryville Coll (TN)
Marywood U (PA)
The Master's Coll and Sem (CA)
McDaniel Coll (MD)
McKendree U (IL)
Medgar Evers Coll of the City U of New York (NY)
Merrimack Coll (MA)
Miami U (OH)
Michigan State U (MI)
MidAmerica Nazarene U (KS)
Middlebury Coll (VT)
Millsaps Coll (MS)
Missouri Baptist U (MO)
Missouri State U (MO)
Molloy Coll (NY)
Monmouth Coll (IL)
Montclair State U (NJ)
Moravian Coll (PA)
Morehouse Coll (GA)
Morningside Coll (IA)
Mountain State U (WV)
Mount Allison U (NB, Canada)
Mount Holyoke Coll (MA)
Mount Marty Coll (SD)
Mount Mercy U (IA)
Mount Olive Coll (NC)
Mount St. Mary's Coll (CA)
Mount Vernon Nazarene U (OH)

Muhlenberg Coll (PA)
Naropa U (CO)
Nazareth Coll of Rochester (NY)
Nebraska Wesleyan U (NE)
Newberry Coll (SC)
New Coll of Florida (FL)
New York U (NY)
Niagara U (NY)
North Carolina State U (NC)
North Central Coll (IL)
Northeastern U (MA)
Northern Arizona U (AZ)
Northwestern Coll (IA)
Northwest Nazarene U (ID)
Northwest U (WA)
Notre Dame de Namur U (CA)
Nyack Coll (NY)
Oberlin Coll (OH)
Ohio U (OH)
Ohio Valley U (WV)
Ohio Wesleyan U (OH)
Oklahoma Christian U (OK)
Oklahoma City U (OK)
Oklahoma Wesleyan U (OK)
Our Lady of the Lake U of San Antonio (TX)
Pacific Lutheran U (WA)
Pacific Union Coll (CA)
Paine Coll (GA)
Palm Beach Atlantic U (FL)
Penn State Abington (PA)
Penn State Altoona (PA)
Penn State Beaver (PA)
Penn State Berks (PA)
Penn State Brandywine (PA)
Penn State DuBois (PA)
Penn State Erie, The Behrend Coll (PA)
Penn State Fayette, The Eberly Campus (PA)
Penn State Greater Allegheny (PA)
Penn State Hazleton (PA)
Penn State Lehigh Valley (PA)
Penn State Mont Alto (PA)
Penn State New Kensington (PA)
Penn State Schuylkill (PA)
Penn State Shenango (PA)
Penn State U Park (PA)
Penn State Wilkes-Barre (PA)
Penn State Worthington Scranton (PA)
Penn State York (PA)
Pepperdine U, Malibu (CA)
Philadelphia Biblical U (PA)
Piedmont Coll (GA)
Pikeville Coll (KY)
Pitzer Coll (CA)
Pomona Coll (CA)
Portland State U (OR)
Presbyterian Coll (SC)
Prescott Coll (AZ)
Princeton U (NJ)
Principia Coll (IL)
Queens Coll of the City U of New York (NY)
Randolph Coll (VA)
Randolph-Macon Coll (VA)
Reed Coll (OR)
Regis U (CO)
Reinhardt U (GA)
Rhodes Coll (TN)
Rice U (TX)
Ripon Coll (WI)
Roanoke Coll (VA)
Rocky Mountain Coll (MT)
Rollins Coll (FL)
Rosemont Coll (PA)
Rutgers, The State U of New Jersey, New Brunswick (NJ)
Sacred Heart U (CT)
Saint Francis U (PA)
St. Francis Xavier U (NS, Canada)
St. John Fisher Coll (NY)
Saint Joseph Coll (CT)
Saint Joseph's Coll of Maine (ME)
Saint Joseph's U (PA)
St. Lawrence U (NY)
Saint Leo U (FL)
Saint Martin's U (WA)
Saint Mary-of-the-Woods Coll (IN)
Saint Mary's Coll (IN)
Saint Mary's Coll of California (CA)
St. Mary's Coll of Maryland (MD)
Saint Michael's Coll (VT)
St. Norbert Coll (WI)
St. Olaf Coll (MN)
St. Thomas Aquinas Coll (NY)
St. Thomas U (FL)
St. Thomas U (NB, Canada)
Saint Xavier U (IL)

Salve Regina U (RI)
Samford U (AL)
San Diego State U (CA)
San Jose State U (CA)
Santa Clara U (CA)
Sarah Lawrence Coll (NY)
Schreiner U (TX)
Scripps Coll (CA)
Seton Hill U (PA)
Sewanee: The U of the South (TN)
Shenandoah U (VA)
Shorter U (GA)
Siena Coll (NY)
Siena Heights U (MI)
Simpson Coll (IA)
Skidmore Coll (NY)
Smith Coll (MA)
Southern Adventist U (TN)
Southern Methodist U (TX)
Southern Wesleyan U (SC)
Southwestern Adventist U (TX)
Spelman Coll (GA)
Spring Arbor U (MI)
Spring Hill Coll (AL)
Stanford U (CA)
State U of New York Coll at Old Westbury (NY)
Stetson U (FL)
Stonehill Coll (MA)
Stony Brook U, State U of New York (NY)
Susquehanna U (PA)
Swarthmore Coll (PA)
Sweet Briar Coll (VA)
Syracuse U (NY)
Tabor Coll (KS)
Temple U (PA)
Tennessee Wesleyan Coll (TN)
Texas Christian U (TX)
Texas Wesleyan U (TX)
Thiel Coll (PA)
Thomas Edison State Coll (NJ)
Thomas More Coll (KY)
Towson U (MD)
Transylvania U (KY)
Trinity Coll (CT)
Trinity U (TX)
Tulane U (LA)
Union Coll (KY)
Union Coll (NE)
Union Coll (NY)
Union U (TN)
The U of Alabama (AL)
The U of Arizona (AZ)
U of Bridgeport (CT)
The U of British Columbia (BC, Canada)
U of California, Berkeley (CA)
U of California, Davis (CA)
U of California, Irvine (CA)
U of California, Los Angeles (CA)
U of California, Santa Barbara (CA)
U of Central Florida (FL)
U of Colorado Boulder (CO)
U of Dayton (OH)
U of Denver (CO)
U of Dubuque (IA)
The U of Findlay (OH)
U of Florida (FL)
U of Georgia (GA)
U of Hawaii at Manoa (HI)
U of Indianapolis (IN)
The U of Iowa (IA)
The U of Kansas (KS)
U of La Verne (CA)
U of Lethbridge (AB, Canada)
U of Manitoba (MB, Canada)
U of Mary Hardin-Baylor (TX)
U of Mary Washington (VA)
U of Miami (FL)
U of Michigan (MI)
U of Minnesota, Twin Cities Campus (MN)
U of Missouri (MO)
U of Mobile (AL)
U of Mount Union (OH)
U of Nebraska at Omaha (NE)
The U of North Carolina at Asheville (NC)
The U of North Carolina at Chapel Hill (NC)
The U of North Carolina at Charlotte (NC)
The U of North Carolina at Greensboro (NC)
U of North Dakota (ND)
U of Northern Iowa (IA)
U of Oklahoma (OK)
U of Oregon (OR)
U of Ottawa (ON, Canada)

U of Pennsylvania (PA)
U of Pittsburgh (PA)
U of Puget Sound (WA)
U of Redlands (CA)
U of Regina (SK, Canada)
U of Richmond (VA)
U of Rochester (NY)
U of St. Thomas (MN)
U of San Diego (CA)
U of San Francisco (CA)
U of Saskatchewan (SK, Canada)
The U of Scranton (PA)
U of South Carolina (SC)
U of Southern California (CA)
U of Southern Mississippi (MS)
U of South Florida (FL)
The U of Tennessee (TN)
The U of Texas at Austin (TX)
U of the Incarnate Word (TX)
U of the Ozarks (AR)
U of the Pacific (CA)
U of the Southwest (NM)
The U of Toledo (OH)
U of Tulsa (OK)
U of Vermont (VT)
U of Virginia (VA)
U of Washington (WA)
U of Waterloo (ON, Canada)
The U of Western Ontario (ON, Canada)
U of West Florida (FL)
U of Wisconsin–Eau Claire (WI)
U of Wisconsin–Madison (WI)
U of Wyoming (WY)
Vanderbilt U (TN)
Vassar Coll (NY)
Villanova U (PA)
Virginia Commonwealth U (VA)
Virginia Intermont Coll (VA)
Virginia Wesleyan Coll (VA)
Viterbo U (WI)
Wabash Coll (IN)
Wake Forest U (NC)
Walla Walla U (WA)
Wartburg Coll (IA)
Washburn U (KS)
Washington and Lee U (VA)
Washington State U (WA)
Washington U in St. Louis (MO)
Webster U (MO)
Wellesley Coll (MA)
Wesleyan Coll (GA)
Wesleyan U (CT)
Western Illinois U (IL)
Western Kentucky U (KY)
Western Michigan U (MI)
Westminster Coll (MO)
Westmont Coll (CA)
Wheaton Coll (MA)
Wheeling Jesuit U (WV)
Whitman Coll (WA)
Wilfrid Laurier U (ON, Canada)
Willamette U (OR)
William Jewell Coll (MO)
Williams Coll (MA)
Wilmington Coll (OH)
Wingate U (NC)
Wittenberg U (OH)
Wofford Coll (SC)
Wright State U (OH)
Xavier U (OH)
Yale U (CT)
Youngstown State U (OH)

RELIGIOUS STUDIES RELATED
Bryn Athyn Coll of the New Church (PA)
Claremont McKenna Coll (CA)
St. Edward's U (TX)
Sarah Lawrence Coll (NY)
Trevecca Nazarene U (TN)
U of Regina (SK, Canada)
U of the West (CA)
The U of Western Ontario (ON, Canada)
Ursuline Coll (OH)

RESEARCH AND EXPERIMENTAL PSYCHOLOGY RELATED
U of Michigan–Flint (MI)

RESORT MANAGEMENT
California State U, Chico (CA)
Coastal Carolina U (SC)
Florida Gulf Coast U (FL)
Mitchell Coll (CT)
Sierra Nevada Coll (NV)
U of Minnesota, Crookston (MN)

RESPIRATORY CARE THERAPY
Armstrong Atlantic State U (GA)
Ball State U (IN)
Baptist Coll of Health Sciences (TN)
Bellarmine U (KY)
Boise State U (ID)
Dakota State U (SD)
Fairleigh Dickinson U, Coll at Florham (NJ)
Florida Ag and Mech U (FL)
Gannon U (PA)
Georgia Health Sciences U (GA)
Georgia State U (GA)
Indiana U Bloomington (IN)
Indiana U East (IN)
Indiana U of Pennsylvania (PA)
Indiana U–Purdue U Indianapolis (IN)
Indiana U South Bend (IN)
Indiana U Southeast (IN)
Long Island U, Brooklyn Campus (NY)
Marshall U (WV)
Midwestern State U (TX)
Missouri State U (MO)
North Dakota State U (ND)
Northern Michigan U (MI)
The Ohio State U (OH)
St. Catherine U (MN)
Salisbury U (MD)
Shenandoah U (VA)
State U of New York Upstate Medical U (NY)
Stony Brook U, State U of New York (NY)
Texas Southern U (TX)
Texas State U–San Marcos (TX)
Thomas Edison State Coll (NJ)
The U of Akron (OH)
The U of Alabama at Birmingham (AL)
U of Hartford (CT)
U of Indianapolis (IN)
The U of Kansas (KS)
U of Missouri (MO)
The U of North Carolina at Charlotte (NC)
U of South Alabama (AL)
U of Waterloo (ON, Canada)
Wheeling Jesuit U (WV)
York Coll of Pennsylvania (PA)
Youngstown State U (OH)

RESTAURANT, CULINARY, AND CATERING MANAGEMENT
The Art Inst of Ohio–Cincinnati (OH)
The Art Inst of Seattle (WA)
Coll of the Ozarks (MO)
Johnson & Wales U (FL)
Johnson & Wales U (RI)
Johnson & Wales U - Charlotte Campus (NC)
Kendall Coll (IL)
Pennsylvania Coll of Technology (PA)
Southeast Missouri State U (MO)
State U of New York Coll of Technology at Delhi (NY)
U of Hawaii–West Oahu (HI)

RESTAURANT/FOOD SERVICES MANAGEMENT
Coll of the Ozarks (MO)
Colorado State U (CO)
The Culinary Inst of America (NY)
ECPI Coll of Technology, Virginia Beach (VA)
Johnson & Wales U (CO)
Johnson & Wales U - Charlotte Campus (NC)
Kendall Coll (IL)
Lindenwood U (MO)
Messiah Coll (PA)
Niagara U (NY)
The Ohio State U (OH)
The Restaurant School at Walnut Hill Coll (PA)
The U of Alabama (AL)
U of Central Florida (FL)
U of Minnesota, Crookston (MN)
U of Missouri (MO)
U of San Francisco (CA)

RETAILING
Central Michigan U (MI)
Stevens Inst of Business & Arts (MO)
U of South Carolina (SC)
U of Wisconsin–Madison (WI)

RETAIL MANAGEMENT
Central Michigan U (MI)

RHETORIC AND COMPOSITION
Albany State U (GA)
Ashland U (OH)
Auburn U (AL)
Augsburg Coll (MN)
Ball State U (IN)
Bates Coll (ME)
Belmont U (TN)
Bemidji State U (MN)
Bloomsburg U of Pennsylvania (PA)
Bob Jones U (SC)
Bowling Green State U (OH)
Brigham Young U (UT)
California Polytechnic State U, San Luis Obispo (CA)
California State U, Fullerton (CA)
California State U, Long Beach (CA)
California State U, Los Angeles (CA)
Calvin Coll (MI)
Carson-Newman Coll (TN)
Clarion U of Pennsylvania (PA)
Clark Atlanta U (GA)
Clemson U (SC)
Coll of Saint Benedict (MN)
Columbus State U (GA)
Cornell Coll (IA)
Creighton U (NE)
Denison U (OH)
Dickinson State U (ND)
Drake U (IA)
Duquesne U (PA)
East Tennessee State U (TN)
East Texas Baptist U (TX)
Evangel U (MO)
Fairmont State U (WV)
Ferris State U (MI)
Georgia Coll & State U (GA)
Georgia Southern U (GA)
Governors State U (IL)
Graceland U (IA)
Greenville Coll (IL)
Hardin-Simmons U (TX)
Humboldt State U (CA)
Illinois Coll (IL)
Iowa State U of Science and Technology (IA)
Ithaca Coll (NY)
Kent State U (OH)
Lehman Coll of the City U of New York (NY)
Lipscomb U (TN)
Lock Haven U of Pennsylvania (PA)
Long Island U, Brooklyn Campus (NY)
Louisiana Coll (LA)
Louisiana State U in Shreveport (LA)
Manchester Coll (IN)
Marietta Coll (OH)
Marshall U (WV)
The Master's Coll and Sem (CA)
McKendree U (IL)
Miami U (OH)
Minnesota State U Mankato (MN)
Minnesota State U Moorhead (MN)
Minot State U (ND)
Mississippi Valley State U (MS)
Newberry Coll (SC)
North Carolina Ag and Tech State U (NC)
North Central Coll (IL)
Northeastern Illinois U (IL)
Northern Arizona U (AZ)
Northern State U (SD)
Northwestern Coll (IA)
Northwestern Oklahoma State U (OK)
Northwest Missouri State U (MO)
Oklahoma Christian U (OK)
Oklahoma City U (OK)
Oregon State U (OR)
Ouachita Baptist U (AR)
Pace U (NY)
Pepperdine U, Malibu (CA)
Portland State U (OR)
Rider U (NJ)
St. Catherine U (MN)
Saint John's U (MN)
St. John's U (NY)
St. Joseph's Coll, Long Island Campus (NY)
St. Joseph's Coll, New York (NY)
San Jose State U (CA)
Shippensburg U of Pennsylvania (PA)
South Dakota State U (SD)
Southern Illinois U Carbondale (IL)
Southern Illinois U Edwardsville (IL)

INDEXES

Southern Utah U (UT)
State U of New York at New Paltz (NY)
State U of New York Coll at Oneonta (NY)
Stephen F. Austin State U (TX)
Syracuse U (NY)
Tarleton State U (TX)
Temple U (PA)
Texas A&M U (TX)
Texas Southern U (TX)
Texas Tech U (TX)
Texas Wesleyan U (TX)
Trinity U (TX)
Troy U (AL)
Union U (TN)
U of Arkansas at Pine Bluff (AR)
U of California, Berkeley (CA)
U of Central Missouri (MO)
U of Cincinnati (OH)
U of Dubuque (IA)
U of Georgia (GA)
The U of Iowa (IA)
U of Minnesota, Twin Cities Campus (MN)
U of Montevallo (AL)
U of Nebraska at Omaha (NE)
The U of North Carolina at Greensboro (NC)
U of North Texas (TX)
U of Pittsburgh (PA)
U of Rhode Island (RI)
U of Richmond (VA)
U of Sioux Falls (SD)
The U of South Dakota (SD)
U of South Florida (FL)
The U of Tennessee (TN)
The U of Texas at Arlington (TX)
The U of Texas at Tyler (TX)
U of the Cumberlands (KY)
U of Waterloo (ON, Canada)
U of Wisconsin–Platteville (WI)
U of Wisconsin–River Falls (WI)
U of Wisconsin–Superior (WI)
U of Wisconsin–Whitewater (WI)
Utah State U (UT)
Wabash Coll (IN)
Walla Walla U (WA)
West Chester U of Pennsylvania (PA)
Willamette U (OR)
William Jewell Coll (MO)
Winona State U (MN)
York Coll of the City U of New York (NY)
Youngstown State U (OH)

RHETORIC AND COMPOSITION/ WRITING RELATED

Syracuse U (NY)

ROBOTICS TECHNOLOGY

Alcorn State U (MS)
Indiana State U (IN)
Indiana U–Purdue U Indianapolis (IN)
Lake Superior State U (MI)
Purdue U (IN)
U of Rio Grande (OH)

ROMANCE LANGUAGES

Bard Coll (NY)
Beloit Coll (WI)
Bowdoin Coll (ME)
Bryn Mawr Coll (PA)
Carleton Coll (MN)
City Coll of the City U of New York (NY)
Colgate U (NY)
Dartmouth Coll (NH)
DePauw U (IN)
Elmira Coll (NY)
Franklin Coll Switzerland (Switzerland)
Gettysburg Coll (PA)
Harvard U (MA)
Haverford Coll (PA)
Hunter Coll of the City U of New York (NY)
Iowa State U of Science and Technology (IA)
Marlboro Coll (VT)
Merrimack Coll (MA)
Mount Allison U (NB, Canada)
Mount Holyoke Coll (MA)
Oberlin Coll (OH)
Pomona Coll (CA)
Ripon Coll (WI)

Rockford Coll (IL)
St. Thomas Aquinas Coll (NY)
Sarah Lawrence Coll (NY)
Truman State U (MO)
Tufts U (MA)
The U of British Columbia (BC, Canada)
U of Georgia (GA)
U of Hawaii at Manoa (HI)
U of Illinois at Chicago (IL)
U of Maine (ME)
U of Maryland, Coll Park (MD)
U of Michigan (MI)
U of Nevada, Las Vegas (NV)
U of New Brunswick Fredericton (NB, Canada)
U of Notre Dame (IN)
U of Oregon (OR)
U of Washington (WA)
Vanderbilt U (TN)
Washington and Lee U (VA)
Washington U in St. Louis (MO)
Wesleyan U (CT)
Wheeling Jesuit U (WV)

ROMANCE LANGUAGES RELATED

Hood Coll (MD)
North Carolina Ag and Tech State U (NC)
U of Lethbridge (AB, Canada)
U of Michigan–Flint (MI)
The U of North Carolina at Chapel Hill (NC)
U of Pennsylvania (PA)

RURAL SOCIOLOGY

U of Wisconsin–Madison (WI)

RUSSIAN

American U (DC)
Amherst Coll (MA)
Arizona State U (AZ)
Bard Coll (NY)
Barnard Coll (NY)
Bates Coll (ME)
Beloit Coll (WI)
Boston Coll (MA)
Boston U (MA)
Bowdoin Coll (ME)
Bowling Green State U (OH)
Brandeis U (MA)
Bryn Mawr Coll (PA)
Bucknell U (PA)
Carleton Coll (MN)
Claremont McKenna Coll (CA)
Colgate U (NY)
Coll of the Holy Cross (MA)
Columbia U, School of General Studies (NY)
Cornell Coll (IA)
Dartmouth Coll (NH)
Dickinson Coll (PA)
Drew U (NJ)
Georgetown U (DC)
Goucher Coll (MD)
Grinnell Coll (IA)
Haverford Coll (PA)
Hofstra U (NY)
Hunter Coll of the City U of New York (NY)
Juniata Coll (PA)
Kent State U (OH)
La Salle U (PA)
Lawrence U (WI)
Lehman Coll of the City U of New York (NY)
Luther Coll (IA)
Macalester Coll (MN)
Michigan State U (MI)
Middlebury Coll (VT)
New Coll of Florida (FL)
New York U (NY)
Northern Illinois U (IL)
Oberlin Coll (OH)
The Ohio State U (OH)
Ohio U (OH)
Oklahoma State U (OK)
Penn State Abington (PA)
Penn State Altoona (PA)
Penn State Beaver (PA)
Penn State Berks (PA)
Penn State Brandywine (PA)
Penn State DuBois (PA)
Penn State Erie, The Behrend Coll (PA)
Penn State Fayette, The Eberly Campus (PA)

Penn State Greater Allegheny (PA)
Penn State Hazleton (PA)
Penn State Lehigh Valley (PA)
Penn State Mont Alto (PA)
Penn State New Kensington (PA)
Penn State Schuylkill (PA)
Penn State Shenango (PA)
Penn State Park (PA)
Penn State Wilkes-Barre (PA)
Penn State Worthington Scranton (PA)
Penn State York (PA)
Pomona Coll (CA)
Portland State U (OR)
Queens Coll of the City U of New York (NY)
Reed Coll (OR)
Rider U (NJ)
Rutgers, The State U of New Jersey, New Brunswick (NJ)
Saint Louis U (MO)
St. Olaf Coll (MN)
San Diego State U (CA)
Sarah Lawrence Coll (NY)
Scripps Coll (CA)
Seattle Pacific U (WA)
Sewanee: The U of the South (TN)
Smith Coll (MA)
Stony Brook U, State U of New York (NY)
Swarthmore Coll (PA)
Syracuse U (NY)
Temple U (PA)
Texas A&M U (TX)
Trinity Coll (CT)
Trinity U (TX)
Truman State U (MO)
Tufts U (MA)
Tulane U (LA)
United States Military Acad (NY)
The U of Arizona (AZ)
The U of British Columbia (BC, Canada)
U of California, Davis (CA)
U of California, Los Angeles (CA)
U of Denver (CO)
U of Florida (FL)
U of Georgia (GA)
U of Hawaii at Manoa (HI)
U of Illinois at Chicago (IL)
The U of Iowa (IA)
U of Manitoba (MB, Canada)
U of Maryland, Coll Park (MD)
U of Michigan (MI)
U of Minnesota, Twin Cities Campus (MN)
U of Missouri (MO)
U of Nebraska–Lincoln (NE)
U of New Brunswick Fredericton (NB, Canada)
U of New Hampshire (NH)
U of Northern Iowa (IA)
U of Notre Dame (IN)
U of Oklahoma (OK)
U of Ottawa (ON, Canada)
U of Pennsylvania (PA)
U of Pittsburgh (PA)
U of Rochester (NY)
U of St. Thomas (MN)
U of Saskatchewan (SK, Canada)
U of South Carolina (SC)
U of Southern California (CA)
U of South Florida (FL)
The U of Tennessee (TN)
The U of Texas at Arlington (TX)
The U of Texas at Austin (TX)
U of Utah (UT)
U of Vermont (VT)
U of Washington (WA)
U of Waterloo (ON, Canada)
U of Wisconsin–Madison (WI)
U of Wyoming (WY)
Vanderbilt U (TN)
Vassar Coll (NY)
Wake Forest U (NC)
Washington U in St. Louis (MO)
Wellesley Coll (MA)
Wesleyan U (CT)
West Chester U of Pennsylvania (PA)
Wheaton Coll (MA)
Williams Coll (MA)
Yale U (CT)

RUSSIAN, CENTRAL EUROPEAN, EAST EUROPEAN AND EURASIAN STUDIES

Bowdoin Coll (ME)

Columbia U, School of General Studies (NY)
Hawai`i Pacific U (HI)
Kent State U (OH)
Marlboro Coll (VT)
Michigan State U (MI)
Middlebury Coll (VT)
Portland State U (OR)
Rutgers, The State U of New Jersey, New Brunswick (NJ)
Sarah Lawrence Coll (NY)
The U of British Columbia (BC, Canada)
U of Missouri (MO)
Wayne State U (MI)
Wesleyan U (CT)

RUSSIAN STUDIES

American U (DC)
Bard Coll (NY)
Beloit Coll (WI)
Boston Coll (MA)
Boston U (MA)
Brown U (RI)
Carleton Coll (MN)
Carnegie Mellon U (PA)
Claremont McKenna Coll (CA)
Colby Coll (ME)
Colgate U (NY)
Coll of the Holy Cross (MA)
The Coll of Wooster (OH)
The Colorado Coll (CO)
Columbia U, School of General Studies (NY)
Cornell Coll (IA)
Dartmouth Coll (NH)
DePauw U (IN)
Grand Valley State U (MI)
Hamilton Coll (NY)
Hobart and William Smith Colls (NY)
Kent State U (OH)
Lafayette Coll (PA)
La Salle U (PA)
Lawrence U (WI)
Marlboro Coll (VT)
Michigan State U (MI)
Middlebury Coll (VT)
Mount Holyoke Coll (MA)
Muhlenberg Coll (PA)
Oberlin Coll (OH)
Rhodes Coll (TN)
Rutgers, The State U of New Jersey, New Brunswick (NJ)
St. Olaf Coll (MN)
San Diego State U (CA)
Scripps Coll (CA)
Sewanee: The U of the South (TN)
Smith Coll (MA)
Stetson U (FL)
Syracuse U (NY)
Texas State U–San Marcos (TX)
Texas Tech U (TX)
Tufts U (MA)
Tulane U (LA)
United States Military Acad (NY)
U of Alaska Fairbanks (AK)
The U of British Columbia (BC, Canada)
U of California, Los Angeles (CA)
U of California, Santa Cruz (CA)
U of Colorado Boulder (CO)
U of Houston (TX)
The U of Kansas (KS)
U of Manitoba (MB, Canada)
U of Maryland, Coll Park (MD)
U of Massachusetts Amherst (MA)
U of Michigan (MI)
U of Minnesota, Twin Cities Campus (MN)
U of Missouri (MO)
U of Northern Iowa (IA)
U of Oregon (OR)
U of Richmond (VA)
U of Rochester (NY)
U of St. Thomas (MN)
U of Southern Maine (ME)
The U of Texas at Austin (TX)
U of Tulsa (OK)
U of Vermont (VT)
U of Washington (WA)
U of Waterloo (ON, Canada)
Washington and Lee U (VA)
Washington U in St. Louis (MO)
Wellesley Coll (MA)
Wesleyan U (CT)
Wheaton Coll (MA)
Wittenberg U (OH)
Yale U (CT)

SALES AND MARKETING/ MARKETING AND DISTRIBUTION TEACHER EDUCATION

Bowling Green State U (OH)
Colorado State U (CO)
Eastern Michigan U (MI)
Eastern New Mexico U (NM)
Fayetteville State U (NC)
Kent State U (OH)
Louisiana State U and Ag and Mech Coll (LA)
Middle Tennessee State U (TN)
New York Inst of Technology (NY)
North Carolina State U (NC)
Rider U (NJ)
State U of New York at Oswego (NY)
U of Minnesota, Twin Cities Campus (MN)
U of Wisconsin–Stout (WI)
Utah State U (UT)
Western Michigan U (MI)
Wright State U (OH)

SALES, DISTRIBUTION, AND MARKETING OPERATIONS

Brock U (ON, Canada)
Champlain Coll (VT)
Cleary U (MI)
Dalton State Coll (GA)
Harding U (AR)
HEC Montreal (QC, Canada)
Husson U (ME)
Kennesaw State U (GA)
McKendree U (IL)
Metropolitan State U (MN)
Middle Tennessee State U (TN)
New York U (NY)
Quinnipiac U (CT)
Seton Hill U (PA)
Texas A&M U (TX)
Tuskegee U (AL)
The U of Akron (OH)
U of Baltimore (MD)
The U of Findlay (OH)
U of Houston (TX)
U of Memphis (TN)
U of North Texas (TX)
U of Pennsylvania (PA)
U of the Incarnate Word (TX)
U of Wisconsin–Stout (WI)
U of Wisconsin–Superior (WI)
West Chester U of Pennsylvania (PA)
Wichita State U (KS)

SANSKRIT AND CLASSICAL INDIAN LANGUAGES

Bard Coll (NY)
Harvard U (MA)

SCANDINAVIAN LANGUAGES

Augsburg Coll (MN)
Augustana Coll (IL)
Luther Coll (IA)
U of California, Berkeley (CA)
U of California, Los Angeles (CA)
U of Minnesota, Twin Cities Campus (MN)
The U of Texas at Austin (TX)
U of Washington (WA)

SCANDINAVIAN STUDIES

Concordia Coll (MN)
Pacific Lutheran U (WA)
U of Washington (WA)
U of Wisconsin–Madison (WI)

SCHOOL LIBRARIAN/SCHOOL LIBRARY MEDIA

The Coll of St. Scholastica (MN)
East Central U (OK)

SCHOOL PSYCHOLOGY

Eastern Washington U (WA)
U of Cincinnati (OH)
U of Wisconsin–River Falls (WI)

SCIENCE TEACHER EDUCATION

Abilene Christian U (TX)
Adams State Coll (CO)
Alfred U (NY)
Alma Coll (MI)
Alvernia U (PA)
Alverno Coll (WI)
Andrews U (MI)
Aquinas Coll (MI)

Arcadia U (PA)
Arkansas Tech U (AR)
Ashland U (OH)
Assumption Coll (MA)
Athens State U (AL)
Auburn U (AL)
Ball State U (IN)
Baptist Bible Coll of Pennsylvania (PA)
Beloit Coll (WI)
Bemidji State U (MN)
Bethel Coll (IN)
Biola U (CA)
Bluefield Coll (VA)
Bob Jones U (SC)
Boise State U (ID)
Boston U (MA)
Bowie State U (MD)
Brewton-Parker Coll (GA)
Brigham Young U (UT)
Brock U (ON, Canada)
Buena Vista U (IA)
California State U, San Marcos (CA)
Calumet Coll of Saint Joseph (IN)
Calvin Coll (MI)
Cameron U (OK)
Campbellsville U (KY)
Capital U (OH)
Carroll U (WI)
Castleton State Coll (VT)
Cedarville U (OH)
Central Michigan U (MI)
Chipola Coll (FL)
City Coll of the City U of New York (NY)
Clarion U of Pennsylvania (PA)
Clemson U (SC)
Coll of Saint Mary (NE)
The Coll of Saint Rose (NY)
Coll of the Atlantic (ME)
Coll of the Ozarks (MO)
Colorado State U (CO)
Columbus State U (GA)
Concordia Coll (MN)
Concordia Coll–New York (NY)
Concordia U Chicago (IL)
Concordia U Wisconsin (WI)
Covenant Coll (GA)
Crown Coll (MN)
Dallas Baptist U (TX)
Defiance Coll (OH)
Delaware State U (DE)
Dickinson State U (ND)
Dixie State Coll of Utah (UT)
Doane Coll (NE)
Dordt Coll (IA)
Dowling Coll (NY)
Eastern Illinois U (IL)
Eastern Michigan U (MI)
Eastern Washington U (WA)
Edgewood Coll (WI)
Elizabethtown Coll (PA)
Elmira Coll (NY)
Elon U (NC)
Evangel U (MO)
Fairmont State U (WV)
Florida Ag and Mech U (FL)
Florida Atlantic U (FL)
Florida Inst of Technology (FL)
Florida State U (FL)
Freed-Hardeman U (TN)
Gettysburg Coll (PA)
Governors State U (IL)
Graceland U (IA)
Grand Valley State U (MI)
Greensboro Coll (NC)
Grove City Coll (PA)
Hannibal-LaGrange U (MO)
Harding U (AR)
Hardin-Simmons U (TX)
Hofstra U (NY)
Hope Coll (MI)
Hunter Coll of the City U of New York (NY)
Huntington U (IN)
Indiana State U (IN)
Indiana U Bloomington (IN)
Indiana U–Purdue U Fort Wayne (IN)
Indiana U South Bend (IN)
Indiana Wesleyan U (IN)
Indian River State Coll (FL)
Inter American U of Puerto Rico, Metropolitan Campus (PR)
Inter American U of Puerto Rico, San Germán Campus (PR)
Ithaca Coll (NY)
Judson Coll (AL)
Juniata Coll (PA)
Keene State Coll (NH)

Kent State U (OH)
Lakehead U (ON, Canada)
La Salle U (PA)
Le Moyne Coll (NY)
Lewis-Clark State Coll (ID)
Lincoln Memorial U (TN)
Lindenwood U (MO)
Longwood U (VA)
Louisiana Coll (LA)
Loyola U Chicago (IL)
Lubbock Christian U (TX)
Lyndon State Coll (VT)
Madonna U (MI)
Malone U (OH)
Manchester Coll (IN)
Mansfield U of Pennsylvania (PA)
Maranatha Baptist Bible Coll (WI)
Marian U (WI)
Mars Hill Coll (NC)
Marywood U (PA)
The Master's Coll and Sem (CA)
Merrimack Coll (MA)
Miami Dade Coll (FL)
Miami U (OH)
Michigan State U (MI)
Midwestern State U (TX)
Millersville U of Pennsylvania (PA)
Minnesota State U Mankato (MN)
Minot State U (ND)
Mississippi Valley State U (MS)
Missouri Baptist U (MO)
Missouri State U (MO)
Montana State U (MT)
Montana State U Billings (MT)
Moravian Coll (PA)
Morningside Coll (IA)
Mount Mercy U (IA)
Mount Vernon Nazarene U (OH)
Nebraska Wesleyan U (NE)
New Mexico Highlands U (NM)
New York U (NY)
Niagara U (NY)
Nicholls State U (LA)
North Carolina Ag and Tech State U (NC)
North Carolina State U (NC)
North Dakota State U (ND)
Northeastern State U (OK)
Northern Arizona U (AZ)
Northern Michigan U (MI)
Northland Coll (WI)
Northwestern Oklahoma State U (OK)
Northwest Missouri State U (MO)
Oklahoma Christian U (OK)
Oklahoma City U (OK)
Oklahoma Wesleyan U (OK)
Ouachita Baptist U (AR)
Pace U (NY)
Rhode Island Coll (RI)
Rider U (NJ)
Sacred Heart U (CT)
St. Ambrose U (IA)
Saint Francis U (PA)
Saint Joseph's U (PA)
St. Petersburg Coll (FL)
Seattle Pacific U (WA)
Shawnee State U (OH)
Southeastern Oklahoma State U (OK)
Southeastern U (FL)
Southeast Missouri State U (MO)
Southern Illinois U Edwardsville (IL)
Southern Nazarene U (OK)
Southern Wesleyan U (SC)
State U of New York at Fredonia (NY)
State U of New York at New Paltz (NY)
State U of New York at Oswego (NY)
State U of New York Coll at Old Westbury (NY)
State U of New York Coll at Oneonta (NY)
State U of New York Coll of Environmental Science and Forestry (NY)
Tabor Coll (KS)
Talladega Coll (AL)
Tarleton State U (TX)
Taylor U (IN)
Temple U (PA)
Texas A&M Intl U (TX)
Texas A&M U–Corpus Christi (TX)
Texas Christian U (TX)
Texas Wesleyan U (TX)
Trine U (IN)
Union U (TN)
The U of Akron (OH)

The U of Arizona (AZ)
The U of British Columbia (BC, Canada)
U of Central Florida (FL)
U of Charleston (WV)
U of Dayton (OH)
U of Evansville (IN)
The U of Findlay (OH)
U of Georgia (GA)
U of Indianapolis (IN)
The U of Iowa (IA)
U of Lethbridge (AB, Canada)
U of Louisiana at Lafayette (LA)
U of Maine (ME)
U of Maine at Farmington (ME)
U of Maine at Presque Isle (ME)
U of Manitoba (MB, Canada)
U of Mary Hardin-Baylor (TX)
U of Maryland, Coll Park (MD)
U of Michigan–Dearborn (MI)
U of Minnesota, Duluth (MN)
U of Minnesota, Twin Cities Campus (MN)
U of Mississippi (MS)
U of Missouri (MO)
U of Nebraska–Lincoln (NE)
U of Nevada, Reno (NV)
U of New Brunswick Fredericton (NB, Canada)
The U of North Carolina at Pembroke (NC)
U of North Dakota (ND)
U of Northern Iowa (IA)
U of North Florida (FL)
U of Notre Dame (IN)
U of Oklahoma (OK)
U of Pittsburgh at Johnstown (PA)
U of Regina (SK, Canada)
U of Rio Grande (OH)
U of St. Francis (IL)
U of St. Thomas (MN)
U of Sioux Falls (SD)
The U of South Dakota (SD)
U of South Florida (FL)
The U of Tennessee at Chattanooga (TN)
The U of Tennessee at Martin (TN)
The U of Toledo (OH)
U of Vermont (VT)
U of Washington (WA)
U of West Florida (FL)
U of Wisconsin–Eau Claire (WI)
U of Wisconsin–La Crosse (WI)
U of Wisconsin–Madison (WI)
U of Wisconsin–Platteville (WI)
U of Wisconsin–River Falls (WI)
U of Wisconsin–Stout (WI)
U of Wisconsin–Superior (WI)
U of Wisconsin–Whitewater (WI)
Upper Iowa U (IA)
Ursuline Coll (OH)
Utah State U (UT)
Utah Valley U (UT)
Valparaiso U (IN)
Viterbo U (WI)
Walsh U (OH)
Washington State U (WA)
Washington U in St. Louis (MO)
Wayland Baptist U (TX)
Waynesburg U (PA)
Wayne State Coll (NE)
Wayne State U (MI)
Weber State U (UT)
Western Carolina U (NC)
Western State Coll of Colorado (CO)
Wichita State U (KS)
Widener U (PA)
Wilmington Coll (OH)
Wilmington U (DE)
Winona State U (MN)
Wright State U (OH)
Xavier U (OH)
Xavier U of Louisiana (LA)
York Coll of Pennsylvania (PA)
Youngstown State U (OH)

SCIENCE TECHNOLOGIES

Marylhurst U (OR)

SCIENCE TECHNOLOGIES RELATED

Arizona State U (AZ)
Athens State U (AL)
Bridgewater State U (MA)
Clemson U (SC)
Kean U (NJ)
Kent State U at Geauga (OH)
Madonna U (MI)
North Carolina State U (NC)
Northern Arizona U (AZ)

U of Wisconsin–Stout (WI)
Willamette U (OR)

SCIENCE, TECHNOLOGY AND SOCIETY

Arizona State U (AZ)
Butler U (IN)
California State Polytechnic U, Pomona (CA)
Colby Coll (ME)
Cornell U (NY)
Eastern Michigan U (MI)
Georgetown U (DC)
Georgia Inst of Technology (GA)
James Madison U (VA)
Lehigh U (PA)
Massachusetts Inst of Technology (MA)
Michigan State U (MI)
New Jersey Inst of Technology (NJ)
North Carolina State U (NC)
Pitzer Coll (CA)
Rensselaer Polytechnic Inst (NY)
Rutgers, The State U of New Jersey, Newark (NJ)
Scripps Coll (CA)
Slippery Rock U of Pennsylvania (PA)
Stanford U (CA)
U of Nevada, Reno (NV)
U of Puget Sound (WA)
U of Washington, Bothell (WA)
Vanderbilt U (TN)
Vassar Coll (NY)
Washington U in St. Louis (MO)
Wesleyan U (CT)
Worcester Polytechnic Inst (MA)

SCULPTURE

Alberta Coll of Art & Design (AB, Canada)
Aquinas Coll (MI)
Bard Coll at Simon's Rock (MA)
Bennington Coll (VT)
Bethany Coll (KS)
Biola U (CA)
Birmingham-Southern Coll (AL)
Boston U (MA)
Brigham Young U (UT)
California Coll of the Arts (CA)
California State U, Long Beach (CA)
The Cleveland Inst of Art (OH)
Colorado State U (CO)
Concordia U (QC, Canada)
Drake U (IA)
Emily Carr U of Art + Design (BC, Canada)
Escuela de Artes Plasticas de Puerto Rico (PR)
Ferris State U (MI)
Indiana U–Purdue U Fort Wayne (IN)
Inter American U of Puerto Rico, San Germán Campus (PR)
Kent State U (OH)
Longwood U (VA)
Lyme Acad Coll of Fine Arts (CT)
Maine Coll of Art (ME)
Marlboro Coll (VT)
Maryland Inst Coll of Art (MD)
Marywood U (PA)
Massachusetts Coll of Art and Design (MA)
Minneapolis Coll of Art and Design (MN)
Minnesota State U Mankato (MN)
Mount Allison U (NB, Canada)
Northern Arizona U (AZ)
Northern Michigan U (MI)
Northwest Nazarene U (ID)
Ohio U (OH)
Otis Coll of Art and Design (CA)
Pacific Northwest Coll of Art (OR)
Portland State U (OR)
Pratt Inst (NY)
Ringling Coll of Art and Design (FL)
Rocky Mountain Coll of Art + Design (CO)
Rutgers, The State U of New Jersey, New Brunswick (NJ)
Salem State U (MA)
Sarah Lawrence Coll (NY)
Savannah Coll of Art and Design (GA)
School of the Museum of Fine Arts, Boston (MA)
School of Visual Arts (NY)
Seton Hill U (PA)
Sonoma State U (CA)

State U of New York at New Paltz (NY)
Temple U (PA)
Texas Christian U (TX)
U of Dallas (TX)
U of Hartford (CT)
U of Houston (TX)
The U of Iowa (IA)
The U of Kansas (KS)
U of Massachusetts Dartmouth (MA)
U of Miami (FL)
U of Michigan (MI)
U of Oregon (OR)
U of Regina (SK, Canada)
The U of the Arts (PA)
U of Washington (WA)
Virginia Commonwealth U (VA)
Virginia Intermont Coll (VA)
Washington U in St. Louis (MO)
Western State Coll of Colorado (CO)

SECONDARY EDUCATION

Abilene Christian U (TX)
Acadia U (NS, Canada)
Alabama Ag and Mech U (AL)
Alabama State U (AL)
Albertus Magnus Coll (CT)
Albion Coll (MI)
Albright Coll (PA)
Alderson-Broaddus Coll (WV)
Alfred U (NY)
Alma Coll (MI)
American U (DC)
Andrews U (MI)
Anna Maria Coll (MA)
Arcadia U (PA)
Arizona State U (AZ)
Ashland U (OH)
Assumption Coll (MA)
Athens State U (AL)
Atlantic Union Coll (MA)
Auburn U (AL)
Auburn U Montgomery (AL)
Augsburg Coll (MN)
Augustana Coll (SD)
Baker U (KS)
Baptist Bible Coll of Pennsylvania (PA)
Beloit Coll (WI)
Bemidji State U (MN)
Benedictine Coll (KS)
Bennington Coll (VT)
Bethel Coll (IN)
Biola U (CA)
Birmingham-Southern Coll (AL)
Blackburn Coll (IL)
Bluefield Coll (VA)
Boise State U (ID)
Boston Coll (MA)
Bowie State U (MD)
Brewton-Parker Coll (GA)
Briar Cliff U (IA)
Brock U (ON, Canada)
Bucknell U (PA)
Butler U (IN)
Calumet Coll of Saint Joseph (IN)
Calvary Bible Coll and Theological Sem (MO)
Calvin Coll (MI)
Campbellsville U (KY)
Canisius Coll (NY)
Carson-Newman Coll (TN)
The Catholic U of America (DC)
Cedar Crest Coll (PA)
Centenary Coll (NJ)
Central State U (OH)
Champlain Coll (VT)
Chipola Coll (FL)
The Citadel, The Military Coll of South Carolina (SC)
City Coll of the City U of New York (NY)
Clarke U (IA)
Clark U (MA)
Clemson U (SC)
Coll of Charleston (SC)
The Coll of New Jersey (NJ)
Coll of Saint Benedict (MN)
Coll of St. Joseph (VT)
Coll of Saint Mary (NE)
Coll of the Atlantic (ME)
Coll of the Ozarks (MO)
Concordia Coll (MN)
Concordia Coll–New York (NY)
Concordia U Chicago (IL)
Concordia U, St. Paul (MN)
Concordia U Wisconsin (WI)
Concord U (WV)
Corban U (OR)
Cornell Coll (IA)

INDEXES

Cumberland U (TN)
Dallas Baptist U (TX)
Daytona State Coll (FL)
Defiance Coll (OH)
Delaware State U (DE)
DePaul U (IL)
Dickinson State U (ND)
Dominican Coll (NY)
Dordt Coll (IA)
Drake U (IA)
Drury U (MO)
Duquesne U (PA)
East Central U (OK)
East Stroudsburg U of Pennsylvania (PA)
Elmhurst Coll (IL)
Elmira Coll (NY)
Elon U (NC)
Emmanuel Coll (MA)
Emporia State U (KS)
Evangel U (MO)
Fairmont State U (WV)
Faulkner U (AL)
Felician Coll (NJ)
Fitchburg State U (MA)
Flagler Coll (FL)
Florida Gulf Coast U (FL)
Florida Southern Coll (FL)
Fontbonne U (MO)
Fort Lewis Coll (CO)
Franklin Pierce U (NH)
Freed-Hardeman U (TN)
Free Will Baptist Bible Coll (TN)
Furman U (SC)
Gannon U (PA)
Gardner-Webb U (NC)
Gettysburg Coll (PA)
Grace Bible Coll (MI)
Graceland U (IA)
Grand Canyon U (AZ)
Grand Valley State U (MI)
Great Basin Coll (NV)
Greensboro Coll (NC)
Grove City Coll (PA)
Guilford Coll (NC)
Hamline U (MN)
Hannibal-LaGrange U (MO)
Harding U (AR)
Hillsdale Coll (MI)
Hillsdale Free Will Baptist Coll (OK)
Hofstra U (NY)
Holy Family U (PA)
Houghton Coll (NY)
Humboldt State U (CA)
Hunter Coll of the City U of New York (NY)
Huntington U (IN)
Huston-Tillotson U (TX)
Idaho State U (ID)
Illinois Coll (IL)
Indiana U Bloomington (IN)
Indiana U East (IN)
Indiana U Kokomo (IN)
Indiana U Northwest (IN)
Indiana U–Purdue U Fort Wayne (IN)
Indiana U South Bend (IN)
Indiana U Southeast (IN)
Indiana Wesleyan U (IN)
Inter American U of Puerto Rico, San Germán Campus (PR)
Iowa State U of Science and Technology (IA)
Iowa Wesleyan Coll (IA)
Ithaca Coll (NY)
Jacksonville State U (AL)
Jarvis Christian Coll (TX)
John Brown U (AR)
John Carroll U (OH)
Johnson State Coll (VT)
Juniata Coll (PA)
Kansas State U (KS)
Keene State Coll (NH)
Kentucky Wesleyan Coll (KY)
Keuka Coll (NY)
King's Coll (PA)
The King's U Coll (AB, Canada)
Kutztown U of Pennsylvania (PA)
Kuyper Coll (MI)
Lakehead U (ON, Canada)
Lake Superior State U (MI)
Lamar U (TX)
La Salle U (PA)
Lasell Coll (MA)
Lawrence U (WI)
Lee U (TN)
Le Moyne Coll (NY)
Lesley U (MA)

LeTourneau U (TX)
Lewis U (IL)
Lincoln Christian U (IL)
Lincoln Memorial U (TN)
Lindenwood U (MO)
Lindsey Wilson Coll (KY)
Lock Haven U of Pennsylvania (PA)
Long Island U, Brooklyn Campus (NY)
Long Island U, C.W. Post Campus (NY)
Longwood U (VA)
Loras Coll (IA)
Louisiana Coll (LA)
Lourdes Coll (OH)
Loyola U Chicago (IL)
Lubbock Christian U (TX)
MacMurray Coll (IL)
Maharishi U of Management (IA)
Manchester Coll (IN)
Manhattanville Coll (NY)
Mansfield U of Pennsylvania (PA)
Marian U (WI)
Marietta Coll (OH)
Marist Coll (NY)
Marquette U (WI)
Marshall U (WV)
Mars Hill Coll (NC)
The Master's Coll and Sem (CA)
McKendree U (IL)
McMurry U (TX)
Medaille Coll (NY)
Merrimack Coll (MA)
Miami U (OH)
Michigan State U (MI)
MidAmerica Nazarene U (KS)
Midway U (KY)
Midwestern State U (TX)
Minnesota State U Mankato (MN)
Mississippi State U (MS)
Missouri Southern State U (MO)
Missouri State U (MO)
Missouri U of Science and Technology (MO)
Molloy Coll (NY)
Monmouth U (NJ)
Montana State U Billings (MT)
Moravian Coll (PA)
Mount Aloysius Coll (PA)
Mount Marty Coll (SD)
Mount Mercy U (IA)
Mount Olive Coll (NC)
Mount Saint Mary Coll (NY)
Mount Vernon Nazarene U (OH)
Nazareth Coll of Rochester (NY)
Newberry Coll (SC)
New England Coll (NH)
Newman U (KS)
New Mexico State U (NM)
Niagara U (NY)
North Carolina Ag and Tech State U (NC)
North Central Coll (IL)
Northern Michigan U (MI)
Northern State U (SD)
Northwestern Coll (IA)
Northwestern Oklahoma State U (OK)
Northwest Nazarene U (ID)
Northwest U (WA)
Nova Southeastern U (FL)
Ohio U (OH)
Ohio U–Chillicothe (OH)
Ohio Valley U (WV)
Ohio Wesleyan U (OH)
Oklahoma Christian U (OK)
Oklahoma City U (OK)
Oklahoma State U (OK)
Oklahoma Wesleyan U (OK)
Ouachita Baptist U (AR)
Pacific U (OR)
Penn State Abington (PA)
Penn State Altoona (PA)
Penn State Beaver (PA)
Penn State Berks (PA)
Penn State Brandywine (PA)
Penn State DuBois (PA)
Penn State Erie, The Behrend Coll (PA)
Penn State Fayette, The Eberly Campus (PA)
Penn State Greater Allegheny (PA)
Penn State Hazleton (PA)
Penn State Lehigh Valley (PA)
Penn State Mont Alto (PA)
Penn State New Kensington (PA)
Penn State Schuylkill (PA)
Penn State Shenango (PA)

Penn State U Park (PA)
Penn State Wilkes-Barre (PA)
Penn State Worthington Scranton (PA)
Penn State York (PA)
Pepperdine U, Malibu (CA)
Prescott Coll (AZ)
Presentation Coll (SD)
Providence Coll (RI)
Purdue U Calumet (IN)
Purdue U North Central (IN)
Rhode Island Coll (RI)
Rider U (NJ)
Ripon Coll (WI)
Rivier Coll (NH)
Rockford Coll (IL)
Rockhurst U (MO)
Rocky Mountain Coll (MT)
Sacred Heart U (CT)
St. Ambrose U (IA)
Saint Anselm Coll (NH)
St. Catherine U (MN)
Saint Francis U (PA)
St. Francis Xavier U (NS, Canada)
Saint John's U (MN)
St. John's U (NY)
Saint Joseph's Coll (IN)
Saint Joseph's U (PA)
Saint Martin's U (WA)
Saint Mary-of-the-Woods Coll (IN)
Saint Michael's Coll (VT)
St. Thomas Aquinas Coll (NY)
St. Thomas U (FL)
Salem State U (MA)
Salve Regina U (RI)
San Diego Christian Coll (CA)
Seattle Pacific U (WA)
Shepherd U (WV)
Siena Coll (NY)
Siena Heights U (MI)
Simmons Coll (MA)
Simpson Coll (IA)
Slippery Rock U of Pennsylvania (PA)
Southern Connecticut State U (CT)
Southern Utah U (UT)
Southwestern Assemblies of God U (TX)
Spring Arbor U (MI)
Springfield Coll (MA)
Spring Hill Coll (AL)
State U of New York at Fredonia (NY)
State U of New York at New Paltz (NY)
State U of New York at Oswego (NY)
State U of New York Coll at Old Westbury (NY)
State U of New York Coll at Oneonta (NY)
Stetson U (FL)
Susquehanna U (PA)
Tabor Coll (KS)
Tarleton State U (TX)
Tennessee Technological U (TN)
Tennessee Wesleyan Coll (TN)
Texas Christian U (TX)
Thiel Coll (PA)
Thomas More Coll (KY)
Thomas U (GA)
Trent U (ON, Canada)
Trine U (IN)
Troy U (AL)
Union Coll (KY)
Union Coll (NE)
Union Inst & U (OH)
Union U (TN)
Université de Sherbrooke (QC, Canada)
Université du Québec en Outaouais (QC, Canada)
The U of Alabama (AL)
The U of Alabama at Birmingham (AL)
The U of Arizona (AZ)
U of Arkansas at Pine Bluff (AR)
The U of British Columbia (BC, Canada)
U of Central Missouri (MO)
U of Cincinnati (OH)
U of Dallas (TX)
U of Dayton (OH)
U of Dubuque (IA)
The U of Findlay (OH)
U of Hartford (CT)
U of Hawaii at Hilo (HI)
U of Hawaii at Manoa (HI)

U of Idaho (ID)
U of Indianapolis (IN)
The U of Iowa (IA)
The U of Kansas (KS)
U of Louisiana at Lafayette (LA)
U of Maine (ME)
U of Maine at Farmington (ME)
U of Maine at Presque Isle (ME)
U of Manitoba (MB, Canada)
U of Maryland, Coll Park (MD)
U of Michigan (MI)
U of Michigan–Dearborn (MI)
U of Minnesota, Twin Cities Campus (MN)
U of Missouri (MO)
U of Missouri–St. Louis (MO)
U of Montevallo (AL)
U of Nebraska at Omaha (NE)
U of Nevada, Las Vegas (NV)
U of New Brunswick Fredericton (NB, Canada)
U of North Florida (FL)
U of Pittsburgh at Bradford (PA)
U of Pittsburgh at Johnstown (PA)
U of Portland (OR)
U of Redlands (CA)
U of Regina (SK, Canada)
U of Rhode Island (RI)
U of Rio Grande (OH)
U of St. Thomas (TX)
U of San Francisco (CA)
U of Saskatchewan (SK, Canada)
The U of Scranton (PA)
U of Sioux Falls (SD)
U of South Alabama (AL)
U of South Carolina Aiken (SC)
U of South Carolina Upstate (SC)
The U of South Dakota (SD)
The U of Tampa (FL)
The U of Tennessee at Chattanooga (TN)
U of the Cumberlands (KY)
U of the Ozarks (AR)
U of the Southwest (NM)
The U of Toledo (OH)
U of Vermont (VT)
U of Washington (WA)
The U of Western Ontario (ON, Canada)
U of West Georgia (GA)
U of Wisconsin–Platteville (WI)
U of Wisconsin–River Falls (WI)
U of Wisconsin–Stevens Point (WI)
U of Wisconsin–Whitewater (WI)
U of Wyoming (WY)
Utah State U (UT)
Valparaiso U (IN)
Vanderbilt U (TN)
Victory U (TN)
Villanova U (PA)
Virginia Intermont Coll (VA)
Virginia Polytechnic Inst and State U (VA)
Virginia Wesleyan Coll (VA)
Wagner Coll (NY)
Walsh U (OH)
Wartburg Coll (IA)
Washburn U (KS)
Washington State U (WA)
Washington U in St. Louis (MO)
Waynesburg U (PA)
Weber State U (UT)
Wells Coll (NY)
Western Connecticut State U (CT)
Western New England U (MA)
Western Oregon U (OR)
West Liberty U (WV)
Westminster Coll (MO)
Westmont Coll (CA)
Wheaton Coll (IL)
Wheeling Jesuit U (WV)
Wichita State U (KS)
William Jewell Coll (MO)
William Paterson U of New Jersey (NJ)
Wilmington Coll (OH)
Winona State U (MN)
Wright State U (OH)
Xavier U of Louisiana (LA)
York Coll of the City U of New York (NY)
Youngstown State U (OH)

SECONDARY SCHOOL ADMINISTRATION/ PRINCIPALSHIP

The U of North Carolina at Pembroke (NC)

SECURITIES SERVICES ADMINISTRATION

American Public U System (WV)
Central Pennsylvania Coll (PA)
Davenport U, Grand Rapids (MI)
Herzing U (GA)
St. John's U (NY)
Webber Intl U (FL)

SECURITY AND LOSS PREVENTION

Johnson & Wales U (RI)
Lewis U (IL)
Northern Michigan U (MI)

SELLING SKILLS AND SALES

U of Memphis (TN)

SIGN LANGUAGE INTERPRETATION AND TRANSLATION

Augustana Coll (SD)
Bethel Coll (IN)
Bloomsburg U of Pennsylvania (PA)
Columbia Coll Chicago (IL)
Gallaudet U (DC)
Idaho State U (ID)
Indiana U–Purdue U Indianapolis (IN)
MacMurray Coll (IL)
Maryville Coll (TN)
Mount Aloysius Coll (PA)
Quincy U (IL)
Troy U (AL)
U of Louisville (KY)
U of New Hampshire at Manchester (NH)
U of Northern Colorado (CO)
U of North Florida (FL)
Valdosta State U (GA)
Western Oregon U (OR)
Wright State U (OH)

SLAVIC, BALTIC, AND ALBANIAN LANGUAGES RELATED

Rutgers, The State U of New Jersey, Newark (NJ)

SLAVIC LANGUAGES

Boston Coll (MA)
Columbia U, School of General Studies (NY)
Harvard U (MA)
Indiana U Bloomington (IN)
Princeton U (NJ)
Stanford U (CA)
The U of British Columbia (BC, Canada)
U of California, Berkeley (CA)
U of California, Los Angeles (CA)
U of California, Santa Barbara (CA)
U of Illinois at Chicago (IL)
The U of Kansas (KS)
U of Manitoba (MB, Canada)
U of Minnesota, Twin Cities Campus (MN)
U of Pittsburgh (PA)
U of Virginia (VA)
U of Washington (WA)
Wayne State U (MI)

SLAVIC STUDIES

Barnard Coll (NY)
Columbia U, School of General Studies (NY)
Connecticut Coll (CT)
Lawrence U (WI)
U of Ottawa (ON, Canada)
U of Waterloo (ON, Canada)

SMALL BUSINESS ADMINISTRATION

Adams State Coll (CO)
Arcadia U (PA)
Avila U (MO)
Carroll U (WI)
Carson-Newman Coll (TN)
Huntington U (IN)
Husson U (ME)
Kendall Coll (IL)
Lewis-Clark State Coll (ID)
North Central Coll (IL)
Northern Michigan U (MI)
U of Nebraska at Omaha (NE)

SOCIAL AND PHILOSOPHICAL FOUNDATIONS OF EDUCATION

Eastern Washington U (WA)
Transylvania U (KY)
Washington U in St. Louis (MO)

SOCIAL PSYCHOLOGY

Bennington Coll (VT)
Brigham Young U (UT)
Clarion U of Pennsylvania (PA)
Florida Atlantic U (FL)
Grand Valley State U (MI)
Lawrence U (WI)
Maryville U of Saint Louis (MO)
Moravian Coll (PA)
Northwest Missouri State U (MO)
Paine Coll (GA)
Penn State Abington (PA)
U of California, Irvine (CA)
U of Nevada, Reno (NV)
U of New England (ME)
U of Wisconsin–Superior (WI)
Western Michigan U (MI)

SOCIAL SCIENCES

Adelphi U (NY)
Albertus Magnus Coll (CT)
Alma Coll (MI)
Alvernia U (PA)
Alverno Coll (WI)
Andrews U (MI)
Aquinas Coll (MI)
Arizona State U (AZ)
Asbury U (KY)
Ashland U (OH)
Atlanta Christian Coll (GA)
Augsburg Coll (MN)
Azusa Pacific U (CA)
Ball State U (IN)
Belhaven U (MS)
Bemidji State U (MN)
Benedictine Coll (KS)
Benedictine U (IL)
Bennington Coll (VT)
Berry Coll (GA)
Bethany Lutheran Coll (MN)
Bethel Coll (IN)
Bethel U (MN)
Biola U (CA)
Bluefield Coll (VA)
Bluefield State Coll (WV)
Blue Mountain Coll (MS)
Bluffton U (OH)
Boise State U (ID)
Brewton-Parker Coll (GA)
Brock U (ON, Canada)
Buena Vista U (IA)
California Polytechnic State U, San Luis Obispo (CA)
California State Polytechnic U, Pomona (CA)
California State U, Los Angeles (CA)
California State U, Monterey Bay (CA)
California State U, San Bernardino (CA)
California State U, San Marcos (CA)
California State U, Stanislaus (CA)
Calvin Coll (MI)
Campbellsville U (KY)
Castleton State Coll (VT)
Central Coll (IA)
Central Connecticut State U (CT)
Central Michigan U (MI)
Clarion U of Pennsylvania (PA)
Clarkson U (NY)
Cleveland State U (OH)
Colgate U (NY)
Coll of Saint Benedict (MN)
Coll of Saint Mary (NE)
The Coll of St. Scholastica (MN)
Coll of the Humanities and Sciences, Harrison Middleton U (AZ)
Colorado State U (CO)
Concordia Coll (MN)
Concordia Coll–New York (NY)
Coppin State U (MD)
Corban U (OR)
Cumberland U (TN)
Daniel Webster Coll (NH)
Defiance Coll (OH)
Delta State U (MS)
DePaul U (IL)
Dickinson State U (ND)
Divine Word Coll (IA)
Doane Coll (NE)
Dominican Coll (NY)
Dominican U (IL)

Dordt Coll (IA)
Dowling Coll (NY)
Eastern Michigan U (MI)
Eastern New Mexico U (NM)
East Stroudsburg U of Pennsylvania (PA)
Edgewood Coll (WI)
Edinboro U of Pennsylvania (PA)
Elizabethtown Coll (PA)
Elmira Coll (NY)
Embry-Riddle Aeronautical U–Prescott (AZ)
Emporia State U (KS)
Eugene Lang Coll The New School for Liberal Arts (NY)
Faulkner U (AL)
Ferrum Coll (VA)
Florida Atlantic U (FL)
Florida Southern Coll (FL)
Florida State U (FL)
Fontbonne U (MO)
Freed-Hardeman U (TN)
Gannon U (PA)
Gardner-Webb U (NC)
Gettysburg Coll (PA)
Governors State U (IL)
Grand Valley State U (MI)
Great Basin Coll (NV)
Harding U (AR)
Harvard U (MA)
Hawai`i Pacific U (HI)
Holy Apostles Coll and Sem (CT)
Holy Family U (PA)
Humboldt State U (CA)
Inter American U of Puerto Rico, San Germán Campus (PR)
Ithaca Coll (NY)
James Madison U (VA)
The Johns Hopkins U (MD)
Johnson C. Smith U (NC)
Juniata Coll (PA)
Kansas State U (KS)
Keene State Coll (NH)
Kent State U (OH)
Kentucky State U (KY)
Keuka Coll (NY)
Keystone Coll (PA)
The King's U Coll (AB, Canada)
Kutztown U of Pennsylvania (PA)
Lake Superior State U (MI)
La Salle U (PA)
Lehigh U (PA)
Lesley U (MA)
Lewis-Clark State Coll (ID)
Liberty U (VA)
Lock Haven U of Pennsylvania (PA)
Long Island U, Brooklyn Campus (NY)
Loyola U New Orleans (LA)
Lyndon State Coll (VT)
Manchester Coll (IN)
Mansfield U of Pennsylvania (PA)
Marlboro Coll (VT)
Mars Hill Coll (NC)
Marylhurst U (OR)
Marywood U (PA)
Mayville State U (ND)
McKendree U (IL)
Mesa State Coll (CO)
Metropolitan State U (MN)
Michigan State U (MI)
Mid-Continent U (KY)
Minnesota State U Mankato (MN)
Minot State U (ND)
Mississippi U for Women (MS)
Missouri Baptist U (MO)
Montreat Coll, Montreat (NC)
Moravian Coll (PA)
Morehead State U (KY)
Mount Saint Mary Coll (NY)
Mount St. Mary's Coll (CA)
Mount Vernon Nazarene U (OH)
Muhlenberg Coll (PA)
National-Louis U (IL)
Nazareth Coll of Rochester (NY)
New Coll of Florida (FL)
New York Inst of Technology (NY)
New York U (NY)
Niagara U (NY)
North Carolina Ag and Tech State U (NC)
North Central Coll (IL)
North Dakota State U (ND)
Northern Kentucky U (KY)
North Georgia Coll & State U (GA)
Northwestern Oklahoma State U (OK)
Northwest Nazarene U (ID)
Notre Dame de Namur U (CA)
Oklahoma Panhandle State U (OK)

Oklahoma Wesleyan U (OK)
Our Lady of the Lake U of San Antonio (TX)
Pace U (NY)
Pacific Union Coll (CA)
Piedmont Coll (GA)
Point Park U (PA)
Portland State U (OR)
Prescott Coll (AZ)
Providence Coll (RI)
Purdue U (IN)
Quinnipiac U (CT)
Radford U (VA)
Ramapo Coll of New Jersey (NJ)
Regis U (CO)
Rhode Island Coll (RI)
Robert Morris U (PA)
Rockford Coll (IL)
Rogers State U (OK)
Roosevelt U (IL)
Rosemont Coll (PA)
Rust Coll (MS)
Sage Coll of Albany (NY)
St. Andrews Presbyterian Coll (NC)
St. Catherine U (MN)
Saint John's U (MN)
St. John's U (NY)
St. Joseph's Coll, Long Island Campus (NY)
St. Joseph's Coll, New York (NY)
Saint Mary-of-the-Woods Coll (IN)
Saint Mary's Coll of California (CA)
Saint Mary's U of Minnesota (MN)
St. Thomas Aquinas Coll (NY)
Saint Xavier U (IL)
San Diego Christian Coll (CA)
San Diego State U (CA)
San Jose State U (CA)
Sarah Lawrence Coll (NY)
Sewanee: The U of the South (TN)
Shawnee State U (OH)
Shimer Coll (IL)
Shorter U (GA)
Siena Heights U (MI)
Southern Arkansas U–Magnolia (AR)
Southern Illinois U Carbondale (IL)
Southern Methodist U (TX)
Southern Oregon U (OR)
Southern Utah U (UT)
Southern Wesleyan U (SC)
Southwestern Adventist U (TX)
Spalding U (KY)
Spring Arbor U (MI)
Spring Hill Coll (AL)
State U of New York at Binghamton (NY)
State U of New York at New Paltz (NY)
State U of New York Coll at Old Westbury (NY)
State U of New York Empire State Coll (NY)
Stetson U (FL)
Suffolk U (MA)
Sul Ross State U (TX)
Tabor Coll (KS)
Texas A&M Intl U (TX)
Texas Wesleyan U (TX)
Thomas Edison State Coll (NJ)
Thomas U (GA)
Towson U (MD)
Trent U (ON, Canada)
Trine U (IN)
Troy U (AL)
Union Coll (KY)
Union Coll (NE)
Union Coll (NY)
United States Air Force Acad (CO)
Université du Québec en Outaouais (QC, Canada)
U at Buffalo, the State U of New York (NY)
The U of Akron (OH)
U of Alaska Southeast (AK)
U of Arkansas at Pine Bluff (AR)
U of Bridgeport (CT)
The U of British Columbia (BC, Canada)
U of California, Irvine (CA)
U of Central Florida (FL)
U of Dallas (TX)
U of Denver (CO)
The U of Findlay (OH)
U of Hawaii–West Oahu (HI)
U of Houston–Downtown (TX)
U of Houston–Victoria (TX)
U of La Verne (CA)
U of Lethbridge (AB, Canada)
U of Maine at Fort Kent (ME)

U of Maryland U Coll (MD)
U of Massachusetts Boston (MA)
U of Michigan (MI)
U of Michigan–Dearborn (MI)
U of Mobile (AL)
The U of Montana Western (MT)
U of Montevallo (AL)
U of Nevada, Las Vegas (NV)
U of North Dakota (ND)
U of Northern Colorado (CO)
U of North Texas (TX)
U of Oregon (OR)
U of Ottawa (ON, Canada)
U of Pennsylvania (PA)
U of Pittsburgh (PA)
U of Pittsburgh at Bradford (PA)
U of Pittsburgh at Greensburg (PA)
U of Pittsburgh at Johnstown (PA)
U of Puerto Rico at Humacao (PR)
U of Regina (SK, Canada)
U of Rio Grande (OH)
U of St. Thomas (MN)
U of South Carolina Beaufort (SC)
U of Southern Indiana (IN)
U of Southern Maine (ME)
U of South Florida (FL)
The U of Texas–Pan American (TX)
U of the Pacific (CA)
U of the Southwest (NM)
U of the Virgin Islands (VI)
U of Utah (UT)
U of Washington (WA)
U of West Florida (FL)
U of Wisconsin–Platteville (WI)
U of Wisconsin–River Falls (WI)
U of Wisconsin–Stevens Point (WI)
U of Wisconsin–Stout (WI)
U of Wisconsin–Superior (WI)
U of Wisconsin–Whitewater (WI)
U of Wyoming (WY)
Upper Iowa U (IA)
Valparaiso U (IN)
Vanderbilt U (TN)
Virginia Wesleyan Coll (VA)
Viterbo U (WI)
Washington State U (WA)
Washington U in St. Louis (MO)
Wayland Baptist U (TX)
Waynesburg U (PA)
Wayne State Coll (NE)
Webster U (MO)
Wesleyan Coll (GA)
Wesleyan U (CT)
Western Connecticut State U (CT)
Western Kentucky U (KY)
Western Oregon U (OR)
West Liberty U (WV)
Westminster Coll (UT)
Westmont Coll (CA)
Widener U (PA)
William Paterson U of New Jersey (NJ)
Wilmington Coll (OH)
Winona State U (MN)
Worcester Polytechnic Inst (MA)
Wright State U (OH)
Youngstown State U (OH)

SOCIAL SCIENCES RELATED

Abilene Christian U (TX)
Adelphi U (NY)
Anna Maria Coll (MA)
Bard Coll at Simon's Rock (MA)
Bennington Coll (VT)
Bloomsburg U of Pennsylvania (PA)
Boston U (MA)
California Polytechnic State U, San Luis Obispo (CA)
Central Michigan U (MI)
Cleveland State U (OH)
Coll of Staten Island of the City U of New York (NY)
Concordia U (QC, Canada)
Covenant Coll (GA)
Eastern Oregon U (OR)
Elizabethtown Coll (PA)
The Evergreen State Coll (WA)
Georgetown U (DC)
Gettysburg Coll (PA)
Hamline U (MN)
Indiana U Bloomington (IN)
Indiana U Kokomo (IN)
Indiana U of Pennsylvania (PA)
John Jay Coll of Criminal Justice of the City U of New York (NY)
Mary Baldwin Coll (VA)
Marywood U (PA)
Midwestern State U (TX)
Millersville U of Pennsylvania (PA)
Monmouth U (NJ)

Mount Holyoke Coll (MA)
New Mexico Highlands U (NM)
New York U (NY)
Northern Arizona U (AZ)
Northwest Missouri State U (MO)
Prescott Coll (AZ)
Purchase Coll, State U of New York (NY)
Rutgers, The State U of New Jersey, New Brunswick (NJ)
Saint Mary's Coll of California (CA)
Sarah Lawrence Coll (NY)
Simon Fraser U (BC, Canada)
Skidmore Coll (NY)
Towson U (MD)
United States Military Acad (NY)
The U of Akron (OH)
The U of Alabama at Birmingham (AL)
U of California, Berkeley (CA)
U of Denver (CO)
U of Illinois at Springfield (IL)
U of Massachusetts Amherst (MA)
U of New England (ME)
U of Pittsburgh (PA)
U of Regina (SK, Canada)
U of Rhode Island (RI)
U of Rochester (NY)
The U of Tennessee at Chattanooga (TN)
U of Waterloo (ON, Canada)
The U of Western Ontario (ON, Canada)
U of West Florida (FL)
U of Wisconsin–Green Bay (WI)
Washington U in St. Louis (MO)
Whitman Coll (WA)

SOCIAL SCIENCE TEACHER EDUCATION

Alma Coll (MI)
Arkansas State U (AR)
Auburn U (AL)
Averett U (VA)
Biola U (CA)
Blackburn Coll (IL)
Blue Mountain Coll (MS)
Bridgewater Coll (VA)
Brigham Young U (UT)
Buena Vista U (IA)
Campbellsville U (KY)
Carroll U (WI)
Concordia U Chicago (IL)
Corban U (OR)
Delta State U (MS)
Dominican Coll (NY)
Dordt Coll (IA)
Dowling Coll (NY)
Eastern Illinois U (IL)
Eastern Michigan U (MI)
Eastern Washington U (WA)
East Stroudsburg U of Pennsylvania (PA)
Elmira Coll (NY)
Emmanuel Coll (GA)
Emporia State U (KS)
Fayetteville State U (NC)
Ferris State U (MI)
Florida Ag and Mech U (FL)
Florida Atlantic U (FL)
Gardner-Webb U (NC)
Johnson State Coll (VT)
Judson Coll (AL)
Lewis-Clark State Coll (ID)
Liberty U (VA)
Lincoln U (MO)
Lindenwood U (MO)
Lindsey Wilson Coll (KY)
Lyndon State Coll (VT)
Manchester Coll (IN)
Mansfield U of Pennsylvania (PA)
Marquette U (WI)
Marywood U (PA)
Mayville State U (ND)
McKendree U (IL)
Medaille Coll (NY)
Michigan State U (MI)
Millikin U (IL)
Minot State U (ND)
Mississippi Valley State U (MS)
Montana State U (MT)
Montana State U Billings (MT)
Mount St. Mary's U (MD)
Nebraska Wesleyan U (NE)
Northern Michigan U (MI)
Northwest Missouri State U (MO)
Northwest Nazarene U (ID)
Pacific Union Coll (CA)
Rhode Island Coll (RI)
Rust Coll (MS)

Sacred Heart U (CT)
St. Ambrose U (IA)
Saint Mary's U of Minnesota (MN)
Seattle Pacific U (WA)
Shawnee State U (OH)
Simpson U (CA)
Southeastern U (FL)
State U of New York at New Paltz (NY)
State U of New York Coll at Oneonta (NY)
Tabor Coll (KS)
Union Coll (NE)
The U of Arizona (AZ)
U of Central Florida (FL)
U of Evansville (IN)
U of Maine at Farmington (ME)
U of Maine at Fort Kent (ME)
The U of Montana Western (MT)
U of Nebraska–Lincoln (NE)
U of Nevada, Reno (NV)
The U of North Carolina at Greensboro (NC)
U of North Dakota (ND)
U of Northern Iowa (IA)
U of Rio Grande (OH)
The U of South Dakota (SD)
U of South Florida (FL)
U of Utah (UT)
U of West Florida (FL)
U of Wisconsin–River Falls (WI)
U of Wisconsin–Superior (WI)
Upper Iowa U (IA)
Valparaiso U (IN)
Wartburg Coll (IA)
Washington U in St. Louis (MO)
Wayne State Coll (NE)
Weber State U (UT)
Western Michigan U (MI)
Western State Coll of Colorado (CO)
Westmont Coll (CA)
Winona State U (MN)
Youngstown State U (OH)

SOCIAL STUDIES TEACHER EDUCATION

Abilene Christian U (TX)
Adams State Coll (CO)
Alma Coll (MI)
Alvernia U (PA)
Alverno Coll (WI)
Anderson U (IN)
Aquinas Coll (MI)
Arkansas Tech U (AR)
Augustana Coll (SD)
Averett U (VA)
Baptist Bible Coll of Pennsylvania (PA)
The Baptist Coll of Florida (FL)
Bethany Coll (KS)
Bethel Coll (IN)
Bethel U (MN)
Bethune-Cookman U (FL)
Bluefield Coll (VA)
Bob Jones U (SC)
Boston U (MA)
Cabrini Coll (PA)
Calumet Coll of Saint Joseph (IN)
Calvin Coll (MI)
Cameron U (OK)
Campbellsville U (KY)
Capital U (OH)
Carroll U (WI)
Castleton State Coll (VT)
Cedarville U (OH)
Central Michigan U (MI)
City Coll of the City U of New York (NY)
Clarion U of Pennsylvania (PA)
Clearwater Christian Coll (FL)
The Coll of Saint Rose (NY)
Coll of the Ozarks (MO)
Colorado State U (CO)
Columbus State U (GA)
Concordia Coll (MN)
Concordia U, St. Paul (MN)
Corban U (OR)
Crown Coll (MN)
Dordt Coll (IA)
Dowling Coll (NY)
Duquesne U (PA)
Eastern Michigan U (MI)
Eastern Washington U (WA)
East Texas Baptist U (TX)
Elmira Coll (NY)
Erskine Coll (SC)
Ferris State U (MI)

Franklin Coll (IN)
Gannon U (PA)
Grace Coll (IN)
Grand Valley State U (MI)
Greensboro Coll (NC)
Harding U (AR)
Hardin-Simmons U (TX)
Hofstra U (NY)
Holy Family U (PA)
Hope Coll (MI)
Huntington U (IN)
Huston-Tillotson U (TX)
Illinois State U (IL)
Indiana State U (IN)
Indiana U Bloomington (IN)
Indiana U Northwest (IN)
Indiana–Purdue U Fort Wayne (IN)
Indiana U–Purdue U Indianapolis (IN)
Indiana U South Bend (IN)
Indiana U Southeast (IN)
Indiana Wesleyan U (IN)
Inter American U of Puerto Rico, Metropolitan Campus (PR)
Inter American U of Puerto Rico, San Germán Campus (PR)
Iowa Wesleyan Coll (IA)
Ithaca Coll (NY)
John Brown U (AR)
Johnson State Coll (VT)
Juniata Coll (PA)
Keene State Coll (NH)
Kennesaw State U (GA)
Kent State U (OH)
Kentucky Wesleyan Coll (KY)
Keuka Coll (NY)
Keystone Coll (PA)
Le Moyne Coll (NY)
Limestone Coll (SC)
Long Island U, Brooklyn Campus (NY)
Long Island U, C.W. Post Campus (NY)
Louisiana State U in Shreveport (LA)
Lubbock Christian U (TX)
Madonna U (MI)
Malone U (OH)
Manchester Coll (IN)
Manhattanville Coll (NY)
Mansfield U of Pennsylvania (PA)
Maranatha Baptist Bible Coll (WI)
Marian U (WI)
Marist Coll (NY)
Maryville Coll (TN)
Merrimack Coll (MA)
Messiah Coll (PA)
Metropolitan State U (MN)
Miami U (OH)
Michigan State U (MI)
MidAmerica Nazarene U (KS)
Midwestern State U (TX)
Millersville U of Pennsylvania (PA)
Minnesota State U Mankato (MN)
Minnesota State U Moorhead (MN)
Molloy Coll (NY)
Moravian Coll (PA)
Morris Coll (SC)
Mount Vernon Nazarene U (OH)
Nazareth Coll of Rochester (NY)
New York Inst of Technology (NY)
New York U (NY)
Niagara U (NY)
Nicholls State U (LA)
North Carolina State U (NC)
North Dakota State U (ND)
Northeastern State U (OK)
Northern Michigan U (MI)
North Greenville U (SC)
Northland Coll (WI)
Northwestern Coll (MN)
Northwestern State U of Louisiana (LA)
Northwest U (WA)
Nyack Coll (NY)
Ohio Wesleyan U (OH)
Oklahoma Christian U (OK)
Ouachita Baptist U (AR)
Pace U (NY)
Penn State Harrisburg (PA)
Philadelphia Biblical U (PA)
Pittsburg State U (KS)
Queens Coll of the City U of New York (NY)
Rhode Island Coll (RI)
Rivier Coll (NH)
Rocky Mountain Coll (MT)

St. Catherine U (MN)
St. Edward's U (TX)
Saint Francis U (PA)
St. John Fisher Coll (NY)
St. John's U (NY)
St. Joseph's Coll, Long Island Campus (NY)
St. Joseph's Coll, New York (NY)
St. Olaf Coll (MN)
St. Thomas U (FL)
Siena Heights U (MI)
Southeastern Louisiana U (LA)
Southeastern Oklahoma State U (OK)
Southeast Missouri State U (MO)
Southern Nazarene U (OK)
Southwestern Assemblies of God U (TX)
Spring Arbor U (MI)
State U of New York at New Paltz (NY)
State U of New York Coll at Old Westbury (NY)
State U of New York Coll at Potsdam (NY)
Syracuse U (NY)
Tabor Coll (KS)
Taylor U (IN)
Temple U (PA)
Texas A&M Intl U (TX)
Texas A&M U–Corpus Christi (TX)
Texas Christian U (TX)
Texas Lutheran U (TX)
Texas Wesleyan U (TX)
Trine U (IN)
The U of Akron (OH)
The U of Arizona (AZ)
U of Charleston (WV)
U of Evansville (IN)
U of Georgia (GA)
U of Indianapolis (IN)
The U of Iowa (IA)
U of Lethbridge (AB, Canada)
U of Louisiana at Lafayette (LA)
U of Louisiana at Monroe (LA)
U of Maine (ME)
U of Mary Hardin-Baylor (TX)
U of Maryland, Coll Park (MD)
U of Michigan–Dearborn (MI)
U of Michigan–Flint (MI)
U of Minnesota, Duluth (MN)
U of Minnesota, Twin Cities Campus (MN)
U of Mississippi (MS)
U of Missouri (MO)
U of Missouri–St. Louis (MO)
U of Nevada, Reno (NV)
The U of North Carolina at Greensboro (NC)
The U of North Carolina at Pembroke (NC)
U of Oklahoma (OK)
U of Pittsburgh at Johnstown (PA)
U of Regina (SK, Canada)
U of St. Francis (IL)
U of St. Thomas (MN)
The U of Tennessee at Chattanooga (TN)
U of the Cumberlands (KY)
The U of Toledo (OH)
U of Vermont (VT)
U of Wisconsin–Eau Claire (WI)
U of Wisconsin–La Crosse (WI)
U of Wisconsin–Madison (WI)
U of Wisconsin–River Falls (WI)
U of Wisconsin–Superior (WI)
Ursuline Coll (OH)
Utah State U (UT)
Virginia Intermont Coll (VA)
Virginia Wesleyan Coll (VA)
Viterbo U (WI)
Washington State U (WA)
Washington U in St. Louis (MO)
Wayland Baptist U (TX)
Wayne State U (MI)
Weber State U (UT)
Western Carolina U (NC)
Western Michigan U (MI)
Wheaton Coll (IL)
Wheeling Jesuit U (WV)
Widener U (PA)
Wingate U (NC)
Xavier U of Louisiana (LA)
York Coll of Pennsylvania (PA)
Youngstown State U (OH)

SOCIAL WORK

Abilene Christian U (TX)
Adams State Coll (CO)
Adelphi U (NY)
Alabama Ag and Mech U (AL)
Alabama State U (AL)
Albany State U (GA)
Albertus Magnus Coll (CT)
Alvernia U (PA)
Anderson U (IN)
Andrews U (MI)
Anna Maria Coll (MA)
Appalachian State U (NC)
Arizona State U (AZ)
Arkansas State U (AR)
Asbury U (KY)
Ashland U (OH)
Auburn U (AL)
Augsburg Coll (MN)
Austin Peay State U (TN)
Avila U (MO)
Azusa Pacific U (CA)
Ball State U (IN)
Barton Coll (NC)
Belmont U (TN)
Bemidji State U (MN)
Bethany Coll (KS)
Bethany Coll (WV)
Bethel U (MN)
Biola U (CA)
Bloomsburg U of Pennsylvania (PA)
Bluffton U (OH)
Boise State U (ID)
Bowie State U (MD)
Bowling Green State U (OH)
Briar Cliff U (IA)
Bridgewater State U (MA)
Buena Vista U (IA)
Cabrini Coll (PA)
California State U, Long Beach (CA)
California State U, Los Angeles (CA)
California State U, San Bernardino (CA)
Calvin Coll (MI)
Campbellsville U (KY)
Capital U (OH)
Carlow U (PA)
Castleton State Coll (VT)
The Catholic U of America (DC)
Cedar Crest Coll (PA)
Cedarville U (OH)
Centenary Coll (NJ)
Central Connecticut State U (CT)
Central Michigan U (MI)
Central State U (OH)
Champlain Coll (VT)
Chapman U (CA)
Chatham U (PA)
Christopher Newport U (VA)
Clark Atlanta U (GA)
Clarke U (IA)
Cleveland State U (OH)
Coker Coll (SC)
Coll of Mount St. Joseph (OH)
The Coll of Saint Rose (NY)
The Coll of St. Scholastica (MN)
Coll of Staten Island of the City U of New York (NY)
Coll of the Ozarks (MO)
Colorado State U (CO)
Columbia Coll (SC)
Concordia Coll (MN)
Concordia Coll–New York (NY)
Concordia U Chicago (IL)
Concordia U Wisconsin (WI)
Concord U (WV)
Coppin State U (MD)
Creighton U (NE)
Dalton State Coll (GA)
Defiance Coll (OH)
Delaware State U (DE)
Delta State U (MS)
Dickinson State U (ND)
Dominican Coll (NY)
Dordt Coll (IA)
East Central U (OK)
Eastern Michigan U (MI)
Eastern New Mexico U (NM)
Eastern Washington U (WA)
East Tennessee State U (TN)
Edinboro U of Pennsylvania (PA)
Elizabeth City State U (NC)
Elizabethtown Coll (PA)
Elmira Coll (NY)
Evangel U (MO)
Ferris State U (MI)
Ferrum Coll (VA)

Florida Ag and Mech U (FL)
Florida Atlantic U (FL)
Florida Gulf Coast U (FL)
Florida Intl U (FL)
Florida State U (FL)
Fontbonne U (MO)
Franklin Pierce U (NH)
Freed-Hardeman U (TN)
Gannon U (PA)
George Fox U (OR)
Georgian Court U (NJ)
Georgia State U (GA)
Gordon Coll (MA)
Governors State U (IL)
Graceland U (IA)
Grand Valley State U (MI)
Great Basin Coll (NV)
Greenville Coll (IL)
Harding U (AR)
Hardin-Simmons U (TX)
Hawai`i Pacific U (HI)
Holy Family U (PA)
Hood Coll (MD)
Hope Coll (MI)
Humboldt State U (CA)
Huntington U (IN)
Idaho State U (ID)
Illinois State U (IL)
Indiana State U (IN)
Indiana U Bloomington (IN)
Indiana U East (IN)
Indiana U Northwest (IN)
Indiana U–Purdue U Indianapolis (IN)
Indiana Wesleyan U (IN)
Inter American U of Puerto Rico, Metropolitan Campus (PR)
Jacksonville State U (AL)
James Madison U (VA)
Johnson C. Smith U (NC)
Judson Coll (AL)
Juniata Coll (PA)
Kansas State U (KS)
Kent State U (OH)
Kentucky State U (KY)
Keuka Coll (NY)
Kutztown U of Pennsylvania (PA)
Kuyper Coll (MI)
Lakehead U (ON, Canada)
Lamar U (TX)
La Salle U (PA)
Laurentian U (ON, Canada)
Lebanese American U (Lebanon)
Lehman Coll of the City U of New York (NY)
Lewis-Clark State Coll (ID)
Lewis U (IL)
Limestone Coll (SC)
Lincoln Memorial U (TN)
Lincoln U (MO)
Lindenwood U (MO)
Lipscomb U (TN)
Lock Haven U of Pennsylvania (PA)
Long Island U, Brooklyn Campus (NY)
Long Island U, C.W. Post Campus (NY)
Longwood U (VA)
Loras Coll (IA)
Louisiana Coll (LA)
Lourdes Coll (OH)
Loyola U Chicago (IL)
Lubbock Christian U (TX)
Luther Coll (IA)
MacMurray Coll (IL)
Madonna U (MI)
Malone U (OH)
Manchester Coll (IN)
Mansfield U of Pennsylvania (PA)
Marian U (WI)
Marist Coll (NY)
Marshall U (WV)
Mars Hill Coll (NC)
Mary Baldwin Coll (VA)
Marywood U (PA)
McDaniel Coll (MD)
McKendree U (IL)
Medgar Evers Coll of the City U of New York (NY)
Messiah Coll (PA)
Metropolitan State U (MN)
Miami U (OH)
Michigan State U (MI)
Middle Tennessee State U (TN)
Midwestern State U (TX)
Millersville U of Pennsylvania (PA)
Millikin U (IL)
Minnesota State U Mankato (MN)

Ferris State U (MI)
Fitchburg State U (MA)
Flagler Coll (FL)
Florida Ag and Mech U (FL)
Florida Atlantic U (FL)
Florida Gulf Coast U (FL)
Florida Intl U (FL)
Florida Southern Coll (FL)
Florida State U (FL)
Fontbonne U (MO)
Fort Lewis Coll (CO)
Framingham State U (MA)
Francis Marion U (SC)
Franklin & Marshall Coll (PA)
Franklin Coll (IN)
Franklin Pierce U (NH)
Friends U (KS)
Furman U (SC)
Gallaudet U (DC)
Gardner-Webb U (NC)
Geneva Coll (PA)
George Fox U (OR)
Georgetown Coll (KY)
Georgetown U (DC)
Georgia Coll & State U (GA)
Georgian Court U (NJ)
Georgia Southern U (GA)
Georgia State U (GA)
Gettysburg Coll (PA)
Gordon Coll (MA)
Goucher Coll (MD)
Grace Coll (IN)
Grand Canyon U (AZ)
Grand Valley State U (MI)
Greensboro Coll (NC)
Greenville Coll (IL)
Grinnell Coll (IA)
Grove City Coll (PA)
Guilford Coll (NC)
Hamilton Coll (NY)
Hamline U (MN)
Hampshire Coll (MA)
Hannibal-LaGrange U (MO)
Hanover Coll (IN)
Hardin-Simmons U (TX)
Hartwick Coll (NY)
Harvard U (MA)
Haverford Coll (PA)
Hawai'i Pacific U (HI)
Hendrix Coll (AR)
Hillsdale Coll (MI)
Hobart and William Smith Colls (NY)
Hofstra U (NY)
Hollins U (VA)
Holy Family U (PA)
Holy Names U (CA)
Hood Coll (MD)
Hope Coll (MI)
Houghton Coll (NY)
Humboldt State U (CA)
Hunter Coll of the City U of New York (NY)
Huntington U (IN)
Huston-Tillotson U (TX)
Idaho State U (ID)
Illinois Coll (IL)
Illinois State U (IL)
Illinois Wesleyan U (IL)
Immaculata U (PA)
Indiana U Bloomington (IN)
Indiana U East (IN)
Indiana U Kokomo (IN)
Indiana U Northwest (IN)
Indiana U of Pennsylvania (PA)
Indiana U–Purdue U Fort Wayne (IN)
Indiana U–Purdue U Indianapolis (IN)
Indiana U South Bend (IN)
Indiana U Southeast (IN)
Indiana Wesleyan U (IN)
Inter American U of Puerto Rico, Metropolitan Campus (PR)
Inter American U of Puerto Rico, San Germán Campus (PR)
Iowa State U of Science and Technology (IA)
Iowa Wesleyan Coll (IA)
Ithaca Coll (NY)
Jacksonville State U (AL)
James Madison U (VA)
Jarvis Christian Coll (TX)
John Carroll U (OH)
The Johns Hopkins U (MD)
Johnson State Coll (VT)
Juniata Coll (PA)
Kalamazoo Coll (MI)
Kansas State U (KS)

Kean U (NJ)
Keene State Coll (NH)
Kennesaw State U (GA)
Kent State U (OH)
Kentucky Wesleyan Coll (KY)
Kenyon Coll (OH)
Keuka Coll (NY)
King's Coll (PA)
The King's U Coll (AB, Canada)
Knox Coll (IL)
Kutztown U of Pennsylvania (PA)
Lafayette Coll (PA)
LaGrange Coll (GA)
Lake Forest Coll (IL)
Lakehead U (ON, Canada)
Lake Superior State U (MI)
Lamar U (TX)
Lane Coll (TN)
La Roche Coll (PA)
La Salle U (PA)
Lasell Coll (MA)
Laurentian U (ON, Canada)
Lebanon Valley Coll (PA)
Lee U (TN)
Lehigh U (PA)
Lehman Coll of the City U of New York (NY)
Le Moyne Coll (NY)
Lewis & Clark Coll (OR)
Lewis U (IL)
Lincoln U (MO)
Lindenwood U (MO)
Linfield Coll (OR)
Lock Haven U of Pennsylvania (PA)
Long Island U, Brooklyn Campus (NY)
Long Island U, C.W. Post Campus (NY)
Longwood U (VA)
Loras Coll (IA)
Louisiana Coll (LA)
Louisiana State U and Ag and Mech Coll (LA)
Louisiana State U in Shreveport (LA)
Lourdes Coll (OH)
Loyola Marymount U (CA)
Loyola U Chicago (IL)
Loyola U Maryland (MD)
Loyola U New Orleans (LA)
Luther Coll (IA)
Lycoming Coll (PA)
Lynchburg Coll (VA)
Macalester Coll (MN)
Madonna U (MI)
Manchester Coll (IN)
Manhattan Coll (NY)
Manhattanville Coll (NY)
Mansfield U of Pennsylvania (PA)
Marlboro Coll (VT)
Marquette U (WI)
Marshall U (WV)
Mars Hill Coll (NC)
Mary Baldwin Coll (VA)
Marymount U (VA)
Maryville Coll (TN)
Maryville U of Saint Louis (MO)
Massachusetts Coll of Liberal Arts (MA)
McDaniel Coll (MD)
McKendree U (IL)
McMurry U (TX)
Mercer U (GA)
Merrimack Coll (MA)
Mesa State Coll (CO)
Messiah Coll (PA)
Miami U (OH)
Michigan State U (MI)
MidAmerica Nazarene U (KS)
Middlebury Coll (VT)
Middle Tennessee State U (TN)
Midwestern State U (TX)
Millersville U of Pennsylvania (PA)
Milligan Coll (TN)
Millikin U (IL)
Millsaps Coll (MS)
Mills Coll (CA)
Minnesota State U Mankato (MN)
Minnesota State U Moorhead (MN)
Minot State U (ND)
Mississippi State U (MS)
Mississippi Valley State U (MS)
Missouri Southern State U (MO)
Missouri State U (MO)
Molloy Coll (NY)
Monmouth Coll (IL)
Monmouth U (NJ)
Montana State U (MT)

Montana State U Billings (MT)
Montclair State U (NJ)
Moravian Coll (PA)
Morehead State U (KY)
Morehouse Coll (GA)
Morris Coll (SC)
Mount Allison U (NB, Canada)
Mount Holyoke Coll (MA)
Mount Mercy U (IA)
Mount Saint Mary Coll (NY)
Mount St. Mary's Coll (CA)
Mount St. Mary's U (MD)
Mount Vernon Nazarene U (OH)
Muhlenberg Coll (PA)
Murray State U (KY)
National U (CA)
Nazareth Coll of Rochester (NY)
Nebraska Wesleyan U (NE)
Newberry Coll (SC)
New Coll of Florida (FL)
New England Coll (NH)
New Jersey City U (NJ)
Newman U (KS)
New Mexico State U (NM)
New York Inst of Technology (NY)
New York U (NY)
Niagara U (NY)
Nicholls State U (LA)
North Carolina Ag and Tech State U (NC)
North Carolina State U (NC)
North Central Coll (IL)
North Dakota State U (ND)
Northeastern Illinois U (IL)
Northeastern State U (OK)
Northeastern U (MA)
Northern Arizona U (AZ)
Northern Illinois U (IL)
Northern Kentucky U (KY)
Northern Michigan U (MI)
Northern State U (SD)
North Georgia Coll & State U (GA)
Northland Coll (WI)
Northwestern Coll (IA)
Northwestern Oklahoma State U (OK)
Northwest Missouri State U (MO)
Notre Dame de Namur U (CA)
Nova Southeastern U (FL)
Nyack Coll (NY)
Oberlin Coll (OH)
Oglethorpe U (GA)
The Ohio State U (OH)
Ohio U (OH)
Ohio Wesleyan U (OH)
Oklahoma City U (OK)
Oklahoma State U (OK)
Old Dominion U (VA)
Oregon State U (OR)
Ouachita Baptist U (AR)
Our Lady of the Lake U of San Antonio (TX)
Pacific Lutheran U (WA)
Pacific U (OR)
Paine Coll (GA)
Penn State Abington (PA)
Penn State Altoona (PA)
Penn State Beaver (PA)
Penn State Berks (PA)
Penn State Brandywine (PA)
Penn State DuBois (PA)
Penn State Erie, The Behrend Coll (PA)
Penn State Fayette, The Eberly Campus (PA)
Penn State Greater Allegheny (PA)
Penn State Harrisburg (PA)
Penn State Hazleton (PA)
Penn State Lehigh Valley (PA)
Penn State Mont Alto (PA)
Penn State New Kensington (PA)
Penn State Schuylkill (PA)
Penn State Shenango (PA)
Penn State U Park (PA)
Penn State Wilkes-Barre (PA)
Penn State Worthington Scranton (PA)
Penn State York (PA)
Pepperdine U, Malibu (CA)
Piedmont Coll (GA)
Pikeville Coll (KY)
Pittsburg State U (KS)
Pitzer Coll (CA)
Pomona Coll (CA)
Portland State U (OR)
Prairie View A&M U (TX)
Presbyterian Coll (SC)
Prescott Coll (AZ)

Princeton U (NJ)
Principia Coll (IL)
Providence Coll (RI)
Purchase Coll, State U of New York (NY)
Purdue U (IN)
Purdue U Calumet (IN)
Queens Coll of the City U of New York (NY)
Quinnipiac U (CT)
Radford U (VA)
Ramapo Coll of New Jersey (NJ)
Randolph Coll (VA)
Randolph-Macon Coll (VA)
Reed Coll (OR)
Regis Coll (MA)
Regis U (CO)
Reinhardt U (GA)
Rhode Island Coll (RI)
Rhodes Coll (TN)
Rice U (TX)
The Richard Stockton Coll of New Jersey (NJ)
Rider U (NJ)
Ripon Coll (WI)
Rivier Coll (NH)
Roanoke Coll (VA)
Rockford Coll (IL)
Rocky Mountain Coll (MT)
Rollins Coll (FL)
Roosevelt U (IL)
Rosemont Coll (PA)
Rowan U (NJ)
Russell Sage Coll (NY)
Rust Coll (MS)
Rutgers, The State U of New Jersey, Camden (NJ)
Rutgers, The State U of New Jersey, Newark (NJ)
Rutgers, The State U of New Jersey, New Brunswick (NJ)
Sacred Heart U (CT)
Saginaw Valley State U (MI)
St. Ambrose U (IA)
Saint Anselm Coll (NH)
St. Bonaventure U (NY)
St. Catherine U (MN)
St. Edward's U (TX)
Saint Francis U (PA)
St. Francis Xavier U (NS, Canada)
St. John Fisher Coll (NY)
Saint John's U (MN)
St. John's U (NY)
Saint Joseph's Coll (IN)
Saint Joseph's Coll of Maine (ME)
Saint Joseph's U (PA)
St. Lawrence U (NY)
Saint Leo U (FL)
Saint Louis U (MO)
Saint Mary's Coll (IN)
Saint Mary's Coll of California (CA)
St. Mary's Coll of Maryland (MD)
Saint Mary's U of Minnesota (MN)
Saint Michael's Coll (VT)
St. Norbert Coll (WI)
St. Olaf Coll (MN)
St. Thomas U (NB, Canada)
Saint Xavier U (IL)
Salem State U (MA)
Salisbury U (MD)
Salve Regina U (RI)
Samford U (AL)
Sam Houston State U (TX)
San Diego State U (CA)
San Francisco State U (CA)
San Jose State U (CA)
Santa Clara U (CA)
Sarah Lawrence Coll (NY)
Savannah State U (GA)
Scripps Coll (CA)
Seattle Pacific U (WA)
Seton Hill U (PA)
Shawnee State U (OH)
Shenandoah U (VA)
Shepherd U (WV)
Shippensburg U of Pennsylvania (PA)
Shorter U (GA)
Siena Coll (NY)
Simmons Coll (MA)
Simon Fraser U (BC, Canada)
Simpson Coll (IA)
Skidmore Coll (NY)
Smith Coll (MA)
Sonoma State U (CA)
South Dakota State U (SD)
Southeastern Louisiana U (LA)

Southeastern Oklahoma State U (OK)
Southern Arkansas U–Magnolia (AR)
Southern Connecticut State U (CT)
Southern Illinois U Carbondale (IL)
Southern Illinois U Edwardsville (IL)
Southern Methodist U (TX)
Southern Nazarene U (OK)
Southern Oregon U (OR)
Southern Utah U (UT)
Spelman Coll (GA)
Spring Arbor U (MI)
Springfield Coll (MA)
Stanford U (CA)
State U of New York at Binghamton (NY)
State U of New York at Fredonia (NY)
State U of New York at New Paltz (NY)
State U of New York at Oswego (NY)
State U of New York at Plattsburgh (NY)
State U of New York Coll at Geneseo (NY)
State U of New York Coll at Old Westbury (NY)
State U of New York Coll at Oneonta (NY)
State U of New York Coll at Potsdam (NY)
Stephen F. Austin State U (TX)
Stetson U (FL)
Stonehill Coll (MA)
Stony Brook U, State U of New York (NY)
Suffolk U (MA)
Susquehanna U (PA)
Sweet Briar Coll (VA)
Syracuse U (NY)
Tabor Coll (KS)
Talladega Coll (AL)
Tarleton State U (TX)
Taylor U (IN)
Temple U (PA)
Tennessee Technological U (TN)
Texas A&M Intl U (TX)
Texas A&M U (TX)
Texas A&M U–Corpus Christi (TX)
Texas A&M U–Kingsville (TX)
Texas Christian U (TX)
Texas Lutheran U (TX)
Texas Southern U (TX)
Texas State U–San Marcos (TX)
Texas Tech U (TX)
Texas Wesleyan U (TX)
Texas Woman's U (TX)
Thiel Coll (PA)
Thomas Edison State Coll (NJ)
Thomas More Coll (KY)
Thomas U (GA)
Transylvania U (KY)
Trent U (ON, Canada)
Trevecca Nazarene U (TN)
Trinity Coll (CT)
Trinity U (TX)
Troy U (AL)
Truman State U (MO)
Tufts U (MA)
Tulane U (LA)
Tuskegee U (AL)
Union Coll (NY)
Union U (TN)
United States Military Acad (NY)
Université du Québec en Outaouais (QC, Canada)
U at Buffalo, the State U of New York (NY)
The U of Akron (OH)
The U of Alabama (AL)
The U of Alabama at Birmingham (AL)
The U of Alabama in Huntsville (AL)
U of Alaska Fairbanks (AK)
The U of Arizona (AZ)
U of Arkansas (AR)
U of Arkansas at Pine Bluff (AR)
The U of British Columbia (BC, Canada)
The U of British Columbia–Okanagan (BC, Canada)
U of California, Berkeley (CA)
U of California, Davis (CA)
U of California, Irvine (CA)
U of California, Los Angeles (CA)
U of California, Merced (CA)

U of California, Santa Barbara (CA)
U of California, Santa Cruz (CA)
U of Central Florida (FL)
U of Central Missouri (MO)
U of Cincinnati (OH)
U of Colorado at Colorado Springs (CO)
U of Colorado Boulder (CO)
U of Colorado Denver (CO)
U of Dayton (OH)
U of Delaware (DE)
U of Denver (CO)
U of Dubuque (IA)
U of Evansville (IN)
The U of Findlay (OH)
U of Florida (FL)
U of Georgia (GA)
U of Guelph (ON, Canada)
U of Hartford (CT)
U of Hawaii at Hilo (HI)
U of Hawaii at Manoa (HI)
U of Hawaii–West Oahu (HI)
U of Houston (TX)
U of Houston–Clear Lake (TX)
U of Houston–Downtown (TX)
U of Idaho (ID)
U of Illinois at Chicago (IL)
U of Indianapolis (IN)
The U of Iowa (IA)
The U of Kansas (KS)
U of La Verne (CA)
U of Lethbridge (AB, Canada)
U of Louisiana at Lafayette (LA)
U of Louisiana at Monroe (LA)
U of Louisville (KY)
U of Maine (ME)
U of Maine at Farmington (ME)
U of Maine at Presque Isle (ME)
U of Manitoba (MB, Canada)
U of Mary Hardin-Baylor (TX)
U of Maryland, Baltimore County (MD)
U of Maryland, Coll Park (MD)
U of Mary Washington (VA)
U of Massachusetts Amherst (MA)
U of Massachusetts Boston (MA)
U of Massachusetts Dartmouth (MA)
U of Massachusetts Lowell (MA)
U of Memphis (TN)
U of Miami (FL)
U of Michigan (MI)
U of Michigan–Dearborn (MI)
U of Michigan–Flint (MI)
U of Minnesota, Duluth (MN)
U of Minnesota, Twin Cities Campus (MN)
U of Mississippi (MS)
U of Missouri (MO)
U of Missouri–St. Louis (MO)
U of Mobile (AL)
U of Montevallo (AL)
U of Mount Union (OH)
U of Nebraska at Omaha (NE)
U of Nebraska–Lincoln (NE)
U of Nevada, Las Vegas (NV)
U of Nevada, Reno (NV)
U of New Brunswick Fredericton (NB, Canada)
U of New Brunswick Saint John (NB, Canada)
U of New England (ME)
U of New Hampshire (NH)
The U of North Carolina at Asheville (NC)
The U of North Carolina at Chapel Hill (NC)
The U of North Carolina at Greensboro (NC)
The U of North Carolina at Pembroke (NC)
The U of North Carolina Wilmington (NC)
U of North Dakota (ND)
U of Northern Colorado (CO)
U of Northern Iowa (IA)
U of North Florida (FL)
U of North Texas (TX)
U of Notre Dame (IN)
U of Oklahoma (OK)
U of Oregon (OR)
U of Ottawa (ON, Canada)
U of Pennsylvania (PA)
U of Pittsburgh (PA)
U of Pittsburgh at Bradford (PA)
U of Pittsburgh at Johnstown (PA)
U of Portland (OR)
U of Puget Sound (WA)
U of Redlands (CA)
U of Regina (SK, Canada)
U of Rhode Island (RI)

U of Richmond (VA)
U of Rio Grande (OH)
U of St. Thomas (MN)
U of San Diego (CA)
U of San Francisco (CA)
U of Saskatchewan (SK, Canada)
U of Science and Arts of Oklahoma (OK)
The U of Scranton (PA)
U of Sioux Falls (SD)
U of South Alabama (AL)
U of South Carolina (SC)
U of South Carolina Aiken (SC)
U of South Carolina Beaufort (SC)
U of South Carolina Upstate (SC)
The U of South Dakota (SD)
U of Southern California (CA)
U of Southern Indiana (IN)
U of Southern Maine (ME)
U of Southern Mississippi (MS)
U of South Florida (FL)
The U of Tampa (FL)
The U of Tennessee (TN)
The U of Tennessee at Martin (TN)
The U of Texas at Arlington (TX)
The U of Texas at Austin (TX)
The U of Texas at Dallas (TX)
The U of Texas at San Antonio (TX)
The U of Texas at Tyler (TX)
The U of Texas of the Permian Basin (TX)
The U of Texas–Pan American (TX)
U of the District of Columbia (DC)
U of the Incarnate Word (TX)
U of the Ozarks (AR)
U of the Pacific (CA)
The U of Toledo (OH)
U of Tulsa (OK)
U of Utah (UT)
U of Vermont (VT)
U of Virginia (VA)
U of Washington (WA)
U of Waterloo (ON, Canada)
The U of Western Ontario (ON, Canada)
U of West Florida (FL)
U of West Georgia (GA)
U of Wisconsin–Eau Claire (WI)
U of Wisconsin–La Crosse (WI)
U of Wisconsin–Madison (WI)
U of Wisconsin–Parkside (WI)
U of Wisconsin–River Falls (WI)
U of Wisconsin–Stevens Point (WI)
U of Wisconsin–Superior (WI)
U of Wisconsin–Whitewater (WI)
U of Wyoming (WY)
Upper Iowa U (IA)
Ursuline Coll (OH)
Utah State U (UT)
Valdosta State U (GA)
Valparaiso U (IN)
Vanderbilt U (TN)
Vassar Coll (NY)
Villanova U (PA)
Virginia Commonwealth U (VA)
Virginia Polytechnic Inst and State U (VA)
Virginia State U (VA)
Virginia Wesleyan Coll (VA)
Viterbo U (WI)
Wagner Coll (NY)
Wake Forest U (NC)
Walla Walla U (WA)
Walsh U (OH)
Wartburg Coll (IA)
Washburn U (KS)
Washington & Jefferson Coll (PA)
Washington and Lee U (VA)
Washington Coll (MD)
Washington State U (WA)
Wayland Baptist U (TX)
Waynesburg U (PA)
Wayne State Coll (NE)
Wayne State U (MI)
Weber State U (UT)
Webster U (MO)
Wellesley Coll (MA)
Wells Coll (NY)
Wesleyan U (CT)
West Chester U of Pennsylvania (PA)
Western Carolina U (NC)
Western Connecticut State U (CT)
Western Illinois U (IL)
Western Kentucky U (KY)
Western Michigan U (MI)
Western New England U (MA)
Western Oregon U (OR)
Western State Coll of Colorado (CO)
Westfield State U (MA)

West Liberty U (WV)
Westminster Coll (MO)
Westminster Coll (UT)
Westmont Coll (CA)
West Virginia U (WV)
Wheaton Coll (IL)
Wheaton Coll (MA)
Whitman Coll (WA)
Wichita State U (KS)
Widener U (PA)
Wilfrid Laurier U (ON, Canada)
Wilkes U (PA)
Willamette U (OR)
William Paterson U of New Jersey (NJ)
Williams Coll (MA)
Wingate U (NC)
Winona State U (MN)
Winthrop U (SC)
Wittenberg U (OH)
Wofford Coll (SC)
Worcester State U (MA)
Wright State U (OH)
Xavier U (OH)
Xavier U of Louisiana (LA)
Yale U (CT)
York Coll of Pennsylvania (PA)
York Coll of the City U of New York (NY)
Youngstown State U (OH)

SOCIOLOGY AND ANTHROPOLOGY
Alma Coll (MI)
Pace U (NY)
Swarthmore Coll (PA)
Transylvania U (KY)

SOIL CHEMISTRY AND PHYSICS
The U of Tennessee (TN)

SOIL SCIENCE AND AGRONOMY
California Polytechnic State U, San Luis Obispo (CA)
Colorado State U (CO)
Michigan State U (MI)
New Mexico State U (NM)
North Dakota State U (ND)
Oklahoma State U (OK)
Penn State Abington (PA)
Penn State Altoona (PA)
Penn State Beaver (PA)
Penn State Berks (PA)
Penn State Brandywine (PA)
Penn State DuBois (PA)
Penn State Erie, The Behrend Coll (PA)
Penn State Fayette, The Eberly Campus (PA)
Penn State Greater Allegheny (PA)
Penn State Hazleton (PA)
Penn State Lehigh Valley (PA)
Penn State Mont Alto (PA)
Penn State New Kensington (PA)
Penn State Schuylkill (PA)
Penn State Shenango (PA)
Penn State Wilkes-Barre (PA)
Penn State Worthington Scranton (PA)
Penn State York (PA)
The U of British Columbia (BC, Canada)
U of California, Davis (CA)
U of Delaware (DE)
U of Florida (FL)
U of Maine (ME)
U of Minnesota, Twin Cities Campus (MN)
U of Nebraska–Lincoln (NE)
U of New Hampshire (NH)
U of Saskatchewan (SK, Canada)
The U of Tennessee at Martin (TN)
U of Wisconsin–Madison (WI)
U of Wisconsin–River Falls (WI)
U of Wisconsin–Stevens Point (WI)
Utah State U (UT)
Washington State U (WA)

SOIL SCIENCES RELATED
Brigham Young U (UT)
North Carolina State U (NC)
U of Hawaii at Manoa (HI)

SOLAR ENERGY TECHNOLOGY
Appalachian State U (NC)

SOUTH ASIAN LANGUAGES
The U of British Columbia (BC, Canada)

U of Minnesota, Twin Cities Campus (MN)
Yale U (CT)

SPANISH
Abilene Christian U (TX)
Adams State Coll (CO)
Adelphi U (NY)
Albany State U (GA)
Albertus Magnus Coll (CT)
Albion Coll (MI)
Albright Coll (PA)
Alfred U (NY)
Allegheny Coll (PA)
Alma Coll (MI)
American U (DC)
Amherst Coll (MA)
Anderson U (IN)
Anderson U (SC)
Andrews U (MI)
Angelo State U (TX)
Anna Maria Coll (MA)
Appalachian State U (NC)
Aquinas Coll (MI)
Arcadia U (PA)
Arizona State U (AZ)
Armstrong Atlantic State U (GA)
Asbury U (KY)
Ashland U (OH)
Assumption Coll (MA)
Auburn U (AL)
Augsburg Coll (MN)
Augustana Coll (IL)
Augustana Coll (SD)
Austin Coll (TX)
Austin Peay State U (TN)
Azusa Pacific U (CA)
Baker U (KS)
Baldwin-Wallace Coll (OH)
Ball State U (IN)
Bard Coll (NY)
Bard Coll at Simon's Rock (MA)
Barnard Coll (NY)
Barry U (FL)
Barton Coll (NC)
Bates Coll (ME)
Bellarmine U (KY)
Belmont U (TN)
Beloit Coll (WI)
Bemidji State U (MN)
Benedictine Coll (KS)
Benedictine U (IL)
Bennington Coll (VT)
Berea Coll (KY)
Berry Coll (GA)
Bethany Coll (WV)
Bethel Coll (IN)
Bethel U (MN)
Biola U (CA)
Birmingham-Southern Coll (AL)
Blackburn Coll (IL)
Bloomsburg U of Pennsylvania (PA)
Blue Mountain Coll (MS)
Bluffton U (OH)
Bob Jones U (SC)
Boise State U (ID)
Boston Coll (MA)
Boston U (MA)
Bowdoin Coll (ME)
Bowling Green State U (OH)
Brandeis U (MA)
Briar Cliff U (IA)
Bridgewater Coll (VA)
Bridgewater State U (MA)
Brock U (ON, Canada)
Brown U (RI)
Bryan Coll (TN)
Bryn Mawr Coll (PA)
Bucknell U (PA)
Buena Vista U (IA)
Butler U (IN)
Cabrini Coll (PA)
California Baptist U (CA)
California State Polytechnic U, Pomona (CA)
California State U, Bakersfield (CA)
California State U, Dominguez Hills (CA)
California State U, Fullerton (CA)
California State U, Long Beach (CA)
California State U, Los Angeles (CA)
California State U, San Bernardino (CA)
California State U, San Marcos (CA)
California State U, Stanislaus (CA)
Calvin Coll (MI)
Canisius Coll (NY)
Capital U (OH)
Carleton Coll (MN)

Carnegie Mellon U (PA)
Carroll U (WI)
Carson-Newman Coll (TN)
Case Western Reserve U (OH)
Castleton State Coll (VT)
The Catholic U of America (DC)
Cedarville U (OH)
Central Coll (IA)
Central Connecticut State U (CT)
Central Michigan U (MI)
Centre Coll (KY)
Chapman U (CA)
Chatham U (PA)
Chestnut Hill Coll (PA)
Christopher Newport U (VA)
City Coll of the City U of New York (NY)
Claremont McKenna Coll (CA)
Clarion U of Pennsylvania (PA)
Clark Atlanta U (GA)
Clarke U (IA)
Clark U (MA)
Cleveland State U (OH)
Coastal Carolina U (SC)
Colby Coll (ME)
Colgate U (NY)
Coll of Charleston (SC)
The Coll of New Jersey (NJ)
Coll of Saint Benedict (MN)
Coll of Saint Elizabeth (NJ)
The Coll of Saint Rose (NY)
The Coll of St. Scholastica (MN)
Coll of Staten Island of the City U of New York (NY)
Coll of the Holy Cross (MA)
Coll of the Ozarks (MO)
The Coll of Wooster (OH)
The Colorado Coll (CO)
Colorado State U (CO)
Columbia Coll (SC)
Columbia U, School of General Studies (NY)
Columbus State U (GA)
Concordia Coll (MN)
Concordia U (QC, Canada)
Concordia U Chicago (IL)
Concordia U Wisconsin (WI)
Connecticut Coll (CT)
Cornell Coll (IA)
Cornell U (NY)
Creighton U (NE)
Dartmouth Coll (NH)
Davidson Coll (NC)
Delaware State U (DE)
Denison U (OH)
DePaul U (IL)
DePauw U (IN)
DeSales U (PA)
Dickinson Coll (PA)
Dickinson State U (ND)
Doane Coll (NE)
Dominican Coll (NY)
Dominican U (IL)
Dordt Coll (IA)
Drew U (NJ)
Drury U (MO)
Duquesne U (PA)
Earlham Coll (IN)
East Central U (OK)
Eastern Michigan U (MI)
Eastern New Mexico U (NM)
Eastern Washington U (WA)
East Stroudsburg U of Pennsylvania (PA)
East Texas Baptist U (TX)
Eckerd Coll (FL)
Edgewood Coll (WI)
Edinboro U of Pennsylvania (PA)
Elizabethtown Coll (PA)
Elmhurst Coll (IL)
Elmira Coll (NY)
Elon U (NC)
Emmanuel Coll (MA)
Emory & Henry Coll (VA)
Endicott Coll (MA)
Erskine Coll (SC)
Evangel U (MO)
Fairfield U (CT)
Fairleigh Dickinson U, Coll at Florham (NJ)
Fairleigh Dickinson U, Metropolitan Campus (NJ)
Fayetteville State U (NC)
Ferrum Coll (VA)
Flagler Coll (FL)
Florida Ag and Mech U (FL)
Florida Atlantic U (FL)
Florida Gulf Coast U (FL)
Florida Intl U (FL)
Florida Southern Coll (FL)

Fort Lewis Coll (CO)
Francis Marion U (SC)
Franklin & Marshall Coll (PA)
Franklin Coll (IN)
Friends U (KS)
Furman U (SC)
Gallaudet U (DC)
Gardner-Webb U (NC)
George Fox U (OR)
Georgetown Coll (KY)
Georgetown U (DC)
Georgia Coll & State U (GA)
Georgian Court U (NJ)
Georgia State U (GA)
Gettysburg Coll (PA)
Gordon Coll (MA)
Goucher Coll (MD)
Grace Coll (IN)
Grand Valley State U (MI)
Greensboro Coll (NC)
Greenville Coll (IL)
Grinnell Coll (IA)
Grove City Coll (PA)
Guilford Coll (NC)
Hamline U (MN)
Hampden-Sydney Coll (VA)
Hanover Coll (IN)
Harding U (AR)
Hardin-Simmons U (TX)
Hartwick Coll (NY)
Haverford Coll (PA)
Hendrix Coll (AR)
Hillsdale Coll (MI)
Hobart and William Smith Colls (NY)
Hofstra U (NY)
Hollins U (VA)
Holy Family U (PA)
Holy Names U (CA)
Hood Coll (MD)
Hope Coll (MI)
Houghton Coll (NY)
Humboldt State U (CA)
Hunter Coll of the City U of New
   York (NY)
Idaho State U (ID)
Illinois Coll (IL)
Illinois State U (IL)
Illinois Wesleyan U (IL)
Immaculata U (PA)
Indiana U Bloomington (IN)
Indiana U Northwest (IN)
Indiana U of Pennsylvania (PA)
Indiana U–Purdue U Fort Wayne
   (IN)
Indiana U–Purdue U Indianapolis
   (IN)
Indiana U South Bend (IN)
Indiana U Southeast (IN)
Indiana Wesleyan U (IN)
Inter American U of Puerto Rico,
   Metropolitan Campus (PR)
Inter American U of Puerto Rico,
   San Germán Campus (PR)
Iowa State U of Science and
   Technology (IA)
Ithaca Coll (NY)
Jacksonville State U (AL)
Jamestown Coll (ND)
John Brown U (AR)
John Carroll U (OH)
The Johns Hopkins U (MD)
Johnson C. Smith U (NC)
Judson Coll (AL)
Juniata Coll (PA)
Kalamazoo Coll (MI)
Kean U (NJ)
Keene State Coll (NH)
Kent State U (OH)
Kentucky State U (KY)
Kentucky Wesleyan Coll (KY)
Kenyon Coll (OH)
King Coll (TN)
King's Coll (PA)
Knox Coll (IL)
Kutztown U of Pennsylvania (PA)
Lafayette Coll (PA)
LaGrange Coll (GA)
Lake Forest Coll (IL)
Lamar U (TX)
La Roche Coll (PA)
La Salle U (PA)
Laurentian U (ON, Canada)
Lawrence U (WI)
Lebanon Valley Coll (PA)
Lee U (TN)
Lehigh U (PA)
Lehman Coll of the City U of New
   York (NY)

Le Moyne Coll (NY)
Lewis & Clark Coll (OR)
Liberty U (VA)
Lincoln U (MO)
Lindenwood U (MO)
Linfield Coll (OR)
Lipscomb U (TN)
Lock Haven U of Pennsylvania (PA)
Long Island U, C.W. Post Campus
   (NY)
Longwood U (VA)
Loras Coll (IA)
Louisiana Coll (LA)
Louisiana State U and Ag and Mech
   Coll (LA)
Louisiana State U in Shreveport
   (LA)
Loyola Marymount U (CA)
Loyola U Chicago (IL)
Loyola U Maryland (MD)
Loyola U New Orleans (LA)
Luther Coll (IA)
Lycoming Coll (PA)
Lynchburg Coll (VA)
Lyon Coll (AR)
Macalester Coll (MN)
MacMurray Coll (IL)
Madonna U (MI)
Malone U (OH)
Manchester Coll (IN)
Manhattan Coll (NY)
Manhattanville Coll (NY)
Mansfield U of Pennsylvania (PA)
Marian U (WI)
Marietta Coll (OH)
Marist Coll (NY)
Marlboro Coll (VT)
Marquette U (WI)
Mars Hill Coll (NC)
Mary Baldwin Coll (VA)
Maryville Coll (TN)
Marywood U (PA)
McDaniel Coll (MD)
McMurry U (TX)
Mercer U (GA)
Merrimack Coll (MA)
Mesa State Coll (CO)
Messiah Coll (PA)
Miami U (OH)
Michigan State U (MI)
MidAmerica Nazarene U (KS)
Middlebury Coll (VT)
Midwestern State U (TX)
Millersville U of Pennsylvania (PA)
Millikin U (IL)
Millsaps Coll (MS)
Mills Coll (CA)
Minnesota State U Mankato (MN)
Minnesota State U Moorhead (MN)
Minot State U (ND)
Mississippi U for Women (MS)
Missouri Southern State U (MO)
Missouri State U (MO)
Molloy Coll (NY)
Monmouth Coll (IL)
Montana State U Billings (MT)
Montclair State U (NJ)
Moravian Coll (PA)
Morehead State U (KY)
Morehouse Coll (GA)
Morningside Coll (IA)
Mount Allison U (NB, Canada)
Mount Holyoke Coll (MA)
Mount Saint Mary Coll (NY)
Mount St. Mary's Coll (CA)
Mount St. Mary's U (MD)
Mount Vernon Nazarene U (OH)
Muhlenberg Coll (PA)
Murray State U (KY)
Nazareth Coll of Rochester (NY)
Nebraska Wesleyan U (NE)
New Coll of Florida (FL)
New Jersey City U (NJ)
New Mexico Highlands U (NM)
New York U (NY)
Niagara U (NY)
North Carolina State U (NC)
North Central Coll (IL)
North Dakota State U (ND)
Northeastern Illinois U (IL)
Northeastern State U (OK)
Northeastern U (MA)
Northern Arizona U (AZ)
Northern Illinois U (IL)
Northern Kentucky U (KY)
Northern Michigan U (MI)
Northern State U (SD)
North Georgia Coll & State U (GA)

Northwestern Coll (IA)
Northwestern Coll (MN)
Northwestern Oklahoma State U
   (OK)
Northwest Missouri State U (MO)
Northwest Nazarene U (ID)
Oberlin Coll (OH)
Oglethorpe U (GA)
The Ohio State U (OH)
Ohio U (OH)
Ohio Wesleyan U (OH)
Oklahoma Christian U (OK)
Oklahoma City U (OK)
Oklahoma State U (OK)
Oregon State U (OR)
Ouachita Baptist U (AR)
Our Lady of the Lake U of San
   Antonio (TX)
Pace U (NY)
Pacific Lutheran U (WA)
Pacific Union Coll (CA)
Pacific U (OR)
Penn State Abington (PA)
Penn State Altoona (PA)
Penn State Beaver (PA)
Penn State Berks (PA)
Penn State Brandywine (PA)
Penn State DuBois (PA)
Penn State Erie, The Behrend Coll
   (PA)
Penn State Fayette, The Eberly
   Campus (PA)
Penn State Greater Allegheny (PA)
Penn State Hazleton (PA)
Penn State Lehigh Valley (PA)
Penn State Mont Alto (PA)
Penn State New Kensington (PA)
Penn State Schuylkill (PA)
Penn State Shenango (PA)
Penn State U Park (PA)
Penn State Wilkes-Barre (PA)
Penn State Worthington Scranton
   (PA)
Penn State York (PA)
Pepperdine U, Malibu (CA)
Piedmont Coll (GA)
Pittsburg State U (KS)
Pitzer Coll (CA)
Pomona Coll (CA)
Portland State U (OR)
Prairie View A&M U (TX)
Presbyterian Coll (SC)
Prescott Coll (AZ)
Princeton U (NJ)
Principia Coll (IL)
Providence Coll (RI)
Purchase Coll, State U of New York
   (NY)
Queens Coll of the City U of New
   York (NY)
Quinnipiac U (CT)
Ramapo Coll of New Jersey (NJ)
Randolph Coll (VA)
Randolph-Macon Coll (VA)
Reed Coll (OR)
Regis Coll (MA)
Regis U (CO)
Rhode Island Coll (RI)
Rhodes Coll (TN)
Rice U (TX)
Rider U (NJ)
Ripon Coll (WI)
Rivier Coll (NH)
Roanoke Coll (VA)
Rockford Coll (IL)
Rockhurst U (MO)
Rollins Coll (FL)
Rosemont Coll (PA)
Rowan U (NJ)
Russell Sage Coll (NY)
Rutgers, The State U of New
   Jersey, Camden (NJ)
Rutgers, The State U of New
   Jersey, Newark (NJ)
Rutgers, The State U of New
   Jersey, New Brunswick (NJ)
Sacred Heart U (CT)
Saginaw Valley State U (MI)
St. Ambrose U (IA)
Saint Anselm Coll (NH)
St. Bonaventure U (NY)
St. Catherine U (MN)
St. Edward's U (TX)
Saint Francis U (PA)
St. John Fisher Coll (NY)
Saint John's U (MN)
St. John's U (NY)
Saint Joseph Coll (CT)

St. Joseph's Coll, Long Island
   Campus (NY)
St. Joseph's Coll, New York (NY)
Saint Joseph's U (PA)
St. Lawrence U (NY)
Saint Louis U (MO)
Saint Mary's Coll (IN)
Saint Mary's Coll of California (CA)
Saint Mary's U of Minnesota (MN)
Saint Michael's Coll (VT)
St. Norbert Coll (WI)
St. Olaf Coll (MN)
St. Thomas Aquinas Coll (NY)
St. Thomas U (NB, Canada)
Saint Xavier U (IL)
Salem State U (MA)
Salisbury U (MD)
Salve Regina U (RI)
Samford U (AL)
Sam Houston State U (TX)
San Diego State U (CA)
San Francisco State U (CA)
San Jose State U (CA)
Santa Clara U (CA)
Sarah Lawrence Coll (NY)
Scripps Coll (CA)
Seattle Pacific U (WA)
Seton Hill U (PA)
Sewanee: The U of the South (TN)
Shenandoah U (VA)
Shepherd U (WV)
Shippensburg U of Pennsylvania
   (PA)
Shorter U (GA)
Siena Coll (NY)
Siena Heights U (MI)
Simmons Coll (MA)
Simpson Coll (IA)
Skidmore Coll (NY)
Slippery Rock U of Pennsylvania
   (PA)
Smith Coll (MA)
Sonoma State U (CA)
South Dakota State U (SD)
Southeastern Louisiana U (LA)
Southeastern Oklahoma State U
   (OK)
Southeast Missouri State U (MO)
Southern Adventist U (TN)
Southern Arkansas U–Magnolia
   (AR)
Southern Connecticut State U (CT)
Southern Illinois U Carbondale (IL)
Southern Methodist U (TX)
Southern Nazarene U (OK)
Southern Oregon U (OR)
Southern Utah U (UT)
Spelman Coll (GA)
Spring Arbor U (MI)
Spring Hill Coll (AL)
Stanford U (CA)
State U of New York at Binghamton
   (NY)
State U of New York at Fredonia
   (NY)
State U of New York at New Paltz
   (NY)
State U of New York at Oswego
   (NY)
State U of New York at Plattsburgh
   (NY)
State U of New York Coll at
   Geneseo (NY)
State U of New York Coll at Old
   Westbury (NY)
State U of New York Coll at
   Oneonta (NY)
State U of New York Coll at
   Potsdam (NY)
Stephen F. Austin State U (TX)
Stetson U (FL)
Stonehill Coll (MA)
Stony Brook U, State U of New York
   (NY)
Suffolk U (MA)
Sul Ross State U (TX)
Susquehanna U (PA)
Swarthmore Coll (PA)
Sweet Briar Coll (VA)
Syracuse U (NY)
Tarleton State U (TX)
Taylor U (IN)
Temple U (PA)
Tennessee Technological U (TN)
Tennessee Wesleyan Coll (TN)
Texas A&M Intl U (TX)
Texas A&M U (TX)
Texas A&M U–Corpus Christi (TX)

Texas A&M U–Kingsville (TX)
Texas Christian U (TX)
Texas Lutheran U (TX)
Texas Southern U (TX)
Texas State U–San Marcos (TX)
Texas Tech U (TX)
Texas Wesleyan U (TX)
Thomas More Coll (KY)
Transylvania U (KY)
Trinity Coll (CT)
Trinity U (TX)
Truman State U (MO)
Tufts U (MA)
Tulane U (LA)
Union Coll (NE)
Union Coll (NY)
Union U (TN)
United States Military Acad (NY)
U at Buffalo, the State U of New
   York (NY)
The U of Akron (OH)
The U of Alabama (AL)
The U of Arizona (AZ)
U of Arkansas (AR)
U of Arkansas–Fort Smith (AR)
The U of British Columbia (BC,
   Canada)
The U of British Columbia–
   Okanagan (BC, Canada)
U of California, Berkeley (CA)
U of California, Davis (CA)
U of California, Irvine (CA)
U of California, Los Angeles (CA)
U of California, Santa Barbara (CA)
U of Central Florida (FL)
U of Central Missouri (MO)
U of Cincinnati (OH)
U of Colorado at Colorado Springs
   (CO)
U of Colorado Boulder (CO)
U of Colorado Denver (CO)
U of Dallas (TX)
U of Dayton (OH)
U of Delaware (DE)
U of Denver (CO)
U of Evansville (IN)
The U of Findlay (OH)
U of Florida (FL)
U of Georgia (GA)
U of Guelph (ON, Canada)
U of Hawaii at Manoa (HI)
U of Houston (TX)
U of Houston–Downtown (TX)
U of Idaho (ID)
U of Illinois at Chicago (IL)
U of Indianapolis (IN)
The U of Iowa (IA)
The U of Kansas (KS)
U of La Verne (CA)
U of Louisiana at Lafayette (LA)
U of Louisiana at Monroe (LA)
U of Louisville (KY)
U of Maine (ME)
U of Manitoba (MB, Canada)
U of Mary Hardin-Baylor (TX)
U of Maryland, Coll Park (MD)
U of Massachusetts Amherst (MA)
U of Massachusetts Boston (MA)
U of Massachusetts Dartmouth
   (MA)
U of Miami (FL)
U of Michigan (MI)
U of Michigan–Dearborn (MI)
U of Michigan–Flint (MI)
U of Minnesota, Duluth (MN)
U of Minnesota, Twin Cities
   Campus (MN)
U of Mississippi (MS)
U of Missouri (MO)
U of Missouri–St. Louis (MO)
U of Mount Union (OH)
U of Nebraska at Omaha (NE)
U of Nebraska–Lincoln (NE)
U of Nevada, Las Vegas (NV)
U of Nevada, Reno (NV)
U of New Brunswick Fredericton
   (NB, Canada)
U of New Brunswick Saint John
   (NB, Canada)
U of New Hampshire (NH)
The U of North Carolina at Asheville
   (NC)
The U of North Carolina at Charlotte
   (NC)
The U of North Carolina at
   Greensboro (NC)
The U of North Carolina at
   Pembroke (NC)

The U of North Carolina Wilmington (NC)
U of North Dakota (ND)
U of Northern Colorado (CO)
U of Northern Iowa (IA)
U of North Florida (FL)
U of North Texas (TX)
U of Notre Dame (IN)
U of Oklahoma (OK)
U of Oregon (OR)
U of Ottawa (ON, Canada)
U of Pennsylvania (PA)
U of Pittsburgh (PA)
U of Pittsburgh at Greensburg (PA)
U of Portland (OR)
U of Puget Sound (WA)
U of Redlands (CA)
U of Regina (SK, Canada)
U of Rhode Island (RI)
U of Richmond (VA)
U of Rochester (NY)
U of St. Thomas (MN)
U of St. Thomas (TX)
U of San Diego (CA)
U of San Francisco (CA)
U of Saskatchewan (SK, Canada)
The U of Scranton (PA)
U of South Carolina (SC)
U of South Carolina Upstate (SC)
The U of South Dakota (SD)
U of Southern California (CA)
U of Southern Indiana (IN)
U of South Florida (FL)
The U of Tampa (FL)
The U of Tennessee (TN)
The U of Tennessee at Martin (TN)
The U of Texas at Arlington (TX)
The U of Texas at Austin (TX)
The U of Texas at San Antonio (TX)
The U of Texas at Tyler (TX)
The U of Texas of the Permian Basin (TX)
The U of Texas–Pan American (TX)
U of the Cumberlands (KY)
U of the District of Columbia (DC)
U of the Incarnate Word (TX)
U of the Ozarks (AR)
U of the Pacific (CA)
The U of Toledo (OH)
U of Tulsa (OK)
U of Utah (UT)
U of Vermont (VT)
U of Virginia (VA)
U of Washington (WA)
U of Waterloo (ON, Canada)
The U of Western Ontario (ON, Canada)
U of West Florida (FL)
U of West Georgia (GA)
U of Wisconsin–Eau Claire (WI)
U of Wisconsin–Green Bay (WI)
U of Wisconsin–La Crosse (WI)
U of Wisconsin–Madison (WI)
U of Wisconsin–Parkside (WI)
U of Wisconsin–Platteville (WI)
U of Wisconsin–River Falls (WI)
U of Wisconsin–Stevens Point (WI)
U of Wisconsin–Whitewater (WI)
U of Wyoming (WY)
Utah State U (UT)
Utah Valley U (UT)
Valdosta State U (GA)
Valparaiso U (IN)
Vanderbilt U (TN)
Vassar Coll (NY)
Villanova U (PA)
Virginia Polytechnic Inst and State U (VA)
Virginia Wesleyan Coll (VA)
Viterbo U (WI)
Wabash Coll (IN)
Wagner Coll (NY)
Wake Forest U (NC)
Walla Walla U (WA)
Walsh U (OH)
Wartburg Coll (IA)
Washburn U (KS)
Washington & Jefferson Coll (PA)
Washington and Lee U (VA)
Washington Coll (MD)
Washington State U (WA)
Washington U in St. Louis (MO)
Wayland Baptist U (TX)
Wayne State Coll (NE)
Weber State U (UT)
Webster U (MO)
Wellesley Coll (MA)
Wells Coll (NY)
Wesleyan Coll (GA)
Wesleyan U (CT)

West Chester U of Pennsylvania (PA)
Western Carolina U (NC)
Western Connecticut State U (CT)
Western Illinois U (IL)
Western Kentucky U (KY)
Western Michigan U (MI)
Western Oregon U (OR)
Westfield State U (MA)
Westminster Coll (MO)
Westmont Coll (CA)
Wheaton Coll (IL)
Wheeling Jesuit U (WV)
Whitman Coll (WA)
Wichita State U (KS)
Widener U (PA)
Wilfrid Laurier U (ON, Canada)
Wilkes U (PA)
Willamette U (OR)
William Jewell Coll (MO)
William Paterson U of New Jersey (NJ)
Williams Coll (MA)
Wilmington Coll (OH)
Winona State U (MN)
Wittenberg U (OH)
Wofford Coll (SC)
Worcester State U (MA)
Wright State U (OH)
Xavier U (OH)
Xavier U of Louisiana (LA)
Yale U (CT)
York Coll of Pennsylvania (PA)
York Coll of the City U of New York (NY)
Youngstown State U (OH)

SPANISH AND IBERIAN STUDIES
Bard Coll (NY)
Bard Coll at Simon's Rock (MA)
The U of Western Ontario (ON, Canada)

SPANISH LANGUAGE TEACHER EDUCATION
Abilene Christian U (TX)
Adams State Coll (CO)
Alma Coll (MI)
Anderson U (IN)
Appalachian State U (NC)
Assumption Coll (MA)
Auburn U (AL)
Augustana Coll (IL)
Bethel Coll (IN)
Bethel U (MN)
Blue Mountain Coll (MS)
Bob Jones U (SC)
Bridgewater Coll (VA)
Bryan Coll (TN)
Buena Vista U (IA)
Calvin Coll (MI)
Carroll U (WI)
The Catholic U of America (DC)
Cedarville U (OH)
Central Michigan U (MI)
Coll of Saint Mary (NE)
The Coll of Saint Rose (NY)
Colorado State U (CO)
Concordia Coll (MN)
Concordia U Wisconsin (WI)
Delaware State U (DE)
Dordt Coll (IA)
Dowling Coll (NY)
Duquesne U (PA)
Eastern Michigan U (MI)
Eastern Washington U (WA)
East Texas Baptist U (TX)
Edgewood Coll (WI)
Elmhurst Coll (IL)
Elmira Coll (NY)
Evangel U (MO)
Fayetteville State U (NC)
Franklin Coll (IN)
Friends U (KS)
Gardner-Webb U (NC)
Georgia Southern U (GA)
Grace Coll (IN)
Grand Valley State U (MI)
Greensboro Coll (NC)
Greenville Coll (IL)
Harding U (AR)
Hardin-Simmons U (TX)
Hofstra U (NY)
Hope Coll (MI)
Indiana U Bloomington (IN)
Indiana U Northwest (IN)
Indiana U–Purdue U Fort Wayne (IN)

Indiana U–Purdue U Indianapolis (IN)
Indiana U South Bend (IN)
Indiana Wesleyan U (IN)
Inter American U of Puerto Rico, Metropolitan Campus (PR)
Inter American U of Puerto Rico, San Germán Campus (PR)
Ithaca Coll (NY)
Juniata Coll (PA)
Keene State Coll (NH)
Kent State U (OH)
Kentucky Wesleyan Coll (KY)
King Coll (TN)
Lee U (TN)
Le Moyne Coll (NY)
Liberty U (VA)
Lindenwood U (MO)
Lipscomb U (TN)
Long Island U, Brooklyn Campus (NY)
Long Island U, C.W. Post Campus (NY)
Lubbock Christian U (TX)
Malone U (OH)
Manchester Coll (IN)
Manhattanville Coll (NY)
Mansfield U of Pennsylvania (PA)
Marian U (WI)
Marist Coll (NY)
Marquette U (WI)
Maryville Coll (TN)
Marywood U (PA)
McMurry U (TX)
Messiah Coll (PA)
Miami U (OH)
Michigan State U (MI)
MidAmerica Nazarene U (KS)
Millersville U of Pennsylvania (PA)
Minnesota State U Moorhead (MN)
Minot State U (ND)
Missouri State U (MO)
Molloy Coll (NY)
Montana State U Billings (MT)
Moravian Coll (PA)
Morningside Coll (IA)
Mount Vernon Nazarene U (OH)
Niagara U (NY)
North Carolina Ag and Tech State U (NC)
North Carolina State U (NC)
North Dakota State U (ND)
Northeastern State U (OK)
Northern Arizona U (AZ)
Northern Michigan U (MI)
Northwest Missouri State U (MO)
Northwest Nazarene U (ID)
Ohio U (OH)
Ohio Wesleyan U (OH)
Pace U (NY)
Pittsburg State U (KS)
Rhode Island Coll (RI)
Sacred Heart U (CT)
Saginaw Valley State U (MI)
St. Ambrose U (IA)
St. Catherine U (MN)
St. Edward's U (TX)
St. John Fisher Coll (NY)
St. John's U (NY)
St. Joseph's Coll, Long Island Campus (NY)
St. Joseph's Coll, New York (NY)
Saint Mary's U of Minnesota (MN)
Saint Xavier U (IL)
Salem State U (MA)
Salve Regina U (RI)
Southeastern Louisiana U (LA)
Southeastern Oklahoma State U (OK)
State U of New York at New Paltz (NY)
State U of New York at Plattsburgh (NY)
State U of New York Coll at Old Westbury (NY)
State U of New York Coll at Oneonta (NY)
Taylor U (IN)
Texas A&M Intl U (TX)
Texas A&M U–Corpus Christi (TX)
Texas Christian U (TX)
The U of Akron (OH)
The U of Arizona (AZ)
U of Arkansas–Fort Smith (AR)
U of Evansville (IN)
U of Illinois at Chicago (IL)
U of Indianapolis (IN)
The U of Iowa (IA)
U of Louisiana at Lafayette (LA)
U of Louisiana at Monroe (LA)

U of Maine (ME)
U of Michigan–Flint (MI)
U of Minnesota, Duluth (MN)
U of Missouri–St. Louis (MO)
U of Nebraska–Lincoln (NE)
The U of North Carolina at Charlotte (NC)
The U of North Carolina at Greensboro (NC)
The U of North Carolina Wilmington (NC)
The U of South Dakota (SD)
The U of Tennessee at Martin (TN)
U of the Cumberlands (KY)
The U of Toledo (OH)
U of Wisconsin–River Falls (WI)
Utah Valley U (UT)
Valdosta State U (GA)
Valparaiso U (IN)
Viterbo U (WI)
Washington State U (WA)
Washington U in St. Louis (MO)
Weber State U (UT)
Western Carolina U (NC)
Western Michigan U (MI)
Western State Coll of Colorado (CO)
Wheeling Jesuit U (WV)
Widener U (PA)
William Jewell Coll (MO)
Winona State U (MN)
Xavier U of Louisiana (LA)
York Coll of Pennsylvania (PA)
Youngstown State U (OH)

SPECIAL EDUCATION
Abilene Christian U (TX)
Adams State Coll (CO)
Alabama Ag and Mech U (AL)
Alabama State U (AL)
Albany State U (GA)
Albright Coll (PA)
Alvernia U (PA)
Anderson U (SC)
Arizona State U (AZ)
Armstrong Atlantic State U (GA)
Asbury U (KY)
Ashland U (OH)
Athens State U (AL)
Auburn U (AL)
Augustana Coll (SD)
Austin Peay State U (TN)
Avila U (MO)
Barry U (FL)
Barton Coll (NC)
Bellarmine U (KY)
Belmont U (TN)
Benedictine Coll (KS)
Benedictine U (IL)
Bethel U (TN)
Bloomsburg U of Pennsylvania (PA)
Bob Jones U (SC)
Boise State U (ID)
Boston U (MA)
Bowie State U (MD)
Bowling Green State U (OH)
Bridgewater State U (MA)
Brigham Young U (UT)
Buena Vista U (IA)
Cabrini Coll (PA)
Calvin Coll (MI)
Canisius Coll (NY)
Capital U (OH)
Carlow U (PA)
Carson-Newman Coll (TN)
Cedarville U (OH)
Centenary Coll (NJ)
Central State U (OH)
Christian Brothers U (TN)
Clarion U of Pennsylvania (PA)
Clemson U (SC)
Cleveland State U (OH)
Coastal Carolina U (SC)
Coll of Charleston (SC)
Coll of Mount St. Joseph (OH)
The Coll of New Jersey (NJ)
Coll of Saint Mary (NE)
The Coll of Saint Rose (NY)
Columbia Coll (SC)
Concordia U Chicago (IL)
Concord U (WV)
Coppin State U (MD)
Cumberland U (TN)
Curry Coll (MA)
Dakota Wesleyan U (SD)
Delaware State U (DE)
DePaul U (IL)
Doane Coll (NE)
Dominican Coll (NY)
Dowling Coll (NY)
East Central U (OK)

Eastern Illinois U (IL)
Eastern New Mexico U (NM)
Eastern Washington U (WA)
East Stroudsburg U of Pennsylvania (PA)
East Tennessee State U (TN)
Edinboro U of Pennsylvania (PA)
Elizabeth City State U (NC)
Elmhurst Coll (IL)
Elon U (NC)
Erskine Coll (SC)
Evangel U (MO)
Fairmont State U (WV)
Felician Coll (NJ)
Fitchburg State U (MA)
Florida Atlantic U (FL)
Florida Gulf Coast U (FL)
Florida Intl U (FL)
Fontbonne U (MO)
Freed-Hardeman U (TN)
Furman U (SC)
Gannon U (PA)
Geneva Coll (PA)
Georgia Coll & State U (GA)
Georgia Southern U (GA)
Gordon Coll (MA)
Goucher Coll (MD)
Grace Coll (IN)
Grand Canyon U (AZ)
Grand Valley State U (MI)
Greensboro Coll (NC)
Greenville Coll (IL)
Holy Family U (PA)
Houghton Coll (NY)
Huntington U (IN)
Idaho State U (ID)
Illinois State U (IL)
Indiana State U (IN)
Indiana U Bloomington (IN)
Indiana U of Pennsylvania (PA)
Indiana U South Bend (IN)
Indiana U Southeast (IN)
Indiana Wesleyan U (IN)
Indian River State Coll (FL)
Inter American U of Puerto Rico, Metropolitan Campus (PR)
Inter American U of Puerto Rico, Ponce Campus (PR)
Inter American U of Puerto Rico, San Germán Campus (PR)
Iowa Wesleyan Coll (IA)
Jacksonville State U (AL)
John Brown U (AR)
John Carroll U (OH)
Kean U (NJ)
Kent State U (OH)
Keuka Coll (NY)
King's Coll (PA)
Kutztown U of Pennsylvania (PA)
Lamar U (TX)
La Salle U (PA)
Lebanon Valley Coll (PA)
Lee U (TN)
Le Moyne Coll (NY)
Lesley U (MA)
Lewis U (IL)
Liberty U (VA)
Lindenwood U (MO)
Lock Haven U of Pennsylvania (PA)
Longwood U (VA)
Louisiana Coll (LA)
Louisiana State U in Shreveport (LA)
Loyola U Chicago (IL)
Loyola U Maryland (MD)
Lubbock Christian U (TX)
Lyndon State Coll (VT)
MacMurray Coll (IL)
Manchester Coll (IN)
Manhattan Coll (NY)
Mansfield U of Pennsylvania (PA)
Marist Coll (NY)
Mars Hill Coll (NC)
Marywood U (PA)
Medaille Coll (NY)
Medgar Evers Coll of the City U of New York (NY)
Miami Dade Coll (FL)
Miami U (OH)
Michigan State U (MI)
Middle Tennessee State U (TN)
Midway Coll (KY)
Midwestern State U (TX)
Millersville U of Pennsylvania (PA)
Minnesota State U Moorhead (MN)
Misericordia U (PA)
Mississippi State U (MS)
Missouri State U (MO)
Molloy Coll (NY)
Monmouth U (NJ)
Montana State U Billings (MT)

SPEECH-LANGUAGE PATHOLOGY

Rockhurst U (MO)
Saint Xavier U (IL)
Texas Christian U (TX)
Towson U (MD)
U of Central Missouri (MO)
U of Maryland, Coll Park (MD)
U of Montevallo (AL)
U of Nebraska–Lincoln (NE)
U of Nevada, Reno (NV)
U of Northern Colorado (CO)
U of Northern Iowa (IA)
U of Oklahoma Health Sciences Center (OK)
U of Science and Arts of Oklahoma (OK)
The U of Toledo (OH)
The U of Western Ontario (ON, Canada)
U of West Georgia (GA)
U of Wisconsin–Whitewater (WI)
Valdosta State U (GA)
Xavier U of Louisiana (LA)

SPEECH TEACHER EDUCATION

Anderson U (IN)
Arkansas Tech U (AR)
Augustana Coll (SD)
Baptist Bible Coll of Pennsylvania (PA)
Bemidji State U (MN)
Boston U (MA)
Brigham Young U (UT)
Buena Vista U (IA)
Capital U (OH)
Central Michigan U (MI)
Colorado State U (CO)
Culver-Stockton Coll (MO)
Dickinson State U (ND)
Dordt Coll (IA)
East Texas Baptist U (TX)
Elmira Coll (NY)
Evangel U (MO)
Harding U (AR)
Hardin-Simmons U (TX)
Indiana U Bloomington (IN)
Indiana U–Purdue U Fort Wayne (IN)
Indiana U–Purdue U Indianapolis (IN)
King Coll (TN)
Lubbock Christian U (TX)
McKendree U (IL)
Northeastern State U (OK)
Northwestern Coll (IA)
Northwestern State U of Louisiana (LA)
Northwest U (WA)
Oklahoma City U (OK)
Saginaw Valley State U (MI)
St. Ambrose U (IA)
St. Catherine U (MN)
Southeastern Louisiana U (LA)
Southeast Missouri State U (MO)
Southern Nazarene U (OK)
Southwestern Coll (KS)
State U of New York at New Paltz (NY)
Texas A&M U–Corpus Christi (TX)
Texas Wesleyan U (TX)
Trevecca Nazarene U (TN)
The U of Arizona (AZ)
U of Indianapolis (IN)
The U of Iowa (IA)
U of Louisiana at Lafayette (LA)
U of Louisiana at Monroe (LA)
U of Maine (ME)
U of Michigan–Flint (MI)
U of Northern Iowa (IA)
U of Rio Grande (OH)
U of St. Thomas (MN)
The U of South Dakota (SD)
Wartburg Coll (IA)
Wayne State Coll (NE)
William Jewell Coll (MO)

SPORT AND FITNESS ADMINISTRATION/ MANAGEMENT

Abilene Christian U (TX)
Adelphi U (NY)
Albertus Magnus Coll (CT)
Alderson-Broaddus Coll (WV)
Alvernia U (PA)
American Public U System (WV)
American U (DC)
Anna Maria Coll (MA)
Arkansas State U (AR)
Asbury U (KY)

Augustana Coll (SD)
Averett U (VA)
Baker U (KS)
Baldwin-Wallace Coll (OH)
Barry U (FL)
Barton Coll (NC)
Belhaven U (MS)
Bemidji State U (MN)
Bethany Coll (KS)
Bethany Coll (WV)
Bethel Coll (IN)
Blackburn Coll (IL)
Bluffton U (OH)
Bowling Green State U (OH)
Bridgewater State U (MA)
Brock U (ON, Canada)
Buena Vista U (IA)
Calvin Coll (MI)
Canisius Coll (NY)
Cedarville U (OH)
Centenary Coll (NJ)
Claflin U (SC)
Clarke U (IA)
Clayton State U (GA)
Cleveland State U (OH)
Coastal Carolina U (SC)
Coker Coll (SC)
Coll of Mount St. Joseph (OH)
Columbia Coll (MO)
Columbia Southern U (AL)
Concordia Coll–New York (NY)
Concordia U Chicago (IL)
Concordia U Wisconsin (WI)
Coppin State U (MD)
Corban U (OR)
Crown Coll (MN)
Culver-Stockton Coll (MO)
Dakota Wesleyan U (SD)
Daniel Webster Coll (NH)
Davenport U, Grand Rapids (MI)
Defiance Coll (OH)
Delaware State U (DE)
DeSales U (PA)
Drury U (MO)
Eastern Michigan U (MI)
East Tennessee State U (TN)
Edinboro U of Pennsylvania (PA)
Elmhurst Coll (IL)
Elon U (NC)
Emmanuel Coll (GA)
Endicott Coll (MA)
Erskine Coll (SC)
Faulkner U (AL)
Ferrum Coll (VA)
Fitchburg State U (MA)
Flagler Coll (FL)
Fontbonne U (MO)
Fort Lewis Coll (CO)
Franklin Pierce U (NH)
Gannon U (PA)
Gardner-Webb U (NC)
Geneva Coll (PA)
Georgia Southern U (GA)
Goldey-Beacom Coll (DE)
Grace Coll (IN)
Grand Canyon U (AZ)
Greensboro Coll (NC)
Greenville Coll (IL)
Guilford Coll (NC)
Hamline U (MN)
Harding U (AR)
Holy Family U (PA)
Huntingdon Coll (AL)
Husson U (ME)
Indiana Tech (IN)
Indiana Wesleyan U (IN)
Ithaca Coll (NY)
Jamestown Coll (ND)
John Brown U (AR)
Johnson & Wales U (CO)
Johnson & Wales U (FL)
Johnson & Wales U (RI)
Johnson & Wales U - Charlotte Campus (NC)
Johnson C. Smith U (NC)
Johnson State Coll (VT)
Kennesaw State U (GA)
Kentucky Wesleyan Coll (KY)
Keystone Coll (PA)
King Coll (TN)
Lasell Coll (MA)
Laurentian U (ON, Canada)
LeTourneau U (TX)
Lewis U (IL)
Liberty U (VA)
Limestone Coll (SC)
Lindenwood U (MO)
Lock Haven U of Pennsylvania (PA)

Longwood U (VA)
Loras Coll (IA)
Louisiana State U and Ag and Mech Coll (LA)
Lubbock Christian U (TX)
Lynchburg Coll (VA)
Lyndon State Coll (VT)
MacMurray Coll (IL)
Madonna U (MI)
Malone U (OH)
Manchester Coll (IN)
Maranatha Baptist Bible Coll (WI)
Marian U (WI)
Mars Hill Coll (NC)
Marymount U (VA)
Maryville U of Saint Louis (MO)
Medaille Coll (NY)
Menlo Coll (CA)
Mesa State Coll (CO)
Messiah Coll (PA)
Miami U (OH)
MidAmerica Nazarene U (KS)
Midway Coll (KY)
Midwestern State U (TX)
Millikin U (IL)
Minnesota State U Mankato (MN)
Minot State U (ND)
Misericordia U (PA)
Missouri Baptist U (MO)
Mitchell Coll (CT)
Montana State U (MT)
Montana State U Billings (MT)
Morehead State U (KY)
Mount Ida Coll (MA)
Mount St. Mary's U (MD)
Mount Vernon Nazarene U (OH)
National U (CA)
Nebraska Wesleyan U (NE)
Neumann U (PA)
Newbury Coll (MA)
New England Coll (NH)
Niagara U (NY)
North Carolina Ag and Tech State U (NC)
North Carolina State U (NC)
North Central Coll (IL)
North Dakota State U (ND)
Northern Kentucky U (KY)
Northern Michigan U (MI)
Northern State U (SD)
North Greenville U (SC)
Nova Southeastern U (FL)
Oklahoma Christian U (OK)
Principia Coll (IL)
Quincy U (IL)
Reinhardt U (GA)
Rice U (TX)
Roanoke Coll (VA)
Robert Morris U (PA)
Rockhurst U (MO)
Rocky Mountain Coll (MT)
Rogers State U (OK)
Sacred Heart U (CT)
St. Ambrose U (IA)
St. Bonaventure U (NY)
St. John Fisher Coll (NY)
St. John's U (NY)
Saint Joseph's Coll (IN)
Saint Joseph's Coll of Maine (ME)
Saint Leo U (FL)
Saint Mary's Coll of California (CA)
St. Thomas Aquinas Coll (NY)
St. Thomas U (FL)
Salem State U (MA)
Samford U (AL)
Schreiner U (TX)
Seattle Pacific U (WA)
Seton Hill U (PA)
Shawnee State U (OH)
Siena Heights U (MI)
Simpson Coll (IA)
Slippery Rock U of Pennsylvania (PA)
Southeastern Louisiana U (LA)
Southeastern U (FL)
Southeast Missouri State U (MO)
Southern Adventist U (TN)
Southern Illinois U Carbondale (IL)
Southern Methodist U (TX)
Southern Nazarene U (OK)
Southern Vermont Coll (VT)
Southwestern Assemblies of God U (TX)
Southwestern Coll (KS)
Spring Arbor U (MI)
Springfield Coll (MA)
State U of New York at Oswego (NY)

Stetson U (FL)
Tabor Coll (KS)
Taylor U (IN)
Tennessee Wesleyan Coll (TN)
Texas A&M U (TX)
Texas Lutheran U (TX)
Texas State U–San Marcos (TX)
Texas Wesleyan U (TX)
Thomas More Coll (KY)
Tiffin U (OH)
Towson U (MD)
Trevecca Nazarene U (TN)
Trine U (IN)
Troy U (AL)
Union Coll (KY)
Union Coll (NE)
Union U (TN)
The U of Akron (OH)
U of Cincinnati (OH)
U of Dayton (OH)
U of Delaware (DE)
U of Evansville (IN)
U of Florida (FL)
U of Georgia (GA)
U of Houston (TX)
U of Indianapolis (IN)
The U of Iowa (IA)
U of Louisville (KY)
U of Mary Hardin-Baylor (TX)
U of Massachusetts Amherst (MA)
U of Memphis (TN)
U of Miami (FL)
U of Michigan (MI)
U of Minnesota, Crookston (MN)
U of Minnesota, Twin Cities Campus (MN)
U of Mount Union (OH)
U of Nevada, Las Vegas (NV)
U of New England (ME)
U of North Florida (FL)
U of Pittsburgh at Bradford (PA)
U of Regina (SK, Canada)
U of Saint Mary (KS)
U of South Carolina (SC)
The U of Tampa (FL)
The U of Tennessee (TN)
The U of Texas at Austin (TX)
U of the Cumberlands (KY)
U of the Incarnate Word (TX)
U of the Sciences in Philadelphia (PA)
U of Tulsa (OK)
U of Wisconsin–Parkside (WI)
Valparaiso U (IN)
Virginia Intermont Coll (VA)
Viterbo U (WI)
Walla Walla U (WA)
Wartburg Coll (IA)
Washington State U (WA)
Wayland Baptist U (TX)
Wayne State Coll (NE)
Western Carolina U (NC)
Western New England U (MA)
Western State Coll of Colorado (CO)
West Virginia U (WV)
Wichita State U (KS)
Widener U (PA)
Wilmington Coll (OH)
Wilmington U (DE)
Wingate U (NC)
Winona State U (MN)
Winthrop U (SC)
Xavier U (OH)
York Coll of Pennsylvania (PA)

SPORTS COMMUNICATION

Lasell Coll (MA)
Oklahoma State U (OK)
U of Evansville (IN)

SPORTS STUDIES

Central Michigan U (MI)
Huntington U (IN)
Southwestern Coll (KS)
Trevecca Nazarene U (TN)
Western Kentucky U (KY)

STATISTICS

American U (DC)
American U of Beirut (Lebanon)
Appalachian State U (NC)
Barnard Coll (NY)
Bowling Green State U (OH)
Brock U (ON, Canada)
California Polytechnic State U, San Luis Obispo (CA)
California State U, Fullerton (CA)

California State U, Long Beach (CA)
Carnegie Mellon U (PA)
Case Western Reserve U (OH)
Central Michigan U (MI)
Colorado State U (CO)
Columbia U, School of General Studies (NY)
Concordia U (QC, Canada)
Cornell U (NY)
Eastern Michigan U (MI)
Ferris State U (MI)
Florida Intl U (FL)
Florida State U (FL)
Grand Valley State U (MI)
Harvard U (MA)
Hunter Coll of the City U of New York (NY)
Idaho State U (ID)
Indiana U Bloomington (IN)
Indiana U–Purdue U Fort Wayne (IN)
Iowa State U of Science and Technology (IA)
Kansas State U (KS)
Lehigh U (PA)
Loyola U Chicago (IL)
Miami U (OH)
Michigan State U (MI)
Montana State U (MT)
Mount Holyoke Coll (MA)
North Carolina State U (NC)
North Dakota State U (ND)
Northwest Missouri State U (MO)
Ohio Wesleyan U (OH)
Oklahoma State U (OK)
Penn State Abington (PA)
Penn State Altoona (PA)
Penn State Beaver (PA)
Penn State Berks (PA)
Penn State Brandywine (PA)
Penn State DuBois (PA)
Penn State Erie, The Behrend Coll (PA)
Penn State Fayette, The Eberly Campus (PA)
Penn State Greater Allegheny (PA)
Penn State Hazleton (PA)
Penn State Lehigh Valley (PA)
Penn State Mont Alto (PA)
Penn State New Kensington (PA)
Penn State Schuylkill (PA)
Penn State Shenango (PA)
Penn State York Park (PA)
Penn State Wilkes-Barre (PA)
Penn State Worthington Scranton (PA)
Penn State York (PA)
Purdue U (IN)
Rice U (TX)
Rutgers, The State U of New Jersey, New Brunswick (NJ)
St. John Fisher Coll (NY)
San Diego State U (CA)
San Francisco State U (CA)
Simon Fraser U (BC, Canada)
Slippery Rock U of Pennsylvania (PA)
Sonoma State U (CA)
Southern Methodist U (TX)
Stanford U (CA)
State U of New York Coll at Oneonta (NY)
U at Buffalo, the State U of New York (NY)
The U of Akron (OH)
The U of British Columbia (BC, Canada)
U of California, Berkeley (CA)
U of California, Davis (CA)
U of California, Los Angeles (CA)
U of California, Santa Barbara (CA)
U of Central Florida (FL)
U of Florida (FL)
U of Georgia (GA)
U of Guelph (ON, Canada)
U of Illinois at Chicago (IL)
The U of Iowa (IA)
U of Manitoba (MB, Canada)
U of Maryland, Baltimore County (MD)
U of Michigan (MI)
U of Minnesota, Duluth (MN)
U of Minnesota, Twin Cities Campus (MN)
U of Missouri (MO)
U of Nevada, Las Vegas (NV)
U of New Brunswick Fredericton (NB, Canada)

U of New Brunswick Saint John (NB, Canada)
The U of North Carolina Wilmington (NC)
U of North Florida (FL)
U of Ottawa (ON, Canada)
U of Pennsylvania (PA)
U of Pittsburgh (PA)
U of Regina (SK, Canada)
U of Rochester (NY)
U of Saskatchewan (SK, Canada)
U of South Carolina (SC)
U of South Florida (FL)
The U of Tennessee (TN)
The U of Tennessee at Martin (TN)
The U of Texas at Dallas (TX)
The U of Texas at San Antonio (TX)
U of Vermont (VT)
U of Washington (WA)
U of Waterloo (ON, Canada)
The U of Western Ontario (ON, Canada)
U of Wisconsin–Madison (WI)
U of Wyoming (WY)
Utah State U (UT)
Virginia Polytechnic Inst and State U (VA)
Washington U in St. Louis (MO)
Western Michigan U (MI)
Winona State U (MN)
Wright State U (OH)
Xavier U of Louisiana (LA)

STATISTICS RELATED
Carnegie Mellon U (PA)
Saint Mary's Coll (IN)
United States Military Acad (NY)

STRINGED INSTRUMENTS
Acadia U (NS, Canada)
Bard Coll (NY)
Bennington Coll (VT)
Brigham Young U (UT)
Butler U (IN)
Carnegie Mellon U (PA)
The Colburn School Conservatory of Music (CA)
Five Towns Coll (NY)
Hardin-Simmons U (TX)
Hope Coll (MI)
Houghton Coll (NY)
Inter American U of Puerto Rico, San Germán Campus (PR)
Lamar U (TX)
Lawrence U (WI)
Mannes Coll The New School for Music (NY)
Mount Allison U (NB, Canada)
New England Conservatory of Music (MA)
The New School for Jazz and Contemporary Music (NY)
Northwestern Coll (MN)
Oberlin Coll (OH)
Oklahoma City U (OK)
Peabody Conservatory of The Johns Hopkins U (MD)
Roosevelt U (IL)
San Francisco Conservatory of Music (CA)
Sarah Lawrence Coll (NY)
State U of New York at Fredonia (NY)
Stetson U (FL)
The U of British Columbia (BC, Canada)
The U of Iowa (IA)
The U of Kansas (KS)
U of Nebraska at Omaha (NE)
U of Southern California (CA)
U of Washington (WA)
The U of Western Ontario (ON, Canada)
Vanderbilt U (TN)
Willamette U (OR)
Xavier U of Louisiana (LA)

STRUCTURAL ENGINEERING
Penn State Harrisburg (PA)
U at Buffalo, the State U of New York (NY)
U of Central Florida (FL)
U of Southern California (CA)
The U of Toledo (OH)
Western Michigan U (MI)

SUBSTANCE ABUSE/ADDICTION COUNSELING
Alvernia U (PA)
Calumet Coll of Saint Joseph (IN)

Coll of St. Joseph (VT)
Hawai'i Pacific U (HI)
Indiana U–Purdue U Fort Wayne (IN)
Indiana Wesleyan U (IN)
Metropolitan State U (MN)
Minot State U (ND)
Newman U (KS)
Northwestern State U of Louisiana (LA)
Rhode Island Coll (RI)
Tiffin U (OH)
U of Cincinnati (OH)
U of Lethbridge (AB, Canada)
The U of South Dakota (SD)
The U of Texas–Pan American (TX)
Viterbo U (WI)
Washburn U (KS)

SURVEYING ENGINEERING
Ferris State U (MI)
Florida Atlantic U (FL)
North Carolina Ag and Tech State U (NC)
U of Maine (ME)

SURVEYING TECHNOLOGY
East Tennessee State U (TN)
Great Basin Coll (NV)
Idaho State U (ID)
New Mexico State U (NM)
Nicholls State U (LA)
Penn State Wilkes-Barre (PA)
Polytechnic U of Puerto Rico (PR)
Southern Polytechnic State U (GA)
Texas A&M U–Corpus Christi (TX)
Troy U (AL)
The U of Akron (OH)
U of Florida (FL)
U of Maine (ME)
U of New Brunswick Fredericton (NB, Canada)

SUSTAINABILITY STUDIES
Aquinas Coll (MI)
Cleary U (MI)
Dominican U of California (CA)
The Evergreen State Coll (WA)
Goddard Coll (VT)
Messiah Coll (PA)
Sierra Nevada Coll (NV)
Stony Brook U, State U of New York (NY)
Western New England U (MA)
Wheeling Jesuit U (WV)

SWEDISH
Brigham Young U (UT)

SYSTEM, NETWORKING, AND LAN/WAN MANAGEMENT
Alcorn State U (MS)
Champlain Coll (VT)
Dakota State U (SD)
Herzing U (GA)
Intl Business Coll, Fort Wayne (IN)
Northern Michigan U (MI)
Southern Nazarene U (OK)
Texas A&M U (TX)
U of Hawaii–West Oahu (HI)

SYSTEMS ENGINEERING
Case Western Reserve U (OH)
Delaware State U (DE)
Ferris State U (MI)
Johnson & Wales U (RI)
Providence Coll (RI)
Southern Polytechnic State U (GA)
United States Military Acad (NY)
United States Naval Acad (MD)
The U of Arizona (AZ)
U of Florida (FL)
U of Maine (ME)
The U of North Carolina at Charlotte (NC)
U of Pennsylvania (PA)
U of Southern California (CA)
U of Virginia (VA)
U of Waterloo (ON, Canada)
U of Wyoming (WY)
Washington U in St. Louis (MO)

SYSTEMS SCIENCE AND THEORY
Boston U (MA)
Carnegie Mellon U (PA)
Indiana U Bloomington (IN)
James Madison U (VA)
Marshall U (WV)

Stanford U (CA)
United States Military Acad (NY)
Washington U in St. Louis (MO)
Yale U (CT)

TAXATION
Fontbonne U (MO)
Grand Valley State U (MI)

TECHNICAL AND SCIENTIFIC COMMUNICATION
Lehigh U (PA)

TECHNICAL TEACHER EDUCATION
Auburn U (AL)
Bowling Green State U (OH)
Eastern Illinois U (IL)
Ferris State U (MI)
Inter American U of Puerto Rico, San Germán Campus (PR)
Montana State U (MT)
New York Inst of Technology (NY)
Northern Arizona U (AZ)
The Ohio State U (OH)
Oklahoma State U (OK)
Pittsburg State U (KS)
Rhode Island Coll (RI)
South Dakota State U (SD)
The U of Akron (OH)
U of Arkansas (AR)
U of Georgia (GA)
U of Idaho (ID)
U of Minnesota, Twin Cities Campus (MN)
U of Missouri (MO)
U of Saskatchewan (SK, Canada)
U of Wisconsin–Stout (WI)
Utah State U (UT)
Wayne State U (MI)
Western Michigan U (MI)
Wright State U (OH)

TECHNOLOGY/INDUSTRIAL ARTS TEACHER EDUCATION
Appalachian State U (NC)
Ball State U (IN)
Bemidji State U (MN)
Berea Coll (KY)
Central Connecticut State U (CT)
Central Michigan U (MI)
The Coll of New Jersey (NJ)
Colorado State U (CO)
Drury U (MO)
Eastern Michigan U (MI)
Fitchburg State U (MA)
Georgia Southern U (GA)
Humboldt State U (CA)
Illinois State U (IL)
Keene State Coll (NH)
Kent State U (OH)
Lindenwood U (MO)
Middle Tennessee State U (TN)
Millersville U of Pennsylvania (PA)
Mississippi State U (MS)
Missouri State U (MO)
New Mexico Highlands U (NM)
New York City Coll of Technology of the City U of New York (NY)
North Carolina Ag and Tech State U (NC)
North Carolina State U (NC)
Northern Arizona U (AZ)
The Ohio State U (OH)
Pittsburg State U (KS)
Purdue U (IN)
Rhode Island Coll (RI)
St. Petersburg Coll (FL)
Southeast Missouri State U (MO)
State U of New York at Oswego (NY)
Texas A&M U–Corpus Christi (TX)
Texas Wesleyan U (TX)
U of Idaho (ID)
U of Minnesota, Crookston (MN)
U of Minnesota, Twin Cities Campus (MN)
U of Nevada, Reno (NV)
U of Northern Iowa (IA)
U of Southern Mississippi (MS)
U of the Ozarks (AR)
U of Wisconsin–Stout (WI)
U of Wyoming (WY)
Utah State U (UT)
Viterbo U (WI)
Wayland Baptist U (TX)
Wayne State Coll (NE)
Western Michigan U (MI)
Westfield State U (MA)

TELECOMMUNICATIONS TECHNOLOGY
Ferris State U (MI)
Inter American U of Puerto Rico, Bayamón Campus (PR)
Ithaca Coll (NY)
Lawrence Technological U (MI)
National U (CA)
New York City Coll of Technology of the City U of New York (NY)
New York Inst of Technology (NY)
Pace U (NY)
Pacific U (OR)
Pepperdine U, Malibu (CA)
St. John's U (NY)
Southern Polytechnic State U (GA)
U of Wisconsin–Platteville (WI)

TEXTILE SCIENCE
Michigan State U (MI)

TEXTILE SCIENCES AND ENGINEERING
Auburn U (AL)
Clemson U (SC)
Georgia Inst of Technology (GA)
North Carolina State U (NC)
Philadelphia U (PA)
U of Massachusetts Dartmouth (MA)

THEATER DESIGN AND TECHNOLOGY
Bard Coll at Simon's Rock (MA)
Bennington Coll (VT)
Biola U (CA)
Boston U (MA)
Brenau U (GA)
Brigham Young U (UT)
California Inst of the Arts (CA)
Centenary Coll (NJ)
Central Michigan U (MI)
Coker Coll (SC)
Coll of the Ozarks (MO)
Columbia Coll Chicago (IL)
Concordia U (QC, Canada)
DePaul U (IL)
Dixie State Coll of Utah (UT)
Doane Coll (NE)
Elon U (NC)
Fitchburg State U (MA)
Five Towns Coll (NY)
Florida Southern Coll (FL)
Greensboro Coll (NC)
Huntington U (IN)
Illinois Wesleyan U (IL)
Ithaca Coll (NY)
Kean U (NJ)
Keene State Coll (NH)
Lindenwood U (MO)
Millikin U (IL)
New York City Coll of Technology of the City U of New York (NY)
Northwest Missouri State U (MO)
Oklahoma City U (OK)
Penn State Abington (PA)
Penn State Altoona (PA)
Penn State Beaver (PA)
Penn State Berks (PA)
Penn State Brandywine (PA)
Penn State DuBois (PA)
Penn State Erie, The Behrend Coll (PA)
Penn State Fayette, The Eberly Campus (PA)
Penn State Greater Allegheny (PA)
Penn State Hazleton (PA)
Penn State Lehigh Valley (PA)
Penn State Mont Alto (PA)
Penn State New Kensington (PA)
Penn State Schuylkill (PA)
Penn State Shenango (PA)
Penn State U Park (PA)
Penn State Wilkes-Barre (PA)
Penn State Worthington Scranton (PA)
Penn State York (PA)
Purchase Coll, State U of New York (NY)
Rocky Mountain Coll (MT)
Salem State U (MA)
Seton Hill U (PA)
Shenandoah U (VA)
Slippery Rock U of Pennsylvania (PA)
Southwestern Coll (KS)
State U of New York at Binghamton (NY)
State U of New York at New Paltz (NY)

Stephens Coll (MO)
Texas Tech U (TX)
Trinity U (TX)
U of Alaska Fairbanks (AK)
The U of Arizona (AZ)
U of Cincinnati (OH)
U of Delaware (DE)
The U of Kansas (KS)
U of Lethbridge (AB, Canada)
U of Miami (FL)
U of Michigan (MI)
U of Michigan–Flint (MI)
U of North Carolina School of the Arts (NC)
U of Regina (SK, Canada)
U of Southern California (CA)
The U of the Arts (PA)
Virginia Intermont Coll (VA)
Webster U (MO)
Western Michigan U (MI)
Western State Coll of Colorado (CO)
Wright State U (OH)

THEATER LITERATURE, HISTORY AND CRITICISM
Albertus Magnus Coll (CT)
Averett U (VA)
Bard Coll (NY)
Bard Coll at Simon's Rock (MA)
Bennington Coll (VT)
Bowdoin Coll (ME)
Buena Vista U (IA)
Clark Atlanta U (GA)
DePaul U (IL)
Eugene Lang Coll The New School for Liberal Arts (NY)
Keene State Coll (NH)
Moravian Coll (PA)
Saint Mary's Coll of California (CA)
Salem State U (MA)
State U of New York at New Paltz (NY)
Suffolk U (MA)
Texas Christian U (TX)
U of Saskatchewan (SK, Canada)
Washington & Jefferson Coll (PA)
Washington U in St. Louis (MO)
Western Michigan U (MI)
West Virginia U (WV)

THEATER/THEATER ARTS MANAGEMENT
Berry Coll (GA)
Bethany Coll (KS)
Biola U (CA)
Cedarville U (OH)
DEREE - The American Coll of Greece (Greece)
Juniata Coll (PA)
Massachusetts Coll of Liberal Arts (MA)
Michigan State U (MI)
Nazareth Coll of Rochester (NY)
Oglethorpe U (GA)
Ohio U (OH)
Pittsburg State U (KS)
Regent U (VA)
Reinhardt U (GA)
Rowan U (NJ)
Seton Hill U (PA)
Slippery Rock U of Pennsylvania (PA)
Stephens Coll (MO)
The U of British Columbia (BC, Canada)
U of Evansville (IN)
U of Miami (FL)
U of Minnesota, Duluth (MN)
U of Regina (SK, Canada)
U of Richmond (VA)
U of Southern California (CA)

THEOLOGICAL AND MINISTERIAL STUDIES RELATED
Baptist Bible Coll of Pennsylvania (PA)
California Christian Coll (CA)
Concordia U (QC, Canada)
Hardin-Simmons U (TX)
Huntington U (IN)
John Brown U (AR)
Lincoln Christian U (IL)
Marquette U (WI)
Northwest Christian U (OR)
Northwestern Coll (MN)
Trevecca Nazarene U (TN)
Trinity Coll of Florida (FL)
Viterbo U (WI)

THEOLOGY

Alvernia U (PA)
Anderson U (IN)
Andrews U (MI)
Anna Maria Coll (MA)
Apex School of Theology (NC)
Appalachian Bible Coll (WV)
Aquinas Coll (TN)
Assumption Coll (MA)
Atlanta Christian Coll (GA)
Atlantic Union Coll (MA)
Augsburg Coll (MN)
Azusa Pacific U (CA)
Barry U (FL)
Bellarmine U (KY)
Belmont Abbey Coll (NC)
Benedictine U (IL)
Biola U (CA)
Bluefield Coll (VA)
Bob Jones U (SC)
Boston Coll (MA)
Brewton-Parker Coll (GA)
Briar Cliff U (IA)
Calumet Coll of Saint Joseph (IN)
Calvin Coll (MI)
Carlow U (PA)
Cedarville U (OH)
Christendom Coll (VA)
Coll of Saint Benedict (MN)
Coll of Saint Elizabeth (NJ)
Coll of Saint Mary (NE)
Concordia U (CA)
Concordia U (QC, Canada)
Concordia U Chicago (IL)
Concordia U, St. Paul (MN)
Concordia U Wisconsin (WI)
Creighton U (NE)
Crown Coll (MN)
DeSales U (PA)
Dominican U (IL)
Dordt Coll (IA)
Duquesne U (PA)
Elmhurst Coll (IL)
Faulkner U (AL)
Gannon U (PA)
Georgetown U (DC)
Grace Bible Coll (MI)
Hanover Coll (IN)
Hardin-Simmons U (TX)
Hellenic Coll (MA)
Hillsdale Free Will Baptist Coll (OK)
Holy Cross Coll (IN)
Holy Trinity Orthodox Sem (NY)
Houghton Coll (NY)
Huntington U (IN)
Immaculata U (PA)
Indiana Wesleyan U (IN)
John Brown U (AR)
King's Coll (PA)
The King's U Coll (AB, Canada)
Kuyper Coll (MI)
Lee U (TN)
Lincoln Christian U (IL)
Louisiana Coll (LA)
Loyola Marymount U (CA)
Loyola U Chicago (IL)
Lubbock Christian U (TX)
Marquette U (WI)
Martin Luther Coll (MN)
The Master's Coll and Sem (CA)
Master's Coll and Sem (ON, Canada)
MidAmerica Nazarene U (KS)
Morris Coll (SC)
Mount St. Mary's U (MD)
Mount Vernon Nazarene U (OH)
Multnomah U (OR)
Newman U (KS)
Northwest Nazarene U (ID)
Oklahoma Wesleyan U (OK)
Ouachita Baptist U (AR)
Pacific Lutheran U (WA)
Pacific Union Coll (CA)
Palm Beach Atlantic U (FL)
Providence Coll (RI)
Rockhurst U (MO)
St. Ambrose U (IA)
Saint Anselm Coll (NH)
St. Bonaventure U (NY)
St. Catherine U (MN)
Saint John's U (MN)
St. John's U (NY)
Saint Joseph's Coll of Maine (ME)
St. Louis Christian Coll (MO)
Saint Louis U (MO)
Saint Mary-of-the-Woods Coll (IN)
Saint Mary's Coll of California (CA)
Saint Mary's U of Minnesota (MN)

San Diego Christian Coll (CA)
Seattle Pacific U (WA)
Silver Lake Coll (WI)
Southeastern Baptist Theological Sem (NC)
Southern Adventist U (TN)
Southern Nazarene U (OK)
Southwestern Adventist U (TX)
Southwestern Assemblies of God U (TX)
Spring Arbor U (MI)
Tabor Coll (KS)
Texas Lutheran U (TX)
Union Coll (NE)
Union U (TN)
U of Dallas (TX)
U of Dubuque (IA)
U of Evansville (IN)
U of Mary Hardin-Baylor (TX)
U of Minnesota, Twin Cities Campus (MN)
U of Notre Dame (IN)
U of Portland (OR)
U of St. Francis (IL)
U of Saint Mary (KS)
U of St. Thomas (MN)
U of San Francisco (CA)
The U of Western Ontario (ON, Canada)
Valparaiso U (IN)
Walla Walla U (WA)
Walsh U (OH)
Washington Adventist U (MD)
Wheeling Jesuit U (WV)
Xavier U of Louisiana (LA)

THEOLOGY AND RELIGIOUS VOCATIONS RELATED

Abilene Christian U (TX)
Arlington Baptist Coll (TX)
Baptist Bible Coll of Pennsylvania (PA)
Cedarville U (OH)
Concordia Coll–New York (NY)
Master's Coll and Sem (ON, Canada)
Missouri Baptist U (MO)
Newman U (KS)
Ouachita Baptist U (AR)
St. Edward's U (TX)
Simpson U (CA)
Southeastern U (FL)
Southern Nazarene U (OK)
Thiel Coll (PA)
Union U (TN)
U of St. Thomas (TX)

THEORETICAL AND MATHEMATICAL PHYSICS

Chapman U (CA)
Oregon State U (OR)
Sweet Briar Coll (VA)
U at Buffalo, the State U of New York (NY)
U of Guelph (ON, Canada)
U of Ottawa (ON, Canada)
U of Saskatchewan (SK, Canada)
The U of Western Ontario (ON, Canada)

THERAPEUTIC RECREATION

Alderson-Broaddus Coll (WV)
Ashland U (OH)
Brigham Young U (UT)
California State U, Chico (CA)
Calvin Coll (MI)
Central Michigan U (MI)
Coker Coll (SC)
Concordia U (QC, Canada)
Eastern Michigan U (MI)
Eastern Washington U (WA)
Grand Valley State U (MI)
Indiana Tech (IN)
Ithaca Coll (NY)
Longwood U (VA)
Minnesota State U Mankato (MN)
Pittsburg State U (KS)
Prescott Coll (AZ)
St. Andrews Presbyterian Coll (NC)
Shorter U (GA)
Slippery Rock U of Pennsylvania (PA)
Springfield Coll (MA)
Temple U (PA)
The U of Akron (OH)
The U of Iowa (IA)
The U of North Carolina Wilmington (NC)

U of Southern Maine (ME)
U of Waterloo (ON, Canada)
U of Wisconsin–La Crosse (WI)
Western Carolina U (NC)
Winona State U (MN)

TOOL AND DIE TECHNOLOGY

Utah State U (UT)

TOURISM AND TRAVEL SERVICES MANAGEMENT

Arizona State U (AZ)
Bowling Green State U (OH)
Brock U (ON, Canada)
California State U, Chico (CA)
Concord U (WV)
Delaware State U (DE)
Fort Lewis Coll (CO)
Hawai'i Pacific U (HI)
Indiana U East (IN)
Indiana U–Purdue U Indianapolis (IN)
Intl Business Coll, Fort Wayne (IN)
Johnson & Wales U (FL)
Johnson & Wales U (RI)
Johnson State Coll (VT)
Mansfield U of Pennsylvania (PA)
Niagara U (NY)
Northeastern State U (OK)
St. Thomas U (FL)
Salem State U (MA)
State U of New York Coll of Technology at Delhi (NY)
State U of New York Maritime Coll (NY)
Texas A&M U (TX)
United States Intl U (Kenya)
U of Central Florida (FL)
U of Guelph (ON, Canada)
U of Hawaii at Manoa (HI)
The U of Montana Western (MT)
U of Nevada, Las Vegas (NV)
U of South Carolina (SC)
The U of Texas at San Antonio (TX)

TOURISM AND TRAVEL SERVICES MARKETING

Johnson & Wales U (RI)
Mitchell Coll (CT)
U of Central Missouri (MO)
Western Michigan U (MI)

TOURISM PROMOTION

Bowling Green State U (OH)

TOXICOLOGY

Ashland U (OH)
Eastern Michigan U (MI)
Northeastern U (MA)
Penn State Beaver (PA)
Penn State Berks (PA)
Penn State DuBois (PA)
Penn State Fayette, The Eberly Campus (PA)
Penn State Greater Allegheny (PA)
Penn State Hazleton (PA)
Penn State Mont Alto (PA)
Penn State New Kensington (PA)
Penn State Shenango (PA)
Penn State U Park (PA)
Penn State Wilkes-Barre (PA)
Penn State York (PA)
St. John's U (NY)
U of California, Berkeley (CA)
U of Louisiana at Monroe (LA)
U of Saskatchewan (SK, Canada)
The U of Western Ontario (ON, Canada)

TRADE AND INDUSTRIAL TEACHER EDUCATION

Athens State U (AL)
Auburn U (AL)
Bemidji State U (MN)
California State U, Long Beach (CA)
California State U, San Bernardino (CA)
The Coll of Saint Rose (NY)
Colorado State U (CO)
Delaware State U (DE)
Eastern New Mexico U (NM)
Fitchburg State U (MA)
Florida Ag and Mech U (FL)
Indiana State U (IN)
Indiana U of Pennsylvania (PA)
Iowa State U of Science and Technology (IA)
Kent State U (OH)

Lindenwood U (MO)
New York Inst of Technology (NY)
Northern Kentucky U (KY)
Prairie View A&M U (TX)
San Diego State U (CA)
Southern Illinois U Carbondale (IL)
State U of New York at Oswego (NY)
Temple U (PA)
Texas A&M U–Corpus Christi (TX)
U of Arkansas at Pine Bluff (AR)
U of Central Florida (FL)
U of Louisville (KY)
U of Minnesota, Twin Cities Campus (MN)
U of Nevada, Reno (NV)
U of North Florida (FL)
U of Saskatchewan (SK, Canada)
U of Southern Maine (ME)
U of South Florida (FL)
U of the District of Columbia (DC)
The U of Toledo (OH)
U of West Florida (FL)
U of Wyoming (WY)
Upper Iowa U (IA)
Valdosta State U (GA)
Virginia State U (VA)
Wayland Baptist U (TX)
Western Kentucky U (KY)
Western Michigan U (MI)

TRANSPORTATION AND MATERIALS MOVING RELATED

Lewis U (IL)
Niagara U (NY)
Syracuse U (NY)
United States Merchant Marine Acad (NY)
The U of British Columbia (BC, Canada)

TRANSPORTATION/MOBILITY MANAGEMENT

American Public U System (WV)
Bridgewater State U (MA)
North Carolina Ag and Tech State U (NC)
U of North Florida (FL)
U of Pennsylvania (PA)
U of Wisconsin–Superior (WI)

TURF AND TURFGRASS MANAGEMENT

Clemson U (SC)
Florida Southern Coll (FL)
New Mexico State U (NM)
North Carolina State U (NC)
North Dakota State U (ND)
The Ohio State U (OH)
Penn State Abington (PA)
Penn State Altoona (PA)
Penn State Beaver (PA)
Penn State Berks (PA)
Penn State Brandywine (PA)
Penn State DuBois (PA)
Penn State Erie, The Behrend Coll (PA)
Penn State Fayette, The Eberly Campus (PA)
Penn State Greater Allegheny (PA)
Penn State Hazleton (PA)
Penn State Lehigh Valley (PA)
Penn State Mont Alto (PA)
Penn State New Kensington (PA)
Penn State Schuylkill (PA)
Penn State Shenango (PA)
Penn State U Park (PA)
Penn State Wilkes-Barre (PA)
Penn State Worthington Scranton (PA)
Penn State York (PA)
Rutgers, The State U of New Jersey, New Brunswick (NJ)
Tennessee Technological U (TN)
Texas A&M U (TX)
U of Georgia (GA)
U of Minnesota, Crookston (MN)
U of Nebraska–Lincoln (NE)
U of Rhode Island (RI)

TURKISH

The U of Texas at Austin (TX)
U of Utah (UT)

UKRAINIAN

U of Saskatchewan (SK, Canada)

URBAN EDUCATION AND LEADERSHIP

The Coll of New Jersey (NJ)

URBAN FORESTRY

Texas A&M U (TX)
U of California, Davis (CA)
U of Minnesota, Crookston (MN)

URBAN MINISTRY

Crossroads Bible Coll (IN)
Crown Coll (MN)

URBAN STUDIES/AFFAIRS

Albertus Magnus Coll (CT)
The American U of Paris (France)
Aquinas Coll (MI)
Arizona State U (AZ)
Augsburg Coll (MN)
Ball State U (IN)
Barnard Coll (NY)
Boston U (MA)
Brown U (RI)
Bryn Mawr Coll (PA)
Butler U (IN)
California State U, Dominguez Hills (CA)
California State U, Northridge (CA)
Calvary Bible Coll and Theological Sem (MO)
Canisius Coll (NY)
Cleveland State U (OH)
Coll of Charleston (SC)
The Coll of Wooster (OH)
Columbia U, School of General Studies (NY)
Concordia U (QC, Canada)
Connecticut Coll (CT)
Coppin State U (MD)
Delaware State U (DE)
DePaul U (IL)
Dillard U (LA)
Elmhurst Coll (IL)
Eugene Lang Coll The New School for Liberal Arts (NY)
Furman U (SC)
Hamline U (MN)
Hampshire Coll (MA)
Haverford Coll (PA)
Hobart and William Smith Colls (NY)
Hunter Coll of the City U of New York (NY)
Lipscomb U (TN)
Loyola Marymount U (CA)
Manhattan Coll (NY)
Minnesota State U Mankato (MN)
Morehouse Coll (GA)
New Coll of Florida (FL)
New Jersey City U (NJ)
New York U (NY)
Northeastern Illinois U (IL)
Oglethorpe U (GA)
Ohio U (OH)
Ohio Wesleyan U (OH)
Portland State U (OR)
Purchase Coll, State U of New York (NY)
Queens Coll of the City U of New York (NY)
Rhodes Coll (TN)
Rutgers, The State U of New Jersey, Camden (NJ)
Rutgers, The State U of New Jersey, New Brunswick (NJ)
Saint Louis U (MO)
San Diego State U (CA)
San Francisco State U (CA)
Sarah Lawrence Coll (NY)
Stanford U (CA)
Temple U (PA)
Towson U (MD)
Trinity U (TX)
Tufts U (MA)
The U of British Columbia (BC, Canada)
U of California, Berkeley (CA)
U of California, Irvine (CA)
U of Cincinnati (OH)
U of Illinois at Chicago (IL)
U of Lethbridge (AB, Canada)
U of Minnesota, Duluth (MN)
U of Minnesota, Twin Cities Campus (MN)
U of Pennsylvania (PA)
U of Pittsburgh (PA)
The U of Texas at Austin (TX)
The U of Toledo (OH)
U of Utah (UT)

The U of Western Ontario (ON, Canada)
U of Wisconsin–Green Bay (WI)
Vassar Coll (NY)
Virginia Commonwealth U (VA)
Washington U in St. Louis (MO)
Wayne State U (MI)
Worcester State U (MA)
Wright State U (OH)

VETERINARY/ANIMAL HEALTH TECHNOLOGY

Brigham Young U (UT)
Intl Business Coll, Fort Wayne (IN)
Medaille Coll (NY)
Michigan State U (MI)
Mississippi State U (MS)
Mount Ida Coll (MA)
Murray State U (KY)
North Dakota State U (ND)
Purdue U (IN)
St. Petersburg Coll (FL)
State U of New York Coll of Technology at Delhi (NY)
Thomas Edison State Coll (NJ)
U of Nebraska–Lincoln (NE)

VISION SCIENCE/ PHYSIOLOGICAL OPTICS

U of the Incarnate Word (TX)

VISUAL AND PERFORMING ARTS

Alderson-Broaddus Coll (WV)
American U (DC)
Angelo State U (TX)
Arizona State U (AZ)
Armstrong Atlantic State U (GA)
Art Center Coll of Design (CA)
Assumption Coll (MA)
Baldwin-Wallace Coll (OH)
Bard Coll at Simon's Rock (MA)
Barnard Coll (NY)
Bennington Coll (VT)
Blackburn Coll (IL)
Bloomfield Coll (NJ)
Blue Mountain Coll (MS)
Brown U (RI)
Bucknell U (PA)
California Baptist U (CA)
California State U, San Marcos (CA)
Centenary Coll of Louisiana (LA)
Claremont McKenna Coll (CA)
Clemson U (SC)
Columbia U, School of General Studies (NY)
Concordia U (QC, Canada)
Cooper Union for the Advancement of Science and Art (NY)
Delta State U (MS)
DEREE - The American Coll of Greece (Greece)
Dowling Coll (NY)
East Stroudsburg U of Pennsylvania (PA)
Eckerd Coll (FL)
Eugene Lang Coll The New School for Liberal Arts (NY)
Fairleigh Dickinson U, Coll at Florham (NJ)
Fairleigh Dickinson U, Metropolitan Campus (NJ)
Ferrum Coll (VA)
Gannon U (PA)
Gettysburg Coll (PA)
Harvard U (MA)
Indiana U of Pennsylvania (PA)
Inter American U of Puerto Rico, San Germán Campus (PR)
Iowa State U of Science and Technology (IA)
Ithaca Coll (NY)
Johnson C. Smith U (NC)
Johnson State Coll (VT)
King Coll (TN)
LaGrange Coll (GA)
Lindenwood U (MO)
Long Island U, C.W. Post Campus (NY)
Loras Coll (IA)
Maryland Inst Coll of Art (MD)
Massachusetts Coll of Liberal Arts (MA)
Mississippi State U (MS)
Mississippi U for Women (MS)
Missouri State U (MO)
Mount Olive Coll (NC)
Naropa U (CO)
New Mexico Highlands U (NM)
New Mexico State U (NM)

Oregon State U (OR)
Penn State Abington (PA)
Penn State Altoona (PA)
Penn State Beaver (PA)
Penn State Berks (PA)
Penn State Brandywine (PA)
Penn State DuBois (PA)
Penn State Erie, The Behrend Coll (PA)
Penn State Fayette, The Eberly Campus (PA)
Penn State Greater Allegheny (PA)
Penn State Hazleton (PA)
Penn State Lehigh Valley (PA)
Penn State Mont Alto (PA)
Penn State New Kensington (PA)
Penn State Schuylkill (PA)
Penn State Shenango (PA)
Penn State U Park (PA)
Penn State Wilkes-Barre (PA)
Penn State Worthington Scranton (PA)
Penn State York (PA)
Prescott Coll (AZ)
Providence Coll (RI)
Purchase Coll, State U of New York (NY)
Ramapo Coll of New Jersey (NJ)
Regis U (CO)
Rensselaer Polytechnic Inst (NY)
The Richard Stockton Coll of New Jersey (NJ)
Rogers State U (OK)
Rutgers, The State U of New Jersey, New Brunswick (NJ)
St. Bonaventure U (NY)
Saint Joseph's U (PA)
San Jose State U (CA)
Sarah Lawrence Coll (NY)
Savannah Coll of Art and Design (GA)
Savannah State U (GA)
Shenandoah U (VA)
South Dakota State U (SD)
Southeast Missouri State U (MO)
State U of New York at New Paltz (NY)
State U of New York Coll at Old Westbury (NY)
State U of New York Coll at Potsdam (NY)
Stonehill Coll (MA)
Suffolk U (MA)
Texas Wesleyan U (TX)
The U of Arizona (AZ)
The U of British Columbia (BC, Canada)
The U of British Columbia– Okanagan (BC, Canada)
U of Colorado at Colorado Springs (CO)
U of Houston–Downtown (TX)
U of Louisiana at Lafayette (LA)
U of Maryland, Baltimore County (MD)
U of Mary Washington (VA)
U of North Carolina School of the Arts (NC)
U of Pennsylvania (PA)
U of Regina (SK, Canada)
U of Rio Grande (OH)
U of St. Francis (IL)
U of Saint Mary (KS)
U of San Francisco (CA)
The U of South Dakota (SD)
U of Southern California (CA)
U of Southern Mississippi (MS)
The U of Tennessee at Martin (TN)
The U of Texas at Austin (TX)
The U of Texas at Dallas (TX)
U of Utah (UT)
U of Wisconsin–Superior (WI)
Valdosta State U (GA)
Vassar Coll (NY)
Virginia State U (VA)
Viterbo U (WI)
Wheelock Coll (MA)
Wichita State U (KS)
Worcester State U (MA)

VISUAL AND PERFORMING ARTS RELATED

Adelphi U (NY)
Baldwin-Wallace Coll (OH)
The Baptist Coll of Florida (FL)
Bard Coll at Simon's Rock (MA)
Brigham Young U (UT)
California Inst of the Arts (CA)
Cameron U (OK)
Claremont McKenna Coll (CA)

Clemson U (SC)
Columbia U, School of General Studies (NY)
Cumberland U (TN)
The Evergreen State Coll (WA)
Illinois State U (IL)
Illinois Wesleyan U (IL)
Indiana U Bloomington (IN)
Maine Coll of Art (ME)
Marywood U (PA)
Millikin U (IL)
New York U (NY)
Penn State Altoona (PA)
Providence Coll (RI)
Purchase Coll, State U of New York (NY)
Rice U (TX)
Sacred Heart U (CT)
Saint Mary's Coll of California (CA)
Samford U (AL)
Sarah Lawrence Coll (NY)
School of the Museum of Fine Arts, Boston (MA)
Seton Hill U (PA)
Simon Fraser U (BC, Canada)
Spring Arbor U (MI)
State U of New York Coll at Geneseo (NY)
Stetson U (FL)
Syracuse U (NY)
U of California, Davis (CA)
U of Lethbridge (AB, Canada)
U of Michigan (MI)
U of New Haven (CT)
U of South Florida (FL)
U of Washington, Bothell (WA)
U of Wisconsin–Green Bay (WI)
Webster U (MO)
Western State Coll of Colorado (CO)

VITICULTURE AND ENOLOGY

Cornell U (NY)

VOCATIONAL REHABILITATION COUNSELING

Emporia State U (KS)
Maryville U of Saint Louis (MO)
U of Wisconsin–Madison (WI)
U of Wisconsin–Stout (WI)
Wright State U (OH)

VOICE AND OPERA

Abilene Christian U (TX)
Acadia U (NS, Canada)
Andrews U (MI)
Anna Maria Coll (MA)
Baldwin-Wallace Coll (OH)
Bard Coll (NY)
Barry U (FL)
Belmont U (TN)
Bennington Coll (VT)
Biola U (CA)
Birmingham-Southern Coll (AL)
Boston U (MA)
Bowling Green State U (OH)
Brigham Young U (UT)
Butler U (IN)
California Baptist U (CA)
California State U, Long Beach (CA)
Calvary Bible Coll and Theological Sem (MO)
Calvin Coll (MI)
Campbellsville U (KY)
Capital U (OH)
Carnegie Mellon U (PA)
Carson-Newman Coll (TN)
The Catholic U of America (DC)
Chapman U (CA)
Cincinnati Christian U (OH)
Coker Coll (SC)
Delaware State U (DE)
Dordt Coll (IA)
Drake U (IA)
East Texas Baptist U (TX)
Five Towns Coll (NY)
Furman U (SC)
Hannibal-LaGrange U (MO)
Hardin-Simmons U (TX)
Hope Coll (MI)
Houghton Coll (NY)
Illinois Wesleyan U (IL)
Indiana U–Purdue U Fort Wayne (IN)
Inter American U of Puerto Rico, San Germán Campus (PR)
Ithaca Coll (NY)
Lamar U (TX)
Lawrence U (WI)
Lee U (TN)
Lincoln Christian U (IL)

Lipscomb U (TN)
Long Island U, C.W. Post Campus (NY)
Louisiana Coll (LA)
Mannes Coll The New School for Music (NY)
Maryville Coll (TN)
The Master's Coll and Sem (CA)
McMurry U (TX)
MidAmerica Nazarene U (KS)
Millikin U (IL)
Minnesota State U Mankato (MN)
Mount Allison U (NB, Canada)
Newberry Coll (SC)
New England Conservatory of Music (MA)
Northern Arizona U (AZ)
Northern State U (SD)
Northwestern U (MN)
Notre Dame de Namur U (CA)
Nyack Coll (NY)
Oberlin Coll (OH)
The Ohio State U (OH)
Ohio U (OH)
Oklahoma Christian U (OK)
Oklahoma City U (OK)
Ouachita Baptist U (AR)
Palm Beach Atlantic U (FL)
Peabody Conservatory of The Johns Hopkins U (MD)
Rider U (NJ)
Roosevelt U (IL)
Samford U (AL)
San Diego Christian Coll (CA)
San Francisco Conservatory of Music (CA)
Sarah Lawrence Coll (NY)
Shorter U (GA)
Southeastern U (FL)
Southern Methodist U (TX)
State U of New York at Fredonia (NY)
State U of New York at New Paltz (NY)
Stetson U (FL)
Talladega Coll (AL)
Temple U (PA)
Texas Wesleyan U (TX)
Trinity U (TX)
Union U (TN)
The U of British Columbia (BC, Canada)
U of Cincinnati (OH)
U of Idaho (ID)
The U of Iowa (IA)
The U of Kansas (KS)
U of Miami (FL)
U of Mobile (AL)
U of Nebraska at Omaha (NE)
U of North Carolina School of the Arts (NC)
U of Redlands (CA)
U of Southern California (CA)
The U of Tennessee at Martin (TN)
U of the Pacific (CA)
U of Tulsa (OK)
U of Washington (WA)
The U of Western Ontario (ON, Canada)
Valparaiso U (IN)
Vanderbilt U (TN)
Walla Walla U (WA)
Washington U in St. Louis (MO)
Western Michigan U (MI)
Willamette U (OR)
William Paterson U of New Jersey (NJ)

WALDORF/STEINER TEACHER EDUCATION

Prescott Coll (AZ)

WATER QUALITY AND WASTEWATER TREATMENT MANAGEMENT AND RECYCLING TECHNOLOGY

Mississippi Valley State U (MS)
Murray State U (KY)

WATER RESOURCES ENGINEERING

Central State U (OH)
State U of New York Coll of Environmental Science and Forestry (NY)
The U of Arizona (AZ)
U of Guelph (ON, Canada)
U of Nevada, Reno (NV)

WATER, WETLANDS, AND MARINE RESOURCES MANAGEMENT

Colorado State U (CO)
Florida Gulf Coast U (FL)
Sterling Coll (VT)
Stony Brook U, State U of New York (NY)
Texas State U–San Marcos (TX)
U of Georgia (GA)
U of Minnesota, Crookston (MN)
U of New Hampshire (NH)
Western State Coll of Colorado (CO)

WEB/MULTIMEDIA MANAGEMENT AND WEBMASTER

Champlain Coll (VT)
ECPI Coll of Technology, Virginia Beach (VA)
Hawai`i Pacific U (HI)
Indiana Tech (IN)
Lewis-Clark State Coll (ID)
Limestone Coll (SC)
Mars Hill Coll (NC)
Neumont U (UT)
Northern Michigan U (MI)
Trevecca Nazarene U (TN)
U of Dubuque (IA)
U of St. Francis (IL)

WEB PAGE, DIGITAL/ MULTIMEDIA AND INFORMATION RESOURCES DESIGN

The Art Inst of Ohio–Cincinnati (OH)
The Art Inst of Seattle (WA)
The Art Inst of York–Pennsylvania (PA)
Azusa Pacific U (CA)
Champlain Coll (VT)
The Cleveland Inst of Art (OH)
Columbia Coll Chicago (IL)
Concordia U (QC, Canada)
Dakota Wesleyan U (SD)
DeVry U, Phoenix (AZ)
DeVry U, Pomona (CA)
DeVry U, Westminster (CO)
DeVry U, Miramar (FL)
DeVry U, Orlando (FL)
DeVry U, Decatur (GA)
DeVry U, Chicago (IL)
DeVry U, Kansas City (MO)
DeVry U, North Brunswick (NJ)
DeVry U, Columbus (OH)
DeVry U, Fort Washington (PA)
DeVry U, Houston (TX)
DeVry U, Irving (TX)
DeVry U, Arlington (VA)
DeVry U, Federal Way (WA)
DeVry U Online (IL)
Duquesne U (PA)
Emily Carr U of Art + Design (BC, Canada)
Franklin U (OH)
Grace Coll (IN)
Hampshire Coll (MA)
Harding U (AR)
Indiana Wesleyan U (IN)
Intl Acad of Design & Technology (FL)
Iowa Wesleyan Coll (IA)
Johnson & Wales U (RI)
Lasell Coll (MA)
Liberty U (VA)
Neumont U (UT)
New Jersey Inst of Technology (NJ)
New York City Coll of Technology of the City of New York (NY)
Northwest Missouri State U (MO)
Pennsylvania Coll of Technology (PA)
Quinnipiac U (CT)
Santa Clara U (CA)
Silver Lake Coll (WI)
State U of New York Coll of Technology at Delhi (NY)
Tennessee Technological U (TN)
Thiel Coll (PA)
Trevecca Nazarene U (TN)
U of Dubuque (IA)
U of Mount Union (OH)
The U of North Carolina at Asheville (NC)
U of Wisconsin–Stevens Point (WI)
Utah Valley U (UT)

WELDING TECHNOLOGY

LeTourneau U (TX)

Northland Coll (WI)
Northwest U (WA)
Perelandra Coll (CA)
St. Edward's U (TX)
Salem State U (MA)
Spring Hill Coll (AL)
Thiel Coll (PA)
U of Colorado Denver (CO)
U of Evansville (IN)
U of Michigan–Flint (MI)
U of Minnesota, Twin Cities Campus (MN)
U of Nevada, Reno (NV)
The U of Tampa (FL)
The U of Texas at Austin (TX)
Wartburg Coll (IA)
Western Michigan U (MI)

YOUTH MINISTRY
Abilene Christian U (TX)
Anderson U (IN)
Andrews U (MI)
Asbury U (KY)
Baptist Bible Coll of Pennsylvania (PA)
Benedictine Coll (KS)
Bethel Coll (IN)
Bethel U (MN)
Bluffton U (OH)
Calvary Bible Coll and Theological Sem (MO)
Cedarville U (OH)

Concordia U Wisconsin (WI)
Corban U (OR)
Crown Coll (MN)
Dordt Coll (IA)
East Texas Baptist U (TX)
Geneva Coll (PA)
Gordon Coll (MA)
Grace Bible Coll (MI)
Grace Coll (IN)
Great Lakes Christian Coll (MI)
Greenville Coll (IL)
Harding U (AR)
Hardin-Simmons U (TX)
Hillsdale Free Will Baptist Coll (OK)
Huntingdon Coll (AL)
Huntington U (IN)
Indiana Wesleyan U (IN)
John Brown U (AR)
King Coll (TN)
Kuyper Coll (MI)
Lee U (TN)
Lincoln Christian U (IL)
Lipscomb U (TN)
Lubbock Christian U (TX)
Malone U (OH)
Maranatha Baptist Bible Coll (WI)
Master's Coll and Sem (ON, Canada)
MidAmerica Nazarene U (KS)
Mid-Atlantic Christian U (NC)
Mount Vernon Nazarene U (OH)
Multnomah U (OR)

New Hope Christian Coll (OR)
North Greenville U (SC)
Northwestern Coll (MN)
Northwest U (WA)
Nyack Coll (NY)
Oak Hills Christian Coll (MN)
Ouachita Baptist U (AR)
Saint Mary's U of Minnesota (MN)
Simpson U (CA)
Southern Nazarene U (OK)
Southwestern Assemblies of God U (TX)
Spring Arbor U (MI)
Tabor Coll (KS)
Trevecca Nazarene U (TN)
Trinity Coll of Florida (FL)
U of Indianapolis (IN)
U of Sioux Falls (SD)
William Jessup U (CA)

YOUTH SERVICES
Stony Brook U, State U of New York (NY)
U of Hawaii at Manoa (HI)
The U of Western Ontario (ON, Canada)
Wheelock Coll (MA)

ZOOLOGY/ANIMAL BIOLOGY
Andrews U (MI)
Auburn U (AL)
Bennington Coll (VT)

California State U, Long Beach (CA)
Coll of the Atlantic (ME)
Colorado State U (CO)
Humboldt State U (CA)
Idaho State U (ID)
Juniata Coll (PA)
Kent State U (OH)
Malone U (OH)
Mars Hill Coll (NC)
Miami U (OH)
Michigan State U (MI)
North Carolina State U (NC)
North Dakota State U (ND)
Northern Arizona U (AZ)
Northern Michigan U (MI)
The Ohio State U (OH)
Ohio U (OH)
Ohio Wesleyan U (OH)
Oklahoma State U (OK)
Oregon State U (OR)
Prescott Coll (AZ)
Rutgers, The State U of New Jersey, Newark (NJ)
San Francisco State U (CA)
Sonoma State U (CA)
Southern Illinois U Carbondale (IL)
Southern Utah U (UT)
State U of New York at Oswego (NY)
State U of New York Coll of Environmental Science and Forestry (NY)

Tarleton State U (TX)
Texas A&M U (TX)
Texas State U–San Marcos (TX)
Texas Tech U (TX)
The U of Akron (OH)
The U of British Columbia (BC, Canada)
The U of British Columbia–Okanagan (BC, Canada)
U of California, Davis (CA)
U of California, Santa Barbara (CA)
U of Florida (FL)
U of Guelph (ON, Canada)
U of Hawaii at Manoa (HI)
U of Maine (ME)
U of Manitoba (MB, Canada)
U of Minnesota, Twin Cities Campus (MN)
U of New Brunswick Fredericton (NB, Canada)
U of New Hampshire (NH)
U of Oklahoma (OK)
U of Rhode Island (RI)
U of Vermont (VT)
U of Washington (WA)
U of Wisconsin–Madison (WI)
U of Wyoming (WY)
Utah State U (UT)
Washington State U (WA)
Weber State U (UT)
Winona State U (MN)

Entrance Difficulty

This index groups colleges by their own assessment of their entrance difficulty level. The colleges were asked to select the level that most closely corresponds to their entrance difficulty, according to the guidelines below. Institutions for which high school class rank and/or standardized test scores do not apply as admission criteria were asked to select the level that best indicates their entrance difficulty as compared to other institutions.

MOST DIFFICULT

More than 75 percent of the freshmen were in the top 10 percent of their high school class and scored over 1310 on the SAT (critical reading and mathematical combined) or over 29 on the ACT (composite); about 30 percent or fewer of the applicants were accepted.

Amherst Coll (MA)
Barnard Coll (NY)
Bates Coll (ME)
Bowdoin Coll (ME)
Brandeis U (MA)
Brown U (RI)
Bryn Mawr Coll (PA)
Bucknell U (PA)
California Inst of Technology (CA)
Carnegie Mellon U (PA)
Claremont McKenna Coll (CA)
The Colburn School Conservatory of Music (CA)
Colby Coll (ME)
Colgate U (NY)
The Coll of William and Mary (VA)
Columbia U, School of General Studies (NY)
Cooper Union for the Advancement of Science and Art (NY)
Cornell U (NY)
Dartmouth Coll (NH)
Franklin W. Olin Coll of Eng (MA)
Georgetown U (DC)
Gettysburg Coll (PA)
Harvard U (MA)
Harvey Mudd Coll (CA)
Haverford Coll (PA)
The Johns Hopkins U (MD)
The Juilliard School (NY)
Lafayette Coll (PA)
Lehigh U (PA)
Massachusetts Inst of Technology (MA)
Middlebury Coll (VT)
New York U (NY)
Pomona Coll (CA)
Princeton U (NJ)
Reed Coll (OR)
Rice U (TX)
Stanford U (CA)
Swarthmore Coll (PA)
Trinity Coll (CT)
Tufts U (MA)
United States Air Force Acad (CO)
United States Military Acad (NY)
U of Notre Dame (IN)
U of Pennsylvania (PA)
U of Southern California (CA)
Washington and Lee U (VA)
Washington U in St. Louis (MO)
Wellesley Coll (MA)
Wesleyan U (CT)
Williams Coll (MA)
Yale U (CT)

VERY DIFFICULT

More than 50 percent of the freshmen were in the top 10 percent of their high school class and scored over 1230 on the SAT or over 26 on the ACT; about 60 percent or fewer applicants were accepted.

Albany Coll of Pharmacy and Health Sciences (NY)
Allegheny Coll (PA)
American U (DC)
American U in Bulgaria (Bulgaria)
Art Center Coll of Design (CA)
Austin Coll (TX)
Bard Coll (NY)
Beloit Coll (WI)
Bennington Coll (VT)
Bentley U (MA)
Boston Coll (MA)
Boston U (MA)
California Inst of the Arts (CA)
Carleton Coll (MN)
Case Western Reserve U (OH)
Centre Coll (KY)
Chapman U (CA)
Christendom Coll (VA)
Clarkson U (NY)
The Coll of New Jersey (NJ)
Coll of the Atlantic (ME)
Coll of the Holy Cross (MA)
The Colorado Coll (CO)
Colorado School of Mines (CO)
Connecticut Coll (CT)
Davidson Coll (NC)
Denison U (OH)
Dickinson Coll (PA)
Earlham Coll (IN)
Eugene Lang Coll The New School for Liberal Arts (NY)
Florida State U (FL)
Franklin & Marshall Coll (PA)
Furman U (SC)
Georgia Inst of Technology (GA)
Grinnell Coll (IA)
Grove City Coll (PA)
Hamilton Coll (NY)
Hendrix Coll (AR)
Hillsdale Coll (MI)
Hobart and William Smith Colls (NY)
Illinois Inst of Technology (IL)
Illinois Wesleyan U (IL)
James Madison U (VA)
Kalamazoo Coll (MI)
Kenyon Coll (OH)
Kettering U (MI)
Lake Forest Coll (IL)
Lawrence U (WI)
Lewis & Clark Coll (OR)
Loyola Marymount U (CA)
Macalester Coll (MN)
Mannes Coll The New School for Music (NY)
Marist Coll (NY)
Maryland Inst Coll of Art (MD)
Massachusetts Coll of Art and Design (MA)
Medical U of South Carolina (SC)
Missouri U of Science and Technology (MO)
Mount Holyoke Coll (MA)
Muhlenberg Coll (PA)
New Coll of Florida (FL)
New England Conservatory of Music (MA)
The New School for Jazz and Contemporary Music (NY)
North Carolina State U (NC)
Northeastern U (MA)
Oberlin Coll (OH)
Oglethorpe U (GA)
The Ohio State U (OH)
Ohio Wesleyan U (OH)
Parsons The New School for Design (NY)
Patrick Henry Coll (VA)
Peabody Conservatory of The Johns Hopkins U (MD)
Penn State Abington (PA)
Penn State Altoona (PA)
Penn State Berks (PA)
Penn State Erie, The Behrend Coll (PA)
Penn State Harrisburg (PA)
Penn State U Park (PA)
Pepperdine U, Malibu (CA)
Polytechnic Inst of NYU (NY)

Pratt Inst (NY)
Presbyterian Coll (SC)
Providence Coll (RI)
Queens Coll of the City U of New York (NY)
Rensselaer Polytechnic Inst (NY)
Rhodes Coll (TN)
The Richard Stockton Coll of New Jersey (NJ)
Rollins Coll (FL)
Rose-Hulman Inst of Technology (IN)
St. John's Coll (NM)
St. Lawrence U (NY)
Saint Luke's Coll of Health Sciences (MO)
St. Mary's Coll of Maryland (MD)
St. Olaf Coll (MN)
San Jose State U (CA)
Sarah Lawrence Coll (NY)
Scripps Coll (CA)
Sewanee: The U of the South (TN)
Skidmore Coll (NY)
Smith Coll (MA)
Spelman Coll (GA)
State U of New York at Binghamton (NY)
State U of New York at New Paltz (NY)
State U of New York Coll at Geneseo (NY)
State U of New York Coll at Oneonta (NY)
State U of New York Maritime Coll (NY)
Stonehill Coll (MA)
Stony Brook U, State U of New York (NY)
Thomas Aquinas Coll (CA)
Transylvania U (KY)
Trinity U (TX)
Tulane U (LA)
Union Coll (NY)
United States Coast Guard Acad (CT)
United States Merchant Marine Acad (NY)
United States Naval Acad (MD)
The U of British Columbia (BC, Canada)
U of California, Berkeley (CA)
U of California, Davis (CA)
U of California, Irvine (CA)
U of California, Los Angeles (CA)
U of California, Santa Barbara (CA)
U of California, Santa Cruz (CA)
U of Florida (FL)
U of Mary Washington (VA)
U of Miami (FL)
U of Michigan (MI)
The U of North Carolina at Chapel Hill (NC)
U of North Carolina School of the Arts (NC)
U of North Florida (FL)
U of Puget Sound (WA)
U of Richmond (VA)
U of Rochester (NY)
U of San Diego (CA)
The U of Texas at Austin (TX)
The U of Texas at Dallas (TX)
U of Tulsa (OK)
U of Virginia (VA)
The U of Western Ontario (ON, Canada)
U of Wisconsin–Madison (WI)
Vanderbilt U (TN)
Vassar Coll (NY)
Villanova U (PA)
Wake Forest U (NC)
Washington & Jefferson Coll (PA)
Wheaton Coll (IL)
Wheaton Coll (MA)
Whitman Coll (WA)
Willamette U (OR)
Wofford Coll (SC)
Worcester Polytechnic Inst (MA)

MODERATELY DIFFICULT

More than 75 percent of the freshmen were in the top half of their high school class and scored over 1010 on the SAT or over 18 on the ACT; about 85 percent or fewer of the applicants were accepted.

Hampshire Coll (MA)
Hanover Coll (IN)
Harding U (AR)
Hardin-Simmons U (TX)
Harrison Coll, Indianapolis (IN)
Harrison Coll, Lafayette (IN)
Harrison Coll, Muncie (IN)
Hartwick Coll (NY)
Hawai'i Pacific U (HI)
HEC Montreal (QC, Canada)
Herzing U (GA)
Hofstra U (NY)
Hollins U (VA)
Holy Cross Coll (IN)
Holy Family U (PA)
Holy Names U (CA)
Hood Coll (MD)
Hope Coll (MI)
Houghton Coll (NY)
Humboldt State U (CA)
Hunter Coll of the City U of New York (NY)
Huntingdon Coll (AL)
Huntington U (IN)
Husson U (ME)
Huston-Tillotson U (TX)
Illinois Coll (IL)
Illinois State U (IL)
Immaculata U (PA)
Indiana State U (IN)
Indiana Tech (IN)
Indiana U Bloomington (IN)
Indiana U East (IN)
Indiana U of Pennsylvania (PA)
Indiana U–Purdue U Indianapolis (IN)
Indiana U South Bend (IN)
Indiana Wesleyan U (IN)
Inter American U of Puerto Rico, Guayama Campus (PR)
Inter American U of Puerto Rico, Metropolitan Campus (PR)
Inter American U of Puerto Rico, Ponce Campus (PR)
Inter American U of Puerto Rico, San Germán Campus (PR)
Iowa State U of Science and Technology (IA)
Iowa Wesleyan Coll (IA)
Ithaca Coll (NY)
Jefferson Coll of Health Sciences (VA)
John Brown U (AR)
John Carroll U (OH)
John Jay Coll of Criminal Justice of the City U of New York (NY)
Johnson & Wales U (CO)
Johnson & Wales U (FL)
Johnson & Wales U (RI)
Johnson & Wales U - Charlotte Campus (NC)
Johnson Bible Coll (TN)
Johnson C. Smith U (NC)
Johnson State Coll (VT)
Judson Coll (AL)
Juniata Coll (PA)
Kean U (NJ)
Kennesaw State U (GA)
Kent State U (OH)
Kentucky Wesleyan Coll (KY)
Keuka Coll (NY)
King Coll (TN)
The King's Coll (NY)
King's Coll (PA)
The King's U Coll (AB, Canada)
Knox Coll (IL)
Kutztown U of Pennsylvania (PA)
Kuyper Coll (MI)
LaGrange Coll (GA)
Lakehead U (ON, Canada)
Lake Superior State U (MI)
La Salle U (PA)
Lasell Coll (MA)
Lawrence Technological U (MI)
Lebanese American U (Lebanon)
Lebanon Valley Coll (PA)
Lehman Coll of the City U of New York (NY)
Le Moyne Coll (NY)
LeTourneau U (TX)
Lewis U (IL)
Lincoln Christian U (IL)
Lincoln Memorial U (TN)
Lindenwood U (MO)
Linfield Coll (OR)
Lipscomb U (TN)

Lock Haven U of Pennsylvania (PA)
Logan U–Coll of Chiropractic (MO)
Long Island U, C.W. Post Campus (NY)
Longwood U (VA)
Loras Coll (IA)
Louisiana Coll (LA)
Louisiana State U and Ag and Mech Coll (LA)
Louisiana State U in Shreveport (LA)
Loyola U Chicago (IL)
Loyola U Maryland (MD)
Loyola U New Orleans (LA)
Lubbock Christian U (TX)
Luther Coll (IA)
Lycoming Coll (PA)
Lyme Acad Coll of Fine Arts (CT)
Lynchburg Coll (VA)
Lyndon State Coll (VT)
Lynn U (FL)
Lyon Coll (AR)
MacMurray Coll (IL)
Madonna U (MI)
Maharishi U of Management (IA)
Maine Coll of Art (ME)
Malone U (OH)
Manchester Coll (IN)
Manhattan Coll (NY)
Manhattanville Coll (NY)
Mansfield U of Pennsylvania (PA)
Marian U (WI)
Marietta Coll (OH)
Marlboro Coll (VT)
Marquette U (WI)
Marshall U (WV)
Mars Hill Coll (NC)
Martin Luther Coll (MN)
Mary Baldwin Coll (VA)
Marymount U (VA)
Maryville Coll (TN)
Maryville U of Saint Louis (MO)
Marywood U (PA)
Massachusetts Coll of Liberal Arts (MA)
Massachusetts Maritime Acad (MA)
The Master's Coll and Sem (CA)
McDaniel Coll (MD)
McKendree U (IL)
McMurry U (TX)
McNally Smith Coll of Music (MN)
Medaille Coll (NY)
Medcenter One Coll of Nursing (ND)
Menlo Coll (CA)
Mercer U (GA)
Mercy Coll of Northwest Ohio (OH)
Merrimack Coll (MA)
Messiah Coll (PA)
Miami U (OH)
Michigan State U (MI)
MidAmerica Nazarene U (KS)
Middle Tennessee State U (TN)
Midwestern State U (TX)
Millersville U of Pennsylvania (PA)
Milligan Coll (TN)
Millikin U (IL)
Millsaps Coll (MS)
Mills Coll (CA)
Milwaukee School of Eng (WI)
Minneapolis Coll of Art and Design (MN)
Minnesota School of Business–Blaine (MN)
Minnesota State U Mankato (MN)
Minnesota State U Moorhead (MN)
Minot State U (ND)
Misericordia U (PA)
Mississippi State U (MS)
Mississippi U for Women (MS)
Missouri Baptist U (MO)
Missouri Southern State U (MO)
Missouri State U (MO)
Mitchell Coll (CT)
Molloy Coll (NY)
Monmouth Coll (IL)
Monmouth U (NJ)
Montana State U (MT)
Montana State U Billings (MT)
Montana Tech of The U of Montana (MT)
Montclair State U (NJ)
Montreat Coll, Montreat (NC)
Moravian Coll (PA)

Morehouse Coll (GA)
Morningside Coll (IA)
Mount Allison U (NB, Canada)
Mount Carmel Coll of Nursing (OH)
Mount Ida Coll (MA)
Mount Mercy U (IA)
Mount Saint Mary Coll (NY)
Mount St. Mary's Coll (CA)
Mount St. Mary's U (MD)
Mount Vernon Nazarene U (OH)
Multnomah U (OR)
Murray State U (KY)
Naropa U (CO)
Nazareth Coll of Rochester (NY)
Nebraska Wesleyan U (NE)
Neumann U (PA)
Neumont U (UT)
Newberry Coll (SC)
New Hampshire Inst of Art (NH)
New Jersey City U (NJ)
New Jersey Inst of Technology (NJ)
New Mexico Inst of Mining and Technology (NM)
New Mexico State U (NM)
New Saint Andrews Coll (ID)
The New School for General Studies (NY)
New York Inst of Technology (NY)
New York School of Interior Design (NY)
Niagara U (NY)
North Carolina Ag and Tech State U (NC)
North Central Coll (IL)
North Dakota State U (ND)
Northeastern State U (OK)
Northern Arizona U (AZ)
Northern Illinois U (IL)
Northern Kentucky U (KY)
North Georgia Coll & State U (GA)
Northland Coll (WI)
Northwest Christian U (OR)
Northwestern Coll (IA)
Northwestern Coll (MN)
Northwestern Oklahoma State U (OK)
Northwestern State U of Louisiana (LA)
Northwest Missouri State U (MO)
Northwest Nazarene U (ID)
Northwest U (WA)
Nova Southeastern U (FL)
Ohio U (OH)
Oklahoma City U (OK)
Oklahoma State U (OK)
Old Dominion U (VA)
O'More Coll of Design (TN)
Oregon State U (OR)
Otis Coll of Art and Design (CA)
Ouachita Baptist U (AR)
Our Lady of the Lake U of San Antonio (TX)
Pace U (NY)
Pacific Lutheran U (WA)
Pacific Union Coll (CA)
Pacific U (OR)
Palm Beach Atlantic U (FL)
Penn State Beaver (PA)
Penn State Brandywine (PA)
Penn State DuBois (PA)
Penn State Fayette, The Eberly Campus (PA)
Penn State Greater Allegheny (PA)
Penn State Hazleton (PA)
Penn State Lehigh Valley (PA)
Penn State Mont Alto (PA)
Penn State New Kensington (PA)
Penn State Schuylkill (PA)
Penn State Shenango (PA)
Penn State Wilkes-Barre (PA)
Penn State Worthington Scranton (PA)
Penn State York (PA)
Pennsylvania Coll of Art & Design (PA)
Philadelphia Biblical U (PA)
Philadelphia U (PA)
Piedmont Coll (GA)
Pima Medical Inst (NV)
Pitzer Coll (CA)
Point Park U (PA)
Portland State U (OR)
Prairie View A&M U (TX)
Prescott Coll (AZ)
Principia Coll (IL)
Purchase Coll, State U of New York (NY)

INDEXES

Purdue U (IN)
Purdue U Calumet (IN)
Quincy U (IL)
Quinnipiac U (CT)
Radford U (VA)
Ramapo Coll of New Jersey (NJ)
Randolph Coll (VA)
Randolph-Macon Coll (VA)
Regis Coll (MA)
Regis U (CO)
Reinhardt U (GA)
Research Coll of Nursing (MO)
Resurrection U (IL)
Rhode Island Coll (RI)
Rider U (NJ)
Ringling Coll of Art and Design (FL)
Ripon Coll (WI)
Rivier Coll (NH)
Roanoke Coll (VA)
Rockford Coll (IL)
Rockhurst U (MO)
Rocky Mountain Coll (MT)
Rocky Mountain Coll of Art + Design (CO)
Roosevelt U (IL)
Rosemont Coll (PA)
Rowan U (NJ)
Russell Sage Coll (NY)
Rust Coll (MS)
Rutgers, The State U of New Jersey, Camden (NJ)
Rutgers, The State U of New Jersey, Newark (NJ)
Rutgers, The State U of New Jersey, New Brunswick (NJ)
Sacred Heart Major Sem (MI)
Sacred Heart U (CT)
Saginaw Valley State U (MI)
St. Ambrose U (IA)
St. Andrews Presbyterian Coll (NC)
Saint Anselm Coll (NH)
St. Bonaventure U (NY)
St. Catherine U (MN)
St. Charles Borromeo Sem, Overbrook (PA)
St. Edward's U (TX)
Saint Francis U (PA)
St. Francis Xavier U (NS, Canada)
St. John Fisher Coll (NY)
St. John's Coll (MD)
Saint John's U (MN)
St. John's U (NY)
Saint Joseph's Coll (IN)
St. Joseph's Coll, Long Island Campus (NY)
St. Joseph's Coll, New York (NY)
Saint Joseph's Coll of Maine (ME)
Saint Joseph's U (PA)
St. Louis Coll of Pharmacy (MO)
Saint Louis U (MO)
Saint Louis U–Madrid Campus (Spain)
Saint Martin's U (WA)
Saint Mary-of-the-Woods Coll (IN)
Saint Mary's Coll (IN)
Saint Mary's Coll of California (CA)
Saint Mary's U of Minnesota (MN)
Saint Michael's Coll (VT)
St. Norbert Coll (WI)
St. Thomas Aquinas Coll (NY)
St. Thomas U (NB, Canada)
Saint Xavier U (IL)
Salisbury U (MD)
Salve Regina U (RI)
Samford U (AL)
Sam Houston State U (TX)
Samuel Merritt U (CA)
San Diego Christian Coll (CA)
San Diego State U (CA)
San Francisco Conservatory of Music (CA)
San Francisco State U (CA)
Santa Clara U (CA)
Savannah Coll of Art and Design (GA)
School of the Museum of Fine Arts, Boston (MA)
School of Visual Arts (NY)
Schreiner U (TX)
Seattle Pacific U (WA)
Seton Hill U (PA)
Shenandoah U (VA)
Shepherd U (WV)
Shimer Coll (IL)
Shippensburg U of Pennsylvania (PA)

Shorter U (GA)
Siena Coll (NY)
Siena Heights U (MI)
Sierra Nevada Coll (NV)
Simmons Coll (MA)
Simon Fraser U (BC, Canada)
Simpson Coll (IA)
Simpson U (CA)
Skyline Coll (VA)
Slippery Rock U of Pennsylvania (PA)
Soka U of America (CA)
Sonoma State U (CA)
South Dakota School of Mines and Technology (SD)
Southeastern Louisiana U (LA)
Southeastern Oklahoma State U (OK)
Southeast Missouri State U (MO)
Southern Adventist U (TN)
Southern Arkansas U–Magnolia (AR)
Southern Connecticut State U (CT)
Southern Illinois U Carbondale (IL)
Southern Illinois U Edwardsville (IL)
Southern Methodist U (TX)
Southern Oregon U (OR)
Southern Polytechnic State U (GA)
Southern Utah U (UT)
Spalding U (KY)
Spring Arbor U (MI)
Springfield Coll (MA)
Spring Hill Coll (AL)
State U of New York at Fredonia (NY)
State U of New York at Oswego (NY)
State U of New York at Plattsburgh (NY)
State U of New York Coll at Old Westbury (NY)
State U of New York Coll at Potsdam (NY)
State U of New York Coll of Environmental Science and
    Forestry (NY)
State U of New York Coll of Technology at Alfred (NY)
State U of New York Coll of Technology at Delhi (NY)
State U of New York Downstate Medical Center (NY)
State U of New York Upstate Medical U (NY)
Stephen F. Austin State U (TX)
Stephens Coll (MO)
Sterling Coll (VT)
Stetson U (FL)
Stevens Inst of Business & Arts (MO)
Stevenson U (MD)
Suffolk U (MA)
Sullivan Coll of Technology and Design (KY)
Susquehanna U (PA)
Sweet Briar Coll (VA)
Syracuse U (NY)
Tabor Coll (KS)
Talladega Coll (AL)
Tarleton State U (TX)
Taylor U (IN)
Temple U (PA)
Tennessee Technological U (TN)
Texas A&M Intl U (TX)
Texas A&M U (TX)
Texas A&M U–Corpus Christi (TX)
Texas A&M U–Kingsville (TX)
Texas Christian U (TX)
Texas Lutheran U (TX)
Texas State U–San Marcos (TX)
Texas Tech U (TX)
Texas Wesleyan U (TX)
Thiel Coll (PA)
Thomas More Coll (KY)
Thomas More Coll of Liberal Arts (NH)
Tiffin U (OH)
Towson U (MD)
Trent U (ON, Canada)
Trevecca Nazarene U (TN)
Trine U (IN)
Trinity Coll of Nursing and Health Sciences (IL)
Troy U (AL)
Truman State U (MO)
Tuskegee U (AL)
Union Coll (KY)
Union Coll (NE)
Union U (TN)
United States Intl U (Kenya)
Université de Sherbrooke (QC, Canada)
U at Buffalo, the State U of New York (NY)
The U of Akron (OH)

The U of Alabama (AL)
The U of Alabama at Birmingham (AL)
The U of Alabama in Huntsville (AL)
The U of Arizona (AZ)
U of Arkansas (AR)
U of Bridgeport (CT)
The U of British Columbia–Okanagan (BC, Canada)
U of California, Merced (CA)
U of Central Florida (FL)
U of Central Missouri (MO)
U of Charleston (WV)
U of Cincinnati (OH)
U of Colorado at Colorado Springs (CO)
U of Colorado Boulder (CO)
U of Colorado Denver (CO)
U of Dallas (TX)
U of Dayton (OH)
U of Delaware (DE)
U of Denver (CO)
U of Dubuque (IA)
U of Evansville (IN)
The U of Findlay (OH)
U of Georgia (GA)
U of Guelph (ON, Canada)
U of Hartford (CT)
U of Hawaii at Hilo (HI)
U of Hawaii at Manoa (HI)
U of Hawaii–West Oahu (HI)
U of Houston (TX)
U of Idaho (ID)
U of Illinois at Chicago (IL)
U of Illinois at Springfield (IL)
U of Indianapolis (IN)
The U of Iowa (IA)
The U of Kansas (KS)
U of La Verne (CA)
U of Lethbridge (AB, Canada)
U of Louisiana at Lafayette (LA)
U of Louisville (KY)
U of Maine (ME)
U of Maine at Farmington (ME)
U of Manitoba (MB, Canada)
U of Mary Hardin-Baylor (TX)
U of Maryland, Baltimore County (MD)
U of Maryland, Coll Park (MD)
U of Massachusetts Amherst (MA)
U of Massachusetts Boston (MA)
U of Massachusetts Dartmouth (MA)
U of Massachusetts Lowell (MA)
U of Memphis (TN)
U of Michigan–Dearborn (MI)
U of Michigan–Flint (MI)
U of Minnesota, Crookston (MN)
U of Minnesota, Duluth (MN)
U of Minnesota, Twin Cities Campus (MN)
U of Mississippi (MS)
U of Missouri (MO)
U of Missouri–St. Louis (MO)
U of Mobile (AL)
U of Montevallo (AL)
U of Mount Union (OH)
U of Nebraska–Lincoln (NE)
U of Nevada, Las Vegas (NV)
U of Nevada, Reno (NV)
U of New Brunswick Fredericton (NB, Canada)
U of New Brunswick Saint John (NB, Canada)
U of New England (ME)
U of New Hampshire (NH)
U of New Hampshire at Manchester (NH)
U of New Haven (CT)
The U of North Carolina at Asheville (NC)
The U of North Carolina at Charlotte (NC)
The U of North Carolina at Greensboro (NC)
The U of North Carolina at Pembroke (NC)
The U of North Carolina Wilmington (NC)
U of Northern Colorado (CO)
U of Northern Iowa (IA)
U of North Texas (TX)
U of Oklahoma (OK)
U of Oregon (OR)
U of Ottawa (ON, Canada)
U of Pittsburgh (PA)
U of Pittsburgh at Greensburg (PA)
U of Pittsburgh at Johnstown (PA)
U of Portland (OR)

U of Puerto Rico at Humacao (PR)
U of Redlands (CA)
U of Rhode Island (RI)
U of St. Francis (IL)
U of Saint Mary (KS)
U of St. Thomas (MN)
U of St. Thomas (TX)
U of San Francisco (CA)
U of Science and Arts of Oklahoma (OK)
The U of Scranton (PA)
U of Sioux Falls (SD)
U of South Alabama (AL)
U of South Carolina (SC)
U of South Carolina Aiken (SC)
U of South Carolina Upstate (SC)
The U of South Dakota (SD)
U of Southern Indiana (IN)
U of Southern Maine (ME)
U of Southern Mississippi (MS)
U of South Florida (FL)
The U of Tampa (FL)
The U of Tennessee (TN)
The U of Tennessee at Chattanooga (TN)
The U of Tennessee at Martin (TN)
The U of Texas at Arlington (TX)
The U of Texas at San Antonio (TX)
The U of Texas at Tyler (TX)
The U of Texas of the Permian Basin (TX)
The U of Texas Southwestern Medical Center at Dallas (TX)
The U of the Arts (PA)
U of the Cumberlands (KY)
U of the Incarnate Word (TX)
U of the Ozarks (AR)
U of the Pacific (CA)
U of the Sciences in Philadelphia (PA)
U of the Southwest (NM)
U of the West (CA)
U of Utah (UT)
U of Vermont (VT)
U of Washington (WA)
U of Washington, Bothell (WA)
U of Waterloo (ON, Canada)
U of West Florida (FL)
U of Wisconsin–Eau Claire (WI)
U of Wisconsin–Green Bay (WI)
U of Wisconsin–La Crosse (WI)
U of Wisconsin–Parkside (WI)
U of Wisconsin–River Falls (WI)
U of Wisconsin–Stevens Point (WI)
U of Wisconsin–Stout (WI)
U of Wisconsin–Superior (WI)
U of Wisconsin–Whitewater (WI)
U of Wyoming (WY)
Upper Iowa U (IA)
Utah State U (UT)
Valdosta State U (GA)
Valparaiso U (IN)
VanderCook Coll of Music (IL)
Vaughn Coll of Aeronautics and Technology (NY)
Vermont Tech Coll (VT)
Virginia Military Inst (VA)
Virginia Polytechnic Inst and State U (VA)
Virginia Wesleyan Coll (VA)
Viterbo U (WI)
Wabash Coll (IN)
Wagner Coll (NY)
Walla Walla U (WA)
Walsh U (OH)
Wartburg Coll (IA)
Washington Adventist U (MD)
Washington Coll (MD)
Washington State U (WA)
Watkins Coll of Art, Design, & Film (TN)
Waynesburg U (PA)
Wayne State U (MI)
Webber Intl U (FL)
Webster U (MO)
Wells Coll (NY)
Wentworth Inst of Technology (MA)
Wesleyan Coll (GA)
West Chester U of Pennsylvania (PA)
Western Carolina U (NC)
Western Connecticut State U (CT)
Western Illinois U (IL)
Western Intl U (AZ)
Western Michigan U (MI)

Western New England U (MA)
Western Oregon U (OR)
Western State Coll of Colorado (CO)
Westfield State U (MA)
Westminster Coll (MO)
Westminster Coll (UT)
Westmont Coll (CA)
West Virginia U (WV)
Wheeling Jesuit U (WV)
Widener U (PA)
Wilkes U (PA)
William Jessup U (CA)
William Jewell Coll (MO)
William Paterson U of New Jersey (NJ)
Wilmington Coll (OH)
Wingate U (NC)
Winona State U (MN)
Winthrop U (SC)
Wittenberg U (OH)
Woodbury U (CA)
Worcester State U (MA)
Xavier U (OH)
Xavier U of Louisiana (LA)
York Coll of Pennsylvania (PA)
York Coll of the City U of New York (NY)
Young Harris Coll (GA)

MINIMALLY DIFFICULT

Most freshmen were not in the top half of their high school class and scored somewhat below 1010 on the SAT or below 19 on the ACT; up to 95 percent of the applicants were accepted.

AIB Coll of Business (IA)
Alabama Ag and Mech U (AL)
Alabama State U (AL)
Albany State U (GA)
Amberton U (TX)
American Coll of Thessaloniki (Greece)
Amridge U (AL)
Anderson U (SC)
Anna Maria Coll (MA)
Aquinas Coll (TN)
Armstrong Atlantic State U (GA)
Avila U (MO)
Baker Coll of Allen Park (MI)
Baker Coll of Auburn Hills (MI)
Baker Coll of Cadillac (MI)
Baker Coll of Clinton Township (MI)
Baker Coll of Flint (MI)
Baker Coll of Jackson (MI)
Baker Coll of Muskegon (MI)
Baker Coll of Owosso (MI)
Baker Coll of Port Huron (MI)
Baptist Bible Coll of Pennsylvania (PA)
Barclay Coll (KS)
Barton Coll (NC)
Beacon Coll (FL)
Bethel Coll (IN)
Bethel U (TN)
Bethune-Cookman U (FL)
Bob Jones U (SC)
Bowie State U (MD)
Brevard Coll (NC)
Brewton-Parker Coll (GA)
Bryant & Stratton Coll (WI)
Bryn Athyn Coll of the New Church (PA)
California Baptist U (CA)
Calvary Bible Coll and Theological Sem (MO)
Central Pennsylvania Coll (PA)
Central State U (OH)
Cincinnati Christian U (OH)
Claflin U (SC)
Clarion U of Pennsylvania (PA)
Clayton State U (GA)
Clearwater Christian Coll (FL)
Cleveland Chiropractic Coll–Los Angeles Campus (CA)
Coll of Coastal Georgia (GA)
Coll of St. Joseph (VT)
Coll of Saint Mary (NE)
Columbus State U (GA)
Concordia U, St. Paul (MN)
Concord U (WV)
Crandall U (NB, Canada)
Crown Coll (MN)

Dakota State U (SD)
Davenport U, Grand Rapids (MI)
DeVry Coll of New York (NY)
DeVry U, Phoenix (AZ)
DeVry U, Pomona (CA)
DeVry U, Miramar (FL)
DeVry U, Orlando (FL)
DeVry U, Decatur (GA)
DeVry U, Chicago (IL)
DeVry U, Kansas City (MO)
DeVry U, North Brunswick (NJ)
DeVry U, Columbus (OH)
DeVry U, Fort Washington (PA)
DeVry U, Houston (TX)
DeVry U, Irving (TX)
DeVry U, Arlington (VA)
DeVry U, Federal Way (WA)
DeVry U Online (IL)
Dickinson State U (ND)
DigiPen Inst of Technology (WA)
East Central U (OK)
Eastern New Mexico U (NM)
Embry-Riddle Aeronautical U–Worldwide (FL)
Emmanuel Coll (GA)
Everest U, Lakeland (FL)
Everest U, Tampa (FL)
Everest U, Tampa (FL)
Fairmont State U (WV)
Faith Baptist Bible Coll and Theological Sem (IA)
Faulkner U (AL)
Fayetteville State U (NC)
Ferris State U (MI)
Ferrum Coll (VA)
Fisher Coll (MA)
Franklin Pierce U (NH)
Goodwin Coll (CT)
Grace Bible Coll (MI)
Grand View U (IA)
Hannibal-LaGrange U (MO)
Harrisburg U of Science and Technology (PA)
Hebrew Coll (MA)
Hellenic Coll (MA)
Idaho State U (ID)
Indiana U Kokomo (IN)
Indiana U Northwest (IN)
Indiana U–Purdue U Fort Wayne (IN)
Indiana U Southeast (IN)
ITT Tech Inst, Bessemer (AL)
ITT Tech Inst, Madison (AL)
ITT Tech Inst, Mobile (AL)
ITT Tech Inst, Phoenix (AZ)
ITT Tech Inst, Tempe (AZ)
ITT Tech Inst, Tucson (AZ)
ITT Tech Inst (AR)
ITT Tech Inst, Anaheim (CA)
ITT Tech Inst, Clovis (CA)
ITT Tech Inst, Concord (CA)
ITT Tech Inst, Corona (CA)
ITT Tech Inst, Lathrop (CA)
ITT Tech Inst, Oxnard (CA)
ITT Tech Inst, Rancho Cordova (CA)
ITT Tech Inst, San Bernardino (CA)
ITT Tech Inst, San Diego (CA)
ITT Tech Inst, San Dimas (CA)
ITT Tech Inst, Sylmar (CA)
ITT Tech Inst, Torrance (CA)
ITT Tech Inst, Aurora (CO)
ITT Tech Inst, Thornton (CO)
ITT Tech Inst, Fort Lauderdale (FL)
ITT Tech Inst, Fort Myers (FL)
ITT Tech Inst, Jacksonville (FL)
ITT Tech Inst, Lake Mary (FL)
ITT Tech Inst, Miami (FL)
ITT Tech Inst, Pinellas Park (FL)
ITT Tech Inst, Tallahassee (FL)
ITT Tech Inst, Tampa (FL)
ITT Tech Inst, Atlanta (GA)
ITT Tech Inst, Duluth (GA)
ITT Tech Inst, Kennesaw (GA)
ITT Tech Inst (ID)
ITT Tech Inst, Burr Ridge (IL)
ITT Tech Inst, Mount Prospect (IL)
ITT Tech Inst, Orland Park (IL)
ITT Tech Inst, Fort Wayne (IN)
ITT Tech Inst, Indianapolis (IN)
ITT Tech Inst, Merrillville (IN)

INDEXES

ITT Tech Inst, Newburgh (IN)
ITT Tech Inst, South Bend (IN)
ITT Tech Inst, Cedar Rapids (IA)
ITT Tech Inst, Clive (IA)
ITT Tech Inst (KS)
ITT Tech Inst, Lexington (KY)
ITT Tech Inst, Louisville (KY)
ITT Tech Inst, St. Rose (LA)
ITT Tech Inst (MD)
ITT Tech Inst, Norwood (MA)
ITT Tech Inst, Woburn (MA)
ITT Tech Inst, Canton (MI)
ITT Tech Inst, Swartz Creek (MI)
ITT Tech Inst, Troy (MI)
ITT Tech Inst, Wyoming (MI)
ITT Tech Inst (MN)
ITT Tech Inst (MS)
ITT Tech Inst, Arnold (MO)
ITT Tech Inst, Earth City (MO)
ITT Tech Inst, Kansas City (MO)
ITT Tech Inst, Springfield (MO)
ITT Tech Inst (NE)
ITT Tech Inst (NV)
ITT Tech Inst (NM)
ITT Tech Inst, Charlotte (NC)
ITT Tech Inst, Charlotte (NC)
ITT Tech Inst, High Point (NC)
ITT Tech Inst, Morrisville (NC)
ITT Tech Inst, Akron (OH)
ITT Tech Inst, Dayton (OH)
ITT Tech Inst, Hilliard (OH)
ITT Tech Inst, Norwood (OH)
ITT Tech Inst, Strongsville (OH)
ITT Tech Inst, Warrensville Heights (OH)
ITT Tech Inst, Youngstown (OH)
ITT Tech Inst, Oklahoma City (OK)
ITT Tech Inst, Tulsa (OK)
ITT Tech Inst (OR)
ITT Tech Inst, Greenville (SC)
ITT Tech Inst, Chattanooga (TN)
ITT Tech Inst, Cordova (TN)
ITT Tech Inst, Johnson City (TN)
ITT Tech Inst, Knoxville (TN)
ITT Tech Inst, Nashville (TN)
ITT Tech Inst, Arlington (TX)
ITT Tech Inst, Austin (TX)
ITT Tech Inst, DeSoto (TX)
ITT Tech Inst, Houston (TX)
ITT Tech Inst, Houston (TX)
ITT Tech Inst, Richardson (TX)
ITT Tech Inst, San Antonio (TX)
ITT Tech Inst, Webster (TX)
ITT Tech Inst (UT)
ITT Tech Inst, Chantilly (VA)
ITT Tech Inst, Norfolk (VA)
ITT Tech Inst, Richmond (VA)
ITT Tech Inst, Salem (VA)
ITT Tech Inst, Springfield (VA)
ITT Tech Inst, Everett (WA)
ITT Tech Inst, Seattle (WA)
ITT Tech Inst, Spokane Valley (WA)
ITT Tech Inst, Green Bay (WI)
ITT Tech Inst, Greenfield (WI)
ITT Tech Inst, Madison (WI)
Jacksonville State U (AL)
Jamestown Business Coll (NY)
Jamestown Coll (ND)
Jarvis Christian Coll (TX)
Kendall Coll (IL)
Kentucky State U (KY)
Keystone Coll (PA)
Lamar U (TX)
Lane Coll (TN)
La Roche Coll (PA)
Lee U (TN)
Lewis-Clark State Coll (ID)
Liberty U (VA)
Life U (GA)
Limestone Coll (SC)
Lindsey Wilson Coll (KY)
Long Island U, Brooklyn Campus (NY)
Lourdes Coll (OH)
Maple Springs Baptist Bible Coll and Sem (MD)
Maria Coll (NY)
Marymount Coll, Palos Verdes, California (CA)

Mesa State Coll (CO)
Metropolitan State U (MN)
Mid-Atlantic Christian U (NC)
Mid-Continent U (KY)
Midway Coll (KY)
Mississippi Valley State U (MS)
Morehead State U (KY)
Mount Aloysius Coll (PA)
Mount Marty Coll (SD)
Mount Olive Coll (NC)
Musicians Inst (CA)
National-Louis U (IL)
National U (CA)
Nevada State Coll at Henderson (NV)
Newbury Coll (MA)
New England Coll (NH)
New Hope Christian Coll (OR)
Newman U (KS)
New Mexico Highlands U (NM)
Northcentral U (AZ)
Northeastern Illinois U (IL)
Northern Michigan U (MI)
Northern State U (SD)
North Greenville U (SC)
Notre Dame de Namur U (CA)
Oak Hills Christian Coll (MN)
Ohio Valley U (WV)
Oklahoma Wesleyan U (OK)
Our Lady of the Lake Coll (LA)
Pacific Northwest Coll of Art (OR)
Paier Coll of Art, Inc. (CT)
Paine Coll (GA)
Perelandra Coll (CA)
Pima Medical Inst, Mesa (AZ)
Pima Medical Inst, Tucson (AZ)
Pima Medical Inst (CA)
Pima Medical Inst, Denver (CO)
Pima Medical Inst (NM)
Pima Medical Inst (WA)
Pittsburg State U (KS)
Polytechnic U of Puerto Rico (PR)
Purdue U North Central (IN)
Regent U (VA)
Robert Morris U (PA)
Robert Morris U Illinois (IL)
Sage Coll of Albany (NY)
Saint Joseph Sem Coll (LA)
Saint Leo U (FL)
St. Louis Christian Coll (MO)
St. Thomas U (FL)
Salem State U (MA)
Savannah State U (GA)
Silver Lake Coll (WI)
South Dakota State U (SD)
Southeastern Baptist Theological Sem (NC)
Southeastern U (FL)
Southern Vermont Coll (VT)
Southern Wesleyan U (SC)
Southwestern Adventist U (TX)
Southwestern Coll (KS)
State U of New York Empire State Coll (NY)
Stratford U, Falls Church (VA)
Tennessee Wesleyan Coll (TN)
Texas Woman's U (TX)
Trinity Coll of Florida (FL)
Trinity Lutheran Coll (WA)
Truett-McConnell Coll (GA)
TUI U (CA)
U of Alaska Fairbanks (AK)
U of Arkansas–Fort Smith (AR)
U of Baltimore (MD)
U of Houston–Clear Lake (TX)
U of Houston–Victoria (TX)
U of Louisiana at Monroe (LA)
U of Maine at Fort Kent (ME)
U of Maine at Presque Isle (ME)
The U of Montana Western (MT)
U of Nebraska at Omaha (NE)
U of North Dakota (ND)
U of Pittsburgh at Bradford (PA)
U of Pittsburgh at Titusville (PA)
U of Regina (SK, Canada)
U of South Carolina Beaufort (SC)
U of the Virgin Islands (VI)
U of West Georgia (GA)

U of Wisconsin–Platteville (WI)
Ursuline Coll (OH)
Victory U (TN)
Villa Maria Coll of Buffalo (NY)
Virginia Intermont Coll (VA)
Virginia State U (VA)
Wade Coll (TX)
Wayland Baptist U (TX)
Western Kentucky U (KY)
West Liberty U (WV)
Wheelock Coll (MA)
Wilfrid Laurier U (ON, Canada)
Wright State U (OH)

NONCOMPETITIVE

Virtually all applicants were accepted regardless of high school rank or test scores.

American Public U System (WV)
Andrew Jackson U (AL)
Antioch U Midwest (OH)
Appalachian Bible Coll (WV)
Arlington Baptist Coll (TX)
Ashworth Coll (GA)
Athabasca U (AB, Canada)
Athens State U (AL)
The Baptist Coll of Florida (FL)
Beulah Heights U (GA)
Bluefield State Coll (WV)
Boston Architectural Coll (MA)
Brookline Coll, Phoenix (AZ)
Brookline Coll, Tempe (AZ)
Brookline Coll, Tucson (AZ)
Brookline Coll (NM)
California Christian Coll (CA)
Calumet Coll of Saint Joseph (IN)
Cambridge Coll (MA)
Cameron U (OK)
Carolina Christian Coll (NC)
Chipola Coll (FL)
Christian Life Coll (IL)
Clear Creek Baptist Bible Coll (KY)
Cleveland Chiropractic Coll–Kansas City Campus (KS)
CollAmerica–Flagstaff (AZ)
Coll of Central Florida (FL)
Columbia Bible Coll (BC, Canada)
Columbia Coll (PR)
Columbia Southern U (AL)
Crossroads Bible Coll (IN)
Dalton State Coll (GA)
Daytona State Coll (FL)
Delta State U (MS)
DeVry U, Westminster (CO)
Dixie State Coll of Utah (UT)
Dominican Coll (NY)
Emmaus Bible Coll (IA)
Emporia State U (KS)
Florida State Coll at Jacksonville (FL)
Franklin U (OH)
Free Will Baptist Bible Coll (TN)
Granite State Coll (NH)
Great Basin Coll (NV)
Gulf Coast Comm Coll (FL)
Hamilton Tech Coll (IA)
Heritage Christian U (AL)
Hillsdale Free Will Baptist Coll (OK)
Holy Apostles Coll and Sem (CT)
Holy Trinity Orthodox Sem (NY)
Huntington Coll of Health Sciences (TN)
Indian River State Coll (FL)
Intl Acad of Design & Technology (FL)
Jones Coll, Jacksonville (FL)
Jones Intl U (CO)
Kansas State U (KS)
Kent State U at Ashtabula (OH)
Kent State U at East Liverpool (OH)
Kent State U at Geauga (OH)
Kent State U at Salem (OH)
Kent State U at Stark (OH)
Kent State U at Trumbull (OH)
Kent State U at Tuscarawas (OH)
LA Coll Intl (CA)
Lexington Coll (IL)

Lincoln U (MO)
Maranatha Baptist Bible Coll (WI)
Marylhurst U (OR)
Master's Coll and Sem (ON, Canada)
Mayville State U (ND)
Medgar Evers Coll of the City U of New York (NY)
Miami Dade Coll (FL)
Morris Coll (SC)
Mountain State U (WV)
New England Inst of Technology (RI)
New York City Coll of Technology of the City U of New York (NY)
Nicholls State U (LA)
The Ohio State U at Lima (OH)
The Ohio State U at Marion (OH)
The Ohio State U–Mansfield Campus (OH)
The Ohio State U–Newark Campus (OH)
Ohio U–Chillicothe (OH)
Ohio U–Zanesville (OH)
Oklahoma Christian U (OK)
Oklahoma Panhandle State U (OK)

Oklahoma State U, Oklahoma City (OK)
Olympic Coll (WA)
Pacific States U (CA)
Palm Beach State Coll (FL)
Palmer Coll of Chiropractic (IA)
Peirce Coll (PA)
Pennsylvania Coll of Technology (PA)
Pensacola State Coll (FL)
Pikeville Coll (KY)
Polk State Coll (FL)
Potomac State Coll of West Virginia U (WV)
Presentation Coll (SD)
Rogers State U (OK)
St. Petersburg Coll (FL)
Santa Fe Coll (FL)
Seminole State Coll of Florida (FL)
Shawnee State U (OH)
Southern Nazarene U (OK)
Southwestern Assemblies of God U (TX)
Sul Ross State U (TX)
Texas Southern U (TX)

Thomas Edison State Coll (NJ)
Thomas U (GA)
Union Inst & U (OH)
Université du Québec en Outaouais (QC, Canada)
U of Alaska Southeast (AK)
U of Houston–Downtown (TX)
U of Maine at Augusta (ME)
U of Maryland U Coll (MD)
U of Rio Grande (OH)
The U of Texas–Pan American (TX)
U of the District of Columbia (DC)
The U of Toledo (OH)
Utah Valley U (UT)
Vincennes U Jasper Campus (IN)
Washburn U (KS)
Wayne State Coll (NE)
Weber State U (UT)
Wichita State U (KS)
Wilmington U (DE)
World Coll (VA)
Youngstown State U (OH)

Cost Ranges

Southeastern Louisiana U (LA)
Southern Arkansas U–Magnolia (AR)
Texas A&M U–Kingsville (TX)
The U of North Carolina at Asheville (NC)
The U of North Carolina at Greensboro (NC)
The U of North Carolina at Pembroke (NC)
U of Puerto Rico at Humacao (PR)
U of Southern Mississippi (MS)
The U of Tennessee at Martin (TN)
Utah State U (UT)
Valdosta State U (GA)
Wayne State Coll (NE)
Weber State U (UT)
Western Carolina U (NC)

$12,000–$13,999

Colleges with No Room and Board or with Room Only

Brookline Coll, Phoenix (AZ)
Brookline Coll, Tempe (AZ)
Brookline Coll, Tucson (AZ)
Brookline Coll (NM)
California State U, San Marcos (CA) **(room only)**
Cambridge Coll (MA)
Carlos Albizu U, Miami Campus (FL)
Clemson U (SC)
Crossroads Bible Coll (IN) **(room only)**
Florida National Coll (FL)
Indiana U–Purdue U Fort Wayne (IN) **(room only)**
Mercy Coll of Health Sciences (IA)
Penn State Abington (PA)
Penn State Brandywine (PA)
Penn State DuBois (PA)
Penn State Fayette, The Eberly Campus (PA)
Penn State Lehigh Valley (PA)
Penn State New Kensington (PA)
Penn State Schuylkill (PA)
Penn State Shenango (PA)
Penn State Wilkes-Barre (PA)
Penn State Worthington Scranton (PA)
Penn State York (PA)
Strayer U - Akron Campus (OH)
Strayer U - Alexandria Campus (VA)
Strayer U - Allentown Campus (PA)
Strayer U - Anne Arundel Campus (MD)
Strayer U - Arlington Campus (VA)
Strayer U - Augusta Campus (GA)
Strayer U - Baymeadows Campus (FL)
Strayer U - Birmingham Campus (AL)
Strayer U - Brickell Campus (FL)
Strayer U - Center City Campus (PA)
Strayer U - Chamblee Campus (GA)
Strayer U - Charleston Campus (SC)
Strayer U - Cherry Hill Campus (NJ)
Strayer U - Chesapeake Campus (VA)
Strayer U - Chesterfield Campus (VA)
Strayer U - Christiana Campus (DE)
Strayer U - Cobb County Campus (GA)
Strayer U - Columbia Campus (SC)
Strayer U - Columbus Campus (OH)
Strayer U - Coral Springs Campus (FL)
Strayer U - Cranberry Woods Campus (PA)
Strayer U - Delaware County Campus (PA)
Strayer U - Doral Campus (FL)
Strayer U - Douglasville Campus (GA)
Strayer U - Fairview Park Campus (OH)
Strayer U - Florence Campus (KY)
Strayer U - Fort Lauderdale Campus (FL)
Strayer U - Fredericksburg Campus (VA)
Strayer U - Greensboro Campus (NC)
Strayer U - Greenville Campus (SC)
Strayer U - Henrico Campus (VA)
Strayer U - Huntersville Campus (NC)
Strayer U - Huntsville Campus (AL)
Strayer U - Irving Campus (TX)
Strayer U - Jackson Campus (MS)
Strayer U - King of Prussia Campus (PA)
Strayer U - Knoxville Campus (TN)
Strayer U - Lawrenceville Campus (NJ)
Strayer U - Lexington Campus (KY)
Strayer U - Lithonia Campus (GA)
Strayer U - Little Rock Campus (AR)

Strayer U - Loudoun Campus (VA)
Strayer U - Louisville Campus (KY)
Strayer U - Lower Bucks County Campus (PA)
Strayer U - Maitland Campus (FL)
Strayer U - Manassas Campus (VA)
Strayer U - Mason Campus (OH)
Strayer U - Metairie Campus (LA)
Strayer U - Miramar Campus (FL)
Strayer U - Morrow Campus (GA)
Strayer U - Newport News Campus (VA)
Strayer U - North Austin Campus (TX)
Strayer U - North Charlotte Campus (NC)
Strayer U - North Raleigh Campus (NC)
Strayer U - Northwest Houston Campus (TX)
Strayer U - Orlando East Campus (FL)
Strayer U - Owings Mills Campus (MD)
Strayer U - Palm Beach Gardens Campus (FL)
Strayer U - Penn Center West Campus (PA)
Strayer U - Piscataway Campus (NJ)
Strayer U - Plano Campus (TX)
Strayer U - Prince George's Campus (MD)
Strayer U - Rockville Campus (MD)
Strayer U - Roswell Campus (GA)
Strayer U - RTP Campus (NC)
Strayer U - Salt Lake Campus (UT)
Strayer U - Sand Lake Campus (FL)
Strayer U - Savannah Campus (GA)
Strayer U - South Charlotte Campus (NC)
Strayer U - South Raleigh Campus (NC)
Strayer U - Takoma Park Campus (DC)
Strayer U - Tampa East Campus (FL)
Strayer U - Tampa Westshore Campus (FL)
Strayer U - Teays Valley Campus (WV)
Strayer U - Virginia Beach Campus (VA)
Strayer U - Washington Campus (DC)
Strayer U - White Marsh Campus (MD)
Strayer U - Willingboro Campus (NJ)
Strayer U - Woodbridge Campus (VA)
U of Arkansas for Medical Sciences (AR) **(room only)**
Western Connecticut State U (CT) **(room only)**

Colleges with Room and Board

Adams State Coll (CO)
Alabama Ag and Mech U (AL)
Alcorn State U (MS)
Angelo State U (TX)
Appalachian State U (NC)
Arkansas State U (AR)
Armstrong Atlantic State U (GA)
Austin Peay State U (TN)
The Baptist Coll of Florida (FL)
Bemidji State U (MN)
Bethany Bible Coll (NB, Canada)
Blue Mountain Coll (MS)
Brock U (ON, Canada)
California State U, Bakersfield (CA)
California State U, Los Angeles (CA)
California State U, Monterey Bay (CA)
Central State U (OH)
Clayton State U (GA)
Columbus State U (GA)
Coppin State U (MD)
Crandall U (NB, Canada)
Dakota State U (SD)
Fairmont State U (WV)
Florida Ag and Mech U (FL)
Fort Lewis Coll (CO)
Jacksonville State U (AL)
Kennesaw State U (GA)
Kentucky State U (KY)
Lakehead U (ON, Canada)
Lamar U (TX)
Lane Coll (TN)
Louisiana State U and Ag and Mech Coll (LA)
Marshall U (WV)
Middle Tennessee State U (TN)
Midwestern State U (TX)
Minnesota State U Mankato (MN)
Minnesota State U Moorhead (MN)
Mississippi State U (MS)
Missouri State U (MO)
Montana Tech of The U of Montana (MT)
Morehead State U (KY)
Murray State U (KY)
New Coll of Florida (FL)

Nicholls State U (LA)
North Dakota State U (ND)
Northern Kentucky U (KY)
North Georgia Coll & State U (GA)
The Ohio State U–Newark Campus (OH)
Oklahoma State U (OK)
Prairie View A&M U (TX)
Purdue U Calumet (IN)
Shepherd U (WV)
Simon Fraser U (BC, Canada)
South Dakota School of Mines and Technology (SD)
South Dakota State U (SD)
Southeast Missouri State U (MO)
Southern Polytechnic State U (GA)
Tarleton State U (TX)
Tennessee Technological U (TN)
Texas A&M Intl U (TX)
Texas Woman's U (TX)
Troy U (AL)
Truman State U (MO)
U of Alaska Fairbanks (AK)
U of Alaska Southeast (AK)
The U of British Columbia (BC, Canada)
The U of British Columbia–Okanagan (BC, Canada)
U of Central Florida (FL)
U of Central Missouri (MO)
U of Florida (FL)
U of Houston–Victoria (TX)
U of Idaho (ID)
U of Memphis (TN)
U of Mississippi (MS)
U of Montevallo (AL)
The U of North Carolina at Charlotte (NC)
U of North Carolina School of the Arts (NC)
The U of North Carolina Wilmington (NC)
U of North Dakota (ND)
U of North Florida (FL)
U of Oklahoma (OK)
U of Ottawa (ON, Canada)
U of South Alabama (AL)
The U of South Dakota (SD)
U of Southern Indiana (IN)
The U of Texas of the Permian Basin (TX)
U of the District of Columbia (DC)
U of the Virgin Islands (VI)
U of Utah (UT)
U of Waterloo (ON, Canada)
U of West Florida (FL)
U of West Georgia (GA)
U of Wisconsin–Eau Claire (WI)
U of Wisconsin–La Crosse (WI)
U of Wisconsin–Platteville (WI)
U of Wisconsin–River Falls (WI)
U of Wisconsin–Stevens Point (WI)
U of Wisconsin–Stout (WI)
U of Wisconsin–Superior (WI)
U of Wisconsin–Whitewater (WI)
U of Wyoming (WY)
Utah Valley U (UT)
Washburn U (KS)
Western State Coll of Colorado (CO)
West Liberty U (WV)
West Virginia U (WV)
Wichita State U (KS)

$14,000–$15,999

Colleges with No Room and Board or with Room Only

Calumet Coll of Saint Joseph (IN)
Chamberlain Coll of Nursing (MO)
DeVry Coll of New York (NY)
DeVry U, Phoenix (AZ)
DeVry U, Pomona (CA)
DeVry U, Westminster (CO)
DeVry U, Miramar (FL)
DeVry U, Orlando (FL)
DeVry U, Decatur (GA)
DeVry U, Chicago (IL)
DeVry U, Kansas City (MO)
DeVry U, North Brunswick (NJ)
DeVry U, Columbus (OH)
DeVry U, Fort Washington (PA)

DeVry U, Houston (TX)
DeVry U, Irving (TX)
DeVry U, Arlington (VA)
DeVry U, Federal Way (WA)
DeVry U Online (IL)
Jarvis Christian Coll (TX) **(room only)**
Medical U of South Carolina (SC)
Peirce Coll (PA)
Salem State U (MA) **(room only)**
Southeastern Bible Coll (AL) **(room only)**
Strayer U - Nashville Campus (TN)
Strayer U - Shelby Oaks Campus (TN)
Strayer U - Thousand Oaks Campus (TN)
Thomas U (GA) **(room only)**
U of Colorado at Colorado Springs (CO) **(room only)**

Colleges with Room and Board

Acadia U (NS, Canada)
Bloomsburg U of Pennsylvania (PA)
Bowie State U (MD)
California State Polytechnic U, Pomona (CA)
California State U, Chico (CA)
California State U, Dominguez Hills (CA)
California State U, Fullerton (CA)
California State U, Long Beach (CA)
California State U, Stanislaus (CA)
Calvary Bible Coll and Theological Sem (MO)
Clarion U of Pennsylvania (PA)
Colorado State U (CO)
Columbia Bible Coll (BC, Canada)
Divine Word Coll (IA)
Eastern Oregon U (OR)
Eastern Washington U (WA)
East Stroudsburg U of Pennsylvania (PA)
Edinboro U of Pennsylvania (PA)
The Evergreen State Coll (WA)
Fitchburg State U (MA)
Florida Atlantic U (FL)
Florida Gulf Coast U (FL)
Florida State U (FL)
Framingham State U (MA)
Francis Marion U (SC)
Georgia Southern U (GA)
Goddard Coll (VT)
Hillsdale Free Will Baptist Coll (OK)
Humboldt State U (CA)
Indiana State U (IN)
Indiana U–Purdue U Indianapolis (IN)
Iowa State U of Science and Technology (IA)
James Madison U (VA)
Johnson Bible Coll (TN)
Kansas State U (KS)
Kutztown U of Pennsylvania (PA)
Lincoln U (MO)
Lock Haven U of Pennsylvania (PA)
Mansfield U of Pennsylvania (PA)
Martin Luther Coll (MN)
Massachusetts Coll of Liberal Arts (MA)
Mesa State Coll (CO)
Millersville U of Pennsylvania (PA)
Montana State U (MT)
Morris Coll (SC)
Mountain State U (WV)
North Carolina State U (NC)
Northern Arizona U (AZ)
Northwest Missouri State U (MO)
Radford U (VA)
Saginaw Valley State U (MI)
Salisbury U (MD)
Sam Houston State U (TX)
Shawnee State U (OH)
Shippensburg U of Pennsylvania (PA)
Southern Oregon U (OR)
State U of New York at New Paltz (NY)
State U of New York at Plattsburgh (NY)
State U of New York Coll at Old Westbury (NY)
State U of New York Coll at Oneonta (NY)
State U of New York Coll at Potsdam (NY)
State U of New York Coll of Technology at Alfred (NY)
State U of New York Upstate Medical U (NY)
Stephen F. Austin State U (TX)
Texas A&M U–Corpus Christi (TX)
Texas State U–San Marcos (TX)
The U of Alabama at Birmingham (AL)
The U of Alabama in Huntsville (AL)
U of Arkansas (AR)

U of Guelph (ON, Canada)
The U of Iowa (IA)
The U of Kansas (KS)
U of Louisville (KY)
U of Maine at Fort Kent (ME)
U of Maine at Presque Isle (ME)
U of Mary Washington (VA)
U of Michigan–Flint (MI)
U of Nebraska at Omaha (NE)
U of Nebraska–Lincoln (NE)
U of Nevada, Reno (NV)
U of New Brunswick Fredericton (NB, Canada)
The U of North Carolina at Chapel Hill (NC)
U of Northern Colorado (CO)
U of Northern Iowa (IA)
U of North Texas (TX)
U of South Carolina Aiken (SC)
U of South Carolina Beaufort (SC)
U of South Carolina Upstate (SC)
U of South Florida (FL)
The U of Tennessee (TN)
The U of Tennessee at Chattanooga (TN)
The U of Texas at Arlington (TX)
The U of Texas at Tyler (TX)
U of Washington, Bothell (WA)
U of Wisconsin–Green Bay (WI)
U of Wisconsin–Parkside (WI)
Virginia Polytechnic Inst and State U (VA)
Virginia State U (VA)
West Chester U of Pennsylvania (PA)
Western Kentucky U (KY)
Western Oregon U (OR)
Westfield State U (MA)
Winona State U (MN)
Wright State U (OH)
Youngstown State U (OH)

$16,000–$17,999

Colleges with No Room and Board or with Room Only

AIB Coll of Business (IA) **(room only)**
American U of Beirut (Lebanon) **(room only)**
Boston Architectural Coll (MA)
Clarkson Coll (NE) **(room only)**
Cleary U (MI)
Goldfarb School of Nursing at Barnes-Jewish Coll (MO)
Marylhurst U (OR)
Minnesota School of Business–Blaine (MN)
Saint Francis Medical Center Coll of Nursing (IL) **(room only)**
St. Joseph's Coll, Long Island Campus (NY)
St. Joseph's Coll, New York (NY)
State U of New York Downstate Medical Center (NY) **(room only)**
Wade Coll (TX) **(room only)**

Colleges with Room and Board

Appalachian Bible Coll (WV)
Arizona State U (AZ)
Auburn U (AL)
Ball State U (IN)
Bob Jones U (SC)
Bowling Green State U (OH)
Bridgewater State U (MA)
California Polytechnic State U, San Luis Obispo (CA)
California State U, Northridge (CA)
Castleton State Coll (VT)
Central Connecticut State U (CT)
The Citadel, The Military Coll of South Carolina (SC)
Coastal Carolina U (SC)
Eastern Michigan U (MI)
Fashion Inst of Technology (NY)
Florida Intl U (FL)
Georgia Coll & State U (GA)
Georgia Inst of Technology (GA)
Grand Valley State U (MI)
Heritage Christian U (AL)
Indiana U Bloomington (IN)
Indiana U of Pennsylvania (PA)
Johnson State Coll (VT)
Kent State U (OH)
Lake Superior State U (MI)
Longwood U (VA)

Louisiana Coll (LA)
Lyndon State Coll (VT)
Maranatha Baptist Bible Coll (WI)
Mid-Atlantic Christian U (NC)
Missouri U of Science and Technology (MO)
Northern Michigan U (MI)
Old Dominion U (VA)
Paine Coll (GA)
Portland State U (OR)
Purchase Coll, State U of New York (NY)
Queens Coll of the City U of New York (NY)
Rhode Island Coll (RI)
San Diego State U (CA)
San Francisco State U (CA)
San Jose State U (CA)
Slippery Rock U of Pennsylvania (PA)
Sonoma State U (CA)
Southern Illinois U Edwardsville (IL)
State U of New York at Fredonia (NY)
State U of New York at Oswego (NY)
State U of New York Coll at Geneseo (NY)
State U of New York Coll of Technology at Delhi (NY)
State U of New York Maritime Coll (NY)
Stony Brook U, State U of New York (NY)
Talladega Coll (AL)
Texas A&M U (TX)
Texas Tech U (TX)
Towson U (MD)
U at Buffalo, the State U of New York (NY)
The U of Alabama (AL)
The U of Arizona (AZ)
U of Georgia (GA)
U of Hawaii at Manoa (HI)
U of Houston (TX)
U of Maine at Farmington (ME)
U of Minnesota, Crookston (MN)
U of Missouri (MO)
U of Missouri–St. Louis (MO)
U of Nevada, Las Vegas (NV)
U of Oregon (OR)
U of South Carolina (SC)
U of Southern Maine (ME)
The U of Texas at San Antonio (TX)
The U of Texas Southwestern Medical Center at Dallas (TX)
The U of Toledo (OH)
U of Wisconsin–Madison (WI)
Virginia Commonwealth U (VA)
Wayland Baptist U (TX)
Wayne State U (MI)
Western Illinois U (IL)
Western Michigan U (MI)
Worcester State U (MA)

$18,000–$19,999

Colleges with No Room and Board or with Room Only

Aquinas Coll (TN)
Bastyr U (WA)
Everest U, Tampa (FL)
Goodwin Coll (CT)
Grand Canyon U (AZ)
Harrisburg U of Science and Technology (PA)
National-Louis U (IL)
New England Inst of Technology (RI)
Pennsylvania Coll of Art & Design (PA)

Colleges with Room and Board

Blackburn Coll (IL)
Boston Baptist Coll (MA)
Central Michigan U (MI)
Cleveland State U (OH)
Eastern Illinois U (IL)
Emmanuel Coll (GA)
Emmaus Bible Coll (IA)
Faith Baptist Bible Coll and Theological Sem (IA)
Ferris State U (MI)
Florida Coll (FL)
Georgia State U (GA)
Harding U (AR)
Huston-Tillotson U (TX)
Illinois State U (IL)
Keene State Coll (NH)
Lee U (TN)

INDEXES

Lincoln Christian U (IL)
Michigan State U (MI)
Mid-Continent U (KY)
Montclair State U (NJ)
New Hope Christian Coll (OR)
New Jersey City U (NJ)
Oak Hills Christian Coll (MN)
The Ohio State U (OH)
Ohio U (OH)
Polytechnic U of Puerto Rico (PR)
Purdue U (IN)
St. Louis Christian Coll (MO)
Southern Connecticut State U (CT)
Southern Illinois U Carbondale (IL)
State U of New York at Binghamton (NY)
State U of New York Coll of Environmental Science and Forestry (NY)
Texas Southern U (TX)
Trinity Coll of Florida (FL)
The U of Akron (OH)
U of Cincinnati (OH)
U of Colorado Boulder (CO)
U of Colorado Denver (CO)
U of Delaware (DE)
U of Illinois at Springfield (IL)
U of Maine (ME)
U of Maryland, Baltimore County (MD)
U of Maryland, Coll Park (MD)
U of Massachusetts Dartmouth (MA)
U of Massachusetts Lowell (MA)
U of Minnesota, Duluth (MN)
U of Minnesota, Twin Cities Campus (MN)
U of Pittsburgh at Bradford (PA)
U of Pittsburgh at Johnstown (PA)
U of Pittsburgh at Titusville (PA)
U of Rhode Island (RI)
The U of Texas at Austin (TX)
The U of Texas at Dallas (TX)
U of the Southwest (NM)
U of Virginia (VA)
U of Washington (WA)
Vermont Tech Coll (VT)
Virginia Military Inst (VA)
Washington State U (WA)
Winthrop U (SC)

$20,000–$24,999

Colleges with No Room and Board or with Room Only

Antioch U Midwest (OH)
Cincinnati Coll of Mortuary Science (OH)
Columbia Coll of Nursing (WI)
Creative Center (NE)
DigiPen Inst of Technology (WA)
Goldey-Beacom Coll (DE) **(room only)**
Hebrew Coll (MA)
Jefferson Coll of Health Sciences (VA) **(room only)**
Johnson & Wales U (RI)
Lexington Coll (IL)
McNally Smith Coll of Music (MN)
Molloy Coll (NY)
Mount Carmel Coll of Nursing (OH) **(room only)**
O'More Coll of Design (TN)
Pacific Oaks Coll (CA)
Pacific States U (CA) **(room only)**
Regent U (VA) **(room only)**
The Restaurant School at Walnut Hill Coll (PA) **(room only)**
Resurrection U (IL)
Saint Louis U–Madrid Campus (Spain) **(room only)**
Villa Maria Coll of Buffalo (NY) **(room only)**
Wheeling Jesuit U (WV)

Colleges with Room and Board

Allen Coll (IA)
Atlanta Christian Coll (GA)
Atlantic Union Coll (MA)
Baptist Bible Coll of Pennsylvania (PA)
Barclay Coll (KS)
Belhaven U (MS)
Bethel U (TN)
Bethune-Cookman U (FL)

Brewton-Parker Coll (GA)
Bryan Coll (TN)
Bryn Athyn Coll of the New Church (PA)
Central Pennsylvania Coll (PA)
Christopher Newport U (VA)
Cincinnati Christian U (OH)
Claflin U (SC)
Clearwater Christian Coll (FL)
Coll of Charleston (SC)
The Coll of New Jersey (NJ)
The Coll of William and Mary (VA)
Colorado School of Mines (CO)
Columbia Coll (MO)
Cumberland U (TN)
Dallas Baptist U (TX)
Daniel Webster Coll (NH)
Daniel Webster Coll–Portsmouth Campus (NH)
Davenport U, Grand Rapids (MI)
Dillard U (LA)
East Texas Baptist U (TX)
Evangel U (MO)
Faulkner U (AL)
Flagler Coll (FL)
Freed-Hardeman U (TN)
Free Will Baptist Bible Coll (TN)
Gallaudet U (DC)
Grace Bible Coll (MI)
Great Lakes Christian Coll (MI)
Grove City Coll (PA)
Hannibal-LaGrange U (MO)
Husson U (ME)
Intl Acad of Design & Technology (FL)
Jamestown Coll (ND)
Johnson C. Smith U (NC)
Judson Coll (AL)
Kean U (NJ)
Kentucky Wesleyan Coll (KY)
Kuyper Coll (MI)
Liberty U (VA)
Life U (GA)
Lincoln Memorial U (TN)
Lindenwood U (MO)
Lourdes Coll (OH)
Lubbock Christian U (TX)
Madonna U (MI)
Massachusetts Coll of Art and Design (MA)
Massachusetts Maritime Acad (MA)
Miami U (OH)
Mount Olive Coll (NC)
Multnomah U (OR)
Northern Illinois U (IL)
North Greenville U (SC)
Ohio Valley U (WV)
Oklahoma Christian U (OK)
Penn State Altoona (PA)
Penn State Beaver (PA)
Penn State Berks (PA)
Penn State Erie, The Behrend Coll (PA)
Penn State Greater Allegheny (PA)
Penn State Harrisburg (PA)
Penn State Hazleton (PA)
Penn State Mont Alto (PA)
Penn State U Park (PA)
Pennsylvania Coll of Technology (PA)
Pikeville Coll (KY)
Presentation Coll (SD)
Ramapo Coll of New Jersey (NJ)
Reinhardt U (GA)
The Richard Stockton Coll of New Jersey (NJ)
Rowan U (NJ)
Rutgers, The State U of New Jersey, Camden (NJ)
Rutgers, The State U of New Jersey, Newark (NJ)
Rutgers, The State U of New Jersey, New Brunswick (NJ)
Sacred Heart Major Sem (MI)
St. Mary's Coll of Maryland (MD)
Southeastern U (FL)
Southern Adventist U (TN)
Southwestern Adventist U (TX)
Southwestern Assemblies of God U (TX)
Spalding U (KY)
Stratford U, Falls Church (VA)
Temple U (PA)
Truett-McConnell Coll (GA)
Tuskegee U (AL)
Union Coll (KY)

Union Coll (NE)
U of California, Davis (CA)
U of California, Irvine (CA)
U of California, Santa Barbara (CA)
U of Illinois at Chicago (IL)
U of Massachusetts Amherst (MA)
U of Michigan (MI)
U of Mobile (AL)
U of New Hampshire (NH)
U of Pittsburgh (PA)
U of Pittsburgh at Greensburg (PA)
U of the Cumberlands (KY)
U of Vermont (VT)
William Paterson U of New Jersey (NJ)
Xavier U of Louisiana (LA)
York Coll of Pennsylvania (PA)

$25,000–$29,999

Colleges with No Room and Board or with Room Only

Burlington Coll (VT) **(room only)**
FIDM/The Fashion Inst of Design & Merchandising, Los Angeles Campus (CA)
Long Island U, Brentwood Campus (NY)
New Hampshire Inst of Art (NH) **(room only)**
Rocky Mountain Coll of Art + Design (CO)
Watkins Coll of Art, Design, & Film (TN) **(room only)**

Colleges with Room and Board

Alderson-Broaddus Coll (WV)
Alverno Coll (WI)
Anderson U (SC)
Andrews U (MI)
Asbury U (KY)
Avila U (MO)
Baker U (KS)
Barton Coll (NC)
Benedictine Coll (KS)
Bethany Coll (KS)
Bethany Lutheran Coll (MN)
Bethel Coll (IN)
Bluefield Coll (VA)
Campbellsville U (KY)
Carson-Newman Coll (TN)
Cedarville U (OH)
Christendom Coll (VA)
Clark Atlanta U (GA)
Cogswell Polytechnical Coll (CA)
Coker Coll (SC)
Coll of St. Joseph (VT)
Coll of Saint Mary (NE)
Crown Coll (MN)
Culver-Stockton Coll (MO)
Dakota Wesleyan U (SD)
Doane Coll (NE)
Dordt Coll (IA)
Drury U (MO)
Edgewood Coll (WI)
Fontbonne U (MO)
Friends U (KS)
Gardner-Webb U (NC)
Grace Coll (IN)
Graceland U (IA)
Grand View U (IA)
Greenville Coll (IL)
Hardin-Simmons U (TX)
Hawai'i Pacific U (HI)
Hillsdale Coll (MI)
Holy Cross Coll (IN)
Huntingdon Coll (AL)
Huntington U (IN)
Indiana Wesleyan U (IN)
Iowa Wesleyan Coll (IA)
John Brown U (AR)
Keystone Coll (PA)
Limestone Coll (SC)
Lindsey Wilson Coll (KY)
Lyon Coll (AR)
MacMurray Coll (IL)
Malone U (OH)
Marian U (WI)
Mars Hill Coll (NC)

McMurry U (TX)
MidAmerica Nazarene U (KS)
Midway Coll (KY)
Milligan Coll (TN)
Missouri Baptist U (MO)
Montreat Coll, Montreat (NC)
Mount Aloysius Coll (PA)
Mount Marty Coll (SD)
Mount Vernon Nazarene U (OH)
Nebraska Wesleyan U (NE)
Newman U (KS)
Northwest Christian U (OR)
Northwest Nazarene U (ID)
Northwest U (WA)
Nyack Coll (NY)
Oklahoma Wesleyan U (OK)
Ouachita Baptist U (AR)
Our Lady of the Lake U of San Antonio (TX)
Philadelphia Biblical U (PA)
Piedmont Coll (GA)
Rocky Mountain Coll (MT)
St. Charles Borromeo Sem, Overbrook (PA)
Saint Joseph Sem Coll (LA)
Saint Leo U (FL)
St. Thomas U (FL)
Samford U (AL)
Schreiner U (TX)
Shorter U (GA)
Siena Heights U (MI)
Silver Lake Coll (WI)
Simpson U (CA)
Southern Nazarene U (OK)
Southern Vermont Coll (VT)
Southern Wesleyan U (SC)
Southwestern Coll (KS)
Spring Arbor U (MI)
Sullivan Coll of Technology and Design (KY)
Tabor Coll (KS)
Tennessee Wesleyan Coll (TN)
Texas Lutheran U (TX)
Texas Wesleyan U (TX)
Thomas Aquinas Coll (CA)
Thomas More Coll of Liberal Arts (NH)
Tiffin U (OH)
Trevecca Nazarene U (TN)
Trinity Lutheran Coll (WA)
Union U (TN)
U of Advancing Technology (AZ)
U of California, Berkeley (CA)
U of California, Los Angeles (CA)
U of California, Santa Cruz (CA)
U of Dubuque (IA)
U of Mary Hardin-Baylor (TX)
U of Rio Grande (OH)
U of Saint Mary (KS)
U of Sioux Falls (SD)
U of the Ozarks (AR)
Upper Iowa U (IA)
Vaughn Coll of Aeronautics and Technology (NY)
Viterbo U (WI)
Walla Walla U (WA)
Washington Adventist U (MD)
Waynesburg U (PA)
Webber Intl U (FL)
Wesleyan Coll (GA)
Westminster Coll (MO)
William Jessup U (CA)
Wingate U (NC)
Young Harris Coll (GA)

$30,000 AND OVER

Colleges with No Room and Board or with Room Only

Art Center Coll of Design (CA)
California Coll of the Arts (CA) **(room only)**
The King's Coll (NY) **(room only)**
LA Coll Intl (CA)
Minneapolis Coll of Art and Design (MN) **(room only)**
Neumont U (UT) **(room only)**
New York School of Interior Design (NY) **(room only)**
Otis Coll of Art and Design (CA)
Prescott Coll (AZ) **(room only)**
Samuel Merritt U (CA)

San Francisco Conservatory of Music (CA)
School of the Museum of Fine Arts, Boston (MA) **(room only)**
The U of the Arts (PA) **(room only)**

Colleges with Room and Board

Abilene Christian U (TX)
Adelphi U (NY)
Albany Coll of Pharmacy and Health Sciences (NY)
Albertus Magnus Coll (CT)
Albright Coll (PA)
Alfred U (NY)
Allegheny Coll (PA)
Alma Coll (MI)
Alvernia U (PA)
American Jewish U (CA)
American U (DC)
Amherst Coll (MA)
Anderson U (IN)
Anna Maria Coll (MA)
Aquinas Coll (MI)
Arcadia U (PA)
The Art Inst of Boston at Lesley U (MA)
Ashland U (OH)
Assumption Coll (MA)
Augsburg Coll (MN)
Augustana Coll (IL)
Augustana Coll (SD)
Austin Coll (TX)
Averett U (VA)
Azusa Pacific U (CA)
Baldwin-Wallace Coll (OH)
Bard Coll (NY)
Bard Coll at Simon's Rock (MA)
Barnard Coll (NY)
Barry U (FL)
Bates Coll (ME)
Beacon Coll (FL)
Bellarmine U (KY)
Belmont Abbey Coll (NC)
Belmont U (TN)
Beloit Coll (WI)
Benedictine U (IL)
Bennington Coll (VT)
Bentley U (MA)
Berry Coll (GA)
Bethany Coll (WV)
Bethel U (MN)
Biola U (CA)
Birmingham-Southern Coll (AL)
Bloomfield Coll (NJ)
Bluffton U (OH)
Boston Coll (MA)
Boston U (MA)
Bowdoin Coll (ME)
Brandeis U (MA)
Brenau U (GA)
Brevard Coll (NC)
Briar Cliff U (IA)
Bridgewater Coll (VA)
Brown U (RI)
Bryant U (RI)
Bryn Mawr Coll (PA)
Bucknell U (PA)
Buena Vista U (IA)
Butler U (IN)
Cabrini Coll (PA)
California Baptist U (CA)
California Inst of Technology (CA)
California Inst of the Arts (CA)
Calvin Coll (MI)
Canisius Coll (NY)
Capital U (OH)
Carleton Coll (MN)
Carlow U (PA)
Carnegie Mellon U (PA)
Carroll U (WI)
Case Western Reserve U (OH)
The Catholic U of America (DC)
Cedar Crest Coll (PA)
Centenary Coll (NJ)
Centenary Coll of Louisiana (LA)
Central Coll (IA)
Centre Coll (KY)
Champlain Coll (VT)
Chapman U (CA)

Chatham U (PA)
Chestnut Hill Coll (PA)
Christian Brothers U (TN)
Claremont McKenna Coll (CA)
Clarke U (IA)
Clarkson U (NY)
Clark U (MA)
The Cleveland Inst of Art (OH)
Colby Coll (ME)
Colgate U (NY)
Coll for Creative Studies (MI)
Coll of Mount St. Joseph (OH)
Coll of Saint Benedict (MN)
Coll of Saint Elizabeth (NJ)
The Coll of Saint Rose (NY)
The Coll of St. Scholastica (MN)
Coll of the Atlantic (ME)
Coll of the Holy Cross (MA)
The Coll of Wooster (OH)
The Colorado Coll (CO)
Columbia Coll (SC)
Columbia Coll Chicago (IL)
Columbia U, School of General Studies (NY)
Columbus Coll of Art & Design (OH)
Concordia Coll (MN)
Concordia Coll–New York (NY)
Concordia U (CA)
Concordia U Chicago (IL)
Concordia U, St. Paul (MN)
Concordia U Wisconsin (WI)
Connecticut Coll (CT)
Corban U (OR)
Corcoran Coll of Art and Design (DC)
Cornell Coll (IA)
Cornell U (NY)
Covenant Coll (GA)
Creighton U (NE)
The Culinary Inst of America (NY)
Curry Coll (MA)
Dartmouth Coll (NH)
Davidson Coll (NC)
Defiance Coll (OH)
Denison U (OH)
DePaul U (IL)
DePauw U (IN)
DeSales U (PA)
Dickinson Coll (PA)
Dominican Coll (NY)
Dominican U (IL)
Dominican U of California (CA)
Dowling Coll (NY)
Drake U (IA)
Drew U (NJ)
Duquesne U (PA)
Earlham Coll (IN)
Eckerd Coll (FL)
Elizabethtown Coll (PA)
Elmhurst Coll (IL)
Elmira Coll (NY)
Elon U (NC)
Embry-Riddle Aeronautical U–Daytona (FL)
Embry-Riddle Aeronautical U–Prescott (AZ)
Emmanuel Coll (MA)
Emory & Henry Coll (VA)
Endicott Coll (MA)
Erskine Coll (SC)
Eugene Lang Coll The New School for Liberal Arts (NY)
Fairfield U (CT)
Fairleigh Dickinson U, Coll at Florham (NJ)
Fairleigh Dickinson U, Metropolitan Campus (NJ)
Felician Coll (NJ)
Ferrum Coll (VA)
Fisher Coll (MA)
Five Towns Coll (NY)
Florida Inst of Technology (FL)
Florida Southern Coll (FL)
Franklin & Marshall Coll (PA)
Franklin Coll (IN)
Franklin Coll Switzerland (Switzerland)
Franklin Pierce U (NH)
Franklin W. Olin Coll of Eng (MA)
Furman U (SC)
Gannon U (PA)
Geneva Coll (PA)
George Fox U (OR)
Georgetown Coll (KY)

Georgetown U (DC)
Georgian Court U (NJ)
Gettysburg Coll (PA)
Gordon Coll (MA)
Goucher Coll (MD)
Greensboro Coll (NC)
Grinnell Coll (IA)
Guilford Coll (NC)
Hamilton Coll (NY)
Hamline U (MN)
Hampden-Sydney Coll (VA)
Hampshire Coll (MA)
Hanover Coll (IN)
Hartwick Coll (NY)
Harvard U (MA)
Harvey Mudd Coll (CA)
Haverford Coll (PA)
Hellenic Coll (MA)
Hendrix Coll (AR)
Hobart and William Smith Colls (NY)
Hofstra U (NY)
Hollins U (VA)
Holy Family U (PA)
Holy Names U (CA)
Hood Coll (MD)
Hope Coll (MI)
Houghton Coll (NY)
Illinois Coll (IL)
Illinois Inst of Technology (IL)
Illinois Wesleyan U (IL)
Immaculata U (PA)
Indiana Tech (IN)
Ithaca Coll (NY)
John Carroll U (OH)
The Johns Hopkins U (MD)
Johnson & Wales U (CO)
Johnson & Wales U (FL)
Johnson & Wales U - Charlotte Campus (NC)
The Juilliard School (NY)
Juniata Coll (PA)
Kalamazoo Coll (MI)
Kendall Coll (IL)
Kenyon Coll (OH)
Kettering U (MI)
Keuka Coll (NY)
King Coll (TN)
King's Coll (PA)
Knox Coll (IL)
Lafayette Coll (PA)
LaGrange Coll (GA)
Lake Forest Coll (IL)
La Roche Coll (PA)
La Salle U (PA)
Lawrence Technological U (MI)
Lawrence U (WI)
Lebanon Valley Coll (PA)
Lehigh U (PA)
Le Moyne Coll (NY)
Lesley U (MA)
LeTourneau U (TX)
Lewis & Clark Coll (OR)
Lewis U (IL)
Linfield Coll (OR)
Lipscomb U (TN)
Long Island U, Brooklyn Campus (NY)
Long Island U, C.W. Post Campus (NY)
Loras Coll (IA)
Loyola Marymount U (CA)
Loyola U Chicago (IL)
Loyola U Maryland (MD)
Loyola U New Orleans (LA)
Luther Coll (IA)
Lycoming Coll (PA)
Lyme Acad Coll of Fine Arts (CT)
Lynchburg Coll (VA)
Lynn U (FL)
Macalester Coll (MN)
Maharishi U of Management (IA)
Maine Coll of Art (ME)
Manchester Coll (IN)
Manhattan Coll (NY)
Manhattanville Coll (NY)
Mannes Coll The New School for Music (NY)
Marietta Coll (OH)
Marist Coll (NY)

Marlboro Coll (VT)
Marquette U (WI)
Mary Baldwin Coll (VA)
Maryland Inst Coll of Art (MD)
Marymount Coll, Palos Verdes, California (CA)
Marymount U (VA)
Maryville Coll (TN)
Maryville U of Saint Louis (MO)
Marywood U (PA)
Massachusetts Inst of Technology (MA)
The Master's Coll and Sem (CA)
McDaniel Coll (MD)
McKendree U (IL)
Medaille Coll (NY)
Menlo Coll (CA)
Mercer U (GA)
Merrimack Coll (MA)
Messiah Coll (PA)
Middlebury Coll (VT)
Millikin U (IL)
Millsaps Coll (MS)
Mills Coll (CA)
Milwaukee School of Eng (WI)
Misericordia U (PA)
Mitchell Coll (CT)
Monmouth Coll (IL)
Monmouth U (NJ)
Moravian Coll (PA)
Morehouse Coll (GA)
Morningside Coll (IA)
Mount Holyoke Coll (MA)
Mount Ida Coll (MA)
Mount Mercy U (IA)
Mount Saint Mary Coll (NY)
Mount St. Mary's Coll (CA)
Mount St. Mary's U (MD)
Muhlenberg Coll (PA)
Naropa U (CO)
Nazareth Coll of Rochester (NY)
Neumann U (PA)
Newberry Coll (SC)
Newbury Coll (MA)
New England Coll (NH)
New England Conservatory of Music (MA)
The New School for General Studies (NY)
The New School for Jazz and Contemporary Music (NY)
New York Inst of Technology (NY)
New York U (NY)
Niagara U (NY)
North Central Coll (IL)
Northeastern U (MA)
Northland Coll (WI)
Northwestern Coll (IA)
Northwestern Coll (MN)
Notre Dame de Namur U (CA)
Nova Southeastern U (FL)
Oberlin Coll (OH)
Oglethorpe U (GA)
Ohio Wesleyan U (OH)
Oklahoma City U (OK)
Pace U (NY)
Pacific Lutheran U (WA)
Pacific Northwest Coll of Art (OR)
Pacific Union Coll (CA)
Pacific U (OR)
Palm Beach Atlantic U (FL)
Parsons The New School for Design (NY)
Patrick Henry Coll (VA)
Peabody Conservatory of The Johns Hopkins U (MD)
Pepperdine U, Malibu (CA)
Philadelphia U (PA)
Pitzer Coll (CA)
Point Park U (PA)
Polytechnic Inst of NYU (NY)
Pomona Coll (CA)
Pratt Inst (NY)
Presbyterian Coll (SC)
Princeton U (NJ)
Principia Coll (IL)
Providence Coll (RI)
Quincy U (IL)
Quinnipiac U (CT)
Randolph Coll (VA)
Randolph-Macon Coll (VA)
Reed Coll (OR)

Regis Coll (MA)
Regis U (CO)
Rensselaer Polytechnic Inst (NY)
Research Coll of Nursing (MO)
Rhodes Coll (TN)
Rice U (TX)
Rider U (NJ)
Ringling Coll of Art and Design (FL)
Ripon Coll (WI)
Rivier Coll (NH)
Roanoke Coll (VA)
Robert Morris U (PA)
Robert Morris U Illinois (IL)
Rockford Coll (IL)
Rockhurst U (MO)
Rollins Coll (FL)
Roosevelt U (IL)
Rose-Hulman Inst of Technology (IN)
Rosemont Coll (PA)
Russell Sage Coll (NY)
Sacred Heart U (CT)
Sage Coll of Albany (NY)
St. Ambrose U (IA)
St. Andrews Presbyterian Coll (NC)
Saint Anselm Coll (NH)
St. Bonaventure U (NY)
St. Catherine U (MN)
St. Edward's U (TX)
Saint Francis U (PA)
St. John Fisher Coll (NY)
St. John's Coll (MD)
St. John's Coll (NM)
Saint John's U (MN)
St. John's U (NY)
Saint Joseph Coll (CT)
Saint Joseph's Coll (IN)
Saint Joseph's Coll of Maine (ME)
Saint Joseph's U (PA)
St. Lawrence U (NY)
St. Louis Coll of Pharmacy (MO)
Saint Louis U (MO)
Saint Martin's U (WA)
Saint Mary-of-the-Woods Coll (IN)
Saint Mary's Coll (IN)
Saint Mary's Coll of California (CA)
Saint Mary's of Minnesota (MN)
Saint Michael's Coll (VT)
St. Norbert Coll (WI)
St. Olaf Coll (MN)
St. Thomas Aquinas Coll (NY)
Saint Xavier U (IL)
Salve Regina U (RI)
San Diego Christian Coll (CA)
Santa Clara U (CA)
Sarah Lawrence Coll (NY)
Savannah Coll of Art and Design (GA)
School of Visual Arts (NY)
Scripps Coll (CA)
Seattle Pacific U (WA)
Seton Hill U (PA)
Sewanee: The U of the South (TN)
Shenandoah U (VA)
Shimer Coll (IL)
Siena Coll (NY)
Sierra Nevada Coll (NV)
Simmons Coll (MA)
Simpson Coll (IA)
Skidmore Coll (NY)
Smith Coll (MA)
Soka U of America (CA)
Southern Methodist U (TX)
Spelman Coll (GA)
Springfield Coll (MA)
Spring Hill Coll (AL)
Stanford U (CA)
Stephens Coll (MO)
Sterling Coll (VT)
Stetson U (FL)
Stevenson U (MD)
Stonehill Coll (MA)
Suffolk U (MA)
Susquehanna U (PA)
Swarthmore Coll (PA)
Sweet Briar Coll (VA)
Syracuse U (NY)

Taylor U (IN)
Texas Christian U (TX)
Thiel Coll (PA)
Thomas More Coll (KY)
Transylvania U (KY)
Trine U (IN)
Trinity Coll (CT)
Trinity U (TX)
Tufts U (MA)
Tulane U (LA)
Union Coll (NY)
U of Bridgeport (CT)
U of Charleston (WV)
U of Dallas (TX)
U of Dayton (OH)
U of Denver (CO)
U of Evansville (IN)
The U of Findlay (OH)
U of Hartford (CT)
U of Indianapolis (IN)
U of La Verne (CA)
U of Miami (FL)
U of Mount Union (OH)
U of New England (ME)
U of New Haven (CT)
U of Notre Dame (IN)
U of Pennsylvania (PA)
U of Portland (OR)

U of Puget Sound (WA)
U of Redlands (CA)
U of Richmond (VA)
U of Rochester (NY)
U of St. Francis (IL)
U of St. Thomas (MN)
U of St. Thomas (TX)
U of San Diego (CA)
U of San Francisco (CA)
The U of Scranton (PA)
U of Southern California (CA)
The U of Tampa (FL)
U of the Incarnate Word (TX)
U of the Pacific (CA)
U of the Sciences in Philadelphia (PA)
U of Tulsa (OK)
Ursuline Coll (OH)
Valparaiso U (IN)
Vanderbilt U (TN)
VanderCook Coll of Music (IL)
Vassar Coll (NY)
Villanova U (PA)
Virginia Intermont Coll (VA)
Virginia Wesleyan Coll (VA)
Wabash Coll (IN)
Wagner Coll (NY)
Wake Forest U (NC)
Walsh U (OH)

Wartburg Coll (IA)
Washington & Jefferson Coll (PA)
Washington and Lee U (VA)
Washington Coll (MD)
Washington U in St. Louis (MO)
Webster U (MO)
Wellesley Coll (MA)
Wells Coll (NY)
Wentworth Inst of Technology (MA)
Wesleyan U (CT)
Western New England U (MA)
Westminster Coll (UT)
Westmont Coll (CA)
Wheaton Coll (IL)
Wheaton Coll (MA)
Whitman Coll (WA)
Widener U (PA)
Wilkes U (PA)
Willamette U (OR)
William Jewell Coll (MO)
Williams Coll (MA)
Wilmington Coll (OH)
Wittenberg U (OH)
Wofford Coll (SC)
Woodbury U (CA)
Worcester Polytechnic Inst (MA)
Xavier U (OH)
Yale U (CT)

INDEXES

Advertisers Index

The following schools have provided and paid for a half-page or full-page display ad, which appears in the **Profiles** section on the page noted in this index.

Advertisers Index

Alphabetical Listing

INDEXES

INDEXES

INDEXES

INDEXES

INDEXES

INDEXES

INDEXES

INDEXES

Alphabetical Listing

Geographical Listing of Close-Ups

INDEXES

Special Advertising Section

Thomas Jefferson University School of Population Health

University of Medicine & Dentistry of New Jersey

Saint Louis University

St. Mary's University

The Winston Preparatory Schools